MW01180874

Corporate Giving Directory 2001

ISSN 1055-0623

Corporate Giving Directory 2001

22nd Edition

LySandra C. Hill,
Editor

TAFT
AN IMPRINT OF
THE GALE GROUP

DETROIT
NEW YORK
SAN FRANCISCO
LONDON
BOSTON
WOODBRIDGE, CT

Corporate Giving Directory

Matthew Brisbois,
Laurie Fundukian,
LySandra C. Hill,
Editors

Pamela Kalte,
Carolyn Swift-Muschott,
Associate Editors

Kathryn Wandzel,
Assistant Editor

Bohdan Romaniuk,
Senior Editor

Anthony L. Gerring,
Technical Editor

Monica M. Hubbard,
Contributing Senior Editor

Lori Schoenenberger,
Managing Editor

Theresa Rocklin,
Manager, Technical Support Services

Emmanuel T. Barrido,
Senior Programmer/Analyst

Pamela A.E. Galbreath,
Senior Art Director

Mike Logusz,
Graphic Artist

Mary Beth Trimper,
Composition Manager

Evi Seoud,
Assistant Production Manager

Nekita McKee,
Production Assistant

Ron Montgomery,
Data Capture Manager

Gwendolyn Tucker,
Data Capture Project Administrator

Cynthia Jones,
Data Capture Associate

Copyright © 2000 by
The Taft Group
27500 Drake Rd.
Farmington Hills, MI 48331-3535

While every effort has been made to ensure the reliability of the information presented in this publication, The Taft Group does not guarantee the accuracy of the data contained herein. The Taft Group accepts no payment for this listing; and inclusion in the publication of any organization, agency, institution, publication, service, or individual does not imply endorsement of the editors or publisher. Errors brought to the attention of the publisher and verified to the satisfaction of the publisher will be corrected in future editions.

This publication is a creative work protected by all applicable copyright laws, as well as by misappropriation, trade secret, unfair competition, and other applicable laws. The authors and editors of this work have added value to the underlying factual matter herein through one or more of the following: unique and original selection, coordination, expression, arrangement, and classification of the information. All rights to this publication will be rigorously defended.

All rights reserved including the right of reproduction in whole or in part in any form.

ISBN: 1-56995-404-6
ISSN: 1055-4998

Printed in the United States of America
Published In the United States by the Gale Group

The Taft Group is the nation's leading publisher of reference, how-to, and professional information for nonprofit organizations and institutions. For further information or for a catalog, contact 800-877-TAFT (Sales) or 248-699-4253 (Editorial Offices).

Table of Contents

PREFACE

The Taft Group's *Corporate Giving Directory (CGD)* is the premier source of information on corporate philanthropy. Fundraisers and other nonprofit executives seeking a share of corporate funding depend upon *CGD* as a primary tool in finding and securing charitable support for their nonprofit organizations. The 22nd edition of this unique, single-volume source provides detailed descriptive profiles of 1,082 of the top corporate charitable giving programs in the United States.

CGD 2001 delivers the latest information on program priorities; cash, nonmonetary, and corporate sponsorship giving; corporate matching gift and company-sponsored volunteer programs; corporate operating locations; geographic giving preferences; corporate and foundation officers and directors; application procedures and evaluative criteria; and recently awarded grants data that helps your nonprofit organization gain a crucial edge as corporate philanthropy budgets tighten. Also included in this edition are more than 750 e-mail and web addresses for companies and their giving programs.

Noteworthy Features

Collectively, the companies profiled in this edition awarded nearly $4.8 billion in cash and nonmonetary support to nonprofit organizations during their most recent reporting period. Each company profiled makes contributions of at least $200,000 annually, including nonmonetary support.

Approximately 50 percent of the companies featured in this edition cover difficult-to-research direct giving programs, which are often untapped sources of support. Information on direct giving programs is not available from IRS Forms 990, corporate annual reports, or directories limited to foundation philanthropy. However, through direct contact with corporate giving programs, the Taft Group provides this valuable information.

Another unique feature is the special emphasis on detailing hard-to-track nonmonetary support. More than one third of the featured corporations reported approximate values of nonmonetary support.

Corporations profiled in *CGD 2001* are arranged in alphabetical order by sponsoring company name. Immediately following the company name is descriptive information about that company, which can include a star with number ranking 1-100 if that company ranks among the top 100 givers in *CGD*, a company contact, company description, and operating locations. If the company has a direct giving program, that information directly follows the company-related information and may include recent giving figures, nonmonetary support, corporate sponsorship, and giving contact. The "Nonmonetary Support" section indicates the type of support offered and an estimated value, if available. The "Corporate Sponsorship" section notes the type of events or causes that the company sponsors, contact information, and the estimated value (if available) of such support. If the company administers a foundation, the foundation name immediately follows the aforementioned company information. The "Restrictions" section helps fundraisers identify organizations and activities not funded by particular philanthropic programs, helping to save valuable research time and effort. Besides describing which kinds of grants a funder makes, each giving program has a grant "Type" section, which notes information on what kinds of grants, products or volunteer time a company will support and can also include a company's employee matching gift program, including ratios, restrictions, and ranges of gifts that the company will match.

Method of Compilation

Principles at each corporation and giving program profiled in the previous edition of *CGD* were given several opportunities to update and verify the information appearing in their profiles. Data was gathered from Taft's extensive in-house research collection for corporate foundations and giving programs appearing in this edition. Additional data was gathered through mail and telephone surveys, company web sites and through the examination of such primary documents as IRS Forms 990, corporate and foundation annual reports, proxy statements, and other publications provided by the corporations.

Available in Electronic Formats

Corporate Giving Directory is available for licensing on magnetic tape or diskette in a fielded format. The database is available only for internal data processing and nonpublishing purposes. For more information, call 800-877-TAFT.

Comments and Suggestions Are Welcome

We encourage your comments and suggestions on how future editions may be enhanced to meet your prospecting needs. Please submit comments to:

Editor, *Corporate Giving Directory*
The Taft Group
27500 Drake Road
Farmington Hills, MI 48331-3535
www.taftgroup.com

Top Ten Givers By Category

Each year, Taft's *Corporate Giving Watch* newsletter profiles the top corporate givers in the following eight categories: arts & humanities, civic & public affairs, education, environment, health, international giving, science (top 5), and social services. This list of top ten corporate givers is taken from the July 2000 supplement issue of *Corporate Giving Watch*.

Provided by phone and written surveys of company/foundation representatives, Form 990 federal tax returns, company web sites, and annual reports, these figures represent the companies'/foundations' most complete financial information for the fiscal year 1998. Companies/foundations that did not provide giving figures through one of the aforementioned sources were not included.

Arts & Humanities

Dayton Hudson Corp.
Eli Lilly and Co.
Sara Lee Corp.
IBM Corp.
Ford Motor Co.
AT&T Corp.
Bell Atlantic Corp.
DaimlerChrysler Corp.
Ameritech Corp.
General Electric Co.

Civic & Public Affairs

Fannie Mae
AT&T Corp.
General Motors Corp.
Citibank
Eli Lilly and Co.
Bell Atlantic Corp.
Merck & Co., Inc.
Ford Motor Co.
IBM Corp.
Johnson and Johnson

Education

Intel Corp.
IBM Corp.
Bank of America
Hewlett-Packard Co.
Microsoft Corp.
Exxon Corp.
The Boeing Co.
AT&T Corp.
General Motors Corp.
Merck & Co., Inc.

Environment

Exxon Corp.
Patagonia Inc.
General Motors Corp.
Chevron Corp.
IBM Corp.
Hewlett-Packard Co.
Wal-Mart Stores, Inc.
Pfizer Inc.
Toyota USA
J.P. Morgan & Co.

Health

Merck & Co., Inc.
Johnson and Johnson
Pfizer Inc.
Eli Lilly & Co.
Bristol-Myers Squibb Co.
General Motors Corp.
Procter and Gamble Co.
Bell Atlantic Corp.
Ford Motor Co.
IBM Corp.

International

Procter & Gamble Co.
Hewlett-Packard Co.
Merck & Co., Inc.
Johnson & Johnson
Exxon Corp.
Eli Lilly & Co.
General Electric Co.
IBM Corp.
Microsoft Corp.
Chevron Corp.

Science

Procter & Gamble Co.
Merck & Co.
Monsanto Co.
Toyota U.S.A.
IBM Corp.

Social Services

Microsoft Corp.
Dayton Hudson Corp.
Sara Lee Corp.
Hewlett-Packard Co.
IBM Corp.
General Mills, Inc.
Merrill Lynch & Co., Inc.
General Electric Co.
Merck & Co., Inc.
Pillsbury Co.

Corporations New to This Edition

The corporations listed below are new to this edition of the *Corporate Giving Directory*.

- AirTouch Communications
- Albany International Corp.
- AMCORE Bank Rockford
- American Fidelity Corp.
- Atlantic Investment Co.
- Auburn Foundry
- BankAtlantic Bancorp
- R.G. Barry Corp.
- Bassett Furniture Industries
- BellSouth Telecommunications
- Boler Co.
- Cantor, Fitzgerald Securities Corp.
- Carris Reels
- CCB Financial Corp.
- Centex Corp.
- Central Vermont Public Service Corp.
- Chicago Board of Trade
- Chemed Corp.
- Chicago Sun-Times, Inc.
- Clark Refining & Marketing
- Colonial Oil Industries, Inc.
- Comdisco, Inc.
- Continental Grain Co.
- Conwood Co. LP
- Crane Co.
- Croft-Leominster
- Crown Books
- Daily News
- Danis Companies
- DeKalb Genetics Corp.
- Dreyer's Grand Ice Cream
- Duriron Co., Inc.
- Erb Lumber Co.
- Extendicare Health Services
- Fabri-Kal Corp.
- Federated Mutual Insurance Co.
- First American Corp.
- Florida Rock Industries
- Franklin Electric Co.
- First National Bank of Evergreen Park
- First Financial Bank
- Galter Corp.
- Giddings & Lewis
- Gosiger, Inc.
- Grede Foundries
- Griffith Laboratories U.S.A.
- Group Health Plan
- Guess?
- GuideOne Insurance
- Gulf Power Co.
- Harnischfeger Industries
- Heilig-Meyers Co.
- IBP
- Idaho Power Co.
- Indiana Mills & Manufacturing
- Keesal, Young & Logan PC
- Kelly Services
- Green Bay Packaging
- LandAmerica Financial Services
- LG&E Energy Corp.
- Liberty Diversified Industries
- Lowe's Companies
- Madison Gas & Electric Co.
- Manor Care Health SVS, Inc.
- Marathon Cheese Corp.
- Monarch Machine Tool Co.
- MTS Systems Corp.
- NASDAQ Stock Market
- National Life of Vermont
- Navcom Systems
- National Bank of Commerce Trust & Savings
- Newport News Shipbuilding
- North American Royalties
- Procter & Gamble Co. Cosmetics Division
- Nucor Corp.
- New York Mercantile Exchange
- Ohio National Life Insurance Co.
- Old Kent Bank
- ONEOK, Inc.
- Osborne Enterprises
- Outboard Marine Corp.
- Pacific Enterprises
- Park National Bank
- Pheonix Financial Group
- Pioneer Group
- Praxair
- Quanex Corp.
- Regions Bank
- Safeguard Scientifics
- South Bend Tribune Corp.
- Marcus Schloss & Co.
- Schwebel Baking Co.
- Servco Pacific
- J.R. Simplot Co.
- SIT Investment Associates, Inc.
- S&T Bancorp
- Sovereign Bank
- Standard Register Co.
- Sverdrup Corp.
- Teleflex Inc.
- Toledo Blade Co.
- Vanguard Group
- Ticketmaster Corp.
- The Timken Co.
- Toro Co.
- Union Planters Corp.
- UPN Channel 50
- Webster Bank
- John Wiley & Sons
- Wiremold Co.
- Wolverine World Wide

Corporations Not Profiled in This Edition

The following companies were profiled in the 21st edition of *Corporate Giving Directory* but are not included in this edition for one or more of the following reasons: the company was bought or merged with another company and no longer maintains a separate foundation or giving program; the company went out of business; the corporate foundation became defunct; or the corporation's most recently disclosed contributions figures do not meet the criteria for inclusion in *CGD*.

- Aeroquip-Vickers, Inc.
- Allendale Insurance Co.
- ARCO Chemical Co.
- Arkwright Mutual Insurance Co.
- Armco, Inc.
- Bankers Trust Corp.
- BHP Copper North America
- Coltec Industries, Inc.
- Commonwealth General Corp.
- Echlin, Inc.
- Enron Corp.
- Entex
- First Commercial Bank NA
- Hoechst Corp.
- Marquette Medical Systems
- Moorman Manufacturing Co.
- National City Bank
- Pacific Telesis Group
- Republic New York Corp.
- Rhone-Poulenc Rorer-U.S.
- Rhone-Poulenc, Inc.
- Sonat, Inc.
- Stockham Valves & Fittings, Inc.
- Stroh Brewery Co.
- Unum Corp.
- Vencor, Inc.
- Western Atlas, Inc.

Corporations That Support Preselected Organizations

In an effort to help researchers save valuable time and effort, *Corporate Giving Directory* now lists the corporations and foundations that support preselected organizations. Even though these corporations generally do not accept unsolicited proposals, they still have a full profile within the directory. The information that is found within each profile could help researchers decide to stop researching a particular corporation or to attempt a different approach.

- AEGON U.S.A. Inc./AEGON U.S.A. Charitable Foundation
- Alma Piston Co./Emmet and Frances Tracy Fund
- American General Finance/American General Finance Foundation
- APL Limited
- Arizona Public Service Co./ APS Foundation, Inc.
- Armstrong World Industries, Inc./ Armstrong Foundation
- Associated Food Stores/Associated Food Stores Charitable Foundation
- Autodesk Inc./Autodesk Foundation
- Baird & Co. (Robert W.)/ Baird & Co. Foundation (Robert W.)
- Barclays Capital
- Bassett Furniture Industries/ Bassett Furniture Industries Foundation
- Becton Dickinson & Co.
- Bernstein & Co., Inc. (Sanford C.)/ Bernstein & Co. Foundation, Inc. (Sanford C.)
- BFGoodrich Co./ Goodrich Foundation, Inc. (B.F.)
- Boler Co./ Boler Co. Foundation
- BP Amoco Corp./BP Amoco Foundation
- Bradford & Co. (J.C.)/ Bradford & Co. Foundation (J.C.)
- Burress (J.W.)/ Burress Foundation (J.W.)
- Business Improvement/ Schoeneckers Foundation
- Butler Capital Corp./ Butler Foundation
- Cantor, Fitzgerald Securities Corp./ Cantor, Fitzgerald Foundation
- Carter-Wallace, Inc./ Carter-Wallace Foundation
- Central Newspapers, Inc./ Central Newspapers Foundation
- Century 21/ Century 21 Associations Foundation
- CGU Insurance/ General Accident Charitable Trust
- Charter Manufacturing Co./ Charter Manufacturing Co. Foundation
- Circuit City Stores, Inc./ Circuit City Foundation
- Cowen (S.G.)/ Cowen Foundation
- CSR Rinker Materials Corp.
- Cummings Properties Management/ Cummings Properties Foundation
- Dial Corp./Viad Corp. Fund
- Domino's Pizza Inc.
- Erb Lumber Corp./Erb Foundation
- Ethyl Corp.
- Extendicare Health Services/ Extendicare Foundation
- Federal-Mogul Corp.
- Fisher Brothers Cleaning Services/ Fisher Brothers Foundation, Inc.
- Forbes Inc./ Forbes Foundation
- General Dynamics Corp.
- General Electric Co./GE Fund
- Globe Corp./ Globe Foundation
- Goldman Sachs Group/ Goldman Sachs Foundation
- Gosiger, Inc./ Gosiger Foundation
- Harnischfeger Industries/ Harnischfeger Industries Foundation
- Harris Corp./ Harris Foundation
- Heilig-Meyers Co./ Heilig-Meyers Foundation
- Hitachi America Limited/ Hitachi Foundation
- HON Industries Inc./ HON Industries Charitable Foundation
- Hubbard Broadcasting, Inc./Hubbard Foundation
- Inman Mills/ Inman-Riverdale Foundation
- International Flavors & Fragrances Inc./ IFF Foundation Inc.
- Jacobs Engineering Corp./ Jacobs Engineering Foundation
- Jacobson & Sons (Benjamin)/ Jacobson & Sons Foundation (Benjamin)
- Jones & Co. (Edward D.)/ Jones & Co. Foundation (Edward D.)
- Kennametal, Inc./ Kennametal Foundation
- Kirkland & Ellis/ Kirkland & Ellis Foundation
- Laclede Gas Co./ Laclede Gas Charitable Trust
- Ladish Co., Inc./ Ladish Co. Foundation
- Lancaster Lens, Inc./ Lancaster Lens Foundation
- LandAmerica Financial Services/ LandAmerica Foundation
- Leigh Fibers, Inc./ Orchard Foundation
- Lennox International, Inc./ Lennox Foundation
- Leviton Manufacturing Co. Inc./ Leviton Foundation New York
- MacMillan Bloedel Inc./ MacMillan Bloedel Foundation
- Mazda North America Operations/ Mazda Foundation (USA), Inc.
- Milliken & Co./Milliken Foundation
- MTD Products Inc./ Jochum-Moll Foundation (The)
- MTS Systems Corp.
- NASDAQ Stock Market/ NASDAQ Stock Market Educational Foundation
- Nestle U.S.A. Inc.
- Oklahoma Publishing Co./ Oklahoma Foundation (The)
- Old National Bank Evansville/ Old National Bank Charitable Trust
- Overseas Shipholding Group Inc./ OSG Foundation
- PACCAR Inc./ PACCAR Foundation
- Pacific Century Financial Corp./ Pacific Century Financial Corp. Foundation
- Park National Bank/ Park National Corp. Foundation
- Parker Hannifin Corp./ Parker Hannifin Foundation
- Pheonix Financial Group/Pheonix Foundation
- Premier Dental Products Co./ Charlestein Foundation (Julius & Ray)
- PriceWaterhouseCoopers/ PriceWaterhouseCoopers Foundation
- Progressive Corp.
- Putnam Investments/ Putnam Investors Fund

- Reinhart Industrial Foods/ Reinhart Family Foundation (D.B. and Marjorie)
- Revlon Inc./ Revlon Foundation Inc.
- Safeguard Securities/ Safeguard Securities Foundation
- Schloss & Co. (Marcus)/ Rexford Fund
- ServiceMaster Co./ ServiceMaster Foundation
- Shea Co. (John F.)/ Shea Co. Foundation (J.F.)
- Sierra Pacific Industries/ Sierra Pacific Foundation
- Simplot Co. (J.R.)/ Simplot Foundation (J.R.)
- SIT Investment Associates, Inc./ SIT Investment Associates Foundation
- Slant/Fin Corp./ Slant/Fin Foundation
- Standard Register Co./ Sherman-Standard Register Foundation
- Strear Farms Co./ Strear Family Foundation
- Stupp Brothers Bridge & Iron Co./ Stupp Brothers Bridge & Iron Co. Foundation
- Sunmark Capital Corp./ Sunmark Foundation
- Tamko Roofing Products/ Craig Foundation (E.L.)
- Teleflex Inc./ Teleflex Foundation
- Ticketmaster Corp./ Ticketmaster Foundation
- Titan Industrial Corp./ Titan Industrial Foundation
- Trace International Holdings, Inc./ Trace International Holdings, Inc. Foundation
- True Oil Co./True Foundation
- Trustmark Insurance Co./ Trustmark Foundation
- United Co./ United Coal Co. Charitable Foundation
- United Services Automobile Association/ USAA Foundation, A Charitable Trust
- Universal Foods Corp./ Universal Foods Foundation
- Van Leer Holding/ Van Leer U.S. Foundation
- Vesper Corp./ Vesper Foundation
- Wachtell, Lipton, Rosen & Katz/ Wachtell, Lipton, Rosen & Katz Foundation
- Webster Bank/Smith Foundation Inc. (Harold Webster)
- Whitman Corp./ Whitman Corp. Foundation
- Wilbur-Ellis Co. & Connell Brothers Co./ Wilbur Foundation (Brayton)
- Wolverine World Wide/ Wolverine World Wide Foundation
- Young & Rubicam/ Young & Rubicam Foundation
- Zilkha & Sons/ Zilkha Foundation, Inc.

XYZ Stores

1 ★ Number 35 of top 100 givers

2 Company Contact

Montgomery Burns
700 Haywood Rd.
Greenville, SC 29607
Phone: (555) 297-3200
Web: www.xyz.com

3 Company Description

Revenue: US$4,000,000,000 (1999)
Employees: 5,000 (1999)
Fortune Rank: 200, per FORTUNE Magazine's list of 500 Largest U.S. Corporations (1999).
SIC(s): 5555 Department stores

4 Operating Locations

CA: XYZ Limited, Los Angeles, San Diego; CT: XYZ Limited, New Haven; ME: XYZ Limited, Bangor; Australia: XYZ Limited, Sydney
Nonmonetary Support
Value: $9,000,000 (1998); $4,000,000 (1997)
Type: Donated Products
Note: Product donations are directed primarily to organizations that support overseas educational programs.

5 Nonmonetary Support

Value: $9,000,000 (1998); $4,000,000 (1997)
Type: Donated Products
Note: Product donations are directed primarily to organizations that support overseas educational programs.

6 Corporate Sponsorship

Value: $5,000 (1998); $4,000 (1997)
Type: Arts & cultural events; Music & entertainment events

XYZ Foundation

7 Giving Contact

Emmit Roman, Executive Director
555 Haywood Rd., Ste. 200
Greenville, SC 29607
Phone: (555) 297-3203
Email: eroman@xyz.com

8 Foundation Description

Founded: 1944
EIN: 576020261
Organization Type: Corporate Foundation
Giving Locations: headquarters and operating communities.
Grant Types: General Support.
Note: Employee matching gift ratio: 2 to 1 for contributions over $25 to colleges and universities, up to $2,000 annually; 1 to 1 for gifts to hospitals and cultural institutions, up to $500 annually.

9 Giving Philosophy

'The XYZ Foundation is dedicated to establishing educational programs through cash grants. Recipients are generally U.S.-based and focus on the areas of art, education, and human services.'
1999 Fact Sheet

10 Financial Summary

Total Giving: $591,800 (1998); $479,500 (1997); $351,750 (1996).
Giving Analysis: Giving for 1998 includes: foundation ($554,300); foundation grants to United Way ($37,500).
Assets: $13,426,773 (1998); $12,777,075 (1997); $9,640,239 (1996).
Gifts Received: $242,355 (1998); $224,794 (1997); $99,749 (1996). Note: Contributions are received from various XYZ Stores.

11 Typical Recipient:

Arts & Humanities: Arts Centers, Museums/ Galleries, Music, Performing Arts
Civic & Public Affairs: African American Affairs, Chambers of Commerce, Civic & Public Affairs-General, Parades/Festivals
Education: Arts/Humanities Education, Colleges & Universities, Medical Education, Religious Education
Environment: Resource Conservation
Health: Cancer, Clinics/Medical Centers, Emergency/Ambulance Services, Health Organizations, Hospitals, Medical Research, Single-Disease Health Associations
Religion: Churches, Religious Organizations, Religious Welfare, Seminaries
Social Services: Community Service Organizations, Food/Clothing Distribution, Homes, United Funds/United Ways, YMCA/YWCA/YMHA/ YWHA, Youth Organizations

12 Contributions Analysis

Giving Priorities: The arts, education, social services, and the environment.
Arts & Humanities: 29%. Funds museums, performing arts, and historical societies.
Civic & Public Affairs: 1%.
Education: 20%. Supports private pre-college and higher education.
Environment: 17%. Funds conservation efforts.
Health: 7%. Supports hospitals, clinics, and cancer research.
Religion: 7%. Christian groups, churches, and welfare organizations are supported.
Social Services: 19%. Funds United Way, youth groups, and social services.

13 Application Procedures

Initial Contact: Send a brief letter on organization's letterhead describing program.
Application Requirements: Send copy of most recent audited financial statement and proof of tax-exempt status.
Deadlines: May 1; November 1.
Evaluative Criteria: Priority is given to organizations serving XYZ employees.
Decision Notification: Final decisions are usually made within eight to ten weeks of receipt.

14 Restrictions

Does not award grants to individuals, political or lobbying groups, or religious organizations for sectarian purposes.

15 Additional Information

XYZ Stores acquired ACME Products in 1999.
Publications: Annual Report; Guidelines

16 Corporate Officials

John C. Belk: chairman B Charlotte, NC 1920. ED Davidson College (1943). PRIM CORP EMPL chairman: Belk Stores Services Inc. CORP AFFIL director: Lowes Home Centers Inc.; chairman: Parks-Belk Co. Northern Virginia; vice president: Leggett Realty South Boston Virginia; director: Lowes Companies; chairman: Charlotte Belk Inc.; director: Coca-Cola Bottling Co. Consolidated; director: Brothers Investment Co.; director: Chaparral Steel Co.
Montgomery Burns: pres B Springfield, IL 1900. ED Henderson Univ (1922). PRIM CORP EMPL pres: XYZ Stores Services Inc. CORP AFFIL director: Lowes Home Centers Inc.; vice president: Parks-Belk Co. Northern Virginia

SAMPLE ENTRY

Foundation Officials

John A. Kuhne: director
Emmit Roman: executive director
Kate M. Simpson: director

17 Grants Analysis

Disclosure Period: calendar year ending 1998
Total Grants: $554,300*
Number of Grants: 117
Average Grant: $4,738
Highest Grant: $100,000
Typical Range: $200 to $20,000
***Note:** Giving excludes United Way.

18 Recent Grants

NOTE: Grants derived from a 1999 Form 990.

Arts & Humanities

5,000	Greenville Symphony Orchestra, Greenville, SC

Civic & Public Affairs

7,500	Greenville Urban League, Greenville, SC

Education

50,000	Converse College, Spartanburg, SC
25,000	Converse College, Spartanburg, SC
15,000	University of South Carolina Lancaster, Lancaster, SC
10,000	Furman University, Greenville, SC
10,000	University of South Carolina Lancaster, Lancaster, SC
6,500	Brevard College, Owensboro, KY
6,000	Anderson College, Anderson, SC

Environment

10,000	Highlands Land Trust

Health

10,000	Greenville Free Medical Clinic, Greenville, SC
10,000	Presbyterian Hospital, Charlotte, NC

Religion

15,000	Fourth Presbyterian Church

Social Services

5,000	Pickens County YMCA, Easley, SC

User's Guide

Entries are arranged in alphabetical order by the name of the company that sponsors the contributions program. A company may give directly, through a foundation, or both; if no foundation exists, the company gives directly.

Sample Entry

The abbreviated sample entry shown at left illustrates the standard elements of information typically provided in a profile. Numbered items in the sample are explained in the corresponding numbered paragraphs below.

1 *Star Ratings System*

The top 100 companies (ranked according to the most recent overall giving information in the Taft database at the time of production) have a black star below the company name with the corresponding number rank.

2 *Company Contact*

The name of the person responsible for answering inquiries and receiving grant applications for corporate direct giving programs, as well as the individual's title, organization name, mailing address, telephone number, and fax number, when available, as reported by the company. If there is more than one contact, the name of that person is listed in a note immediately after the telephone number or fax number. The note also contains the corporation's World Wide Web or e-mail address when available.

3 *Company Description*

Includes financial and other statistical information as reported in the April 17, 2000 issue of *Fortune* magazine (Time, Inc., New York, NY), and several corporate databases available on-line.

If the sponsoring company is a subsidiary of or affiliated with another company, this information is listed under "Parent Company." Revenue/Sales, profits, number of employees, Fortune rank, and SIC information as reported by the company or major business publications, give a capsule look at the financial health and business interests of the profiled company. Corporate giving levels are closely tied to a company's sales and profits: the more profitable a company, the greater its philanthropic potential. Many companies base their giving on a percentage of pretax profits, typically 0.5% to 2.5%, but occasionally as high as 5%. Fortune rank is a classic indicator of how a company compares to its peers. The number of employees also provides a quick measure of a company's size, and corporate programs are usually interested in seeing charitable contributions affect the largest number of corporate employees. Fortune rank, as well as company sales, profits, and number of employees are given for 1999, where available. SIC information helps identify corporations with a special interest in a particular activity due to the nature of their business.

4 *Operating Locations*

Company business typically revolves around corporate headquarters and operating locations, and charitable giving information reflects this orientation. Headquarters information is indexed in the index to "Companies by Headquarters State." Operating locations are indexed in the "Companies by Operating Location" index. A company's field of business or marketing orientation often influences its charitable objectives.

5 *Nonmonetary Support*

Lists seven types of nonmonetary support offered: cause-related marketing & promotion, donated equipment, donated products, in-kind services, loaned employees, loaned executives, and workplace solicitation. Also includes the value of such support and whom to contact, if available. This information is indexed in the "Companies by Nonmonetary Support Type" index.

6 *Corporate Sponsorship*

Lists information on the types of events or causes sponsored, as estimated budget for sponsorship, and the name and title of the person to contact for more information.

7 *Giving Contact*

The name of the person responsible for answering inquiries and receiving grant applications for the corporate foundation, as well as the individual's title, organization name, mailing address, telephone number, and fax number, when available, as reported by the company. If there is more than one contact, the name of that person is listed in a note immediately after the telephone number or fax number. The note also contains the corporation's World Wide Web or e-mail address when available.

8 *Foundation Description*

Listed here is general information about the foundation, such as year **Founded**, its **Employer Identification Number (EIN)**, the unique nine digit number assigned to a philanthropic institution by the Internal Revenue Service, **Organization Type**, **Giving Locations**, **Former Names** and **Grant Types**. Foundations are grouped into four general categories (or **Organization Type**): **Family, General Purpose, Institutional,** or **Special Purpose**. **GrantTypes** lists the financial support typically offered by the foundation using nineteen standard categories ranging from award to seed money. Companies that consider requests for specific types of funding are indexed in the index to "Companies by Grant Type." **Giving Locations**

indicates the geographic preference for disbursing funds as reported by the foundation or based on analysis of grants lists. Users should review the index to "Companies by Headquarters" and the index to "Companies by Location of Grant Recipient" to gain a greater understanding of a foundation's geographic giving interests. The **Note** section offers any other relevant information pertaining to Grant Types or employee matching gift programs.

9 *Giving Philosophy*

Provides a quotation from the corporation or foundation that best represents the rationale used by corporate leadership to justify or evaluate corporate contributions.

10 *Financial Summary*

Lists giving figures for the three most recent years available, as reported by the company. Also includes information on the scope of the program, including whether the company gives directly, through a foundation, or both. If the company has a foundation, this section lists foundation assets and any gifts the foundation received for the three most recent years available. Use this information to qualify a corporation according to its giving potential and to spot trends in its overall corporate giving.

11 *Typical Recipients*

Lists the organizations and issues that a corporation has supported in recent years, using 215 standard recipient categories under nine broad categories: Arts & Humanities, Civic & Public Affairs, Education, Environment, Health, International, Religion, Science, and Social Services. This section is designed to catalog the kinds of activities supported, rather than indicate priority. The "Companies by Recipient Type" index provides a comprehensive list of all companies identified as supporting a particular type of organization. A complete list of the 215 recipient organization types, arranged under the 9 major categories, is available starting on page xix; a complete listing of the 215 recipient types, arranged in alphabetical order and cross-referenced to major categories, starts on page xxi.

12 *Contributions Analysis*

Describes philanthropic priorities as reported by the sponsoring company; these priorities are based on an analysis of giving patterns during the most recent period for which the information was available. Giving priorities are usually described in terms of percentage ranges that indicate continuing patterns of philanthropic activity. Percentages may not total 100% due to rounding of figures and use of ranges. This section also describes program initiatives and special areas of focus within a general category of giving, as well as providing details on company-sponsored employee volunteer programs.

13 *Application Procedures*

Initial Contact, **Application Requirements**, and **Deadlines** outline the preferred methods of contacting the company, meeting requirements for proposals, and sending requests within specific time frames, respectively. Deadlines are indexed in the "Companies by Application Deadline" index. **Evaluative Criteria** and **Decision Notification** describe the decision-making process companies follow when reviewing requests, including procedures, the criteria upon which requests are evaluated, and when decisions are made.

14 *Restrictions*

A brief description of restrictions on eligibility, or types of programs, campaigns, or organizations that are not funded.

15 *Additional Information*

Reports additional procedures, significant changes in the company's status, or policies that could influence solicitation efforts. The **Publications** section lists any printed material provided by the foundation or giving program.

16 *Corporate Officials/Foundation Officials*

Provides biographical information on principal corporate officers and contributions program officers, directors, or trustees. When available, includes year and place of birth, education (school, program, degree, and year of graduation), current employment, corporate affiliations, nonprofit affiliations, and club affiliations. The biographical information is indexed six ways: by name, place of birth, alma mater, corporate affiliation, nonprofit affiliation, and club affiliation. This background biographical information helps nonprofits discover connections to development teams and boards of directors, as well as uncover opportunities to cultivate relationships with these decision makers.

17 *Grants Analysis*

An analytical section which calculates **Total Grants**, **Number of Grants, Average Grant, Highest Grant**, and **Typical Range**. The **Disclosure Period** indicates the year (actual or fiscal) from which the analytical information was derived. The **Note** contains information on large grants that may skew the average, or any other relevant information pertaining to the grants analysis.

18 *Recent Grants*

When available, provides a listing of the top 50 recently awarded grants. Grants are listed in descending order based on dollar amount within the general categories of Arts & Humanities, Civic & Public Affairs, Education, Environment, Health, International, Religion, Science, and Social Services. The **Note** at the top of this section indicates the year of the Recent Grants listings.

List of Abbreviations

&	And
AA	Associate of Arts
AB	Arts, Bachelor of
acct	accountant
admin	administration, administrative, administrator
adv	advisor, advisory
AFB	Air Force Base
Aff	Affairs
affil	affiliation
AG	Aktiengesellschaft
Am	America, American
AM	Arts, Master of
Apt	Apartment
APO	Army Post Office
archt	architect
Assn	Association
Assoc(s)	Associate(s), Associated
asst	assistant
atty	attorney
Ave	Avenue
b	born
BA	Bachelor of Arts
BBA	Bachelor of Business Administration
bd	board
BD	Bachelor of Divinity
BE	Bachelor of Engineering
BFT	Bachelor of Foreign Trade
Bldg	Building
Blvd	Boulevard
Bros	Brothers
BS	Bachelor of Science
BSChE	Bachelor of Science in Chemical Engineering
BSME	Bachelor of Science in Mechanical Engineering
Bur	Bureau
Bus	Business
c/o	care of
CC	Country Club
ceo	chief executive officer
cfo	chief financial officer
Chap	Chapter
Chem	Chemical, Chemist, Chemistry
chmn	chairman
chp	chairperson
chwm	chairwoman
Co	Company
Coll	College
comm	committee
commn	commission
commnr	commissioner
Commun	Communication(s), Community
comptr	comptroller
Conf	Conference
Confed	Confederation
Cong	Congress
Consult	Consultant, Consulting
contr	controller
coo	chief operating officer
Coop	Cooperating, Cooperative, Cooperation
Corp	Corporate, Corporation
Counc	Council
couns	counsel, counseling, counselor
CPA	Certified Public Accountant
Ct	Court
Ctr	Center, Centre
curr	current
cust	customer
DB	Divinity, Bachelor of
del	delegate
Dem	Democrat
dep	deputy
Dept	Department
Devel	Development
dir	director
Distr	Distributor, Distribution, Distributing
Div	Division
don	donor
Dr	Doctor
Dr	Drive
E	East
Econ	Economic, Economics
Ed	Education, Educational, Educated
EIN	Employer Identification Number
empl	employment
Engg	Engineering
engr	engineer
exec	executive
Expy	Expressway
f/b/o	for the benefit of
Fdn	Foundation
fdr	founder
Fed	Federal, Federation, Federated
Fin	Finance, Financial
Fl	Floor
FPO	Fleet Post Office
Ft	Fort
Fwy	Freeway
GC	Golf Club
gen	general
gov	governing, governor
govt	government
grad	graduate
hon	honorable, honorary
Hosp	Hospital
Hwy	Highway
Inc	Incorporated
Indus	Industrial, Industries, Industry
Ins	Insurance
Inst	Institute, Institution
Intl	International
JD	Juris Doctor
Jr	Junior
Legis	Legislation, Legislative, Legislator
LLB	Laws, Bachelor of
LLD	Laws, Doctor of
Ln	Lane
LP	Limited Partnership
Ltd	Limited
MA	Master of Arts
MBA	Master of Business Administration
Med	Medical
mem	member
Meml	Memorial
Metro	Metropolitan
Mfg	Manufacturing
Mfr	Manufacturer
Mgmt	Management
mgr	manager
misc	miscellaneous
Mktg	Marketing
Mng	Managing
MS	Master of Science
Mt	Mount
Mus	Museum
N	North
NAACP	National Association for the Advancement of ColoredPeople
N. Ap.	Not Applicable
N. Av.	Not Available
Natl	National
NE	North East
No	Number
nonpr	nonprofit
NW	North West
off	office, officer
oper	operating, operations
Org	Organization
pers	personnel
PhB	Philosophy, Bachelor of

PhD	Philosophy, Doctor of
phil	philanthropic
Pk	Park
Pke	Pike
Pkwy	Parkway
Pl	Place
Plz	Plaza
PO	Post Office
Polytech	Polytechnic, Polytechnical
pres	president
prin	principal
prof	professor
Prov	Province, Provincial
Ptnr	Partner
pub(s)	publication(s)
pub	public
publ(s)	published, publisher, publishing
Pvt	Private
Rd	Road
RD	Rural Delivery
rehab	rehabilitation
rel	religious, religion
rels	relations
rep	representative
Repbl	Republican
Res	Research, Researcher
ret	retired
RFD	Rural Free Delivery
Rm	Room
RR	railroad
RR	Rural Route
Rte	Route
RY	Railway
S	South
SB	Science, Bachelor of
Sch	School
SE	South East
secy	secretary
sen	senator
SM	Science, Master of
Soc	Society
Sq	Square
Sr	Senior
SR	Star/State Route
St	Saint, State, Street
Sta	Station
Ste	Sainte, Suite
Sub(s)	Subsidiary(ies)
supt	superintendent
supvr	supervisor
Svc(s)	Service(s)
SW	South West
Sys	System(s)
Tech	Technological, Technical, Technology
Tel & Tel	Telephone and Telegraph
Terr	Terrace
Tpke	Turnpike
treas	treasurer
trust	trustee
Un	United
Univ	University
US	United States
u/w/o	under the will of
vchmn	vice chairman
vp	vice president
W	West
YC	Yacht Club
YMCA	Young Men's Christian Association
YMHA	Young Men's Hebrew Association
YWCA	Young Women's Christian Association
YWHA	Young Women's Hebrew Association

Nonprofit Recipient Categories

Categories	Recipient Organization Types
Arts & Humanities	Art History, Arts Appreciation, Arts Associations & Councils, Arts Centers, Arts Festivals, Arts Funds, Arts Institutes, Arts Outreach, Ballet, Community Arts, Dance, Ethnic & Folk Art, Film & Video, Historic Preservation, History & Archeology, Libraries, Literary Arts, Museums/Galleries, Music, Opera, Performing Arts, Public Broadcasting, Theater, Visual Arts
Civic & Public Affairs	African American Affairs, Asian American Affairs, Botanical Gardens/Parks, Business/Free Enterprise, Chambers of Commerce, Civil Rights, Clubs, Community Foundations, Economic Development, Economic Policy, Employment/Job Training, Ethnic Organizations, First Amendment Issues, Gay/Lesbian Issues, Hispanic Affairs, Housing, Inner-City Development, Law & Justice, Legal Aid, Minority Business, Municipalities/Towns, Native American Affairs, Nonprofit Management, Parades/Festivals, Philanthropic Organizations, Professional/Trade Associations, Public Policy, Rural Affairs, Safety, Urban/Community Affairs, Women's Affairs, Zoos/Aquariums
Education	Afterschool Enrichment Programs, Agricultural Education, Arts/Humanities Education, Business Education, Business-School Partnerships, Colleges & Universities, Community/Junior Colleges, Continuing Education, Economic Education, Education Associations, Education Funds, Education Reform, Elementary Education (private), Elementary Education (public), Engineering Education, Environmental Education, Faculty Development, Gifted & Talented Programs, Health & Physical Education, International Exchange, International Studies, Journalism/Media Education, Leadership Training, Legal Education, Literacy, Medical Education, Minority Education, Preschool Education, Private Education (precollege), Public Education (precollege), Religious Education, School Volunteerism, Science/Mathematics Education, Secondary Education (private), Secondary Education (public), Social Sciences Education, Special Education, Student Aid, Vocational/Technical Education
Environment	Air/Water Quality, Energy, Forestry, Protection, Research, Resource Conservation, Sanitary Systems, Watershed, Wildlife Protection
Health	Adolescent Health Issues, AIDS/HIV, Alzheimer's Disease, Arthritis, Cancer, Children's Health/Hospitals, Clinics/Medical Centers, Diabetes, Emergency/Ambulance Services, Eyes/Blindness, Geriatric Health, Health Funds, Health Organizations, Health Policy/Cost Containment, Heart, Home-Care Services, Hospices, Hospitals, Hospitals (university affiliated), Kidney, Long-Term Care, Medical Rehabilitation, Medical Research, Medical Training, Mental Health, Multiple Sclerosis, Nursing Services, Nutrition, Outpatient Health Care, Prenatal Health Issues, Preventive Medicine/Wellness Organizations, Public Health, Research/Studies Institutes, Respiratory, Single-Disease Health Associations, Speech & Hearing, Transplant Networks/Donor Banks, Trauma Treatment
International	Foreign Arts Organizations, Foreign Education Institutions, Health Care/Hospitals, Human Rights, International Affairs, International Development, International Environmental Issues, International Law, International Organizations, International Peace & Security Issues, International Relations, International Relief Efforts, Missionary/Religious Activities, Trade
Religion	Bible Study/Translation, Churches, Dioceses, Jewish Causes, Ministries, Missionary Activities (domestic), Religious Organizations, Religious Welfare, Seminaries, Social/Policy Issues, Synagogues/Temples
Science	Observatories/planetariums, science exhibits/fairs, scientific institutes, scientific organizations
Social Services	Animal Protection, At-Risk Youth, Big Brother/Big Sister, Camps, Child Abuse, Child Welfare, Community Centers, Community Service Organizations, Counseling, Crime Prevention, Day Care, Delinquency/Criminal Rehabilitation, Domestic Violence, Emergency Relief, Family Planning, Family Services, Food & Clothing Distribution, Homes, People With Disabilities, Recreation & Athletics, Refugee Assistance, Scouts, Senior Services, Sexual Abuse, Shelters/Homeless, Special Olympics, Substance Abuse, United Funds/United Way, Veterans, Volunteer Services, YMCA/YMHA/YWCA/YWHA, Youth Organizations

Recipient Organization Types

How to Use the Indexes: Funder Indexes

There are eight indexes to corporations/foundations in Taft's *Corporate Giving Directory*. These indexes can be used to target specific philanthropic institutions, such as those with headquarters and charitable interests in certain regions of the country, or those that support specific nonprofit fields of activity or provide certain types of grants. The following example illustrates how to use the indexes to narrow your research: A prospect researcher needs a contribution to support a scholarship fund at a college in California.

The researcher can use the **Index to Companies by Headquarters State** or the **Index to Companies by Location of Grant Recipient** to locate a philanthropic organization that funds projects in California. The researcher then cross-checks the California corporations with the **Index to Companies by Grant Type** to find which ones contribute to scholarship funds. Next, the researcher cross-references those California companies that have supported scholarship funds with the **Index to Companies by Recipient Type** for organizations that have a history of giving to colleges and universities. Finally, the researcher can check the new **Index to Companies by Application Deadline** to see which organizations meet his/her campaign deadline needs.

In the sample indexes provided, one prospective funding possibility is the Chevron Corporation located in San Francisco. The researcher can now contact the foundation and initiate the application process; however, he or she can strengthen the funding proposal by discovering links, if there are any, between their organization and the Chevron Corporation by using the six Biography Indexes included in the *Corporate Giving Directory* (please see the next section for more information on these indexes). The eight corporate/foundation indexes are:

- **Index to Companies by Headquarters State:** Arranges companies by the state in which their main office is located.
- **Index to Companies by Operating Locations:** Lists corporations alphabetically within the states of their major operating locations.
- **Index to Companies by Location of Grant Recipient:** Arranges companies by the states in which they have allocated their funds, both within the United States and abroad (generated by the location of grants made by the corporation/foundation).
- **Index to Companies by Grant Type:** Lists corporations by the types of funding they generally prefer or are required by their charters to endorse.
- **Index to Companies by Nonmonetary Support Type:** Classifies companies by the type of non-financial support they generally fund.
- **Index to Companies by Recipient Type:** Arranges companies by the types of nonprofit programs and organizations they currently support or have a history of funding.
- **Index to Companies by Application Deadline:** Arranged by month, this index alphabetically lists the companies according to their application deadlines.
- **Master Index to Corporations/Foundations:** Alphabetically arranges all corporations/foundations profiled in the directory with page numbers.

Companies by Headquarters State

California

Caesar's World, Inc.
California Federal Bank
Chevron Corporation
Clorox Co.
Consolidated Freightways, Inc.
Copley Press, Inc.
Deutsch Co.
Disney Co. (Walt)
EMI Records Group North America
Esprit Holdings
Farmer's Group, Inc.

Companies by Location of Grant Recipient

California

Los Angeles
CertainTeed Corp.
Cessna Aircraft Company (The)
Chase Manhattan Bank, NA
Chevron Corporation
Chicago Title & Trust Co.
Chicago Tribune Co.
Chrysler Corp.
CIGNA Corporation
Circuit City Stores, Inc.
Citicorp

Companies by Grant Type

Scholarship

Chesapeake Corp.
Chevron Corporation
Chubb Corp. (The)
CIGNA Corporation
Cincinnati Milacron, Inc.
CINergy
Circuit City Stores, Inc.
CIT Group Holdings, Inc. (The)
Cleveland-Cliffs, Inc.

Companies by Recipient Type

Education

COLLEGES & UNIVERSITIES
Chesapeake Corp.
Chesebrough-Pond's USA Co.
Chevron Corporation
Chicago Title and Trust Co.
Chicago Tribune Co.
Chrysler Corp.
Chubb Corp. (The)
Church & Dwight Co., Inc.
CIBA-GEIGY Corp.
CIBA-GEIGY Corp Pharmaceuticals Division
CIGNA Corporation
Cincinnati Bell Inc.
Cincinnati Milacron, Inc.

Companies by Application Deadline

January

Bausch & Lomb
Boatmen's Bancshares, Inc.

How to Use the Indexes: Biography Indexes

There are six biographical indexes in Taft's *Corporate Giving Directory*. These indexes list corporate/foundation executives who can influence grant decisions. In addition to an alphabetical listing of names, the indexes identify alma maters, important affiliations, and places of birth.

Researchers can use this critical information to identify common areas of interest between the company decision makers and advocates for the proposed project at the nonprofit – for example, a shared membership in another nonprofit organization. The researcher can then use these links to establish a network between his or her organization and one or more corporations or corporate foundations. The following example illustrates how to use the indexes to narrow your research.

A prospect researcher needs a contribution to support a scholarship fund at a college in California. By using the various indexes to corporation/foundation, the researcher identifies the Chevron Corporation as a prospective funding possibility. The researcher can then strengthen the funding proposal by discovering if there are any links between his or her organization and the company.

Kenneth Tindall Derr, chairman, CEO, and director of the Chevron Corp., belongs to several nonprofit organizations including the California Business Roundtable. The researcher discovers a link between the corporation and his or her nonprofit: a nonprofit board member or a project advocate also belongs to the California Business Roundtable. With knowledge of this shared interest, the board member can approach the corporation's chairman on a first-hand basis.

Any of the biographical indexes can be used to uncover common interests between the board members and advocates of the nonprofit and the decision-makers at a philanthropy. For example, a nonprofit organization located in Montana needs funding for a proposed project. There are a limited number of corporate grant-makers that give to Montana-based nonprofit projects and virtually no large corporations located in the state.

The researcher can use the indexes to reveal an interest for the welfare of Montana and its citizens. Using the Index to Officers and Directors by Alma Mater, the researcher discovers that Douglas Beighle, senior vice president for Boeing, graduated from the University of Montana.

Referring back to Mr. Beighle's biography in the company's profile, the researcher further discovers that he also serves as a trustee of the University of Montana Foundation and is a member of the Montana Bar Association. In addition, the profile reveals that the company has recently supported a Montana-based organization even though it primarily gives to organizations in Philadelphia, PA; Wichita, KS; and Seattle, WA.

Officers and Directors by Nonprofit Affiliation

CA Bankers Assn

Johnson, Lloyd Peter, chmn, ceo, dir: Norwest Corp.; dir: Norwest Foundation
Mullane, Donald A., exec vp: BankAmerica Corp.

CA Bar Assn

Bryson, John E. chmn, ceo: Southern California Edison Co.
Clarke, Richard A., chmn, ceo, dir: Pacific Gas & Electric Co.
Farman, Richard Donald, chmn, ceo, dir: Southern California Gas Co.

CA Business Roundtable

Clarke, Richard A., chmn, deo, dir: Pacific Gas & Electric Co.
Derr, Kenneth Tindall, chmn, ceo: Chevron Corp

Officers and Directors by Alma Mater

Univ MS

Barnett, Robert Glenn, secy: Deposit Guaranty Foundation
Hattox, Brock Alan, sr vp, cfo: McDermott Inc
Lackey, S. Allen, dir: Shell Oil Co. Foundation

Univ MT

Beighle, Douglas Paul, sr vp: Boeing Co. (The)
Cole, Perry J., treas: MPCo/Entech Foundation
Dickey, Boh A., exec vp, cfo, dir: SAFECO Corp.

- The six biographical indexes are:
- **Index to Officers and Directors by Name:** Arranges officers, trustees, directors, managers, staff, and contact people in alphabetical order with the name of the corporations.
- **Index to Officers and Directors by Place of Birth:** Lists individuals by the state or country in which they were born.
- **Index to Officers and Directors by Alma Mater:** Lists individuals by the colleges or universities that they attended or received a degree.
- **Index to Officers and Directors by Corporate Affiliation:** Lists individuals by corporations to which they belong.
- **Index to Officers and Directors by Nonprofit Affiliation:** Lists individuals by nonprofit organizations to which they belong.
- **Index to Officers and Directors by Club Affiliation:** Lists individuals by clubs to which they belong.

TYPICAL RECIPIENTS DEFINITIONS

ARTS & HUMANITIES: direct aid to support or promote arts organizations, facilities, or performances

Art History: organizations or programs promoting the study of art history

- Archives of American Art of the Smithsonian Institution, Washington, DC
- Arizona State University College of Fine Arts, Tempe, AZ - in support of - The Historical Organ in America Symposium -

Arts Appreciation: organizations or programs promoting recognition of artistic and cultural values

- Friends of Humanities, New York, NY

Arts Associations & Councils: advocacy or membership organizations dealing with the arts; includes national, state, and regional councils, commissions, and organizations

- Arts Council of Greater Chicago, Chicago, IL
- Atlanta Arts Alliance, Atlanta, GA
- Pittsburgh Cultural Trust, Pittsburgh, PA

Arts Centers: facilities where a variety of arts programs are staged

- Midland Center for the Arts, Midland, MI
- Salina Art Center, Salina, KS
- Garde Art Center, New Haven, CT

Arts Festivals: general cultural celebrations and festivals

- Peter Britt Gardens Music and Arts Festival Association, Medford, OR
- Columbia Festival of the Arts, Columbia, MD

Arts Funds: organizations whose primary purpose is to raise money and distribute it to more than one arts group

- United Performing Arts Fund, Milwaukee, WI
- Business Fund for the Arts, Springfield, MA

Arts Institutes: organizations or institutions whose purpose is to offer general artistic training and various arts programs (See also **Arts/Humanities Education**)

- Minneapolis Institute of Arts, Minneapolis, MN
- Art Institute of Chicago, Chicago, IL

Arts Outreach: organizations or programs promoting exposure to the arts for underserved populations including children, the aged, the disabled, the disadvantaged, and the hospitalized

- Hospital Audiences, New York, NY
- Young Audiences of Houston, Houston, TX

Ballet: organizations and groups focused on ballet

- American Ballet Theatre, New York, NY
- Ballet Oklahoma, Oklahoma City, OK - funds for a touring Nutcracker
- Carlisle Project, Carlisle, PA - for an artistic affiliation with the Pittsburgh Ballet Theatre

Community Arts: arts groups or organizations specifically concerned with community arts activities

- Association of Community Arts Council of Kansas, Salina, KS
- Central Philadelphia Development Corporation, Philadelphia, PA - Avenue of the Arts corridor project

Dance: organizations performing or promoting dance, excluding ballet

- Alvin Ailey American Dance Theater, New York, NY
- Dance Umbrella, Boston, MA
- National Dance Institute, New York, NY

Ethnic & Folk Art: arts groups serving or comprising of members of a particular ethnic group or folk art

- American Folklore Society, Arlington, VA
- Museum of African American Life and Culture, Dallas, TX
- Tambouritzans Eastern European Dance Troupe, Cleveland, OH

Film & Video: groups concerned with film or video as media

- America Film Institute, Washington, DC
- West Virginia Film History Project, Charleston, WV
- Film Society of Lincoln Center, New York, NY

General: arts organizations or programs that do not fall into other categories

- Muse Film and Television, New York, NY
- US Department of State Fine Arts, Washington, DC

Historic Preservation: organizations concerned with the preservation of historical buildings, landmarks, and/or artifacts

- Central Arizona Land Trust, Prescott, AZ - toward the purchase/preservation of landmarks
- Plimoth Plantation, Plymouth, MA
- Preservation Society of Newport County, Newport, RI

History & Archeology: organizations concerned with the study of history and/or archeology, including local historical societies and professional organizations

- Castleton Historical Society, Castleton, VT
- Historical Society of Western Pennsylvania, Pittsburgh, PA

Libraries: institutions housing collections of books, organizations and associations concerned with libraries, and the establishment of libraries at various types of organizations

- Extra Mile Education Foundation, Pittsburgh, PA - library facilities
- New York Public Library, New York, NY

Literary Arts: funding, advancement, publication, and appreciation of literature and writing

- Poetry in the Streets, New York, NY
- Writers Guild of Los Angeles, Los Angeles, CA

Museums & Galleries: places where art objects are collected and displayed

- Metropolitan Museum of Art, New York, NY
- North Carolina Museum of History, Charlotte, NC

Music: groups concerned with the promotion, appreciation, or performance of music

- Aspen Music Festival, Aspen, CO
- Pacific Symphony Orchestra, Irvine, CA

Opera: organizations dealing specifically with opera

- Lyric Opera of Houston, Houston, TX
- Metropolitan Opera Centennial Fund, New York, NY

Performing Arts: centers, organizations, and groups concerned with general staged arts programs

- John F. Kennedy Center for the Performing Arts, Washington, DC
- Big Apple Circus, New York, NY

Public Broadcasting: publicly supported television and radio

- National Public Radio, Washington, DC
- Smoky Hill Public Television Corporation, KOOD 9, Bunker Hill, KS

Theater: buildings or companies concerned with stage productions

- Guthrie Theater, Minneapolis, MN
- Kentucky Shakespeare Festival, Louisville, KY

Visual Arts: organizations and programs concerned with shows, exhibits, artists, and/or the production of paintings, sculptures, and photographs

- Center for Visual Arts, New York, NY
- Hirschorn Sculpture Garden, Washington, DC - to exhibit the touring Rodin collection

CIVIC & PUBLIC AFFAIRS: support of issues and activities related to the community at the national, regional, and local levels; recipients generally are not social service-oriented; rather, they are concerned with promoting the public good as it applies to policies and programs

African American Affairs: organizations and groups specifically concerned with African American social and political issues

- NAACP Legal Defense and Education Fund, New York, NY - support of fair housing work
- California Commission on African American Males, San Francisco, CA

Asian American Affairs: organizations and groups concerned with Asian American social and political issues

- Cambodian Association of Greater Philadelphia, Philadelphia, PA - to support the mentor/tutorial program
- Committee Against Anti-Asian Violence, New York, NY

Botanical Gardens/Parks: organizations that support community parks as well as institutional gardens

- Central Park Conservancy, New York, NY

- Friends of the Topiary Park, Columbus, OH - topiary garden

Business & Free Enterprise: organizations promoting advancement and understanding of the free-market system or business associations

- Conference Board, New York, NY
- National Alliance of Business, New York, NY
- Southern California Entrepreneurship Academy, Los Angeles, CA

Chambers of Commerce: specific chambers of commerce for civic support grants; special programs that fall outside the civic area are coded within their area (e.g., a chamber-sponsored scholarship program would be found under **Student Aid**)

- Angelina Chamber of Commerce Foundation, Lufkin, TX - purchase land
- South Orange County Chamber of Commerce, Irvine, CA

Civil Rights: organizations promoting equal rights and civil liberties

- American Civil Liberties Union Foundation, New York, NY
- Center for Constitutional Rights, New York, NY - Mississippi voting rights project
- Center for Individual Rights, Washington, DC

Clubs: general civic organizations active in the community

- Junior League of Dallas, Dallas, TX
- Kiwanis Foundation of South Bend, South Bend, IN
- Memphis Rotary Foundation, Memphis, TN

Community Foundations: publicly sponsored organizations that make grants in geographically restricted areas for social, educational, religious or other charitable purposes

- Community Foundation of Western Massachusetts, Springfield, MA
- Limestone Area Community Foundation, Athens, AL

Economic Development: groups of projects designed to encourage/enhance economic growth in a community, includes organizations meeting multiple community development needs

- Borough of Bristol, Bristol, PA - improvements to Riverfront Park Wharf
- Downtown Ft. Worth Initiatives, Ft. Worth, TX - downtown strategic action plan
- Rutgers University, Piscataway, NJ - project support for the documentation and evaluation of the Minneapolis Neighborhood Revitalization Program

Economic Policy: organizations dealing with research or issues related to finance and the economy

- Center for the Study of Market Process, Fairfax, VA
- Citizens for a Sound Economy Education Foundation, Washington, DC
- Pennsylvania Economy League, Philadelphia, PA

Employment/Job Training: organizations providing employment and job training or conducting research on employment issues and trends

- Children's Storefront Foundation, New York, NY - teen employment
- Fresh Start Farms, San Francisco, CA - to create a demonstration urban micro-farm to provide homeless individuals with training and employment in bio-intensive organic farming
- Midwest Center for Labor Research, Chicago, IL - renewal support for the Chicago Project, an effort focused primarily on job creation/retention on Chicago's west side

Ethnic Organizations: support to ethnic groups not covered by more specific categories

- Cuban American Committee Research and Education Fund, Miami, FL
- Project on Ethnic Relations, Princeton, NJ

First Amendment Issues: groups concerned with freedom of speech

- Free Speech Council, Santa Clara, CA

Gay/Lesbian Issues: groups concerned with policies and initiatives affecting the Gay/Lesbian community

- Equality Colorado, Denver, CO - for general support and religious outreach on gay, lesbian, and bisexual issues
- Los Angeles Gay and Lesbian Community Services Center, Los Angeles, CA - purchase and renovation of headquarters facility

General: civic organizations or programs that do not fall into other categories

- CES of Minneapolis, Minneapolis, MN
- Values In Practice, Los Angeles, CA

- Mission Economic and Cultural Association, San Francisco, CA - support of its volunteer coordinator position

Hispanic Affairs: organizations concerned with issues affecting the Hispanic community or providing services limited to the Hispanic community

- Hispanic Women's Network of Texas, Ft. Worth, TX - mentoring program for young Hispanic women
- Latino Civil Rights Task Force, Washington, DC - to undertake a community assets assessment

Housing: organizations working for the creation of adequate low-cost homes and housing projects, and exploring issues related to housing (See also **People with Disabilities** and **Shelters/Homelessness**)

- East Akron Neighborhood, Akron, OH - to the home improvement program for low-income East Akron homeowners
- Enterprise Foundation, Columbia, MD - fulfills three-year pledge of $300,000, to support large-scale development of affordable housing in Washington, DC
- Habitat for Humanity, New York, NY

Law & Justice: organizations concerned with the judicial system or with dispute resolution, mediation, or arbitration (See also **Delinquency & Crime Rehabilitation**)

- American Bar Association Fund for Justice and Education, New York, NY - standing committee on Law and National Security
- Western Justice Center, Pasadena, CA - toward renovation expenses of the Dispute-Resolution Centers Keating Memorial Building

Legal Aid: organizations and programs providing legal assistance

- Landmark Legal Foundation, Kansas City, MO
- Legal Aid Society of Milwaukee, WI
- Southern Minnesota Regional Legal Services, St. Paul, MN

Minority Business: organizations and programs supporting minority business development

- Arkansas Regional Minority Purchasing Council, Little Rock, AR

Municipalities: aid to cities, towns, or counties for unspecified purposes

- City of Hartford, CT
- Downtown Ft. Worth Initiatives, Ft. Worth, TX - maintenance and landscaping of Burnett Park
- Village of Armonk, NY

Native American Affairs: organizations or programs focusing on the needs of the Native American community

- Native American Rights Fund, St. Paul, MN - Water Resources Project
- Seventh Generation Fund for Indian Development, Forestville, CA

Nonprofit Management: organizations designed to assist nonprofit organizations in administration, management, and/or fund raising

- Foundation Center, New York, NY
- Independent Sector, Washington, DC
- National Charities Information Bureau, New York, NY
- National Society of Fund-Raising Executives, Washington, DC

Parades/Festivals: community celebratory events

- Clark County Fair Association, Arkadelphia, PA
- Memphis in May International Festival, Memphis, TN

Philanthropic Organizations: organizations concerned with grant making and the philanthropic process or that make direct grants to nonprofit organizations

- Fidelity Investments Charitable Gift Fund, New York, NY
- Hyatt Foundation, Chicago, IL

Professional & Trade Associations: membership or other organizations concerned with a particular profession or business

- American Society of Newspaper Editors, Washington, DC
- Cosmetic, Toiletry, and Fragrance Association, New York, NY
- National Association of Manufacturers, Washington, DC

Public Policy: groups concerned with broad public issues or national policy, including general support to think tanks

- American Enterprise Institute for Public Policy Research, Washington, DC
- Brookings Institute, Washington, DC

- Carnegie Mellon University, Pittsburgh, PA - to Center for the Study of Public Policy

Rural Affairs: organizations concerned with issues or activities specific to non-urban environments

- Community and Shelter Assistance, Newberg, OR - to develop farm worker housing projects in Oregon rural communities
- Tri-County United Action, Orangeburg, SC - organizing rural counties to develop a membership-based, direct-action community empowerment organization

Safety: agencies promoting or protecting public safety, including fire departments, 911, and police (See also **Emergency/Ambulance Services**)

- Kansas City 911, Kansas City, MO
- Mothers Against Drunk Driving, Washington, DC
- National Fire Safety Council, Boca Raton, FL

Urban & Community Affairs: suppport for prgrams and organizations concerned with improving broad-based community initiatives, improving community life, or urban affairs or planning

- Change - to promote community partnerships to strengthen and empower low-income, inner-city residents
- Lenox Hill Neighborhood Association, New York, NY
- National Urban Coalition, Washington, DC

Women 's Affairs: groups concerned with the advancement and equal rights; includes employment and job training programs focused on women only and organizations concerned with issues of abortion that are not church-related

- Business and Professional Women's Foundation, Washington, DC
- Catalyst for Women, New York, NY
- National Organization for Women, New York, NY
- Women's Resource Center of Northern Michigan, Petosky, MI

Zoos/Aquariums: includes zoos, zoological societies and support associations, and aquariums

- Bronx Zoo, New York, NY
- Friends of the National Zoo, Washington, DC

EDUCATION: aid to organizations, institutions, and programs with an academic or school-based focus

Afterschool/Enrichment Programs: school-based programs designed to enhance, enrich, and/or augment a student's education

- San Francisco University High School, San Francisco, CA - Summer Bridge program
- Tuba City Unified School District, Tuba City, AZ - enrichment studies for high-achieving, predominantly Navajo, seventh and eighth grade students

Agricultural Education: programs in farming, animal husbandry, or food production

- Iowa State University, Ames, IA - corn farming genetics program
- Michigan 4-H Foundation, East Lansing, MI - for programs to teach young people about high technology, stress management, and global issues
- University of Vermont, Burlington, VT - dairy farming program

Arts/Humanities Education: institution-based educational programs or studies concerned with the arts and humanities, including music, visual arts, and writing (See also **Art Institutes**)

- Center for Creative Studies, Detroit, MI
- Newark Community School of the Arts, Newark, NJ - scholarships
- Teachers and Writers Collaborative, New York, NY

Business Education: programs in any aspect of business, marketing, finance, or administration, including pre- and post-college

- American Graduate School of International Management, Phoenix, AZ
- Harvard University Graduate School of Business, Cambridge, MA
- Junior Achievement of Greater Topeka, Topeka, KS

Business-School Partnerships: collaborative efforts between schools and the business community

- Texas Business and Education Coalition, Houston, TX
- Private Industry Council, Charelston, WV

Colleges & Universities: accredited institutions of postsecondary education, including their component parts and departments if not covered by another educational subcategory

- Beloit College, Beloit, WI

- Cornell University, Ithaca, NY - toward a study of interethnic conflict
- Northeastern University, Boston, MA

Community & Junior Colleges: two-year or nonresidential postsecondary institutions

- Cuyahoga Community College, Cleveland, OH
- San Jacinto Junior College, San Jacinto, TX
- St. Augustine Community College, FL

Continuing Education: remedial or continuing education for adults, not necessarily degree-oriented

- Boston Center for Adult Education, Boston, MA
- LaFarge Lifelong Learning Institute, Milwaukee, WI
- Open University, Washington, DC

Economic Education: academic study of the science of economics

- Foundation for American Communications, Los Angeles, CA - two-year supplement, for economics training for journalists in policies related to urban poverty, international economics, and social welfare
- Indiana Council for Economic Education, Indianapolis, IN - annual/challenge grant

Education Associations: organizations concerned with educational issues, including professional associations for educators

- American Association of School Administrators, Arlington, VA
- National Board for Professional Teaching Standards, Detroit, MI
- International Foundation for Education and Self Help, Phoenix, AZ

Education Funds: groups whose purpose is to raise money for more than one educational institution

- Independent Colleges of Southern California, Los Angeles, CA
- San Francisco Education Fund, San Francisco, CA - support, over two years, of its organizational development
- Strom Thurmond Educational Fund, Washington, DC

Education Reform: organizations, schools concerned with reforming and revitalizing school systems, including alternative programming, advocacy, and policy reform

- Alabama Arise, Montgomery, AL - to allow organization to intensify its citizens - education and advocacy efforts around educational reform in Alabama
- Center for Leadership in School Reform, Louisville, KY
- Teach for America, West Helena, AR

Elementary Education (Private): private elementary schools, programs, or groups concerned with education at the primary level (Grades K-8)

- Extra Mile Education Foundation, Pittsburgh, PA - operating support for three inner-city parochial schools
- Interfaith Elementary School, Oakland, CA
- St. John's Educational Thresholds, San Francisco, CA

Elementary Education (Public): public elementary schools, programs, or groups concerned with education at the primary level (Grades K-8)

- Bloomfield Grade School, Bloomfield, MN
- Heath Springs Elementary School, Heath Springs, SC

Engineering Education: any program, organization, or institution concerned with the study of engineering and technology; includes institutes of technology

- DeVry Institute of Technology, Lombard, IL
- Florida A&M University, Tallahassee, FL
- Massachusetts Institute of Technology, Cambridge, MA

Environmental Education: school-based environmental studies programs

- Chesapeake Bay Foundation, Annapolis, MD - to provide scholarship money for Washington, DC, area students participating in field experience programs
- Visions United, Atlanta, GA - environmental education program for elementary and secondary school students

Faculty Development: aid for the improvement and advancement of working teachers and professors

- Southern Regional Education Board, Atlanta, GA - professional development program for 600 teachers and school leaders at 20 Georgia - High Schools that Work -
- Westminster College, Wilmington, PA - five-year pledge, toward expansion of faculty development program

General: support for educational organizations not covered by other categories

- IMPAC Learning Systems, Little Rock, AR
- Institute for Contemporary Studies, San Francisco, CA
- San Diego School of Success, San Diego, CA
- Student Advocacy, White Plains, NY
- Yale Review, New Haven, CT

Gifted & Talented: programs designed for gifted and talented students

- Society for Advancement of Gifted Children, Chicago, IL

Health & Physical Education: programs in health maintenance, nutrition, and physical fitness

- Classroom, Inc., New York, NY - second installment of three-year grant totaling $300,000 in support of the development of a hospital/health care simulation
- Sewickley Academy, Sewickley, PA - for physical education equipment

International Exchange: programs or organizations that support or promote exchange of students and faculty between the U.S. and other countries; includes training foreign researchers and faculty at U.S. higher education institutions

- Canajoharie American Field Service, Canajoharie, NY - general support of programs
- LaGrange International Friendship Exchange, LaGrange, GA
- Middlebury College, Middlebury, VT - toward Consortium for East-West Cultural and Academic Exchange

International Studies: programs concerned with the study of other countries or foreign affairs in general

- George Washington University, Washington, DC - to Elliott School of International Affairs
- Georgetown University School of Foreign Service, Washington, DC - Southeast Asian Studies program
- Southern Center for International Studies, Atlanta, GA
- World Learning, Brattleboro, VT

Journalism Education: school-based organizations, programs, and departments concerned with various news media

- Editorial Projects in Education, Washington, DC
- Indiana University Foundation - final support for minority scholarship program participants in the School of Journalism
- University of Oregon School of Journalism, Portland, OR

Leadership Training: institutions, organizations, and programs that promote leadership and self-esteem

- Colorado Outward Bound School, Denver, CO
- Community Development Institute, East Palo Alto, CA - for the Leadership Training Academy, which seeks to prepare East Palo Alto youth to assume community leadership roles

Legal Education: institutions or programs concerned with the study of law

- Columbia University School of Law, New York, NY - scholarship fund
- Tufts University, Medford, MA - to endow a professorship in the legal studies program
- William Mitchell College of Law, St. Paul, MN

Literacy: remedial education in reading for children or adults

- Barbara Bush Foundation for Family Literacy, Houston, TX - A Celebration of Reading program
- Central Detroit Community Center, Detroit, MI - adult literacy program
- Literacy Services of Greater Milwaukee, Milwaukee, WI

Medical Education: institutions or programs concerned with the study medicine, nursing, pharmacology, dentistry, psychiatry, etc.

- Baylor College of Medicine, Waco, TX
- Cornell University, Ithaca, NY - fellowship program for graduate veterinary students interested in academic careers
- Helene Fuld School for Nursing, Camden, NJ - to purchase classroom furniture and for scholarships

Minority Education: promoting educational opportunities for members of minority groups

- American Indian College Fund, New York, NY
- Ft. Worth Hispanic Chamber of Commerce, Ft. Worth, TX - college scholarships for Hispanic students
- United Negro College Fund, New York, NY

Preschool Education: institutions or organizations concerned with pre-elementary education; includes nursery schools that teach (See also **Day Care**)

- Bucks County Head Start - roof repairs at Bensalem Head Start Center

- City of Minneapolis, Minneapolis, MN - capital funds for construction of the Sheridan Neighborhood Early Learning Center
- Grafton Playschool, Grafton, VT

Private Education (Precollege): private elementary and secondary schools or organizations, or programs designed for private school systems

- Akiba Hebrew Academy, Merion Station, PA
- Archbishop Stepinac High School, White Plains, NY
- Phillips Exeter Academy, Exeter, NH
- St. George's School, Newport, RI

Public Education (Precollege): public elementary and secondary schools or organizations, or programs designed for public school systems

- Memphis City Schools, Memphis, TN
- New Haven Board of Education, New Haven, CT
- Public School #41, New York, NY
- State of Hawaii Department of Education, Lihue, HI - career-oriented field trips for Waianae Coast students

Religious Education: programs or institutions primarily concerned with teaching religion (either comparative or doctrine) or training clergy

- Calvary Bible College, Cheyenne, WY
- Christian Theological Seminary, Indianapolis, IN
- Stanford University Jewish Studies Program, Stanford, CA

School Volunteerism: organizations and programs that encourage school-based volunteer activities, including students, parents, schools, and communities

- New York City School Volunteer Program, New York, NY
- Parents-Teachers Association Arkansas Congress, Springdale, AR
- World Vision, Seattle, WA - for the startup costs of the Seattle Student Mentor Program, which links volunteers with at-risk students in central city schools

Science/Technology Education: programs, organizations, or institutions concerned with the scientific or technical disciplines, (i.e., math, chemistry, computer sciences, and physics) at all levels

- Life Lab Science Program, Santa Clara, CA - over two years, to expand the Bay Area Science Innovation and Leadership Project (BASIL), through which students are taught hands-on physical and earth sciences by growing and experimenting with a Life Lab garden
- Oberlin College, Oberlin, OH - to match the grant of the National Science Foundation to renovate the ground floor for the Wright Physics Laboratory
- Purdue University, West Lafayette, IN - campaign for the advancement of science and technology

Secondary Education (Private): private secondary schools, programs, or groups concerned with education at the middle or high school level

- Archbishop Carroll High , Washington, DC
- Crespi Carmelite High School, Encino, CA
- St. Vincent St. Mary High School, Houston, TX - for scholarship endowment

Secondary Education (Public): public secondary schools, programs, or groups concerned with education at the middle or high level

- Lancaster County Schools, Lancaster, PA - Barr Street Junior High School
- New Bedford Public Schools, New Bedford, MA - Project HELP, information on health-related topics and careers for high school students
- Wilmington Middle-High School, Wilmington, DE - soccer field lights

Social Sciences Education: school-based organizations, programs, and departments concerned with social sciences, including anthropology, history, sociology, political science, etc.

- Case Western Reserve University School of Applied Social Science, Cleveland, OH
- New School for Social Research, New York, NY
- University of Wisconsin Madison Department of Political Science, Madison, WI - over one year, research grant for study - Racial Conflict and Cultural Politics in the United States: An Examination of Black Cultural Projection

Special Education: education for the disabled or learning-impaired

- Action Centered Tutoring Services, Hartford, CT

- American School for the Deaf, Hartford, CT
- Foundation for Children with Learning Disabilities
- Hadley School for the Blind, Winnetka, IL

Student Aid: direct financial aid such as scholarships based on academic achievement, broadly defined, or organizations providing scholarships; scholarship programs in specific areas covered above (e.g., law and medicine are included with their recipient respective category)

- Call to College Fund, Newark, NJ - scholarship fund
- Clemson University, Clemson, SC - scholarship program
- National Merit Scholarship Corporation, Evanston, IL

Vocational/Technical Education: institutions and programs that train individuals for a particular field or skill

- Don Bosco Technical Institute, Rosemead, CA
- General Motors Institute for Automotive Training, Pontiac, MI
- Mankato Area Vocational Technical Institute, Mankato, MN

ENVIRONMENT: support for organizations concerned with environmental stewardship and issues

Air/Water Quality: organizations concerned with air and water quality

- American Rivers, Washington, DC
- Clean Water Fund, Washington, DC
- University of California Los Angeles Foundation, Los Angeles, CA - additional support toward the Water Reclamation Project

Energy: energy conservation and efficiency

- Izaak Walton League of America, Minneapolis, MN - funds for the Midwest Energy Efficiency Program, promoting energy efficiency and renewable energy
- Southern Environmental Law Center, Charlotte, NC - over three years, to promote increased utility investments in energy efficiency in the southeastern US

Forestry: issues affecting forests

- Cradle of Forestry, Asheville, NC
- Institute for Sustainable Forestry, Redway, CA
- National Forest Foundation, Washington, DC

General: support for multipurpose environmental organizations or organizations and projects not covered by specific categories

- 1,000 Friends of Oregon, Portland, OR - capital building project
- Environmental Defense Fund, New York, NY
- National Audubon Society, New York, NY

Protection: organizations or projects whose primarly goal is to protect the environment or protect the public from harmful environmental practices

- Ecotrust, Portland, OR - to support the Willapa Bay program, which assists local residents to protect the environment and promote sustainable economic development projects
- Mothers and Others for a Livable Planet, New York, NY - for the Safe Food Program to broaden and strengthen the constituency for foods raised without chemical additives; $50,000 over two years

Research: organizations and projects focused on researching environmental impacts

- Desert Research Institute, Tucson, AZ
- Princeton University, Princeton, NJ - first installment of $285,000 grant, for continued support of the Center for Energy and Environmental studies for research on fuel cell technology

Resource Conservation: organizations and projects broadly working to preserve resources affecting numerous environmental topics

- Conservation Law Foundation, Boston, MA
- Land and Water Fund of the Rockies, Boulder, CO
- Nature Conservancy, Washington, DC

Sanitary Systems: organizations or projects concerned with waste management

- Dakota Resource Council Education Project, Dickinson, ND - to build the capacity of North Dakota citizens to participate in the formulation of waste management policies

- Dakota Rural Action, Bookings, SD - to build the capacity of South Dakota citizens to participate in the formulation and implementation of statewide solid waste management

Watershed: projects and organizations with a specific focus on watershed protection

- Chesapeake Bay Foundation, Annapolis, MD - support for a program to provide long-term protection of the Nanticoke River Watershed in Delaware and Maryland
- Urban Creeks Council, Berkeley, CA - funds to train local river conservation groups about ways to revitalize urban waterways in the Upper Mississippi watershed

Wildlife Protection: organizations and projects designed to protect wildlife and their habitats

- Defenders of Wildlife, Washington, DC - to support a pilot GAP Analysis project to restore the states natural heritage
- National Fish and Wildlife Foundation, Washington, DC
- New York Zoological Society, New York, NY - continued support of the Wildlife Survival Center on St. Catherine's Island, GA

HEALTH: support for organizations that provide medical or health-related services, care, research, and training

Adolescent Health Issues: health issues affecting teens and youths

- Alliance for Young Families, Boston, MA - final support for the Health Adolescent Project
- Coalition for School-Based Primary Health Care, Bronx, NY - to strengthen and institutionalize school-based adolescent clinics in New York state
- Teen Health Center, Galveston, TX

AIDS/HIV: medical research and organizations concerned with AIDS/HIV

- AIDS Outreach Center, Galveston, TX - development/implementation of fundraising program
- Design Industries Foundation for AIDS, New York, NY
- RAIN Arkansas, Little Rock, AR
- Shelter Resources, New Orleans, LA - support two AIDS shelter houses

Alzheimers Disease: medical research and organizations concerned with patients with Alzheimer's

- Alzheimer's Resource Center, Winter Park, FL
- Medical College of Georgia, Augusta, GA - for Alzheimers Disease project

Arthritis: medical research and organizations concerned with patients with arthritis

- Arthritis Foundation, Atlanta, GA
- Arthritis Research Institute, West Palm Beach, FL

Cancer: medical research and organizations concerned with patients with cancer

- American Cancer Society, Salt Lake City, UT
- Boca Raton Community Hospital, Boca Raton, FL - Lynn Regional Cancer Center
- Dana Farber Cancer Institute, Boston, MA

Children's Health/Hospitals: hospitals, medical research, and organizations concerned with children's health issues

- Children's Hospital Foundation, Denver, CO
- Easter Seal Society-Dallas Center, Dallas, TX
- Make-A-Wish Foundation, Phoenix, AZ
- Ronald McDonald House, Jamestown, NY - toward expenses of families unable to pay for lodging while child is in a hospital nearby

Clinics/Medical Centers: medical centers and community-based clinics

- Cedars-Sinai Medical Center, Los Angeles, CA
- Church Health Center, Memphis, TN
- Los Angeles Free Clinic, Los Angeles, CA
- Montefiore Medical Center, New York, NY

Diabetes: medical research and organizations concerned with patients with diabetes

- Joslin Diabetes Center, Boston, MA
- Juvenile Diabetes Foundation, Dallas, TX - medical research

Emergency/Ambulance Services: rescue squads, emergency first aid, and/or transportation to medical facilities

- American Red Cross, New York, NY

- Rescue Squad, Sparta, TN
- Utah Emergency Medical Training, Midvale, UT

Eyes/Blindness: medical research and organizations concerned with patients with vision problems

- Eye Bank for Sight Restoration, New York, NY
- Retina Research Foundation, Houston, TX - funds for research

Geriatric Health: health and medical care of the aged, including gerontology

- Adler School of Professional Psychology, Chicago, IL - to expand gerontology specialization certificate program to include a master's degree program in gerontological psychology
- Buehler Center on Aging, Chicago, IL
- Council for Jewish Elderly, Lieberman Geriatric Health Center, Chicago, IL
- Long Beach Area Geriatric Health Care Council, Long Beach, CA

Health Policy/ Cost Containment: programs and organizations concerned with health care policy, the efficient management of health facilities, or the reduction or containment of health care costs

- Cato Institute, Washington, DC - toward policy research and educational activities on health care reform; second-year and final support of the Connecticut Health Care Coalition
- Tax Foundation, Washington, DC - for research and public education on the tax implications of health care reform proposals

Health Funds: organizations that primarily raise money for distribution to other health organizations and organizations that support health-related interests

- Combined Health Agency Drive, Laguna Beach, CA
- Grantmakers in Health, Washington, DC - for general support
- United Hospital Fund of New York, Bronx, NY

Health Organizations: local or national organizations concerned with health care and services, including health care organizations not covered elsewhere

- American Council on Science and Health, Washington, DC
- Blue Ridge Community Health Service, Buffalo, NY
- Latino Health Network, Boston, MA - to support the Latino Health Initiative

Heart: medical research and organizations concerned with patients with heart problems

- American Heart Association, Tucson, AZ
- Children's Heart Fund, New York, NY
- New York Hospital Cornell Medical Center, New York, NY - to establish the H. Lawrence Bogert Fund in Cardiology

Home-Care Services: organizations or programs concerned with providing in-home health care

- Coalition for Independence, Washington, DC - three-year grant in partial support of a homemaker retention and advancement program developed by a local consortium, the Home-Care Alliance
- Hospice Care of DC, Washington, DC - to train specialty care staff for the Home Care Nursing Program
- Little Sisters of the Assumption Family Health Service, New York, NY - to help underwrite the costs of the Community-Based Home Health Care Program for needy families in East Harlem

Hospices: facilities providing supportive care for the terminally ill and organizations concerned with such care

- Hospice of Midland, Midland, MI
- Kentucky Association of Hospices, Nicholasville, KY
- United Hospice Fund, New York, NY

Hospitals: organizations providing medical and surgical care that may require patients to stay more than 24 hours for treatment and recovery

- Brigham and Women's Hospital, Boston, MA
- St. Joseph Hospital, Providence, RI
- Washington Hospital Center, Washington, DC

Kidney: medical research and organizations concerned with patients with kidney problems

- National Kidney Foundation, Washington, DC
- National Kidney Foundation of Upper Midwest, St. Paul, MN

Long-Term Care: organizations or programs providing extended health-care services

- Grace Presbyterian Village, Dallas, TX - care for the aged and infirm

- Life Services Network of Illinois, Hinsdale, IL - for research to identify the characteristics of residents in assisted living facilities in Illinois and to determine their level of impairment
- Northwestern University, Evanston, IL - to examine how long-term care providers plan to participate in an environment emphasizing integration and collaboration with other health care providers
- Verona House Corporation, Pittsburgh, PA - two-year pledge, toward renovation of Corpus Christi Residence as a personal care boarding home for young adults who have chronic illnesses, including individuals who have been diagnosed HIV positive

Medical Rehabilitation: programs and organizations primarily concerned with restoring people (especially those with chronic conditions) to a more normal life

- Allegheny Valley MH/MR Program, Pittsburgh, PA - summer therapeutic recreation program
- Rehabilitation Institute of Chicago, Chicago, IL
- St. Mary's Rehabilitation Center, Minneapolis, MN
- Steere House Nursing and Rehabilitation Center, Providence, RI

Medical Research: programs and organizations concerned with discovering causes of and treatment for medical problems and diseases

- City of Hope, Los Angeles, CA
- Foundation for Neurological Diseases, New York, NY
- National Jewish Center for Immunology and Respiratory Medicine, Denver, CO
- University of Minnesota, Minneapolis, MN - funds for an anorexia nervosa relapse prevention project, for the bulimia nervosa treatment project, and for a follow-up study of patients treated for eating disorders

Medical Training: professional training offered by health organizations to doctors, nurses, and other health care and rescue/ emergency personnel who have already completed their basic medical education, which is designed to supplement, extend, or update their basic medical education

- Wisconsin Institute of Family Medicine, WI - externship
- Training Exchange, Foxboro, MA - medical education

Mental Health: organizations concerned with researching, alleviating, or curing mental and psychological disorders

- Anxiety Disorders Association of America, Rockville, MD - for establishment of library
- Mental Health Association, New York, NY
- Phoenix South Community Mental Health Center, Phoenix, AZ
- Richard H. Young Psychiatric Hospital, Omaha, NE

Multiple Sclerosis: medical research and organizations concerned with patients with Multiple Sclerosis

- National Multiple Sclerosis Society, Chicago, IL
- National Multiple Sclerosis West Texas Chapter, Midland, TX

Nursing Services: care provided by practical or registered nurses in private homes or medical facilities

- Nursing Services of the Ohio Valley, Columbus, OH
- Prospect Park Block Nurse Program, Minneapolis, MN
- Visiting Nurse Health System, Atlanta, GA
- Visiting Nurses Association of Chicago, Chicago, IL

Nutrition: programs and organizations concerned with preventive care as opposed to treatment of illness

- Nutrition Foundation, Washington, DC
- FPSP/Kiribati Vitamin Deficiency, New York, NY

Outpatient Health Care: organizations providing medical or surgical care not requiring the patient to stay for more than 24 hours

- Northern Itasca Health Care Center, Grand Rapids, MN - for expansion and remodeling of outpatient services
- Scotland Health Group, Laurinburg, NC - to expand the outpatient surgery department

Prenatal Health Issues: medical services for pregnant women and new-born infants

- California Medical Center Foundation, Los Angeles, CA - toward acquisition of networked computerized fetal monitoring system
- Minneapolis Crisis Nursery, Minneapolis, MN
- Parents of Premature and High-Risk Infants, New York, NY
- Utah Department of Health Baby Your Baby, Salt Lake City, UT

Preventive Medicine/Wellness Organizations: programs and organizations concerned with preventive care as opposed to treatment of illness

- Addison County Community Action Group, Middlebury, VT - second-year support to expand and strengthen prevention and primary medical care for low-income people
- Wellness Community, Pasadena, CA

Public Health: programs and organizations concerned with health matters of broad community or national import, such as containing the spread of communicable diseases; also includes public awareness training and education

- College of Medicine and Dentistry Department of Community Health, Princeton, NJ
- National Center for Disease Control, Bethesda, MD
- Western Consortium for Public Health, Center for Integrated Services for Families and Neighborhoods, Sacramento, CA

Research/Studies Institutes: medical institutions primarily involved in research, with no discipline specified, including child development research

- Biomedical Research Institute, Los Angeles, CA
- Louisiana Children's Research Center, New Orleans, LA
- Psoriasis Research Institute, Stanford, CA - computer technology
- Scripps Research Institute Graduate Program Fellowship, La Jolla, CA

Respiratory: medical research and organizations concerned with patients with lung and other respiratory problems

- American Lung Association, Washington, DC

Single-Disease Health Associations: organizations concerned with research, treatment, and other aspects of a single diseases not included in specific categories within Health

- Midland Cerebral Palsy Center, Midland, TX
- Muscular Dystrophy Association, New York, NY
- National Downs Syndrome Society, New York, NY

Speech & Hearing: medical research and organizations concerned with patients with medical problems affecting speech and hearing

- Central Institute for the Deaf, St. Louis, MO - research on regeneration of inner ear
- Deafness Research Foundation, New York, NY
- Houston Ear Research Foundation, Houston, TX

Transplant Networks/Donor Banks: organizations that collect and distribute blood and various organs

- Central Kentucky Blood Center, Lexington, KY
- Children's Blood Foundation, New York, NY
- Georgia Eye Bank, Atlanta, GA - for fund-raising campaign

Trauma Treatment: organizations that treat trauma injuries

- Burn Clinic Foundation, Detroit, MI
- Foundation for Memorial Medical Center, Savannah, GA - trauma care center
- National Head Injury Foundation, Vermont Chapter, Rutland, VT

INTERNATIONAL: aid to organizations that are international in scope, as well as organizations that provide education and training, development assistance and research, emergency relief, health care, and related services to countries, communities, and institutions outside the United States

Foreign Arts Institutions: arts institutions located outside the United States

- American Friends of Israel Philharmonic, New York, NY
- American Friends of the Israel Museum, Los Angeles, CA
- Musee Bartholdi, Colmar, France - remodel exhibition room

Foreign Educational Institutions: educational institutions located outside the United States

- American Academy in Rome, New York, NY
- Charles University, Prague, Czech Republic
- University of Wroclaw, Wroclaw, Poland - for use over two years in automating its library system
- Universidad Centroamericana Jose - for use over three years toward the development of its library

General: support for multipurpose international organizations or organizations and projects not covered by specific category

- Friends of Mauritschas, New York, NY

- National Public Radio, Washington, DC - to support the third year of the establishment of Tokyo burearu

International Health Care: organizations providing health care located outside the United States or concerned with international health care issues on a global scale

- Project HOPE, Millwood, NJ
- Health Volunteers Overseas, Washington, DC
- CARE International, Atlanta, GA - acquisition and renovation of 151 Ellis Building
- Haddad Hospital, Lebanon - purchase equipment

Human Rights: organizations addressing human rights issues on a global scale

- American Association for the Advancement of Science, Washington, DC - documentation and database analysis of human rights violations in Guatemala
- Center for Victims of Torture, Minneapolis, MN - support for an organization that treats people who have been tortured by foreign governments
- Human Rights Watch, New York, NY

International Affairs: organizations and programs concerned with issues affecting a broad spectrum of countries and/or multidimensional relationships

- Carnegie Council on Ethics and International Affairs, New York, NY - general program support
- Center for Strategic and International Studies, Washington, DC
- Near East Foundation, New York, NY

International Development: organizations and programs involved with the global economic and social development activities

- Accion International, Cambridge, MA
- Fund for Democracy and Development, Washington, DC - renewed support of efforts to help stimulate entrepreneurship among Russian citizens
- International Service for the Acquisition of Agri-Biotech Applications, Ithaca, NY - International Biotechnology Collaboration Program to transfer biotechnology from industrial countries to the Third World

International Environmental Issues: organizations and programs involved with environmental stewardship on a global scale or projects underway outside the United States

- Conservation International Foundation, Washington, DD
- Friends of the Earth (France) - over two years, for a program to improve the lending policies of multilateral development banks in East Central Europe with respect to sustainable development
- Sierra Legal Defense Fund, Vancouver, Canada - in support of litigation work to protect the ancient forests of British Columbia
- Worldwatch Institute, Washington, DC

International Law: organizations and programs involoved with the international legal process

- United Nations, New York, NY - for a study on international law

International Organizations: organizations that are multinational in scope, usually with headquarters overseas although occasionally they may be based in the United States

- Center for Foreign Journalists, Arlington, VA - fulfills pledge of $75,000, to provide administrative support for the center's training and technical assistance programs for foreign journalists
- Colmar Municipality, Colmar, France - equipment for skating rink
- University of Sussex, Sussex, England - over two years, for Science Policy Research Unit's project, - European and Japanese Plutonium Policies: Toward a New Consensus -

International Peace & Security Issues: programs and organizations concerned with global peace and security, including nuclear nonproliferation

- Hemisphere Initiatives - monitoring negotiations, peace implementation, and political transformation
- Hoover Institution on War, Revolution, and Peace, Stanford, CA - special archive project
- International Peace Academy, New York, NY - support for the promotion of improved international conflict management and resolution

International Relations: organizations concerned primarily with issues affecting relationships among countries

- China Institute in America, New York, NY
- Council on Foreign Relations, New York, NY
- United Nations Institute for Training and Development, New York, NY
- World Neighbors, Oklahoma City, OK

International Relief Efforts: organizations that seek to relieve human suffering and devastation due to environmental and social upheaval

- International Rescue Committee, New York, NY
- Save the Children Federation, Westport, CT - funds for the Poverty Alleviation and Nutrition Program, and to establish a training center for the model in Vietnam
- US Committee for UNICEF, New York, NY

Missionary/Religious Activities: religious organizations, churches, and communities outside the United States

- Archdiocese Concepcion, Chile - purchase vehicle
- Jerusalem Foundation, New York, NY
- Presbyterian Church, USA Presbyterian World Service, Louisville, KY

Trade: organizations and activities concerned with international trade or the development of free market economies in third world countries and emerging democracies

- Global Exchange, San Francisco, CA - Freedom to Travel Campaign/Association for Free Trade with Cuba
- Institute for East-West Studies, New York, NY - Banking and Finance Assistance Center Budapest, Hungary
- US ASEAN Council for Business and Technology, Washington, DC

RELIGION: aid to organizations centered around religious beliefs or practices

Bible Study/Translation: organizations focused on study of the Bible

- Ancient Biblical Manuscript Center for Preservation and Research, Claremont, CA

Churches: Christian houses of worship and chapels, and organizations concerned with church affairs

- Armenian Apostolic Holy Cross Church, Los Angeles, CA
- Bendersville Lutheran Church, Bendersville, NY
- Church Federation of Greater Indianapolis, Indianapolis, IN

Dioceses: programs and projects at specific dioceses

- Archdiocese of Los Angeles, Los Angeles, CA - to enhance the computer capabilities of the Chancery complex and Pastoral Regional Offices

General: general support for unspecified religious organizations or organizations that do not fall into one of the specific categories

- Southern Christian Leadership Conference, GA

Jewish Causes: Jewish causes and activities

- Anti-Defamation League of B' nai B'irth, Miami, FL
- Hadassah, Los Angeles, CA
- Hebrew Union College Jewish Institute of Religion, New York, NY
- Jewish Community Center, White Plains, NY
- Jewish Theological Seminary, New York, NY

Mininsties: ministries providing health, education, social, and/or religious services to communities in the United States

- Good Works, Downington, PA - for expansion of ministry
- Light of Life Ministries, Pittsburgh, PA - toward the Resident Counseling Component
- New Horizons Ministries, Atlanta, GA

Missionary Activities (Domestic): evangelical missions providing health, education, social, and/or religious services to communities in the United States

- Light of Life Ministries - toward the Resident Counseling Component
- St. Paul's Catholic Mission, Crownpoint, New Mexico - religious education for the Navajo
- Society for the Propagation of the Faith, New York - pastoral missionary work

Religious Organizations: organizations whose primary purpose is religious in nature

- Christophers, New York, NY
- Archbishops Community Appeal, New Orleans, LA
- St. Croix Valley Chaplaincy Association, Stillwater, MN

Religious Welfare: organizations or projects affiliated with religious organizations or institutions that provide community services or that advocate on behalf of communities, includes Salvation Army

- Catholic Charities, Pittsburgh, PA - counseling services to African American students
- Greater Minneapolis Interfaith Network, Minneapolis, MN - for a shelter for homeless families and single women

- Interfaith Housing Coalition, Dallas, TX - toward transitional apartment improvements
- Lutheran Family Service of Oregon and Southwest Washington, Portland, OR - to replicate the Nurturing Family, a parenting and pre-parenting education program
- Salvation Army, New York, NY

Seminaries: seminaries and theological schools

- Austin Presbyterian Theological Seminary, Austin, TX - to help fund the construction of a community center
- Bethel College and Seminary, St. Paul, MN
- Union Theological Seminary, Richmond, VA

Social/Policy Issues: organizations and projects concerned with religion and religious organizations and their relationships with broader social and policy issues

- Institute on Religion and Public Life, New York, NY
- National Conference of Christians and Jews, New York, NY
- University of California Santa Barbara, Santa Barbara, CA - religious and public life in Los Angeles

Synagogues: Jewish houses of worship

- Congregation Emanu-El, New York, NY
- Temple B' nai Israel, Galveston, TX
- United Synagogue of America, New York, NY

SCIENCE: aid to scientific research organizations and institutes which are not affiliated with a university or based in an academic setting

General: general support for unspecified science organizations or organizations that do not fall into one of the specific categories

Observatories and Planetariums: scientific and astronomical research into the solar system

- Fairbanks Museum and Planetarium, St. Johnsbury, VT
- University of Arizona Kitts Peak National Observatory, Tucson, AZ

Science Exhibits and Fairs: temporary and permanent science displays, fairs, and competitions

- Chicago Student Science Fair, Chicago, IL

Science Museums: museums devoted to science and natural history

- Pacific Northwest Museum of Natural History, Ashland, OR - for the development of this new natural history museum
- California Museum of Science and Industry Foundation - children's science projects

Scientific Centers/Institutes: institutions primarily devoted to scientific research and/or the advancement or practice of science

- Maryland Academy of Science, Annapolis, MD
- National Academy of Sciences, Washington, DC
- Woods Hole Oceanographic Institution, Woods Hole, MA

Scientific Labs: scientific research laboratories

- Cold Spring Harbor Laboratory, Cold Spring, NY

Scientific Organizations: organizations associated with the field of science

- American Chemical Society, New York, NY
- Empire State College, Saratoga Springs, NY - Western European Genetic Engineering project

SOCIAL SERVICES: aid to organizations that provide direct or indirect assistance or services to individuals and communities , with a focus on meeting basic needs, providing support networks, and issue-specific advocacy

Animal Protection: organizations and programs that promote the humane treatment of animals

- Humane Society of Missouri, Lincoln, MO
- Society for the Prevention of Cruelty to Animals of Lorain County Animal Medical Center, New York, NY

At-Risk Youth: organizations and programs focused on the needs of youth most in need of support services and the issues affecting their lives, including violence, runaway services, school dropout prevention programs, and multiservice agencies

- Covenant House, New Orleans, LA
- Harambee House for Youth, Washington, DC
- Progressive Youth Center, St. Louis, MO - Stay-In School Program

- Save Our Sons and Daughters, Detroit, MI - to launch the Youth Action Initiatives for Peace Program, a youth organizing effort targeting selected high schools in Detroit

Big Brothers/Big Sisters: support for this organization, which provides a range of services for youth

- Big Brothers and Big Sisters, New York, NY
- Big Brothers Association of Greater Boston, Boston, MA - Project 2X

Camps: broad range of organizations that provide recreational opportunities for youth, as well as residential facilities

- Camp Penuel, St. Louis, MO - pool table
- Committed Partners for Youth - residential camp
- Ft. Wayne State Developmental Center, Ft. Wayne, IN - capital grant for Camp Samaritan

Child Abuse: organizations that help children and families overcome and prevent physical and sexual child abuse (See also **Domestic Violence** and **Sexual Abuse**)

- Chance Center, Dallas, TX - child abuse community assistance
- National Committee for Prevention of Child Abuse, Chicago, IL - partial support for Healthy Families America, a project to develop a network of statewide systems for voluntary home visitor services for all new parents
- Oklahoma Committee to Prevent Child Abuse, Oklahoma City, OK

Child Welfare: broad spectrum of organizations concerned with the well-being of children, including advocacy as well as the provision of services

- Advocates for Children of New York City, Long Island City, NY - to support implementation of a parent organizing and training program focused on Chapter 1 compliance and systemwide reform
- Borrego Springs Children's Center, Borrego Springs, CA
- Children's Aid Society, New York, NY
- Children's Defense Fund, Washington, DC
- St. Mary's Home for Children, Providence, RI

Community Centers: organizations and facilities serving many community groups and offering a variety of activities

- Bronx River Neighborhood Centers, Bronx, NY
- Curtis Park Community Center, Denver, CO
- Open Door Community Center, Columbus, GA
- Phoenix Community Center, Phoenix, AZ

Community Service Organizations: multipurpose organizations providing human services

- Assistance League of Reno-Sparks, Reno, NV
- Brooklyn Bureau of Community Service, Brooklyn, NY
- Pillsbury Neighborhood Services, Minneapolis, MN
- South Carolina Department of Social Services, Columbia, SC
- Union Settlement Association, New York, NY

Counseling: personal or group guidance services

- Family Counseling and Guidance Centers, Boston, MA
- Mattie Rhodes Counseling and Art Center, Kansas City, MO - for agency staffing and other support services for Project Early Families
- Suicide Prevention and Crisis Call Center, Reno, NV

Crime Prevention: organizations and programs addressing crime and violence prevention, as well as the impact of crime and violence on communities; includes support for police departments (See also **Safety**)

- Crime Stoppers of Midland, Midland, TX
- Dispute Resolution Center, Minneapolis, MN - project funds to establish a pilot youth mediation training project
- Juvenile Protection Association, Chicago, IL - development program
- Lancaster Police Department, Lancaster, SC
- National Crime Prevention Council, Washington, DC - for SMAD Program
- Sheriffs Youth Foundation, Los Angeles, CA - Anti-Gang/Drug Education

Day Care: organizations providing day care for children and/or adults, as well as advocacy organizations addressing day care policies (See also **Preschool Education**)

- Day Care Action Council of Illinois
- The City, Minneapolis, MN - on-site day care for children of students attending an alternative school
- Martin Luther King Day Care Center, Camden, NJ - Sikora Center for Child Development

- Vista Del Mar, Los Angeles, CA

Delinquency/Criminal Rehabilitation: organizations and programs concerned with the rehabilitation of juvenile and adult offenders

- Alternative Life Paths Program, Atlanta, GA - capital improvements and program support for facility serving youth referred by the juvenile justice system
- Citizens Advisory to Probation and Parole, St. Louis, MO - aggressive offender counseling program
- Program for Female Offenders, Pittsburgh, PA - over three years, development of a parenting program
- South Carolina Department of Probation, Parole, and Pardon Services, Columbia, SC

Domestic Violence: programs for battered or abused spouses and family members; this category includes the broadest code comprising child abuse and sexual abuse

- Family Violence Network, Elkhart, IN
- Independence House, Hyannis, MA - support for shelter for battered women
- Parents Anonymous, Albuquerque, NM - for abusive parents
- Women's Center and Shelter, Pittsburgh. PA - over three years, integrated domestic violence intervention

Emergency Relief: emergency aid to the poor, the disadvantaged, and/or the victims of disasters in the United States, exclusive of the Red Cross, which appears under emergency/ambulance services

- Community Emergency Assistance Program, Brooklyn Center, NY
- Hurricane Allen-St. Lucie Rebuilding Fund, St. Lucie, FL
- World Vision, Monrovia, CA - toward the Volunteer Mobilization, Rehabilitation, and Recovery Program supporting the Mid-West flood crisis in 1993

Family Planning: organizations concerned with planned pregnancy and population control including educational programs

- Advocates for Youth, Washington, DC - teen pregnancy prevention
- Center for Population Options, Washington, DC
- Inwood House, New York - pregnancy prevention project in junior and senior high schools
- National Family Planning and Reproductive Health Association, Washington, DC
- Planned Parenthood, New York, NY

Family Services: organizations providing general family services, including adoption and foster care counseling and networks

- Brooklyn Services for Families and Children, New York, NY
- Effective Parenting Information for Children, Rochester, NY
- Family Counseling Center, Columbus, GA
- Family Services of Jamestown, Jamestown, NY - toward a - Comprehensive Play Therapy - program
- Parental Stress Center, Pittsburgh, PA - Begin Again Program

Food & Clothing Distribution: associations providing aid in the form of food and/or clothing, including recycling of used clothing and surplus food

- Martha's Table, Washington, DC
- Meals on Wheels of Northampton, Bethlehem, PA
- Second Harvest Food Bank, Savannah, GA
- West Noble Food and Clothing Pantry, Ligonier, IN

General: human service organizations or programs that do not fall into other categories

- HEART, Santa Clara, CA
- SABAH, Snyder, NY

Homes: group residential facilities, including orphanages, homes for youth, and unspecified service providers

- Hope House of Savannah, Savannah, GA - to assist with the day-to-day operations of the home
- Mt. St. Vincent Home, Denver, CO
- New England Home for Little Wanderers, Boston, MA

People with Disabilities: organizations, programs, and support networks that aid physically and mentally disabled individuals

- Accessible Living, Beaverton, OR
- Competitive Employment Opportunities, Pittsburgh, PA - purchase of computer to serve a growing list of severely disabled clients
- Goodwill Industries, Tulsa, OK
- Guiding Eyes for the Blind, New York, NY
- Recording for the Blind, Princeton, NJ

- Sheltered Workshop Fund, Akron, OH - workshops for the disabled

Recreation & Athletics: recreational and athletic activities, programs, or facilities provided for public use and benefit, including sports facilities, athletic events, and the promotion of recreation and athletics

- City of LaGrange, LaGrange, GA - for neighborhood water playgrounds
- Mid-Fairfield Youth Hockey, Greenwich, CT
- St. Louis Soccer Park Fund, St. Louis, MO
- U.S. Figure Skating Association, Colorado Springs, CO
- U.S. Olympic Committee, Atlanta, GA

Refugee Assistance: organizations concerned with the welfare of refugees in the United States

- American Refugee Committee, St. Paul, MN - Hmong family project
- Minneapolis Care Society, MN - aid to newly arrived Laotian refugees
- Refugee Resources, San Francisco, CA
- Refugee Voices, Washington, DC - office skills training for refugees

Scouts: support for boys and girls scouting troops, regardless of the purpose of the grant

- Boy Scouts of America, Philadelphia, PA
- Girl Scout Council of St. Croix Valley, St. Paul, MN
- Conifer Council Girl Scouts, Arkadelphia, AR - summer camp

Senior Services: programs, organizations, and advocy groups focused on the elderly

- Bronx Community College Project Save Our Seniors, Bronx, NY
- Center for Social Gerontology, Ann Arbor, MI
- Kennett Area Senior Center, Kennett, PA - building addition
- Seniors with Power United for Rights (SPUR), New Orleans, LA

Sexual Abuse: organizations and programs focused strictly on sexual abuse

- CARE Centers, Pittsburgh, PA - over three years, expanded services for sexually abused adults
- Midland Rape Crises Center, Midland, TX
- Terry Reilly Health Services, Boise, ID - for a sexual abuse prevention demonstration project

Shelters/Homelessness: temporary residential facilities for the homeless or those in need of shelter, as well as services for homeless individuals

- Coalition for the Homeless, New York, NY
- Genesis Shelter, Atlanta, GA - cost of remodeling facility to house homeless families with newborn children

Special Olympics: recreational program for the disabled

- Louisiana Special Olympics, Lake Charles, LA
- Texas Special Olympics, Area 22, Austin, TX

Substance Abuse: organizations concerned with the prevention of substance abuse, including drugs and alcohol, and rehabilitation of abusers

- Challenge, Inc., Ft. Worth, TX - community-based neighborhood organizing and substance abuse prevention programs
- Drug Abuse Foundation of Palm Beach County, Delray, FL
- Nexus, Dallas, TX - substance abuse rehabilitation for women
- OnTrack, Medford, OR - for an intensive substance abuse treatment program for single fathers and their children

United Funds/United Way: conduit organizations set up primarily to raise funds for distribution to other service organizations, regardless of purpose of support

- Federation of Protestant Welfare Agencies, New York, NY
- United Fund of Greater New York, New York, NY - partial support for staffing and printing costs for the Minority Foster Care Development Project
- United Way Crusade of Mercy, Chicago, IL
- United Way of Tri-State, New York, NY

Veterans: organizations serving veterans or addressing veterans - issues

- Del-Mar Paralyzed Vets Association, Christiana, DE - prosthetics fund
- Permian Basin Vietnam Veterans Memorial Committee, Midland, TX
- Vietnam Veterans Memorial, Washington, DC

Volunteer Services: organizations established to promote voluntarism and/or to refer volunteers to organizations needing support

- Executive Service Corps, Chicago, IL
- Family Friends of the National Capital Area, Washington, DC - training senior volunteers
- Volunteers of America, Metairie, LA
- Youth Service Opportunities Project, New York, NY

YMCA/YMHA/YWCA/YWHA: support for Ys regardless of purpose

- YMCA of Bethlehem, Bethelehem, PA
- YMCA of Brandywine, Coatsville, PA - to provide financial assistance to low-income families requiring services of preschool and school-age child care
- YWCA, Bethesda, MD - over two years, support for the women's counseling service

Youth Organizations: organizations whose activities are primarily directed to youth, exclusive of such specific categories as scouts and big brothers and sisters

- Boys and Girls Club, Greenwich, CTGeorgia Academy for Children and Youth Professionals, Atlanta, GA - training programs for professionals serving children and youth
- Girls, Incorporated, New York, NY
- New Bedford Summer Fund, New Bedford, MA - startup for pooled fund for summer youth activities
- Project Reach, New York, NY - startup support of the Youth-Organizing-Youth project on the Lower East side

Glossary

501(C)3: Section of the Internal Revenue Code that defines nonprofit, charitable, tax-exempt organizations. Organizations qualifying under this section of the Code include religious, educational, charitable, amateur athletic, scientific or literary groups, and private foundations.

990-PF: See *Form 990-PF*

ACTION GRANT: A grant made to examine an operating program or project, as opposed to a research grant.

ANNUAL REPORT: Voluntary yearly report of financial and structural conditions prepared by the management of an organization. Although the term is sometimes used to refer to a report on the contributions activities of a foundation or corporation, "annual report" is more frequently applied to a corporation's annual report to shareholders.

ASSETS: The overall property or resources of the funding organization, including cash, real property, stocks, bonds, etc.

AWARD GRANT: A specific type of grant bestowed as an award for meeting a goal or other special accomplishment.

BENEFACTOR: Donor, usually at the highest level.

BENEFICIARY: Person or organization named by an insured to receive benefits upon death of insured—either primary or secondary.

BEQUEST: Cash, securities, or other personal property, transferred by will. A bequest may consist of a set amount, a percentage, or a residual amount of tangible property.

BRICKS AND MORTAR: Describes construction materials, equipment, and/or funds used to provide the basic "building blocks" for a building or construction project. See also *capital grant.*

CAPITAL EXPENDITURE: An expenditure to acquire an asset with an expected useful life of more than one year.

CAPITAL GRANT: Grant provided to fund a *capital expenditure,* usually for physical plant construction or equipment. See also *bricks and mortar.*

CAUSE-RELATED MARKETING AND PROMOTION: Support provided by a for-profit corporation in which the company's donations are directly linked to marketing efforts to benefit the company. One example would be a case in which an airline contributed $5 to a city's symphony orchestra for every passenger who booked a flight on the airline from that city; another example would be a company-sponsored foot race in which part of the fee for entering the race helps support a local charity.

CHALLENGE GRANT: A grant that is paid on the condition that the recipient organization is able to raise additional funds from other donors.

CHARITABLE REMAINDER ANNUITY TRUST: Provides a fixed amount of income to donor for life or for a term of years; upon death, the remainder reverts to the named charity.

CHARITY: Non-profit organization, institution or agency created to carry out programs or projects or to operate activities for the public good. Under section 501(c)3 of the Internal Revenue Code, organizations applying for tax-exempt status are required to meet certain criteria that distinguish them as a "public charity" rather than a private foundation.

COMBINED GIVING PROGRAM: A corporate contributions program that consists of both a *corporate direct giving program* and a *corporate foundation.* Because the direct giving program and the corporate foundation may each have distinct fields of interest, it is important to target proposals to the individual program or foundation based on its explicit funding priorities.

COMMUNITY FOUNDATION: An organization established to provide grants in a specific community or geographic area; typically, funds are pooled from multiple donors and donor organizations and independently administered.

COMMUNITY FUND: An organization or program that conducts annual campaigns to support local health and social service agencies. See also *united fund.*

COMPANY-SPONSORED FOUNDATION: See *corporate foundation.*

CONFERENCE/SEMINAR GRANT: A grant awarded to fund a conference or seminar.

CONTRIBUTION: Gift or donation in various forms to a non-profit organization for which no tangible value is received.

CONTRIBUTIONS COMMITTEE: The board responsible for making the grant decisions in a company or foundation.

CORPORATE DIRECT GIVING PROGRAM: A program established within the body of a for-profit corporation to coordinate the charitable interests of the corporation. Unlike a *corporate foundation*, a corporate direct giving program typically does not exist as a 501(c)(3) organization and is not subject to the same laws/regulations as a corporate or independent foundation.

CORPORATE FOUNDATION: Philanthropic organization established to coordinate the charitable interests of a sponsoring corporation. Most corporate foundations are themselves 501(c)(3) organizations and, as such, are legally required to file a 990-PF each year.

CORPORATE GIVING PROGRAM: A *corporate direct giving program, foundation*, or *combined giving program* sponsored by a for-profit company. The giving program may be sponsored by a private or publicly-owned corporation.

DEFERRED GIVING: Contributions to an organization other than through current gifts; fund reverts to organization at a later date.

DEPARTMENT GRANT: A grant awarded on the basis that it be used to support a specific academic department, usually in a college or university.

DIRECT GRANT: A monetary award made directly to the recipient organization, as contrasted with noncash support, in-kind contributions, or other nonmonetary grants.

DISCLOSURE PERIOD: Period of time to which the source information in a profile applies; may be based on fiscal or calendar year. Data provided in a Form 990-PF whose disclosure period is January 1 through December 31 of a given year refer to the financial and organizational condition of the foundation during that particular calendar year.

DISTRIBUTION COMMITTEE: See *contributions committee*.

DONATED EQUIPMENT: Equipment donated by a company to a nonprofit organization.

DONATED PRODUCTS: Products donated by a company to a nonprofit organization.

DONEE: The grant recipient.

DONOR: Person who contributes to a non-profit organization; synonymous with contributor or giver.

EMERGENCY GRANT: Funds provided for emergency purposes, such as disaster aid.

EMPLOYEE MATCHING GIFT: A contribution made by a company employee and matched by a like gift from the employer.

EMPLOYER IDENTIFICATION NUMBER (EIN): A nine-digit code used to identify a foundation on its annual 990-PF filing.

ENDOWMENT: The process whereby a donor provides funds to an organization or institution to run a program or facility; typically, the program or facility is named after the donor.

ENDOWMENT CAMPAIGN: A campaign to solicit funds to establish or supplement an organization's endowment fund.

ESTATE: Degree, quality, nature and extent of one's interest in, or ownership of, land, property, real estate, securities, royalties, insurance, cash, treasures, etc.

FAMILY FOUNDATION: A foundation that receives its funds solely from members of a single family. Generally, family members serve as officers or board members and influence grantmaking decisions.

FEDERATED CAMPAIGN: Fund raising campaign conducted by one agency or group for many participating or member organizations. See also *united fund*.

FEDERATED GIVING PROGRAM: See *united fund*.

FELLOWSHIP: An endowment, or money paid from such an endowment, for the support of a graduate student in a university or college.

FORM 990-PF: Financial report filed annually by a private or corporate foundation in accordance with federal and state tax laws. Items listed in the 990-PF include foundation assets, receipts, expenditures, compensation of officers, and grants.

FUNDING ORGANIZATION: Any type of donor organization — corporate foundation or direct giving program; community, independent, family, private, or operating foundation; charitable trust, etc.

GENERAL PURPOSE FOUNDATION: An independent private foundation that awards grants in many different fields of interest.

GENERAL SUPPORT: A grant made to support the general work of an organization, rather than a specific project or goal. (Opposite of a *restricted grant*.)

GRANT: Allocation of money by foundation, corporation, government, or organization to a person, agency, or institution for a general or specific purpose.

IN-KIND CONTRIBUTION: A contribution of equipment, supplies, or other property. See also *nonmonetary support*.

IN-KIND SERVICES: Contribution of services, such as printing, data processing, or technical assistance.

INDEPENDENT FOUNDATION: Any grantmaking, non-operating foundation.

LOAN: Funds awarded with the understanding that the amount of the loan be repaid over a period of time.

LOANED EMPLOYEES: Company employees whose time is donated.

LOANED EXECUTIVES: Company executives whose time is donated.

MEMORIAL: A gift intended to preserve the memory of a person or event. Memorial gifts are made to nonprofit organizations to memorialize deceased individuals; memorial trusts are established as an interest-bearing investment to memorialize the deceased.

MISSION STATEMENT: Concise description of the purpose of an organization.

MULTIYEAR/CONTINUING SUPPORT: Grants awarded in several installments over a period of two or more years.

NONMONETARY SUPPORT: Contributions such as equipment, supplies, and services. See also *donated equipment, donated products, in-kind contributions, in-kind services, loaned employees, and loaned executives.*

OPERATING EXPENSE GRANT: A grant to support the day-to-day administrative, staffing, and other operational costs of a program or organization.

OPERATING FOUNDATION: A foundation established for the purpose of conducting scientific research or other highly focused programs, usually within the aegis of its own organizational structure. Funds are generally restricted to the foundation's own projects and not provided as grants to other organizations.

PLEDGE: Promise made by a potential donor to pay a specific sum over a set period; property or fund paid at a later date.

PRIVATE FOUNDATION: An independent grantmaking organization operated by a private group, such as a family or private board. The Taft Group defines private foundations as family and general purpose foundations, rather than corporate, community, or operating foundations.

PROFESSORSHIP GRANT: Funds that help establish or support an ongoing professorship position within a college or university.

PROFILE: A description of pertinent details about a prospective donor gathered through prospect research.

PROGRAM-RELATED INVESTMENT: A loan or other investment made for a project related to the donor's specific interests, usually with the agreement that the recipient repay the funds over a period of time.

PROJECT GRANT: Funding for a stated project.

PROPOSAL: A written request or application for a gift or grant that includes why the project or progam is needed, who will carry it out, and how much it will cost.

PUBLIC CHARITY: A nonprofit organization that solicits funds from the general public and uses the funds to sponsor or aid social, educational, or religious activities, or engage in activities that provide relief for distressed or underprivileged individuals. Public charities are defined in Section 509(a)(1-4) of the Internal Revenue Code. Some public charities use the term "foundation" in their names but are not classified by the Internal Revenue Service as a foundation.

QUERY LETTER: Brief, preliminary letter describing an organization and proposed grant request, usually sent prior to initiating a full proposal.

RECENT GRANT: In Taft publications, a listing of recent grants may include grants awarded and paid during the *disclosure period* or 2-3 years immediately preceding the disclosure period.

RESEARCH GRANT: Funds awarded for specific research projects, usually at a college or university.

RESTRICTED GRANT: A contribution that specifies the purposes of the gift or how it must be used.

RFP: Request for Proposal. A solicitation of grant proposals. RFPs are used mainly by government agencies and are not often issued by corporate or private foundations.

SCHOLARSHIP GRANT: Funds provided to support a scholarship or scholarship program at a college or university.

SEED MONEY: Funds given for the support of a new program or organization.

SINGLE-DISEASE HEALTH ASSOCIATION: A nonprofit organization devoted to addressing a specific health care issue, such as heart disease, leukemia, etc.

SPECIAL PURPOSE FOUNDATION: A private foundation established to support specific areas of interest.

TECHNICAL ASSISTANCE: Support in the form of expert aid or advice, sometimes donated to a nonprofit.

TESTAMENTARY TRUST: A trust established by a last will and testament.

TRUST FUND: Everything (real or personal property, money or any assets) held by one entity for management by another.

TRUSTEE: Member of a board appointed to manage the affairs of a foundation, corporation, trust, or nonprofit.

UNITED FUND: A fundraising program administered by one agency or group for many participating or member organizations.

WORKPLACE SOLICITATION: An organized program that makes appeals to the employees of a corporation or other organization in the workplace.

PROFILES

GIVING PROFILES

ABB INC.

Company Contact

Norwalk, CT
Web: http://www.abb.com/usa

Company Description

Former Name: Asea Brown Boveri Inc.
Employees: 22,000
SIC(s): 3511 Turbines & Turbine Generator Sets, 3612 Transformers Except Electronic, 3613 Switchgear & Switchboard Apparatus, 5063 Electrical Apparatus & Equipment.
Parent Company: ABB ASEA Brown Boveri (Holding) Ltd., Affolternstrasse 44, PO Box 8131, Zurich, Switzerland

Operating Locations

CA: ABB Inc., Los Angeles; ABB Hafo Inc., San Diego; ABB Inc., San Ramon; CT: ABB Inc., Norwalk; ABB Financial Services Inc., Stamford; ABB Inc., Stamford, Windsor; FL: ABB Kent Meters, Ocala; ABB CEAG Power Supplies Inc, Palm Coast; Medium Voltage Equipment, Sanford; IN: Power Transformers & Components, Muncie; ME: ABB Environmental Services Inc., Portland; ABB Inc., Portland; MI: ABB Paint Finishing, Auburn Hills; NC: ABB Power T&D Co. Inc., Raleigh; NJ: ABB Inc., Bloomfield; ABB Lummus Global Inc., Bloomfield; ABB Lummus Heat Transfer, Bloomfield; ABB Simcon Inc., Bloomfield; ABB K-Flow Inc., Millville; ABB Trubocharger Co., North Brunswick; ABB Inc., Roseland, Union; NY: ABB Traction Inc., Elmira; ABB Inc., Rochester, Wellsville; OH: ABB Inc., Columbus; ABB Industrial Systems Inc, Columbus; PA: ABB STAL Refrigeration, Bensalem; ABB Inc., King of Prussia; TX: ABB Randall Corp., Houston; ABB Kent Taylor Inc., Laredo; ABB Control Inc., Wichita Falls; VA: ABB Power Generation, Inc., Midlothian; WI: ABB Flexible Automation, New Berlin; ABB Garden City Fan, New Berlin; WV: ABB Inc., Lewisburg

Nonmonetary Support

Type: Workplace Solicitation

Corporate Sponsorship

Type: Sports events; Arts & cultural events
Note: Sponsors Olympic events.

Giving Contact

Eleanor Anton, Director, Corporate Communications
ABB Inc.
501 Merritt 7
PO Box 06856
Norwalk, CT 06856-5308
Phone: (203)750-2461
Fax: (203)750-7788

Alternate Contact

Eleanore Anton
Phone: (203)750-2461

Description

Organization Type: Corporate Giving Program
Giving Locations: headquarters and operating communities.
Grant Types: Employee Matching Gifts, General Support, Project, Research.

Giving Philosophy

'As a corporate citizen, ABB Inc. and its companies or divisions' operations (ABB) has a responsibility to encourage and support charitable, educational, cultural, and civic activities that contribute to the well being of the United States in general and of the communities in which the Company is located in particular. Through these contributions, the Company seeks to share in society's common responsibility for improvements of health and welfare and the advancement of education and culture, as well as protection of the environment.' ABB Policy Statement

Financial Summary

Total Giving: Contributes through corporate direct giving program only. Company does not disclose contributions figures.

Typical Recipients

Arts & Humanities: Public Broadcasting
Education: Colleges & Universities, Community & Junior Colleges, Science/Mathematics Education
Health: Hospitals
Science: Science Exhibits & Fairs
Social Services: Child Welfare, Counseling, Family Services, Homes, Substance Abuse, United Funds/United Ways, Volunteer Services, Youth Organizations

Application Procedures

Initial Contact: letter of inquiry and a full proposal
Application Requirements: name and address of contact person, a description of organization, amount requested, purpose for which funds are sought, demonstration of community support and involvement, history of past support, method of meeting goals, overview of proposed budget, and statement relating purpose to interests and priorities of program
Deadlines: None.
Decision Notification: contributions committee meets once per month; responses to proposals mailed after each meeting

Restrictions

Does not support individuals; political or lobbying groups; religious organizations for sectarian purposes; fraternal or labor organizations; trips, tours, or member agencies of United Way, unless for capital purposes and approved by United Way; foundations that are primarily grantmaking bodies; hospital capital improvement campaigns, unless cost-effectiveness of total program can be clearly demonstrated; organizations located outside the United States; organizations located outside operating locations; organizations without 501(c)(3) status; private foundations; private secondary schools; publications; salaries; secondary education; organizations whose sale function is entertainment; or organizations submitting more than one proposal in a 12-month period.

Corporate Officials

Peter S. Janson: president, chief executive officer PRIM CORP EMPL president, chief executive officer: ABB Inc. CORP AFFIL chairman: ABB Power T & D Co. Inc.

Grants Analysis

Disclosure Period: calendar year ending
Typical Range: $1,000 to $5,000

ABBOTT LABORATORIES

 Number 75 of Top 100 Corporate Givers

Company Contact

100 Abbott Park Road
Abbott Park, IL 60064-6400
Phone: (847)936-1000
Fax: (847)937-1511
Web: http://www.abbott.com

Company Description

Revenue: US$13,178,000 (1999)
Employees: 56,236 (1999)
Fortune Rank: 135, per FORTUNE Magazine's list of 500 Largest U.S. Corporations (1999).
FF 135
SIC(s): 2833 Medicinals & Botanicals, 2834 Pharmaceutical Preparations, 2844 Toilet Preparations, 3841 Surgical & Medical Instruments.

Operating Locations

Argentina: Abbott Laboratories Argentina SA, Florencio Varela, Buenos Aires; Australia: Medisense Australia Pty. Ltd., Balwyn; Abbott Australasia Pty. Ltd., Kurnell; Abbott Australian Holdings Pty. Ltd., Sydney; Austria: Abbott GmbH, Vienna; Belgium: Abbott SA, Ottignies-Louvain-La-Nueve; Medisense Belgie BVBA, Wommelgem, Anvers; Brazil: Abbott Laboratories do Brasil Ltda., Sao Paulo; Canada: Medisense Canada, Mississauga; Abbott Laboratories Ltd., Montreal; Chile: Abbott Laboratories de Chile Ltda., Santa Cruz; Colombia: Abbott Laboratories de Columbia SA, Bogota, Cundinamarco; Denmark: Medisense Danmark AS, Snedsted, Viborg; Abbott Laboratories AS, Vedbaek, Copenhagen; Ecuador: Abbott Laboratories del Ecuador SA, Guayaquil, Guayas; France: Abbott Laboratories SA, Neuilly-sur-Seine; Abbott France SA, Rungis, Val-de-Marne; Medisense France SA, Schiltigheim, Bas-Rhin; Alcyon Analyseur, St. Mathieu de Treviers; Germany: Medisense (Deutschland) GmbH, Taufkirchen, Bayern; Greece: Abbott Laboratories (Hellas) SA, Athens, Attiki; Guatemala: Abbott Laboratories SA, Guatemala City; India: Abbott Laboratories Ltd., Mumbai; Ireland: Abbott Laboratories Ireland Ltd., Dublin; Abbott Ireland Ltd., Sligo; Italy: Abbott SpA, Aprilia, Lazio; Japan: Dinabot Co. Ltd., Tokyo; Mexico: Abbott Laboratories de Mexico SA de CV, Ciudad de Mexico; Malaysia: Abbott Laboratories Sdn. Bhd., Shah Alam, Selangor; Netherlands: Medisense Nederland BV, Amersfoort, Utrecht; Medisense Europe BV, Nieuwegein, Utrecht; Norway: Medisense Norge AS, Billingstad, Akershus; New Zealand: Abbott Laboratories (New Zealand) Ltd., Terrace Naenae, Wellington; Pakistan: Abbott Laboratories Pakistan Ltd., Landhi; Peru: Abbott Laboratorios SA, Lima; Portugal: Abbott Laboratorios Lda., Alfragide, Amadora; Singapore: Abbott Laboratories (Singapore) Pte. Ltd., Singapore; Spain: Abbott Cientifica SA, Madrid; Abbott Laboratories SA, Madrid; Sweden: Abbott Scandinavia AB, Kisa, Ostergotland; Medisense Sverige AB, Kisa, Ostergotland; Switzerland: Medisense AG, Basel, Basel-Stadt; Abbott Laboratories SA, Cham, Zug; Thailand: Abbott Laboratories Ltd., Pathumwan; United Kingdom: Medisense Contract Manufacturing Ltd., Abingdon, Oxfordshire; Medisense UK Ltd., Abingdon, Oxfordshire; Uruguay: Abbott Laboratories Uruguay Ltda., Montevideo; Venezuela: Abbott Laboratories CA, Caracas

Nonmonetary Support

Value: $9,000,000 (1992); $19,200,000 (1991); $5,000,000 (1989)
Type: Donated Products
Note: Product donations are directed primarily to organizations that support overseas medical missions and hospitals.

Corporate Sponsorship

Range: less than $5,000
Type: Arts & cultural events; Music & entertainment events

Abbott Laboratories Fund(Bud)

Giving Contact

Cindy Schwab, Vice President
Abbott Laboratories Fund
Dept. 379, Building AP14C
100 Abbott Park Road
Abbott Park, IL 60064-3500
Phone: (847)937-7075
Fax: (847)935-5051

Description

Founded: 1951
EIN: 366069793
Organization Type: Corporate Foundation
Giving Locations: headquarters and operating communities.
Grant Types: Employee Matching Gifts, General Support, Research.
Note: Employee matching gift ratio: 1 to 1 for elementary and secondary schools and higher education ; public broadcasting; foundations (meeting criteria); and hospitals. Contact Rhonda Rudolph, Matching Grant Coordinator.

Giving Philosophy

'The Abbott Laboratories Fund (The Fund) is an Illinois not-for-profit philanthropic corporation established by Abbott Laboratories, a leading worldwide company devoted the discovery, development, manufacture, and sale of health-care products and services. Abbott Laboratories provides the primary financial support of The Fund. The Fund is primarily designed to provide support through cash grants to United States-based recipients who operate in the areas of health and welfare, education, culture, art, civic, and public policy.' *1996 Fact Sheet*

Financial Summary

Total Giving: $10,530,134 (1998); $9,464,200 (1997); $8,900,000 (1996 approx)
Giving Analysis: Giving for 1997 includes: foundation ($7,497,362); foundation matching gifts ($1,439,381); foundation grants to United Way ($527,457); 1998: foundation ($7,631,749); foundation matching gifts ($1,606,063); foundation grants to United Way ($1,292,322)
Assets: $128,519,680 (1998); $94,695,258 (1997); $48,448,427 (1993)
Gifts Received: $9,300,000 (1998); $2,700,000 (1997)

Typical Recipients

Arts & Humanities: Arts Institutes, Community Arts, Dance, Arts & Humanities-General, Historic Preservation, Libraries, Museums/Galleries, Music, Opera, Performing Arts, Public Broadcasting, Theater
Civic & Public Affairs: Botanical Gardens/Parks, Clubs, Community Foundations, Economic Development, Economic Policy, Civic & Public Affairs-General, Hispanic Affairs, Housing, Law & Justice, Professional & Trade Associations, Public Policy, Safety, Urban & Community Affairs, Women's Affairs, Zoos/Aquariums
Education: Business Education, Colleges & Universities, Community & Junior Colleges, Continuing Education, Education Associations, Engineering/Technological Education, Health & Physical Education, Health & Physical Education, Legal Education, Medical Education, Minority Education, Private Education (Precollege), Public Education (Precollege), Religious Education, Science/Mathematics Education, Student Aid
Environment: Forestry, Environment-General
Health: Children's Health/Hospitals, Clinics/Medical Centers, Emergency/Ambulance Services, Geriatric Health, Health Organizations, Heart, Hospices, Hospitals, Hospitals (University Affiliated), Kidney, Medical Rehabilitation, Medical Research, Medical Training, Nursing Services, Nutrition, Public Health, Research/Studies Institutes, Single-Disease Health Associations
International: Health Care/Hospitals, International Development
Religion: Religious Welfare
Science: Observatories & Planetariums, Science Museums, Science Museums, Scientific Centers & Institutes, Scientific Research
Social Services: Child Welfare, Community Centers, Community Service Organizations, Delinquency & Criminal Rehabilitation, Emergency Relief, Family Services, People with Disabilities, Scouts, Sexual Abuse, Shelters/Homelessness, Substance Abuse, United Funds/United Ways, Volunteer Services, YMCA/YWCA/YMHA/YWHA, Youth Organizations

Contributions Analysis

Giving Priorities: United funds, community programs, agencies supporting disadvantaged individuals, and health care institutions. Product donations are directed primarily toward organizations that support overseas medical missions and hospitals. Major support goes to Puerto Rican community organizations, funds, and health and educational organizations. Some support for U.S.-based organizations with an international focus in the areas of international health care, education, and relations.
Arts & Humanities: 9%. Supports organizations providing cultural enrichment in operating communities. Interests include art, music, and museums. Operates matching gifts programs for public broadcasting.
Civic & Public Affairs: 6%. Interests include community improvement projects and groups involved in the fields of administration of justice, public policy, safety, and business.
Education: 20%. Concentrates on colleges and universities possessing the potential to benefit the health-care industry, including basic research programs in physical and biological sciences, medicine, pharmacology, nutrition, and diagnostics. Also supports institutions that are potential sources of personnel for the health-care industry. Operates matching gifts program for education.
Health: 50%. Supports united funds and community drives funding local institutions, or other specific, well-defined programs in communities where company has a significant number of employees. Supports agencies working with disadvantaged youth and senior citizens and agencies seeking to improve the socioeconomic position of women, minorities, and immigrant populations. Also supports individual hospitals and health-care institutions used frequently by company employees. Maintains an employee matching gifts program for hospitals.
Note: 15% of giving is in the form of matching grants. Total contributions in 1998.

Application Procedures

Initial Contact: Send written request.
Application Requirements: Send a description of organization's mission; geographic area served; description of project, outlining needs and goals; amount requested; budget information; copy of 501(c)(3) tax-exempt letter; most recent audited financial statement; annual report and other supporting materials; and list of current supporters and donors.
Deadlines: None; Contributions committee meets continuously throughout the year.
Evaluative Criteria: Priority is given to organizations serving communities in which Abbott has significant operations or employees; organizations whose activities support professions in health-care fields related to Abbott's primary areas of operation; institutions of higher learning which benefit the health care industry and its employees.
Decision Notification: Final decisions are usually made within eight weeks of receipt.

Restrictions

Does not award grants to individuals, political or lobbying groups, or religious organizations for sectarian purposes; purely social organizations; symposiums or conferences; memberships, or business-related purposes; does not support dinners, special events, ticket purchases, or goodwill advertising.

Additional Information

The fund gives preference to requests for one-time contributions and for programmatic and operating purposes; multiyear and capital requests are considered as exceptions.
Abbott Laboratories Fund is supported by contributions from Abbott Laboratories employees, retirees, and the corporation.
Publications: Abbott Laboratories Fund Contributions Policy; Annual Report

Corporate Officials

Duane Lee Burnham: chairman, chief executive officer, director B Excelsior, MN 1942. ED University of Minnesota BS (1963); University of Minnesota MBA (1972). PRIM CORP EMPL chairman, chief executive officer, director: Abbott Laboratories ADD CORP EMPL chairman: Abbott Diagnostics Inc. CORP AFFIL director: Sara Lee Corp.; chairman: Oximetrix De Puerto Rico Inc.; director: NCR Corp.; director: North Trust Corp. NONPR AFFIL trustee: Northwestern University; member advisory board, director: Northwestern University Kellogg Graduate School Business Management; life trustee: Museum Science & Industry; director: Healthcare Leadership Council; director: Lyric Opera Chicago; director: Evanston Northwestern Healthcare; chairman: Chicago Council Fgn Relationss.
Gary Patrick Coughlan: chief financial officer, senior vice president finance B Fresno, CA 1944. ED Saint Mary's College BA (1966); University of California, Los Angeles MA (1967); Wayne State University MBA (1971). PRIM CORP EMPL chief financial officer, senior vice president finance: Abbott Laboratories ADD CORP EMPL chief financial officer: Abbott Health Products Inc. CORP AFFIL director: Fort James Corp. NONPR AFFIL member: Financial Executives Institute; member advisory council: University Illinois Chicago; member advisory council: De Paul University College Commerce; member: Council Financial Executives; member advisory council: Council Foreign Relations; director: Chicago Horticultural Society; member: Conference Board Inc. CLUB AFFIL Economic Club Chicago.
Thomas Richard Hodgson: president, chief operating officer, director B Lakewood, OH 1941. ED Purdue University BSChE (1963); University of Michigan MSE (1964); Harvard University MBA (1969). PRIM CORP EMPL president, chief operating officer, director: Abbott Laboratories ADD CORP EMPL president: Abbott Chemistrys Inc.; president: Abbott Diagnostics Inc.; president: Oximetrix de Puerto Rico Inc. CORP AFFIL director: MacLean Fogg Co.; director: Case Corp. NONPR AFFIL trustee, member executive committee: Rush-Presbyterian-Saint Lukes Medical Center; member: Tau Beta Pi; member engineering visiting committee: Purdue University; member: Chicago Council Foreign Relations; member: Phi Eta Sigma. CLUB AFFIL Shoreacres Club; Knollwood Club; Economic Club; Harvard Business School Chicago Club; Chicago Club.

Foundation Officials

Gary Patrick Coughlan: director (see above)
Kenneth W. Farmer: president, director PRIM CORP EMPL vice president management information service & administration: Abbott Laboratories.
Cindy A. Schwab: vice president
Carol A. Sebesta: treasurer
J. Smith: secretary

Ellen M. Walvoord: director PRIM CORP EMPL senior vice president human resources: Abbott Laboratories.

Grants Analysis

Disclosure Period: calendar year ending 1998
Total Grants: $8,930,134*
Number of Grants: 5,000 (approx)
Average Grant: $1,786 (approx)
Highest Grant: $500,000
Typical Range: $1,000 to $5,000
***Note:** Giving excludes matching gifts; Grants analysis excludes highest grant figure.

Recent Grants

Note: Grants derived from 1998 Form 990.

Arts & Humanities

175,000 Lyric Opera of Chicago, Chicago, IL
125,000 Chicago Symphony Orchestra, Chicago, IL
100,000 World War II Memorial Fund/American Battle Monuments Commission, Arlington, VA
45,000 Museum of Contemporary Art, Chicago, IL

Civic & Public Affairs

55,000 Tri-County Industries, Rocky Mount, NC
35,000 Allendale Association, Lake Villa, IL
30,000 Women's Board of Ravinia Festival Association, Highland Park, IL
5,000 Commercial Club Foundation, Chicago, IL

Education

100,000 Barat College, Lake Forest, IL
92,625 National Merit Scholarship Corporation, Chicago, IL
65,000 Association of University Programs in Health Administration, Arlington, VA
50,000 College of Lake County Foundation, Grayslake, IL
50,000 University of Arizona-Department of Anesthesia, Tucson, AR
40,000 University of Illinois at Urbana-Champaign, Urbana, IL
34,000 University of California/Berkeley, Berkeley, CA
32,066 St. Anastasla School, Waukegan, IL
31,835 University of Illinois Foundation, Champaign, IL
31,185 University of Notre Dame, Notre Dame, IN
27,118 Moody Bible Institute, Chicago, IL
25,000 American Foundation for Pharmaceutical Education, Rockville, MD
25,000 Chicago Academy of Sciences, Chicago, IL
25,000 Lake Forest College, Lake Forest, IL
25,000 Lake Forest Graduate School of Management, Lake Forest, IL
25,000 Northwestern University Medical School, Chicago, IL
24,102 University of Wisconsin Foundation, Madison, WI
24,000 DePaul University, Chicago, IL

Environment

117,000 Lake County Forest Preserve, Libertyville, IL

Health

500,000 American Red Cross, Washington, DC
100,000 American Red Cross Disaster Relief Fund, Washington, DC
75,000 American Social Health Association, Triangle Park, NC
50,000 American Dietetic Association Foundation, Chicago, IL
50,000 American Society of Health System Pharmacists Research & Education, Bethesda, MD
50,000 American Society of Parenteral and Enteral Nutrition, Silver Spring, MD
50,000 Children's Hospital Foundation, Columbus, OH
30,000 Harvard University/Brigham & Womens Hospital, Boston, MA

International

74,921 Fondos Unidos, San Juan, Costa Rica

Religion

40,000 Catholic Charities of Lake County, Waukegan, IL

Science

110,000 Field Museum of Natural History, Chicago, IL
35,000 Museum Campus, Chicago, IL

Social Services

1,226,328 United Way Lake County, Green Oaks, IL
242,442 United Way of Franklin County, Columbus, OH
78,255 United Way of Kenosha County, Kenosha, WI
77,890 Nash/Rocky Mount United Way, Rocky Mount, NC
76,758 United Way of the Great Salt Lake Area, Salt Lake City, UT
51,253 United Way Crusade of Mercy, Chicago, IL
43,000 Northern Illinois Council on Alcoholism & Substance Abuse, Round Lake, IL
39,282 United Way of Ashland County, Ashland, KY
36,923 United Way of Santa Clara County, Santa Clara, CA
31,918 United Way of Scotland County, Laurinburg, NC
31,063 United Way of Metropolitan Dallas, Inc., Dallas, TX

ABC

Company Contact

New York, NY
Web: http://www.abc.com

Company Description

Former Name: Capital Cities/ABC.
Employees: 20,200
SIC(s): 2711 Newspapers, 2731 Book Publishing, 4832 Radio Broadcasting Stations, 4833 Television Broadcasting Stations.

Operating Locations

Australia: Capital Cities/ABC Video Systems, Sydney; France: Worldwide Television News France SA, Paris, Ville-de-Paris; Germany: Worldwide Television News GmbH, Frankfurt, Hessen; Hong Kong: ESPN Asia Ltd., Causeway Bay; ABC News Intercontinental, Central District; Italy:, Roma, Lazio; United Kingdom: Starbird Satellite Services Ltd., London; Worldwide Television News Corp., London; Worldwide Television News United Kingdom Ltd., London

ABC Foundation

Giving Contact

Ms. Bernadette Longford, Manager of Corporate Giving
ABC Foundation
77 W 66th St., 20th Fl.
New York, NY 10023
Phone: (212)456-7498
Fax: (212)456-7909

Alternate Contact

Andrew Jackson, Vice President, Corporate Affairs

Description

EIN: 237443020
Organization Type: Corporate Foundation
Former Name: Capital Cities/ABC Foundation.
Giving Locations: headquarters and operating communities.
Grant Types: Employee Matching Gifts, General Support.

Financial Summary

Total Giving: $3,082,616 (1997); $3,725,947 (1995); $3,037,511 (1994). Note: Contributes through foundation only.
Assets: $2,781,459 (1997); $1,999,069 (1995); $1,020,635 (1994)
Gifts Received: $2,000,000 (1997); $4,500,000 (1995); $2,500,000 (1994)

Typical Recipients

Arts & Humanities: Arts Associations & Councils, Arts Centers, Arts Funds, Ballet, Dance, Ethnic & Folk Arts, Film & Video, Arts & Humanities-General, Historic Preservation, History & Archaeology, Libraries, Museums/Galleries, Performing Arts, Public Broadcasting, Theater
Civic & Public Affairs: African American Affairs, Botanical Gardens/Parks, Business/Free Enterprise, Chambers of Commerce, Community Foundations, Economic Development, Employment/Job Training, First Amendment Issues, Civic & Public Affairs-General, Housing, Minority Business, Municipalities/Towns, Philanthropic Organizations, Professional & Trade Associations, Public Policy, Safety, Urban & Community Affairs, Women's Affairs
Education: Business Education, Colleges & Universities, Education Reform, Engineering/Technological Education, Journalism/Media Education, Legal Education, Literacy, Medical Education, Minority Education, Private Education (Precollege), Public Education (Precollege), Student Aid
Environment: Environment-General
Health: Cancer, Children's Health/Hospitals, Clinics/Medical Centers, Health Organizations, Heart, Hospitals, Hospitals (University Affiliated), Medical Research, Medical Training, Single-Disease Health Associations, Transplant Networks/Donor Banks
International: Foreign Arts Organizations, International Affairs, International Relief Efforts
Religion: Jewish Causes, Religious Welfare
Science: Science Museums
Social Services: At-Risk Youth, Child Welfare, Community Service Organizations, Family Services, Food/Clothing Distribution, Homes, People with Disabilities, Scouts, Senior Services, Substance Abuse, Volunteer Services, YMCA/YWCA/YMHA/YWHA, Youth Organizations

Contributions Analysis

Giving Priorities: Education, social services, civic organizations, arts funds, and health organizations. Very limited support to U.S.-based organizations with an international focus; primarily concerned with children, journalism, and the free press.
Arts & Humanities: 33%. Emphasis is on programs which encourage culturally diverse forms of expression which work to broaden their audiences. Other interests include museums, public broadcasting, film institutes, dance, music, arts associations, theater, and performing arts centers.
Civic & Public Affairs: 39%. Funding supports professional and trade associations, particularly those related to the news media. Other interests include business, civil rights, women's issues, and public policy.

Education: 13%. Supports efforts to bolster private education with emphasis on access and equity. Majority of funding supports colleges and universities, especially in the New York area. Interests include business, medical, journalism, and legal education. Other areas of interest include public education, literacy, minority education, and student aid.
Environment: 2%. Support environmental concerns.
Health: 2%. Funds single-disease health associations, health centers, and hospitals.
International: 3%.
Religion: 2%. Supports religious organizations and Jewish causes.
Science: About 1%.
Social Services: 5%. Emphasizes youth organizations. Child welfare, family services, community service organizations, employment, the aged, and religious welfare are also supported.
Note: Total contributions made in 1997.

Application Procedures

Initial Contact: Send a brief letter or proposal.
Application Requirements: Include a description of organization; amount requested; purpose of funds sought; recently audited financial statement; proof of tax-exempt status.
Deadlines: First of February, May, August, or November.
Decision Notification: Decisions are generally made on a quarterly basis.

Restrictions

Does not make contributions to individuals.

Corporate Officials

Ronald J. Doerfler: senior vice president, chief financial officer B Jersey City, NJ 1941. ED Fairleigh Dickinson University BS (1965); Fairleigh Dickinson University MBA (1973). PRIM CORP EMPL senior vice president, chief financial officer: Capital Cities ABC Inc. ADD CORP EMPL senior vice president: American Broadcasting Companies; director, vice president: ABC News Inc.; vice president. chief financial officer: Hearst Corp.; vice president: WABC-AM Radio Inc. NONPR AFFIL member: Institute Newspaper Fin Executives; member: International Radio & Television Society; member: American Institute CPAs; member: Broadcast Fin Management Association.
Philip Richeson Farnsworth: secretary B New Orleans, LA 1941. ED Washington & Lee University BA (1964); Tulane University JD (1967); New York University LLM (1968). PRIM CORP EMPL secretary: ABC, Inc. ADD CORP EMPL secretary: ABC Holding Co. Inc.; secretary, director: ABC News Inc.; secretary: TV Connection Inc. CLUB AFFIL University Club.
Michael Patrick Mallardi: senior vice president B New York, NY 1934. ED University of Notre Dame BA (1956). PRIM CORP EMPL senior vice president: ABC.
Thomas Sawyer Murphy: B Brooklyn, NY 1925. ED Cornell University BS (1945); Harvard University MBA (1949). CORP AFFIL director: Walt Disney Co.; chairman, director: WPLJ-FM Radio Inc.; chairman, director: WABC-AM Radio Inc.; director: Columbia/HCA Healthcare Corp.; director: Double Click; director: America Broadcasting Companies.

Foundation Officials

Daniel Barnett Burke: vice president, treasurer, director B Albany, NY 1929. ED University of Vermont AB (1950); Harvard University MBA (1955). PRIM CORP EMPL director: ABC. CORP AFFIL director: Rohm & Haas Co.; director: Washington Post Co.; director: Darden Restaurants Inc.; director: Morgan Stanley Group Inc.; director: Conrail Inc.; director: Consolidated Rail Corp. NONPR AFFIL director: Partnership Drug Free America; trustee: Presbyterian Hospital; chairman: International Executive Service Corps.
Ronald J. Doerfler: vice president, director (see above)
Philip Richeson Farnsworth: secretary (see above)
Andrew Jackson: vice president PRIM CORP EMPL vice president corporate affairs: ABC.
Bernadette Williams Longford: manager corporate giving
Michael Patrick Mallardi: vice president, director (see above)
David Westin: vice president, director B Flint, MI 1952. ED University of Michigan BA (1974); University of Michigan JD (1977). PRIM CORP EMPL president: ABC TV Network ADD CORP EMPL president, director: America Broadcasting Companies Television Network Group; president: ABC News Holding Co. Inc. CORP AFFIL vice president: KTRK TV Inc.

Grants Analysis

Disclosure Period: calendar year ending 1997
Total Grants: $3,082,616
Number of Grants: 229
Average Grant: $13,461
Highest Grant: $500,000
Typical Range: $2,000 to $15,000

Recent Grants

Note: Grants derived from 1997 Form 990.

Arts & Humanities

200,000	Academy of Television Arts and Sciences, North Hollywood, CA
100,000	New York Science, Industry, and Business Library, New York, NY
90,000	Museum of Television and Radio, New York, NY
75,000	Lincoln Center for the Performing Arts, New York, NY
50,000	Museum of Television and Radio, New York, NY
50,000	Performing Arts, Fort Worth, TX
25,000	American Film Institute, Los Angeles, CA
25,000	Lincoln Center for the Performing Arts, New York, NY
15,000	Acting Company, New York, NY
15,000	Dance Theater of Harlem, New York, NY
15,000	Metropolitan Museum of Art, New York, NY
15,000	New York City Ballet, New York, NY

Civic & Public Affairs

500,000	Greater Kansas City Community Foundation, Kansas City, MO
50,000	Central Park Conservancy, New York, NY
50,000	Enterprise Foundation, Columbia, MD
33,333	American Press Institute, Reston, VA
25,000	American Women's Economic Development Corporation, New York, NY
20,000	Committee for Economic Development, New York, NY
20,000	Habitat for Humanity, Kansas City, MO
20,000	J.P. McCarthy Foundation, Southfield, MI
20,000	Public Allies, Chicago, IL
18,000	Foundation for Minority Interests in Media, New York, NY
15,000	Center for Communication, New York, NY
15,000	Citizens Advice Bureau, New York, NY
12,500	National Black Media Coalition, Silver Spring, MD

Education

50,000	Columbia University School of Journalism, New York, NY
50,000	Communities in Schools, Alexandria, VA
50,000	Inner-City Scholarship Fund, New York, NY
25,000	Junior Achievement, New York, NY
20,000	St. John's University, Jamaica, NY
20,000	University of Missouri School of Journalism, Columbia, MO
15,000	College Fund/UNCF, New York, NY
15,000	Reading is Fundamental, Washington, DC
12,500	University of North Carolina School of Journalism, Chapel Hill, NC

Environment

25,000	Open Space Institute, New York, NY -- Conservation Partnership project
22,500	River Legacy Foundation, Fort Worth, TX

Health

20,000	New York Blood Center, New York, NY
15,000	Herbert G. Birch Services, New York, NY
12,500	Georgetown University Medical Center, Washington, DC

International

25,000	UNICEF, New York, NY
25,000	UNICEF, New York, NY
20,000	International Radio and Television Foundation, New York, NY
20,000	International Radio and Television Foundation, New York, NY
15,000	International Executive Service Corps, Stamford, CT
15,000	International Executive Service Corps, Stamford, CT

Religion

25,000	University of Notre Dame, Notre Dame, IN -- Holocaust Conference project
15,000	Jewish Museum, New York, NY

Science

20,000	American Museum of Natural History, New York, NY

Social Services

30,000	Madison Square Boys and Girls Club, New York, NY
25,000	Hazelden, Center City, MN
25,000	Westside YMCA, New York, NY
15,000	Boys Hope, Bridgeton, MO
13,500	Girl Scouts of America, New York, NY

ACE HARDWARE CORP.

Company Contact

2200 Kensington Ct.
Oak Brook, IL 60523
Phone: (630)990-6600
Fax: (630)990-6838
Web: http://www.acehardware.com

Company Description

Revenue: US$3,181,800,000 (1999)
Employees: 4,352
Fortune Rank: 482, per FORTUNE Magazine's list of 500 Largest U.S. Corporations (1999).
FF 482
SIC(s): 5072 Hardware, 5251 Hardware Stores.

Operating Locations

Ace Hardware operates in all 50 U.S. states and 62 foreign countries.

Corporate Sponsorship

Value: $3,100,000 (1999); $3,000,000 (1998)
Type: Sports events; Other
Contact: Jane Murphy
Care of Children's Miracle Network
2200 Kensington Court
OakBrook, IL 60523-2100

Ace Hardware Foundation

Giving Contact

Paula K. Erickson, Manager, Corporate Communication and Public Relations
2200 Kensington Court
Oak Brook, IL 60523-2100
Phone: (630)990-6444
Fax: (630)990-1742
Email: pthom@memo.acehardware.com

Description

EIN: 363820478
Organization Type: Corporate Foundation
Giving Locations: nationally.

Financial Summary

Total Giving: $3,016,000 (1998 approx); $40,040 (1997); $1,500,000 (1996 approx)
Giving Analysis: Giving for 1997 includes: foundation ($40,040); 1998: corporate direct giving (approx $3,000,000); foundation (approx $16,000)
Assets: $415,481 (1998); $3,703 (1997); $8,939 (1996)
Gifts Received: $420,561 (1998); $34,195 (1997); $32,963 (1996)

Typical Recipients

Health: Children's Health/Hospitals, Emergency/Ambulance Services

Contributions Analysis

Health: 100%. Corporate sponsorship includes funding to The Children's Miracle Network. Through the foundation, funding is given to The American Red Cross.

Application Procedures

Initial Contact: Send a brief letter.
Application Requirements: Provide name and purpose of organization, name and address of contact person, a detailed description of why funds are needed, and proof of tax-exempt status.
Deadlines: December 31.

Restrictions

Company is restricted by federal guidelines from making charitable contributions since it is a dealer-owned cooperative. However, Ace Hardware employees, dealers, and vendors do support the Children's Miracle Network through various fund-raising activities. Disaster relief efforts are also supported.
Company supports 501 (c) (3) organizations only.

Additional Information

Publications: Annual Report

Corporate Officials

David F. Hodnik: president, chief executive officer B Waukegan, IL 1947. ED Western Illinois University BS (1970). PRIM CORP EMPL president, chief executive officer: Ace Hardware Corp. CORP AFFIL president, director: ACE Insurance Agency Inc.
Howard J. Jung: chairman, director PRIM CORP EMPL chairman, director: Ace Hardware Corp.

Grants Analysis

Disclosure Period: calendar year ending 1998
Total Grants: $16,000*
Number of Grants: 1
***Note:** Giving excludes corporate direct giving.

Recent Grants

Note: Grants derived from 1999 Form 990.

Health
American Red Cross National Headquarters, Washington, DC -- Flood, Hurricane Tornado, and Disaster Victims

Advanced Micro Devices, Inc.

Company Contact

1 AMD Place
Sunnyvale, CA 94086
Web: http://www.amd.com

Company Description

Founded: 1969
Foreign Name: AMD
Revenue: US$2,857,600 (1999)
Employees: 13,800 (1998)
SIC(s): 3672 Printed Circuit Boards.

Operating Locations

Japan: Atsugi; Malaysia: Penang, Pulau Pinang; Singapore; Thailand: Bangkok; United Kingdom: Basingstoke, Hampshire

Nonmonetary Support

Type: Donated Equipment; Donated Products; In-kind Services
Volunteer Programs: AMD organizes group volunteer activites that provide hundreds of AMD employees with the opportunity to participate in local community events. The company's Grant Incentives for Volunteer Efforts (GIVE) program provides minigrants to eligible organizations for which AMD employees volunteer.
Contact: Jeanette Nagashima, University Relations Manager
Note: Alternate Contact: Allyson Peerman, Corporate Community Affairs.

Corporate Sponsorship

Value: $200,000
Type: Festivals/fairs; Sports events; Other
Contact: Dyan, Community Affairs Site Manager Sunnyvale, CA
Note: Sponsors education-related events, festivals, volunteer recognition, and special olympics.

Giving Contact

Allyson Peerman, Manager, Corporate Community Affairs
AMD Charitable Giving Program
5204 E. Ben White Blvd.
MailStop 529
Austin, TX 78741
Phone: (512)602-5501
Email: allyson.peerman@AMD.com

Description

Organization Type: Corporate Giving Program
Former Name: Advanced Micro Devices Charitable Foundation.
Giving Locations: CA; TX headquarters and operating communities.
Grant Types: Emergency, Employee Matching Gifts, General Support, Project.

Giving Philosophy

'Advanced Micro Devices is committed to being a good neighbor, and a responsible, conscientious and involved corporate citizen of our local communities. Through community involvement and philanthropic investments, AMD strives to positively impact the health and prosperity of the region, to create a prepared and adaptable current and future workforce and support well-managed nonprofit providers in their efforts to effectively serve disadvantaged members of the local population. These actions are designed to enrich the communities in which we operate, making them better places to live, work, and conduct business.' Corporate Philosophy, Corporate Contributions Program Guidelines and Application

Financial Summary

Total Giving: $2,500,000 (2000 approx); $2,500,000 (1999); $2,500,000 (1998). Note: Contributes through corporate direct giving program only.
Giving Analysis: Giving for 1998 includes: corporate direct giving (approx $2,500,000); 1999: corporate direct giving (approx $2,500,000); 2000: corporate direct giving (approx $2,500,000)

Typical Recipients

Civic & Public Affairs: Employment/Job Training, Civic & Public Affairs-General
Education: Colleges & Universities, Private Education (Precollege), Public Education (Precollege), Science/Mathematics Education
Health: Clinics/Medical Centers, Hospitals
Social Services: Child Welfare, Community Centers, Community Service Organizations, Food/Clothing Distribution, People with Disabilities, Shelters/Homelessness, United Funds/United Ways, Youth Organizations

Contributions Analysis

Giving Priorities: Contributions are allocated to education, civic betterment, health and human services, and the United Way.
Civic & Public Affairs: 3%.
Education: 40%.
Social Services: 57%. Includes health and human services funding.
Note: Total contributions made in 1997.

Application Procedures

Initial Contact: Send a letter requesting guidelines and an AMD grant application form.
Application Requirements: Include specific amount requested, with an explanation of how the funds will be used; a description of organization that will be receiving the grant, with a statement of its purposes and objectives and scope; description of how funds will be used, including project goals, method for measuring results, and a timetable for program implementation; the names and qualifications of the person(s) who will administer the grant; proof of tax-exempt status; financial statement or annual report; project budget; and list of board members, and contributors.
Deadlines: May 1 for decisions made by September; December 1 for decisions made by March.
Review Process: Organizations are contacted by phone or letter when decision is made.
Evaluative Criteria: Ability of the agency to be self-supporting; whether AMD funds will be used to 'lever' for other funding, particularly from other companies; whether request for support is for a specific project and generally not for on-going operating expenses; whether AMD funds will be used to enhance existing programs by funding special projects or providing seed funds for a new component of an organization; and impact on AMD employees, families, and general community.
Decision Notification: Reply given within six weeks of receipt of proposal.

Restrictions

Grants ordinarily are not given for fund-raising events such as dinners or golf tournaments. They are never given to political, religious, or fraternal organizations; individuals; capital or endowment fund-raising drives; or national, advocacy, research, or cultural programs. Athletic teams, recreational programs, public broadcasting and scouting troops are also excluded from funding.

Additional Information

Receiving a grant one year does not ensure eligibility the following year.
Organizations receiving funding are requested to share their progress with the contributions committee through written reports at least once each year
The foundation has been dissolved; the company only gives directly.

The company allocates 1% of its pretax profits to its charitable contributions program.
The company allocates 1% of its pretax profits to its charitable contributions program.
Publications: Corporate Contributions Guidelines

Corporate Officials

Richard Previte: president, chief operating officer, director B Boston, MA 1935. ED San Jose State University BS (1956); San Jose State University MA (1957). PRIM CORP EMPL vice chairman: Advanced Micro Devices Inc. ADD CORP EMPL president: AMD Travel Ltd. CORP AFFIL director: Robinson Nugent Inc.; acting chief executive officer: Vantis.
Walter Jeremiah Sanders, III: chairman, chief executive officer, director B Chicago, IL 1936. ED University of Illinois BEE (1958). PRIM CORP EMPL chairman, chief executive officer, director: AMD. CORP AFFIL director: Donaldson Lufkin & Jenrette Inc. NONPR AFFIL co-founder, director, member: Santa Clara County Manufacturing Group; co-founder, director, member: Semiconductor Industry Association.

Giving Program Officials

Brenda Hendrickson: manager corporate affairs and corporate giving

Grants Analysis

Disclosure Period: calendar year ending

Recent Grants

Note: Grants derived from 1993 Form 990.

Health
10,000 VMC Foundation, San Jose, CA -- Valley Medical Center

AEGON U.S.A. INC.

Company Contact

1111 North Charles St.
Baltimore, MD 21201-5574
Phone: (410)576-4571
Fax: (410)347-8685
Web: http://www.aegon.com

Company Description

Employees: 6,000
SIC(s): 6311 Life Insurance, 6719 Holding Companies Nec.
Parent Company: AEGON NV, Mariahoeveplein 50, The Hague, Netherlands

Operating Locations

FL: Idex Investor Services, Largo; Idex Management, Largo; Intersecurities, Largo; GA: Creditor Resources, Atlanta; IA: AEGON USA, Cedar Rapids; AEGON U.S.A. Inc., Cedar Rapids; Hawkeye Holding, Cedar Rapids; IN: JLW Financial Management Systems, Inc., Merrillville; KY: AEGON USA, Louisville; Commonwealth General Corp., Louisville; MD: AEGON USA, Inc., Baltimore; AUSA Holding Co., Baltimore; AUSA Life Insurance Co., Baltimore; NJ: AEGON Reinsurance Co. of America, Short Hills; AEGON U.S. Holding Corp., Short Hills; CORPA Reinsurance Co., Short Hills

Nonmonetary Support

Type: In-kind Services; Loaned Executives

Corporate Sponsorship

Type: Arts & cultural events; Festivals/fairs; Music & entertainment events; Sports events

AEGON U.S.A. Charitable Foundation

Giving Contact

Rosmary Kostmayer, Director, Public Relations and Colorados
AEGON USA, Inc.
1111 N. Charles St.
Baltimore, MD 21201
Phone: (410)576-4576
Fax: (410)347-8685

Alternate Contact

Marie Swope
4333 Edgewood Road Northeast
Cedar Rapids, IA 52499
Phone: (319)398-8935

Description

Founded: 1988
EIN: 421415998
Organization Type: Corporate Foundation. Supports preselected organizations only.
Giving Locations: IA: eastern; KY; MD: central headquarters and operating communities.
Grant Types: Capital, Employee Matching Gifts, General Support, Project, Scholarship.

Financial Summary

Total Giving: $2,261,985 (1998); $1,266,783 (1997); $1,153,374 (1996). Note: Contributes through corporate direct giving program and foundation.
Giving Analysis: Giving for 1997 includes: foundation ($822,427); foundation grants to United Way ($385,323); foundation matching gifts ($59,033); 1998: foundation ($1,397,191); foundation grants to United Way ($797,843); foundation matching gifts ($66,951)
Assets: $51,853,774 (1998); $49,153,723 (1997); $23,762,499 (1996)
Gifts Received: $3,592,021 (1998); $17,762,876 (1997); $29,477 (1996). Note: In 1998, contributions were received from Life Investors Insurance Co. of America, Leo Barry, Mr. and Mrs. Donald Shepard, and others. In 1997, contributions were received from PLF Insurance, Commonwealth General Corp., Reading Fun Ltd., Leo Barry, Life Investors Industry Co. of America, Bankers United Life Assurance Co., Monumental Life Industry Co., Larry Brown, Mr. & Mrs. Donald Shephard, and Rex Eno.

Typical Recipients

Arts & Humanities: Arts Institutes, Community Arts, Dance, Ethnic & Folk Arts, Historic Preservation, History & Archaeology, Libraries, Museums/Galleries, Music, Public Broadcasting, Theater
Civic & Public Affairs: Chambers of Commerce, Clubs, Community Foundations, Civic & Public Affairs-General, Housing, Philanthropic Organizations, Public Policy, Zoos/Aquariums
Education: Business Education, Colleges & Universities, Community & Junior Colleges, Education Funds, Education-General, Private Education (Precollege), Public Education (Precollege), Secondary Education (Public), Student Aid
Environment: Resource Conservation
Health: Alzheimers Disease, Arthritis, Children's Health/Hospitals, Diabetes, Heart, Hospitals, Public Health, Single-Disease Health Associations
International: Health Care/Hospitals
Religion: Dioceses, Religious Welfare
Science: Scientific Centers & Institutes
Social Services: Child Welfare, Community Service Organizations, Domestic Violence, Family Services, Recreation & Athletics, United Funds/United Ways, YMCA/YWCA/YMHA/YWHA

Contributions Analysis

Giving Priorities: Supports education, health, and cultural and civic organizations.
Arts & Humanities: 5%.
Civic & Public Affairs: 6%. Supports chamber of commerce and community development.
Education: 18%. Gives to Junior Achievement, colleges and university and other education concerns.
Health: 4%.
Religion: 6%. Funds Catholic concerns.
Social Services: 60%. Supports United Way, YMCAs/YWCAs, and youth groups.
Note: Total contributions made in 1998.

Application Procedures

Deadlines: None.
Notes: Foundation allocates some funding to its subsidiary, Commonwealth General Corporation. Commonwealth does does not make direct grants but may be contacted for grant consideration through Aegon.

Additional Information

AEGON merged with Providian Corp. in June 1997.

Corporate Officials

Patrick S. Baird: chief operating officer, chief financial officer, chief executive officer B 1954. ED University of Iowa BS (1976). PRIM CORP EMPL chief operating officer, chief financial officer: AEGON United States of America Inc. CORP AFFIL director: Capital Security Insurance; chief operating officer: Life Investors Insurance America; chief financial officer: AUSA Holding Co.
Bart Herbert, Jr.: executive vice president, chief marketing officer B Ogden, UT 1955. ED University of Utah (1978); Emory University (1992). PRIM CORP EMPL executive vice president, chief marketing officer: AEGON U.S.A. Inc. CORP AFFIL president: Monumental General Casualty Co.; president, chief executive officer: Monumental General Insurance Group; president: Monumental General Administrator.
Douglas C. Kolsrud: executive vice president, chief investment officer B 1955. ED University of Iowa BS (1978). PRIM CORP EMPL executive vice president, chief investment officer: AEGON U.S.A. Inc. CORP AFFIL vice president: Life Investors Insurance of America; vice president: PFL Life Insurance Co.; vice president: First AUSA Life Insurance Co.; executive vice president: AEGON United States of America Investment Management; vice president: Bankers United Life Assurance Co.
Donald James Shepard: chairman, president, chief executive officer B Cedar Rapids, IA 1946. ED University of Chicago MBA (1981). PRIM CORP EMPL chairman, president, chief executive officer: AEGON U.S.A. Inc. CORP AFFIL trustee: Walters Art Gallery; director: Mercantile Safe Deposit Trust Co.; director: PHH Corp.; director: Mercantile Bankshares Corp. NONPR AFFIL trustee: Johns Hopkins Health System Corp./Johns Hopkins Hospital; trustee: Johns Hopkins University; director: Baltimore Symphony Orchestra.

Giving Program Officials

Rosmary Kostmayer: manager PRIM CORP EMPL director communications: AEGON U.S.A. Inc.

Grants Analysis

Disclosure Period: calendar year ending 1998
Total Grants: $1,397,194*
Number of Grants: 179
Average Grant: $7,806
Highest Grant: $240,000
Typical Range: $500 to $25,000
***Note:** Grant analysis excludes matching gifts; United Way.

Recent Grants

Note: Grants derived from 1998 Form 990.

Arts & Humanities

35,000 Baltimore Symphony Orchestra, Baltimore, MD
19,500 Cedar Rapids Symphony, Cedar Rapids, IA
11,101 Baltimore Symphony Orchestra, Baltimore, MD
10,000 Maryland Historical Society, Baltimore, MD
10,000 Maryland Institute, Baltimore, MD

Civic & Public Affairs

50,000 Congressional Award Foundation, Washington, DC
15,000 Cedar Rapids Area Chamber Of Commerce/Priority One, Cedar Rapids
10,000 Greater Baltimore Community Foundation, Baltimore, MD
10,000 Greater Cedar Rapids Foundation Skate Inc., Cedar Rapids, IA
10,000 Revisions Community Housing Development, Catonville, MD
10,000 Variety Club of Iowa, Cedar Rapids, IA
7,500 National Aquarium in Baltimore, Baltimore, MD

Education

89,375 University of Northern Iowa, Cedar Falls, IA
80,000 Jefferson County Public Education Foundation, Louisville, KY
20,000 Mt. Saint Mary's College, Emmitsburg, MD
20,000 University of Baltimore, Baltimore, MD
20,000 University of Maryland Foundation, Baltimore, MD
20,000 Villa Julie College, Stevenson, MD
16,405 Transylvania University, Lexington, KY
15,000 Junior Achievement of ECI, Cedar Rapids, IA
15,000 Regis-LaSalle Foundation, Cedar Rapids, IA
10,060 Kirkwood Community College Foundation, Cedar Rapids, IA
10,000 Junior Achievement, Louisville, KY
10,000 Junior Achievement of Central Maryland, Hunt Valley, MD

Health

40,000 Copper Ridge, Sykesville, MD
15,000 Mt. Washington Pediatric Hospital, Baltimore, MD
10,000 Arkansas Children's Hospital Fund, Little Rock, AR
7,500 American Diabetes Association, Cedar Rapids, IA

Religion

100,000 Archdiocese of Baltimore, Baltimore, MD
7,500 St. Luke's Foundation, Cedar Rapids, IA

Social Services

240,000 Metro United Way, Louisville, KY
165,573 United Way of Central Md., Baltimore, MD
125,000 YMCA of Greater Louisville Project Safe Place, Louisville, KY
67,500 Police Athletic League, Baltimore, MD
52,817 United Way of East Central Ia, Cedar Rapids, IA
52,817 United Way of ECI, Cedar Rapids, IA
52,817 United Way of ECI, Cedar Rapids, IA
52,817 United Way of ECI, Cedar Rapiuds, IA
44,073 United Way of Pinellas County, Largo, FL
33,542 United Way of Westchester & Putnam, White Plains, NY
33,542 United Way of Westchester Putnam, White Plains, NY
32,334 Triangle United Way, Charlotte, NY
30,000 Family & Children's Counseling Center, Louisville, KY
20,354 United Way of Pulaski County, Little Rock, AR
15,000 Alternative Services, Cedar Rapids, IA
15,000 YMCA of Central Maryland, Baltimore, MD
12,500 Four Oaks Foundation, Cedar Rapids, IA
12,000 United Way of Pulaski County, Little Rock, AR
10,000 The Family Tree, Baltimore, MD

AETNA, INC.

 Number 31 of Top 100 Corporate Givers

Company Contact

151 Farmington Ave.
Hartford, CT 06156
Phone: (860)273-0123
Fax: (860)273-3971
Web: http://www.aetna.com

Company Description

Former Name: Aetna Life & Casualty Co.
Revenue: US$26,453,000,000 (1999)
Profit: US$848,100,000
Employees: 55,900 (1999)
Fortune Rank: 49, per FORTUNE Magazine's list of 500 Largest U.S. Corporations (1999).
FF 49
SIC(s): 6311 Life Insurance, 6321 Accident & Health Insurance, 6331 Fire, Marine & Casualty Insurance, 6411 Insurance Agents, Brokers & Service.

Operating Locations

Australia: Aetna International (Australia) Ltd., Chatswood; Canada: Aetna Benefits Management, Toronto; Aetna Canada Holdings Ltd., Toronto; Aetna Life Insurance Co. of Canada, Toronto; Equinox Financial Group, Toronto; Mount Batten Properties Ltd., Toronto; Hong Kong: East Asia Aetna Insurance Co. Hong Kong, Central District; East Asta Aetna Services Co. Ltd., Central District; New Zealand: Aetna International (New Zealand) Ltd.; Aetna Health (New Zealand) Ltd., Auckland; Taiwan: Aetna Life Insurance Co. of America (ALICA), Taipei; United Kingdom: Aetna Capital Management International Ltd., London; Imperial Fire & Marine Reinsurance Co. Ltd., London
Note: Operates in more than 100 cities nationwide.

Nonmonetary Support

Value: $2,000 (1999 approx); $10,000 (1998 approx); $30,000 (1997)
Type: In-kind Services
Volunteer Programs: The company sponsors the Aetna Volunteer Council.

Corporate Sponsorship

Value: $1,533,000 (1998); $1,275,954 (1997); $1,540,159 (1996)
Type: Sports events; Other

Aetna Foundation

Giving Contact

Ms. Marilda G. Alfonso, President & Executive Director
Aetna Foundation
151 Farmington Ave., RE1B
Hartford, CT 06156-3180
Phone: (860)273-4770
Fax: (860)273-4764

Alternate Contact

Phone: (860)273-6382

Description

EIN: 237241940
Organization Type: Corporate Foundation
Giving Locations: CT: Hartford principally near operating locations and to national organizations.
Grant Types: Employee Matching Gifts, General Support, Matching, Multiyear/Continuing Support.
Note: Employee matching gift ratio: 1 to 1 for gifts to eligible organization, up to $5,000 per employee annually. Also makes loans/investments for social purposes. Matching grants will be pro-rated when the maximum is exceeded.

Financial Summary

Total Giving: $25,771,876 (1999 approx); $29,395,344 (1998); $17,860,750 (1997). Note: Contributes through corporate direct giving program and foundation. 1999 Giving includes corporate direct giving ($16,109,484); foundation ($8,819,242); domestic subsidiaries ($141,150); international subsidiaries ($700,000); nonmonetary support. 1997 Giving includes foundation ($6,944,641).
Giving Analysis: Giving for 1998 includes: domestic subsidiaries ($13,869,002); corporate direct giving ($7,441,035); foundation ($7,256,637); international subsidiaries ($828,670)
Assets: $4,600,000 (1999); $12,909,213 (1998); $18,595,515 (1997)
Gifts Received: $5,550,629 (1997); $5,255,007 (1996); $212,629 (1995). Note: Foundation receives contributions from Aetna, Inc.

Typical Recipients

Arts & Humanities: Arts Associations & Councils, Arts Centers, Arts Outreach, Ballet, Arts & Humanities-General, Historic Preservation, History & Archaeology, Libraries, Opera
Civic & Public Affairs: African American Affairs, Business/Free Enterprise, Chambers of Commerce, Economic Development, Employment/Job Training, Hispanic Affairs, Law & Justice, Minority Business, Public Policy, Urban & Community Affairs
Education: Afterschool/Enrichment Programs, Arts/Humanities Education, Business Education, Business-School Partnerships, Colleges & Universities, Education Associations, Education Funds, Education Reform, Education-General, Health & Physical Education, International Studies, Leadership Training, Medical Education, Minority Education, Public Education (Precollege), Science/Mathematics Education, Secondary Education (Private), Secondary Education (Public), Student Aid, Vocational & Technical Education
Health: AIDS/HIV, Cancer, Children's Health/Hospitals, Clinics/Medical Centers, Emergency/Ambulance Services, Health Organizations, Heart, Hospitals, Nursing Services, Nutrition, Prenatal Health Issues, Public Health, Respiratory
International: Foreign Educational Institutions, Health Care/Hospitals, International Development, International Organizations, International Relief Efforts
Religion: Seminaries
Science: Scientific Centers & Institutes
Social Services: At-Risk Youth, Child Abuse, Child Welfare, Family Services, People with Disabilities, Scouts, United Funds/United Ways, Volunteer Services, Youth Organizations

Contributions Analysis

Giving Priorities: Educational achievement for minorities especially in higher education, programs in low-income urban communities, united funds, AIDS and other health programs. An international grants program was created in 1988 to make contributions in countries where Aetna is expanding operations. Foundation programs are under way in Canada (with

over $140,000 disbursed in 1997), Hong Kong, Malaysia, China, South Africa, and Chile. Local management plays a key role in identifying promising grant candidates. Priorities are immunization and primary health-care for children, and educational scholarships.
Arts & Humanities: 6%.
Civic & Public Affairs: About 10%. General giving program, with grants to national and local organizations through field offices, international offices, departments, and headquarters office. Supports public affairs, community development, and workforce development programs.
Education: 19%. supports college preparation, school-to-career initiatives and Junior Achievement.
Health: 25%. Supports cardiovascular disease prevention and detection initiatives.
International: 8%.
Religion: 1%.
Social Services: 31%. Supports the United Way and other social service organizations.
Note: Above priorities are for foundation and corporate grants. Aetna also gives Voice of Conscience Awards, and contributes through Aetna US Healthcare and Aetna Canada. Total contributions made in 1997.

Application Procedures

Initial Contact: most grants are in an invitation-only basis; contact local field office or headquarters office for current policy

Restrictions

Foundation does not support individuals; capital building, endowment or debt reduction drives; political activities; religious organizations; scholarships; fundraising dinners, advertising or other similar special events, sporting events or conferences; and organizations that do not have tax-exempt status.

Additional Information

Aetna sponsors the Quality Care Research Fund, which makes grants to participants in the Academic and Managed Care Forum for medical research and education of forum participants. Contact Dennis Oakes, (215)654-5964.
For information on the Voice of Conscience Awards, call (860)273-6382.
Publications: Annual Report

Corporate Officials

John Roger Bolton: senior vice president corporate communications B Saint Louis, MO 1950. ED Iowa State University (1968-1970); Ohio State University BJ (1972). PRIM CORP EMPL senior vice president corporate communications: Aetna, Inc.
Earl Gilbert Graves: director B Brooklyn, NY 1935. ED Morgan State University BA (1958). PRIM CORP EMPL chairman: Earl G. Graves Ltd. ADD CORP EMPL chairman: Earl G. Graves Publishing; chairman, chief executive officer: Pepsi-Cola Washington DC. CORP AFFIL director: Federated Department Stores Inc.; director: Rohm & Haas Co.; director: AMR Corp.; director: Aetna Inc.; director: Aetna Life & Casualty Co. Inc. NONPR AFFIL member president council business administration: University Vermont; director: Young President Organization; director: Steadman-Hawkins Sports Medicine; director: TransAfrica Forum; member: Sigma Pi Phi; member: Southern Christian Leadership Conference; member: President Commission Small & Minority Business; director: New York State Urban Development Corp.; member: Omega Psi Phi; director: National Supplier Development Council; director: New American Schools Development Corp.; director: Magazine Publishers Association; member: NAACP; member: Interracial Council Business Opportunity; member visitors committee: Harvard University John F Kennedy School Government; trustee: Howard University; director: Business Marketing Corp.; director: Glass Ceiling Commission; trustee: American Museum Natural History & Planetarium Authority; national commissioner scouting: Boy Scouts America; director: Advertising Council. CLUB AFFIL trustee: New York Economic Club.
Richard Leslie Huber: chairman, president, chief executive officer, director B Brevard, NC 1936. ED Harvard University BA (1958). PRIM CORP EMPL chairman, president, chief executive officer, director: Aetna, Inc. ADD CORP EMPL vice chairman: Aetna Services Inc.; vice chairman: Aetna Life Insurance Co. CORP AFFIL vice chairman: Aetna Life & Casualty Co. Inc.; director: Re Corp. NONPR AFFIL director: Hartford Ballet; trustee: Mark Twain House; member: Council Foreign Relations. CLUB AFFIL Harvard Club.
Lucille M. Nickerson: vice president, corporate secretary B Canaan, CT 1947. ED Connecticut College BA (1968); University of Connecticut JD (1980); University of Connecticut MS (1980). PRIM CORP EMPL vice president, corporate secretary: Aetna, Inc. ADD CORP EMPL vice president: Aetna Life Insurance Co.
L. Edward Shaw, Jr.: general counsel B Elmira, NY 1944. ED Georgetown University BA (1966); Yale University JD (1969). PRIM CORP EMPL general counsel: Aetna Inc. ADD CORP EMPL chief cor officer: National Westminster Bank North America. NONPR AFFIL member: Association Bar New York City; member: Phi Beta Kappa. CLUB AFFIL Winged Foot Golf Club.
Arnold B. West: assistant secretary counsel PRIM CORP EMPL assistant secretary counsel: Aetna, Inc.

Giving Program Officials

Diana Kinosh: director PRIM CORP EMPL consultant: Aetna, Inc.

Foundation Officials

Marilda G. Alfonso: president, executive director
Rub Apatoff: director
John Roger Bolton: senior vice president (see above)
Ronald E. Compton: chairman, president (see above)
Frederick C. Copeland, Jr.: director ED Columbia University (1967). PRIM CORP EMPL president: Aetna International Inc.
Earl Gilbert Graves: director (see above)
John Y. Kim: director PRIM CORP EMPL vice president: Aetna Life Insurance & Annuity Co. CORP AFFIL president: Aeltus Investment Management.
Lucille M. Nickerson: secretary (see above)
Arnold B. West: counsel (see above)
Elease E. Wright: director B Queens, NY 1954. ED University of Connecticut (1976). PRIM CORP EMPL senior vice president: Aetna Inc.

Grants Analysis

Disclosure Period: calendar year ending 1998
Total Grants: $14,697,672*
Number of Grants: 800 (approx)
Average Grant: $18,372 (approx)
Highest Grant: $1,265,000
Typical Range: $5,000 to $25,000
***Note:** Giving excludes domestic and international subsidiaries.

Recent Grants

Note: Grants derived from 1997 Form 990.

Arts & Humanities

200,000	Greater Hartford Arts Council, Hartford, CT -- United Arts Campaign
50,000	Hartford Ballet, Hartford, CT -- Major Gifts Campaign
50,000	Hartford Ballet, Hartford, CT -- general operating support for programming and contribution toward challenge grant to ensure long-term financial stability
25,000	Connecticut Opera, Hartford, CT -- to sponsor production of Hansel and Gretel

Civic & Public Affairs

100,000	Arthur Ashe Foundation, New York, NY -- general funding for the endowment of a new foundation
100,000	Welfare to Work Partnership, Washington, DC -- general operating support
50,000	Capital Region Workforce Development Board, Hartford, CT -- Mayor Mike's Working Wonders Program
50,000	Connecticut Capital Region Growth Council, Hartford, CT -- annual investment
50,000	National Conference, New York, NY -- diversity program
43,509	Arthur Ashe Foundation, New York, NY -- balance of $65,000 commitment
37,500	Greater Hartford Transit District, Hartford, CT -- support next planning stages of Griffin Line, a light rail transit project focused on Hartford/Windsor corridor
36,000	Connecticut Forum, Hartford, CT -- annual funding and an additional $21,000 to become Lifetime Patron
33,000	US Small Business Administration, Hartford, CT -- minority business development program
30,000	National Foundation for Teaching Entrepreneurship, New York, NY -- SummerBiz Camp for at-risk, low-income youth

Education

100,000	Outward Bound USA, Garrison, NY -- Saturday Academy
100,000	University of Connecticut Foundation, Storrs, CT
50,000	St. Joseph College, Hartford, CT -- Saturday Academy
50,000	Trinity College, Hartford, CT -- Saturday Academy
50,000	Trinity College, Hartford, CT -- fall Saturday Academy
50,000	Yale University School of Medicine, New Haven, CT -- to study the effectiveness of a volunteer-based mentoring program on the health of at-risk, inner-city infants
44,760	Stanford University, Stanford, CA -- for a program for management of chronic disease-creating health care value by transforming patients into partners
42,000	Johnson C. Smith University, Charlotte, NC -- fall Saturday Academy
42,000	Johnson C. Smith University, Charlotte, NC -- spring Saturday Academy
40,300	Clark Atlanta University, Atlanta, GA -- fall Saturday Academy
40,300	Clark Atlanta University, Atlanta, GA -- spring Saturday Academy
40,000	Howard University, Washington, DC -- spring Saturday Academy
40,000	Howard University, Washington, DC -- fall Saturday Academy
40,000	Middlesex Community Technical College, Middletown, CT -- fall Saturday Academy
40,000	Middlesex Community Technical College, Middletown, CT -- spring Saturday Academy
40,000	University of Southern California, Los Angeles, CA -- spring Saturday Academy
40,000	University of Southern California, Los Angeles, CA -- fall Saturday Academy
35,000	University of Wisconsin Milwaukee, Milwaukee, WI -- spring Saturday Academy
35,000	University of Wisconsin Milwaukee, Milwaukee, WI -- fall Saturday Academy
34,555	University of Southern California, Los Angeles, CA -- transportation for USC Pre-College Enrichment Academy scholars to their home schools

30,000 Gwynedd-Mercy College, Gwynedd Valley, PA -- health science center project
25,000 University of Pennsylvania School of Nursing, Philadelphia, PA -- for 'A Woman's Point of View: A Self-Help Program for Women's Cardiovascular Health'

Health
1,000,000 American Heart Association, Dallas, TX -- National Women's Heart Disease and Stroke Campaign
100,000 Connecticut Children's Medical Center, Hartford, CT -- to establish Child Health Data Center to collect, manage, analyze, and disseminate child health information
100,000 Delmarva Foundation for Medical Care, Easton, MD -- SmartStart Child Health Initiative
75,000 St. Francis Hospital and Medical Center, Hartford, CT -- Children's Advocacy Center
30,050 American Heart Association, Conshohocken, PA -- 'The Silent Epidemic: Women and Heart Disease' sponsorship
25,000 California Kids Healthcare Foundation, Encino, CA -- expand healthcare coverage in San Diego County to uninsured children

International
440,000 Shanghai Jiao Tong University, Shanghai, People's Republic of China -- to restructure and strengthen Management School's graduate programs
440,000 Shanghai Jiao Tong University, Shanghai, People's Republic of China -- to restructure and strengthen Management School's graduate programs

Religion
35,000 Hartford Seminary, Hartford, CT -- preservation of the Seminary building

Social Services
632,500 United Way of the Capital Area Combined Health Appeal, Hartford, CT
316,250 United Way of the Capital Area Combined Health Appeal, Hartford, CT
316,250 United Way of the Capital Area Combined Health Appeal, Hartford, CT
200,000 Trinity College, Hartford, CT -- Aetna Center for Families
100,000 Trinity College, Hartford, CT -- Aetna Center for Families
50,000 Middlesex United Way, Middletown, CT

AFLAC INC.

Company Contact
1932 Wynnton Road
Columbus, GA 31999
Phone: (706)323-3431
Fax: (706)324-6330
Web: http://www.aflac.com

Company Description
Former Name: American Family Corp.
Revenue: US$8,640,000,000 (1999)
Employees: 2,639 (1999)
Fortune Rank: 205, per FORTUNE Magazine's list of 500 Largest U.S. Corporations (1999).
FF 205
SIC(s): 6321 Accident & Health Insurance, 6399 Insurance Carriers Nec.

Operating Locations
Canada: AFLAC Insurance Co. of Canada, Mississauga; United Kingdom: Wessex Family Ltd., London; Wessex Insurance Co. Ltd., Winchester; Wessex Life Assurance Co. Ltd., Winchester; Jewry Street Properties Ltd., Winchester, Hampshire

Nonmonetary Support
Type: Donated Equipment; Donated Products; Loaned Employees; Loaned Executives

Giving Contact
Linda Ledbetter, Administrator, Corp. Contributions
1932 Wynnton Road
Columbus, GA 31999
Phone: (706)323-3431
Fax: (706)596-3908

Description
Organization Type: Corporate Giving Program
Giving Locations: GA
Grant Types: General Support.

Financial Summary
Total Giving: $850,000 (1991); $800,000 (1990)

Typical Recipients
Arts & Humanities: Community Arts, Historic Preservation, Museums/Galleries
Civic & Public Affairs: Economic Development, Professional & Trade Associations, Public Policy
Education: Business Education, Colleges & Universities, Community & Junior Colleges, Elementary Education (Private), Health & Physical Education, Special Education
Health: Health Organizations, Hospices, Medical Research, Single-Disease Health Associations
Social Services: Child Welfare, Homes, Shelters/Homelessness, Substance Abuse, United Funds/United Ways

Contributions Analysis
Giving Priorities: Major support for health organizations and medical research, also supports civic concerns and the arts.
Arts & Humanities: About 10%. Supports community arts, historic preservation, and museums.
Civic & Public Affairs: About 20%. Interests include better government, economic development, public policy, ethnic and minority organizations, and professional associations.
Education: About 5%. Favors colleges and universities, community and junior colleges, business education, elementary education, and special education.
Health: About 65% of total contributions. Recipients include health organizations, medical research, hospices, single-disease health organizations, shelters, child welfare, and united funds. Also supports cancer research and treatment, including recent grants to fund chairs in cancer research at various hospitals and to support children's hospitals.

Application Procedures
Initial Contact: Send a brief letter of inquiry.
Application Requirements: Include a description of organization, amount requested, purpose of funds sought, recently audited financial statements, and proof of tax-exempt status.
Deadlines: None.

Restrictions
Does not support individuals, religious organizations for sectarian purposes, or political or lobbying groups. Organizations must be charitable and nonprofit.

Additional Information
The company reports that through the late 1990s, contributions will primarily support cancer research and health-related projects. International contributions are driven by the personal interests of the company's senior officers, Paul and Daniel Amos. Giving is unstructured.

Corporate Officials
Daniel P. Amos: president, chief executive officer, director treasurer B Pensacola, FL 1951. ED University of Georgia BS (1973). PRIM CORP EMPL president, chief executive officer, director: AFLAC Inc. CORP AFFIL director: Columbus Bank & Trust Co.; director: Synorris Fin Corp.; deputy chief executive officer, vice chairman, president: America Family Corp.
Paul Shelby Amos: co-founder, chairman, director B Enterprise, AL 1926. PRIM CORP EMPL co-founder, chairman, director: AFLAC Inc. NONPR AFFIL trustee: Asbury Theological Seminary. CLUB AFFIL Country Club Columbus; Big Eddy Club.
Kriss Cloninger, III: executive vice president, chief financial officer, treasurer B Houston, TX 1947. ED University of Texas BBA (1969); University of Texas MBA (1971). PRIM CORP EMPL executive vice president, chief financial officer, treasurer: AFLAC Inc.
Yoshiki Otake: chairman PRIM CORP EMPL chairman: AFLAC Japan. CORP AFFIL officer: AFLAC Inc.; vice chairman: AFLAC International.

Giving Program Officials
Michael E. Henry: senior vice president PRIM CORP EMPL senior vice president, director government relations: AFLAC Inc.

Foundation Officials
Daniel P. Amos: secretary, treasurer, trustee (see above)
Paul Shelby Amos: president, trustee (see above)

Grants Analysis
Disclosure Period: calendar year ending
Typical Range: $1,000 to $2,500

AGL RESOURCES INC.

Company Contact
PO Box 4569
Atlanta, GA 30302-4569
Phone: (404)584-3491
Fax: (404)584-3479
Web: http://www.aglresources.com

Company Description
Revenue: US$1,068,600,000 (1999)
Employees: 2,892 (1999)

Nonmonetary Support
Type: Cause-related Marketing & Promotion; Donated Equipment; In-kind Services; Loaned Employees; Loaned Executives; Workplace Solicitation

Corporate Sponsorship
Type: Arts & cultural events; Music & entertainment events; Festivals/fairs; Sports events
Contact: Katrina Graham, Director of Civic Affairs
Note: Sponsors Walk America.

Giving Contact
Peter L. Banks, Vice President, External Affairs
Atlanta, GA
Email: pbanks@aglresources.com

Description
Organization Type: Corporate Giving Program
Giving Locations: GA
Grant Types: Capital, Conference/Seminar, Employee Matching Gifts, Scholarship, Seed Money.

Financial Summary
Total Giving: $505,268 (1996); $498,127 (1995); $445,000 (1994). Note: Contributes through corporate direct giving program only.

Typical Recipients
Arts & Humanities: Arts Associations & Councils, Arts Centers, Arts Festivals, Arts Institutes, Community Arts, Ethnic & Folk Arts, Historic Preservation, Museums/Galleries, Music, Opera, Performing Arts, Public Broadcasting, Theater

Civic & Public Affairs: Civil Rights, Economic Development, Employment/Job Training, Housing, Law & Justice, Professional & Trade Associations, Rural Affairs, Safety, Women's Affairs
Education: Agricultural Education, Business Education, Colleges & Universities, Community & Junior Colleges, Continuing Education, Economic Education, Education Associations, Education Funds, Elementary Education (Private), Engineering/Technological Education, Journalism/Media Education, Literacy, Minority Education, Special Education
Environment: Environment-General
Health: Health Organizations, Hospices, Medical Research, Mental Health, Nutrition, Public Health
Science: Observatories & Planetariums, Science Exhibits & Fairs, Scientific Organizations
Social Services: Child Welfare, Community Centers, Community Service Organizations, Delinquency & Criminal Rehabilitation, Family Services, Food/Clothing Distribution, Homes, People with Disabilities, Senior Services, Shelters/Homelessness, Substance Abuse, United Funds/United Ways, Volunteer Services, Youth Organizations

Contributions Analysis

Arts & Humanities: 5% to 10%. Includes arts festivals, music, museums, arts organizations, historic preservation, public broadcasting, and theater arts.
Civic & Public Affairs: 45% to 50%. Supports better government campaigns, civil rights, consumer affairs, housing, law and justice, professional and trade associations, miscellaneous organizations, community development, economics, and environmental organizations.
Education: 25% to 30%. Funding favors higher education, agricultural education, secondary, minority, engineering, and journalism education.
Health: About 15%. Recipients include mental health, health organizations, community service organizations, child welfare, youth organizations, and senior services.
Note: Company also supports United Way.

Application Procedures

Initial Contact: Send a a brief letter of inquiry.
Application Requirements: Information should include a description of organization, amount requested, purpose of funds sought, and proof of tax-exempt status.
Deadlines: None.

Restrictions

Company usually only considers giving within state. Company does not support individuals, religious organizations for sectarian purposes, or political or lobbying groups.

Corporate Officials

Peter L. Banks: vice president external affairs B Barnesville, GA 1938. PRIM CORP EMPL vice president external affairs: AGL Resources Inc. NONPR AFFIL director: Gordon College Foundation Inc.; director: Smithsall Woods Foundation Inc.; director: American Gas Association; director: Children's Museum Atlanta.
Ralph Bankston: director community affairs PRIM CORP EMPL director community affairs: Atlanta Gas Light Co. CORP AFFIL director community civic affairs: AGL Resources Inc.
David R. Jones: principal B Atlanta, GA 1937. ED Georgia Institute of Technology BS (1959). PRIM CORP EMPL principal: Atlanta Gas & Light Co. ADD CORP EMPL chief executive officer: AGI Resources Inc.; chief executive officer, president, director: AGL Investments Inc.; chairman: Chattanooga Gas Co. CORP AFFIL chairman: Chattanooga Gas Co.; director: Federation Reserve Bank Atlanta; director: AGL Investment Inc.; director: AGL Resources Inc.

Giving Program Officials

Peter L. Banks: (see above)

Grants Analysis

Disclosure Period: calendar year ending
Typical Range: $500 to $5,000

AGRILINK FOODS, INC.

Company Contact

Rochester, NY

Company Description

Former Name: (Parent) Agway, Inc.
Employees: 3,363
SIC(s): 2032 Canned Specialties, 2033 Canned Fruits & Vegetables, 2037 Frozen Fruits & Vegetables, 2038 Frozen Specialties Nec.
Parent Company: Pro-Fac Cooperative

Nonmonetary Support

Value: $120,000 (1989)
Type: Donated Products
Note: Nonmonetary support requests are handled individually by each division.

Agrilink Foods/Pro-Fac Foundation

Giving Contact

Ms. Susan C. Riker, Secretary
Agrilink Foods/Pro-Fac Foundation
PO Box 20670
Rochester, NY 14602
Phone: (716)264-3155
Fax: (716)383-1606

Description

EIN: 166071142
Organization Type: Corporate Foundation
Giving Locations: headquarters and operating communities.
Grant Types: Capital, Emergency, Endowment, General Support.

Financial Summary

Total Giving: $300,000 (fiscal year ending June 26, 1999 approx); $275,000 (fiscal 1998 approx); $185,000 (fiscal 1997 approx). Note: Contributes through foundation only.
Giving Analysis: Giving for fiscal 1996 includes: foundation ($201,725); foundation grants to United Way ($76,175); fiscal 1999: foundation (approx $300,000)
Assets: $300,000 (fiscal 1999 approx); $300,000 (fiscal 1998 approx); $111,048 (fiscal 1996)
Gifts Received: $300,000 (fiscal 1996); $175,000 (fiscal 1995); $300,000 (fiscal 1993). Note: Contributions are received from Curtice-Burns Foods Inc.

Typical Recipients

Arts & Humanities: Arts Associations & Councils, Arts Centers, Community Arts, Libraries, Museums/Galleries, Music, Performing Arts, Public Broadcasting, Theater
Civic & Public Affairs: African American Affairs, Business/Free Enterprise, Civil Rights, Clubs, Community Foundations, Economic Development, Employment/Job Training, Civic & Public Affairs-General, Housing, Rural Affairs, Safety, Urban & Community Affairs, Women's Affairs
Education: Agricultural Education, Business Education, Colleges & Universities, Community & Junior Colleges, Education Funds, Literacy, Minority Education, Private Education (Precollege), Special Education, Student Aid
Environment: Environment-General, Resource Conservation
Health: Cancer, Children's Health/Hospitals, Clinics/Medical Centers, Emergency/Ambulance Services, Geriatric Health, Health Organizations, Heart, Hospices, Hospitals, Medical Rehabilitation, Mental Health, Nursing Services, Public Health, Single-Disease Health Associations
Religion: Religious Welfare
Science: Science Museums, Scientific Research
Social Services: Animal Protection, Child Welfare, Community Centers, Community Service Organizations, Delinquency & Criminal Rehabilitation, Domestic Violence, Emergency Relief, Family Planning, Family Services, Food/Clothing Distribution, Homes, People with Disabilities, Recreation & Athletics, Scouts, Senior Services, Shelters/Homelessness, Substance Abuse, United Funds/United Ways, Veterans, Volunteer Services, YMCA/YWCA/YMHA/YWHA, Youth Organizations

Contributions Analysis

Arts & Humanities: About 10%. Emphasis is on music. Other interests include libraries, theater, public broadcasting, and arts centers and associations.
Education: 5% to 10%. Highest priorities are agricultural education, education funds, and colleges and universities.
Health: 5% to 10%. Grants primarily support hospitals and single-diseasehealth associations.
Social Services: 60% to 65%. Majority of funding supports the United Way. Other interests include youth organizations, child welfare, organizations for the handicapped, recreation and athletics, and community service organizations.

Application Procedures

Initial Contact: brief letter or proposal
Application Requirements: a description of organization, amount requested, purpose of funds sought, recently audited financial statement, and copy of IRS 501(c)(3) letter
Deadlines: None.

Restrictions

Contributions are not made to individuals, political groups, dinners or special events, international projects, fraternal organizations, goodwill advertising, or religious activities for sectarian purposes.

Corporate Officials

Dennis M. Mullen: president, chief executive officer, director B Newark, NJ 1953. ED Saint Leo College BA. PRIM CORP EMPL president, chief executive officer, director: Agrilink Foods, Inc.
William D. Rice: senior vice president, chief financial officer, secretary B Saint Paul, MN 1934. ED Harvard University AB (1956); Harvard University Graduate School of Business Administration MBA (1961). PRIM CORP EMPL senior vice president, chief financial officer, secretary: Agrilink Foods, Inc. CORP AFFIL regional director: Chase Lincoln First Bank NA; senior vice president strategic development,secretary: Agrilink Foods Inc. NONPR AFFIL trustee: National Food Processors Association.
Bea B. Slizewski: vice president corporate communications B Rochester, NY 1943. ED State University of New York (1986). PRIM CORP EMPL vice president corporate communications: Agrilink Foods, Inc.

Foundation Officials

Robert V. Call, Jr.: chairman, trustee B Batavia, NY 1926. ED Cornell University (1950); Harvard University (1981). PRIM CORP EMPL chairman, director: Agrilink Foods, Inc. ADD CORP EMPL vice president, director: Call Farms Inc.; vice president: Genesee Farms Inc.; president, director: My-T Acres Inc.
Virginia Ford: trustee CORP AFFIL director: Agrilink Foods, Inc.
William D. Rice: trustee (see above)

Grants Analysis

Disclosure Period: fiscal year ending June 26, 1998
Total Grants: $275,000
Number of Grants: 235
Average Grant: $1,170
Highest Grant: $25,000
Typical Range: $500 to $5,000

Recent Grants

Note: Grants derived from fiscal 1996 Form 990.

Arts & Humanities

5,000 Rundel Library Foundation, Rochester, NY -- capital expansion project
4,000 WXXI, Rochester, NY -- program underwriting
4,000 WXXI Public Broadcasting Council, Rochester, NY -- underwrite the Nature Series
3,000 Corporate Council for the Arts, Tacoma, WA
2,500 Geva Theater, Rochester, NY
2,500 Memorial Art Gallery, Rochester, NY
2,000 Rochester Philharmonic Orchestra, Rochester, NY
1,500 Pantages Centre for Performing Arts, Tacoma, WA
1,500 Southeast Michigan Library Coop, Paw Paw, MI

Civic & Public Affairs

2,000 Corner Stone Alliance, Benton Harbor, MI -- community economic development projects
2,000 National Junior Horticultural Association, Fremont, MI

Education

5,500 Independent Colleges of Washington, Seattle, WA -- support for 10 colleges
5,000 Pennsylvania State University, University Park, PA -- potato research program
5,000 Pennsylvania State University, University Park, PA -- potato research program
2,500 LEAD New York, Ithaca, NY -- agriculture leadership classes
2,000 Darwin Turner Minority Scholars, Cincinnati, OH -- scholarships for black students
2,000 Future Farmers of America, Wichita, KS -- agriculture scholarships
2,000 Oregon Independent College Foundation, Portland, OR -- support for eight colleges
2,000 University of Georgia, Tifton, GA -- research
2,000 University of Georgia 4-H, Tifton, GA -- research
1,500 Junior Achievement, Tacoma, WA
1,500 School of the Holy Childhood, Rochester, NY
1,500 United Negro College Fund, Buffalo, NY -- scholarships for 41 black colleges

Health

5,000 Crestwood Children's Center, Clifton Springs, NY -- funds for cancer center
2,000 Al Sigl Center, Rochester, NY -- upgrade and modernize Elmwood Avenue campus
1,500 University of Rochester Medical Center, Rochester, NY -- Hugh Cumming Memorial Teaching Day
1,200 Farmedic, Alfred, NY -- training for farm emergencies
1,000 American Red Cross, Rochester, NY -- Disaster Relief Fund

Religion

21,000 Saints Peter and Paul's Church, Rochester, NY -- provide space for nonprofit organizations
3,000 Open Door Mission, Rochester, NY -- Samaritan House project
1,500 Rogers House, Rochester, NY -- outreach programs for Corpus Christi church

Science

5,000 Rochester Museum and Science Center, Rochester, NY -- capital campaign for upgrade of building and systems
2,000 Boyce Thompson Institute for Plant Research, Ithaca, NY

Social Services

25,000 United Way, Rochester, NY
16,000 United Way Pierce County, Tacoma, WA
12,000 United Way Blossomland, Benton Harbor, MI
4,000 United Way, Genesee, NY
3,800 United Way Henry County, New Castle, IN
3,375 United Way, Rochester, NY
3,000 United Way Wayne County, Rochester, NY
3,000 YMCA, St. Joseph, MI -- expansion of facilities
2,500 Boy Scouts of America Otetiana Council, Rochester, NY -- capital campaign for new cub scout camp
2,500 Macon County United Givers, Montezuma, GA
2,000 Alamo Boys and Girls Club, Alamo, TX
2,000 Alamo Boys and Girls Club, Alamo, TX -- to build natural interpretive trail
2,000 Boys and Girls Club, Tacoma, WA -- renovation of four facilities
2,000 Macon County United Givers, Montezuma, GA
1,500 Lifespan, Rochester, NY -- eldercare resource center project
1,500 Macon County Recreation Department, Montezuma, GA
1,500 Macon County Recreation Department, Montezuma, GA

AIR PRODUCTS AND CHEMICALS, INC.

Company Contact

Allentown, PA
Web: http://www.airproducts.com

Company Description

Revenue: US$5,020,000,000 (1999)
Employees: 17,400 (1999)
Fortune Rank: 324, per FORTUNE Magazine's list of 500 Largest U.S. Corporations (1999).
FF 324
SIC(s): 2813 Industrial Gases, 2819 Industrial Inorganic Chemicals Nec, 2873 Nitrogenous Fertilizers, 3443 Fabricated Plate Work--Boiler Shops.

Operating Locations

Australia: Anchor Chemical Australia Pty. Ltd., Parramatta; Belgium: Air Products Management SA, Brussels, Brabant; Air Products SA, Brussels, Brabant; Airprochem Inc., Brussels, Brabant; Brazil: Air Products Gases Industriais Ltda., Sao Paulo; Canada: Air Products Canada, Brampton; Ram Wheel Welding Supplies Ltd., Edmonton; Czech Republic: Ferox Akciova Spolecnost, Decin; France: Prodair et Cie, Centre Paris Pleyel, St. Denis; Air Products, Paris, Ville-de-Paris; Prodair SA, Paris, Ville-de-Paris; Union Mobiliere Industrielle, Strasbourg, Bas-Rhin; Germany: Air Products GmbH, Hattingen, Nordrhein-Westfalen; Air Products and Chemical Pura Verwaltungs GmbH, Norderstedt, Hamburg; Ireland: Air Products Ireland Ltd., Dublin; Italy: Anchor Italiana SpA, Dorno, Lombardia; Air Products Italia Sud SRL, Monza, Lombardia; Japan: Air Products Pacific, Osaka; Air Products Japan Inc., Tokyo; Mexico: Air Products and Chemicals de Mexico SA de CV, Mexico; Netherlands: Air Products (Pernis) BV, Vondelingenplaat, Zuid-Holland; Air Products Nederland BV, Waddinxveen, Zuid-Holland; Norway: Air Products AS, Kristiansand, Vest-Agder; Singapore: Anchor Chemical Asia Pacific Pte. Ltd., Singapore; Spain: Air Products Iberica SA, Barcelona, Cataluna; Air Products Ventas y Servicios SA, Barcelona, Cataluna; Carburos Metalicos Soldadura SA, Barcelona, Cataluna; Gases Medicinales E Industriales SA, Barcelona, Cataluna; Sociedad Espanola de Carburos Metalicos SA, Barcelona, Cataluna; Ashdo SA, Madrid; Oxigasa SA, Zaragoza, Aragon; United Kingdom: Air Products Cryogenic Services Ltd., Aberdeen, Grampian; Gardner Cryogenics, Aberdeen, Grampian; Air Products (Chemicals) Plc, Manchester, Greater Manchester; Anchor Chemical International Ltd., Manchester, Greater Manchester; Anchor Chemical (United Kingdom) Ltd., Manchester, Greater Manchester; Ancomer Ltd., Manchester, Greater Manchester; Air Products (Great Britain) Ltd., Walton-on-Thames, Surrey; Air Products Group Ltd., Walton-on-Thames, Surrey; Air Products Plc, Walton-on-Thames, Surrey; Air Products (United Kingdom) Ltd., Walton-on-Thames, Surrey; Onsite Engineering Services Ltd., Walton-on-Thames, Surrey

Nonmonetary Support

Value: $325,000 (1989); $250,000 (1988); $350,000 (1987)
Type: Donated Equipment; In-kind Services; Loaned Employees
Volunteer Programs: Seventy percent of employees volunteer in community activities. Volunteerism is encouraged and recognized by the company, but it does not have a formal volunteer program.
Contact: Mary Jo Aggrevay, Community Relations Report

Air Products Foundation

Giving Contact

Timothy J. Holt
Air Products Foundation
7201 Hamilton Boulevard
Allentown, PA 18195-1501
Phone: (610)481-6349
Fax: (610)481-6642

Description

EIN: 232130928
Organization Type: Corporate Foundation
Giving Locations: headquarters and operating communities.
Grant Types: Capital, Employee Matching Gifts, General Support, Multiyear/Continuing Support, Operating Expenses, Project.
Note: Matching gifts are for higher education, arts and cultural organisation.

Giving Philosophy

'The bottom line of the company's concern with social responsibility is this: business needs a healthy society if it is to survive and prosper. Although the company recognizes its first responsibility is to succeed in its business and make a profit, it also recognizes that it can no longer simply respond to the demands of the marketplace. It has a responsibility to also respond to the broader expectations of society, fostering an environment conducive to growth and opportunity for all.' *Air Products & Chemicals, Inc.*

Financial Summary

Total Giving: $2,560,925 (fiscal year ending September 30, 1998); $2,273,306 (fiscal 1997); $908,466 (fiscal 1996). Note: Fiscal 1997 Giving includes matching gifts; United Way. Fiscal 1996 Giving includes foundation; matching gifts.

Giving Analysis: Giving for fiscal 1998 includes: foundation matching gifts ($1,809,626); foundation ($597,775); foundation grants to United Way ($153,526)
Assets: $13,684,909 (fiscal 1997); $14,276,352 (fiscal 1996); $15,090,842 (fiscal 1994)
Gifts Received: $13,237,500 (fiscal 1994). Note: In 1994, the Foundation received contributions from the Prodair Corporation.

Typical Recipients

Arts & Humanities: Arts Festivals, Arts Funds, Community Arts, Dance, Historic Preservation, Libraries, Museums/Galleries, Music, Opera, Performing Arts, Public Broadcasting, Theater
Civic & Public Affairs: Business/Free Enterprise, Civil Rights, Economic Development, Economic Policy, Civic & Public Affairs-General, Housing, Municipalities/Towns, Public Policy, Safety, Urban & Community Affairs, Women's Affairs
Education: Arts/Humanities Education, Business Education, Colleges & Universities, Economic Education, Education Associations, Education Funds, Education Reform, Engineering/Technological Education, Education-General, Legal Education, Literacy, Minority Education, Science/Mathematics Education
Environment: Air/Water Quality, Environment-General, Resource Conservation
Health: Cancer, Children's Health/Hospitals, Emergency/Ambulance Services, Health Organizations, Heart, Multiple Sclerosis, Nutrition, Single-Disease Health Associations
International: International Peace & Security Issues
Religion: Religious Welfare
Science: Science Exhibits & Fairs
Social Services: Child Welfare, Community Service Organizations, Counseling, Day Care, Delinquency & Criminal Rehabilitation, Domestic Violence, Emergency Relief, Family Services, Food/Clothing Distribution, Homes, People with Disabilities, Recreation & Athletics, Scouts, Senior Services, Shelters/Homelessness, Substance Abuse, United Funds/United Ways, Volunteer Services, Youth Organizations

Contributions Analysis

Giving Priorities: Engineering and business education, independent college funds, united way, and single disease health associations. Foreign subsidiaries make contributions directly in-country. These contributions are not tracked and are handled independently of corporate headquarters. Domestically, the foundation provides limited support to organizations with international interests.
Arts & Humanities: 14%. Supports museums, music, and the performing arts. Other areas of interest include theaters, festivals, and public broadcasting.
Civic & Public Affairs: 7%. Economic development is a major concern, as are environmental affairs, business and free enterprise organizations, and housing rehabilitation. Also supports safety organizations.
Education: 29%. Supports engineering and business departments of colleges and universities. Also interested in independent college funds and minority, economic, and arts education. Majority of education funds are in the form of matching gifts.
Health: 10%. Health Interests include single-disease health associations and emergency services.
International: Company donates an unspecified amount of money to international organizations through foreign subsidiaries.
Social Services: 40%. Fund United Way. Also supports food distribution, programs for the disabled, and programs for the prevention of drug and alcohol abuse.
Note: Above percentages represent foundation contributions only. Direct giving program priorities are similar. Matching gifts are included in the analysis.

Application Procedures

Initial Contact: Send brief letter and one copy of full proposal.
Application Requirements: Provide a description of the organization, including history, activities, purpose, constituency served, and governing board; purpose of grant; details on how purpose will be achieved; total amount of fund-raising campaign; amount requested and, if the request is for a specific project, description of project with applicable budget; proof of tax-exempt status; copy of most recent Form 990; copy of operating budget for current fiscal year; and list of current contributions or commitments received from companies, foundations, and government bodies, including amounts.
Deadlines: None.
Review Process: Requests are screened by contributions officer, then the committee reviews for approval or denial.
Evaluative Criteria: Committee examines need, population served, benefit to Air Products community, and funding sources.
Decision Notification: Usually made within 60 to 90 days of receipt of request.

Restrictions

Does not support fraternal organizations, labor groups, service clubs, individuals, operating funds for member agencies of the United Way, political or lobbying groups, religious organizations, veterans organizations, hospitals, or elementary or secondary schools.

Additional Information

Company has participated in public/private ventures to rehabilitate abandoned and condemned properties in Allentown, PA.

Corporate Officials

James Harrington Agger: senior vice president, secretary, general counsel B Philadelphia, PA 1936. ED Saint Joseph's University AB (1958); University of Pennsylvania JD (1961). PRIM CORP EMPL senior vice president, secretary, general counsel: Air Products and Chemicals, Inc. NONPR AFFIL member: American Bar Association.
Leo J. Daley: vice president, treasurer B Shenandoa, PA 1946. ED Pennsylvania State University (1968); Widener University (1979). PRIM CORP EMPL vice president, treasurer: Air Products and Chemicals, Inc. ADD CORP EMPL treasurer: Air Products Inc.; treasurer: Air Products Helium Inc.; gov: Lehigh Northampton Airport Authority. NONPR AFFIL member: National Association of Corporate Treasurers; member: Society International Treasurers; member: Financial Executives Institute; member: Institute of Management Accountants.
William J. Kendrick: vice president public affairs B Boston, MA 1932. ED Boston College BSBA (1956); New England School of Law LLB (1959). PRIM CORP EMPL vice president public affairs: Air Products and Chemicals, Inc.
Harold A. Wagner: chairman, president, chief executive officer, director B Oakland, CA 1935. ED Stanford University BS (1958); Harvard University MBA (1963); Stanford University SEP (1982). PRIM CORP EMPL chairman, president, chief executive officer, director: Air Products and Chemicals, Inc. CORP AFFIL director: PACCAR Inc.; director: United Technologies Corp.

Foundation Officials

James Harrington Agger: director (see above)
Pierre Leonce Thibaut Brian: trustee B New Orleans, LA 1930. ED Louisiana State University BS (1951); Massachusetts Institute of Technology ScD (1956).
R.G. Cherrington: secretary
Leo J. Daley: vice president, treasurer (see above)
Ruth Margaret Davis: trustee B Sharpsville, PA 1928. ED American University BA (1950); University of Maryland MA (1952); University of Maryland PhD (1955). PRIM CORP EMPL founder, president, chief executive officer: Pymatuning Group Inc. CORP AFFIL director: Varian Associates Inc.; director: Tupperware Corp. Inc.; director: Prin Finance Group Inc.; director: SSDS Inc.; director: Premark International Inc.; director,trustee: Consolidated Edison Co. New York Inc.; director: Consolidated Edison Inc.; director: Ceridian Corp.; director: Air Products & Chemicals Inc.; director: BTG Inc.; chairman: Aerospace Corp. NONPR AFFIL member: Tau Beta Pi; member: Washington Philosophical Society; fellow: Society Information Display; member: Phi Kappa Phi; member: Sigma Pi Sigma; member: National Academy Public Administration; member: National Academy Arts & Sciences; member: National Academy Engineering; trustee: Institute Defense Analysts; member: American Mathematical Society; board visitors: Catholic University America; fellow: American Institute Aeronautics & Astronautics; member: American Association Advancement Science.
William J. Kendrick: chairman (see above)
Terry Robert Lautenbach: trustee B Cincinnati, OH 1938. ED Xavier University BS (1959). CORP AFFIL director: Varian Associates Inc.; director: Footstar Inc.; director: Loomis Sayles Mutual Funds; director: Air Products & Chemicals Inc.; director: CVS Corp. NONPR AFFIL director: Xavier University. CLUB AFFIL Sanctuary Golf Club; Wee Burn Country Club.
Walter Frederick Light: trustee B Cobalt, ON Canada 1923. ED Queens College BS (1949). CORP AFFIL director: Rockcliffe Research & Technology Inc.; director: Transtream Inc.; director: Procter & Gamble Co. NONPR AFFIL fellow: Engineering Institute Canada; fellow: Montreal Museum Fine Arts; member: Corp. Engineers Quebec; fellow: Canada Academy Engineering; member associates: Carleton University; member: Association Professional Engineers. CLUB AFFIL Mount Royal Club; York Club.
L. G. Long: assistant secretary
John Robert Lovett: director B Norristown, PA 1931. ED Ursinus College BS (1953); University of Delaware MS (1955); University of Delaware PhD (1957). NONPR AFFIL member: Institute Chemical Engineers (UK); member: Society Chemical Industry; member: Chemical Manufacturers Association; member: American Chemical Society; member: American Institute Chemical Engineers.
Cornelius Patrick Powell: president B Saint Paul, MN 1931. ED University of Minnesota BBA (1955); Wayne State University LLM (1961). PRIM CORP EMPL vice president taxes: Air Products and Chemicals, Inc.
Gerald Andrew White: director B Long Island, NY 1934. ED Villanova University BChE (1957); Harvard Business School (1975). NONPR AFFIL member: Financial Executives Institute; member: Tau Beta Pi; member: American Institute Chemical Engineers; member: Fin Executives Research Foundation.

Grants Analysis

Disclosure Period: fiscal year ending September 30, 1998
Total Grants: $597,775*
Number of Grants: 565 (approx)
Average Grant: $2,256
Typical Range: $500 to $5,000
***Note:** Giving excludes matching gifts and United Way.

Recent Grants

Note: Grants derived from fiscal 1997 Form 990.

Arts & Humanities

26,200	WLVT-TV/Channel 39, Bethlehem, PA -- program support
10,000	Bethlehem Musikfest Association, Bethlehem, PA -- Banana Factory
10,000	Bethlehem Musikfest Association, Bethlehem, PA -- operating support
10,000	Mayfair, Allentown, PA -- operating support
9,200	Allentown Art Museum, Allentown, PA -- program support

7,000 Lehigh Valley Chamber Orchestra, Lehigh Valley, PA -- operating support
6,000 WVIA, Pittston, PA -- operating support

Civic & Public Affairs
42,000 Velodrome Fund, Allentown, PA -- operating support
25,000 Team Pennsylvania Foundation, Harrisburg, PA -- multiyear grant
10,000 PA 2000, Harrisburg, PA -- operating support
10,000 Pennsylvanians for Effective Government Education Committee, Harrisburg, PA -- special assessment
5,000 City of Allentown, Allentown, PA -- operating support

Education
50,000 University of Pennsylvania, Philadelphia, PA
50,000 Ursinus College, Collegeville, PA
25,000 Purdue University, West Lafayette, IN
20,000 Muhlenberg College, Allentown, PA -- multiyear grant
15,000 United Negro College Fund, New York, NY
12,500 Foundation for Independent Colleges, Harrisburg, PA
10,000 Carnegie Mellon University, Pittsburgh, PA
10,000 Cornell University, Ithaca, NY
10,000 Junior Achievement of the Lehigh Valley, Bethlehem, PA -- operating support
10,000 Lehigh University Alumni Memorial Building, Bethlehem, PA -- operating support
10,000 Manhattan College, Riverdale, NY
10,000 Massachusetts Institute of Technology, Cambridge, MA
10,000 National Action Council for Minorities in Engineering, New York, NY
10,000 Pennsylvania Council on Economic Education, Harrisburg, PA -- operating support
10,000 Pennsylvania State University, University Park, PA
10,000 University of Delaware, Newark, DE
10,000 University of Pennsylvania, Philadelphia, PA
10,000 Villanova University, Villanova, PA
7,500 Carnegie Mellon University, Pittsburgh, PA
7,500 Consortium for Graduate Study in Management, St. Louis, MO
7,500 Cornell University, Ithaca, NY
7,500 Purdue University, West Lafayette, IN
7,500 Purdue University, West Lafayette, IN
7,500 University of Minnesota, Minneapolis, MN
6,000 Baum School of Art, Allentown, PA -- operating support
5,000 Teach for America, New York, NY -- program support

Environment
5,000 Wildlands Conservancy, Emmaus, PA -- operating support
5,000 Wintergreen Nature Foundation, Wintergreen, VA -- operating support

Health
10,000 Easter Seal Society of the Northeastern Counties, Scranton, PA -- operating support
7,000 American Cancer Society, Allentown, PA -- operating support
7,000 American Heart Association, Bethlehem, PA -- operating support
6,000 Easter Seal Society of the Lehigh Valley and the Poconos, Allentown, PA -- operating support

Religion
25,000 Salvation Army, Allentown, PA -- multiyear grant

Social Services
25,000 Boys and Girls Club, Allentown, PA -- multiyear grant
25,000 Camelot for Children, Allentown, PA -- operating support
15,000 Pace Soccer Club, Pace, FL -- program support
9,000 Teens Who Care, Martinez, CA -- operating support
7,000 Lehigh County Meals on Wheels, Bethlehem, PA -- operating support

Airborne Freight Corp.

Company Contact

3101 Western Avenue
Seattle, WA 98121
Phone: (206)285-4600
Fax: (206)281-1444
Web: http://www.airborne.com

Company Description

Revenue: US$3,074,500,000
Employees: 20,700
Fortune Rank: 489, per FORTUNE Magazine's list of 500 Largest U.S. Corporations (1999).
FF 489
SIC(s): 4513 Air Courier Services, 4731 Freight Transportation Arrangement.

Corporate Sponsorship

Range: less than $700,000

Giving Contact

Dianne Fessler, Vice President, Tax Accounting
Airborne Freight Corp.
PO Box 662
Seattle, WA 98111
Phone: (206)285-4600 ext 1595
Fax: (206)281-4438

Alternate Contact

Sheryl Marquardt
Phone: (206)286-1595
Fax: (206)281-4438
Email: sheryl.marquardt@airborne.com

Description

Organization Type: Corporate Giving Program
Giving Locations: WA: western Washington
Grant Types: Award, Capital, Emergency, Employee Matching Gifts, Fellowship, General Support, Multiyear/Continuing Support.

Giving Philosophy

'Airborne Express provides support to non-profit organizations that are making a significant difference in the quality of life for the communities in the Pacific Northwest.'
Charitable areas supported by Airborne Express: Culture & Arts, including capital campaigns, one-time grants to support equipment purchases, enhancements and special projects; Civic, including capital campaigns, operating support, and corporate memberships; Education, including scholarship and program support, capital campaign for higher education, special needs education, and diversity programs: and Human Services, which Airborne Express supports through direct program support. Significant Human Services support areas include disaster relief, domestic abuse, elder care, family support services, health support services, homelessness, hunger and food programs, United Way, and youth. *Airborne Express Charitable Giving Guidelines*

Financial Summary

Total Giving: $800,000 (2000 approx); $750,000 (1999 approx); $720,000 (1998 approx). Note: Contributes through corporate direct giving program.

Typical Recipients

Arts & Humanities: Arts & Humanities-General
Civic & Public Affairs: Civic & Public Affairs-General
Education: Education-General
Health: Health-General
Social Services: Social Services-General

Contributions Analysis

Giving Priorities: Contributions program is unstructured, responding to requests on a case-by-case basis. Company reports the following approximate giving percentages.
Arts & Humanities: 10%.
Civic & Public Affairs: 10%.
Education: 20%.
Social Services: 55%.

Application Procedures

Initial Contact: Request applications guidelines.
Application Requirements: Send a concise written request including: organization name and address; project name and purpose; amount requested; contact person, title, and phone number; primary purpose of the organization; constituency served; number of people served last year; and geographic area served; number employees, including full-and part-time employees and volunteers; percentage of agency's budget that is used for administration and solicitation; regular funding sources and major commitments organization has already received, with names and amounts; statement regarding why request deserves special consideration by Airborne for funding. Attach proof of non-profit status, financial statements and budgets, and list of board of directors.
Deadlines: None.
Review Process: Application are reviewed for funding in February, May, and November.

Restrictions

Company generally does not fund religious organizations for theological purposes, political organizations, social/fraternal organizations, team sponsorships, conventions or conferences, personal or individual sponsorships, organizations providing services outside the state of Washington, corporate advertising, organizations spending in excess of 30% on fundraising activities, endowments or memorials, operating funds for art performances, or in-kind donations.

Additional Information

Company also operates under the name Airborne Express Co.

Corporate Officials

Robert George Brazier: president, chief operating officer, director B Chicago, IL 1937. ED Stanford University BA (1959). PRIM CORP EMPL president, chief operating officer, director: Airborne Freight Corp. ADD CORP EMPL vice president: Airborne Forwarding Corp.

Robert Stanley Cline: chairman, chief executive officer, director B Urbana, IL 1937. ED New York University; Dartmouth College BA (1959). PRIM CORP EMPL chairman, chief executive officer, director: Airborne Freight Corp. ADD CORP EMPL president, director: Airborne Forwarding Corp. CORP AFFIL director: Seattle First National Bank; director: Ranier Ice & Cold Storage; director: SAFECO Corp.; president, director: Awawego Delivery Inc.; director: Metricom Corp. NONPR AFFIL trustee: Corporate Council Arts; director: Washington Roundtable; trustee: Childrens Hospital Foundation.

Roy C. Liljebeck: executive vice president, chief financial officer B Tacoma, WA 1937. ED University of Puget Sound BA (1961). PRIM CORP EMPL executive vice president, chief financial officer: Airborne

Freight Corp. CORP AFFIL vice president: Solid Visions Inc.

Giving Program Officials

Dianne Fessler: vice president

AK STEEL CORP.

Company Contact

Middletown, OH
Web: http://www.aksteel.com

Company Description

Former Name: Empire-Detroit Steel and Armco Steel Co.
Employees: 5,762
SIC(s): 3312 Blast Furnaces & Steel Mills, 3316 Cold-Finishing of Steel Shapes, 3339 Primary Nonferrous Metals Nec.
Parent Company: Kawasaki Steel Corp., 2-3, Uchi Saiwaicho 2-chome, Chiyoda-ku, Tokyo, Japan

Operating Locations

KY: AK Steel Corp., Ashland; OH: AK Steel Corp., Middletown; AK Steel Corp., Middletown

Nonmonetary Support

Type: Workplace Solicitation

Corporate Sponsorship

Type: Arts & cultural events; Music & entertainment events
Note: Sponsors events in operating communities.

AK Steel Foundation

Giving Contact

Brian T. Coughlin, Government Affairs Manager; Executive Director
703 Curtis St.
Middletown, OH 45043
Phone: (513)425-2826
Fax: (513)425-2676

Description

Founded: 1990
EIN: 311284344
Organization Type: Corporate Foundation
Formed by Merger of: Armco Inc. (1999).
Giving Locations: operating locations.
Grant Types: Award, Employee Matching Gifts, Matching, Scholarship.
Note: Employee matching gift ratio: 1 to 1 for educational and cultural institutions.

Financial Summary

Total Giving: $991,930 (1997); $381,160 (1996); $295,746 (1995). Note: Contributes through foundation only. 1996 Giving includes scholarship; United Way ($164,500).
Giving Analysis: Giving for 1997 includes: foundation ($676,217); foundation grants to United Way ($191,500); foundation scholarships ($112,000); foundation matching gifts ($12,213)
Assets: $7,799,575 (1997); $7,242,671 (1996); $6,589,491 (1995)
Gifts Received: $1,000,000 (1995); $3,035,025 (1990). Note: Gifts are received from Armco, Inc., Kawasaki Steel Investments, Inc, Armco Steel Co., L.P. and Breed, Abbott & Morgan.

Typical Recipients

Arts & Humanities: Arts Associations & Councils, Arts Centers, Arts Institutes, Community Arts, Dance, Film & Video, History & Archaeology, Museums/Galleries, Music, Opera, Performing Arts, Public Broadcasting, Theater
Civic & Public Affairs: Business/Free Enterprise, Chambers of Commerce, Clubs, Community Foundations, Civic & Public Affairs-General, Housing, Parades/Festivals, Public Policy, Safety, Urban & Community Affairs
Education: Business Education, Colleges & Universities, Economic Education, Education Funds, Engineering/Technological Education, Education-General, International Studies, Public Education (Precollege), Student Aid
Environment: Wildlife Protection
Health: Cancer, Clinics/Medical Centers, Emergency/Ambulance Services, Heart, Hospices, Hospitals, Public Health, Single-Disease Health Associations
International: Foreign Arts Organizations
Religion: Religious Welfare
Social Services: Child Welfare, Community Service Organizations, Crime Prevention, Family Services, Homes, People with Disabilities, Recreation & Athletics, Scouts, Senior Services, United Funds/United Ways, YMCA/YWCA/YMHA/YWHA, Youth Organizations

Contributions Analysis

Giving Priorities: Supports single-disease health associations; community arts; a symphony orchestra; and various health, civic, social service, and religious organizations. Company matches employee gifts to a wide range of charitable, cultural, and educational organizations.
Arts & Humanities: 6%.
Civic & Public Affairs: 2%. Support is directed to community foundations and Junior Achievement chapters.
Education: 5%. Primary interests include colleges and universities, secondary education, and education associations. Also sponsors a scholarship program for children of employees.
Environment: 12%. Supports the Ohio River Mussel Migration Trust Fund.
Health: 46%. Supports hospitals and medical centers.
International: 1%.
Religion: 1%.
Social Services: 27%. Primary support includes funding for the United Ways in Ohio and Pennsylvania.
Note: Total contributions made in 1997.

Application Procedures

Initial Contact: Send a brief letter of inquiry.
Application Requirements: a description of organization, amount requested, project description, and proof of tax-exempt status
Deadlines: None.
Notes: For scholarship or matching grant programs, applicants can request application forms, which include specific criteria for each program.

Additional Information

In 1995, the company reported it changed its name from Armco Steel Company to AK Steel Corporation. The foundation has also undergone a name change; it is now called the AK Steel Foundation. Kawasaki owns approximately 15-16% of AK Steel Corp.'s stock.
AK Steel announced, its merger with Armco Inc. would take effect September 30, 1999. As a result of the merger, the business and operations of Armco will be conducted by and in the name of AK Steel. Armco shares will cease to trade on the New York Stock Exchange as of close of business on September 30, 1999.
Publications: Application Forms; Sons and Daughters of Alaska Steel Corporate Employees Scholarship Program; Employee Matching Gift Program Informational Brochure

Corporate Officials

Gary Melampy: vice president, chief executive officer, director PRIM CORP EMPL vice president: Alaska Steel Corp.
Richard E. Newsted: executive vice president PRIM CORP EMPL executive vice president: AK Steel Corp.
Richard M. Wardrop, Jr.: chairman, chief executive officer, director B McKeesport, PA 1945. ED Pennsylvania State University (1968). PRIM CORP EMPL chairman, chief executive officer, director: Alaska Steel Corp. ADD CORP EMPL chairman: AK Steel Holding Corp.
James Lyman Wareham: president B Clinton, IA 1939. ED University of Notre Dame BSEE (1961). PRIM CORP EMPL president: AK Steel Holding Corp. CORP AFFIL president, director: Wheeling-Pitts Corp.; director: Laidlaw Environmental Service Inc.; director: Wesbanco; president: AK Steel Corp.; director: Bliss-Salem Inc. NONPR AFFIL director: Wheeling Hospital; director: Wheeling Jesuit College; member: West Virginia Manufacturing Association; member: Ohio Steel Industry Advisory Commission; director: United Way Upper Ohio Valley; member: International Iron & Steel Institute; member: Manufacturing Association; member: Chamber of Commerce Wheeling; member: Institute Mining & Metallurgy Engineers; member: Association of Iron & Mettallurgical Engineers; member: Association Iron & Steel Engineers; director: American Iron & Steel Institute.

Foundation Officials

Thomas Carlisle Graham: trustee B Greensburg, PA 1927. ED University of Louisville BCE (1947). CORP AFFIL director: Mellon National Corp.; director: Texas Oil & Gas Corp.; director: Marathon Oil Co.; director: Mellon Bank NA; director: Hershey Foods Corp.; director: International Paper Co.; director: Hammermill Paper Co. NONPR AFFIL trustee: Committee for Economic Development; board visitors: University Pittsburgh Joseph M. Katz Graduate School of Business; chairman: American Iron & Steel Institute; trustee: Carnegie Institute. CLUB AFFIL Rolling Rock Club; Fox Chapel Golf Club; Laurel Valley Country Club; Duquesne Club.
Randall F. Preheim: president, trustee PRIM CORP EMPL vice president, secretary: Alaska Steel Corp. CORP AFFIL vice president, secretary: AK Steel Holding Corp.
James A. Weyers: executive secretary PRIM CORP EMPL communication manager: Alaska Steel Corp.

Grants Analysis

Disclosure Period: calendar year ending 1997
Total Grants: $676,217*
Number of Grants: 52
Average Grant: $5,906*
Highest Grant: $375,000
Typical Range: $1,000 to $15,000
***Note:** Giving excludes matching gifts; scholarship; United Way. Average grant figure excludes highest grant.

Recent Grants

Note: Grants derived from 1997 Form 990.

Arts & Humanities

25,000	Television Middletown, Middletown, OH -- Capital Phase I
10,000	Paramount Arts Center, Ashland, KY -- Great Expectations campaign
6,000	Middletown Symphony Orchestra, Middletown, OH
5,000	Arts in Middletown, Middletown, OH
3,000	Historic Newburgh, Newburgh, IN
3,000	Sorg Opera Company, Middletown, OH
2,000	Paramount Arts Center, Ashland, KY
1,000	Huntington Museum of Art, Huntington, WV

Civic & Public Affairs

5,000	Lebanon Habitat for Humanity, Lebanon, OH
4,200	Ashland Kiwanis, Ashland, KY -- Sebald Self-Reliance Awards
3,102	Habitat for Humanity -- framing
2,765	Ashland Kiwanis, Ashland, KY -- Sebald Self-Reliance Award Banquet
2,500	Monroe Community Foundation
1,000	Ashland Tri-State Fair and Regatta, Ashland, KY
1,000	Middletown All-American Weekend, Middletown, OH
1,000	Tri-State Foundation -- winter wonderland
500	Mothers Against Drunk Driving, Dallas, TX

Education

20,000	Southern Indiana Japanese School, IN
10,000	Junior Achievement, Middletown, OH
3,000	Colorado State University, Fort Collins, CO
3,000	University of Pittsburgh, Pittsburgh, PA
2,000	Junior Achievement of Ohio Valley, Ashland, KY
2,000	Middletown Community Foundation, Middletown, OH -- Sebald Awards
500	Greater Cincinnati Center for Economic Education, Cincinnati, OH

Environment

100,000	Ohio River Mussel Migration Trust Fund

Health

375,000	Kings Daughters Medical Center Foundation
10,000	Ashland Red Cross, Ashland, KY
2,000	Middletown Regional Hospital Foundation, Middletown, OH
500	Shriners Hospital, Ashland, KY

International

10,000	Middfest International, Middletown, OH

Religion

6,000	Salvation Army -- capital campaign

Social Services

37,500	Middletown Area United Way, Middletown, OH
36,500	Boyd County United Way, Ashland, KY
25,000	Middletown Area United Way, Middletown, OH
25,000	Middletown Area United Way, Middletown, OH
25,000	Ohio Presbyterian Retirement Services, Columbus, OH
12,500	Middletown Area United Way, Middletown, OH
12,500	Middletown Area United Way, Middletown, OH
12,500	Middletown Area United Way, Middletown, OH
12,500	Middletown Area United Way, Middletown, OH
10,000	Gertrude Ramey Children's Home, Ashland, KY
5,000	Abilities First Foundation, Middletown, OH -- Steel on Wheels
5,000	United Way of Southwestern Indiana, Evansville, IN
4,000	YMCA, Middletown, OH -- corporate cup
2,500	Greenup County United Way, Russell, KY
2,100	Butler County Sheriffs Office Bagpipe Band
1,500	River Cities United Way
1,000	Middletown Area United Way, Middletown, OH -- Festival of Trees
500	Spencer County Sheriff -- charity fund
500	Vanderburgh County Sheriff, Evansville, IN -- charity fund

Alabama Power Co.

Company Contact

Birmingham, AL

Company Description

Assets: US$8,734,000,000
Employees: 6,865
SIC(s): 4911 Electric Services.
Parent Company: Southern Co., Atlanta, GA, United States

Nonmonetary Support

Type: In-kind Services; Loaned Employees; Workplace Solicitation
Note: Co. reports that nonmonetary support is limited.

Corporate Sponsorship

Type: Arts & cultural events; Pledge-a-thon; Music & entertainment events; Festivals/fairs; Sports events

Alabama Power Foundation

Giving Contact

Jacquelyn S. Shaia, President
Alabama Power Foundation
PO Box 2641, 600 N. 18th St.
Birmingham, AL 35291
Phone: (205)257-2508
Fax: (205)257-1860
Note: Proposals should be sent to the manager of the nearest Alabama Power Business Office.

Description

Founded: 1990
EIN: 570901832
Organization Type: Corporate Foundation
Giving Locations: headquarters and operating communities.
Grant Types: Capital, Employee Matching Gifts, Endowment, General Support, Matching, Multiyear/Continuing Support, Project, Scholarship, Seed Money.

Giving Philosophy

'People make communities what they are and develop communities into what they can become. People are the key to the success of every community. Their energy, innovation and ideas spark excitement and new projects that enhance the standard of living for everyone.

The Alabama Power Foundation is dedicated to helping people who, in turn, provide their time and resources to the improvement of their communities. Since its beginning in 1989, the Alabama Power Foundation has worked to become a catalyst in the communities served by Alabama Power and throughout our state.

We pursue this involvement through the work of Alabama Power employees, who are integral players in the communities where they live and work. To Alabama Power employees, living in a community means working in the community, bettering the community, and seeking to improve the quality of life for everyone in the community.

The Alabama Power Foundation provides funds to assist employees' community involvement. Foundation grants become substantial mechanisms for community development when combined with the enthusiasm and spirit of community leaders, funding from other areas within the community, and the resources and energy of Alabama Power's employees.

Behind every grant provided by the Foundation, there is a story that involves community needs, caring people, and an effort to provide sufficient funding to make a dream of improvement into a reality..We are proud to be Alabamians, and consider ourselves fortunate to be in a position to invest in people and the communities where they live.' *Alabama Power Foundation, Inc. Annual Report 1995*

Financial Summary

Total Giving: $6,835,294 (1997); $5,631,573 (1996); $5,280,844 (1995). Note: Contributes through corporate direct giving program and foundation. 1997 Giving includes foundation. 1996 Giving includes scholarship ($246,850); matching gifts ($85,782).
Assets: $156,135 (1998); $140,298,994 (1997); $122,616,905 (1996)
Gifts Received: $2,418,851 (1997); $9,453,802 (1996); $11,555,056 (1995). Note: The foundation receives funds from Alabama Power Co., APSO, Birmingham Urban, E.B. Harris, and Robert O'Finley Foundation.

Typical Recipients

Arts & Humanities: Arts Associations & Councils, Arts Centers, Arts Festivals, Community Arts, Dance, Historic Preservation, History & Archaeology, Libraries, Museums/Galleries, Music, Performing Arts, Theater, Visual Arts
Civic & Public Affairs: African American Affairs, Botanical Gardens/Parks, Business/Free Enterprise, Civil Rights, Community Foundations, Economic Development, Civic & Public Affairs-General, Urban & Community Affairs, Zoos/Aquariums
Education: Business Education, Colleges & Universities, Community & Junior Colleges, Education Funds, Education Reform, Elementary Education (Private), Engineering/Technological Education, Education-General, Literacy, Minority Education, Public Education (Precollege), Science/Mathematics Education
Environment: Environment-General
Health: Cancer, Diabetes, Eyes/Blindness, Health Organizations, Heart, Mental Health, Single-Disease Health Associations
Religion: Jewish Causes, Missionary Activities (Domestic)
Science: Science Exhibits & Fairs, Science Museums, Scientific Labs
Social Services: Child Welfare, Community Centers, Community Service Organizations, Delinquency & Criminal Rehabilitation, Family Services, Food/Clothing Distribution, People with Disabilities, Scouts, Senior Services, Shelters/Homelessness, Substance Abuse, United Funds/United Ways, Youth Organizations

Contributions Analysis

Giving Priorities: Health and human services, civic and community activities, education, and culture and the arts.
Arts & Humanities: 5% to 10%. Art associations, libraries, and symphonies and ballets receive art support along with public broadcasting.
Civic & Public Affairs: 10% to 15%. Supports urban and community affairs and business and free enterprise. Environmental affairs and zoos also receivegifts.
Education: 40% to 45%. Primarily supports colleges and universities and K-12 education. Continuing education, economic education, education funds, Junior Achievement, and literacy also receive gifts.
Health: About 35% to 40% of gifts. Pediatric health, mental health associations, health funds, and single-disease health associations all receive support.

Application Procedures

Initial Contact: Send a letter no longer than four pages.
Application Requirements: Include a description of organization, and its mission; previous support from foundation; projects goals and objectives; need project is trying to meet; expected results of project; key staff members, including those directly involved in project; list of board of directors; amount requested; description of use and evidence of need; how results

will be measured; how project may be used by others; how project will be sustained once foundation's funding is gone; recently audited financial statements; and proof of tax-exempt status.
Deadlines: None.
Review Process: Manager at local plant will review request and decide whether or not to refer it to the foundation with a recommendation. Foundation will review forwarded proposals and make the final decision.
Evaluative Criteria: Preference is given to programs that have a long-term effect, can be replicated, and respond to issues that concern the customers, employees, and shareholders of Alabama Power Co.; provide opportunities for achievement and leadership to youth, minorities, and elderly; support community development; promote understanding of public issues; identify new programs which can adapt to other communities; or stimulate giving by other organizations.
Decision Notification: Six to eight weeks after application is received.

Restrictions

Does not support individuals, religious organizations for sectarian purposes, political or lobbying groups, or organizations which lack 501(c)(3) status.
Also does not fund organizations which discriminate on the basis of race, color, creed, gender, or national origin or operating expenses which duplicate United Way funding (capital or special project funding will be considered).

Additional Information

Publications: Charitable Giving Pamphlet; Foundation Annual Report

Corporate Officials

Art P. Beattie: vice president, secretary, treasurer B Pittsburgh, PA 1954. ED University of Tennessee BS (1975); University of Alabama MBA (1979). PRIM CORP EMPL vice president, secretary, treasurer: Alabama Power Co. ADD CORP EMPL secretary: Southern Electric Generating Co.
Elmer Beseler Harris: president, chief executive officer, director B Chilton County, AL 1939. ED Auburn University BS (1962); Auburn University MS (1968); Auburn University MBA (1970). PRIM CORP EMPL president, chief executive officer, director: Alabama Power Co. CORP AFFIL director: Southern Energy Resources Inc.; director: Southern Co. Services Inc.; president, director: Southern Electric Generating Co.; executive vice president, director: Southern Co. Inc.; director: AmSouth Bank NA; director: SCI Holdings Inc.; director: Alabama Property Co.; director: AmSouth Bancorp. NONPR AFFIL trustee: Southern Research Institute; director: United Way America; member: Southeast Electric Exchange; trustee: Samford University; member: Society American Military Engineers; member advisory board: Saint Vincent Hospital; member: Edison Electric Institute; director: Public Affairs Research Council Alabama; director: Boy Scouts America Birmingham Area Council; director: Alabama Council Economic Education. CLUB AFFIL Summit Club; Montgomery Club; Rotary Club.
James H. Miller, III: senior vice president PRIM CORP EMPL senior vice president: Alabama Power Co.

Foundation Officials

Art P. Beattie: treasurer (see above)
Thomas E. Chappell: executive vice president, director
Banks H. Farris: chairman B 1935. ED Auburn University BCE (1958); Jones Law School LLB (1968). PRIM CORP EMPL executive vice president: Alabama Power Co.
Michael D. Garrett: director PRIM CORP EMPL executive vice president: Alabama Power Co.
William Bruce Hutchins, III: director B Tuscaloosa, AL 1943. PRIM CORP EMPL executive vice president, chief financial officer: Alabama Power Co. CORP AFFIL director: Southern Electronic Generating Co. NONPR AFFIL member: National Association Accts; member: National Management Association; member: Financial Executive Institute; member: Micron Delta Epsilon; member: Beta Alpha Psi; member: Beta Gamma Sigma.
James H. Miller, III: director (see above)
Michael L. Scott: director
Jacquelyn S. Shaia: president, director
Pat L. Southerland: secretary, treasurer

Grants Analysis

Disclosure Period: calendar year ending 1997
Total Grants: $6,835,294
Number of Grants: 227
Typical Range: $500 to $7,500

Recent Grants

Note: Grants derived from 1997 Form 990.

Arts & Humanities

190,600	Metropolitan Arts Council, Birmingham, AL
30,000	Birmingham Festival of the Arts, Birmingham, AL
30,000	Colonial Williamsburg Foundation, Williamsburg, VA
25,000	Birmingham Landmarks, Birmingham, AL
20,000	Birmingham Festival of the Arts, Birmingham, AL

Civic & Public Affairs

144,774	Alabama Power Service Organization, Birmingham, AL
132,525	Alabama Power Service Organization, Birmingham, AL
40,000	Birmingham Urban Revitalization Partnership, Birmingham, AL
35,000	Jesse Owens Memorial Park, Moulton, AL
25,000	Alabama Power Energizers, Birmingham, AL
25,000	Alabama Power Energizers, Birmingham, AL
25,000	Montgomery Area Community Foundation, Montgomery, AL
23,505	Alabama Power Energizers, Birmingham, AL
20,583	Alabama Power Energizers, Birmingham, AL
15,000	Bethel Ensue Action Task, Birmingham, AL
15,000	Community Foundation for South Alabama, Mobile, AL
15,000	Pace, Greensboro, AL

Education

62,500	Mobile College, Mobile, AL
40,000	University of West Alabama Foundation, Livingston, AL
32,500	Stillman College, Tuscaloosa, AL
31,250	University of Alabama, Birmingham, AL
30,000	United Negro College Fund, Birmingham, AL
25,200	Auburn University, Auburn, AL
20,000	Alabama Association of Independent Colleges and Universities, Birmingham, AL
15,000	Chilton Education Foundation, Clanton, AL
15,000	Chilton Education Foundation, Clanton, AL
15,000	Dallas County Education Fund, Selma, AL
15,000	Dekalb Educational Foundation, Fort Payne, AL
15,000	Dekalb Educational Foundation, Fort Payne, AL
15,000	Lowdes County Public School Foundation, Wayneville, AL
15,000	Partners in Education, Roanoke, VA
15,000	Talladega City Schools Foundation, Talladega, AL
13,300	Junior Achievement, Birmingham, AL
12,700	Wilcox County Student Education Enhancement Program, Camden, AL
10,000	University of Alabama, AL

Health

100,000	Helen Keller Eye Research Foundation, Birmingham, AL
25,000	American Cancer Society, Birmingham, AL

Social Services

297,476	United Way of Central Alabama, Birmingham, AL
164,650	United Way of Central Alabama, Birmingham, AL
82,136	United Way of Southwest Alabama, Mobile, AL
43,775	United Way of Calhoun County, Anniston, AL
41,905	Montgomery Area United Way, Montgomery, AL
30,657	United Way of West Alabama, Tuscaloosa, AL
30,000	Service Guild, Birmingham, AL
26,780	United Way of Etowah County, Gadsen, AL
25,862	Wiregrass United Way, Dothan, AL
25,000	Alabama Child Caring Foundation, Birmingham, AL
25,000	Boys and Girls Club of Central Alabama, Birmingham, AL
15,000	Etowah Youth Services, Attalla, AL
10,162	United Way of Central Alabama, Birmingham, AL

Alaska Airlines, Inc.

Company Contact

Seattle, WA
Web: http://www.alaskaair.com

Company Description

Revenue: US$906,810,000
Employees: 10,467
SIC(s): 4512 Air Transportation--Scheduled.
Parent Company: Alaska Air Group

Nonmonetary Support

Value: $855,975 (1994)
Type: In-kind Services
Note: All support in this area is in the form of airline tickets.

Corporate Sponsorship

Type: Sports events
Note: Sponsors the Iditarod dog sled race.

Giving Contact

Donna Hartman, Assistant to Vice President, Public Affairs
Alaska Airlines, Inc.
PO Box 68900
Seattle, WA 98168
Phone: (206)433-3383

Description

Organization Type: Corporate Giving Program
Giving Locations: headquarters and operating communities.
Grant Types: Emergency, General Support.

Financial Summary

Total Giving: $2,000,000 (1999 approx); $1,200,000 (1996 approx); $900,000 (1994)

Assets: $1,313,000 (1995); $1,315,000 (1994)

Typical Recipients

Arts & Humanities: Arts & Humanities-General
Civic & Public Affairs: Civic & Public Affairs-General
Education: Business Education, Education Funds, Education-General
Environment: Environment-General
Health: Health-General, Heart
Social Services: Social Services-General

Contributions Analysis

Giving Priorities: Supports local arts, civic, education, health, and social service organizations. Promotes volunteerism through the United Way and its sponsored projects.

Application Procedures

Initial Contact: Submit a full proposal.
Application Requirements: On organization's letterhead, provide a description of organization, amount requested, purpose of funds sought, and proof of tax-exempt status.
Deadlines: None.
Decision Notification: Six weeks after receipt of applications.

Restrictions

Company does not give directly to individuals or Schools.

Corporate Officials

William S. Ayer: president public affairs PRIM CORP EMPL president: Alaska Airlines, Inc.
John F. Kelly: chairman, chief executive officer, director B 1944. ED University of Puget Sound BA (1967). PRIM CORP EMPL chairman, chief executive officer, director: Alaska Airlines, Inc. CORP AFFIL chairman, director: Horizon Air Industries Inc.; director: Washington Water Power Co.; chairman, president, chief executive officer, director: Alaska Air Group Inc.; vice president, controller: Anheuser-Busch Companies Inc.
William L. MacKay: vice president public affairs PRIM CORP EMPL vice president public affairs: Alaska Airlines, Inc.

Giving Program Officials

Donna Ellenga Hartman: (see above)
William L. MacKay: vice president (see above)

Grants Analysis

Disclosure Period: calendar year ending 1999
Total Grants: $2,000,000 (approx)

Recent Grants

Note: Grants derived from 1994 grants list.

Civic & Public Affairs
Shriners, Seattle, WA

Education
Alaskan Students, AK
Independent College Foundation, Portland, OR
Independent College Foundation, Seattle, WA
Junior Achievment, Seattle, WA

Environment
Nature Conservancy, Anchorage, AK

Health
Airlifeline, Sacramento, CA
American Heart Society, Seattle, WA
Cystic Fibrosis, Seattle, WA
Northwest Medical Teams, OR

Albany International Corp.

Company Contact

Menands, NY
Web: http://www.albint.com

Company Description

Profit: US$10,300,000
Employees: 5,404
SIC(s): 2299 Textile Goods Nec, 2431 Millwork, 3554 Paper Industries Machinery.

Nonmonetary Support

Type: Donated Products; Loaned Executives

Giving Contact

Ken Paulver, Vice President, Corporate Communications
PO Box 1907
Albany, NY 12201-1907
Phone: (518)445-2200
Fax: (518)447-6343
Email: ken_pauler@albint.com

Description

Organization Type: Corporate Giving Program
Giving Locations: headquarters and operating communities.
Grant Types: Award, Capital, Employee Matching Gifts, Multiyear/Continuing Support.

Giving Philosophy

'The mission of Albany's charitable giving is to improve the quality of life in the communities in which our employees live and work. While we support local chapters of national organizations, we focus primarily on organizations that are locally based and operated.' Charitable Contribution Guidelines

Financial Summary

Total Giving: $250,000 (1991); $250,000 (1990). Note: Company does not disclose contributions figures. Contributes through corporate direct giving program only.

Typical Recipients

Arts & Humanities: Community Arts, Dance, Museums/Galleries, Music, Performing Arts, Theater
Education: Economic Education
Health: Hospices

Contributions Analysis

Arts & Humanities: Funds cultural organizations that further the fine and performing arts.
Education: Supports capital campaigns for colleges and universities, and paper schools from which company draws employees; also provides scholarships.
Health: Supports hospital capital campaigns.
Social Services: Funds United Way and human service organizations.

Application Procedures

Initial Contact: Company generally preselects organizations; however, a letter of inquiry should include a description of organization, amount requested, purpose of funds sought, and proof of tax-exempt status.

Restrictions

Does not support individuals, religious organizations for sectarian purposes, political or lobbying groups, or organizations outside operating areas.

Corporate Officials

Francis L. McKone: president, chief executive officer, director B Lowell, MA 1934. ED Lowell Technological Institute (1956); Rensselaer Polytechnic Institute (1963). PRIM CORP EMPL president, chief executive officer, director: Albany International Corp. CORP AFFIL director: Albany International Canada. NONPR AFFIL member: Canadian Pulp Paper Association; member: Tech Association Pulp & Paper Industry.
Michael C. Nahl: chief financial officer PRIM CORP EMPL chief financial officer: Albany International Corp.
J. Spencer Standish: chairman, director B Albany, NY 1925. ED Massachusetts Institute of Technology BS (1945). PRIM CORP EMPL chairman, director: Albany International Corp. CORP AFFIL director: Berkshire Life Insurance Co. NONPR AFFIL president: University Albany Foundation; member: World Economic Forum; trustee: Siena College; trustee: Albany Medical Center; member: American Management Association; trustee: Albany Academy. CLUB AFFIL Wolferts Roost Country Club; Schuyler Meadows Country Club; Fort Orange Club; member: Johns Island Club.

Grants Analysis

Disclosure Period: calendar year ending
Typical Range: $1,000 to $2,500

Albertson's Inc.

Company Contact

Boise, ID
Web: http://www.albertsons.com

Company Description

Acquired: American Stores (1999).
Revenue: US$37,478,100,000 (1999)
Profit: US$404,100,000 (1999)
Employees: 88,000
Fortune Rank: 24, per FORTUNE Magazine's list of 500 Largest U.S. Corporations (1999).
FF 24
SIC(s): 5411 Grocery Stores, 5912 Drug Stores & Proprietary Stores.

Operating Locations

Operates 15 divisions in locations.

Nonmonetary Support

Value: $1,300,000 (1994)
Type: Cause-related Marketing & Promotion; Donated Products; In-kind Services

Corporate Sponsorship

Type: Arts & cultural events; Festivals/fairs; Sports events

Giving Contact

Renee Bergquist, Director of Investor Relations
Albertson's Inc.
250 Parkcenter Blvd.
PO Box 20
Boise, ID 83726
Phone: (208)395-5949
Fax: (208)395-6631

Description

Organization Type: Corporate Giving Program
Giving Locations: headquarters and operating communities.
Grant Types: Award, Capital, Conference/Seminar, Emergency, Employee Matching Gifts, Endowment, General Support, Matching, Multiyear/Continuing Support.
Note: Employee matching gift ratio: 1 to 1 for higher education only, up to $1000.

Financial Summary

Total Giving: $3,000,000 (1998 approx); $2,945,000 (1997); $2,500,000 (1996 approx)
Giving Analysis: Giving for 1998 includes: corporate direct giving (approx $3,000,000)
Assets: $6,233,968 (1999); $5,218,590 (1998)

Typical Recipients

Arts & Humanities: Arts Appreciation, Arts Centers, Community Arts, Historic Preservation, Libraries, Music, Opera, Performing Arts, Public Broadcasting
Education: Business Education, Colleges & Universities, Community & Junior Colleges, Economic Education, Elementary Education (Private), Minority Education
Health: Emergency/Ambulance Services, Geriatric Health, Hospitals, Medical Rehabilitation, Mental Health, Public Health
Social Services: Child Welfare, Community Centers, Community Service Organizations, Emergency Relief, Food/Clothing Distribution, Senior Services, Shelters/Homelessness, Substance Abuse, United Funds/ United Ways, Youth Organizations

Contributions Analysis

Arts & Humanities: Goal is to assure the availability of a pool of creative resources and services in the visual, performing, and written arts for the enrichment and enjoyment of employees and other corporateconstituents, and to provide standards of excellence in culture and the arts. Includes assistance to performing arts programs, museums, public broadcasting cultural programs, and non-academic libraries.
Education: Seeks to assure the availability of a pool of trained and educated men and women from which to draw employees; to encourage continuing research and development in academic specialities relevantto the business corporation; and to promote standards of educational excellence. Support includes assistance to public and private higher education institutions, employee matching grants, scholarship programs and related organizations, including those which seek to increase public knowledge of economics and other subjects of special importance to the company.
Health: Goals are to assure the availability of adequate health care and human service support for employees and other corporate constituents; and to promote the development of new, workable responses to human health and welfare needs. Support includes assistance to federated drives, hospitals, youth agencies, and other local health and welfare groups. Customers and employees raise money to support the Muscular Dystrosphy Association.

Application Procedures

Initial Contact: Call or write for guidelines and application form.
Application Requirements: Submit completed application form, including a description of organization, amount requested, purpose of funds sought, recently audited financial statement, and proof of tax-exempt status.
Deadlines: None.
Evaluative Criteria: Present an identifiable community need, tax-exempt status, efficient and effective administration, plentiful volunteer support, serves large population, programs have long-term effects, employee participation, participants encouraged to be self-sufficient, wide community support.

Restrictions

Does not support religious organizations for sectarian purposes, or political or lobbying groups.

Additional Information

In community fund drives, company generally contributes on a pro rata basis, figuring the number of Albertson's employees as a percentage of private employment in the area.
Publications: Contributions Policy and Procedures

Corporate Officials

Richard L. King: president, chief operating officeraffairs ED Utah State University BS (1971). PRIM CORP EMPL president, chief operating officer: Albertson's Inc. CORP AFFIL director: TJ International Inc.
Gary Glenn Michael: chairman, chief executive officer, director B Laurel, MT 1940. ED University of Idaho BS (1962). PRIM CORP EMPL chairman, chief executive officer, director: Albertson's Inc. CORP AFFIL director: Questar Corp.; director: Questar Gas Co.; director: Boise Cascade Corp.; chairman: Buttrey Food & Drug Stores Co.
A. Craig Olson: senior vice president finance, chief financial officer B Twin Falls, ID 1951. ED University of Idaho BS (1974). PRIM CORP EMPL senior vice president finance, chief financial officer: Albertson's Inc. NONPR AFFIL member: American Institute CPAs; member: Financial Executives Institute.
Michael Read: vice president public affairs PRIM CORP EMPL vice president public affairs: Albertson's Inc.

Giving Program Officials

Renee Bergquist: director investor relations
John G. Danielson: vice president, treasurer PRIM CORP EMPL vice president, treasurer: Albertson's Inc.

Grants Analysis

Disclosure Period: calendar year ending 1996
Total Grants: $2,500,000 (approx)

ALCOA INC.

 Number 52 of Top 100 Corporate Givers

Company Contact

Pittsburgh, PA
Web: http://www.alcoa.com

Company Description

Former Name: Aluminum Co. of America.
Revenue: US$15,489,400,000
Profit: US$853,000,000
Employees: 103,500
Fortune Rank: 106, per FORTUNE Magazine's list of 500 Largest U.S. Corporations (1999).
FF 106
SIC(s): 2819 Industrial Inorganic Chemicals Nec, 3334 Primary Aluminum, 3353 Aluminum Sheet, Plate & Foil, 3354 Aluminum Extruded Products.

Operating Locations

Argentina: Alusud Argentina SA Industrial y Comercial, Buenos Aires; Feroscar SA Industrial y Comercial, La Plata; Australia: Alcoa of Australia Ltd., Boddington, Huntly, Jarrahdale, Willowdale, Kwinana, Pinjarra, Point Henry; Kaal Australia Ltd., Point Henry; Alcoa of Australia Ltd., Portland; Australian Fused Materials Pty. Ltd., Rockingham; Alcoa of Australia Ltd., Wagerup; Kaal Australia Pty. Ltd., Yennora; Bahrain: Gulf Closures W.L.L., Manama; Brazil: Alcoa Aluminio SA, Barueri, Cotia; AFL do Brazil Ltda., Itajuba; Alcoa Aluminio SA, Itapissuma, Lages, Pindamonhangaba, Sorocaba, Pocos de Caldas, Queimados, Salto, Sao Caetano, Turbarao, Utinga; Consorcio de Aluminio do Maranhao, Sao Luis; Mineracao Rio do Norte SA, Trombetas; Canada: DBM Industries Ltd., Montreal; Alcoa Fujikura Ltd., Owen Sound; Chile: Alusud Embalajes Chile Ltda., Santiago; People's Republic of China: Alcoa Shanghai Aluminum Products Co. Ltd., Shanghai, Chiba; Asian-American Packaging Systems Co. Ltd., Tianjin; Asian-American Containers Manufacturing Co. Ltd., Tianjin, Chiba; Colombia: Alusud Embalajes Colombia Ltda., Bogota, Cundinamarco; Germany: Alcoa Automotive Structures GmbH, Esslingen, Soest; Stribel GmbH, Frickenhausen; Alcoa Extrusions Hannover GmbH & Co. KG, Hannover, Niedersachsen; Michels GmbH & Co. KG, Herzebrock, St. Vit; Alcoa Chemie GmbH, Ludwigshafen, Rheinland-Pfalz; Alcoa Deutschland GmbH, Viernheim, Worms am Rhein; Guinea: Halco (Mining) Inc., Sangaredi; Hungary: AFL/Michels GmbH, Enying, Mor, Salgotarjan; AFL/Stribel GmbH, Mor; AFL/Michels GmbH, Szekesfehervar; Alcoa Kofem KFT, Szekesfehervar; Alcoa Wheel Products-Europe, Szekesfehervar; CSI Hungary Manufacturing and Trading LLC, Szekesfehervar; India: Alcoa-ACC Industrial Chemicals Ltd.; Ireland: AFL Ireland Ltd., Dundalk; Italy: Alcoa Italia SpA, Bolzano, Feltre, Fossanova, Fusina, Iglesias, Mori, Portovesme; Jamaica: Alcoa Minerals of Jamaica, Clarendon; Japan: Shibazaki Seisakusho Ltd., Ichikawa, Nogi; Moralco Ltd., Iwakuni, Yamaguchi; KSL Alcoa Aluminum Company Ltd. (Kaal), Moka; Alcoa Kasei Ltd., Naoetsu; Mexico: Alcoa Fujikura Ltd., Acuna, Juarez, Monterrey, Piedras Negras; HC Industries de Mexico SA de CV, Saltillo; Malaysia: Unified Accord Sdn. Bhd., Kuala Lumpur, Selangor; Netherlands: Alcoa Nederland BV, Cuijk, DeLier; Alcoa Nederland Holding BV, Drunen, Noord-Brabant; Alcoa Nederland BV, Geldermalsen, Giessen; Alcoa Moerdijk BV, Moerdijk, Rotterdam; Alcoa Chemie Nederland BV, Rotterdam, Zuid-Holland; Norway: A-CMI, Lista, Mosjoen; Elkem Aluminium ANS, Lista, Mosjoen; Peru: Alusud Peru SA, Lima; Russia: CSI Vostok Ltd., Lyubachany; Aluminum East-Building Systems International, Moscow; Aluminum East-Closure Systems International, Moscow; Singapore: ACAP Singapore Pte. Ltd., Singapore; Spain: Alcoa Inespal SA, Alicante, Amorebieta, Aviles, La Coruna, San Ciprian; Capsulas Metalicas SA, Barcelona, Cataluna; Alcoa Inespal SA, La Coruna, Noblejas, San Ciprian; Extrusion de Aluminio SA, Valls, Cataluna; Suriname: Suriname Aluminum Company LLC, Moengo; Suriname Aluminum Co., Paranam; United Kingdom: Alcoa Systems (United Kingdom) Ltd., Stratford-Upon-Avon; Alcoa Extruded Products (United Kingdom) Ltd., Swansea, West Glamorgan; Alcoa Manufacturing (Great Britain) Ltd., Swansea, West Glamorgan

Alcoa Foundation

Giving Contact

Kathleen W. Buechel, President
Alcoa Foundation
3002 Alcoa Building
425 6th Avenue
Pittsburgh, PA 15219-1850
Phone: (412)553-2348
Fax: (412)553-4532

Description

Founded: 1952
EIN: 251128857
Organization Type: Corporate Foundation
Giving Locations: principally near operating locations and to national organizations.
Grant Types: Award, Capital, Challenge, Conference/Seminar, Emergency, Employee Matching Gifts, Fellowship, General Support, Matching, Multiyear/Continuing Support, Research, Scholarship, Seed Money.
Note: Employee matching gift ratio: 2 to 1 for higher education.

Giving Philosophy

'Alcoa Foundation was founded in 1952 in order to help people and programs in communities where Alcoa operates facilities, in the United States and abroad. .. We have been committed first and foremost to supporting programs in education. Increasingly, however, we are contributing to a variety of human service programs that are essential in today's economic environment. Another growing segment is in support given to international programs and organizations, particularly in the area of health and welfare.'
Alcoa Foundation Annual Report

Financial Summary

Total Giving: $16,400,000 (1999 approx); $16,400,000 (1998 approx); $14,997,460 (1997). Note: Contributes through foundation only.

Giving Analysis: Giving for 1996 includes: foundation ($10,729,330); foundation matching gifts ($1,605,320); foundation scholarships ($540,000)

Assets: $353,479,141 (1997); $323,436,171 (1996); $306,204,319 (1995)

Gifts Received: $4,251 (1992)

Typical Recipients

Arts & Humanities: Arts Associations & Councils, Arts Centers, Arts Festivals, Arts Funds, Arts Institutes, Ballet, Community Arts, Dance, Arts & Humanities-General, Historic Preservation, History & Archaeology, Libraries, Literary Arts, Museums/Galleries, Music, Opera, Performing Arts, Public Broadcasting, Theater, Visual Arts

Civic & Public Affairs: African American Affairs, Botanical Gardens/Parks, Business/Free Enterprise, Civil Rights, Community Foundations, Economic Development, Economic Policy, Employment/Job Training, Hispanic Affairs, Housing, Law & Justice, Legal Aid, Municipalities/Towns, Parades/Festivals, Philanthropic Organizations, Professional & Trade Associations, Public Policy, Safety, Urban & Community Affairs, Women's Affairs, Zoos/Aquariums

Education: Agricultural Education, Arts/Humanities Education, Business Education, Colleges & Universities, Community & Junior Colleges, Economic Education, Education Associations, Education Funds, Education Reform, Elementary Education (Private), Engineering/Technological Education, Faculty Development, Education-General, Gifted & Talented Programs, International Exchange, International Studies, Journalism/Media Education, Legal Education, Literacy, Medical Education, Minority Education, Preschool Education, Private Education (Precollege), Public Education (Precollege), Science/Mathematics Education, Student Aid

Environment: Environment-General, Resource Conservation

Health: AIDS/HIV, Cancer, Children's Health/Hospitals, Emergency/Ambulance Services, Geriatric Health, Health Policy/Cost Containment, Health Funds, Health Organizations, Hospices, Hospitals, Medical Rehabilitation, Medical Research, Medical Training, Mental Health, Prenatal Health Issues, Public Health, Single-Disease Health Associations, Speech & Hearing

International: Foreign Arts Organizations, Foreign Educational Institutions, Health Care/Hospitals, International Development, International Environmental Issues, International Organizations, International Peace & Security Issues, International Relations, International Relief Efforts, Missionary/Religious Activities

Religion: Jewish Causes, Religious Organizations, Religious Welfare, Seminaries

Science: Science Exhibits & Fairs, Science Museums, Scientific Organizations

Social Services: At-Risk Youth, Big Brother/Big Sister, Child Welfare, Community Centers, Community Service Organizations, Counseling, Day Care, Delinquency & Criminal Rehabilitation, Domestic Violence, Emergency Relief, Family Planning, Family Services, Food/Clothing Distribution, Homes, People with Disabilities, Recreation & Athletics, Senior Services, Shelters/Homelessness, Social Services-General, Special Olympics, Substance Abuse, United Funds/United Ways, Volunteer Services, YMCA/YWCA/YMHA/YWHA, Youth Organizations

Contributions Analysis

Giving Priorities: Educational grants in the form of matching gifts, special purpose grants, development and building grants, and scholorships; United Way; hospitals; and arts. Company gives to U.S.-based organizations with an international focus and in overseas operating locations through the foundation. Priorities generally follow foundation guidelines. In 1996, 44% of contributions went to education, 24% went to health and human services, 14% went to organizations outside the U.S., 11% went to civic and community, and 5% went to culture and the arts. According to the foundation's 1996 annual report, 'The geography of grantmaking presents an expanding frontier.. In recent years, Alcoa has pursued growth opportunities on five continents until, today, more than half of the corporation's employees are living and working in countries other than the United States. In quantitative terms, the trend to globalization is clear from the growth of our international grantmaking over the past few years. While our support for programs in U.S. locations has remained strong, our non-U.S. grants tripled in three years, from $600,000 in 1994 to $1.8 million in 1996, advancing the work of international and community organizations in 15 countries. This year and next, based on programs we are currently developing, the total may exceed $2 million, and the number of locations will grow apace.'

Arts & Humanities: About 5%.

Civic & Public Affairs: About 15%. Funds organizations that work to improve community services and quality of life. Interests include civil rights, economic development, law and justice, public policy, public safety, urban affairs organizations, and housing and community development.

Education: 40% to 45%. Supports matching gifts, higher education organizations, higher education scholarships and fellowships, and scholarships for children of Alcoa employees. Limited program of unrestricted funding. Support of quality education and research in public and private educational institutions. Historical interests in engineering and economics; supports newer specialized areas such as ceramics, polymers, and fiber optics. Grants are awarded to help improve both facilities and the quality of teaching at the secondary education level, particularly in the areas of economics, math, and science.

Health: About 5%. Supports, hospitals, and medical organizations. In addition, the foundation supports single-disease health associations, medical research, and community service organizations.

International: 10% to 15%. Gives to communities where company has a presence; priorities differ depending on community needs.

Social Services: 15%. Emphasis on United Ways and to indigent and handicapped persons, battered women and abused children.

Application Procedures

Initial Contact: Submit a letter of inquiry and proposal.

Application Requirements: Include description of specific project, purpose and objective, procedure to be followed (for research requests), amount requested, budget information, list of other corporate and foundation donors; recently audited financial statement; and proof of tax-exempt status.

Deadlines: None; requests acknowledged upon receipt.

Decision Notification: Foundation directors usually meet once a month.

Notes: Applicants are encouraged to contact the management of the local Alcoa facility.

Restrictions

In general, foundation does not fund the following: organizations or causes in states or countries where company does not have operating locations; deficit reduction or operating reserves; political or lobbying groups; fraternal organizations; individuals (except the scholarship program for children of Alcoa employees); sectarian or religious groups for services limited to their members; endowments; trips or tours; student exchanges; golf outings, fundraising dinners, tickets, tables, or advertising for benefit purposes; documentaries or videos; or hospitals for capital campaigns (unless cost-effectiveness of total capital program can be clearly demonstrated).

Only organizations classified as public charities that are tax-exempt under the Internal Revenue Code are considered for grants.

Additional Information

Alcoa merged with Alumax Inc. in 1998.

Recommendations from local Alcoa personnel are important in determining awards.

The foundation reports a growing interest in international giving; international grants tripled between 1993 and 1996.

Publications: Foundation Annual Report

Corporate Officials

Richard Lawrence Fischer: executive vice president, chairman counselcois B Pittsburgh, PA 1936. ED University of Pittsburgh AB (1958); University of Pittsburgh JD (1961); Georgetown University LLM (1965). PRIM CORP EMPL executive vice president, chairman counsel: Alcoa Inc. ADD CORP EMPL president: Alcoa International Holdings Co.

Robert F. Slagle: executive vice president human resources and communications B Rahway, NJ 1940. ED Cornell University (1963); Cornell University (1964). PRIM CORP EMPL executive vice president human resources and communications: Aluminum Co. of America.

Foundation Officials

Kathleen W. Buechel: president, treasurer B 1955. ED Harvard University MPA (1988).

Earnest Jonathan Edwards: director B Pamplin, VA 1938. ED Virginia State University (1961); Duquesne University (1975). CORP AFFIL director: Duracell International Inc. NONPR AFFIL director: LaRoche College; member: National Association Black Accountants; member: Institute of Management Accountants; member: Financial Executives Institute.

Richard Lawrence Fischer: director (see above)

Patricia L. Higgins: director PRIM CORP EMPL vice president, chief information officer: Allcoa Inc. CORP AFFIL director: The Williams Co. Inc.

Barbara S. Jeremiah: director B Pittsburgh, PA 1952. PRIM CORP EMPL vice president corporate development: Alcoa Inc. NONPR AFFIL member: American Corp. Counsel Association; member: Federal Energy Bar Association.

Richard B. Kelson: director B Pittsburgh, PA 1946. ED University of Pennsylvania BA (1968); University of Pittsburgh JD (1972). PRIM CORP EMPL executive vice president, chief financial officer: Aluminum Co. of America ADD CORP EMPL executive vice president, chief financial officer: Alcoa Inc. NONPR AFFIL member: Private Sector Councils CFPs; director: University Pittsburgh Law School Board Visitors; member: Pennsylvania Economic League; member: Financial Executives Institute Officers Conference Group; director: Pennsylvania Business Roundtable; director: Conference Board Council Financial Executives; member: Financial Executives Institute; member: American Bar Association; member: American Corp. Counsel Association.

Robert F. Slagle: director (see above)

Grace Smith: secretary, assistant treasurer

Grants Analysis

Disclosure Period: calendar year ending 1996

Total Grants: $12,874,650

Number of Grants: 2,262

Average Grant: $5,692

Typical Range: $500 to $25,000

Note: Grants are derived from a partial grants list.

Recent Grants

Note: Grants derived from 1997 Form 990.

Arts & Humanities

1,000 Miller Dance Theatre Byrne, SC

Education

25,000 Public Schools Pittsburgh, Pittsburgh, PA

15,000 Community College Stanly, Albemarle, NC

50 Univerdity Belmont, TN

Social Services

3,000 United Fund Appeal Pexin, Pekin, IL

Alcon Laboratories, Inc.

Company Contact

Fort Worth, TX
Web: http://www.alconlabs.com

Company Description

Employees: 5,037 (1999)
SIC(s): 2834 Pharmaceutical Preparations, 3841 Surgical & Medical Instruments, 3851 Ophthalmic Goods.
Parent Company: Nestle S.A., Avenue Nestle 55, Vevey, Switzerland

Operating Locations

HI: Alcon Laboratories, Inc., Honolulu; MD: Alcon Laboratories, Inc., Elkridge; PA: Alcon Laboratories, Inc., Sinking Spring; TX: Alcon Eye Care, Fort Worth; Alcon Laboratories, Fort Worth; Alcon Pharma, Fort Worth; Alcon Surgical, Fort Worth; Alcon Systems, Fort Worth

Nonmonetary Support

Value: $10,000,000 (1998); $10,000,000 (1997 approx); $10,000,000 (1996)
Type: Donated Products
Contact: Winona Mueller, Manager Medical Missions
Note: Co. provides nonmonetary support. Products are donated to vision care specialists participating in medical mission trips.

Alcon Foundation

Giving Contact

Mary Dulle, Director, Corporate Communications
Alcon Laboratories, Inc.
6201 S Fwy.
Ft. Worth, TX 76134
Phone: (817)293-0450
Fax: (817)568-7128
Email: Mary.Dulle@Alconlabs.com

Description

Founded: 1962
EIN: 756034736
Organization Type: Corporate Foundation
Giving Locations: TX: Fort Worth nationally.
Grant Types: General Support.

Giving Philosophy

'The foundation focuses its efforts on programs that advance the education or skill levels of opthalmologists or optometrists. In addition, we make our products available to eye care professionals who are planning medical mission trips to third world countries.' In areas where the company has a facility, funding is available for community organizations, social services, and the arts.

Financial Summary

Total Giving: $277,194 (1998); $400,000 (1997 approx); $356,000 (1996). Note: Contributes through corporate direct giving program and foundation.
Giving Analysis: Giving for 1996 includes: foundation ($312,836); 1997: foundation ($550,695); 1998: foundation ($277,194)
Assets: $1,293 (1998); $147 (1996); $24,881 (1994)
Gifts Received: $277,000 (1998); $313,062 (1996); $395,000 (1994). Note: The foundation receives donations from Alcon Laboratories, Inc.

Typical Recipients

Arts & Humanities: Arts Associations & Councils, Arts Outreach, Ballet, Libraries, Museums/Galleries, Music, Opera, Performing Arts, Public Broadcasting, Theater
Civic & Public Affairs: African American Affairs, Business/Free Enterprise, Clubs, Civic & Public Affairs-General, Hispanic Affairs, Philanthropic Organizations, Urban & Community Affairs, Women's Affairs, Zoos/Aquariums
Education: Business Education, Colleges & Universities, Community & Junior Colleges, Education Associations, Health & Physical Education, Medical Education, Minority Education, Private Education (Precollege), Public Education (Precollege), Science/Mathematics Education, Secondary Education (Private), Secondary Education (Public), Student Aid
Health: Cancer, Children's Health/Hospitals, Children's Health/Hospitals, Clinics/Medical Centers, Emergency/Ambulance Services, Eyes/Blindness, Health Funds, Health Organizations, Hospitals, Medical Research, Mental Health, Prenatal Health Issues, Public Health, Single-Disease Health Associations
International: Foreign Educational Institutions, Health Care/Hospitals, International Peace & Security Issues
Religion: Ministries, Religious Welfare, Seminaries
Science: Science-General, Science Museums
Social Services: Camps, Child Welfare, Community Centers, Community Service Organizations, Counseling, Family Services, Food/Clothing Distribution, Homes, People with Disabilities, Shelters/Homelessness, Social Services-General, YMCA/YWCA/YMHA/YWHA, Youth Organizations

Contributions Analysis

Giving Priorities: Education and research organizations specializing in ophtalmology and optometry.
Arts & Humanities: 26%. Major support goes to theaters, music, symphonies, and opera in the Ft. Worth area. Also contributes to libraries and public broadcasting.
Civic & Public Affairs: About 3%. Supports a variety of community organizations.
Education: 17%. Funding supports colleges, universities, and education associations for ophthalmic or optometric research. Also funds minority education, and secondary public and private education. Supports Junior Achievement and the Adopt-a-School program.
Health: 38%. Majority of contributions support eye-related health funds and health associations.
Social Services: 16%. Supports a variety of social service organizations in the Ft. Worth, TX, area with grants ranging from $250 to $1,000. Majority of contributions fund child welfare and youth organizations. Other priorities include community centers, food distribution, homes, shelters, and religious welfare.
Note: Total contributions in 1998.

Application Procedures

Initial Contact: Submit a letter or proposal.
Application Requirements: Include a description of organization, amount requested, purpose of funds sought, a recently audited financial statement including list of other major contributors, and proof of tax-exempt status.
Deadlines: None; decisions are announced bimonthly.

Restrictions

Alcon limits contributions to education and research institutions within Alcon's areas of specialization: ophthalmology, optometry, and vision care. Arts, civic and public affairs, and social services are limited to headquarters area.

Corporate Officials

C. Allen Baker: executive vice presidento B 1942. PRIM CORP EMPL executive vice president: Alcon Laboratories, Inc.
Timothy R. G. Sear: president, chief executive officer B 1937. ED Manchester University (1962). PRIM CORP EMPL president, chief executive officer: Alcon Laboratories, Inc. CORP AFFIL president: Alcon Puerto Rico Inc.

Foundation Officials

C. Allen Baker: trustee (see above)
Barry Caldwell: trustee
Mary Dulle: chairman PRIM CORP EMPL director professional relations: Alcon Laboratories, Inc.
J. Hiddeman: trustee
Fred Pettinato: trustee
Timothy R. G. Sear: trustee (see above)
John Alexander Walters: trustee B Philadelphia, PA 1938. ED Wagner College BA (1960). PRIM CORP EMPL corporate vice president human resources: Alcon Laboratories, Inc.

Grants Analysis

Disclosure Period: calendar year ending 1998
Total Grants: $277,194
Number of Grants: 188
Average Grant: $1,474
Highest Grant: $50,000
Typical Range: $250 to $2,000

Recent Grants

Note: Grants derived from 1998 Form 990.

Arts & Humanities

50,000 Performing Arts Fort Worth, Ft. Worth, TX -- Goodwill

7,500 Fort Worth Ballet, Ft. Worth, TX -- Goodwill

1,500 Modern Art Museum, Ft. Worth, TX -- Goodwill

1,500 Stage West, Ft. Worth, TX -- Goodwill

1,000 Ft. Worth Public Library Foundation, Ft. Worth, TX -- Goodwill

1,000 Jubilee Theater, Ft. Worth, TX -- Goodwill

1,000 Jubilee Theater, Ft. Worth, TX -- Goodwill

Civic & Public Affairs

10,000 Casa Manana, Ft. Worth, TX -- Goodwill

10,000 Michels Foundation, Philadelphia, PA -- Goodwill

1,500 Ft. Worth Zoo, Ft. Worth, TX -- Goodwill

1,500 Women's Shelter of Arlington, Arlington, TX -- Goodwill

1,000 Colleyville Lion's Club, Colleyville, TX -- Goodwill

1,000 Mayfest, Ft. Worth, TX -- Goodwill

1,000 Sturge-Weber Foundation, Gillette, NJ -- Goodwill

Education

10,000 Association Of University Professors in Ophthalmology, San Francisco, CA -- Goodwill

10,000 Country Day School, Ft. Worth, TX -- Goodwill

10,000 Trinity Valley School, Ft. Worth, TX -- Goodwill

10,000 University of North Texas Health Science Center, Ft. Worth, TX -- Goodwill

8,000 Texas Christian University, Ft. Worth, TX -- Goodwill

3,000 Association of Schools and Colleges of Optometry, Rockville, MD -- Goodwill

3,000 Texas Christian University, Ft. Worth, TX -- Goodwill

1,500 Nolan High School, Ft. Worth, TX -- Goodwill

1,250 Everman ISD, Everman, TX -- Goodwill

1,000 Emory University, Atlanta, GA -- Goodwill

1,000	Medical College of Wisconsin, Milwaukee, WI -- Goodwill
Health	
15,000	Association For Research in Vision & Ophthalmology, Bethesda, MD -- Goodwill
10,000	Johns Hopkins Hospital - Wilmer, Baltimore, MD -- Goodwill
7,000	Harris Methodist Health Foundation, Ft. Worth, TX -- Goodwill
5,000	American Red Cross Tarrant County Chapter, Ft. Worth, TX -- Goodwill
5,000	Kresge Eye Institute, Detroit, MI -- Goodwill
5,000	National Alliance For the Eye and Vision Research, Washington, DC -- Goodwill
3,384	Susan G. Komen Breast Cancer Foundation, Ft. Worth, TX -- Goodwill
3,000	Pan-American Association Of Ophthalmology, Arlington, TX -- Goodwill
2,500	Cooks Children's Medical Center, Ft. Worth, TX -- Goodwill
1,000	Cancer Research Foundation, Arlington, TX -- Goodwill
1,000	Southwestern Medical Center - UT, Dallas, TX -- Goodwill
750	National Ophthalmology Prayer Breakfast, Tampa, FL -- Goodwill
750	Regions Hospital, St. Paul, MN -- Goodwill
International	
3,000	International Society of Refractive Keratoplasty, Atlanta, GA -- Goodwill
1,500	Orbis, New York, NY -- Goodwill
Religion	
1,000	Salvation Army, Ft. Worth, TX -- Goodwill
750	Burleson Ministries Alliance, Burleson, TX -- Goodwill
Science	
1,500	Ocular Cell & Molecular Biology Symposium, Cleveland, OH -- Goodwill
Social Services	
7,500	Goodwill Industries of Ft. Worth, Ft. Worth, TX -- Goodwill
4,000	Arlington Boys & Girls Clubs, Arlington, TX -- Goodwill
2,500	Camp Carter, Ft. Worth, TX -- Goodwill
2,500	YWCA, Ft. Worth, TX -- Goodwill
2,000	Goodfellows, Ft. Worth, TX -- Goodwill
1,000	Lena Pope Home, Ft. Worth, TX -- Goodwill
1,000	Warm Place, Ft. Worth, TX -- Goodwill

ALEXANDER &BALDWIN, INC.

Company Contact

Honolulu, HI
Web: http://www.alexanderbaldwin.com

Company Description

Revenue: US$959,300,000 (1999)
Employees: 2,331 (1999)
SIC(s): 2062 Cane Sugar Refining, 4214 Local Trucking With Storage, 4412 Deep Sea Foreign Transportation of Freight, 4481 Deep Sea Passenger Transportation Except Ferry.

Nonmonetary Support

Value: $25,000 (1995); $100,000 (1994); $50,000 (1993)
Type: Donated Equipment; Donated Products
Contact: Paul Merwin
Matson Navigation
PO Box 7452
San Francisco, CA 94125
Note: Company reports that it donates used shipping containers.

Alexander & Baldwin Foundation

Giving Contact

Ms. Meredith J. Ching, Senior Vice President
Alexander & Baldwin Foundation
PO Box 3440
Honolulu, HI 96801-3440
Phone: (808)525-6642
Fax: (808)525-6677

Alternate Contact

Linda Howe, Vice President

Description

Founded: 1992
EIN: 990291942
Organization Type: Corporate Foundation
Giving Locations: CA: San Francisco including bay area; HI west coast.
Grant Types: Capital, Employee Matching Gifts, General Support, Operating Expenses, Project.
Note: Employee matching gift ratio: 1 to 1 for cultural gifts, up to $1,000 annually; for education gifts, up to $2,000 annually.

Giving Philosophy

'The Alexander & Baldwin Foundation supports qualified not-for-profit community organizations and projects with cash contributions. These contributions are primarily intended to benefit communities in which A&B companies operate or where A&B employees reside. It is the policy of the Foundation to selectively support organizations and projects that address significant community needs in the following categories: health & human services, education, culture & arts, community, maritime, and the environment' *Alexander & Baldwin Foundation grant application*

Financial Summary

Total Giving: $1,300,000 (1999); $1,276,690 (1998); $1,364,930 (1997). Note: Contributes through foundation only.
Giving Analysis: Giving for 1995 includes: foundation ($1,106,941); foundation grants to United Way ($223,900); 1997: foundation ($1,268,280); foundation grants to United Way ($96,650); 1998: foundation ($990,040); foundation grants to United Way ($277,650)
Assets: $1,765,000 (1998); $3,436,352 (1997)
Gifts Received: $2,000 (1998); $1,722,000 (1997). Note: 1997 contributions were received from Alexander and Baldwin, Inc. ($1,720,000) and miscellaneous donors ($2,000).

Typical Recipients

Arts & Humanities: Arts Centers, Historic Preservation, History & Archaeology, Museums/Galleries, Music, Opera, Performing Arts, Public Broadcasting, Theater
Civic & Public Affairs: Asian American Affairs, Economic Development, Economic Policy, Civic & Public Affairs-General, Housing, Philanthropic Organizations, Public Policy, Urban & Community Affairs, Women's Affairs
Education: Arts/Humanities Education, Colleges & Universities, Elementary Education (Private), Gifted & Talented Programs, Private Education (Precollege), Public Education (Precollege), Secondary Education (Private), Secondary Education (Public)
Environment: Environment-General, Resource Conservation
Health: AIDS/HIV, Children's Health/Hospitals, Clinics/Medical Centers, Emergency/Ambulance Services, Health Organizations, Heart, Heart, Hospitals, Medical Rehabilitation, Nutrition, Single-Disease Health Associations
International: International Peace & Security Issues
Religion: Religious Organizations, Religious Welfare
Science: Science Museums
Social Services: Big Brother/Big Sister, Child Welfare, Community Centers, Food/Clothing Distribution, Homes, Scouts, Special Olympics, Substance Abuse, United Funds/United Ways, YMCA/YWCA/YMHA/YWHA, Youth Organizations

Contributions Analysis

Giving Priorities: Education, culture and arts, social health and welfare, and community projects.
Arts & Humanities: 14%. Recipients include the performing arts, theater, historical societies, and museums.
Civic & Public Affairs: 4%. Supports local civic affairs, including economic develoment, housing, safety programs, minorities, youth groups, humane societies, and cultural festivals.
Education: 16%. Contributes to colleges and universities and private and public education.
Environment: Funds such organizations as the Conservation Council for Hawaii, and the Hawaii Nature Center.
Health: 7%. Support for hospitals, health services, and single-disease organizations.
Social Services: 56%. Emphasis on United Way. Also support youth organizations, child welfare, and the disabled.

Application Procedures

Initial Contact: Submit proposal in writing with Grant Application Cover Sheet.
Application Requirements: Include purpose of organization, with history and accomplishments; primary objective of the proposed project; how it will be administered and how the population will be served, and the plan for project evaluation; amount requested from A&B and why A&B was asked for support; financial information on the organization, including other sources of revenue, planned expenses, contributions already received, donor list, project's budget (if applicable), and percent of total that is requested by the foundation; list of the organization's board of directors and company employees involved with the organization; letter or copy of the IRS tax-exempt status notification; contact name and daytime phone number. daytime phone number.
Deadlines: 15th of the month prior to the meeting for which the grant will be considered; major capital and other requests of $20,000 and over considered in March and September.
Review Process: Contributions committee evaluates all applications on a case-by-case basis.
Evaluative Criteria: Committee only considers requests from the following types of organizations: those whose activities are located where the company has operations; those which have active volunteer support of company employees; those which minimize administrative costs so that those served receive the largest benefit from A&B's support; and those which provide some form of recognition for the contribution received.
Decision Notification: Committee meets in odd numbered months.
Notes: Organizations in Hawaii should contact Ms. Meredith J. Ching, Chair, Hawaii Contributions Committee, at the above address. Organizations on the U.S. mainland should contact Mr. Paul Stevens, Chair, Mainland Contributions Committee, c/o Matson Navigation Co., PO Box 7452, San Francisco, CA 94120. Contributions are one-time grants per calendar year. Notification will be done in writing generally within two weeks of meeting. Acknowledgement of receiving a proposal will only be done if a self-addressed stamped envelope or post card is made available.

Restrictions

Foundation doesn't fund individuals, religious organizations for religious purposes, events, travel, entertainment, or dinners.
Foundation does not make multi-year pledges and prefers not to be sole donor to a cause.
Foundation does not give to scholarship programs.

Additional Information

The Alexander & Baldwin Foundation was organized and is funded by Alexander & Baldwin, Inc., and its subsidiaries, A&B-Hawaii, Inc. and Matson Navigation Co., Inc.
The company also operates a political action committee for political contributions. Scott Matsuura and Meredith Ching, vice president, are contacts for the committee.
A&B also supports the Alexander & Baldwin Sugar Museum.
Publications: Grant Guidelines; Review of Giving

Corporate Officials

Meredith J. Ching: vice president government & community relations B Honolulu, HI 1956. ED Stanford University BS (1978); University of California, Los Angeles MBA (1980). PRIM CORP EMPL vice president government & community relations: Alexander & Baldwin, Inc. CORP AFFIL vice president: A& B Hawaii Inc.
W. Allen Doane: president, chief executive officer, director B 1947. ED Brigham Young University; Harvard University MBA (1975). PRIM CORP EMPL president, chief executive officer, director: Alexander & Baldwin Inc. ADD CORP EMPL president, chief executive officer: A & B Hawaii Inc.; vice chairman: A & B Properties Inc.; chairman: Kahului Trucking and Storage; president: Kauai Coffee Inc.
G. Stephen Holaday: senior vice president B 1944. ED Iowa State University BS (1971); Iowa State University MBA (1971). PRIM CORP EMPL senior vice president: A & B Hawaii, Inc. CORP AFFIL senior vice president, treasurer, chief financial officer: A&B-HI; treasurer: Nova Chemicals Inc.
John B. Kelley: vice president investor relations B 1945. ED University of Michigan BS (1965); University of Michigan MS (1970); Stanford University MBA (1976); Stanford University (1976-1979). PRIM CORP EMPL vice president investor relations: Alexander & Baldwin, Inc. ADD CORP EMPL vice president: AB Hawaii Inc.
Michael J. Marks: vice president, general counsel, secretary B 1938. ED Cornell University AB (1960); University of Chicago JD (1963). PRIM CORP EMPL vice president, general counsel, secretary: Alexander & Baldwin, Inc. ADD CORP EMPL senior vice president, general counsel: A&B-Hawaii Inc.; secretary: Matson Navigation Co. CORP AFFIL senior vice president, general counsel, assistant secretary: A & B Hawaii Inc.
Charles Bradley Mulholland: executive vice president B Los Angeles, CA 1941. ED University of Southern California BA (1965); Columbia University School of Business Administration (1980). PRIM CORP EMPL executive vice president: Alexander & Baldwin Inc. ADD CORP EMPL president, chief executive officer: Matson Navigation Co. Inc.
Alyson J. Nakamura: secretary B Honolulu, HI 1965. ED University of Hawaii (1987); University of California (1991). PRIM CORP EMPL secretary: A & B Hawaii Inc. CORP AFFIL secretary: A & B Properties Inc.
Thomas A. Wellman: controller, assistant treasurer B Casper, WY 1958. ED Brigham Young University BS (1983); University of Hawaii at Manoa MS (1984). PRIM CORP EMPL controller, assistant treasurer: Alexander & Baldwin, Inc. CORP AFFIL controller: A & B Properties Inc.; treasurer: Kahului Trucking Storage; vice president, controller: A & B Hawaii Inc. NONPR AFFIL director: Finance Executive Institute; member: Institute of Management Accountants; member: American Institute CPAs.

Foundation Officials

Meredith J. Ching: senior vice president, director, chairman HI committee (see above)
Branton B. Dreyfus: director B San Francisco, CA 1953. ED University of San Francisco (1975). PRIM CORP EMPL vice president, area manager Hawaii: Matson Navigation Co. Inc. NONPR AFFIL director: Seamen's Church Institute of Los Angeles; director: Steamship Association of Southern California.
Charles Bradley Mulholland: executive vice president, director (see above)
Alyson J. Nakamura: secretary (see above)
Robert K. Sasaki: director B Honolulu, HI 1941. ED Pomona College (1963); University of California at Berkeley (1965). PRIM CORP EMPL president, director: A&B Properties Inc. CORP AFFIL vice president, director: South Shore Resources, Inc.; executive vice president, director: WDCI Inc.; vice president, director: South Shore Community Services, Inc.; senior vice president: Kukui'ula Development Co., Inc.; director: Ohanui Corp.; vice president: Alexander & Baldwin Inc.; director: East Maui Irrigation Co.; president, director: A&B Development Co. (California); senior vice president: A&B-HI.
Paul E. Stevens: chairman mainland committee PRIM CORP EMPL senior vice president: Matson Navigation Co.

Grants Analysis

Disclosure Period: calendar year ending 1998
Total Grants: $990,040*
Number of Grants: 380
Average Grant: $2,629
Highest Grant: $130,000
Typical Range: $100 to $10,000
*Note: Giving excludes matching gifts; United Way.

Recent Grants

Note: Grants derived from 1998 Form 990.

Arts & Humanities

15,000	Maui Arts & Cultural Center, Maui, HI
15,000	National Maritime Museum-SFO, San Francisco, CA
12,500	U.S.S. Missouri Memorial Association, Honolulu, HI
10,000	A&B Sugar Museum, Maui, HI
10,000	A&B Sugar Museum, Maui, HI
10,000	A&B Sugar Museum, Maui, HI
10,000	Hawaii Opera Theatre, Honolulu, HI
5,000	Bishop Museum, Honolulu, HI
5,000	Hawaii Maritime Center, Honolulu, HI
5,000	Historic Hawaii Foundation, Honolulu, HI
5,000	Honolulu Theatre for Youth, Honolulu, HI
5,000	Manoa Valley Theatre, Honolulu, HI

Civic & Public Affairs

25,000	Habitat for Humanity, San Francisco, CA
5,000	Community Work Day/Teens on Call, Honolulu, HI
5,000	Maui Economic Development, Maui, HI

Education

25,000	Hawaii Pacific University, Honolulu, HI
25,000	UH Foundation - Maui Community College, Maui, HI
16,000	Kamehameha School Song Contest, Honolulu, HI
10,000	Island School, Honolulu, HI
10,000	Le Jardin Academy, Honolulu, HI
10,000	Oceanic Institute, The, Honolulu, HI
7,000	John Swett High School, Crockett, CA
5,000	Carquinez Middle School, Crockett, CA
5,000	College Park High School, Pleasant Hill, CA
5,000	Hawaii Pacific University, Honolulu, HI
5,000	Honolulu Academy of Arts, Honolulu, HI
5,000	Public Schools of Hawaii Foundation, Honolulu, HI

Environment

10,000	Nature Conservancy of Hawaii, Honolulu, HI

Health

25,000	Maui County Nutrition Project, Maui, HI
6,000	American Heart Association, Honolulu, HI
5,000	American Red Cross, Honolulu, HI
5,000	Hana Community Health Center, Hana, HI
5,000	Ho' Omana' Olana, Honolulu, HI
5,000	Kahuku Hospital, Kahuku, HI
5,000	Rehab Hospital of the Pacific Foundation, Honolulu, HI

Religion

5,000	Maui Salvation Army, Maui, HI
5,000	Maui Salvation Army, Maui, HI

Social Services

130,000	Aloha United Way, Honolulu, HI
120,000	Maui United Way, Maui, HI
55,000	Aloha United Way, Honolulu, HI
32,000	United Way (Bay Area), San Rafael, CA
20,000	United Way (Kauai-Matson), Kauai, HI
20,000	United Way (Napa/Solano), Napa, CA
15,000	Big Brothers/Big Sisters-Maui, Maui, HI
15,000	YWCA - Kauai, Kauai, HI
15,000	YWCA - Oahu, Oahu, HI
8,000	United Way of Greater L.A., Los Angeles, CA
5,000	Boy Scouts of America-Aloha, Honolulu, HI
5,000	Boy Scouts of America-Bay Area, San Francisco, CA
5,000	Girl Scout Council of Hawaii, Honolulu, HI

Allegheny Technologies Inc.

Company Contact

1000 Six PPG Place
Pittsburgh, PA 15222-5479
Phone: (412)394-2800
Fax: (412)394-3034
Web: http://www.alleghenytechnologies.com

Company Description

Former Name: Allegheny Ludlum Corp.; Allegheny Teledyne Inc. (1999).
Revenue: US$3,923,400,000
Employees: 24,000
Fortune Rank: 444, per FORTUNE Magazine's list of 500 Largest U.S. Corporations (1999).
FF 444
SIC(s): 3312 Blast Furnaces & Steel Mills.

Allegheny Technologies Inc. Charitable Trust

Giving Contact

Jon D. Walton, Senior Vice President, Secretary & General Counsel
Allegheny Technologies Inc.
Pittsburgh, PA
Phone: (412)394-2836
Fax: (412)394-3010

Description

EIN: 256228755
Organization Type: Corporate Foundation
Former Name: Allegheny Teledyne Inc. (1999).
Giving Locations: PA: Pittsburgh including greater metropolitan area headquarters and operating communities.

Grant Types: Capital, Employee Matching Gifts, General Support.
Note: Employee matching gift ratio: 1 to 1 for secondary, composite secondary or elementary education, up to $500 annually; for higher education up to $2,000 annually.

Giving Philosophy

'Allegheny Ludlum recognizes its role as a neighbor in our plant communities. We support many educational, civic and charitable causes. As a commitment to education, area high schools are awarded math and science grants. In addition, we support and work closely with the Penn State New Kensington Campus, the University of Pittsburgh, and Carnegie Mellon University. .. Perhaps the public spirit and caring of Allegheny Ludlum employees is best demonstrated through employee contributions to the United Way. In addition, many employees participated in two Days of Caring, a time when volunteers learn firsthand about how the United Way serves local needs. Such activities represent the dedication of Allegheny Ludlum and our people to our plant communities.' *Allegheny Ludlum Corp. 1992 Annual Report*

Financial Summary

Total Giving: $1,000,000 (fiscal year ending May 30, 1998 approx); $1,698,863 (fiscal 1997); $1,096,881 (fiscal 1996). Note: Contributes through corporate direct giving program and foundation. Giving includes foundation.
Assets: $1,664,028 (fiscal 1996); $2,604,342 (fiscal 1992); $2,963,170 (fiscal 1990)
Gifts Received: $750,000 (fiscal 1996); $500,000 (fiscal 1992)

Typical Recipients

Arts & Humanities: Arts Centers, Arts Festivals, Dance, Historic Preservation, History & Archaeology, Libraries, Museums/Galleries, Music, Opera, Performing Arts, Public Broadcasting, Theater
Civic & Public Affairs: Business/Free Enterprise, Chambers of Commerce, Economic Development, Economic Policy, Employment/Job Training, Civic & Public Affairs-General, Law & Justice, Legal Aid, Philanthropic Organizations, Professional & Trade Associations, Urban & Community Affairs, Women's Affairs, Zoos/Aquariums
Education: Arts/Humanities Education, Business Education, Colleges & Universities, Community & Junior Colleges, Economic Education, Education Associations, Education Funds, Engineering/Technological Education, Minority Education, Public Education (Precollege), Science/Mathematics Education, Secondary Education (Private), Student Aid
Environment: Environment-General
Health: Children's Health/Hospitals, Emergency/Ambulance Services, Hospitals, Medical Rehabilitation, Mental Health, Nursing Services, Single-Disease Health Associations
International: International Affairs, International Relations
Religion: Churches, Jewish Causes, Ministries, Religious Organizations, Religious Welfare
Science: Scientific Centers & Institutes
Social Services: Child Welfare, Community Centers, Community Service Organizations, Counseling, Family Services, Food/Clothing Distribution, Homes, People with Disabilities, Recreation & Athletics, Scouts, Senior Services, Sexual Abuse, United Funds/United Ways, YMCA/YWCA/YMHA/YWHA, Youth Organizations

Contributions Analysis

Giving Priorities: United funds, youth organizations, child welfare, public broadcasting, higher education, and community development.
Arts & Humanities: About 20%. Grants are made to musical organizations, libraries, theaters and arts centers.
Civic & Public Affairs: 10% to 15%. Primarily supports community and economic development and philanthropic organizations. Interest also shown in professional and trade associations.
Education: About 15%. Supports colleges and universities, schooladministrations, and high schools in the Pittsburgh area. Also provides employee matching gifts.
Health: About 5%. Supports medical rehabilitation, hospitals, and single-disease health associations.
Social Services: 50% to 55%. Major support to the United Way in the Northeast and to traditional youth organizations such as the YMCA, Big Brothers and Big Sisters, Boys and Girls Clubs, and the Boy Scouts of America. Limited support also to child welfare organizations, food and clothing distribution, and children's homes.

Application Procedures

Initial Contact: brief letter or proposal
Application Requirements: history of organization, amount requested, purpose of funds sought, and proof of tax-exempt status
Deadlines: None.
Notes: Foundation prefers grant requests forwarded by operating locations with the recommendation of local corporate officers or employees.

Restrictions

Foundation does not make contributions to individuals or private foundations.
Contributions are made primarily in operating locations.

Additional Information

On November 29, 1999 the transformation initiatives at Allegheny Teledyne Inc. were completed. Two companies, Teledyne Technologies Inc. and WaterPik Technologies Inc. were spun-off. Allegheny Teledyne Inc. was renamed Allegheny Technologies Inc.

Corporate Officials

Robert P. Bozzone: vice chairman, director, chief executive officer B Glens Falls, NY 1933. ED Rensselaer Polytechnic Institute BS (1955). PRIM CORP EMPL vice chairman, director: Allegheny Teledyne Inc. CORP AFFIL director: DQE Inc.; director: Duquesne Light Co.; vice chairman: Allegheny Ludlum Corp.; chairman: Alstrip Inc.
Judd R. Cool: senior vice president human resources B Saint Louis, MO 1935. ED Washington State University (1957); Stanford University (1985). PRIM CORP EMPL senior vice president human resources: Allegheny Teledyne Inc.
James L. Murdy: executive vice president finance and administration, chief financial officer B Aberdeen, SD 1938. ED Loyola University BBA (1960). PRIM CORP EMPL executive vice president finance and administration, chief financial officer: Allegheny Teledyne Inc. CORP AFFIL director: United Meridian Corp.; vice president, director: All Acquisition Corp. NONPR AFFIL director: Childrens Hospital Pittsburgh.
Richard Paul Simmons: chairman, president, chief executive officer B Bridgeport, CT 1931. ED Massachusetts Institute of Technology BS (1953). PRIM CORP EMPL chairman, president, chief executive officer: Allegheny Teledyne Inc. ADD CORP EMPL president: Teledyne Inc. CORP AFFIL director: HCS Inc.; director: PNC Bank Corp.; director: Consolidated Natural Gas Co.

Foundation Officials

Robert P. Bozzone: trustee (see above)
James L. Murdy: trustee (see above)
Jon David Walton: trustee B Clairton, PA 1942. ED Purdue University BS (1964); Valparaiso University JD (1969). PRIM CORP EMPL senior vice president, secretary, general counsel: Allegheny Teledyne Inc. CORP AFFIL vice president, section: All Acquisition Corp. NONPR AFFIL chairman: Pittsburgh Youth Golf Foundation; trustee: Westminster College; member: Pennsylvania Bar Association; member: Pennsylvania Chamber Business & Industry; member: American Society of Corporate Secretaries; president, director: Music Mt Lebanon; member: American Corporate Counsel Association; member: American Arbitration Association; member: American Bar Association; member: Allegheny County Bar Association. CLUB AFFIL Rolling Rock Club; Valley Brook Country Club; Duquesne Club.

Grants Analysis

Disclosure Period: fiscal year ending May 30, 1997
Total Grants: $1,698,863
Number of Grants: 32
Average Grant: $10,842*
Highest Grant: $1,362,755
Typical Range: $500 to $20,000
***Note:** Average grant excludes highest grant.

Recent Grants

Note: Grants derived from fiscal 1997 Form 990.

Arts & Humanities

50,000	Pittsburgh Symphony Society, Pittsburgh, PA
11,500	Civic Light Opera, Pittsburgh, PA
5,000	Pittsburgh Regional History Center, Pittsburgh, PA
4,000	Community Library, Tarentum, PA
2,500	Pittsburgh Center for the Arts, Pittsburgh, PA
2,500	Pittsburgh Dance Council, Pittsburgh, PA
1,000	Opera Theater, Pittsburgh, PA

Civic & Public Affairs

1,362,755	Allegheny Teledyne Incorporated Charitable Trust, Pittsburgh, PA
25,000	Allegheny Conference on Community Development, Pittsburgh, PA
5,000	Engineers Society of Western Pennsylvania, Pittsburgh, PA
5,000	Institute for Research on the Economics of Taxation, Washington, DC
3,000	National Legal Center for the Public Interest, Washington, DC
2,500	Pennsylvanians for Modern Courts, Pittsburgh, PA
1,000	Allegheny Judicature Society, Chicago, IL
1,000	Tax Foundation, Washington, DC

Education

10,000	Inroads, Hartford, CT
8,250	St. Vincent College Campaign 150, Latrobe, PA
5,000	Waynesburg College, Waynesburg, PA

Health

10,000	Washington Hospital Capital Campaign, Washington, PA
5,000	Gateway Rehabilitation Center, Aliquippa, PA
1,000	Medical Rescue Team South Authority, Pittsburgh, PA

Religion

15,000	Salvation Army, Pittsburgh, PA
10,000	Holy Family Institute, Pittsburgh, PA
5,000	Catholic Charities, Pittsburgh, PA
1,000	Jewish National Fund, Pittsburgh, PA

Science

20,000	Carnegie Science Center, Pittsburgh, PA

Social Services

102,524	United Way Southwestern Pennsylvania, Pittsburgh, PA
8,334	Pittsburgh Blind Association, Pittsburgh, PA

7,000 Girl Scouts of America, Pittsburgh, PA
5,000 Butler County Family YMCA, Butler, PA
3,000 Boy Scouts of America, Pittsburgh, PA
1,000 Variety the Children's Charity, Long Island, NY

ALLIANT TECHSYSTEMS

Company Contact

Hopkins, MN
Web: http://www.atk.com/

Company Description

Employees: 7,700
SIC(s): 3483 Ammunition Except for Small Arms, 3669 Communications Equipment Nec, 3812 Search & Navigation Equipment.

Nonmonetary Support

Note: The foundation donates equipment from Alliant Techsystems to schools and other nonprofit agencies in several Minnesota locations.

Alliant Techsystems Community Investment Foundation

Giving Contact

Wayne Gilbert, Secretary & Treasurer
Alliant Techsystems Community Investment Foundation
600 2nd Street, NE
Hopkins, MN 55343
Phone: (612)931-5422
Fax: (612)931-5423

Description

Founded: 1992
EIN: 411683475
Organization Type: Corporate Foundation
Giving Locations: MN: Minneapolis; UT: Magna; WA: Seattle headquarters and operating communities.
Grant Types: Employee Matching Gifts, General Support.
Note: Employee matching gift ratio: 1 to 1 up to $200 annually.

Giving Philosophy

'The Alliant Techsystems Community Investment Foundation seeks diversity and caliber of technically trained workers. Focus is placed on initiatives that: enlarge the pool of technical talent, with an emphasis on increasing participation of under-represented groups; improve the quality of math and science education by addressing human service needs that are barriers to learning; and equip math and science teachers to improve student achievement.' Alliant Techsystems Community Foundation Grant Guidelines.

Financial Summary

Total Giving: $321,362 (fiscal year ending March 31, 1998); $300,000 (fiscal 1996 approx); $268,712 (fiscal 1994). Note: Contributes through foundation only.
Assets: $86,301 (fiscal 1998); $262,271 (fiscal 1993); $438,658 (fiscal 1992)
Gifts Received: $275,300 (fiscal 1998); $369,750 (fiscal 1993); $451,500 (fiscal 1992). Note: Contributions were received from Alliant Techsystems.

Typical Recipients

Arts & Humanities: History & Archaeology, Museums/Galleries, Music, Public Broadcasting
Civic & Public Affairs: African American Affairs, Business/Free Enterprise, Economic Development, Economic Policy, Employment/Job Training, Ethnic Organizations, Civic & Public Affairs-General, Philanthropic Organizations, Professional & Trade Associations, Public Policy, Women's Affairs
Education: Business Education, Colleges & Universities, Economic Education, Education Associations, Elementary Education (Public), Engineering/Technological Education, Faculty Development, International Studies, Medical Education, Minority Education, Private Education (Precollege), Public Education (Precollege), Science/Mathematics Education, Student Aid
Health: Cancer, Children's Health/Hospitals, Emergency/Ambulance Services, Medical Research, Single-Disease Health Associations
Social Services: Child Welfare, Counseling, Family Services, Food/Clothing Distribution, Homes, People with Disabilities, Recreation & Athletics, United Funds/United Ways, Volunteer Services

Contributions Analysis

Giving Priorities: Focus on social services and education.
Arts & Humanities: Less than 5%. Funds museums, including the Naval Undersea Museum, and orchestras.
Civic & Public Affairs: About 5%. Recipients include minorityassociations, public affairs, civic leagues, management improvement, economic development, and recreation.
Education: 30% to 35%. Supports business, economic, math, and science education. Public education, colleges and universities, and scholarship funds are other recipients. Focus is on programs that overcome education barriers and equip math and science teachers to improve student performance. Also supports Junior Achievement.
Health: Less than 5%. Supports single-disease associations, children's hospitals, and ambulance services.
Social Services: 60% to 65%. Primarily supports United Way chapters. Funds Special Olympics and child welfare organizations.
Note: The giving categories promote the foundation's overall goals, which are to enlarge the pool of technical talent, with emphasis on under-represented groups; improve the quality of math and science education by addressing human service needs that serve as barriers to learning; and to help math and science teachers to improve student achievement.

Application Procedures

Initial Contact: Send a brief letter.
Application Requirements: mission of organization; description of project, its purpose and expected outcomes; amount requested and project budget; copy of IRS 501(c)(3) letter; list of board of directors; and a copy of most recent audited financial statement.
Deadlines: None.
Evaluative Criteria: prefers to fund programs that reflect the foundation's overall goals
Decision Notification: proposals are reviewed as they are received

Restrictions

Generally, the foundation will not support religious organizations for sectarian purposes; capital or endowment drives; political campaigns or lobbying activities; individuals; travel by groups or individuals; meetings, conferences, or seminars; fundraising events or benefits; or advertising or printing.

Additional Information

In the next year, Alliant Techsystems will begin to focus more of its financial resources on math and science education for under-represented groups. Over time, the goal is to drive math and science education investment to 40% of total contributions through gradual redirection of funding and an increase in the amounts contributed.
Publications: Application Guidelines

Corporate Officials

Peter A. Bukowick: president, chief operating officer, director B 1944. ED Lafayette College BA (1965); University of Virginia PhD (1969). PRIM CORP EMPL president, chief operating officer, director: Alliant Techsystems Inc.
Scott Meyers: vice president, treasurer, chief financial officer ED Elmhurst BA. PRIM CORP EMPL vice president, treasurer, chief financial officer: Alliant Techsystems.
Richard Schwartz: chairman, president, chief executive officer, director B 1936. ED Cooper Union BS (1957); Pepperdine University MBA (1972). PRIM CORP EMPL chairman, president, chief executive officer, director: Alliant Techsystems.
Kristi Rollag Wangstad: vice president public affairs B Sioux Falls, SD 1955. ED Luther College BA (1977); Boston University MA (1982). PRIM CORP EMPL vice president public affairs: Alliant Techsystems.

Foundation Officials

Wayne E Gilbert: secretary-treasurer, director PRIM CORP EMPL director, state & community lc: Alliant Techsystems Inc.
Kristi Rollag Wangstad: president (see above)

Grants Analysis

Disclosure Period: fiscal year ending March 31, 1994
Total Grants: $210,618*
Number of Grants: 22*
Average Grant: $9,574
Highest Grant: $155,153
Typical Range: $1,000 to $10,000
*Note: Giving excludes matching gifts.

Recent Grants

Note: Grants derived from 1994 Annual Report.

Arts & Humanities

1,000 Johnstown Symphony Orchestra, Johnstown, PA -- for key community relationships
500 Minnesota Air National Guard Historic Foundation, Minneapolis, MN -- for key community relationships

Civic & Public Affairs

7,400 Metropolitan Economic Development Association (MEDA), Minneapolis, MN -- for key community relationships
3,346 Women in Technology and Science (WITS), Minneapolis, MN -- to increase the US pool of technical talent
2,500 Minnesota Cultural Diversity Center, Minneapolis, MN -- for key community relationships
1,000 NAACP, Minneapolis, MN -- for key community relationships
260 National Society of Black Engineers, Seattle, WA -- to increase the US pool of technical talent

Education

27,400 University of Minnesota Project Technology Power, Minneapolis, MN -- to increase the US pool of technical talent
13,780 Minorities in Technology and Science (MITS), Minneapolis, MN -- to increase the US pool of technical talent
12,000 Math Engineering Science Achievement (MESA), Seattle, WA -- to increase the US pool of technical talent
10,000 Teachers Academy, Minneapolis, MN -- to increase the US pool of technical talent
7,109 North Carolina A&T State University, Greensboro, NC -- to increase the US pool of technical talent

5,875	Minnesota International Center, Minneapolis, MN -- for key community relationships
5,125	LINK, Seattle, WA -- to increase the US pool of technical talent
5,000	University of Washington Minority Student Engineering Program (UWMSEP), Seattle, WA -- to increase the US pool of technical talent
2,000	Junior Engineering Technical Society (JETS), Minneapolis, MN -- to increase the US pool of technical talent
450	Junior Achievement, Minneapolis, MN -- to increase the US pool of technical talent

Health

500	Leukemia Society, Minneapolis, MN -- to eliminate barriers to learning
500	St. Paul Children's Hospital, St. Paul, MN -- to eliminate barriers to learning
314	Horsham Ambulance Corps, Horsham, PA -- for key community relationships

Social Services

155,153	United Way, Minneapolis, MN -- to eliminate barriers to learning
7,500	Danny Thomas Memorial Golf Tournament, Minneapolis, MN -- to support employee-directed volunteerism

Allianz Life Insurance Co. Of North America

Company Contact

Minneapolis, MN
Web: http://www.allianz.com

Company Description

Assets: US$1,050,000,000
Employees: 440
SIC(s): 6311 Life Insurance.
Parent Company: Allianz of America, Inc.
Parent Revenue: US$25,879,000,000

Operating Locations

CA: Allianz Underwriters Insurance Co., Burbank; CT: Allianz of America Corp., Westport; MN: Allianz Life Insurance Co. of North America, Minneapolis; Allianz Life Insurance Co. of North America, Minneapolis; TX: Allianz Life Insurance Co., Dallas

Nonmonetary Support

Type: Loaned Employees; Workplace Solicitation

Giving Contact

Jack LoSapio, Vice President, Human Resources
1750 Hennepin Ave.
Minneapolis, MN 55403
Phone: (612)347-6500
Fax: (612)337-6299

Description

Organization Type: Corporate Giving Program
Giving Locations: near headquarters only.
Grant Types: Capital, General Support, Matching.

Financial Summary

Total Giving: $230,000 (1994)

Typical Recipients

Arts & Humanities: Libraries, Museums/Galleries, Music
Civic & Public Affairs: Economic Development, Housing, Urban & Community Affairs
Education: Colleges & Universities, Economic Education, Education Funds
Health: Health Organizations, Heart, Hospitals
Religion: Churches, Religious Organizations
Social Services: People with Disabilities, Scouts, United Funds/United Ways, YMCA/YWCA/YMHA/YWHA, Youth Organizations

Application Procedures

Initial Contact: Send a brief letter of inquiry and a full proposal. Include a description of organization, amount requested, and purpose of funds sought. It is best to apply by the end of the third quarter, as the review board meets in the fall.

Restrictions

Company does not support individuals, political or lobbying groups, or religious organizations for sectarian purposes.

Additional Information

According to Allianz of America, Inc., each local office administers independent contributions programs, with Allianz Life's being the largest. Local offices decide on recipients and support levels, with nonmonetary support such as loaned employees included in programs.

Corporate Officials

Lowell Carlton Anderson: chairman, director treasurer, chief financial officer B Minneapolis, MN 1937. ED Macalester College BSBA (1963). PRIM CORP EMPL chairman, director: Allianz Life Insurance Co. North America. CORP AFFIL chairman, chief executive officer, director: Preferred Life Insurance Co. New York; president, director: NALAC Fin Plans; advisor director: Continuum Co. NONPR AFFIL director, member: Greater Minneapolis Chamber of Commerce. CLUB AFFIL Pool & Yacht Club; Minneapolis Club.

Edward J. Bonachi: senior vice president, treasurer, chief financial officer PRIM CORP EMPL senior vice president, treasurer, chief financial officer: Allianz Life Insurance Co. North America.

Grants Analysis

Disclosure Period: calendar year ending
Typical Range: $1,000 to $2,500

Recent Grants

Note: Grants derived from 1995 grants list.

Arts & Humanities
Augsburg College Library Fund, Minneapolis, MN
St. Paul Chamber Orchestra, Saint Paul, MN

Civic & Public Affairs
Minneapolis/St Paul Housing Fund, Minneapolis, MN

Education
Minnesota Private College Fund, Minneapolis, MN

Health
Minneapolis Heart Institute, Minneapolis, MN

Religion
Basilica, Minneapolis, MN
St. John's Capital Fund, Minneapolis, MN

Social Services
Boy Scouts of America, Minneapolis, MN
United Way, Minneapolis, MN
YMCA, Minneapolis, MN

AlliedSignal Inc.

Company Contact

Morristown, NJ
Web: http://www.honeywell.com

Company Description

Revenue: US$15,128,000,000
Profit: US$1,331,000,000
Employees: 70,400

Operating Locations

Australia: Bendix Group Superannuation Pty. Ltd., Ballarat; Bendix Mintex Pty. Ltd., Ballarat; AlliedSignal Aerospace Ltd., Waterloo; Austria: Jurid Vertriebs GmbH, Vienna; Belgium: AlliedSignal Aftermarket Europe NV, Leuven, Brabant; AlliedSignal Europe NV, Leuven, Brabant; Brazil: AlliedSignal Automotive Ltda., Guarulhos; Canada: AlliedSignal Canada, Etobicoke; AlliedSignal Aerospace Canada, Montreal; AlliedSignal Aerospatiale Canada, Montreal; Prestone Products (Canada) Ltd., Toronto; People's Republic of China: AlliedSignal China, Beijing; Denmark: AlliedSignal Aftermarket Europe APS I Likvidation, Tastrup, Arhus; France: AlliedSignal Deutschland GmbH, Blagnac, Haute Garonne; AlliedSignal Materiaux de Friction, Drancy, Seine-St.-Denis; AlliedSignal Catalyseurs Pour L'Environement SA, Florange, Moselle; AlliedSignal Aftermarket Europe BV, Levallois Perret; AlliedSignal Automotive Europe, Levallois Perret; AlliedSignal Europe Services Techniques, Levallois Perret; AlliedSignal Systemes de Freinage, Levallois Perret; AlliedSignal Fibers Europe, Longlaville; AlliedSignal Industrial Fibers SA, Longlaville; Bendix SVI, St. Fargeau Ponthierry; AlliedSignal Turbo SA, Thaon les Vosges, Vosges; Financiere Allied Signal, Thaon les Vosges, Vosges; Garrett Finances SA, Thaon les Vosges, Vosges; AlliedSignal Laminate Systems (SA), Villebon Sur Yvette, Essonne; Germany: AlliedSignal Bremsbelag GmbH, Glinde, Schleswig-Holstein; AlliedSignal Environmental Catalysts GmbH, Hannover, Niedersachsen; AlliedSignal Aftermarket Europe GmbH, Neunkirchen, Saarland; AlliedSignal Bremssysteme GmbH, Neunkirchen, Saarland; AlliedSignal Aerospace GmbH, Raunheim, Hessen; AlliedSignal Deutschland GmbH, Raunheim, Hessen; ICSRD Rueckhaltesysteme Fuer Fahrzeugsicherheit GmbH, Raunheim, Hessen; AlliedSignal Polymers GmbH, Rudolstadt, De-Ost; AlliedSignal Chemical Holding AG, Seelze, Niedersachsen; AlliedSignal Specialty Chemicals GmbH, Seelze, Niedersachsen; Riedelde AG, Seelze, Niedersachsen; AlliedSignal Laminate Systems GmbH, Wipperfuerth; Hong Kong: Norplex Oak Pacific Ltd., Kwai Chung; Oak Industries Hong Kong Ltd., Tsim Sha Tsui East, Kowloon; Allied Chemical International Corp., Tsim Sha Tsui, Kowloon; Ireland: AlliedSignal Ireland Ltd., Waterford; AlliedSignal Ireland Software Ltd., Waterford; Italy: AlliedSignal Turbo SpA, Atessa, Abruzzi; AlliedSignal Automotive Italia SpA, Crema, Lombardia; AlliedSignal Italia SpA, Milano, Lombardia; AlliedSignal Freni SpA, Modugno, Puglia; Jurid Italia SRL, Roma, Lazio; Japan: AlliedSignal Inc Japan, Tokyo; Garrett Turbo, Tokyo; Netherlands: AlliedSignal Carpet Fibers BV, Emmen, Drenthe; Grimes Aerospace Co., Hoofddorp, Noord-Holland; Jurid Handel Maatschappij BV, Rotterdam, Zuid-Holland; Frye International BV, Soest, Utrecht; Frye Intl. BV, Soest, Utrecht; AlliedSignal Fluorochemicals Europe BV, Weert, Limburg; AlliedSignal Aftermarket Europe BV, Weesp, Noord-Holland; Singapore: AlliedSignal Performance Additives (Singapore) Pte. Ltd., Singapore; AlliedSignal Singapore (Pte.) Ltd., Singapore; Spain: AlliedSignal Materiales de Friccion SA, Barcelona, Cataluna; AlliedSignal Automotive Espana SA, Granollers, Cataluna; Stop Iberica SA, Lezo, La Rioja; Greyco SA, Los Corrales de Buelna; La Industrial Plastica y Metalurgica SA, Madrid; AlliedSignal Sistemas de Seguridad SA, Sant Just Desvern, Cataluna; Sweden: AlliedSignal Aftermarket Europe Sverige AB, Bandhagen, Stockholm; Taiwan: Norplex Oak Materials Taiwan Ltd., Taipei; AlliedSignal Laminate Systems, Tao-yuan; United Kingdom: Cheshire Castings Ltd., Altrincham, Cheshire; AlliedSignal Holdings Ltd., Bristol, Avon; AlliedSignal Ltd., Bristol, Avon; Dexbin Ltd., Bristol, Avon; BSRD Ltd., Carlisle, Cumbria; Garett Turbo Service Ltd., Cheadle, Cheshire; Turbocare Ltd., Cheadle, Cheshire; Allied Corp. Pensions Investments Ltd., Cheltenham, Gloucestershire; Fortin Laminating Ltd., Glossop, Derby; Klippan Automotive Products (UK) Ltd., London; Norplex/Oak (UK) Ltd.,

Northampton, Northamptonshire; Ferranti-Bendix Power Generation Ltd., Oldham, Lancashire; Garrett Automotive Ltd., Skelmersdale, Lancashire; AlliedSignal Aerospace (UK) Ltd., Southall, Middlesex

Nonmonetary Support

Value: $7,800,000 (1997)
Type: Donated Equipment; Donated Products
Note: Support is provided by the company at internal cost.

AlliedSignal Foundation Inc.

Giving Contact

Alan S. Painter, Vice President & Executive Director
AlliedSignal Foundation Inc.
PO Box 2245
Morristown, NJ 07962-2245
Phone: (973)455-5876
Fax: (973)455-3632

Description

EIN: 222416651
Organization Type: Corporate Foundation
Giving Locations: headquarters and operating communities.
Grant Types: Capital, Department, Employee Matching Gifts, General Support, Multiyear/Continuing Support.
Note: Employee matching gift ratio: 1 to 1.

Giving Philosophy

'For many years, AlliedSignal has carried out a program of financial contributions to various nonprofit educational, community, and cultural organizations. On a local level, these funds go to recognized organizations in communities where our plants are situated and our employees live. Nationally, our grants are concentrated in the education area, where the corporation has a responsibility to assist colleges and universities upon which it depends for its future engineers, scientists, and professional managers.' *AlliedSignal Contributions Program*

Financial Summary

Total Giving: $10,000,000 (1999 approx); $10,000,000 (1998 approx); $9,959,390 (1997). Note: Contributes through corporate direct giving program and foundation. 1997 Giving includes corporate direct giving ($728,601); foundation ($1,430,789); nonmonetary support.
Assets: $326,267 (1991); $282,940 (1990); $268,715 (1989)
Gifts Received: $9,027,542 (1995); $8,982,188 (1993); $8,881,324 (1992). Note: The foundation receives gifts from AlliedSignal.

Typical Recipients

Arts & Humanities: Arts Associations & Councils, Arts Centers, Arts Institutes, Community Arts, Dance, Historic Preservation, Libraries, Museums/Galleries, Music, Opera, Performing Arts, Public Broadcasting, Theater
Civic & Public Affairs: African American Affairs, Chambers of Commerce, Economic Development, Employment/Job Training, Civic & Public Affairs-General, Housing, Law & Justice, Professional & Trade Associations, Public Policy, Safety, Urban & Community Affairs, Women's Affairs
Education: Arts/Humanities Education, Business Education, Business-School Partnerships, Colleges & Universities, Community & Junior Colleges, Continuing Education, Education Funds, Education Reform, Elementary Education (Public), Engineering/Technological Education, Environmental Education, Faculty Development, Education-General, Health & Physical Education, International Exchange, Legal Education, Literacy, Medical Education, Minority Education, Private Education (Precollege), Public Education (Precollege), Science/Mathematics Education, Social Sciences Education, Special Education, Student Aid
Environment: Environment-General
Health: Alzheimers Disease, Cancer, Children's Health/Hospitals, Clinics/Medical Centers, Diabetes, Geriatric Health, Health Organizations, Heart, Hospitals, Medical Rehabilitation, Medical Research, Multiple Sclerosis, Nursing Services, Public Health, Single-Disease Health Associations, Transplant Networks/Donor Banks
International: Foreign Educational Institutions, International Affairs
Religion: Churches, Dioceses, Jewish Causes, Ministries, Religious Welfare
Science: Scientific Centers & Institutes
Social Services: At-Risk Youth, Child Welfare, Community Centers, Community Service Organizations, Counseling, Delinquency & Criminal Rehabilitation, Domestic Violence, Family Services, Food/Clothing Distribution, Homes, People with Disabilities, Recreation & Athletics, Senior Services, Sexual Abuse, Shelters/Homelessness, Substance Abuse, United Funds/United Ways, Volunteer Services, Youth Organizations

Contributions Analysis

Giving Priorities: Higher education; United Way; hospitals; medical research, espe cially on aging; and performing arts. Company does not make contributions specifically for international purposes. On a select basis, has supported the domestic operations of organizations with an international focus through AlliedSignal Inc. Major suport has gone to Youth for Understanding. The company and foundation do not track information on the activities of overseas operating companies.
Arts & Humanities: 5% to10%. Supports performing arts, museums, and galleries. Other arts recipients include theater, dance, and community arts groups. Also matches employee gifts to arts organizations.
Civic & Public Affairs: Less than 5%. Supports economic development, business, law and justice, and community and minority affairs organizations.
Education: 55% to 60%. Support goes primarily to colleges and universities; interests include business, technical, engineering, and science education. Other recipients include state associations of independent colleges, minority education, and higher education associations. Also supports innovative K-12 programs in plant communities and administers matching gifts program to education.
Health: 30% to 35%. Major support to United Ways, hospitals, and medical research programs. Human service interests include the disabled, employment and job training, youth organizations, and child welfare groups. Also matches employee gifts to hospitals and first aid squads.

Application Procedures

Initial Contact: brief letter
Application Requirements: a description of organization, including name, address, primary mission, and contact person; description of proposed project; amount of grant request, including plans for implementation and benefits expected; copy of 501(c)(3) exemption letter; budget information (i.e. annual report, audited financial statement, proposed project budget); list of board members; list of other corporate support; and any additional information that may be helpful
Deadlines: applications accepted from May to August
Evaluative Criteria: whether recipient's activities relate to company's interests, if organization is near company's location
Decision Notification: decisions generally made during fall quarter
Notes: Requests from community-based organizations should be submitted through local plants or facilities. Requests from national organizations and colleges and universities should be directed to the foundation itself.

Restrictions

Generally does not support member agencies of the United Way, individuals, political or lobbying groups, religious organizations for sectarian purposes, dinners or special events, fraternal organizations, or goodwill advertising.
The foundation only funds organizations with tax-exempt status.

Additional Information

The foundation also sponsors a number of programs, including matching gifts for active employees and directors of AlliedSignal; Challenge 2000 Program, which supports innovative K-12 programs to improve literacy and science and math skills; Targeted University Program, which awards $100,000 grants to universities that conduct research on technologies key to AlliedSignal's business activities; and a number of scholarship programs for employee children.
On December 2, 1999 Honeywell International Inc. announced that the merger involving AlliedSignal Inc. and Honeywell Inc. became effective after the close of trading on the New York Stock Exchange on December 1st. In connection with the merger, AlliedSignal Inc. changed its name to Honeywell International Inc.
Publications: Alliedsignal Contributions Program

Corporate Officials

Lawrence Arthur Bossidy: chairman, chief executive officer, director communications B Pittsfield, MA 1935. ED Colgate University BA (1957). PRIM CORP EMPL chairman, chief executive officer, director: AlliedSignal Inc. CORP AFFIL vice chairman, director: Ladd Petroleum Corp.; director: Merck & Co. Inc.; vice chairman, director: General Electric Motors; vice chairman, director: Kidder Peabody & Co. Inc.; vice chairman, director: General Electric Lighting; vice chairman, director: General Electric Industries & Power System; vice chairman, director: General Electric Investment Corp.; vice chairman, director: General Electric Financial Services; vice chairman, director: Employers Reins Corp.; vice chairman, director: General Electric Communications & Services; director: Champion International Corp. NONPR AFFIL member: Business Roundtable; member: Elfun.
Larry E. Kittelberger: senior vice president, chief information officer PRIM CORP EMPL senior vice president, chief information officer: AlliedSignal Inc.
Peter Michael Kreindler: senior vice president, general counsel, secretary B Liberty, NY 1945. ED Harvard University BA (1967); Harvard University JD (1971). PRIM CORP EMPL senior vice president, general counsel, secretary: AlliedSignal Inc.
Frederick M. Poses: president, chief operating officer B New York, NY 1942. ED New York University BBA (1965). PRIM CORP EMPL president, chief operating officer: AlliedSignal Inc. ADD CORP EMPL president, director: EM Sector Holdings Inc. CORP AFFIL chairman, chief executive officer, director: American Standard Co. Inc.
Donald J. Redlinger: senior vice president human resources & communications PRIM CORP EMPL senior vice president human resources & communications: AlliedSignal Inc.

Foundation Officials

Lawrence Arthur Bossidy: chairman, director (see above)
Ken Cole: secretary
Peter Michael Kreindler: president, director (see above)
Alan Sproul Painter: vice president, executive director B Flemington, NJ 1935. ED Middlebury College AB (1957); Stanford University (1974). PRIM CORP

EMPL director corporate affairs: AlliedSignal Inc. NONPR AFFIL trustee: Saint Elizabeth College; trustee: Tri-County Scholarship Fund; member advisor board: Morris County Fire Police Training Academy.

Frederick M. Poses: director (see above)

Donald J. Redlinger: director (see above)

Grants Analysis

Disclosure Period: calendar year ending 1996
Total Grants: $10,000,000*
Number of Grants: 720
Average Grant: $13,888
Highest Grant: $100,000
Typical Range: $1,000 to $20,000
***Note:** Giving excludes nonmonetary support. Figures are approximate.

Recent Grants

Note: Grants derived from 1996 Form 990.

Arts & Humanities

100,000	New Jersey Performing Arts Center, Newark, NJ

Education

100,000	Carnegie Mellon University, Pittsburgh, PA -- brake noise and vibration research
100,000	Catholic University, Washington, DC -- capital grant for School of Engineering chemistry lab upgrade
100,000	Purdue University, West Lafayette, IN -- AlliedSignal Partnership Program
100,000	University of Michigan Ann Arbor, Ann Arbor, MI -- to support Michigan Joint Manufacturing Initiative
75,000	Massachusetts Institute of Technology, Cambridge, MA -- for Leaders in Manufacturing program
75,000	United Negro College Fund, New York, NY -- scholarship fund for Black students
65,130	Youth for Understanding, Washington, DC -- scholarships for AlliedSignal employee children
65,000	Arizona State University, Tempe, AZ -- Engineering Excellence Program
62,600	National Merit Scholarship Corporation, Chicago, IL -- scholarships
50,000	Challenger Learning Center, Carson, CA -- final of four payments, to provide equipment for simulated space station
50,000	Duke University Fuqua Graduate School of Business, Durham, NC -- AlliedSignal Integrated Learning Experience Course
50,000	Science City at Union Station, Kansas City, MO -- second of five payments on $500,000 grant, for creation of science museum
50,000	University of Arizona Foundation, Tucson, AZ -- Engineering Excellence and Aerospace Mechanical Engineering programs
45,000	Columbia University School of Business, New York, NY -- fellowships for minorities and women
44,500	North Carolina A&T University Foundation, Greensboro, NC -- scholarships for the Imagine the Possibilities Program
40,000	California Academy of Math and Science, Carson, CA -- AlliedSignal Computer Technology Lab at Magnet High School
30,000	California Institute of Technology, Pasadena, CA -- Industrial Associates Program
30,000	Independent College Fund of New Jersey, Summit, NJ
30,000	Stanford University School of Business, Stanford, CA -- corporate affiliates program
30,000	Stanford University School of Engineering, Stanford, CA
30,000	University of Illinois Foundation Department of Mechanical and Industrial Engineering, Urbana, IL -- fracture control program
27,500	Georgia Tech Foundation, Atlanta, GA -- Center for Engineering Tribology
25,000	Northwestern University, Evanston, IL -- Kellogg MBA/MMM Affiliates Program
25,000	Pennsylvania State University, University Park, PA -- Learning Factory
25,000	Spelman College, Atlanta, GA -- second of three payments, for science laboratory
25,000	University of Maryland Foundation, College Park, MD -- AlliedSignal Graduate Fellowship in micro electronics
25,000	University of Notre Dame, Notre Dame, IN -- combination five-year program with arts and letters
25,000	University of Pennsylvania Wharton School of Business, Philadelphia, PA
25,000	University of Southern California Graduate School of Business, Los Angeles, CA -- business affiliates program
25,000	University of Southern California School of Engineering, Los Angeles, CA -- industrial associates program

Health

120,000	American Federation for Aging Research, New York, NY -- creative investigator grants
100,000	Aging Research Award 4 -- research in aging
100,000	Aging Research Award 5 -- final of two payments on grant
100,000	St. Clare-Riverside Foundation, Denville, NJ -- final payment on $500,000 grant, for capital grant for same day surgery
40,000	Alliance for Aging Research, Washington, DC -- Research Award Administration
40,000	University of Virginia Chemical Engineering Department, Charlottesville, VA -- research

International

40,000	University of Toronto Engineering Department, Toronto, ON, Canada
40,000	University of Toronto Engineering Department, Toronto, ON, Canada

Social Services

331,000	United Way, Los Angeles, CA
190,000	United Way Tri-State, New York, NY -- for Morris County
120,000	United Way Valley of the Sun, Phoenix, AZ
90,000	Heart of America United Way, Kansas City, MO
65,000	United Way Tri-State, New York, NY -- for east Fairfield County, CT
62,500	United Way Bergen County, Oradell, NJ
55,000	United Way Central Maryland, Baltimore, MD
42,000	United Way St. Joseph County, South Bend, IN
40,000	United Way Southeastern Michigan, Detroit, MI
37,000	United Way Midlands, Columbia, SC
30,000	United Way North Angeles Region I, Van Nuys, CA
25,000	United Way Southeastern Michigan, Detroit, MI -- second of three payments on grant

ALLMERICA FINANCIAL CORP.

Company Contact

Worcester, MA
Web: http://www.allmerica.com

Company Description

Former Name: State Mutual Life Assurance Co.; Hanover Insurance Co.
Revenue: US$3,432,500,000 (1999)
Employees: 6,300 (1999)
Fortune Rank: 440, per FORTUNE Magazine's list of 500 Largest U.S. Corporations (1999).
FF 440
SIC(s): 6726 Investment Offices Nec.

Operating Locations

Operates offices in 22 states and the District of Columbia.

Nonmonetary Support

Type: Donated Equipment; In-kind Services; Loaned Executives; Workplace Solicitation

Allmerica Financial Charitable Foundation, Inc.

Giving Contact

David C. Portney, President
440 Lincoln Street
Worcester, MA 01653
Phone: (508)855-2757
Fax: (508)855-6332

Description

Founded: 1991
EIN: 043105650
Organization Type: Corporate Foundation
Giving Locations: MA: Worcester
Grant Types: Employee Matching Gifts, General Support.

Financial Summary

Total Giving: $922,343 (1998); $822,973 (1997); $611,637 (1996). Note: Contributes through corporate direct giving program and foundation.
Giving Analysis: Giving for 1996 includes: foundation ($405,743); foundation matching gifts ($120,626); foundation grants to United Way ($85,268); 1997: foundation ($420,080); foundation grants to United Way ($290,000); foundation matching gifts ($112,893); 1998: foundation ($555,835); foundation grants to United Way ($271,700); foundation matching gifts ($94,808)
Assets: $5,801,041 (1998); $4,080,098 (1997); $3,348,249 (1996)
Gifts Received: $1,326,661 (1998); $433,662 (1997); $259,760 (1996). Note: Foundation receives contributions from the First Allmerica Financial Life Insurance Company, the Hanover Insurance Company, and Citizens Insurance Company of America.

Typical Recipients

Arts & Humanities: Arts Associations & Councils, Arts Festivals, Arts Outreach, Arts & Humanities-General, History & Archaeology, Libraries, Museums/Galleries, Music, Performing Arts, Theater
Civic & Public Affairs: Business/Free Enterprise, Clubs, Community Foundations, Economic Development, Civic & Public Affairs-General, Hispanic Affairs, Housing, Parades/Festivals, Philanthropic Organizations, Public Policy, Safety, Urban & Community Affairs, Women's Affairs

Education: Business Education, Business-School Partnerships, Colleges & Universities, Community & Junior Colleges, Education Reform, Engineering/Technological Education, Faculty Development, Education-General, Medical Education, Preschool Education, Private Education (Precollege), Private Education (Precollege), Public Education (Precollege), Religious Education, School Volunteerism, Student Aid
Environment: Environment-General
Health: AIDS/HIV, Cancer, Children's Health/Hospitals, Clinics/Medical Centers, Emergency/Ambulance Services, Eyes/Blindness, Health-General, Health Organizations, Heart, Hospitals, Hospitals (University Affiliated), Medical Research, Nursing Services, Public Health, Single-Disease Health Associations
Religion: Religious Welfare
Science: Scientific Centers & Institutes
Social Services: Big Brother/Big Sister, Child Welfare, Community Centers, Community Service Organizations, Day Care, Domestic Violence, Family Services, Food/Clothing Distribution, Recreation & Athletics, Scouts, Sexual Abuse, Sexual Abuse, Shelters/Homelessness, Social Services-General, Special Olympics, Substance Abuse, United Funds/United Ways, Volunteer Services, YMCA/YWCA/YMHA/YWHA, Youth Organizations

Contributions Analysis

Arts & Humanities: 12%. Supports performing arts and public broadcasting.
Civic & Public Affairs: 12%. Supports minority affairs, urban and community programs, and community development.
Education: 14%. Recipients include community colleges, education reform, school volunteerism programs, and universities.
Health: 10%. Funding supports clinics, single-disease health associations, nursing services, and medical research.
Social Services: 52%. Includes giving to United Way. Also supports community centers, youth organizations, food and clothing distribution, substance abuse prevention, Special Olympics, scouting, and homeless shelters.

Application Procedures

Initial Contact: Send a brief letter of inquiry.
Application Requirements: Include a description of organization, amount requested, purpose of funds sought, audited financial statement, and proof of tax-exempt status.
Deadlines: None.

Restrictions

The foundation's efforts focus soley on giving in Worcester, MA.

Corporate Officials

John Francis O'Brien, Jr.: president, chief executive officer, director B Brockton, MA 1943. ED Harvard College (1965); Harvard University MBA (1968). PRIM CORP EMPL president, chief executive officer: Allmerica Financial Corp. CORP AFFIL director: State Mutual Life Assurance Co.; director: TJX Co. Inc.; chairman: Hanover Insurance Co. Inc.; member, executive committee: Massachusetts Capital Resource Co.; director: First Allamerica Life Insurance Co.; president,ceo: First Allmerica Financial Life Insurance Co.; chairman: Citizens Insurance Co. of America; director: Cabot Corp.; chief executive officer, director, president: Citizens Corp.; president, chief executive officer: Allmerica Financial Corp.; president, chief executive officer, director: Allmerica Property & Casualty Companies Inc.; director: Abiomed Inc.; president: Allamerica Financial Life Insurance and Annuity Co. NONPR AFFIL director: Life Insurance Association of Massachusetts; trustee: Worcester Polytech Institute; visitors committee board overseers: Harvard College; director: American Council Life Insurance; executive committee: Harvard Alumni Association.

David Portney: second vice president public relations PRIM CORP EMPL second vice president public relations: Allmerica Securities Trust.

Theodore J. Rupley: president, chief executive officer, director B Sacramento, CA 1939. ED University of Nevada BS Economics (1962). PRIM CORP EMPL president, chief executive officer, director: Allmerica Securities Trust. CORP AFFIL vice president: American International Group Inc.; vice president: Allmerica Financial Corp. NONPR AFFIL trustee: Insurance Institute America; trustee: Republican Leadership Council; trustee: Association California Insurance Companies; director: Insurance Information Institute; director: Alliance American Insurers.

Foundation Officials

M.J. Pearle: contact PRIM CORP EMPL director community relations: Allmerica Securities Trust.

Grants Analysis

Disclosure Period: calendar year ending 1998
Total Grants: $555,835*
Number of Grants: 97
Average Grant: $5,730*
Highest Grant: $222,000
Typical Range: $500 to $5,000
***Note:** Giving excludes matching gifts; United Way. Average grant figure excludes highest grant.

Recent Grants

Note: Grants derived from 1998 Form 990.

Arts & Humanities

25,000	Mechanics Hall, Worcester, MA -- Youth Concerts
25,000	Worcester Art Museum, Worcester, MA
10,000	Forum Theatre, Worcester, MA
10,000	Performing Arts School of Worcester, Worcester, MA
7,500	Worcester Foothills Theatre, Worcester, MA
5,400	Very Special Arts Massachusetts, Boston, MA
5,000	Music Worcester, Worcester, MA

Civic & Public Affairs

25,000	Fidelity Inv. Ch. Gift Fund, Boston, MA
15,000	Girls, Inc., Worcester, MA
14,000	Worcester Police - D.A.R.E., Worcester, MA
10,000	Community Foundation of Livingston County, Detroit, MI
10,000	Main South Community Development Center
5,000	First Night Worcester, Worcester, MA
5,000	Women's Conference, Worcester, MA
5,000	Worcester Community Housing Resources, Worcester, MA

Education

20,000	Volunteer Incentive Program, Austin, TX
19,200	Junior Achievement of Central MA, Worcester, MA
14,000	Roy Westran Scholarship Foundation, Lansing, MI
11,075	Thorndyke Road School, Worcester, MA
10,000	Elm Park Center for ECE, Worcester, MA
9,200	Columbus Park Prep. School, Worcester, MA
9,000	Canterbury Street School, Worcester, MA
5,000	MSPCC, Worcester, MA
5,000	Tufts University, Medford, MA
3,500	Olivet College, Olivet, MI

Health

20,000	Memorial Foundation, Worcester, MA
10,000	American Red Cross Disaster Relief, Worcester, MA
10,000	Epilepsy Foundation of Michigan, Southfield, MI
10,000	Interfaith Hospitality Network, Worcester, MA
10,000	Worcester Foundation for Biomedical Research, Worcester, MA
5,000	AIDS Project Worcester, Worcester, MA
5,000	Ronald McDonald House of New York, New York, NY
3,000	American Cancer Society, Worcester, MA
3,000	American Heart Association, Framingham, MA

Social Services

222,000	United Way of Central Massachusetts, Worcester, MA
42,000	Livingston County United Way, Howell, MI
25,000	Big Brothers/Big Sisters, Worcester, MA
16,100	Sports Alive, Worcester, MA
10,000	Henry Lee Wills Community Center, Worcester, MA
10,000	YMCA Family Fest, Worcester, MA
10,000	YOU, Inc., Worcester, MA
8,160	LACASA, Howell, MI
7,500	Boys & Girls Club of Worcester, Worcester, MA
5,000	Atlanta Community Food Bank, Atlanta, GA
5,000	Rape Crisis Center, Worcester, MA
5,000	Worcester County Food Bank, Shrewsbury, MA
5,000	Worcester Youth Center, Worcester, MA
5,000	YouthNet, Worcester, MA
5,000	YWCA, Worcester, MA
4,800	Heart of West Michigan United Way, Grand Rapids, MI

ALLSTATE INSURANCE CO.

Company Contact

Northbrook, IL
Web: http://www.allstate.com

Company Description

Employees: 48,200
Fortune Rank: 47, per FORTUNE Magazine's list of 500 Largest U.S. Corporations (1999).
FF 47
SIC(s): 6331 Fire, Marine & Casualty Insurance, 6399 Insurance Carriers Nec.
Parent Company: Allstate Corp.

Operating Locations

Operates throughout the USA.

Nonmonetary Support

Type: Donated Equipment; In-kind Services
Volunteer Programs: Allstate's formal volunteer program, Helping Hands, provides opportunities for employees and agents to volunteer in the community. More than 200 committees nationally and 54 percent of employees and agents partake in volunteer activities.

Corporate Sponsorship

Type: Sports events; Other

Allstate Foundation

Giving Contact

Ron Mori, Executive Director
Allstate Foundation
2775 Sanders Rd., Suite F-4
Northbrook, IL 60062-6127
Phone: (847)402-5502
Fax: (847)326-7517
Email: rmori@allstate.com
Web: http://www.allstate.com/foundation

Alternate Contact

Laurie Stinson, Director of Corporate Relations
Phone: (847)402-8941

Description

EIN: 366116535
Organization Type: Corporate Foundation
Giving Locations: nationally.
Grant Types: Award, Employee Matching Gifts, General Support, Project, Scholarship.
Note: Allstate matches 20% pf employee funds pledge during the analysis giving campaign. Foundation matches contributions of employers to institutions of higher education, gifts should be at least $25, foundation will not exceed $1,000.

Giving Philosophy

'Allstate Insurance Company has offered quality insurance products and services since its founding in 1931. It has also demonstrated a social commitment of the highest order--a commitment embraced by the founder of Allstate Insurance Company, General Robert E. Wood, and strengthened by employees throughout the years. Symbolic of this commitment is The Allstate Foundation. Established in 1952, the Foundation's generous grantmaking and innovative programs have complemented the Company's extensive volunteer program, in-kind contributions and civic leadership projects.' The Allstate Foundation Guidelines for Giving

Financial Summary

Total Giving: $9,400,000 (1999 approx); $7,802,010 (1997); $7,100,378 (1996)
Giving Analysis: Giving for 1997 includes: foundation ($7,252,510); foundation grants to United Way ($549,500); 1999: foundation ($9,400,000)
Assets: $327,000 (1998 approx); $1,507,415 (1997); $2,259,370 (1996)
Gifts Received: $7,886,081 (1997); $7,095,313 (1996); $11,499,844 (1994). Note: Foundation receives contributions from Allstate Insurance Company.

Typical Recipients

Arts & Humanities: Museums/Galleries
Civic & Public Affairs: African American Affairs, Asian American Affairs, Business/Free Enterprise, Chambers of Commerce, Clubs, Community Foundations, Economic Development, Employment/Job Training, Civic & Public Affairs-General, Hispanic Affairs, Housing, Inner-City Development, Law & Justice, Professional & Trade Associations, Public Policy, Safety, Urban & Community Affairs, Women's Affairs
Education: Business Education, Colleges & Universities, Community & Junior Colleges, Economic Education, Education Associations, Education Funds, Elementary Education (Public), Education-General, Medical Education, Minority Education, School Volunteerism, Student Aid
Health: Children's Health/Hospitals, Clinics/Medical Centers, Emergency/Ambulance Services, Emergency/Ambulance Services, Health Policy/Cost Containment, Health Funds, Health Organizations, Hospitals, Hospitals (University Affiliated), Medical Research, Prenatal Health Issues, Public Health
International: International Development, International Organizations
Religion: Religious Welfare
Science: Science Museums
Social Services: Community Service Organizations, Counseling, Crime Prevention, Domestic Violence, Emergency Relief, Family Services, Recreation & Athletics, Scouts, Substance Abuse, United Funds/United Ways, Volunteer Services, YMCA/YWCA/YMHA/YWHA, Youth Organizations

Contributions Analysis

Giving Priorities: Health and fitness programs; healthcare cost containment; nonprofit community organizations; civic organizations; and higher education, especially institutions that have insurance programs.
Civic & Public Affairs: (Housing & Neighborhood Revitalization) Programs include home fire prevention tips, encourage usage of smoke detectors, security information against burglary, accident prevention within and around the home, and small business safety awareness. Supports affordable housing, building rehabilitation, economic growth, home ownership, and neighborhood improvement. Foundation supports the All-America City Awards program. Company participates in a Neighborhood Partnership Program, partnering with organizations to build stronger and safer neighborhoods.

Application Procedures

Initial Contact: Send one copy of request in letter form; consult foundation guidelines before submitting.
Application Requirements: Provide a summary of organization's project or program need (two-page maximum), amount requested and funding period; organization's and contact person's name, address, and phone number; explanation of how proposal addresses needs not met by other nonprofits and why applicant organization is qualified to address these needs; implementation timetable, communications plan, and evaluative criteria; explanation of how program relates to foundation's goals; statement of history, purpose, and goals of organization; number of members, constituents, and geographic area served; use of volunteers and accomplishments to date; operating budget for past two years and for proposed project; sources of financial support; audited financial statement for previous year; copy of most recent annual report; proof of tax-exempt status; list of officers and board members and their affiliations; background of executive director and key staff involved in project; and list of other donors.
Deadlines: None.
Review Process: Site visits or interviews are scheduled only if the foundation staff requires additional information.
Decision Notification: Written notification of preliminary turn down sent within 30 days of receipt.
Notes: The Allstate Foundation delegates decision making to 17 Field Office Grant Committees throughout the country. Eligible non-profit organizations should contact the main office for a guidelines brochure that outlines the regions and offices to send requests. Non-profit groups that service multiple regions of the United States, the City of Chicago, or have a proposal with national scope, should submit their proposals directly to the foundation's home office. Organizations wishing to receive written notification of receipt of proposals should enclose a self-addressed, stamped envelope. If funding is approved, a grant letter will outline the terms of the grant and propose a payment schedule.

Restrictions

Foundation does not award grants to individuals; athletic events or bands; scouting groups; capital funds for building and equipment; endowment funds; travel funds; films, videotapes, or audio productions; fundraising events; sponsorships; memorials; groups or organizations that will re-grant the Foundation's gift to other organizations or individuals; non-domestic causes; medical research; private secondary schools; volunteer fire departments; or multi-year pledge requests.

Additional Information

A grant given by the foundation in any one year does not ensure future funding; if renewed funding is desired, agencies should submit an additional, formal request.

The foundation operates a decentralized program. The metro-Chicago budget is reserved for nonprofits in the headquarters area. The field office budget is disbursed among city, state, and regional Field Office Grant Committees in communities where the company has a significant employee base. The company-wide budget is allocated for support of employee matching gifts and programs designed to serve a national audience or several field office communities.
Publications: Guidelines; Matching Grant Guidelines; Community Report (annually)

Corporate Officials

Edward M. Liddy: president, chief operating officer, director investment officer B 1947. PRIM CORP EMPL president, chief operating officer, director: Allstate Insurance Co. CORP AFFIL chairman: PMI; chairman: PMI Group Inc.; director: Kroger Co.; director: Allstate Indemnity Co.; director: Allstate Motor Club Inc.; president, chief operating officer: Allstate Corp.
Robert William Pike: senior vice president, secretary, general counsel, director B Lorain, OH 1941. ED Bowling Green State University BA (1963); University of Toledo JD (1966). PRIM CORP EMPL senior vice president, secretary, general counsel, director: Allstate Corp. CORP AFFIL secretary, general csl, director: Allstate Insurance Co.; vice president: Allstate Indemnity Co. NONPR AFFIL executive committee: National Association Independent Insurers; member: Ohio Bar Association; director executive committee: Association California Insurance Companies; member: Illinois Bar Association; member: American Bar Association.
Casey J. Sylla: senior vice president, chief investment officer PRIM CORP EMPL senior vice president, chief investment officer: Allstate Insurance Co. CORP AFFIL senior vice president: Allstate Corp.; senior vice president: Allstate Indemnity Co.

Giving Program Officials

Ron Mori: executive director

Foundation Officials

Jerry D. Choate: chairman, chief executive officer, director B Talihina, OK 1938. ED San Jose State University (1961). PRIM CORP EMPL chief executive officer, chairman, director: Allstate Corp. CORP AFFIL chairman: Northbrook Property & Casualty Insurance; director: Allstate Motor Club Inc.; director: Amgen Inc.; chairman: Allstate Insurance Co.; chairman: Allstate Indemnity Co. NONPR AFFIL member advisory board: Northwestern University Kellogg Graduate School Business Management; director: Saint Francis Hospital; director: Insurance Institute Highway Safety; trustee: AICPCU; director: Highway Users Federation Safety Mobility. CLUB AFFIL member: Commercial Club Colorado.
Robert W. Gary: vice president, trustee PRIM CORP EMPL senior vice president, director: Allstate Insurance Co. CORP AFFIL vice president: Allstate Indemnity Co.; director: Allstate Motor Club Inc.; senior vice president: Allstate Corp.
Edward M. Liddy: vice president, trustee (see above)
H. Louis Gordon Lower, II: vice president, trustee B New York, NY 1945. ED Yale University BA (1967); Harvard University MBA (1970). PRIM CORP EMPL president: Allstate Life Insurance Co. CORP AFFIL director: Allstate Insurance Co.; president: Glenbrook Life Annuity Co.; director: Allstate Indemnity Co.
Robert William Pike: vice president, secretary (see above)
Myron J. Resnick: vice president, treasurer, trustee B Louisville, KY 1931. ED University of Pennsylvania BS (1953); University of Michigan JD (1956). PRIM CORP EMPL senior vice president, treasurer, director: Allstate Insurance Co. CORP AFFIL director: American Horizon Property Casualty Insurance Co.; treasurer: Glenbrook Life Annuity Co.; director: Allstate Insurance Co. Ltd. (United Kingdom); president:

Allstate Investment Management Co. NONPR AFFIL member: Illinois Bar Association; board advisors: University Pennsylvania Institute Law & Economics; member: Chicago Mortgage Attorneys Association; director: Chicago Urban League; trustee: Aurora University; member: Chicago Bar Association; member: Association Life Insurance Council; member: American Bar Association; member Chicago executive committee: Anti-Defamation League B'nai B'rith. CLUB AFFIL Reform Club.

Grants Analysis

Disclosure Period: calendar year ending 1999
Total Grants: $9,000,000 (approx)*
Number of Grants: 1200 (approx)
Average Grant: $7,500 (approx)
Highest Grant: $535,000
Typical Range: $500 to $10,000
*Note: Giving excludes United Way.

Recent Grants

Note: Grants derived from 1998 Form 990.

Arts & Humanities

50,000	Chicago Children's Museum, Chicago, IL

Civic & Public Affairs

125,000	Claretian Associates, Inc., Chicago, IL
125,000	South Dallas Fair Park Inner City Development Corporation, Dallas, TX
100,000	National Training and Information Center, Chicago, IL
86,800	National Center for Neighborhood Enterprise, Washington, DC
85,000	Neighborhood Housing Services of Chicago, Chicago, IL
77,000	General Federation of Women's Clubs, Washington, DC
76,000	Neighborhood Housing Services of Los Angeles, Los Angeles, CA
73,500	East Bay Community Foundation, Oakland, CA
67,000	Organization of Chinese Americans, Inc., Washington, DC
65,000	100 Black Men of Atlanta, Inc., Atlanta, GA
65,000	Neighborhood Partnership of Montclair, Inc., Montclair, CA
60,000	Neighborhood Housing Servies of New York City, New York, NY
60,000	Urban League of New York, New York, NY
53,312	Neighborhood Housing Services of New York City (Brooklyn), Brooklyn, NY
50,000	Neighborhood Housing Services of America, Chevy Chase, MD
50,000	Roadway Safety Foundation, Washington, DC
42,500	East Bay Community Foundation, Oakland, CA
35,000	Survive Alive House, Chicago, IL
32,000	Neighborhood Housing Services of New Haven, CT, New Haven, CT
30,000	Center for Auto Safety, Washington, DC
30,000	National Council of Laraza, Washington, DC
30,000	Ser-Jobs for Progress National Inc., Irving, TX

Education

392,400	Citizens' Scholarship Foundation of America, St. Peter, MN
45,000	Junior Achievement of Chicago, Chicago, IL
39,500	Township High School District 214 Community Education Foundation, Arlington Heights, IL
36,500	American Academy of Pediatrics, Elk Grove Village, IL
35,000	I-Car Education Foundation, Rolling Meadows, IL
35,000	Illinois State University, Normal, IL
30,000	Howard University, Center for Insurance Education, Washington, DC
30,000	Insurance Education Foundation, Inc., Indianapolis, IN
26,000	National Hispanic Scholarship Fund, CA, San Francisco, CA
25,000	Trustees of Columbia University in the City of New York, New York, NY
25,000	United Negro College Fund, Chicago, IL

Health

535,000	American Red Cross, Falls Church, VA
150,000	American Health Foundation, New York, NY
35,000	University of Chicago Childrens Hospital-Safe Kids Buckle Up, Chicago, IL

Religion

200,000	Home of the Sparrow, McHenry, IL
25,000	Lutheran Social Services of Illinois, Des Plaines, IL

Science

40,000	Field Museum of Natural History, Chicago, IL

Social Services

475,000	United Way-Crusade of Mercy, Chicago, IL
225,000	Boys & Girls Clubs of America, Streamwood, IL
150,000	Points of Light Foundation, Washington, DC
110,500	National Crime Prevention Council, Washington, DC
50,000	Family Violence Prevention Fund, San Francisco, CA
50,000	Points of Light Foundation, Washington, DC
35,000	United Way of Lake County, Green Oaks, IL
30,000	South Side Help Center, Chicago, IL
25,000	Metropolitan Family Services, Chicago, IL

ALLTEL CORP.

Company Contact

Little Rock, AR
Web: http://www.alltel.com

Company Description

Revenue: US$6,302,000,000 (1999)
Employees: 21,504 (1999)
Fortune Rank: 276, per FORTUNE Magazine's list of 500 Largest U.S. Corporations (1999).
FF 276
SIC(s): 4812 Radiotelephone Communications, 4813 Telephone Communications Except Radiotelephone, 7372 Prepackaged Software, 7374 Data Processing & Preparation.

Giving Contact

Andrea Peel, Corporate Communications Supervisor
One Allied Dr.
Little Rock, AR 72202
Phone: (501)661-8000
Fax: (501)905-6424

Description

Organization Type: Corporate Giving Program
Formed by Merger of: Aliant Communications (1999).
Formed by Merger of: ALLTEL (1999).

Contributions Analysis

Giving Priorities: Interests include education, health, and community betterment.

Application Procedures

Initial Contact: Write or call for an application form.

Restrictions

Does not fund religious organizations or political groups.

Additional Information

Aliant Communications merged with ALLTEL in July 1999.

Corporate Officials

Joseph 'Joe' Ford: chairman, chief executive officer, president B Conway, AR 1937. ED University of Arkansas BS (1959). PRIM CORP EMPL chairman, chief executive officer, president: ALLTEL Corp. CORP AFFIL director: Systematics Information Services; director: LDDS Communications; chairman: Security Savings Bank; director: Dial Corp.; director: Duke Power Co.; director: Advanced Telecommunications Corp.; director: Beverly Enterprises. NONPR AFFIL trustee: Baptist Medical Center; member: Greater Little Rock Chamber of Commerce.
Jeff Gardner: chief financial officer ED College William & Mary MBA; Purdue University BS. PRIM CORP EMPL chief financial officer: ALLTEL Corp.

Grants Analysis

Disclosure Period: calendar year ending

ALMA PISTON CO.

Company Contact

Alma, MI

Company Description

Employees: 750
SIC(s): 3563 Air & Gas Compressors, 3714 Motor Vehicle Parts & Accessories.

Emmet and Frances Tracy Fund

Giving Contact

Emmet E. Tracy, Jr., President
Alma Piston Co.
21 Kercheval Avenue
Grosse Pointe Farms, MI 48236
Phone: (313)881-5007
Fax: (313)881-3495

Description

EIN: 386057796
Organization Type: Corporate Foundation. Supports preselected organizations only.
Giving Locations: MI: Detroit
Grant Types: General Support.

Financial Summary

Total Giving: $2,000,000 (fiscal year ending November 30, 1998); $1,700,022 (fiscal 1997); $1,250,040 (fiscal 1996). Note: Contributes through foundation only. 1996 Giving includes United Way ($17,500).
Assets: $3,063,515 (fiscal 1997); $3,216,350 (fiscal 1996); $3,072,012 (fiscal 1995)
Gifts Received: $1,050,000 (fiscal 1997); $1,050,000 (fiscal 1996); $1,000,000 (fiscal 1995). Note: In 1995 and 1996, gifts were received from Alma Piston Co.

Typical Recipients

Arts & Humanities: Arts & Humanities-General, History & Archaeology, Libraries
Civic & Public Affairs: Clubs, Civic & Public Affairs-General, Public Policy

Education: Colleges & Universities, Education-General, Gifted & Talented Programs, Minority Education, Private Education (Precollege), Secondary Education (Private), Student Aid
Health: Cancer, Children's Health/Hospitals, Emergency/Ambulance Services, Heart, Hospitals, Long-Term Care, Medical Research, Prenatal Health Issues, Single-Disease Health Associations
International: Health Care/Hospitals, International Affairs, International Organizations, International Relief Efforts, Missionary/Religious Activities
Religion: Churches, Missionary Activities (Domestic), Religious Organizations, Religious Welfare, Seminaries, Social/Policy Issues
Social Services: At-Risk Youth, Child Abuse, Child Welfare, Community Service Organizations, Food/Clothing Distribution, People with Disabilities, Recreation & Athletics, Senior Services, United Funds/United Ways, Youth Organizations

Contributions Analysis

Giving Priorities: About 15% of foundation contributions support international missionary organizations and relief agencies.

Corporate Officials

Emmet E. Tracy, Jr.: president, chief executive officer, director B 1933. ED College of the Holy Cross AB (1955); University of Michigan JD (1958). PRIM CORP EMPL president, chief executive officer, director: Alma Piston Co. CORP AFFIL president: GPP Inc.; counsel: Riley Roumell.

Foundation Officials

Walter B. Fisher: treasurer
David M. Rosenberger: secretary B 1949. ED Princeton University AB (1972); Harvard University JD (1975). PRIM CORP EMPL attorney: Dy Kema Gossett.
Emmet E. Tracy, Jr.: president (see above)

Grants Analysis

Disclosure Period: fiscal year ending November 30, 1996
Total Grants: $1,232,540*
Number of Grants: 197
Average Grant: $6,257
Highest Grant: $118,000
Typical Range: $200 to $25,000
***Note:** Giving excludes United Way.

Recent Grants

Note: Grants derived from fiscal 1996 Form 990.

Arts & Humanities

39,395	City of Alma, Alma, MI -- Tracy Memorial
15,000	Michigan Supreme Court Historical Society, Lansing, MI

Civic & Public Affairs

7,500	Morality in Media, New York, NY
7,500	Trigg-C.M. Russell Foundation, Great Falls, MT

Education

28,000	Regis University, Denver, CO
25,000	Northwood University, Troy, MI
15,000	Holy Cross College, Worcester, MA
15,000	Hotchkiss School, Lakeville, CT
10,000	Boston College, Boston, MA -- Irish Papers Account
10,000	Dominican High School, Detroit, MI
10,000	Harvard University, Cambridge, MA
10,000	Madonna College, Livonia, MI
10,000	Manhattanville College of the Sacred Heart, Purchase, NY
10,000	Portsmouth Abbey School, Portsmouth, RI
10,000	Regis University, Denver, CO
10,000	University of Detroit, Detroit, MI
10,000	Valley View School, North Brookfield, MA
6,000	University Liggett School, Grosse Pointe Woods, MI

Health

50,000	Hospital for Special Surgery, New York, NY
12,500	Northern Michigan Hospital, Petoskey, MI
10,000	American Red Cross, Detroit, MI
10,000	Children's Hospital, Detroit, MI
10,000	Gratiot Community Hospital, Alma, MI
10,000	Henry Ford Hospital, Detroit, MI
10,000	Northern Michigan Hospital, Petoskey, MI
10,000	Orthopedic Research and Education Foundation, Chicago, IL
10,000	Rose Hill Center, Holly, MI
10,000	Wilson Cancer Center, Royal Oak, MI
7,500	Ruth Jackson Orthopedic Society, Rosemont, IL

International

118,000	American Ireland Fund, San Francisco, CA
50,000	American Ireland Fund, Boston, MA
15,000	CARE Foundation, Chicago, IL
12,500	UNICEF, New York, NY
10,500	American Ireland Fund, San Francisco, CA
10,000	Glenmary Missions, Cincinnati, OH

Religion

100,000	Genesis Foundation, Grosse Pointe Farms, MI
75,000	Genesis Foundation, Grosse Pointe Farms, MI
25,000	Gleaners, Detroit, MI
25,000	Holy Childhood Church, Harbor Springs, MI
25,000	Support Our Aging Religious, Silver Spring, MD
15,000	Right to Life, Grand Rapids, MI
12,500	Discalced Carmelite Nuns Monastery of St. Therese, Clinton Township, MI
10,000	Catholic Youth Organization, Detroit, MI
10,000	Equestrian Order, New York, NY
10,000	FADICA, Washington, DC
10,000	Jesuit Seminary and Mission Bureau, Boston, MA
10,000	Life Directions, Detroit, MI
10,000	Little Sisters of the Poor, Oregon, OH

Social Services

10,000	United Way, Detroit, MI
6,000	National Committee to Prevent Child Abuse, Chicago, IL

Alyeska Pipeline Service Co.

Company Contact

Anchorage, AK
Web: http://www.alyeska-pipe.com

Company Description

Employees: 900
SIC(s): 4612 Crude Petroleum Pipelines.

Nonmonetary Support

Value: $50,000 (1994)
Type: Donated Equipment; In-kind Services
Volunteer Programs: Co. provides nonmonetary support to institutions where employees volunteer.

Giving Contact

Janie Leask, Manager, Community Relations
Alyeska Pipeline Service Co.
1835 S Bragaw St.
Anchorage, AK 99512
Phone: (907)787-8865
Fax: (907)787-8240
Email: leaskjp@alyeska-pipeline.com

Description

Organization Type: Corporate Giving Program
Giving Locations: AK: statewide, Anchorage, Fairbanks, Prince William Sound, Valdez
Grant Types: Employee Matching Gifts, General Support.
Note: Employee matching gift ratio: 1 to 1. Maximum of $2,000 per employee and $5,000 maximum to any one institution.

Giving Philosophy

'Alyeska contributes for the benefit of the community because we believe sound communities help all of us. The emphasis is on community benefit because Alyeska (as with many other companies) recognizes its responsibility to contribute to the quality of life in its communities. Alyeska also recognizes that its ability to attract, motivate and retain good people depends upon there being good communities in which those employees can live and work.' Alyeska Pipeline Contributions Guidelines

Financial Summary

Total Giving: $380,000 (2000 approx); $406,000 (1999 approx); $1,200,000 (1996 approx). Note: Contributes through corporate direct giving program only. 1996 Giving includes corporate direct giving; nonmonetary support.

Typical Recipients

Arts & Humanities: Arts & Humanities-General
Civic & Public Affairs: Economic Development, Civic & Public Affairs-General, Rural Affairs, Urban & Community Affairs
Education: Education-General
Environment: Environment-General
Social Services: Emergency Relief, Social Services-General, United Funds/United Ways, Youth Organizations

Contributions Analysis

Civic & Public Affairs: (United Funds & United Way) Most of the company's health and human services support is made through large contributions to United Way, which generally account for about 80% of total contributions.

Application Procedures

Initial Contact: call or send a brief letter of inquiry
Application Requirements: a description of organization, amount requested, a description of organization's beneficiaries, operating budget with amount of revenue received from the government or the United Way, background of each board member, IRS 501(c)(3) tax-determination letter, list of corporate contributors, indication of how organization assists Alyeska people, and list of Alyeska people associated with the organization
Deadlines: None.
Decision Notification: contributions committee meets monthly

Restrictions

Grants are made only to organizations that have been designated tax-exempt by the Internal Revenue Service.
Does not award grants to religious organizations, partisan political groups, individual winner programs such as pageants, governmental organizations, capital campaigns, endowments, scholarships to individuals, or transportation expenses.

Additional Information

Alyeska is particularly interested in the following types of programs: those that encourage people to participate in civic processes; those that attract young people to serve actively for the betterment of their community; those that support a balance in resource development and environmental protection; those

that help with educational and economic development for Alaska natives; those that promote health and safety; and those programs that provide emergency support for the relief of human suffering.
Proposals endorsed by an employee of Alyeska with a written statement are given preference over other requests.

Corporate Officials

R. Malone: president
W. H. Newbold: senior vice president PRIM CORP EMPL senior vice president: Alyeska Pipeline Service Co.
P. J. Ptacek: vice president human resources PRIM CORP EMPL vice president human resources: Alyeska Pipeline Service Co.

Giving Program Officials

J. Meidinger: manager community relations

AMCORE BANK ROCKFORD

Company Contact

Rockford, IL

Company Description

Deposits: US$976,000,000
Employees: 420
SIC(s): 6021 National Commercial Banks.
Parent Company: AMCORE Financial, Inc.

AMCORE Foundation

Giving Contact

James Waddell, Chairman
AMCORE Foundation
501 7th St., PO Box 1537
Rockford, IL 61110
Phone: (815)968-2241
Fax: (815)961-7530
Web: http://www.amcore.com

Description

EIN: 366042947
Organization Type: Corporate Foundation
Giving Locations: IL: Rockford including surrounding communities
Grant Types: Capital, General Support.

Financial Summary

Total Giving: $290,000 (1998 approx); $244,250 (1996); $190,700 (1994)
Assets: $4,147,833 (1998); $3,667,690 (1997); $3,331,995 (1996)
Gifts Received: $238,156 (1996); $193,000 (1994); $156,700 (1993). Note: In 1996, contributions were received from Amcore Investment Group NA.

Typical Recipients

Arts & Humanities: Arts Associations & Councils, Dance, Arts & Humanities-General, Historic Preservation, Libraries, Literary Arts, Museums/Galleries, Music, Performing Arts, Public Broadcasting, Theater
Civic & Public Affairs: African American Affairs, Botanical Gardens/Parks, Business/Free Enterprise, Chambers of Commerce, Clubs, Economic Development, Employment/Job Training, Civic & Public Affairs-General, Hispanic Affairs, Housing, Minority Business, Parades/Festivals, Philanthropic Organizations, Public Policy, Safety, Urban & Community Affairs, Women's Affairs
Education: Business Education, Colleges & Universities, Community & Junior Colleges, Economic Education, Education-General, Health & Physical Education, Literacy, Medical Education, Minority Education, Preschool Education, Private Education (Precollege), Public Education (Precollege), Science/Mathematics Education, Secondary Education (Private), Secondary Education (Public), Special Education
Environment: Environment-General
Health: AIDS/HIV, Alzheimers Disease, Cancer, Clinics/Medical Centers, Emergency/Ambulance Services, Health-General, Health Organizations, Hospices, Hospitals, Long-Term Care, Mental Health, Nursing Services, Nutrition, Public Health, Single-Disease Health Associations
Religion: Jewish Causes, Religious Welfare
Science: Science Museums
Social Services: Child Welfare, Community Centers, Community Service Organizations, Counseling, Crime Prevention, Day Care, Delinquency & Criminal Rehabilitation, Domestic Violence, Emergency Relief, Family Services, Food/Clothing Distribution, Homes, People with Disabilities, Recreation & Athletics, Scouts, Senior Services, Shelters/Homelessness, Social Services-General, Substance Abuse, United Funds/United Ways, Veterans, Volunteer Services, YMCA/YWCA/YMHA/YWHA, Youth Organizations

Application Procedures

Initial Contact: Send a brief letter of inquiry.
Application Requirements: name and a description of organization, number of members, amount requested, purpose of funds sought, recently audited financial statement, proof of tax-exempt status, a list of officers and board members, most recent annual report, operating budget for last two years, a statement as to how the organization benefits the community, and a list of other donors.
Deadlines: None.

Restrictions

Does not support individuals, religious organizations for sectarian purposes, political or lobbying groups, organizations outside operating areas, or loans of any kind. Foundation does support organizations located in the company's immediate market area.

Corporate Officials

Charles E. Gagnier: chairman, chief executive officer, director PRIM CORP EMPL chairman: AMCORE Bank Rockford.
John Hecht: chief financial officer PRIM CORP EMPL chief financial officer: AMCORE Bank Rockford.
James Warsaw: president, chief executive officer, director PRIM CORP EMPL president, chief executive officer, director: AMCORE Bank Rockford.

Foundation Officials

E. Taylor Carlin: director
Carl J. Dargene: director B Rockford, IL 1930. ED University of Illinois; University of South Carolina (1951). PRIM CORP EMPL chairman: AMCORE Financial Inc. PRIM NONPR EMPL dir: AMCORE Bank of Rockford. CORP AFFIL director: AMCORE Bank Rockford.
Robert A. Doyle: director
Charles E. Gagnier: president, director (see above)
Mary E. Gerber: secretary
Robert A. Henry, MD: director
Robert Joseph Meuleman: director B South Bend, IN 1939. ED University of Notre Dame BA (1961); Michigan State University MBA (1962). PRIM CORP EMPL president, chief executive officer: Amcore Bank North America. CORP AFFIL director: AMCORE Financial Inc.; director: Rockford Pro - America. NONPR AFFIL mem: Rockford Chamber of Commerce; director: Swedish America Hosp Foundation; mem: Chartered Financial Analysts; mem: Milwaukee Financial Analysts. CLUB AFFIL Rockford Country Club.
William O. Nelson: director

Grants Analysis

Disclosure Period: calendar year ending 1996
Total Grants: $244,250
Number of Grants: 70
Highest Grant: $63,000
Typical Range: $100 to $10,000

Recent Grants

Note: Grants derived from 1997 Form 990.

Arts & Humanities

9,752	Northern Public Radio, Rockford, IL
2,500	Rockford Symphony Orchestra, Rockford, IL
2,500	Woodstock Mozart Festival, Woodstock, IL

Civic & Public Affairs

10,000	Davis Park, Rockford, IL
2,500	Horizon House Foundation, Rockford, IL
2,300	Rockford Neighborhood Redevelopment, Rockford, IL

Education

8,000	Boylan Catholic High School, Rockford, IL
7,000	Rockford College, Rockford, IL
5,000	Christian Life Schools, Rockford, IL
3,000	Luther Academy, Lutheran High School, Rockford, IL
3,000	University of Illinois College of Medicine, Rockford, IL
2,500	Community Education Foundation, Rockford, IL
2,000	Junior Achievement, Rockford, IL
2,000	Keith School, Rockford, IL
2,000	Rockford Christian School, Rockford, IL

Health

10,000	Crusader Clinic, Rockford, IL
10,000	Northern Illinois AIDS Center, Rockford, IL
2,500	Janet Wattles Center, Rockford, IL

Religion

20,000	Rockford Rescue Mission, Rockford, IL
5,000	Zion Community Center Corporation, Rockford, IL
5,000	Zion Development Corporation, Rockford, IL

Social Services

66,000	United Way Rock River Valley, Rockford, IL
10,000	YMCA, Rockford, IL
5,000	Family Advocate, Rockford, IL
5,000	Rocvale Children's Home, Rockford, IL
5,000	Vietnam Veteran's Honor Society, Rockford, IL
3,200	YMCA Partners With Youth, Rockford, IL
3,000	United Way, Elgin, IL
2,500	Implementation Task Force to Benefit Children, Rockford, IL
2,000	Center for Sight and Hearing Impaired, Rockford, IL

AMEREN CORP.

Company Contact

St. Louis, MO
Web: http://www.ameren.com

Company Description

Former Name: Union Electric Co.
Assets: US$6,870,800,000
Employees: 6,035
SIC(s): 4931 Electric & Other Services Combined.

Nonmonetary Support

Value: $96,312 (1998); $220,000 (1997); $119,000 (1996)
Type: Donated Equipment
Volunteer Programs: Ameren Helping Hands where employees and their families volunteer. VIP/TEAMS

Program in which small grants ($50-$500) are given to nonprofits for which Ameren employees volunteer.

Corporate Sponsorship

Value: $5,000

Type: Arts & cultural events; Festivals/fairs; Sports events

Note: Sponsors Fair Saint Louis, Holiday Parade and First-Nite Saint Louis.

Ameren Corp. Charitable Trust

Giving Contact

Susan M. Bell, Senior Supervisor, Community Relations
PO Box 66149, Mail Code 100
St. Louis, MO 63166-6149
Phone: (314)554-2817
Fax: (314)554-2888
Email: susan_m_bell@ameren.com
Note: for nonprofits in Ameren VE service area.

Alternate Contact

Public Affairs
Ameren CIPS
607 East Adams Street, C1301
Springfield, IL 62739
Note: for nonprofits in Ameren CIPS service area.

Description

EIN: 436022693

Organization Type: Corporate Foundation

Giving Locations: limited to Ameren VE and Ameren CIPS local district offices.; near headquarters and service areas.

Grant Types: Capital, Employee Matching Gifts, General Support, Multiyear/Continuing Support, Project, Scholarship.

Note: Employee matching gift ratio: 1 to 1 between $10 and $500 annually per employee, for accredited colleges and universities only.

Giving Philosophy

'As a private enterprise entrusted with an essential public service, we recognize our civic responsibility in the communities we serve. We shall strive to advance the growth and welfare of these communities and shall participate in civic activities which fulfill that goal..for we believe this is both good citizenship and good business.'

'Union Electric's history of community involvement dates back to our company's early days. Through contributions to local and non-profit groups and a variety of other services, we have worked toward improving the quality of life in our communities. Our employees also have an impressive record of service to the community.' *Statement of Policy and Report to the Community*

Financial Summary

Total Giving: $2,847,399 (1998); $2,860,077 (1997); $2,752,357 (1996)

Giving Analysis: Giving for 1997 includes: foundation ($2,431,000); corporate direct giving ($429,000); 1998: foundation ($2,168,830); corporate direct giving ($582,257); nonmonetary support ($96,312)

Assets: $10,702,561 (1999); $11,458,746 (1998); $11,036,438 (1997)

Typical Recipients

Arts & Humanities: Arts Associations & Councils, Arts Centers, Arts Festivals, Arts Funds, Arts Institutes, Dance, Historic Preservation, History & Archaeology, Libraries, Museums/Galleries, Music, Opera, Performing Arts, Public Broadcasting, Theater, Visual Arts

Civic & Public Affairs: African American Affairs, Botanical Gardens/Parks, Chambers of Commerce, Economic Development, Housing, Safety, Urban & Community Affairs

Education: Arts/Humanities Education, Business Education, Colleges & Universities, Community & Junior Colleges, Economic Education, Education Funds, Education Reform, Elementary Education (Private), Engineering/Technological Education, Education-General, Minority Education, Private Education (Precollege), Public Education (Precollege), Science/Mathematics Education, Student Aid

Environment: Forestry, Environment-General

Health: Children's Health/Hospitals, Emergency/Ambulance Services, Health Organizations

Religion: Dioceses, Jewish Causes, Ministries, Religious Organizations, Religious Welfare

Science: Scientific Centers & Institutes

Social Services: Child Welfare, Community Centers, Community Service Organizations, Counseling, Delinquency & Criminal Rehabilitation, Emergency Relief, Family Services, Food/Clothing Distribution, Homes, People with Disabilities, Recreation & Athletics, Scouts, Senior Services, Shelters/Homelessness, United Funds/United Ways, Volunteer Services, YMCA/YWCA/YMHA/YWHA, Youth Organizations

Contributions Analysis

Giving Priorities: Education, services for the youth and elderly, and the environment.

Arts & Humanities: 10% to 15%. Supports theater, opera, and the Arts and Education fund.

Civic & Public Affairs: 20% to 25%. Supports botanical gardens, parks, and historical societies.

Education: 25% to 30%. The majority supports the 'Ameren Scholarship' program.

Social Services: 45% to 50%. Principal support goes to the United Way of Greater St. Louis.

Application Procedures

Initial Contact: Send a letter or proposal on organization's letterhead.

Application Requirements: Include an explanation of project for which funds are requested, along with projected outcome, statement of organization's mission and how project fits organization's purpose; current status of fundraising for project and end goal; organization's current board-approved operating budget, and audited financial statement; specific amount requested; proof of tax-exempt status; and roster of organization's governing board and staff.

Deadlines: None.

Review Process: Proposals reviewed by contributions committee. Requests for contributions exceeding $25,000 are reviewed and approved by the contributions committee of the Ameren board of directors; contributions of less than $25,000 are awarded directly by the Ameren VE or Ameren CIPS.

Evaluative Criteria: Determining factors include the location of organization in area in which company operates; conformity to company's priorities; overall benefit to community; qualifications, including management experience, of individuals who administer program; total level of support sought by organization throughout community and prospects for obtaining that support; Ameren's current operating situation and priorities relative to overall amount available for contributions.

Decision Notification: Two to three months after biannual meeting.

Notes: Outside the Saint Louis area, request should be sent to Ameren UE and Ameren CIPS local district offices.

Restrictions

Does not support individuals; political, fraternal, veterans', religious organizations; or social or similar groups.

The company never contributes electric or natural gas service.

Additional Information

Ameren was formed at the end of 1997 as the result of the merger of Union Electric Co. and Central Illinois Public Service Co.

Grantees must submit reports indicating project results.

Items of salvage from company stock are sometimes donated to nonprofit organizations, including utility poles, office furnishings, and other surplus items. Organizations receiving such material must arrange pickup. Same general policies and procedures prevail as with monetary contributions. monetary contributions.

Publications: Community Report; Giving Guidelines; Annual Report

Corporate Officials

M. Patricia Barrett: vice president corporate communicationso B Saint Louis, MO 1937. ED Saint Louis University (1959); Washington University (1995). PRIM CORP EMPL vice president corporate communications: Ameren Corp.

Susan M. Bell: senior supervisor-corporate communications PRIM CORP EMPL senior supervisor-corporate communications: Ameren Corp.

Charles William Mueller: chairman, president, chief executive officer B Belleville, IL 1938. ED Saint Louis University BSEE (1961); Saint Louis University MBA (1966). PRIM CORP EMPL chairman, president, chief executive officer: Ameren Corp. ADD CORP EMPL president: Union Electric Co. CORP AFFIL director: Kiel Center Corp.; director: Electric Energy Inc.; department chairman: Federation Reserve Bank Saint Louis; director: Angelica Corp.; director: BJC Health System. NONPR AFFIL director: Saint Louis Childrens Hospital; director: United Way Greater Saint Louis; director: Regional Commerce & Growth Association; member: Institute Electrical & Electronics Engineers; director: Municipal Theatre Association; director: Civic Progress; director: Edison Electric Institute; director: Association of Edison Illuminating Companies. CLUB AFFIL Saint Clair Country Club; Saint Louis Club; Bogey Club; Missouri Athletic Club.

Foundation Officials

Susan M. Bell: senior supervisor-corporate communications (see above)

Charles William Mueller: trustee (see above)

Grants Analysis

Disclosure Period: calendar year ending 1998

Total Grants: $2,751,087*

Highest Grant: $705,000

Typical Range: $5,000 to $25,000

***Note:** Grants analysis provided by the company. Highest grant to United Way of Greater Saint Louis.

Recent Grants

Note: Grants derived from 1996 Annual Report.

Arts & Humanities

75,000	Muny-Student Theater Project Company, Saint Louis, MO
75,000	St. Louis Symphony, Saint Louis, MO
50,000	KETC/Channel 9
10,000	Missouri Historical Society, Saint Louis, MO
5,000	Capitol City Council on the Arts, Jefferson City, MO
5,000	Opera Theater, Saint Louis, MO

Civic & Public Affairs

200,000	Forest Park Forever, Saint Louis, MO
50,000	Missouri Botanical Garden, Saint Louis, MO
25,000	Lake Area Chamber of Commerce
10,000	Urban League, Saint Louis, MO
10,000	Urban League, Saint Louis, MO

Education

110,000	Washington University, Saint Louis, MO
55,000	Arts and Education Fund, Saint Louis, MO

55,000 St. Louis University, Saint Louis, MO
54,000 University of Missouri Rolla, Rolla, MO
50,000 University of Missouri St. Louis, Saint Louis, MO
34,000 University of Missouri Columbia, Columbia, MO
23,960 National Merit Scholarship Program, Cleveland, OH
11,000 Junior Achievement Mississippi Valley
10,000 Webster University, Webster Groves, MO
7,000 Lincoln University, Philadelphia, PA
6,500 Lindenwood College, Saint Charles, MO
6,500 Maryville University, Saint Louis, MO
5,000 United Negro College Fund, New York, NY

Health
25,000 Ronald McDonald House
15,000 St. Charles County Emergency Management Agency
15,000 Saints Joachim and Ann Care Service
10,000 American Red Cross Adair County Chapter
10,000 St. Joachim and Ann Care Service

Religion
35,000 St. Vincent de Paul Society, Saint Louis, MO
7,000 Jewish Federation, Philadelphia, PA
5,000 Good Samaritan Center, Excelsior Springs, MO
5,000 Lake Area Ministries, Camdenton, MO

Social Services
705,000 United Way, Saint Louis, MO
60,000 Magic House, Saint Louis, MO
55,000 Provident Counseling, Saint Louis, MO
50,000 Girl Scout Council
50,000 YWCA, Saint Louis, MO
25,000 St. Louis Community Foundation, Saint Louis, MO -- Teens Care Fund
15,000 Boy Scouts of America Great Rivers Council, Columbia, MO
11,500 United Way Partnership
10,000 FISH Volunteers, Cape Girardeau, MO
10,000 Grace Hill Neighborhood Services, Saint Louis, MO
10,000 Paraquad, Saint Louis, MO
10,000 Samaritan Center, Jefferson City, MO
10,000 United Way, Cape Girardeau, MO
10,000 United Way, Jefferson City, MO
7,000 United Way Callaway County, Fulton, MO
5,000 Audrain County Human Development Corp, Columbia, MO
5,000 Helping Hands, Potosi, MO

AMERICA WEST AIRLINES, INC.

Company Contact
Phoenix, AZ
Web: http://www.americawest.com

Company Description
Revenue: US$1,739,500,000
Employees: 10,866
SIC(s): 4512 Air Transportation--Scheduled.

Nonmonetary Support
Value: $3,000,000 (1994); $2,900,000 (1993); $2,700,000 (1992)
Type: Donated Products; In-kind Services
Volunteer Programs: In 1999, over 2,100 volunteers supported communities where America West services.
Co. sponsors the 'DO-CREW' volunteer corps.
Note: Gifts in-kind include travel vouchers.

Corporate Sponsorship
Type: Arts & cultural events

America West Airlines Foundation

Giving Contact
Ann Vry, Coordinator, Community Relations Directory
America West Airlines Foundation
Corporate Headquarters, 4000 East Sky Harbor Boulevard
Phoenix, AZ 85034
Phone: (805)693-3652
Fax: (805)693-3715
Email: ann.vry@americawest.com

Description
Founded: 1991
Organization Type: Corporate Foundation
Giving Locations: headquarters and operating communities.
Grant Types: General Support.

Giving Philosophy
'The spirit of commitment is in the air. All around us, a renewed sense of responsibility is on the rise; a rededication to the selfless values that define our society at its best. This spirit is integral to America West Airlines. Since initiating service a decade ago, our airline has been deeply involved in the communities we serve. .. During times that have challenged the resolve of corporate giving, America West has increased its scope of community support. The force that drives this commitment is unmistakable. At the heart of our airline, you'll find the men and women of America West, their dedication constantly soaring to new heights.' America West Airlines

Financial Summary
Total Giving: $3,500,000 (fiscal year ending September 30, 1995 approx); $3,000,000 (fiscal 1994 approx); $2,500,000 (fiscal 1993 approx). Note: Contributes through corporate direct giving program and foundation. Giving includes nonmonetary support. 1996 Giving includes corporate direct giving; foundation ($50,000). 1995 Giving includes corporate direct giving; foundation ($75,500).

Typical Recipients
Arts & Humanities: Community Arts, Performing Arts
Civic & Public Affairs: Business/Free Enterprise, Economic Development, Professional & Trade Associations, Urban & Community Affairs, Zoos/Aquariums
Education: Business Education, Colleges & Universities, Economic Education, Elementary Education (Private), Faculty Development, Literacy, Minority Education, Preschool Education, Private Education (Precollege), Public Education (Precollege)
Environment: Environment-General
Health: Health Organizations, Hospitals, Single-Disease Health Associations
Social Services: Community Service Organizations, Emergency Relief, Recreation & Athletics, Volunteer Services, Youth Organizations

Contributions Analysis
Arts & Humanities: About 15%.
Civic & Public Affairs: About 15%.
Education: 20% to 25%.
Environment: 10%.
Health: 35% to 40%.

Application Procedures
Initial Contact: Information requests about donations, grants, or scholarships can be obtained from co.'s website. Submit a full proposal on organization's letterhead.
Application Requirements: Include a summary of the organization's objectives and purpose; date of the event, a description of the event, and applicant's specific request; details of the type of exposure America West Airlines Inc. will receive as a sponsor.
Deadlines: Eight to ten weeks before the event and any print deadlines.
Decision Notification: A written response is generally made within four weeks.
Notes: Company requests that this information be confirmed prior to submitting a request.

Restrictions
The Air Transportation Donation Program does not include AmeriWest Vacation packages. In addition, it is not designed to provide support for the following: building funds/capital projects; cargo shipments; religious, political, or labor/fraternal organizations; celebrity travel; discount travel; individual and group travel, including athletic teams or school projects.

Additional Information
Company also establishes community partnerships with civic and industry groups such as chambers of commerce, convention and visitors' bureaus, and travel associations. The purpose of these partnerships is to bolster local economic development. In turn, these groups help to stimulate the economy and generate business for the airline. Company also sponsors various sporting, cultural, and civic events. America West can support only one annual event for any single organization.
Complimentary travel donations may not be used for nonprofit administrative travel. administrative travel.
Publications: Community Relations Report; Program Guidelines

Corporate Officials
William Augustus Franke: chairman, president, chief executive officerars B Bryan, TX 1937. ED Stanford University BA (1959); Stanford University LLB (1961). PRIM CORP EMPL chairman, president, chief executive officer: America West Airlines Inc. ADD CORP EMPL chairman, chief executive officer: America West Holdings Corp.; president, owner: Franke & Inc. CORP AFFIL director: Phelps Dodge Corp.; chairman: Engineer and Fabricators Co.; managing partner: Newbridge Latin American LLP; director: Beringer Wine Estates; director: Central Newspapers Inc.; director: Airplanes Ltd.; chairman, trustee: Airplanes United States Trust. NONPR AFFIL member: Chief Executives Organization; member: Washington Bar Association; member: American Bar Association; member: Arizona State University School Business; director: Air Transport Association. CLUB AFFIL Paradise Valley Country Club; Phoenix Country Club; Arizona Club; Desert Mountain Country Club.
C. A. Howlett: senior vice president public affairs PRIM CORP EMPL senior vice president public affairs: America West Airlines, Inc. ADD CORP EMPL vice president public affairs: America West Holdings Corp.

Foundation Officials
Wil Counts: vice president, scholarships and grants committee
Anna Dahl: secretary
Marlene Klotz-Collins: vice president community rels
Charles P. Thompson: manager community relations
Ann Vry: director community relations

Grants Analysis
Disclosure Period: fiscal year ending September 30, 1994
Total Grants: $59,000
Number of Grants: 10
Average Grant: $5,900
Highest Grant: $5,000

Typical Range: $2,500 to $10,000

Recent Grants

Note: Grants derived from fiscal 1993 grants list.

Arts & Humanities

2,000 Arts Genesis, Inc., Tucson, AZ -- Old Pascua Youth Artists

Education

5,000 University of Nevada Las Vegas, Las Vegas, NV -- Accelerated School Satellite Center Project

4,000 Cave Creek Unified School District 93 and Maricopa County Sheriff's Department, Phoenix, AZ -- Midnight Madness

2,850 Brophy College Preparatory, Phoenix, AZ -- The Loyola Project

2,000 Tacoma Community College, Seattle, WA -- Academic Career Prep 2000 Leadership

825 Phoenix Newspapers, Inc., Phoenix, AZ -- Newspapers In Education Program

325 Columbus Dispatch, Columbus, OH -- Newspapers In Education Program

Social Services

4,000 Wilson Elementary School District, Phoenix, AZ -- Parents and Teachers: Together We Can Make A Difference

2,000 Ballet Metropolitan, Inc., Columbus, OH -- Community Outreach Program

2,000 Mesa Unified School District, Phoenix, AZ -- Respect Program

AMERICAN ELECTRIC POWER

Company Contact

Columbus, OH
Web: http://www.aep.com

Company Description

Also Known As: AEP.
Revenue: US$6,345,900,000
Employees: 17,951
Fortune Rank: 253, per FORTUNE Magazine's list of 500 Largest U.S. Corporations (1999).
FF 253
SIC(s): 4911 Electric Services, 6719 Holding Companies Nec.

Nonmonetary Support

Type: Donated Equipment; In-kind Services; Loaned Executives
Volunteer Programs: In Ohio, grants may be made to organizations where employees provide a substantial commitment to volunteering.
Note: Workplace solicitation is for United Way and Operation Feed only.

Corporate Sponsorship

Type: Arts & cultural events; Music & entertainment events
Note: Sponsors business and award luncheons.

Giving Contact

Ms. Rody Woischke, Contributions Administrator
American ElectricPower
1 Riverside Plaza
Corporate Communications
Columbus, OH 43215
Phone: (614)223-1697
Fax: (614)223-1676
Email: rody-woischke@aep.com

Description

Organization Type: Corporate Giving Program
Giving Locations: IN; KY; MI; OH; TN; VA; WV headquarters and operating communities.
Grant Types: Capital, Employee Matching Gifts, General Support, Multiyear/Continuing Support, Scholarship.
Note: Employee matching gift ratio: 1 to 1 for education only.

Giving Philosophy

'We are a citizen of each community we serve and take an active part in its affairs. Like any other citizen, we want our neighbors to think well of us. We prosper only ad the community prospers; so we help it thrive in every way we can.' Guidelines Brochure

Financial Summary

Total Giving: $4,000,000 (1999 approx); $4,000,000 (1998 approx); $3,540,000 (1997 approx). Note: Contributes through corporate direct giving program only.
Assets: $19,483,000 (1998 approx); $16,615,000 (1997 approx)

Contributions Analysis

Giving Priorities: Higher education with focus on math and science, economic development, environmental affairs, and health care cost containment.
Civic & Public Affairs: Funds programs to encourage economic development.
Education: Funds K-12 programs in the fields of math, science, and technology. Company also sponsors the American Electric Power System Educational Trust Fund for children of employees. Children of eligible employees may win up to $6,000 over a three-year period. Through its matching gifts program, supports universities, colleges, and secondary schools. Supports higher education with scholarship program for employees' children.

Application Procedures

Initial Contact: Send a letter of proposal.
Application Requirements: a description of organization, including purpose and goals; description of intended use of requested funds, who will benefit from the services rendered, and overall budget of related program; proof of 501(c)(3) status; description of how the organization will validate its use of funds; and reference to the 'Guidelines for Corporate Giving' brochure.
Deadlines: November 1
Evaluative Criteria: Applications are judged individually based on perceived overall benefit to communities in the company's service area.
Decision Notification: Decisions generally made in the fourth quarter for the following year. Committee may refer requests to local operating company for consideration.
Notes: Requests for more information should be addressed to William J. Lhota, Executive Vice President.

Restrictions

Company will not fund religious or national organizations that do not benefit the general public in its seven-state service area, trips or tours, individuals, or fraternal organizations.

Additional Information

Much of the company's giving takes place at the local level. As of April, 2000, company is expecting approval for merger with American Electric Power.
Publications: Guidelines; Annual Report, Giving Guidelines

Corporate Officials

Ernest Linn Draper, Jr.: chairman, president, chief executive officer, director B Houston, TX 1942. ED Williams College BA (1960-1962); Rice University BSChE (1965); Cornell University PhD (1970). PRIM CORP EMPL chairman, president, chief executive officer, director: American Electric Power. CORP AFFIL chairman, chief executive officer: Windsor Coal Co.; chairman: Yorkshire Electricity Group; chairman, chief executive officer: Wheeling Power Co.; director: Vectra Technologies Inc.; president, chief executive officer, director: West Virginia Power Co.; chairman, chief executive officer: Southern Appalachian Coal Co.; chairman, chief executive officer: Southern Ohio Coal Co.; chairman, chief executive officer: Price River Coal Co. Inc.; chairman, chief executive officer: Simco Inc.; chairman, chief executive officer: Ohio Power Co.; president, director: Ohio Valley Electric Corp.; chairman, chief executive officer: Kingsport Power Co.; president, chief executive officer, director: Kanawha Valley Power Co.; chairman, chief executive officer: Kentucky Power Co.; president, director: Indiana-Kentucky Electric Corp.; chairman, chief executive officer: Indiana Michigan Power Co.; president, chief executive officer, director: Franklin Real Estate Co.; president, chief executive officer, director: Indiana Franklin Realty Co.; chairman, chief executive officer, director: Columbus Southern Power Co.; chairman, chief executive officer: Conesville Coal Preparation Co.; president, chief executive officer, director: Colomet Inc.; chairman, chief executive officer: Central Ohio Coal Co.; chief executive officer, president: Central Operating Co.; chairman, chief executive officer: Central Appalachian Coal Co.; chairman, chief executive officer: Central Coal Co.; president, director: Cardinal Operating Co.; chairman, chief executive officer: Cedar Coal Co.; chairman, chief executive officer: Blackhawk Coal Co.; director: Borden Chemicals Plastics; chairman, president, chief executive officer: America Electric Power Service Corp.; chairman, chief executive officer: Appalachian Power Co.; chairman, chief executive officer: AEP Investment Inc.; chairman, chief executive officer: AEP Resources Inc.; chairman, chief executive officer: AEP Energy Services Inc.; president, chief executive officer, director: AEP Generating Co.
William J. Lhota: executive vice president B 1939. ED Ohio State University BCE (1964); Massachusetts Institute of Technology MS (1978). PRIM CORP EMPL executive vice president: American Electric Power Service Corp. CORP AFFIL State Auto Financial Corp.; president, chief operating officer: Wheeling Power Co.; director: Ohio Valley Electric Corp.; president, chief operating officer: Kingsport Power Co.; president, chief operating officer: Ohio Power Co.; president, chief operating officer: Kentucky Power Co.; director: Huntington Bancshares Inc.; president, chief operating officer: Indiana Michigan Power Co.; president, chief operating officer: Columbus Southern Power Co.; president, chief operating officer: Appalachian Power Co.; vice president: Cardinal Operating Co.

Giving Program Officials

Ms. Rody Woischke: contributions administrator

Grants Analysis

Disclosure Period: calendar year ending 1999
Total Grants: $4,000,000 (approx)

AMERICAN EXPRESS CO.

 Number 54 of Top 100 Corporate Givers

Company Contact

New York, NY
Web: http://www.americanexpress.com/corp

Company Description

Revenue: US$21,278,000,000 (1999)
Employees: 51,012 (1999)
Fortune Rank: 71, per FORTUNE Magazine's list of 500 Largest U.S. Corporations (1999).
FF 71

SIC(s): 4724 Travel Agencies, 4731 Freight Transportation Arrangement, 6082 Foreign Trade & International Banks, 6719 Holding Companies Nec.

Operating Locations

Argentina: American Express Bank Ltd. SA, Buenos Aires; Australia: AELC Australia P/L, North Ryde; Austria: American Express Bank Ltd., Vienna; Belgium: American Express International Inc.Soc de Droit Americain, Brussels, Brabant; American Express Overseas Credit Corp. SA, Brussels, Brabant; Amexco Inc., Brussels, Brabant; Wings Aircraft Leasing Corp. SA, Brussels, Brabant; Brazil: American Express do Brasil S/A Turismo, Sao Paulo; American Express do Brasil Servicos Internacionais SA, Sao Paulo; Intercapital Comercio E Participacoes Ltda., Sao Paulo; Canada: Amex Bank of Canada, Markham; Amex Canada Inc., Markham; Chile: American Express Bank Ltda., Quillota; France: American Express Bank (France) SA, Paris, Ville-de-Paris; Amex Gestion, Paris, Ville-de-Paris; Col Venice Simplon-Orient Expr., Paris, Ville-de-Paris; American Express Carte France, Rueil Malmaison; American Express Voyages Tourisme, Rueil Malmaison; Germany: Venice-Simplon-Orient-Express Deutschland GmbH, Duesseldorf; American Express Bank GmbH, Frankfurt, Hessen; American Express International Inc. Deutschland, Frankfurt, Hessen; Amex Grundstuecksverwaltung GmbH, Frankfurt, Hessen; Schenkerrhenus Reisen Verwaltungs GmbH, Frankfurt, Hessen; Hong Kong: American Espress Bank Ltd., Central District; Amex Asia Ltd., Central District; American Express International, Quarry Bay; Hungary: American Express Magyarorszag Utazasi Szolgaltatasok KFT, Budapest; Ireland: American Express Ireland Ltd., Blackrock; Italy: Alberghiera Fiesolana SpA, Fiesole, Toscana; American Express Co. SpA, Roma, Lazio; American Express Services Europe Ltd., Roma, Lazio; Luxembourg: American Express Bank (Luxembourg) SA, Luxembourg; American Express International Inc., Luxembourg; Multistakes Co. SA, Luxembourg; Mexico: American Express Co. (Mexico) SA de CV, Ciudad de Mexico; Malaysia: American Express (Malaysia) Sdn. Bhd., Kuala Lumpur, Selangor; Netherlands: American Express International Inc., Amsterdam, Noord-Holland; American Express Ltd., Amsterdam, Noord-Holland; American Express Services Europe Ltd., Amsterdam, Noord-Holland; Norway: American Express Comp. AS, Oslo, Akershus; Bordewick Reisebya AS, Oslo, Akershus; Nyman & Schultz Norge AS, Oslo, Akershus; Singapore: American Express International, Singapore; Spain: American Express de Espana SA, Madrid; American Express Viajer SA, Madrid; Sweden: Nyman and Schultz Group AB; Ostanan Fastighets AB; Resespecialisterna Helsingborg AB, Helsingborg, Malmohus; Resespecialisterna Syd AB, Malmo, Malmohus; American Express Co. AB, Stockholm; American Express Resebyra AB, Stockholm; Amex Services Sweden AB, Stockholm; Bookhotel AB, Stockholm; First Card AB, Stockholm; Forstkrings AD Viator, Stockholm; Nyman & Schultz AB, Stockholm; Nyman and Schultz Grupp and Konferens AB, Stockholm; Nyman and Schultz Resebyraer AB, Stockholm; Scandanavian Express AB, Stockholm; Stockholm Central Hotel AB, Stockholm; Thailand: American Express (Thailand) Co. Ltd., Samsennai Phyathai; Taiwan: American Express International (Taiwan), Taipei; United Kingdom: American Express Europe Ltd., Brighton, East Sussex; American Express Services Europe Ltd., Brighton, East Sussex; Travellers Cheque Associates Ltd., Brighton, East Sussex; American Express Insurance Services Ltd., Burgess Hill, West Sussex; American Express Europe Ltd., Glasgow, Strathclyde; AEOCC Management Co. Ltd., Jersey, Channel Islands; American Express Bank Asset Management (Jersey) Ltd., Jersey, Channel Islands; American Express Overseas Credit Corp. Ltd., Jersey, Channel Islands; Cardmember Financial Services Ltd., Jersey, Channel Islands; Acuma Ltd., London; AEB (UK) Plc, London; American Express Asset Management Ltd., London; American Express Bank Ltd., London; American Express Nominees Ltd., London; Amex Services Europe Ltd., London; Venice Simplon-Orient-Express Ltd., London

Nonmonetary Support

Note: Nonmonetary support is provided by the company, but on an ad hoc basis only.

American Express Foundation

Giving Contact

Anne Wickham, Director, Cultural Heritage Program
American Express Foundation/Philanthrophic Program
American Express Tower
World Financial Center
200 Vesey St.
New York, NY 10285-4803
Phone: (212)640-5660
Fax: (212)693-1033

Alternate Contact

Terry Savage, Director, Economic Independence Program

Description

EIN: 136123529
Organization Type: Corporate Foundation
Giving Locations: AZ; CA; DC; FL; GA; IL; MA; MN; NY; NC; TX; UT headquarters and operating communities; international committees South Pacific, South Asia, East Asia, Europe,Middle East, Africa and Latin America/Caribbean;;.
Grant Types: Employee Matching Gifts, Project.

Giving Philosophy

'Since it was established in 1954, the American Express Foundation implemented an ambitious philanthropic program aimed at providing funds to cultural, educational and community organizations around the world. Since then, and through these organizations, the Foundation has given support to a series of projects carried out in different communities where employees, customers, and shareholders of American Express live and work.

The philanthropic activities carried out by the company through the Foundation were consolidated in decentralized projects, whereby in spite of the fact that the outlines, policies and programs are established by the Headquarters, each country identifies and determines the local needs, suggests projects and develops the donation's proposals.

The American Express Philanthropic Program thus becomes an essential part of the company's business strategy, by improving the conditions of the communities where it operates and turning them into suitable places to make business. At the same time, and in order to complement the Program's financial support, American Express employees contribute part of their time to participate in community organizations and voluntary projects. The American Express Philanthropic Program is forever gaining more significance and interest throughout the world.' *The American Express Foundation and its Philanthropic Program*

Financial Summary

Total Giving: $15,828,062 (1998); $21,600,000 (1996 approx); $20,400,000 (1995 approx). Note: Contributes through corporate direct giving program and foundation. Giving includes foundation.
Giving Analysis: Giving for 1995 includes: foundation ($11,713,394); corporate direct giving (approx $8,686,606); 1996: foundation ($12,596,335); corporate direct giving (approx $9,003,665); 1998: corporate direct giving (approx $9,871,974); foundation ($8,798,275); foundation matching gifts ($4,498,951); foundation grants to United Way ($2,530,800)
Assets: $33,831,168 (1998); $32,644,709 (1996); $42,452,988 (1995)
Gifts Received: $25,293 (1998); $1,407,973 (1996); $143,157 (1995). Note: Gifts are received from American Express Travel Related Services, American Express Bank Ltd., IDS Financial Services, and American Express Company.

Typical Recipients

Arts & Humanities: Arts Centers, Arts Festivals, Arts Outreach, Dance, Historic Preservation, Museums/Galleries, Music, Opera, Performing Arts, Theater, Visual Arts
Civic & Public Affairs: African American Affairs, Botanical Gardens/Parks, Civil Rights, Economic Development, Employment/Job Training, Hispanic Affairs, Housing, Minority Business, Nonprofit Management, Philanthropic Organizations, Public Policy, Urban & Community Affairs, Women's Affairs, Zoos/Aquariums
Education: Arts/Humanities Education, Business Education, Colleges & Universities, Community & Junior Colleges, Continuing Education, Economic Education, Education Funds, Education Reform, Faculty Development, Education-General, International Exchange, International Studies, Literacy, Minority Education, Preschool Education, Public Education (Precollege), Social Sciences Education, Vocational & Technical Education
Environment: Resource Conservation
Health: AIDS/HIV, Children's Health/Hospitals, Emergency/Ambulance Services, Health Organizations, Hospitals, Hospitals (University Affiliated), Single-Disease Health Associations
International: Foreign Arts Organizations, Foreign Educational Institutions, Health Care/Hospitals, International Affairs, International Development, International Environmental Issues, International Organizations, International Peace & Security Issues, International Relations, International Relief Efforts, Missionary/Religious Activities
Social Services: At-Risk Youth, Big Brother/Big Sister, Child Welfare, Community Centers, Community Service Organizations, Counseling, Day Care, Delinquency & Criminal Rehabilitation, Domestic Violence, Family Services, Food/Clothing Distribution, People with Disabilities, Senior Services, Shelters/Homelessness, Substance Abuse, United Funds/United Ways, Volunteer Services, Youth Organizations

Contributions Analysis

Giving Priorities: Currently supports three primary categories: community service, cultural heritage, and economic independence.
Arts & Humanities: 1%. Includes grants made in support of the cultural heritage program.
Civic & Public Affairs: 29%. Includes the economic independence program. Support is given to economic education, college funds, the Urban league, and global initiatives.
International: 13%. Suppors international foundations, the arts, health concerns, and business development.
Social Services: 26%. Supports community service, including foundations, hospital causes, the Red Cross, YWCAs and YMCAs, children's concerns, homeless shelters, and domestic peace.
Note: Total contributions made in 1998. Analysis based on foundation giving only.

Application Procedures

Initial Contact: See website for guidelines, then send a proposal in the form of a letter, of not more than two to three pages.
Application Requirements: Include the name and address of organization; contact person, title, telephone and fax numbers; funds requested; geographic area served; amount requested; description of project, including objectives, target groups to be served, needs to be addressed, activities to be undertaken, expected outcomes, current involvement of American

Express employees and advisors, project timetable, and future plans for including American Express volunteers, if applicable; detailed project budget; plans for evaluating results; and history of previous support from the American Express Philanthropic Program, American Express Foundation, the American Express Minnesota Philanthropic Program, American Express Cultural Affairs, an American Express business unit or subsidiary, or the American Express Volunteer Action Fund.

Deadlines: None.

Review Process: The initial review of proposals is completed by program officers.

Evaluative Criteria: Priority is given to projects rather than general support; projects supported by public/private partnerships (for example, business/school/parent coalitions); efforts that involve American Express beyond grant support (for example, employee and management participation, promotion); and distinctive projects in which American Express involvement and expertise can make a difference.

Notes: U.S. organizations must include the following attachments: copy of IRS 501(c)(3) and 509(a) (1), (2), or (3) tax-exemption letters; latest audited financial statement; list of organization's board of directors or similar governing body, including their affiliations; and list of funding sources, including a list of contributors. Outside the United States, grants are made to organizations able to document not-for-profit status. Unless requested, do not include videos, books or bulky materials, which will not be considered or returned. The grant review process takes several months.

Restrictions

The philanthropic program does not support individual needs, including scholarships; fundraising activities such as benefits, charitable dinners, galas, or sporting events; good-will advertising, souvenir journals, or dinner programs; travel for individuals or groups; sectarian activities of religious organizations; political causes, candidates, organizations, or campaigns; books, magazines, or articles published in professional journals; endowments or capital campaigns, traveling exhibitions; or sports sponsorships.

Additional Information

Grants are made on behalf of the American Express Co. and its subsidiaries, which include American Express Travel Related Services, American Express Financial Advisors, and American Express Bank. Proposals should be forwarded to the appropriate person for national, local, or international grantmaking. A contact list is available in the guidelines brochure.

Publications: Guidelines Brochure

Corporate Officials

Kenneth Irvine Chenault: president, chief operating officer, directorars & communications B New York, NY 1951. ED Bowdoin College BA (1973); Harvard University JD (1976). PRIM CORP EMPL president, chief operating officer, director: American Express Co. CORP AFFIL director: Quaker Oats Co.; director: International Business Machines Corp. NONPR AFFIL director: New York University Downtown Hospital; director: New York University Medical Center; director: CASA; director: NCAA; member: American Bar Association.

Richard Karl Goeltz: vice chairman, chief financial officer B Chicago, IL 1942. ED Brown University AB (1964); Columbia University MBA (1966). PRIM CORP EMPL vice chairman, chief financial officer: American Express Co. NONPR AFFIL chairman: American Express Credit Corp.; director: New Germany Fund.

Harvey Golub: chairman, chief executive officer, director B Brooklyn, NY 1939. ED Cornell University (1956-1958); New York University BS (1961). PRIM CORP EMPL chairman, chief executive officer, director: American Express Co. ADD CORP EMPL director: America Express Bank Ltd.; chairman, chief executive officer: America Express Travel Related Services; director: American Express Financial Advisors; director: American Express Financial Corp.; director: American Express Banking Corp. CORP AFFIL director: IDS Extra Income Fund Inc.; chief executive officer: Investors Syndicate Development Corp.; director: IDS Bond Fund Inc.; director: IDS Discovery Fund Inc.; director: Campbell Soup Co.; director: Dow Jones & Co. Inc. NONPR AFFIL director: United Way New York City; member: World Travel Tourism Council; member: President Committee Arts & Humanities; director: New York City Partnership; member: President Advisory Committee Trade Policy & Negotiations; director: Columbia Presbyterian Hospital; director: New York Chamber of Commerce; director: Business Roundtable; director: Carnegie Hall; director: American Enterprise Institute; member: Bretton Woods Committee.

Jonathan S. Linen: vice chairman B 1944. PRIM CORP EMPL vice chairman: American Express Co. ADD CORP EMPL director: American Expres Financial Corp. CORP AFFIL director: Bausch & Lomb Inc.

Mike O'Neill: senior vice president public affairs PRIM CORP EMPL senior vice president public affairs: American Express Co.

Thomas E. Schick: executive vice president corporate affairs & communications B 1947. PRIM CORP EMPL executive vice president corporate affairs & communications: American Express Co.

Foundation Officials

Kenneth Irvine Chenault: trustee (see above)

Mary Ellen Craig: senior manager

Harvey Golub: trustee (see above)

Cornelia W. Higginson: vice president international programs, secretary

Jonathan S. Linen: trustee (see above)

Mary Beth Salerno: president, trustee PRIM CORP EMPL vice president domestic programs: American Express Co.

Terry Savage: director

Thomas E. Schick: trustee (see above)

Grants Analysis

Disclosure Period: calendar year ending 1998

Total Grants: $8,430,200*

Number of Grants: 775 (approx)

Average Grant: $10,878 (approx)

Typical Range: $200 to $30,000

***Note:** Giving excludes scholarship; matching gifts; United Way and corporate giving.

Recent Grants

Note: Grants derived from 1996 Form 990.

Arts & Humanities

50,000	Boys Choir of Harlem, New York, NY
50,000	Young Audiences National Chapter, New York, NY -- payment on $150,000 three-year grant, for Meet the Artists educational CD-ROM

Civic & Public Affairs

75,000	New York City Partnership Foundation, New York, NY
65,000	National Urban League, New York, NY -- support and the Black Executive Exchange Program
50,000	Central Park Conservancy, New York, NY -- payment on $150,000 three year grant, for Historic Preservation Program
50,000	Manhattan Institute for Policy Research Center for Civic Innovation, New York, NY
50,000	Ronald H. Brown Foundation, Washington, DC -- payment on $100,000 two-year grant

Education

200,000	Reach and Teach, White Plains, NY -- payment on $650,000 three year, for travel and tourism programs in South Africa
130,000	National Retail Institute, Washington, DC -- payment on $390,000 three-year grant
40,000	United Negro College Fund, New York, NY -- payment on $200,000 five-year grant

Health

400,000	American National Red Cross, Washington, DC -- American Express Foundation Disaster Relief Fund
200,000	Presbyterian Hospital in the City of New York, New York, NY -- Capital Campaign for the 21st Century
34,000	New York University Medical Center Foundation, New York, NY -- for new corporate health alliance

International

350,000	National Academy Foundation Academies of Travel and Tourism, New York, NY
350,000	National Academy Foundation Academies of Travel and Tourism, New York, NY
300,000	National Academy Foundation Academies of Travel and Tourism, New York, NY
265,000	Travel and Tourism Education Program, Princes Risborough, England -- to fund travel and tourism program in the United Kingdom
215,000	Travel and Tourism Education Program, Princes Risborough, England -- continued support of travel and tourism program
215,000	Travel and Tourism Education Program, Princes Risborough, England -- to fund travel and tourism program in the United Kingdom
200,000	Reach and Teach USA, White Plains, NY -- to support implementation of a travel and tourism program in South Africa
150,000	National Academy Foundation Academies of Travel and Tourism, New York, NY
100,000	Academia de Viajes Y Turismo, Sao Paolo, SP, Brazil -- to enable development of travel and tourism education at secondary school and equivalent levels prior to career choice and vocational training
65,000	Academia de Viajes Y Turismo, Mexico City, DF, Mexico -- to fund expansion of travel and tourism education in Mexico
56,500	Women Aid Federation, Bristol, England -- to fund travel and tourism program in Russia
55,000	Fundacion Caspicara, Quito, Ecuador -- restoration of historic building to be used as foundation's headquarters
50,000	Academia de Viajes Y Turismo, Mexico City, DF, Mexico -- to fund expansion of travel and tourism education in Mexico
50,000	Center for Strategic and International Studies, Washington, DC -- Values and Leadership Fellowship Program
50,000	Colombo Eye Hospital, Colombo, Sri Lanka -- Sri Lanka disaster relief grant
50,000	Fundacao Roberto Marinho, Rio de Janeiro, RJ, Brazil -- restoration of historic church
50,000	Instituto de Academias Professionalizantes, Sao Paolo, SP, Brazil -- travel and tourism program
50,000	Instituto de Academies Professionalizantes, Sao Paolo, SP, Brazil -- travel and tourism programs

50,000 National Gallery of Canada, Ottawa, ON, Canada -- payment on $300,000 three-year grant, for learning center
50,000 Ocean Park Corporation, Ocean Park, Hong Kong -- primary school education program
50,000 Ocean Park Corporation, Ocean Park, Hong Kong -- to fund educational outreach program
50,000 Travel and Tourism Education Program, Hong Kong -- continued support
50,000 Travel and Tourism Education Program, Quarry Bay, Hong Kong -- to fund travel and tourism program
46,200 Charities Aid Foundation, England -- Global Volunteer Action fund
43,000 Banff Centre for Continuing Education, Banff, AB, Canada -- summer festival
40,000 Kurogene Kosakurko, Tokyo, Japan -- payment on $85,000 two-year grant, for Kamakura City signage project
40,000 Sociedad Defensora Del Tesoro Artistico de Mexico, Mexico City, DF, Mexico -- to fund Heritage Walking Trail in Mexico City
40,000 Sociedad Defensora del Tesoro Artistico de Mexico, Col del Valle, DF, Mexico -- Mexico City Historic Walking Tour
40,000 Travel and Tourism Education Program, Budapest, Hungary -- to fund the Hungary Travel and Tourism Programme
40,000 UNESCO Paris, Paris, France -- publication on world heritage sites in China
36,500 Opera Atelier, Toronto, ON, Canada
33,189 Charities Aid Foundation, England -- small grants program
30,000 Canadian Tourism Human Resource Council, Ottawa, ON, Canada -- second payment on $100,000 grant, to fund development of travel and tourism education in Canada
30,000 Canadian Tourism Human Resource Council, Ottawa, ON, Canada -- payment on $100,000 three-year grant
30,000 Friends of Czech Greenways, New York, NY -- American Express Fund for central and eastern Europe
30,000 Travel and Tourism Education Program, Dublin, Ireland -- to fund travel and tourism program in Ireland
30,000 Travel and Tourism Education Program, Dublin, Ireland -- to fund Ireland Travel and Tourism Programme

Social Services

560,000 United Way Tri-State Area, New York, NY
220,000 Valley of the Sun United Way, Phoenix, AZ
155,000 United Way Broward County, Fort Lauderdale, FL
95,000 United Way, Greensboro, NC
75,000 City Harvest Honor Roll, New York, NY -- payment on $150,000 two-year grant
75,000 United Way, Salt Lake City, UT
65,000 United Way Massachusetts Bay, Boston, MA
50,000 United Way International, Alexandria, VA -- payment on $100,000 two year grant
45,000 United Way, Atlanta, GA
45,000 United Way, Chicago, IL
40,000 Valley of the Sun United Way, Phoenix, AZ
35,000 United Way Bay Area, San Francisco, CA
30,000 United Way, Los Angeles, CA
30,000 United Way Southeastern Michigan, Detroit, MI

American Fidelity Corp.

Company Contact

Oklahoma City, OK

Company Description

Employees: 1,100

Corporate Sponsorship

Type: Arts & cultural events

American Fidelity Corp. Founders Fund

Giving Contact

Jo Ella Ramsey, Secretary
American Fidelity Corp. Founders Fund
2000 Classen Boulevard
Oklahoma City, OK 73106
Phone: (405)523-5111
Fax: (405)523-5421

Description

EIN: 731236059
Organization Type: Corporate Foundation
Giving Locations: OK
Grant Types: General Support.

Financial Summary

Total Giving: $250,000 (fiscal year ending June 30, 1998 approx); $2,874 (fiscal 1997); $135,483 (fiscal 1996). Note: Contributes through corporate direct giving program and foundation. 1998 Giving includes foundation. 1995 Giving includes foundation ($99,316).
Assets: $4,074,604 (fiscal 1997); $3,490,999 (fiscal 1996); $3,066,316 (fiscal 1994)
Gifts Received: $5,722 (fiscal 1994); $200,000 (fiscal 1993); $85,607 (fiscal 1992). Note: In fiscal 1994, contributions were received from Lenice B. Cameron 1980 Trust for William M. Cameron; Lenice B. Cameron 1980 Trust for Lynda L. Cameron; C. W. Cameron 1980 Trust for William M. Cameron; C. W. Cameron 1980 Trust for Lynda L. Cameron ($907 each); and Jo Carol Cameron 1980 Trust for William M. Cameron and Jo Carol Cameron 1980 Trust for Lynda L. Cameron ($1,047 each).

Typical Recipients

Arts & Humanities: Arts Associations & Councils, Arts Funds, Arts Institutes, Ballet, Historic Preservation, History & Archaeology, Libraries, Museums/Galleries, Music, Theater
Civic & Public Affairs: Clubs, Community Foundations, Economic Development, Civic & Public Affairs-General, Municipalities/Towns, Native American Affairs, Nonprofit Management, Public Policy, Urban & Community Affairs, Women's Affairs, Zoos/Aquariums
Education: Business Education, Colleges & Universities, Community & Junior Colleges, Economic Education, Education Funds, Faculty Development, Education-General, Private Education (Precollege), Public Education (Precollege), Science/Mathematics Education
Environment: Environment-General, Resource Conservation
Health: AIDS/HIV, Arthritis, Children's Health/Hospitals, Clinics/Medical Centers, Emergency/Ambulance Services, Health Organizations, Heart, Hospitals, Hospitals (University Affiliated), Prenatal Health Issues, Single-Disease Health Associations
International: International Relief Efforts
Religion: Churches, Ministries, Religious Welfare
Science: Science Museums
Social Services: Big Brother/Big Sister, Child Abuse, Child Welfare, Community Service Organizations, Family Services, Food/Clothing Distribution, People with Disabilities, Recreation & Athletics, Scouts, Substance Abuse, United Funds/United Ways, YMCA/YWCA/YMHA/YWHA, Youth Organizations

Application Procedures

Initial Contact: letter requesting application form

Restrictions

Does not support political or lobbying groups or organizations which discriminate on the basis of race, color, national origin, sex, or physical disability or impairment.

Corporate Officials

Brett Browman: assistant vice president PRIM CORP EMPL assistant vice president: American Fidelity Corp.
William E. Durrett: senior chairman B 1930. ED University of Oklahoma. PRIM CORP EMPL senior chairman: American Fidelity Corp. CORP AFFIL director: OGE Energy Corp.
John Rex: president B 1933. PRIM CORP EMPL president: American Fidelity Corp. CORP AFFIL president, chief operating officer: American Fidelity Assurance Co.; president: American Fidelity Securities.

Foundation Officials

Brett Browman: member (see above)
Joe Carroll Cambrom: member
Laura Cambrom: member
William M. Cambrom: chairman
William E. Durrett: president (see above)
JoElla Ramsey: secretary
John Rex: treasurer (see above)

Grants Analysis

Disclosure Period: fiscal year ending June 30, 1997
Total Grants: $2,874
Number of Grants: 3
Average Grant: $958
Highest Grant: $2,500
Typical Range: $250 to $5,000

Recent Grants

Note: Grants derived from fiscal 1997 Form 990.

Arts & Humanities

24 Allied Arts Foundation, Oklahoma City, OK

Environment

2,500 Ethnobiology and Conservation Team, Arlington, VA

Health

500 St. Anthony Hospital Foundation, Oklahoma City, OK

American General Corp.

Company Contact

2929 Allen Parkway
Houston, TX 77019
Phone: (713)522-1111
Fax: (713)523-8531
Web: http://www.agc.com

Company Description

Revenue: US$10,679,000,000 (1999)
Profit: US$1,131,000,000 (1999)
Employees: 15,747
Fortune Rank: 162, per FORTUNE Magazine's list of 500 Largest U.S. Corporations (1999).
FF 162

SIC(s): 6162 Mortgage Bankers & Correspondents, 6211 Security Brokers & Dealers, 6311 Life Insurance, 6719 Holding Companies Nec.

Operating Locations
Through its subsidiaries, the company maintains 1,576 branch and regional offices throughout the USA.

Nonmonetary Support
Value: $165,000 (1993); $100,000 (1992); $100,000 (1991)
Type: Donated Equipment; In-kind Services; Loaned Employees; Loaned Executives
Note: Company reports that it also donates printing, used furniture, and computers.

Corporate Sponsorship
Type: Arts & cultural events; Festivals/fairs; Sports events
Contact: Robert Merlick, Senior Vice President, Corp. Relations

Giving Contact
Virginia Tomlinson, Director, Community Relations
Houston, TX
Email: virginia_tomlinson@agc.com

Description
Organization Type: Corporate Giving Program
Grant Types: Employee Matching Gifts.
Note: Employee matching gift ratio: 2 to 1 for higher education only, up to $4,000.

Financial Summary
Total Giving: $4,000,000 (1999 approx); $3,700,000 (1997 approx); $2,000,000 (1996 approx). Note: Contributes through corporate direct giving program only.

Typical Recipients
Arts & Humanities: Arts & Humanities-General
Civic & Public Affairs: Civic & Public Affairs-General
Education: Colleges & Universities, Education-General
Health: Health-General
Social Services: Social Services-General, United Funds/United Ways

Contributions Analysis
Arts & Humanities: 20% to 25%.
Civic & Public Affairs: 10% to 15%.
Education: 15% to 20%.
Social Services: 45% to 50%. United Way and health care.

Application Procedures
Initial Contact: written request
Application Requirements: brief a description of organization, clearly stating its objectives, activities, accomplishments, and geographic scope; purpose for which contribution is requested; amount requested and list of other sources of financial support (show fund-raising costs as a percentage of the budgeted revenues); list of the names and business or professional affiliations of officers and board of directors or trustees; and copy of the IRS determination letter indicating 501(c)(3) tax-exempt status
Deadlines: None.
Evaluative Criteria: top priority given to organizations that provide the greatest good for the largest number of people in the community in the long term
Decision Notification: requests accepted and reviewed throughout the year

Restrictions
The company makes contributions only to organizations that have been granted exemption from federal income tax for at least three years.
Contributions will not be provided for organizations without 501(c)(3) public charity status; organizations supported by United Way; veterans, labor, religious, political, fraternal, or external athletic groups, except in special cases in which such groups provide needed service to the community at large; capital campaigns and national organizations not located near a major company facility; private foundations; direct donations to individuals; hospital operating expenses, unless it is a teaching institution; start-up programs; secondary or elementary schools; state universities, unless a matching gift; grants to national organizations solely concerned with a specific disease; museums, art centers, and performing arts institutions in communities where the company has no major facility; activities generally considered to be the responsibility of the government; local chapters if already giving to national organization; organizations whose activities are mainly international; or courtesy advertising and telephone solicitations.

Corporate Officials
Susan A. Jacobs: senior vice president, deputy general counsel, secretary B 1947. PRIM CORP EMPL senior vice president, deputy general counsel, secretary: American General Corp.

Giving Program Officials
Robert D. Mrlik: senior vice president corporate relations PRIM CORP EMPL senior vice president: American General Corp.

AMERICAN GENERAL FINANCE

Company Contact
Evansville, IN

Company Description
Former Name: Credithrift Financial.
Assets: US$7,641,000,000
Employees: 6,500
SIC(s): 6141 Personal Credit Institutions, 6411 Insurance Agents, Brokers & Service.
Parent Company: American General Financial Inc., United States

Operating Locations
Operates offices in 40 states.

American General Finance Foundation

Giving Contact
Michelle Dixon, Community Relations Coordinator
American General Finance Corp.
601 NW Second St.
Evansville, IN 47708
Phone: (812)468-5413
Fax: (812)468-5682

Alternate Contact
PO Box 59
Evansville, IN 47701-0059
Note: Inquiries regarding scholarships should be directed to the University of Evansville, Director of Financial Aid.

Description
Founded: 1958
EIN: 356042566
Organization Type: Corporate Foundation. Supports preselected organizations only.
Giving Locations: IN: Evansville including statewide
Grant Types: General Support, Matching, Scholarship.

Giving Philosophy
'The American General Finance Foundation, Inc. contributes to nonprofit, tax-exempt organizations. The Foundation was formed primarily to engage in, assist, and contribute to the support of education, civic, literary and scientific activities and projects. Priority will be given to those nonprofit organizations supporting youth, human services, patriotic, civic, and community actitivies.' Grant Proposal Guidelines

Financial Summary
Total Giving: $317,909 (1998); $357,187 (1997); $415,824 (1996). Note: Contributes through foundation only.
Giving Analysis: Giving for 1996 includes: foundation grants to United Way ($224,915); foundation ($144,909); foundation scholarships ($46,000); 1997: foundation grants to United Way ($163,204); foundation ($145,983); foundation scholarships ($48,000); 1998: foundation grants to United Way ($139,102); foundation ($117,524); foundation scholarships ($46,000); foundation matching gifts ($15,283)
Assets: $119,080 (1998); $196,464 (1997); $120,033 (1996)
Gifts Received: $239,000 (1998); $432,390 (1997); $405,000 (1996). Note: In 1998, contributions were received from American General Finance, Inc. and its subsidiaries.

Typical Recipients
Arts & Humanities: Arts Associations & Councils, Dance, Historic Preservation, Libraries, Museums/Galleries, Music, Public Broadcasting, Theater
Civic & Public Affairs: Botanical Gardens/Parks, Business/Free Enterprise, Clubs, Community Foundations, Economic Development, Civic & Public Affairs-General, Housing, Municipalities/Towns, Parades/Festivals, Safety, Urban & Community Affairs
Education: Agricultural Education, Business Education, Colleges & Universities, Education Funds, Education-General, Literacy, Private Education (Precollege), Public Education (Precollege), Secondary Education (Public), Student Aid
Health: AIDS/HIV, Alzheimers Disease, Arthritis, Cancer, Children's Health/Hospitals, Diabetes, Emergency/Ambulance Services, Heart, Hospices, Hospitals, Medical Rehabilitation, Mental Health, Prenatal Health Issues, Single-Disease Health Associations
Religion: Religious Organizations, Religious Welfare
Science: Science Museums
Social Services: Big Brother/Big Sister, Community Service Organizations, Day Care, Domestic Violence, Emergency Relief, Family Services, Food/Clothing Distribution, People with Disabilities, Recreation & Athletics, Scouts, Senior Services, Shelters/Homelessness, Special Olympics, Substance Abuse, United Funds/United Ways, Volunteer Services, YMCA/YWCA/YMHA/YWHA, Youth Organizations

Contributions Analysis
Arts & Humanities: 8%. Supports Evansville area performing arts organizations, including dance, theater, and the philharmonic.
Civic & Public Affairs: 6%. Supports community organizations that promote civic pride, as well as improved housing.
Education: 12%. Primarily supports Indiana colleges and universities. Secondary support is allocated to scholarships for children of employees and a matching gift program. Also supports secondary education.
Health: 2%. Supports emergency services and local chapters of national single-diseasehealth organizations in contributions generally less than $1,000.
Religion: Less than 1%. Contributions support religious welfare organizations.
Social Services: 71%. More than half supports the United Way and related agencies. Also provides support to a company-sponsored employee volunteer program. The remainder goes to youth organizations and organizations helping the disabled and elderly.
Note: Total contributions made in 1998.

Application Procedures

Initial Contact: letter, then proposal for grants; request application form for scholarships
Application Requirements: for proposal description of project/activity, including purpose, objective, geographic area to be served, timetable/length of program/activity, impact, volunteer needs and resources, and contact person; a description of organization, including statement of purpose, objectives, governing members/board of directors; itemized budget and contingency plans; current list of corporate and foundation donors, with amounts; description of other funding requirements during current operating year; copy of 501(c)(3) tax-exempt ruling from the IRS; letter from officer of the organization affirming that the determination letter has not been revoked and that the present operation of the organization and its support continue to be consistent with its exempt status as established in the determination letter; current audited financial statement; other community organizations providing similar service/project/activity; amount of funds requested; and the name(s) and qualifications of person(s) administering funds
Deadlines: June 1 for scholarships; grant proposals are reviewed throughout the year
Review Process: Committee of senior management personnel reviews proposals each quarter, and notifies potential grantees of their decision.

Corporate Officials

Robert A. Cole: chief financial officer, senior vice president B Cleveland, OH 1951. ED Purdue University (1974); DePaul University (1981). PRIM CORP EMPL chief financial officer, senior vice president: American General Financial Corp.
Michelle Dixon: community relations coordinator PRIM CORP EMPL community relations coordinator: American General Finance.
Frederick Geissinger: chairman, chief executive officer, prs B Huntington, PA 1945. ED Dartmouth College BA (1967); University of Chicago MBA (1969). PRIM CORP EMPL chairman, chief executive officer, prs: American General Finance Inc. CORP AFFIL chairman: Yosemite Insurance Co.; president, chief executive officer: American General Finance Corp. NONPR AFFIL member: Urban Land Institute.
Philip M. Hanley: senior vice president, chief financial officer B Matton, IL 1945. PRIM CORP EMPL senior vice president, chief financial officer: American General Finance Inc. ADD CORP EMPL chief financial officer: Merit Life Insurance Co.; chief financial officer: Yosemite Insurance Co.
George W. Schmidt: controller, assistant secretary PRIM CORP EMPL controller, assistant secretary: American General Finance Inc. ADD CORP EMPL controller: American General Finance Corp.
James R. Tuerff: president, director B Gary, IN 1941. ED Saint Joseph's College BA (1963). PRIM CORP EMPL president, director: American General Finance. CORP AFFIL president, chief executive officer: American General Property Insurance Co. NONPR AFFIL member advisory committee: Saint Josephs College; director: YMCA Greater Houston; fellow: Life Management Institute Society Houston; director: Saint Joseph Hospital Foundation; director: American Council Life Insurance; director: Boy Scouts America Sam Houston Area Council.

Foundation Officials

Bryan A. Binyon: treasurer B North Hollywood, CA 1956. ED University of the Pacific (1978); University of Pennsylvania (1980). PRIM CORP EMPL treasurer: American General Finance. NONPR AFFIL member: American Fin SVCs Association.
W. Tal Bratton: senior vice president
Robert A. Cole: senior vice president, chief financial officer, director (see above)
Mary R. Deig: assistant secretary
Frederick Wallace Geissinger: chairman, chief executive officer, president, director B Huntington, PA 1945. ED Dartmouth College AB (1967); University of Chicago MBA (1969). PRIM CORP EMPL chairman, chief executive officer: American General Finance Inc. NONPR AFFIL member: Real Estate Board New York; member: Urban Land Institute. CLUB AFFIL member: Pelham Country Club.
Jerry L. Gilpin: senior vice president
James Leslie Gleaves: assistant treasurer B Dallas, TX 1952. ED University of Texas BBA (1974); University of Texas Graduate School of Business MBA (1977). PRIM CORP EMPL vice president, treasurer: American General Corp. NONPR AFFIL director: Houston Arts Fund; member: Houston Society Financial Analysts; member: Financial Analysts Federation. CLUB AFFIL University Club Texas.
Philip M. Hanley: senior vice president (see above)
Roy L. Hardison: assistant secretary
Bennie D. Hendrix: executive vice president
David M. McManigal: assistant treasurer
George W. Schmidt: controller, assistant secretary (see above)
Raymond J. Sims: executive vice president ED Lehigh University (1971); Harvard University (1976). PRIM CORP EMPL chief financial officer, senior vice president: Raychem Corp. ADD CORP EMPL chief financial officer: Raychem International Corp.
Leonard J. Winiger: assistant treasurer, assistant controller

Grants Analysis

Disclosure Period: calendar year ending 1998
Total Grants: $93,324*
Number of Grants: 33
Average Grant: $2,828
Highest Grant: $15,000
Typical Range: $1,000 to $10,000
***Note:** Giving excludes scholarship, matching gifts and community involvement programs.

Recent Grants

Note: Grants derived from 1997 Form 990.

Arts & Humanities

10,000	Evansville Philharmonic Orchestra, Evansville, IN
2,500	Arts Council of Southwest Indiana, Evansville, IN
1,700	WNIN Southwest Indiana Public Broadcasting, Evansville, IN
1,000	Reitz Home Preservation Society, Evansville, IN

Civic & Public Affairs

5,000	Center City Corporation, Evansville, IN
2,000	Operation City Beautiful, Evansville, IN
1,000	Junior League, Evansville, IN
750	Evansville Park Foundation, Evansville, IN

Education

10,000	University of Southern Indiana, Evansville, IN
2,500	University of Evansville, Evansville, IN
1,000	Junior Achievement of Southwestern Indiana, Evansville, IN
500	Reitz High School, Evansville, IN

Health

25,000	American Red Cross, Evansville, IN

Religion

1,000	Salvation Army, Evansville, IN

Science

1,500	Evansville Museum of Arts and Science, Evansville, IN

Social Services

163,203	United Way, Evansville, IN
30,240	Field Community Involvement Program, Evansville, IN
5,000	Crisis Prevention Center, Evansville, IN
2,500	Evansville FC Soccer Club, Evansville, IN
2,000	Boy Scouts of America Buffalo Trace Council, Evansville, IN
2,000	Boys and Girls Club, Evansville, IN
2,000	Park Foundation, Henderson, KY
2,000	Raintree Girl Scout Council, Evansville, IN
2,000	YWCA, Evansville, IN
500	Allied Fellows Bacon Center, Evansville, IN
500	Big Brothers and Big Sisters, Evansville, IN

American Honda Motor Co., Inc.

Company Contact

1919 Torrance Boulevard
Torrance, CA 90501-2746
Phone: (310)783-2000
Fax: (310)783-3900
Web: http://www.hondacorp.com

Company Description

Employees: 13,774
SIC(s): 3711 Motor Vehicles & Car Bodies, 3714 Motor Vehicle Parts & Accessories, 3751 Motorcycles, Bicycles & Parts, 5012 Automobiles & Other Motor Vehicles.
Parent Company: Honda Motor Co. Ltd., 1-1, 2-chome, Minami-Aoyama, Minato-ku, Tokyo, Japan

Operating Locations

CA: American Honda Motor Co., Inc., Cerritos; Calhac, Cerritos; American Honda Motor Co., Torrance; American Honda Motor Co. Automobile Sales Division, Torrance; American Honda Motor Co., Inc., Torrance; American Honda Motor Co. Motorcycle Division, Torrance; Honda International Trading Co., Torrance; Honda North America, Torrance; Honda R&D North America, Torrance; NC: Honda Power Equipment Manufacturing, Swepsonville; OH: American Honda Motor Co., Inc., Marysville; Honda of America Manufacturing, Marysville

American Honda Foundation

Giving Contact

Kathryn Carey, Foundation Manager
American Honda Foundation
PO Box 2205
Torrance, CA 90509-2205
Phone: (310)781-4090
Fax: (310)781-4270

Alternate Contact

Corporate Community Relations Division
American Honda Motor Co.
1919 Torrance Boulevard
Torrance, CA 90501
Phone: (310)783-2000

Description

EIN: 953924667
Organization Type: Corporate Foundation
Giving Locations: nationally.
Grant Types: Challenge, Fellowship, General Support, Matching, Multiyear/Continuing Support, Operating Expenses, Project, Scholarship, Seed Money.

Giving Philosophy

'American Honda Motor Co., Inc., is committed to conducting an enterprise that is of real and continuing value to society. One of the most powerful ways American Honda Motor Co., Inc., can demonstrate this commitment is by effectively fulfilling its basic role as

a business enterprise. .. This corporate policy recognizes that the success of the business is affected by the vitality of the communities in which it operates and the society at large. Accordingly, the establishment of the American Honda Foundation is in the interests of the company, its employees, clients, stockholders, and the general public. It is the policy of the American Honda Motor Co., Inc., to be a good corporate citizen and to be responsive to the broad needs of society. Through a program of responsible investment (of contributions funds) in organizations meeting the needs of the American society in the areas of youth and scientific education, the American Honda Foundation strives to assist in deriving long term benefits for the communities in which it operates and the society as a whole.' *American Honda Foundation Contributions Policy*

Financial Summary

Total Giving: $940,000 (fiscal year ending March 31, 2000 approx); $748,000 (fiscal 1999 approx); $700,000 (fiscal 1998 approx). Note: Contributes through corporate direct giving program and foundation. Giving includes foundation.
Assets: $18,939,154 (fiscal 1997); $17,370,979 (fiscal 1996); $15,260,159 (fiscal 1995)
Gifts Received: $1,000,000 (fiscal 1997); $500,000 (fiscal 1996); $500,000 (fiscal 1995). Note: Foundation receives contributions from American Honda Motor Co., Inc.

Typical Recipients

Civic & Public Affairs: Employment/Job Training
Education: Colleges & Universities, Economic Education, Education Reform, Elementary Education (Private), Elementary Education (Public), Engineering/Technological Education, Environmental Education, Gifted & Talented Programs, Health & Physical Education, Leadership Training, Literacy, Minority Education, Preschool Education, Private Education (Precollege), Public Education (Precollege), Science/Mathematics Education, Secondary Education (Public), Student Aid
Environment: Environment-General, Resource Conservation
Science: Science Museums, Scientific Centers & Institutes

Contributions Analysis

Giving Priorities: Higher education and scientific programs that emphasize scientific education, especially for youth.
Education: Almost 100%. Supports national organizations working in the areas of youth and scientific education. Gives to colleges and universities, K-12 educational institutions, community colleges, and vocational or trade organizations. Also funds organizations with programs for scientific education, scholarship and fellowship programs, and gifted student programs. Also supports national programs for academic or curriculum development that emphasize innovative educational methods and techniques; educational radio and television stations; short-subject films, movies, and slides about scientific education; and other organizations which fall under thefoundation's focus.
Note: Above priorities are for the American Honda Foundation only. Company gives directly across a range of focus areas.

Application Procedures

Initial Contact: request application form, then full proposal
Application Requirements: statement of organization's purpose; description of program for which grant is requested; proof of tax-exempt status; copy of most recent Form 990; list of board of directors and a resolution from the board that authorizes request; copy of organization's current budget with comparisons to previous budget and with significant changes reconciled; two most recently audited financial statements; list of current contributions with amounts for each; three- to five-year plan for organization; proposed budget utilizing the grant funds requested with line item detail; and supporting materials
Deadlines: applications must be received by November 1 for grants awarded February 1, February 1 for grants awarded May 1, May 1 for grants awarded August 1, and August 1 for grants awarded November 1
Review Process: in the first month of the quarter, grants are evaluated and approximately 10% of proposals continue in the review process; in the second month, a site visit is conducted; board of directors meets at the end of each quarter to make final decisions on proposals
Evaluative Criteria: board looks for proposals that are imaginative, creative, youthful, scientific, humanistic, innovative, and forward thinking; also considered in funding are programs that are: national in scope, broad, soundly managed, financially sound and have a high potential for success, a low degree of duplication of effort, an urgency of need (not merely financial), and a minimal risk for venture capital investment
Decision Notification: at quarterly board meetings in January, April, July, and October
Notes: Grant applications can be requested in writing at above address. Mark the request Attn: Grant Application Request, and include a self-addressed, stamped envelope. For direct corporate contributions, send a letter of inquiry to Community Relations Department at American Honda Motor Co. No application form is required.

Restrictions

The foundation does not support individuals; for-profit organizations; small, local, community and/or regional projects; scholarships; loans for small businesses; advocacy; foreign exchange programs; sponsorships, conferences, or seminars; veterans or fraternal organizations; labor groups; service club activities; propaganda statements; environmental issues; arts and culture; health, social, or welfare issues; research papers; medical and/or educational research; disaster relief; annual fund drives; corporate memberships; trips or tours; direct support of churches, religious groups, or sectarian organizations; attempts to influence legislation; advertising in charitable publications; hospital operating funds; private foundations; beauty or talent contests; groups serving special interests of their constituencies; marathon-type fundraising; political organizations, programs, campaigns, or candidates; dinners or special events; or organizations outside the United States. Also does not make grants considered to be in the company's self-interest. Organizations should not submit an application more than once in a 12-month period; repeat requests are not considered in the same year. In addition, the foundation does not make gifts or donations of any Honda products for any purpose.

Additional Information

In 1993, company announced a ten-year, $40 million commitment to establish a special alternative secondary school and teacher development center--Eagle Rock School and Professional Development Center, in Estes Park, CO. This school operates independently of the foundation.
Also, Honda of America Manufacturing Co., a subsidiary of American Honda Motor Co., gives through the Honda of America Foundation.
Publications: Policy Statement; Grant Application Form; Guidelines; Newsletter

Corporate Officials

Koichi Amemiya: president, chief executive officer, director B 1941. PRIM CORP EMPL president, chief executive officer, director: American Honda Motor Co., Inc. CORP AFFIL president: Honda North America; president: Honda Trading America Corp.

Foundation Officials

Kathryn Ann Carey: foundation manager B Los Angeles, CA 1949. ED California State University BA (1971). NONPR AFFIL member: Public Relations Society America; member: Southern California Association Philanthropy; member: Ninety-Nines; member: Ocicats International; member: Humane Society U.S.; member: Los Angeles Society Prevention Cruelty Animals; member: Elsa Wild Animal Appeal; member: Greenpeace; member: American Quarter Horse Association; member: Council Foundations; member: Aircraft Owners & Pilots Association; member: American Humane Association; director: Advocates Nursing Home Reform; president: Affinity Group Japanese Philanthropy. CLUB AFFIL mem: Advertising Los Angeles Club.
Donna Hammond: senior program officer
Tadao Kebayashi: president PRIM CORP EMPL executive vice president: American Honda Motor Co., Inc.
John Petas: vice president, director
Tom Ross: secretary, treasurer

Grants Analysis

Disclosure Period: fiscal year ending March 31, 1996
Total Grants: $312,100
Number of Grants: 8
Average Grant: $39,013
Highest Grant: $50,000
Typical Range: $20,000 to $50,000

Recent Grants

Note: Grants derived from 1996 Form 990.

Education

50,000	California Academy of Math and Science, Carson, CA -- scientific equipment, materials for science curriculum
50,000	Futures for Children, Albuquerque, NM -- support Bridge to the Future program
50,000	United Negro College Fund, Los Angeles, CA -- support Ladders of Hope program
46,000	Loma Linda University, Loma Linda, CA -- summer research program for minority students and teachers
40,000	Rolling Readers, San Diego, CA -- literacy program for low-income children
35,000	First Nations Development Institute, Fredericksburg, VA -- for Indigenous Economics Curriculum program
21,100	Fort Defiance Elementary School, Fort Defiance, AZ -- support Project HOPE
20,000	Children's Storefront, New York, NY -- support tuition-free preschool through eighth grade Harlem school

AMERICAN RETAIL GROUP

Company Contact

New York, NY

Company Description

Employees: 16,000
SIC(s): 5611 Men's & Boys' Clothing Stores, 5621 Women's Clothing Stores, 5630 Women's Accessory & Specialty Stores.

Humanitas Foundation

Giving Contact

Peter S. Robinson, Executive Director, Vice President
Humanitas Foundation
1114 Avenue of the Americas, 28th Floor
New York, NY 10036
Phone: (212)704-2300

Fax: (212)704-2301

Description

Founded: 1979
EIN: 133005012
Organization Type: Corporate Foundation
Giving Locations: nationally.
Grant Types: Conference/Seminar, Emergency, Multiyear/Continuing Support, Operating Expenses, Project, Seed Money.

Financial Summary

Total Giving: $680,400 (1998); $950,250 (1996); $1,744,348 (1995). Note: Contributes through foundation only.
Giving Analysis: Giving for 1998 includes: foundation matching gifts ($10,000)
Assets: $452,825 (1998); $269,236 (1996); $362,831 (1995)
Gifts Received: $671,850 (1998); $739,850 (1996); $1,289,850 (1995). Note: Contributions were received from American Retail Group.

Typical Recipients

Arts & Humanities: Arts & Humanities-General, History & Archaeology
Civic & Public Affairs: Business/Free Enterprise, Employment/Job Training, Civic & Public Affairs-General, Hispanic Affairs, Housing, Public Policy, Urban & Community Affairs, Women's Affairs
Education: Afterschool/Enrichment Programs, Colleges & Universities, Elementary Education (Private), Education-General, Leadership Training, Legal Education, Literacy, Medical Education, Private Education (Precollege), Religious Education, School Volunteerism, Secondary Education (Private), Secondary Education (Public), Student Aid
Health: AIDS/HIV, Children's Health/Hospitals, Health-General, Geriatric Health, Health Organizations, Long-Term Care, Outpatient Health Care, Prenatal Health Issues, Public Health
International: Foreign Educational Institutions, Health Care/Hospitals, International Development, International Organizations, Missionary/Religious Activities
Religion: Churches, Dioceses, Ministries, Religious Organizations, Religious Welfare, Social/Policy Issues
Social Services: At-Risk Youth, Community Centers, Community Service Organizations, Counseling, Day Care, Domestic Violence, Family Planning, Family Services, Refugee Assistance, Senior Services, Shelters/Homelessness, Youth Organizations

Application Procedures

Initial Contact: Send a written request for guidelines.
Deadlines: January 30, May 30, and September 30.

Restrictions

Limited to projects within the United States that are sponsored by organizations of the Roman Catholic Church.

Additional Information

Publications: Application Guidelines

Corporate Officials

Roland M. Brenninkmeyer: president, chief executive officer, director PRIM CORP EMPL president, chief executive officer, director: American Retail Group Inc. CORP AFFIL chairman: Maurice's Inc.

Foundation Officials

Kenneth R. Allex: vice president, treasurer
Anthony Brenninkmeyer: director
Louis Brenninkmeyer: president, chief executive officer, director
Roland M. Brenninkmeyer: president, director (see above)
Miles P. Fischer: secretary PRIM CORP EMPL vice president: Cambrian Corp.
George M. Gillan: assistant treasurer
Peter S. Robinson: director
David J. Vezeris: assistant secretary

Grants Analysis

Disclosure Period: calendar year ending 1998
Total Grants: $670,400*
Number of Grants: 41
Average Grant: $16,351
Highest Grant: $30,000
Typical Range: $2,000 to $40,000
*Note: Giving excludes matching gifts.

Recent Grants

Note: Grants derived from 1998 Form 990.

Civic & Public Affairs

15,000 Maura Clarke-Ita Ford Center, Brooklyn, NY -- Towards first year expenses of a training center for women in transition to paid employment

14,600 Centro San Francisco, Ponce, PR -- To re-start the San Francisco medical dispensary

10,000 Caroline House, Wilton, CA -- General Support of Caroline House

1,000 Mercy Center for Women, Erie, PA -- To purchase tools for the Mercy Center for Women

Education

25,000 Seton Hall University- College of Nursing, South Orange, NJ -- For year two of a three year effort to develop and implement a way of providing health care in parishes using nurse practitioners and nurse case manag

7,750 Saint Mary's Academy of the Holy Family, New Orleans, LA -- Final grant to send five students to the 1998 Oracle National Summer Institute

Health

20,500 National Catholic AIDS Network, Sebastopol, CA -- $15,000 for financial aid program, $2,500 for publication of HIV/AIDS in the Catholic workplace and $3,000 towards development of regional networks of

Religion

50,000 Catholic Campaign for Human Development, Washington, DC -- Towards the creation of child day care centers and home health aide businesses that will train and employ former recipients of public assistance and o

34,300 Religious of Jesus and Mary, Mt. Rainier, MD -- For a social outreach worker during The Washington Middle School for Girls' 1st Year starting in 9/98

30,000 FADICA, Washington, DC -- Up to $25,000 in general support and up to $5,000 in project support

30,000 Fall River Diocese, Fall River, MA -- As a final grant for the second year of the effort to introduce parish social ministry into the Diocese of Fall River

30,000 Ursuline Social Outreach, New Rochelle, NY -- One-time only grant to hire a new staff person for position of Director of the Adult Learning Center

25,000 Catholic Charities Maine, Portland, ME -- To develop an Information and Referral System of licensed counselors, social workers, pastoral counselors and psychotherapists who respect Catholic va

25,000 Miami Archdiocese, Miami Shores, FL -- Towards the salaries of social ministers in the parishes of Notre Dame d'Haiti and Mision de Altagracia at Corpous Christi parish

25,000 New York Archdiocese Catholic Charities, NY, NY -- For a new Vicariate Coordinators of Parish Social Ministry

22,000 Palm Beach Diocese, Palm Beach Gardens, LA -- $12,000 for the Orita Mentoring Program & $10,000 towards youth and adult leaders' attendance at the 1998 Unity Explosion Conference, Dallas

20,000 Catholic Legal Immigration Network, Inc., Washington, DC -- For two national covenings for Catholic legal immigration programs and for monthly conference calls on legal and operational issues.

20,000 Hope Community Services, Inc., New Rochelle, NY -- For the Community Self-Sufficiency Program.

20,000 St. Camillus Ministries, Inc., Milwaukee, WI -- Renovation of the 1st Floor of Raphael House to create a Sensitive Care Unit for the care of people with HIV

15,000 Fall River Diocese Catholic Social Services, Fall River, MA -- Towards the purchase of a van

15,000 Juneau Catholic Community Services, Inc., Juneau, AK -- To expand the Care Coordination Program for the Elderly to rural villages

15,000 Most Holy Trinity Catholic Church, Yonkers, NY -- General Support of "The Shepherd's Place"

15,000 Oakland Diocese- Khmmu/Latin Catholic Community, Oakland, CA -- Towards a pilot program to teach English to adults in the Khmmu of Northern California

15,000 Saint Martin de Porres Residence, Inc., Lewiston, ME -- For the renovation of basement space at 23 Bartlett Street, Lewiston, to provide a multi-purpose room for use by programs of the recipient

10,000 Albany Diocese Catholic Charities, Saratoga Springs, NY -- One-time only grant for the Center for Counseling, Psychotherapy and Consultative

10,000 Community of Holy Rosary and St. John, Columbus, OH -- $4000 for repairs to the Children's Room and $6,000 towards the 1998 salary of the newly hired custodian for the St. John's Center

10,000 Congregation of St. Dominic, Blauvelt, NY -- One-time only grant for the Center for Counseling, Psychotherapy and Consultative services at the Highbridge Community Life Center, Bronx, NY

10,000 Franciscan Sisters of the Poor, Brooklyn, NY -- One time grant for the first year of the Frances Residence of Park Slope Christian Help, Inc., Brooklyn, New York.

10,000 Lubbock Diocese Catholic Family Service, Lubbock, TX -- As a final grant for the Youth Counseling Incentive program

6,000 Sisters of the Presentation of the Blessed Virgin Mary, Aderdeen, SD -- To offer courses of the "Personality and Human Relations Program" to women at the South Dakota State Prison, Pierre, South Dakota.

5,000 Catholic Social Services of Central and Southern Indiana, Indianapolis, IA -- $5,000 for the Family Growth Program and $5,000 to match funds raised locally for the program from businesses, corporations, individuals or religious

5,000 Little Rock Diocese Catholic Social Services, Little Rock, AR -- For expenses of developing HIV/AIDS Care teams among Spanish speaking Catholics

5,000 St. Elizabeth Ann Seton Catholic

	Church, Hiawatha, IA -- As a one-time only for the Hiawatha Habitat for Humanity Project
5,000	St. Joseph Social Service Center, Elizabeth, NJ -- For job training program, "Project Ready"
4,500	Northeast Catholic Counseling Center, Portland, OR -- To hire a development consultant
3,900	Toledo Diocese Catholic Charities, Toledo, OH -- To Provide mediation training for three people
3,850	FADICA, Washington, DC -- To publish the proceedings of the FADICA symposium, "Signs of Hope" on Catholic inner-city schools.
2,000	St. Ignatius Church, Brooklyn, NY -- Towards the purchase of recreational equipment for the "Open Books/Open Gym" program.

Social Services

25,000	Marguerite's Place, Nashua, NH -- General Support of Marguerite's Place
25,000	Resources, Inc., Brooklyn, NY -- To develop a managerial training component of Resources
20,000	Ozanam Center, Brownsville, TX -- Towards the cost of materials to construct five family units
10,000	Harvest House, South Buffalo, NY -- For materials to build a storage facility for baby items distributed to low income people
10,000	Mercy Center Inc., Bronx, NY -- Matching grant for donations from individuals donors given in general support of the Center in response to its Christmas 1997 direct mail appeal

AMERICAN STANDARD INC.

Company Contact

Piscataway, NJ
Web: http://www.americanstandard.com

Company Description

Revenue: US$6,653,900,000
Employees: 38,000
Fortune Rank: 242, per FORTUNE Magazine's list of 500 Largest U.S. Corporations (1999).
FF 242
SIC(s): 3261 Vitreous Plumbing Fixtures, 3431 Metal Sanitary Ware, 3432 Plumbing Fixtures Fittings & Trim, 3585 Refrigeration & Heating Equipment.
Parent Company: ASI Holding Corp.

Operating Locations

Austria; Belgium; Brazil; Canada; Costa Rica; Dominican Republic; France; Germany; Greece; Guatemala; Italy; Mexico; Nicaragua; Netherlands; Sweden; United Kingdom

Corporate Sponsorship

Type: Pledge-a-thon
Contact: John Adams, Human Resources
Note: Sponsors March of Dimes Walk-a-thon.

American Standard Foundation

Giving Contact

Adrian B. Deshotel, Vice President, Human Resources
American Standard Foundation
One Centennial Ave.
PO Box 6820
Piscataway, NJ 08855-6820
Phone: (732)980-6000
Fax: (732)980-6121

Description

EIN: 256018911
Organization Type: Corporate Foundation
Giving Locations: headquarters and operating communities.
Grant Types: Employee Matching Gifts, General Support, Scholarship.

Financial Summary

Total Giving: $2,526,244 (1998); $1,874,874 (1997); $2,444,442 (1996). Note: Contributes through foundation only. 1997 Giving includes matching gifts ($490,983); scholarship ($40,073); United Way ($684,566). 1996 Giving includes matching gifts ($384,755); scholarship ($115,990); United Way ($688,072).
Giving Analysis: Giving for 1996 includes: foundation grants to United Way ($688,072); foundation matching gifts ($384,755); foundation scholarships ($115,990); 1997: foundation grants to United Way ($684,566); foundation matching gifts ($490,983); foundation scholarships ($40,073); 1998: foundation grants to United Way ($739,785); foundation matching gifts ($508,186); foundation scholarships ($113,310)
Assets: $11,060,796 (1997); $10,592,979 (1996); $11,785,557 (1995)

Typical Recipients

Arts & Humanities: Dance, Libraries
Civic & Public Affairs: Business/Free Enterprise, Community Foundations, Economic Policy, Employment/Job Training, Housing, Legal Aid
Education: Agricultural Education, Business Education, Colleges & Universities, Education Funds, Education Reform, Environmental Education, Education-General, International Exchange, Private Education (Precollege), Public Education (Precollege), Secondary Education (Private), Secondary Education (Public), Student Aid
Health: Emergency/Ambulance Services
International: Foreign Educational Institutions, International Affairs, International Development, International Relations
Religion: Religious Organizations, Religious Welfare
Science: Scientific Centers & Institutes
Social Services: Community Service Organizations, United Funds/United Ways

Contributions Analysis

Giving Priorities: United Way, precollege education, and higher education.
Civic & Public Affairs: 29%. Supports employment programs, job training, science centers and other community organizations and initiatives.
Education: 34%. Majority of support takes the form of matching gifts to precollege and higher education. Also makes gifts to colleges and universities.
Social Services: 37%. Supports United Ways in company communities.
Note: Total contributions in 1998.

Application Procedures

Initial Contact: Send a brief letter or proposal to the president of foundation.
Application Requirements: Include purpose, history, and scope of organization; amount requested; purpose for which funds are sought; recently audited financial statement; and proof of tax-exempt status.
Deadlines: None.

Corporate Officials

Fred A. Allardyce: senior vice president medical products sector B Rahway, NJ 1941. ED Yale University BA (1963); University of Chicago Graduate School of Business Administration MBA (1965). PRIM CORP EMPL senior vice president medical products sector: American Standard Inc.
Adrian B. Deshotel: vice president human resources PRIM CORP EMPL vice president human resources: American Standard Companies Inc.
Horst Hinrichs: vice chairman, director B 1933. ED University of Stuttgart (1958). PRIM CORP EMPL vice chairman, director: American Standard Inc.
Richard A. Kalaher: vice president, secretary, general counsel B Milwaukee, WI 1940. ED Union College AB (1962); Northwestern University JD (1965). PRIM CORP EMPL vice president, secretary, general counsel: American Standard Inc. NONPR AFFIL chairman, legal officer: Conference Board; member: International Bar Association; member: American Bar Association; member: Association Bar City NYK.
Emmanuel Andrew Kampouris: chairman, president, chief executive officer, director B Alexandria, Egypt 1934. ED King's College (1953); Oxford University BA (1957); North Staffforshire College Technology (1962). PRIM CORP EMPL chairman, president, chief executive officer, director: American Standard Inc. ADD CORP EMPL president: Facs Facility Services Inc. CORP AFFIL director: Ideal Standard Mexico; director: INCESA; director: Hoxan Corp.; director: Ideal Refractories SAI; director: America Standard Sanitaryware Thailand Ltd. NONPR AFFIL member: Oxford Law Society; member: Young President Organization; director: Federation Greek Industries; member: American Hellenic Chamber of Commerce; member: Chief Executives Organization. CLUB AFFIL Spring Brook Country Club; Quogue Beach Club; Quogue Field Club; Laurel Valley Golf Club; Oxford University Club; Chemists Club; Economic Club New York.
George H. Kerckhove: vice president, chief financial officer B 1937. ED University of Wisconsin MA (1962); University of Wisconsin MBA (1972). PRIM CORP EMPL vice president, chief financial officer: American Standard Inc. ADD CORP EMPL vice president, chief financial officer: American Standard Co.s Inc. NONPR AFFIL chairman: Air Conditioning Refrigeration Institute; member advisory board: Gunderson Medicine Foundation.

Foundation Officials

Fred A. Allardyce: director (see above)
Thomas S. Battaglia: director B 1958. ED University of Michigan (1981). PRIM CORP EMPL vice president, treasurer: American Standard Inc. CORP AFFIL president: GKN Westland Inc.; vice president: Visual Productions Inc.
Adrian B. Deshotel: secretary, treasurer (see above)
Richard A. Kalaher: president (see above)

Grants Analysis

Disclosure Period: calendar year ending 1998
Total Grants: $1,164,963*
Number of Grants: 25
Average Grant: $46,599*
Highest Grant: $407,631
Typical Range: $4,000 to $50,000
***Note:** Giving excludes matching gifts; scholarships; United Way.

Recent Grants

Note: Grants derived from 1998 Form 990.

Arts & Humanities

15,000	National Dance institute, New York, NY

Civic & Public Affairs

50,000	Citizens for a Sound Economy, Washington, DC
10,000	National Legal Center, Washington, DC
10,000	Pacific Legal Foundation, Sacramento, CA
8,000	Business Council for International Understanding, New York, NY
5,000	Washington Legal Foundation, Washington, DC
2,500	Employment Policy Foundation, Washington, DC

Education

75,000	Ashrae Reuben Trane Schirshp, Atlanta, GA
38,310	National Merit Scholarship Corp, Chicago, IL
30,000	Eisenhower Exchange Fellowship, Philadelphia, PA
5,000	Environmental Literacy Council, Washington, DC
5,000	Seneca Area Career System, Tiffin, OH
1,000	Young Scholars' Institute, Trenton, NJ

Health

300,000	American Red Cross Hurricane Mitch Relief, Washington, DC

International

40,763	University of Oxford, Oxford, England
40,000	National Endowment for Democracy, Washington, DC
16,000	University of Oxford, Oxford, England
15,000	Executive Council on Diplomacy, Armonk, NY
10,000	Council on Foreign Relations, New York, NY
10,000	University of Oxford, Oxford, England
6,500	Executive Council on Diplomacy, Armonk, NY
5,000	Trilateral Commission, New York, NY
2,000	Campaign to Preserve U.S. Global Leadership, Washington, DC

Religion

50,000	New Life of New York, New York, NY
50,000	New Life of New York, New York, NY

Social Services

322,417	United Way, New York, NY -- August - 2nd & 3rd Quarter '98
322,338	United Way, New York, NY -- February -4th Quarter '97
100,000	Best Friends Foundation, Washington, DC
95,009	United Way, New York, NY -- April - 1st Quarter '98
11,352	Best Friends Foundation, Washington, DC

American Stock Exchange, Inc.

Company Contact

New York, NY
Web: http://www.amex.com

Company Description

Revenue: US$144,000,000
Employees: 679
SIC(s): 6231 Security & Commodity Exchanges.

Nonmonetary Support

Type: In-kind Services

Corporate Sponsorship

Type: Arts & cultural events

Giving Contact

Richard F. Syron, Chairman
American Stock Exchange, Inc.
86 Trinity Place
New York, NY 10006-1881
Phone: (212)306-1100
Fax: (212)306-1152

Description

Organization Type: Corporate Giving Program
Giving Locations: NY: New York including the metropolitan area
Grant Types: General Support, Project.

Financial Summary

Total Giving: $400,000 (1998 approx); $350,000 (1997 approx); $250,000 (1996 approx). Note: Contributes through corporate direct giving program only.

Typical Recipients

Arts & Humanities: Museums/Galleries, Performing Arts
Civic & Public Affairs: Civic & Public Affairs-General, Public Policy, Urban & Community Affairs, Women's Affairs
Health: Health-General
Social Services: Child Welfare, Youth Organizations

Contributions Analysis

Arts & Humanities: Museums and the performing arts.
Health: Health care, child welfare, and youth organizations.

Application Procedures

Initial Contact: Send short written proposal.
Application Requirements: Include purpose, objectives, and goals of the organization; current budget; most recent audited financial statement; and a tax-exempt status letter.
Deadlines: None.
Review Process: Contributions committee meets quarterly.

Restrictions

The company does not make grants to individuals or schools, and does not make loans for any purpose.

Additional Information

Publications: Application Guidelines

Corporate Officials

Thomas Ryan: president, chief operating officer, director PRIM CORP EMPL president, chief operating officer: American Stock Exchange Inc.
Richard F. Syron: chairman, chief executive officer, director B Boston, MA 1943. ED Boston College BS (1966); Tufts University MA (1969); Tufts University PhD (1971). PRIM CORP EMPL chairman, chief executive officer, director: American Stock Exchange Inc. CORP AFFIL director: Thermo Electron Corp.; director: John Hancock Mutual Life Insurance Co.; director: Park Saint Corp.; director: Dreyfus Corp.; director: John Hancock. NONPR AFFIL chairman: Boston College; director: Boston Municipal Research Bureau; chairman: American Business Conference.

Giving Program Officials

Suzanne Johnson: human resources consultant

American United Life Insurance Co.

Company Contact

Indianapolis, IN
Web: http://www.aul.com

Company Description

Income: US$1,195,175,000
Employees: 880
SIC(s): 6311 Life Insurance.

Nonmonetary Support

Value: $5,000 (1998); $100,000 (1994); $20,000 (1993)
Type: Donated Equipment
Contact: Kim Pekarek, Real Estate Department
Note: Co. currently sponsors a United Way Day of Caring for employees that volunteer.

Corporate Sponsorship

Type: Arts & cultural events; Music & entertainment events; Pledge-a-thon; Sports events
Contact: Kelli Walker, Corporate Contributions Administrator
Note: Annual Sponsorship Budget: about 2% of anticipated net income.

AUL Foundation Inc.

Giving Contact

James W. Freeman, Chairman, Committee
American United Life Insurance Co.
One American Square
PO Box 368
Indianapolis, IN 46206-0368
Phone: (317)285-1609
Fax: (317)285-1979

Alternate Contact

Phone: (317)285-1489

Description

EIN: 311146437
Organization Type: Corporate Foundation
Giving Locations: IN headquarters and operating communities.
Grant Types: Capital, Employee Matching Gifts, Endowment, General Support.
Note: Matching gifts for higher education only.

Giving Philosophy

'We have become a global society, or, as Marshall McLuhan called it, 'the global village.' And the technology that links the global village together, and drives commerce today, is changing at a phenomenal rate.'
'If we in the United States are to keep pace, we must see that our young people get the best education possible. For that reason, we at American United Life find ourselves giving more attention--and more money--to educational programs and institutions.'
'As a life and health insurance company, we have had a particular interest in health and fitness. And we still do. Also, as a major Indianapolis-based company, we feel an obligation to help as many as possible of the institutions that contribute to the quality of life in central Indiana..' Jerry D. Semler, Chairman, President, and CEO, American United Life Insurance Co.

Financial Summary

Total Giving: $2,077,000 (1998); $1,930,000 (1997); $1,696,000 (1996). Note: Contributes through corporate direct giving program and foundation.
Giving Analysis: Giving for 1996 includes: corporate direct giving ($1,141,000); foundation ($589,340); 1997: corporate direct giving ($1,143,438); foundation ($786,562); 1998: corporate direct giving ($1,314,000); foundation ($758,000); nonmonetary support ($5,000)
Assets: $6,222,000 (1998); $5,774,551 (1997); $5,654,278 (1996)
Gifts Received: $370,500 (1997); $1,757,416 (1996); $531,300 (1994). Note: The foundation receives contributions from American United Life Insurance Company.

Typical Recipients

Arts & Humanities: Arts Associations & Councils, Arts Centers, Ethnic & Folk Arts, Libraries, Museums/Galleries, Music, Opera, Performing Arts, Public Broadcasting, Theater, Visual Arts
Civic & Public Affairs: Business/Free Enterprise, Economic Development, Employment/Job Training, Legal Aid, Professional & Trade Associations, Public Policy, Urban & Community Affairs, Zoos/Aquariums
Education: Business Education, Colleges & Universities, Economic Education, Education Funds, Education Reform, Faculty Development, Education-General, Leadership Training, Legal Education, Medical

Education, Minority Education, Private Education (Precollege), Student Aid
Health: AIDS/HIV, Cancer, Cancer, Health Organizations, Hospitals, Medical Research, Medical Training, Mental Health, Nursing Services, Public Health, Single-Disease Health Associations
International: Health Care/Hospitals
Religion: Jewish Causes, Seminaries
Social Services: Animal Protection, Child Welfare, Community Centers, Community Service Organizations, Counseling, Day Care, Delinquency & Criminal Rehabilitation, Domestic Violence, Emergency Relief, Family Services, Food/Clothing Distribution, People with Disabilities, Recreation & Athletics, Scouts, Senior Services, Shelters/Homelessness, Special Olympics, Substance Abuse, United Funds/United Ways, Volunteer Services, YMCA/YWCA/YMHA/YWHA, Youth Organizations

Contributions Analysis

Arts & Humanities: 10% to 15%. Provides grants for arts associations, libraries, music, and theater, among other interests.
Civic & Public Affairs: 10% to 15%. Contributions go to organizations involved with public policy, especially those concerned with minority groups and labor organizations. Interests also include urban and local affairs, and zoos and botanical gardens.
Education: 35% to 40%. Includes donations to college associations, colleges, universities, and at least one seminary. Economics, law, and physical education are of particular interest.
Health: 30% to 35%. Majority of funding supports the United Way. Also supports hospitals, medical research, health organizations, and social services for the homeless and aged.

Application Procedures

Initial Contact: Submit a written request.
Application Requirements: Include description and purpose of the organization, amount requested, purpose of funds sought, recently audited financial statement, other sources of funding, and proof of tax-exempt status.
Deadlines: By the first of each month.
Evaluative Criteria: Based on how request impacts Indianapolis area; requesting organization is generally accepted and respected and provides a needed service to a wide segment of population.

Restrictions

Does not support individuals, religious organizations for sectarian purposes, service clubs, youth groups, organizations with many similar counterparts, or political or lobbying groups.
Generally does not support tax-supported organizations.

Additional Information

Company donates at least 2% of its pre-tax income to support charitable organizations.
Publications: Guidelines

Corporate Officials

Jim Freeman: vice president, chairman corporate contributions committee PRIM CORP EMPL vice president, chairman corporate contributions committee: American United Life Insurance Co.
James W. Murphy: senior vice president corporate finance B Milan, MD 1936. ED Rockhurst College BSBA (1957). PRIM CORP EMPL senior vice president corporate finance: American United Life Insurance Co. NONPR AFFIL member: Financial Executives Institute; fellow: LOMA.
R. Stephen Radcliffe: executive vice president B Winamac, IN 1945. ED Michigan State University BSc (1967); University of Michigan MA (1968). PRIM CORP EMPL executive vice president: American United Life Insurance Co.
Jerry D. Semler: chairman, president, chief executive officer, director B Indianapolis, IN 1937. ED Purdue University BS (1958). PRIM CORP EMPL chairman, president, chief executive officer, director: American United Life Insurance Co. CORP AFFIL chairman, chief executive officer: State Life Insurance Co.; director: IWC Resources Corp.; director: LIMRA International. NONPR AFFIL director: American Council Life Insurance.

Foundation Officials

Judy Boyle: secretary
James M. Cornelius: director B Kalamazoo, MI 1943. ED Michigan State University BA (1965); Michigan State University MBA (1967). PRIM CORP EMPL chairman: Guidant Corp. CORP AFFIL director: National Bank Indianapolis; director: American United Life Insurance Co.; director: Lilly Industries Inc. NONPR AFFIL trustee: Indiana Repertory Theatre; trustee: Indianapolis Museum Art.
James E. Dora: director B 1936. ED Purdue University (1958). CORP AFFIL ltd. partner: Holiday Inn North; partner: I-70 East Inn Devel; chairman, manager: General Hotels Corp.; director: America United Life Insurance Co.; partner: B&D Associates; partner: Airport Inn Developers.
James Thomas Morris: director B Terre Haute, IN 1943. ED Indiana University AB (1965); Butler University MBA (1970). PRIM CORP EMPL chairman: Indianapolis Water Co. CORP AFFIL director: Paul Harris Stores Inc.; director: NiSource Inc.
James W. Murphy: treasurer (see above)
William R. Riggs: director CORP AFFIL director: American United Life Insurance Co.
Jerry D. Semler: chairman, director (see above)

Grants Analysis

Disclosure Period: calendar year ending 1998
Total Grants: $2,072,000
Number of Grants: 223*
Average Grant: $9,241
Highest Grant: $150,000
Typical Range: $1,000 to $50,000
***Note:** Number of grants exclude matching grants. Grants analysis provided by the foundation.

Recent Grants

Note: Grants derived from 1998 Form 990.

Arts & Humanities

50,000	Indiana Repertory Theatre, Inc., Indianapolis, IN -- Capital and Endowment Campaign
25,000	Elteljorg Museum, Indianapolis, IN -- "Eye on the Future" Campaign
8,090	Metropolitan Indianapolis Public Broadcasting, Indianapolis, IN -- WFYI TelePhlex Campaign
8,000	Indianapolis Museum of Art, Indianapolis, IN -- Operating Fund

Civic & Public Affairs

10,000	Sigma Theta Tau International, Indianapolis, IN -- Capital Campaign

Education

150,000	Purdue University, West Lafayette, IN -- Endow a Professorship
100,000	Indiana University Foundation, Bloomington, IN -- Endow a Chair
25,000	Marian College, Indianapolis, IN -- Capital Campaign
20,000	Educational Choice Charitable Trust, Indianapolis, IN -- Ed Choice Program
20,000	Independent Colleges of Indiana Foundation, Indianapolis, IN -- Undesignated Funds
20,000	Independent Colleges of Indiana Foundation, Indianapolis, IN -- Indiana Wesleyan University
15,000	Indiana University Foundation, Bloomington, IN -- Scholarship Fund
12,500	Center for Leadership Development, Indianapolis, IN -- Operating Fund
10,000	Indiana University Foundation, Bloomington, IN -- Memorial Gift
5,000	Independent Colleges of Indiana Foundation, Indianapolis, IN -- Butler University
5,000	Junior Achievement of Central Indiana, Indianapolis, IN -- Exchange City
5,000	Purdue University, West Lafayette, IN -- Charter Sponsorship Ins Marketing Institute
4,800	Junior Achievement of Central Indiana, Indianapolis, IN -- Operating Fund
3,500	Independent Colleges of Indiana Foundation, Indianapolis, IN -- Marian College
3,000	Independent Colleges of Indiana Foundation, Indianapolis, IN -- University of Indianapolis

Health

5,000	American Cancer Society, Indianapolis, IN -- Hoosier Commitment Campaign

Religion

10,000	Christian Theological Seminary, Indianapolis, IN -- Capital Campaign
8,000	Jewish Federation of Greater Indianapolis, Indianapolis, IN -- Capital Campaign

Social Services

100,000	Indiana Sports Corporation, Indianapolis, IN -- NCAA Relocation Fund
20,000	Pleasant Run Children's Home Foundation, Indianapolis, IN -- Capital Campaign
6,666	Hoosier Capital Girl Scout Council, Indianapolis, IN -- Capital Campaign
4,700	Class, Indianapolis, IN -- Indiana Coalition for Education Progress
1,000	United Way of Central Indiana, Indianapolis, IN -- Winter Assistance Fund

AMERITAS LIFE INSURANCE CORP.

Company Contact

Lincoln, NE

Company Description

Assets: US$5,399,000,000
Employees: 800
SIC(s): 6311 Life Insurance, 6321 Accident & Health Insurance, 6324 Hospital & Medical Service Plans.

Ameritas Charitable Foundation

Giving Contact

Scott Stuckey, Assistant Vice President of Corporate Communications
Ameritas Life Insurance Corp.
PO Box 81889
Lincoln, NE 68501
Phone: (402)467-1122
Fax: (402)467-7939

Description

Founded: 1985
EIN: 363428705
Organization Type: Corporate Foundation
Giving Locations: NE: Lincoln
Grant Types: Capital, General Support, Multiyear/Continuing Support, Professorship, Project, Research.

Financial Summary

Total Giving: $275,000 (1998 approx); $245,475 (1997); $260,000 (1996 approx)

Giving Analysis: Giving for 1996 includes: foundation ($154,725); corporate direct giving ($105,275); 1997: foundation ($245,475)
Assets: $6,591,748 (1997); $6,097,375 (1996); $3,990,594 (1995)
Gifts Received: $1,999,937 (1996); $497,700 (1992); $760,575 (1989). Note: Contributions are received from Ameritas Life Insurance Corp.

Typical Recipients

Arts & Humanities: Arts Associations & Councils, Ballet, Dance, History & Archaeology, Libraries, Museums/Galleries, Music, Performing Arts, Public Broadcasting, Theater
Civic & Public Affairs: Clubs, Community Foundations, Economic Development, Economic Policy, Employment/Job Training, Civic & Public Affairs-General, Housing, Parades/Festivals, Professional & Trade Associations, Urban & Community Affairs
Education: Business Education, Colleges & Universities, Continuing Education, Economic Education, Education Funds, Faculty Development, Education-General, Health & Physical Education, Leadership Training, Medical Education, Minority Education, Private Education (Precollege), Public Education (Precollege), Religious Education, Science/Mathematics Education, Secondary Education (Private)
Environment: Environment-General, Resource Conservation
Health: AIDS/HIV, Children's Health/Hospitals, Clinics/Medical Centers, Emergency/Ambulance Services, Health Organizations, Hospitals, Medical Research, Public Health, Research/Studies Institutes, Single-Disease Health Associations
Religion: Religious Organizations, Religious Welfare
Social Services: Animal Protection, At-Risk Youth, Community Service Organizations, Family Services, Food/Clothing Distribution, Homes, People with Disabilities, Scouts, Senior Services, Substance Abuse, United Funds/United Ways, YMCA/YWCA/YMHA/YWHA, Youth Organizations

Contributions Analysis

Giving Priorities: Major focus on education, civic concerns, the arts, and health.
Arts & Humanities: 10% to 15%. Public broadcasting, museums, and performing arts.
Civic & Public Affairs: 15% to 20%. Economic development and research.
Education: 40% to 45%. Colleges and universitites, secondary education, and education associations in Nebraska.
Health: 5% to 10%. Medical research, hospitals, and single-disease health associations.
Social Services: About 15%. Youth organizations, YMCAs, United Way, and food banks.

Application Procedures

Initial Contact: Send a written application.
Application Requirements: Include purpose for funding; names of the board of directors; recently audited financial statement; a proposed budget; proof of tax-exempt status; and amount requested.
Deadlines: None.
Notes: Additional information may be requested as necessary.

Restrictions

Does not support individuals, religious organizations for sectarian purposes, political or lobbying groups, or organizations that require a major portion of budget for administration and solicitation.

Corporate Officials

Lawrence Joseph Arth: chairman, chief executive officer, director chief financial officer B Lincoln, NE 1943. ED University of Nebraska BBA (1965); University of Nebraska MA (1969). PRIM CORP EMPL chairman, chief executive officer, director: Ameritas Life Insurance Corp. CORP AFFIL chairman, president, chief executive officer: AMAL Corp.; president, director: Ameritas Investment Advisors Inc. NONPR AFFIL member: Lincoln Chamber of Commerce; member: Omaha/Lincoln Society; member: Financial Analysts Federation. CLUB AFFIL Lincoln Country Club.
Kenneth C. Louis: president, chief operating officer, director B Pittsburgh, PA 1938. ED Pennsylvania State University (1961). PRIM CORP EMPL president, chief operating officer, director: Ameritas Life Insurance Corp. CORP AFFIL director: Pathmark Assurance Co.; director: Veritas Corp.; director: Lincoln Gateway Shopping Center Inc.; executive vice president, director: Ameritas Variable Life Insurance Co.; director: First Ameritas Life Insurance Corp. New York; senior vice president, director: Ameritas Investment Corp.; director: Ameritas Managed Dental Plan Inc.; vice president, director: AMAI Corp.; director: Ameritas Investment Advisors Inc.
JoAnn M. Martin: senior vice president, partner, chief financial officer B Plainview, NE 1954. ED University of Nebraska (1975); Colorado State University (1982). PRIM CORP EMPL senior vice president, partner, chief financial officer: Ameritas Life Insurance Corp. ADD CORP EMPL senior vice president, chief financial officer, corporate treasurer: Ameritas Acacia Mutual Holding Co.; chief financial officer, director: Ameritas Managed Dental Plan. CORP AFFIL compt, director: Pathmark Assurance Co.; fellow, member: Life Management Institute; director, controller: Lincoln Gateway Shopping Center Inc.; comptroller, director: Ameritas Variable Life Insurance Co.; vice president, controller: First Ameritas Life Insurance Corp.; director: Acacia National Life; comptroller: Ameritas Marketing Group. NONPR AFFIL member: American Institute CPAs.

Foundation Officials

Lawrence Joseph Arth: vice president, director (see above)
JoAnn M. Martin: controller (see above)
William C. Smith: president, director
Neal Edward Tyner: treasurer, director B Grand Island, NE 1930. ED University of Nebraska (1951); University of Nebraska BBA (1956).

Grants Analysis

Disclosure Period: calendar year ending 1997
Total Grants: $245,475
Number of Grants: 80
Average Grant: $3,068
Highest Grant: $20,000
Typical Range: $200 to $25,000

Recent Grants

Note: Grants derived from 1997 Form 990.

Arts & Humanities

8,500	Strategic Air Command Museum, Omaha, NE
6,000	Lincoln Symphony Orchestra, Lincoln, NE
5,000	Lincoln Community Playhouse, Lincoln, NE
4,000	Lincoln Children's Museum, Lincoln, NE
2,500	Constitutional Heritage Institute, Omaha, NE
1,000	Nebraskans for Public Television, Lincoln, NE -- Grand Benefactor

Civic & Public Affairs

25,000	Nebraska Community Foundation, Lincoln, NE
5,000	Lincoln Community Foundation, Lincoln, NE
3,000	Lincoln Community Foundation, Lincoln, NE
2,500	Nebraska Council on Economic Education, Lincoln, NE
2,000	Bright Lights, Lincoln, NE

Education

20,000	Nebraska Wesleyan University, Lincoln, NE -- Great Teaching program
17,000	Lincoln Medical Education Foundation, Lincoln, NE
10,000	Nebraska Wesleyan University, Lincoln, NE -- Ameritas Faculty Fellowship
5,450	American College, Bryn Mawr, PA
5,000	Christian Urban Education Service, Omaha, NE
5,000	Lincoln Lutheran High School, Lincoln, NE
5,000	Lincoln Public Schools Foundation, Lincoln, NE
5,000	Pius X High School, Lincoln, NE
5,000	University of Nebraska, Lincoln, NE -- Ameritas Professorship Fund
4,500	Junior Achievement, Lincoln, NE -- operating fund investment
4,400	University of Nebraska, Lincoln, NE
3,000	Beatrice Educational Foundation, Beatrice, NE
2,500	Doane College, Crete, NE -- academic leadership fund
2,500	Wayne State Foundation, Wayne, NE
1,800	College of St. Mary, Omaha, NE
1,700	S.S. Huebner Foundation, Philadelphia, PA
1,500	Nebraska Independent College Foundation, Omaha, NE
1,000	Nebraska Wesleyan University, Lincoln, NE -- White tribute

Environment

1,000	Nature Conservancy, Lincoln, NE

Health

6,000	Mayo Foundation, Rochester, MN
5,000	Life and Health Insurance, Washington, DC
5,000	University of Nebraska, Lincoln, NE -- Center for Dental Research
3,000	American Red Cross, Lincoln, NE
1,500	Tabitha Foundation, Lincoln, NE
1,000	Nebraska Easter Seal Society, Lincoln, NE

Religion

4,500	Peoples City Mission Foundation, Lincoln, NE
1,000	St. Monica's Home, Lincoln, NE
1,000	Samaritan Counseling, Lincoln, NE

Social Services

12,500	Friendship Home, Lincoln, NE
5,000	Youth Services Systems, Lincoln, NE
4,000	Girl Scouts of America Homestead Council, Lincoln, NE
3,400	Capital Humane Society, Lincoln, NE -- capital campaign
2,500	Child Advocacy Center, Lincoln, NE
2,000	Food Bank, Lincoln, NE
2,000	Summer Youth Program, Lincoln, NE
1,500	Lighthouse, Lincoln, NE
1,500	YMCA, Beatrice, NE
1,000	Nebraska Council to Prevent Alcohol and Drugs, Lincoln, NE
1,000	York Area Senior Center, York, NE

AMERITECH CORP.

Number 33 of Top 100 Corporate Givers

Company Contact

Chicago, IL
Web: http://www.ameritech.com

Company Description

Revenue: US$17,154,000,000
Profit: US$3,606,000,000
Employees: 66,128
SIC(s): 4813 Telephone Communications Except Radiotelephone, 6719 Holding Companies Nec.

Parent Company: SBC Communications Inc., San Antonio, TX, United States

Nonmonetary Support

Note: Nonmonetary support is offered only by Ameritech's Bell-company subsidiaries.

Corporate Sponsorship

Type: Arts & cultural events; Festivals/fairs; Music & entertainment events; Sports events

Ameritech Foundation

Giving Contact

Michael E. Kuhlin, Senior Director, Corporate Contributions
Ameritech Corporate
30 South Wacker Drive, 34th Floor
Chicago, IL 60606
Phone: (312)750-5037
Note: Foundation serves as the regional, national, and international contact; Illinois, Indiana, Michigan, Ohio, and Wisconsin also have a director of corporate contributions

Description

Founded: 1984
EIN: 363350561
Organization Type: Corporate Foundation
Giving Locations: IL; IN; MI; MO; OH; WI headquarters and operating communities.
Grant Types: Employee Matching Gifts, Project.
Note: Employee matching gift ratio: 1 to 1 to eligible educational, arts and cultural organisation.

Giving Philosophy

'Education, economic development, the quality of life and employee volunteerism - these are Ameritech's cornerstones for providing enhanced telecommunications technologies and networking capabilities to be the world's premier provider of full-service communications for people at work, at home or on the move. 'Customers, first and foremost, are paramount to Ameritech. The company looks at its customers' desires as opportunities, and invests billions of dollars each year to provide them with high quality state-of-the-art communications products and services. As a responsible corporate citizen, Ameritech also invested more than $25 million of its earnings last year (1996) in selected educational, civic, health and human services, and cultural organizations.' *Contributions Guidelines*

Financial Summary

Total Giving: $28,113,500 (1998 approx); $19,814,196 (1997); $12,688,950 (1996). Note: Contributes through corporate direct giving program and foundation.
Giving Analysis: Giving for 1996 includes: foundation ($11,971,382); foundation matching gifts ($717,568); 1997: foundation ($14,114,196); corporate grants to United Way ($5,700,000); 1998: foundation ($22,613,500); foundation grants to United Way ($5,500,000); foundation matching gifts ($3,600,000)
Assets: $143,937,056 (1997); $121,194,904 (1996); $5,000,000 (1993)
Gifts Received: $5,000,000 (1997); $5,000,000 (1996). Note: Contributions are received from Ameritech Corp.

Typical Recipients

Arts & Humanities: Arts Associations & Councils, Arts Festivals, Arts Institutes, History & Archaeology, Libraries, Museums/Galleries, Music, Opera, Performing Arts
Civic & Public Affairs: African American Affairs, Business/Free Enterprise, Civil Rights, Community Foundations, Economic Development, Economic Policy, Employment/Job Training, Civic & Public Affairs-General, Hispanic Affairs, Housing, Public Policy, Urban & Community Affairs, Women's Affairs
Education: Arts/Humanities Education, Business Education, Colleges & Universities, Economic Education, Education Associations, Education Funds, Education Reform, Faculty Development, Education-General, Literacy, Minority Education, Public Education (Precollege), Science/Mathematics Education, Social Sciences Education
Environment: Environment-General
Health: Emergency/Ambulance Services, Medical Rehabilitation
International: Foreign Educational Institutions
Religion: Religious Welfare
Science: Observatories & Planetariums, Science Museums, Scientific Centers & Institutes
Social Services: Day Care, Senior Services, Special Olympics, United Funds/United Ways

Contributions Analysis

Giving Priorities: Education, economic development, quality of life in communities and volunteerism.
Arts & Humanities: 23%. Priority is given to: projects and programs that are rich in cultural diversity, provide broad educational experiences and enhance the economic vitality where Ameritech has a significant business presence; exhibits, events and performances on a selected and limited basis, and all with a strong educational component; and title sponsorships.
Civic & Public Affairs: 14%. Priority is given to: projects which stimulate urban renewal in partnership with key civic and community leaders and organizations; initiatives which address crime prevention and safety issues; programs that address environmental issues where company's outputs impact community needs and interest--e.g., recycling phone directories, cable, computer, telecommuting; projects which advance diversity, affirmative action and equal employment access; and a limited number of public policy organizations that address telecommunications, economic development, and regulation.
Education: 33%. Higher education priorities are: staffing and programs that advance state-of-the-art telecommunications technologies and their applications on campuses; faculty training programs for utilizing technology in the classroom; research, training and innovative applications of communications technologies; public policy that contributes to the understanding of communications and technology; and programs for colleges to attract and retain minority faculty and students. Elementary and secondary education priorities are: reading and economic literacy programs as basic educational needs; programs that help school administrators and teachers understand the use of telecommunications technologies; initiatives which encourage professional development for teachers to incorporate communications technologies into the classroom; programs that recognize and reward teachers who apply telecommunications technologies in teaching and learning; and alliances among schools to introduce new telecommunications technologies where it would otherwise be unaffordable.
Health: 27%. Majority of funding goes to United Ways in operating locations. Among other health and human service agencies, priority is given to: human service organizations that work collaboratively with educational and/or health institutions on clearly defined community needs; nonprofits that help seniors, the disabled and other health-related groups for programs that enhance the quality of life through the deployment of advanced telecommunications technologies; disaster relief efforts on a case-by-case basis; Special Olympics; and hospitals in limited, targeted, and proactive ways, to advance innovative uses of telecommunications technologies in measurable ways other health care providers can benefit from or emulate.
Note: Total contributions in 1998.

Application Procedures

Initial Contact: Send a brief letter of inquiry to director of contributions.
Application Requirements: Include a description of organization, its history and purpose; a list of the organization's board of directors and their affiliations; overview of proposed project for which funding is sought, including evidence of need; summary of the project's budget showing anticipated sources of revenue and expenses; amount requested; plans for publicizing grant and project; beneficiaries of program; measurements to evaluate the grant's effectiveness; population and geographic area served by organization and/or project; other corporate or foundation support, including a list of the organization's top 12 contributors and amounts they contribute on an annual basis; proof of 501(c)(3) status.
Deadlines: None.
Evaluative Criteria: Funded programs are unique and innovative; could serve as a model; and have the participation of Ameritech volunteers. Also considered are the rationale for request for support; constituencies served; benefits derived from organization's services; stated objectives, long-range planning, active participation and financial support by the governing body, professional staff, and volunteers; accountability through regular evaluation and public reporting; reliable financial information, including annual, audited financial statements; information to support fund-raising goals, time tables, and administrative expenses; lack of dependence on any single source of assistance; level of support from other corporations; priority is given to programs that are communications technology based.
Decision Notification: Board meets quarterly; initial response is typically within 6 weeks of receipt of request.
Notes: Each participating state has its own contributions committee. See separate entries for information.

Restrictions

Contributions are restricted to project support, except for the United Way.
The foundation does not support individuals; operating or annual support; hospitals or health centers; the purchase of computers or related equipment; religious organizations using funds for denominational or sectarian purposes; political organizations, candidates for political office, or organizations whose purpose is to influence legislation; discriminatory organizations; labor, veterans', military, or international organizations; athletic or sports programs (excluding Special Olympics and U.S. Olympics); foundations that are themselves grant-making bodies; individuals or organizations with a very limited constituency; service clubs raising money for community purposes; national health organizations (except for United Way); agencies supported by United Way; building capital campaigns; medical research; nursing or retirement homes; travel funds; organizations that receive considerable support from city, county, state or federal government; or organizations without 501(c)(3) public charity status from the Internal Revenue Service. The foundation also does not contribute toward special-occasion or goodwill advertising, benefit tickets, or fundraising events.
Company cannot donate or discount telecommunications services.

Additional Information

Priority is given to making larger, focused grants to fewer organizations, rather than many smaller grants. The Ameritech Foundation is designed to complement the philanthropic programs of the Ameritech family of companies. It focuses on innovative national and regional programs in economic development, public policy issues, and ways that communications can help improve society.
Requests are considered for unique and innovative projects and programs where Ameritech maintains services, maintenance, or corporate facilities. Priority

is given to communications technology-based projects and programs. Ameritech does not award grants to fund its own products and services.
Subsidiaries manage charitable giving programs that award additional contributions annually, principally to state and local organizations.
Only one contribution is generally made to an organization per year.
Ameritech is currently being bought by SBC Communications.
For current guidelines call (312)750-5037.
Publications: Contribution Guidelines; Community Service Report

Corporate Officials

Barry K. Allen: president regulatory & wholesale operation B Indianapolis, IN 1948. ED University of Kentucky BBA (1970); Boston College MBA (1974). PRIM CORP EMPL president regulatory & wholesale operation: Ameritech Corp. CORP AFFIL director: Harley-Davidson Inc.
Ronald L. Blake: president general business services ED University of Cincinnati MBA. PRIM CORP EMPL president general business services: Ameritech Corp.
W. Patrick Campbell: executive vice president corporate strategy & business development B 1946. ED LaSalle University BA (1968). PRIM CORP EMPL executive vice president corporate strategy & business development: Ameritech Corp.
Walter S. Catlow: executive vice president B 1944. ED Ball State University BA; Pace University MM. PRIM CORP EMPL executive vice president: Ameritech Corp.
Joel Stanley Engel: vice president technology B New York, NY 1936. ED City University of New York City College BSEE (1957); Massachusetts Institute of Technology MSEE (1959); Polytechnic Institute Brooklyn PhD (1964). PRIM CORP EMPL vice president technology: Ameritech Corp. NONPR AFFIL director: Syracuse Research Corp.; advisory board: University Illinois College of Engineering; member: National Academy Engineering; member: Sigma Xi; fellow: Institute Electrical & Electronics Engineers; executive advisory council: International Communications Forum; director: Alliance for Telecommunication Industry Solutions.
Melvin Russell Goodes: chairman, chief executive officer, director B Hamilton, ON Canada 1935. ED Queens University BComm (1957); University of Chicago MBA (1960). PRIM CORP EMPL chairman, chief executive officer, director: Warner-Lambert Co. ADD CORP EMPL president: Warner-Lambert Ltd. CORP AFFIL director: Unisys Corp.; officer: Chase Manhattan Bank; director: Chase Manhattan Corp.; director: Ameritech Corp. NONPR AFFIL member: Proprietary Association; trustee: Queens University; member: National Wholesale Druggists Association; member: Pharmaceutical Manufacturer Association; member: National Association Retail Druggists; member finance committee: National Council Economic Education; director: National Alliance Business; member: International Executive Service Corps. CLUB AFFIL Plainfield Country Club; Pine Valley Golf Club.
James Alan Henderson: vice chairman, chief executive officer, director B South Bend, IN 1934. ED Princeton University AB (1956); Harvard University MBA (1963). PRIM CORP EMPL chairman, chief executive officer, director: Cummins Engine Co. Inc. CORP AFFIL director: Rohm & Haas Co.; director: Inland Steel Industries Inc.; director: Landmark Communications Inc.; director: Ameritech Corp. NONPR AFFIL member policy commission: Business Roundtable; president board trustee: Culver Education Foundation; member: Business Council.
Bruce Bradshaw Howat, Jr.: secretary, corporate counsel B Fresno, CA 1945. ED University of Illinois (1967); University of Illinois JD (1970). PRIM CORP EMPL secretary, corporate counsel: Ameritech Corp. ADD CORP EMPL secretary: Ameritech Monitoring Services Inc.
Barbara A. Klein: vice president, comptroller B Pittsburgh, PA 1954. ED Loyola University MBA; Marquette University BA (1976). PRIM CORP EMPL vice president, comptroller: Ameritech Corp.
Sheldon B. Lubar: chairman B Milwaukee, WI 1929. ED University of Wisconsin BA (1951); University of Wisconsin LLB (1953); University of Wisconsin DSc (1988). PRIM CORP EMPL chairman: Christiana Companies, Inc. CORP AFFIL director: MGIC Investment Corp.; director: Weatherford International Inc.; chairman: Lubar & Co.; director: Massachusetts Mutual Life Insurance Co.; director: EVI Weatherford Inc.; director: Firstar Bank Corp.; director: Ameritech Corp.
Gary R. Lytle: vice president federal relations B Detroit, MI 1943. ED Michigan State University MBA (1966). PRIM CORP EMPL vice president federal relations: Ameritech Corp. NONPR AFFIL member: United States Tel Association.
Sari Macrie: vice president investor relations ED Arizona State University MBA; University of Maryland BS. PRIM CORP EMPL vice president investor relations: Ameritech Corp.
John Bonnet McCoy: president, chief executive officer B Columbus, OH 1943. ED Williams College (1965); Stanford University (1967). PRIM CORP EMPL president, chief executive officer: Bank One Corp. CORP AFFIL director: Tenneco Inc.; director: Cardinal Health Inc.; director: Federal Home Loan Mortgage Corp.; director: Ameritech Corp.; chairman: Capitol South Urdan Redev Corp. NONPR AFFIL trustee: Stanford University; member: Young President Organization; director: Senior PGA Tour; director: Federal National Mortgage Association; trustee: Kenyon College; president: Columbus Area Growth Foundation; member: Columbus Chamber of Commerce; active: Boy Scouts America; member: Bankers Roundtable; trustee: Battelle Memorial Institute; member: American Bankers Association; member: Association Bank Holding Companies. CLUB AFFIL Seminole Golf Club; Cypress Point Club; Links Club New York.
Richard C. Notebaert: chairman, chief executive officer B Montreal, PQ Canada 1948. ED University of Wisconsin BA (1969); University of Wisconsin MBA (1983). PRIM CORP EMPL chairman, chief executive officer: Ameritech Corp. CORP AFFIL director: SBC Communications Inc.; director: Sears, Roebuck & Co.; director: AON Corp.
Walter Maurice Oliver: senior vice president human resources B Decatur, IL 1945. ED Whitworth College BA (1967); Gonzaga University MS (1977). PRIM CORP EMPL senior vice president human resources: Ameritech Corp.
John Doyle Ong: chairman board, director B Uhrichsville, OH 1933. ED Ohio State University BA (1954); Ohio State University MA (1954); Harvard University LLB (1957); Kent State University LHD (1982); Ohio State University H (1996); University of Akron H (1996). CORP AFFIL director: Marsh & McLennan Companies Inc.; director: TRW Inc.; director: Geon Co.; chairman emeritus: B.F. Goodrich Co.; director: Cooper Industries Inc.; director: ASARCO Inc.; director: Ameritech Corp. NONPR AFFIL member: Rubber Manufacturer Association; trustee: University Chicago; member: Phi Alpha Theta; member: Phi Beta Kappa; member: Ohio Bar Association; chairman: Ohio Historic Society; member: Conference Board; chairman: Business Roundtable Ohio; member: Chemical Manufacturers Association; member: Business Council. CLUB AFFIL Union League Club; Union Club; Portage Country Club; Rolling Rock Club; Ottawa Shooting Club; The Links Club; Metro Club; Castalia Trout Club.
Richard W. Pehlke: vice president, treasurer B Oak Park, IL 1953. ED Valparaiso University BS (1975); DePaul University MS (1983). PRIM CORP EMPL vice president, treasurer: Ameritech Corp. CORP AFFIL director: Ideal Industries Inc.; director: Telecom New Zealand Ltd. NONPR AFFIL member: National Association of Corporate Treasurers; member: National Investor Relations Institute; member: Financial Executives Institute.
Thomas Jay Reiman: senior vice president public policy B Chicago, IL 1949. ED Georgia State University (1971); Mercer University (1974). PRIM CORP EMPL senior vice president public policy: Ameritech Corp. CORP AFFIL director: Anicom Inc.
Thomas E. Richards: executive vice president communications information products sector B 1954. ED University of Pittsburgh BA (1976); Massachusetts Institute of Technology MS (1991). PRIM CORP EMPL executive vice president communications information products sector: Ameritech Corp.
Oren G. Shaffer: executive vice president, chief financial officer B Sharpsville, PA 1942. ED University of California BS (1968); Massachusetts Institute of Technology MS (1985). PRIM CORP EMPL executive vice president, chief financial officer: Ameritech Corp. CORP AFFIL director: Sunshine Mining Ref Co. NONPR AFFIL member: National Association Accts; member: Officers Conference Group; member: Financial Executives Institute. CLUB AFFIL Portage Country Club; Firestone Country Club.
Lawrence E. Strickling: vice president, president public policy ED Harvard University LLB; University of Maryland BA. PRIM CORP EMPL vice president, president public policy: Ameritech Corp.
John Vaughn: vice president unit development & strategy ED Purdue University BS; University of Notre Dame MBA. PRIM CORP EMPL vice president unit development & strategy: Ameritech Corp.
Joan H. Walker: senior vice president corporate communications B 1947. ED Douglass College BA (1968); Rutgers University MA (1973). PRIM CORP EMPL senior vice president corporate communications: Ameritech Corp.
Kelly Raymond Welsh: executive vice president, general counsel B Chicago, IL 1952. ED Harvard University AB (1974); Sussex University (England) MA (1975); Harvard University JD (1978). PRIM CORP EMPL executive vice president, general counsel: Ameritech Corp. NONPR AFFIL member: Council Foreign Relations Chicago; chairman: Metropolitan Pier & Exposition Authority; member: Chicago Council Lawyers; member: American Bar Association; member: Chicago Bar Association. CLUB AFFIL Legal Club.

Giving Program Officials

Michael E. Kuhlin: manager PRIM CORP EMPL director corporate contributions: Ameritech Corp.

Foundation Officials

Robert L. Barnett: director B 1940. ED Oberlin College BA (1961); Case Western Reserve University BSEE (1963); Xavier University MSEE (1964). PRIM CORP EMPL executive vice president, president: iDen Group, Motorola Inc. CORP AFFIL director: Johnson Controls Inc.; director: USG Corp.
Ronald L. Blake: director (see above)
Lynn M. Martin: director CORP AFFIL director: TRW Inc.; director: Ryder System Inc.; director: Harcourt General Inc.; director: Procter & Gamble Co. NONPR AFFIL Davee Chair: Northwestern University Kellogg Graduate School Business Management.
Arthur Naravjo: treasurer
Richard C. Notebaert: director (see above)
Laura D'Andrea Tyson: director B Bayonne, NJ 1947. ED Smith College BA (1968); Massachusetts Institute of Technology PhD (1974). PRIM NONPR EMPL professor economics: University of California, Berkeley. CORP AFFIL director: Ameritech Corp.; director: Eastman Kodak Co.
James Arlen Unruh: director B Goodrich, ND 1941. ED Jamestown College BSBA (1963); University of Denver MBA (1964). CORP AFFIL director: Ameritech Corp.; director: Prudential Insurance Co. America. NONPR AFFIL member: President National Security Telecommunications Advisory Committee; member, board overseers: University Pennsylvania Wharton School Business; member: Pennsylvania Business Roundtable; vice chairman: Greater Philadelphia First Corp.; trustee: Jamestown College;

member executive committee: Computer Systems Policy Project; chairman: Franklin Institute.

Grants Analysis

Disclosure Period: calendar year ending 1997
Typical Range: $10,000 to $100,000

Recent Grants

Note: Grants derived from 1997 Form 990.

Arts & Humanities

500,000	Library of Congress, Washington, DC
500,000	Library of Congress, Washington, DC
500,000	Library of Congress, Washington, DC
350,000	Chicago Symphony Orchestra, Chicago, IL
350,000	Orchestral Association
200,000	Art Institute of Chicago, Chicago, IL
200,000	Art Institute of Chicago, Chicago, IL

Civic & Public Affairs

1,532,681	Matching Gift Program
1,402,916	Matching Gift Center - Employee, NJ
1,212,414	Matching Gift Center - Employee, NJ
1,139,678	Matching Gift Program
923,026	Matching Gift Center - Employee, NJ
853,724	Matching Gift Program
674,718	Matching Gift Center - Employee, NJ
495,622	Matching Gift Center - Employee, NJ
450,000	Pioneering Partners Foundation, Centerville, MA
407,686	Matching Gift Center - Employee, NJ
391,425	Matching Gift Center - Employee, NJ
373,889	Matching Gift Center - Employee, NJ
340,592	Matching Gift Center - Employee, NJ
325,367	Matching Gift Center - Employee, NJ
320,512	Matching Gift Center - Employee, NJ
208,545	Matching Gift Center - Employee, NJ

Education

428,000	Northwestern University, Evanston, IL
428,000	Northwestern University, Evanston, IL
360,000	Northwestern University, Evanston, IL
325,000	Foundation for Independent Higher Education, Chicago, IL
325,000	Foundation for Independent Higher Education, Chicago, IL
300,000	Michigan State University, East Lansing, MI
300,000	Michigan State University, East Lansing, MI
300,000	Michigan State University, East Lansing, MI
261,000	University of Wisconsin - Madison, Madison, WI
250,000	Case Western Reserve University, Cleveland, OH
250,000	Case Western Reserve University, Cleveland, OH
250,000	Western Illinois University, Macomb, IL
240,000	Case Western Reserve University, Cleveland, OH
240,000	Ohio State University, Columbus, OH
240,000	Purdue University, West Lafayette, IN
240,000	Purdue University, West Lafayette, IN
240,000	University, West Lafayette, IN
200,000	Ohio State University, Columbus, OH
200,000	Reading is Fundamental - National, Washington, DC
200,000	University of Illinois Foundation, Champaign, IL
200,000	University of Wisconsin Foundation, Madison, WI
100,000	University of Illinois Chicago, Chicago, IL

Environment

755,742	Miscellaneous Awards

Social Services

270,000	National Council on the Aging, Washington, DC
270,000	National Council on the Aging, Washington, DC

AMERITECH ILLINOIS

Company Contact

Chicago, IL
Web: http://www.ameritech.com

Company Description

Former Name: Illinois Bell Telephone Co.
SIC(s): 4813 Telephone Communications Except Radiotelephone.
Parent Company: Ameritech Corp., Chicago, IL, United States
Parent Revenue: US$49,489,000,000 (1999)

Nonmonetary Support

Value: $175,000 (1991); $200,000 (1987)
Type: Donated Equipment; In-kind Services; Loaned Executives
Note: Nonmonetary support is provided through the company.

Giving Contact

Donna Jernigan, Director of Corporate Contributions
Ameritech Illinois
225 West Randolph, 30-A
Chicago, IL 60606

Alternate Contact

Mike Kuhlin, Senior Director of Corporate Contributions
Ameritech Corp.
30 South Wacker Drive, 34th Floor
Chicago, IL 60606
Phone: (312)750-5037

Description

Organization Type: Corporate Giving Program
Giving Locations: IL
Grant Types: Employee Matching Gifts, General Support, Project.
Note: Employee matching gift ratio: 1 to 1 for gifts to eligible educational and arts and cultural organisation.

Financial Summary

Total Giving: Contributes through corporate direct giving program and foundation. See Ameritech Corp. entry for details.

Typical Recipients

Arts & Humanities: Community Arts, Dance, Museums/Galleries, Music, Opera, Theater
Civic & Public Affairs: Civil Rights, Economic Development, Housing, Law & Justice, Public Policy, Urban & Community Affairs, Zoos/Aquariums
Education: Colleges & Universities, Economic Education, Engineering/Technological Education, Science/Mathematics Education
Health: Health Policy/Cost Containment, Health Organizations
Social Services: Community Service Organizations, People with Disabilities, Substance Abuse, United Funds/United Ways, Youth Organizations

Contributions Analysis

Giving Priorities: Health, social welfare, higher education, culture, and civic interests.

Application Procedures

Initial Contact: a brief letter of inquiry to Donna Jernigan, director of contributions
Application Requirements: description of the organization, its history and purpose; list of board members and affiliations; overview of project, including evidence of need; summary of project budget, showing anticipated sources of revenue and expenses; amount requested; measurements to evaluate grant's effectiveness; plans for publicizing the grant and project; geographic area served by organization and project; beneficiaries of program; other corporate or foundation support, including a list of organization's top 12 contributors, and amounts contributed annually; copy of IRS tax-exempt determination letter
Deadlines: None.
Evaluative Criteria: unique and innovative project, which could serve as a model; participation of Ameritech volunteers; projects serve Ameritech operating area; projects and programs are measurable, where stated goals and objectives can be measured against established criteria; priority is given to communications technology-based projects
Decision Notification: board meets quarterly; initial response usually within six weeks of receipt of letter of inquiry

Restrictions

Contributions are restricted to project support, except for the United Way.
Company cannot donate or discount telecommunications services.
Ameritech will not consider requests from: organizations which are not tax-exempt; discriminatory organizations; political organizations, candidates for political office, or groups whose primary purpose is to influence legislation; religious organizations when denominational or sectarian in purpose; affiliates of labor organizations; national health organizations, other than United Way; building capital campaigns; medical research; nursing or retirement homes; local athletic or sports programs, excluding Special Olympics and U.S. Olympics; organizations benefiting only a few people; service organizations raising money for community purposes, or second-party giving; special occasion, good will, program advertising, or special interest magazines; annual support for United Way agencies; individuals; travel funds for tours, expeditions, or trips; or organizations which receive sizable portions of their support through municipal, county, state, or federal dollars.

Additional Information

Ameritech Illinois was formerly known as Illinois Bell.

Giving Program Officials

Donna Jernigan: manager PRIM CORP EMPL director corporate contributions: Ameritech Illinois.

AMERITECH INDIANA

Company Contact

Indianapolis, IN
Web: http://www.ameritech.com

Company Description

Former Name: Indiana Bell Telephone Co.
SIC(s): 4813 Telephone Communications Except Radiotelephone.
Parent Company: Ameritech Corp., Chicago, IL, United States
Parent Revenue: US$49,489,000,000 (1999)

Nonmonetary Support

Type: Loaned Executives

Giving Contact

LeeAnn Hoy, Director, Corporate Contributions
240 North Meridian, 1811
Indianapolis, IN 46204
Phone: (317)265-5339
Fax: (317)265-4354

Alternate Contact

Mike Kuhlin, Senior Director of Corporate Contributions
Ameritech Corp.
30 South Wacker Drive, 34th Floor
Chicago, IL 60606

Phone: (312)750-5037

Description

Organization Type: Corporate Giving Program
Giving Locations: IN: principally near operating locations and to national organizations
Grant Types: Employee Matching Gifts, Project.
Note: Employee matching gift ratio: 1 to 1 for gifts to eligible educational, arts or cultural organisation.

Financial Summary

Total Giving: Contributes through corporate direct giving program and foundation. See Ameritech Corp. entry for details.

Typical Recipients

Arts & Humanities: Arts Appreciation, Arts Associations & Councils, Arts Centers, Arts Festivals, Arts Funds, Arts Institutes, Community Arts, Dance, Ethnic & Folk Arts, Historic Preservation, Literary Arts, Museums/Galleries, Music, Opera, Theater, Visual Arts
Civic & Public Affairs: Business/Free Enterprise, Economic Development, Economic Policy, Employment/Job Training, Philanthropic Organizations, Urban & Community Affairs, Women's Affairs, Zoos/Aquariums
Education: Arts/Humanities Education, Business Education, Colleges & Universities, Continuing Education, Economic Education, Elementary Education (Private), Engineering/Technological Education, Faculty Development, Journalism/Media Education, Legal Education, Literacy, Minority Education, Private Education (Precollege), Public Education (Precollege), Science/Mathematics Education, Social Sciences Education
Health: Health Policy/Cost Containment
Science: Science Exhibits & Fairs, Scientific Organizations
Social Services: Community Centers, Community Service Organizations, People with Disabilities, Senior Services, Substance Abuse, United Funds/United Ways, Youth Organizations

Application Procedures

Initial Contact: a brief letter of inquiry to director of contributions
Application Requirements: a description of organization, its history and purpose; list of board members and affiliations; overview of project, including evidence of need; summary of project budget, showing anticipated sources of revenue and expenses; amount requested; measurements to evaluate grant's effectiveness; plans for publicizing the grant and project; geographic area served by organization and project; beneficiaries of program; other corporate or foundation support, including a list of organization's top 12 contributors and amounts contributed annually; copy of IRS tax-exempt determination letter
Deadlines: None.
Evaluative Criteria: unique and innovative project, which could serve as a model; participation of Ameritech volunteers; projects serve Ameritech operating areas; projects and programs are measurable, where stated goals and objectives can be measured against established criteria; priority is given to communications technology-based projects
Decision Notification: board meets quarterly; initial response usually within six weeks of receipt of letter of inquiry

Restrictions

Contributions are restricted to project support, except for the United Way.
Company cannot donate or discount telecommunications services.
Ameritech will not consider requests from: organizations which are not tax-exempt; discriminatory organizations; political organizations, candidates for political office, or groups whose primary purpose is to influence legislation; religious organizations when denominational or sectarian in purpose; affiliates of labor organizations; national health organizations, other than United Way; building capital campaigns; medical research; nursing or retirement homes; local athletic or sports programs, excluding Special Olympics and U.S. Olympics; organizations benefiting only a few people; service organizations raising money for community purposes, or second-party giving; special occasion, good will, program advertising, or special interest magazines; annual support for United Way agencies; individuals; travel funds for tours, expeditions, or trips; or organizations which receive sizable portions of their support through municipal, county, state, or federal dollars.

Additional Information

Ameritech Indiana was formerly known as Indiana Bell.

Corporate Officials

Lee Ann Hoy: director corporate contributions
Kent A. Lebherz: president PRIM CORP EMPL president: Ameritech Indiana. CORP AFFIL director: Ameritech Services Inc. Delaware.

AMERITECH MICHIGAN

Company Contact

Detroit, MI
Web: http://www.ameritech.com

Company Description

Former Name: Michigan Bell Telephone Co.
Employees: 66,128
SIC(s): 4813 Telephone Communications Except Radiotelephone.
Parent Company: Ameritech Corp., Chicago, IL, United States
Parent Revenue: US$49,489,000,000 (1999)

Nonmonetary Support

Type: Donated Products; In-kind Services; Loaned Executives

Corporate Sponsorship

Type: Arts & cultural events; Festivals/fairs; Music & entertainment events; Sports events
Contact: Lisa Bellford, Sponsorship Manager

Giving Contact

Lisa Hamway, Director, Corporate Contributions
Ameritech Michigan
444 Michigan Avenue, Room 1550
Detroit, MI 48226
Phone: (313)223-5747
Fax: (313)496-9332

Alternate Contact

Mike Kuhlin, Senior Director of Corporate Contributions
Ameritech
30 South Wacker Drive, 34th Floor
Chicago, IL 60606
Phone: (312)750-5037
Fax: (312)207-1098

Description

Organization Type: Corporate Giving Program
Giving Locations: MI: emphasis on the Detroit metropolitan area
Grant Types: Award, Employee Matching Gifts, Project.
Note: Employee matching gift ratio: 1 to 1 for gifts to eligible educational, arts and cultural organisation.

Financial Summary

Total Giving: Contributes through corporate direct giving program and foundation. See Ameritech Corp. entry for details.

Typical Recipients

Arts & Humanities: Arts Associations & Councils, Arts Centers, Community Arts, Historic Preservation, Museums/Galleries, Music, Opera, Performing Arts, Public Broadcasting, Theater
Civic & Public Affairs: Business/Free Enterprise, Civil Rights, Economic Development, Law & Justice, Safety, Urban & Community Affairs, Zoos/Aquariums
Education: Arts/Humanities Education, Business Education, Colleges & Universities, Education Associations, Education Funds, Engineering/Technological Education, Science/Mathematics Education
Environment: Environment-General
Health: Geriatric Health, Hospitals
International: Health Care/Hospitals
Religion: Religious Organizations, Religious Welfare
Science: Science Exhibits & Fairs
Social Services: Community Service Organizations, Family Planning, Family Services, Food/Clothing Distribution, Recreation & Athletics, Senior Services, United Funds/United Ways, Youth Organizations

Contributions Analysis

Giving Priorities: Public and private two- and four-year colleges in Michigan, economic development, united funds and other social service organizations, and performing arts.

Application Procedures

Initial Contact: a brief letter of inquiry to Lisa Hamway, director of contributions
Application Requirements: a description of organization, its history and purpose; list of board members and affiliations; overview of project, including evidence of need; summary of project budget, showing anticipated sources of revenue and expenses; amount requested; measurements to evaluate grant's effectiveness; plans for publicizing the grant and project; geographic area served by organization and project; beneficiaries of program; other corporate or foundation support, including a list of organization's top 12 contributors, and amounts contributed annually; copy of IRS tax-exempt determination letter
Deadlines: None.
Evaluative Criteria: unique and innovative project, which could serve as a model; participation of Ameritech volunteers; projects serve Ameritech operating areas; projects and programs are measurable, where stated goals and objectives can be measured against established criteria; priority is given to communications technology-based projects
Decision Notification: board meets quarterly; initial response usually within six weeks of receipt of letter of inquiry

Restrictions

Contributions are restricted to project support, except for the United Way.
Company cannot donate or discount telecommunications services.
Ameritech will not consider requests from: organizations which are not tax-exempt; discriminatory organizations; political organizations, candidates for political office, or groups whose primary purpose is to influence legislation; religious organizations when denominational or sectarian in purpose; affiliates of labor organizations; national health organizations, other than United Way; building capital campaigns; medical research; nursing or retirement homes; local athletic or sports programs, excluding Special Olympics and U.S. Olympics; organizations benefiting only a few people; service organizations raising money for community purposes, or second-party giving; special occasion, good will, program advertising, or special interest magazines; annual support for United Way

agencies; individuals; travel funds for tours, expeditions, or trips; or organizations which receive sizable portions of their support through municipal, county, state, or federal dollars.

Additional Information

Ameritech Michigan was formerly known as Michigan Bell.

Corporate Officials

Robert N. Cooper: president corporate contributions PRIM CORP EMPL president: Ameritech Michigan. CORP AFFIL director: Ameritech Service Inc.
Lisa Hamway: director corporate contributions PRIM CORP EMPL director corporate contributions: Ameritech Michigan.

Giving Program Officials

Lyn Allen: PRIM CORP EMPL director corporate contributions: Ameritech Michigan.

AMERITECH OHIO

Company Contact

Cleveland, OH
Web: http://www.ameritech.com

Company Description

Former Name: Ohio Bell Telephone Co.
SIC(s): 4813 Telephone Communications Except Radiotelephone.
Parent Company: Ameritech Corp., Chicago, IL, United States
Parent Revenue: US$49,489,000,000 (1999)

Nonmonetary Support

Value: $39,000 (1992); $11,706 (1991); $94,701 (1990)
Type: Donated Equipment
Note: Nonmonetary support is supplied by the company.

Corporate Sponsorship

Type: Arts & cultural events; Music & entertainment events

Giving Contact

William W. Boag, Jr., Director, Corporate Contributions
Ameritech Ohio
45 Erieview Plaza, Room 1457
Cleveland, OH 44114
Phone: (216)822-2423
Fax: (216)822-5522

Alternate Contact

Mike Kuhlin, Senior Director of Corporate Contributions
Ameritech Corp.
30 South Wacker Drive, 34th Floor
Chicago, IL 60606
Phone: (312)750-5154
Fax: (312)207-1098

Description

Organization Type: Corporate Giving Program
Former Name: Ameritech Ohio Foundation.
Giving Locations: OH: company's service area
Grant Types: Employee Matching Gifts, Project.
Note: Employee matching gift ratio: 1 to 1 for gifts to eligible educational, arts and cultural organisation.

Financial Summary

Total Giving: Contributes through corporate direct giving program only. See Ameritech Corp. entry for details.

Typical Recipients

Arts & Humanities: Arts Institutes, Arts & Humanities-General, Museums/Galleries, Music, Opera, Performing Arts, Public Broadcasting, Theater
Civic & Public Affairs: African American Affairs, Botanical Gardens/Parks, Civic & Public Affairs-General, Parades/Festivals, Public Policy, Urban & Community Affairs, Zoos/Aquariums
Education: Business Education, Colleges & Universities, Economic Education, Education Funds, Literacy, Private Education (Precollege), Public Education (Precollege), Science/Mathematics Education, Student Aid
Health: Clinics/Medical Centers, Health Policy/Cost Containment, Speech & Hearing
Science: Science Exhibits & Fairs, Science Museums, Scientific Centers & Institutes
Social Services: Animal Protection, Community Service Organizations, Recreation & Athletics, Scouts, United Funds/United Ways, Volunteer Services, YMCA/YWCA/YMHA/YWHA

Contributions Analysis

Giving Priorities: United Way, program funds for private, independent colleges of Ohio, leading cultural institutions in operating cities, and civic and community projects.

Application Procedures

Initial Contact: a brief letter of inquiry to Bill Boag, director of contributions
Application Requirements: a description of organization, its history and purpose; list of board members and affiliations; overview of project, including evidence of need; summary of project budget, showing anticipated sources of revenue and expenses; amount requested; measurements to evaluate grant's effectiveness; plans for publicizing the grant and project; geographic area served by organization and project; beneficiaries of program; other corporate or foundation support, including a list of organization's top 12 contributors, and amounts contributed annually; copy of IRS tax-exempt determination letter
Deadlines: None.
Evaluative Criteria: unique and innovative project, which could serve as a model; participation of Ameritech volunteers; projects serve Ameritech operating areas; projects and programs are measurable, where stated goals and objectives can be measured against established criteria; priority is given to communications technology-based projects
Decision Notification: board meets quarterly; initial response usually within six weeks of receipt of letter of inquiry

Restrictions

Contributions are restricted to project support, except for the United Way.
Company cannot donate or discount telecommunications services.
Ameritech will not consider requests from: organizations which are not tax-exempt; discriminatory organizations; political organizations, candidates for political office, or groups whose primary purpose is to influence legislation; religious organizations when denominational or sectarian in purpose; affiliates of labor organizations; national health organizations, other than United Way; building capital campaigns; medical research; nursing or retirement homes; local athletic or sports programs, excluding Special Olympics and U.S. Olympics; organizations benefiting only a few people; service organizations raising money for community purposes, or second-party giving; special occasion, good will, program advertising, or special interest magazines; annual support for United Way agencies; individuals; travel funds for tours, expeditions, or trips; or organizations which receive sizable portions of their support through municipal, county, state, or federal dollars.

Additional Information

Ameritech Ohio was formerly known as Ohio Bell.
Publications: Guidelines

Corporate Officials

Jacqueline F. Woods: president PRIM CORP EMPL president: Ameritech Ohio. NONPR AFFIL vice chairman: Great Lakes Museum Science Environment.

Giving Program Officials

William W. Boag, Jr.: PRIM CORP EMPL director corporate contributions: Ameritech Ohio.

Grants Analysis

Disclosure Period: calendar year ending

Recent Grants

Note: Grants derived from 1994 Form 990.

Arts & Humanities

83,000	Musical Arts Association, Cleveland, OH
83,000	Musical Arts Association, Cleveland, OH
70,000	Rock-N-Roll Hall of Fame and Museum, Cleveland, OH
15,000	Karamu House, Cleveland, OH
14,900	Columbus Symphony Orchestra, Columbus, OH
14,000	Columbus Association for Performing Arts, Columbus, OH
10,000	Playhouse Square Foundation, Cleveland, OH
6,527	Educational Television Association of Metro Cleveland, Cleveland, OH
5,930	Cleveland Museum of Art, Cleveland, OH
5,500	Victoria Theater Association, Dayton, OH

Civic & Public Affairs

25,000	Greater Cleveland Roundtable, Cleveland, OH
16,700	Cleveland Bicentennial Commission, Cleveland, OH
6,250	Columbus Urban League, Columbus, OH
5,000	Urban League of Greater Cleveland, Cleveland, OH
5,000	Wilds, Columbus, OH

Education

250,000	University of Findlay, Findlay, OH
250,000	University of Findlay, Findlay, OH
144,000	Ohio Department of Education, Cleveland, OH
125,000	Ohio Foundation of Independent Colleges, Columbus, OH
60,000	Cleveland State University Development Foundation, Cleveland, OH
60,000	Cleveland State University Development Foundation, Cleveland, OH
50,000	Cleveland Development Foundation, Inner-City Schools Fund, Cleveland, OH
40,000	Case Western Reserve University, Cleveland, OH
40,000	Case Western Reserve University, Cleveland, OH
20,000	Cleveland City Schools Fund, Cleveland, OH
20,000	John Carroll University, University Heights, OH
15,000	University of Rio Grande, Rio Grande, OH
11,000	Junior Achievement of Greater Cleveland, Cleveland, OH
10,000	Read for Literacy, Toledo, OH
9,230	Ohio State University Development Fund, Columbus, OH
5,700	Dartmouth College, Hanover, NH
5,500	University of Virginia, Charlottesville, VA
5,000	Findlay City Schools, Findlay, OH

Health

75,000 Cleveland Clinic Foundation, Cleveland, OH

25,000 Central Ohio Speech and Hearing Center, Columbus, OH

Science

200,000 Inventure Place, Cleveland, OH

100,000 Great Lakes Museum of Science, Environment, and Technology, Cleveland, OH

100,000 Great Lakes Museum of Science, Environment, and Technology, Cleveland, OH

25,000 Center of Science and Industry, Toledo, OH

Social Services

262,500 United Way Services, Cleveland, OH

131,250 United Way Services, Cleveland, OH

90,950 United Way Franklin County, Columbus, OH

45,475 United Way Franklin County, Columbus, OH

30,000 United Way Greater Toledo, Toledo, OH

15,000 United Way Greater Toledo, Toledo, OH

10,000 Business Volunteerism Council, Cleveland, OH

10,000 Business Volunteerism Council, Cleveland, OH

5,000 Boy Scouts of America Central Ohio Council, Columbus, OH

5,000 Family YMCA Lancaster and Fairfield County, Lancaster, OH

5,000 Timber House, Columbus, OH

AMERITECH WISCONSIN

Company Contact

Milwaukee, WI
Web: http://www.ameritech.com

Company Description

Former Name: Wisconsin Bell, Inc.
SIC(s): 4813 Telephone Communications Except Radiotelephone.
Parent Company: Ameritech Corp., Chicago, IL, United States
Parent Revenue: US$49,489,000,000 (1999)

Giving Contact

Peggy Larson, Director, Corporate Contributions
Ameritech Wisconsin
722 North Broadway, 13th Floor
Milwaukee, WI 53202
Phone: (414)678-2310
Fax: (414)678-2756

Alternate Contact

Mike Kuhlin, Senior Director of Corporate Contributions
Ameritech Corp.
30 South Wacker Drive, 34th Floor
Chicago, IL 60606
Phone: (312)750-5154
Fax: (312)207-1098

Description

Organization Type: Corporate Giving Program
Giving Locations: WI: operating locations in Wisconsin
Grant Types: Employee Matching Gifts, Project.
Note: Employee matching gift ratio: 1 to 1 for gifts to eligible educational, arts and cultural organisation.

Financial Summary

Total Giving: Contributes through corporate direct giving program and foundation. See Ameritech Corp. entry for details.

Typical Recipients

Arts & Humanities: Arts Associations & Councils, Arts Centers, Arts Festivals, Historic Preservation, Museums/Galleries, Music, Performing Arts, Public Broadcasting
Civic & Public Affairs: African American Affairs, Employment/Job Training, Civic & Public Affairs-General, Law & Justice, Parades/Festivals, Urban & Community Affairs, Zoos/Aquariums
Education: Business Education, Colleges & Universities, Economic Education, Education-General, Public Education (Precollege), Science/Mathematics Education
Environment: Environment-General
Health: AIDS/HIV, Cancer, Clinics/Medical Centers, Health-General, Hospitals
Religion: Religious Welfare
Social Services: At-Risk Youth, Community Centers, Community Service Organizations, People with Disabilities, Recreation & Athletics, Social Services-General, Substance Abuse, United Funds/United Ways, Youth Organizations

Application Procedures

Initial Contact: a brief letter of inquiry to Peggy Larson, director of contributions
Application Requirements: a description of organization, its history and purpose; list of board members and affiliations; overview of project, including evidence of need; summary of project budget, showing anticipated sources of revenue and expenses; amount requested; measurements to evaluate grant's effectiveness; plans for publicizing the grant and project; geographic area served by organization and project; beneficiaries of program; other corporate or foundation support, including a list of organization's top 12 contributors, and amounts contributed annually; copy of IRS tax-exempt determination letter
Deadlines: None.
Evaluative Criteria: unique and innovative project, which could serve as a model; participation of Ameritech volunteers; projects serve Ameritech operating areas; projects and programs are measurable, where stated goals and objectives can be measured against established criteria; priority is given to communications technology-based projects
Decision Notification: board meets quarterly; initial response usually within six weeks of receipt of letter of inquiry

Restrictions

Contributions are restricted to project support, except for the United Way.
Company cannot donate or discount telecommunications services.
Ameritech will not consider requests from: organizations which are not tax-exempt; discriminatory organizations; political organizations, candidates for political office, or groups whose primary purpose is to influence legislation; religious organizations when denominational or sectarian in purpose; affiliates of labor organizations; national health organizations, other than United Way; building capital campaigns; medical research; nursing or retirement homes; local athletic or sports programs, excluding Special Olympics and U.S. Olympics; organizations benefiting only a few people; service organizations raising money for community purposes, or second-party giving; special occasion, good will, program advertising, or special interest magazines; annual support for United Way agencies; individuals; travel funds for tours, expeditions, or trips; or organizations which receive sizable portions of their support through municipal, county, state, or federal dollars.

Additional Information

Ameritech Wisconsin was formerly known as Wisconsin Bell.

Corporate Officials

Bronson J. Haase: president, chief executive officer B 1943. PRIM CORP EMPL president, chief executive officer: WICOR Energy Service Co. CORP AFFIL vice president: WICOR Inc.; president, chief executive officer: Wisconsin Gas Co.; president, chief executive officer: Field Tech Inc.

Giving Program Officials

Peggy Larson: manager PRIM CORP EMPL director corporate contributions: Ameritech Wisconsin. NONPR AFFIL director: Easter Seal Society Milwaukee.

Grants Analysis

Disclosure Period: calendar year ending

Recent Grants

Note: Grants derived from 1994 grants list.

Arts & Humanities

95,000 United Performing Arts Fund, Milwaukee, WI

25,000 Children's Museum

7,500 Madison Civic Music Association, Madison, WI

AMERUS GROUP

Company Contact

Des Moines, IA

Company Description

Former Name: American Mutual Life Insurance Co., Central Companies.
Employees: 179
SIC(s): 6311 Life Insurance.

Nonmonetary Support

Value: $75,000 (1997 approx); $65,000 (1994); $40,000 (1993)
Type: Donated Equipment; In-kind Services; Loaned Employees; Loaned Executives
Note: Co. provides nonmonetary support.

Giving Contact

Director, Community Relations
699 Walnut Street
Des Moines, IA 50309
Phone: (515)557-3910
Fax: (515)283-3269

Description

Organization Type: Corporate Giving Program
Giving Locations: IA
Grant Types: Capital, Employee Matching Gifts, General Support.
Note: Employee matching gifts have a $500 maximum.

Financial Summary

Total Giving: $1,400,000 (1998 approx); $1,400,000 (1997 approx); $1,400,000 (1996 approx). Note: Contributes through corporate direct giving program only. 1997 Giving includes nonmonetary support.

Typical Recipients

Arts & Humanities: Arts Associations & Councils, Arts Centers, Community Arts, Arts & Humanities-General, Music, Opera, Performing Arts
Civic & Public Affairs: Business/Free Enterprise, Economic Development, Housing
Education: Community & Junior Colleges, Education-General, Public Education (Precollege)
Health: Health-General, Hospices

Social Services: Community Centers, Counseling, Day Care, Family Services, Food/Clothing Distribution, Homes, Shelters/Homelessness, Social Services-General, Substance Abuse, United Funds/United Ways, Volunteer Services

Contributions Analysis

Arts & Humanities: 5% to 10%. Arts centers, music, the performing arts, art associations, and community arts.
Civic & Public Affairs: 5% to 10%. Economic development, housing, business interests, and other foundation-related issues.
Education: 15% to 20%. Public education, community colleges, and general educational programs.
Health: 50% to 55%. Health organizations and hospices.
Social Services: 10% to 15%. Community services, family services, the homeless, substance abuse programs, volunteer services, and counseling.

Application Procedures

Initial Contact: a brief letter of inquiry and a full proposal
Application Requirements: overview of organization, amount requested, purpose of funds sought, recently audited financial statements, sources and uses of funds statement, list of board members, a contact individual, and proof of tax-exempt status
Deadlines: None.

Restrictions

Does not support individuals, religious organizations for sectarian purposes, or political or lobbying groups.

Additional Information

Company reports that it underwent a merger and a name change in January 1995. Formerly Central Companies, it was known as the American Mutual Life Insurance Company, now known as the AmerUS Group.
Publications: Annual Report

Corporate Officials

Roger Kay Brooks: chairman, director B Clarion, IA 1937. ED University of Iowa BA (1959). PRIM CORP EMPL chairman: AmerUS Group. CORP AFFIL chairman: Amer US Savings Bank; chairman: Central Life Assurance Co. NONPR AFFIL member: Phi Beta Kappa; fellow: Society Actuaries; member: Greater Des Moines Chamber of Commerce; member: Iowa Insurance Hall Fame. CLUB AFFIL Actuaries Des Moines Club; Des Moines Club.
Tom Godlasky: executive vice president, chief investment officer B Tyrone, PA 1955. ED Indiana University of Pennsylvania (1977); University of Pittsburgh (1979). PRIM CORP EMPL executive vice president, chief investment officer: AmerUS Life Holdings Inc.
Sam Charles Kalainov: chairman, president, chief executive officer B Steele, ND 1930. ED North Dakota State University BS (1956); American College Life Underwriters (1966). PRIM CORP EMPL chairman, president, chief executive officer: AmerUS Group. CORP AFFIL director: Bankers Trust Co.; director: Des Moines International Airport; director: AmerUS Life Insurance Co.; chairman: American Mutual Holding Corp.; officer: AmerUS Life Holdings Inc. NONPR AFFIL member: Greater Des Moines Chamber of Commerce; member: National Association Life Underwriters; trustee: Drake University; member: American Legion; chairman: Corporate International Trade; director: American Council Life Insurance. CLUB AFFIL Rotary Club.
Gary McPhail: president emeritus PRIM CORP EMPL president emeritus: AmerUS Group.
Michael E. Sproule: chief financial officer, director PRIM CORP EMPL chief financial officer, director: Central Life Assurance Co.

Giving Program Officials

Ted W. Wheat: PRIM CORP EMPL director committee relations: AmerUS Group.

Grants Analysis

Disclosure Period: calendar year ending
Typical Range: $1,000 to $2,500

AMETEK, INC.

Company Contact

Paoli, PA
Web: http://www.ametek.com

Company Description

Employees: 6,300
SIC(s): 3316 Cold-Finishing of Steel Shapes, 3621 Motors & Generators, 3823 Process Control Instruments, 3829 Measuring & Controlling Devices Nec.

AMETEK Foundation

Giving Contact

Kathryn E. Londra, Corporate Secretary
AMETEK Foundation
2 Station Square
Paoli, PA 19301
Phone: (610)647-2121

Description

Founded: 1960
EIN: 136095939
Organization Type: Corporate Foundation
Giving Locations: headquarters and operating communities; nationally.
Grant Types: General Support, Research.

Financial Summary

Total Giving: $1,513,536 (1998); $628,980 (1997); $629,397 (1996). Note: Contributes through foundation only.
Giving Analysis: Giving for 1997 includes: foundation grants to United Way ($150,975); 1998: foundation ($1,360,322); foundation grants to United Way ($153,214)
Assets: $7,887,928 (1998); $8,064,726 (1997); $8,108,612 (1996)
Gifts Received: $650,100 (1996); $650,000 (1995); $650,000 (1994). Note: The foundation receives contributions from AMETEK, Inc.

Typical Recipients

Arts & Humanities: Arts Centers, Arts Funds, Ballet, Dance, Ethnic & Folk Arts, Historic Preservation, History & Archaeology, Libraries, Museums/Galleries, Music
Civic & Public Affairs: Botanical Gardens/Parks, Civic & Public Affairs-General, Municipalities/Towns, Professional & Trade Associations, Safety, Urban & Community Affairs, Women's Affairs, Zoos/Aquariums
Education: Business Education, Colleges & Universities, Education Associations, Education Funds, Elementary Education (Private), Engineering/Technological Education, Education-General, International Exchange, Legal Education, Literacy, Medical Education, Private Education (Precollege), Public Education (Precollege), Science/Mathematics Education, Student Aid, Vocational & Technical Education, Vocational & Technical Education
Environment: Environment-General, Resource Conservation
Health: Cancer, Clinics/Medical Centers, Diabetes, Emergency/Ambulance Services, Health Funds, Health Organizations, Hospitals, Medical Rehabilitation, Medical Research, Mental Health, Preventive Medicine/Wellness Organizations, Public Health
International: International Affairs
Religion: Jewish Causes, Ministries
Science: Science Museums, Scientific Centers & Institutes
Social Services: Child Welfare, Community Service Organizations, Food/Clothing Distribution, Homes, People with Disabilities, Scouts, Senior Services, Shelters/Homelessness, United Funds/United Ways, YMCA/YWCA/YMHA/YWHA, Youth Organizations

Contributions Analysis

Giving Priorities: Secondary and higher education, hospitals, medical research, united funds, and religious welfare.
Arts & Humanities: 15%. Supports libraries primarily.
Education: 23%. Primarily colleges and universities and technical and engineering institutions and organizations. Other interests include student aid, private secondary education, education funds, and literacy.
Health: 13%. Health services, cancer centers, and single-disease health associations. 5%. Hospitals.
Religion: 4%. Fund religious philanthropic programs.
Social Services: 32%. YMCA and Junior Achievement.

Application Procedures

Initial Contact: Submit brief letter or proposal.
Application Requirements: Submit a description of organization, amount requested, purpose of funds sought, recently audited financial statement, and proof of tax-exempt status.
Deadlines: March 1 for May meeting, or by October 1 for November meeting.

Restrictions

The foundation does not support political or lobbying groups.

Corporate Officials

Walter Elwood Blankley: chairman, director, director B Philadelphia, PA 1935. ED Princeton University (1957). PRIM CORP EMPL chairman, director: AMETEK, Inc. CORP AFFIL director: Technical Council Greater Philadelphia; director: Manufacturers Alliance Productivity & Innovation Inc.; director: Ametek Aerospace Products; director: CDI Corp.; director: Amcast Industries Corp. NONPR AFFIL member: American Society Mechanical Engineers.
Frank S. Hermance: president, chief executive officer, director ED Rochester Institute Technology BSEE (1971); Rochester Institute Technology MSEE (1973). PRIM CORP EMPL president, chief executive officer, director: AMETEK, Inc.
Elizabeth Rosenwald Varet: director ED Harvard University AB (1965). PRIM CORP EMPL chairman: American Securities LP. CORP AFFIL director: Schutte & Koerting Inc.; partner: W R Family Associates; director: Ametek Inc.

Foundation Officials

Walter Elwood Blankley: president, director (see above)
Lewis George Cole: director B New York, NY 1931. ED University of Pennsylvania BS (1951); Yale University LLB (1954). PRIM CORP EMPL partner: Stroock & Stroock & Lavan. CORP AFFIL director: Ametek Inc. NONPR AFFIL member: Association Bar New York City; member: New York State Bar Association; member: American Bar Association.
Helmut N. Friedlaender: director CORP AFFIL director: Ametek Inc.
Kathryn E. Londra: secretary, treasurer
Elizabeth Rosenwald Varet: vice president, director (see above)

Grants Analysis

Disclosure Period: calendar year ending 1997
Total Grants: $1,360,322*
Number of Grants: 82
Average Grant: $16,589

Highest Grant: $222,591
Typical Range: $1,000 to $10,000
***Note:** Giving excludes United Way.

Recent Grants

Note: Grants derived from 1998 Form 990.

Arts & Humanities

50,000	The Free Library of Philadelphia, Philadelphia, PA
15,000	Gibsonville Public Library Early Childhood Programs, Gibsonville, NC
10,000	Free Library of Philadelphia Foundation, Philadelphia, PA
10,000	The Pierpont Morgan Library, New York, NY
7,500	Alamance Public Library, Burlington, NC
5,000	The Free Library of Philadelphia, Philadelphia, PA -- Summer Reading Program
5,000	Museum of Western Colorado, Grand Junction, CO

Education

28,660	National Merit Scholarship Corporation, Evanston, IL
27,500	Yale Law School, New Haven, CT
18,700	Youth for Understanding International Exchange, Washington, DC
15,000	Beaver College, Glenside, PA
15,000	Binghamton School District, Binghamton, NY
15,000	Kent State University Foundation, Kent, OH
10,000	Bard College Annandale-On-The, Hudson, NY
10,000	Eckert College, St. Petersburg, FL
7,500	Alamance School District High School, Burlington, NC
5,000	Polk Education Foundation, Lakeland, FL
5,000	Princeton University, Princeton, NJ
5,000	Upper Bucks Vocational/Technical School, Paoli, PA

Environment

25,000	Central Park Conservancy, New York, NY
17,500	Natural Resources Defense Council, New York, NY

Health

25,000	Memorial Sloan-Kettering Cancer Center, New York, NY
25,000	Paoli Memorial Hospital, Paoli, PA
12,500	Cornell Cooperative Extension, Binghamton, NY
10,000	Alamance Regional Medical Center, Burlington, NC
7,500	Juvenile Diabetes Foundation, New York, NY
6,000	Philadelphia Hospitality, Inc., Philadelphia, PA
5,000	Community Hospital Foundation, Grand Junction, CO

International

45,000	World Affairs Council of Philadelphia, Philadelphia, PA

Religion

25,000	Anti-Defamation League, Philadelphia, PA

Science

10,000	The Franklin Institute Science Museum, Philadelphia, PA -- Corporate Partner Program

Social Services

25,000	Coalition for the Homeless, New York, NY
23,500	United Way of Portage County, Stevens Point, WI
23,256	United Way of Southeastern Pennsylvania, Philadelphia, PA
16,430	United Way of Ulster County, Kingston, NY
15,202	United Way of Southwestern Pennsylvania, Pittsburgh, PA
15,000	Abilities, Inc. of Florida, Clearwater, FL
14,555	United Way of Racine, Racine, WI
12,500	Eagles Youth Partnership, Philadelphia, PA
12,250	Wapakoneta Family YMCA, Wapakoneta, OH
12,062	United Way of Delaware, Wilmington, DE
11,100	United Way of Alamance County, Burlington, NC
6,859	United Way of Meriden-Wallingford, Meriden, CT
6,000	United Way of Massachusetts Bay, Boston, MA
6,000	United Way of Merrimack Valley, Lawrence, MA
6,000	Upper Pinellas Association for Retarded Citizens, Clearwater, FL
5,200	United Way of Greater Greensboro, Greensboro, NC
5,000	Adoption Center of Delaware Valley, Philadelphia, PA
5,000	United Way of Central Florida, Highland City, FL
5,000	Upper Main Line YMCA Association, Berwyn, PA

AMGEN, INC.

Company Contact

Houston, TX
Web: http://www.amgen.com

Company Description

Revenue: US$3,340,100,000 (1999)
Employees: 4,594 (1999)
Fortune Rank: 463, per FORTUNE Magazine's list of 500 Largest U.S. Corporations (1999).
FF 463
SIC(s): 5122 Drugs, Proprietaries & Sundries.

Nonmonetary Support

Type: Donated Equipment; Donated Products

Amgen Foundation

Giving Contact

Annette Chavez, Administrator
Amgen Foundation
Mailstop 27-4-A
One Amgen Center Drive
Thousand Oaks, CA 91320-1799
Phone: (805)447-4056
Fax: (805)499-6751
Web: http://www.amgen.com/corporate/AmgenCommunity.html

Description

EIN: 770252898
Organization Type: Corporate Foundation
Giving Locations: headquarters; nationally.
Grant Types: Employee Matching Gifts, General Support.
Note: Employee matching gift ratio: 1 to 1 from $50 to $10,000.

Financial Summary

Total Giving: $1,500,000 (1999 approx); $1,532,237 (1998); $1,200,000 (1997 approx). Note: Contributes through corporate direct giving program and foundation. Giving includes foundation.
Giving Analysis: Giving for 1998 includes: foundation ($1,532,237)
Assets: $4,878,296 (1998); $12,321 (1995); $174,762 (1994)
Gifts Received: $6,303,500 (1998); $821,000 (1995); $480,000 (1994). Note: Contributions are received from Amgen, Inc.

Typical Recipients

Arts & Humanities: Arts Associations & Councils, Arts & Humanities-General, Historic Preservation, Libraries, Museums/Galleries, Music
Civic & Public Affairs: Asian American Affairs, Botanical Gardens/Parks, Community Foundations, Gay/Lesbian Issues, Civic & Public Affairs-General, Hispanic Affairs, Housing, Public Policy
Education: Business Education, Colleges & Universities, Education Funds, Education Reform, Education-General, Literacy, Medical Education, Private Education (Precollege), Public Education (Precollege), Science/Mathematics Education, Secondary Education (Public), Student Aid, Vocational & Technical Education
Environment: Environment-General, Resource Conservation
Health: AIDS/HIV, Alzheimers Disease, Cancer, Children's Health/Hospitals, Clinics/Medical Centers, Emergency/Ambulance Services, Health Organizations, Heart, Hospices, Hospitals, Medical Research, Preventive Medicine/Wellness Organizations, Single-Disease Health Associations
International: Health Care/Hospitals
Religion: Religious Welfare
Science: Science Museums, Scientific Centers & Institutes
Social Services: At-Risk Youth, Child Abuse, Child Welfare, Community Service Organizations, Day Care, Family Services, People with Disabilities, Recreation & Athletics, Senior Services, Social Services-General, United Funds/United Ways, YMCA/YWCA/YMHA/YWHA, Youth Organizations

Contributions Analysis

Giving Priorities: Supports educational programs with focus on biological sciences, health and service organizations, and arts and culture within the greater Los Angeles and Ventura County areas.
Arts & Humanities: 22%. Gives to museums, visual and performing arts.
Education: 20%. Supports precollege and higher education, especially those with a focus on biological science. Scholarships.
Health: 25%. Supports free clinics, the Red Cross, hospice, and research.
Social Services: 20%. Funds senior concerns, the United Way, and youth programs.

Application Procedures

Initial Contact: Send a one- to two-page written request.
Application Requirements: Include name, address, and a description of organization; amount requested; purpose of grant; contact person, title, and telephone number; background of organization; target population served by organization; geographic area served by organization; and proof of tax-exempt status.
Deadlines: None.

Restrictions

Does not support alumni drives or teacher organizations; construction or building improvements; capital campaigns; city/municipal/federal government departments; endowments and foundations; individuals, charitable dinners or sporting events; labor unions; municipal or for-profit hospitals; religious organizations; professional sports events or athletes; civic organizations that do not serve the areas in which Amgen is located; overseas organizations or sponsorship for overseas events.

Additional Information

Company has established a series of programs that provide its products, including Epogen and Neupogen, to medically needy patients with no insurance or with limited financial resources.

Company's commitment to education extends beyond basic science and the local community to include users of its products. Company also provides educational programs and tools to assist the medical community to better understand its products.

Company also sponsors an annual Teacher Excellence Award.

Company also sponsors an annual Teacher Excellence Award.

Corporate Officials

Gordon M. Binder: chairman, chief executive officer, directorchief financial officer B Saint Louis, MO 1935. ED Purdue University BS (1957); Harvard University MBA (1962). PRIM CORP EMPL chairman, chief executive officer, director: Amgen, Inc. CORP AFFIL president: Amgen International Inc. NONPR AFFIL director: Ronald Reagan Presidential Library.

Kathryn E. Falberg: senior vice president finance, chief financial officer ED University of California, Los Angeles MBA (1981). PRIM CORP EMPL senior vice president finance, chief financial officer: Amgen, Inc.

Foundation Officials

Annette Chavez: administrator

Linda J. Hodge: president PRIM CORP EMPL secretary, director: Amgen Puerto Rico Inc.

Grants Analysis

Disclosure Period: calendar year ending 1998
Total Grants: $1,532,237*
Number of Grants: 1,200 (approx)
Average Grant: $1,277 (approx)
Highest Grant: $50,000
Typical Range: $100 to $3,000
***Note:** Giving includes matching gifts, scholarships, and United Way.

Recent Grants

Note: Grants derived from 1998 Form 990.

Arts & Humanities

25,000 Alliance For The Arts, Thousand Oaks, CA
25,000 Alliance For The Arts, Thousand Oaks, CA
25,000 New West Symphony, Thousand Oaks, CA
10,000 Los Angeles County Museum Of Art, Los Angeles, CA
10,000 Music Center Unified Fund, Los Angeles, CA
10,000 Natural History Museum Of Los Angeles, Los Angeles, CA
9,000 Seattle Symphony, Seattle, WA
8,000 Conejo Valley Symphony Orchestra, Thousand Oaks, CA
7,500 Los Angeles Philharmonic, Los Angeles, CA
7,500 Many Mansions, Thousand Oaks, CA

Civic & Public Affairs

10,000 Chinese Christian Herald Crusades, New York, NY
7,500 Many Mansions, Thousand Oaks, CA
5,774 Los Angeles Gay & Lesbian Center, Los Angeles, CA

Education

45,740 National Merit Scholarship Corporation, Evanston, IL
10,000 ARCS Foundation, Inc., Oak Brook, IL
10,000 Conejo Valley Unified School District, Thousand Oaks, CA
10,000 Crane School, Santa Barbara, CA
10,000 Faith Heritage School, Syracuse, NY
10,000 Junior League Of Los Angeles, Los Angeles, CA
10,000 Williams College, Williamstown, MA
7,545 KCLU - California Lutheran University, Thousand Oaks, CA
7,368 Southwest Texas State University, San Marcos, TX
6,000 Atma Vidya Educational Foundation, Austin, TX

Health

25,000 American Red Cross, Ventura, CA
25,000 National Race For The Cure, Washington, DC
15,000 Wellness Community - Valley Ventura, Ventura, CA
12,500 American Cancer Society, Los Angeles, CA
10,374 American Cancer Society, Los Angeles, CA
10,000 American Red Cross- Disaster Relief Fund, Los Angeles, CA
10,000 Conejo Free Clinic, Conejo, CA
10,000 Santa Barbara Breast Resource Center, Santa Barbara, CA
10,000 The Wellness Community, Pasadena, CA
8,072 American Heart Association, Los Angeles, CA
7,500 Conejo Free Clinic, Thousand Oaks, CA
7,500 Hospice Of Conejo, Thousand Oaks, CA
7,500 Hospice Of The Conejo, Thousand Oaks, CA

International

15,567 Hope Worldwide Ltd., Ridge wood, NJ
15,000 Doctors Without Borders, New York, NY

Religion

10,000 Samaritan House - Catholic Charities, San Francisco, CA

Science

15,000 California Science Center Foundation, Los Angeles, CA
10,000 California Science Center Foundation, Los Angeles, CA

Social Services

50,000 United Way Of Ventura County, Ventura, CA
17,301 United Way Of Ventura County, Ventura, CA
15,180 United Way Of Puerto Rico, San Juan, PR
8,950 Young People Of Watts, Inc., Los Angeles, CA
7,500 Conejo Valley Senior Concerns, Thousand Oaks, CA
7,500 Conejo Valley Senior Concerns, Thousand Oaks, CA
7,490 United Way Of Ventura County, Ventura, CA
7,000 Save The Children, New York, NY

AMP INC.

Company Contact

Harrisburg, PA
Web: http://www.amp.com

Company Description

Revenue: US$5,500,000,000
Employees: 40,000
SIC(s): 3423 Hand & Edge Tools Nec, 3629 Electrical Industrial Apparatus Nec, 3643 Current-Carrying Wiring Devices, 3678 Electronic Connectors.
Parent Company: Tyco International Ltd.

Operating Locations

Argentina: AMP SA Argentina, Martinez, Buenos Aires; Australia: Australian AMP Pty. Ltd., Castle Hill; Austria: AMP Osterreich Handels GmbH, Vienna; Belgium: AMP Holland BV Vennootschap Naar Nederlands Recht, Zaventem, Brabant; Canada: AMP of Canada Ltd., Markham; People's Republic of China: AMP Shanghai Ltd., Shanghai, Chiba; France: AMP Simel, Gevrey Chambertin, Cote d'Or; Toucheboeuf (Etablissements), Montlouis Sur Loire; AMP Export SARL, Pontoise, Val d'Oise; AMP de France (ste), Pontoise, Val d'Oise; Germany: AMP Deutschland GmbH, Langen, Hessen; Hong Kong: AMP Products Pacific Ltd., Kowloon; Ireland: AMP Ireland Ltd., Dublin; Italy: AMP Italia SpA, Collegno, Piemonte; Japan: AMP Technology Japan, Kawasaki, Kanagawa; JWP Businessland Japan Co. Ltd., Tokyo; Republic of Korea: AMP Korea Ltd., Seoul; Mexico: AMP de Mexico SA, Tlalnepantla; Malaysia: AMP Products (Malaysia) Sdn. Bhd., Shah Alam, Selangor; Netherlands: AMP Holland BV, S'Hertogenbosch; AMP Laminates BV, S'Hertogenbosch; AMP Plus BV, S'Hertogenbosch; AMP Taiwan BV, S'Hertogenbosch; AMP Technology Europe BV, S'Hertogenbosch; Norway: AMP Norge AS, Nesbru, Akershus; New Zealand: New Zealand AMP Ltd., Mangere Bridge; Portugal: AMP Portugal Conectores Electricos E Electronicos Lda., Lisboa; Singapore: AMP Singapore Pte. Ltd., Singapore; Spain: AMP Espanola SA, Barcelona, Cataluna; Sweden: AMP Svenska AB; Switzerland: Decolletage SA St. Maurice, St. Maurice, Grisons; AMP (Schweiz) HFI AG, Steinach, Saint Gallen; Taiwan: AMP Manufacturing Taiwan Ltd., Hsin-chu; AMP Taiwan BV, Taipei; United Kingdom: Madison Cable Ltd., Dundee, Tayside; AMP of Great Britain Ltd., Stanmore, Middlesex

Nonmonetary Support

Value: $5,000 (1989); $25,000 (1988)
Type: Cause-related Marketing & Promotion; Donated Products; In-kind Services; Loaned Employees; Workplace Solicitation
Volunteer Programs: After employees complete 100 hours of volunteer services in a calendar year with a nonprofit organization, the Dollars for Doers program will authorize a $250 contribution from the Foundation to that organization. This is a yearly maximum of $2,000 to one eligible organization.
Contact: Mary Rakoczy
Phone: (717)592-4869
Note: Nonmonetary support is provided by the company. Workplace solicitation applies to United Way only.

Corporate Sponsorship

Type: Arts & cultural events; Music & entertainment events

AMP Foundation

Giving Contact

Dianna Wills, Manager, Community Relations & Contributions
AMP Inc.
PO Box 3608 (176-042)
Harrisburg, PA 17105-3608
Phone: (717)592-4812
Fax: (717)592-6130
Email: dkwills@amp.com

Description

EIN: 232022928
Organization Type: Corporate Foundation
Giving Locations: NC: Triad; PA: central Pennsylvania; VA headquarters and operating communities.
Grant Types: Capital, Employee Matching Gifts, Multiyear/Continuing Support.
Note: Employee matching gift ratio: 1 to 1 for PAC contributions; 2 to 1 for education, for the first $100 of employee gift, then 1 to 1 up to maximum of $5,000.

Giving Philosophy

'The AMP Foundation is dedicated to fostering a society that enhances the quality of life and in which all people can fully participate. We believe this is made possible through a broad range of the highest quality educational opportunities.' *The AMP Foundation brochure*

Financial Summary

Total Giving: $1,658,357 (1998); $1,400,000 (1997); $1,400,000 (1996)
Giving Analysis: Giving for 1996 includes: foundation ($894,636); foundation grants to United Way ($295,061); 1997: foundation ($966,958); foundation grants to United Way ($328,082); 1998: foundation ($1,284,842); foundation grants to United Way ($373,515)
Assets: $20,784,759 (1998); $20,080,343 (1997); $18,350,873 (1996 approx)

Typical Recipients

Arts & Humanities: Arts Associations & Councils, Arts Centers, Arts Funds, Libraries, Museums/Galleries, Music, Public Broadcasting, Theater
Civic & Public Affairs: African American Affairs, Business/Free Enterprise, Civil Rights, Clubs, Economic Development, Employment/Job Training, Hispanic Affairs, Housing, Minority Business, Municipalities/Towns, Professional & Trade Associations, Safety, Urban & Community Affairs
Education: Colleges & Universities, Community & Junior Colleges, Education Associations, Elementary Education (Public), Engineering/Technological Education, Environmental Education, Education-General, Literacy, Minority Education, Private Education (Precollege), Public Education (Precollege), School Volunteerism, Science/Mathematics Education, Secondary Education (Private), Vocational & Technical Education
Environment: Environment-General
Health: Cancer, Children's Health/Hospitals, Clinics/Medical Centers, Emergency/Ambulance Services, Health Organizations, Hospices, Hospitals, Mental Health, Single-Disease Health Associations
International: International Relations
Religion: Ministries
Science: Science Museums, Scientific Centers & Institutes
Social Services: Big Brother/Big Sister, Child Abuse, Child Welfare, Community Centers, Community Service Organizations, Family Services, Food/Clothing Distribution, People with Disabilities, Recreation & Athletics, Scouts, Shelters/Homelessness, Substance Abuse, United Funds/United Ways, YMCA/YWCA/YMHA/YWHA, Youth Organizations

Contributions Analysis

Giving Priorities: Higher education and organizations that have an education component. Subsidiaries outside the U.S. make unspecified contributions in local communities.
Arts & Humanities: 10%. Provides funding for art societies, music, museums, and arts festivals and associations.
Civic & Public Affairs: 10%. Funds agencies that promote personal growth, career opportunities, and economic self-sufficiency.
Education: 57%. Support goes to accredited educational institutions, public and private, particularly when grant addresses business or community concern of AMP. Also supports an employee matching gift fund that donates to accredited high schools, colleges, and universities.
Social Services: 23%. Supports United Way.

Application Procedures

Initial Contact: Send brief letter or proposal.
Application Requirements: Provide a description of organization and its purposes; description of the project, including costs, proposed budget, and source of funding; list of board members; proof of IRS section 501(c)(3) status; most recent IRS Form 990.
Deadlines: Applications are accepted throughout the year and decisions are made on a quarterly basis; the majority of grants are budgeted in the first quarter of the year; deadlines are December 15, March 15, June 15, and September 15.
Evaluative Criteria: Preference is given to organizations where AMP employees volunteer; organizations must be non-profit, and operate within geographic areas where AMP has employees; organizations should support AMP's corporate objectives in education, community development and arts and culture.
Notes: Requests over $2,500 must fill out the foundation's application for corporate contributions.

Restrictions

Foundation does not support organizations in geographic areas where AMP has few or no employees; individuals; private foundations; national organizations; general operating needs of United Way agencies; service clubs; social, labor, or veterans organizations; political campaigns; organizations or programs that pose a potential conflict of interest for AMP; organizations that discriminate based on race, religion, color, nationality, age, sex, physical or mental conditions, veteran status or marital status; programs of churches or religious organizations with the exception of nondenominational programs such as food banks, youth centers or non-sectarian education programs. Foundation may not support courtesy advertising; testimonial or fund-raising dinners, loans or investments; capital campaigns or other fund-raising of national organizations.

Additional Information

Grant recipients must submit a final report which evaluates the results of the funded program.

Corporate Officials

Robert M. Ripp: chairman, chief executive officer, director B New York, NY 1941. ED Iona College BA (1963); New York University MBA (1967). PRIM CORP EMPL chairman, chief executive officer, director: AMP Inc. CORP AFFIL chairman: AMP Investments Inc.; director: Network Imaging Corp.; director: ACE Ltd.

Giving Program Officials

Dianna K. Wills: assistant chairman contributions committee PRIM CORP EMPL manager community relations & contributions: AMP Inc.
Merrill A. Yohe, Jr.: chairman contributions committee B Hanover, PA 1934. ED Gettysburg College AB (1958); Dickinson School of Law LLB (1964). PRIM CORP EMPL vice president public affairs: AMP Inc.

Foundation Officials

Harris T. Booker, Junior: director
Joseph C. Overbaugh: director B Hanover, PA 1945. ED Villanova University (1967). PRIM CORP EMPL treasurer: AMP Inc. NONPR AFFIL member: American Institute CPAs; member: National Association of Corporate Treasurers.
Ray J. Thomas: director

Grants Analysis

Disclosure Period: calendar year ending 1997
Total Grants: $1,284,842*
Number of Grants: 573
Average Grant: $2,242
Highest Grant: $208,115
Typical Range: $500 to $5,000
***Note:** Giving excludes United Way.

Recent Grants

Note: Grants derived from 1997 Form 990.

Arts & Humanities

30,000	Allied Arts Fund, Harrisburg, PA
16,775	Harrisburg Symphony, Harrisburg, PA
10,000	Rockingham Public Library
5,500	United Arts Council, Greensboro, NC
5,364	Susquehanna Art Museum, Harrisburg, PA

Civic & Public Affairs

5,250	South Central Pennsylvania Development, PA

Education

40,000	Council of the Great City Schools, Washington, DC
39,661	Pennsylvania State University, University Park, PA
26,000	Schulylkill Training and Technology Center, PA
22,500	Guilford County Schools, Greensboro, NC
17,500	Guilford Tech Community College, Jamestown, NC
15,000	Middletown Area School District, Middletown, PA
13,000	Forsyth Technical Community College, Winston-Salem, NC
10,000	Council for Public Education, Harrisburg, PA
10,000	Danville Community College, Danville, VA
10,000	Penn College of Technology, Williamsport, PA
9,241	Bloomsburg University Foundation, Bloomsburg, PA
9,175	Wilson College, Chambersburg, PA
7,280	Millersville University, Millersville, PA
7,000	Davidson County Community College, Lexington, KY
6,885	Shippensburg University Foundation, Shippensburg, PA
6,500	Rhyne Elementary School, Gastonia, NC
6,500	Sedge Garden Parent-Teacher Association, Winston-Salem, NC
6,500	Wallburg Elementary School Parent-Teachers Organization, Wallburg, NC
6,250	Pennsylvania State University Harrisburg, Middletown, PA
6,250	Pennsylvania State University Harrisburg Environmental Programs, Harrisburg, PA
6,000	Inroads, Baltimore, MD

Environment

62,000	Piedmont Environmental Center, High Point, NC

Health

15,000	United Cerebral Palsy of the Capital Area, Camp Hill, PA
11,378	American Red Cross, Harrisburg, PA
8,363	Hospice of Lancaster County, Enola, PA
3,217	American Cancer Society, Harrisburg, PA

International

23,000	Asia Foundation, San Francisco, CA
23,000	Asia Foundation, San Francisco, CA

Science

10,000	Museum of Scientific Discovery, Harrisburg, PA

Social Services

207,832	United Way Capital Region, Harrisburg, PA
28,000	United Way, Greensboro, NC
18,000	United Way Roanoke Valley, Roanoke, VA
17,750	ARC, Camp Hill, PA
15,500	United Way Forsyth County, Winston-Salem, NC

12,550	United Way, Lancaster, PA
11,000	United Way York County, York, PA
10,650	Big Brothers and Big Sisters, Harrisburg, PA
10,592	Bethesda Mission, Harrisburg, PA
10,000	Friendship Community Center
8,500	Goodwill Industries Central Pennsylvania, Harrisburg, PA
7,500	Gaudenzia, Philadelphia, PA
7,000	Second Mile, Harrisburg, PA
7,000	United Way Gaston County, Gastonia, NC
6,600	United Way Southeastern Pennsylvania, Philadelphia, PA
5,096	Boy Scouts of America Keystone Area Council, Mechanicsburg, PA

AMR CORP.

Company Contact

Fort Worth, TX
Web: http://www.amrcorp.com

Company Description

Revenue: US$15,192,000,000 (1999)
Profit: US$1,314,000,000
Employees: 92,000 (1999)
Fortune Rank: 77, per FORTUNE Magazine's list of 500 Largest U.S. Corporations (1999).
FF 77
SIC(s): 4512 Air Transportation--Scheduled, 6719 Holding Companies Nec.

Nonmonetary Support

Type: Donated Products; In-kind Services
Note: Sales Department provides in-kind services for nonprofits. Company also donates travel vouchers to organizations.

AMR/American Airlines Foundation

Giving Contact

Kathy Andersen, Administrator, Corporate Contributions
AMR/American Airlines Foundation
PO Box 619616
Mail Drop 5575
Dallas, TX 75261-9616
Phone: (817)967-3545
Fax: (817)967-9784
Note: Facsimiles should be limited to one page plus transmittal sheet.

Description

EIN: 762086656
Organization Type: Corporate Foundation
Giving Locations: nationally and internationally.
Grant Types: General Support, Multiyear/Continuing Support, Project, Scholarship.

Financial Summary

Total Giving: $1,167,429 (1998); $980,844 (1997); $1,156,270 (1996). Note: 1997 Giving includes United Way ($450,600).
Giving Analysis: Giving for 1996 includes: foundation ($750,170); foundation grants to United Way ($406,100); 1997: foundation ($530,244); foundation grants to United Way ($450,600); 1998: foundation ($801,579); foundation grants to United Way ($365,850)
Assets: $3,743,805 (1998); $4,801,367 (1997); $5,093,383 (1996)
Gifts Received: $291,727 (1998); $291,946 (1997); $5,260,749 (1996). Note: In 1998 contributions were received from Flagship Charities ($286,727) and Chicago Charities ($5,000).

Typical Recipients

Arts & Humanities: Arts Associations & Councils, Arts Centers, Community Arts, Historic Preservation, History & Archaeology, Libraries, Museums/Galleries, Music, Opera, Performing Arts, Public Broadcasting
Civic & Public Affairs: African American Affairs, Botanical Gardens/Parks, Business/Free Enterprise, Civil Rights, Clubs, Community Foundations, Civic & Public Affairs-General, Hispanic Affairs, Minority Business, Municipalities/Towns, Parades/Festivals, Philanthropic Organizations, Professional & Trade Associations, Public Policy, Safety, Urban & Community Affairs, Women's Affairs, Zoos/Aquariums
Education: Arts/Humanities Education, Business Education, Colleges & Universities, Education Reform, Education-General, Minority Education, Private Education (Precollege), Public Education (Precollege), School Volunteerism, Science/Mathematics Education, Secondary Education (Public), Student Aid
Environment: Resource Conservation
Health: AIDS/HIV, Cancer, Children's Health/Hospitals, Clinics/Medical Centers, Diabetes, Emergency/Ambulance Services, Eyes/Blindness, Health Funds, Health Organizations, Hospitals, Hospitals (University Affiliated), Kidney, Multiple Sclerosis, Public Health, Single-Disease Health Associations
International: Foreign Educational Institutions, Human Rights, International Relations, International Relief Efforts
Religion: Jewish Causes, Religious Organizations, Religious Welfare
Science: Science Museums
Social Services: At-Risk Youth, Big Brother/Big Sister, Child Welfare, Child Welfare, Community Service Organizations, Counseling, Crime Prevention, Family Services, Food/Clothing Distribution, Recreation & Athletics, Scouts, Senior Services, Social Services-General, Substance Abuse, United Funds/United Ways, Volunteer Services, YMCA/YWCA/YMHA/YWHA, Youth Organizations

Contributions Analysis

Giving Priorities: Higher education; arts; United Way; youth, disabled, elderly and homeless organizations; hospitals; and civic organizations. International giving interests of AMR and its foundation are projects designed to preserve environmentally sensitive property throughout the world; partnerships that promote economic development in AMR communities; performances or programs that promote a higher level of understanding of the arts from countries where AMR/American Airlines has a presence; specific programs designed to highlight the world's diversity of cultures, ethnic backgrounds, and national origins; and events or activities aimed at educating students and adults about world geography.
Arts & Humanities: Less than 5%. Funds activities that exemplify excellence in the visual and/or performing art, including performances or programs that promote a higher level of understanding of the arts from countries where AMR/American Airlines has a presence. Also aids specific programs designed to highlight the world's diversity of cultures, ethnic background, and national origins. Also gives to art funds that make a significant contribution to the creation of high quality art programs in local communities.
Civic & Public Affairs: 20%. Funds educational programs aimed at increasing awareness and involvement in recycling and other environmental protection activities and projects designed to preserve environmentally sensitive property throughout the world. Partners with environmental organizations, such as the Nature Conservancy. Also sponsors initiatives that promote economic development in company's communities.
Education: 23%. Supports programs aimed at providing higher education and business career training opportunities to minorities, in particular those that support American's existing national partnership with the United Negro College Fund. Supports efforts to create greater understanding and cooperation between various ethnic groups. Also funds events and activities aimed at educating young adults about world geography.
Health: 18%. United Way receives highest percentage of foundation grants. Funding also supports the American Cancer Society, American Red Cross, and Give the Kids the World Foundation.
International: 5%. Funds International habitat for Humanity.
Religion: Less than 5%.
Social Services: 33%. Funds social services, youth services, meals on wheels, volunteerism, and the United Way.

Application Procedures

Initial Contact: Send a brief letter or proposal.
Application Requirements: Submit purpose of organization, intended use of funds, proof of tax-exempt status, list of names of officers, key staff members and board members, project budget including sources of funding already committed or expected, timetable of the project, method of measuring success of the project, most recent audited financial statement, and any additional support materials that may provide a more thorough understanding of the organization.
Deadlines: None.
Decision Notification: Notice of a decision or request for more information is usually sent within two months of receipt of proposal.
Notes: Foundation requests that organizations contact foundation administrator only.

Restrictions

Does not contribute to the support of organizations lacking proof of 501(c)(3) tax-exempt status; endowments; annual operating support fund drives; organizations that discriminate on the basis of race, religion, sex or national origin; religious, fraternal, social or veterans' organizations; political or partisan organizations established to influence legislation or specific elections; individuals; organizations receiving support from United Way drives; basic academic or scientific research; athletic events or sponsorships; or social functions or advertising in commemorative journals, yearbooks or special event publications. journals, yearbooks or special event publications.

Corporate Officials

Robert Woodward Baker: executive vice president, general counsel B Bronxville, NY 1944. ED Trinity College BA (1966); University of Pennsylvania Wharton School MBA (1968). PRIM CORP EMPL executive vice president: AMR Corp. CORP AFFIL executive vice president operations: American Airlines Inc.; vice chairman: AMR Eagle Inc.; vice president: American Airlines Fuel Corp.
Donald J. Carty: president, chairman, chief executive officer, director B 1946. ED Queene University Kingston BA (1968); Harvard University MBA (1971). PRIM CORP EMPL president, chairman, chief executive officer, director: AMR Corp. CORP AFFIL director: Dell Computer Corp.; director: Brinker International Inc.; chairman, chief executive officer: America Airlines Inc.; chairman: AMR Training Consult Group; advisory board: Allendale Mutual Insurance Co. NONPR AFFIL trustee: Queens University.
Robert Lloyd Crandall: director B Westerly, RI 1935. ED College of William & Mary (1953-1955); University of Rhode Island BS (1957); University of Pennsylvania Wharton School MBA (1960). PRIM CORP EMPL director: AMR Corp. CORP AFFIL director: Media One Group; director: The Sabre Group; director: Canadian Airlines; director: Halliburton Co.
Anne H. McNamara: senior vice president, general counsel B Shanghai, People's Republic of China 1947. ED Vassar College AB (1969); Cornell University JD (1972). PRIM CORP EMPL senior vice president, general counsel: AMR Corp. CORP AFFIL director: Louisville Gas & Electric Co.; director: Sabre Group Holdings Inc.; director: LG&E Energy Corp.

Foundation Officials

Kathy Andersen: administrator corporate contributions

Robert A. Britton: secretary, manager CORP AFFIL managing director: American Airlines Inc.

Donald J. Carty: vice president, treasurer (see above)

Grants Analysis

Disclosure Period: calendar year ending 1998
Total Grants: $801,579*
Number of Grants: 76
Average Grant: $10,547
Highest Grant: $150,000
Typical Range: $100 to $10,000
***Note:** Giving excludes United Way.

Recent Grants

Note: Grants derived from 1997 Form 990.

Arts & Humanities

5,000	Friends of Dallas Public Library, Dallas, TX
3,000	Oklahoma Simfonia, Tulsa, OK
2,700	Dallas Symphony Orchestra, Dallas, TX
2,500	Fort Worth Symphony Orchestra Association, Fort Worth, TX
2,000	Nashville Symphony, Nashville, TN
1,390	North Texas Public Broadcasting, Dallas, TX
800	Westfield High School Band Boosters, Houston, TX

Civic & Public Affairs

2,000	Honor Legion of the Fire Department, New York, NY
1,500	Chicago Zoological Society, Brookfield, IL
1,500	Tuskegee Airmen, Arlington, VA
1,000	Dallas Helps, Dallas, TX
1,000	National Minority Supplier Development Council Conference, New York, NY
1,000	North Beach Club, Flushing, NY

Education

150,000	Paul Quinn College, Dallas, TX
22,444	National Merit Scholarship Corporation, Evanston, IL
20,000	University of Oklahoma Foundation, Norman, OK
2,500	Communities in Schools, Fort Worth, TX
2,500	I Have a Dream Foundation, Fort Worth, TX
2,500	Southern Methodist University, Dallas, TX
2,000	University of Texas Arlington, Arlington, TX
1,000	Texas Christian University, Fort Worth, TX

Health

43,000	Concern Foundation, Culver City, CA
25,000	Easter Seal Society, Miami, FL
10,000	Make-A-Wish Foundation, Dallas, TX
1,400	American Red Cross, Tulsa, OK
1,000	Make-A-Wish Foundation, Phoenix, AZ
800	American Cancer Society, Forest Hills, NY
500	Zale Lipshy University Hospital, Dallas, TX

International

50,000	Habitat for Humanity International, Americus, GA
50,000	Habitat for Humanity International, Americus, GA

Religion

10,000	Salvation Army, Dallas, TX
1,000	Angel Flight, Lancaster, TX

Social Services

225,000	United Way, Dallas, TX
108,000	Tulsa Area United Way, Tulsa, OK
100,000	United Way of Dade County, Miami, FL
43,000	Big Sisters, Los Angeles, CA
43,000	Community Trust Fund of Volunteer League of San Fernando Valley, Studio City, CA
43,000	Friends of Child Advocates, Monterey Park, CA
10,000	United Way Crusade of Mercy, Chicago, IL
5,000	Big Shoulders Fund, Chicago, IL
5,000	United Way Tri-State, Stamford, CT
4,500	Tulsa Boys Home, Tulsa, OK
3,000	Alliance for Children, Fort Worth, TX
3,000	Greater Dallas Crime Commission, Dallas, TX
2,000	Big Brothers and Big Sisters, Dallas, TX
2,000	Tulsa Meals on Wheels, Tulsa, OK
1,500	United Way of Massachusetts Bay, Boston, MA
1,100	Tulsa Boys Home, Tulsa, OK
1,000	Bryan's House, Dallas, TX
1,000	Compassionate Friends, Oak Brook, IL
1,000	Family Gateway, Dallas, TX

AMSTED INDUSTRIES INC.

Company Contact

Chicago, IL
Web: http://www.amsted.com

Company Description

Revenue: US$1,000,000,000
Employees: 9,000
SIC(s): 3315 Steel Wire & Related Products, 3321 Gray & Ductile Iron Foundries, 3325 Steel Foundries Nec, 3493 Steel Springs Except Wire.

Amsted Industries Foundation

Giving Contact

Jerry W. Gura, Director, Public Affairs
Amsted Industries Foundation
205 North Michigan Ave., 44th Floor
Boulevard Towers South
Chicago, IL 60601
Phone: (312)819-8518
Fax: (312)819-8523

Description

Founded: 1953
EIN: 366050609
Organization Type: Corporate Foundation
Giving Locations: IL: Chicago headquarters and operating communities.
Grant Types: Employee Matching Gifts, General Support.
Note: Employee matching gift ratio: 1 to 1 for gifts to education, civic and cultural groups.

Financial Summary

Total Giving: $531,176 (fiscal year ending September 30, 1998); $568,000 (fiscal 1997 approx); $518,144 (fiscal 1996). Note: Contributes through corporate direct giving program and foundation.
Giving Analysis: Giving for fiscal 1996 includes: foundation ($432,094); foundation grants to United Way ($86,050); fiscal 1998: foundation ($448,576); foundation grants to United Way ($82,600)
Assets: $3,379,206 (fiscal 1998); $2,777,327 (fiscal 1994); $3,798,625 (fiscal 1991)
Gifts Received: $500,000 (fiscal 1998)

Typical Recipients

Arts & Humanities: Arts Associations & Councils, Arts Centers, Arts Festivals, Arts Institutes, Ballet, Historic Preservation, History & Archaeology, Museums/Galleries, Music, Opera, Public Broadcasting
Civic & Public Affairs: Asian American Affairs, Botanical Gardens/Parks, Business/Free Enterprise, Clubs, Community Foundations, Civic & Public Affairs-General, Housing, Law & Justice, Legal Aid, Parades/Festivals, Philanthropic Organizations, Professional & Trade Associations, Safety, Urban & Community Affairs, Women's Affairs, Zoos/Aquariums
Education: Business-School Partnerships, Colleges & Universities, Community & Junior Colleges, Education Funds, Engineering/Technological Education, International Studies, Literacy, Minority Education, Private Education (Precollege), Religious Education, Science/Mathematics Education, Vocational & Technical Education
Health: Alzheimers Disease, Clinics/Medical Centers, Health Organizations, Hospitals, Medical Rehabilitation
International: International Affairs, International Relations
Religion: Religious Welfare
Science: Observatories & Planetariums, Science Museums, Scientific Centers & Institutes, Scientific Labs
Social Services: Big Brother/Big Sister, Child Welfare, Delinquency & Criminal Rehabilitation, Emergency Relief, Family Planning, Family Services, Recreation & Athletics, United Funds/United Ways, YMCA/YWCA/YMHA/YWHA, Youth Organizations

Contributions Analysis

Arts & Humanities: 12%. Arts funding is given to arts associations (particularly music), institutes, opera, museums, and public broadcasting.
Civic & Public Affairs: 8%. Focus on civic institutions, such as planetariums and arboretums.
Education: 44%. Major support is given to education, including science and technology at the university level, math and science academies, foundations and universities. Also supports scholarships and matching gifts.
Health: 3%. Funds research and teaching hospitals, community hospitals serving employees, and special care facilities.
Science: 3%. Supports Museum of Science and Industry.
Social Services: 30%. Funds United Way chapters and youth organziations.
Note: Total contributions made in fiscal 1998.

Application Procedures

Initial Contact: Send a written request.
Application Requirements: Include organization's objectives, the project/activity requiring support, and the amount requested, list of donors and directors, financial statement, and evidence of tax status.
Deadlines: Requests are reviewed montly.
Decision Notification: Organizations are notified of decision approximately 15 days after receipt.
Notes: Budgeting begins for fiscal year on October 1.

Restrictions

The foundation will not support political organizations or candidates, sectarian or denominational organizations, veterans' groups, or commemorative advertising.

Additional Information

The foundation reports that its contributions program is taking a more employee-directed approach. Matching gifts account for 90% of the funding. Contributions to charitable organizations account for 10%. The only direct grants currently made are to educational institutions from which employees are recruited and to a pre-selected number of Chicago cultural institutions.

Corporate Officials

Thomas C. Berg: vice president, general counsel, secretary B 1950. ED University of Chicago BA (1972); DePaul University JD (1975). PRIM CORP EMPL vice president, general counsel, secretary: Amsted Industries Inc.

Robert A. Chiappetta: vice president, chief financial officer PRIM CORP EMPL vice president, chief financial officer: Amsted Indiana Inc.

Arthur W. Goetschel: chairman, president, chief executive officer PRIM CORP EMPL chairman, president, chief executive officer: Amsted Industries Inc.

Jerry W. Gura: director, public affairs PRIM CORP EMPL director, public affairs: AMSTED Industries Inc.

Matthew J. Hower: treasurer PRIM CORP EMPL treasurer: Amsted Indiana Inc.

Raymond A. Jean: corporate vice president PRIM CORP EMPL corporate vice president: Amsted Industries Inc.

Gordon Russell Lohman: director B Chicago, IL 1934. ED Massachusetts Institute of Technology BS (1955). PRIM CORP EMPL director: Amsted Industries Inc. CORP AFFIL director: Fortune Brands Inc.; director: Central Illinois Public Service Co; director: America Brands Inc.; outside director: Baltimore Aircoil Co. Inc.; director: Ameren Corp. NONPR AFFIL trustee: Illinois Institute Technology.

Joseph W. Newman: controller PRIM CORP EMPL controller: Amsted Indiana Inc.

Orpheus Javaras Sopranos: corporate vice president B Evanston, IL 1935. ED University of Chicago AB (1957); University of Chicago MBA (1957). PRIM CORP EMPL corporate vice president: Amsted Industries Inc. NONPR AFFIL member: American Institute CPAs; member: Illinois CPAs Society. CLUB AFFIL University Club; Mid-America Club; Skokie Country Club.

Byron D. Speice: corporate vice president PRIM CORP EMPL corporate vice president: Amsted Indiana Inc.

David B. Whitehurst: corporate vice president PRIM CORP EMPL corporate vice president: Amsted Indiana Inc.

Giving Program Officials

Jerry W. Gura: contact (see above)

Foundation Officials

Robert A. Chiappetta: trustee (see above)
Jerry W. Gura: contact (see above)
Gordon Russell Lohman: trustee (see above)

Grants Analysis

Disclosure Period: fiscal year ending September 30, 1996
Total Grants: $448,576*
Number of Grants: 349
Average Grant: $1,285
Highest Grant: $24,000
Typical Range: $100 to $3,000
***Note:** Giving excludes United Way.

Recent Grants

Note: Grants derived from fiscal 1998 Form 990.

Arts & Humanities

100,000 Salisbury House, Des Moines, IA
75,000 Terrace Hill Foundation, Des Moines, IA -- for reacreation and tourism
55,000 Des Moines Art Center, Des Moines, IA
50,000 Iowa Natural Heritage Foundation, Des Moines, IA
40,000 Des Moines Symphony Orchestra Association, Des Moines, IA
35,000 Civic Center of Greater Des Moines, Des Moines, IA
25,000 Des Moines Art Center, Des Moines, IA
25,000 Des Moines Metro Opera, Indianola, IA
25,000 Living History Farms, Urbandale, IA -- for recreation and tourism
10,000 Lyric Opera of Chicago, Chicago, IL
10,000 The Orchestral Association, Chicago, IL
5,000 Art Institute of Chicago, Chicago, IL
4,000 Ballet Chicago, Chicago, IL
4,000 Field Museum of Natural History, Chicago, IL
4,000 George W. Brown Jr. Ojibwe Museum & Cultural Center, Lac du Flambeau, WI

Civic & Public Affairs

150,000 Chinese Cultural Center of America, Ames, IA
66,667 Blank Park Zoo, Des Moines, IA
66,666 Greater Des Moines Housing Trust Fund, Des Moines, IA
30,000 Greater Des Moines Foundation, Des Moines, IA
25,000 Variety Club of Iowa, Inc., Des Moines, IA -- Huma
15,000 HOME, Inc., Des Moines, IA
15,000 Young Women's Resource Center, Des Moines, IA
14,000 Legal Aid Society of Polk County, Des Moines, IA
13,000 Legacy 150 Foundation, Des Moines, IA
5,000 The Oriental Institute, Chicago, IL
4,000 Community Chest, Geneva, IL
3,334 Morton Arboretum, Lisle, IL
3,000 Adler Planetarium, Chicago, IL
2,500 Financial Accounting Foundation, Norwalk, CT
2,500 National Aquarium in Baltimore, Baltimore, MD
2,500 Ravinia Festival, Highland Park, IL
2,500 Washington Legal Foundation, Washington, DC

Education

200,000 Drake University, Des Moines, IA
75,000 Grand View College, Des Moines, IA
72,500 Grand View College, Des Moines, IA
70,000 Iowa College Foundation, Des Moines, IA
51,000 Drake University, Des Moines, IA
50,000 Des Moines Business/Education Alliance, Des Moines, IA
30,500 Central College, Pella, IA
30,000 Grand View College, Des Moines, IA
30,000 Simpson College, Indianola, IA
24,000 IIT Trustee Challenge Campaign, Chicago, IL
20,000 Illinois Institute of Technology, Chicago, IL
20,000 United Negro College Fund, New York, NY
15,000 William Penn College, Oskaloosa, IA
10,000 Illinois Math and Science Academy, Aurora, IL
10,000 Massachusetts Institute of Technology, Cambridge, MA
8,000 North Carolina State University, Raleigh, NC
7,000 University of Chicago, Chicago, IL
5,000 Northwestern University, Evanston, IL
5,000 Purdue University, West Lafayette, IN
5,000 University of Illinois Foundation, Urbana, IL
4,100 Our Lady of the Westside School, Chicago, IL
4,000 Hanover College, Hanover, IN
4,000 Illinois Institute of Technology, Chicago, IL
4,000 St. Norbert College, DePere, WI
4,000 University of Chicago, Chicago, IL
3,434 Elgin Academy, Elgin, IL
3,400 University of Maryland Foundation, Adelphi, MD
3,000 Cornell College, Mount Vernon, IA
3,000 Foundry Educational Foundation, Des Plaines, IL
3,000 Lynchburg Christian Academy, Lynchburg, VA
3,000 Metro East Lutheran High School, Edwardsville, IL
2,400 Rosemont College, Rosemont, PA

Health

12,500 Alzheimer's Association - Iowa Golden Chapter, Des Moines, IA
10,000 Rehabilitation Institute of Chicago, Chicago, IL

International

20,000 Iowa Council for International Understanding, Des Moines, IA

Religion

25,000 Lutheran Social Service of Iowa, Des Moines, IA
20,000 House of Mercy, Des Moines, IA

Science

20,000 Science Center of Iowa, Des Moines, IA -- Arts & Culture
5,000 J. Engalitcheff Thermal Fluids Lab, Baltimore, MD
4,000 Museum of Science and Industry, Chicago, IL

Social Services

220,138 United Way of Central Iowa, Des Moines, IA
209,367 United Way of Central Iowa, Des Moines, IA
208,876 United Way of Central Iowa, Des Moines, IA
181,626 United Way of Central Iowa, Des Moines, IA
57,000 YMCA of Greater Des Moines, Des Moines, IA
44,389 United Way of Central Iowa, Des Moines, IA
34,600 American Red Cross Central Iowa Chapter, Des Moines, IA
30,000 United Way of Central Iowa, Des Moines, IA
25,000 Youth Emergency Services and Shelter, Des Moines, IA
25,000 YWCA of Greater Des Moines/Des Moines Register Learning Center, Des Moines, IA
24,600 United Way of Central Maryland, Baltimore, MD
20,000 Planned Parenthood of Greater Iowa, Inc., Des Moines, IA
20,000 United Way, Chicago, IL
20,000 YMCA of Greater Des Moines, Des Moines, IA
20,000 YMCA of Greater Des Moines, Des Moines, IA
15,000 The Foundation for Children & Families of Iowa, Des Moines, IA
15,000 Youth Law Center, Des Moines, IA
15,000 YWCA of Greater Des Moines, Des Moines, IA
12,500 Big Brothers Big Sisters of Greater Des Moines, Inc., Des Moines, IA
7,500 Alliance Area United Way, Alliance, OH
7,400 United Way of Central Delaware, Wilmington, DE
6,000 United Way of Central Indiana, Inc., Indianapolis, IN
5,000 Blue Springs Little League Baseball Inc., Blue Springs, MO
5,000 Boys & Girls Clubs of Chicago, Chicago, IL
5,000 United Way of Kenosha County, Kenosha, WI
3,300 United Way of Petis County, Sedalia, MO
2,600 United Way of Madera County, Madera, CA
2,500 Boys & Girls Clubs of America, Richardson, TX
2,500 Olathe Youth Baseball, Olathe, KS

ANALOG DEVICES, INC.

Company Contact

Norwood, MA
Web: http://www.analog.com

Company Description

Employees: 6,900
SIC(s): 3674 Semiconductors & Related Devices.

Nonmonetary Support

Value: $25,000 (1990); $150,000 (1989); $100,000 (1988)
Type: Donated Equipment; Donated Products

Corporate Sponsorship

Type: Arts & cultural events

Giving Contact

Human Resources Manager
Analog Devices, Inc.
One Technology Way
PO Box 9106
Norwood, MA 02062-9106
Phone: (781)461-3682
Fax: (781)461-4496

Description

Organization Type: Corporate Giving Program
Giving Locations: near company's major research and manufacturing sites.
Grant Types: Employee Matching Gifts, General Support, Project.

Giving Philosophy

'In the area of community responsibility, our goal is to be an asset to every community in which we operate. We strive to satisfy the goal by dealing with our customers and suppliers with honesty and integrity; by offering employees a stable work environment; by donating a portion of our profits to support worthy causes; by encouraging and supporting employees in their efforts to make their communities better places to live and work; by cultivating relationships and collaborations with other private and public concerns in our communities; and by supporting and complementing our status as an equal opportunity/affirmative action employer.' The Corporate Contributions Program at Analog Devices

Financial Summary

Total Giving: Contributes through corporate direct giving program only.

Typical Recipients

Arts & Humanities: Museums/Galleries, Public Broadcasting
Civic & Public Affairs: Zoos/Aquariums
Education: Colleges & Universities, Minority Education, Science/Mathematics Education
Environment: Environment-General
Health: Hospitals
Social Services: Community Service Organizations, United Funds/United Ways

Contributions Analysis

Giving Priorities: Higher education with emphasis on graduate education in areas of electrical engineering and computer science; arts; social service organizations; and health organizations.
Civic & Public Affairs: 10% of contributions. Supports a wide variety of local organizations in the arts, social services, civic and public affairs,and health.
Education: 90% of contributions. Supports higher education in the areas of electrical engineering and computer science with the purpose of increasing the number of engineering and computer science graduates. Emphasis on graduate level programs. Supports professorships, graduate student fellowships, facilities renovation, equipment purchases, sponsored research, and summer institutes. Also sponsors programs for employee education, cooperative students, summer interns, and matching gifts.

Application Procedures

Initial Contact: Send a brief letter or call.
Application Requirements: Provide a clear, concise, and comprehensive description of the project; explanation of project's significance to community and what the project expects to accomplish; a brief description of the organization's background and purpose; and a list of officers and directors.
Deadlines: None.
Review Process: Decisions are made throughout the year by committee of company employees representing various functions within the company.
Evaluative Criteria: The quality and quantity of technical education that the school is able to provide; quality and relevance of faculty-sponsored research in field of electronics; potential for program to be self-renewing; area of technical interest to the company; geographic proximity of institution to major company development facilities; benefit to communities where employees live and work.
Decision Notification: The education support committee meets twice a year; corporate contributions committee meets quarterly.

Restrictions

Company does not support religious or political organizations; advertising space, dinners, or other fund-raising events; professional organizations or societies; national or regional organizations; or societies or foundations for specific diseases or conditions.

Additional Information

Company prefers to support a few major activities with significant funding rather than offering many small donations.
All requests for funding are considered in light of the level of United Way support and other funding already available.
Publications: Guidelines

Corporate Officials

Russ Brown: vice president human resourceso, director B 1934. PRIM CORP EMPL vice president human resources: Analog Devices Inc.
Jerald G. Fishman: president, chief executive officer, director B 1945. ED Northeastern University MSEE; City College of New York BSEE (1967); Boston University MBA (1972). PRIM CORP EMPL president, chief executive officer, director: Analog Devices Inc. CORP AFFIL director: Kollmorgen Corp.
John Francis: manager human resources PRIM CORP EMPL manager human resources: Analog Devices Inc.
William A. Martin: treasurer PRIM CORP EMPL treasurer: Analog Devices Inc.
Brian McAloon: vice president sales PRIM CORP EMPL vice president sales: Analog Devices Inc.
Joseph E. McDonough: vice president finance, chief financial officer B 1947. ED Georgetown University BS; University of Pennsylvania MBA. PRIM CORP EMPL vice president finance, chief financial officer: Analog Devices Inc.
Ray S. Stata: chairman, chief executive officer, director B Coatesville, PA 1934. ED Massachusetts Institute of Technology BS (1957); Massachusetts Institute of Technology MS (1958). PRIM CORP EMPL chairman, chief executive officer, director: Analog Devices Inc.

Giving Program Officials

Dennis Buss: director (see above)
John Francis: community & education grant coordinator (see above)

Grants Analysis

Disclosure Period: calendar year ending
Typical Range: $5,000 to $20,000*
***Note:** Typical range for community grants is $500 to $5,000.

ANDERSEN CORP.

Company Contact

Bayport, MN

Company Description

Employees: 3,600
SIC(s): 2431 Millwork.

Corporate Sponsorship

Contact: Keith Olson, Secretary & Treasurer

Bayport Foundation

Giving Contact

Chloette Haley, Grant Consultant
Bayport Foundation
PO Box 204
Bayport, MN 55003-0204
Phone: (651)439-1557
Fax: (651)439-9480
Email: chloettehaley@scenicriver.org

Alternate Contact

Phone: 888-439-9508

Description

EIN: 416020912
Organization Type: Corporate Foundation
Giving Locations: MN: East Metro area, Washington County; WI: Pierce County, Polk County, St. Croix County
Grant Types: Capital, General Support, Multiyear/Continuing Support.

Financial Summary

Total Giving: $1,500,000 (fiscal year ending November 30, 2000 approx); $1,417,000 (fiscal 1999); $1,988,280 (fiscal 1997). Note: Contributes through foundation only. Fiscal 1997 Giving includes foundation ($1,988,280 (includes United Way $63,000)).
Assets: $41,449,505 (fiscal 1997); $36,162,244 (fiscal 1996); $32,416,287 (fiscal 1995). Note: Contributions were received from the Anderson Corporation.
Gifts Received: $620,744 (fiscal 1997); $1,400,000 (fiscal 1996); $500,000 (fiscal 1994)

Typical Recipients

Arts & Humanities: Arts Centers, Arts Institutes, Arts & Humanities-General, Historic Preservation, History & Archaeology, Libraries, Museums/Galleries, Music, Public Broadcasting, Theater
Civic & Public Affairs: Business/Free Enterprise, Civil Rights, Clubs, Community Foundations, Economic Policy, Civic & Public Affairs-General, Housing, Legal Aid, Municipalities/Towns, Public Policy, Safety, Urban & Community Affairs, Zoos/Aquariums
Education: Arts/Humanities Education, Colleges & Universities, Economic Education, Education Associations, Education Funds, Elementary Education (Private), Elementary Education (Public), Engineering/Technological Education, Education-General, Minority Education, Preschool Education, Private Education (Precollege), Public Education (Precollege), Religious Education, Science/Mathematics Education, Special Education, Student Aid, Vocational & Technical Education
Environment: Environment-General, Resource Conservation
Health: Cancer, Children's Health/Hospitals, Clinics/Medical Centers, Emergency/Ambulance Services,

Eyes/Blindness, Health Funds, Health Organizations, Hospitals, Kidney, Medical Rehabilitation, Medical Research, Public Health, Single-Disease Health Associations, Speech & Hearing
International: International Peace & Security Issues
Religion: Churches, Religious Organizations, Religious Welfare
Science: Science Museums
Social Services: Animal Protection, Camps, Child Welfare, Community Centers, Community Service Organizations, Emergency Relief, Family Planning, Family Services, Food/Clothing Distribution, Homes, People with Disabilities, Recreation & Athletics, Refugee Assistance, Scouts, Substance Abuse, United Funds/United Ways, Volunteer Services, YMCA/YWCA/YMHA/YWHA, Youth Organizations

Contributions Analysis

Giving Priorities: Youth organizations, united way, education, health organizations, arts, churches, and civic organizations.
Arts & Humanities: 5% to 10%. Funding priorities include orchestras, music camps, and art centers.
Civic & Public Affairs: 5% to 10%. Most funding benefits local fire and rescue departments and libraries.
Education: About 5%. Focus is on precollege education, with major support typically given to school districts, public and private elementary schools, and arts educationfor children. Educational television, colleges and universities, and education associations also receive support.
Health: 30% to 35%. Supports local hospitals, medical research, and single-disease health organizations.
Religion: About 5%. Predominantly supports local churches with capital grants.
Social Services: 25% to 30%. Emphasis on youth organizations. Awards major grants to the United Way and the Salvation Army. Other interests include the aged, community service organizations, recreation and athletics, and volunteer services.

Application Procedures

Initial Contact: brief written request
Application Requirements: a description of organization, amount requested, purpose of funds sought, recently audited financial statement, and proof of tax-exempt status
Deadlines: None.

Foundation Officials

Mary Andersen Hulings: vice president CORP AFFIL director: Andersen Corp.; director: Andersen Windows.
Harold C. Meissner: vice president B 1917. PRIM CORP EMPL assistant chairman, chief executive officer, director: Andersen Corp.
Keith D. Olson: secretary, treasurer
Pat Riley: director
W. Arvid Wellman: president, director B 1918. PRIM CORP EMPL chairman, chief executive officer, director: Andersen Corp.

Grants Analysis

Disclosure Period: fiscal year ending November 30, 1997
Total Grants: $1,925,280*
Number of Grants: 140
Average Grant: $13,752
Highest Grant: $250,000
Typical Range: $1,000 to $20,000
***Note:** Giving excludes United Way.

Recent Grants

Note: Grants derived from fiscal 1998 Form 990.

Arts & Humanities

36,000 Twin Cities Public TV, St. Paul, MN
26,000 St. Paul Chamber Orchestra, St. Paul, MN
22,000 Minnesota Orchestral Association, Minneapolis, MN
15,000 St. Croix Center for Arts, St. Croix, MN
11,000 Bayport Public Library Foundation, Bayport, MN
10,000 Hudson Band Backers, Inc., Hudson, WI
9,500 Minnesota Public Radio, Inc., St. Paul, MN
9,000 Phipps Center for the Arts, Minneapolis, MN

Civic & Public Affairs

65,000 National Right to Work Legal Defense Foundation, Washington, DC
25,000 St. Croix Valley Community Foundation, Stillwater, MN
10,000 Kiwanas of St. Paul Foundation, St. Paul, MN
7,500 Marine Volunteer Fire Department, Edwardsville, IL

Education

30,000 Independent School District 834, Stillwater, MN
25,000 University of Minnesota, St. Paul, MN
12,000 Learning Disabilities Association, St. Paul, MN
8,000 Minnesota Council on Economic Education, St. Paul, MN

Environment

10,000 Carpenter SCV Nature Center, Hastings, MN

Health

150,000 Courage Center, St. Paul, MN
25,000 Gillette Children's Hospital, St. Paul, MN
15,000 Hazelden Foundation, Center City, MN
10,000 St. Croix County Department of Health, St. Croix, MN
10,000 Vision Loss Resources, Inc., Minneapolis, MN
6,500 Research & Development - Camp Avanti, St. Croix, MN
5,000 Pierce Country Public Health, Ellsworth, WI

Religion

250,000 Presbyterian Homes, Arden Hills, MN
25,000 Salvation Army, St. Paul, MN
10,000 Mt. Zion Lutheran Church, Alexandria, MN
10,000 St. Paul's Episcopal Church, Virginia, MN
6,500 St. Croix Valley Chaplaincy Association, St. Croix, MN
6,000 First Lutheran Church, Westby, WI
5,000 Christ Lutheran Church, Minneapolis, MN
5,000 First Evangelical Lutheran, Pillager, MN
5,000 Immanuel Evangelical Lutheran, Gaylord, MN
5,000 St. John's Lutheran Church, Chaska, MN

Science

10,800 Science Museum of Minnesota, St. Paul, MN

Social Services

140,000 Girl Scout Council of St. Croix Valley, St. Croix, MN
61,000 Boy Scouts of America, Indianhead Council, St. Paul, MN
17,500 Family Service of St. Croix Area, St. Croix, MN
15,000 YMCA, Hudson, WI -- Camp St. Croix
10,500 YMCA of Minneapolis, Minneapolis, MN
10,000 Amery Youth Hockey Association, Amery, WI
10,000 Blackhawk Hockey Association, Baldwin, WI
10,000 Community Volunteer Service, St. Paul, MN
10,000 St. Croix Animal Shelter, St. Croix, MN
8,000 Youth Leadership, Minneapolis, MN
7,000 Young Life, St. Croix Valley Chapter, Stillwater, MN
6,000 St. Croix Valley Teen Center, Stillwater, MN
5,000 Family Resource Center, Lindstrom, MN
5,000 YWCA of St. Paul, St. Paul, MN

Andersons Inc.

Company Contact

Maumee, OH

Company Description

Former Name: The Andersons.
Employees: 3,024
SIC(s): 0119 Cash Grains Nec, 5153 Grain & Field Beans, 5191 Farm Supplies, 7389 Business Services Nec.

Anderson Foundation

Giving Contact

Beverly J. Lange, Secretary to the Chairman
Anderson Foundation
PO Box 119
Maumee, OH 43537
Phone: (419)891-6404
Fax: (419)891-6695

Description

EIN: 346528868
Organization Type: Corporate Foundation
Giving Locations: headquarters and operating communities, including plant locations.
Grant Types: Capital, Employee Matching Gifts, General Support, Project, Seed Money.
Note: Employee matching gift ratio: 1 to 1.

Giving Philosophy

'The Anderson Foundation strives to enhance the quality of life in communities where facilities owned and/or operated by the Andersons are located. There is a tendency to select donees located in communities where the trustees and donors of the foundation are best acquainted with the specific charitable programs under consideration..' *Anderson Foundation*

Financial Summary

Total Giving: $726,000 (1998); $723,189 (1997); $969,000 (1996). Note: Contributes through corporate direct giving program and foundation.
Giving Analysis: Giving for 1995 includes: foundation ($589,419); foundation grants to United Way ($240,135); 1996: foundation ($602,694); foundation grants to United Way ($248,461); 1997: foundation ($470,971); foundation grants to United Way ($252,218)
Assets: $5,159,335 (1997); $4,990,520 (1996); $5,267,394 (1995)
Gifts Received: $750,369 (1994); $520,847 (1993); $209,153 (1992). Note: Foundation receives contributions from The Andersons.

Typical Recipients

Arts & Humanities: Arts Associations & Councils, Arts Centers, Historic Preservation, History & Archaeology, Libraries, Museums/Galleries, Music, Opera, Public Broadcasting, Theater
Civic & Public Affairs: African American Affairs, Botanical Gardens/Parks, Clubs, Economic Development, Economic Policy, Housing, Municipalities/Towns, Parades/Festivals, Public Policy, Rural Affairs, Safety, Urban & Community Affairs, Zoos/Aquariums

Education: Agricultural Education, Business Education, Colleges & Universities, Education Associations, Education Funds, Education Reform, Education-General, Literacy, Minority Education, Private Education (Precollege), Public Education (Precollege), Science/Mathematics Education, Secondary Education (Private), Secondary Education (Public), Vocational & Technical Education
Environment: Environment-General, Wildlife Protection
Health: Clinics/Medical Centers, Emergency/Ambulance Services, Hospices, Hospitals, Medical Research, Mental Health, Nursing Services, Preventive Medicine/Wellness Organizations, Single-Disease Health Associations
Religion: Churches, Ministries, Religious Organizations, Religious Welfare
Science: Scientific Centers & Institutes, Scientific Organizations, Scientific Research
Social Services: Animal Protection, Camps, Child Welfare, Community Centers, Community Service Organizations, Family Services, Food/Clothing Distribution, People with Disabilities, Recreation & Athletics, Refugee Assistance, Scouts, Senior Services, United Funds/United Ways, YMCA/YWCA/YMHA/YWHA, Youth Organizations

Contributions Analysis

Giving Priorities: Major support for United Way, social services, the arts, and civic causes.
Arts & Humanities: About 15%. Primarily supports orchestras and operas. Also funds libraries, museums, public broadcasting, and arts associations.
Civic & Public Affairs: 10% to 15%. Supports economic development, zoos, botanical gardens, and local and community organizations.
Education: 5% to 10%. Supports colleges and universities. Also funds public and private precollege education and agricultural education.
Religion: 5% to 10%. Supports a variety of churches, missionary activities, and church auxiliaries. Funds Catholic, Protestant, and nonsectarian organizations.
Science: Less than 5%. Contributes funds to science and research institutes.
Social Services: About 50% of total contributions. The majority of social service grants support United Way chapters. Also, foundation gives to youth activities, food banks, community service organizations, YMCA's and shelters.
Note: Total contributions in 1997.

Application Procedures

Initial Contact: Send a brief letter of inquiry, not more than five pages.
Application Requirements: Include a description of the organization, with organization's purpose and objectives; need the project intends to address; geographical area and population to be served; timetable for the project; name(s) and qualifications of the person who will administer the grant; how the success of the project will be evaluated; amount requested; purpose of funds sought; recently audited financial statements; proof of tax-exempt status; list of officers and directors; and list of major donors.
Deadlines: At least three weeks before quarterly board meetings, which are in March, June, September, and December.

Restrictions

Does not support individuals, or political or lobbying groups. Also not funded are endowments, church building or operating funds, or building or operating funds for elementary schools.
Generally, does not serve as major, or sole, funder of project.

Additional Information

The foundation's major donor is The Andersons, Inc., but the foundation reports that its activities are separate. The company does offer a very limited amount of direct giving in its headquarters area.

Corporate Officials

Thomas Harold Anderson: chairman, director B Toledo, OH 1924. PRIM CORP EMPL chairman, director: The Andersons Inc.

Foundation Officials

Charles D. Anderson: trustee B Detroit, MI 1931. ED Michigan School of Mines (1953). PRIM CORP EMPL chairman, president: Anderson Tool Sales Inc. CORP AFFIL chairman: ATD Tools Corp. NONPR AFFIL member: Fraternal Order Eagles.
Jeffrey W. Anderson: trustee
Kevin Anderson: trustee
Mary Anderson: trustee
Thomas Harold Anderson: chairman, trustee (see above)
Martha Corcoran: trustee
John P. Kraus: trustee
Beverly J. Lange: secretary PRIM CORP EMPL secretary: Andersons Management Corp.

Grants Analysis

Disclosure Period: calendar year ending 1997
Total Grants: $470,971*
Number of Grants: 155
Average Grant: $3,039
Highest Grant: $207,340
Typical Range: $100 to $5,500
***Note:** Giving excludes United Way.

Recent Grants

Note: Grants derived from 1997 Form 990.

Arts & Humanities

50,000	Toledo Orchestra Association, Toledo, OH
16,667	Toledo Cultural Arts Center, Toledo, OH
10,400	WOSU/Public Broadcasting, Columbus, OH
10,150	Toledo Lucas County Public Library, Toledo, OH
5,685	WGTE-TV 30/Public Broadcasting Foundation of Northwest Ohio, Toledo, OH
5,000	Jay County Library, Portland, IN
5,000	Stranahan Theater Trust, Toledo, OH
3,110	WGBU-TV/PBS at Bowling Green State University, Bowling Green, OH
2,500	Arts Commission, Toledo, OH

Civic & Public Affairs

51,000	Toledo Zoological Society, Toledo, OH
10,000	Farm Labor Research Project, Toledo, OH
10,000	Greater Toledo Urban League, Toledo, OH
5,200	Connecting Point, Toledo, OH
5,000	Local Initiatives Support Corporation, Toledo, OH
3,333	Fulton County Agriculture Society, Fayette, OH
3,000	Corporation for Effective Government, Toledo, OH
2,000	Keep Toledo/Lucas County Beautiful, Toledo, OH

Education

25,100	Ohio State University, Columbus, OH
5,800	University of Toledo, Toledo, OH
5,250	Future Farmers of America Foundation, Alexandria, VA
5,000	4-H Camp Palmer, Fayette, OH
5,000	Ohio Foundation of Independent Colleges, Columbus, OH
5,000	Wells County 4-H, Bluffton, IN
3,000	Junior Achievement of Northwest Ohio, Toledo, OH

Environment

2,000	The Wilds, Columbus, OH

Health

5,000	Northwest Ohio Hospice Association, Toledo, OH
4,000	Wellness Community, Perrysburg, OH
1,800	Mercy and St. Charles Hospitals, Oregon, OH
1,667	Visiting Nurses Association, Toledo, OH
1,200	American Red Cross, Toledo, OH

Religion

40,000	Sisters of Notre Dame, Toledo, OH
8,333	Catholic Youth Organization, Toledo, OH
5,000	Central City Ministries, Toledo, OH
3,433	St. Thomas More University Parish, Bowling Green, OH
2,750	Davids House of Compassion, Toledo, OH

Science

3,334	Edison Industrial Systems Center, Toledo, OH
1,200	Agricultural Research Institute, Bethesda, MD

Social Services

207,340	United Way, Toledo, OH
91,553	YMCA, Toledo, OH
13,121	United Way of Franklin County, Columbus, OH
5,489	United Way, Lima, OH
5,384	United Way of Cass County, Logansport, IN
5,000	YMCA, Lima, OH
3,455	United Way of Champaign County, Savoy, IL
3,050	United Way of Monroe County, Monroe, MI
2,500	AASK Midwest, Toledo, OH -- aid to adoption of special kids
1,992	United Way of Delaware County, Muncie, IN
1,343	United Way of Wells County, Bluffton, IN
1,293	United Way of Western St. Joseph County, Three Rivers, MI
1,174	United Way, Delta, OH

ANHEUSER-BUSCH COMPANIES, INC.

Company Contact

St. Louis, MO
Web: http://www.anheuser-busch.com

Company Description

Revenue: US$11,704,000,000 (1999)
Employees: 23,344 (1999)
Fortune Rank: 151, per FORTUNE Magazine's list of 500 Largest U.S. Corporations (1999).
FF 151
SIC(s): 2046 Wet Corn Milling, 2051 Bread, Cake & Related Products, 2082 Malt Beverages, 6719 Holding Companies Nec.

Nonmonetary Support

Type: Donated Products
Volunteer Programs: Through the Anheuser-Busch Employee Volunteer Grant Program, the company supports and recognizes its employees who actively volunteer their time and talents to nonprofit organizations by making grants to these organizations for unusual or special projects. An Employee Matching Gifts Program for educational institutions is also offered through the company's charitable foundation.
Note: The company has donated cans of fresh drinking water to victims of natural disasters.

Corporate Sponsorship

Type: Sports events; Arts & cultural events
Contact: Tony Ponturo, Vice President, Corporate Media & Sports Marketing

Anheuser-Busch Foundation/Anheuser-Busch Charitable Trust

Giving Contact

Jayne Nicholson, Contributions Specialist
Anheuser-Busch Companies
1 Busch Place
St. Louis, MO 63118-1852
Phone: (314)577-2453
Fax: (314)577-3251

Description

Founded: 1975
EIN: 510168084
Organization Type: Corporate Foundation
Giving Locations: principally near operating locations and to national organizations.
Grant Types: Capital, Employee Matching Gifts, General Support.

Giving Philosophy

'Since its earliest days, Anheuser-Busch has been deeply concerned with human needs and the quality of life. In fact, after the San Francisco earthquake in 1906, Adolphus Busch donated $100,000 to aid the victims of the disaster. Anheuser-Busch believes strongly in giving back to the communities in which it does business, and this is why the company and its charitable foundation donate funds to hundreds of charitable organizations each year. In 1995, Anheuser-Busch provided disaster relief after the Oklahoma City bombing, flooding in California, Missouri, and Louisiana, and hurricanes in Florida, Georgia, the Virgin Islands, and Puerto Rico.

'Anheuser-Busch supports many organizations that work for minority economic development, preservation of cultural heritage, educational opportunities, and leadership development. Anheuser-Busch and its family of wholesalers are also the largest corporate supporters of the National Hispanic Scholarship Fund, contributing more than $26,000,000 in the past 13 years.

'Anheuser-Busch has a long-standing commitment to the communities where it operates breweries and other major facilities. The company's corporate contributions program is designed to benefit, support and strengthen those communities through donations to a broad range of local nonprofit organizations, including colleges and universities, health care institutions, social service agencies, civic organizations, and arts and cultural groups.

'Anheuser-Busch informs consumers of its support of various national and local organizations through its 'Glad to be Your Neighbor, Proud to be Your Friend' advertising campaign. This effort encourages others to lend their support to these worthwhile endeavors.'
Anheuser-Busch Companies 1996/1997 Fact Book

Financial Summary

Total Giving: $6,270,907 (1997); $9,646,319 (1996); $13,608,809 (1994). Note: Contributes through corporate direct giving program and foundation.
Giving Analysis: Giving for 1996 includes: foundation ($7,620,879); foundation grants to United Way ($2,025,440); 1997: foundation ($6,270,907)
Assets: $49,286,482 (1997); $46,306,638 (1996); $69,150,927 (1994 approx)
Gifts Received: $1,024,131 (1997); $62,522 (1994); $7,287 (1993)

Typical Recipients

Arts & Humanities: Arts Associations & Councils, Arts Centers, Arts Funds, Community Arts, Historic Preservation, History & Archaeology, Libraries, Museums/Galleries, Music, Performing Arts, Public Broadcasting, Theater
Civic & Public Affairs: African American Affairs, Botanical Gardens/Parks, Civil Rights, Clubs, Employment/Job Training, Hispanic Affairs, Housing, Law & Justice, Public Policy, Rural Affairs, Urban & Community Affairs, Zoos/Aquariums
Education: Agricultural Education, Arts/Humanities Education, Business Education, Colleges & Universities, Continuing Education, Education Funds, Education Reform, Engineering/Technological Education, Education-General, Health & Physical Education, International Exchange, Literacy, Medical Education, Minority Education, Private Education (Precollege), Public Education (Precollege), Science/Mathematics Education, Secondary Education (Private), Secondary Education (Public), Special Education, Student Aid, Vocational & Technical Education
Environment: Air/Water Quality, Environment-General, Resource Conservation, Wildlife Protection
Health: AIDS/HIV, Alzheimers Disease, Cancer, Children's Health/Hospitals, Emergency/Ambulance Services, Health Policy/Cost Containment, Health Organizations, Heart, Hospitals, Medical Research, Public Health, Single-Disease Health Associations
Religion: Jewish Causes, Religious Welfare, Seminaries
Science: Scientific Centers & Institutes, Scientific Organizations, Scientific Research
Social Services: At-Risk Youth, Child Welfare, Community Service Organizations, Counseling, Delinquency & Criminal Rehabilitation, Emergency Relief, Food/Clothing Distribution, People with Disabilities, Recreation & Athletics, Scouts, Senior Services, Shelters/Homelessness, Substance Abuse, United Funds/United Ways, Volunteer Services, YMCA/YWCA/YMHA/YWHA, Youth Organizations

Contributions Analysis

Giving Priorities: Education, Health Care, Human Services, Minorities and Youth, Cultural Enrichment, and Environemntal Protection.
Arts & Humanities: About 5%. Supports music groups, television, and libraries.
Civic & Public Affairs: 5% to 10%.
Education: 25% to 30%. Primarily supports colleges and universities near company's major facilities.
Environment: About 10%. Supports such organizations as The Nature Conservancy, The Conservation Fund, National Fish and Wildlife Foundation, Center for Marine Conservation, The National Wildlife Foundation, and the World Bird Sanctuary.
Health: 10% to 15%. Major support to American Red Cross. Also supports hospitals and single-disease health organizations.
Social Services: About 30%. Primarily supports the United Way, programs for minorities, and organizations serving youth.

Application Procedures

Initial Contact: Write or call to request guidelines form.
Application Requirements: Include information on the organization such as official name, complete mailing address, phone number, brief general description of purpose and major activities, amount and purpose of request, your affiliation with United Way, and does your organization have a permanent liquor license; most recent audited financial statement; current operating budget; annual report; list of board members, with affiliations; proof of tax-exempt status; and list of current funders.
Deadlines: None.
Decision Notification: Review takes approximately six to eight weeks.

Restrictions

Does not support individuals, political organizations, organizations whose activities are primarily religious, social or fraternal groups, athletic organizations, hospital operating budgets, or organizations that do not have tax-exempt status.

Additional Information

As the world's largest brewer, Anheuser-Busch works to encourage responsible drinking among adults who choose to drink and to fight alcohol abuse, drunk driving, and underage drinking. Anheuser-Busch is a major supporter of alcohol education efforts on college campuses, including the BACHUS (Boost Alcohol Consciousness Concerning the Health of University Students) peer-education network, the National Collegiate Athletic Association Foundation's 'Choices' grant program, 'TIPS for the University' program, and National Collegiate Alcohol Awareness Week.

The company's Busch Gardens and Sea World parks care for endangered and threatened species, such as manatees. The Sea World Parks are known for their rescue and rehabilitation programs. The Anheuser-Busch Theme Parks also support 'A Pledge and a Promise' environmental awards program. Established in 1993, the program is held in cooperation with national conservation organizations to honor outstanding efforts of school groups that have made positive contributions to the environment. It offers 13 awards totaling $100,000. The company sponsors an innovative urban beautification program, Operation Brightside, in 12 communities where its breweries are located. The program is based on a public/private partnership designed to involve citizens in cleaning up their cities and, more importantly, in keeping them clean.
Publications: Guidelines; Application Form

Corporate Officials

August Adolphus Busch, III: chairman, president, chief executive officer B Saint Louis, MO 1937. ED University of Arizona (1957-1958); Siebel Institute of Technology (1960-1961). PRIM CORP EMPL chairman, president, chief executive officer: Anheuser-Busch Companies, Inc. CORP AFFIL director: Save Mart Supermarkets; director: Southwest Bell Corp.; director: Manufacturers Railway Co.; director: Saint Louis Refrigerator Co.; director: Emerson Electric Co.; director: General America Life Insurance Co.; officer: Busch Media Group Inc.; director: Civic Center Corp. NONPR AFFIL director: SBC Community Inc.; director: United Way of Saint Louis; vice president: Greater Saint Louis Area; president executive board: Saint Louis Boy Scouts America. CLUB AFFIL Noonday Club; Saint Louis Country Club; Log Cabin Club.

Giving Program Officials

JoBeth Goode Brown: trustee B Oakdale, LA 1950. ED Tulane University Newcomb College BA (1972); Washington University JD (1979). PRIM CORP EMPL vice president, secretary: Anheuser-Busch Companies, Inc. CORP AFFIL secretary: Busch Mechanical Services Inc. NONPR AFFIL member: Order Coif; director: Saint Louis Zoo Friends; member: Missouri Womens Forum; secretary: International Womens Forum; member: Missouri Bar Association; member: American Society of Corporate Secretaries; member: Bar Association Metropolitan Saint Louis; member: American Bar Association.
August Adolphus Busch, III: trustee B Saint Louis, MO 1937. ED University of Arizona (1957-1958); Siebel Institute of Technology (1960-1961). PRIM CORP EMPL chairman, president, chief executive officer: Anheuser-Busch Companies, Inc. CORP AFFIL director: Save Mart Supermarkets; director: Southwest Bell Corp.; director: Manufacturers Railway Co.; director: Saint Louis Refrigerator Co.; director: Emerson Electric Co.; director: General America Life Insurance Co.; officer: Busch Media Group Inc.; director: Civic Center Corp. NONPR AFFIL director: SBC Community Inc.; director: United Way of Saint Louis; vice president: Greater Saint Louis Area; president executive board: Saint Louis Boy Scouts America. CLUB AFFIL Noonday Club; Saint Louis Country Club; Log Cabin Club.
Jayne Nicholson: contributions specialist

Grants Analysis

Disclosure Period: calendar year ending 1996
Total Grants: $7,620,879*
Number of Grants: 582
Average Grant: $13,094
Highest Grant: $500,000
Typical Range: $5,000 to $50,000
***Note:** Giving excludes United Way.

Recent Grants

Note: Grants derived from 1998 Form 990.

Arts & Humanities

250,000 American Battle Monuments, Arlington, VA
250,000 Missouri Historical Society, St. Louis, MO
8,333 De Menil House Foundation, Houston, TX

Civic & Public Affairs

500,000 St Louis Zoo Foundation, St. Louis, MO
50,000 Welfare to Work Partnership, Washington, DC

Education

100,000 Ranken Technical College, St. Louis, MO
40,000 Stetson University, Miami, FL
36,807 Washington University, St. Louis, MO
34,640 Saint Louis University, St. Louis, MO
25,000 University of North Florida, Jacksonville, FL
15,725 Cornell University, Ithaca, NY
15,121 University of Florida Foundation, Inc., Gainesville, FL
12,348 Saint Louis University High School, St. Louis, MO
11,500 Westminster Christian Academy, St. Louis, MO
8,450 University of Missouri-Columbia, Columbia, MO
6,760 Maryville University, St. Louis, MO
6,635 Whitfield School, St. Louis, MO
6,195 Mary Institute/Saint Louis Country Day, St. Louis, MO
475 The Kansas State University Foundation, Manhattan, KS

Environment

20,000 New England Water Works Association Inc, Milford, MA

Health

100,000 American Red Cross National Disaster Relief Fund, St. Louis, MO

Religion

71,429 The Salvation Army, St. Louis, MO
50,000 Jewish Community Centers Association, St. Louis, MO
10,150 Concordia Seminary, St. Louis, MO

Social Services

200,000 YMCA of Greater St Louis, St. Louis, MO
100,000 American Red Cross National Disaster Fund, St. Louis, MO
100,000 Girl Scout Council of Greater St Louis, St. Louis, MO
70,000 YWCA-Houston, Houston, TX
20,000 Washington Tennis Foundation Inc, St. Louis, MO
10,000 Kids Under Twenty-One, St. Louis, MO
10,000 YMCA-North Valley, Mission Hills, CA

AON CORP.

Company Contact

Chicago, IL
Web: http://www.aon.com

Company Description

Revenue: US$6,492,900,000
Employees: 40,000
Fortune Rank: 248, per FORTUNE Magazine's list of 500 Largest U.S. Corporations (1999).
FF 248
SIC(s): 6411 Insurance Agents, Brokers & Service, 6719 Holding Companies Nec.

Operating Locations

Cyprus: Hellenic Bain Clarkson EPE, Nicosia; Denmark: Aon Danmark A/S, Copenhagen; Aon Holdings Scandinavia A/S, Copenhagen; Aon Pensionsradgivning A/S, Copenhagen; Aon Risk Management Services Scandinavia A/S, Copenhagen; Aon Specialty Denmark A/S, Copenhagen; Germany: Aon Deutschland GmbH, Hamburg; Aon Wacus Verwaltungs GmbH, Hamburg; Carstens and Schuees GmbH & Co. KG, Hamburg; Carstens and Schuees Verwaltungs GmbH, Hamburg; CIA Deutschland Kreditversicherungsmakler und Beratungs GmbH, Hamburg; Hanseatisches Assekuranz Kontor GmbH, Hamburg; Havag Hudiglangefeldt GmbH, Hamburg; Jonny Pape GmbH, Hamburg; Rollins Hudig Hall Holdings (Deutschland) GmbH, Hamburg; London General Holdings Ltd. Zweigniederlassung Wiesbaden, Wiesbaden, Hessen; Vereinigte Versicherungsges von Amerika Unfallversicherungen Zweigndl der Combined Insurance Co. of America, Wiesbaden, Hessen; Greece: Hellenic Bain Clarkson SA, Athens, Attiki; Hong Kong: Bain Clarkson (Hong Kong) Ltd., Central District; Captive Management Services Ltd., Central District; Gilman (Life and Pensions) Ltd., Central District; Inchcape Insurance Holdings (Hong Kong) Ltd., Central District; Ireland: Clarkson Puckle (Ireland) Ltd., Dublin; Combined Insurance Co. of Ireland Ltd., Dublin; Combined Life Assurance Co. of Europe Ltd., Dublin; Kenya: Insurance Holdings (Africa) Ltd., Nairobi; Mexico: Alexander and Alexander Mexico, Ciudad de Mexico; Asesores Kennedy Agentes de Seguro y de Fianzas SA de CV, Ciudad de Mexico; Inmuebles Niagara SA de CV, Ciudad de Mexico; Grupo Kena SA de CV, Naucalpan; Netherlands: Aon Re Netherlands CV Reinsurance Brokers, Amsterdam, Noord-Holland; BH Insurance Holdings BV, Amsterdam, Noord-Holland; Blom En Van der AA Holding BV, Amsterdam, Noord-Holland; BV Assurantiekantoor Langeveldt-Schroder, Amsterdam, Noord-Holland; Hudig Langeveldt Reinsurance CV, Amsterdam, Noord-Holland; Langeveldt Groep BV, Amsterdam, Noord-Holland; London General Holdings Ltd., Amsterdam, Noord-Holland; Paribas Assurantien BV, Amsterdam, Noord-Holland; Pat Ryan & Associates, Amsterdam, Noord-Holland; Hudig Langeveldt Merwestad BV, Dordrecht, Zuid-Holland; Aon Hudig Groningen BV, Groningen; Aon Hudig Hengelo BV, Hengelo, Overijssel; Aon Hudig Nijmegen BV, Nijmegen, Gelderland; Ascom Nijmegen BV, Nijmegen, Gelderland; Aon Hudig Noordwijk BV, Noordwijk, Zuid-Holland; Saat Van Marwijk Beheer BV, Noordwijk, Zuid-Holland; Saat Van Marwijk Noordwijk BV, Noordwijk, Zuid-Holland; Aon BV, Rotterdam, Zuid-Holland; Aon Captive Services (Nederland) BV, Rotterdam, Zuid-Holland; Aon Groep Nederland BV, Rotterdam, Zuid-Holland; Aon Holdings Asia BV, Rotterdam, Zuid-Holland; Aon Holdings BV, Rotterdam, Zuid-Holland; Aon Intl BV, Rotterdam, Zuid-Holland; Aon Makelaars in Assurantien BV, Rotterdam, Zuid-Holland; Aon Risk Consultants BV, Rotterdam, Zuid-Holland; Bloemers and Co. Herverzekering BV, Rotterdam, Zuid-Holland; Hudig Langeveldt Janson Elffers BV, Rotterdam, Zuid-Holland; Hudig Langeveldt Makelaardij in Assurantien BV, Rotterdam, Zuid-Holland; Hudig Langeveldt (Pensioenbureau) BV, Rotterdam, Zuid-Holland; Langeveldt de Vos BV, Rotterdam, Zuid-Holland; Rollins Hudig Hall Netherlands BV, Rotterdam, Zuid-Holland; AH Laseur BV, S'Gravenhage, Zuid-Holland; Aon Hudig Tilburg BV, Tilburg, Noord-Brabant; Aon Hudig Venlo BV, Venlo, Limburg; Norway: Aon Norway AS, Oslo, Akershus; Duo A/S, Oslo, Akershus; New Zealand: Harvey Trinder (New Zealand) Ltd., Auckland; Singapore: Bain Clarkson Insurance Brokers Pte. Ltd., Singapore; Credit Insurance Association (S) Pte. Ltd., Singapore; Spain: Aon Warranty Group SA, Barcelona, Cataluna; Sweden: Aon Sweden Syd AB; Bain Clarkson Consulting AB; Bain Clarkson Smaland AB; Industri Risk Management AB; Bain Clarkson Sweden AB, Stockholm; United Kingdom: Aon Trustee Services Ltd., Birmingham, West Midlands; Clarkson Puckle Construction Insurance Consultants Ltd., Birmingham, West Midlands; HRGM (UK) Ltd., Birmingham, West Midlands; Bain Hogg Group Ltd., Bristol, Avon; United Rental Group Ltd., Chesterfield, Derbyshire; Broadgate Holding Ltd., Coventry, West Midlands; Clarkson Puckle Scotland Ltd., Edinburgh, Lothian; Hogg Robinson (Scotland) Ltd., Edinburgh, Lothian; Nigel Morris and Associates Ltd., Edinburgh, Lothian; Godwins Ltd., Farnborough, Hampshire; Godwins (Trustees) Ltd., Farnborough, Hampshire; Burlington Insurance Services Ltd., Folkestone, Kent; Aon Surety & Guarantee Ltd., Forest Row, East Sussex; Assuco Holdings Ltd., Guernsey, Channel Islands; Hogg Insurance Management Ltd., Guernsey, Channel Islands; Leslie and Godwin (CI) Ltd., Guernsey, Channel Islands; Aon Entertainment Risk Services Ltd., Iver, Buckingham; Combined Insurance Co. of America, Kingston-Upon-Thames, Surrey; Combined Life Assurance Co. Ltd., Kingston-Upon-Thames, Surrey; London General Holdings Ltd., Kingston-Upon-Thames, Surrey; London General Insurance Co. Ltd., Kingston-Upon-Thames, Surrey; Poland Puckle Insurance Brokers Ltd., Liphook, Hampshire; A1 Insurance Agency Ltd., London; Agricola Training Ltd., London; Agricola Underwriting Ltd., London; Agricultural Risk Control Ltd., London; Agricultural Risk Management Ltd., London; Airscope Ltd., London; Alexander and Alexander Ltd., London; Aon Advisors (United Kingdom) Ltd., London; Aon Alexander Howden Ltd., London; Aon Alexander Ltd., London; Aon Bain Hogg Ltd., London; Aon Construction Services Intl Ltd., London; Aon Consulting Group Ltd., London; Aon India Ltd., London; Aon Overseas Holdings Ltd., London; Aon Pyramid International Ltd., London; Aon Re Special Risks Ltd., London; Aon Re UK Ltd., London; Aon Risk Consultants (Europe) Ltd., London; Aon Risk Resources Ltd., London; Aon Risk Services Holdings United Kingdom Ltd., London; Aon UK Holdings Ltd., London; Artscope Insurance Services Ltd., London; Artscope International Insurance Services Ltd., London; Asset Security Managers Ltd., London; Bain Clarkson Ltd., London; Bain Clarkson RB Ltd., London; Bain Clarkson Underwriting Management Ltd., London; Bain Dawes Services Ltd., London; Bain Hogg (Hellas) Ltd., London; Bain Hogg Holdings Ltd., London; Bain Hogg Intl Holdings Ltd., London; Bain Hogg Intl Ltd., London; Bain Hogg Ltd., London; Bain Hogg Management Ltd., London; Bainsons and Golmick Ltd., London; Bankassure Insurance Services Ltd., London; Bec Insurance Services Ltd., London; Bevington Lowndes Ltd., London; BL Carnie Hogg Robinson Ltd., London; Camperdown Ltd., London; CIA Link Ltd., London; Clarkson Bain Japan Ltd., London; Clarkson Puckle Aviation Insurance Ltd., London; Clarkson Puckle Group Ltd., London; Clarkson Puckle Holding Ltd., London; Clarkson Puckle Home Ltd., London; Clarkson Puckle International Reinsurances Ltd., London; Clarkson Puckle International Risks Ltd., London; Clarkson Puckle North America Ltd., London; Clarkson Puckle Overseas Ltd., London; Clarkson Puckle UK Ltd., London; Clarkson Reinsurance and Underwriting Consultants Ltd., London; Clay and Patners Pension Trustees Ltd., London; Commercial and Political Risk Consultants Ltd., London; Commercial and Political Risk Services Ltd., London; Contract and Investment Recoveries Ltd., London; Credit Indemnity and Financial Services Ltd., London; Credit Insurance Association Ltd., London; Credit Insurance Research Unit Ltd., London; Credit and Political Insurance Services Ltd., London; Credit and Political Risks Reinsurance Consultants Ltd., London; Document Risk Management Ltd., London; Downes and Burke (Special Risks) Ltd., London; Eastaf Holdings Ltd., London; Edward Lumley Financial

Services Ltd., London; Edward Lumley and Sons (Underwriting Agencies) Ltd., London; Ernest A. Notcutt (Overseas) Ltd., London; Ernest Notcutt Insurance Services Ltd., London; Figurecheck Ltd., London; Fortis Hogg Robinson Ltd., London; Gardner Mountain and Capel-Cure Agencies Ltd., London; Gardner Mountain Management Services Ltd., London; HARB Ltd., London; HGRM Marine Ltd., London; HIB Ltd., London; Highplain Ltd., London; Hobbs and Partners Ltd., London; Hodgson McCreery & Co. Ltd., London; Hogg Automotive Insurance Services Ltd., London; Hogg Group Plc, London; Hogg Properties Ltd., London; Hogg Robinson and Gardner Mountain (Insurance) Ltd., London; HRGM (101) Ltd., London; HRGM (102) Ltd., London; HRGM (103) Ltd., London; HRGM (107) Ltd., London; HRGM (108) Ltd., London; HRGM Cargo Ltd., London; HRGM Intl and Reinsurance Ltd., London; HRGM Management Services Ltd., London; HRGM Midlands Ltd., London; HRGM North America Ltd., London; HRGM Reinsurance and Non-Marine Ltd., London; HRGM Services Ltd., London; HRGM Southern Ltd., London; Industrial Overseas Ltd., London; Industrial Risk Management Advisers Ltd., London; Insurance Management Services Intl Ltd., London; Investment Insurance Intl (Managers) Ltd., London; Leslie and Godwin Energy Resources Ltd., London; Leslie and Godwin Group Ltd., London; Leslie and Godwin Investments Ltd., London; Leslie and Godwin Ltd., London; Lylehead Ltd., London; Macey Clifton Walters Ltd., London; Macey Williams Ltd., London; Markgrant Ltd., London; Media/Professional Insurance Agency Ltd., London; Mercia Insurance Brokers Ltd., London; Motorguard Ltd., London; Motorplan Ltd., London; Nicholson Jenner Leslie Group Ltd., London; Nicholson Leslie Agencies Ltd., London; Nicholson Leslie Aviation Ltd., London; Nicholson Leslie Aviation Reinsurance Brokers Ltd., London; Nicholson Leslie Bankassure Ltd., London; Nicholson Leslie Financial Institutions Ltd., London; Nicholson Leslie International Ltd., London; Nicholson Leslie International Reinsurance Brokers Ltd., London; Nicholson Leslie Investments Ltd., London; Nicholson Leslie Ltd., London; Nicholson Leslie Management Services Ltd., London; Nicholson Leslie Marine Ltd., London; Nicholson Leslie Nonmarine Reinsurance Brokers Ltd., London; Nicholson Leslie North America Ltd., London; Nicholson Leslie North American Reinsurance Brokers Ltd., London; Pension Fund Administration and Management Ltd., London; Property Owners Database Ltd., London; Punchcliff Ltd., London; RHA Insurance Services Ltd., London; RHH Surety and Guarantee Ltd., London; Risk Management Consultants Ltd., London; Rollins Hudig Hall (Nederland) Ltd., London; Rostron Hancock Ltd., London; Saxonbeech Ltd., London; Seascope Insurance Services Ltd., London; SLE Worldwide Ltd., London; Staple Hall Trading and Finance Co. Ltd., London; Structured Compensation Ltd., London; Tethercrest Ltd., London; TTF Insurance Services Ltd., London; United Car and Van Rental Ltd., London; Leslie and Godwin (WFG) Ltd., Manchester, Greater Manchester; MAB Insurance Services Ltd., Manchester, Greater Manchester; John Scott Insurance Brokers Ltd., Marlow, Buckinghamshire; Greyfriars Administrative Services Ltd., Reading, Berkshire; Homestead Finance Ltd., Reading, Berkshire; Aon Alexander Clay Ltd., Swansea, West Glamorgan; Commercial Credit Corp. Ltd., Wallington, Surrey

Corporate Sponsorship

Type: Music & entertainment events; Pledge-a-thon

Aon Foundation

Giving Contact

Carolyn E. Labutka, Executive Director, AON Foundation
AON Corp.
123 North Wacker Drive
Chicago, IL 60606
Phone: (312)701-3035
Fax: (312)701-4533

Description

EIN: 363337340
Organization Type: Corporate Foundation
Giving Locations: internationally; operating locations.
Grant Types: Award, Capital, Challenge, Department, Employee Matching Gifts, Endowment, General Support, Operating Expenses, Research.
Note: Employee matching gift ratio: 1 to 1.

Financial Summary

Total Giving: $5,000,000 (1999 approx); $5,000,000 (1998); $4,208,171 (1996 approx). Note: Contributes through foundation only.
Giving Analysis: Giving for 1996 includes: foundation ($3,464,129); foundation grants to United Way ($377,700); foundation matching gifts ($366,342)
Assets: $427,910 (1996); $288,198 (1993); $1,575,703 (1992)
Gifts Received: $4,318,445 (1996); $3,000,000 (1992). Note: In 1992, contributions were received from AON Corporation and its subsidiaries.

Typical Recipients

Arts & Humanities: Arts Associations & Councils, Arts Centers, Arts Festivals, Arts Institutes, Dance, Historic Preservation, History & Archaeology, Libraries, Museums/Galleries, Music, Opera, Performing Arts, Public Broadcasting, Theater
Civic & Public Affairs: Business/Free Enterprise, Civil Rights, Economic Development, Economic Policy, Employment/Job Training, Law & Justice, Parades/Festivals, Philanthropic Organizations, Public Policy, Safety, Urban & Community Affairs, Women's Affairs, Zoos/Aquariums
Education: Arts/Humanities Education, Business Education, Business-School Partnerships, Colleges & Universities, Education Associations, Education Funds, Elementary Education (Private), Faculty Development, Education-General, Health & Physical Education, Legal Education, Preschool Education, Private Education (Precollege), Public Education (Precollege), Religious Education, Science/Mathematics Education, Student Aid
Environment: Environment-General, Resource Conservation
Health: AIDS/HIV, Alzheimers Disease, Children's Health/Hospitals, Clinics/Medical Centers, Emergency/Ambulance Services, Health Funds, Hospitals, Medical Rehabilitation, Medical Research, Single-Disease Health Associations
International: Foreign Educational Institutions, International Affairs, International Relations
Religion: Churches, Jewish Causes, Religious Organizations, Religious Welfare
Science: Science Museums, Scientific Centers & Institutes
Social Services: At-Risk Youth, Child Welfare, Community Centers, Community Service Organizations, Counseling, Food/Clothing Distribution, Homes, People with Disabilities, Recreation & Athletics, Refugee Assistance, Senior Services, United Funds/United Ways, Volunteer Services, Youth Organizations

Contributions Analysis

Giving Priorities: Youth organizations, United Way, community service programs, colleges and universities, secondary education, arts, urban and community affairs, and hospitals. Most contributions are made to U.S.-based nonprofit organizations that address international affairs, primarily cultural and community affairs. Health care, especially pediatric, is a major concern for contributions made by foreign subsidiaries. The foundation also makes matching gifts to international organizations through employees of AON.
Arts & Humanities: 15% to 20%. Museums, historical societies, and performing arts groups. Interests include symphonies, theater, and ballet.
Civic & Public Affairs: 15% to 20%. Urban and community affairs, public policy groups, conservation efforts, and philanthropic organizations.
Education: 10% to 15%. Colleges and universities, including arts, technology, and legal education. Also supports high schools, religious institutions, and elementary education.
Health: 5% to 10%. Hospitals, single-disease health organizations, pediatric health, research, and health funds.
Social Services: About 45%. More than half of funding supports child development efforts and organizations, including United Way funds, child welfare organizations, volunteer groups, and various community service programs.

Application Procedures

Initial Contact: Send a letter or proposal.
Application Requirements: Provide name, address, phone number of organization, and name of executive director; one paragraph a description of organization; description of project, including specific objectives, evidence of need, proof that program would not duplicate existing services, and history of organization with such projects; amount requested and purpose of request; list of other potential funding sources and amounts; description of the greatest challenges facing organization in the next two or three years, and evaluation of organization's strengths and weaknesses; list of current contributors and amounts; proof of 501(c)(3) status, and annual report.
Deadlines: Quarterly: March 31, June 30, September 30, December 31.

Restrictions

Grants are not made to individuals or political organizations.

Additional Information

AON Corporation was formerly Combined International Corporation. The AON Foundation was formerly the Combined International Foundation.
Publications: Foundation Annual Report

Corporate Officials

Daniel T. Cox: executive vice president, chief counsel, director B 1946. ED University of North Carolina (1968); Vanderbilt University MA (1971). PRIM CORP EMPL executive vice president: Aon Corp.
Harvey Norman Medvin: executive vice president, treasurer, chief financial officer B Chicago, IL 1936. ED University of Illinois BS (1958). PRIM CORP EMPL executive vice president, treasurer, chief financial officer: Aon Corp. CORP AFFIL director: Ryan Insurance Group DE; president, treasurer, director: Ryan Warranty Services; director: Combined Insurance Co.
Patrick G. Ryan: chairman, president, chief executive officer B Milwaukee, WI 1937. ED Northwestern University BS (1959). PRIM CORP EMPL chairman, president, chief executive officer: Aon Corp. CORP AFFIL director: Tribune Co.; president: Ryan Properties Inc.; director: Sears, Roebuck & Co.; president: Ryan Companies United States Inc.; chairman, director: Pat Ryan & Associates; president: Ryan Builders Inc.; director: Combined Insurance Co.; director: AON Risk Services Companies; officer: AON Warranty Group; chairman: AON Group Inc. NONPR AFFIL trustee: Northwestern University; trustee: Rush-Presbyterian-Saint Lukes Medical Center; trustee: Field Museum Natural History.
Raymond Inwood Skilling: executive vice president, chief counsel, director B Enniskillen, England 1939. ED Queens University LLB (1961); University of Chicago JD (1962). PRIM CORP EMPL executive vice president, chief counsel, director: Aon Corp. CORP AFFIL executive vice president, chief couns, director: Combined Insurance Co. NONPR AFFIL member:

Chicago Bar Association; member: Illinois Bar Association; member: American Bar Association. CLUB AFFIL Racquet Club Chicago; City London Club; Economic Club; Chicago Club; Carlton Club London; Casino Club.

Foundation Officials

Franklin Alan Cole: chairman B Park Falls, WI 1926. ED University of Illinois BA (1947); Northwestern University JD (1950). PRIM CORP EMPL chairman: Croesus Corp. CORP AFFIL vice president, director: AON Corp.; director: GATX Corp.; director: America National Bank & Trust Co. Chicago.

Carolyn E. Labutka: executive director

Andrew James McKenna: director B Chicago, IL 1929. ED University of Notre Dame BS (1951); DePaul University JD (1954). PRIM CORP EMPL chairman, president, chief executive officer: Schwarz Paper Co. CORP AFFIL director: Skyline Corp.; director: Tribune Co.; director: McDonald's Corp.; director: First Chicago NBD Corp.; director: First National Bank Chicago; director: Childrens Memorial Hospital; director: Dean Foods Co.; director: Chicago Bears Football Club; director: Chicago National League Baseball Club; director: AON Corp. NONPR AFFIL chairman board trustees: Museum Science & Industry; chairman board trustees: University Notre Dame; director: Catholic Charities Chicago; director: Childrens Memorial Medical Center.

Harvey Norman Medvin: treasurer (see above)

Patrick G. Ryan: president (see above)

Raymond Inwood Skilling: director (see above)

Grants Analysis

Disclosure Period: calendar year ending 1996
Total Grants: $3,464,129*
Number of Grants: 325
Average Grant: $10,659
Highest Grant: $500,000
Typical Range: $1,000 to $10,000
***Note:** Giving excludes matching gifts, United Way.

Recent Grants

Note: Grants derived from 1996 Form 990.

Arts & Humanities

500,000	Chicago Symphony, Lyric Opera Facility Fund, Chicago, IL -- support renovation projects
90,000	Ravinia Festival Association, Highland Park, IL -- program support
60,000	Lyric Opera, Chicago, IL -- program support, for Opening Night
50,000	Chicago Children's Museum, Chicago, IL
50,000	WTTW/Channel 11, Chicago, IL -- support Window to the World
40,000	Museum of Contemporary Art, Chicago, IL -- support Chicago Contemporary Campaign for the MCA
30,000	Carnegie Hall Corporate Fund, New York, NY -- concert support
30,000	Metropolitan Museum of Art, New York, NY -- program support
25,000	Chicago Cultural Center Foundation, Chicago, IL -- support Gala Opening of McCormick Place Grand Concourse
25,000	Chicago Historical Society, Chicago, IL
25,000	Chicago Music and Dance Theater, Chicago, IL -- second of six payments on pledge

Civic & Public Affairs

50,000	Chicago '96, Chicago, IL -- one of two payments
30,000	Lincoln Park Zoological Society, Chicago, IL -- final of five payments on pledge
30,000	Lincoln Park Zoological Society, Chicago, IL -- payment on five-year pledge for program support
28,500	Employee Benefit Research Institute, Washington, DC -- for 1997 membership dues
25,000	Women's Legal Defense Fund, Washington, DC -- for 25th Anniversary Luncheon
20,000	Manhattan Institute for Policy Research, New York, NY
20,000	New York Partnership Foundation, New York, NY

Education

100,000	Archdiocese of Chicago School System, Chicago, IL -- first payment of five-year pledge
100,000	El Valor, Chicago, IL
55,000	College of Insurance, New York, NY -- annual awards dinner
50,000	Midtown Educational Foundation, Chicago, IL
35,861	National Merit Scholarship Corporation, Evanston, IL
25,000	Associated Colleges of Illinois, Chicago, IL -- annual grant
25,000	Consortium for the MBA Enterprise Corps, Chapel Hill, NC -- program support
25,000	Golden Apple Foundation, Chicago, IL -- 1996 annual support, program support
25,000	Golden Apple Foundation, Chicago, IL -- 1995 annual support, program support
20,000	Chicago Foundation for Education, Chicago, IL -- annual grant, program support
20,000	Providence-St. Mel School, Chicago, IL -- scholarships fund

Environment

20,000	Natural Ties, Evanston, IL

Health

25,000	City of Hope, Des Plaines, IL -- support Spirit of Life honoring Kathryn J. McIntyre
20,000	Children's Memorial Hospital, Chicago, IL -- support Campaign for Children
20,000	Eire Family Health Center, Chicago, IL
20,000	Rush Presbyterian-St. Luke's Medical Center, Chicago, IL -- support Campaign for Rush

International

20,000	INSEAD, France
20,000	INSEAD, France

Religion

50,000	United Jewish Appeal Federation, New York, NY -- first of two payments for program support
30,000	Jewish United Fund, Chicago, IL -- for 1994 payment
30,000	Jewish United Fund, Chicago, IL -- for Israel Emergency Fund

Science

50,000	Museum of Science and Industry, Chicago, IL -- support for Campaign 2000

Social Services

327,700	United Way Crusade of Mercy, Chicago, IL -- annual support, program support
95,000	Boys and Girls Club, Chicago, IL -- annual grant, program support
50,000	American Refugee Committee, Chicago, IL -- program support
50,000	Human Relations Foundation, Chicago, IL -- program support
40,000	Maryville City of Youth, Des Plaines, IL -- annual grant
35,700	Chicago United, Chicago, IL -- annual grant
33,000	Boys and Girls Club Robert R. McCormick Women's Auxiliary, Chicago, IL -- annual grant, program support
30,000	Huggy Bears, New York, NY -- for 1996 Huggy Bears Invitational Tennis Tournament
28,000	United Way Forsyth County, Winston-Salem, NC -- program support
20,000	Special Children's Charities, Chicago, IL -- support Cheers for Children Charities Gala
18,000	Chicago United, Chicago, IL -- for 1996 membership dues

APL LTD.

Company Contact

Oakland, CA
Web: http://www.apl.com

Company Description

Former Name: APL Corp.; American President Companies, Ltd.
Revenue: US$2,739,000,000
Profit: US$30,300,000
Employees: 5,174
SIC(s): 4212 Local Trucking Without Storage, 4213 Trucking Except Local, 4412 Deep Sea Foreign Transportation of Freight.

Nonmonetary Support

Type: Donated Equipment; Loaned Employees; Loaned Executives

Volunteer Programs: Employees in the Bay Area are eligible for the pilot volunteer program. They are allowed four hours per month of co. time to volunteer. Co. gives funds through its employee matching gifts volunteer services grant program. Grants of $500 per employee are given to organizations at which employees volunteer their time, limited to four grants per year.

Giving Contact

John Pachtner, Director Corporate Communications
APL Ltd.
1111 Broadway
Oakland, CA 94607
Phone: (510)272-8181
Fax: (510)272-8930

Description

Organization Type: Corporate Giving Program. Supports preselected organizations only.

Giving Locations: CA: Oakland, San Francisco including Bay area locations where APL subsidiaries have regional or district offices.

Grant Types: Employee Matching Gifts, Matching.

Note: Minimum gift matched is $25; maximum is $5,000 per year.

Financial Summary

Total Giving: $320,067 (1997); $349,614 (1996); $540,000 (1995). Note: Contributes through corporate direct giving program only.

Giving Analysis: Giving for 1997 includes: foundation ($200,365); foundation grants to United Way ($119,702)

Assets: $134,948 (1997); $215,459 (1996); $209,938 (1995)

Gifts Received: $325,600 (1997); $389,059 (1996); $435,000 (1995). Note: Foundation receives contributions from APL.

Typical Recipients

Arts & Humanities: Arts Associations & Councils, Arts Festivals, Arts Funds, Ballet, Dance, Arts & Humanities-General, Historic Preservation, History & Archaeology, Libraries, Museums/Galleries, Music, Opera, Performing Arts, Theater

Civic & Public Affairs: African American Affairs, Civil Rights, Clubs, Community Foundations, Economic

Development, Employment/Job Training, Ethnic Organizations, Municipalities/Towns, Parades/Festivals, Professional & Trade Associations, Urban & Community Affairs
Education: Arts/Humanities Education, Business Education, Colleges & Universities, Continuing Education, Education Associations, Education Funds, Education Reform, Elementary Education (Private), Education-General, International Exchange, International Studies, Leadership Training, Legal Education, Minority Education, Private Education (Precollege), Public Education (Precollege), Religious Education, School Volunteerism, Secondary Education (Private)
Environment: Environment-General, Resource Conservation
Health: AIDS/HIV, Cancer, Children's Health/Hospitals, Clinics/Medical Centers, Heart, Hospitals, Medical Research, Multiple Sclerosis, Prenatal Health Issues, Public Health, Single-Disease Health Associations
International: International-General, Health Care/Hospitals, International Relief Efforts, Trade
Religion: Religious Welfare
Science: Science Museums
Social Services: Child Abuse, Child Welfare, Community Centers, Community Service Organizations, Domestic Violence, Family Services, Food/Clothing Distribution, People with Disabilities, Recreation & Athletics, Refugee Assistance, Scouts, Social Services-General, United Funds/United Ways, Volunteer Services, YMCA/YWCA/YMHA/YWHA, Youth Organizations

Contributions Analysis

Giving Priorities: United Way, American Red Cross, higher education, museums, performing arts, municipal organizations, hospitals, single-disease health associations.
Arts & Humanities: 5% to 10%. Funds ballet, theater and the performing arts.
Civic & Public Affairs: Less than 5%.
Education: 20% to 25%. Supports colleges, universities and education associations.
Health: 5% to 10%.
Social Services: 50% to 55%. Funds united funds, and youth groups.
Note: Total contributions in 1997.

Restrictions

The following organizations are not eligible: religious, veteran, labor, or fraternal organizations (except for programs which benefit the community-at-large), political parties, organizations, candidates, or issues.

Additional Information

The APL Ltd. Foundation has recently ceased operations. The company maintains a direct giving program. Matching employee's contribution is the primary focus of the giving program. APL Ltd. merged with Singapore-based Neptune Orient Lines in 1997.

Corporate Officials

Timothy James Rhein: president, chief executive officer, chief acct officer B San Francisco, CA 1941. ED University of Santa Clara BS (1962). PRIM CORP EMPL president, chief executive officer: APL Ltd. CORP AFFIL president, chief executive officer: American President Lines Ltd.; chairman: APL Land Transport Services.
William J. Stuebgen: vice president, controller, chief acct officer B Denver, CO 1947. ED Colorado State University BS (1969). PRIM CORP EMPL vice president, controller, chief acct officer: APL Ltd. CORP AFFIL vice president: APL Land Transport Services.

Giving Program Officials

John Pachtner: director corporate communications
Timothy J. Windle: assistant secretary

Grants Analysis

Disclosure Period: calendar year ending 1997
Total Grants: $200,365*
Number of Grants: 201
Average Grant: $997
Highest Grant: $119,702
Typical Range: $100 to $10,000
***Note:** Giving excludes United Way.

Recent Grants

Note: Grants derived from 1997 Form 990.

Arts & Humanities

6,910	National Maritime Museum Association, San Francisco, CA
5,000	Museum of Contemporary Art San Diego, San Diego, CA
4,000	Oakland Ballet, Oakland, CA
3,000	Old Globe Theatre, San Diego, CA
2,500	Orange County Performing Arts Center, Costa Mesa, CA
2,500	US Capitol Historical Society, Washington, DC
2,100	American Conservatory Theater, San Francisco, CA
1,075	San Francisco Ballet, San Francisco, CA
1,000	Friends of DCI

Civic & Public Affairs

5,000	Oakland NAACP, Oakland, CA
3,650	Oakland Strokes, Oakland, CA
2,500	Mayor's Summer Jobs Program
1,200	National Italian-American Foundation, Washington, DC
1,000	Oakland Sharing the Vision, Oakland, CA
1,000	Two/Ten International Footwear Foundation, St. Watertown, MA

Education

6,200	University of California Berkeley Foundation, Berkeley, CA
6,000	Head-Royce School, Oakland, CA
5,000	Katherine Delmar Burk Scool, San Francisco, CA
5,000	Students in Free Enterprise, Springfield, MO
3,500	Next Step Center, Oakland, CA
3,335	Christian Educators Association, Pasadena, CA
3,300	St George's School, Newport, RI
3,150	Lycee Francais La Perouse, San Francisco
2,750	Mann Catholic High School, Kentfield, CA
2,500	The Japan-America Student Conference, Washington, DC
1,700	Roanoke College, Roanoke, VA
1,350	Claremont McKenna College, Claremont, CA
1,250	Lincoln Child Center, Oakland, CA
1,250	University of Washington Foundation, Seattle, WA
1,000	Ben Lippen School, Columbia, SC
1,000	Brigham Young University, Provo, UT
1,000	Holy Names College Symposium, Oakland, CA
1,000	Junior achievement, San Francisco, CA
1,000	Lakeside School, Seattle, WA
1,000	Leadership Education for Asian Pacifics, Inc.
1,000	Mills College, Oakland, CA
1,000	Oakland 2000 Ready to Learn, Oakland, CA
1,000	Santa Clara University, Santa Clara, CA

Health

4,668	American Heart Association, San Francisco, CA
3,883	Leukemia Society of America, San Francisco, CA
3,627	American Cancer Society, San Francisco, CA
2,849	AID Atlanta, Atlanta, GA
2,500	San Francisco Free Clinic, San Francisco, CA
1,500	Healthy City, Oakland Fund, Oakland, CA
1,500	Nebraska AIDS Project, Omaha, NE
1,000	Alameda County Cancer League
1,000	Bay Area Tumor Institute, Oakland, CA
1,000	Cancer Care of NCW
1,000	Children's Hospital Foundation

International

5,000	Baytrade, Oakland, CA
1,000	International Maritime Center

Religion

2,500	Littlest Angel Guild, Glenwood Springs, CO

Social Services

119,702	United Way, Oakland, CA
5,000	Child Assault Prevention, Oakland, CA
4,995	People Helping People
2,500	Boy Scouts of America-Marin Council
2,000	Meals on Wheels, San Francisco, CA
1,500	The Kennedy Institute, Washington, DC
1,000	Boys and Girls Club of Oakland, Oakland, CA
1,000	Fremont Tennis Association, Fremont, CA
1,000	Rosalie Dold Center for Children

APPLE COMPUTER, INC.

Company Contact

Cupertino, CA
Web: http://www.apple.com

Company Description

Revenue: US$6,134,000,000 (1999)
Employees: 9,736 (1999)
Fortune Rank: 285, per FORTUNE Magazine's list of 500 Largest U.S. Corporations (1999).
FF 285
SIC(s): 3571 Electronic Computers, 5045 Computers, Peripherals & Software.

Operating Locations

Australia: Apple Computer Australia Pty. Ltd., Frenchs Forest; Austria: Apple Computer GmbH, Vienna; Belgium: Apple Computer Benelux BV, Brussels, Brabant; Apple Computer SA, Brussels, Brabant; Bangladesh: Ananda Computers, Dhaka; Citech Co. Ltd., Dhaka; Canada: Apple Canada Ltd., Markham; Claris Canada, Toronto; Croatia: ACS Adria Computer Systems DOO, Maksimirska, Zagreb; Denmark: Apple Computer, Allerod, Frederiksborg; Ecuador: Inteleq SA, Quito, Pichincha; Egypt: Pan Arab Computer Center, Cairo, Al Qahirah; France: Claris France, Issy Les Moulineaux; Apple Computer Europe, Les Ulis, Essonne; Apple Computer France, Les Ulis, Essonne; Micro Conseil International, Orly, Val-de-Marne; Polaris Informatique, Orly, Val-de-Marne; Germany: Apple Computer GmbH, Ismaning, Bayern; Claris GmbH, Unterschleissheim, Bayern; Hong Kong: Apple Computer International Ltd., Causeway Bay; Iceland: Apple Umbooio HF, Reykjavik, Gullbringusysla; Radiobudin HF, Reykjavik, Gullbringusysla; Ireland: Apple Computer Ltd., Cork; Apple Computer Accessories, Dublin; Claris Ireland, Dublin; Claris Ireland Holdings Ltd., Dublin; Italy: Apple Computer SpA, Cologno Monzese, Lombardia; Japan: Apple Japan, Tokyo; Kazakhstan: Absys Asian Business Systems, Almaty; Republic of Korea: Elex Computer, Yongsan-Gu; Mexico: Apple Computer Mexico SA de CV, Ciudad de Mexico; Netherlands: Next Computer Software BV, Amstelveen, Noord-Holland; Apple Computer BV, Apeldoorn, Gelderland; Apple Computer

Benelux BV, Bunnik, Utrecht; Pakistan: UDL Computers Pvt. Ltd., Karachi, Sindh; Paraguay: Corporacion Technologica Saeca, Asuncion; Peru: Amicro SA, Lima; Philippines: Distributed Processing Systems, Makati, Rizal; Saudi Arabia: Jeraisy Tech Est., Riyadh; Singapore: Apple Computer Ltd., Singapore; Spain: Apple Computer Espana SA, Barcelona, Cataluna; Apple Computer Fondo de Pensiones, Barcelona, Cataluna; Sweden: Apple Computer AB, Kisa, Ostergotland; Switzerland: Apple Computer AG, Wallisellen, Zurich; Thailand: Sahaviriya Infortech Computer Co. Ltd., Bangpongpang, Bangkok; Sahaviriya Oa Public Co. Ltd., Bangpongpang, Bangkok; Tanawat Information Systems Co. Ltd., Thungmahamek, Bangkok; Sahaviriya Advanced Products Co. Ltd., Yannawa, Bangkok; Turkey: Bilkom Bilgisayar Ve Ozel Egitim Hizmetleri AS, Istanbul; Taiwan: Apple Computer Asia Taiwan Branch (USA), Taipei; United Arab Emirates: Arab Business Machines, Dubai; United Kingdom: Mayfield International Computers Ltd., East Molesey, Surrey; Apple Computer (UK) Ltd., Uxbridge, Middlesex; Claris International, Uxbridge, Middlesex; Uzbekistan: Absys Asian Business Systems, Tashkent; Vietnam: Peace Tour Co. Ltd., Ho Chi Minh City

Nonmonetary Support

Value: $7,000,000 (1993); $8,000,000 (1991); $8,620,000 (1990)
Type: Donated Equipment

Giving Contact

Fred Silverman, Manager, Community Affairs
Apple Computer Inc.
1 Infinite Loop
Cupertino, CA 95014-2084
Phone: (408)974-2974
Fax: (408)974-5870

Description

Organization Type: Corporate Giving Program
Giving Locations: nationally.
Grant Types: Employee Matching Gifts, General Support, Project.
Note: Employee matching gift ratio: 1 to 1 up to $1,000.

Giving Philosophy

'At Apple Computer we are in the unique position of being able to contribute, beyond philanthropic dollars, the tools people need to meet the challenges of a rapidly changing world. When we give Apple computers, and our expertise, to programs in our schools and communities, we are essentially investing in people learning to apply technology to new generations of ideas that can enrich education and make communities healthier. Through its community affairs program, Apple strives to direct its resources to projects that help people meet future, as well as current, needs in their schools and communities.' *The Way We Give*, Philanthropic programs of Apple Computer, Inc.

Financial Summary

Total Giving: Contributes through corporate direct giving program only. Majority of giving is nonmonetary support.

Typical Recipients

Arts & Humanities: Community Arts, Museums/Galleries, Music, Performing Arts, Theater
Education: Elementary Education (Private), Minority Education, Public Education (Precollege)
Environment: Environment-General
Health: Single-Disease Health Associations

Contributions Analysis

Giving Priorities: Computer grants and education. Contributions primarily are in the form of donated computers. Highest priority is grants to support educational projects that use microcomputers to create new ways of learning and teaching. The company's goal is to develop curriculum strategies that incorporate computers as tools to address a range of educational restructuring. These include creating student-centered learning experiences, developing interdisciplinary curricula, making connections between learning in and out of school, and changing the role of teachers from deliverers to facilitators of learning. The company reported that it gives about 15% of gifts to international organizations.
Arts & Humanities: About 15%.
Education: 40% to 45%. These grants support educational projects that use computers to create new ways of learning and teaching. The company's goal is to develop curriculum strategies that incorporate computers as tools to address a range of educational restructuring. These include creating student-centered learning experiences, developing interdisciplinary curricula, making connections between learning in and out of school, and changing the role of teachers from deliverers to facilitators of learning. Current focus is partnerships between K-12 schools and institutions of professional development for teachers. Partnerships must be between U.S. public or private elementary, secondary, or middle schools and either a single accredited university or college school of education or other department, teacher college, or nonprofit organization that provides ongoing pre- and in-service K-12 teacher training.
Environment: 10% to 15%.
Health: 5% to 10%.

Application Procedures

Initial Contact: Call or write the Community Affairs department, or visit www.apple.com for latest guidelines, which outline proposal requirements.
Deadlines: February.
Review Process: Different program officers handle each area of giving.
Evaluative Criteria: For nonprofit grant: community benefit, organizational need, sustainability, innovation, potential use as model. For education grants: well-articulated needs, goals, and implementation plans that benefit the students and both partners; well-conceived framework for changing delivery for teacher professional development; creative use of distributed learning tools; relevance of learning activities to students; creative strategies that promote diversity and access to curriculum by students with different backgrounds and abilities; strong administrative support and commitment for the plan; clear dissemination plan that will benefit the community; creative assessment strategies; and compelling case that grant will further the vision in ways that are not otherwise available.
Decision Notification: Varies with each program, usually eight to ten weeks after deadline; for education grants, by May.
Notes: Guidelines and projects may differ from year to year. In 1998, company supported partnerships between K-12 education and teacher development institutions.

Restrictions

Individuals, government agencies (except those serving as a vital link in a network of private nonprofit groups), and religious or political organizations are ineligible for corporate grants.
Company reports that it does not make equipment loans or donate used computers.
Does not make grants for endowment funds, building construction or acquisition, publications, salaries, sponsorship of athletic events, fundraising events, raffles, auctions, door prizes, or traditionally parent-supported activities, such as P.T.A., Scouts, Little League, etc.
Recipients must adhere to Apple's internal nondiscrimination policies.

Additional Information

Currently the giving program has ceased operations. In keeping with its mission and corporate responsibility activities, Apple has implemented programs that allow customers to return computer batteries and laser printer toner cartridges to Apple for recycling or disposal. Overseas companies also follow suit: Apple Germany started a program in 1992 that allows customers to return used products and product packaging.

Corporate Officials

Timothy D. Cook: senior vice president worldwide operations
Nancy R. Heinen: senior vice president, general counsel
Steven Paul Jobs: interim chief executive officer B 1955. ED Reed College. PRIM CORP EMPL interim chief executive officer: Apple Computer Inc. ADD CORP EMPL co-founder: NeXT Software Inc. CORP AFFIL chairman, chief executive officer: Pixar.
Siobann Kenny: corporate contributions
Mitch Mandich: senior vice president
Armas Clifford Markkula, Jr.: chairman, director B 1942. ED University of Southern California MS. PRIM CORP EMPL chairman, director: Apple Computer, Inc. CORP AFFIL chairman: ACM Aviation Inc.; founder director: Echelon Corp.
Jon Rubenstein: senior vice president
Dr. Avadis Tevanian, Jr.: senior vice president

Giving Program Officials

Andrea Gooden: PRIM CORP EMPL program manager education grants: Apple Computer, Inc.
Anne McMullin: PRIM CORP EMPL program manager regional & international programs: Apple Computer, Inc.
Fred Silverman: PRIM CORP EMPL manager community affairs: Apple Computer, Inc.

Grants Analysis

Disclosure Period: fiscal year ending September 30,
Typical Range: $5,000 to $10,000

APPLETON PAPERS INC.

Company Contact

Appleton, WI

Company Description

Employees: 3,700
SIC(s): 2621 Paper Mills, 2672 Coated & Laminated Paper Nec.
Parent Company: Arjo Wiggins Appleton Plc

Operating Locations

AZ: Appleton Papers Inc., Phoenix; CA: Appleton Papers Inc., Auburn, San Leandro; CO: Appleton Papers Inc., Englewood; GA: Appleton Papers Inc., Roswell; IL: Appleton Papers Inc., West Chicago; KS: Appleton Papers Inc., Kansas City; MN: Appleton Papers Inc., Saint Paul; NY: Appleton Papers Inc., Elmsford, Feura Bush, Newton Falls; OH: Appleton Papers Inc., West Carrollton, Cleveland; Appleton Papers-West Carrollton Mill, Dayton; OR: Appleton Papers Inc., Portland; PA: Appleton Papers-Harrisburg, Camp Hill; Appleton Papers Inc., Camp Hill, Roaring Spring; Appleton Papers-Spring Mill, Roaring Spring; TN: Appleton Papers Inc., Kingsport; TX: Appleton Papers Inc., Lewisville; WI: Appleton Papers, Inc., Appleton; Appleton Papers Inc., Appleton, Combined Locks; Appleton Papers-Locks Mills, Combined Locks; Appleton Papers-Portage Plant, Portage

Nonmonetary Support

Value: $15,000 (1996); $25,000 (1993); $20,000 (1992)
Type: Donated Equipment; Donated Products
Contact: Billy Van Den Brandt, Staff Public Relations Representative

Corporate Sponsorship

Type: Arts & cultural events; Music & entertainment events; Sports events; Pledge-a-thon
Note: Company budgets up to $10,000 per event and sponsors marathons, concerts, and bowl-a-thons.

Giving Contact

Dennis N. Hultgren, Director, Environmental & Public Affairs
Appleton Papers Inc.
825 East Wisconsin Avenue
PO Box 359
Appleton, WI 54912
Phone: (920)991-8600
Fax: (920)991-8407
Email: dhultgren@appletonpapers.com

Description

Organization Type: Corporate Giving Program
Giving Locations: NY: Newton Falls; OH: Dayton; PA: Harrisburg, Roaring Spring; WI: Appleton headquarters and operating communities.
Grant Types: Award, Capital, Employee Matching Gifts, General Support, Multiyear/Continuing Support, Project, Scholarship.
Note: Employee matching gift ratio: 1 to 1 for education only.

Financial Summary

Total Giving: $650,000 (1999 approx); $650,000 (1998 approx); $600,000 (1997 approx). Note: Contributes through corporate direct giving program only. Giving includes nonmonetary support.

Typical Recipients

Arts & Humanities: Arts Associations & Councils, Libraries, Museums/Galleries, Music, Performing Arts, Visual Arts
Civic & Public Affairs: Business/Free Enterprise
Education: Colleges & Universities, Economic Education, Engineering/Technological Education, Faculty Development, Minority Education, Science/Mathematics Education, Student Aid
Environment: Environment-General
Health: Single-Disease Health Associations
Social Services: Child Welfare, Community Service Organizations, Counseling, Domestic Violence, Emergency Relief, Food/Clothing Distribution, People with Disabilities, Recreation & Athletics, Senior Services, Shelters/Homelessness, Substance Abuse, United Funds/United Ways, Youth Organizations

Application Procedures

Initial Contact: a brief letter of inquiry and proposal
Application Requirements: a description of organization, amount requested, purpose of funds sought, recently audited financial statement, proof of tax-exempt status, number of people benefiting from the project, and extent of Appleton employees' involvement
Deadlines: None

Restrictions

The company does not consider funding for the following: dinners or special events, goodwill advertising, member agencies of united funds, individuals, hospitals, fraternal organizations, political or lobbying groups, religious organizations for sectarian purposes, or groups whose agendas differ from the goals of the company.

Giving Program Officials

Dennis N. Hultgren: director B Milwaukee, WI 1946. ED University of Wisconsin (1969); University of Wisconsin (1973). PRIM CORP EMPL director environmental & public affairs: Appleton Papers Inc. CORP AFFIL director: Norwest Bank. NONPR AFFIL member: Rotary International.

Grants Analysis

Disclosure Period: calendar year ending 1997
Total Grants: $600,000 (approx)
Typical Range: $5,000 to $10,000

ARCHER-DANIELS-MIDLAND CO.

 Number 96 of Top 100 Corporate Givers

Company Contact

Decatur, IL
Web: http://www.admworld.com

Company Description

Revenue: US$16,108,600,000
Profit: US$403,600,000
Employees: 23,132
Fortune Rank: 120, per FORTUNE Magazine's list of 500 Largest U.S. Corporations (1999).
FF 120
SIC(s): 2041 Flour & Other Grain Mill Products, 2045 Prepared Flour Mixes & Doughs, 2046 Wet Corn Milling, 2074 Cottonseed Oil Mills.

Operating Locations

Australia: ADM Australia Pty. Ltd., Bondi Junction; Canada: Ambrosia Chocolates Ltd., Georgetown; ADM Agriindustries Ltd., Windsor; Cayman Islands: Archer Daniels Midland Int SA, George Town, Grand Cayman; France: Charton Patisserie Industrielle, Grande Synthe, Nord; Oleagineux (Societe Industrielle Des), St. Laurent Blangy; Germany: ADM Oelmuehlen Beteiligungs GmbH, Hamburg; Belegschaftsunter Stuetzungs Ein Richtung GmbH der Oelmuehle Hamburg, Hamburg; Hanseatic Trading Co. GmbH, Hamburg; Neuhof Hafen GmbH, Hamburg; Noblee & Thoerl GmbH, Hamburg; Oelmuehle Hamburg AG, Hamburg; Phospholipid GmbH, Hamburg; Silo-Betriebs GmbH, Hamburg; Silo P Kruse Betriebs GmbH & Co. KG, Hamburg; ADM Beteiligungs GmbH, Kleve, Nordrhein-Westfalen; ADM Oelmuehlen GmbH and Co. KG, Kleve, Nordrhein-Westfalen; Oelmuehle Leer Connemann GmbH and Co., Leer, Niedersachsen; Verwaltungs Gesellschaft Oelmuehle Leer Connemann GmbH, Leer, Niedersachsen; Beteiligungs Gesellschaft Oelmuehle Rothensee GmbH, Magdeburg, De-Ost; Oelmuehle Rothensee GmbH and Co. KG, Magdeburg, De-Ost; Silo Rothensee GmbH & Co. KG, Magdeburg, De-Ost; ADM Soya Mainz GmbH and Co. KG, Mainz, Rheinland-Pfalz; Leicoma Zucht-Und Handels GmbH, Verden, Niedersachsen; Ireland: ADM Ireland Holdings Ltd., Cork; ADM Ringaskiddy, Cork; Southern Milling Ltd., Cork; Arkady Feed Ltd., Dublin; Arkady Grain Ltd., Dublin; Paul & Vincent Ltd., Edgeworthstown; Netherlands: ADM Ireland Holdings Ltd., Europoort Rotterdam; Archer Daniels Midland Europe BV, Europoort Rotterdam; Archer Daniels Midland Europoort BV, Europoort Rotterdam; Archer Daniels Midland Finance BV, Europoort Rotterdam; Archer Daniels Midland Nederland BV, Europoort Rotterdam; Archer Daniels Midland Specialty Ingredien BV, Europoort Rotterdam; ADM Cocoa BV, Koog Aan De Zaan; ADM Cocoa International BV, Koog Aan De Zaan; Targhee Holding BV, Koog Aan De Zaan; Twincon BV, Koog Aan De Zaan; Twincon Intl BV, Wormer, Noord-Holland; J.G. Van Bruinessen BV, Zaandam, Noord-Holland; United Kingdom: Archer Daniels Midland Ingredients Ltd., Erith, Kent; Archer Daniels Midland International Ltd., Erith, Kent; Archer Daniels Midland Intl Ltd., Erith, Kent; Archer Daniels Midland Investments (United Kingdom) Ltd., Erith, Kent; Erith Oil Works Trading Ltd., Erith, Kent; Haldane Foods Ltd., Newport Pagnell; Snackmasters Ltd., Newport Pagnell; Happidog Pet Foods Ltd., Preston, Lancashire; Kwality Foods Ltd., Southampton, Hampshire; House of Natural Food Ltd., Watford, Hertfordshire

Nonmonetary Support

Type: Donated Equipment; Loaned Employees
Note: Company also loans workspace.

Corporate Sponsorship

Type: Arts & cultural events; Festivals/fairs; Music & entertainment events

Archer-Daniels-Midland Foundation

Giving Contact

Archer-Daniels-Midland Foundation
4666 Faries Parkway
PO Box 1470
Decatur, IL 62526
Phone: (217)424-2570
Fax: (217)424-5581
Note: Telephone inquiries are strongly discouraged. A contact person is not listed.

Description

Founded: 1953
EIN: 416023126
Organization Type: Corporate Foundation
Giving Locations: IL nationally; principally near operating locations and to national organizations.
Grant Types: Employee Matching Gifts, General Support.
Note: Employee matching gift ratio: 1 to 1.

Financial Summary

Total Giving: $7,237,662 (fiscal year ending June 30, 1998); $4,645,816 (fiscal 1996); $5,879,623 (fiscal 1994). Note: Contributes through foundation only.
Giving Analysis: Giving for fiscal 1994 includes: foundation ($5,407,532); foundation matching gifts ($4,484,086); fiscal 1996: foundation ($4,150,436); foundation matching gifts ($490,380); foundation grants to United Way ($5,000); fiscal 1998: foundation ($6,629,851); foundation matching gifts ($520,702); foundation grants to United Way ($87,109)
Assets: $4,095,231 (fiscal 1998); $4,552,771 (fiscal 1996); $2,907,425 (fiscal 1994)
Gifts Received: $7,000,000 (fiscal 1998); $9,002,438 (fiscal 1993). Note: In fiscal 1993, the foundation received 252,700 shares of Saloman, Inc., stock from Archer-Daniels-Midland Co. In fiscal 1998, contributions were received from Archer Daniels Midland Company.

Typical Recipients

Arts & Humanities: Arts Associations & Councils, Arts Centers, Arts Festivals, Arts Funds, Arts Institutes, Ethnic & Folk Arts, Historic Preservation, History & Archaeology, Libraries, Museums/Galleries, Music, Opera, Performing Arts, Public Broadcasting, Theater
Civic & Public Affairs: African American Affairs, Business/Free Enterprise, Civil Rights, Clubs, Community Foundations, Economic Development, Economic Policy, Hispanic Affairs, Law & Justice, Legal Aid, Native American Affairs, Professional & Trade Associations, Public Policy, Rural Affairs, Safety, Urban & Community Affairs, Women's Affairs, Zoos/Aquariums
Education: Agricultural Education, Arts/Humanities Education, Business Education, Colleges & Universities, Community & Junior Colleges, Economic Education, Education Associations, Education Funds, Faculty Development, Education-General, Health & Physical Education, International Exchange, International Studies, Legal Education, Medical Education, Minority Education, Private Education (Precollege),

Religious Education, Science/Mathematics Education, Secondary Education (Private), Student Aid
Environment: Forestry, Environment-General, Resource Conservation
Health: Cancer, Children's Health/Hospitals, Health Organizations, Hospitals
International: Foreign Educational Institutions, Health Care/Hospitals, Human Rights, International Affairs, International Development, International Environmental Issues, International Organizations, International Peace & Security Issues, International Relations, International Relief Efforts, Missionary/Religious Activities, Trade
Religion: Churches, Jewish Causes, Missionary Activities (Domestic), Religious Organizations, Religious Welfare
Science: Science-General, Scientific Centers & Institutes
Social Services: Child Welfare, Community Service Organizations, Day Care, Emergency Relief, Family Planning, Food/Clothing Distribution, People with Disabilities, Recreation & Athletics, Scouts, Senior Services, Shelters/Homelessness, Substance Abuse, United Funds/United Ways, Volunteer Services, YMCA/YWCA/YMHA/YWHA, Youth Organizations

Contributions Analysis

Giving Priorities: Public policy organizations, urban affairs groups, higher education, united funds, youth organizations, and performing arts. Primarily supports U.S.-based organizations with interests in international relations, business, and public policy. Major support goes to education and legal issues involving agriculture in developing countries. Also supports national security and diplomatic relations.
Arts & Humanities: 10%. Recipients include historic preservation programs, historical societies, public broadcasting, libraries, museums, music, and theater.
Civic & Public Affairs: 10% to 15%. Primary interests include public policy organizations, urban affairs groups, and international affairs. Also supports economic development, government improvement, safety, civil rights, and business organizations.
Education: 10%. Majority supports colleges and universities. Also supports religious, agricultural, business, and legal education, as well as education funds and associations.
International: 10% to 15%. Supports international public policy organizations.
Religion: 30% to 35%. Primarily for Jewish concerns.
Social Services: 10% to 15%. Major support goes to united funds and youthorganizations. Other interests include child and family welfare, emergency relief, religious welfare, and recreation.
Note: Total contributions in fiscal 1998.

Application Procedures

Initial Contact: Send a brief letter or proposal.
Application Requirements: Include a description of organization, amount requested, purpose of funds sought, recently audited financial statement, and proof of tax-exempt status.
Deadlines: None.
Notes: The foundation does not accept phone inquiries.

Restrictions

Grants are not made to individuals.
Generally does not give to united funds except in the form of matching gifts.

Corporate Officials

Dwayne Orville Andreas: chairman, chief executive officer general counsel, secretary B Worthington, MN 1918. ED Wheaton College (1935-1936). PRIM CORP EMPL chairman, chief executive officer: Archer-Daniels-Midland Co. CORP AFFIL chairman: Seaview Hotel Corp.; chief executive officer: Independent Soy Processors; director: Salomon Inc.; director: Hollinger International Inc. NONPR AFFIL member: Trilateral Commission; vice chairman: Woodrow Wilson Center International Scholars; member: Foreign Policy Association; trustee: Hoover Institute; director: Boys Club America. CLUB AFFIL The Links Club; director: Indian Creek Country Club; Knickerbocker Club; chairman: Economic Club New York; Friars Club; Blind Brook Country Club.
Lowell Willard Andreas: chairman audit committee, member executive & finance committee B Lisbon, IA 1922. ED University of Iowa; Wheaton College (1941). PRIM CORP EMPL chairman audit committee, member executive & finance committee: Archer-Daniels-Midland Co. CORP AFFIL director: National City Bank.
James R. Randall: president, director B 1924. ED University of Wisconsin BScE (1948). PRIM CORP EMPL president, director: Archer-Daniels-Midland Co.
Richard P. Reising: senior vice president, general counsel, secretary B 1944. ED Stanford University BA; University of Missouri JD (1969). PRIM CORP EMPL senior vice president, general counsel, secretary: Archer-Daniels-Midland Co. ADD CORP EMPL president: Agrinational Insurance Co.; secretary: Coeval Inc. CORP AFFIL director: Hickory Point Bank & Trust.

Foundation Officials

John Hancock Daniels: chairman B Saint Paul, MN 1921. ED Saint Paul Academy (1932-1937); Phillips Exeter Academy (1939); Yale University BA (1943); Harvard University Advanced Management Program (1957). CORP AFFIL officer: Mulberry Resources Inc. NONPR AFFIL director: National Sporting Library; trustee: Yale Library Association; member: Masters Foxhounds Association America; director: Business Council; trustee: Committee for Economic Development. CLUB AFFIL Springdale Hall Club; Woodhill Country Club; Minneapolis Club; Grolier Club; The Links Club; Elizabethan Club.
Claudia Madding: president
Richard P. Reising: secretary (see above)

Grants Analysis

Disclosure Period: fiscal year ending June 30, 1998
Total Grants: $6,629,851*
Number of Grants: 481
Average Grant: $13,783
Highest Grant: $1,000,000
Typical Range: $1,000 to $25,000
***Note:** Giving excludes matching gifts and United Way.

Recent Grants

Note: Grants derived from fiscal 1998 Form 990.

Arts & Humanities

100,000	Chicago Historical Society, Chicago, IL
100,000	Georgia Public Television, Atlanta, GA
100,000	Lyric Opera of Chicago, Chicago, IL
60,000	Decatur Public Library, Decatur, IL
50,000	Bush Presidential Library Foundation, College Station, TX
40,000	Children's Museum of Illinois, Chicago, IL

Civic & Public Affairs

125,000	Citizens for a Sound Economy Foundation, Washington, DC
100,000	Horatio Alger Association of Distinguished Americans, Inc., Alexandria, VA
100,000	NAACP, Washington, DC
50,000	The Economic Club of New York, New York, NY
50,000	The Economic Club of New York, New York, NY
50,000	Institute for Political Economy, Washington, DC
48,140	Illinois Agricultural Leadership Foundation, Macomb, IL
25,000	Citizens for a Sound Economy Foundation, Washington, DC
10,000	National Center for APEC, Seattle, WA

Education

100,000	The School For Field Studies, Beverly, MA
50,000	Auburn University, Birmingham, AL
50,000	Champion Economics & Business Association, Lynchburg, VA
50,000	Dakota Wesleyan University, Mitchell, SD
50,000	Dakota Wesleyan University, Mitchell, SD
50,000	Institute For EastWest Studies, New York, NY
40,000	Millikin University, Decatur, IL
40,000	Richland Community College Foundation, Decatur, IL
36,000	University of Illinois-College of Aces, Chicago, IL
25,000	William Marsh Rice University, Houston, TX

Health

100,000	Roberto C Goizueta Cancer Research Fund, Atlanta, GA
50,000	Easter Seal Society of Central Illinois. Inc, Decatur, IL

International

100,000	International Life Sciences Institute, Washington, DC
50,000	America - Israel Friendship League, New York, NY
50,000	Council on Foreign Relations, New York, NY
50,000	The Forum for International Policy, Washington, DC
50,000	The Nixon Center for Peace and Freedom, Washington, DC
26,000	Woodrow Wilson International Center For Scholars, Washington, DC
25,000	Africare, Washington, DC
25,000	Center for Strategic & International Studies, Washington, DC
25,000	Council on Foreign Relations, New York, NY
25,000	International Arid Lands Consortium, Tucson, AZ
25,000	International Policy Council on Agriculture Food & Trade, Washington, DC
20,000	The Trilateral Commission, New York, NY
15,000	The Citizens Network for Foreign Affairs, Washington, DC
10,000	American Friends of Bilderberg, Inc., New York, NY
10,000	Anti Defamation League, New York, NY
10,000	Asia Society, New York, NY
10,000	Business Council For The United Nations, New York, NY
10,000	Business Executives for National Security, Inc., New York, NY
10,000	CARE Foundation, New York, NY
10,000	Center for Security Policy, Washington, DC
10,000	Council on Foreign Relations, New York, NY
10,000	Executive Council on Diplomacy, Washington, DC
10,000	International Policy Council on Agriculture Food & Trade, Washington, DC
10,000	International Rescue Committee, New York, NY
10,000	National Committee on American Foreign Policy, Inc., New York, NY
10,000	National Peace Foundation, Washington, DC
10,000	Project Mexico of the Orthodox Church, Irvine, CA
7,000	Asia Society, New York, NY
5,000	American University in Bulgaria, Bulgaria

5,000	CARE Foundation, New York, NY
5,000	Constituency for Africa, Washington, DC
5,000	National Foreign Trade Council Inc, New York, NY
5,000	National Policy Association, Washington, DC
5,000	Project Concern International, San Diego, CA
5,000	The World Food Prize, Washington, DC
1,000	International Agricultural Association, Oak Brook, IL
250	Chicago Council on Foreign Relations, Chicago, IL
150	World Wildlife Fund, Washington, DC -- CON
100	World Affairs Council of Central Illinois, Peoria, IL

Religion

1,000,000	Anti Defamation League of B'Nai B'rith, New York, NY
250,000	Russian Orthodox Church in America, Decatur, IL
200,000	National Council of the Churches of Christ in the USA, New York, NY
36,000	The Jewish Theological Seminary, New York, NY
25,000	The Edgar M. Bronfman Fund-World Jewish Congress, New York, NY

Science

37,500	National Corn Growers Association, St. Louis, MO
37,500	National Corn Growers Association, St. Louis, MO
37,500	National Corn Growers Association, St. Louis, MO

Social Services

250,000	American Red Cross, New York, NY
250,000	American Red Cross, New York, NY
59,297	United Way of Decatur & Macon County, Decatur, IL -- ORG
50,000	Boys & Girls Clubs of America, New York, NY
50,000	YMCA-YWCA Capital Campaign, New York, NY
40,000	YMCA-YWCA Capital Campaign, New York, NY
30,000	The Emerald Coast Classic Foundation, Birmingham, AL
27,812	United Way of Decatur & Macon County, Decatur, IL -- ORG

ARISTECH CHEMICAL CORP.

Company Contact

Pittsburgh, PA
Web: http://www.aristechchem.com

Company Description

Employees: 1,550
SIC(s): 2821 Plastics Materials & Resins, 2865 Cyclic Crudes & Intermediates, 2869 Industrial Organic Chemicals Nec, 3081 Unsupported Plastics Film & Sheet.
Parent Company: ACC Holdings Corp.

Corporate Sponsorship

Type: Arts & cultural events; Music & entertainment events; Pledge-a-thon
Contact: Mrs. S. Vandreak, Manager, Employee Communications & Relations

Aristech Foundation

Giving Contact

John S. (Jack) Maurer, Executive Director
Aristech Foundation
600 Grant Street, Suite 1170
Pittsburgh, PA 15219-2704
Phone: (412)433-2747
Fax: (412)433-7721

Description

Founded: 1988
EIN: 256298142
Organization Type: Corporate Foundation
Giving Locations: headquarters and operating communities.
Grant Types: Capital, Conference/Seminar, Emergency, Employee Matching Gifts, Endowment, General Support, Multiyear/Continuing Support.
Note: Employee matching gift ratio: 1 to 1 for higher education only, up to $3,000 per institution annually.

Giving Philosophy

The foundation focuses its giving in four principal areas:
'Education: Support of higher education, with particular emphasis on business administration, chemical engineering and the globalization of commerce. Programs which prepare young people to enter the workforce of tomorrow. Educational programs and activities which promote and enhance the mutual understanding of the peoples, cultures and business practices of the United States and Japan.
'Community Services: Enhancing economic development in and promoting the general health and welfare of Aristech communities. Programs which broaden opportunities for the youth of Aristech communities, with particular emphasis on the underprivileged, disadvantaged and disabled.
'Arts and Cultural: To help ensure a strong foundation of arts and cultural institutions/programs in Aristech communities. This would include the support of well-established as well as start-up cultural organizations. Programs which introduce young people, the disadvantaged and the disabled to the arts through well-developed outreach and participatory methods. Activities which promote and enhance of arts and cultural programs between the United States and Japan.
'Environmental: Programs involved in the conservation of natural resources and public health, and which couple their efforts with the concepts of sound science, risk assessment and sustainable economic development.' 1995 Aristech Foundation Annual Report.

Financial Summary

Total Giving: $272,880 (1997); $375,000 (1996); $750,000 (1995). Note: Contributes through corporate direct giving program and foundation.
Giving Analysis: Giving for 1995 includes: foundation ($352,800); foundation matching gifts ($30,450); 1996: foundation ($300,350); foundation grants to United Way ($74,650); 1997: foundation ($202,880); foundation grants to United Way ($70,000)
Assets: $437,749 (1997); $473,409 (1995); $444,098 (1994)
Gifts Received: $300,000 (1997); $375,000 (1995); $500,000 (1989). Note: Contributions are received from Aristech Chemical Corp.

Typical Recipients

Arts & Humanities: Arts Associations & Councils, Arts Centers, Arts Institutes, Ballet, Dance, Arts & Humanities-General, History & Archaeology, Libraries, Museums/Galleries, Music, Opera, Public Broadcasting, Theater
Civic & Public Affairs: Business/Free Enterprise, Civil Rights, Economic Development, Economic Policy, Employment/Job Training, Civic & Public Affairs-General, Law & Justice, Professional & Trade Associations, Urban & Community Affairs, Women's Affairs, Zoos/Aquariums
Education: Business Education, Colleges & Universities, Economic Education, Education Funds, Education Reform, Engineering/Technological Education, Environmental Education, Education-General, Science/Mathematics Education, Student Aid
Environment: Environment-General, Resource Conservation, Wildlife Protection
Health: Clinics/Medical Centers, Emergency/Ambulance Services, Hospices, Single-Disease Health Associations
Religion: Religious Welfare
Science: Scientific Centers & Institutes, Scientific Organizations
Social Services: Community Service Organizations, Family Services, Food/Clothing Distribution, People with Disabilities, Recreation & Athletics, Scouts, Shelters/Homelessness, Special Olympics, United Funds/United Ways, Youth Organizations

Contributions Analysis

Giving Priorities: Higher education, youth organizations, united funds, and the arts.
Arts & Humanities: About 15%. Art institutes; performing arts; public broadcasting in Pittsburgh; libraries; and historical societies.
Civic & Public Affairs: 15% to 20%. Funds economic development, women's concerns, and zoological societies.
Education: About 20%. Higher education, especially universities located in Pittsburgh, PA; education foundations and funds; and small colleges nationwide.
Environment: Less than 5%. Protection and conservation of natural resources and public health.
Social Services: 35% to 40%. United Way chapters; youth organizations, including boys and girls clubs and the Boy Scouts; and community service organizations.
Note: Total contributions in 1997.

Application Procedures

Initial Contact: Send concise written proposal with a cover letter, signed by an authorized executive of the organization.
Application Requirements: Include need and objectives of program; plan of action; list of other organizations involved with similar programs, and how the proposed project is similar or different from those programs; a line-item budget for the project; the amount of funding requested; organization's budget with income sources; IRS tax/exemption letter; and a list of board of directors.
Deadlines: At least one month prior to trustee meetings, held in early January and early July.

Restrictions

The foundation does not make grants to individuals, special events or dinners, religious organizations for sectarian purposes, hospitals, or political groups. Grants generally are not awarded for conferences, seminars, symposia, travel purposes, or for the publishing of books, films, or television productions.

Additional Information

Publications: Annual Report

Corporate Officials

Patrick Jack: president, chief operating officer PRIM CORP EMPL president, chief operating officer: Aristech Chemical Corp.
Mark K. McNally: senior vice president, general counsel, secretary B Pittsburgh, PA 1946. ED Georgetown University (1968); University of Pittsburgh (1972). PRIM CORP EMPL senior vice president, general counsel, secretary: Aristech Chemical Corp.

Michael J. Prendergast: vice president, chief financial officer B Annapolis, MD 1948. ED University of Virginia BA (1973); University of Virginia School of Law JD (1976). PRIM CORP EMPL vice president, chief financial officer: Aristech Chemical Corp.

Foundation Officials

John S. Maurer: executive director

Grants Analysis

Disclosure Period: calendar year ending 1997
Total Grants: $202,880*
Number of Grants: 76
Average Grant: $2,669
Highest Grant: $65,000
Typical Range: $1,000 to $10,000
***Note:** Giving excludes United Way.

Recent Grants

Note: Grants derived from 1997 Form 990.

Arts & Humanities

10,000	Pittsburgh Symphony Society, Pittsburgh, PA
5,000	Carnegie Museums, Pittsburgh, PA
5,000	Historical Society of Western Pennsylvania, Pittsburgh, PA
5,000	Pittsburgh Ballet, Pittsburgh, PA -- capital campaign
5,000	Pittsburgh Cultural Trust, Pittsburgh, PA
5,000	Pittsburgh Opera, Pittsburgh, PA
2,500	Pittsburgh Ballet, Pittsburgh, PA
1,000	Pittsburgh Public Theater, Pittsburgh, PA

Civic & Public Affairs

17,750	Allegheny Conference on Community Development, Pittsburgh, PA
15,000	Chemical Heritage Foundation, Philadelphia, PA
5,250	Penn Southwest Association, Pittsburgh, PA
5,000	Women's Center and Shelter, Pittsburgh, PA
3,000	Pennsylvania Free Enterprise Week, Pittsburgh, PA
3,000	Zoological Society, Pittsburgh, PA
1,000	Pennsylvanians for Modern Courts, Pittsburgh, PA

Education

10,000	Junior Achievement of Southwestern Pennsylvania, Pittsburgh, PA
10,000	Robert Morris College, Coraopolis, PA
5,700	Lehigh University, Bethlehem, PA
5,000	University of Pittsburgh, Pittsburgh, PA
3,100	Junior Achievement of Ohio Valley, Ashland, KY
3,000	Carnegie Mellon University, Pittsburgh, PA
3,000	Grove City College, Grove City, PA
2,600	Junior Achievement of Southeast Texas, Houston, TX
2,500	Shawnee State University, Portsmouth, OH
1,800	Pennsylvania Chemical Industry Education Foundation, Harrisburg, PA
1,310	Texas A&M University, College Station, TX
1,000	Mississippi State University, Mississippi State, MS
700	Thiel College, Greenville, PA
600	Pennsylvania State University, University Park, PA
550	Carnegie Mellon University, Pittsburgh, PA
550	Gig Green Scholarship Fund, Huntington, WV
500	Ashland University, Ashland, OH
500	University of Missouri Columbia, Columbia, MO

Environment

10,000	Wildlife Habitat Council, New York, NY

Health

2,500	American Red Cross, Pittsburgh, PA
2,000	Bradley Center, Pittsburgh, PA

Religion

3,000	Salvation Army, Pittsburgh, PA

Science

7,500	Carnegie Science Center, Pittsburgh, PA

Social Services

65,000	United Way of Southwestern Pennsylvania, Pittsburgh, PA
6,000	Boy Scouts of America, Pittsburgh, PA
5,150	United Way of Texas Gulf Coast, Houston, TX
5,000	Family Resources, Pittsburgh, PA
5,000	Girl Scouts of America of Southwestern Pennsylvania, Pittsburgh, PA
5,000	United Way of the River Cities, Huntington, WV
2,500	Greater Pittsburgh Community Food Bank, McKeesport, PA
2,500	Three Rivers Youth, Pittsburgh, PA
2,000	Goodwill Industries, Pittsburgh, PA
2,000	Pittsburgh Blind Association, Pittsburgh, PA
1,500	Special Olympics, Norristown, PA
1,000	Youth Guidance, Sewickley, PA

ARIZONA PUBLIC SERVICE CO.

Company Contact

Phoenix, AZ
Web: http://www.apsc.com

Company Description

Assets: US$6,418,200,000
Employees: 6,484
SIC(s): 4911 Electric Services.
Parent Company: Pinnacle West Capital Corp.

Nonmonetary Support

Type: Donated Equipment; In-kind Services; Loaned Executives
Volunteer Programs: The company matches employee volunteer hours given to nonprofit organizations that provide a service in one of their giving areas. Each hour an APS employee or retiree volunteers is matched at $5, if at least 25 hours in single calendar year have been spent volunteering.

APS Foundation, Inc.

Giving Contact

Ms. Terry DeValle, Community Relations Representative
Arizona Public Service Co.
PO Box 53999
M/S 8510
Phoenix, AZ 85072-3999
Phone: (602)250-2259
Fax: (602)250-2419

Description

EIN: 953735903
Organization Type: Corporate Foundation. Supports preselected organizations only.
Giving Locations: AZ: primarily Arizona and New Mexico, near the Four Corners Power Plant; NM near Four Corners Power Plant.
Grant Types: Capital, Conference/Seminar, Employee Matching Gifts, Matching, Multiyear/Continuing Support.
Note: Company administers two matching gifts programs: $5 for each hour an employee or retiree volunteers at a nonprofit organization located within the company's giving area; Employee matching gift program for cultural organizations in Arizona and New Mexico, near the Four Corners Power Plant. Alumni gifts to accredited colleges and universities in the U.S. are matched by the APS.

Giving Philosophy

'As one of Arizona's major corporations, we believe we have a responsibility to our communities. We would like to help them achieve their full potential. 'Our goal is to help create a better educated workforce, a cleaner, safer environment and a stronger cultural community. By doing so, we'll attract new business and citizens to our state, and our communities will thrive..We know that corporate citizenship is a necessity, not an option, and we are committed to being Arizona's premier corporate citizen.' *Arizona Public Service Company Corporate Responsibility Report*

Financial Summary

Total Giving: $1,424,239 (1998); $1,044,544 (1997); $1,192,693 (1996). Note: Contributes through corporate direct giving program and foundation.
Giving Analysis: Giving for 1995 includes: foundation ($1,269,577); foundation matching gifts ($25,016); corporate direct giving ($1,230); 1996: foundation grants to United Way ($210,346); foundation matching gifts ($32,992); 1997: foundation ($1,014,740); foundation matching gifts ($29,804);
Assets: $23,829,461 (1998); $22,650,336 (1997); $19,776,281 (1996)
Gifts Received: $1,000,000 (1998); $2,000,000 (1997); $3,000,000 (1996). Note: Contributions are received from Arizona Public Service Co.

Typical Recipients

Arts & Humanities: Arts Associations & Councils, Arts Centers, Arts Funds, Ballet, Dance, Ethnic & Folk Arts, History & Archaeology, Libraries, Museums/Galleries, Music, Opera, Performing Arts, Public Broadcasting, Theater
Civic & Public Affairs: African American Affairs, Botanical Gardens/Parks, Civil Rights, Economic Development, Civic & Public Affairs-General, Hispanic Affairs, Housing, Municipalities/Towns, Native American Affairs, Professional & Trade Associations, Urban & Community Affairs, Women's Affairs, Zoos/Aquariums
Education: Agricultural Education, Business Education, Colleges & Universities, Community & Junior Colleges, Education Reform, Education-General, Medical Education, Public Education (Precollege), Science/Mathematics Education, Secondary Education (Public)
Environment: Environment-General, Resource Conservation
Health: Cancer, Children's Health/Hospitals, Emergency/Ambulance Services, Eyes/Blindness, Health Funds, Heart, Hospices, Hospitals, Medical Research, Prenatal Health Issues, Public Health, Research/Studies Institutes
Religion: Religious Welfare
Science: Observatories & Planetariums, Science Museums, Scientific Centers & Institutes
Social Services: Child Welfare, Community Service Organizations, Domestic Violence, Family Services, Food/Clothing Distribution, People with Disabilities, Recreation & Athletics, Scouts, Shelters/Homelessness, United Funds/United Ways, Volunteer Services, YMCA/YWCA/YMHA/YWHA, Youth Organizations

Contributions Analysis

Giving Priorities: Supports health and human services, community development, arts and culture, education, and the environment.
Arts & Humanities: 34%. Recipients include local theaters, dance companies, museums, and arts centers.

Civic & Public Affairs: 8%. Recipients include local Chamber of Commerce offices, the YMCA, the Arizona Women Employment and Education, Junior Achievment, Boys and Girls Clubs, leadership organizations, and community organizations.
Education: 15%. Recipients are area schools and school programs.
Environment: 1%.
Health: 7%. Recipients are primarily throughout Arizona and New Mexico. Recipients include hospices, the American Cancer Society, the Arizona AIDS Project, and medical centers.
Religion: 3%.
Science: 3%.
Social Services: 29%. Supports food banks, youth groups, YMCA/YWCAs, and United Way.

Application Procedures

Initial Contact: Send a brief letter or proposal.
Application Requirements: Include a description of organization, purpose, and history; contact person, address, and phone; amount requested; purpose of funds sought, including percentage of total need; proof of tax-exempt status; list of board of directors and description of staff organization; names and amounts of other corporate contributions; names of any company employees involved with organization; one-page line item budget for the project; annual budget or audited financial statement; percentage of budget funded by United Way; other corporate contributors, with amounts; information on APS employee volunteers.
Deadlines: None; budget is set in October.
Evaluative Criteria: Favors proposals with a well-defined program need rather than general operating support requests.
Notes: Guidelines are for the corporate direct giving program. Organizations outside Phoenix should send requests to local APS representatives.

Restrictions

The company does not fund individuals or individual scholarships; religious, political, fraternal, legislative or lobbying efforts; travel or hotel expenses.

Additional Information

Publications: Community Investment Report

Corporate Officials

Ms. Terry DeValle: community relations representativeeo, director PRIM CORP EMPL community relations representative: Arizona Public Service Co.
William J. Hemelt: controller B Baltimore, MD 1954. ED Lehigh University BS (1974); Lehigh University MBA (1976). PRIM CORP EMPL controller: Arizona Public Service Co. CORP AFFIL chief financial officer, secretary, treasurer: Gum Tech International Inc. NONPR AFFIL member: Financial Executives Institute.
Nancy Carol Loftin: vice president, general counsel B Phoenix, AZ 1954. ED Arizona State University BS (1976); University of Arizona JD (1979). PRIM CORP EMPL vice president, general counsel: Arizona Public Service Co. CORP AFFIL treasurer: Loftin Equipment Co. Inc.
Jaron B. Norberg: director B 1937. ED Brigham Young University; University of Utah JD (1967). PRIM CORP EMPL director: Arizona Public Service Co.
William J. Post: president, chief executive officer B Salem, OH 1950. ED Arizona State University BS (1972). PRIM CORP EMPL president, chief executive officer: Arizona Public Service Co. ADD CORP EMPL president, director: Pinnacle West Capital Corp.
Shirley A. Richard: executive vice president customer service marketing & corporate relations B Tipton, KS 1947. ED Fort Hays State University BS (1971). PRIM CORP EMPL executive vice president customer service marketing & corporate relations: Arizona Public Service Co.
Richard Snell: chairman, president, chief executive officer, director B Phoenix, AZ 1930. ED Stanford University BA (1952); Stanford University JD (1954). PRIM CORP EMPL chairman, president, chief executive officer, director: Pinnacle West Capital Corp. CORP AFFIL chairman: Suncor Development Co.; director: Suncor Homes Inc.; chairman: El Dorado Investment Co.; director: Bank One Arizona NA; director: Central Newspapers Inc.; director: Aztar Corp.; chairman: AR Public Service Co. NONPR AFFIL member: Arizona Bar Association; trustee: YMCA Metropolitan Phoenix & Sun Valley; member: American Bar Association; trustee: American Graduate School International Management. CLUB AFFIL Phoenix Country Club; Paradise Valley Country Club.

Foundation Officials

William J. Hemelt: treasurer, director (see above)
Nancy Carol Loftin: secretary, director (see above)
Jaron B. Norberg: vice president, director (see above)
William J. Post: vice president, director (see above)
Shirley A. Richard: vice president, director (see above)
Charles P. Thompson: manager

Grants Analysis

Disclosure Period: calendar year ending 1997
Total Grants: $1,037,428*
Number of Grants: 105
Average Grant: $9,880
Highest Grant: $60,000
Typical Range: $1,000 to $20,000
***Note:** Giving excludes matching gifts.

Recent Grants

Note: Grants derived from 1997 Form 990.

Arts & Humanities

60,000	Phoenix Symphony, Phoenix, AZ
28,000	Friends of the Phoenix Public Library, Phoenix, AZ
25,000	Heard Museum, Phoenix, AZ
25,000	Orpheum Theater Foundation, Phoenix, AZ
25,000	Phoenix Art Museum, Phoenix, AZ
20,000	Phoenix Art Museum, Phoenix, AZ
15,000	Arizona Community Foundation/Historical Society, Phoenix, AZ
15,000	Arizona Theater Company, Phoenix, AZ
15,000	Phoenix Theater, Phoenix, AZ
10,000	Ballet Arizona, Phoenix, AZ
10,000	Centro Cultural Mexicano, Phoenix, AZ
10,000	Scottsdale Cultural Council, Scottsdale, AZ
10,000	Scottsdale Cultural Council, Scottsdale, AZ
10,000	West Valley Fine Arts Council, Litchfield Park, AZ
7,500	Arizona Wolf Trap Program, Phoenix, AZ
7,000	Phoenix Theater, Phoenix, AZ
5,000	Actors Theater, Phoenix, AZ
5,000	Actors Theater, Phoenix, AZ
5,000	Arizona Opera Company, Phoenix, AZ

Civic & Public Affairs

20,000	Southwest Leadership Foundation, Phoenix, AZ
6,250	National Park Foundation, Washington, DC
5,000	Corporation for Supportive Housing, Phoenix, AZ

Education

30,000	Challenger Learning Center, Phoenix, AZ
25,000	Pinal County University Foundation, Coolidge, AZ
25,000	University of Arizona College of Agriculture, Phoenix, AZ
20,000	Maricopa Community Colleges Foundation, Phoenix, AZ
20,000	Northern Arizona University Ralph M. Bilby Fund for Excellence, Flagstaff, AZ
13,000	Junior Achievement of Central Arizona, Phoenix, AZ
10,000	Communities in Schools of the Valley of the Sun, Phoenix, AZ
7,500	Sedona Medical Campus, Sedona, AZ

Environment

35,000	Nature Conservancy, Tucson, AZ
5,000	Arizona Clean and Beautiful, Phoenix, AZ

Health

50,000	University of Arizona Foundation, Tucson, AZ -- Arizona Cancer Center
30,000	St. Joseph's Hospital Barrow Neurological Foundation, Phoenix, AZ
20,000	American Red Cross, Phoenix, AZ
10,000	Hospice of the Valley, Phoenix, AZ
7,500	Phoenix Memorial Hospital Foundation, Phoenix, AZ

Religion

15,000	Salvation Army Southwest Division, Phoenix, AZ
7,500	St. Vincent de Paul Society, Phoenix, AZ

Science

30,000	Arizona Science Center, Phoenix, AZ

Social Services

50,000	YMCA of Phoenix and Valley of the Sun, Phoenix, AZ
12,500	YWCA of Maricopa County, Phoenix, AZ
10,000	Arizona Academic Decathlon Association, Phoenix, AZ
10,000	Central Arizona Shelter Service, Phoenix, AZ
10,000	Goodwill Industries of Central Arizona, Phoenix, AZ
7,500	Camp Fire Council, Phoenix, AZ
7,500	Childsplay, Tempe, AZ
5,000	Association of Arizona Food Banks, Phoenix, AZ
5,000	Boy Scouts of America Western Region, Sunnyvale, CA
5,000	Carl Hayden Community Youth Center, Phoenix, AZ

ARMSTRONG WORLD INDUSTRIES, INC.

Company Contact

Lancaster, PA
Web: http://www.armstrong.com

Company Description

Profit: US$14,300,000 (1999)
Employees: 18,900 (1999)
Fortune Rank: 449, per FORTUNE Magazine's list of 500 Largest U.S. Corporations (1999).
FF 449
SIC(s): 2511 Wood Household Furniture, 3253 Ceramic Wall & Floor Tile, 3996 Hard Surface Floor Coverings Nec.

Operating Locations

Australia: Armstrong-Nylex Pty. Ltd., Breaside; Armstrong World Industries Pty. Ltd., Silverwater; Canada: Armstrong World Industries Canada Ltd., Montreal; France: Bois et Panneaux Sud, Bagneux; Armstrong Building Products, Pontarlier, Doubs; Worthington Armstrong Venture Europe SA, Rouvignies, Nord; Germany: Armstrong Building Products GmbH, Muenster, Nordrhein-Westfalen; Armstrong Europa GmbH, Muenster, Nordrhein-Westfalen; Armstrong Insulation Products GmbH, Muenster, Nordrhein-Westfalen; Armstrong Textile Products GmbH, Muenster, Nordrhein-Westfalen; Armstrong World Industries GmbH, Muenster, Nordrhein-Westfalen; Hong

Kong: Armstrong AWI Ltd., Central District; Italy: Armstrong Insulation Products SRL, Trazzano Rosa, Lombardia; Netherlands: Armstrong Building Products BV, Hoogezand, Groningen; Armstrong World Idustries ACI BV, Hoogezand, Groningen; Singapore: Armstrong Singapore Pte. Ltd., Singapore; Spain: Armstrong Insulation Products SA, Madrid; Switzerland: Armstrong Insulation Products AG, Pfaffnau, Lucerne; ISO Holding AG, Schwyz; United Kingdom: Armstrong World Industries Ltd., Stockton-on-Tees, Cleveland; Armstrong Building Products, Uxbridge, Middlesex; Armstrong Europe Services, Uxbridge, Middlesex; Armstrong Floor Products Europe Ltd., Uxbridge, Middlesex; Armstrong Hunter Douglas Ltd., Uxbridge, Middlesex; Armstrong (UK) Investments, Uxbridge, Middlesex
Note: Includes plant locations.

Armstrong Foundation

Giving Contact

Cathy R. Witmer, Contributions Administrator
Armstrong World Industries Inc.
2500 Columbia Ave.
PO Box 3001
Lancaster, PA 17604
Phone: (717)397-0611

Description

EIN: 232387950
Organization Type: Corporate Foundation. Supports preselected organizations only.
Giving Locations: PA: Lancaster
Grant Types: Employee Matching Gifts, General Support, Scholarship.

Financial Summary

Total Giving: $1,821,618 (1995); $1,587,517 (1994); $1,429,385 (1993). Note: Contributes through foundation only.
Assets: $13,161,280 (1995); $12,312,267 (1994); $12,947,645 (1993)
Gifts Received: $1,504,000 (1994); $850,000 (1993); $802,000 (1992). Note: The foundation receives contributions from Armstrong World Industries. In 1992, Applied Color Systems also gave to the foundation.

Typical Recipients

Arts & Humanities: Arts Festivals, Historic Preservation, Libraries, Opera
Civic & Public Affairs: African American Affairs, Business/Free Enterprise, Chambers of Commerce, Economic Development, Economic Policy, Ethnic Organizations, Housing, Parades/Festivals, Philanthropic Organizations, Professional & Trade Associations, Public Policy, Safety, Urban & Community Affairs
Education: Afterschool/Enrichment Programs, Arts/Humanities Education, Business Education, Colleges & Universities, Education Funds, Engineering/Technological Education, Medical Education, Minority Education, Private Education (Precollege), Public Education (Precollege), Science/Mathematics Education, Student Aid
Environment: Resource Conservation
Health: Cancer, Clinics/Medical Centers, Emergency/Ambulance Services, Eyes/Blindness, Health Organizations, Hospices, Hospitals, Medical Research, Nursing Services, Public Health, Single-Disease Health Associations
International: Health Care/Hospitals, International Relations
Religion: Religious Welfare, Social/Policy Issues
Science: Scientific Centers & Institutes
Social Services: Child Welfare, Community Service Organizations, Family Planning, Food/Clothing Distribution, People with Disabilities, Recreation & Athletics, Scouts, Shelters/Homelessness, Substance Abuse, United Funds/United Ways, YMCA/YWCA/YMHA/YWHA, Youth Organizations

Contributions Analysis

Giving Priorities: The foundation has supported medical Project Hope in the U.S. and for a project in China.
Arts & Humanities: 5% to 10%. Support emphasizes libraries and historic preservation.
Civic & Public Affairs: 15% to 20%. Funding supports the Pennsylvania Chamber of Commerce, civic associations, and various research foundations.
Education: About 25%. Funding supports the National Merit Scholarship Corporation, universities, colleges and educational foundations.
Health: 5% to 10%. Funding supports health-care associations and hospitals.
Social Services: 35% to 40% of total contributions. Funding supports various United Way chapters, local youth organizations, and local family support services.

Corporate Officials

George A. Lorch: chairman, chief executive officer, director B Glen Ridge, NJ 1941. ED Virginia Polytechnic Institute & State University BS (1963). PRIM CORP EMPL chairman, chief executive officer, director: Armstrong World Industries. CORP AFFIL director: Household International Inc.; director: Stanley Works; director: Dal-Tile International Inc.; director: RR Donnelley & Sons Co.
Frank A. Riddick, III: senior vice president, chief financial officer PRIM CORP EMPL senior vice president, chief financial officer: Armstrong World Industries.

Foundation Officials

M. William Jones: secretary, assistant to president
John N. Jordin: vice president, director
Warren M. Posey, Jr.: treasurer B New Orleans, LA 1940. ED University of California at Berkeley (1963); University of Pennsylvania Wharton School (1965).
R. A. Sills: assistant secretary
G. P. Walker: assistant treasurer
Cathy R. Witmer: contributions admin

Grants Analysis

Disclosure Period: calendar year ending 1995
Total Grants: $1,821,618
Number of Grants: 629*
Average Grant: $2,896*
Highest Grant: $360,000
Typical Range: $100 to $5,000
***Note:** Total grants, number of grants, and average grants include matching gifts for education.

Recent Grants

Note: Grants derived from 1997 Form 990.

Arts & Humanities

25,000	Lancaster County Library, Lancaster, PA

Civic & Public Affairs

30,000	Lancaster Housing Opportunity Partnership, Lancaster, PA
25,000	Lancaster Alliance, Lancaster, PA
11,000	Pennsylvania Economy League, Wilkes-Barre, PA
10,000	West Lancaster Fire Company 1, Lancaster, PA
10,000	Maytown East Donegal Township Fire Department, Maytown, PA

Education

161,545	National Merit Scholarship Corporation, Chicago, IL
95,000	Millersville University, Millersville, PA
50,000	Franklin and Marshall College, Lancaster, PA
40,000	Millersville University, Millersville, PA
20,000	Citizens Scholarship Foundation of Lancaster County, Lancaster, PA
20,000	Elizabethtown College, Elizabethtown, PA
17,100	Junior Achievement of Central Pennsylvania, Lancaster, PA
15,000	Pennsylvania State University Harrisburg, Middletown, PA
12,000	Foundation for Independent Colleges, Harrisburg, PA
10,000	Lebanon Valley College, Annville, PA -- Toward 2001 project
10,000	Pennsylvania Academy of Music, Lancaster, PA
5,000	Morehouse School of Medicine, Atlanta, GA

Environment

15,000	Chesapeake Bay Foundation, Annapolis, MD

Health

50,000	Lancaster Health Alliance, Lancaster, PA
40,000	City of Hope, Los Angeles, CA
25,000	Southeast Lancaster Health Services, Lancaster, PA
20,000	Community Hospital Foundation, Lancaster, PA
10,000	City of Hope, Los Angeles, CA

Science

13,000	National Institute of Building Sciences, Washington, DC

Social Services

550,000	United Way of Lancaster County, Lancaster, PA
12,250	United Way of Central Georgia, Macon, GA
10,195	United Way of Escambia County, Pensacola, FL
10,000	Foundation for A Drug Free Pennsylvania, Harrisburg, PA
10,000	Susquehanna Association for the Blind, Lancaster, PA

Arvin Industries, Inc.

Company Contact

Columbus, IN
Web: http://www.arvin.com

Company Description

Profit: US$91,100,000 (1999)
Employees: 12,982
Fortune Rank: 494, per FORTUNE Magazine's list of 500 Largest U.S. Corporations (1999).
FF 494
SIC(s): 3465 Automotive Stampings, 3469 Metal Stampings Nec, 3479 Metal Coating & Allied Services, 3714 Motor Vehicle Parts & Accessories.

Arvin Foundation

Giving Contact

E.H. Dawson, Contributions Committee Chairman
Arvin Foundation
One Noblitt Plz.
PO Box 3000
Columbus, IN 47202-3000
Fax: (812)379-3688

Description

EIN: 356020798
Organization Type: Corporate Foundation
Giving Locations: AL; IN; MI; MO; OK; SC; TN headquarters and operating communities.
Grant Types: Capital, General Support.

Giving Philosophy

'Arvin financially supports charitable, educational and youth activities and other community needs on a continuing basis through the Arvin Foundation, Inc. Established in 1951, the Foundation is funded from Arvin earnings in such a way that a continuous stream of gifts can be maintained even during years when the economy is weak. Since the Foundation's gifts traditionally have been made to the basic operating funds of charities to which tax dollars and government funds are not available, this policy has proven sound and responsible in supporting those organizations in times when money is difficult to raise.' Arvin Foundation, Inc., Review

Financial Summary

Total Giving: $603,619 (1997); $843,962 (1996); $1,036,886 (1995). Note: Contributes through foundation only. 1997 Giving includes United Way ($85,800).
Assets: $4,573,463 (1997); $4,063,696 (1995); $3,642,709 (1994)
Gifts Received: $1,012,065 (1994); $1,239,475 (1992); $1,229,359 (1991). Note: Contributions received from Arvin Industries, Inc.

Typical Recipients

Arts & Humanities: Arts Associations & Councils, Arts Centers, Arts Funds, Arts & Humanities-General, History & Archaeology, Libraries, Museums/Galleries, Music
Civic & Public Affairs: Botanical Gardens/Parks, Business/Free Enterprise, Chambers of Commerce, Clubs, Community Foundations, Economic Development, Employment/Job Training, Ethnic Organizations, Hispanic Affairs, Housing, Municipalities/Towns, Parades/Festivals, Philanthropic Organizations, Urban & Community Affairs
Education: Business Education, Business-School Partnerships, Colleges & Universities, Community & Junior Colleges, Economic Education, Education Associations, Education Funds, Education Reform, Elementary Education (Private), Elementary Education (Public), Engineering/Technological Education, Faculty Development, Education-General, International Exchange, Literacy, Minority Education, Private Education (Precollege), Public Education (Precollege), Science/Mathematics Education, Secondary Education (Public), Student Aid
Environment: Resource Conservation
Health: Cancer, Children's Health/Hospitals, Clinics/Medical Centers, Emergency/Ambulance Services, Eyes/Blindness, Health Organizations, Hospices, Hospitals, Public Health, Research/Studies Institutes, Respiratory, Single-Disease Health Associations
International: Foreign Educational Institutions, Health Care/Hospitals, International Affairs, International Organizations
Science: Science Museums, Scientific Centers & Institutes
Social Services: Animal Protection, Camps, Community Service Organizations, Day Care, Family Services, Food/Clothing Distribution, People with Disabilities, Recreation & Athletics, Scouts, United Funds/United Ways, Youth Organizations

Contributions Analysis

Giving Priorities: Higher education, technical training, United Way, hospitals, museums, arts funds, and youth organizations.
Arts & Humanities: 5% to 10%. Supports orchestras, museums, libraries, and several other arts and music groups.
Civic & Public Affairs: 30% to 35%. Grants are made to hospitals, health organizations, environmental projects, as well as support for hospice and home care. Single-disease organizations receive support. Civic concerns include fire departments, historical museums, booster clubs, and public broadcasting.
Education: 40% to 45%. Major support for colleges and universities. Also supports educational foundations, K-12 education, scholarship funds, economic education, and vocational training.
Social Services: 15% to 20%. Primarily supports United Way organizations and youth organizations.

Application Procedures

Initial Contact: one- or two-page letter
Application Requirements: list of board of directors; purpose and needs of program; budget; duration, goals, and leadership; amount requested and date contribution needed; recently audited financial statement; and proof of tax-exempt status
Deadlines: None.
Review Process: contributions committee meets approximately every six to eight weeks to review requests; replies usually sent within 30-60 days of receipt of request

Restrictions

Arvin Foundation does not make loans or grants to individuals, for endowments, or to religious organizations for sectarian purposes.

Additional Information

As of 1995, Arvin Industries Inc. had sold divisions in California, Ohio, New York, and North Carolina.
Publications: Foundation Annual Review

Corporate Officials

James Kendrick Baker: vice chairman, director B Wabash, IN 1931. ED DePauw University AB (1953); Harvard University MBA (1958). PRIM CORP EMPL vice chairman, director: Arvin Industries, Inc. CORP AFFIL director: Vinyl-Metal Laminators Institute; director: Space Industries; director: Tokheim Corp.; director: INB Finance Corp.; director: Roll Coater Inc.; director: Geon Co.; director: Carlspan SRL; director: Cinergy Corp.; director: 1st Chicago NBD; director: Ancast Industries Corp. NONPR AFFIL vice chairman, director: New American Schools Development Corp.; member advisory board, trustee: Northwestern University Kellogg Graduate School Business Management; trustee: Institute Global Ethics; founding chairman: Indiana Center Philanthropy; member: Indiana Chamber of Commerce; director: Associated Colleges Indiana; member: Columbus Area Chamber of Commerce. CLUB AFFIL Rotary Club; DePauw University Alumni Club; Harrison Lake Country Club.
V. William Hunt: chief executive officer, chairman, president, director B Washington, DC 1944. ED Indiana University AB (1966); Indiana University JD (1969). PRIM CORP EMPL chief executive officer, chairman, president, director: Arvin Industries, Inc. ADD CORP EMPL secretary: Roll Coater.
Raymond Phillip Mack: vice president human resources B Chicago, IL 1940. ED DePaul University (1968); Loyola University Chicago (1973). PRIM CORP EMPL vice president human resources: Arvin Industries, Inc. NONPR AFFIL member: American Compensation Association; member: Manufacturer Alliance Productivity & Innovation Human Resources Council.
Byron O. Pond: chairman, chief executive officer, director B Royal Oak, MI 1936. ED Wayne State University BS (1961). CORP AFFIL director: Cooper Tire & Rubber Co.; chief executive officer: Maremont Corp.
A. R. Sales: treasurer B Holguin, Cuba 1948. ED Indiana University BS (1972); Indiana University MBA (1977). PRIM CORP EMPL treasurer: Arvin Industries, Inc. NONPR AFFIL member: National Association of Corporate Treasurers; member advisory board: Purdue University; member: Financial Executives Institute; member advisory board: Indiana University; director: Columbus Economic Development Board; director: Columbus Regional Hospital Foundation; chairman, director: Bartholomew County United Way; member: Beta Gamma Sigma.

Foundation Officials

James Kendrick Baker: chairman, director (see above)
Edwin H. Dawson: director PRIM CORP EMPL vice president & general manager components group: Arvin Exhaust.
V. William Hunt: director (see above)
J. William Kendall: chairman, director B Ashland, KY 1932. ED DePauw University (1954). PRIM CORP EMPL vice president community relations: Arvin Industries, Inc. CORP AFFIL vice president: Arvin Industries Inc.
Raymond Phillip Mack: director (see above)
David M. Main: secretary, director PRIM CORP EMPL assistant secretary: Arvin Industries, Inc.
W. Frederick Meyer: president B 1933. ED Wabash College AB (1955); Indiana University MBA (1958).
A. R. Sales: director (see above)
Richard Alan Smith: treasurer, director B Boston, MA 1924. ED Harvard University BS (1946). PRIM CORP EMPL chairman, director, chief executive officer: Harcourt General, Inc. CORP AFFIL chairman: GC Co. Inc.; chairman, chief executive officer: Neiman Marcus Group Inc.
Charles H. Watson: director

Grants Analysis

Disclosure Period: calendar year ending 1997
Total Grants: $517,819*
Number of Grants: 87
Average Grant: $5,952
Highest Grant: $50,000
Typical Range: $1,000 to $15,000
***Note:** Giving excludes United Way.

Recent Grants

Note: Grants derived from 1997 Form 990.

Arts & Humanities

25,000	Veterans Memorial Fund, Columbus, IN
20,000	Heritage Fund Focus Group, Columbus, IN
10,000	Indianapolis Symphony, Indianapolis, IN
7,000	Columbus Pro Musica, Columbus, IN
6,250	Columbus Area Arts Council, Columbus, IN
5,000	Indianapolis Museum of Art, Indianapolis, IN
2,500	Ethall Expo, Columbus, IN
2,000	Detroit Symphony Orchestra, Detroit, MI
2,000	Fayette County Public Library, Fayette, AL
1,500	Heritage of Hope, Hope, IN

Civic & Public Affairs

25,000	Heritage Fund of Bartholomew County, Columbus, IN
10,000	INFOCUS Indiana, Indianapolis, IN
5,000	Columbus Arts Chamber Foundation, Columbus, IN
5,000	Housing Partnership, Columbus, IN
3,000	Columbus Enterprise Development Corporation, Columbus, IN
2,500	National Hispanic Partnership, Novato, CA

Education

10,000	AWBA University Foundation, Kansas City, MO
10,000	Indiana Council for Higher Education, West Lafayette, IN
8,000	AWBA University Foundation, Kansas City, MO
8,000	Bartholomew Consolidated School Corp, Columbus, IN
6,000	Junior Achievement of Central Indiana, Indianapolis, IN
5,000	Foundation for Independent Higher Education, Chicago, IL
5,000	Independent Colleges Foundation, Indianapolis, IN

5,000	University of Alabama, Birmingham, AL
2,000	Fayette County Local Education Advancement Foundation, Fayette, AL
2,000	Martin Methodist College, Pulaski, TN
2,000	Seading Academy, Birmingham, AL
1,000	Fayette Elementary School, Fayette, AL
1,000	GMI Engineering and Management Institute, Flint, MI
1,000	Hauser Community Scholarship Foundation, Hope, IN

Environment

1,000	Nature Conservancy, Indianapolis, IN

Health

20,000	Columbus Regional Hospital Foundation, Columbus, IN
15,000	Hospice and Home Care, Columbus, IN
5,000	Fort Chanders Loudon Medical Center, Loudon, TN
2,500	Tennessee Lions Eye Center, Nashville, TN
1,200	Ronald McDonald House, Knoxville, TN
1,000	American Red Cross Disaster Relief, Louisville, KY

Social Services

50,000	Foundation for Youth, Columbus, IN
23,300	United Way of Bartholomew County, Columbus, IN
23,000	United Way of Bartholomew County, Columbus, IN
23,000	United Way of Bartholomew County, Columbus, IN
8,000	United Way of Johnson County, Franklin, IN
5,000	United Way of Bartholomew County, Columbus, IN
2,500	Hope Summer Playground, Hope, IN
2,000	Greenfield K-9 Fund, Greenfield, IN
2,000	United Way of Shelby County, Sidney, OH
1,500	Association of Retarded Citizens of Hancock County, Greenfield, IN
1,500	United Way, Chickasha, OK
1,200	Boy Scouts of America, Indianapolis, IN
1,000	Columbus Parks and Recreation Department, Columbus, IN

ASARCO INC.

Company Contact

New York, NY
Web: http://www.asarco.com

Company Description

Profit: US$169,200,000
Employees: 11,800
SIC(s): 2879 Agricultural Chemicals Nec, 3272 Concrete Products Nec, 3331 Primary Copper, 3339 Primary Nonferrous Metals Nec.

Nonmonetary Support

Type: Donated Equipment; In-kind Services

Corporate Sponsorship

Contact: Richard Osborne, Director

ASARCO Foundation

Giving Contact

Don M. Noyes, Vice President
ASARCO Foundation
180 Maiden Lane
New York, NY 10038
Phone: (212)510-1813
Fax: (212)510-1835

Description

Founded: 1956
EIN: 136089860
Organization Type: Corporate Foundation
Giving Locations: headquarters and operating communities.
Grant Types: Fellowship, General Support, Matching, Multiyear/Continuing Support, Scholarship.

Financial Summary

Total Giving: $200,000 (1998 approx); $200,000 (1997 approx); $77,896 (1996). Note: Contributes through corporate direct giving program and foundation.
Giving Analysis: Giving for 1996 includes: foundation ($66,096); foundation grants to United Way ($11,800)
Assets: $492,599 (1996); $544,767 (1995); $592,220 (1994)
Gifts Received: $650,000 (1989)

Typical Recipients

Arts & Humanities: History & Archaeology, Performing Arts
Civic & Public Affairs: Public Policy
Education: Colleges & Universities, Economic Education, Engineering/Technological Education, Legal Education, Private Education (Precollege), Public Education (Precollege), Religious Education, Science/Mathematics Education, Secondary Education (Private), Student Aid
Environment: Environment-General
Health: Hospices
International: International Development, International Peace & Security Issues
Religion: Jewish Causes, Religious Organizations
Social Services: People with Disabilities, United Funds/United Ways, Youth Organizations

Contributions Analysis

Giving Priorities: Scholarships and matching gifts to colleges and universities; United Way.
Education: About 40%. Majority of funding supports higher education. Also funds science and technology education and private secondary schools through grants and matching gifts.
Health: About 40%. Supports United Way.

Application Procedures

Initial Contact: Send a brief letter.
Application Requirements: Include a description of the purpose and objectives of the grant; proof of tax-exempt status.
Deadlines: None.
Decision Notification: Primary meeting is usually held in February.

Restrictions

The foundation does not support individuals, political campaigns, lobbying groups, or propaganda activities.

Corporate Officials

William Dowd: controller, chief executive officer, director PRIM CORP EMPL controller: ASARCO Inc.
Francis R. McAllister: president, chief executive officer B Saint George, UT 1942. ED University of Utah BS (1966); New York University MBA (1971). PRIM CORP EMPL president, chief executive officer: ASARCO Inc. CORP AFFIL director: Mexico Desarrollo Industries Minero SA; director: Southern Peru Copper Corp.
Richard de Jongh Osborne: chairman, chief executive officer, director B Bronxville, NY 1934. ED Princeton University BA (1956). PRIM CORP EMPL chairman, chief executive officer, director: ASARCO Inc. CORP AFFIL director: Vacco Industries Inc.; chairman: Federated Metals Corp.; director: Southern Peru Copper Corp.; president: Encycle Inc.; director: B.F. Goodrich Co.; director: Birmingham Steel Corp.; president: ASARCO Exploration Co.; president: ASARCO International Corp.; chairman: Ar Mexican Explorations Inc. NONPR AFFIL director: National Mining Association; director: Tinker Foundation; director: International Copper Association; member: Council Foreign Relations; member: Downtown Association; director: Copper Development Association; member: Council Americas; director: Ams Society; director: American Australian Association. CLUB AFFIL Economic Club; Sakonnet Golf Club.

Foundation Officials

William Dowd: vice president (see above)
Carmen D. Gonzalez: assistant secretary PRIM CORP EMPL assistant secretary, director: ASARCO Inc. Oil & Gas Co. CORP AFFIL assistant secretary: Federated Metals Corp.
Augustus Blagden Kinsolving: director B Boston, MA 1940. ED Yale University BA (1961); Oxford University MA (1963); Harvard University LLB (1965). PRIM CORP EMPL vice president, general counsel: ASARCO Inc. CORP AFFIL director, secretary: Southern Peru Copper Corp.; president: AR Mexican Holdings Inc. NONPR AFFIL member: Downtown Association; member: National Association for State Court; member: American Bar Association; member: Council Americas; member: American Association Rhodes Scholars. CLUB AFFIL New York Yacht Club.
Francis R. McAllister: vice president, director (see above)
Robert James Muth: president, director B Philadelphia, PA 1933. ED Lafayette College BA (1954); Yale University Divinity School (1954-1955); Columbia University LLB (1960). PRIM CORP EMPL vice president government & public affairs: ASARCO Inc. CORP AFFIL director: Southern Peru Copper Corp.; vice president, director: ASARCO Inc. Oil & Gas Co. NONPR AFFIL member: New York State Bar Association; director: Northern Lights Institute; chairman: Lead Industry Association; member: George School Comm; secretary, director: International Copper Association; member: American Bar Association; member: American Institute Mining Metallurgical Petroleum Engineers. CLUB AFFIL Metropolitan Club.
Don M. Noyes: vice president PRIM CORP EMPL manager advertising and public relations: ASARCO Inc.
Richard de Jongh Osborne: director (see above)
Christopher F. Schultz: treasurer PRIM CORP EMPL treasurer: ASARCO Inc.

Grants Analysis

Disclosure Period: calendar year ending 1996
Total Grants: $66,096*
Number of Grants: 135
Average Grant: $490
Highest Grant: $13,180
Typical Range: $50 to $1,000
***Note:** Giving excludes United Way. Giving includes matching gifts.

Recent Grants

Note: Grants derived from 1996 Form 990.

Education

13,180	National Merit Scholarship Corporation, Evanston, IL
5,000	Joint Council of Economic Education
25	Montana Tech Foundation, Butte, MT

Social Services

10,000	United Way Tri-State Area, New York, NY
1,000	United Way, Salt Lake City, UT
800	United Way Jefferson County, Charles Town, WV

ASHLAND, INC.

Company Contact

Ashland, KY

Web: http://www.ashland.com

Company Description

Former Name: Ashland Oil, Inc.
Revenue: US$6,801,000,000 (1999)
Employees: 23,000 (1999)
Fortune Rank: 245, per FORTUNE Magazine's list of 500 Largest U.S. Corporations (1999).
FF 245
SIC(s): 1221 Bituminous Coal & Lignite--Surface, 1311 Crude Petroleum & Natural Gas, 1629 Heavy Construction Nec, 2911 Petroleum Refining.

Operating Locations

Australia: Valvoline Australia Pty. Ltd., Smithfield; Brazil: Ashland Participacoes Ltd., Sao Paulo; Canada: Ashland Chemicals, Mississauga; Valvoline Oil & Chemicals Ltd., Mississauga; France: Ashland-Avebene, Moulineaux; Germany: Ashland-Suedchemie-Kernfest GmbH, Hilden; Ashland Coal Saarbergwerke A.G., Saarbruecken; Italy: Ashland Chemical Italiana SpA, Milan; Mexico: Ashland de Mexico SA de CV; Nigeria: Ashland Oil Co., Lagos; Ashland Oil (Nigeria) Co., Lagos; Netherlands: Valvoline Oil Nederland B.V., Dordrecht, Zuid-Holland; B.V. Ashland-Suedchemie V.H. Necof, Geertruidenberg, Noord-Brabant; Saudi Arabia: Saudi Industrial Resins Ltd., Jeddah; United Kingdom: Valvoline Oil Co. Ltd., Birkenhead; Ashland Oil International Ltd., London; Ashland Chemical Ltd., Worcestershire

Nonmonetary Support

Value: $400,000 (1990); $400,000 (1989); $400,000 (1988)
Type: Donated Equipment; Donated Products; In-kind Services
Volunteer Programs: The company encourages employee volunteerism through activities such as the annual River Sweep, a clean-up of the Ohio River.
Note: Value of nonmonetary support is less than $50,000 annually.

Corporate Sponsorship

Type: Arts & cultural events
Contact: C. Whitehead, President
Note: Sponsors various events.

Ashland Inc. Foundation

Giving Contact

Mrs. Judy B. Thomas, President
Ashland Inc. Foundation
50 East RiverCenter Boulevard
PO Box 391
Ashland, KY 41114
Phone: (606)329-4525
Fax: (606)815-4496
Web: http://www.ashland.com/community/foundation

Description

EIN: 616057900
Organization Type: Corporate Foundation
Giving Locations: KY; MN; OH; WV headquarters and operating communities.
Grant Types: Employee Matching Gifts, General Support, Scholarship.
Note: Scholarships for children of employees only.

Financial Summary

Total Giving: $3,000,000 (fiscal year ending September 30, 2000 approx); $3,000,000 (fiscal 1999 approx); $5,000,000 (fiscal 1996 approx). Note: Contributes through corporate direct giving program and foundation. While the foundation still exists, grants come directly from the company.
Giving Analysis: Giving for fiscal 1996 includes: foundation matching gifts ($1,338,901)
Assets: $593 (fiscal 1993); $8,609 (fiscal 1992); $360,022 (fiscal 1991)
Gifts Received: $4,737,559 (fiscal 1993); $4,900,000 (fiscal 1992). Note: In fiscal 1993, the foundation received contributions from Ashland Oil.

Typical Recipients

Arts & Humanities: Arts Associations & Councils, Arts Centers, Arts Funds, Community Arts, Dance, Historic Preservation, History & Archaeology, Museums/Galleries, Music, Opera, Performing Arts, Public Broadcasting, Theater
Civic & Public Affairs: African American Affairs, Botanical Gardens/Parks, Business/Free Enterprise, Community Foundations, Economic Development, Civic & Public Affairs-General, Law & Justice, Municipalities/Towns, Philanthropic Organizations, Public Policy, Urban & Community Affairs
Education: Business Education, Colleges & Universities, Community & Junior Colleges, Economic Education, Education Associations, Education Funds, Education Reform, Engineering/Technological Education, Education-General, International Studies, Literacy, Private Education (Precollege), Public Education (Precollege), Student Aid
Environment: Environment-General, Resource Conservation
Health: Cancer, Clinics/Medical Centers, Health Organizations, Hospitals, Single-Disease Health Associations, Speech & Hearing
International: International Development
Religion: Religious Welfare
Social Services: Child Welfare, People with Disabilities, Senior Services, United Funds/United Ways, Youth Organizations

Contributions Analysis

Giving Priorities: Education, united funds, hospitals and health organizations, arts centers, and civic and economic development, and environmental concerns.
Arts & Humanities: 8%. Funding supports art centers, funds, associations, museums, public broadcasting, and music.
Civic & Public Affairs: 14%. Funding supports economic development; community affairs; and law and justice.
Education: 61%. Funding supports colleges, universities, and secondary schools, primarily in operating areas, with a focus on schools preparing students for a career in the industry. Literacy, educational foundations, and community and junior colleges are also of interest. Foundation sponsors scholarships for children of employees, employee matching gifts program to educational institutions, and runs print and broadcast ads promoting education.
Health: 13%. Funds United Way; other recipients include youth organizations, groups concerned with the aged and child welfare, community centers and service agencies, and hospitals and health groups.
Note: Total contributions made in 1995.

Application Procedures

Initial Contact: See Web site for guidelines, then send a full proposal.
Application Requirements: Each proposal must contain a cover letter of no more than one page, which should: outline the need; show how the project addresses that need; demonstrate how the proposal meets the foundation's priorities; indicate amount requested requested and total project budget; specify funding period; list key program or deadline dates. Proposals should include: organization name, address, phone number, and the name and phone number of a contact person; brief description of how the proposal address identified needs not met by other nonprofits, number of individuals served, and expected results; list of company employee volunteers and nature of involvement; timetable for project implementation, communication, and evaluation; statement of the history, purpose, and goals of the organization, number of members, constituents served, geographic service area, volunteer involvement, related accomplishments and qualifications; operating budget for the past two years, with percentages for program, administrative, fundraising, and other expenses; project budget, with all sources of financial support, committed and pending; audited financial statement; most recent annual report; proof of tax-exempt status; list of officers and board members, with affiliations; background statement on executive director and key staff; list of other donors, including United Way or other federated funds, corporations, foundations, individuals, and government sources.
Deadlines: None.
Review Process: Foundation staff reviews proposals, and may schedule site visits or interviews if more information is needed.
Decision Notification: Decisions are made quarterly; notification is by letter.

Restrictions

Foundation does not support individual; organizations that received United Way funding; fraternal, veteran, labor, athletic, or sectarian organizations serving a limited group; political or lobbying organizations; capital campaigns for building or equipment; endowment funds; travel funds; films, videotapes, or audio production; projects outside the United States; sponsorship, tickets, or goodwill advertising; or organizations that conflict with the company's goals, programs, products, or employees.

Additional Information

Foundation changed its name from Ashland Oil Foundation Inc. to Ashland, Inc. Foundation.

Corporate Officials

Paul Wilbur Chellgren: chief executive officer, chairman, director B Tullahoma, TN 1943. ED University of Kentucky BS (1964); Harvard University MBA (1966); Oxford University MBA (1967). PRIM CORP EMPL chief executive officer, chairman, director: Ashland Inc. CORP AFFIL director: PNC Bank Corp.; director: PNC Bank Kentucky Inc.; director: Arch Coal Inc.; director: Medtronic Inc. NONPR AFFIL member: Society Chemical Industry; trustee: University Kentucky; vice chairman, trustee: National Foundation Advancement Arts; member: National Petroleum Refiners Association; director: Marshall University Foundation; trustee: Museum of Art; director: Foundation Tri-State Community; chairman: Leadership Tri State; trustee: Centre College; member: Chemical Manufacturers Association; sec, treasurer, director: American Friends University College Oxford Inc.; director: American Petroleum Institute.

Foundation Officials

John Alfred 'Fred' Brothers: trustee B Huntington, WV 1940. ED Virginia Polytechnic Institute & State University BS (1962); Virginia Polytechnic Institute & State University MS (1965); Virginia Polytechnic Institute & State University PhD (1966); Harvard University Advanced Management Program (1981). PRIM CORP EMPL executive vice president: Ashland Inc. CORP AFFIL director: GTS Duratk Inc.; director: The Geon Co. NONPR AFFIL member, director: Phi Kappa Phi; member: Tau Beta Pi; director: Ohio Dominican College; adj professor engineering: Ohio State University; director: Columbus Children's Hospital; director: Columbus Museum Art; member: Chemical Manufacturers Association; member: Columbus Chamber of Commerce; member: American Petroleum Institute. CLUB AFFIL Sciotto Country Club; Muirfield Country Club; Rolling Rock Club; Columbus Club; Mill Reef Club.
Paul Wilbur Chellgren: member (see above)
Sue G. Dowdy: manager
Fred M. Greenwood: secretary
Terry L. McKinley: assistant secretary
Rick E. Music: trustee PRIM CORP EMPL administrative vice president: SuperAmerica.

Joseph Marvin Quin: trustee B Vicksburg, MS 1947. ED University of Mississippi BBA (1969); University of Virginia MBA (1972). PRIM CORP EMPL senior vice president, chief financial officer: Ashland Inc. CORP AFFIL director: Ashland Coal Inc.; director: Kentucky Electric Steel; director: Arch Coal Inc.
Larry K. Wessel: assistant treasurer
Charles Whitehead: president
Harry M. Zachem: chairman, trustee B Ironton, OH 1944. ED University of Kentucky BA (1968); Harvard University AMP (1985). PRIM CORP EMPL senior vice president public affairs: Ashland Inc. CORP AFFIL director: Kentucky Bank & Trust. NONPR AFFIL member: National Association Manufacturer; member: Thunderbird-America Graduate School International Management.

Grants Analysis

Disclosure Period: fiscal year ending September 30, 1993
Total Grants: $3,407,884*
Number of Grants: 146
Average Grant: $23,341
Highest Grant: $263,500
Typical Range: $1,000 to $25,000
***Note:** Giving excludes matching gifts.

Recent Grants

Note: Grants derived from fiscal 1993 Form 990.

Arts & Humanities

5,000 Minnesota Orchestral Association, Minneapolis, MN

Civic & Public Affairs

5,000 American Chemical Society, Washington, DC

Education

263,500 Ashland Public Schools, Ashland, KY
207,500 Marshall University Foundation, Huntington, WV
200,000 College of Business and Economics, Lexington, KY
155,900 Russell Independent Schools, Russell, KY
150,000 Transylvania University, Lexington, KY
120,148 Boyd County Schools, Ashland, KY
100,000 New American Schools Development Corp, Washington, DC
88,000 Greenup County Schools, Greenup, KY
75,000 Morehead State University Foundation, Morehead, KY
62,500 Kentucky School Reform Corp, Lexington, KY
60,000 Vanderbilt University, Nashville, TN
60,000 West Virginia University Foundation, Morgantown, WV
54,000 Berea College, Berea, KY
52,000 Fairview Independent Schools, Ashland, KY
50,000 Centre College, Danville, KY
50,000 Eastern Kentucky University, Richmond, KY
50,000 University of Louisville, Louisville, KY
35,000 Kentucky Independent College Fund, Louisville, KY
35,000 Raceland Independent Schools, Raceland, KY
25,000 Governor's Honors Academy Foundation, Morgantown, WV
25,000 Governor's Scholars Program, Frankfort, KY
25,000 Northern Kentucky University, Highland Heights, KY
25,000 West Virginia Education Fund, Charleston, WV
20,000 Pikeville College, Pikeville, KY
20,000 Rose Hill Christian School, Ashland, KY
18,800 Ohio Foundation for Independent Colleges, Columbus, OH
17,500 Holy Family Schools, Ashland, KY
15,000 Ohio State University, Columbus, OH
15,000 West Virginia State College Foundation, Institute, WV
13,500 University of Kentucky, Lexington, KY
11,250 Business Higher Education Forum, Washington, DC
10,700 Marshall University Research Corp, Huntington, WV
10,000 Midway College, Midway, KY
10,000 West Virginia University, Morgantown, WV
7,200 West Virginia Foundation for Independent Colleges, Charleston, WV
6,000 University of Charleston, Charleston, WV
5,000 Alice Lloyd College, Pippa Passes, KY
5,000 Asbury College, Wilmore, KY
5,000 Business Economics Education Foundation of Minnesota, Minneapolis, MN
5,000 Franklin University, Columbus, OH
5,000 National Foundation for the Improvement of Education, Washington, DC
4,500 West Virginia Governors Honors Academy Foundation, Charleston, WV
4,000 National Society of Professional Engineers Education Foundation, Alexandria, VA
3,000 West Virginia Secondary School Activities Commission, Parksburg, WV

International

25,000 Center for Strategic International Studies, Washington, DC

Science

88,255 Marshall University, Huntington, WV
10,000 Kentucky Science and Technology Council, Lexington, KY

Social Services

5,000 Children's Place, Huntington, WV

Associated Food Stores

Company Contact

Jamaica, NY

Company Description

Employees: 31
SIC(s): 5141 Groceries--General Line.

Associated Food Stores Charitable Foundation

Giving Contact

Harry Laufer, President & Chief Executive Officer
Associated Food Stores Charitable Foundation
122-20 Merrick Blvd.
Jamaica, NY 11434
Phone: (718)978-0764

Description

Founded: 1987
EIN: 112866371
Organization Type: Corporate Foundation. Supports preselected organizations only.
Giving Locations: NY: including metropolitan area
Grant Types: General Support.

Financial Summary

Total Giving: $171,250 (1998); $199,024 (1996); $286,106 (1995). Note: Contributes through foundation only.
Giving Analysis: Giving for 1998 includes: foundation ($171,250)
Assets: $933,220 (1998); $864,135 (1996); $853,712 (1995)
Gifts Received: $201,750 (1998); $200,000 (1996); $200,000 (1995). Note: Contributions are received from Associated Food Stores.

Typical Recipients

Arts & Humanities: History & Archaeology
Civic & Public Affairs: Employment/Job Training, Civic & Public Affairs-General
Education: Business Education, Colleges & Universities, Education-General, Private Education (Precollege), Special Education, Student Aid
Environment: Wildlife Protection
Health: Cancer, Children's Health/Hospitals, Clinics/Medical Centers, Diabetes, Eyes/Blindness, Geriatric Health, Hospitals, Long-Term Care, Medical Research, Nursing Services, Single-Disease Health Associations
International: Health Care/Hospitals, International Relief Efforts, Missionary/Religious Activities
Religion: Jewish Causes, Religious Organizations, Religious Welfare, Seminaries
Social Services: Community Service Organizations, People with Disabilities, Recreation & Athletics, Scouts, Social Services-General, YMCA/YWCA/YMHA/YWHA, Youth Organizations

Contributions Analysis

Giving Priorities: Major support given to Jewish causes. Also supports civic organizations, scholarship funds, secondary schools, universities, wildlife conservation, and healthcare and geriatric health.
Education: 33%. Supports secondary schools, univerities, and communication education.
Religion: 63%. Supports Jewish organizations and religious welfare.
Social Services: 3%. Supports organizations that benefit youth.
Note: Total contributions made in 1998.

Corporate Officials

Ira Gober: chairman, chief financial officer, partner, director B 1943. ED City College of New York BA (1964); Bernard Baruch School BBA (1966). PRIM CORP EMPL chairman, chief financial officer, partner, director: Associated Food Stores.
Harry Laufer: president, chief executive officer, partner, director B 1933. PRIM CORP EMPL president, chief executive officer, partner, director: Associated Food Stores. NONPR AFFIL chairman: Brandeis School.

Foundation Officials

Harvey Berg: director
Ira Gober: director (see above)
Harry Laufer: director (see above)

Grants Analysis

Disclosure Period: calendar year ending 1998
Total Grants: $171,250
Number of Grants: 26
Average Grant: $6,587
Highest Grant: $30,100
Typical Range: $100 to $30,000

Recent Grants

Note: Grants derived from 1997 Form 990.

Civic & Public Affairs

800 Workmens Circle Building Fund
500 Harold Schneiderman Memorial Fund, Howard Beach, NY

Education

17,000 Brandeis School
11,000 Ramaz School, New York, NY
10,000 Yeshiva University, New York, NY
5,000 School for Language and Communication, North Bellmore, NY
5,000 Solomon Schechter School of Long Island

300 Junior Achievement

Health

1,000 New York Eye and Ear Infirmary, New York, NY
500 United Cerebral Palsy Association, Los Angeles, CA
450 Daughters of Miriam, Clifton, NJ
300 Sephardic Geriatric Foundation, Brooklyn, NY
150 American Cancer Society

Religion

28,150 Hewlett Rockaway Jewish Center
24,800 United Jewish Appeal Federation, New York, NY
23,000 Jewish Theological Seminary of America, New York, NY
15,000 Congregation Bach Jan Eisenstein
12,000 Congregation Kehilath Jeshurun, New York, NY
5,000 Hewlett Hadassah
5,000 Lubavitch Youth Organization
2,000 Jewish Foundation for the Righteous, New York, NY
1,800 Foundation for Conservative Judaism
1,800 Yeshiva and Mesivta Toras of South Shore
1,500 Mesivta of Long Beach, Long Beach, NY
1,000 Beth Malca Yeshiva
1,000 Upper East Side Hatzolah, New York, NY
500 Beth Abraham Foundation, Bronx, NY
500 Chabad Lubavitch
500 Suffolk Youth Jewish Community Center, Commack, NY
300 Parker Jewish Geriatric Institute, New York, NY
250 Yeshiva Karlin Stolin
100 Boro Park Progressive Synagogue, Brooklyn, NY
50 Lido Beach Synagogue, Lido Beach, NY

Social Services

1,350 Boy Scouts of America Greater New York Council

AT&T CORP.

 Number 12 of Top 100 Corporate Givers

Company Contact

Basking Ridge, NJ
Web: http://www.att.com

Company Description

Revenue: US$62,391,000,000 (1999)
Profit: US$6,398,000,000
Employees: 107,800 (1999)
Fortune Rank: 8, per FORTUNE Magazine's list of 500 Largest U.S. Corporations (1999).
FF 8
SIC(s): 4812 Radiotelephone Communications, 4813 Telephone Communications Except Radiotelephone, 4899 Communications Services Nec.

Operating Locations

Australia: AT&T Easylink Services Australia Ltd., Lane Cove; Teradata Australia Pty. Ltd., North Sydney; Belgium: AT&T ISTEL Belgium SA, Brussels, Brabant; Brazil: Lucent Technologies Brasil Ltda., Sao Paulo; Canada: AT&T Security Products, Maple Ridge; International Systems Group Inc., Markham; AT&T Communications Canada, Ottawa; AT&T Paradyne Canada Ltd., Richmond Hill; AT&T Canada, Toronto; AT&T Capital Canada, Toronto; People's Republic of China: AT&T China (FC), Beijing; AT&T of Shanghai Ltd., Shanghai, Chiba; Colombia: AT&T Communication Services of Colombia SA, Bogota, Cundinamarco; Czech Republic: AT&T Business Communication Systems Spol SRO, Prague; Denmark: AT&T SA en Liquidation, Brussels, Brabant; France: Gretag Imaging France SA, Carrieres Sur Seine, Yvelines; AT&T ISTEL France, Issy Les Moulineaux; Dataid SA, Issy Les Moulineaux; Germany: AT&T American Telecommunication und Telefonservice GmbH, Dortmund, Nordrhein-Westfalen; AT&T Network Systems, Mannheim, Baden-Wuerttemberg; Hotel-und Freizeit GmbH, Neuhaus, De-Ost; Hong Kong: AT&T, Causeway Bay; AT&T Hong Kong Ltd., Causeway Bay; Lucent Technologies Asia/Pacific Inc., Causeway Bay; AT&T Asia/Pacific, Central District; AT&T China, Central District; AT&T International East Asia (Central District), Central District; AT&T Technologies International Purchasing Co., Central District; Italy: Capita Corp. Italy SpA, Milano, Lombardia; Japan: AT&T Japan Ltd., Tokyo; AT&T Jens Corp., Tokyo; AT&T Paradyne Japan Corp., Tokyo; AT&T Unix Pacific Co. Ltd., Tokyo; Republic of Korea: AT&T Communications Korea Ltd., Seoul; AT&T Korea Ltd., Seoul; Luxembourg: AT&T Luxembourg SA, Colmar, Berg; Dataid Eurosoft Luxembourg SA, Strassen; Mexico: AT&T Mexico SA de CV, Ciudad de Mexico; NCR de Mexico SA de CV, Ciudad de Mexico; Malaysia: American Telephone & Telegraph (Malaysia) Sdn. Bhd., Ampang, Kuala Lumpur; Norway: AT&T Norge AS, Oslo, Akershus; Philippines: AT&T Philippines, Makati, Rizal; Portugal: American Telephone & Telegraph Portugal-Communicacoes SA, Lisboa; NCR Portugal Informatica Lda., Lisboa; NCR Portuguesa-Gestao e Investimentos Lda., Lisboa; Singapore: AT&T Consumer Products Pte. Ltd., Singapore; AT&T Technologies International Purchasing Co., Singapore; Teradata Singapore Pte. Ltd., Singapore; Spain: AT&T Espana SA, Madrid; Lucent Technologies Microelectronica SA, Tres Cantos, Madrid; Sweden: Lucent Technologies Sweden AB, Stockholm; Switzerland: AT&T International, Geneva; Gretacoder Data Systems AG, Regensdorf, Zurich; NCR (Schweiz), Wallisellen, Zurich; Lucent Technologies SA, Zurich; Thailand: AT&T Networks Technology (Thailand) Co. Ltd., Chachoengsao; Alphasource Manufacturing Solutions Public Co. Ltd., Pathum Thani; AT&T (Thailand) Inc., Pathumwan; Taiwan: AT&T Global Information Solutions Taiwan Ltd., Taipei; United Kingdom: Terradat (United Kingdom) Ltd., Cardiff, South Glamorgan; Sharebase Europe Ltd., Chertsey, Surrey; Teradata Europe Ltd., Chertsey, Surrey; AT&T Capital Ltd., London; AT&T Communications (United Kingdom) Ltd., London; AT&T Capital (Automotive Services) Ltd., Manchester, Greater Manchester; AT&T (United Kingdom) Holdings Ltd., Redditch, Worcestershire; Paradyne International Ltd., Slough, Berkshire; Venezuela: AT&T Andinos SA, Caracas

Nonmonetary Support

Value: $16,269,246 (1997); $377,459 (1996); $7,000,000 (1993)
Type: Cause-related Marketing & Promotion; Donated Products; In-kind Services; Loaned Employees; Loaned Executives
Contact: Jo-Ann Greene, Director, AT&T University Equipment Donation Program
Note: Co. does not accept unsolicited requests for nonmonetary support.

Corporate Sponsorship

Type: Music & entertainment events; Sports events

AT&T Foundation

Giving Contact

Ronald Dabney, Communications Manager
AT&T Foundation
32 Avenue of the Americas, 24th Fl.
New York, NY 10013
Phone: (212)387-4801
Fax: (212)387-5098
Email: rdabney@attmail.com

Description

EIN: 133166495
Organization Type: Corporate Foundation
Giving Locations: headquarters and operating communities; nationally and internationally.
Grant Types: Award, Conference/Seminar, Emergency, Employee Matching Gifts, Fellowship, Matching, Multiyear/Continuing Support, Operating Expenses, Project.
Note: Employee matching gift ratio: 1 to 1 for tax-deductible gifts to higher education and cultural institutions with grants from $25 to $10,000 and a maximum of $50,000 per organization. Foundation alsosponsors the AT&T Cares program to provide grants to organisation where employees volunteer at least 50 hours of time.

Giving Philosophy

'The AT&T Foundation is the principal instrument for AT&T philanthropy in the United States and throughout the world. We give cash grants to nonprofit institutions for innovative programs that focus on helping people achieve self-sufficiency and lead productive lives.

'We seek projects that meet society's needs and relate to AT&T's business interests. We are particularly inclined toward projects that employ innovative technological solutions. The AT&T Foundation awards grants in the following three program areas: education, arts and culture, and civic and community services.

'The scope of the AT&T Foundation is global, although the majority of our funds support U.S.-based institutions. In addition, AT&T maintains a corporate contributions program to serve communities with a major AT&T presence.' *AT&T Foundation Guidelines*

Financial Summary

Total Giving: $61,100,000 (1998); $64,641,666 (1997); $48,516,228 (1996). Note: Contributes through corporate direct giving program and foundation. 1998 Giving includes foundation. 1997 Giving includes corporate direct giving ($11,549,857); foundation ($36,822,563); nonmonetary support. 1996 Giving includes corporate direct giving ($9,500,000); foundation ($37,736,769); international subsidiaries ($900,000); nonmonetary support.
Assets: $88,572,927 (1997); $109,928,319 (1996); $124,058,989 (1995)
Gifts Received: $12,759,922 (1997); $34,508,452 (1996); $12,033,547 (1995)

Typical Recipients

Arts & Humanities: Arts Associations & Councils, Arts Centers, Arts Festivals, Ballet, Dance, Libraries, Museums/Galleries, Music, Opera, Performing Arts, Theater, Visual Arts
Civic & Public Affairs: African American Affairs, Civil Rights, Community Foundations, Economic Development, Economic Policy, Employment/Job Training, Hispanic Affairs, Housing, Nonprofit Management, Professional & Trade Associations, Public Policy, Urban & Community Affairs, Women's Affairs
Education: Arts/Humanities Education, Business Education, Colleges & Universities, Education Associations, Education Funds, Education Reform, Elementary Education (Public), Engineering/Technological Education, Faculty Development, Education-General, International Exchange, International Studies, Medical Education, Minority Education, Preschool Education, Public Education (Precollege), Science/Mathematics Education, Secondary Education (Public), Social Sciences Education, Student Aid
Environment: Environment-General
Health: Children's Health/Hospitals, Emergency/Ambulance Services, Health Policy/Cost Containment, Hospitals, Speech & Hearing

International: Foreign Arts Organizations, Foreign Educational Institutions, International Affairs, International Relations
Science: Science Museums
Social Services: Child Welfare, Community Service Organizations, Day Care, Emergency Relief, Family Services, People with Disabilities, Substance Abuse, United Funds/United Ways, Youth Organizations

Contributions Analysis

Giving Priorities: Education, United Way, arts institutions, performing arts, and nonprofit organizations. The AT&T Foundation 'invests globally in undertakings that address a range of public concerns.' In the area of education, company makes grants that support lifelong learning, as well as teacher training and parent participation in children's education. Foundation looks for initiatives that use technology to connect students, teachers, and institutions of learning and that encourage efforts toward involving students in mathematics, science, and engineering. In its arts and culture program area, company supports artistic work that fosters communication, builds diverse audiences, and inspires innovation and learning in communities. It also targets initiatives that help women and artists of diverse cultures bring their work to wider audiences. In the civic and community service program area, company gives to initiatives that promote diversity and advance equal opportunity. It backs projects that promote economic capacity building in local communities, and it supports organizations that aim to protect the environment. AT&T assists programs designed to give children a sound start in life and to equip parents to better balance the demands of work and family life. Also contributes to organizations that deliver social and health services to people in need, particulary children, mothers, and people living with HIV/AIDS. The foundation also matches employee contributions to educational and cultural organizations and provides grants to recognize employee volunteer efforts. Outside the United States, AT&T bases its consideration of proposals from nonprofit institutions (or their equivalents) primarily on the advice and counsel of in-country managers and employees who have established strong community links in countries where it has a significiant presence. Regional contributions offices for organizations outside the U.S. are as follows:
For organizations in Australia, China, India, Indonesia, Japan, Philippines, South Korea, Taiwan, and Thailand, contact AT&T Asia/Pacific Inc., Shell Tower, Times Sq., 1 Matheson St., 30th Fl., Causeway Bay, Hong Kong, 011-852-2-506-5051.
For organizations in France, contact AT&T France SA, Tour Horizon, 52 quai de Dion-Bouton, 92806 Puteaux, Cedex, France, 011-33-1-4767-4709.
For organizations in Germany, contact AT&T Deutschland, Eschersheimer Landstrasse 14, D-60322, Frankfurt, Germany, 011-49-69-153-06-431.
For organizations in Italy, The Netherlands, Poland, South Africa, and Spain, contact AT&T Communications Service SA, Chaussee de Wavre 1943, B-1160 Brussels, Belgium.
For organizations in Russia, contact AT&T CIS Ltd., Toko Tower,11th Fl., 6, Krasnopresnenskaya, 123242 Moscow, Russia, 011-7-095-974-1462.
For organizations in the United Kingdom, contact AT&T England, Norfolk House, 31 St. James' Sq., London, SW1 4JR, United Kingdom, 011-44-171-925-8116.
For organizations in Canada, c/o AT&T Canada, 320 Front St. West, 17th Fl., Toronto, Ontario, Canada M5V 3B6, 416-204-2908.
For organizations in Argentina, Brazil, Chile, Colombia, Mexico, Puerto Rico, and Venezuela, contact AT&T, 233 Ponce de Leon Blvd., Rm. 941-10, Coral Gables, FL 33134, 305-569-3753.
Arts & Humanities: About 20%. Support to nationally and internationally recognized arts and cultural institutions that foster communication and promote cross-cultural understanding. Organizations must have been professionally managed for at least five years and compensate both artistic and managerial personnel. National arts service organizations are also funded, particularly those that offer technical assistance or professional services to foundation-eligible institutions. Particular interest in the creation, production, and presentation of new work and initiatives that provide access to the arts to all segments of society by bringing the work of women and artists of diverse cultures to wider audiences.
Civic & Public Affairs: About 30%. Support to organizations and projects that enhance the effectiveness of the nonprofit sector and promote public policy formulation in matters of children and families, accessibility of health and social services to those in need, the advancement of diversity, and the protection of the environment. Projects should serve as models for other organizations and lend themselves to measurable evaluation, with results that can be disseminated to a wide audience.
Education: 50% to 55%. Supports projects that assist and facilitate lifelong learning, teacher training, and parent participation in education. Emphasis on initiatives that use technology to connect students, teachers, and institutions of learning; and which stimulate student interests and involvement in mathematics, science and engineering. Through the AT&T Learning Network, funding is provided to organizations that help teachers, students, parents and communities capitalize on technology to enhance education. As part of this effort, funding is provided for the innovative use of technology to foster family involvement in education and provide professionaldevelopment opportunities for preparation of new teachers. Collaboration among institutions and across communities to promote lifelong learning is encouraged.

Application Procedures

Initial Contact: write for guidelines and application form, then brief letter with completed application
Application Requirements: brief history of the organization and description of mission; statement relating purpose to interests and priorities of foundation; detailed description of purpose for which grant is sought and amount requested; operating and/or project budget for current year showing anticipated sources of revenue and expenses (if project support sought, include a detailed budget for the project); and proof of 501(c)(3) status
Deadlines: None.
Review Process: staff members make recommendations to board of trustees
Evaluative Criteria: supports programs that advance the personal and professional prospects of families, children, women, and minorities; to strengthen the capacity of public and nonprofit institutions to deliver high-quality services; promote diversity and equal opportunity; are accessible to all segments of society; offer systemic change to redress inequities rooted in socioeconomic, historic, geographic, racial, and sexual differences; support public and nonprofit leadership at the regional and national levels; encourage and reinforce excellence and innovation where it is found; assist efforts to keep America competitive by addressing education, especially in the sciences and engineering; enhance the quality of life in communities where AT&T employees live and work; utilize technology in inventive ways; or involve employee volunteers
Decision Notification: in trustees meet monthly
Notes: For U.S.-based national organizations, apply to foundation. For local projects, apply to Regional Contributions Manager in area; contact information is included in guidelines.

Restrictions

Foundation does not make grants to individuals; organizations that practice discrimination; political organizations, campaigns, or lobbying groups; religious groups for sectarian purposes; operating expenses or capital campaigns of local health and human service organizations other than hospitals; endowments or memorials; building projects; local chapters of national organizations; sports teams or athletic events; or goodwill advertising, banquets, or other fundraising events; the purchase or installation of computers, modems, printers, etc.; non-academic extracurricular activities; single disease research organizations; medical research; child-care or elderly care facilities; video and film production; programs to alleviate homelessness and drug abuse; student or amateur arts groups; competitions; zoos, historical societies or planetariums; arts programs designed primarily for rehabilitation or therapy; public radio and television stations for unrestricted purposes; equipment acquisition or program underwriting; or science museum or science/technology exhibitions except through special AT&T programs.
The foundation does not donate any AT&T goods or services.

Additional Information

Guidelines may be obtained by either calling (212) 387-4868, or sending a fax message to (212) 387-4906.
Guidelines include extensive restrictions by program area, and should be carefully reviewed before submitting a request.
The company's nonmonetary support program provides AT&T computer laboratories to selected colleges and universities. This is an invitational program not open to unsolicited requests.
Publications: Foundation Report; Guidelines

Corporate Officials

C. Michael Armstrong: chairman, chief executive officerceo wireless group B Detroit, MI 1938. ED Miami University BS (1961); Dartmouth College (1976). PRIM CORP EMPL chairman, chief executive officer: AT&T Corp. CORP AFFIL director: Times Mirror Co.; chairman, chief executive officer: Hughes Electronics Corp.; director: LA CitiCorp.; chairman board: AT&T Broadband Internet Services; director: Citigroup Inc. NONPR AFFIL vice chairman: World Affairs Council; member advisory board: Yale School Management; member board advisors: University Southern California Business School; vice chairman: Sabriyas Castle Fun Foundation; member supervisory board: Thyssen-Bornemisza Group; member: National Security Telecommunications Advisory Committee; chairman: President's Export Council; member business advisory council: Miami University; chairman advisory board: Johns Hopkins School Medicine; trustee: Johns Hopkins University; member: Defense Policy Advisory Committee Trade; member: GM President Council; member: Council Foreign Relations; trustee: Carnegie Hall.
Harold W. Burlingame: executive vice president merger integration B Zaynesville, OH. PRIM CORP EMPL executive vice president wireless group: AT&T Corp.
Richard J. Martin: executive vice president public relations employee communications ED Ohio State University BS. PRIM CORP EMPL executive vice president public relations employee communications: AT&T Corp.
Charles H. Noski: senior executive vice president, chief financial officer PRIM CORP EMPL senior executive vice president, chief financial officer: AT&T Corp.
Daniel E. Somers: senior executive vice president, chief financial officer ED Stonehill College BS (1969). PRIM CORP EMPL senior executive vice president, chief financial officer: AT&T Corp.
John D. Zeglis: chairman and chief executive officer wireless group PRIM CORP EMPL chairman and chief executive officer wireless group: AT&T Corp.

Foundation Officials

Robert Angelica: treasurer
Harold W. Burlingame: trustee (see above)
R. Steven Davis: trustee
Richard J. Martin: chairman, trustee (see above)
Timothy J. McClimon: executive director B Clinton, IA 1953. ED Luther College BA (1975); Saint Cloud State College MS (1976); Georgetown University J.D.

(1986). NONPR AFFIL director: Theatre Committees Group; member: Volunteer Lawyers Arts; director: Second Stage Theatre; adjunct professor: New York University; director: Performance Space 122; member: New York State Bar Association; consult: National Endowment Arts; member: New York City Bar Association; director: Merce Cunningham Dance Foundation; member: American Bar Association; director: Field Papers.
Vivian Nero: secretary
William H. Oliver: trustee
Marilyn Reznick: vice president education program
Suzanne M. Sato: vice president arts & culture program
Esther Silver-Parker: president, trustee
Maureen Tart: trustee
Mitzi Vaimberg: vice president civic community services

Grants Analysis

Disclosure Period: calendar year ending 1996
Total Grants: $37,738,769*
Number of Grants: 1,031
Average Grant: $36,604
Highest Grant: $1,900,000
Typical Range: $1,000 to $50,000
***Note:** Giving excludes international subsidiaries; nonmonetary support.

Recent Grants

Note: Grants derived from 1996 grants list.

Arts & Humanities

250,000 Queens Borough Public Library, Jamaica, NY
150,000 New York Public Library, New York, NY
125,000 Arena Stage, Washington, DC
125,000 Joffrey Ballet, Chicago, IL

Civic & Public Affairs

500,000 Center for Occupational Research and Development, Waco, TX
468,000 Center for Occupational Research and Development, Waco, TX
250,000 Center for Occupational Research and Development, Waco, TX
200,000 New England Governors Conference, Boston, MA
250 California Community Foundation LAARF, Los Angeles, CA

Education

500,000 Detwiler Foundation Computers for Schools Program, La Jolla, CA
500,000 United Negro College Fund, New York, NY
275,000 Exploris, Raleigh, NC
200,000 National Center for Restructuring Education, Schools, and Teaching, New York, NY
200,000 National Council for Accreditation of Teacher Education, Washington, DC
200,000 Penn State University Center for Academic Computing, University Park, PA
200,000 University of Texas Institute of Texan Cultures, San Antonio, TX
180,000 Lehigh University College of Engineering and Applied Science, Bethlehem, PA
170,000 National Commission on Teaching and America's Future, New York, NY
150,000 Foundation for Joint Venture, San Jose, CA
150,000 Galef Institute, Los Angeles, CA
150,000 National Action Council for Minorities in Engineering, New York, NY
150,000 New Jersey Institute of Technology, Newark, NJ
150,000 Rensselaer Polytechnic Institute, Troy, NY
150,000 University of California Los Angeles, Los Angeles, CA
140,000 United Negro College Fund, New York, NY
135,000 National Foundation for the Improvement of Education, Washington, DC
135,000 University of Texas San Antonio, San Antonio, TX
125,000 Purdue University School of Engineering, West Lafayette, IN
125,000 Technology for Results in Elementary Education, Los Angeles, CA
120,000 Lehigh University, Bethlehem, PA
105,000 Massachusetts Institute of Technology, Electrical Engineering, and Computer Science, Cambridge, MA
100,000 Georgia Research Alliance, Athens, GA

International

120,000 Malaysian-American Commission on Educational Exchange, Kuala Lumpur, Malaysia

Science

150,000 Franklin Institute of Science Museum, Philadelphia, PA

Social Services

1,900,000 United Way Tri-State, New York, NY
537,460 United Way Crusade of Mercy, Chicago, IL
525,000 United Way, Atlanta, GA
400,000 United Way, Dayton, OH
225,000 United Way National Capital Area, Washington, DC
213,000 Mile High United Way, Denver, CO
212,000 United Way, Dallas, TX
172,000 United Way Franklin County, Columbus, OH
170,000 Merrimack Valley United Funds, Lawrence, MA
162,000 Heart of America United Way, Kansas City, MO
155,000 Heart of Florida United Way, Orlando, FL
140,000 United Way, Jacksonville, FL
122,500 United Fund of Lehigh County, Allentown, PA
120,200 United Way, Oklahoma City, OK
115,000 United Way Bay Area, San Francisco, CA

Atlantic Investment Co.

Company Contact

Atlanta, GA

Company Description

Former Name: Atlantic Realty Co.
Revenue: US$8,700,000
Employees: 17
SIC(s): 6500 Real Estate.

Courts Foundation

Giving Contact

John W. Stephenson, Executive Director
Courts Foundation
1530 SunTrust Tower
25 Park Pl., NE
Atlanta, GA 30303-2917
Phone: (404)658-9066
Fax: (404)659-4802

Description

Founded: 1950
EIN: 586036859
Organization Type: Corporate Foundation
Giving Locations: headquarters and operating communities.
Grant Types: Capital, Challenge, Conference/Seminar, Endowment, General Support, Operating Expenses, Professorship, Project.

Financial Summary

Total Giving: $3,063,728 (1998); $1,144,979 (1997); $925,932 (1996)
Giving Analysis: Giving for 1998 includes: foundation ($3,033,728); foundation grants to United Way ($30,000)
Assets: $28,006,499 (1998); $27,056,938 (1997)
Gifts Received: $150,000 (1998); $1,737,725 (1997). Note: IN 1998, contributions were received from R.W. Courts, II.

Typical Recipients

Arts & Humanities: Arts Appreciation, Arts Centers, Arts Festivals, Ballet, Community Arts, Museums/Galleries, Music, Performing Arts
Civic & Public Affairs: Botanical Gardens/Parks, Business/Free Enterprise, Chambers of Commerce, Community Foundations, Employment/Job Training, Civic & Public Affairs-General, Housing, Inner-City Development, Law & Justice, Nonprofit Management, Philanthropic Organizations, Public Policy, Urban & Community Affairs, Zoos/Aquariums
Education: Business Education, Colleges & Universities, Elementary Education (Private), Engineering/Technological Education, Faculty Development, Education-General, Private Education (Precollege), Religious Education, Science/Mathematics Education, Secondary Education (Private), Special Education, Student Aid
Environment: Environment-General
Health: Cancer, Children's Health/Hospitals, Clinics/Medical Centers, Diabetes, Emergency/Ambulance Services, Eyes/Blindness, Health Organizations, Hospices, Hospitals, Mental Health
Religion: Churches, Religion-General, Ministries, Religious Organizations, Religious Welfare, Seminaries
Social Services: Animal Protection, Big Brother/Big Sister, Camps, Child Welfare, Community Service Organizations, Emergency Relief, Family Services, People with Disabilities, Scouts, Shelters/Homelessness, United Funds/United Ways, YMCA/YWCA/YMHA/YWHA, Youth Organizations

Contributions Analysis

Arts & Humanities: 21%. Funds arts centers and festivals, museums, and dance.
Civic & Public Affairs: 35%. Supports community foundations, a botanical garden, and legal affairs.
Education: 20%. Funds pre-college and higher education.
Environment: 3%.
Health: 5%.
Religion: 11%. Funds Christian groups.
Social Services: 4%.
Note: Total contributions made in 1998.

Application Procedures

Initial Contact: Submit a letter of request of no more than three pages in length.
Application Requirements: Letter should include the following: the full legal name of the organization; a summary statement describing the organization, its history, its mission or purpose, and its program and recent service statistics; specific amount of money requested; a clearly stated proposed use of the funds requested and a detailed budget of the total cost of the project; brief biographical information about the organization's chief administrative officer; a brief statement advising how the grant, if made would be evaluated for effectiveness; total of other gifts and grants received to date toward the purpose of the request; a timetable for successful completion of the project; and the signature of the chief administrative officer of the institution. As separate attachments, please include an audited financial statement reflecting results from the organization's most recent

fiscal year; a list of members of the governing board and their principal occupations; and a copy of the organization's most recent IRS Letter of determination. A copy of a case statement or more detailed of the project may also be included with the Letter of request.

Deadlines: Letters of request should be received no later than March 1, June 1, September 1, or December 1 in order to be considered at the respective quarterly meeting.

Decision Notification: The trustees meet quarterly, in March, June, September, and December.

Restrictions

Requests should be for support of capital projects or programs that can anticipate self-sufficiency in later years. Only occasionally are grants made for current budget support. The foundation gives first priority to grant requests from organizations serving metropolitan Atlanta and limits its grants almost exclusively to organizations headquartered in Georgia, benefiting Georgians.

Additionally, the foundation considers grants only to institutions determined by the IRS to be tax-exempt and classified as 'not a private foundation.' It does not make grants or loans to individuals. Priority is given to agencies and organizations having a program of acknowledged quality and giving evidence or promise of leadership within their field.

Additional Information

All applicants are asked to wait at least one year from the date of any previous application before submitting a new request. The trustees prefer to support a relatively small number of significant, carefully planned projects. The board precludes personal appearances by applicants, and trustees should not be contacted personally concerning a proposal or request made or to be made to the foundation. Personal interviews with the foundation's staff are granted when appropriate, but applicants should first correspond in writing to the foundation when submitting a formal grant proposal. The foundation does not publish an analysis report. The board of trustees reviews the material submitted in support of the application and, through the executive director, may seek additional information about the organization, the project, and specific plans for achieving the success of the project.

Publications: General Information; Application Guidelines

Corporate Officials

Donald Ray Barron: president, director B Macon, GA 1947. ED University of Georgia (1969); Atlanta Law School (1979). PRIM CORP EMPL president, director: Atlantic Investment Co. CORP AFFIL vice president, director: Second Corp.

Richard Winn Courts, II: chairman, director B Atlanta, GA. PRIM CORP EMPL chairman, director: Atlantic Investment Co. CORP AFFIL director: Southern Mills Inc.; director: SunTrust Banks Georgia Inc.; director: NAPA Distribution Center; director: Genuine Parts Co.; director: NAPA Auto Parts; director: Cousins Properties Inc.

Paul S. Watcher: vice president financial PRIM CORP EMPL vice president financial: Atlantic Investment Co.

Grants Analysis

Disclosure Period: calendar year ending 1998
Total Grants: $3,033,728*
Number of Grants: 55
Average Grant: $37,662*
Highest Grant: $1,000,000
Typical Range: $15,000 to $50,000
***Note:** Giving excludes United Way. Average grant excludes highest grant.

Recent Grants

Note: Grants derived from 1998 Form 990.

Arts & Humanities

600,000 The Atlanta Ballet, Atlanta, GA -- Capital support: Capital campaigns
25,000 Arts Festival Association of Atlanta, Inc., Atlanta, GA -- Capital support: Capital campaigns
10,000 Robert W. Woodruff Arts Center, Atlanta, GA -- General support
5,000 The Children's Museum of Atlanta, Atlanta, GA -- General support: Operating Support
5,000 Robert W. Woodruff Arts Center, Atlanta, GA -- General support
5,000 Robert W. Woodruff Arts Center, Atlanta, GA -- General support

Civic & Public Affairs

1,000,000 East Lake Community Foundation, Inc., Atlanta, GA -- Capital support: New construction
25,000 Atlanta Botanical Garden, Inc., Atlanta, GA -- Capital support: Capital campaigns
20,000 Atlanta Chamber of Commerce, Atlanta, GA -- General support
15,000 Free Bytes NP, Inc., Atlanta, GA -- General support: Operating Support
5,000 Atlanta Resource Foundation, Inc., Atlanta, GA -- General support
5,000 Georgia Justice Project, Inc., Atlanta, GA -- General support
1,000 Southeastern Council of Foundations, Atlanta, GA -- Capital support: Endowments

Education

500,000 Wesleyan School, Atlanta, GA -- Student Aid: Scholarships
50,000 The University of Georgia, Athens, GA -- Student Aid
30,000 Computers for Classrooms, Inc., East Point, GA -- General support: Operating Support
25,000 The Schenck School, Inc., Atlanta, GA -- Capital support: Capital campaigns
10,000 Birmingham-Southern College, Birmingham, AL -- General support
10,000 Pace Academy, Atlanta, GA -- Capital support: Capital campaigns
1,000 Atlanta Speech School, Atlanta, GA -- General support

Environment

100,000 Path Foundation, Atlanta, GA -- Capital support

Health

75,000 The Good Samaritan Health Center, Inc., Atlanta, GA -- Capital support: Equipment
25,000 Metropolitan Atlanta Chapter, American National Red Cross, Atlanta, GA -- Capital support: Building/renovation
15,000 Piedmont Hospital, Inc., Atlanta, GA -- Capital support: Equipment
10,000 Shepherd Spinal Center, Atlanta, GA -- General support
10,000 Shepherd Spinal Center, Atlanta, GA -- General support
5,000 American Cancer Society, Atlanta, GA -- Capital support: New construction
5,000 Shephred Spinal Center, Atlanta, GA -- General support
2,000 CDC Foundation, Atlanta, GA -- General support
1,000 Juvenile Diabetes Foundation, Atlanta, GA -- General support

Religion

175,107 Leading the Way, Atlanta, GA -- Capital support: Equipment
47,000 Second Ponce De Leon Baptist Church, Atlanta, GA -- Capital support
31,000 Reflections Ministries, Atlanta, GA -- General support
25,000 Fellowship of Christian Athletes, Watkinsville, GA -- Capital support: Endowments
15,000 Reflections Ministries, Atlanta, GA -- General support
10,000 Reflections Ministries, Atlanta, GA -- General support
10,000 Reflections Ministries, Atlanta, GA -- General support
10,000 Youth Ministry Resources, Inc., Alpharetta, GA -- Program development: Conferences/Seminars
5,835 Reflections Ministries, Atlanta, GA -- Program development: Seed money
5,000 Columbia Theological Seminary, Decatur, GA -- General support
4,116 Reflections Ministries, Atlanta, GA -- Program development: Seed money
3,270 Reflections Ministries, Atlanta, GA -- Program development: Seed money
2,500 Reflections Ministries, Atlanta, GA -- Program development: Seed money
1,000 Northside United Methodist Church, Atlanta, GA -- General support

Social Services

50,000 YMCA of Metropolitan Atlanta, Atlanta, GA -- Capital support: Building/renovation
25,000 Boys & Girls Clubs of Metro Atlanta, Inc., Atlanta, GA -- Capital support: Capital campaigns
20,000 United Way of Metropolitan Atlanta, Inc., Atlanta, GA -- General support
10,400 Canine Assistants, Inc., Alpharetta, GA -- General support: Operating Support
10,000 United Way of Metropolitan Atlanta, Inc., Atlanta, GA -- General support: Operating Support
2,500 Boy Scouts of America, Inc. Atlanta Area Council, Atlanta, GA -- General support: Annual campaigns

ATLANTIC RICHFIELD CO.

Number 87 of Top 100 Corporate Givers

Company Contact

Los Angeles, CA
Web: http://www.arco.com

Company Description

Also Known As: ARCO.
Revenue: US$13,055,000,000
Profit: US$452,000,000
Employees: 18,400 (1999)
Fortune Rank: 136, per FORTUNE Magazine's list of 500 Largest U.S. Corporations (1999).
FF 136
SIC(s): 1221 Bituminous Coal & Lignite--Surface, 1222 Bituminous Coal--Underground, 1311 Crude Petroleum & Natural Gas, 1321 Natural Gas Liquids.

Operating Locations

Australia: ARCO Coal Australia, Brisbane; ARCO Resources Ltd., Brisbane; Coal Resources of Queensland Ltd., Brisbane; Curragh Coal Sales Co. Pty. Ltd., Brisbane; Curragh Queensland Mining Ltd., Brisbane; Gordonstone Coal Management Pty. Ltd., Brisbane; ARCO Chemical Australia P/L, Chatswood; Belgium: ARCO Chemical Products Europe, Gent, Flandre-Orientale; Canada: ARCO Chemicals Canada, Scarborough; Canada Ltd., Toronto; France: ARCO Chimie France SNC, Fos Sur Mer, Bouches-de-Rhone;

ARCO Chimie TDI, Fos Sur Mer, Bouches-de-Rhone; Germany: ARCO Chemical (Deutschland) GmbH, Duesseldorf; Hong Kong: ARCO Chemical Asia Pacific Ltd., Admiralty; ARCO Chemical China Ltd., Central District; ARCO China, Central District; Indonesia: Atlantic Richfield Indonesia, Jakarta, Jakarta Raya; Netherlands: ARCO Chemie Investment Nederland BV, Botlek Rotterdam; ARCO Chemie Nederland Ltd., Botlek Rotterdam; ARCO Chemie Technologie Nederland BV, Botlek Rotterdam; ARCO Chemie Utilities BV, Rotterdam, Zuid-Holland; New Zealand: ARCO Petroleum Taranaki Ltd., Wellington; Singapore: ARCO Chemical (Singapore) Pte. Ltd., Singapore; Taiwan: ARCO Chemical Taiwan Co. Ltd., Taipei; Chiunglong Petrochemical Co. Ltd., Taipei; United Kingdom: ARCO British Ltd., Guildford, Surrey; Tricentrol Plc, Guildford, Surrey; ARCO Chemical Europe, Maidenhead, Berkshire

Nonmonetary Support

Value: $100,000 (1992); $100,000 (1991); $100,000 (1990)
Type: Donated Equipment; In-kind Services; Loaned Employees; Loaned Executives
Note: Requests for nonmonetary support are handled by each local company's public affairs office.

ARCO Foundation

Giving Contact

Russell G. Sakaguchi, President
ARCO Foundation
333 South Hope
Los Angeles, CA 90071
Phone: (213)486-3342
Fax: (213)486-0113

Description

EIN: 953222292
Organization Type: Corporate Foundation
Giving Locations: AK Southwestern United States; Western United States.
Grant Types: Employee Matching Gifts, General Support.
Note: Employee matching gift ratio: 1 to 1.

Giving Philosophy

'ARCO communities--where company headquarters or operations are located in the West and Southwest--are more than ever multicultural and multiracial. Many of the activities we support respond to these new realities, particularly the need to nourish the skills and ambitions of minority children. These youngsters will be a crucial part of tomorrow's America and they need our help now to prepare for that future.'
'We've discovered that there is no shortage of opportunities for corporate support of the arts, community involvement, environmental programs, and much more in this country today. Because need is unlimited and our funds are not, we are forced to make difficult choices. The challenge is always to find imaginative new ways to use the dollars we have available and to support strongly the things that work.' Lodwrick M. Cook, Chairman, ARCO
'Key components for the ARCO Foundation's grantmaking strategy are: remaining responsive to changing community needs and business objectives; targeting a limited number of grantmaking program areas of deepest concern to ARCO communities and the company's business operations; setting and articulating clear objectives an guidelines in each program area; focusing grantmaking on geographic areas within close proximity to ARCO's business activities; forming and nurturing long-term relationships with grantees and maintaining consistency in grantmaking to achieve desired results; encouraging the broadest possible participation of active and retired ARCO employees in the nonprofit sector through contributions of money and time; sharing foundation grantmaking responsibilities with ARCO operating companies in a carefully coordinated effort; seeking out synergistic grantmaking opportunities for joint foundation and ARCO operating company participation; remaining accountable to ARCO stakeholders.' ARCO Foundation web site.

Financial Summary

Total Giving: $10,800,000 (2000 approx); $11,800,000 (1999 approx); $8,323,802 (1998). Note: Contributes through corporate direct giving program and foundation.
Giving Analysis: Giving for 1996 includes: foundation matching gifts ($5,939,737); foundation ($4,060,263); 1997: foundation ($7,826,212); foundation matching gifts ($5,973,788); 1998: foundation ($7,950,473); foundation grants to United Way ($1,898,685)
Assets: $2,130,913 (1998); $2,100,000 (1996); $2,621,009 (1995)
Gifts Received: $8,355,492 (1998); $5,457,195 (1996); $4,983,999 (1995). Note: In 1998, contributions were received from Atlantic Richfield Co.

Typical Recipients

Arts & Humanities: Arts Centers, Community Arts, Dance, Ethnic & Folk Arts, Historic Preservation, Libraries, Music, Performing Arts, Public Broadcasting, Theater
Civic & Public Affairs: Asian American Affairs, Civil Rights, Community Foundations, Economic Development, Employment/Job Training, Ethnic Organizations, Civic & Public Affairs-General, Hispanic Affairs, Housing, Minority Business, Nonprofit Management, Public Policy, Urban & Community Affairs, Women's Affairs, Zoos/Aquariums
Education: Agricultural Education, Business Education, Colleges & Universities, Continuing Education, Economic Education, Education Funds, Education Reform, Elementary Education (Public), Engineering/Technological Education, Engineering/Technological Education, Faculty Development, Education-General, Literacy, Minority Education, Preschool Education, Private Education (Precollege), Public Education (Precollege), Science/Mathematics Education, Student Aid, Vocational & Technical Education
Environment: Environment-General, Resource Conservation, Wildlife Protection
Health: Children's Health/Hospitals, Research/Studies Institutes
Science: Science Museums
Social Services: At-Risk Youth, Child Welfare, Community Service Organizations, Domestic Violence, Family Services, Food/Clothing Distribution, Recreation & Athletics, Scouts, Senior Services, United Funds/United Ways, Volunteer Services, YMCA/YWCA/YMHA/YWHA, Youth Organizations

Contributions Analysis

Giving Priorities: Precollege education, especially for minorities; national social and economic organizations; health care; elderly programs; art organizations; and environmental organizations. Domestic interests include public policy and international development. Support to U.S.-based organizations must be used in the United States. Support for nonprofit organizations by overseas locations, considered a business expense, are administered independently of corporate headquarters.
Arts & Humanities: 40%. Supports programs which offer cultural experiences to diverse ethnic groups, or which assist emerging arts organizations in underserved neighborhoods.
Civic & Public Affairs: 6%.
Education: 22%. Precollege programs supported are aimed at promoting: readiness-for-school services, including parent training and early childhood curricula for at-risk children; academic achievement through improvements in school attendance, grades and school-completion levels; increased interest and achievement in mathematics and science resulting in higher enrollment and success rates in college preparatory course-work and in plans to pursue math/science careers; parent effectiveness through increased involvement in public school education, especially among low-income families; professional staff preparation and development through programs that incorporate school restructuring issues as part of the curriculum for teachers, counselors and administrators; programs that improve the qualifications and effectiveness of math and science teachers; and teacher-training curricula on language development and English-language acquisition. Supported higher education programs include special projects at selected research universities and programs that increase the number of minority students entering and completing degree programs in fields related to the energy industry. Also supports policy analysis and scholarship programs.
Environment: 1%. Supports environmental education. Also supports land preservation for ecologically unique land, ecological restoration, conservation of wildlife, and community recycling programs.
Science: 1%.
Social Services: 30%. Supports United Way and social services.
Note: Total contributions made in 1998.

Application Procedures

Initial Contact: See foundation web site for guidelines, then submit a written proposal, if appropriate.
Application Requirements: One-page proposal summary, including mission statement, grant amount requested and purpose of grant, legal name of organization, and any past Arco support (with dates and amounts); proposal of not more than five pages, including: mission and history of organization, need for project in view of related work by others, project description, goals, objectives, action plan, expected outcomes or results, method of evaluation, plan for continuing activity; financial information, including financial statement, income and expense budget, list of other current and projected sources of funding; most recent Form 990; and list of board members, with affiliations.
Deadlines: None.
Evaluative Criteria: Priority of project within Foundation's goals, anticipated results, resources requested and available funds.
Decision Notification: Bimonthly meetings are held for most requests; directors review major education requests in December, and all other major requests periodically.
Notes: Faxed applications and videos are not accepted. Local and regional applicants should apply directly to nearest company field office.

Restrictions

Only nonprofit, tax-exempt public charities as defined in Section 501(c)(3) of the IRS Code are eligible.
Does not support individuals; organizations whose services are not provided in a geographic area of interest to ARCO; film or video projects; religious activities or organizations; specialized single-issue health organizations, except under Foundation's Matching Grants or Volunteer Grants programs; fraternal, professional, or veterans' organizations or similar membership groups; endowments; annual, automatically renewable, or multiyear grants; organizations that discriminate on the basis of race, color, sex, or national origin; or benefit dinners, advertisements, or tables at fund-raising events.

Additional Information

Details regarding the Matching Grants, Volunteer Grants, and United Way programs can be obtained by contacting the ARCO Foundation offices in California, Arkansas, or Texas.
Vastar Resources is a separate corporate entity in Texas that administers grants to qualified nonprofit organizations in the Gulf Coast area.
Publications: Annual Report

Corporate Officials

Michael Ray Bowlin: chairman, chief executive officer, director B Amarillo, TX 1943. ED North Texas State University BBA (1965); North Texas State University MBA (1967). PRIM CORP EMPL chairman, chief executive officer, director: Atlantic Richfield Co. CORP AFFIL chairman, chief executive officer: ARCO International Oil & Gas Co.; officer: Wells Fargo & Co.
Marie L. Knowles: executive vice president, chief financial officer PRIM CORP EMPL executive vice president, chief financial officer: Atlantic Richfield Co. CORP AFFIL director: Phelps Dodge Corp.

Foundation Officials

Michael Ray Bowlin: chairman, director (see above)
Glenn M. Pastrana: research assistant, matching gifts coordinator
Russell G. Sakaguchi: president
Michael E. Wiley: president B 1950. ED University of Texas at Dallas MBA; University of Tulsa BS. PRIM CORP EMPL president, chief operating officer: Atlantic Richfield Co. ADD CORP EMPL chairman: Union Texas Petroleum Holdings; chairman: Vastar Gas Marketing Inc.; chairman: Vastar Resources Inc.

Grants Analysis

Disclosure Period: calendar year ending 1998
Total Grants: $7,950,473*
Number of Grants: 840 (approx)
Average Grant: $7,092*
Highest Grant: $2,000,000
Typical Range: $1,000 to $25,000
***Note:** Grants analysis based on approved and paid grants. GEX United Way. Average grant figure excludes highest grant.

Recent Grants

Note: Grants derived from 1998 Form 990.

Arts & Humanities

2,000,000 Music Center of Los Angeles, Los Angeles, CA
175,000 Music Center Unified Fund, Los Angeles, CA
100,000 KCET, Los Angeles, CA
40,000 East Los Angeles Classic, Monterey Park, CA
37,500 Los Angeles County Public Library, Downey, CA

Civic & Public Affairs

250,000 Los Angeles Annenberg, Los Angeles, CA
37,500 Los Angeles Urban Funders, Los Angeles, CA
35,000 Community Partners, Los Angeles, CA
30,000 Low Income Housing Fund, Los Angeles, CA
25,000 Project 180, New York, NY

Education

250,000 Stanford University, Stanford, CA
100,000 Puente Learning Center, Los Angeles, CA
75,000 Los Angeles Educational, Los Angeles, CA
50,000 University of North Texas, Denton, TX
48,500 Claremont Mckenna College, Claremont, CA
47,350 LSU Foundation, Baton Rouge, LA
47,000 The Achievement Council, Los Angeles, CA
46,800 UC Regents, Davis, CA
45,000 California State Polytechnic, Pomona, CA
45,000 California State University, Long Beach, CA
45,000 California State University, Los Angeles, CA
45,000 California State University, Los Angeles, CA
45,000 California State University, Los Angeles, CA
45,000 Texas A & M University, College Station, TX
43,900 National Merit Scholarship Corp, Evanston, IL
40,000 Claremont Graduate University, Claremont, CA
40,000 University of Houston, Houston, TX
40,000 University Texas at Austin, Austin, TX
38,000 California Maritime Academy, Vallejo, CA
38,000 Colorado School of Mines Foundation, Golden, CO
36,200 University of Southern California, Los Angeles, CA
35,000 Los Angeles Parent Institute, Los Angeles, CA
35,000 University of Missouri-, Rolla, MO
35,000 The University of Oklahoma Foundation, Norman, OK
32,000 University of California Los Angeles, Los Angeles, CA
25,000 Montana Tech, Butte, MT
25,000 Reading is Fundamental, Washington, DC

Environment

40,000 Sustainable Conservation, San Francisco, CA

Science

25,000 SW Museum of Science & Technology, Dallas, TX

Social Services

750,000 United Way of Los Angeles, Los Angeles, CA
487,885 United Way of Anchorage, Anchorage, AK
224,273 United Way of Metropolitan, Dallas, TX
101,454 United Way of Whatcom County, Bellingham, WA
70,469 United Way of Midland, Midland, TX
59,555 Metro United Way, Louisville, KY
54,730 Kenai Peninsula United Way, Kenai, AK
47,000 United Way of Anchorage, Anchorage, AK
43,844 United Way of Anchorage, Anchorage, AK
30,750 Boys and Girls Clubs, Anchorage, AK
30,000 Boy Scouts of America, Pasadena, CA

AUBURN FOUNDRY

Company Contact

Auburn, IN

Company Description

Employees: 615
SIC(s): 3300 Primary Metal Industries.

Auburn Foundry Foundation

Giving Contact

David Fink, President
PO Box 471
Auburn, IN 46706
Phone: (219)925-0900
Fax: (219)925-5137

Description

EIN: 356019220
Organization Type: Corporate Foundation
Giving Locations: headquarters area only.
Grant Types: General Support.

Financial Summary

Total Giving: $223,834 (fiscal year ending February 28, 1997); $110,000 (fiscal 1995); $85,025 (fiscal 1994). Note: Fiscal 1997 Giving includes scholarship ($12,000); United Way ($8,500).
Assets: $1,431,079 (fiscal 1997); $844,566 (fiscal 1995); $847,951 (fiscal 1994)
Gifts Received: $250,000 (fiscal 1997); $50,000 (fiscal 1995); $550,000 (fiscal 1994). Note: In 1997, contributions were received from Auburn Foundry.

Typical Recipients

Arts & Humanities: Arts Associations & Councils, Libraries, Music
Civic & Public Affairs: Housing
Education: Business Education, Colleges & Universities, Education Funds, Private Education (Precollege), Public Education (Precollege), Science/Mathematics Education
Health: Prenatal Health Issues
Religion: Religious Welfare
Social Services: Food/Clothing Distribution, People with Disabilities, Scouts, United Funds/United Ways, YMCA/YWCA/YMHA/YWHA

Application Procedures

Initial Contact: The foundation requests applications be made in writing. Include purpose of funds sought and proof of tax-exempt status.
Deadlines: None.

Additional Information

Trust(s): Fort Wayne Natl Bank

Corporate Officials

David Fink: president financial PRIM CORP EMPL president: Auburn Foundry.
William E. Fink: chairman PRIM CORP EMPL chairman: Auburn Foundry.
John Neiger: vice president financial PRIM CORP EMPL vice president financial: Auburn Foundry.

Foundation Officials

Walt Bienz: trustee
William E. Fink: trustee (see above)

Grants Analysis

Disclosure Period: fiscal year ending February 28, 1997
Total Grants: $203,334*
Number of Grants: 16
Average Grant: $8,000*
Highest Grant: $83,334
Typical Range: $500 to $15,000
***Note:** Giving excludes scholarship; United Way. Average grant figure excludes highest grant.

Recent Grants

Note: Grants derived from fiscal 1997 Form 990.

Arts & Humanities

50,000 Eckhart Public Library, Auburn, IN
1,000 Arts United, Fort Wayne, IN
500 Dekalb Community Concert Association, Auburn, IN

Civic & Public Affairs

30,000 Dekalb County Operation Shelter, Auburn, IN

Education

18,000 Independent Colleges of Indiana, Indianapolis, IN
5,000 Science Central, Fort Wayne, IN
4,000 Tri-State University, Angola, IN
2,500 Junior Achievement, Fort Wayne, IN
2,200 St. Francis College, Fort Wayne, IN
1,500 Foundry Educational Foundation, Des Plaines, IL

Health

500 March of Dimes, Auburn, IN

Religion

2,500 Youth for Christ, Auburn, IN

Social Services

83,334 YMCA Dekalb County, Auburn, IN
8,500 United Way Dekalb County, Auburn, IN
1,000 Community Harvest Food Bank, Fort Wayne, IN
800 Boy Scouts of America Anthony Wayne Council, Fort Wayne, IN
500 Dekalb County Association for Retarded Children, Auburn, IN

AUTODESK INC.

Company Contact

San Rafael, CA
Web: http://www.autodesk.com

Company Description

Employees: 1,894
SIC(s): 7371 Computer Programming Services.

Nonmonetary Support

Value: $1,000,000 (1994)
Type: Donated Products

Autodesk Foundation

Giving Contact

Elizabeth Share, Chief Financial Officer
Autodesk Foundation
111 McInnis Parkway
San Rafael, CA 94903
Phone: (415)507-6336
Fax: (415)507-6339

Alternate Contact

Walt Spevak
Note: Mr. Spevak is the contact for educational software requests.

Description

Organization Type: Corporate Foundation. Supports preselected organizations only.
Giving Locations: CA: San Francisco including the Bay Area nationally; Marin County; Sonoma County.
Grant Types: General Support.

Giving Philosophy

'The Audodesk Foundation creates a unique bridge between the business and education communities engaged in school reform in order to provide vision, leadership, and incubation of new and expanding initiatives and collaborations.
'The goal of our work is to improve education for all students; the tool we use to help meet this goal is project-based learning. At the heart of project-based learning is the conviction that all children must have an excellent education in order to lead this nation forward into the next century--an education that prepares them to use their minds well, apply what they learn in school to lifelong endeavors, be technologically literate, and have the skills and self-confidence to succeed in the globally competitive workforce.' Autodesk Foundation web site.

Financial Summary

Total Giving: $200,000 (1996 approx); $150,000 (1995 approx); $1,280,000 (1994 approx). Note: Contributes through corporate direct giving program and foundation. Giving includes foundation.

Typical Recipients

Arts & Humanities: Arts & Humanities-General
Civic & Public Affairs: Civic & Public Affairs-General
Education: Education-General
Environment: Environment-General
Social Services: Social Services-General

Contributions Analysis

Education: 100% of foundation support funds K-12 educational programs.

Restrictions

Does not support political or religious organizations.

Additional Information

Company is developing an employee matching gifts program for 501(c)(3) organizations.

Corporate Officials

Carol A. Bartz: chairman, chief executive officer B Alma, WI 1948. ED University of Wisconsin BS (1971). PRIM CORP EMPL chairman, chief executive officer: Autodesk Inc. CORP AFFIL president: Sun Federal; director: Cisco Systems Inc.; director: Bea Systems; director: Cadence Design Systems Inc.; director: AirTouch Communications Inc. NONPR AFFIL director: National Breast Cancer Research Foundation; director: University Wisconsin School Business; member: National Association Securities Dealers; member: Committee 200; director: Federation National Medals Science & Technology; member: California Chamber of Commerce; member: Advisory Council Stanford University Business School.
Eric B. Herr: president, chief operating officer B 1948. ED Indiana University; Kenyon College. PRIM CORP EMPL president, chief operating officer: Autodesk Inc.

Foundation Officials

Carol A. Bartz: director (see above)
Patricia Clark: director
Robert Hughes: director
Tom King: director
Steve McMahon: director ED Harvard University; University of Notre Dame. PRIM CORP EMPL vice president human resources facilities: Autodesk Inc.
Judy Morgan: program director, School-to-Career
Kathleen Mullin: director
Bob Pearlman: president
Sanna Randolph: director professional development
Elizabeth Share: vice president, chief financial officer
Kendall Starkweather: director
Kendall N. Starkweather: director B 1945. PRIM NONPR EMPL director: International Technology Education Association. CORP AFFIL director: Autodesk Inc.
Joyce Winterton: director

Grants Analysis

Disclosure Period: calendar year ending
Typical Range: $1,000 to $2,500

AVERY DENNISON CORP.

Company Contact

Pasadena, CA
Web: http://www.averydennison.com

Company Description

Revenue: US$3,768,200,000 (1999)
Employees: 16,100 (1999)
Fortune Rank: 429, per FORTUNE Magazine's list of 500 Largest U.S. Corporations (1999).
FF 429
SIC(s): 2672 Coated & Laminated Paper Nec, 2899 Chemical Preparations Nec, 3569 General Industrial Machinery Nec.

Operating Locations

Avery International Converting Group operates 6 divisions in locations. Sodabar Products Group operates 3 divisions in locations.

Nonmonetary Support

Type: Donated Products

Avery Dennison Foundation

Giving Contact

Joyce M. Reid, Director, Corporate Programs
Avery Dennison Corp.
150 North Orange Grove Boulevard
Pasadena, CA 91103
Phone: (626)304-2000
Fax: (626)577-9587

Description

EIN: 953251844
Organization Type: Corporate Foundation
Giving Locations: headquarters and operating communities.
Grant Types: General Support.

Financial Summary

Total Giving: $200,000 (1999 approx); $135,000 (1998); $253,000 (1997). Note: Contributes through corporate direct giving program and foundation.
Giving Analysis: Giving for 1998 includes: foundation ($110,000); foundation grants to United Way ($25,000)
Assets: $8,244,864 (1998); $6,258,909 (1997); $3,935,066 (1996)

Typical Recipients

Arts & Humanities: Arts & Humanities-General, Museums/Galleries, Music
Civic & Public Affairs: Civic & Public Affairs-General, Women's Affairs
Education: Colleges & Universities, Education-General
Health: Children's Health/Hospitals, Health-General
Social Services: Recreation & Athletics, Social Services-General, United Funds/United Ways

Contributions Analysis

Giving Priorities: Primary giving to the arts and social services.
Arts & Humanities: 74%. Supports the Music Center of Los Angeles County.
Social Services: 26%. Funds the United Way and Pasadena Southwest Little League.
Note: Total foundation giving in 1998.

Application Procedures

Initial Contact: Send a written request.
Application Requirements: Include organization's purpose and background, project goals and methods, project itemized budget, amount requested, project timetable, standards for evaluating the effectiveness of project, tax-exemption letter from IRS and ruling that the organization is not a private foundation, current financial statement, list of board of directors, and a list of current contributors with giving levels.
Deadlines: None.
Evaluative Criteria: Supports projects that address specific community needs, are action-oriented and develop opportunities for life enrichment, and in which self-support or broad-based community support is the ultimate objective; special consideration given to organizations near company facilities or in which company employees actively participate.
Decision Notification: Final decision can be given within three to six months.
Notes: Multiple requests from one organization in a calendar year are discouraged. Grants will be made on an annual basis with no renewals implied.

Restrictions

No contributions are made to individuals; service clubs, fraternal organizations, or veterans groups; churches or religious organizations; advertising; private foundations; beauty or talent contests; political organizations, candidates, ballot measures, or other

political activities; operating funds for hospitals; or United Way agencies.
The program supports nonprofit organizations with IRS 501(c)(3) tax-exempt status only.

Additional Information

Publications: Annual Report

Corporate Officials

Robert M. Calderoni: chief financial officer, senior vice president finance ED Fordham University BS (1981). PRIM CORP EMPL chief financial officer, senior vice president finance: Avery Dennison Corp.
Charles Daly Miller: chairman, director B Hartford, CT 1928. ED Johns Hopkins University (1949). PRIM CORP EMPL chairman, director: Avery Dennison Corp. CORP AFFIL director: Pacific Mutual Life Insurance Co.; director: Nationwide Health Properties Inc.; director: Davidson & Associates Inc.; director: Great Western Finance Corp.; chairman, director: Avery Dennison Decorative Films. NONPR AFFIL director: Edison International.
Philip Mark Neal: president, chief executive officer, director B San Diego, CA 1940. ED Pomona College BA (1962); Stanford University MBA (1964). PRIM CORP EMPL president, chief executive officer, director: Avery Dennison Corp. CORP AFFIL president: Avery Dennison Office Privates Co. NONPR AFFIL trustee: Pomona College; government: Town Hall California; director: Independent Colleges Southern California; member: Financial Executives Institute.

Giving Program Officials

Joyce M. Reid: PRIM CORP EMPL director communications: Avery Dennison Corp.

Grants Analysis

Disclosure Period: calendar year ending 1998
Total Grants: $135,000*
Number of Grants: 3
Average Grant: $45,000
Highest Grant: $100,000
Typical Range: $10,000 to $100,000
***Note:** Giving includes United Way.

Recent Grants

Note: Grants derived from 1998 Form 990.

Arts & Humanities
100,000 The Music Center of Los Angeles County, Los Angeles, CA

Social Services
25,000 United Way of Greater Los Angeles, Los Angeles, CA
10,000 Pasadena Southwest Little League, Pasadena, CA

AVISTA CORPORATION

Company Contact

Spokane, WA
Web: http://www.avistacorp.com

Company Description

Former Name: Washington Water Power Co. (WWP).
Assets: US$3,713,500,000 (1999)
Profit: US$26,000,000 (1999)
Employees: 3,303
Fortune Rank: 223, per FORTUNE Magazine's list of 500 Largest U.S. Corporations (1999).
FF 223
SIC(s): 4931 Electric & Other Services Combined.

Nonmonetary Support

Type: Donated Equipment; In-kind Services; Loaned Employees

Corporate Sponsorship

Type: Arts & cultural events; Festivals/fairs; Pledge-a-thon; Sports events

Giving Contact

Debbie Simock, Community Relations Coordinator
Avista Corp.
PO Box 3727
Spokane, WA 99220
Phone: (509)495-8031
Fax: (509)495-8725
Email: dsimock@avistacorp.com

Description

Organization Type: Corporate Giving Program
Giving Locations: ID: Northern Idaho service area; WA: Eastern Washington service area
Grant Types: General Support, Matching, Multiyear/Continuing Support, Project.

Financial Summary

Total Giving: $511,146 (1998). Note: Contributes through corporate direct giving program only.
Giving Analysis: Giving for 1998 includes: corporate direct giving ($511,146)

Typical Recipients

Arts & Humanities: Arts & Humanities-General, Libraries, Museums/Galleries, Performing Arts, Public Broadcasting, Theater
Civic & Public Affairs: Civic & Public Affairs-General, Safety, Women's Affairs
Education: Colleges & Universities, Community & Junior Colleges, Economic Education, Elementary Education (Private), Engineering/Technological Education, Faculty Development, Minority Education, Public Education (Precollege)
Environment: Environment-General
Social Services: Community Service Organizations, Senior Services, United Funds/United Ways, Youth Organizations

Contributions Analysis

Arts & Humanities: Educational programs of orchestras, museums, theaters, the performing arts, visual art programs and exhibits, and public radio and television.
Civic & Public Affairs: Organizations that provide services for housing and local civic and community projects and observances.
Education: Supports educational programs for elementary and secondary schools through its 'Investing in Education' program. Several components of this program include Good Ideas Grants for Teachers, the Viewpoint speaker series, and Partners in Safety. Also supports public and private higher education institutions. Energy and environmental awareness education programs are another focus.
Environment: Supports energy and awareness programs, programs dealing with energy efficiency, air and water quality, fish and wildlifeenhancement, and wise use of land resources.
Social Services: Majority of support is disbursed through corporate and employee contributions to federated drives. Also supports other organizations and programs focusing on senior citizens, limited-income individuals, public safety, children's and women's issues, and youthorganizations. A special initiative is 'Project Share,' a fuel-blind heating assistance program for low-income residents with utility bills.
Note: Contributes to areas of education, economic and community affairs, and cultrual diversity.

Application Procedures

Initial Contact: Requests must be submitted in writing.
Application Requirements: Include a brief summary of the organization including date of establishment, history, mission statement, and objectives; copy of IRS letter designating the organization's 501(c)(3) status; current financial statement; list of board of directors and key staff; a brief overview of the program/project for which funding is requested including purpose, targeted population, evaluation strategies, anticipated results, budget, other organizations providing support, and timeline; and current or past corporate involvement, if any, in the organization or program, including employee volunteers, board members, etc.
Deadlines: None.
Review Process: Proposals reviewed by corporate contributions committee.
Evaluative Criteria: Organizations must be tax-exempt and must provide documentation confirming 501(c)(3) status; be located within areas where company operates; show evidence of sound fiscal policies and responsible financial management; have a competent, knowledgeable, and broad-based board of directors with policy-making authority that represents the organization and its members; show a method to evaluate the results of the proposed project; describe collaborative efforts, if applicable, with similar programs/providers and show the project does not represent an unnecessary duplication of effort; and be relevant to company's business interests.
Decision Notification: Requests in excess of $5,000 are reviewed quarterly in February, May, August, and November; requests under $5,000 are usually processed within 30 days.
Notes: Applicants outside Spokane are encouraged to submit requests to regional offices. Contact headquarters for further information. Special attention is given to organizations and programs that serve a large number of people, have long-term benefits, include the company's employees, have broad community support, and are consistent with Avista Corp.'s business interests.

Restrictions

Generally does not contribute to individuals, team or extra-curricular school events, tournament fund raisers, trips or tours, churches or other religious organizations, organizations that discriminate for any reason, endowments or foundations, or hospital or patient care institution operating funds.
Restricts giving to eastern Washington and northern Idaho.

Additional Information

Priority is given to requests that demonstrate partnerships and cooperative efforts between organizations and agencies and which directly benefit people within areas where company conducts business.
Publications: Contributions Guidelines

Corporate Officials

Paul Anthony Redmond: chairman, chief executive officer, director B Lakeview, OR 1937. ED Gonzaga University BSEE (1965). PRIM CORP EMPL chairman, chief executive officer, director: Washington Water Power Co. CORP AFFIL director: US Bancorp; director: Washington Irrigation & Development Co.; director: Pentzer Fin Services Corp.; director: Pentzer Jefferson Corp.; chairman: Pentzer Corp.; chairman: Pentzer Development Corp.; chairman: Itron Inc.

Giving Program Officials

Debbie Simock: manager community relations

Grants Analysis

Disclosure Period: calendar year ending
Typical Range: $500 to $1,000

AVON PRODUCTS, INC.

Company Contact

New York, NY
Web: http://www.avon.com

Company Description

Revenue: US$5,212,700,000
Employees: 33,900
Fortune Rank: 312, per FORTUNE Magazine's list of 500 Largest U.S. Corporations (1999).
FF 312
SIC(s): 2844 Toilet Preparations, 3961 Costume Jewelry, 5122 Drugs, Proprietaries & Sundries.

Operating Locations

Argentina: Cosmeticos Avon SACI, Victoria, Buenos Aires; Australia: Avon Products Pty. Ltd., Brookvale; Austria: Avon Cosmetics Vertriebs GmbH, Vienna; Belgium: Avon SA, Wavre, Brabant; Bolivia: Productos Avon Ltda. Bolivia, Sato Cruz; Brazil: Avon Cosmeticos Ltda., Sao Paulo; Avon Industrial Ltda., Sao Paulo; Canada: Avon Canada, Pointe-Claire-Dorval; France: Avon, Paris, Ville-de-Paris; Germany: Avon Cosmetics GmbH, Neufahrn, Bayern; Hong Kong: Avon Products, Central District; Avon Cosmetics (Febo) Ltd., Kowloon Bay, Kowloon; Hungary: Avon Cosmetics Hungary, Godollo, Pest; Indonesia: PT Avon Indonesia, Cilandak, Jakarta Raya; Italy: Avon Cosmetics SpA, Olgiate Comasco, Lombardia; Japan: Avon Products Co. Ltd., Tokyo; Mexico: Avonova SA de CV, Celaya; Avon Cosmetics SA de CV, Ciudad de Mexico; Malaysia: Avon Cosmetics (Malaysia) Sdn. Bhd., Petaling Jaya, Selangor; Norway: Avon Cosmetics AS, Oslo, Akershus; New Zealand: Avon Cosmetics Ltd., Auckland; Peru: Productos Avon SA, Lima; Philippines: Avon Products Manufacturing, Quezon City, Manila; Portugal: Avon Cosmeticos Lda., Lisboa; Spain: Avon Cosmetics SA, Madrid; Thailand: Avon Cosmetics Ltd., Hua Mak; Taiwan: Avon Cosmetics (Taiwan) Ltd., Taipei; United Kingdom: Avon Cosmetics Ltd., Northampton, Northamptonshire; Avon European Holdings Ltd., Northampton, Northamptonshire; Langtrees Ltd., Northampton, Northamptonshire; Parfums Stern Overseas Ltd., Northampton, Northamptonshire; Venezuela: Avon Cosmetics de Venezuela CA, Guatire, Miranda

Nonmonetary Support

Value: $9,000,000 (1993); $3,000,000 (1988); $3,500,000 (1987)
Type: Donated Equipment; Donated Products; In-kind Services
Note: Products are distributed through a partnership with Gifts In Kind.

Avon Products Foundation, Inc.

Giving Contact

Judy Barker, President
Avon Products Foundation, Inc.
1345 Avenue of the Americas
New York, NY 10105
Phone: (212)282-5525
Fax: (212)282-6049

Description

Founded: 1955
EIN: 136128447
Organization Type: Corporate Foundation
Giving Locations: headquarters and operating communities.
Grant Types: Capital, Employee Matching Gifts, Scholarship.

Giving Philosophy

'The Avon Products Foundation, Inc., supports the vision of its corporate parent, Avon Products, Inc.: To be the company that best understands and satisfies the product, service and self-fulfillment needs of women, globally. To help Avon fulfill that vision, the Foundation is dedicated to supporting endeavors that understand and respond to the unique needs of women and their families, and enable women to reach their full potential.' Avon Product Foundation website.

Financial Summary

Total Giving: $2,485,464 (1997); $1,981,118 (1996); $1,686,035 (1995). Note: Contributes through foundation only.
Giving Analysis: Giving for 1996 includes: foundation ($1,686,605); foundation matching gifts ($166,054); foundation scholarships ($128,459); 1997: foundation ($1,510,905); foundation scholarships ($708,550); foundation matching gifts ($155,509); foundation grants to United Way ($110,500)
Assets: $39,261 (1997); $49,482 (1996); $67,176 (1995)
Gifts Received: $2,500,000 (1997); $2,000,000 (1996); $1,730,000 (1995). Note: Contributions are received from Avon Products, Inc.

Typical Recipients

Arts & Humanities: Arts Associations & Councils, Arts Centers, Arts Festivals, Arts Funds, Arts Institutes, Arts Outreach, Community Arts, Ethnic & Folk Arts, Libraries, Museums/Galleries, Music, Opera, Performing Arts, Public Broadcasting, Theater
Civic & Public Affairs: African American Affairs, Asian American Affairs, Business/Free Enterprise, Chambers of Commerce, Civil Rights, Clubs, Economic Development, Economic Policy, Employment/Job Training, Hispanic Affairs, Law & Justice, Legal Aid, Native American Affairs, Nonprofit Management, Philanthropic Organizations, Public Policy, Urban & Community Affairs, Women's Affairs, Zoos/Aquariums
Education: Arts/Humanities Education, Business Education, Colleges & Universities, Community & Junior Colleges, Economic Education, Education Funds, Leadership Training, Literacy, Medical Education, Minority Education, Science/Mathematics Education, Special Education, Student Aid
Environment: Environment-General
Health: Cancer, Children's Health/Hospitals, Emergency/Ambulance Services, Health Funds, Health Organizations, Hospices, Hospitals, Medical Rehabilitation, Medical Research, Mental Health, Outpatient Health Care, Prenatal Health Issues, Single-Disease Health Associations
International: Foreign Educational Institutions, Health Care/Hospitals, International Development, International Organizations, International Relief Efforts
Religion: Religious Welfare
Science: Science Museums, Scientific Centers & Institutes
Social Services: Animal Protection, At-Risk Youth, Child Abuse, Child Welfare, Community Centers, Community Service Organizations, Delinquency & Criminal Rehabilitation, Domestic Violence, Family Services, Food/Clothing Distribution, People with Disabilities, Recreation & Athletics, Refugee Assistance, Senior Services, Shelters/Homelessness, Special Olympics, Substance Abuse, United Funds/United Ways, Volunteer Services, YMCA/YWCA/YMHA/YWHA, Youth Organizations

Contributions Analysis

Giving Priorities: United funds, programs for the economically deprived, education, civil rights programs, hospitals, and arts. Avon sponsors worldwide programs that focus on women's concerns, primarily through cause-related marketing programs. Since 1992, Avon and its sales representatives in the U.S., U.K., Canada, Mexico, Venezuela, the Philippines, and other countries have spearheaded a grass-roots breast cancer awareness campaign to educate women about the importance of early detection and to improve access to mammography exams and breast cancer education. Money raised through the sale of products supports community-based programs worldwide. The company has established a Worldwide Fund for Women's Health, which addresses breast cancer efforts, as well as such other health-related issues as AIDS in Thailand and elder care in Japan, and emotional and financial support for mothers in need in Germany. The company also has awards programs that recognize women's achievements in many fields in Avon countries around the world. The foundation, which has traditionally limited support to U.S. organizations, is expanding its support of women worldwide. Working in partnership with Avon Russia, the foundation agreed to underwrite a series of events in Russia on behalf of Magee Womancare International. Affiliated with the Magee-Women's Hospital of Pittsburgh, PA, this organization seeks to improve the quality of healthcare for women around the world. The first event was a wellness festival held in Moscow in March 1997. In addition, the foundation is sponsoring 18 two-minute Womancare infomercials that will air in Russia, as well as various other educational materials that will focus on women's health issues.
Arts & Humanities: 5% to 10%. Supports a variety of arts interests, including arts associations and centers, theater, music, opera, and public broadcasting.
Civic & Public Affairs: 25% to 30%. Priorities include programs concerned with civil rights, minority business, and women's affairs.
Education: 30% to 35%. Primarily supports scholarships to students attending high schools in certain corporate operating locations and scholarship programs targeting women and minorities. Interests also include general support to colleges and universities; education funds; organizations concerned with youth leadership development; minority, business, and economic education; and literacy. Sponsors employee matching gifts program that supports educational institutions.
Health: 10% to 15%. Funds women's health organizations and programs that deal with early detection of breast cancer and hospitals.
International: About 15%. Supports international women's organizations.
Social Services: About 10%. Primarily supports united fund drives. Other areas of interest include social services programs for women and general community, family, and social service organizations.
Note: Supports international women organizations.

Application Procedures

Initial Contact: Write or call the Foundation to receive their information and guidelines brochure.
Application Requirements: Proposals should include amount requested; statement of objectives; history; goals; accomplishments; current annual report; current budget; IRS tax-exemption letter; list of current funding sources; recently audited financial statements; list of board members; and list of accrediting agencies.
Deadlines: None.

Restrictions

Foundation does not support individuals for educational or other purposes; political causes or candidates; religious, fraternal, or veteran organizations, unless they are engaged in significant projects benefiting the entire community; fundraising events, telethons, marathons, races, or benefits; or courtesy advertising.

Additional Information

Avon also supports research into alternatives to the use of animal testing in new product development.
To strengthen its Global Supplier Code of Conduct, Avon in 1997 implemented a certification and monitoring program to ensure that all suppliers meet and conform to the code. According to the 1996 annual report, 'Together with other major corporations and with the guidance of the Council on Economic Priorities, Avon is working to create cooperative certification and monitoring programs that will aid in endorsing those suppliers who meet the agreed-upon criteria.'
The Avon breast Cancer Awareness Crusade, founded in 1993, is one of the largest supporters of

breast health programs in America. Its mission is to provide more women, particularly low-income, minority, and older women, with direct access to breast cancer education and early detection screening services, at minimal or no cost.

The Avon Women of Enterprise Awards program is a partnership between Avon Products, Inc. and the U.S. Small Business administration. The program recognizes and honors women entrepreneurs who have overcome personal and professional challenges or exhibited exceptional entrepreneurialship.

Publications: Information and Guidelines Brochure

Corporate Officials

James Edward Preston: chairman, chief executive officer, director B Cleveland, OH 1933. ED Temple University; Northwestern University BS (1955). PRIM CORP EMPL chairman, chief executive officer, director: Avon Products, Inc. CORP AFFIL director: Venator Group Inc.; director: FW Woolworth Co.; chairman: Avon-Lomalinda Inc.; director: Readers Digest Association Inc.; director: Aramark Corp.; chairman: Avon International Operations. NONPR AFFIL director: ARA Services; director: Cosmetic Toiletry Fragrance Association.

Edward Joseph Robinson: president, chief operating officer, director B White Plains, NY 1940. ED Iona College BBA (1962). PRIM CORP EMPL president, chief operating officer, director: Avon Products, Inc. NONPR AFFIL trustee: Iona College; member: New York Society CPA's; member: American Institute CPAs. CLUB AFFIL New York Athletic Club; Winged Foot Country Club; Metro Club.

Foundation Officials

Gail Ann Blanke: vice president B Cleveland, OH 1941. ED Sweet Briar College AB. PRIM CORP EMPL senior vice president: Avon Products Inc. NONPR AFFIL member: Society Mayflower Descendants; member: Women's Forum New York; member: National Advertisers; member: American Women in Radio & Television; member: International Association of Business Communications. CLUB AFFIL Metropolitan Club; Rockaway Hunt Club; Doubles Club; Lawrence Beach Club.

Glenn S. Clarke: president, director

Maria Montoya: director

James Edward Preston: vice president, director (see above)

Mary Quinn: program officer

Grants Analysis

Disclosure Period: calendar year ending 1997

Total Grants: $1,510,905*

Number of Grants: 107

Average Grant: $14,121

Highest Grant: $161,250

Typical Range: $1,000 to $20,000

***Note:** Giving excludes matching gifts; scholarships; United Way.

Recent Grants

Note: Grants derived from 1997 Form 990.

Arts & Humanities

105,000 Best Friends Foundation, Washington, DC -- for expansion of educational program and transportation for girls to perform at Lamb's Theater

15,000 Lincoln Center for the Performing Arts, New York, NY -- support for Consolidated Corporate Fund

6,480 Young Audiences, New York, NY -- early childhood literacy programming at PS 25

Civic & Public Affairs

355,000 Washington Center, Washington, DC -- Women as Leaders seminar

50,000 American Women's Economic Development Corporation, New York, NY -- establishment of alumnae association

50,000 Hispanic Federation, New York, NY -- Latino CORE Initiative

50,000 Support Center for Nonprofit Management, San Francisco, CA -- management assistance programs for nonprofit women's organizations

10,000 Trickle Up Program, New York, NY -- support for microenterprise program

10,000 Women's Center for Education and Career Advancement -- provide services to women seeking employment

5,000 Business for Social Responsibility -- educational programs

5,000 Gildas Club, New York, NY -- free psychological support for people with cancer and their families

5,000 Women in Need, New York, NY -- support for Candlelight Project

5,000 Women at Work, Pasadena, CA -- fund free job information services program

Education

161,250 National Merit Scholarship Corporation Presidents Club Program, Evanston, IL -- scholarships for children and grandchildren of President's club members

100,000 Hostos Community College, Bronx, NY -- emergency financial assistance to students

100,000 Spelman College, Atlanta, GA

75,000 Business and Professional Women's Foundation, Washington, DC -- scholarship program for women in business studies

50,000 College Fund/UNCF -- support for Avon Capital WISE Scholarship Fund

30,000 American Indian College Fund, New York, NY -- emergency financial aid scholarships

19,000 Eleanor Roosevelt Center at Val-Kill, Hyde Park, NY -- Girls Leadership workshop

12,500 Adelphi University, Garden City, NY -- scholarships for minority women

12,500 Iona College, New York, NY -- scholarships for women of African American, Hispanic, and Asian heritage

10,000 Hispanic Women's Center -- provide training for women entering the job market

10,000 International Association of Approved Basketball Officials, Newark, NJ -- scholarships for female high school seniors

10,000 Junior Achievement, NY -- support programs at Bilingual School PS 25

10,000 National Hispanic Scholarship Fund, Baltimore, MD

10,000 Ohio Foundation of Independent Colleges, Columbus, OH -- scholarships for women majoring in business

10,000 Organization of Chinese Americans, Riverside, CT -- Avon college scholarship program

9,000 Women's Research and Education Fund, Washington, DC -- scholarships for women

7,000 Laubach Literacy Council -- support for a pilot Women's Learning and Entrepreneurial Development program

5,000 Pasadena City College, Pasadena, CA -- funding of cosmetology lab construction

Health

140,000 Memorial Sloan-Kettering Cancer Center, New York, NY

20,000 Good Samaritan Hospital -- Avon-named labor and delivery room

5,000 American Cancer Society, Pasadena, CA -- support for cancer patients

5,000 National Foundation for Facial Reconstruction, New York, NY

International

111,000 Magee Womencare International -- consumer health education materials and development of a series of women's health infomercials to be broadcast in Russia

111,000 Magee Womencare International -- consumer health education materials and development of a series of women's health infomercials to be broadcast in Russia

91,425 Reach and Teach USA, White Plains, NY -- entrepreneurial training program for South African women

91,425 Reach and Teach USA, White Plains, NY -- entrepreneurial training program for South African women

50,000 Gifts in Kind International, Alexandria, VA -- donation of merchandise to nonprofit organizations for the direct use by their clients

50,000 Gifts in Kind International, Alexandria, VA -- donation of merchandise to nonprofit organizations for the direct use by their clients

10,000 Rutgers University, New Brunswick, NJ -- funding for the Leadership Development Institute for Women in Mexico

10,000 Rutgers University, New Brunswick, NJ -- funding for the Leadership Development Institute for Women in Mexico

Science

5,000 New York Hall of Science, Flushing, NY -- support for programs at PS 25 and Avon-sponsored Girl Scout troop

Social Services

75,000 United Way, New York, NY -- support for the Women with HIV/AIDS initiative, the Strategic Alliance Fund, and the Hollis Community Service Center

45,000 Helen Keller Services for the Blind, Brooklyn, NY -- support for summer camp and Braille library program

13,500 United Way, DE -- support programs for women and children

10,000 Children's Aid Society, New York, NY -- support of annual meeting and symposium

10,000 Dole Foundation, Washington, DC -- support for programs for the disabled to become employed

10,000 Girls, Inc. -- support Urban Girls Initiative program

10,000 Women's Commission for Refugee Women and Children -- support for general public education and advocacy efforts

7,500 Center for Enriched Living, Deerfield, IL -- providing skills for people with disabilities

7,000 United Way, Atlanta, GA

5,000 Aid Gwinnett, Atlanta, GA -- education and youth prevention

BADGER METER, INC.

Company Contact

Milwaukee, WI

Web: http://www.badgermeter.com

Company Description

Employees: 940

SIC(s): 3823 Process Control Instruments, 3824 Fluid Meters & Counting Devices.

Corporate Sponsorship

Contact: James Wright, Director

Badger Meter Foundation

Giving Contact

Beth McCallister, Secretary
Badger Meter Foundation
PO Box 245036
Milwaukee, WI 53224-9536
Phone: (414)355-0400
Fax: (414)371-5956

Description

EIN: 396043635
Organization Type: Corporate Foundation
Giving Locations: WI: Milwaukee
Grant Types: General Support.

Financial Summary

Total Giving: $280,000 (2000 approx); $346,000 (1999 approx); $276,158 (1998). Note: Contributes through foundation only. 1997 Giving includes United Way ($44,000). 1996 Giving includes United Way ($45,000).
Giving Analysis: Giving for 1998 includes: foundation grants to United Way ($55,158); foundation matching gifts ($350)
Assets: $2,081,354 (1998); $1,873,756 (1997); $1,605,872 (1996)
Gifts Received: $265,271 (1998); $207,000 (1997); $165,000 (1996). Note: In 1998, contributions were received from Badger Meter, Inc.

Typical Recipients

Arts & Humanities: Arts & Humanities-General, Libraries, Museums/Galleries, Music, Opera, Performing Arts, Theater
Civic & Public Affairs: Botanical Gardens/Parks, Economic Development, Employment/Job Training, Civic & Public Affairs-General, Hispanic Affairs, Housing, Law & Justice, Municipalities/Towns, Parades/Festivals, Public Policy, Urban & Community Affairs, Zoos/Aquariums
Education: Arts/Humanities Education, Business Education, Business-School Partnerships, Colleges & Universities, Education Funds, Engineering/Technological Education, Faculty Development, Education-General, Health & Physical Education, Literacy, Medical Education, Minority Education, Private Education (Precollege), Public Education (Precollege), Religious Education, Science/Mathematics Education, Secondary Education (Private), Secondary Education (Public), Student Aid
Environment: Environment-General, Resource Conservation
Health: Arthritis, Cancer, Health Organizations, Heart, Hospitals, Medical Research, Mental Health, Preventive Medicine/Wellness Organizations, Single-Disease Health Associations, Speech & Hearing, Transplant Networks/Donor Banks
Religion: Religious Welfare
Social Services: Child Welfare, Community Centers, Community Service Organizations, Day Care, Food/Clothing Distribution, Homes, People with Disabilities, Recreation & Athletics, Scouts, Shelters/Homelessness, Substance Abuse, United Funds/United Ways, YMCA/YWCA/YMHA/YWHA, Youth Organizations

Contributions Analysis

Giving Priorities: Education and community service organizations.
Arts & Humanities: About 15%. Interests include festivals, opera, music, the performing arts, and theater.
Civic & Public Affairs: 35% to 40%. Supports a diverse group of community services, including youth organizations, homes, children's centers, museums, and youth recreational activities.
Education: 30% to 35%. Foundation supports colleges, universities, day schools, education funds, engineering education, continuing education, and scholarship funds.
Environment: Less than 5%. Supports zoological societies and conservationgroups.
Health: 10% to 15%. Support favors single-disease health associations and hospitals. Also supports pediatric health care, emergency services, community hospitals, and health organizations.
Social Services: 15% to 20%. Recipients include rescue missions, aid for the mentally retarded, and food and clothing distribution. Majority ofsupport funds Goodwill Industries.

Application Procedures

Initial Contact: Send a brief letter of inquiry on applicant's letterhead.
Application Requirements: Information should include purpose of funds sought; amount requested; and an attached copy of an IRS 501(c)(3) determination letter.
Deadlines: None.
Decision Notification: Board meets in April, August, and December.

Corporate Officials

Ronald H. Dix: vice president administration & human resources B 1944. ED University of Wisconsin BS (1969). PRIM CORP EMPL vice president administration & human resources: Badger Meter, Inc.
Richard A. Meeusen: vice president, chief financial officer, treasurer B 1954. ED University of Wisconsin, Whitewater BS (1976). PRIM CORP EMPL vice president, chief financial officer, treasurer: Badger Meter, Inc.
James O. Wright: chairman, director B Milwaukee, WI 1921. ED Yale University BS (1944). PRIM CORP EMPL chairman, director: Badger Meter, Inc. CORP AFFIL director: Northwestern Mutual Life Insurance Co.; director: Wisconsin Natural Gas Co.; director: Marshall & Ilsley Corp.; director: Grede Foundries Inc.; director: Marshall & Ilsley Bank; director: Becor Western Inc.

Foundation Officials

John P. Biver: treasurer
Peter Wayne Bruce: director B Rome, NY 1945. ED University of Wisconsin BA (1967); University of Chicago JD (1970). PRIM CORP EMPL executive vice president chief compliance officer general: Northwest Mutual Life Insurance Co. NONPR AFFIL member: Village Shorewood Community Development Association; member: Wisconsin Bar Association; chairman, director: Saint Marys Hill Hospital Curative Foundation; member: American Law Institute; member: Milwaukee Bar Association; director: Alverno College.
Ronald H. Dix: director (see above)
Richard S. Gallagher: director B Minot, ND 1942. ED Northwestern University BSBA (1964); Harvard University JD (1967). PRIM CORP EMPL partner: Foley & Lardner. NONPR AFFIL member: Memorial Park Committee; director: United Performing Arts Fund; fellow: American Law Institute; director: Donors Forum Wisconsin; fellow: American College Tax Counsel; fellow: American College Trust & Estate Counsel; member: American Bar Association.
Patrick A. Jones: director
Beth McCallister: secretary
Barbara M. Wiley: director
James O. Wright: president, director (see above)

Grants Analysis

Disclosure Period: calendar year ending 1998
Total Grants: $220,650*
Number of Grants: 64*
Average Grant: $3,448
Highest Grant: $44,750
Typical Range: $500 to $5,000
***Note:** Giving excludes United Way and matching gifts.

Recent Grants

Note: Grants derived from 1998 Form 990.

Arts & Humanities

10,000	Marcus Center for Performing Arts, Milwaukee, WI
5,000	United Performing Arts Fund, Milwaukee, WI
3,000	The Children's Museum, Milwaukee, WI
3,000	Milwaukee Public Library, Milwaukee, WI
2,900	Wisconsin Conservatory of Music, Milwaukee, WI
2,000	Milwaukee Art Museum, Milwaukee, WI
1,500	Florentine Opera Company, Milwaukee, WI
1,500	Milwaukee Public Museum, Milwaukee, WI
1,000	Milwaukee Symphony Orchestra, Milwaukee, WI
1,000	Skylight Opera Theatre, Milwaukee, WI

Civic & Public Affairs

5,000	Brown Deer Village, Brown Deer, WI
5,000	Neighborhood House, Milwaukee, WI
2,500	Esperanza Unida, Milwaukee, WI
1,000	The Park People, Milwaukee, WI
1,000	Zoological Society of Milwaukee, Milwaukee, WI

Education

40,000	University School Milwaukee, Milwaukee, WI
25,500	Alverno College, Milwaukee, WI
8,333	UWM-Foundation, Milwaukee, WI
5,000	Messmer High School, Milwaukee, WI
5,000	PAVE, Milwaukee, WI
5,000	Puelicher Center, Madison, WI
5,000	Urban Day School, Milwaukee, WI
2,500	Brookfield Academy, Milwaukee, WI
1,500	Brown Deer Scholarships, Brown Deer, WI
1,500	Brown Deer Teacher Awards, Brown Deer, WI
1,500	Marquette University, Milwaukee, WI
1,000	Milwaukee Institute of Art & Design, Milwaukee, WI

Environment

1,000	Riveredge Nature Center, Newburg, WI

Health

5,000	Columbia Hospital, Milwaukee, WI
5,000	Health Education Center, Milwaukee, WI
2,500	Community Memorial Hospital, Milwaukee, WI
2,500	Froedtert Memorial Hospital, Milwaukee, WI
1,000	American Heart Association, Milwaukee, WI
1,000	Center for Deaf & Hard of Hearing, Milwaukee, WI
500	American Cancer Society, Milwaukee, WI

Religion

1,000	Bethany Christian Services, Milwaukee, WI

Social Services

44,750	United Way - Milwaukee, Milwaukee, WI
25,000	Goodwill Industries, Milwaukee, WI
5,000	Second Harvest, Milwaukee, WI
5,000	YMCA - Schroeder Aquatic Center, Milwaukee, WI
3,000	Ozaukee Ice Center, Mequon, WI
2,500	St. Francis Children's Center, Milwaukee, WI
2,500	Silver Spring Neighborhood Center, Milwaukee, WI
2,500	United Community Center, Milwaukee, WI

2,000	Portal Industries, Grafton, WI
1,000	Milwaukee Kickers, Milwaukee, WI
1,000	United Way-Nogales, Rio Rico, AZ
1,000	United Way-Tulsa, Tulsa, OK
500	Benedict Center, Milwaukee, WI

ROBERT W. BAIRD &CO.

Company Contact
Milwaukee, WI
Web: http://www.rwbaird.com

Company Description
Operating Revenue: US$350,000,000
Employees: 1,150
SIC(s): 6200 Security & Commodity Brokers, 6282 Investment Advice.
Parent Company: Northwestern Mutual Life Insurance, Milwaukee, WI, United States

Corporate Sponsorship
Type: Arts & cultural events; Music & entertainment events

Robert W. Baird & Co. Foundation

Giving Contact
G. Frederick Kasten, Jr., Chairman & Chief Executive Officer
Robert W. Baird & Co. Foundation
777 East Wisconsin Avenue, 28th Floor
Milwaukee, WI 53202
Phone: (414)765-3500
Fax: (414)765-3600

Description
Founded: 1967
EIN: 396107937
Organization Type: Corporate Foundation. Supports preselected organizations only.
Giving Locations: headquarters and operating communities.
Grant Types: Capital, Conference/Seminar, Endowment, General Support.

Financial Summary
Total Giving: $650,000 (1999 approx); $650,000 (1998); $450,912 (1996). Note: Contributes through corporate direct giving program and foundation. 1998 Giving includes foundation. 1996 Giving includes United Way ($29,550); 1995 Giving includes foundation ($385,063); United Way ($34,950).
Assets: $5,644,477 (1996); $4,057,073 (1995); $3,774,827 (1993)
Gifts Received: $1,022,136 (1996); $75,000 (1995); $500,000 (1993). Note: In 1995, contributions were received from Robert W. Baird & Co.

Typical Recipients
Arts & Humanities: Arts Institutes, Ballet, Arts & Humanities-General, History & Archaeology, Libraries, Museums/Galleries, Music, Opera, Performing Arts, Public Broadcasting, Theater
Civic & Public Affairs: Business/Free Enterprise, Clubs, Economic Development, Economic Policy, Employment/Job Training, Civic & Public Affairs-General, Law & Justice, Municipalities/Towns, Parades/Festivals, Public Policy, Urban & Community Affairs, Zoos/Aquariums
Education: Business Education, Business-School Partnerships, Colleges & Universities, Economic Education, Education Reform, Engineering/Technological Education, Education-General, Medical Education, Minority Education, Private Education (Precollege), Vocational & Technical Education
Health: Cancer, Children's Health/Hospitals, Emergency/Ambulance Services, Health-General, Health Organizations, Heart, Hospitals, Medical Rehabilitation, Medical Research, Public Health
Religion: Jewish Causes, Religious Organizations, Religious Welfare
Science: Science Museums
Social Services: Child Welfare, Community Centers, Community Service Organizations, Delinquency & Criminal Rehabilitation, Domestic Violence, People with Disabilities, Scouts, Social Services-General, United Funds/United Ways, YMCA/YWCA/YMHA/YWHA, Youth Organizations

Contributions Analysis
Arts & Humanities: 20% to 25%. Funding goes to art institutions and museums, the performing arts, theater and libraries.
Civic & Public Affairs: 15% to 20%. Interests include economic development and policy, job training, business groups for free enterprise, and public policy.
Education: 30% to 35%. Supports business education, colleges and universities, education reform, minority education and private education.
Health: 5% to 10%. Funding goes to cancer research, children's health issues, health organizations, hospitals, and medical research.
Science: Less than 5%. Supports science museums.
Social Services: About 20%. Supports child welfare issues, scouting, the United Way, youth organizations, and delinquency and criminal rehabilitation.

Restrictions
Does not support individuals, religious organizations for sectarian purposes, and political or lobbying groups.

Corporate Officials
James D. Bell: executive vice president PRIM CORP EMPL executive vice president: Baird Financial Corp.
G. Frederick Kasten, Jr.: chairman, chief executive officer, director PRIM CORP EMPL chairman, chief executive officer, director: Robert W. Baird & Co. CORP AFFIL director: Columbia Health System Inc.; director: Regal-Beloit Corp.
Paul E. Purcell: president PRIM CORP EMPL president: Robert W. Baird & Co. CORP AFFIL president: Baird Finance Corp.
James M. Vemlyak: chief financial officer PRIM CORP EMPL chief financial officer: Robert W. Baird & Co.

Foundation Officials
James D. Bell: trustee (see above)
G. Frederick Kasten, Jr.: trustee (see above)

Grants Analysis
Disclosure Period: calendar year ending 1996
Total Grants: $421,362*
Number of Grants: 214
Average Grant: $1,969
Highest Grant: $29,000
Typical Range: $100 to $15,000
***Note:** Giving excludes United Way.

Recent Grants
Note: Grants derived from 1996 Form 990.

Arts & Humanities

29,000	United Performing Arts Fund
25,000	Florida Orchestra, Tampa, FL
6,000	Milwaukee Redevelopment Corporation, Milwaukee, WI
5,000	Chicago Opera Theater, Chicago, IL
5,000	Florida Orchestra, Tampa, FL
5,000	Marcus Center for Performing Arts
5,000	Wisconsin History Foundation, Madison, WI
4,000	Milwaukee Ballet, Milwaukee, WI
4,000	Milwaukee Repertory Theater, Milwaukee, WI
3,250	Marcus Center for Performing Arts
3,000	Channel 10/36 Friends, Milwaukee, WI
3,000	Milwaukee Public Museum, Milwaukee, WI
3,000	Milwaukee Symphony Orchestra League, Milwaukee, WI
2,750	Friends of the Milwaukee Public Museum, Milwaukee, WI
2,500	Skylight Opera Theater, Milwaukee, WI

Civic & Public Affairs

5,000	Future Neenah Development Corporation, Neenah, WI
5,000	Great Circus Parade, Milwaukee, WI
5,000	Greater Milwaukee Committee, Milwaukee, WI
5,000	Milwaukee Enterprise Center, Milwaukee, WI
5,000	New Hope Project, Milwaukee, WI
4,000	Public Policy Forum, Milwaukee, WI
3,000	Hull House Association, Chicago, IL
2,500	Forward Wisconsin, Milwaukee, WI
2,500	GMC Inner-City Task Force

Education

10,000	Florida Council on Economic Education, Tampa, FL
10,000	PAVE, San Diego, CA
10,000	Western Wisconsin Technical College Foundation, La Crosse, WI
8,000	University of Southern Florida Foundation
5,000	Hope College, Holland, MI
5,000	Lawrence University, Appleton, WI
5,000	St. Norbert College
5,000	University of Wisconsin Milwaukee Foundation Enhancing Academic Excellence, Milwaukee, WI
4,000	Milwaukee School of Engineering, Milwaukee, WI
3,000	Medical College of Wisconsin, Milwaukee, WI

Health

10,000	Luther Hospital, Eau Claire, WI
5,500	Karen Yontz Women's Cardiac Awareness Center
4,000	Children's Hospital Foundation, Seattle, WA
3,000	American Cancer Society, Milwaukee, WI
3,000	Make-A-Wish Foundation

Religion

5,000	St. Josaphat Basillica, Milwaukee, WI
4,000	Milwaukee Catholic Home Foundation, Milwaukee, WI
3,200	St. Aemilian-Lakeside, Milwaukee, WI
3,000	St. Aemilian-Lakeside, Milwaukee, WI

Social Services

21,000	United Way, Milwaukee, WI
10,000	YMCA
8,000	Boys and Girls Clubs, Milwaukee, WI
7,000	United Way, Milwaukee, WI
5,000	Crisis Center of Hillsborough County
4,000	Boy Scouts of America Milwaukee County Council, Milwaukee, WI
4,000	Goodwill Industries

BAKER HUGHES INC.

Company Contact
3900 Essex Lane, Suite 210
Houston, TX 77027
Phone: (713)439-8600
Fax: (713)439-8699
Web: http://www.bakerhughes.com

Company Description
Acquired: Western Atlas Inc. (1998).
Revenue: US$4,546,700,000 (1999)

Employees: 32,300 (1998)
Fortune Rank: 329, per FORTUNE Magazine's list of 500 Largest U.S. Corporations (1999).
FF 329
SIC(s): 2819 Industrial Inorganic Chemicals Nec, 3532 Mining Machinery, 3533 Oil & Gas Field Machinery, 3556 Food Products Machinery, 3571 Electronic Computers.

Baker Hughes Foundation

Giving Contact
Isaac C. Kerridge, Executive Director
Houston, TX
Email: paulette.peoples@bakerhughes.com

Description
Organization Type: Corporate Foundation
Giving Locations: TX
Grant Types: Matching.

Typical Recipients
Arts & Humanities: Museums/Galleries, Performing Arts
Education: Engineering/Technological Education
Health: Medical Research

Application Procedures
Initial Contact: Send brief letter of inquiry, including a description of organization, amount requested, purpose of funds sought, recently audited financial statements, and proof of tax-exempt status. There are no deadlines.

Restrictions
Does not support individuals, religious organizations for sectarian purposes, or political or lobbying groups.

Additional Information
Baker Hughes Foundation giving program has ceased. The foundation doesn't know when they will resume their giving.

Corporate Officials
Max L. Lukens: president, chairman, chief executive officer, chief operating officer PRIM CORP EMPL president, chairman, chief executive officer, chief operating officer: Baker Hughes Inc.
Eric Leonard Mattson: senior vice president, chief financial officer B Pittsburgh, PA 1951. ED Pennsylvania State University (1973); Pennsylvania State University (1974). PRIM CORP EMPL senior vice president, chief financial officer: Baker Hughes Inc.

Foundation Officials
Isaac C. Kerridge: executive director

Grants Analysis
Disclosure Period: calendar year ending

Recent Grants
Note: Grants derived from 1999 grants list.

Arts & Humanities
Children's Museum of Houston, Houston, TX

Civic & Public Affairs
Friends of the Stehun Foundation, Houston, TX

Education
Junior Achievement of Southeast Texas, Houston, TX

Health
American Heart Association, Houston, TX
Hermann Children's Hospital, Houston, TX
Juvenile Diabetes Foundation, Houston, TX

Science
Houston Museum of Natural Science, Houston, TX

Social Services
Boy Scouts of America, Houston, TX
Boys & Girls Clubs of America, Houston, TX
United Way, Houston, TX

Ball Corp.

Company Contact
10 Longs Peak Drive
PO Box 5000
Broomfield, CO 80021-2510
Phone: (303)469-3131
Web: http://www.ball.com

Company Description
Revenue: US$3,584,200,000 (1999)
Profit: US$104,200,000 (1999)
Employees: 13,000
Fortune Rank: 438, per FORTUNE Magazine's list of 500 Largest U.S. Corporations (1999).
FF 438
SIC(s): 3089 Plastics Products Nec, 3411 Metal Cans, 3542 Machine Tools--Metal Forming Types, 3661 Telephone & Telegraph Apparatus, 3812 Search & Navigation Equipment.

Nonmonetary Support
Type: Donated Equipment; Donated Products; Loaned Executives; Workplace Solicitation

Giving Contact
Harold Sohn, Vice President, Corporate Relations
PO Box 5000
Broomfield, CO 80038-5000
Phone: (303)460-2126
Fax: (303)460-2127

Description
Organization Type: Corporate Giving Program
Giving Locations: IN
Grant Types: Employee Matching Gifts, General Support, Multiyear/Continuing Support, Project.

Financial Summary
Total Giving: Company does not disclose contributions figures.

Typical Recipients
Arts & Humanities: Arts & Humanities-General
Civic & Public Affairs: Civic & Public Affairs-General
Education: Education-General
Health: Health-General
Social Services: Social Services-General

Application Procedures
Initial Contact: Send a brief letter of inquiry and a full proposal. Include a description of organization, amount requested, purpose of funds sought, recently audited financial statement, and proof of tax-exempt status.

Restrictions
Does not support individuals, religious organizations for sectarian purposes, or political or lobbying groups.

Corporate Officials
R. David Hoover: executive vice president, chief financial officero, director PRIM CORP EMPL executive vice president, chief financial officer: Ball Corp.
George A. Sissel: chairman, president, chief executive officer, director B Chicago, IL 1936. ED University of Colorado BS (1958); University of Minnesota JD (1966). PRIM CORP EMPL chairman, president, chief executive officer, director: Ball Corp. CORP AFFIL director: First Merchants Corp.; board advisor: First Chicago Equity Capital; director: First Merchants Bank NA; chairman: Ball Aerospace & Technology Corp. NONPR AFFIL member: Sigma Chi; member: Sigma Tau; member: Order Coif; member: Massachusetts Institute Technology Society Senior Executives; director: National Association Manufacturers; member: Indiana Bar Association; director: Indiana Chamber of Commerce; member: Colorado Bar Association; member: Eta Kappa Nu; member: American Society of Corporate Secretaries; chairman: Can Manufacturers Institute; member: American Bar Association. CLUB AFFIL Rotary Club.

Grants Analysis
Disclosure Period: calendar year ending
Typical Range: $50 to $1,000

Bandag, Inc.

Company Contact
Muscatine, IA
Web: http://www.bandag.com

Company Description
Employees: 4,791 (1999)
SIC(s): 3011 Tires & Inner Tubes, 3069 Fabricated Rubber Products Nec, 3559 Special Industry Machinery Nec.

Operating Locations
Belgium: Bandag Eastern Hemisphere Rubber Division, Lanklaar; Bandag N.V., Zaventem; Brazil: Campinas Mafra; Canada: Bandag Canada, Shawinigan; Mexico: Leon; Malaysia: Bandag Malaysia Sdn. Bhd., Kuala Lumpur; Republic of South Africa: Bandag South Africa, Johannesburg; Venezuela: Caracas

Nonmonetary Support
Value: $200,000 (1996)
Type: Loaned Employees; Loaned Executives; Workplace Solicitation

Corporate Sponsorship
Value: $500,000
Type: Sports events
Contact: Janet Sichterman, Vice President, Peoples Service
Note: Sponsors only local events or causes.

Giving Contact
Doug Herlein, Manager, Development Consultant
Bandag, Inc.
2905 N Hwy. 61
Muscatine, IA 52761-5886
Phone: (319)262-1400
Fax: (319)262-1069

Description
Organization Type: Corporate Giving Program
Giving Locations: headquarters and operating communities.
Grant Types: Award, Capital, Challenge, Emergency, Employee Matching Gifts, General Support, Multiyear/Continuing Support, Project, Research, Scholarship, Seed Money.

Financial Summary
Total Giving: $500,000 (2000 approx); $500,000 (1999 approx); $550,000 (1997 approx). Note: Contributes through corporate direct giving program only.

Typical Recipients
Arts & Humanities: Arts Associations & Councils, Community Arts, Performing Arts
Civic & Public Affairs: African American Affairs, Business/Free Enterprise, Chambers of Commerce, Clubs, Community Foundations, Ethnic Organizations, Hispanic Affairs, Housing, Inner-City Development, Municipalities/Towns, Native American Affairs, Parades/Festivals, Philanthropic Organizations, Professional & Trade Associations, Safety, Urban & Community Affairs, Women's Affairs

Education: Arts/Humanities Education, Business Education, Business-School Partnerships, Colleges & Universities, Community & Junior Colleges, Continuing Education, Elementary Education (Public), Engineering/Technological Education, Faculty Development, Education-General, Health & Physical Education, Literacy, Minority Education, Student Aid, Vocational & Technical Education
Environment: Air/Water Quality, Resource Conservation
Health: Adolescent Health Issues, Children's Health/ Hospitals, Clinics/Medical Centers, Eyes/Blindness, Health-General, Health Policy/Cost Containment, Health Funds, Health Organizations, Hospices, Hospitals, Hospitals (University Affiliated), Prenatal Health Issues, Preventive Medicine/Wellness Organizations, Public Health, Speech & Hearing
Science: Scientific Centers & Institutes
Social Services: At-Risk Youth, Camps, Child Welfare, Community Centers, Community Service Organizations, Counseling, Domestic Violence, Emergency Relief, Recreation & Athletics, Social Services-General, Substance Abuse, United Funds/United Ways, Volunteer Services, Youth Organizations

Contributions Analysis

Arts & Humanities: Less than 5%. Supports arts associations, the performing arts, and community art programs.
Civic & Public Affairs: About 30%. Contributes to environmental efforts, AfricanAmerican and Hispanic affairs, women's issues, and safety and urban concerns.
Education: About 40%. Funding is awarded to colleges and universities, business and engineering educational programs, and public education and student aid programs.
Health: About 30%. Supports single-disease health organizations and issues, public health, health care cost containment, and hospitals. Additional support is for community activities and services, child welfare, counseling, and the United Way.

Application Procedures

Initial Contact: letter or proposal, telephone requests are not accepted
Application Requirements: a description of organization, amount requested, purpose of funds sought, and proof of tax-exempt status

Restrictions

The vast majority of giving is limited to within the county and city of Muscatine, IA.
Company does not support religious organizations or political or lobbying groups.

Corporate Officials

Martin Gregory Carver: chairman, president, chief executive officer B Davenport, IA 1948. ED University of Iowa BA (1970); University of Indiana MBA (1972). PRIM CORP EMPL chairman, president, chief executive officer: Bandag, Inc. ADD CORP EMPL president: Bandag Licensing Corp. NONPR AFFIL member: National Association Manufacturer; member: University Iowa School Business; director: Augustana College. CLUB AFFIL Rotary International Club.

Giving Program Officials

John Lodge: PRIM CORP EMPL vice president employee services: Bandag, Inc.

BANFI VINTNERS

Company Contact

1111 Cedar Swamp Road
Old Brookville, NY 11545
Phone: (516)626-9200
Fax: (516)626-9218
Web: http://www.banfivintners.com

Company Description

Employees: 130
SIC(s): 2084 Wines, Brandy & Brandy Spirits.
Parent Company: Castello Banfi SRL, Tenuto Poggio All'oro, Sant'Angelo Scalo, Siena, Italy

Operating Locations

DC: Banfi Vintners, Washington; NY: Banfi Vintners, Farmingdale, Glen Head, Old Brookville; House of Banfi, Old Brookville; Villadco, Old Brookville; Vinum, Old Brookville

Banfi Vintners Foundation

Giving Contact

Phillip D. Calderone, Executive Director
Banfi Vintners Foundation

Description

Founded: 1982
EIN: 112622792
Organization Type: Corporate Foundation
Giving Locations: NY: New York Metropolitan Area
Grant Types: General Support, Operating Expenses.

Financial Summary

Total Giving: $593,415 (1997); $427,087 (1996); $725,000 (1995). Note: Contributes through foundation only.
Giving Analysis: Giving for 1997 includes: foundation ($593,415)
Assets: $13,079,053 (1997); $12,976,610 (1996); $12,870,897 (1995)

Typical Recipients

Arts & Humanities: Arts Associations & Councils, Arts Centers, Ballet, Ethnic & Folk Arts, Historic Preservation, Museums/Galleries, Music, Opera, Performing Arts, Public Broadcasting, Theater
Civic & Public Affairs: Chambers of Commerce, Clubs, Community Foundations, Economic Development, Ethnic Organizations, Civic & Public Affairs-General, Hispanic Affairs, Parades/Festivals, Professional & Trade Associations, Public Policy, Safety
Education: Business Education, Colleges & Universities, Continuing Education, Education Associations, Education Funds, Gifted & Talented Programs, Legal Education, Minority Education, Private Education (Precollege), Secondary Education (Public), Special Education, Student Aid
Environment: Wildlife Protection
Health: Cancer, Eyes/Blindness, Health Organizations, Hospitals, Medical Research, Multiple Sclerosis, Single-Disease Health Associations, Trauma Treatment
International: Foreign Arts Organizations, International Organizations, International Relations, International Relief Efforts
Religion: Churches, Religious Organizations, Religious Welfare, Seminaries, Social/Policy Issues
Science: Scientific Organizations
Social Services: Child Welfare, Community Centers, Community Service Organizations, Family Services, Food/Clothing Distribution, People with Disabilities, Recreation & Athletics, Senior Services, Substance Abuse, United Funds/United Ways, Youth Organizations

Contributions Analysis

Arts & Humanities: 24%. A ballet company, the Smithsonian, and the Seattle Symphony Orchestra.
Civic & Public Affairs: 17% Professional associations.
Education: 37%. Colleges, universities, and specialty schools nationwide.
Health: 9%. Hospitals and disease research and prevention.
International: 1%. Recently gave to landmark preservation in Bermuda.
Religion: 6%. Supports churches and Christian and Jewish organizations.
Social Services: 6%. United Way, people with disabilities, and family services.
Note: Total contributions made in 1997.

Application Procedures

Deadlines: None.
Notes: The foundation does not have a specific application procedure or form.

Restrictions

Does not support dinners or special events, fraternal organizations, goodwill advertising, individuals, political or lobbying groups, or religious groups for sectarian purposes.

Corporate Officials

Harry F. Mariani: president, treasurer, director B 1937. ED Colgate University (1959). PRIM CORP EMPL president, treasurer, director: Banfi Products Corp.
John J. Mariani: chairman, chief executive officer, director B 1932. ED Cornell University (1954). PRIM CORP EMPL chairman, chief executive officer, director: Banfi Products Corp.

Foundation Officials

Phillip D. Calderone: treasurer
Harry F. Mariani: director (see above)
John J. Mariani: director (see above)
John G. Troiano: executive director

Grants Analysis

Disclosure Period: calendar year ending 1997
Total Grants: $593,415
Number of Grants: 150 (approx)
Average Grant: $4,000 (approx)
Highest Grant: $75,000
Typical Range: $500 to $5,000
Note: Grants analysis derived from 1997 partial grants list.

Recent Grants

Note: Grants derived from 1997 Form 990.

Arts & Humanities

62,500	WHYY, Philadelphia, PA
10,000	Seattle Symphony Orchestra, Seattle, WA
5,000	Italian American National Hall of Fame, Trenton, NJ
5,000	John and Mabel Kingling Museum of Art
1,500	Educational Television Association, Cleveland, OH
1,500	Nashville Symphony Guild, Nashville, TN
1,000	Sarasota Ballet, Sarasota, FL

Civic & Public Affairs

12,500	Federation of Italian American Organizations, Houston, TX
10,000	American Institute of Wine and Food, San Francisco, CA
10,000	American Institute of Wine and Food, San Francisco, CA
10,000	Aspen Foundation, Aspen, CO
6,500	American Institute of Wine and Food, San Francisco, CA
5,000	Cornell Society of Hotelmen Foundation, Ithaca, NY
4,000	Society of Wine Educators, East Longmeadow, MA
2,000	American Institute of Wine and Food, San Francisco, CA
1,200	Italian American Foundation
1,000	Anthony and Claire Pace Foundation
1,000	Dante Foundation of Nassau County, Uniondale, NY

Education

75,000	Colgate University, Hamilton, NY
10,000	Cornell Johnson School of Management
10,000	Pace University, White Plains, NY
5,000	Cardinal Mooney High School, Sarasota, FL
5,000	Colgate University, Hamilton, NY
5,000	Cornell School of Hotel Administration
5,000	Long Island Caddie Scholarship Fund, Wheatley Heights, NY
5,000	St. Martha's Catholic School
5,000	University Foundation
3,800	CMIIS Tuition Assistance Trust
1,950	University of Arizona Foundation, Tucson, AZ
1,250	Molloy College
1,000	Georgetown University, Washington, DC
1,000	St. Edward Confessor School
900	Wine Spectator California Scholarship Foundation, New York, NY

Health

25,000	Huntington Hospital Association, Huntington, NY
5,000	St. Francis Hospital Foundation, New York, NY
3,500	St. Francis Hospital Foundation, New York, NY
1,000	William Heiser Foundation for the Cure of Spinal Cord Injuries, Wantagh, NY

International

3,000	International Charitable Fund of Bermuda, New York, NY

Religion

15,000	St. Patrick's Church, Cleveland, OH
5,000	St. Patrick Church, Terre Haute, IN
1,000	Bishops Annual Appeal
700	National Conference of Christians and Jews

Social Services

10,000	Italian Community Center
5,000	Glenville Baker Boys and Girls Club
3,000	Classic Charities of Orange County
1,000	Assistance League of Newport Mesa, Costa Mesa, CA
900	Help for the Poor, Portland, OR
750	Food for the Poor, Pompano Beach, FL
750	Long Island Cares, West Brentwood, NY
700	Children's House

Bank Of America

★ Number 8 of Top 100 Corporate Givers

Company Contact

Charlotte, NC

Web: http://www.bankamerica.com

Company Description

Former Name: BankAmerica Corp. (1999).

Profit: US$5,165,000,000

Employees: 170,975

Fortune Rank: 11, per FORTUNE Magazine's list of 500 Largest U.S. Corporations (1999).

FF 11

SIC(s): 6021 National Commercial Banks, 6712 Bank Holding Companies.

Operating Locations

Australia: Absentia Nominees Pty. Ltd., Sydney; BA (Australia) Holdings, Sydney; BA Australia Ltd., Sydney; BA Investors Managment Ltd., Sydney; BA Leasing Ltd., Sydney; BA Nominees Ltd., Sydney; BA Securities Ltd., Sydney; BA Staff Super-Annuation Ltd., Sydney; Belgium: Bank of America National Trust & Savings Assn., Antwerpen, Anvers; Brazil: BankAmerica Representacao e Servicos Ltda., Sao Paulo; Canada: Bank of America Canada, Toronto; Bank of America Canada Leasing Corp., Toronto; Chile: Inversiones Financieras Sp Chile SA, Coquimbo; Continental International Finance Corp. Ltda., Santiago; Cayman Islands: BankAmerica Fund Management Ltd., George Town, Grand Cayman; Harbour Nominees Ltd., George Town, Grand Cayman; BankAmerica Insurance Co., Road Town, Grand Cayman; France: BA Futures SA, Paris, Ville-de-Paris; Germany: Bank of America National Trust & Savings Assn., Frankfurt, Hessen; Hong Kong: Bank of America (Asia) Ltd., Admiralty; Appold Japan Ltd. (AKA Hoare Govett Japan Ltd.), Central District; BankAmerica Nominees (Hong Kong) Ltd., Central District; BankAmerica Trust Co. (Hong Kong) Ltd., Central District; BATCO Nominees Ltd., Central District; Canton Pacific Fund Managers Ltd., Central District; Canton Pacific Systems Ltd., Central District; Continental Euro-Asia Finance Ltd., Central District; Continental Illinois Asia Ltd., Central District; Continental Illinois (Nominees) Ltd., Central District; Continental International Securities Ltd., Central District; Fiduciary Services Ltd., Central District; ITG Secretaries Ltd., Central District; Renfrew Services Ltd., Central District; Security Pacific Hong Kong Holdings Ltd., Central District; BA Asia Ltd., Quarry Bay; BA Finance (Hong Kong) Ltd., Wan Chai; BankAmerica Intl Trustee (BVI) Ltd., Wan Chai; Luxembourg: BA Holding Co. SA, Luxembourg; Mexico: Bank of America Mexico SA, Ciudad de Mexico; Netherlands: Bank of America National Trust & Savings Assn., Amsterdam, Noord-Holland; BankAmerica Overseas Finance Corp. NV, Willemstad, Noord-Brabant; Singapore: Bank of America Singapore Ltd., Singapore; BankAmerica Nominees (1993) Pte. Ltd., Singapore; Hoare Govett Securities (Singapore) Pte. Ltd., Singapore; Thailand: BA Finance & Securities (Thailand) Ltd., Bangkok; United Kingdom: Severn River Crossing Plc, Bristol, Avon; Shamrock Leasing Ltd., Bromley, Kent; Dartford River Crossing Ltd., Dartford, Kent; Skye Bridge Ltd., Edinburgh, Lothian; Bank of America (Jersey) Ltd., Jersey, Channel Islands; BankAmerica Properties (Jersey) Ltd., Jersey, Channel Islands; BankAmerica Trust Co. (Jersey) Ltd., Jersey, Channel Islands; BA Futures, London; BA Netting Ltd., London; BA Swallow Business Systems Ltd., London; Bank of America Intl Ltd., London; Bank of America National Trust & Savings Assn., London; Bank America Nominees Ltd., London; CINB Nominees (London) Ltd., London; Normtrace Ltd., London; Seattle-First National Bank, London; Securilease Ltd., London; Security Pacific Euro-Finance, London; Security Pacific Leasing Corp., London; SP Insurance Services, London; Swallow Business Systems Ltd., London; Trumpmove Ltd., London; Venezuela: Bamerinvest CA, Caracas

Nonmonetary Support

Value: $2,000,000 (1989); $2,000,000 (1988); $3,000,000 (1987)

Type: Cause-related Marketing & Promotion; Donated Equipment; Loaned Employees

Corporate Sponsorship

Type: Arts & cultural events; Festivals/fairs; Music & entertainment events; Pledge-a-thon

Bank of America Foundation

Giving Contact

Caroline O. Boitano, President & Executive Director
Bank of America Foundation
PO Box 37000
Dept. 3246
CA5-704-08-03
San Francisco, CA 94137
Phone: (415)953-3175
Fax: (415)622-3469
Web: http://www.bankofamerica.com/foundation

Description

EIN: 941670382

Organization Type: Corporate Foundation

Giving Locations: headquarters and operating communities, except in Washington State.

Grant Types: Capital, General Support, Project, Seed Money.

Giving Philosophy

'Since 1968, BankAmerica Foundation has built on the long tradition of service to the community which has always been a part of Bank of America's history. The foundation views its contributions as an investment in the community. Through its grants program, the foundation hopes to improve the quality of life, to address the needs of education, and to create an atmosphere which will result in a stronger and richer community.' *BankAmerica Foundation Guidelines*

Financial Summary

Total Giving: $100,000,000 (1999 approx); $91,500,000 (1998); $20,000,000 (1997). Note: Contributes through corporate direct giving program and foundation. 1996 Giving includes foundation ($18,633,872); domestic subsidiaries ($2,350,000).

Assets: $5,048,445 (1996); $3,023,670 (1995); $1,934,434 (1994)

Gifts Received: $20,174,021 (1996); $19,793,583 (1995); $11,228,449 (1994). Note: In 1994, gifts were received from BankAmerica Corp. and Seafirst Bank Matching Gifts Program.

Typical Recipients

Arts & Humanities: Arts Appreciation, Arts Associations & Councils, Arts Centers, Arts Festivals, Arts Funds, Arts Institutes, Ballet, Community Arts, Ethnic & Folk Arts, Historic Preservation, Libraries, Museums/Galleries, Music, Opera, Performing Arts, Public Broadcasting, Theater

Civic & Public Affairs: Asian American Affairs, Botanical Gardens/Parks, Business/Free Enterprise, Civil Rights, Community Foundations, Economic Development, Employment/Job Training, Hispanic Affairs, Housing, Legal Aid, Native American Affairs, Nonprofit Management, Professional & Trade Associations, Public Policy, Rural Affairs, Urban & Community Affairs, Women's Affairs, Zoos/Aquariums

Education: Afterschool/Enrichment Programs, Agricultural Education, Business Education, Colleges & Universities, Community & Junior Colleges, Economic Education, Education Funds, Education Reform, Elementary Education (Private), Engineering/Technological Education, Environmental Education, Faculty Development, Education-General, Health & Physical Education, International Exchange, International Studies, Leadership Training, Medical Education, Minority Education, Science/Mathematics Education, Student Aid

Environment: Environment-General, Resource Conservation

Health: Children's Health/Hospitals, Clinics/Medical Centers, Emergency/Ambulance Services, Health Organizations, Hospitals, Medical Research, Prenatal Health Issues

International: International Environmental Issues, International Relations

Science: Science Museums, Scientific Centers & Institutes

Social Services: Child Abuse, Child Welfare, Community Service Organizations, Family Services, Food/Clothing Distribution, People with Disabilities, Substance Abuse, United Funds/United Ways, YMCA/YWCA/YMHA/YWHA, Youth Organizations

Contributions Analysis

Giving Priorities: Education, community development, health and human services, and art and culture.

Arts & Humanities: 15% to 20%. Interests include music, arts centers, museums, public broadcasting, libraries, and theater.
Civic & Public Affairs: 28%. Supports community development and economic initiatives. Also funds housing corporations and women's affairs.
Education: 25%. Gives at the college and university level, as well as the elementary level. Major support goes to scholarship programs and public education. Other interests include economic, medical, and minority education, aswell as business/education partnerships.
Health: 29%. Primary distribution is through the United Way in operating locations. Also supports hospitals, youth and family service organizations, and various other health, community service, and social service organizations.

Application Procedures

Initial Contact: Send a brief letter of inquiry
Application Requirements: Information should include: purpose of funds sought; correct mailing address, name and phone number of contact person; amount requested; brief statement of mission; copy of IRS letter of designation; current list of board members with affiliations; operating budget and project budget if applicable; population and geographic area served; list of sources and amounts of other funding obtained, pledged or requested for this purpose; and financial information for the previous two years, with an audited financial statement, if available.
Deadlines: None.
Evaluative Criteria: Organizations must demonstrate fiscal and administrative stability, good management policies and practices, and the ability to produce a budget and organizational financial statement
Decision Notification: Decisions regarding funding requests are ongoing. All requests will be reviewed in a competitive process.

Restrictions

Generally not receptive to individuals, organizations without 501(c)(3) public charity status, memorial campaigns, fund-raising events, political activities, religious organizations for sectarian purposes, research, athletic events and programs, endowment campaigns, advertising, member agencies of united funds, book or film or video projects, public or private education (K-12), disease advocacy organizations, or organizations that discriminate on the basis of age, culture, race, gender, or sexual orientation.

Additional Information

In 1992, BankAmerica Corp. and BankAmerica Foundation acquired, respectively, Security Pacific Corp. and Security Pacific Foundation and related entities, Security Pacific Foundation Northwest and Security Pacific Bank Arizona Foundation. The foundations associated with Security Pacific completely dissolved; the giving program for BankAmerica Corp. and its subsidiaries continues to be contained completely within BankAmerica Foundation.
BankAmerica Corp. and NationsBank have merged to create Bank of America.
BankAmerica Corp. and NationsBank have merged to create Bank of America.

Corporate Officials

David A. Coulter: president, director (retired) B Pittsburgh, PA 1948. ED Carnegie Mellon University BS; Carnegie Mellon University MS (1971). PRIM CORP EMPL president, director: BankAmerica Corp. ADD CORP EMPL president: BankAmerica National Trust & Savings Association. CORP AFFIL director: Pacific Gas & Electric Co.; director: PG&E Corp.; member: Opportunity Capital Partners; chairman: Continental Illinois Venture Del; director: Local Initiatives Support Corp.; chairman: Bank American FSB. NONPR AFFIL director: San Francisco Art Institute; member: University California San Diego Graduate School International Relations; member: LP Advisory Comm; member: Pacific Studies Advisory Board; director: Institute International Finance Inc.; director: Joint Venture Silicon Valley Network Board; member: Bay Area Council.
Donald A. Mullane: executive vice president B Los Angeles, CA 1938. ED University of Southern California. PRIM CORP EMPL executive vice president: Bank of America. CLUB AFFIL City Bunker Hill Club; Hacienda Golf Club; Bankers San Francisco Club.
Richard Morris Rosenberg: chairman, chief executive officer (retired) B Fall River, MA 1930. ED Suffolk University BS (1952); Golden Gate University MBA (1963); Golden Gate College LLB (1966). PRIM CORP EMPL chairman, chief executive officer (retired): BankAmerica Corp. CORP AFFIL director: Potlatch Corp.; director: SBC Corp.; director: Airborne Freight Corp.; director: Northrop Grumman Corp. NONPR AFFIL director: San Francisco Symphony; director: United Way America; trustee: California Institute Technology. CLUB AFFIL Hillcrest Country Club; Rainier Club.

Foundation Officials

Caroline O. Boitano: president, executive director
Kathleen J. Burke: trustee B 1952. PRIM CORP EMPL vice chairman, personnel relations officer: BankAmerica Corp.
Sandra Cohen: secretary
William M. Goodyear: trustee B 1948. ED University of Notre Dame BA (1970); Dartmouth College MBA (1972). PRIM CORP EMPL chairman, chief executive officer, director: Bank of America-Illinois. CORP AFFIL director: Continental Illinois Venture Del.
Raymond M. McKee: trustee
Donald A. Mullane: chairman (see above)
Judy Tufo: finance officer
James Wagele: senior vice president

Grants Analysis

Disclosure Period: calendar year ending 1996
Total Grants: $18,633,872*
Number of Grants: 1,260*
Average Grant: $14,789
Highest Grant: $1,750,000
Typical Range: $1,000 to $25,000
***Note:** Giving includes foundation.

Recent Grants

Note: Grants derived from 1996 Form 990.

Arts & Humanities

100,000 Chicago Symphony Orchestra, Chicago, IL
100,000 Music Center of Los Angeles County, Los Angeles, CA
100,000 San Francisco Symphony Association, San Francisco, CA
75,000 National Trust for Historic Preservation, Washington, DC
50,000 American Conservatory Theater, San Francisco, CA
50,000 California Museum Foundation, Los Angeles, CA
50,000 KCET Community Television of Southern California, Los Angeles, CA
50,000 Library Foundation, San Francisco, CA
50,000 Oregon Public Broadcasting, Portland, OR
50,000 San Francisco Opera Association, San Francisco, CA

Civic & Public Affairs

335,000 Neighborhood Housing Services, Chicago, IL
100,000 Local Initiatives Support Corporation, San Francisco, CA
50,000 Housing Association for Napa Development, Napa, CA
50,000 Monterey Bay Aquarium, Monterey, CA
30,000 Humboldt Park Family and Community Development Council, Chicago, IL

Education

276,500 Citizens Scholarship Foundation of America Achievement Awards, St. Peter, MN
114,725 Citizens Scholarship Foundation of America, St. Peter, MN
100,000 University of San Francisco, San Francisco, CA
85,000 DePaul University, Chicago, IL
80,000 Independent Colleges of Southern California, Los Angeles, CA
54,315 Junior Achievement Southern Californian, Los Angeles, CA
50,000 University of California San Francisco, San Francisco, CA
50,000 University of Nevada Reno Foundation, Reno, NV
40,000 Los Angeles Educational Partnership, Los Angeles, CA

Environment

50,000 Greenlining Institute, San Francisco, CA

Health

100,000 City of Hope, Duarte, CA
50,000 American Red Cross San Diego Imperial Counties Chapter, San Diego, CA

International

50,000 Asia Foundation, San Francisco, CA
50,000 Asia Foundation, San Francisco, CA
50,000 Conservation International, Washington, DC
50,000 Conservation International, Washington, DC

Social Services

1,750,000 United Way Bay Area, San Francisco, CA
1,250,000 United Way, Los Angeles, CA
446,000 United Way Crusade of Mercy, Chicago, IL
285,000 Valley of the Sun United Way, Phoenix, AZ
250,000 United Way Orange County, Irvine, CA
155,000 United Way San Benito County, CA
140,000 United Way, Sacramento, CA
100,000 Friendly House, Portland, OR
81,300 United Way Columbia Willamette
70,000 United Way Southern Nevada, Las Vegas, NV
65,000 United Way, Dallas, TX
60,000 United Way, Tucson, AZ
60,000 United Way Santa Clara County, Santa Clara, CA
50,000 United Way, Fresno, CA
50,000 United Way, New York, NY
50,000 Valley of the Sun YMCA, Phoenix, AZ
47,000 Aloha United Way, Honolulu, HI
30,000 United Way Northern Nevada and the Sierra, Reno, NV
30,000 United Way Texas Gulf Coast, Houston, TX
30,000 Urban Gateways, Chicago, IL
30,000 YMCA, Los Angeles, CA

BANK OF NEW YORK CO., INC.

Company Contact

New York, NY
Web: http://www.bankofny.com/

Company Description

Revenue: US$5,793,000,000
Employees: 15,810
Fortune Rank: 251, per FORTUNE Magazine's list of 500 Largest U.S. Corporations (1999).
FF 251
SIC(s): 6022 State Commercial Banks, 6712 Bank Holding Companies.

Giving Contact

Pat Bicket, Vice President and Assistant Secretary
Bank of New York Co., Inc.
1 Wall St.
13th Floor
New York, NY 10286
Phone: (212)742-7039
Fax: (212)635-1799

Description

Organization Type: Corporate Giving Program
Giving Locations: DE; NJ; NY
Grant Types: Award, Capital, Conference/Seminar, Emergency, Employee Matching Gifts, Endowment, Fellowship, General Support, Multiyear/Continuing Support.
Note: Employee matching gift ratio: 1 to 1.

Financial Summary

Total Giving: $4,700,000 (1997 approx); $4,680,000 (1996 approx); $4,680,000 (1995 approx). Note: Contributes through corporate direct giving program only.

Typical Recipients

Arts & Humanities: Arts Appreciation, Arts Associations & Councils, Arts Centers, Historic Preservation, Libraries, Literary Arts, Museums/Galleries, Music, Opera, Performing Arts, Public Broadcasting
Civic & Public Affairs: Business/Free Enterprise, Civil Rights, Economic Development, Housing, Zoos/Aquariums
Education: Education Associations, Elementary Education (Private), Minority Education, Private Education (Precollege)
Environment: Environment-General
Health: Health Organizations, Hospitals, Nursing Services, Single-Disease Health Associations
Social Services: Child Welfare, Community Service Organizations, Family Services, Shelters/Homelessness, Substance Abuse, United Funds/United Ways, Volunteer Services, Youth Organizations

Contributions Analysis

Giving Priorities: Social welfare, education, arts and humanities, and civic groups.
Arts & Humanities: About 20%. Support goes to museums, culturalgroups, historic preservation and restoration, public broadcasting, libraries, and the performing arts.
Civic & Public Affairs: About 60%. Emphasis is on grants supporting housing, youth organizations, drug and alcohol abuse programs, and family and community services. Less than 5%. Emphasis on economic development, civil rights, business and free enterprise, international affairs, and national security.
Education: About 20%. Private educational institutions receive considerable funding through the company's matching gift program. Support also goes to educational associations, elementary, minority, and liberal arts education.
Health: Less than 5%. Especially supports hospitals, health organizations and nursing services.

Application Procedures

Initial Contact: letter with proposal attached
Application Requirements: goals and financial statement for organization and project; tax identification number
Deadlines: None, but prefers to receive proposals in the fall
Notes: Regional branches have discretionary budgets for contributions to local nonprofits. The headquarters office handles requests from statewide groups.

Restrictions

*Company does not support religious or political organizations or individuals.

Additional Information

Majority of recipients are organizations the company traditionally supports, though policy does not restrict first-time requests.

Corporate Officials

Alan Richard Griffith: vice chairman, chief executive officer, director B Mineola, NY 1941. ED Lafayette College BA (1964); City University of New York MBA (1971). PRIM CORP EMPL vice chairman: Bank of New York Co., Inc. CORP AFFIL vice chairman: Bank New York Co. Inc. NONPR AFFIL trustee: Chesapeake Bay Foundation; trustee: Lafayette College; trustee: Amyotrophic Lateral Sclerosis Association. CLUB AFFIL University Club New York; Marco Polo Club.
Thomas A. Renyi: president, chief executive officer, director B Passaic, NJ 1946. ED Rutgers University BA (1967); Rutgers University MBA (1968). PRIM CORP EMPL president, chief executive officer, director: Bank of New York Co., Inc. CORP AFFIL president, director: Bank New York Co. Inc.; chairman: BNY Mortgage Co. Inc.

Giving Program Officials

Pat Bicket: vice president, assistant secretary

Grants Analysis

Disclosure Period: calendar year ending
Typical Range: $1,000 to $10,000

Bank One Corp.

Company Contact

One First National Plaza
Chicago, IL 60670
Phone: (312)732-4000
Fax: (312)732-3366
Web: http://www.bankone.com

Company Description

Acquired: Premier Bank Lafayette.
Revenue: US$25,986,000,000 (1999)
Profit: US$3,479,000,000 (1999)
Employees: 7,500
Fortune Rank: 50, per FORTUNE Magazine's list of 500 Largest U.S. Corporations (1999).
FF 50
SIC(s): 6000 Depository Institutions, 6021 National Commercial Banks, 6700 Holding & Other Investment Offices.

Nonmonetary Support

Value: $1,300,000 (1990); $800,000 (1988); $1,400,000 (1987)
Type: Donated Equipment; In-kind Services; Loaned Executives

First National Bank of Chicago Foundation

Giving Contact

Diane M. Smith, Vice President
First National Bank of Chicago Foundation
1 First National Plaza, Suite 0356
Chicago, IL 60670
Phone: (312)732-6948
Fax: (312)732-2437

Description

EIN: 366033828
Organization Type: Corporate Foundation
Giving Locations: IL: Chicago
Grant Types: Capital, Employee Matching Gifts, Endowment, Fellowship, General Support, Operating Expenses, Project.

Giving Philosophy

'In making contributions, we seek to be a corporate leader in bettering the social, economic, and cultural lives of the people of Chicago, thereby serving as an exemplary corporate citizen and supporting the growth of the corporation.' *First Chicago Contributions*

Financial Summary

Total Giving: $3,180,992 (1998); $1,717,162 (1997); $2,213,046 (1996). Note: Contributes through foundation only.
Giving Analysis: Giving for 1996 includes: foundation grants to United Way ($1,320,000); foundation matching gifts ($422,436); 1997: foundation matching gifts ($167,999); 1998: foundation grants to United Way ($1,835,642); foundation program-related investments ($537,500); foundation matching gifts ($20,350)
Assets: $15,663,737 (1998); $11,441,186 (1997); $10,210,998 (1996)
Gifts Received: $7,099,993 (1998); $2,000,000 (1997). Note: The foundation receives contributions from First Chicago Equity Corp.

Typical Recipients

Arts & Humanities: Arts Centers, Arts Festivals, Arts Institutes, Community Arts, Dance, Ethnic & Folk Arts, Arts & Humanities-General, Historic Preservation, History & Archaeology, Libraries, Museums/Galleries, Music, Opera, Performing Arts, Public Broadcasting, Theater
Civic & Public Affairs: African American Affairs, Asian American Affairs, Botanical Gardens/Parks, Business/Free Enterprise, Civil Rights, Clubs, Economic Development, Hispanic Affairs, Housing, Law & Justice, Public Policy, Urban & Community Affairs, Zoos/Aquariums
Education: Arts/Humanities Education, Business Education, Colleges & Universities, Economic Education, Education Associations, Education Funds, Engineering/Technological Education, International Studies, Minority Education, Private Education (Precollege), Science/Mathematics Education
Environment: Environment-General
Health: Children's Health/Hospitals, Hospitals
Science: Observatories & Planetariums, Science Museums, Scientific Centers & Institutes
Social Services: At-Risk Youth, Child Welfare, Community Service Organizations, Family Services, People with Disabilities, United Funds/United Ways, YMCA/YWCA/YMHA/YWHA, Youth Organizations

Contributions Analysis

Giving Priorities: United way, community improvement, civics, higher education, and the arts.
Arts & Humanities: 9%. Contributes to a variety of arts organizations in the Chicago area, including music, theater, museums, and libraries.
Civic & Public Affairs: 5%. Supports civic organizations concerned with better government; economic and housing development; crime, justice, and law; environment and ecology; race and ethnic relations; and improvement of the public sector. Prefers to fund specific projects/programs and favors programs that promotes self-sufficiency. Also supports organizations that reinforce Chicago's reputation as a world class city and have active employee involvement.
Education: 14%. Education support is primarily disbursed through matching gifts and general support for colleges and universities.
Health: 3%. Supports hospitals and medical centers.
Science: 3%. Supports science museums, natural history museums, and planetariums.
Social Services: 65%. Major support to the United Way/Crusade of Mercy as principal means of addressing a broad variety of social welfare needs.
Note: Total contributions in 1998.

Application Procedures

Initial Contact: Send cover letter and proposal.

Application Requirements: Include goals and objectives of requesting organization, list of recent achievements, description of programs, list of board members and key personnel, background information on organization and specific project, purpose for which funds are sought, current budget and principal funding sources, recently audited financial statement or annual report, proof of tax-exempt status.

Deadlines: None.

Evaluative Criteria: Clear definition of goals and responsibilities; demonstration of effective organizational, programmatic, and financial objective setting and management; evidence of broad-based support; evidence that the service is a response to a valid need and is superior to existing competitors; documentation of past success or sound reasons to expect success in the future.

Restrictions

In general, the foundation does not support individuals; religious or fraternal organizations; preschool, elementary, or secondary schools; agencies receiving United Way/Crusade of Mercy funds; public agencies; multiyear operating pledges; or consecutive multiyear capital pledges.

Corporate Officials

David J. Vitale: vice chairman B Beverly, MA 1946. ED Harvard University (1968); University of Chicago (1976). PRIM CORP EMPL vice chairman: Bank One Corp. CORP AFFIL vice chairman, president: First National Bank Chicago; chairman: American National Bank; chairman: American National Bank Tr Chicago. NONPR AFFIL vice chairman: Glenwood School Boys.

Foundation Officials

Ilona M. Berry: secretary ED Bradley University (1977); University of Illinois (1980). PRIM CORP EMPL secretary, director: First Chicago Finance Corp. CORP AFFIL secretary: First Chicago Futures Inc.; secretary, director: First Chicago National Processing; secretary, director: First Capital Corp. Chicago.

Clark D. Burrus: vice president, director B Chicago, IL 1928. ED Roosevelt University BS (1954); Roosevelt University MPA (1972). PRIM CORP EMPL senior vice president: First Chicago NBD Corp. CORP AFFIL chairman: Chicago Transit Authority.

Diane M. Smith: vice president, director

Richard Lee Thomas: vice president B Marion, OH 1931. ED Kenyon College BA (1953); Harvard University MBA (1958). CORP AFFIL director: Sara Lee Corp.; director: Unicom Corp.; director: IMC Global Inc.; director: CNA Financial Corp.; director: First National Bank Chicago; director: Bank One Corp.

David J. Vitale: vice president, director (see above)

Grants Analysis

Disclosure Period: calendar year ending 1998
Total Grants: $787,500*
Number of Grants: 40
Average Grant: $19,688
Highest Grant: $100,000
Typical Range: $10,000 to $50,000
***Note:** Giving excludes United Way, matching gifts, and program-related investments.

Recent Grants

Note: Grants derived from 1998 Form 990.

Arts & Humanities

70,000	Chicago Theatre Group-Goodman Theatre, Chicago, IL
50,000	The Art Institute of Chicago, Chicago, IL
30,000	Ravinia Festival Association, Chicago, IL
25,000	Chicago Public Library Foundation, Chicago, IL
20,000	Chicago Children's Museum, Chicago, IL
20,000	Chicago Historical Society, Chicago, IL
20,000	Hubbard Street Dance Chicago, Chicago, IL
15,000	Mexican Fine Arts Center, Chicago, IL
12,500	Newberry Library, Chicago, IL
10,000	Wabash "Y" Renaissance Corporation, Chicago, IL
10,000	WBEZ Alliance, Inc., Chicago, IL
5,000	Old Town School of Folk Music, Chicago, IL

Civic & Public Affairs

100,000	Center for Neighborhood Technology, Chicago, IL
30,000	Linclon Park Zoological Society, Chicago, IL
15,000	Oriental Institute, Chicago, IL
10,000	The Commercial Club Foundation, Chicago, IL
10,000	Metropolitan Planning Council, Chicago, IL
5,000	El Valor, Chicago, IL

Education

125,000	University of Chicago, Chicago, IL
100,000	Northwestern University, Chicago, IL
50,000	De Paul University, Chicago, IL
40,000	Illinois Institute of Technology, Chicago, IL
40,000	Roosevelt University, Chicago, IL
20,000	Chicago Academy of Sciences, Chicago, IL
20,000	Glenwood School for Boys, Chicago, IL
20,000	Saint Xavier University, Chicago, IL
5,000	Harvard University, Cambridge, MA
5,000	Midtown Educational Foundation, Chicago, IL
5,000	Stanford University, Stanford, CA
5,000	Williams College, Williamstown, MA
2,728	Brown University, Brown, RI
2,622	Trinity College, Hartford, CT

Health

60,000	Core Foundation-Rush St. Luke's Hospital, Chicago, IL
30,000	Children's Memorial Medical Center, Chicago, IL
15,000	Northwestern Memorial Hospital, Chicago, IL

Science

50,000	The Field Museum, Chicago, IL
35,000	Museum of Science & Industry, Chicago, IL
20,000	The Adler Planetarium, Chicago, IL

Social Services

1,835,642	United Way/Crusade of Mercy, Chicago, IL
100,000	Big Shoulders Fund, Chicago, IL
80,000	YMCA of Metropolitan Chicago, Chicago, IL
15,000	Metropolitan Family Services, Portland, OR
12,500	Urban Gateways, Chicago, IL
10,000	Bethel New Life, Chicago, IL
10,000	The Children's Place Association, Chicago, IL
10,000	Lester and Rosalie Anixter Center, Chicago, IL

BANK ONE, TEXAS-HOUSTON OFFICE

Company Contact

Houston, TX

Company Description

Employees: 1,660
SIC(s): 6021 National Commercial Banks.
Parent Company: Bank One, Texas, NA, Fort Worth, TX, United States
Parent Revenue: US$10,272,000,000

Nonmonetary Support

Type: Donated Equipment; Donated Products

Corporate Sponsorship

Type: Other
Contact: Mary Gibbs, Vice President, Market Development/Public Relations
Note: Sponsors African American Business Achievement Awards (Pinnacle); The Spirit of Christmas.

Giving Contact

Teresa Hill, Charitable Contributions Coordinator
Bank One, Texas-Houston Office
910 Travis TX2-4240
Houston, TX 77002
Phone: (713)751-3526
Fax: (713)751-3870

Alternate Contact

Phone: (713)751-3501

Description

Organization Type: Corporate Giving Program
Giving Locations: TX: Houston
Grant Types: Capital, Employee Matching Gifts, General Support, Multiyear/Continuing Support.

Financial Summary

Total Giving: $737,000 (2000 approx); $737,000 (1999 approx); $635,000 (1998 approx). Note: Contributes through corporate direct giving program only.

Typical Recipients

Arts & Humanities: Arts Associations & Councils, Ethnic & Folk Arts, Arts & Humanities-General, Libraries, Museums/Galleries, Performing Arts, Public Broadcasting

Civic & Public Affairs: Business/Free Enterprise, Civil Rights, Economic Development, Civic & Public Affairs-General, Housing, Law & Justice, Municipalities/Towns, Urban & Community Affairs

Education: Colleges & Universities, Continuing Education, Elementary Education (Private), Education-General, Private Education (Precollege), Public Education (Precollege), Student Aid

Environment: Environment-General

Health: Health-General, Health Organizations, Hospitals, Medical Research

Social Services: Community Service Organizations, Social Services-General, Substance Abuse, United Funds/United Ways, Youth Organizations

Contributions Analysis

Arts & Humanities: About 15%. Contributes to performing arts programs, museums, public radio and television, and cultural programs.

Civic & Public Affairs: About 10%. Interests include business, voter registration and education, civil rights, justice and law, and non-academic research. About 10%. Supports programs and projects in the areas of community and neighborhood improvement, community development, housing and urban revitalization, community-based education, and economic development in low- to moderate-income neighborhoods.

Education: About 20%. Interests include primary and secondary schools, public and private higher education institutions, adult education programs, scholarship programs, public library systems, and other related organizations. Also operates employee matching gift program to educational institutions.

Environment: About 5%. Recipients include environmental conservation, energy conservation, visual pollution, air pollution, and recycling.

Health: About 40% of total contributions. Includes assistance to federated drives such as United Way;

hospitals; local health and welfare groups; health research organizations; and youth agencies. Also supports nonprofit drug abuse and rehabilitation programs in Houston, and a matching gift program for employee contributions to health and welfare organizations.

Application Procedures

Initial Contact: written proposal
Application Requirements: brief summary of organization, its activities and mission; current executive staff and board of directors; statement of the specific amount requested and purpose of the funds; copy of IRS 501(c)(3) statement; audited financial statements; and level of United Way funding and application of those funds
Deadlines: 15th of every month
Evaluative Criteria: evidence that the project, event, or program will address an important need in the community; maintain or improve key elements of Houston's cultural, educational, environmental, civic, or health services; does not duplicate existing program or project; has direct relevance to the bank's goals and objectives; has impact consistent with the proposed expenditure; and has demonstrated competence among those guiding or staffing the project, event, or program
Decision Notification: requests responded to within 60 days

Restrictions

Requests are not approved to support partisan political organizations, to fraternal organizations, to individuals, to hospitals' or other patient care institutions' operating funds, to any customer or supplier directly for general operating purposes, or for community services outside Houston's operating area.
Company only supports private, nonprofit, and tax-exempt organizations with certified 501(c)(3) status.

Additional Information

Bank One's other regional offices have budgets for corporate giving.
Publications: Community Relations and Contributions Policies; Guidelines

Grants Analysis

Disclosure Period: calendar year ending
Typical Range: $1,000 to $2,500

BANK ONE, TEXAS, NA

Company Contact

Fort Worth, TX
Web: http://www.bankoneonline.com

Company Description

Former Name: Team Bank Fort Worth Region.
SIC(s): 6021 National Commercial Banks, 6712 Bank Holding Companies.
Parent Company: Banc One Corp., Columbus, OH, United States

Nonmonetary Support

Type: Donated Products; Loaned Employees; Loaned Executives; Workplace Solicitation
Note: Workplace solicitation is limited to the United Way.
Note: Workplace Solicitation is limited to the United Way.

Corporate Sponsorship

Type: Arts & cultural events; Festivals/fairs

Giving Contact

Susan Stahl, Vice President, Community Affairs
Bank One, TX 1-2463
1717 Main St.
Dallas, TX 75201
Phone: (214)290-2249
Fax: (214)290-7979
Email: susan_stahl@mail.bankone.com

Description

Organization Type: Corporate Giving Program
Giving Locations: TX: Dallas
Grant Types: Capital, General Support, Matching, Multiyear/Continuing Support.

Financial Summary

Total Giving: Contributes through corporate direct giving program only.

Typical Recipients

Arts & Humanities: Arts & Humanities-General
Civic & Public Affairs: Civic & Public Affairs-General
Education: Colleges & Universities
Social Services: Social Services-General, United Funds/United Ways

Application Procedures

Initial Contact: Send a brief letter of inquiry.
Application Requirements: Include a description of organization, amount requested, purpose of funds sought, audited financial statement, and proof of tax-exempt status.
Deadlines: Requests for support should be received at least two months prior to the date of the event.
Decision Notification: Requests for funding are reviewed as they are received.
Notes: All requests for contributions must be made in writing.

Restrictions

Does not support individuals, religious organizations for sectarian purposes, political or lobbying groups, organizations outside operating areas, or operating or administration expenses.

Corporate Officials

Ty Miller: president PRIM CORP EMPL president: Bank One Texas.

Giving Program Officials

Susan Stahl: PRIM CORP EMPL vice president community affairs: Bank One Texas NA.

BANKATLANTIC BANCORP

Company Contact

Fort Lauderdale, FL

Company Description

Assets: US$3,700,000,000
Employees: 1,100
SIC(s): 6035 Federal Savings Institutions, 6712 Bank Holding Companies.

BankAtlantic Foundation

Giving Contact

Shelley Levan, Vice President
1750 East Sunrise Boulevard
Ft. Lauderdale, FL 33304-3013
Phone: (954)760-5458

Description

Founded: 1994
EIN: 650499150
Organization Type: Corporate Foundation
Giving Locations: FL: Southern Florida

Financial Summary

Total Giving: $300,000 (1999 approx); $282,900 (1998); $282,000 (1997)
Giving Analysis: Giving for 1998 includes: foundation grants to United Way ($10,000)
Assets: $1,007,791 (1998); $498,950 (1997); $364,972 (1994)
Gifts Received: $768,000 (1998); $891,766 (1997); $410,050 (1994). Note: In 1998, contributions were received from BankAtlantic.

Typical Recipients

Arts & Humanities: Arts Associations & Councils, Ballet, Dance, Film & Video, History & Archaeology, Libraries, Museums/Galleries, Music, Opera, Performing Arts, Public Broadcasting, Theater
Civic & Public Affairs: African American Affairs, Business/Free Enterprise, Civil Rights, Community Foundations, Economic Development, Civic & Public Affairs-General, Housing, Nonprofit Management, Urban & Community Affairs
Education: Arts/Humanities Education, Business Education, Business-School Partnerships, Colleges & Universities, Community & Junior Colleges, Economic Education, Education Reform, Legal Education, Minority Education
Health: Emergency/Ambulance Services
Science: Science Museums
Social Services: At-Risk Youth, Child Welfare, Child Welfare, Community Service Organizations, Day Care, Domestic Violence, Family Services, People with Disabilities, Scouts, Senior Services, Shelters/Homelessness, United Funds/United Ways, Volunteer Services, YMCA/YWCA/YMHA/YWHA, Youth Organizations

Contributions Analysis

Giving Priorities: Social services, art and culture, education, and civics.
Arts & Humanities: Supports fine arts, libraries, museums, and music.
Civic & Public Affairs: 19%. Supports urban/community affairs, housing, civil rights, and community foundations.
Education: 22%. Supports continuing studies, literacy programs, and higher education.
Environment: 1%.
Health: 3%. Supports prenatal health, children's health, and hearing & deaf services.
Science: 3%. Funds the South Florida Science Museum and the Museum of Discovery & Science.
Social Services: 29%. Supports child and youth services, United Way, elder care, and human services.
Note: Total contributions made in 1998.

Application Procedures

Initial Contact: Submit typewritten proposal on organization's letterhead. Include the name, address, telephone number, and a description of organization; name of the director; project description and proposed dates; proposed income and expense budgets; total amount requested; project director's name, address, and telephone number (if different); project location; proof of tax-exempt status; copy of charitable solicitation license; anticipated benefits of project; list of board members; and the signature of the executive director acknowledging application.
Deadlines: None.

Restrictions

Does not support social functions or sporting events, national health-related organizations, religious schools or organizations, capital or endowment campaigns, individuals, purchase of ads or tickets, or hospitals or medical research.

Additional Information

Support goes to education, human services, arts, civic organizations, public policy, economic development, and affordable housing.

Corporate Officials

Alan Levan: chairman, president, chief executive officer PRIM CORP EMPL chairman, president, chief executive officer: BankAtlantic Bancorp.

Foundation Officials

Alan Levan: president, trustee (see above)
Robin Reiter: treasurer, trustee PRIM CORP EMPL senior vice president: BankAtlantic Bancorp.
Mary Rutigliano: program officer
Lew Saricea: secretary, trustee

Grants Analysis

Disclosure Period: calendar year ending 1998
Total Grants: $272,900*
Number of Grants: 104*
Average Grant: $2,624*
Highest Grant: $25,000
Typical Range: $500 to $10,000
***Note:** Giving excludes United Way.

Recent Grants

Note: Grants derived from 1998 Form 990.

Arts & Humanities

10,000	Florida Philharmonic, Fort Lauderdale, FL
10,000	Miami City Ballet, Miami Beach, FL
8,000	Florida Grand Opera, Miami, FL
5,000	Broward Public Library Foundation, Inc., Fort Lauderdale, FL
3,500	Ballet Florida, West Palm Beach, FL
3,500	Caldwell Theatre Company, Boca Raton, FL
3,000	City Theatre, Coral Gables, FL
2,500	ArtServe, Fort Lauderdale, FL
2,500	Maximum Dance Company, Miami, FL
2,500	Miami Art Museum, Miami, FL
2,500	Museum of Art-Fort Lauderdale, Fort Lauderdale, FL
1,500	Broward Performing Arts Foundation, Inc., Fort Lauderdale, FL

Civic & Public Affairs

7,500	Greater Miami Local Initiatives Support Corporation, Miami, FL
5,000	Greater Miami Neighborhoods, Miami, FL
5,000	Urban League of Broward County, Fort Lauderdale, FL
3,000	Broward Community Foundation, Fort Lauderdale, FL
2,000	People Engaged in Active Community Efforts, Inc., West Palm Beach, FL
1,500	Migrant Association of South Florida, Inc., Boynton Beach, FL
1,500	The Urban League of Greater Miami, Miami, FL
1,500	Working Capital, Florida, Miami, FL

Education

25,000	South Florida Annenberg Challenge, Fort Lauderdale, FL
10,000	Broward Community College Foundation, Fort Lauderdale, FL
5,000	Florida Council on Economic Education, Tampa, FL
5,000	University of Miami School of Law, Coral Gables, FL
2,500	Barry University, Miami Shores, FL
2,500	Partners In Education, Fort Lauderdale, FL
2,500	United Negro College Fund, Coral Springs, FL
2,000	Center for Creative Education, West Palm Beach, FL
2,000	Junior Achievement of Palm Beach, Martin & Hendry Counties, Riviera Beach, FL
1,500	Communities In Schools of Palm Beach County, Inc., Lake Worth, FL
1,500	Junior Achievement of South Florida, Pompano Beach, FL

Health

2,500	American Red Cross-Broward Chapter, Fort Lauderdale, FL

Science

5,000	Museum of Discovery & Science, Fort Lauderdale, FL
2,500	South Florida Science Museum, West Palm Beach, FL

Social Services

20,000	Broward Partnership For The Homeless, Inc., Fort Lauderdale, FL
5,000	United Way of Dade County, Miami, FL
5,000	United Way of Dade-WAGES Coalition, Miami, FL
3,000	Children's Home Society/Coastal Division-Palm Beach County, West Palm Beach, FL
3,000	Elderly Interest Fund, Fort Lauderdale, FL
3,000	Girl Scouts of Broward County, Inc., Oakland Park, FL
3,000	Kids In Distress, Fort Lauderdale, FL
2,500	Greater Miami Progress Foundation, Miami, FL
2,500	The Hope Center, Miami, FL
2,500	Lighthouse of Broward County, Fort Lauderdale, FL
2,500	SOS Children's Village of Florida, Coconut Creek, FL
2,500	Women In Distress of Broward County, Fort Lauderdale, FL
2,000	ARC Broward, Sunrise, FL
2,000	Broward Coalition for the Homeless, Fort Lauderdale, FL
2,000	Carrfour Corporation, Miami, FL
2,000	Do The Right Thing, Inc., Miami, FL
2,000	YMCA of Broward County, Fort Lauderdale, FL
1,500	Child Care Resource & Referral, Inc., Deiray Beach, FL
1,500	The Making of a Champion Youth Program, North Miami, FL

BankBoston-Connecticut Region

Company Contact

Hartford, CT
Web: http://www.bankboston.com

Company Description

Former Name: Bank of Boston Connecticut; Bank of Boston; Connecticut Bancorp.
Assets: US$2,300,000,000
Employees: 1,400
Parent Company: BankBoston Corp., Boston, MA, United States

Nonmonetary Support

Value: $50,000 (1998)
Type: Donated Equipment; Donated Products; In-kind Services; Loaned Employees; Loaned Executives; Workplace Solicitation
Note: Company also provides space and technical assistance. Support for in-kind services ranges from $5,000 to $10,000 annually.

Corporate Sponsorship

Range: less than $400,000
Type: Arts & cultural events; Festivals/fairs; Music & entertainment events; Sports events
Contact: Phillip Margolis, Director, Corporate Relations

BankBoston Charitable Foundation

Giving Contact

Brooke Dorweiler Polley, Director Community Relations
BankBoston-Connecticut Region
100 Pearl Street
Hartford, CT 06103
Phone: (860)727-5204
Fax: (860)727-5444
Email: bpolley@bkb.com

Description

Organization Type: Corporate Foundation
Giving Locations: CT headquarters area only; operating locations.
Grant Types: Employee Matching Gifts, General Support, Project.

Financial Summary

Total Giving: $750,000 (2000 approx); $800,000 (1999 approx); $700,000 (1998 approx). Note: Contributes through corporate direct giving program and foundation.

Typical Recipients

Arts & Humanities: Arts & Humanities-General
Civic & Public Affairs: Employment/Job Training, Civic & Public Affairs-General, Housing
Education: Colleges & Universities, Continuing Education, Education Funds, Education-General, Literacy, Public Education (Precollege)
Environment: Environment-General
Health: Health-General, Hospitals, Public Health
Social Services: Food/Clothing Distribution, Shelters/Homelessness, Social Services-General, United Funds/United Ways, Volunteer Services

Contributions Analysis

Arts & Humanities: About 5%. Emphasis on arts service organizations that increase the impact of individual artists and arts organizations. Also supports organizations that bring affordable programs to the community.
Civic & Public Affairs: About 30%. Focus on improving neighborhoods, restoring or creating affordable housing, supporting entrepreneurship and small business development, consumer credit counseling, and volunteer involvement.
Education: About 30%. Supports public education through company's partnership school program.
Health: About 5%. Emphasis on delivery of health care services to the inner city. Support for hospitals directed to campaigns benefittingthe hospital as a whole.
Social Services: About 30%. Each year, the largest contribution is made to the United Way. Also supports programs helping people become independent,including employment, job training, food distribution, shelter assistance, and independent living assistance.

Application Procedures

Initial Contact: Call or write for guidelines, then send written request.
Application Requirements: Proposals will include a cover letter on organization's letterhead, including: amount requested, purpose of funds sought, name and telephone number of contact person, number of individuals to be served; proposal including: brief history and a description of organization, with mission and accomplishments; recently audited financial statement of most recent fiscal year; operating budgets for current year and proposed budget for next

year; project budget; list of corporations and foundations supporting project and amounts; IRS tax-determination letter; names and affiliations of board of directors; percentage of funding from the United Way; and report on last grant received from BankBoston.
Deadlines: None.
Review Process: Contributions is committee meets monthly.
Evaluative Criteria: Emphasis on programs which provide opportunities for involvement of banking expertise and employees; interest in programs that help individuals become productive citizens.
Decision Notification: Payouts are made quarterly.
Notes: Request from Connecticut organizations should be sent to the above address; requests from other New England organizations should be directed to Michele Courton Brown, Director, Corporate Contributions, Government & Community Affairs, BankBoston, 01-28-04, PO Box 2016, Boston, MA 02106-2016, (617)434-2171.

Restrictions

The company does not support individuals; religious, fraternal, political, or veterans' organizations; national organizations, including state and local chapters, excluding United Way; basic research projects; or travel expenses.

Additional Information

Requests also can be sent to offices in Boston, MA; Portland, ME; Providence, RI; and Burlington, VT. See BankBoston entry for more information.
Publications: Application Guidelines

Corporate Officials

R. Nelson Griebel: president, chief executive officer, director PRIM CORP EMPL president, chief executive officer, director: BankBoston-Connecticut Region. CORP AFFIL president, chief executive officer, director: Colonial Bancorp Inc.
Carol Heller: manager government affairs & community investments PRIM CORP EMPL manager government affairs & community investments: BankBoston-Connecticut Region.
Phil Margolis: manager external affairs PRIM CORP EMPL manager external affairs: BankBoston-Connecticut Region.
Bruce A. Wilson: senior vice president B 1941. ED Bryant College BS (1961-1965). PRIM CORP EMPL senior vice president: BankBoston-Connecticut Region. CORP AFFIL executive vice president, director: Colonial Bancorp Inc.

Foundation Officials

R. Nelson Griebel: vice chairman (see above)
Brooke Polley: senior communication relations specialist

BankBoston Corp.

 Number 72 of Top 100 Corporate Givers

Company Contact

Boston, MA
Web: http://www.bkb.com

Company Description

Formed by Merger of: Fleet Financial Group, Inc. (1999).
Revenue: US$75,700,000 (1999)
Employees: 25,000 (1999)

Operating Locations

France: Bureau Investissement Location Bilsa, Paris, Ville-de-Paris; Germany: Bank Boston NA Zweigniederlassung, Frankfurt am Main; Hong Kong: Bank of Boston Asia/Pacific Region Headquarters, Central District; Haiti: Bank of Boston, Port-au-Prince; Luxembourg: Bank of Boston SA, Luxembourg; Boston Overseas Holding SA, Luxembourg; Boston Overseas Holdings SA, Luxembourg; Mexico: Banco de Boston SA, Ciudad de Mexico; United Kingdom: SEV Holdings Ltd., Birmingham, West Midlands; STF Management Ltd., Birmingham, West Midlands; Sumit Equity Ventures Ltd., Birmingham, West Midlands; MJPAP (Syndications) Ltd., Bristol, Avon; Murray Johnstone Asset Management Ltd., Glasgow, Strathclyde; Murray Johnstone Holdings Ltd., Glasgow, Strathclyde; Murray Johnstone Investment Management Ltd., Glasgow, Strathclyde; Murray Johnstone Ltd., Glasgow, Strathclyde; Murray Johnstone Marketing Services Ltd., Glasgow, Strathclyde; Murray Johnstone (Poland) Ltd., Glasgow, Strathclyde; Murray Johnstone Private Equity Ltd., Glasgow, Strathclyde; Murray Johnstone Private Investors Ltd., Glasgow, Strathclyde; Murray Johnstone Unit Trust Management Ltd., Glasgow, Strathclyde; First National Bank of Boston (Guernsey) Ltd., Guernsey, Channel Islands; BancBoston Capital Ltd., London; Bank of Boston Money Markets Ltd., London; Bank of Boston NA, London; Firnabos Nominees Ltd., London; Murray Johnstone (General Partner) Ltd., London; Old Colony Nominees Ltd., London

Nonmonetary Support

Value: $860,000 (1995); $100,000 (1993); $1,500,000 (1990)
Type: Donated Equipment; In-kind Services; Loaned Executives
Note: Co. provides nonmonetary support, meeting space and technical support. In-kind contributions requests must be on letterhead stationary & sent to the Massachusetts office.

Corporate Sponsorship

Type: Arts & cultural events; Music & entertainment events
Contact: Daniel Salera, Director, Corp. Contributions & Community Service

BankBoston Charitable Foundation

Giving Contact

Ms. Michele Courton Brown, Director, Corporate Contributions
BankBoston Corp.
MS 01-28-05
PO Box 2016
Boston, MA 02106-2016
Phone: (617)434-2804
Fax: (617)434-8905

Description

EIN: 042748070
Organization Type: Corporate Foundation
Formed by Merger of: Fleet Bank (1999).
Formed by Merger of: BankBoston (1999).
Giving Locations: CT; MA; NH: Southern New Hampshire; RI
Grant Types: Employee Matching Gifts, General Support, Project.

Giving Philosophy

'The decisions we make to commit our charitable resources to communities are as hard and as thoughtful as the ones we make every day to commit our financial resources to customers. We especially seek, as we review the dozens of grant requests that arrive every week, to identify those where a major and multifaceted relationship is possible. We look for opportunities where our grant investment can make a difference, where an issue of key importance to us is involved, where we can act as a catalyst in creating a model, and where we can help an organization to take the next step in fulfilling its mandate, to grow and prosper and perhaps even become self-sustaining. In short, we seek to put our strength to work in the community in situations where we can have the most impact, just as we seek to put our financial strengths to work for our customers.' Ira Stepanian, Chairman and CEO, Bank Boston Corp.

Financial Summary

Total Giving: $11,000,000 (1998 approx); $8,622,097 (1997); $6,500,000 (1996 approx). Note: Contributes through corporate direct giving program and foundation.
Assets: $7,719,409 (1997); $4,427,504 (1995); $9,174,918 (1994)
Gifts Received: $2,892,756 (1997); $10,000,450 (1994). Note: Contributions are received from BankBoston.

Typical Recipients

Arts & Humanities: Arts Associations & Councils, Arts Institutes, Community Arts, Ethnic & Folk Arts, Arts & Humanities-General, Historic Preservation, History & Archaeology, Libraries, Museums/Galleries, Music, Performing Arts, Public Broadcasting, Theater, Visual Arts
Civic & Public Affairs: Botanical Gardens/Parks, Business/Free Enterprise, Chambers of Commerce, Economic Development, Employment/Job Training, Civic & Public Affairs-General, Hispanic Affairs, Housing, Municipalities/Towns, Philanthropic Organizations, Public Policy, Urban & Community Affairs, Women's Affairs
Education: Business Education, Colleges & Universities, Community & Junior Colleges, Engineering/Technological Education, Health & Physical Education, Literacy, Preschool Education, Private Education (Precollege), Public Education (Precollege), Vocational & Technical Education
Environment: Air/Water Quality, Environment-General, Resource Conservation
Health: AIDS/HIV, Cancer, Clinics/Medical Centers, Health Organizations, Hospitals, Long-Term Care, Public Health
International: Foreign Educational Institutions, International Development
Religion: Dioceses, Jewish Causes, Social/Policy Issues
Science: Science Museums
Social Services: Child Abuse, Child Welfare, Community Centers, Community Service Organizations, Family Services, Food/Clothing Distribution, People with Disabilities, Recreation & Athletics, Senior Services, Shelters/Homelessness, United Funds/United Ways, Volunteer Services, Youth Organizations

Contributions Analysis

Giving Priorities: Social services, education, civic groups, performing arts, and health care for the disadvantaged. International contributions follow general guidelines as domestic giving, although programs are independently administered. High priorities are education, community development, and community services. Contributions overseas are more than $1 million annually. No support through domestic program for internationally focused organizations.
Arts & Humanities: 10% to 15%. Supports performing arts organizations and institutions. Emphasis is on arts services, organizations, and museums that bring affordable programs to local communities.
Civic & Public Affairs: 30%. Support for economic development, community development, affordable housing programs, as well as some other services to low- and moderate-income communities. Specific interest in small business development and job creation programs.
Education: 10% to 15%. Major support to public education, particularly in Boston. Other interests include education funds and associations and pre-collegiate business education.

Health: 5%. Emphasis on delivery of health care services to underserved populations. Also provides ongoing support to urban community health centers and organizations that help families with health care planning and treatment.
Social Services: 25% to 30%. Majority of funding is awarded to the United Way. Other interests include youth services.

Application Procedures

Initial Contact: Call or write for guidelines, then send written proposal.
Application Requirements: Include cover letter on organization's letterhead, including amount requested, purpose of grant, and contact person and phone number; brief history and description of the organization, including purpose and accomplishments; current and proposed organizational budgets; sources and amounts of support for most recently completed year; total project budget (if request is for a project); recently audited financial statements; most recent Form 990; IRS determination letter of tax-exempt charitable status under section 501(c)(3) and proof that the organization is not a private foundation as defined in Section 509(a) of the IRS Code; names and affiliations of the Board of Directors; and a report on the last grant received from BankBoston.
Deadlines: Last business day in January, March, May, August, and October.
Review Process: Corporate Contribution Committee meets in February, April, June, September, and November to consider requests.
Evaluative Criteria: Focus on BankBoston's three priority giving areas: economic opportunity, public education, and services to youth; interested in helping communities help themselves become better places to live and work, supporting entrepreneurship and small business development, and increasing volunteer involvement in community life.
Notes: Massachusetts proposals should be sent to above address. Connecticut proposals should be sent to: Carol Heller, Manager, Public Affairs, BankBoston-CT, 100 Pearl Street, Hartford, CT 06103, (860) 727-5481. Rhode Island proposals should be sent to: Frederick C. Lohrum, Regional President, BankBoston, One BankBoston Plaza, Providence, RI 02903, (401)278-8508.

Restrictions

Does not support individuals, religious programs, fraternal organizations, political or lobbying groups, veterans' groups, national organizations, research projects, conferences, forums, benefits, goodwill advertising, or travel expenses.
Program support grants must be applied for yearly. Support of any program or project during one period is not a guarantee of continued support by BankBoston. Organizations may submit only one request for support of any kind during a calendar year. Organizations submitting proposals may not submit requests during the year for fundraising events, membership, conferences, and other special events to benefit their organizations. (Requests for in-kind contributions are an exception to this rule.)
Organizations that have been denied support must wait a full calendar year before submitting a new request.

Additional Information

BankBoston and Fleet Bank have merged to become FleetBank Financial. The company reports for now (according to web info. dated 1/1/2000) both companies are joined but separate.
Publications: Guidelines

Corporate Officials

Michele Courton Brown: director corporate contributions PRIM CORP EMPL director corporate contributions: Bank of Boston Corp.
Charles Kilvert Gifford: chairman, chief executive officer B Providence, RI 1942. ED Princeton University BA (1964). PRIM CORP EMPL chairman, chief executive officer: Bank of Boston Corp. CORP AFFIL director: Massachusetts Mutual Life Insurance Co.; director: WGBH; chief executive officer, president: First National Bank Boston; trustee: FleetBoston Financial Corp.; director: BEC Energy; director: Boston Edison Co.; president, director: Bank Boston NA; chairman: Baybanks Inc.; president: BancBoston Capital Corp. NONPR AFFIL director: Northwestern University; member, executive, committee: United Way; director: Boston Private Industries Council; director: Junior Achievement; member: Boston Chamber of Commerce; chairman: Boston Plan for Excellence in Public Schools.
Henrique deCampos Meirelles: president, chief operating officer

Foundation Officials

Michele Courton Brown: director (see above)
Charles Kilvert Gifford: trustee (see above)
Ira A. Jackson: trustee PRIM CORP EMPL executive director: Bankboston NA.
Susannah Swihart: trustee B 1956. CORP AFFIL director: BancBoston Ventures Inc.; chief financial officer: FleetBoston Financial Corp.

Grants Analysis

Disclosure Period: calendar year ending 1997
Total Grants: $8,622,097
Number of Grants: 1,745 (approx)
Average Grant: $4,941
Typical Range: $1,000 to $5,000 and $25,000 to $50,000

Recent Grants

Note: Grants derived from 1997 Form 990.

Arts & Humanities

6,400	Long Wharf, New Haven, CT
2,500	Boston Conservatory, Boston, MA

Civic & Public Affairs

50,000	Boston Enterprise Fund, Boston, MA
25,000	Community Economic Development
25,000	Massachusetts Association of Community Development, MA
20,000	Citizens Research, Hartford, CT
20,000	The Partnership, Boston, MA
10,000	Connecticut Small Business
5,120	Matching Gift Center
5,000	Hispanic Coalition of Waterbury, Waterbury, CT
5,000	Massachusetts Career Development
3,000	Urban Edge
2,500	Broad Park Development, Hartford, CT
2,500	N.O.W. Inc., New York, NY

Education

10,000	University of Massachusetts/Amherst, Amherst, MA
6,800	Community Prepatory School, Providence, RI
5,250	Boston Educational Development Foundation, Boston, MA
3,780	University of Massachusetts, Amherst, MA

Environment

5,035	The Nature Center for the Environment, Westport, CT
5,000	Boston Citywide Land Trust, Boston, MA
5,000	Boston Citywide Land Trust, Boston, MA
5,000	Save the Harbor, Boston, MA

Health

6,000	Dana-Farber Cancer Institute, Boston, MA
4,000	Marian Manor, Pittsburgh, PA

Religion

10,000	Christian Economic Coalition, Borchester, MA
10,000	Jewish Federation of Rhode Island, Providence, RI
5,000	Jewish Foundation

Social Services

366,667	United Way of New England
90,000	Community United Way
8,300	United Way of New Hampshire, NH
5,000	Executive Service Corps of New England, Boston, MA
2,500	Stand for Children, New York, NY

BANTA CORP.

Company Contact

Menasha, WI
Web: http://www.banta.com

Company Description

Profit: US$20,600,000
Employees: 6,100
SIC(s): 2732 Book Printing, 2752 Commercial Printing--Lithographic, 2759 Commercial Printing Nec, 7336 Commercial Art & Graphic Design.

Operating Locations

Includes division locations

Corporate Sponsorship

Type: Arts & cultural events; Music & entertainment events; Other; Sports events
Note: Sponsors the Arts Alliance Event, Chamber of Commerce Events (local chapter), and the Sweet Adelaines (music group).

Banta Corp. Foundation

Giving Contact

Gerald A. Henseler, President
Banta Corp. Foundation
225 Main St., Box 8003
Menasha, WI 54952-8003
Phone: (920)751-7777
Fax: (920)751-7790

Description

Founded: 1953
EIN: 396050779
Organization Type: Corporate Foundation
Giving Locations: WI operating locations.
Grant Types: Award, Capital, Employee Matching Gifts, General Support, Multiyear/Continuing Support.

Financial Summary

Total Giving: $300,000 (2000 approx); $300,000 (1999 approx); $355,642 (1998). Note: Contributes through corporate direct giving program and foundation.
Giving Analysis: Giving for 1997 includes: foundation ($295,671); foundation scholarships ($50,000); foundation matching gifts ($21,678); 1998: foundation ($336,450); foundation scholarships ($82,500); foundation matching gifts ($19,192)
Assets: $2,339 (1998); $2,143 (1997); $71,373 (1996)
Gifts Received: $358,200 (1998); $309,000 (1997); $244,500 (1996). Note: Contributions are received from the Banta Corp.

Typical Recipients

Arts & Humanities: Arts Centers, Arts & Humanities-General, History & Archaeology, Libraries, Museums/Galleries, Music, Performing Arts, Public Broadcasting, Theater, Visual Arts

Civic & Public Affairs: Botanical Gardens/Parks, Business/Free Enterprise, Chambers of Commerce, Economic Development, Civic & Public Affairs-General, Parades/Festivals, Urban & Community Affairs
Education: Arts/Humanities Education, Colleges & Universities, Education Funds, Engineering/Technological Education, Education-General, Gifted & Talented Programs, International Studies, Medical Education, Minority Education, Preschool Education, Science/Mathematics Education, Secondary Education (Private), Student Aid, Vocational & Technical Education
Environment: Resource Conservation
Health: AIDS/HIV, Cancer, Children's Health/Hospitals, Clinics/Medical Centers, Emergency/Ambulance Services, Heart, Hospitals, Nursing Services
Religion: Religious Organizations, Religious Welfare
Social Services: Child Welfare, Community Service Organizations, Counseling, Domestic Violence, Food/Clothing Distribution, People with Disabilities, Recreation & Athletics, Scouts, Substance Abuse, United Funds/United Ways, YMCA/YWCA/YMHA/YWHA, Youth Organizations

Contributions Analysis

Arts & Humanities: 9%. Supports performing arts, theater, libraries, public radio, children's museum, and the arts.
Civic & Public Affairs: 4%.
Education: 69%. Funds educational programs, scholarship programs, colleges, and universities.
Health: 4%. Funds the American Red Cross Disaster Relief, community clinics, medical centers, visiting nurse association, and children's hospitals.
Social Services: 14%. Supports Goodwill Industries, domestic abuse services, and youth services.
Note: Total contributions in 1998.

Application Procedures

Initial Contact: Send a brief letter of inquiry.
Application Requirements: Include a description of organization, amount requested, purpose of funds sought, recently audited financial statement, and proof of tax exempt status.
Deadlines: November 1.
Decision Notification: board meets twice annually, in the spring and fall

Corporate Officials

Donald D. Belcher: chairman, president, chief executive officer, director B Kansas City, MO 1938. ED Dartmouth College BA (1960); Stanford University MBA (1964). PRIM CORP EMPL chairman, president, chief executive officer, director: Banta Corp. CORP AFFIL chairman: Packaging Fulfillment Specialists; director: Hunt Manufacturing Co. NONPR AFFIL trustee: Lawrence University.
Gerald A. Henseler: executive vice president, chief financial officer, director B Marshfield, WI 1940. ED University of Wisconsin, Madison BS (1962). PRIM CORP EMPL executive vice president, chief financial officer, director: Banta Corp. CORP AFFIL director: First National Bancshares Corp.; vice president: Tidi Products Inc.; director: Banta Healthcare Products Inc.

Foundation Officials

Rosalie N. Barbera: vice president, director
Donald D. Belcher: vice president, director (see above)
Gerald A. Henseler: president (see above)
Margaret Banta Humleker: vice president, director
Henry G. Wells: vice president, director

Grants Analysis

Disclosure Period: calendar year ending 1998
Total Grants: $336,450*
Number of Grants: 80
Average Grant: $4,206
Highest Grant: $82,500
Typical Range: $1,000 to $15,000
***Note:** Giving excludes matching gifts; scholarships.

Recent Grants

Note: Grants derived from 1997 Form 990.

Arts & Humanities

5,000	Bergstrom-Mahler Campaign Fund
5,000	Gunston Hall Regents Fund, Lorton, VA
3,500	Fox Cities Children's Museum, Appleton, WI
3,500	Paine Art Center and Arboretum, Oshkosh, WI
3,500	Wisconsin Public Radio Association, Madison, WI
3,000	Fox Valley Symphony Orchestra, Menasha, WI
3,000	Milwaukee Graphic Arts Institute, Milwaukee, WI
2,500	Wisconsin History Foundation, Madison, WI
2,500	Wisconsin Library Association, Madison, WI
1,500	American Player's Theater
1,500	United Performing Arts Fund, Milwaukee, WI

Civic & Public Affairs

5,000	Grand Prix of Minnesota, MN
5,000	Quality Fox Cities
2,000	Future Neenah Development Corporation, Neenah, WI
1,000	Heritage Hill Foundation, Grand Rapids, MI

Education

50,000	Banta Scholarship Program, Menasha, WI
50,000	Lawrence University, Appleton, WI
18,000	St. Norbert College, Depere, WI
12,000	Wisconsin Foundation of Independent Colleges, Milwaukee, WI
10,000	St. Mary's Central High School
7,700	WMC Foundation, Madison, WI
7,500	Lawrence University, Appleton, WI
5,000	Lakeland College, Sheboygan, WI
5,000	Printing Industry of Minnesota Scholarships, St. Paul, MN
5,000	University of Wisconsin Fox Cities, Fox City, WI
4,500	National Scholarship Trust Fund, Pittsburgh, PA
4,345	University of Wisconsin Stout Advanced Technology Systems, Stout, WI
4,000	St. Norbert College, Depere, WI
3,000	Milwaukee School of Engineering, Milwaukee, WI
2,300	Fox Valley Technical College Foundation, Appleton, WI
2,000	United Negro College Fund, New York, NY
1,500	Lakeland College, Sheboygan, WI

Health

10,000	Visiting Nurse Association
6,000	Children's Hospital Foundation, Seattle, WA
5,000	American Red Cross Disaster Relief -- support for North Dakota flood
5,000	Give Kids the World, Washington, PA
3,000	Minneapolis Children's Medical Center, Minneapolis, MN
2,500	Fox Cities Community Clinic, Appleton, WI
1,500	Boston to New York AIDS Ride
1,500	Valley Visiting Nurse Association Health System
1,000	Appleton Medical Center Foundation, Appleton, WI
1,000	Make-A-Wish Foundation, Butler, WI

Social Services

20,000	Goodwill Industries of North Central Wisconsin, Menasha, WI
5,000	Hanley-Hazelden Foundation, West Palm Beach, FL
5,000	United Community Services, Orwell, OH
2,500	Boy Scouts of America Bay-Lakes Council
2,500	Fox River Area Girl Scout Council, Appleton, WI
2,500	Menasha Youth Sports, Menasha, WI
2,500	Regional Domestic Abuse Services, Neenah, WI
2,000	Rawhide Boys Ranch, New London, WI

BARCLAYS CAPITAL

Company Contact

Charlotte, NC
Web: http://www.barcap.com

Company Description

Former Name: Barclays American Corp.; Barclays Bank/Barclays Capital.
Employees: 1,225
SIC(s): 6021 National Commercial Banks, 6153 Short-Term Business Credit.
Parent Company: Barclays Bank Plc, 54 Lombard Street, London, England

Operating Locations

NC: Barclays Capital, Charlotte; NY: Barclays Capital, New York

Corporate Sponsorship

Range: $125,000 - $175,000 (1999)
Contact: Denise Brenner, Charitable Gifts Coordinator

Giving Contact

Linda Wynns, Associate Director, Corporate Communications
Barclays Capital
222 Broadway, 10th Floor
New York, NY 10038
Phone: (212)412-3825
Fax: (212)412-7300
Email: LindaWynns@barcap.com

Description

Organization Type: Corporate Giving Program. Supports preselected organizations only.
Former Name: Barclays Bank Foundation (1999).
Giving Locations: NY: New York
Grant Types: Employee Matching Gifts, General Support.

Financial Summary

Total Giving: $250,000 (2000 approx); $220,000 (1999 approx); $0 (1998)
Giving Analysis: Giving for 1996 includes: foundation matching gifts ($66,732); foundation grants to United Way ($5,000); 1997: foundation ($120,960); foundation matching gifts ($42,023)
Assets: $8,356 (1997); $181,645 (1994); $221,753 (1993). Note: Company assets for 1999 is approximately $413 billion.
Gifts Received: $220,000 (1999 approx); $285,000 (1994); $128,196 (1992)

Typical Recipients

Arts & Humanities: Arts Associations & Councils, Arts Centers, Ballet, Dance, Museums/Galleries, Music, Performing Arts, Theater
Civic & Public Affairs: Chambers of Commerce, Civil Rights, Clubs, Civic & Public Affairs-General, Housing, Public Policy, Urban & Community Affairs, Women's Affairs, Zoos/Aquariums
Education: Arts/Humanities Education, Business Education, Colleges & Universities, Community & Junior

Colleges, Economic Education, Elementary Education (Private), Literacy, Minority Education, Student Aid
Health: AIDS/HIV, Cancer, Children's Health/Hospitals, Diabetes, Hospices, Hospitals, Medical Research, Single-Disease Health Associations
International: International Organizations, International Relief Efforts
Religion: Jewish Causes, Ministries, Religious Welfare, Synagogues/Temples
Social Services: Animal Protection, Child Welfare, Community Service Organizations, Family Services, Food/Clothing Distribution, Homes, Scouts, Special Olympics, United Funds/United Ways, YMCA/YWCA/YMHA/YWHA, Youth Organizations

Contributions Analysis

Giving Priorities: Major emphasis on education and the arts.
Arts & Humanities: 33%. Donates to performing arts.
Civic & Public Affairs: 7%. Focuses on improving the community through local community organizations, and neighborhood sports teams.
Education: 42%. Primarily supports through matching gifts. Also donates to universities, specialized art schools and Junior Achievement.
Health: 11%. Funds the Amyotropic Lateral Sclerosis Association, other disease-specific groups, and hospitals.
Religion: 2%. Primarily funds Jewish causes.
Social Services: 5%. Majority of support goes to family services and youth organizations.
Note: Total contributions in 1997.

Restrictions

Applicants must be within the tristate New York area or within areas of corporate offices outside New York.

Additional Information

In 1999, Barclays Bank Foundation was dissolved. The company now has a direct giving program.

Corporate Officials

Thomas Kalaris: chief executive americas PRIM CORP EMPL chief executive americas: Barclays Bank/Barclays Capital.
Graham McGahen: credit risk manager PRIM CORP EMPL credit risk manager: Barclays Bank/Barclays Capital.
Michael Prior: managing director

Foundation Officials

Graham McGahen: director (see above)

Grants Analysis

Disclosure Period: calendar year ending 1997
Total Grants: $120,960*
Number of Grants: 21
Average Grant: $3,548*
Highest Grant: $50,000
Typical Range: $500 to $15,000
***Note:** Giving excludes matching gifts. Average grant figure excludes highest grant.

Recent Grants

Note: Grants derived from 1997 Form 990.

Arts & Humanities

30,000	Circle in the Square Theater, New York, NY
10,000	Kennedy Center for the Performing Arts, Washington, DC

Civic & Public Affairs

5,000	The Point/The Heroes Foundation
1,750	Junior Fortnightly Club, Summit, NJ
1,000	Odyssey Foundation, New York, NY
1,000	OICW, Menlo Park, CA

Education

50,000	Union Settlement Association, New York, NY
500	A Better Chance, Boston, MA

Health

5,000	AIDS Walk, New York, NY
3,760	Leukemia Society of America, New York, NY
2,000	ALS Association, New York, NY
1,000	New York Downtown Hospital, New York, NY
1,000	T.J. Martell Foundation, New York, NY
500	Breast Cancer Resource Center Race for the Cure, Princeton, NJ
200	American Diabetes Association, Washington, DC

Religion

1,000	National Conference of Synagogues, Teaneck, NJ
500	St. George's Society, New York, NY
500	Wall Street Synagogue, New York, NY

Social Services

5,000	American Public Welfare Association, Washington, DC
1,000	Directions for Our Youth, New York, NY
250	YWCA, Summit, NJ

C.R. Bard, Inc.

Company Contact

Murray Hill, NJ
Web: http://www.crbard.com

Company Description

Employees: 7,700
SIC(s): 3841 Surgical & Medical Instruments, 3842 Surgical Appliances & Supplies, 3845 Electromedical Equipment, 5047 Medical & Hospital Equipment.

Operating Locations

Canada: Bard Canada, Mississauga; Vascath, Mississauga; Italy: Bard SpA, Roma, Lazio; Japan: Medicon, Osaka; Bard Japan Co. Ltd., Tokyo; Malaysia: Bard Sdn. Bhd., Kulim, Kedah; United Kingdom: Davol International Ltd., Clacton-On-Sea, East Sussex; Bard Holdings Ltd., Crawley, West Sussex; Bard Ltd., Crawley, West Sussex

Nonmonetary Support

Value: $1,873,252 (1996); $1,850,000 (1993)
Type: Donated Products
Contact: George N. Thayer, Corp. Tax Manager
Note: Products are donated to disaster relief and humanitarian aid organizations worldwide.

C.R. Bard Foundation

Giving Contact

Ms. Linda A. Hrevnack, Manager, Community Affairs & Contributions
Bard Foundation
730 Central Ave.
Murray Hill, NJ 07974
Phone: (908)277-8182
Fax: (908)277-8098

Description

Founded: 1988
EIN: 222840708
Organization Type: Corporate Foundation
Giving Locations: headquarters and operating communities.
Grant Types: Employee Matching Gifts, General Support.
Note: Employee matching gift ratio: 1 to 1 to arts and culture, education, health-care, the United Way, and social welfare organization, up to $25,000 annually per employee, or up to $5,000 annually per director.Grants are also made for programs.

Giving Philosophy

'C.R. Bard, Inc., a leading multinational developer, manufacturer and marketer of technologically-advanced health care products, is committed to its role as a responsible corporate citizen. This commitment is the basis of the Company's relationship with customers, employees, and the communities in which they live and work.'
'The Company has therefore established the C.R. Bard Foundation, Inc., which supports a corporate contributions program that provides financial support to organizations in which societal needs coincide with corporate interests.' *C. R. Bard Foundation Corporate Giving Guidelines*

Financial Summary

Total Giving: $1,054,645 (1998); $2,621,337 (1997); $846,041 (1996). Note: Contributes through corporate direct giving program and foundation. 1997 Giving includes corporate direct giving ($227,597); foundation ($520,488); nonmonetary support. 1996 Giving includes foundation. 1995 Giving includes corporate direct giving ($187,062); foundation ($478,508); matching gifts ($226,335).
Giving Analysis: Giving for 1998 includes: foundation ($677,898); corporate direct giving ($376,747)
Assets: $1,147,377 (1998); $1,752,876 (1997); $1,374,060 (1996)
Gifts Received: $1,005,012 (1997); $7,000 (1993). Note: Foundation receives gifts from C.R. Bard, Inc.

Typical Recipients

Arts & Humanities: Museums/Galleries, Music, Performing Arts, Public Broadcasting, Theater, Visual Arts
Civic & Public Affairs: Community Foundations, Employment/Job Training, Civic & Public Affairs-General, Hispanic Affairs, Housing, Municipalities/Towns, Philanthropic Organizations, Safety, Urban & Community Affairs
Education: Colleges & Universities, Economic Education, Education Funds, Elementary Education (Private), Education-General, Gifted & Talented Programs, Leadership Training, Medical Education, Minority Education, Private Education (Precollege), Special Education, Student Aid
Health: AIDS/HIV, Cancer, Children's Health/Hospitals, Clinics/Medical Centers, Emergency/Ambulance Services, Health-General, Geriatric Health, Health Funds, Health Organizations, Heart, Hospices, Hospitals, Hospitals (University Affiliated), Medical Rehabilitation, Medical Research, Preventive Medicine/Wellness Organizations, Public Health, Single-Disease Health Associations, Speech & Hearing
International: Health Care/Hospitals, Human Rights, International Affairs, International Relief Efforts
Religion: Religious Welfare
Science: Scientific Centers & Institutes
Social Services: Community Service Organizations, Domestic Violence, Family Services, Recreation & Athletics, Scouts, Special Olympics, Substance Abuse, United Funds/United Ways, YMCA/YWCA/YMHA/YWHA, Youth Organizations

Contributions Analysis

Giving Priorities: Company supports disaster relief efforts and Co-Operation Ireland. Support is estimated at $100,000 to $150,000 annually. Supports a variety of causes, including minority and business organizations and philanthropic organizations. Consideration is given to organizations where employees are active volunteers.
Arts & Humanities: 6%. Funds public television, music, museums, arts education, and local civic, recreational, and youth organizations.
Civic & Public Affairs: 4%.
Education: 30%. Emphasis is on colleges, universities, and independent college funds. Focus on medical education and research, and programs which benefit the health-care industry.

Health: 33%. Majority of funding supports health-related united funds. Primarily supports programs specializing in cardiology, urology, and oncology. Other interests include health care associations, hospitals, and emergency services.
International: 6%.
Religion: Less than 1%.
Science: Less than 1%.
Social Services: 21%. Supports United Way, Boys and Girls Clubs, and Special Olympics.

Application Procedures

Initial Contact: written proposal
Application Requirements: name, address, history, and mission of organization; the amount requested including the purpose for which funds are sought; a copy of the organization's operating budget; a copy of its most recent audited financial statement; a list of the organization's directors; a copy of the organization's IRS document confirming its tax-exempt status; and a statement indicating degree of support received from the United Way
Deadlines: None.
Decision Notification: contributions committee meets quarterly; applicants informed of the status of their requests after each meeting

Restrictions

Does not contribute to individuals, capital campaigns, private foundations, political parties, fraternal groups, religious groups, or sectarian or veterans' organizations.
Also does not fund organizations which receive major support from the United Way or similar programs.

Corporate Officials

Hope Greenfield: vice president human resourceso, director B 1951. PRIM CORP EMPL vice president human resources: C.R. Bard, Inc.
William H. Longfield: chairman, chief executive officer, director B Chicago, IL 1938. ED Drake University BS (1960); Northwestern University MS (1972). PRIM CORP EMPL chairman, chief executive officer, director: C.R. Bard, Inc. CORP AFFIL director: West Co. Inc.; director: Horizon Health Corp.; director: United Dental Care Inc.; director: Atlantic Health System; director: HCR Manor Care Inc. NONPR AFFIL director: Centerary College; director: Health Industry Manufacturers Association. CLUB AFFIL Metedeconk Country Club; Baltusrol Golf Club; Echo Lake Country Club.

Giving Program Officials

Linda A. Hrevnack: manager community affairs & contributions

Foundation Officials

Donna Dennis: secretary
William H. Longfield: president (see above)
James Natale: vice president PRIM CORP EMPL vice president, healthcare services: C. R. Bard, Inc.

Grants Analysis

Disclosure Period: calendar year ending 1998
Total Grants: $1,054,645
Number of Grants: 184
Average Grant: $4,717
Highest Grant: $100,000
Typical Range: $1,000 to $10,000
Note: Grants analysis provided by foundation.

Recent Grants

Note: Grants derived from 1997 Form 990.

Arts & Humanities

20,000	New Jersey Performing Arts Center, Newark, NJ
10,000	Newark Symphony Orchestra, Newark, NJ
5,000	National Plastics Center and Museum, Leominster, MA

Civic & Public Affairs

14,863	Henry H. Kessler Foundation, Inc., West Orange, NJ
5,900	SAGE, Inc., Summit, NJ
3,000	New Jersey Network, NJ

Education

100,000	University of Texas Houston, Houston, TX
12,500	Independent College Fund of New Jersey, Summit, NJ
10,000	Allentown College of Saint Francis De Sales, Allentown, PA
10,000	Foundation of the University of Medicine and Dentistry of New Jersey, Newark, NJ
10,000	Independent College Fund of New Jersey, Summit, NJ
10,000	The Washington Center, Washington, DC
7,500	West of Ireland Education Fund, New York, NY
6,000	Carmen School, Las Piedras, PR
5,000	New England Colleges Fund, Woburn, MA
5,000	New Jersey SEEDS, Rightstown, NJ
5,000	Oxford College at Emory University, Oxford, GA
2,500	Lake Educational Assistance Foundation, Menton, OH

Health

26,000	National Association For Continence, Spartanburg, SC
25,000	Cardiovascular and Interventional Radiology Research and Education Foundation, Fairfax, VA
25,000	Children's Specialized Hospital Foundation, Mountainside, NJ
24,200	American Foundation for Urologic Disease, Baltimore, MD
13,375	Summit Speech School, New Providence, NJ
10,000	Healing Hands Inc, Conyers, GA
10,000	Overlook Hospital Foundation, Summit, NJ
10,000	Robert E. Wise Research & Education Institute, Burlington, MA
10,000	Society for the Advancement of Women's Health Research, Washington, DC
8,000	Cystic Fibrosis Foundation Northeastern New York Chapter, Albany, NY
5,528	Combined Health Appeal of New Jersey, Spotswood, NJ
5,000	Glens Falls Hospital, Glens Falls, NY
5,000	Morristown Memorial Health Foundation, Morristown, NJ
5,000	St. Joseph Health Services of Rhode Island Robert P. Garni Fund for Family Medicine, North Providence, RI
4,000	Camp Sunshine, Casco, ME
3,000	Consolidated Products & Services, Inc, Braintree, MA
2,500	Cottonwood Inc, Lawrence, KS
2,500	Fisher House, Inc, Lackland, TX
2,500	March of Dimes Birth Defects Foundation Greater Utah Chapter, Salt Lake City, UT
2,500	Primary Children's Medical Center Foundation, Salt Lake City, UT
2,500	Rhode Island Hospital Foundation, Providence, RI

International

25,000	Worldwide Fund for Mothers Injured in Childbirth, Chicago, IL
10,000	Project Hope, Bethesda, MD
5,000	Freedom House, Glen Gardner, NJ

Religion

2,500	Shepherd's Gate Hospice, Inc., Covington, GA

Science

2,500	Science Center, Jersey City

Social Services

29,075	United Way of Southeastern New England, Providence, RI
23,774	United Way of Union County, Elizabeth, NJ
21,433	Fondos Unidos De Puerto Rico, San Juan, PR
17,197	Covington-Newton County United Fund, Covington, GA
15,117	United Way of Douglas County, Lawrence, KS
11,476	Tri-County United Way, Inc., Queensbury, NY
6,407	United Way of The Great Salt Lake Area, Salt Lake City, UT
2,500	Boys and Girls Club of Greater Billerica, Billerica, MA
2,500	New Jersey Special Olympics, Princeton, NJ

BARDEN CORP.

Company Contact

Danbury, CT

Company Description

Employees: 850
SIC(s): 3469 Metal Stampings Nec, 3562 Ball & Roller Bearings, 3568 Power Transmission Equipment Nec.

Barden Foundation, Inc.

Giving Contact

Thomas F. Loughman, Treasurer & Trustee
Barden Foundation, Inc.
1146 Barnum Avenue
Bridgeport, CT 06610
Phone: (203)336-0121
Fax: (203)336-6440

Alternate Contact

Scholarship Committe
Barden Foundation, Inc.
200 Park Ave.
Danbury, CT 06810
Phone: (203)744-2211
Note: Application address for scholarship requests.

Description

Founded: 1959
EIN: 066054855
Organization Type: Corporate Foundation
Giving Locations: CT: Bridgeport, Danbury, Winsted
Grant Types: General Support, Scholarship.

Financial Summary

Total Giving: $425,625 (fiscal year ending October 31, 1998); $486,685 (fiscal 1996); $440,550 (fiscal 1995). Note: Contributes through foundation only.
Giving Analysis: Giving for fiscal 1996 includes: foundation grants to United Way ($290,000); foundation ($169,685); foundation scholarships ($27,000); fiscal 1998: foundation ($267,125); foundation grants to United Way ($133,500); foundation scholarships ($25,000)
Assets: $7,060,517 (fiscal 1998); $6,256,186 (fiscal 1996); $5,724,841 (fiscal 1995)
Gifts Received: $8,000 (fiscal 1992); $8,877 (fiscal 1991); $81,000 (fiscal 1989). Note: Contributions were received from the Barden Corp.

Typical Recipients

Arts & Humanities: Arts Centers, Museums/Galleries, Music, Theater

Civic & Public Affairs: African American Affairs, Civil Rights, Clubs, Civic & Public Affairs-General, Municipalities/Towns, Parades/Festivals, Safety, Urban & Community Affairs, Zoos/Aquariums
Education: Business Education, Colleges & Universities, Community & Junior Colleges, Education Funds, Engineering/Technological Education, Education-General, Private Education (Precollege), Public Education (Precollege), Student Aid, Vocational & Technical Education
Health: Cancer, Children's Health/Hospitals, Emergency/Ambulance Services, Health Organizations, Hospices, Hospitals, Medical Rehabilitation, Nursing Services, Single-Disease Health Associations
Religion: Religious Organizations, Religious Welfare
Science: Science Exhibits & Fairs, Science Museums, Scientific Organizations
Social Services: Child Welfare, Community Centers, Community Service Organizations, Day Care, Emergency Relief, Family Services, People with Disabilities, Recreation & Athletics, Scouts, Special Olympics, United Funds/United Ways, Volunteer Services, YMCA/YWCA/YMHA/YWHA, Youth Organizations

Contributions Analysis

Arts & Humanities: 4%.
Civic & Public Affairs: 1%.
Education: 8%. Funding goes to science education, public education in the headquarters area, and scholarships.
Health: 41%. Supports national health agencies, hospitals and nursing homes, and local health organizations.
Religion: 2%.
Social Services: 44%. Funds the United Way, youth agencies, and local social welfare organizations.
Note: Total contributions in fiscal 1998.

Application Procedures

Initial Contact: Send a letter of request for grants; request an application for scholarships.
Application Requirements: Include a description of organization, goals and requirements, amount requested, purpose of grant, recent financial statement, and copy of IRS determination letter.
Deadlines: By December for grant award in following year; April 1 for scholarships.
Decision Notification: Trustees meet in February.

Restrictions

Most scholarships are restricted to children of employees of the Barden Corp.
Organizations must be tax-exempt charities.

Additional Information

Publications: Informational Brochure

Corporate Officials

John Emling: vice president B 1956. ED Saint Bonaventure University BBA Marketing. PRIM CORP EMPL vice president: Barden Corp.

Foundation Officials

Robert M. Davis: trustee
John Emling: trustee (see above)
Thomas F. Loughman: treasurer, trustee
Robert P. Moore: trustee B 1924. CORP AFFIL president: Lacey Manufacturing Co. Division.
Stanley Noss: trustee

Grants Analysis

Disclosure Period: fiscal year ending October 31, 1998
Total Grants: $169,685*
Number of Grants: 48
Average Grant: $5,565
Highest Grant: $65,500
Typical Range: $1,000 to $15,000
***Note:** Giving excludes scholarship; United Way.

Recent Grants

Note: Grants derived from 1999 Form 990.

Arts & Humanities

2,000	Discovery Museum, Bridgeport, CT
2,000	Downtown Cabaret Theatre, Bridgeport, CT
1,000	Barnum Museum, Bridgeport, CT
999	Charles Ives Center for the Arts, Dabury, CT
500	The Greater Brideport Symphony Youth Orchestras, Fairfield, CT
500	Scott-Fanton Museum, Danbury, CT

Civic & Public Affairs

2,000	Ct Zoologial Society, Bridgeport, CT
500	Water Witch Hose Co. No. 2, Bridgeport, CT
125	The Hundred Club Of Connecticut, Glastonbury, CT

Education

3,000	Junior Achievement of Western Connecticut, Inc., Bridgeport, CT
3,000	Mercy Learning Center, Bridgeport, CT
2,000	Bridgeport Public Education Fund, Bridgeport, CT
1,000	Danbury Public Schools and Business Collaborative, Danbury, CT

Health

37,500	Bridgeport Hospital, Bridgeport, CT
37,500	Danbury Hospital Development Fund, Inc., Danbury, CT
30,000	Datahr, Brookfield, CT
12,500	M C C A, Danbury, CT
10,000	Charlotte Hungerford Hospital, Torrington, CT
10,000	The Regional Hospice of Western Connecticut, Danbury, CT
9,000	New Milford Hospital, New Milford, CT
7,000	Hanahoe Children's Clinic, Danbury, CT
5,000	American Cancer Society - Bridgeport, Westport, CT
5,000	American Cancer Society - Danbury, Danbury, CT
4,000	Connecticut Hospice, Branford, CT
4,000	Make-A-Wish Foundation of Connecticut, Inc., Trumbull, CT
3,000	Connecticut Childrens Hospital, Newington, CT
2,000	Winsted Volunteer Ambulance Service, Winsted, CT
1,000	Foothills Visiting Nurse Service, Winsted, CT
1,000	Visiting Nurse Services of Connecticut, Inc., Bridgeport, CT

Religion

8,000	Pope John Paul II Foundation, Danbury, CT
1,000	Cardinal Shehan Center, Bridgeport, CT

Social Services

75,000	United Way of Northern Fairfield County, Danbury, CT
31,000	United Way of Northwest Connecticut, Inc., Winsted, CT
27,500	United Way of Eastern Fairfield County, Bridgeport, CT
12,500	Regional Y M C A of Western Connecticut, Danbury, CT
9,000	Girl Scout Council of Southwestern Connecticut, Inc., Wilton, CT
7,000	Winsted Area Public Day Care, Inc., Winsted, CT
6,000	American Red Cross - Fairfied County, Westport, CT
5,000	Danbury Rotary Trust, Danbury, CT
3,000	Child Guidance Center of Bridgeport, Bridgeport, CT
3,000	McGiveney Community Center, Bridgeport, CT
3,000	Prime Time House, Torrington, CT
2,000	BAYM, Inc., Bridgeport, CT
2,000	Connecticut Special Olympics, Inc., Hamden, CT
2,000	Hall Neighborhood House, Bridgeport, CT
2,000	Northwest CT Family Y M C A, Winsted, CT
2,000	Town of Winchester Youth Service Bureau, Winsted, CT
1,000	Bridgeport Police Activities League, Inc., Bridgeport, CT
1,000	Danbury Police Athletic League, Inc., Danbury, CT
500	The Volunteer Center, Danbury, CT

BARDES CORP.

Company Contact

Cincinnati, OH

Company Description

Employees: 700
SIC(s): 3451 Screw Machine Products, 3643 Current-Carrying Wiring Devices.

Corporate Sponsorship

Type: Arts & cultural events; Music & entertainment events

Bardes Fund

Giving Contact

Rebecca Autry
Bardes Fund
4730 Madison Road
Cincinnati, OH 45227-1426
Phone: (513)533-6279
Fax: (513)871-4084
Email: rautry@ilsco.com

Description

Founded: 1955
EIN: 316036206
Organization Type: Corporate Foundation
Giving Locations: OH: Cincinnati
Grant Types: General Support.

Financial Summary

Total Giving: $180,000 (2000 approx); $180,000 (1999 approx); $180,000 (1998 approx). Note: Contributes through corporate direct giving program and foundation. Giving includes foundation. 1996 Giving includes foundation ($144,545); United Way ($28,000).
Assets: $5,000,000 (2000 approx); $5,000,000 (1999 approx); $3,007,786 (1996)
Gifts Received: $600,000 (1999 approx); $150,000 (1996); $215,000 (1995). Note: Contributions are received from Bardes Corp.

Typical Recipients

Arts & Humanities: Arts Associations & Councils, Arts Funds, Community Arts, Historic Preservation, History & Archaeology, Libraries, Museums/Galleries, Music, Performing Arts, Public Broadcasting, Theater
Civic & Public Affairs: Botanical Gardens/Parks, Clubs, Civic & Public Affairs-General, Public Policy, Urban & Community Affairs, Zoos/Aquariums
Education: Business Education, Colleges & Universities, Education Funds, Education-General, Private Education (Precollege), Student Aid, Vocational & Technical Education
Environment: Environment-General

Health: AIDS/HIV, Cancer, Emergency/Ambulance Services, Eyes/Blindness, Heart, Hospices, Hospitals, Medical Rehabilitation, Medical Research, Preventive Medicine/Wellness Organizations, Public Health, Single-Disease Health Associations
International: Foreign Arts Organizations, International Affairs
Religion: Churches, Religious Organizations, Religious Welfare
Social Services: Child Welfare, Community Service Organizations, Family Planning, Family Services, Recreation & Athletics, United Funds/United Ways, Youth Organizations

Application Procedures

Initial Contact: written request
Deadlines: None.

Corporate Officials

Merrilyn B. Bardes: president B 1945. PRIM CORP EMPL president: Bardes Corp.
Brittain B. Cudlip: chairman B 1948. PRIM CORP EMPL chairman: Bardes Corp. CORP AFFIL president: WRB Inc.; chairman: Walnut Hill Properties Inc.; vice president: Kentucky Connector Corp.; president: New Horizons Madonna Hall; vice president: Ilsco Corp. NONPR AFFIL trustee: Tufts University.
David J. FitzGibbon: president, chief executive officer B 1944. ED Thomas More College (1965). PRIM CORP EMPL president, chief executive officer: Bardes Corp. CORP AFFIL chief operating officer: Ilsco Corp.; president: Kentucky Connector Corp.
J. E. Valentine: chief financial officer PRIM CORP EMPL chief financial officer: Bardes Corp.

Foundation Officials

Rebecca Autry: secretary

Grants Analysis

Disclosure Period: calendar year ending 1997
Total Grants: $178,121
Number of Grants: 85
Average Grant: $2,096
Highest Grant: $29,000
Typical Range: $100 to $25,000

Recent Grants

Note: Grants derived from 1996 Form 990.

Arts & Humanities

11,000	Fine Arts Fund, Cincinnati, OH
5,750	Cincinnati Symphony Orchestra, Cincinnati, OH
5,000	Playhouse in the Park, Cincinnati, OH
5,000	Preservation Society, Newport, RI
5,000	Society of Four Arts, Palm Beach, FL
5,000	USCT Preservation Foundation, Washington, DC
2,500	Preservation Society, Newport, RI
2,000	New York Historical Society, New York, NY
1,750	University of Virginia Historic Preservation, Charlottesville, VA
1,500	Preservation Foundation, Palm Beach, FL
1,200	Preservation Society, Newport, RI
1,000	National Gallery Circle, Washington, DC
1,000	Preservation Society, Newport, RI
1,000	Redwood Library and Athenaeum, Newport, RI

Civic & Public Affairs

5,000	Cincinnati Zoo, Cincinnati, OH
2,200	WRC, Cincinnati, OH
1,000	Circles, Washington, DC
1,000	Heritage Foundation, Palm Beach, FL
1,000	National Zoo, Washington, DC
1,000	NESF, Rosslyn, VA
1,000	Rollins Fund, Winter Park, FL
500	Hyde Park Center, Cincinnati, OH

Education

16,500	Citizens Scholarship Foundation, St. Peter, MN
10,000	Jefferson Scholars Program, Charlottesville, VA
5,000	Boston College, Chestnut Hill, MA
3,000	Lawrenceville School, Lawrenceville, NJ -- annual giving
2,000	Hill School, Palm Beach, FL
1,500	University of Virginia Alumni Association, Charlottesville, VA
750	Xavier University, Cincinnati, OH
690	Stone Ridge School, Washington, DC
500	Junior Achievement, Cincinnati, OH

Health

5,000	Schepens Eye Research Institute, Boston, MA
2,000	American Cancer Society, Palm Beach, FL
1,400	American Red Cross, West Palm Beach, FL
1,000	American Red Cross, Palm Beach, FL
1,000	Hospice Guild, Palm Beach, FL
1,000	Intra-Coastal Health Foundation, New York, NY
1,000	Paracare Association, Palm Beach, FL
1,000	Rehabilitation Center for Children, Palm Beach, FL
1,000	Wellness Community, Cincinnati, OH
500	Vincent T. Lombardi Cancer Center, Washington, DC

International

2,500	International Tennis Hall of Fame, New York, NY
1,000	International Tennis Hall of Fame, New York, NY
750	International Tennis Hall of Fame, New York, NY

Religion

5,000	Royal Poinciana Chapel, Palm Beach, FL
1,000	Salvation Army, Palm Beach, FL
500	Mother of Mercy, Cincinnati, OH -- capital campaign

Social Services

27,500	United Way, Cincinnati, OH
1,000	Planned Parenthood, West Palm Beach, FL
525	Thrift Shop Charities, Washington, DC

BARNES GROUP INC.

Company Contact

123 Main St.
PO Box 489
Bristol, CT 06011-0489
Phone: (860)583-7070
Fax: (860)589-7466
Web: http://www.barnesgroupinc.com

Company Description

Employees: 3,800 (1998)
SIC(s): 3465 Automotive Stampings, 3493 Steel Springs Except Wire, 3495 Wire Springs, 3496 Miscellaneous Fabricated Wire Products.

Barnes Group Foundation Inc.

Giving Contact

Thomas Barnes, Secretary
Barnes Group Foundation Inc.
123 Main St.
PO Box 489
Bristol, CT 06011-0489
Phone: (860)583-7070
Fax: (860)589-7466

Description

EIN: 237339727
Organization Type: Corporate Foundation
Giving Locations: opearting communities.
Grant Types: General Support.

Financial Summary

Total Giving: $450,000 (2000 approx); $450,000 (1999 approx); $526,809 (1998). Note: Contributes through foundation only.
Giving Analysis: Giving for 1996 includes: foundation grants to United Way ($37,603); 1997: foundation grants to United Way ($30,140)
Assets: $3,587,835 (1998); $3,096,755 (1997); $2,349,799 (1996)
Gifts Received: $500,000 (1998); $750,000 (1997); $500,000 (1996). Note: In 1998, contributions were received from Barnes Group Inc.

Typical Recipients

Arts & Humanities: Arts Associations & Councils, Arts Centers, Arts Festivals, Community Arts, Dance, Historic Preservation, Libraries, Museums/Galleries, Music, Opera, Public Broadcasting, Theater
Civic & Public Affairs: African American Affairs, Clubs, Community Foundations, Civic & Public Affairs-General, Housing, Legal Aid, Minority Business, Municipalities/Towns, Public Policy, Safety, Urban & Community Affairs, Zoos/Aquariums
Education: Afterschool/Enrichment Programs, Business Education, Colleges & Universities, Community & Junior Colleges, Education Funds, Engineering/Technological Education, Education-General, Minority Education, Private Education (Precollege), Public Education (Precollege), Religious Education, Science/Mathematics Education, Secondary Education (Private), Special Education, Student Aid, Vocational & Technical Education
Environment: Air/Water Quality, Environment-General
Health: Cancer, Children's Health/Hospitals, Emergency/Ambulance Services, Hospitals, Medical Research, Single-Disease Health Associations, Trauma Treatment
International: International Relief Efforts
Science: Science Museums
Social Services: Big Brother/Big Sister, Child Welfare, Community Service Organizations, Crime Prevention, Family Services, Homes, People with Disabilities, Recreation & Athletics, Scouts, Senior Services, Special Olympics, Substance Abuse, United Funds/United Ways, YMCA/YWCA/YMHA/YWHA, Youth Organizations

Contributions Analysis

Giving Priorities: Primary support for education, health, social services. Limited support for religious causes, arts and humanities, civic, environmental causes, and science.
Arts & Humanities: 7%. Contributes to arts centers, museums, libraries, and public broadcasting.
Civic & Public Affairs: 6%. Recipients include urban affairs, municipalities, leadership councils, and community foundations.
Education: 36%. About three-fifths of funds supports Citizens Scholarship Foundation for college tuition for children of employees. Also supports colleges and universities, private education, business education, religious high schools, and college funds.
Environment: 1%. Supports the Bristol Regional Environmental Centers, Inc.
Health: 24%. Funds hospitals, cancer centers, and health organizations.
Religion: 24%. Supports religious education, YMCA, and other religious organizations.
Science: 1%. Supports the Science Center of Connecticut.

Social Services: 17%. Supports youth organizations, homes for children, guide dogs for the blind, Focus Hope, and family services. Also supports United Way.
Note: Total contributions made in 1998.

Application Procedures

Initial Contact: Write or call an operating division of the company requesting application form.
Application Requirements: State purpose, history of organization, describe project, annual itemized budget, project budget, foundation and corporate donors, and 501(c)(3) exemption letter.
Deadlines: March 1.
Decision Notification: Board meets four times per year.

Restrictions

To be an eligible candidate for the scholarship grant, applicants must be a child of either a current Barnes Group employee in the US or Canada who has worked for the company at least one year by the application deadline, or a retired employee.
The foundation does not support political or lobbying efforts.

Additional Information

Contact Citizen Scholarship Foundation of America, Inc. at 1505 Riverview Rd., PO Box 297, St. Peter, MN 56082 or phone (603) 627-3870.
Publications: Contributions Policy; Guidelines

Corporate Officials

John Edward Besser: senior vice president finance & law B Iowa City, IA 1942. ED University of Rochester AB (1964); Northwestern University JD (1967). PRIM CORP EMPL senior vice president finance & law: Barnes Group Inc. NONPR AFFIL member: Missouri Bar Association; board electors: Wadsworth Atheneum; member: American Bar Association; director: Greater Hartford Arts Council.
John J. Locher: vice president, treasurer B 1944. ED Fordham University BA (1966); New York University Leonard N. Stern School of Business MBA (1971). PRIM CORP EMPL vice president, treasurer: Barnes Group Inc.

Foundation Officials

Thomas O. Barnes: secretary B 1949. PRIM CORP EMPL board chairman: Barnes Group Inc. CORP AFFIL chairman: Chapman Machine Co. Inc.
Wallace W. Barnes: director B Bristol, CT 1926. ED Williams College BA (1949); Yale University LLB (1952); Harvard University Advanced Management Program (1973); Harvard University LLD (1988). CORP AFFIL chairman, director: Tradewind Turbines Corp.; director: Loctite Corp.; director: Rogers Corp.; director: Connecticut Innovations Inc.; director: DeMaria Electro Optics Inc.; director executive committee: Aetna Life & Casualty Co. Inc. NONPR AFFIL director: Great Hartford Chamber of Commerce; member: Newcomen Society; member: Connecticut Business & Industry Association; member: Bristol Historical Society; member: Connecticut Bar Association; member: American Judicature Society; member: American Arbitration Association; member: American Bar Association. CLUB AFFIL Williams Club; Yale Club; Elks Club; Farmington Country Club; Economic Club; American Legion Club; Chippance Golf Club.
John Edward Besser: director (see above)
John J. Locher: treasurer (see above)

Grants Analysis

Disclosure Period: calendar year ending 1998
Total Grants: $487,779*
Number of Grants: 278
Average Grant: $1,755*
Highest Grant: $100,000
Typical Range: $50 to $4,000
***Note:** Giving excludes United Way.

Recent Grants

Note: Grants derived from 1998 Form 990.

Arts & Humanities

14,000 Bushnell - 1998 Connecticut Arts Gala, Hartford, CT
11,000 Greater Hartford Arts Center, Hartford, CT
4,000 Hollis Brookline Auditorium Fund, Inc., Hollis, NH
2,500 New England Carousel Museum, Bristol, CT

Civic & Public Affairs

5,000 Main Street Community Foundation, Bristol, CT
4,500 Miracles, Hartford, CT
3,792 The National Conference, Los Angeles, CA
3,700 City of Saline, Saline, MI
2,260 Urban League of Greater Hartford, Hartford, CT

Education

54,475 Citizens' Scholarship Foundation of America, St. Peter, MN
54,475 Citizens' Scholarship Foundation of America, St. Peter, MN
8,000 University of Hartford Associates, Hartford, CT
7,000 Edgewood School, Hamden, CT
5,000 Tunxis Community College Annual Economic Conference, Farmington, CT
4,000 Bishop Garrigan High, Corpus Christi, TX
4,000 Drew University, Los Angeles, CA
4,000 Renbrook School, Hartford, CT
4,000 St. Paul's Catholic High School, Highland, IL
4,000 Utica College Of Syracuse University, Utica, NY
3,800 Junior Achievement of Southeasten Michigan, Detroit, MI
3,650 Saint Matthew School, Spokane, WA
3,600 American Islamic Academy, Dearborn, MI
3,500 Inroads/Greater Hartford, Hartford, CT
3,400 Gettysburg College, Gettysburg, PA
3,000 St. John's Jesuit High School, Toledo, OH
2,500 American School for the Deaf, Hartford, CT
2,500 United Negro College Fund, Hartford, CT
2,400 Michigan State University, Detroit, MI
2,310 Toledo Christian Schools, Toledo, OH

Environment

4,995 Bristol Regional Environmental Centers, Bristol, CT

Health

100,000 Bristol Hospital - Capital Campaign, Bristol, CT
12,500 Connecticut Children's Hospital Center, New Haven, CT
5,000 Saint Francis/Mount Sinai Hospital, Hartford, CT
4,350 American Paralysis Association, Los Angeles, CA

Social Services

10,000 United Way - Cleveland, Cleveland, OH
9,000 Family Center Capital Campaign, Bristol, CT
6,500 United Way - Corry Area, Corry, PA
5,000 Big Brothers/Big Sisters, Hartford, CT
5,000 Drugs Don't Work, Hartford, CT
5,000 McLean Home, Canton, CT
4,400 Boy Scouts Of America-Connecticut Rivers Council, Hartford, CT
3,700 Washtenaw United Way, Washtenaw, MI
3,080 Boy Scouts Of America-Connecticut Rivers Council, Hartford, CT
3,000 Fidelco Guide Dog Foundation, Bloomfield, CT
3,000 United Way - Hartford, Hartford, CT
2,500 United Way - Detroit, Detroit, MI
2,500 YMCA Of Corry, Corry, PA
2,030 United Way West Central Connecticut
2,000 United Way - Hartford, Hartford, CT

R.G. BARRY CORP.

Company Contact

13405 Yarmouth Road NW
Pickerington, OH 43147
Phone: (614)864-6400
Fax: (614)864-3129
Email: ryoust@rgbarry.com
Web: http://www.rgbarry.com

Company Description

Founded: 1947
Revenue: US$150,700,000 (1998)
Employees: 2,400
SIC(s): 2211 Broadwoven Fabric Mills--Cotton, 3142 House Slippers, 3143 Men's Footwear Except Athletic, 3144 Women's Footwear Except Athletic.

Nonmonetary Support

Type: Donated Products

Barry Foundation

Giving Contact

Marilyn Thomas, Corporate Finance Administrator
Barry Foundation

Description

Founded: 1963
EIN: 316051086
Organization Type: Corporate Foundation
Giving Locations: nationally.
Grant Types: General Support.

Financial Summary

Total Giving: $250,000 (1999 approx); $449,223 (1998); $250,000 (1997 approx)
Assets: $3,398 (1998); $5,494 (1996); $20,107 (1995)
Gifts Received: $425,000 (1998); $225,000 (1996); $25,000 (1995). Note: In 1995, contributions were received from the R.G. Barry Corp.

Typical Recipients

Arts & Humanities: Arts Centers, Arts Funds, Arts Institutes, Ballet, Community Arts, Dance, Ethnic & Folk Arts, Arts & Humanities-General, History & Archaeology, Libraries, Museums/Galleries, Music, Opera, Performing Arts, Public Broadcasting, Theater
Civic & Public Affairs: Business/Free Enterprise, Clubs, Community Foundations, Economic Development, Civic & Public Affairs-General, Urban & Community Affairs
Education: Arts/Humanities Education, Business Education, Colleges & Universities, Community & Junior Colleges, Education Associations, Education Funds, Education-General, Private Education (Precollege), Religious Education, Student Aid
Health: AIDS/HIV, Cancer, Diabetes, Health-General, Health Funds, Health Organizations, Medical Research, Single-Disease Health Associations, Speech & Hearing
International: International Affairs, International Development, International Relief Efforts, Missionary/Religious Activities
Religion: Churches, Jewish Causes, Religious Organizations, Religious Welfare, Synagogues/Temples
Social Services: Child Welfare, Community Centers, Community Service Organizations, Family Planning,

Family Services, People with Disabilities, Scouts, Senior Services, Shelters/Homelessness, Social Services-General, Substance Abuse, United Funds/United Ways, YMCA/YWCA/YMHA/YWHA, Youth Organizations

Contributions Analysis

Giving Priorities: Education, civic organizations, health, arts, religious causes, and youth and social services.
Arts & Humanities: 4%. Supports museums and cultural programs.
Civic & Public Affairs: 41%. Funds community development, chambers of commerce, and public policy.
Education: 30%. Supports higher education, educational programs.
Health: 2%. Funds health care organizations and concerns.
Religion: 4%. Supports Jewish causes and education.
Social Services: 18%. Funds youth and social services.
Note: Total contributions made in 1998.

Application Procedures

Initial Contact: Send a brief letter of inquiry.
Application Requirements: Information should include a description of organization, amount requested, purpose of funds sought, and proof of tax-exempt status.
Deadlines: None.

Restrictions

Does not support individuals, religious organizations for sectarian purposes, or political or lobbying groups.

Additional Information

Publications: Financial Statements

Corporate Officials

Richard L. Burrell: senator vice president finance, secretary, treasurer B Union City, OH 1933. ED Miami University BS (1955); Xavier University MBA (1965). PRIM CORP EMPL senator vice president finance, secretary, treasurer: R.G. Barry Corp. CORP AFFIL director: Lord, Sullivan, Yoder, Worthington, Ohio, ZeeMed Services. NONPR AFFIL member: Financial Executives Institute.
Gordon Benjamin Zacks: chairman, president, chief executive officer, director B Terre Haute, IN 1933. ED Ohio State University BA (1955). PRIM CORP EMPL chairman, president, chief executive officer, director: R.G. Barry Corp. NONPR AFFIL member: National Republican Senatorial Committee; honorary chairman: Un Jewish Appeal; member: American Management Association; member: Chief Executives Organization.

Foundation Officials

Richard L. Burrell: treasurer (see above)
William Edward Ellis, Jr.: secretary B Statesville, NC 1948. ED University of North Carolina; North Carolina State University (1973). PRIM CORP EMPL executive vice president marketing: Monex Resources.
Harvey M. Krueger: trustee B Jersey City, NJ 1929. ED Columbia College (1951); Columbia University (1953). PRIM CORP EMPL managing director: Shearson Lehman Brothers. CORP AFFIL director: Ivax Corp.; director: Manhattan Industries; director: Chaus; director: Automatic Data Processing Corp.; director: RG Barry Corp.; director: Ampal Corp.
Florence Melton: chairman
Gordon Benjamin Zacks: president (see above)

Grants Analysis

Disclosure Period: calendar year ending 1998
Total Grants: $377,048*
Number of Grants: 51*
Average Grant: $7,393*
Highest Grant: $85,000
Typical Range: $500 to $25,000

*Note: Grant analysis excludes United Way.

Recent Grants

Note: Grants derived from 1996 Form 990.

Arts & Humanities
17,000 George Bush Presidential Library Center, College Station, TX
2,000 Ballet Met, Columbus, OH
2,000 Columbus Museum of Art, Columbus, OH

Civic & Public Affairs
2,000 Columbus Foundation Trilogy Campaign, Columbus, OH

Education
8,333 Bexley Education Foundation, Bexley, OH

Health
5,000 Children's Hospital Surgical Cancer Research Fund, Boston, MA -- cancer research
1,200 Columbus Speech and Hearing Center, Columbus, OH

International
50,000 American Friends of Shalom Hartman Institute, Englewood, NJ -- research and Jewish studies
10,000 American Friends of Shalom Hartman Institute, Englewood, NJ -- endowment fund
6,667 Israel Tennis Centers Association, New York, NY
5,000 American-Israel Chamber of Commerce, New York, NY -- research and education
5,000 Israel Leadership and Education Foundation, New York, NY
1,500 Two/Ten Foundation, Watertown, MA

Religion
50,000 Columbus Jewish Federation, Columbus, OH
8,000 US Holocaust Memorial Museum, Washington, DC
3,000 Anti-Defamation League, New York, NY

Social Services
18,247 United Way Franklin County, Columbus, OH
17,316 United Way Franklin County, Columbus, OH
10,000 Gladney Fund, Fort Worth, TX
9,794 United Way Concho Valley, San Angelo, TX

BASSETT FURNITURE INDUSTRIES

Company Contact

Bassett, VA

Company Description

Employees: 7,850
SIC(s): 2511 Wood Household Furniture, 2512 Upholstered Household Furniture.

Bassett Furniture Industries Fdn.

Giving Contact

James Philpott, Vice President & Personnel Director
PO Box 626
Bassett, VA 24055-0626
Phone: (540)629-6200

Description

Founded: 1993
EIN: 541652381
Organization Type: Corporate Foundation. Supports preselected organizations only.
Grant Types: General Support.

Financial Summary

Total Giving: $212,320 (fiscal year ending November 30, 1994); $158,752 (fiscal 1993)
Assets: $781,453 (fiscal 1994); $936,079 (fiscal 1993)
Gifts Received: $154,500 (fiscal 1994); $1,092,678 (fiscal 1993). Note: In fiscal 1994, contributions were received from Bassett Furniture Industries.

Typical Recipients

Arts & Humanities: Arts Associations & Councils, History & Archaeology, Museums/Galleries, Theater
Civic & Public Affairs: Chambers of Commerce, Economic Development, Employment/Job Training, Safety, Urban & Community Affairs
Education: Arts/Humanities Education, Business Education, Colleges & Universities, Community & Junior Colleges, Education Funds, Minority Education, Private Education (Precollege), Secondary Education (Public)
Environment: Resource Conservation
Health: Cancer, Emergency/Ambulance Services, Single-Disease Health Associations
Social Services: Animal Protection, Camps, Community Centers, Recreation & Athletics, Scouts, YMCA/YWCA/YMHA/YWHA

Corporate Officials

Glenn A. Hunsucker: president, chief operating officer PRIM CORP EMPL president, chief operating officer: Bassett Furniture Industries.
Robert H. Spilman: chairman, chief executive officer B Knoxville, TN 1927. ED North Carolina State University BS (1950). PRIM CORP EMPL chairman, chief executive officer: Bassett Furniture Industries. CORP AFFIL director: Richmond Virginia Electric & Power Co.; director: TRINOVirginia Corp.; director: Pittston Co.; chairman: NC International Home Furnishings Center; director: NCNB Corp.; chairman: Jefferson-Pilot Corp.; director: Dominion Energy Inc.; director: Dominion Resources Inc.; director: Blue Ridge Airport. NONPR AFFIL trustee: Virginia Foundation Independent Colleges; member: Virginia Manufacturers Association; member: National Furniture Manufacturer Association; trustee: Darden School Foundation; member: Furniture Factories Marketing Association; member: American Furniture Manufacturer Association. CLUB AFFIL Linville Golf Club; Waterfront Golf Club; Hunting Hills Country Club; Commonwealth Club; Grandfather Golf Club & Country Club; Chatmoss Country Club; Bassett Country Club; Brook Club.

Foundation Officials

Billy M. Brammer: treasurer, director
Glenn A. Hunsucker: president, director (see above)
J. Stanley Payne: secretary
Robert H. Spilman: chairman, director (see above)

Grants Analysis

Disclosure Period: fiscal year ending November 30, 1994
Total Grants: $212,320
Number of Grants: 25
Highest Grant: $105,000
Typical Range: $50 to $25,000

Recent Grants

Note: Grants derived from fiscal 1996 Form 990.

Arts & Humanities
25,000 Piedmont Arts Association, Martinsville, VA -- Shared Vision program

6,000	Virginia Museum of Fine Arts Foundation, Richmond, VA -- Giving Fund Drive
2,000	Jamestown-Yorktown Foundation, Williamsburg, VA
1,000	Theater IV, Richmond, VA
Civic & Public Affairs	
3,000	Bassett Volunteer Fire Department, Bassett, VA
2,000	Dublin and Laurens Chamber of Commerce, Dublin, GA
1,000	Jobs for Virginia Graduates, Richmond, VA
250	Concord Coalition, Roanoke, VA
Education	
8,000	Independent Colleges of North Carolina, Winston-Salem, NC
5,000	Bassett High School Art Department, Bassett, VA
3,000	Ferrum College, Ferrum, VA
2,500	Junior Achievement, Colorado Springs, CO
1,000	Hillsdale College, Hillsdale, MI
1,000	United Negro College Fund, Fairfax, VA
Environment	
10,000	Nature Conservancy, Charlottesville, VA
Health	
3,000	Bassett Rescue Squad, Bassett, VA
600	American Cancer Society, Dublin, GA
Social Services	
3,000	YMCA Martinsville and Henry County, Martinsville, VA
500	Boy Scouts of America Blue Ridge Mountain Council, Roanoke, VA
500	Camp Holiday Trails, Charlottesville, VA

BATTELLE MEMORIAL INSTITUTE

Company Contact

505 King Avenue
Columbus, OH 43201-2693
Phone: 800-201-2011
Email: solutions@battelle.org
Web: http://www.battelle.org

Company Description

Revenue: US$710,100,000 (1999)
Employees: 8,600
SIC(s): 8731 Commercial Physical Research.

Operating Locations

Germany: Battelle Memorial Institute, Frankfurt; Switzerland: Battelle MML Institute, Geneva
Note: Operates internationally.

Nonmonetary Support

Value: $432,000 (1990); $390,000 (1988)
Type: Donated Equipment; Loaned Employees

Corporate Sponsorship

Type: Arts & cultural events; Other
Note: Sponsors education events and causes.

Giving Contact

Karen Hollern, Director, Community Relations
Battelle Memorial Institute
505 King Ave.
Columbus, OH 43201
Phone: (614)424-7980
Fax: (614)424-3301

Description

Organization Type: Corporate Giving Program
Giving Locations: headquarters and operating communities.
Grant Types: Capital, Challenge, Conference/Seminar, Emergency, Fellowship, General Support, Matching, Multiyear/Continuing Support.

Giving Philosophy

'We at Battelle believe that.. we should be an active partner in the broad technical and societal communities in which we work, as well as in the geographic communities in which we have operations and our staff members live. As a responsible corporate citizen, we strive, by both deeds and dollars, to assist a wide range of activities designed to enhance the human condition that we believe are deserving of Battelle's support.' *A Few Words About Charitable Distributions*, Battelle Memorial Institute

Financial Summary

Total Giving: Contributes through corporate direct giving program only.

Typical Recipients

Arts & Humanities: Arts Associations & Councils, Community Arts, Dance, Libraries, Museums/Galleries, Music, Opera, Performing Arts, Public Broadcasting, Theater
Civic & Public Affairs: Business/Free Enterprise, Economic Development, Employment/Job Training, Professional & Trade Associations, Zoos/Aquariums
Education: Business Education, Colleges & Universities, Community & Junior Colleges, Economic Education, Elementary Education (Private), Engineering/Technological Education, Faculty Development, Literacy, Medical Education, Minority Education, Public Education (Precollege), Science/Mathematics Education
Health: Geriatric Health, Health Policy/Cost Containment, Hospitals, Medical Research, Nursing Services, Nutrition, Single-Disease Health Associations
Social Services: Child Welfare, Family Planning, Family Services, People with Disabilities, Recreation & Athletics, Senior Services, Substance Abuse, United Funds/United Ways, Youth Organizations

Contributions Analysis

Giving Priorities: Education, cultural and arts organizatios, hospitals, and United Way.
Arts & Humanities: 22%. Supports a variety of cultural and arts organizations,including museums, dance and music groups, libraries and theater.
Civic & Public Affairs: 7%. Interests include civic betterment organizations.
Education: 42%. Majority of funds support colleges and universities in company operating locations. Emphasis on engineering education, science and math. Also supports professional societies; literacy; and business, elementary, minority, and public precollege education.
Health: 29%. Supports community charitable institutions such as hospitals, and United Ways; and agencies assisting people with disabilites and the disadvantaged.

Application Procedures

Initial Contact: letter requesting an appointment for an informal meeting
Application Requirements: a description of organization; amount requested; purpose for which funds are sought; recently audited financial statement; and proof of tax-exempt status
Deadlines: None.
Review Process: member of the community relations department meets with requesting organization; if mutual interest exists, suggestions for preparing written proposal are given; proposals are then presented to the distributions committee
Decision Notification: distributions committee meets four to six times per year, depending upon volume of requests

Restrictions

Does not support fraternal organizations, goodwill advertising, individuals, political or lobbying groups, or religious organizations.

Corporate Officials

William J. Madia: executive vice president, manager B Pittsburgh, PA 1947. ED Indiana University of Pennsylvania (1971); Virginia Polytechnic Institute & State University (1975). PRIM CORP EMPL executive vice president, manager: Battelle Memorial Institute.
Douglas Eugene Olesen, PhD: president, chief executive officer B Tonasket, WA 1939. ED University of Washington BS (1962); University of Washington MS (1963); University of Washington PhD (1972). PRIM CORP EMPL president, chief executive officer: Battelle Memorial Institute. CORP AFFIL director: B.F. Goodrich Co.; director: Columbia Gas Systems Inc. NONPR AFFIL trustee: Riverside Hospital Foundation; trustee: United Way Franklin; director: Ohio State University Foundation; trustee: Ohio Business Roundtable; member: Ohio Chamber of Commerce; trustee: INROADS/Columbus; director: Columbia Energy Group; trustee: Columbus Museum Art; trustee: Capital University.

Giving Program Officials

Jon Buesman: assistant director

Grants Analysis

Disclosure Period: calendar year ending
Typical Range: $1,000 to $2,500

BAUSCH & LOMB INC.

Company Contact

Rochester, NY
Web: http://www.bausch.com

Company Description

Employees: 13,000
SIC(s): 3479 Metal Coating & Allied Services, 3634 Electric Housewares & Fans, 3827 Optical Instruments & Lenses, 3851 Ophthalmic Goods.

Operating Locations

Operates in Canada, the Caribbean, Latin America, Europe, Australia, and Asia.

Nonmonetary Support

Value: $10,000 (1994); $250,000 (1991); $506,000 (1989)
Type: In-kind Services

Corporate Sponsorship

Type: Arts & cultural events; Sports events; Festivals/fairs
Note: Provides sponsorship through the divisions of Bausch & Lomb.

Bausch & Lomb Foundation, Inc.

Giving Contact

Barbara M. Kelley, Vice President
Bausch & Lomb Foundation, Inc.
One Bausch & Lomb Place
Rochester, NY 14604
Phone: (716)338-6000
Fax: (716)338-6007

Description

EIN: 166039442
Organization Type: Corporate Foundation
Giving Locations: NY: Rochester
Grant Types: General Support.

Financial Summary

Total Giving: $902,500 (1997); $1,600,000 (1996); $1,570,500 (1995). Note: Contributes through corporate direct giving program and foundation.
Assets: $2,381,233 (1997); $1,984,818 (1996); $1,770,916 (1995)
Gifts Received: $901,500 (1997); $1,000,000 (1996); $250,000 (1995). Note: Contributions are received from Bausch & Lomb Inc.

Typical Recipients

Arts & Humanities: Libraries, Museums/Galleries, Music, Performing Arts, Theater
Civic & Public Affairs: Botanical Gardens/Parks, Business/Free Enterprise, Economic Development, Employment/Job Training, Housing, Public Policy, Urban & Community Affairs, Women's Affairs, Zoos/Aquariums
Education: Colleges & Universities, Community & Junior Colleges, Minority Education, Science/Mathematics Education
Environment: Environment-General
Health: Clinics/Medical Centers, Geriatric Health, Nursing Services
Science: Scientific Centers & Institutes
Social Services: Child Welfare, Community Centers, Community Service Organizations, Homes, People with Disabilities, Recreation & Athletics, United Funds/United Ways, Youth Organizations

Contributions Analysis

Giving Priorities: Higher education, housing and economic development, youth organizations, united funds, and cultural organizations.
Arts & Humanities: 29%. Funds a library and a museum.
Civic & Public Affairs: 15%. Housing and economic development. International affairs, public policy, and women's affairs have also received support.
Education: 50%. Colleges and universities are funded.
Health: 4%. Supports visiting nurses and elder care.
Social Services: 2%. Funds a children's center.
Note: Total contributions made in 1997.

Application Procedures

Initial Contact: Send a written letter proposal.
Application Requirements: Include a description of organization; amount requested; purpose of funds sought; recently audited financial statement; budget showing revenue and expenses; proof of tax-exempt status; and list of board of directors.
Deadlines: None.

Additional Information

Company is currently reviewing its policy on international giving.

Corporate Officials

William M. Carpenter: chief executive officer, director, chairman B 1952. ED Dartmouth College BA; Northwestern University MBA. PRIM CORP EMPL chief executive officer, director, chairman: Bausch & Lomb Inc.
Alan H. Resnick: vice president, treasurer B Boston, MA 1943. ED Tufts University BS (1965); Columbia University MBA (1967). PRIM CORP EMPL vice president, treasurer: Bausch & Lomb Inc. NONPR AFFIL treasurer: Visiting Nurse Foundation Inc.
William H. Waltrip: chairman, director B 1937. PRIM CORP EMPL chairman, director: Bausch & Lomb Inc. CORP AFFIL chairman: Technology Solutions Co.; director: Thomas & Betts Corp.

Foundation Officials

Barbara M. Kelley: vice president PRIM CORP EMPL vice president corporate communications: Bausch & Lomb Inc.
Alan H. Resnick: treasurer (see above)

Grants Analysis

Disclosure Period: calendar year ending 1997
Total Grants: $902,500
Number of Grants: 10
Average Grant: $90,250
Highest Grant: $300,000
Typical Range: $50,000 to $100,000

Recent Grants

Note: Grants derived from 1997 Form 990.

Arts & Humanities

250,000	Rundel Library, Rochester, NY
10,000	Strong Museam, Rochester, NY

Civic & Public Affairs

100,000	UNCGR Foundation, Rochester, NY
37,500	Wilson Commencement Park, Rochester, NY

Education

300,000	University of Rochester, Rochester, NY
100,000	Monroe Community College, Rochester, NY
50,000	Nazareth College, Rochester, NY

Health

25,000	Visiting Nurse Foundation, Rochester, NY
10,000	Eldersource, Rochester, NY

Social Services

20,000	Crestwood Children's Center, Rochester, NY

BAXTER INTERNATIONAL INC.

Company Contact

One Baxter Parkway
Deerfield, IL 60015-4633
Phone: (847)948-2000
Fax: (847)948-3948
Web: http://www.baxter.com

Company Description

Founded: 1931
Former Name: Baxter and Allegiance Corp.
Revenue: US$6,599,000,000
Employees: 42,000
Fortune Rank: 243, per FORTUNE Magazine's list of 500 Largest U.S. Corporations (1999).
FF 243
SIC(s): 2297 Nonwoven Fabrics, 2389 Apparel & Accessories Nec, 3841 Surgical & Medical Instruments, 3842 Surgical Appliances & Supplies.

Operating Locations

Australia: Baxter Healthcare Pty. Ltd., Old Toongabbie; Belgium: Dade SA, Brussels, Brabant; Baxter Distribution Center Europe SA, Lessines; Baxter SA, Lessines; Canada: Baxter Corp., Mississauga; Colombia: Laboratorios Baxter SA, Bogota, Cundinamarco; Travenol Industrial y Comercial SA, Palmira; Denmark: Baxter A/S, Allerod, Frederiksborg; France: Societe Baxter Travenol, Coignieres, Yvelines; Baxter SA, Maurepas; Germany: Baxter Deutschland GmbH, Unterschleissheim, Bayern; Pas Palzer GmbH, Woerrstadt, Rheinland-Pfalz; Ireland: Baxter Healthcare Ltd., Dun Laoghaire; Italy: Baxter SpA, Roma, Lazio; Clintec SRL, Roma, Lazio; Japan: Baxter Ltd., Tokyo; Mexico: Baxter SA de CV, Jiutepec; Malaysia: Euromedical Industries Sdn. Bhd., Sungei Petani, Kedah; Netherlands: Dade NV, Amersfoort, Utrecht; Baxter BV, Uden, Noord-Brabant; Norway: Baxter AS, Oslo, Akershus; New Zealand: Baxter Diagnostics PL, Auckland; Baxter Healthcare Ltd., Auckland; Portugal: Baxter Medico Farmaceutica Lda., Cacem, Sintra; Singapore: Baxter Healthcare Far East Pte. Ltd., Singapore; Spain: Baxter SA, Valencia, Communidad Valencia; Switzerland: Baxter Edwards AG, Horw, Lucerne; Xenomedica AG, Horw, Lucerne; United Kingdom: Danby Medical Ltd., Colchester, Essex; Unicare Medical Services Ltd., Harlow, Essex; Baxter Healthcare Ltd., Thetford, Norfolk; Baxter Laboratories (1960) Ltd., Thetford, Norfolk

Nonmonetary Support

Value: $5,000,000 (1998); $21,000,000 (1996); $10,000,000 (1995)
Type: Donated Products
Note: Product donations are listed at wholesale value. Donates medical supplies internationally.

Baxter Allegiance Foundation

Giving Contact

Ms. Patricia A. Morgan, Executive Director & Secretary
Baxter Allegiance Foundation

Description

EIN: 363159396
Organization Type: Corporate Foundation
Giving Locations: IL: Chicago nationally; Europe; Latin America; Puerto Rico;.
Grant Types: Employee Matching Gifts, General Support.
Note: Employee matching gift ratio: 1 to 1.

Giving Philosophy

'The Baxter Allegiance Foundation is the philanthropic arm of Baxter International Allegiance Corp., which, through its subsidiaries, is the world's leading manufacturer and marketer of health-care products and services. Both Baxter International Allegiance Corp. and the foundation support the development of better, more accessible health care, delivered as economically as possible. To this end, the foundation has developed several continuing priorities and programs. Through its grant program, The Baxter Allegiance Foundation places special emphasis on initiatives that benefit the entire health field. These include policy and advocacy efforts; early-stage research; and projects that emphasize access, quality, cost-effectiveness or education and are designed to be models for larger programs. Each year, the foundation sponsors a number of prizes recognizing excellence in service, research or innovation in the health-care field..these include the nation's leading hospital award, the Foster G. McGaw award, which recognizes outstanding commitment to the community, and the Baxter Health Service Research Award, which recognizes the best original research on health-care delivery. Together, these prizes celebrate distinguished work in health-care delivery and highlight opportunities for positive change. The foundation also supports the philanthropic efforts of Baxter International Allegiance Corporation employees through a number of important programs. Among the most far-reaching is the Dollars for Doers program, which makes grants to organizations where U.S. Baxter employees volunteer. In all these efforts, The Baxter Allegiance Foundation's fundamental purpose is to make a positive and long lasting impact on health care and the health of our communities - in Illinois where Baxter International Allegiance Corp. is headquartered, across the United States and around the world.' The Baxter Foundation Report

Financial Summary

Total Giving: $4,884,366 (1998); $3,794,786 (1997); $4,529,668 (1996)
Giving Analysis: Giving for 1996 includes: foundation ($3,883,925); foundation grants to United Way ($456,400); foundation matching gifts ($189,343); 1997: foundation ($3,221,474); foundation grants to

United Way ($384,711); foundation matching gifts ($188,601)
Assets: $5,395,546 (1998); $4,619,127 (1997); $6,441,834 (1996)
Gifts Received: $5,166,674 (1998); $2,100,000 (1997); $2,900,000 (1996)

Typical Recipients

Arts & Humanities: Arts Institutes, Museums/Galleries, Music, Opera
Civic & Public Affairs: Asian American Affairs, Business/Free Enterprise, Clubs, Community Foundations, Economic Development, Employment/Job Training, Civic & Public Affairs-General, Hispanic Affairs, Housing, Municipalities/Towns, Native American Affairs, Nonprofit Management, Philanthropic Organizations, Professional & Trade Associations, Urban & Community Affairs, Zoos/Aquariums
Education: Business Education, Colleges & Universities, Education Associations, Education Funds, Education Reform, Elementary Education (Public), Education-General, Health & Physical Education, Medical Education, Minority Education, Preschool Education, Public Education (Precollege), Science/Mathematics Education, Secondary Education (Private), Student Aid
Health: AIDS/HIV, Children's Health/Hospitals, Clinics/Medical Centers, Emergency/Ambulance Services, Eyes/Blindness, Health Policy/Cost Containment, Health Organizations, Heart, Home-Care Services, Hospitals, Hospitals (University Affiliated), Long-Term Care, Medical Rehabilitation, Medical Research, Nursing Services, Preventive Medicine/Wellness Organizations, Public Health, Research/Studies Institutes, Respiratory
International: Foreign Educational Institutions, International-General, Health Care/Hospitals, International Organizations, International Relief Efforts, Missionary/Religious Activities
Religion: Jewish Causes, Religious Welfare
Science: Observatories & Planetariums, Science Museums, Scientific Research
Social Services: At-Risk Youth, Camps, Child Abuse, Child Welfare, Community Service Organizations, Counseling, Day Care, Domestic Violence, Family Services, Food/Clothing Distribution, People with Disabilities, Recreation & Athletics, Refugee Assistance, Senior Services, Sexual Abuse, Shelters/Homelessness, Substance Abuse, United Funds/United Ways, YMCA/YWCA/YMHA/YWHA, Youth Organizations

Contributions Analysis

Giving Priorities: Health care, health education, United Way, and youth organizations. Domestically, does not make contributions to organizations with an international focus as a general practice. Has supported some health-related organizations with programs overseas and is expanding into Europe, Mexico, and Latin America. It also donates products to international relief agencies.
Civic & Public Affairs: 6%. Supports local community organizations.
Education: 26%. Supports higher education.
Health: 25%. Supports health care access, improving the quality of the health-care delivery system, and increasing the availability of resources to health-care providers. Also supports improved cost effectiveness of the delivery system, immunization, and sponsors employees matching gifts to hospitals.
International: 13%. Funds International relief organizations and international causes.
Religion: 2%. Funds YMCA and religious organizations.
Social Services: 28%. Support goes to community service and youth organizations.
Note: Total contributions made in 1998.

Application Procedures

Initial Contact: Send a written proposal or request.
Application Requirements: Include a description of organization and its purpose, history, programs, and achievements; audited financial statement; operating and program budgets; list of board members and affiliations; a statement describing the purpose of requested grant, including how it meets the foundation's priorities; a plan for measuring results, periodically reporting on progress, as well as a final evaluation; a copy of organization's IRS form 501(c)(3) or equivalent; and list of sources of support, with amounts given, including corporate donors, the United Way, foundations and the government.
Deadlines: None.
Review Process: Proposals are reviewed continuously.
Evaluative Criteria: Eligibility under foundation guidelines; evidence that project is a response to a valid need and is superior to competing projects; evidence of organization's capacity to achieve goals.
Decision Notification: The board meets in February, April, July, October, and December.

Restrictions

The foundation does not support individuals; religious, social, fraternal, or veterans' groups; capital or endowment campaigns; hospitals; educational institutions, except when a grant would increase skills or availability of health care or enhance the community where company employees live; advertising, promotional materials, trips, tours, dances, tables, or tickets. No grants are made to disease-specific organizations.

Additional Information

In 1988, the Baxter American Foundation changed its name to The Baxter Foundation. Also in 1988, Baxter Travenol changed its name to Baxter International, Inc., and Baxter Travenol Laboratories changed its name to Baxter Healthcare Corporation. In 1996, Baxter divided into two companies--Baxter International, a global medical technology company; and Allegiance Corporation, a cost-management company. The foundation is now called the Baxter Allegiance Foundation.
The foundation runs a **Dollars for Doers** program, which donates grants between $100 and $500 to organizations where full-time or part-time U.S. employees volunteer. Employees must have been an active volunteer for at least six months. IRS 501(c)(3) or 170(c) organizations are eligible.
Publications: Foundation Annual Report

Corporate Officials

William B. Graham: chairman emerituso, chairman B Chicago, IL 1911. ED University of Chicago SB (1932); University of Chicago JD (1936); Carthage College LLD (1974); Lake Forest College LLD (1983). PRIM CORP EMPL chairman emeritus: Baxter International Inc. NONPR AFFIL member: Sigma Xi; director: Wendy Will Care Federation; member: Phi Delta Phi; member: Pharmaceutical Manufacturer Association; member: Phi Beta Kappa; trustee: Orchestral Association; member: Illinois Manufacturer Association; president, director: Lyric Opera Chicago; trustee: Evanston Hospital; director: Big Shoulders Fund; director: Chicago Horticultural Society; member: American Pharmaceutical Association. CLUB AFFIL Seminole Club; Old Elm Club; Indian Hills Country Club; The Links Club; Everglades Club; Commercial Club; Commonwealth Club; Chicago Club; Bath & Tennis Club; Casino Club.
Harry M. Jansen Kraemer, Jr.: president, chief executive officer, chairman B January 16, 1955. PRIM CORP EMPL president, chief executive officer, chairman: Baxter International Inc.
Jack L. McGinley: group vice president PRIM CORP EMPL group vice president: Baxter Healthcare Corp.

Foundation Officials

Jill H. Carter: director
Joseph F. Damico: director B 1954. ED James Madison University BS (1976); James Madison University MBA (1977). PRIM CORP EMPL president, chief operating officer, director: Allegiance Corp. CORP AFFIL president: Allegiance Healthcare Corp.
William B. Graham: chairman, director (see above)
Wilfred J. Lucas: director
Jack L. McGinley: president, director (see above)
Patricia A. Morgan: executive director, secretary
William E. Saxelby: director
Charles W. Thurman: director, treasurer

Grants Analysis

Disclosure Period: calendar year ending 1997
Total Grants: $3,221,474*
Number of Grants: 108
Average Grant: $29,828
Highest Grant: $309,389
Typical Range: $5,000 to $50,000
***Note:** Giving excludes matching gifts; United Way.

Recent Grants

Note: Grants derived from 1998 Form 990.

Civic & Public Affairs

50,000 The Commercial Club Foundation, Chicago, IL
50,000 San Diego American Indian Health Center, San Diego, CA -- Supports mental health services for American Indian children
31,550 Project Vida, El Paso, TX -- Supports a community training program for health aides and medical assistants

Education

344,263 Citizens' Scholarship Foundation of America Inc, St. Peter, MN -- Supports The Baxter Allegiance Foundation Scholarship Program
166,667 University of Iowa College of Medicine, Iowa City, IA -- Supports participation in the Commonwealth Fund's Healthy Steps for Young Children Program
150,000 Charles R. Drew University of Medicine and Science, Los Angeles, CA -- Supports seed money for indigent care clinics
100,000 Rush Medical College, Chicago, IL -- Supports research on the heart-failure patient
75,264 Indiana University for the Shalom Health Care Center, Indianapolis, IN -- Supports expansion of services at the Shalom Health Care Center
70,944 Barat College, Lake Forest, IL -- Supports the collaborative program to train science education teachers
63,000 AUPHA, Washington, IL -- Supports the 1998 Health Services Research Prize
50,000 College of Lake County, Grayslake, IL -- Supports the "Access to Success" program
37,911 Delta State University, Cleveland, MS -- Supports a faculty position in the School of Nursing to train nurse practitioners
29,000 Waukegan Schools Foundation, Waukegan, IL -- Supports a collaborative program to train science education teachers

Health

172,800 Hospital Research and Educational Trust, Chicago, IL -- Supports the Foster G. McGaw Prize
78,540 Children's Memorial Institute for Education and Research, Chicago, IL -- Supports pediatric liver research
78,298 Mountain Area Health Education Center, Asheville, NC -- Supports a preventive education program to decrease birth defects
67,700 Wallkill Valley Health Center, Walden, NY -- Supports care for children under

five and for the elderly and creates a health education program

65,775 American Lung Association of Orange County, Santa Ana, CA -- Supports the A is for Asthma Head Start Project

65,500 Metropolitan Visiting Nurse Association, Minneapolis, MN -- Supports home-health programs for the elderly

58,650 Social Action Community Health Systems, San Bernardino, CA -- Supports the development of a children's clinic in Ontario

50,000 Renaissance West Community Health Services, Inc., Detroit, MI -- Supports a substance abuse prevention program for children

46,608 Alberque Karire Kaniniga A. C., Cuauhtemoc, Mexico -- Supports a respite care program

43,749 Grace Hill Wellness Initiative, St. Louis, MO -- Supports a wellness program to reduce diabetes among the poor

40,000 Health and Medicine Policy Research Group, Chicago, IL -- Supports the Chicago Schweitzer Fellows Program

37,100 Ambulatory Surgery Access Coalition, San Francisco, CA -- Supports program replication and recognition of volunteer participants

32,000 San Francisco Community Clinic Consortium, San Francisco, CA -- Supports the Volunteer Services Program

30,000 The Free Clinic of Greater Cleveland, Cleveland, OH -- Supports expansion of the Clinic's capacity to serve the medically indigent

30,000 People's Clinic, Boulder, CO -- Supports the Prenatal Program for low-income women

28,561 Albuquerque Health Care for the Homeless, Inc., Albuquerque, NM -- Supports expansion of the children's Outreach Program

25,000 American Red Cross-Ashville Mountain Area Chapter, Asheville, NC -- Supports disaster relief in Western North Carolina and Eastern Tennessee

International

100,000 Instituto Down De Cuernavaca, A. C., Cuernavaca, MO, Mexico -- Supports a new residence

57,097 Ludwig Boltzmann Institute for Clinical Anesthesiology, Vienna, Austria -- Supports the training of anesthesiologists from the former Eastern Bloc

50,000 Asociacion Industrias Zona Franca San Cristobal, Inc., Haina, Dominican Republic -- Supports disaster relief efforts in the Dominican Republic

50,000 Cruz Roja Americana, Trujillo Alto, Puerto Rico -- Supports disaster relief efforts in Puerto Rico

50,000 Doctor's Without Borders USA, Inc., New York, NY -- Supports medical care in Central America for victims of Hurricane Mitch

50,000 Escuela Para Personas Con Impedimento, Inc., Guayama, Puerto Rico -- Supports the development of a special learning program for individuals with disabilities

32,360 Community of St. Egidio USA, Inc., New York, NY -- Supports health care for the frail elderly in Rome, Italy

25,000 Family Life Services, Castlebar, Ireland -- Supports expanded mental health, family and addiction counseling

20,000 Instituto Del Hogar Celia Y Harris Bunker, Rio Piedras, Puerto Rico -- Supports expansion of prevention programs and family therapy for domestic violence victims

17,000 Misioneras De Cristo Salvador, Inc., Guaynabo, Puerto Rico -- Supports the agency's counseling and educational programs

16,000 Asociacion Mayaguezana De Personas Con Impedimentos, Inc., Mayaguez, Puerto Rico -- Supports improved access to care for disabled residents of Mayaquez

15,000 Fundacion John Douglas, A.C., Cuernavaca, Mexico -- Supports a health clinic at Casa Hogar Douglas

10,000 Pusat Harian Harapan Bakti, Balik Pulau, Malaysia -- Supports expanded health and education programs

9,500 Escuela Carmen Salas De Torrado, Jayuya, Puerto Rico -- Supports curriculum improvement for the special education program

8,000 Casa Hogar De Nuestra Sma. Trinidad, A. C., Cuernavaca, Mexico -- Supports a computer training program

Social Services

330,927 United Way of Lake County, Green Oaks, IL

80,509 United Way/Crusade of Mercy, Chicago, IL

66,667 Hole in the Wall Gang Fund for Barretstown Gang Camp Fund, New Haven, CT -- Supports the recruitment and training of camp counselors

64,832 Children's Home Society of Florida, Fort Lauderdale, FL -- Supports expansion of family foster care services in Broward County, Florida

57,750 Travelers Aid Society of Pittsburgh, Pittsburgh, PA -- Support the Mobile Moms project

50,000 Providence House, Inc., Cleveland, OH -- Supports program expansion

50,000 St. Louis Crisis Nursery, St. Louis, MO -- Supports the S.O.S. for Kids program

49,732 Rincon Del Amor Home for the Elderly, Chihuahua, Mexico -- Supports medical care for children and the elderly

32,638 The Exchange Club Family Center, Memphis, TN -- Supports expanded counseling services

30,000 Hope Shelter, Inc., Cypress, TX -- Supports expansion of services for abused and neglected children

29,520 The Alabama Child Caring Foundation, Birmingham, AL -- Supports the Caring Program for Children in the cities of Bessemer and Hoover

26,900 YMCA of Metropolitan Chicago, Chicago, IL -- Supports Camp Duncan's specialized health-care camps

25,755 YWCA of Glendale, Glendale, CA -- Supports expanded services to women and children

BAYER CORP.

Company Contact

100 Bayer Rd.
Pittsburgh, PA 15205-9741
Phone: (412)777-2000
Fax: (412)777-2034
Web: http://www.bayerus.com

Company Description

Former Name: Miles Inc.
Employees: 23,504
SIC(s): 2833 Medicinals & Botanicals, 2834 Pharmaceutical Preparations, 2836 Biological Products Except Diagnostic, 2842 Polishes & Sanitation Goods.
Parent Company: Bayer Group, Leverkusen, Germany

Operating Locations

CA: Bayer Corp., Berkeley; Bayer Corp. Pharmaceuticals, Berkeley; Bayer Corp., Irvine, Laguna Hills, Lake Forest, Sacramento, Stockton, Tustin; CO: Bayer Corp., Aurora; CT: Bayer Corp. Pharmaceutical Division, West Haven; DC: Bayer Corp., Washington; Bayer Corp., Washington; FL: Bayer Corp., Vero Beach; IL: Bayer Corp., Kankakee; Florasynth, Skokie; IN: Bayer Corp., Elkhart; MA: CheMarketing International, Fitchburg; ChemDesign Corp., Fitchburg; NRC, Newton; Deerfield Urethane, South Deerfield; Polysar, Springfield; AGFA EPS Division, Wilmington; MI: Bayer Corp., Troy; MO: Bayer Corp., Kansas City; Bayer Group Agriculture Division, Kansas City; Bayer Corp., Shawnee; MS: Bayer Corp., Jackson; NC: Cutter Laboratories, Clayton; NJ: Bayer Group Flavors Division, Branchburg; Bayer Group Consumer Care Division, Morristown; Bayer Corp., Parsippany; Cutter Biologicals, Pompton Plains; AGFA Division of Bayer Corp., Ridgefield Park; Bayer Corp., Ridgefield Park; Bayer Group Fragrance Division, Springfield; Haarmann & Reimer Corp., Springfield; Florasynth, Teterboro; Rhein Chemie Corp., Trenton; NY: Bayer Corp., New York; H.C. Starck, New York; Bayer Corp., Tarrytown; Bayer Corp. Diagnostics Division, Tarrytown; OH: Bayer Corp., Addyston; PA: Bayer Corp., Pittsburgh; Bayer Group Polymers Division, Pittsburgh; PR: Bayer Corp.; SC: Bayer Corp., Columbia; TX: Bayer Corp., Houston; WI: SpecialtyChem Products Corp., Marinette

Nonmonetary Support

Value: $200,000 (1991)
Type: Donated Products
Note: Company provides nonmonetary support. Annual nonmonetary support is approximately $200,000.

Bayer Foundation

Giving Contact

Sande Deitch, Executive Director
Bayer Foundation
100 Bayer Road, Building 4
Pittsburgh, PA 15205-9741
Phone: (412)777-5791
Fax: (412)778-4432

Description

EIN: 356026510
Organization Type: Corporate Foundation
Giving Locations: headquarters and operating communities.
Grant Types: Capital, Endowment, General Support.

Giving Philosophy

'Bayer Corporation is committed to taking an active role in its business communities. Through the Bayer Foundation, the company works with community leaders to enhance the quality of life for its employees and their neighbors. The foundation makes grants in three areas: civic and community programs; science education and workforce development; and the arts, arts education, and culture.'

Financial Summary

Total Giving: $4,500,000 (1997 approx); $3,400,000 (1996 approx); $2,685,644 (1995 approx). Note: Contributes through foundation only.
Giving Analysis: Giving for 1997 includes: foundation (approx $4,500,000)
Assets: $34,000,000 (1995 approx); $30,047,406 (1994); $28,873,763 (1993)

Typical Recipients

Arts & Humanities: Arts Associations & Councils, Arts Centers, Arts Festivals, Community Arts, Museums/Galleries, Music, Opera, Performing Arts, Public Broadcasting
Civic & Public Affairs: Professional & Trade Associations, Public Policy, Safety, Urban & Community Affairs
Education: Business Education, Colleges & Universities, Education-General, Medical Education, Minority Education, Private Education (Precollege), Public Education (Precollege), Science/Mathematics Education, Secondary Education (Public)
Health: Clinics/Medical Centers, Health Funds, Health Organizations, Hospitals, Single-Disease Health Associations
International: International Organizations
Religion: Religious Welfare
Social Services: Community Service Organizations, People with Disabilities, United Funds/United Ways, Youth Organizations

Contributions Analysis

Giving Priorities: Programs that address science literacy, science education or science-oriented vocational education; science programs at colleges and universities; cultural activities that are accessible to a majority of community resident; arts education programs; and broad-based civic and community programs.
Note: Twice a year written notification of decisions will be made within a few weeks of the meeting at which the proposal is reviewed.

Application Procedures

Initial Contact: See corporate website for guidelines, then send written proposal to Site Contributions Committee at the Bayer site nearest your organization.
Application Requirements: Include organization's name, contact person, title, address, phone number, and federal I.D. number; whether your organization receives operating funds from the United Way; organization's history and purpose, including the services it provides and the people and geographic areas it serves; purpose for which funding is requested, including what issue, problem or need is being addressed by the project or activity, how it answers a need in the community, how it provides broad community access, a plan for achieving the stated objectives, expected outcomes, how results will be measured, how the program relates to priorities of the Bayer Foundation, the city or region the program targets, who the program will serve, project timetable, and similar programs or services your organization offers; and your organization's total annual budget and the total budget for the project, clearly indicating support request from foundation and support obtained from other funders. Attach a board-approved budget and year-to-date actuals for current year; most recent audited financial report and Form 990; proof of tax-exempt status; list of board of directors, with addresses and affiliations; and list of significant funding for the past two year.
Deadlines: March 15 and September 15.
Review Process: Site Contributions Committee reviews proposals and forwards them to the foundation; if additional information is needed, staff will contact applicant.
Decision Notification: Written notification of decisions will be made within a few weeks of the meeting at which the proposal is reviewed.

Restrictions

Company does not make grants to organizations without 501(c)(3) status; individuals; charitable dinners and events; student trips or exchange programs; religious organizations; organizations that discriminate by race, color, creed, gender, or national origin; United Way agencies for operating support; endowment funds; political or lobbying groups; deficit reduction or operating reserves; community advertising; athletic sponsorships; telephone solicitations; or organizations located outside of the U.S.

Additional Information

Bayer Inc. Pharmaceutical Division also has a small grant program in West Have, CT.
Publications: Application Guidelines

Corporate Officials

Margo Barnes: senior vice president, treasurer PRIM CORP EMPL senior vice president: Bayer Corp.
Gerd Dieter Mueller: executive vice president, chief financial officer, director, chief administrative officer B Hannover, Germany 1936. ED University of Munich (1957-1959); University of Cologne LLB (1961); Nordhein-Westfalen (Germany) LLM (1965). PRIM CORP EMPL executive vice president, chief financial officer, director, chief administrative officer: Bayer Corp. CORP AFFIL president: CDS International. NONPR AFFIL member: National Association Manufacturer; trustee: Robert Morris College.
Helge H. Wehmeier: president, chief executive officer, director B Goettingen, Germany 1943. PRIM CORP EMPL president, chief executive officer, director: Bayer Corp. CORP AFFIL director: PNC Bank Corp.; member: Trilateral Commission; president, chief executive officer: Bayer AG; member: Conference Board. NONPR AFFIL member: Chemical Manufacturers Association; director: Pittsburgh Symphony Society; trustee: Carnegie Mellon University; member executive committee: Allegheny Conference on Community Development; business committee member: Arts Inc. New York.
Jon R. Wyne: senior vice president, treasurer B 1944. ED University of California, Santa Barbara BA (1966); University of California, Los Angeles MBA (1968). PRIM CORP EMPL senior vice president, treasurer: Bayer Corp. CORP AFFIL treasurer, director: Deerfield Urethane Inc.

Foundation Officials

Margo Barnes: vice president (see above)
Sande Deitch: executive director
Thomas Kerr: secretary
Gerd Dieter Mueller: president (see above)
Jon R. Wyne: treasurer (see above)

Grants Analysis

Disclosure Period: calendar year ending
Typical Range: $500 to $10,000

L.L. BEAN, INC.

Company Contact

Freeport, ME
Web: http://www.llbean.com/

Company Description

Employees: 3,500
SIC(s): 5961 Catalog & Mail-Order Houses.

Nonmonetary Support

Type: Cause-related Marketing & Promotion; Donated Products; Loaned Employees
Note: Nonmonetary support is provided by the company. Company also provides facilities for meetings.

Corporate Sponsorship

Type: Arts & cultural events

Giving Contact

Janet Wyper, Manager, Community Relations
L.L. Bean, Inc.
Casco Street
Freeport, ME 04033
Phone: (207)865-4761
Fax: (207)552-6821

Description

Organization Type: Corporate Giving Program
Giving Locations: ME: Brunswick, Freeport, Lewiston, Portland nationally.
Grant Types: Award, Capital, General Support, Multiyear/Continuing Support.

Giving Philosophy

'L.L. Bean is an active and committed corporate citizen, forming relationships with national, state, regional and local not for profit and civic organizations. The company's corporate philosophy is rooted in the spirit of giving back to the community and has concentrated efforts on being a good neighbor through philanthropic and civic leadership.
Long term relationships are the core of L.L. Bean's giving philosophy, and the company has several partnerships that date back more than twenty years. Many of these relationships have benefited from resources that include expertise and goods in kind as well as dollars. Financial contributions are made in the form of grants, capital campaign pledges and product or gift certificate donations. Inherent to its strong belief in community leadership is L.L. Bean's encouragement of volunteerism and the company's support and organization of a number of community activities. Hundreds of L.L. Bean employees have helped to maintain the largest section of the Appalachian Trail in Maine. Events such as the local children's fishing derby and the 4th of July Family Fun Run and 10K race, as well as the lead corporate contributor to the American Red Cross blood drives in the state of Maine are traditions dating back decades.'
L.L. Bean focuses charitable giving in four major categories: Conservation and Recreation, Education, Health and Human Services, and Culture and the Arts. *L.L. Bean Corporate Citizenship*

Financial Summary

Total Giving: $1,000,000 (1997 approx); $1,000,000 (1996 approx); $1,000,000 (1995 approx). Note: Contributes through corporate direct giving program only.

Typical Recipients

Arts & Humanities: Museums/Galleries, Performing Arts, Public Broadcasting, Theater
Education: Education Reform, Elementary Education (Public), Education-General, Science/Mathematics Education, Vocational & Technical Education
Environment: Environment-General, Resource Conservation, Wildlife Protection
Health: Hospitals
Social Services: Community Service Organizations, Recreation & Athletics, Volunteer Services

Contributions Analysis

Giving Priorities: Conservation, education, health, social services, and the arts.
Arts & Humanities: Limited funding is available for local cultural and arts organizations, such as the Portland Museum of Art and the Maine State Music Theater.
Education: Eduational reform in local public schools (K-12) in Maine is the second priority. Focus is on curriculum development and restructuring efforts to improve the quality of education and life choices of children of employees and their neighbors. Organizations that have been supported include: the Maine Aspirations Foundation, Main Math and Science Alliance, and the Maine Career Advantage Program.
Environment: Conservation and recreation receive the majority of grants with emphasis on recreational activities that encourage responsible use of the outdoors. For example, funds have been awarded to the Appalachian Mountain Club, Appalachian Trail Conference, Ducks Unlimited, and the Student Conservation Association.
Social Services: Support is also given to health and human services in the local area, including major support to the United Way.

Application Procedures

Initial Contact: Submit a brief proposal.
Application Requirements: Include a brief statement of organization's goals and accomplishments; purpose of project, population served and timeframe; amount requested and how it will be used; itemized budget including all sources of committed and anticipated funding; and proof of tax-exempt status.
Deadlines: June 30.
Review Process: Acknowledgement of proposal will be sent within two weeks of receipt.
Decision Notification: Proposals that have been processed for further consideration will be reviewed in December by board of directors.
Notes: The company previously did not accept applications and prefers to fund organizations with which it has long-standing relationships.

Restrictions

Contributions are not made to individuals; political, sectarian or religious groups; team sponsorships or sporting events; conference sponsorships; advertising in programs, bulletins, yearbooks or brochures; or film or television underwriting

Additional Information

Company donates 2% to 3% of pretax earnings to charity.
Company reports that grants are awarded in December.

Corporate Officials

Leon A. Gorman: president, chief executive officeraffairs B Nashua, NH 1934. ED Bowdoin College BA (1956). PRIM CORP EMPL president, chief executive officer: L.L. Bean, Inc. CORP AFFIL director: Depositors Corp.; director: Carrol Reed Ski Shops; director: Central ME Power Co. NONPR AFFIL trustee: Outward Bound School Hurricane Island; director: Pine Tree County Boy Scouts; corporate: Maine Medical Center; member, director: Greater Portland Chamber of Commerce; advisor, trustee: Maine Audubon Society; member alumni council: Bowdoin College.
John Oliver: director public affairs PRIM CORP EMPL director public affairs: L.L. Bean, Inc.

Giving Program Officials

Janet Wyper: PRIM CORP EMPL senior community relations specialist: L.L. Bean, Inc.

BECHTEL GROUP, INC.

Company Contact

San Francisco, CA
Web: http://www.bechtel.com

Company Description

Revenue: US$8,500,000,000
Employees: 30,000
SIC(s): 1522 Residential Construction Nec, 1541 Industrial Buildings & Warehouses, 1542 Nonresidential Construction Nec, 1611 Highway & Street Construction.

Operating Locations

Australia: Bechtel Australia Proprietary Ltd., Melbourne; Minenco Pty. Ltd., South Melbourne; Oakden Pty. Ltd., South Melbourne; York Town Corp. Pty., South Melbourne; Canada: Seauanda Ventures, Don Mills; Bechtel Quebec Ltd., Montreal; Bechtel Canada, Toronto; France: Bechtel France, Paris, Ville-de-Paris; Japan: Overseas Bechtel Japan Branch, Tokyo; Republic of Korea: Bechtel International, Kangnam-Gu, Seoul; Singapore:, Singapore; Bechtel Singapore (Pte.) Ltd., Singapore; Spain: Bechtel Espana SA, Madrid; Thailand: Bechtel International, Bangkok; Taiwan: Pacific Engineers & Constructors Ltd., Taipei; United Kingdom: Bechtel Holdings Ltd., London; Bechtel Ltd., London; Bechtel Personnel & Operational Services Ltd., London; Bechtel Risk Management Ltd., London; Bechtel Water Technology Ltd., London

Nonmonetary Support

Value: $100,000 (1997)
Type: In-kind Services
Note: Co. provides limited nonmonetary support.

Bechtel Foundation

Giving Contact

Leeanne Lang, Assistant Secretary
Bechtel Foundation
PO Box 193965
San Francisco, CA 94119-3965
Phone: (415)768-5974
Fax: (415)768-0263
Email: lmlang@bechtel.com

Description

EIN: 946078120
Organization Type: Corporate Foundation
Giving Locations: internationally, in major operating locations.
Grant Types: Employee Matching Gifts, General Support.
Note: Foundation matches employee gifts to colleges and universities in the United States.

Financial Summary

Total Giving: $3,000,000 (2000 approx); $2,900,000 (1999 approx); $2,017,000 (1998). Note: Contributes through foundation only.
Giving Analysis: Giving for 1998 includes: foundation ($2,017,000); 1999: foundation (approx $2,900,000); 2000: foundation (approx $3,000,000)
Assets: $20,504,000 (1999); $20,960,000 (1998); $21,522,000 (1997)

Typical Recipients

Arts & Humanities: Ethnic & Folk Arts, Libraries, Museums/Galleries
Civic & Public Affairs: African American Affairs, Business/Free Enterprise, Chambers of Commerce, Clubs, Economic Development, Economic Policy, Ethnic Organizations, Hispanic Affairs, Legal Aid, Minority Business, Nonprofit Management, Philanthropic Organizations, Professional & Trade Associations, Public Policy, Urban & Community Affairs, Zoos/Aquariums
Education: Business-School Partnerships, Colleges & Universities, Education Funds, Education Reform, Elementary Education (Public), Engineering/Technological Education, Education-General, International Studies, Legal Education, Minority Education, Private Education (Precollege), Public Education (Precollege), Science/Mathematics Education, Secondary Education (Public), Student Aid, Vocational & Technical Education
Health: Cancer, Emergency/Ambulance Services, Hospitals, Research/Studies Institutes
International: Foreign Educational Institutions, International Affairs, International Development, International Organizations, International Peace & Security Issues, International Relations, Missionary/Religious Activities
Religion: Jewish Causes, Religious Welfare
Science: Science Exhibits & Fairs, Science Museums, Scientific Centers & Institutes, Scientific Organizations, Scientific Research
Social Services: Child Welfare, Emergency Relief, Food/Clothing Distribution, Recreation & Athletics, Scouts, Substance Abuse, United Funds/United Ways, Youth Organizations

Contributions Analysis

Giving Priorities: Education, social welfare organizations, civic organiztions, arts groups, and health organizations. Limited support to U.S.-based organizations with an international focus; interests include economics and policy organizations.
Education: About 70%. Support is given for educational enrichment programs such as local science fairs, special educational activities, or regional museum programs, in math or science, for young people around the world; and engineering and business schools at selected colleges and universities around the world (divided between unrestricted support and support for scholarship programs).
Social Services: About 15%. Social service programs, primarily United Way or similar campaigns in the communities with Bechtel offices or major projects.

Application Procedures

Initial Contact: Send a brief letter of inquiry; if foundation is interested, a full proposal will be requested.
Application Requirements: Include a description of organization; amount requested; purpose for which funds are sought; recently audited financial statement; and proof of tax-exempt status.
Deadlines: None.

Restrictions

Foundation does not support religious, fraternal, or social organizations; individuals; conferences and events; media productions; fellowships; fellowships; internships, or residencies; endowed or named chairs; or catalogs and publications.
Foundation rarely makes grants to individual schools or school districts.

Additional Information

In all cases, local Bechtel managers make the grants for their geographic areas. Nearly all grants are initiated by the local management team.

Corporate Officials

Riley Peart Bechtel: chairman, chief executive officer, director B 1952. ED University of California, Davis BA (1975); Stanford University MBA (1980); Stanford University JD (1980). PRIM CORP EMPL chairman, chief executive officer, director: Bechtel Corp., Inc. CORP AFFIL director: Sequoia Ventures Inc.; director: JP Morgan & Co. Inc.; chairman, director: Overseas Bechtel Inc.; director: Fremont Group LLC; director: Fremont Investors Inc.; chairman, director: Bechtel Power Corp.; chairman, director: Bechtel Operating Services Corp.; chairman, director: Bechtel Overseas Corp.; chairman: Bechtel Leasing Services Inc.; president: Bechtel Financial Services Co.; chairman, director: Bechtel International Inc.; chairman, director: Bechtel Energy Corp.; chairman, director: America Bechtel Inc.; chairman: Bechtel Construction Operations Inc. NONPR AFFIL member deans advisory council: Stanford University Law School; trustee: Thacher School; member advisory council: Stanford University Graduate School Business; member: California Business Roundtable; member: JP Morgan International Advisory Council; member policy committee: Business Roundtable; member: American Bar Association; member: Business Council.
John Douglas Carter: executive vice president, director B Pendleton, OR 1946. ED Harvard University LLB; Stanford University AB (1968); Harvard University JD (1971). PRIM CORP EMPL executive vice president, director: Bechtel Group, Inc. ADD CORP EMPL senior vice president: america Bechtel Inc.; senior vice president: Bechtel Corp.; director: Bechtel Overseas Corp.; director: Bechtel Power Corp.; director: Overseas Bechtel Inc. CORP AFFIL president: Bechtel Enterprises Inc. NONPR AFFIL member: San Francisco Bar Association; member: San Francisco Chamber of Commerce; member: California Bar Association; member: International Bar Association; member: American Bar Association. CLUB AFFIL Bankers Club; Olympic Club.
Donald J. Gunther: director B 1938. ED University of Missouri BScE (1960). PRIM CORP EMPL director:

Bechtel Group, Inc. CORP AFFIL president: Bechtel Americas; executive vice president: Bechtel Corp.
Adrian Zaccaria: president, chief operating officer, director B 1944. ED United States Merchant Marine Academy BS (1966). PRIM CORP EMPL president, chief operating officer, director: Bechtel Group, Inc. CORP AFFIL officer: Bechtel Systems Infrastructure; administration: International Bechtel S De RL; president: Bechtel Overseas Corp.; president: Bechtel Leasing Services Inc.; president: Bechtel North America Power Corp.; executive vice president, director: Bechtel Corp.; president: Bechtel International Inc.; president: America Bechtel Inc.; vice chairman: Bechtel Construction Operations Inc.

Foundation Officials

Riley Peart Bechtel: chairman (see above)
M. E. Martello: assistant treasurer
Georgeanne Proctor: treasurer
Charles E. Redman: president

Grants Analysis

Disclosure Period: calendar year ending 1998
Total Grants: $2,017,000
Number of Grants: 327
Average Grant: $5,000 (approx)
Highest Grant: $150,000
Typical Range: $1,000 to $10,000
Note: Grants analysis provided by the company.

Recent Grants

Note: Grants derived from 1996 Form 990.

Arts & Humanities

10,000 Pierpont Morgan Library, New York, NY

Civic & Public Affairs

50,000 American Society of Civil Engineers, New York, NY
35,000 National Association of Minority Contractors, Washington, DC
30,000 Committee for Economic Development, New York, NY
14,900 Society of Women Engineers, New York, NY
10,000 East Bay Zoological Society, Oakland, CA

Education

275,000 Jason Foundation for Education, Waltham, MA
180,000 Oakland Unified School District, Oakland, CA
100,000 Castilleja School, Palo Alto, CA
60,000 National Action Council for Minorities in Engineering, New York, NY
55,000 Pennsylvania State University, University Park, PA
30,500 University of California Berkeley, Berkeley, CA
28,500 University of Houston, Houston, TX
22,150 Houston Baptist University, Houston, TX
20,000 National Society of Professional Engineers Educational Foundation, Alexandria, VA
20,000 Yale University, New Haven, CT
18,500 University of California Berkeley, Berkeley, CA
16,500 Stanford University, Stanford, CA
15,000 Partners in School Innovation
15,000 San Francisco State University, San Francisco, CA
13,895 National Merit Scholarship Corporation, Evanston, IL
13,100 University of Maryland, College Park, MD
13,000 Colorado School of Mines, Golden, CO
13,000 Junior Engineering Technical Society, Alexandria, VA
12,334 Montgomery College Foundation, Rockville, MD
11,000 North Carolina A&T State University, Greensboro, NC
10,000 Bel Air High School, Bel Air, CA
10,000 Cunningham Elementary School
10,000 International Road Educational Foundation, Washington, DC
10,000 Lewis T. Preston Education Program for Girls
10,000 Montana Tech Foundation, Butte, MT
10,000 Teach for America, New York, NY
10,000 Virginia Polytechnic Institute and State University, Blacksburg, VA

Health

25,000 Meyer Friedman Institute, San Francisco, CA

International

60,000 American University of Beirut, Beirut, Lebanon
30,000 International House, Berkeley, CA
23,500 Laspau Academic and Professional Programs for the Americas, Cambridge, MA
23,000 Hoover Institution on War, Peace, and Revolution, Stanford, CA
20,000 Hong Kong University of Science and Technology, Hong Kong
20,000 National University of Singapore, Singapore
10,000 American University in Cairo, Cairo, Egypt
10,000 Malaysian-American Commission

Religion

10,000 US Holocaust Memorial Museum, Washington, DC

Science

10,000 Exploratorium, San Francisco, CA
10,000 San Francisco Bay Area Science Fair, San Francisco, CA
10,000 US Space Foundation, Colorado Springs, CO

Social Services

214,000 United Way Bay Area, San Francisco, CA
25,000 Houston Golf Association, Houston, TX
15,625 United Way Benton and Franklin Counties, Tri-Cities, WA
10,000 Oregon's Children Foundation, OR

BECKMAN COULTER, INC.

Company Contact

Fullerton, CA
Web: http://www.beckmancoulter.com

Company Description

Former Name: Beckman Instruments, Inc.
Employees: 10,000 (1999)
SIC(s): 2833 Medicinals & Botanicals, 3826 Analytical Instruments, 8071 Medical Laboratories.

Nonmonetary Support

Type: Donated Equipment
Note: The company also has a mentor program.

Corporate Sponsorship

Type: Pledge-a-thon

Giving Contact

Elke Eastman, Manager, Community Affairs
Beckman Coulter, Inc.
4300 N. Harbor Boulevard
PO Box 3100
Fullerton, CA 92834-3100
Phone: (714)871-4848
Fax: (714)773-7743

Description

Organization Type: Corporate Giving Program
Giving Locations: headquarters and operating communities.
Grant Types: Challenge, Conference/Seminar, Employee Matching Gifts, Project, Research, Seed Money.

Financial Summary

Total Giving: $500,000 (2000 approx); $500,000 (1999 approx); $400,000 (1998 approx). Note: Contributes through corporate direct giving program only. Giving includes nonmonetary support.

Typical Recipients

Education: Afterschool/Enrichment Programs, Business-School Partnerships, Colleges & Universities, Community & Junior Colleges, Elementary Education (Public), Engineering/Technological Education, Faculty Development, Education-General, Science/Mathematics Education
Health: AIDS/HIV, Alzheimers Disease, Arthritis, Cancer, Diabetes, Heart, Kidney, Medical Research, Multiple Sclerosis, Respiratory
Science: Science-General, Observatories & Planetariums, Science Exhibits & Fairs, Science Museums, Scientific Centers & Institutes, Scientific Labs, Scientific Organizations, Scientific Research
Social Services: Food/Clothing Distribution, United Funds/United Ways, Volunteer Services

Contributions Analysis

Education: Scientific education, science, and research-related healthcare.

Application Procedures

Initial Contact: Requests must be in writing
Application Requirements: Send a one-page letter of request. Include a description of organization, amount requested, and purpose of funds sought.
Review Process: The Employees Contributions Task Force Committee meets at least 10 times per year.
Notes: All requests are acknowledged.

Restrictions

Does not support individuals, religious organizations for sectarian purposes, or political or lobbying groups.

Additional Information

The Arnold and Mabel Beckman Foundation (Irvine, CA) is not associated with Beckman Coulter, Inc.
Publications: Guidelines Sheet

Corporate Officials

John P. Wareham: president, chief executive officer, director B 1941. PRIM CORP EMPL president, chief executive officer, director: Beckman Coulter Inc. CORP AFFIL president: Hybritech Inc.
Dennis K. Wilson: vice president finance, chief financial officer PRIM CORP EMPL vice president finance, chief financial officer: Beckman Instruments Inc. CORP AFFIL vice president finance, chief executive officer: Beckman Coulter Inc.; vice president: Hybritech Inc.

Grants Analysis

Disclosure Period: calendar year ending

Recent Grants

Note: Grants derived from 1996 grants list.

Education

California State University, Fullerton, CA
Fullerton School District and Fullerton Union High School District, Fullerton, CA
Irvine Unified School District, Irvine, CA

Health

AIDS Walk of Orange County
American Cancer Society
March of Dimes
National Multiple Sclerosis Society
Pediatric Cancer Research Foundation

Science
Keystone Science Center
Orange County Science and Engineering Fair

BECTON DICKINSON &CO.

Company Contact

Franklin Lakes, NJ
Web: http://bd.com

Company Description

Revenue: US$3,116,900,000
Employees: 18,900
Fortune Rank: 451, per FORTUNE Magazine's list of 500 Largest U.S. Corporations (1999).
FF 451
SIC(s): 2381 Fabric Dress & Work Gloves, 2812 Alkalies & Chlorine, 2834 Pharmaceutical Preparations, 3841 Surgical & Medical Instruments.

Operating Locations

Austria: Becton Dickinson Warenvertriebs GmbH, Vienna; Belgium: Becton Dickinson Benelux NV, Aalst, Flandre-Orientale; Becton Dickinson Buitven, Aalst, Flandre-Orientale; Becton Dickinson France SA, Aalst, Flandre-Orientale; Becton Dickinson Distribution Center NV, Temse, Flandre-Orientale; Brazil: Becton Dickinson Industrias Cirurgicas Ltda., Juiz de Fora; Canada: Becton Dickinson Canada, Mississauga; France: Becton Dickinson & Co., Le Pont de Claix, Isere; Becton Dickinson France, Le Pont de Claix, Isere; Becton Dickinson Laboratory Products-Europe, Meylan; Germany: Becton Dickinson GmbH, Heidelberg, Baden-Wuerttemberg; Hong Kong: Asia Becton Dickinson, Wan Chai; Becton Dickinson & Co. Ltd., Wan Chai; Ireland:, Dun Laoghaire; Benex Ltd., Shannon; Italy: Becton Dickinson Italia SpA, Milano, Lombardia; Japan: Nippon Becton Dickinson Co. Ltd., Tokyo; Netherlands: Becton Dickinson BV, Leiden, Zuid-Holland; Becton Dickinson Cellular Imaging Systems BV, Leiden, Zuid-Holland; Panama: Becton Dickinson & Co. SA, Panama City; Singapore: Becton Dickinson Medical Products Pte. Ltd., Singapore; Becton Dickinson Worldwide, Singapore; Spain: Becton Dickinson SA, San Agustin de Guadalix; Sweden: Becton Dickinson AB, Stockholm; Switzerland: Becton Dickinson AG, Basel, Basel-Stadt; United Kingdom: B-D UK Holdings Ltd., Oxford, Oxfordshire; Becton Dickinson (Royston) Ltd., Oxford, Oxfordshire; B-D (Cambridge UK) Ltd., Royston, Hertfordshire

Nonmonetary Support

Type: Donated Equipment; Donated Products; Inkind Services
Volunteer Programs: BD employees and retirees who volunteer their time to charitable organizations are honored through the company's Community Service Awards Program. The program provides financial contributions to the non-profit organization to which BD associates have donated their time.

Giving Contact

Elizabeth Scott, Manager, Community Relations
Becton Dickinson & Co.
1 Becton Dr.
Franklin Lakes, NJ 07417
Phone: (201)847-6651
Fax: (201)847-5305
Web: http://www.bd.com/community

Description

Organization Type: Corporate Giving Program. Supports preselected organizations only.
Giving Locations: principally near operating locations and to national organizations.
Grant Types: Capital, Challenge, Employee Matching Gifts, Project, Scholarship, Seed Money.
Note: Capital grants are for hospitals only. The company sponsors a Matching Gifts Program, through which it matches donations of employees and retirees to eligible non-profit organizations. BD also matches specified hours of employee and volunteer service with a financial donation.

Giving Philosophy

'BD is a global medical technology firm whose goal is to fundamentally improve the health and well-being of the world's population. Our comprehensive corporate giving efforts make available financial resources, BD products and services, gifts in-kind, and, most importantly, the talen and integrity of our people in the support of non-profit programs that make a real difference in the health of people around the world.
'We work closely with non-profit partners who share our purpose and vision. We have a keen sense of social responsibility and the belief that strong community relationships serve to further our purpose and progress as an organization.
'Together . . . we work to create stronger and healthier communities around the world; we build strong relationships to address the critical needs of people worldwide; we are committed to action.' *BD Community Partnerships*

Financial Summary

Total Giving: $3,500,000 (1998 approx). Note: Company does not disclose contributions figures.

Typical Recipients

Civic & Public Affairs: Public Policy
Education: Colleges & Universities, Education Associations, Engineering/Technological Education, Medical Education, Science/Mathematics Education
Health: Hospitals, Medical Research, Medical Training, Nursing Services
International: Health Care/Hospitals
Science: Scientific Organizations
Social Services: Family Services, United Funds/United Ways, Volunteer Services, Youth Organizations

Contributions Analysis

Giving Priorities: Becton Dickinson & Co. manages a corporate contributions program as part of the company's community relations program. Direct support is provided, with a focus on support of health care related initiatives at the national and international levels. Support is offered through two separate programs. The Health Care Fund focuses on public and preventive health care programs throughout the world that address unmet needs in the areas of medical and technological concentrations. The Local Initiatives Fund supports community intiatives in areas where Becton Dickinson has a presence.

Restrictions

The BD Global Healthcare Fund does not support fund-raising events and prefers to donate directly to health care programs and operations. The Fund does not contribute to workshops, sporting events, or dinners. Only qualified charitable/non-profit organizations are eligible for funding. Healthcare proposals are accepted by invitation only.
The BD Local Initiatives Fund provides support for the underwriting of programs and operating costs of qualified charitable/non-profit organizations only. Event-driven activities are not supported.

Additional Information

BD provides product donations, including medical supplies and devises and diagnostic systems, through several relief organizations. Contact directly any of the following agencies which partner with BD to distribute product donations if interested in receiving general medical relief information: AmeriCares, 800-486-HELP; MAP International, 800-225-8550; Project Hope, 800-544-HOPE.

Corporate Officials

Clateo Castellini: chairman, president, chief executive officer B Milan, Italy 1935. ED Bocconi University BA (1958); Harvard University MBA (1973). PRIM CORP EMPL chairman, president, chief executive officer: Becton Dickinson & Co. CORP AFFIL director: Bestfoods. NONPR AFFIL member: Economic Development Board.
Wesley Jackson Howe: chairman emeritus, director B Jersey City, NJ 1921. ED Stevens Institute of Technology ME (1943); Stevens Institute of Technology MS (1953). PRIM CORP EMPL chairman emeritus, director: Becton Dickinson & Co. CORP AFFIL chairman: Reins Co.; chairman: New Jersey Business & Industry; director: New Jersey Manufacturers Insurance Co. NONPR AFFIL member: New Jersey Chamber of Commerce; chairman emeritus board trustee: Stevens Institute Technology. CLUB AFFIL Arcola Country Club.

Giving Program Officials

Elizabeth Scott: manager community relations

Grants Analysis

Disclosure Period: calendar year ending
Typical Range: $2,500 to $5,000

BELK-SIMPSON DEPARTMENT STORES

Company Contact

Greenville, SC

Company Description

Employees: 850

Belk-Simpson Foundation

Giving Contact

Maryanne Senior Vice President and Foundation Coordinator Hartman
700 Haywood Rd.
Greenville, SC 29607
Phone: (864)235-3148
Fax: (864)232-1061
Note: Extension for Ms. Hartman is 213

Description

Founded: 1944
EIN: 576020261
Organization Type: Corporate Foundation
Giving Locations: headquarters and operating communities.
Grant Types: General Support.

Financial Summary

Total Giving: $591,800 (1998); $479,500 (1997); $351,750 (1996)
Giving Analysis: Giving for 1998 includes: foundation ($554,300); foundation grants to United Way ($37,500)
Assets: $13,426,773 (1998); $12,777,075 (1997); $9,640,239 (1996)
Gifts Received: $242,355 (1998); $224,794 (1997); $99,749 (1996). Note: Contributions are received from various Belks Stores.

Typical Recipients

Arts & Humanities: Arts Centers, History & Archaeology, Museums/Galleries, Music, Performing Arts
Civic & Public Affairs: African American Affairs, Chambers of Commerce, Civic & Public Affairs-General, Parades/Festivals

Education: Arts/Humanities Education, Colleges & Universities, Medical Education, Private Education (Precollege), Religious Education
Environment: Environment-General, Resource Conservation
Health: Cancer, Clinics/Medical Centers, Emergency/Ambulance Services, Health Organizations, Hospitals, Medical Research, Single-Disease Health Associations
Religion: Churches, Religious Organizations, Religious Welfare, Seminaries
Social Services: Child Welfare, Community Service Organizations, Food/Clothing Distribution, Homes, Senior Services, Shelters/Homelessness, United Funds/United Ways, United Funds/United Ways, YMCA/YWCA/YMHA/YWHA, Youth Organizations

Contributions Analysis

Giving Priorities: Religion, education, social services, and the environment.
Arts & Humanities: 7%. Funds museums, performing arts, and historical society.
Civic & Public Affairs: 1%.
Education: 20%. Supports private pre-college and higher education.
Environment: 17%. Funds conservation efforts.
Health: 7%. Supports hospitals, clinics, and cancer research.
Religion: 29%. Christian groups, churches, and welfare organizations are supported.
Social Services: 19%. Funds United Way, youth groups, and social services.
Note: Total contributions in 1998.

Application Procedures

Initial Contact: Send brief letter on organization's letterhead describing program.
Deadlines: May 1; November 1.

Corporate Officials

John Montgomery Belk: chairman B Charlotte, NC 1920. ED Davidson College (1943). PRIM CORP EMPL chairman: Belk Stores Services Inc. CORP AFFIL director: Lowes Home Centers Inc.; chairman: Parks-Belk Co. Northern Virginia; vice president: Leggett Realty South Boston Virginia; director: Lowes Companies; chairman: Charlotte Belk Inc.; director: Coca-Cola Bottling Co. Consolidated; director: Brothers Investment Co.; director: Chaparral Steel Co.; chairman: Belk-Hudson Inc. Spartanburg SC; chairman: Belk-Hudson-Leggett; chairman: Belk Enterprises Inc.; chairman: Belk-Gallant, La Grange Georgia; chairman: Belk Center Inc.; chairman: Belk Department Store, Greensboro NC; chairman: Belk Brothers Co.

Foundation Officials

John A. Kuhne: director
Lucy S. Kuhne: director
Nell M. Rice: director
Kate M. Simpson: director

Grants Analysis

Disclosure Period: calendar year ending 1998
Total Grants: $554,300*
Number of Grants: 117
Average Grant: $4,738
Highest Grant: $100,000
Typical Range: $200 to $20,000
*Note: Giving excludes United Way.

Recent Grants

Note: Grants derived from 1998 Form 990.

Arts & Humanities

25,000 Greenville County Art Museum, Greenville, SC
5,000 Greenville Symphony Orchestra, Greenville, SC
5,000 Imaginenation Children's Museum
2,000 Greenville County Historical Society, Greenville, SC

Civic & Public Affairs

5,000 Greenville Urban League, Greenville, SC

Education

50,000 Converse College, Columbia, SC
10,000 Furman University, Greenville, SC
10,000 Governor's School for the Arts, Louisville, KY
10,000 Presbyterian College, Clinton, SC
5,000 Converse College, Columbia, SC
5,000 South Carolina Governor's School For the Arts, Greenville, SC
5,000 Southside Christian School, Greenville, SC
5,000 St Josephs High School, New York, NY
2,500 Brevard College, Brevard, NC
2,500 King College, Bristol, TN
2,500 North Greenville College, Greenville, SC
2,000 Anderson College, Anderson, SC
2,000 Clemson University (Nurses School), Clemson, SC
1,000 Awarded November 1998 North Greenville College, Greenville, SC
1,000 Columbia International University, Columbia, SC

Environment

50,000 Highlands Land Trust, Highlands, NC
45,000 Montreat Cottager's Wilderness Fund, Montreat, NC

Health

25,000 Memorial Mission Hospital, Asheville, NC
10,000 Greenville Free Medical Clinic, Greenville, SC
1,500 Cancer Research Instituite, New York, NY
1,500 Cancer Research Institute, New York, NY

Religion

100,000 Montreat Presbyterian Church, Montreat, NC
25,000 Buncomb St United Methodist Church
10,000 Montreat Presbyterian Church, Montreat, NC
5,000 Bonclarken Assembly, Greenville, SC
5,000 Trinity Presbyterian Church, Asheville, NC
4,500 Fellowship of Christian Athletes-KY, Louisville, KY
4,500 Fellowship of Christian Athletes-KY, Louisville, KY
2,500 Salvation Army of Greenville, Greenville, SC
2,000 Changed Lives, Inc., Chattanooga, TN
2,000 Salvation Army, Greenville, SC
1,500 Greenville Rescue Mission, Greenville, SC

Social Services

25,000 Pendleton Place, Greenville, SC
25,000 United Way of Greenville County, Greenville, SC
25,000 Ymca of Greater Greenville, Greenville, SC
5,000 Presbyterian Home for Children, Charlotte, NC
5,000 United Way Greenville County, Greenville, SC
2,500 United Way of Kershaw County, Camden, SC
2,000 Cobb County Meals on Wheels, Marietta, GA
2,000 Cobb County Meals on Wheels, Marietta, GA
2,000 Meals on Wheels, Greenville, SC
2,000 Meals on Wheels-Greenville, Greenville, SC
2,000 Senior Action, Greenville, SC
2,000 Young Life, Inc., Raleigh, NC
2,000 Young Life, Inc., Raleigh, NC
2,000 Young Life, Inc., Raleigh, NC

Belk Stores Services Inc.

Company Contact

Charlotte, NC
Web: http://www.belk.com

Company Description

Employees: 2,300
SIC(s): 7389 Business Services Nec, 8721 Accounting, Auditing & Bookkeeping.

Nonmonetary Support

Note: In 1998, 10,681 shares of North Carolina Railroad (NCRR) were contributed to 12 different charities at fair market value.

Belk Foundation

Giving Contact

Paul B. Wyche, Jr., Trustee
Belk Foundation
2801 West Tyvola Road
Charlotte, NC 28217-4500
Phone: (704)357-1000
Fax: (704)357-1883

Description

Founded: 1988
EIN: 566046450
Organization Type: Corporate Foundation
Giving Locations: GA; NC; SC
Grant Types: Capital, Endowment, General Support, Operating Expenses, Professorship.

Financial Summary

Total Giving: $2,504,914 (fiscal year ending May 31, 1999); $1,950,156 (fiscal 1998)
Giving Analysis: Giving for fiscal 1998 includes: foundation ($1,944,556); foundation grants to United Way ($5,600); fiscal 1999: foundation ($2,497,914); foundation grants to United Way ($7,000)
Assets: $55,643,005 (fiscal 1998)
Gifts Received: $1,008,100 (fiscal 1998); $1,024,026 (fiscal 1994). Note: In 1994, contributions were received from Belk stores throughout Georgia and North and South Carolina.

Typical Recipients

Arts & Humanities: Arts Associations & Councils, Libraries, Museums/Galleries, Opera, Public Broadcasting
Civic & Public Affairs: Botanical Gardens/Parks, Business/Free Enterprise, Employment/Job Training, Civic & Public Affairs-General, Housing, Parades/Festivals, Urban & Community Affairs, Women's Affairs
Education: Afterschool/Enrichment Programs, Business Education, Colleges & Universities, Community & Junior Colleges, Economic Education, Education Associations, Education Funds, Elementary Education (Public), Literacy, Medical Education, Minority Education, Preschool Education, Private Education (Precollege), Public Education (Precollege), Science/Mathematics Education
Environment: Environment-General, Resource Conservation
Health: Children's Health/Hospitals, Emergency/Ambulance Services, Health Funds, Health Organizations, Hospitals, Hospitals (University Affiliated), Medical Rehabilitation
Religion: Churches, Ministries, Religious Organizations, Religious Welfare, Seminaries
Social Services: Child Welfare, Emergency Relief, Family Planning, Family Services, Recreation & Athletics, Scouts, Senior Services, Shelters/Homelessness, Substance Abuse, United Funds/United

Ways, YMCA/YWCA/YMHA/YWHA, Youth Organizations

Contributions Analysis

Giving Priorities: Education, social welfare organizations, health-care funds, community organizations, and the arts.

Arts & Humanities: 11%. Interests include museums and the performing arts.

Civic & Public Affairs: 4%. Supports community-oriented organizations.

Education: 63%. More than three-fourths generally supports colleges and universities in North Carolina, South Carolina, and Georgia. Other interests include child care, education funds, economic education, and precollege public education.

Health: 3%. Grants support building funds at North Carolina hospitals.

Religion: 9%. Funds seminaries, churches and ministries, and religious welfare.

Social Services: 10%. More than one-fourth supports united funds. Remaining funds support recreation, youth organizations, and family planning.

Note: Total contributions in fiscal 1998.

Application Procedures

Initial Contact: Send a brief written proposal.

Application Requirements: Include a description of organization; amount requested; purpose of funds sought; recently audited financial statement; proof of tax-exempt status; and whether single-year or multi-year grant is requested.

Deadlines: None.

Additional Information

Each of the Belk stores operate as an individual corp., but contributes through the foundation, including the Belk-Tyler Foundation in Rocky Mountain, NC and Belk-Simpson Foundation in Greenville, SC.

Corporate Officials

John Montgomery Belk: chairman B Charlotte, NC 1920. ED Davidson College (1943). PRIM CORP EMPL chairman: Belk Stores Services Inc. CORP AFFIL director: Lowes Home Centers Inc.; chairman: Parks-Belk Co. Northern Virginia; vice president: Leggett Realty South Boston Virginia; director: Lowes Companies; chairman: Charlotte Belk Inc.; director: Coca-Cola Bottling Co. Consolidated; director: Brothers Investment Co.; director: Chaparral Steel Co.; chairman: Belk-Hudson Inc. Spartanburg SC; chairman: Belk-Hudson-Leggett; chairman: Belk Enterprises Inc.; chairman: Belk-Gallant, La Grange Georgia; chairman: Belk Center Inc.; chairman: Belk Department Store, Greensboro NC; chairman: Belk Brothers Co.

Foundation Officials

Claudia Belk: member board advisors PRIM CORP EMPL director: Park Meridian Bank.

John Montgomery Belk: member board advisors (see above)

Katherine McKay Belk: member board advisors

B. Frank Matthews, II: member board advisors B 1928. PRIM CORP EMPL executive vice president, director: Matthews-Belk Co. CORP AFFIL officer: Public Service Co. NC.

Leroy Robinson: member board advisors CORP AFFIL director: Belk-Gallant, La Grange Georgia; director: Charlotte Belk Inc.; director: Belk Department Store, Rock Hill.

Grants Analysis

Disclosure Period: fiscal year ending May 31, 1999

Total Grants: $2,497,914*

Number of Grants: 67

Average Grant: $22,696*

Highest Grant: $1,000,000

Typical Range: $5,000 to $50,000

***Note:** Giving excludes United Way. Average grant excludes highest grant.

Recent Grants

Note: Grants derived from 1999 Form 990.

Arts & Humanities

100,000	Arts & Science Council, Charlotte, NC -- General
50,000	Museum Of The New South, Charlotte, NC -- General
25,000	Greensboro Children's Museum, Greensboro, NC -- Capital Campaign
12,000	WTVI Educational TV Station, Charlotte, NC -- General
10,000	Mint Museum of Art, Charlotte, NC -- General
7,000	Airborne & Special Operations Museum Foundation, Fayetteville, NC -- General

Civic & Public Affairs

44,000	Partners For Parks, Inc., Charlotte, NC -- General
10,000	Central Carolinas Choices, Charlotte, NC -- General
10,000	Festival In The Park, Charlotte, NC -- General
10,000	Junior Woman's Club, Charlotte, NC -- General
10,000	Wing Haven Foundation, Charlotte, NC -- General

Education

1,000,000	Davidson College, Charlotte, NC -- Scholarship Fund
175,000	Roanoke College, Roanoke, VA -- General
100,000	Mars Mill College -- Endowment Fund
40,000	Gaston County Literacy Council, Charlotte, NC -- General
30,000	Virginia Foundation For Independent Colleges, Richmond, VA -- Scholarship Fund
25,000	Appalachian State University, Boone, NC -- Endowment Fund
25,000	Wake Forest University, Winston-Salem, NC -- Scholarship Fund
20,000	Christ School, Arden, NC -- General
16,420	Charlotte Latin School, Charlotte, NC -- General
16,420	Gaston College, Dallas, NC -- General
15,000	Crossnore School, Crossnore, NC -- General
15,000	The Independent College Fund of North Carolina, Charlotte, NC -- Scholarship Fund
14,340	Belmont Abbey College, Belmont, NC -- General
10,000	Forestview High School, Gastonia, NC -- General
10,000	Junior Achievement of the Carolinas, Charlotte, NC -- General
7,000	Shaw University -- General
7,000	Shaw University, Raleigh, NC -- General

Health

50,000	Presbyterian Hospital Foundation, Charlotte, NC -- General
50,000	Ronald McDonald House, Jacksonville, FL -- General
50,000	Wake Forest University Baptist Medical Center, Winston-Salem, NC -- Capital Campaign
20,000	Cannon/Sloop Health Care Foundation, Newland, NC -- General
15,000	Presbyterian Hemby Children's Hospital, Charlotte, NC -- General

Religion

75,000	Union Theological Seminary, New York, NY -- Scholarship Fund
50,000	The Salvation Army, Charlotte, NC -- Capital Campaign
10,000	The Salvation Army, Gastonia, NC -- General
10,000	Wee Kirk Presbyterian Church, Montreat, NC -- Building Fund

Social Services

50,000	Boy Scouts of America-Mecklenburg County Council, Charlotte, NC -- General
50,000	CPCC Foundation, Charlotte, NC -- Capital Campaign
50,000	Sharon Towers, Charlotte, NC -- General
30,000	Kinder-Mourn, Charlotte, NC -- General
25,000	Lincoln County YMCA, Damariscotta, ME -- Capital Campaign
20,000	YMCA, Summerville, SC -- General
15,000	Charlotte Regional Sports Commission, Charlotte, NC -- Scholarship Fund
10,000	Boy Scouts of America - Northeast Georgia, Jefferson, GA -- General
10,000	Charlotte Mecklenburg Senior Centers, Charlotte, NC -- General
10,000	Charlotte Touchdown Club, Charlotte, NC -- Scholarship Fund
10,000	Lowcountry Senior Coalition, Inc., Charleston, SC -- Capital Campaign
7,000	Gaston County Family YMCA, Gastonia, NC -- General
7,000	United Way, Greensboro, NC -- General

BELL ATLANTIC CORP.

 Number 28 of Top 100 Corporate Givers

Company Contact

1095 Avenue of the Americas
New York, NY 10036
Phone: (212)395-2121
Web: http://www.bell-atl.com

Company Description

Revenue: US$33,174,000,000 (1999)
Profit: US$2,965,300,000 (1998)
Employees: 140,000 (1999)
Fortune Rank: 33, per FORTUNE Magazine's list of 500 Largest U.S. Corporations (1999).
FF 33
SIC(s): 4813 Telephone Communications Except Radiotelephone, 6719 Holding Companies Nec.

Nonmonetary Support

Type: Donated Equipment; Loaned Executives

Volunteer Programs: The foundation offers a variety of volunteerism opportunities through their Good Citizen programs. In 1999, employees donated over seven million hours and $11.7 million in monetary support.

Corporate Sponsorship

Type: Arts & cultural events; Festivals/fairs; Music & entertainment events; Pledge-a-thon; Sports events

Note: Sponsors golf-a-thons, walk-a-thons, museum exhibits, and concerts.

Bell Atlantic Foundation

Giving Contact

Suzanne DuBose, President
Bell Atlantic Foundation
1095 Avenue of the Americas, Room 3200
New York, NY 10036
Phone: 800-360-7955
Fax: (212)398-0951
Email: suzanne.a.dubose@bellatlantic.com
Web: http://www.bellatlanticfoundation.com

Alternate Contact

Juan Rodriguez
Phone: 800-621-9900

Email: juan.n.rodriguez@bellatlantic.com

Description

EIN: 232502809
Organization Type: Corporate Foundation
Giving Locations: DE; DC: Washington; ME; MD; MA; NH; NJ; NY; PA; RI; VT; VA; WV principally near operating locations and to national organizations.
Grant Types: Employee Matching Gifts, General Support.
Note: Employee matching gift ratio: 1 to 1 for education, arts & humanities, health & human services, and the environment.

Giving Philosophy

'New communication technologies have the power to improve the lives of people in our communities. The goal of the Bell Atlantic Foundation is to provide opportunities for nonprofit organizations to apply new technology to the programs and services they offer, advance their mission and give people in our communities the tools and means to improve their lives and achieve their goals.'
'We cannot solve every problem, of course. Nor can we possibly fund every worthwhile program. So we have chosen to focus our efforts on the cities and towns we serve from Maine to Virginia, and especially on the children and young people from these communities. And since information technology is what we are about, most of our philanthropic support will continue to be centered on making technology more available to students, as well as teachers, services organizations, and cultural institutions with youth programs.'
'The Bell Atlantic Foundation supports quality projects and programs that directly address community needs through effective communications and information management technology. Priority will be given to activities that facilitate collaborations through network solutions and enhanced communication systems in education; health and human services; arts and humanities; and communities.' From the Bell Atlantic Web Site

Financial Summary

Total Giving: $36,301,876 (1999); $31,672,396 (1998); $24,509,399 (1997). Note: Contributes through corporate direct giving program and foundation.
Giving Analysis: Giving for 1998 includes: foundation ($29,064,395); corporate direct giving ($2,414,173); nonmonetary support ($193,828); 1999: foundation ($31,123,819); corporate direct giving ($4,878,057); nonmonetary support ($300,000)
Assets: $33,000,000 (1999 approx); $20,940,703 (1996)
Gifts Received: $13,000,000 (1996)

Typical Recipients

Arts & Humanities: Arts Associations & Councils, Arts & Humanities-General, History & Archaeology, Libraries, Museums/Galleries, Music, Public Broadcasting, Theater
Civic & Public Affairs: African American Affairs, Civic & Public Affairs-General
Education: Arts/Humanities Education, Business Education, Colleges & Universities, Education Reform, Engineering/Technological Education, Education-General, Literacy, Minority Education, Public Education (Precollege), Science/Mathematics Education, Student Aid, Vocational & Technical Education
International: International Environmental Issues
Science: Scientific Organizations
Social Services: Child Welfare, United Funds/United Ways, Volunteer Services, Youth Organizations

Contributions Analysis

Giving Priorities: Currently supports creative programs that integrate technology into the community.
Arts & Humanities: 18%. Focus is on extending telecommunications power to the arts to broaden audiences and reach young people. Funds regional and statewide sponsorships, memberships in arts organizations, arts and education programs directed for grades 5-12, and technology applications such as web site development, digital archives, and distance learning.
Civic & Public Affairs: 25%. Supports grants that address local community needs, applications of new technology for community-based organizations, employee volunteer programs, and community technology centers.
Education: 37%. Focus is on incorporating technology into education. Funds technology applications such as distance learning, web-based curriculum development, and collaborative community networking. Also supports building technology infrastructure such as wiring, modem development, computers and internet access; and teacher training on integration of technology into the classroom, including web content.
Health: 19%. Focus is on integrating new technology in the provision of needed services. Supports the United Way; Junior Achievement; pediatric AIDS service organizations; after-school programs including the Girls and Boys Clubs, YMCA, Boy Scouts, Girl Scouts, Girls Inc., Police Athletic League, and Urban League. Funding also goes to the prevention of substance abuse, homelessness, hunger, and other societal problems.

Application Procedures

Initial Contact: Effective 01/01/2000, the foundation only accepts online applications. Visit the Foundation's web site for an application.
Application Requirements: Refer to the web site for a complete list of application guidelines.
Deadlines: None.
Review Process: Proposals are continuously reviewed.

Additional Information

Bell Atlantic merged with NYNEX in 1997. As of April 2000, Bell Atlantic is scheduled to merge with GTE following the formal merger approval process. Bell Atlantic and GTE have selected Verizon as the new name of the combined company.
Publications: Application Form

Corporate Officials

Raymond W. Smith: chairman, chief executive officer, director B Pittsburgh, PA 1937. ED Carnegie Mellon University BS (1959); University of Pittsburgh MBA (1967). PRIM CORP EMPL chairman, chief executive officer, director: Bell Atlantic Corp. CORP AFFIL director: USAirways Group Inc.; director: Westinghouse Electric Corp.; chairman: Bell Atlantic Maryland. NONPR AFFIL member: Library Congress James Madison National Council; member national advisory board: Private Sector Councils; member board advisors: Arden Theatre Co.; member: Business Roundtable.

Foundation Officials

Patrick C. G. Coulter: president B Seattle, WA 1941. ED California State University, Northridge BS (1975); University of Southern California MPA (1980). PRIM CORP EMPL senior vice president, corporate communications: Gulfstream Aerospace Corp. NONPR AFFIL member: Public Relations Society America; member: Society Professional Journalists.
Suzanne A. DuBose: president

Grants Analysis

Disclosure Period: calendar year ending 1999
Total Grants: $36,001,876*
Number of Grants: 3,900 (approx)
Average Grant: $9,231
Highest Grant: $2,100,000
Typical Range: $1,000 to $30,000
***Note:** Giving includes United Way.

Recent Grants

Note: Grants derived from 1997 Form 990.

Arts & Humanities

400,000 National Gallery of Art, Washington, DC
300,000 Library of Congress, Washington, DC
50,000 American Music Theater Festival, Philadelphia, PA
10,000 Vice Presidents Residence Foundation, Alexandria, VA
7,600 Arts Power, Ridgewood, NJ

Civic & Public Affairs

35,000 ODC, San Francisco, CA

Education

320,000 Council of the Great City Schools, Washington, DC
250,000 Virginia Tech and State University, Blacksburg, VA
200,000 Delaware Center for Educational Technology, Wilmington, DE
120,000 Galludet University, Washington, DC
100,000 Junior Achievement of the National Capital Area
50,000 University of Maryland Baltimore Center for Marine Biology, Baltimore, MD
45,000 Learning Independence Through Computers, Baltimore, MD
34,450 Educational Opportunity Fund Program, Camden, NJ
20,000 Restoration Community Music and Arts Academy
10,000 Hampton University, Hampton, VA
10,000 Lincoln University, Lincoln University, PA

International

75,000 Earthwatch, Watertown, MA

Social Services

300,000 Points of Light Foundation, Washington, DC
50,000 Washington Area Project for Youth, Washington, DC

BELL ATLANTIC CORP.-WEST VIRGINIA

Company Contact

Charleston, WV
Web: http://www.bell-atl.com

Company Description

Former Name: Chesapeake & Potomac Telephone Co. of West Virginia.
Revenue: US$585,190,000
Employees: 1,800
SIC(s): 2741 Miscellaneous Publishing, 4813 Telephone Communications Except Radiotelephone.
Parent Company: Bell Atlantic Corp., 1095 Avenue of the Americas, New York, NY, United States

Nonmonetary Support

Type: In-kind Services

Corporate Sponsorship

Value: $500,000 (1998)
Type: Arts & cultural events; Festivals/fairs; Music & entertainment events; Pledge-a-thon
Contact: John Golden, Manager, Corporate Communications

Giving Contact

Stan Cavindish, Director, External Affairs
1500 MacCorkle Avenue, Room 500
Charleston, WV 25314
Phone: (304)344-7445
Fax: (304)344-6123
Email: hugh.s.cavendish@bellatlantic.com
Web: http://www.bell-atl.com/ba-wv

Description
Organization Type: Corporate Giving Program
Giving Locations: WV
Grant Types: Award, General Support, Multiyear/Continuing Support, Operating Expenses, Project.

Financial Summary
Total Giving: $600,000 (2000 approx); $600,000 (1999 approx); $628,000 (1998). Note: Figures are for Bell Atlantic West Virginia regional office.
Assets: $1,500,000 (2000); $1,500,000 (1999)

Typical Recipients
Arts & Humanities: Arts & Humanities-General
Civic & Public Affairs: Civic & Public Affairs-General
Education: Education-General
Environment: Environment-General
Health: Health-General
International: International-General
Science: Science-General
Social Services: Social Services-General

Application Procedures
Application Requirements: Company suggests all applicants apply online.

Restrictions
Does not support individuals, religious organizations for sectarian purposes, political or lobbying groups, or organizations outside operating areas.

Corporate Officials
Dennis M. Bone: president, chief executive officer PRIM CORP EMPL president, chief executive officer: Bell Atlantic-West Virginia.
R. A. Ireland, II: vice president, consultant PRIM CORP EMPL vice president, consultant: Bell Atlantic-West Virginia.

Grants Analysis
Disclosure Period: calendar year ending
Typical Range: $1,000 to $2,500

BELL ATLANTIC-DELAWARE, INC.

Company Contact
Wilmington, DE
Web: http://www.bellatlanticfoundation.com

Company Description
Former Name: Diamond State Telephone Co.
Employees: 900
SIC(s): 4813 Telephone Communications Except Radiotelephone.
Parent Company: Bell Atlantic Corp., 1095 Avenue of the Americas, New York, NY, United States

Corporate Sponsorship
Type: Arts & cultural events; Festivals/fairs; Music & entertainment events; Other; Sports events
Note: Sponsors AIDS walk, Easter Seals Golf, McDonald's LPGA, galas, a mini grand prix, and educational initiatives.

Giving Contact
Lauren Petrusky, Co-Manager, Corporate Contributions/Events
Bell Atlantic-Delaware, Inc.
901 Tatnall St., 2nd Fl.
Wilmington, DE 19801
Phone: (302)576-5322
Fax: (302)576-1132
Email: lauren.a.petrusky@bell-atl.com

Alternate Contact
Luanne Baratta, Co-Manager, Corporate Contributions/Events
Email: luanne.k.baratta@bell-atl.com

Description
Organization Type: Corporate Giving Program
Giving Locations: DE; DC; ME; MD; MA; NH; NJ; NY; PA; RI; VT; VI; WV
Grant Types: Employee Matching Gifts, General Support.

Financial Summary
Total Giving: $340,000 (2000 approx); $340,000 (1999 approx); $340,000 (1998 approx). Note: Contributes through corporate direct giving program only.
Giving Analysis: Giving for 1997 includes: foundation ($2,387,050); foundation grants to United Way ($707,813); 1999: foundation (approx $340,000)

Typical Recipients
Arts & Humanities: Arts & Humanities-General
Civic & Public Affairs: Civic & Public Affairs-General
Education: Education-General
Health: Health-General
Social Services: Social Services-General

Contributions Analysis
Giving Priorities: Company primarily supports K-12 education. Also supports health and human services, social and economic development, and the arts and humanities. Company also encourages employees to participate in volunteer activities, including mentoring, through an active community relations team.
Arts & Humanities: 32%.
Civic & Public Affairs: 2%.
Education: 48%.
International: 3%.
Social Services: 15%.

Application Procedures
Initial Contact: Visit the website at: http://www.bellatlanticfoundation.com for application form.
Deadlines: None.
Evaluative Criteria: Preference is given to programs that provide opportunities for teachers to remedy gaps in prior training and keep up-to-date in science disciplines; introduce and prepare teachers to use technology as an effective teaching tool in all disciplines (i.e. distance learning); motivate students to pursue academic preparation for careers in science and technology; and change the attitudes of students by enriching experiences that students have with math and science. Organizations should provide evidence of sound management, active boards, competent leadership and continuity of efficient administration, request funding for a specific project, and not operating support, and have a demonstrated record of successful performance.

Restrictions
Does not support individuals, religious organizations for sectarian purposes, or political or lobbying groups, organizations not eligible for tax-deductible support, organizations not exempt under section 501(3)(c) of the Internal Revenue Codes organizations with discriminate on the basis of sex, religion, or color, organizations whose primary purpose is to influence legislation, good-will advertising, operating expenses or organizations supported by United Way, endowments or capital campaigns, film and media production projects or broadcast program underwriting, research studies, or organizations that have received a grant from Bell Atlantic in the last three consecutive years. Will no longer accept paper applications, application form necessary or apply on-line. Does not accept videos.

Corporate Officials
Gilbert H. Smith, Jr.: director PRIM CORP EMPL director: Bell Atlantic-Delaware, Inc.

Giving Program Officials
Luanne Baratta: PRIM CORP EMPL manager corporate contributions/events: Bell Atlantic-Delaware, Inc.
Lauren Petrusky: PRIM CORP EMPL manager corporate contributions/events: Bell Atlantic-Delaware, Inc.

Grants Analysis
Disclosure Period: calendar year ending 1997
Total Grants: $2,387,050*
Number of Grants: 20
Average Grant: $119,252
Typical Range: $500 to $2,500 and $100,000 to $200,000
***Note:** Giving excludes matching gifts.

BELLSOUTH CORP.

Company Contact
1155 Peachtree St. NE
Atlanta, GA 30309-3610
Phone: (404)249-2000
Fax: (404)249-5599
Web: http://www.bellsouthcorp.com

Company Description
Revenue: US$25,224,000,000 (1999)
Profit: US$3,448,000,000 (1999)
Employees: 96,200 (1999)
Fortune Rank: 58, per FORTUNE Magazine's list of 500 Largest U.S. Corporations (1999).
FF 58
SIC(s): 4813 Telephone Communications Except Radiotelephone, 6719 Holding Companies Nec.

Nonmonetary Support
Value: $500,000 (1995); $550,000 (1994); $500,000 (1993)
Type: Loaned Executives
Note: Co. also offers corporate leadership and management training conferences.

BellSouth Foundation

Giving Contact
Greg Norton, Grants Administrator
BellSouth Foundation
1155 Peachtree Street, NE, Room 7H08
Atlanta, GA 30309-3610
Phone: (404)249-2396
Fax: (404)249-5696
Email: grants.manager@bsc.bellsouth.net

Description
Founded: 1986
EIN: 581708046
Organization Type: Corporate Foundation
Giving Locations: principally near operating locations and to national organizations.
Grant Types: Capital, Conference/Seminar, Emergency, Employee Matching Gifts, Endowment, Fellowship, General Support, Matching, Multiyear/Continuing Support.
Note: Employee matching gift ratio: 2 to 1 for education gifts; 1 to 1 for cultural gifts. Corporate contributions fund operating expenses, employee matching gifts, and conference/seminar gifts. Foundation funds policy studies.

Giving Philosophy
'In our 1996-2000 operating program, we redefined our mission and identified key areas in which we would focus our efforts. Simply put, our five-year focus is as follows:
'Mission: To improve education in the South by stimulating fundamental change in primary and secondary

education that will result in active learning and improved outcomes for all students.
'I. Developing Individual Capacity to Improve Learning: Promoting Capable Teachers; Developing Educators for Leadership; Supporting Families.
'II. Creating Environments to Improve Learning: Rethinking Institutional Roles and Relationships; Encouraging Community Involvement.
'III. Promoting Partnerships Through Technology to Improve Learning: Linking Schools with Other Learning Environments; Providing Technical Assistance to Organizations and Communities.'
'In addition to open grants, we developed eight special initiatives to achieve our 1996-2000 goals. They are: recreate colleges of teacher education; increase teachers' knowledge of the workplace; sponsor a Superintendents Leadership Institute; promote family involvement in children's learning; link health initiatives with education reform; identify emerging state issues and policy opportunities to spur greater commitment to education reform; ensure that higher education is involved in preK-12 improvement; help schools make the best use of telecommunications applications for student learning by mobilizing company-wide commitment, resources and technical assistance.' 1996 Annual Report

Financial Summary

Total Giving: $2,517,386 (1998); $3,015,440 (1997); $2,600,000 (1996). Note: Contributes through corporate direct giving program and foundation.
Giving Analysis: Giving for 1996 includes: foundation ($2,600,000); 1997: foundation ($3,015,440); 1998: foundation ($2,517,386)
Assets: $67,384,551 (1998); $62,192,125 (1997); $58,782,447 (1996)
Gifts Received: $14,000,000 (1996). Note: 1996 Contributions received from BellSouth Corp.

Typical Recipients

Arts & Humanities: Libraries, Museums/Galleries
Civic & Public Affairs: Chambers of Commerce, Public Policy, Urban & Community Affairs
Education: Arts/Humanities Education, Business Education, Business-School Partnerships, Colleges & Universities, Community & Junior Colleges, Education Associations, Education Reform, Elementary Education (Private), Engineering/Technological Education, Faculty Development, Education-General, Health & Physical Education, International Exchange, Leadership Training, Legal Education, Medical Education, Minority Education, Preschool Education, Public Education (Precollege), School Volunteerism, Science/Mathematics Education, Special Education, Vocational & Technical Education
Environment: Resource Conservation
Science: Science Museums
Social Services: Day Care, Family Services

Contributions Analysis

Giving Priorities: All areas of education.
Education: 100%. The foundation has the sole priority of improving the quality of education in its Southeastern service area. Emphasis is on the initiation of educational reform programs; recipients include educational organizations, four-year universities, two-year colleges, and K-12 schools. Foundation seeks to relate education policy to the changing needs of the region, and to encourage collaboration between institutions. Also important is the use of technology, especially information technology, to bring about improvements. BellSouth Corp. prefers to fund organizations which can obtain sustaining support from other sources, or whose initiatives will in time come underpublic sector funding.
The Foundation has set its course through the year 2000, embracing a systemic approach that focuses on improved learning from pre-kindergarten through high school. All aspects of work must be geared toward improving learning; active learning will emphasize outcomes, skills, and an ability to engage in self-directed learning; a commitment to equity will suffuse all funded programs; and the Foundation will promote collaboration among institutions and individuals as a strategy to produce results in student learning.
Giving is distributed between three focus areas: Technology receives 30%; Building Capacity of Educators and Families, 35%; and Improving Learning Environments, 35%.
Note: Company also maintains a substantial direct giving program, which makes contributions within the company's service area in the categories of education, 51%; health and human services, 29%; arts and culture, 13%; civic and community, 6%; and miscellaneous interests, 1%.

Application Procedures

Initial Contact: Call for guidelines and cover sheet, then send written proposal.
Application Requirements: Include purpose of project, timeframe, and program design; background of effort and issue addressed; learning focus for preK-12 students; results and outcomes; evaluation measures and benchmarks; future sustainability, dissemination, and/or replication; total cost and amount requested; organizational information; proof of tax-exempt status; and Foundation cover sheet.
Deadlines: February 1 or September 1 for foundation grants; the corporation reviews requests on a continuous basis.
Evaluative Criteria: Funded programs have an impact in Alabama, Florida, Georgia, Kentucky, Louisiana, Mississippi, North Carolina, South Carolina, and/or Tennessee; focus on learning outcomes; lead to comprehensive, systemic change; have a broad and positive impact on diverse populations, with special attention to racial and other minorities, and to students at risk; involve collaborative partnerships; link learning to work opportunities and workplace requirements; use technology to forge new connections, even when technology is not the primary focus of the program; demonstrate the capacity to gain continuing support and to link with other reform efforts; will result in dissemination of lessons learned and in replication of successful practices; and are most likely to produce measurable results.
Decision Notification: Board meets in April and November to make final decisions.
Notes: Foundation requests that applicants send one original proposal and one copy; do not send video or audio tapes, photographs, artwork or other bulky materials. If brochures are necessary to explain an integral part of the program, only one copy should be submitted. Refrain from calling during the review process.

Restrictions

The foundation does not support capital or building campaigns; endowments; general operating expenses; education product development; individuals for study, research, or travel; fundraising events or dinners; scholarships; single discipline curricula unrelated to comprehensive school reform; equipment acquisition; programs that are primarily recreational; any organization that discriminates on the basis of race, creed, gender or national origin; programs outside of operating locations; or non-tax-exempt organizations.

Additional Information

Grantmaking was suspended during 2000 as the foundation reviewed its giving program. New guidelines were expected to be available for the 2001 grantmaking cycle.
Publications: Bellsouth Foundation Grant Guidelines 1996-2000; New Strategies for the Bellsouth Foundation; Annual Report on Grantmaking Activity of the Bellsouth Foundation

Corporate Officials

F. Duane Ackerman: president, chief executive officerdevelopment B Dade City, FL 1942. ED Rollins College BA (1964); Rollins College MA (1970). PRIM CORP EMPL president, chief executive officer: BellSouth Corp. CORP AFFIL director: Wachovia Bank of Georgia, NA; director: American Business Products Inc.; director: American Heritage Life. NONPR AFFIL trustee: Rollins College.
Keith O. Cowan: vice president corporate development B Hartford, CT 1956. ED University of North Carolina BS (1978); University of Virginia School of Law JD (1982). PRIM CORP EMPL vice president corporate development: BellSouth Corp. CORP AFFIL director: Medirisk Inc.

Foundation Officials

Suzanne H. Detlefs: trustee PRIM CORP EMPL president: BellSouth Advertising & Publishing Corp.
Mark E. Droege: trustee
Mark L. Feidler: trustee PRIM CORP EMPL president: BellSouth Telecommunications Inc. ADD CORP EMPL president: BellSouth Mobility Inc.
Salin Geevarghese: associate director, grant maker
Leslie Graitcer: executive director
Margaret H Green: trustee PRIM CORP EMPL group president: Bell South Telecommunications Inc.
Sue A. McLaughlin: trustee
William C. Pate: chairman PRIM CORP EMPL vice president advertising and Public Relations: BellSouth Corp.
Kin Patterson: treasurer
Chuck Shewbridge: vice president
Patricia Willis: president CORP AFFIL director: BellSouth Corp.

Grants Analysis

Disclosure Period: calendar year ending 1998
Total Grants: $2,517,386
Number of Grants: 99 (approx)
Average Grant: $25,428
Highest Grant: $50,000
Typical Range: $10,000 to $50,000

Recent Grants

Note: Grants derived from 1998 Form 990.

Education

200,000	CLSR, Louisville, KY
50,000	Board of Regents of University System of Georgia, Atlanta, GA
50,000	Board of Regents of the University System of Georgia, Atlanta, GA
50,000	Board of Regents of the University System of Georgia, Atlanta, GA
50,000	Board of Regents of University System of Georgia, Atlanta, GA
50,000	Board of Regents of the University System of Georgia, Atlanta, GA
50,000	Commonwealth Institute for Parent Leadership, Louisville, KY
50,000	Entary/Professional Development/ School of Development & Teacher Training, Tampa, FL
50,000	Louisiana Forum for Educational Excellence, Baton Rouge, LA
50,000	Metro Atlanta Partnership/Visual Arts and Learning, Atlanta, GA
50,000	North Carolina Institute for Educational Policymakers, Winston-Salem, NC
50,000	University System of Georgia, Atlanta, GA
40,000	Born to Learn, Tupelo, MS
40,000	Born to Learn, Tupelo, MS
40,000	Recreating College of Teacher Education, Gainesville, FL
40,000	Recreating Colleges of Teacher Education, Birmingham, AL
35,000	The Chalk Project, Charlotte, NC
35,000	East Carolina University, Greenville, SC
35,000	Re-Create Colleges of Teacher Education, Louisville, KY
35,000	Re-Create Colleges of Teachers Education, Gainesville, FL
35,000	Teachers as Leaders, Lawrenceville, GA -- Summer Scholars Program

30,000	Educators in the Workplace, Charlotte, NC
30,000	Educators in the Workplace, Greenville, SC
30,000	Educators in the Workplace, Memphis, TN
30,000	Educators in the Workplace, Mobile, AL
30,000	Educators in the Workplace, Winston-Salem, NC
30,000	Internet Education Project, Knoxiville, TN
30,000	Learning Will Never be the Same, San Francisco, CA
30,000	Linking Education and Health, Charlotte, NC
30,000	Linking Health and Education, Charlotte, NC
30,000	Linking Health and Education, Shelby, NC
30,000	Louisiana Network for Teaching Resources & Renewal, Shreveport, LA
30,000	Orange County Public Schools, Orlando, FL
30,000	Re-Create Colleges of Teacher Education, Birmingham, AL
30,000	Re-Create Colleges of Teacher Education, Bowling Green, KY
30,000	Recreate Colleges of Teacher Education Initiative, Charlotte, NC
30,000	Recreating Colleges of Teacher Education, Bowling Green, KY
30,000	Recreating Colleges of Teacher Education, Louisville, KY
30,000	Recreating Colleges of Teacher Education Initiative, Birmingham, AL
30,000	Standard Bearer, Louisville, KY
30,000	University of Georgia, Athens, GA -- Internet Education Project: Secondary
25,000	Outgoing Wire Transfer Intech 2000 Wire Funds to Nationsbank, Miami, FL
25,000	Re-Create Colleges of Teacher Education, San Francisco, CA
25,000	Recreate Colleges of Teacher Education Initiative, Jackson, MS
25,000	Recreating College of Teacher Education, Bowling Green, KY
25,000	Recreating Colleges of Teacher Education, Louisville, KY
25,000	Recreating Colleges of Teacher Education, San Francisco, CA
25,000	Teaching Wth Technology: Success in the Classroom, Charlotte, NC
25,000	University of Georgia, Atlanta, GA -- To Support the Program for School Improvement
25,000	Urban School Boards Initiative, Winston-Salem, NC
Environment	
50,000	Rural Initiative Project, Winston-Salem, NC

BellSouth Telecommunications

 Number 47 of Top 100 Corporate Givers

Company Contact

Atlanta, GA

Company Description

Revenue: US$20,000,000,000
Employees: 68,600
SIC(s): 4800 Communications, 4813 Telephone Communications Except Radiotelephone.
Parent Company: BellSouth Corp., 1155 Peachtree St. NE, Atlanta, GA, United States

Nonmonetary Support

Type: Donated Equipment; Donated Products; In-kind Services; Loaned Employees

Giving Contact

Emily Holley, Contributions Manager
SU700 BellSouth Center
675 W. Peachtree St., NE
Atlanta, GA 30375
Phone: (404)529-7777

Description

Organization Type: Corporate Giving Program
Giving Locations: headquarters and operating communities.

Financial Summary

Total Giving: $20,000,000 (1999 approx); $18,000,000 (1998 approx); $18,000,000 (1997 approx)

Contributions Analysis

Arts & Humanities: 15%.
Civic & Public Affairs: 10%.
Education: 38%.
Health: 36%.

Application Procedures

Initial Contact: send a brief letter of inquiry
Application Requirements: a description of organization, amount requested, purpose of funds sought, recently audited financial statement, and proof of tax-exempt status

Restrictions

Company does not make contributions to individuals or families; organizations that are not eligible for tax-exempt status or do not hold a 501(c)(3) tax-exempt letter from the federal government; organizations that discriminate based on race, color, religion, gender, disability, or national origin; political organizations, fundraising, or campaigns; organizations whose prime purpose is to influence legislation; special occasion or goodwill advertising; churches or religious organizations; however, requests for church-affiliated hospitals or clinics, educational institutions or programs, and community outreach programs or projects will be considered; fraternal or veterans organizations; labor organizations; or organizations performing primarily medical research, which must be monitored or evaluated for performance results.

Additional Information

The objective of the corporate contributions program for BellSouth Telecommunications is to provide financial, program development, and leadership support to projects and organizations where company and community objectives intersect, deriving maximum benefit for each investment.
Publications: Contributions Philosophy; Guidelines Sheet

Corporate Officials

Ike Harris: controller PRIM CORP EMPL controller: BellSouth Telecommunications Inc.

Grants Analysis

Disclosure Period: calendar year ending
Typical Range: $1,000 to $2,500

A.H. Belo Corp.

Company Contact

400 S. Record St.
Dallas, TX 75202
Phone: (214)977-6606
Fax: (214)977-7655
Web: http://www.belo.com

Company Description

Revenue: US$178,300,000 (1999)
Employees: 6,920 (1998)
SIC(s): 2711 Newspapers, 4833 Television Broadcasting Stations.

Corporate Sponsorship

Type: Arts & cultural events
Contact: Regina Sullivan, Vice President, Govenment & Public Affairs

A.H. Belo Corp. Foundation

Giving Contact

Judith M. Garrett Sequra, President, Executive Director
PO Box 655237
Dallas, TX 75265-5237
Phone: (214)977-6802
Fax: (214)977-6620

Alternate Contact

Phone: (214)977-6661

Description

Founded: 1952
EIN: 756012569
Organization Type: Corporate Foundation
Former Name: Dallas Morning News-WFAA Foundation.
Giving Locations: CA: Sacramento; KY: Owensboro; LA: New Orleans; OK: Tulsa; TX: Bryan, College Station, Dallas, Ft. Worth, Houston; VA: Hampton, Norfolk; WA: Seattle, Tacoma headquarters area only; principally near operating locations and to national organizations.
Grant Types: Capital, Endowment.

Financial Summary

Total Giving: $2,000,000 (1999 approx); $1,800,000 (1998 approx); $900,000 (1996 approx). Note: Contributes through corporate direct giving program and foundation. 1996 Giving includes foundation.
Assets: $25,000,000 (1996 approx); $23,000,000 (1995 approx); $7,600,000 (1994)
Gifts Received: $250,000 (1993). Note: Contributions are received from A.H. Belo Corp.

Typical Recipients

Arts & Humanities: Ethnic & Folk Arts, Historic Preservation, Museums/Galleries
Civic & Public Affairs: Botanical Gardens/Parks, Municipalities/Towns, Urban & Community Affairs
Education: Education Funds, Journalism/Media Education, Literacy
Health: Health Organizations, Hospitals

Contributions Analysis

Civic & Public Affairs: The foundation's giving currently is focused on two areas of long-time interest to the company, its founders, and management. One area is the enhancement of urban parks and open spaces, which the trustees have chosen because these areas offer the greatest benefit to the most citizens in large US cities. Contributions support parks, open spaces, city planning, and public improvements.
Education: The second area of interest is journalism education, which serves to promote an informed citizenry. Scholarships in journalism have been endowed by the foundation at the University of Texas at Austin and Southern Methodist University.
Note: While the foundation focuses on the areas above, it also makes community service grants year-round to qualified organizations in operating cities.

Application Procedures

Initial Contact: Send a brief letter of inquiry.

Application Requirements: minimum background material, a list of officers and directors, copy of IRS proof of tax-exempt status

Deadlines: None.

Review Process: the foundation is governed by four trustees who also are directors of Belo Corp.; smaller requests are reviewed year-round for community service support; however, capital and endowment grants in the foundation's focus areas are considered three times a year

Notes: The foundation encourages calls and letters of inquiry before the submission of a full proposal.

Additional Information

A.H. Belo Corp.'s companion philanthropic foundation was established in 1952, named in honor of G.P. Dealey, founder of *The Dallas Morning News* and majority owner of Belo from 1926 until his death in 1946. Its name changed to the Dallas Morning News-WFAA Foundation in 1983, and in 1995, it was renamed the A.H. Belo Corp. Foundation. The above profile reflects contributions by A.H. Belo Corp., *The Dallas Morning News,* and WFAA-TV. Wholly-owned operating companies handle local requests for support and public service announcements independently. Contact the appropriate company directly. announcements independently. Contact the appropriate company directly.

Corporate Officials

Robert William Decherd: chairman, president, chief executive officer, director B Dallas, TX 1951. ED Harvard University BA (1973). PRIM CORP EMPL chairman, president, chief executive officer, director: A.H. Belo Corp. CORP AFFIL chairman: Owensboro Messenger Inquirer; chairman: Henderson Gleaner; director: Kimberly-Clark Corp.; chairman, chief executive officer: Audubon Printers Ink Ltd. NONPR AFFIL member: Newspaper Association America; trustee: Tomas Rivera Policy Institute.

Ward L. Huey, Jr.: president broadcast division, vice chairman, director B Dallas, TX 1938. ED Southern Methodist University BA (1960). PRIM CORP EMPL president broadcast division, vice chairman, director: A.H. Belo Corp. CORP AFFIL president: WWL TV Inc.; vice chairman: Maxium Service Television; president: 3rd Avenue Television Inc. NONPR AFFIL member executive committee: State Fair Texas; member: TV Bureau Advertising; trustee: Southern Methodist University; member executive committee: Southern Methodist University Meadows School Arts; director: Dallas Foundation; member: Maxium Service TV Association; Member: Dallas Advertising League; member: Association Broadcast Executives Texas. CLUB AFFIL Salesmanship Club Dallas; Dallas Country Club.

Burl Osborne: president publishing division, director B Jenkins, KY 1937. ED University of Kentucky (1955-1957); Marshall University BA (1960); Harvard University Graduate School of Business Administration AMP (1984); Long Island University MBA (1984). PRIM CORP EMPL president publishing division, director: A.H. Belo Corp. CORP AFFIL director, publisher, editor: Dallas Morning News. NONPR AFFIL member: Organization Professional Journalists; member: Southern Newspaper Publishers Association; director: Newspaper Association America; board member: Nieman Foundation; board member: Harvard University; member journalism advisory committee: Knight Foundation; member: American Society Newspaper Editors.

Foundation Officials

Robert William Decherd: chairman, trustee (see above)

Judith M. Garrett: vice president, secretary, executive director

Ward L. Huey, Jr.: vice president, trustee (see above)

James McQueen Moroney, Jr.: trustee B Dallas, TX 1921. ED University of Texas BBA (1943). CORP AFFIL director: A.H. Belo Corp. NONPR AFFIL chairman: University Dallas.

Burl Osborne: president, trustee (see above)

Grants Analysis

Disclosure Period: calendar year ending

Typical Range: $2,000 to $100,000

Bemis Co., Inc.

Company Contact

222 S. Ninth St.
Suite 2300
Minneapolis, MN 55402-4099
Phone: (612)376-3000
Web: http://www.bemis.com

Company Description

Employees: 7,950

SIC(s): 2672 Coated & Laminated Paper Nec, 3565 Packaging Machinery.

Bemis Co. Foundation

Giving Contact

Lawrence E. Schwanke, Trustee
Bemis Co. Foundation
Phone: (612)376-3008
Fax: (612)376-3150

Description

EIN: 416038616

Organization Type: Corporate Foundation

Giving Locations: MN: Minneapolis principally near operating locations and to national organizations.

Grant Types: Award, Capital, Employee Matching Gifts, General Support, Matching, Multiyear/Continuing Support.

Note: Employee matching gift ratio: 2 to 1 for education and Food Shelves. Annual budget is commintted to multi-year grants and no more than 20% of annual budget is committed to capital programs.

Giving Philosophy

'The aim of the foundation is to match the available funds with those public needs where the interests of the company and our employees are inseparable. Priorities in grants will be given to those organizations and/or programs that will contribute the most to advancing the quality of life for all people in the communities in which we operate. Emphasis will be on those programs that encourage the development of our human resources, education programs, and in a lesser degree civic and art institutions that encourage participation by the general public.' Bemis Company Foundation Purpose and Guidelines

Financial Summary

Total Giving: $3,000,000 (1999 approx); $2,615,592 (1998); $5,787,387 (1997). Note: Contributes through corporate direct giving program and foundation.

Giving Analysis: Giving for 1997 includes: foundation ($2,396,237); foundation grants to United Way ($241,943); foundation matching gifts ($153,988); 1998: foundation ($2,211,513); foundation grants to United Way ($251,279); foundation matching gifts ($152,800)

Assets: $1,300,000 (1999 approx); $1,113,879 (1998); $1,184,689 (1997)

Gifts Received: $2,562,000 (1998); $2,735,000 (1997); $1,775,000 (1996). Note: Foundation receives contributions from Bemis Company, Inc.

Typical Recipients

Arts & Humanities: Arts Appreciation, Arts Associations & Councils, Arts Centers, Arts Institutes, History & Archaeology, Libraries, Museums/Galleries, Music, Opera, Performing Arts, Public Broadcasting, Theater, Visual Arts

Civic & Public Affairs: African American Affairs, Business/Free Enterprise, Community Foundations, Economic Development, Employment/Job Training, Public Policy, Safety, Urban & Community Affairs, Women's Affairs, Zoos/Aquariums

Education: Business Education, Colleges & Universities, Community & Junior Colleges, Education Associations, Education Funds, Education Reform, Elementary Education (Private), Engineering/Technological Education, Education-General, Health & Physical Education, International Studies, Legal Education, Medical Education, Minority Education, Preschool Education, Private Education (Precollege), Public Education (Precollege), Religious Education, Student Aid, Vocational & Technical Education

Environment: Environment-General

Health: Clinics/Medical Centers, Emergency/Ambulance Services, Health Policy/Cost Containment, Health Funds, Health Organizations, Hospitals, Nursing Services, Prenatal Health Issues, Public Health, Single-Disease Health Associations, Speech & Hearing

International: International Environmental Issues, International Peace & Security Issues

Religion: Religious Welfare

Science: Science Museums

Social Services: Child Welfare, Community Centers, Community Service Organizations, Counseling, Day Care, Domestic Violence, Emergency Relief, Family Planning, Family Services, Family Services, Food/Clothing Distribution, Homes, People with Disabilities, Recreation & Athletics, Scouts, Senior Services, Shelters/Homelessness, Substance Abuse, United Funds/United Ways, YMCA/YWCA/YMHA/YWHA, Youth Organizations

Contributions Analysis

Giving Priorities: Social welfare; education; cultural organizations; civic groups.

Arts & Humanities: About 1%. Emphasis on programs with which company employees are involved. Cultural interests include public broadcasting, theater, arts centers, music, and museums.

Civic & Public Affairs: 9%. Civic concerns include economic development, environmental affairs, safety, and business and free enterprise groups.

Education: 52%. Funding supports employee educational matching gifts, scholarship programs for children of employees, and independent college associations in states where company facilities are located.

Health: 7%. Health interests include hospitals and single-disease health organizations.

Social Services: 26%. Major support goes to united fund drives in operating locations. Another priority is food shelves and food banks (the company also sponsors an employee matching gifts program to food banks). Other social welfare interests include child welfare and youth organizations, the aged, employment, and community service organizations.

Note: Total foundation contributions in 1998.

Application Procedures

Initial Contact: Send a brief letter or proposal.

Application Requirements: Include a description of organization; amount requested; purpose of funds sought; budget including existing and possible sources of income; officers and board members; details on how objectives will be attained; budget, including information on existing and anticipated sources of support; list of board members and officers; and proof of tax-exempt status.

Deadlines: None.

Evaluative Criteria: Project is within giving categories; involvement of company employees; and proposal display an innovative approach to problem solving.

Restrictions

Grants do not support non tax-exempt organizations, individuals, organizations for religious or political purposes, or lobbying efforts or campaigns. Company prefers not to give to educational capital funds, endowments, or trips or tours.

Grants will not exceed 5% of total requirements of any organization or campaign.

No grants are approved for more than three years.

No grants are approved for more than three years.

Additional Information

The basis for charitable contributions is 2% of company's domestic pretax profits.

Publications: Annual Community Relations Report

Corporate Officials

Benjamin R. Field, III: senior vice president, chief financial officer, treasurer B Hartford, CT 1938. ED Williams College BA (1961); Harvard University Graduate School of Business Administration MBA (1963). PRIM CORP EMPL senior vice president, chief financial officer, treasurer: Bemis Co., Inc.

Scott W. Johnson: senior vice president, secretary, general counsel B Saint Paul, MN 1940. ED Harvard University AB (1962); University of Minnesota JD (1966). PRIM CORP EMPL senior vice president, secretary, general counsel: Bemis Co., Inc. NONPR AFFIL chairman: Minneapolis Coalition Educational Reform & Accountability; member: Minnesota Bar Association. CLUB AFFIL Interlochen Country Club; Minneapolis Club.

John H. Roe: chairman, director B Saint Paul, MN 1939. ED Williams College BA (1962); Harvard University MBA (1964). PRIM CORP EMPL chairman, director: Bemis Co., Inc.

Foundation Officials

Audrey Kirchner: secretary PRIM CORP EMPL administrative assistant: Bemis Co. Inc.

Lawrence E. Schwanke: trustee PRIM CORP EMPL vice president human resources: Bemis Co., Inc.

Gene C. Wulf: vice president, controller B 1950. PRIM CORP EMPL vice president, controller: Bemis Co. Inc. CORP AFFIL vice president: Curwood Inc.; treasurer: Perfecseal Inc.

Grants Analysis

Disclosure Period: calendar year ending 1998
Total Grants: $2,211,513*
Number of Grants: 248
Average Grant: $8,917
Highest Grant: $250,000
Typical Range: $100 to $50,000
***Note:** Giving excludes matching gifts; United Way.

Recent Grants

Note: Grants derived from 1998 Form 990.

Arts & Humanities

12,000 Minnesota Orchestral Association, Minneapolis, MN

Civic & Public Affairs

50,000 The Campaign for the Minnesota Zoo, Apple Valley, MN
50,000 Minnesota Diversified Industries, St Paul, MN
25,000 Saint Paul Riverfront Corp, St Paul, MN
20,000 Project for Pride in Living Inc, Minneapolis, MN
10,000 Good News Home for Women, Flemington, NJ
10,000 Harriet Tubman Center, Minneapolis, MN

Education

274,350 Citizens Scholarship Foundation of America, St Peter, MN
250,000 University of Wisconsin Foundation, Madison, WI
100,000 Fox Valley Technical College, Appleton, WI
50,000 A Chance to Grow Inc, Minneapolis, MN
50,000 Minneapolis Public Schools Foundation, Minneapolis, MN
50,000 Rebuild Academy, Minneapolis, MN
30,000 Wisconsin Foundation for Independent Colleges, Milwaukee, WI
25,000 Seed Academy/Harvest Preparatory School, Minneapolis, MN
25,000 University of Wisconsin Milwaukee Foundation, Milwaukee, WI
20,000 The Institute for Education & Advocacy, Minneapolis, MN
15,000 Tips Center, Crossett, AR
13,000 Assn of Independent Colleges/Universities PA, Harrisburg, PA
12,150 Citizens Scholarship Foundation of America, St Peter, MN
11,000 Independent Colleges of Indiana Foundation, Indianapolis, IN
10,000 Mankato State University, Mankato, MN
10,000 Terra Community College, Fremont, OH

Health

100,000 Mercy Medical Center, Oshkosh, WI
30,000 The Northern Lakes Health Consortium, Duluth, MN
10,000 Valley Visiting Nurse Association, Neenah, WI

Religion

25,000 Salvation Army, Mankato, MN

Science

50,000 Science Museum of Minnesota, St Paul, MN
12,000 Science Museum of Minnesota, St Paul, MN

Social Services

100,000 YWCA Community and Urban Sports Center, Minneapolis, MN
60,000 United Way of Minneapolis Area, Minneapolis, MN
39,248 United Way of Wabash Valley, Terre Haute, IN
25,000 Akron Metropolitan YMCA, Akron, OH
25,000 American Red Cross, Mankato, MN
25,000 St Davids Child Development & Family Services, Minnetonka, MN
25,000 Wabash Valley Family Sports Center, Terre Haute, IN
22,000 Community Development Center, Shelbyville, TN
17,228 United Way of Lebanon County, Lebanon, PA
15,000 Cap Services Inc, Appleton, WI
15,000 Greater Hazleton Area United Way, Hazleton, PA
15,000 Greater Minneapolis Crisis Nursery, Minneapolis, MN
15,000 United Way, Oshkosh, WI
12,000 United Way of Summit County, Akron, OH
11,390 Minnesota Food Bank Network, Arden Hills, MN
11,000 Greater Mankato Area United Way Inc, Mankato, MN
10,900 Akron-Canton Regional Food Bank, Akron, OH
10,125 Emergency Shelters of the Fox Valley, Appleton, WI
10,000 Emergency Foodshelf Network (EFN), Minneapolis, MN
10,000 Hunterdon Prevention Resources, Flemington, NJ
10,000 Sabathani Community Center Inc, Minneapolis, MN

BEMIS MANUFACTURING CO.

Company Contact

300 Mill Street
PO Box 901
Sheboygan Falls, WI 53085
Phone: 800-558-7651
Fax: (920)467-8573
Email: corp@BemisMfg.com
Web: http://www.bemismfg.com

Company Description

Employees: 1,200
SIC(s): 2499 Wood Products Nec, 2511 Wood Household Furniture, 3084 Plastics Pipe, 3089 Plastics Products Nec, 3944 Games, Toys & Children's Vehicles, 3991 Brooms & Brushes.

F.K. Bemis Family Foundation

Giving Contact

Karen Hoefler, Director
Bemis Manufacturing Co.
PO Box 901
300 Mill Street
Sheboygan Falls, WI 53085-0901
Phone: (920)467-4621
Fax: (920)467-8573
Email: corp@BemisMfg.com

Description

Founded: 1953
EIN: 396067930
Organization Type: Corporate Foundation
Giving Locations: WI: Sheboygan County
Grant Types: General Support, Scholarship.

Financial Summary

Total Giving: $346,266 (1998); $297,438 (1997); $294,305 (1996). Note: Contributes through foundation only.

Giving Analysis: Giving for 1997 includes: foundation ($290,938); foundation scholarships ($4,500); foundation grants to United Way ($2,000); 1998: foundation ($332,766); foundation scholarships ($11,500); foundation grants to United Way ($2,000)

Assets: $17 (1998); $27 (1997); $25 (1996)

Gifts Received: $346,266 (1998); $297,450 (1997); $293,240 (1996). Note: Contributions received from Bemis Manufacturing Co.

Typical Recipients

Arts & Humanities: Arts Associations & Councils, Arts Centers, Arts Festivals, History & Archaeology, Libraries, Museums/Galleries, Music, Performing Arts, Public Broadcasting, Theater

Civic & Public Affairs: Business/Free Enterprise, Clubs, Employment/Job Training, Civic & Public Affairs-General, Urban & Community Affairs

Education: Business Education, Colleges & Universities, Private Education (Precollege), Public Education (Precollege), Vocational & Technical Education

Environment: Environment-General

Health: Cancer, Children's Health/Hospitals, Hospitals, Medical Research

International: Foreign Educational Institutions

Religion: Churches, Religious Welfare

Social Services: Camps, Child Welfare, Community Service Organizations, Recreation & Athletics, Scouts, United Funds/United Ways, YMCA/YWCA/YMHA/YWHA

Contributions Analysis

Giving Priorities: Supports arts organizations, colleges and universities, hospitals, and social services organizations, including those benefiting youth.
Arts & Humanities: 27%. Funds arts centers, museums, libraries, and public broadcasting.
Civic & Public Affairs: 1%.
Education: 36%. Supports colleges and universities.
Health: 12%. Funds hospitals and single-disease associations.
Social Services: 25%. Supports United Way and activities for youth.
Note: Total contributions in 1998.

Application Procedures

Initial Contact: Send a brief letter of inquiry.
Application Requirements: Include purpose of funds sought and proof of tax-exempt status.
Deadlines: None.

Corporate Officials

Richard A. Bemis: president, chief executive officer, director B 1941. ED Denison College BA (1963). PRIM CORP EMPL president, chief executive officer, director: Bemis Manufacturing Co. CORP AFFIL director: WPS Resources Corp.
Peter Lukaszewicz: treasurer, director PRIM CORP EMPL treasurer, director: Bemis Manufacturing Co.

Foundation Officials

Peter F. Bemis: vice president B 1947. ED Carroll College BS (1969). PRIM CORP EMPL vice president, secretary: Bemis Manufacturing Co. NONPR AFFIL chairman: Lakeland College.
Richard A. Bemis: president (see above)
Peter Lukaszewicz: treasurer (see above)
Mary Parent: secretary, director

Grants Analysis

Disclosure Period: calendar year ending 1998
Total Grants: $332,766*
Number of Grants: 30
Average Grant: $9,751*
Highest Grant: $50,000
Typical Range: $1,000 to $10,000
***Note:** Giving excludes scholarship; United Way. Average grant figure excludes highest grant.

Recent Grants

Note: Grants derived from 1997 Form 990.

Arts & Humanities

22,250 Sheboygan County Historical Museum, Sheboygan, WI
12,500 Barrie Library
5,500 John Michael Kohler Arts Center, Sheboygan, WI
5,000 Mead Library, Sheboygan, WI
1,200 Channel 10/36, Milwaukee, WI
1,000 Sheboygan County Historical Research Center, Sheboygan Falls, WI
1,000 Sheboygan Symphony, Sheboygan, WI
500 James Madison Very Special Arts, Madison, WI

Civic & Public Affairs

5,000 Milwaukee Neighborhood, Milwaukee, WI
5,000 Wilson House Project, Sheboygan, WI
2,500 Workbound, Sheboygan, WI
2,000 Falls Jaycees, Sheboygan, WI
750 Sheboygan Service Club, Sheboygan, WI
288 Main Street Loan Fund, Sheboygan Falls, WI

Education

50,000 Lakeland College Building Fund, Sheboygan, WI
10,000 Lakeland College Annual, Sheboygan, WI
4,500 University of Wisconsin Madison, Madison, WI
1,000 Carnegie Mellon University, Pittsburgh, PA
1,000 Junior Achievement Wisconsin, Milwaukee, WI
1,000 Marquette University, Milwaukee, WI
1,000 University of Wisconsin Oshkosh, Oshkosh, WI
500 Lakeshore Technical College, Cleveland, WI

Health

37,500 St. Nicholas Hospital, Sheboygan, WI
15,000 Children's Hospital, Milwaukee, WI
2,000 City of Hope, Los Angeles, CA
500 American Cancer Society, Sheboygan, WI

International

1,000 Trinity International University, Deerfield, IL

Religion

50,000 St. Norbert, De Pere, WI

Social Services

30,000 YMCA Building Fund, Sheboygan, WI
10,000 Girl Scouts of America Manitou Council, Sheboygan, WI
9,600 YMCA Annual Combined, Sheboygan, WI
2,500 Youth Athletic Field, Sheboygan, WI
2,000 Camp Evergreen Kiddie Camp, Sheboygan, WI
2,000 United Way, Sheboygan Falls, WI
1,100 Boy Scouts of America, Sheboygan, WI
500 Rainbow Kids, Sheboygan, WI
250 Reach, Sheboygan, WI

BEN &JERRY'S HOMEMADE INC.

Company Contact

Waterbury, VT
Web: http://www.benjerry.com

Company Description

Employees: 751 (1999)
SIC(s): 2024 Ice Cream & Frozen Desserts, 5143 Dairy Products Except Dried or Canned, 5812 Eating Places, 6794 Patent Owners & Lessors.

Nonmonetary Support

Type: Donated Products
Note: Company provides nonmonetary support.

Corporate Sponsorship

Type: Festivals/fairs

Ben & Jerry's Foundation

Giving Contact

Rebecca Golden, Director
Ben & Jerry's Foundation
30 Community Drive
South Burlington, VT 05403-6828
Phone: (802)651-9600
Note: Phone extension for Ms. Golden is 7485.

Alternate Contact

Debbie Kessler
Phone: (802)846-1500
Fax: (802)846-1558
Note: Phone extention is 7567.

Description

Founded: 1977
EIN: 030300865
Organization Type: Corporate Foundation
Giving Locations: VT: focusing on Community Action Teams U.S.-based organizations.
Grant Types: General Support, Project.

Giving Philosophy

'The Ben & Jerry's Foundation mission is to support and contribute to progressive social change in the United States. By progressive social change we mean efforts to change the underlying conditions that create social problems such as racism, sexism, poverty and environmental destruction. We primarily fund small grassroots organizations, and are willing to take risks funding new projects and small organizations struggling to survive.' Ben & Jerry's Foundation 1996 Annual Report

Financial Summary

Total Giving: $500,000 (2000 approx); $283,000 (1999 approx); $278,000 (1998 approx). Note: Contributes through corporate direct giving program and foundation.
Giving Analysis: Giving for 1996 includes: foundation ($323,143); domestic subsidiaries ($115,415); corporate direct giving ($70,711); 1997: foundation ($456,350)
Assets: $1,078,701 (1997); $1,408,091 (1996); $1,145,262 (1995)
Gifts Received: $86,883 (1997); $834,621 (1996); $120,750 (1995). Note: Contributions are received from Ben & Jerry's, Inc., Ben Cohen, and Jerry Greenfield.

Typical Recipients

Arts & Humanities: Arts Associations & Councils, Ethnic & Folk Arts, Film & Video, Historic Preservation, Libraries, Music, Public Broadcasting
Civic & Public Affairs: African American Affairs, Asian American Affairs, Business/Free Enterprise, Civil Rights, Community Foundations, Economic Development, Economic Policy, Employment/Job Training, Ethnic Organizations, Gay/Lesbian Issues, Civic & Public Affairs-General, Hispanic Affairs, Housing, Law & Justice, Municipalities/Towns, Native American Affairs, Professional & Trade Associations, Public Policy, Rural Affairs, Safety, Urban & Community Affairs, Women's Affairs
Education: Elementary Education (Public), Education-General, Private Education (Precollege)
Environment: Air/Water Quality, Forestry, Environment-General, Protection, Resource Conservation, Wildlife Protection
Health: AIDS/HIV, Cancer, Mental Health
International: Human Rights, International Development, International Environmental Issues, International Peace & Security Issues, International Relief Efforts
Religion: Religious Welfare
Social Services: Animal Protection, Child Welfare, Community Centers, Community Service Organizations, Crime Prevention, Emergency Relief, Food/Clothing Distribution, People with Disabilities, Recreation & Athletics, Senior Services, Shelters/Homelessness, YMCA/YWCA/YMHA/YWHA, Youth Organizations

Contributions Analysis

Giving Priorities: Supports progressive social change in the areas of disadvantaged groups, children and families, and the environment. Primarily funds small grassroots organizations. Priority is projects which are models of systemic change and examples of creative problem solving.
Arts & Humanities: 5%. Funds filmmaking, public broadcasting, and libraries.
Civic & Public Affairs: 47%. Focus on minority and legal affairs.

Environment: 22%. Supports resource management.
Health: 1%. Funds Vermont AIDS Council.
Social Services: 25%. Supports food banks, antipoverty initiatives, and youth organizations.
Note: Total foundation contributions in 1997.

Application Procedures

Initial Contact: Call or write for guidelines, then send one-page letter of inquiry (2 copies).
Application Requirements: Letter of inquiry should be copied onto the Foundation's cover sheet, and should include: a description of organization and indication of competence in the area of proposal; outline of the project, including who will benefit, design of project, and outcomes expected; brief overview of your budget, income sources, and expenses for the project.
Deadlines: None, for initial inquiries; applications should be submitted by the first of March, July or November for invited full proposals.
Review Process: Foundation reviews initial requests, and then invites full proposals for large grants (using the National Network of Grantmakers Common Grant Application); full proposals and small requests (less than $1,000) are reviewed quarterly.
Decision Notification: Initial letters are reviewed within six weeks of receipt; final decisions are announced within ten weeks after quarterly meetings.
Notes: Express delivery of packages is strongly discouraged; faxed proposals and inquiries are not accepted. The Foundation encourages the use of recycled paper and double-sided copying; avoid using plastic covers, sheet protectors, and glossy photos. Do not send additional backup materials, videos, or cassettes.

Restrictions

Grants are not made to support basic or direct service programs.
Foundation does not fund: discretionary or emergency requests, colleges or universities, individuals, scholarship programs, research projects, religious projects, state agencies, or international or foreign programs, or direct services programs.

Additional Information

The Foundation generally supports organizations with budgets under $250,000.
Ben and Jerry's Foundation was established in 1985 through a donation of stock in Ben and Jerry's Homemade, Inc.
Approximately 7.5% of pre-tax profits is set aside annually for philanthropy; the foundation, the Community Action Team, and corporate philanthropy each receive a portion of this total.
In April 2000, an agreement was made to sell Ben & Jerry's Homemade, Inc. to Unilever. As part of the terms of agreement, Ben & Jerry's will operate separately from Unilever's existing U.S. ice cream business. In addition, Ben & Jerry's will have an independent board of directors which will concentrate on maintaining Ben & Jerry's social mission and brand integrity.
Publications: Application Packet; Annual Report

Corporate Officials

Jerry Greenfield: co-founder, vice chairman B New York, NY 1950. ED Oberlin College BA (1973). PRIM CORP EMPL co-founder, vice chairman: Ben & Jerry's Homemade Inc.

Foundation Officials

Elizabeth Bankowski: secretary B Boston, MA 1947. ED Boston College (1970). PRIM CORP EMPL director: Ben & Jerry's Homemade, Inc.
Jeffrey Furman: treasurer, trustee PRIM CORP EMPL director: Ben & Jerry's Homemade Inc.
Rebecca Golden: director

Grants Analysis

Disclosure Period: calendar year ending 1997
Total Grants: $456,350
Number of Grants: 206
Average Grant: $2,215
Highest Grant: $10,000
Typical Range: $1,000 to $10,000

Recent Grants

Note: Grants derived from 1997 Form 990.

Arts & Humanities

7,500	Arkansas Broadcasting Foundation, Little Rock, AR
4,000	Brookfield Free Public Library
4,000	Women Making Movies, New York, NY

Civic & Public Affairs

10,000	Calumet Project, Hammond, IN
10,000	Centro Independiente de Trabajadores Agricolas, Florida, NY
10,000	Coalition LA, San Pedro, CA
10,000	Community Action Development Corporation, Boulder, CO
10,000	Cooperative Ownership Development Corporation
10,000	Farmworker Association, Apopka, FL
10,000	Latino Workers Center, New York, NY
10,000	REACH Project, Chicago, IL
10,000	Timbisha Shoshone, Death Valley, CA
9,500	United Indian Nations Community Development, Oakland, CA
5,500	Chinese Staff and Workers Association, Brooklyn, NY
5,000	Asian Immigrant Women Advocates, Oakland, CA
5,000	Commercial Sexual Exploitation Resource Institute, Minneapolis, MN
5,000	Equality Colorado, Denver, CO
5,000	Idaho Rural Council, Boise, ID
5,000	Massachusetts Tenants Resource Center, Boston, MA
5,000	River Alliance, Madison, WI
5,000	Safer Pest Control Project, Chicago, IL
5,000	Strategic Actions for a Just Economy, Los Angeles, CA
5,000	Workers Awaaz, Long Island City, NY
4,000	Black Men for Eradication of Sexism, Atlanta, GA
4,000	Welfare Rights Organizing Coalition, Seattle, WA

Environment

10,000	Bay Area Nuclear Waste Coalition, San Francisco, CA
10,000	Maine Forest Biodiversity Project, Rockland, ME
10,000	Save Our Cumberland Mountains, Lake City, TN
7,500	Citizens for Safe Water Around Badger, Merrimac, WI
5,000	Alternatives for Community and Environment, Roxbury, MA
5,000	Buckeye Forest Council, Athens, OH
5,000	Klamath Siskiyou Wildlands Center, Williams, OR
5,000	Powder River Basin Resource Council, Douglas, WI
4,000	Alaska Forum for Environmental Responsibility, Valdez, AK
4,000	Ascutney Mountain Audubon Society, Saxtons River, VT -- cleaning and restoration of bird watching area and installation of picnic tables
4,000	Rogue Institute for Ecology and Economy, Ashland, OR
3,000	Wildlands Project, Tucson, AZ

Health

5,000	Vermont AIDS Council, Montpelier, VT

Social Services

10,000	Bellows Falls Recreation Department, Bellows Falls, VT
10,000	Center for Young Women's Development, San Francisco, CA
10,000	Project Phoenix, St. Albans, VT
10,000	Town of Reading, Reading, VT -- Batley Field Project
7,500	9 to 5s Poverty Network Initiative, Waukesha, WI
7,000	Williamstown Community Baseball/Softball
5,000	Child Welfare Organizing Project, New York, NY
5,000	Food Project, Lincoln, MA
5,000	Greater Boston Regional Youth Council, Boston, MA
5,000	Greater Ithaca Activities Center Food From the Hood, Ithaca, NY
5,000	Vermont Lions Charities, South Strafford, VT -- Montgomery flood relief
5,000	Youth United for Community Action, Oakland, CA

Sanford C. Bernstein & co., Inc.

Company Contact

New York, NY

Company Description

Revenue: US$73,000,000
Employees: 985
SIC(s): 6211 Security Brokers & Dealers, 6282 Investment Advice, 8742 Management Consulting Services.

Corporate Sponsorship

Type: Arts & cultural events; Music & entertainment events; Sports events
Contact: Neil Kuttner, Chief Financial Officer
Note: Provides sponsorship only when a staff member is directly involved or requests sponsorship. Sponsors two-thirds of cost when employee pays one-third.

Sanford C. Bernstein & Co. Foundation, Inc.

Giving Contact

Zalman C. Bernstein, Trustee
Sanford C. Bernstein & Co. Foundation
767 5th Ave., 22nd Fl.
New York, NY 10153-0185
Phone: (212)486-5800
Fax: (212)486-8430

Description

EIN: 136277976
Organization Type: Corporate Foundation. Supports preselected organizations only.
Giving Locations: CA: Los Agneles, San Francisco; CT; FL; NJ; NY; TX: Dallas
Grant Types: Award, Capital, General Support.

Financial Summary

Total Giving: $437,345 (1998); $464,265 (1997); $407,934 (1996). Note: Contributes through corporate direct giving program and foundation. Giving includes foundation.
Assets: $5,154,301 (1998); $5,146,975 (1997); $4,940,544 (1996)
Gifts Received: $250,000 (1992); $304,000 (1991); $567,500 (1990). Note: Contributions were received from Sanford C. Bernstein & Co.

Typical Recipients

Arts & Humanities: Arts Associations & Councils, Arts Centers, Arts Institutes, Community Arts, Arts &

Humanities-General, History & Archaeology, Libraries, Museums/Galleries, Music, Opera, Performing Arts, Public Broadcasting, Theater
Civic & Public Affairs: Business/Free Enterprise, Civil Rights, Clubs, Economic Development, Employment/Job Training, Gay/Lesbian Issues, Civic & Public Affairs-General, Housing, Legal Aid, Public Policy, Urban & Community Affairs, Women's Affairs
Education: Arts/Humanities Education, Business Education, Colleges & Universities, Economic Education, Education Funds, Education Reform, Education-General, International Exchange, Minority Education, Minority Education, Private Education (Precollege), Public Education (Precollege), Religious Education, Science/Mathematics Education, Special Education, Student Aid
Health: AIDS/HIV, Arthritis, Cancer, Children's Health/Hospitals, Clinics/Medical Centers, Diabetes, Eyes/Blindness, Geriatric Health, Health Organizations, Heart, Hospitals, Long-Term Care, Medical Research, Nursing Services, Prenatal Health Issues, Preventive Medicine/Wellness Organizations, Single-Disease Health Associations, Speech & Hearing
International: Foreign Arts Organizations, Foreign Educational Institutions, International Environmental Issues, International Organizations, International Peace & Security Issues, International Relations, Missionary/Religious Activities
Religion: Jewish Causes, Religious Organizations, Religious Welfare, Synagogues/Temples
Social Services: Big Brother/Big Sister, Child Abuse, Child Welfare, Community Centers, Community Service Organizations, Counseling, Family Planning, Family Services, Homes, People with Disabilities, Recreation & Athletics, Refugee Assistance, Senior Services, Shelters/Homelessness, United Funds/United Ways, Volunteer Services, YMCA/YWCA/YMHA/YWHA, Youth Organizations

Contributions Analysis

Giving Priorities: Jewish religious organizations and health services. Supports religious, educational, and cultural organizations in Israel.
Arts & Humanities: 15%. Supports historical preservation, opera, arts institutes, and the performing arts.
Civic & Public Affairs: 12%. Supports business and civic clubs.
Education: 16%. Mostly supports pre-college education, including inner-city scholarship funds, tutoring, minority education, Jewish schools, day schools, and high schools.
Health: 20%. Support favors hospitals, medical research, single-disease associations, nursing homes, camps for the disabled, and pediatric health.
International: 2%. Supports organizations for the disabled, community centers, religious, and cultural organizations in Israel.
Religion: 15%. Emphasis on Jewish religious organizations and synagogues.
Social Services: 19%. Supports youth programs with emphasis on disadvantaged youth, as well as shelters and immigration projects.
Note: Total contributions in 1998.

Restrictions

The foundation and company support only organizations with which employees and their spouses have direct involvement. Each employee may submit one application.

Corporate Officials

Lewis A. Sanders: chairman, chief executive officer B New York, NY 1946. ED Columbia University (1968). PRIM CORP EMPL chairman, chief executive officer: Sanford C. Bernstein & Co. Inc.

Foundation Officials

Andrew Adelson: trustee PRIM CORP EMPL senior vice president, director: Sanford C. Bernstein & Co. Inc.
Kevin R. Brine: trustee B Port Chester, NY 1950. ED University of Wisconsin (1975); New York University (1981). PRIM CORP EMPL senior vice president, director: Sanford C. Bernstein & Co. Inc.
Charles C. Cahn: trustee PRIM CORP EMPL senior vice president, director: Sanford C. Bernstein & Co.
Roger Hertog: trustee B 1941. PRIM CORP EMPL president, chief operating officer, director: Sanford C. Bernstein & Co. Inc.
Lewis A. Sanders: trustee (see above)
Francis H. Trainer, Jr.: trustee PRIM CORP EMPL senior vice president, director: Sanford C. Bernstein & Co.

Grants Analysis

Disclosure Period: calendar year ending 1998
Total Grants: $437,345
Number of Grants: 115
Average Grant: $3,803
Highest Grant: $28,400
Typical Range: $1,000 to $5,500

Recent Grants

Note: Grants derived from 1998 Form 990.

Arts & Humanities

6,790	Park Performing Arts Center, Union City, NJ -- Cultural
4,755	Long Island Philharmonic Society Inc., Melville, NY -- Cultural
4,755	Love Creek Productions, Inc., New York, NY -- Cultural
4,755	Theater Development Fund, Inc., New York, NY -- Cultural
4,075	Caramoor Center for Music & The Arts, Katonah, NY -- Cultural
4,075	CityArts, Inc., New York, NY -- Cultural
4,075	Jewish Museum - Judaica Acquisitions Fund, New York, NY -- Cultural

Civic & Public Affairs

6,790	Congressional Award Foundation, Washington, DC -- Social Welfare
6,115	The Hetrick-Martin Institute, New York, NY -- Social Welfare
6,115	Stratford Arms Community Council, New York, NY -- Social Welfare
5,435	Emunah of America, New York, NY -- Social Welfare
4,755	Habitat for Humanity of Westchester, White Plains, NY -- Social Welfare
4,755	Women's Venture Fund Inc, New York, NY -- Social Welfare
4,075	Junior League of Elizabeth/Plainfield, Cranford, NJ -- Social Welfare
4,075	Long Island Citizens for Community Values, Huntington, NY -- Social Welfare

Education

28,400	East Harlem Tutorial Program, New York, NY -- Educational
6,790	Diller-Quaile School of Music, New York, NY -- Cultural
6,790	Sinai, Special Needs Institute, Teaneck, NJ -- Social Welfare
6,115	Teach for America, Los Angeles, CA -- Educational
5,435	Friends of Bezalel Academy of Arts & Design, Inc., New York, NY -- Cultural
4,755	AIESEC United States, New York, NY -- Social Welfare
4,755	Hoff-Barthelson Music School, Scarsdale, NY -- Cultural
4,755	Westminster School, Simsbury, CT -- Educational
4,260	Link Community School, Newark, NJ -- Educational
4,075	School of the Arts Foundation, Inc., Palm Beach, FL -- Cultural

Health

6,790	Auxiliary of St. Vincent's Hospital, New York, NY
6,790	Concerned Parents for AIDS Research, New York, NY -- Medical Research
6,790	Juvenile Diabetes Foundation, New Canaan, CT -- Social Welfare
6,790	League for the Hard of Hearing, New York, NY -- Social Welfare
6,790	National Down Syndrome Society, New York, NY -- Medical Research
6,790	The Wellness Community, Santa Monica, CA -- Social Welfare
6,115	Long Island Jewish Medical Center, New Hyde Park, NY -- Social Welfare
4,755	American Heart Association, Irvine, CA -- Medical Research
4,755	Fight for Sight, Inc., New York, NY -- Social Welfare
4,755	Valley Presbyterian Hospital, Van Nuys, CA -- Medical Research

International

6,790	Seeds of Peace, New York, NY -- Social Welfare
4,755	International Center in New York, Inc., New York, NY -- Social Welfare

Religion

5,435	Catholic Big Sisters Inc., New York, NY -- Social Welfare
4,755	Jewish Community Center-Upper West Side, New York, NY -- Social Welfare
4,755	Jewish Federation of Palm Beach County, West Palm Beach, FL -- Social Welfare
4,755	Union for Traditional Judasim, Teaneck, NJ -- Religious
4,075	Ezras Torah Fund, Inc., New York, NY -- Religious

Social Services

6,790	Burden Center for the Aging, New York, NY -- Social We are
6,790	Connecticut Counseling Centers, Inc., Waterbury, CT -- Social Welfare
6,790	Edwin Gould Services for Children, New York, NY -- Social Welfare
6,790	Project Ezra, New York, NY -- Social Welfare
6,390	Planned Parenthood Hudson Peconic, Inc., Hawthorne, NY -- Social Welfare
5,435	YMCA of Tarrytown, Tarrytown, NY -- Social Welfare
4,755	Association for Retarted Citizens (ARC), Greenwich, CT -- Social Welfare
4,075	Big Brothers/Big Sisters of Palm Beach County, West Palm Beach, FL -- Social Welfare

BERWIND GROUP

Company Contact

3000 Centre Square West
1500 Market St.
Philadelphia, PA 19102
Phone: (215)563-2800
Fax: (215)563-8347
Web: http://www.berwind.com

Company Description

Founded: 1874
Employees: 4,800 (1998)
SIC(s): 2834 Pharmaceutical Preparations, 2865 Cyclic Crudes & Intermediates, 3441 Fabricated Structural Metal, 6519 Real Property Lessors Nec.

Nonmonetary Support

Type: Donated Equipment

Corporate Sponsorship

Type: Pledge-a-thon
Note: Sponsors walk-a-thons for breast cancer and juvenile diabetes.

Giving Contact
Mary LaRue, Chairperson, Contributions Committee
Berwind Corp.
Philadelphia, PA

Description
Organization Type: Corporate Giving Program
Giving Locations: headquarters area only.
Grant Types: Capital, Employee Matching Gifts, General Support.
Note: Employee matching gift ratio: 1 to 1 up to $1,000.

Financial Summary
Total Giving: $500,000 (2000 approx); $500,000 (1999 approx); $800,000 (1996 approx). Note: Contributes through corporate direct giving program only.

Typical Recipients
Arts & Humanities: Arts Institutes, Arts & Humanities-General, Libraries, Museums/Galleries, Music, Performing Arts, Public Broadcasting, Theater
Civic & Public Affairs: Civic & Public Affairs-General, Women's Affairs, Zoos/Aquariums
Education: Business Education, Colleges & Universities, Education-General, Legal Education, Minority Education
Environment: Environment-General
Health: Health-General, Hospitals
Science: Scientific Centers & Institutes
Social Services: Child Welfare, Community Centers, Delinquency & Criminal Rehabilitation, Family Planning, Food/Clothing Distribution, Senior Services, United Funds/United Ways

Application Procedures
Initial Contact: letter of inquiry
Application Requirements: a description of organization, amount requested, purpose of funds sought, list of organizations which support the work done by your organization, list of board of directors, and IRS 501(c)(3) tax-determination letter
Deadlines: by November for proceeding year

Restrictions
Does not support political or lobbying groups.

Corporate Officials
C. Graham Berwind, Jr.: chairman, president, chief executive officer B Bryn Mawr, PA 1928. ED University of Vermont BA (1951); Harvard University MBA (1953). PRIM CORP EMPL chairman, president, chief executive officer: Berwind Corp. CORP AFFIL director: CRC Industries Inc.

Giving Program Officials
Mary A. LaRue: chairman contributions committee PRIM CORP EMPL secretary: Berwind Corp.

Grants Analysis
Disclosure Period: calendar year ending
Typical Range: $1,000 to $2,500

BESTFOODS

Company Contact
Englewood Cliffs, NJ
Web: http://www.bestfoods.com

Company Description
Former Name: CPC International Inc.
Revenue: US$8,374,000,000
Employees: 55,300
Fortune Rank: 207, per FORTUNE Magazine's list of 500 Largest U.S. Corporations (1999).
FF 207
SIC(s): 2022 Cheese--Natural & Processed, 2032 Canned Specialties, 2033 Canned Fruits & Vegetables, 2046 Wet Corn Milling.

Operating Locations
Australia: Starch Australasia, Sydney; Austria: C.H. Knorr Nahrungsmittelfabrik, Ges.mbH, Wels; Belgium: CPC-Monda N.V./S.A., Antwerp; CPC Europe Consumer Foods Division, Brussels; People's Republic of China: CPC Foods Co. Ltd. Beijing, Beijing; Bestfoods Guanzhou Ltd., Guangzhou; CPC (Shanghai) Foods Ltd., Shanghai; Czech Republic: CPC Foods A.S., Prague; Denmark: CPC Foods A/S, Skovlunde; Dominican Republic: Knorr Alimentaria, S.A., Santo Domingo; Finland: CPC Foods Oy, Espoo; France: CPC France, Clamart; Germany: CPC Deutschland GmbH, Heilbronn; Greece: CPC (Hellas) A.B.E.E., Kifissia; Hong Kong: Bestfoods Asia, Hong Kong; CPC/AJI (Asia) Ltd., Hong Kong; CPC/AJI (Hong Kong) Ltd., Hong Kong; Hungary: CPC Hungary Ltd., Budaors; Indonesia: P.T. Knorr Indonesia, Jakarta; India: Corn Products Co. (India) Ltd., Mumbai; Ireland: Knorr Bestfoods Ltd., Inchicore; Israel: Israel Edible Products Ltd., Pituach; Italy: CPC Italia S.p.A., Cinisello Balsamo; Jordan: Bestfoods Jordan, Amman; Kenya: CPC Industrial Products, Nairobi; CPC Kenya Ltd., Nairobi; Morocco: CPC Maghreb S.A., Casablanca; Malaysia: CPC/AJI (Malaysia) Sdn Berhad, Kuala Lumpur; Netherlands: CPC Benelux B.V., Hilversum; Norway: CPC Foods A/S, Billingstad; Pakistan: CPC Rafhan Ltd., Faisalabad; CPC Rufhan Ltd., Faisalabad; CPC Refhan Ltd., Lahore; Philippines: California Mfg. Co. Inc., Manila; Poland: CPC Amino S.P. ZO.O, Poznan; Portugal: Knorr Portuguesa-Produtos Alimentares S.A., Lisbon; Romania: CPC Romania, Bucharest; Russia: CPC Foods Company Ltd., Moscow; Saudi Arabia: Bestfoods Saudia Arabia Co. Ltd., Jeddah; Singapore: CPC/AJI (Singaport) Pte. Ltd., Singapore; Spain: Bestfoods Espana, S.A., Barcelona; Starlux, Barcelona; Sri Lanka: CPC (Lanka) Ltd., Colombo; Sweden: CPC Foods AB, Kristianstad; Switzerland: Knorr-Nahrmittel Aktiengesellschraft, Thayngen; CPC Export (Africa/Middle East) AG, Zurich; Thailand: CPC/AJI (Thailand) Ltd., Bangkok; Turkey: Besan-Besin Sanayi ve Ticaret A.S., Istanbul; Taiwan: CPC/AJI (Taiwan) Ltd., Taipei; United Kingdom: Bestfoods UK Ltd., Esher, Surrey

Nonmonetary Support
Value: $12,700,000 (1994); $7,200,000 (1992); $15,000,000 (1991)
Type: Donated Equipment; Donated Products; In-kind Services
Note: Co. provides product donations mainly through its divisions. Support goes primarily to Second Harvest and other food banks.

Corporate Sponsorship
Type: Arts & cultural events; Festivals/fairs; Music & entertainment events; Pledge-a-thon; Sports events
Contact: Richard Bergeman, chairperson
Note: Sponsors events through a matching gift program.

Giving Contact
Ms. Patricia Biale, Manager, Personnel Services
Bestfoods
International Plz.
700 Sylvan Ave.
Englewood Cliffs, NJ 07632
Phone: (201)894-2521
Fax: (201)894-2457

Description
Organization Type: Corporate Giving Program
Giving Locations: international organizations; principally near operating locations and to national organizations.
Grant Types: Employee Matching Gifts, General Support.
Note: Company matches employee gifts to all non-profit organisation except fraternal organisation or organisation concerned with religion or politics.

Giving Philosophy
'CPC's Contribution Program is a demonstration of its sincere belief that a healthy and prosperous social and economic climate serves the best interest of its customers, employees, stockholders, communities and the general public. As a multi-national corporation, it is in our best interests to be as helpful as possible consistent with our resources to provide meaningful support for our communities both local and national. In short, we deem it is good business to be an enlightened corporate citizen.' *Contributions Policy and Guidelines, CPC International Inc.*

Financial Summary
Total Giving: $4,000,000 (2000 approx); $4,000,000 (1999 approx); $4,000,000 (1998 approx). Note: Contributes through corporate direct giving program only. Giving includes corporate direct giving; domestic subsidiaries; international subsidiaries; matching gifts.

Typical Recipients
Arts & Humanities: Arts Associations & Councils, Arts Centers, Arts Festivals, Arts Funds, Community Arts, Dance, Ethnic & Folk Arts, Historic Preservation, Libraries, Museums/Galleries, Music, Performing Arts, Public Broadcasting, Theater
Civic & Public Affairs: Business/Free Enterprise, Civil Rights, Economic Development, Employment/ Job Training, Law & Justice, Municipalities/Towns, Professional & Trade Associations, Public Policy, Safety, Urban & Community Affairs, Zoos/Aquariums
Education: Business Education, Colleges & Universities, Community & Junior Colleges, Economic Education, Education Associations, Faculty Development, International Exchange, International Studies, Literacy, Minority Education, Private Education (Precollege), Public Education (Precollege), Science/ Mathematics Education, Student Aid
Environment: Environment-General
Health: Health Policy/Cost Containment, Health Funds, Health Organizations, Hospitals, Medical Research, Mental Health, Nursing Services, Single-Disease Health Associations
International: International Peace & Security Issues, International Relations
Social Services: Child Welfare, Community Centers, Community Service Organizations, Domestic Violence, Family Services, People with Disabilities, Refugee Assistance, Senior Services, Substance Abuse, United Funds/United Ways, Youth Organizations

Contributions Analysis
Giving Priorities: Education, social welfare, health, the arts, civics, and international organizations. About 5% of domestic contributions support international affairs organizations. Figures on international contributions are not tracked by corporate headquarters. Overseas subsidiaries address needs of local communities and do not report contributions to the corporate level.
Arts & Humanities: 5% to 10%. Primary arts support is donated to community arts organizations, museums, and theaters. Other interests include musicand public broadcasting.
Civic & Public Affairs: 5% to 10%. Interests include urban improvement projects centering on economic development, law and justice, environmental concerns, civil rights, and public safety.
Education: 40% to 45%. Emphasis is on higher education. Other educational interests include economic programs, literacy projects, and minority education.
Health: 15% to 20%. Most contributions go to local chapters of national health organizations, with additional support to hospitals, single-disease health organizations, and mental health programs.
International: 5% to 10%. Provides limited support to international affairs organizations.

Social Services: 15% to 20%. Support includes United Way, child and family service organizations, substance abuse prevention, and community service centers.

Application Procedures

Initial Contact: letter and proposal
Application Requirements: cover letter should include reason for request, specific amount sought, and name of contact person; proposal should include purpose and history of organization, objectives for coming year, client population and geographic scope, current board membership, projected income and expenses for current year, audited financial statement of previous year, proof of tax-exempt status, list of current supporters
Deadlines: None.
Decision Notification: committee meets four times per year

Restrictions

Company does not support individuals; political, fraternal, or religious organizations; goodwill advertising, or special events.

Additional Information

Company also sponsors the CPC Education Foundation, which awards scholarships to children of employees.

Corporate Officials

Harry Elliott: senior vice president finance, administration
Diani Santucci: vice president health & safety
Luis Schuchinski: vice president taxes
Charles Richard Shoemate: chairman, president, chief executive officer B La Harpe, IL 1939. ED Western Illinois University BS (1962); University of Chicago MBA (1971). PRIM CORP EMPL chairman, president, chief executive officer: Best Foods. CORP AFFIL director: CIGNA Corp.; director: International Paper Co. NONPR AFFIL vice chairman: Conference Board Inc.; director: Grocery Manufacturer America; trustee: Committee for Economic Development.

Giving Program Officials

Richard P. Bergeman: chairman contributions committee (see above)
Patricia Biale: member contributions committee (see above)
Harry Elliott: senior vice president (see above)

Grants Analysis

Disclosure Period: calendar year ending
Typical Range: $1,000 to $5,000

BETHLEHEM STEEL CORP.

Company Contact

Bethlehem, PA
Web: http://www.bethsteel.com

Company Description

Revenue: US$4,477,800,000
Employees: 17,800
Fortune Rank: 412, per FORTUNE Magazine's list of 500 Largest U.S. Corporations (1999).
FF 412
SIC(s): 1221 Bituminous Coal & Lignite--Surface, 3312 Blast Furnaces & Steel Mills, 3315 Steel Wire & Related Products.

Nonmonetary Support

Value: $30,000 (1998); $30,000 (1993); $30,000 (1992)
Type: Donated Equipment; Donated Products; In-kind Services
Note: Support is provided by the company and the foundation.

Corporate Sponsorship

Value: $1,000
Type: Arts & cultural events; Festivals/fairs

Bethlehem Steel Foundation

Giving Contact

James F. Kostecky, Executive Director
Bethlehem Steel Foundation
1170 Eighth Avenue
Rm. 1711, Martin Tower
Bethlehem, PA 18016-7699
Phone: (610)694-6940
Fax: (610)694-1509
Email: kostecky@bethsteel.com

Alternate Contact

Email: pubaffrs@bethsteel.com

Description

Organization Type: Corporate Foundation
Giving Locations: headquarters and operating communities.
Grant Types: Capital, Conference/Seminar, Employee Matching Gifts, General Support, Multiyear/Continuing Support.

Giving Philosophy

'The Bethlehem Steel Foundation was formed by Bethlehem Steel Corporation for the purpose of developing and implementing a program of grants for charitable activities that contribute to the achievement of corporate strategic objectives and help enhance shareholder value in the company..The Foundation concentrates its grantmaking in the areas of education, human services, health care, economic education, public policy research, culture and the arts, and civic and community improvement. The objectives of the Foundation are to: (1) enhance the quality of life in communities where Bethlehem Steel has operations or other important interests and where its employees and their families live; (2) promote excellence in education, (3) advance the discussion and development of public policy; and (4) strengthen and sustain the economic, social, and political environment necessary to nurture our free society.' *Bethlehem Steel Foundation 1996 Annual Report*

Financial Summary

Total Giving: $1,620,987 (1998); $1,308,842 (1997); $1,169,035 (1996). Note: Contributes through foundation only.
Giving Analysis: Giving for 1998 includes: foundation ($1,620,687); foundation grants to United Way ($838,850); corporate direct giving ($340,000); foundation matching gifts ($45,187)
Gifts Received: $1,623,747 (1998); $1,310,638 (1997); $1,189,303 (1996). Note: Contributions received from Bethlehem Steel Corp.

Typical Recipients

Arts & Humanities: Arts Associations & Councils, Arts Centers, Arts Festivals, Community Arts, Historic Preservation, History & Archaeology, Libraries, Museums/Galleries, Music, Performing Arts, Public Broadcasting, Theater, Visual Arts
Civic & Public Affairs: African American Affairs, Botanical Gardens/Parks, Business/Free Enterprise, Civil Rights, Community Foundations, Economic Development, Economic Policy, Employment/Job Training, Civic & Public Affairs-General, Hispanic Affairs, Housing, Law & Justice, Legal Aid, Minority Business, Municipalities/Towns, Philanthropic Organizations, Professional & Trade Associations, Public Policy, Safety, Urban & Community Affairs
Education: Arts/Humanities Education, Business Education, Business-School Partnerships, Colleges & Universities, Economic Education, Engineering/Technological Education, Education-General, Legal Education, Literacy, Minority Education, Private Education (Precollege), Public Education (Precollege), Science/Mathematics Education, Student Aid, Vocational & Technical Education
Environment: Air/Water Quality, Environment-General, Resource Conservation, Wildlife Protection
Health: Emergency/Ambulance Services, Geriatric Health, Health Policy/Cost Containment, Health Organizations, Hospitals, Nursing Services, Nutrition, Public Health
Science: Scientific Centers & Institutes
Social Services: Child Welfare, Community Centers, Community Service Organizations, Counseling, Day Care, Delinquency & Criminal Rehabilitation, Domestic Violence, Emergency Relief, Family Services, Food/Clothing Distribution, People with Disabilities, Recreation & Athletics, Senior Services, Shelters/Homelessness, Substance Abuse, United Funds/United Ways, Volunteer Services, Youth Organizations

Contributions Analysis

Giving Priorities: Education, public policy research, culture and the arts and civic and community improvement.
Arts & Humanities: 12%. Contributes to the performing arts and public broadcasting.
Civic & Public Affairs: 3%. Funds local civic foundations including parks and neighborhood clean-up projects. (Public Policy) 9%.
Education: 12%. Emphasis on minority-based and business education, as well as Junior Achievement.
Environment: 5%.
Health: 2%. Supports hospitals, medical centers, and health clinics.
Social Services: 58%. Supports United Way, urban renewal groups, boys and girls clubs, substance abuse clinics, disease-specific organizations and community organizations.
Note: Above percentages reflect foundation giving only. Total contributions made in 1998.

Application Procedures

Initial Contact: brief letter and proposal
Application Requirements: a complete a description of organization and a statement of objectives; an explanation of why support is requested; a description of the benefits and geographic area to be served; financial information, including an explanation of disbursements as well as contributions and other sources of revenue; plans for reporting and measuring results; amount requested, description of how funding will be used, justification for request; proof of tax-exempt status
Evaluative Criteria: Foundation prefers to fund organizations that enhance the community where the company operates and the employees live; promote excellence in education; sustain and strengthen economic, social and political structures; and advance the discussion and development of public policy
Decision Notification: initial response to funding usually takes up to four weeks

Restrictions

Does not support organizations not exempt from taxation under Section 501(c)(3), individuals, religious organizations for sectarian purposes, political or lobbying groups, or foreign institutions and organizations.

Additional Information

Contributions are given solely by Bethlehem Steel Corp.
Bethlehem Steel acquired Lukens, Inc. in June of 1998.
Publications: Foundation Annual Report; Guidelines for Giving

Corporate Officials

Curtis Handley Barnette: chairman, chief executive officer, director administrative officer B Saint Albans, WV 1935. ED West Virginia University AB (1956); University of Manchester (1956-1957); Yale University JD (1962); Harvard University Advanced Management Program (1975). PRIM CORP EMPL chairman, chief executive officer, director: Bethlehem Steel Corp. CORP AFFIL director: Lehigh Valley Partnership; director: Met Life Insurance Co. NONPR AFFIL member: WV Bar Association; chairman: WV University Foundation; director: WLVT-TV; member: Phi Delta Phi; member advisory council: Trade Policy & Negotiations; member: Phi Alpha Theta; member: Phi Beta Kappa; member: Pennsylvania Chamber Business & Industry; director: Pennsylvania Society; member: Pennsylvania Bar Association; chairman: Pennsylvania Business Roundtable; member: Northampton County Bar Association; trustee: Lehigh University; director: National Legal Center Public Interest; member: Fed Bar Association; director: International Iron & Steel Institute; member: Connecticut Bar Association; member: DC Bar Association; member: Beta Theta Pi; member policy committee: Business Roundtable; member: Association General Counsel; member: American Law Institute; member: American Society of Corporate Secretaries; director: American Iron & Steel Institute; member: American Judicature Society; member: American Bar Association; member: American Corporate Secretarys Association. CLUB AFFIL Yale Club; Saucon Valley Country Club; University Club Washington; The Links Club; Loblolly Bay Yacht Club; Bethlehem Club; Blooming Grove Hunting & Fishing Club.

Steven G. Donches: vice president public affairs B Bethlehem, PA 1945. ED Saint Joseph's University (1967). PRIM CORP EMPL vice president public affairs: Bethlehem Steel Corp.

Duane R. Dunham: president, Sparrows Point Division

Gary Lee Millenbruch: executive vice president, chief financial officer, director, trustee B Marysville, KS 1937. ED Kansas State University BS (1959). PRIM CORP EMPL executive vice president, chief financial officer, director, trustee: Bethlehem Steel Corp. NONPR AFFIL member: Financial Executives Institute; Free Accepted Masons; member: American Iron & Steel Institute.

Dr. A. E. Moffitt, Junior: senior vice president, chief administrative officer

Roger Pratt Penny: president, chief operating officer, director B Buffalo, NY 1936. ED Union College BA (1958). PRIM CORP EMPL president, chief operating officer, director: Bethlehem Steel Corp. CORP AFFIL director: Walbridge Coatings; director: Double G Coatings. NONPR AFFIL treasurer: Saint Lukes Hospital; member: Valparaiso Chamber of Commerce; member: Orchard Park Chamber of Commerce; vice president exploring: Boy Scouts America Lehigh Valley; member: Buffalo Chamber of Commerce; member: American Iron & Steel Institute; member: American Iron & Steel Engineers. CLUB AFFIL Sand Creek Club; Saucon Valley Country Club; Buffalo Soccer Club.

Giving Program Officials

James Frank Kostecky: executive director B Ephrata, PA 1943. ED Villanova University BCE (1965); Carnegie Mellon University MScE (1967); Lehigh University MS (1971). PRIM CORP EMPL director corporate support programs: Bethlehem Steel Corp.

Foundation Officials

Steven G. Donches: president (see above)
Duane R. Dunham: director (see above)
James Frank Kostecky: executive director (see above)
Dr. A. E. Moffitt, Junior: director (see above)

Grants Analysis

Disclosure Period: calendar year ending 1998
Total Grants: $736,650*
Number of Grants: 161
Average Grant: $4,575
Highest Grant: $250,000
Typical Range: $200 to $25,000
***Note:** Giving excludes matching gifts, United Way.

Recent Grants

Note: Grants derived from 1996 Annual Report.

Arts & Humanities

50,000	Smithsonian Institution, Baltimore, MD -- capital campaign
7,500	Historic Bethlehem Partnership, Bethlehem, PA
5,500	Allentown Art Museum, Allentown, PA
5,000	John F. Kennedy Center for Performing Arts, Washington, DC
4,250	WLVT-TV/Channel 39, Bethlehem, PA
4,000	Ned Smith Center for Nature and Art, Millersburg, PA
3,500	Bethlehem Musikfest Association, Bethlehem, PA
3,000	Bach Choir of Bethlehem, Bethlehem, PA
3,000	Baltimore Museum of Industry, Baltimore, MD -- first payment on $9,000 three-year grant, for capital campaign
3,000	Hugh Moore Historical Park and Museums, Easton, PA -- first payment on $9,000 three-year grant, for capital campaign
2,500	Burnside Plantation, Bethlehem, PA -- second payment on $7,500 three-year grant, for capital campaign
2,500	Lincoln Center for Performing Arts, New York, NY
2,500	Touchstone Theater, Bethlehem, PA -- second payment on $10,000 four-year grant, for capital campaign

Civic & Public Affairs

30,000	Burn Prevention Foundation, Allentown, PA
30,000	Northwest Indiana Forum, Portage, IN -- first payment on $150,000 five-year grant, for capital campaign for Envision 2000 program
11,500	National Minority Suppliers Development Council, New York, NY
10,000	Economic Strategy Institute, Washington, DC
5,000	American Council for Capital Formation Center for Policy Research, Washington, DC
5,000	Campaign for Greater Michigan City, Michigan City, IN -- second payment on $20,000 four-year grant, for capital campaign
5,000	Community Foundation of Greater Johnstown, Johnstown, PA -- third payment on $25,000 four-year grant
5,000	Pennsylvania 2000, Harrisburg, PA
3,330	Turning Point of the Lehigh Valley, Bethlehem, PA -- second payment on $10,000 three-year grant, for capital campaign
3,000	Eastern Baltimore Area Community Development Corp, Baltimore, MD
3,000	Employment Policy Foundation, Washington, DC

Education

25,000	Valparaiso University, Valparaiso, IN -- first payment on $75,000 three-year grant, for capital campaign
15,000	Harvard Center for Risk Analysis, Boston, MA
13,480	Citizens Scholarship Foundation of America, St. Peter, MN
12,500	National Action Council for Minorities in Engineering, New York, NY
7,500	United Negro College Fund, Fairfax, VA
5,000	Allentown College, Center Valley, PA -- second payment on $15,000 three-year grant, for capital campaign
5,000	Baltimore County Public Schools Education Foundation, Baltimore, MD
3,600	Southeastern Technical Magnet School, Baltimore, MD
2,500	Maryland Business Roundtable for Education, Baltimore, MD

Environment

10,000	Keep America Beautiful, Stamford, CT
10,000	National Environmental Policy Institute, Washington, DC
5,000	Indiana Environmental Institute, Indianapolis, IN
3,500	Wildlands Conservancy of the Lehigh Valley, Emmaus, PA
3,500	Wildlife Habitat Enhancement Council, Silver Spring, MD

Health

10,000	St. Luke's Hospital, Fountain Hill, PA -- second payment on $50,000 five-year grant, for capital campaign

Social Services

238,500	United Way Central Maryland, Baltimore, MD
224,000	United Way Greater Lehigh Valley, Bethlehem, PA
127,450	United Way Porter County, Valparaiso, IN
40,000	United Way Capital Region, Harrisburg, PA
26,850	United Way Greater LaPorte County, La Porte, IN
26,000	United Way Buffalo and Erie County, Buffalo, NY
19,800	Lake Area United Way, Griffith, IN
15,000	United Way, Johnstown, PA
12,000	Foundation for a Drug-Free Pennsylvania, Harrisburg, PA
10,000	Boys and Girls Clubs of Porter County, Portage, IN -- first payment on $40,000 four-year grant, for capital campaign
2,500	Valley Youth House, Bethlehem, PA -- second payment on $7,500 three-year grant, for capital campaign

BFGOODRICH CO.

Company Contact

3 Coliseum Center
2550 West Tyvola Road
Charlotte, NC 28217-3597
Phone: (704)423-7000
Email: communications@corp.bfg.com
Web: http://www.bfgoodrich.com

Company Description

Formed by Merger of: Coltec Industries, Inc. (1999).
Revenue: US$3,950,800,000
Employees: 13,143
Fortune Rank: 300, per FORTUNE Magazine's list of 500 Largest U.S. Corporations (1999).
FF 300
SIC(s): 2812 Alkalies & Chlorine, 2821 Plastics Materials & Resins, 2822 Synthetic Rubber, 2869 Industrial Organic Chemicals Nec.

Operating Locations

Operates in Canada, Europe, South America, and Australia.

Corporate Sponsorship

Type: Arts & cultural events
Contact: Marty Viser, Manager
B.F. Goodrich Foundation

B.F. Goodrich Foundation, Inc.

Giving Contact

Patricia Meinecke, Director, Corporate Communications
The BF Goodrich Foundation
2550 W. Tyvola Road
Charlotte, NC 28217
Phone: (704)423-7080
Fax: (704)423-7127
Email: mviser@corp.bfg.com
Web: http://www.bfgoodrich.com/corporate/giving.asp

Description

EIN: 341601879
Organization Type: Corporate Foundation. Supports preselected organizations only.
Giving Locations: OH nationally; operating locations.
Grant Types: Award, Capital, Employee Matching Gifts, General Support.
Note: Matching gifts are given to educational and cultural organisation. For education employees must be an alumus, board member or faculty member of educational institution. Cultural institutions must be regional.

Financial Summary

Total Giving: $1,718,280 (2000 approx); $2,198,953 (1999); $1,116,409 (1998 approx). Note: Contributes through corporate direct giving program and foundation. 1998 Giving includes foundation ($1,116,409). 1997 Giving includes foundation ($934,805); matching gifts ($204,500); United Way ($110,000).
Assets: $15,294,386 (1997); $14,983,868 (1996); $15,619,245 (1995)
Gifts Received: $218,680 (1997); $107,000 (1996); $2,577,990 (1995). Note: In 1997, contributions were received from Goodrich.

Typical Recipients

Arts & Humanities: Arts Centers, Ballet, Community Arts, Dance, Historic Preservation, History & Archaeology, Libraries, Museums/Galleries, Music, Opera, Performing Arts, Public Broadcasting, Theater, Visual Arts
Civic & Public Affairs: Botanical Gardens/Parks, Business/Free Enterprise, Chambers of Commerce, Economic Development, Economic Policy, Employment/Job Training, Civic & Public Affairs-General, Law & Justice, Municipalities/Towns, Parades/Festivals, Professional & Trade Associations, Public Policy, Urban & Community Affairs, Women's Affairs
Education: Afterschool/Enrichment Programs, Business Education, Colleges & Universities, Community & Junior Colleges, Economic Education, Education Associations, Education Funds, Education Reform, Engineering/Technological Education, Education-General, Minority Education, Public Education (Precollege), Science/Mathematics Education, Student Aid
Health: Children's Health/Hospitals, Emergency/Ambulance Services, Geriatric Health, Health Organizations, Hospices, Hospitals, Nursing Services
Religion: Religious Organizations
Science: Science Exhibits & Fairs, Science Museums, Scientific Centers & Institutes, Scientific Organizations
Social Services: Community Centers, Community Service Organizations, Emergency Relief, People with Disabilities, Recreation & Athletics, Scouts, Senior Services, Substance Abuse, United Funds/United Ways, Youth Organizations

Contributions Analysis

Giving Priorities: Hospitals, human services, education, culture, and public policy research.
Arts & Humanities: 25% to 30%. Supports a variety of interests in major plant communities, including the performing arts, public radio and television, museums, preservation organizations, and historicalsocieties. Sponsors matching gifts programs for cultural organizations located in communities where employees live or work.
Civic & Public Affairs: 10% to 15%. Supports municipalities, trade associations, civic and nonacademic public policy research organizations in plant communities.
Education: About 30%. Emphasizes support to educational institutions located in major plant locations that provide technical research in areas of company interests or that serve as a major source of personnel. Sponsors matching gifts program and scholarships for children of employees. Also supports education-related public policy research organizations.
Health: 20% to 25%. Gifts to hospitals are for capital grants only and are given in communities in which company has operating facilities. Gives preference to organizations in Northeast Ohio.
Science: 15%to 20%. Supports science museums.
Social Services: 10% to 15%. Emphasis on United Ways in communities where company has operating facilities. Also supports privately financed agencies directed to basic human needs, such as youth development and family care.

Restrictions

Company does not support individuals; dinners or special events; religious, fraternal, labor, political, or tax-supported organizations; operating costs of hospitals; educational institutions, except for specific needs; United Way recipients, except for capital needs; or national organizations, except for programs important to the company.
Generally grants will not be made to endowment funds, to other foundations, or to non-tax-exempt organizations.

Additional Information

BF Goodrich Foundation was established in January 1989. The foundation is the sole source of funding for organizations in Northeast Ohio and for national organizations. BF Goodrich manufacturing plants administer their own charitable giving budgets.

Corporate Officials

David L. Burner: chairman, president, chief executive officer, director B Lodi, OH 1939. ED Ohio University BS (1962). PRIM CORP EMPL chairman, president, chief executive officer, director: B.F. Goodrich Co. ADD CORP EMPL officer: Jcair Inc.; chairman: Simmonds Precision Products. CORP AFFIL director: Brush Wellman Inc. NONPR AFFIL director: Salvation Army Greater Cleveland; director: Summit Education Initiative; director: Greater Cleveland Growth Association; board governor: Aerospace Institute America; director: Cleveland Scholarship Program Inc.
Nicholas James Calise: vice president, associate general counsel, secretary B New York, NY 1941. ED Middlebury College AB (1962); Columbia University LLB (1965); Columbia University MBA (1965). PRIM CORP EMPL vice president, associate general counsel, secretary: B.F. Goodrich Co. ADD CORP EMPL secretary: B.F. Goodrich Areo Comp Overhaul; secretary: B.F. Goodrich Freedpm Chemical Co.; treasurer: Jcair Inc.; secretary: Mitech Corp.; secretary: Simmonds Precision Montion Controls. NONPR AFFIL life member: Reserve Officers Association; member: U.S. Naval Institute; member: Ohio Bar Association; life member: Navy League U.S.; member: New York State Bar Association; life member: Judge Advocates Association; life member: Naval Reserve Association; member: Cleveland Bar Association; member: Connecticut Bar Association; member: American Society of Corporate Secretaries; member: Association Bar New York City; member: American Corporate Counsel Association; member: American Legion; member: American Bar Association. CLUB AFFIL Country Club Hudson; Akron City Club; Cordillera Club.
Gary L. Habegger: vice president human resources B Decatur, IN 1944. ED Seattle Pacific University (1966); University of Michigan (1978). PRIM CORP EMPL vice president human resources: B.F. Goodrich Co. ADD CORP EMPL vice president: Simmonds Precision Products.
Robert Jewell: vice president communications PRIM CORP EMPL vice president communications: B.F. Goodrich Co.
Scott E. Kuechle: vice president treasurer PRIM CORP EMPL vice president treasurer: B.F. Goodrich Co.
Les C. Vinney: senior vice president, chief financial officer B Cleveland, OH 1948. ED Cornell University BA (1970); Cornell University MBA (1972). PRIM CORP EMPL senior vice president, chief financial officer: B.F. Goodrich Co. CORP AFFIL president, director: Tremco Autobody Technologies; president: Tremco Inc.; treasurer: B.F. Performance Freedom Chem Co.

Foundation Officials

Nicholas James Calise: secretary (see above)
Gary L. Habegger: president (see above)
Scott E. Kuechle: treasurer (see above)
Terry Leonard: vice president
David B. Price, Jr.: vice president ED University of Missouri BS (1968); Harvard University MBA (1976). PRIM CORP EMPL executive vice president: BF Goodrich Co. CORP AFFIL president: B.F. Performance Freedom Chem Co.; president, chief operating officer: B.F. Performance Materials.
Lois Sumegi: administrator

Grants Analysis

Disclosure Period: calendar year ending 1997
Total Grants: $934,805*
Number of Grants: 56 (approx)
Average Grant: $16,996
Highest Grant: $150,000
Typical Range: $10,000 to $20,000
***Note:** Giving excludes matching gifts; United Way.

Recent Grants

Note: Grants derived from 1997 Form 990.

Arts & Humanities

150,000	Cleveland Orchestra, Cleveland, OH -- capital, operating support, multiyear support
20,000	National Corporate Theater Fund, New York, NY
15,000	Metropolitan Opera Association, New York, NY
10,000	Allen Theater, Cleveland, OH -- capital campaign
10,000	Cleveland Museum of Art, Cleveland, OH
10,000	Cleveland Opera, Cleveland, OH
10,000	Ohio Ballet, Akron, OH
7,500	Cleveland Playhouse, Cleveland, OH
6,500	Phoenix Symphony, Phoenix, AZ -- capital campaign, multiyear pledge
6,200	Cleveland Playhouse Square, Cleveland, OH
6,000	Great Lakes Theater Festival, Cleveland, OH -- support educational program, multiyear support
5,000	Akron Art Museum, Akron, OH
5,000	Akron Symphony Orchestra, Akron, OH
5,000	Lincoln Center for Performing Arts, New York, NY

5,000	National History Day, College Park, MD
1,000	Akron Civic Center, Akron, OH
750	Children's Concert Society, Akron, OH
Civic & Public Affairs	
41,000	GEM Consortium, Notre Dame, IN
20,000	City Year, Cleveland, OH -- city, community youth program multiyear support
20,000	Cuyahoga Valley Scenic Railroad, Gate Mills, OH -- support civic, community operating fund
10,000	Goodrich Park, York, ME
10,000	Hiram Village, Hiram, OH -- capital campaign, multiyear support
10,000	Ohio Chamber of Commerce, Columbus, OH -- support civic and community capital campaign
5,000	First Night, Akron, OH
5,000	Vocational Guidance Services, Cleveland, OH
Education	
100,000	University of Akron, Akron, OH -- support Scholars Program, multiyear support
38,000	Ohio Foundation of Independent Colleges, Columbus, OH
30,000	Tougaloo College, Tougaloo, MS -- capital campaign support
23,355	National Merit Scholarship Corporation, Evanston, IL
20,000	University of Akron College of Polymer Science and Engineering, Akron, OH -- support Waldo Semon Symposium
15,000	University Circle Endowment Fund, Cleveland, OH -- civic, community endowment, multiyear support
10,000	Case Western Reserve University, Cleveland, OH -- Ambassadors Program
10,000	E.J. Thomas Enrichment Fund, Akron, OH
10,000	Gallaudet University, Washington, DC -- project support, multiyear support
10,000	Summit Education Initiative, Everett Building, Akron, OH
10,000	Urban Community School, Cleveland, OH -- civic, community capital campaign, multiyear support
9,500	Junior Achievement, Akron, OH
7,000	United Negro College Fund, Cleveland, OH
5,000	Foundation for Student Communications, Princeton, NJ
5,000	University of Akron, Akron, OH -- support special program fund
5,000	University Circle, Cleveland, OH
Health	
10,000	Visiting Nurse and Hospice, Akron, OH
5,000	Hospice of Chenango County, Norwich, NY -- capital campaign, multiyear support
Science	
150,000	Inventure Place, Akron, OH -- support special project, civic and community multiyear support
25,000	Great Lakes Science Center, Cleveland, OH -- capital campaign, multiyear support
10,000	Cleveland Museum of Natural History, Cleveland, OH -- capital campaign, multiyear support
Social Services	
110,000	United Way of Summit County, Akron, OH
10,500	Great Trail Council Boy Scouts of America, Akron, OH
10,000	Hope Lodge, Cleveland, OH -- capital campaign, multiyear support
5,000	All American Soap Box Derby, Akron, OH

Binney & Smith Inc.

Company Contact

1100 Church Lane
Easton, PA 18042
Phone: (610)559-6610
Fax: (610)559-6691
Web: http://www.crayola.com

Company Description

Employees: 1,600
SIC(s): 2891 Adhesives & Sealants, 3944 Games, Toys & Children's Vehicles, 3952 Lead Pencils & Art Goods.
Parent Company: Hallmark Cards Inc., 2501 McGee St., Kansas City, MO, United States

Nonmonetary Support

Value: $3,600 (1996)
Type: Donated Products

Corporate Sponsorship

Type: Arts & cultural events; Festivals/fairs
Note: Sponsors events in the Easton, Pennsylvania community.

Giving Contact

Marta Boulos Gabriel, Community Affairs Manager
Binney & Smith Inc.
PO Box 431
Easton, PA 18044-0431

Description

Organization Type: Corporate Giving Program
Giving Locations: PA: Easton CAN: Linsay, ON
Grant Types: Capital, Employee Matching Gifts, Matching.

Financial Summary

Total Giving: $300,000 (2000 approx); $305,000 (1999 approx); $305,000 (1998 approx). Note: Contributes through corporate direct giving program only.

Typical Recipients

Arts & Humanities: Arts Appreciation, Arts Associations & Councils, Arts Centers, Arts Festivals, Arts Funds, Arts Institutes, Community Arts, Dance, Film & Video, Historic Preservation, Libraries, Literary Arts, Museums/Galleries, Music, Opera, Performing Arts, Public Broadcasting, Theater, Visual Arts
Civic & Public Affairs: Business/Free Enterprise, Civil Rights, Community Foundations, Economic Development, Economic Policy, First Amendment Issues, Civic & Public Affairs-General, Hispanic Affairs, Philanthropic Organizations
Education: Afterschool/Enrichment Programs, Arts/Humanities Education, Business Education, Colleges & Universities, Community & Junior Colleges, Continuing Education, Economic Education, Education Associations, Education Funds, Elementary Education (Private), Education-General, Literacy, Preschool Education, Private Education (Precollege), Public Education (Precollege), Secondary Education (Private), Secondary Education (Public), Social Sciences Education, Special Education, Student Aid
Environment: Environment-General, Wildlife Protection
Health: Children's Health/Hospitals, Emergency/Ambulance Services, Health-General, Speech & Hearing
International: International Relations
Social Services: At-Risk Youth, Child Welfare, Community Centers, Domestic Violence, Family Services, Sexual Abuse, Shelters/Homelessness, Social Services-General, United Funds/United Ways, Volunteer Services, Youth Organizations

Contributions Analysis

Arts & Humanities: Supports art organizations that help ensure a higher qulaity of life for all citizens. Considers requests to organizations that stress excellence and community participation, especially with children. Also considers support for performing arts and public broadcasting.
Civic & Public Affairs: Funds organizations that encourage a better working relationship between business and the community. Also funds local environmental and ecological issues.
Education: Focus on early childhood development and quality arts in education initatives. Grants may be made for start-up programs. Limited support for special programs. Assistance is given to programs for the physically and mentally disabled.
Health: Majority of contributions go to the United Way. Limited support towards preventive health measures. Funding also given to human serviceprograms, services for children, the elderly and the disabled, and programs that assist disadvantaged children.

Application Procedures

Initial Contact: letter of request on organization letterhead
Application Requirements: purpose and background information of the organization, amount requested, purpose of funds sought, recently audited financial statements, copy of IRS 501 (c)(3) tax determination letter, population served, time frame in which contribution is needed, planned use of contributions, and follow-up evaluation of contributions impact
Deadlines: September 1 prior to the year for which funding is sought
Review Process: major contributions are reviewed annually by corporate contributions committee; contributions under $1,000 are reviewed weekly

Restrictions

The company does not support individuals, individual schools, religious organizations for sectarian purposes, athletic groups, fraternal organizations, national or international organizations, individual child care centers, nursing and convalescent homes, prisoners, conventions, hospitals, endowment funds, labor groups, social clubs, or veteran's organizations. Generally, funding is not given for past operating deficits, travel, conferences, non-product goodwill advertising, or undefined operational support.
Gives to local organizations only. Does not have out of state beneficiaries.

Additional Information

Publications: Informational Brochure (including Guidelines)

Giving Program Officials

Marta Boulos Gabriel: PRIM CORP EMPL community affairs manager: Binney & Smith Inc.

Grants Analysis

Disclosure Period: calendar year ending
Typical Range: $1,000 to $2,500

Binswanger Companies

Company Contact

Philadelphia, PA
Web: http://www.cbbi.com

Company Description

Employees: 150
SIC(s): 6531 Real Estate Agents & Managers, 6799 Investors Nec.

Binswanger Foundation

Giving Contact

John K. Binswanger
Binswanger Foundation
2 Logan Square, 4th Floor
Philadelphia, PA 19103

Phone: (215)448-6000
Fax: (215)448-6238
Email: info@cbbi.com

Description

EIN: 236296506
Organization Type: Corporate Foundation
Giving Locations: PA
Grant Types: General Support.

Financial Summary

Total Giving: $328,241 (1996); $234,073 (1995); $408,365 (1994). Note: Contributes through foundation only.
Giving Analysis: Giving for 1995 includes: foundation ($183,573); foundation grants to United Way ($50,000); 1996: foundation grants to United Way ($40,000)
Assets: $991,413 (1996); $1,117,169 (1995); $177,362 (1994)
Gifts Received: $50,000 (1996); $941,550 (1995); $25,000 (1992)

Typical Recipients

Arts & Humanities: Arts Associations & Councils, Arts Festivals, Community Arts, Arts & Humanities-General, Historic Preservation, History & Archaeology, Libraries, Museums/Galleries, Music, Theater
Civic & Public Affairs: African American Affairs, Botanical Gardens/Parks, Business/Free Enterprise, Clubs, Employment/Job Training, Civic & Public Affairs-General, Public Policy, Urban & Community Affairs, Zoos/Aquariums
Education: Arts/Humanities Education, Business-School Partnerships, Colleges & Universities, Education-General, Minority Education, Private Education (Precollege)
Health: Cancer, Children's Health/Hospitals, Health Organizations, Hospitals, Hospitals (University Affiliated), Medical Research, Mental Health, Public Health, Single-Disease Health Associations
International: Foreign Educational Institutions, International Affairs, International Organizations, Missionary/Religious Activities
Religion: Jewish Causes, Religious Organizations, Religious Welfare, Social/Policy Issues
Science: Science Museums, Scientific Centers & Institutes
Social Services: Child Welfare, Community Service Organizations, Crime Prevention, Day Care, Delinquency & Criminal Rehabilitation, Family Services, People with Disabilities, Recreation & Athletics, Scouts, Substance Abuse, United Funds/United Ways, Youth Organizations

Application Procedures

Initial Contact: Send a brief letter of inquiry.
Deadlines: None.
Notes: The foundation has no formal grant application procedure or application form.

Additional Information

Foundation reports their grant making is suspended, but they are still in operation.

Corporate Officials

David R. Binswanger: president, chief executive officer B Abington, PA 1956. ED Bowdoin College (1978); Harvard University MBA (1982). PRIM CORP EMPL president, chief executive officer: Binswanger Companies. CORP AFFIL president: Binswanger International; president: Binswanger Management Corp.
Frank G. Binswanger, Jr.: co-chairman, director B Philadelphia, PA 1928. ED Wesleyan University (1950). PRIM CORP EMPL co-chairman, director: Binswanger Companies. CORP AFFIL cochairman: Binswanger International; chairman: Binswanger Management Corp.
John K. Binswanger: co-chairman, director B Philadelphia, PA 1932. ED Wesleyan University (1954). PRIM CORP EMPL co-chairman, director: Binswanger Companies. CORP AFFIL chairman: Binswanger Management Corp.; co-chairman: Chesterton Blumenauer Binswanger.
Michael J. Brennan: chief financial officer, senior vice president B Philadelphia, PA 1958. ED LaSalle University (1979); Villanova University (1989). PRIM CORP EMPL chief financial officer, senior vice president: Binswanger Companies. CORP AFFIL senior vice president, chief financial officer: Binswanger Management Corp.

Foundation Officials

David R. Binswanger: treasurer (see above)
Frank G. Binswanger, III: secretary CORP AFFIL chief executive officer: Binswanger International Ltd.; president: Binswanger Management Corp.
John K. Binswanger: chairman (see above)
Robert B. Binswanger: vice chairman

Grants Analysis

Disclosure Period: calendar year ending 1996
Total Grants: $328,241
Number of Grants: 60
Average Grant: $5,471
Highest Grant: $75,000
Typical Range: $100 to $6,000

Recent Grants

Note: Grants derived from 1996 Form 990.

Arts & Humanities

11,200 Philadelphia Museum of Art, Philadelphia, PA
3,000 Avenue of the Arts, Philadelphia, PA
2,060 Free Library of Philadelphia Foundation, Philadelphia, PA
2,000 Children's Museum, Boston, MA
1,584 Philadelphia Orchestra, Philadelphia, PA
1,000 Annenberg Center, Philadelphia, PA
1,000 Massachusetts Museum of Contemporary Art, North Adams, MA
1,000 PECO Energy Jazz Festival, Philadelphia, PA
500 Citizen's for Restoration of Historic La Mott, La Mott, PA

Civic & Public Affairs

5,000 Welcome America, Philadelphia, PA
4,000 Greater Philadelphia Urban Affairs Coalition, Philadelphia, PA
2,500 National Constitution, Philadelphia, PA
1,240 Zoological Society, Philadelphia, PA
1,000 Arthur Ashe Tribute Endowment Fund, Devon, PA

Education

50,000 Deerfield Academy, Deerfield, MA
17,800 Wesleyan University, Middletown, CT
9,816 Germantown Academy, Fort Washington, PA
2,500 Thomas Jefferson University, Philadelphia, PA
2,000 Shady Hill School, Cambridge, MA
2,000 Valley Forge Specialized Educational Service Corporation, Paoli, PA
1,500 Hampshire College, Amherst, MA
1,250 Germantown Friends School, Philadelphia, PA
1,000 Stratford Friends School, Havertown, PA
620 Pennsylvania Academy of Fine Arts, Philadelphia, PA
500 Abington Friends School, Jenkintown, PA

Health

33,333 Children's Hospital, Philadelphia, PA
10,000 Abington Memorial Hospital Foundation, Abington, PA
6,000 Center for Autistic Children, Philadelphia, PA
1,000 Harvard Center for Children's Health, Boston, MA
1,000 Leukemia Society National Capital Area, Alexandria, VA
1,000 Los Angeles Child Guidance Clinic, Los Angeles, CA
1,000 Mercy Health Corporation, Bala Cynwyd, PA
560 Hospital of the University of Pennsylvania Philadelphia Antiques Show, Philadelphia, PA

International

5,000 Keneseth Israel, Elkins Park, PA
2,000 World Affairs Council, Philadelphia, PA
1,000 American Committee for Weizmann Institute of Science, New York, NY

Religion

75,000 Federation of Allied Jewish Appeal, Philadelphia, PA
5,000 Rodeph Shalom Congregation, Philadelphia, PA
1,000 Jewish Family and Children's Service of Greater Philadelphia, Philadelphia, PA
500 American Jewish Committee, New York, NY

Science

2,500 Franklin Institute, Philadelphia, PA

Social Services

40,000 United Way SEPA, Philadelphia, PA
5,328 Boy Scouts of America Cradle of Liberty Council 525, Philadelphia, PA
2,000 Center City Crime Victim Services, Philadelphia, PA
1,670 Abraxas Foundation, Philadelphia, PA
1,480 Police Athletic League, Philadelphia, PA
1,140 Children's Seashore House, Philadelphia, PA
1,100 Horton's Kids, Washington, DC
1,000 Citizen's Crime Commission of Delaware Valley, Philadelphia, PA
500 Anti-Violence Partnership, Philadelphia, PA

WILLIAM BLAIR &CO.

Company Contact

Chicago, IL
Web: http://www.wmblair.com

Company Description

Revenue: US$140,000,000
Employees: 620
SIC(s): 6211 Security Brokers & Dealers, 6282 Investment Advice.

Corporate Sponsorship

Type: Arts & cultural events

William Blair & Co. Foundation

Giving Contact

E. David Coolidge, III, Chief Executive Officer
William Blair and Co. Foundation
222 West Adams Street
Chicago, IL 60606
Phone: (312)236-1600

Description

Founded: 1980
EIN: 363092291
Organization Type: Corporate Foundation
Giving Locations: IL: Chicago
Grant Types: Award, General Support.

Note: There are no restrictions on the type of grants awarded.

Financial Summary

Total Giving: $750,000 (fiscal year ending August 31, 1999 approx); $660,410 (fiscal 1998); $710,600 (fiscal 1997). Note: Contributes through corporate direct giving program and foundation.
Assets: $5,000,000 (fiscal 1999 approx); $4,366,998 (fiscal 1998); $4,498,943 (fiscal 1997)
Gifts Received: $500,050 (fiscal 1998); $750,000 (fiscal 1997); $600,000 (fiscal 1996). Note: Contributions are received from William Blair & Co.

Typical Recipients

Arts & Humanities: Arts Appreciation, Arts Centers, Arts Festivals, Arts Institutes, Dance, Arts & Humanities-General, History & Archaeology, Libraries, Museums/Galleries, Music, Opera, Performing Arts, Public Broadcasting, Theater
Civic & Public Affairs: Business/Free Enterprise, Clubs, Economic Development, Employment/Job Training, Civic & Public Affairs-General, Law & Justice, Municipalities/Towns, Parades/Festivals, Philanthropic Organizations, Professional & Trade Associations, Public Policy, Safety, Urban & Community Affairs, Zoos/Aquariums
Education: Business Education, Colleges & Universities, Economic Education, Education Funds, Elementary Education (Private), Faculty Development, Education-General, Literacy, Private Education (Precollege), Public Education (Precollege), Religious Education, School Volunteerism, Secondary Education (Private), Special Education, Student Aid
Environment: Resource Conservation
Health: Children's Health/Hospitals, Clinics/Medical Centers, Health-General, Health Organizations, Hospitals, Hospitals (University Affiliated), Medical Rehabilitation, Medical Research, Single-Disease Health Associations
International: International Affairs, International Relations, Missionary/Religious Activities
Religion: Jewish Causes, Ministries, Religious Organizations, Religious Welfare
Science: Observatories & Planetariums, Science Museums, Scientific Organizations
Social Services: Child Welfare, Community Centers, Community Service Organizations, Counseling, Day Care, Delinquency & Criminal Rehabilitation, Family Services, Food/Clothing Distribution, People with Disabilities, Recreation & Athletics, Refugee Assistance, Scouts, Senior Services, Shelters/Homelessness, Social Services-General, Substance Abuse, Youth Organizations

Contributions Analysis

Giving Priorities: Support for social services, the arts, education, civic causes, and health organizations.
Arts & Humanities: 18%. Arts institutes, dance, museums, historical societies, opera, and theater.
Civic & Public Affairs: 16%. Primarily for community affairs prgrams, zoos, and a horticultural society.
Education: 25%. Emphasis on colleges and universities, secondary schools, and education associations.
Environment: 1%.
Health: 10%. Hospitals, medical centers, and medical rehabilitation.
International: 1%.
Religion: 10%. Supports religious welfare.
Social Services: 19%. Focus on youth organizations, child welfare, and recreation projects.
Note: Total contributions for fiscal 1998.

Application Procedures

Initial Contact: Submit a brief letter of inquiry and full proposal.
Application Requirements: Include a description of organization, amount requested, proof of tax-exempt status.
Deadlines: None.

Restrictions

Does not support individuals or political or lobbying groups.

Additional Information

The general activities of the organization or the specific purpose should have significant impact on the Chicago area.

Corporate Officials

E. David Coolidge, III: chief executive officer B 1943. ED Williams College (1965); Harvard University (1967). PRIM CORP EMPL chief executive officer: William Blair & Co. CORP AFFIL director: Pittway Corp.
Edgar D. Jannotta: senior director B Evanston, IL 1931. ED Princeton University (1953); Harvard University MBA (1959). PRIM CORP EMPL senior director: William Blair & Co. LLC. CORP AFFIL director: Sloan Valve Co.; director: Unicom Corp.; director: Safety-Kleen Corp.; director: New York Stock Exchange Inc.; director: Oil-Dri Corp. America; director: Commonwealth Edison Co.; director: Molex Inc.; director: Bandag Inc.; director: AAR Corp.; director: AON Corp.
John P. Kayser: chief financial officer PRIM CORP EMPL chief financial officer: William Blair & Co. LLC.

Foundation Officials

Stephen Campbell: treasurer
E. David Coolidge, III: vice president (see above)
Edgar D. Jannotta: president (see above)
John P. Kayser: chief financial officer, secretary (see above)
James M. McMullan: vice president

Grants Analysis

Disclosure Period: fiscal year ending August 31, 1998
Total Grants: $660,410
Number of Grants: 248
Average Grant: $2,663
Highest Grant: $20,000
Typical Range: $500 to $5,000
Note: Grant Analysis provided by foundation.

Recent Grants

Note: Grants derived from 1998 Form 990.

Arts & Humanities

10,000 Art Institute of Chicago, The, Chicago, IL
7,500 Chicago Historical Society, Chicago, IL
5,000 Art Institute of Chicago, The, Chicago, IL
5,000 Chicago Children's Museum, Chicago, IL
5,000 Chicago Sinfonietta, Chicago, IL
5,000 Chicago Symphony Orchestra, Chicago, IL
5,000 Hubbard Street Dance, Chicago, IL
5,000 Lyric Opera of Chicago, Chicago, IL
5,000 Museum Campus, The, Chicago, IL
5,000 Steppenwolf Theatre Company, Chicago, IL

Civic & Public Affairs

20,000 Commerical Club Foundation, The, Chicago, IL
6,000 Ravinia Festival, Highland Park, IL
5,000 Better Government Association, Chicago, IL
5,000 Chicago Horticultural Society, Chicago, IL
5,000 Hull House Association, Chicago, IL
5,000 Lincoln Park Zoological Society, Chicago, IL
5,000 Ravinia Festival, Highland Park, IL

Education

17,400 Hebrew Academy of Cleveland, Cleveland, OH
10,000 Citizen Education Fund, Columbus, OH
5,000 Chicago Communities In Schools, Chicago, IL
5,000 Chicago Foundation For Education, Chicago, IL
5,000 Chicago State University, Chicago, IL
5,000 Daniel Murphy Scholarship Foundation, Chicago, IL
5,000 Illinois Council on Economic Education, Dekalb, IL
5,000 Northwestern Settlement House, Evanston, IL
5,000 Providence-St. Mel School, Chicago, IL
5,000 St. Ignatius College Prep, Chicago, IL
5,000 Shenandoah University, Winchester, VA
5,000 STAC Fund, Sparkill, NY

Environment

5,000 Lake Forest Open Lands Association, Lake Forest, IL

Health

5,500 Lake Forest Hospital, Lake Forest, IL
5,500 Lake Forest Hospital, Lake Forest, IL
5,000 Illinois Masonic Medical Center, Chicago, IL
5,000 Rehabilitation Institute, Chicago, IL
5,000 Rush-Presbyterian-St. Luke's Medical Center For The Cook County-Rush Health Center, Chicago, IL
5,000 University of Chicago Hospitals, Chicago, IL

International

5,000 Chicago Council on Foreign Relations, Chicago, IL

Religion

20,000 Presbyterian Homes, The, Evanston, IL
5,000 Rest Haven Christian Services, Chicago, IL
5,000 Spertus Institute of Jewish Studies, Chicago, IL

Social Services

10,000 AON-Maryville Golf Classic, Northbrook, IL
8,500 Maryville City of Youth, Des Plaines, IL
5,000 Abraham Lincoln Centre, Chicago, IL
5,000 American Refugee Committee, Minnea polis, MN
5,000 Boy Scouts of America, Chicago, IL
5,000 Chicago Platform Tennis Charities, Inc., Chicago, IL
5,000 Chicago Youth Programs, Inc., Chicago, IL
5,000 Children First Fund, New York, NY
5,000 Hazelden, New York, NY
5,000 Hazelden, New York, NY

H&R Block, Inc.

Company Contact

Kansas City, MO
Web: http://www.handrblock.com

Company Description

Revenue: US$1,521,500,000 (1999)
Employees: 86,500 (1999)
SIC(s): 7291 Tax Return Preparation Services, 8721 Accounting, Auditing & Bookkeeping.

Operating Locations

List includes headquarters offices for Personnel Pool of America, an H&R Block operating company.

H&R Block Foundation

Giving Contact

Ms. Barbara Lebedun, President
The H&R Block Foundation
4435 Main Street, Suite 500
Kansas City, MO 64111
Phone: (816)932-8324
Fax: (816)753-1585

Alternate Contact

Kay Pearson-Boyd
Note: For general inquiries and contributions requests for the Kansas City, MO area.

Description

Founded: 1974
EIN: 237378232
Organization Type: Corporate Foundation
Giving Locations: MO: Kansas City nationally.
Grant Types: Capital, Employee Matching Gifts, General Support, Multiyear/Continuing Support.
Note: Employee matching gift ratio: 1 to 1 for gifts to education institutions and the United Way.

Giving Philosophy

'In making contribution decisions, the directors are concerned both about the corporate responsibilities of H&R Block, Inc. and about its commitment, through the Foundation, to help enhance the quality of life in the Kansas City area.' The H&R Block Foundation

Financial Summary

Total Giving: $1,865,213 (1998); $1,646,881 (1997); $1,455,964 (1996). Note: Contributes through corporate direct giving program and foundation.
Assets: $46,764,980 (1998); $42,175,588 (1997); $37,105,082 (1996)
Gifts Received: $511,618 (1996); $304,000 (1995); $2,883,322 (1994). Note: Contributions given by H&R Block, Inc.

Typical Recipients

Arts & Humanities: Arts Appreciation, Arts Associations & Councils, Arts Centers, Arts Festivals, Arts Funds, Arts Institutes, Arts Outreach, Ballet, Community Arts, Dance, Ethnic & Folk Arts, Libraries, Literary Arts, Museums/Galleries, Music, Opera, Performing Arts, Public Broadcasting, Theater, Visual Arts
Civic & Public Affairs: Botanical Gardens/Parks, Business/Free Enterprise, Civil Rights, Clubs, Community Foundations, Economic Development, Employment/Job Training, Housing, Law & Justice, Legal Aid, Nonprofit Management, Public Policy, Safety, Urban & Community Affairs, Women's Affairs, Zoos/Aquariums
Education: Afterschool/Enrichment Programs, Agricultural Education, Arts/Humanities Education, Business Education, Colleges & Universities, Community & Junior Colleges, Continuing Education, Economic Education, Education Funds, Education Reform, Environmental Education, Education-General, Legal Education, Literacy, Minority Education, Preschool Education, Private Education (Precollege), Public Education (Precollege), Science/Mathematics Education, Social Sciences Education, Special Education, Student Aid
Environment: Environment-General, Watershed
Health: AIDS/HIV, Cancer, Children's Health/Hospitals, Clinics/Medical Centers, Geriatric Health, Health Funds, Health Organizations, Heart, Hospices, Hospitals, Medical Rehabilitation, Mental Health, Multiple Sclerosis, Prenatal Health Issues, Public Health, Research/Studies Institutes, Single-Disease Health Associations
International: International Relations
Religion: Jewish Causes, Religious Organizations, Religious Welfare, Social/Policy Issues
Science: Science Exhibits & Fairs
Social Services: At-Risk Youth, Camps, Child Welfare, Community Centers, Community Service Organizations, Counseling, Crime Prevention, Day Care, Delinquency & Criminal Rehabilitation, Domestic Violence, Emergency Relief, Family Planning, Family Services, Food/Clothing Distribution, Homes, People with Disabilities, Recreation & Athletics, Refugee Assistance, Scouts, Senior Services, Shelters/Homelessness, Special Olympics, Substance Abuse, United Funds/United Ways, Volunteer Services, YMCA/YWCA/YMHA/YWHA, Youth Organizations

Contributions Analysis

Giving Priorities: Education, performing arts, gallaries, community improvement projects, hospitals, elderly, disabled, high risk youth, and United Way.
Arts & Humanities: About 10% to 15%. The foundation provides support for opportunities for expression by artists of all ages in every medium. As grants in other areas, arts and culture grants result in important-partnerships with community organizations and enrichment for company communities.
Civic & Public Affairs: About 5%. Foundation efforts to support neighborhood development focus on grassroots needs, community activities, environmental improvements, and safety in core city neighborhoods of Greater Kansas City, MO. (United Funds & United Way) About 5%.
Education: 30% to 35%. Major interest in supporting education through H&R Block Foundation scholarship grants (to children of company employees) and through Kansas and Missouri college funds. Considers requests for specific projects and capital improvements from higher education institutions and independent primary and secondary schools. Also interested in special education programs for at-risk youths and job training. Does not ordinarily provide additional scholarship assistance outside of the foundation-sponsored program described above. Public and private colleges and private secondary schools eligible for matching gifts.
Environment: Less than 5%.
Health: 10% to 15%. Considers requests for special projects from hospitals and neighborhood health centers, especially programs focused on indigent care. Also interested in mental health centers and educational programs to prevent mental illness. Focus on access to health care, substance abuse treatment, counseling services, and shelter for abused women and children. Supports job training and placement programs for the chronically mentally ill.
Social Services: 10% to 15%. Emphasizes programs for high-risk, vulnerable, or emotionally disturbed youth.

Application Procedures

Initial Contact: request guidelines, then submit a formal written proposal.
Application Requirements: Information should include a cover letter detailing amount requested and grant period; project description (including an explanation of why the project is needed, who will be served and what will be accomplished during a specific time period); information on the sustainability of the project and its lasting benefits to the participants, organization and community; a specific plan for evaluating and reporting outcomes; budget and projected sources of funds for the grant period; recently audited financial statement or Form 990; proof of tax-exempt status; and a description of organization (including staff, board of directors, history and accomplishments).
Deadlines: None.
Evaluative Criteria: relevance to foundation's focus areas; 501(c)(3) status; location within metropolitan areas of Kansas City, MO; stability of organization's management; financial planning; fiscal soundness; long- and short-range goals and objectives
Decision Notification: board of directors considers requests at quarterly meetings in September (annual meeting), December, March, and June; written notification of grants awarded follows each meeting
Notes: Organizations may be asked to submit additional information or to meet with a member of the foundation's board of directors or staff.

Restrictions

Foundation does not make grants projects for which foundation must exercise expenditure responsibility; single-disease agencies; travel, or conferences; publications; historic preservation projects; telethons, dinners, advertising or other fundraising events; individuals, or businesses.

Additional Information

Foundation favors making proportionately significant grants to relatively few activities, rather than relatively minor grants to a great many activities. Generally, grants of less than $500 are not made.
Foundation usually makes one-year grants but, in appropriate circumstances, will consider requests for up to five years for special project funding.
H&R Block is no longer affiliated with CompuServe.
The foundation does not have grant application forms.
H&R Block is no longer affiliated with CompuServe.
The foundation does not have grant application forms.
Publications: Annual Report

Corporate Officials

Henry Wollman Bloch: chairman, director, director B Kansas City, MO 1922. ED University of Michigan BS (1944). PRIM CORP EMPL chairman, director: H&R Block Inc. CORP AFFIL director: CompuServe Inc.; director: Commerce Bancshares Inc. NONPR AFFIL general chairman: United Negro College Fund; president trustees: University Kansas City; director: Saint Lukes Foundation; director: Saint Lukes Hospital; vice chairman, director: Midwest Research Institute; director, trustee: Nelson-Atkins Museum Art; director: Mid-American Coalition Health Care; vice chairman corporate fund: Kennedy Center; director: Menorah Medical Center Foundation; director: Kansas City Symphony; trustee: Junior Achievement Mid-America; vice president, director: Kansas City Area Health Planning Council; director: International Public Relations Council; member: Greater Kansas City Chamber of Commerce; director: HRB Management Inc.; member: Golden Key National Honor Society; member: Academy Squires. CLUB AFFIL Oakwood Country Club; River Club; Kansas City Racquet Club; John Gardiners Tennis Ranch; Kansas City Country Club; Carriage Club.
Frank L. Salizzoni: president, chief executive officer, director B 1938. ED Pennsylvania State University BS (1960); George Washington University MS (1964). PRIM CORP EMPL president, chief executive officer, director: H&R Block Inc. CORP AFFIL director: Orbital Sciences Corp.; director: SKF U.S.A. Inc.; president: Block Financial Corp.; president: Block HR Group Inc.

Foundation Officials

Henry Wollman Bloch: chairman (see above)
Robert L. Bloch: secretary, program officer
Charles E. Curran: director
Barbara Lebedun: president
Edward Taylor Matheny, Junior: director B Chicago, IL 1923. ED University of Missouri BA (1944); Harvard University JD (1949). PRIM CORP EMPL of counsel: Blackwell, Sanders, Matheny, Weary & Lombardi LLP. NONPR AFFIL Phi Beta Kappa; Sigma Chi; member: Kansas City Bar Association; member: Missouri Bar Association; trustee: Eye Foundation; trustee: Jacob L. and Ella C. Louse Foundation. CLUB AFFIL Mission Hills Country Club; River Club.
Frank L. Salizzoni: vice chairman (see above)
Morton Irvin Sosland: director B Kansas City, MO 1925. ED Harvard University (1946). PRIM CORP EMPL chairman: Sosland Publishing Co. CORP AFFIL director: Kansas City Southern Industries; director: H&R Block Inc. NONPR AFFIL director: Greater Kansas City Community Foundation.

Grants Analysis

Disclosure Period: calendar year ending 1997
Total Grants: $1,646,881
Number of Grants: 382
Average Grant: $4,000
Highest Grant: $100,000
Typical Range: $1,000 to $20,000

Recent Grants

Note: Grants derived from 1996 Form 990.

Arts & Humanities

18,000 State Ballet of Missouri, Kansas City, MO -- to underwrite 1997 spring performance
12,000 Kansas City Symphony, Kansas City, MO -- support 1996-97 season
12,000 Mid-America Arts Alliance, Kansas City, MO -- for Exhibits USA
10,000 Columbus Symphony Orchestra, Columbus, OH -- to underwrite Young People's Concerts
10,000 John F. Kennedy Center for Performing Arts, Washington, DC -- operating support
10,000 Kansas City Art Institute, Kansas City, MO -- to renovate Living Center
10,000 Kansas City Symphony, Kansas City, MO -- operating support
7,500 Balletmet, Columbus, OH -- support Dance Academy Reaching Out programs
7,500 Kansas City Friends of Alvin Ailey, Kansas City, MO -- support Ailey Camp

Civic & Public Affairs

375,000 Royals Succession Plan, Kansas City, MO -- for Greater Kansas City Community Foundation Royal Succession Plan
20,000 Maine Street Corridor Development Corporation, Kansas City, MO -- operating support
7,500 Greater Kansas City Community Foundation, Kansas City, MO -- operating support

Education

108,580 Citizens Scholarship Foundation of America, St. Peter, MN -- for H&R Block Foundation Scholarship Program
20,000 Greater Kansas City Community Foundation, Kansas City, MO -- to help establish UMKC Law School, Edward A. Smith Chair of Law and Society
20,000 I Know I Can, Columbus, OH -- to sustain last dollar scholarship programs
20,000 University of Missouri Kansas City Henry W. Block School of Business, Kansas City, MO -- to fund new position
11,100 Citizens Scholarship Foundation of America, St. Peter, MN -- scholarships
10,000 Central City School Fund, Kansas City, MO -- scholarship assistance
10,000 I Know I Can, Columbus, OH -- to sustain last dollar scholarship programs
10,000 Learning Exchange, Kansas City, MO -- operating support, purchase computer equipment for Exchange City
10,000 National Future Farmers of American Foundation, Madison, WI -- to underwrite 1996 FFA National Convention
10,000 Rockhurst College, Kansas City, MO -- for Freshman in Science Program
7,500 Missouri Humanities Council, St. Louis, MO -- support READ from the START program
7,000 De la Salle Education Centers, Kansas City, MO -- operating support

Environment

65,000 Earthworks, Kansas City, MO -- capital campaign
10,000 Friends of Lakeside Nature Center, Kansas City, MO -- to construct new educational facility

Health

40,000 Children's Mercy Hospital, Kansas City, MO -- support for Centennial Fund
12,000 Carot Westside Clinic, Kansas City, MO -- support for Bilingual Volunteer Data Program
12,000 Commcare-Community Network for Behavioral Healthcare, Kansas City, MO -- staff training
10,000 Health Partnership Clinic of Johnson County, Overland Park, KS -- to establish community relations group
10,000 KCMC Child Development Corporation, Kansas City, MO -- to construct new child development center
10,000 Network Rehabilitative Services, Kansas City, MO -- underwrite costs of vocational programs
8,000 Truman Medical Center Charitable Foundation, Kansas City, MO -- to increase outreach programs, provide medicare to low-income high risk obstetric patients

Religion

10,000 National Conference of Christians and Jews, Kansas City, MO -- support The People Puzzle

Social Services

25,000 YMCA, Kansas City, MO -- capital campaign
15,625 Heart of America United Way, Kansas City, MO -- agency support
15,625 Heart of America United Way, Kansas City, MO -- agency support
15,625 Heart of America United Way, Kansas City, MO -- agency support
15,625 Heart of America United Way, Kansas City, MO -- agency support
15,000 Boy Scouts of America Heart of America, Kansas City, MO -- to renovate swimming pool at Bartle Scout Reservation
15,000 Rotary Youth Camp Association, Kansas City, MO -- to replace swimming pool
10,250 Associated Youth Services, Kansas City, MO -- computer hardware, software
10,000 Children's Place, Kansas City, MO -- new telephone system
10,000 Foodchain, Kansas City, MO -- support moving headquarters to Kansas City
10,000 Heart of America United Way, Kansas City, MO -- for Jackson County Division of Family Services
10,000 Kaw Valley Center of Wyandotte House, Kansas City, MO -- underwrite Aggression Replacement Training to teachers
10,000 Youth Opportunities Unlimited, Kansas City, MO -- support Outreach Program
7,500 Mid Continent Council of Girl Scouts, Kansas City, MO -- support TeamWorks Program
7,500 YMCA, Kansas City, MO -- capital campaign
7,000 Friendship House, Kansas City, MO -- support for Continuing Care Program

BLOUNT INTERNATIONAL, INC.

Company Contact

Montgomery, AL
Web: http://www.blount.com

Company Description

Employees: 4,400
SIC(s): 3523 Farm Machinery & Equipment, 3531 Construction Machinery, 3537 Industrial Trucks & Tractors, 3949 Sporting & Athletic Goods Nec.

Giving Contact

Pat McGee, Jr.
PO Box 949
Montgomery, AL 36101-0949
Phone: (334)244-4211
Fax: (334)271-8188
Email: classysam@aol.com

Description

Founded: 1970
Organization Type: Corporate Giving Program
Giving Locations: AL: Montgomery principally near operating locations and to national organizations.
Grant Types: Capital, Department, Employee Matching Gifts, Endowment, Fellowship, General Support, Project, Research, Scholarship.
Note: Gifts to education and cultural enrichment are matched up to $2,500 annually.

Giving Philosophy

'The Blount organization has a strong commitment to corporate citizenship and endorses the concept that companies, as well as individuals, must contribute to the well-being of society. We believe that a corporation today has institutional responsibilities that go beyond its primary economic role. These responsibilities include a broad concern for social, civic, cultural and educational enrichment, particularly in the communities in which Blount has a major presence.' Blount International, Inc.

Financial Summary

Total Giving: $2,198,347 (1998); $475,110 (1995); $441,604 (1994). Note: Contributes through corporate direct giving program only. According to the co., foundation became defunct in 1999.
Giving Analysis: Giving for 1998 includes: foundation ($2,164,417); foundation matching gifts ($33,930)
Assets: $1,351,669 (1998); $110,346 (1995); $95,001 (1993)
Gifts Received: $1,244,000 (1998); $491,000 (1995); $380,000 (1993). Note: Contributions were received from Blount, Inc.

Typical Recipients

Arts & Humanities: Arts Associations & Councils, Arts Centers, Arts Festivals, Arts Institutes, Ballet, Dance, Ethnic & Folk Arts, Film & Video, Historic Preservation, History & Archaeology, Libraries, Literary Arts, Museums/Galleries, Music, Opera, Performing Arts, Public Broadcasting, Theater, Visual Arts
Civic & Public Affairs: Community Foundations, Economic Development, Economic Policy, Municipalities/Towns, Parades/Festivals, Philanthropic Organizations, Public Policy, Safety, Urban & Community Affairs, Women's Affairs, Zoos/Aquariums
Education: Arts/Humanities Education, Business Education, Colleges & Universities, Economic Education, Education Associations, Education Funds, Education Reform, Engineering/Technological Education, Education-General, Literacy, Medical Education, Minority Education, Preschool Education, Private Education (Precollege), Public Education (Precollege), Religious Education, Science/Mathematics Education, Secondary Education (Private), Special Education, Student Aid
Environment: Forestry, Environment-General, Wildlife Protection
Health: Arthritis, Cancer, Health Organizations, Hospices, Hospitals, Mental Health, Single-Disease Health Associations
International: Foreign Educational Institutions
Religion: Religious Organizations, Religious Welfare

Social Services: Animal Protection, Child Welfare, Community Centers, Community Service Organizations, Domestic Violence, Family Services, Food/Clothing Distribution, Homes, Recreation & Athletics, Scouts, Senior Services, Substance Abuse, United Funds/United Ways, YMCA/YWCA/YMHA/YWHA, Youth Organizations

Contributions Analysis

Giving Priorities: Health, education, civic affairs and cultural activities.

Arts & Humanities: 21%. Interests include historic preservation, opera, ballet, museums, and arts associations. Grants typically range from $100 to $5,000. A small percentage of funds is disbursed through a matching grants program.

Civic & Public Affairs: 13%. Interests include economic development, municipalities, and safety organizations. Sponsors small matching grants program.

Education: 57%. General goals of education grants are to prepare students for careers in business, government, and education; to advance knowledge in science and technology; and to enhance educational opportunities for minorities and the disadvantaged. One-half of contributions support colleges and universities. Also shows interest in economic education, private and public education, and education associations. Matching grants comprise about one third of education funding.

Health: 8%. Includes health and welfare giving. Interests include hospitals and health associations.

Application Procedures

Initial Contact: Send a brief letter, no longer than two or three pages.

Application Requirements: Include the name of the organization and contact person; the purpose, history, activities, and programs of the organization; evidence of need for the activity or project; benefits expected; plans for evaluation; evidence of ability to carry the project to completion; the projected budget; projected sources and amounts of funding needed; copy of latest financial statement; and proof of tax-exempt status. Any additional factual material related to the organization or the request that may be helpful during evaluation of the proposal may also be included.

Deadlines: None.

Restrictions

Support is limited to organizations in the areas of health, education, civic affairs, and cultural activities. Only organizations that have been granted tax-exemption from federal income tax under section 501(c)(3) and ruled to be publicly supported under section 509(a) of the Internal Revenue Code will be funded.

Corporate Officials

Winton Malcolm Blount, Jr.: chairman, chief executive officer, director, chairman B Union Springs, AL 1921. ED University of Alabama (1939-1941); Seattle Pacific University PhD (1971). PRIM CORP EMPL chairman: Blount International, Inc. CORP AFFIL officer: Gear Products Inc.; chairman: B I Industries Inc.; chairman: Blount Industries Power Equipment Group; chairman: B I Holdings Corp. NONPR AFFIL trustee emeritus: University Alabama; director: YMCA Montgomery; member: U.S. Chamber of Commerce; trustee: Southern Center International Studies; member advisory council: U.S. Army Aviation Museum; member: Newcomen Society North America; trustee: Rhodes College; member: Conference Board; member: NAM; member: American Management Association; member: Business Council; member: American Enterprise Institute; member: Alabama Chamber of Commerce. CLUB AFFIL Rotary Club.

Duncan Joseph McInnes: executive vice president administration, chief administrative officer B Mobile, AL 1943. ED University of Alabama BS (1965); Jones Law School LLB (1973). PRIM CORP EMPL executive vice president administration, chief administrative officer: Blount International, Inc. NONPR AFFIL member: American Society of Corporate Secretaries.

John Michael Panettiere: president, chief executive officer, director, chairman B Kansas City, MO 1937. ED Rockhurst College; University of Kansas; West Minster College BA (1959). PRIM CORP EMPL president, chief executive officer, director, chairman: Blount International Inc. ADD CORP EMPL chairman: Federal Manufacturing Corp.; chairman: Federal Cartridge Co.; president: BI Holdings Corp.; president, chief executive officer, director: Blount Inc.; chairman: Dixon Industries Inc.; chairman: Gear Products Inc.

Grants Analysis

Disclosure Period: calendar year ending 1998
Total Grants: $2,164,417*
Number of Grants: 119
Average Grant: $9,868*
Highest Grant: $1,000,000
Typical Range: $5,000 to $50,000
***Note:** Giving excludes matching gifts. Average grant figure excludes highest grant.

Recent Grants

Note: Grants derived from 1997 Form 990.

Arts & Humanities

125,000	Alabama Shakespeare Festival, Montgomery, AL
32,000	Montgomery Symphony, Montgomery, AL
27,000	Alabama Shakespeare Festival, Montgomery, AL
25,000	Alabama Shakespeare Festival, Montgomery, AL
20,000	Birmingham Festival of Arts, Birmingham, AL
20,000	Metropolitan Arts Guild, New York, NY
15,000	Alabama Public Television, Birmingham, AL -- educational
10,000	Alabama Public Television, Birmingham, AL -- educational
10,000	Folger Shakespeare Library, Washington, DC
10,000	Landmarks Foundation, Montgomery, AL -- civic, community
10,000	Montgomery Ballet, Montgomery, AL
7,500	Jubilee City Fest, Montgomery, AL
7,500	Jubilee City Fest, Montgomery, AL
7,000	Alabama Humanities Foundation, Birmingham, AL -- civic, community
7,000	Alabama Shakespeare Festival, Montgomery, AL
5,000	Landmarks Foundation, Montgomery, AL -- civic, community

Civic & Public Affairs

25,000	American Enterprise Institute for Public Policy Research, Washington, DC -- civic, community
15,000	Montgomery Area Zoological Society, Montgomery, AL -- civic, community
5,000	Leadership Coffeyville, Coffeyville, KS -- civic, community
5,000	Voices, Birmingham, AL -- civic, community

Education

25,000	Bryant Jordan Scholar Athlete Foundation, Selma, AL -- educational
20,000	Montgomery Academy, Montgomery, AL
15,000	Alabama Institute for Education in Arts, Montgomery, AL
10,000	Alabama Institute for Deaf and Blind, Talladega, AL -- health, welfare
10,000	Alabama School of Fine Arts Foundation, Birmingham, AL
10,000	Alabama School of Math and Science Foundation, Mobile, AL
10,000	Capstone Foundation, Tuscaloosa, AL -- culture, art
10,000	Success by Six, Montgomery, AL -- educational
10,000	University of Alabama, University, AL
10,000	University of Alabama College of Engineering, Tuscaloosa, AL
8,333	Spelman College, Atlanta, GA
8,000	Clackamas Community College, Montgomery, AL -- culture, art
8,000	Montgomery Academy, Montgomery, AL
7,500	Wetumpka High School, Montgomery, AL
7,000	Junior Achievement Columbia Empire, Portland, OR -- health, welfare

Health

25,000	Memorial Sloan-Kettering Cancer Center, New York, NY -- health, welfare
16,055	Hospice, Montgomery, AL -- health, welfare
14,035	Foundation of Guelph General Hospital

Religion

5,000	North Florida Fellowship of Christian Athletes, Tallahassee, FL -- civic, community

Social Services

100,000	YMCA, Montgomery, AL -- health, welfare
12,500	Substance Abuse Youth Networking Organization, Montgomery, AL -- civic, community
12,500	Valley Boys and Girls Club, Lewiston, ID -- health, welfare
10,000	Alabama Highland Games, Montgomery, AL
7,389	Guelph Civic Center, Portland, OR -- civic, community
6,250	Montgomery Humane Society, Montgomery, AL -- civic, community
5,000	Blue-Gray National Tennis Classic, Montgomery, AL -- civic, community
5,000	Boy Scouts of America, Montgomery, AL -- civic, community
5,000	Boy Scouts of America, Montgomery, AL -- civic, community
5,000	Children's Harbor, Childrens Harbor, AL -- civic, community
5,000	Girl Scouts of America, Montgomery, AL -- civic, community

Blue Bell, Inc.

Company Contact

Greensboro, NC
Web: http://www.bluebell.com

Company Description

SIC(s): 2253 Knit Outerwear Mills, 2311 Men's/Boys' Suits & Coats, 2321 Men's/Boys' Shirts, 2325 Men's/Boys' Trousers & Slacks.
Parent Company: VF Corp., Greensboro, NC, United States

Blue Bell Foundation

Giving Contact

Edward Heim, Secretary, Advisory Committee
Blue Bell Foundation
PO Box 21488
Greensboro, NC 27420-1488
Phone: (336)332-4106
Fax: (336)332-4259

Description

EIN: 566041057
Organization Type: Corporate Foundation
Giving Locations: principally near operating locations and to national organizations.
Grant Types: Employee Matching Gifts, General Support.

Financial Summary

Total Giving: $198,169 (1998); $266,252 (1997); $290,539 (1996). Note: Contributes through corporate direct giving program and foundation. 1998 Giving includes Foundation.

Giving Analysis: Giving for 1996 includes: foundation ($259,860); foundation matching gifts ($30,679); 1997: foundation ($191,318); foundation grants to United Way ($45,000); foundation matching gifts ($29,934); 1998: foundation ($168,894); foundation matching gifts ($29,275)

Assets: $6,375,166 (1998); $5,075,010 (1996); $4,018,570 (1992)

Typical Recipients

Arts & Humanities: Arts Associations & Councils, Arts Centers, Arts Festivals, Arts Funds, Community Arts, Historic Preservation, Libraries, Museums/Galleries, Music, Theater

Civic & Public Affairs: Botanical Gardens/Parks, Chambers of Commerce, Clubs, Employment/Job Training, Civic & Public Affairs-General, Housing, Law & Justice, Municipalities/Towns, Public Policy, Safety, Urban & Community Affairs, Zoos/Aquariums

Education: Agricultural Education, Arts/Humanities Education, Business Education, Colleges & Universities, Community & Junior Colleges, Economic Education, Education Associations, Education Funds, Elementary Education (Public), Engineering/ Technological Education, Literacy, Minority Education, Private Education (Precollege), Public Education (Precollege), Secondary Education (Public), Student Aid

Environment: Resource Conservation, Wildlife Protection

Health: Cancer, Children's Health/Hospitals, Diabetes, Emergency/Ambulance Services, Heart, Hospices, Hospitals, Medical Rehabilitation, Medical Research, Prenatal Health Issues, Public Health, Respiratory, Single-Disease Health Associations

International: Health Care/Hospitals, International Development

Religion: Churches, Jewish Causes, Ministries, Religious Organizations, Religious Welfare, Social/Policy Issues

Science: Scientific Centers & Institutes

Social Services: At-Risk Youth, Child Abuse, Child Welfare, Community Centers, Community Service Organizations, Counseling, Day Care, Domestic Violence, Emergency Relief, Food/Clothing Distribution, Homes, People with Disabilities, Recreation & Athletics, Scouts, Special Olympics, Substance Abuse, United Funds/United Ways, YMCA/YWCA/YMHA/ YWHA, Youth Organizations

Contributions Analysis

Giving Priorities: Education and social services.

Arts & Humanities: 10% to 15%. Supports arts councils, historical museums, and some performing arts.

Civic & Public Affairs: About 10%. Recipients include municipalities, environmental efforts, and community affairs.

Education: 35% to 40%. Emphasis is on the National Merit Scholarship Corporation, colleges and universities. Also supports preschools, high schools (public and private), education funds, and community education programs. The foundation operates a large matching gift program for company employees who wish to contribute to educational institutions.

Health: Less than 5%. Favors hospitals, cancer treatment, hospices, and science centers.

Religion: 5% to 10%. Churches and religious organizations receive funding.

Social Services: 25% to 30%. Supports United Way chapters and community service organizations. Housing, food distribution, and youth activities are also major priorities.

Application Procedures

Initial Contact: Send a letter of request.

Application Requirements: Include a description of organization; IRS tax determination letter; and amount requested.

Deadlines: None.

Decision Notification: Board meets two times per year.

Restrictions

Foundation does not support individuals; grants made to organizations that directly benefit company's employees.

Corporate Officials

Lawrence R. Pugh: chairman, director jeanswear coalition B 1933. PRIM CORP EMPL chairman, director: VF Corp. CORP AFFIL director: Vanity Fair Intimates Inc.; chairman: Vanity Fair Jeans Wear Inc.; officer: Jansport Inc.; chairman: President Trustees Colby.

John P. Schamberger: president, chairman jeanswear coalition B 1948. ED Saint John's University BS (1969); Saint John's University MBA (1974). PRIM CORP EMPL president, chairman jeanswear coalition: VF Corp.

Foundation Officials

Ed Heim: secretary advisory committee

Donald P. Laws: member advisory committee PRIM CORP EMPL president, Wrangler Westernwear: VF Jeanswear Inc. CORP AFFIL president: VF Corp.

John P. Schamberger: member advisory board (see above)

Grants Analysis

Disclosure Period: calendar year ending 1998

Total Grants: $168,894*

Number of Grants: 94

Average Grant: $1,797

Highest Grant: $10,000

Typical Range: $100 to $5,000

***Note:** Giving excludes matching gifts.

Recent Grants

Note: Grants derived from 1998 Form 990.

Civic & Public Affairs

2,500 Nashville Chamber of Commerce, Nashville, TN -- 1st Pymnt of $10,000 Pledge PD Over 4 Years Time

2,000 Madison County Fire Department, Richmond, KY -- Contribution from the Blue Bell Foundation (1998)

1,000 Columbus Police Department, Columbus, OH -- Contribution from Blue Bell FOUNDATION 1998

1,000 North Carolina Zoological Society, Asheboro, NC -- Corporate Seal Sponsorship

Education

23,015 Citizen's Scholarship Foundation, St. Peter, MN -- 1998 Contribution

5,000 Guilford College, Greensboro, NC -- 1998 Contribution

3,000 Junior Achievement, Winston - Salem, NC -- 1998 Blue Bell FOUNDATION Contribution

2,000 The College of William & Mary, Williamsburg, VA -- Matching Gift of $2000.00 FRM Ron Martin

2,000 North Carolina State University, Raleigh, NC -- Matching Gift of $2000.00 from Roger Graves

2,000 Tennessee Foundation for Independent Colleges, Nashville, TN -- Contribution from the Blue Bell Foundation 1998

1,870 Wake Forest University, Winston-Salem, NC -- Matching of $1870.00 from Clarke Doster

1,300 Donelson Christian Academy, Nashville, TN -- Matching Gift of $1300.00 from Gary Swindell

1,200 Junior Achievement, Greensboro, NC -- Contribution from Blue Bell FOUNDATION 1998

1,155 Greensboro Montessori School, Greensboro, NC -- Matching Gift of $1150.00 FRM Sandra F. Mayfield

1,000 Agenes Scott College, Decatur, GA -- Matching of $1000.00 FRM Bona Allen

1,000 Baylor University, Waco, TX -- Matching of $1000.00 from Fred S. Barber

1,000 Georgia Tech Alumni Association, Atlanta, GA -- Matching of $1000.00 FRM Bona Allen

1,000 Greensboro Music Academy, Greensboro, NC -- 1998 Contribution

1,000 Happy Hill Farm and Academy, Granbury, TX -- Matching Gift of $1000.00 from Casey Jones

1,000 ST. Pius X School, Greensboro, NC -- 1998 Contribution

1,000 Students in Free Enterprise, Springfield, MO -- Contribution

1,000 Wake Forest University, Winston-Salem, NC -- Matching Gift of $1000.00 FRM Terry Weatherford

1,000 West Virginia University, Morgantown, WV -- Matching of $1000.00 from Michael T. Barrett

700 Guilford College, Greensboro, NC -- Matching Gift of $700.00 from Ellen Martin

650 UNC-Greensboro, Greensboro, NC -- Matching Gift of $650.00 from Ruth Ellen Luck

500 The University of Tennessee, Knoxville, TN -- Matching Gift of $500.00 from Keith Mcpeters

Health

5,000 American Red Cross, Greensboro, NC -- 1998 Contribution

5,000 West Texas Rehabilitation Center, Abilene, TX -- Contribution

1,000 American Cancer Society's Relay for Life, Goodlettsville, TN -- Contribution

1,000 American Heart Association, Durham, NC -- Contribution from the Blue Bell

1,000 American Heart Association, Greensboro, NC -- Contribution from the Blue Bell Foundation 1998

1,000 American Lung Association, Raleigh, NC -- 1998 Contribution

800 Ronald McDonald House, Winston-Salem, NC -- Contribution from Blue Bell FOUNDATION 1998

750 Epilepsy Foundation, Landover, MD -- 1998 Blue Bell Contribution

Religion

1,550 Templo Elim, Fabens, TX -- Contribution

1,000 Heal Thserve Ministry, Greensboro, NC -- Contribution

750 Galilee Baptist Church, Seminole, OK -- Contribution from the Blue Bell Foundation 1998

Social Services

5,000 Bertie County YMCA, Windsor, NC -- Contribution

5,000 Horsepower Therapeutic Learning Center, NC

5,000 Old North State Council, Greensboro, NC -- 1998 Contribution

4,500 Community Resource Center, Nashville, TN -- Contribution from the Blue Bell Foundation 1998

2,000 Cardinal Amateur, Greensboro, NC -- 1998 Contribution

2,000 Charles Davis Foundation, Nashville, TN -- Contribution from the Blue Bell Foundation 1998

1,000 Community Swim Association, Mobile, AL -- 1998 Contribution
1,000 Goodwill Industries, Winston-Salem, NC -- Good Turn for Goodwill Clothing Drive
1,000 Special Olympics of Raleigh, Raleigh, NC -- 1998 Contribution
1,000 Tarheel Triad Girl Scout Council, Inc, Colfax, NC -- Contribution from Blue Bell Foundation 1998 (for Denim After Dark 1998)
750 Greensboro Wildcats Association, Greensboro, NC -- 1998 Contribution

Blue Cross &Blue Shield Of Alabama

Company Contact

Birmingham, AL
Web: http://www.bcbsal.com

Company Description

Employees: 2,200
SIC(s): 6324 Hospital & Medical Service Plans.

Caring Foundation

Giving Contact

James M. Brown, Vice President
Caring Foundation
450 Riverchase Pkwy. East
Birmingham, AL 35298
Phone: (205)988-2503
Fax: (205)444-6555
Email: jbrown@bcbsal.org

Description

EIN: 631035261
Organization Type: Corporate Foundation
Giving Locations: AL
Grant Types: General Support.

Financial Summary

Total Giving: $1,394,801 (1998); $1,471,195 (1997); $1,491,047 (1996). Note: Contributes through foundation only.
Giving Analysis: Giving for 1998 includes: foundation grants to United Way ($10,700)
Assets: $33,971,399 (1998); $28,764,310 (1996); $23,872,926 (1994)
Gifts Received: $13,500,000 (1994)

Typical Recipients

Arts & Humanities: Arts Associations & Councils, Arts Festivals, Ballet, Historic Preservation, History & Archaeology, Music, Opera, Public Broadcasting, Theater
Civic & Public Affairs: Business/Free Enterprise, Clubs, Civic & Public Affairs-General, Housing, Parades/Festivals, Safety, Urban & Community Affairs, Women's Affairs, Zoos/Aquariums
Education: Arts/Humanities Education, Business Education, Colleges & Universities, Economic Education, Education Funds, Education-General, Literacy, Minority Education, Private Education (Precollege), Public Education (Precollege), Secondary Education (Private), Special Education, Student Aid
Environment: Protection
Health: AIDS/HIV, Alzheimers Disease, Arthritis, Cancer, Children's Health/Hospitals, Emergency/Ambulance Services, Eyes/Blindness, Health Organizations, Heart, Hospitals, Multiple Sclerosis, Prenatal Health Issues, Respiratory, Single-Disease Health Associations, Speech & Hearing, Trauma Treatment
Religion: Jewish Causes, Religious Organizations, Religious Welfare, Social/Policy Issues
Social Services: Camps, Child Welfare, Community Service Organizations, Day Care, People with Disabilities, Recreation & Athletics, Scouts, Shelters/Homelessness, Substance Abuse, United Funds/United Ways, Volunteer Services, YMCA/YWCA/YMHA/YWHA, Youth Organizations

Contributions Analysis

Arts & Humanities: 6%. Emphasis on the symphony, ballet, and opera.
Education: 9%. Supports educational groups in Alabama, including colleges and universities.
Health: 25%. Primarily supports single-disease health organizations.
Religion: 1%. Religious welfare.
Social Services: 59%. Supports youth agencies and child welfare.
Note: Total contributions in 1998.

Application Procedures

Initial Contact: Submit application in writing.
Application Requirements: Include the name of the organization, charitable purpose, and amount requested.
Deadlines: None.

Corporate Officials

G. Phillip Pope: chief financial officer B 1946. ED Jacksonville State University (1968). PRIM CORP EMPL chief financial officer: Blue Cross Blue Shield of Alabama.

Giving Program Officials

James M. Brown: vice president PRIM CORP EMPL vice president: Blue Cross & Blue Shield Alabama.

Foundation Officials

H. L. Jones: vice president B 1938. PRIM CORP EMPL president: Blue Cross Blue Shield Alabama.
Terry Kellogg: treasurer PRIM CORP EMPL senior vice president: Blue Cross Blue Shield of Alabama.
G. Phillip Pope: vice president (see above)
A. Grey Till, Jr.: secretary PRIM CORP EMPL secretary: Blue Cross Blue Shield of Alabama.

Grants Analysis

Disclosure Period: calendar year ending 1997
Total Grants: $1,471,195
Number of Grants: 93
Average Grant: $15,819
Highest Grant: $695,891
Typical Range: $500 to $20,000
Note: Grant Analysis was provided by foundation.

Recent Grants

Note: Grants derived from 1998 Form 990.

Arts & Humanities

60,000 Alabama Symphony, Birmingham, AL
10,000 Alabama Ballet, Birmingham, AL
10,000 Opera Birmingham, Birmingham, AL

Education

33,334 Reading Alabama Inc., Montgomery, AL
30,000 Auburn University, Birmingham, AL
25,000 Hoover City Schools, Hoover, AL
10,000 Birmingham Southern College, Birmingham, AL
6,766 University of Alabama, Birmingham, AL
6,250 Junior Achievement, Birmingham, AL
2,500 Alabama Independent Colleges and Universities, Birmingham, AL
2,500 Alabama School of Fine Arts, Birmingham, AL
2,000 Troy State University, Montgomery, AL
1,500 College Fund UNCF, Birmingham, AL
1,440 Hoover City Schools Foundation, Hoover, AL
1,250 Holy Family High School, Birmingham, AL

Health

153,750 Children's Hospital of Alabama Poison Control, Birmingham, AL
127,500 Alabama Poison Center in Tuscaloosa, Tuscaloosa, AL
15,000 Alabama Lion's Sight Conservation Program, Birmingham, AL
10,000 Amercan Red Cross, Birmingham, AL
6,522 Leukemia Society of America, Birmingham, AL
5,195 American Heart Association, Birmingham, AL
3,750 Cystic Fibrosis Foundation, Birmingham, AL
3,600 Birmingham Ear Institute, Birmingham, AL
3,500 Alabama Kidney Foundation, Birmingham, AL
2,700 American Liver Association, Birmingham, AL
2,500 American Lung Association, Birmingham, AL
2,250 Crohn's and Colitis Foundation, Birmingham, AL
2,000 Aids Task Force of Alabama, Birmingham
2,000 Make-A-Wish Foundation of Alabama, AL -- *GCI Mobile
1,650 Arthritis Foundation, Birmingham, AL
1,350 National Multiple Sclerosis Society, Birmingham, AL

Religion

10,000 Discovery 2000, Birmingham, AL
5,678 Salvation Army, Birmingham, AL
1,300 National Conference of Christians and Jews, Birmingham, AL

Social Services

700,059 Alabama Child Caring Foundation, Birmingham, AL
25,000 UAB Athletics, Birmingham, AL
10,700 United Way, Birmingham, AL
10,000 Greater Alabama Council of Boy Scouts, Birmingham, AL
10,000 Tukabatchee Boy Scouts, Montgomery, AL
10,000 Voices for Alabama Children, Montgomery, AL
6,750 Boyscouts of America, Birmingham, AL
5,880 Cahaba Girl Scout Council, Birmingham, AL
5,000 Children's Harbor Inc., Birmingham, AL
3,000 Alabama Sports Festival Inc., Birmingham, AL
2,500 St Anne's Home, Birmingham, AL
2,500 YMCA, Birmingham, AL
2,250 Camp Fire Boys & Girls, Birmingham, AL
2,000 Service Guild of Birmingham, Birmingham, AL
1,100 Big Oak Ranch, Gadsden, AL

Blue Cross &Blue Shield Of Iowa

Company Contact

Des Moines, IA

Company Description

Assets: US$550,300,000
Employees: 2,000
SIC(s): 6321 Accident & Health Insurance, 6324 Hospital & Medical Service Plans.

Wellmark Foundation

Giving Contact

Mary Kramer, Executive Director
Wellmark Foundation
Ruan Building
636 Grand Avenue, Station 150
Des Moines, IA 50309-2502
Phone: (515)245-4500
Fax: (515)323-7648

Description

Founded: 1991
EIN: 421368650
Organization Type: Corporate Foundation
Giving Locations: IA; SD
Grant Types: General Support, Scholarship.

Giving Philosophy

'In Iowa and South Dakota, as across the nation, there are pressing health care needs that currently are not being met due to limited local, state and federal resources. In response, the Wellmark Foundation, a tax-exempt charitable foundation, was established in 1990 for the purpose of improving the cost, quality and accessibility of health care in both states. The foundation concentrates its grantmaking in these three areas of health care.'

'In most cases, the foundation provides first-dollar funds, or seed money, to nonprofit organizations to help local communities establish or expand health care projects. Preference is given to projects that are co-funded in the first year by other community organizations and/or health care providers. Programs that are successful on the local level and show promise for being replicated or adopted by the mainstream health care system will be given priority consideration.'

'The foundation also gives priority consideration to programs that address the health care needs of at-risk Iowans and South Dakotans. Based on the social, economic and demographic makeup of both states, three key populations --children (and pregnant women), elderly residents and rural residents-- have been identified as being most at-risk for falling outside the current capacity of the health care system. The majority of the foundation's grants will be awarded to programs that target the specific health care needs of these special populations. In most cases, the foundation will not be the sole funder of the project. Most awards are provided for one year only.'

'Thus, the foundation will give preference to programs most likely to stay operational and financially viable after the foundation's financial assistance ends. Programs should demonstrate strong community support and evidence of ongoing support.' Information Sheet

Financial Summary

Total Giving: $1,089,586 (1996); $786,405 (1995); $575,784 (1994). Note: Contributes through foundation only.
Giving Analysis: Giving for 1998 includes: foundation (approx $4,685,560); foundation grants to United Way (approx $197,000)
Assets: $16,087,910 (1996); $15,860,049 (1995); $15,438,362 (1994)
Gifts Received: $14,294 (1996); $42,504 (1995); $5,000,000 (1994). Note: Contributions are received from Blue Cross and Blue Shield of Iowa.

Typical Recipients

Arts & Humanities: Arts Centers, Libraries, Music, Opera, Theater
Civic & Public Affairs: Clubs, Civic & Public Affairs-General, Public Policy, Rural Affairs, Safety, Zoos/Aquariums
Education: Afterschool/Enrichment Programs, Agricultural Education, Business Education, Colleges & Universities, Education-General, Medical Education, Preschool Education, Public Education (Precollege), Student Aid
Environment: Resource Conservation
Health: Alzheimers Disease, Cancer, Children's Health/Hospitals, Clinics/Medical Centers, Emergency/Ambulance Services, Health Organizations, Hospices, Hospitals, Hospitals (University Affiliated), Multiple Sclerosis, Prenatal Health Issues, Public Health, Respiratory
Religion: Religious Welfare
Social Services: Child Abuse, Child Welfare, Community Service Organizations, Day Care, Domestic Violence, Family Services, Food/Clothing Distribution, People with Disabilities, Recreation & Athletics, Scouts, Senior Services, Substance Abuse, United Funds/United Ways, YMCA/YWCA/YMHA/YWHA, Youth Organizations

Contributions Analysis

Health: 100%. Funding is given for the purpose of improving the cost, quality and accessibility of health care.

Application Procedures

Initial Contact: Include a description of organization, amount requested, purpose of funds sought, recently audited financial statement, and proof of tax-exempt status.
Deadlines: None.

Additional Information

Publications: Information Sheet

Corporate Officials

Rich Anderson: chief financial officer, chief executive officer PRIM CORP EMPL chief financial officer: Blue Cross Blue Shield of Iowa.
John D. Forsyth: president, chief executive officer PRIM CORP EMPL president, chief executive officer: Blue Cross Blue Shield of Iowa. NONPR AFFIL member: National Association State Universities & Land-Grant Colleges; director: United Way Michigan; member: Association American Universities; member: Leadership Giving Comm; member: Ann Arbor Chamber of Commerce; member: Association American Medicine Colleges Council Teaching Hospitals; member: American Council Education.

Foundation Officials

Mary Elizabeth Kramer: vice president B Burlington, IA 1935. PRIM NONPR EMPL president: Iowa State Senate. NONPR AFFIL member: Rotary International; member: Society Human Resources Management; member: Nexus; member: Greater Des Moines Chamber of Commerce; member: Iowa Management Association.

Grants Analysis

Disclosure Period: calendar year ending 1996
Total Grants: $1,089,586
Number of Grants: 57
Average Grant: $19,116
Highest Grant: $94,300
Typical Range: $1,000 to $50,000

Recent Grants

Note: Grants derived from 1997 Form 990.

Civic & Public Affairs

40,000	Lions Club, SD

Education

87,799	Saydel Consolidated School District, Des Moines, IA
26,000	Iowa State University, Ames, IA

Health

132,500	Polk County Department of Health, IA
112,000	Montgomery County Memorial Hospital Foundation, Red Oak, IA
97,777	Sioux Valley Health System Foundation, IA
70,000	Iowa Department of Public Health, IA
36,000	Iowa Tobacco Free Action Team, IA
20,000	Lee County Health Department, IA

Social Services

175,000	United Way of Central Iowa, Des Moines, IA
50,000	Rock in Prevention, Des Moines, IA
50,000	Young Parents Network, Cedar Rapids, IA
25,000	South Dakota Caring Program, SD
22,100	United Way, IA
18,500	South Dakota United Ways, SD

Blue Cross &Blue Shield Of Michigan

Company Contact

Detroit, MI
Web: http://www.bcbsm.com

Company Description

Employees: 6,500
SIC(s): 6300 Insurance Carriers.

Blue Cross & Blue Shield of Michigan Foundation

Giving Contact

Nancy Szydlowski, Executive Assistant
Blue Cross & Blue Shield of Michigan Foundation
600 Lafayette E., X520
Detroit, MI 48226-2927
Phone: (313)225-8706
Fax: (313)225-7730
Email: nmaloy@bcbsm.com

Description

Organization Type: Corporate Foundation
Giving Locations: MI
Grant Types: Award, Conference/Seminar, Matching, Research.
Note: Company supports healthcare research and proposal development.

Giving Philosophy

'The BCBSM Foundation is dedicated to improving the health of Michigan citizens through research and service. The diversity, relevance and practical application of the research and service delivery projects we fund has earned the Foundation a reputation for excellence in health philanthropy..Foundation makes grants to: enhance the quality and appropriate use of health care services, improve access to appropriate health services, control health care costs and support a socially responsible health agenda. 1998 Analysis Report.'

Financial Summary

Total Giving: $2,300,000 (1999 approx); $1,205,258 (1998 approx); $1,510,355 (1997). Note: Contributes through foundation only.
Assets: $56,000,000 (1999 approx); $58,587,448 (1998); $52,288,023 (1997)

Typical Recipients

Health: Cancer, Diabetes, Health-General, Geriatric Health, Health Policy/Cost Containment, Heart, Hospitals, Medical Research, Mental Health, Prenatal Health Issues, Preventive Medicine/Wellness Organizations, Single-Disease Health Associations

Contributions Analysis

Health: 100%. Goals for giving are to enhance the quality and appropriate use of health-care services,

improve access to appropriate health services, and control health-care costs. Supports the following programs: the Investigator Initiated Research Program, which supports health care researchers interested in finding ways to improve health-care in Michigan by funding projects which address health-care costs, quality, and access to services; the Matching Initiative Program, which supports a variety of innovative health service projects and attempts to foster collaboration among foundations and other funding organizations, and which matches grants for conferences and seminars; the Request for Proposals Program; the Physician Investigator Research Award, for projects that include physician-led pilot studies, feasibility studies, or small research studies in clinical or health services research; the Student Award Program, which offers one-year grants for health-care research to doctoral and medical students in Michigan universities; the Proposal Development Award, which helps community nonprofit organizations develop proposals for improving health- care delivery; and the Excellence in Research Awards, which honors researchers who make significant contributions toward improving health care delivery in Michigan.

Application Procedures

Initial Contact: Contact foundation for guidelines.
Review Process: Proposals are reviewed by staff, then sent to Grants Advisory Panel for external review; based on Grant Advisory Panel and staff reviews, funding recommendations are presented for review by the foundation board of directors.
Evaluative Criteria: Based on significance of project, contribution of new information not otherwise available, technical quality of proposed project, qualifications of project staff, and feasibility of the project.
Notes: Each program has extensive, detailed guidelines for application, and some programs have specific application forms.

Restrictions

All funds go to health-care related concerns in Michigan.
Foundation does not support religious organizations for sectarian purposes, or political or lobbying groups.

Additional Information

Publications: Foundation Annual Report (including Guidelines)

Foundation Officials

Ira Strumwasser, PhD.: executive director

Grants Analysis

Disclosure Period: calendar year ending 1998
Total Grants: $1,205,258*
Number of Grants: 33
Average Grant: $36,523
Typical Range: $2,500 to $75,000
***Note:** Giving excludes grants to individuals.

Recent Grants

Note: Grants derived from 1996 Annual Report.

Health

100,053	University of Michigan Medical Center, Ann Arbor, MI -- first year of three-year pledge for Effectiveness of Shared Decision-Making Program for Women with Breast Cancer
86,178	University of Michigan Medical Center, Ann Arbor, MI -- first payment on five-year pledge for Cardiovascular Centers of Excellence program
75,000	Wayne State University School of Medicine, Detroit, MI -- for Pathways to Mammography Follow-up
70,674	University of Michigan Institute of Gerontology, Ann Arbor, MI -- second and final payment for Survival, Health Care Utilization, and Dementia program
66,553	Michigan State University, East Lansing, MI -- first payment on two-year pledge for Greater Flint Standard Decision Project
48,000	University of Michigan Medical Center, Ann Arbor, MI -- support Preoperative Cardiac Risk Assessment program
35,890	Catherine McAuley Health System -- second payment on three-year pledge for Screening and Follow-Up Protocol for Outpatient Initiation of Continuous Insulin Infusion Therapy program
29,210	University of Michigan Medical Center, Ann Arbor, MI -- for Community Physicians Response to Cesarean Section Guidelines
10,000	New England Journal of Medicine -- for health policy
10,000	Otolaryngology, Head and Neck Surgery -- clinical research
10,000	University of Michigan, Ann Arbor, MI -- support Collaborative Care of Depressed Patients in the Community
10,000	Wayne State University, Detroit, MI -- support Evidence for Apoptosis in Inflammatory Myopathies
10,000	Wayne State University Harper Hospital, Detroit, MI -- for Left Ventricular Dysfunction in Diabetes
9,950	Michigan State University Kalamazoo Center for Medical Studies, Kalamazoo, MI -- for Comparison of Combined Urine Dipstick, Clinical Scoring System
9,919	St. Joseph Mercy Hospital -- for preoperative predictors of mortality
9,833	Hutzel Hospital Center for Rheumatic Diseases, Detroit, MI -- support Pregnancies Complicated by Systemic Lupus Erythematosus program
9,410	Wayne State University, Detroit, MI -- supplemental award to supplement two-year funding for Predictors of the Kept Postpartum Appointment by Medicaid Eligible Women
8,405	Wayne State University, Detroit, MI -- first payment on three-year pledge for Distribution of Complications Related to Prostate Cancer Treatment
2,500	Scheurer Hospital, Pigeon Michigan Project 4 HEALTH, Pigeon, MI -- support Comprehensive Senior Wellness Program
2,500	Scheurer Hospital, Pigeon Michigan Rural Health Care Delivery System, Pigeon, MI -- for building roads to improve access to medical services in Thumb Area
800	Michigan State University Department of Psychiatry, East Lansing, MI -- supplemental award for Mental Health in the Nursing Home program

Blue Cross &blue Shield Of Minnesota

Company Contact

St. Paul, MN
Web: http://www.bluecrossmn.com

Company Description

Assets: US$630,700,000
Employees: 3,000
SIC(s): 6300 Insurance Carriers.

Nonmonetary Support

Value: $300,000 (1998 approx)
Type: Cause-related Marketing & Promotion; Donated Equipment; In-kind Services; Loaned Employees; Loaned Executives

Corporate Sponsorship

Type: Pledge-a-thon
Note: Sponsors health-related events.

Blue Cross & Blue Shield of Minnesota Foundation Inc.

Giving Contact

Daniel Johnson, Director, Community Affairs
PO Box 64560
St. Paul, MN 55164-0560
Phone: (612)456-1580
Fax: (612)456-1570
Web: http://www.bluecrossmn.com/community/index.shtml

Description

Founded: 1986
EIN: 363525653
Organization Type: Corporate Foundation
Giving Locations: MN
Grant Types: Conference/Seminar, Employee Matching Gifts, General Support, Operating Expenses, Research, Scholarship.

Financial Summary

Total Giving: $1,900,000 (1999 approx); $1,500,000 (1998 approx); $1,311,613 (1997). Note: Contributes through corporate direct giving program and foundation.
Giving Analysis: Giving for 1997 includes: nonmonetary support ($745,533); foundation ($531,613); corporate direct giving ($20,000); foundation grants to United Way ($14,467)
Assets: $33,937,146 (1999); $13,115,958 (1998); $13,439,244 (1997)
Gifts Received: $6,737 (1997); $1,081 (1996); $2,000,000 (1993). Note: Contributions were received from Blue Cross and Blue Shield of Minnesota and HMO Minnesota Blue Plus.

Typical Recipients

Arts & Humanities: Museums/Galleries, Theater
Civic & Public Affairs: African American Affairs, Asian American Affairs, Community Foundations, Economic Development, Civic & Public Affairs-General, Housing, Nonprofit Management, Public Policy, Urban & Community Affairs
Education: Business Education, Colleges & Universities, Economic Education, Faculty Development, Health & Physical Education, Leadership Training, Medical Education, Minority Education, Student Aid
Environment: Environment-General
Health: AIDS/HIV, Cancer, Children's Health/Hospitals, Clinics/Medical Centers, Diabetes, Emergency/ Ambulance Services, Health-General, Health Policy/ Cost Containment, Health Funds, Health Organizations, Heart, Hospitals, Kidney, Medical Rehabilitation, Medical Research, Medical Training, Mental Health, Multiple Sclerosis, Nutrition, Prenatal Health Issues, Preventive Medicine/Wellness Organizations, Public Health, Respiratory, Single-Disease Health Associations, Trauma Treatment
Religion: Churches, Religious Welfare
Social Services: At-Risk Youth, Child Welfare, Community Service Organizations, Crime Prevention, Day Care, Domestic Violence, Family Services, Food/ Clothing Distribution, People with Disabilities, Scouts, Senior Services, Shelters/Homelessness, United Funds/United Ways

Contributions Analysis

Health: 100%. Priority is given to projects that improve the health status of Minnesotans by reducing the use of tobacco as an underlying cause of illness and premature death; individual fitness; nutritional

safety; childhood immunization; and helping select populations navigate the health care system.

Application Procedures

Initial Contact: Submit letter of inquiry.
Application Requirements: Include with letter of inquiry, summary of proposed project and amount requested.
Deadlines: None.
Review Process: Foundation provides informal indication of likelihood of support in response to letter of inquiry; if favorable, formal proposal is requested.
Decision Notification: Grants are approved periodically during year.

Restrictions

Does not support individuals, religious organizations for sectarian purposes, political or lobbying groups, or organizations outside operating areas.

Additional Information

Publications: Giving Guidelines; Annual Report

Corporate Officials

Marie Banks, MD: president PRIM CORP EMPL president: Blue Cross & Blue Shield of Minnesota.
Joan Cleary: administrator PRIM CORP EMPL administrator: Blue Cross & Blue Shield Minnesota.
Andrew P. Czajkowski: chief executive officer PRIM CORP EMPL chief executive officer: Blue Cross & Blue Shield of Minnesota. CORP AFFIL president: HMO Minnesota.

Foundation Officials

Norris Anderson, MD: director
Karen Brohn: director
Andrew P. Czajkowski: chairman, director (see above)
Deborah Glass: director
Daniel Johnson: executive director
Carol Laurent: secretary, director
Deborah Montgomery: director
Richard M. Niemiec: treasurer, director PRIM CORP EMPL senior vice president: BCBSM Inc.
Steve Richards, MD: director
Maryann Stump: director PRIM CORP EMPL vice president: Blue Cross & Blue Shield of Minnesota.
Francis Windsor: director

Grants Analysis

Disclosure Period: calendar year ending 1998
Total Grants: $1,500,000
Number of Grants: 40
Average Grant: $36,000
Typical Range: $3,000 to $100,000
Note: Grants analysis provided by the foundation.

Recent Grants

Note: Grants derived from 1998 Form 990.

Arts & Humanities

500 Penumbra Theatre, St. Paul, MN -- Aferican-American Theatre Support

Civic & Public Affairs

7,500 Fairview Foundation, Edina, MN -- Pharmacy Benefits Program for Seniors and Support of Starry Night Gala
5,000 Corporation for Supportive Housing, Minneapolis, MN -- Supportive housing and Managed Care pilot program
2,500 PACER Center, Inc., Minneapolis, MN -- General support
1,500 Lyndale Neighborhood Association, Minneapolis, MN -- Charles Horn Terrace Cooperative Health Promotion Campaign
1,000 Central Minnesota Community Foundation, St. Cloud, MN -- Lend A Hand Fund following Explosion

Education

125,000 The C. Everett Koop Institute of Dartmouth, Hanover, NH -- Tobacco Never Dies project
75,000 University of Minnesota, Minneapolis, MN -- Minnesota Health Care Access Survey
26,000 University of Minnesota Continuing Medical Education, Minneapolis, MN -- Statewide Tobacco Cessation Conference
10,000 Fairview Institute for Leadership Development, Minneapolis, MN -- Fairview Quality Leadership Conference
10,000 Northwest Technical College, East Grand Forks, MN -- Support of nursing scholarships
10,000 William Mitchell College of Law, St. Paul, MN -- Support for "Tobacco Regulation: A Convergence of Law, Medicine and Public Policy" symposium
1,000 David M. Winfield Awards, Inc., West St. Paul, MN -- Minority Student Athlete Awards
500 Minnesota Council on Economic Education, St. Paul, MN -- General support

Health

98,500 Minnesota Institute of Public Health, Anoka, MN -- Minnesota Decides-tobacco use and prevention cessation initiative
60,000 Mayo Clinic, Rochester, MN -- Quit and Win Pilot Cessation Project
57,500 Northwestern Mental Health Center, Inc., Crookston, MN -- Flood Rsponse - Red River Valley
41,000 ACHN Foundation, Willmar, MN -- Prenatal Care Initiative
20,000 American Cancer Society, Minneapolis, MN -- Anti-smoking video support
20,000 Health Start, Inc., St. Paul, MN -- Health education and risk prevention for high-risk males
20,000 Neighborhood Health Care Network, St. Paul, MN -- Support for Underinsured and uninsured residents of the Twin Cities
15,000 Workers Compensation Health Initiative, St. Paul, MN -- Workers Compensation Health Initiative
12,000 The Health Fund of Minnesota, Minneapolis, MN -- General Support to the Health Fund
12,000 St. Luke's Hospital and Regional Trauma Center, Duluth, MN -- Pediatric nursing emergency courses in four Northeastern MN communities
5,000 American Lung Association, Washington, DC -- General support
5,000 Association of Nonsmokers Minnesota, St. Paul, MN -- Smoke free restaurants guide for 'MN
5,000 Minnesota Smoke Free 2000 Coalition, Minneapolis, MN -- Promote a smoke-free society by the year 2000
5,000 National Kidney Foundation of MN, Inc., Minneapolis, MN -- Support for Kidney House
1,000 Children's Hospital Association, St. Paul, MN -- General support
1,000 Mark A. Nugent Medical Research Foundation, St. Paul, MN -- Research causes and treatments of depression
500 AIDS Events Minnesota, Chicago, IL -- AIDS Bike Ride
500 Mid-Minnesota Health Clinic, St. Cloud, MN -- General support
250 Northwestern Mental Health Center, Crookston, MN -- General support

Religion

5,000 Greater Minneapolis Council of Churches, Minneapolis, MN -- Teen Indian Parent Program

Social Services

31,750 Duluth Family Practice, Duluth, MN -- Development of U of M Duluth program for practicing medicine in a managed care environment
10,000 Children Are People Support Groups, Inc., St. Paul, MN -- Smoking and chemical dependency curriculum for adolescents
10,000 Greater Minneapolis Crisis Nursery, Minneapolis, MN -- Health services for vulnerable children
5,000 Health Care Coalition on Violence, Anoka, MN -- Task Force on Violence
4,000 Greater St. Paul Retired and Senior Volunteer, St. Paul, MN -- General Program Support
2,500 Washburn Child Guidance Center, Minneapolis, MN -- Family Focused Therapeutic Program
2,000 Mary's Shelter, Eagan, MN -- Homeless shelter for women
1,000 Gillette Children's Foundation, St. Paul, MN -- Free Care Fund

BOEING CO.

★ Number 17 of Top 100 Corporate Givers

Company Contact

PO Box 3707
Seattle, WA 98124-2207
Web: http://www.boeing.com

Company Description

Revenue: US$57,993,000,000 (1999)
Profit: US$1,120,000,000
Employees: 231,000 (1999)
Fortune Rank: 10, per FORTUNE Magazine's list of 500 Largest U.S. Corporations (1999).
FF 10
SIC(s): 3679 Electronic Components Nec, 3721 Aircraft, 3728 Aircraft Parts & Equipment Nec, 3812 Search & Navigation Equipment.

Operating Locations

Australia: Allen-Bradley Pty. Ltd., Blackburn; McDonnell Douglas (Australia) P/L, Lara; Boeing International Corp., Mascot; Boeing Australia, North Ryde; Aerospace Technologies of Australia Ltd., Port Melbourne; Meritor Light Vehicle Systems Australia Pty. Ltd., Preston; Rockwell Standard of Australia Ltd., Sunshine; Austria: Rockwell Automation GesmbH, Linz, Oberosterreich; Belgium: Rockwell Automation NV, Mechelen, Brabant; Brazil: Meritor do Brasil Ltda., Limeira; Rockwell Participa Aes Ltda., Limeira; Logicos Sistemas de Controle Industrial Ltda., Sao Paulo; Canada: McDonnell Douglas Canada Ltd., Mississauga; Boeing of Canada Ltd., Winnipeg; Boeing Canada Technology, Winnipeg; Manitoba Ltd., Winnipeg; England: Henry Butcher Industrial Finance Ltd., London; McDonnell Douglas Aerospace UK Ltd., London; MDFC Industrial Finance Ltd., London; Private and Commercial Finance Group Ltd., London; France: Meritor France, Courbevoie, Hauts-de-Seine; Meritor Light Vehicle Systems, Courbevoie, Hauts-de-Seine; Ror Rockwell SA, Mitry Mory, Seine-et-Marne; Meritor Heavy Vehicule Systems ST Etienne SA, St. Etienne; Germany: Meritor Automotive GmbH, Frankfurt, Hessen; Rockwell Golde GmbH, Frankfurt, Hessen; Boeing International Cooperation, Munich, Bavaria; Hong Kong: McDonnell Douglas Information Systems Ltd., Admiralty; McDonnell Douglas Pacific & Asia Ltd., Central District; Rockwell Collins Internationalasia Pacific Ltd., Central District; Rockwell Intl (Asia Pacific) Ltd., Wan Chai; Ireland: Ror Rockwell (Ireland) Ltd., Naas; Italy: Meritor Italiana SpA, Albese Con Cassano, Lombardia; Boeing International Corp., Roma, Lazio; Japan: BT Network Information Service

Co. Ltd., Tokyo; McDonnell Douglas Japan Ltd., Tokyo; Rockwell Intl Japan Co. Ltd., Tokyo; Republic of Korea: Rockwell-Collins Intl Inc., Yonddungpo-Gu, Soul-t'ukpyolsi; Mexico: Rockwell Semiconductos Systems SA de CV, Mexicali; Rockwell Fumagalli SA de CV, Pozos; Malaysia: Rockwell Electronics (Austral-Asia) Pty. Ltd., Kuala Lumpur, Selangor; Northern Ireland: Wescom (UK) Ltd., Newry, Down; Netherlands: Meritor Heavy Vehicle Systems BV, Helmond, Noord-Brabant; Rockwell Collins (UK) Ltd., Hoofddorp, Noord-Holland; McDonnell Douglas Support Services, Luchthaven Schiphol; McDonnell BV, S'Gravenhage, Zuid-Holland; New Zealand: Rockwell Automation (New Zealand) Ltd., Auckland; Singapore: Rockwell-Collins Intl Inc., Singapore; Rockwell Intl Manufacturing Pte. Ltd., Singapore; Spain: Rockwell Automation SA, Hospitalet de Llobregat; Meritor Heavy Vehicle Systems Espana SA, Llica de Vall, Cataluna; Boeing International Corp. (Sucursal en Espana), Madrid; McDonnell Douglas Information Systems SA, Madrid; Rockwell Light Vehicle Systems Espana SA, Santa Maria de Palautordera; Taiwan: Rockwell Intl Taiwan Co. Ltd., Taipei; United Kingdom: Meritor Maudslay Ltd., Alcester, Warwickshire; Meritor Light Vehicle Systems (UK) Ltd., Birmingham, West Midlands; Boeing Defence UK, Glasgow, Strathclyde; Rockwell Intl Pension Trustees, Hounslow, Greater London; Wilmot-Breeden (Holdings) Ltd., Hounslow, Greater London; AMC Equipment Leasing Ltd., London; AMC Leasing Ltd., London; AMC Trust Ltd., London; Rockwell Charitable Trustees Ltd., London; Allen-Bradley (Overseas) Ltd., Milton Keynes, Buckinghamshire; Rockwell Intl Ltd., Milton Keynes, Buckinghamshire; Rockwell European Holdings Ltd., Preston, Lancashire; Rockwell Collins (UK) Ltd., Reading, Berkshire; Meritor Automotive Ltd., Slough, Berkshire; Rockwell Intl Holdings Ltd., Slough, Berkshire; Rockwell Semiconductor Systems Ltd., Slough, Berkshire; Rockwell Switching Systems Ltd., Slough, Berkshire; Tyseley Estates Ltd., Slough, Berkshire; Ror Meritor (Manufacturing) Ltd., Wednesbury, West Midlands; Meritor Heavy Vehicle Systems Ltd., Wrexham, Clwyd

Nonmonetary Support

Value: $7,500,000 (1996); $7,300,000 (1994); $6,300,000 (1993)
Type: Donated Equipment; Donated Products; In-kind Services; Loaned Employees
Note: Boeing will also provide services, such as printing, graphics, technical support, and transportation.

Corporate Sponsorship

Value: $200
Type: Arts & cultural events; Festivals/fairs

The Boeing Co. Charitable Trust

Giving Contact

Christine G. Jones, Manager, Corporate Contributions
The Boeing Co.
PO Box 3707 MS 14-04
Seattle, WA 98124-2207
Phone: (206)655-1131
Fax: (206)655-2000

Description

Founded: 1964
EIN: 916056738
Organization Type: Corporate Foundation
Giving Locations: headquarters and operating communities where Boeing employees work and reside; national.
Grant Types: Capital, Employee Matching Gifts, Multiyear/Continuing Support, Project, Scholarship, Seed Money.
Note: Employee matching gift ratio: 1 to 1 for current employees; .50 to 1 for retired emloyees. Gifts are matched to educational, arts, cultural, and civic organizations. Requests for matching gifts are employee initiated.

Giving Philosophy

'While the chief concern of any publicly held corporation must be to provide a fair return to its shareholders, Boeing will continue to have a strong commitment to being a good corporate neighbor, enhancing the quality of life in communities across the nation where our employees live and work.' *Family, Friends, and Good Neighbors: Boeing Community Involvement Report*

Financial Summary

Total Giving: $53,818,314 (1998); $44,335,800 (1996); $36,400,000 (1995 approx). Note: Co. gives directly and through a trust.
Giving Analysis: Giving for 1996 includes: corporate direct giving ($23,300,000); nonmonetary support ($7,500,000); foundation ($7,306,250); corporate grants to United Way ($3,393,550); international subsidiaries ($36,000); 1998: corporate direct giving ($46,800,000); nonmonetary support ($7,000,000); foundation ($18,314)
Assets: $31,074,973 (1998); $18,805,611 (1996)
Gifts Received: $5,000,000 (1998). Note: The trust receives contributions from Boeing Co.

Typical Recipients

Arts & Humanities: Arts Centers, Arts Funds, Community Arts, Dance, Ethnic & Folk Arts, History & Archaeology, Libraries, Museums/Galleries, Music, Opera, Performing Arts, Theater
Civic & Public Affairs: Asian American Affairs, Botanical Gardens/Parks, Business/Free Enterprise, Economic Development, Civic & Public Affairs-General, Housing, Professional & Trade Associations, Urban & Community Affairs, Zoos/Aquariums
Education: Business Education, Colleges & Universities, Community & Junior Colleges, Continuing Education, Economic Education, Education Funds, Elementary Education (Private), Engineering/Technological Education, Faculty Development, Education-General, Legal Education, Literacy, Minority Education, Preschool Education, Private Education (Precollege), Public Education (Precollege), Science/Mathematics Education, Special Education, Student Aid
Environment: Environment-General
Health: Clinics/Medical Centers, Emergency/Ambulance Services, Hospices, Mental Health
International: International Relief Efforts
Religion: Jewish Causes, Religious Welfare
Science: Science Museums, Scientific Centers & Institutes
Social Services: Child Welfare, Community Centers, Community Service Organizations, Delinquency & Criminal Rehabilitation, Domestic Violence, Food/Clothing Distribution, Homes, People with Disabilities, Recreation & Athletics, Senior Services, Shelters/Homelessness, Substance Abuse, United Funds/United Ways, Volunteer Services, YMCA/YWCA/YMHA/YWHA, Youth Organizations

Contributions Analysis

Giving Priorities: Boeing targets four core areas of support: education, health and human services, arts and cultural organizations, and civic and environmental organizations.
Arts & Humanities: 19%. Supports arts, music, drama, and dance. Especially interested in projects that explore the relationships between art, science, and technology.
Civic & Public Affairs: 8%. Includes environmental grants. Funds initiatives concerned with long-term community growth. Also interested in projects that aid communities and the environment at the same time. Supports youth corps, aquariums, student conservation clubs, and the Arkansas Riverwalk.
Education: 41%. Supports K-12 and higher education. Funds curriculum enhancement; minority education, especially in technical and engineering fields; academic research in technical areas; and lifelong learning.
Health: 32%. Includes human service organizations and United Way. Supports agencies that ease mental and physical suffering, addiction or substance abuse, and family problems. Funds basic needs for housing and nutrition, boys and girls clubs, and programs for the homeless.
Note: Total contributions made in 1998.

Application Procedures

Initial Contact: Send a one- to two-page proposal letter.
Application Requirements: Include a description of organization; history of service; statement of purpose and organizational objectives; definition of project describing community need, goals for project, specific activities, timeline, and plan for measuring results; itemized budget, list of committed financial supporters, plans for multiyear funding, if appropriate; evidence of nonprofit status; most recent audited financial statements; and list of board of directors, officers, and their affiliations.
Deadlines: None.
Review Process: Initial review is conducted by the manager of company contributions.
Decision Notification: Review process is continuous; contributions committee meets quarterly; contributions budget for following year is prepared by late October for final approval by company board of directors in December.

Restrictions

No support given to individuals; political candidates, committees, or organizations; fraternal organizations; goodwill advertising; or religious organizations.
Company does not support hospitals or medical research organizations. The company will not consider requests for travel expenses, athletic events, or agency-sponsored walks, runs or golf tournaments.

Additional Information

In 1997 McDonnell Douglas Corp. was acquired by the Boeing Co. The four McDonnell Douglas Employees Community Funds (East, West, Mesa and Canada) are in the process of changing their names to Boeing and being incorporated into the giving program.
Publications: Corporate Citizenship Report; Contributions Request Guidelines

Corporate Officials

Jim F. Albaugh: senior vice president, president space and communications systems PRIM CORP EMPL senior vice president, president space and communications systems: Boeing Co.
Theodore J. Collins: senior vice president law and contracts PRIM CORP EMPL senior vice president law and contracts: Boeing Co.
Philip Murray Condit: chairman, chief executive officer, director B Berkeley, CA 1941. ED University of California at Berkeley BS (1963); Princeton University MS (1965); Massachusetts Institute of Technology MS (1975); University of Tokyo (1997). PRIM CORP EMPL chairman, chief executive officer, director: Boeing Co. ADD CORP EMPL president: Boeing Irving Co. CORP AFFIL director: Nordstrom Inc.; director: Fluke Corp.; director: Hewlett Packard Co.; chairman: Boeing Corinth Co. NONPR AFFIL member: Society Sloan Fellows; member: United States National Academy Engineering; fellow: Royal Aeronautical Society; member: Society Automotive Engineers; trustee: Museum Flight; member advisory council: Princeton University Department Mechanical & Aerospace Engineering; fellow: American Institute Aeronautics &

Astronautics; fellow: AIAA. CLUB AFFIL Rainier Club; Columbia Tower Club.
James B. Dagnon: senior vice president people PRIM CORP EMPL senior vice president people: Boeing Co.
Christopher W. Hansen: senior vice president operations PRIM CORP EMPL senior vice president operations: Boeing Co.
Deborah C. Hopkins: senior vice president, chief financial officer PRIM CORP EMPL senior vice president, chief financial officer: Boeing Co.
Harry C. Stonecipher: president, chief operating officer, director B Scott County, TN 1936. ED Tennessee Technical Institute BS (1960). PRIM CORP EMPL president, chief operating officer, director: Boeing Co. CORP AFFIL director: Cincinnati Milacron Inc.

Grants Analysis

Disclosure Period: calendar year ending 1998
Total Grants: $53,818,314*
Typical Range: $10,000 to $150,000
***Note:** Giving includes corporate; foundation; nonmonetary support.

Recent Grants

Note: Grants derived from 1996 Form 990.

Arts & Humanities

1,000,000	Seattle Symphony, Seattle, WA
150,000	Seattle Opera, Seattle, WA
100,000	Avenue of the Arts, Philadelphia, PA
52,250	Henry Art Gallery, Seattle, WA
25,000	American Helicopter Museum and Education Center, West Chester, PA
15,000	Tacoma Symphony Orchestra Guild, Tacoma, WA

Civic & Public Affairs

100,000	Office of Research Administration, Seattle, WA
100,000	Point Defiance Zoo and Aquarium, Tacoma, WA
82,500	Seattle Chinatown International Village, Seattle, WA
75,000	Fremont Public Association, Fremont, WA
55,000	Tuckwilla Pond Park, Bellevue, WA
25,000	Neighborhood House, Seattle, WA
12,000	Housing Resources Corp, Bainbridge Island, WA

Education

2,000,000	Washington State University, Pullman, WA
500,000	California Institute of Technology, Pasadena, CA
500,000	Seattle University, Seattle, WA
300,000	Purdue University, West Lafayette, IN
300,000	Seattle Pacific University, Seattle, WA
150,000	Seattle Community College District, Seattle, WA
100,000	North Carolina A&T State University, Greensboro, NC
87,500	Stanford University, Stanford, CA
70,000	University of Notre Dame, Notre Dame, IN
60,000	Heritage College, Toppenish, WA
50,000	University of Maryland Foundation, Adelphi, MD

Environment

25,000	Mountains to Sound Greenway, Seattle, WA

Health

110,000	Puget Sound Neighborhood Health Centers, Seattle, WA
50,000	American Red Cross Seattle King County, Seattle, WA
17,500	45th Street Clinic, Seattle, WA

Religion

182,000	Salvation Army, Wichita, KS
45,000	Jewish Family Services, Seattle, WA

Science

300,000	Exploration Place, Seattle, WA
300,000	Pacific Science Center, Seattle, WA
10,000	Oregon Museum of Science and Industry, Portland, OR

Social Services

3,393,550	United Way King County, Seattle, WA
200,000	YMCA of Snohomish County, Okanogan, WA
82,500	Children's Home Society of Washington, Seattle, WA
75,000	Seattle Mariners Little League Fields, Seattle, WA

BOISE CASCADE CORP.

Company Contact

Boise, ID
Web: http://www.bc.com

Company Description

Revenue: US$6,953,000,000 (1999)
Employees: 23,726 (1999)
Fortune Rank: 252, per FORTUNE Magazine's list of 500 Largest U.S. Corporations (1999).
FF 252
SIC(s): 2421 Sawmills & Planing Mills--General, 2436 Softwood Veneer & Plywood, 2439 Structural Wood Members Nec, 2493 Reconstituted Wood Products.

Operating Locations

Canada: Boise Cascade Canada Ltd., Toronto; United Kingdom: Boise Cascade Sales Ltd., Amersham, Buckinghamshire; Virgin Islands of the United States: Boise Cascade Foreign Sales Corp., St. Thomas

Nonmonetary Support

Range: $50,000 - $400,000
Type: Donated Equipment; Donated Products

Giving Contact

Connie E. Weaver, Contributions Administrator
Boise Cascade Corp.
1111 West Jefferson Street
PO Box 50
Boise, ID 83728-0001
Phone: (208)384-7673
Fax: (208)384-7224

Description

Organization Type: Corporate Giving Program
Giving Locations: headquarters and operating communities.
Grant Types: Capital, Employee Matching Gifts, Project.
Note: Matching gifts for education only.

Giving Philosophy

'To help achieve Boise Cascade's goal of optimizing its long term value to shareholders and society, the company provides support for charitable activities designed to enhance the living environments of the communities in which it operates. Efforts are made to support programs which not only benefit the recipients but also have the potential to positively impact our employees and the company.' Report of Contributions, Boise Cascade Corporation

Financial Summary

Total Giving: $1,500,000 (1997 approx); $500,000 (1993 approx); $1,000,000 (1992). Note: Contributes through corporate direct giving program only.

Typical Recipients

Arts & Humanities: Community Arts, Dance, Libraries, Museums/Galleries, Music, Opera, Performing Arts, Theater
Civic & Public Affairs: Business/Free Enterprise, Civil Rights, Economic Development, Economic Policy, Public Policy, Women's Affairs, Zoos/Aquariums
Education: Business Education, Colleges & Universities, Community & Junior Colleges, Economic Education, Engineering/Technological Education, Literacy, Minority Education, Special Education
Environment: Environment-General
Health: Emergency/Ambulance Services, Hospitals
Social Services: Community Centers, Homes, Recreation & Athletics, Senior Services, Substance Abuse, United Funds/United Ways, Youth Organizations

Contributions Analysis

Giving Priorities: Emphasis is on culture, education, and the environment. Health and human service programs are supported through the United Way.

Application Procedures

Initial Contact: Write to nearest Boise Cascade facility.
Application Requirements: Include a description of the organization and its purpose; proof of tax-exempt status; list of officers a directors; current operating budget and sources of funding; recently audited financial statement or most recent Form 990; purpose of grant; project budget and estimated fund-raising costs; and sources of funding, both committed and proposed.
Deadlines: None.
Decision Notification: Proposals are reviewed on an ongoing basis.

Restrictions

Company does not support organizations located in areas where the company has few or no operations; individuals; private foundations; international organizations; fraternal, social, labor, or veterans' organizations; requests of a political nature and organizations or programs that are sensitive, controversial, harmful, or which pose a potential conflict of interest for the company; operating expenses of United Way member agencies; school trips or tours; athletic teams, scholarships, or sport vehicles; courtesy advertising; testimonial dinners; loans or investments; or churches or religious organizations.
Company generally will not arrange loans, or support memorials, grants to cover operating deficits, or projects that are primarily fund-raising events; organizations that channel funds to donee agencies, except for United Way; or endowments at educational institutions or funds or associations whose sole purpose is to raise funds for educational institutions or other organizations.

Additional Information

Priority is given to organizations and programs in communities where the company operates and to those in which company employees are involved.
Operating locations manage and distribute their own funds. Grant seekers should contact the location nearest them.
Publications: Guidelines

Corporate Officials

Vincent Thomas Hannity: vice president corporate communications & investor relations B Tacoma, WA 1944. ED Gonzaga University (1967); Stanford University (1989). PRIM CORP EMPL vice president corporate communications & investor relations: Boise Cascade Corp.
George Jay Harad: chairman, chief executive officer, director B Newark, NJ 1944. ED Franklin and Marshall College BA (1965); Harvard University MBA (1971). PRIM CORP EMPL chairman, chief executive officer, director: Boise Cascade Corp. ADD CORP EMPL chairman: Boise Cascade Office Products Corp. CORP AFFIL director: United States West Inc.; director: Allendale Insurance Co.; director: KartoffelSoft Inc. NONPR AFFIL board governors: National Council

Paper Industry Air & Stream Improvement; member: Phi Beta Kappa; member: NAM; director: American Forest & Paper Association; director: Institute Paper Science Technology. CLUB AFFIL Crane Creek Country Club; Arid Club; Century Boston Club.

Giving Program Officials

Connie Weaver: contributions administrator

Grants Analysis

Disclosure Period: calendar year ending
Typical Range: $1,000 to $10,000

Boler Co.

Company Contact

Itasca, IL

Company Description

Employees: 1,500
SIC(s): 3713 Truck & Bus Bodies, 3714 Motor Vehicle Parts & Accessories, 3715 Truck Trailers.

Boler Co. Foundation

Giving Contact

John M. Boler, Chairman, President & Chief Executive Officer
500 Park Blvd., Suite 1010
Itasca, IL 60143-1285
Phone: (630)773-9111
Fax: (630)773-9121

Description

Founded: 1987
EIN: 366854134
Organization Type: Corporate Foundation. Supports preselected organizations only.
Giving Locations: IL; IN; OH
Grant Types: General Support.

Financial Summary

Total Giving: $31,000 (1998); $361,000 (1995); $7,000 (1994)
Assets: $1,385,194 (1998); $905,666 (1995); $1,197,968 (1994)
Gifts Received: $120,000 (1998); $150,000 (1994). Note: In 1998, contributions were received from the Boler Co.

Typical Recipients

Arts & Humanities: Arts Festivals, Arts Funds, Dance, Opera
Civic & Public Affairs: Civic & Public Affairs-General
Education: Business Education, Colleges & Universities, Education Associations, Education Funds, Elementary Education (Private), Faculty Development, Education-General, Private Education (Precollege), Secondary Education (Private), Student Aid
Health: Cancer, Children's Health/Hospitals, Hospices, Hospitals, Long-Term Care
Social Services: Community Service Organizations

Contributions Analysis

Education: 100%. Primary support for a religions high school; also funds universities.
Note: Total contributions in 1998.

Corporate Officials

John M. Boler: chairman, president, chief executive officer, owner, director B 1934. PRIM CORP EMPL chairman, president, chief executive officer, owner, director: Boler Co.
John M. Gaynor: chief financial officer, treasurer, assistant secretary, controller PRIM CORP EMPL chief financial officer, treasurer, assistant secretary, controller: Boler Co.

Foundation Officials

John M. Boler: trustee (see above)
John M. Gaynor: trustee (see above)

Grants Analysis

Disclosure Period: calendar year ending 1998
Total Grants: $31,000
Number of Grants: 3
Average Grant: $10,333
Highest Grant: $25,000
Typical Range: $1,000 to $15,000

Recent Grants

Note: Grants derived from 1998 Form 990.

Education

25,000	Bishop Verot High School, Fort Myers, FL -- General Fund
5,000	John Carroll University Presidential Forum, Cleveland, OH -- General Fund
1,000	Depaul University, Chicago, IL -- General Fund

Borden, Inc.

Company Contact

Columbus, OH

Company Description

Employees: 4,200
SIC(s): 2022 Cheese--Natural & Processed, 2023 Dry, Condensed & Evaporated Dairy Products, 2024 Ice Cream & Frozen Desserts, 2026 Fluid Milk.

Operating Locations

Argentina: Compania Casco SA Industrial y Comercial, Olivos, Buenos Aires; Australia: Abbott Packaging, Kirrawee; Borden Chemical Australia Pty. Ltd., Laverton; Wrapping Specialists Pty. Ltd., Prestons; Belgium: Biscuiterie Muguet NV, Kapelle-Op-Den-Bos, Brabant; AEP Belgium SA, Mons, Hainaut; Brazil: Alba Quimica Industria e Comercio Ltda., Sao Paulo; Canada: Borden Co. Ltd., Etobicoke; Colombia: Alisa SA, Bogota, Cundinamarco; Compania Colombiana de Alimentos Lacteos SA, Santa Fe de Bogota; Costa Rica: Borden de Costa Rica SA, San Jose; Denmark: Borden Co. A/S, Esbjerg, Ribe; Borden Ost A/S, Esbjerg, Ribe; Cocio Chokoladem LK A/S, Esbjerg, Ribe; Ecuador: Nutrinsa SA, Quito, Pichincha; Quimica Borden Ecuatoriana SA, Quito, Pichincha; France: Borden Chimie SA, Deville Les Rouen; Borden France SA, Deville Les Rouen; AEP Borden Packaging France, Fecamp, Seine-Maritime; Manufacturing, Fecamp, Seine-Maritime; Pami Immobiliere, Les Ulis, Essonne; Borden SFPO (Ste.), Paris, Ville-de-Paris; Germany: Fiap Deutschland GmbH, Remscheid, Nordrhein-Westfalen; Cofin Kunststoffhandel GmbH, Witten, Nordrhein-Westfalen; Ireland: Borden International Packaging Ltd., Athy; Borden Co. Ltd., Mallow; Borden Foods Ltd., Mallow; Italy: Termofin SpA, Foggia, Puglia; Albadoro SpA, Guarene, Piemonte; Cistefra SRL, Manfredonia, Puglia; Maite SpA, Manfredonia, Puglia; Monder Aliment SpA, Peschiera Borromeo, Lombardia; Fiap Fabbrica Italiana Articoli Plastici SpA, Turate, Lombardia; Luxembourg: International Packaging SA, Luxembourg; Malaysia: Borden Chemical (Malaysia) Sdn. Bhd., Kuala Lumpur, Selangor; Netherlands: Borden Belgium NV, Kapelle-Op-Den-Bos, Brabant; Norway: Borden Scandinavia AS, Gjovik, Oppland; New Zealand: AEP Industries (New Zealand) Ltd., Ellerslie, Auckland; Panama: Compania Chiricana de Leche SA, Panama City; Compania Internacional de Ventas SA, Panama City; Fabrica de Productos Borden SA, Panama City; Helados Borden SA, Panama City; Spain: Quimica Borden Espana SA, Erandio, Vizcaya; United Kingdom: Borden International (Europe) Ltd., Bagshot, Surrey; Borden Chemical Finance Ltd., Southampton, Hampshire; Borden Chemical UK Ltd., Southampton, Hampshire; Borden Realty United Kingdom Ltd., Southampton, Hampshire; Vanguard Plastics Ltd., Southampton, Hampshire

Nonmonetary Support

Value: $1,800,000 (1990); $1,800,000 (1989); $500,000 (1988)
Type: Donated Products; In-kind Services

Corporate Sponsorship

Type: Sports events
Contact: Robert Boyer, Vice President, Marketing

Borden Foundation, Inc.

Giving Contact

Ms. Frankie Nowland, President, Director of Social Responsibilities
Borden Foundation, Inc.
180 East Broad Street
Columbus, OH 43215-3799
Phone: (614)225-4580
Fax: (614)225-4066

Alternate Contact

Note: Alternate phone number is a recorded message that provides information for grant seekers.

Description

Founded: 1944
EIN: 136089941
Organization Type: Corporate Foundation
Giving Locations: principally near operating locations and to national organizations.
Grant Types: Challenge, Department, Employee Matching Gifts, General Support, Multiyear/Continuing Support.
Note: Matches gifts for higher education, health care, and youth and arts organisation.

Giving Philosophy

'Through its philanthropic and business endeavors, Borden, Inc., continues to demonstrate its commitment to social responsibility. The corporation views its contribution program as an investment; one which will help to improve the lives of community residents, especially where Borden is a corporate citizen. The Borden Foundation, the principal conduit for corporate contributions of Borden, Inc., is responsive to human needs through its support of projects and programs of quality within its priority areas of funding. The Foundation's grant program currently focuses on giving disadvantaged children in Borden communities a better chance.' Guidelines for Grant Consideration

Financial Summary

Total Giving: $1,000,000 (2000 approx); $1,000,000 (1999 approx); $1,187,044 (1996). Note: Contributes through foundation only. 1995 Giving includes foundation ($1,043,661); United Way ($145,455).
Assets: $1,706,045 (1996); $93,925 (1995); $73,443 (1994)
Gifts Received: $677,076 (1996); $1,200,750 (1995); $1,300,000 (1994)

Typical Recipients

Arts & Humanities: Arts Associations & Councils, Arts Centers, Arts Institutes, Ballet, Community Arts, Dance, Historic Preservation, Libraries, Museums/Galleries, Music, Opera, Performing Arts, Theater
Civic & Public Affairs: African American Affairs, Botanical Gardens/Parks, Business/Free Enterprise, Chambers of Commerce, Civil Rights, Clubs, Community Foundations, Economic Development, Economic Policy, Ethnic Organizations, Hispanic Affairs, Law & Justice, Municipalities/Towns, Nonprofit Management, Parades/Festivals, Philanthropic Organizations, Professional & Trade Associations, Public Policy, Urban & Community Affairs, Women's Affairs

Education: Business Education, Colleges & Universities, Continuing Education, Education Associations, Education Funds, Engineering/Technological Education, Education-General, Literacy, Minority Education, Private Education (Precollege), Public Education (Precollege), Science/Mathematics Education, Special Education, Student Aid
Environment: Environment-General
Health: AIDS/HIV, Arthritis, Cancer, Children's Health/Hospitals, Emergency/Ambulance Services, Eyes/Blindness, Hospitals, Medical Research, Mental Health, Prenatal Health Issues, Public Health, Single-Disease Health Associations
International: International Relations, International Relief Efforts, Missionary/Religious Activities
Religion: Churches, Dioceses, Religious Organizations, Religious Welfare
Science: Science Museums, Scientific Centers & Institutes, Scientific Organizations
Social Services: At-Risk Youth, Big Brother/Big Sister, Child Welfare, Community Service Organizations, Domestic Violence, Emergency Relief, Family Services, Food/Clothing Distribution, Homes, People with Disabilities, Recreation & Athletics, Scouts, Shelters/Homelessness, United Funds/United Ways, Volunteer Services, YMCA/YWCA/YMHA/YWHA, Youth Organizations

Contributions Analysis

Giving Priorities: Social welfare, eduction, urban affairs organizations, hospitals, arts funds. The foundation supports international causes through American-based 501(c)(3) organizations whose activities reflect the foundation's area of primary interest: giving disadvantaged children in Borden communities a better chance. Funding emphasis is given to nutrition education and food programs focused on meeting the needs of disadvantaged children; programs that improve conditions where children live, provide emergency shelter and services to children without homes and/or develop housing suited to children's special needs; and programs that provide children with adequate health care. The foundation also is interested in supporting the following areasto benefit disadvantaged children: prevention and early intervention programs, including parenting education and early childhood education programs, as well as school-based programs that improve early educational opportunities; sports, recreation, and camping programs sponsored by youth-serving agencies; and programs that make possible the participation of disadvantaged children in the arts through programming by community arts institutions. Criteria for support include exemplary programs in communities where Borden has facilities and employees; national programs assisting local direct service projects; and model programs operating anywhere in the United Statesor Canada. Overseas operations make contributions in-country to charitable organizations, the level of which is not tracked. Managers are autonomous in choosing recipients for support, with no coordination or budget approval coming from the U.S. headquarters. Company also makes product donations on a local basis within specific countries or from the U.S.
Arts & Humanities: About 10%. Contributions are considered for arts organizations and activities within budgetary limitations.
Civic & Public Affairs: 15 to 20%. Grants for selected community activities are considered within budgetary limitations.
Education: 5 to 10%. Supports post-secondary educational institutions through grants to select national umbrella agencies.
International: Less than 5%. Support is provided to international causes through American-based 501(c)(3) organizations whose activities reflect area of primary interest.
Science: 20 to 25%. Gives to science centers and museums.
Social Services: 40 to 45%. Majority of support funds large grants to united funds and youth organizations, and considerable support to religious welfare organizations. Special consideration given to nutrition education and food programs for children and projects that improve living conditions for children or provide them with adequate shelter and/or health care. Foundation also supports parenting and early childhood education programs; sports, recreation, and camping programs sponsored by youth-serving agencies; and programs that enable disadvantaged children to participate in the arts through programming by community arts institutions. Interests also includecommunity services, shelters, and aid to the homeless.
Note: The foundation focuses on funding direct services and programs for disadvantaged youth across all program areas.

Application Procedures

Initial Contact: preliminary letter of inquiry to the foundation
Application Requirements: for letter, include name, address, telephone number, and IRS tax-exempt classification, description of objectives and programs, the specific amount of request, and its proposed use; full proposals must include responses, in numerical order, to the following: (1) name, affiliation, address, and phone number of organization and its contact person; (2) how long organization has existed and geographical area and number of people served; (3) principal staff and board of trustees, and how often board meets; (4) members of board associated with or employed by organization and whether the board has authorized grant request; (5) amount of compensation, if any, for board members; (6) current sources of income, with percentages, for the past three years; (7) amount and percentage of total income expended for fund raising, program, administrative, and general operations for the past two years; (8) copy of IRS tax-exemption letter, current financial statement, and most recent financial audit; (9) information on Philanthropic Advisory Service rating; (10) a description of organization's affiliations; (11) purpose of project or request, including whether problem area to be addressed is a special project or part of general operating support; (12) why organization should be the vehicle of support for project and how this project will benefit recipients and total community; (13) how project will be carried out; (14) principal project staff, with brief summaries of education and work experience; (15) distinguishing characteristics of this project from others in the same field; (16) proposed budget; (17) amount requested and time frame for disbursement; (18) percentage of total budget supplied by government, if any; (19) all organizations to be approached for funding of project and amounts requested from each; (20) organizations that have committed support and at what levels; (21) how project will be sustained after foundation support is completed; (22) what review and evaluation procedures will determine success of project
Deadlines: 1st of March, July, October
Review Process: initial screening, research, and evaluation conducted by foundation staff to ensure compliance with grant criteria
Decision Notification: board meets in April, August, and November; written notification of the decision will be sent to the requesting organization within two weeks following the meeting
Notes: Preliminary letters are reviewed within 60 days of receipt. The foundation will notify organization if a formal proposal is needed.

Restrictions

Foundation does not support individuals; endowments; memberships; lobbying organizations; conferences, workshops, or seminars; building or renovation; journal advertisements; political activities or organizations; organizations deriving major support from government funding; or organizations that discriminate in any way consistent with national equal opportunity policies.

Requests to consider a portion of the support for a project will generally receive greater priority generally receive greater priority

Additional Information

Foundation requires status reports on the success of project.

Corporate Officials

C. Robert Kidder: chairman, president, chief executive officer, director B Freeport, NY 1943. ED University of Michigan BS (1966); Iowa State University MS (1968). PRIM CORP EMPL chairman, president, chief executive officer, director: Borden, Inc. CORP AFFIL director: Morgan Stanley Dean Witter Co.; director: Resource Partners Inc.; director: Electronic Data Systems Corp.; chairman: Corning Consumer Products Co.; director: Dean Witter Reynolds Inc.; chairman: Borden Foods Corp.; chairman: Borden Holdings Inc.; chairman: Borden Chemical Inc.; director: AEP Industries Inc.; director: B.F. Processing Corp.

Foundation Officials

Richard Hays Byrd: treasurer B Wheeling, WV 1939. ED Michigan State University BA (1960); Michigan State University MBA (1961). PRIM CORP EMPL assistant treasurer: Borden, Inc. CORP AFFIL assistant treasurer: BCP Management Inc.; assistant treasurer: BDH One Inc.
Anthony S. D'Amato: chairman B Brooklyn, NY 1930. ED Polytechnic Institute Brooklyn BS (1952). PRIM CORP EMPL chairman, chief executive officer: Borden, Inc. CORP AFFIL president: Borden Chemical Co.; director: Bank New York Co. Inc. NONPR AFFIL member: American Chemical Society.
H. C. Doughty, Jr.: secretary
Frankie Nowland: president, director social responsibilities

Grants Analysis

Disclosure Period: calendar year ending 1996
Total Grants: $1,187,044
Number of Grants: 487
Average Grant: $2,437
Highest Grant: $200,000
Typical Range: $500 to $10,000

Recent Grants

Note: Grants derived from 1996 Form 990.

Arts & Humanities

25,000	Columbus Museum of Art, Columbus, OH
15,000	King Arts Complex, Columbus, OH
10,000	Ballet Met, Columbus, OH
10,000	Wexner Center for the Arts, Columbus, OH
7,500	Opera Columbus, Columbus, OH
5,000	Art for Community Expression, Columbus, OH
5,000	Wexner Center for the Arts, Columbus, OH
3,000	ProMusica, Columbus, OH

Civic & Public Affairs

110,000	National Urban League, New York, NY
25,000	Columbus Urban League, Columbus, OH
5,000	Center for New Directions, Columbus, OH
5,000	Greater Columbus Chamber of Commerce, Columbus, OH
5,000	Philippine American Foundation, Washington, DC
3,500	Merrymakers Foundation, Columbus, OH

Education

20,000	Ohio State University Young Scholars Program, Columbus, OH
15,000	Ohio Foundation for Independent Colleges, Columbus, OH

10,000 Polytechnic University, Brooklyn, NY
5,000 Students in Free Enterprise, Springfield, MO
5,000 Students in Free Enterprise, Springfield, MO
5,000 Students in Free Enterprise, Springfield, MO
3,000 Council for Advancement and Support of Education, Washington, DC

Environment

5,000 Keep America Beautiful, Stamford, CT

Health

20,000 March of Dimes Birth Defects Foundation, Columbus, OH
11,313 Prevent Blindness Ohio, Columbus, OH
8,548 Grace Health Care Foundation, Morganton, NC
5,000 American Red Cross, Louisville, KY
5,000 Easter Seal Society, Columbus, OH
3,000 American Cancer Society, Plymouth, WI

International

3,500 Franciscan Missionary Sisters of the Sacred Heart, New York, NY
3,500 Franciscan Missionary Sisters of the Sacred Heart, New York, NY

Religion

5,000 National Christ Child Safety, Washington, DC
3,500 Diocese of Worcester Apostolate of Prayer and Healing, Worcester, MA

Science

200,000 Center of Science and Industry, Columbus, OH
3,000 Museum of Science, Boston, MA

Social Services

163,378 United Way Franklin County, Columbus, OH
25,000 I Know I Can, Columbus, OH
25,000 YMCA, Columbus, OH
25,000 YWCA, Columbus, OH
20,000 Boy Scouts of America, Brady, TX
12,500 Mid-Ohio Food Bank, Columbus, OH
10,000 Food Industry Crusade Against Hunger, Washington, DC
10,000 Mid Ohio-Food Bank, Columbus, OH
5,000 Big Brothers and Big Sisters, Cleveland, OH
5,000 Childhood League Center, Columbus, OH
5,000 Hannah Neil Center for Children, Columbus, OH
4,000 YMCA Central Ohio, Columbus, OH
3,536 United Way Merrimack Valley, Lawrence, MA
3,000 Columbus Youth Corps, Columbus, OH
3,000 Food for All, Redlands, CA
3,000 Minority Youth Link, Columbus, OH
3,000 United Way, Detroit, MI

BORMAN'S INC.

Company Contact

Detroit, MI

Company Description

Employees: 8,500
SIC(s): 5411 Grocery Stores, 5912 Drug Stores & Proprietary Stores.
Parent Company: Tengelmann Warenhandels Gesellschaft, Wissollstrasse 5-43, Mulheim an der Ruhr, Germany

Operating Locations

Operates 2 divisions in Detroit, MI.

The Borman Fund

Giving Contact

Gilbert Borman, Secretary & Treasurer
The Borman Fund
20500 Civic Center Drive, Suite 2750
Southfield, MI 48076
Phone: (248)350-0300
Fax: (248)350-2920

Description

EIN: 386069267
Organization Type: Corporate Foundation
Giving Locations: MI: Southeastern Michigan
Grant Types: Award, General Support, Project.

Financial Summary

Total Giving: $400,000 (2000 approx); $400,000 (1999 approx); $400,000 (1998 approx). Note: Contributes through corporate direct giving program and foundation. 1995 Giving includes foundation; United Way ($1,250).
Assets: $689,538 (1995); $616,714 (1994); $609,849 (1993)
Gifts Received: $311,984 (1995); $322,554 (1994); $310,840 (1993). Note: In 1995, contributions were received from Great Atlantic & Pacific Tea Company ($300,000), Paul Borman ($5,000), and other sources ($6,984).

Typical Recipients

Arts & Humanities: Arts Associations & Councils, Arts Centers, Arts Institutes, Community Arts, Dance, Ethnic & Folk Arts, Historic Preservation, Libraries, Literary Arts, Museums/Galleries, Music, Performing Arts, Theater
Civic & Public Affairs: Civil Rights, Civic & Public Affairs-General, Housing, Parades/Festivals, Philanthropic Organizations, Public Policy, Urban & Community Affairs, Zoos/Aquariums
Education: Colleges & Universities, International Exchange, Minority Education, Private Education (Precollege), Religious Education, Science/Mathematics Education, Secondary Education (Public)
Environment: Environment-General
Health: AIDS/HIV, Alzheimers Disease, Cancer, Children's Health/Hospitals, Emergency/Ambulance Services, Eyes/Blindness, Geriatric Health, Health Organizations, Hospices, Hospitals, Long-Term Care, Mental Health, Multiple Sclerosis, Single-Disease Health Associations
International: Foreign Educational Institutions, Health Care/Hospitals, International Affairs, International Organizations, International Relief Efforts, Missionary/Religious Activities
Religion: Churches, Jewish Causes, Religious Organizations, Religious Welfare, Seminaries, Synagogues/Temples
Science: Scientific Centers & Institutes, Scientific Organizations
Social Services: Animal Protection, Child Welfare, Community Centers, Community Service Organizations, Day Care, Delinquency & Criminal Rehabilitation, Domestic Violence, Emergency Relief, Family Planning, Family Services, Food/Clothing Distribution, People with Disabilities, Recreation & Athletics, Senior Services, Shelters/Homelessness, Substance Abuse, United Funds/United Ways, Youth Organizations

Contributions Analysis

Giving Priorities: Jewish religious organizations.
Arts & Humanities: About 5%. Supports museums, arts institutes, the Detroit Symphony Orchestra, and the Detroit Public Library.
Civic & Public Affairs: 10% to 15%. Supports civil liberties, zoological societies, and public policy institutes.
Education: 10% to 15%. Colleges and universities, religious education, and private precollege education are funded.
Health: 15% to 20%. Primarily funds single-disease health organizations and national health societies.
International: Less than 5%. International affairs and missionary activities are funded.
Religion: 55% to 60%. Support goes to Jewish religious organizations.

Application Procedures

Initial Contact: written request
Application Requirements: amount needed, purpose of the grant, and organizational and financial information
Deadlines: None.

Restrictions

The company does not support individuals, political or lobbying groups.

Corporate Officials

Paul Borman: chairman B Detroit, MI 1932. ED Michigan State University (1954). PRIM CORP EMPL chairman: Borman's Inc. CORP AFFIL director: First Federal Michigan.

Foundation Officials

Gilbert Borman: secretary, treasurer, director
Marlene Borman: vice president, director B Grant County, ND 1936. ED Cleveland Institute of Technology; United States Air Force Institute of Technology. PRIM CORP EMPL vice president research & engineering: Disc Instruments. NONPR AFFIL member: American Management Association; member: National Society Professional Engineers.
Paul Borman: president, director (see above)

Grants Analysis

Disclosure Period: calendar year ending 1995
Total Grants: $510,322*
Number of Grants: 94
Average Grant: $5,429
Highest Grant: $113,960
Typical Range: $100 to $5,000
***Note:** Giving excludes United Way.

Recent Grants

Note: Grants derived from 1995 Form 990.

Arts & Humanities

10,000 Greenfield Village/Henry Ford Museum, Dearborn, MI
2,500 Detroit Symphony, Detroit, MI
1,580 Henry Ford Museum, Dearborn, MI
1,100 Detroit Institute of Arts Founders Society, Detroit, MI

Civic & Public Affairs

26,100 Civil Liberties Action League, New York, NY
7,500 Michigan Thanksgiving Day Parade, Detroit, MI
1,500 Haven, Pontiac, MI

Education

25,000 University of Michigan, Ann Arbor, MI
3,000 University of Detroit High School, Detroit, OH
1,600 Detroit Country Day Schools, Detroit, MI
500 Hillel Day School, Farmington Hills, MI

Health

52,500 Karamanos Cancer Foundation, Detroit, MI
11,049 Michigan Cancer Foundation, Birmingham, MI
3,930 Cystic Fibrosis Foundation, Southfield, MI

2,700	Alzheimer's Disease and Related Disorders Association, Southfield, MI
2,000	Michigan Parkinsons Foundation, Detroit, MI
1,018	Sinai Hospital, Detroit, MI
1,000	Children's Leukemia Foundation, Southfield, MI
1,000	Hospice for Southeastern Michigan, Southfield, MI
1,000	Michigan Psychoanalytic Foundation, Southfield, MI
784	Jewish Home for the Aged, Detroit, MI
International	
5,000	Edgar M. Bronfman Fund World Jewish Congress, New York, NY
3,000	Weizmann Institute of Science, Israel
1,000	Bar Ilan University in Israel, Southfield, MI
1,000	One Israel Fund, New York, NY
Religion	
113,960	United Jewish Appeal, New York, NY
47,895	American ORT Federation, New York, NY
35,180	Yeshiva Beth Yehudah, Southfield, MI
35,000	Allied Jewish Campaign, Bloomfield Hills, MI
30,000	United Jewish Foundation, Bloomfield Hills, MI
12,500	Council of Orthodox Rabbis, Southfield, MI
10,000	Jewish Policy Center, Washington, DC
7,000	Jewish Family Services, West Bloomfield, MI
5,400	Congregation Shaarey Zedek, Southfield, MI
5,000	Lautenberg Center, New York, NY
5,000	Temple Israel, West Bloomfield, MI
2,500	Kollel Institute, Oak Park, MI
2,000	Masorti, Hyattsville, MD
1,500	American Jewish Joint District, New York, NY
1,400	Jewish Theological Seminary, New York, NY
1,000	JARC, Southfield, MI
1,000	KADIMA, Southfield, MI
875	Capuchin Charity Guild, Detroit, MI
600	Hebrew Free Loan Association, Southfield, MI
500	JESNA, Southfield, MI
Social Services	
10,062	Operational Independence, New York, NY
2,500	Spaulding for Children, Southfield, MI
1,250	United Way, Detroit, MI
1,000	Detroit Institute for Children, Detroit, MI
1,000	Michigan Humane Society, Auburn Hills, MI

BOSTON EDISON CO.

Company Contact

Boston, MA
Web: http://bostonedison.com

Company Description

Assets: US$3,729,300,000
Employees: 3,367
SIC(s): 4911 Electric Services.
Parent Company: NSTAR, 800 Boylston St., Boston, MA, United States

Nonmonetary Support

Type: Donated Equipment; Workplace Solicitation
Note: Co. donates used furniture. Co. donated approximately $20,000 in equipment in 1998.

Corporate Sponsorship

Value: $100,000 (1998)
Type: Arts & cultural events; Music & entertainment events
Contact: Ann Cardello, Administrator
Note: Boston Symphony Orchestra, American Ireland Fund Dinner and Batterd Women fundraiser.

Boston Edison Foundation

Giving Contact

Ann Cardello, Foundation Administrator
Boston Edison Foundation
800 Boylston St. (P-1701)
Boston, MA 02199-2599
Phone: (617)424-2235
Fax: (617)424-2736
Email: Ann_Cardello@bedison.com
Web: http://www.bedison.com/community/index.htm

Description

EIN: 042754285
Organization Type: Corporate Foundation
Giving Locations: MA: Eastern Massachusetts, Boston
Grant Types: Capital, Challenge, Employee Matching Gifts, General Support, Matching, Project, Seed Money.
Note: Employee matching gift ratio: 1 to 1 to education.

Giving Philosophy

'It is the intention of The Boston Edison Foundation to be involved in and aware of the concerns and needs facing the communities of which the Company is a part. The Foundation will marshal available resources of funds, manpower, goods and services to address positively local, high-priority concerns and needs that meet with Foundation priorities and guidelines.' *Contributions Guidelines, Boston Edison Foundation*

Financial Summary

Total Giving: $1,300,000 (1999 approx); $1,085,000 (1998 approx); $1,099,000 (1997). Note: Contributes through corporate direct giving program and foundation.
Assets: $1,800,000 (1999 approx); $1,700,000 (1998 approx); $1,400,000 (1997 approx)
Gifts Received: $1,100,000 (1994); $1,100,000 (1993); $700,000 (1992). Note: Contributions are received from the Boston Edison Co.

Typical Recipients

Arts & Humanities: Arts Institutes, Arts Outreach, Ballet, Dance, Historic Preservation, Libraries, Museums/Galleries, Music, Performing Arts
Civic & Public Affairs: Economic Development, Employment/Job Training, Housing, Law & Justice, Municipalities/Towns, Philanthropic Organizations, Professional & Trade Associations, Safety, Urban & Community Affairs, Zoos/Aquariums
Education: Afterschool/Enrichment Programs, Business-School Partnerships, Colleges & Universities, Education Reform, Elementary Education (Public), Engineering/Technological Education, Leadership Training, Minority Education, Preschool Education, Private Education (Precollege), Religious Education, Science/Mathematics Education, Student Aid
Health: AIDS/HIV, Alzheimers Disease, Cancer, Clinics/Medical Centers, Emergency/Ambulance Services, Health Organizations, Hospices, Hospitals, Long-Term Care, Nursing Services, Single-Disease Health Associations
Religion: Religious Welfare, Social/Policy Issues
Science: Science Museums
Social Services: Community Centers, Community Service Organizations, Counseling, Emergency Relief, Family Services, Food/Clothing Distribution, People with Disabilities, Recreation & Athletics, Senior Services, Shelters/Homelessness, United Funds/United Ways, Youth Organizations

Contributions Analysis

Giving Priorities: Education, united way, youth organizations, arts funds, and hospitals.
Arts & Humanities: 5% to 10%. Supports area museums, art centers, and cultural organizations that enhance the quality of life in the Boston area, that generally attract a broad segment of the public, and that are of interest to the company's employees.
Civic & Public Affairs: 10% to 15%. Main concern is economic development and business and free enterprise, but also supports environmental efforts, civil rights, and minority organizations. Also, supports science museums and local churches.
Education: 30% to 35%. Major support awarded to private colleges and universities and higher education associations located within company's service area that supply an appreciable number of employees, or have a significant relationship to the company or the electric utility industry. Other areas of interest include student aid; business, arts, legal, religious, and continuing education; education funds; and faculty development. Educational programs that address significant community needs (particularly those related to the unemployed, handicapped,minorities, and women) are also supported.
Health: 40% to 45%. Supports hospitals, health centers, nursing services, United Way, Youth organizations, and hospices.

Application Procedures

Initial Contact: All proposals must be submitted using an Associated Grantmakers of Massachusetts Common Proposal Format; guidelines revised in 1998.
Application Requirements: Include recent annual report, budget for organization and specific project requiring funding, specific amount of funding requested, other funding sources either at hand or anticipated, provision for accountability to project sponsors, and proof of tax-exempt status.
Deadlines: February 15 (for April assessment), July 15 (for September), and October 1 (for December).
Review Process: Company volunteers serve on the Foundation Task Force and review requests, make site visits, and conduct interviews; Task Force makes recommendations to foundation trustees.
Evaluative Criteria: Organization is tax-exempt and serves an Edison community; program has measurable goals and objectives that relate to a foundation concern; realistic strategy for achieving goals; provide company with appropriate recognition; employee volunteer involvement; funding is for a specific project, not general support; positive impact on the community; demonstrated need; non-duplication of services; plans for continued operation; long-term solutions.
Decision Notification: Trustees assess proposals in April, September, and December.

Restrictions

Proposals for same project will not be considered more than once within a one-year period. The foundation does not usually support capital campaigns (building as well as renovation); commitments beyond one year; events such as dinners, conferences, workshops, symposiums, etc.; and programs receiving substantial support from others. The foundation also limits its consideration of contributions to third party organizations, preferring to support direct program grants.

Additional Information

In 1999, Boston Edison's holding company, BEC Energy, and Commonwealth Energy System merged to

form NSTAR. Boston Edison is a subsidiary of NSTAR.
Publications: Foundation Annual Report; Guidelines

Corporate Officials

Alison Alden: senior vice president sales, service, human resources PRIM CORP EMPL senior vice president sales, service, human resources: Boston Edison Co. CORP AFFIL senior vice president sales, services, human resources: BEC Energy.
John J. Connolly: director corporate relations PRIM CORP EMPL director corporate relations: Boston Edison Co.
Douglas S. Horan: senior vice president, general counsel ED Case Western Reserve University BS; Johns Hopkins University MA; Northeastern University JD. PRIM CORP EMPL senior vice president, general counsel: NSTAR ADD CORP EMPL senior vice president, general counsel: BEC Energy.
James J. Judge: senior vice president corporate service business unit, treasurer ED Babson College. PRIM CORP EMPL senior vice president corporate service business unit, treasurer: Boston Edison Co. ADD CORP EMPL vice president, treasurer: BEC Energy Inc.; treasurer: Boston Energy Technology Group Inc.; treasurer: Harbor Electric Energy Co.; senior vice president, chief financial officer: NSTAR.
Ronald A. Ledgett: executive vice president B 1938. ED Stanford University. PRIM CORP EMPL executive vice president: Boston Edison Co.
Leon J. Olivier: Chief nuclear office PRIM CORP EMPL chief nuclear office: Northeast Utilities.
Robert J. Weafee, Jr.: vice president, controller PRIM CORP EMPL vice president, controller: Boston Edison Co.

Foundation Officials

Alison Alden: trustee (see above)
Ann L. Cardello: administrator
John J. Connolly: director (see above)
Theodora S. Convisser: trustee B New York, NY 1947. ED Brandeis University BA (1969); Northeastern University JD (1975); Boston University LLM (1979). PRIM CORP EMPL assistant general counsel clerk: BEC Energy ADD CORP EMPL clerk: Boston Energy Technology Group Inc.; clerk: Coneco Corp.; clerk, director: Harbor Electric Energy Electric Energy Co.; clerk: Northwind Boston LLC; clerk: Rez-Tek International Corp.
Lester Carl Gustin: trustee B 1942. ED Boston University BS (1967). PRIM CORP EMPL senior vice president corporate relations: Boston Edison Co.
Douglas S. Horan: trustee (see above)
C. S. Daisy Jao: tax advisor
James J. Judge: trustee (see above)
Catherine J. Keuthen: legal adv
Ronald A. Ledgett: trustee (see above)
Emilie F. O'Neill: treasurer
Leon J. Olivier: trustee (see above)
Walter E. Salvi: manager

Grants Analysis

Disclosure Period: calendar year ending 1998
Total Grants: $1,085,000
Number of Grants: 115
Average Grant: $9,435
Typical Range: $1000 to $10,000
Note: Grant Analysis provided by foundation.

Recent Grants

Note: Grants derived from 1996 Form 990.

Civic & Public Affairs

1,743 Associate Grant Making Baystate, Boston, MA -- operating support

BOSTON GAS CO.

Company Contact

Boston, MA
Web: http://www.naturalgas.com/bostongas

Company Description

Assets: US$705,500,000
Employees: 1,300
SIC(s): 4924 Natural Gas Distribution.
Parent Company: Eastern Enterprises, 9 Riverside Rd., Weston, MA, United States

Nonmonetary Support

Type: Loaned Employees

Giving Contact

Michael Bruno, Community Relations Coordinator
Boston Gas Co.
One Beacon St.
Boston, MA 02108
Phone: (617)723-5512 ext 2443
Fax: (617)742-3042

Description

Organization Type: Corporate Giving Program
Giving Locations: MA: Central Massachusetts, Eastern Massachusetts
Grant Types: General Support.
Note: Employee matching gift ratio: 2 to 1.

Financial Summary

Total Giving: $270,000 (2000 approx); $270,000 (1999 approx); $262,363 (1998). Note: Contributes through corporate direct giving program only.

Typical Recipients

Arts & Humanities: Arts & Humanities-General
Civic & Public Affairs: Civic & Public Affairs-General
Education: Education-General
Health: Health-General
Social Services: United Funds/United Ways

Application Procedures

Initial Contact: letter of inquiry and proposal on organization's letterhead
Application Requirements: summary of need, including background, objective, time period, key staff, and budget; most recent financial statement; membership of the governing board; copy of IRS tax-exemption certification, and IRS letter establishing that the organization is not a private foundation; list of other sources of support; and approval and signature of organization's chief executive officer or development director
Deadlines: between 30 to 90 days before actual need

Restrictions

The company does not support political or religious groups, private foundations, or individuals.

Additional Information

The company's maximum single contribution is $5,000 over a three-year period. Requests for funding larger than $5,000 should be directed to Boston Gas Company's parent, Eastern Enterprises.
Publications: Application Guidelines

Corporate Officials

J. Atwood Ives: chairman, chief executive officer B Atlanta, GA 1936. ED Yale University BA (1959); Stanford University Graduate School of Business Administration MBA (1961); Harvard University Advanced Management Program AMP (1975). PRIM CORP EMPL chairman, chief executive officer, trustee: Eastern Enterprises. CORP AFFIL director: Neiman Marcus Group Inc.; trustee Mutual Funds, director: Massachusetts Finance Services Co. NONPR AFFIL corporate advisory board: Stanford University Graduate School Business; director: United Way Massachusetts Bay; director: Massachusetts Business Roundtable; trustee: Museum Fine Arts; corporate advisory board: Boston College School of Management.
Chester R. Messer: president, chief operating officer B Concord, NH 1942. ED Harvard University Advanced Management Program; Northeastern University; University of New Hampshire BA (1963). PRIM CORP EMPL president, chief operating officer: Boston Gas Co. ADD CORP EMPL senior vice president: Establishmentern Enterprises. NONPR AFFIL director: Institute Gas Technology; director: New England Gas Association; director: American Gas Association.

Giving Program Officials

Kathleen Hearn: manager PRIM CORP EMPL manager community & government relations: Boston Gas Co.

Grants Analysis

Disclosure Period: calendar year ending
Typical Range: $250 to $1,000

THE BOSTON GLOBE

Company Contact

Boston, MA
Web: http://www.boston.com

Company Description

Employees: 2,101
SIC(s): 2711 Newspapers.
Parent Company: New York Times Co., 229 West 43rd Street, New York, NY, United States

Nonmonetary Support

Type: Cause-related Marketing & Promotion; In-kind Services
Note: Co. provides nonmonetary support. Supports the Globe Santa Program, which raises funds from readers to provide Christmas donations to needy families.

Boston Globe Foundation

Giving Contact

Klare E. Shaw, Executive Director
The Boston Globe Foundation
PO Box 2378
Boston, MA 02107-2378
Phone: (617)929-2895
Fax: (617)929-2041
Email: foundation@globe.com

Description

EIN: 222821421
Organization Type: Corporate Foundation
Giving Locations: MA: Boston, Cambridge, Chelsea, Somerville
Grant Types: Capital, Employee Matching Gifts, General Support, Multiyear/Continuing Support.
Note: Employee matching gift ratio: 1 to 1 to education.

Giving Philosophy

'Our goal is to empower low income children, teens and families. We hope our funding will have a special impact on children and teens in communities of color and those who have been excluded from equal participation in our society (these could include, as examples: children and youth with disabilities, children and youth with AIDS, refugees, low-birth-rate babies and pregnant/nursing mothers, immigrants and incarcerated youth.)

'In order to promote empowerment, we support community-based agencies as our highest priority. The Boston Globe Foundation defines a community-based agency as an agency with roots in the community served, in which board and staff reflect the diversity and interests of that community. To empower,

we are interested in programs and agencies which provide active self-determined roles for participants, and in which input from directly affected constituents is essential to project design and implementation. It is our hope that funded activities will alter the social isolation of program participants. For example, young people should play a meaningful and pro-active role in programs that wish to foster self-direction and self-esteem in youth.

'As a second priority, we fund advocacy agencies which influence public policy around needs of low-income populations. We also will consider agencies which are not community-based but have responsive staff and governance and are willing to, and capable of, serving the articulated interests of a given community.' *Letter from the Executive Director of the Foundation*

Financial Summary

Total Giving: $2,000,000 (fiscal year ending June 30, 2000 approx); $2,000,000 (fiscal 1999 approx); $2,212,561 (fiscal 1998). Note: Contributes through foundation only.

Giving Analysis: Giving for fiscal 1996 includes: foundation ($1,506,487); foundation matching gifts ($61,235); fiscal 1997: foundation ($2,516,032); fiscal 1998: foundation ($2,212,561)

Assets: $816,766 (fiscal 1998); $1,039,295 (fiscal 1997); $992,101 (fiscal 1996)

Gifts Received: $2,307,726 (fiscal 1998); $2,333,193 (fiscal 1997); $2,297,814 (fiscal 1996). Note: Contributions received from Globe Newspaper Company.

Typical Recipients

Arts & Humanities: Arts Associations & Councils, Arts Festivals, Arts Funds, Arts Outreach, Ballet, Dance, Ethnic & Folk Arts, Arts & Humanities-General, Libraries, Museums/Galleries, Music, Performing Arts, Public Broadcasting, Theater, Visual Arts

Civic & Public Affairs: Botanical Gardens/Parks, Business/Free Enterprise, Economic Development, Employment/Job Training, Hispanic Affairs, Housing, Nonprofit Management, Philanthropic Organizations, Professional & Trade Associations, Safety, Urban & Community Affairs, Women's Affairs, Zoos/Aquariums

Education: Afterschool/Enrichment Programs, Business-School Partnerships, Colleges & Universities, Education Reform, Elementary Education (Private), Environmental Education, Faculty Development, Education-General, Journalism/Media Education, Literacy, Medical Education, Minority Education, Preschool Education, Private Education (Precollege), Public Education (Precollege), Science/Mathematics Education, Special Education, Student Aid

Environment: Environment-General, Protection

Health: AIDS/HIV, Children's Health/Hospitals, Clinics/Medical Centers, Health Organizations, Hospitals, Medical Research, Mental Health, Nutrition

International: Foreign Arts Organizations, Human Rights

Religion: Religious Welfare

Science: Science Museums

Social Services: Camps, Child Welfare, Community Centers, Community Service Organizations, Counseling, Crime Prevention, Day Care, Domestic Violence, Family Services, Food/Clothing Distribution, Homes, People with Disabilities, Recreation & Athletics, Shelters/Homelessness, Substance Abuse, United Funds/United Ways, Youth Organizations

Contributions Analysis

Giving Priorities: Social services, civic programs, education, cultural and arts funds, hopitals, health organizations, and summer camps.

Arts & Humanities: 15%. Funds support libraries, dance and other performing arts, museums, public broadcasting, and visual arts. Focus onpromoting the artistic expression and creativity of youth.

Civic & Public Affairs: 14%. Highest priority is supporting community-building programs that support children and teens. Grants go to a wide variety of organizations, including disability awareness, urban development groups and community affairs programs, parenting skills, decreasing racism and bias, youth leadership development, youth welfare and recreation programs, food assistance, shelters, legal assistance, job training, and other social services and civic programs.

Education: 22%. Funding supports scholarship funds, student aid, colleges and universities. Major funder of the Boston Schoolyard Initiative. Other interests are media education, science education, and afterschool enrichment programs. Supports eliminating barriers to educational and employment opportunities, improving public education, family literacy, and English language skills. Foundation also administers a matching gifts program.

Environment: 2%. Supports lead poisoning prevention, environmental education, and open space initiatives.

Health: 4%. Supports community-based health centers andgrassroots organizing and advocacy efforts for increased access to health care in the Boston area. Supports youth with disabilities, and substance abuse and HIV/AIDs programs.

Science: 7%. Supports science initiatives.

Social Services: 36%. Supports youth groups, adoption/foster care, volunteerism, dependent care, emergency assistance, and food distribution.

Note: Total contributions made in 1998.

Application Procedures

Initial Contact: Apply using the Associated Grantmakers of Massachusetts (AGM) Common Proposal Format and a Boston Globe Foundation Addendum. Contact the AGM and Boston Globe Foundation for forms.

Application Requirements: Completed proposal following the AGM Common Proposal Format and answers to all questions asked on the Boston Globe Foundation's Addendum.

Deadlines: None.

Review Process: Proposals reviewed by foundation staff, agencies investigated, budgetary requirements evaluated, and recommendation made to foundation board which meets February, June and in the fall.

Evaluative Criteria: The foundation's primary funding criteria is to support programs and operations of well-managed, financially viable charitable organizations based in Boston, Cambridge, Somerville and Chelsea, MA that serve youth ages 0-22 who live primarily in low-income neighborhoods. Secondary funding criteria include a preference for programs that foster inclusion of youth not participating fully in society; build bridges for youth across divides (neighborhood borders, varied backgrounds); link youth programs with other neighborhood initiatives, as participants in an integrated community effort; and demonstrate effective and consistent constituency involvement in creation and implementation of programs. The foundation also evaluates whether an agency values inclusion and diversity among staff, clientele and decision-makers; has active governing bodies knowledgeable about the organization's mission and constituents; addresses systemic causes of a problem, or educates the public on important issues.

Decision Notification: Allow four to six months for processing.

Notes: Foundation sponsors meetings on how to shape proposals. Call the foundation for more information regarding community information meetings.

Restrictions

The foundation does not make grants to individuals or for the purchase of tables, tickets, or advertising. The foundation does not make more than one grant per fiscal year to any one organization.

Additional Information

The Globe Santa Fund solicits through advertising and publicity contributions to purchase Christmas gifts for needy children. The company also administers several scholarship programs, including the L.L. Winship Scholarship Fund (for children of full-time company employees), the I. Arthur Seigel Scholarship Fund (athletic), the Marjorie L. Adams Scholarship Fund (for children of employees), and the Louis Shriber Scholarship Fund (for Globe newsboys). The company also sponsors scholastic art awards and the Globe Interscholastic Festival.

The foundation holds bi-weekly informational meetings for grantsseekers to help shape proposals. Staff explains funding priorities and application procedures. The contact for these meetings is Sylvia Payton, at (617)929-2895.

The New York Times Company acquired the Globe Newspaper Co.'s parent corporation, Affiliated Publications, in 1993.

Publications: Application; Guidelines; Report to the Community

Corporate Officials

Paul R. Norman: controller, chief executive officer, director PRIM CORP EMPL controller: Globe Newspaper Co.

William Osgood Taylor: chairman, chief executive officer, director B Boston, MA 1932. ED Harvard University BA (1954). PRIM CORP EMPL chairman, emeritus chief executive officer, director: Globe Newspaper Co. ADD CORP EMPL president: Affiliated Publishers Inc. CORP AFFIL director: New York Times Co.; chairman emeritus: Boston Globe Publishing; vice chairman: Federation Reserve Bank Boston. NONPR AFFIL member director: International Center Journalists; trustee: International Crisis Group; chairman: Freedom Trail Foundation; trustee: Boston Public Library; trustee: Boston Public Library Foundation; director: Boston Adult Literacy Fund.

Foundation Officials

Leslie Griffin: director

Alexander Boyd Hawes, Jr.: treasurer B Washington, DC 1947. ED University of Denver (1965-1969). PRIM CORP EMPL assistant to president: Globe Newspaper Co. NONPR AFFIL director: Friends of Sakonnet Lighthouse.

Catherine Emily Campbell Henn: president B Saint Louis, MO 1942. ED Wellesley College (1964); Harvard University (1969). PRIM CORP EMPL vice president Legal affairs, clerk, counsel: Globe Newspaper Co. CORP AFFIL vice president, clerk, counsel: Affiliated Publications Inc.; treasurer, clerk: Globe SPLty Products Inc.

Suzanne W. Maas: executive director

Mary Marty: assistant treasurer B 1942. ED Marycrest College (1964). PRIM CORP EMPL treasurer: Affiliated Publications Inc. ADD CORP EMPL treasurer: Globe SPLty Products Inc.

Loretta McLaughlin: director

Paul R. Norman: comptroller (see above)

Sylvia Payton: executive secretary

Mariella Puerto: project director

Cathy Rawlings: bookkeeper

Klare E. Shaw: assistant director

Benjamin B. Taylor: director B 1947. ED Harvard University. PRIM CORP EMPL president, publisher chairman: Globe Newspaper Co. NONPR AFFIL trustee: Park School; trustee: Radcliffe College.

William Osgood Taylor: chairman, director (see above)

Grants Analysis

Disclosure Period: fiscal year ending June 30, 1998

Total Grants: $2,299,981

Number of Grants: 250 (approx)

Average Grant: $9,200

Typical Range: $3,000 to $10,000

Recent Grants

Note: Grants derived from fiscal 1996 Form 990.

Arts & Humanities

15,000	HSPC Diversity Initiative -- support arts and humanities organizations
15,000	WGBH Educational Foundation, Springfield, MA -- for National Center for Accessible Media
10,000	Boston Ballet, Boston, MA -- for CityDance
10,000	Children's Museum -- multiyear pledge for Urban Environmental Education and Exhibition Center
10,000	Wang Center for Performing Arts, Boston, MA -- multiyear pledge in memory of John I. Taylor
9,500	Federated Dorchester Neighborhood Houses, Dorchester, MA -- for Art Express, art programming
8,000	Very Special Arts Massachusetts, Boston, MA -- for Support Curriculum and Inclusion through the Arts program
7,500	Community Music Center, Boston, MA -- for Community Arts Education Initiative
7,000	Museum of African American History, Detroit, MI -- for youth programs

Civic & Public Affairs

50,000	Boston Globe Foundation, Boston, MA -- for Lead Action Plan
20,000	New England Aquarium, Boston, MA -- program support, capital campaign
13,400	Associated Grantmakers of Massachusetts, Boston, MA -- support services
12,350	Boston Globe Foundation, Boston, MA -- for DATP
10,000	Local Initiatives Support Corporation, Boston, MA -- to build low-income housing in Boston
8,000	Chelsea's Commission on Hispanic Affairs, Chelsea, MA -- operating support, support parent organization
7,510	American Press Institute, Reston, VA -- operating support
7,000	Citizens for Safety, Boston, MA -- for youth programming
7,000	Codman Square Neighborhood Development, Boston, MA -- for Resident Development Program
7,000	Fenway Community Development Corporation, Boston, MA -- for Fenway Family Coalition
7,000	ICA Group, Boston, MA -- for Community Jobs Program in Boston
7,000	La Alianza Hispana, Los Angeles, CA -- operating support
7,000	Women's Institute for Housing and Economic Development, Boston, MA -- housing support

Education

70,000	University of Massachusetts Boston, Boston, MA -- support 1996 Taylor Scholars Program
12,000	Boston Partners in Education, Boston, MA -- operating support
11,000	Boston Partners in Education, Boston, MA -- support Books and Kids literacy initiative
10,000	Citywide Educational Coalition, Boston, MA -- support parental involvement, teacher workshops
10,000	Fund for Boston Schoolyards, Boston, MA
10,000	University of Massachusetts Boston, Boston, MA -- operating support for Urban Scholars Program
8,000	United South End Settlements, Boston, MA -- for youth development, computer programs for youth
8,000	Urban College of Boston/Action for Boston Community Development, Boston, MA -- for High School to College Bridge Program

Environment

10,000	Boston Greenspace Alliance, Boston, MA -- for advocacy, community service agenda
10,000	Conservation Law Foundation, Boston, MA -- for Lead Poisoning Prevention Project
9,000	Boston Natural Areas Fund, Boston, MA -- operating support
7,000	Boston Greenspace Alliance, Boston, MA -- support administering the Boston Schoolyard Initiative

Health

10,000	Boston Freedom Summer/Codman Square Health Center, Boston, MA -- for Boston Freedom Summer '95
8,500	Trustees of Health and Hospitals Fund for Excellence, Boston, MA -- support for Failure to Thrive Clinic at Boston City Hospital
7,500	Health Care for All, Boston, MA -- support Children's Health Access Project

International

7,000	World Music -- for Sharing the Rhythm project

Religion

15,000	Black Church Capacity Building Project -- support of Black Church Capacity Building Project
9,000	East Boston Ecumenical Community Council, Boston, MA -- for youth programs
9,000	El Centro Del Cardenal/Catholic Charities -- support Lazos Comunales Program

Social Services

39,000	Project Bread, Boston, MA -- for Emergency Feeding Network
15,000	Boston Children's Services, Boston, MA -- for Project Excel
15,000	Roca, Inc., Chelsea, MA -- renovations
11,000	Dorchester Youth Collaborative, Dorchester, MA -- support CUE program
10,000	Boys and Girls Clubs, Boston, MA -- five-year pledge for capital campaign
9,000	Special Adoption Family Services, Boston, MA -- operating support
8,000	Uphams Corner Community Center/Bird Street Community Center, Dorchester, MA -- for Teen Organizing Project
7,000	Asian Task Force Against Domestic Violence, Boston, MA -- for Asian Shelter and Advocacy Project
7,000	Emerge -- for Date Violence Intervention Program

BOURNS, INC.

Company Contact

1200 Columbia Ave.
Riverside, CA 92507
Phone: (909)781-5500
Fax: (909)781-5006
Web: http://www.bourns.com

Company Description

Employees: 4,000
SIC(s): 3676 Electronic Resistors, 3679 Electronic Components Nec, 3699 Electrical Equipment & Supplies Nec.

Nonmonetary Support

Type: Donated Equipment

Bourns Foundation

Giving Contact

Gordon L. Bourns, President
1200 Columbia Ave.
Riverside, CA 92507
Phone: (909)781-5690
Fax: (909)781-5273

Description

EIN: 956044472
Organization Type: Corporate Foundation
Giving Locations: CA: focusing on Inland Empire area of Southern California; UT
Grant Types: Capital, Endowment, Multiyear/Continuing Support, Scholarship.

Financial Summary

Total Giving: $1,696,539 (fiscal year ending November 30, 1998); $295,770 (fiscal 1997); $1,120,122 (fiscal 1996). Note: Contributes through foundation only.
Giving Analysis: Giving for fiscal 1996 includes: foundation ($1,117,122); foundation grants to United Way ($3,000); fiscal 1998: foundation ($1,696,539)
Assets: $433,320 (fiscal 1998); $316,779 (fiscal 1997); $339,477 (fiscal 1996)
Gifts Received: $1,800,000 (fiscal 1998); $256,875 (fiscal 1997); $1,100,000 (fiscal 1996). Note: Contributions were received from Bourns, Inc.

Typical Recipients

Arts & Humanities: Arts & Humanities-General, Museums/Galleries
Civic & Public Affairs: Clubs, Economic Development, Civic & Public Affairs-General
Education: Arts/Humanities Education, Business Education, Colleges & Universities, Education Funds, Engineering/Technological Education, Education-General, Private Education (Precollege), Public Education (Precollege), Religious Education, Science/Mathematics Education, Student Aid
Health: Cancer, Children's Health/Hospitals, Diabetes, Health-General, Hospices, Hospitals
Religion: Religious Welfare
Social Services: Community Service Organizations, Recreation & Athletics, Scouts, Shelters/Homelessness, Social Services-General, United Funds/United Ways, YMCA/YWCA/YMHA/YWHA, Youth Organizations

Contributions Analysis

Education: 98%. Funds public and private pre-college education and major support for colleges and universities focusing on engineering.
Note: Total contributions in fiscal 1998.

Application Procedures

Initial Contact: Send a brief letter of inquiry.
Application Requirements: Include description of program, including benefits, and purpose of funds sought.
Deadlines: None.

Corporate Officials

Gordon L. Bourns: chairman finance, chief financial officer, treasurer B 1949. ED University of California, Los Angeles BSEE (1971); University of California, Los Angeles MBA (1973). PRIM CORP EMPL chairman: Bourns, Inc.
William P. McKenna: vice president finance, chief financial officer, treasurer B 1947. ED College of the Holy Cross MA (1968); University of Southern California MBA (1976). PRIM CORP EMPL vice president finance, chief financial officer, treasurer: Bourns, Inc.

Foundation Officials

Gordon L. Bourns: president, trustee (see above)
Linda Bourns Hill: vice president, trustee
Anita L. MacBeth: trustee CORP AFFIL director: Bourns Inc.
Denise L. Moyles: trustee
Gerald T. Young: secretary, treasurer, trustee

Grants Analysis

Disclosure Period: fiscal year ending November 30, 1998
Total Grants: $1,696,539
Number of Grants: 20
Average Grant: $5,319*
Highest Grant: $1,595,469
Typical Range: $1,000 to $5,000
***Note:** Average grant excludes highest grant.

Recent Grants

Note: Grants derived from fiscal 1998 Form 990.

Arts & Humanities

6,000 Riverside Youth Museum, Riverside, CA -- Youth Programs

Civic & Public Affairs

15,000 Junior League of Riverside, Riverside, CA -- Youth Programs

Education

1,595,469 UC Riverside Foundation, Riverside, CA -- College of Engineering
20,000 St. Andrews School, Saratoga, CA -- Educational Programs
11,000 Newport Harbor Educational Foundation, Newport Beach, CA -- Youth/Educational Programs
10,000 Orange Coast College Foundation, Costa Mesa, CA -- Educational Program
7,170 UC Riverside Foundation, Riverside, CA -- Educational Program
5,000 California Baptist College, Riverside, CA -- Educational Programs/Future Development
5,000 Utah State University, Logan, UT -- Engineering Scholarships
4,000 UC Riverside Foundation, Riverside, CA -- Educational Programs
3,000 UC Riverside Foundation, Riverside, CA -- Engineering Scholarships
2,500 Newport Harbor High School PTA, Newport Beach, CA -- Educational Programs
2,000 Regents of UC Riverside, Riverside, CA -- Educational Program
500 Riverside Christian School System, Riverside, CA -- Educational Programs

Health

2,500 Parkview Community Hospital Foundation, Riverside, CA -- Future Development
1,500 Juvenile Diabetes Foundation, Riverside, CA -- Diabetes Research
1,000 Loma Linda University Children's Hospital Fdtn., Loma Linda, CA -- Philanthropic Services

Social Services

3,000 Inland Empire Boy Scouts of America, Riverside, CA -- Youth Programs
1,500 Assistance League of Riverside, Riverside, CA -- Philanthropic Services
400 Riverside YMCA, Riverside, CA -- Philanthropic Services

BOWATER INC.

Company Contact

55 East Camperdown Way
PO Box 1028
Greenville, SC 29602
Phone: (864)282-9559
Fax: (864)282-9482
Web: http://www.bowater.com

Company Description

Employees: 8,300
SIC(s): 2421 Sawmills & Planing Mills--General, 2611 Pulp Mills, 2621 Paper Mills, 2672 Coated & Laminated Paper Nec.

Operating Locations

Canada: Bowater Canadian Ltd., Hamilton; Bowater Mersey Paper Co. Ltd., Liverpool, Merseyside
Note: Also operates in Halifax, Nova Scotia, Canada.

Nonmonetary Support

Value: $21,500 (1993)
Type: Donated Products

Corporate Sponsorship

Type: Festivals/fairs; Music & entertainment events
Contact: David Maffucci, Senior Vice President & Chief Financial Officer
Note: Sponsorship is subject to annual board approval.

Giving Contact

Gordon Manuel, Director, Government Affairs
Greenville, SC

Description

Organization Type: Corporate Giving Program
Giving Locations: headquarters and operating communities.
Grant Types: Capital, Employee Matching Gifts, General Support.
Note: Employee matching gift ratio: 1 to 1.

Financial Summary

Total Giving: $550,000 (1996 approx); $550,000 (1995 approx); $452,000 (1994). Note: Contributes through corporate direct giving program only.

Typical Recipients

Arts & Humanities: Arts Associations & Councils, Arts Centers, Community Arts, Libraries, Music, Performing Arts, Public Broadcasting
Civic & Public Affairs: Economic Development, Urban & Community Affairs
Education: Business Education, Colleges & Universities, Community & Junior Colleges, Continuing Education, Economic Education, Engineering/Technological Education, Minority Education
Environment: Environment-General
Health: Health Organizations, Hospitals
Social Services: United Funds/United Ways, Youth Organizations

Contributions Analysis

Giving Priorities: Company's Canadian subsidiary makes contributions locally. Priorities are health and human services and education.
Arts & Humanities: 10% to 15%. Museums, libraries, community arts, theater, and the performing arts.
Civic & Public Affairs: About 5%. Supports economic development, environmental affairs, urban and community affairs, and zoos and botanical gardens.
Education: About 25%. Colleges, universities, community colleges, continuing education programs, economic education, business education, and education for minorities.
Health: 45% to 50%. Hospitals, hospices, health organizations, aid for the disabled, community centers, drug abuse programs, shelters, and community service organizations. A large portion of funds in this category support the United Way.

Application Procedures

Initial Contact: letter of inquiry
Application Requirements: a description of organization, amount requested, purpose of funds sought, recently audited financial statement, and IRS tax-determination letter
Deadlines: for small grants, None; for larger grants, July 31.
Evaluative Criteria: requires that the organization requesting funds truly needs the money; that the donation ultimately benefits the company, a significant number of employees, or the operating community; that the contribution must meet the standards of the community and be an appropriate amount; and, whenever possible, donations should be backed by appropriate community participation

Restrictions

Does not support individuals, religious organizations for sectarian purposes, or political or lobbying groups. If the organization requesting a donation is supported by a united fund or if an agency which the contributions committee believes should be a member of a united fund, company will not make a donation.

Additional Information

Each company division has its own contributions budget, with varying application procedures.
Publications: Bowater Incorporated Criteria for Corporate Giving

Corporate Officials

David G. Maffucci: senior vice president, chief financial officer B Stamford, CT 1950. ED Sacred Heart University BA (1972). PRIM CORP EMPL senior vice president, chief financial officer: Bowater Inc. NONPR AFFIL member: Financial Executives Institute; member: National Association Accts; member: American Institute CPAs.

Giving Program Officials

Michelle Day: PRIM CORP EMPL manager office services: Bowater Inc.
Deborah L. Humphrey: director PRIM CORP EMPL director corporate relations: Bowater Inc.

Grants Analysis

Disclosure Period: calendar year ending
Typical Range: $250 to $1,000

BP AMOCO CORP.

 Number 46 of Top 100 Corporate Givers

Company Contact

Chicago, IL
Web: http://www.bpamoco.com

Company Description

Former Name: Amoco Corp.;
Acquired:.
Profit: US$1,862,000,000
Employees: 56,450
SIC(s): 1311 Crude Petroleum & Natural Gas, 1321 Natural Gas Liquids, 2221 Broadwoven Fabric Mills--Manmade, 6719 Holding Companies Nec.
Parent Company: BP Amoco Plc, Britannic House, 1 Finsbury Circus, London, United Kingdom

Operating Locations

AL: BP Amoco Corp., Tuscaloosa; CO: BP Amoco Corp., Denver, Salida; GA: BP Amoco Corp., Atlanta, Norcross; IL: BP Amoco Corp., Chicago, Naperville, Urbana; IN: BP Amoco Corp., Winamac; LA: BP Amoco Corp., New Orleans; MI: BP Amoco Corp., Flint; MS: BP Amoco Corp., Moss Point; NJ: BP Amoco Corp., Madison; NY: BP Amoco Corp., New York, Pelham; OK: BP Amoco Corp., Tulsa; TX: BP Amoco Corp., Houston, Texas City; VA: BP Amoco Corp., Grafton, Yorktown

Nonmonetary Support

Value: $588,230 (1989); $148,900 (1988); $494,000 (1987)
Type: Donated Equipment; Donated Products
Note: Nonmonetary gifts are distributed through local corporate divisions.

Corporate Sponsorship

Type: Arts & cultural events; Festivals/fairs
Contact: Iris Walker, Coordinator, Corporate Relations
Note: Sponsorship support is limited.

BP Amoco Foundation

Giving Contact

Sonya Jackson, President
BP Amoco Foundation
200 E. Randolph Dr.
Chicago, IL 60601
Phone: (312)856-6306
Fax: (312)616-0826

Description

EIN: 366046879
Organization Type: Corporate Foundation. Supports preselected organizations only.
Former Name: Amoco Foundation (1998).
Giving Locations: headquarters and operating communities, nationally and internationally.
Grant Types: Capital, Emergency, Employee Matching Gifts, Fellowship, General Support, Loan, Scholarship.
Note: Employee matching gift ratio: 1 to 1 for precollege math, science, or technology programs, or to educational institutions.

Giving Philosophy

'We will provide our employees and partners with counsel and resources that promote the continuous improvement of communities where we have a presence. We will be an integral part of making Amoco preeminent and of strengthening our global business strategies. We will support innovative community-involvement programs and initiatives that respond to change, create opportunity and address needs in the communities where we operate. Our financial support will also reflect Amoco's business success and strategic direction. We value Integrity; People; Technology; Environment, Health and Safety; Business Relationships; and Progress. These will be our reference points as we use our resources to make an impact. Our resources include current employees, retired employees, technical know-how and financial assistance. Quality education; healthy, vibrant communities with solid infrastructure; the development of our youth; and environmental stewardship are all strategic to Amoco's mission of conducting business responsibly and fulfilling our role as a good corporate citizen.'*Amoco Guidelines*

Financial Summary

Total Giving: $21,000,000 (2000 approx); $37,000,000 (1999 approx); $19,000,000 (1998 approx). Note: Contributes through corporate direct giving program and foundation. 1997 Giving includes foundation ($15,143,883); United Way ($1,995,000).
Assets: $42,000,500 (1999 approx); $74,245,741 (1997); $76,506,121 (1996)
Gifts Received: $40,165,067 (1996); $24,606,250 (1993); $27,047,546 (1992). Note: Foundation receives contributions from BP Amoco Corp.

Typical Recipients

Arts & Humanities: Arts Centers, Arts Institutes, Ethnic & Folk Arts, Libraries, Museums/Galleries, Music, Performing Arts
Civic & Public Affairs: African American Affairs, Asian American Affairs, Business/Free Enterprise, Chambers of Commerce, Community Foundations, Economic Development, Economic Policy, Employment/Job Training, Hispanic Affairs, Housing, Law & Justice, Nonprofit Management, Professional & Trade Associations, Public Policy, Urban & Community Affairs, Women's Affairs, Zoos/Aquariums
Education: Agricultural Education, Business Education, Colleges & Universities, Community & Junior Colleges, Continuing Education, Education Associations, Education Funds, Engineering/Technological Education, Education-General, International Exchange, Minority Education, Public Education (Precollege), Science/Mathematics Education, Student Aid
Environment: Air/Water Quality, Environment-General, Resource Conservation, Wildlife Protection
Health: Children's Health/Hospitals, Clinics/Medical Centers, Emergency/Ambulance Services, Hospitals, Public Health, Research/Studies Institutes, Single-Disease Health Associations
International: Foreign Educational Institutions, Health Care/Hospitals, International Affairs, International Environmental Issues, International Organizations, International Relations, Missionary/Religious Activities
Religion: Ministries, Religious Welfare
Science: Science Museums, Scientific Organizations
Social Services: At-Risk Youth, Child Welfare, Community Centers, Community Service Organizations, Delinquency & Criminal Rehabilitation, Family Services, Homes, People with Disabilities, Recreation & Athletics, Social Services-General, United Funds/ United Ways, Volunteer Services, YMCA/YWCA/ YMHA/YWHA, Youth Organizations

Contributions Analysis

Giving Priorities: Individual business units work with their local community to choose partners and programs. Interests include sustainable jobs, wealth creation, and financial stability.
Arts & Humanities: 15% to 20%. Supports museums, music, art, theaters, and artscenters. Also funds visual and performing arts when these organizations enhance the quality of life, strengthen neighborhoods by bringing art to disadvantaged individuals and communities, and present performances and instructions in schools, community centers, and neighborhoods.
Civic & Public Affairs: About 10%. Interests include employment, economic growth, public policy groups, government and tax issues, public safety, housing, youth leadership, and urban redevelopment issues. Supports programs that strengthen communities by promoting and investing in economic growth, and a healthy environment. Programs that promote minorities, emergency relief efforts, and the United Way receive funding under this category. Also supports major health facilities, programs that help the disadvantged receive health-care, and hospices when these programs reflect the educational and community objectives of the foundation.
Education: 30% to 35%. To foster an effective educational system and adequate workforce pool that reflects the diversity of the people in Amoco communities. Supports university programs that target disciplines required in Amoco's business; precollege programs that focus on math, science, and economic education; programs that promote minority participation in technical fields; and national and local school reform efforts. Also supports precollege and higher education through matching gifts and volunteer efforts.
Health: Less than 5%.
International: 5%. Supports hospitals, schools, museums, and other institutions in Amoco's overseas operating locations. Also contributes to local and national groups dedicated to improving conditions for the citizens in the host country.
Science: About 1%.
Social Services: 30% to 35%. Includes United Way and family and community service organizations.

Application Procedures

Initial Contact: Call to request guidelines; then one- or two-page letter with application.
Application Requirements: Brief a description of organization (including legal name, primary purpose, and history); specific purpose of grant request and expected benefits; amount requested and evaluative criteria; budget information, including annual report or financial statement listing sources of support; copy of IRS 501(c)(3) determination letter; list of board members.
Deadlines: Varies, depending on local committee.
Review Process: Budget for grants are reviewed August through November by the local contribution committees; Board of Directors gives final approval on budget in late December.
Evaluative Criteria: For a request to be approved it must adhere to the company's giving priorities and benefit the local business community.
Notes: Local area contributions committees evaluate and recommend proposals to the foundation. Contact information is included in guidelines.

Restrictions

Foundation does not provide grants for endowments. Foundation does not support individuals, private foundations, or religious, fraternal, social, or athletic programs or sports. Ordinarily does not make grants to member agencies of the United Way, except for occasional capital funding. Unsolicited requests in the areas of higher education and public policy are not accepted.

Additional Information

Amoco and BP America merged in 1998 to form BP Amoco.
Contacts for specific programs include the following: for National Programs in Education and Youth, Annie Smith (312) 856-5063; for Matching Gifts, Susan Carpen (312) 856-2050; for International, Patricia Wright (312) 856-6305; for Community, Irene Brown (312) 856- 6355; for Community Relations and Employee/ Retiree Volunteer Programs, Iris Walker (312) 856-6651; for Constituency Relations and Enviromental, Glanna Zelaya Bem (312) 856-2051.
Local Amoco dealers also provide the Amoco Community Scholarship program for high school students.
Publications: Foundation Annual Report; Corp. Annual Report

Corporate Officials

Sir John Browne: chief executive officer PRIM CORP EMPL chief executive officer: BP Amoco Corp.
John L. Carl: executive vice president, chief financial officer B Huntington, IN 1948. ED Purdue University BS (1970); Indiana University MBA (1972). PRIM CORP EMPL executive vice president, chief financial officer: BP Amoco. NONPR AFFIL member: Indiana University School Business Deans Advisory Council; director: United Way Chicago County; member: Financial Executives Institute; member: American Petroleum Institute; director: Evanston Hospital.
James E. Fligg: executive vice president B Sydney, NW Australia 1936. ED University of New South Wales BS (1968); Harvard University AMP (1980). PRIM CORP EMPL president: Amoco Corp. CORP AFFIL director: First Mississippi Corp.; director: Chemfirst Inc. NONPR AFFIL member executive committee: Society Chemical Industry; board managers: YMCA Chicago; member: National Petroleum Refiners Association; director: Chemical Manufacturers Association. CLUB AFFIL Mid-America Club; Chicago Club; Club International.
L. Richard Flury: executive vice president CORP AFFIL director: Illinois Tool Works Inc.
W. Douglas Ford: executive vice president PRIM CORP EMPL executive vice president: Amoco Corp. CORP AFFIL executive vice president: Amoco Oil Co.; director: USG Corp.
Harry Laurance Fuller: cochairman, director B Moline, IL 1938. ED Cornell University BSChE (1961);

DePaul University JD (1965). PRIM CORP EMPL co-chairman,: BP Amoco p.lc. CORP AFFIL director: Motorola Inc.; director: Chase Manhattan Corp.; director: Abbott Laboratories; director: Chase Manhattan Bank NA Inc. NONPR AFFIL director: Chicago Rehabilitation Institute; trustee: Orchestral Association; director: Catalyst for Women Inc.; director: American Petroleum Institute. CLUB AFFIL Mid-America Club; Chicago Club; Chicago Golf Club.

William G. Lowrie: president, deputy chief executive officer, director B Painesville, OH 1943. ED Ohio State University BS (1966). PRIM CORP EMPL president, deputy chief executive officer, director: BP Amoco Corp. CORP AFFIL director: Bank One Corp. NONPR AFFIL president: Northwestern Memorial Corp.; member: Society Petroleum Engineers; director: Junior Achievement; trustee, director: National 4-H Council; member: American Petroleum Institute. CLUB AFFIL Mid-America Club.

George S. Spindler: senior vice president law & corporate affairs B Omaha, NE 1938. ED Georgia Institute of Technology BCE (1961); DePaul University JD (1966). PRIM CORP EMPL senior vice president law & corporate affairs: Amoco Corp.

David F. Work: senior vice president shared service B 1945. ED Wesleyan University BA (1968); University of California MS (1970). PRIM CORP EMPL senior vice president shared service: Amoco Corp. CORP AFFIL vice president: Amoco Production Co.

Foundation Officials

Paula Banks: chairman, board member
James E. Boyajian: director
John L. Carl: director (see above)
Inge B. Fretheim: director PRIM CORP EMPL president: Amoco Power Resources Corp.
Richard L. McNeel: director PRIM CORP EMPL group vice president: Amoco Chemical Co.
George S. Spindler: chairman, director (see above)
David F. Work: director (see above)

Grants Analysis

Disclosure Period: calendar year ending 1997
Total Grants: $15,143,883*
Number of Grants: 1,350 (approx)
Average Grant: $10,485 (approx)*
Highest Grant: $1,000,000
Typical Range: $1,000 to $100,000
***Note:** Giving excludes United Way. Average grant excludes highest grant.

Recent Grants

Note: Grants derived from 1997 Form 990.

Arts & Humanities

1,000,000 Chicago Symphony Orchestra, Chicago, IL

Civic & Public Affairs

108,000 Philanthropic Research Center, Naperville, IL
100,000 South Carolina Aquarium, Charleston, SC
70,000 Charis Housing
70,000 National Council of La Raza, Washington, DC
65,000 National Urban League, New York, NY
63,000 Cosmopolitan Chamber of Commerce, Chicago, IL
56,000 Chinese Mutual Aid Association, Chicago, IL
50,000 Riverdale Redevelopment Corporation

Education

591,000 Celebrating Science, Houston, TX
145,968 National Merit Scholarship Corporation, Evanston, IL
136,000 National Action Council for Minorities in Engineering, New York, NY
100,000 College of the Mainland, Texas City, TX
100,000 Educational Resources Foundation for Technical Education and Economic Development, Columbia, SC
98,000 Junior Achievement, Colorado Springs, CO
94,500 Texas A&M University, College Station, TX
92,200 Purdue University, West Lafayette, IN
68,100 University of Oklahoma, Norman, OK
67,700 University of Texas, Austin, TX
65,000 Binational Fulbright Commission
63,750 Georgia Institute of Technology, Atlanta, GA
61,130 Florida A&M University, Sarasota, FL
60,000 National Consortium for Graduate Degrees, Notre Dame, IN
52,771 Jeff Davis High School Computer Lab Enhancements
50,000 Academy for Mathematics and Science Teachers, Chicago, IL
50,000 Keystone Science School, Keystone, CO
50,000 National Center for Construction Education
50,000 Spelman College, Atlanta, GA
50,000 United Negro College Fund, New York, NY
22,500 Midtown Educational Foundation, Chicago, IL

Environment

55,000 Wildlife Habitat Council, Silver Spring, MD

Health

100,000 Northwestern Memorial Hospital, Chicago, IL
68,000 Cimitarra Municipal Hospital
50,000 Near North Health Service Corporation, Chicago, IL

International

200,000 American University in Cairo, New York, NY
200,000 American University in Cairo, New York, NY
75,000 Center for Strategic and International Studies, Washington, DC
75,000 Center for Strategic and International Studies, Washington, DC
70,000 Americares Foundation, New Canaan, CT
70,000 Americares Foundation, New Canaan, CT

Religion

50,000 FCS Urban Ministries, Atlanta, GA

Science

50,000 Field Museum of Natural History, Chicago, IL

Social Services

950,000 United Way, Chicago, IL
318,000 United Way, Houston, TX
150,000 United Way, Tulsa, OK
120,000 City of Texas Conference Center
110,000 United Way, Texas City, TX
102,500 Metropolitan Family Services
100,500 Westside Holistic Family Services, Chicago, IL
70,000 United Way, Griffith, IN
55,000 Rose Garden Community Services, Chicago, IL
54,000 United Way, Denver, CO
50,000 Paternal Involvement Project

J.C. BRADFORD &CO.

Company Contact

330 Commerce St.
Nashville, TN 37201
Phone: (615)748-9000
Fax: (615)748-9287
Web: http://www.jcbradford.com

Company Description

Revenue: US$462,000,000
Employees: 2,000
SIC(s): 6211 Security Brokers & Dealers.

Corporate Sponsorship

Type: Arts & cultural events; Festivals/fairs; Music & entertainment events; Sports events; Pledge-a-thon

J.C. Bradford and Co. Foundation

Giving Contact

James C. Bradford, Jr., Senior Partner
Nashville, TN
Email: jimmy@jcbradford.com

Alternate Contact

Luke Simons, Managing Partner

Description

Founded: 1986
EIN: 621303221
Organization Type: Corporate Foundation. Supports preselected organizations only.
Giving Locations: TN: Nashville
Grant Types: General Support.

Financial Summary

Total Giving: $733,856 (1998); $583,041 (1997); $462,022 (1996)
Giving Analysis: Giving for 1997 includes: foundation grants to United Way ($128,490); 1998: foundation grants to United Way ($117,807)
Assets: $774,266 (1998); $1,294,239 (1997); $1,133,375 (1996)
Gifts Received: $158,548 (1998); $691,841 (1997); $1,046,429 (1996). Note: In 1998, contributions were received from J.C. Bradford and Co., Robert Doolittle, Davidson Partners, Techni Source, Skipper Bowles, Tom Wylly, R. Patrick Shepherd, and Mike Lowe.

Typical Recipients

Arts & Humanities: Arts Centers, Arts Institutes, Ballet, Dance, Arts & Humanities-General, History & Archaeology, Libraries, Museums/Galleries, Music, Opera, Performing Arts, Theater
Civic & Public Affairs: Botanical Gardens/Parks, Clubs, Community Foundations, Economic Development, Civic & Public Affairs-General, Housing, Urban & Community Affairs
Education: Arts/Humanities Education, Business Education, Colleges & Universities, Continuing Education, Economic Education, Education Associations, Education Funds, Elementary Education (Private), Elementary Education (Public), Education-General, Leadership Training, Legal Education, Private Education (Precollege), Secondary Education (Private), Student Aid, Vocational & Technical Education
Environment: Resource Conservation
Health: Arthritis, Cancer, Children's Health/Hospitals, Health Funds, Heart, Hospitals, Single-Disease Health Associations
Religion: Churches, Ministries, Religious Welfare
Social Services: Community Centers, Community Service Organizations, Crime Prevention, Family Services, Food/Clothing Distribution, Homes, Scouts, Sexual Abuse, United Funds/United Ways, YMCA/YWCA/YMHA/YWHA, Youth Organizations

Contributions Analysis

Giving Priorities: Arts and humanities, education, health, social services, religion, and civic and public policy
Arts & Humanities: 6%. Supports public broadcasting, historic preservation, museums, and the theater.
Civic & Public Affairs: 34%. Supports community foundations, neighborhood development, zoos,

parks, botanical gardens, public policy and civic affairs.
Education: 11%. Supports educational programs and higher education.
Health: 7%. Supports American Red Cross, hospitals, single-disease health associations, and health care concerns.
Religion: 19%. Supports churches, seminaries, religious education, and the YMCA.
Social Services: 23%. Supports child and family services, United Way, humane society, drug and sexual abuse centers.
Note: Total contributions made in 1998.

Restrictions

Grants are not made to individuals.

Corporate Officials

James C. Bradford, Jr.: senior partnerr B Nashville, TN 1933. ED Princeton University BA (1955). PRIM CORP EMPL senior partner: J.C. Bradford & Co. NONPR AFFIL trustee: Montgomery Bell Academy; member: National Association Securities Dealers. CLUB AFFIL Belle Meade Country Club.
R. Randall Harness: chief financial officer PRIM CORP EMPL chief financial officer: J.C. Bradford & Co.
C. Taxon Malott: part owner PRIM CORP EMPL part owner: J.C. Bradford & Co.

Foundation Officials

James C. Bradford, Jr.: president (see above)
C. Taxon Malott: secretary, treasurer (see above)
W. Lucas Simons: vice president

Grants Analysis

Disclosure Period: calendar year ending 1998
Total Grants: $616,049*
Number of Grants: 132*
Average Grant: $4,667*
Highest Grant: $107,500
Typical Range: $500 to $5,000
***Note:** Giving excludes United Way.

Recent Grants

Note: Grants derived from 1997 Form 990.

Arts & Humanities
25,250 Nashville Symphony, Nashville, TN
15,000 Cheekwood, Nashville, TN
15,000 Leonard Bernstein Center, Nashville, TN
10,000 Nashville Institute for the Arts, Nashville, TN
7,500 Nashville Opera Association, Nashville, TN

Education
30,000 Lehigh University, Lehigh, PA
25,000 University of Tennessee Chattanooga, Chattanooga, TN
15,000 University of Georgia, Athens, GA
10,000 North Carolina Outward Bound School, Morgantown, NC
10,000 Tennessee State University School of Business, TN
10,000 USC Development Foundation
8,500 Montgomery Bell Academy, Nashville, TN
6,250 Westminster School, Simsbury, CT
6,000 Cassidy Elementary School
6,000 Knoxville Catholic High School, Knoxville, TN

Health
22,643 Cystic Fibrosis Foundation, Philadelphia, PA

Religion
16,000 Westminster Presbyterian Church
10,000 Christ Episcopal Church, San Antonio, TX

Social Services
128,490 United Way
28,126 Martha O'Bryan Center, Nashville, TN

BRANCH BANKING & TRUST CO.

Company Contact

Winston-Salem, NC
Web: http://www.bbandt.com

Company Description

Income: US$179,200,000
Employees: 3,138
SIC(s): 6022 State Commercial Banks.
Parent Company: BB&T Financial Corp., Winston-Salem, NC, United States

Nonmonetary Support

Type: Cause-related Marketing & Promotion; Donated Equipment; Donated Products; In-kind Services

Corporate Sponsorship

Type: Arts & cultural events; Festivals/fairs; Music & entertainment events

Giving Contact

Rodney Clapp, City Executive
Branch Banking & Trust Co.
351 South Churton Street
P.O. Box 1269
Hillsboro, NC 27278
Phone: (336)733-2000
Fax: (336)644-2003

Description

Organization Type: Corporate Giving Program
Giving Locations: NC; SC; VA
Grant Types: Conference/Seminar, Emergency, General Support.

Financial Summary

Total Giving: Contributes through corporate direct giving program only.

Typical Recipients

Arts & Humanities: Arts & Humanities-General
Civic & Public Affairs: Civic & Public Affairs-General
Education: Education-General
Health: Health-General
Social Services: Social Services-General

Application Procedures

Initial Contact: letter of inquiry
Application Requirements: a description of organization, amount requested, purpose of funds sought, recently audited financial statement, and proof of tax-exempt status
Deadlines: None.

Restrictions

Company gives locally only.

Corporate Officials

John Andrew Allison, IV: chairman, chief executive officer, director B Charlotte, NC 1948. ED University of North Carolina BBA (1971); Duke University (1973); Rutgers University Stonier Graduate School of Banking (1981). PRIM CORP EMPL chairman, chief executive officer, director: BB&T Corp. CORP AFFIL chairman, chief executive officer: BB&T Financial Corp.; chairman, chief executive officer, director: Branch Banking & Trust Co. NONPR AFFIL member: American Bankers Association; member: Bankers Roundtable.
Scott Eldridge Reed: senior executive vice president, chief financial officer B Chicago, IL 1948. ED Wake Forest University BS (1970); University of North Carolina MBA (1972). PRIM CORP EMPL senior executive vice president, chief financial officer: Branch Banking & Trust Co. CORP AFFIL director: Craigie Inc.; director: Goddard Technology Corp.; treasurer, director: BB&T Savings Corp.; treasurer: Carba Realty Inc.; senior executive vice president, chief financial officer: BB&T Corp.; treasurer: BB&T Financial Corp. of SC; treasurer: 150 Corp.
Henry Gaston Williamson, Jr.: chief operating officer B Whiteville, NC 1947. ED East Carolina University BSBA (1969); East Carolina University MBA (1972); University of North Carolina (1979). PRIM CORP EMPL chief operating officer: Branch Banking & Trust Co. CORP AFFIL president: BB&T Financial Corp. of SC; director: BB&T Financial Corp. NONPR AFFIL director: East Carolina University; member: Omicron Delta Epsilon; member executive committee, director: Boy Scouts America East Carolina Council; director: BB&T Center Leadership Development; member: Beta Gamma Sigma; director: ARC, Wilson County Chapter. CLUB AFFIL Kiwanis Club; Wilson Country Club.

BRIDGESTONE/ FIRESTONE, INC.

Company Contact

Nashville, TN
Web: http://www.bridgestone-firestone.com

Company Description

Employees: 45,000
SIC(s): 2296 Tire Cord & Fabrics, 3011 Tires & Inner Tubes, 3069 Fabricated Rubber Products Nec, 5014 Tires & Tubes.
Parent Company: Bridgestone Corp., 10-1 Kyobashi 1-chome, chuo-ku, Tokyo, 104, Japan

Operating Locations

AR: Bridgestone/Firestone, Inc., Russellville; Firestone Tube Co., Russellville; CA: Bridgestone/Firestone, Inc., Irvine; Bridgestone Cycle (U.S.A.), San Leandro; FL: Bridgestone/Firestone, Inc., Mary Esther, West Palm Beach; GA: Bridgestone/Firestone, Inc., Marietta, Norcross, Tucker; IA: Bridgestone/Firestone, Inc., Des Moines; Firestone Agricultural Tire Co., Des Moines; IL: Bridgestone/Firestone, Inc., Bloomington, Decatur; American Tire & Service Co., Rolling Meadows; Bridgestone/Firestone, Inc., Rolling Meadows; Bridgestone/Firestone Retail Operations, Rolling Meadows; IN: Firestone Building Products Co., Carmel; Firestone Industrial Products Co., Carmel; Bridgestone/Firestone, Inc., Indianapolis; MA: Bridgestone/Firestone, Inc., Quincy; MI: Bridgestone/Firestone, Inc., Southfield; Bridgestone/Firestone Original Equipment Tire Sales Co., Southfield; MN: Bridgestone/Firestone, Inc., Minneapolis; NC: Firestone Fibers & Textiles Co., Kings Mountain; Bridgestone/Firestone, Inc., Wilson; NY: Bridgestone/Firestone, Inc., Clifton Park; OH: Bridgestone/Firestone, Inc., Akron; Bridgestone/Firestone Information Services Co., Akron; Bridgestone/Firestone Research Laboratories, Akron; Bridgestone/Firestone Technology Co., Akron; Firestone Synthetic Rubber & Latex Co., Akron; Bridgestone/Firestone Credit Services Co., Brook Park; OK: Bridgestone/Firestone, Inc., Oklahoma City; Dayton Tire, Oklahoma City; TN: Bridgestone/Firestone, Inc., LaVergne; Bridgestone/Firestone, Nashville; Bridgestone/Firestone, Inc., Nashville; Bridgestone/Firestone Off Road Tire Co., Nashville; Bridgestone/Firestone Tire Manufacturing Operations, Nashville; Bridgestone/Firestone Tire Sales Co., Nashville; TX: Bridgestone/Firestone, Inc., Corpus Christi, Grand Prairie, Houston
Note: Also operate in Canada, Mexico, Europe, South and Central America, Liberia, and Singapore.

Corporate Sponsorship

Type: Sports events
Note: Sponsors motor sports racing.

The Bridgestone/ Firestone Trust Fund

Giving Contact

Bernice Csaszar, Administrator
Bridgestone/Firestone Trust Fund
50 Century Boulevard
Nashville, TN 37214
Phone: (615)872-1415
Fax: (615)872-1414
Email: bfstrustfund@bfsusa.com

Description

Founded: 1952
EIN: 346505181
Organization Type: Corporate Foundation
Giving Locations: headquarters and operating communities.
Grant Types: Capital, Challenge, Employee Matching Gifts, General Support, Operating Expenses, Project, Scholarship, Seed Money.

Giving Philosophy

'Bridgestone/Firestone is committed to being a good corporate citizen nationally, regionally and, especially, in the communities where it has manufacturing plants, sales facilities and offices. .. Contributions are made to achieve the corporate objectives of the company, while increasing goodwill and positive awareness of the company and its employees. Special consideration is given to organizations to which employees give their money and volunteer their time to improve the communities where they live and work.'
Guidelines for Charitable Giving

Financial Summary

Total Giving: $5,000,000 (2000 approx); $3,500,000 (1999 approx); $2,611,336 (1998). Note: Contributes through foundation only.
Giving Analysis: Giving for 1997 includes: foundation ($1,538,677); foundation grants to United Way ($409,837); 1998: foundation ($2,139,548); foundation grants to United Way ($471,788)
Assets: $67,994,672 (1998); $37,495,099 (1997); $30,450,551 (1996)

Typical Recipients

Arts & Humanities: Arts Associations & Councils, Arts Institutes, Arts Outreach, Ballet, Community Arts, Dance, Arts & Humanities-General, Historic Preservation, Libraries, Museums/Galleries, Music, Opera, Public Broadcasting, Theater
Civic & Public Affairs: African American Affairs, Business/Free Enterprise, Civil Rights, Community Foundations, Economic Development, Employment/Job Training, Civic & Public Affairs-General, Housing, Law & Justice, Professional & Trade Associations, Public Policy, Rural Affairs, Urban & Community Affairs, Zoos/Aquariums
Education: Agricultural Education, Arts/Humanities Education, Business Education, Colleges & Universities, Community & Junior Colleges, Economic Education, Education Funds, Engineering/Technological Education, International Studies, Medical Education, Minority Education, Public Education (Precollege), Religious Education, Science/Mathematics Education, Special Education, Student Aid, Vocational & Technical Education
Environment: Environment-General
Health: Children's Health/Hospitals, Emergency/Ambulance Services, Health Organizations, Hospices, Hospitals, Medical Research, Nursing Services, Single-Disease Health Associations
Religion: Ministries
Science: Scientific Centers & Institutes, Scientific Organizations
Social Services: At-Risk Youth, Child Welfare, Community Centers, Community Service Organizations, Emergency Relief, Family Planning, Family Services, People with Disabilities, Recreation & Athletics, Scouts, Senior Services, Substance Abuse, United Funds/United Ways, Volunteer Services, Youth Organizations

Contributions Analysis

Giving Priorities: Education, hospitals, united funds, welfare programs, civic and environmental improvement, and cultural programs.
Arts & Humanities: 16%. Primarily gives to arts councils and institutions.
Civic & Public Affairs: 7%. Supports community and neighborhood improvement, environment and energy conservation, law and justice, housing and urban revitalization, civil rights and equal opportunity, voter registration and education, and job training.
Education: 25%. Priorities include colleges, universities, and youth development programs. Contributions support programs that assure availability of trained persons, encourage research in areas relevant to the corporation, and promote excellence. Other interests include education-related organizations that expand public knowledge of the free enterprise system; public and private higher education; adult education programs; fellowships; and scholarships. Also sponsors employee matching gifts program.
Health: 4%. Contributes to organizations that provide adequate health care for employees and their communities, and that promote the development of new approaches to health needs.
Science: 3%.
Social Services: 45%. Supports the United Way, youth and community groups.
Note: Total contributions made in 1998.

Application Procedures

Initial Contact: Send a brief letter or proposal; organizations in communities where Bridgestone/Firestone operates should write to local major facility.
Application Requirements: Include a description of organization, amount requested, purpose of funds sought, recently audited financial statement, proof of tax-exempt status, 501(C)(3) Federation IRS Form 990 or letter, board of directors, current operating budget, and list of major donors, including each of their contributions.
Deadlines: None.
Review Process: proposals are reviewed upon receipt; those proposals meeting basic criteria are held for review by the committee that meets several times a year; applicants are notified of committee's decision

Restrictions

Recipients must have 501(c)(3) status and must operate in accordance with the principle of equal opportunity.
Grants do not support groups that discriminate, partisan political organizations, or groups limited to a single religious organization.

Additional Information

In 1992, the company relocated its corporate headquarters from Akron, OH, to Nashville, TN.
In 1989, Bridgestone U.S.A., Inc., merged with Firestone Tire & Rubber Co. to become Bridgestone/Firestone, Inc., a wholly owned subsidiary of Bridgestone Corp. of Japan.
Publications: Guidelines

Corporate Officials

Tetsuo Ando: chief financial officer, executive vice president, treasurer B Tokyo, Japan 1941. ED Keio Gijyuka University (1964). PRIM CORP EMPL chief financial officer, executive vice president, treasurer: Bridgestone/Firestone, Inc.
Masatoshi Ono: chairman, chief executive officer B 1937. ED Kumamoto University (Japan) BS (1959). PRIM CORP EMPL chairman, chief executive officer: Bridgestone/Firestone, Inc.
Kenji Shibata: president PRIM CORP EMPL president: Bridgestone/Firestone, Inc.

Foundation Officials

Bernice Csaszar: administrator

Grants Analysis

Disclosure Period: calendar year ending 1998
Total Grants: $2,139,548*
Number of Grants: 1,128 (approx)
Average Grant: $1,897
Highest Grant: $125,000
Typical Range: $100 to $5,000
***Note:** Giving excludes United Way.

Recent Grants

Note: Grants derived from 1997 Form 990.

Arts & Humanities

54,000 Educational Television Association, Cleveland, OH
20,000 Cleveland Museum of Art, Cleveland, OH
15,000 Nashville Opera Association, Nashville, TN
15,000 National Public Radio, Washington, DC
12,500 Nashville Symphony Association, Nashville, TN
12,500 Tennessee Repertory Theater, Nashville, TN
10,000 Nashville Ballet, Nashville, TN
10,000 Tennessee State Museum, Nashville, TN
7,500 Automotive Hall of Fame, Midland, MI
5,500 Lake Charles Symphony, Lake Charles, LA

Civic & Public Affairs

30,000 American Truck Stop Foundation, Alexandria, VA
25,000 Los Angeles Urban League, Los Angeles, CA
20,000 Society of Automotive Engineers, Warrendale, PA
12,000 Arkansas Agriculture Development Council, AR
10,000 Middle Tennessee Community Foundation, Nashville, TN
10,000 National Future Farmers of America Foundation, Madison, WI
10,000 Tennessee Foundation, TN
10,000 Tennessee Ocoee Development Agency, TN

Education

48,175 National Merit Scholarship Corporation, Evanston, IL
38,000 National Future Farmers of America Foundation, Madison, WI
35,000 National 4-H Council, Chevy Chase, MD
16,000 McNeese State University Foundation, Lake Charles, LA
11,400 National Future Farmers of America Foundation, Madison, WI
10,000 College Fund
10,000 Jef Krosnoff Memorial Trust Scholarship
10,000 Junior Achievement, Akron, OH
10,000 Motlow College Foundation, Tullahoma, TN
10,000 University of Washington Foundation, Seattle, WA
9,600 Accreditation Board
6,000 University of Akron, Akron, OH
5,050 Ursinus College, Collegeville, PA

Social Services

100,000 Akron Golf Charities Foundation, Akron, OH
55,000 United Way Central Iowa, Des Moines, IA

55,000 United Way Summit County, Akron, OH
50,700 United Way Middle Tennessee, Nashville, TN
40,000 Springhouse Golf Classic Corporation, Nashville, TN
35,000 United Way, Oklahoma City, OK
35,000 United Way Decatur/Macon County, Decatur, IL
35,000 United Way Wilson County, Wilson, NC
20,379 United Way Southeastern Michigan, MI
19,500 United Way, Oklahoma City, OK
19,400 United Way Southeastern Michigan, MI
12,000 Warren County United Way
11,000 United Way Crusade of Mercy, Chicago, IL
10,000 United Way Gaston County, Gastonia, NC
8,300 United Way Central Indiana, Indianapolis, IN
8,000 United Way McLean County, Bloomington, IL
7,000 United Way Southwest Louisiana, Lake Charles, LA
6,000 United Way Orange County
5,000 Boy Scouts of America Great Trail Council

BRIGGS &STRATTON CORP.

Company Contact

Milwaukee, WI
Web: http://www.briggsandstratton.com

Company Description

Employees: 7,615 (1999)
SIC(s): 3519 Internal Combustion Engines Nec.

Nonmonetary Support

Value: $89,807 (1994); $109,485 (1989); $117,638 (1988)
Type: Donated Products
Note: Nonmonetary support has been provided in the past by the company. Support is primarily donated engines.

Briggs & Stratton Corp. Foundation

Giving Contact

Kasandra K. Preston, Secretary & Treasurer
Briggs & Stratton Corp. Foundation
12301 W Wirth St.
Wauwatosa, WI 53222
Phone: (414)259-5333
Fax: (414)259-5773

Description

EIN: 396040377
Organization Type: Corporate Foundation
Giving Locations: WI: Milwaukee principally near operating locations and to national organizations.
Grant Types: Capital, General Support, Scholarship.
Note: Scholarships are for children of employees only.

Financial Summary

Total Giving: $1,304,930 (fiscal year ending November 30, 1998); $1,462,800 (fiscal 1997); $2,363,325 (fiscal 1996). Note: Contributes through corporate direct giving program and foundation.
Giving Analysis: Giving for fiscal 1996 includes: foundation ($2,125,325); foundation grants to United Way ($238,000); fiscal 1997: foundation ($1,060,300); foundation grants to United Way ($266,000); foundation scholarships ($136,500); fiscal 1998: foundation ($1,038,930); foundation grants to United Way ($266,000)
Assets: $15,594,110 (fiscal 1998); $15,614,708 (fiscal 1997); $112,673,419 (fiscal 1996)
Gifts Received: $1,100,000 (fiscal 1998); $1,250,000 (fiscal 1997); $298,800 (fiscal 1991). Note: Contributions are received from Briggs & Stratton Corp.

Typical Recipients

Arts & Humanities: Arts Festivals, Arts Funds, Arts Institutes, Ballet, Community Arts, Dance, Arts & Humanities-General, Historic Preservation, Museums/Galleries, Music, Performing Arts, Public Broadcasting, Theater
Civic & Public Affairs: African American Affairs, Community Foundations, Economic Development, Civic & Public Affairs-General, Municipalities/Towns, Parades/Festivals, Philanthropic Organizations, Professional & Trade Associations, Rural Affairs, Safety, Urban & Community Affairs
Education: Agricultural Education, Business Education, Colleges & Universities, Community & Junior Colleges, Education Associations, Education Reform, Engineering/Technological Education, Education-General, Leadership Training, Medical Education, Minority Education, Private Education (Precollege), Public Education (Precollege), Science/Mathematics Education, Social Sciences Education, Student Aid, Vocational & Technical Education
Environment: Environment-General, Resource Conservation
Health: Children's Health/Hospitals, Health-General, Health Funds, Health Organizations, Heart, Long-Term Care, Nursing Services, Speech & Hearing, Trauma Treatment
International: International Peace & Security Issues, International Relations
Science: Science Exhibits & Fairs, Science Museums, Scientific Centers & Institutes, Scientific Organizations
Social Services: Animal Protection, Big Brother/Big Sister, Child Welfare, Community Centers, Community Service Organizations, Counseling, Day Care, Food/Clothing Distribution, Scouts, Social Services-General, Substance Abuse, United Funds/United Ways, YMCA/YWCA/YMHA/YWHA, Youth Organizations

Contributions Analysis

Giving Priorities: United funds and the performing arts.
Arts & Humanities: 30% to 35%. Supports the United Performing Arts Fund, museums and public television.
Civic & Public Affairs: 5% to 10%. Supports development projects in Milwaukee encompassing economic development and public policy. Other interests include business and free enterprise.
Education: About 25%. Support includes funding for scholarships to employees' children. Other interests include colleges and universities, schools in communities where the company has plants, precollege programs, and agricultural education.
Health: Less than 1%. Supports united funds.
Social Services: About 30%.
Note: Total contributions in fiscal 1998.

Application Procedures

Initial Contact: Send brief letter or proposal.
Application Requirements: Include a description of organization and purpose, amount requested, income statement, and balance sheet information, as well as forecasts, if possible; include proof of tax-exempt status.
Deadlines: May and October.
Decision Notification: Decisions are generally made at the end of June and November.

Restrictions

Contributions are not made to individuals, religious organizations, dinners or special events, fraternal organizations, goodwill advertising, or political or lobbying groups.

Additional Information

Foundation is in the process of restructuring its giving program.

Corporate Officials

John Stephen Shiely: president, chief operating officer, director B Saint Paul, MN 1952. ED University of Notre Dame BBA (1974); Marquette University JD (1977); Northwestern University MBA (1990). PRIM CORP EMPL president, chief operating officer, director: Briggs & Stratton Corp. CORP AFFIL director: Quad Graphics Inc.; director: Saint Charles Inc.; director: Consolidated Papers Inc.; director: MI Marshall Ilsley Bank. NONPR AFFIL director: Childrens Hospital Wisconsin; board regents: Milwaukee School Engineering; member: American Corporate Counsel Association; member: Association for Corporate Growth.
Frederick Prescott Stratton, Jr.: chairman, chief executive officer, director B Milwaukee, WI 1939. ED Yale University BS (1961); Stanford University MBA (1963). PRIM CORP EMPL chairman, chief executive officer, director: Briggs & Stratton Corp. CORP AFFIL director: WI Electric Power Co.; director: WI Energy Corp.; director: Weyco Group Inc.; director: Midwest Express Airlines Inc.; director: Midwest Express Holdings Inc.; director: Banc One Corp.

Foundation Officials

Kasandra K. Preston: secretary, treasurer, director
John Stephen Shiely: vice president, director (see above)
Frederick Prescott Stratton, Jr.: president, director (see above)

Grants Analysis

Disclosure Period: fiscal year ending November 30, 1998
Total Grants: $1,038,930*
Number of Grants: 108
Average Grant: $9,620
Highest Grant: $212,500
Typical Range: $500 to $10,000
***Note:** Giving excludes United Way.

Recent Grants

Note: Grants derived from fiscal 1998 Form 990.

Arts & Humanities

125,400 United Performing Arts Fund, Milwaukee, WI -- arts groups
100,000 Milwaukee Art Museum, Milwaukee, WI -- Capital contribution
32,500 Milwaukee Ballet, Milwaukee, WI
25,000 Milwaukee Symphony Orchestra, Milwaukee, WI
20,000 Milwaukee Repertory Theater, Milwaukee, WI
15,000 Milwaukee Public Museum, Inc., Milwaukee, WI
10,000 Milwaukee Art Museum, Milwaukee, WI
7,800 Channel 10/36 Friends, Milwaukee, WI -- Support public television
7,500 Milwaukee Chamber Theater, Milwaukee, WI

Civic & Public Affairs

25,000 Village Foundation, Alexandria, VA
20,200 National FFA Foundation, Madison, WI -- Fruit & Proficiency Awards
15,000 EAA Aviation Foundation, Inc., Oshkosh, WI -- Program support
10,000 Milwaukee Redevelopment Corporation, Milwaukee, WI -- Economic Development

7,500 Milwaukee World Festival, Inc., Milwaukee, WI -- Summerfest

Education

100,000 Youth Leadership Academy, Inc., Milwaukee, WI
50,000 Partners Advancing Values in Education, Inc. (PAVE), St. Francis, WI -- scholarship program
12,500 Three Rivers Community College, Poplar Bluff, MO -- capital contribution
10,000 Greater Milwaukee Education, Inc., Milwaukee, WI
10,000 Inroads, Inc., St. Louis, MO
10,000 Marquette University, Milwaukee, WI -- Washington Center for Covernment
10,000 Milwaukee School of Engineering, Milwaukee, WI
10,000 Mount Mary College, Milwaukee, WI -- Capital contribution
10,000 Murray State University Foundation, Murray, KY -- College of Industry & Technology
10,000 University School Milwaukee Corporation, Milwaukee, WI -- tuition scholarship for minority student
10,000 UWM Foundation, Milwaukee, WI
7,500 Junior Achievement of SE Wisconsin Foundation, Milwaukee, WI
7,500 Poplar Bluff Public Schools, Poplar Bluff, MO
6,000 Ogeechee Tech Foundation, Inc., GA -- *GCI Statesboro
5,000 Connecticut College, New London, CT
5,000 George Mason University Foundation, Haverford, PA -- Project support
5,000 Georgia Southern College, Statesboro, GA -- Program support
5,000 Yale University, New Haven, CT

Environment

12,500 Natural Resources Foundation of Wisconsin, Madison, WI -- besadny conservation grants program
10,000 Taliesin Preservation Commission, Inc., Spring Green, WI -- preservation program

Health

6,000 Wisconsin Society for Brain Injured Children, Milwaukee, WI
5,000 Center for the Deaf and Hard of Hearing, Brookfield, WI

International

30,000 Hoover Institution on War, Revolution & Peace, Stanford, CA -- Economic research

Science

10,000 Science, Economics & Tech. Center, Milwaukee, WI -- Discovery World Museum

Social Services

212,500 United Way of Greater Milwaukee, Inc., Milwaukee, WI -- Assist agencies providing health & social services
15,000 St. Ann Center for Intergenerational Care, Milwaukee, WI -- Capital contribution
15,000 United Fund of Poplar Bluff & Butler County, Poplar Bluff, MO -- Assist agencies providing health & social services
15,000 United Way - Murray/Calloway County, Murray, KY -- Assist agencies providing health & social services
14,500 United Way - Lee County, Inc., Auburn, AL -- Assist agencies providing health & social services
12,500 Wisconsin Humane Society, Milwaukee, WI -- Capital contribution
11,500 United Way - Rolla, Rolla, MO -- Assist agencies providing health & social services
10,000 Big Brothers/Big Sisters of Metropolitan Milwaukee, Milwaukee, WI -- Program support
10,000 United Way - Statesboro, Statesboro, GA -- Assist agencies providing health & social services
10,000 YMCA, Milwaukee, WI -- Capital contribution
7,500 United Community Center, Inc., Milwaukee, WI -- Capital contribution
5,680 Girl Scouts of Milwaukee Area, Milwaukee, WI -- Program support

Bristol-Myers Squibb Co.

★ Number 41 of Top 100 Corporate Givers

Company Contact

345 Park Avenue
New York, NY 10154
Phone: (212)546-4000
Fax: (212)546-9574
Web: http://www.bms.com

Company Description

Revenue: US$18,283,600,000
Profit: US$3,141,200,000
Employees: 54,000
Fortune Rank: 78, per FORTUNE Magazine's list of 500 Largest U.S. Corporations (1999).
FF 78
SIC(s): 2099 Food Preparations Nec, 2834 Pharmaceutical Preparations, 3841 Surgical & Medical Instruments, 3999 Manufacturing Industries Nec.

Operating Locations

Australia: Bristol-Myers Squibb Australia Pty. Ltd., Noble Park; Bristol-Myers Superannuation Ltd., Noble Park; Belgium: Bristol-Myers Squibb International Corp. Societe de Droit Americain, Brussels, Brabant; Canada: Zimmer of Canada Ltd., Mississauga; Bristol-Myers Squibb Canada, Montreal; Colombia: Mead Johnson Intl Ltd., Bogota, Cundinamarco; Bristol-Myers Squibb SA, Cali, Valle del Cauca; Czech Republic: Convatec, Prague; Ecuador: Bristol-Myers Ecuatoriana SA, Guayaquil, Guayas; Mead Johnson (Ecuador) SA, Guayaquil, Guayas; Egypt: Bristol-Myers Squibb Egypt SAE, Cairo, Al Qahirah; France: Laboratoires Guieu France, Nanterre, Hauts-de-Seine; Orpex, Paris, Ville-de-Paris; Complements Alimentaires (Ste. Francaise de), Puteaux, Hauts-de-Seine; Greece: Mead Johnson SA, Athens, Attiki; Hong Kong: Squibb (Far East) Ltd., Aberdeen, Grampian; Bristol-Myers Squibb (Hong Kong) Ltd., North Point; Carmen (Hong Kong) Ltd., Wong Chuk Hang; Hungary: Pharmavit Gyogyszer-es Elemiszeripariresvenytarsasag, Veresegyhaz, Pest; Indonesia: PT Squibb Indonesia, Jakarta, Jakarta Raya; Italy: Mead Johnson SpA, Anagni, Lazio; Clairol International SRL, Milano, Lombardia; Laboratori Guieu SpA, Milano, Lombardia; Bristol-Myers Squibb SpA, Roma, Lazio; Zimmer SRL, San Giuliano Milanese; Jamaica: Mead Johnson Jamaica Ltd., Kingston; Japan: Bristol-Myers (Japan) Ltd., Tokyo; Bristol-Myers Squibb KK, Tokyo; Mexico: Clairol de Mexico SA de CV, Ciudad de Mexico; Bristol-Myers de Mexico SA de CV, Mexico; Mead Johnson de Mexico SA de CV, Mexico; Malaysia: Bristol-Myers Squibb (Malaysia) Sdn. Bhd., Shah Alam, Selangor; Netherlands: Zimmer BV, Amersfoort, Utrecht; Listo BV, Amsterdam, Noord-Holland; Mead Johnson BV, Nijmegen, Gelderland; Bristol-Myers BV, Weesp, Noord-Holland; Apothecon BV, Woerden, Utrecht; Bristol-Myers Squibb Holdings BV, Woerden, Utrecht; New Zealand: Bristol-Myers Squibb (New Zealand) Ltd., Auckland; Panama: Bristol Laboratories International SA, Colon; Peru: Bristol-Myers Squibb Peru SA, Lima; Manufactureros Quimicos Farmaceuticos SA, Lima; Philippines: ER Squibb & Sons Philippines Corp., Makati, Rizal; Bristol Laboratories, Manino, Manila; Portugal: Heyden Farmaceutica Portuguesa Lda., Lisboa; Mead Johnson Farmaceutica Lda., Lisboa; Bristol-Myers Squibb Farmaceutica Portuguesa Lda., Paco de Arcos, Oeiras; Singapore: Bristol-Myers Squibb (Singapore) Pte. Ltd., Singapore; Zimmer Pte. Ltd., Singapore; Spain: Zimmer SA, Barcelona, Cataluna; Bristol-Myers SA, Madrid; Immobiliaria y de Construcciones SA, Madrid; Squibb Industria Farmaceutica SA, Madrid; Convatec SA, Sant Just Desvern, Cataluna; Sweden: Bristol Laboratorier AB; Bristol-Myers Squibb AB, Bromma, Stockholm; Switzerland: Bristol-Myers Squibb AG, Baar, Zug; Bristol-Myers Squibb Products SA, Baar, Zug; Intrafin SA, Baar, Zug; Thailand: Squibb (Thailand) Ltd., Bangkok; Trinidad and Tobago: Bristol-Myers Co., Trincity; Taiwan: Bristol-Myers Squibb (Taiwan) Ltd., Taipei; Venezuela: Bristol-Myers Squibb de Venezuela SA, Caracas; Laboraros Bristol de Venezuela SA, Caracas; Mead Johnson de Venezuela SA, Caracas

Nonmonetary Support

Value: $35,000,000 (2000 approx); $30,000,000 (1997); $40,000,000 (1996)
Type: Donated Products
Note: Contact local operating facilities for local nonmonetary giving. Contact Frank Cifuni at the Edition, NJ, facility for international product requests.

Bristol-Myers Squibb Foundation Inc.

Giving Contact

Bristol-Myers Squibb Foundation, Inc.
Web: http://www.bms.com/aboutbms/founda/data/founda.html

Description

Founded: 1990
EIN: 133127947
Organization Type: Corporate Foundation
Giving Locations: headquarters and operating communities; internationally; nationally.
Grant Types: Employee Matching Gifts, General Support, Project, Research.
Note: Employee matching gift ratio: 1 to 1.

Giving Philosophy

'The Bristol-Myers Squibb Foundation, Inc., through philanthropic giving supports the Bristol-Myers Squibb Company's mission to help extend and enhance human life. For over 40 years, the Foundation has invested in a broad range of programs that address important health and social issues, and that help serve the needs of society, particularly in communities where the company's employees live and work. Key funding initiatives include the Unrestricted Biomedical Research Grants Program, which supports leading research institutions throughout the world; Women's Health Education, which seeks to improve the quality of math and science education; and a broad range of programs in communities where Bristol-Myers Squibb offices, manufacturing facilities and research centers are located.' *1996 Report of Charitable Contributions*

Financial Summary

Total Giving: $29,122,295 (1999); $24,728,932 (1998); $54,728,932 (1997). Note: Contributes through corporate direct giving program and foundation. Giving includes corporate direct giving, foundation, domestic subsidiaries, international subsidiaries, nonmonetary support.
Giving Analysis: Giving for 1998 includes: corporate direct giving ($12,790,571); foundation ($11,938,361)
Assets: $1,478,576 (1997); $1,824,922 (1995); $5,161,540 (1994)
Gifts Received: $8,000,000 (1997); $8,500,000 (1995); $12,000,000 (1994)

Typical Recipients

Arts & Humanities: Arts Associations & Councils, Arts Centers, Arts Funds, Arts Institutes, Arts Outreach, Historic Preservation, Libraries, Museums/Galleries, Music, Opera, Performing Arts, Public Broadcasting, Theater

Civic & Public Affairs: African American Affairs, Botanical Gardens/Parks, Business/Free Enterprise, Community Foundations, Economic Development, Employment/Job Training, Civic & Public Affairs-General, Housing, Law & Justice, Municipalities/Towns, Professional & Trade Associations, Public Policy, Rural Affairs, Safety, Urban & Community Affairs, Zoos/Aquariums

Education: Arts/Humanities Education, Business Education, Colleges & Universities, Education Funds, Education Reform, Legal Education, Medical Education, Minority Education, Private Education (Precollege), Religious Education, Social Sciences Education, Special Education, Student Aid

Environment: Air/Water Quality, Environment-General

Health: AIDS/HIV, Cancer, Children's Health/Hospitals, Clinics/Medical Centers, Diabetes, Emergency/Ambulance Services, Geriatric Health, Health Organizations, Heart, Hospitals, Medical Rehabilitation, Medical Research, Medical Training, Nutrition, Research/Studies Institutes, Transplant Networks/Donor Banks

International: Foreign Educational Institutions, Health Care/Hospitals, International Affairs, International Organizations, International Relations, Missionary/Religious Activities

Religion: Jewish Causes, Missionary Activities (Domestic), Religious Welfare

Science: Science Museums, Scientific Centers & Institutes, Scientific Organizations, Scientific Research

Social Services: Community Service Organizations, Crime Prevention, Food/Clothing Distribution, People with Disabilities, Recreation & Athletics, Shelters/Homelessness, Substance Abuse, United Funds/United Ways, Volunteer Services, Youth Organizations

Contributions Analysis

Giving Priorities: Medical research, health care, education, community development, cultural institutions, and international affairs. Company is committed to charitable contributions where company does business. It's international business managers provide direct support to appropriate local institutions and organizations. Recipient organizations are not tracked. Requests from U.S.-based organizations for support of activities with a global focus are reviewed by the foundation. Support is limited to special programs or individual projects which relate to existing areas of interest, which include medical research and health. Research facilities throughout the world have received grants through the Nutrition Research Grant Program and the Cancer Research Grant Program. In 1995, approximately 25% of contributions were to international organizations.

Arts & Humanities: 5% to 10%. Provides support on very selective basis to prominent cultural institutions. Emphasis is on nationally recognized performing arts centers and major natural history, science, and art museums. Also considers organizations with broad appeal in operating communities.

Civic & Public Affairs: 20% to 25%. Seeks to support organizations that help strengthen economic and community development and provide equal opportunity and job training for socially disadvantaged groups, as well as to improve operation of our system of law and justice. Also supports united funds and public policy research that advances understanding of the free enterprise system. Other interests include youth, the aged, and the disabled.

Education: 25% to 30%. Directs support toward: advancement of higher education; math and science education; independent state and regional associations; graduate schools of business with which company coordinates recruitment programs; programs widening opportunities for minorities and women; schools with programs of special interest to company and divisions; and selected national programs to advance and improve quality of education and broaden educational opportunities. Also emphasizes support for secondary education, particularly programs that focus onmath, science, and health education, and the shortage of qualified teachers in these subjects.

Health: 35% to 40%. Select grants to support unrestricted medical research at leading national and international institutions. Since 1977, company has committed funding through its unrestricted grant programs to support research in cancer, nutrition, orthopedics, cardiovascular medicine and related metabolic diseases, infectious diseases, and neuroscience. Has established a Women's Health Education Initiative. Funding also goes to research into alternatives to the use of animals in testing. Other health interests include hospitals, and organizations working to solve administrative, economic, and public policy problems in health care in areas ofcompany operations. No grants are made available for individual research projects.

International: About 20%. Spread across all categories. International business managers provide support for appropriate local institutions and organizations.

Application Procedures

Initial Contact: brief letter or proposal

Application Requirements: brief statement of history, goals, and accomplishments to date; amount requested; purpose of funds sought; list of current funding sources; recently audited financial statement; current year's operating budget; current annual report; list of board members; proof of tax-exempt status; most recent IRS Form 990

Deadlines: by October 1; organizations should not submit more than one grant application in a 12-month period

Restrictions

The foundation does not support individual medical research; conferences, special events, or videos; sponsorships; political, fraternal, social, or veterans organizations; religious or sectarian activities, unless they benefit entire community; organizations funded through federated campaigns; endowments; or courtesy advertising.

Additional Information

Organizations located in communities where the company maintains facilities may apply directly to the local office.

Publications: Report of Charitable Contributions

Corporate Officials

Harrison MacKellar Bains, Jr.: vice president, treasurercorporate environmental affairs B Pasadena, CA 1943. ED University of Redlands BA (1964); University of California MBA (1966); Harvard University Graduate School of Business Administration (1983). PRIM CORP EMPL vice president, treasurer: Bristol-Myers Squibb Co. ADD CORP EMPL treasurer: Boclaro Inc.; treasurer: Bristol Caribbean Inc.; treasurer: Bristol-Myers Squibb Laboratories; treasurer: Squibb Manufacturing Inc. NONPR AFFIL treasurer: Food Safety Council; member: National Association of Corporate Treasurers; member: Financial Executives Institute.

Alice C. Brennan: vice president, secretary B Ilion, NY 1953. ED Columbia University MA; Skidmore College BA (1975); Hofstra University JD (1981). PRIM CORP EMPL vice president, secretary: Bristol-Myers Squibb Co. NONPR AFFIL director: American Society of Corporate Secretaries.

Charles Andreas Heimbold, Jr.: chairman, president, chief executive officer B Newark, NJ 1933. ED Villanova University BA (1954); The Hague Academy of International Law (1959); University of Pennsylvania LLB (1960); New York University LLM (1966). PRIM CORP EMPL chairman, president, chief executive officer: Bristol-Myers Squibb Co. CORP AFFIL director: ExxonMobil Corp. NONPR AFFIL member, board: University Pennsylvania; chairman board overseers: University Pennsylvania Law School; chairman: Phoenix House Foundation Inc.; member: Commonwealth Fund Commission on Womens Health; trustee: International House; member: Association Bar New York City; trustee: American Museum Natural History. CLUB AFFIL Riverside Yacht Club; member: Causeway Club; River Club.

Michael F. Mee: senior vice president, chief financial officer B Boston, MA 1942. ED Bentley College (1966); University Minnesota MBA (1968); Massachusetts Institute of Technology (1984). PRIM CORP EMPL senior vice president, chief financial officer: Bristol-Myers Squibb Co. NONPR AFFIL member: Conference Boards Council Financial Executives; member board overseers: University Minnesota Carlson School Management. CLUB AFFIL Economic Club New York.

John L. Skule, III: senior vice president corporate environmental affairs PRIM CORP EMPL senior vice president corporate environmental affairs: Bristol-Myers Squibb Co.

Foundation Officials

Harrison MacKellar Bains, Jr.: treasurer (see above)

Alice C. Brennan: secretary (see above)

John L. Damonti: president PRIM CORP EMPL corporate contributions contact: Bristo Myers Squibb Co.

John L. Skule, III: director (see above)

Grants Analysis

Disclosure Period: calendar year ending 1997
Total Grants: $24,728,932*
Number of Grants: 2,000 (approx)
Average Grant: $12,364 (approx)
Typical Range: $1,000 to $10,000
***Note:** Giving excludes nonmonetary support.

Recent Grants

Note: Grants derived from 1997 Form 990.

Arts & Humanities

150,000 Lincoln Center for the Performing Arts, New York, NY
75,000 Kennedy, J.F., Center for the Performing Arts, Washington, DC

Civic & Public Affairs

100,000 New York Botanical Garden, Bronx, NY
50,000 Puerto Rico Foundation, Hato Ray, Puerto Rico

Education

250,000 University of Pennsylvania - Women's Health Report Card, Philadelphia, PA
238,476 National Merit Scholarship, Evanston, IL
100,000 Federal University Rio Grande do Sul-better health for women
100,000 Harvard School of Public Health-better health for women, Boston, MA
100,000 Johns Hopkins School of Public Health-better health for women, Baltimore, MD
100,000 Morehouse Medical School - Medical & Health, Atlanta, GA
100,000 Morehouse Medical School - capital campaign for women's health, Atlanta, GA
100,000 Morehouse School of Medicine - National Campaign-Fundraiser, Atlanta, GA
100,000 Rockefeller University - (BARG/IDC), New York, NY
100,000 University of California, San Diego-Women's Health Initiative, La Jolla, CA
100,000 University of New Mexico School of Medicine-Women's Health, Albuquerque, NM

100,000 University of WA School of Medicine-Better Health for Women, Seattle, WA
50,000 Classroom, Inc., New York, NY
50,000 United Negro College Fund, New York, NY
50,000 University of Pennsylvania - Capital campaign, Philadelphia, PA
25,000 University of Pennsylvania Law School, Philadelphia, PA

Health
160,000 Pharmaceutical Research & Manuf, of America Foundation, Washington, DC
140,000 American Red Cross - Disaster Relief, Washington, DC
130,000 American Italian Cancer Foundation, New York, NY
100,000 Aichi Cancer Center Hospital, Nagoya, Japan
100,000 American Foundation for AIDS Research (AMFAR)-women's health, New York, NY
100,000 Hammersmith Hospital-Royal Postgraduate School/London-cardio, London, England
100,000 Max Planck Institute for Medical Research - Neuroscience, Heidelberg, Germany

International
250,000 China Initiative - Dept. of Int'l Cooperation (MOH), Beijing, People's Republic of China
100,000 Chinese University of Hong Kong - nutrition, Shatin, Hong Kong
100,000 Finsen Institute/Rigshopitalet, Denmark - cancer, Copenhagen, Denmark
100,000 Institute Pasteur, Paris/Infectious disease, Paris, France
100,000 Instituto de Nutricion y Technologia (INTA)/Chile-nutrition, Casilda, Argentina
100,000 Istituto Nazionale Tumori - cancer, Milano, Italy
100,000 Karolinska Insti JTET-Sweden/Infectious Disease, Stockholm, Sweden
100,000 MRC Dunn Nutrition Centre/England Centre, London, England
100,000 University of Lausanne, Switzerland-Cardiovascular, Lausanne, Switzerland
100,000 University of Lausanne, Switzerland-Infectious Disease, Lausanne, Switzerland
100,000 University of Lund/Sweden-Infectious Disease, Lund, Sweden
100,000 University of Nice, France - Neuroscience, Nice, France
100,000 Weizmann Institute, Rehovot, Israel
50,000 Istitute Oriopedici Rizzoli Italy/Orthopaedic, Bologna, Italy
50,000 Universidad de Santiago de Compostela/Spain Ortho, Spain
50,000 University of Adelaide - Australia, Adelaide, SA, Australia
50,000 University of Tokyo - Orthodaedic, Tokyo, Japan

Religion
60,000 Franciscan Sisters of the Poor, New York, NY

Science
400,000 American Museum of Natural History, New York, NY

Social Services
1,020,000 United Way of Tristate, New York, NY -- New York City
150,000 Center on Addiction and Substance Abuse - women's health, New York, NY
75,000 Employee Volunteer Award Program, New York, NY
50,000 Boys and Girls Clubs of America, New York, NY
50,000 Partnership for Drug Free America, New York, NY

Broderbund Software, Inc.

Company Contact
Novato, CA
Web: http://www.broderbund.com

Company Description
Former Name: Broderbund Corp.
Employees: 1,129
SIC(s): 3944 Games, Toys & Children's Vehicles, 7372 Prepackaged Software.
Parent Company: The Learning Co.

Broderbund Foundation

Giving Contact
Nancy Klussman
PO Box 10162
San Rafael, CA 94912
Phone: (415)721-4653
Fax: (415)382-4500

Description
Founded: 1988
EIN: 680154752
Organization Type: Corporate Foundation
Giving Locations: CA: San Francisco Bay area
Grant Types: General Support.

Financial Summary
Total Giving: $153,926 (1998); $258,187 (1997); $368,507 (1996). Note: Contributes through foundation only.
Giving Analysis: Giving for 1996 includes: foundation ($341,957); foundation grants to United Way ($26,550); 1997: foundation ($216,012); foundation grants to United Way ($31,750); foundation matching gifts ($10,425); 1998: foundation ($139,416); foundation matching gifts ($14,432); foundation grants to United Way ($78)
Assets: $3,737,711 (1998); $3,677,147 (1997); $3,530,216 (1996)
Gifts Received: $220,216 (1997); $918,000 (1996); $1,419,360 (1995). Note: Contributions were received from the Broderbund Corp.

Typical Recipients
Arts & Humanities: Ethnic & Folk Arts, Libraries, Music, Theater
Civic & Public Affairs: Business/Free Enterprise, Employment/Job Training, Civic & Public Affairs-General, Hispanic Affairs, Native American Affairs, Parades/Festivals, Rural Affairs, Zoos/Aquariums
Education: Arts/Humanities Education, Leadership Training, Literacy, Medical Education, Minority Education, Preschool Education, Public Education (Precollege), Science/Mathematics Education, Secondary Education (Private), Student Aid
Environment: Forestry, Environment-General, Resource Conservation, Wildlife Protection
Health: AIDS/HIV, Cancer, Children's Health/Hospitals, Emergency/Ambulance Services, Hospices, Hospitals, Mental Health, Preventive Medicine/Wellness Organizations, Public Health, Respiratory, Single-Disease Health Associations
International: International Environmental Issues, International Peace & Security Issues
Religion: Ministries, Religious Welfare
Science: Science Museums, Scientific Centers & Institutes
Social Services: Animal Protection, At-Risk Youth, Big Brother/Big Sister, Child Abuse, Child Welfare, Community Service Organizations, Counseling, Day Care, Domestic Violence, Family Services, Food/Clothing Distribution, People with Disabilities, Senior Services, Sexual Abuse, Shelters/Homelessness, Special Olympics, Substance Abuse, United Funds/United Ways, Volunteer Services, Youth Organizations

Contributions Analysis
Giving Priorities: Social Services, health, and education.
Arts & Humanities: 4%. Supports orchestras and museums.
Civic & Public Affairs: 4%. Funds festivals and general civil service organizations.
Education: 11%. Supports primary and secondary education, colleges, and literacy initiatives.
Environment: 4%. Funds animal and environmental protection organizations.
Health: 37%. Supports single-disease health organizations.
Religion: 1%. Supports religious welfare organizations.
Social Services: 39%. Funds youth organizations, food bank, and family services.
Note: Total contributions made in 1998.

Application Procedures
Initial Contact: Send a brief letter of inquiry.
Application Requirements: Include the organization's statement of purpose, amount requested, and proof of tax-exempt status.
Deadlines: None.
Evaluative Criteria: Employee involvement is a consideration. Preference is given to health, social welfare, and environmental organizations in the San Francisco Bay area.

Corporate Officials
Douglas G. Carlston: chairman, chief operating officer PRIM CORP EMPL chairman: Broderbund Software Inc.
Joseph P. Durrett: chief executive officer B 1945. ED Duke University BA; University of Pennsylvania MBA. PRIM CORP EMPL chief executive officer: Broderbund Software Inc.
William M. McDonagh: president, chief operating officer PRIM CORP EMPL president, chief operating officer: Broderbund Software Inc.

Foundation Officials
Douglas G. Carlston: president, director (see above)
Erin G. Carlston: director
William M. McDonagh: director (see above)
Patsy Murphy: secretary, director

Grants Analysis
Disclosure Period: calendar year ending 1998
Total Grants: $139,416*
Number of Grants: 37
Average Grant: $3,768
Highest Grant: $16,667
Typical Range: $100 to $10,000
***Note:** Giving excludes matching gifts; United Way.

Recent Grants
Note: Grants derived from 1997 Form 990.

Arts & Humanities
3,000 Marin Museum of the American Indian, Novato, CA -- support educational programs
1,000 Alhambra Chamber Orchestra, Novato, CA -- for medical expenditures for underprivileged kids
1,000 Shakespeare at the Beach, Stinson Beach, CA -- support Marin City Project program taking kids to a play

Civic & Public Affairs
3,000 Frankie Poulos Foundation, Novato, CA -- support for Angelfest

1,000 Arete, Larkspur, CA
1,000 United Indian Nations, Oakland, CA -- for affordable housing project

Education

10,000 North Bay Children's Center, Novato, CA -- for facility renovations
2,500 Dominican College, San Rafael, CA -- support Nursing Education Outreach Program
2,500 Hoby, Los Angeles, CA -- support youth leadership seminars
2,500 Marin County Office of Education, San Rafael, CA -- support Marin Literacy Program
2,500 Teen Inspiration, San Rafael, CA -- support after school art programs for teens

Environment

10,000 Marin Conservation Corps, San Rafael, CA -- purchase and set up of computer system
5,000 Marine Mammal Center, Sausalito, CA -- support radio telemetry of released animals
2,500 Bay Institute, San Francisco, CA -- for restoration projects
2,500 Bay Institute, San Francisco, CA -- for installation of voicemail system
2,500 Point Reyes Bird Observatory, Stinson Beach, CA -- support 20th annual Bird-A-Thon

Health

10,000 Children's Miracle Network, Salt Lake City, UT -- for 1997 broadcast underwriting
10,000 Marin General Hospital Foundation, San Rafael, CA -- support special events
2,500 Early Childhood Mental Health, Richmond, CA -- purchase IntelliKeys keyboard
2,500 Hospice of the Grand Valley, Grand Junction, CO
2,500 Novato Human Needs Center, Novato, CA -- support Center Place Relief Fund
2,000 Marin AIDS Project, San Rafael, CA -- support Dinner and Art Auction
1,500 Asthma Education and Resource Council of Marin, Mill Valley, CA -- support community outreach, health education programs
1,500 Center for Attitudinal Healing, Sausalito, CA -- corporate sponsor of Fall Fantasia benefit
1,000 AIDS Project of the East Bay, Oakland, CA -- for educational programs, prevention programs
1,000 Meals of Marin, San Rafael, CA -- provide kitchen tent for homeless people with AIDS

International

10,000 Earth Options Institute, Sebastopola, CA -- support Marin County Electric Bicycle Demonstration Program

Religion

2,500 San Rafael Canal Ministry, San Rafael, CA

Science

2,000 Marine Science Institute, Redwood City, CA -- support combination of 12 Discovery Voyages and land-on programs to 480 students

Social Services

24,350 United Way Bay Area, San Francisco, CA -- for annual holiday grant
10,000 Full Circle, San Rafael, CA -- for Multi-Systemic Latino Family Support Program
10,000 Human Concern Center Ritter House, San Rafael, CA -- to upgrade computer system
10,000 Lincoln Child Center, Oakland, CA -- support Phase II of Technology Expansion
10,000 Novato Youth Center, Novato, CA -- support child care scholarships to low-income parents
8,800 Big Brothers and Big Sisters, San Rafael, CA -- to recruit big brothers
7,500 Drawbridge, San Rafael, CA -- support art programs for homeless children
7,500 Fairfax-San Anselmo Children's Center, San Anselmo, CA -- to purchase a van
7,500 Meals of Marin, San Rafael, CA -- support Food Project
5,000 Marin Concerned Citizens, San Rafael, CA -- support Adopt-A-Family Program
3,750 United Way Sonoma, Santa Rosa, CA -- annual holiday grant
3,650 United Way Alameda County, Oakland, CA -- annual holiday grant
3,500 Micrografx Chili for Children, Richardson, TX -- support fundraiser for National Center for Missing and Exploited Children
3,260 Volunteer Center of Marion, San Rafael, CA -- support Human Race fundraising
2,500 Goodwill Industries, San Francisco, CA -- support Marin Employment Collaboratives
2,500 Marion Association of Retarded Citizens, San Rafael, CA -- sponsor table at Great Chefs of Marin benefit
2,500 Volunteer Center of Marin, San Rafael, CA -- corporate sponsor for 1997 Human Race
2,500 Working Essentials, San Francisco, CA -- provide homeless people with personal care packages
1,000 Family Law Center, San Rafael, CA
1,000 Marin Association of Retarded Citizens, San Rafael, CA
1,000 San Francisco Food Bank, San Francisco, CA -- additional food for agencies assisting needy

BROOKLYN UNION

Company Contact

Brooklyn, NY
Web: http://www.bug.com

Company Description

Former Name: Brooklyn Union Gas Co.
Assets: US$2,289,600,000
Employees: 3,336
SIC(s): 4924 Natural Gas Distribution.
Parent Company: KeySpan Energy Corp.

Nonmonetary Support

Type: Donated Equipment; Donated Products; In-kind Services
Contact: Marie Cutrone, Inquiry Management Coordinator

Corporate Sponsorship

Type: Arts & cultural events; Festivals/fairs; Music & entertainment events; Pledge-a-thon; Sports events
Contact: Marie Cutrone, Inquiry Management Coordinator

Giving Contact

Audra Fox, Community Development
Brooklyn Union Community Development
One Metrotech Ctr.
Brooklyn, NY 11201-3850
Phone: (718)403-2000
Fax: (718)488-1778
Email: webmaster@bug.com

Description

Organization Type: Corporate Giving Program
Giving Locations: NY: Brooklyn, Queens, Staten Island
Grant Types: Award, Employee Matching Gifts, Endowment, Fellowship, General Support, Matching, Multiyear/Continuing Support.

Financial Summary

Total Giving: Contributes through corporate direct giving program only.

Typical Recipients

Arts & Humanities: Arts & Humanities-General
Civic & Public Affairs: Civic & Public Affairs-General
Education: Education Funds, Education-General
Environment: Environment-General
Health: Health-General
Social Services: Social Services-General, Youth Organizations

Application Procedures

Initial Contact: brief letter no more than two pages in length
Application Requirements: description of the organization, amount requested, and purpose of funds
Deadlines: None.

Restrictions

The foundation supports 501(c)(3) organizations only.

Additional Information

The program funds projects that prove to have an impact on the lives of its customers. The program managers are interested in organizations that have a proven ability to reach out to the community. Preference is given to letters that are less than two pages and 'to the point.'

Corporate Officials

Robert Barry Catell: chairman, chief executive officer B Brooklyn, NY 1937. ED City University of New York BME (1958); City University of New York MME (1964). PRIM CORP EMPL chairman, chief executive officer: KeySpan Energy Corp. CORP AFFIL chairman, chief executive officer, director: MarketSpan Corp.; director: Star Energy Inc.; chairman: Keyspan Energy Corp.; director: The Houston Exploration Co.; trustee: Independence Savings Bank; director: Fuel Resources Inc.; director: Gas Energy Inc.; director: Alberta Northeast Inc.; chairman: Boundary Gas Inc. NONPR AFFIL member: New York State Business Council; member: Society Gas Lighting; member: New York Serda Board; director: New York Energy Research & Development Authority; member executive committee: New York Gas Group; director: Gas Research Institute; member: New York City Partnership; director: American Gas Association; chairman: Business Council for a Sustainable Energy Future.
Jan C. Childress: vice president PRIM CORP EMPL vice president: Brooklyn Union. NONPR AFFIL director: Non Profit Facilities Fund.
Robert J. Fani: senior vice president PRIM CORP EMPL senior vice president: Brooklyn Union.
Craig Gerard Matthews: president, chief operating officer B Brooklyn, NY 1943. ED Rutgers University BCE (1965); Polytechnic Institute Brooklyn MS (1971). PRIM CORP EMPL president, chief operating officer: KeySpan Energy Corp. PRIM NONPR EMPL president, chief operating officer: Brooklyn Union. NONPR AFFIL director: Regional Plan Association; director: Salvation Army; director: Public Utility Report Inc.; director: Poly University; director: Prospect Park Alliance; director: Neighborhood Housing Services America; director: Greater Jamaica Development Corp.; director: Inform; director: Brooklyn Philharmonic; member: Brooklyn Chamber of Commerce;

director: Brooklyn College Advisory Board; director: American Gas Association.

Foundation Officials

Anne Jordan: director PRIM CORP EMPL vice president financial planning: Brooklyn Union.

BROWN SHOE CO., INC.

Company Contact

8300 Maryland Avenue
St. Louis, MO 63105-3693
Phone: (314)854-4084
Fax: (314)854-4205
Web: http://www.brownshoe.com

Company Description

Employees: 11,000 (1999)
SIC(s): 5661 Shoe Stores.

Nonmonetary Support

Value: $400,000 (1993); $400,000 (1990); $400,000 (1989)
Type: Donated Equipment; Donated Products; In-kind Services; Loaned Employees; Loaned Executives; Workplace Solicitation

Corporate Sponsorship

Type: Arts & cultural events; Festivals/fairs; Music & entertainment events; Other
Note: Sponsors fund-raising walks and educational events.

Brown Shoe Co. Charitable Trust

Giving Contact

Thomas G. Malecek, Secretary, Board of Control
Brown Shoe Co. Charitable Trust
c/o Suntrust Bank, Atlanta
PO Box 4655
Atlanta, GA 30302
Email: tmalecek@brownshoe.com

Description

EIN: 237443082
Organization Type: Corporate Foundation
Giving Locations: MO: St. Louis principally near operating locations and to national organizations.
Grant Types: Capital, Employee Matching Gifts, General Support.
Note: Employee matching gift ratio: 2 to 1.

Financial Summary

Total Giving: $712,000 (2000 approx); $676,850 (1999 approx); $676,498 (1998). Note: Contributes through foundation only.
Giving Analysis: Giving for 1997 includes: foundation ($435,686); foundation grants to United Way ($243,500)
Assets: $3,558,000 (1999 approx); $3,568,242 (1998); $3,814,694 (1997)
Gifts Received: $449,190 (1995)

Typical Recipients

Arts & Humanities: Arts Associations & Councils, Arts Outreach, Dance, Ethnic & Folk Arts, Museums/Galleries, Music, Opera, Performing Arts, Public Broadcasting, Theater
Civic & Public Affairs: African American Affairs, Botanical Gardens/Parks, Clubs, Community Foundations, Ethnic Organizations, Housing, Parades/Festivals, Philanthropic Organizations, Professional & Trade Associations, Public Policy, Urban & Community Affairs, Zoos/Aquariums
Education: Business Education, Colleges & Universities, Economic Education, Education Associations, Leadership Training, Minority Education, Special Education, Student Aid
Environment: Environment-General
Health: Alzheimers Disease, Children's Health/Hospitals, Emergency/Ambulance Services, Eyes/Blindness, Hospitals, Multiple Sclerosis, Preventive Medicine/Wellness Organizations
International: Foreign Arts Organizations, International Organizations, International Relations, International Relief Efforts
Religion: Religion-General, Jewish Causes, Religious Welfare, Seminaries, Social/Policy Issues
Science: Science Museums, Scientific Centers & Institutes
Social Services: At-Risk Youth, Community Service Organizations, Domestic Violence, Family Services, People with Disabilities, Scouts, United Funds/United Ways, YMCA/YWCA/YMHA/YWHA, Youth Organizations

Contributions Analysis

Giving Priorities: United funds, youth organizations, community service, higher education, arts organizations, and civic interests.
Arts & Humanities: 25%. Funds symphony and opera societies in the St. Louis, MO, area. Other interests include public broadcasting, historic preservation, art museums, and theater. Matches employee gifts to cultural organizations.
Civic & Public Affairs: 13%. Interests include botanical gardens, housing, zoos, the environment, and economic development, with grants generally less than $500.
Education: 12%. Primarily supports private colleges and universities with degree programs. Recipients also include minority college funds and seminaries. Also matches employee gifts to private colleges and universities.
International: 4%. Supports the Two-Ten International Footwear Foundation.
Religion: 5%. Supports Jewish causes and Salvation Army.
Science: 1%. Supports science and natural history museums.
Social Services: 40%. Primarily supports united funds and youth organizations. Also supports recreation and athletics and community service organizations.
Note: Total contributions made in 1997.

Application Procedures

Initial Contact: brief letter or proposal
Application Requirements: a description of organization; proposed budget for the project; amount requested; purpose for which funds are sought; recently audited financial statement; proof of tax-exempt status; and list of board members and senior staff
Deadlines: None.

Restrictions

Qualifying organizations must be located in areas of employee concentration; expenditures are restricted to the United States.
Does not support individuals or endowment campaigns; national charities; elementary and secondary education; or state-sponsored institutions of higher education.

Additional Information

The Brown Group shareholders approved name change to Brown Shoe Co., Inc. in May of 1999.

Corporate Officials

Bernard Adolphus Bridgewater, Jr.: chairman, president, chief executive officer, director B Tulsa, OK 1934. ED West Minster College AB (1955); Harvard University MBA (1964). PRIM CORP EMPL chairman, president, chief executive officer, director: Brown Group, Inc. CORP AFFIL director: NationsBank Corp.; director: FMC Corp.; director: McDonnell Douglas Corp.; director: Enserch Exploration Inc.; director: Enserch Corp. NONPR AFFIL member: Phi Alpha Delta; trustee: Washington University; member: Omicron Delta Kappa. CLUB AFFIL Saint Louis Country Club; River Club; Indian Hills Country Club; Log Cabin Club; Chicago Club.
Ronald A. Fromm: vice president PRIM CORP EMPL vice president: Brown Group, Inc. CORP AFFIL president: Brown Shoe Co. Inc.; chairman: Pagoda Trading Co. Inc.

Foundation Officials

Bernard Adolphus Bridgewater, Jr.: member board control (see above)

Grants Analysis

Disclosure Period: calendar year ending 1998
Total Grants: $434,998*
Number of Grants: 71*
Average Grant: $6,126*
Highest Grant: $225,000
Typical Range: $500 to $10,000 and $15,000 to $25,000
***Note:** Giving excludes United Way.

Recent Grants

Note: Grants derived from 1998 Form 990.

Arts & Humanities

72,200	St. Louis Symphony Orchestra, St. Louis, MO -- Operating Grant
28,928	KETC-TV, St. Louis, MO -- Operating Grant
25,000	Arts and Education Council of Greater St. Louis, St. Louis, MO -- Operating Grant
15,600	Repertory Theater of St. Louis, St. Louis, MO -- Operating Grant
15,000	St. Louis Art Museum, St. Louis, MO -- Operating Grant
5,000	American Museum of Natural History, New York, NY -- Operating Grant
5,000	The Muny, St. Louis, MO -- Operating Grant
4,000	New England Conservatory of Music, Boston, MA -- Operating Grant
1,000	Dance St. Louis, St. Louis, MO -- Operating Grant

Civic & Public Affairs

31,628	St. Louis Zoo Friends Association, St. Louis, MO -- Operating Grant
24,000	Two/Ten International Footwear Foundation, Watertown, MA -- Operating Grant
22,310	Missouri Botanical Garden, St. Louis, MO -- Operating Grant
15,000	Fair St. Louis, St. Louis, MO -- Operating Grant
5,000	Vail Valley Foundation, Vail, CO -- Operating Grant
2,500	St. Louis County Fair and Air Show, St. Louis, MO -- Operating Grant
2,000	American Enterprise Institute for Public Policy Research, Washington, DC -- Operating Grant
1,500	The Brookings Institute, Washington, DC -- Operating Grant
1,000	Christmas in St. Louis Foundation, St. Louis, MO -- Operating Grant
1,000	Ethics Resource Center, Washington, DC -- Operating Grant
1,000	Laclede's Landing Foundation, St. Louis, MO -- Operating Grant
800	St. Louis Variety Club, St. Louis, MO -- Operating Grant

Education

31,194	St. Louis University, St. Louis, MO -- Operating Grant
27,490	Washington University, St. Louis, MO -- Operating Grant

10,500	Junior Achievement of Mississippi Valley, Inc., St. Louis, MO -- Operating Grant
5,200	Stanford University, Stanford, CA -- Operating Grant
5,000	Princeton University, Princeton, NJ -- Operating Grant
2,100	Vanderbilt University, Nashville, TN -- Operating Grant
1,700	Harvard University, Cambridge, MA -- Operating Grant
1,666	Fontbonne College, St. Louis, MO -- Operating Grant
1,400	Middlebury College, Middlebury, VT -- Operating Grant
1,000	Character Education Partnership, Alexandria, VA -- Operating Grant
1,000	Westminster College, Fulton, MO -- Operating Grant
Environment	
1,100	The Nature Conservancy, Arlington, VA -- Operating Grant
Health	
2,500	Alzheimer's Disease Association St. Louis, St. Louis, MO -- Operating Grant
1,000	Multiple Sclerosis Society, St. Louis, MO -- Operating Grant
1,000	Wellness Community, St. Louis, MO -- Operating Grant
Religion	
10,000	The Papal Visit 1999, St. Louis, MO -- Operating Grant
6,000	Jewish Community Center, St. Louis, MO -- Operating Grant
3,080	Kenrick-Glennon Seninary, St. Louis, MO -- Operating Grant
2,500	Salvation Army St. Louis, St. Louis, MO -- Operating Grant
1,000	National Council of Christians & Jews, St. Louis, MO -- Operating Grant
Science	
6,882	St. Louis Science Center, St. Louis, MO -- Operating Grant
Social Services	
225,000	United Way of Greater St. Louis, St. Louis, MO -- Operating Grant
16,500	United Way of Dane County, Wisconsin, Madison, WI -- Operating Grant
10,650	YMCA of Greater St. Louis, St. Louis, MO -- Operating Grant
10,000	Girl Scouts of Greater St. Louis, St. Louis, MO -- Operating Grant
1,500	National Council on Youth Leadership, St. Louis, MO -- Operating Grant
1,000	Boys Scouts St. Louis, St. Louis, MO -- Operating Grant
1,000	Mathews-Dickey Boys' Club, St. Louis, MO -- Operating Grant
1,000	Missouri Goodwill Industries, St. Louis, MO -- Operating Grant

BROWN &WILLIAMSON TOBACCO CORP.

Company Contact

401 South 4th Avenue, Suite 200
PO Box 35090
Louisville, KY 40232-5090
Phone: (502)568-7000
Fax: (502)568-7494
Web: http://www.bw.com

Company Description

Employees: 6,600
SIC(s): 2111 Cigarettes, 2131 Chewing & Smoking Tobacco.
Parent Company: British American Tobacco Plc, Globe House, Four Temple Place, London, England

Operating Locations

GA: Brown & Williamson Tobacco Corp., Macon; Brown & Williamson Tobacco Corp., Macon Plant, Macon; KY: Brown & Williamson Tobacco Corp., Louisville; Brown & Williamson Tobacco Corp., Louisville; NC: Brown & Williamson Tobacco Corp., Wilson, Winston-Salem

Nonmonetary Support

Type: Donated Equipment; Workplace Solicitation

Giving Contact

Joseph Helewicz, Vice President, Public Affairs, Chairman of Contributions Committee
Brown & Williamson Tobacco Corp.
1500 Brown & Williamson Tower
PO Box 35090
Louisville, KY 40202
Phone: (502)568-7000
Fax: (502)568-7494

Alternate Contact

Donna S. Bohn, Secretary

Description

Organization Type: Corporate Giving Program
Giving Locations: headquarters and operating communities.
Grant Types: Award, Capital, Employee Matching Gifts, General Support, Operating Expenses, Research, Scholarship.

Financial Summary

Total Giving: $3,000,000 (2000 approx); $3,000,000 (1999 approx); $4,500,000 (1998 approx). Note: Contributes through corporate direct giving program only.

Typical Recipients

Arts & Humanities: Arts Associations & Councils, Dance, Ethnic & Folk Arts, Historic Preservation, Libraries, Museums/Galleries, Public Broadcasting
Civic & Public Affairs: Business/Free Enterprise, Economic Development, Employment/Job Training, Law & Justice, Public Policy, Urban & Community Affairs, Women's Affairs, Zoos/Aquariums
Education: Colleges & Universities, Education Associations, Minority Education, Science/Mathematics Education
Environment: Environment-General
Science: Scientific Organizations
Social Services: Child Welfare, Community Centers, Community Service Organizations, Family Services, Senior Services, Substance Abuse, United Funds/ United Ways

Application Procedures

Initial Contact: letter requesting formal application form
Application Requirements: description of the organization, amount requested, purpose of funds sought, recently audited financial statement, and proof of tax-exempt status
Deadlines: August.

Restrictions

The company does not support individuals, dinners or special events, fraternal organizations, goodwill advertising, member agencies of united funds, political or lobbying groups, or religious organizations for sectarian purposes.

Corporate Officials

Nick Brookes: chairman, president, chief executive officerhuman resources PRIM CORP EMPL chairman, president, chief executive officer: Brown & Williamson Tobacco Corp.
Joseph S. Helewicz: vice president public affairs PRIM CORP EMPL vice president public affairs: Brown & Williamson Tobacco Corp.
Michael J. McGraw: senior vice president law & human resources PRIM CORP EMPL senior vice president law & human resources: Brown & Williamson Tobacco Corp.

Giving Program Officials

Joseph S. Helewicz: chairman contributions committee (see above)

Grants Analysis

Disclosure Period: calendar year ending
Typical Range: $2,500 to $5,000

Recent Grants

Note: Grants derived from 1994 partial grants list.

Civic & Public Affairs	
5,000	American Indian College Fund, Louisville, KY -- to ensure the survival and growth of their institutions, all of which are located on or near reservations in 12 western and midwestern states

BROWNING-FERRIS INDUSTRIES INC.

Company Contact

757 N. Eldridge
Houston, TX 77079
Phone: (281)870-8100
Fax: (281)870-7844
Web: http://www.bfi.com

Company Description

Foreign Name: BFI
Revenue: US$4,745,700,000 (1999)
Employees: 26,000 (1999)
Fortune Rank: 373, per FORTUNE Magazine's list of 500 Largest U.S. Corporations (1999).
FF 373
SIC(s): 4953 Refuse Systems, 4959 Sanitary Services Nec.
Parent Company: Allied Waste Industries, Scottsdale, AZ, United States

Nonmonetary Support

Type: Cause-related Marketing & Promotion; In-kind Services; Loaned Employees; Loaned Executives

Corporate Sponsorship

Type: Festivals/fairs
Contact: Bonnie Moss, Director Community Affairs

Giving Contact

Argentina James, Director Corporate Affairs
Browning-Ferris Industries Inc.
757 N. Eldridge
Houston, TX 77079
Phone: (281)870-7135
Fax: (281)870-7182
Email: argentina.james@bfi.com

Description

Organization Type: Corporate Giving Program
Giving Locations: headquarters and operating communities.
Grant Types: Capital, Challenge, General Support, Multiyear/Continuing Support, Project, Research.

Financial Summary

Total Giving: $750,000 (1999 approx); $1,000,000 (1998); $860,000 (1997 approx). Note: Contributes through corporate direct giving program only.

Typical Recipients

Arts & Humanities: Arts Associations & Councils, Museums/Galleries, Music, Performing Arts
Civic & Public Affairs: Civil Rights, Municipalities/Towns, Public Policy
Education: Business Education, Colleges & Universities, Literacy
Environment: Environment-General
Health: Health Funds, Health Organizations, Hospices, Single-Disease Health Associations
Social Services: Community Service Organizations, Shelters/Homelessness, United Funds/United Ways, Youth Organizations

Application Procedures

Initial Contact: written proposal
Application Requirements: a description of organization, amount requested, purpose of funds sought, recently audited financial statements, and proof of tax-exempt status
Deadlines: None.

Restrictions

Does not support individuals, religious organizations for sectarian purposes, or political or lobbying groups.

Corporate Officials

Eric Graves: vice president corporate communications
Bruce E. Ranck: president, chief executive officer, director B Toronto, ON Canada 1949. ED Michigan State University BS (1970). PRIM CORP EMPL president, chief executive officer, director: Browning-Ferris Industries Inc. CORP AFFIL president: Niagara Recycling Inc.; director: Texas Commerce Bank; director: Memorial Healthcare System; president: New Morgan Landfill Co.; president: International Disposal Corp. California; president: Lake Area Disposal Inc.; director: Furon Co.; president, director: Browning-Ferris Industries Colorado; president: Browning-Ferris Industries Idaho; president: BFI Waste System North America; president: BFI Disposal System North Carolina; president: BFI Disposal System Ohio; chief executive officer: BFI Disposal System North America.
William Doyle Ruckelshaus: chairman, director B Indianapolis, IN 1932. ED Princeton University BA (1957); Harvard University LLB (1960). PRIM CORP EMPL chairman, director: Browning-Ferris Industries Inc. CORP AFFIL director: Weyerhaeuser Co.; director: Solutia Inc.; director: Monsanto Co.; director: Nordstrom Inc.; principal, director, founder: Madrona Investment Group LLC; director: Cummins Engine Co. Inc.; director: Gargoyles Inc.; director: Coinstar Inc. NONPR AFFIL member: Indianapolis Bar Association; chairman: University Wyoming Institute Environment & Natural Resources & Policy; member: Fed Bar Association; member: Indiana Bar Association; member: District of Columbia Bar Association.

Giving Program Officials

Argentina James: director corporate affairs
Bonnie Moss: director corporate affairs

Grants Analysis

Disclosure Period: calendar year ending
Typical Range: $1,000 to $2,500

BRUNSWICK CORP.

Company Contact

1 North Field Court
Lake Forest, IL 60045
Phone: (847)735-4469
Fax: (847)735-4481
Web: http://www.brunswickcorp.com

Company Description

Revenue: US$3,945,200,000
Employees: 22,800
SIC(s): 3519 Internal Combustion Engines Nec, 3732 Boat Building & Repairing, 3949 Sporting & Athletic Goods Nec.

Brunswick Foundation

Giving Contact

Mary Kay Bottorff, President
Brunswick Foundation

Description

EIN: 366033576
Organization Type: Corporate Foundation
Giving Locations: principally near operating locations and to national organizations.
Grant Types: Fellowship, Project, Research, Scholarship.

Giving Philosophy

'Established in 1957 by Brunswick Corporation, Brunswick Foundation provides financial support to nonprofit organizations directly and through special programs. Special program grants are designed to encourage individual support of nonprofit organizations, volunteerism and undergraduate studies, and primary grants are focused towards specific areas where we believe the Foundation can do some good.'
Brunswick Foundation Annual Report

Financial Summary

Total Giving: $744,389 (1998); $799,998 (1997); $806,540 (1996). Note: Contributes through foundation only.
Giving Analysis: Giving for 1998 includes: foundation ($733,047)
Assets: $7,753,110 (1998); $7,698,513 (1997); $9,561,646 (1996)
Gifts Received: $100,000 (1998); $3,895,243 (1996); $1,984,000 (1995). Note: In 1998, contributions were received from Brunswick Corp.

Typical Recipients

Arts & Humanities: Arts Festivals, Arts Funds, Arts Institutes, Community Arts, Dance, Historic Preservation, Libraries, Museums/Galleries, Music, Performing Arts, Theater
Civic & Public Affairs: Asian American Affairs, Botanical Gardens/Parks, Civil Rights, Clubs, Community Foundations, Economic Development, Legal Aid, Professional & Trade Associations, Rural Affairs, Urban & Community Affairs, Women's Affairs, Zoos/Aquariums
Education: Business Education, Colleges & Universities, Community & Junior Colleges, Education Associations, Engineering/Technological Education, Environmental Education, Leadership Training, Literacy, Minority Education, Private Education (Precollege), Science/Mathematics Education, Secondary Education (Private), Student Aid
Environment: Environment-General, Wildlife Protection
Health: Children's Health/Hospitals, Clinics/Medical Centers, Emergency/Ambulance Services, Health Organizations, Hospices, Hospitals, Mental Health, Nursing Services, Prenatal Health Issues, Single-Disease Health Associations
International: International Affairs, International Relations
Religion: Ministries, Religious Welfare
Social Services: At-Risk Youth, Big Brother/Big Sister, Child Welfare, Community Centers, Community Service Organizations, Day Care, Delinquency & Criminal Rehabilitation, Emergency Relief, Family Planning, Family Services, Food/Clothing Distribution, People with Disabilities, Recreation & Athletics, Scouts, Senior Services, Shelters/Homelessness, Special Olympics, Substance Abuse, United Funds/United Ways, Volunteer Services, YMCA/YWCA/YMHA/YWHA, Youth Organizations

Contributions Analysis

Giving Priorities: Higher education, civic groups, youth organizations, united funds, museums, libraries, and hospitals.
Arts & Humanities: 4%. Support given to arts, museums, and memorial foundations.
Civic & Public Affairs: 2%. Supports clubs and community foundations.
Education: 58%. Majority of funding supports scholarships to children of company employees.
Health: 4%. Support American Red Cross Disaster Relief Fund, hospitals, and health care organizations.
Religion: 4%. Supports religious causes and organizations.
Social Services: 28%. Supports youth and child services, volunteer programs and United Way.
Note: Total contributions made in 1998.

Application Procedures

Initial Contact: brief letter
Application Requirements: objectives and purpose for which grant is sought; plans for implementation and evaluation of project; benefits expected; evidence of need for project; budget; IRS 501(c)(3) verification; and most recently audited financial statement
Deadlines: None.
Decision Notification: Committee meets as needed.
Notes: Foundation does not accept telephone solicitations.

Restrictions

Foundation does not make grants to individuals or provide loans. Does not support organizations that are not tax-exempt; religious or political organizations, veterans' groups, fraternal orders; labor groups; preschool, primary or secondary schools; trips, tours, tickets, dinners, special events or advertising; or capital or endowment grants. Does not donate company equipment.

Additional Information

Foundation is in the process of reorganization.
Publications: Annual Report

Corporate Officials

Peter N. Larson: chairman, chief executive officer, director B Los Angeles, CA 1939. ED Oregon State University BS (1960); Seton Hall University JD (1972). PRIM CORP EMPL chairman, chief executive officer, director: Brunswick Corp. CORP AFFIL director: Coty Corp.; Kimberly-Clark; director: CIGNA Corp.; director: Compaq Computer Corp.

Foundation Officials

Mary Kay Bottorff: president
Peter Bannerman Hamilton: director B Philadelphia, PA 1946. ED Princeton University AB (1968); Yale University JD (1971). PRIM CORP EMPL senior vice president, chief financial officer: Brunswick Corp. CORP AFFIL director: Fidelity Life Association; director: Kemper National Insurance Co.; director: American Motorists Insurance Co.
Michael D. Schmitz: secretary PRIM CORP EMPL assistant secretary: Brunswick Corp.
Geoffrey Smith: treasurer
Kenneth B. Zeigler: director PRIM CORP EMPL vice president, chief human resources officer: Brunswick Corp.

Grants Analysis

Disclosure Period: calendar year ending 1998
Total Grants: $245,300*
Number of Grants: 104*
Average Grant: $2,359*
Highest Grant: $40,000
Typical Range: $100 to $5,000
***Note:** Giving excludes scholarships and United Way.

Recent Grants

Note: Grants derived from 1998 Form 990.

Arts & Humanities

5,000 Oklahoma City National Memorial Foundation, Oklahoma City, OK

Civic & Public Affairs

10,000 Every Womans Place Inc., Muskegon, MI
2,500 Ijams Nature Park, Knoxville, TN
2,000 Linking Business and Education, Everett, WA
500 Northside Men's Club, Inc., Washburn, TN
200 American Business Women's Association, Kansas City, MO
200 Filipino Families of Skokie, Skokie, IL
200 Junior Womans League of Waukegan, Waukegan, IL

Education

7,500 Junior Achievement of Chicago, Chicago, IL
1,500 Michigan Dunes Montessori, Muskegon, MI

Environment

5,000 OpenLands Project, Chicago, IL

Health

5,000 American Red Cross Disaster Relief Fund, Spencer, SD

Religion

1,500 Knoxville Area Rescue Ministries, Knoxville, TN
1,000 Holy Family House Inc, Churchville, MD

Social Services

40,000 United Way of Fond du Lac, Fond du Lac, WI
34,000 Tulsa Area United Way, Tulsa, OK
25,000 Child and Family Services of Knox County Inc, Knoxville, TN
25,000 Ela Area YMCA, Chicago, IL
23,300 Stillwater Area United Way, Stillwater, OK
10,000 Big Brothers/Big Sisters of Stillwater, Stillwater, OK
10,000 Freshwater Angler Association Inc., Dallas, TX
10,000 Pedals for Progress, High Ridge, NJ
7,800 Heart of Florida United Way, Orlando, FL
7,500 Great Lakes Sport Fishing Council, Elmhurst, IL
5,000 Big Brothers/Big Sisters of the Lakeshore, Inc., Muskegon, MI
3,500 Volunteer Muskegon, Muskegon, MI
3,000 Boys & Girls Clubs of America, Chicago, IL
2,000 Big Brothers/Big Sisters of Lake County, Gurnee, IL
2,000 The Boggy Creek Gang A Hole In the Wall, Orlando, FL
2,000 Oklahoma Special Olympics, Tulsa, OK
1,750 United Way Oshkosh, Oshkosh, WI
1,000 Toys for Tots - USMC Palm Coast, Palm Coast, FL
1,000 United Way Milwaukee, Milwaukee, WI
1,000 United Way Washington County, Hartford, WI
700 Southern Appalachian Volunteer Effort, Knoxville, TN
500 Arden Shore Child and Family Services, Lake Bluff, IL
500 Connection Resource Services, Inc., Libertyville, IL
350 Jefferson City Little League, Jefferson City, TN
250 Boy Scouts of America Troop 0073 (Short Gap), Ridgeley, WV
250 Boy Scouts of America Troop 0641, Oshkosh, WI
200 Boy Scouts of America Cub Scout Pack 704, Port St. John, FL
200 Boy Scouts of America - Troup 481, Tutusville, FL
200 Carter HS Athletic Boosters Club, Strawberry Plains, TN
200 Family Matters, Chicago, IL
200 Farragut Baseball Inc., Farragut, TN
200 Girl Scouts of America, 771 - Magic Empire Council, Stillwater, OK
150 Big Brothers/Big Sisters of Fond du Lac Company, Fond du Lac, WI
150 Big Brothers/Big Sisters of Fond du Lac Company, Fond du Lac, WI
150 Big Brothers/Big Sisters of Stillwater, Stillwater, OK
150 Big Brothers/Big Sisters of Stillwater, Stillwater, OK

BUCYRUS-ERIE CO.

Company Contact

South Milwaukee, WI
Web: http://www.bucyrus.com

Company Description

Revenue: US$233,220,000
Employees: 1,166
SIC(s): 3532 Mining Machinery, 3533 Oil & Gas Field Machinery.
Parent Company: B-E Holding, Inc.

Bucyrus-Erie Foundation

Giving Contact

Mr. Sitgfredo Gutieriez, Administrator, Program Officer
Bucyrus-Erie Foundation
1020 Broadway
Milwaukee, WI 53202
Phone: (414)272-5805
Fax: (414)272-6235
Email: milwfdn@execpc.com

Description

EIN: 396075537
Organization Type: Corporate Foundation
Giving Locations: WI: Milwaukee County, Milwaukee South Milwaukee
Grant Types: Capital, Employee Matching Gifts, General Support, Project.
Note: Matching gifts are for education, health and social services, and the arts.

Financial Summary

Total Giving: $850,000 (1999 approx); $890,000 (1998 approx); $778,722 (1997). Note: Contributes through foundation only.
Giving Analysis: Giving for 1997 includes: foundation ($547,943); foundation grants to United Way ($109,840); foundation matching gifts ($65,196); foundation scholarships ($55,743)
Assets: $15,260,827 (1997); $13,531,574 (1996)

Typical Recipients

Arts & Humanities: Arts Associations & Councils, Arts Funds, Ballet, Dance, Historic Preservation, Libraries, Museums/Galleries, Music, Opera, Performing Arts, Public Broadcasting, Theater
Civic & Public Affairs: African American Affairs, Business/Free Enterprise, Economic Development, Economic Policy, Employment/Job Training, Hispanic Affairs, Housing, Municipalities/Towns, Native American Affairs, Parades/Festivals, Professional & Trade Associations, Public Policy, Safety, Urban & Community Affairs, Zoos/Aquariums
Education: Business Education, Colleges & Universities, Economic Education, Education Funds, Elementary Education (Private), Engineering/Technological Education, Education-General, Literacy, Medical Education, Minority Education, Private Education (Precollege), Public Education (Precollege), Religious Education, Science/Mathematics Education, Student Aid
Environment: Energy, Resource Conservation
Health: Children's Health/Hospitals, Clinics/Medical Centers, Health Organizations, Hospitals, Medical Rehabilitation, Medical Research, Single-Disease Health Associations
International: Foreign Arts Organizations
Religion: Religious Welfare
Social Services: Big Brother/Big Sister, Child Welfare, Community Centers, Community Service Organizations, Day Care, Domestic Violence, Family Services, Food/Clothing Distribution, Homes, People with Disabilities, Recreation & Athletics, Scouts, Senior Services, Shelters/Homelessness, Substance Abuse, United Funds/United Ways, YMCA/YWCA/YMHA/YWHA, Youth Organizations

Contributions Analysis

Giving Priorities: Social welfare programs, education, hospitals, arts funds, and civic concerns.
Arts & Humanities: 24%. Museums and performing arts receive support. Other areas of interest include public broadcasting and libraries.
Civic & Public Affairs: 3%. Supports public policy, environmental affairs, business/free enterprise, and urban and community affairs.
Education: 11%. Emphasis on higher education institutions. Interests include technical and engineering education at the university level. Also supports education funds, arts education, student aid, literacy programs, and public and private precollege education.
Environment: 2%.
Health: 5%. Focus on hospitals, pediatric health and single-disease associations.
Religion: 8%. Funds religious social service organizations.
Social Services: 47%. Majority of funding supports united funds, youth programs, and community service organizations in Milwaukee County. Other interests include the handicapped, the prevention of domestic violence, homes, employment programs, and family service organizations.
Note: Total contributions in 1997.

Application Procedures

Initial Contact: Send a brief outline on organization's letterhead.
Application Requirements: Include a description of organization; amount requested; purpose of funds sought; size and characteristics of target population; recently audited financial statement; most recent IRS Form 990; and proof of tax-exempt status under IRS code 501(c)(3).
Deadlines: None.
Review Process: Staff reviews proposal, investigates agencies (sometimes involving site visits), evaluates budgetary requirements, and makes recommendations to the board of directors; directors make all final funding decisions.
Decision Notification: Decisions generally are made within three months from the time a proposal is received.
Notes: Contact foundation for complete guidelines before submitting a full proposal.

Restrictions

Does not give to individuals, purchase tickets or tables at dinners or other functions, or purchase goodwill advertising.
Generally does not make more than one grant per fiscal year to any one organization.
Company does not make contributions of equipment or supplies.

Additional Information

Scholarship eligibility requirements are as follows: Applicants must be children or legal wards of active full-time employees of Bucyrus-Erie Co. and any of its divisions or domestic subsidiaries; scholarship recipients must be enrolled in an accredited university or college; children and legal wards of officers and directors of Bucyrus-Erie Co. and any of its divisions or domestic subsidiaries are ineligible. Contact the foundation for more information and for application forms. The Milwaukee Foundation manages the Bucyrus Foundation for the company.
Grants are focused in Milwaukee County only; plant locations of the Bucyrus International companies may also contribute to organizations.
Specific guidelines determine eligibility under matching programs.
Grant inquiries should be directed to the grants manager at (414)272-5805.
Publications: Application Guidelines

Corporate Officials

Norbert J. Verville: vice president, chief financial officer, treasurer, director PRIM CORP EMPL vice president, chief financial officer, treasurer, director: Bucyrus-Erie Co.
William Bergford Winter: president B LaCrosse, WI 1928. ED University of Wisconsin (1951). PRIM CORP EMPL president: Bucyrus-Erie Co. CORP AFFIL director: WICOR Inc.; director: WI Gas Co. NONPR AFFIL member executive board: YMCA Metropolitan Milwaukee. CLUB AFFIL University Club; Western Racquet Club; Milwaukee Country Club.

Foundation Officials

Stephen Ney Graff: director B Granville, IA 1934. ED Marquette University BSBA (1956). PRIM CORP EMPL managing partner: Arthur Andersen & Co. CORP AFFIL director: Regal-Beloit Corp.; director: Northwestern Mutual Life Insurance Co. NONPR AFFIL treasurer, member: Metropolitan Milwaukee Chamber of Commerce; member: Wisconsin Institute CPA's; member advisory board: Inroads Wisconsin; president: Competitive Wisconsin Inc.; director: Friends Milwaukee Public Museum; member: American Institute CPAs. CLUB AFFIL Milwaukee Club; University Club.
Stigfredo Guiterrez: secretary, manager, trustee
Mary Ann W. Labahn: director
Donald E. Porter: director
Brenton H. Rupple: director B Waukesha, WI 1924. ED University of Wisconsin (1948). CORP AFFIL director: Roundy's Inc.
Norbert J. Verville: treasurer (see above)
William Bergford Winter: chairman, president, director (see above)

Grants Analysis

Disclosure Period: calendar year ending 1997
Total Grants: $547,943*
Number of Grants: 98
Average Grant: $5,591
Highest Grant: $16,250
Typical Range: $100 to $10,000
***Note:** Giving excludes United Way; matching gifts; scholarships.

Recent Grants

Note: Grants derived from 1997 Form 990.

Arts & Humanities

16,250	United Performing Arts Fund, Milwaukee, WI -- operating
16,250	United Performing Arts Fund, Milwaukee, WI -- operating
16,250	United Performing Arts Fund, Milwaukee, WI -- operating
16,250	United Performing Arts Fund, Milwaukee, WI -- operating
12,000	Florentine Opera Club, Milwaukee, WI -- operating
11,000	Florentine Opera Company, Milwaukee, WI -- operating
10,000	Florentine Opera Company, Milwaukee, WI -- capital
7,500	Milwaukee Public Museum, Milwaukee, WI -- operating
6,000	Pabst Theater, Milwaukee, WI -- capital
5,000	South Milwaukee Public Library, Milwaukee, WI -- capital

Civic & Public Affairs

7,500	Neighborhood House, Milwaukee, WI -- capital
5,000	South Milwaukee Centennial Project, Milwaukee, WI -- operating
5,000	Zoological Society of Milwaukee County, Milwaukee, WI -- operating

Education

10,000	Milwaukee School of Engineering, Milwaukee, WI -- operating
7,500	University of Wisconsin College of Engineering, WI -- capital
7,500	University of Wisconsin Foundation, Madison, WI -- capital
6,000	Alverno College, Milwaukee, WI -- capital
5,000	Bruce Guadalupe Community School, Milwaukee, WI -- capital
5,000	Junior Achievement of Southeastern Wisconsin, Milwaukee, WI -- operating
5,000	Marquette University, Milwaukee, WI -- capital
5,000	Medical College of Wisconsin, Milwaukee, WI -- operating
5,000	Wisconsin Lake Schooner Education Association, Milwaukee, WI -- capital

Environment

10,000	Council of Energy Resource Tribes, Denver, CO -- operating

Health

7,500	Children's Hospital, WI -- capital
7,500	Children's Hospital Foundation, Seattle, WA -- capital
7,500	St. Luke's Medical Center, Phoenix, AZ -- capital

Religion

12,500	St. Ann's Adult Day Care -- operating
12,500	St. Ann's Adult Day Care -- operating
7,500	St. Luke's South Shore -- capital
5,000	St. Francis Children's Center -- operating

Social Services

24,000	United Way, Milwaukee, WI -- operating
24,000	United Way, Milwaukee, WI -- operating
24,000	United Way, Milwaukee, WI -- operating
24,000	United Way, Milwaukee, WI -- operating
12,500	YMCA, Milwaukee, WI -- capital
12,500	YMCA, Milwaukee, WI -- capital
12,340	United Way, Milwaukee, WI -- operating
11,000	South Milwaukee Police Department Project DARE, Milwaukee, WI -- operating
11,000	South Milwaukee Police Department Project DARE, Milwaukee, WI -- operating
10,000	YWCA, Milwaukee, WI -- capital
9,000	YMCA South Shore Branch -- operating
9,000	YMCA South Shore Branch -- operating
7,500	Children's Outing Association, Milwaukee, WI -- operating
7,500	Children's Outing Association, Milwaukee, WI -- operating
7,500	Parenting Network, Milwaukee, WI -- operating
6,000	Goodwill Industries -- capital
6,000	South Milwaukee Human Concerns, Milwaukee, WI -- operating
6,000	YMCA South Shore Branch Partner of Youth -- operating
5,500	Boy Scouts of America Milwaukee County Council, WI -- operating
5,500	Boy Scouts of America Milwaukee County Council, WI -- operating

BURGER KING CORP.

Company Contact

17777 Old Cutter Rd.
Miami, FL 33157
Phone: (305)378-7011
Fax: (305)378-7262
Web: http://www.burgerking.com

Company Description

Employees: 42,000
SIC(s): 5812 Eating Places, 6719 Holding Companies Nec.
Parent Company: Diageo Plc, 8 Henrietta Place, London, United Kingdom

Operating Locations

FL: Burger King Corp., Miami
Note: Operates more than 7,000 restaurants nationally and internationally.

Nonmonetary Support

Value: $200,000 (1995)
Type: Donated Equipment; Donated Products; In-kind Services; Loaned Employees; Loaned Executives; Workplace Solicitation

Corporate Sponsorship

Note: Sponsors educational programs for K-12 and a drop-out prevention program.

Burger King Foundation

Giving Contact

Marion Hoffman, Manager, Government & Community Affairs
Burger King Corp.
Attn: Community Affairs Department
PO Box 020783
Miami, FL 33102
Phone: (305)378-3000
Fax: (305)378-3290

Alternate Contact

Robert Ackley
Phone: (305)378-7159

Description

Founded: 1993
Organization Type: Corporate Foundation
Grant Types: Award, Conference/Seminar, General Support, Multiyear/Continuing Support.

Financial Summary

Total Giving: $2,300,000 (1998 approx); $2,300,000 (1997 approx); $3,000,000 (1996 approx). Note: Contributes through corporate direct giving program and foundation. 1997 Giving includes corporate direct giving ($1,300,000); scholarship ($1,000,000).

Contributions Analysis

Education: 100% of contributions. Main emphasis is the Burger King Academy. The academy provides services to at-risk high school students or high school students functioning below their potential in a traditional school setting. The Burger King Academy, in conjunction with Cities in Schools and local school boards and nonprofit organizations, offers such services as drop-out prevention programs, child care, employment skills, on-the-job training, and internships. Each student who graduates receives a fully accredited high school diploma from the partner school district.

Application Procedures

Initial Contact: written request
Application Requirements: a description of organization, amount requested, budget, and description of the project for which funds are requested
Deadlines: None.
Decision Notification: committee usually meets three times per year; allow twelve weeks to process request; foundation will contact only those applicant organizations to which it would like to offer support

Additional Information

Company assists franchise groups in community involvement. It offers assistance to community fundraising programs, adopt-a-school programs, and cause-related marketing programs. pa1In May 2000, applications were not being accepted for remainder of the year.

Corporate Officials

Vincent L. Berkeley, Jr: senior vice president PRIM CORP EMPL senior vice president: Burger King Corp.
Paul Clayton: president PRIM CORP EMPL president: Burger King Corp.
Mark Giresi: senior vice president PRIM CORP EMPL senior vice president: Burger King Corp.
Colin Heggie: chief financial officer PRIM CORP EMPL chief financial officer: Burger King Corp.
Marion Hoffman: manager government & community affairs PRIM CORP EMPL manager government & community affairs: Burger King Corp.
Yvonne Jackson: senior vice president PRIM CORP EMPL senior vice president: Burger King Corp.
Dennis Malamatinas: chief executive officer B 1955. PRIM CORP EMPL chief executive officer: Burger King Corp.

Foundation Officials

Rick Falcon: director community affairs
Mark Giresi: (see above)
Colin Heggie: director (see above)
Yvonne Jackson: director (see above)

BURLINGTON INDUSTRIES, INC.

Company Contact

Greensboro, NC
Web: http://www.burlington-ind.com

Company Description

Employees: 20,100
SIC(s): 2211 Broadwoven Fabric Mills--Cotton, 2221 Broadwoven Fabric Mills--Manmade, 2231 Broadwoven Fabric Mills--Wool, 2273 Carpets & Rugs.

Operating Locations

Mexico
Note: Operates in 10 states and 42 communities and maintains plants in Mexico.

Nonmonetary Support

Value: $250,000 (1994); $200,000 (1989); $300,000 (1988)
Type: Donated Products; Loaned Executives
Volunteer Programs: Company does not have a formal employee volunteer program, but it provides meeting space on the premises or time off to individual employees who volunteer for Junior Achievement. Company also sponsors two Red Cross Blood Drives annually.
Note: Co. provides nonmonetary support

Corporate Sponsorship

Type: Arts & cultural events; Music & entertainment events

Burlington Industries Foundation

Giving Contact

C. Richard Windham, Executive Director
Burlington Industries Foundation
PO Box 21207
Greensboro, NC 27420-1207
Phone: (336)379-2303
Fax: (336)379-4504
Email: windham.dick@burlington.com

Description

EIN: 566043142
Organization Type: Corporate Foundation
Giving Locations: NC; SC; VA principally near operating locations and to national organizations.
Grant Types: Award, Capital, Conference/Seminar, Employee Matching Gifts, General Support.
Note: Employee matching gift ratio: 1 to 1 up to $5,000 for current employees; up to $1,000 for retired employees.

Giving Philosophy

'Burlington Industries has long recognized its responsibilities as a good corporate citizen, and as a major part of this commitment, the company established the Burlington Industries Foundation in 1943.. The foundation is supported entirely by contributions from the company. It gives priority to aid to higher education and to projects which make life better in communities where Burlington employees live.' Burlington Industries Foundation

Financial Summary

Total Giving: $1,000,000 (fiscal year ending September 30, 2000 approx); $1,000,000 (fiscal 1999 approx); $986,191 (fiscal 1998). Note: Contributes through foundation only.
Giving Analysis: Giving for fiscal 1996 includes: foundation ($1,359,614); foundation matching gifts ($224,946); corporate direct giving ($171,687); foundation gifts to individuals ($23,050); fiscal 1998: foundation ($510,215); foundation matching gifts ($254,226); foundation grants to United Way ($162,250); foundation gifts to individuals ($29,750)
Assets: $3,290,740 (fiscal 1998); $4,177,354 (fiscal 1997); $4,389,497 (fiscal 1996)
Gifts Received: $100 (fiscal 1998)

Typical Recipients

Arts & Humanities: Arts Associations & Councils, Arts Funds, Historic Preservation, Libraries, Museums/Galleries
Civic & Public Affairs: Botanical Gardens/Parks, Business/Free Enterprise, Clubs, Community Foundations, Employment/Job Training, Civic & Public Affairs-General, Housing, Law & Justice, Minority Business, Municipalities/Towns, Nonprofit Management, Philanthropic Organizations, Public Policy, Safety, Urban & Community Affairs
Education: Agricultural Education, Business Education, Colleges & Universities, Community & Junior Colleges, Education Associations, Education Funds, Education Reform, Elementary Education (Public), Engineering/Technological Education, Faculty Development, Education-General, Literacy, Minority Education, Private Education (Precollege), Private Education (Precollege), Public Education (Precollege), Science/Mathematics Education, Student Aid, Vocational & Technical Education
Environment: Environment-General
Health: AIDS/HIV, Children's Health/Hospitals, Clinics/Medical Centers, Emergency/Ambulance Services, Health Organizations, Hospitals, Multiple Sclerosis, Outpatient Health Care, Preventive Medicine/Wellness Organizations, Respiratory, Single-Disease Health Associations
International: International Affairs, International Relations
Religion: Jewish Causes, Ministries, Religious Welfare
Science: Science Museums, Scientific Centers & Institutes
Social Services: Community Centers, Community Service Organizations, Delinquency & Criminal Rehabilitation, Family Services, People with Disabilities, Recreation & Athletics, Scouts, Shelters/Homelessness, Special Olympics, Substance Abuse, United Funds/United Ways, YMCA/YWCA/YMHA/YWHA, Youth Organizations

Contributions Analysis

Giving Priorities: Education, social welfare organizations, hospitals, community development, environmental improvement, and arts councils.
Arts & Humanities: 5%. Contributions primarily channeled through local arts councils. Interests include museums, libraries, music, and public broadcasting.
Civic & Public Affairs: 10%. Supports programs that benefit employees and the community, with interests in environmental concerns; civil rights; law and justice; economic development; safety; and business and free enterprise.
Education: 33%. Primarily supports colleges and universities located in areas where there is a high concentration of employees and from which the company recruits. Interests include textiles-related education, and technological, engineering, and business education. Education associations and funds; public secondary education; university libraries; and economic, arts, fashion design, and math education all receive funding. Grants in this field, awarded in the Southeast and nationally, generally range between $1,000 and $10,000.
Health: 8%. Supports local hospitals, generally preferring capital projects rather than operating expenses. Also supports local health care facilities in operating locations. Generally does not support other health-related organizations.
Religion: 1%. Major support for Greensboro Urban Ministry with additional funding for Jewish causes.
Science: 2%.
Social Services: 40%. Primarily supports united funds and youth organizations. Interests also include crime and delinquency prevention, employment, and community service organizations. Also supports organizations where employees volunteer.
Note: About 1% of foundation's giving provides funds for employees in distress. Total contributions in fiscal 1998.

Application Procedures

Initial Contact: Send a brief letter or proposal.
Application Requirements: Include a description of organization, including its aims and purpose; need and justification for program; evidence that organization and its programs are developed and have direction; information on organization's reputation, efficiency, management ability, financial status, and other income sources; proof that organization is tax-exempt and is not a private foundation.
Deadlines: None.
Notes: Foundation may request additional information.

Restrictions

Contributions generally are not made to national organizations; organizations that are not tax-exempt; fraternal, labor, or veterans' organizations; churches; endowment funds; organizations supported through federated campaigns; private secondary schools; historic preservation projects; outdoor dramas; individuals; workshops, conferences, or seminars; production of films, documentaries, or other similar projects; operating expenses; political organizations, parties, or candidates; or medical research.

Corporate Officials

James M. Guin: vice president human resources & public relations B 1943. ED North Carolina State University BS (1966). PRIM CORP EMPL vice president human resources & public relations: Burlington Industries, Inc.

George W. Henderson, III: president, chief executive officer, director B Roanoke, VA 1948. ED University of North Carolina BA (1970); Emory University MBA (1974). PRIM CORP EMPL president, chief executive officer, director: Burlington Industries, Inc. CORP AFFIL director: Wachovia Corp.; director: Washovia Bank NA; director: Jefferson Pilot Corp.; director: Jefferson Pilot Life Insurance Co.

Lynn L. Lane: treasurer B 1951. PRIM CORP EMPL treasurer: Burlington Industries, Inc. ADD CORP EMPL treasurer: BI Transportation Inc.

Dick Windham: director public relations PRIM CORP EMPL director public relations: Burlington Industries, Inc.

Foundation Officials

Park R. Davidson: trustee B Keosauqua, IA 1934. ED University of Iowa (1955); University of Iowa Law School (1957). PRIM CORP EMPL treasurer: Burlington Industries, Inc.

George W. Henderson, III: trustee (see above)

Charles A. McLendon: trustee ED University of North Carolina (1946).

Dick Windham: executive director (see above)

Grants Analysis

Disclosure Period: fiscal year ending September 30, 1998

Total Grants: $510,215*

Number of Grants: 97

Average Grant: $5,260

Highest Grant: $75,000

Typical Range: $500 to $15,000

***Note:** Giving excludes United Way; matching gifts; and gifts to employees in distress.

Recent Grants

Note: Grants derived from fiscal 1998 Form 990.

Arts & Humanities

15,000	United Arts Council, Greensboro, NC
7,500	Greensboro Children's Museum, Greensboro, NC
7,500	North Carolina Museum of Art, Raleigh, NC

Civic & Public Affairs

25,000	Pavillon Foundation, Greensboro, NC
10,000	Community Foundation of Greater Greensboro Inc., Greensboro, NC
10,000	The Jesse Helms Center, Wingate, NC
5,000	Community Foundation of Greater Greensboro Inc., Greensboro, NC
5,000	Employment Policy Foundation, Washington, DC

Education

25,000	North Carolina School of Science and Mathematics, Durham, NC
25,000	UNC-Greensboro Excellence Foundation, Greensboro, NC
25,000	Virginia Polytechnic Institute, Blacksburg, VA
20,000	North Carolina Textile Foundation, Raleigh, NC
15,000	Independent College Fund of North Carolina, Charlotte, NC
10,000	Canterbury School, Greensboro, NC
10,000	Wake Forest University, Salem, NC
7,500	Bennett College, Greensboro, NC
7,500	Richmond Community College, Richmond, VA
7,500	Virginia Foundation for Independent Colleges, Richmond, VA
6,500	St. Pauls Elementary School, San Francisco, CA
5,000	Alamance Community College, Graham, NC
5,000	Alamance Community College, Graham, NC
5,000	Junior Achievement of Central North Carolina, Inc., Gaston, NC
5,000	North Carolina A & T University, Greensboro, NC
5,000	Reading Connections, Greensboro, NC
5,000	Saint Mary's College, Raleigh, NC

Environment

5,000	The Nature Conservancy of North Carolina, Carrboro, NC

Health

20,000	NC Partnership For Children, Raleigh, NC
10,000	Spartanburg Regional Medical Center Foundation, Spartanburg, SC
6,015	National Multiple Sclerosis Society, Greensboro, NC
5,000	Carroll Wellness Center Inc., Hillsville, VA
5,000	Granville Hospital Foundation Inc., Oxford, NC

Religion

5,000	Salvation Army - Gaston County, Gaston, NC

Science

5,000	Natural Science Center of Greensboro, Greensboro, NC
5,000	Natural Science Center of Greensboro, Greensboro, NC

Social Services

75,000	Hope for Philadelphia Homeless Inc, Philadelphia, PA
55,000	United Way of Greater Greensboro Inc., Greensboro, NC
12,500	Alamance County United Way, Burlington, NC
11,500	United Way of Mooresville/South Iredell, Mooresville, NC
10,000	Reidsville Community Pool Association, Reidsville, NC
8,400	The Center For Community Self-Help, Durham, NC
6,800	YMCA - East Gaston, Gaston, NC
6,000	Drew County United Way, Monticello, AR
6,000	United Way of Richmond County, Rockingham, NC
5,500	Lexington/Rockbridge County United Way, Lexington, NC
5,000	1999 Special Olympics World Games, Raleigh, NC
5,000	BSA-Old North State Council, Greensboro, NC
5,000	Greensboro Tennis Foundation, Greensboro, NC
5,000	Halifax United Way, Halifax, NC
5,000	United Way of Mecklenburg County, Charlotte, NC
5,000	United Way of Rutherford County, Rutherford, NC

BURLINGTON NORTHERN SANTA FE CORP.

Company Contact

2650 Lou Menk Drive, 2nd Floor
PO Box 961057
Fort Worth, TX 76161-0057
Phone: (817)333-2000
Web: http://www.bnsf.com

Company Description

Revenue: US$8,941,000,000

Employees: 43,000

Fortune Rank: 188, per FORTUNE Magazine's list of 500 Largest U.S. Corporations (1999).
FF 188

SIC(s): 4011 Railroads--Line-Haul Operating, 4613 Refined Petroleum Pipelines.

Nonmonetary Support

Type: Donated Equipment

Note: Company provides nonmonetary support.

Burlington Northern Santa Fe Foundation

Giving Contact

Richard Russack, President
Burlington Northern Santa Fe Foundation
5601 West 26th Street
Cicero, IL 60804
Phone: (708)222-4815
Fax: (708)222-4857
Email: sharon.heft@bnsf.com

Description

Organization Type: Corporate Foundation

Giving Locations: principally near operating locations and to national organizations.

Grant Types: Capital, Employee Matching Gifts, General Support, Matching, Multiyear/Continuing Support.

Financial Summary

Total Giving: $3,900,000 (fiscal year ending , 1999 approx); $3,994,228 (fiscal 1998); $4,050,890 (fiscal 1997). Note: Contributes through corporate direct giving program and foundation.

Giving Analysis: Giving for fiscal 1998 includes: foundation (approx $3,744,228); corporate direct giving (approx $250,000)

Assets: $904,163 (fiscal 1998); $2,075,062 (fiscal 1996)

Application Procedures

Initial Contact: brief letter requesting application form; application packet will be sent pending determination of eligibility.

Application Requirements: description of the organization, amount requested, copy of IRS tax-exempt ruling, current budget, principal sources and amounts of ongoing annual support, copy of most recently filed Form 990, information on the purpose, need for and relevance of the project, the approach to implementing the project, description of local support and coordination; method of project evaluation; how grant funds will be used; the competence of the organization and its personnel, and outside contractors in a direct or indirect supervisory position over the project; outline of future funding of on-going projects, list of other sources of support.

Deadlines: None.

Review Process: consideration is given to each proposal to determine eligibility; declined organizations receive notification by mail; approved organizations receive funds shortly after approval

Evaluative Criteria: relevance to community needs, management capability, ability to achieve program's objectives, impact on community, level of volunteer participation, current and future sources of financial support

Decision Notification: As long as six months after application.

Restrictions

In general, the foundation does not support individuals; political, religious, fraternal, or veterans organizations; national health organizations or their local chapters; computers or computer-related projects; goodwill advertising; tours, conferences, dinners, seminars, workshops, testimonials, or endowment funds; corporate memberships or contributions to

Chambers of Commerce, taxpayer associations, state railroad associations, and other bodies whose activities are expected to directly benefit the company; or programs beyond stated geographic areas of interest. beyond stated geographic areas of interest.

Additional Information

Burlington Northern Santa Fe Corporation was formed by the merger of Burlington Northern Inc. and Santa Fe Pacific Corporation

Corporate Officials

Matthew K. Rose: senior vice president, chief executive officer

Denis E. Springer: senior vice president, chief financial officer B South Bend, IN 1946. ED University of Notre Dame BS (1967); University of Chicago MBA (1969). PRIM CORP EMPL senior vice president, chief financial officer: Santa Fe Pacific Corp. CORP AFFIL director: Santa Fe Minerals Inc.; director: Santa Fe Pacific Pipelines Inc.; director: Atchison, Topeka & Santa Fe Railroad Co.; senior vice president, chief financial officer: Burlington Northern Santa Fe Corp.; director: ACE Ltd. NONPR AFFIL member: American Institute CPAs; member: Financial Executives Institute.

Foundation Officials

Douglas Babs: director

Jeffrey Moreland: director

Richard A. Russack: president ED Union College BS (1959); New York University BA (1960). PRIM CORP EMPL vice president corporate relations: Burlington Northern Santa Fe Corp.

Denis E. Springer: director (see above)

Grants Analysis

Total Grants: $3,994,228

Burlington Resources, Inc.

Company Contact

Houston, TX

Company Description

Employees: 1,423

SIC(s): 1311 Crude Petroleum & Natural Gas, 1321 Natural Gas Liquids.

Burlington Resources Foundation

Giving Contact

Susan Baer, Treasurer
Burlington Resources Foundation
PO Box 4239
Houston, TX 77210
Phone: (713)624-9364
Fax: (713)624-9635

Description

EIN: 943096534

Organization Type: Corporate Foundation

Grant Types: Capital, Employee Matching Gifts, General Support.

Giving Philosophy

'The Foundation administers a consistent contributions program in recognition of the company's opportunity to support and improve the general welfare and quality of life in communities it serves.' *How to Apply, Burlington Resources Foundation*

Financial Summary

Total Giving: Contributes through corporate direct giving program and foundation.

Assets: Annual Asset Range: $650,000 to $6,000,000.

Gifts Received: $1,698,000 (1994); $3,815,000 (1993); $2,897,992 (1992). Note: Contributions received from Meridian Oil Inc.

Typical Recipients

Arts & Humanities: Arts Associations & Councils, Arts Festivals, Arts Funds, Community Arts, Dance, Libraries, Museums/Galleries, Music, Opera, Public Broadcasting, Theater

Civic & Public Affairs: Clubs, Economic Policy, Hispanic Affairs, Housing, Native American Affairs, Philanthropic Organizations, Urban & Community Affairs, Zoos/Aquariums

Education: Arts/Humanities Education, Business Education, Colleges & Universities, Education Associations, Education Funds, Elementary Education (Public), Engineering/Technological Education, International Studies, Literacy, Minority Education, Private Education (Precollege), Public Education (Precollege), Science/Mathematics Education, Student Aid

Environment: Environment-General, Resource Conservation

Health: Children's Health/Hospitals, Emergency/Ambulance Services, Nursing Services, Prenatal Health Issues, Preventive Medicine/Wellness Organizations, Public Health, Single-Disease Health Associations

International: International Organizations

Religion: Religious Welfare, Seminaries

Science: Science Museums

Social Services: At-Risk Youth, Child Welfare, Family Services, Food/Clothing Distribution, Homes, People with Disabilities, Recreation & Athletics, United Funds/United Ways, Volunteer Services, YMCA/YWCA/YMHA/YWHA, Youth Organizations

Contributions Analysis

Giving Priorities: Education, United Way, social organizations, arts, health care centers, and civic organizations.

Arts & Humanities: 10% to 15%. Interests include theatre, performing arts, visual arts, historical centers, public and educational broadcasting, and other related activities.

Civic & Public Affairs: 5% to 10%. Supports community and other civic affairs. Other eligible recipients include organizations that are government related or are concerned with such activities as crime prevention, parks and recreation facilities, minority interests, the environment, and community development.

Education: 45% to 50%. High priority to technical colleges and educational programs addressing the mining industry. Grants of an exceptional nature may be made to vocational and noncollege schools. Support will not be provided for the expansion of a student body or the payment of scholarships.

Health: Less than 5%. Supports family health centers, crisis pregnancycenters, and rehabilitation centers. Interests include hospitals, medical facilities and programs focusing on hospital buildings and equipment and improvement campaigns.

Social Services: About 30%. Primarily supports child welfare, youth camps and organizations, community service oranizations, and the United Way.

Application Procedures

Initial Contact: request application form

Application Requirements: completed application should include, total project cost and period; amount and source of pledges and commitments to date; current budget; amount requested from foundation and other sources; copy of tax-exempt letter; names and addresses of board of directors; project purpose; needs to be addressed; relevance to foundation; approach to implement project; local support for project; coordination with others working on problem; plans for evaluation; how funds will be used; future support plans for project; and ability of organization and personnel to implement project

Deadlines: None.

Review Process: applicants should enclose a self-addressed stamped envelope if they want notification that application was received

Decision Notification: allow four months for a decision

Notes: Foundation discourages telephone calls or personal visits. Copies of application forms are not accepted. Forms should not be placed in binders or other types of covers.

Restrictions

Does not support religious organizations for religious purposes; veteran or fraternal organizations; general endowment funds; national health organizations or programs; individuals; fund-raising events; corporate memberships, chambers of commerce, taxpayer associations, and other bodies whose activities are not expected to directly benefit the company; political organizations, campaigns, or candidates; and computers or related computer related projects.

Additional Information

Burlington Resources was separated from Burlington Northern Inc. in 1988. It operates its own foundation out of Ft. Worth, TX.

Burlington Resources Foundation gives on behalf of El Paso Natural Gas Co., El Paso, TX; Glacier Park Co., Seattle, WA; Meridian Oil Inc., Houston, TX; and Meridian Minerals Co., Englewood, CO.

Corporate Officials

Everett D. Dubois: senior vice president, treasurer B 1944. ED South Dakota State University MS; South Dakota State University BS. PRIM CORP EMPL senior vice president, treasurer: Burlington Resources Inc. CORP AFFIL treasurer: Burlington Research Hydrocarb; senior vice president, treasurer: Meridian Oil Inc.

Foundation Officials

Everett D. Dubois: treasurer (see above)

John E. Hagale: vice president finance B Springfield, MO 1956. ED University of Notre Dame BBA (1979). PRIM CORP EMPL chief financial officer, executive vice president: Burlington Resources Inc. ADD CORP EMPL executive vice president: Burlington Resource Oil Gas Co.; executive vice president: Burlington Resource Trading Del.

L. David Hanower: assistant secretary B New York, NY 1959. ED Harvard University (1981); University of Chicago Law School (1985). PRIM CORP EMPL senior vice president law: Burlington Resources Inc.

George Everett Howison: vice president B Bridgeport, CT 1944. ED Massachusetts Institute of Technology BS (1967); Dartmouth College MBA (1969). PRIM CORP EMPL vice president, treasurer: Burlington Northern Inc. CORP AFFIL president, director: Meridian Oil Marketing Inc. NONPR AFFIL member: Financial Executives Institute.

Leslie S. Leland: secretary PRIM CORP EMPL secretary: Burlington Resources Inc.

Donald K. North: president B Bemidji, MN 1934.

Thomas Howard O'Leary: chairman B New York, NY 1934. ED College of the Holy Cross AB (1954); University of Pennsylvania Wharton School MBA (1961). PRIM CORP EMPL chairman, president, chief executive officer: Burlington Resources Inc. CORP AFFIL director: B.F. Goodrich Co.; director: Kroger Co.

Grants Analysis

Disclosure Period: calendar year ending

Typical Range: $5,000 to $50,000

Recent Grants

Note: Grants derived from 1994 Form 990.

Arts & Humanities

25,000 Seattle International Music Festival, Seattle, WA
20,000 Bloomfield Community Library
20,000 Museum of Fine Arts, Boston, MA
15,000 Houston Symphony Society, Houston, TX

Civic & Public Affairs

25,000 Foundation for Research on Economics, Seattle, WA
25,000 Lake City Chapter of the Washington of Emblem Clubs
15,000 Habitat for Humanity International Midland Habitat for Humanity, Midland, TX
15,000 Political Economy Research Center
12,500 Intertribal Indian Cermonial Association

Education

250,000 University of Montana Foundation, MT
100,000 Heritage College, Toppenish, WA
100,000 Oregon State University, Corvallis, OR
50,000 Colorado School of Mines, Golden, CO
50,000 Louisiana State University, Baton Rouge, LA
50,000 Montana Tech Foundation, Butte, MT
50,000 Southern California College, Costa Mesa, CA
50,000 Texas A&M University, College Station, TX
50,000 Texas Tech University, Lubbock, TX
50,000 University of New Mexico, Albuquerque, NM
50,000 University of Texas Austin, Austin, TX
50,000 University of Texas Austin, Austin, TX
25,000 Jewish Day School of Metropolitan Seattle, Seattle, WA
25,000 University of Oklahoma, Norman, OK
18,000 Aztec Municipal School District 2
18,000 Bloomfield Schools Naaba Ani Elementary
17,000 New Mexico State University, Las Cruces, NM
15,000 Junior Achievement
11,940 Briarwood-Brookwood, Houston, TX

Environment

20,000 National Tree Trust, Washington, DC
10,640 Dakota West Resource Conservation and Development Area

Health

20,000 Wellness Community of Greater St. Louis, St. Louis, MO
15,000 Ambulance Fund
15,000 Local Infant Formula for Emergencies Houston
15,000 Make-A-Wish Foundation of the Texas Gulf Coast, TX

Religion

25,000 Christian Community Service, Houston, TX
20,000 I am Third Foundation

Science

50,000 Houston Museum of Natural Science, Houston, TX

Social Services

48,500 United Way Texas Gulf Coast, Houston, TX
27,200 United Way Metropolitan Tarrant County, Fort Worth, TX
25,600 San Juan United Way, Farmington, NM
25,000 Boys Country of Houston, Houston, TX
18,700 United Way Texas Gulf Coast, Houston, TX
15,000 Avondale House, Houston, TX
15,000 Center for the Retarded
15,000 Child Advocates
15,000 Family Service Center of Houston and Harris county, Houston, TX
15,000 High Sky Children's Ranch, Midland, TX
15,000 YMCA Greater Seattle, Seattle, WA
14,000 Spaulding for Children
12,500 United Way Midland, Midland, TX

LEO BURNETT CO.

Company Contact

Chicago, IL
Web: http://www.leoburnett.com

Company Description

Billings: US$5,980,000,000
Employees: 9,029
SIC(s): 7311 Advertising Agencies.

Operating Locations

United Kingdom: Leo Burnett Ltd., London; Leo Burnett Moradpour Ltd., London

Nonmonetary Support

Value: $2,000,000 (1997 approx); $2,000,000 (1996)
Type: Cause-related Marketing & Promotion

Leo Burnett Co. Charitable Foundation

Giving Contact

Kristin Anderson, Vice President & Director, Community Affairs
Leo Burnett Co.
35 W Wacker Dr.
Chicago, IL 60601
Phone: (312)220-5959
Fax: (312)220-6523

Description

EIN: 363379336
Organization Type: Corporate Foundation
Giving Locations: IL: Chicago
Grant Types: Employee Matching Gifts, General Support, Operating Expenses, Project.

Financial Summary

Total Giving: $1,000,000 (1998 approx); $1,100,000 (1997 approx); $614,090 (1996). Note: Contributes through corporate direct giving program and foundation. 1996 Giving includes foundation ($464,090); United Way ($150,000).
Assets: $3,513,788 (1996); $3,995,671 (1995); $2,077,969 (1994)
Gifts Received: $106 (1996); $2,325,000 (1995); $1,502,053 (1994). Note: Contributions are received from the Leo Burnett Co.

Typical Recipients

Arts & Humanities: Arts Centers, Arts Funds, Arts Institutes, Ballet, Film & Video, Arts & Humanities-General, Historic Preservation, History & Archaeology, Libraries, Museums/Galleries, Music, Opera, Performing Arts, Public Broadcasting, Theater
Civic & Public Affairs: African American Affairs, Business/Free Enterprise, Chambers of Commerce, Civil Rights, Economic Development, Civic & Public Affairs-General, Hispanic Affairs, Housing, Law & Justice, Municipalities/Towns, Professional & Trade Associations, Public Policy, Rural Affairs, Urban & Community Affairs, Zoos/Aquariums
Education: Agricultural Education, Arts/Humanities Education, Business Education, Colleges & Universities, Community & Junior Colleges, Education Funds, Education Reform, Engineering/Technological Education, Minority Education, Preschool Education, Private Education (Precollege), Public Education (Precollege), Science/Mathematics Education, Student Aid
Environment: Environment-General, Wildlife Protection
Health: Cancer, Children's Health/Hospitals, Clinics/Medical Centers, Health Organizations, Hospices, Hospitals, Multiple Sclerosis, Single-Disease Health Associations
International: Foreign Arts Organizations, Health Care/Hospitals, International Affairs, International Environmental Issues, International Organizations, International Relations, International Relief Efforts, Missionary/Religious Activities
Religion: Jewish Causes, Religious Welfare
Science: Science Museums
Social Services: At-Risk Youth, Child Welfare, Community Centers, Community Service Organizations, Family Services, Food/Clothing Distribution, Recreation & Athletics, Scouts, United Funds/United Ways, Youth Organizations

Contributions Analysis

Giving Priorities: Youth and welfare organizations, education, art groups, urban improvements, and health organizations. Has supported environmental affairs, relief work, and the United Nations.
Arts & Humanities: 15% to 20%. Supports art institutes, museums, art funds, andgroups such as symphonies and theater players in the Chicago area.
Civic & Public Affairs: 5% to 10%. Contributions go to groups in the field of advertising and organizations that benefit the Chicago area, including anti-defamation groups and projects devoted to urban safety and improvement. Also funds environmental groups.
Education: 25% to 30%. Funds support colleges, universities, and business education. Also supports educational funds; high schools and other institutes in the Chicago region; and independent programs such as literacy promotion campaigns. Emphasis is placed on programs that support the field of advertising.
Social Services: 40% to 45%. Majority of funds support United Way. Also supports youth recreation and welfare organizations.

Application Procedures

Initial Contact: Send a brief letter of inquiry.
Application Requirements: Include a description of organization, financial statement, listing of board of directors and IRS statement.
Deadlines: None.
Evaluative Criteria: Supports disadvantaged groups in the Chicago area; supports social and economic structure of Chicago; supports education in the creative fields.
Decision Notification: After bi-annual meetings.

Restrictions

The foundation does not provide grants to individuals or religious groups.

Corporate Officials

Kristin Anderson: vice president, director community affairs PRIM CORP EMPL vice president, director community affairs: Leo Burnett Co.
Richard B. Fizdale: chairman, chief executive officer, director B 1938. PRIM CORP EMPL chairman, chief executive officer, director: Leo Burnett Co. Inc. CORP AFFIL chairman: Leo Burnett Worldwide Inc.

Foundation Officials

Kristin Anderson: secretary, contact (see above)

Grants Analysis

Disclosure Period: calendar year ending 1996
Total Grants: $464,090
Number of Grants: 160
Average Grant: $2,900
Highest Grant: $150,000
Typical Range: $200 to $10,000

Recent Grants

Note: Grants derived from 1997 Form 990.

Education

16,614 University of Michigan, Ann Arbor, MI -- scholarship

J.W. Burress

Company Contact

Roanoke, VA

Company Description

Employees: 130

J.W. Burress Foundation

Giving Contact

John W. Burress, III, President & Treasurer
J.W. Burress Foundation
3760 N. Liberty St.
Winston-Salem, NC 27105
Phone: (336)767-6900

Description

Founded: 1986
EIN: 561554131
Organization Type: Corporate Foundation. Supports preselected organizations only.
Giving Locations: NC
Grant Types: General Support.

Financial Summary

Total Giving: $204,950 (1997); $181,000 (1996); $58,500 (1994)
Assets: $1,784,789 (1997); $447,987 (1996); $286,269 (1994)
Gifts Received: $1,357,773 (1997); $300,000 (1996); $20,000 (1993). Note: In 1996, contributions were received from J.W. Burress Inc.

Typical Recipients

Arts & Humanities: Arts Associations & Councils, Arts Institutes, History & Archaeology, Museums/Galleries, Public Broadcasting, Theater
Civic & Public Affairs: Botanical Gardens/Parks, Civil Rights, Clubs, Civic & Public Affairs-General, Philanthropic Organizations
Education: Arts/Humanities Education, Business Education, Colleges & Universities, Education Funds, Education-General, Private Education (Precollege), Public Education (Precollege), Religious Education, Secondary Education (Private), Special Education
Health: Cancer, Eyes/Blindness, Single-Disease Health Associations, Transplant Networks/Donor Banks
Religion: Churches, Ministries, Religious Organizations, Religious Welfare
Social Services: Child Welfare, Community Centers, Family Services, Homes, Senior Services, YMCA/YWCA/YMHA/YWHA, Youth Organizations

Application Procedures

Initial Contact: The foundation has no formal grant application procedure or application form.
Deadlines: None.

Corporate Officials

John W. Burress, III: chairman, president, chief executive officer PRIM CORP EMPL chairman, president, chief executive officer: J.W. Burress.

Foundation Officials

John W. Burress, III: president, treasurer (see above)
R. C. Vaughn: assistant secretary

Grants Analysis

Disclosure Period: calendar year ending 1997
Total Grants: $204,950
Number of Grants: 26
Typical Range: $1,000 to $5,000

Recent Grants

Note: Grants derived from 1997 Form 990.

Arts & Humanities

6,500 Institute of Arts and Humanities
5,500 Reynolda House, Winston-Salem, NC
1,000 Arts Council, Winston-Salem, NC

Civic & Public Affairs

50,000 Winston-Salem Foundation, Winston-Salem, NC
1,000 Blue Ridge Institute
1,000 Cabell Brand Center
1,000 Reynolda Gardens

Education

77,000 Episcopal High School, Alexandria, VA
19,000 University of North Carolina Chapel Hill, Chapel Hill, NC
10,000 Salem Virginia Education Foundation
5,000 Stuart Hall School, Staunton, VA
2,500 North Carolina School of the Arts, Winston-Salem, NC
2,000 University of North Carolina Chapel Hill, Chapel Hill, NC
1,000 St. Mary's School, Owatonna, MN

Health

14,000 University of North Carolina Lineberger Cancer Center, NC
1,250 Cystic Fibrosis

Religion

1,000 Winston-Salem Downtown Church Center, Winston-Salem, NC
500 Trinity Center

Social Services

2,000 Jordan Institute for Families
1,000 Senior Services

Business Improvement

Company Contact

Edina, MN
Web: http://www.biperformance.com

Company Description

Foreign Name: BI
Former Name: Business Incentives.
Employees: 1,150
SIC(s): 8742 Management Consulting Services.
Parent Company: Schoeneckers, Inc.

Schoeneckers Foundation

Giving Contact

L. Guy Schoenecker, President
Schoeneckers Foundation
PO Box 1610
Minneapolis, MN 55440
Phone: (612)835-4800
Fax: (612)844-4033

Description

Founded: 1979
EIN: 411369001
Organization Type: Corporate Foundation. Supports preselected organizations only.
Giving Locations: MN
Grant Types: General Support.

Financial Summary

Total Giving: $1,000,000 (fiscal year ending September 30, 1999 approx); $571,180 (fiscal 1998); $350,000 (fiscal 1997 approx). Note: Contributes through foundation only.
Assets: $239,060 (fiscal 1998); $193,475 (fiscal 1996); $16,698 (fiscal 1992)
Gifts Received: $681,250 (fiscal 1998); $360,000 (fiscal 1996); $273,000 (fiscal 1992). Note: In fiscal 1998, contributions were received from Schoeneckers, Inc.

Typical Recipients

Civic & Public Affairs: Civic & Public Affairs-General, Law & Justice, Nonprofit Management, Parades/Festivals, Women's Affairs
Education: Business Education, Colleges & Universities, Economic Education, Education-General, Legal Education, Private Education (Precollege)
Health: Alzheimers Disease, Cancer, Children's Health/Hospitals, Diabetes, Emergency/Ambulance Services, Health Organizations, Heart, Hospices, Hospitals, Multiple Sclerosis, Respiratory, Single-Disease Health Associations
Religion: Churches, Ministries, Religious Organizations, Religious Welfare
Social Services: Community Centers, Community Service Organizations, Day Care, Emergency Relief, Food/Clothing Distribution, Homes, United Funds/United Ways, United Funds/United Ways, Volunteer Services, Youth Organizations

Contributions Analysis

Giving Priorities: Higher education.
Education: 95%. Funds the foundation's highest grant of $538,050 to the University of St. Thomas.
Note: Total contributions made in fiscal 1998.

Additional Information

The company and foundation changed their names from Business Incentives and Business Incentives Foundation to B. I. Performance Services and Schoeneckers Foundation, respectively.

Corporate Officials

Guy Schoenecker: president, chief executive officer B 1927. ED University of Minnesota Law School BSL; Saint Thomas College BA (1949). PRIM CORP EMPL president, chief executive officer: Shoeneckers Inc.

Foundation Officials

James E. O'Brien: director ED University of Alaska BA (1962); University of Minnesota JD (1965). PRIM CORP EMPL chairman, chief executive officer: Moss & Barnett. NONPR AFFIL director: Opportunity Partners; chairman: Unilaw; director: Kiwanis Minneapolis; director: Fund Legal Aid Society; member: Kiwanis International.
Guy Schoenecker: president (see above)
Larry Schoenecker: director B 1954. ED University of Saint Thomas. PRIM CORP EMPL senior vice president: Shoeneckers Inc.

Grants Analysis

Disclosure Period: fiscal year ending September 30, 1998
Total Grants: $571,180
Number of Grants: 14
Average Grant: $2,548*
Highest Grant: $538,050
Typical Range: $50 to $2,400
***Note:** Average grant figure excludes largest grant.

Recent Grants

Note: Grants derived from fiscal 1998 Form 990.

Civic & Public Affairs

12,000 Bridging Inc., Bloomington, MN

Education

538,050 University of St. Thomas, St. Paul, MN -- Development Service

10,000	Hamline University School of Law, St. Paul, MN

Health

100	Cystic Fibrosis Foundation, Grafton, WI
100	Leukemia Society of America, Minneapolis, MN
40	Make-a-Wish Foundation of Wisconsin, Butler, WI

Religion

4,500	Partners in Mission, Minneapolis, MN
2,000	Hilltop Samaritan Center, Sioux Falls, SD
1,250	Catholic Charities, Minneapolis, MN -- Hats & Mittens Campaign (Corp Match)
1,000	Loaves and Fishes Too, Minneapolis, MN
100	Sisters Of The Carmelite Ministry, Lake Elmo, MN

Social Services

1,000	Salvation Army, Brooklyn Center, MN -- Flood Relief Fund
1,000	United Way of Minnesota Area, Minneapolis, MN -- Annual Campaign
40	Minnesota Masonic Home, Bloomington, MN

Business Men's Assurance Co. Of America

Company Contact

Kansas City, MO

Company Description

Assets: US$2,200,000
Employees: 600
SIC(s): 6311 Life Insurance, 6321 Accident & Health Insurance, 6399 Insurance Carriers Nec, 6411 Insurance Agents, Brokers & Service.

Nonmonetary Support

Value: $10,000 (1993)
Type: Donated Products; In-kind Services; Loaned Employees; Workplace Solicitation

Corporate Sponsorship

Type: Arts & cultural events; Music & entertainment events; Other
Contact: Lisa Buss, Community Affairs Coordinator
Note: Company-sponsored events include auctions and dinners. Also sponsors Health and Human Services

Giving Contact

Libby Buss, Community Affairs Coordinator
BMA
BMA Tower, PO Box 419458
Kansas City, MO 64141
Phone: (816)751-5420
Fax: (816)751-5710
Note: Toll free: (800)262-5433

Description

Organization Type: Corporate Giving Program
Giving Locations: MO: Kansas City metropolitan area headquarters.
Grant Types: Employee Matching Gifts, General Support.
Note: Employee matching gift ratio: 1 to 1.

Financial Summary

Total Giving: $600,000 (2000 approx); $600,000 (1999 approx); $600,000 (1998 approx). Note: Contributes through corporate direct giving program only.

Typical Recipients

Arts & Humanities: Arts & Humanities-General
Civic & Public Affairs: Civic & Public Affairs-General
Education: Education-General
Health: Health-General
Social Services: Social Services-General

Application Procedures

Initial Contact: a brief letter of inquiry
Application Requirements: a description of organization, list of staff and board members, list of any BMA employees who volunteer for the organization, amount requested, purpose of funds sought, recently audited financial statements, and proof of tax-exempt status
Deadlines: None.

Restrictions

Does not support individuals or religious organizations for sectarian purposes.

Corporate Officials

Giorgio Balzer: chairman, chief executive officer ED University of Rome (1963). PRIM CORP EMPL chairman, chief executive officer: Business Men's Assurance Co. of America. CORP AFFIL president, United States branch: Generali Insurance Co. Trieste Venice; director: Jones & Babson Inc.; United States representative: Generali Assicurazioni Generali SPA.

Giving Program Officials

Vernon W. Voorhees, II: PRIM CORP EMPL senior vice president corporate service, secretary: Business Men's Assurance Co. of America.

Butler Capital Corp.

Company Contact

New York, NY

Company Description

Employees: 400
SIC(s): 6211 Security Brokers & Dealers.

Butler Foundation

Giving Contact

Gilbert Butler, President
767 5th Ave.
New York, NY 10153
Phone: (212)980-0606
Fax: (212)759-0876

Description

Founded: 1988
EIN: 043032409
Organization Type: Corporate Foundation. Supports preselected organizations only.
Giving Locations: headquarters area only.
Grant Types: General Support.

Financial Summary

Total Giving: $246,150 (1996); $133,500 (1995); $56,687 (1993). Note: Giving includes scholarship.
Assets: $4,114,382 (1996); $3,144,860 (1995); $1,606,313 (1993)
Gifts Received: $1,109,090 (1996)

Typical Recipients

Arts & Humanities: Historic Preservation, History & Archaeology, Libraries, Museums/Galleries, Music
Education: Private Education (Precollege), Secondary Education (Private)
Environment: Air/Water Quality, Environment-General, Resource Conservation, Wildlife Protection
Health: Cancer, Eyes/Blindness, Mental Health
International: Foreign Educational Institutions
Social Services: United Funds/United Ways

Corporate Officials

Gilbert Butler: president PRIM CORP EMPL president: Butler Capital Corp.
Neil Weiss: chief financial officer PRIM CORP EMPL chief financial officer: Butler Capital Corp.

Foundation Officials

Gilbert Butler: president, treasurer, director (see above)
R. Bradford Malt: vice president, clerk, director
Howard A. Matlin: treasurer
Emily Kernan Rafferty: director
Winthrop Rutherford, Jr.: director

Grants Analysis

Disclosure Period: calendar year ending 1996
Total Grants: $226,150*
Number of Grants: 32
Average Grant: $7,067
Highest Grant: $30,000
Typical Range: $1,000 to $15,000
***Note:** Giving excludes scholarship.

Recent Grants

Note: Grants derived from 1996 Form 990.

Arts & Humanities

15,000	Metropolitan Museum of Art, New York, NY -- Fund for the Met grant
7,000	Metropolitan Museum of Art, New York, NY -- drawing exhibition
6,000	Chamber Music Society of Utica, New Hartford, NY
5,000	Historic Old St. John's Church, Utica, NY
5,000	Preservation League, Albany, NY

Education

10,000	Milton Academy, Milton, MA

Environment

15,000	Environmental Defense Fund, New York, NY
15,000	Wildlife Conservation Society, Bronx, NY
10,000	Natural Resources Defense Council, New York, NY
10,000	New York Rivers Unified, Rome, NY
10,000	Wildlife Conservation Society, Bronx, NY
5,000	Adirondack Nature Conservancy, New York, NY
5,000	American Rivers, Washington, DC -- challenge grant for membership development
5,000	American Rivers, Washington, DC
5,000	Natural Resources Council of Maine, Augusta, ME

Health

30,000	Schepens Eye Research Institute, Boston, MA -- research
20,000	National Association for Research on Schizophrenia and the Depressions, Great Neck, NY
10,000	Memorial Sloan-Kettering Cancer Center, New York, NY
9,900	Cancer Research Fund, New York, NY

Social Services

10,000	United Way, New York, NY

Butler Manufacturing Co.

Company Contact

Kansas City, MO
Web: http://www.butlermfg.com

Company Description

Employees: 5,171 (1999)
SIC(s): 1542 Nonresidential Construction Nec, 2452 Prefabricated Wood Buildings, 2542 Partitions & Fixtures Except Wood, 3448 Prefabricated Metal Buildings.

Nonmonetary Support

Value: $70,000 (1998); $30,000 (1993)
Type: Donated Products

Butler Manufacturing Co. Foundation

Giving Contact

Barbara Lee Fay, Foundation Administrator
Butler Manufacturing Co. Foundation
PO Box 419917, BMA Tower
Kansas City, MO 64141-0917
Phone: (816)968-3208
Fax: (816)968-3211
Email: blfay@butlermfg.com

Description

EIN: 440663648
Organization Type: Corporate Foundation
Giving Locations: MO: Kansas City
Grant Types: Award, Capital, Emergency, Employee Matching Gifts, General Support, Scholarship.
Note: Employee matching gift ratio: 1 to 1 for higher education and culture.

Giving Philosophy

'The Foundation's purpose is to provide sustained financial assistance to worthy charitable, educational, and health and welfare programs in the United States, and to enhance the quality of life in those U.S. communities where Butler Manufacturing Company and its wholly owned subsidiaries operate facilities.' *Butler Manufacturing Company Foundation*

Financial Summary

Total Giving: $800,000 (1999 approx); $915,457 (1998); $700,000 (1997 approx). Note: Contributes through corporate direct giving program and foundation.
Giving Analysis: Giving for 1997 includes: foundation (approx $500,000); corporate direct giving (approx $200,000); 1998: foundation ($563,092); corporate direct giving ($282,365); nonmonetary support ($70,000)
Assets: $7,000,000 (1998 approx); $6,900,000 (1997 approx); $5,500,000 (1996 approx)
Gifts Received: $300,000 (1989)

Typical Recipients

Arts & Humanities: Arts Institutes, Ballet, Dance, Museums/Galleries, Music, Opera, Performing Arts, Theater
Civic & Public Affairs: Employment/Job Training, Professional & Trade Associations, Urban & Community Affairs
Education: Agricultural Education, Colleges & Universities, Education Associations, Engineering/Technological Education, Education-General, Minority Education, Private Education (Precollege), Public Education (Precollege), Student Aid
Health: Children's Health/Hospitals, Clinics/Medical Centers, Emergency/Ambulance Services, Health Policy/Cost Containment, Health Organizations, Hospitals
Religion: Religious Welfare
Social Services: At-Risk Youth, Big Brother/Big Sister, Child Welfare, Community Service Organizations, Crime Prevention, Family Services, Scouts, United Funds/United Ways, YMCA/YWCA/YMHA/YWHA, Youth Organizations

Contributions Analysis

Giving Priorities: Youth programs, minority development, neighborhoods and support of non-residential building programs using the company's products; scholarships for children of employees, and grants to colleges and universities serving locations where employees reside; and the community's principal arts organizations.
Arts & Humanities: About 15%. Primarily supports major art groups that broaden the cultural experience where Butler has a presence. Recipients include museums, theater, arts associations, symphonies, and ballet. Some interest in minority groups and cultural opportunities for the economically disadvantaged. Foundation also operates an employee matching gift program for arts interests.
Civic & Public Affairs: 55% to 60%. Foundation makes contributions to communities where company has employees and significant capital investment. Supports the United Way. Also supports minority assistance, youth programs, special-interest hospitals and health care programs, and neighborhoods and non-residential building.
Education: 20% to 25%. Majority of funding supports scholarship programs operated by the foundation. Awards are given to children of Butler employees attending four-year accredited colleges. Also provides matching gifts to colleges and universities. Institutions receiving grants must supply significant numbers of employees to Butler, provide opportunities for continuing education to Butler employees, or have programs that provide education to residents of the city where a Butler plant operates. Foundation also gives assistance to minority education and marketable career skills for youth.

Application Procedures

Initial Contact: Call or write for guidelines, then written proposal.
Application Requirements: Include a description of program and clear statement of purpose; evidence o effective program management and reasonable fundraising expenses; an annual report with financial statements authorized by a public accountant, detailed annual budget; names and addresses of an active and responsive governing body holding regular meetings, whose members have no material conflict of interest and who serve the organization without compensation; names of principal donors giving $500 or more and the amounts received from each in the preceding year; copy of 501 (c)(3) filing.
Deadlines: None.
Review Process: Trustees adopt a grant plan in December of each year, then meet quarterly to approve grants.
Evaluative Criteria: Proportionately significant financial assistance will be given in relatively few areas of need as opposed to relatively minor assistance in a great many areas; the long-range responsibility of Butler and its employees within the community will be evaluated in part by taking into account the number of Butler employees in the community and the scope of operations that Butler has in the community; the significant personal contributions of time, finances, and leadership responsibilities by employees of Butler to nonprofit organizations will be recognized by the foundation where possible; the favorable comparison of the foundation's contribution to those of other corporations and foundations in the United States--grants and distribution patterns will be compared in relation to earnings, net worth, asset value, sales volume, and employment; the simple and clear responsibility to give financial assistance to the institutions and individuals meeting the great human needs of our society; the ability of the foundation to afford contributions without substantial invasion of invested assets.

Restrictions

Grants normally are not made to individuals (except current Butler employees or retirees to cover a hardship); political organizations; religious organizations for sectarian purposes; preschool, primary, and secondary institutions; organizations receiving operating expenses from the United Way; or fraternal or veterans' organizations.
The foundation also does not support national health organizations, hospitals (except those providing unique services like burn treatment or pediatric care); tours, conferences, seminars, or workshops; testimonial activities, including dinners, tables, tickets, advertisements, or walk-a-thons; endowment funds; other foundations providing grants to nonprofits; and programs beyond the foundation's purpose.
Support of capital campaigns for buildings and facilities generally will be considered only when the products of Butler Manufacturing Company are used in the project.

Additional Information

Grants are made to charitable activities which bear directly or indirectly on the activities and social environment of the company and the people with whom it interacts. Foundation favors significant giving rather than many gifts resulting in minor assistance.
Grants and distribution patterns will be compared to company earnings, net worth, asset value, sales volume, and employment. Total grants in any one year will be approximately 2% of the annual average of the company's domestic pretax income in the preceding five years. of the company's domestic pretax income in the preceding five years.
Publications: Guidelines

Corporate Officials

Richard O. Ballentine: vice president, secretary, general counsel B Springfield, OH 1936. ED Wittenberg University AB (1958); University of Michigan JD (1961). PRIM CORP EMPL vice president, secretary, general counsel: Butler Manufacturing Co. ADD CORP EMPL secretary: BMC Real Estate Inc.
Hans G. Berger: managing director PRIM CORP EMPL managing director: Butler Europe.
John T. Cole: corporate controller PRIM CORP EMPL corporate controller: Butler Manufacturing Co.
Thomas J. Hall: vice president B 1945. PRIM CORP EMPL president: Butler Real Estate, Inc. ADD CORP EMPL vice president: Butler Manufacturing Co.
John J. Holland: president, chief executive officer, director B 1950. ED University of Kansas BS (1972); University of Kansas MBA (1980). PRIM CORP EMPL president, chief executive officer, director: Butler Manufacturing Co.
John W. Huey: vice president administration B Washington, DC 1947. ED University of Kansas (1969); University of Kansas (1972). PRIM CORP EMPL vice president administration: Butler Manufacturing Co.
Richard Sinclair Jarman: executive vice president B Omaha, NE 1947. ED United States Military Academy (1969); University of Missouri (1977). PRIM CORP EMPL executive vice president: Butler Manufacturing Co. NONPR AFFIL director: Rehabilitation Institute.
Larry C. Miller: vice president finance, chief financial officer B 1956. ED University of Kansas (1978). PRIM CORP EMPL vice president finance, chief financial officer: Butler Manufacturing Co.
Robert J. Novello: chairman PRIM CORP EMPL chairman: Copeland Corp. CORP AFFIL director: Butler Manufacturing Co.
Donald Henry Pratt: chairman B Hays, KS 1937. ED Wichita State University BS (1960); Harvard University MBA (1965). PRIM CORP EMPL chairman: Butler Manufacturing Co. CORP AFFIL vice president: BMC Real Estate Inc.; director: Bucon Inc.; director: American Century Companies Inc.; director: Atlas Copco North America.
Robert J. Reintjes, Sr.: director B 1932. PRIM CORP EMPL president, director: NUCO International Inc. ADD CORP EMPL president, chief executive officer: George P Reintjes Co. Inc. CORP AFFIL director: Butler Manufacturing Co.; director: Midwest Grain Products Inc.; director: Berkel & Co. Contractors Inc.
Ronald E. Rutledge: executive PRIM CORP EMPL executive: Butler Manufacturing Co. CORP AFFIL

president: Naturalite; president: Vistawall Architectural Products.

Foundation Officials

Richard O. Ballentine: secretary (see above)
Barbara Lee Fay: foundation administrator
C. L. William Haw: member PRIM CORP EMPL president, chief executive officer: National Farms Inc. CORP AFFIL director: Butler Manufacturing Co.
John W. Huey: trustee (see above)
Richard Sinclair Jarman: trustee (see above)
William L. Johnsmeyer: trustee B 1947. ED Purdue University MS (1978); Long Island University MBA (1979). PRIM CORP EMPL president: Bucon Inc. ADD CORP EMPL president: Butler Construction.
Larry C. Miller: treasurer (see above)
Robert J. Novello: member (see above)
Donald Henry Pratt: vice president, trustee (see above)
Robert J. Reintjes, Sr.: member (see above)
Judith A. Rogala: member ED Roosevelt University (1976); University of New Mexico (1982). PRIM CORP EMPL executive vice president business service division: Office Depot Inc. CORP AFFIL president: Aramark Uniform Services; director: Red Roof Inns Inc.

Grants Analysis

Disclosure Period: calendar year ending 1997
Total Grants: $500,000
Number of Grants: 216
Average Grant: $2,510
Highest Grant: $100,000
Typical Range: $250 to $5,000
Note: Grants analysis supplied by foundation.

Recent Grants

Note: Grants derived from 1994 grants list.

Arts & Humanities

23,000	Kansas City Art Institute, Kansas City, MO -- higher education
10,000	Nelson-Atkins Museum of Art, Kansas City, MO -- museum
5,000	Missouri Repertory Theater, Kansas City, MO -- theater
3,779	Missouri Repertory Theater, Kansas City, MO -- theater
2,500	Kansas City Symphony, Kansas City, MO -- music
2,500	Lyric Opera of Kansas City, Kansas City, MO -- music
2,500	State Ballet of Missouri, Kansas City, MO -- dance

Civic & Public Affairs

5,000	Kansas City Neighborhood Alliance, Kansas City, MO -- neighborhood improvement
2,500	Full Employment Council, Kansas City, MO -- youth job training

Education

25,837	National Future Farmers of America Foundation, Madison, WI -- agriculture education
11,000	Rockhurst College, Kansas City, MO -- higher education
10,000	Galesburg Public Schools Foundation, Galesburg, IL -- public education
3,500	DeLaSalle Education Center, Kansas City, MO -- alternative education
3,300	Inroads, Kansas City, MO -- minority education
3,000	University of Missouri Kansas City, Kansas City, MO -- higher education
2,500	Learning Exchange, Kansas City, MO -- student/teacher education
2,050	University of Illinois Foundation, Champaign, IL -- higher education
2,000	Auburn University, Auburn, AL -- higher education
2,000	California Institute of Technology, Pasadena, CA -- higher education
2,000	Cornell College, Mount Vernon, IA -- higher education
2,000	Hampton University, Hampton, VT -- higher education
2,000	Marietta College, Marietta, OH -- higher education
2,000	Monmouth College, Monmouth, IL -- higher education
2,000	Morehouse College, Atlanta, GA -- higher education
2,000	Northeast Missouri State University, Kirksville, MO -- higher education
2,000	Pembroke State University, Pembroke, SC -- higher education
2,000	University of Notre Dame, Notre Dame, IN -- higher education
1,000	Iowa State University, Ames, IA -- higher education

Health

10,000	Children's Mercy Hospital, Kansas City, MO -- health care
5,000	Kaweah Delta Hospital Foundation, Visalia, CA -- health care
5,000	Swope Parkway Health Center, Kansas City, MO -- public health care
2,471	Mid-America Coalition on Health Care, Kansas City, MO -- health care

Religion

2,500	Metropolitan Lutheran Ministries, Kansas City, MO -- social services
2,000	City Union Mission, Kansas City, MO -- social services

Social Services

61,000	Heart of America United Way, Kansas City, MO -- social services
50,000	Children's Benefit Fund, Paramus, NJ -- health care for youth
13,000	United Way Knox County, Galesburg, IL -- social services
8,000	Boy Scouts of America Allohak Council, Kansas City, MO -- youth development
5,000	Ad Hoc Group Against Crime, Kansas City, MO -- crime prevention
5,000	Greater Terrell United Way, Terrell, TX -- social services
3,000	Boy Scouts of America Heart of America, Kansas City, MO -- youth development
3,000	Boys and Girls Clubs Greater Kansas City, Kansas City, MO -- youth development
3,000	Lebanon County United Way, Lebanon, PA -- social services
2,500	Big Brothers and Big Sisters, Kansas City, MO -- youth development
2,500	Scotland County United Way, Laurinburg, NC -- social services
2,500	United Way Central Alabama, Birmingham, AL -- social services
2,500	YOUTHNET, Kansas City, MO -- youth development
2,000	Heart of America Family Services, Kansas City, KS -- social services
2,000	United Way Hays County, San Marcos, TX -- social services
2,000	YMCA Greater Kansas City, Kansas City, MO -- youth development

CABOT CORP.

Company Contact

Boston, MA
Web: http://www.cabot-corp.com

Company Description

Employees: 4,800
SIC(s): 2819 Industrial Inorganic Chemicals Nec, 2821 Plastics Materials & Resins, 2895 Carbon Black, 3061 Mechanical Rubber Goods.

Nonmonetary Support

Value: $200,000 (1994); $300,000 (1993); $200,000 (1992)
Type: Donated Equipment; Donated Products; In-kind Services; Loaned Employees; Loaned Executives
Note: Nonmonetary support is provided by the co. and the foundation. For information on nonmonetary support, contact local Cabot facilities manager.

Corporate Sponsorship

Value: $200,000

Cabot Corp. Foundation

Giving Contact

Ms. Dorothy L. Forbes, Executive Director, Vice President
Cabot Corp. Foundation
75 State Street
Boston, MA 02109
Phone: (617)342-6004

Alternate Contact

Phone: (617)342-6002
Note: The alternate phone number is to answer preliminary inquiries. Organizations can also contact local Cabot facilities.

Description

EIN: 046035227
Organization Type: Corporate Foundation
Giving Locations: principally near operating locations and to national organizations.
Grant Types: Capital, Challenge, Employee Matching Gifts, Fellowship, General Support, Professorship, Project, Research, Scholarship, Seed Money.
Note: Employee matching gift ratio: 1 to 1 for schools and united funds only.

Giving Philosophy

'Cabot's businesses are based on science and are technology-driven, but the company's desire to advance science and technology far exceeds our immediate business interests. It is critical, we believe, that more people around the world understand the importance of science and technology in their everyday lives. It is vital that our policymakers consider scientific and technological complexities when deciding major national issues. It is essential that we train skilled educators in mathematics, engineering and other sciences and that these educators motivate those young people who can develop the new technology that will be required to meet the industrial demands of tomorrow.' *Cabot Corporation Foundation*

Financial Summary

Total Giving: $587,473 (fiscal year ending September 30, 1998); $883,773 (fiscal 1997); $732,900 (fiscal 1996 approx). Note: Contributes through corporate direct giving program and foundation. Giving includes foundation.
Giving Analysis: Giving for fiscal 1998 includes: foundation matching gifts ($327,809); foundation gifts to individuals ($17,700)
Assets: $2,095,188 (fiscal 1998); $2,745,608 (fiscal 1997); $2,533,310 (fiscal 1996)
Gifts Received: $1,059,655 (fiscal 1997); $1,435,620 (fiscal 1996); $1,512,366 (fiscal 1995)

Typical Recipients

Arts & Humanities: Arts Appreciation, Arts Associations & Councils, Arts Centers, Arts Funds, Arts Institutes, Arts Outreach, Community Arts, Dance, Ethnic & Folk Arts, Historic Preservation, Libraries, Literary Arts, Museums/Galleries, Music, Opera, Performing Arts, Theater
Civic & Public Affairs: African American Affairs, Botanical Gardens/Parks, Business/Free Enterprise, Community Foundations, Economic Development, Economic Policy, Employment/Job Training, Law & Justice, Legal Aid, Municipalities/Towns, Public Policy, Safety, Urban & Community Affairs, Women's Affairs, Zoos/Aquariums
Education: Business Education, Colleges & Universities, Colleges & Universities, Community & Junior Colleges, Economic Education, Education Funds, Elementary Education (Private), Engineering/Technological Education, Faculty Development, Education-General, Health & Physical Education, International Exchange, International Studies, Literacy, Minority Education, Preschool Education, Private Education (Precollege), Public Education (Precollege), Science/Mathematics Education, Special Education, Student Aid
Environment: Air/Water Quality, Environment-General, Wildlife Protection
Health: Cancer, Clinics/Medical Centers, Diabetes, Health Organizations, Heart, Hospitals, Prenatal Health Issues
International: Foreign Arts Organizations, Foreign Educational Institutions, International-General, Health Care/Hospitals, International Development, International Organizations, International Relations, International Relief Efforts
Religion: Ministries
Science: Science Exhibits & Fairs, Science Museums, Scientific Organizations
Social Services: At-Risk Youth, Camps, Child Welfare, Community Centers, Community Service Organizations, Counseling, Day Care, Domestic Violence, Emergency Relief, Food/Clothing Distribution, Homes, People with Disabilities, Recreation & Athletics, Senior Services, Substance Abuse, United Funds/United Ways, Volunteer Services, YMCA/YWCA/YMHA/YWHA, Youth Organizations

Contributions Analysis

Giving Priorities: Education, civic, health, and welfare improvements; culture; public policy research; nonprofit international organizations. International giving is very decentralized among approximately 20 operating locations. Managing directors are relatively autonomous in supporting local organizations (approximately $2,000 to $5,000 U.S. dollars per location). The foundation makes a few grants to foreign organizations that meet U.S. IRS regulations. In 1997, contributions for international purposes were more than $130,000. Communities receiving grants were Bombay, India; Sarnia and Lac du Bonnet, Canada; Maua, Brazil; Port Dickson, Malaysia; Stanlow, England; and Valasske Mezirici, Czech Republic. Company also sponsors volunteer community service awards open to application by overseas employees and their spouses wherein company provides $1,000 to organizations where employees/spouses volunteer.
Arts & Humanities: 11%. Supports museums that promote science education and community arts organizations, including visual and performing arts groups in company operating communities.
Civic & Public Affairs: 16%. Includes civic, health and welfare concerns. Priority is given to community projects involving company employees and retirees. Typical recipients include youth organizations, urban and community affairs groups, safety organizations, the handicapped, and hospitals.
Education: 36%. Supports higher educational science and technology programs, placing priority on mathematics, physics, chemistry, and special disciplines, including ceramics, materials and polymer sciences, and chemical and metallurgical engineering. Special interest is in schools that encourage research by students and junior faculty. Also supports secondary school science and mathematics education, particularly programs focused on gifted students. Other interests include colleges and universities in company operating communities; skills development and occupational retraining, especially for minorities, women, and the handicapped; and, to a lesser degree, applied economics programs at all levels of education. Also supports educational public broadcasting and Junior Achievement.
Environment: 3%. Supports environmental education and conservation.
Health: 3%. Supports hospitals, medical centers and single-disease concerns.
International: 24%. Supports international causes.
Science: 2%.
Social Services: 5%. Supports child and youth services, and the United Way.
Note: Total contributions in 1998.

Application Procedures

Initial Contact: Send a written proposal.
Application Requirements: Include statement of proposed project (no more than two pages), including its purpose, uniqueness, long-term goals, specific short-term objectives, estimated time required for completion, and manner by which results are measured; brief background information on organization, board of directors, and those leading proposed effort; proof of tax-exempt status; total project cost, present and potential funding sources, and amount requested of Cabot; include latest audited financial statement if organization's budget exceeds $100,000.
Deadlines: Proposals must be received at least one month before board meetings held in March, June, September, and December.
Review Process: Grant requests for/from communities where Cabot has operations are reviewed at the local level by community relations teams; if appropriate for foundation funding, they are forwarded to the executive director; further information and site visits may be necessary; approval is made by the directors of the foundation.
Evaluative Criteria: Year-end reports, audits, community relations team recommendation, employee involvement.
Decision Notification: Quarterly.

Restrictions

Cabot Corporation Foundation does not make contributions to individuals, political or fraternal organizations, religious institutions for sectarian purposes, advertising, or dinner-table sponsorship.

Additional Information

Cabot strongly encourages requests from projects under way in plant locations. The contributions program has expanded its involvement in plant communities, tying contributions more closely to the nature of business, encouraging greater employee participation in community volunteer activities, and addressing significant societal concerns. Foundation particularly considers recommendations from teams formed by local employees, which initiate community projects and consider local requests for support.
Company prefers to support specific projects or programs rather than general operating expenses.
Strong consideration is given to projects that combine financial support with company manpower, technical assistance, or in-kind support to achieve objectives.
Company often conducts 'needs assessments' surveys to determine if projects will have a long-term effect on the community they serve.
Cabot is especially interested in projects involved with science and technology.
Organizations receiving grants are expected to provide periodic progress reports.

Publications: Guidelines

Corporate Officials

Samuel Wright Bodman, III: chairman, chief executive officer, director B Chicago, IL 1938. ED Cornell University BS (1961); Massachusetts Institute of Technology PhD (1964). PRIM CORP EMPL chairman, chief executive officer, director: Cabot Corp. ADD CORP EMPL director: Cabot Oil & Gas Corp.; director: Distrigas Massachusetts Corp. CORP AFFIL director: Westvaco Corp.; director: Security Capital Group Inc.; director: Thermo Electron Corp.; director: John Hancock Mutual Life Insurance Co. NONPR AFFIL trustee, member executive committee: Massachusetts Institute Technology; trustee: New England Aquarium; trustee: Isabella Stewart Gardner Museum.
Charles Agustus Gray: vice president technology B Washington, DC 1938. ED Cornell University BSChE (1961); Massachusetts Institute of Technology PhD (1965). PRIM CORP EMPL vice president technology: Cabot Corp.
Robert Rothberg: vice president, general counsel B 1949. ED Cornell University BS (1970); Cornell University MS (1971); Harvard University JD (1974). PRIM CORP EMPL vice president, general counsel: Cabot Corp.

Foundation Officials

Samuel Wright Bodman, III: president, director (see above)
Dorothy L. Forbes: executive director
Charles Agustus Gray: director (see above)
Karen M. Morressey: director
Robert Rothberg: director (see above)

Grants Analysis

Disclosure Period: fiscal year ending September 30, 1998
Total Grants: $587,473*
Number of Grants: 50
Average Grant: $11,749
Highest Grant: $75,000
Typical Range: $1,000 to $10,000
***Note:** Giving excludes matching gifts and volunteer grants.

Recent Grants

Note: Grants derived from fiscal 1999 Form 990.

International

25,000	Lambton County Board of Education, Canada -- to expand science programs in schools
25,000	Obec Mesto Valasske Mezirici, Czech Republic -- to repair local schools damaged by summer floods
20,000	Family YMCA of Sarnia Lambton, Canada -- final payment on two-year pledge for capital campaign
15,000	Cancer Patients Aid Association, India -- training for volunteers and educational program for patients
15,000	Sage, Lac du Bonnet, MB, Canada -- to renovate building for multipurpose use
10,000	Lac du Bonnet Regional Library, Lac du Bonnet, MB, Canada -- support automated library system
6,000	Massachusetts State Science Fair, Boston, MA -- to send students to International Science Fair in Louisville, KY
5,000	Babson College, Wellesley, MA -- support Center for Global Entrepreneurial Leadership
5,000	Sociedade Amigos do Jardim Oratorio, Brazil -- for additional space school

Cadence Designs Systems, Inc.

Company Contact
San Jose, CA
Web: http://www.cadence.com/community.html

Company Description
Employees: 3,028
SIC(s): 7371 Computer Programming Services, 7372 Prepackaged Software, 7389 Business Services Nec.

Operating Locations
Operates sales, research and development, and distribution offices in 17 countries.

Nonmonetary Support
Type: Donated Products
Note: Nonmonetary support budget is approximately $36,000,000 annually.

Giving Contact
Kathy L. Wheeler, Communication Affairs
Cadence Design Systems, Inc.
2655 Seely Ave., MS5A1
San Jose, CA 95134
Phone: (408)428-5993
Fax: (408)954-8766

Description
Organization Type: Corporate Giving Program
Giving Locations: CA: Santa Clara Valley area headquarters and major operating locations.
Grant Types: General Support.

Giving Philosophy
'Cadence Design Systems, Inc. is the worldwide leader in the development and marketing of software used to accelerate and advance the creation of electronic systems. One of the ten largest software companies in the world, with the company headquarters in San Jose and additional facilities dispersed globally, Cadence is firmly committed to supporting the communities where its employees live and work.' *Cadence Charitable Contributions Guidelines*

Financial Summary
Total Giving: Contributes through corporate direct giving program only.

Typical Recipients
Arts & Humanities: Arts & Humanities-General
Civic & Public Affairs: Civic & Public Affairs-General
Education: Colleges & Universities, Education-General, Science/Mathematics Education
Social Services: Youth Organizations

Contributions Analysis
Education: Focus is currently on K-12 education. However, Stars & Strikes, a community grants program, is not limited to K-12 education.

Application Procedures
Initial Contact: brief letter of application
Application Requirements: issue to be addressed and population to be served by the project; list of objectives that will be accomplished by the project and how success will be measured; timeline for implementation; amount of funds requested and how they will be expended (please be specific); names of any Cadence employees who are active with the organization; brief a description of organization's history, current goals, and accomplishments; proof of nonprofit status (copy of IRS 501(c)(3) letter); itemized budget for project, including funds that have already been committed; current balance sheet and detailed budget for the organization; copy of agency's nondiscrimination policy
Deadlines: before November 15 for support in the following calendar year
Evaluative Criteria: opportunity creates major impact on projects or initiatives addressing community needs; opportunity leverages Cadence contribution to generate significantly greater return for charity; request cites direct employee involvement in charity (especially board membership); opportunity provides new chance for active participation by Cadence employee volunteers; opportunity provides means to enhance visibility for Cadence in local community; support avoids dependencies on Cadence; charity provides infrastructure to enable input, oversight, and evaluation, while diminishing resource commitments required from Cadence; charity maintains 501(c)(3) status and is nonsecular; and charity minimizes overhead as percentage of costs

Restrictions
Funding is not considered for individuals, political or lobbying groups, religious organizations for sectarian purposes, or courtesy advertising. In addition, funding will not be provided for sports leagues or sporting events, 'goodwill' trips, equipment for use in private residences, or production of television, movies, or multimedia programs. Groups that practice or promote unlawful discriminatory policies will not be eligible for funding.

Additional Information
Matching Program serves all areas where Cadence employees live and work, domestically.
Corporate grants typically range from $5,000 to $20,000, but requests outside this area may also be considered.

Corporate Officials
Jack R. Harding: president, chief executive officer B 1955. ED Drew University BA (1977). PRIM CORP EMPL president, chief executive officer: Cadence Design Systems, Inc.
Donald Leo Lucas: chairman B Upland, CA 1930. ED Stanford University BA (1951); Stanford University Graduate School of Business Administration MBA (1953). PRIM CORP EMPL chairman: Cadence Design Systems, Inc. CORP AFFIL director: TriCord System Inc.; chairman: Transcend Services Inc.; director: Oracle Corp.; director: Quantum Health Resources Inc.; director: Coulter Pham Inc.; director: Macromedia Inc. NONPR AFFIL regent emeritus: University Santa Clara; member: Zeta Psi; member: Stanford University Alumni Association; member: Order Malta; member: Stanford Graduate Business Alumni Association; Independent Order Sons Malta; member: American Council Capital Formation. CLUB AFFIL Vintage Club; Stanford Buck Club; Teton Pines Club; Menlo Country Club; Sand Hills Golf Club; Menlo Circus Club; Bighorn Country Club; Jackson Hole Golf & Tennis Club.

Giving Program Officials
Kathryn Lillard Wheeler: PRIM CORP EMPL employee service representative: Cadence Design Systems, Inc.

Grants Analysis
Disclosure Period: calendar year ending

Recent Grants
Note: Grants derived from 1993 grants list.

Education
36,000,000 Carnegie-Mellon University, Pittsburgh, PA -- in computer software to assist engineering students in designing electronic circuits

Caesar's World, Inc.

Company Contact
Los Angeles, CA
Web: http://www.caesar.com

Company Description
Revenue: US$1,015,766,000
Employees: 9,700
SIC(s): 5812 Eating Places, 7011 Hotels & Motels, 7389 Business Services Nec, 7999 Amusement & Recreation Nec.

Nonmonetary Support
Type: Donated Equipment; Donated Products

Corporate Sponsorship
Type: Arts & cultural events; Music & entertainment events; Sports events

Giving Contact
John Shigley, Executive Vice President
Caesar's World, Inc.
3570 Las Vegas Boulevard South
PO Box 14382
Las Vegas, NV 89109
Phone: (702)731-7639
Fax: (702)731-7933

Description
Organization Type: Corporate Giving Program
Giving Locations: headquarters and operating communities.
Grant Types: General Support.

Financial Summary
Total Giving: Contributes through corporate direct giving program only.

Typical Recipients
Arts & Humanities: Arts & Humanities-General
Civic & Public Affairs: Civic & Public Affairs-General
Education: Education-General
Health: Health-General
Social Services: Social Services-General

Application Procedures
Initial Contact: written proposal
Application Requirements: a description of organization, amount requested, purpose of funds sought, recently audited financial statement, and proof of tax-exempt status
Deadlines: by July 31 for next fiscal year
Notes: Each operation handles their own contributions, with the corporate charitable contributions committee approving major donations and periodically reviewing the contributions made.

Restrictions
Company does not support packages such as door prizes or auctions, organizations other than those that are nonprofit and charitable as determined by the IRS, or organization outside of operating areas.

Corporate Officials
John Shigley: executive vice president PRIM CORP EMPL executive vice president: Caesar's World Inc.

California Bank & Trust

Company Contact
San Francisco, CA
Web: http://www.calbanktrust.com

Company Description
Former Name: Sumitomo Bank of California.
Revenue: US$415,677,000
Employees: 1,500
SIC(s): 6082 Foreign Trade & International Banks.
Parent Company: Sumitomo Bank, Ltd., 6-5 Kitahama 4-chome, Chuo-ku, Osaka, Japan

Operating Locations

CA: California Bank & Trust, Mountain View, Albany, Alhambra, Anaheim, Brea, Claremont, Costa Mesa, Cupertino, Fresno, Gardena, Hacienda Heights, Hayward Millbrae, La Palma, Long Beach, Los Angeles; Sumitomo Bank, Ltd., Los Angeles Branch, Los Angeles; California Bank & Trust, Monterey, Oxnard, Pleasant Hill, Pomona, Sacramento, San Francisco; Sumitomo Bank of California, San Francisco; Sumitomo Bank, Ltd., San Francisco Branch, San Francisco; California Bank & Trust, San Jose, San Mateo, Santa Monica, Stockton, Torrance, Watsonville, West Hollywood; GA: Sumitomo Bank, Ltd.-Atlanta Agency, Atlanta; IL: Sumitomo Bank, Ltd., Chicago Branch, Chicago; NY: Sumitomo Bank Capital Markets, New York; Sumitomo Bank Financial Services, New York; Sumitomo Bank Investment Management, New York; Sumitomo Bank Leasing & Finance, New York; Sumitomo Bank, Ltd., New York Branch, New York; Sumitomo Bank of New York Trust Co., New York; Sumitomo Bank Securities, New York; TX: Sumitomo Bank, Ltd.-Houston Agency, Houston; WA: Sumitomo Bank, Ltd.-Seattle Representative Office, Seattle

Nonmonetary Support

Value: $134,000 (1997 approx)
Type: Donated Equipment; In-kind Services; Loaned Employees
Volunteer Programs: Employees are encouraged to become involved in their communities through participation in local civic and government groups and whose primary focus is to improve economic development in the community.
Contact: Steve Nelson

Corporate Sponsorship

Type: Arts & cultural events; Festivals/fairs; Other
Note: Sponsors workshops to target small business lending and technical assistance, and home ownership for low and moderate income individuals.

Giving Contact

Ms. Linda Buckner, Vice President and Manager
California Bank & Trust
Community Development Department
11622 El Camino Real, Suite 200
San Diego, CA 92130
Phone: (858)793-7470
Fax: (858)793-7438

Description

Organization Type: Corporate Giving Program
Giving Locations: CA: Southern and Northern regions headquarters area only.
Grant Types: Capital, Conference/Seminar, Employee Matching Gifts, General Support, Loan, Project.
Note: Employee matching gift ratio: 1 to 1.

Giving Philosophy

CB&T makes monetary contributions to bonafide nonprofit entities, philanthropic foundations, local development groups, institutions of higher learning and local governing bodies whose work improves the lives of citizens in the CB&T community. 1998 Annual Report

Financial Summary

Total Giving: $800,000 (1999 approx); $890,000 (1998 approx); $818,000 (1997 approx)

Typical Recipients

Arts & Humanities: Community Arts, Libraries, Museums/Galleries, Music
Civic & Public Affairs: Economic Development, Employment/Job Training, Housing, Urban & Community Affairs
Education: Colleges & Universities, Public Education (Precollege)
Health: Health Organizations
Social Services: Community Service Organizations, Family Services, People with Disabilities, United Funds/United Ways, Youth Organizations

Contributions Analysis

Giving Priorities: Co. supports local community development, providing grants for educational and philanthropic efforts. Also provides financial opportunities for low and moderate-income neighborhoods in the way of extension of credit and provision of other lending-related Services.

Application Procedures

Initial Contact: Send a written proposal.
Application Requirements: Send a a description of organization and name of contact person, a statement of purpose, a request for a specific amount of funding, an explanation of why funds are needed and how they will be used, a list of contributors, list of board of directors and their business affiliations, a recently audited financial statement including income and expenses, proof of tax-exempt status.
Deadlines: None.
Notes: Individual branches administer small budgets; large grants are referred to the Community Development Department or the Regional Headquarters in San Francisco, Los Angeles, or San Diego.

Restrictions

Does not support individuals, religious organizations for sectarian purposes, or organizations outside operating areas.

Additional Information

In March 1997, Sumitomo Bank announced its 1997 Community Outreach Plan, which contains the bank's CRA (Community Reinvestment Act) goals. The bank has doubled a commitment made in 1993 and will target $1 billion in CRA loans by the year 2003. In addition, the company expanded its Community Advisory Board from five to ten members, and expects to aim for greater diversity in its use of vendors and in its philanthropic support of community organizations. In 1997, the company's goal was to donate 2% of net income, with a greater emphasis given to educational, business, and job development needs in the communities it serves.
Publications: Guidelines Sheet; Annual Report

Grants Analysis

Disclosure Period: calendar year ending 1998
Total Grants: $890,000 (approx)
Number of Grants: 125 (approx)
Average Grant: $6,400
Typical Range: $1,000 to $25,000
Note: Grants analysis is approximate.

CALIFORNIA FEDERAL BANK, FSB

Company Contact

Los Angeles, CA
Web: http://www.calfed.com

Company Description

Assets: US$14,320,600,000
Employees: 2,100
SIC(s): 6035 Federal Savings Institutions.

Nonmonetary Support

Value: $85,000 (1998 approx)
Type: Donated Equipment
Note: Volunteer recognition program allows employees to volunteer 4 hrs/month on co. time. Co. gives gifts & grants to nonprofits where Cal Fed employees volunteer.

Giving Contact

Sue Avila, Associate Community Relations Officer
California Federal Bank, FSB
3900 Lennane Dr., Suite 102
Sacramento, CA 95834
Phone: (916)614-2334
Fax: (916)614-2800

Description

Organization Type: Corporate Giving Program
Giving Locations: CA; NV headquarters and operating locations.
Grant Types: Employee Matching Gifts, General Support.

Giving Philosophy

'California Federal Bank recognizes a responsibility to respond to the needs of the communities in which we conduct business by:
Contributing to the quality of life and well being of society
Encouraging and supporting employee volunteers in community affairs
'California Federal Bank's WE CARE program was created to support tax-exempt organizations that have maximum impact on housing, education, and community developments with an emphasis on inner cities where we operate.' Program Guidelines

Financial Summary

Total Giving: $2,000,000 (1999 approx); $2,000,000 (1998 approx); $250,000 (1995 approx). Note: Contributes through corporate direct giving program only.
Giving Analysis: Giving for 1999 includes: corporate direct giving (approx $2,000,000)

Contributions Analysis

Civic & Public Affairs: Supports the development of affordable housing, housing rehabilitation improvements, and urban renewal. Also supports inner-city programs that promote job training, and development. Programs that provide positive alternatives to at-risk children are also funded.
Education: Funds educational programs, with emphasis on basic skills, and business and financial education to students of all ages in the low-income census tract neighborhoods served by California Federal Bank.

Application Procedures

Initial Contact: Send a written inquiry.
Application Requirements: Include name, address and contact information; amount requested; purpose of which funds will be used; project details, proof of 501(c)(3) status, current annual report (if available), mission statement; population served; and current budget.
Deadlines: None.
Decision Notification: Proposals are reviewed regularly; organizations are notified of decisions as soon as possible.

Restrictions

Company does not support groups that discriminate on basis of race, religious, sex, age, or national origin. Does not support political parties, individuals, sports events, capital campaigns, religious concerns, or international organizations.

Additional Information

California Federal Bank does not guarantee contributions year to year; organizations must reapply for funding consideration.
Publications: guidelines, application form.

Giving Program Officials
Mary Hogarty: vice president community relations

CALLAWAY GOLF CO.

Company Contact
Carlsbad, CA
Web: http://www.callawaygolf.com

Company Description
Employees: 2,252 (1999)
SIC(s): 3940 Toys & Sporting Goods, 3949 Sporting & Athletic Goods Nec.

Callaway Golf Co. Foundation

Giving Contact
Karen Smelkinson, Executive Director
Callaway Golf Co. Foundation
2285 Rutherford Rd.
Carlsbad, CA 92008-8815
Phone: (760)930-8686
Fax: (760)929-9780

Description
Founded: 1994
EIN: 330590291
Organization Type: Corporate Foundation
Giving Locations: CA: San Diego County
Grant Types: General Support, Matching.

Giving Philosophy
The Callaway Golf Company Foundation's purpose is to improve the human condition primarily as it exists in the community in which Callaway Golf Company operates and its employees live, focusing on programs which help people in need; provide access to health care for those who cannot afford it; and improve our community.

'We believe that people are the most precious resource.'

'Our goal is to help people and be a resource to those in need. For us, people are the most highest priority.'

New Initiatives: The Callaway Golf Company Foundation announced in July 1999 that it had reassessed its giving strategy. The Board of Directors decided to cease funding for programs serving the elderly and homeless populations. The Foundation's three main areas of support are currently: family, focusing on the prevention and intervention of domestic violence, including child abuse, and support for those afflicted by it; health, providing access to quality medical care in the community, especially for those who cannot afford it and for the physically challenged; and youth, including support for the children of the company's community who are in need, with emphasis on juvenile violence prevention.

Financial Summary
Total Giving: $535,215 (1998); $869,675 (1996); $804,047 (1995). Note: Contributes through corporate direct giving program and foundation.
Giving Analysis: Giving for 1998 includes: foundation ($535,215)
Assets: $858,977 (1998); $3,497,245 (1996); $3,701,830 (1995)
Gifts Received: $155,555 (1996); $2,084,672 (1995); $73,085 (1994). Note: In 1996, contributions were received from Callaway Golf Co., Michael Sherwin, Bruce Parker, and Steve McKracken.

Typical Recipients
Arts & Humanities: Museums/Galleries
Civic & Public Affairs: Employment/Job Training
Education: Literacy
Health: Alzheimers Disease, Cancer, Children's Health/Hospitals, Eyes/Blindness, Health Organizations, Medical Rehabilitation, Prenatal Health Issues
Religion: Religious Welfare
Social Services: At-Risk Youth, Big Brother/Big Sister, Child Abuse, Child Welfare, Community Service Organizations, Domestic Violence, People with Disabilities, Recreation & Athletics, Shelters/Homelessness, Youth Organizations

Contributions Analysis
Health: 36%. Supports hospitals and hospices.
Social Services: 64%. Major support for at-risk youth. Also funds family violence prevention and services, and organizations helping the disadvantaged.
Note: Total contributions in 1998.

Application Procedures
Initial Contact: Request application guidelines, then submit application.
Application Requirements: Provide a brief history of organization, the goals of the organization, and how the organization has met these goals in the past; a description of the need that the organization and the proposed project fulfills; a description of the proposed project, including objectives and timelines; the qualifications of leadership personnel involved with the project, with a list of the Board of Directors and their affiliations; and a detailed budget for the project, including the specific request for funding from the Foundation. The following supporting documents must be included with an application: IRS letter confirming 501(c)(3) status; most recent audited financial statement and management letter; most recent Form 990; and current proposed budget for the following fiscal year; if available.
Deadlines: March 1 and September 1 to receive contributions in July and January, respectively
Decision Notification: Applicants are informed of the Board's decision by letter.

Restrictions
The Foundation does not support applicants that discriminate on the basis of gender, race, color, religion, national origin, ancestry, age, marital status, medical condition or physical disability, neither in the services they provide nor in the hiring of their staff; or that promote political or particular religious doctrines.

Additional Information
Publications: Application Guidelines

Corporate Officials
Ely Reeves Callaway, Jr.: chairman vice president, chief financial officer B La Grange, GA 1919. ED Emory University AB (1940). PRIM CORP EMPL chairman: Callaway Golf Co. CORP AFFIL principal: Callaway Editions Inc.
Donald H. Dye: president, chief executive officer B Riverside, CA 1942. ED University of Redlands; University of California, Los Angeles BA (1964); University of California, Los Angeles JD (1967). PRIM CORP EMPL president, chief executive officer: Callaway Golf Co.
Elizabeth O'Mea: senior vice president PRIM CORP EMPL senior vice president: Callaway Golf Co.
Frederick R. Port: executive vice president PRIM CORP EMPL executive vice president: Callaway Golf Co.
David A. Rane: executive vice president, chief financial officer ED Brigham Young University (1978). PRIM CORP EMPL executive vice president, chief financial officer: Callaway Golf Co.

Foundation Officials
Ely Reeves Callaway, Jr.: chairman (see above)
John Duffy: director CORP AFFIL senior executive vice president: Callaway Golf Co.
Donald H. Dye: president, chief executive officer (see above)
Michael Haynes: director
Richard Helmstetter: director PRIM CORP EMPL senior executive vice president: Callaway Golf Co.
Julie Malloy: director
Steve McCracken: director, secretary B Artesia, CA 1950. PRIM CORP EMPL executive vice president, chief legal officer, secretary: Callaway Golf Co.
Elizabeth O'Mea: director (see above)
Bruce Parker: director PRIM CORP EMPL senior executive vice president: Callaway Golf Co.
Frederick R. Port: director (see above)
David A. Rane: chief financial officer (see above)
Karen Smelkinson: executive director

Grants Analysis
Disclosure Period: calendar year ending 1998
Total Grants: $535,215
Number of Grants: 43
Average Grant: $12,447
Highest Grant: $40,000
Typical Range: $5,000 to $15,000
Note: Grants analysis provided by foundation.

Recent Grants
Note: Grants derived from 1996 Form 990.

Arts & Humanities

25,000	Children's Museum Museo De Los Ninos, San Diego, CA -- support 1996 School Group Visit Program

Health

50,000	Children's Hospital Foundation, San Diego, CA -- provide assistance to victims of domestic violence
50,000	Scripps Medical Foundation, Encinitas, CA -- Perinatal Services Program for indigent women
25,000	Vista Community Clinic, Vista, CA -- support Kare For Kids Fund
20,000	Christina's Smile Children's Dental Clinic, Austin, TX -- provide free dental care for disadvantaged
15,000	Sharp Healthcare Foundation, San Diego, CA -- support for rehabilitation services
13,000	Hospice of the North Coast, Carlsbad, CA -- support children's bereavement program
10,000	Conner's Cause for Children, Encinitas, CA -- assist families who have children with diseases
6,486	Alzheimer's Family, San Diego, CA -- help for Alzheimer's Disease
5,000	Alzheimer's Association, Pittsburgh, PA -- help for Alzheimer's Disease
2,000	Prevent Blindness of Southern California, San Diego, CA -- emergency fund for eye care

Religion

20,000	St. Clare's Home, Escondido, CA -- provide shelter for homeless women

Social Services

250,000	LPGA Foundation, Daytona Beach, FL -- golf instructions to inner-city youth
100,000	Pro Kids Golf, San Diego, CA -- golf instruction for inner-city youth
55,000	Project Restore, San Diego, CA -- gang intervention and prevention program
50,000	National Alliance for Youth Sports, West Palm Beach, FL -- promoting community sharing
30,000	Boys and Girls Club, Vista, CA -- build a soccer field for gang prevention
25,000	Chi Chi Rodriguez Youth Foundation, Clearwater, FL -- provide assistance and education to at-risk children
20,000	Second Chance, San Diego, CA -- assist homeless with housing and job training
15,000	TERI, Oceanside, CA -- for van purchase

14,407 Casa De Amparo, San Luis Rey, CA -- support educational program for abused
11,232 Community Resource Center, Encinitas, CA -- provide shelter for abused women with children
10,000 Boys and Girls Club, Carlsbad, CA -- support Teen Scene Program
10,000 Boys and Girls Club, Oceanside, CA -- support Project Gangbusters
10,000 Canine Companions for Independence, Oceanside, CA -- enhance the quality of life for disabled
10,000 Escondido Youth Encounter, San Marcos, CA -- treatment for indigent youth
5,300 Children's Home Society of California, San Diego, CA -- provide assistance to at-risk children
5,000 Big Sister League, San Diego, CA -- support mentor program
5,000 Boys and Girls Club, Escondido, CA -- support Street-Safe Program
2,250 Cleveland Sight Center, Cleveland, OH -- support Blind Golf Program

CALVIN KLEIN

Company Contact

New York, NY

Company Description

Employees: 1,500
SIC(s): 2329 Men's/Boys' Clothing Nec, 2339 Women's/Misses' Outerwear Nec, 2844 Toilet Preparations.

Nonmonetary Support

Contact: Laurie Kaufmann, Public Relations Assistant

Corporate Sponsorship

Type: Other

Calvin Klein Foundation

Giving Contact

Joel Semel, Foundation Manager
Calvin Klein Foundation
205 West 39th Street
New York, NY 10018
Phone: (212)719-2600
Fax: (212)292-9787

Description

EIN: 133094765
Organization Type: Corporate Foundation
Grant Types: General Support.

Financial Summary

Total Giving: $484,720 (fiscal year ending June 30, 1998); $664,297 (fiscal 1996); $350,799 (fiscal 1995). Note: Contributes through foundation only. Giving includes foundation.
Assets: $320,325 (fiscal 1998); $435,466 (fiscal 1996); $546,980 (fiscal 1995)
Gifts Received: $526,500 (fiscal 1996); $867,100 (fiscal 1995); $260,000 (fiscal 1994). Note: Contributions are received from Calvin Klein, Inc.

Typical Recipients

Arts & Humanities: Arts Associations & Councils, Arts Centers, Ballet, Dance, Film & Video, Arts & Humanities-General, History & Archaeology, Literary Arts, Museums/Galleries, Music, Performing Arts, Theater
Civic & Public Affairs: Botanical Gardens/Parks, Civil Rights, Economic Development, Ethnic Organizations, Civic & Public Affairs-General, Hispanic Affairs, Housing, Legal Aid, Philanthropic Organizations, Public Policy, Urban & Community Affairs, Women's Affairs
Education: Arts/Humanities Education, Business Education, Colleges & Universities, Education Funds, Education-General, Literacy, Private Education (Precollege)
Environment: Air/Water Quality, Environment-General, Resource Conservation
Health: AIDS/HIV, Alzheimers Disease, Cancer, Children's Health/Hospitals, Clinics/Medical Centers, Health Organizations, Hospitals, Medical Research, Mental Health, Multiple Sclerosis, Single-Disease Health Associations
International: International Environmental Issues, International Organizations, International Peace & Security Issues, International Relief Efforts, Missionary/Religious Activities
Religion: Jewish Causes, Ministries, Religious Organizations, Religious Welfare, Seminaries, Social/Policy Issues
Social Services: Child Welfare, Community Service Organizations, Day Care, Family Services, Food/Clothing Distribution, People with Disabilities, Recreation & Athletics, Scouts, Shelters/Homelessness, Special Olympics, Substance Abuse, United Funds/United Ways

Contributions Analysis

Arts & Humanities: 10% to 15%. Museums, performing arts, and art associations.
Civic & Public Affairs: 15% to 20%. Urban and community affairs, minority affairs, and civil rights organizations.
Education: 5% to 10%. Colleges and universities, religious education associations.
Health: About 30%. Single-disease health associations, hospitals, and children's health.
Social Services: About 25%. Youth organizations, food/clothing distribution, homelessness, and athletic associations.

Application Procedures

Initial Contact: The foundation has no formal grant application procedure or application form.
Deadlines: None.

Corporate Officials

Ricard DiPaola: secretary, chief executive officer, director PRIM CORP EMPL secretary: Calvin Klein Inc.
Gabriella Forte: president, chief operating officer PRIM CORP EMPL president, chief operating officer: Calvin Klein ADD CORP EMPL vice president: Eight Hundred Fifteen Giorgio Armani Boutique. CORP AFFIL officer: Fourteen Fifty Partner Emporio Armani.
Calvin Richard Klein: president B Bronx, NY 1942. ED Fashion Institute of Technology AA (1962). PRIM CORP EMPL president: Calvin Klein. CORP AFFIL vice chairman: Calvin Klein Sport. NONPR AFFIL member: Museum Modern Art; member: Whitney Museum American Art; member: Metropolitan Museum Art; member: Council Fashion Designers America; member: Guggenheim Museum.
Richard Martin: president finance & administration PRIM CORP EMPL president finance & administration: Calvin Klein.
Barry K. Schwartz: chairman, chief executive officer, director B Bronx, NY 1942. ED New York University. PRIM CORP EMPL chairman, chief executive officer, director: Calvin Klein. CORP AFFIL chairman: Calvin Klein Jeanswear Co. NONPR AFFIL director: New York Racing Association.

Foundation Officials

Ricard DiPaola: trustee (see above)
Richard Martin: trustee (see above)
Kristen Vigrass: coordinator

Grants Analysis

Disclosure Period: fiscal year ending June 30, 1996
Total Grants: $644,294
Number of Grants: 93
Average Grant: $7,143
Highest Grant: $75,000
Typical Range: $1,000 to $25,000

Recent Grants

Note: Grants derived from fiscal 1998 Form 990.

Arts & Humanities

32,000 Metropolitan Museum of Art, New York, NY
12,000 American Museum of Moving Image, New York, NY
10,000 Whitney Museum of American Art, New York, NY
8,500 Ballet Theatre Foundation, New York, NY
7,500 Guild Hall, New York, NY
5,000 Classical Action, New York, NY
5,000 National Museum of Dance, Saratoga Springs, NY
5,000 National Museum of Dance, Saratoga Springs, NY
5,000 Smithsonian Institution, Washington, DC
3,250 Underfashion Club Inc, New York, NY

Civic & Public Affairs

25,000 CFDA, New York, NY
7,500 GMHC, New York, NY
5,000 City Parks Foundation, New York, NY
5,000 N.I.A.F., Washington, DC
5,000 Now Defense League, New York, NY
5,000 Rock The Vote Education Fund, Los Angeles, CA
2,500 New York Restoration Project, TN
2,500 Princess Ball, Beverly Hills, CA

Education

10,000 School of American Ballet, New York, NY
10,000 Yale University, New Haven, CT
7,500 St John's University, New York, NY
5,000 Educational Foundation For The Fashion Industry, New York, NY
5,000 Parsons School of Design, New York, NY
5,000 Skowhegan School of Painting & Sculpture, New York, NY
2,520 Royal College of Art, Chicago, IL
2,500 Brooklyn Academy of Music, Brooklyn, NY

Health

15,000 Elizabeth Glaser Pediatric Aids Foundation, Santa Monica, CA
15,000 March of Dimes, New York, NY
14,500 American Italian Cancer Foundation, New York, NY
11,200 Mount Sinai Medical Center, New York, NY
10,000 Health Crisis Network, Miami, FL
10,000 Ovarian Cancer Research Foundation, Los Angeles, CA
7,500 CRIA, New York, NY
5,000 March of Dimes, New York, NY
5,000 Mount Sinai Medical Center, New York, NY
3,500 DIFFA, Chicago, IL
3,400 American Italian Cancer Foundation, New York, NY

Religion

10,000 American Jewish Committee, New York, NY
5,000 Divine Design Ministries, Whitley City, KY
5,000 National Jewish Fund, New York, NY

Social Services

25,000	Mothers Voices, New York, NY
15,000	Hampton Classic Horse Show, NY
11,500	Lighthouse, Inc, New York, NY
10,000	Hazeldon, New York, NY
5,000	CASA, New York, NY
5,000	Casa Concert of Hope
5,000	Child Care Action Campaign, New York, NY
5,000	Citymeals on Wheels, Inc, New York, NY
5,000	New York Special Olympics, New York, NY
5,000	Partnership For The Homeless, New York, NY
3,000	Boy Scouts of America, New York, NY

Campbell Soup Co.

Company Contact

Camden, NJ
Web: http://www.campbellsoup.com

Company Description

Revenue: US$6,424,000,000 (1999)
Employees: 24,500 (1999)
Fortune Rank: 269, per FORTUNE Magazine's list of 500 Largest U.S. Corporations (1999).
FF 269
SIC(s): 2032 Canned Specialties, 2037 Frozen Fruits & Vegetables, 2051 Bread, Cake & Related Products, 2052 Cookies & Crackers.

Operating Locations

Australia; Canada; Japan; Mexico
Note: Operates in Europe and South America.

Nonmonetary Support

Value: $800,000 (1989)
Type: Donated Equipment; Donated Products; In-kind Services; Workplace Solicitation
Contact: Joan Berger, Grant Administrator

Corporate Sponsorship

Type: Arts & cultural events; Festivals/fairs; Music & entertainment events; Sports events
Contact: Robert Desatnick, Director of Advertising
Note: Sponsors figure skating and auto racing events.

Campbell Soup Foundation

Giving Contact

Wendy Milanesa, Program Director
Campbell Soup Foundation
Campbell Pl.
Camden, NJ 08103-1799
Phone: (856)342-6429
Fax: (856)541-8185

Description

EIN: 216019196
Organization Type: Corporate Foundation
Giving Locations: headquarters and operating locations.
Grant Types: Challenge, Employee Matching Gifts, General Support, Project.
Note: Employee matching gift ratio: 1 to 1 for education and United Ways.

Giving Philosophy

'We're committed to making measurable differences in.. specific areas: our hometown and birthplace, Camden, New Jersey, .. and improving the quality of life in areas where we have plant facilities.

'.. we look for projects meeting three criteria: They are well led. Their plans are clear and compelling.. and include commitments to real, measurable results. Finally, they are well calculated, not only to light the lives of people served, but also to shine like beacons and thereby attract additional support and expand opportunities throughout the community.

'Our philosophy gives high priority to bearing the risks others fear to embrace . . . proving out infant ideas with bright potential.' The Campbell Soup Foundation *Building Results.*

Financial Summary

Total Giving: $1,876,800 (fiscal year ending June 30, 1999 approx); $1,875,000 (fiscal 1998 approx); $1,970,186 (fiscal 1997). Note: Contributes through corporate direct giving program and foundation. 1997 Giving includes foundation ($1,269,841); matching gifts ($280,345); United Way ($420,000).
Assets: $24,000,000 (fiscal 1998 approx); $21,937,589 (fiscal 1997); $19,430,687 (fiscal 1996)
Gifts Received: $1,000,000 (fiscal 1995); $2,000,000 (fiscal 1994). Note: Foundation receives contributions from the Campbell Soup Company.

Typical Recipients

Arts & Humanities: Arts Centers, Community Arts, Arts & Humanities-General, Historic Preservation, Museums/Galleries, Music, Performing Arts, Visual Arts
Civic & Public Affairs: African American Affairs, Botanical Gardens/Parks, Business/Free Enterprise, Chambers of Commerce, Economic Development, Economic Policy, Employment/Job Training, Hispanic Affairs, Housing, Law & Justice, Minority Business, Professional & Trade Associations, Urban & Community Affairs, Zoos/Aquariums
Education: Afterschool/Enrichment Programs, Business Education, Colleges & Universities, Community & Junior Colleges, Education Reform, Faculty Development, Education-General, Literacy, Medical Education, Minority Education, Private Education (Precollege), Public Education (Precollege), Science/Mathematics Education, Vocational & Technical Education
Health: Cancer, Children's Health/Hospitals, Diabetes, Emergency/Ambulance Services, Eyes/Blindness, Heart, Hospitals, Kidney, Medical Research, Nutrition, Single-Disease Health Associations
International: International Development, International Relief Efforts
Religion: Churches, Religious Welfare
Science: Science Museums
Social Services: Community Centers, Community Service Organizations, Crime Prevention, Family Services, Food/Clothing Distribution, Recreation & Athletics, Scouts, Shelters/Homelessness, Social Services-General, Special Olympics, United Funds/United Ways, YMCA/YWCA/YMHA/YWHA, Youth Organizations

Contributions Analysis

Giving Priorities: Education, medical research, hospitals, economic development, arts, and social welfare organizations.
Arts & Humanities: 7%. Supports arts centers in Camden and plant communities.
Civic & Public Affairs: 14%. Major support to the City of Camden. Family centers, trade associations, housing, economic development, and minority affairs also receive funding.
Education: 2%. Emphasis on Camden area public education. Also supports colleges and universities that specialize in medical, engineering, and business education.
Social Services: 36%. Grants support Camden youth organizations and the United Way. Also funds family services, recreation, and people and disabilities.

Application Procedures

Initial Contact: Submit application form, then written proposal.
Application Requirements: Summary grant proposal and full narrative proposal, including: description of the organization, including name, address, and telephone number of contact; project objective; target population; major activities planned; timetable; project staff; means of measuring goals; historical sketch of agency and statement of current goals; project budget; other sources of funding; and proof of tax-exempt status.
Deadlines: None.
Review Process: An initial review is conducted by foundation staff; qualifying proposals are forwarded to board of trustees for a final decision. The review process may take up to three months.
Evaluative Criteria: Proposal must apply to one of the foundation's giving areas; organization must demonstrate it has a positive history and strong leadership; proposal must be clear and compelling as well as produce measurable results; project must be visible enough to solicit additional support from other funding sources.
Decision Notification: Applicant will be notified of any delays. Decision is received in writing.

Restrictions

The foundation does not make multiyear grants.
The foundation only accepts proposals submitted in writing. An organization can only submit similar proposals once in a 12-month period. Grants do not exceed $100,000.
The foundation does not support individuals; organizations outside the United States; discriminatory organizations; organizations not defined as tax-exempt under Section 501(c)(3) of the Internal Revenue Code; fraternal, political, or lobbying organizations; or goodwill advertising, dinners, or special events. tax-exempt under Section 501(c)(3) of the Internal Revenue Code; fraternal, political, or lobbying organizations; or goodwill advertising, dinners, or special events.

Additional Information

The foundation is increasing emphasis on reinforcing employee charitable activities. Because of this increased emphasis, the foundation is no longer funding initiatives in the area of diet and health.
Publications: Foundation Annual Report

Corporate Officials

David L. Albright: president finance B 1947. ED Indiana University MA; Villanova University BA (1969). PRIM CORP EMPL president: Pepperidge Farm Inc.
Basil L. Anderson: executive vice president, chief financial officer B 1946. ED Israeli Institute of Technology BS; University of Chicago MBA; University of Illinois MS (1969). PRIM CORP EMPL executive vice president, chief financial officer: Campbell Soup Co. CORP AFFIL president: Campbell Investment Co.; director: Staples Inc.
Roger D. Berry: vice president, chief information officer PRIM CORP EMPL vice president, chief information officer: Campbell Soup Co.
Anthony P. DiSilvestro: vice president, treasurer B Norwalk, CT 1958. ED Dartmouth College (1981); University of Pennsylvania Wharton School (1985). PRIM CORP EMPL vice president, treasurer: Campbell Soup Co.
Bennett Dorrance: vice chairman, director B 1945. PRIM CORP EMPL chairman, managing partner: DMB Associates Inc. ADD CORP EMPL trustee: DMB Ltd.; ltd. partner: DMB Property Ventures LP. CORP AFFIL director: Banc One Corp.; vice chairman, director: Campbell Soup Co.
Brenda Evans Edgerton: vice president business development B Halifax, VA 1949. ED Pennsylvania State University (1966-1969); Rutgers University BA (1970); Temple University MBA (1976). PRIM CORP EMPL vice president business development: Campbell Soup Co. ADD CORP EMPL treasurer: Campbell Sales Co.; treasurer: Herider Farms Inc.; treasurer:

Joseph Campbell Co. CORP AFFIL director: Frontier Corp.; treasurer: Herider Farms Inc.

John J. Furey: corporate secretary, corporate counsel B Coaldale, PA 1949. ED Villanova University BS (1971); Villanova University JD (1975); Villanova University LLM (1984). PRIM CORP EMPL corporate secretary, corporate counsel: Campbell Soup Co. ADD CORP EMPL secretary, director: Campbell Investment Co.; secretary, director: Campbell Sales Co.; secretary, director: Godiva Chocolatier Inc.; secretary, director: Joseph Campbell Co.

Ralph A. Harris: vice president corporate development B New York, NY 1946. ED Brown University BA (1968); Harvard University Graduate School of Business Administration MBA (1970). PRIM CORP EMPL vice president corporate development: Campbell Soup Co. CORP AFFIL vice president: Campbell Investment Co.

David Willis Johnson: chairman, director B Tumut, NW Australia 1932. ED University of Sydney BS (1954); University of Sidney (1955); University of Chicago MBA (1958). PRIM CORP EMPL chairman, director: Campbell Soup Co. CORP AFFIL director: Duane Reade Inc.; director: Colgate-Palmolive Co.; member executive advisory board: Donaldson Lufkin Jenrette Mcht Banking Partners. NONPR AFFIL member advisory council: University Chicago School Business; member advisory council: University Notre Dame College Business Administration; member: Grocery Manufacturer America; member: national Food Products Association; member: American Bakers Association.

Donald R. Lanning: vice president grocery operations PRIM CORP EMPL vice president grocery operations: Campbell Soup Co. CORP AFFIL president: Campbell's Fresh Inc.

Gerald S. Lord: vice president, controller B 1946. PRIM CORP EMPL vice president, controller: Campbell Soup Co. CORP AFFIL vice president, treasurer: Campbell Investment Co. NONPR AFFIL member: Financial Executives Institute; member: National Association of Corporate Treasurers.

Robert Subin: senior vice president B 1938. ED University of Pennsylvania BS (1960). PRIM CORP EMPL senior vice president: Campbell Soup Co. CORP AFFIL director: PECO Energy Co.

F. Martin Thrasher: senior vice president ED University of Western Ontario (1973). PRIM CORP EMPL senior vice president: Campbell Soup Co. CORP AFFIL president: Campbell Soup Co. International Grocery Europe/Canada.

Edward F. Walsh: vice president human resources B 1941. PRIM CORP EMPL vice president human resources: Campbell Soup Co.

Robert J. Zatta: vice president finance PRIM CORP EMPL vice president finance: Campbell Soup Co.

Foundation Officials

Jerry S. Buckley: vice chairman B 1954. PRIM CORP EMPL vice president public affairs: Campbell Soup Co.

Carlos del Sol: trustee

Anthony P. DiSilvestro: treasurer (see above)

Brenda Evans Edgerton: treasurer, trustee (see above)

A. Fred George: trustee PRIM CORP EMPL Branch manager: Campbell Soup Co.

Steve Jander: trustee

April Jeffries: trustee

Ellen O. Kaden: trustee B New York, NY 1951. ED Cornell University BA (1972); Chicago State University MA (1973); Columbia University JD (1977). PRIM CORP EMPL senior vice president Law & government: Campbell Soup Co. NONPR AFFIL trustee: Institute Judicial Administration; member: National Legal Aid & Defender Association; trustee: Columbia University; member: Committee Civil Rights.

Sally G. Robling: trustee

Craig Rydin: trustee B 1953. PRIM CORP EMPL president: Campbell Away from Home. CORP AFFIL vice president: Campbell Soup Co.

William D. Toler: trustee PRIM CORP EMPL president: Campbell Sales Co.

Bertram C. Willis: secretary PRIM CORP EMPL group director government relations: Campbell Soup Co.

Grants Analysis

Disclosure Period: fiscal year ending June 30, 1997
Total Grants: $1,269,841*
Number of Grants: 94
Average Grant: $13,509
Highest Grant: $105,000
Typical Range: $500 to $25,000
***Note:** Giving excludes matching gifts; United Way.

Recent Grants

Note: Grants derived from fiscal 1997 Form 990.

Arts & Humanities

20,000	Perkins Center for the Arts, Morristown, NJ -- for summer program
18,000	Walt Whitman Cultural Arts Center, Camden, NJ -- for summer program
16,000	Stedman Art Gallery -- for summer program
11,000	Independence Seaport Museum, Philadelphia, PA -- for summer program
10,045	Appel Farm Arts and Music Center, Elmer, NJ -- support Dollars for Doers
9,000	Haddonfield Symphony, Haddonfield, NJ -- for summer program
5,000	Clay Studio, Philadelphia, PA -- for summer program

Civic & Public Affairs

90,000	Latin American Economic Development Association, Camden, NJ -- for training project
25,200	Hispanic Family Center for Southern New Jersey, Camden, NJ -- for summer program
25,000	Cooper's Ferry Development Association, Camden, NJ -- support Waterfront initiatives
17,000	NAACP Camden County East Branch, Camden, NJ -- for summer program
15,000	Camden County Council on Economic Opportunity, Camden, NJ -- for summer program
10,000	Christmas in April, Camden, NJ -- support Dollars for Doers

Education

16,000	Rowan College Foundation, Camden, NJ -- for summer program
4,800	Prime, Philadelphia, PA -- for summer program

Health

100,000	American Diabetes Association, Alexandria, VA -- first payment on two-year pledge
100,000	American Dietetic Association, Chicago, IL -- first payment on two-year $160,000 pledge
100,000	American Heart Association, Dallas, TX -- final payment on two-year pledge for web site
60,000	American Diabetes Association, Alexandria, VA -- payment on two-year pledge
5,260	Camden Optometric Eye Center, Camden, NJ -- support Dollars for Doers
4,200	American Red Cross, Camden, NJ -- support Dollars for Doers
3,298	Camden Optometric Eye Center, Camden, NJ -- support Dollars for Doers

Religion

100,000	St. Joseph's Carpenter Society, Camden, NJ -- for Homeowners Academy
25,000	Camden Churches Organized for People, Camden, NJ -- for abandoned buildings in Camden
10,000	Lazarus at the Gate, Moorestown, NJ -- support Dollars for Doers
10,000	Parkside United Methodist Church, Camden, NJ -- support Dollars for Doers
8,975	Fellowship House, Camden, NJ -- support Dollars for Doers
5,000	St. Joseph's Carpenter Society, Camden, NJ -- for summer program
5,000	Trinity Episcopal Church Outreach Commission, Moorestown, NJ -- support Dollars for Doers
5,000	Victory Temple Community Church, Camden, NJ -- support Dollars for Doers
3,500	Cathedral Kitchen, Camden, NJ -- support Dollars for Doers
2,650	Dagsboro Church of God, Dagsboro, DE -- for Millsboro Plant DFD

Social Services

105,000	United Way Camden County, Camden, NJ
105,000	United Way Camden County, Camden, NJ
90,000	United Way Camden County, Camden, NJ
40,000	Client Community Services, Worthington, MN -- for Worthington Plant
20,000	Urbanpromise, Camden, NJ -- for summer program
19,000	Neighborhood Center, Camden, NJ -- for summer program
18,050	Respond, Camden, NJ -- for summer program
13,950	YMCA Camden County, Voorhees, NJ -- for summer program
11,000	Boy Scouts of America Camden County Council, Collingswood, NJ -- for summer program
10,000	Girl Scouts of America, Cherry Hill, NJ -- support Dollars for Doers
10,000	Juvenile Resources Center, Camden, NJ -- support Dollars for Doers
10,000	Philadelphia Youth Tennis, Philadelphia, PA -- for summer program
10,000	Respond, Camden, NJ -- for summer program, Campbell Internship
9,700	YWCA Camden Center, Camden, NJ
8,000	Girl Scouts of America Camden County Council, Cherry Hill, NJ -- for summer program
7,000	Dooley House, Camden, NJ -- support Dollars for Doers
5,000	Concerned Citizens for the Rehabilitation of the Homeless, Laurinburg, NC -- for Maxton Plant DFD
3,000	YWCA Camden County, Stratford, NJ -- for summer program

Cantor, Fitzgerald Securities Corp.

Company Contact

New York, NY

Company Description

Revenue: US$100,000,000
Employees: 400
SIC(s): 6211 Security Brokers & Dealers, 6719 Holding Companies Nec.

Cantor, Fitzgerald Foundation

Giving Contact

B. Gerald Cantor, President
Cantor, Fitzgerald Foundation
One World Trade Center, Suite 10500
New York, NY 10048

Phone: (212)938-5113

Description

EIN: 133117872
Organization Type: Corporate Foundation. Supports preselected organizations only.
Giving Locations: NY
Grant Types: General Support.

Financial Summary

Total Giving: $970,011 (1996); $269,730 (1991); $338,925 (1990)
Assets: $2,545,581 (1996); $1,593,459 (1991); $1,413,847 (1990)
Gifts Received: $300,000 (1991); $600,000 (1990); $625,000 (1989)

Typical Recipients

Arts & Humanities: Community Arts, Arts & Humanities-General, Historic Preservation, History & Archaeology, Museums/Galleries, Music, Performing Arts, Theater
Civic & Public Affairs: Botanical Gardens/Parks, Civic & Public Affairs-General, Law & Justice, Parades/Festivals
Education: Colleges & Universities, Private Education (Precollege)
Environment: Environment-General
Health: Cancer, Diabetes, Eyes/Blindness, Hospitals, Medical Research, Single-Disease Health Associations
International: Foreign Arts Organizations, International Peace & Security Issues
Religion: Jewish Causes, Religious Organizations, Synagogues/Temples
Social Services: Community Service Organizations, Family Services, Food/Clothing Distribution, People with Disabilities, United Funds/United Ways

Contributions Analysis

Note: Grants list for 1991 was not provided.

Corporate Officials

Bernard Gerald Cantor: chairman, director general counsel B New York, NY 1916. ED New York University. PRIM CORP EMPL chairman, director: Cantor Fitzgerald. NONPR AFFIL regent's president council: Holy Cross College; fellow, trustee: Metropolitan Museum Art; member: Fine Arts Society San Diego; member: Business Committee Arts; fellow: Cleveland Museum Art; member: American Federation Arts.
Joseph Malvasio: chief financial officer PRIM CORP EMPL chief financial officer: Cantor Fitzgerald Securities Corp.
Harry Needleman: executive vice president, general counsel B New York, NY 1949. ED City University of New York BA (1970); Saint John's University JD (1975). PRIM CORP EMPL executive vice president, general counsel: Cantor Fitzgerald.

Foundation Officials

Bernard Gerald Cantor: president, director (see above)
Iris Cantor: trustee
Howard W. Lutnick: director
Harry Needleman: secretary (see above)
Joel Rothstein: treasurer, director

Grants Analysis

Disclosure Period: calendar year ending 1996
Total Grants: $970,010
Number of Grants: 157
Average Grant: $4,930*
Highest Grant: $201,000
Typical Range: $100 to $10,000 and $15,000 to $100,000
***Note:** Average grant figure excludes highest grant.

Recent Grants

Note: Grants derived from 1996 Form 990.

Arts & Humanities

17,000	New York Historical Society, New York, NY
10,000	Cabaret '96
5,000	Brooklyn Museum, Brooklyn, NY
5,000	John F. Kennedy Center for Performing Arts, Washington, DC
5,000	Museum Mile Festival

Civic & Public Affairs

5,000	Geranium Ball
5,000	Parks Council, New York, NY
4,000	John Thomas Grazlano Fund

Education

200,000	Haverford College, Haverford, PA

Health

50,000	New York Hospital Cornell Medical Center, New York, NY
31,800	Glaucoma Foundation, New York, NY
25,000	Strang Cancer Prevention Center, New York, NY
6,600	Juvenile Diabetes Foundation, New York, NY
5,000	United Cerebral Palsy Spastic Children's, Van Nuys, CA
4,100	Cystic Fibrosis Foundation, Philadelphia, PA

International

10,000	American Friends of the Israel Museum, New York, NY

Religion

201,000	Anti-Defamation League, New York, NY

Social Services

137,700	Boomer Esiason Heros Benevolent Fund, Bethesda, MD
119,002	City Harvest, New York, NY
4,165	Boomer Esiason Heros Benevolent Fund, Bethesda, MD

CARGILL INC.

 Number 60 of Top 100 Corporate Givers

Company Contact

Minneapolis, MN
Web: http://www.cargill.com

Company Description

Employees: 80,600
SIC(s): 2041 Flour & Other Grain Mill Products, 4424 Deep Sea Domestic Transportation of Freight, 5153 Grain & Field Beans, 6221 Commodity Contracts Brokers & Dealers.

Operating Locations

Australia: Queensland Oilseed Crushers Pty. Ltd., Carole Park; Cargill Processing Ltd., Melbourne; Belgium: Cargill France Vennootschap Naar Frans Recht, Herent, Brabant; Canada: Shaver Poultry Breeding Farms Ltd., Cambridge, Cambridgeshire; Cargill Ltd., Winnipeg; France: Cargill Investor Services SNC, Paris, Ville-de-Paris; Cargill Foods France, St. Germain en Laye, Yvelines; Cargill France, St. Germain en Laye, Yvelines; Standart, St. Germain en Laye, Yvelines; Germany: Cargill Germany Zweigniederlassung Frankfurt, Frankfurt, Hessen; Deutsche Cargill GmbH, Salzgitter, Niedersachsen; Netherlands: Breber Holding BV, Amsterdam, Noord-Holland; Cargill BV, Amsterdam, Noord-Holland; Cargill Eurofinance BV, Amsterdam, Noord-Holland; Cargill Export BV, Amsterdam, Noord-Holland; Cargill Financing BV, Amsterdam, Noord-Holland; Cargill Holdings BV, Amsterdam, Noord-Holland; Cargill Juice Trading BV, Amsterdam, Noord-Holland; Internationale Graanoverslag Maatschappij Amsterdam BV, Amsterdam, Noord-Holland; Fennema BV, Deventer, Overijssel; Gerkens Cacao BV, Wormer, Noord-Holland; Instant Holding BV, Wormer, Noord-Holland; Zaanlandse Olieraffinaderij BV, Zaandam, Noord-Holland; Russia: Russian-American Joint Venture Cargill Private Joint Stock Co., Moscow; Singapore: Cargill International Trading Pte. Ltd., Singapore; Spain: Cargill Espana SA, Sant Cugat del Valles, Catalun; Venezuela: Cargill de Venezuela CA, Caracas; Comestibles Populares SA, Caracas; Fabrica de Pastas Milani Hermanos CA, Caracas; Milani de Venezuela SA, Caracas

Nonmonetary Support

Type: Donated Equipment; Donated Products; Loaned Executives
Contact: Mark Murphy
Note: Co. provides nonmonetary support.

Corporate Sponsorship

Type: Arts & cultural events

Cargill Foundation

Giving Contact

Denise M. Lotton, Program and Grants Manager
Cargill Inc.
PO Box 5650
Minneapolis, MN 55440-5650
Phone: (612)742-6122
Fax: (612)742-7224
Email: denise_lotton@cargill.com

Alternate Contact

Ms. Toni Green, Foundation Contact

Description

EIN: 416020221
Organization Type: Corporate Foundation
Giving Locations: MN: Minneapolis including western and northern suburbs headquarters and operating locations; internationally; nationally.
Grant Types: Capital, Emergency, Employee Matching Gifts, General Support, Multiyear/Continuing Support, Project.

Giving Philosophy

'Cargill builds businesses that contribute to economic growth and better living standards. This is Cargill's basic vision, and from it grows the company's commitment to its communities. Building relationships with the communities that are home to our plants, offices, employees, and customers is an integral part of our business plan. In the future, Cargill will expand its grantmaking program to reflect continued growth in this shared investment.'

'Under the theme 'Cargill Cares', the company strives to alleviate hunger, promote literacy, sustain the arts and improve health and human services. It supports the Special Olympics and works to protect farm children from accidents. Cargill devotes resources to strengthen secondary and higher education and improve the environment. It gives to local fire and police departments, hospitals and day-care centers, schools and libraries. Contributions, whether provided by the Cargill Foundation, individual Cargill businesses or the Cargill Contributions Committee, often are accompanied by the skills and time volunteered by its employees and retirees around the world.'

'To improve our decision-making and achieve greater impact with our limited dollars, we have narrowed the scope of our grantmaking and established criteria against which we will screen and evaluate requests. Our criteria center around Cargill's grantmaking mission, guidelines, focus areas and priorities, and the performance of past grant recipients.'

'Cargill's grantmaking mission is: We will make grants that foster economic, social and human development in each of the communities where Cargill has a presence in order to enable people to achieve their full potential as individuals and as contributing members of society.' *Cargill Grantmaking Guidelines*

Financial Summary

Total Giving: $15,152,000 (1999); $14,153,000 (1998); $11,986,000 (1997). Note: Contributes through corporate direct giving program and foundation. 1999 Giving includes corporate giving; foundation; domestic subsidiary giving; and international subsidiary giving. 1998 Giving includes corporate direct giving ($9,650,000); foundation ($4,500,000). 1997 Giving includes corporate direct giving ($3,651,386); foundation ($4,608,399); domestic subsidiaries ($3,000,000).
Assets: $68,401,382 (1997); $56,541,779 (1996); $39,735,987 (1994)
Gifts Received: $2,600,000 (1997); $3,000,000 (1996); $2,000,000 (1994). Note: Contributions were received from Cargill, Inc., Cargill Financial Services Corp., and North Star Steel Co.

Typical Recipients

Arts & Humanities: Arts Centers, Arts Institutes, Arts Outreach, Arts & Humanities-General, History & Archaeology, Libraries, Museums/Galleries, Music, Opera, Public Broadcasting, Theater
Civic & Public Affairs: African American Affairs, Botanical Gardens/Parks, Chambers of Commerce, Economic Development, Employment/Job Training, Civic & Public Affairs-General, Housing, Law & Justice, Legal Aid, Minority Business, Native American Affairs, Nonprofit Management, Public Policy, Urban & Community Affairs, Women's Affairs, Zoos/Aquariums
Education: Agricultural Education, Arts/Humanities Education, Business Education, Colleges & Universities, Community & Junior Colleges, Economic Education, Education Funds, Education Reform, Elementary Education (Private), Engineering/Technological Education, Faculty Development, Education-General, Leadership Training, Medical Education, Minority Education, Preschool Education, Private Education (Precollege), Public Education (Precollege), Religious Education, Social Sciences Education, Special Education, Student Aid, Vocational & Technical Education
Environment: Environment-General, Resource Conservation
Health: AIDS/HIV, Cancer, Children's Health/Hospitals, Clinics/Medical Centers, Emergency/Ambulance Services, Eyes/Blindness, Health Organizations, Hospitals
International: International Environmental Issues
Religion: Religious Welfare
Science: Science Museums, Scientific Centers & Institutes
Social Services: At-Risk Youth, Big Brother/Big Sister, Child Welfare, Community Centers, Community Service Organizations, Crime Prevention, Day Care, Domestic Violence, Family Planning, Family Services, Food/Clothing Distribution, People with Disabilities, Recreation & Athletics, Scouts, Senior Services, Substance Abuse, United Funds/United Ways, YMCA/YWCA/YMHA/YWHA, Youth Organizations

Contributions Analysis

Giving Priorities: Education, community programs, youth groups, food distribution, health care organizations, and cultural institutions. Domestic contributions support such organizations as AFS International, Consumers for World Trade, Overseas Development Council, Institute for East-West Secutiry Studies, the Japan Society, the U.S. Council for International Business, and the US-USSR Trade and Economic Council. Foreign contributions come directly from businesses in-country (no funds from corporation). Current interests include initiatives that help build partnerships with national/international organizations with experience in community-based programming. In 1997, contributions by Cargill's international businesses totaled $1.9 million.

Application Procedures

Initial Contact: Call foundation to request a copy of their grantmaking guidelines.
Application Requirements: organization's history, mission, programs and services, and staffing support; description of intended use of funds requested, including dollar amount, goals, objectives, and timetable; evidence of IRS 501(c)(3) tax-exempt status; an application cover sheet available form the foundation and answers to questions available in the foundation's guidelines.
Deadlines: None.
Review Process: grants are reviewed as they are received, applicants are notified within 6-8 weeks as to whether their requests have been denied or referred to the Contributions Committee or the foundation; committee meets regularly and reviews grant requests in any category; proposals must be received at least one month prior to committee meetings.
Evaluative Criteria: organizations with effective leadership and significant impact on community; well-managed programs with clear goals and sufficient resources to accomplish objective; and organizations with a full year of operating experience

Restrictions

Foundation does not support political organizations or campaigns; organizations designed primarily for lobbying and advocacy; individuals and their projects; religious organizations for direct religious activities; endowment campaigns; fraternal organizations, societies, or orders; veterans' or professional organizations; travel, either by groups or by individuals.
Foundation generally does not support conferences, seminars, workshops, or symposia; national or local campaigns to eliminate or control specific diseases; athletic scholarships; benefits, fundraisers, or testimonial, recognition, or honoring dinners; membership in civic organizations or trade associations; or organizations or programs that primarily serve adults.
Foundation does not provide seed money or start-up funding for new organizations.

Additional Information

Cargill is taking steps toward achieving a target of two percent of domestic pre-tax earnings for its U.S.-based contributions.
Publications: Guidelines Sheet

Corporate Officials

Robbin S. Johnson: corporate vice president public affairs PRIM CORP EMPL corporate vice president public affairs: Cargill Inc.
James D. Moe: corporate vice president, general counsel, secretary ED Stanford University AB (1962); University of Minnesota LLB (1965). PRIM CORP EMPL corporate vice president, general counsel, secretary: Cargill Inc.
Warren R. Staley: president, chief executive officer ED Kansas State University BA (1965); Cornell University MBA (1967). PRIM CORP EMPL president, chief executive officer: Cargill Inc.
Tyrone K. Thayer: corp. vice president PRIM CORP EMPL corp. vice president: Cargill Inc. CORP AFFIL director: North Star Steel Co.

Giving Program Officials

Larry DeWitt: member contributions committee
James S. Hield: executive director PRIM CORP EMPL secretary: Cargill Inc.
Whitney MacMillan: member contributions committee B 1929. CORP AFFIL director: Deluxe Corp.
James D. Moe: member contributions committee ED Stanford University AB (1962); University of Minnesota LLB (1965). PRIM CORP EMPL corporate vice president, general counsel, secretary: Cargill Inc.
Nancy P. Siska: member contributions committee (see above)
Warren R. Staley: member contributions committee ED Kansas State University BA (1965); Cornell University MBA (1967). PRIM CORP EMPL president, chief executive officer: Cargill Inc.
Tyrone K. Thayer: member contributions committee (see above)

Foundation Officials

James S. Hield: executive director (see above)
Robbin S. Johnson: vice president (see above)
Katherine Kersten: director PRIM NONPR EMPL chairman: Center for the American Experiment.
Frank Sims: director

Grants Analysis

Disclosure Period: calendar year ending 1998
Total Grants: $6,902,300*
Number of Grants: 160
Average Grant: $20,000*
Highest Grant: $600,000
Typical Range: $5,000 to $50,000 and $50,000 to $150,000
***Note:** Grants analysis provided by foundation. Giving excludes corporate direct giving; domestic subsidiaries. Average grant figure excludes highest grant.

Recent Grants

Note: Grants derived from 1998 Form 990.

Arts & Humanities

250,000	The Minnesota Orchestral Association, Minneapolis, MN -- Capital
250,000	The Minnesota Orchestral Association, Minneapolis, MN -- Capital
100,000	The Children's Theatre Company, Minneapolis, MN -- General
100,000	The Minneapolis Institute of Arts, Minneapolis, MN -- Capital
100,000	The Minneapolis Institute of Arts, Minneapolis, MN -- Capital
100,000	The Minneapolis Institute of Arts, Minneapolis, MN -- Capital
100,000	The Minneapolis Institute of Arts, Minneapolis, MN -- Capital
100,000	Minnesota Children's Museum, St. Paul, MN -- Program/Project Development
90,000	Twin Cities Public Television, St. Paul, MN -- Program/Project Development
70,000	The Minnesota Orchestral Association, Minneapolis, MN -- General
65,000	The Minneapolis Institute of Arts, Minneapolis, MN -- General
55,000	Minnesota Public Radio, St. Paul, MN -- General
50,000	Minnesota Public Radio, St. Paul, MN -- Capital
50,000	Twin Cities Public Television, St. Paul, MN -- Capital
50,000	Twin Cities Public Television, St. Paul, MN -- Capital

Civic & Public Affairs

200,000	Habitat for Humanity International, Americus, GA -- General
85,000	Minneapolis American Indian Center, Minneapolis, MN -- Capital
83,334	Courage Center, Golden Valley, MN -- Capital
83,333	Courage Center, Golden Valley, MN -- Capital
60,000	Metropolitan Economic Development Association, Minneapolis, MN -- General
60,000	Progressive Farmer Foundation, Birmingham, AL -- Program/Project Development
50,000	African American Family Services, Minneapolis, MN -- Capital
50,000	Family Housing Fund of Minneapolis and St. Paul, Minneapolis, MN -- General

50,000 Greater Minneapolis Chamber of Commerce, Minneapolis, MN -- Program/Project Development
50,000 The Greater Minneapolis Metropolitan Housing Corporation, Minneapolis, MN -- General
50,000 Pillsbury Neighborhood Services, Minneapolis, MN -- Capital
45,000 Minneapolis Park and Recreation Board, Minneapolis, MN -- Program/Project Development
35,000 Twin Cities Habitat for Humanity, Minneapolis, MN -- General

Education
100,000 The Iowa State University Foundation, Ames, IA -- Program/Project Development
100,000 Kansas State University Foundation, Manhattan, KS -- Program/Project Development
100,000 Metropolitan State University Foundation, St. Paul, MN -- Capital
100,000 University of Illinois Foundation at Urbana-Champaign, Champaign, IL -- Program/Project Development
100,000 University of Minnesota Foundation, Minneapolis, MN -- Program/Project Development
100,000 University of Minnesota, Institute of Technology, Minneapoli, MN -- Capital
100,000 University of Wisconsin Foundation, Madison, Madison, WI -- Program/Project Development
75,000 Minnesota Private College Fund, St. Paul, MN -- Program/Project Development
75,000 Minnesota Private College Fund, St. Paul, MN -- General
50,000 United Negro College Fund, Inc., Minneapolis, MN -- General
50,000 University of Texas Foundation, College of Business, Austin, TX -- Capital
50,000 University of Texas Foundation, College of Business, Austin, TX -- Program/Project Development
45,000 Junior Achievement of the Upper Midwest, Inc., Minneapolis, MN -- General
35,000 Augsburg College, Minneapolis, MN -- Program/Project Development

Science
40,000 Science Museum of Minnesota, St. Paul, MN -- Program/Project Development

Social Services
600,000 United Way of Minneapolis Area, Minneapolis, MN -- General
100,000 Minneapolis YWCA, Minneapolis, MN -- Capital
100,000 Minneapolis YWCA, Minneapolis, MN -- Capital
75,000 Boys & Girls Club of Minneapolis, Minneapolis, MN -- Capital
75,000 Boys & Girls Club of Minneapolis, Minneapolis, MN -- Capital
75,000 National FFA Foundation, Indianapolis, IN -- Program/Project Development
35,000 YMCA of Metropolitan Minneapolis, Minneapolis, MN -- Program/Project Development

CARILLON IMPORTERS, LTD.

Company Contact
Teaneck, NJ

Company Description
Employees: 54
SIC(s): 2084 Wines, Brandy & Brandy Spirits, 2085 Distilled & Blended Liquors.
Parent Company: Diageo Plc, 8 Henrietta Place, London, United Kingdom

Operating Locations
NJ: Carillon Importers, Teaneck

Grand Marnier Foundation

Giving Contact
Sandy Adler, Executive Administrative Assistant
Grand Marnier Foundation
1 Whitman Ct.
Teaneck, NJ 07666
Phone: (201)342-4663

Description
EIN: 133258414
Organization Type: Corporate Foundation
Giving Locations: CA; MD; NY nationally.
Grant Types: General Support.

Financial Summary
Total Giving: $332,100 (1998); $352,400 (1997); $425,590 (1995). Note: Contributes through foundation only.
Assets: $7,015,933 (1998); $7,090,590 (1997); $8,644,907 (1995)
Gifts Received: $613,997 (1991)

Typical Recipients
Arts & Humanities: Arts Associations & Councils, Arts Centers, Arts Outreach, Dance, Ethnic & Folk Arts, Film & Video, Arts & Humanities-General, History & Archaeology, Libraries, Museums/Galleries, Music, Performing Arts, Public Broadcasting, Theater
Civic & Public Affairs: Clubs, Employment/Job Training, Civic & Public Affairs-General, Hispanic Affairs, Native American Affairs, Parades/Festivals, Professional & Trade Associations, Women's Affairs
Education: Arts/Humanities Education, Business Education, Colleges & Universities, Continuing Education, Education-General, International Studies, Leadership Training, Medical Education, Private Education (Precollege), Public Education (Precollege), Science/ Mathematics Education, Student Aid
Environment: Air/Water Quality
Health: AIDS/HIV, Cancer, Children's Health/Hospitals, Clinics/Medical Centers, Emergency/Ambulance Services, Health Organizations, Hospitals, Medical Research, Nutrition, Single-Disease Health Associations
International: Foreign Arts Organizations, Foreign Educational Institutions, International Development, International Organizations, International Peace & Security Issues, International Relations, Missionary/ Religious Activities
Religion: Churches, Jewish Causes, Religious Welfare
Social Services: Child Abuse, Child Welfare, Community Service Organizations, Crime Prevention, Emergency Relief, Family Services, Food/Clothing Distribution, Recreation & Athletics, Shelters/Homelessness

Contributions Analysis
Giving Priorities: The arts, civic organizations, and social services.
Arts & Humanities: 52%. Funds given to performing arts, repertory theater, public television, fine arts museum, and film festivals.
Civic & Public Affairs: 17%.
Education: 6%. Funds educational programs, colleges, and universities.
Environment: 2%.
Health: 5%. Support goes to single-disease organizations, medical centers, and hospitals.
International: 5%. International causes.
Religion: 1%.
Social Services: 12%. Youth and child services, Meals on Wheels, social services, and youth and family counseling services.
Note: Total contributions made in 1998.

Application Procedures
Initial Contact: Submit a brief letter.
Application Requirements: Include a description of organization, amount requested, purpose of funds sought, recently audited financial statement, and proof of tax-exempt status.
Deadlines: None.

Corporate Officials
Michel Roux: president, chief executive officer, director B 1941. PRIM CORP EMPL president, chief executive officer, director: Carillon Importers, Ltd.

Foundation Officials
Joel Buchman: secretary, director
Jerry Ciraulo: treasurer, director PRIM CORP EMPL senior vice president: Carillon Importers Ltd.
Maxime Coury: director
Francois de Gasperis: director
Jacques Marnier: director
Michel Roux: president, director (see above)

Grants Analysis
Disclosure Period: calendar year ending 1998
Total Grants: $332,100
Number of Grants: 72
Average Grant: $4,613
Highest Grant: $150,000
Typical Range: $200 to $10,000

Recent Grants
Note: Grants derived from 1997 Form 990.

Arts & Humanities
175,000 Maryland Public Television, Owings Mills, MD -- to underwrite production
5,000 Theater for a New Audience, New York, NY -- to underwrite fundraising event
3,000 Harmonia Dance, New York, NY -- to underwrite performance reception
3,000 Manhattan Cultural Studios, New York, NY -- to underwrite theater production
2,500 Cornell Fine Arts Museum at Rollins College, Winter Park, FL
1,500 St. Barth Festival de Cinema, New York, NY -- sponsor program
1,000 John Harms Center for the Arts, Englewood, NJ -- support arts education programs
1,000 New York Baroque Dance Company, New York, NY -- to underwrite performance
500 Circum Arts Foundation, New York, NY -- project sponsorship
500 Dreamcatcher Repertory Theater, Weehawken, NJ
500 Momentary Theater, New York, NY -- to underwrite theater production
500 Park Performing Arts Center, Union City, NJ -- sponsor production
500 Thalia Spanish Theater, Sunnyside, NY -- to underwrite production expenses
500 Young Audiences, Princeton, NJ -- to sponsor project
300 Young Playwrights, New York, NY
200 New/Fourth WORLL Movement, New York, NY -- support Library Festival

Civic & Public Affairs
5,000 Tribute to the Pierre Franey Foundation, New York, NY -- to sponsor fundraising event

200	Minority Contractors and Coalition of Trade Workers, Jersey City, NJ
Education	
15,000	Culinary Institute of America, Hyde Park, NY -- scholarships
12,000	New York University, New York, NY
5,000	Florida International University, Miami, FL -- educational program support
2,000	National Book Foundation, New York, NY -- project sponsorship
2,000	Paul Smith's College of Arts and Sciences, Paul Smiths, NY -- sponsor internship program
2,000	Pilchuck Glass School, Seattle, WA -- scholarship fund
1,000	Southwest Learning Center, Santa Fe, NM -- to underwrite arts festival
200	Foundation of the University of Medicine and Dentistry of New Jersey, Newark, NJ
200	IGIA Leadership Academy, Columbia, SC
200	Technotots, New Brunswick, NJ
Health	
10,000	Muscular Dystrophy Foundation for Women, New York, NY -- to underwrite fundraising event
5,000	United Cerebral Palsy Association of Central Florida, Orlando, FL -- to sponsor fundraising gala
1,000	Chemotherapy Foundation, New York, NY -- to underwrite fundraising event
1,000	Lupus Foundation of America, Bronx, NY
500	Doctors Without Borders, New York, NY
500	Memorial Sloan-Kettering Cancer Center, New York, NY
500	National Ataxia Foundation, Minneapolis, MN
500	University of Colorado Colorado Springs, Colorado Springs, CO -- for breast cancer research
300	Corpus Christi Ministries, Jersey City, NJ -- general support, housing for AIDS patients
300	Friends of the Colorado Center for Human Nutrition, Parker, CO
International	
35,000	French Institute Alliance, New York, NY
10,000	Friends of the Israel Defense Forces, New York, NY
5,000	Federation of Alliance Francaise, Washington, DC
Religion	
500	Little Sisters of the Poor, Totowa, NJ
Social Services	
25,000	City Meals on Wheels, New York, NY -- fundraising event sponsorship
2,000	Friends of Olana, Hudson, NY -- to underwrite reception
1,000	Florida Sheriffs Youth Ranches, Boys Ranch, FL
300	Green Chimneys Children's Services, Brewster, NY
200	Children's Hope Foundation, New York, NY -- medical services
200	Youth and Family Counseling Service, Westfield, NJ -- to underwrite concert

CARLSON COMPANIES, INC.

Company Contact

Minneapolis, MN
Web: http://www.carlson.com

Company Description

Revenue: US$11,600,000,000
Employees: 130,000
SIC(s): 4729 Passenger Transportation Arrangement Nec, 5812 Eating Places, 5961 Catalog & Mail-Order Houses, 7359 Equipment Rental & Leasing Nec.
Parent Company: Carlson Holdings

Curtis L. Carlson Family Foundation

Giving Contact

Donna Snyder, Secretary
Curtis L. Carlson Family Foundation
Two Carlson Parkway, 475
Plymouth, MN 55447
Phone: (612)404-5604
Fax: (612)404-5601

Description

Founded: 1959
EIN: 416028973
Organization Type: Corporate Foundation
Giving Locations: MN
Grant Types: General Support.

Financial Summary

Total Giving: $200,000 (2000 approx); $194,318 (1999 approx); $212,244 (1998 approx). Note: Contributes through corporate direct giving program and foundation. 1997 Giving includes foundation ($1,724,200); United Way ($2,600).
Assets: $29,846,027 (1997); $27,138,866 (1996); $4,412,469 (1995)
Gifts Received: $204,384 (1997); $21,189,188 (1996); $3,939,750 (1995). Note: 1997 contributions were received from Edwin C. Gage and Barbara C. Gage.

Typical Recipients

Arts & Humanities: Arts Centers, Arts Funds, Arts Institutes, Community Arts, Libraries, Museums/Galleries, Music, Opera, Public Broadcasting, Theater
Civic & Public Affairs: Business/Free Enterprise, Ethnic Organizations, Civic & Public Affairs-General, Urban & Community Affairs
Education: Colleges & Universities, Education Funds, Education-General, International Studies, Minority Education, Private Education (Precollege), Student Aid
Environment: Forestry, Wildlife Protection
Health: Cancer, Children's Health/Hospitals, Clinics/Medical Centers, Eyes/Blindness, Heart, Hospitals, Medical Research, Public Health, Single-Disease Health Associations
International: Health Care/Hospitals, International Organizations, International Relations
Religion: Churches, Ministries, Religious Organizations, Religious Welfare, Seminaries
Social Services: Child Welfare, Community Service Organizations, People with Disabilities, Scouts, United Funds/United Ways, Youth Organizations

Contributions Analysis

Arts & Humanities: Less than 1%.
Education: 95% to 100%. Major grant to the University of Minnesota Foundation. Also supports other colleges and educational funds.
Religion: Less than 5%.
Social Services: Less than 5%.

Application Procedures

Initial Contact: written request
Application Requirements: for foundation: name of organization, address, and contact information; history and general purpose of the organization; three-year budget history and projected budget of organization; copy of IRS tax-exempt ruling; copy of most recent Form 990; list of board of directors and their affiliations; purpose of request; amount requested; program budget; evidence of cooperation with other similar agencies; evidence of evaluation system for program; and description of how program will be funded on an ongoing basis
Deadlines: September 1 for organizations seeking grants before the end of the calendar year
Review Process: contributions committee reviews requests
Evaluative Criteria: purpose of grant, other sources of support, practicality of proposed plan, plans for future support
Decision Notification: quarterly

Restrictions

Foundation generally does not fund dinners, benefits, or conferences; travel costs; individuals; political activities or causes; athletic events; endowments; and organizations that are not tax-exempt.

Additional Information

Company has operating locations in nearly all 50 states.
Publications: Guidelines and Policy

Corporate Officials

Curtis Leroy Carlson: chairman, director chief financial officer B Minneapolis, MN 1914. ED University of Minnesota BA (1937). PRIM CORP EMPL chairman, director: Carlson Companies Inc. CORP AFFIL chairman: TGI Fridays Inc.; chairman: Tonkawa Inc.; director: Radisson Moscow Corp.; director: Radisson Minneapolis Corp.; chairman: Radisson Missouri Corp.; chairman: Radisson Group Inc.; chairman: Radisson Hotel Corp.; chairman: Premiums International Ltd.; chairman: Nordic-America Travel Inc.; chairman: North America Finance Corp.; president, Chief Executive Officer: MIP Agency Inc.; chairman: Naegele Co. Inc.; chairman, director: K-Promotions Inc.; chairman: CRC Leasing & Management Inc.; director: Gold Points Corp.; chairman: Carlson Real Estate Co. Inc.; chairman: Carlson Travel Group; chairman: Carlson Properties Inc.; chairman: Carlson Leasing Inc.; chairman: Carlson Marketing Group Inc.; chairman, chief executive officer: Carlson Holdings Inc.; chairman: Carlson Hospitality Group. NONPR AFFIL member advisory board: University Minnesota Curtis L Carlson School Management; senior vice president: University Minnesota Foundation; director: University Minnesota; chairman emeritus: Swedish Council America; member: Trading Stamp Institute America; vice chairman board trustee: Sigma Phi Epsilon; director: Swedish-American Chamber of Commerce Honors Comm; director: Minnesota Meetings; foundation: Boys Club Mpls; member: Masons. CLUB AFFIL Shriners Club; Ocean Reef Club; Palm Bay Club; Minneapolis Club; Northland Country Club; Jesters; Minikahda Club.
Barbara C Gage: director PRIM CORP EMPL director: Carlson Companies Inc. ADD CORP EMPL director: Carlson Holdings Inc. CORP AFFIL director: Gage Marketing Group LLC.
Marilyn Carlson Nelson: chairman, chief executive officer, president B Minneapolis, MN 1939. ED Smith College BA (1961). PRIM CORP EMPL chairman, chief executive officer, president: Carlson Companies Inc. CORP AFFIL director: ExxonMobil Corp.; director: US West Inc.; chairman, director: Citizens State Bank Waterville; director, president: Carlson Holdings Inc.; chairman: Citizens State Bank of Montogemery; president: Adams Martin & Nelson Inc.
Martyn R. Redgrave: executive vice president, chief financial officer B 1952. ED New York University MBA; Princeton University BA. PRIM CORP EMPL executive vice president, chief financial officer: Carlson Companies Inc. CORP AFFIL chief financial officer: Carlson Holdings Inc.

Foundation Officials

Arleen M. Carlson: vice president
Curtis Leroy Carlson: president, treasurer (see above)

Barbara C Gage: president (see above)
Donna D. Snyder: secretary

Grants Analysis

Disclosure Period: calendar year ending 1997
Total Grants: $1,726,800*
Number of Grants: 23
Average Grant: $12,582*
Highest Grant: $1,450,000
Typical Range: $50 to $100,000
***Note:** Giving excludes United Way ($2,600). Average grant excludes highest grant.

Recent Grants

Note: Grants derived from 1997 Form 990.

Arts & Humanities

2,500 Plymouth Music Series, Minneapolis, MN
1,050 KTCA-TV/Channel 2, St. Paul, MN -- educational
250 Minnesota Children's Museum, St. Paul, MN
50 Friends of the Minneapolis Public Library, Minneapolis, MN -- educational

Education

1,450,000 University of Minnesota Foundation, Minneapolis, MN -- educational
122,200 Gustavus Adolphus College, St. Peter, MN -- educational
100,000 Sigma Phi Epsilon Education Fund -- educational
10,000 Augsburg College, Minneapolis, MN
2,000 Blake School, Hopkins, MN -- educational
1,000 Cornell Fund -- educational
500 St. David's -- educational
100 Gustavus Engelsma Fund -- educational

Religion

25,300 HAUMC -- religious
1,000 Garrett Evangelical Theological Seminary, Evanston, IL -- religious
500 HAUMC -- religious
50 East End Cooperative Ministry -- religious
25 HAUMC -- support Pat Toschak Offering
25 United Methodist Union -- educational

Social Services

5,000 Boy Scouts of America, New York, NY -- social
2,600 United Way -- social
1,500 ACES -- educational
1,000 Boys and Girls Club -- social
150 Boy Scouts of America Handicapped -- social

CARNIVAL CORP.

Company Contact

3655 Northwest 87th Avenue
Miami, FL 33178-2428
Phone: (305)599-2600
Fax: (305)406-4758
Web: http://www.carnivalcorp.com

Company Description

Revenue: US$3,009,300,000
Employees: 22,000
SIC(s): 7999 Amusement & Recreation Nec.

Arison Foundation

Giving Contact

Matty Rosenburg, Assistant to the President
Arison Foundation
Miami, FL

Description

Founded: 1981
EIN: 592128429
Organization Type: Corporate Foundation
Giving Locations: FL: Miami including surrounding area
Grant Types: General Support.

Financial Summary

Total Giving: $12,500,000 (fiscal year ending June 30, 2000 approx); $10,000,000 (fiscal 1999 approx); $8,183,000 (fiscal 1997). Note: Contributes through corporate direct giving program and foundation. Giving includes foundation.
Assets: $120,934,217 (fiscal 1997)

Typical Recipients

Arts & Humanities: Arts Associations & Councils, Arts Festivals, Arts Funds, History & Archaeology, Museums/Galleries, Music
Civic & Public Affairs: Civil Rights, Municipalities/Towns, Public Policy, Urban & Community Affairs
Education: Education Associations, Education Funds, International Studies, Religious Education
Health: Clinics/Medical Centers, Geriatric Health, Health Organizations, Hospices, Medical Research, Public Health, Single-Disease Health Associations
International: Foreign Educational Institutions, Health Care/Hospitals, International Peace & Security Issues, International Relations, Missionary/Religious Activities
Religion: Jewish Causes, Religious Welfare, Social/Policy Issues, Synagogues/Temples
Social Services: Community Service Organizations, People with Disabilities, Shelters/Homelessness, Youth Organizations

Contributions Analysis

Giving Priorities: Museums, arts organizations, performing arts, international and Jewish programs, medical centers, health associations, and education associations. The Arison Foundation is a private foundation affiliated with the publicly owned Carnival Corp. The foundation gives less than 10% of its total contributions to U.S.-based nonprofit organizations with an international focus. International contributions support Middle East relations and Jewish organizations.
Education: 10% to 15%. Primarily for higher education.
Health: About 1%. Clinics and health organizations.
International: About 70%. Supports medical, educational, and Jewish welfare organizations in Israel.
Religion: 10% to 15%. Majority of funding supports Jewish organizations.
Social Services: About 2%. Focus on the homeless and youth organizations.

Application Procedures

Initial Contact: brief letter or proposal
Application Requirements: a description of organization, amount requested, purpose of funds sought, recently audited financial statement, and proof of tax-exempt status
Deadlines: None.

Additional Information

Foundation's giving is very limited in scope and frequently committed well in advance.

Corporate Officials

M. Micky Arison: chairman, president, chief executive officer secretary B Tel Aviv, Israel 1949. ED University of Miami. PRIM CORP EMPL chairman, president, chief executive officer: Carnival Corp. CORP AFFIL director: CHC International Inc.; general partner: Miami Heat; chairman: Air Holding Co.; chairman, chief executive officer, managing partner: Carnival Cruise Lines.
Shari Arison: director PRIM CORP EMPL director: Carnival Corp.
Arnaldo Perez: vice president, general counsel, secretary ED Miami University BBA (1982); Columbia University JD (1985). PRIM CORP EMPL vice president, general counsel, secretary: Carnival Corp.

Foundation Officials

M. Micky Arison: trustee (see above)
Marilyn Arison: trustee
Shari Arison: president (see above)
Arnaldo Perez: assistant vice president, secretary (see above)
Robert Sturges: vice president

Grants Analysis

Disclosure Period: fiscal year ending June 30, 1997
Total Grants: $8,183,000
Number of Grants: 18
Average Grant: $454,611
Highest Grant: $4,500,000
Typical Range: $100,000 to $500,000

Recent Grants

Note: Grants derived from fiscal 1997 Form 990.

Arts & Humanities

10,000 National Foundation for Advancement in the Arts, Miami, FL
5,000 Florida History Associates, Tallahassee, FL

Education

1,200,000 Friends of the College of Judea and Samaria, Rochelle Park, NJ

Health

50,000 Cleveland Clinic Foundation, Cleveland, OH
1,000 Health Crisis Network, Miami, FL

International

4,500,000 American Friends of Tel Aviv Foundation, New York, NY
4,500,000 American Friends of Tel Aviv Foundation, New York, NY
1,000,000 Friends of Sheba Medical Center of Tel Hashomer, New York, NY
1,000,000 Friends of Sheba Medical Center of Tel Hashomer, New York, NY
100,000 Friends of Tel Aviv Sourasky Medical Center
100,000 Friends of Tel Aviv Sourasky Medical Center
90,000 US Middle East Foundation for Academic Exchange, Coral Gables, FL
90,000 US Middle East Foundation for Academic Exchange, Coral Gables, FL
25,000 Center for Security Policy, Washington, DC
25,000 Center for Security Policy, Washington, DC
10,000 American Friends of Beth Hatefutshoth, New York, NY
10,000 American Friends of Beth Hatefutshoth, New York, NY
10,000 Maccabi USA Sports for Israel, Los Angeles, CA
10,000 Maccabi USA Sports for Israel, Los Angeles, CA

Religion

1,000,000 American Society for Technion, New York, NY
10,000 Simon Wiesenthal Center, Los Angeles, CA
1,000 Holon Foundation
1,000 Temple Beth Shalom

Social Services

150,000 Community Partnership for Homeless, Coral Gables, FL
20,000 Betar Educational Youth Organization, New York, NY

Carolina Power & Light Co.

 Number 98 of Top 100 Corporate Givers

Company Contact

Raleigh, NC
Web: http://www.cplc.com

Company Description

Revenue: US$3,357,600,000 (1999)
Employees: 7,200 (1999)
Fortune Rank: 459, per FORTUNE Magazine's list of 500 Largest U.S. Corporations (1999).
FF 459
SIC(s): 4911 Electric Services.

Nonmonetary Support

Value: $1,010,000 (2000 approx); $50,000 (1990)
Type: Donated Equipment; In-kind Services

Corporate Sponsorship

Value: $1,000
Type: Arts & cultural events; Festivals/fairs; Music & entertainment events
Contact: Merrilee Jacobson, Contributions Coordinator
Note: Also sponsors education on environmental conferences. Annual budget various from $100 to $10,000.

CP&L Foundation

Giving Contact

Tammy Brown, Manager, Corporate Community Relations
Carolina Power & Light Co.
PO Box 1551
Raleigh, NC 27602
Phone: (919)546-4112
Fax: (919)546-4338

Description

EIN: 561720636
Organization Type: Corporate Foundation
Giving Locations: principally near operating locations and to national organizations.
Grant Types: Capital, Employee Matching Gifts, General Support, Scholarship.

Giving Philosophy

'We are committed to more than providing electric service and promoting the economic health of the Carolinas, CP&L seeks ways to improve the quality of life for the communities we serve. In 1991, we once again set records as a United Way pacesetter company.. we further demonstrated our commitment to environmental values by adopting state parks--providing support for educational publications, symposiums, and park volunteer activities. In recent years, we have steadily increased our contributions to education at all levels and placed great emphasis on workforce training programs.' *Carolina Power & Light Company 1991 Annual Report*

Financial Summary

Total Giving: $7,500,000 (2000 approx); $7,000,000 (1998 approx); $3,000,000 (1996 approx). Note: Contributes through corporate direct giving program and foundation.
Giving Analysis: Giving for 1998 includes: corporate direct giving ($3,100,000); foundation ($2,700,000); nonmonetary support ($1,000,000)

Typical Recipients

Arts & Humanities: Arts Associations & Councils, Arts Centers, Historic Preservation, History & Archaeology, Libraries, Museums/Galleries, Music, Public Broadcasting
Civic & Public Affairs: Business/Free Enterprise, Chambers of Commerce, Economic Development, Housing, Municipalities/Towns, Nonprofit Management, Professional & Trade Associations, Urban & Community Affairs
Education: Agricultural Education, Business Education, Business-School Partnerships, Colleges & Universities, Community & Junior Colleges, Education Funds, Engineering/Technological Education, School Volunteerism
Environment: Environment-General
Health: Hospitals, Single-Disease Health Associations
Social Services: Child Welfare, Community Service Organizations, Recreation & Athletics, United Funds/ United Ways, YMCA/YWCA/YMHA/YWHA

Contributions Analysis

Giving Priorities: Education, civic and economic organizations, health organizations, and art and cultural organizations.
Arts & Humanities: 5% to 10%. Supports a variety of local arts and cultural organizations, including museums and arts centers and associations.
Civic & Public Affairs: 10% to 15%. Priorities include business and free enterprise andeconomic development organizations. Professional and trade associations and groups concerned with public policy and environmental affairs are also of interest.
Education: About 45%. Supports colleges and universities, both through general grants and through college funds. Also supports engineering, minority, liberal arts, science, and math.
Health: 25% to 30%. Major recipients for welfare include North Carolina Division of Social Services and the United Way.

Application Procedures

Initial Contact: Call or write for brochure.
Application Requirements: Include description of the organization, amount requested, purpose of funds sought, recently audited financial statement, proof of tax-exempt status, and list of board of directors.
Deadlines: Foundation board meets quarterly: February 1; May 1; August 1; and November 1.

Restrictions

Does not support individuals, religious organizations for sectarian purposes, or goodwill advertising.

Corporate Officials

William Cavanaugh, III: chairman, president, chief executive officer supply B New Orleans, LA 1939. ED Tulane University BSME (1961). PRIM CORP EMPL chairman, president, chief executive officer: Carolina Power & Light Co.
Glen Harden: executive vice president, chief financial officer B Falfurrias, TX 1951. ED Tulane University (1973); Tulane University (1975). PRIM CORP EMPL executive vice president, chief financial officer: Carolina Power & Light Co.
Robert B. McGehee: executive vice president, general counsel B Vicksburg, MS 1943. ED United States Naval Academy (1966); University of Texas JD (1973). PRIM CORP EMPL executive vice president, general counsel: Carolina Power & Light Co.
William Stanley Orser: executive vice president energy supply B New London, CT 1945. ED United States Naval Academy BS (1966); United States Naval Academy MS (1971). PRIM CORP EMPL executive vice president energy supply: Carolina Power & Light Co. NONPR AFFIL member: National Nuclear Accrediting board; member: Nuclear Energy Institute.

Giving Program Officials

Tammy Brown: manager community relations

Foundation Officials

Tammy Brown: secretary (see above)
William Cavanaugh, III: president (see above)
Glen Harden: treasurer (see above)
Robert B. McGehee: trustee (see above)
Mark Mulhern: assistant treasurer

Grants Analysis

Disclosure Period: calendar year ending
Typical Range: $10,000 to $50,000

Recent Grants

Note: Grants derived from 1998 Form 990.

Arts & Humanities

250,000	State Capitol Foundation, Inc, Raleigh, NC
75,000	Friends of the Battleship, Wilmington, NC
75,000	The Historic Preservation Foundation, Raleigh, NC
50,000	United Arts Council of Raleigh, Raleigh, NC
25,000	Asheville Art Museum Inc, Asheville, NC
25,000	Black Mountain - Swannanoa Center for the Arts, Black Mountain, NC
25,000	Friends of the Museum of the North Carolina Handicrafts, Clyde, NC
24,350	North Carolina Museum of History, Raleigh, NC
22,000	Community Arts Council of Western North Carolina, Asherille, NC
20,000	University of North Carolina Center for Public Television, Chapel Hill, NC
15,000	New Hanover Friends of the Public Library, Wilmington, NC
15,000	North Carolina Symphony Society, Inc., Raleigh, NC
15,000	Wayne County Public Library, Inc., Goldsboro, NC
12,500	Airborne & Special Operations, Fayetteville, NC

Civic & Public Affairs

200,000	North Carolina Partnership, Raleigh, NC
100,000	Global Transpark Foundation Inc.,, Kinston, NC
100,000	World Center Foundation, Miami, FL
50,000	City of Hartsville, Hartsville, SC
30,000	Council for Entrepreneurial Development, Research Triangle Park, NC
25,000	Asheville Area Chamber of Commerce, Asheville, NC
20,000	Town of Wallace, Wallace, NC
15,000	North Carolina Center for Nonprofits, Raleigh, NC

Education

120,000	North Carolina State University, Raleigh, NC
105,000	University of South Carolina, Columbia, SC
100,000	Educational Foundation Incorporation, Chapel Hill, NC
60,000	North Carolina Community College Foundation, Raleigh, NC
55,000	Independent College Fund of North Carolina, Charlotte, NC
50,000	Clemson University Public Foundation, Clemson, SC
50,000	Explornet, Raleigh, NC
50,000	North Carolina 4-H Development Fund, Inc., Raleigh, NC
50,000	University of North Carolina Arts and Sciences Foundation, Chapel Hill, NC
50,000	University of North Carolina Kenan-Flagler Business School, Chapel Hill, NC

50,000 University of North Carolina Kenan-Flagler Business School, Chapel Hill, NC
50,000 University of North Carolina - School of Law, Chapel Hill, NC
50,000 University of South Carolina, Columbia, SC
40,000 Medical University of South Carolina, Charleston, SC
40,000 University of North Carolina - Lineberger Cancer Center, Charlotte, NC
30,000 East Carolina University, Greenville, SC
27,489 North Carolina 4-H Development, Raleigh, NC
25,000 Fayetteville State University, Fayetteville, NC
25,000 South Carolina Business Center for Excellence in Education, Columbia, SC
25,000 University of North Carolina, Chapel Hill, NC
25,000 Wake County Communities in Schools, Raleigh, NC
25,000 Wake County Educational Foundation, Raleigh, NC
15,000 Coker College, Darlington, SC
15,000 Independent Colleges & Universities, Chapel Hill, NC
10,500 Junior Achievement of Western North Carolina, Asherille, NC
10,000 Francis Marion University, Florence, SC

Social Services

50,000 The Southeastern Partnership, Inc., Elizabethtown, NC
25,000 Young Mens Christian Association, Raleigh, NC
20,000 North Carolina Amateur Sports, Research Triangle Park, NC

CARPENTER TECHNOLOGY CORP.

Company Contact

Reading, PA

Company Description

Employees: 5,081
SIC(s): 3312 Blast Furnaces & Steel Mills.

Operating Locations

Includes plant and division locations.

Nonmonetary Support

Type: In-kind Services; Loaned Employees

Corporate Sponsorship

Type: Arts & cultural events; Festivals/fairs; Music & entertainment events
Note: Sponsors health and welfare events.

Carpenter Technology Corp. Foundation

Giving Contact

Robert W. Lodge, Vice President
Carpenter Technology Corp. Foundation
PO Box 14662
Reading, PA 19612-4662
Phone: (610)208-2294
Fax: (610)208-3256

Alternate Contact

101 West Bern Street
Reading, PA 19612

Description

EIN: 232191214
Organization Type: Corporate Foundation
Giving Locations: primarily headquarters and operating communities.
Grant Types: Capital, Employee Matching Gifts, General Support, Operating Expenses, Scholarship.
Note: Employee matching gift ratio: 1 to 1 up to $3,000 annually per employee.

Financial Summary

Total Giving: $411,763 (fiscal year ending September 30, 1998); $455,000 (fiscal 1997 approx); $402,609 (fiscal 1996). Note: Contributes through corporate direct giving program and foundation.
Giving Analysis: Giving for fiscal 1996 includes: foundation ($158,575); foundation grants to United Way ($146,320); foundation matching gifts ($82,034); foundation scholarships ($15,680); fiscal 1998: foundation grants to United Way ($164,199); foundation ($145,906); foundation matching gifts ($83,358); foundation scholarships ($18,300)
Assets: $225,848 (fiscal 1998); $623,724 (fiscal 1996); $373,569 (fiscal 1994)
Gifts Received: $400,000 (fiscal 1998); $550,000 (fiscal 1996); $200,000 (fiscal 1994). Note: The foundation receives contributions from Carpenter Technology Corp.

Typical Recipients

Arts & Humanities: Arts Associations & Councils, Arts Festivals, Arts Institutes, Community Arts, History & Archaeology, Libraries, Museums/Galleries, Music, Performing Arts, Public Broadcasting
Civic & Public Affairs: African American Affairs, Business/Free Enterprise, Chambers of Commerce, Community Foundations, Economic Development, Employment/Job Training, Hispanic Affairs, Housing, Legal Aid, Parades/Festivals, Professional & Trade Associations, Public Policy, Safety
Education: Arts/Humanities Education, Business Education, Business-School Partnerships, Colleges & Universities, Community & Junior Colleges, Economic Education, Education Associations, Education Funds, Elementary Education (Private), Faculty Development, Education-General, Education-General, Literacy, Minority Education, Preschool Education, Science/Mathematics Education, Secondary Education (Private), Social Sciences Education, Student Aid, Vocational & Technical Education
Environment: Air/Water Quality, Environment-General, Resource Conservation
Health: AIDS/HIV, Cancer, Clinics/Medical Centers, Emergency/Ambulance Services, Health Funds, Health Organizations, Heart, Hospitals
International: Foreign Educational Institutions
Religion: Churches, Jewish Causes, Religious Welfare
Science: Science Exhibits & Fairs
Social Services: Child Welfare, Community Service Organizations, Emergency Relief, Family Services, Food/Clothing Distribution, Homes, People with Disabilities, Recreation & Athletics, Scouts, Shelters/Homelessness, Special Olympics, Substance Abuse, United Funds/United Ways, YMCA/YWCA/YMHA/YWHA, Youth Organizations

Contributions Analysis

Giving Priorities: Primary support for the United Way, social services, education, and the arts.
Arts & Humanities: 18%. Funds ballet, theater, arts councils, historical preservation, and music.
Civic & Public Affairs: 5%. Funds libraries, public policy research institutes, legal aid foundations, urban leagues, and environmental groups.
Education: 20%. Supports colleges and universities, Junior Achievement, community colleges, and career development. Provides operational as well as capital support, a scholarship program, and matching gifts.
Health: 1%. Supports single-disease health associations, chemical abuse counseling, health organizations, and hospitals.
Social Services: 55%. Gives to united funds, youth groups, and various human service programs including housing, shelters, and food banks.
Note: Total contributions in fiscal 1998.

Application Procedures

Initial Contact: Send a letter of inquiry.
Application Requirements: Include name and address of contact person; a description of organization, including history and purpose; amount requested; purpose of funds sought; recently audited financial statement; proof of tax-exempt status; current annual budget with amount spent on program services, fundraising, administration, and general operating expenses; detailed project budget; donor list indicating contributions received, pledged, or requested within the past year; history of past support; how project will be sustained upon completion of support; list of board of directors and their affiliations; goals and objectives of project; similarity to or differences from other area projects; statement of need; and time frame for completion.
Deadlines: None.
Decision Notification: Contributions are distributed monthly; matching gifts to higher education are made in September.

Restrictions

The foundation does not support individuals, political or lobbying groups, religious organizations for sectarian purposes, endowments, foundations that are primarily grant-making bodies, organizations outside the United States, organizations without 501(c)(3) status, or sports or athletics.

Corporate Officials

Robert Willard Cardy: chairman, president, chief executive officer, director B Saginaw, MI 1936. ED University of Cincinnati BBA (1959). PRIM CORP EMPL chairman, president, chief executive officer, director: Carpenter Technology Corp. CORP AFFIL member executive committee, director: Specialty Steel Industry North America; director: CoreStates Financial Corp. NONPR AFFIL director: Reading Hospital & Medical Center.
G. Walton Cottrell: senior vice president, chief financial officer B Auburn, NY 1939. ED Cornell University BSME (1962); Cornell University MBA (1963). PRIM CORP EMPL senior vice president, chief financial officer: Carpenter Technology Corp. CORP AFFIL director: Talley Manufacturing Technology Inc.; director: Parmatech Corp.; director: Talley Industries Inc.; director: Andersen Laboratories Inc. NONPR AFFIL member: Financial Executives Institute; director: National Association of Corporate Treasurers; director: Cornell University Council.

Giving Program Officials

Patricia A. Weaver: PRIM CORP EMPL administrator contributions program: Carpenter Technology Corp.

Foundation Officials

Robert Willard Cardy: president (see above)
Robert W. Lodge: vice president ED University of Michigan BA (1965); Indiana University MA (1971). PRIM CORP EMPL vice president human resources: Carpenter Technology Corp. CORP AFFIL director: Talley Industries Inc.; director: Talley Manufacturing Technology Inc.
John Rider Welty: secretary B Waynesboro, PA 1948. ED Shippensburg University of Pennsylvania BA (1970); American University JD (1975). PRIM CORP EMPL vice president, secretary, general counsel: Carpenter Technology Corp. CORP AFFIL director: Talley Manufacturing Technology Inc.; director: Talley Metals Technology Inc.; director: Talley Industries Inc.; secretary: Carpentar Advanced Ceramics;

treasurer: Parmatech Corp. NONPR AFFIL member: Pennsylvania Self Insurers Association; member: Phi Alpha Delta; member: Pennsylvania Bar Association; member: American Bar Association; member: American Corporate Counsel Association; member: Alpha Phi Omega.

Grants Analysis

Disclosure Period: fiscal year ending September 30, 1998
Total Grants: $145,906*
Number of Grants: 42
Average Grant: $3,474
Highest Grant: $30,000
Typical Range: $250 to $5,000
***Note:** Giving excludes matching gifts; scholarships; United Way.

Recent Grants

Note: Grants derived from fiscal 1998 Form 990.

Arts & Humanities

25,000	Reading Public Museum, Reading, PA
7,500	Berks Arts Council, Reading, PA
7,500	Reading Symphony Orchestra, Reading, PA
6,500	Reading Musical Foundation, Reading, PA
6,000	Wyomissing Institute/Fine Arts, Wyomissing, PA
5,000	Berks Community Television, Reading, PA
1,000	Reading Pops Orchestra, Reading, PA
600	Reading Symphony Orchestra, Reading, PA
500	Historical Society of Berks County, Reading, PA

Civic & Public Affairs

10,000	Berks County Community Foundation, Reading, PA
5,000	Employment Policy Foundation, Washington, DC
1,050	Foundation for Free Enterprise Education, Erie, PA
1,000	Spanish Speaking Council, Oakland, CA
500	Washington Legal Foundation, Washington, DC
250	Financial Executives Research Fdn., Richmond, VA

Education

30,000	Penn State University, University Park, PA
18,300	National Merit Scholarships, Chicago, IL
8,000	Alvernia College, Reading, PA
3,000	Berks Business Education Coalition, Reading, PA
1,700	BCIU - Educator Internship Program, Reading, PA
1,200	Claflin College, Orangeburg, SC
1,200	Jr. Achievement of Berks County, Inc., Reading, PA
1,200	Orangeburg Calhoun Technical College Foundation, Orangeburg, PA
1,000	Albright College, Reading, PA
750	Alvernia College, Reading, PA
500	Reading Education Center, Reading, PA
356	Kutztown University, Kutztown, PA

Health

1,000	St. Joseph Medical Center, Los Angeles, CA
800	American Cancer Society, Philadelphia, PA

International

500	SAE International, Warrendale, PA

Science

1,000	Reading-Berks Science/Engineering Fair, Reading, PA

Social Services

135,000	United Way of Berks County, Reading, PA
14,779	United Way, Philadelphia, PA
8,000	Police Athletic League, Philadelphia, PA
5,920	Service Centers, San Diego, CA
5,000	Berks Talkline, Reading, PA
5,000	United Way/Chad of San Diego County, San Diego, CA
3,500	Edisto United Way, Orangeburg, SC
1,500	Reading Berks Emergency Shelter, Reading, PA
1,000	American Red Cross, Philadelphia, PA
300	Berks County Special Olympics, Reading, PA
250	Children's Home of Reading, Reading, PA
250	Greater Berks Food Bank, Reading, PA

CARRIER CORP.

Company Contact

Farmington, CT
Web: http://www.carrier.com

Company Description

SIC(s): 3585 Refrigeration & Heating Equipment.
Parent Company: United Technologies Corp., One Financial Plaza, Hartford, CT, United States

Nonmonetary Support

Range: $6,000 - $10,000
Type: In-kind Services; Loaned Executives

Giving Contact

Margaret Martin, Director, Community Relations
Carrier Corp.
PO Box 4808
Syracuse, NY 13221
Phone: (315)432-7559
Fax: (315)432-7898

Description

Organization Type: Corporate Giving Program
Giving Locations: principally near operating locations and to national organizations.
Grant Types: Capital, Employee Matching Gifts, General Support, Project, Scholarship.
Note: Matches gifts for higher education.

Financial Summary

Total Giving: $15,500,000 (2000 approx); $16,400,000 (1999 approx); $14,000,000 (1997 approx). Note: Contributes through corporate direct giving program only.

Typical Recipients

Arts & Humanities: Arts Centers, Community Arts, Historic Preservation, Museums/Galleries, Music, Opera, Performing Arts, Public Broadcasting, Theater
Civic & Public Affairs: Business/Free Enterprise, Civil Rights
Education: Colleges & Universities, Economic Education, Education Associations, Engineering/Technological Education, Literacy, Minority Education, Science/Mathematics Education
Health: Health Organizations, Hospitals, Medical Rehabilitation, Mental Health
Social Services: Child Welfare, Community Centers, People with Disabilities, Senior Services, United Funds/United Ways, Volunteer Services, Youth Organizations

Contributions Analysis

Giving Priorities: Education, social and health organizations, museums, and civic groups.
Arts & Humanities: 5% to 10%. Interests include performing arts groups and museums.
Civic & Public Affairs: 5% to 10%. Limited support goes to civic organizations in local manufacturing areas.
Education: About 50%. Supports various colleges and universities through company's matching gifts program. Also supports educational funds for scholarships and student aid. Emphasis is on engineering education, especially at colleges with a high minority enrollment. Provides some support for elementary and secondary schools through adopt-a-school programs and other activities.
Health: 30% to 35%. Supports united funds, health organizations, rehabilitation, and programs for the mentally retarded. Emphasis is also on geriatric care and programs for the disabled. Some support is provided for youth groups and community service organizations.

Application Procedures

Initial Contact: Check the guidelines and download an application from website.
Application Requirements: Include a a description of organization, amount requested, purpose of funds sought, recently audited financial statement, and proof of tax-exempt status.
Deadlines: None; budget is usually prepared in August or September.

Additional Information

United Technologies Corp, the parent company of Carrier Corp., also sponsors a contributions program (see separate entry).
In April 1999, Carrier Corporation and Toshiba Corporation announced the formation of a global strategic alliance in the heating, ventilation, air conditioning, and refrigeration industry.

Giving Program Officials

Margaret Martin: PRIM CORP EMPL director community relations: Carrier Corp.

Grants Analysis

Disclosure Period: calendar year ending
Typical Range: $500 to $5,000

CARRIS REELS

Company Contact

Rutland, VT

Company Description

Employees: 750
SIC(s): 2499 Wood Products Nec, 3089 Plastics Products Nec, 3499 Fabricated Metal Products Nec.
Parent Company: Carris Financial Corp.

Carris Corp. Foundation

Giving Contact

David Fitz-Gerald, Chief Financial Officer
439 West Street
Rutland, VT 05702
Phone: (802)773-9111

Description

Founded: 1990
EIN: 030326934
Organization Type: Corporate Foundation
Giving Locations: headquarters and operating communities.
Grant Types: General Support.

Financial Summary

Total Giving: $309,180 (1999 approx); $297,288 (1998); $285,854 (1997)
Assets: $1,260,907 (1996); $994,638 (1995); $349,825 (1993)

Gifts Received: $357,161 (1996); $403,980 (1995); $316,161 (1993). Note: In 1996, contributions were received from Carris Reels ($209,679), Carris Reels of Connecticut ($92,351), Vermont Tubbs ($53,630), and Carris Reels of California ($1,502).

Typical Recipients

Arts & Humanities: Arts Associations & Councils, Arts Centers, Libraries, Music, Public Broadcasting, Theater, Visual Arts
Civic & Public Affairs: Civil Rights, Clubs, Employment/Job Training, Civic & Public Affairs-General, Native American Affairs, Parades/Festivals
Education: Colleges & Universities, Education-General, Private Education (Precollege), Science/Mathematics Education, Secondary Education (Public)
Environment: Environment-General
Health: AIDS/HIV, Cancer, Children's Health/Hospitals, Emergency/Ambulance Services, Health Organizations, Nursing Services, Public Health, Single-Disease Health Associations
Religion: Churches, Jewish Causes, Religious Welfare
Science: Scientific Centers & Institutes
Social Services: Animal Protection, Child Abuse, Child Welfare, Community Service Organizations, Delinquency & Criminal Rehabilitation, Family Services, Food/Clothing Distribution, Recreation & Athletics, Scouts, Senior Services, Special Olympics, Substance Abuse, United Funds/United Ways, Veterans

Application Procedures

Initial Contact: The foundation supports organizations nominated by committees of employee owners.

Corporate Officials

William H. Carris: chairman, president, chief executive officer PRIM CORP EMPL chairman, president, chief executive officer: Carris Reels.
David Fitz-Gerald: chief financial officer PRIM CORP EMPL chief financial officer: Carris Reels.

Foundation Officials

Barbara T. Carris: vice president PRIM CORP EMPL vice president, director: Carris Reels.
William H. Carris: president (see above)
Thomas Dowling: secretary
David Fitz-Gerald: treasurer (see above)

Grants Analysis

Disclosure Period: calendar year ending 1996
Number of Grants: 48
Highest Grant: $49,550
Typical Range: $100 to $10,000

Recent Grants

Note: Grants derived from 1996 Form 990.

Arts & Humanities

13,277 Carving Studio, West Rutland, VT
12,000 Chaffee Art Center
2,000 Crossroads Arts Council, Rutland, VT
2,000 Northstar Theater Arts
2,000 Vermont Educational Telecommunications Consortium, South Burlington, VT
1,500 Killington Musical Festival, Killington, VT
1,000 Vermont Symphony Orchestra, Burlington, VT
250 Jeh Julu Drum and Dance Theater
125 Capitol Chamber Artists, Albany, NY

Civic & Public Affairs

1,000 American Civil Liberties Foundation, Montpelier, VT
1,000 Crazy Horse Memorial Foundation, Custer, SD
600 Killington Pico Rotary Club, Killington, VT
500 First Night, Rutland, VT
150 Rutland Lions Club, Rutland, VT

Education

49,550 Augsburg College Full Circle, Minneapolis, MN
13,900 College of St. Joseph, VT
3,500 Mount St. Joseph Academy
3,000 Vermont Achievement Center, Rutland, VT
1,300 Rutland High School, Rutland, VT
750 College of St. Joseph Mayflower Conference
250 Sacred Heart School Endowment Fund
150 Rutland High School Project Graduation, Rutland, VT

Health

5,100 American Red Cross, Rutland, VT
1,000 Children's Brittle Bone Foundation, Highland Park, IL
1,000 Metrowest Fights AIDS, Wayland, MA
1,000 Rutland Health Foundation, Rutland, VT
500 Epilepsy Association
500 Utah AIDS Foundation, Salt Lake City, UT
400 American Cancer Society
200 Muscular Dystrophy Association

Religion

200 Rutland Jewish Center, Rutland, VT

Social Services

11,580 United Way Rutland County, Rutland, VT
5,000 Dismas House
3,100 Rutland County Humane Society, Rutland, VT
1,725 Girl Scout Council of America Vermont Council, Essex Junction, VT
500 Nobody's Children, Windham, NH
500 Prime Family Resources
400 Rutland Recreation Department, Rutland, VT
305 Prevent Child Abuse in Vermont, VT
250 Jimmy Heuga Center
250 Rutland Community Cupboard, Rutland, VT
200 Mary Bridge Children's Trust Fund, Tacoma, WA
200 Vermont Special Olympics, Williston, VT
150 Rutland Area Child Advocacy Team, Rutland, VT
150 Southwestern Vermont Council on Aging, Rutland, VT
100 Proctor Youth League, Proctor, VT
100 Rutland City DARE, Rutland, VT
50 Veterans of Foreign Wars

CARTER-WALLACE, INC.

Company Contact

New York, NY
Web: http://www.carter-wallace.com

Company Description

Employees: 3,360
SIC(s): 2047 Dog & Cat Food, 2834 Pharmaceutical Preparations, 2835 Diagnostic Substances, 2844 Toilet Preparations.

Carter-Wallace Foundation

Giving Contact

Mr. James L. Wagar, Vice President & Treasurer
Carter-Wallace Foundation
1345 Avenue of the Americas
New York, NY 10105
Phone: (212)339-5010
Fax: (212)339-5100

Description

EIN: 133359226
Organization Type: Corporate Foundation. Supports preselected organizations only.
Giving Locations: CT; IL: Decatur; NJ; NY
Grant Types: Employee Matching Gifts, General Support.

Financial Summary

Total Giving: $752,522 (fiscal year ending March 31, 1997); $724,380 (fiscal 1996); $1,133,595 (fiscal 1995). Note: Contributes through foundation only. Fiscal 1997 Giving includes foundation ($727,272); United Way ($24,750).
Assets: $80,383 (fiscal 1997); $178,223 (fiscal 1996); $135,372 (fiscal 1995)
Gifts Received: $650,000 (fiscal 1997); $765,000 (fiscal 1996); $2,400,000 (fiscal 1994). Note: The foundation receives contributions from Carter-Wallace, Inc.

Typical Recipients

Arts & Humanities: Arts Centers, Arts Institutes, Historic Preservation, Libraries, Museums/Galleries, Music, Opera, Performing Arts, Public Broadcasting, Theater
Civic & Public Affairs: Botanical Gardens/Parks, Housing, Law & Justice, Professional & Trade Associations, Urban & Community Affairs, Zoos/Aquariums
Education: Colleges & Universities, Education Associations, Education Funds, Medical Education, Minority Education, Private Education (Precollege), Student Aid
Environment: Environment-General
Health: Arthritis, Cancer, Clinics/Medical Centers, Eyes/Blindness, Health Organizations, Hospitals, Hospitals (University Affiliated), Medical Research, Mental Health, Public Health, Single-Disease Health Associations, Speech & Hearing
International: Foreign Educational Institutions, Health Care/Hospitals, International Relief Efforts
Science: Science Museums
Social Services: Counseling, Crime Prevention, Family Planning, People with Disabilities, Recreation & Athletics, Substance Abuse, United Funds/ United Ways, Youth Organizations

Contributions Analysis

Giving Priorities: Education, hospitals, arts institutions, civic affairs, United Way, youth organizations, and international health organizations.
Arts & Humanities: 15% to 20%. Grants benefit a wide variety of recipient types. Interests include opera and other music-oriented organizations,performing arts centers, libraries, and museums.
Civic & Public Affairs: 5% to 10%. Funds zoos, botanical gardens, and professional associations.
Education: 35% to 40%. Supports colleges and universities in northeastern United States. Medical and dental education are among the highest priorities. Grants are also made to education funds, scholarship funds, and Junior Achievement.
Health: 30% to 35%. Priority is given to hospitals, medical centers, and single-disease health associations.

Corporate Officials

Daniel James Black: president, chief operating officer, director B Asbury Park, NJ 1931. ED Saint John's University (1950-1952); New York University BS (1956). PRIM CORP EMPL president, chief operating officer, director: Carter-Wallace, Inc. CLUB AFFIL Sands Point Golf Club; University Club; Manhasset Bay Yacht Club; Metro Club.
Charles Orcutt Hoyt: chairman executive committee, director B Orange, NJ 1929. ED Princeton University AB (1951); Columbia University MBA (1953). PRIM CORP EMPL chairman executive committee, director: Carter-Wallace, Inc. ADD CORP EMPL vice chairman: Denver Chemical.

Henry Hamilton Hoyt, Jr.: chairman, chief executive officer, director B Orange, NJ 1927. ED Princeton University AB (1949). PRIM CORP EMPL chairman, chief executive officer, director: Carter-Wallace, Inc. ADD CORP EMPL president: International Biological Labs; chairman: Denver Chemical. NONPR AFFIL director: Deafness Research Foundation.
Ralph Levine: president, chief operating officer, director B New York, NY 1936. ED City University of New York BA (1958); New York University JD (1961). PRIM CORP EMPL president, chief operating officer, director: Carter-Wallace, Inc.

Foundation Officials

Daniel James Black: treasurer (see above)
Charles Orcutt Hoyt: director (see above)
Henry Hamilton Hoyt, Jr.: president (see above)
James Lee Wagar: manager B Port Chester, NY 1934. ED Fordham University (1956); New York University MBA (1966). PRIM CORP EMPL vice president, treasurer: Carter-Wallace, Inc. CORP AFFIL treasurer: Denver Chemical.

Grants Analysis

Disclosure Period: fiscal year ending March 31, 1997
Total Grants: $727,272*
Number of Grants: 121
Average Grant: $6,011
Highest Grant: $50,000
Typical Range: $1,000 to $25,000
***Note:** Giving excludes United Way.

Recent Grants

Note: Grants derived from 1997 Form 990.

Arts & Humanities
25,000 Metropolitan Opera Association, New York, NY
15,000 New York Philharmonic, New York, NY
15,000 New York Public Library, New York, NY
7,500 Lincoln Center for Performing Arts, New York, NY
7,500 Metropolitan Museum of Art, New York, NY
7,500 Museum of Modern Art, New York, NY
7,000 WNET/Channel 13, New York, NY
6,000 Carnegie Hall, New York, NY
5,000 Boston Museum of Fine Arts, Boston, MA
5,000 New York City Opera, New York, NY

Civic & Public Affairs
5,000 Central Park Conservancy, New York, NY
5,000 New York Botanical Society, Bronx, NY
5,000 New York Zoological Society, Bronx, NY

Education
50,000 United Negro College Fund, New York, NY
25,000 Princeton University, Princeton, NJ
20,000 Fordham University, New York, NY
15,000 Mount Holyoke College, South Hadley, MA
15,000 University of Medicine and Dentistry of New Jersey Foundation, Newark, NJ
12,500 Independent College Fund of New Jersey, East Orange, NJ
12,500 Independent College Fund of New York, New York, NY
10,000 Johns Hopkins University, Baltimore, MD
7,500 Pingry School, Martinsville, NJ
5,000 American Foundation for Pharmaceutical Education, Rockville, MD
5,000 Greenvale School, New York, NY

Health
41,500 New York Hospital Cornell Medical Center, New York, NY
41,250 Columbia Presbyterian Medical Center, New York, NY
25,000 American Paralysis Association, Short Hills, NJ -- for Henry G. Stifell III Spinal Cord Injury Fund
25,000 Memorial Sloan-Kettering Cancer Center, New York, NY
25,000 Overlook Hospital, Summit, NJ
10,000 Brown University Rhode Island Hospital Department of Medicine, Providence, RI
10,000 Deafness Research Foundation, New York, NY
10,000 Duke University Duke Hospital, Durham, NC
10,000 Massachusetts General Hospital, Boston, MA
10,000 St. Luke's Roosevelt Hospital Center, New York, NY
10,000 Strang Clinic, New York, NY
7,500 Council on Family Health, New York, NY
7,500 Lenox Hill Hospital, New York, NY
7,500 Medical Center at Princeton, Princeton, NJ
7,000 National Arthritis Foundation New York Chapter, New York, NY
5,000 Greenwich Hospital, Greenwich, CT
5,000 Jersey Shore Medical Center, Neptune, NJ
5,000 Mount Sinai Hospital, New York, NY
5,000 North Shore University Hospital, Manhasset, NY

International
20,000 McGill University, Montreal, PQ, Canada
5,000 International Rescue Committee, New York, NY

Science
7,500 American Museum of Natural History, New York, NY

Social Services
22,500 United Way Tri-State, New York, NY
16,500 Planned Parenthood of New York City, New York, NY
12,500 Partnership for a Drug-Free America, New York, NY
6,500 New York City Police Foundation, New York, NY

CASTLE &COOKE PROPERTIES INC.

Company Contact

Honolulu, HI

Company Description

Former Name: Oceanic Properties.
Employees: 1,400
SIC(s): 1521 Single-Family Housing Construction, 4725 Tour Operators, 6531 Real Estate Agents & Managers, 6552 Subdividers & Developers Nec.
Parent Company: Oceanic Properties

Nonmonetary Support

Type: Donated Products

Giving Contact

Beverly Hayashi, Secretary to Management Committee
Castle & Cooke Properties Inc.
PO Box 898900
Mililani, HI 96789-8900
Phone: (808)548-4811
Fax: (808)548-2975

Description

Organization Type: Corporate Giving Program
Giving Locations: HI
Grant Types: Employee Matching Gifts, General Support.

Financial Summary

Total Giving: Contributes through corporate direct giving program only.

Typical Recipients

Arts & Humanities: Arts & Humanities-General
Civic & Public Affairs: Civic & Public Affairs-General
Education: Education-General
Health: Health-General
Social Services: Social Services-General

Application Procedures

Initial Contact: written proposal
Application Requirements: a description of organization, amount requested, purpose of funds sought, recently audited financial statement, and proof of tax-exempt status
Deadlines: None.
Decision Notification: management committee meets weekly

Restrictions

The company only contributes to nonprofit organizations.

Additional Information

Company officials report that the company has merged with the Dole Food Corporation.

Corporate Officials

Wally Miyahara: president, chief executive officer, director PRIM CORP EMPL president, chief executive officer, director: Castle & Cooke Properties Inc.

Giving Program Officials

Beverly Hayashi: secretary PRIM CORP EMPL secretary management & donations committee: Castle & Cooke Properties Inc.

CATERPILLAR INC.

 Number 65 of Top 100 Corporate Givers

Company Contact

Peoria, IL
Web: http://www.cat.com

Company Description

Revenue: US$19,702,000,000 (1999)
Profit: US$1,513,000,000
Employees: 65,824 (1999)
Fortune Rank: 85, per FORTUNE Magazine's list of 500 Largest U.S. Corporations (1999).
FF 85
SIC(s): 3272 Concrete Products Nec, 3511 Turbines & Turbine Generator Sets, 3519 Internal Combustion Engines Nec, 3531 Construction Machinery.

Operating Locations

Australia: Caterpillar of Australia Ltd., Tullamarine; Belgium: Caterpillar Belgium SA, Charleroi, Hainaut; Solar Turbines Overseas Ltd. Societe de Droit Americain, Charleroi, Hainaut; Carterpillar Group Services NV, Grimbergen, Brabant; Caterpillar Commercial NV, Grimbergen, Brabant; Caterpillar Overseas NV Naar Zwitsers Recht, Grimbergen, Brabant; Caterpillar Logistic Services Venn Naar Amerikaans Recht V/D Staat Delaware, Zaventem, Brabant; Brazil: Caterpillar Brasil SA, Piracicaba; Canada: Solar Turbines Canada Ltd., Edmonton; Canadian Diesel Power, Mississauga; Caterpillar of Canada Ltd., Mississauga; MAK Americas, Mississauga; Caterpillar Financial Services Ltd., Oakville; Caterpillar Commercial Services Ltd., Woodbridge; Denmark: MAK Scandanavian AS, Tastrup, Arhus; France: Caterpillar Logistics Services, Ennery; Caterpillar France SA,

Grenoble, Isere; MAK Mediterranee, Marseille; Caterpillar Materiels Routiers, Rantigny, Oise; Caterpillar Commercial, St. Denis; Caterpillar Finance France, St. Denis; Germany: Caterpillar Financial Services Holding GmbH, Ismaning, Bayern; Caterpillar Leasing GmbH, Ismaning, Bayern; MAK Motoren GmbH and Co. KG, Kiel, Schleswig-Holstein; MAK Wohnurisbau GmbH, Kiel, Schleswig-Holstein; Caterpillar Leasing GmbH, Leipzig, De-Ost; Hong Kong: Caterpillar Far East Commercial Ltd., Admiralty; Caterpillar Far East Ltd., Admiralty; Indonesia: PT Natra Raya, Cileungsi, Wjv; Ireland: Energy Services International Ltd., Bray; Caterpillar International Finance Public Ltd. Co., Dublin; Italy: Caterpillar Logistics Services, Castel Maggiore; Caaterpillar Commerciale SRL, Roma, Lazio; Mexico: Caterpillar Arrenadora Financiera SA de CV, Ciudad de Mexico; Caterpillar Credito SA de CV, Ciudad de Mexico; Caterpillar Factoraje Financiero SA de CV, Ciudad de Mexico; GFCM Servicios SA de CV, Ciudad de Mexico; Grupo Financiero Caterpillar Mexico SA de CV, Ciudad de Mexico; Turbinas Solar SA de CV, Ciudad de Mexico; Tecnologia Modificado SA de CV, Nuevo Laredo; Caterpillar Mexico SA de CV, Santa Catarina; Conek SA de CV, Santa Catarina; Immobiliaria Conek SA, Santa Catarina; Turbo Tecnologas de Reparacion SA de CV, Tijuana; Netherlands: Caterpillar Financial Services Corp., Amsterdam, Noord-Holland; Balderson, Vught, Noord-Brabant; Solar Turbines Europe SA, Zwijndrecht, Anvers; Singapore: Caterpillar Asia Pte. Ltd., Singapore; Spain: Caterpillar Logistics Services Spain SA, Guadalajara, Madrid, Madrid; Caterpillar Financial Corpfinanciera SA, Pozuelo de Alarcon, Madrid; Caterpillar Financial Renting SA, Pozuelo de Alarcon, Madrid; Caterpillar Overseas AG, Santa Rosalia, Malaga; Sweden: Caterpillar Financial Nordic Services AB, Danderyd, Stockholm; Switzerland: Caterpillar Overseas SA, Geneva; United Kingdom: Caterpillar Logistics Services Ltd., Leicester, Leicestershire; Caterpillar Overseas SA, Leicester, Leicestershire; Caterpillar (United Kingdom) Ltd., Leicester, Leicestershire; Archer Components Ltd., Peterlee, Durham; Brown Group Holdings Ltd., Peterlee, Durham; Caterpillar Peterlee Ltd., Peterlee, Durham; Charter & Transport Services Ltd., Peterlee, Durham; Caterpillar Financial Services (United Kingdom) Ltd., Slough, Berkshire; Caterpillar Stockton Ltd., Stockton-on-Tees, Cleveland; DJ Industries Ltd., Stockton-on-Tees, Cleveland; Turner Powertrain Systems Ltd., Wolverhampton, West Midlands

Nonmonetary Support

Value: $600,000 (1996)
Type: Donated Equipment; In-kind Services; Loaned Executives

Corporate Sponsorship

Type: Arts & cultural events; Music & entertainment events

Caterpillar Foundation

Giving Contact

Henry Holling
Caterpillar Foundation
100 Northeast Adams Street
Peoria, IL 61629-1480
Phone: (309)675-4418
Fax: (309)675-5815

Description

Founded: 1952
EIN: 376022314
Organization Type: Corporate Foundation
Giving Locations: operating locations; educational matching gifts program is international.
Grant Types: Capital, Department, Employee Matching Gifts, General Support, Operating Expenses, Project.
Note: Employee matching gift ratio: 1 to 1 for higher education only.

Giving Philosophy

'Because of the company's presence in certain communities, there is a benefit to investing in programs and organizations that add to the quality of life and economic development in those communities. We also recognize our responsibility as a corporate citizen to be supportive of these worthwhile activities.' Caterpillar Corporate Support Programs

Financial Summary

Total Giving: $12,895,775 (1998); $11,626,952 (1997); $13,792,353 (1996)
Assets: $21,689,380 (1998); $21,749,936 (1997); $21,679,797 (1996)
Gifts Received: $13,000,000 (1998); $11,814,000 (1997); $10,799,000 (1996). Note: Contributions are received from Caterpillar, Inc.

Typical Recipients

Arts & Humanities: Arts Centers, Community Arts, Arts & Humanities-General, Historic Preservation, Museums/Galleries, Music, Performing Arts, Public Broadcasting, Theater
Civic & Public Affairs: African American Affairs, Botanical Gardens/Parks, Business/Free Enterprise, Civil Rights, Community Foundations, Economic Development, Economic Policy, Ethnic Organizations, Civic & Public Affairs-General, Housing, Law & Justice, Municipalities/Towns, Nonprofit Management, Public Policy, Safety, Urban & Community Affairs
Education: Business Education, Colleges & Universities, Community & Junior Colleges, Economic Education, Education Funds, Education Reform, Engineering/Technological Education, Faculty Development, Education-General, International Studies, Medical Education, Minority Education, Public Education (Precollege), Science/Mathematics Education, Student Aid, Vocational & Technical Education
Environment: Environment-General, Resource Conservation
Health: Cancer, Emergency/Ambulance Services, Health Organizations, Hospices, Hospitals, Mental Health, Single-Disease Health Associations
International: International Peace & Security Issues, Trade
Religion: Religious Welfare
Social Services: Child Welfare, Community Centers, Community Service Organizations, Family Services, Homes, People with Disabilities, Sexual Abuse, Substance Abuse, United Funds/United Ways, YMCA/YWCA/YMHA/YWHA, Youth Organizations

Contributions Analysis

Giving Priorities: Education, health, social welfare, civic improvement, culture, and international economic development. Limited support through foundation to international public policy and economic development-oriented organizations.
Arts & Humanities: 5% to 10%. Provides capital and operating grants. Recipients include music groups, public broadcasting, arts centers, and theaters. Also sponsors matching gifts program, which accounts for the largest share of cultural giving.
Civic & Public Affairs: 10% to 15%. Supports community and economic development programs, environmental organizations, criminal justice, and race relations. The majority of funding in this area is awarded directly by the company and primarily goes to public policy issues and urban affairs.
Education: 40% to 45%. Supports colleges and universities, business, economic, and engineering education; student aid; universities and colleges; and education funds.
Health: 25% to 30%. United Ways in plant communities receive the majority of funding. Also makes capital grants to local health institutions and human service agencies, including youth and religious welfare organizations, homes, and programs for drug and alcohol abuse prevention.

Application Procedures

Initial Contact: short cover letter or proposal
Application Requirements: a description of organization; need and proposed use of funds; operating budget for current year showing breakdown of anticipated expenses and sources of income; copy of most recently audited financial statement; list of members of governing board; copy of 501(c)(3) letter
Deadlines: None.
Decision Notification: notice of approval or rejection is usually sent within one month

Restrictions

In general, company does not support individuals, fraternal organizations, religious organizations whose services are limited to any one sectarian group, political activity, tickets or advertising for fund-raising benefits, or general operations or ongoing programs of agencies funded by the United Way.

Corporate Officials

Gerald S. Flaherty: group president B Spring Valley, IL 1938. ED Northern Illinois University BS (1964); Northern Illinois University MS (1967). PRIM CORP EMPL group president: Caterpillar Inc. CORP AFFIL director: Caterpillar Paving Products; director: Heartland Partners. NONPR AFFIL director: Greater Peoria Airport Authority; trustee: Manufacturer Alliance; trustee: Bradley University.

Foundation Officials

Donald Vester Fites: director (see above)
Gerald S. Flaherty: trustee (see above)
Henry W. Holling: vice president
Alan J. Rassi: trustee PRIM CORP EMPL vice president: Caterpillar Inc.
T. Thorstenson: vice president
Wayne M. Zimmerman: trustee PRIM CORP EMPL vice president employer relations: Caterpillar Inc.

Grants Analysis

Disclosure Period: calendar year ending
Typical Range: $1,000 to $25,000

Recent Grants

Note: Grants derived from 1997 Form 990.

Arts & Humanities

247,812	Cultural
50,000	Bertha Frank Performing Arts Center, Morton, IL
50,000	Corn Stock Theater
50,000	Smithsonian Institution, Washington, DC
50,000	White House Fund, Washington, DC

Civic & Public Affairs

118,000	Municipalities/Towns, Decatur, IL
109,470	Will County
100,000	City of San Diego, San Diego, CA
60,000	City of Lafayette, Lafayette, IN
50,000	Peoria Area Community Foundation, Peoria, IL
50,000	Peoria Area Community Foundation, Peoria, IL
50,000	SAE Vision 2000
50,000	Three Sisters Park, Evergreen, CO
40,000	Sun Star Botanical Garden, Macon, IL

Education

1,463,886	University of Minnesota, MN
1,000,000	Bradley University, Peoria, IL
973,380	University of Illinois, Champaign, IL
600,000	Bradley University, Peoria, IL
405,861	Educational
300,000	Knox College, Galesburg, IL
250,000	Purdue University, West Lafayette, IN
150,000	University
100,000	Construction Education Foundation
75,000	Illinois Central College Foundation

62,500 York College Capital Campaign
60,000 Illinois State University
50,000 Carnegie Mellon University
50,000 Community College
50,000 Monmouth College
50,000 Pennsylvania College of Technology
50,000 University of Illinois
50,000 Valparaiso University-Diversity Excellence Fund
47,000 Education
45,000 TSTM Scholarships (Tri-County Urban League)
40,000 Institute of the Americas
40,000 Occupational Physicians Scholarship Fund (OPSF)
36,000 Iowa State University
30,000 University

Health
100,000 American Red Cross
100,000 Methodist Medical Center Hospice
50,000 Community Cancer Center
35,000 Decatur Mental Health Association

Social Services
750,000 United Way HOIUW Excellence Fund
100,000 Peoria Association of Retarded Citizens PARC
75,000 United Way
50,000 Carver Community Center
50,000 Common Place
50,000 Salem Children's Home
50,000 YMCA
50,000 YWCA

CBS CORP.

Company Contact
51 West 52nd Street
New York, NY 10019
Phone: (212)975-4321
Fax: (212)975-4516
Web: http://www.cbs.com

Company Description
Revenue: US$7,373,000,000 (1999)
Profit: US$780,000,000 (1999)
Employees: 28,900 (1999)
Fortune Rank: 237, per FORTUNE Magazine's list of 500 Largest U.S. Corporations (1999).
FF 237
Parent Company: Viacom Inc., 1515 Broadway, New York, NY, United States

Nonmonetary Support
Type: In-kind Services

CBS Foundation

Giving Contact
New York, NY

Description
EIN: 136099759
Organization Type: Corporate Foundation
Grant Types: Employee Matching Gifts, General Support, Multiyear/Continuing Support, Operating Expenses, Project, Scholarship.

Financial Summary
Total Giving: $2,385,428 (1998); $1,909,051 (1997)
Giving Analysis: Giving for 1997 includes: foundation ($1,585,600); foundation matching gifts ($196,426); foundation grants to United Way ($127,025); 1998: foundation ($2,047,245); foundation matching gifts ($215,183); foundation grants to United Way ($123,000)
Assets: $4,771,159 (1998); $6,730,117 (1997)

Typical Recipients
Arts & Humanities: Film & Video, Libraries, Museums/Galleries, Performing Arts, Public Broadcasting, Theater
Civic & Public Affairs: Chambers of Commerce
Education: Journalism/Media Education, Minority Education, Social Sciences Education, Special Education, Student Aid
Religion: Religious Welfare
Social Services: Community Service Organizations, United Funds/United Ways

Restrictions
Company only supports charitable organizations with IRS 501(c)(3) tax-exempt status.
Does not support projects that are directly associated with the internal operations of divisions of CBS; organizations via advertisements in journals; endowment or capital costs, including construction, renovation, and/or equipment; internal programs and institutions; or individuals.

Additional Information
In December 1997, the corporation changed its name from Westinghouse Electric Corp. to CBS Corp., recognizing it was nearing completion of its transformation to a pure media company.

Corporate Officials
Laurence Alan Tisch: chairman, co-chief executive officer B New York, NY 1923. ED New York University BS (1942); University of Pennsylvania MA (1943); Harvard University Law School (1946). PRIM CORP EMPL chairman, co-chief executive officer: Loews Corp. ADD CORP EMPL chief executive officer: CNA Financial Corp.; chief executive officer: Continental Loss Adjusting Service. CORP AFFIL director: Petrie Stores Corp.; director: Transcontinental Insurance Co. New York; chairman: CNA Financial Corp.; director: Automatic Data Processing Inc.; director: Bulova Corp. NONPR AFFIL chairman board trustees: New York University; director: United Jewish Appeal Federation; trustee: New York Public Library; member: Council Foreign Relations; trustee: Metropolitan Museum Art.

Foundation Officials
Michel Christian Bergerac: director B Biarritz, France 1932. ED Sorbonne University MA (1953); University of California, Los Angeles MBA (1955). PRIM CORP EMPL chairman, chief executive officer: MC Bergerac & Co. CORP AFFIL director: Vion Pharmaceuticals Inc.; director: Topps Co.; director: ICN Pharmaceuticals; director: International Telecharge; director: CBS Inc. NONPR AFFIL trustee: New York Zoological Society.
Joseph Castellano: secretary
Kathryn L. Edmundson: president
Henry Alfred Kissinger: director B Fuerth, Germany 1923. ED Harvard University AB (1950); Harvard University MA (1952); Harvard University PhD (1954). PRIM CORP EMPL founder, chairman: Kissinger Associates ADD CORP EMPL president: Henry A. Kissinger Consulting Co. CORP AFFIL director: Hollinger International Inc.; director: Revlon Inc.; member international advisor committee: Chase Bank; director: Freeport-McMoRan Copper Gold Inc. NONPR AFFIL member: Phi Beta Kappa; director: World Cup USA Inc.; member: Council Foreign Relations; trustee: Metropolitan Museum Art; member: American Academy of Arts & Sciences; member: American Political Science Association. CLUB AFFIL Metro DC Club; River Club; Brook Club; Century Club; Bohemian Club.
Louis J. Rauchenberger, Jr.: treasurer
Linda Richter: assistant treasurer
Franklin Augustine Thomas: director B Brooklyn, NY 1934. ED Columbia University BA (1956); Columbia University LLB (1963). CORP AFFIL director: PepsiCo Inc.; consul: TFF Study Group; director: Lucent Technologies Inc.; director: Conoco Inc.; director: Cummins Engine Co. Inc.; director: Citigroup.
Preston Robert Tisch: chairman, director B Brooklyn, NY 1926. ED Bucknell University (1943-1944); University of Michigan BA (1948). PRIM CORP EMPL co-chairman, co-chief executive officer, director: Loews Corp. ADD CORP EMPL owner, chief executive officer, chairman: New York Football Giants Inc. CORP AFFIL director: Transcontinental Insurance Co. New York; director: Rite Aid Corp.; director: CNA Financial Corp.; director: Hasbro Inc.; director: Bulova Watch Corp.; director: Bulova Corp. NONPR AFFIL trustee: New York University; member: Sigma Alpha Mu; member: Governments Business Advisory Council New York; chairman emeritus: New York Convention & Visit Bureau; president: Citymeals Wheels. CLUB AFFIL Rye Racquet Club; Century Country Club.
David Zemelman: trustee

Grants Analysis
Disclosure Period: calendar year ending 1997
Total Grants: $1,585,600*
Number of Grants: 86
Average Grant: $18,437
Highest Grant: $250,000
***Note:** Giving excludes matching gifts; United Way.

Recent Grants
Note: Grants derived from 1997 Form 990.

Arts & Humanities
100,000 Museum of Television and Radio, New York, NY -- program support, outreach, maintenance of archives
83,000 Museum of Television and Radio, New York, NY -- capital campaign for Los Angeles chapter
75,000 Lincoln Center for Performing Arts, New York, NY -- support outreach activities
50,000 Library Foundation of Los Angeles, Los Angeles, CA -- to implement library card campaign
35,000 John F. Kennedy Center for Performing Arts, Washington, DC -- support national performing arts education classroom program
35,000 New York Public Library, New York, NY -- support Page Program
35,000 WCBS TV Holiday Project -- project support
25,000 American Film Institute, Washington, DC -- educational, training programs
25,000 National Corporate Theater Fund, New York, NY -- operating support
15,000 Museum of Modern Art, New York, NY -- operating support

Civic & Public Affairs
167,000 New York City Partnership and Chamber of Commerce, New York, NY -- support investment fund

Education
250,000 United Negro College Fund, Fairfax, VA -- operating support, curriculum development, scholarships
66,000 University of Miami, Miami, FL -- support three-year visiting Latin American Journalism Program
50,000 Foundation for Independent High Education, Chicago, IL -- scholarship program
25,000 University of St. Thomas, St. Paul, MN -- payment on three-year pledge for Whalen Symposium on Media Ethics
20,000 New York University, New York, NY -- support Metro Center for Urban Education Mentoring and Tutoring Program

Religion
50,000 Good Samaritan Program, Chicago, IL -- program support

Social Services

127,025	United Way USA -- program support
25,000	Neighbors Helping Neighbors, Miami, FL -- support phone bank, emergency services
20,000	All of Us, Pittsburgh, PA -- support for community empowerment campaign

CCB FINANCIAL CORP.

Company Contact

Durham, NC
Web: http://www.ccbonline.com

Company Description

Net Income: US$282,260,000
Employees: 2,891
SIC(s): 6022 State Commercial Banks, 6712 Bank Holding Companies.

CCB Foundation

Giving Contact

John D. Ramsey, President
CCB Foundation
PO Box 931
Durham, NC 27702-0931
Phone: (919)683-7251
Fax: (919)682-3870

Description

Founded: 1985
EIN: 581611223
Organization Type: Corporate Foundation
Giving Locations: headquarters area only.
Grant Types: General Support.

Financial Summary

Total Giving: $955,657 (1998); $768,196 (1997); $662,454 (1996)
Giving Analysis: Giving for 1997 includes: foundation grants to United Way ($172,835); foundation matching gifts ($37,694); 1998: foundation grants to United Way ($194,506); foundation matching gifts ($47,692)
Assets: $1,616,995 (1998); $1,378,459 (1997); $862,833 (1996)
Gifts Received: $1,123,300 (1998); $984,000 (1997); $929,000 (1996). Note: In 1998, contributions were received from Central Carolina Bank.

Typical Recipients

Arts & Humanities: Arts Associations & Councils, Arts & Humanities-General, Libraries, Performing Arts, Theater
Civic & Public Affairs: Business/Free Enterprise, Civic & Public Affairs-General, Housing, Urban & Community Affairs
Education: Arts/Humanities Education, Colleges & Universities, Education-General, Public Education (Precollege)
Health: Emergency/Ambulance Services, Health-General, Hospitals
Science: Science Museums
Social Services: Child Welfare, Crime Prevention, Social Services-General, United Funds/United Ways

Application Procedures

Initial Contact: Send a full proposal. Include a description of organization, amount requested, purpose of funds sought, and proof of tax-exempt status.
Deadlines: None.

Restrictions

Does not support individuals, religious organizations for sectarian purposes, political or lobbying groups, or organizations outside operating areas.

Corporate Officials

Ernest C. Roessler-Alsoa: president, chief executive officer, director B Pittsburgh, PA 1941. ED Dartmouth College (1962); Dartmouth College Amos Tuck Graduate School of Business Administration (1963). PRIM CORP EMPL president, chief executive officer, director: CCB Financial Corp. CORP AFFIL president, chief executive officer, director: CCB & Trust Co. NONPR AFFIL president: Financial Executives Institute.

Foundation Officials

John D. Ramsey: president

Grants Analysis

Disclosure Period: calendar year ending 1997
Total Grants: $557,667*
Number of Grants: 218
Average Grant: $2,788
Highest Grant: $80,000
Typical Range: $2,500 to $5,000
***Note:** Giving excludes matching gifts; United Way.

Recent Grants

Note: Grants derived from 1997 Form 990.

Arts & Humanities

15,000	Carolina Theater, NC -- support for the arts
11,000	Durham Arts Council, Durham, NC -- support the arts
10,000	Durham County Library, Durham, NC
10,000	Piedmont Players-Meroney -- support the arts

Civic & Public Affairs

25,000	Light Up Durham, Durham, NC
10,000	Habitat for Humanity, Greensboro, NC -- for housing
10,000	North Carolina Bankers Association Foundation, NC -- educational

Education

15,850	Durham Public Education Network, Durham, NC -- educational
15,000	Campbell University, Buies Creek, NC
10,000	Carolina College -- for Boiler Fund
10,000	Duke University, Durham, NC
10,000	NCCU, NC -- educational
10,000	University of North Carolina Center for Dramatic Arts, Chapel Hill, NC -- support the arts

Science

28,000	North Carolina Museum of Life and Science-BioQuest, Durham, NC -- educational

Social Services

80,000	United Way Triangle Area, NC
15,000	United Way Guilford, Guilford, NC
10,000	Durham Crimestoppers, Durham, NC
10,000	North Carolina Child Advocacy Institute, Raleigh, NC -- for health, welfare
8,000	United Way Central Carolinas, Charlotte, NC
7,868	United Way Alamance County, Burlington, NC

CENEX HARVEST STATES

Company Contact

5500 Cenex Dr.
Inver Grove Heights, MN 55077
Phone: (651)451-5151
Fax: (651)451-5566
Web: http://www.cenexharveststates.com

Company Description

Formed by Merger of: CENEX and Harvest States Cooperatives (1998).
Revenue: US$6,434,500,000 (1999)
Employees: 2,576 (1999)
Fortune Rank: 267, per FORTUNE Magazine's list of 500 Largest U.S. Corporations (1999).
FF 267
SIC(s): 2911 Petroleum Refining, 5083 Farm & Garden Machinery.

Nonmonetary Support

Type: In-kind Services

Cenex Harvest States Foundation

Giving Contact

William Nelson, President
Cenex Harvest Foundation
Email: wnels@cenexharveststates.com

Alternate Contact

5500 CENEX Dr.
Inver Grove Heights, MN 55077

Description

Founded: 1947
EIN: 416025858
Organization Type: Corporate Foundation
Giving Locations: CO; ID; IA; KS; MN; MT; NE; ND; OR; SD; UT; WA; WI
Grant Types: Emergency, Scholarship.

Financial Summary

Total Giving: $1,400,000 (fiscal year ending November 30, 2000 approx); $1,200,000 (fiscal 1999 approx); $902,848 (fiscal 1997)
Assets: $20,000,000 (fiscal 2000 approx); $20,000,000 (fiscal 1999 approx); $17,157,462 (fiscal 1997)
Gifts Received: $1,829,779 (fiscal 1997); $3,743,281 (fiscal 1996); $4,005,465 (fiscal 1995). Note: In fiscal 1996, contributions were received from CENEX.

Typical Recipients

Arts & Humanities: Arts & Humanities-General
Civic & Public Affairs: Civic & Public Affairs-General, Rural Affairs, Safety, Urban & Community Affairs
Education: Agricultural Education, Colleges & Universities, Community & Junior Colleges, Education-General, Science/Mathematics Education, Student Aid, Vocational & Technical Education
Health: Health-General, Medical Research
International: International-General
Religion: Religion-General, Religious Welfare
Science: Science-General
Social Services: Social Services-General

Application Procedures

Initial Contact: Send a brief letter of inquiry.
Deadlines: None.

Additional Information

Foundation generally support agriculturally related programs. Company reports that 60% of contributions go to education and 40% support rural youth programs and emergency assistance.

Corporate Officials

Lloyd Allen: vice chairman, director PRIM CORP EMPL vice chairman: CENEX.
Noel Keith Estenson: president, chief executive officer B Climax, MN 1938. ED North Dakota State University BS (1961). PRIM CORP EMPL president, chief executive officer: CENEX.
Joel Koonce: chief financial officer, group vice president financial PRIM CORP EMPL chief financial officer, group vice president financial: CENEX.
Elroy Webster: chairman, director PRIM CORP EMPL chairman, director: CENEX.

Foundation Officials

Lloyd Allen: vchairman (see above)
Bruce Anderson: trust
David Baker: executive vice president
Robert Bass: trustee
Curt Eischens: trustee
Aaron Glanzer: trustee CORP AFFIL director: CENEX Inc.
Andrew Hansen: assistant secretary-treasurer
Fred Harris: trustee CORP AFFIL director: CENEX Inc.
Douglas Johnson: trustee CORP AFFIL director: CENEX Inc.
Mary Kaste: mgr, assistant secretary-treasurer
James Kile: trustee
Gaylord Olson: secretary-treasurer PRIM CORP EMPL assistant secretary, treasurer: CENEX.
Bernard Saul: trustee
Denis Schilmoeller: trustee
Michael Toelle: trustee
Richard Traphagen: trustee CORP AFFIL director: CENEX Inc.
Elroy Webster: chairman (see above)
Arnold Weisenbeck: trustee

Grants Analysis

Disclosure Period: fiscal year ending November 30, 1997
Total Grants: $902,848
Typical Range: $125 to $7,500

Recent Grants

Note: Grants derived from fiscal 1997 Form 990.

Civic & Public Affairs

162,500	North Dakota Farmers Union, ND
106,199	South Dakota Farmers Union, SD
89,685	Minnesota Farmers Union, MN
65,425	Wisconsin Farmers Union, WI
57,930	Kansas Farmers Union, KS
47,188	Montana Farmers Union, MT
25,145	Rocky Mountain Farmers Union
18,985	Nebraska Farmers Union, Lincoln, NE
18,400	Iowa Farmers Union, IA
12,000	Executive Institute for Northwest Cooperatives, Olympia, WA
8,450	Washington State Grange, Olympia, WA
7,500	Oregon State Grange, Salem, OR
6,200	Agricultural Cooperative Council of Oregon, OR

Education

9,000	South Dakota State University, Brookings, SD
8,250	University of Idaho Moscow, Moscow, ID
6,750	Montana State University, Bozeman, MT
6,000	North Dakota State University, Fargo, ND
6,000	Southwest State University, Marshall, MN
6,000	University of Nebraska Lincoln, Lincoln, NE

Religion

10,000	Salvation Army -- for emergency assistance

CENTEX CORP.

Company Contact

Dallas, TX

Company Description

Revenue: US$3,975,500,000
Employees: 10,000
Fortune Rank: 318, per FORTUNE Magazine's list of 500 Largest U.S. Corporations (1999).
FF 318
SIC(s): 1521 Single-Family Housing Construction, 2493 Reconstituted Wood Products, 3241 Cement--Hydraulic, 3272 Concrete Products Nec, 3273 Ready-Mixed Concrete, 3275 Gypsum Products, 6552 Subdividers & Developers Nec.

Operating Locations

Operates in states.

Nonmonetary Support

Type: Donated Products; Loaned Employees

Giving Contact

Amy Nation, Secretary to the Chairman & Chief Executive Officer
PO Box 199000
Dallas, TX 75219
Phone: (214)981-5000

Description

Organization Type: Corporate Giving Program
Giving Locations: TX: Dallas including metropolitan area
Grant Types: General Support.

Financial Summary

Total Giving: $332,820 (1999); $298,517 (1998); $292,972 (1997)

Typical Recipients

Arts & Humanities: Arts & Humanities-General
Civic & Public Affairs: Civic & Public Affairs-General
Education: Education-General
Health: Health-General
Social Services: Social Services-General, United Funds/United Ways, Youth Organizations

Contributions Analysis

Arts & Humanities: 15%.
Civic & Public Affairs: 59%. The Company supports Habitat for Humanity and Hearts and Hammers.
Education: 12%.
Health: 14%.

Application Procedures

Initial Contact: Send a brief letter of inquiry and a full proposal.
Application Requirements: a description of organization, amount requested, purpose of funds sought, recently audited financial statement, and proof of tax-exempt status. Also, information on geographic distribution and constituency served.

Restrictions

Does not support individuals, religious organizations for sectarian purposes, or organizations outside operating areas.

Corporate Officials

Laurence E. Hirsch: chairman, chief executive officer, director director B New York, NY 1945. ED University of Pennsylvania Wharton School BS (1968); Villanova University Law School JD (1971). PRIM CORP EMPL chairman, chief executive officer, director: Centex Corp. CORP AFFIL director: Envoy Corp.; director: Heisklberger Zement AG; chairman: Centex Construction Products; director: Commercial Metals Corp.; trustee: Blackrock Group. NONPR AFFIL member undergraduate executive board: University Pennsylvania Wharton School; member, board consults: Villanova University Law School.
David W. Quinn: executive vice president, chief financial officer, director B Stamford, TX 1942. ED Midwestern University (1967). PRIM CORP EMPL executive vice president, chief financial officer, director: Centex Corp. CORP AFFIL chairman, chief executive officer: Texas Trust Savings Bank FSB.

Grants Analysis

Disclosure Period: calendar year ending
Typical Range: $500 to $1,000

CENTRAL MAINE POWER CO.

Company Contact

Augusta, ME
Web: http://www.cmpco.com

Company Description

Assets: US$992,700,000 (1999)
Employees: 1,607 (1999)
SIC(s): 4931 Electric & Other Services Combined.

Operating Locations

Operates 14 district offices throughout Maine.

Nonmonetary Support

Range: $25,000 - $50,000
Type: Donated Equipment; Donated Products; In-kind Services
Note: Provides mentoring-engineering help with science program. Portland employees employees donate time in elementary schools.

Corporate Sponsorship

Type: Music & entertainment events; Sports events; Arts & cultural events; Pledge-a-thon; Festivals/fairs
Contact: Mark Ishkenian, Manager Corporate Communications
Note: Sponsors an electric car race and golf tournaments.

Giving Contact

Harry Lanphear, Managing, Director Customer Operations
Central Maine Power Co.
83 Edison Dr.
Augusta, ME 04336
Phone: (207)623-3521
Fax: (207)626-9561
Email: harry.lanphear@cmpco.com

Description

Organization Type: Corporate Giving Program
Giving Locations: ME: primarily central and southern Maine
Grant Types: Award, Capital, Challenge, Conference/Seminar, Emergency, Employee Matching Gifts, General Support, Matching, Multiyear/Continuing Support, Project, Research, Scholarship, Seed Money.
Note: Employee matching gift ratio: 1 to 1.

Financial Summary

Total Giving: $100,000 (2000 approx); $100,000 (1999 approx); $100,000 (1998 approx). Note: Contributes through corporate direct giving program only.
Giving Analysis: Giving for 2000 includes: foundation (approx $75,000); nonmonetary support (approx $25,000)

Typical Recipients

Arts & Humanities: Arts Associations & Councils, Arts Festivals, Arts Institutes, Community Arts, Dance, Ethnic & Folk Arts, Arts & Humanities-General, Historic Preservation, Libraries, Literary Arts, Museums/Galleries, Music, Performing Arts, Public Broadcasting, Theater, Visual Arts
Civic & Public Affairs: Civil Rights, Economic Development, Economic Policy, Employment/Job Training, Housing, Professional & Trade Associations, Public Policy, Rural Affairs, Safety, Urban & Community Affairs, Women's Affairs
Education: Arts/Humanities Education, Business Education, Colleges & Universities, Community & Junior

Colleges, Continuing Education, Economic Education, Education Associations, Education Funds, Elementary Education (Private), Engineering/Technological Education, Faculty Development, Literacy, Minority Education, Preschool Education, Public Education (Precollege), Science/Mathematics Education, Social Sciences Education, Student Aid
Environment: Environment-General
Health: Emergency/Ambulance Services, Health-General, Geriatric Health, Health Organizations, Hospices, Hospitals, Medical Rehabilitation, Mental Health, Nutrition, Public Health, Single-Disease Health Associations
Science: Science Exhibits & Fairs, Scientific Centers & Institutes
Social Services: Child Welfare, Community Centers, Community Service Organizations, Counseling, Day Care, Delinquency & Criminal Rehabilitation, Domestic Violence, Emergency Relief, Family Planning, Family Services, Food/Clothing Distribution, People with Disabilities, Recreation & Athletics, Senior Services, Shelters/Homelessness, Social Services-General, Substance Abuse, United Funds/United Ways, Volunteer Services, Youth Organizations

Contributions Analysis

Giving Priorities: Focus on homelessness and science and technology education.
Civic & Public Affairs: (United Funds & United Way) About 30%. Company favors contributions to organizations such as United Ways which channel assistance to agencies active in service area. Employee involvement, number of customers served, population density, plus the number of organizations, communities, and services provided by each United Way will determine amount of support. 5% to 10%. General support to groups improving the quality of life in areas where employees work and live.
Education: About 15%. Supports colleges, universities, and technical schools in Maine on a case-by-case basis. Also supports educational programs outside Maine offering programs of interest to company, such as: energy seminars; secondary schools, including public and private institutions for special programs; economic education; and a limited scholarship program.
Health: About 20%. Supports capital campaigns conducted by hospitals and health care centers in service area for new facilities, expansion or renovation, or specialized equipment. Also supports annual operating gifts, single-disease health associations, and health organizations active in service area.
Social Services: Less than 5%. Supports youth organizations and activities that guide, counsel, and enrich the lives of young people. Recipients include 4-H, community centers, scouting, Junior Achievement, summer camps, camps for disabled children, child welfare, and children's homes.
Note: Company reports that 15% of its contributions budget is given at the discretion of its local divisions.

Application Procedures

Initial Contact: Send a brief letter of inquiry.
Application Requirements: Include a description of organization, amount requested, purpose of funds sought, recently audited financial statement, and proof of tax-exempt status.
Deadlines: None.
Decision Notification: Proposals are reviewed monthly.

Restrictions

Company does not support individuals, religious organizations for sectarian purposes, political or lobbying groups, or organizations outside operating areas.

Additional Information

In December 1999, the company's future merge with Energy East was approved.

Corporate Officials

Sara Burns: president, CMP
David T. Flanagan: president, chief executive officer, director B Bangor, ME 1947. ED Harvard University BA (1969); University of London Kings College MA (1970); Boston College Law School JD (1973). PRIM CORP EMPL president, chief executive officer, director: CMP Group Inc. CORP AFFIL director: Maine Electric Power Co.; chairman: Maine Yankee Atomic Power Co.
Mark Ishkenian: director corporate communications PRIM CORP EMPL director corporate communications: Central Maine Power Co.
David E. Marsh: chief financial officer B 1948. ED New Hampshire College BS (1971). PRIM CORP EMPL chief financial officer: CMP Group Inc. CORP AFFIL chief financial officer: Central Maine Power Co.

Giving Program Officials

David F. Allen: PRIM CORP EMPL manager government affairs: CMP Group Inc.

Grants Analysis

Disclosure Period: calendar year ending 2000
Total Grants: $100,000 (approx)
Typical Range: $250 to $5,000

CENTRAL NATIONAL-GOTTESMAN

Company Contact

New York, NY

Company Description

Employees: 800
SIC(s): 5031 Lumber, Plywood & Millwork.

Central National-Gottesman Foundation

Giving Contact

Joshua J. Eisentein, Treasurer
Central National-Gotesman Foundation
3 Manhattanville Road
Purchase, NY 10577
Phone: (914)696-9153
Fax: (914)696-1066

Description

Founded: 1981
EIN: 133047546
Organization Type: Corporate Foundation
Giving Locations: NY
Grant Types: General Support, Scholarship.
Note: Scholarships are for children of employees only.

Financial Summary

Total Giving: $312,246 (1997); $236,352 (1996); $285,530 (1995). Note: Contributes through foundation only. 1997 Giving includes foundation ($160,675); scholarship ($151,071); United Way ($500). 1996 Giving includes foundation ($124,500); scholarship ($107,852); United Way ($4,000).
Assets: $9,281,481 (1997); $7,260,281 (1996); $6,311,743 (1995)

Typical Recipients

Arts & Humanities: Arts Centers, Ballet, Dance, History & Archaeology, Museums/Galleries
Civic & Public Affairs: Economic Development, Civic & Public Affairs-General, Urban & Community Affairs
Education: Arts/Humanities Education, Business Education, Colleges & Universities, Economic Education, Engineering/Technological Education, Education-General, Journalism/Media Education, Literacy, Medical Education, Minority Education, Private Education (Precollege), Religious Education, Science/Mathematics Education, Secondary Education (Private), Secondary Education (Public), Special Education, Student Aid
Health: Cancer, Children's Health/Hospitals, Diabetes, Health Funds, Heart, Hospices, Hospitals, Mental Health, Multiple Sclerosis, Research/Studies Institutes, Single-Disease Health Associations
International: Foreign Arts Organizations, Foreign Educational Institutions, International Relations
Religion: Jewish Causes, Religious Organizations, Synagogues/Temples
Social Services: Camps, Child Welfare, Community Service Organizations, People with Disabilities, Recreation & Athletics, Scouts, Shelters/Homelessness, United Funds/United Ways, Youth Organizations

Application Procedures

Application Requirements: Supplies financial assistance for education to children of company's full-time employees only.

Restrictions

Does not accept outside applications.

Additional Information

Provides scholarships to children of full-time employees of Central National Gottesman.

Corporate Officials

Joshua J. Eisenstein: treasurer PRIM CORP EMPL treasurer: Central National-Gottesman Inc.
Arthur Ross: senior vice president B New York, NY 1910. ED University of Pennsylvania Wharton School (1930); Columbia University BS (1931). PRIM CORP EMPL senior vice president: Central National Gottesman Inc. CORP AFFIL director: Dreyfus Corp.; director: Lazard Special Equities Fund. NONPR AFFIL vice chairman: United Nations Association; member, board overseers: University Pennsylvania Graduate School Fine Arts; trustee, vice president: Spanish Institute; member: International Institute Strategic Studies; director: New York Landmarks Conservancy; member: Council Foreign Relations; member: Foreign Policy Association; director: Central Park Conservancy; member council: Cooper-Hewitt Museum; director: Bryant Park Restoration Corp.; director: Central Park Community Fund; member: Asia Society; director: Barnard College; member: American Association Advancement Science; trustee: American Museum Natural History.
Ira D. Wallach: chairman B New York, NY 1909. ED Columbia University AB (1929); Columbia University JD (1931). PRIM CORP EMPL chairman: Central National-Gottesman Inc. CORP AFFIL executive vice president, director: Cenro Corp.; president, director: Sejak Corp. NONPR AFFIL member: New York Co. Lawyers Association; director: People American Way; member: New York City Bar Association; co-founder, chairman emeritus: Institute East-West Studies; director: Intl Peace Academy; member: American Bar Association; president, director: DS & RH Gottesman Foundation.

Foundation Officials

Joshua J. Eisenstein: treasurer (see above)
Arthur Ross: director (see above)
Ira D. Wallach: executive vice president (see above)
Kenneth L. Wallach: vice president PRIM CORP EMPL vice president: Central National-Gottesman. NONPR AFFIL vice president: YM-YWHA New York.

Grants Analysis

Disclosure Period: calendar year ending 1997
Total Grants: $160,675*
Number of Grants: 40

Average Grant: $4,017
Highest Grant: $23,000
Typical Range: $250 to $15,000
***Note:** Giving excludes scholarship; United Way.

Recent Grants

Note: Grants derived from 1997 Form 990.

Arts & Humanities

10,000 Historic Deerfield, Deerfield, MA
10,000 Wexner Center Foundation, Columbus, OH
1,000 New York City Ballet, New York, NY

Civic & Public Affairs

500 Northwalk Seaport Association, Norwalk, CT

Education

15,000 University of Maine Pulp and Paper Foundation, Orono, ME
10,000 Paper Technology Foundation Western Michigan University, Purchase, NY
5,000 National Book Foundation, New York, NY
4,000 Syracuse Pulp and Paper Foundation, Syracuse, NY
3,600 Cardinal Hayes High School, Bronx, NY
3,500 University of Maine Pulp and Paper Foundation, Orono, ME
2,500 Princeton University, Princeton, NJ
2,500 St. Joseph's University, Philadelphia, PA
2,500 Thomas Jefferson University, Philadelphia, PA
2,500 University of Pennsylvania, Philadelphia, PA
1,250 Junior Achievement, Colorado Springs, CO
1,000 Newspapers in Education, Beverly, MA
1,000 Spurnwink School, Cumberland Fireside, ME
500 National Council on Economic Education, New York, NY

Health

15,000 White Plains Hospital Center, White Plains, NY
5,000 American Heart Association, New York, NY
2,500 Connecticut Children's Medical Center Foundation, Hartford, CT
2,000 Juvenile Diabetes Foundation, Wellesley Hills, MA
1,500 VNS Hospice, Northport, NY
500 Leukemia Society of America, New York, NY
500 United Cerebral Palsy, Hauppauge, NY
250 American Cancer Society, New York, NY
75 Multiple Sclerosis Society, Norwalk, CT

International

2,500 American Friends of Israel Philharmonic, New York, NY

Religion

18,000 United Jewish Appeal Federation, New York, NY
10,000 American Jewish Committee, New York, NY
5,000 United Jewish Appeal Federation, New York, NY

Social Services

3,500 Boy Scouts of America, New York, NY
2,500 Connecticut Special Olympics, Hamden, CT
2,500 Friends of Boston Homeless, Boston, MA
2,500 Hartford Camp Council, Hartford, CT
2,500 Jimmy Fund, Boston, MA
1,500 Association for the Help of Retarded Children, New York, NY
1,500 Children's Village, Dobbs Ferry, NY
1,500 Outreach Project, Woodhaven, NY
1,000 Alpine Learning Group, River Edge, NJ
1,000 Northside Center for Child Development, New York, NY
1,000 Rick Fox-Ed Pinckney Baseball Camp, Boston, MA
1,000 United Way West Putnam, White Plains, NY

Central Newspapers, Inc.

Company Contact

200 E. Van Buren Street
Phoenix, AZ 85004
Phone: (602)444-1100
Web: http://www.centralnews.com

Company Description

Employees: 5,341
SIC(s): 2711 Newspapers.

Corporate Sponsorship

Type: Sports events
Note: Sponsors an all-star basketball game fundraising event for the benefit of Indianapolis Star Fund for the Blind.

Central Newspapers Foundation

Giving Contact

Sandy Harless, Executive Director
Central Newspapers Foundation
307 North Pennsylvania Street
Indianapolis, IN 46204
Phone: (317)633-1299
Fax: (317)656-1435

Description

Founded: 1935
EIN: 356013720
Organization Type: Corporate Foundation. Supports preselected organizations only.
Giving Locations: AZ; IN
Grant Types: Project, Scholarship.

Financial Summary

Total Giving: $330,000 (fiscal year ending April 30, 1999 approx); $314,816 (fiscal 1998); $325,825 (fiscal 1996). Note: Contributes through foundation only.
Giving Analysis: Giving for fiscal 1996 includes: foundation ($191,908); foundation scholarships ($133,917); fiscal 1998: foundation scholarships ($190,216); foundation ($124,600)
Assets: $137,045 (fiscal 1998); $47,155 (fiscal 1996); $122,384 (fiscal 1995)
Gifts Received: $249,789 (fiscal 1998); $205,000 (fiscal 1996); $219,000 (fiscal 1995). Note: Contributions were received from Central Newspapers, Indianapolis Newspapers, Phoenix Newspapers, and Muncie Newspapers.

Typical Recipients

Arts & Humanities: Libraries
Civic & Public Affairs: Philanthropic Organizations
Education: Colleges & Universities, Engineering/Technological Education, Education-General, Journalism/Media Education, Minority Education, Special Education, Student Aid
Health: Cancer, Eyes/Blindness, Preventive Medicine/Wellness Organizations
Social Services: Community Service Organizations, Family Services, People with Disabilities

Contributions Analysis

Arts & Humanities: 1%.
Civic & Public Affairs: 14%. Supports INI Charities.
Education: 68%. The majority of the foundation's support goes to grants and scholarship programs in journalism education at major colleges and universities in Indiana and Arizona. Also provides higher education scholarships to children of employees and paper carriers.
Health: 5%. Funds blindness prevention.
Social Services: 12%. Supports service for the blind.
Note: Total contributions in fiscal 1998.

Corporate Officials

Thomas K. Gillivray: treasurer secretary, vice president, general counsel PRIM CORP EMPL treasurer: Central Newspapers, Inc. CORP AFFIL treasurer: Indianapolis Newspapers Inc.
Frank Eli Russell: chairman B Kokomo, IN 1920. ED Evansville College AB (1942); Indiana University JD (1951). PRIM CORP EMPL chairman: Central Newspapers, Inc. CORP AFFIL director: Muncie Newspapers Inc.; director: Phoenix Newspapers Inc.; chairman retirement committee: Hoosier State Press; director: Indianapolis Newspapers Inc.; president, director: Bradley Paper Co.; president, director: Central Newsprint. NONPR AFFIL member: Sigma Alpha Epsilon; member: Tax Executives Institute; member: Salvation Army; member: Shriners; member: Order Coif; member: Phi Delta Phi; member, director: Newspaper Advertising Bureau; director: Nina Mason Pulliam Charitable Trust; member: Masons; member: Midwest Pension Conference; member: Indianapolis Bar Association; member, director: Institute Newspaper Contrs & Fin Offs; director, vice president: Indiana Association Credit Management; member: Indiana Bar Association; member: Indiana Association Colleges; member: Indiana Association CPA's; director: Eiteljorg Museum; member: Free Accepted Masons; member: Ancient Accepted Scottish Rite; director: Central Newspapers Foundation; member: American Bar Association; member: American Institute CPAs. CLUB AFFIL Meridian Hills Country Club; Skyline Club; Columbia Club; Indianapolis Athletic Club.
Eric S. Tooker: corporate secretary, vice president, general counsel ED University of Michigan JD (1987). PRIM CORP EMPL corporate secretary, vice president, general counsel: Central Newspapers, Inc.

Foundation Officials

Sandra K. Harless: executive director
Robert L. Lowry: assistant treasurer
Eugene Smith Pulliam: vice president, director B Atchison, KS 1914. ED DePauw University AB (1935); DePauw University LLD (1973). PRIM CORP EMPL publisher: Indianapolis Newspaper Inc. CORP AFFIL publisher, president: Phoenix Newspapers Inc.; publisher: Indianapolis News; publisher: Indianapolis Star; director: Central Newspaper Inc. NONPR AFFIL member: Delta Kappa Epsilon; member: Society Professional Journalists; member: American Society Newspaper Editors; member: American Newspaper Publishers Association Foundation. CLUB AFFIL Crooked Stick Golf Club.
Frank Eli Russell: president (see above)
Gene Elwood Sease: director B Portage, PA 1931. ED Juniata College AB (1952); Pittsburgh Theological Seminary BD (1956); University of Pittsburgh MED (1958); Pittsburgh Theological Seminary ThM (1959); University of Pittsburgh PhD (1965). PRIM CORP EMPL chairman: Sease, Gerig & Associates. CORP AFFIL director: National City Bank Indiana; director: Bankers Life Insurance New York; director: Indianapolis Life Insurance Co. NONPR AFFIL member: Phi Delta Kappa; director: Saint Francis Hospital; member: Japan-American Society Indiana; president: Marion County Sheriffs Merit Board; director: Indianapolis Convention Bureau; member: International Platform Association; director: Indianapolis Chamber of Commerce; member: Indiana Scholarship Commission;

member: Indiana Schoolmen's Club; member, director: Indiana Chamber of Commerce; director: Indiana Law Enforcement Training Academy; director: Economic Club Indianapolis; member: English Speaking Union; director: Community Hospital Indianapolis; director: Boy Scouts America Crossroads Council; director: Central Newspaper Federation; member: Alpha Psi Omega; consultant: American Cablevision Indianapolis; director: 500 Festival Associate; member: Alpha Phi Omega. CLUB AFFIL Skyline Club; Indianapolis Kiwanis Club; Indianapolis Masons Club; Columbia Club.

Shirley Ann Williams Shideler: director B Mishawaka, IN 1930. ED Indiana University LLB (1964). PRIM CORP EMPL counsel: Barnes & Thornburg. NONPR AFFIL member: Indianapolis Bar Foundation; member: National Conference Bar Foundations; member: Indianapolis Bar Association; member: Indiana Bar Association. CLUB AFFIL Womens Rotary Club.

Eric S. Tooker: secretary (see above)

Grants Analysis

Disclosure Period: fiscal year ending April 30, 1998
Total Grants: $124,600*
Number of Grants: 9
Average Grant: $13,844
Highest Grant: $45,000
Typical Range: $2,200 to $20,000
***Note:** Giving excludes scholarship.

Recent Grants

Note: Grants derived from fiscal 1998 Form 990.

Arts & Humanities

1,000	Indianapolis Marion County Public Library, Indianapolis, IN

Civic & Public Affairs

45,000	INI Charities, Indianapolis, IN

Education

20,000	Indiana School for Blind, Indianapolis, IN -- Benefit of the Blind
7,500	Arizona State University -- Five ECPulliam Memorial Journalism Scholarships
7,500	University of Arizona -- Five ECPulliam Memorial Journalism Scholarships
6,000	Butler University -- Four Hilton U. Brown awards
6,000	Indiana University(Indiana University Foundation) -- Two Kent Cooper Journalism Scholarships and two Sally Cooper Journalism Scholarships
6,000	Northern Arizona University -- Four ECPulliam Memorial Journalism awards
5,000	University of Indianapolis, Indianapolis, IN
4,500	Ball State University -- Three ECPulliam Memorial Journalism Scholarships
4,500	Depauw University -- Three ECPulliam Memorial Journalism awards
4,500	IUPUI - Journalism Scholarship - Indianapolis -- Two ECPulliam Memorial Journalism Scholarships One ECPulliam Memorial Journalism Scholarship
3,000	Indiana State University (ISU Foundation) -- Two ECPulliam Memorial Journalism awards
3,000	Purdue University -- Two ECPulliam Memorial Journalism awards
3,000	University of Evansville -- Two ECPulliam Memorial Journalism Scholarships
3,000	University of Indianapolis -- Two ECPulliam Memorial Journalism Scholarships
2,000	Vincennes University -- Four ECPulliam Memorial Journalism Scholarships
2,000	Walther Cancer Foundation, Inc. -- Education programs.
1,500	Franklin College -- One Nina Mason Pulliam award
1,500	Huntington College -- One ECPulliam Memorial Journalism award
1,500	Marian College -- One ECPulliam Memorial Journalism Scholarship
1,500	University of Notre Dame -- One William F. Fox award
1,500	Wabash College -- One ECPulliam Memorial Journalism Scholarship
1,000	Baker University -- One Eugene C. Pulliam Memorial Scholarship
1,000	University of Kansas -- One ECPulliam Memorial Journalism Scholarship

Health

15,000	Prevent Blindness, Indiana, Indianapolis, IN

Social Services

20,000	Central Indiana Radio Reading, Indianapolis, IN -- Benefit of the Blind
12,000	Wishard Glasses Program, Indianapolis, IN -- Benefit of the Blind
3,600	Family Service Association of Central Indiana, Inc, Indianapolis, IN
3,000	Northeast Indiana Radio Reading Services, Fort Wayne, IN

Central &South West Services

Company Contact

Dallas, TX
Web: http://www.csw.com

Company Description

Revenue: US$5,482,000,000
Employees: 8,055
Fortune Rank: 301, per FORTUNE Magazine's list of 500 Largest U.S. Corporations (1999).
FF 301
SIC(s): 7374 Data Processing & Preparation, 8721 Accounting, Auditing & Bookkeeping, 8741 Management Services.
Parent Company: Central & South West Corp.

Operating Locations

Includes Bedford Wire Division.

Nonmonetary Support

Type: Loaned Employees; Loaned Executives

Corporate Sponsorship

Value: $350,000
Type: Arts & cultural events; Music & entertainment events; Pledge-a-thon; Sports events
Contact: Connie True, Committee Relations Coordinator

Central & South West Foundation

Giving Contact

Kenneth C. Raney, Vice President, Associate General Counsel, Corporate Secretary
Central & South West Services
PO Box 660164
Dallas, TX 75266-0164
Phone: (214)777-1115
Fax: (214)777-3067

Description

EIN: 366031631
Organization Type: Corporate Foundation
Giving Locations: nationally.
Grant Types: Employee Matching Gifts, General Support.

Financial Summary

Total Giving: $700,000 (fiscal year ending October 31, 2000 approx); $700,000 (fiscal 1999 approx); $637,634 (fiscal 1997). Note: Contributes through foundation only.
Assets: $3,024,776 (fiscal 1997); $3,439,937 (fiscal 1995); $2,422,433 (fiscal 1994)
Gifts Received: $280,000 (fiscal 1996); $1,100,000 (fiscal 1995); $12,000 (fiscal 1994). Note: Contributions were received from CSW Energy.

Typical Recipients

Arts & Humanities: Arts Institutes, Ethnic & Folk Arts, History & Archaeology, Libraries, Museums/Galleries, Performing Arts
Civic & Public Affairs: Chambers of Commerce, Clubs, Community Foundations, Civic & Public Affairs-General, Housing, Philanthropic Organizations, Urban & Community Affairs, Zoos/Aquariums
Education: Business Education, Colleges & Universities, Community & Junior Colleges, Education Associations, Education Funds, Engineering/Technological Education, Legal Education, Medical Education, Minority Education, Religious Education, Science/ Mathematics Education, Student Aid
Environment: Environment-General
Health: Clinics/Medical Centers, Emergency/Ambulance Services, Health Organizations, Medical Research, Nursing Services, Public Health
Religion: Religious Organizations, Religious Welfare, Seminaries
Social Services: Community Service Organizations, Crime Prevention, Substance Abuse, United Funds/ United Ways, YMCA/YWCA/YMHA/YWHA, Youth Organizations

Contributions Analysis

Arts & Humanities: 10% to 15%. Primarily supports museums.
Civic & Public Affairs: 55% to 60%. Support includes community foundations, public policy and youth organizations.
Education: 25% to 30%. Funds numerous colleges and universities. Majority of support is donated through matching gifts.
Health: less than 5%. Funds medical research.
Religion: Less than 5%. Includes support to seminaries.

Application Procedures

Initial Contact: letter and proposal
Application Requirements: purpose, amount requested, and organization's history
Deadlines: None.

Restrictions

Company gives in local operating areas only.
Company provides limited funding outside the service areas of Arkansas, Louisiana, Oklahoma, and Texas.
Company does not provide funding for administrative costs or to individuals.

Additional Information

Foundation places emphasis on supporting organizations for which employees volunteer and serve as board members.
The foundation lists Mellon Bank, Pittsburgh, PA, as a trustee.

Corporate Officials

E. Richard 'Dick' Brooks: chairman, chief executive officer, director B Slaton, TX 1937. ED University of Michigan; Texas Technology University BSEE (1961); Harvard University (1985). PRIM CORP EMPL chairman, chief executive officer, director: Central & South West Services. CORP AFFIL chairman, president, chief executive officer: Transok Inc.; director: Hubbell Inc. NONPR AFFIL member: Texas Research League; executive board: United Way Metropolitan Dallas; member: Texas Chamber of Commerce; member: Texas Council Economic Education;

trustee: North American Electrical Reliability Council; deacon: Park Cities Baptist Church; member executive committee: Edison Electric Institute; trustee: Dallas Symphony Association; trustee: Dallas Theater Center; chairman executive board: Boy Scouts America Circle Ten Council; member executive board: Association Electrical Companies Texas.
Glenn D. Rosilier: executive vice president, chief financial officer B Houston, TX 1948. ED University of Saint Thomas BBA (1970); University of Houston MS (1972). PRIM CORP EMPL executive vice president, chief financial officer: Central & South West Services. CORP AFFIL president: CSW Credit Inc.; director: Enershop Inc. NONPR AFFIL chief executive officer steering committee: Edison Electric Institute; member: Financial Executives Institute; member: American Institute CPAs.

Foundation Officials

Connie True: community relations coordinator

Grants Analysis

Disclosure Period: fiscal year ending October 31, 1997
Total Grants: $637,634
Number of Grants: 198 (approx)
Average Grant: $3,220
Highest Grant: $100,000
Typical Range: $100 to $5,000

Recent Grants

Note: Grants derived from 1997 Form 990.

Arts & Humanities

6,600	Library Information Network, Corpus Christi, TX
2,500	Harlingen Performing Arts, Harlingen, TX

Civic & Public Affairs

100,000	Phillips Visitors Center, Oklahoma City, OK
25,000	Abilene Chamber of Commerce, Abilene, TX
10,000	Habitat for Humanity, Corpus Christi, TX
5,000	Gladys Porter Zoo's Endowment Enhancement
5,000	Leamanship Club, Dallas, TX
1,500	Community Foundation, Abilene, TX

Education

50,000	Laredo Community College Sports, Laredo, TX
40,000	Paul Quinn College, Dallas, TX
30,000	University of Oklahoma, Norman, OK
25,000	Eastern Oklahoma State University, Wilburton, OK
25,000	University of Texas Law School Foundation, Austin, TX
25,000	Wesleyan College, Bartlesville, OK
20,000	Hardin-Simmons University, Abilene, TX
15,600	Hardin-Simmons University, Abilene, TX
10,000	Oklahoma State University Foundation, Stillwater, OK
10,000	Texas A&M University, College Station, TX
7,692	Texas A&M University, College Station, TX
7,537	Abilene Christian University, Abilene, TX
7,500	Freed-Hardeman University, Henderson, TN
7,500	Harwick College, Oneonta, NY
7,500	University of Dallas, Dallas, TX
7,000	Central Baptist College, Conway, AZ
6,000	University of Tulsa, Tulsa, OK
5,550	Oklahoma State University Foundation, Stillwater, OK
4,905	Texas A&M University, College Station, TX
4,650	University of Tulsa, Tulsa, OK
3,750	Hardin-Simmons University, Abilene, TX
3,525	Oklahoma City University Girls Softball, Pittsburg, KS
3,187	Hardin-Simmons University, Abilene, TX
3,000	Abilene Christian University, Abilene, TX
3,000	East Central University Foundation, Ada, OK
3,000	University of Arkansas, Fayetteville, AR
2,565	University of Arkansas Razorback Foundation, Fayetteville, AR
1,500	Louisiana Tech University, Ruston, LA
1,500	McMurry University, Abilene, TX
1,500	Oklahoma City University, Oklahoma City, OK
1,500	University of Arkansas, Fayetteville, AR
1,500	University of Texas San Antonio, San Antonio, TX
1,500	Wellesley College, Wellesley, MA
1,500	Westminster College, Salt Lake City, UT
1,431	Texas A&M University Association of Former Students, College Station, TX
1,300	Ohio State University, Columbus, OH

Religion

15,000	Victoria Presbyterian
1,500	Episcopal Theological Seminary of the Southwest, Austin, TX

Social Services

50,000	Bringing Dreams to Life, Stillwater, OK
15,000	Okmulgee 1997 Summer Youth, Okmulgee, OK
4,000	YWCA Golden Crescent
2,500	Palmer Drug Abuse Program, McAllen, TX

Central Soya Co.

Company Contact

Fort Wayne, IN

Company Description

Employees: 1,200
SIC(s): 2075 Soybean Oil Mills, 5153 Grain & Field Beans.
Parent Company: Eridania Beghin-Say

Operating Locations

GA: Central Soya Co.; Intermarine USA, Savannah; IA: Central Soya Co.; IL: Central Soya Co.; IN: Central Soya Co., Fort Wayne; Central Soya Co., Fort Wayne; Cerestar USA, Hammond; NE: Central Soya Co.; OH: Central Soya Co.; SC: Central Soya Co.

Central Soya Foundation

Giving Contact

Carl L. Hausman, President
PO Box 1400
Ft. Wayne, IN 46801-1400
Phone: (219)425-5100
Fax: (219)425-5330
Email: carl.hausman@centralsoya.com

Description

Founded: 1954
EIN: 356020624
Organization Type: Corporate Foundation
Giving Locations: operating locations.
Grant Types: Capital, General Support, Matching, Operating Expenses, Research, Scholarship.

Financial Summary

Total Giving: $217,858 (1997); $192,688 (1996); $192,503 (1995). Note: Contributes through foundation only.
Assets: $156,423 (1997); $162,467 (1996); $342,724 (1995)
Gifts Received: $200,000 (1997); $400,000 (1993); $400,000 (1992)

Typical Recipients

Arts & Humanities: Arts Appreciation, Arts Associations & Councils, Arts Funds, History & Archaeology, Museums/Galleries, Music, Opera, Public Broadcasting, Theater, Visual Arts
Civic & Public Affairs: African American Affairs, Clubs, Community Foundations, Economic Development, Municipalities/Towns, Parades/Festivals, Philanthropic Organizations, Professional & Trade Associations, Rural Affairs, Safety, Urban & Community Affairs, Women's Affairs, Zoos/Aquariums
Education: Agricultural Education, Business Education, Colleges & Universities, Education Associations, Education Funds, Education-General, Health & Physical Education, Minority Education, Public Education (Precollege), Religious Education, Science/Mathematics Education, Special Education, Student Aid
Environment: Environment-General
Health: Children's Health/Hospitals, Emergency/Ambulance Services, Health Funds, Health Organizations, Hospitals, Medical Rehabilitation, Prenatal Health Issues, Public Health, Single-Disease Health Associations
Religion: Churches, Ministries, Religious Organizations, Religious Welfare
Science: Scientific Centers & Institutes
Social Services: Child Welfare, Community Service Organizations, Day Care, Food/Clothing Distribution, People with Disabilities, Recreation & Athletics, Scouts, United Funds/United Ways, YMCA/YWCA/YMHA/YWHA, Youth Organizations

Application Procedures

Initial Contact: Send a letter that includes a description of organization and its goals, outline of proposed project, and proof of tax-exempt status.
Deadlines: None.

Restrictions

Does not support individuals.

Additional Information

Trust(s): Ft Wayne Natl Bank

Corporate Officials

Carl L. Hausmann: chairman, president, chief executive officer B 1946. ED Boston College BS (1968). PRIM CORP EMPL chairman, president, chief executive officer: Central Soya Co. CORP AFFIL president, chief executive officer: Cerestar USA.

Grants Analysis

Disclosure Period: calendar year ending 1997
Total Grants: $217,858
Number of Grants: 45
Average Grant: $4,841
Highest Grant: $35,000
Typical Range: $1,000 to $5,000

Recent Grants

Note: Grants derived from 1997 Form 990.

Arts & Humanities

14,000	Arts Unlimited, Fort Wayne, IN
9,500	Embassy Theater Foundation, Fort Wayne, IN
6,500	Fort Wayne Philharmonic, Fort Wayne, IN
5,000	Fort Wayne Public Television, Fort Wayne, IN

Education

13,382	National Merit Scholarship Corporation, Evanston, IL -- educational
12,000	Independent Colleges of Indiana, Indianapolis, IN

11,000	Science Central, Fort Wayne, IN
6,000	Junior Achievement, Fort Wayne, IN
6,000	Ohio Foundation for Independent Colleges, Columbus, OH
5,000	Indiana-Purdue Foundation, Fort Wayne, IN -- educational
Health	
5,000	Anthony Wayne Rehabilitation Center for Red Cedar Center, Fort Wayne, IN
5,000	St. Joseph's Health Foundation, Fort Wayne, IN
Religion	
5,000	West Central Neighborhood Ministry, Fort Wayne, IN
Social Services	
35,000	United Way Allen County, Fort Wayne, IN
11,830	United Way Adams County, Decatur, IN
8,000	YMCA, Fort Wayne, IN
7,500	Remington Park and Recreation Board, Remington, IN
5,215	Bellevue United Selective Fund, Bellevue, OH
5,000	Boys and Girls Club, Fort Wayne, IN
5,000	Boys and Girls Club, Fort Wayne, IN

CENTRAL VERMONT PUBLIC SERVICE CORP.

Company Contact
Rutland, VT
Web: http://www.cvps.com

Company Description
Revenue: US$288,280,000
Employees: 670
SIC(s): 4911 Electric Services.

Giving Contact
Hilde Sparrow, Community Relations Representative
77 Grove Street
Rutland, VT 05701
Phone: (802)229-9448

Description
Organization Type: Corporate Giving Program
Giving Locations: VT
Grant Types: Emergency, Endowment, General Support, Multiyear/Continuing Support.

Financial Summary
Total Giving: $202,332 (1994)

Typical Recipients
Arts & Humanities: Community Arts, Libraries, Museums/Galleries, Music, Public Broadcasting
Civic & Public Affairs: Economic Development, Nonprofit Management
Education: Colleges & Universities
Environment: Environment-General
Health: Mental Health
Science: Science Exhibits & Fairs
Social Services: Community Service Organizations

Application Procedures
Initial Contact: Send brief letter of inquiry, including a description of organization, amount requested, and purpose of funds sought. Deadline for January 1 Fiscal year is August 15th.

Restrictions
Does not support individuals, religious organizations for sectarian purposes, political or lobbying groups, or organizations outside operating areas.

Corporate Officials
Frederic Howard Bertrand: chairman, chief executive officer B Montpelier, VT 1936. ED Norwich University BScE (1958); Georgetown University Law Center (1961-1963); College of William & Mary JD (1967); Carnegie Mellon University (1967-1968). PRIM CORP EMPL chairman: Central Vermont Public Service Corp. CORP AFFIL director: Union Mutual Fire Insurance Co.; director: New England Guaranty Insurance Co.; director: Chittenden Trust Co.; chairman, chief executive officer: National Life Insurance Co.; director: Central Vermont Public Services Corp. NONPR AFFIL director: Vermont Business Roundtable; member: Washington County Bar Association; member: Vermont Bar Association; member: Epsilon Tau Sigma; member: Theta Chi; director: Central Vermont Economic Development Corp.; member: American Council Life Insurance.

Francis J. Boyle: vice president, chief financial officer PRIM CORP EMPL vice president, chief financial officer: Central Vermont Public Service Corp.

F. Ray Keyser, Jr.: chairman, director B Chelsea, VT 1927. ED Boston University Law School LLB (1952); Tufts University LLD (1961); Norwich University LLD (1962). PRIM CORP EMPL chairman, director: Central Vermont Public Service Corp. CORP AFFIL director: Vermont Yankee Nuclear Power Co.; director: Vermont Electric Power Corp.; director: Lakey Hitchcock Clinic; director: Union Mutual Fire Insurance Co.; director: Keystone Custodian Funds; director: ICI Mutual Insurance Co.; of counsel: Keyser Crowley Meub Zayden Kulig & Sullivan PC; director: Grand Trunk Corp. NONPR AFFIL member: Masons; member: Vermont Bar Association; member: American Legion; member: American Bar Association.

Robert Harris Young: president, chief executive officer B New York, NY 1947. ED Beloit College (1970); Stanford University (1975). PRIM CORP EMPL president, chief executive officer: Central Vermont Public Service Corp. CORP AFFIL president, chief executive officer, director: SmartEnergy Services; president, chief executive officer, director: Summersville Hydro Corp.; director: Rutland Regional Medical Center; president, chief executive officer, director: Gauley River Management Corp.; director: Green Mountain Bank; president, chief executive officer, director: East Barnet Hydroelectric; president, chief executive officer, director: Equinox Vermont Corp.; president, chief executive officer, director: CV Energy Resources; president, chief executive officer, director: CV Realty; president, chief executive officer, director: Catamount Williams Lake Ltd.; president, chief executive officer, director: Connecticut Valley Electric Co.; president, chief executive officer, director: Catamount Thetford Corp.; president, chief executive officer, director: Catamount Rumford; president, chief executive officer, director: Catamount Rupert Corp.; president, chief executive officer, director: Catamount Energy Corp.; president, chief executive officer, director: Catamount Glenns Ferry Corp.; president, chief executive officer, director: Appomattox Vermont Corp.; director: Associated Industries Vermont.

Grants Analysis
Disclosure Period: calendar year ending
Typical Range: $1,000 to $2,500

CENTURY 21

Company Contact
New York, NY

Company Description
Former Name: Gindi Associatess Foundation.
Employees: 800

Century 21 Associates Foundation

Giving Contact
Abraham Gindi, Trustee
22 Cortland St.
New York, NY 10007

Description
Founded: 1982
EIN: 222412138
Organization Type: Corporate Foundation. Supports preselected organizations only.
Giving Locations: NJ; NY
Grant Types: General Support.

Financial Summary
Total Giving: $424,355 (fiscal year ending May 31, 1999); $307,917 (fiscal 1996); $307,917 (fiscal 1995). Note: Contributes through foundation only.
Assets: $545,951 (fiscal 1999); $612,313 (fiscal 1996); $652,236 (fiscal 1995)
Gifts Received: $305,000 (fiscal 1999); $252,490 (fiscal 1996); $250,000 (fiscal 1995). Note: In fiscal 1999 and fiscal 1995, contributions were received from Century 21.

Typical Recipients
Arts & Humanities: History & Archaeology, Visual Arts
Civic & Public Affairs: Civic & Public Affairs-General, Parades/Festivals
Education: Education-General, Private Education (Precollege), Religious Education, Secondary Education (Private), Student Aid
Health: Cancer, Diabetes, Hospitals, Long-Term Care
International: Foreign Educational Institutions, Missionary/Religious Activities
Religion: Jewish Causes, Religious Organizations, Synagogues/Temples
Social Services: Child Welfare, Community Centers, Community Service Organizations, Homes, Scouts, United Funds/United Ways, Youth Organizations

Foundation Officials
Abraham Gindi: trustee B 1922. PRIM CORP EMPL chief executive officer: Century 21 Inc. CORP AFFIL president: GB Distributors. NONPR AFFIL vice president: Hall Westwood Hebrew Home.

Sam Gindi: trustee B 1924. PRIM CORP EMPL vice president: GB Distributors. CORP AFFIL treasurer: Lollytogs; treasurer: Beatrice Home Fashions; vice president: Century 21 Inc. NONPR AFFIL president: Hall Westwood Hebrew Home.

Grants Analysis
Disclosure Period: fiscal year ending May 31, 1996
Total Grants: $307,917
Number of Grants: 115
Average Grant: $2,678
Highest Grant: $70,000
Typical Range: $250 to $5,000

Recent Grants
Note: Grants derived from 1997 Form 990.

Arts & Humanities	
1,000	Camera, Brooklyn, NY
Education	
10,000	Foundation for Sephardic Studies, Brooklyn, NY
1,500	Foundation for Sephardic Studies, Brooklyn, NY
Health	
3,600	American Diabetes Association, New York, NY
2,000	Sephardic Friends of Mamondes Hospital, Brooklyn, NY

1,000	Central New Jersey Jewish Home for the Aged, Somerset, NJ
1,000	Pediatric Cancer Research Foundation, New York, NY

International

18,000	Magen David Yeshiva, Tiberias, Israel
10,000	Magen David Yeshiva, Tiberias, Israel
7,500	Yeshivat Amegie Torah, Israel
5,000	American Friends of Nezer Hatorah, New York, NY
3,500	Yeshivat Amegie Torah, Israel
2,000	Colelout Rabbi Meir Baal Hanes Sefarm, Efrat, Israel
1,800	American Friends of Megdhal Ohr, New York, NY
1,800	American Friends of Merkaz Historah, New York, NY
1,500	Friend of Yechave Daat, Elberon, NJ
1,250	American Friends of Central Committee for Taharns Hisrshpache in Israel, New York, NY
1,000	Jerusalem Fund, New York, NY

Religion

70,000	United Jewish Appeal, Garden City, NY
18,000	Sephardic Community Center, Brooklyn, NY
15,000	Congregation Zvi Lazedeek, Deal, NJ
15,000	Hillel Yeshiva, Ocean, NJ
15,000	Ozar Hatorah, Albany, NY
15,000	Sephardic Bikur Holim, Brooklyn, NY
10,000	Obel Moshe Society Building Fund, New York, NY
7,500	Ahi Ezer Yeshiva, Brooklyn, NY
6,000	Gesher Yebuda, Brooklyn, NY
5,000	Ahi Ezer Yeshiva, Brooklyn, NY
5,000	ISEF, New York, NY
5,000	ISEF, New York, NY
3,500	Yeshivat Aleret Torah, Springfield, VA
3,200	Sephardic Bikur Holim, Brooklyn, NY
3,000	Sephardic Study Center
2,500	Ateret Moshe, Brooklyn, NY
2,500	ISEF, New York, NY
2,500	Wall Street Synogogue, New York, NY
2,500	Yeshiva of Kings Bay, Brooklyn, NY
2,400	Sephardic Torah Center, Deal, NJ
2,000	Magen David of Turnberry, North Miami Beach, FL
2,000	Sephardic Institute, Brooklyn, NY
2,000	Shaare Torah, Brooklyn, NY
2,000	Yeshivat Hechal Ezra, New York, NY
1,800	Kefer David, Brooklyn, NY
1,600	Sephardic Torah Center, Deal, NJ
1,500	Historical Jewish Center, New York, NY
1,000	Geve Eretz, New York, NY
1,000	Havat Visraei Yeshiva, New York, NY
1,000	Porat Yoseph, Broadway, NY
1,000	Yeshiva Hahaim Vehashalom, New York, NY

Social Services

1,000	Boy Scouts of America, New York, NY

CERTAINTEED CORP.

Company Contact

Valley Forge, PA
Web: http://www.certainteed.com

Company Description

Employees: 6,581
SIC(s): 2421 Sawmills & Planing Mills--General, 2426 Hardwood Dimension & Flooring Mills, 3087 Custom Compound of Purchased Resins, 3271 Concrete Block & Brick.
Parent Company: Compagnie de Saint-Gobain, Les Miroirs, 18 Avenue d'Alsace, Courbevoie, France

Operating Locations

CA: Maxitile, Carson; CertainTeed Corp., Chowchilla, Placentia; DE: Bay Mills (Delaware), Wilmington; FL: CertainTeed Corp., Gainesville; GA: CertainTeed Corp., Social Circle; IA: Wolverine Technologies, Grinnell; IL: Air Vent, Peoria Heights; KS: CertainTeed Corp., Kansas City, McPherson; LA: CertainTeed Corp., Westlake; MA: Diamond Film Divison, Northborough; Bird Inc., Norwood; Bird Roofing Products, Norwood; MI: Wolverine Technologies, Jackson; Ashland-Davis Co., Livonia; MN: CertainTeed Corp., Alberta Lea; NY: Bayex, Albion; OH: Perma Glas-Mesh, Dover; Ludowici Celedon, New Lexington; Ludowici Roof Tile, New Lexington; PA: CertainTeed Corp., Mountain Top, Nesquehoning, Valley Forge; CertainTeed Corp., Valley Forge; CertainTeed Foreign Sales Corp., Valley Forge; CertainTeed International, Valley Forge; CertainTeed Ventures, Valley Forge; CertainTeed Weaving Corp., Valley Forge; Ecophon CertainTeed, Valley Forge; Lake Keowee Country Club, Inc., Valley Forge; Wolverine Vinyl Siding, Valley Forge; SC: CertainTeed Corp., Spartanburg; TX: Pro-Cut Products, Inc, Dallas; CertainTeed Corp., Waco; Cerbay Co., Wichita Falls; Vetrotex CertainTeed Corp., Wichita Falls; WA: Insulate LLC, Auburn

Nonmonetary Support

Value: $64,000 (1997)
Type: Cause-related Marketing & Promotion; Donated Equipment; Donated Products; In-kind Services; Loaned Employees; Workplace Solicitation
Note: Volunteer recognition award program is designed to ackowledge the volunteer activities of these groups for the benefit of their communities.

Corporate Sponsorship

Type: Arts & cultural events
Contact: Dorothy Wackerman, Vice President, Colorados

CertainTeed Corp. Foundation

Giving Contact

Patty Iacono, Communications Coordinator
CertainTeed Corp. Foundation
PO Box 860
Valley Forge, PA 19482-0101
Phone: (610)341-7000
Fax: (610)341-7777

Description

Founded: 1955
EIN: 236242991
Organization Type: Corporate Foundation
Giving Locations: principally near operating locations and to national organizations.
Grant Types: Award, Department, Employee Matching Gifts, Endowment, Fellowship, General Support, Project.

Financial Summary

Total Giving: $500,000 (2000 approx); $500,000 (1999 approx); $424,418 (1998). Note: Contributes through foundation only.
Giving Analysis: Giving for 1996 includes: foundation matching gifts ($96,500); foundation grants to United Way ($21,600); 1998: foundation matching gifts ($126,795); foundation grants to United Way ($24,450)
Assets: $261,448 (1998); $207,665 (1996); $156,219 (1995)
Gifts Received: $465,702 (1998); $369,575 (1996); $311,578 (1995)

Typical Recipients

Arts & Humanities: Arts Associations & Councils, Arts Institutes, Ballet, Community Arts, Film & Video, Arts & Humanities-General, Historic Preservation, History & Archaeology, Libraries, Museums/Galleries, Music, Performing Arts, Theater
Civic & Public Affairs: Business/Free Enterprise, Clubs, Community Foundations, Economic Development, Economic Policy, Employment/Job Training, Ethnic Organizations, Civic & Public Affairs-General, Hispanic Affairs, Housing, Law & Justice, Legal Aid, Municipalities/Towns, Professional & Trade Associations, Public Policy, Safety, Urban & Community Affairs, Women's Affairs, Zoos/Aquariums
Education: Arts/Humanities Education, Colleges & Universities, Colleges & Universities, Community & Junior Colleges, Education Funds, Education Reform, Elementary Education (Private), Elementary Education (Public), Engineering/Technological Education, International Exchange, International Studies, Legal Education, Literacy, Medical Education, Minority Education, Private Education (Precollege), Public Education (Precollege), Religious Education, Secondary Education (Private), Secondary Education (Public)
Environment: Environment-General, Resource Conservation, Wildlife Protection
Health: Alzheimers Disease, Cancer, Children's Health/Hospitals, Clinics/Medical Centers, Emergency/Ambulance Services, Health Organizations, Heart, Hospices, Hospitals, Medical Research, Multiple Sclerosis, Prenatal Health Issues, Public Health, Single-Disease Health Associations
International: Foreign Arts Organizations, Foreign Educational Institutions, Health Care/Hospitals, International Development, International Organizations, International Relations
Religion: Churches, Religious Organizations, Religious Welfare, Seminaries
Science: Science Museums
Social Services: At-Risk Youth, Big Brother/Big Sister, Child Abuse, Child Welfare, Community Centers, Community Service Organizations, Domestic Violence, Food/Clothing Distribution, Homes, People with Disabilities, Recreation & Athletics, Scouts, Shelters/Homelessness, Substance Abuse, United Funds/ United Ways, Volunteer Services, YMCA/YWCA/ YMHA/YWHA, Youth Organizations

Contributions Analysis

Arts & Humanities: 50%. Funds museums, historical societies, and the performing arts.
Civic & Public Affairs: 4%. Supports community centers and community services.
Education: 18%. Supports colleges and universities.
Environment: 1%.
Health: 6%. Funding supports health organizations, hospitals, pediatric healthcare and single-disease associations.
International: 2%.
Religion: 1%.
Social Services: 18%. Funds United Way, youth organizations, and social services.
Note: Approximately 30% of total contributions are for matching gifts. Total contributions in 1998.

Application Procedures

Initial Contact: Send a brief letter requesting application form, specifying whether request is for direct or in-kind/product support.
Application Requirements: Include proof of tax-exempt status, a description of organization, amount requested, purpose for which funds are sought, and a recently audited financial statement.
Deadlines: None.
Notes: Matching gifts are for the homeless, education, and charitable programs and require formal applications. Organizations must have IRS determination as a 501(c)(3) organization.

Restrictions

Foundation does not make grants to individuals, religious organizations for sectarian purposes, or organizations receiving more than 20% of support from United Way or government agencies.

Additional Information

As noted above, Caccini is president of Saint-Gobain NA and, therefore, oversees the company's U.S. holdings, which include Certainteed Corp.

Corporate Officials

Lloyd Ambler: vice president, director PRIM CORP EMPL vice president, director: CertainTeed Corp.

George B. Amoss: vice president finance, chief financial officer B 1941. ED Mount Saint Mary's College BS (1963); University Maryland MBA (1965). PRIM CORP EMPL vice president finance, chief financial officer: CertainTeed Corp. CORP AFFIL chief financial officer: Norton Co.; chief financial officer: Saint-Gobain Corp.; vice president finance: Carborundum Specialty Products.

Robert C. Ayotte: executive vice president, director B 1939. ED Harvard University Graduate School of Business Administration PMD; University of Rhode Island BS (1959). PRIM CORP EMPL executive vice president, director: CertainTeed Corp. CORP AFFIL president: Saint-Gobain Advanced Materials Corp.; president: Saint-Gobain Industrial Ceramics; president: Norton Performance Plastics; president: Carborundum Specialty Products; chairman: Norton Chemical Process Products Corp.

Dennis J. Baker: vice president, director PRIM CORP EMPL vice president, director: CertainTeed Corp.

Stephen L. Borst: assistant secretary PRIM CORP EMPL assistant secretary: CertainTeed Corp. CORP AFFIL secretary: Carborundum Specialty CP.

Gianpaolo Caccini: chairman, chief executive officer, director ED University of Pavia PhD. PRIM CORP EMPL chairman, chief executive officer, director: CertainTeed Corp. CORP AFFIL chairman: Norton Co.; president: Saint-Gobain Corp.

Bruce H. Cowgill: president PRIM CORP EMPL president: CertainTeed Corp.

Jean-Paul Dalle: vice president PRIM CORP EMPL vice president: CertainTeed Corp.

F. Lee Faust: vice president B New Orleans, LA 1943. ED Loyola University (1964); New York University (1971). PRIM CORP EMPL vice president: CertainTeed Corp.

Robert W. Fenton: vice president, controller PRIM CORP EMPL vice president, controller: CertainTeed Corp.

James E. Hilyard: president B New Castle, PA 1941. ED Carnegie Mellon University BS (1963); Case Western Reserve University MBA (1970). PRIM CORP EMPL president: CertainTeed Corp. CORP AFFIL vice chairman, president, director: Ludowici Roof Tile Inc.; president: Celadon; president: Bird Inc. NONPR AFFIL member: National Tile Roofing Manufacturer Association; member: Philadelphia Council on World Affairs; member: National Roofing Contractors Association; member: Asphalt Roofing Manufacturing Association; admissions counselor: Carnegie Mellon University; member: America Production Control Society; member: America AICE. CLUB AFFIL Chesapeake Bay Yacht Club Association; Castle Harbor Yacht Club.

Thomas G. Kinisky: vice president, director PRIM CORP EMPL vice president, director: CertainTeed Corp.

Thomas Milton Landin: vice president, director B Bradford, PA 1937. ED Grove City College BS (1959); University of Denver JD (1967). PRIM CORP EMPL vice president, director: CertainTeed Corp. PRIM NONPR EMPL former vp (govt & pub aff): SmithKline Beecham. NONPR AFFIL member: Washington DC Bar Association; director: YMCA Greater Philadelphia; director: Manufacturer Association Delaware Valley; director: Public Affairs Council; trustee: Caribbean/Latin American Action; director: Citizens Crime Commission; director: American Music Theatre Festival; member: American Bar Association. CLUB AFFIL Vesper Club; Union League Club Philadelphia; Capital Hill Club; Georgetown Club; Army-Navy Country Club.

Bradford C. Mattson: executive vice president exterior building products B Duluth, MN 1952. ED University of Nebraska (1974); Stanford University (1976). PRIM CORP EMPL executive vice president exterior building products: CertainTeed Corp. CORP AFFIL executive vice president: Saint-Gobain Corp.; president: Vetrotex CertainTeed Corp.; chairman: Bird Inc.

John P. Mikulak: vice president, director PRIM CORP EMPL vice president, director: CertainTeed Corp. CORP AFFIL secretary: Japanese Weekend Inc.

John J. Sweeney, III: vice president B Philadelphia, PA 1955. ED West Chester University (1977); Drexel University (1987). PRIM CORP EMPL vice president: CertainTeed Corp. CORP AFFIL vice president benefit investment: Saint-Gobain Corp. NONPR AFFIL member: American Institute CPAs; member: Association Investment Management & Research.

Michael J. Walsh: vice president B Portland, OR 1932. ED University of Portland BA (1954); Georgetown University JD (1959-1959). PRIM CORP EMPL vice president: CertainTeed Corp. NONPR AFFIL member: Oregon Bar Association; member: Portland Chamber of Commerce; member: National Association College & University Attorneys; chairman: Employees Compensation Appeals Board; member: Multnomah County Bar Association; member: American Trial Lawyers Association; member: DC Bar Association; member: American Judicature Society; member: American Arbitration Association. CLUB AFFIL Georgetown University Club.

Foundation Officials

D. Chris Altmansburger: vice president, director

Lloyd Ambler: vice president, director (see above)

George B. Amoss: chief financial officer (see above)

Robert C. Ayotte: executive vice president, director (see above)

Dennis J. Baker: director (see above)

Gianpaolo Caccini: chairman (see above)

Bruce H. Cowgill: director (see above)

Carol M. Gray: assistant secretary

James F. Harkins, Jr.: treasurer B 1953. ED Villanova University BA. PRIM CORP EMPL vice president, treasurer: CertainTeed Corp. CORP AFFIL treasurer: Saint-Gobain Corp.; treasurer: Vetrotex CertainTeed Corp.; treasurer: Norton Performance Plastics; treasurer: Carborundum Specialty Products; treasurer: Norton Co.; treasurer: Ball-Foster Glass Container Co. LLC.

James E. Hilyard: director (see above)

John R. Mesher: assistant secretary B 1952. ED Duquesne University; Indiana University of Pennsylvania BA. PRIM CORP EMPL vice president, secretary, deputy general counsel: CertainTeed Corp. CORP AFFIL officer: Saint-Gobain Corp.

Curtis M. Pontz: assistant secretary

Dorothy C. Wackerman: vice president, secretary, director

Janet Wolf: communications coordinator

Grants Analysis

Disclosure Period: calendar year ending 1998
Total Grants: $273,173*
Number of Grants: 156
Average Grant: $1,751
Highest Grant: $50,000
Typical Range: $100 to $5,000
***Note:** Giving excludes matching gifts; United Way.

Recent Grants

Note: Grants derived from 1998 Form 990.

Arts & Humanities

50,000	Avenue of the Arts, Philadelphia, PA -- Corporate Direct Charitable Contribution
40,000	Regional Performing Arts Center, Philadelphia, PA -- Corporate Direct Charitable Contribution
12,500	Warwick Township Historical Society, Hartsville, PA -- Corporate Direct Charitable Contribution
10,000	The John F. Kennedy Center for the Performing Arts, Washington, DC -- Corporate Direct Charitable Contribution
9,000	Wichita Falls Symphony Orchestra, Inc., Wichita Falls, TX -- Plant Community Charitable Contribution
5,000	Philadelphia Museum of Art, Philadelphia, PA -- Corporate Direct Charitable Contribution
1,000	The End of the Runway Players at Grapevine's Runway Theater, Grapevine, TX -- Plant Community Charitable Contribution

Civic & Public Affairs

7,750	Local Initiatives Support Corporation, Kansas City, MO -- Plant Community Charitable Contribution
1,000	Community Action Council, Hagerstown, MD -- Plant Community Charitable Contribution
1,000	Daemion House, Berwyn, PA -- Corporate Direct Charitable Contribution
1,000	Public Interest Law Center of Philadelphia (PILCOP), Philadelphia, PA -- Corporate Direct Charitable Contribution

Education

20,000	French International School of Philadelphia, Bala Cynwyd, PA -- Corporate Direct Charitable Contribution
5,823	Berlin-Milan Local Schools, Milan, OH -- Plant Community Charitable Contribution
5,000	Penn Literacy Network, Philadelphia, PA -- Corporate Direct Charitable Contribution
3,025	Buffalo State College Foundation, Inc., Buffalo, NY -- Plant Community Charitable Contribution
3,000	Penn Literacy Network, Philadelphia, PA -- Corporate Direct
2,600	Shakopee Senior High School, Shakopee, MN -- Plant Community Charitable Contribution
2,000	Granville Education Foundation, Inc., Oxford, NC -- Plant Community Charitable Contribution
2,000	New Hope Elementary School, Henderson, NC -- Plant Community Charitable Contribution
1,575	Stovall Shaw Elementary School, Stovall, NC -- Plant Community Charitable Contribution
1,000	Bailey Park Elementary, Grinnell, IA -- Plant Community Charitable Contribution

Environment

1,000	Friends of the Wissahickon, Philadelphia, PA -- Corporate Direct Charitable Contribution

Health

5,000	American Cancer Society, Phila. Div., Inc., Philadelphia, PA -- Corporate Direct Charitable Contribution
3,000	Grinnell Regional Medical Center, Grinnell, IA -- Corporate Direct
3,000	Main Line Health System, Bryn Mawr, PA -- Corporate Direct Charitable Contribution
2,000	Grinnell Regional Medical Center, Grinnell, IA -- Plant Community
1,300	Make-A-Wish Foundation of Michigan, Lansing, MI -- Plant Community Charitable Contribution
1,000	Cystic Fibrosis Foundation, Whitehall, PA -- Plant Community Charitable Contribution
1,000	NE GA Ch. Autism Society of America, Athens, GA -- Plant Community Charitable Contribution

International

5,000 Institute for International Economics, Washington, DC -- Corporate Direct Charitable Contribution

Religion

1,500 St. Joaquims Church, Madera, CA -- Plant Community Charitable Contribution

1,000 Jackson Interfaith Shelter, Jackson, MI -- Plant Community Charitable Contribution

1,000 Paynes Chapel UMC, Ridgeway, WV -- Plant Community Charitable Contribution

Social Services

10,000 United Way of Chester County, Exton, PA -- Corporate Direct Charitable Contribution

10,000 United Way of Greater Wichita Falls, Inc., Wichita Falls, TX -- Plant Community Charitable Contribution

5,200 Baker Industries, Paoli, PA -- Corporate Direct

3,000 Pennsylvania Home of the Sparrow, Malvern, PA -- Corporate Direct Charitable Contribution

2,500 Gaudenzia, Inc., Norristown, PA -- Corporate Direct Charitable Contribution

2,000 Jackson N.W. Little League, Jackson, MI -- Plant Community Charitable Contribution

1,500 Multi Community Diversified Services, Inc., McPherson, KS -- Plant Community Charitable Contribution

1,500 United Way of Jackson, Jackson, MI -- Plant Community Charitable Contribution

1,400 United Way of McPherson, Inc., McPherson, KS -- Plant Community Charitable Contribution

1,250 Kentucky Food Bank, Inc., Elizabethtown, KY -- Plant Community Charitable Contribution

1,000 Athens Area Council For The Prevention of Child Abuse and Neglect, Inc., Bogart, GA -- Plant Community Charitable Contribution

1,000 Athens-Clarke CASA Program, Inc., Athens, GA -- Plant Community Charitable Contribution

1,000 Big Brothers/Big Sisters of Washington County, Hagerstown, MD -- Plant Community Charitable Contribution

1,000 Camp Fire Boys and Girls, St. Paul, MN -- Plant Community Charitable Contribution

1,000 The MBF Center, Norristown, PA -- Corporate Direct Charitable Contribution

1,000 Mountaintop Area Little League, Mountaintop, PA -- Plant Community Charitable Contribution

1,000 Northwest Texas Council, BSA, Wichita falls, TX -- Corporate Direct Charitable Contribution

Cessna Aircraft Co.

Company Contact

Wichita, KS

Company Description

Employees: 6,900

SIC(s): 3721 Aircraft, 3728 Aircraft Parts & Equipment Nec.

Cessna Foundation, Inc.

Giving Contact

Marilyn Richwine, Secretary & Treasurer
Cessna Foundation
PO Box 7706
Wichita, KS 67277-7706
Phone: (316)517-7810
Fax: (316)517-7812

Description

Founded: 1952
EIN: 486108801
Organization Type: Corporate Foundation
Giving Locations: KS: Wichita including surrounding area principally near operating locations and to national organizations.
Grant Types: Capital, Employee Matching Gifts.
Note: Employee matching gift ratio: 2 to 1.

Financial Summary

Total Giving: $1,435,524 (1998); $1,134,361 (1997); $1,246,260 (1996). Note: Contributes through foundation only. 1997 Giving includes foundation ($665,634); matching gifts ($120,077); scholarship ($71,300); United Way ($277,350).
Assets: $10,439,870 (1998); $9,151,660 (1997); $11,787,221 (1996)
Gifts Received: $600,000 (1997); $850,000 (1996); $750,000 (1995). Note: Contributions are received from Cessna Aircraft Co.

Typical Recipients

Arts & Humanities: Arts Associations & Councils, Arts Centers, Arts Outreach, Libraries, Museums/Galleries, Music, Theater
Civic & Public Affairs: African American Affairs, Employment/Job Training, Housing, Professional & Trade Associations, Safety, Urban & Community Affairs, Zoos/Aquariums
Education: Agricultural Education, Business Education, Colleges & Universities, Economic Education, Education Funds, Education Reform, Engineering/Technological Education, Medical Education, Private Education (Precollege), Public Education (Precollege), Science/Mathematics Education, Special Education, Student Aid, Vocational & Technical Education
Health: AIDS/HIV, Cancer, Children's Health/Hospitals, Clinics/Medical Centers, Emergency/Ambulance Services, Health Funds, Health Organizations, Heart, Hospices, Hospitals, Multiple Sclerosis, Preventive Medicine/Wellness Organizations, Single-Disease Health Associations
International: Missionary/Religious Activities
Religion: Churches, Ministries, Missionary Activities (Domestic), Religious Organizations, Religious Welfare, Social/Policy Issues
Science: Science Museums, Scientific Centers & Institutes
Social Services: Big Brother/Big Sister, Child Welfare, Community Service Organizations, Family Services, Food/Clothing Distribution, People with Disabilities, Recreation & Athletics, Scouts, Special Olympics, Substance Abuse, United Funds/United Ways, YMCA/YWCA/YMHA/YWHA, Youth Organizations

Contributions Analysis

Arts & Humanities: 10%. Supports arts associations, museums, history, music, and theater.
Civic & Public Affairs: Less than 5%. Supports urban and community affairs and Habitat for Humanity.
Education: 30% to 35%. Funding supports colleges and universities, primarily in Kansas. Other interests include vocational, economic, and medical education. Administers employee matching gifts program to education. Also administers Del Roskam Scholarship program for children or grandchildren of Cessna employees.
Health: About 5%. Funding supports health, including mental health and single disease health associations.
Religion: Less than 5%.
Social Services: 40% to 50%. Funding supports united funds and youth organizations. Other interests include athletic programs, people with disabilities, emergency relief, and food and clothing distribution.

Application Procedures

Initial Contact: Send a brief letter or proposal.
Application Requirements: Include a description of organization, amount requested, purpose of funds sought, recently audited financial statement, and proof of tax-exempt status.
Deadlines: None; board meets quarterly.

Corporate Officials

Gary W. Hay: vice chairman, chief executive officer B Denver, CO 1943. ED Wichita State University BA (1968). PRIM CORP EMPL vice chairman: Cessna Aircraft Co.
Charles B. Johnson: executive vice president operation B 1949. ED Simpson College. PRIM CORP EMPL executive vice president operation: Cessna Aircraft Co.
Russell William Meyer, Jr.: chairman, chief executive officer B Davenport, IA 1932. ED Yale University BA (1954); Harvard University LLB (1961). PRIM CORP EMPL chairman, chief executive officer: Cessna Aircraft Co. CORP AFFIL director: Western Resources Inc.; director: Public Broadcasting System; director: Cessna Finance Corp.; director: Nationsbank Inc. NONPR AFFIL trustee: Wesley Hospital Endowment Association; chairman, director: Wichita Chamber of Commerce; trustee: Wake Forest University; board governors: United Way America; director: United Way Wichita & Sedgwick County; member: Ohio Bar Association; member: Kansas Bar Association; member: Latrobe Chamber of Commerce; member: Gen Aviation Manufacturer Association; president appointee: Aviation Safety Commission; member: Cleveland Bar Association; member: American Bar Association. CLUB AFFIL Wichita Country Club; Pine Valley Club; Wichita Club; Flint Hills National Club; Cypress Hunt Club; Double Eagle Chamber of Commerce.
John E. Moore: executive vice president human resources B Charleston, WV 1943. ED Washington & Lee University BS (1965); University of Kentucky JD (1968). PRIM CORP EMPL executive vice president human resources: Cessna Aircraft Co.

Foundation Officials

Jordan L. Haines: trustee CORP AFFIL director: KN Energy Inc.; director: Q'west Communication International Inc.
Gary W. Hay: trustee (see above)
Charles B. Johnson: trustee (see above)
Russell William Meyer, Jr.: president (see above)
John E. Moore: vice president (see above)
Marilyn Richwine: secretary, treasurer
Kenneth J. Wagnon: trustee

Grants Analysis

Disclosure Period: calendar year ending 1997
Total Grants: $665,634*
Number of Grants: 180 (approx)
Average Grant: $17,452
Highest Grant: $257,250*
Typical Range: $200 to $10,000
***Note:** Giving excludes matching gifts; scholarships; United Way. Highest grant paid quarterly to United Way, Wichita, KS.

Recent Grants

Note: Grants derived from 1998 Form 990.

Arts & Humanities

24,000 Wichita Symphony Society, Inc., Wichita, KS -- Second payment of 5-year, $125,000 pledge

20,000 Music Theatre of Wichita Endowment

Campaign, Wichita, KS -- 2nd payment of 5-Year, $100,000 pledge

11,000 Music Theatre of Wichita, Wichita, KS -- Second payment of 5-year, $60,000 pledge

10,000 Arts Partners, Inc., Wichita, KS -- One-time grant for "Run for the Arts" program

10,000 Friends of the Wichita Art Museum, Inc., Wichita, KS -- One-time grant toward Great Plains Show

10,000 Wichita Public Library Foundation, Wichita, KS -- 1st payment of $3-Year, $30,000 pledge

Civic & Public Affairs

5,000 Urban League of Wichita, Inc., Wichita, KS -- First payment of 3-year, $15,000 pledge

Education

50,000 The Kansas University Endowment Association, Lawrence, KS -- Second payment of 5-year, $250,000 pledge

40,000 Wichita State University - Cessna Stadium, Wichita, KS -- 2nd payment of 5-year, $200,000 pledge

37,500 Wichita State University - Engineering, Wichita, KS -- 15 Scholarships at $2,500 each

33,333 Friends University, Wichita, KS -- First payment of 3-year, $100,000 pledge

33,333 Friends University, Wichita, KS -- 2nd payment of 3-Year, $100,000 pledge

20,000 The Kansas University Endowment Association, Lawrence, KS -- Final payment of 8-year, $125,000 pledge

20,000 Newman University, Wichita, KS -- Final payment of 5-year, $100,000 pledge

15,000 Kansas Independent College Fund, Topeka, KS -- 2nd payment of 3-year, $45,000 pledge

14,063 Ozark Christian College, Joplin, MO -- Matching gift

10,000 Embry-Riddle Aeronautical University, Daytona Beach, FL -- First payment of 12-year, $120,000 pledge

10,000 Junior Achievement of Wichita, Inc., Wichita, KS -- 2nd payment of 5-year, $50,000 pledge

10,000 Wichita State University, Wichita, KS -- 1998 contribution Del Roskam Scholarship

6,000 Wichita State University, Wichita, KS -- Matching gift for 1997 & 1998 - B. Peterman

5,000 Wichita State University, Wichita, KS -- 3rd payment toward Peterman Scholarship Fund

4,000 University of North Dakota - John D. Odegard School of Aerospace, Grand Forks, ND -- Two $2,000.00 scholarships

Health

85,000 Heartspring, Wichita, KS -- 5th payment of 6-Year, $510,000 pledge

20,000 Center for Health and Wellness, Witchita, KS -- First payment of 5-year, $100,000 pledge

20,000 Goodwill/Easter Seal Society of Kansas, Wichita, KS -- Final payment of 5-year, $100,000 pledge

10,000 Cerebral Palsy Research Foundation, Wichita, KS -- Final payment of 5-year, $50,000 pledge

10,000 Hospice, Inc., Wichita, KS -- First payment of 3-year, $30,000 pledge

8,000 Heartspring, Wichita, KS -- Matching Gift for 1998 - Gary Hay

5,000 The AIDS Fund of Wichita/Sedgwick County, Wichita, KS -- Final payment of 3-year, $15,000 pledge

Religion

50,000 The Salvation Army, Wichita, KS -- 5th & final payment of 5-Year, $250,000

25,000 Inter-Faith Ministries - Wichita, Wichita, KS -- Second payment of 3-year, $75,000 pledge

Social Services

100,000 YMCA, Wichita, KS -- 1st payment of 5-year, $500,000 pledge

100,000 YMCA - Wichita, Wichita, KS -- 2nd payment of 5-Year, $500,000 pledge

68,750 United Way of the Plains, Wichita, KS -- 2nd Qtr payment of 1997/98 pledge

68,750 United Way of the Plains, Wichita, KS -- Third quarter payment of 1997/98 pledge

68,750 United Way of the Plains, Wichita, KS -- First quarter payment for 1997/98 pledge

68,750 United Way of the Plains, Wichita, KS -- 4th Qtr payment

20,000 Rainbows United, Inc., Wichita, KS -- Third payment of 5-year, $100,000 pledge

17,000 Midtown Community Resource Center, Wichita, KS -- 1st payment of 3-Year, $50,000 pledge

15,000 United Way of the Plains, Wichita, KS -- 3rd payment of 5-Year, $75,000 pledge

10,000 The Arc of Sedgwick County, Wichita, KS -- First payment of 3-year, $30,000 pledge

10,000 Family Consultation Service, Wichita, KS -- Fourth payment of 5-year, $50,000 pledge

10,000 Friends of Recovery Association, Mission, KS -- Second payment of 3-year, $30,000 pledge

10,000 Youth Entrepreneurs of Kansas, Wichita, KS -- Second payment of 3-year, $30,000 pledge

8,333 Wichita Child Guidance Center, Wichita, KS -- Final payment of 3-year, $25,000 pledge

7,500 Big Brothers & Sisters of Sedgwick County, Wichita, KS -- First payment of 3-year, $22,500 pledge

7,500 Boy Scouts of America - Quivira Council, Wichita, KS -- Annual contribution for 1998

5,000 Big Brothers - Big Sisters of Montgomery County, Independence, KS -- First payment of 3-year, $15,000 pledge

5,000 Scout Council, Wichita, KS -- toward the Urban Campout

3,000 United Way of the Dayton Area, Dayton, OH -- Annual contribution for McCauley Division

CGU Insurance

Company Contact

Philadelphia, PA

Company Description

Former Name: General Accident Insurance.
Assets: US$6,051,101,000
Employees: 4,420
SIC(s): 6331 Fire, Marine & Casualty Insurance.
Parent Company: CGU plc, St. Helen's 1, Undershaft, London, United Kingdom

Operating Locations

IA: Hawkeye Security Insurance Co., West Des Moines; MO: Silvey Corp., Columbia; NY: General Assurance Co., Melville; General Assurance Insurance Co. of New York, Melville; Pennsylvania General Insurance Co. of New York, Melville; OR: CGU Insurance; North Pacific Insurance Co., Portland; Oregon Automobile Insurance Co., Portland; PA: Camden Fire Insurance Assn., Philadelphia; CGU Insurance, Philadelphia; General Accident Insurance, Philadelphia; Pennsylvania General Insurance Co., Philadelphia; Potomac Insurance Co. of Illinois, Philadelphia

Nonmonetary Support

Type: Loaned Executives

General Accident Charitable Trust

Giving Contact

Tom Ford, Vice President of Association Relationss
CGU Insurance
One Beacon Street
Boston, MA 02108
Phone: (617)725-6000

Description

Founded: 1987
EIN: 232441567
Organization Type: Corporate Foundation. Supports preselected organizations only.
Giving Locations: nationally.
Grant Types: Capital, Employee Matching Gifts, General Support.

Financial Summary

Total Giving: $538,031 (1997); $500,000 (1996 approx); $533,653 (1995). Note: Contributes through corporate direct giving program and foundation. 1997 Giving includes matching gifts and United Way.
Giving Analysis: Giving for 1997 includes: corporate grants to United Way ($340,293); corporate matching gifts ($117,521); corporate direct giving ($80,217)
Assets: $5,792,574 (1997); $6,239,096 (1995); $5,505,424 (1994)
Gifts Received: $7,000 (1995); $152,500 (1994); $146,700 (1993). Note: Contributions are received from the General Accident Insurance Company of America.

Typical Recipients

Arts & Humanities: Ballet, Dance, History & Archaeology, Libraries, Museums/Galleries, Music, Performing Arts, Theater
Civic & Public Affairs: Business/Free Enterprise, Clubs, Community Foundations, Economic Development, Economic Policy, Civic & Public Affairs-General, Housing, Philanthropic Organizations, Professional & Trade Associations, Public Policy, Safety, Urban & Community Affairs, Zoos/Aquariums
Education: Agricultural Education, Business Education, Colleges & Universities, Education Funds, Education Reform, Education-General, Minority Education, Private Education (Precollege), Public Education (Precollege), Religious Education, Science/Mathematics Education, Secondary Education (Private), Secondary Education (Public), Student Aid
Health: Cancer, Children's Health/Hospitals, Clinics/Medical Centers, Diabetes, Emergency/Ambulance Services, Hospitals, Long-Term Care, Medical Research, Multiple Sclerosis, Prenatal Health Issues, Single-Disease Health Associations
International: Health Care/Hospitals, International Relief Efforts, Missionary/Religious Activities
Religion: Churches, Jewish Causes, Missionary Activities (Domestic), Religious Organizations, Religious Welfare
Science: Scientific Centers & Institutes
Social Services: Child Welfare, Community Service Organizations, Crime Prevention, Delinquency & Criminal Rehabilitation, Emergency Relief, Homes, People with Disabilities, Scouts, Senior Services, Shelters/Homelessness, Social Services-General, Substance Abuse, United Funds/United Ways, Volunteer Services, Youth Organizations

Contributions Analysis

Arts & Humanities: 3%. Support goes to art museums, the ballet, zoos and conservation societies.
Civic & Public Affairs: 2%. Supports community development, economics, and public policy.
Education: 7%. Gives to private schools and seminaries. Also supports colleges, universities, education funds, and high schools.
Health: 88%. Majority of support goes to united funds. Also supports youth organizations.
Note: The above analysis excludes employee matching gifts.

Corporate Officials

Robert Gowdy: president, chief executive officer PRIM CORP EMPL president, chief executive officer: CGU Insurance ADD CORP EMPL chief executive officer: CGU Corp.; president: Houston General Insurance Co.

Giving Program Officials

Tom Ford: vice president association relations

Grants Analysis

Disclosure Period: calendar year ending 1997
Total Grants: $80,217*
Number of Grants: 51
Average Grant: $1,573
Highest Grant: $12,000
Typical Range: $500 to $5,000
***Note:** Giving excludes matching gifts; United Way.

Recent Grants

Note: Grants derived from 1997 Form 990.

Arts & Humanities

5,000	Pennsylvania Ballet, Philadelphia, PA
2,500	Philadelphia Museum of Art, Philadelphia, PA
1,000	Free Library of Philadelphia Foundation, Philadelphia, PA

Civic & Public Affairs

5,000	Central Philadelphia Development Corporation, Philadelphia, PA
5,000	Fund for Philadelphia, Philadelphia, PA
1,500	Pennsylvania Driving Under the Influence Association, Harrisburg, PA
1,000	Associated General Contractors, Washington, DC
1,000	Committee of Seventy, Philadelphia, PA
1,000	Geheris Center, Mount Holly, NJ
1,000	Habitat for Humanity, Philadelphia, PA
1,000	Pennsylvania Horticultural Society, Philadelphia, PA
1,000	Zoological Society, Philadelphia, PA

Education

12,000	Philadelphia Foundation Sponsor A Scholar, Philadelphia, PA
7,000	Foundation for Independent Colleges, Harrisburg, PA
7,000	Oregon Independent College Foundation, Portland, OR
5,000	Washington State University College of Business and Economics, Pullman, WA
1,000	Executive Service Corps of the Delaware Valley, Ardmore, PA
1,000	Independent College Fund, Albany, NY
1,000	Temple University, Philadelphia, PA

Health

3,500	National Multiple Sclerosis Society, Philadelphia, PA
1,000	Providence Medical Center, Providence, RI
1,000	University of Pennsylvania Cancer Center, Philadelphia, PA

Religion

1,000	St. Andrew's Society, Philadelphia, PA

Science

1,000	Academy of Natural Sciences, Philadelphia, PA

Social Services

245,015	United Way of Southeastern Pennsylvania, Philadelphia, PA
33,500	United Way of the Columbia-Willamette, Portland, OR
7,291	United Way, Rochester, NY
6,344	United Way, New York, NY
5,865	United Way of Burlington County, Mount Holly, NJ
4,190	United Way of Central New York, Syracuse, NY
4,074	United Way of Long Island, Deer Park, NY
3,315	United Way of Middle Tennessee, Nashville, TN
2,516	United Way of Northeast New York, Albany, NY
2,279	United Way of the Bay Area, San Francisco, CA
2,198	United Way of Franklin County, Columbus, OH
2,127	United Way of Buffalo and Erie County, Buffalo, NY
2,000	Boy Scouts of America Cradle of Liberty Council, Philadelphia, PA
1,901	United Way of Central Florida, Orlando, FL
1,834	United Way of the Greater Lehigh Valley, Bethlehem, PA
1,802	United Way of Central Indiana, Indianapolis, IN
1,738	United Way, Dallas, TX
1,623	United Way, New Haven, CT
1,500	Bridge, Philadelphia, PA
1,500	United Way of King County, Seattle, WA
1,416	United Way of the National Capital Region, Washington, DC
1,344	United Way, St. Louis, MO
1,276	United Way of the Capital Region, Harrisburg, PA
1,248	United Way of Southeastern New England, Providence, RI
1,200	Citizens Crime Commission of Delaware Valley, Philadelphia, PA
1,000	United Way, Boise, ID

Champion International Corp.

Company Contact

Stamford, CT
Web: http://www.championinternational.com

Company Description

Revenue: US$5,268,000,000 (1999)
Employees: 21,137 (1999)
Fortune Rank: 314, per FORTUNE Magazine's list of 500 Largest U.S. Corporations (1999).
FF 314
SIC(s): 2499 Wood Products Nec, 2621 Paper Mills.

Nonmonetary Support

Value: $100,000 (1996); $100,000 (1995); $105,000 (1993)
Type: Donated Products
Volunteer Programs: Champion fund for community service awards on analysis gift up to $1,000 for an employee's volunteer organization.

Corporate Sponsorship

Type: Sports events
Contact: John Idenbiddle, Vice President, Creative Services
Note: Sponsored the U.S. Canoe, Kayak, and Rowing teams, and the NCAA.

Giving Contact

Eileen McSweeney, Director of Contributions
Champion International Corp.
1 Champion Plaza
Stamford, CT 06921
Phone: (203)358-7000
Fax: (203)358-6622
Email: mcswee@champint.com

Description

Organization Type: Corporate Giving Program
Giving Locations: headquarters and operating communities.
Grant Types: Employee Matching Gifts, General Support.
Note: Employee matching gift ratio: 1 to 1.

Giving Philosophy

'Champion believes that responsible corporate citizenship is good business, and this belief supports our corporate mission of industry leadership and profitable growth. We know that to maintain such a position requires excellence in every undertaking including our contributions and community support activities. We are also very much aware that the world in which we all function has grown complex and demanding. Throughout the country in the cities and towns with Champion facilities, decisions are regularly made that often have an impact on both business operations and on the quality of life of those communities. We encourage all employees to take an active part in the affairs of their communities, and we support their volunteer efforts. We believe that through these volunteer efforts, along with donated funds, both the interests of our company and our various constituencies can best be met and thus contribute to a healthy, functioning society where everyone benefits.' Guidelines for Giving

Financial Summary

Total Giving: $7,000,000 (2000 approx); $7,000,000 (1999 approx); $8,000,000 (1998 approx). Note: Contributes through corporate direct giving program only. Giving includes corporate direct giving; domestic subsidiaries; nonmonetary support.
Assets: $8,840,000 (1998); $9,111,000 (1997); $9,820,000 (1996)

Typical Recipients

Arts & Humanities: Libraries, Museums/Galleries, Visual Arts
Civic & Public Affairs: Community Foundations, Public Policy, Urban & Community Affairs, Women's Affairs
Education: Colleges & Universities, Engineering/Technological Education, Literacy, Minority Education, Public Education (Precollege)
Environment: Environment-General, Resource Conservation
Health: Hospices, Hospitals
Science: Scientific Centers & Institutes, Scientific Organizations
Social Services: Community Service Organizations, Substance Abuse, United Funds/United Ways

Contributions Analysis

Giving Priorities: United Way, community programs, education, environment, disadvantaged, visual arts.
Arts & Humanities: About 5%. Company's involvement in the paper industry leads tointerest in related arts. Major support to the Fairfield County branch of the Whitney Museum of American Art, located at company headquarters.
Civic & Public Affairs: About 50%. Area of community support is the highest priority, with major facilities in over twenty-five locations administering contributions programs targeted to community needs. Commitment to local United Ways is a mainstay of community support activities. In addition, a separate budget enables local managers to support, on a case-by-case basis, organizations that fall outside the United

Way umbrella. Company also sponsors the Champion Fund for Community Service (see below). This program supports employee volunteerism with company contributions. The company has also expanded the matching gift program beyond education to include contributions to health and humanservices, civic and community programs, and arts and cultural organizations.

Education: About 35%. Support focuses on institutions where the company recruits employees, education and research relating to the pulp and paper industry, and science and technology education. Also supports scholarships for children of employees and middle-school reform and restructure efforts in plant communities.

Environment: Less than 5%. Supports programs dedicated to natural resources, wildlife, and public education on environmental issues.

Social Services: Less than 5%. Focus is on skills development for the disadvantaged, with emphasis on programs concerned with literacy and job training.

Application Procedures

Initial Contact: preliminary letter

Application Requirements: name, address, and telephone number of organization; contact person and title; names of executive director, directors, and their affiliations; copy of IRS exemption letter; description of how proposed project relates to company giving guidelines; description of how project's success will be determined; description of experience and qualifications organization has for implementing project; copy of most recent audited financial statement; sources of income; and budget for organization and proposed project

Deadlines: None.

Review Process: contributions planned one year in advance and based on calendar year budget

Decision Notification: contributions committee meets several times per year; final notification of grants made within ten days of each meeting; preliminary response indicating whether request is being considered made within three weeks of receipt

Notes: Grant requests may be submitted to headquarters or to the contributions coordinator at the nearest Champion facility. A complete list of operating facility addresses is available from the company.

Restrictions

Grants are not made to individuals; organizations without 501(c)(3) status; political candidates or organizations; religious, fraternal, or veterans organizations unless they furnish services to benefit the general public; dinners, benefits, exhibits, conferences, sports events, and other one-time, short-term activities; journal advertisements and the purchase of tickets; supplementary operating funds for agencies in a United Way already supported by company; and community organizations not located within a company location. Unsolicited requests to Corporate Headquarters are rarely granted. Unsolicited requests to Corporate Headquarters are rarely granted.

Additional Information

The Champion International Foundation has ceased to function. In 1995, the foundation paid out all of its assets to organizations that would normally receive grants from the corporate giving program.

All future giving will be exclusively through the company.

Publications: Giving Guidelines; Volunteer Pamphlet; Annual Report

Corporate Officials

Kenwood C. Nichols: vice chairman, executive officer B 1940. ED Auburn University BS (1961); Duke University MS (1964). PRIM CORP EMPL vice chairman, executive officer: Champion International Corp.

Richard E. Olson: chairman, chief executive officer, director B 1937. ED Knox College AB (1959); Paper Science & Technology MA (1961); Paper Science & Technology PhD (1967). PRIM CORP EMPL chairman, chief executive officer, director: Champion International Corp. CORP AFFIL director: Weldwood Can Ltd. NONPR AFFIL member technical association: Pulp and Paper Industry.

Robert W. Turner: vice president public affairs PRIM CORP EMPL vice president public affairs: Champion International Corp.

Giving Program Officials

Eileen McSweeney: director contributions community support program

Foundation Officials

Eileen McSweeney: director contributions community support program (see above)

Grants Analysis

Disclosure Period: calendar year ending 1998

Total Grants: $7,000,000*

Number of Grants: 500 (approx)

Average Grant: $21,500 (approx)

Highest Grant: $150,000

Typical Range: $2,500 to $10,000 and $50,000 to $100,000

***Note:** Giving excludes nonmonetary support.

Recent Grants

Note: Grants derived from 1995 Form 990.

Civic & Public Affairs

75,000	Lawrence County, Moulton, AL
11,000	Public Policy Institute of New York State, Albany, NY
5,000	League of Women Voters Educational Fund, Washington, DC

Environment

20,000	Student Conservation Association, Charlestown, NH

Health

20,000	Hospice of Stamford, Stamford, CT

Science

15,000	Maritime Center, Norwalk, CT
4,500	University of Wisconsin Stevens Point Paper Science Foundation, Stevens Point, WI

Social Services

112,800	United Way Stamford, Stamford, CT
109,000	Butler County United Way, Hamilton, OH

CHARTER MANUFACTURING CO.

Company Contact

Mequon, WI

Company Description

Employees: 800

SIC(s): 3312 Blast Furnaces & Steel Mills, 3496 Miscellaneous Fabricated Wire Products.

Charter Manufacturing Co. Foundation

Giving Contact

Linda T. Mellowes, President
Charter Manufacturing Co. Foundation
PO Box 217
Mequon, WI 53092-0217
Phone: (414)243-4700

Description

EIN: 391486363

Organization Type: Corporate Foundation. Supports preselected organizations only.

Giving Locations: WI: WI

Grant Types: General Support.

Financial Summary

Total Giving: $350,000 (1999 approx); $289,250 (1998); $419,750 (1997). Note: Contributes through foundation only.

Giving Analysis: Giving for 1997 includes: foundation ($369,750); foundation grants to United Way ($50,000); 1998: foundation ($239,250); foundation grants to United Way ($50,000)

Assets: $533,286 (1998); $431,228 (1997); $205,075 (1995)

Gifts Received: $400,000 (1998); $600,000 (1997); $300,000 (1994). Note: Contributions were received from Charter Manufacturing Co.

Typical Recipients

Arts & Humanities: Arts Funds, Community Arts, Museums/Galleries, Music, Performing Arts, Theater

Civic & Public Affairs: Botanical Gardens/Parks, Community Foundations, Civic & Public Affairs-General, Hispanic Affairs, Nonprofit Management, Urban & Community Affairs

Education: Business Education, Colleges & Universities, Engineering/Technological Education, Medical Education, Private Education (Precollege)

Environment: Environment-General, Wildlife Protection

Health: Cancer, Children's Health/Hospitals, Health Organizations, Medical Research, Single-Disease Health Associations, Transplant Networks/Donor Banks

Science: Science Museums

Social Services: Domestic Violence, Family Planning, People with Disabilities, Scouts, United Funds/ United Ways, YMCA/YWCA/YMHA/YWHA, Youth Organizations

Contributions Analysis

Arts & Humanities: 19%. Funds performing arts and art museums.

Civic & Public Affairs: 5%. Funds community and nieghborhood development, and community foundations.

Education: 7%. Supports higher education.

Environment: 2%. Supports environmental concerns.

Health: 5%. Supports hospitals and medical centers.

Science: 2%.

Social Services: 25%. Support for United Way and family planning.

Note: Total contributions in 1998.

Additional Information

The foundation changed its fiscal year to a calendar year.

Corporate Officials

John A. Mellowes: chairman, chief executive officer, director B 1938. ED Cornell University. PRIM CORP EMPL chairman, chief executive officer, director: Charter Manufacturing Co.

Foundation Officials

Henry J. Loos: secretary B 1940. ED Colgate University BA (1962); Harvard University LLB (1965). PRIM CORP EMPL secretary: Charter Manufacturing Co. CORP AFFIL director: Wisconsin Paper Products Co.; director: Young Radiator Co.; secretary: Olsten Milwaukee Inc. NONPR AFFIL member: Milwaukee Bar Association; member: Wisconsin Bar Association; member: American Bar Association; member: Florida Bar Association.

John A. Mellowes: vice president, treasurer (see above)

Linda T. Mellowes: president

Grants Analysis

Disclosure Period: calendar year ending 1998
Total Grants: $293,250*
Number of Grants: 24
Average Grant: $9,969
Highest Grant: $100,000
Typical Range: $1,000 to $50,000
***Note:** Giving excludes United Way.

Recent Grants

Note: Grants derived from 1998 Form 990.

Arts & Humanities

50,000 Milwaukee Art Museum Inc, Milwaukee, WI -- General
5,000 United Performing Arts Fund, Inc., Milwaukee, WI -- General
1,000 Milwaukee Art Museum, Inc, Milwaukee, WI -- General

Civic & Public Affairs

15,000 Milwaukee Foundation, Milwaukee, WI -- General
500 The Gathering on the Green Inc, Thiensville, WI -- General
200 Boerner Botanical Gardens, Milwaukee, WI -- General

Education

10,000 Milwaukee School of Engineering, Milwaukee, WI -- General
5,000 Junior Achievement of Wisconsin, Milwaukee, WI -- General
5,000 Medical College of Wisconsin Inc., Milwaukee, WI -- General
2,500 University School of Milwaukee, Milwaukee, WI -- General
1,000 Smith College, Northampton, MA -- General
500 University School of Milwaukee, Milwaukee, WI -- Christmas & Holiday Shop
400 Junior Achievement Womens Association, Milwaukee, WI -- General
400 Medical College of Wisconsin, Inc., Milwaukee, WI -- General

Environment

5,000 Riveredge Nature Center, Milwaukee, WI -- General
750 Ducks Unlimited of Milwaukee, Milwaukee, WI -- General
500 Schlitz Audubon Center, Milwaukee, WI -- General

Health

10,000 Childrens Hospital Foundation, Milwaukee, WI -- General
5,000 Childrens Hospital Foundation, Milwaukee, WI -- General
500 Expedition Inspiration Fund, Ketchum, ID -- Climb for a Cure

Science

5,000 Museum of Science and Industry, Chicago, IL -- General

Social Services

100,000 YMCA, Saukville, WI -- Capital Campaign
50,000 United Way of Greater Milwaukee, Inc., Milwaukee, WI -- General
15,000 Planned Parenthood of Wisconsin, Inc., Milwaukke, WI -- General
1,000 Planned Parenthood of Wisconsin, Inc., Milwaukee, WI -- General

Chase Bank Of Texas

Company Contact

Houston, TX
Web: http://www.chase.com

Company Description

Former Name: Texas Commerce Bank-Houston NA.
Assets: US$19,804,600,000
Employees: 9,201
SIC(s): 6022 State Commercial Banks.
Parent Company: Chase Manhattan Corp.

Nonmonetary Support

Type: Donated Equipment

Corporate Sponsorship

Value: $1,000
Type: Arts & cultural events; Festivals/fairs; Pledge-a-thon

Chase Bank of Texas Foundation, Inc.

Giving Contact

Ms. Jana Gunter, Secretary, Manager, Community Relations
Chase Bank of Texas
PO Box 2558
Houston, TX 77252-8353
Phone: (713)216-4004
Fax: (713)216-5115

Description

EIN: 746036696
Organization Type: Corporate Foundation
Giving Locations: TX: Houston
Grant Types: Capital, General Support, Multiyear/Continuing Support.
Note: General Support for non-United Way agencies only.

Financial Summary

Total Giving: $1,500,000 (1998 approx); $764,500 (1997); $1,229,441 (1996). Note: Contributes through corporate direct giving program and foundation.
Giving Analysis: Giving for 1997 includes: foundation grants to United Way ($515,000); foundation ($249,500)
Assets: $209,934 (1997); $442,988 (1996); $281,018 (1995)
Gifts Received: $515,000 (1997); $1,347,594 (1996); $1,042,781 (1995). Note: Contributions are received from Texas Commerce Bank.

Typical Recipients

Arts & Humanities: Arts Associations & Councils, Arts Centers, Arts Funds, Ballet, Community Arts, Historic Preservation, Libraries, Museums/Galleries, Music, Opera, Performing Arts, Public Broadcasting, Theater
Civic & Public Affairs: African American Affairs, Botanical Gardens/Parks, Clubs, Community Foundations, Economic Development, Economic Policy, Employment/Job Training, Civic & Public Affairs-General, Hispanic Affairs, Housing, Municipalities/Towns, Nonprofit Management, Professional & Trade Associations, Rural Affairs, Urban & Community Affairs, Women's Affairs, Zoos/Aquariums
Education: Business Education, Colleges & Universities, Community & Junior Colleges, Continuing Education, Education Funds, Engineering/Technological Education, Education-General, Health & Physical Education, Legal Education, Literacy, Medical Education, Minority Education, Public Education (Precollege)
Environment: Resource Conservation
Health: Cancer, Children's Health/Hospitals, Clinics/Medical Centers, Diabetes, Emergency/Ambulance Services, Health Organizations, Heart, Hospices, Hospitals, Medical Research, Medical Training, Mental Health, Prenatal Health Issues, Single-Disease Health Associations
International: International Development
Religion: Jewish Causes, Ministries, Religious Welfare
Science: Science Exhibits & Fairs, Science Museums
Social Services: Big Brother/Big Sister, Child Welfare, Community Centers, Community Service Organizations, Delinquency & Criminal Rehabilitation, Family Planning, Food/Clothing Distribution, Homes, People with Disabilities, Recreation & Athletics, Scouts, Senior Services, Shelters/Homelessness, Substance Abuse, United Funds/United Ways, Volunteer Services, YMCA/YWCA/YMHA/YWHA, Youth Organizations

Contributions Analysis

Giving Priorities: Social welfare, higher education, and the arts.
Arts & Humanities: 5%. Performing arts groups, arts funds, and other localorganizations.
Civic & Public Affairs: 8%. Urban and community affairs organizations, economic development, and environmental affairs.
Education: 14%. Colleges and universities. Interests include business education and education funds.
Health: 1%. Grants are directed toward hospitals, pediatric health, substance abuse care, and single-disease health organizations.
Religion: 2%. Funds religious philanthropic organizations.
Social Services: 70%. Major support to the United Way of the Texas Gulf Coast. Funds youth programs.

Application Procedures

Initial Contact: proposal
Application Requirements: a description of organization, budget, amount requested, purpose of funds sought, recently audited financial statement, copy of 501(c)(3) letter of tax-exempt status, list of board members, and recent contributions
Deadlines: by the 15th of each month
Review Process: committee review system whereby each person receives copies of the requests one week in advance of the meeting
Decision Notification: contributions meetings are held on the last Thursday of the month

Restrictions

Grants are not made to support political or lobbying groups, individuals, or for scholarships. Religious organizations are not supported, except for non-sectarian programs.

Additional Information

In January, 1998, Texas Commerce Bank changed its name to Chase Bank of Texas. The bank's former parent company, Chemical Bank, merged with the Chase Manhattan Corp. in 1995.

Corporate Officials

Alan Roland Buckwalter, III: chief executive officer B New York, NY 1947. ED Fairleigh Dickinson University BA (1970); Stanford University (1985). PRIM CORP EMPL chief executive officer: Chase Bank of Texas. CORP AFFIL director: Western National Corp. NONPR AFFIL director: Salvation Army Houston; trustee: Valley Forge Military Academy & College; director: Houston Symphony; director: American Energy Partners Ltd.; member: ARC. CLUB AFFIL River Oaks Country Club; Sweetwater Country Club; Houston Club; Briar Club; Coronado Club.
Jana Gunter: manager community relations PRIM CORP EMPL manager community relations: Chase Bank of Texas.
Beverly H. McCaskill: secretary PRIM CORP EMPL secretary: Chase Bank of Texas.

Foundation Officials

Alan Roland Buckwalter, III: president (see above)
Jana Gunter: secretary (see above)
Beverly H. McCaskill: vice president, treasurer (see above)
Larry Shyrock: director

Grants Analysis

Disclosure Period: calendar year ending 1997
Total Grants: $249,500*
Number of Grants: 29
Average Grant: $8,604
Highest Grant: $33,000
Typical Range: $100 to $5,000
***Note:** Giving excludes United Way.

Recent Grants

Note: Grants derived from 1997 Form 990.

Arts & Humanities

20,000	Museum of Fine Arts, Houston, TX
10,000	Houston Grand Opera, Houston, TX
5,000	State Preservation Board, Austin, TX

Civic & Public Affairs

33,000	Local Initiatives Support Corporation, Houston, TX
9,000	Association for the Advancement of Mexican Americans, Houston, TX
5,000	Greater Houston Community Foundation, Houston, TX
5,000	Houston Area Women's Center, Houston, TX
5,000	New Hope Housing, Houston, TX

Education

25,000	University of Texas Austin, Austin, TX
20,000	University of Houston, Houston, TX
15,000	South Texas College of Law, Houston, TX
10,000	Baylor College of Medicine, Houston, TX
10,000	Texas A&M University, College Station, TX
5,000	Junior Achievement, Houston, TX
5,000	Texas Southern University, Houston, TX
5,000	University of St. Thomas, Houston, TX
5,000	University of Texas Austin, Austin, TX
5,000	University of Texas Health Sciences, Houston, TX
2,500	Houston Baptist University, Houston, TX
2,000	Rice-Jones Graduate School Partners, Houston, TX

Health

5,000	Memorial Hospital System Foundation, Houston, TX
5,000	Ronald McDonald House, Houston, TX

Religion

10,000	Salvation Army, Houston, TX
5,000	Holocaust Education Center, Houston, TX
3,000	Triangle Ministries, Houston, TX

Social Services

515,000	United Way of the Texas Gulf Coast, Houston, TX
5,000	Big Brothers and Big Sisters, Houston, TX
5,000	Girl Scouts of America San Jacinto Council, Houston, TX
5,000	Star of Hope Recovery Centers, Houston, TX
5,000	YWCA, Houston, TX

Chase Manhattan Bank, NA

Company Contact

New York, NY
Web: http://www.chase.com

Company Description

Employees: 72,700
SIC(s): 6021 National Commercial Banks.
Parent Company: Chase Manhattan Corp.

Operating Locations

Australia: Chemical Australia Securities Ltd., Sydney; Belgium: Chase Manhattan Bank NA Societe de Droit Americain, Brussels, Brabant; Brazil: Banco Chase Manhattan SA, Sao Paulo; Canada: Chase Manhattan Bank of Canada, Toronto; Chemical Bank of Canada, Toronto; Chemical Bank of Canada Lease Inc., Toronto; Chile: Inversiones Chase Manhattan Ltda., Santiago; Cayman Islands: Chemical Intl (Cayman Islands II) Ltd., George Town, Grand Cayman; Chemical Intl (Cayman Islands) Ltd., George Town, Grand Cayman; Chemical Intl Trust Co. Ltd., Grand Cayman; France: Chase Gestion SNC, Paris, Ville-de-Paris; Chase Manhattan Bank NA, Paris, Ville-de-Paris; Chase Manhattan SA, Paris, Ville-de-Paris; Chemical Bank France, Paris, Ville-de-Paris; Germany: CB Trade Services GmbH, Frankfurt, Hessen; Chase Manhattan Bank AG, Frankfurt, Hessen; Chase Manhattan Bank New York Zweigniederlassung Frankfurt am Main, Frankfurt, Hessen; Chase Manhattan Beteiligungs und Verwaltungs GmbH, Frankfurt, Hessen; Chase Manhattan Leasing GmbH, Frankfurt, Hessen; Chemical Bank New York Zweigniederlassung Frankfurt, Frankfurt, Hessen; Hong Kong: Chase Manhattan Financial Services (Hong Kong) Ltd., Causeway Bay; Chase Manhattan Asia Ltd., Central District; Chase Manhattan Investment Services (Hong Kong) Ltd., Central District; Chase Manhattan Trust Co. (Hong Kong) Ltd., Central District; Chemical Asia Ltd., Central District; Chemical Bank, Central District; Chemical Far East Ltd., Central District; Chemical Securities Asia Ltd., Central District; Jordache International (Hong Kong) Ltd., To Kwa Wan, Kowloon; Indonesia: PT Chase Leasing Indonesia, Jakarta, Jakarta Raya; Ireland: Cable Managment (Ireland) Ltd., Dublin; Chase Manhattan Bank (Ireland) Plc, Dublin; Revlon Realistic International Ltd., Dublin; Italy: Chase Manhattan Bank Assoc., Milano, Lombardia; ChaseInvest SpA, Milano, Lombardia; Luxembourg: Capital International Emerging Markets Fund SICAV, Luxembourg; Chase Manhattan Bank Luxembourg SA, Luxembourg; New Europe East Investment Fund SA, Luxembourg; Malaysia: Chase Manhattan Bank (M) BHD, Kuala Lumpur, Selangor; Netherlands: Bancroft Holdings BV, Amsterdam, Noord-Holland; Spain: Chemical Bank CB SA, Bilbao, Pais Vasco; Chase Manhattan Valores Sociedad de Valores SA, Madrid; Corporacion Financiera Chase Manhattan SA, Madrid; Switzerland: Chase Manhattan Private Bank (Switzerland), Geneva; Thailand: Chase Manhattan (Thailand) Ltd., Bangkok; United Kingdom: Trane Ltd., Basingstoke, Hampshire; Chase Bank (Ireland) Plc, Belfast; Chase Manhattan Trustees Ltd., Bournemouth, Dorset; Chemco Equipment Finance Ltd., Cardiff, South Glamorgan; Tantofex (Engineers) Ltd., East Grinstead, West Sussex; Tantofex Ltd., East Grinstead, West Sussex; Chemical Asset Management Ltd., Guernsey, Channel Islands; Chemical Custody (Guernsey) Ltd., Guernsey, Channel Islands; Chemical Holdings (Guernsey) Ltd., Guernsey, Channel Islands; Chemical Investmenst (Guernsey) Ltd., Guernsey, Channel Islands; Chemical Nominees (Guernsey) Ltd., Guernsey, Channel Islands; Chemical Trust (Guernsey) Ltd., Guernsey, Channel Islands; Edwards of Hull Ltd., Hull, North Humberside; Idealstandard Ltd., Hull, North Humberside; Rollosrank Ltd., Hull, North Humberside; Sottini Bathrooms Ltd., Hull, North Humberside; Trevi Showers Ltd., Hull, North Humberside; Chase Bank (Channel Islands) Trust Co. Ltd., Jersey, Channel Islands; Clayton Dewandre Co. Ltd., Leeds, West Yorkshire; Clayton Hydraulics Ltd., Leeds, West Yorkshire; Wabco Automotive Leeds Ltd., Leeds, West Yorkshire; Wabco Automotive UK Ltd., Leeds, West Yorkshire; Perrot Brakes (UK) Ltd., Leicester, Leicestershire; CCP Europe Ltd., London; Chase Asset Management (London) Ltd., London; Chase Capital Financing, London; Chase CS Central Nominees Ltd., London; Chase Export Finance Ltd., London; Chase Manhattan Bank NA, London; Chase Manhattan International Ltd., London; Chase Manhattan Plc, London; Chase Manhattan (United Kingdom) Holdings Ltd., London; Chase Netting (UK) Ltd., London; Chase Nominees Ltd., London; Chembank Depository Nominees Ltd., London; Chembank Nominees Ltd., London; Chemical Bank (UK) Pension Plan Trustee Ltd., London; Chemical Finance Ltd., London; Chemsecurities Ltd., London; Church Commissioners for England (Chase GIS) Nominees Limite, London; CW Property Holdings Ltd., London; Equitable Nominees Ltd., London; Goldway Ltd., London; Laurie Milbank Intl Ltd., London; Littledown Nominees Ltd., London; SGF (UK) Ltd., London; Stanlife Nominees Ltd., London; Texas Commerce Bank NA, London; Trueshare Ltd., London; John Steventon & Sons Ltd., Middlewich, Cheshire; Wabco Automotive Portsmouth Ltd., Portsmouth, Hampshire; American Standard (UK) Co., Rugby, Warwickshire; Wabco Westinghouse Automotive Ltd., Rugby, Warwickshire; City Mortgage Holdings Ltd., Watford, Hertfordshire; City Mortgage Receivables 1 Plc, Watford, Hertfordshire; Bridge Foundry Co. Ltd., Wednesbury, West Midlands

Nonmonetary Support

Value: $2,124,911 (1991); $43,769 (1990); $12,875 (1989)
Type: Donated Equipment; In-kind Services
Note: Co. donates equipment and surplus furniture, and supplies *pro bono* printing.

Chase Manhattan Foundation

Giving Contact

Stephen Gelston
Chase Manhattan Foundation
52 Broadway
New York, NY 10004

Description

EIN: 237049738
Organization Type: Corporate Foundation
Giving Locations: CT; NJ; NY internationally; nationally; primarily headquarters and operating communities.
Grant Types: Award, Capital, Challenge, Department, Employee Matching Gifts, Fellowship, General Support, Multiyear/Continuing Support, Operating Expenses, Professorship, Project.
Note: Employee matching gifts are made to educational and cultural institutions, and for health and human services, housing, and the environment.

Giving Philosophy

'Through its philanthropy program, The Chase Manhattan Corporation aims to enhance the well-being of the communities it serves. Chase understands its responsibilities to its customers, employees, stockholders and the citizenry at large. .. Specific objectives (of the philanthropic program) are: (1.) To improve the quality of life in the communities Chase serves..; (2.) To support the development and promotion of public policies and economic education conducive to growth and community development; (3.) To promote economic development and human well-being in the countries where Chase operates overseas, and to support organizations whose purpose is to foster international understanding; (4.) To encourage charitable giving by the Corporation's employees through matching gift programs; and (5.) To encourage Chase employees to volunteer their non-business time and energies to nonprofit organizations and the people they serve.' *Chase Manhattan Corporate Responsibility Annual Report, Statement of Purpose, 1991*

Financial Summary

Total Giving: $31,339,472 (1997); $19,372,491 (1996); $8,996,887 (1995). Note: Contributes through corporate direct giving program and foundation.

Giving Analysis: Giving for 1996 includes: foundation ($15,116,261); foundation matching gifts ($4,256,230); 1997: foundation ($24,410,544); foundation matching gifts ($6,928,928)
Assets: $52,929,679 (1997); $32,924,078 (1996); $5,095,542 (1995)
Gifts Received: $49,969,314 (1997); $22,788,588 (1996); $12,691,800 (1994). Note: Foundation receives funds from Chase Manhattan Bank and Chase Manhattan Capital Capital Corp.

Typical Recipients

Arts & Humanities: Arts Appreciation, Arts Associations & Councils, Arts Centers, Arts Festivals, Arts Funds, Community Arts, Dance, Ethnic & Folk Arts, Libraries, Literary Arts, Museums/Galleries, Music, Opera, Performing Arts, Public Broadcasting, Theater, Visual Arts
Civic & Public Affairs: African American Affairs, Asian American Affairs, Botanical Gardens/Parks, Business/Free Enterprise, Civil Rights, Economic Development, Economic Policy, Employment/Job Training, Civic & Public Affairs-General, Housing, Law & Justice, Legal Aid, Municipalities/Towns, Nonprofit Management, Philanthropic Organizations, Professional & Trade Associations, Public Policy, Rural Affairs, Safety, Urban & Community Affairs, Women's Affairs
Education: Business Education, Business-School Partnerships, Colleges & Universities, Economic Education, Education Associations, Education Funds, Education Reform, Elementary Education (Private), Engineering/Technological Education, Faculty Development, Education-General, Health & Physical Education, International Studies, Leadership Training, Literacy, Minority Education, Preschool Education, Private Education (Precollege), Public Education (Precollege), Science/Mathematics Education, Special Education, Student Aid, Vocational & Technical Education
Environment: Environment-General, Wildlife Protection
Health: Children's Health/Hospitals, Clinics/Medical Centers, Eyes/Blindness, Geriatric Health, Health Policy/Cost Containment, Health Organizations, Hospitals, Medical Rehabilitation, Public Health, Transplant Networks/Donor Banks
International: Foreign Educational Institutions, Health Care/Hospitals, International Affairs, International Development, International Organizations, International Peace & Security Issues, International Relations
Religion: Churches, Dioceses, Jewish Causes, Ministries, Religious Organizations, Religious Welfare
Science: Science Museums, Scientific Centers & Institutes, Scientific Organizations
Social Services: At-Risk Youth, Child Welfare, Community Centers, Community Service Organizations, Counseling, Day Care, Delinquency & Criminal Rehabilitation, Domestic Violence, Emergency Relief, Family Planning, Family Services, Food/Clothing Distribution, Homes, People with Disabilities, Recreation & Athletics, Scouts, Senior Services, Sexual Abuse, Shelters/Homelessness, Substance Abuse, United Funds/United Ways, Volunteer Services, YMCA/YWCA/YMHA/YWHA, Youth Organizations

Contributions Analysis

Giving Priorities: Social welfare, United Way, health care, education, international organizations, culture and arts, and civics. Contributions to U.S. organizations and contributions of an international nature are made by the Chase Manhattan Corp; contributions to organizations either headquartered outside the United States or seeking funds for programs abroad generally are made by the Chase Manhattan Foundation. Chase considers proposals from organizations in 45 countries. Both general operating and program support are provided in the areas of economic development, aid to children, healthcare and disease prevention, disaster relief, international affairs, the environment, and education. These contributions are monitored at corporate headquarters, but recipients are chosen independently by subsidiaries.
Arts & Humanities: 5%. Major recipients include arts centers and programs in the visual arts. Other support goes to dance and music groups, arts councils, museums, and zoos. The company seeks to support effective arts in education programs, strong audience development and community outreach programs, and programs which encourage the emerging artist and the creative process through the creation and presentation of new work or through the support of developing artists.
Civic & Public Affairs: 34%. A portion of its philanthropic budget goes to stabilize distressed neighborhoods and improve the lives of those community's residents. Focus is on developing housing and jobs for low- and moderate-income people and addressing the diverse needs of the homeless. Other recipients include hospitals, youth organizations, aid to the aged and handicapped, recreation and athletic programs, community service organizations, and employment programs. Recipients include groups concerned with economic development, urban affairs, economic education, and the homeless and hungry. Funds an assortment of nonprofit organizations in the New York area, Connecticut, the U.S. Virgin Islands, and Hong Kong. The grants support local neighborhood projects and nonprofits.
Education: 12%. Supports development funds of colleges and universities. Other interests include graduate and undergraduate education, literacy programs, and minority education. Precollege education is a major priority. The company supports preK-12 programs, primarily in the public school arena, which: provide research and advocacy promoting education reform; develop the leadership skills of school administrators; increase effective pedagogy; or collaborate with schools to address the social, emotional and health needs of children so as to remove barriers to learning. Foundation also sponsors scholarships for children of employees.
Health: 2%. Supports healthcare organizations.
Religion: 4%. Supports religious organizations.
Social Services: 43%. Supports youth and social services and United Way.
Note: Several thousand company employees volunteer in programs serving the communities in which they live and work, in a diverse set of activities that range from serving as mentors for at-risk teenagers to working as 'huggers' for hospital boarder babies, from delivering meals to the homebound elderly to serving on numerous nonprofit boards. Total contributions made in 1997.

Application Procedures

Initial Contact: Send written request for application guidelines.
Application Requirements: Include brief statement of history, goals, and accomplishments; synopsis of current activities; purpose or objective of proposal; amount requested; proof of 501(c)(3) status; current budget showing anticipated expenses and income; current funding sources (and donations); most recently audited financial statement; most recent annual report; number of staff and name and title of highest paid staff member; and list of board of directors.
Deadlines: For arts and culture grants, March 14; for pre-collegiate education, June 9; for community revitalization, June 16; for foundation grants, October 1.
Decision Notification: Foundation board meets three times per year; final notification is within six months; for competitive grants, within three or four months.

Restrictions

Does not support member organizations of the United Way; religious, fraternal, or veterans organizations; political or lobbying groups; dinners, special events, or goodwill advertising; endowment purposes; or individuals except under National Merit Scholarship Program, Educational Testing Service, or Chase Manhattan Foundation.

Additional Information

In 1995, Chase Manhattan Bank and Chemical Bank merged under the name Chase Manhattan Bank.
Contributions are made through one of three programs:
The Chase Manhattan Foundation contributes to organizations outside the tri-state area (New York, New Jersey, and Connecticut) in areas where the company maintains a significant business presence.
Chase Manhattan's corporate responsibility office provides philanthropic and technical support under the Competitive Grants Program to nonprofit organizations in the tri-state area (New York, New Jersey, Connecticut). Areas of concern include culture and art, community revitalization, and pre-college education. Contact: 600 5th Ave., 3rd Fl., New York, NY 10020, (212)332-4100, fax: (212)332-4080.
Chase Manhattan's community relations office develops programs to address community needs and provides assistance to community-based organizations. Contact: 600 5th Ave., 3rd Fl, (212)332-4100, fax: (212)332-4105.
Foundation may make grants to foreign-based organizations that have never applied for, or received, an IRS tax-exempt ruling if applicant organization provides information sufficient to prove that it is a charitable, educational, or scientific organization within the meaning of Section 501(c)(3).
Community-based nonprofit 501(c)(3) organizations located in New York City, Long Island, Dutchess County, Orange County, Putnam County, Rockland County, or Westchester County are eligible for the Neighborhood Grants Program, which provides funds for projects in culture and the arts, education, health and human services, and housing and economic development. The application deadline is mid-February.

Corporate Officials

Richard James Boyle: vice chairman, director B Brooklyn, NY 1943. ED College of the Holy Cross (1965); New York University (1969). PRIM CORP EMPL vice chairman, director: Chase Manhattan Bank, NA.
Thomas Goulet Labrecque: president, chief operating officer, director B Long Branch, NJ 1938. ED Villanova University BA (1960); American University (1962-1964); New York University (1965). PRIM CORP EMPL president, chief operating officer, director: Chase Manhattan Bank, NA ADD CORP EMPL president: Chase Bank Texas; president: Chase Manhattan Corp.; chief executive officer: Chase Manhattan National Holding. CORP AFFIL director: Federal Reserve Bank New York; director: Pfizer Inc.; director: Delphi Automotive Systems Corp. NONPR AFFIL member: Trilateral Commission; treasurer: United Negro College Fund; director: New Visions Public Schools; director: New York Clearing House Association; member: Council Foreign Relations; member board visitors: Duke University Fuqua School Business; trustee: Central Park Conservancy; member: Business Higher Education Forum; member: Business Roundtable; trustee: Brookings Institution; member: Business Council.
Arjun K. Mathruni: executive vice president, chief financial officer B 1945. PRIM CORP EMPL executive vice president, chief financial officer: Chase Manhattan Corp.
Michael Urkowitz: senior vice president B Bronx, NY 1943. ED City University of New York BE (1965); City University of New York MME (1967). PRIM CORP EMPL senior vice president: Chase Manhattan Bank, NA. CORP AFFIL credit card business executive: Chase InfoServ International; director: Master Card United States; director: Cedel SA. NONPR AFFIL member: Pi Tau Sigma; member: Tau Beta Pi; member advisory board: New York City Salvation Army.

James W. Zeigon: executive vice president PRIM CORP EMPL executive vice president: Chase Manhattan Bank, NA.

Giving Program Officials

Steven Gelston: PRIM CORP EMPL contributions officer: Chase Manhattan Bank, NA.

Foundation Officials

Donald L. Boudreau: vice president, trustee B White Plains, NY 1940. ED Pace University (1970). PRIM CORP EMPL executive vice president: Chase Manhattan Bank, NA. NONPR AFFIL trustee: Marymount College; trustee: Pace University.

Richard James Boyle: trustee (see above)

Robert Royal Douglass: trustee B Binghamton, NY 1931. ED Dartmouth College BA (1953); Cornell University LLB (1959). PRIM CORP EMPL counsel: Milbank, Tweed, Hadly & McCloy. CORP AFFIL counsel: Melbank, Tweed, Hadly & McCloy; director: Home Insurance Co.; director: HRE Properties; director: Gryphon Holdings Inc.; director: Gryphon Inc.; chairman: Cedel (Luxembourg). NONPR AFFIL member, board editors: New York Law Journal; member: New York State Bar Association; chairman: Downtown-Lower Manhattan Association; member: American Bar Association; member: Council Foreign Relations; member: Alliance for Downtown New York. CLUB AFFIL World Trade Center Club; Round Hill Club; Seal Harbor Club; Blind Brook Country Club; Century Association.

Anson Wright Elliott: vice president, trustee B New Orleans, LA 1935. ED Princeton University BA (1957); Cornell University MA (1964). PRIM CORP EMPL executive vice president corporate marketing & communications: Chase Manhattan Bank, NA. NONPR AFFIL member government relations council: American Bankers Association; director: Manhattan Institute Public Policy Research.

Michael Patrick Esposito, Jr.: trustee B Hackensack, NJ 1939. ED University of Notre Dame BBA (1961); New York University MBA (1967). PRIM CORP EMPL vice chairman: Inter Atlantic Capital Partners. CORP AFFIL director: Inter Atlantic Securities; director: Risk Capital Reinsurance Co.; director: Forest City Enterprises Inc.; treasurer: Chase Manhattan Overseas Banking; chairman: Exel Ltd.

John B. Evans: assistant secretary, assistant treasurer CORP AFFIL officer: Chase Manhattan Overseas Banking.

Hughlyn F. Fierce: trustee B New York, NY 1935. ED Morgan State University BA (1961); New York University MBA (1967). PRIM CORP EMPL senior vice president: Chase Bank of Arizona. CORP AFFIL vice chairman: Chase Manhattan Overseas Banking. NONPR AFFIL member: American Chamber of Commerce.

David S. Ford: vice president, director

Robert D. Hunter: trustee ED Columbia University; Manhattan College. PRIM CORP EMPL president: Standard & Poors ADD CORP EMPL chairman: Standard & Poors Securities Inc.

Thomas Goulet Labrecque: president (see above)

Maria Elena Lagomasino: trustee PRIM CORP EMPL senior managing director: Chase Manhattan Bank. CORP AFFIL director: Phillips-Van Heusen Corp.

Thomas C. Lynch: trustee PRIM CORP EMPL executive vice president: Chase Manhattan Bank, NA.

Arjun K. Mathruni: trustee (see above)

Arthur Frederick Ryan: trustee B Brooklyn, NY 1942. ED Providence College BA (1963). PRIM CORP EMPL chairman, chief executive officer: The Prudential Insurance Co. of America. CORP AFFIL director, member policy & planning committee, chairman: Depository Trust Co. NONPR AFFIL vice chairman operations division, vice chairman government relations council: American Bankers Association; program manager: CHIPS Same Day Settlement New York Clearing House.

Susan Wylie Schoon: trustee B Brooklyn, IA 1948. ED University of Iowa BA (1970); New York University MBA (1978).

John Vincent Scicutella: trustee B New York, NY 1949. ED Fordham University (1971); Columbia University (1979). PRIM CORP EMPL executive vice president operations: Chase Manhattan Bank, NA. CORP AFFIL chief executive officer: Prudential Insurance of America Inc.

L. Edward Shaw, Jr.: trustee B Elmira, NY 1944. ED Georgetown University BA (1966); Yale University JD (1969). PRIM CORP EMPL general counsel: Aetna Inc. ADD CORP EMPL chief cor officer: National Westminster Bank North America. NONPR AFFIL member: Association Bar New York City; member: Phi Beta Kappa. CLUB AFFIL Winged Foot Golf Club.

Deborah L. Talbot: trustee PRIM CORP EMPL executive vice president, treasurer: Chase Manhattan Bank, NA.

Michael Urkowitz: trustee (see above)

James W. Zeigon: trustee (see above)

Grants Analysis

Disclosure Period: calendar year ending 1997
Total Grants: $24,410,544*
Number of Grants: 1,840 (approx)
Average Grant: $8,215
Highest Grant: $2,099,160
Typical Range: $1,000 to $5,000
*Note: Giving excludes matching gifts.

Recent Grants

Note: Grants derived from 1997 Form 990.

Arts & Humanities

379,200	Public Education Network, NY -- Chase Active Learning National Program
75,000	Whitney Museum of American Art, New York, NY -- first payment on a two-year, $150,000 grant

Civic & Public Affairs

237,500	Greater Jamaica Local Development Corporation, Jamaica, NY
215,000	Central Brooklyn Partnership, Brooklyn, NY
175,000	ACCION, New York, NY
160,000	Nonprofit Facilities Fund, New York, NY
150,000	Corporation for Supportive Housing, New York, NY
150,000	Enterprise Foundation, Columbia, MD
135,000	Parodneck Foundation for Self-Help Housing and Community Development, New York, NY
120,000	Community Loan Fund, Trenton, NJ
110,000	ACORN Housing Corporation, Chicago, IL
100,000	Capital District Community Loan Fund, Albany, NY
100,000	Low-Income Housing Fund, NY
100,000	Neighborhood Housing Services, New York, NY
95,000	Habitat for Humanity International, Denver, CO -- for Brazil, Colombia, Ecuador, Egypt, Korea, Mexico, Peru, the Philippines, and Thailand
87,500	Washington Heights and Inwood Development Corporation, New York, NY
85,000	Brookings Institution, Washington, DC
85,000	Connecticut Housing Investment Fund, Hartford, CT
82,500	Syracuse Neighborhood Housing Services, Syracuse, NY
80,200	Women's Venture Fund, New York, NY
75,000	American Enterprise Institute for Public Policy Research, Washington, DC
75,000	BEC New Communities HDFC, NY
75,000	First State Community Loan Fund, Wilmington, DE -- Community Development Financial Institution Award
75,000	Greater New Haven Community Loan Fund, New Haven, CT
75,000	National Federation of Community Development Credit Unions, New York, NY
65,000	CCRP, New York, NY
65,000	Credit, Inc., Bronx, NY
63,500	Housing Development Assistance Fund, Stamford, CT
60,000	Good Old Lower East Side, New York, NY
57,500	Union County Economic Development Corporation, Union, NJ
55,000	City Parks Foundation, New York, NY

Education

300,000	Newark School District, Newark, NJ -- Principals Leadership Institute
265,000	New Visions for Public Schools, New York, NY -- Chase Active Learning Program VII
150,000	New Visions for Public Schools, New York, NY -- second payment on a $750,000 grant
115,000	Union Settlement Association, New York, NY
100,000	Inner-City Scholarship Fund, New York, NY
100,000	New Visions for Public Schools, New York, NY -- second payment on a $500,000 grant

Health

100,000	New York Hospital-Cornell Medical Center Fund, New York, NY -- second payment on a $500,000 grant
100,000	Primary Care Development Corporation, New York, NY

International

100,000	Peace Corps, New York, NY -- for Chile, China, the Czech Republic, Ecuador, Panama, the Philippines, Poland, Romania, Russia, South Africa, Thailand, and Uzbekistan
100,000	Peace Corps, New York, NY -- for Chile, China, the Czech Republic, Ecuador, Panama, the Philippines, Poland, Romania, Russia, South Africa, Thailand, and Uzbekistan

Religion

135,000	Leviticus 25:21 Alternative Fund, NY
100,000	Second Congregational Church -- for Heart Care International-Guatemala
85,000	Catholic Charities Diocese of Brooklyn/ Queens, New York, NY -- first payment on a three-year, $250,000 grant

Social Services

2,099,160	United Way of Tri-State, New York, NY
1,081,880	United Way of Tri-State, NJ
218,960	United Way of Tri-State, CT
100,000	Cooperative Fund of New England, CT
100,000	United Way, Rochester, NY
62,500	Phoenix House Development Fund, New York, NY -- first payment on a four-year, $250,000 grant
60,000	Boys Club, New York, NY -- first payment on a five-year, $260,000 grant

CHEMED CORP.

Company Contact

Cincinnati, OH

Company Description

Employees: 7,671
SIC(s): 2841 Soap & Other Detergents, 3842 Surgical Appliances & Supplies, 4952 Sewerage Systems, 5047 Medical & Hospital Equipment.

Nonmonetary Support

Type: Donated Equipment; In-kind Services

Chemed Foundation

Giving Contact

Sandra E. Laney, President & Director
255 East 5th Street, Suite 2600
Cincinnati, OH 45202
Phone: (513)721-4300

Description

Founded: 1993
EIN: 311326421
Organization Type: Corporate Foundation
Giving Locations: headquarters and operating communities.
Grant Types: Capital, General Support, Operating Expenses, Project, Scholarship, Seed Money.

Financial Summary

Total Giving: $225,000 (2000 approx); $325,000 (1999 approx); $203,906 (1998)
Giving Analysis: Giving for 1997 includes: foundation grants to United Way ($8,600); foundation gifts to individuals ($150); 1998: foundation ($192,706); foundation grants to United Way ($11,200)
Assets: $3,042,524 (1998); $3,306,084 (1997); $2,836,266 (1996)
Gifts Received: $200,102 (1998); $106,000 (1997); $201,398 (1996). Note: In 1997 and 1998, contributions were received from the Chemed Corp.

Typical Recipients

Arts & Humanities: Arts Funds, Arts & Humanities-General, Museums/Galleries, Music, Opera, Public Broadcasting, Theater
Civic & Public Affairs: Botanical Gardens/Parks, Civic & Public Affairs-General, Housing, Zoos/Aquariums
Education: Arts/Humanities Education, Business Education, Colleges & Universities, Education-General, Private Education (Precollege), Public Education (Precollege), Student Aid
Environment: Environment-General
Health: Cancer, Children's Health/Hospitals, Emergency/Ambulance Services, Eyes/Blindness, Health-General, Single-Disease Health Associations, Speech & Hearing
Religion: Churches, Religion-General, Religious Organizations, Religious Welfare, Social/Policy Issues
Social Services: Child Welfare, Counseling, Day Care, Emergency Relief, Family Services, Food/Clothing Distribution, People with Disabilities, Shelters/Homelessness, Social Services-General, United Funds/United Ways, YMCA/YWCA/YMHA/YWHA

Contributions Analysis

Arts & Humanities: 15%. Supports arts funds, public broadcasting, and the performing arts.
Civic & Public Affairs: 9%. Funds housing and parks.
Education: 50%. Higher education and pre-college enrichment programs are funded.
Environment: 21%. Supports conservation.
Health: 2%.
Religion: 1%.
Social Services: 2%.
Note: Total contributions in 1998.

Application Procedures

Initial Contact: Send a brief letter of inquiry and a full proposal.
Application Requirements: Include a description of organization, amount requested, purpose of funds sought, a financial analysis of the project, and the person in charge of the project.
Deadlines: None.

Restrictions

Does not support individuals or national organizations.

Corporate Officials

Edward L. Hutton: chairman, chief executive officer, director director B Bedford, IN 1919. ED Indiana University BS (1940); Indiana University MS (1941). PRIM CORP EMPL chairman, chief executive officer, director: Chemed Corp. CORP AFFIL chairman, director: Omnicare; chairman, director: National Sanitary Supply Co. NONPR AFFIL member, government board director: American Association University Professors; co-chairman: President Private Sector Survey Cost Control. CLUB AFFIL University Club; Princeton Club; Queen City Club; Bankers Club; Economic Club.
Kevin J. McNamara: president, director B Cleveland, OH 1953. ED Denison University (1975); Cornell University (1978). PRIM CORP EMPL president, director: Chemed Corp. CORP AFFIL director: Omnicare; secretary, general couns, director: Roto-Rooter; assistant secretary, general couns, director: National Sanitary Supply Co.
Timothy S. O'Toole: executive vice president, treasurer, director PRIM CORP EMPL executive vice president, treasurer, director: Chemed Corp.

Foundation Officials

Thomas C. Hutton, Esq.: director
Sandra E. Laney: president PRIM CORP EMPL vice president, administration officer: Chemed Corp.
David J. Lohbeck: treasurer
Kevin J. McNamara: secretary, trustee (see above)
Paul C. Voet: trustee B Cincinnati, OH 1946. ED University of Cincinnati BA (1968); University of Pennsylvania MBA (1970). PRIM CORP EMPL president, chief executive officer, director: National Sanitary Supply Co. CORP AFFIL executive vice president, director: Chemed Corp. NONPR AFFIL member: Phi Eta Sigma; member: Young President Association; member: Phi Alpha Theta; member: Phi Beta Kappa; member: Beta Gamma Sigma; member: Omicron Delta Epsilon; member: American Management Association.

Grants Analysis

Disclosure Period: calendar year ending 1998
Total Grants: $192,706*
Number of Grants: 99
Average Grant: $1,947
Highest Grant: $50,000
Typical Range: $200 to $5,000
*Note: Giving excludes United Way.

Recent Grants

Note: Grants derived from 1998 Form 990.

Arts & Humanities

6,529	Cincinnati Symphony Orchestra, Cincinnati, OH -- 1997-1998 Sponsorship
5,000	The Cam Cameron Show, New Albany, IN -- Cam Cameron Show Advertising
5,000	Crouse Entertainment Group, Lake Forest, IL -- An American Story: One Town's Journey (Documentary)
5,000	Fine Arts Fund, Cincinnati, OH -- Program Support
4,000	Cincinnati Opera, Cincinnati, OH -- Program Support
1,000	WCET, Channel 48, Cincinnati, OH -- Fund for Children's Programming
750	WVXU, Cincinnati, OH -- Program Support
300	Children's Theater, Cincinnati, OH -- Endowment Campaign

Civic & Public Affairs

12,500	Cincinnati Zoo & Botanical Garden, Cincinnati, OH -- Circle of Life Campaign
1,500	Cincinnati Habitat for Humanity, Hamilton, OH -- Program Support
1,500	Southwestern Ohio & Northern Kentucky Habitat for Humanity, Cincinnati, OH -- Program Support

Education

50,000	Indiana University Foundation, Bloomington, IN -- Walt Robbins/Ed Hutton Scholarship
6,667	Thomas More College, Crestview Hills, KY -- 1996 Capital Campaign
6,000	Cumberland College, Williamsburg, KY -- Townhouse 2
5,650	Cumberland College, Williamsburg, KY -- Townhouse 1
5,000	Indiana University Foundation, Bloomington, IN -- Neal Gilliatt Scholarship Fund
5,000	Lower Price Hill Community School, Cincinnati, OH -- Program Support
4,200	U.C. College of Nursing & Health, Cincinnati, OH -- Scholarship Fund
1,500	U.C. Foundation, Cincinnati, OH -- Annual Business Campaign
1,200	Junior Achievement, Cincinnati, OH -- Program Support
1,000	Hebrew Union College, Cincinnati, OH -- Annual Tribute Dinner
1,000	U.C.Foundation, Cincinnati, OH -- Campaign for the Campus
750	College of Mt. St. Joseph, Cincinnati, OH -- Annual Fund
750	U.C.Foundation, Cincinnati, OH -- Friends of CCM
600	Art Academy of Cincinnati, Cincinnati, OH -- Program Support
550	Springer School, Cincinnati, OH -- Program Support
500	Junior Achievement, Cincinnati, OH -- Tri-State Leaders' Classic
500	U.C. College of Nursing & Health, Cincinnati, OH -- Florence Nightingale Banquet
250	Catholic Inner-City Schools Educational Fund, Cincinnati, OH -- Corporate Campaign
250	College of Mt. St. Joseph, Cincinnati, OH -- Student Center Fund

Environment

20,000	Community Land Cooperative, Cincinnati, OH -- Rehab Chemed VI
17,500	Community Land Cooperative, Cincinnati, OH -- Rehab Chemed V
500	Cincinnati Nature Center, Milford, OH -- Gorman Heritage Farm

Health

1,250	American Cancer Society, Cincinnati, OH -- Program Support
1,000	Children's Hospital Medical Center, Cincinnati, OH -- Campaign for Children
1,000	Cincinnati Speech & Hearing Center, Cincinnati, OH -- Program Support
1,000	Prevent Blindness, Cincinnati, OH -- People of Vision Award

Religion

1,500	National Conference of Christians & Jews, Cincinnati, OH -- Annual Awards Dinner
1,000	White Oak Christian Church, Cincinnati, OH -- FBO Jill Wilson

Social Services

1,000	Freestore Foodbank, Cincinnati, OH -- Program Support
500	YMCA of Greater Cincinnati, Cincinnati, OH -- Summer Camp Program
500	YWCA, Cincinnati, OH -- Capital Campaign
400	Family Service of Cincinnati, Cincinnati, OH -- Friends '98 Campaign
300	Neediest Kids of All, Cincinnati, OH -- Program Support

250 Drop Inn Shelterhouse, Cincinnati, OH -- Holiday Fund

CHESAPEAKE CORP.

Company Contact
Richmond, VA
Web: http://www.cskcorp.com

Company Description
Employees: 5,557
SIC(s): 2435 Hardwood Veneer & Plywood, 2621 Paper Mills, 2631 Paperboard Mills, 2653 Corrugated & Solid Fiber Boxes.

Operating Locations
Canada: Chesapeake Display & Packaging (Canada) Ltd., Toronto; France: Chesapeake Coffrets, Ezy Sur Eure, Eure; Plastiphane, Migennes, Yonne; Chesapeake Europe SA, Paris, Ville-de-Paris; Raab Pige, St. Pierre des Corps

Nonmonetary Support
Note: Co. provides nonmonetary support to nonprofits.

Corporate Sponsorship
Type: Arts & cultural events
Contact: J. Causey, Foundation President

Chesapeake Corp. Foundation

Giving Contact
Louis Matherne, Secretary & Treasurer
Chesapeake Corp. Foundation
PO Box 2350
Richmond, VA 23218-2350
Phone: (804)697-1000
Fax: (804)697-1199

Alternate Contact
Fran Boroughs, Assistant Secretary

Description
EIN: 540605823
Organization Type: Corporate Foundation
Giving Locations: operating locations.
Grant Types: Capital, Employee Matching Gifts, Scholarship.

Giving Philosophy
'Chesapeake Corporation Foundation was established in 1955 for the distribution of educational and philanthropic funds for Chesapeake Corporation.. The Foundation has a limited budget and its areas of interest are primarily oriented toward organizations where the majority of the corporation's employees and their families live, work, and procure their educational, medical and social services. A budget is adopted annually in January to include those projects and organizations to which the Foundation contributes regularly: scholarships; direct educational contributions to elementary, secondary and higher educational institutions and associations; health and medical service organizations; community service and cultural organizations. Capital improvement grants are considered in limited amounts for specific medical, social, scientific, educational, and cultural or historical endeavors.' *Chesapeake Corporation Foundation Fields of Interest and Guidelines for Submitting Proposals*

Financial Summary
Total Giving: $300,000 (2000 approx); $500,000 (1999 approx); $583,195 (1998). Note: Contributes through corporate direct giving program and foundation.
Giving Analysis: Giving for 1996 includes: foundation ($443,984); foundation grants to United Way ($82,500); foundation matching gifts ($59,154); 1997: foundation ($434,882); foundation grants to United Way ($113,250); foundation matching gifts ($72,816); 1998: foundation ($345,450); foundation grants to United Way ($101,450); foundation scholarships ($73,366); foundation matching gifts ($62,929)
Assets: $1,981,116 (1998); $1,938,931 (1997); $2,497,614 (1996)
Gifts Received: $600,000 (1999 approx); $540,000 (1998); $512,500 (1996). Note: Contributions are received from the Chesapeake Corporation.

Typical Recipients
Arts & Humanities: Arts Associations & Councils, Arts Funds, Community Arts, Historic Preservation, History & Archaeology, Libraries, Museums/Galleries, Music, Theater
Civic & Public Affairs: African American Affairs, Asian American Affairs, Botanical Gardens/Parks, Community Foundations, Economic Development, Employment/Job Training, Housing, Municipalities/ Towns, Nonprofit Management, Philanthropic Organizations, Professional & Trade Associations, Public Policy, Safety, Urban & Community Affairs
Education: Agricultural Education, Business Education, Colleges & Universities, Community & Junior Colleges, Continuing Education, Education Associations, Education Funds, Engineering/Technological Education, Environmental Education, Education-General, Literacy, Minority Education, Private Education (Precollege), Public Education (Precollege), School Volunteerism, Science/Mathematics Education, Secondary Education (Private), Special Education, Student Aid, Vocational & Technical Education
Environment: Air/Water Quality, Forestry, Environment-General, Resource Conservation
Health: Children's Health/Hospitals, Diabetes, Emergency/Ambulance Services, Health Organizations, Hospitals, Medical Rehabilitation, Mental Health, Research/Studies Institutes
International: Health Care/Hospitals, International Relief Efforts
Religion: Religious Welfare
Science: Observatories & Planetariums, Science Museums, Scientific Centers & Institutes
Social Services: Community Service Organizations, Domestic Violence, Family Services, Homes, People with Disabilities, Recreation & Athletics, Scouts, Scouts, United Funds/United Ways, YMCA/YWCA/ YMHA/YWHA, Youth Organizations

Contributions Analysis
Giving Priorities: Education, United Way, food banks, civic organizations, health care, and art funds. Has supported international relief efforts.
Arts & Humanities: 5%. Funding emphasizes libraries, museums, and historical societies. Funds also support arts councils, symphonies, and theater groups.
Civic & Public Affairs: 8%. Grants support environmental projects, housing coalitions, fire departments, and other community services.
Education: 34%. Funding supports colleges, universities, educational funds and trusts, education councils, scholarship services, high schools, and various educational programs. In addition, foundation has a matching funds program.
Health: 8%. Foundation supports hospitals, health councils, general health organizations, and single-disease associations.
Social Services: 35%. The vast majority of these funds go to United Way organizations in various communities. Other recipients include children's recreational groups, food banks, and animal protection organizations.
Note: Total contributions in 1998.

Application Procedures
Initial Contact: Send a letter of inquiry with a brief statement of the applicant's need for funds.
Application Requirements: Include specific purpose of request and results sought; budget for project including the month in which it is requested that the grant be paid; recently audited financial statement; personnel involved in project; members of governing body; amounts requested from other funding sources; evidence of tax-exempt status; statement that application has been reviewed and approved by organization's governing body.
Deadlines: December 1; foundation trustees meet in January.
Decision Notification: Decisions are made at trustee meetings; secretary attempts to promptly notify organizations that do not fall within the foundation's scope.
Notes: Applications for operating grants should be for amounts not less than $1,000. Applications for capital grants should be for amounts not less than $5,000 and should not be payable over more than five years.

Restrictions
Foundation does not support individuals, organizations which are not tax-exempt under IRS standards, athletic organizations or events, or organizations outside the foundation's geographical or philosophical areas of responsibility.

Additional Information
After the organization has received a grant, the Foundation requires an accounting of the distribution of funds and recent financial statements.
The Foundation reviews all specific requests for funds but does not respond to routine fund-raising appeals. A budget for the year is finalized in January and includes grants to education, health, community service, and cultural organizations to which the foundation regularly contributes.
Company gives directly through marketing or public affairs departments within each operating group.

Corporate Officials
Christopher R. Burgess: assistant vice president PRIM CORP EMPL assistant vice president: Chesapeake Corp.
John Paul Causey, Jr.: senior vice president, secretary, general counsel B Takoma Park, MD 1943. ED Davidson College AB (1965); University of Richmond TC Williams School of Law JD (1968). PRIM CORP EMPL senior vice president, secretary, general counsel: Chesapeake Corp. NONPR AFFIL member: American Corporate Counsel Association; member: American Society of Corporate Secretaries.
Joseph Carter Fox: chairman, president, chief executive officer B Petersburg, VA 1939. ED Washington & Lee University BS (1961); University of Virginia MBA (1963). PRIM CORP EMPL chairman, president, chief executive officer: Chesapeake Corp. CORP AFFIL director: Crestar Financial Corp. NONPR AFFIL director: American Forest & Paper Association.
Louis K. Matherne: treasurer B Brownsville, TN 1951. ED University of Virginia (1973); University of Pennsylvania (1978). PRIM CORP EMPL treasurer: Chesapeake Corp.

Foundation Officials
John Paul Causey, Jr.: chairman, trustee (see above)
Charles Sal Cianciola: trustee B Milwaukee, WI 1933. ED Lawrence University BS (1955). CORP AFFIL director: Associate First Bank of Neenah. CLUB AFFIL Viking Beach Club; Elks Club.
T. G. Harris: trustee
Bruce M. Pinover: trustee PRIM CORP EMPL vice president: Chesapeake Display & Packaging Co.
Brenda L. Skidmore: trustee
E. Massey Valentine: trustee ED University of Virginia (1956).

Grants Analysis
Disclosure Period: calendar year ending 1998
Total Grants: $345,450*

Number of Grants: 92
Average Grant: $3,755
Highest Grant: $37,500
Typical Range: $1,000 to $10,000
***Note:** Giving excludes matching gifts; scholarship; United Way.

Recent Grants

Note: Grants derived from 1998 Form 990.

Arts & Humanities

5,000	Bergstrom-Mahler Museum, Neenah, WI
5,000	Virginia Foundation for the Humanities, Charlottesville, VA
3,500	The Elis Olsson Memorial Library Fund, West Point, VA
3,000	Arts Council of Winston-Salem, Winston-Salem, NC
2,500	Fox Cities Children's Museum, Fox Cities, WI

Civic & Public Affairs

7,500	Town of Menasha Fire Department, Menasha, WI
5,000	Hmong-American Partnership, Minneapolis, MN
5,000	Menasha Action Council, Providing Vision for Tomorrow, Menasha, WI
4,500	Habitat for Humanity, Richmond, VA
3,000	Richmond Renaissance, Richmond, VA
2,700	Wayne County Foundation, Richmond, VA

Education

37,500	Virginia Commonwealth University Foundation, Richmond, VA
20,000	Menasha Joint School District, Menasha, WI
12,500	Holiday Lake 4-H Education Center, Inc., VA
10,000	Johnson & Wales University, Providence, RI
7,500	Virginia Foundation for Independent Colleges, Richmond, VA
5,000	Boone County Education Foundation, Boone, KY
5,000	Lakeland College Kellett Center for Lifelong Learning, Sheboygar, WI
5,000	St. Mary Central High School, Menasha, WI
5,000	University of Wisconsin - Fox Valley Planetarium, Appleton, WI
3,500	Lawrence University, Appleton, WI
3,000	Junior Achievement of Neenah/Menasha, Neenah, WI
3,000	United Negro College Fund (St. Paul's and Virginia Union), Richmond, VA
2,500	Christa McAuliffe Academy, Yakima, WA
2,500	Menasha Education Endowment Fund, Menasha, WI
2,500	University of Wisconsin - Oshkosh College of Business Administration, Osh Kosh, WI
2,500	The Virginia College Fund, Richmond, VA

Environment

10,000	Chesapeake Bay Foundation, Annapolis, MO
2,500	Natural Resources Foundation of Wisconsin, Inc., Madison, WI

Health

7,500	Parent-Child Development Center, West Point, VA
5,000	American Red Cross, West Point, VA
5,000	Dream Catchers Therapeutic Riding, Conway, SC
5,000	Juvenile Diabetes Foundation, VA
5,000	St. Elizabeth Hospital Community Foundation, Appleton, WI
3,000	American Red Cross, West Point, VA
2,500	Children's Hospital, Richmond, VA

Science

20,000	Science Museum of Virginia, Richmond, VA

Social Services

53,000	Fox Cities, Fox Cities, WI
11,500	Forsyth County, Winston-Salem, NC
10,000	Bay-Lakes Council, BSA, Minneapolis, MN
8,000	Broome County, NY
7,500	Youth Sports, Lawrence, KS
5,000	Flagstaff / Bellmont, Flagstaff, AZ
5,000	Goodwill Industries of North Central Wisconsin, Menasha, WI
5,000	Regional Domestic Abuse Services, Neenah, WI
5,000	United Community Services, Inc., Neenah, WI
4,500	Greater Richmond, Richmond, VA
3,500	Tri-County, Queensbury, NY
3,000	Appleton Ice, Appleton, WI
1,000	Boys' and Girls' Brigade, Neenah, WI

CHEVRON CORP.

 Number 42 of Top 100 Corporate Givers

Company Contact

San Francisco, CA
Web: http://www.chevron.com/community

Company Description

Revenue: US$26,801,000,000
Profit: US$1,976,000,000
Employees: 34,000
Fortune Rank: 35, per FORTUNE Magazine's list of 500 Largest U.S. Corporations (1999).
FF 35
SIC(s): 1311 Crude Petroleum & Natural Gas, 1382 Oil & Gas Exploration Services, 2911 Petroleum Refining, 2992 Lubricating Oils & Greases.

Operating Locations

Belgium: Chevron Corp., Brussels, Brabant; Brazil: Chevron do Brasil Ltda., Sao Paulo; Canada: Chevron Chemical (Canada) Ltd., Burlington; Chevron Canada Enterprises Ltd., Calgary; Chevron Canada Resources Ltd., Calgary; Chevron Hibernia Holding Co. Ltd., Calgary; Chevron Standard Ltd., Calgary; Cornwallis Arctic Oils Ltd., Calgary; Chevron Canada Ltd., Vancouver; Cote d'Ivoire: Chevron International Trading Company, Abidjan; Ecuador: Plastigama SA, Guayaquil, Guayas; France: Chevron Chemical SA, Neuilly-sur-Seine; Germany: Chevron Chemical GmbH, Frankfurt, Hessen; Chevron Germany Zweigniederlassung Fuer Deutschland, Hamburg; Netherlands: Chevron Centrale Laboratoria BV, Rijswijk, Zuid-Holland; Norway: Norwegian Gulf Exploration Co. AS, Oslo, Akershus; Spain: Chevron Oil SA, Barcelona, Cataluna; United Kingdom: Action Services Stations Ltd., Cheltenham, Gloucestershire; Britama Tankers Ltd., Cheltenham, Gloucestershire; Chevron & Gulf UK Pension Plan Trustee Co. Ltd., Cheltenham, Gloucestershire; Curran Petroleum Ltd., Cheltenham, Gloucestershire; Gulf Oil (Great Britain) Ltd., Cheltenham, Gloucestershire; Sovereign Pension Trustees Ltd., Cheltenham, Gloucestershire; Perlmans Petroleum Ltd., Hereford, Hereford & Worcester; De La Pena Lubricants Ltd., Liverpool, Merseyside; Telegraph Garages Ltd., Liverpool, Merseyside; Telegraph Service Stations Ltd., Liverpool, Merseyside; Chevron Europe Ltd., London; Chevron International Oil Co. Ltd., London; Chevron Petroleum Co. Ltd., London; Chevron UK Ltd., London; Chevron United Kingdom Offshore Investments Ltd., London; Gulf Oil (Ireland) Ltd., London; Gulf Service Stations Ltd., London; Gulf Oil Refining Ltd., Milford Haven, Dyfed; Kimreel Ltd., Stockport, Cheshire; Montland Ltd., Stockport, Cheshire; Venezuela: Chevron Global Technology Service Co., Caracas

Nonmonetary Support

Value: $700,000 (1996); $2,700,000 (1995); $395,341 (1992)
Type: Donated Equipment
Note: Equipment is book value. Chevron has also donated land. Contact Chevron operating locations for local nonmonetary support.

Giving Contact

Skip Rhodes, Jr., Manager, Corporate Contributions
Chevron Corp.
575 Market St.
San Francisco, CA 94105
Phone: (415)894-7700
Fax: (415)894-5447
Note: Mr. Rhodes handles applications for national and international organizations.

Alternate Contact

Mylene Chan
Phone: (415)894-4616

Description

Organization Type: Corporate Giving Program
Giving Locations: corporate operating locations nationally and internationally.
Grant Types: Award, Employee Matching Gifts, General Support.
Note: Employee/director/retiree matching programs are available for educational institutions and arts and cultural organisation. Gifts to higher educational institutions will be matched up to $5,000 for employees, and up to $1,000 for retirees. Arts-related cultural gifts and gifts to precollege educational institutions will be matched up to $500 per individual annually.

Giving Philosophy

'At Chevron, our concern for the communities in which we operate extends far beyond our own employees and plant gates. We know that a vibrant community is one of the major factors attracting a top-notch workforce, resulting in a burgeoning local economy and a more successful business environment overall. By contributing to these communities, we are investing in our future. Besides dollars, we contribute the time and talent of our employees as well as encourage their active participation as volunteers.' *Values In Action,* Chevron Corporation philanthropy report

Financial Summary

Total Giving: $21,000,000 (2001 approx); $21,000,000 (2000 approx); $20,900,000 (1999 approx). Note: Contributes through corporate direct giving program only. Giving includes corporate direct giving; domestic and international subsidiaries; nonmonetary support.
Assets: $34,300,000 (1995 approx); $34,400,000 (1994 approx)

Typical Recipients

Arts & Humanities: Arts Associations & Councils, Arts Centers, Arts Festivals, Arts Funds, Ballet, Community Arts, Dance, Film & Video, Historic Preservation, Libraries, Museums/Galleries, Music, Opera, Performing Arts, Public Broadcasting, Theater
Civic & Public Affairs: African American Affairs, Business/Free Enterprise, Economic Development, Economic Policy, Employment/Job Training, Hispanic Affairs, Housing, Law & Justice, Legal Aid, Municipalities/Towns, Nonprofit Management, Professional & Trade Associations, Public Policy, Rural Affairs, Safety, Urban & Community Affairs, Women's Affairs, Zoos/Aquariums
Education: Agricultural Education, Arts/Humanities Education, Business Education, Colleges & Universities, Economic Education, Education Associations,

Education Funds, Education Reform, Elementary Education (Private), Engineering/Technological Education, Faculty Development, Education-General, International Studies, Journalism/Media Education, Literacy, Minority Education, Public Education (Precollege), Science/Mathematics Education, Student Aid
Environment: Environment-General, Resource Conservation, Wildlife Protection
Health: AIDS/HIV, Clinics/Medical Centers, Emergency/Ambulance Services, Health Policy/Cost Containment, Health Funds, Health Organizations, Hospices, Hospitals, Medical Rehabilitation, Mental Health, Public Health, Single-Disease Health Associations
International: Foreign Educational Institutions, Health Care/Hospitals, International Affairs, International Environmental Issues, International Peace & Security Issues, International Relations, International Relief Efforts
Science: Observatories & Planetariums, Science Exhibits & Fairs, Scientific Centers & Institutes, Scientific Organizations
Social Services: Child Welfare, Community Centers, Community Service Organizations, Crime Prevention, Day Care, Delinquency & Criminal Rehabilitation, Domestic Violence, Emergency Relief, Family Services, Food/Clothing Distribution, Homes, People with Disabilities, Refugee Assistance, Senior Services, Shelters/Homelessness, Substance Abuse, United Funds/United Ways, Volunteer Services, Youth Organizations

Contributions Analysis

Giving Priorities: Education and environmental concerns. Chevron supports U.S.-based nonprofit organizations with an international focus and organizations located in foreign operating locations. Requests for contributions from international organizations based in the United States are handled at corporate headquarters. Requests from foreign organizations are handled by the appropriate operating company. Budgets are formulated at headquarters for domestic and international subsidiaries.
Arts & Humanities: 5% to 10%. Supports visual, literary, performing arts and cultural institutions in communities where company has significant operations, principally in California. Also supports local arts funds and councils, community concerts, historic preservation, libraries, national and regional art associations, cultural centers, and theaters.
Civic & Public Affairs: About 15%. Contributes to policy research and planning organizations and business/free enterprise groups; organizations that deal with individual initiatives, volunteerism, and philanthropy; and groups that promote community involvement and civic pride, law and justice, better government, and public safety. Other interests include urban planning and development programs and agriculturalexpositions and fairs.
Education: 35% to 40%. Colleges and universities in fields of science, engineering, computer science, business, economics, communications, human resource development, equal access and quality in schools, and other disciplines of interest to the company. Funds are for scholarships, fellowships, department support, and research. Also supports a variety ofeducational organizations and funds. While most contributions continue to go to higher education, support for targeted programs that improve the quality of public education at the primary and secondary levels is increasing. Provides support for disadvantaged and under-represented minority students requiring accelerated instruction in grades K-12. Also matches gifts to education.
Environment: 5% to 10%. Supports conservation programs, wildlife preservation, and environmental education, primarily in California. Includes grants to educational and research institutions withemphasis on environmental affairs. Administers the Chevron Conservation Awards Program in a variety of locations nationwide.
Health: 20% to 25%. Youth organizations; united funds; social welfare organizations that meet the needs of the homeless and abused and neglected children; groups that promote equal opportunity, equity,and access to the mainstream of society; job-readiness and employment programs; and programs targeted to the elderly. Health funding emphasizes hospitals and various local health organizations.
Note: International giving is included in above categories.

Application Procedures

Initial Contact: For Chevron Community Grant, contact a local Chevron field staff representative; for Chevron Corporate Grant, contact J. W. Rhodes, Jr., for application.
Application Requirements: For Chevron Corporate Grant: application form; mission statement; purpose of the program for which support is sought; amount requested with rationale; schedule for implementing project; population served; evaluation plan and method of reporting results; brief qualifications of key staff; names/affiliations of board members; evidence of sound management practices and reasonable fund-raising/staffing costs; evidence of organization's 501(c)(3) status.
Deadlines: For Chevron Corporate Grants: March 1 for announcement date of May 31, July 1 for September 30, November 1 for January 31; for Chevron Community Grants: None.
Decision Notification: Within three months for Community Grants; generally two months after the application deadline for Corporate Grants.
Notes: All funds have been allocated through 2001.

Restrictions

Chevron is currently not accepting grant requests from states in the North Central and Northeastern sections of the U.S.
Chevron does not support individuals; religious, veterans, labor, fraternal, athletic, or political organizations; capital funds for buildings or equipment; endowment funds; operating expenses for organizations receiving support through the United Way; school-related bands and sports events; national health, medical, and human service organizations; travel funds; fund-raising events or benefit tickets; courtesy advertising; secondary funding where funds are pooled to make contributions to others; product requests; conferences or seminars; or freelance films or videos.
The company has recently narrowed its focus to the areas of education and the environment. Other areas may be considered via the Chevron Community Grant, if the request is beneficial to the company's operating areas.
Chevron also sponsors to Chevron Conservation Awards program to recognize outstanding contributions of individuals and organizations to the conservation of natural resources.

Additional Information

Funds have been allocated through 2001. No applications will be accepted until then.
When grants are approved, Chevron requires recipients to sign grant agreements which state that financial and progress reports will be submitted to Chevron to help it monitor the effectiveness of its program. Chevron also requires completion of a substantiation form for grants totaling $250 or more.
Please do not send video or audio tapes. Submitted materials will not be returned.
No organization board members may receive compensation for their services.
If request is for support in a specific community where Chevron operates, apply for a Chevron Community Grant. Grants that support education or the environment will be given priority, but proposals outside these areas that will be beneficial to Chevron's communities or employees are welcome. Only some field offices may require a completed application form; however, it is recommended for use as a guide for proposals.
If funding is sought for the environment or education, and it is broad in scope, requests for a Chevron Investment Grant application form should be made. Unsolicited proposals outside these two areas of emphasis are not encouraged by this grant program.
Publications: Philanthropy Report

Corporate Officials

Lydia I. Beebe: corporate secretary B McPherson, KS 1952. ED University of Kansas (1974); Golden Gate University (1980). PRIM CORP EMPL corporate secretary: Chevron Corp.
Aldo M. Caccamo: vice president public affairs B 1937. ED New Jersey Institute of Technology (1960); Harvard Business School (1964). PRIM CORP EMPL vice president public affairs: Chevron Corp. CORP AFFIL director: Caltex Petroleum Corp. NONPR AFFIL director: San Francisco Chamber of Commerce; director: San Francisco Friends Urban Forest; director: San Francisco Academy; director: Global Climate Coalition.
George Kent Carter: vice president, treasurer B Toledo, OH 1935. ED Stanford University AB (1957); Stanford University MBA (1961). PRIM CORP EMPL vice president, treasurer: Chevron Corp. NONPR AFFIL member: Stanford Business School Association; member: Stanford University Alumni Association; member: Financial Executives Institute. CLUB AFFIL Bankers Club.
Lloyd Edwin Elkins, Junior: vice president B Tulsa, OK 1943. ED Colorado School of Mines (1965). PRIM CORP EMPL vice president: Chevron Corp. CORP AFFIL president: Chevron Services Co.; director: Caltex Pacific Indonesia; director: Caltex Petroleum Corp.; director: American Overseas Ltd. NONPR AFFIL trustee: Center Resource Management; member: Society Petroleum Engineers; member: American Petroleum Institute.
Martin R. Klitten: vice president, chief financial officer B Los Angeles, CA 1944. ED University of California at Berkeley BA; University of Southern California MBA. PRIM CORP EMPL vice president, chief financial officer: Chevron Corp. NONPR AFFIL member: Financial Executives Institute.
R. Bruce Marsh: general tax counsel B New Orleans, LA 1942. ED University of Texas (1966). PRIM CORP EMPL general tax counsel: Chevron Corp. NONPR AFFIL member: Mid-Continent Oil Gas Association; member: Tax Executives Institute; member: American Petroleum Institute.
Richard H. Matzke: vice chairman PRIM CORP EMPL vice chairman: Chevron Corp.
David J. O'Reilly: chairman, chief executive officer ED University College Dublin (1968). PRIM CORP EMPL chairman, chief executive officer: Chevron Corp. NONPR AFFIL director: American Petroleum Institute; member: Western Studies Petroleum Association.
James Norman Sullivan: vice chairman, director B San Francisco, CA 1937. ED University of Notre Dame BS (1959). PRIM CORP EMPL vice chairman, director: Chevron Corp.

Giving Program Officials

Skip Rhodes: PRIM CORP EMPL manager corporate contributions: Chevron Corp.

Grants Analysis

Disclosure Period: calendar year ending 1995
Total Grants: $19,000,000*
Number of Grants: 7,946
Average Grant: $2,391
Highest Grant: $375,000
Typical Range: $2,000 to $10,000
***Note:** Grants analysis is approximate.

Recent Grants

Note: Grants derived from 1994 grants list.

Arts & Humanities

152,061 KQED/Channel 2, San Francisco, CA
86,810 San Francisco Opera Association, San Francisco, CA

75,000 Chevron ENCORE Program, St. Peter, MN

Civic & Public Affairs

100,000 San Francisco Zoological Society, San Francisco, CA
90,000 African American Institute, New York, NY
86,000 City of Richmond, Richmond, CA
70,000 American Enterprise Institute for Public Policy Research, Washington, DC
65,000 Foundation for American Communication, Los Angeles, CA

Education

342,077 University of California, Berkeley, CA
271,300 REACH Program
200,000 Stanford University, Stanford, CA
189,000 Stanford University, Stanford, CA
150,065 Texas A&M University, College Station, TX
131,033 Stanford University, Stanford, CA
120,076 University of Austin, Austin, TX
110,535 University of California, Davis, CA
95,500 Inroads, San Francisco, CA
95,479 Louisiana State University, Baton Rouge, LA
90,040 California Polytechnic State University, San Luis Obispo, CA
87,330 Massachusetts Institute of Technology, Cambridge, MA
83,875 Oregon State University, Corvallis, OR
83,025 University of Washington, Seattle, WA
80,844 Cornell University, Ithaca, NY
76,223 Colorado School of Mines, Golden, CO
75,000 Mathematics, Engineering, and Science Achievement, Oakland, CA
75,000 National Action Council for Minorities in Engineering, New York, NY
75,000 Stanford University Institute for International Studies, Stanford, CA
64,035 Mississippi State University, Mississippi State, MI
64,000 Independent Colleges, Los Angeles, CA

Environment

205,000 Environmental Education Video and Print Material
94,400 Chevron Conservation Awards Program, San Francisco, CA
75,000 Marine World Foundation, Vallejo, CA

Health

1,000,000 Martin Luther King, Jr. Health Clinic, Richmond, CA
128,000 American Red Cross, Los Angeles, CA
95,000 United Way Bay Area, San Francisco, CA -- AIDS programs

International

125,000 Hoover Institute on War, Peace, and Revolution, Stanford, CA
110,000 Professional Scholarships, Nigeria
101,250 World Wildlife Fund, Port Moresby, Papua New Guinea
100,000 Center for Strategic and International Studies, Washington, DC
63,437 United Way, Vancouver, BC, Canada

Social Services

1,050,000 United Way Bay Area, San Francisco, CA
215,000 United Way, Houston, TX
200,000 American Family Entertainment Group, Mill Valley, CA
185,000 United Way, New Orleans, LA
160,000 United Way Bay Area, San Francisco, CA -- youth programs
118,000 United Way Bay Area, San Francisco, CA
105,000 Richmond Police Activities League, Richmond, CA
100,000 United Way, Los Angeles, CA
100,000 United Way Bay Area, San Francisco, CA -- childcare programs
70,000 United Way Bay Area, San Francisco, CA -- homelessness programs

CHICAGO BOARD OF TRADE

Company Contact

Chicago, IL
Web: http://www.cbot.com

Company Description

Employees: 864
SIC(s): 6231 Security & Commodity Exchanges.

Chicago Board of Trade Foundation

Giving Contact

Dena R.S. Cooperman, Assistant Manager, Corporate & Community Relations
141 W. Jackson Blvd.
Chicago, IL 60604
Phone: (312)435-3500

Description

Founded: 1984
EIN: 363348469
Organization Type: Corporate Foundation
Giving Locations: IL
Grant Types: General Support.

Financial Summary

Total Giving: $350,550 (fiscal year ending June 30, 1994); $134,000 (fiscal 1992); $120,000 (fiscal 1991)
Assets: $2,926,662 (fiscal 1994); $2,677,597 (fiscal 1992); $2,554,806 (fiscal 1991)
Gifts Received: $203,010 (fiscal 1994); $100,000 (fiscal 1992); $500,000 (fiscal 1991). Note: In 1992, contributions were received from the Chicago Board of Trade.

Typical Recipients

Arts & Humanities: Arts Festivals, Arts Institutes, Ballet, Community Arts, History & Archaeology, Libraries, Museums/Galleries, Music, Opera, Public Broadcasting
Civic & Public Affairs: Employment/Job Training, Civic & Public Affairs-General, Parades/Festivals, Philanthropic Organizations, Zoos/Aquariums
Education: Business-School Partnerships, Education Associations, Private Education (Precollege), Special Education, Student Aid
Health: Cancer, Clinics/Medical Centers, Multiple Sclerosis, Single-Disease Health Associations
Religion: Religious Welfare
Science: Observatories & Planetariums, Science Museums
Social Services: At-Risk Youth, Child Welfare, Community Service Organizations, Emergency Relief, Food/Clothing Distribution, Homes, People with Disabilities, Scouts, Shelters/Homelessness, United Funds/United Ways, Youth Organizations

Application Procedures

Initial Contact: Send brief letter describing program.
Deadlines: None.

Restrictions

Does not support: individuals, religious organizations for sectarian purposes, political or lobbying groups, or hospitals.

Corporate Officials

Patrick H. Arbor: chairman, chief executive officer PRIM CORP EMPL chairman: Chicago Board of Trade.
Thomas Roy Donovan: president, chief executive officer B Chicago, IL 1937. ED Illinois Institute of Technology BA (1972); Illinois Institute of Technology MPA (1975). PRIM CORP EMPL president, chief executive officer: Chicago Board of Trade. CORP AFFIL director: MidAm. NONPR AFFIL director, member: National Futures Association; council: Northwestern University Associates; director: Illinois Leadership Council Agricultural Education; director, member: De La Salle Institute; council: Grad School Business University; director, member executive committee: Chicago Association Commerce Industry; member: Chicago Central Area Comm. CLUB AFFIL Communal Chicago Club; Executive Club Chicago.

Foundation Officials

David P. Brennan: chairman
Thomas P. Cunningham: director
David J. Fisher: director
Glen M. Johnson: treasurer
Francis X. O'Donnell: director

Grants Analysis

Disclosure Period: fiscal year ending June 30, 1994
Total Grants: $350,550
Number of Grants: 32
Highest Grant: $202,550
Typical Range: $3,000 to $8,000

Recent Grants

Note: Grants derived from fiscal 1997 Form 990.

Arts & Humanities

5,000 Art Institute of Chicago, Chicago, IL
5,000 Chicago Historical Society, Chicago, IL
5,000 Chicago Symphony Orchestra, Chicago, IL
5,000 Lyric Opera, Chicago, IL

Civic & Public Affairs

5,000 Brookfield Zoo, Brookfield, IL
5,000 Lincoln Park Zoo, Chicago, IL
5,000 Little City Foundation, Chicago, IL
5,000 Putts for Peter
5,000 Shedd Aquarium, Chicago, IL

Education

5,000 Glenwood School for Boys, Glenwood, IL
5,000 Visitation Scholarship Fund, Chicago, IL

Health

5,000 American Cancer Society, Chicago, IL
5,000 Erie Family Health Center, Chicago, IL

Science

20,000 Adler Planetarium, Chicago, IL
20,000 Field Museum of Natural History, Chicago, IL

Social Services

5,000 Boy Scouts of America, Chicago, IL
5,000 Girl Scouts of America, Chicago, IL
5,000 Lambs Farms Foundation
5,000 Neighborhood Boys and Girls Clubs, Chicago, IL
4,000 Better Boys Foundation, Chicago, IL

CHICAGO SUN-TIMES, INC.

Company Contact

Chicago, IL

Company Description

Employees: 3,000
SIC(s): 2711 Newspapers.
Parent Company: Hollinger International, Inc.

Nonmonetary Support

Type: In-kind Services

Chicago Sun-Times Charity Trust

Giving Contact

Patricia L. Dudek, Vice President and Manager, Community & Client Services
401 N. Wabash Ave., Rm. 740
Chicago, IL 60611
Phone: (312)321-2213
Web: http://www.suntimes.com

Description

Founded: 1936
EIN: 366059459
Organization Type: Corporate Foundation
Giving Locations: IL: Chicago including metropolitan area
Grant Types: Project, Seed Money.

Financial Summary

Total Giving: $300,000 (fiscal year ending September 30, 1999 approx); $206,712 (fiscal 1998); $140,000 (fiscal 1996)
Assets: $762,907 (fiscal 1998); $380,168 (fiscal 1996); $397,510 (fiscal 1992)
Gifts Received: $353,413 (fiscal 1998); $242,416 (fiscal 1996); $209,003 (fiscal 1992)

Typical Recipients

Arts & Humanities: Arts Outreach, Community Arts, Arts & Humanities-General, Museums/Galleries, Music, Performing Arts, Theater
Civic & Public Affairs: Economic Development, Employment/Job Training, Ethnic Organizations, Urban & Community Affairs
Education: Afterschool/Enrichment Programs, Arts/Humanities Education, Business Education, Business-School Partnerships, Education-General, Journalism/Media Education, Literacy, Public Education (Precollege)
Health: Children's Health/Hospitals, Health-General
Social Services: At-Risk Youth, Child Abuse, Child Welfare, Community Service Organizations, Crime Prevention, Domestic Violence, People with Disabilities, Youth Organizations

Contributions Analysis

Arts & Humanities: 44%. Funds opera, art museums, ballet, and theater.
Civic & Public Affairs: 1%. Support community development and women services.
Education: 19%. Funds pre-college education and literacy.
Religion: 2%. Supports YMCA.
Social Services: 33%. Primary support for youth groups, food banks, and social services.
Note: Total contributions in fiscal 1998.

Application Procedures

Initial Contact: Send a full proposal.
Application Requirements: Include a description of organization and its history, primary functions and goals, list of board members, and professional staff, list of major funders, amount requested, purpose of funds sought, research, proof of tax-exempt status, operating and project budgets, and plans for evaluating the program.
Deadlines: Trustees meet in March and September.

Restrictions

Does not support individuals, religious organizations for sectarian purposes, political or lobbying groups, organizations outside operating areas, or organizations that receive 25% or more of funding from the government or the United Way.

Additional Information

Publications: Policies and Procedures Fact Sheet

Corporate Officials

F. David Radler: chairman, publisher publisher PRIM CORP EMPL chairman, publisher: Chicago Sun-Times.
Joseph Sherman: vice president, assistant publisher PRIM CORP EMPL vice president, assistant publisher: Chicago Sun-Times.

Foundation Officials

Patricia L. Dudek: vice president, trustee PRIM CORP EMPL vice president, manager community & client service: Chicago Sun-Times.
Mark Kipnis: trustee
Linda Loye: secretary
Helen D. McCarthy: treasurer, trustee
Rona Radler: president, trustee
Joseph Sherman: trustee (see above)
Nigel Wade: trustee

Grants Analysis

Disclosure Period: fiscal year ending September 30, 1998
Total Grants: $206,712
Number of Grants: 24
Average Grant: $8,613
Highest Grant: $40,000
Typical Range: $5,000 to $10,000

Recent Grants

Note: Grants derived from fiscal 1996 Form 990.

Arts & Humanities

50,000	Steppenwolf Theater, Chicago, IL
20,000	Museum of Contemporary Art, Chicago, IL
5,000	Chicago Symphony Orchestra, Chicago, IL
1,000	Music Theater Workshop, Chicago, IL

Civic & Public Affairs

15,000	Chicago Neighborhood Development Awards, Chicago, IL

Education

7,500	Reading is Fundamental, Chicago, IL
2,000	Suzuki-Orff School for Young Musicians, Chicago, IL
1,000	Chicago Public Schools, Chicago, IL
1,000	Junior Achievement, Chicago, IL
1,000	Project Education Plus, Chicago, IL

Health

500	DuPage Easter Seal Society, DuPage, IL

International

25,000	Weizmann Institute of Science, Washington, DC

Social Services

3,000	Illinois Action for Children, Chicago, IL
2,000	Chicago Network for Battered Women, Chicago, IL
2,000	Christopher House
2,000	Youth Communications, Chicago, IL
1,000	Center for Conflict Resolution, Chicago, IL
1,000	Union League Boys and Girls Club, Chicago, IL

CHICAGO TITLE CORP.

Company Contact

171 N. Clark St.
Chicago, IL 60601
Phone: (312)630-2000
Fax: (312)223-5955
Web: http://www.ctt.com

Company Description

Revenue: US$1,926,700,000 (1998)
Profit: US$97,000,000 (1998)
Employees: 10,550 (1998)
Parent Company: Fidelity National Financial Inc., 3916 State St., Suite 300, Santa Barbara, CA, United States

Corporate Sponsorship

Type: Arts & cultural events

Chicago Title and Trust Co. Foundation

Giving Contact

Nancy Labik, Foundation Coordinator
Chicago Title and Trust Co. Foundation
171 N. Clark St., 9TF
Chicago, IL 60601-3294
Phone: (312)223-2911
Fax: (312)223-4829

Description

Founded: 1951
EIN: 366036809
Organization Type: Corporate Foundation
Giving Locations: IL: Chicago
Grant Types: Award, Employee Matching Gifts, General Support, Matching.

Giving Philosophy

'The Chicago Title and Trust Company Foundation is the philanthropic arm of Chicago Title and Trust Company and Chicago Title Insurance Company. The Foundation exists to manifest Chicago Title and Trust's goal of good corporate citizenship and is the vehicle by which we support the communities of our employees and customers. Based in Chicago, the Foundation concentrates on serving the Metropolitan Chicago area; however, Chicago Title and Trust Company operations throughout the United States call upon the Foundation to support their local communities.' *Chicago Title & Trust Company Foundation Guide and Application Procedures*

Financial Summary

Total Giving: $678,009 (1998); $731,140 (1997); $575,946 (1996). Note: Contributes through corporate direct giving program and foundation.
Giving Analysis: Giving for 1998 includes: foundation ($439,880); foundation grants to United Way ($147,639); foundation matching gifts ($90,490)
Assets: $2,540,103 (1998); $2,382,819 (1997); $2,498,588 (1996)
Gifts Received: $360,000 (1998); $180,000 (1997); $830,941 (1994). Note: In 1998, contributions were received from Chicago Title and Trust Co.

Typical Recipients

Arts & Humanities: Arts Appreciation, Arts Festivals, Arts Institutes, Community Arts, Arts & Humanities-General, Libraries, Museums/Galleries, Music, Opera, Performing Arts, Public Broadcasting, Theater
Civic & Public Affairs: African American Affairs, Asian American Affairs, Botanical Gardens/Parks, Business/Free Enterprise, Clubs, Economic Development, Employment/Job Training, Civic & Public Affairs-General, Housing, Law & Justice, Legal Aid, Nonprofit Management, Urban & Community Affairs, Women's Affairs, Zoos/Aquariums
Education: Business Education, Colleges & Universities, Economic Education, Education-General, Journalism/Media Education, Legal Education, Literacy, Medical Education, Minority Education, Public Education (Precollege), School Volunteerism, Student Aid

Health: Cancer, Children's Health/Hospitals, Diabetes, Emergency/Ambulance Services, Eyes/Blindness, Health Organizations, Hospitals, Multiple Sclerosis, Respiratory, Single-Disease Health Associations, Trauma Treatment
Social Services: At-Risk Youth, Big Brother/Big Sister, Child Welfare, Community Service Organizations, Crime Prevention, Delinquency & Criminal Rehabilitation, Family Planning, Food/Clothing Distribution, Scouts, Senior Services, Shelters/Homelessness, United Funds/United Ways, YMCA/YWCA/YMHA/YWHA, Youth Organizations

Contributions Analysis

Arts & Humanities: 42%. Supports major cultural institutions such as theaters, art institutes, and libraries. Also operates an Employee Matching Gift for PBS Programs with grants to Chicago stations and others throughout the United States.
Civic & Public Affairs: 12%. Focus on strengthening the social and economic position of the community. Funds housing projects, services for the disadvantaged through job training, mentoring, and help programs. Supports parks, cultural diversity, and economic development.
Education: 4%. Supports higher education, primarily through an employee matching gift program. Other education support includes Junior Achievement, grants for improvement of existing facilities, and for specific objectives with established needs evidenced by stable or growing enrollment.
Health: 7%. Limited funding supports American Red Cross, disease-specific organizations, and hospitals.
Social Services: 35%. Emphasis on supporting youth throuth developing mentoring programs and youth groups. Recipients include United Way, youth programs, and Planned Parenthood.
Note: Total contributions made in 1998.

Application Procedures

Initial Contact: Send a written proposal.
Application Requirements: Include a description of organization, its purpose, history, programs, and achievements; statement describing the specific purpose of grant request; a plan for evaluating program; current operating budget and budget for proposed project; audited financial statement; copy of certificate of tax exemption; list of officers and board members; and sources of income.
Deadlines: March 1 and September 1.
Evaluative Criteria: Applicant organization contributes to improving the quality of community life, with an emphasis on the urban community; organization is tax-exempt; organization does not show evidence of discrimination; and program qualifies under established priorities of foundation.
Decision Notification: The board meets in April and October.
Notes: Proposals should generally not exceed 10 pages in length. Elaborate, costly proposals are discouraged.

Restrictions

Foundation does not support religious or political activities, funds for reducing or eliminating a budget deficit, or individuals.

Additional Information

Although multi-year grants may be made, grants are not automatically renewed. Requests must be submitted annually, along with a financial statement and an account of accomplishments with the expenditure of funds.
Publications: Application Guidelines

Corporate Officials

Stuart Douglas Bilton: president, chief executive officerhuman resources B Croydon, England 1946. ED London School of Economics (1967); University of Wisconsin (1970). PRIM CORP EMPL president, chief executive officer: Chicago Trust Co. CORP AFFIL executive vice president: Chicago Title & Trust Co.; director: Security Trust Co.; president: Alleghany Asset Management Inc.; director: Baldwin & Lyons Inc.
Richard L. Pollay: vice chairman, director B 1932. ED University of Chicago BS (1952); University of Chicago JD (1955). PRIM CORP EMPL vice chairman, director: Chicago Title and Trust Co.
Richard Paul Toft: chairman B Saint Louis County, MO 1936. ED University of Missouri (1958). PRIM CORP EMPL chairman: Chicago Title and Trust Co. CORP AFFIL director: Cologne Life Reinsurance Co.; director: Peoples Energy Corp.; chairman, chief executive officer: Alleghany Asset Management Inc.; chairman: Chicago Title Insurance Co.
S. LaNette Zimmerman: senior vice president human resources B Newark, AR 1944. ED University of Wisconsin (1969); University of Wisconsin (1975). PRIM CORP EMPL senior vice president human resources: Chicago Title and Trust Co.

Foundation Officials

Stuart Douglas Bilton: trustee (see above)
Nancy Labik: foundation coord
Marguerite Leanne Lachman: trustee B Vancouver, BC Canada 1943. ED University of Southern California BA (1964); Claremont Graduate School MA (1966). PRIM CORP EMPL managing director: Schroder Real Estate Associates. CORP AFFIL managing director: Schroder Mortgage Associates; director: Liberty Property Trust; director: Lincoln National Corp.; director: Chicago Title Corp. NONPR AFFIL trustee, vice president: Urban Land Foundation; trustee, vice president: Urban Land Institute; member: New York Womens Forum. CLUB AFFIL Commercial Club Chicago.
Margaret (Pontius) 'Mardie' Mac Kimm: trustee B Chicago, IL 1933. ED College of William & Mary BA (1955). PRIM CORP EMPL senior vice president corporate communications: Kraft Foods, Inc. CORP AFFIL director: FW Woolworth Co.; director: El du Pont de Nemours & Co.; director: Venator Group Inc.; director: Chicago Title Insurance Co.; director: Chicago Title & Trust Co. NONPR AFFIL executive committee: Chicago Community Trust. CLUB AFFIL Womens Athletic Club.
Richard L. Pollay: trustee (see above)
John E. Rau: trustee B Milwaukee, WI 1948. ED Boston College BS (1970); Harvard University Graduate School of Business Administration MBA (1972). PRIM CORP EMPL president, chief executive officer: Chicago Title Corp. ADD CORP EMPL president: Chicago Title & Trust Co.; president: Chicago Title Insurance Co. MO; president: Security Union Title Insurance Co.; president, chief executive officer: Ticor Title Insurance Co. CORP AFFIL director: LaSalle National Bank; director: Nicor Inc.; director: Borg-Warner Automotive Inc.; director: First Industrial Realty Corp.
Richard Paul Toft: trustee (see above)
S. LaNette Zimmerman: trustee (see above)

Grants Analysis

Disclosure Period: calendar year ending 1998
Total Grants: $439,880*
Number of Grants: 125
Average Grant: $3,519
Highest Grant: $50,000
Typical Range: $500 to $5,000
***Note:** Giving excludes matching gifts; United Way.

Recent Grants

Note: Grants derived from 1998 Form 990.

Arts & Humanities

50,000	Chicago Symphony/Lyric Opera Facilities Fund, Chicago, IL
50,000	Goodman Theatre, Chicago, IL
30,000	Shakespeare Repretory Company, Chicago, IL
12,500	The Art Institute of Chicago, Chicago, IL -- 4th installment to second century fund
11,000	Chicago Symphony Orchestra, Chicago, IL
10,000	The Art Institute of Chicago, Chicago, IL
6,000	women's board of ravinia festival, Chicago, IL -- For the Ravinia Gala
5,000	Lyric Opera of Chicago, Chicago
5,000	Marian Sutherland Kirby Library, Chicago, IL
5,000	The Museum Campus, Chicago, IL
5,000	Musiic Center of the North Shore, Chicago, IL -- 1998 recognition dinner
5,000	Ravinia Festival, Chicago, IL
5,000	Shakespeare Repertory Theater, Chicago, IL
5,000	Yea Highland Park Celebration at Ravinia, Chicago, IL

Civic & Public Affairs

25,000	The Commercial Club Foundation, Chicago, IL
10,000	Neighborhood Housing Services of Chicago, Inc., Chicago, IL
7,500	Lincoln Park Zoological Society Womens Board, Chicago, IL
5,000	Jane Addams Hull House Association, Chicago, IL
5,000	Lincoln Park Zoo, Chicago, IL
3,500	Metropolitan Planning Council, Chicago, IL
2,500	Local Initiatives Support Corporation in Chicago, Chicago, IL

Education

6,500	Junior Achievement of Chicago, Chicago, IL
5,000	John Marshall Law School, Chicago, IL -- kratovil seminar
5,000	Wilkes University, Wilkes-Barre, PA -- allan p. kirby center
3,500	Chicago Communities in Schools, Inc., Chicago, IL

Health

5,000	American Cancer Society, Chicago, IL
5,000	Children's Brain Tumor Foundation, Chappagua, NY
5,000	Evanston Northwestern Healthcare, Evanston, IL
5,000	Good Shepard Hospital, Chicago, IL
5,000	Make a Wish Foundation, Chicago, IL
5,000	National Multiple Sclerosis Society, Chicago, IL
3,000	Sids Alliance, Chicago, IL
3,000	Sids Alliance of Illinois, Glenview, IL

Social Services

91,000	United Way, Chicago, IL
11,611	United Way of King County, Seattle, WA
10,000	Big Brothers Big Sisters of of King County, Kirkland, WA
10,000	Boys & Girls Clubs of Chicago, Chicago, IL
6,000	Greater Chicago Food Depository, Chicago, IL
5,000	Boys and Girls Clubs of Chicago, Chicago, IL
5,000	Illinois Facilities Fund, Chicago, IL -- provides real estate loan & consulting
4,179	The New United Way, Chicago, IL
4,060	United Way of Minneapolis, Minneapolis, MN
4,005	United Way of Minneapolis, Minneapolis, MN
3,000	Children's Benefit Fund, Inc., New York, NY
3,000	Greater Chicago Food Depository, Chicago, IL
3,000	Voices for Illinois Children, Chicago, IL
2,758	United Way of Pierce County, Tacoma, WA
2,658	United Way of Columbia-Willamette, Portland, OR

2,634 United Way of King County, Seattle, WA
2,525 United Way of Snohomish County, Everett, WA

Chicago Tribune Co.

Company Contact

Chicago, IL

Company Description

Employees: 10,700
SIC(s): 2711 Newspapers.
Parent Company: Tribune Co.

Nonmonetary Support

Value: $1,500,000 (1989)
Note: Nonmonetary support is no longer offered.

Corporate Sponsorship

Type: Arts & cultural events; Festivals/fairs; Music & entertainment events; Sports events
Contact: Marcy Keno, Community Events Manager
Note: Sponsorship is given through in-kind donations.

Chicago Tribune Foundation

Giving Contact

Marguerite Brannon, President and Contributions Manager
Chicago Tribune Foundation
435 N. Michigan Ave., Suite 200
Chicago, IL 60611-4041
Phone: (312)222-4300
Fax: (312)222-3751

Description

EIN: 366050792
Organization Type: Corporate Foundation
Giving Locations: IL: Chicago including metropolitan area
Grant Types: Employee Matching Gifts, General Support, Project.
Note: Employee matching gift ratio: 2 to 1.

Giving Philosophy

'The mission of Chicago Tribune Company is helping people master their world through knowledge. Eight values--integrity, customer satisfaction, innovation, employee involvement, citizenship, diversity, and teamwork--guide us as we pursue our mission. These values, particularly the values of employee involvement, citizenship, and diversity also guide our corporate contributions.'
'The mission of Chicago Tribune Foundation is to promote public knowledge and strengthen the Chicago metropolitan community by encouraging journalistic excellence, diversity and liberty; supporting cultural institutions, civic efforts and the United Way; and providing employees the opportunity to direct the Foundation's contributions via a matching gift program.'

Financial Summary

Total Giving: $5,887,095 (1997); $1,548,498 (1996); $1,469,732 (1995). Note: Contributes through corporate direct giving program and foundation.
Giving Analysis: Giving for 1996 includes: foundation ($1,415,800); foundation matching gifts ($132,698); 1997: corporate direct giving ($4,423,579); foundation ($1,355,800); foundation matching gifts ($107,716)
Assets: $7,208,751 (1997); $3,932,614 (1996); $1,453,533 (1995)
Gifts Received: $1,475,000 (1996). Note: The foundation is supported by funds from the Chicago Tribune Company.

Typical Recipients

Arts & Humanities: Arts Funds, Arts Institutes, Ethnic & Folk Arts, History & Archaeology, Literary Arts, Museums/Galleries, Music, Opera, Performing Arts, Theater
Civic & Public Affairs: African American Affairs, Asian American Affairs, Civil Rights, Clubs, Economic Development, Employment/Job Training, Civic & Public Affairs-General, Hispanic Affairs, Housing, Minority Business, Municipalities/Towns, Native American Affairs, Professional & Trade Associations, Public Policy, Urban & Community Affairs, Zoos/Aquariums
Education: Colleges & Universities, Education-General, Journalism/Media Education, Literacy, Public Education (Precollege), Secondary Education (Public), Vocational & Technical Education
Environment: Environment-General
Health: AIDS/HIV, Children's Health/Hospitals, Health Organizations, Prenatal Health Issues, Transplant Networks/Donor Banks
International: Human Rights
Religion: Jewish Causes, Religious Organizations, Religious Welfare
Science: Science Museums
Social Services: Child Abuse, Child Welfare, Community Service Organizations, Delinquency & Criminal Rehabilitation, Domestic Violence, Family Services, Food/Clothing Distribution, People with Disabilities, Senior Services, Shelters/Homelessness, Substance Abuse, United Funds/United Ways, Youth Organizations

Contributions Analysis

Giving Priorities: United Way, performing arts, arts education, journalism, and government improvement.
Arts & Humanities: 11%. Support is directed to programs for disadvantaged children who would not otherwise have access to the arts, and to organizations that foster diversity. Some general support is given to select cultural institutions in Chicago. Grants support programs that lead to journalistic excellence, promote diversity in the newspaper industry, and protect press freedoms. Support goes to professional associations, including minority associations; student groups and universities; and public policy institutes.
Civic & Public Affairs: 75%. Grants support civic efforts in the Chicago area led by the business community. Major support goes to the United Way/Crusade of Mercy. Grants in this area are by invitation only.
Education: 12%. Supports programs that provide basic literacy and employment skills and GED preparation.
Note: The company also helps raise money for Chicago area causes through the Chicago Tribune Charities Program by sponsoring local fundraising events. The program works in partnership with the Robert R. McCormick Tribune Foundation; focuses are employment and literacy. The Chicago Tribune Holiday Fund generates contributions from the public to address basic human needs for children, people withdevelopmental disabilities, the homeless, and the hungry. Total contributions made in 1997.

Application Procedures

Initial Contact: Send cover letter and grant proposal, preferably using the Chicago Area Grant Application Form. For application forms and information, call (312) 222-4033 or (312) 222-4300.
Application Requirements: A one-sided, one-page list of board of directors; copy of the most recent IRS tax-exempt status form; audited financial statements or Form 990 from the most recent fiscal year; organization budget for year in which funding is being sought; sources of support, listing which funds have been committed; annual report or other literature on the organization's programmatic, financial, and managerial accomplishments.
Deadlines: February 1 for culture proposals, June 1 for journalism proposals.
Decision Notification: Board meeting for culture proposals is held in late May and for journalism proposals in late August.

Additional Information

The Chicago Tribune Company works in partnership with the Robert R. McCormick Tribune Foundation to assist local philanthropy. Company assists foundation in raising monies for two of its funds: Chicago Tribune Charities and the Chicago Tribune Holiday Fund. The Chicago Tribune uses articles, columns, and other aspects of the newspaper to solicit donations from its readers to finance the Chicago Tribune Holiday Fund, which addresses the needs of children, the homeless, hunger and developmental disability in metropolitan Chicago. These funds are matched by the McCormick Tribune Foundation and used to disburse gifts of toys and books to children during the holiday season. Support also goes to organizations that combat child abuse and developmental delay. Other areas of support include programs or organizations that provide immediate shelter needs for the homeless, and hunger programs that subsidize food banks or alleviate hunger. Chicago Tribune Charities receives funds from the sponsorship endeavors of the Chicago Tribune Company. These monies are used to combat illiteracy and unemployment in the Chicago area. Eligible programs include job preparation and training as well as adult education programs, GED preparation and English as a Second Language programs. The Robert R. McCormick Tribune Foundation also supports programs that enhance the independence of persons with debilitating mental and physical disabilities. All money donated by the public or raised through sponsorship by the Chicago Tribune is matched by the Robert R. McCormick Tribune Foundation. Requests for support in these areas require a completed application form to be sent to the foundation in care of the Chicago Tribune Charities or the Chicago Tribune Holiday Fund at 435 North Michigan Avenue, Chicago, Illinois, 60611. Fund at 435 North Michigan Avenue, Chicago, Illinois, 60611.
Publications: Annual Report; Grantmaking Guidelines

Corporate Officials

Denise Palmer: vice president, strategy & finance B 1957. ED Northwestern University Kellogg Graduate School of Business Administration; University of Dayton BS. PRIM CORP EMPL vice president, strategy & finance: Chicago Tribune Co.

Foundation Officials

Marguerite Brannon: president
Sheila C. Davidson: director
Robert Paul Delo: director B Fremont, MI 1952. ED DePaul University BA (1974); Keller Graduate School of Management MBA (1983). PRIM CORP EMPL senior accountant: Chicago Tribune Co. NONPR AFFIL member: American Institute CPAs; member: CPA Society.
Paulette Dodson: secretary
Dianne Francys Donovan: director B Houston, TX 1948. ED Spring Hill College BA (1970); University of Missouri MA (1975); University of Chicago MA (1982). PRIM CORP EMPL member editorial board: Chicago Tribune Co.
Liza Gross: director
Claudette Hadley: director
Marcy Keno: director
Denise Palmer: treasurer (see above)
Ken Santiago: director
Ken Santiga: director
Susan Zukrou: director

Grants Analysis

Disclosure Period: calendar year ending 1997
Total Grants: $5,779,379*
Number of Grants: 280
Average Grant: $20,641
Highest Grant: $455,000

Typical Range: $5,000 to $25,000
***Note:** Giving excludes matching gifts.

Recent Grants

Note: Grants derived from 1997 Annual Report.

Civic & Public Affairs

30,000 El Valor Corporation, Chicago, IL -- bilingual early intervention program for Hispanic families with special needs children
30,000 Lakefront Single Room Occupancy, Chicago, IL -- affordable housing, comprehensive services
25,000 Latin United Community Housing Association, Chicago, IL -- homeless assistance, prevention programs
25,000 Latin United Community Housing Association, Chicago, IL -- homeless assistance, prevention programs
25,000 Shelter, Arlington Heights, IL -- emergency and temporary care and housing for adolescents

Education

25,000 Park Lawn School and Activity Center, Oak Lawn, IL -- vocations programs

Health

65,000 Open Hand, Chicago, IL -- nutrition network for people with HIV/AIDS
30,000 HIV Coalition, Mount Prospect, IL -- food distribution
25,000 Alivio, Chicago, IL -- prenatal and postnatal classes for low-income Hispanic mothers
25,000 Night Ministry, Chicago, IL -- open door youth emergency shelter, comprehensive services

International

35,000 Heartland Alliance for Human Needs and Human Rights, Chicago, IL -- for Neon Street comprehensive programs

Religion

50,000 Catholic Charities of the Archdiocese of Chicago, Chicago, IL -- child abuse prevention program for mothers in drug treatment program
50,000 Interfaith Council for the Homeless, Aurora, IL -- meals for warming centers and shelters
40,000 Chicago Christian Industrial League, Chicago, IL -- shelters, comprehensive programs for homeless
35,000 Catholic Charities of the Archdiocese of Chicago, Chicago, IL -- parish emergency assistance, food network
30,000 Hesed House, Aurora, IL -- church-based food pantry
25,000 Christian Outreach of Lutherans, Waukegan, IL -- food distribution
25,000 Good News Partners, Chicago, IL -- networking to provide food, support services
25,000 Lutheran Child and Family Services of Illinois, River Forest, IL -- Hispanic food network

Social Services

153,500 ARC, Homewood, IL -- for personal items for recreation for residents of community group homes
125,000 Greater Chicago Food Depository, Chicago, IL -- food distribution in Cook County
95,000 Bethlehem Center Food Bank, St. Charles, IL -- food distribution
75,000 Women's Treatment Center, Chicago, IL -- parenting programs, counseling programs
50,000 Chicago Coalition for the Homeless, Chicago, IL -- support for organizational members who provide homeless shelters and services
50,000 Northern Illinois Council on Alcoholism and Substance Abuse, Gurnee, IL -- child abuse prevention program for mothers in substance abuse program
50,000 Second Harvest, Chicago, IL -- evaluation of food donations for homeless population
45,000 Inspiration Corporation, Chicago, IL -- meals served in cafe setting in Uptown
40,000 Chicago Anti-Hunger Federation, Chicago, IL -- distributes food, training
40,000 Chicago Fund on Aging and Disability, Chicago, IL -- emergency meal delivery programs
40,000 Illinois Hunger Coalition, Springfield, IL -- for child nutrition project
35,000 Northwestern University Settlement, Chicago, IL -- food distribution network
33,000 Seguin Services, Cicero, IL -- comprehensive services for children and their families
30,000 Community Crisis Center, Elgin, IL -- emergency shelter for women and children of domestic violence
30,000 National Committee to Prevent Child Abuse, Chicago, IL -- home visitation services to prevent child abuse
30,000 Port -- hunger relief programs
30,000 Residents for Emergency Shelter, Chicago, IL -- shelters, warming center, comprehensive services
26,775 Shapiro Developmental Center -- to purchase personal items or recreation to residents of group homes
25,000 Association House, Chicago, IL -- family shelter program for Hispanic families
25,000 Chicago Abused Women's Coalition, Chicago, IL -- emergency shelter, assistance for women affected by domestic violence
25,000 Community Support Services, Chicago, IL -- support services
25,000 Filmore Center for Human Services, Berwyn, IL -- bilingual social worker for child abuse prevention services
25,000 Northpointe Achievement Center, Zion, IL -- for community integrated living arrangement in homes in Lake County
25,000 Northwest Indiana Food Bank, Gary, IN -- food distribution
25,000 Proviso Association for Retarded Citizens, Westchester, IL -- comprehensive services for children and adults
25,000 Ray Graham Association for People with Disabilities, Elmhurst, IL -- support Anna Hanson Center
25,000 West Side Mentally Retarded Children's Aid, Chicago, IL -- transportation services for clients
20,000 Chicago Lighthouse for the Blind, Chicago, IL -- for in-home intervention programs for families
20,000 Children's Advocacy Center, Hoffman Estates, IL -- bilingual child advocate for Latino clients
20,000 Circle Family Care, Chicago, IL -- child abuse prevention services
20,000 Esperanza Community Services, Chicago, IL -- support services for families of developmentally delayed children

CHUBB CORP.

Company Contact

Warren, NJ
Web: http://www.chubb.com/

Company Description

Revenue: US$6,729,600,000 (1999)
Employees: 6,931 (1999)
Fortune Rank: 257, per FORTUNE Magazine's list of 500 Largest U.S. Corporations (1999).
FF 257
SIC(s): 6311 Life Insurance, 6321 Accident & Health Insurance, 6331 Fire, Marine & Casualty Insurance, 6719 Holding Companies Nec.

Chubb Foundation

Giving Contact

Ms. Kathleen B. Travinsky, Secretary
Chubb Foundation
15 Mountain View Road
Warren, NJ 07059
Phone: (908)903-3580
Fax: (908)903-2955

Description

EIN: 226058567
Organization Type: Corporate Foundation
Giving Locations: nationally.
Grant Types: Scholarship.

Financial Summary

Total Giving: $816,017 (1997); $766,400 (1996); $676,166 (1995). Note: Contributes through foundation only.
Assets: $16,530,129 (1996); $15,876,215 (1995); $13,713,610 (1994)
Gifts Received: $3,000 (1996); $3,000 (1995); $2,000 (1994)

Typical Recipients

Arts & Humanities: Museums/Galleries
Education: Colleges & Universities, Student Aid

Contributions Analysis

Education: 100% of total contributions. Foundation was established to provide scholarships to employees' family members wishing to attend four-year educational institutions.

Application Procedures

Initial Contact: letter requesting application
Application Requirements: name, address, and zip code; school or college student is attending and what class; and employee information
Deadlines: applications by December 31, student financial statements by March 1
Notes: Scholarship information is available at branches and affiliated companies. Applications should be addressed to Educational Consultant, PO Box 250861, Columbia University Station, New York, New York 10025.

Restrictions

Scholarships are limited to employees' children and family members.

Corporate Officials

Dean Raymond O'Hare: chairman, treasurer B Jersey City, NJ 1942. ED New York University BS (1963); Pace University MBA (1968). PRIM CORP EMPL chairman: Chubb Life Insurance Co. North America. CORP AFFIL director: Fluor Corp.; chairman, president: Vigilant Insurance Co.; director: Federal Insurance Co.; chairman, vice president: Chubb & Son Inc.; chairman: Colonial Life Insurance Co. North America; chairman, chief executive officer: Chubb Corp.; director: Chubb Insurance Co. Canada; chairman, director: Bellemead Development Corp. NONPR AFFIL director: New Jersey Partnership; trustee: WDC; member: American Insurance Association; director: Coalition Service Industry. CLUB AFFIL The Links Club; India House Club.

Philip J. Sempier: vice president, treasurer B 1946. PRIM CORP EMPL vice president, treasurer: Chubb Corp. ADD CORP EMPL treasurer: Federation Insurance Co.; treasurer: Chubb Custom Insurance Co.
Richard Donald Smith: president, director B 1928. ED Fordham University BA (1948); Fordham University JD (1952). PRIM CORP EMPL president, director: Chubb Corp.

Foundation Officials

Elizabeth T. Gildersleeve: chairman ED Trinity College BA. PRIM CORP EMPL executive vice president: D'Arcy Masius Benton & Bowles.
Philip J. Sempier: president, treasurer (see above)
Kathleen B. Travinsky: secretary

Grants Analysis

Disclosure Period: calendar year ending 1996
Total Grants: $766,400
Number of Grants: 386
Average Grant: $1,985
Highest Grant: $5,000
Typical Range: $1,000 to $5,000
Note: All foundation grants are scholarship awards to individuals.

Recent Grants

Note: Grants derived from 1994 grants list.

Arts & Humanities

300,000 Smithsonian Institution, National Museum of American History, Washington, DC

CHURCH &DWIGHT CO., INC.

Company Contact

Princeton, NJ

Company Description

Employees: 937
SIC(s): 2812 Alkalies & Chlorine, 2819 Industrial Inorganic Chemicals Nec, 2841 Soap & Other Detergents, 2842 Polishes & Sanitation Goods.

Operating Locations

Canada; United Kingdom

Nonmonetary Support

Type: Donated Equipment; Donated Products; In-kind Services; Loaned Employees; Loaned Executives

Corporate Sponsorship

Type: Music & entertainment events

Giving Contact

Steven Cugini, Vice President, Human Resources
Church & Dwight Co., Inc.
469 North Harrison Street
Princeton, NJ 08543-5297
Phone: (609)683-5900
Fax: (609)497-7269

Description

Organization Type: Corporate Giving Program
Giving Locations: NJ
Grant Types: Employee Matching Gifts, Research.

Financial Summary

Total Giving: $100,000 (2000 approx); $100,000 (1999 approx); $100,000 (1998 approx). Note: Contributes through corporate direct giving program only. Giving includes corporate direct giving; domestic subsidiaries.

Typical Recipients

Arts & Humanities: Community Arts, Historic Preservation, Libraries, Museums/Galleries, Music, Public Broadcasting
Civic & Public Affairs: Urban & Community Affairs
Education: Agricultural Education, Arts/Humanities Education, Business Education, Colleges & Universities
Environment: Environment-General
Health: Emergency/Ambulance Services, Health Funds, Health Organizations, Hospitals, Medical Research, Mental Health
Science: Scientific Organizations
Social Services: Animal Protection, Community Service Organizations, Emergency Relief, Food/Clothing Distribution, United Funds/United Ways, Youth Organizations

Application Procedures

Initial Contact: letter of inquiry
Application Requirements: a description of organization, amount requested, purpose of funds sought, recently audited financial statements, and proof of tax-exempt status
Deadlines: None.

Restrictions

Does not support individuals, religious organizations for sectarian purposes, or political or lobbying groups.

Corporate Officials

Dwight Church Minton: chairman, director B North Hills, NY 1934. ED Yale University BA (1959); Stanford University Graduate School of Business Administration MBA (1961). PRIM CORP EMPL chairman, director: Church & Dwight Co., Inc. CORP AFFIL director: Medusa Corp.; director: Medusa Cement Corp.; director: Crane Co.; director: First Brands Corp. NONPR AFFIL trustee: Morehouse College; trustee: National Environmental Education & Training Foundation; chairman: Greater Yellowstone Coalition; member: Grocery Manufacturer America; member: Chemical Manufacturers Association. CLUB AFFIL Yale Club; Racquet & Tennis Club; Seawanhaka Corinthian Yacht Club; Lotos Club.

CIBC OPPENHEIMER

Company Contact

New York, NY
Web: http://www.cibc.com

Company Description

Former Name: Canadian Imperial Bank of Commerce; CIBC Wood Gundy Securities Corp.
Revenue: US$34,000,000
Employees: 185
SIC(s): 6211 Security Brokers & Dealers, 6221 Commodity Contracts Brokers & Dealers.
Parent Company: Woody Gundy Holdings
Parent Assets: US$191,740,000,000

Operating Locations

CA: Canadian Imperial Bank of Commerce (California), Los Angeles; CIBC Oppenheimer, Los Angeles; Canadian Imperial Bank of Commerce (California), San Francisco; CIBC Oppenheimer, San Francisco; DE: Canadian Imperial Holdings, Wilmington; GA: CIBC, Atlanta; CIBC Oppenheimer, Atlanta; IL: CIBC Oppenheimer, Chicago; NY: Canadian Imperial Holding Co., New York; Canadian Imperial Service Co., New York; CIBC, New York; CIBC Aviation, New York; CIBC Oppenheimer Corp., New York; CIBC Wood Gundy Securities Corp., New York; Oppenheimer Capital, New York; TX: CIBC Oppenheimer, Houston

Nonmonetary Support

Type: Cause-related Marketing & Promotion; Donated Equipment

Corporate Sponsorship

Note: Sponsors 'Children's Miracle Day;' one day's earnings are donated to create openings in day care in the five burroughs area.

Giving Contact

Deborah Douglas, Managing Directory of Marketing & Communication
CIBC Oppenheimer
425 Lexington Avenue, 9th Floor
New York, NY 10017
Phone: (212)856-4009
Fax: (212)856-3996

Description

Organization Type: Corporate Giving Program
Giving Locations: CA: Los Angeles, Menlo Park, San Francisco; DC; FL: Boca Raton, Fort Lauderdale, Miami; GA: Atlanta; IL: Chicago; MA: Boston; MO: Saint Louis; NY: New York City; TX: Dallas, Houston; WA: Seattle headquarters and operating communities.
Grant Types: General Support, Loan, Operating Expenses, Project, Seed Money.

Financial Summary

Total Giving: $1,216,441 (1997); $450,000 (1995); $250,000 (1994). Note: Contributes through corporate direct giving program only.

Typical Recipients

Arts & Humanities: Libraries
Civic & Public Affairs: Chambers of Commerce, Economic Development, Employment/Job Training, Housing, Inner-City Development, Legal Aid, Municipalities/Towns, Urban & Community Affairs
Education: Business Education
Social Services: United Funds/United Ways, YMCA/YWCA/YMHA/YWHA

Restrictions

Does not support individuals, religious organizations for sectarian purposes, political or lobbying groups, or organizations outside operating areas.

Additional Information

The company is restructuring its giving program.

Corporate Officials

Al Flood: chairman, chief executive officer B Monkton, ON Canada 1935. ED Harvard University. PRIM CORP EMPL chairman, chief executive officer: Canadian Imperial Bank of Commerce. CORP AFFIL chairman, chief executive officer: CIBC Subs. NONPR AFFIL director: Council for Canadian Unity; trustee: Hospital for Sick Children; chairman: Business Council National Issues.
John Hunkin: president B Toronto, ON Canada 1945. ED University of Manitoba BS (1967); York University MBA (1969). PRIM CORP EMPL president: CIBC Oppenheimer.
Michael Rulle: chief executive officer PRIM CORP EMPL chief executive officer: Canadian Imperial Holdings.
Matt Singleton: managing director PRIM CORP EMPL managing director: CIBC Oppenheimer.

Grants Analysis

Disclosure Period: calendar year ending
Typical Range: $1,000 to $2,500

Recent Grants

Note: Grants derived from 1995 grants list.

Arts & Humanities

New York Public Library, New York, NY

Civic & Public Affairs

Banana Kelly Community Improvement Association, Bronx, NY
Greater Jamaica Development Corp

Housing Partnership Development Corp, New York, NY
Local Initiatives Support Corp
Neighborhood Housing Services, New York, NY
New York City Partnership, New York, NY
South Bronx Overall Economic Development Corp, Bronx, NY

Social Services
United Way New York, New York, NY
YMCA New York, New York, NY

CIGNA CORP.

 Number 79 of Top 100 Corporate Givers

Company Contact
Philadelphia, PA
Web: http://www.cigna.com

Company Description
Revenue: US$21,437,000,000
Profit: US$1,292,000,000
Employees: 44,707
Fortune Rank: 75, per FORTUNE Magazine's list of 500 Largest U.S. Corporations (1999).
FF 75
SIC(s): 6282 Investment Advice, 6311 Life Insurance, 6331 Fire, Marine & Casualty Insurance, 6719 Holding Companies Nec.

Operating Locations
New Zealand: CIGNA Insurance New Zealand Ltd., Auckland; CIGNA Life Insurance New Zealand Ltd., Wellington; Spain: CIGNA Insurance Co. of Europe SA-NV (Delegacion General en Espana), Madrid; Taiwan: Connecticut General Life Insurance Co. (Taiwan Branch), Taipei; United Kingdom: CIGNA GB Holdings Ltd., London; CIGNA Insurance Co. of Europe SA-NV, London; CIGNA International Investment Advisors Ltd., London; CIGNA Services United Kingdom Ltd., London; CIGNA Reinsurance Co. (United Kingdom) Ltd., Maidstone, Kent; Ernest Linsdell Ltd., Maidstone, Kent

Nonmonetary Support
Value: $47,250 (1998); $47,250 (1997)
Type: Donated Equipment
Contact: Ronald Dykas, Technical Consultant

Corporate Sponsorship
Type: Other; Arts & cultural events
Note: Sponsors fundraising events for women's health and infant/maternal care, March of Dimes-WalkAmerica, Race for the Cure, and Denim Day.

CIGNA Foundation

Giving Contact
Deborah Veney Robinson, Director, Civic Affairs
CIGNA Contributions and Civic Affairs
2 Liberty Place
1601 Chestnut Street, TL06B
Philadelphia, PA 19192-2066
Phone: (215)761-4881
Fax: (215)761-5632

Alternate Contact
Arnold W. Wright, Jr., Director of Civic Affairs
900 Cottage Grove Road, W-A
Hartford, CT 06152-5001
Note: Alternate contact is for the Hartford area only.

Description
EIN: 236261726
Organization Type: Corporate Foundation
Giving Locations: CT: Hartford including metropolitan area; PA: Philadelphia including metropolitan area
Grant Types: Conference/Seminar, Emergency, Employee Matching Gifts, Fellowship, General Support.
Note: Employee matching gift ratio: 1 to 1 for culture and art organisation.

Giving Philosophy
'The basic mission of CIGNA is to strengthen CIGNA Corporation by supporting organizations and activities that improve the overall climate for business. Contributions and civic Affairs to programs and activities that encourage a strong educational, economic, social, and cultural climate in the communities in which we operate are recognized as good for business, since they benefit the Corporation, our customers, our shareholders and our employees. We focus our attention on activities of specific concern to CIGNA and the insurance and financial services industry in general. We also support programs that improve the corporate image and position the Corporation and employees of the CIGNA companies as concerned and responsible citizens.' *CIGNA Foundation Annual Report*

Financial Summary
Total Giving: $9,851,647 (1998); $10,210,913 (1997); $6,271,064 (1996). Note: Contributes through corporate direct giving program and foundation.
Giving Analysis: Giving for 1997 includes: foundation ($6,788,373); corporate direct giving ($3,422,540); 1998: foundation ($7,129,523); corporate direct giving ($2,722,124)
Assets: $2,093,497 (1997); $1,839,543 (1996); $821,261 (1995)
Gifts Received: $7,336,227 (1996); $6,855,471 (1995)

Typical Recipients
Arts & Humanities: Arts Associations & Councils, Arts Festivals, Ballet, History & Archaeology, Libraries, Museums/Galleries, Music, Opera, Public Broadcasting, Theater
Civic & Public Affairs: African American Affairs, Business/Free Enterprise, Chambers of Commerce, Economic Development, Economic Policy, Civic & Public Affairs-General, Hispanic Affairs, Law & Justice, Nonprofit Management, Philanthropic Organizations, Professional & Trade Associations, Public Policy, Safety, Urban & Community Affairs, Women's Affairs, Zoos/Aquariums
Education: Arts/Humanities Education, Business Education, Colleges & Universities, Education Reform, Elementary Education (Private), Faculty Development, Education-General, Health & Physical Education, International Exchange, Legal Education, Literacy, Medical Education, Private Education (Precollege), Public Education (Precollege), Secondary Education (Public), Special Education, Student Aid
Environment: Energy, Resource Conservation
Health: Adolescent Health Issues, Cancer, Children's Health/Hospitals, Clinics/Medical Centers, Health Organizations, Prenatal Health Issues, Public Health
International: Human Rights
Religion: Religious Welfare
Science: Science Museums, Scientific Centers & Institutes
Social Services: Child Welfare, Community Service Organizations, Crime Prevention, Food/Clothing Distribution, People with Disabilities, United Funds/ United Ways, Volunteer Services

Contributions Analysis
Giving Priorities: Education, human services, health, culture and arts, and civics. As a rule, the company and the foundation do not make contributions for international purposes, either domestically or through foreign operating companies. Consideration is given to cultural institutions, including the Philadelphia Orchestra Association for its European tour; education organizations such as the World Association for Cooperative Education; and public policy organizations such as the World Affairs Council of Philadelphia.
Arts & Humanities: About 13%. Major grants go to arts councils, ballet, museums, orchestras, science academies, and theaters in Philadelphia and Hartford. Significant portion of funding supports the foundation's matching gifts program.
Civic & Public Affairs: About 17%. Emphasis on public policy research, urban and minority affairs groups, safety, and the environment.
Education: About 25%. Support is provided to colleges and universities, with a special interest in minority education and insurance-related curricula. Limited support given to literacy and arts education projects. Substantial support is given to the foundation's matching gifts program, and also to two corporate tutorial programs. 'My Friend Taught Me' and 'Learning, Friends, and Fun.' The programs host local elementary school students weekly for one-on-one tutoring/ mentoring by employee volunteers.
Health: About 45%. CIGNA's primary focus is on women's health and infant maternal care, with an emphasis on programs that reduce infant mortality and low-birthweight.

Application Procedures
Initial Contact: one- or two-page letter
Application Requirements: a description of organization (including name, history, activities, purpose, and board members); description of program for which grant is requested; objectives and evaluative criteria; most recently audited financial statement; copy of IRS 501(c)(3) letter; copy of the most recent Form 990
Deadlines: None; however, the foundation recommends that proposals be submitted by September 1 for funding in the next year.
Decision Notification: ongoing; allow six weeks for initial review

Restrictions
CIGNA Foundation generally will not provide funds to the following categories: individuals, political organizations, religious activities or organizations that are denominational or sectarian, organizations receiving substantial support through United Way or other CIGNA-supported federated funding agencies, endowment drives or capital campaigns, or hospital capital improvements or expansions.

Additional Information
Publications: Annual Report; Contributions Report

Corporate Officials
H. Edward Hanway: president, chief executive officerliance officer B West Chester, PA 1952. ED Loyola College BA (1974); Widener University MBA (1984). PRIM CORP EMPL president, chief executive officer: CIGNA Corp. NONPR AFFIL member: PICPA; member: World Affairs Council Philadelphia; member: American Institute of CPA's.
Paul H. Rohrkemper: treasurer PRIM CORP EMPL treasurer: CIGNA Corp. CORP AFFIL vice president: INA Corp.; secretary: Peoples Light Theatre Co. Inc.
James Gathings Stewart: executive vice president, chief financial officer B Fort Wayne, IN 1942. ED DePauw University BA (1964); University of Michigan MAS (1965). PRIM CORP EMPL executive vice president, chief financial officer: CIGNA Corp. NONPR AFFIL member: American Academy of Actuaries; member: Society Actuaries.
Carol J. Ward: secretary, compliance officer B 1957. ED Yale University (1978); Emory University School of Law (1983). PRIM CORP EMPL secretary, compliance officer: CIGNA Corp. ADD CORP EMPL CIGNA Eagle Lodge Properties. NONPR AFFIL member: American Corporate Counsel Association; member: American Society of Corporate Secretaries; member: American Bar Association.

Giving Program Officials

Donald M. Levinson: director B 1946. ED Columbia University (1967); Columbia University (1968). PRIM CORP EMPL executive vice president human resources: CIGNA Corp. NONPR AFFIL member: American Psychological Society.

Foundation Officials

Paul Bergsteinsson: assistant treasurer PRIM CORP EMPL treasurer: Insurance Co. of North America. CORP AFFIL vice president: Recovery Services International.
John J. Corcoran: assistant secretary
Lauren M. Hartman: director civic affairs
Lee R. Hoffman: assistant secretary
David C. Kopp: assistant secretary B Oak Park, IL 1945. ED Northern Illinois University BA (1967); University of Illinois JD (1970). PRIM CORP EMPL secretary: Connecticut General Life Insurance Co. ADD CORP EMPL secretary: Connecticut General Corp.; secretary: Healthsource Inc.; secretary: CIGNA Health Corp.; secretary: CIGNA Healthcare Florida; secretary: CIGNA Healthcare Tennessee; secretary: Cigna Life Insurance Co.; secretary: Ina Life Insurance Co. New York ADD NONPR EMPL secretary: International Rehabilitation Association.
Michael Kuchs: assistant secretary
Paul H. Rohrkemper: vice president, treasurer (see above)
Thomas Joseph Wagner: chairman B Jackson, MI 1939. ED Earlham College BA (1957); University of Chicago JD (1965). PRIM CORP EMPL executive vice president, general counsel: CIGNA Corp. NONPR AFFIL vice president finance: United States Pacific Economic Corp. Council; director: University Pennsylvania Institute Law & Economics; trustee: Eisenhower Exchange Fellowships; member: American Bar Association; member: American Corporate Counsel Association.
Carol J. Ward: secretary (see above)
Barry Frank Wiksten: president B Seattle, WA 1935. ED Miami University BA (1960); Tufts University Fletcher School of Law & Diplomacy MA (1961). PRIM CORP EMPL senior vice president public affairs: CIGNA Corp. NONPR AFFIL member: Public Relations Seminars New York; director: WHYY Philadelphia; member public affairs research council: Conference Board; director: Independence Hall Association; member public information committee: Business Roundtable. CLUB AFFIL Union League Club; Athenaeum Club.
Arnold W. Wright, Jr.: vice president, executive director

Grants Analysis

Disclosure Period: calendar year ending 1998
Total Grants: $7,129,523*
Number of Grants: 376
Average Grant: $18,962
Highest Grant: $700,000
Typical Range: $2,000 to $30,000
***Note:** Grant analysis provided by foundation.

Recent Grants

Note: Grants derived from 1997 Form 990.

Arts & Humanities

75,000	KVIE-TV/Channel 6, Sacramento, CA
55,000	Greater Hartford Arts Council, Hartford, CT
40,000	Bushnell Memorial Hall, Hartford, CT
25,000	Pennsylvania Ballet, Philadelphia, PA
25,000	Peoples Light and Theater Company, Malvern, PA -- education program
25,000	Philadelphia Museum of Art, Philadelphia, PA
25,000	Wadsworth Athenaeum, Hartford, CT

Civic & Public Affairs

150,000	American Enterprise Institute for Public Policy Research, Washington, DC
72,000	Greater Hartford Chamber of Commerce Foundation, Hartford, CT
35,000	Conference Board, New York, NY
25,000	American Bar Association Fund for Justice and Education, Chicago, IL
25,000	Brookings Institution, Washington, DC
25,000	Cato Institute, Washington, DC
25,000	Committee for a Responsible Federal Budget, Washington, DC
25,000	Competitive Enterprise Institute, Washington, DC
25,000	Greater Philadelphia Chamber of Commerce Regional Foundation, Philadelphia, PA
25,000	Insurance Industry Charitable Foundation, Moraga, CA
25,000	PICPA Foundation for Education and Research, Philadelphia, PA
25,000	Zoological Society, Philadelphia, PA
20,000	1807 and Friends, Philadelphia, PA

Education

330,000	Morehouse School of Medicine, Atlanta, GA
105,631	National Merit Scholarship Corporation, Evanston, IL
80,740	Citizens Scholarship Foundation of America, St. Peter, MN
73,000	University of Connecticut Foundation, Storrs, CT
50,000	Philadelphia High School Academies, Philadelphia, PA
30,000	Eisenhower Exchange Fellowships, Philadelphia, PA
25,000	District II Superintendent Neighborhood School Partnership, Philadelphia, PA
25,000	Junior Achievement of North Central Connecticut, Hartford, CT
25,000	National Center for Health Education, New York, NY
25,000	University of Richmond, Richmond, VA

Health

125,000	St. Francis/Mount Sinai Medical Center, Hartford, CT
75,000	Hartford Action Plan on Infant Health, Hartford, CT
50,000	Maternity Care Coalition, Philadelphia, PA
50,000	University of California Los Angeles Department of Pediatrics and School of Public Health, Los Angeles, CA
30,000	Susan G. Komen Breast Cancer Foundation, Dallas, TX
25,000	Charlotte Race for the Cure, Charlotte, NC
25,000	CHILD Council, Hartford, CT
25,000	Core Foundation, Chicago, IL
25,000	Healthy Mothers, Healthy Babies Coalition, Washington, DC
25,000	March of Dimes Birth Defects Foundation, East Hartford, CT
25,000	March of Dimes Birth Defects Foundation, Wayne, PA
25,000	Resources for Human Development, Philadelphia, PA

Religion

25,000	Salvation Army, Hartford, CT

Science

65,000	Franklin Institute Science Museum, Philadelphia, PA
20,000	Academy of Natural Sciences, Philadelphia, PA

Social Services

700,000	United Way of Southeastern Pennsylvania, Philadelphia, PA
542,500	United Way of the Capital Area, Hartford, CT
402,625	United Way Field Agencies, Alexandria, VA
65,000	CPR Institute for Dispute Resolution, New York, NY
30,000	My Friend Taught Me

CINCINNATI BELL INC.

Company Contact

Cincinnati, OH
Web: http://www.cinbellinc.com

Company Description

Revenue: US$1,573,700,000
Employees: 19,700
SIC(s): 4813 Telephone Communications Except Radiotelephone, 6719 Holding Companies Nec.

Nonmonetary Support

Value: $550,000 (1994)
Type: Donated Equipment; In-kind Services; Loaned Employees; Loaned Executives; Workplace Solicitation

Corporate Sponsorship

Type: Arts & cultural events; Festivals/fairs; Music & entertainment events; Sports events

Cincinnati Bell Foundation, Inc.

Giving Contact

Robert Horine, Directory, Public Affairs
Cincinnati Bell Foundation
201 East Fourth Street, Room 102-890
Cincinnati, OH 45202
Phone: (513)397-7545
Fax: (513)723-9815

Description

EIN: 311125542
Organization Type: Corporate Foundation
Giving Locations: areas where employees live and work.
Grant Types: Capital, Employee Matching Gifts, General Support, Matching, Multiyear/Continuing Support, Project.

Giving Philosophy

'Cincinnati Bell reinforces (its) commitment to the community by supporting its employees in their endeavors and by contributing financial support to worthwhile causes and programs. To demonstrate that commitment, Cincinnati Bell Inc. established the Cincinnati Bell Foundation in 1984 as the philanthropic arm of the community.' *The Cincinnati Bell Foundation Brochure*

Financial Summary

Total Giving: $974,000 (1999 approx); $1,678,754 (1998); $1,187,228 (1997). Note: Contributes through corporate direct giving program and foundation.
Giving Analysis: Giving for 1996 includes: foundation ($662,996); foundation grants to United Way ($340,488); foundation matching gifts ($1,740); 1997: foundation ($774,939); foundation grants to United Way ($380,500); foundation matching gifts ($31,789); 1998: foundation ($1,257,437); foundation grants to United Way ($382,500); foundation matching gifts ($38,817)
Assets: $2,567,136 (1998); $4,034,185 (1997); $5,644,651 (1995)
Gifts Received: $4,000,000 (1995); $2,500,000 (1994); $500,000 (1993). Note: Contributions are received from Cincinnati Bell Inc.

Typical Recipients

Arts & Humanities: Arts Centers, Arts Festivals, Arts Funds, Arts Institutes, Museums/Galleries, Music, Opera, Performing Arts, Public Broadcasting, Theater
Civic & Public Affairs: African American Affairs, Business/Free Enterprise, Chambers of Commerce, Community Foundations, Economic Development, Employment/Job Training, Civic & Public Affairs-General, Housing, Municipalities/Towns, Professional & Trade Associations, Public Policy, Urban & Community Affairs, Women's Affairs, Zoos/Aquariums
Education: Business Education, Colleges & Universities, Community & Junior Colleges, Continuing Education, Economic Education, Education Funds, Education Reform, Elementary Education (Private), Engineering/Technological Education, Faculty Development, Education-General, Literacy, Medical Education, Minority Education, Private Education (Precollege), Public Education (Precollege), Religious Education, Special Education, Student Aid, Vocational & Technical Education
Health: Cancer, Clinics/Medical Centers, Emergency/Ambulance Services, Hospices, Hospitals, Public Health, Single-Disease Health Associations, Speech & Hearing
International: International Affairs
Religion: Dioceses, Religious Welfare, Synagogues/Temples
Science: Scientific Organizations
Social Services: Child Welfare, Community Centers, Community Service Organizations, Food/Clothing Distribution, Homes, People with Disabilities, Recreation & Athletics, Scouts, United Funds/United Ways, Youth Organizations

Contributions Analysis

Giving Priorities: Social service, civics, education, performing arts, and health.
Arts & Humanities: 37%. Performing arts, museums, music, and arts funds.
Civic & Public Affairs: 6%. Funds community foundations, and community development.
Education: 18%. Majority to colleges and universities in communities where Cincinnati Bell operates. Other recipients include educational funds which help disadvantaged youth. Many grants are part of the matching gifts program.
Health: 8%. Supports hospitals, Hospice, medical centers, and American Red Cross Disaster Relief Fund.
Social Services: 31%. Supports youth organizations, Habitat for Humanity, work and rehabilitation centers, and United Way.
Note: Total contributions made in 1998.

Application Procedures

Initial Contact: in writing
Application Requirements: summary of the organization's needs, financial report, and IRS letter which verifies organization's tax-exempt standing
Deadlines: None.
Evaluative Criteria: foundation favors organizations and groups that work in education, cultural enrichment, and health and welfare
Decision Notification: foundation board generally meets at the end of each quarter; decisions announced within three months
Notes: The foundation emphasizes that there is no set application procedure and no specific forms.

Restrictions

Foundation does not fund organizations that are non tax-exempt under IRS standards; organizations that discriminate on the basis of race, color, creed, or national origin; political organizations; religious groups for sectarian purposes; operational expenses for groups supported by the United Way, other than through the United Way; local chapters of national health agencies that are not funded by the United Way.

Additional Information

Due to budget restrictions, the foundation will be funding mostly repeat recipients. Not accepting applications until July 1, 1999. Under review on Foundation & Mission.

Corporate Officials

Cheryl Nichols Campbell: operation service advisory group B Ocala, FL 1948. ED Dartmouth College; University of Pennsylvania; University of Hawaii (1969); Purdue University BA (1970). PRIM CORP EMPL operation service advisory group: Bell Communications Research. NONPR AFFIL chairman: Mayor's Commission Children; member: Telephone Pioneers America; member: Junior League; trustee: Children Protective Services Greater Cincinnati; member: Junior Achievement Cincinnati.
Richard G. Ellenberger: president, chief executive officer, director B 1953. ED Old Dominion University. PRIM CORP EMPL president, chief executive officer, director: Cincinnati Bell Inc. CORP AFFIL president, chief executive officer, director: Cincinnati Bell Telephone Co.
John Thomas LaMacchia: president, chief executive officer, director B Washington, DC 1941. ED Catholic University America BS (1963); Indiana University PhD (1966); Indiana University JD (1976). PRIM CORP EMPL president, chief executive officer, director: Cincinnati Bell Inc. CORP AFFIL director: Multimedia Inc.; director: Burlington Resources Inc.; director: Kroger Co. NONPR AFFIL trustee: University Cincinnati Foundation; trustee: University Cincinnati Medical Center Fund; member: Institute Electrical & Electronics Engineers; trustee: Saint Joseph Infant Maternity Home; member: American Bar Association; trustee: Cincinnati Chamber of Commerce. CLUB AFFIL Queen City Club; Commonwealth Club; Kenwood Country Club; Bankers Club.
Barbara J. Stonebraker: senior vice president B Dayton, OH 1944. ED University of Cincinnati (1978). PRIM CORP EMPL senior vice president: Cincinnati Bell Inc. NONPR AFFIL director: Ohio Telephone Association; director: U.S. Telephone Association.

Foundation Officials

John Thomas LaMacchia: trustee (see above)
Barbara J. Stonebraker: executive vice president (see above)

Grants Analysis

Disclosure Period: calendar year ending 1998
Total Grants: $1,257,437*
Number of Grants: 79*
Average Grant: $15,917
Highest Grant: $330,000
Typical Range: $1,000 to $8,000 and $10,000 to $25,000
***Note:** Giving excludes matching gifts; United Way.

Recent Grants

Note: Grants derived from 1997 Form 990.

Arts & Humanities

70,000	Fine Arts Fund, Cincinnati, OH
60,000	Cincinnati Symphony Orchestra, Cincinnati, OH
20,000	Cincinnati Art Museum, Cincinnati, OH
10,000	Sundance Children's Theater, Sundance, UT
10,000	Utah Arts Festival Foundation, Salt Lake City, UT
5,000	Utah Opera Company, Salt Lake City, UT

Civic & Public Affairs

50,000	Cincinnati Zoo, Cincinnati, OH
15,000	Urban League, Jacksonville, FL
11,500	Work and Rehabilitation Centers, Cincinnati, OH
10,000	Cincinnati Works, Cincinnati, OH
10,000	Southwestern Ohio and Northern Kentucky Habitat for Humanity
5,000	Greater Cincinnati Foundation, Cincinnati, OH
4,000	Yes/Youth Employment Service, Cincinnati, OH
3,000	Jobs for Cincinnati Graduates, Cincinnati, OH

Education

100,000	University of Cincinnati College of Engineering, Cincinnati, OH
25,000	Central State University, Wilberforce, OK
25,000	Greater Cincinnati Scholarship Fund, Cincinnati, OH
10,500	Thomas More College, Crestview Hills, KY
10,000	Joy Outdoor Education Center, Clarksville, OH
7,500	Junior Achievement, Cincinnati, OH
7,000	College of Mount St. Joseph, Mount St. Joseph, OH
5,000	Catholic Inner-City Schools Education Fund, Cincinnati, OH
5,000	University of Notre Dame, South Bend, IN
5,000	Xavier University, Cincinnati, OH
4,500	Northern Kentucky University Foundation, Highland Heights, KY
4,000	University of Cincinnati Foundation, Cincinnati, OH
3,000	Center for Economic Education

Health

35,000	American Red Cross Disaster Relief Fund
18,607	Hospice, Cincinnati, OH
15,000	St. Elizabeth Medical Center Foundation, Dayton, OH

Religion

33,334	St. Joseph Home, Cincinnati, OH
15,000	Good Samaritan Foundation, Cincinnati, OH
15,000	Mount St. Joseph Vision 2000 Campaign
10,000	Franciscan at St. John
6,000	Friends of Plum Street Temple

Social Services

300,000	United Way, Cincinnati, OH
25,000	Greater Cincinnati 2008 Amateur Sports Association, Cincinnati, OH
20,000	Girl Scouts of America Great Rivers Council
18,000	Heart of Florida United Way, Orlando, FL
17,300	United Way Crusade of Mercy, Chicago, IL
10,000	Cincinnati Youth Collaborative, Cincinnati, OH
8,500	United Way, Salt Lake City, UT
6,000	United Way, Pueblo, CO
5,000	Children's Center, Salt Lake City, UT
4,000	United Way Midlands, Columbia, SC
3,000	Cincinnati Youth Collaborative, Cincinnati, OH
3,000	United Way, Tucson, AZ
2,000	United Way Butler County, Butler, PA
2,000	United Way Central Southern Utah, UT
2,000	United Way Iron County, Cedar City, UT

CINERGY CORP.

Company Contact

Cincinnati, OH
Web: http://www.cinergy.com

Company Description

Former Name: PSI Energy.
Revenue: US$5,876,300,000
Employees: 8,600

Fortune Rank: 289, per FORTUNE Magazine's list of 500 Largest U.S. Corporations (1999).
FF 289
SIC(s): 4911 Electric Services, 4924 Natural Gas Distribution.

Nonmonetary Support

Value: $30,000 (1998 approx)
Type: Donated Equipment; In-kind Services; Workplace Solicitation
Contact: Joe Hale, President

Corporate Sponsorship

Range: less than $6,000,000
Type: Arts & cultural events; Festivals/fairs; Music & entertainment events; Pledge-a-thon
Contact: Joe Hale, President, Cinergy Foundation
Note: The company sponsors events for the March of Dimes and the Diabetes Foundation.

Cinergy Foundation

Giving Contact

Karol King, Foundation Manager
Cinergy Foundation
139 E. 4th St.
Cincinnati, OH 45202
Phone: (513)287-1251
Fax: (513)651-9196
Email: kking@cinergy.com
Web: http://www.cinergy.com/foundation

Alternate Contact

Phone: 800-262-3000

Description

Founded: 1992
EIN: 351755088
Organization Type: Corporate Foundation
Former Name: PSI Energy Foundation.
Giving Locations: IN: company service area; KY: Northern Kentucky (company service area); OH: company service area
Grant Types: Conference/Seminar, Employee Matching Gifts, Project, Scholarship, Seed Money.

Giving Philosophy

'Community service is a way of life . .. the Foundation is to be a national leader in community development by creating proactive, innovative partnerships that improve the quality of life by reinvesting in the communities we serve. For decades, we've supported worthy endeavors in all communities we serve. We extend our hand to charitable organizations in education, community development, arts and culture, health and human services, the environment, youth, and many other valuable activities. And our support takes many forms. As a corporation we provide both funding and in-kind resources. As concerned individuals, we give freely of our own personal time and resources.' *Foundation Grant Application Guidelines*

Financial Summary

Total Giving: $5,200,000 (2000 approx); $5,571,237 (1999); $5,700,000 (1998 approx)
Giving Analysis: Giving for 1997 includes: foundation ($4,458,170); foundation grants to United Way ($562,019)
Assets: $14,426 (1997); $468,821 (1996); $105,270 (1995)
Gifts Received: $4,675,368 (1997); $6,209,653 (1996); $3,496,026 (1995)

Typical Recipients

Arts & Humanities: Arts Associations & Councils, Arts Centers, Arts Festivals, Arts Funds, Ballet, Community Arts, Arts & Humanities-General, Historic Preservation, History & Archaeology, Libraries, Museums/Galleries, Music, Opera, Performing Arts, Public Broadcasting, Theater
Civic & Public Affairs: African American Affairs, Botanical Gardens/Parks, Chambers of Commerce, Community Foundations, Economic Development, Civic & Public Affairs-General, Municipalities/Towns, Nonprofit Management, Public Policy, Urban & Community Affairs, Zoos/Aquariums
Education: Arts/Humanities Education, Business Education, Business-School Partnerships, Colleges & Universities, Education Funds, Education Reform, Elementary Education (Private), Engineering/Technological Education, Faculty Development, Education-General, Leadership Training, Literacy, Private Education (Precollege), Public Education (Precollege), Student Aid
Environment: Environment-General, Resource Conservation
Health: Children's Health/Hospitals, Emergency/Ambulance Services, Health-General, Hospitals, Mental Health, Prenatal Health Issues
Religion: Religious Welfare
Social Services: Child Welfare, People with Disabilities, Recreation & Athletics, Scouts, Social Services-General, Special Olympics, Substance Abuse, United Funds/United Ways, YMCA/YWCA/YMHA/YWHA, Youth Organizations

Contributions Analysis

Arts & Humanities: Supports visual and performing arts, cultural programs, and arts education in company's service area.
Civic & Public Affairs: Supports projects that help communities help themselves. Supports the environment through environmental education, park development and enhancement, resource preservation, reforestation, and recycling; youth development, including the Youth Environmental Service (YES) program.
Education: Supports two primary areas: workforce development and staff development. Workforce development projects create a fundamental, seamless, results-based system that enhances the way youth are prepared to meet the demands of a highly skilled workforce, including school-to-work and career development initiatives; increase academic standards; and encourage lifelong learning. Staff development projects encourage continuous improvement in teaching and expanded leadership roles for all teachers, including providing peer assistance and review; training for teachers to take on new roles within the school as mentors, facilitators, community liaisons,curriculum development and assessment experts; enhance educators' ability to observe exemplary teaching practices, conduct and review research, plan for school improvement, and integrate technlogy; individualize instruction; and facilitate schools' efforts to reach out effectively to parents and the community.
Health: Supports health and social service programs which promotehealthy lifestyles and preventative medical care. Major support to the United Way.

Application Procedures

Initial Contact: phone call to request application guidelines and grant application form, then full proposal
Application Requirements: grant application form requests the following information: organization name, address, phone number, and federal tax identification number; name and title of contact person; a brief a description of organization's mission, goals, and objectives; and project information, including name and dates of project, total project cost, dollar amount requested, number of people project benefits, county within which project is located, additional counties benefiting from project, plan for recognizing contributors, project description, a list of Cinergy employees involved in the project and a description of their roles; attachments requested include a copy of 501(c)(3) tax exemption letter; a copy of organization's current budget and the project budget, showing all project revenues and expenses; timetable for becoming self-sufficient; plan for project evaluation; the names and addresses of the organization's board of directors; clear, measurable project objectives; and other supplementary material that describe the organization
Deadlines: the 15th of March, June, and September
Review Process: grant requests are reviewed on a quarterly basis; applicants are encouraged to submit grant applications as far in advance of the project dates above as possible
Evaluative Criteria: how project benefits citizens and communities, especially within company's service area
Decision Notification: organizations receive notification of grant approximately six weeks after submission deadline; applications received after the deadline will automatically be considered at the next grant application deadline
Notes: Applicants are encouraged to call the foundation to discuss their proposals prior to submission. Applicants are requested to submit their grant application to the district office closest to them for review and endorsement by the district manager. Managers and employees are involved in the decision-making process, and the foundation reports it is important for the Cinergy district manager in applicant's service area to be well informed about project.

Restrictions

The foundation does not fund capital campaigns; advertising; membership dues; non-tax exempt organizations; post-prom or post-graduation activities; programs posing a conflict of interest; recognition or academic awards programs (unless part of a staff or workforce development program); technology and audiovisual equipment; travel expenses; uniforms; post-event funding; organizations benefiting an individual or a few persons; capital or endowment campaigns; construction projects; auctions, textbooks purchases, for schools or fundraising events; or veterans, labor, religious, political, or fraternal groups.
Generally, gifts for competitions, golf events, and athletic programs and facilities are beyond the scope of foundation's program.

Additional Information

Company is looking for partnerships between the company and organizations that enhance the future of Indiana communities. Grants are for specific projects or designated programs. Grants are made on a one-year basis. Re-application is necessary for consideration of a grant renewal. Special consideration is given to programs with a statewide scope that benefit citizens in company's service area. Some organizations receiving grants from the Cinergy Foundation will be offered the added benefit of an energy audit of their facilities at Cinergy's expense. The audit provides the organization with recommendations to save on energy costs. Cinergy's expense. The audit provides the organization with recommendations to save on energy costs.
Publications: Guidelines; Annual Report

Corporate Officials

E. Renae Conley: president, chief financial officer B Muncie, IN. ED Ball State University (1981). PRIM CORP EMPL president: Cincinnati Gas & Electric.
Cheryl M. Foley: vice president, secretary, general counsel B Warren, OH 1947. ED Mount Holyoke College (1969); Capital University Law School (1978). PRIM CORP EMPL vice president, secretary, general counsel: Cinergy Corp. ADD CORP EMPL vice president, secretary, director, general counsel: Cincinnati Gas & Electric Co. Inc.; vice president, secretary, director, general counsel: Cinergy Investments Inc.; secretary: Cinergy Resources Inc.; vice president, secretary, director, general counsel: Cinergy Services Inc.; treasurer: Cinergy Capital Trading Inc. CORP AFFIL vice president, secretary, general counsel: Tri-State Improvement Co.; vice president, general secretary, director: West Harrison Gas & Electric Co.; vice president, secretary, director, general counsel:

PSI Energy Inc.; secretary, director: South Construction Co. Inc.; vice president, secretary, general counsel: Miami Power Corp.; secretary, director: PSI Energy Argentina Inc.; vice president, secretary, general counsel: KO Transmission Co.; vice president, secretary, general counsel: Lawrenceburg Gas Co.

William J. Grealis: vice president B Olmsted Falls, OH 1945. ED Ohio University (1967); University of Akron (1972). PRIM CORP EMPL vice president: Cinergy Corp. ADD CORP EMPL president, director: Cincergy Investments; president, director: Cinergy Communication Inc.; president: Lawrenceburg Gas Co. CORP AFFIL president corp. development, chief strategic officer: Cincinnati Gas & Electric Co. Inc.

Donald B. Ingle, Jr.: president energy services business unit, vice president PRIM CORP EMPL president energy services business unit, vice president: Cinergy Corp.

Jerry W. Liggett: vice president human resources PRIM CORP EMPL vice president human resources: Cinergy Corp.

Madaleine W. Ludlow: vice president, chief financial officer PRIM CORP EMPL vice president, chief financial officer: Cinergy Corp. CORP AFFIL president: Cinergy Marketing & Trading LLC.

John M. Mutz: vice president B Indianapolis, IN 1935. ED Northwestern University BS (1957); Northwestern University MS (1958). PRIM CORP EMPL vice president: Cinergy Corp. CORP AFFIL president, director: PSI Resources Inc.; president: PSI Energy Inc. NONPR AFFIL vice chairman board, director: Indianapolis Zoological Society.

Jackson Harold Randolph: chairman B Cincinnati, OH 1930. ED University of Cincinnati BBA (1958); University of Cincinnati MBA (1968). PRIM CORP EMPL chairman: Cinergy Corp. CORP AFFIL chairman, chief executive officer: YGK Inc.; chairman, chief executive officer: Union Light Heat & Power Co.; chairman, chief executive officer: West Harrison Gas & Electric Co.; chairman, chief executive officer: Tri-State Improvement Co.; director: PNC Bank Corp.; director: PNC Corp.; chairman, chief executive officer: Lawrenceburg Gas Co.; chairman, chief executive officer: Miami Power Corp.; chairman, chief executive officer: Enertech Associates International Inc.; chairman: Cincinnati Gas Electric Co.; director: Energy Inc.; director: Cincinnati Financial Corp.; director: Cen Trust Bank NA. NONPR AFFIL member: Delta Sigma Pi; member: Phi Eta Sigma; member advisory committee: Catherine Booth Home; director: ARC; member: Beta Gamma Sigma. CLUB AFFIL Queen City Club; Metro Club; Bankers Club; Cincinnati Country Club.

James E. Rogers, Jr.: vice chairman, president, chief executive officer B Birmingham, AL 1947. ED University of Kentucky BBA (1970); University of Kentucky JD (1974). PRIM CORP EMPL vice chairman, president, chief executive officer: Cinergy Corp. CORP AFFIL director: Owens & Minor Inc.; director: Wellman Inc.; director: Duke Realty Investments Inc.; director: Fifth Third Bank; director: Bankers Life Holding Inc.; director: AO Irkutsk Energo. NONPR AFFIL member: Washington DC Bar Association; member: Young President Organization; director: University Kentucky Business Partnership Foundation; trustee: National Symphony Orchestra; director: Nature Conservancy Indiana Chapter Butler University; member: Kentucky Bar Association; director: Edison Electric Institute; member: FBA; director: Cincinnati Museum Association. CLUB AFFIL Skyline Club; Metropolitan Club; Queen City Club; Meridian Hills Country Club; Bankers Club; Crooked Stick Golf Club.

William L. Sheafer: vice president, treasurer B Huntsville, AL 1943. ED University of Cincinnati (1966); Xavier University (1976). PRIM CORP EMPL vice president, treasurer: Cinergy Corp. ADD CORP EMPL treasurer: West Harrison Gas Electric Co.; treasurer: CGE Resources Marketing Inc.; treasurer: CGE Eck Inc.; treasurer: Cincinnati Gas Electric Co.; treasurer: Cinergy Capital Trading Inc.; treasurer: Cinergy Services Inc.; treasurer: Enertech Associates International Inc.; treasurer: Lawrenceburg Gas Co.; treasurer: Miami Power Corp.; treasurer: Psi Energy Inc.; treasurer: TriState Improvement Co.

Larry Thomas: president delivery business unit PRIM CORP EMPL president delivery business unit: Cinergy Corp.

Charles Joseph (Chuck) Winger: vice president, chief financial officer B Hartford City, IN 1945. ED Manchester College (1967). PRIM CORP EMPL vice president, chief financial officer: Cinergy Corp. NONPR AFFIL member: American Institute CPAs; member: Financial Executive Institute.

Foundation Officials

Phillip R. Cox: director B 1946. ED Xavier University (1967-1969). PRIM CORP EMPL president: Cox Financial Corp. ADD CORP EMPL secretary: Crown Mortgage Services Inc. CORP AFFIL director: Cincinnati Bell Inc.; director: Cinergy Corp.

Kenneth Duberstein: director PRIM CORP EMPL officer: The Duberstein Group. CORP AFFIL director: Saint Paul Co.s Inc.; director: Boeing Co.; director: Cinergy Corp. NONPR AFFIL director: Federation National Mortgage Association.

Cheryl M. Foley: vice president, secretary, director (see above)

William J. Grealis: director (see above)

J. Joseph Hale, Jr.: president, director PRIM CORP EMPL vice president corporate communications: Cinergy Corp.

John A. Hillenbrand, II: director B 1932. PRIM CORP EMPL chairman, president, chief executive officer: Glynnadam, Inc. CORP AFFIL director: Hillenbrand Industries; vice chairman: Pri Pak Inc.; director: Able Body Corp.; director: Cinergy Corp.

George C. Juilfs: director B 1939. PRIM CORP EMPL president, chief executive officer: SENCORP. CORP AFFIL director: Cinergy Corp.; chairman: SENCO Products Inc.

Elizabeth K. Lanier: director PRIM CORP EMPL officer: Cinergy Corp.

John M. Mutz: director (see above)

Jackson Harold Randolph: chairman, director (see above)

James E. Rogers, Jr.: vice chairman, director (see above)

William L. Sheafer: treasurer, director (see above)

Grants Analysis

Disclosure Period: calendar year ending 1997
Total Grants: $4,458,170*
Number of Grants: 1,300*
Average Grant: $3,500
Highest Grant: $510,000*
Typical Range: $200 to $5,000
***Note:** Giving excludes United Way. Highest grant was given to United Way Community Services, Detroit, Michigan, therefore was excluded in grants analysis.

Recent Grants

Note: Grants derived from 1997 Form 990.

Arts & Humanities

100,000	Cincinnati Arts Association, Cincinnati, OH
100,000	Cincinnati Arts Association, Cincinnati, OH
100,000	Cincinnati Symphony Orchestra, Cincinnati, OH
87,500	Fine Arts Fund, Cincinnati, OH
62,500	Cincinnati Arts Association, Cincinnati, OH
50,000	Children's Museum, Cincinnati, OH -- community enhancement
50,000	Cincinnati Art Museum, Cincinnati, OH
50,000	Cincinnati Art Museum, Cincinnati, OH
50,000	Cincinnati Arts Association, Cincinnati, OH
50,000	Cincinnati Arts Association, Cincinnati, OH
50,000	Cincinnati Ballet, Cincinnati, OH
50,000	Fine Arts Fund, Cincinnati, OH
30,000	Contemporary Arts Center, New Orleans, LA
30,000	Indiana Repertory Theater, Indianapolis, IN
25,000	Children's Museum
25,000	Cincinnati Museum, Cincinnati, OH
25,000	Conner Prairie, Fishers, IN
25,000	Eitelboro Museum
25,000	Historical Landmarks, Grass Valley, CA -- community enhancement
25,000	Playhouse in the Park, Cincinnati, OH
22,100	WGUC FM Cincinnati, Cincinnati, OH
20,000	Cincinnati Art Museum, Cincinnati, OH
20,000	Cincinnati Musical Foundation, Cincinnati, OH
20,000	Indiana Humanities Council, Indianapolis, IN -- community enhancement
20,000	Indianapolis Symphony, Indianapolis, IN
20,000	Playhouse in the Park, Cincinnati, OH

Civic & Public Affairs

100,000	Cincinnati Zoo and Botanical Garden, Cincinnati, OH
50,000	Cincinnati Zoo and Botanical Garden, Cincinnati, OH -- community enhancement
50,000	National Underground Railroad Freedom Center, Cincinnati, OH -- educational
33,333	Greater Cincinnati Tall Stacks Commission, Cincinnati, OH -- community enhancement
30,000	Cincinnati Parks Foundation, Cincinnati, OH
25,000	Cincinnati Horticulture, Cincinnati, OH
25,000	Indianapolis Zoological Society, Indianapolis, IN -- educational
25,000	Indianapolis Zoological Society, Indianapolis, IN -- community enhancement
20,000	Urban League -- community enhancement

Education

59,200	USA Group Guarantee -- educational
50,000	Foundation for Independent Colleges -- educational
50,000	Independent Colleges, Los Angeles, CA -- educational
35,000	Greater Cincinnati, Cincinnati, OH -- educational
30,000	NKU Foundation -- educational
30,000	University of Cincinnati Engineering Center, Cincinnati, OH -- educational
25,000	Harmony School Education -- educational
25,000	Mayerson Academy -- educational

Health

50,000	American Red Cross -- human services
30,000	March of Dimes Birth Defects Foundation -- human services

Social Services

510,000	United Way Community Services, Detroit, MI -- community enhancement
75,000	Greater Cincinnati 2008 Amateur Sports Association, Cincinnati, OH
33,333	YMCA -- community enhancement
25,000	NCAA Women's -- community enhancement
25,000	USA Gymnastics Foundation -- community enhancement

CIRCUIT CITY STORES, INC.

Company Contact

Richmond, VA
Web: http://www.circuitcity.com

Company Description

Revenue: US$8,870,800,000
Employees: 36,430
Fortune Rank: 160, per FORTUNE Magazine's list of 500 Largest U.S. Corporations (1999).
FF 160
SIC(s): 5722 Household Appliance Stores, 5731 Radio, Television & Electronics Stores.

Nonmonetary Support

Value: $380,000 (1995); $308,581 (1992); $23,421 (1988)
Type: Donated Products
Note: Foundation provides nonmonetary support.

Circuit City Foundation

Giving Contact

Cassandra O. Stoddart, Co-EXE Director
Circuit City Foundation
9950 Mayland Dr.
Richmond, VA 23233
Phone: (804)527-4000
Fax: (804)527-4173

Alternate Contact

Jane Guganus, Co-Executive Director

Description

EIN: 546048660
Organization Type: Corporate Foundation. Supports preselected organizations only.
Giving Locations: communities where employees live and work.
Grant Types: Challenge, Employee Matching Gifts, General Support, Scholarship.
Note: Matching gifts are limited to education and art and culture. Challenge grants are limited to public broadcasting. Scholarships are limited to spouses and children of employees.

Giving Philosophy

'Circuit City has made a commitment to responsible corporate citizenship in the communities which have supported our stores. In addition to our basic responsibility to provide the highest quality goods and service to our customers at the lowest possible prices, we wish to contribute to the support of worthy charitable endeavors in areas where we have stores.' *Letter to potential applicants from foundation executive director*

Financial Summary

Total Giving: $1,909,491 (fiscal year ending February 28, 1999); $2,500,000 (fiscal 1998 approx); $1,843,990 (fiscal 1997). Note: Contributes through corporate direct giving program and foundation.
Giving Analysis: Giving for fiscal 1996 includes: foundation ($1,460,295); foundation scholarships ($211,588); fiscal 1997: foundation ($1,275,727); foundation grants to United Way ($337,000); foundation scholarships ($231,263); fiscal 1999: foundation ($1,392,991); foundation grants to United Way ($282,600); foundation scholarships ($233,900)
Assets: $192,032 (fiscal 1999); $1,786,952 (fiscal 1997); $1,991,485 (fiscal 1996)
Gifts Received: $1,000,000 (fiscal 1999); $1,621,385 (fiscal 1997); $1,634,307 (fiscal 1996). Note: Contributions received from Circuit City Stores, Inc.

Typical Recipients

Arts & Humanities: Arts Associations & Councils, Ethnic & Folk Arts, History & Archaeology, Museums/Galleries, Music, Performing Arts, Public Broadcasting, Theater
Civic & Public Affairs: Business/Free Enterprise, Economic Development, Housing, Urban & Community Affairs
Education: Business Education, Colleges & Universities, Community & Junior Colleges, Education Reform, Education-General, Minority Education, Private Education (Precollege), Public Education (Precollege), Social Sciences Education, Student Aid
Environment: Environment-General
Health: Emergency/Ambulance Services, Heart, Single-Disease Health Associations, Transplant Networks/Donor Banks
International: Missionary/Religious Activities
Religion: Jewish Causes, Religious Welfare
Science: Science Museums, Scientific Centers & Institutes
Social Services: Child Welfare, Community Centers, Recreation & Athletics, Shelters/Homelessness, United Funds/United Ways, YMCA/YWCA/YMHA/YWHA, Youth Organizations

Contributions Analysis

Giving Priorities: United Way, social service, arts education, health organizations, and civics.
Arts & Humanities: 18%. Major emphasis is on public broadcasting, which typically accounts for nearly three-quarters of total arts giving. Considerable support also goes to symphonies and museums.
Civic & Public Affairs: 24%. Funding is provided to community affairs organizations, police agencies and volunteer fire departments, environmental organizations, African-American affairs, and women's groups.
Education: 24%. Foundation focused its education giving to concentrate on public education reform; support also goes to higher education.
Health: 1%. Grants generally benefit hospitals, single-disease health organizations, and the American Red Cross.
International: 4%.
Religion: 5%.
Science: 9%. Funds science museums.
Social Services: 15%. United Ways throughout the Eastern states and California receive the majority of this support. Other interests include youth organizations and aid to persons with disabilities.
Note: Total contributions made in 1998.

Application Procedures

Initial Contact: There is no specific application format.
Application Requirements: Include background of organization, people served, specific project for which support is desired, plans for recognizing company's contribution, and proof of 501(c)(3) status for cash requests.
Deadlines: None, for grants and product donations; June 15 for scholarships.
Review Process: Board of trustees meets in spring and fall; exact dates vary from year to year.
Decision Notification: Requests for cash or major products take at least six weeks for consideration; minor product donation decisions usually made within 2 or 3 weeks.
Notes: Foundation may request additional information.

Restrictions

Company does not support individuals, fraternal organizations; or political or lobbying groups.
Company does not make grants to national organizations or provide cash to religious organizations for sectarian purposes.

Corporate Officials

Richard L. Sharp: chairman, chief executive officer, director B Washington, DC 1947. ED University of Virginia (1965-1966); College of William & Mary (1968-1970). PRIM CORP EMPL chairman, chief executive officer, director: Circuit City Stores, Inc. CORP AFFIL director: Flextronics International; director: Fort James Corp.; chairman: Carmax Auto Superstores Inc.
Alan Leon Wurtzel: chairman, trustee B Mount Vernon, NY 1933. ED Oberlin College AB (1955); London School of Economics (1955-1956); Yale University LLB (1959). PRIM CORP EMPL chairman, trustee: Circuit City Stores, Inc. CORP AFFIL director: Dollar Tree Stores. NONPR AFFIL member: National Skills Studies Board; member: Virginia State Board Education; director: National Alliance Business; member: Gov Economic Advisory Council.

Foundation Officials

Adrienne Bank: member scholarship committee
Robert Lewis Burrus, Jr.: trustee B Richmond, VA 1934. ED University of Richmond BA (1955); Duke University LLB (1958). PRIM CORP EMPL partner, chairman: McGuire, Woods, Battle & Boothe, LLP. CORP AFFIL director: Smithfield Foods Inc.; director, member audit committee: Riverton Investment Corp.; director, chairman comptr committee, member audit committee: S&K Famous Brands Inc.; director: O'Sullivan Corp.; trustee: Richmond Renaissance Inc.; secretary: Genicom Corp.; director: Heilig-Meyers Co.; director: CSX Corp.; director: Capitol Cement Corp.; director: Concepts Direct Inc. NONPR AFFIL member building committee: Virginia Museum; trustee: Virginia Museum Fine Arts; member: Virginia Bar Association; fellow: Virginia Law Foundation; trustee: University Richmond; trustee: Valentine Museum; director: Richmond Childrens Museum; member: Omicron Delta Kappa; member: Richmond Bar Association; board visitors: Duke University Law School; trustee: Historic Richmond Foundation; member: American Bar Association; fellow: American Bar Foundation. CLUB AFFIL Forum Club; Commonwealth Club; Country Club Virginia; Bull & Bear Club.
Grace Harris: member scholarship committee PRIM NONPR EMPL provost, vice president academic affairs: Virginia Commonwealth University. CORP AFFIL director: Rich Food Holdings.
Frances Aaronson Lewis: trustee B Brooklyn, NY 1922. ED University of Michigan BA (1942). PRIM CORP EMPL vice chairman, executive vice president: Best Products Co., Inc. NONPR AFFIL member: Virginia State Board Education; trustee: Washington & Lee University; member: Virginia Retail Merchants Association; trustee: Virginia Environmental Endowment; member exhibition committee: Virginia Museum Fine Arts; member capital funds board: United Way America; member legislative aff committee: Richmond Chamber of Commerce; member: Richmond Public School Board; member judaic culture advisory committee: Commonwealth University; member advisory board: Garfield F Childs Memorial Fund; trustee: Circle City Foundation; member: Beta Gamma Sigma.
Hyman Meyers: trustee B 1911. PRIM CORP EMPL vice president, director: Meyers & Tabakin Inc. CORP AFFIL director: Heilig-Meyers Co.
Frances Rosi: trustee
Richard L. Sharp: trustee (see above)
Cassandra Stoddart: executive director
Edward Villanueva: trustee B New York, NY 1935. ED Columbia College (1956); Columbia College (1960). CORP AFFIL director: Circuit City Stores Inc.; director: Richfood Holdings Inc.
Alan Leon Wurtzel: chairman (see above)

Grants Analysis

Disclosure Period: fiscal year ending February 28, 1998
Total Grants: $1,110,391*
Number of Grants: 683
Average Grant: $1,626
Highest Grant: $120,000
Typical Range: $1,000 to $5,000
***Note:** Giving excludes United Way.

Recent Grants

Note: Grants derived from fiscal 1997 Form 990.

Arts & Humanities

100,000	Valentine Museum, Richmond, VA
52,000	National Public Radio, Washington, DC
52,000	National Public Radio, Washington, DC

20,000 KQED, San Francisco, CA
20,000 WETA/Public Television, Washington, DC
10,000 Downtown Presents, Richmond, VA
10,000 Virginia Historical Society, Richmond, VA
10,000 Virginia Museum, Richmond, VA
5,000 Arena Stage, Washington, DC
5,000 Jamestown Yorktown Fund, Williamsburg, VA
5,000 Phillips Collection, Richmond, VA
3,500 WCVE FM, Richmond, VA
2,500 Phillips Collection, Richmond, VA

Civic & Public Affairs
15,000 National Alliance of Business, Washington, DC
10,000 Metropolitan Business Foundation, Richmond, VA
5,000 Carver Promise, Richmond, VA

Education
25,000 An Achievable Dream, Newport News, VA
20,000 University of Richmond, Richmond, VA
11,500 Virginia State University, Petersburg, VA
10,000 Communities in Schools, Richmond, VA
10,000 Students in Free Enterprise, Springfield, MO
7,500 Harvard Business School, Cambridge, MA
5,000 Project Nishma, Washington, DC
5,000 United Negro College Fund, Richmond, VA
5,000 Virginia Institute of Political Science, Charlottesville, VA
2,500 Longwood College Inaugural, Farmville, VA
2,500 United Negro College Fund, Richmond, VA

Health
5,000 American Heart Association, Glen Allen, VA
5,000 Richmond Blood Services, Richmond, VA

International
25,000 New Israel Fund, Washington, DC

Religion
60,000 Jewish Community Federation, Richmond, VA
4,000 United Jewish Appeal Federation, New York, NY

Science
10,000 Weizmann Institute of Science, New York, NY

Social Services
35,000 Dallas Youth Services Corps, Dallas, TX
20,500 United Way, Los Angeles, CA
20,000 YMCA, Richmond, VA
15,500 United Way Suburban Chicago, Hinsdale, IL
9,000 United Way, Atlanta, GA
9,000 United Way Bay Area, San Francisco, CA
8,000 United Way Texas Gulf Coast, Houston, TX
7,500 United Way Orange County, Irvine, CA
7,000 United Way, Dallas, TX
7,000 United Way, St. Louis, MO
6,000 United Way Dade County, Miami, FL
6,000 United Way Massachusetts Bay, Boston, MA
5,000 Boys and Girls Club, Richmond, VA
5,000 Daily Planet, Richmond, VA
5,000 YMCA, Richmond, VA
4,500 United Way, Minneapolis, MN
4,000 Heart of Florida United Way, Orlando, FL

The CIT Group, Inc.

Company Contact

New York, NY

Company Description

Assets: US$18,932,500,000
Employees: 2,950
SIC(s): 6141 Personal Credit Institutions, 6153 Short-Term Business Credit, 6159 Miscellaneous Business Credit Institutions, 6719 Holding Companies Nec.
Parent Company: Dai-Ichi Kangyo Bank, Ltd., 1-1-5 Uchi-Saiwaicho, Chiyoda-ku, Tokyo, Japan

Operating Locations

CA: Dai-Ichi Kangyo Bank of California-Los Angeles, Los Angeles; Dai-Ichi Kangyo Bank, Limited-Los Angeles, Los Angeles; Dai-Ichi Kangyo Bank, Limited-San Francisco, San Francisco; Dai-Ichi Kangyo Bank of California, San Jose, Torrance; GA: Dai-Ichi Kangyo Bank, Limited-Atlanta, Atlanta; IL: Dai-Ichi Kangyo Bank, Limited-Chicago, Chicago; DKB Financial Futures Corp., Chicago; NJ: DKB Data Services (USA), Jersey City; CIT Group/Equipment Financing, Livingston; CIT Group/Equity Investments, Livingston; The CIT Group, Inc., Livingston; CIT Group/Industrial Financing, Livingston; CIT Group/Sales Financing, Livingston; NY: CIT Group/Business Credit, New York; CIT Group/Capital Finance, New York; CIT Group/Commercial Services, New York; CIT Group/Credit Finance, New York; CIT Group Holdings, New York; The CIT Group, Inc., New York; Dai-Ichi Kangyo Bank, Limited-New York, New York; Dai-Ichi Kangyo Trust Co. of New York, New York; DKB Financial Products, New York; DKB Securities Corp., New York; TX: Dai-Ichi Kangyo Bank, Limited-Houston, Houston

Corporate Sponsorship

Type: Arts & cultural events; Festivals/fairs
Contact: Joan Woods, Contact
Note: Sponsored events raise funds for cancer care in New Jersey.

CIT Group Foundation

Giving Contact

Albert R. Gamper, Jr., President & Chief Executive Officer
CIT Group Foundation
650 CIT Dr.
Livingston, NJ 07039
Phone: (973)740-5000
Fax: (973)740-5264

Description

EIN: 136083856
Organization Type: Corporate Foundation
Giving Locations: nationally, with an emphasis on headquarters area only.
Grant Types: General Support, Scholarship.

Financial Summary

Total Giving: $1,700,000 (1999 approx); $1,902,364 (1998); $1,718,952 (1997). Note: Contributes through corporate direct giving program and foundation.
Giving Analysis: Giving for 1996 includes: foundation grants to United Way ($263,185); foundation scholarships ($92,989); foundation matching gifts ($54,315); 1997: foundation ($1,024,571); foundation scholarships ($327,615); foundation grants to United Way ($300,060); foundation matching gifts ($66,706); 1998: foundation ($1,437,633); foundation grants to United Way ($300,000); foundation scholarships ($97,027); foundation matching gifts ($67,704)
Assets: $10,017 (1998); $62,643 (1997); $555,126 (1996)
Gifts Received: $1,850,000 (1998); $1,250,000 (1997); $1,860,040 (1996). Note: Contributions received from company.

Typical Recipients

Arts & Humanities: Arts Funds, Community Arts, Libraries, Museums/Galleries, Music, Performing Arts, Public Broadcasting, Theater
Civic & Public Affairs: African American Affairs, Business/Free Enterprise, Economic Development, Economic Policy, Civic & Public Affairs-General, Housing, Municipalities/Towns, Philanthropic Organizations, Professional & Trade Associations, Urban & Community Affairs, Women's Affairs
Education: Business Education, Colleges & Universities, Continuing Education, Education Funds, Education Reform, Engineering/Technological Education, Education-General, Journalism/Media Education, Legal Education, Minority Education, Private Education (Precollege), Public Education (Precollege), Secondary Education (Private), Secondary Education (Public), Special Education, Student Aid
Health: AIDS/HIV, Arthritis, Cancer, Children's Health/Hospitals, Clinics/Medical Centers, Emergency/Ambulance Services, Health Organizations, Heart, Hospitals, Medical Research, Mental Health, Single-Disease Health Associations, Transplant Networks/Donor Banks, Trauma Treatment
International: International Peace & Security Issues, International Relations, Missionary/Religious Activities
Religion: Dioceses, Jewish Causes, Religious Organizations, Religious Welfare
Social Services: Child Welfare, Community Centers, Community Service Organizations, Food/Clothing Distribution, Homes, People with Disabilities, Recreation & Athletics, Scouts, Shelters/Homelessness, Substance Abuse, United Funds/United Ways, Veterans, Volunteer Services, YMCA/YWCA/YMHA/YWHA, Youth Organizations

Contributions Analysis

Giving Priorities: Music, arts, museums, education, religious organizations, healthcare, and civic organizations.
Arts & Humanities: 25%. Supports music, performing arts, and museums.
Civic & Public Affairs: 16%. Emphasis is on economic development, African-American affairs, and community affairs.
Education: 16%. Supports business education, student aid, private education, and education reform. Other interests include minority education and education funds.
Health: 9%. Supports clinics, mental health care, single-disease associations, emergency care, and children's health care.
Religion: 9%. Religious welfare and Jewish and Christian causes.
Social Services: 25%. Majority of funding supports United Way and youth organizations. Also supports community centers, people with disabilities, and substance abuse organizations.
Note: Total contributions made in 1998.

Application Procedures

Initial Contact: Send a written proposal.
Application Requirements: Include a description of organization, amount requested, purpose of funds sought, audited financial statement, annual report, and proof of tax-exempt status.
Deadlines: None.

Restrictions

Does not support political or lobbying groups, or individual grants.

Corporate Officials

Albert R. Gamper, Jr.: president, chief executive officer, chairman B 1942. ED Harvard University PMD; Rutgers University BA. PRIM CORP EMPL president, chief executive officer, chairman: The CIT Group, Inc.
Janet Herowitz: director community affairs PRIM CORP EMPL director community affairs: The CIT Group, Inc.

Joseph Laone: executive vice president PRIM CORP EMPL executive vice president: The CIT Group, Inc.
Thomas J. O'Rourke: senior vice president PRIM CORP EMPL senior vice president: The CIT Group, Inc.
Joseph Anthony Pollicino: vice chairman, director B New York, NY 1939. ED Dartmouth College Graduate School of Credit & Finance Management (1977). PRIM CORP EMPL vice chairman, director: The CIT Group, Inc. CORP AFFIL director: CIT Group/Commercial Services Inc.; vice chairman: CIT Group/Credit Finance.

Foundation Officials

Albert R. Gamper, Jr.: president, chief executive officer, director (see above)
Susan Mitchell: senior vice president
Joseph Anthony Pollicino: executive vice chairman (see above)

Grants Analysis

Disclosure Period: calendar year ending 1998
Total Grants: $37,633*
Number of Grants: 326
Average Grant: $4,410
Highest Grant: $258,185
Typical Range: $500 to $10,000
***Note:** Giving excludes matching gifts, scholarship, and United Way. Grants analysis derived from 1998 Form 990.

Recent Grants

Note: Grants derived from 1997 Form 990.

Arts & Humanities

200,000 New Jersey Performing Arts Center, Livingston, NJ
200,000 New Jersey Performing Arts Center, Newark, NJ
48,750 Thirteen/WNET, New York, NY
48,750 Thirteen/WNET, New York, NY
22,000 New Jersey Performing Arts Center, Newark, NJ

Education

100,000 United Way of Tri-State, New York, NY
36,000 Newark Academy, Livingston, NJ
36,000 Newark Academy, Newark, NJ
30,000 Junior Achievement of New York, New York, NY
30,000 Junior Achievement of New York, New York, NY

Health

50,000 Saint Barnabas Medical Centers, Livingston, NJ
50,000 Saint Barnabas Medical Centers, Livingston, NJ
23,500 Pediatric Foundation, New York, NY
23,500 Pediatric Foundation, New York, NY

Religion

24,000 Catholic Community Services, Newark, NJ

Social Services

100,000 United Way of Tri-State, New York, NY
100,000 United Way of Tri-State, New York, NY
100,000 United Way of Tri-State, New York, NY
100,000 United Way of Tri-State, New York, NY
100,000 United Way of Tri-State, New York, NY

CITIBANK CORP.

 Number 34 of Top 100 Corporate Givers

Company Contact

New York, NY
Web: http://www.citi.com

Company Description

Former Name: Citicorp.
Revenue: US$32,605,000,000
Profit: US$3,464,000,000
Employees: 170,000
SIC(s): 6021 National Commercial Banks, 6712 Bank Holding Companies.
Parent Company: Citigroup, New York, NY, United States

Operating Locations

Argentina: Diners Club Argentina Sociedad Anonima Comercial y de Turismo, Buenos Aires; Celulosa Argentina SA, Capitan Bermudez, Santa Fe; Australia: ACS Financial Services Ltd., Melbourne; Clarke Vickers Services Pty. Ltd., Melbourne; Premium Fleet Charge Pty. Ltd., Melbourne; Fuelcard Pty. Ltd., Port Melbourne; Aratula P/L, Sydney; Boonah P/L, Sydney; Carindale P/L, Sydney; Citibank Ltd., Sydney; Citicorp Australia Intl Finance Ltd., Sydney; Citicorp Australia Ltd., Sydney; Citicorp Australia Overseas Finance Ltd., Sydney; Citicorp Canberra P/L, Sydney; Citicorp Capital Markets Australia Ltd., Sydney; Citicorp Financial Services Ltd., Sydney; Citicorp General Insurance Ltd., Sydney; Citicorp Insurance Brokers Australia Ltd., Sydney; Citicorp Investments Ltd., Sydney; Citicorp Life Insurance Ltd., Sydney; Citicorp Ltd., Sydney; Citicorp Nominees Pty. Ltd., Sydney; Citicorp Wholesale P/L, Sydney; Citifunds Investment Services Ltd., Sydney; Citifutures Ltd., Sydney; Citisecurities Ltd., Sydney; CVS Nominees P/L, Sydney; Margaret Street Nominees Pty. Ltd., Sydney; Remitance Collection Services Ltd., Sydney; Tarwood Pty. Ltd., Sydney; Belgium: Citibank Belgium SA, Brussels, Brabant; Citibank NA Societe de Droit Americain, Brussels, Brabant; Citicorp Insurance Service SA, Brussels, Brabant; Citilease SA, Brussels, Brabant; Citilife SA, Brussels, Brabant; Diners Club Benelux SA, Brussels, Brabant; Dinshopping SA, Brussels, Brabant; Bahamas: Citibank Colombia (Nassau) Ltd., Nassau, New Providence; Bermuda: Citicorp Insurance (Bermuda) Ltd., Hamilton; Brazil: Citibank Leasing SA Arrendamento Mercantil, Barueri; Citibank Distribuidora de Titulos e Valores Mobiliarios SA, Rio de Janeiro; Banco Crefisul de Investimento SA, Sao Paulo; CITC Brasil Comerico Exterior SA, Sao Paulo; FNC Comercio e Participacoes Ltda., Sao Paulo; Canada: Alberta Ltd., Toronto; Chudleigh Funding, Toronto; Citibank Canada, Toronto; Citibank Canada Leasing Inc., Toronto; Citibank Canada Securities Ltd., Toronto; Citibank Nominee Ltd., Toronto; Citicorp Capital Investors Ltd., Toronto; Ontario Inc., Toronto; Chile: Citicorp Chile SA Agente de Valores, Ovalle; Tarjetas de Chile SA, Rengo; Colombia: Banco Internacional de Columbia SA, Bogota, Cundinamarco; Citibank Columbia, Bogota, Cundinamarco; Cititrust Colombia SA Sociedad Fiduciaria Cititrust SA, Bogota, Cundinamarco; Costa Rica: Asesores Corporativos de Costa Rica SA, San Jose; Citivalores Puesta de Bolsa SA, San Jose; Cayman Islands: Citibank Capital Corp., George Town, Grand Cayman; Mighty Ltd. Partnership, George Town, Grand Cayman; Czech Republic: Citibank AS, Prague; Denmark: Citibank Intl Plc, Copenhagen; Dominican Republic: Banco de Desarrolo Citicorp SA, Santo Domingo; France: Citibank International Plc, Courbevoie, Hauts-de-Seine; Citi Chanzy, Puteaux, Hauts-de-Seine; Citi Churchill, Puteaux, Hauts-de-Seine; Citi Gestion, Puteaux, Hauts-de-Seine; Citi Immobilier SA, Puteaux, Hauts-de-Seine; Citi les Tilleuls SA, Puteaux, Hauts-de-Seine; Citibank SA, Puteaux, Hauts-de-Seine; Paris Citicorp Center, Puteaux, Hauts-de-Seine; Germany: Citi Services GmbH, Aachen, Nordrhein-Westfalen; Citibank Privatkunden AG, Duesseldorf; Citifinanzberatung GmbH-Beratungs- und Vermittlungsgesellschaft fuer Bank- und Versicherungsdienstleistungen, Duesseldorf; Alpha Trans Leasing Verwaltungs GmbH, Frankfurt, Hessen; Beta Trans Leasing Verwaltungsgesellschaft mbH, Frankfurt, Hessen; Citibank AG, Frankfurt, Hessen; Citibank Beteiligungen AG, Frankfurt, Hessen; Citibank Invest Kapitalanlage GmbH, Frankfurt, Hessen; Citibank NA in New York Filiale Frankfurt, Frankfurt, Hessen; Citicorp Kartenservice GmbH, Frankfurt, Hessen; Citicorp Leasing (Deutschland) GmbH, Frankfurt, Hessen; Citicorp Venture Capital Beratungs GmbH, Frankfurt, Hessen; Diners Club Deutschland GmbH, Frankfurt, Hessen; Fairchild Semiconductor GmbH, Fuerstenfeldbruck, Bayern; Citicorp Operations Consulting GmbH, Meerbusch, Nordrhein-Westfalen; Gamma Trans Leasing Verwaltun GmbH, Nidderau, Hessen; Guam: Citicorp Credit, Agana; Hong Kong: Asia Pacific Capital Corp. Ltd., Causeway Bay; Citibank VA (Nominees) Ltd., Causeway Bay; Citicorp Insurance Agency Ltd., Causeway Bay; Citicorp Investment Services Ltd., Causeway Bay; Citibank Global Asset Management (Asia) Ltd., Central District; Citicorp Asia Pacific Ltd., Central District; Citicorp International Ltd., Central District; Citicorp International Nominees Ltd., Central District; Mercantile Bank Ltd., Central District; Citicorp Hong Kong Ltd., Kennedy Town; Network Foods (Hong Kong) Ltd., North Point; Citibank Investment Services Ltd., Quarry Bay; Citicorp Commercial Finance (Hong Kong) Ltd., Tsim Sha Tsui, Kowloon; Fairchild Semiconductor Hong Kong Ltd., Tsim Sha Tsui, Kowloon; Carte Blanche International (Hong Kong) Ltd., Wan Chai; Honduras: Banco de Honduras SA, Tegucigalpa; Hungary: Citibank RT, Budapest; Indonesia: PT Citicorp Finance Indonesia, Jakarta, Jakarta Raya; PT Citicorp Securities Indonesia, Jakarta, Jakarta Raya; India: Citicorp Information Technology Industries Ltd., Mumbai; Citicorp Overseas Software Ltd., Mumbai; City Corp Overseas Software Ltd., Mumbai; Ireland: Citibank Holdings Ireland Ltd., Dublin; Citibank NA, Dublin; Citibank Trustees (Ireland) Ltd., Dublin; Citicorp (Dublin) Finance, Dublin; Citicorp Finance Ireland Ltd., Dublin; Citicorp Investments Managers Ireland Ltd., Dublin; Citilux Ireland, Dublin; Pavec Ltd., Dublin; Scottish Provident (Irish Holdings) Ltd., Dublin; Pope Brothers (Mallow) Ltd., Mallow; Italy: Citicorp Finanziaria Citifin SpA, Milano, Lombardia; Citinvest SpA, Milano, Lombardia; Citiservice SpA, Milano, Lombardia; Cititrust SpA Istituto Fiduciario, Milano, Lombardia; Jamaica: First National Citibank, Kingston; Japan: Citicorp Credit, Tokyo; Citilease Co. Ltd., Tokyo; Cititrust & Banking Corp., Tokyo; Fairchild Semiconductor Japan Ltd., Tokyo; Republic of Korea: First Citicorp Leasing, Chongno-Gu; Luxembourg: Citibank Luxembourg SA, Luxembourg; Citicurrencies SA, Luxembourg; Citilandmark SA, Luxembourg; Citimarkets SA, Luxembourg; Citinvest SA, Luxembourg; Citiporfolios SA, Luxembourg; Femos Holding SA, Luxembourg; Mexico: Arrendadora Financiera Reforma SA de CV, Ciudad de Mexico; Citi Info SA de CV, Ciudad de Mexico; Citi Promotora de Fondos SA de CV, Ciudad de Mexico; Diners Club de Mexico SA de CV, Ciudad de Mexico; Imref SA de CV, Ciudad de Mexico; Malaysia: Citicorp Capital Sdn. Bhd., Kuala Lumpur, Selangor; Citicorp International Trading Co. Sdn. Bhd., Kuala Lumpur, Selangor; Netherlands: Berlin Real Estate BV, Amsterdam, Noord-Holland; Castellana 21 BV, Amsterdam, Noord-Holland; Citibank NA, Amsterdam, Noord-Holland; Creinvest BV, Amsterdam, Noord-Holland; Diners Club Benelux SA, Amsterdam, Noord-Holland; Dinshopping NV, Amsterdam, Noord-Holland; Hanseatic Real Estate BV, Amsterdam, Noord-Holland; Citicorp Financia BV, Arnhem, Gelderland; New Zealand: Advance Futures Ltd., Auckland; Pakistan: Citicorp Investment Bank (Pakistan) Ltd., Islamabad; Paraguay: Citifinanciera SA, Asuncion; Peru: Citicorp Servium SA, Lima; Sociedad Entermediaria de Valgres Inversiones Citicorp, Lima; Philippines: Fairchild Semiconductor Authority (Hong Kong) Ltd. (Philippines), Lapu City, Cebu; Citi Center Building Corp., Manila; Portfolio Holdings, Manila; Poland: Citibank Poland SA, Warsaw, Warszawa; Portugal: Citibank Portugal SA, Lisboa; Singapore: Citibank Consumers Nominee Pte. Ltd., Singapore; Citibank Finance Ltd., Singapore; Citibank Nominees Singapore Pte. Ltd., Singapore; Citicorp Futures Ltd., Singapore; Citicorp Investment Bank (Singapore) Pte.

Ltd., Singapore; Citicorp Vickers Singapore Pte. Ltd., Singapore; Diners Club Asia, Singapore; Fairchild Semiconductor Asia Pacific Pte. Ltd., Singapore; Federal Express Pacific Inc., Singapore; Le Chocolatier Boutique Pte. Ltd., Singapore; Network Foods Distribution Pte. Ltd., Singapore; Pengkalen Investments Ltd., Singapore; SCI Manufacturing Singaport Pte. Ltd., Singapore; Specialist Food Retailers Pte. Ltd., Singapore; Spain: Citibank Broker Correduria de Seguros SA, Alcobendas, Madrid; Citibank Espana SA, Alcobendas, Madrid; Citifin Espana Establecimiento Financiero de Credito SA, Alcobendas, Madrid; Citigestion Sociedad Gestora de Instituciones de Inversion Colectiva SA, Alcobendas, Madrid; Citihouse SA, Alcobendas, Madrid; Citipensiones Entidad Gestora de Fondo de Pensiones SA, Alcobendas, Madrid; Citibank NA Sucursal en Espana, Madrid; Citifondo Lider Fondo de Inversion Mobiliaria, Madrid; Sweden: Citibank NA, Stockholm; Switzerland: Confidas Finance et Placement SA, Geneva; Citibank (Switzerland), Zurich; Thailand: Citicapital Ltd., Bangkok; Citicorp Finance & Securities (Thailand) Ltd., Bangkok; Citicorp Leasing (Thailand) Ltd., Bangkok; Diners Club Thailand Ltd., Bangkok; Trinidad and Tobago: Citibank (Trinidad & Tobago) Ltd., Port-of-Spain; Citicorp Merchant Bank Ltd., Port-of-Spain; Taiwan: Citibank NA Taiwan Branch, Taipei; Diners Club International (Taiwan) Ltd., Taipei; United Kingdom: Cardholder Services Ltd., Farnborough, Hampshire; Diners Club Ltd., Farnborough, Hampshire; SCI Development Ltd., Irvine, Strathclyde; Assuritas Corp., Jersey, Channel Islands; CCIL Nominees Ltd., Jersey, Channel Islands; Citibank (Channel Islands) Ltd., Jersey, Channel Islands; Citicorp (Jersey) Ltd., Jersey, Channel Islands; Finch Ltd., Jersey, Channel Islands; Jersey Corporate Trade Services Ltd., Jersey, Channel Islands; Primus Nominees (Jersey) Ltd., Jersey, Channel Islands; Channel Collections Ltd., London; CIB Properties Ltd., London; Citi Pensions & Trustees Ltd., London; Citibank Financial Trust Ltd., London; Citibank Intl Plc, London; Citibank Investments Ltd., London; Citibank Leasing Ltd., London; Citibank NA, London; Citibank Trust Ltd., London; Citicorp, London; Citicorp Diners Club Ltd., London; Citicorp Finance Ltd., London; Citicorp Scrimgeour Vickers Securities Ltd., London; Citicorp Trustee Co. Ltd., London; Citicorporate Ltd., London; Citifriends Nominee Ltd., London; Citifutures Ltd., London; Citiloans Plc, London; Citinet Ltd., London; CVC Capital Partners Ltd., London; National City Nominees Ltd., London; NCB Trust Ltd., London; Norwich Property Trust Ltd., London; Vidacos Nominees Ltd., London; Blenheim House Hotel, North Berwick, East Lothian; Lee International Film Studios Ltd., Shepperton, Middlesex; Rush Lane Investments Ltd., Shepperton, Middlesex; Uruguay: Citicorp Inversiones SAIF, Montevideo; Diners Club Uruguay SA, Montevideo; Venezuela: Citibank NA, Caracas; Citicorp Mercado de Capitales CA, Caracas; Citidata CA, Caracas

Nonmonetary Support

Type: Donated Equipment
Note: In Miami, the Citibank Family Tech Program donated 1,000 computers to students.
Volunteer Programs: The corporation's volunteer incentive program provides up to $500 for organizations to which employees volunteer.

Corporate Sponsorship

Type: Music & entertainment events

Citigroup Foundation

Giving Contact

Paul Michael Ostergard, Vice President, Director, Corporate Contributions & Civic Responsibility
Citibank
153 East 53rd Street, 3rd Floor
New York, NY 10043
Phone: (212)559-9547
Fax: (212)793-5944

Description

EIN: 133781879
Organization Type: Corporate Foundation
Giving Locations: NY: New York headquarters and operating communities.
Grant Types: Employee Matching Gifts, Fellowship, General Support, Multiyear/Continuing Support, Project.
Note: Employee matching gift ratio: 1 to 1.

Giving Philosophy

'Economic vitality, business growth and strong societies go together. Citibank's Contributions program reflects that basic understanding of how the world works. .. In towns, cities and countries all over the globe, we use our contributions to stimulate broader participation. We look for ways to give that multiply the impact of the funds we provide. We try to nurture human imagination and to solve problems. We look for innovators, and particularly for people who understand that involvement and commitment often make the difference between a good idea and a good idea that works. We look for projects that will attract and involve thousands of Citibank employees who join with organizations we support and add their own time, energy and resources to produce measurable results.'
Report on Citicorp's Contributions and Guidelines

Financial Summary

Total Giving: $27,000,000 (1999 approx); $28,014,058 (1998); $35,000,000 (1997 approx). Note: Contributes through corporate direct giving program and foundation. Giving includes corporate direct giving; foundation; domestic and international subsidiaries.
Giving Analysis: Giving for 1996 includes: foundation ($11,004,261); domestic subsidiaries ($6,772,439); foundation matching gifts ($5,234,246); international subsidiaries ($4,772,554); corporate direct giving ($3,326,000); 1998: foundation ($17,040,571); foundation matching gifts ($8,454,987); corporate direct giving ($2,293,500); foundation grants to United Way ($780,000)
Assets: $136,206,912 (1998); $12,435,172 (1996)
Gifts Received: $122,917,264 (1998); $19,699,658 (1996). Note: Foundation receives contributions from Citicorp and Citibank.

Typical Recipients

Arts & Humanities: Arts Appreciation, Arts Associations & Councils, Arts Centers, Arts Festivals, Arts Funds, Arts Institutes, Dance, Ethnic & Folk Arts, Historic Preservation, Libraries, Museums/Galleries, Music, Opera, Performing Arts, Public Broadcasting, Theater
Civic & Public Affairs: Business/Free Enterprise, Civil Rights, Economic Development, Economic Policy, Employment/Job Training, Nonprofit Management, Public Policy, Urban & Community Affairs, Women's Affairs, Zoos/Aquariums
Education: Arts/Humanities Education, Business Education, Colleges & Universities, Community & Junior Colleges, Continuing Education, Economic Education, Education Associations, Education Funds, Elementary Education (Private), International Exchange, International Studies, Literacy, Minority Education, Private Education (Precollege), Public Education (Precollege), Science/Mathematics Education, Special Education
Environment: Environment-General
Health: Emergency/Ambulance Services, Health Policy/Cost Containment, Health Organizations, Hospices, Hospitals, Medical Research, Single-Disease Health Associations
International: Foreign Educational Institutions, Health Care/Hospitals, International Peace & Security Issues, International Relations
Social Services: Child Welfare, Community Centers, Community Service Organizations, Day Care, Emergency Relief, Family Services, Food/Clothing Distribution, Homes, People with Disabilities, Shelters/Homelessness, United Funds/United Ways, Volunteer Services, Youth Organizations

Contributions Analysis

Giving Priorities: Education, civic development, culture, health, and United Way. Company gives to U.S.-based nonprofits with an international focus, as well as to local organizations through foreign subsidiaries. Support to U.S.-based organizations is handled at corporate headquarters. Grants for developed countries are made in the same categories as in the United States, including research on critical issues in the global economy; education; and communication among leaders in countries in which company operates, as well as culture and the arts. Grants for developing countries focus on technical assistance for development, specialized medical training and treatment, as well as disaster relief efforts. Overseas corporate officers and contribtuions committees develop priorities that address local interest. Budgets are derived from operating earnings. The two major functions overseas include education and community revitalization.
Arts & Humanities: 6%. Museums and performing arts groups receive significant support. Special interest in groups that encourage new talent and outreach programs that bring the arts to broad audiences,including public schools and the disadvantaged. Cultural support also includes historical preservation, libraries, public broadcasting, arts councils, zoos, botanical gardens, and arts education. Matches employee contributions to cultural groups.
Civic & Public Affairs: 46%. Funds neighborhood development, including groups concerned with economic development and affordable housing. Increasing emphasis is on community development financial institutions. Also supports employment training, civic groups, nonprofit technical assistance, and groups concerned with urban issues.
Education: 41%. Supports efforts to improve education at all levels. Increasing efforts on K-12 programs within inner-city schools; early childhood and public education; and programs that focus on equal access to quality education for minorities and women. Also interested in programs to prepare young people for employment. Supports organizations conducting research on free enterprise, economics, and public policy; graduate schools of business; and other institutions from which employees are recruited. Matches employees' gifts to education.
Environment: 2%. Supports national conservation efforts.
Health: 5%. Focuses on education to prevent health problems and health care cost containment. Support goes largely to the United Way of the Tri-State Area. Other united funds in major operating locations also receive support.
International: Overseas business units award grants to qualified local charities. The company also awards funds to U.S.-based nonprofit organizations with an international focus.

Application Procedures

Initial Contact: Call for guidelines.
Application Requirements: Proposal should include a brief statement of history, goals, and accomplishments; purpose and objective of project; current annual report; amount requested; proof of tax-exempt status; current year's budget showing anticipated expenses and income; list of funding sources and amounts contributed; most recently audited financial statement; list of governing board members; and list of accrediting agencies, when appropriate; cultural organizations should include audience statistics.
Deadlines: Small requests are handled regularly; other requests have various deadlines available from the contact person.

Review Process: Initial review by contributions staff and committee members, who may deny a request or make a recommendation to the full committee or policy committee.
Evaluative Criteria: Provide evidence of clearly delineated goals and effective, innovative programs that conform to bank's giving priorities; have stable management, and sound financial status; strong leadership to strengthen communities in which bank operates and serve as a model for other nonprofits; and opportunities for employee volunteer involvement.
Decision Notification: Ongoing; contributions committee meets as required; in most cases, applicants learn of a decision in writing within sixty to ninety days.
Notes: Many contributions committees use a proposal application form, available from local contact person. Citibank and Citicorp Foundation initiate majority of funding, but unsolicited proposals are accepted.

Restrictions

The company does not support individuals; political causes or candidates; religious, veterans', or fraternal organizations, unless project significantly benefits entire community; fund-raising dinners, benefits, or events; or courtesy advertising.

Additional Information

Citicorp Foundation and Travelers Foundation merged to form the Citigroup Foundation in 1999.
Company and foundation prefer to initiate grants, but will consider unsolicited proposals.
The company generally prefers to support specific, one-year programs in areas of charitable interest.
Potential for combination with volunteers, in-kind services, or other direct Citibank involvement is frequently a deciding factor in grant decisions. Citibank also makes housing, small business, and student loans; is involved with programs to hire minority youth and to pay summer interns at community nonprofit organizations; provides technical assistance; and encourages employees to participate in the matching gifts program.
Publications: Public Responsibility at Citibank; Guidelines

Corporate Officials

Paul John Collins: vice chairman, director B West Bend, WI 1936. ED University of Wisconsin BBA (1958); Harvard University MBA (1961). PRIM CORP EMPL vice chairman, director: Citibank. CORP AFFIL director: Kimberly-Clark Corp.; director: Nokia Corp. NONPR AFFIL trustee: Central Park Conservancy; trustee: Glyndebume Arts Trust; trustee: Carnegie Hall. CLUB AFFIL River Club.
Paul Michael Ostergard: vice president, director corporate contributions B Akron, OH 1939. ED University of Madrid (1959-1960); Case Western Reserve University AB (1961); University of Michigan JD (1964); Harvard University MPA (1969). PRIM CORP EMPL vice president, director corporate contributions: Citibank. NONPR AFFIL member: Omicron Delta Kappa; member: Phi Beta Kappa; director: ARC Greater Greater New York; director: Junior Achievement New York; member, board: American Council Arts. CLUB AFFIL Wexford Plantation Club; Harvard Club.
John Shepard Reed: co-chairman B Chicago, IL 1939. ED Massachusetts Institute of Technology BA (1961); Massachusetts Institute of Technology BS (1961); Massachusetts Institute of Technology MS (1965). PRIM CORP EMPL co-chairman: CitiGroup Inc. ADD CORP EMPL chairman, chief executive officer: Citibank NA. CORP AFFIL director: Rand Corp.; director: Philip Morris Inc.; director: Monsanto Co.; director: Philip Morris Companies Inc. NONPR AFFIL member: Memorial Sloan-Kettering Cancer Center; member services policy advisory committee: U.S. Trade Report; director: Massachusetts Institute Technology; member policy committee: Business Roundtable; chairman: Coalition Service Industry; member: Business Council; member: American Museum Natural History.
William Reginald Rhodes: vice chairman B New York, NY 1935. ED Brown University BA History (1957). PRIM CORP EMPL vice chairman: Citibank. CORP AFFIL director: Conoco Inc.; vice chairman: Citigroup Inc. NONPR AFFIL member: Venezuela-American Chamber of Commerce; board overseers: Watson Institute International Studies; member executive committee: United States-Russia Business Council; member: United States-Egyptian President Council; founding member: United States National Council International Management Center Budapest; director: Private Export Funding Corp.; government: New York Presbyterian Hospital; chairman: Northfield Mt Hermon School; director: New York City Partnership; member: Lincoln Center Corporate Leadership Committee; vice chairman: Metropolitan Museum Business Committee; vice chairman: Institute International Finance Inc.; director: Foreign Policy Association; director: Institute East-West Studies; member: Council Foreign Relations; trustee: Brown University; trustee: Council Americas; member executive committee: Bretton Woods Committee; member: Bankers Association Foreign Trade; member: Bankers Roundtable; director: Americas Society; director: African-American Institute.
Herman Onno Ruding: vice chairman, director B Breda, Netherlands 1939. ED Erasmus University (Netherlands) School of Economics MA (1964); Erasmus University (Netherlands) School of Economics PhD (1969). PRIM CORP EMPL vice chairman, director: Citibank. CORP AFFIL director: Corning Inc.; vice chairman, director: Citicorp. NONPR AFFIL director: Sinai Hospital; member: Trilateral Commission; member: Committee Monetary Union Europe; member: Christian Democratic Alliance.
Sanford I. Weill: chairman, chief executive officer B New York, NY 1933. ED Cornell University BA (1955); Cornell University Graduate School Business & Public Administration (1954-1955). PRIM CORP EMPL chairman, chief executive officer: Citigroup. CORP AFFIL director: E.I. du Pont de Nemours and Co.; director: IDS Mutual Fund Group; director: AT&T Corp. NONPR AFFIL member business committee: Museum Modern Art; member: New York Society Security Analysts; member, board overseers: Cornell University Medicine College; chairman: Carnegie Hall Society Inc.; vice chairman advisory council: Cornell University Johnson Graduate School Management; founder: Academy Fin. CLUB AFFIL Cornell Club; Harmonie Club; Century Country Club.

Giving Program Officials

Alan Okada: PRIM CORP EMPL vice president health programs: Citibank. CORP AFFIL vice president health programs: Citibank NA.
Peter C. Thorp: PRIM CORP EMPL vice president university relations: Citibank. CORP AFFIL vice president univ rels: Citibank NA.

Foundation Officials

Paul Michael Ostergard: president (see above)

Grants Analysis

Disclosure Period: calendar year ending 1998
Total Grants: $19,334,071*
Number of Grants: 700 (approx)
Average Grant: $27,620*
Highest Grant: $225,000
Typical Range: $5,000 to $50,000
*Note: Giving excludes United Way and matching gifts.

CITIGROUP

Company Contact

New York, NY
Web: http://www.citi.com

Company Description

Former Name: Primerica Corp.; Travelers Inc.; Travelers Group.
Assets: US$716,900,000,000 (1999)
Profit: US$9,867,000,000 (1999)
Employees: 56,200
Fortune Rank: 7, per FORTUNE Magazine's list of 500 Largest U.S. Corporations (1999).
FF 7
SIC(s): 6022 State Commercial Banks, 6141 Personal Credit Institutions, 6153 Short-Term Business Credit, 6159 Miscellaneous Business Credit Institutions.

Operating Locations

Travelers has branch offices throughout the U.S. Its main business subsidiaries include: Smith Barney Shearson; Primerica Financial Services; Commerical Credit Co.; American Capital Management & Research; RCM; Transport Life Insurance Co.; Primerica Bank; and Gulf Insurance Co.; and The Travelers Insurance Companies.

Nonmonetary Support

Value: $500,000 (1990)

Corporate Sponsorship

Note: Sponsors a limited number of fundraising dinners and events annually.

Citigroup Foundation

Giving Contact

Paul M. Ostergard, Chairman, Chief Executive Officer
Citigroup Foundation
153 E. 53rd St., 3rd Floor
New York, NY 10043
Phone: (212)559-9163

Alternate Contact

Ms. Patricia R. Byrne, Grants Manager

Description

Organization Type: Corporate Foundation
Former Name: Primerica Foundation.
Giving Locations: headquarters and operating communities.
Grant Types: General Support, Project.

Giving Philosophy

'The Travelers Foundation is the principal philanthropic program of Travelers Group. Through our efforts nationwide, we stand on the vanguard of an established trend: supporting programs that serve the critical needs of children and families.
'Grants from the Foundation support public education. They serve to expand and promote career education opportunities; to assure readiness of young children to enter and succeed in school; and to foster arts education programs.
'In every project we fund, the key to making a difference is 'the people ingredient'--the participation of Travelers Group employees. Spread throughout the country in a wide network of subsidiary offices, our people volunteer their time and expertise to organizations that they determine work most effectively to solve local problems. This hands-on involvement, coupled with financial support from the Foundation, is a powerful synergy that can effect positive change both locally and nationally.' *A Face Behind Every Grant, Travelers Foundation 1996 Annual Report*

Financial Summary

Total Giving: $12,475,656 (1997); $10,817,765 (1996); $9,631,501 (1995). Note: Contributes through corporate direct giving program and foundation. 1997

Giving includes foundation, including local contributions ($6,492,785); general grants (5,312,470); Volunteer Incentive program (670,401). 1996 Giving includes foundation, including local contributions ($5,680,172); general grants ($4,462,579); Volunteer Incentive program ($675,014).
Assets: $9,932,321 (1995); $4,525,873 (1993); $2,600,906 (1991)

Typical Recipients

Arts & Humanities: Arts Associations & Councils, Arts Centers, Arts Outreach, Ballet, Community Arts, Dance, History & Archaeology, Libraries, Museums/Galleries, Music, Opera, Performing Arts, Public Broadcasting, Theater, Visual Arts
Civic & Public Affairs: African American Affairs, Botanical Gardens/Parks, Business/Free Enterprise, Economic Development, Employment/Job Training, Hispanic Affairs, Housing, Municipalities/Towns, Parades/Festivals, Public Policy, Safety, Women's Affairs
Education: Afterschool/Enrichment Programs, Arts/Humanities Education, Business Education, Business-School Partnerships, Colleges & Universities, Economic Education, Education Funds, Education Reform, Education-General, Literacy, Medical Education, Minority Education, Preschool Education, Private Education (Precollege), Public Education (Precollege), Science/Mathematics Education, Secondary Education (Public), Student Aid
Environment: Environment-General, Resource Conservation
Health: AIDS/HIV, Cancer, Children's Health/Hospitals, Clinics/Medical Centers, Diabetes, Geriatric Health, Health Organizations, Home-Care Services, Hospitals, Hospitals (University Affiliated), Medical Rehabilitation, Medical Research, Prenatal Health Issues, Preventive Medicine/Wellness Organizations, Public Health
International: Missionary/Religious Activities
Religion: Churches, Jewish Causes, Religious Organizations, Religious Welfare, Seminaries
Social Services: At-Risk Youth, Child Abuse, Child Welfare, Community Centers, Community Service Organizations, Day Care, Domestic Violence, Family Services, Food/Clothing Distribution, Recreation & Athletics, Scouts, Shelters/Homelessness, Substance Abuse, United Funds/United Ways, YMCA/YWCA/YMHA/YWHA, Youth Organizations

Contributions Analysis

Giving Priorities: Public education, human service, health, civic development, and culture.
Arts & Humanities: 10% to 15%. Supports performing art centers and groups, art foundations, galleries, and libraries. Also supports art education programs.
Civic & Public Affairs: 5% to 10%. Housing programs, community foundations and public policy research receive funding.
Education: About 45%. Focus is on improving public education, particularly in the areas of school to work transition and preparing children to enter and succeed in school. Recipients include public schools, preschool education and care programs, and minority education projects. Also supports literacy projects, arts education, afterschool programs, and economic education. A major focus is the Academy of Finance Program.
Social Services: About 35%. Supports medical foundations, health centers, single-disease associations, hospitals, and infant health organizations. Human service interests include United Ways, other youth organizations, child welfare and safetygroups, and food distribution. Emphasis is on improving the quality of life for families and children.

Application Procedures

Initial Contact: one- to three-page preliminary proposal, either to the contact for national and New York City organizations, or to the nearest Travelers Group office
Application Requirements: description of and purpose of organization; name, title, address, and phone number of contact person; description of project to be funded (include objectives, target groups, needs, activities, budget, and timespan); copy of IRS tax-exempt letter; recent financial information, including a recently audited financial statement, list of recent contributors, and an annual report, if available; list of organization's governing board; description of staff; and proof that organization and services are not discriminatory in any way
Deadlines: None.
Review Process: review takes two to three months; foundation may need to call to obtain additional information
Notes: Foundation uses four categories to classify its grants: general grants, local contributions, Volunteer Incentive Program, and the Smith Barney Community Investment program. Each category has its own requirements.

Restrictions

The foundation does not support individuals; political organizations; religious bodies; labor organizations; agencies whose sole purpose is social or recreational; and professional marketing or trade organizations.
The following activities are not eligible for support: courtesy advertising; special events; books, magazines, or articles in professional journals; or fundraising activities such as benefits, charitable dinners or sporting events.
The foundation does not support capital or endowment fund drives, except under special circumstances with a waiver from the foundation's board of directors; nor does it provide general operating funds for member agencies of United Way in areas where Travelers Group or its affiliates give to those united fund drives.

Additional Information

Citigroup Foundation was created in 1999 by the merger of the Citicorp Foundation and the Travelers Foundation. Profile grants reflect those of the Travelers Foundation for 1996.

Corporate Officials

Robert Irving Lipp: chief executive officer B 1938. ED Williams College (1960); Harvard University MBA (1963); New York University JD (1969). PRIM CORP EMPL chief executive officer: Citigroup ADD CORP EMPL chairman: Automobile Insurance Co. of Hartford; chairman: Standard Fire Insurance Co.; president: Travco Insurance Co.; group chief executive officer, vice chairman: Travelers Group Inc.; chairman: Travelers Casualty Surety Co. America; chairman: Travelers Casualty Surety Co. Illinois; chairman: Travelers Indemnity Co.; chairman: Travelers Indemnity of Connecticut; chairman: Travelers Property Casualty. CORP AFFIL director: Commercial Credit Co.; president: Phoenix Insurance Co.; director: CCC Holdings Inc.
Joseph James Plumeri, II: president B Trenton, NJ 1943. ED College of William & Mary BA (1966); New York Law School (1969-1969). PRIM CORP EMPL president: Primerica Financial Services. CORP AFFIL vice chairman, group chief executive officer: Travelers Group Inc.; vice chairman: Citigroup Inc. NONPR AFFIL director, trustee endowment association: College William & Mary. CLUB AFFIL Columbus Club.
Charles O. Prince, III: senior vice president, general counsel, secretary B 1950. ED University of Southern California BA (1971); University of Southern California MA (1975); University of Southern California JD (1975). PRIM CORP EMPL executive vice president, general counsel, secretary: Travelers Group.
Todd Thomson: chief financial officer PRIM CORP EMPL chief financial officer: Citigroup.
Sanford I. Weill: chairman, chief executive officer B New York, NY 1933. ED Cornell University BA (1955); Cornell University Graduate School Business & Public Administration (1954-1955). PRIM CORP EMPL chairman, chief executive officer: Citigroup. CORP AFFIL director: E.I. du Pont de Nemours and Co.; director: IDS Mutual Fund Group; director: AT&T Corp. NONPR AFFIL member business committee: Museum Modern Art; member: New York Society Security Analysts; member, board overseers: Cornell University Medicine College; chairman: Carnegie Hall Society Inc.; vice chairman advisory council: Cornell University Johnson Graduate School Management; founder: Academy Fin. CLUB AFFIL Cornell Club; Harmonie Club; Century Country Club.

Foundation Officials

Patricia R. Bryne: assistant treasurer, grants manager
James R. Dimon: trustee B New York, NY 1956. ED Tufts University BA (1978); Harvard University Graduate School of Business Administration MBA (1982). PRIM CORP EMPL president, chief operating officer, chief financial officer: The Travelers Inc. ADD CORP EMPL president: Primerica Corp.; president: Travelers Group Inc. CORP AFFIL director: Tricon Global Restaurants Inc.
Robert Irving Lipp: vice president, treasurer, trustee (see above)
Charles O. Prince, III: secretary, trustee (see above)
Charles V. Raymond: president
Sanford I. Weill: chairman (see above)

Grants Analysis

Disclosure Period: calendar year ending 1997
Total Grants: $11,805,255*
Number of Grants: 1,625
Average Grant: $7,265
Highest Grant: $1,200,000
Typical Range: $1,000 to $20,000
***Note:** Giving excludes Volunteer Incentive program.

Recent Grants

Note: Grants derived from 1997 Form 990.

Arts & Humanities

300,000	Carnegie Hall
250,000	OLD STATE HOUSE ASSOC.
110,000	Greater Hartford Arts Council Inc.
75,000	Connecticut Public Television and Radio
72,000	Robert W Woodruff Arts Center, Inc
60,000	City of New York Department of Cultural Affairs
50,000	Baltimore Childrens Museum
50,000	Bushnell Memorial Hall
50,000	Children's Television Workshop
50,000	Gerald R. Ford Foundation
50,000	National Symphony Orchestra
45,000	New York City Ballet

Civic & Public Affairs

75,000	Families and Work Institute
50,000	Center for Career Development in Early Care and Education

Education

350,000	National Academy Foundation
300,000	National Academy Foundation
300,000	National Academy Foundation
200,000	National Academy Foundation
115,000	United Negro College Fund, Inc
102,000	Fund for Public Schools, Inc.
75,000	Center City Churches, Inc.
70,000	Berkmar Cluster Schools
50,000	Center for Arts Education
50,000	Citizenship Education Fund
50,000	INNER CITY SCHOLARSHIP
45,000	Williams College
40,000	Fund for Public Schools, Inc.
35,000	Florida State University Foundation
30,000	Fund for Educational Excellence
30,000	Junior Achievement of North Central Connecticut
30,000	New Visions for Public Schools
30,000	University of Connecticut

Health

200,000	New York University Medical Center
50,000	New York Downtown Hospital
35,000	Hartford Action Plan on Infant Health
30,000	VNA Health Care Inc., Plainville, CT

Religion

250,000	ASYLUM HILL
250,000	CONGREGATIONAL CHURCH

Social Services

300,000	United Way of the Capital Area, Inc.
135,000	Center on Addiction and Substance Abuse
66,667	NATIONAL COMMITTEE TO
65,000	Childrens Defense Fund
55,000	DARE New Jersey
50,000	Child Care Action Campaign
50,000	Child Care, Inc.
50,000	National Assoc. of Child Care Resource & Referral Agencies
50,000	YMCA OF GREATER NEW YORK
40,000	United Neighborhood Houses
38,762	Emory Egleston Children's Research Center
30,000	KIDSGYM, USA
30,000	New York State Child Care Coordinating Council

CITIZENS BANK-FLINT

Company Contact

Flint, MI
Web: http://www.cbcf.com

Company Description

SIC(s): 6036 Savings Institutions Except Federal.
Parent Company: Citizens Banking Corp.
Parent Assets: US$132,880,000,000

Nonmonetary Support

Type: Cause-related Marketing & Promotion; Donated Equipment; In-kind Services; Loaned Executives

Corporate Sponsorship

Type: Arts & cultural events; Festivals/fairs; Music & entertainment events; Sports events
Note: Supports auctions and dinners for all areas.

Giving Contact

David Albert, Assistant Vice President
328 South Saginaw Street
Flint, MI 48502
Phone: (810)766-7500
Fax: (810)766-7634

Description

Organization Type: Corporate Giving Program
Giving Locations: headquarters and operating communities.
Grant Types: Challenge, Employee Matching Gifts, General Support, Project, Scholarship, Seed Money.

Financial Summary

Total Giving: $450,000 (2000 approx); $300,000 (1999 approx); $300,000 (1998 approx). Note: Contributes through corporate direct giving program only.

Typical Recipients

Arts & Humanities: Arts Associations & Councils, Arts Centers, Arts Festivals, Arts Outreach, Community Arts, Arts & Humanities-General
Civic & Public Affairs: African American Affairs, Asian American Affairs, Botanical Gardens/Parks, Business/Free Enterprise, Chambers of Commerce, Community Foundations, Economic Development, Civic & Public Affairs-General, Housing, Inner-City Development, Nonprofit Management, Urban & Community Affairs
Education: Afterschool/Enrichment Programs, Arts/Humanities Education, Business Education, Business-School Partnerships, Colleges & Universities, Community & Junior Colleges, Education-General, Health & Physical Education, Medical Education, Minority Education
Health: Adolescent Health Issues, Children's Health/Hospitals, Clinics/Medical Centers, Health-General
Social Services: At-Risk Youth, Camps, Child Welfare, Community Service Organizations, Day Care, Family Planning, People with Disabilities, Shelters/Homelessness, Social Services-General, United Funds/United Ways, Volunteer Services, Youth Organizations

Application Procedures

Initial Contact: written request to marketing department
Application Requirements: background and financial information of the organization and name, telephone number, and address of a contact person; copy of the organization's determination of IRS 501(c)(3) status; an explanation of the organization's purpose and philosophy; evidence of managerial skill, expertise, knowledge, commitment and support from a policy board or from the community; and the amount requested and intended use of the funds
Evaluative Criteria: support from other sources, scope and effectiveness of the proposed program
Notes: The amount requested must be reasonable in relation to the total funds required for the project.

Restrictions

Grants for operating purposes including budget deficits and daily expenses incurred for the operation of the organization will generally not be considered. Pledges for longer-term capital projects may be considered.
Bank will not make contributions for the purpose or with the intent of obtaining or retaining business. Organizations receiving support from general community fund campaigns, which already receive support from the bank, are not eligible to receive additional funding support. Contributions are not normally made to national health organizations. Support may be provided to local agencies of national organizations to meet local needs.
Also does not support political organizations or candidates; sectarian organizations whose services are limited to members of any one religious group; fraternal or veterans organizations unless the gift is in support of a recognized community project; or the operating funds of hospitals or other patient care institutions (capital programs may be considered).

Additional Information

Citizens Bank is the lead bank of Citizens Banking Corp. This profile relates to information for Citizens Bank of Flint, MI, only. Citizens Bank-Flint recognizes that its obligations to meet the credit and other banking needs of the low and moderate-income areas of its community under the Community Reinvestment Act are separate and distinct from its obligations relative to charitable contributions. Contributions will not be made to meet, or to provide a substitute for, providing banking services under the Community Reinvestment Act.
The major portion of contributions will be allocated to established organizations with reputations of excellence, cost-effectiveness and meeting community needs; some contributions may be granted to newly established, innovative organizations where the probability of success is likely.
Publications: Guidelines Sheet

Corporate Officials

John William Ennest: chief financial officer president B Bad Axe, MI 1942. ED University of Detroit (1964); Michigan State University (1965). PRIM CORP EMPL chief financial officer: Citizens Bank-Flint.
Karen Magidsohn: vice president PRIM CORP EMPL vice president: Citizens Bank-Flint.
Wayne G. Schaeffer: community president B Saginaw, MI 1946. ED Western Michigan University (1969). PRIM CORP EMPL community president: Citizens Bank-Flint. CORP AFFIL president: Citizens Bank Michigan; executive vice president: Citizens Banking Corp. NONPR AFFIL member: American Institute CPAs; member: Financial Executives Institute.

Giving Program Officials

David Albert: trustee

Foundation Officials

Karen Magidsohn: trustee (see above)

Grants Analysis

Disclosure Period: calendar year ending
Typical Range: $1,000 to $20,000

CITIZENS FINANCIAL GROUP, INC.

Company Contact

Providence, RI

Company Description

Assets: US$17,300,000,000 (1998)
Employees: 2,167
SIC(s): 6022 State Commercial Banks.
Parent Company: Royal Bank of Scotland Plc, 42 St. Andrew Sq., Edinburgh, Scotland

Operating Locations

CA: Royal Bank of Scotland Plc, San Francisco; CT: Citizens Bank of Connecticut, New London; GA: Citizens Mortgage Corp., Atlanta; Gulf State Mortgage, Atlanta; MA: Citizens Bank of Massachusetts, Fairhaven; NY: Royal Bank of Scotland Plc, New York; RI: Citizens Financial Group, Providence; Citizens Financial Services Corp., Providence; Citizens Leasing Corp., Providence; Citizens Savings Bank, Providence; Citizens Trust Co., Providence

Nonmonetary Support

Type: Cause-related Marketing & Promotion; Donated Equipment; Loaned Employees

Citizens Charitable Foundation

Giving Contact

D. Faye Sanders, Senior Vice President
Citizens Charitable Foundation
1 Citizens Plaza
Providence, RI 02903-1339
Phone: (401)456-7285
Fax: (401)456-7644

Description

EIN: 056022653
Organization Type: Corporate Foundation
Giving Locations: RI
Grant Types: General Support.

Financial Summary

Total Giving: $969,326 (1998); $513,320 (1996); $422,650 (1995). Note: Contributes through foundation only.
Giving Analysis: Giving for 1996 includes: foundation grants to United Way ($220,020); foundation scholarships ($8,000); 1998: foundation ($692,826); foundation grants to United Way ($276,500)
Assets: $5,207,337 (1998); $1,408,586 (1996); $1,463,921 (1995)

Gifts Received: $4,457,162 (1998); $234,169 (1996); $356,042 (1995). Note: The foundation receives contributions from Citizens Bank of Rhode Island.

Typical Recipients

Arts & Humanities: Arts Centers, Arts Funds, Arts Institutes, History & Archaeology, Libraries, Literary Arts, Museums/Galleries, Music, Performing Arts, Theater

Civic & Public Affairs: African American Affairs, Botanical Gardens/Parks, Economic Development, Employment/Job Training, Civic & Public Affairs-General, Hispanic Affairs, Housing, Law & Justice, Philanthropic Organizations, Urban & Community Affairs, Women's Affairs, Zoos/Aquariums

Education: Afterschool/Enrichment Programs, Arts/Humanities Education, Business Education, Colleges & Universities, Community & Junior Colleges, Economic Education, Education Associations, Education Funds, Medical Education, Private Education (Precollege), Secondary Education (Public), Student Aid

Environment: Environment-General

Health: AIDS/HIV, Clinics/Medical Centers, Emergency/Ambulance Services, Geriatric Health, Health Organizations, Hospices, Hospitals, Medical Rehabilitation, Medical Research, Mental Health, Nursing Services, Public Health, Single-Disease Health Associations

International: Health Care/Hospitals

Religion: Churches, Dioceses, Jewish Causes, Ministries, Missionary Activities (Domestic), Religious Organizations, Religious Welfare

Science: Science Museums, Scientific Centers & Institutes

Social Services: Camps, Child Welfare, Community Centers, Community Service Organizations, Day Care, Family Services, Food/Clothing Distribution, Homes, People with Disabilities, Recreation & Athletics, Scouts, Senior Services, Sexual Abuse, Shelters/Homelessness, Substance Abuse, United Funds/United Ways, YMCA/YWCA/YMHA/YWHA, Youth Organizations

Contributions Analysis

Arts & Humanities: 10%. Museums, music, and the performing arts are funded.

Civic & Public Affairs: 16%. Supports zoological societies, community affairs, and philanthropic organizations.

Education: 26%. Funds colleges and universities, medical schools, economic education, and programs for community education.

Health: 5%. Hospitals and ambulatory health care centers received support.

Religion: 7%. Funds religious welfare.

Science: 2%.

Social Services: 33%. Supports United Way, child welfare, youth organizations, community centers, day care, and community service organizations.

Note: Total contributions in 1998.

Application Procedures

Initial Contact: Send a written proposal.

Application Requirements: Include a description of agency, its purpose, history, and programs; summary of need, amount requested, and description of agencies providing similar services; financial data on organization, such as independent audit, budget with sources of income, breakdown of expenditures by program, administration, and personnel; brief explanation why Citizens Charitable Foundation would be an appropriate donor; list of board of directors; copy of IRS tax-determination letter; and copy of affirmative action/equal opportunity policy.

Deadlines: None.

Decision Notification: Board meets quarterly; allow 60 to 90 days for a reply.

Restrictions

The foundation does not award grants to the following: member agencies of federated organizations, including United Way agencies, except for major capital campaigns; government and quasi-governmental agencies and organizations including commissions and task forces; local affiliates of national health organizations; agencies outside the foundation's geographic area; labor, fraternal and veterans organizations, and programs or projects of a political nature. The foundation also does not provide funding to individuals, religious bodies, operating deficits, annual campaigns, conferences or seminars, endowments, general operating support, research projects, trips and tours, loans, or advertising and fund-raising activities. tours, loans, or advertising and fund-raising activities.

Additional Information

All organizations requesting funding must agree to evaluation procedures including on-site visits and community interviews. The foundation may request periodic reports from organizations receiving funding. The foundation will not contribute in excess of 1% of the total goal to capital fund campaigns. Generally, payments are made within a three- to five-year period in order to eliminate an accumulation of substantial pledges in future years.

Publications: Annual Report (including Application Guidelines)

Corporate Officials

Lawrence K. Fish: chairman, chief executive officer B Chicago, IL 1944. ED Drake University (1966); Harvard University Graduate School of Business Administration MBA (1968). PRIM CORP EMPL chairman, chief executive officer, president: Citizens Financial Group Inc. CORP AFFIL director: MasterCard Inc.; director: Textron Inc.; chairman: Citizens Bank Massachusetts; director: John Hancock Mutual Life Insurance Co.; chairman, chief executive officer: Bank New England. NONPR AFFIL president: Institute Contemporary Art Boston; overseer: New England Conservatory Music. CLUB AFFIL Longwood Club.

Mark J. Formica: president B 1948. PRIM CORP EMPL president: Citizens Bank Rhode Island.

Foundation Officials

Lawrence K. Fish: trustee (see above)
Mark J. Formica: trustee (see above)
D. Faye Sanders: senior vice president

Grants Analysis

Disclosure Period: calendar year ending 1998
Total Grants: $692,826*
Number of Grants: 88
Average Grant: $7,873
Highest Grant: $100,000
Typical Range: $1,000 to $10,000
***Note:** Giving excludes United Way.

Recent Grants

Note: Grants derived from 1998 Form 990.

Arts & Humanities

25,000	Rhode Island Philharmonic, Providence, RI
15,000	Garde Arts Center, New London, CT
10,000	Oddfellows Playhouse, Hartford, CT
6,000	Mark Twain House, Hannibal, MO
5,000	Children's Museum Center of Rhode Island, Providence, RI
5,000	Children's Museum of Southeastern Connecticut, New London, CT
5,000	Lyman Allyn Art Museum, New London, CT
5,000	Shubert Performing Arts Center, New Haven, CT
5,000	Shubert Performing Arts Center, New Haven, CT

Civic & Public Affairs

25,000	Providence Plan, Providence, RI
20,000	Urban Collaborative Accelerated Program, Providence, RI
15,000	Elmwood Neighborhood Housing, Providence, RI
10,000	Eastern Connecticut Housing Opportunities, New London, CT
10,000	Local Initiatives Support Organization, Providence, RI
5,000	Connecticut Housing Investment Fund, Hartford, CT
5,000	The Connection Fund, Middletown, CT
5,000	Eastern Connecticut Housing Opportunities, New London, CT
5,000	Edgewood Village, Inc, New Haven, CT
5,000	Fund for Community Progress, Providence, RI
5,000	Greater Dwight Development Corp, New Haven, CT
5,000	Greater New Haven Community Loan Fund, New Haven, CT
5,000	Leap Inc, New Haven, CT
5,000	Opportunities Industrialization Center, Charleston, WV
5,000	The Rockfall Foundation, Middletown, CT
5,000	Woman's Center of Rhode Island, Providence, RI

Education

100,000	Johnson and Wales University, Providence, RI
97,000	Providence College, Providence, RI
10,000	Rhode Island School of Design, Providence, RI
6,800	Community Preparatory School, Providence, RI

Environment

4,000	Massachusetts Audobon Society, Boston, MA

Health

15,000	Rhode Island Hospital, Providence, RI
10,506	Alliance for Living, New London, CT
5,000	Alderhouse, Centralia, WA
5,000	American Red Cross - Middlesex, New London, CT
5,000	New Haven Aids Project, New Haven, CT

Religion

50,000	Vision of Hope, NC
6,000	Catholic Charity Fund, Providence, RI
5,000	Billings P Learned Mission Inc, New London, CT

Science

5,000	Kid City Children's Museum, Princeton, NJ
5,000	Kid City Childrens Museum, Princeton, NJ
5,000	Submarine Force Library and Museum, Groton, CT

Social Services

230,000	United Way of Southeastern New England, Providence, RI
10,000	The Children's Home, Cromwell, CT
5,000	Alder House Residential Communities, Arroyo Grande, CA
5,000	Child and Family Agency of Southeastern Connecticut, New London, CT
5,000	Columbus House, New Haven, CT
5,000	Rushford Center, Inc., Middletown, CT
4,875	United Way, Providence, RI
4,875	United Way of Southeastern Connecticut, Gales Ferry, CT
4,750	Middlesex United Way, Middlesex, RI -- '98 Pledge

CLARCOR INC.

Company Contact
Rockford, IL
Web: http://www.clarcor.com

Company Description
Employees: 2,562
SIC(s): 3411 Metal Cans, 3564 Blowers & Fans, 3569 General Industrial Machinery Nec, 3714 Motor Vehicle Parts & Accessories.

Nonmonetary Support
Value: $20,000 (1991); $20,000 (1990)
Type: Loaned Executives
Note: Nonmonetary support is for United Way only, and is approximately $20,000 annually.

Corporate Sponsorship
Type: Music & entertainment events; Arts & cultural events

CLARCOR Foundation

Giving Contact
Mr. David J. Lindsay, Chairman
CLARCOR Foundation
PO Box 7007
Rockford, IL 61125
Phone: (815)962-8867
Fax: (815)962-0417

Alternate Contact
Sue Berg, Foundation Secretary

Description
EIN: 366032573
Organization Type: Corporate Foundation
Giving Locations: operating locations only.
Grant Types: Capital, Employee Matching Gifts, General Support, Multiyear/Continuing Support.
Note: Employee matching gift ratio: 1 to 1 to educational institutions.

Giving Philosophy
'CLARCOR is committed, as a fundamental element of its corporate goals, to its role as a good corporate citizen. Each of the CLARCOR businesses is committed to this role through efforts to improve the quality of life in, and remain sensitive to, the communities in which these businesses are located. The CLARCOR Foundation, as the charitable trust of CLARCOR, seeks to fulfill this role by funding, within its means, chosen agencies and organizations serving the public good.' *Foundation Guidelines*

Financial Summary
Total Giving: $500,000 (2000 approx); $500,000 (1999 approx); $494,942 (1998). Note: Contributes through corporate direct giving program and foundation.
Giving Analysis: Giving for 1996 includes: foundation ($461,046); foundation grants to United Way ($91,871); 1997: foundation ($452,195); foundation grants to United Way ($87,640); 1998: foundation ($385,730); foundation grants to United Way ($109,212)
Assets: $8,469,720 (1997); $7,434,326 (1996); $7,284,291 (1995)

Typical Recipients
Arts & Humanities: Arts Associations & Councils, Dance, Ethnic & Folk Arts, Arts & Humanities-General, History & Archaeology, Libraries, Museums/Galleries, Music, Opera, Theater
Civic & Public Affairs: Botanical Gardens/Parks, Economic Development, Employment/Job Training, Civic & Public Affairs-General, Hispanic Affairs, Housing, Minority Business, Parades/Festivals, Women's Affairs
Education: Business Education, Colleges & Universities, Economic Education, Faculty Development, Education-General, Legal Education, Literacy, Private Education (Precollege), Public Education (Precollege)
Health: Cancer, Clinics/Medical Centers, Emergency/Ambulance Services, Health Funds, Health Organizations, Hospices, Hospitals, Long-Term Care, Mental Health, Nursing Services, Public Health, Respiratory
Religion: Churches, Religion-General, Religious Welfare
Science: Science Museums
Social Services: At-Risk Youth, Big Brother/Big Sister, Child Welfare, Community Centers, Community Service Organizations, Crime Prevention, Day Care, Emergency Relief, Family Services, Food/Clothing Distribution, Homes, People with Disabilities, Recreation & Athletics, Scouts, United Funds/United Ways, YMCA/YWCA/YMHA/YWHA, Youth Organizations

Contributions Analysis
Giving Priorities: Social welfare, the arts, hospitals, education, and international nonprofit organizations.
Arts & Humanities: Less than 5%. Includes support for music, theater, and dance groups.
Civic & Public Affairs: 15% to 20%. Primarily supports civic concerns in local communities.
Education: About 55%. Supports business education and colleges and universities.
Health: 10% to 15%. Recipients include health organizations andhospitals.
Social Services: 15% to 20%. Recipients include child welfare and youth organizations, as well as community organizations.
Note: Total contributions made in 1997.

Application Procedures
Initial Contact: brief letter; grant application
Application Requirements: amount requested, purpose for which funds are sought, a description of organization, recently audited financial statement, and proof of tax-exempt status
Deadlines: None.
Decision Notification: quarterly

Additional Information
In 1988, J.L. Clark Manufacturing Co. was reincorporated as CLARCOR Inc. The foundation name was changed from the Clark Foundation to the CLARCOR Foundation.
Publications: Foundation Guidelines

Corporate Officials
Lawrence Eugene Gloyd: chairman, chief executive officer, director B Milan, IN 1932. ED Hanover College BA (1954). PRIM CORP EMPL chairman, chief executive officer, director: CLARCOR Inc. ADD CORP EMPL chairman: Airguard industries Inc.; chairman: Baldwin Filters Inc.; chairman, chief executive officer: Clark Filter Inc.; director: J.L. Clark Inc. CORP AFFIL director: United Air Specialists Inc.; director: Woodward Governor Co.; director: Ruppman Marketing Inc.; director: Thomas Industries Inc.; director: AMCORE Financial Inc.; director: GUD Holdings Ltd. NONPR AFFIL member: National Association Manufacturer; member: President Association; director: Illinois Council Economic Education; member: Illinois Manufacturer Association; director: Council 100; member: Hardware Group Association; member: American Hardware Manufacturer Association; national director: Big Brotherss/Big Sisters. CLUB AFFIL Masons Club.
Bruce A. Klein: chief financial officer B Louisville, KY 1947. ED University of Louisville BA (1973); University of Chicago MBA (1976). PRIM CORP EMPL chief financial officer: CLARCOR Inc. ADD CORP EMPL treasurer: J.L. Clark Inc. Delaware. CORP AFFIL director: Peoples Insurance Agency; director: Suntec Industries Inc.
William F. Knese: vice president, treasurer B 1948. PRIM CORP EMPL vice president, treasurer: CLARCOR Inc.
David J. Lindsay: vice president B 1955. ED University of Illinois BS (1977). PRIM CORP EMPL vice president: CLARCOR Inc.

Foundation Officials
Sue M. Berg: secretary
Lawrence Eugene Gloyd: trustee (see above)
Norman E. Johnson: trustee B Lake Mills, IA 1948. ED University of Iowa (1970); Drake University (1972). PRIM CORP EMPL president: Clarcor Inc. CORP AFFIL president: Baldwin Filters Inc.; chairman: JL Clark Inc.
Bruce A. Klein: trustee (see above)
William F. Knese: chairman, trustee (see above)
David J. Lindsay: trustee (see above)

Grants Analysis
Disclosure Period: calendar year ending 1998
Total Grants: $385,730*
Number of Grants: 63*
Average Grant: $6,123
Typical Range: $1,000 to $10,000
***Note:** Giving excludes United Way.

Recent Grants
Note: Grants derived from 1996 Form 990.

Arts & Humanities

25,000	Burpee Museum, Rockford, IL
10,000	Tinker Swiss Cottage Museum, Rockford, IL
8,000	Fulton Opera House, Lancaster, PA
6,000	New American Theater, Rockford, IL
5,000	Rockford Art Museum, Rockford, IL
3,000	Rockford Area Arts Council, Rockford, IL

Civic & Public Affairs

10,000	RAMP, Rockford, IL
5,000	Opportunities Industrialization Corps Vocational Institute
2,000	Promised Land Employment Services, Rockford, IL
2,000	Rockford Neighborhood Redevelopment, Rockford, IL
1,000	Little Friends, Naperville, IL

Education

10,000	Yankton Public Schools, Yankton, SD
5,000	Kearney Public Schools, Kearney, NE
5,000	Rockford College, Rockford, IL
4,000	Keith Country Day School, Rockford, IL
3,000	Gothenberg Public Schools, Gothenburg, NE
3,000	Junior Achievement Rock River Valley
2,500	Elizabethtown College, Elizabethtown, PA
2,500	Golden Apple Teaching Award
2,000	Barbara Olson School of Hope, Rockford, IL
1,750	Illinois Council on Economic Education, Dekalb, IL
1,000	Harlem Schools, New York, NY

Health

10,000	Crusaders Health Foundation
10,000	Northern Illinois Hospice Association, Rockford, IL
10,000	Rosecrance Health Network, Rockford, IL
5,000	Wesley Willows, Rockford, IL
3,000	Janet Wattles Center, Rockford, IL
2,500	American Red Cross, Rockford, IL
1,500	St. Anthony Medical Center
1,000	American Lung Association, Rockford, IL

Religion

2,500	Lancaster Theological Society, Lancaster, PA
2,500	Salvation Army, Rockford, IL
1,000	Emmanuel Lutheran Church

Science

2,000	Discovery Center Museum, Rockford, IL

Social Services

91,870	United Way, Rockford, IL
62,500	YMCA, Rockford, IL
35,000	YMCA, Kearney, NE
30,000	Big Brothers and Big Sisters, Rockford, IL
13,250	Children's Justice Center, Tulsa, OK
10,000	Stepping Stones, Rockford, IL
6,600	RocVale Children's Foundation
5,000	Boy Scouts of America, Rockford, IL
5,000	Hunger Connection, Rockford, IL
3,000	Boys and Girls Club, Rockford, IL
3,000	Martin House, Trenton, NJ
3,000	Mill, Millville, NJ
2,500	Center for Sight and Hearing Impaired, Rockford, IL
2,500	Girl Scouts of America Rock River Valley Council
2,500	Youth Services Network, Rockford, IL
2,000	Rockford Area Crime Stoppers, Rockford, IL

CLARK REFINING & MARKETING

Company Contact

St. Louis, MO
Web: http://www.clarkusa.com

Company Description

Former Name: Clark Oil & Refining Corp.
Employees: 7,500
SIC(s): 2911 Petroleum Refining.
Parent Company: AOC Holdings Inc.

Nonmonetary Support

Type: Donated Products; Loaned Employees

Giving Contact

Suzanne Miller, Charitable Contributions Coordinator
8182 Maryland Ave.
St. Louis, MO 63105
Phone: (314)854-9804
Fax: (314)854-1580

Description

Organization Type: Corporate Giving Program
Giving Locations: headquarters and operating communities.
Grant Types: Award, Employee Matching Gifts, Matching, Scholarship.

Financial Summary

Total Giving: $250,000 (1999 approx); $200,000 (1998 approx); $160,000 (1997)

Typical Recipients

Arts & Humanities: Museums/Galleries, Performing Arts
Civic & Public Affairs: African American Affairs, Legal Aid, Minority Business, Safety, Urban & Community Affairs
Education: Continuing Education, International Exchange, Literacy
Environment: Air/Water Quality, Energy, Environment-General, Protection
Health: AIDS/HIV, Alzheimers Disease, Arthritis, Cancer, Children's Health/Hospitals, Clinics/Medical Centers, Diabetes, Eyes/Blindness, Health-General, Multiple Sclerosis
Social Services: Community Centers, Community Service Organizations, Special Olympics, United Funds/United Ways, Youth Organizations

Application Procedures

Initial Contact: Send a brief letter of inquiry. Include a description of organization, amount requested, purpose of funds sought, recently audited financial statement, and proof of tax-exempt status.

Corporate Officials

Maura Clark: chief financial officer, chief executive officer PRIM CORP EMPL chief financial officer: Clark Refining & Marketing.
Paul D. Melnuk: president, chief executive officer B Winnipeg, MB Canada 1954. ED University of Manitoba BA (1976). PRIM CORP EMPL president, chief executive officer: Clark Refining & Marketing. CORP AFFIL director: Trizec Corp.; director: Horsham Corp.; director: Bracknell Corp.; president, chief executive officer: Clark USA. NONPR AFFIL member: Canadian Institute Chartered Accts.

Grants Analysis

Disclosure Period: calendar year ending

CLEVELAND-CLIFFS, INC.

Company Contact

Cleveland, OH

Company Description

Employees: 5,006 (1999)
SIC(s): 1011 Iron Ores.

Nonmonetary Support

Type: Loaned Executives; Workplace Solicitation
Note: Co. provides nonmonetary support.

The Cleveland-Cliffs Foundation

Giving Contact

David L. Gardner, Vice President, Assistant Treasurer
The Cleveland-Cliffs Foundation
1100 Superior Avenue
Cleveland, OH 44114
Phone: (216)694-5407
Fax: (216)694-6741

Description

EIN: 346525124
Organization Type: Corporate Foundation
Giving Locations: MI; MN; OH nationally; nationally.
Grant Types: Capital, Employee Matching Gifts, General Support, Matching, Multiyear/Continuing Support.

Financial Summary

Total Giving: $575,000 (1999 approx); $624,384 (1998); $607,260 (1997). Note: Contributes through foundation only.
Giving Analysis: Giving for 1996 includes: foundation ($362,550); foundation matching gifts ($81,023); foundation grants to United Way ($50,466); 1997: foundation ($487,000); foundation matching gifts ($65,268); foundation grants to United Way ($54,992); 1998: foundation ($483,675); foundation matching gifts ($84,410); foundation grants to United Way ($56,109)
Assets: $1,502,619 (1998); $1,653,982 (1997); $1,435,340 (1996)
Gifts Received: $400,000 (1998); $500,000 (1996); $500,000 (1995). Note: The foundation receives contributions from Cleveland-Cliffs, Inc.

Typical Recipients

Arts & Humanities: Arts Associations & Councils, Ballet, Historic Preservation, History & Archaeology, Libraries, Museums/Galleries, Music, Opera, Performing Arts, Theater
Civic & Public Affairs: Botanical Gardens/Parks, Business/Free Enterprise, Chambers of Commerce, Clubs, Community Foundations, Economic Development, Employment/Job Training, Civic & Public Affairs-General, Municipalities/Towns, Parades/Festivals, Philanthropic Organizations, Public Policy, Urban & Community Affairs, Zoos/Aquariums
Education: Business Education, Colleges & Universities, Community & Junior Colleges, Continuing Education, Economic Education, Education Associations, Education Funds, Education Reform, Engineering/Technological Education, Education-General, Minority Education, Private Education (Precollege), Public Education (Precollege), Science/Mathematics Education, Secondary Education (Private), Secondary Education (Public), Student Aid
Environment: Environment-General, Resource Conservation, Wildlife Protection
Health: Cancer, Children's Health/Hospitals, Clinics/Medical Centers, Emergency/Ambulance Services, Health Organizations, Heart, Hospitals, Preventive Medicine/Wellness Organizations, Public Health
International: Health Care/Hospitals
Religion: Religious Welfare
Science: Science Museums, Scientific Centers & Institutes
Social Services: Child Welfare, Community Service Organizations, Counseling, Delinquency & Criminal Rehabilitation, Emergency Relief, Family Services, Food/Clothing Distribution, People with Disabilities, Recreation & Athletics, Scouts, Senior Services, United Funds/United Ways, YMCA/YWCA/YMHA/YWHA, Youth Organizations

Contributions Analysis

Arts & Humanities: 15% to 20%. Supports natural history museums, music, theater, public libraries, and art funds.
Civic & Public Affairs: 15% to 20%. Interests include municipalities, urban leagues, legal foundations, better business, and economic development.
Education: 40% to 45%. Education foundations and college funds, including business, economic, minority, private, and public education. Supports matching gifts to education institutions.
Health: 20% to 25%. Largest contribution supports United Way. Other recipients include health foundations, community child care services, cancer society, hospitals, the aged, youth organizations, athletics, and community service organizations.
Note: Total contributions in 1998.

Application Procedures

Initial Contact: Submit a brief letter of inquiry.
Application Requirements: Include a description of organization, amount requested, purpose of funds sought, recently audited financial statements, and proof of tax-exempt status.
Deadlines: None.
Review Process: Vice president evaluates requests and submits them to distribution committee for their approval; a letter is sent regarding final decision.

Restrictions

Foundation does not support individuals or political or lobbying groups.

Additional Information

Publications: Guidelines Sheet

Corporate Officials

Joseph H. Ballway, Jr.: vice president, general counsel PRIM CORP EMPL vice president, general counsel: Cleveland-Cliffs, Inc.

Cynthia B. Bezik: senior vice president, finance B Youngstown, OH 1953. ED Youngstown State University (1970); Case Western Reserve University (1980). PRIM CORP EMPL senior vice president, finance: Cleveland-Cliffs, Inc. CORP AFFIL manager financial analysis: Pickands Mather; chief financial officer: Cliffs Resources Inc. NONPR AFFIL member: National Association Accts; member: Planning Forum; member: Financial Executives Institute; member: American Society Women Accountants; member: Cleveland Cliffs Iron Co.; member: American Iron & Steel Institute. CLUB AFFIL Womens City Club.

John S. Brinzo: president, chief executive officer B Cleveland, OH 1942. ED Kent State University BS,BA (1964); Case Western Reserve University MBA (1968). PRIM CORP EMPL president, chief executive officer: Cleveland-Cliffs, Inc. NONPR AFFIL member: American Iron & Steel Institute; director: National Mining Association.

William Rushton Calfee: executive vice president, commercial B Cleveland, OH 1946. ED Williams College BA (1968); Harvard University Advanced Management Program (1984). PRIM CORP EMPL executive vice president, commercial: Cleveland-Cliffs, Inc. ADD CORP EMPL executive vice president: Ceveland-Cliffs Iron Co.

George N. Chandler, II: vice president, reduced iron PRIM CORP EMPL vice president, reduced iron: Cleveland-Cliffs, Inc.

Edward C. Dowling: senior vice president, operations PRIM CORP EMPL senior vice president, operations: Cleveland-Cliffs, Inc.

Robert Emmet: vice president financial planning, treasurer B 1945. ED Yale University BA (1967); Harvard University MBA (1973). PRIM CORP EMPL vice president financial planning, treasurer: Cleveland-Cliffs, Inc. ADD CORP EMPL vice president: Clevelabd-Cliffs Iron Co.

Donald J. Gallagher: vice president, sales PRIM CORP EMPL vice president, sales: Cleveland-Cliffs, Inc.

John E. Lenhard: secretary, associate general counsel PRIM CORP EMPL secretary, associate general counsel: Cleveland-Cliffs, Inc.

Robert J. Leroux: controller PRIM CORP EMPL controller: Cleveland-Cliffs, Inc.

Richard F. Novak: vice president, human resources PRIM CORP EMPL vice president, human resources: Cleveland-Cliffs, Inc.

Thomas J. O'Neil: executive vice president, operations PRIM CORP EMPL executive vice president, operations: Cleveland-Cliffs, Inc.

John W. Sanders: senior vice president, international development PRIM CORP EMPL senior vice president, international development: Cleveland-Cliffs, Inc.

James A. Trethewey: senior vice president, operations services PRIM CORP EMPL senior vice president, operations services: Cleveland-Cliffs, Inc.

A. Stanley West: senior vice president, sales & commercial planning PRIM CORP EMPL senior vice president, sales & commercial planning: Cleveland-Cliffs, Inc.

Foundation Officials

John S. Brinzo: trustee (see above)
William Rushton Calfee: trustee (see above)
D. L. Gardner: vice president, assistant treasurer
Thomas J. O'Neil: trustee (see above)
John W. Sanders: trustee (see above)
A. Stanley West: trustee (see above)

Grants Analysis

Disclosure Period: calendar year ending 1998
Total Grants: $483,675*
Number of Grants: 145
Average Grant: $3,336
Highest Grant: $50,000
Typical Range: $250 to $5,000
***Note:** Giving excludes matching gifts; United Way.

Recent Grants

Note: Grants derived from 1998 Form 990.

Arts & Humanities

40,000	Republic Area Historical Area, Republic, MI -- Capital
25,000	Cleveland Orchestra, Cleveland, OH -- Capital
15,000	Great Lakes Museum, Cleveland, OH -- Capital
15,000	Great Lakes Museum STEP Program, Cleveland, OH -- Operating
10,000	Playhouse Square, Cleveland, OH -- Capital
5,000	Cleveland Museum of Natural History, Cleveland, OH -- Capital
3,000	Cleveland Museum of Art, Cleveland, OH -- Capital

Civic & Public Affairs

10,000	William G. Mather, Cleveland, OH -- Operating
8,750	Cleveland Tomorrow, Cleveland, OH -- Operating
5,000	Cleveland Zoological Society, Cleveland, OH -- Capital
3,000	Minnesota Association of Commerce and Industry Foundation, St. Paul, MN -- Work Ready Minnesota

Education

25,000	Michigan Technological University, Houghton, MI -- Capital
20,000	University Circle, Cleveland, OH -- Capital
14,349	Northern Michigan University, Marquette, MI
10,000	Cleveland Public Schools, Cleveland, OH -- Operating
10,000	Cleveland State University - Industrial History Collection Library Fund, Cleveland, OH -- Operating
10,000	Northern Michigan University, Marquette, MI -- Ice Arena
8,350	University School, Hunting Valley, OH
7,700	Massachusetts Institute of Technology, Cambridge, MA
5,955	Michigan Technological University, Houghton, MI
5,000	Campaign for Advanced Manufacturing Program, Cleveland, OH -- Operating
5,000	Cleveland Initiative for Education, Cleveland, OH -- Operating
5,000	Cleveland State University - French/American Library Fund, Cleveland, OH -- Operating
5,000	Magnificat High School, Rocky River, OH
5,000	Marquette County Partners for Education, Marquette, MI -- Operating
5,000	Michigan Tech/Mining Engineering and Mineral Process Scholarships, Houghton, MI -- Operating
5,000	Minnesota Partners for Education/Iron Country Schools, Duluth, MN -- Operating
5,000	Negaunee Public Schools, Negaunee, MI -- Operating
4,785	Lake Superior School District, Two Harbors, MN -- Operating
4,150	University of Minnesota Foundation, Minneapolis, MN
3,800	Case Western Reserve University, Cleveland, OH
3,000	American Institute of Mining, Metallurgical and Petroleum, New York, NY -- Minnesota Minerals Workshop
3,000	Cleveland Scholarship Program, Cleveland, OH -- Operating
3,000	Julie Billiart School, Lyndhurst, OH -- Operating
3,000	Magnificat High School, Rocky River, OH -- Capital
100	University of Waterloo, Waterloo, Canada

Health

9,000	Fairview General Hospital, Cleveland, OH -- Capital
7,500	American Cancer Society/Hope Lodge, Cleveland, OH -- Capital
5,000	American Red Cross, Cleveland, OH -- Operating
5,000	Captain West Jackman Hospital, Labrador City, Canada
5,000	Sept. Iles Hospital Foundation, Sept-Iles, Canada
3,000	Ronald McDonald House, Cleveland, OH -- Capital

Religion

10,000	Salvation Army - Marquette, Marquette, MI -- Capital

Social Services

50,000	Superior Nordic Training and Recreation Complex, Ishpeming, MI -- Capital
49,409	United Way - Cleveland, Cleveland, OH -- Fund drive
15,000	U.S. Ski Hall of Fame, Ishpeming, MI -- Capital
10,000	YMCA - Marquette, Marquette, MI -- Capital
5,000	YMCA - Cleveland, Cleveland, OH
3,400	United Way - Minnesota, Chisholm, MN -- Fund drive
3,300	United Way - Marquette County, Marquette, MI -- Fund drive
3,000	Center for Families and Children, Cleveland, OH -- Capital

Clorox Co.

Company Contact

1221 Broadway
Oakland, CA 94612-1888
Phone: (510)271-7000
Fax: (510)832-1463
Web: http://www.clorox.com

Company Description

Acquired: First Brands Corp. (1999).
Revenue: US$4,003,000,000 (1999)
Profit: US$246,000,000 (1999)
Employees: 11,000 (1999)
Fortune Rank: 399, per FORTUNE Magazine's list of 500 Largest U.S. Corporations (1999).
FF 399
SIC(s): 2033 Canned Fruits & Vegetables, 2034 Dehydrated Fruits, Vegetables & Soups, 2035 Pickles, Sauces & Salad Dressings, 2842 Polishes & Sanitation Goods.
Parent Company: Henkel KGAA, Henkelstrasse 67, Dusseldorf, Germany

Operating Locations

AL: Clorox Co., Birmingham; CA: Clorox Co., Laguna Hills, Los Angeles, Oakland; Clorox Co., Oakland; GA: Clorox Co., Forest Park; IL: Clorox Co., Chicago, Naperville; MD: Clorox Co., Aberdeen; MN: Clorox Co., Bloomington; MO: Clorox Co., Kansas City; MS: Clorox Co., Pearl; NH: Clorox Co., Nashua; OH: Clorox Co., Cleveland; TX: Clorox Co., Farmers Branch, Houston
Note: Operates over 30 plants in the USA and internationally.

Nonmonetary Support

Value: $90,000 (1997); $1,800,000 (1996); $1,000,000 (1995)
Type: Donated Equipment; Donated Products; In-kind Services; Workplace Solicitation
Note: Support is given to Second Harvest Food Bank and for disaster relief.

Corporate Sponsorship

Note: 1995 sponsorships included 42 local events. Contact the nearest operating facility for information.

Clorox Co. Foundation

Giving Contact

Ms. Carmella J. Johnson, Contributions Manager
Clorox Co. Foundation
PO Box 24305
Oakland, CA 94623
Phone: (510)271-2199
Web: http://www.clorox.com/company/foundation

Description

Founded: 1980
EIN: 942674980
Organization Type: Corporate Foundation
Giving Locations: CA: Oakland, San Francisco including metropolitan area operating locations.
Grant Types: Capital, Employee Matching Gifts, Endowment, General Support, Operating Expenses, Project, Scholarship.
Note: Employee matching gift ratio: 1 to 1 for educational institutions and the United Way.

Giving Philosophy

'The Clorox Company Foundation's mission is to fulfill Clorox's commitment to responsible corporate citizenship by helping to improve the quality of life in communities in which Clorox employees live and work. The work of the Foundation is accomplished through grantmaking, mobilization of employee volunteers, and collaborative efforts with other funders and community leaders.' *Clorox Company Foundation's Mission Statement*

Financial Summary

Total Giving: $3,160,611 (fiscal year ending June 30, 1998); $1,538,758 (fiscal 1997); $4,551,656 (fiscal 1996)
Giving Analysis: Giving for fiscal 1997 includes: foundation ($1,528,758); foundation grants to United Way ($187,340); foundation matching gifts ($50,860); fiscal 1998: foundation matching gifts ($1,770,000); foundation ($1,574,334); foundation grants to United Way ($129,000)
Assets: $8,083,227 (fiscal 1998); $6,419,110 (fiscal 1997); $4,940,819 (fiscal 1995)
Gifts Received: $2,753,102 (fiscal 1998); $81,634,970 (fiscal 1997); $1,520,000 (fiscal 1995)

Typical Recipients

Arts & Humanities: Arts Appreciation, Arts Associations & Councils, Arts Centers, Arts Festivals, Arts Outreach, Ballet, Community Arts, Dance, Ethnic & Folk Arts, Film & Video, Arts & Humanities-General, Historic Preservation, Libraries, Literary Arts, Museums/Galleries, Music, Opera, Performing Arts, Public Broadcasting, Theater, Visual Arts
Civic & Public Affairs: African American Affairs, Asian American Affairs, Chambers of Commerce, Civil Rights, Clubs, Community Foundations, Economic Development, Employment/Job Training, Civic & Public Affairs-General, Hispanic Affairs, Law & Justice, Legal Aid, Municipalities/Towns, Nonprofit Management, Safety, Urban & Community Affairs, Women's Affairs, Zoos/Aquariums
Education: Arts/Humanities Education, Business Education, Colleges & Universities, Community & Junior Colleges, Continuing Education, Economic Education, Education Associations, Education Funds, Education Reform, Elementary Education (Private), Elementary Education (Public), Environmental Education, Faculty Development, Education-General, Journalism/Media Education, Literacy, Minority Education, Preschool Education, Private Education (Precollege), Public Education (Precollege), School Volunteerism, Science/Mathematics Education, Secondary Education (Public), Special Education, Student Aid
Environment: Environment-General, Resource Conservation, Wildlife Protection
Health: Children's Health/Hospitals, Clinics/Medical Centers, Emergency/Ambulance Services, Geriatric Health, Health Funds, Health Organizations, Hospices, Hospitals, Mental Health, Prenatal Health Issues, Public Health, Research/Studies Institutes, Single-Disease Health Associations
International: International Affairs, International Development
Religion: Ministries, Religious Organizations, Religious Welfare
Science: Science Exhibits & Fairs
Social Services: At-Risk Youth, Big Brother/Big Sister, Child Welfare, Community Centers, Community Service Organizations, Counseling, Day Care, Delinquency & Criminal Rehabilitation, Domestic Violence, Family Planning, Family Services, Food/Clothing Distribution, People with Disabilities, Recreation & Athletics, Scouts, Senior Services, Shelters/Homelessness, Substance Abuse, United Funds/United Ways, Volunteer Services, YMCA/YWCA/YMHA/YWHA, Youth Organizations

Contributions Analysis

Giving Priorities: Youth, social welfare, education, employment training, the arts, civics, and health.
Arts & Humanities: 1%. Funding is awarded to music, theater, community arts, and dance organizations in California. Other interests include museums, opera, painting/sculpture, ethnic arts, and arts festivals and centers.
Civic & Public Affairs: 2%. Civic interests include civil rights, low-income housing, law and justice, parks and the environment, technical assistance, volunteer development, and conflict resolution programs.
Education: 79%. Emphasis is on quality of education for all young people from kindergarten through college, with attention to minority and low-income youth. Education grants will increasingly focus on K-12, as well as preschool and early childhood development programs that emphasize prevention and intervention through mentoring, tutoring, and parent involvement. Of special interest are drop-out prevention, programs designed to help students develop tools for learning, programs that actively involve parents and the community in the educational process, and programs that provide for and nurture students from infancy through high school and beyond. Matches employee contributions to higher education. Supports programs such as the East Oakland Youth Development Center, which provide a place for youth to go for recreation and personal and intellectual enrichment. Also supports arts outreach activities, reading camps, family counseling, and leadership development programs.
Health: 1%.
Science: 1%.
Social Services: 16%.
Note: Foundation also supports disaster relief, the Clorox Commitment Awards, and Clorox Partners Scholarships for college education. Total contributions made in 1998.

Application Procedures

Initial Contact: Send a brief letter of inquiry or phone call to request application guidelines and application form.
Application Requirements: Include a completed standard form; a description of organization; project summary; list of board of directors; staff list, with demographic information; organizational and project budget information; constituency served; plans for project evaluation; other sources of support; recently audited financial statement; proof of tax-exempt status.
Deadlines: Applications for foundation grants are accepted August 1 to June 1 of each fiscal year ending June 30; deadlines are July 1, October 1, January 1, and April 1; requests for special events sponsorship should be submitted in writing at least sixty days prior to the event.
Review Process: For grants in excess of $2,500, applications are reviewed by contributions committee, which advises the board of trustees; grants in excess of $10,000 must be reviewed by the board.
Evaluative Criteria: Foundation favors applicants whose programs focus on direct delivery of services; launch programs or services in an innovative manner; promote volunteer participation and citizen involvement; encourage self-reliance and personal growth among individuals served; have a broad base of financial support and a reasonable fund development plan; include Clorox employee involvement; have sound evaluation procedures; clarity of purpose; outcomes related to performance; sound fiscal and management practices; involvement of board members; demonstrated collaborative relationships; and diversity of board, staff, clients, etc.
Decision Notification: Contributions committee meets quarterly.
Notes: Endowment/capital campaign requests include building funds, purchase of major equipment, or general operating reserve funds. However, the foundation discourages contributions to endowments. The company's operating facilities each have their own particular funding priorities and independent review processes. A complete list of contributions programs at Clorox locations is contained within the guidelines.

Restrictions

The foundation will not provide grants to political parties, organizations, candidates, or issues; exclusive membership organizations; religious causes, except nonsectarian activities available to the community at large; field trips, tours, or travel; individuals; benefit or raffle tickets; conferences; conventions or meetings; media productions; athletic leagues or events; national projects; advertising; association or membership dues; fundraising events; deficits or retroactive funding; or organizations which receive more than 15% of funding from United Way or government sources.
Only one grant request per organization will be considered within a fiscal year time period (July 1 through June 30).

Additional Information

First-time grants generally range from $1,000 to $5,000 for general operating support and special projects. The foundation considers itself to be a supplemental funding source, seeking points of intervention where modest grants can be leveraged for greater change.
In addition to cash contributions by the company and foundation, Clorox has invested more than $60 million in low-income housing projects nationwide. Such investments are expected to increase to approximately $100 million.
The Clorox Co. is a U.S. affiliate of Henkel KGAA, which has a 28% investment in Clorox. Other U.S. affiliates are Loctite Corp. (29%) and Ecolab (25%).
Publications: Guidelines; Application Form; Foundation Annual Report

Corporate Officials

Karen M. Rose: vice president, treasurer, chief executive officer, director B 1949. PRIM CORP EMPL vice president, treasurer: Clorox Co. CORP AFFIL treasurer: Brita Products Co.; treasurer: Clorox International Co. Inc.
G. Craig Sullivan: chairman, president, chief executive officer, director B 1940. ED Boston College BS (1964). PRIM CORP EMPL chairman, president, chief executive officer, director: Clorox Co. CORP AFFIL officer: Clorox International Co. Inc.

Giving Program Officials

James A. Hasler: member contributions committee PRIM CORP EMPL member contributions committee: Clorox Co.

Joel J. Hayashida: member contributions committee PRIM CORP EMPL member contributions committee: Clorox Co.
Carmella J. Johnson: manager PRIM CORP EMPL contributions manager: Clorox Co.
Karen M. Rose: member contributions committee B 1949. PRIM CORP EMPL vice president, treasurer: Clorox Co. CORP AFFIL treasurer: Brita Products Co.; treasurer: Clorox International Co. Inc.
Jean Scanlon: member contributions committee
Andy Zwemer: PRIM CORP EMPL member contributions committee: Clorox Co.

Foundation Officials

Peter D. Bewley: vice president, secretary B Atlantic City, NJ 1946. ED Princeton University BA (1968); Stanford University JD (1971). PRIM CORP EMPL senior vice president, general counsel, secretary: The Clorox Co. CORP AFFIL secretary: Atlantic Health Group Inc.; senior vice president, secretary, general secretary: Nova Care Inc.
Gerald E. Johnston: trustee B 1947. PRIM CORP EMPL group vice president: Clorox Co.
Peter N. Louras: vice president B 1950. PRIM CORP EMPL group vice president: Clorox Co. ADD CORP EMPL chairman: Brita Products Co.; chairman: Clorox International Co. Inc.
G. Craig Sullivan: chairman (see above)

Grants Analysis

Disclosure Period: fiscal year ending June 30, 1998
Total Grants: $1,574,334*
Number of Grants: 200 (approx)
Average Grant: $7,900 (approx)
Typical Range: $2,500 to $10,000
***Note:** Giving excludes matching gifts and United Way.

Recent Grants

Note: Grants derived from fiscal 1997 Form 990.

Arts & Humanities

50,000 Oakland Ballet Company, Oakland, CA
50,000 Oakland Museum of California Foundation, Oakland, CA
25,000 Oakland Ballet Company, Oakland, CA
13,334 Oakland Ballet Company, Oakland, CA
12,000 California Shakespeare Festival, Berkeley, CA
10,000 Berkeley Repertory Theater, Berkeley, CA
10,000 Oakland East Bay Symphony, Oakland, CA
7,500 Oakland Community Fund, Oakland, CA
7,000 Oakland Asian Culture Center, Oakland, CA
5,000 Oakland Youth Orchestra, Oakland, CA

Education

150,000 Marcus A. Foster Educational Institute, Oakland, CA
100,000 University of California Berkeley Incentive Awards Program, Berkeley, CA
42,500 Citizens Scholarship Foundation of America, St. Peter, MN
20,000 Marcus A. Foster Educational Institute, Oakland, CA
17,000 Marcus A. Foster Educational Institute, Oakland, CA
15,000 National Merit Scholarship Corporation, Evanston, IL
15,000 Reading is Fundamental, Chicago, IL
14,000 California State University, Hayward, CA
12,842 National Merit Scholarship Corporation, Evanston, IL
11,300 University of California Berkeley Foundation, Berkeley, CA
10,000 California College of Arts and Crafts, Oakland, CA
10,000 Harford Community College Foundation, Bel Air, MD
10,000 Louisville Deaf Deal School, Louisville, KY
10,000 Oakland Unified School District, Oakland, CA

Health

10,000 Healthy City Oakland Fund, Oakland, CA
10,000 Highland Foundation, Oakland, CA
10,000 Mount Diablo Hospital Foundation, Concord, CA
10,000 Summit Medical Center Foundation, Oakland, CA
10,000 White Bird Clinic, Eugene, OR

Religion

8,000 West Side Ecumenical Ministry, Cleveland, OH

Social Services

187,340 United Way, Oakland, CA
25,000 East Oakland Youth Development Foundation, Oakland, CA
25,000 East Oakland Youth Development Foundation, Oakland, CA
25,000 East Oakland Youth Development Foundation, Oakland, CA
25,000 East Oakland Youth Development Foundation, Oakland, CA
24,058 United Way, Atlanta, GA
15,000 Oakland Chinese Community Council, Oakland, CA
15,000 Omni Youth Services, Buffalo Grove, IL
10,280 United Way Capital Area, Jackson, MS
10,000 East Oakland Youth Development Foundation, Oakland, CA
10,000 Lincoln Child Center, Oakland, CA
10,000 Mississippi Lifeline, Jackson, MI
10,000 Oakland Children's Fairyland, Oakland, CA
8,172 Vanstar, Pasadena, CA
7,989 United Way Lane County, Eugene, OH
7,800 United Way, Atlanta, GA
7,500 Big Brothers and Big Sisters, Houston, TX
7,202 United Way Central Maryland, Baltimore, MD
7,042 United Way
6,198 United Way Capital Area, Jackson, MS

CNA

Company Contact

Chicago, IL
Web: http://www.cna.com

Company Description

Former Name: CNA Financial Corp./CNA Insurance Companies.
Assets: US$60,734,700,000
Employees: 24,300
SIC(s): 6311 Life Insurance, 6321 Accident & Health Insurance, 6331 Fire, Marine & Casualty Insurance.

Nonmonetary Support

Type: Donated Equipment; In-kind Services
Note: Co. provides nonmonetary support.

CNA Foundation

Giving Contact

Sarada Amani, Community Relations Manager
CNA Foundation
CNA Plaza, 15 South
Chicago, IL 60685
Phone: (312)822-5318
Fax: (312)822-2418

Description

Founded: 1995
EIN: 364029026
Organization Type: Corporate Foundation
Giving Locations: in communities where co. has a presence.
Grant Types: Employee Matching Gifts, General Support, Multiyear/Continuing Support, Operating Expenses, Scholarship.
Note: Employee matching gift ratio: 1 to 1.

Financial Summary

Total Giving: $2,358,431 (1998); $3,429,979 (1997); $3,500,000 (1996 approx). Note: Contributes through corporate direct giving program and foundation.
Giving Analysis: Giving for 1997 includes: foundation ($3,429,979); 1998: foundation ($1,445,501); foundation matching gifts ($552,430); foundation grants to United Way ($360,500)
Assets: $28,280,946 (1998); $27,334,185 (1997); $2,737,127 (1995)
Gifts Received: $1,000,000 (1998); $481,000 (1997); $284,694 (1995). Note: Contributions were received from CNA.

Typical Recipients

Arts & Humanities: Arts Institutes, Dance, Historic Preservation, Libraries, Literary Arts, Museums/Galleries, Music, Opera, Performing Arts, Theater
Civic & Public Affairs: Business/Free Enterprise, Clubs, Employment/Job Training, Civic & Public Affairs-General, Housing, Law & Justice, Philanthropic Organizations, Professional & Trade Associations, Public Policy, Safety, Urban & Community Affairs, Women's Affairs, Zoos/Aquariums
Education: Arts/Humanities Education, Business Education, Colleges & Universities, Continuing Education, Economic Education, Education Associations, Education Funds, Faculty Development, Education-General, Literacy, Minority Education, Minority Education, Preschool Education, Private Education (Precollege), Public Education (Precollege), Science/Mathematics Education, Student Aid
Health: AIDS/HIV, Children's Health/Hospitals, Health-General, Health Organizations, Hospitals, Medical Research
Religion: Religious Welfare
Social Services: Child Abuse, Child Welfare, Community Service Organizations, Counseling, Delinquency & Criminal Rehabilitation, Family Services, Food/Clothing Distribution, People with Disabilities, Scouts, Shelters/Homelessness, Social Services-General, United Funds/United Ways, Youth Organizations

Contributions Analysis

Giving Priorities: Education, health and human services, culture and the arts, civic and community.
Arts & Humanities: 15%. Provides funding to a variety of causes, including music, theater, and art institutes. The majority of support goes to outreach programs for school children, the economic disadvantaged and the elderly.
Civic & Public Affairs: 7%. Grants encourage community economic development, the advancement of sound civic policy, and special interest programs that address affordable housing, leadership development, job creation and overall economic development in depressed neighborhoods.
Education: 55%. The company encourages pre-collegiate education programs that strengthen public schools and school reform through the advancement of basic curriculum, enhanced learning opportunities and faculty development. Another area of interest is pre-collegiate mathematics and science. Emphasis is placed on programs that encourage innovations in the teaching and learning of mathematics and science. Provides matching gifts to higher education institutions.

Health: About 2%. Supports health organizations located in communities where the company has a presence.
Social Services: 20%. Primary support for the United Way.
Note: Total contributions in 1998.

Application Procedures

Initial Contact: Request guidelines; then submit proposal.
Application Requirements: Include a description of the organization with its mission and project to be supported, a needs statement and objectives; amount requested and rationale; latest audited financial statement; proof of tax-exempt status; and names and amounts of other contributors; description of benefits to be realized and population to be served; plans for evaluating and reporting results; a current budget; and the names and affiliations of trustees or board of directors.
Deadlines: None.

Restrictions

Does not support individuals; religious organizations for sectarian purposes; capital campaigns; political or lobbying groups; veterans, labor, alumni, military, or fraternal organizations; social clubs; professional associations; organizations that discriminate by race, color, creed, gender, national origin or disability; endowed chairs or professorships; general endowments; United Way affiliated agencies; ad books, goodwill advertising, raffles, etc.; tickets for testimonials or benefits; documentaries, films, videos, or media projects; national groups whose local chapters receive support; foundations that make grants; trips or travel by student groups; or organizations, programs or projects that pose a conflict of interest.

Additional Information

All giving through foundation is in the form of matching gifts. Information above is for corporate grant program.
Matching gifts are available only to company employees.
Company publishes a corporate contribution guidelines sheet.
CNA Insurance Companies is affiliated with CNA Financial Corporation, Continental Casualty Company, and Continental Assurance Company. Company.

Corporate Officials

Bernard L. Henges Bauge: chairman
Antoinette Cook Bush: partner PRIM CORP EMPL partner: Skadden, Arps, Slate, Meagher & Flom. CORP AFFIL director: CNA Financial Corp.
Dennis Haig Chookaszian: chairman, chief executive officer B Chicago, IL 1943. ED Northwestern University BSChE (1965); University of Chicago MBA (1967); London School of Economics MS (1968). PRIM CORP EMPL chairman, chief executive officer: CNA Insurance Co. CORP AFFIL chairman: Valley Forge Life Insurance Co.; chairman: Transcontinental Insurance Canada New York; chairman: Transportation Insurance Co.; chairman: National Fire Insurance Hartford; chairman: Niagara Fire Insurance Co.; director: Mercury Fin; chairman: Firemens Insurance Newark New Jersey; director: Loews Corp.; chairman: Continental Corp.; chairman: Continental Insurance Co. New Jersey; chairman: Columbia Casualty Corp.; chairman: Continental Assurance Co.; director: CNA Financial Corp.; chairman: American Casualty Reading Pennsylvania; chairman: CNA Casualty California; chairman: Agency Management Services. NONPR AFFIL member: Insurance Service Office; trustee: Northwestern University; chairman: Foundation Health Enhancement; member: Illinois CPAs Society; member: Beta Gamma Sigma; executive vice president, director: Boy Scouts America Chicago Area Council; member: American Institute Association; member: American Institute CPAs; member: American Council Life Insurance. CLUB AFFIL member: Westmoreland Country Club; member: Economic Club Chicago; Executive Club Chicago; member: East Bank Club.
Peter E. Jokiel: senior vice president, chief financial officer B 1947. ED Northern Illinois University (1972). PRIM CORP EMPL senior vice president, chief financial officer: CNA Financial Corp. CORP AFFIL chief financial officer: Transportation Insurance Co.; vice president: Valley Forge Life Insurance Co.; chief financial officer: Transcontinental Insurance Co. New York; chief financial officer: Continental Loss Adjusting Services; vice president: Firemens Insurance Newark New Jersey; vice president: Continental Insurance Co. New Jersey; chief financial officer: Continental Casualty Co.; vice president: Continental Corp.; senior vice president: Continental Assurance Co.; chief financial officer: CNA Casualty California; chief financial officer: Columbia Casualty Co.; senior vice president: American Casualty Reading Pennsylvania.
James S. Tisch: president, chief executive officer, director B Atlantic City, NJ 1953. ED Cornell University BA (1975); University of Pennsylvania Wharton School MBA (1976). PRIM CORP EMPL president, chief executive officer, director: Loews Corp. CORP AFFIL chairman: Diamond Offshore Drilling Inc.; director: Vail Resorts Inc.; director: CNA Financial Corp. NONPR AFFIL trustee: Mount Sinai Medical Center New York; president elect: United Jewish Appeal Federation New York; trustee: Dalton School New York; director: Federation Employment & Guidance Service.
Laurence Alan Tisch: chairman, co-chief executive officer B New York, NY 1923. ED New York University BS (1942); University of Pennsylvania MA (1943); Harvard University Law School (1946). PRIM CORP EMPL chairman, co-chief executive officer: Loews Corp. ADD CORP EMPL chief executive officer: CNA Financial Corp.; chief executive officer: Continental Loss Adjusting Service. CORP AFFIL director: Petrie Stores Corp.; director: Transcontinental Insurance Co. New York; chairman: CNA Financial Corp.; director: Automatic Data Processing Inc.; director: Bulova Corp. NONPR AFFIL chairman board trustees: New York University; director: United Jewish Appeal Federation; trustee: New York Public Library; member: Council Foreign Relations; trustee: Metropolitan Museum Art.
Preston Robert Tisch: co-chairman, co-chief executive officer, director B Brooklyn, NY 1926. ED Bucknell University (1943-1944); University of Michigan BA (1948). PRIM CORP EMPL co-chairman, co-chief executive officer, director: Loews Corp. ADD CORP EMPL owner, chief executive officer, chairman: New York Football Giants Inc. CORP AFFIL director: Transcontinental Insurance Co. New York; director: Rite Aid Corp.; director: CNA Financial Corp.; director: Hasbro Inc.; director: Bulova Watch Corp.; director: Bulova Corp. NONPR AFFIL trustee: New York University; member: Sigma Alpha Mu; member: Governments Business Advisory Council New York; chairman emeritus: New York Convention & Visit Bureau; president: Citymeals Wheels. CLUB AFFIL Rye Racquet Club; Century Country Club.

Giving Program Officials

Sarada Amani: PRIM CORP EMPL manager community relations: CNA Insurance Companies.

Foundation Officials

Edward J. Noha: director B New York, NY 1926. ED Pace University BBA (1951). CORP AFFIL director: Loews Corp.; chairman: National Fire Insurance Co. Hartford; chief executive officer, director: CNA Financial Corp.; chairman: Continental Loss Adjusting Services.
William Henry Sharkey, Jr.: director PRIM CORP EMPL director, senior vice president: CNA Casualty of California. CORP AFFIL officer: Transportation Insurance Co.; officer: Valley Forge Life Insurance Co.; senior vice president: Transcontinental Insurance Co. New York; officer: Firemans Insurance Newark New Jersey; director: Niagara Fire Insurance Co.; director: Continental Insurance Canada; officer: Continental Insurance Co. New Jersey; officer: Continental Casualty Canada; senior vice president: American Casualty Reading Pennsylvania; senior vice president: Continental Assurance Canada.

Grants Analysis

Disclosure Period: calendar year ending 1998
Total Grants: $1,445,501*
Number of Grants: 88
Average Grant: $16,426
Highest Grant: $686,961
Typical Range: $1,000 to $25,000
***Note:** Giving excludes United Way; matching gifts.

Recent Grants

Note: Grants derived from 1998 Form 990.

Arts & Humanities

187,500	Lincoln Center for the Performing Arts, Washington, DC
50,000	Whitney Museum of American Art, New York, NY
15,000	Shakespeare Repertory, Chicago, IL
11,000	The Goodman Theatre, Chicago, IL
10,000	The Chicago Symphony Orchestra, Chicago, IL
7,500	Steppenwolf Theatre Company, Chicago, IL
5,000	Friends of the Chicago Public Library, Chicago, IL
5,000	Hubbard Street Dance Chicago, Chicago, IL
5,000	Lyric Opera of Chicago, Chicago, IL

Civic & Public Affairs

50,000	Civic Committee of the Commercial Club, Chicago, IL
50,000	Neighborhood Housing Service of Chicago, Chicago, IL
10,440	Charitabulls, Chicago, IL
10,000	American Enterprise Institute for Public Policy Research, Washington, DC
10,000	Financial Accounting Foundation, Columbus, OH
6,500	Neighborhood Housing Service, Chicago, IL
5,000	Designs for Change, Chicago, IL
5,000	National Training & Information Center, Chicago, IL
5,000	Streetwise Newspaper, Chicago, IL

Education

686,961	Mathcounts, Alexandria, VA
138,695	The National Merit Scholarship, Chicago, IL
41,500	Illinois State University, Normal, IL
26,000	DePaul University, Chicago, IL
25,000	University of Illinois Foundation, Chicago, IL
20,000	Illinois Council of Teachers of Math, Springfield, IL
20,000	Indiana University Foundation, Bloomington, IN
15,000	Howard University, Washington, DC
15,000	Junior Achievement Of Chicago, Chicago, IL
15,000	Skinner School, Chicago, IL
15,000	University of Wisconsin Foundation, Madison, WI
10,000	Citizenship Education Fund, Washington, DC
10,000	Inner City Teaching Corp, Chicago, IL
8,500	Society of Actuaries Minority Scholarship, Schaumburg, IL
5,000	Chicago Association of Local School Councils, Chicago, IL
5,000	JL Kellogg Graduate School of Management, Boston, MA
5,000	University Of Chicago, Chicago, IL

Health

11,000 Children's Memorial Medical Center, Chicago, IL
7,500 Chicago House, Chicago, IL
5,000 Glenview Evangelical Free Church, Glenview, IL
5,000 Mayo Foundation, Rochester, MN

Religion

25,000 Misericordia Heart of Mercy, Chicago, IL

Social Services

360,500 United Way of Chicago, Chicago, IL
10,000 Girl Scouts - IL Linois Crossroads, IL
10,000 Voices for Illinois Children, Chicago, IL
7,193 Boy Scouts of America, Chicago, IL
5,000 Boys & Girls Clubs of Chicago, Chicago, IL
5,000 Chicago Cares, Chicago, IL
5,000 Chris Zorich Foundation, Chicago, IL
5,000 National Committee to Prevent Child Abuse, Chicago, IL
5,000 People's Resource Center Du Page, Du Page, IL
5,000 Second Harvest National Food Bank, Chicago, IL

CNF TRANSPORTATION, INC.

Company Contact

Palo Alto, CA
Web: http://www.cnf.com

Company Description

Former Name: Consolidated Freightways, Inc.
Revenue: US$4,941,500,000
Employees: 25,100
Fortune Rank: 296, per FORTUNE Magazine's list of 500 Largest U.S. Corporations (1999).
FF 296
SIC(s): 4213 Trucking Except Local.

Corporate Sponsorship

Type: Arts & cultural events; Festivals/fairs; Music & entertainment events; Sports events; Pledge-a-thon
Note: Sponsorship is considered on an individual basis.

Giving Contact

Chris Kidwell, Vice President, Corporate Benefits
CNF Transportation, Inc.
3240 Hillview Ave.
Palo Alto, CA 94304
Phone: (650)494-2900
Fax: (650)813-5311

Description

Organization Type: Corporate Giving Program
Giving Locations: nationally, with an emphasis on areas where company operates.
Grant Types: Employee Matching Gifts, General Support.

Giving Philosophy

CNF Transportation, Inc. '. . . is committed to a program providing financial support to selected organizations which endeavor to improve our economic and social well-being. While the primary business ..is to provide quality transportation services, the Company also believes its responsibilities extend beyond that objective. The . . . Company has an obligation to be sensitive to broad areas of need and concern to society in general and to participate in the private sector of philanthropy, particularly where private programs can be especially effective. In carrying out its obligation, . . . intends to benefit not only the organizations receiving support but also our employees and the communities in which they live and work, our shareholders and our entire society.' *Corporate Contributions Program Guidelines*

Financial Summary

Total Giving: $836,000 (1996 approx); $836,000 (1995 approx). Note: Contributes through corporate direct giving program only.

Typical Recipients

Arts & Humanities: Arts Institutes, Museums/Galleries, Performing Arts, Public Broadcasting, Visual Arts
Education: Colleges & Universities, Economic Education, Student Aid
Social Services: Community Service Organizations, People with Disabilities, Senior Services, United Funds/United Ways, Youth Organizations

Contributions Analysis

Civic & Public Affairs: Supports organizations involved in the community and public well-being similar to United Way.
Education: Supports scholarship programs.

Application Procedures

Initial Contact: Submit a written request.
Application Requirements: Include legal name of organization and official contact person; brief a description of organization, with history and purpose; purpose for which grant is requested and anticipated benefits of program or project; amount needed; expected sources of other funding; program budget; statement that organization is not a recipient of any United Way or other similar federated organization (if organization is a recipient, list what percentage of funding); copy of latest annual financial statement; and evidence of tax-exempt status.
Deadlines: None.
Review Process: Proposals are first reviewed by contributions screening committee; if appropriate, proposal is passed to board of directors of contributions committee.
Evaluative Criteria: Objectives, programs, and effectiveness of requesting organization, and need are considered.
Decision Notification: Usually three months after receiving request.
Notes: The contributions committee must approve all requests of $1,000 or more.

Restrictions

The company does not support individuals; organizations that are not tax-exempt; organizations that discriminate by race, color, creed, or national origin; capital programs, except in pre-selected locations; hospital or other patient care operating funds; organizations outside the United States; political parties, candidates, or partisan political organizations; organizations influencing legislation; or religious organizations for sectarian purposes.

The company also does not support veterans' and labor organizations, fraternal associations, athletic groups, social clubs, and similar groups; organizations receiving United Way or federated campaign support; endowment funds; testimonial dinners or benefit programs involving the purchase of tables, tickets, or advertising; or travel expenses related to tours, conferences, seminars, etc.

Additional Information

The company changed its name in December 1996; the company was formerly known as Consolidated Freightways, Inc.
Publications: Corporate Contributions Program Guidelines

Corporate Officials

Donald Eugene Moffitt: chairman, director, director B Terre Haute, IN 1932. ED Indiana State University BA (1954); Indiana University (1956); Harvard University Advanced Management Program (1970). PRIM CORP EMPL chairman, director: CNF Transportation, Inc. CORP AFFIL chairman: Williamette Sales Co.; chairman, director: Menlo Logistics Inc.; executive vice president fin, director: Road System Inc.; chairman, director: Emery Air Freight Corp.; chairman, director: Emery Distr System; chairman, director: Con-Way Truckload Services; director, director: Consolidated Freightways Corp. DE. NONPR AFFIL member, director, vice chairman: National Chamber of Commerce; business advisory council: Northwestern University Transportation Center; director: Hoover Institute; director: Conference Board; director, executive committee: Highway Users Federation Safety Mobility; director: Boy Scouts America; director: California Business Roundtable; trustee: Automotive Safety Foundation; director: Bay Area Council; director: American Red Cross.
Gregory L. Quesnel: president, chief executive officer, director B Woodburn, OR 1948. ED Columbia University Graduate Executive Program in Business Administration; University of Oregon BS (1970); University of Portland MBA (1975). PRIM CORP EMPL president, chief executive officer, director: CNF Transportation, Inc. CORP AFFIL treasurer, director: Emery Distr System; president, director: Vantageparts.

Giving Program Officials

Henry A. Schmitt: PRIM CORP EMPL vice president corporate relations: CNF Transportation, Inc.

Foundation Officials

Donald Eugene Moffitt: president (see above)
Gregory L. Quesnel: vice president (see above)

COACHMEN INDUSTRIES, INC.

Company Contact

Elkhart, IN
Web: http://www.coachmen.com

Company Description

Employees: 3,813
SIC(s): 3448 Prefabricated Metal Buildings, 3711 Motor Vehicles & Car Bodies, 3713 Truck & Bus Bodies, 3792 Travel Trailers & Campers.

Nonmonetary Support

Type: Donated Equipment; Donated Products

Corporate Sponsorship

Type: Arts & cultural events; Festivals/fairs; Music & entertainment events
Note: Supports symphony orchestras.

Giving Contact

Bill Angelo, Corporate Controller
Coachmen Industries, Inc.
PO Box 3300
Elkhart, IN 46515
Phone: (219)206-1700
Fax: (219)262-8823

Description

Organization Type: Corporate Giving Program
Giving Locations: headquarters area only.
Grant Types: General Support.

Financial Summary

Total Giving: Contributes through corporate direct giving program only.

Typical Recipients

Arts & Humanities: Arts & Humanities-General
Civic & Public Affairs: Economic Development, Civic & Public Affairs-General
Education: Economic Education, Education-General

Health: Health-General
Social Services: Social Services-General

Application Procedures

Initial Contact: a brief letter of inquiry
Application Requirements: a description of organization, amount requested, purpose of funds sought, recently audited financial statement, and proof of tax-exempt status
Deadlines: None.

Corporate Officials

Keith Daniel Corson: president, chief operating officer B South Bend, IN 1935. ED Wichita State University (1958-1959). PRIM CORP EMPL president, chief operating officer: Coachmen Industries, Inc. CORP AFFIL president: Michiana Easy Livin' Country; president: Northwoods RV Country Inc.; president: Gulfcoast Easy Living Country; president: Marietta RV WInc.; president: Colfax Country RV Sales Inc.; president: Freeway Easy Living Country; president: All American Homes North Carolina; president: Coachmen Industries Georgia.
Claire Corson Skinner: chairman, chief executive officer B Dallas, TX 1954. ED Southern Methodist University BA (1976); University of Notre Dame JD (1981). PRIM CORP EMPL chairman, chief executive officer: Coachmen Industries, Inc. CORP AFFIL chief executive officer: Michiana Easy Livin' Country; chairman: Coachmen Industries Georgia. NONPR AFFIL director: Florida RV Trade Association; director: Recreational Vehicle Industry Association; member: American Management Association; member: American Bar Association.

Giving Program Officials

Bill Angelo: PRIM CORP EMPL corporate controller: Coachmen Industries, Inc.

Coca-cola Co.

 Number 68 of Top 100 Corporate Givers

Company Contact

Atlanta, GA
Web: http://www.thecoca-colacompany.com

Company Description

Revenue: US$19,805,000,000 (1999)
Profit: US$2,431,000,000 (1999)
Employees: 26,000
Fortune Rank: 83, per FORTUNE Magazine's list of 500 Largest U.S. Corporations (1999).
FF 83
SIC(s): 2037 Frozen Fruits & Vegetables, 2086 Bottled & Canned Soft Drinks, 2087 Flavoring Extracts & Syrups Nec, 2099 Food Preparations Nec.

Operating Locations

Italy: Coca-Cola Bevande Italia SRL, Milano, Lombardia; Coca-Cola Export Corp., Milano, Lombardia; Japan: Coca-Cola Japan Co. Ltd., Tokyo; Nigeria: Coca-Cola Nigeria Ltd., Lagos; Netherlands: Bottling Holdings (Netherlands) BV, Schiedam, Zuid-Holland; Coca-Cola Finance (Nederland) BV, Schiedam, Zuid-Holland; Coca-Cola Nederland BV, Schiedam, Zuid-Holland; Norway: Coca-Cola Norge A/S, Lysaker, Akershus; Russia: Coca-Cola Refreshments Moscow Private Joint Stock Co., Moscow; Coca-Cola Private Joint Stock Co., Orel; Spain: Campania de Servicios de Bebidas Refrescantes SL, Madrid; Refrescos Envasados SA, Madrid; Switzerland: Minute Maid SA, Pfaeffikon, Schwyz; Coca-Cola AG, Zurich; Turkey: Coca-Cola Export Corp. Merkezi Atlanta Turkiye Istanbul Subesi, Istanbul; Maksan Manisa Mesrubat Kutulama Sanayi AS, Istanbul; Mepa Mesrubat Pazarlama Dagitim ve Ticaret AS, Istanbul; United Kingdom: Beverage Services Ltd., London; Coca-Cola Holdings (United Kingdom) Ltd., London; Coca-Cola International Sales Ltd., London; Refreshment Spectrum Ltd., London; Coca-Cola Export Corp., Uxbridge, Middlesex; Uruguay: Montevideo Refrescos SA, Montevideo

Nonmonetary Support

Value: $500,000 (1990)
Type: Donated Equipment

Corporate Sponsorship

Type: Arts & cultural events; Festivals/fairs; Music & entertainment events; Sports events
Contact: Kirk Glaze, Contact

Coca-Cola Foundation

Giving Contact

Donald Ray Greene, President
Coca-Cola Foundation
PO Drawer 1734
Atlanta, GA 30301
Phone: (404)676-2568
Fax: (404)676-8804

Description

Founded: 1984
EIN: 581574705
Organization Type: Corporate Foundation
Giving Locations: internationally; nationally.
Grant Types: Capital, Challenge, Employee Matching Gifts, Endowment, Fellowship, General Support, Project, Scholarship.
Note: Employee matching gift ratio: 2 to 1.

Giving Philosophy

'The Coca-Cola Foundation's mission is to foster and promote a favorable environment for business growth by supporting educational and related community needs.
'The Coca-Cola Foundation's objectives are to provide youth with the educational opportunities and support systems they need to become knowledgeable and productive citizens. Education is a fundamental means to help individuals reach their full potential. The foundation, by committing its resources to education, can help to address society's greatest educational challenges and to provide quality learning opportunities.
'The Coca-Cola Foundation's focus on education continues a tradition of more than a century of corporate philanthropy. The Foundation's support of quality education is one way The Coca-Cola Company fulfills its responsibilities as a corporate citizen.' *Always Touching The Future,* The Coca-Cola Foundation 1994

Financial Summary

Total Giving: $12,000,000 (2000 approx); $12,000,000 (1999 approx); $12,497,561 (1998).
Note: Contributes through corporate direct giving program and foundation. 1997 Giving includes foundation. 1996 Giving includes foundation. 1995 Giving includes foundation; scholarship ($238,150).
Assets: $23,823,325 (1996); $21,118,000 (1993); $19,300,000 (1992)
Gifts Received: $4,928,297 (1996)

Typical Recipients

Arts & Humanities: Arts Festivals, Ballet, Historic Preservation, History & Archaeology, Libraries, Museums/Galleries, Theater
Civic & Public Affairs: African American Affairs, Hispanic Affairs, Native American Affairs, Public Policy
Education: Afterschool/Enrichment Programs, Arts/Humanities Education, Business Education, Colleges & Universities, Education Associations, Education Funds, Education Reform, Elementary Education (Private), Engineering/Technological Education, Environmental Education, Faculty Development, Education-General, Health & Physical Education, International Exchange, International Studies, Leadership Training, Literacy, Medical Education, Minority Education, Private Education (Precollege), Public Education (Precollege), Science/Mathematics Education, Social Sciences Education, Student Aid, Vocational & Technical Education
International: Foreign Educational Institutions, Health Care/Hospitals, International Affairs, International Development, International Environmental Issues, International Relief Efforts
Science: Science Museums, Scientific Centers & Institutes
Social Services: Recreation & Athletics, YMCA/YWCA/YMHA/YWHA, Youth Organizations

Contributions Analysis

Giving Priorities: Higher education, classroom teaching & learning, and global education.
Education: 100% of foundation giving. Coca-Cola has allocated over $100 million for the decade of the 1990s--$5,000,000 per year--to be used solely for the purpose of supporting education. Supports public and private colleges and universities, elementary and secondary schools, teacher training programs, educational programs for minority students, arts and environmental education programs and educational programs that serve a global constituency. Grants will still span the traditional areas of giving--arts, civic, health, and social service--but projects must have some basis in education. Special interests include pipeline programs that encourage students to stay in school andproceed on to college and graduate school, scholarship programs that support graduate and undergraduate students, minority advancement through scholarships, urban and cultural diversity programs and global exchange programs which encourage international studies, global understanding or student exchange. The foundation is also interested in programs that introduce art education curricula into public schools and programs which collaborate between higher education, cultural institutions and K-12 public schools.

Application Procedures

Initial Contact: call to request application form
Application Requirements: Completed application with program summary of no more than five pages. Information should include organization's mission; general program description, an explanation of why it is appropriate for Coca-Cola Foundation to help fund the project; financial statement; board of directors; proof of tax-exempt status; a statement on letterhead indicating that there is no change in purpose of organization since the issuance of the IRS letters; total project cost and amount requested; and a plan for measuring the success of the project.
Deadlines: None.
Decision Notification: Applications are accepted and reviewed continuously; notification is made within 30 days
Notes: If proposal is being considered for funding, further communication may be required.

Restrictions

Foundation does not make grants to individuals; religious organizations or endeavors; political, legislative, lobbying or fraternal organizations; or organizations that do not have tax-exempt status under IRS Code Section 501(c)(3).

Additional Information

Foundation prefers to support direct service projects and programs rather than making contributions to intermediary funding agencies.
Preference is given to proposals that identify clearly defined need, describe an innovative way to meet that need, demonstrate the applicant's ability to implement

the process, and show how the program will benefit the general community.
Special consideration is given to organizations that effectively engage volunteers in reaching their goals. engage volunteers in reaching their goals.

Corporate Officials

Douglas Daft: chairman, chief executive officer PRIM CORP EMPL chairman, chief executive officer: Coca-Cola Co.
Randal W. Donaldson: vice president PRIM CORP EMPL vice president: The Coca-Cola Co.
Donald Ray Greene: assistant vice president B Macon, GA 1948. ED University of Georgia AB (1970); Ball State University MA (1973). PRIM CORP EMPL assistant vice president: The Coca-Cola Co. NONPR AFFIL chairman: American Council Arts.
Jack L. Stahl: president PRIM CORP EMPL president: Coca-Cola Co.

Foundation Officials

John Richard Alm: director B Jamestown, NY 1946. ED State University of New York BS (1972). PRIM CORP EMPL senior vice president, chief financial officer: Coca-Cola Enterprises Inc. CORP AFFIL senior vice president: Bluegrass Coca-Cola Bottling Co.; senior vice president: Johnston Coca-Cola Bottling Group. NONPR AFFIL member: Financial Executives Institute; member: Minnesota Society CPA's.
Michelle Beale: director PRIM CORP EMPL senior vice president: Coca-Cola Foods. CORP AFFIL senior vice president: Coca-Cola Co.
Frank Bifuco, Junior: director
Randal W. Donaldson: director (see above)
Donald Ray Greene: president, director (see above)
Ingrid Saunders Jones: chairman, director B Detroit, MI 1945. ED Michigan State University BA (1968); Eastern Michigan University MA (1972). PRIM CORP EMPL vice president: The Coca-Cola Co.
Joseph West Jones: secretary, director B Georgetown, DE 1912. ED Beacom College BA (1932). PRIM CORP EMPL chairman: Ichauway Inc.

Grants Analysis

Disclosure Period: calendar year ending 1998
Total Grants: $12,497,561
Number of Grants: 207
Average Grant: $60,375
Highest Grant: $350,000
Typical Range: $10,000 to $100,000

Recent Grants

Note: Grants derived from 1997 Form 990.

Arts & Humanities

100,000	Capital Theater, Atlanta, GA -- support Atlanta Project
75,000	Atlanta Ballet, Atlanta, GA -- support 1996-97 Bravo! Campaign
75,000	Atlanta Historical Society, Atlanta, GA -- support Fellows Program
65,000	Spoleto Festival USA, Charleston, SC -- support 1997 EducationSpoleto

Education

300,000	Morehouse College, Atlanta, GA -- to establish Leadership Center
250,000	Ohio State University Foundation, Columbus, OH -- support Critical Difference for Women Program
240,110	Duke University, Durham, NC -- support Solid Waste Minimization and Management Program
200,000	100 Black Men of America, Atlanta, GA -- support National Scholarship Program
200,000	Clemson University Foundation, Clemson, SC -- support five-year partnership to maintain Minority Scholars Program
200,000	Clemson University Research Foundation, Clemson, SC -- support La Amistad Conservation and Development Initiative
200,000	Georgetown University School of Foreign Service, Washington, DC -- support Minority Student Educational Programs
200,000	Georgia State University Foundation, Atlanta, GA -- support Rialto Project
200,000	University of Georgia College of Business Administration, Athens, GA -- support for Coca-Cola Student Lounge
185,000	Independent Colleges of Southern California, Los Angeles, CA -- support for Southern and Northern Independent Colleges of California
150,000	University of Oklahoma Foundation, Norman, OK -- support Coca-Cola Professorship in Native American Studies, Coca-Cola outreach programs
130,000	Jacksonville University, Jacksonville, FL -- support Career Corridor Initiative
105,000	Georgia Tech Foundation, Atlanta, GA -- support Sam Nunn School of International Affairs
100,000	Auburn University Foundation, Auburn University, AL -- support minority students in Science and Engineering and Mathematics Partner program
100,000	DePaul University, Chicago, IL -- support Career Corridor Initiative Program
100,000	Florida A&M University, Sarasota, FL -- support Second Century Campaign
100,000	Morehouse School of Medicine, Atlanta, GA -- support Clinical Training and Residency Program
100,000	North Carolina A&T State University, Greensboro, NC -- support Career Corridor Initiative
100,000	United Negro College Fund, New York, NY -- for national support
100,000	University of Arizona Foundation, Tucson, AZ -- support Project Soar Career Corridor Initiative
100,000	University of Arkansas Foundation, Fayetteville, AR -- support Coca-Cola Scholarship Program
100,000	University of Georgia College of Business Administration, Athens, GA -- support Coca-Cola Student Lounge
100,000	University of Kingston, WA -- support Career Corridor Initiative
100,000	University of Michigan College of Literature, Science Development, and External Relations, Ann Arbor, MI -- support Coca-Cola UROP Scholars
100,000	University of Minnesota, Minneapolis, MN -- support Career Corridor Initiative
100,000	University of Missouri Columbia, Columbia, MO -- support Coca-Cola Ambassadors Program
100,000	University of North Carolina Kenan-Flagler Business School, Chapel Hill, NC -- support Coca-Cola MBA Fellowships
100,000	University of Pennsylvania, Philadelphia, PA -- support Career Corridor Initiative
100,000	West Virginia University Foundation, Morgantown, WV -- support Health Sciences and Technology Academy
100,000	White House Fellows Foundation, Washington, DC -- capital campaign
75,000	University of Alabama, Tuscaloosa, AL -- support Multiple Abilities Program
65,000	Florida Independent College Fund, Lakeland, FL -- support Coca-Cola First Generation Scholarship Program
62,500	International Foundation for Education and Self-Help, Phoenix, AZ
60,000	American Council on Education, Washington, DC -- support 15th anniversary status report on minorities in higher education
60,000	Georgia Foundation for Independent Colleges, Atlanta, GA -- support Coca-Cola Minority Achievement Award Program
50,000	Wake Forest University Babcock Graduate School of Management, Winston-Salem, NC -- support Coca-Cola Scholars Program
50,000	Winston-Salem State University, Winston-Salem, NC -- to endow Merit Scholarship

International

125,000	Friends of McGill University, New York, NY -- support Coca-Cola International Student Center
125,000	Friends of McGill University, New York, NY -- support Coca-Cola International Student Center
100,000	Foundation for Community Development, Mozambique -- support Socio-Economic Reconstruction of Rural Communities program
100,000	Foundation for Community Development, Mozambique -- support Socio-Economic Reconstruction of Rural Communities program
75,000	Africare, Washington, DC -- support Rural Development Program for Eastern Transvaal South Africa
75,000	Africare, Washington, DC -- support Rural Development Program for Eastern Transvaal South Africa

Science

100,000	International Life Sciences Institute, Washington, DC -- support Research Foundation
75,000	American Museum of Natural History, New York, NY -- support Moveable Museum

Social Services

251,250	Intercultural Development Research Association, San Antonio, TX -- support national expansion of Coca Cola Valued Youth Program
200,000	Healthsouth Sports Medicine Council, Birmingham, AL -- support Go For It Curriculum
100,000	Boys and Girls Clubs, Atlanta, GA -- support Power Hour Program
100,000	YMCA, Atlanta, GA -- support Techwood Village, campaign initiatives

COLGATE-PALMOLIVE CO.

 Number 70 of Top 100 Corporate Givers

Company Contact

New York, NY
Web: http://www.colgate.com

Company Description

Revenue: US$8,971,600,000
Employees: 38,000
Fortune Rank: 187, per FORTUNE Magazine's list of 500 Largest U.S. Corporations (1999).
FF 187
SIC(s): 2047 Dog & Cat Food, 2841 Soap & Other Detergents, 2844 Toilet Preparations.

Operating Locations

Argentina: Colgate Palmolive SAIC, Llavallol, Buenos Aires; Australia: Colgate Palmolive Pty. Ltd., Sydney; Austria: Colgate Palmolive GmbH, Vienna; Belgium: Colgate Palmolive Belgium SA, Brussels, Brabant; Colgate Palmolive Europe SA, Brussels, Brabant; Colgate-Palmolive Research & Development Inc., Brussels, Brabant; CKR SC, Verviers, Liege; Brazil: CP Industria e Comercio Ltda., Sao Paulo; Canada:

Colgate Palmolive Canada, Toronto; People's Republic of China: Colgate (Guangzhou) Co. Ltd., Guangzhou, Chiba; Cote d'Ivoire: Colgate Palmolive Cote D'Ivoire SA, Abidjan; Costa Rica: Colgate Palmolive (Central America), San Jose; Czech Republic: Colgate Palmolive Spol SRO, Prague; Denmark: Colgate Palmolive A/S, Glostrup, Copenhagen; Colgate Palmolive Nordic A/S, Glostrup, Copenhagen; Dominica: Dominica Coconut Products Ltd., Roseau; Ecuador: Colgate Palmolive del Ecuador SA, Guayaquil, Guayas; Egypt: Colgate Palmolive Egypt SAE, Alexandria; Fiji: Colgate Palmolive (Fiji) Ltd., Suva; France: Bella, Courbevoie, Hauts-de-Seine; Colgate Palmolive, Courbevoie, Hauts-de-Seine; Cotelle ETS, Courbevoie, Hauts-de-Seine; Cotelle SA, Courbevoie, Hauts-de-Seine; Delpha, Courbevoie, Hauts-de-Seine; Hill's Pet Products SNC, Valbonne, Alpes-Maritimes; Germany: Colgate Palmolive GmbH, Hamburg; Hill's Pet Nutrition GmbH, Hamburg; Guatemala: Colgate Palmolive (Central America) SA, Guatemala City; Guyana: Colgate Palmolive (Guyana) Ltd., Georgetown, Demerara-Mahaica; Hong Kong: Colgate Palmolive Hong Kong Ltd., Causeway Bay; Hungary: Colgate Palmolive (Magyarorszag) KFT, Budapest; India: Colgate Palmolive (India) Ltd., Mumbai; Ireland: Colgate Palmolive, Dublin; Italy: Colgate Palmolive SpA, Anzio, Lazio; Hill's Pet Nutrition SpA, Roma, Lazio; Jamaica: Colgate Palmolive Co. (Jamaica) Ltd., Kingston; Japan: Hill's Colgate (Japan) Ltd., Tokyo; Kenya: Colgate Palmolive (East Africa) Ltd., Nairobi; Mexico: Demi SA de CV, Lerma; Colgate Palmolive SA de CV, Mexico; Mennen de Mexico SA de CV, Naucalpan; Mission Hills SA de CV, San Jose Iturbide; Morocco: Colgate Palmolive Maroc, Casablanca; Malaysia: Gervas Corp. Sdn. Bhd., Kuala Lumpur, Selangor; Colgate Palmolive (Malaysia) Sdn. Bhd., Petaling Jaya, Selangor; Colgate Palmolive Marketing Sdn. Bhd., Petaling Jaya, Selangor; Netherlands: Hill's International Sales FSC BV, Breda, Noord-Brabant; Hill's Pet Nutrition BV, Breda, Noord-Brabant; Hill's Pet Nutrition Manufacturing BV, Etten Leur, Noord-Brabant; Hamol BV, Klundert, Noord-Brabant; Colgate Palmolive Nederland BV, Weesp, Noord-Holland; Hamol BV, Weesp, Noord-Holland; Norway: Colgate Palmolive Norge AS, Lysaker, Akershus; New Zealand: Colgate Palmolive Ltd., Petone, Wellington; Panama: Colgate Palmolive CA, Panama City; Philippines: Colgate Palmolive Philippines, Manila; Papua New Guinea: Colgate Palmolive Investments (Papua New Guinea) Pty. Ltd., Lae; Poland: Colgate Palmolive (Poland) Sp Zoo, Warsaw, Warszawa; Portugal: Colprogeca Sociedade Geral de Fibras Cafes e Produtos Coloniais Lda., Lisboa; Romania: Colgate Palmolive Romania SRL, Bucharest; Senegal: Nouvelles Savonneries de L'Ouest Africain SA, Dakar; Singapore: Colgate Palmolive (Eastern) Pte. Ltd., Singapore; Thailand: Colgate Palmolive (Thailand) Co. Ltd., Klongtoey, Bangkok; Turkey: Colgate Palmolive Haci Sakir Sabun Sanayi Ve Ticaret AS, Istanbul; Colgate-Palmolive Temizlik Urunleri Sanayi Ve Ticaret AS, Istanbul; Taiwan: Hawley & Hazel Taiwan Corp., Taipei; United Republic of Tanzania: Body Care Ltd., Dar Es Salaam; United Kingdom: Colgate Palmolive Mennen Ltd., Guildford, Surrey; Colgate Palmolive United Kingdom Ltd., Guildford, Surrey; Colgate (UK) Ltd., Guildford, Surrey; Hill's Pet Nutrition Ltd., Hatfield, Hertfordshire; Venezuela: Colgate Palmolive CA, Caracas; Zambia: Colgate Palmolive (Zambia) Ltd., Ndola, Copperbelt

Nonmonetary Support

Value: $5,150,000 (1998); $627,000 (1996); $650,000 (1994)
Type: Cause-related Marketing & Promotion; Donated Equipment; Donated Products; In-kind Services

Corporate Sponsorship

Type: Arts & cultural events; Sports events
Note: Supports the Colgate Women's Games.

Giving Contact

Sally Phipps, Contributions Manager
Colgate-Palmolive Co.
300 Park Avenue
New York, NY 10022
Phone: (212)310-2175
Fax: (212)310-2873

Description

Organization Type: Corporate Giving Program
Grant Types: Employee Matching Gifts, General Support, Multiyear/Continuing Support.
Note: Employee matching gift ratio: 1 to 1 for education, hospitals, United Way, and specified youth and minorityorganisation.

Giving Philosophy

'Colgate-Palmolive Company is committed to supporting through its charitable contributions program the health, education and welfare needs of people throughout the worldwide communities in which it operates. The Company's philanthropic activities are diverse, ranging from programs which provide oral care education to youth athletic and scholarship programs.' *Charitable Contributions Information & Guidelines*

Financial Summary

Total Giving: $12,000,000 (2000 approx); $12,000,000 (1999 approx); $11,692,000 (1998). Note: Contributes through corporate direct giving program only. 1998 Giving includes corporate direct giving ($6,242,000); foundation ($300,000); domestic and international subsidiaries ($5,316,000); international subsidiaries (6,376,000); nonmonetary support. 1996 Giving includes corporate direct giving ($4,783,000); international subsidiaries ($7,598,000); nonmonetary support.

Typical Recipients

Arts & Humanities: Arts & Humanities-General
Civic & Public Affairs: Civic & Public Affairs-General
Education: Education-General
Health: Health-General
Social Services: Social Services-General

Contributions Analysis

Giving Priorities: Priority to improve and enhance educational needs of youth and minorities; also gives to edcuation, health, welfare, arts, and civic organizations. Company supports organizations whose primary activities are dedicated to youth, women and minorities, education, health and welfare, cultural arts, and civic and community activities, with priority given programs that enhance and service the educational needs of youth and minorities. Foreign subsidiaries have independent contributions budgets and do not have to report giving to headquarters.
International: Colgate-Palmolive's foreign subsidiaries also contribute funds to nonprofits, and the Colgate-Palmolive Company maintains a foundationin South Africa, which gave $1,600,000 in 1996.

Application Procedures

Initial Contact: one- to two-page letter
Application Requirements: background information on organization; statement of major programs and services rendered; specific purpose for funding sought; proof of tax-exempt status; current operating budget
Deadlines: None.
Review Process: each request is evaluated individually to determine eligibility within current budget and giving priorities; renewals of contributions are not automatic and cannot be guaranteed from year to year
Decision Notification: within four to six weeks of receipt of request

Corporate Officials

Jann Coles: manager corporate education PRIM CORP EMPL manager corporate education: Colgate-Palmolive Co.
Lois Juliber: chief operating officer PRIM CORP EMPL chief operating officer: Colgate-Palmolive Co.
Reuben Mark: chairman, chief executive officer B Jersey City, NJ 1939. ED Middlebury College AB (1960); Harvard University MBA (1963). PRIM CORP EMPL chairman, chief executive officer: Colgate-Palmolive Co. CORP AFFIL director: Toys R Us; director: New York Stock Exchange Inc.; director: Time Warner Inc.; director: Citicorp. NONPR AFFIL member: National Executive Service Corps; director: Soap & Detergent Association; director: Grocery Manufacturer America.
William Shanahan: president PRIM CORP EMPL president: Colgate-Palmolive Co.

Giving Program Officials

Lexanne Hamilton: contributions administrator

Collins &Aikman Corp.

Company Contact

Charlotte, NC

Company Description

Former Name: Wickes Companies.
Employees: 11,700
SIC(s): 2679 Converted Paper Products Nec, 3714 Motor Vehicle Parts & Accessories, 5013 Motor Vehicle Supplies & New Parts, 5023 Homefurnishings.

Collins & Aikman Foundation

Giving Contact

Ms. Arlene Bookman, Administrator
Collins & Aikman Foundation
701 McCullough Drive
Charlotte, NC 28262
Phone: (704)548-2389
Fax: (704)548-2391

Description

EIN: 954085655
Organization Type: Corporate Foundation
Giving Locations: operating locations.
Grant Types: Employee Matching Gifts, General Support.

Financial Summary

Total Giving: $467,729 (1998); $497,995 (1997); $621,589 (1996). Note: Contributes through foundation only.
Giving Analysis: Giving for 1996 includes: foundation grants to United Way ($83,250); foundation matching gifts ($15,715); foundation scholarships ($12,100); 1997: foundation grants to United Way ($32,250); foundation scholarships ($26,830); foundation matching gifts ($9,735); 1998: foundation grants to United Way ($60,473); foundation scholarships ($26,440); foundation matching gifts ($15,831)
Assets: $3,527,010 (1998); $3,820,024 (1997); $4,144,417 (1996)

Typical Recipients

Arts & Humanities: Arts Associations & Councils, Arts Centers, Arts & Humanities-General, Libraries, Museums/Galleries, Music
Civic & Public Affairs: Economic Development, Municipalities/Towns, Professional & Trade Associations, Urban & Community Affairs, Zoos/Aquariums
Education: Business Education, Business-School Partnerships, Colleges & Universities, Community & Junior Colleges, Education Funds, Education Reform, Education-General, Literacy, Science/Mathematics Education, Vocational & Technical Education
Environment: Environment-General

Health: AIDS/HIV, Cancer, Clinics/Medical Centers, Eyes/Blindness, Health Organizations, Hospices, Hospitals, Medical Research, Nursing Services, Public Health, Single-Disease Health Associations, Trauma Treatment
Religion: Jewish Causes, Missionary Activities (Domestic), Religious Welfare
Science: Scientific Centers & Institutes
Social Services: Animal Protection, Emergency Relief, Food/Clothing Distribution, People with Disabilities, Recreation & Athletics, Scouts, Shelters/Homelessness, Substance Abuse, United Funds/United Ways, YMCA/YWCA/YMHA/YWHA, Youth Organizations

Contributions Analysis

Giving Priorities: Social welfare and education.
Arts & Humanities: 17%. Major interests are music, arts outreach programs, and performing arts.
Civic & Public Affairs: 5%. Supports civic foundations and urban affairs.
Education: 34%. Majority of grants benefit colleges and universities, with limited support to Junior Achievement. Also funds educational matching gifts and scholarships.
Health: 5%. Funding supports hospitals and single-disease health organizations.
Social Services: 32%. Majority of funding supports United Ways in various communities. Remaining funds generally support youth organizations, family services, and crime prevention.
Note: Total contributions in 1998.

Application Procedures

Initial Contact: Send a brief letter or proposal.
Application Requirements: Include a description of organization; amount requested and purpose of funds sought; recently audited financial statement; and proof of tax-exempt status.

Corporate Officials

David A. Stockman: co-chairman, director B Fort Hood, TX 1946. ED Michigan State University BA (1968); Harvard University Divinity School (1968-1970). PRIM CORP EMPL co-chairman, director: Collins & Aikman Corp. CORP AFFIL president: RES Holding Corp.; director: Collins Aikman Plastics Inc.; director: Clark United States of America Inc.; co-chairman, co-chief executive officer, director: Collins & Aikman Group Inc.; senior managing director: Blackstone Group. NONPR AFFIL member: Council Foreign Relations.

Giving Program Officials

Eugene A. White: vice president, secretary PRIM CORP EMPL vice president, taxation: Collins & Aikuran Corp.

Foundation Officials

Arlene Bookman: administrator
Roger Eads: assistant vice president
David A. Stockman: president, director (see above)
Eugene A. White: vice president, secretary (see above)

Grants Analysis

Disclosure Period: calendar year ending 1998
Total Grants: $364,985*
Number of Grants: 88
Average Grant: $4,148
Highest Grant: $25,000
Typical Range: $500 to $5,000
***Note:** Giving excludes matching gifts; scholarship; United Way.

Recent Grants

Note: Grants derived from 1997 Form 990.

Arts & Humanities

10,000	Arts Partnership, Spartanburg, SC
10,000	Automotive Hall of Fame, Midland, MI
5,000	Arts and Science Council Charlotte Mecklenburg, Charlotte, NC -- endowment
5,000	Arts and Science Council Charlotte Mecklenburg, Charlotte, NC -- support fund drive
5,000	Brevard Music Center, Brevard, NC
5,000	Mint Museum of Art, Charlotte, NC
5,000	Spartanburg County Public Library, Spartanburg, SC
4,000	Cultural Center for the Arts, Canton, OH

Civic & Public Affairs

22,813	American Textile Foundation, Washington, DC
3,000	Echoing Hills Village, Warsaw, OH
3,000	Stark Development Board, Canton, OH

Education

25,000	Converse College, Spartanburg, SC
20,000	Wharton Fund
16,667	Isothermal Community College, Spindale, NC
12,500	Person County Partners in Education
10,000	University of South Carolina Business Partnership Foundation, Columbia, SC
6,000	Independent College Fund, Winston-Salem, NC
5,000	Lenoir-Rhyne College, Hickory, NC
5,000	Limestone College, Gaffney, SC
5,000	Spartanburg Technical College Foundation, Spartanburg, SC
2,500	Piedmont Community College Foundation
2,500	Union Settlement Association, New York, NY

Health

25,000	Pavilion Recovery Center, Greensboro, NC
10,000	Spartanburg Regional Medical Center Foundation, Spartanburg, SC
7,000	City of Hope
5,000	City of Hope, Los Angeles, CA
5,000	Detroit Institute of Ophthalmology, Detroit, MI
5,000	Hospice, Forest City, NC
3,000	Cystic Fibrosis Foundation, Philadelphia, PA

Religion

7,000	Anti-Defamation League, New York, NY
5,000	Salvation Army
3,000	Chinmaya Mission, Houston, TX
2,500	First Priority, Charlotte, NC

Science

10,000	Institute of Textile Technology, Charlottesville, VA -- support Graduate Fellowships Fund

Social Services

25,000	Phoenix House Development Fund, New York, NY
18,900	YMCA of University City
14,000	United Way of Central Carolinas, Charlotte, NC
10,000	YMCA, Charlotte, NC
7,000	Boy Scouts of America Mecklenburg County Council, Charlotte, NC
5,000	Mobile Meal Service of Spartanburg County, Spartanburg, SC
5,000	Spartanburg Animal Welfare League, Spartanburg, SC
5,000	United Way, Cleveland, OH
5,000	United Way of Clinton and Essex Counties
5,000	United Way of Clinton and Essex Counties
5,000	United Way of Person County
5,000	United Way of Pitt County, Greenville, NC
4,500	United Way of Stanly County, Albermarle, NC
3,000	Boy Scouts of America Mecklenburg County Council, Charlotte, NC
3,000	United Way of Southwestern New England
2,500	Boy Scouts of America, New York, NY

COLONIAL LIFE & ACCIDENT INSURANCE CO.

Company Contact

Columbia, SC
Web: http://www.unum.com

Company Description

Revenue: US$515,800,000
Employees: 1,195
SIC(s): 6411 Insurance Agents, Brokers & Service.
Parent Company: Colonial Companies, Inc.

Nonmonetary Support

Value: $63,000 (1993)
Type: Donated Equipment; In-kind Services; Loaned Employees; Loaned Executives

Giving Contact

Maria Kitchens, Public/Community Relations Administrator
Colonial Life & Accident Insurance Co.
1200 Colonial Life Blvd.
PO Box 1365
Columbia, SC 29202
Phone: (803)213-7424
Fax: (803)213-7433

Description

Organization Type: Corporate Giving Program
Giving Locations: SC
Grant Types: General Support.

Giving Philosophy

"From the Heart' is the name Colonial chose for its employee volunteer program. It could also describe our overall corporate community involvement program, including individual and corporate volunteerism, and financial support for more than 50 organizations and projects annually.'
'Colonial's corporate giving mission is to be a good corporate citizen: to be part of the community and to help resolve social and economic problems.' *Colonial Home Page*

Financial Summary

Total Giving: $560,000 (1996 approx); $500,000 (1994 approx); $500,000 (1993 approx). Note: Contributes through corporate direct giving program only.

Typical Recipients

Arts & Humanities: Arts Appreciation, Arts Associations & Councils, Arts Centers, Arts Festivals, Arts Institutes, Community Arts, Dance, Ethnic & Folk Arts, Historic Preservation, Libraries, Museums/Galleries, Music, Opera, Performing Arts, Theater, Visual Arts
Civic & Public Affairs: Business/Free Enterprise, Economic Development, Economic Policy, Employment/Job Training, Housing, Law & Justice, Legal Aid, Nonprofit Management, Philanthropic Organizations, Professional & Trade Associations, Safety, Zoos/Aquariums
Education: Agricultural Education, Arts/Humanities Education, Business Education, Colleges & Universities, Community & Junior Colleges, Economic Education, International Exchange, International Studies, Private Education (Precollege), Public Education (Precollege), Student Aid
Environment: Environment-General
Health: Emergency/Ambulance Services, Geriatric Health, Health Policy/Cost Containment, Hospices, Hospitals, Medical Research, Medical Training, Mental Health, Nursing Services, Public Health, Single-Disease Health Associations

Social Services: Animal Protection, Child Welfare, Community Centers, Community Service Organizations, Counseling, Day Care, Delinquency & Criminal Rehabilitation, Domestic Violence, Emergency Relief, Family Planning, Family Services, Food/Clothing Distribution, Homes, People with Disabilities, Recreation & Athletics, Refugee Assistance, Senior Services, Substance Abuse, United Funds/United Ways, Volunteer Services, Youth Organizations

Contributions Analysis

Arts & Humanities: About 20%. Favors local ballet, symphony, and museums.
Civic & Public Affairs: 20% to 25%. Supports better government, economic development, housing, community affairs, and national security.
Education: 15% to 20%. Interests include teacher training and development programs, college scholarships, K-12 mentoring programs, and colleges, universities, and community colleges.
Environment: 10% to 15%. Interests include better business organizations,free enterprise, conservation and the environment, and zoos and botanical gardens.
Health: 30% to 35%. Interests include homeless shelters, AIDS and drug abuse education projects, child abuse prevention, and elder-care.

Application Procedures

Initial Contact: a brief letter of inquiry
Application Requirements: a description of organization, amount requested, purpose of funds sought, recently audited financial statements, and proof of tax-exempt status
Deadlines: September 1 for the following year

Restrictions

The company does not support beauty contests, fashion shows, adversarial groups, individuals, religious organizations for sectarian purposes, or political or lobbying groups.

Corporate Officials

Paul Hoot Clifton, Jr.: president B Fort Wayne, IN 1947. ED University of South Carolina BA (1971); Harvard University Graduate School of Business Administration (1983). PRIM CORP EMPL president: Colonial Life & Accident Insurance Co. ADD CORP EMPL vice president: Benefitamerica Inc.
Robert Emmett Staton: president B Suffolk, VA 1946. ED Presbyterian College (1968); University of South Carolina (1971). PRIM CORP EMPL president: Colonial Life & Accident Insurance Co. CORP AFFIL director: Benefitamerica Inc.; president: Colonial Co. Inc.

Giving Program Officials

Edwina Carms: PRIM CORP EMPL community service administration: Colonial Life & Accident Insurance Co.

Grants Analysis

Disclosure Period: calendar year ending
Typical Range: $1,000 to $2,500

Colonial Oil Industries, Inc.

Company Contact

Savannah, GA

Company Description

Employees: 75
SIC(s): 2911 Petroleum Refining, 5171 Petroleum Bulk Stations & Terminals, 5541 Gasoline Service Stations.
Parent Company: Colonial Group, Inc.

Colonial Foundation

Giving Contact

Francis A. Brown, Vice President, Finance & Chief Financial Officer
PO Box 576
Savannah, GA 31402
Phone: (912)236-1331

Description

Founded: 1986
EIN: 581693323
Organization Type: Corporate Foundation
Giving Locations: GA
Grant Types: General Support.

Financial Summary

Total Giving: $681,537 (1998); $225,707 (1997); $363,312 (1996)
Giving Analysis: Giving for 1998 includes: foundation ($644,787); foundation grants to United Way ($36,750)
Assets: $4,857,360 (1998); $5,616,837 (1997); $4,499,788 (1996)
Gifts Received: $400,000 (1996); $200,000 (1994); $500,000 (1993). Note: In 1996, contributions were received from the Colonial Group.

Typical Recipients

Arts & Humanities: Arts & Humanities-General, Historic Preservation, History & Archaeology, Museums/Galleries, Music, Performing Arts, Public Broadcasting, Theater
Civic & Public Affairs: Business/Free Enterprise, Chambers of Commerce, Clubs, Community Foundations, Civic & Public Affairs-General, Housing, Law & Justice, Legal Aid, Safety, Urban & Community Affairs
Education: Business Education, Colleges & Universities, Economic Education, Education Associations, Education Funds, Education Reform, Engineering/Technological Education, Education-General, Literacy, Minority Education, Private Education (Precollege), Public Education (Precollege), Secondary Education (Public), Special Education
Environment: Resource Conservation
Health: Arthritis, Cancer, Children's Health/Hospitals, Diabetes, Emergency/Ambulance Services, Health-General, Health Organizations, Hospices, Long-Term Care, Prenatal Health Issues, Respiratory
Religion: Churches, Missionary Activities (Domestic), Religious Welfare
Science: Science Museums, Scientific Organizations
Social Services: Animal Protection, Child Welfare, Community Service Organizations, Family Services, Food/Clothing Distribution, People with Disabilities, Recreation & Athletics, Scouts, Sexual Abuse, United Funds/United Ways, Volunteer Services, YMCA/YWCA/YMHA/YWHA, Youth Organizations

Contributions Analysis

Arts & Humanities: 12%. Supports historical preservation, museums, and performing arts.
Civic & Public Affairs: 1%.
Education: 75%. Funds higher education and private pre-college education.
Environment: 1%.
Health: 2%.
Religion: 1%.
Social Services: 9%. Primarily funds United Way and youth groups.
Note: Total contributions in 1998.

Application Procedures

Initial Contact: Send a brief letter of inquiry.
Application Requirements: Include proof of tax-exempt status.
Deadlines: None.

Corporate Officials

Francis A. Brown: vice president finance, treasurer, director PRIM CORP EMPL vice president finance, treasurer, director: Colonial Oil Industries.
Robert H. Demere, Jr.: president, chief executive officer PRIM CORP EMPL president, chief executive officer: Colonial Oil Industries.
Robert H. Demere: chairman B Savannah, GA 1924. ED Yale University (1945). PRIM CORP EMPL chairman: Colonial Oil Industries. CORP AFFIL director: First Union Corp. Georgia; chairman: Interstate Stations; director: First Union Bank Savannah; chairman: Eagle Carriers; chairman: Enmark Stations; chairman: Colonial Marine Industries; chairman: Colonial Terminals; chairman: Chatham Towing Co.; chairman: Colonial Interstate.

Foundation Officials

W. A. Baker, Jr.: vice president
Francis A. Brown: vice president, treasurer (see above)
Robert H. Demere, Jr.: vice president, secretary (see above)
Robert H. Demere: president (see above)

Grants Analysis

Disclosure Period: calendar year ending 1998
Total Grants: $644,787*
Number of Grants: 52
Average Grant: $4,604*
Highest Grant: $410,000
Typical Range: $500 to $5,000
***Note:** Giving excludes United Way. Average grant figure excludes highest grant.

Recent Grants

Note: Grants derived from 1998 Form 990.

Arts & Humanities

51,500	Telfair Museum of Art, Savannah, GA
50,000	Savannah Onstage, Savannah, GA
10,000	Savannah Symphony, Savannah, GA
5,000	Savannah Theater Co., Savannah, GA
4,500	Historic Savannah Foundation, Savannah, GA
2,500	Georgia Historical Society, Savannah, GA
1,000	Georgia Public Television, Atlanta, GA

Civic & Public Affairs

5,000	Savannah Area Chamber of Commerce, Savannah, GA
1,000	Chatham/Savannah Citizen Advocacy, Savannah, GA
500	Rotary Club of Savannah, Savannah, GA
500	Union Society, Savannah, GA
100	Christmas in July, Saginaw, MI

Education

410,000	Savannah Country Day School, Savannah, GA
5,000	Royce Learning Center, Savannah, GA
4,000	St. Vincent's Academy, Newark, NJ
3,000	Armstrong State College, Armstrong, GA
2,500	Georgia Foundation of Independent Colleges, Atlanta, GA
1,750	Georgia Southern University, Statesboro, GA
1,000	Georgia Council For Economic Education, Atlanta, GA
1,000	Georgia Partnership for Excellence, Atlanta, GA
1,000	Junior Achievement, Atlanta, GA
1,000	Sea Education Association, Woods Hole, MA

Environment

1,000	National Conservancy, Arlington, VA

Health

5,000	Leukemia Society of America, Savannah, GA

4,000	American Red Cross, Savannah, GA
1,000	Hospice Savannah, Savannah, GA
500	Ronald McDonald House of Savannah, Savannah, GA
500	Savannah Health Mission, Savannah, GA
450	American Cancer Society, Savannah, GA
200	Chatham Nursing Home, Savannah, GA
100	March of Dimes, New York, NY
Religion	
2,000	Union Mission, Norfolk, VA
1,000	St. Joseph's Foundation, Savannah, GA
1,000	Salvation Army, Savannah, GA
1,000	Young Life of Savannah, Savannah, GA
Social Services	
36,750	United Way, Savannah, GA
5,000	YMCA of Coastal Georgia, Savannah, GA
2,250	Parent and Child Development, Savannah, GA
2,000	Boy Scouts of America, Savannah, GA
1,000	Girl Scout Council of Savannah, Savannah, GA
1,000	Greenbriar Children Center, Savannah, GA
1,000	YMCA Blue Ridge Assembly, Black Mountain, NC
287	Empty Stocking Fund, Atlanta, GA

Comdisco, Inc.

Company Contact

Rosemont, IL

Company Description

Revenue: US$3,243,000,000
Employees: 2,000
Fortune Rank: 380, per FORTUNE Magazine's list of 500 Largest U.S. Corporations (1999).
FF 380
SIC(s): 7379 Computer Related Services Nec.

Comdisco Foundation

Giving Contact

Barbara Herman, Executive Assistant
6111 North River Road
Rosemont, IL 60018
Phone: (847)698-3000

Alternate Contact

Nick Pontikes, CEO
Note: Mr. Pontikes is the contact for corporate contribution requests.

Description

Founded: 1994
EIN: 363977234
Organization Type: Corporate Foundation
Giving Locations: headquarters area only.
Grant Types: General Support.

Financial Summary

Total Giving: $738,575 (fiscal year ending September 30, 1998); $686,855 (fiscal 1997); $365,675 (fiscal 1996)
Assets: $11,969,295 (fiscal 1998); $15,163,690 (fiscal 1997); $11,802,127 (fiscal 1996)

Typical Recipients

Arts & Humanities: Museums/Galleries
Civic & Public Affairs: Philanthropic Organizations, Urban & Community Affairs, Women's Affairs
Education: Afterschool/Enrichment Programs, Business Education, Education Funds, Education-General, Preschool Education, Science/Mathematics Education, Student Aid
Health: Children's Health/Hospitals, Clinics/Medical Centers, Hospices, Long-Term Care, Single-Disease Health Associations
International: Health Care/Hospitals
Religion: Churches, Religious Organizations, Religious Welfare
Social Services: Big Brother/Big Sister, Child Abuse, Child Welfare, Community Service Organizations, Family Services, Homes, People with Disabilities, Recreation & Athletics, Scouts, Shelters/Homelessness, Special Olympics, YMCA/YWCA/YMHA/YWHA, Youth Organizations

Contributions Analysis

Arts & Humanities: 2%. Funds children's museums.
Civic & Public Affairs: 15%. Supports community foundations and women's issues.
Education: 30%. Funds educatin foundations and Junior Achievement.
Health: 16%. Hospitals nad single-disese health associations receive funding.
International: 2%.
Religion: 7%. Funds Christian groups.
Social Services: 27%. Supports Special Olympics.
Note: Total contributions in fiscal 1998.

Application Procedures

Initial Contact: Send a full proposal.
Application Requirements: Include proof of 501(c)(3) status, a description of organization, amount requested, recently audited financial statement, summary of need and purpose of funds sought, history of organization, current operating budget, list of board members with business affiliations and addresses, and an annual report, if available.
Deadlines: None.

Restrictions

Grants are not given to individuals, schools (public or private), private foundations, corporations, scholarships, gifts in kind, events, capital or endowment campaigns, cultural arts, political or lobbying organizations, organizations with primarily international activity, film, videotape or audio productions.

Additional Information

Company endowed the Comdisco Foundation in 1994.

Corporate Officials

John J. Vosicky: executive vice president finance, chief financial officer PRIM CORP EMPL executive vice president finance, chief financial officer: Comdisco.

Foundation Officials

Philip A. Hewes: secretary, director
Lynne Pontikes: director
Nicholas K. Pontikes: president, director PRIM CORP EMPL executive vice president (CDRS): Comdisco.
John J. Vosicky: treasurer, director (see above)

Grants Analysis

Disclosure Period: fiscal year ending September 30, 1998
Total Grants: $738,575
Number of Grants: 122
Average Grant: $6,054
Highest Grant: $100,000
Typical Range: $1,000 to $10,000

Recent Grants

Note: Grants derived from fiscal 1998 Form 990.

Arts & Humanities	
5,000	Chicago Childrens Museum, Chicago, IL
5,000	Du Page Children's Museum, Chicago, IL
Civic & Public Affairs	
40,000	Reach For Tomorrow, Fairfax, VA
30,000	The Chris Zorich Foundation, Chicago, IL
25,000	Chicago Foundation For Women, Chicago, IL
1,200	Misericordia Wonens League, Chicago, IL
Education	
100,000	Junior Achievement of Chicago, Chicago, IL
100,000	Junior Achievement of Chicago, Chicago, IL
5,000	Have Dreams, Chicago, IL
5,000	Midtown Educational Foundation, Chicago, IL
2,500	Chicago Academy of Sciences, Chicago, IL
2,000	Scholarship And Guidance Association, Chicago, IL
1,250	Junior Achievement of Chicago, Chicago, IL
Health	
100,000	Marklund, Chicago, IL
10,000	Holy Family Medical Center, Des Plaines, IL
2,000	Rainbow Hospice, Park Ridge, IL
1,500	Larabida Childrens Hospital, Chicago, IL
1,250	Illinois Spina Bifida Association, Chicago, IL
1,000	The Ronald McDonald House, Chicago, IL
International	
15,000	Hope Worldwide, Ridge Wood, NJ
Religion	
25,000	Holy Family Church, Chicago, IL
18,750	Maryville, Chicago, IL
5,000	Saint Josephs Corondelet, Chicago, IL
2,000	House of The Good Shepherd, Chicago, IL
2,000	Maryville, Chicago, IL
Social Services	
100,000	Misericordia, Chicago, IL
5,100	Infant Welfare Society of Chicago, Chicago, IL
5,000	Boys Hope Girls Hope, St. Louis, MO
5,000	Family Matters, Chicago, IL
5,000	Help From People to People, Chicago, IL
5,000	Illinois Special Olympics, Chicago, IL
5,000	Illinois Special Olympics, Normal, IL
5,000	Illinois Special Olympics, Normal, IL
5,000	Shelter, Inc., IL
5,000	Youth Guidance, Chicago, IL
2,500	Center For Enriched Living, Deerfield, IL
2,500	Childrens Memorial Foundation, Chicago, IL
2,500	Lawrence Hall Youth Service, Chicago, IL
2,000	The Brass Ring Society, Tulsa, OK
2,000	Juvenile Protective Association, Chicago, IL
2,000	Recording for The Blind & Dislexic, Chicago, IL
1,500	Access Living, Chicago, IL
1,500	New Horizon Center, Chicago, IL
1,200	Pan Massachusetts Challenge, Boston, MA
1,000	Barrington Youth Service, Barrington, IL
1,000	Big Brothers Big Sisters, Chicago, IL
1,000	Cabrini Green Youth & Family Services, Chicago, IL

1,000 Youth Foundation of Skokie, Skokie, IL

COMERICA INC.

Company Contact

Comerica Tower
500 Woodward Avenue
Detroit, MI 48226
Phone: (313)222-7356
Fax: (313)222-3240
Web: http://www.comerica.com

Company Description

Revenue: US$3,219,900,000
Employees: 13,500
Fortune Rank: 455, per FORTUNE Magazine's list of 500 Largest U.S. Corporations (1999).
FF 455
SIC(s): 6022 State Commercial Banks, 6712 Bank Holding Companies.

Nonmonetary Support

Value: $200,000 (1992); $93,000 (1988); $52,000 (1987)
Type: Donated Equipment; In-kind Services; Loaned Employees; Loaned Executives
Contact: Charlene Cole, Education/Volunteer Program Manager

Corporate Sponsorship

Value: $60,000
Type: Arts & cultural events; Festivals/fairs; Music & entertainment events
Note: Sponsors civic/community and health and human services events.

Comerica Foundation

Giving Contact

Caroline Solomon Chambers, Corporate Contributions Assistant Vice President
Email: c_chamber@comerica.com

Alternate Contact

Fax: (313)222-8720

Description

Founded: 1997
Organization Type: Corporate Foundation
Giving Locations: CA; FL; MI: especially southeastern MI; TX
Grant Types: Capital, Emergency, Employee Matching Gifts, General Support, Matching, Multiyear/Continuing Support.
Note: Employee matching gift ratio: 1 to 1 for gifts to colleges and universities, up to $2,000 per employee annually. Company sponsors a special one-time holiday match program.

Giving Philosophy

'Comerica is Michigan's largest bank holding company. .. We are proud of the role we play in bringing quality financial services to individuals, businesses, and units of government, yet our involvement as a corporate citizen goes far beyond these basics. We support, to the greatest extent possible, the economic, health, educational, social, and cultural services that are important to all of us. We realize that no corporation, no matter how large or influential, can answer all the needs that exist. However, by being responsible and working in concert with other organizations and groups, we can contribute significantly toward making the places where we conduct business better places to work and live.' Contributions Policy

Financial Summary

Total Giving: $4,857,422 (1998); $4,705,000 (1997 approx); $4,431,788 (1996)
Giving Analysis: Giving for 1998 includes: foundation ($3,256,448); foundation grants to United Way ($944,333); corporate direct giving ($656,641)
Gifts Received: $2,000,000 (1998). Note: The foundation receives gifts from Comerica, Inc.

Typical Recipients

Arts & Humanities: Arts Institutes, Libraries, Music, Opera, Public Broadcasting
Civic & Public Affairs: Business/Free Enterprise, Economic Development, Urban & Community Affairs
Education: Colleges & Universities, Minority Education, Public Education (Precollege)
Health: Hospitals, Mental Health, Single-Disease Health Associations
Social Services: United Funds/United Ways, Youth Organizations

Contributions Analysis

Giving Priorities: Hospitals, social services, civic activities, education, and the arts.
Arts & Humanities: 14%. Recipients include museums, opera, arts centers and institutes, and libraries.
Civic & Public Affairs: (Housing & Neighborhood Revitalization) 13%. Contributes to revitalize the cities near operating locations, including projects to rehabilitate or construct housing in low- to moderate-income neighborhoods, and efforts to stimulate business growth.
Education: 17%. Supports minority and independent college funds, colleges and universities, United Negro College Fund, public broadcasting, science centers, and business and free enterprise education programs for youth. Matches employee gifts to higher education.
Health: 31%. Recipients include united funds and federated campaigns, youth organizations, organizations concerned with environmental and minority affairs, and food banks. Also supports hospitals and single-disease health associations.
Note: Total contributions made in fiscal 1998.

Application Procedures

Initial Contact: written proposal
Application Requirements: concise statements about project or agency describing programs, need, budget, management, goals, and accomplishments; amount requested; itemized projection of program costs; organizational operating budgets for past two years (preferably audited statements); list of existing funding sources; current board of directors; documentation on the method in which the contribution will be used in the program; and proof of tax-exempt status
Deadlines: None.
Review Process: after initial staff review, proposals go to corporate contributions committee which determines specific amounts or terms of contributions; organizations will receive written notification of funding decision within 60 days of receipt of request
Notes: Organizations in Southeastern Michigan may apply to above address; other organizations should contact nearest bank branch. Comerica Foundation board ratifies final decisions concerning contributions allocations.

Restrictions

The company does not support individuals; religious, fraternal, or political organizations; charitable golf events, recreational and athletic programs; multiyear pledges; endowment funds; non-tax-exempt organizations; or organizations supported by united funds. The company avoids controversial organizations and causes.

Additional Information

The company gives primarily to private and public 501(c)(3) organizations, and prefers innovative organizations which demonstrate the ability to solve problems and provide direct services relating to economic development. Approximately 30% of Comerica's contributions are made through headquarters direct giving and 70% of contributions are made through the Comerica Foundation.
The company reports that three permanent funds have been established with the Community Foundation of Southeastern Michigan to address specific needs of the community in the areas of the arts, youth activities, and economic development. Contact the Community Foundation of Southeastern Michigan at (313) 961-6675, or submit a proposal to Vice President of Programs, 333 W. Fort St., Ste. 2010, Detroit, MI 48226.
Publications: Comerica Contributions Policy

Corporate Officials

John D. Lewis: vice chairman, executive assistant to chief executive officer B 1950. PRIM CORP EMPL vice chairman: Comerica Inc. ADD CORP EMPL vice chairman: Comerica Bank; director: Comerica Bank California.
Eugene A. Miller: chairman, chief executive officer B Detroit, MI 1937. ED Detroit Institute of Technology BBA (1964); University of Wisconsin School of Bank Administration (1968). PRIM CORP EMPL chairman, chief executive officer: Comerica Inc. CORP AFFIL director: Detroit Edison Co.; director: DTE Energy Co.; director: Amerisure Companies; chairman, chief executive officer: Comerica Bank. NONPR AFFIL director: Detroit Medical Center; director: Detroit Symphony Orchestra Hall Inc.; member: Bankers Roundtable; vice chairman, tru: Cranbrook Educational Community.
Albert P. Taylor: vice president, executive assistant to chief executive officer PRIM CORP EMPL vice president, executive assistant to chief executive officer: Comerica Inc.

Foundation Officials

Caroline Solomon Chambers: secretary PRIM CORP EMPL corporate contributions officer: Comerica Inc.

Grants Analysis

Disclosure Period: calendar year ending 1998
Total Grants: $3,913,089*
Typical Range: $500 to $30,000
***Note:** Giving excludes United Way.

COMMERCE BANCSHARES, INC.

Company Contact

Kansas City, MO
Web: http://www.commercebank.com

Company Description

Employees: 4,854
SIC(s): 6021 National Commercial Banks, 6712 Bank Holding Companies.

Nonmonetary Support

Volunteer Programs: The company actively encourages employee volunteerism. Employees and executives also are active in United Way, Habitat for Humanity, and numerous community organizations.

Commerce Bancshares Foundation

Giving Contact

Sheila Rice, Director of Administration
Commerce Bancshares Foundation
PO Box 13095
Kansas City, MO 64199-3095
Phone: (816)234-2985

Description

Founded: 1952
EIN: 446012453
Organization Type: Corporate Foundation
Giving Locations: IL; KS; MO
Grant Types: General Support.

Financial Summary

Total Giving: $1,088,370 (1998); $1,025,252 (1997 approx); $911,831 (1996). Note: Contributes through corporate direct giving program and foundation.
Giving Analysis: Giving for 1997 includes: foundation ($739,366); foundation grants to United Way ($285,886)
Assets: $5,275,530 (1998); $2,905,300 (1997 approx); $3,713,220 (1996)
Gifts Received: $997,639 (1996); $16,453 (1993); $657,899 (1992). Note: In 1996, contributions were received from Commerce Bancshares Inc.

Typical Recipients

Arts & Humanities: Arts Associations & Councils, Arts Centers, Community Arts, Historic Preservation, History & Archaeology, Libraries, Museums/Galleries, Music, Opera, Public Broadcasting, Theater
Civic & Public Affairs: African American Affairs, Botanical Gardens/Parks, Community Foundations, Economic Development, Civic & Public Affairs-General, Housing, Legal Aid, Municipalities/Towns, Parades/Festivals, Urban & Community Affairs, Zoos/Aquariums
Education: Agricultural Education, Arts/Humanities Education, Business Education, Business-School Partnerships, Colleges & Universities, Education Funds, Education-General, Literacy, Private Education (Precollege), Public Education (Precollege), Secondary Education (Private), Secondary Education (Public)
Environment: Environment-General, Resource Conservation
Health: Cancer, Children's Health/Hospitals, Clinics/Medical Centers, Emergency/Ambulance Services, Health Organizations, Hospitals, Public Health, Single-Disease Health Associations
International: International Affairs
Religion: Dioceses, Missionary Activities (Domestic), Religious Organizations, Religious Welfare
Science: Science Exhibits & Fairs, Science Museums, Scientific Centers & Institutes
Social Services: Child Welfare, Community Centers, Community Service Organizations, Counseling, Domestic Violence, Family Planning, Family Services, Food/Clothing Distribution, Scouts, Shelters/Homelessness, Substance Abuse, United Funds/United Ways, YMCA/YWCA/YMHA/YWHA, Youth Organizations

Contributions Analysis

Giving Priorities: Supports arts, civic improvement, education, and health and human services.
Arts & Humanities: 10% to 15%. Supports Kansas City arts organizations, including music, public television, and a museum.
Civic & Public Affairs: 10% to 15%. Supports housing and economic development, civil rights, public protection, employment, and local civic organizations.
Education: 10% to 15%. Supports institutions of higher education in Missouri, including colleges, universities, military schools, and education funds. Provides some support for public education. Also supports science and social science programs.
Social Services: 60% to 65%. Primarily supports the United Way, recreation, youth development, food distribution, and other human service organizations.

Application Procedures

Initial Contact: Address letter of inquiry to local branch president.
Application Requirements: Include a description of organization and its purpose, amount requested, time frame, proof of tax-exempt status, a list of the board of directors, an audited financial statement, specific program budget, a list of other donors and proof of 501(c)(3) status.
Deadlines: None.
Review Process: All requests for support originate from the communities served; local bank presidents forward requests to the foundation; if additional information is required, the foundation requests it.
Evaluative Criteria: Ability to help target constituency.
Decision Notification: Review process is ongoing; organization should set aside at least six months for a specific request.

Restrictions

The foundation does not support private foundations.

Corporate Officials

Daniel Bolen: chairman
David Woods Kemper: chairman, president, chief executive officer, director B Kansas City, MO 1950. ED Harvard University AB (1972); Oxford University Worcester College MA (1974); Stanford University Graduate School of Business Administration MBA (1976). PRIM CORP EMPL chairman, president, chief executive officer, director: Commerce Bancshares, Inc. CORP AFFIL director: SLH Corp.; director: Wave Technologies International Inc.; director: Seafield Capital Corp.; director: Lab Holdings Inc.; director: Ralcorp Holdings Inc.; chairman: City National Bank Pittsburgh; director: Commerce Bank Saint Louis; director: Business Mens Assurance Co. NONPR AFFIL trustee: Saint Louis Symphony Orchestra; trustee: Washington University; trustee: Missouri Botanical Gardens; member: Academy Arts & Sciences; member: Bankers Roundtable. CLUB AFFIL Saint Louis Country Club; University Club; River Club; Saint Louis Club; Racquet Club; Kansas City Country Club; Old Warson Country Club.
James M. Kemper, Jr.: chairman, president, director B Kansas City, MO 1921. ED Yale University BA (1943). PRIM CORP EMPL chairman, president, director: Tower Properties Co. CORP AFFIL director: Commerce Bancshares Inc.; director: Commerce Bank Saint Joseph.
Jonathan McBride Kemper: vice chairman B Kansas City, MO 1953. ED Harvard University AB (1975); Harvard University MBA (1979). PRIM CORP EMPL vice chairman, chief executive officer, director: Commerce Bank, NA ADD CORP EMPL vice chairman: Commerce Bancshares Inc.; president, chief executive officer, director: Commerce Bank Kansas City. NONPR AFFIL director: Greater Kansas City Community Foundation.
Warren W. Weaver: chairman PRIM CORP EMPL chairman: Commerce Bancshares, Inc. CORP AFFIL chairman: Commerce Bank NA.

Foundation Officials

Michael D. Fields: president
James M. Kemper, Jr.: director (see above)
Jonathan McBride Kemper: director (see above)
Edward J. Reardon, II: director PRIM CORP EMPL president: Commerce Bank, NA.
J. Daniel Stinnett: director B Great Falls, MT 1945. ED Vanderbilt University (1967); University of Missouri, Kansas City (1972). PRIM CORP EMPL vice president, general counsel, secretary: Commerce Bancshares, Inc. CORP AFFIL secretary: Commerce Bank NA.

Grants Analysis

Disclosure Period: calendar year ending 1998
Total Grants: $1,088,370
Number of Grants: 623
Average Grant: $1,747
Typical Range: $200 to $5,000

Recent Grants

Note: Grants derived from 1998 Form 990.

Arts & Humanities

10,000	Kansas City Museum Association, Kansas City, MO
6,250	St. Louis Regional Educational & Public-Television Commission, St. Louis, MO
5,000	Allied Arts Council of St. Joseph, St. Joseph, MO
5,000	Allied Arts Council of St. Joseph, St. Joseph, MO
5,000	Arts & Education Council of Greater St. Louis, St. Louis, MO
5,000	Lebanon-Laclede County Library District, Lebanon, MO
5,000	Missouri Historical Society, St. Louis, MO
5,000	St. Louis Symphony Society, St. Louis, MO
4,850	Ozark Public Telecommunications Inc., Springfield, MO

Civic & Public Affairs

10,000	Kansas City Neighborhood Alliance, Kansas City, MO
10,000	St. Louis Zoo Foundation, St. Louis, MO
8,333	Local Initiatives Support Corporation, Kansas City, MO
6,200	McLean County Coalition for Affordable Housing, Bloomington, IL
5,000	Habitat for Humanity Kansas City Inc., Kansas City, MO
5,000	Operation Impact Inc., St. Louis, MO
5,000	Regional Housing Alliance, St. Louis, MO

Education

20,000	Missouri Colleges Fund Inc., Jefferson City, MO
10,000	Harris-Stowe State College, St. Louis, MO
10,000	Missouri Military Academy, Mexico, MO
5,000	Junior Achievement Inc. Mississippi Valley Affiliate, Hazelwood, MO
5,000	St. Louis University, St. Louis, MO

Environment

5,000	Nature Conservancy Inc. Kansas Chapter, Topeka, KS

Health

6,000	Liberty Hospital Foundation, Liberty, MO
5,000	Bromenn Healthcare Inc., Bloomington, IL
5,000	Cerebral Palsy Research Foundation of Kansas Inc., Wichita, KS
5,000	Cox Health Systems, Springfield, MO
5,000	Saint Joseph Health Center, Kansas City, MO

Religion

16,667	Archdiocese of St. Louis, St. Louis, MO
5,000	Interfaith Community Services Inc., St. Joseph, MO

Science

6,500	Lakeview Museum of Arts & Sciences, Peoria, IL

Social Services

46,000	United Way of the Plains, Wichita, KS
40,950	United Way of Greater St. Louis Inc., St. Louis, MO
40,950	United Way of Greater St. Louis Inc., St. Louis, MO
40,950	United Way of Greater St. Louis Inc., St. Louis, MO
40,950	United Way of Greater St. Louis Inc., St. Louis, MO
25,000	Heart of America United Way Inc., Kansas City, MO
25,000	Heart of America United Way Inc., Kansas City, MO
25,000	Heart of America United Way Inc., Kansas City, MO

25,000	Heart of America United Way Inc., Kansas City, MO
20,000	Heart of Illinois United Way Inc., Peoria, IL
15,500	United Way of McLean County, Bloomington, IL
11,000	United Way of the Ozarks, Springfield, MO
8,000	Jackson County United Way, Independence, MO
5,000	Young Mens Christian Association, Pittsburg, KS
5,000	Young Men's Christian Association of Greater St. Louis, St. Louis, MO
4,795	United Way of Riley County Inc., Manhattan, KS
4,750	United Way of Greater St. Joseph Inc., St. Joseph, MO
4,750	United Way of Greater St. Joseph Inc., St. Joseph, MO
4,750	United Way of Greater St. Joseph Inc., St. Joseph, MO
4,750	United Way of Greater St. Joseph Inc., St. Joseph, MO

COMMERCIAL FEDERAL CORP.

Company Contact

Omaha, NE
Web: http://www.comfedbank.com

Company Description

Assets: US$7,096,700,000
Employees: 1,541
SIC(s): 6036 Savings Institutions Except Federal, 6712 Bank Holding Companies.

Nonmonetary Support

Type: Donated Equipment; In-kind Services

Giving Contact

Roger Lewis, Director of Marketing/Executive Vice President
Commercial Federal Corp.
2120 S. 72nd St., 14th Floor
Marketing Department
Omaha, NE 68124
Phone: (402)390-5315
Fax: (402)392-8777

Description

Organization Type: Corporate Giving Program
Giving Locations: operating locations.
Grant Types: General Support.

Financial Summary

Total Giving: Contributes through corporate direct giving program only.

Typical Recipients

Arts & Humanities: Arts & Humanities-General
Civic & Public Affairs: Civic & Public Affairs-General
Education: Education-General
Social Services: Social Services-General

Application Procedures

Initial Contact: written request
Application Requirements: outline of type of contribution, purpose of funds sought, and a description of organization
Deadlines: None.

Restrictions

Company does not make contributions to individuals or religious groups for sectarian purposes.

Corporate Officials

William Allingham Fitzgerald: chairman, director B Omaha, NE 1937. ED Creighton University BSBA (1959); University of Georgia Savings & Loan League Executive Training Program (1962); University of Indiana Savings & Loan League Executive Training Program (1969). PRIM CORP EMPL chairman, director: Commercial Federal Corp. CORP AFFIL chairman: Secure Futures Inc.; chairman, chief executive officer, director: Commercial Federal Bank; vice president: Commercial Federal Service. NONPR AFFIL member: America Community Bankers.

Giving Program Officials

Roger Lewis: PRIM CORP EMPL director marketing: Commercial Federal Corp.

COMMERCIAL INTERTECH CORP.

Company Contact

1775 Logan Ave.
Youngstown, OH 44501-0239
Phone: (330)746-8011

Company Description

Employees: 3,836
SIC(s): 2452 Prefabricated Wood Buildings, 3441 Fabricated Structural Metal, 3443 Fabricated Plate Work--Boiler Shops, 3714 Motor Vehicle Parts & Accessories.

Nonmonetary Support

Type: Loaned Executives

Commercial Intertech Foundation

Giving Contact

Mary Ann Tanner, Executive Assistant to Chief Executive Officer
PO Box 239
Youngstown, OH 44501
Phone: (330)746-8011
Fax: (330)746-0422

Description

EIN: 346517437
Organization Type: Corporate Foundation
Giving Locations: OH
Grant Types: Award, Conference/Seminar, Employee Matching Gifts, Fellowship, General Support.

Financial Summary

Total Giving: $312,758 (fiscal year ending October 31, 1998); $270,849 (fiscal 1997); $399,265 (fiscal 1996). Note: Contributes through corporate direct giving program and foundation.
Giving Analysis: Giving for fiscal 1996 includes: foundation ($364,265); corporate direct giving ($35,000); fiscal 1997: foundation ($138,149); foundation grants to United Way ($132,700); fiscal 1998: foundation ($178,383); foundation grants to United Way ($132,500); foundation matching gifts ($1,875)
Assets: $663,262 (fiscal 1998); $696,678 (fiscal 1997); $685,877 (fiscal 1996)
Gifts Received: $240,000 (fiscal 1998); $240,000 (fiscal 1997); $300,000 (fiscal 1996). Note: Contributions are received from Commercial Intertech Corp.

Typical Recipients

Arts & Humanities: Arts Associations & Councils, Arts Institutes, Arts & Humanities-General, History & Archaeology, Libraries, Music, Performing Arts, Public Broadcasting
Civic & Public Affairs: Botanical Gardens/Parks, Business/Free Enterprise, Economic Development, Civic & Public Affairs-General, Municipalities/Towns, Philanthropic Organizations, Professional & Trade Associations, Public Policy, Urban & Community Affairs
Education: Arts/Humanities Education, Business Education, Colleges & Universities, Economic Education, Education Funds, Engineering/Technological Education, Education-General, Minority Education, Public Education (Precollege), Social Sciences Education, Special Education
Environment: Energy
Health: Cancer, Children's Health/Hospitals, Clinics/Medical Centers, Diabetes, Emergency/Ambulance Services, Health-General, Health Organizations, Heart, Home-Care Services, Hospices, Hospitals, Long-Term Care, Multiple Sclerosis, Public Health, Single-Disease Health Associations, Speech & Hearing
International: International Affairs, International Relations
Religion: Ministries, Religious Welfare
Social Services: Camps, Child Welfare, Day Care, Domestic Violence, Emergency Relief, Family Planning, People with Disabilities, Recreation & Athletics, Scouts, Senior Services, Social Services-General, Substance Abuse, United Funds/United Ways, Volunteer Services, YMCA/YWCA/YMHA/YWHA, Youth Organizations

Contributions Analysis

Arts & Humanities: 8%. Supports symphonies, art associations, public radio, and public television.
Civic & Public Affairs: 6%.
Education: 28%. Gives to colleges and universities, primarily in Ohio.
Health: 7%. Supports hospices and medical centers.
Social Services: 50%. Primarily gives to United Way; also supports drug abuse prevention.
Note: Total foundation contributions in fiscal 1998.

Application Procedures

Initial Contact: Send a brief letter describing program.
Application Requirements: Include a description of organization, amount requested, purpose of funds sought, board of directors, list of management, recently audited financial statement, and proof of tax-exempt status.
Deadlines: None.

Corporate Officials

William Wallace Cushwa: director, president, chief executive officer, director B Youngstown, OH 1937. ED University of Notre Dame; Case Western Reserve University MBA (1975). PRIM CORP EMPL director: Commercial Intertech Corp. CORP AFFIL director: Commercial Shearing Inc. NONPR AFFIL member: Planning Forum.
Steven J. Hewitt: senior vice president, chief financial officer B 1949. PRIM CORP EMPL senior vice president, chief financial officer: Commercial Intertech Corp.
Paul Joseph Powers: chairman, president, chief executive officer, director B Boston, MA 1935. ED Merrimack College BA (1956); George Washington University MBA (1962). PRIM CORP EMPL chairman, president, chief executive officer, director: Commercial Intertech Corp. CORP AFFIL director: Twin Disc Inc.; director: Global Marine Inc.; director: Ohio Edison Co.; president: Gens Component Engineering Co.; chairman: Cylinder City Inc.; director: First Energy Corp.; director: Cuno Inc. NONPR AFFIL member: National Fluid Power Association; director, member: Youngstown Area Chamber of Commerce; director, member: National Association Manufacturer; member: Machinery & Allied Products Institute; member, director: Manufacturer Alliance.

Foundation Officials

Charles Benton Cushwa, III: trustee B Youngstown, OH 1934. ED University of Notre Dame (1956); University of Notre Dame (1961). PRIM NONPR EMPL Director: Youngstown State University, Cushwa Center for Industrial Development. CORP AFFIL director: Home Savings & Loan Co.; director: Commercial Intertech Corp.; director: Cushwa Small Business Development Center. NONPR AFFIL member: Rotary International.

William Wallace Cushwa: trustee (see above)

John Galvin: trustee PRIM CORP EMPL chief financial officer: Factory Mutual Engineering Corp. CORP AFFIL director: Commercial Intertech Corp.

Richard Hill: trustee

Neil Darwin Humphrey: trustee B Idaho Falls, ID 1928. ED Idaho State University BA (1950); University of Denver MS (1951); Brigham Young University EdD (1974). CORP AFFIL director: Commercial Intertech Corp.

Gilbert Mott Manchester: assistant secretary B Youngstown, OH 1944. ED Lafayette College BA (1966); Case Western Reserve University JD (1969). PRIM CORP EMPL vice president, general counsel: Commercial Intertech Corp.

Kenneth William Marcum: treasurer B Detroit, MI 1939. ED Ohio University (1961). PRIM CORP EMPL vice president, treasurer: Commercial Intertech Corp. NONPR AFFIL member: American Institute CPAs.

Gerald C. McDonough: trustee B Cleveland, OH 1928. ED Case Western Reserve University (1953). CORP AFFIL director: Commercial Intertech Corp.; director: York International Corp.

Paul Joseph Powers: president, trustee (see above)

Shirley M. Shields: secretary PRIM CORP EMPL secretary: Commercial Intertech Corp. CORP AFFIL secretary: Cylinder City Inc.

George M. Smart: trustee B Conneaut, OH 1945. ED DeFiance College (1967); University of Pennsylvania Wharton School (1969). PRIM CORP EMPL chairman, president: Phoenix Packaging Corp. CORP AFFIL director: FirstEnergy Corp.; director: Ohio Edison Co.; director: Commercial Intertech Corp.

Don Eugene Tucker: trustee B Rockbridge, OH 1928. ED Aurora College BA (1951); Yale University Law School LLB (1956). CORP AFFIL director: Commercial Intertech Corp.; director: Bank One Youngstown Ohio. NONPR AFFIL member: Ohio Bar Association; member: Youngstown Area Chamber of Commerce; member: Mahoning County Bar Association; trustee: Mahoning County Tuberculosis & Health Association; trustee, president: Butler Institute American Art.

Bruce C. Wheatley: vice president B Du Quoin, IL 1942. ED Southern Illinois University (1963); University of Denver (1966). PRIM CORP EMPL senior vice president administration: Commercial Intertech Corp.

Grants Analysis

Disclosure Period: fiscal year ending October 31, 1997
Total Grants: $178,383*
Number of Grants: 56
Average Grant: $3,185
Highest Grant: $50,000
Typical Range: $25 to $5,000
***Note:** Giving excludes United Way, matching gifts.

Recent Grants

Note: Grants derived from 1999 Form 990.

Arts & Humanities

10,000 Youngstown Symphony Society, Youngstown, OH
5,000 Butler Institute of American Art, Youngstown, OH
5,000 Youngstown Playhouse, Youngstown, OH
5,000 Youngstown Symphony Society, Youngstown, OH
1,000 Northeast Educational Television of Ohio, Kent, OH

Civic & Public Affairs

10,000 Fellows Riverside Garden-Mill Creek Park, Youngstown, OH
5,000 Industrial Information Institute for Education, Youngstown, OH
1,000 Industrial Information Institute for Education, Youngstown, OH
1,000 Potential Development Program, Inc., Youngstown, OH
500 Jubilee Gardens, Youngstown, OH
500 St. Joseph Development Foundation, Warren, OH

Education

50,000 Campaign for YSU, Youngstown, OH
12,000 Ohio Foundation of Independent Colleges, Cleveland, OH
10,000 Case Western Reserve University, Cleveland, OH
2,500 Junior Achievement of Mahoning Valley, Girard, OH
2,500 Youngstown State University Foundation, Youngstown, OH
2,000 Defiance College, Defiance, OH
2,000 Youngstown State University-Wick House, Youngstown, OH
1,690 Youngstown State University - WYSU, Youngstown, OH
1,000 Fluid Power Educational Foundation, Milwaukee, WI
1,000 Idaho State University, Pocatello, ID
500 Mentors for Tomorrow, Youngstown, OH
500 Society of Manufacturing Engineers, Dearborn, MI
500 United Negro College Fund, Inc., Cleveland, OH
500 University of Reno Nevada Foundation, Reno, NV

Health

5,000 St. Elizabeth Health Center, Youngstown, OH
5,000 Western Reserve Care System, Youngstown, OH
5,000 Youngstown Hearing & Speech Center, Youngstown, OH
2,000 Hospice of the Valley, Youngstown, OH
1,500 Angels of Easter Seal, Youngstown, OH
1,000 American Heart Association, Columbus, OH
1,000 Muscular Dystrophy Association, Westlake, OH
500 American Cancer Society, Washington, DC

International

1,000 Executive Council on Diplomacy, Armonk, NY

Religion

1,500 Interfaith Home Maintenance, Youngstown, OH

Social Services

32,500 Youngstown Area United Way, Youngstown, OH
32,500 Youngstown Area United Way, Youngstown, OH
32,500 Youngstown Area United Way, Youngstown, OH
32,500 Youngstown Area United Way, Youngstown, OH
5,760 Youngstown Foundation - YMCA, Youngstown, OH
5,000 Kings Mountain United Fund, Kings Mountain, NC
3,333 YWCA, Youngstown, OH
3,000 Millcreek Children's Center, Youngstown, OH
2,000 United Way of Defiance County, Dayton, OH
1,000 Burdman Group, Youngstown, OH
1,000 Salvation Army, Youngstown, OH
1,000 Volunteer Service to Seniors, Youngstown, OH
500 United Way of Orange County, Los Angeles, CA
500 Youngstown Foundation Support Fund, Youngstown, OH
400 Lake To River Girl Scout Council, Niles, OH

Commonwealth Edison Co.

Company Contact

Chicago, IL
Web: http://www.ceco.com

Company Description

Revenue: US$6,937,000,000
Employees: 16,800
SIC(s): 4911 Electric Services.
Parent Company: Unicom Corp., 10 S. Dearborn St., 37th Floor, Chicago, IL, United States

Nonmonetary Support

Value: $24,000 (1997); $50,000 (1996); $400,000 (1994)
Type: Donated Equipment; In-kind Services

Giving Contact

Mr. Edward M. Peterson, Corporate Responsibility Manager
Commonwealth Edison Co.
PO Box 767
Chicago, IL 60690
Phone: (312)394-3062
Fax: (312)394-5737

Description

Organization Type: Corporate Giving Program
Giving Locations: IL: Chicago including surrounding area
Grant Types: Capital, Employee Matching Gifts, General Support, Matching, Multiyear/Continuing Support.
Note: Employee matching gift ratio: 1 to 1 for education only. The company also reports benefits as a typical grant type.

Financial Summary

Total Giving: $3,800,000 (2000 approx); $3,900,000 (1999 approx); $3,394,000 (1998). Note: Contributes through corporate direct giving program only. Giving includes corporate direct giving; nonmonetary support. 1997 Giving includes corporate direct giving ($3,899,800); matching gifts ($134,800); nonmonetary support.
Giving Analysis: Giving for 1998 includes: corporate direct giving ($3,394,000)

Typical Recipients

Arts & Humanities: Arts Institutes, Community Arts, Dance, Ethnic & Folk Arts, Libraries, Museums/Galleries, Opera, Performing Arts, Public Broadcasting, Theater
Civic & Public Affairs: Civil Rights, Economic Development, Housing, Urban & Community Affairs, Zoos/Aquariums
Education: Colleges & Universities
Health: Health Organizations, Hospitals, Single-Disease Health Associations
Social Services: Community Service Organizations, Substance Abuse, United Funds/United Ways, Youth Organizations

Contributions Analysis

Giving Priorities: United funds, education, the arts, civics, and economic education.
Arts & Humanities: 12%. Supports a wide variety of activities; largest contributions are awarded to major institutions within service area. Offers modest contributions to broad range of smaller organizations.
Civic & Public Affairs: 35%. Primarily United Funds & United Way with emphasis on Metropolitan Crusade of Mercy. Other interest include urban development, particularly in low-income areas of northern Illinois.
Education: 32%. Priority is higher education, particularly private institutions within company's service area.
Health: 3%. Emphasis is on hospitals, which generally receive only capital support; also limited support for other health activities.
Social Services: 18%. Supports various welfare and community organizations.
Note: Total contributions made in 1997.

Application Procedures

Initial Contact: Send a brief letter of inquiry.
Application Requirements: Include outline of proposal, a description of organization, amount requested, and proof of tax-exempt status.
Deadlines: None.
Review Process: Corporate responsibility committee evaluates most requests.
Decision Notification: Committee meets in February, May, August, and November.
Notes: Company accepts the Chicago Area Grant Application Form. Requests of $2,000 or less may be reviewed and decided upon by a subcommittee.

Restrictions

The company does not purchase ads for benefit programs or make grants to religious or political organizations, individuals, or fraternal organizations. Company does not make contributions to Metropolitan Crusade of Mercy-supported agencies. Company does not support elementary or secondary education, endowments, or educational operating expenses. Capital support typically is limited to one-half of 1% of total campaign.

Corporate Officials

John T. Costello: vice president corporate relationsn counsel PRIM CORP EMPL vice president corporate relations: Commonwealth Edison Co.
John W. Rowe: chairman, chief executive officer PRIM CORP EMPL chairman, chief executive officer: Commonwealth Edison Co.
Pamela B. Strobel: senior vice president, general counsel B Chicago, IL 1952. ED University of Illinois BS (1974); University of Illinois JD (1977). PRIM CORP EMPL senior vice president, general counsel: Commonwealth Edison of Indiana. CORP AFFIL senior vice president, general counsel: Commonwealth Edison Co.; senior vice president, general counsel: Unicom Corp.; director: Badger Meter Inc.

Giving Program Officials

John T. Costello: member corporate responsibility committee (see above)
Edward M. Peterson: Corporate responsibility manager (see above)
Pamela B. Strobel: member corporate responsibility committee (see above)

Foundation Officials

John W. Rowe: membership corporate responsibility committee (see above)

Grants Analysis

Disclosure Period: calendar year ending 1998
Total Grants: $3,394,000*
Number of Grants: 400 (approx)
Average Grant: $8,485
Typical Range: $1,000 to $10,000

*Note: Grants analysis provided by the company.

COMPAQ COMPUTER CORP.

Company Contact

Houston, TX
Web: http://www.compaq.com/corporate/community

Company Description

Revenue: US$38,525,000,000 (1999)
Fortune Rank: 20, per FORTUNE Magazine's list of 500 Largest U.S. Corporations (1999).
FF 20
SIC(s): 3571 Electronic Computers, 5045 Computers, Peripherals & Software.

Operating Locations

Australia: Compaq Computer Australia Pty. Ltd., Lane Cove; Olnet Pty. Ltd., Melbourne; Tandem Applied Communications Pty. Ltd., Melbourne; Compaq Computer Australia Pty. Ltd., Pyrmont; Austria: Compaq Computer GmbH, Vienna; Tandem Computer GmbH, Vienna; Belgium: Compaq Computer NV, Zaventem, Brabant; Tandem Computers NV, Zaventem, Brabant; Brazil: Compaq Computer Brasil Industria e Comercio Ltda., Sao Paulo; Canada: Tandem Computers Canada Ltd., Markham; Compaq Canada, Richmond Hill; Denmark: Compaq Computer A/S, Birkerod, Frederiksborg; Tandem Computers A/S, Brondby, Copenhagen; Twinsoft Denmark A/S, Brondby, Copenhagen; France: Compaq Computer France, Issy Les Moulineaux; MNP France, Issy Les Moulineaux; Tandem Computers SA, Sevres, Hauts-de-Seine; Germany: Compaq Computer GmbH, Aschheim, Bayern; Tandem Computers GmbH, Bad Homburg, Hessen; Micro Communication GmbH, Dortmund, Nordrhein-Westfalen; Tandem Computers Europe Inc. Frankfurt Branch, Frankfurt, Hessen; Hong Kong: Compaq Computer Hong Kong Ltd., Admiralty; Tanden Computers (Hong Kong) Ltd., Wan Chai; Italy: Tandem Computers Italia SpA, Milano, Lombardia; Compaq Computer SpA, Rozzano, Lombardia; Japan: Compaq KK, Tokyo; Tandem Computers Japan Ltd., Tokyo; Mexico: Compaq Computer de Mexico SA de CV, Ciudad de Mexico; Tandem Computers de Mexico SA de CV, Ciudad de Mexico; Malaysia: Compaq Computer Malaysia Sdn. Bhd., Petaling Jaya, Selangor; Netherlands: Compaq Computer International Corp., Gorinchem, Zuid-Holland; Compaq Holdings BV, Gorinchem, Zuid-Holland; Compaq Computer BV, Gouda, Zuid-Holland; Tandem Computers BV, Hoofddorp, Noord-Holland; Divacto BV, Oosterhout, Noord-Brabant; Norway: Tandem Computers A/S, Lysaker, Akershus; Twinsoft A/S, Lysaker, Akershus; Compaq Computer Norway AS, Oslo, Akershus; New Zealand: Compaq Computer New Zealand Ltd., Auckland; Portugal: Compaq Computer Portugal Lda., Alges, Lisboa; Singapore: Compaq Computer Asia Pte. Ltd., Singapore; Compaq Holdings Pte. Ltd., Singapore; Spain: Compaq Computer SA, Las Rozas de Madrid, Madrid; Tandem Computers Iberica SA, Madrid; Ungermann Bass Networks Espanola Ltd. Sucursal en Espana, Madrid; Sweden: Compaq Computer AB, Kisa, Ostergotland; Tandem Computers AB, Kisa, Ostergotland; Switzerland: Compaq Computer AG, Bassersdorf, Zurich; Tandem Computers AG, Schlieren, Zurich; United Kingdom: Compaq Computer Manufacturing Ltd., Bishopton, Strathelyde; Tandem Computers Europe Inc., High Wycombe, Buckinghamshire; SA Sucre Export NV, London; Compaq Computer Group Ltd., Richmond, Surrey; Compaq Computer Ltd., Richmond, Surrey; Greenwich Shipping Ltd., Twickenham, Middlesex

Nonmonetary Support

Value: $2,300,000 (1994); $1,700,000 (1993); $3,500,000 (1992)
Type: Cause-related Marketing & Promotion; Donated Equipment; In-kind Services
Note: The company donates computers valued at between $2,000 and $3,500 each.

Corporate Sponsorship

Type: Arts & cultural events; Music & entertainment events; Sports events
Note: Angie Tipton, Manager, Sports Marketing and Sponsorship.

Giving Contact

Linda Guertin, Manager, Corporate Community Relations
Compaq Computer Corp.
PO Box 692000-MS050620
Houston, TX 77269-2000
Phone: (281)370-0670
Fax: (281)514-7024
Email: cpqocontributions@compaq.com

Description

Founded: 1989
Organization Type: Corporate Giving Program
Former Name: Compaq Computer Foundation.
Grant Types: Employee Matching Gifts, General Support.
Note: Employee matching gift ratio: 1 to 1.

Financial Summary

Total Giving: $8,000,000 (fiscal year ending , 1998); $6,500,000 (fiscal 1997 approx); $6,685,505 (fiscal 1996). Note: Contributes through corporate direct giving program only.
Giving Analysis: Giving for fiscal 1996 includes: foundation ($128,500); foundation matching gifts ($57,005); fiscal 1998: corporate direct giving ($8,000,000)
Assets: $1,002 (fiscal 1998); $2,864 (fiscal 1996); $177,600 (fiscal 1995)
Gifts Received: $499,000 (fiscal 1995); $2,275,596 (fiscal 1994); $1,526,061 (fiscal 1993). Note: Foundation received contributions from Compaq Computer Corp.

Typical Recipients

Arts & Humanities: Arts Funds, Arts & Humanities-General, History & Archaeology, Museums/Galleries, Music, Opera, Performing Arts, Public Broadcasting, Theater
Civic & Public Affairs: Botanical Gardens/Parks, Employment/Job Training, Hispanic Affairs, Parades/Festivals, Philanthropic Organizations, Women's Affairs, Zoos/Aquariums
Education: Business Education, Elementary Education (Public), Literacy, Science/Mathematics Education, Social Sciences Education, Student Aid
Health: AIDS/HIV, Cancer, Children's Health/Hospitals, Diabetes, Eyes/Blindness, Heart, Medical Rehabilitation, Medical Research, Mental Health, Multiple Sclerosis, Single-Disease Health Associations
International: International Affairs, International Environmental Issues
Religion: Jewish Causes, Ministries, Religious Welfare
Social Services: Animal Protection, Child Welfare, Community Service Organizations, Counseling, Crime Prevention, Day Care, Food/Clothing Distribution, People with Disabilities, Scouts, Shelters/Homelessness, Special Olympics, Substance Abuse, United Funds/United Ways, Volunteer Services, YMCA/YWCA/YMHA/YWHA, Youth Organizations

Contributions Analysis

Giving Priorities: Provides support to two main program areas: enhancing education and strengthing communities.
Civic & Public Affairs: Community programs focus on healthcare and community services, environment, and arts and culture.

Education: Contributed resources to support education. Continues support to technology in the classroom. Also supports K-12 education for math and science programs, porfession development for teachers, and programs for education enrichment (i.e., mentoring and homework centers).
Note: Call (281) 514-0527 for recent priorities.

Application Procedures

Initial Contact: Submit a 2-3 page letter.
Application Requirements: Include a description of organization, statement of purpose and objectives, details on project scope, itemized budget, proof of tax exemption, and audited financial statement, explanation of programs need, and description on why company should invest support.
Deadlines: None.
Review Process: Contributions committee reviews requests quarterly. Compaq will review initial request; if it meet guidelines, an application will be sent.
Decision Notification: Reply given within 30 days of receipt of letter.
Notes: Call (281)514-0527 or visit the company's Website, for current program guidelines and focus areas.

Restrictions

Organizations must be tax-exempt and must have been in operation for at least two years.
No contributions are made to individuals, religious, political or fraternal organizations, lobbying groups, endowments, grant making private foundations, fundraising events or sponsorships, trips, sporting events, transportation, or organizations that violated Compaq principles and philosophies.

Additional Information

In 1996, the Compaq Computer Foundation ceased operations. The company will continue to give directly, and provide matching gifts and non-monetary support.
In 1997, Tandem Computers Inc. became a subsidiary of the company.
Compaq has also acquired Digital Equipment.

Corporate Officials

Eckhard A. Pfeiffer: president, chief executive officer, director B Lauban, Germany 1941. ED Kaufmaennissche Berufsschule BA (1963); Southern Methodist University MBA (1983). PRIM CORP EMPL president, chief executive officer, director: Compaq Computer Corp. CORP AFFIL director: General Motors Corp.; director: Hughes Electronics Corp.; director: Bell Atlantic Corp.

Giving Program Officials

Julie Vickers: manager community relations

Recent Grants

Note: Grants derived from 1996 Form 990.

Arts & Humanities

10,000	Children's Museum, Houston, TX -- Circus Flora fundraiser
5,000	Houston Children's Chorus, Houston, TX -- golf tournament
5,000	KUHT/Houston Public Television, Houston, TX -- primetime partner
3,000	Orange Show, Houston, TX
2,500	Texas Accountants and Lawyers for Arts, Houston, TX -- gala expenses

Civic & Public Affairs

10,000	Houston Zoological Society, Houston, TX -- Meet the Keeper series
7,000	Tomball Fireworks Committee, Tomball, TX -- fireworks displays
2,500	River Oaks Garden Club Forum, Houston, TX -- for Bayou Bend Garden
1,000	Celebrate Houston 1996, Houston, TX -- gala expenses

Education

10,000	Columbia University Graduate School of Business, New York, NY
5,000	Association for Better Community Schools, Houston, TX -- Matzke Elementary School area park
1,000	Junior Achievement Southeast Texas, Houston, TX -- fundraiser table
500	University of Texas Women in Government Relations, Austin, TX -- Barbara Jordan scholarship luncheon

Health

10,000	Susan G. Komen Foundation Race for the Cure, Houston, TX -- cancer research
10,000	Texas Heart Institute, Houston, TX -- Charlton Heston dinner
5,000	AIDS Project, Los Angeles, CA
5,000	Cancare, Houston, TX
5,000	Mental Health Association, Dallas, TX -- Mental Health Tennis Tour
1,000	American Cancer Society, Tomball, TX -- Tomball golf tournament

Religion

5,000	Trinity Life Center, Houston, TX -- Magic of Carolyn Farb fundraiser

Social Services

10,000	Boy Scouts of America Sam Houston Area Council, Houston, TX
7,500	Cycreek Family YMCA, Houston, TX -- afterschool child care
3,000	Junior League, Houston, TX -- support for volunteer efforts
2,500	National Alliance to End Homelessness, Washington, DC -- European wine tasting
1,000	Crimestoppers, Houston, TX -- Don Bishop memorial fund
1,000	Just for Kids, Austin, TX -- memorial fund

COMPASS BANK

Company Contact

Birmingham, AL

Company Description

Former Name: Central Bank of the South.
Gross Operating Earnings: US$389,000,000
Employees: 4,300
SIC(s): 6022 State Commercial Banks.
Parent Company: Compass Bancshares, Inc.

Operating Locations

Maintains 83 locations throughout Alabama.

Compass Bank Foundation

Giving Contact

E. Lee Harris, Jr., Executive Vice President & Executive Officer of Human Resources
Compass Bank Foundation
PO Box 10566
15 S. 20th Street
Birmingham, AL 35296
Phone: (205)933-3000
Fax: (205)933-3336

Description

Founded: 1981
EIN: 630823545
Organization Type: Corporate Foundation
Giving Locations: AL; TX
Grant Types: Capital, General Support, Scholarship.

Financial Summary

Total Giving: $752,375 (1997); $757,917 (1996); $529,026 (1995). Note: Contributes through foundation only.
Assets: $3,427,463 (1997); $2,960,320 (1996); $2,800,000 (1995)
Gifts Received: $799,290 (1997); $607,959 (1996); $880,318 (1993). Note: Contributions are received from Compass Bank.

Typical Recipients

Arts & Humanities: Arts Associations & Councils, Arts Festivals, Museums/Galleries, Music, Performing Arts, Public Broadcasting, Theater
Civic & Public Affairs: Botanical Gardens/Parks, Business/Free Enterprise, Chambers of Commerce, Civil Rights, Economic Development, Civic & Public Affairs-General, Legal Aid, Municipalities/Towns, Professional & Trade Associations, Public Policy, Rural Affairs, Safety, Urban & Community Affairs, Zoos/Aquariums
Education: Arts/Humanities Education, Business Education, Colleges & Universities, Community & Junior Colleges, Education Funds, Elementary Education (Public), Education-General, Legal Education, Literacy, Private Education (Precollege), Public Education (Precollege), Religious Education, Science/Mathematics Education, Social Sciences Education, Special Education, Student Aid
Environment: Resource Conservation
Health: Cancer, Children's Health/Hospitals, Clinics/Medical Centers, Diabetes, Health Funds, Health Organizations, Heart, Hospices, Hospitals, Mental Health, Transplant Networks/Donor Banks
International: Health Care/Hospitals
Religion: Ministries, Religious Organizations, Religious Welfare
Science: Science Museums
Social Services: Child Welfare, Community Centers, Community Service Organizations, Family Services, Homes, People with Disabilities, Recreation & Athletics, Scouts, United Funds/United Ways, Veterans, YMCA/YWCA/YMHA/YWHA, Youth Organizations

Contributions Analysis

Giving Priorities: Education, the arts, civic organizations, environmental causes, health, international organizations, science, and social services.
Arts & Humanities: 6%. Supports humanities, children's theater, festivals and the arts.
Civic & Public Affairs: 11%. Funs botanical gardens, public affairs, urban revitalization programs, and community foundations.
Education: 50%. Funds higher education and Junior Achievement.
Health: 1%. Funds community health and single-disease associations.
Science: 3%. Supports science museums and organizations.
Social Services: 29%. Primarily supports United Way, youth and social services.
Note: Total contributions made in 1997.

Application Procedures

Initial Contact: brief proposal
Application Requirements: list of board of directors, a description of organization, amount requested, purpose of funds sought, recently audited financial statement, and proof of tax-exempt status
Deadlines: None.

Restrictions

Does not support religious organizations for sectarian purposes, individuals, or political or lobbying groups. Grants are limited to 501(c)(3) organizations.

Corporate Officials

E. Lee Harris, Jr.: senior vice president human resourcesl
Garrett R. Hegel: chief financial officer B Waukegan, IL 1950. ED University of Wisconsin (1973). PRIM

CORP EMPL chief financial officer: Compass Bancshares Inc. ADD CORP EMPL chief financial officer: Compass Bank. NONPR AFFIL member: American Society CPAs; member: Federation Executive Institute; member: American Institute CPAs.

D. Paul Jones, Jr.: chairman, chief executive officer B Birmingham, AL 1942. ED University of Alabama BS (1964); University of Alabama JD (1967); New York University LLM (1968). PRIM CORP EMPL chairman, chief executive officer: Compass Bancshares Inc. CORP AFFIL director: Russell Lands Co.; director: Golden Enterprises Inc.; member: International Financial Conference; director: Federal Reserve Bank Atlanta; director: Compass Bank; partner: Economic Development Partnership Alabama. NONPR AFFIL fellow: Society International Business Fellows; board: University Alabama; member: Service Corp. Ret Executives; director: Business Council Alabama; member: Region 2020 Inc. CLUB AFFIL Rotary Club.

Jerry W. Powell: secretary, general counsel B Montgomery, AL 1950. ED Birmingham-Southern College BA (1972); University of Alabama JD (1975). PRIM CORP EMPL secretary, general counsel: Compass Bancshares Inc. ADD CORP EMPL secretary, general counsel: Compass Bank. CORP AFFIL secretary: Compass Brokerage Inc. NONPR AFFIL member: American Bar Association; member: American Corporate Counsel Association.

Foundation Officials

E. Lee Harris, Jr.: contact (see above)
Garrett R. Hegel: president (see above)
D. Paul Jones, Jr.: trustee (see above)
Jerry W. Powell: secretary (see above)

Grants Analysis

Disclosure Period: calendar year ending 1997
Total Grants: $752,375
Number of Grants: 134
Average Grant: $5,615
Highest Grant: $200,000
Typical Range: $100 to $5,000

Recent Grants

Note: Grants derived from 1997 Form 990.

Arts & Humanities

12,500	Alabama Shakespeare Festival, Montgomery, AL
12,500	Arts Council, Winston-Salem, NC
7,500	Festival of Arts
2,500	Children's Theater
2,500	Humanities Foundation, Mount Pleasant, SC

Civic & Public Affairs

17,500	Urban Revitalization Partnership
15,000	Civil Rights Institute
10,000	Chamber of Commerce Foundation
7,000	Public Affairs Research Council
7,000	Public Affairs Research Council
5,000	Botanical Gardens
5,000	Botanical Gardens
5,000	Operation New Birmingham, Birmingham, AL

Education

200,000	Samford University, Birmingham, AL
50,000	Birmingham Southern College, Birmingham, AL
25,000	Auburn University, Auburn, AL
20,000	Reading Alabama, New York, NY
12,000	Birmingham Southern College, Birmingham, AL
10,000	Jacksonville State University Foundation, Jacksonville, AL
7,718	Citizens Scholarship Foundation of America, St. Peter, MN
3,936	Citizens Scholarship Foundation of America, St. Peter, MN
3,000	Junior Achievement

Environment

2,500	Nature Conservancy, AL

Health

5,000	Juvenile Diabetes Foundation, New York, NY
2,500	Community Blood Bank

International

4,000	PATH, Seattle, WA

Science

20,000	Discovery 2000, Birmingham, AL

Social Services

42,500	United Way
42,500	United Way
12,200	United Way
10,000	YWCA
9,992	Children's Harbor, Birmingham, AL
6,500	United Way
5,000	Boys and Girls Clubs
5,000	Corporate Foundation for Children, Montgomery, AL
5,000	Girl Scouts of America
5,000	Horizons
5,000	Park Foundation, New York, NY
5,000	Park Foundation, New York, NY
4,880	United Way
4,000	United Way
4,000	United Way
3,875	United Way
3,875	United Way
3,875	United Way
3,875	United Way
3,122	Girl Scouts of America
3,000	Assistance League
3,000	United Way
2,500	Loving Hands

Computer Associates International, Inc.

Company Contact

Islandia, NY
Web: http://www.cai.com

Company Description

Revenue: US$5,253,000,000 (1999)
Employees: 14,650 (1999)
Fortune Rank: 315, per FORTUNE Magazine's list of 500 Largest U.S. Corporations (1999).
FF 315
SIC(s): 7372 Prepackaged Software.

Operating Locations

Australia: Tertola Pty. Ltd., Artarmon; Cheyenne Software (Australia) Pty. Ltd., Wantirna South; Austria: Computer Associates International GmbH, Vienna; Belgium: Computer Associates SA, Brussels, Brabant; Nantucket SA, Brussels, Brabant; Canada: Nantucket Software (Canada) Ltd., Mississauga; Computer Associates Canada Ltd., Ottawa; Cheyenne Softward Inc., Richmond Hill; Denmark: Computer Associates Scandinavia A/S, Farum, Frederiksborg; France: Cheyenne Software Inc., Le Chesnay, Yvelines; Computer Associates SA, Nanterre, Hauts-de-Seine; Germany: CA Computer Associates GmbH, Darmstadt, Hessen; Access Technology GmbH, Neuss, Nordrhein-Westfalen; Hong Kong: Computer Associates International Ltd., Wan Chai; Ireland: Computer Associates Ltd., Dublin; Israel: CA Computer Associates Israel Ltd., Tel Aviv; Italy: Computer Associates SpA, Basiglio, Lombardia; Japan: Cheyenne Software KK, Tokyo; Republic of Korea: Computer Associates Korea Ltd., Seoul; Malaysia: Computer Associates (Malaysia) Sdn. Bhd., Kuala Lumpur, Selangor; Netherlands: Compucare BV, Nieuwegein, Utrecht; Computer Associates BV, Nieuwegein, Utrecht; Computer Associates Real Estate BV, Nieuwegein, Utrecht; Pansophic Systems Benelux, Nieuwegein, Utrecht; Norway: Computer Associates Norway AS, Oslo, Akershus; New Zealand: Computer Associates (New Zealand) Ltd., Auckland; Computer Associates (NZ) Ltd., Wellington; Philippines: Philippine Computer Associates International, Makati, Rizal; Portugal: Computer Associates International, Lisboa; Singapore: Computer Associates Pte. Ltd., Singapore; Gstar Pte. Ltd., Singapore; Spain: CA Computer Associates SA, Madrid; Sweden: Computer Associates Sweden AB, Danderyd, Stockholm; Switzerland: Computer Associates AG, Kloten, Zurich; Thailand: Computer Associates (Thailand) Co. Ltd., Bangkok; United Kingdom: Cheyenne Software Inc., London; Ask Group Ltd., Slough, Berkshire; CA Management Ltd., Slough, Berkshire; Cheyenne Software (UK) Ltd., Slough, Berkshire; Computer Associates Plc, Slough, Berkshire; Forcenatural Ltd., Slough, Berkshire; Intelligence Quotient United Kingdom Ltd., Slough, Berkshire; On-Line Software Intl Ltd., Slough, Berkshire; Seekgo Ltd., Slough, Berkshire; Cheyenne Advanced Technology Ltd., Wellington, Somerset

Corporate Sponsorship

Contact: Jayne Mayer, Executive Director Community Relations
Note: Sponsors various charities.

Giving Contact

Debra Coughlin, Senior Vice President, Personnel
Computer Associates International, Inc.
1 Computer Associates Plaza
Islandia, NY 11749
Phone: (516)342-5224
Fax: (516)342-5737

Alternate Contact

Bonnie Burke, Administration Assistant
Phone: (516)342-3562

Description

Organization Type: Corporate Giving Program
Giving Locations: internationally; nationally.
Grant Types: Employee Matching Gifts, Matching.
Note: Employee matching gift ratio: 1 to 1.

Financial Summary

Total Giving: Contributes through corporate direct giving program only.

Typical Recipients

Arts & Humanities: Arts & Humanities-General
Civic & Public Affairs: Civic & Public Affairs-General
Education: Education-General
Health: Health-General
Social Services: Social Services-General

Contributions Analysis

Giving Priorities: Company supports U.S.-based organizations with an international focus.
International: Company gives an unspecified amount in international contributions.

Restrictions

Company does not support religious organizations for sectarian purposes, or political groups.

Additional Information

Company does not disclose contributions figures.

Corporate Officials

Peter A. Schwartz: chief financial officer, consultant B 1943. ED Yale University BA (1965); George Washington University MBA (1970). PRIM CORP EMPL chief financial officer, consultant: Computer Associates International, Inc.

Giving Program Officials

Lisa Mars: PRIM CORP EMPL senior vice president personnel: Computer Associates International, Inc.

CONAGRA, INC.

Company Contact

Omaha, NE
Web: http://www.conagra.com

Company Description

Revenue: US$24,594,300,000 (1999)
Profit: US$613,200,000
Employees: 82,629
Fortune Rank: 60, per FORTUNE Magazine's list of 500 Largest U.S. Corporations (1999).
FF 60
SIC(s): 0212 Beef Cattle Except Feedlots, 0259 Poultry & Eggs Nec, 2013 Sausages & Other Prepared Meats, 2015 Poultry Slaughtering & Processing.

Operating Locations

Australia: ConAgra Wool Pty. Ltd., Altona North; Zenchiku Tancred Pastoral Co. Pty. Ltd., Beaudesert; ConAgra Holdings (Australia) Pty. Ltd., Brisbane; Australia Meat Holdings Pty. Ltd., Dinmore; ConAgra International (Australia) Pty. Ltd., North Sydney; Dr. Johnston Group Pty. Ltd., Pymble; Barrett Burston Malting Co. Pty. Ltd., South Yarra; RW Duncan & Sons Pty. Ltd., South Yarra; Belgium: Hifinance NV, Antwerpen, Anvers; ConAgra-Europe, Brussels, Brabant; Brazil: ConAgra International Ltda., Sao Paulo; Canada: Leaver Mushrooms Co. Ltd., Campbellville; Usen Fisheries Ltd., Liverpool, Merseyside; ConAgra Ltd., Toronto; Swifts Meats & Poultry & Feed Co. Ltd., Toronto; Chile: Bergerco International SA, Santiago; France: Salaisons (Ste. Anonyme Mediterraneenne De), Biot, Alpes-Maritimes; ConAgra France, Paris, Ville-de-Paris; Germany: Kurt A Becher GmbH & Co. KG, Bremen; Beatrice International Food (Deutschland) GmbH, Duesseldorf; Hong Kong: ConAgra International Ltd., Central District; Japan: Woodward Japan, Tokyo; Republic of Korea: Woodward & Dickerson (Far East) Ltd., Seoul; Mexico: UAP Mexico SA de CV, Los Mochis; Netherlands: ConAgra Europe BV, Amsterdam, Noord-Holland; Lamb Weston Holland BV, Eemshaven, Groningen; New Zealand: Dr. Johnston Group Pty. Ltd., Christchurch; Portugal: Sapropor Sociedade Gestora de Participacoes Sociais SA, Cartaxo; ConAgra Internacional Comercio de Produtos Agroalimentares Lda., Lisboa; Damatta Produtos Alimentares Lda., Montijo; Cabral & Oliveiras SA, Rio de Loba, Viseu; HBI-Producoes Agro-Pecuarias Lda., Vila Cha de Ourique, Cartaxo; Saprogal Portugal Agropecuaria SA, Vila Cha de Ourique, Cartaxo; Singapore: ConAgra Asia-Pacific Pte. Ltd., Singapore; ConAgra International Pte. Ltd., Singapore; Spain: Bioter SA, La Coruna, Galicia; Mercampo SL, La Coruna, Galicia; Saprogal SA, La Coruna, Galicia; ConAgra International SA, Madrid; ConAgra SA, Madrid; Thailand: Champagra Co. Ltd., Bangkok; United Kingdom: Kings Horticulture Ltd., Colchester, Essex; Willmot Pertwee Ltd., Maidstone, Kent

Nonmonetary Support

Note: Nonmonetary support is provided by the company. The type and amount of such support varies according to the individual operating subsidiaries.

ConAgra Foundation

Giving Contact

Lynn Phares, Vice President, Corporate Relations
ConAgra Inc.
1 ConAgra Dr.
Omaha, NE 68102-5001
Phone: (402)595-4000
Fax: (402)595-4595

Description

EIN: 362899320
Organization Type: Corporate Foundation
Giving Locations: primarily in locations where there are major ConAgra facilities.
Grant Types: Capital, General Support, Multiyear/Continuing Support, Project.

Financial Summary

Total Giving: $7,500,000 (fiscal year ending May 31, 1997 approx); $7,526,961 (fiscal 1996); $6,600,000 (fiscal 1994). Note: Contributes through corporate direct giving program and foundation. Fiscal 1997 Giving includes foundation. Fiscal 1996 Giving includes corporate direct giving ($2,500,000); foundation ($5,026,961).
Assets: $4,615,477 (fiscal 1996); $11,977,252 (fiscal 1994); $15,000,000 (fiscal 1993 approx)

Typical Recipients

Arts & Humanities: Arts Associations & Councils, Arts Funds, Dance, History & Archaeology, Museums/Galleries, Music, Opera, Performing Arts
Civic & Public Affairs: Chambers of Commerce, Economic Development, Housing, Municipalities/Towns, Parades/Festivals, Public Policy, Rural Affairs, Urban & Community Affairs, Zoos/Aquariums
Education: Agricultural Education, Business Education, Colleges & Universities, Community & Junior Colleges, Education Associations, Engineering/Technological Education, Education-General, Minority Education, Public Education (Precollege), Student Aid, Vocational & Technical Education
Environment: Environment-General
Health: Clinics/Medical Centers, Emergency/Ambulance Services, Health Organizations, Hospices, Nutrition
Religion: Dioceses
Science: Scientific Centers & Institutes, Scientific Organizations
Social Services: Big Brother/Big Sister, Child Welfare, Family Services, Food/Clothing Distribution, People with Disabilities, Scouts, Shelters/Homelessness, Substance Abuse, United Funds/United Ways, YMCA/YWCA/YMHA/YWHA, Youth Organizations

Contributions Analysis

Giving Priorities: Areas of focus include education, health and human services, arts and culture, and civic and community betterment. Current initiatives include Feeding Children Better, consisting of three components: expanding Kids' Cafes to provide hungry children with square meals, streamlining the collection and distribution of donated food to get it to hungry families faster and more cheaply (through a partnership with America's Second Harvest), and raising awareness about the hidden nature of childhood hunger; Home Food Safety; and ConAgra Community Service Awards, which are given to organizations nominated by ConAgra's independent operating companies.

Application Procedures

Initial Contact: Send a brief letter or proposal.
Application Requirements: Include mission of requesting organization; project goals and objectives, including explanation of community need; list of companies being solicited and levels of support requested and received; budget projections and sources of income; list of officers and board of directors; amount requested; proof of tax-exempt status; a brief history of achievements; audited financial statements; if applicable, ConAgra employee involvement; how grant will improve quality of life in a ConAgra community.
Deadlines: Last working day of January, April, July, and October.
Evaluative Criteria: Capacity of program to address specific community needs and suggest solutions designed to meet these needs; how the organization or project seeks self support or broad-based community support as an ultimate goal; organization's ability to state goals, select measurements, and set and meet deadlines.
Notes: Foundation does not accept phone or fax inquiries.

Restrictions

ConAgra generally will not support the following: projects that do not impact ConAgra communities; endowment funds or grant-making organizations; most fundraising and testimonial events/dinners, including tickets, silent auctions, raffles, telethons, etc.; conferences, seminars, workshops, symposia, publication of proceedings and all aspects relating to conferences; grants totaling more than 10% of the organization's campaign goal or annual budget, whichever is smaller; elementary or secondary educational schools, both public and private; underwriting or sponsoring radio or television programming; support for athletic teams or events; and emergency operating support.
ConAgra will not consider funding for individuals; organizations with a limited constituency, such as clubs and fraternal or social organizations; religious groups for religious endeavors; travel or tours for individuals or groups; advertising; and for-profit organizations.
Foundation does not generally consider funding a program or project for more than 3 years. Grants are principally limited to Nebraska and major operating locations.

Additional Information

ConAgra requests that applicant organizations have been in operation for at least one year.
Publications: Corporate Contributions Program Guidelines

Corporate Officials

Bruce Rohde: vice chairman, chief executive officer ED Creighton University BS (1971); Creighton University JD (1973). PRIM CORP EMPL vice chairman, chief executive officer: ConAgra, Inc. NONPR AFFIL officer: Creighton University.

Foundation Officials

James P. O'Donnell: treasurer B 1947. ED University of Kentucky BS (1969); Xavier University MBA (1974). PRIM CORP EMPL senior vice president, chief financial officer: ConAgra, Inc. CORP AFFIL director: Commercial Federal Bank Omaha.
Lynn Levisay Phares: president, fund manager, director B Brownwood, TX 1947. ED Louisiana State University BA (1970); University of Nebraska MA (1987). PRIM CORP EMPL vice president corporate relations: ConAgra Inc.

Grants Analysis

Disclosure Period: fiscal year ending May 31, 1996
Total Grants: $5,026,961
Number of Grants: 484
Average Grant: $10,386
Highest Grant: $1,000,000
Typical Range: $500 to $50,000

Recent Grants

Note: Grants derived from 1996 Form 990.

Arts & Humanities

1,000,000	SAC Museum Memorial Society, Omaha, NE
300,000	Heritage Joslyn Foundation, Omaha, NE
230,400	Heritage Joslyn Foundation, Omaha, NE
130,000	United Arts Omaha, Omaha, NE
33,000	Omaha Community Playhouse, Omaha, NE
33,000	Omaha Community Playhouse, Omaha, NE
30,000	Omaha Symphony, Omaha, NE

Civic & Public Affairs

300,000 Omaha 2000 Education Foundation, Omaha, NE
50,000 Greater Omaha Chamber Foundation, Omaha, NE
30,000 Ak-Sar-Ben Foundation, Omaha, NE
27,500 Ak-Sar-Ben Foundation, Omaha, NE
25,000 City of Quincy, Quincy, CO
25,000 Manufacturing Institute, Washington, DC
25,000 River City Roundup, Omaha, NE
25,000 Southwest Minority Economic Development Council, Fullerton, CA
17,000 Omaha Zoo Foundation, Omaha, NE
15,000 Habitat for Humanity International, St. James, MN

Education

333,335 Creighton University, Omaha, NE
60,000 College of St. Mary, Omaha, NE
50,000 Bellevue University Foundation, Bellevue, NE
38,500 National Future Farmers of America Foundation, Madison, WI
33,533 National Merit Scholarship Corp, Evanston, IL
31,000 Metropolitan Community College Foundation, Omaha, NE
25,000 Council of Independent Colleges, Washington, DC
25,000 Dana College, Blair, NE
23,500 Horatio Alger Association, Washington, DC
20,000 Institute of Food Technologists, Chicago, IL
20,000 Junior Achievement Central Arizona, Phoenix, AZ
17,150 Junior Achievement Midlands, Omaha, NE
16,500 Omaha Schools Foundation, Omaha, NE
15,000 Chadron State Foundation, Chadron, NE
15,000 Midland Lutheran College, Omaha, NE
15,000 Midtown Educational Foundation, Chicago, IL

Health

50,000 American Red Cross Heartland Chapter, Omaha, NE
50,000 Hospice House, Omaha, NE
25,000 North Colorado Medical Center Foundation, Greeley, CO
15,000 Micah House Corp, Council Bluffs, IA

Social Services

200,000 Quality Living, Omaha, NE
100,000 Omaha Council Bluffs Metro YMCA, Omaha, NE
90,750 United Way Midlands, Omaha, NE
90,750 United Way Midlands, Omaha, NE
90,708 Boys Clubs, Omaha, NE
70,000 Family Service, Omaha, NE
47,633 Boys Clubs, Omaha, NE
47,632 Boys Clubs, Omaha, NE
25,000 Boy Scouts of America Mid-American Council, Omaha, NE
25,000 Salt Fork YMCA, Marshall, MO
20,000 Boys and Girls Club, Athens, AL
20,000 YMCA Omaha Council Bluffs Metro Area, Omaha, NE
15,000 Boy Scouts of America Mid-America Council, Omaha, NE

CONE MILLS CORP.

Company Contact

Greensboro, NC
Web: http://www.cone.com

Company Description

Employees: 6,600
SIC(s): 2211 Broadwoven Fabric Mills--Cotton, 2396 Automotive & Apparel Trimmings, 3086 Plastics Foam Products.

Nonmonetary Support

Type: Donated Equipment

Corporate Sponsorship

Contact: Mike Horrigan, Vice President of Human Resources

ABC Foundation

Giving Contact

ABC Foundation
3101 North Elm Street
Greensboro, NC 27415
Phone: (336)379-6459
Fax: (336)379-6832

Description

EIN: 581504894
Organization Type: Corporate Foundation
Giving Locations: NC: Greensboro operating locations.
Grant Types: Capital.

Financial Summary

Total Giving: $332,000 (fiscal year ending October 31, 2000 approx); $384,000 (fiscal 1999 approx); $424,694 (fiscal 1997). Note: Contributes through corporate direct giving program and foundation.
Giving Analysis: Giving for fiscal 1997 includes: foundation ($212,844); foundation grants to United Way ($145,850); foundation scholarships ($66,000)
Assets: $4,811,857 (fiscal 1997); $4,828,418 (fiscal 1994); $5,267,072 (fiscal 1993)
Gifts Received: $1,000,000 (fiscal 1993). Note: Foundation receives contributions from Cone Mills Corp.

Typical Recipients

Arts & Humanities: Arts Associations & Councils, Arts Funds
Civic & Public Affairs: Business/Free Enterprise, Clubs, Community Foundations, Economic Policy, Housing, Municipalities/Towns, Public Policy, Urban & Community Affairs
Education: Business Education, Business-School Partnerships, Colleges & Universities, Economic Education, Education Funds, Engineering/Technological Education, Education-General, Literacy, Minority Education, Public Education (Precollege), Student Aid, Vocational & Technical Education
Environment: Resource Conservation
Health: Emergency/Ambulance Services, Health Organizations, Hospices, Multiple Sclerosis
International: International Organizations
Religion: Ministries, Religious Welfare
Social Services: Child Welfare, People with Disabilities, Recreation & Athletics, Substance Abuse, United Funds/United Ways, YMCA/YWCA/YMHA/YWHA, Youth Organizations

Contributions Analysis

Arts & Humanities: About 5%. Supports the United Arts Council of North Carolina.
Civic & Public Affairs: 5% to 10%. Favors textile foundations, business foundations, and civic organizations.
Education: About 30%. Supports college funds, scholarship services, Junior Achievement, colleges, public education, vocational technical schools, and literacy.
Social Services: 55% to 65%. Primarily supports various United Ways located in North Carolina, South Carolina and Mississippi. Other support goes to Goodwill Industries, YMCA, and youth organizations.

Application Procedures

Initial Contact: a brief letter of inquiry
Application Requirements: a description of organization, amount requested, and purpose of funds sought
Deadlines: None.
Notes: The foundation is not currently accepting new for funds.

Restrictions

Does not support organizations outside of operating areas.

Corporate Officials

John L. Bakane: president, chief executive officer, director B Birmingham, AL 1951. ED University of Alabama BS (1973); University of Virginia MBA (1975). PRIM CORP EMPL president, chief executive officer, director: Cone Mills Corp. NONPR AFFIL chairman accounting subcommittee: American Textile Manufacturer Association; member: Financial Executives Institute.
Dewey Leonard Trogdon, Jr.: chairman B Summerfield, NC 1932. ED Guilford College AB (1958); University of North Carolina (1967-1968); University of Virginia (1970); Harvard University Advanced Management Program (1978). PRIM CORP EMPL chairman: Cone Mills Corp. CORP AFFIL director: First Union Corp.

Foundation Officials

Dewey Leonard Trogdon, Jr.: director (see above)

Grants Analysis

Disclosure Period: fiscal year ending October 31, 1997
Total Grants: $212,844*
Number of Grants: 43
Average Grant: $84,950
Highest Grant: $120,000
Typical Range: $300 to $5,000
***Note:** Giving excludes scholarships; United Way.

Recent Grants

Note: Grants derived from 1997 Form 990.

Arts & Humanities

17,000 United Arts Council, Greensboro, NC

Civic & Public Affairs

10,000 Sit-In Movement, Greensboro, NC
6,666 Greensboro Housing Authority, Greensboro, NC -- for Eastside Project
5,000 Bell House, Greensboro, NC
5,000 Junior League, Greensboro, NC
2,000 Business Foundation of North Carolina, Chapel Hill, NC
1,650 National Conference
750 Haw River Civic Association, Haw River, NC

Education

22,000 University of North Carolina Greensboro, Greensboro, NC -- scholarships, general support
15,000 Independent College Fund of North Carolina, Raleigh, NC
12,000 Isothermal Community College and Foundation, Spindale, NC -- scholarships, general support
10,345 Educational Testing Service, Princeton, NJ
9,833 North Carolina Business Committee for Education, Raleigh, NC
9,000 United Way Rowan County, Rowan County, NC -- scholarships awards
8,333 Greensboro College, Greensboro, NC -- scholarships awards
7,000 North Carolina State University, Raleigh, NC -- scholarships awards

5,500 Winthrop University, Rock Hill, SC -- scholarships awards
5,000 Cities in School of North Carolina, Raleigh, NC
5,000 Independent Colleges and Universities of South Carolina, Taylors, SC
5,000 University of North Carolina Greensboro Bryan School of Business, Greensboro, NC
3,500 Bennett College, Greensboro, NC
3,000 Junior Achievement, Greensboro, NC
2,500 Boston College, Chestnut Hill, MA -- scholarships awards
2,500 College of Charleston, Charleston, SC -- scholarships awards
2,500 Gardner-Webb University, Boiling Springs, NC -- scholarships awards
2,500 Johns Hopkins University, Baltimore, MD -- scholarships awards
2,500 Meredith College, Raleigh, NC -- scholarships awards
2,500 North Carolina A&T State University, Raleigh, NC -- scholarships awards
2,500 University of Maryland, Baltimore, MD -- scholarships awards
2,500 Villanova University, Villanova, PA -- scholarships awards
2,000 North Carolina Council on Economic Education, Greensboro, NC
1,500 University of North Carolina Chapel Hill, Chapel Hill, NC -- scholarships awards
1,000 Clemson University, Clemson, SC -- scholarships awards
1,000 Spartanburg Technical College, Spartanburg, SC -- scholarships awards
500 Greenville Technical College, Greenville, SC -- scholarships awards

Health
8,334 American Red Cross, Greensboro, NC -- capital campaign
6,467 National Multiple Sclerosis Society, Buffalo, NY
5,000 Hospice of Rutherford County, Rutherford County, NC
2,500 American Red Cross, Rowan County, NC

International
33,333 Pavillon International, Bloomfield Hills, MI

Religion
1,000 Baptist Children's Homes of North Carolina, Thomasville, NC

Social Services
120,000 United Way, Greensboro, NC
22,000 United Appeal of Rutherford County, Rutherford County, NC
11,000 United Way Union County, Union County, SC
5,000 Greensboro Ice Sports, Greensboro, NC
5,000 YMCA Blue Ridge Assembly, Black Mountain, NC
2,850 United Way Marion County, Marion, SC
2,000 United Way Alamance County, Burlington, NC
1,000 United Way Tri-State, New York, NY
500 Elon Homes for Children, Elon, NC

CONECTIV

Company Contact
Wilmington, DE
Web: http://www.conectiv.com

Company Description
Former Name: Delmarva Power & Light Co.
Assets: US$2,979,200,000
Employees: 2,963
SIC(s): 4931 Electric & Other Services Combined.

Nonmonetary Support
Type: In-kind Services; Loaned Employees; Loaned Executives; Workplace Solicitation

Corporate Sponsorship
Contact: Erin Keller

Giving Contact
Vince Jacono
Conectiv
PO Box 231
Wilmington, DE 19899
Phone: (302)429-3528
Fax: (302)429-3141

Description
Organization Type: Corporate Giving Program
Giving Locations: restricted to service territory.
Grant Types: Capital, General Support.

Giving Philosophy
'It's not unusual for companies to think their employees are special. But there's something about providing a vital community service that seems to attract people with an uncommon need to serve . . . So it's not wonder that when the community reaches out for special support that Connectiv and its employees are right there. You'll find us at work in our schools, as volunteers in community organizations, working to better the environment, and preserving natural resources.
'You'll see it reflected in our products and services and how we provide them. Recycling 100% of our fly ash, which reduces the need for landfills, is one good example. Partnering with business and government in economic development efforts is another.
'Recognizing the need for a strong workforce, Conectiv is also involved in a number of educational initiatives to provide companies with the skilled labor they'll need to compete in the 21st century. Our employees bring 'real life' lessons into the classroom through such programs as Junior Achievement. They help in many other ways, too, such as raising funds for scholarship programs, judging science fairs, wiring classrooms for the Internet, and serving as tutors, mentors and role models for students at dozens of schools throughout the region.'

Financial Summary
Total Giving: $700,000 (1997 approx); $425,000 (1994 approx); $410,000 (1993). Note: Contributes through corporate direct giving program only.

Typical Recipients
Arts & Humanities: Arts & Humanities-General
Civic & Public Affairs: Civic & Public Affairs-General
Education: Education-General
Health: Health-General
Social Services: Social Services-General

Application Procedures
Initial Contact: Call or write for a formal application form.
Application Requirements: Include name and address of organization, contact name, organization's purpose, list of officers and directors, description of program, annual operating budget, number of full-time employees, purpose of funds sought, how program will be evaluated, other sources of funding, and amount requested.
Deadlines: None.
Evaluative Criteria: Well-planned and structured programs that allow the company to meet the needs of the community, programs providing a rationale for giving, programs that enhance the quality of life in Conectiv's service area, and programs that apportion available funds to secure the most beneficial impact.

Restrictions
The company does not support individuals, religious organizations for sectarian purposes, organizations outside of service area, or political or lobbying groups.

Additional Information
Contributions should meet the needs of people in the company's service area, and the company should receive appropriate recognition for contributions made.
Publications: Informational Brochure; Application Form

Corporate Officials
Vince Jacono: manager public affairss
Mike Ratchford: director corporate communications

CONOCO, INC.

Company Contact
Houston, TX

Company Description
Profit: US$744,000,000 (1999)
Fortune Rank: 74, per FORTUNE Magazine's list of 500 Largest U.S. Corporations (1999).
FF 74
SIC(s): 1311 Crude Petroleum & Natural Gas, 2819 Industrial Inorganic Chemicals Nec, 2899 Chemical Preparations Nec, 2911 Petroleum Refining.

Nonmonetary Support
Value: $67,500 (1993)
Type: Donated Equipment; In-kind Services

Corporate Sponsorship
Type: Arts & cultural events; Festivals/fairs
Contact: Sue Collier, Director, Houston Community Relations

Giving Contact
Sue S. Collier, Director, Houston Community Affairs
Conoco Inc.
Box 2197
Houston, TX 77252
Phone: (281)293-1039
Fax: (281)293-1961

Alternate Contact
Judi Burleson, Assistant Director Community Affairs
Phone: (281)293-2685

Description
Organization Type: Corporate Giving Program
Giving Locations: geographical areas where facilities and employees are located.
Grant Types: Employee Matching Gifts, Project.
Note: Employee matching gift ratio: 1 to 1.

Giving Philosophy
'At Conoco, we hold it a privilege to serve society as a responsible corporate citizen, and we commit to operate as a valued neighbor in the communities in which we work and live. Conoco's Corporate Contributions Program supports organizations and projects which exhibit commitment to lasting, measurable progress, financial accountability, traditional family values, broad community benefit, and potential as a model which can be replicated successfully. Beforehand, such organizations must show significant planning and progress relative to a demonstrated broadly-defined need. In essence, Conoco requires excellence in its philanthropic initiatives, emphasizing those which serve as a catalyst to help people help themselves.' *Conoco Giving Guidelines*

Financial Summary

Total Giving: Contributes through corporate direct giving program only.

Typical Recipients

Civic & Public Affairs: Economic Development, Safety, Urban & Community Affairs
Education: Business Education, Colleges & Universities, Economic Education, Engineering/Technological Education, Minority Education, Public Education (Precollege), Science/Mathematics Education
Environment: Environment-General
Health: Nutrition
Social Services: United Funds/United Ways

Contributions Analysis

Arts & Humanities: 25%. Supports cultural and arts institutions in directly pursuing their traditional missions. Company often sponsors culturally-diverse programs.
Civic & Public Affairs: 25%. Focus is on neighborhood revitalization, safety issues, and other community improvement activities. Support reflects the cultural diversity of the metropolitan Houston area.
Education: 25%. Grants are made to selected colleges and universities to improve academic resources. Also supports higher education funds for academicresearch on a technical, social, or economic level. Other interests include summer scholarship and co-op programs, and opportunities for minorities in engineering, business, and geoscience. Precollege interests include reduction of absenteeism and dropout rates, with an emphasis on programs developing critical thinking skills, math, and science. Also supports employee matching gift program and funding for the education of employee family members.
Health: 25%. Focus is on preventive programs with direct benefit to the community and the disadvantaged, as opposed to medical research or the treatment of individuals. Also makes large donations to the United Way on an annual basis.
Note: Total contributions made in 1998.

Application Procedures

Initial Contact: written proposal
Application Requirements: name, address, and telephone number of organization; type of organization (independent local, national, or national affiliate); contact person and title; general purpose of organization; constituencies and number of people served; IRS exemption letter; annual operating budget; percent salaries within overhead; administration and fund raising costs; audited statements for the previous two years, sources of funding (corporate, foundation, government, United Way, individual, other); top five corporate contributors and amounts contributed; name of executive director; names and affiliations of directors and trustees; names of Conoco employees directly involved in the organization; purpose, goals, and objectives of the grant; need for program or project; benefit to the community; number of people affected; plans and timetable to reach stated objective; evaluation mechanism; line-item budget for program or project; and amount requested
Deadlines: None.

Restrictions

Company does not fund alumni drives or teacher organizations; any government departments; individuals; labor unions; research; for-profit hospitals; operating expenses or deficits; political organizations; religious or sectarian causes, projects, schools; professional sports events or athletes; or service, fraternal, or veteran organizations.

Additional Information

Philanthropic commitments generally are for a year or less, or until the end of a program or project.
No contribution is automatically renewable.
Conoco receives close to 1,000 grant requests per year.
Applications may be sent to local offices; however, large requests and requests from organizations located in the Houston area should be sent directly to the headquarters office. sent directly to the headquarters office.

Corporate Officials

Archie W. Dunham: president, chief executive officer B Durant, OK 1938. ED Harvard University Executive Management Program; Stanford University Executive Management Program; University of Oklahoma BS (1956-1960); University of Oklahoma MBA (1966). PRIM CORP EMPL president, chief executive officer: Conoco, Inc. CORP AFFIL director: Louisiana-Pacific Corp.; director: Phelps Dodge Corp.; director: El du Pont de Nemours & Co. NONPR AFFIL member: Energy Institute Americas; vice chairman: United States Energy Association; member: American Petroleum Institute; member: Bretton Woods Committee.

Giving Program Officials

Sue S. Collier: PRIM CORP EMPL director Houston community affairs: Conoco, Inc.

Consolidated Electrical Distributors

Company Contact

Westlake Village, CA

Company Description

Employees: 2,500
SIC(s): 3629 Electrical Industrial Apparatus Nec, 5063 Electrical Apparatus & Equipment.

Dunard Fund U.S.A., Ltd.

Giving Contact

Chris Ann3 Barker, Assistant to the President
31356 Via Colinas, Suite 107
Westlake Village, CA 91362
Phone: (818)991-9000
Fax: (818)991-6842

Description

EIN: 980087034
Organization Type: Corporate Foundation

Financial Summary

Total Giving: $808,500 (1997); $610,936 (1996)
Assets: $3,503,364 (1997); $2,764,542 (1996)
Gifts Received: $1,370,000 (1997); $1,057,070 (1996). Note: In 1996, contributions were received from Rolled Alloys ($250,000) and Consolidated Electrical Distributors ($800,000).

Typical Recipients

Arts & Humanities: Arts Associations & Councils
Education: Arts/Humanities Education, Colleges & Universities
International: Foreign Arts Organizations, International Environmental Issues, International Organizations, International Relations
Social Services: Child Welfare

Contributions Analysis

Giving Priorities: Arts, higher education and civics.
Arts & Humanities: 15%. Supports conservancy, and museums.
Civic & Public Affairs: 34%. Supports community foundations.
Education: 51%. Supports higher education.
Note: Total contributions made in 1997.

Application Procedures

Initial Contact: Send a letter at anytime to either headquarters or any of the other 400 locations throughout the US.
Deadlines: None.

Additional Information

Company has operating locations in nearly all 50 states. Also supported by U.S. Rental, Inc.

Corporate Officials

Keith W. Colburn: chairman, chief executive officer PRIM CORP EMPL chairman, chief executive officer: Consolidated Electrical Distr.
Tom Luloo: chief financial officer PRIM CORP EMPL chief financial officer: Consolidated Electrical Distr.
Antonio Monis, Jr.: president PRIM CORP EMPL chairman: Consolidated Electrical Distr.

Foundation Officials

Carol C. Hogel: president, director
Jens C. Hogel: vice president, director
Bernard E. Lyons: secretary, director

Grants Analysis

Disclosure Period: calendar year ending 1997
Total Grants: $808,500
Number of Grants: 12
Average Grant: $67,375
Highest Grant: $300,000
Typical Range: $1,000 to $100,000

Recent Grants

Note: Grants derived from 1996 Form 990.

Arts & Humanities

20,000 Cal Arts, Sacramento, CA

Education

116,626 Yale University School of Music, New Haven, CT
10,000 Yale University, New Haven, CT
7,070 Yale University, New Haven, CT
1,216 Yale University, New Haven, CT
1,000 Kneisel Hall, Blue Hill, ME

International

271,850 American Friends of Edinburgh Festival, Edinburgh, Scotland
160,000 National Trust for Scotland, Scotland
40,000 American Friends of National Galleries of Scotland, Scotland -- exhibition
30,924 Centre Canadian Architecture -- support for film
20,000 Crown Prince Frederik Fund, Boston, MA
10,000 International Festival Society, Los Angeles, CA -- support for Edinburgh Festival
5,250 Yale Center for British Art, New Haven, CT
5,000 American Scandinavian Foundation, New York, NY -- student exchange program

Social Services

17,000 Beginning with Children Foundation, New York, NY

Consolidated Natural Gas Co.

Company Contact

Pittsburgh, PA
Web: http://www.cng.com

Company Description

Revenue: US$3,074,400,000 (1999)
Profit: US$136,800,000 (1999)

Fortune Rank: 496, per FORTUNE Magazine's list of 500 Largest U.S. Corporations (1999).
FF 496
SIC(s): 1311 Crude Petroleum & Natural Gas, 1381 Drilling Oil & Gas Wells, 4923 Gas Transmission & Distribution, 6719 Holding Companies Nec.
Parent Company: Dominion Resources, Inc., 120 Tredegar Street, Richmond, VA, United States

Nonmonetary Support
Type: Donated Equipment
Note: Nonmonetary support is provided by the foundation and the co.

Corporate Sponsorship
Type: Arts & cultural events; Festivals/fairs; Music & entertainment events
Note: Sponsors conventions.

Consolidated Natural Gas System Foundation

Giving Contact
Mr. Jim Mesltoh, Executive, Directory
Consolidated Natural Gas System Foundation
CNG Tower
625 Liberty Avenue
Pittsburgh, PA 15222-3199
Phone: (412)690-1231
Fax: (412)690-7608

Description
EIN: 136077762
Organization Type: Corporate Foundation
Giving Locations: DC: Washington; LA; OH; OK; PA; VA; WV national organizations.
Grant Types: Award, Capital, Employee Matching Gifts, General Support, Project.
Note: Employee matching gift ratio: 1 to 1.

Financial Summary
Total Giving: $3,352,232 (1998); $3,000,000 (1997 approx); $2,734,587 (1996). Note: Contributes through foundation only.
Giving Analysis: Giving for 1996 includes: foundation ($1,871,725); foundation grants to United Way ($559,462); foundation matching gifts ($303,400); 1998: foundation ($2,465,213); foundation grants to United Way ($572,452); foundation matching gifts ($314,567)
Assets: $4,922,384 (1998); $10,324,171 (1996); $12,683,115 (1995)
Gifts Received: $14,525,000 (1995); $3,025,000 (1994); $3,475,000 (1993). Note: Contributions are received from Consolidated Natural Gas, CNG Transmission Corporation, East Ohio Gas Company, Peoples Natural Gas Company, Virginia Natural Gas Company, Hope Gas Co., West Ohio Gas Company, and CNG Producing Company.

Typical Recipients
Arts & Humanities: Arts Associations & Councils, Arts Centers, Arts Festivals, Arts Funds, Arts Institutes, Arts Outreach, Ballet, Dance, Historic Preservation, History & Archaeology, Libraries, Museums/Galleries, Music, Opera, Performing Arts, Public Broadcasting, Theater
Civic & Public Affairs: Business/Free Enterprise, Economic Development, Civic & Public Affairs-General, Housing, Municipalities/Towns, Professional & Trade Associations, Public Policy, Urban & Community Affairs, Women's Affairs, Zoos/Aquariums
Education: Business Education, Colleges & Universities, Community & Junior Colleges, Economic Education, Education Funds, Elementary Education (Private), Elementary Education (Public), Engineering/Technological Education, Education-General, Literacy, Minority Education, Preschool Education, Public Education (Precollege), Science/Mathematics Education
Environment: Air/Water Quality, Energy, Environment-General, Protection, Resource Conservation
Health: Cancer, Children's Health/Hospitals, Clinics/Medical Centers, Emergency/Ambulance Services, Health Policy/Cost Containment, Health Organizations, Hospitals
Religion: Religious Welfare
Science: Science Museums, Scientific Centers & Institutes
Social Services: Child Welfare, Community Centers, Community Service Organizations, Counseling, Domestic Violence, Food/Clothing Distribution, Homes, People with Disabilities, Recreation & Athletics, Senior Services, Substance Abuse, United Funds/United Ways, YMCA/YWCA/YMHA/YWHA, Youth Organizations

Contributions Analysis
Giving Priorities: Education, civics, the arts, health, and human services.
Arts & Humanities: 36%. Funds music, public broadcasting, historic groups, and museums and galleries.
Civic & Public Affairs: 13%. Supports municipalities and towns, urban and community affairs, and economic development.
Education: 10%. Supports colleges and universities, education funds, and secondary education.
Environment: 8%. Supports energy issues and general environment.
Health: 2%. Emergency health organizations and health policy foundations.
Religion: 2%. Funds religious welfare.
Social Services: 30%. Primarily supports the United Way in operating areas.
Note: Total contributions in 1998.

Application Procedures
Initial Contact: letter of inquiry
Application Requirements: a description of organization, including legal name, history, activities, and governing board; amount requested and list of other sources of funding; purpose of funds sought; recently audited financial statement; proof of tax-exempt status; and narrative statement describing the project's objectives, need addressed, impact on community, and method of accomplishing objectives
Deadlines: None.
Review Process: requests should be submitted to local operating company
Evaluative Criteria: the project is within company's operating area and benefits health and social services, education, culture and art, community development or the United Way

Restrictions
Foundation does not support dinners or special events, fraternal organizations, labor groups, goodwill advertising, individuals, member agencies of united funds, political or lobbying groups, or religious organizations for sectarian purposes.
Grants are limited to organizations which are tax exempt under section 501 (c)(3) of the IRS Code. Organizations involved in the activities listed above and located within Consolidated's service area receive consideration. Grants to organizations outside service areas are rare. receive consideration. Grants to organizations outside service areas are rare.

Additional Information
Consolidated Gas merged with Dominion Resources, Inc. in January 2000. Under the terms of the merger agreement, Consolidated Natural Gas became a direct subsidiary of Dominion. Changes to the Consolidated Natural Gas giving program have not been announced.
Each operating company sets its own giving priorities. Company reports nonmonetary support; however, types of support vary among regional operating companies.

Corporate Officials
George A. Davidson, Jr.: chairman, chief executive officer, director B Pittsburgh, PA 1938. ED University of Pittsburgh BS (1960). PRIM CORP EMPL chairman, chief executive officer, director: Consolidated Natural Gas Co. CORP AFFIL director: B.F. Goodrich Co.
Stephen R. McGreevy: vice president accounting & financial control PRIM CORP EMPL vice president accounting & financial control: Consolidated Natural Gas Co.
David M. Westfall: senior vice president, chief financial officer ED Fairmont State College BA; Stanford University. PRIM CORP EMPL senior vice president, chief financial officer: Consolidated Natural Gas Co.
Stephen E. Williams: senior vice president, general counsel B 1949. ED Harvard University BS; West Virginia University JD (1974). PRIM CORP EMPL senior vice president, general counsel: Consolidated Natural Gas Co. CORP AFFIL interim president: CNG Power Co.; interim president: CNG Storage Service Co.

Foundation Officials
Ronald Adam: director
Jerry L. Causey: director B 1944. ED North Carolina State University BS (1966). PRIM CORP EMPL president: Virginia Natural Gas Inc.
Bill Fox: director PRIM CORP EMPL president Virginia Gas: Consolidated Natural Gas Co.
Ray N. Ivey: director PRIM CORP EMPL chairman public affairs: Consolidated Natural Gas Co.
Stephen R. McGreevy: director (see above)
Jim Mesloh: executive director
Thomas D. Newland: director PRIM CORP EMPL president, chief executive officer: East Ohio Gas Co.
Pat Riley: director
Jim Thomson: director PRIM CORP EMPL president: CNG International Corp.
Stephen E. Williams: president (see above)

Grants Analysis
Disclosure Period: calendar year ending 1998
Total Grants: $2,465,213*
Number of Grants: 362
Average Grant: $6,810
Highest Grant: $70,000
Typical Range: $500 to $10,000
***Note:** Giving excludes matching gifts; United Way.

Recent Grants
Note: Grants derived from 1998 Form 990.

Arts & Humanities

50,000	National Museum of American Art, Washington, DC -- Operating
50,000	National Museum of American Art, Washington, DC -- Operating
50,000	Ohio Historical Society, Columbus, OH -- Operating
50,000	Ohio Historical Society, Columbus, OH -- Operating
50,000	Pittsburgh Cultural Trust, Pittsburgh, PA -- Operating
50,000	Pittsburgh Symphony Society, Pittsburgh, PA -- Operating
45,000	First Ladies' Fund, Canton, OH -- Operating
41,000	Ohio Historical Society, Columbus, OH -- Operating
39,000	Wqed Pittsburgh, Pittsburgh, PA -- Operating
34,000	Civic Light Opera, Pittsburgh, PA -- Operating
33,000	Pittsburgh Ballet Theatre, Pittsburgh, PA -- Operating
33,000	Pittsburgh Opera, Pittsburgh, PA -- Operating
25,000	Colonial Williamsburg Foundation, Williamsburg, VA -- Operating
25,000	Playhouse Square Foundation - Allen Theatre, Cleveland, OH -- Operating

25,000	Westmoreland Museum of American Art, Greensburg, PA -- Operating
20,000	Benedum Center Library, Bridgeport, WV -- Operating
20,000	Great Lakes Museum, Cleveland, OH -- Operating
20,000	Historical Society of Western Pennsylvania, Pittsburgh, PA -- Operating
20,000	West Virginia Public Theatre, Morgantown, WV -- Operating

Civic & Public Affairs

25,000	American Council of Young Political Leaders, Washington, DC -- Operating
25,000	American Council of Young Political Leaders, Washington, DC -- Operating
25,000	Congressional Award Foundation, Washington, DC -- Operating
25,000	Pittsburgh Regional Alliance, Pittsburgh, PA -- Operating
25,000	Progress & Freedom Foundation, Washington, DC -- Operating
20,000	Camp - Campaign for Manufacturing Advancement, Cleveland, OH -- Operating

Education

50,000	Fairmont State College, Fairmont, WV -- Operating
50,000	Graduate School of Industrial Administration, Pittsburgh, PA -- Operating
50,000	Old Dominion University, Norfolk, VA -- Operating
33,000	Early Childhood Initiative, Pittsburgh, PA -- Operating
21,000	Syracuse University, Syracuse, NY -- Operating

Environment

70,000	Dollar Energy Fund, Pittsburgh, PA -- Operating
57,500	Audubon Society of Western Pennsylvania, Pittsburgh, PA -- Operating
25,000	Inform, Inc., New York, NY -- Operating
25,000	Keystone Center, Vandergrift, PA -- Operating

Health

25,000	American Red Cross Disaster Relief Fund, Syracuse, NY -- Operating
25,000	National Race for the Cure, Washington, DC -- Operating
20,000	Children's Hospital Medical Center of Akron, Akron, OH -- Operating

Religion

47,500	Salvation Army/Northeast Ohio/People Helping People Fuel Fund, Cleveland, OH -- Operating
25,000	Salvation Army, Cleveland, OH -- Operating
20,000	Salvation Army, Pittsburgh, PA -- Operating

Social Services

80,195	United Way - Cleveland, Cleveland, OH -- Operating
80,195	United Way Services, Cleveland, OH -- Operating
41,500	United Way of Harrison County, Inc., Clarksburg, WV -- Operating
35,939	United Way of Southwestern PA, Pittsburgh, PA -- Operating
25,000	Achievable Dream, Inc., Newport News, VA -- Operating
25,000	Hill House Association, Pittsburgh, PA -- Operating
24,700	United Way of South Hampton Roads, Norfolk, VA -- Operating
24,000	Harrison County YMCA, Clarksburg, WV -- Operating
20,000	United Way of Greater New Orleans, New Orleans, LA -- Operating
4,000	United Way of South Louisiana, Houma, LA -- Operating

CONSOLIDATED PAPERS, INC.

Company Contact

Wisconsin Rapids, WI

Company Description

Employees: 7,261 (1999)
SIC(s): 2611 Pulp Mills, 2621 Paper Mills, 2631 Paperboard Mills, 2653 Corrugated & Solid Fiber Boxes.

Consolidated Papers Foundation, Inc.

Giving Contact

Susan Feith, President
Consolidated Papers Foundation, Inc.
PO Box 3
Wisconsin Rapids, WI 54495-0003
Phone: (715)424-3004
Fax: (715)424-1314

Description

Founded: 1951
EIN: 396040071
Organization Type: Corporate Foundation
Giving Locations: WI: headquarters and operating communities
Grant Types: Capital, Employee Matching Gifts, Endowment, General Support, Project, Scholarship.
Note: Employee matching gift ratio: 1 to 1 for gifts to higher education, social service organisation, and the arts.

Financial Summary

Total Giving: $2,500,000 (2000 approx); $2,200,000 (1999 approx); $1,580,672 (1998)
Giving Analysis: Giving for 1997 includes: foundation ($1,710,680); foundation grants to United Way ($249,425); foundation matching gifts ($176,803); 1998: foundation grants to United Way ($288,795); foundation matching gifts ($192,855)
Assets: $50,779,527 (1998); $46,947,937 (1997); $42,524,746 (1996)
Gifts Received: $729,000 (1998); $1,056,000 (1997); $1,054,000 (1996). Note: 1998 contributions Consolidated Papers, Inc. ($680,000), Ruth Barker ($25,000), and Sally Hands (24,000).

Typical Recipients

Arts & Humanities: Arts Associations & Councils, Arts Institutes, Ballet, Community Arts, Historic Preservation, History & Archaeology, Libraries, Museums/Galleries, Music, Performing Arts, Public Broadcasting, Theater, Visual Arts
Civic & Public Affairs: Botanical Gardens/Parks, Community Foundations, Economic Development, Employment/Job Training, Civic & Public Affairs-General, Housing, Municipalities/Towns, Professional & Trade Associations, Public Policy, Safety, Zoos/Aquariums
Education: Afterschool/Enrichment Programs, Arts/Humanities Education, Business Education, Colleges & Universities, Continuing Education, Economic Education, Education Funds, Engineering/Technological Education, Education-General, Gifted & Talented Programs, Literacy, Medical Education, Minority Education, Private Education (Precollege), Science/Mathematics Education, Secondary Education (Private), Secondary Education (Public), Student Aid, Vocational & Technical Education
Environment: Air/Water Quality, Environment-General, Wildlife Protection
Health: Emergency/Ambulance Services, Eyes/Blindness, Health Organizations, Hospices, Hospitals, Medical Rehabilitation, Preventive Medicine/Wellness Organizations, Trauma Treatment
International: International Relations
Religion: Religious Welfare
Science: Science Museums, Scientific Centers & Institutes
Social Services: Animal Protection, Camps, Community Service Organizations, Crime Prevention, Family Planning, People with Disabilities, Recreation & Athletics, Scouts, Senior Services, Shelters/Homelessness, United Funds/United Ways, YMCA/YWCA/YMHA/YWHA, Youth Organizations

Contributions Analysis

Giving Priorities: Education, social welfare, civics, the arts, hospitals, united funds, United Way, and environmental concerns.
Arts & Humanities: 13%. Supports public broadcasting, public libraries, arts councils, and historic preservation and renovation, primarily in Wisconsin.
Civic & Public Affairs: 9%. Funds zoos, economic development, community affairs and public policy.
Education: 53%. Primarily independent, accredited four-year colleges and universities in Wisconsin. Support includes unrestricted and capital grants. Special interests include science, technology, and engineering education relating to the pulp and paper industry. Also supports minority and independent college funds and merit scholarship programs.
Environment: 2%. Funds nature conservancy, and environmental concerns.
Health: 1%. Primarily supports united funds. Remaining contributions fund groups concerned with youth, recreation, the aged, community services, hospitals, and health interests.
Social Services: 22%. Funds Planned Parenthood, youth services, women's shelters, and the United Way.
Note: Total contributions made in 1998.

Application Procedures

Initial Contact: Send a brief letter of inquiry.
Application Requirements: Information should include a description of organization, amount requested, purpose of funds sought, recently audited financial statement, and proof of IRS nonprofit status
Deadlines: March 1 for board of directors meeting in June; September 1 for fall meeting.

Restrictions

There are no restrictions or limitations on grants. However, educational institutions and charities geographically close to corporate installations of Consolidated Papers, Inc. have been favored in the past.

Corporate Officials

Gorton M. Evans, Jr.: president, chief executive officer, director B 1938. ED Michigan State University BS (1960). PRIM CORP EMPL president, chief executive officer, director: Consolidated Papers, Inc. ADD CORP EMPL president: Inter Lake Wisconsin Inc.; president: Inter Lake Papers Inc.
Richard John Kenney: senior vice president finance B Evanston, IL 1941. ED Loras College BA (1963); Indiana University MBA (1965). PRIM CORP EMPL senior vice president finance: Consolidated Papers, Inc. ADD CORP EMPL vice president: Walker Parking Consult/Engrs. NONPR AFFIL member: American Forest & Paper Association. CLUB AFFIL Bulls Eye Club.
George Wilson Mead, II: chairman, director B Milwaukee, WI 1927. ED Yale University BS (1950); Institute of Paper Chemistry MS (1952). PRIM CORP EMPL chairman, director: Consolidated Papers, Inc. CORP AFFIL director: Newaygo Timber Co. Ltd.; director: Snap-On Tools Inc.; chairman, director: Consolidated Water Power Co. NONPR AFFIL director, president: Consolidated Civic Foundation; trustee: Institute Paper Chemistry; director: American Forest & Paper Association; member: American Paper Institute.

Foundation Officials

Susan Feith: vice president, executive director
Richard John Kenney: director (see above)
David A. Krommenacker: director PRIM CORP EMPL vice president packaging operations: Consolidated Papers, Inc.
Carl R. Lemke: secretary ED University of Wisconsin BBA (1965). PRIM CORP EMPL assistant secretary: Consolidated Papers, Inc.
J. Richard Matsch: treasurer PRIM CORP EMPL assistant treasurer: Consolidated Papers, Inc.
Emily B. McKay: director
George Wilson Mead, II: president, director (see above)

Grants Analysis

Disclosure Period: calendar year ending 1998
Total Grants: $1,099,022*
Number of Grants: 143*
Average Grant: $11,053
Highest Grant: $160,000
Typical Range: $1,000 to $15,000
***Note:** Giving excludes matching gifts; United Way.

Recent Grants

Note: Grants derived from 1998 Form 990.

Arts & Humanities

31,250	Wisconsin Public Broadcasting Foundation-TV, Madison, WI -- Underwrite
13,500	American Players Theatre, Spring Green, WI -- Underwrite
10,000	Arts Council of South Wood County, Wisconsin Rapids, WI -- Unrestricted/Underwrite
10,000	Kimberly Public Library, Kimberly, WI -- Unrestricted
10,000	Minnesota Ballet, Duluth, MN -- Capital/Underwrite
8,000	Wisconsin Rapids, City of/McMillan Memorial Library, Wisconsin Rapids, WI -- Equipment
7,900	Central Wisconsin Symphony Orchestra, Stevens Point, WI -- Underwrite
5,000	Irma Stein Memorial Library/Presque Isle, Presque Isle, WI -- Unrestricted
5,000	Ogema Public Library, Ogema, WI -- Unrestricted

Civic & Public Affairs

15,000	Ice Age Park & Trail Foundation, Madiscon, WI -- Capital
8,000	Portage County Sheriff's Department Rescue, Stevens Point, WI -- Capital

Education

149,400	Carroll College, Waukesha, WI -- Unrestricted/Capital
105,190	National Merit Scholarship Corporation, Evanston, IL -- Scholarships
50,000	Community Christian Academy, Wisconsin Rapids, WI -- Capital
50,000	Duluth Graduate Medical Education Council, Duluth, MN -- Capital
44,000	Marquette University, Milwaukee, WI -- Unrestricted
35,000	University of MN Foundation/Paper Science & Eng Lab, Minneapolis, MN -- Capital
30,100	Beloit College, Beloit, WI -- Unrestricted
30,000	Lawrence University, Appleton, WI -- Unrestricted
25,000	Pulp & Paper Foundation - Miami University, Oxford, OH -- Scholarships
20,700	Ripon College, Ripon, WI -- Unrestricted
20,200	Milwaukee School of Engineering, Milwaukee, WI -- Unrestricted
17,000	Northland College, Ashland, WI -- Unrestricted
15,000	Assumption High School, Wisconsin Rapids, WI -- Unrestricted/Capital
13,800	St. Norbert College, De Pere, WI -- Unrestricted
13,500	Pulp & Paper - University of WI - Stevens Point, Stevens Point, WI -- Scholarships
13,250	UW-Stevens Point/Odyssey of the Mind, Stevens Point, WI -- Underwrite
12,800	Milwaukee Institute of Art & Design, Milwaukee, WI -- Unrestricted
12,300	Lakeland College, Sheboygan, WI -- Unrestricted
12,000	Institute of Paper Science & Technology, Atlanta, GA -- Unrestricted
10,100	United Negro College Fund, New York, NY -- Scholarships
10,000	Carthage College, Kenosha, WI -- Unrestricted
10,000	Medical College of Wisconsin, Milwaukee, WI -- Untrestricted
9,500	Alverno College, Milwaukee, WI -- Unrestricted
8,250	Mid-State Technical College Foundation, Wisconsin Rapids, WI -- Scholarships
8,000	Wisconsin Center for Academically Talented Youth, Madison, WI -- Partial Underwrite
7,100	Viterbo College, La Crosse, WI -- Unrestricted
5,000	Pulp & Paper Foundation - University of Minnesota, St. Paul, MN -- Unrestricted

Environment

10,000	Friends of Horicon Marsh, Horicon, WI -- Capital
10,000	Wisconsin Society of Ornithology, Hartland, WI -- Underwrite

Health

15,000	Airlifeline LTD, Republic, MI -- Capital

Social Services

160,000	United Way of South Wood County, Wisconsin Rapids, WI -- Unrestricted
39,270	United Way of Portage County, Stevens Point, WI -- Unrestricted
37,000	United Way of Greater Duluth, Duluth, MN -- Unrestricted
16,300	United Way of Fox Cities, Inc., Menasha, WI -- Unrestricted
13,000	Rawhide Boys Ranch, New London, WI -- Capital
10,000	Appleton Ice, Inc., Appleton, WI -- Capital
10,000	Kellner Youth Sports Association, Inc., Wisconsin Rapids, WI -- Capital
10,000	Wisconsin Rapids Youth Baseball Association, Inc., Wisconsin Rapids, WI -- Capital
8,500	Badger State Games, Madison, WI -- Unrestricted

Constellation Energy Group, Inc.

Company Contact

39 W. Lexington St.
Baltimore, MD 21201
Phone: (410)234-5678
Fax: (410)234-5220
Web: http://www.constellationgroup.com

Company Description

Former Name: Baltimore Gas & Electric (1999).
Revenue: US$3,786,200,000 (1999)
Profit: US$273,600,000 (1999)
Employees: 9,000 (1999)
Fortune Rank: 424, per FORTUNE Magazine's list of 500 Largest U.S. Corporations (1999).
FF 424
SIC(s): 4931 Electric & Other Services Combined, 4932 Gas & Other Services Combined, 5722 Household Appliance Stores.

Nonmonetary Support

Value: $110,000 (1997 approx); $145,400 (1995); $200,000 (1994)
Type: Donated Equipment; Donated Products; In-kind Services
Contact: Connie Wingfield, Contributions Coordinator

Corporate Sponsorship

Type: Arts & cultural events; Pledge-a-thon; Festivals/fairs
Note: Sponsors events that aid children's causes and health disorders.

Baltimore Gas & Electric Foundation

Giving Contact

Malinda B. Smallon, Director, Corporate Contributions
Baltimore Gas & ElectricFoundation
PO Box 1475
1003 G&E Building
Baltimore, MD 21203-1475
Phone: (410)234-7481
Fax: (410)234-7471
Email: Malinda.B.Small@BGE.com

Description

Founded: 1986
EIN: 521452037
Organization Type: Corporate Foundation
Giving Locations: MD: Central Maryland service areas
Grant Types: Capital, Conference/Seminar, Employee Matching Gifts, General Support, Multiyear/Continuing Support.
Note: Employee matching gift ratio: 1 to 1 between $25 and $2,000 annually per employee.

Giving Philosophy

'BGE's Contributions Program is based on the recognition that our vitality as an organization depends on the well being of the communities in which we operate. Through thoughtful social investments, the company strives to enhance the health, welfare, financial strength, and the quality of life of our employees and all who live in those communities.

'Program Objectives: to assist those organizations that play significant roles in education, health and welfare, cultural enrichment, civic and environmental improvement, and economic development in the communities where we have significant business interests; to allocate available funds and other resources in accordance with genuine needs with the expectation of accomplishing worthwhile missions; to provide support for organizations in which BGE has designated management and employee involvement.' Corporate Contributions Program guidelines

Financial Summary

Total Giving: $5,000,000 (1999 approx); $4,700,000 (1997); $4,300,000 (1996). Note: Contributes through corporate direct giving program and foundation. 1997 corporate direct giving; foundation ($1,756,500); United Way ($756,000). Giving includes 1996 Giving includes corporate direct giving; foundation ($1,698,898); United Way ($753,000). 1995 Giving includes corporate direct giving ($2,038,172); foundation ($2,351,055); nonmonetary support.
Assets: $429,405 (1997); $888,422 (1996); $1,932,704 (1995)

Gifts Received: $2,035,162 (1997); $1,500,000 (1996); $973,900 (1995). Note: The foundation receives gifts from the Baltimore Gas and Electric Company.

Typical Recipients

Arts & Humanities: Arts Festivals, Dance, Historic Preservation, History & Archaeology, Libraries, Museums/Galleries, Music, Performing Arts, Theater
Civic & Public Affairs: Business/Free Enterprise, Economic Development, Housing, Law & Justice, Professional & Trade Associations, Urban & Community Affairs, Zoos/Aquariums
Education: Arts/Humanities Education, Colleges & Universities, Continuing Education, Education Funds, Faculty Development, Education-General, Health & Physical Education, Literacy, Medical Education, Minority Education, Preschool Education, Religious Education, Science/Mathematics Education, Social Sciences Education, Special Education, Student Aid
Environment: Air/Water Quality, Environment-General, Resource Conservation
Health: Clinics/Medical Centers, Hospices, Hospitals, Public Health
Religion: Jewish Causes, Religious Welfare, Seminaries
Science: Science Museums, Scientific Centers & Institutes, Scientific Research
Social Services: At-Risk Youth, Child Abuse, Child Welfare, Community Service Organizations, Family Services, People with Disabilities, Scouts, Senior Services, Special Olympics, United Funds/United Ways, Volunteer Services, YMCA/YWCA/YMHA/YWHA, Youth Organizations

Contributions Analysis

Giving Priorities: Arts, environmental affairs, minority issues, higher education, hospitals, housing for the elderly and disabled, and youth programs.
Arts & Humanities: About 13%. Supports institutions that enrich the culturaldevelopment of children and youth, provide enjoyment for employees and public, and attract favorable national and international attention to the Baltimore area.
Civic & Public Affairs: About 18%. Supports programs designed to achieve business and civic goals, such as creating jobs for people of all levels of skill and training. Also supports efforts to create affordable housing and stable communities in the Central Maryland area.
Education: 35%. Primarily supports elementary and secondary education programs that prepare students to leave school ready to work. Also supports the national and state education goal that children will start school ready to learn.
Environment: Less than 5%. Focus is on conservation and environmental education.
Health: 32%. Focus is on support services for families and children that promote self-sufficiency and provide prevention and health education services.
Note: Company places special emphasis on organizations whose services contribute, at least in part, to early childhood development, whether in education, health and welfare, or cultural enrichment.

Application Procedures

Initial Contact: two copies of cover letter written on the requesting organization's letterhead and signed by the executive director and/or board president and written proposal
Application Requirements: narrative proposal of no more than five pages, including a brief summary and history of the agency, its mission, goals, and objectives; description of current programs, activities, and accomplishments; overall agency plans for the coming year; a description of organizational structure, staff responsibilities, and level of volunteer involvement; any affiliation with federated funds or public agencies; statement of need to be addressed, description of constituency served and how they will benefit; description of project goals and measurable objectives; description o f programs/activities planned to accomplish these goals, and whether or not this is an ongoing activity; timetable for implementation; any other organizations participating in the project; list of names and qualifications of key staff and volunteers responsible for project implementation; other sources of funding and a projected budget; expected results during the funding period and how the project's results and success will be measured; list of board committee assignments, occupations, community affiliations, and criteria for board selection; agency's annual report, most recent financial statement, and current annual operating budget, including a summary of itemized expenses and revenue; funding sources and listing of past major contributors with amounts and anticipated future funding sources; and a copy of the original IRS determination letter indicating 501(c)(3) status
Deadlines: None.
Review Process: after Corporate Contributions committee meeting, company may arrange for interviews or site visits
Evaluative Criteria: projects demonstrate broad base of community support, support from other foundations and corporations, and are non-discriminatory
Decision Notification: committee meets in March, June, September, and December; organizations are usually notified six to eight weeks after receipt of proposal

Restrictions

Does not normally fund member agencies of the United Way. Company does not contribute to churches for religious causes, sports teams, organizations in conflict with company goals, health research programs, activities, nor provide start-up funding.

Additional Information

Publications: Guidelines

Corporate Officials

Edward A. Crooke: president B 1938. ED University of Maryland BS (1968); Loyola College MBA (1971). PRIM CORP EMPL president: Baltimore Gas & Electric Co. CORP AFFIL director: First Maryland Bancorp; director: First National Bank Maryland Inc.; director: Constellation Energy Group Inc.; chairman: BGE Energy Projects & Services; chairman: BGE Home Products & Services Inc.
Christian Herndon Poindexter: chairman, chief executive officer, director B Evansville, IN 1938. ED United States Naval Academy BS (1960); Loyola College MBA (1976). PRIM CORP EMPL chairman, chief executive officer, director: Baltimore Gas & Electric Co. ADD CORP EMPL director, president, chairman, chief executive officer: Constellation Energy Group Inc. CORP AFFIL director: Mercantile Bankshares Corp.; director: Dome Corp.; director: KMS Group Inc.; chairman, chief executive officer: Constellation Investments Inc.; chairman, chief executive officer: Constellation Properties Inc.; chairman, chief executive officer: Constellation Biogas Inc. NONPR AFFIL trustee: Villa Julie College; secretary, director: YMCA Anne Arundel County; trustee: Morgan State University; president, director: Scholarships Scholars Inc.; trustee: John Hopkins University; trustee: Maryland Academy Science; member: Engineering Society Baltimore; member: Institute Electrical & Electronics Engineers; member executive board: Boy Scouts America Baltimore Area Council.
Thomas E. Ruszin, Jr.: treasurer PRIM CORP EMPL treasurer: Baltimore Gas & Electric Co. CORP AFFIL treasurer: Constellation Energy Corp.

Foundation Officials

David A. Brune: secretary, treasurer ED University of Detroit JD (1969). PRIM CORP EMPL vice president finance & accounting, chief financial officer secretary: Baltimore Gas & Electric Co.
Edward A. Crooke: president (see above)
Gary R. Fuhrman: vice president
Anita M. Jackson: assistant secretary, assistant treasurer
Christian Herndon Poindexter: chairman (see above)
Thomas E. Ruszin, Jr.: assistant secretary, assistant treasurer (see above)

Grants Analysis

Disclosure Period: calendar year ending 1997
Total Grants: $1,756,500*
Number of Grants: 41
Average Grant: $42,841
Highest Grant: $725,000
Typical Range: $10,000 to $75,000
***Note:** Giving excludes corporate direct giving; United Way.

Recent Grants

Note: Grants derived from 1997 Form 990.

Arts & Humanities

110,000	Baltimore Children's Museum, Baltimore, MD -- capital campaign
70,000	Maryland Historical Society, Baltimore, MD -- capital campaign for Education/ Public Programs Center
62,500	Baltimore Center for Performing Arts, Baltimore, MD -- operating support
60,000	Walters Art Gallery Endowment Foundation, Baltimore, MD -- capital campaign for Family Art Center
40,000	Baltimore Museum of Art, Baltimore, MD -- for campaign to acquire Lucas Collection
25,000	Great Blacks in Wax Museum, Baltimore, MD -- capital campaign for museum expansion
25,000	St. John's College, Annapolis, MD -- capital campaign for college library
10,000	Baltimore City Life Museums, Baltimore, MD -- capital campaign

Civic & Public Affairs

25,000	Enterprise Foundation, Columbia, MD -- for Sandtown/Winchester Transformation project
25,000	National Aquarium in Baltimore, Baltimore, MD -- capital improvements
25,000	Neighborhood Housing Service, Baltimore, MD -- program support

Education

300,000	Johns Hopkins University, Baltimore, MD -- for Medical Discovery Fund
200,000	Johns Hopkins University, Baltimore, MD -- for School of Continuing Studies
75,000	Goucher College, Baltimore, MD -- for Legacy Campaign
50,000	University of Maryland Foundation, Adelphi, MD -- support Campaign for Maryland
50,000	University of Maryland Medical System, Baltimore, MD -- capital campaign
50,000	Western Maryland College, Westminster, MD -- capital campaign for new science center
45,000	Loyola College of Maryland, Baltimore, MD -- support Renewing the Promise Capital Campaign
40,000	Maryland Institute College of Art, Baltimore, MD -- capital campaign
30,000	Independent College Fund of Maryland, Baltimore, MD -- capital campaign
29,000	Towson State University Foundation, Towson, MD -- capital campaign for teacher recruitment/mentor program
25,000	Villa Julie College, Stevenson, MD -- capital campaign for science center construction
12,000	Learning Bank of Coil, Baltimore, MD -- capital campaign for building renovations

10,000 Living Classrooms Foundation, Baltimore, MD -- capital campaign for Weinberg Center

Environment

10,000 Nature Conservancy, Chevy Chase, MD -- support Campaign for Chesapeake Rivers

Health

33,000 North Arundel Hospital Foundation, Glen Burnie, MD -- support Emergency Care for Life Capital Campaign

25,000 St. Joseph Hospital Foundation, Towson, MD -- capital campaign

20,000 Greater Baltimore Medical Center, Baltimore, MD -- capital campaign

20,000 Mercy Medical Center, Baltimore, MD -- capital campaign

20,000 Sinai Hospital, Baltimore, MD -- support Second Century Capital Campaign

15,000 Bon Secours of Maryland Foundation, Baltimore, MD -- capital campaign for Community Support Center

12,500 Carroll County General Hospital, Westminster, MD -- capital campaign for Women's Center

10,000 Greater Baltimore Medical Center, Baltimore, MD -- capital campaign for Health Center and Hospice

Religion

20,000 Institute of Jewish and Christian Studies, Baltimore, MD -- endowment fund

12,500 St. Ambrose Housing Aid Center, Baltimore, MD -- capital campaign

Science

50,000 Christopher Columbus Development Center, Baltimore, MD -- capital campaign

Social Services

725,000 United Way Central Maryland, Baltimore, MD -- corporate pledge

31,000 United Way Calvert County, Huntington, MD -- corporate pledge

30,000 Kennedy Krieger Institute, Baltimore, MD -- capital campaign

30,000 Volunteer Maryland, Crownsville, MD -- operating support

25,000 Woodbourne Foundation, Baltimore, MD -- capital campaign for program support

20,000 Boy Scouts of America, Baltimore, MD -- for Renaissance Campaign

10,000 Maryland Special Olympics, Columbia, MD -- capital campaign

Consumers Energy Co.

Company Contact

Jackson, MI
Web: http://www.consumersenergy.com

Company Description

Former Name: Consumers Power Co.
Assets: US$7,025,000,000
Employees: 8,907
SIC(s): 4931 Electric & Other Services Combined.
Parent Company: CMS Energy Corp.

Nonmonetary Support

Type: In-kind Services

Corporate Sponsorship

Type: Arts & cultural events; Festivals/fairs; Music & entertainment events

Consumers Energy Foundation

Giving Contact

Carolyn Bloodworth, Secretary/Treasurer
Consumers Energy Foundation
212 W. Michigan Ave.
Jackson, MI 49201
Phone: (517)788-0432
Fax: (517)788-2281
Email: foundation@consumersenergy.com

Alternate Contact

Phone: 877-501-4952

Description

EIN: 382935534
Organization Type: Corporate Foundation
Giving Locations: MI nationally.
Grant Types: Capital, Employee Matching Gifts, General Support, Operating Expenses, Project.
Note: Employee matching gift ratio: 1 to 1 for donations to colleges, universities, and Michigan food banks and community foundations, up to $5,000 per employee or retiree annually.

Giving Philosophy

Consumers Energy views contributions to the communities in which they operate as a responsibility. It is the company's philanthropic policy to improve Michigan's quality of life, and in doing so, build a foundation of responsibility and trust.

'The Foundation awards grants in five major fields of interest: Social Welfare initiatives that provide solutions to problems faced by individuals and families who are unable to address their needs without help; Michigan Growth and Environmental Enhancement efforts that protect and enhance Michigan's physical environment; Education initiatives that coordinate and develop partnerships for systemic reform in grades K-12 and programs that support schools of higher learning with special interest in curricula and capital improvements in the study of business, political science, economics, engineering and natural/physical sciences; Community and Civic endeavors that support programs focusing on Michigan's economic development at the community, regional and statewide levels, with a preference given to volunteer-driven efforts, public/private partnerships and short- or long-term projects with significant evaluation components; Culture and Arts programs that increase awareness of the values of artistic and cultural achievements and encourage their growth.'

Financial Summary

Total Giving: $1,500,000 (1998 approx); $1,320,512 (1997); $1,256,343 (1996). Note: Contributes through corporate direct giving program and foundation. 1997 Giving includes foundation ($654,261); volunteer investment grants-VIP ($91,725); matching gifts ($199,635); United Way ($374,892). 1996 Giving includes foundation ($657,330); volunteer investment grants-VIP ($60,625); matching gifts ($178,651); United Way ($359,737). 1995 Giving includes foundation ($1,056,639); matching gifts ($188,625).
Assets: $1,021,831 (1997); $895,723 (1996); $922,543 (1995)
Gifts Received: $1,950,000 (1997); $1,400,050 (1996); $1,400,000 (1995). Note: Contributions are received from Consumers Energy Company.

Typical Recipients

Arts & Humanities: Arts Associations & Councils, Arts Funds, Arts Institutes, Community Arts, Arts & Humanities-General, Historic Preservation, History & Archaeology, Libraries, Museums/Galleries, Music, Opera, Performing Arts, Public Broadcasting, Theater
Civic & Public Affairs: Botanical Gardens/Parks, Chambers of Commerce, Community Foundations, Economic Development, Employment/Job Training, Civic & Public Affairs-General, Housing, Parades/Festivals, Philanthropic Organizations, Professional & Trade Associations, Public Policy, Urban & Community Affairs, Zoos/Aquariums
Education: Agricultural Education, Arts/Humanities Education, Business Education, Business-School Partnerships, Colleges & Universities, Community & Junior Colleges, Economic Education, Engineering/Technological Education, Legal Education, Minority Education, Public Education (Precollege), Science/Mathematics Education, Secondary Education (Public)
Environment: Energy, Environment-General, Resource Conservation, Watershed, Wildlife Protection
Health: Alzheimers Disease, Cancer, Children's Health/Hospitals, Emergency/Ambulance Services, Hospitals
International: International Relations
Religion: Religious Welfare
Science: Scientific Centers & Institutes
Social Services: Camps, Community Centers, Community Service Organizations, Family Services, Food/Clothing Distribution, People with Disabilities, Recreation & Athletics, Scouts, Senior Services, Shelters/Homelessness, Substance Abuse, United Funds/United Ways, Volunteer Services, YMCA/YWCA/YMHA/YWHA, Youth Organizations, Youth Organizations

Contributions Analysis

Giving Priorities: Social welfare, education, civics, the arts, community development, and health care.
Arts & Humanities: 10% to 15%. Interests include museums, opera, public broadcasting, symphonies, and theater.
Civic & Public Affairs: 15% to 20%. Supports economic development and job training, housing, and public affairs.
Education: 10% to 15%. Supports Michigan colleges and universities, K-12 education, specialized educational foundations, and programs that improve the curricula for business, economics, engineering, math, and the natural and physical sciences.
Environment: Less than 5%. Foundation supports the Great Lakes Regional Corporate Enviromental Council, habitat and land preservation, and air and water quality.
Health: Less than 5%. Supports American Red Cross.
Religion: Less than 5%. Religious causes.
Social Services: 50% to 55%. Majority of support goes to the United Way. Other interests include family and children services, YMCAs, volunteer programs, senior services, and food distribution programs.

Application Procedures

Initial Contact: Send a cover letter and the Council of Michigan Foundation's Common Grant Application.
Application Requirements: Cover letter should include a description of organization, and make a strategic link between proposal and foundation's interests. Attachments to completed application should include current budget including other sources of funding, most recent audited financial statement, list of board of directors, and proof of tax-exempt status.
Deadlines: None; requests reviewed quarterly.
Review Process: Applications are reviewed locally and at company headquarters, then sent to foundation board for consideration; after preliminary review, applicant may be asked to provide additional information. Small grants of less than $5,000 can be approved at any time; larger grants need prior board approval.
Evaluative Criteria: Indications of effective governing board, realistic budget, clearly defined program that is supported by the public, business, and other foundations (if appropriate); and record of accomplishment.
Decision Notification: The foundation tries to respond within six to eight weeks.

Restrictions

Funds only groups to which donations are tax-deductible.

Does not support individuals, political or lobbying groups, endowments, organizations whose operating status is supported by the United Way, religious organizations for sectarian purposes, or labor, veterans, fraternal and social clubs.

Also does not contribute to organizations which discriminate on the basis of sex, age, height, weight, marital status, race, religion, creed, color, national or origin, ancestry, disability, handicap, or veteran status. The Foundation does not buy tickets or make payments to events or celebrations to raise funds or charitable purposes, or sponsor advertising to support these efforts.

Additional Information

Consumers Energy Foundation looks for grant recipients that provide solutions to problems faced by individuals and families who are unable to address their own needs without help; protect and enhance the natural environment; improve the availability and quality of education while stressing cost effectiveness; back the improvement and effectiveness of the public's health care systems, with special emphasis on reducing patient costs; participate in community and civic activities for the betterment of the citizenry and their governments; and increase an awareness of the values of artistic and cultural achievements and encourage their growth.

The foundation considers requests from qualified organizations to support operating budgets and capital fund programs for construction, refurbishment or purchase of buildings, structures, equipment or other physical enhancements.

A contribution from Consumers Energy Foundation is more likely to be approved when grant seekers' programs are focused on high priority needs which they are capable of addressing successfully.

The foundation will not respond to telephone requests. Facsimile requests are discouraged.

Corporate Officials

Paul A. Elbert: president, chief executive officer natural gas B 1950. ED Ohio State University BA; University of Illinois MA. PRIM CORP EMPL president, chief executive officer natural gas: Consumers Energy Co. CORP AFFIL chairman: Michigan Gas Storage Co.; director: Sugar Monitor Co.

David W. Joos: president, chief executive officer electric, executive vice president B Fargo, ND 1953. ED Iowa State University of Science & Technology (1975); Iowa State University of Science & Technology (1976). PRIM CORP EMPL president, chief executive officer electric, executive vice president: Consumers Energy Co. NONPR AFFIL member: American Society Mechanical Engineers; member: Registered Professional Engineers; member: American Nuclear Society.

William Thomas McCormick, Jr.: chairman, chief executive officer, director B Washington, DC 1944. ED Cornell University BS (1966); Massachusetts Institute of Technology PhD (1969). PRIM CORP EMPL chairman, chief executive officer, director: CMS Energy Corp. ADD CORP EMPL chairman: Consumers Energy Co.; chairman: Consumers Power Co. CORP AFFIL director: First Chicago NBD Inc.; director: Rockwell International Corp.; director: Bank One Corp.; chairman, chief executive officer: CMS Enterprises Co. NONPR AFFIL director, member: Greater Detroit Chamber of Commerce; director: Schumberger; director: American Gas Association; director: Edison Electric Institute.

Giving Program Officials

Carolyn A. Bloodworth: secretary-trs PRIM CORP EMPL director community relations: CMS Energy Corp.

Foundation Officials

Carolyn A. Bloodworth: secretary-trs (see above)

John W. Clark: president B 1945. ED Indiana University (1968). PRIM CORP EMPL senior vice president communications: CMS Energy Corp. ADD CORP EMPL senior vice president commission: Consumers Energy Co.

Victor J. Fryling: director B 1948. ED Wayne State University BS (1970). PRIM CORP EMPL president, chief operating officer: CMS Energy Corp. ADD CORP EMPL chairman: CMS Marketing Service Trading Co.; president: CMS Enterprises Co.; chairman: CMS Gas Transmission & Storage Co.; chairman: CMS Generation Co.; chairman: CMS Generation Operating Co.; chairman: CMS Generation Filer City; president: CMS Generation Filer Cy Operating Co.; principal: CMS Generation Grayling Co.; chairman: CMS Generation Recycling Co.; president: CMS Midland Inc.; chairman: CMS NOMECO Oil & Gas Co.; president: Consumers Energy Co.; chairman: Panhandle Eastern Pipe Line Co.

William Thomas McCormick, Jr.: chairman (see above)

Grants Analysis

Disclosure Period: calendar year ending 1997
Total Grants: $654,261*
Number of Grants: 109
Average Grant: $6,002
Highest Grant: $25,000
Typical Range: $1,000 to $10,000
***Note:** Giving excludes volunteerism; matching gifts; United Way.

Recent Grants

Note: Grants derived from 1998 Form 990.

Arts & Humanities

17,000	Michigan State University WKAR TV, East Lansing, MI
15,000	Grand Rapids Public Museum, Grand Rapids, MI
14,000	Detroit Symphony Orchestra, Detroit, MI
10,000	Detroit Institute of Arts, Detroit, MI
10,000	Ella Sharp Museum, Jackson, MI
10,000	Michigan Opera Theatre, Detroit, MI
5,000	Historical Society of Saginaw County Inc, Saginaw, MI
5,000	Kalamazoo Civic Players, Kalamazoo, MI
5,000	Michigan Artrain, Ann Arbor, MI
5,000	Michigan Council for the Humanities, Lansing, MI

Civic & Public Affairs

25,000	Detroit Renaissance Inc, Detroit, MI
15,000	Jackson Community Foundation, Jackson, MI
10,000	Campaign for Greater Detroit, Detroit, MI
10,000	Detroit Regional Economic Partnership, Detroit, MI
10,000	Gerald R Ford Foundation, Grand Rapids, MI
10,000	Local Initiatives Support Corp, Lansing, MI
10,000	R.E.A.D.Y. Project, Mt Pleasant, MI
8,000	Aspen Institute, Bethesda, MD
6,300	Detroit Renaissance Foundation, Detroit, MI
6,000	Detroit Zoological Society, Royal Oak, MI
5,000	Charlevoix State Bank, T.I.C.Fund, Charlevoix, MI
5,000	Frederik Meijer Gardens, Grand Rapids, MI

Education

11,250	Michigan Technological University, Houghton, MI
10,000	Detroit College of Law at Michigan State University, East Lansing, MI
10,000	Grand Valley State University Foundation - (Grand Design 2000 Campaign), Grand Rapids, MI
10,000	Michigan State University College of Engineering, East Lansing, MI
10,000	United Negro College Fund, New York, NY
10,000	Western Michigan University Foundation, Kalamazoo, MI
8,000	Close Up Foundation, Alexandria, VA
5,000	Interlochen Arts Academy, Interlochen, MI
5,000	Interlochen Arts Academy, Interlochen, MI
5,000	Kettering University, Flint, MI
5,000	Madonna University, Livonia, MI
5,000	Michigan Colleges Foundation, Southfield, MI

Environment

7,000	Saginaw Bay Watershed Initiative, Saginaw, MI
5,000	Kellogg Bird Sanctuary, Augusta, MI
5,000	Michigan Envirothon, Lake City, MI

Health

10,000	Barbara Ann Karmanos Cancer Institute, Lathrup Village, MI

Religion

10,000	The Salvation Army, Grand Rapids, MI
5,000	City Rescue Mission of Saginaw, Inc, Saginaw, MI

Social Services

15,000	United Way Capital Campaign, Detroit, MI
10,000	Grand Action Foundation/Grand Rapids Arena, Grand Rapids, MI
10,000	Michigan Harvest Gathering, Lansing, MI
5,000	Boys & Girls Club of Saginaw County, Inc, Saginaw, MI
5,000	Camp Blodgett, Grand Rapids, MI
5,000	City of Jackson Human Relations Commission, Jackson, MI
5,000	Fair Winds Girl Scout Council, Swartz Creek, MI
5,000	George W Romney Fund for Volunteerism in Michigan, East Lansing, MI
5,000	Handicapped Children & Adults Foundation of Jackson County, Jackson, MI
5,000	Jackson Y Center, Jackson, MI

CONTINENTAL GRAIN CO.

Company Contact

New York, NY

Company Description

Employees: 17,500
SIC(s): 0211 Beef Cattle Feedlots, 0213 Hogs, 0251 Broiler, Fryer & Roaster Chickens, 2041 Flour & Other Grain Mill Products, 2048 Prepared Feeds Nec, 6159 Miscellaneous Business Credit Institutions.

Continental Grain Foundation

Giving Contact

Dwight C. Coffin, Vice President, Human Resources
277 Park Ave.
New York, NY 10172
Phone: (212)207-5100
Fax: (212)207-5163

Description

EIN: 136160912
Organization Type: Corporate Foundation
Giving Locations: NY midwest.

Grant Types: General Support, Scholarship.

Financial Summary

Total Giving: $414,130 (fiscal year ending January 31, 1997); $109,990 (fiscal 1996); $152,325 (fiscal 1995)
Assets: $3,254 (fiscal 1997); $839 (fiscal 1996); $1,014 (fiscal 1995)
Gifts Received: $416,630 (fiscal 1997); $109,890 (fiscal 1996); $152,975 (fiscal 1995). Note: In fiscal 1997, contributions were received from Continental Grain Co.

Typical Recipients

Arts & Humanities: Historic Preservation, Museums/Galleries, Music, Opera, Performing Arts
Civic & Public Affairs: African American Affairs, Chambers of Commerce, Legal Aid, Urban & Community Affairs, Women's Affairs
Education: Agricultural Education, Business Education, Colleges & Universities, Education Funds, Education Reform, International Studies, Legal Education, Minority Education, Student Aid
Health: Cancer, Children's Health/Hospitals, Emergency/Ambulance Services, Hospitals, Multiple Sclerosis, Nursing Services, Single-Disease Health Associations
International: Health Care/Hospitals, Human Rights, International Development, International Organizations, International Peace & Security Issues, International Relations, International Relief Efforts
Religion: Churches, Jewish Causes, Seminaries
Science: Science Museums
Social Services: Child Welfare, Community Service Organizations, Family Services, People with Disabilities, United Funds/United Ways, Volunteer Services, YMCA/YWCA/YMHA/YWHA, Youth Organizations

Application Procedures

Initial Contact: Send a brief letter of inquiry detailing purpose for which grant is requested. There are no deadlines.

Corporate Officials

James John Bigham: executive vice president, chief financial officer, director B Waterbury, CT 1937. ED Fairfield University BS (1959); Columbia University MBA (1961); Harvard University Graduate School of Business Administration (1970). PRIM CORP EMPL executive vice president, chief financial officer, director: Continental Grain Co.
Dwight C. Coffin: vice president human resources PRIM CORP EMPL vice president human resources: Continental Grain Co.
Michel Fribourg: chairman emeritus, director B 1913. PRIM CORP EMPL chairman emeritus, director: Continental Grain Co. CORP AFFIL director: Overseas Shipholding Group Inc.
Donald L. Staheli: chairman, director B Hurricane, UT 1931. ED University of Illinois MS; University of Illinois PhD; Utah State University BS. PRIM CORP EMPL chairman, director: Continental Grain Co.

Foundation Officials

Dwight C. Coffin: vice president, secretary, director (see above)
Gerald Frenchman: vice president
Michel Fribourg: president, director (see above)
Donald L. Staheli: vice president, director (see above)
Lawrence G. Weppler: assistant secretary
Daniel J. Willet: treasurer

Grants Analysis

Disclosure Period: fiscal year ending January 31, 1997
Total Grants: $414,130
Number of Grants: 51*
Highest Grant: $70,000
Typical Range: $250 to $15,000
***Note:** Number of grants does not include a contribution to an individual.

Recent Grants

Note: Grants derived from 1997 Form 990.

Arts & Humanities

15,000	Museum of Modern Art, New York, NY
10,000	Carnegie Hall Society, New York, NY
10,000	Metropolitan Opera Association, New York, NY

Civic & Public Affairs

10,000	New York Partnership and Chamber of Commerce, New York, NY

Education

70,000	Yale University Law School, New Haven, CT
15,000	Ohio State University, Columbus, OH
14,180	National Merit Scholarship Corporation, Evanston, IL
10,000	Columbia Business School, New York, NY
10,000	Joseph H. Lauder Institute of Management and International Studies, Philadelphia, PA
7,500	Columbia Business School, New York, NY
5,000	Prep for Prep, New York, NY

Health

10,000	SLE Foundation, New York, NY

International

25,000	Appeal of Conscience Foundation, New York, NY
25,000	Council on Foreign Relations, New York, NY
20,000	America-China Society
10,000	Asia Society, New York, NY
10,000	International Rescue Committee, New York, NY

Religion

15,000	Jewish Theological Seminary, New York, NY

Social Services

10,000	Points of Light Foundation, Washington, DC
10,000	YMCA, New York, NY

CONTRAN CORP.

Company Contact

Dallas, TX

Company Description

Revenue: US$2,360,000,000
Employees: 8,500
SIC(s): 1311 Crude Petroleum & Natural Gas, 2063 Beet Sugar, 2421 Sawmills & Planing Mills--General, 5812 Eating Places.

Operating Locations

Operates internationally.

Harold Simmons Foundation, Inc.

Giving Contact

Ms. Lisa Simmons Epstein, President
Harold Simmons Foundation, Inc.
5430 LBJ Fwy., Suite 1700
Dallas, TX 75240-2697
Phone: (972)991-2400
Fax: (972)448-1456

Description

Founded: 1988
EIN: 752222091
Organization Type: Corporate Foundation
Giving Locations: TX: Dallas including metropolitan area
Grant Types: Capital, General Support.

Giving Philosophy

'Grants are made by the Harold Simmons Foundation to fulfill an important aspect of its funding corporations' role as responsible corporate citizens. Our aim is to improve the quality of life of all citizens in the Dallas area where our employees live and work. In implementing this program, we try to respond to current community needs by looking for grant proposals that are timely and well researched. We are particularly interested in supporting programs that complement, rather than duplicate, other private and public efforts.'
Foundation Grant Application Information

Financial Summary

Total Giving: $1,112,348 (1997); $1,313,155 (1996); $1,292,491 (1995). Note: Contributes through foundation only.
Assets: $21,777,719 (1997); $10,714,277 (1996); $2,882,432 (1995)
Gifts Received: $6,800,000 (1997); $9,960,000 (1996); $1,285,000 (1995). Note: Contributions are received from Contran Corp.

Typical Recipients

Arts & Humanities: Arts Centers, Arts Outreach, Dance, Historic Preservation, Libraries, Museums/Galleries, Music, Performing Arts, Public Broadcasting, Theater
Civic & Public Affairs: Botanical Gardens/Parks, Community Foundations, Economic Development, Employment/Job Training, Civic & Public Affairs-General, Housing, Nonprofit Management, Philanthropic Organizations, Professional & Trade Associations, Public Policy, Urban & Community Affairs, Women's Affairs, Zoos/Aquariums
Education: Arts/Humanities Education, Business Education, Colleges & Universities, Education Reform, Faculty Development, Education-General, Leadership Training, Literacy, Medical Education, Private Education (Precollege), Public Education (Precollege), Religious Education, Secondary Education (Public)
Environment: Environment-General
Health: AIDS/HIV, Cancer, Children's Health/Hospitals, Clinics/Medical Centers, Health Organizations, Hospitals, Hospitals (University Affiliated), Kidney, Medical Research, Mental Health, Multiple Sclerosis, Nursing Services, Prenatal Health Issues, Public Health, Single-Disease Health Associations, Transplant Networks/Donor Banks
International: Health Care/Hospitals, International Development, International Relief Efforts
Religion: Churches, Jewish Causes, Ministries, Religious Welfare, Social/Policy Issues
Science: Science Museums
Social Services: At-Risk Youth, Camps, Child Welfare, Community Service Organizations, Counseling, Crime Prevention, Domestic Violence, Family Planning, Family Services, Food/Clothing Distribution, Shelters/Homelessness, Substance Abuse, United Funds/United Ways, Volunteer Services, YMCA/YWCA/YMHA/YWHA, Youth Organizations

Contributions Analysis

Giving Priorities: Health, social servics, education, civics, and the arts.
Arts & Humanities: 5%. Recipients include symphonies, opera, public broadcasting, theater, and museums.
Civic & Public Affairs: 20%. Funding supports philanthropic organizations, economic development, botanical gardens, and housing.
Education: 7%. Funding supports colleges and universities, public and private secondary schools, and education reform.

Health: 12%. Recipients include medical facilities and prenatal health institutes.
Religion: 28%. Religious welfare and ministries receive support.
Social Services: 29%. Funding supports United Way, the disabled, youth organizations, child welfare, substance abuse policy, and community service.
Note: Total contributions made in 1997.

Application Procedures

Initial Contact: Send a written proposal.
Application Requirements: Include a brief history of organization and its purpose; explanation of proposed project, and amount of funds requested; plans for evaluation of project; list of foundation's directors, including professional affiliations; description of staff; description of use of volunteers; list of major donors; copy of organization's tax determination letter from IRS; financial information; most recent audited statement or Form 990; current year's budget for organization and project; fundraising costs and total fundraising goal.
Deadlines: None.
Review Process: If initial criteria are met, further information may be requested.
Decision Notification: Two to three months after receipt of proposal.

Restrictions

Foundation does not support individuals, endowments, deficit financing, or organizations that discriminate on the basis of race, religion, or sex. Multiyear grants are limited in number.

Corporate Officials

Eugene Karl Anderson: vice president, secretary B Omaha, NE 1935. ED Wayne State University (1958); University of Nebraska (1962). PRIM CORP EMPL vice president: Contran Corp. CORP AFFIL vice president: Valhi Group Inc.; vice president, assistant treasurer: Valhi Inc.; vice president: National City Lines Inc.
Glenn Reuben Simmons: vice chairman B Golden, TX 1928. ED Texas Christian University; East Texas State University BS (1950). PRIM CORP EMPL vice chairman: Contran Corp. CORP AFFIL director: Valhi Group Inc.; vice chairman: Valhi Inc.; vice chairman: Valcor Inc.; director: NL Industries Inc.; chairman: Sherman Wire Caldwell Inc.; chairman, chief executive officer, director: Keystone Consolidated Industries; vice chairman: National City Lines Inc.; chief executive officer: Fox Valley Steel Wire Co.; chairman: DeSoto Inc.; president: Flight Proficiency Service Inc.
Steven L. Watson: vice president, secretary PRIM CORP EMPL vice president, secretary: Contran Corp. CORP AFFIL secretary: Flight Proficiency Service Inc.; secretary: National City Lines Inc.; secretary: Dallas Compressor Co.

Foundation Officials

Eugene Karl Anderson: treasurer (see above)
Lisa K. Simmons Epstein: president
John Mark Hollingsworth: assistant secretary B Dallas, TX 1951. ED Rhodes College BA (1973); Southern Methodist University JD (1977). PRIM CORP EMPL general corporate counsel: Valhi Inc.
Harold Clark Simmons: chairman, director B Alba, TX 1931. ED University of Texas BA (1951); University of Texas MA (1952). PRIM CORP EMPL chairman, chief executive officer: Valhi Inc. ADD CORP EMPL chairman, chief executive officer: Contran Corp. CORP AFFIL chairman: Valcor Inc.; trustee: Harold C Simmons Family Trust; director: Kronos; chairman: NL Industries Inc. NONPR AFFIL member: Phi Beta Kappa.
Steven L. Watson: vice president, secretary, director (see above)

Grants Analysis

Disclosure Period: calendar year ending 1997
Total Grants: $1,034,848*
Number of Grants: 136
Average Grant: $7,609
Highest Grant: $100,000
Typical Range: $1,000 to $25,000
***Note:** Grant analysis excludes United Way.

Recent Grants

Note: Grants derived from 1997 Form 990.

Arts & Humanities

15,000 Van Cliburn Foundation, Fort Worth, TX -- Cliburn concerts at Meyerson Symphony Center
10,000 Dallas Symphony Association, Dallas, TX -- community outreach programs
10,000 Sammons Center for the Arts, Dallas, TX -- capital campaign to renovate Historic Turtle Creek Pump House
7,500 Dallas Children's Theater, Dallas, TX -- Curtains Up On Reading program
5,000 Dallas Black Dance Theater, Dallas, TX -- 20th Anniversary
5,000 Dallas Theater Center, Dallas, TX -- for a new arts education initiative that involves teacher training and in-classroom participation by teaching artists

Civic & Public Affairs

100,000 Crystal Charity Ball, Dallas, TX
50,000 Dallas Zoological Society, Dallas, TX -- capital campaign for children's zoo
15,000 Enterprise Foundation, Dallas, TX -- operating expenses to promote housing development programs
10,000 Dallas Women's Foundation, Dallas, TX -- cooperative funding
10,000 Vecinos Unidos, Dallas, TX -- establishing low-income housing in West Dallas
10,000 Women Helping Women, Houston, TX -- operating expenses
5,000 Maple Avenue Economic Development Corporation, Dallas, TX -- salary support for staff

Education

33,000 Greenhill School, Dallas, TX -- capital campaign
10,000 Communities in Schools, Dallas, TX -- North Dallas High School program
5,000 East Dallas Community School, Dallas, TX -- Parent Involvement Replication project
5,000 Notre Dame of Dallas Schools, Dallas, TX -- kitchen repairs and equipment

Health

25,000 Marrow Foundation, Arlington, VA -- two-year pledge
25,000 National Tuberous Sclerosis Association, Landover, MD
10,000 Turtle Creek Manor, Dallas, TX -- women's outpatient program
10,000 University of Texas Southwestern Medical Center, Dallas, TX -- Dallas Heart Ball
5,000 AIDS Arms, Dallas, TX -- early intervention program
5,000 AIDS Services, Dallas, TX -- operating expenses
5,000 Mental Health Association, Dallas, TX -- 50th anniversary celebration
5,000 National Tuberous Sclerosis Association, Landover, MD -- Texas Scottish Rite Hospital for Children Treasure Street Benefit
5,000 Parkland Foundation, Dallas, TX -- Healthy Start and Lifespan joint project to assist teen parents in Pleasant Grove
5,000 Southwestern Ball, Dallas, TX -- paralysis research

International

50,000 Care Foundation, Dallas, TX -- first payment on a five-year pledge for Global Initiative for Girls Education
50,000 Care Foundation, Dallas, TX -- first payment on a five-year pledge for Global Initiative for Girls Education

Religion

100,000 Fellowship of Christian Athletes, Dallas, TX -- 20th Annual Tom Landry FCA Open
50,000 Salvation Army, Dallas, TX -- capital campaign
25,000 Salvation Army School for Officer Training, Atlanta, GA -- five-year pledge to support School for Officers Training Southern Territory
10,000 Salvation Army, Dallas, TX -- end-of-year needs
5,000 Hour of Power, Garden Grove, CA -- general expenses
5,000 Hour of Power, Garden Grove, CA
5,000 Nations Ministries, Honobia, OK -- operating expenses
5,000 Northwest Bible Church, Dallas, TX -- unrestricted
5,000 Santa Barbara Rescue Mission, Santa Barbara, CA -- expansion of women's and children's shelter and recovery center

Social Services

50,000 Genesis Women's Shelter, Dallas, TX -- building a new transitional facility
50,000 YWCA, Dallas, TX -- capital campaign
25,000 Dallas Children's Advocacy Center, Dallas, TX -- first of two payments for capital campaign to expand facility
25,000 United Way, Dallas, TX -- Alexis de Tocqueville Society
20,000 Girls, Inc., Dallas, TX -- operating expenses for Preventing Adolescent Pregnancy program
20,000 YMCA, Dallas, TX -- capital campaign for Lakewest branch operations
12,500 United Way of Santa Barbara County, Santa Barbara, CA -- capital needs at headquarters building
10,000 Habilitat, Kaneohe, HI -- operating expenses
10,000 Pine Cove, Tyler, TX -- high school youth camp
10,000 United Way of Santa Barbara County, Santa Barbara, CA -- Alexis de Tocqueville Society
7,500 Attitudes and Attire, Dallas, TX -- staff salaries
7,500 Dispute Mediation Service, Dallas, TX -- implementation of Young Men's Work, a ten-week curriculum for older adolescent boys to promote nonviolent behavior and attitudes
5,000 Outreach Foundation, Dallas, TX -- first-year operation expenses for shelter for homeless men

Conwood Co. Lp

Company Contact

Memphis, TN

Company Description

SIC(s): 2131 Chewing & Smoking Tobacco.

American Snuff Co. Charitable Trust

Giving Contact

David Simpson, III, General Counsel
PO Box 217
Memphis, TN 38101
Phone: (901)761-2050

Description

Founded: 1952
EIN: 626036034
Organization Type: Corporate Foundation
Giving Locations: headquarters area only.
Grant Types: General Support.

Financial Summary

Total Giving: $291,602 (1998); $253,035 (1997); $222,900 (1996)
Giving Analysis: Giving for 1997 includes: foundation grants to United Way ($222,035); foundation grants to United Way ($31,000); 1998: foundation ($265,852); foundation grants to United Way ($25,750)
Assets: $8,026,922 (1998); $6,651,580 (1997); $5,615,141 (1996)

Typical Recipients

Arts & Humanities: Arts Associations & Councils, Arts Institutes, Ballet, Arts & Humanities-General, Museums/Galleries, Public Broadcasting
Civic & Public Affairs: Botanical Gardens/Parks, Clubs, Employment/Job Training, Civic & Public Affairs-General, Housing, Safety, Urban & Community Affairs
Education: Business Education, Colleges & Universities, Education Funds, Education-General, Literacy, Public Education (Precollege)
Health: Children's Health/Hospitals, Clinics/Medical Centers, Health-General, Kidney, Single-Disease Health Associations
Religion: Jewish Causes, Religious Organizations, Religious Welfare
Social Services: Child Welfare, Community Service Organizations, Food/Clothing Distribution, Homes, Scouts, Social Services-General, United Funds/United Ways, Volunteer Services, Youth Organizations

Contributions Analysis

Arts & Humanities: 18%. Funds museums and arts councils, public broadcasting, and ballet.
Civic & Public Affairs: 5%. Supports housing, leadership, and gardens.
Education: 23%. Colleges, universities, public grade schools, and Junior Achievement are funded.
Health: 13%. Supports hospitals and single-disease associations.
Religion: 20%. Funds Christian groups.
Social Services: 20%. Youth organizations and the United Way receive support.
Note: Total contributions in 1998.

Application Procedures

Initial Contact: Send a brief letter of inquiry including a description of organization, amount requested, purpose of funds sought, and proof of tax-exempt status.
Deadlines: None.

Restrictions

Does not support individuals, religious organizations for sectarian purposes, political or lobbying groups, or organizations outside operating areas.

Corporate Officials

W. E. Ingram: president, chief executive officer PRIM CORP EMPL president, chief executive officer: Conwood Colt LP.
E. S. Robertson: vice president, chief financial officer PRIM CORP EMPL vice president, chief financial officer: Conwood Co. LP.
William Mimms Rosson: chairman B Springfield, TN 1922. ED Vanderbilt University (1944). PRIM CORP EMPL chairman: Conwood Co. LP. CORP AFFIL president, director: Taylor Bros; chief executive officer, director: Scott Tobacco Co.; president, director: Conwood Capital Corp.; president, director: GP Corp. NONPR AFFIL director: Smokeless Tobacco Council.

Giving Program Officials

David Louis Simpson, III: B Memphis, TN 1936. ED Southwestern Memphis University (1958); Vanderbilt University (1961). PRIM CORP EMPL secretary, general counsel: Conwood Co. LP.

Grants Analysis

Disclosure Period: calendar year ending 1998
Total Grants: $265,852*
Number of Grants: 76
Average Grant: $3,498
Highest Grant: $25,000
Typical Range: $2,000 to $5,000
***Note:** Giving excludes United Way.

Recent Grants

Note: Grants derived from 1998 Form 990.

Arts & Humanities

10,000	Memphis Museums, Inc., Memphis, TN
10,000	Mifa, Memphis, TN
7,500	WKNO-TV/FM, Memphis, TN
7,000	Memphis Arts Council, Memphis, TN
5,000	Dixon Gallery & Gardens, Memphis, TN
2,500	Memphis Brooks Museum of Art, Memphis, TN
1,000	Ballet Memphis, Memphis, TN
1,000	The Children's Museum of Memphis, Memphis, TN

Civic & Public Affairs

5,000	Habitat for Humanity, Memphis, TN
1,500	Memphis Botanic Garden, Memphis, TN
1,000	Boys & Girls Clubs of Greater Memphis, Memphis, TN
1,000	Leadership Memphis, Memphis, TN
1,000	Leadership Memphis, Memphis, TN

Education

25,000	Rhodes College, Memphis, TN
6,500	Tennessee Foundation for Independent Colleges, Brentwood, TN
3,000	Junior Achievement of Greater Memphis, Inc., Memphis, TN
3,000	Rhodes College, Memphis, TN
2,000	Independent College Fund of North Carolina, Winston-Salem, NC
2,000	Lemoyne -Owen College, Memphis, TN
1,000	Independent College Fund, Winston-Salem, NC
1,000	University of Memphis Foundation, Memphis, TN
1,000	University of Memphis Foundation, Memphis, TN
950	White Station Middle School, Memphis, TN
700	White Station Middle School, Memphis, TN
663	White Station Middle School, Memphis, TN

Health

17,500	Church Health Center, Memphis, TN
10,000	Lebonheur Children's Medical Center, Memphis, TN
5,000	National Kidney Foundation of West Tennessee, Baltimore, MD
5,000	St. Jude Children's Research Hospital, Memphis, TN
3,000	Lebonheur Club, Inc., Memphis, TN
2,000	National Kidney Foundation of West Tennessee, Inc., Baltimore, MD
800	Tennessee Hemophilia Foundation, Memphis, TN
200	Tennessee Hemophilia Foundation, Memphis, TN

Religion

10,000	Young Life Memphis Metro, Memphis, TN
9,000	Neighborhood Christian Center, Memphis, TN
6,500	Baddour Memorial Center, Senatobia, MS
6,000	Tennessee Baptist Children's Home, Brentwood, TN
3,000	Associated Catholic Charities, Inc., Washington, DC
3,000	Tennessee Baptist Children's Homes. Inc., Brentwood, TN
2,500	Neighborhood Christian Centers, Inc., Memphis, TN
40	Memphis Hadassah, Memphis, TN

Social Services

10,000	Mary Galloway Home, Memphis, TN
5,000	Food Bank, Memphis, TN
5,000	Kings Daughters & Sons Home, Midland, MI
4,000	Volunteer Center of Memphis, Memphis, TN
2,500	Boy Scouts of America, Memphis, TN
2,500	Boy Scouts of America, Memphis, TN
2,500	Memphis Child Advocacy Center, Memphis, TN
2,200	Memphis Child Advocacy Center, Memphis, TN
2,000	Boy Scouts of America, Memphis, TN
2,000	Youth Villages, Arlington, TN
1,500	Hands on Memphis, Memphis, TN
1,000	Volunteer Center of Memphis, Memphis, TN
500	Boy Scouts of America, Memphis, TN
300	Memphis Child Advocacy Center, Memphis, TN

COOK INLET REGION

Company Contact

Anchorage, AK
Web: http://www.ciri.com

Company Description

Employees: 180
SIC(s): 1300 Oil & Gas Extraction, 4400 Water Transportation, 4800 Communications, 6500 Real Estate.

Nonmonetary Support

Type: In-kind Services

Corporate Sponsorship

Type: Arts & cultural events
Note: Sponsors daily Alaskan native cultural programs in the summer.

CIRI Foundation

Giving Contact

Lydia Hays
CIRI Foundation
2600 Cordova Street, Suite 206
Anchorage, AK 99503
Phone: (907)263-5582
Fax: (907)263-5588
Email: tcf@ciri.com
Web: http://www.ciri.com/about_ciri/tcs
Note: Toll Free: (800)764-3382

Description

Founded: 1982
EIN: 920087914
Organization Type: Corporate Foundation
Giving Locations: national.
Grant Types: Scholarship.
Note: Foundation provides educational scholarships and grants, and education and heritage grants for special projects.

Financial Summary

Total Giving: $735,000 (2000 approx); $673,000 (1999 approx); $512,099 (1998). Note: Contributes through foundation only.

Giving Analysis: Giving for 1998 includes: foundation ($512,099)
Assets: $17,900,000 (1999 approx); $17,442,842 (1998); $11,500,000 (1997 approx)
Gifts Received: $100,000 (1999 approx); $1,045,473 (1998); $1,548,088 (1994). Note: In 1998, contributions were received from Cook Inlet Region, KPMG Peat Marwick, South Central Foundation and other miscellaneous contributors.

Typical Recipients

Arts & Humanities: Arts Centers, Ethnic & Folk Arts, Arts & Humanities-General, Historic Preservation, Museums/Galleries, Public Broadcasting
Civic & Public Affairs: Civic & Public Affairs-General, Native American Affairs
Education: Afterschool/Enrichment Programs, Education-General, Minority Education

Contributions Analysis

Education: 100%. Funding interests include internship/job training programs, student financial aid and scholarships, and support of colleges and universities.
Note: Total contributions made in 1998.

Application Procedures

Initial Contact: Send a brief letter of inquiry.
Application Requirements: Include a description of organization, amount requested, purpose of funds sought, recently audited financial statement and proof of tax-exempt status.
Deadlines: March 1, June 1, September 1, and Novermber 1; scholarship deadlines: June 1 and December 1; student education grants: March 31, June 30, September 30, and December 1.

Additional Information

Provides scholarships for Alaska native (Eskimo, Indian, and Aleut) enrollees of Cook Inlet Region and their descendants. Special project grants also are limited to activities affiliated with Alaska natives.
Publications: Guidelines; Application form

Corporate Officials

Craig A. Floerchinger: vice president, chief executive officer PRIM CORP EMPL vice president: Cook Inlet Region Inc. CORP AFFIL treasurer: Construction Machinery Inc.
Carl H. Marrs: president, chief executive officer B 1949. PRIM CORP EMPL president, chief executive officer: Cook Inlet Region Inc.

Foundation Officials

Margaret S. Brown: director
Esther Combs: secretary, treasurer
Britton E. Crosley: director
William D. English: director CORP AFFIL director: Cook Inlet Region Inc.
Craig A. Floerchinger: director (see above)
Sharon Gagnon: director
Bart Garber: director
Dr. Jeff Gonnason: director
Carol Gore: director
Robert Gottstein: director
Lydia L. Hays: executive director
Roy M. Huhndorf: president NONPR AFFIL director: Cook Inlet Tribal Council.
Sharon John: director
Don Karabelnikoff: vice president
Janie Leask: director CORP AFFIL director: Cook Inlet Region Inc.
Carl H. Marrs: director (see above)
John Monfor: president
Edward B. Rasmuson: director B Houston, TX 1940. ED Harvard University BA (1962). PRIM CORP EMPL chairman, director: National Bank of Alaska. CORP AFFIL chairman, director: National Bancorp of AK.

Grants Analysis

Disclosure Period: calendar year ending 1998
Total Grants: $512,099*
Number of Grants: 243
Average Grant: $2,107
Highest Grant: $11,959
Typical Range: $300 to $8,000
***Note:** In 1998, all grants were made to individuals.

Recent Grants

Note: Grants derived from 1993 Form 990.

Civic & Public Affairs

1,000 Motorcycle Mechanics Institute, Anchorage, AK -- vocational training
825 Safety Training Corp, Anchorage, AK -- vocational training

Education

1,000 Kenai Peninsula College, Soldotna, AK -- vocational training

COOPER INDUSTRIES, INC.

Company Contact

Houston, TX
Web: http://www.cooperindustries.com

Company Description

Revenue: US$3,670,000,000 (1999)
Employees: 28,100 (1999)
Fortune Rank: 418, per FORTUNE Magazine's list of 500 Largest U.S. Corporations (1999).
FF 418
SIC(s): 3357 Nonferrous Wiredrawing & Insulating, 3423 Hand & Edge Tools Nec, 3491 Industrial Valves, 3612 Transformers Except Electronic.
Parent Company: INFINT SA, 2 Boulevard Royale, Luxembourg, Luxembourg

Operating Locations

Australia: Cooper Tools Pty. Ltd., Albury; Cameron Australasia Pty. Ltd., Cheltenham, Gloucestershire; Cooper Industries Australia Pty. Ltd., Circular Quay; Crousehinds (Australia) Pty. Ltd., Regents Park; Austria: CEAG Sicherheitstechnik Osterreich GmbH, Linz, Oberosterreich; Belgium: Champion Spark Plug Belgium SA, Binche, Hainaut; Brunei Darussalam: Syarikat Rajah Sdn. Bhd., Kuala Belait; Brazil: Cooper Tools Industrial Ltda., Sorocaba; Canada: Cooper Industries Canada, Mississauga; Costa Rica: Cortek Internacional SA, Alajuela; Denmark: Acrimo Danmark A/S, Risskov, Arhus; France: Cameron France SA, Beziers, Herault; Cooper Automotive France, Paris, Ville-de-Paris; Belden Electronics Sarl, Puteaux, Hauts-de-Seine; Acrimo Stores SA, Vaux le Penil, Seine-et-Marne; Roussel SA, Vaux le Penil, Seine-et-Marne; Germany: Champion Zuendkerzen Deutschland GmbH, Bad Homburg, Hessen; Ireland: Champion Spark Plug Ireland Ltd., Naas; CSP Industries BV, Naas; Italy: Cooper Automotive Filtration SpA, Casarza Ligure, Liguria; Cooper Industries Italia SpA Champion Spark Plug Div., Druento, Piemonte; Mexico: Arrow Hart SA de CV, Ciudad de Mexico; Cooper Automotive de Mexico SA de CV, Ciudad de Mexico; Crousehinds Domex SA de CV, Ciudad de Mexico; Netherlands: Lufkin Europa BV, Emmen, Drenthe; CEAG Benelux BV, Rotterdam, Zuid-Holland; Norway: Acrimo Norge AS, Drobak, Akershus; New Zealand: Champion Spark Plugs NZ Ltd., Auckland; Singapore: Cameron Iron Works (Singapore) Pte. Ltd., Singapore; Spain: CEAG Nortem SA, Tarrasa, Cataluna; Sweden: Sani Sweden AB; Sani Sweden Realty AB; Sanimaskiner AB; Acrimo Sverige AB, Anderstorp, Jonkoping; Acrimo AB, Helsingborg, Malmohus; Emweco AB, Helsingborg, Malmohus; Metallhyttans AB, Helsingborg, Malmohus; Witreco AB, Helsingborg, Malmohus; Taiwan: RTE Far East Corp., Chungli; United Kingdom: B&S Fuses Ltd., Brigend, Mid Glamorgan; Bussmann (United Kingdom) Ltd., Loughborough, Leicestershire; Cooper (United Kingdom) Ltd., Loughborough, Leicestershire; DFL Fusegear Ltd., Workington, Cumbria; Venezuela: Cooper Automotive de Venezuela CA, Los Guayos, Carabobo

Nonmonetary Support

Value: $150,000 (1997 approx); $20,000 (1996); $30,000 (1995)
Type: Donated Equipment; Donated Products; In-kind Services
Note: Nonmonetary support is handled through local contacts.

Corporate Sponsorship

Value: $150,000
Type: Arts & cultural events; Music & entertainment events; Pledge-a-thon
Note: Sponsors arts organization productions.

Cooper Industries Foundation

Giving Contact

Ms. Jennifer L. Evans, Manager, Corporate Giving Programs
Cooper Industries Foundation
PO Box 4446
Houston, TX 77210-4446
Phone: (713)209-8800
Fax: (713)209-8982
Email: evans@cooperindustries.com
Note: Subsidiaries have separate contact persons; call the foundation office for information.

Description

EIN: 316060698
Organization Type: Corporate Foundation
Giving Locations: operating locations.
Grant Types: Capital, Challenge, Emergency, Employee Matching Gifts, General Support, Matching, Multiyear/Continuing Support.
Note: Employee matching gift ratio: 1 to 1; 2 to 1 for volunteer services.

Giving Philosophy

'At Cooper Industries, good citizenship takes many forms. .. The company contributes to the quality of life in communities where we are a significant employer by providing financial support to various nonprofit organizations, and by encouraging Cooper employees to support worthwhile efforts with their own gifts of time and money.' *Cooper Industries Foundation, 1993 Annual Report*

Financial Summary

Total Giving: $3,700,000 (1999 approx); $3,447,363 (1998); $3,799,000 (1997). Note: Contributes through corporate direct giving program and foundation.
Giving Analysis: Giving for 1996 includes: foundation ($1,704,630); foundation grants to United Way ($1,294,675); foundation matching gifts ($318,377); 1997: foundation ($1,676,935); foundation grants to United Way ($1,102,115); foundation matching gifts ($315,180); 1998: foundation ($3,074,276); foundation grants to United Way ($745,216); foundation matching gifts ($373,087)
Assets: $7,100,420 (1998); $10,003,753 (1997); $3,635,202 (1996)
Gifts Received: $1,000 (1998); $9,856,410 (1997); $5,694,750 (1996)

Typical Recipients

Arts & Humanities: Arts Associations & Councils, Arts Funds, Dance, Historic Preservation, Libraries, Museums/Galleries, Music, Opera, Performing Arts, Public Broadcasting, Theater

Civic & Public Affairs: Business/Free Enterprise, Economic Development, Economic Policy, Employment/Job Training, Housing, Law & Justice, Municipalities/Towns, Public Policy, Safety, Urban & Community Affairs, Women's Affairs, Zoos/Aquariums
Education: Arts/Humanities Education, Business Education, Colleges & Universities, Community & Junior Colleges, Economic Education, Education Associations, Education Funds, Engineering/Technological Education, Literacy, Medical Education, Private Education (Precollege), Public Education (Precollege), Science/Mathematics Education, Secondary Education (Public), Student Aid, Vocational & Technical Education
Environment: Environment-General
Health: Cancer, Emergency/Ambulance Services, Health Funds, Health Organizations, Heart, Hospices, Hospitals, Mental Health, Single-Disease Health Associations
International: Health Care/Hospitals, International Affairs
Religion: Religious Welfare
Science: Science Museums, Scientific Centers & Institutes
Social Services: Animal Protection, Child Welfare, Community Centers, Community Service Organizations, Emergency Relief, Food/Clothing Distribution, People with Disabilities, Recreation & Athletics, Senior Services, United Funds/United Ways, YMCA/YWCA/YMHA/YWHA, Youth Organizations

Contributions Analysis

Giving Priorities: Education, United Way, civics, health, social welfare, and cultural funds. International funding activities have taken on increasing importance. Division employee relations managers in the U.S. respond to requests from applicable international company. Domestically, the foundation occasionally makes a grant to an internationally focused organization. In 1994, Cooper expanded its volunteer awards programs to include employes at all of its international locations. In 1996, Cooper recognized 31 volunteers in nine countries, enabling them to direct cash contributions totaling $46,500 to the nonprofit organizations of their choice. In 1995, overseas subsidiaries donated about $100,000.
Arts & Humanities: 18%. Majority of support funds museums, music, opera, and theaters. Other beneficiaries include cultural centers, arts associations, arts funds, and libraries.
Civic & Public Affairs: 6%. Primarily supports civic-improvement, environmental affairs organizations, and public policy research organizations. Other interests include business, international, and women's affairs organizations; zoos; and botanical gardens.
Education: 8%. Primarily supports colleges and universities; also scholarships, education funds and associations, and economic education.
Health: 1%.
Religion: 1%.
Social Services: 66%. Funds United Way and social services.

Application Procedures

Initial Contact: brief letter or proposal
Application Requirements: a description of organization and its mission, amount requested, purpose of funds sought, budget information and funding sources, list of board members, and proof of tax-exempt status
Deadlines: None; budget is set in the fall for the following year
Review Process: review team evaluates requests on an ongoing basis; response within four to six weeks of receipt
Notes: Organizations in communities where Cooper has a plant facility should direct their requests to local facilities.

Restrictions

The following types of organizations normally are not eligible for grants: religious organizations (especially for sectarian purposes), national health and welfare organizations (except through a local united fund drive), fraternal or veterans' organizations, goodwill advertising, political candidates or organizations, labor organizations, and lobbying organizations. The company does not support individuals.

Corporate Officials

D. Bradley McWilliams: chief financial officer, senior vice president financerc B 1941. ED New York University; University of Texas BBA (1966); University of Texas JD (1971). PRIM CORP EMPL chief financial officer, senior vice president finance: Cooper Industries, Inc. CORP AFFIL director: Kronos Data Systems Inc.; director: Kronos Inc.
Phyllis J. Piano: vice president public affairs B Milwaukee, WI 1956. ED University of Wisconsin BA (1977). PRIM CORP EMPL vice president public affairs: Cooper Industries, Inc. CORP AFFIL vice president: Raytheon Co.
H. John Riley, Jr.: chairman, president, chief executive officer, director B Syracuse, NY 1940. ED Syracuse University BS (1961); Harvard University (1985). PRIM CORP EMPL chairman, president, chief executive officer, director: Cooper Industries, Inc. CORP AFFIL director: Wyman-Gordon Co.; director: Baker Hughes Inc.; director: Central Houston Inc. NONPR AFFIL trustee: Manufacturer Alliance Productivity & Innovation.

Giving Program Officials

Jennifer L. Evans: manager, secretary PRIM CORP EMPL manager corporate giving programs: Cooper Industries Inc.

Foundation Officials

D. Bradley McWilliams: vice president (see above)
Phyllis J. Piano: president (see above)
H. John Riley, Jr.: chairman, president, chief executive officer (see above)

Grants Analysis

Disclosure Period: calendar year ending 1998
Total Grants: $3,074,276*
Number of Grants: 269
Average Grant: $10,838*
Highest Grant: $169,656
Typical Range: $5,000 to $15,000
***Note:** Giving excludes matching gifts; United Way. Average grant excludes highest grant.

Recent Grants

Note: Grants derived from 1997 Form 990.

Arts & Humanities

30,000	Museum of Fine Arts, Houston, TX
25,000	Texas Aviation Hall of Fame, Galveston, TX
20,000	Alley Theater, Houston, TX
20,000	Houston Grand Opera, Houston, TX
20,000	Houston Symphony Society, Houston, TX
20,000	Syracuse Symphony Orchestra, Syracuse, NY
20,000	WCNY PBS, Liverpool, NY

Civic & Public Affairs

33,000	Central Houston Civic Improvement, Houston, TX
25,000	Women's Home, Houston, TX
20,000	Star of Hope Mission, Houston, TX
15,000	Friends of the Burnet Park Zoo, Syracuse, NY

Education

30,000	Onondaga Community College, Syracuse, NY
25,000	Western Reserve Academy, Hudson, OH
22,260	National Merit Scholarship Corporation, Evanston, IL
20,000	Burlington Community High School, Burlington, IA
20,000	Piedmont Technical College, Greenwood, SC
20,000	University of Houston, Houston, TX
20,000	University of Texas Houston Health Science Center, Houston, TX
15,000	Hinds Community College, Raymond, MS
15,000	Junior Achievement of Southeast Texas, Houston, TX
15,000	Union County Public Schools, Monroe, NC

Health

20,000	M.D. Anderson Cancer Center, Houston, TX

Science

20,000	Houston Museum of Natural Science and B.B. Planetarium, Houston, TX

Social Services

94,005	United Way of Waukesha County, Waukesha, WI
87,650	United Way of the Texas Gulf Coast, Houston, TX
50,715	United Way of West Central Mississippi, Vicksburg, MS
49,770	United Way of Asheville and Buncombe County, Asheville, NC
43,565	United Way, St. Louis, MO
39,650	Burlington Area United Way, Burlington, IA
36,655	Triangle United Way, Morrisville, NC
36,465	United Way, St. Louis, MO
33,760	United Way of Sumter, Clarendon, and Lee, Sumter, SC
33,360	United Way of Greater LaPorte County, Lafayette, IN
31,565	United Way of Elk Grove Village, Elk Grove Village, IL
31,530	United Way of the Midlands, Columbia, SC
29,925	Triangle United Way, Morrisville, NC
25,705	United Way of Central Carolinas, Charlotte, NC
24,790	United Way of Rowan County, Salisbury, NC
22,015	United Way of Cullman County, Cullman, AL
20,540	United Way of Southeastern Mississippi, Hattiesburg, MS
18,625	United Way, Dayton, OH
18,155	United Way, Palestine, TX
18,080	Metro United Way, Louisville, KY
17,570	United Way, St. Louis, MO
16,630	United Way of Wayne County, Goldsboro, NC
16,580	United Way of Sumler County, Americus, GA
16,340	United Way, Milwaukee, WI
15,590	Sturgis United Fund, Sturgis, MI
15,480	United Way of Northern Shenandoah Valley, Winchester, VA
15,000	YMCA/YWCA, Burlington, IA

Cooper Tire &Rubber Co.

Company Contact

Findlay, OH
Web: http://www.coopertire.com

Company Description

Employees: 8,284
SIC(s): 3011 Tires & Inner Tubes, 3069 Fabricated Rubber Products Nec.

Operating Locations
Includes plant locations.

Nonmonetary Support
Type: Donated Equipment; Donated Products

Corporate Sponsorship
Type: Arts & cultural events
Contact: Patricia Brown, Director of Communications
Note: Sponsors an art festival in Findlay.

Restrictions
Company does not award grants to individuals.

Corporate Officials
Patrick W. Rooney: chairman, president, chief executive officer, director B 1935. ED Harvard University Advanced Management Program; University of Findlay BS. PRIM CORP EMPL chairman, president, chief executive officer, director: Cooper Tire & Rubber Co. CORP AFFIL director: Huffy Corp.
Philip G. Weaver: executive vice president, chief financial officer, trustee PRIM CORP EMPL executive vice president, chief financial officer, trustee: Cooper Tire & Rubber Co.

Foundation Officials
William C. Hattendorf: trustee B Fort Wayne, IN 1934. ED Bowling Green State University BS (1960). PRIM CORP EMPL vice president, treasurer: Cooper Tire & Rubber Co.
Philip G. Weaver: trustee (see above)
Eileen White: trustee

Grants Analysis
Disclosure Period: calendar year ending 1997
Total Grants: $650,354*
Number of Grants: 274 (approx)
Average Grant: $2,190
Highest Grant: $74,000
Typical Range: $100 to $15,000
***Note:** Grants analysis is approximate.

Recent Grants
Note: Grants derived from 1994 Form 990.

Arts & Humanities

22,410	Friends of Eckhart Public Library, Eckhart, IN
6,470	Findlay Area Arts Council, Findlay, OH
6,000	Texarkana Regional Arts and Humanities Council, Texarkana, AR
5,350	Public Broadcasting Foundation of Northwest Ohio, Toledo, OH
3,000	National Automotive and Truck Museum of the US, Auburn, IN
2,650	Hancock Historical Museum Association, Findlay, OH

Civic & Public Affairs

6,668	Findlay/Hancock County Community Foundation, Findlay, OH
5,000	Center for Workforce Preparation and Quality Education, Washington, DC
5,000	Opportunities, Chicago, IL

Education

60,652	University of Findlay, Findlay, OH
20,000	Ohio Foundation of Independent Colleges, Columbus, OH
19,000	University of Akron, Akron, OH
15,400	Bowling Green State University, Bowling Green, OH
13,000	Owens Technical College, Findlay, OH
12,000	St. Joseph College, West Hartford, CT
8,230	University of Toledo, Toledo, OH
8,230	University of Toledo, Toledo, OH
7,000	St. Meinrad College, St. Meinrad, IN
6,800	Miami University, Miami, FL
6,400	University of Notre Dame, South Bend, IN
6,100	Purdue University, West Lafayette, IN
6,000	Bethany College, Lindsborg, KS
6,000	Graceland College, Lamoni, IA
6,000	Marian College, Indianapolis, IN
6,000	Mount Union Nazarene College
6,000	St. Francis College, Fort Wayne, IN
6,000	Southern Nazarene University, Bethany, OK
5,060	St. Wendelin School Education Foundation, Fostoria, OH
4,260	Taylor University, Upland, IN
3,334	University of Missouri Columbia College of Business, Columbia, MO
3,118	Ohio State University, Columbus, OH
3,050	Ashland University, Ashland, OH
3,000	Cedar Crest College, Allentown, PA
2,000	Dekalb Central Junior Achievement
2,000	St. Vincent-St. Mary High School, Akron, OH
1,000	University of Findlay, Findlay, OH
100	Rensselaer Polytechnic Institute, Troy, NY

Health

10,000	Betty Jane Memorial Rehabilitation Center, Tiffin, OH
5,000	Area Health Education Center

Religion

6,000	Winebrenner Theological Seminary, Findlay, OH
2,500	Findlay Area Youth for Christ, Findlay, OH

Social Services

71,000	United Way Hancock County, Findlay, OH
16,185	United Way Greater Texarkana, Texarkana, AR
12,000	United Way Lee County, Fort Myers, FL
8,500	United Way Dekalb County, Auburn, IN
6,000	United Way Greater Toledo, Toledo, OH
5,400	United Way Southwest Georgia, Waycross, GA
5,000	Dekalb County Council on Aging, Dekalb, IN
3,581	Clarksdale United Fund
2,500	United Way Union County, Elizabeth, NJ

Cooper Tire & Rubber Foundation

Giving Contact
James Alec Reinhardt, Trustee
Cooper Tire & Rubber Foundation
Lima & Western Ave.
Findlay, OH 45840
Phone: (419)424-4320
Fax: (419)424-4212

Description
EIN: 237025013
Organization Type: Corporate Foundation
Giving Locations: OH operating locations.
Grant Types: Employee Matching Gifts, General Support.

Financial Summary
Total Giving: $600,000 (1999 approx); $575,000 (1998); $650,354 (1997). Note: Contributes through corporate direct giving program and foundation.
Assets: $783,026 (1997); $727,698 (1995); $664,457 (1994)
Gifts Received: $700,000 (1997); $500,000 (1995); $500,000 (1994)

Typical Recipients
Arts & Humanities: Arts Associations & Councils, Arts & Humanities-General, Libraries, Museums/Galleries, Public Broadcasting
Civic & Public Affairs: Community Foundations, Employment/Job Training, Civic & Public Affairs-General
Education: Business Education, Colleges & Universities, Education Funds, Engineering/Technological Education, Faculty Development, Education-General, Private Education (Precollege), Secondary Education (Private), Vocational & Technical Education
Health: Health-General, Medical Rehabilitation, Public Health
Religion: Religious Welfare, Seminaries
Social Services: Senior Services, Social Services-General, United Funds/United Ways

Contributions Analysis
Arts & Humanities: 10%. Supports arts associations, public broadcasting, and museums.
Civic & Public Affairs: 4%. Supports job training and trade associations.
Education: 55%. Funding supports universities, technical colleges, secondary education, and business education.
Social Services: 31%. Emphasis is on united funds, youth organizations, and senior services.
Note: Total contributions made in 1997.

Application Procedures
Initial Contact: Send a brief letter.
Application Requirements: Include a description of organization, amount requested, purpose of funds sought, recently audited financial statement, and proof of tax-exempt status.
Deadlines: None.

Coors Brewing Co.

Company Contact
Golden, CO
Web: http://www.coors.com

Company Description
Employees: 6,200
SIC(s): 2082 Malt Beverages.

Nonmonetary Support
Type: Donated Equipment; Donated Products; In-kind Services
Note: Contact the company for guidelines on product donations.

Corporate Sponsorship
Type: Arts & cultural events; Festivals/fairs; Music & entertainment events; Sports events
Note: Supports conferences.

Giving Contact
Buck Boze, Corporate Relations Manager
Coors Brewing Co. Corp. Contributions
PO Box 4030
Golden, CO 80401
Phone: (303)277-5953
Fax: (303)277-6132

Alternate Contact
Phone: (303)277-6051

Description
Organization Type: Corporate Giving Program
Giving Locations: CO: Denver; TN: Memphis; VA: Elkton
Grant Types: Conference/Seminar, General Support.

Giving Philosophy

'The groups who have benefited from our philosophy of giving are many. They come from all over America, have members of all races and goals covering a wide range of issues. We have created Coors Corporate Contributions as a resource for these groups and as a method for Coors Brewing Company to: (1) actively address the challenges being faced in our communities, (2) be involved in our communities by supporting grass-roots nonprofit organizations, and (3) support issues that are important to our consumers, our retailers, and our industry.' *Coors Brewing Company Corporate Contributions Program Guidelines*

Financial Summary

Total Giving: $2,200,000 (1997 approx); $2,200,000 (1996 approx); $3,000,000 (1995 approx). Note: Contributes through corporate direct giving program only. Giving includes domestic subsidiaries.

Typical Recipients

Arts & Humanities: Arts Associations & Councils, Arts Centers, Community Arts, Dance, Ethnic & Folk Arts, Historic Preservation, Museums/Galleries, Music, Opera, Performing Arts, Public Broadcasting, Theater
Civic & Public Affairs: African American Affairs, Botanical Gardens/Parks, Business/Free Enterprise, Chambers of Commerce, Civil Rights, Economic Policy, Hispanic Affairs, Native American Affairs, Nonprofit Management, Urban & Community Affairs, Women's Affairs
Education: Business Education, Colleges & Universities, Community & Junior Colleges, Economic Education, Literacy, Minority Education, Public Education (Precollege), Science/Mathematics Education
Environment: Environment-General
Health: AIDS/HIV, Emergency/Ambulance Services, Health Funds, Health Organizations, Hospices, Hospitals, Medical Rehabilitation, Mental Health, Respiratory, Single-Disease Health Associations
Religion: Dioceses, Jewish Causes
Social Services: Domestic Violence, Emergency Relief, People with Disabilities, Recreation & Athletics, Senior Services, Shelters/Homelessness, Substance Abuse, Volunteer Services

Contributions Analysis

Giving Priorities: Women's groups, minority groups, social services, health, education, environmental and issues regarding alcohol.

Application Procedures

Initial Contact: written request
Application Requirements: include name, address, telephone number, and contact person of organization; brief a description of organization including its history, goals, and purposes; details on funding request; proof of tax-exempt status; information on opportunities for visibility for Coors Brewing Company
Deadlines: None; allow a minimum of two months for processing application
Review Process: review process takes about two months; notification will be made in writing
Decision Notification: requests are reviewed the first Wednesday of every month except December; requests will be held over until January
Notes: Faxed proposals are accepted. Prefers only to receive one proposal per year from an organization, though it may contain multiple requests.

Restrictions

Grants are generally not made to individuals in personal programs; individual scholarships; teams, groups, races or 'athons'; travel expenses; political activities; or requests by phone.

Additional Information

Company reports they are currently restructuring their giving program--possible time of completion is October 2000.

Coors prefers to evaluate each proposal on its own merits and has not established fixed charitable categories for corporate donations.
Coors Speakers Bureau is designed to serve Denver and its suburbs. Out-of-town requests will be considered on the basis of location, group size, type of function, and availability of speakers. Reimbursement for travel expenses will be accepted.
Company prefers to give small amounts of money to a large number of organizations. All donations granted on a one-time basis with no implied renewals.
Coors distributorships are mostly independently owned and administer their own giving programs. Distributors of Coors products are encouraged to be actively involved with community organizations and events scheduled within their respective market areas.
Publications: Annual Report; Contributions Program Guidelines

Corporate Officials

Peter Hanson Coors: vice president, director B Denver, CO 1946. ED Cornell University BS (1969); University of Denver MBA (1970). PRIM CORP EMPL vice president, director: Adolph Coors Co. CORP AFFIL officer: United States Bancorp; director: Coors Distribution Co.; director: Energy Corp. America; vice chairman, chief executive officer: Coors Brewing Co. NONPR AFFIL director: Wildlife Legislative Fund; member: Young President Organization; honorary director: Special Olympics Colorado; director: Up With People; trustee: Presidents Leadership Committee, University Colorado; trustee: Seeds of Hope Foundation; member: Opportunities Centers America; trustee: Outward Bound Colorado; chairman devel committee, trustee: National Commission Future Regis College; member: National Individuals Advancement Council; member executive committee: Ducks Unlimited Inc. CLUB AFFIL Metro Denver Executives Club.
William K. Coors: chairman, president, director B Golden, CO 1916. ED Princeton University BSChE (1938); Princeton University MSChE (1939). PRIM CORP EMPL chairman, president, chief executive officer, director: Adolph Coors Co.
W. Leo Kiely, III: president, chief operating officer B 1947. ED Harvard University; University of Pennsylvania. PRIM CORP EMPL president, chief operating officer: Coors Brewing Co. ADD CORP EMPL vice president: Adolph Coors Co.; director: Bell Sports Corp. CORP AFFIL director: Signature Resorts Inc.; director: Bell Sports Inc.; chairman: Coors Distribution Co. NONPR AFFIL director: National Association Manufacturers; member: Wharton School Finance.

Giving Program Officials

John Meadows: vice president, director corporate relations PRIM CORP EMPL vice president, director corporate relations: Coors Brewing Co.
Celia Sheneman: manager corporate relations PRIM CORP EMPL national program manager: Coors Brewing Co.

Foundation Officials

Buck Boze: corporate relations manager

Grants Analysis

Disclosure Period: calendar year ending
Typical Range: $100 to $5,000

Recent Grants

Note: Grants derived from 1992 Annual Report.

Arts & Humanities
Dance Theater of Harlem, New York, NY
Denver Museum of Miniatures, Dolls, and Toys, Denver, CO
Denver Public Library Friends Foundation, Denver, CO

Civic & Public Affairs
Dallas Hispanic Chamber of Commerce Foundation, Dallas, TX
Denver Botanical Gardens, Denver, CO
Denver Housing Authority, Denver, CO

Education
Junior Achievement
Literacy Council of Chicago, Chicago, IL
NAACP, New York, NY
University of Denver, Denver, CO
University of Maryland, University Park, MD

Health
AIDS Library of Philadelphia, Philadelphia, PA
AIDS Research
American Lung Association
Colorado AIDS Project, CO
Denver Alliance for the Mentally Ill, Denver, CO

Religion
Archdiocese of Denver, Denver, CO
Salvation Army

Social Services
DC Cares, Washington, DC
Denver Association of Family Child Care, Denver, CO

Copley Press, Inc.

Company Contact

La Jolla, CA

Company Description

Employees: 3,000
SIC(s): 2711 Newspapers.

Corporate Sponsorship

Contact: Ms. Shari Griffin, Contact
Note: Sponsorships are offered through the company, not the foundation, and are handled differently from location to location.

James S. Copley Foundation

Giving Contact

Ms. Anita A. Baumgardner, Secretary & Trustee
James S. Copley Foundation
7776 Ivanhoe Ave.
PO Box 1530
La Jolla, CA 92038-1530
Phone: (858)454-0411

Description

EIN: 956051770
Organization Type: Corporate Foundation
Giving Locations: in immediate circulation areas only.
Grant Types: Capital, Employee Matching Gifts, Endowment, Multiyear/Continuing Support, Scholarship.
Note: Employee matching gift ratio: 1 to 1 for gifts to education institutions, up to $1,000 annually.

Giving Philosophy

'The James S. Copley Foundation, funded solely by The Copley Press, Inc., supports responsible and creative charitable and civic organizations within the immediate circulation areas of the Copley newspapers.'
'Grants will usually fall within these broad areas of concern: education, culture and the arts, medical and health, youth development, human services and urban/civic affairs. The Foundation does not encourage proposals dealing with general operating expenses, budgetary support, 'seed' money and unrestricted purposes.' *Copley Newspapers Program Policies, Guidelines, and Procedures*

Financial Summary

Total Giving: $2,000,000 (2000 approx); $2,000,000 (1999); $2,287,340 (1998). Note: Contributes through corporate direct giving program and foundation.
Giving Analysis: Giving for 1996 includes: foundation ($1,815,076); foundation matching gifts ($44,142); 1997: foundation ($1,107,895); foundation grants to United Way ($364,250); foundation matching gifts ($52,825)
Assets: $25,000,000 (1999 approx); $25,747,501 (1998); $29,877,696 (1997)
Gifts Received: $16,453 (1997); $20,657 (1996); $13,857 (1995). Note: Foundation receives contributions from the San Diego Union Shoe Fund.

Typical Recipients

Arts & Humanities: Arts Centers, Dance, Ethnic & Folk Arts, Arts & Humanities-General, Libraries, Literary Arts, Museums/Galleries, Music, Opera, Performing Arts, Public Broadcasting, Theater, Visual Arts
Civic & Public Affairs: Community Foundations, Civic & Public Affairs-General, Law & Justice, Professional & Trade Associations, Public Policy, Urban & Community Affairs, Zoos/Aquariums
Education: Arts/Humanities Education, Colleges & Universities, Education Funds, Literacy, Medical Education, Private Education (Precollege), Secondary Education (Private), Student Aid
Environment: Resource Conservation
Health: AIDS/HIV, Alzheimers Disease, Children's Health/Hospitals, Clinics/Medical Centers, Hospices, Hospitals, Mental Health, Preventive Medicine/Wellness Organizations, Public Health, Research/Studies Institutes, Single-Disease Health Associations
International: Foreign Educational Institutions, International Organizations
Religion: Dioceses, Religious Welfare
Social Services: Animal Protection, Child Abuse, Child Welfare, Community Centers, Community Service Organizations, Food/Clothing Distribution, Homes, People with Disabilities, Recreation & Athletics, Senior Services, Shelters/Homelessness, Substance Abuse, United Funds/United Ways, YMCA/YWCA/YMHA/YWHA, Youth Organizations

Contributions Analysis

Giving Priorities: Social service, the arts, education, civics, and health.
Arts & Humanities: About 30%. Support goes to San Diego area arts organizations such as the symphony, opera, and museum of art. The remainder, in grants generally less than $5,000, supports arts funds and festivals, historical societies, theaters, and dance.
Education: 10% to 15%. Funds colleges and universities, private precollege education, scholarship programs, and education associations; supports journalism education and literacy. Also gives matching gifts.
Health: 10% to 15%. Funds hospitals and hospices. Occasionally gives to single-disease health associations.
Social Services: 45% to 50%. Primarily to united funds and youth organizations. Also funds recreation, senior programs, assistance for the disadvantaged and various community service organizations. Supports religious organizations that help the disadvantaged.

Application Procedures

Initial Contact: Submit letter.
Application Requirements: Include name of organization, address, telephone number, and name of contact person; statement of purpose and objectives, succinct summary of project, target population and geographic area to be served; anticipated cost of project, amount of request, how funds will be spent, sources of financial support (committed and pending), and plan for sustaining project after the initial funding; list of board of directors and staff; current financial report; and proof of tax-exempt status.
Deadlines: January 1.
Review Process: The board meets sometime in the spring to review requests; usually responds within 30 days.
Notes: The foundation does not accept faxed applications or videotapes.

Restrictions

Foundation does not make grants to individuals, fundraising events, goodwill advertising, or political or lobbying groups. Grants generally are not made for unrestricted purposes, budgetary support, operating expenses, or seed money.
Grants generally are not made to organizations receiving support from United Way; loans; general fund drives or annual appeals; debt retirement or operational deficits; state universities and colleges; grantmaking organizations; national organizations; public elementary and secondary schools; organizations whose activities are mainly international; research projects; government and public agencies; religious, fraternal, or athletic organizations; conferences or seminars; organisation for distribution to beneficiaries of their own choosing; or for production costs of films, videos, television programs, or books.
Scholarship funds are only contributed to colleges and universities for distribution, not to individuals.

Additional Information

Foundation does not grant interviews.
Contributions are made for one year and imply no commitment to repeat donations.
Publications: Giving Guidelines

Corporate Officials

David C. Copley: president, chief executive officer, director, senior management board B 1952. ED Menlo College BSBA. PRIM CORP EMPL president, chief executive officer, director, senior management board: Copley Press, Inc. ADD CORP EMPL publ: Borrego Sun; president: Copley Northwest Inc.; president: Copley News Service; president: Puller Paper Co. CORP AFFIL member editorial Bd: San Diego Union-Tribune; officer: Peoria Journal Star Inc.; chairman, chief executive officer: Fox Valley Press Inc. NONPR AFFIL president: University San Diego President Club; member president associates: Zoological Society San Diego; member: U.S. Humane Society; director: San Diego Museum Art; member president council: Scripps Clinic & Research Foundation; member president council: San Diego Kind Corp.; member: San Diego Hall Science; member: San Diego Historical Society; trustee: San Diego Crew Classic Foundation; member: San Diego Aerospace Museum; member advisory board: San Diego Automotive Museum; member: National Newspaper Association; director: Saint Vincent de Paul Society; trustee emeritus: Museum Photog Arts; member: FOCAS; trustee emeritus: La Jolla Playhouse; trustee: Canterbury School; trustee emeritus: American Craft Council. CLUB AFFIL Bachelor San Diego Club.
Helen K. Copley: chairman, director, senior management board B Cedar Rapids, IA 1922. ED Hunter College (1945). PRIM CORP EMPL chairman, director, senior management board: Copley Press, Inc. ADD CORP EMPL publ: San Diego Union-Tribune. CORP AFFIL officer: Peoria Journal Star Inc.; chairman, editorial board: Union Tribune Publishing Co.; director: Fox Valley Press Inc.; chairman: Copley News Service. NONPR AFFIL honorary chairman: Washington Crossing Foundation; member: YWCA; life member: Scripps Memorial Hospital Auxiliary; life member: Star of India Auxiliary; member: San Diego Symphony Association; life member: San Diego Zoological Society; member: San Diego Society Natural History; life member: San Diego Hall Science; life member: San Diego Opera Association; honorary chairman: San Diego Council Literacy; life patroness: Makua Auxiliary; member: Newspaper Association America; member: La Jolla Town Council; member: Inter-American Press Association; life member: La Jolla Museum Contemp Art; member: California Press Institute; life member: Friends of International Center; member: California Newspaper Publishers Association; member: California Press Association; member: American Press Institute. CLUB AFFIL San Francisco Press Club; LA Press Club.
Dean P. Dwyer: vice president finance, treasurer, senior management board PRIM CORP EMPL vice president finance, treasurer, senior management board: Copley Press, Inc. CORP AFFIL treasurer, director: Fox Valley Press Inc.; assistant secretary: Peoria Journal Star Inc.
Charles F. Patrick: executive vice president, chief operating officer, senior management board PRIM CORP EMPL executive vice president, chief operating officer, senior management board: Copley Press, Inc.

Foundation Officials

Anita A. Baumgardner: secretary, trustee
David C. Copley: president, trustee (see above)
Helen K. Copley: chairman, trustee (see above)
Robert F. Crouch: vice president, trustee CORP AFFIL officer: Fox Valley Press Inc.
Alex De Bakcsy: vice president, trustee CORP AFFIL director: Copley Press Inc.
Charles F. Patrick: treasurer, trustee (see above)
Karl ZoBell: vice president, trustee B La Jolla, CA 1932. ED Utah State University (1949-1951); Columbia University (1951-1952); Columbia University AB (1953); Stanford University JD (1958). PRIM CORP EMPL partner: Gray, Cary, Ames & Frye. CORP AFFIL director, founder: La Jolla Bank & Trust Co.; vice president, director: Geisel-Seuss Enterprises Inc. NONPR AFFIL trustee: Dr Seuss Foundation; member: Lambda Alpha; director: James C Copley Charitable Foundation; fellow: American College Trust & Estate Counsel; member: California Bar Association; member: American Bar Association. CLUB AFFIL La Jolla Beach & Tennis Club.

Grants Analysis

Disclosure Period: calendar year ending 1998
Total Grants: $2,230,144*
Average Grant: $6,554 (approx)
Highest Grant: $250,000
Typical Range: $100 to $10,000
***Note:** Giving excludes matching gifts. Grants analysis is provided by the foundation.

Recent Grants

Note: Grants derived from 1997 Form 990.

Arts & Humanities

125,000	La Jolla Playhouse, La Jolla, CA
100,000	KPBS Public Broadcasting, San Diego, CA
100,000	Museum of Photographic Arts, San Diego, CA
50,000	San Diego Opera, San Diego, CA
10,000	Border Voices Poetry Project
5,000	La Jolla Chamber Music Society, La Jolla, CA
3,000	Malashock Dance Company, San Diego, CA
3,000	San Diego Museum of Man, San Diego, CA
2,500	North Coast Repertory Theater, Solana Beach, CA
2,500	San Diego Repertory Theater, San Diego, CA

Civic & Public Affairs

25,000	Zoological Society, San Diego, CA
10,000	Committee to Protect Journalism, New York, NY
5,000	San Diego Organizing Project, San Diego, CA
3,500	Aurora Foundation, Aurora, IL

Education

16,000	Independent Colleges of Southern California, Los Angeles, CA

11,000	Bishop's School, La Jolla, CA
4,050	University of San Diego, San Diego, CA
3,250	Inter-American Press Association Scholarship Fund
3,195	San Diego State University, San Diego, CA
3,000	Reading Literacy Learning
2,500	Bradley University, Peoria, IL
2,500	California State University, San Marcos, CA
2,000	Menlo College, Atherton, CA
Environment	
50,000	Will County Audubon Society
Health	
100,000	Scripps Foundation for Medicine
30,000	Children's Hospital Foundation, Seattle, WA
30,000	Hospice, San Diego, CA
16,667	Silver Cross Hospital Foundation
10,000	San Diego Grantmakers AIDS Collaboration, San Diego, CA
7,000	North County Health Services
5,000	Palomar Pomerado Health Foundation, Escondido, CA
5,000	Wellness Community, San Diego, CA
3,000	Alzheimer's Family Centers, Margate, FL
3,000	San Diego Parkinson Corporation, San Diego, CA
2,500	Health Reach Clinic
Religion	
100,000	Diocese of San Diego, San Diego, CA
60,000	St. Vincent de Paul Village
Social Services	
364,250	United Way
30,626	San Diego Union Tribune Shoe Fund, San Diego, CA
20,000	Noah Homes, Spring Valley, CA
15,000	San Diego Crew Classic, San Diego, CA
15,000	YMCA Copley Family
7,500	Senior Adult Services, San Diego, CA
6,000	Help Them to Hope
5,000	Hugh O'Brian Youth Foundation, Wichita, KS
5,000	Senior Community Centers, San Diego, CA
5,000	YMCA of San Diego County, San Diego, CA
2,500	Daybreak Shelter Services
2,500	Guardian Angel Home
2,500	YMCA, Naperville, IL

CORNING INC.

Company Contact

Corning, NY
Web: http://www.corning.com

Company Description

Revenue: US$3,578,000,000
Employees: 20,000
Fortune Rank: 334, per FORTUNE Magazine's list of 500 Largest U.S. Corporations (1999).
FF 334
SIC(s): 3229 Pressed & Blown Glass Nec, 3661 Telephone & Telegraph Apparatus, 3821 Laboratory Apparatus & Furniture, 3826 Analytical Instruments.

Nonmonetary Support

Type: Loaned Executives
Note: Co. provides nonmonetary support.

Corning Inc. Foundation

Giving Contact

Kristin A. Swain, President
Corning Inc. Foundation
MP, LB-02
Corning, NY 14831
Phone: (607)974-8746
Fax: (607)974-4756

Alternate Contact

Karen C. Martin, Program Officer
Phone: (607)974-8489

Description

EIN: 166051394
Organization Type: Corporate Foundation
Giving Locations: headquarters and operating communities and nationally; internationally to U.S.-based organizations.
Grant Types: Employee Matching Gifts, Fellowship, Project.
Note: Employee matching gift ratio: 1 to 1 up to $5,000 per employee annually; institutions may receive up to $20,000 in matched payments per calendar year.

Giving Philosophy

'The Corning Foundation, established in 1952, focuses on projects which enhance the quality of life in communities where Corning and its wholly-owned subsidiaries have operations. The Foundation prefers to fund seed projects which can attract other sources of support and which promise to benefit the most persons over the longest period of time.'
'Nationally, emphasis is on higher education. Limited support is given to cultural organizations and to those concerned with social and economic problems.' *Corning Foundation Grant Application Procedures*

Financial Summary

Total Giving: $3,024,527 (1998); $3,501,987 (1997); $2,931,616 (1996). Note: Contributes through corporate direct giving program and foundation.
Giving Analysis: Giving for 1996 includes: foundation ($2,011,408); foundation matching gifts ($920,208); 1997: foundation ($2,137,283); foundation matching gifts ($896,304); foundation grants to United Way ($468,400); 1998: foundation ($1,698,105); foundation matching gifts ($873,222); foundation grants to United Way ($453,200)
Assets: $7,229,109 (1998); $7,317,226 (1997); $3,437,043 (1996)
Gifts Received: $6,663,000 (1997); $3,367,707 (1996); $2,956,148 (1995)

Typical Recipients

Arts & Humanities: Arts Associations & Councils, Arts Outreach, Community Arts, Historic Preservation, Libraries, Museums/Galleries, Music, Performing Arts, Public Broadcasting, Theater, Visual Arts
Civic & Public Affairs: Community Foundations, Economic Development, Employment/Job Training, Municipalities/Towns, Professional & Trade Associations, Public Policy, Urban & Community Affairs, Women's Affairs
Education: Afterschool/Enrichment Programs, Business Education, Business-School Partnerships, Colleges & Universities, Community & Junior Colleges, Education Associations, Education Reform, Engineering/Technological Education, Environmental Education, Faculty Development, Minority Education, Public Education (Precollege), Science/Mathematics Education, Student Aid
Environment: Environment-General, Resource Conservation
Health: Clinics/Medical Centers, Emergency/Ambulance Services, Hospices, Hospitals (University Affiliated)
International: Foreign Educational Institutions
Religion: Jewish Causes
Science: Science Museums, Scientific Centers & Institutes, Scientific Organizations
Social Services: At-Risk Youth, Big Brother/Big Sister, Community Centers, Community Service Organizations, Family Planning, Recreation & Athletics, Scouts, Senior Services, United Funds/United Ways, YMCA/YWCA/YMHA/YWHA, Youth Organizations

Contributions Analysis

Giving Priorities: Education, human services, the arts, and civics. Recipients include colleges and universities, private elementary and secondary schools, public schools, hospitals, nursing homes, hospice programs, performing and visual arts, museusm, libraries, public radio and television, historical societies, nature centers, zoos and botanical gardens, Supports cultural, community, and civic events or organizations. Emphasis is on cultural programs that support the preservation of art, art museums, libraries, performing arts, opera, and art workshops. Usually supports the large cultural organizations. Community and civic issues funding includes natural disaster relief, emergency relief, Boys & Girls Club of America, Partnership for a Drug-Free America, and international organizations that directly benefit the US. Supports U.S.-based organizations with an international focus. Interests include international business education, community development in the Third World, and foreign policy and international relations. Contributions in this area are less than $50,000 annually.
Arts & Humanities: About 60%. Gives to community service, cultural organizations, and education. Support to cultural organizations includes art education, arts organizations, libraries, museums, and public broadcasting. Educational funds go to selected elementary and secondary schools, community colleges, and four-year institutions. Support includes scholarships, pre-college residencies in science and engineering, career awareness programs, scientific lectures and equipment acquisitions. Community service support goes to hospitals, hospices, United Way, literacy councils, community parks, youth and women's centers, YMCA and Girl Scouts and Boy Scouts of America.About 30%. Recipients include colleges and universities, private elmentary and secondary schools, public schools, hospitals, nursing homes, hospice programs, performing and visual arts, museums, libraries, public radio and television, historical societies, nature centers, zoos and botanical gardens. Supports cultural, community, and civic events or organizations. Emphasis is on cultural programs that support the preservation of art, art museums, libraries, performing arts, opera, and art workshops. Usually supports the larger cultural organizations. Community and civic issues funding includes natural disaster relief, emergency relief, Boys & Girls Clubof America, Partnership for a Drug-Free America, and international organizations that directly benefit the US.
Education: 49%. Program supports the engineering grants-in-aid project, which provides assistance to women and other minority students enrolled at selected colleges of engineering. Also supports engineering education and career development projects, predoctoral science fellowships and special projects, with emphasis on the physical sciences.
Note: Overall, the foundation's giving is divided: 50% to 55% toeducation; 25% to cultural programs; 10% to community programs; 10% to 15% to the United Way; and 2% to civic programs.

Application Procedures

Initial Contact: Send a two- to three-page letter of inquiry signed by the senior administrative officer of the organization.
Application Requirements: Send a full proposal; project description, including project's purpose, details on how its objectives are to be attained and evaluated, demonstration of how project promotes cooperation among other organizations in the same field, timetable, amount sought and when funds are needed, itemized project budget, other potential and

secured sources of support, how the project fits foundation interests; a description of organization, list of officers and board members, proof of tax-exempt status, a long-range plan for generating other funding and attaining self-sufficiency, and organization's budget and copy of the organization's latest audited financial statement.
Deadlines: None.
Decision Notification: Written responses usually follow within four weeks of receipt of inquiries; if interested, foundation will ask for a full proposal; board meets in March, June, September, and November.

Restrictions

Grants are not made to individuals; political parties, campaigns, or causes; labor or veterans' organizations; religious groups; fraternal orders; for fundraising events; athletic activities; to volunteer emergency squads; or for goodwill advertising.

Additional Information

Publications: Guidelines; Foundation Annual Report

Corporate Officials

Chesleu Peter Washburn Booth: senior vice president development B Huntington, NY 1939. ED Harvard University BA (1961); Harvard University JD (1965). PRIM CORP EMPL senior vice president development: Corning Inc. CORP AFFIL director: Samcor Glass Ltd.; director: Samsung Corning Co. Inc.; director: Corning International Corp.; chairman: Biosym Technologies Inc. CLUB AFFIL University Club.
Van C. Campbell: vice chairman, chief financial officer, chief administrative officer, director B Charleston, WV 1938. ED Cornell University BA (1960); Harvard University MBA (1963). PRIM CORP EMPL vice chairman, chief financial officer, chief administrative officer, director: Corning Inc. CORP AFFIL director: Quest Diagnostics Inc.; director: Pittsburgh Corning Corp.; director: Dow Corning Corp.; director: General Signal Corp.; director: Corning International Corp.; director: Corning Laboratory Services Inc.; director: Armstrong World Industries Inc.; director: Chase Lincoln First Bank NA. NONPR AFFIL trustee: Corning Glass Works Foundation.
James B. Flaws: senior vice president, chief financial officer, treasurer B 1948. ED Tufts University BS (1971); Dartmouth College MBA (1973). PRIM CORP EMPL senior vice president, chief financial officer, treasurer: Corning Inc.
Norman E. Garrity: executive vice president, director B Homestead, PA 1941. ED Bucknell University AB (1962); Bucknell University MS (1963). PRIM CORP EMPL executive vice president, director: Corning Inc. ADD CORP EMPL president: Corning Technologies. CORP AFFIL director: Dow Corning Corp.
James Richardson Houghton: director B Corning, NY 1936. ED Harvard University AB (1958); Harvard University MBA (1962). PRIM CORP EMPL director: Corning Inc. CORP AFFIL director: JP Morgan & Co. Inc.; director: Harvard Corp.; director: Metropolitan Life Insurance Co.; director: ExxonMobil Corp. NONPR AFFIL trustee: Metropolitan Museum Art; member business council: Trilateral Commission; trustee: Corning Museum Glass. CLUB AFFIL University Club; Rolling Rock Club; Tarratine Club; Laurel Valley Golf Club; River Club; Corning Country Club; Harvard Club; Augusta National Golf Club; Brookline Country Club.
E. Marie McKee: senior vice president B Columbus, IN 1951. ED Purdue University BA (1973); Purdue University MBA (1976). PRIM CORP EMPL senior vice president: Corning Inc. ADD CORP EMPL president: Corning Museum Glass; chairman: Steuben Glass. CORP AFFIL director: Carolina Power Co.
Arthur John Peck, Jr.: secretary, vice president B Trenton, NJ 1940. ED Yale University BA (1962); Washington & Lee University LLB (1968). PRIM CORP EMPL secretary, vice president: Corning Inc. CORP AFFIL director: Wisland SA; assistant secretary: Market Street Restoration Corp.; secretary: Teddington Co. Ltd.; secretary, director: Corning Inc. Foreign Sales Corp.; secretary: Corning International Corp. NONPR AFFIL director: Guthrie Healthcare Sys.; trustee, secretary: Rockwell Museum; assistant secretary, director: Corning Museum Glass; secretary, director: Corning Classic Charities Inc.

Foundation Officials

Roger G. Ackerman: trustee B Paterson, NJ 1938. ED Rutgers University BS (1960); Rutgers University MS (1962). CORP AFFIL director: Pittsburgh Corning Corp.; director: Pittston Co.; director: Dow Corning Corp.; director: Massachusetts Mutual Life Insurance Co.; director: Corning International Corp. NONPR AFFIL trustee: Corning Museum Glass; member executive committee: National Association Manufacturer.
Chesleu Peter Washburn Booth: trustee (see above)
Lindsay W. Brown: treasurer PRIM NONPR EMPL assistant treasurer, director: Corning Museum of Glass.
Thomas Scharman Buechner: trustee B New York, NY 1926. ED Princeton University (1945); Ecole des Beaux Arts (1946); Institut voor Pictologie (1947); University of Paris (1947). PRIM CORP EMPL counsel: Corning Glass Works. NONPR AFFIL trustee: Rockwell Museum; trustee: Tiffany Foundation; trustee: Pilchuck School; trustee: Corning Museum Glass; member: National Collection Fine Arts; member: Brooklyn Institute Arts & Science; member: Century Association; trustee: Arnot Art Museum Arts Southern Finger Lakes; member faculty art school: Bild-Werk Fravenau Germany.
Van C. Campbell: trustee (see above)
James B. Flaws: trustee (see above)
Norman E. Garrity: trustee (see above)
M. Ann Gosnell: assistant secretary PRIM CORP EMPL assistant secretary, director: Corning International Corp. CORP AFFIL assistant secretary, director: Corning Enterprises Inc.
James Richardson Houghton: trustee (see above)
John W. Loose: trustee B Hartford, CT 1942. ED Earlham College BA (1964). PRIM CORP EMPL president: Corning Communications; director: Corning Inc. ADD CORP EMPL chairman board: Siecor Corp. CORP AFFIL director: Polaroid Corp.
Karen C. Martin: program officer
E. Marie McKee: chairman, trustee (see above)
Arthur John Peck, Jr.: secretary (see above)
Richard E. Rahill: trustee B 1934. PRIM CORP EMPL president, director: Corning Enterprises Inc.
Kristin A. Swain: president
William Casper Ughetta: trustee B New York, NY 1933. ED Princeton University AB (1954); Harvard University LLB (1959). CORP AFFIL director: Covance Inc.; director: Siecor Corp.; director: Chemung Canal Trust Co.; director: Corning International Corp. NONPR AFFIL officer: Corning Museum Glass; member: New York State Bar Association; director: Boy Scouts America; officer: Corning Glass Works Foundation; member: American Corporate Counsel Association; member: Association Bar New York City; member: American Bar Association. CLUB AFFIL Princeton Club; University Club; Corning Country Club.

Grants Analysis

Disclosure Period: calendar year ending 1998
Total Grants: $1,598,105*
Number of Grants: 150 (approx)
Average Grant: $9,320*
Highest Grant: $300,000
Typical Range: $1,000 to $15,000
***Note:** Giving excludes matching gifts; United Way. Average grant excludes highest grant.

Recent Grants

Note: Grants derived from 1998 Form 990.

Arts & Humanities

200,000 Chemung County Performing Arts, Elmira, NY -- Renovation/Expansion Project
125,000 Chemung Valley Arts Council, Corning, NY -- Regional cultural plan
30,000 Metropolitan Museum of Art, New York, NY -- General program support
26,000 One Seventy One Cedar, Corning, NY -- Performing and visual arts
25,000 National Warplane Museum of Geneseo, Horseheads, NY -- Exhibition
20,000 Corning-Elmira Musical Arts, Corning, NY -- Concert Series
15,000 Chemung County Performing Arts, Elmira, NY -- General program support
13,000 WSKG Public Telecommunications Council, Binghamton, NY -- Program underwriting
10,000 Corning-Painted Post Civic Music Association, Corning, NY -- Concert series
10,000 The Lyric Council, Blacksburg, VA -- Lyric Theatre

Civic & Public Affairs

20,500 Community Career Development Council, Corning, NY -- Career awareness education
18,000 American Enterprise Institute for Public Policy Research, Washington, DC -- General program support
16,000 Public Policy Institute of New York State, Albany, NY -- General program support
10,000 City of Harrodsburg, Harrodsburg, KY -- Recreation complex
10,000 Women's Center of the Southern Tier, Corning, NY -- General program support

Education

200,000 Harvard University, Cambridge, MA -- Fund for Faculty Development
50,000 The Rutgers University Foundation, New Brunswick, NJ -- Chair in Ceramic Engineering
48,000 Corning City School District, Painted Post, NY
30,000 Corning City School District, Painted Post, NY -- Computerization
26,526 Stanford University, Stanford, CA
25,000 Cornell University, Ithaca, NY
25,000 Corning Community College, Corning, NY -- Palomar prototype telescope refurbishment
25,000 The Rutgers University Foundation, New Brunswick, NJ -- Ceramics/Fiber Optics Program
24,571 New York State College of Ceramics at Alfred University, Alfred, NY
24,477 The Rutgers University Foundation, New Brunswick, NJ
23,750 Massachusetts Institute of Technology, Cambridge, MA
23,621 University of California, Santa Barbara, CA
15,000 Alfred University, Alfred, NY -- Frechette Professorship in Ceramic Science
15,000 The North Carolina A & T University Foundation, Greensboro, NC
15,000 The Pennsylvania State University, University Park, PA
15,000 Rensselaer Polytechnic Institute, Troy, NY -- Multidisciplinary Design Laboratory
15,000 Rensselaer Polytechnic Institute, Troy, NY
15,000 Syracuse University, Syracuse, NY
15,000 Virginia Polytechnic Institute and State University, Blacksburg, VA
11,550 Mon Valley Education Consortium, McKeesport, PA -- Scholarship program

10,000	St. Lawrence University, Canton, NY -- Economic development

Health

120,000	Arnot Ogden Medical Center Foundation, Elmira, NY -- Renovation/expansion project
10,000	Lower Cape Fear Hospice, Wilmington, NC -- Hospice Care Center

Science

150,000	Regional Science and Discovery Center, Corning, NY -- Educational outreach and expansion project

Social Services

300,000	United Way of the Southern Tier, Corning, NY
100,000	YMCA, Corning, NY -- Renovation/ expansion project
31,000	Cape Fear Area United Way, Wilmington, NC
23,000	Centre County United Way, State College, PA
23,000	United Way of Mon Valley, Monessen, PA
18,000	Berkeley County Committee on Aging, Martinsburg, WV -- Senior center
14,500	United Way of Berkeley and Morgan Counties, WVA, Martinsburg, WV
11,000	DeWitt County United Fund, Clinton, IL
10,000	Boy Scouts of America, Wilmington, NC -- Camp development
10,000	YMCA, State College, PA -- Expansion project

Country Curtains, Inc.

Company Contact

Lee, MA

Company Description

Employees: 137
SIC(s): 2299 Textile Goods Nec.

High Meadow Foundation

Giving Contact

Tamara Stevens, Administrator
High Meadow Foundation
PO Box 955
Stockbridge, MA 01262
Phone: (413)243-1474
Fax: (413)243-1067

Description

EIN: 222527419
Organization Type: Corporate Foundation
Giving Locations: MA: Berkshire County, MA
Grant Types: Capital, General Support.

Financial Summary

Total Giving: $1,319,791 (fiscal year ending September 30, 1998); $1,717,323 (fiscal 1996); $1,238,138 (fiscal 1995). Note: Contributes through foundation only.
Giving Analysis: Giving for fiscal 1996 includes: foundation ($1,567,623); foundation scholarships ($112,500); foundation grants to United Way ($37,200)
Assets: $1,948,279 (fiscal 1998); $1,336,424 (fiscal 1996); $912,555 (fiscal 1993)
Gifts Received: $1,477,125 (fiscal 1998); $1,746,140 (fiscal 1996); $673,296 (fiscal 1991). Note: In 1998, contributions were received from Country Curtains Retail, Country Curtains Mail Order, Red Lion Inn, Housatonic Curtain, Mr. and Mrs. John Fitzpatrick, JoAnn Brown, and others.

Typical Recipients

Arts & Humanities: Arts Associations & Councils, Arts Centers, Arts Festivals, Dance, Arts & Humanities-General, Historic Preservation, History & Archaeology, Libraries, Museums/Galleries, Music, Opera, Performing Arts, Public Broadcasting, Theater
Civic & Public Affairs: Botanical Gardens/Parks, Business/Free Enterprise, Community Foundations, Economic Development, Native American Affairs, Parades/Festivals, Professional & Trade Associations, Public Policy, Urban & Community Affairs, Women's Affairs, Zoos/Aquariums
Education: Agricultural Education, Arts/Humanities Education, Colleges & Universities, Community & Junior Colleges, Education Associations, Education Funds, Education-General, International Studies, Legal Education, Minority Education, Private Education (Precollege), Public Education (Precollege), Student Aid
Environment: Resource Conservation
Health: AIDS/HIV, Children's Health/Hospitals, Clinics/Medical Centers, Emergency/Ambulance Services, Hospices, Hospitals, Nursing Services, Public Health
International: Foreign Arts Organizations
Religion: Churches, Religious Welfare
Social Services: Child Welfare, Community Centers, Community Service Organizations, Counseling, Family Planning, Family Services, People with Disabilities, Recreation & Athletics, Shelters/Homelessness, United Funds/United Ways, Youth Organizations

Contributions Analysis

Giving Priorities: Education, social services, arts, civics, and environment causes.
Arts & Humanities: 53%. Over one-half of contributions for the arts support theater and performing arts. Other interests include chamber music, operas, symphonies, museums, art associations, dance, and public broadcasting.
Civic & Public Affairs: 6%. Support community service organizations.
Education: 31%. The majority of giving supports private and public precollege education. Also donates to colleges and universities, including scholarships, agricultural education, arts education, educational associations and funds, international studies, legal education, and minority education.
Environment: 2%. Supports wildlife care and rehabilitations and land preservation.
Health: 19%. Funds pediatric health and medical research. Other interests include hospitals, hospices, and medical centers. Single-disease health associations and outpatient health care also receive support.
Social Services: 8%. Funds child welfare, the diasble, family planning and services, shelters, and united funds.
Note: Total contributions made in 1998.

Application Procedures

Initial Contact: Send a brief letter.
Application Requirements: Information includes a description of program, brief history, and amount sought.
Deadlines: None.

Restrictions

The foundation limits the majority of gifts to charitable organizations in Berkshire County, MA.

Corporate Officials

Jane P. Fitzpatrick: chairman, chief executive officer, treasurer B 1925. PRIM CORP EMPL chairman, chief executive officer, treasurer: Country Curtains, Inc. CORP AFFIL treasurer: Housatonic Curtain Co. Inc.; treasurer: Red Lion Inc.; chairman: Country Curtains Mail Order Inc.; chairman: Fitzpatrick Companies Inc.
Robert B. Trask: president, chief operating officer, director B Springfield, MA 1946. ED Western New England College (1971). PRIM CORP EMPL president, chief operating officer, director: The Fitzpatrick Companies Inc. ADD CORP EMPL vice president, clearing houserk, director: Red Lion Inc. CORP AFFIL director: More Window Ways Inc.; member: New England Mail Order Association; director: Housatonic Curtain Co. Inc.; vice president: Lee Community Development Corp.; director: Fitzpatrick Retail & Realty Co. Inc.; clerk, director: Country Curtains Retail Inc.; member: Direct Marketing Association; trustee: City Savings Bank; president, chief operating officer, director: Country Curtains Mail Order Inc.; director: Berkshire Gas Co., Inc.; corporator: Berkshire Health Systems. NONPR AFFIL member: Knights of Columbus; corporator: North Adams State College Foundation; member: Institute of Management Accountants; trustee: Berkshire Theatre Festival; secretary, treasurer: High Meadow Foundation Inc.; member: American Institute CPAs; trustee: Berkshire Community College.

Foundation Officials

JoAnn Fitzpatrick Brown: director PRIM CORP EMPL vice president: Country Curtains, Inc. CORP AFFIL vice president: Housatonic Curtain Co. Inc.
Jane P. Fitzpatrick: chairman (see above)
John H. Fitzpatrick: president B 1925. PRIM CORP EMPL president, director: Housatonic Curtain Co. Inc. CORP AFFIL vice chairman: Country Curtains Inc.; director: Fitzpatrick Retail & Realty Co. Inc.
Nancy J. Fitzpatrick: president B 1946. PRIM CORP EMPL president, director: Country Curtains, Inc. ADD CORP EMPL treasurer: Berkshire Collections Inc.; vice president, director: Country Curtains Mail Order Inc.; president: Country Curtains Retail Inc.; executive vice president: Fitzpatrick Companies Inc.; treasurer, director: Fitzpatrick Retail & Realty Co. Inc.; vice president,director: Housatonic Curtain Co. Inc.; president,director: Red Lion Inc.
Mary Ann Snyder: director
Tamara Stevens: administrator
Robert B. Trask: clerk, trustee (see above)

Grants Analysis

Disclosure Period: fiscal year ending September 30, 1998
Total Grants: $1,319,791
Number of Grants: 425 (approx)
Average Grant: $3,105
Highest Grant: $161,250
Typical Range: $100 to $5,000

Recent Grants

Note: Grants derived from fiscal 1998 Form 990.

Arts & Humanities

161,250	Berkshire Theatre Festival:, Pittsfield, MA -- Annual - M/M & General
45,000	Guthrie Foundation, Housatonic, MA
40,000	Massachusetts Museum of Contemporary Art:, North Adams, MA -- Pledge - M/M
25,000	Edith Wharton Restoration Inc, Lenox, MA -- pledge
20,000	Historic Deerfield, Inc.:, Deerfield, MA -- Pledge - M/M
20,000	Ventfort Hall Association Inc., Lenox, MA
15,000	Bershire Opera Company:, Lee, MA -- Annual
10,000	Lenox Library Association:, Lenox, MA -- General
10,000	Paramount Center, Inc., Ratland, VT
8,014	Edith Wharton Restoration, Inc.:, Lenox, MA -- Annual - AFB
5,000	Berkshire Children's Chorus, Sheffield, MA
5,000	Berkshire Theatre Festival, Pittsfield, MA -- annual
5,000	Berkshire Theatre Festival, Pittsfield, MA -- Scholarship

5,000	Chesterwood:, Stockbridge, MA -- Annual - M/M
2,500	Berkshire Theatre Festival, Pittsfield, MA -- annual
1,500	Lenox Library Association, Lenox, MA -- pledge
1,000	Chesterwood, Stockbridge, MA -- annual
1,000	Historic Deerfield Inc, Deerfield, MA -- general
1,000	Massachusetts Museum of Contemporary Art, North Adams, MA -- Membership
1,000	Massachusetts Museum of Contemporary Art, North Adams, MA -- Founders Fund
1,000	Massachusetts Museum of Contemporary Art, North Adams, MA -- Founders Fund
1,000	Massachusetts Museum of Contemporary Art, North Adams, MA
300	Historic Deerfield Inc, Deerfield, MA -- pledge
200	Edith Wharton Restoration Inc, Lenox, MA -- annual
100	Chesterwood, Stockbridge, MA -- genaral
50	Berkshire Opera Company, Lee, MA -- general

Civic & Public Affairs

25,000	Berkshire Botanical Garden, Pittsfield, MA -- pledge
5,500	Central Park Conservancy, New York, NY
5,000	Berkshire Botanical Garden:, Pittsfield, MA -- Annual
5,000	Berkshire Taconic Community Foundation, Millerton, NY -- Gould Farm - Documentary
5,000	Pittsfield Parade Committee, Pittsfield, MA
1,000	Berkshire Botanical Garden, Pittsfield, MA -- Membership

Education

52,000	Buckley School:, New York, NY -- Pledge
50,000	Massachusetts College of Liberal Arts:, Boston, MA -- Pledge
34,000	Green Mountain College, Poultney, VT
25,000	Berkshire Community College, Pittsfield, MA
20,000	Emma Willard School, Troy, NY -- pledge
17,500	St. Mary's School:, Poughkeepsie, NY -- Pledge
10,450	Buckley School, New York, NY -- pledge
7,000	Emma Willard School:, Troy, NY -- Annual Fund
5,000	Emma Willard School, Troy, NY -- capital campaign
5,000	St. Mary's School, Poughkeepsie, NY -- general
75	Emma Willard School, Troy, NY -- general

Environment

10,000	Berkshire Natural Resources Council, Inc.:, Pittsfield, MA -- Pledge
600	Berkshire Natural Resources Council Inc, Pittsfield, MA -- NF
500	Berkshire Natural Resources Council Inc, Pittsfield, MA -- pledge

Health

5,000	Children's Health Program, Great Barrington, MA

Social Services

29,000	Berkshire United Way, Inc.:, Pittsfield, MA -- Pledge - Corporate
10,000	Berkshire United Way, Pittsfield, MA -- pledge
10,000	Girls Inc. of Pittsfield, Pittsfield, MA -- capital donation
5,000	Hillcrest Hospital Golf Classic, Pittsfield, MA
2,000	Girls Inc. of Pittsfield, Pittsfield, MA
1,300	Girls Inc. of Pittsfield:, Pittsfield, MA -- Annual - M/M

Cox Enterprises Inc.

Company Contact

Atlanta, GA

Company Description

Employees: 44,000
SIC(s): 2711 Newspapers, 4832 Radio Broadcasting Stations, 4833 Television Broadcasting Stations, 4841 Cable & Other Pay Television Services.

Nonmonetary Support

Type: Cause-related Marketing & Promotion; Donated Equipment; In-kind Services
Note: Each company operating location can be contacted for nonmonetary support.

James M. Cox Foundation

Giving Contact

Ms. Leigh Ann Launius, Assistant Secretary
James M. Cox Foundation
PO Box 105720
Atlanta, GA 30348
Phone: (404)843-7912
Fax: (404)843-5599
Email: LeighAnn.Launius@cox.com

Description

EIN: 586032469
Organization Type: Corporate Foundation
Giving Locations: GA: Atlanta headquarters and operating communities.
Grant Types: Capital, Project.

Financial Summary

Total Giving: $1,857,500 (1998); $1,167,666 (1997); $906,500 (1996). Note: Contributes through corporate direct giving program and foundation.
Giving Analysis: Giving for 1998 includes: foundation ($1,857,500)
Assets: $6,732,828 (1998); $6,522,998 (1997); $6,458,614 (1992)
Gifts Received: $1,550,000 (1998); $800,000 (1997). Note: Conributions received from Cox Enterprises.

Typical Recipients

Arts & Humanities: Arts Associations & Councils, Arts Centers, Arts Festivals, Arts Institutes, Historic Preservation, History & Archaeology, Libraries, Museums/Galleries, Opera, Performing Arts, Theater
Civic & Public Affairs: African American Affairs, Botanical Gardens/Parks, Community Foundations, Economic Development, Ethnic Organizations, Civic & Public Affairs-General, Housing, Urban & Community Affairs, Women's Affairs, Zoos/Aquariums
Education: Colleges & Universities, Education Reform, Engineering/Technological Education, Education-General, Journalism/Media Education, Leadership Training, Literacy, Medical Education, Public Education (Precollege), School Volunteerism, Special Education, Student Aid
Environment: Environment-General, Environment-General, Wildlife Protection
Health: Cancer, Children's Health/Hospitals, Emergency/Ambulance Services, Health Policy/Cost Containment, Hospices, Hospitals, Medical Rehabilitation, Multiple Sclerosis, Preventive Medicine/Wellness Organizations, Public Health, Single-Disease Health Associations
International: Health Care/Hospitals
Religion: Jewish Causes, Religious Organizations, Religious Welfare
Science: Science Museums, Scientific Centers & Institutes
Social Services: Animal Protection, Camps, Community Service Organizations, Counseling, Family Services, Food/Clothing Distribution, Homes, Shelters/Homelessness, Volunteer Services, YMCA/YWCA/YMHA/YWHA, Youth Organizations

Contributions Analysis

Giving Priorities: The performing arts, museums, and education.
Arts & Humanities: 22%. Recipients include museums, arts centers and institutes, and musical groups such as orchestras.
Civic & Public Affairs: 25%. Supports conservancy, zoology, and community services.
Education: 29%. Supports educational programs, universities and colleges.
Environment: 5%. Funds environmental concerns.
Health: 11%. Funds hospitals, medical treatment and medical centers .
Social Services: 5%. Funds philanthropic organizations, youth foundations, recreational groups, councils for victims and shelters.
Note: Total contributions made in 1998.

Application Procedures

Initial Contact: Send three copies of written request.
Application Requirements: Outline of needs and goals; copy of IRS tax-exemption letter; list of recent donors, including dollar amounts; annual report and other financial information, including audited financial statements (or most recent Form 990); list of board members and officers with salaries; copy of current or project budget.
Deadlines: April 1 and October 1.
Review Process: Local management recommends grants; foundation trustees make grant decisions.
Decision Notification: The foundation makes its decision at semi-annual meetings.

Restrictions

All potential recipients must be tax-exempt under IRS standards.
No grants are made to individuals.

Additional Information

The foundation does not accept personal interviews.

Corporate Officials

David E. Easterly: president, chief operating officer affairs, secretary B Denison, TX 1942. ED University of Texas; Austin College BA (1965). PRIM CORP EMPL president, chief operating officer: Cox Enterprises Inc. CORP AFFIL director: Cox Communications Inc.; vice president: Grand Junction Newspapers. NONPR AFFIL member: Newspaper Association America; member, director: Southern Newspaper Publishers Association; member: Associated Press.
Timothy W. Hughes: senior vice president B 1943. ED Bellarmine College AB (1965); Cleveland State University JD (1973). PRIM CORP EMPL senior vice president: Cox Enterprises Inc.
Richard J. Jacobson: vice president, treasurer B 1956. ED Georgia State University (1980). PRIM CORP EMPL vice president, treasurer: Cox Enterprises Inc.
James Cox Kennedy: chairman, chief executive officer, director B 1947. ED University of Denver BBA (1970). PRIM CORP EMPL chairman, chief executive officer, director: Cox Enterprises Inc. ADD CORP

EMPL chairman, president: National Auto Dealers Exchange. CORP AFFIL director: Manheim Auctions Inc.; director: National Service Industries Inc.; Flagler System Inc.; chairman, director: Cox Communications Inc.; director: Cox Radio Inc.; advisory director: Chase Bank Texas.

Andrew Austin Merdek: vice president legal affairs, secretary B Portland, ME 1950. ED Middlebury College AB (1972); University of Virginia JD (1978). PRIM CORP EMPL vice president legal affairs, secretary: Cox Enterprises Inc. ADD CORP EMPL secretary: Cox Texas Pubs Inc.; secretary: Cox Broadcasting Inc.; secretary: Cox Communications Inc.; secretary: Cox Interactive Media Inc.; secretary: Cox NC Pubs Inc.; secretary: Cox Newspapers Inc.; secretary, director: Dayton Newspapers Inc.; secretary: Eagle Research Group Inc.; secretary, director: GA Television Co.; secretary: Hospitality Network Inc.; secretary, director: Manheim Auction Government Service; secretary: Manheim Auctions Inc.; secretary, director: Manheim Metro Detroit Auto Auction; secretary,director: Palm Beach Newspapers Inc.; secretary: WFTV Inc. NONPR AFFIL member: Order Coif; member: Phi Beta Kappa; chairman: Newspaper Association American Legal Affairs Committee; member: American Corporate Counsel Association; member: American Society of Corporate Secretaries; member: American Bar Association.

Foundation Officials

Barbara Cox Anthony: chairman B Honolulu, HI 1923. PRIM CORP EMPL chairman: Dayton Newspapers Inc. CORP AFFIL director: Cox Enterprises Inc.

John G. Boyette: treasurer B 1944. ED Augusta College BBA (1968). PRIM CORP EMPL vice president, controller: Cox Enterprises Inc.

Anne Cox Chambers: chairman, trustee B Dayton, OH 1919. ED Finch Junior College. PRIM CORP EMPL chairman: Atlanta Journal-Constitution. CORP AFFIL director: Cox Enterprises Inc. NONPR AFFIL director: New York Botanical Garden; member national committee: Whitney Museum American Art; director: Metropolitan Museum Art; trustee: Museum Modern Art; member: LaCoste School Arts; director: MacDowell Colony; director: High Museum Art; director: Emory Museum Art & Archaeology; director: Forward Arts Foundation; director: Cities Schs; member: Council Foreign Relations; director: American Ambassadors Chmns Council; director: Atlanta Arts Alliance.

Timothy W. Hughes: trustee (see above)

James Cox Kennedy: trustee (see above)

Leigh Ann (Korns) Launius: assistant secretary PRIM CORP EMPL administration assistant: Cox Enterprises Inc.

Andrew Austin Merdek: secretary (see above)

Grants Analysis

Disclosure Period: calendar year ending 1998
Total Grants: $1,857,500
Number of Grants: 50
Average Grant: $37,150
Highest Grant: $200,000
Typical Range: $10,000 to $50,000

Recent Grants

Note: Grants derived from 1998 Form 990.

Arts & Humanities

50,000	Arts Festival of Atlanta, Atlanta, GA
45,000	Woodruff Arts Center--Annual Fund, Atlanta, GA
40,000	Dayton Art Institute, Dayton, OH
40,000	Georgia State Rialto, Atlanta, GA
34,000	Woodruff Arts Center--Renovation Campaign, Atlanta, GA
25,000	The Atlanta Opera, Atlanta, GA
25,000	Austin Children's Museum, Austin, TX
25,000	Clark County Historical Society, Little Rock, AR
25,000	Florida Gulf Coast Arts Center, Tampa, FL
25,000	International Museum of Cartoon Art, Boca Raton, FL
25,000	Longview Museum of Fine Arts, Longview, TX
25,000	Oklahoma City National Memorial Foundation, Oklahoma City, OK
10,000	Longview Library, Longview, TX
10,000	Norton Museum of Art, West Palm Beach, FL
5,000	Museum of the Albermarle, Elizabeth City, NC

Civic & Public Affairs

150,000	Carter Center, Atlanta, GA
50,000	Atlanta Botanical Garden, Atlanta, GA
50,000	East Lake Revitalization, Atlanta, GA
50,000	Friends of John A. White Park, Inc., Atlanta, GA
35,000	The Atlanta Project, Atlanta, GA
25,000	East Lake Community Foundation--Yates Course, Atlanta, GA
25,000	Fairlie-Poplar Streetscape Project, Atlanta, GA
25,000	French-American Foundation, New York, NY
25,000	Sandy Springs Revitalization, Inc., Atlanta, GA
25,000	Zoo Atlanta, Atlanta, GA
15,000	Women's Protective Services of Lubbock, Lubbock, TX
5,000	Capitol Area Mosaic, Atlanta, GA

Education

200,000	Kennesaw State University Family Enterprise Center, Kennesaw, GA
90,000	University of Central Florida, Orlando, FL
50,000	Michigan State University - Quello Center, East Lansing, MI
50,000	Oglethorpe University, Atlanta, GA
40,000	Communities in Schools of Atlanta, Atlanta, GA
30,000	Study Hall of Emmaus House, Inc., Atlanta, GA
25,000	Morehouse School of Medicine, Atlanta, GA
20,000	Virginia Wesleyan College, Norfolk, VA
16,000	Communities in Schools (National), Atlanta, GA
10,000	Atlanta Outward Bound Center, Atlanta, GA
5,000	Florida A&M University, Tallahassee, FL

Environment

100,000	PATH Foundation, Atlanta, GA

Health

75,000	National MS Society--Georgia Chapter, Atlanta, GA
50,000	Georgia Health Decisions, Atlanta, GA
50,000	Juvenile Diabetes Foundation International, New York, NY
25,000	Auditory Education Center, Inc., Atlanta, GA

Religion

7,500	American ORT, New York, NY
5,000	Jerusalem House, Atlanta, GA

Science

25,000	SciTrek, Atlanta, GA

Social Services

50,000	Camp Twin Lakes, Atlanta, GA
25,000	Atlanta Humane Society, Atlanta, GA
15,000	The Link Counseling Center, Atlanta, GA
5,000	Hands on Atlanta, Atlanta, GA

CPI CORP.

Company Contact

St. Louis, MO

Web: http://www.cpicorp.com

Company Description

Revenue: US$543,300,000
Employees: 12,400
SIC(s): 5999 Miscellaneous Retail Stores Nec, 7221 Photographic Studios--Portrait.

Nonmonetary Support

Value: $68,900 (1996); $143,990 (1994); $162,000 (1993)
Type: Donated Products; In-kind Services

Corporate Sponsorship

Type: Arts & cultural events; Music & entertainment events; Sports events

CPI Corp. Philanthropic Trust

Giving Contact

Fran Scheper, Executive Vice President, Human Resources
CPI Philanthropic Trust
1706 Washington Avenue
St. Louis, MO 63103
Phone: (314)231-1575
Fax: (314)231-2398

Description

EIN: 431334012
Organization Type: Corporate Foundation
Giving Locations: near headquarters.
Grant Types: Award, Capital, Employee Matching Gifts, Fellowship, General Support, Matching.
Note: Employee matching gift ratio: 1 to 1.

Giving Philosophy

'The CPI Philanthropic Programs represent the charitable arm of the CPI Corporation. The Company recognizes that as a free enterprise corporation operating in and at the sufferance of a free society, it has important corporate responsibilities to help build and strengthen that free society.' *CPI Philanthropic Programs Guidelines*

Financial Summary

Total Giving: $81,500 (fiscal year ending January 31, 1998); $350,000 (fiscal 1997); $365,850 (fiscal 1996). Note: Contributes through corporate direct giving program and foundation.

Giving Analysis: Giving for fiscal 1996 includes: corporate direct giving ($296,900); foundation ($68,950); fiscal 1997: corporate direct giving ($281,000); foundation ($69,000); fiscal 1998: foundation ($81,500); corporate direct giving ($5,000)

Assets: $134,935 (fiscal 1998); $207,741 (fiscal 1997); $300,488 (fiscal 1996)

Gifts Received: $400,000 (fiscal 1994); $240,000 (fiscal 1993). Note: The foundation receives contributions from CPI Corporation.

Typical Recipients

Arts & Humanities: Dance, Museums/Galleries, Performing Arts, Theater

Civic & Public Affairs: Business/Free Enterprise, Chambers of Commerce, Community Foundations, Housing, Nonprofit Management, Parades/Festivals, Urban & Community Affairs, Women's Affairs

Education: Afterschool/Enrichment Programs, Colleges & Universities, Education Funds, Education-General, Private Education (Precollege), Secondary Education (Public), Special Education

Health: Children's Health/Hospitals, Eyes/Blindness, Geriatric Health, Hospitals, Multiple Sclerosis, Respiratory

International: Missionary/Religious Activities

Religion: Religious Organizations, Religious Welfare, Social/Policy Issues

Science: Scientific Centers & Institutes
Social Services: At-Risk Youth, Camps, Child Welfare, Community Service Organizations, Community Service Organizations, Counseling, Day Care, Domestic Violence, Family Services, Food/Clothing Distribution, People with Disabilities, Recreation & Athletics, Scouts, Shelters/Homelessness, United Funds/ United Ways, YMCA/YWCA/YMHA/YWHA, Youth Organizations

Contributions Analysis

Giving Priorities: Social welfare, education, civics affairs, and single disease health associations.
Civic & Public Affairs: 15%. Gives to chambers of commerce and various other organizations in St. Louis and the state of Missouri.
Education: 44%. Support goes to education councils, private precollege education, college funds, and colleges and universities.
Social Services: 41%. Supports youth organizations, recreation and child welfare organizations.
Note: Total contributions made in 1998.

Application Procedures

Initial Contact: Send a brief letter of inquiry requesting guidelines.
Application Requirements: Include literature or brochures on agency or organization; description of project, including statement of objectives and mission; proof of tax-exempt status; amount requested, duration of project, and itemized budget; current year's financial statements; and list of current corporate donors.
Deadlines: None.
Review Process: Unsuccessful requests are immediately acknowledged and declined; proposals that receive a favorable review are submitted to the philanthropic committee for consideration.
Evaluative Criteria: Organization or project must have an active board of directors, show financial and managerial competence, show a method for evaluating results of project, be able to describe project in comparison to similar projects, and have wide constituency.
Decision Notification: Grantees are notified as soon as possible of committee's action.

Restrictions

Grants are made only to organizations located in operating locations. Does not support religious organizations for sectarian purposes; individuals; political or veterans' organizations; non-accredited schools; fraternal or labor organizations; organizations that discriminate on the basis of race, color, creed, sex, marital status, or handicap; team raising funds to benefit other organizations; tax-supported organizations, except schools through the matching grant program; operating expenses of United Way or Jewish Federation member agencies; or projects eligible for full government funding or for which full government funding is being sought. agencies; or projects eligible for full government funding or for which full government funding is being sought.

Corporate Officials

Alyn V. Essman: chairman, chief executive officer B Saint Louis, MO 1932. ED Washington University BBA (1953). PRIM CORP EMPL chairman, chief executive officer: CPI Corp. CORP AFFIL chairman: Consumer Programs Inc.

Giving Program Officials

Fran Scheper: chairman, trustee PRIM CORP EMPL vice president human resources: CPI Corp.

Grants Analysis

Disclosure Period: fiscal year ending January 31, 1998
Total Grants: $81,500*
Number of Grants: 15
Average Grant: $5,433
Highest Grant: $30,000
Typical Range: $1,000 to $10,000
***Note:** Giving excludes corporate direct giving.

Recent Grants

Note: Grants derived from 1998 Form 990.

Civic & Public Affairs

5,000	Focus St. Louis, St. Louis, MO -- Grant
5,000	Focus St. Louis, St. Louis, MO -- Grant
1,000	Women's Crisis Center, St. Louis, MO -- Grant

Education

30,000	University of Missouri St. Louis, St. Louis, MO -- Summer Bridge Program
3,000	Today & Tomorrow Education Fund, St. Louis, MO -- Grant
3,000	Webster University, St. Louis, MO -- Grant

Health

500	Cardinal Care Program, Richmond, VA -- Grant

Social Services

20,000	Our Little Haven, St. Louis, MO -- Grant
5,000	Family Resource Center, St. Louis, MO -- Grant
2,500	Camp Happy Day, St. Louis, MO -- Grant
2,000	Epworth Children's Home, St. Louis, MO -- Grant
1,500	Boy Scouts of America, St. Louis, MO -- Grant
1,000	Citizens For Missouri Children, St. Louis, MO -- Grant
1,000	National Jr. Tennis League, San Francisco, CA -- Grant
1,000	Uni-Pres Kinder Cottage, St. Louis, MO -- Grant

CRANE &CO., INC.

Company Contact

Dalton, MA
Web: http://www.crane.com

Company Description

Employees: 1,300
SIC(s): 2621 Paper Mills, 2761 Manifold Business Forms.

Nonmonetary Support

Value: $20,000 (1996); $8,000 (1995)
Type: Cause-related Marketing & Promotion; Donated Products
Note: Co. provides nonmonetary support.

Corporate Sponsorship

Contact: David Crane, Chief Financial Officer

Crane & Co. Fund

Giving Contact

Liz Pomeroy, Executive Secretary
Crane & Co. Fund
30 South Street
Dalton, MA 01226
Phone: (413)684-2600
Fax: (413)684-1820

Description

Founded: 1953
EIN: 046057388
Organization Type: Corporate Foundation
Giving Locations: MA: near headquarters
Grant Types: Capital, General Support.

Financial Summary

Total Giving: $300,000 (2000 approx); $300,000 (1999 approx); $220,700 (1998). Note: Contributes through corporate direct giving program and foundation.
Giving Analysis: Giving for 1997 includes: foundation (approx $300,000); 1998: foundation ($220,700)
Assets: $166,000 (1998); $101,612 (1996); $126,582 (1995)
Gifts Received: $237,426 (1998); $208,424 (1996); $191,413 (1995). Note: Contributions are received from Crane & Co.

Typical Recipients

Arts & Humanities: Arts Associations & Councils, Arts Centers, Arts Festivals, Arts Funds, Arts Institutes, Ballet, Community Arts, Dance, Arts & Humanities-General, Historic Preservation, History & Archaeology, Museums/Galleries, Music, Performing Arts, Public Broadcasting, Theater
Civic & Public Affairs: Botanical Gardens/Parks, Business/Free Enterprise, Chambers of Commerce, Economic Development, Employment/Job Training, Civic & Public Affairs-General, Native American Affairs, Professional & Trade Associations, Safety, Urban & Community Affairs, Women's Affairs
Education: Agricultural Education, Arts/Humanities Education, Business Education, Business-School Partnerships, Colleges & Universities, Community & Junior Colleges, Education Funds, Engineering/Technological Education, Education-General, Literacy, Public Education (Precollege), Science/Mathematics Education, Student Aid
Environment: Air/Water Quality, Environment-General, Resource Conservation, Sanitary Systems, Wildlife Protection
Health: Cancer, Children's Health/Hospitals, Clinics/ Medical Centers, Diabetes, Emergency/Ambulance Services, Eyes/Blindness, Health-General, Health Funds, Health Organizations, Heart, Hospices, Hospitals, Hospitals (University Affiliated), Kidney, Respiratory, Single-Disease Health Associations
Religion: Churches, Religious Welfare
Science: Scientific Research
Social Services: Child Abuse, Child Welfare, Community Centers, Community Service Organizations, Day Care, Family Services, Food/Clothing Distribution, People with Disabilities, Recreation & Athletics, Social Services-General, United Funds/United Ways, Volunteer Services, YMCA/YWCA/YMHA/YWHA, Youth Organizations

Contributions Analysis

Arts & Humanities: 8%. Supports museums, theater, historic preservation, music, and the performing arts.
Civic & Public Affairs: 4%. Supports business organizations, Native American affairs, community affairs, and local trade associations.
Education: 19%. Funds the Zenas Crane Fund for Student Aid. Colleges and universities and educational programs also receive funding.
Health: 11%. A local medical center, health organizations, and emergency services receive funding.
Social Services: 56%. Majority supports youth organizations. Additional recipients include organizations for people with disabilities, religious welfare, and community centers.
Note: Total contributions made in 1998.

Corporate Officials

David W. Crane: chief financial officer B 1959. ED Dartmouth College (1981); University of Chicago (1985). PRIM CORP EMPL chief financial officer: Crane & Co., Inc. ADD CORP EMPL treasurer: Authentication Technicals.
Lansing E. Crane: chairman, president B 1945. ED Yale University BA (1967); Boston University JD (1970). PRIM CORP EMPL chairman, president: Crane & Co., Inc.
Richard C. Kendall: trustee B 1955. PRIM CORP EMPL treasurer: Crane Co. Inc.

Foundation Officials

David W. Crane: trustee (see above)
Richard C. Kendall: trustee (see above)
James D. Manning: trustee B 1940. PRIM CORP EMPL vice president: Crane Co. Inc.

Grants Analysis

Disclosure Period: calendar year ending 1998
Total Grants: $220,700
Number of Grants: 66
Average Grant: $3,344
Highest Grant: $77,000
Typical Range: $200 to $4,000

Recent Grants

Note: Grants derived from 1996 Form 990.

Arts & Humanities

4,000	Hancock Shaker Village, Pittsfield, MA
2,500	Berkshire Museum, Pittsfield, MA
2,000	Williamstown Theater Festival, Williamstown, MA
1,750	Business Friends of Tanglewood
1,000	Berkshire County Historical Society, Pittsfield, MA
1,000	Berkshire Theater Festival, Stockbridge, MA
750	Becket Arts Center, Pittsfield, MA
500	Barrington Stage Company, Great Barrington, MA
500	Jacob's Pillow, Lee, CT
500	Shakespeare and Company, Lenox, MA
500	WGBY/Channel 57, Springfield, MA
400	Berkshire Art Association, Pittsfield, MA
300	Edith Wharton Restoration, Lenox, MA
300	Norman Rockwell Museum, Stockbridge, MA
300	WAMC, Albany, NY

Civic & Public Affairs

5,000	NASC
1,000	Housatonic Valley Association, Cornwall Bridge, CT
500	Trustees of Reservations, Beverly, MA
500	Women's Club, Pittsfield, MA
350	South Mountain Association, Pittsfield, MA
300	Windsor Volunteer Fire Department, Gainesville, FL

Education

11,500	Zenas Crane Fund for Student Aid, Dalton, MA
11,500	Zenas Crane Fund for Student Aid, Dalton, MA
5,000	Quest Quality Education Scholastic
1,200	Syracuse Pulp and Paper Foundation, Syracuse, NY
1,200	University of Maine, Orono, ME
1,000	James J. Mooney Scholarship Fund
1,000	Pittsfield Public Schools, Pittsfield, MA
500	Hancock Central School
500	New England Colleges Fund, Woburn, MA
500	Pittsfield Citizens Scholarship Foundation, Pittsfield, MA
500	Pittsfield Community Music School, Pittsfield, MA
300	Literacy Volunteers of Berkshire County, Pittsfield, MA

Environment

5,000	Massachusetts Audubon Society, Lincoln, MA
3,000	Berkshire Natural Resources Council, Pittsfield, MA

Health

19,500	Berkshire Medical Center, Pittsfield, MA
1,500	Dalton Ambulance Fund, Dalton, MA
875	American Cancer Society, Pittsfield, MA
400	Hinsdale Ambulance Fund, Hinsdale, MA

Religion

1,000	Christian Center, Pittsfield, MA
1,000	First Congregational Church, Geneva, NE

Social Services

72,000	Berkshire United Way, Pittsfield, MA
30,000	Boys and Girls Club, Pittsfield, MA
17,500	W. Murray Crane Community House, Dalton, MA
17,500	W. Murray Crane Community House, Dalton, MA
5,000	Pittsfield YMCA, Pittsfield, MA
1,800	Dalton Community Center, Dalton, MA
1,000	Child Care of the Berkshires, North Adams, MA
500	Recording for Blind and Dyslexic, Princeton, NJ
250	Dalton Community Cable Association, Dalton, MA

Crane Co.

Company Contact

Stamford, CT

Company Description

Acquired: Stockham Valves & Fittings Inc.
Profit: US$22,700,000
Employees: 10,700
SIC(s): 3052 Rubber & Plastics Hose & Belting, 3494 Valves & Pipe Fittings Nec, 3594 Fluid Power Pumps & Motors, 3621 Motors & Generators, 5074 Plumbing & Hydronic Heating Supplies.

Crane Foundation

Giving Contact

Gil Dickoff, Treasurer
100 1st Stamford Pl.
Stamford, CT 06902
Phone: (203)363-7300
Fax: (203)363-7295

Description

Founded: 1951
EIN: 436051752
Organization Type: Corporate Foundation
Giving Locations: NY; PA
Grant Types: Emergency, Employee Matching Gifts, General Support.

Financial Summary

Total Giving: $214,974 (1998); $227,386 (1996); $213,669 (1995)
Giving Analysis: Giving for 1998 includes: foundation ($165,745); foundation matching gifts ($49,230)
Assets: $6,536,757 (1998); $5,346,047 (1996); $4,661,006 (1995)

Typical Recipients

Arts & Humanities: Arts Associations & Councils, Arts Centers, Ballet, Historic Preservation, History & Archaeology, Libraries, Museums/Galleries, Music, Performing Arts, Public Broadcasting, Theater
Civic & Public Affairs: Botanical Gardens/Parks, Business/Free Enterprise, Economic Development, Economic Policy, Civic & Public Affairs-General, Hispanic Affairs, Housing, Law & Justice, Legal Aid, Minority Business, Parades/Festivals, Public Policy, Safety, Urban & Community Affairs, Women's Affairs, Zoos/Aquariums
Education: Arts/Humanities Education, Business Education, Colleges & Universities, Community & Junior Colleges, Economic Education, Education Funds, Education Reform, Elementary Education (Public), Faculty Development, Education-General, International Studies, Legal Education, Literacy, Minority Education, Private Education (Precollege), Public Education (Precollege), Science/Mathematics Education, Secondary Education (Private), Secondary Education (Public), Student Aid
Environment: Environment-General, Wildlife Protection
Health: Cancer, Diabetes, Emergency/Ambulance Services, Eyes/Blindness, Health Organizations, Hospitals, Medical Research, Mental Health, Multiple Sclerosis, Single-Disease Health Associations, Transplant Networks/Donor Banks
International: International-General, Health Care/Hospitals, International Development, International Environmental Issues, International Organizations, International Peace & Security Issues, International Relief Efforts
Religion: Bible Study/Translation, Religious Welfare
Science: Scientific Centers & Institutes
Social Services: At-Risk Youth, Child Abuse, Child Welfare, Community Service Organizations, Domestic Violence, Food/Clothing Distribution, Homes, People with Disabilities, Recreation & Athletics, Special Olympics, Substance Abuse, United Funds/United Ways, Volunteer Services, YMCA/YWCA/YMHA/YWHA, Youth Organizations

Contributions Analysis

Arts & Humanities: 15%. Supports arts councils, libraries, and the performing arts.
Civic & Public Affairs: 21%. Legal affairs, municipalities, zoos and parks receive support.
Education: 33%. Funds colleges, universities, and private pre-college education.
Environment: 3%. Supports Defenders of Wildlife.
Health: 4%. Supports hospitals, medical services, and health care.
International: 7%. Supports international services.
Science: 6%. Supports the Pacific Science Center.
Social Services: 10%. Supports social services and youth services.
Note: Total contributions in 1998.

Application Procedures

Initial Contact: Send brief letter on organization letterhead describing program. Applicants must include proof of tax-exempt status. There are no deadlines.
Deadlines: None.

Restrictions

Grants are not made to individuals.

Corporate Officials

L. Hill Clark: president, chief operating officer chief financial officer PRIM CORP EMPL president, chief operating officer: Crane Co.
Robert Sheldon Evans: chairman, chief executive officer B Pittsburgh, PA 1944. ED University of Pennsylvania BA (1966); Columbia University MBA (1968). PRIM CORP EMPL chairman, chief executive officer: Crane Co. CORP AFFIL director: Mid-Ocean Ltd.; director: HBD Industries; chairman: Medusa Corp.; director: Fansteel. NONPR AFFIL member deans advisory council: Columbia University Graduate School Business; trustee: Eaglebrook School; trustee: Allen Stevenson School.
David S. Smith: vice president finance, chief financial officer PRIM CORP EMPL vice president finance, chief financial officer: Crane Co.

Foundation Officials

Gil A. Dickoff: treasurer B New York, NY 1961. ED State University of New York (1983); State University of New York (1984). PRIM CORP EMPL treasurer: Crane Co.
Augustus I. DuPont: executive vpr, secretary, director
Robert Sheldon Evans: chairman, president, director (see above)
Richard B. Phillips: vice president B Norwich, CT 1944. ED Saint Lawrence University (1967). PRIM CORP EMPL vice president human resources: Crane Co. NONPR AFFIL member: Manufacturer Alliance

Productivity & Innovation; member: Society Human Resources Management.
David S. Smith: executive vice president, controller (see above)
Thomas J. Ungerland: assistant secretary

Grants Analysis

Disclosure Period: calendar year ending 1998
Total Grants: $165,745*
Number of Grants: 62
Average Grant: $2,673
Highest Grant: $20,000
Typical Range: $100 to $10,000
***Note:** Giving excludes matching gifts.

Recent Grants

Note: Grants derived from 1998 Form 990.

Arts & Humanities

6,000	Seattle Symphony/Operating Fund, Seattle, WA
5,000	Lincoln Center for the Performing Arts, New York, NY
5,000	Pierpont Morgan Library, New York, NY
2,000	KCTS 9, Seattle, WA
2,000	New York Public Library, New York, NY
1,500	Rialto Square Theatre, Joliet, IL
1,500	Rogers Public Library, Rogers, AR
1,200	Corporate Council for the Arts, Seattle, WA

Civic & Public Affairs

10,000	National Legal Center for the Public Interest, Washington, DC
7,500	Washington Legal Foundation, Washington, DC
5,500	LEAD Program in Business, Inc., New York, NY
3,000	Will County Bicentennial Park, Inc., Joliet, IL
1,500	Pleasant Gardens Fire Department, Pleasant Gardens, NC
1,500	St. Louis Zoo Friends Association, St. Louis, MO

Education

20,000	Carnegie Mellon University, Pittsburgh, PA
10,000	Columbia Business School/, New York, NY -- 1998 Annual Dinner
5,000	Carnegie Mellon University, PA
5,000	Manhattan Institute/Center for Judicial Studies, New York, NY
5,000	Snohomish County Christian School, WA
3,000	Junior Achievement of Central Ohio, Columbus, OH -- Educational Program
3,000	Junior Achievement of Lorain County
3,000	Junior Achievement of Puget Sound, Seattle, WA
3,000	McDowell Educational Foundation, Erie, PA
3,000	Northside Elementary School, Sacramento, CA -- Partners in Education
2,500	Binghamton University, NY
2,500	Dashew International Student Center at UCLA, Los Angeles, CA
2,500	Fairfield University, CT
2,500	Hebron Academy, ME
2,500	Independent Colleges of Washington, Seattle, WA
2,500	James Madison University, VA
2,500	St. John the Baptist School, OH
2,400	Indiana University, IN
2,000	Junior Achievement of Central Ohio, Columbus, OH -- Scholarship Program
2,000	Rogers Senior High School, Rogers, AR -- Engineering Scholarship
2,000	Wilbraham & Monson Academy, MA
1,500	Colgate University, NY
1,500	Columbia University, NY
1,500	McDowell High School Renaissance Program, Erie, PA
1,500	Pleasant Gardens Elementary School, Pleasant Gardens, NC
1,000	Junior Achievement of Southern California, Los Angeles, CA

Environment

5,000	Defenders of Wildlife, Washington, DC

Health

5,000	Combined Health Appeal of Connecticut, Hartford, CT
1,000	Stamford Emergency Medical Services, Inc., Stamford, CT
1,000	Warrington Community Ambulance Corps, Warrington, CT

International

5,000	West Island Educational Foundation, Montreal, PQ, Canada
2,500	Heart & Stroke Foundation of Quebec, Montreal, PQ, Canada
2,500	Junior Achievement of Canada, Toronto, ON, Canada
2,500	Juvenile Diabetes Foundation of Canada, Richmond Hill, ON, Canada
1,500	Auxiliary of the Montreal General Hospital, Montreal, PQ, Canada
1,000	Bethany Care Society, Calgary, AB, Canada

Science

10,000	Pacific Science Center, Seattle, WA

CRANSTON PRINT WORKS CO.

Company Contact

Cranston, RI

Company Description

Employees: 1,175
SIC(s): 2261 Finishing Plants--Cotton, 3552 Textile Machinery, 3554 Paper Industries Machinery.

Cranston Foundation

Giving Contact

Carolyn Lake, Administrator
Cranston Foundation
1381 Cranston St.
Cranston, RI 02920
Phone: (401)943-4800
Fax: (401)943-3971
Email: cpw@cpw.com

Description

EIN: 056015348
Organization Type: Corporate Foundation
Giving Locations: nationally; operating locations.
Grant Types: Employee Matching Gifts, General Support.

Financial Summary

Total Giving: $238,928 (fiscal year ending June 30, 1999); $235,075 (fiscal 1998); $263,432 (fiscal 1997). Note: Contributes through foundation only.
Giving Analysis: Giving for fiscal 1996 includes: foundation scholarships ($166,225); foundation ($155,157); foundation matching gifts ($24,003); fiscal 1997: foundation scholarships ($147,075); foundation grants to United Way ($43,000); foundation matching gifts ($29,756); fiscal 1998: foundation scholarships ($125,773); foundation ($83,720); foundation matching gifts ($25,582);
Assets: $177,450 (fiscal 1998); $282,467 (fiscal 1997); $501,029 (fiscal 1996)
Gifts Received: $24,902 (fiscal 1997); $323,741 (fiscal 1996); $328,840 (fiscal 1995)

Typical Recipients

Arts & Humanities: Ethnic & Folk Arts, History & Archaeology, Libraries, Museums/Galleries
Civic & Public Affairs: Safety
Education: Arts/Humanities Education, Business Education, Colleges & Universities, Community & Junior Colleges, Engineering/Technological Education, Medical Education, Minority Education, Science/Mathematics Education, Student Aid, Vocational & Technical Education
Environment: Environment-General, Resource Conservation
Health: Emergency/Ambulance Services, Hospitals, Kidney, Prenatal Health Issues
Religion: Jewish Causes, Religious Welfare
Social Services: Big Brother/Big Sister, Community Service Organizations, Scouts, United Funds/United Ways, YMCA/YWCA/YMHA/YWHA, Youth Organizations

Contributions Analysis

Giving Priorities: Education, healthcare associations and organizations, civics, and arts.
Arts & Humanities: 4%. Interests include museums, libraries, music, historic preservation, and arts councils.
Civic & Public Affairs: 8%. Favors housing projects, youth organizations, and ambulance and fire safety services.
Education: 63%. Majority of funding supports scholarships to colleges and universities, primarily for children of company employees. Also, a few direct grants are given to education. Foundation also operates matching grants program.
Health: 25%. Focus on community service organizations, homes for the elderly, and health foundations and associations. One-third supports the United Jewish Appeal. Other interests include community centers, municipal funds for community needs and health.
Note: Total contributions made in 1998.

Application Procedures

Initial Contact: Send a written request.
Application Requirements: Include details of project; funding requirements; budget information; organization's management structure, purpose, operation, and goals; copy of IRS classification letter; and recent financial statements.
Deadlines: Before May 1 for funding during that fiscal year.
Decision Notification: Trustees normally meet twice per year.

Restrictions

The foundation only makes contributions to domestic organizations which have been ruled by the IRS as tax exempt under Section 501(c)(3) of the Internal Revenue Code.

Additional Information

Publications: Guidelines

Corporate Officials

Nancy Kirsch: general counselo, director PRIM CORP EMPL general counsel: Cranston Print Works Co.
Carolyn Lake: administrator PRIM CORP EMPL administrator: Cranston Print Works Co.
Robert Mandeville: chief financial officer, secretary, treasurer B Woonsocket, RI 1943. ED Bryant College (1963). PRIM CORP EMPL chief financial officer, secretary, treasurer: Cranston Print Works Co. CORP AFFIL secretary, treasurer, chief financial officer: Cranston International Sales Corp.; secretary, treasurer, chief financial officer: Cranston Trucking Co.
Frederic Lincoln Rockefeller: B New York, NY 1921. ED Yale University (1947). CORP AFFIL chairman of the board: Cranston Print Works Co. NONPR AFFIL director: American Textile Manufacturer Institute; director: Textile Distr Association.

George Whitcomb Shuster: president, chief executive officer, director B Trenton, NJ 1946. ED Yale University (1967); Yale University Law School (1973). PRIM CORP EMPL president, chief executive officer, director: Cranston Print Works Co. CORP AFFIL director: Ashwright Inc. NONPR AFFIL director: Kent County Memorial Hospital.

Foundation Officials

Ann Baker: trustee
Glenn Carlson: trustee
Mike Emmett: trustee
Carolyn Lake: administrator (see above)
Robert Mandeville: trustee (see above)
William Mason: trustee
Frederic Lincoln Rockefeller: trustee (see above)
George Whitcomb Shuster: trustee (see above)
Pat Strouse: trustee

Grants Analysis

Disclosure Period: fiscal year ending June 30, 1999
Total Grants: $238,928*
Number of Grants: 35
Average Grant: $6,827
Highest Grant: $15,000
Typical Range: $200 to $15,000
***Note:** Grants analysis provided by foundation. Giving excludes scholarship; matching gifts; United Way.

Recent Grants

Note: Grants derived from fiscal 1997 Form 990.

Arts & Humanities
2,000 Slater Mill Historic Site, Pawtucket, RI -- for OSMA 75th Anniversary
2,000 University of Rhode Island, Kingston, RI -- for Textile Gallery
1,000 Museum of Art-RISD, Providence, RI -- for exhibit
500 American Textile History Museum, Lowell, MA -- operating support
500 Providence Public Library, Providence, RI -- operating support

Civic & Public Affairs
1,000 Fletcher Fire and Rescue Department, Fletcher, NC -- operating support
1,000 Webster Fire Department, Webster, MA -- operating support
200 Dudley Firefighters' Association, Dudley, MA -- operating support

Education
10,000 University of Massachusetts Dartmouth, North Dartmouth, MA -- for Textiles Sciences Department
2,000 Educational Foundation, Fashions Industries, New York, NY -- for scholarship awards dinner
500 Blue Ridge College Educational Foundation, Flat Rock, NC -- for Nora A. Gregory Nursing Endowment
500 Students in Free Enterprise, Springfield, MO -- operating support

Environment
1,000 Nature Conservancy, Providence, RI -- operating support
500 Massachusetts Audubon Society, Lincoln, MA -- operating support
500 Save the Bay, Providence, RI -- operating support

Health
10,000 Hubbard Regional Hospital, Webster, MA -- operating support
1,000 Kent County Memorial Hospital, Warwick, RI -- operating support
1,000 Pardee Hospital Foundation, Henderson, NC -- operating support
1,000 Park Ridge Hospital Foundation, Fletcher, NC -- operating support
1,000 Rhode Island Hospital, Providence, RI -- operating support
1,000 Webster Ambulance Squad, Webster, MA -- operating support
1,000 Webster Rescue Squad, Webster, MA -- operating support
1,000 Women and Infants Hospital, Providence, RI -- operating support
100 National Kidney Foundation of Maryland, Baltimore, MD -- in memory of Edward M. Judge

Religion
3,600 United Jewish Appeal Federation, New York, NY -- operating support

Social Services
12,000 United Way Henderson County, Hendersonville, NC -- operating support
12,000 United Way Southeastern New England, Providence, RI -- operating support
12,000 United Way Webster and Dudley, Webster, MA -- operating support
7,000 United Way, New York, NY -- operating support
1,000 YMCA Kent County, Warwick, RI -- for camperships
500 Share-A-Walk, New York, NY
200 Big Brothers, Pawtucket, RI -- operating support

Credit Suisse First Boston

Company Contact

New York, NY
Web: http://www.csfb.com

Company Description

Former Name: First Boston.
Assets: US$133,757,000,000
Employees: 5,033
SIC(s): 6211 Security Brokers & Dealers.
Parent Company: Credit Suisse First Boston, Inc.
Parent Income: US$13,830,000,000

Operating Locations

NY: Credit Suisse First Boston, New York; Swiss American Securities, New York; PR: Credit Suisse First Boston, Hato Rey
Note: Operates throughout the USA.

Corporate Sponsorship

Range: less than $3,000,000
Type: Sports events
Note: Co. sponsors the Willowbend Children's Charity Golf Outing.

Credit Suisse First Boston Foundation Trust

Giving Contact

Mr. Casey Karel, Vice President
Credit Suisse First Boston Foundation Trust
11 Madison Ave.
New York, NY 10010
Phone: (212)325-2389
Fax: (212)325-6665
Email: casey.karel@csfb.com

Description

Founded: 1959
EIN: 046059692
Organization Type: Corporate Foundation
Giving Locations: NY: New York headquarters and operating communities; nationally.
Grant Types: General Support.

Note: The foundation also awards mini-grants to employees.

Financial Summary

Total Giving: $1,000,000 (2000 approx); $1,000,000 (1999); $1,000,000 (1998). Note: Contributes through corporate direct giving program and foundation.
Giving Analysis: Giving for 1998 includes: foundation ($1,000,000)
Assets: $99,530 (1996); $28,125 (1995); $24,995 (1994)
Gifts Received: $557,600 (1996); $581,726 (1995); $775,599 (1994). Note: The foundation received contributions from Credit Suisse First Boston Corporation.

Typical Recipients

Arts & Humanities: Arts Associations & Councils, Arts Centers, Arts Funds, Arts Institutes, Ballet, Dance, Arts & Humanities-General, Libraries, Museums/Galleries, Music, Opera, Performing Arts, Public Broadcasting, Theater
Civic & Public Affairs: African American Affairs, Botanical Gardens/Parks, Business/Free Enterprise, Civil Rights, Clubs, Community Foundations, Economic Development, Economic Policy, Employment/Job Training, Civic & Public Affairs-General, Law & Justice, Municipalities/Towns, Professional & Trade Associations, Public Policy, Urban & Community Affairs, Women's Affairs
Education: Arts/Humanities Education, Business Education, Colleges & Universities, Continuing Education, Economic Education, Education Funds, Education Reform, Engineering/Technological Education, Education-General, Minority Education, Preschool Education, Private Education (Precollege), Public Education (Precollege), School Volunteerism, Special Education, Student Aid, Vocational & Technical Education
Environment: Air/Water Quality
Health: Cancer, Children's Health/Hospitals, Clinics/Medical Centers, Emergency/Ambulance Services, Hospitals, Medical Research, Mental Health, Prenatal Health Issues, Single-Disease Health Associations, Transplant Networks/Donor Banks
International: Health Care/Hospitals, International Relations
Religion: Religious Welfare
Social Services: At-Risk Youth, Child Welfare, Community Centers, Community Service Organizations, Food/Clothing Distribution, People with Disabilities, Recreation & Athletics, Scouts, Shelters/Homelessness, Special Olympics, United Funds/United Ways, Volunteer Services, YMCA/YWCA/YMHA/YWHA, Youth Organizations

Contributions Analysis

Giving Priorities: Higher education, social service, the arts, civic concerns, medical research, single-disease health organizations, international organizations, and scientific organizations.
Arts & Humanities: 10% to 15%. Support is for major nationally oriented groups and community-based organizations. Supports museums and performing arts centers.
Education: About 50%. Grants support educational initiatives and inner-city youth programs.
Health: 10% to 15%.
Social Services: 10% to 15%. Supports organizations in the New York area or in cities where company has branch offices. Other areas of interest include shelters for the homeless, child welfare, volunteer services, and youth organizations, including those serving at-risk youth.
Note: Total contributions made in 1996.

Application Procedures

Initial Contact: Send a brief letter of inquiry requesting guidelines.
Application Requirements: Include a description of organization, amount requested, purpose of funds

sought, recently audited financial statement, annual report, proof of tax-exempt status, names and affiliations of board members.
Deadlines: None.
Decision Notification: Proposals are reviewed on a quarterly basis.

Restrictions

Foundation does not give to political, religious, veterans or fraternal groups, individuals or non-501 (c)(3) organizations.
The foundation reports that most unsolicited proposals are not funded.

Additional Information

In 1994, the company reported that it changed its name. The company was formerly known as First Boston Inc., but is now known as Credit Suisse First Boston Corp. Additionally, the company's trust has changed its name from First Boston Foundation Trust to Credit Suisse First Boston Foundation Trust.
Publications: Guidelines

Corporate Officials

Stephen A. M. Hester: chief financial officer, chairman PRIM CORP EMPL chief financial officer: Credit Suisse First Boston.
David Mulford: chairman B Rockford, IL 1937. ED Lawrence University BA (1959); Boston University MA (1962); Oxford University PhD (1966). PRIM CORP EMPL chairman: Credit Suisse First Boston. NONPR AFFIL trustee: Lawrence University; member: White House Fellows Association; member: Council Fgn Relations. CLUB AFFIL member: Metropolitan Club.
Allen D. Wheat: president, chairman PRIM CORP EMPL president, chairman: Credit Suisse First Boston Corp.

Foundation Officials

Adrian R. T. Cooper: trustee PRIM CORP EMPL managing director: Credit Suisse First Boston.
Joe McLaughlin: trustee
Elisabeth Millard: trustee
Ken Miller: trustee PRIM CORP EMPL vice chairman: Credit Suisse First Boston. CORP AFFIL director: Viacom Inc.
David C. O'Leary: chairman, trustee NONPR AFFIL director: Good Shepherd Services.
Douglas L. Paul: trustee
Ruedi Stalder: trustee B Solothurn, Switzerland 1940. CORP AFFIL director: Credit Suisse First Boston Corp.
Andy Stone: trustee

Grants Analysis

Disclosure Period: calendar year ending 1998
Total Grants: $1,000,000*
Number of Grants: 60
Average Grant: $10,000
Highest Grant: $75,000
Typical Range: $5,000 to $10,000
***Note:** Grants analysis was provided by the foundation.

Recent Grants

Note: Grants derived from 1996 Form 990.

Arts & Humanities

20,000	New York Public Library, New York, NY
5,000	Ballet Hispanico, New York, NY
5,000	Woodruff Arts Center, Atlanta, GA

Civic & Public Affairs

50,000	Pride First Corporation, New York, NY
10,000	Community Impact Corporation, New York, NY
10,000	Cord Foundation, New York, NY
5,000	City Parks Foundation, New York, NY
5,000	Junior League, New York, NY
5,000	Lawyers Alliance, New York, NY
5,000	NAACP Act So, New York, NY
5,000	NAACP Legal Defense Fund, New York, NY
5,000	National Minority Business Council, New York, NY
5,000	Prospect Park Alliance, Brooklyn, NY

Education

25,000	Cities in Schools, New York, NY
25,000	Prep for Prep, New York, NY
10,000	Cooke Center for Learning and Development, New York, NY
10,000	Junior Achievement, New York, NY
10,000	Student and Sponsor Partnership, New York, NY
5,000	Daniel Murphy Scholarship Foundation, Chicago, IL
5,000	East Harlem College and Career Counseling Program, New York, NY
5,000	East Harlem Tutorial Program, New York, NY
5,000	New York City School Volunteer Program, New York, NY

Environment

10,000	Fresh Air Fund, New York, NY

Health

10,000	Leukemia Society of America, New York, NY
10,000	March of Dimes Birth Defects Foundation, New York, NY
10,000	Ronald McDonald House, New York, NY
6,000	New York Hospital Cornell Medical Center, New York, NY
5,000	Children's Blood Foundation, New York, NY
5,000	New York Blood Center, New York, NY

International

10,000	CARE, New York, NY

Religion

5,000	Good Shepherd Services, New York, NY
5,000	Salvation Army, New York, NY

Social Services

25,000	City Kids Foundation, New York, NY
10,000	Boy Scouts of America, New York, NY
10,000	City Kids Foundation, New York, NY
10,000	New York Cares, New York, NY
10,000	New York Special Olympics, New York, NY
10,000	New York Times Neediest Cases Funds, New York, NY
10,000	United Way, New York, NY
10,000	Yorkville Pantry, New York, NY
7,750	United Way Crusade of Mercy, Chicago, IL
5,000	Association to Benefit Children, New York, NY
5,000	Boys and Girls Clubs, New York, NY
5,000	Boys Harbor, New York, NY
5,000	Camphill Foundation, Kimberton, PA
5,000	Children's Storefront, New York, NY
5,000	Henry Street Settlement, New York, NY
5,000	Project Reach Youth, Brooklyn, NY
5,000	YMCA, New York, NY
5,000	YWCA, New York, NY

Crestar Finance Corp.

Company Contact

Richmond, VA
Web: http://www.crestar.com

Company Description

Revenue: US$22,861,900,000
Employees: 8,720
SIC(s): 6022 State Commercial Banks, 6712 Bank Holding Companies.

Nonmonetary Support

Contact: James Warrick, Executive Vice President
Note: Co. provides an unspecified amount of nonmonetary support in the form of donated property or land which is no longer used by banks.

Corporate Sponsorship

Type: Festivals/fairs
Contact: Nancy Greby, Marketing/Advertising

Crestar Foundation

Giving Contact

Ms. Brenda L. Skidmore, President
Crestar Foundation
919 East Main Street
Richmond, VA 23219
Phone: (804)782-5000
Fax: (804)782-5191

Description

EIN: 237336418
Organization Type: Corporate Foundation
Giving Locations: headquarters and operating communities.
Grant Types: Employee Matching Gifts, General Support.
Note: Employee matching gift ratio: 1 to 1. Company will match any employee's contributions of $25 or more up to an aggregate of $3,000 annually, for eligible educational institutions and cultural organizations.

Giving Philosophy

'Private support of nonprofit organizations has become of much greater importance to our society in recent years. In recognition of our belief in the value of corporate philanthropy, Crestar will give primary consideration to those activities which contribute to the social and economic development of the communities it serves.' *Crestar Corporate Contributions Program*

Financial Summary

Total Giving: $4,000,000 (1999 approx); $3,302,448 (1998); $2,860,389 (1997). Note: Contributes through corporate direct giving program and foundation. Giving includes foundation only.
Giving Analysis: Giving for 1997 includes: foundation ($2,290,542); foundation grants to United Way ($388,650); foundation matching gifts ($181,197); 1998: foundation ($2,588,070); foundation grants to United Way ($519,861); foundation matching gifts ($194,517)
Assets: $5,015,823 (1998); $289,345 (1997); $122,652 (1996)
Gifts Received: $8,000,000 (1998); $2,850,000 (1997); $1,255,553 (1996). Note: Gifts received from Crestar Bank.

Typical Recipients

Arts & Humanities: Arts Associations & Councils, Arts Centers, Arts Festivals, Arts Funds, Arts Outreach, Ballet, Community Arts, Ethnic & Folk Arts, Historic Preservation, History & Archaeology, Libraries, Museums/Galleries, Music, Opera, Theater
Civic & Public Affairs: Botanical Gardens/Parks, Business/Free Enterprise, Chambers of Commerce, Economic Development, Economic Policy, Employment/Job Training, Civic & Public Affairs-General, Housing, Parades/Festivals, Philanthropic Organizations, Public Policy, Urban & Community Affairs, Zoos/Aquariums
Education: Arts/Humanities Education, Business Education, Colleges & Universities, Community & Junior Colleges, Economic Education, Education Funds, Engineering/Technological Education, Environmental Education, Faculty Development, Medical Education, Minority Education, Private Education (Precollege),

Public Education (Precollege), Secondary Education (Public), Special Education
Environment: Air/Water Quality, Environment-General, Resource Conservation
Health: AIDS/HIV, Cancer, Children's Health/Hospitals, Clinics/Medical Centers, Emergency/Ambulance Services, Eyes/Blindness, Health Policy/Cost Containment, Health Funds, Health Organizations, Heart, Hospices, Hospitals, Mental Health, Multiple Sclerosis, Speech & Hearing
International: Health Care/Hospitals, International Relations
Religion: Religious Organizations, Religious Welfare, Social/Policy Issues
Science: Science Exhibits & Fairs, Science Museums, Science Museums, Scientific Centers & Institutes, Scientific Research
Social Services: At-Risk Youth, Child Welfare, Community Service Organizations, Domestic Violence, Family Services, Food/Clothing Distribution, People with Disabilities, Recreation & Athletics, Scouts, Senior Services, Shelters/Homelessness, Social Services-General, United Funds/United Ways, YMCA/YWCA/YMHA/YWHA, Youth Organizations

Contributions Analysis

Giving Priorities: Health, human services, education, the arts, and civics.
Arts & Humanities: 15%. Supports museums, performing arts and literary groups, historic preservation, and arts funds and centers. Public broadcasting and libraries are also of interest. Includes matching gifts.
Civic & Public Affairs: 35%. Economic development in operating communities is primary focus. Also supports national organizations that promote public understanding of economics and free enterprise.
Education: 24%. Primarily supports private colleges and universities through independent college funds. Supports private secondary and elementary schools that are important to communities served by Crestar. Support is also provided in the form of employee matching gifts.
Health: 25%. Major emphasis is on United Way organizations serving Crestar communities. Awards capital and other grants to hospitals, religious welfare organizations such as the Salvation Army, youth homes, and scouting.
Note: Total contributions in 1998.

Application Procedures

Initial Contact: Send a written proposal to local Crestar president or to foundation.
Application Requirements: Include project and operating budgets, full description of area of need, reason for request, expected benefits from program.
Deadlines: October 15; budgeting is done in the fourth quarter for the following year.
Review Process: President of foundation or local Crestar facility makes recommendations to contributions committee, which meets in July and December.
Evaluative Criteria: Request conforms to priority areas, corporate presence in geographic area served by organization, program or activity improves economy and quality of life in community, evidence of good management and active involvement of community leaders, and direct or indirect benefits to corporation or its employees.

Restrictions

Does not support individuals; political parties or candidates; religious, veterans', or fraternal organizations, unless activity benefits general community or involves economic education; member agencies of united funds, unless special permission has been granted to solicit funds; organizations that foster or encourage racial, religious, class, or other prejudices; or organizations that do not qualify as tax-exempt under Section 501(c)(3) of the Internal Revenue Code.

Corporate Officials

James M. Wells, III: president B 1946. ED Rutgers University; University of Colorado; University of North Carolina (1968). PRIM CORP EMPL president: Crestar Financial Corp. CORP AFFIL president: Crestar Bank; director: Crestar Mortgage Corp.

Foundation Officials

Brenda L. Skidmore: principal
Shirley Doss Swartwout: secretary, treasurer
Richard Granville Tilghman: chairman, chief executive officer B Norfolk, VA 1940. ED University of Virginia BA (1963). PRIM CORP EMPL chairman, chief executive officer, president: Crestar Financial Corp. CORP AFFIL chairman, chief executive officer: Crestar Bank; director: Chesapeake Corp. NONPR AFFIL director: Virginia Foundation Independent Colleges; trustee: Virginia Music Foundation; principal: Virginia Business Council; director: Richmond Renaissance Inc.; member: Virginia Bankers Association; trustee: Colonial Williamsburg Foundation; member: American Bankers Association; member: Bankers Roundtable. CLUB AFFIL Country Club Virginia; Commonwealth Club.

Grants Analysis

Disclosure Period: calendar year ending 1998
Total Grants: $2,588,070*
Number of Grants: 750 (approx)
Average Grant: $3,451
Typical Range: $1,000 to $10,000
***Note:** Giving excludes United Way, matching gifts.

Recent Grants

Note: Grants derived from 1996 Form 990.

Arts & Humanities
B&O Railroad Museum, Baltimore, MD
Cultural Alliance, Washington, DC
Fine Arts Rockbridge, Lexington, VA
Historic Manassas, Manassas, VA
Preservation Alliance of Virginia, Staunton, VA
Pride of Baltimore, Baltimore, MD
Reynolds Homestead, Critz, VA
Virginia Museum Foundation, Richmond, VA

Civic & Public Affairs
Better Business Bureau, Baltimore, MD
Christmas in April Anne Arundel County, Annapolis, MD
First Night, Annapolis, MD
Orange Downtown Alliance, Orange, VA
Virginia Housing Coalition, Christiansburg, VA
Washington Airports Task Force, Washington, DC

Education
Academy of the Arts, Easton, MD
Averett College, Danville, VA
Carlisle School, Martinsville, VA
Independent College Fund of Maryland, Baltimore, MD
James River Day School, Lynchburg, VA
Junior Achievement, Hunt Valley, MD
Loyola College, Baltimore, MD
Old Dominion University, Norfolk, VA
Randolph Macon College, Ashland, VA
Riverside School, Richmond, VA
Roanoke College, Salem, VA
Teacher's Appreciation, Radford, VA
Virginia Tech, Blacksburg, VA
Virginia Wesleyan College, Norfolk, VA

Environment
Chesapeake Bay Foundation, Annapolis, MD
Nature Conservancy, Virginia Chapter, Charlottesville, MD
River Foundation, Roanoke, VA

Health
American Heart Association, Harrisonburg, VA
Augusta Regional Free Clinic, Fisherville, VA
Children's Hospital of the Kings Daughters, Norfolk, VA
Friends of Hospice, Easton, MD
Full Circle AIDS Hospice Support, Norfolk, VA
Harrisonburg Rescue Squad, Harrisonburg, VA
House of Mercy, Baltimore, MD
Luray Volunteer Rescue Squad, Luray, VA
Memorial Hospital Foundation, Easton, MD
Ronald McDonald House, Charlottesville, VA
Virginians for Health Care Solutions, Richmond, VA
Williamsburg Community Hospital, Williamsburg, VA

Religion
Catholic Charities, Baltimore, MD

Science
Maryland Science Center, Baltimore, MD
Virginia Discovery Museum, Charlottesville, VA

Social Services
Family Services of Central Virginia, Lynchburg, VA
Long Way Home, Radford, VA
United Way Central Maryland, Baltimore, MD
Virginia Voice for the Print Handicapped, Richmond, VA

CROFT-LEOMINSTER

Company Contact

Baltimore, MD
Web: http://www.croft-leominster.com

Company Description

Former Name: Leominister.
Employees: 7

Croft-Leominster Foundation

Giving Contact

L. Gordon Croft, Chairman
300 Water St
Baltimore, MD 21202
Phone: (410)576-0100
Fax: (410)576-8232
Email: jyoo@croft-leominster.com

Description

Founded: 1990
EIN: 521682796
Organization Type: Corporate Foundation
Giving Locations: MD: Baltimore
Grant Types: General Support.

Financial Summary

Total Giving: $199,395 (1998); $134,120 (1997); $57,000 (1996)
Assets: $3,753,884 (1998); $3,744,469 (1997); $2,046,851 (1996)
Gifts Received: $912,801 (1997); $639,087 (1996). Note: In 1996, contributions were received from L. Gordon Croft.

Typical Recipients

Arts & Humanities: Arts & Humanities-General, Museums/Galleries
Civic & Public Affairs: Botanical Gardens/Parks, Clubs, Employment/Job Training, Civic & Public Affairs-General, Housing, Public Policy, Safety, Urban & Community Affairs
Education: Colleges & Universities, Community & Junior Colleges, Education Funds, Education Reform, Private Education (Precollege), Secondary Education (Private), Student Aid
Health: Alzheimers Disease, Emergency/Ambulance Services, Heart, Hospitals
International: Health Care/Hospitals, Missionary/Religious Activities

Religion: Churches, Religious Organizations, Religious Welfare
Social Services: Big Brother/Big Sister, Community Service Organizations, Food/Clothing Distribution, Recreation & Athletics, Shelters/Homelessness, Substance Abuse, Youth Organizations

Contributions Analysis

Giving Priorities: Disadvantaged and homeless people, education of children of all levels of scholarships, and healthcare institutions.
Arts & Humanities: Less than 1%.
Civic & Public Affairs: 5%. Supports foundations, volunteer programs, and housing.
Education: 93%. Major grant to Johns Hopkins University. Supports colleges and education organizations.
Health: Less than 1%.
Religion: 1%. Funds churches and religious good will services.
Social Services: 1%. Supports community programs for the hungry, for senior citizens, and for families.
Note: Total contributions made in 1998.

Application Procedures

Initial Contact: Send a brief letter of inquiry.
Application Requirements: Include a description of charitable purpose of organization, amount requested and purpose of funds sought.
Deadlines: None.

Corporate Officials

Kent G. Croft: president, chief executive officer PRIM CORP EMPL president, chief executive officer: Croft-Leominster.
L. Gordon Croft: chairman PRIM CORP EMPL chairman: Croft-Leominster.

Foundation Officials

Jane A. Croft: secretary
Kent G. Croft: president (see above)
L. Gordon Croft: vice president (see above)

Grants Analysis

Disclosure Period: calendar year ending 1998
Total Grants: $199,395
Number of Grants: 55
Average Grant: $588*
Highest Grant: $167,600
Typical Range: $50 to $1,000
***Note:** Average grant figure excludes highest grant.

Recent Grants

Note: Grants derived from 1997 Form 990.

Civic & Public Affairs

600 Habitat for Humanity, La Plata, MD -- support aid to disadvantaged
500 Roland Park, Baltimore, MD -- support Spirit Campaign
240 Joe Sandusky Fund, Sparks, MD -- for local appeal

Education

43,000 Johns Hopkins University, Baltimore, MD -- for educational assistance
28,225 Washington and Lee University, Lexington, VA -- support educational programs
25,100 St. Paul's School, Brooklandville, MD -- support educational programs
11,000 Randolph-Macon Women's College, Lynchburg, VA -- support educational programs
10,000 Dartmouth College, Hanover, NH -- support educational programs
1,000 Charles County Community College, La Plata, MD -- support educational programs
1,000 Independent College Fund of Maryland, Baltimore, MD -- for educational assistance
1,000 Queen of Peace Cluster School, Baltimore, MD -- support educational programs
1,000 University of Maryland Love of Learning School, College Park, MD -- support educational programs

Health

360 Physicians Memorial Hospital Foundation, La Plata, MD -- for local appeal

International

500 St. Ignatius Church, Port Tobacco, MD -- for local appeal

Religion

1,000 Good Shepherd Church, Ruxton, MD -- support aid to disadvantaged

Social Services

4,000 RAISE, Baltimore, MD -- support aid to disadvantaged
2,000 Homeless Advocacy Association, White Plains, MD -- support aid to disadvantaged
1,000 Genesis Jobs, Baltimore, MD -- support aid to disadvantaged
500 Bags of Plenty, Baltimore, MD -- for local appeal
250 Big Brothers and Big Sisters, Baltimore, MD -- support aid to disadvantaged

CROWN BOOKS

Company Contact

Landover, MD

Company Description

Employees: 2,300
SIC(s): 5942 Book Stores.
Parent Company: Dart Group Corp., Landover, MD, United States

Crown Books Foundation

Giving Contact

Cathy Postelle, Corporate Contributions
3300 75th Ave.
Landover, MD 20785
Phone: (301)226-1251

Description

Founded: 1988
EIN: 521590726
Organization Type: Corporate Foundation
Giving Locations: nationally.
Grant Types: General Support.

Financial Summary

Total Giving: $270,250 (1995); $75,500 (1993); $284,433 (1992)
Assets: $3,471,057 (1995); $3,490,235 (1993); $3,455,694 (1992)

Typical Recipients

Civic & Public Affairs: Economic Development
Education: Education-General, Literacy, Student Aid
Health: Children's Health/Hospitals
Religion: Jewish Causes

Application Procedures

Initial Contact: Send a brief letter of inquiry on organization's letterhead. Include a detailed a description of organization and the purpose of funds sought.
Deadlines: None. Because of the volume of requests, a written reply to request is sent if applicant includes a stamped, self-addressed envelope.

Restrictions

Contributions limited to organizations addressing reading and literacy issues.

Corporate Officials

Mark Flint: co-chief operating officer PRIM CORP EMPL co-chief operating officer: Crown Books.
Donald Pilch: chief financial officer PRIM CORP EMPL chief financial officer: Crown Books.
Bonita Wilson: co-chief operating officer PRIM CORP EMPL co-chief operating officer: Crown Books.

Foundation Officials

Elliot Arditti: director PRIM CORP EMPL general counselor: Dart Group Corp.

Grants Analysis

Disclosure Period: calendar year ending 1995
Number of Grants: 7
Highest Grant: $250,000
Typical Range: $150 to $5,000

Recent Grants

Note: Grants derived from 1995 Form 990.

Civic & Public Affairs

1,250 Flary Small Business Development Center, Manassas, VA

Education

5,000 DC Reading is Fundamental, Washington, DC
5,000 Reading Is Fundamental, Washington, DC
3,000 National Book Foundation, New York, NY
1,000 Washington Scholarship Fund, Washington, DC

Health

5,000 Make-A-Wish Foundation, Rockville, MD

Religion

250,000 US Holocaust Memorial Museum, Washington, DC

CSR RINKER MATERIALS CORP.

Company Contact

West Palm Beach, FL

Company Description

Employees: 2,900
SIC(s): 1422 Crushed & Broken Limestone, 3271 Concrete Block & Brick, 3273 Ready-Mixed Concrete, 3441 Fabricated Structural Metal.
Parent Company: CSR America
Parent Revenue: US$4,803,000,000

Operating Locations

FL: CSR Rinker Materials Corp., Miami; CSR Florida, West Palm Beach; CSR Rinker Materials Corp., West Palm Beach; CSR Rinker Materials Corp., West Palm Beach; GA: CSR America, Atlanta; NV: CSR West, Las Vegas; TX: CSR Central, Houston

Giving Contact

Frank LaPlaca, Administrator
Rinker Materials Corp.
1501 Belvedere Road
West Palm Beach, FL 33406
Phone: (561)833-5555
Fax: (561)820-8359
Email: flaplaca@wpbcentral.csra.com

Description

Founded: 1957
Organization Type: Corporate Giving Program. Supports preselected organizations only.

Giving Locations: FL: Dade County, Palm Beach County
Grant Types: General Support, Multiyear/Continuing Support.

Financial Summary

Total Giving: $422,185 (fiscal year ending March 31, 1998); $597,398 (fiscal 1997); $525,356 (fiscal 1996). Note: Contributes through corporate direct giving program only.
Giving Analysis: Giving for fiscal 1997 includes: foundation ($287,387); foundation grants to United Way ($132,298); foundation gifts to individuals ($2,500); fiscal 1998: foundation ($318,000); foundation grants to United Way ($104,185)
Assets: $8,220,664 (fiscal 1998); $7,400,157 (fiscal 1997); $7,689,597 (fiscal 1996)

Typical Recipients

Arts & Humanities: Arts Centers, Music, Performing Arts
Civic & Public Affairs: Community Foundations, Economic Development, Professional & Trade Associations, Safety, Urban & Community Affairs
Education: Business Education, Colleges & Universities, Community & Junior Colleges, Education-General, Literacy, Preschool Education, Private Education (Precollege), Science/Mathematics Education, Student Aid
Environment: Wildlife Protection
Health: Cancer, Children's Health/Hospitals
International: International Relief Efforts
Social Services: Scouts, Substance Abuse, United Funds/United Ways, YMCA/YWCA/YMHA/YWHA, Youth Organizations

Contributions Analysis

Giving Priorities: Business organizations, private secondary schools, business education, religion, and youth organizations.
Arts & Humanities: 2%. Supports the Raymond F. Kravis Center.
Civic & Public Affairs: 5%. Supports community foundations and other civic organizations.
Education: 59%. Funds universities and colleges.
Environment: 2%. Supports wildlife initiatives.
International: 2%. Supports a children's foundation.
Social Services: 27%. Supports United Way, scouts, and substance abuse initiatives.

Additional Information

The company's foundation has been defunct as of 1996.

Corporate Officials

Bob Capasso: chief financial officer, chief executive officer PRIM CORP EMPL chief financial officer: CSR Rinker Materials Corp.
Bill Snyder: president, chief executive officer PRIM CORP EMPL president, chief executive officer: CSR Rinker Materials Corp.

Giving Program Officials

Frank LaPlaca: administrator

Grants Analysis

Disclosure Period: fiscal year ending March 31, 1998
Total Grants: $318,000*
Number of Grants: 23
Average Grant: $9,909*
Highest Grant: $100,000
Typical Range: $1,000 to $30,000
***Note:** Giving excludes United Way. Average grant figure excludes highest grant.

Recent Grants

Note: Grants derived from 1997 Form 990.

Arts & Humanities
10,000 Raymond F. Kravis Center

Civic & Public Affairs
20,000 Broward Community Foundation
2,000 AGC Washington, Los Vegas, NV

Education
100,000 University of Florida
50,000 Stetson University
25,000 Palm Beach Atlantic College
20,000 University of Miami
10,000 Robert Wesleyan College
10,000 Rollins College
10,000 University of Florida (Rinker)
10,000 UNLV Foundation
6,000 EPI/NAPA
5,000 Florida State University
2,500 University of Washington

Environment
5,000 Washington Wildlife & Recreation
1,000 Survey Wildlife

Health
10,000 MD Anderson Cancer Center
500 The Cancer Institute

International
10,000 Give Kids World Foundation

Social Services
100,000 United Way of Palm Beach County
5,000 Boy Scouts of America - Houston
4,185 United Way So Nevada
4,000 Gulfstream Council of Boy Scouts
1,000 Northern Area Substance Abuse Area

CSS Industries, Inc.

Company Contact

Philadelphia, PA

Company Description

Employees: 3,928
SIC(s): 2679 Converted Paper Products Nec, 2754 Commercial Printing--Gravure, 3497 Metal Foil & Leaf, 6719 Holding Companies Nec.
Parent Company: Philadelphia Industries

Corporate Sponsorship

Type: Arts & cultural events

Farber Foundation

Giving Contact

Jack Farber, Chairman & President
1845 Walnut Street, Suite 800
Philadelphia, PA 19103
Phone: (215)569-9900
Fax: (215)569-9979

Alternate Contact

Jacqueline A. Tullys, Coordinator
Note: For scholarship program information.

Description

EIN: 236254221
Organization Type: Corporate Foundation
Giving Locations: PA
Grant Types: General Support.

Financial Summary

Total Giving: $433,732 (1998); $337,835 (1997); $392,993 (1996)
Giving Analysis: Giving for 1996 includes: foundation ($209,485); foundation scholarships ($168,508); foundation grants to United Way ($15,000); 1997: foundation ($230,335); foundation scholarships ($89,500); foundation grants to United Way ($18,000); 1998: foundation ($215,561); foundation scholarships ($198,171); foundation grants to United Way ($20,000)
Assets: $4,090,217 (1998); $4,479,502 (1997); $4,001,406 (1996)
Gifts Received: $100,000 (1990); $100,000 (1989). Note: In 1990, contributions were received from Philadelphia Industries.

Typical Recipients

Arts & Humanities: Community Arts, Dance, History & Archaeology, Museums/Galleries, Music, Performing Arts, Public Broadcasting
Civic & Public Affairs: Chambers of Commerce, Civil Rights, Economic Policy, Civic & Public Affairs-General, Nonprofit Management, Philanthropic Organizations, Urban & Community Affairs, Women's Affairs
Education: Business Education, Colleges & Universities, Education Funds, Education-General, Health & Physical Education, Legal Education, Special Education, Student Aid
Health: Alzheimers Disease, Arthritis, Cancer, Children's Health/Hospitals, Diabetes, Emergency/Ambulance Services, Health Policy/Cost Containment, Hospitals, Kidney, Long-Term Care, Medical Rehabilitation, Medical Research, Multiple Sclerosis, Single-Disease Health Associations
International: Health Care/Hospitals, International Affairs, Missionary/Religious Activities
Religion: Jewish Causes, Religious Organizations, Religious Welfare, Social/Policy Issues
Science: Science Museums
Social Services: Community Service Organizations, Crime Prevention, Delinquency & Criminal Rehabilitation, Emergency Relief, Family Services, People with Disabilities, Recreation & Athletics, Scouts, Social Services-General, Substance Abuse, United Funds/United Ways, Youth Organizations

Contributions Analysis

Giving Priorities: Social services, with emphasis on Jewish welfare, the arts, health organizations, education, and civic causes.
Arts & Humanities: 14%. Supports museums, music organizations, and the performing arts.
Civic & Public Affairs: 5%. Funds philanthropic and community based organizations.
Education: 4%. Funds colleges and universitites.
Health: 12%. Primarily supports single-disease causes.
International: 2%. Supports organizations that are international in scope.
Religion: 49%. Major grant to the American Jewish Committee.
Social Services: 14%. Funds United Way and youth programs.
Note: Total contributions in 1998.

Application Procedures

Initial Contact: Request application form and guidelines.
Deadlines: Mid April for scholarships.

Additional Information

Provides scholarships to children of employees who have been with CSS Industries or one of its subsidiaries for at least two years.
Publications: Application Guidelines

Corporate Officials

Jack Farber: chairman, president, director B 1933. ED University of Pennsylvania BS (1954-1968). PRIM CORP EMPL chairman, president, director: CSS Industries. CORP AFFIL director: Hunt Co.; director: Paper Magic Group Inc.; chairman: Berwick Industries Inc.
Clifford E. Pietrafitta: vice president finance, treasurer B Philadelphia, PA 1962. ED LaSalle University (1984). PRIM CORP EMPL vice president finance, treasurer: CSS Industries, Inc.

Foundation Officials

James G. Baxter: vice president, treasurer B Audubon, NJ 1948. ED Lehigh University (1970). PRIM CORP EMPL president consumer products division: CSS Industries.

Stephen Victor Dubin: vice president, secretary B Brooklyn, NY 1938. ED Boston University JD (1961); City University of New York BA (1961). PRIM CORP EMPL senior vice president, secretary, general counsel: CSS Industries Inc. NONPR AFFIL member: Pennsylvania Bar Association; member: Philadelphia Bar Association; member: New York State Bar Association; member: Masons; member: Nassau County Bar Association; member: Illinois Bar Association; member: County Lawyers Association; member: Free Accepted Masons; member: Chicago Bar Association; member: American Bar Association; member: American Society of Corporate Secretaries; chairman: America Jewish Committee.

Jack Farber: president (see above)

Grants Analysis

Disclosure Period: calendar year ending 1998
Total Grants: $215,561*
Number of Grants: 39
Average Grant: $5,527
Highest Grant: $112,500
Typical Range: $250 to $50,000
***Note:** Giving excludes scholarship; United Way.

Recent Grants

Note: Grants derived from 1998 Form 990.

Arts & Humanities

25,000 Regional Performing Arts Center, Philadelphia, PA -- General
5,000 Philadelphia Museum of Art, Philadelphia, PA -- General
2,500 The Music Group, Philadelphia, PA -- General

Civic & Public Affairs

3,500 Greater Philadelphia Urban Affairs Coalition, Philadelphia, PA -- General
2,500 Committee of Seventy, Philadelphia, PA -- General
1,800 League of Women Voters of Pennsylvania, Havertown, PA -- General
1,000 Leaque of Women Voters of Pennsylvania, Harrisburg, PA -- General
1,000 Phillies Charities, Inc., Blue Bell, PA -- General
500 Delaware Valley Grantmakers, Philadelphia, PA -- General
500 Pennsylvania Economy League, Inc., Philadelphia, PA -- General
500 Philadelphia - Israel Chamber of Commerce Foundation, Philadelphia, PA -- General
50 F.O.P. General Welfare Fund, Philadelphia, PA -- General

Education

5,000 University of Penna Museum of Archaeology & Anthropology, Philadelphia, PA -- General
2,500 Boston University School of Law, Boston, MA -- General
1,000 Lehigh University, Bethlehem, PA -- General
1,000 Thomas Jefferson University Women's Board of Trustees, Philadelphia, PA -- General
500 Jr. Achievement of Delaware Valley, Newtown Square, PA -- General
500 Queens College Foundation, Flushing, NY -- General

Health

15,000 Eagle Fly for Leukemia, Bala Cynwyd, PA -- General
5,000 Juvenile Diabetes Foundation, Bala Cynwyd, PA -- General
3,000 National Tay-Sachs and Allied Diseases Association of Delaware Valley (NTSAD-DV), Jenkintown, PA -- General
2,500 Magee Rehabilitation, Philadelphia, PA -- General
1,000 ALS Association Greater Philadelphia Chapter, Philadelphia, PA -- General
1,000 Alzheimer's Association, Philadelphia, PA -- General
1,000 American Cancer Society, Philadelphia, PA -- General
650 United Cerebral Palsy Association, Philadelphia, PA -- General
300 Philadelphia Physicians for Social Responsibility, Philadelphia, PA -- General
131 Leukemia Society, Philadelphia, PA -- General

International

3,000 Operation Smile-Philadelphia, Philadelphia, PA -- General
1,500 World Affairs Council of Philadelphia, Philadelphia, PA -- General

Religion

112,500 American Jewish Committee, New York, NY -- General
2,500 Israel 50, Philadelphia, PA -- General

Social Services

20,000 United Way of Southeastern PA, Philadelphia, PA -- General
3,000 Cradle of Liberty Council, BSA, Philadelphia, PA -- General
2,500 The American Camping Association, Martinville, IN -- General
2,500 Eagle Youth Partnership, Philadelphia, PA -- General
2,500 Operation Understanding, Philadelphia, PA -- General
750 Association for Developmental Disabilities, Jenkintown, PA -- General
560 Citizens Crime Commission, Philadelphia, PA -- General
320 Blenheim Athletic, Blackwood, NJ -- General

CSX CORP.

Company Contact

Richmond, VA
Web: http://www.csx.com

Company Description

Revenue: US$9,898,000,000
Employees: 47,314
Fortune Rank: 159, per FORTUNE Magazine's list of 500 Largest U.S. Corporations (1999).
FF 159
SIC(s): 3731 Ship Building & Repairing, 4011 Railroads--Line-Haul Operating, 4489 Water Passenger Transportation Nec, 6719 Holding Companies Nec.

Giving Contact

Alan Rudnick, Vice President, General Counsel, Corporate Secretary
CSX Corp.
1 James Ctr.
901 E. Cary St.
Richmond, VA 23219-5629
Phone: (804)782-1525
Fax: (804)783-1356
Email: alan_rudnick@csx.com

Alternate Contact

Anita Hill, Administrator of Corporate Contributions
Phone: (804)782-1583

Description

Organization Type: Corporate Giving Program
Giving Locations: nationally.
Grant Types: Employee Matching Gifts, Endowment, General Support, Matching.
Note: Employee matching gift ratio: 1 to 1 to institutions of higher education only.

Financial Summary

Total Giving: $3,314,000 (1996 approx). Note: Contributes through corporate direct giving program only.

Typical Recipients

Arts & Humanities: Arts & Humanities-General
Civic & Public Affairs: Civic & Public Affairs-General
Education: Education-General
Health: Health-General
Social Services: Social Services-General

Application Procedures

Initial Contact: letter
Application Requirements: name of organization, purpose of request, amount requested, deadline for funding, and proof of tax-exempt status
Deadlines: None.

Corporate Officials

Alan A. Rudnick: vice president, general counsel, corporate secretary B Cleveland, OH 1947. ED University of Chicago BA (1969); Case Western Reserve University JD (1973). PRIM CORP EMPL vice president, general counsel, corporate secretary: CSX Corp. NONPR AFFIL member: Ohio Bar Association; member: Virginia Bar Association; member: American Bar Association; member: Maryland Bar Association.

John William Snow: chairman, president, chief executive officer B Toledo, OH 1939. ED University of Toledo BA (1962); University of Virginia PhD (1965); George Washington University Law School LLB (1967). PRIM CORP EMPL chairman, president, chief executive officer: CSX Corp. CORP AFFIL director: USX Corp.; chairman, director: Sea-Land Service; director: Textron Inc.; director: Johnson & Johnson; director: NationsBank Corp.; director: Circuit City Stores Inc.; chairman: CSX Transportation. NONPR AFFIL trustee: Johns Hopkins University; member: Virginia Bar Association.

Giving Program Officials

Anita H. Hill: administration assistant PRIM CORP EMPL administrative assistant: CSX Corp.

CUMMINGS PROPERTIES MANAGEMENT

Company Contact

200 West Cummings Park
Woburn, MA 01801
Phone: (781)935-8000
Fax: (781)935-1990
Web: http://www.cummings.com

Company Description

Employees: 350

Cummings Properties Foundation

Giving Contact

Rob Nigro, Managing Trustee
Cummings Properties Foundation
Email: leasing@cummings.com
Web: http://www.cummings.com/mck_info.html

Description

Founded: 1986
EIN: 046541313
Organization Type: Corporate Foundation. Supports preselected organizations only.
Giving Locations: MA: Woburn
Grant Types: General Support.

Financial Summary

Total Giving: $671,453 (1997); $225,000 (1996); $200,000 (1995). Note: Contributes through foundation only.
Giving Analysis: Giving for 1997 includes: foundation ($590,000); foundation scholarships ($81,453)
Assets: $10,340,615 (1997); $8,431,546 (1996); $5,941,259 (1995)
Gifts Received: $115,400 (1997); $1,258,695 (1996); $439,600 (1995). Note: Contributions are received from 50 Concord Street, Lundquist, Anderson Central, Interstate 93, WRB, and other donors who made contributions of less than $10,000.

Typical Recipients

Arts & Humanities: Arts Associations & Councils, History & Archaeology, Libraries, Museums/Galleries, Music, Public Broadcasting
Civic & Public Affairs: Business/Free Enterprise, Clubs, Employment/Job Training, Ethnic Organizations, Civic & Public Affairs-General, Housing, Municipalities/Towns, Philanthropic Organizations, Public Policy, Safety, Urban & Community Affairs, Zoos/Aquariums
Education: Arts/Humanities Education, Business Education, Colleges & Universities, Elementary Education (Private), Education-General, Minority Education, Private Education (Precollege), School Volunteerism, Secondary Education (Private), Secondary Education (Public), Student Aid
Health: Cancer, Children's Health/Hospitals, Clinics/Medical Centers, Diabetes, Heart, Hospices, Hospitals, Medical Research, Nursing Services, Respiratory, Single-Disease Health Associations
International: Health Care/Hospitals, Missionary/Religious Activities
Religion: Churches, Jewish Causes, Religious Organizations, Religious Welfare
Science: Science Museums
Social Services: Animal Protection, At-Risk Youth, Camps, Child Welfare, Community Service Organizations, Crime Prevention, Food/Clothing Distribution, People with Disabilities, Recreation & Athletics, Scouts, Senior Services, Special Olympics, Substance Abuse, United Funds/United Ways, YMCA/YWCA/YMHA/YWHA, Youth Organizations

Contributions Analysis

Civic & Public Affairs: 13%. Supports Fidelity Charitable Gift Fund.
Education: 87%. Provides scholarships and supports Winchester Community Music school.
Note: Total contributions made in 1997.

Restrictions

The foundation does not make multi-year pledges; make contributions to an organization more than once per calendar year; donate to causes or fundraising events which benefit one person or a specific group of people; make donations to marketing or advertising; or sponsors athletic teams.

Additional Information

The foundation has suspended its grant making, but is primarily committed to the ongoing sponsorship of New Horizons, a non-profit retirement community in Woburn. They also sponsor the $1 million McKeown Scholars program in eight local communities.

Corporate Officials

William S. Cummings: chairman, director B 1937. ED Tufts University (1958). PRIM CORP EMPL chairman: Cummings Properties Management. CORP AFFIL president: WRB Inc.; president: New Horizons Madonna Hall; chairman: Walnut Hill Properties Inc. NONPR AFFIL trustee: Tifts University.
James L. McKeown: president, director B 1955. PRIM CORP EMPL president, director: Cummings Properties Management.

Foundation Officials

Susan F. Brand, Esq.: officer
Daniel W. Cummings: trustee
Marilyn D. Cummings, MD: trustee PRIM NONPR EMPL officer: New Horizons at Madonna Hall.
John A. Forsyth: trustee
Marian E. Forsyth: trustee
James L. McKeown: president, trustee (see above)

Grants Analysis

Disclosure Period: calendar year ending 1997
Total Grants: $590,000*
Number of Grants: 2
Average Grant: $295,000
Highest Grant: $500,000
Typical Range: $10,000 to $100,000
***Note:** Average grant figure excludes highest grant.

Recent Grants

Note: Grants derived from 1996 Form 990.

Arts & Humanities

4,000	Boston Symphony Orchestra, Boston, MA
436	North Shore Music Theater
120	New Hampshire Public Television, NH
100	Essex Shipbuilding Museum, Essex, MA
100	Friends of Ipswich Public Library, Ipswich, MA

Civic & Public Affairs

67,575	Fidelity Investments Charitable Gift Fund, Boston, MA
5,000	Beverly Fire Department Fund, Beverly, MA
500	Woburn Council of Social Concern, Woburn, MA
100	Winton Club, Winchester, MA

Education

29,000	Tufts University Parents Fund, Medford, MA
5,000	Winchester Community Music School, Winchester, VA
2,500	A Better Chance, Boston, MA
1,000	Goodyear School
1,000	Winchester Scholarship Foundation, Winchester, VA
750	Milton Academy, Milton, MA
500	Beverly High School, Beverly, MA
500	Edward F. Lang Scholarship Fund
400	Junior Achievement, Boston, MA
135	Hurld School
100	Phillips Academy, Hanover, MA
100	University of Pennsylvania, Philadelphia, PA

Health

30,500	Hospice Care, Boston, MA
20,000	American Cancer Society, Boston, MA
2,000	Boston Regional Medical Center, Boston, MA
800	Massachusetts Easter Seal Society, Worcester, MA
750	Joslin Diabetes Center, Boston, MA
500	ALS Association, MA
250	Winchester Hospital, Winchester, VA
100	Muscular Dystrophy Association, Boston, MA
100	Visiting Nurse Health Care

International

100	Lasalette Foreign Missions

Religion

15,000	St. Eulalias Church
10,000	Cardinal's Appeal, Boston, MA
2,000	Tufts University Hillel Foundation, Medford, MA
1,000	St. Joseph's Church, Boston, MA

Science

1,000	Museum of Science, Boston, MA

Social Services

10,863	Supportive Living, Andover, MA
5,000	YMCA, Boston, MA
1,700	Boys and Girls Club, Woburn, MA
1,000	Kids Kingdom at Leland Park
1,000	YMCA, Beverly, MA
800	Massachusetts Assisted Living Facility Association, MA
500	Winchester Sports Foundation, Winchester, VA
150	United Way Massachusetts Bay, Boston, MA
125	Girls, Incorporated, Boston, MA
100	Friends of Sudbury Senior Citizens, Sudbury, MA
100	Hope
100	Massachusetts Society for Prevention of Cruelty to Animals, Boston, MA
100	New Hampshire Special Olympics, Manchester, NH
100	Northshore Bikeways Coalition

Cummins Engine Co., Inc.

Company Contact

Columbus, IN
Web: http://www.cummins.com

Company Description

Revenue: US$6,266,000,000
Employees: 28,341
Fortune Rank: 262, per FORTUNE Magazine's list of 500 Largest U.S. Corporations (1999).
FF 262
SIC(s): 3519 Internal Combustion Engines Nec, 7549 Automotive Services Nec.

Operating Locations

Australia: Onan Australia Pty. Ltd., Hindmarsh; Cummins Engine Co. Pty. Ltd., Scoresby; Belgium: Cummins Diesel NV, Mechelen, Anvers; Canada: Fleetguard International Corp., Mississauga; Colombia: Cummins de Colombia SA, Barranquilla; France: Mixjet Ile de France, Corbas, Rhone; Mixjet SA, Corbas, Rhone; Cummins France SARL, Quimper, Finistere; Fleetguard (SNC), Quimper, Finistere; Petbow, Quimper, Finistere; SNC Kuss, Quimper, Finistere; Petbow Welding Products Ltd., Sandwich, Kent; Dampers SA, Venissieux, Rhone; Holset Service Societe en Nom Collectif, Venissieux, Rhone; Techniparts SA, Venissieux, Rhone; Germany: Holset Engineering Deutschland GmbH, Bannewitz, De-Ost; Cummins Diesel Deutschland GmbH, Gross Gerau, Hessen; Hong Kong: Cummins Engine Hong Kong Ltd., Sha Tin; India: Kirloskar Cummins Ltd., Pune; Ireland: Cummins Engine Co. Ltd., Dublin; Italy: Cummins Diesel Italia SpA, San Giuliano Milanese; Japan: Cummins Diesel (Japan) Ltd., Tokyo; Mexico: Cummins SA de CV, Ciudad de Mexico; Cummins de Occidente SA de CV, Tlaquepaque; Netherlands: Turbo Europa BV, Hoogland, Utrecht; Onan International BV, Hoorn, Limburg; Norway: Newage Norge AS, Oslo, Akershus; New Zealand: Cummins Engine Co. Ltd., Auckland; Spain: Stamford Iberica SA, Madrid; United Kingdom: Holset Engineering Co. Ltd., Huddersfield, West Yorkshire; Auto Diesels Power Plant Ltd., London; Newage Ltd., London; Cummins Engine Co. Ltd., New Malden, Surrey; Cummins United Kingdom Ltd.,

New Malden, Surrey; Nu-Plant Service Ltd., Sandwich, Kent; Petbow Custom Generators Ltd., Sandwich, Kent; PGI Manufacturing Ltd., Sandwich, Kent; PGI (UK Holding) Ltd., Sandwich, Kent; Power Group International Ltd., Sandwich, Kent; Markon Engineering Co. Ltd., Stamford, Lincolnshire; Newage International Ltd., Stamford, Lincolnshire; Newage Machine Tools Ltd., Stamford, Lincolnshire; Onan International Ltd., Stamford, Lincolnshire

Nonmonetary Support

Value: $35,716 (1995); $95,000 (1990); $200,000 (1989)
Type: Donated Equipment; Donated Products; Loaned Executives

Corporate Sponsorship

Type: Sports events; Other
Note: Also sponsors awards banquets for various nonprofits.

Cummins Engine Foundation

Giving Contact

Tracy H. Souza, Executive Director, President
Cummins Engine Foundation
Box 3005, Mail Code 60909
Columbus, IN 47202-3005
Phone: (812)377-3746
Fax: (812)377-3971

Alternate Contact

500 Jackson Street
Columbus, IN 47201

Description

EIN: 356042373
Organization Type: Corporate Foundation
Giving Locations: operating locations.
Grant Types: Challenge, Employee Matching Gifts, General Support, Project, Scholarship, Seed Money.

Giving Philosophy

'The challenge we face is to find ways to help these communities in their efforts to find new and effective ways to employ their resources. Just as American business is being forced to become leaner and more productive in order to meet tough international competition, so social and human services, facing government budget cuts and tighter philanthropic dollars, must continually reassess priorities and develop new responses to new needs. .. A few years ago, we cut back on our national grants and increased funding on local projects to our plant communities. We reexamined our overall philosophy and reaffirmed the key program areas of youth and education, equity and justice for the underserved, community development and the arts.' *Cummins Contributions Report*

Financial Summary

Total Giving: $3,000,000 (fiscal year ending February 28, 2000 approx); $3,000,000 (fiscal 1999 approx); $3,000,000 (fiscal 1998 approx). Note: Contributes through corporate direct giving program and foundation. 1996 Giving includes foundation. 1995 Giving includes corporate direct giving ($309,805); foundation ($2,449,334); matching gifts ($314,735); scholarship ($98,580).
Assets: $5,694,694 (fiscal 1996); $6,091,595 (fiscal 1995); $600,000 (fiscal 1992)
Gifts Received: $4,702,413 (fiscal 1995); $4,000,000 (fiscal 1994). Note: In fiscal 1995, the foundation received contributions from Fleetguard, Inc.

Typical Recipients

Arts & Humanities: Arts Appreciation, Arts Associations & Councils, Arts Festivals, Arts Funds, Arts Outreach, Community Arts, Dance, Historic Preservation, History & Archaeology, Libraries, Museums/Galleries, Music, Performing Arts, Public Broadcasting
Civic & Public Affairs: African American Affairs, Botanical Gardens/Parks, Chambers of Commerce, Civil Rights, Community Foundations, Economic Development, Economic Policy, Employment/Job Training, Housing, Legal Aid, Municipalities/Towns, Nonprofit Management, Public Policy, Rural Affairs, Urban & Community Affairs, Women's Affairs
Education: Afterschool/Enrichment Programs, Arts/Humanities Education, Business Education, Business-School Partnerships, Colleges & Universities, Community & Junior Colleges, Education Funds, Education Reform, Elementary Education (Private), Engineering/Technological Education, Education-General, International Exchange, Minority Education, Private Education (Precollege), Public Education (Precollege), Science/Mathematics Education, Student Aid
Environment: Environment-General, Resource Conservation, Wildlife Protection
Health: Children's Health/Hospitals, Eyes/Blindness, Hospices, Hospitals, Mental Health, Preventive Medicine/Wellness Organizations, Public Health, Research/Studies Institutes
International: Foreign Arts Organizations, Foreign Educational Institutions, Human Rights, International Peace & Security Issues, International Relations
Religion: Religious Welfare
Social Services: Child Welfare, Community Centers, Community Service Organizations, Counseling, Day Care, Domestic Violence, Emergency Relief, Family Planning, Family Services, Food/Clothing Distribution, Recreation & Athletics, Scouts, Senior Services, Shelters/Homelessness, Substance Abuse, United Funds/United Ways, Volunteer Services, YMCA/YWCA/YMHA/YWHA, Youth Organizations

Contributions Analysis

Giving Priorities: Youth welfare, educatin, civic development, social welfare, united way, justice, public policy, and nonprofit international organizations. Company provides contributions to U.S.-based nonprofits with an international focus. Interests include international business education, South Africa, economics, and foreign relations. Contributions range from $50,000 to $150,000 annually for domestic organizations. Company also contributes through its foreign subsidiaries, but funds are not tracked. In India, the Cummins Diesel India Foundation, with the support of Cummins and Kirlosakr-Cummins Ltd., has helped establish an engineering college for women, the only one in India. In Brazil, Cummins built a local elementary school, named after founder Clessie Cummins, that is now operated by thelocal community. Cummins employees also volunteer their time and ongoing support for more than 350 students at the school. The Cummins Medical Center in Brazil has provided medical services to thousands of people since 1992, when Cummins employees worked with the community to build it.
Civic & Public Affairs: (United Funds & United Way) About 25%. (Public Policy) Less than 5%.
Education: About 40%. Supports private, public, and religious elementary and secondary education, colleges, and universities. Also supports youth groups, Big Brothers/Big Sisters, YMCA's, and community foundations. Provides scholarships and matches employee gifts.
Note: Above priorities reflect foundation giving.

Application Procedures

Initial Contact: written inquiry or proposal; local projects outside Indiana should be sent to local plant manager; proposals from Indiana communities should be directed to the foundation
Application Requirements: brief description of problem being addressed, what program hopes to achieve, operating plan, budget for project and organizational budget, description of key leadership, criteria for evaluating success of program, and documentation of tax-exempt status
Deadlines: None.
Review Process: annual philanthropic plan and budget are set in December
Decision Notification: directors meet three times a year; small grants are made from a discretionary budget between meetings

Restrictions

Does not support political causes or candidates, sectarian religious activities, fraternal organizations, goodwill advertising, or individuals. Scholarships are given only to employees' children.

Additional Information

Cummins contributes 5% of its domestic pretax profits and 1% of its international profits for charitable activities.

Corporate Officials

John Kenneth Edwards: executive president, group president power generation B Erie, PA 1944. ED Claremont McKenna College BA (1966); Vanderbilt University MA (1972). PRIM CORP EMPL president: Cummins Engine Co. Inc.
James Alan Henderson: vice chairman, chief executive officer, director B South Bend, IN 1934. ED Princeton University AB (1956); Harvard University MBA (1963). PRIM CORP EMPL chairman, chief executive officer, director: Cummins Engine Co. Inc. CORP AFFIL director: Rohm & Haas Co.; director: Inland Steel Industries Inc.; director: Landmark Communications Inc.; director: Ameritech Corp. NONPR AFFIL member policy commission: Business Roundtable; president board trustee: Culver Education Foundation; member: Business Council.
F. Joseph Loughrey: group president worldwide operations & technology, vice president B Holyoke, MA 1949. ED University of Notre Dame BS (1971). PRIM CORP EMPL group president, executive vice president: Cummins Engine Co. Inc. ADD CORP EMPL director: Development Services Inc.; director: Onan Corp.; director: Tower Automotive Inc.
Joseph Irwin Miller: director associate B Columbus, IN 1909. ED Yale University AB (1931); Oxford University MA (1933). PRIM CORP EMPL director associate: Cummins Engine Co. Inc. CORP AFFIL director: Irwin Financial Corp. NONPR AFFIL member: Phi Beta Kappa; honorary fellow: Royal Institute British Architects; member: Ind Academy; member: Business Council; member: Conference Board; fellow: Branford College; member: American Philosophical Society; member: Beta Gamma Sigma; honorary member: American Institute Architects; fellow: American Academy of Arts & Sciences.
Theodore Matthew Solso: president, chief operating officer, director B Spokane, WA 1947. ED DePauw University (1969); Harvard University MBA (1971). PRIM CORP EMPL president, chief operating officer, director: Cummins Engine Co. Inc. CORP AFFIL director: Cyprus Amax Minerals Co.; director: Irwin Financial Corp.; director: BP Amoco Corp.; president: Cummins Americas Inc.

Foundation Officials

C. Roberto Cordaro: director
John Kenneth Edwards: director (see above)
Mark R. Gerstle: director
James Alan Henderson: chairman, director (see above)
F. Joseph Loughrey: director (see above)
Ted Leroy Marston: director PRIM CORP EMPL consultant: Cummins Engine Co. Inc.
Joseph Irwin Miller: director (see above)
William Irwin Miller: director B Columbus, IN 1956. ED Yale University BA (1978); Stanford University

MBA (1981). PRIM CORP EMPL chairman: Irwin Financial Corp. CORP AFFIL chairman: Irwin Management Co. Inc.; chairman: Tipton Lakes Co.; director: Cummins Engine Co. Inc. NONPR AFFIL trustee: Christian Theological Seminary; trustee: Taft School; director: American Public Radio Minneapolis.

Kiran M. Patel: director, treasurer

Brenda S. Pitts: director B Madison, IN 1950. ED Indiana University (1972). PRIM CORP EMPL vice president: Cummins Engine Co., Inc.

Henry Brewer Schacht: director B Erie, PA 1934. ED Yale University BS (1956); Harvard University MBA (1962). CORP AFFIL director: Johnson & Johnson; director: Knoll Inc.; director: Chase Manhattan Corp.; chairman executive committee, director: Cummins Engine Co. Inc.; director: CBS Corp.; director: Chase Manhattan Bank NA Inc.; director: ALCOA Inc.; director: AT&T Corp. NONPR AFFIL member: Tau Beta Pi; honorary trustee: Yale Corp.; member: Harvard University Business School; senior member: Conference Board; member: Council Foreign Relations; member: Business Enterprise Trust; honorary trustee: Committee for Economic Development; honorary trustee: Brookings Institution; member: Business Council.

Theodore Matthew Solso: director (see above)

Richard Burkett Stoner, Jr.: director B Indianapolis, IN 1946. ED Yale University (1968); Harvard University (1974). PRIM CORP EMPL vice president: Cummins Engine Co. Inc. CORP AFFIL chairman: Holset Engineering Co. Ltd. UK; partner: Johnson Smith Pence Densborn Wright Health.

Bernard Joseph White: director NONPR AFFIL associate dean, professor: University Michigan School Business Administration.

Grants Analysis

Disclosure Period: fiscal year ending February 28, 1998
Total Grants: $4,729,743*
Number of Grants: 203
Average Grant: $12,625
Highest Grant: $465,851
Typical Range: $1,000 to $15,000
*Note: Grants analysis supplied by foundation.

Recent Grants

Note: Grants derived from fiscal 1998 Form 990.

Arts & Humanities

75,000	Heritage Fund of Bartholomew County, Columbus, IN -- payment on $260,000 grant, for support for Children, Youth, and Families Initiative
50,000	Heritage Fund of Bartholomew County, Columbus, OH -- payment on $150,000 grant, for support of construction of the Veterans Memorial
47,500	Columbus Area Arts Council, Columbus, IN -- payment on $45,000 grant
25,000	Columbus Pro Musica, Columbus, IN
24,744	Bartholomew County Public Library, Columbus, IN -- payment on grant, for architect fees for Hope branch library
21,651	Heritage Fund of Bartholomew County, Columbus, IN -- payment on grant, for fees for design of Veterans Memorial
17,000	Columbus Area Arts Council, Columbus, IN -- payment on grant, for Steward Fund
11,931	Fund for the Arts of Chautauqua County

Civic & Public Affairs

136,540	City of Columbus, Columbus, IN -- payment on $220,000 grant, for architect fees for Woodside Fire Station
38,964	Visitors Center, Columbus, IN -- design fees for architectural exhibit
22,000	Indiana Donors Alliance, Indianapolis, IN
20,000	Madison Community Foundation, Madison, IN -- payment on grant, for operating support
15,000	Jennings County Community Foundation, Mount Vernon, IN -- payment on $25,000 grant, for startup operating support
15,000	NAACP, New York, NY
10,000	Committee for Economic Development, New York, NY

Education

450,000	Bartholomew Consolidated School Corporation, Columbus, IN -- payment on grant, for architect fees for expansion of Richards, Smith, and Cliffy Creek schools
50,000	Bartholomew Consolidated School Corporation, Columbus, IN -- support for Alternative Education Network
50,000	New American Schools Development Corporation, Arlington, VA -- payment on grant, for schoolhouse program in Memphis, TN
40,000	North Carolina Wesleyan College, Rocky Mount, NC -- payment on grant, for capital campaign
35,000	Bartholomew Consolidated School Foundation, Columbus, IN
30,000	United Negro College Fund, Fairfax, VA
20,000	Putnam County Schools -- Fleetguard program
17,000	Partners in Public Education, Memphis, TN -- payment on grant, for support of principals' training program
15,000	Flatrock Haw Creek School Corporation, Hope, IN -- support for student assistance program
15,000	Rose-Hulman Institute of Technology, Terre Haute, IN -- payment on $45,000 grant, for support of graduate students from India

Health

41,963	Visions, Rocky Mount, NC -- payment on grant, for support of Common Ground training
40,000	Columbus Regional Hospital Foundation, Columbus, IN -- payment on grant, for support of Volunteers in Medicine clinic
25,000	Mayo Foundation, Rochester, MN -- payment on $100,000 grant, for capital gift

International

33,000	Public Radio International, Minneapolis, MN -- payment on grant, for support of New Century campaign
12,000	Cummins Bursary Scheme Trust, Johannesburg, Republic of South Africa -- payment on grant, for multiyear scholarship support for disadvantaged Africans

Religion

50,000	National Council of Churches, New York, NY -- support for Burned Churches Fund

Social Services

200,000	United Way Bartholomew County, Columbus, IN
81,125	United Way, Minneapolis, MN
52,049	Foundation for Youth, Columbus, IN -- payment on $500,000 grant, for capital campaign
50,000	YMCA, Fostoria, OH -- capital campaign
33,979	Foundation for Youth, Columbus, IN -- planning for facility renovation
30,960	Heritage Fund of Bartholomew County, Columbus, IN -- challenge grant for the Child Care Fund
30,000	Foundation for Youth, Columbus, IN -- support for youth advocate
25,099	United Way Jackson County
25,000	Scott County Family YMCA, Scottsburg, IN -- capital campaign
21,600	United Way, Memphis, TN
20,000	Boys Club, Seymour, IN -- payment on grant, for capital campaign
20,000	United Way South Chautauqua County
19,227	United Way, Charleston, SC
18,299	United Way Jennings County
18,000	Human Services, Columbus, IN -- payment on $32,600 grant, for support of homeless shelter
17,106	United Way, Fostoria, OH
15,885	United Way, Huntsville, AL
15,000	United Way Bartholomew County, Columbus, IN -- startup support for volunteer center
11,734	United Way Johnson County

CUNA MUTUAL GROUP

Company Contact

Madison, WI
Web: http://www.cunamutual.com

Company Description

Employees: 2,809
SIC(s): 6311 Life Insurance, 6321 Accident & Health Insurance, 6399 Insurance Carriers Nec.

Nonmonetary Support

Type: Donated Equipment
Note: Nonmonetary support budget is approximately $5,000 annually.

CUNA Mutual Group Foundation, Inc.

Giving Contact

Terri J. Fiez, Executive Director
CUNA Mutual Group Foundation
5910 Mineral Point Rd.
PO Box 391
Madison, WI 53701-0391
Phone: (608)231-7908
Fax: (608)238-2449
Note: Toll free: (800)937-2644

Description

EIN: 396105418
Organization Type: Corporate Foundation
Giving Locations: CA: Pomona; GA: Duluth; IA: Waverly; MI: Southfield; MN: Bloomington; NY: Albany; TX: Dallas; WI: Madison generally in communities where CUNA Mutual is located.
Grant Types: Capital, Emergency, Employee Matching Gifts, Matching, Multiyear/Continuing Support.

Giving Philosophy

'Today, our commitment to charitable contributions and other social responsibility programs that promote the general well-being of the communities in which our employees live and work is an integral part of our operations.'
The mission of the CUNA Mutual Group Foundation is to support and create programs that enable individuals to help themselves attain self-sufficiency, and to leverage giving with volunteer activities and partnerships with other organizations:' *CUNA Mutual Group Grant Information: People Helping People*

Financial Summary

Total Giving: $534,141 (1998); $477,349 (1997); $488,000 (1996). Note: Contributes through corporate direct giving program and foundation.
Giving Analysis: Giving for 1995 includes: foundation ($479,000); 1997: foundation grants to United Way ($242,555); foundation ($234,794); 1998: foundation ($534,141)

Assets: $515,372 (1997); $401,385 (1996); $354,640 (1995)
Gifts Received: $563,000 (1997); $488,000 (1996); $492,165 (1995). Note: The foundation receives contributions from CUNA Mutual Group.

Typical Recipients

Arts & Humanities: Arts Associations & Councils, Arts Centers, Arts Festivals, Arts Funds, Community Arts, Dance, Arts & Humanities-General, Historic Preservation, History & Archaeology, Libraries, Museums/Galleries, Music, Opera, Performing Arts, Public Broadcasting, Theater
Civic & Public Affairs: African American Affairs, Botanical Gardens/Parks, Business/Free Enterprise, Community Foundations, Economic Development, Civic & Public Affairs-General, Housing, Minority Business, Municipalities/Towns, Parades/Festivals, Philanthropic Organizations, Public Policy, Safety, Urban & Community Affairs, Zoos/Aquariums
Education: Business Education, Business-School Partnerships, Colleges & Universities, Education Associations, Education Funds, Education-General, Gifted & Talented Programs, Legal Education, Minority Education, Public Education (Precollege), Religious Education, Science/Mathematics Education, Secondary Education (Public), Student Aid, Vocational & Technical Education
Environment: Energy, Resource Conservation
Health: AIDS/HIV, Cancer, Children's Health/Hospitals, Clinics/Medical Centers, Emergency/Ambulance Services, Health Policy/Cost Containment, Health Organizations, Medical Rehabilitation, Medical Research, Mental Health, Nursing Services, Prenatal Health Issues, Public Health, Single-Disease Health Associations
International: International Organizations
Religion: Religious Welfare
Social Services: At-Risk Youth, Big Brother/Big Sister, Camps, Child Welfare, Community Centers, Community Service Organizations, Day Care, Emergency Relief, Family Services, Food/Clothing Distribution, People with Disabilities, Recreation & Athletics, Scouts, Senior Services, Shelters/Homelessness, Social Services-General, Special Olympics, United Funds/United Ways, YMCA/YWCA/YMHA/YWHA, Youth Organizations

Contributions Analysis

Giving Priorities: United Way, education, performing arts, housing, and civic organizations.
Arts & Humanities: 7%. Supports theater, orchestras, pubic broadcasting, and history organizations.
Civic & Public Affairs: 17%. Funds housing, legal and economic concerns, and civic institutions and events.
Education: 11%. Emphasis on minority vocational training, fields related to CUNA Mutual business, employee recruitment, quality projects that do not receive tax support, and projects that link business need with educational development.
Health: 6%. Emphasis is on cost containment, wellness and prevention, family support and services access, and local-level services.
Social Services: 58%. Majority of funding supports United Way. Emphasis is on basic resources (food/shelter/clothing); employment and training; minority and underprivileged youth; transportation; and community assistance.
Note: Total contributions in 1997.

Application Procedures

Initial Contact: Call to request guidelines and application.
Application Requirements: Include completed application form, list of current board of directors, most recent audited financial statement, current operating budget (and project budget, if applicable), copy of annual report, copy of IRS tax exemption letter, and any supporting material.
Deadlines: None, for funding under $5,000; requests over $5,000 must be received six weeks before the board meets to be considered for funding at the meeting; contact the foundation executive director for exact dates of meetings.
Evaluative Criteria: Program serves communities where company employees lives and work or where employees are active volunteers; involves training, management assistance, and involvement by employees and not just monetary assistance; leverages funds through challenge grants, matching funds or cooperative funding from other sources; reduces duplication and provides cost-effective services; proposal benefits a large section of the community at a low per-capita cost; and provides direct services rather than general operations; demonstrates significant, measurable outcomes.
Decision Notification: Board reviews proposals three times annually, in February, May, and October.

Restrictions

The foundation will not provide grants for organizations without IRS 501(c)(3) nonprofit status; individuals; political parties, candidates, or partisan political campaigns; professional associations; religious purposes; endowment funds; the purchase of tickets or items for fund raising events; or for organizations that conflict with the company's goals, products, or policyowners.
The foundation will generally not consider grants for travel funds, benefit tickets, or courtesy advertising; athletic activities; regional or national programs; organizations that receive a major portion of their funding from government sources; grantmaking bodies; service clubs; general operating support; capital campaigns, unless approved by the Capital Fund Raising Committee in Madison, Wisconsin; or programs that receive United Way funding.

Additional Information

Madison, WI; Pomona, CA; and Waverly, IA are considered 'primary locations' for grant consideration.
Publications: Application Guidelines; Application Form

Corporate Officials

Terri Fiez: manager community relationsrc
Michael B. Kitchen: president, chief executive officer, director B Toronto, ON Canada 1945. ED Ryerson Polytechnic Institute (1968). PRIM CORP EMPL president, chief executive officer, director: CUNA Mutual Insurance Group ADD CORP EMPL president: Members Life Insurance Co.; president: CUNA Mutual Insurance Society; president: CUNA Mutual Insurance Agency; president: CUNA Mutual Investment Corp.; president: CUNA Mutual Life Insurance Co. CORP AFFIL director: CUMIS General Insurance Co.; director: CUMIS Life Insurance Co.; director: Canadian Northern Shield Insurance Co.

Foundation Officials

Larry Blanchard: assistant secretary, treasurer
Terri Fiez: executive director (see above)
Michael B. Kitchen: secretary, treasurer, executive officer (see above)
Neil A. Springer: vice president, director PRIM CORP EMPL treasurer: Cuna Mutual Insurance Agency. CORP AFFIL officer: CUNA Mutual Insurance Society; officer: CUNA Mutual Life Insurance Co.
Larry Wilson: president, director CORP AFFIL director: CUNA Mutual Insurance Group.

Grants Analysis

Disclosure Period: calendar year ending 1997
Total Grants: $234,794*
Number of Grants: 148
Average Grant: $1,586
Highest Grant: $35,000
Typical Range: $100 to $5,000
***Note:** Giving excludes United Way.

Recent Grants

Note: Grants derived from 1997 Form 990.

Arts & Humanities

8,000	Friends of WHA-TV, Madison, WI
7,500	Very Special Arts, Muncie, IN
5,000	Gerald A. Bartell Community Theater, Black Earth, WI
5,000	Waverly Public Library
1,500	Wisconsin History Foundation, Madison, WI -- sesquicentennial committee
1,000	American Players Theater, Spring Green, WI
1,000	CTM Productions
1,000	Madison Repertory Theater, Madison, WI
1,000	Wisconsin Chamber Orchestra, Madison, WI
1,000	Wisconsin Youth Symphony Orchestra, Madison, WI

Civic & Public Affairs

35,000	Habitat for Humanity of Dane County, Madison, WI
17,500	Henry Vilas Park Zoological Society, Madison, WI
15,000	Credit Union Foundation
5,000	Community Housing and Services
1,500	Madison Art Center, Madison, WI
1,000	Center for Public Representation, Madison, WI
1,000	NECA/IBEW Holiday Fantasy in Lights
900	People for Parks, Minneapolis, MN
850	Capitol City Parade Association, Middleton, WI

Education

18,000	CUNA Management Schools
7,600	Harvey Williams Memorial Scholarship
5,000	MATC Foundation
5,000	Wisconsin Center for Academically Talented Youth, Madison, WI
5,000	Wisconsin Foundation of Independent Colleges, Milwaukee, WI
2,715	University of Wisconsin Foundation, Madison, WI
2,500	Business and Education Partnership, Madison, WI
1,500	Filene Education Foundation
1,500	University of California Riverside, Riverside, CA
1,010	University of Wisconsin Whitewater Foundation, WI
875	Wartburg College, Waverly, IA

Environment

1,500	Energy Services, Madison, WI

Health

13,000	American Red Cross Dane County Chapter, Madison, WI
5,000	Certified Nursing Assistant Career Alliance
5,000	Madison Area Rehabilitation Centers, Madison, WI
1,500	American Red Cross Pomona Valley Chapter
1,500	Doernbecher Children's Hospital, Portland, OR
1,500	Meriter Foundation, Madison, WI
1,000	Life and Health Insurance Medical Research Fund, Washington, DC

Social Services

195,000	United Way of Dane County, Madison, WI
36,055	United Way Community Services, Detroit, MI
11,500	United Way of Mount Baldy Region
5,000	City of Madison, Madison, WI
5,000	East Madison Community Center
5,000	Second Harvest Food Bank of Southern Wisconsin, Madison, WI
1,500	Children's Center of Wayne County, Detroit, MI

1,500	Girl Scouts of America Black Hawk Council, Madison, WI
1,000	Dane County Youth Connection, Madison, WI
1,000	Madison Metropolitan School District, Madison, WI -- community recreation
1,000	Satellite Family Child Care
1,000	Wheelchair Recycling Project

HELENE CURTIS INDUSTRIES, INC.

Company Contact

Chicago, IL
Web: http://www.yoursalon.com

Company Description

Revenue: US$1,265,600,000
Employees: 3,500
SIC(s): 2844 Toilet Preparations, 6719 Holding Companies Nec.
Parent Company: Unilever NV, Rotterdam, Netherlands
Parent Revenue: US$45,180,000,000

Nonmonetary Support

Type: Cause-related Marketing & Promotion; Donated Products; Loaned Employees

Corporate Sponsorship

Type: Arts & cultural events; Music & entertainment events
Contact: Dr. Eugene Zeffren, Executive Vice President

Giving Contact

Donna Riley, Administration Assistant
Helene Curtis Inc.
325 North Wells Street
Chicago, IL 60610
Phone: (312)661-2571
Fax: (312)527-5103

Description

Organization Type: Corporate Giving Program
Giving Locations: IL
Grant Types: Employee Matching Gifts, General Support.
Note: Employee gifts program matches up to $1,000 per employee.

Financial Summary

Total Giving: Contributes through corporate direct giving program only.

Typical Recipients

Arts & Humanities: Arts & Humanities-General
Civic & Public Affairs: Civic & Public Affairs-General
Education: Education-General
Health: Health-General
Social Services: Community Service Organizations, Social Services-General

Application Procedures

Initial Contact: letter of inquiry
Application Requirements: a description of organization
Deadlines: None.

Restrictions

Applications are accepted from local nonprofit organizations only.

Corporate Officials

Gerald S. Gidwitz: chairman B Memphis, TN 1906. ED University of Chicago PhB (1927). PRIM CORP EMPL chairman: Helene Curtis Industries, Inc. CORP AFFIL partner: Tribros Investment Co.; vice president: Hiniker Co.; partner: Metro Structures. NONPR AFFIL director: Jamestown Foundation; trustee: Roosevelt University; director: Chicago Crime Commission; member: Illinois Manufacturer Association; trustee: Auditorium Theatre Council.

Ronald J. Gidwitz: president, chief executive officer B Chicago, IL 1945. ED Brown University (1967). PRIM CORP EMPL president, chief executive officer: Helene Curtis Industries, Inc. CORP AFFIL president: Helene Curtis Inc.; president: Coster Co.; director: America National Canada Co.; director: Continental Materials Corp. NONPR AFFIL director: Lyric Opera Chicago; director: Museum Science & Industry; director: Field Museum Natural History; member: Chicagoland Chamber of Commerce; chairman board trustee: City College Chicago; member national board directors, governor: Boys & Girls Clubs America.

Giving Program Officials

Eugene Zeffren: executive vice president B St. Louis, MO 1941. ED Washington State University (1963); University of Chicago (1967). PRIM CORP EMPL executive vice president, chief operating officer: Helene Curtis Industries, Inc.

CYPRUS AMAX MINERALS CO.

Company Contact

Englewood, CO
Web: http://www.cyprusamax.com

Company Description

Former Name: Cyprus Minerals Co.
Profit: US$124,000,000
Employees: 11,000

Nonmonetary Support

Value: $5,000 (1998); $1,000 (1994)
Type: Donated Equipment; In-kind Services

Cyprus Amax Foundation

Giving Contact

Lola Ball, Manager, Government Affairs & Charitable Contributions
Cyprus Amax Minerals Co.
9100 E. Mineral Circle
PO Box 3299
Englewood, CO 80112
Phone: (303)643-5000
Fax: (303)643-5988
Email: lball@cyprus.com

Alternate Contact

Phone: (303)643-5090

Description

Founded: 1996
EIN: 841317947
Organization Type: Corporate Foundation
Giving Locations: headquarters and operating communities.
Grant Types: Endowment, General Support.

Giving Philosophy

'The purpose of Cyprus Amax Minerals Company's charitable contribution program is to produce direct benefits for the Company, its subsidiaries, its employees, and the mining industry. Only those charitable, educational, or community requests that have a direct bearing on the Company or the mining industry and its future are appropriate for a publicly held corporation.'
Charitable Contributions Guidelines

Financial Summary

Total Giving: $124,230 (1997); $523,230 (1996 approx); $580,000 (1995 approx). Note: Contributes through corporate direct giving program and foundation. 1996 Giving includes foundation ($477,447); matching gifts (45,783).
Assets: $4,045,521 (1997); $3,427,595 (1996)
Gifts Received: $195,133 (1997); $255,632 (1996)

Typical Recipients

Arts & Humanities: Arts Institutes, Museums/Galleries
Civic & Public Affairs: Zoos/Aquariums
Education: Colleges & Universities, Environmental Education, Science/Mathematics Education, Student Aid
Environment: Environment-General
Health: Emergency/Ambulance Services, Single-Disease Health Associations
Social Services: United Funds/United Ways

Contributions Analysis

Arts & Humanities: 15% to 20%. Contributes to museums, performing and visual arts with the goal ofenriching the quality of life in company communities.
Civic & Public Affairs: 5% to 10%. Supports the environment, economic research, resource study, international affairs, and science and technology.
Education: 40% to 50%. Supports higher education to help prepare tomorrow's generation to understand, contribute, and assume responsibility. Stresses support of scholarships, fellowships, professorships, and other educational activities in fields of interest to the mining industry.
Health & Welfare 25% to 30%. Supports organizations serving youth, minorities, the disadvantaged, and the aged. Also supports some medical programs and hospitals in communities serving employees and their families.

Application Procedures

Initial Contact: brief written proposal
Application Requirements: background, purpose, and program of applicant organization; summary of the need for support and how it will be used; percent of grant that will be applied directly to the project for which funds are sought and percent that will be used for fundraising and central administration; other pledged or paid funding sources, public and/or private; percent of funds that are either raised by or contributed by board of directors; method of evaluating program effectiveness; most recent Form 990; recent financial statement or budget; Federal Employer Identification Number; statement from an officer of organization attesting to the fact that the organization is chartered, registered, or incorporated in the U.S.; proof of tax-exempt status
Deadlines: None.
Review Process: employee gifts are matched January through October, and the remaining funds are disbursed as grants in November and December of each year
Evaluative Criteria: sound management, effective scope and impact, project benefits the natural resources industry, project impacts a community with significant numbers of employees, strong backing from community

Restrictions

Foundation does not generally support: political organizations or candidates, fraternal or similar organizations, or special interest groups attempting to influence legislation; religious or sectarian organizations; memorial funds; individuals; primary and secondary education; sports and athletic events; goodwill advertising; endowments or endowment campaigns; organizations operating outside the United States; municipal, state, federal, or quasi-governmental agencies; fundraising dinners, parties, benefits, balls, or other social fundraising events. fundraising events.

Additional Information
The company generally avoids funding programs requiring significant contributions in future years, and each year's contribution does not ensure similar gifts in the future.
Publications: Guidelines

Corporate Officials
Philip C. Wolf: senior vice president, general counsel, secretary B 1948. ED University of Michigan (1969); Vanderbilt University JD (1972). PRIM CORP EMPL senior vice president, general counsel, secretary: Cyprus Amax Minerals Co. CORP AFFIL secretary: Cyprus Miami Mining Corp.; president, director: Cyprus SPLty Metals Co.

Giving Program Officials
Lola Ball: PRIM CORP EMPL manager, corporate contributions: Cyprus Amax Minerals Co.

Grants Analysis
Disclosure Period: calendar year ending 1997
Total Grants: $124,230*
Number of Grants: 7
Average Grant: $17,747
Highest Grant: $29,832
Typical Range: $5,000 to $50,000
*Note: Giving includes matching gifts, scholarship.

Recent Grants
Note: Grants derived from 1996 Form 990.

Civic & Public Affairs

25,000 Colorado's Ocean Journey, CO -- to build aquarium

Education

400,000 Colorado School of Mines, Golden, CO -- support Amax Chair in Environmental Science

28,800 Educational Testing Service, Princeton, NJ -- scholarships

23,647 Arizona State University Office of Climatology, Tempe, AZ -- research

DAILY NEWS

Company Contact
New York, NY

Company Description
Employees: 1,600
SIC(s): 2711 Newspapers.

Tribune New York Foundation

Giving Contact
John Campi, Vice President, Promotions
450 West 33rd Street, 3rd Floor
New York, NY 10001
Phone: (212)210-2100 ext 1925

Alternate Contact
220 East 42nd Street, 10th Floor
New York, NY 10017
Phone: (212)210-2603

Description
Founded: 1958
EIN: 136161525
Organization Type: Corporate Foundation
Former Name: Daily News Foundation.
Giving Locations: NY: New York
Grant Types: General Support.

Financial Summary
Total Giving: $229,165 (1996); $269,793 (1995); $203,924 (1994). Note: In 1996 Giving includes matching gifts ($9,165).
Assets: $5,487,420 (1996); $5,080,239 (1995); $4,391,726 (1994)
Gifts Received: $2,611 (1991)

Typical Recipients
Arts & Humanities: Arts Associations & Councils, Arts Centers, Arts Funds, Arts Institutes, Arts Outreach, Ballet, Community Arts, Dance, Ethnic & Folk Arts, Film & Video, Arts & Humanities-General, Historic Preservation, Libraries, Museums/Galleries, Music, Performing Arts, Public Broadcasting, Theater, Visual Arts
Civic & Public Affairs: African American Affairs, Botanical Gardens/Parks, Economic Development, Ethnic Organizations, Civic & Public Affairs-General, Hispanic Affairs, Housing, Municipalities/Towns, Public Policy, Women's Affairs, Zoos/Aquariums
Education: Afterschool/Enrichment Programs, Arts/Humanities Education, Colleges & Universities, Education Funds, Journalism/Media Education, Legal Education, Minority Education, Private Education (Precollege), School Volunteerism, Special Education
Environment: Resource Conservation, Wildlife Protection
Health: Cancer, Hospitals, Long-Term Care, Medical Research
International: Foreign Arts Organizations
Religion: Religious Organizations, Religious Welfare
Science: Scientific Centers & Institutes
Social Services: At-Risk Youth, Child Welfare, Community Service Organizations, Family Services, Food/Clothing Distribution, People with Disabilities, Recreation & Athletics, United Funds/United Ways, Volunteer Services, Youth Organizations

Application Procedures
Initial Contact: Return completed application form along with a proposal, no longer than three pages, which includes a description of the project, the community need addressed, and why the program should be funded. Also include an annual report or descriptive brochure, if available, the organization's annual budget, project budget, amount requested, recently audited financial statement, proof of tax-exempt status, a list of current directors with titles and business affiliations, and a list of all major contributors and their level of support.
Deadlines: None.

Additional Information
Contributions were temporarily suspended in early 1998. Profile reflects past priorities.

Corporate Officials
Fred Drasner: co-founder, president, chief executive officer, co-publisher, director PRIM CORP EMPL co-founder, president, chief executive officer, co-publisher, director: U.S. News & World Report.
Mortimer Benjamin Zuckerman: co-founder, chairman, co-publisher, director B Montreal, PQ Canada 1937. ED McGill University BA (1957); McGill University LLB (1961); Harvard University LLM (1962); University of Pennsylvania MBA (1962). PRIM CORP EMPL co-founder, chairman, co-publisher, director: Boston Properties Co. CORP AFFIL owner, chairman, editor-in-chief, director: US News & World Report; owner, chairman, president: Atlantic Monthly Co. NONPR AFFIL advisory board: University Pennsylvania Wharton School; director: Wolf Trap Foundation; director: Tennis Hall Fame; member: Council Foreign Relations; member: Intl Institute Strategic Studies; advisory board: Center Strategic & International Studies. CLUB AFFIL Harmonie Club; Harvard Club.

Foundation Officials
Patrick J. Austin: assistant secretary, treasurer, director
Paul A. Bissonette: vice president, director
Gail Busby: secretary
Michael Eigner: president, director
Gerald P. McCarthy: director
Robert H. Paquette: director
Kathleen Shearen Maynard Shepherd: director B New York, NY 1950. ED Tufts University (1968-1969); Duke University (1972-1973); Westchester Community College (1974-1975); New York University (1975-1977). NONPR AFFIL member: National Academy Television Arts Sciences Private Industry Council; member: Private Industry Council; member: Archdiocese Communications Comm.
Richard Stone: director

Grants Analysis
Disclosure Period: calendar year ending 1996
Total Grants: $220,000*
Number of Grants: 36
Average Grant: $6,111
Highest Grant: $24,000
Typical Range: $1,000 to $10,000
*Note: Giving excludes matching gifts.

Recent Grants
Note: Grants derived from 1996 Form 990.

Arts & Humanities

10,000 Museum of Television and Radio, New York, NY

5,000 American Ballet Theater, New York, NY

5,000 Boys Choir of Harlem, New York, NY

5,000 Broadcasters Foundation, Greenwich, CT

5,000 Caribbean Cultural Center, New York, NY

5,000 Dance Theater of Harlem, New York, NY

5,000 Jersey City Museum, Jersey City, NJ

5,000 Katonah Museum of Art, Katonah, NY

5,000 Long Island Children's Museum, Garden City, NY

Civic & Public Affairs

10,000 Foundation for Minority Interests in Media, New York, NY

5,000 Foundation of American Women in Radio and Television, New York, NY

5,000 Midtown Management Group, New York, NY

Education

10,000 Columbia University Graduate School of Journalism, New York, NY

6,000 New York Law School, New York, NY

5,000 Art Education for the Blind, New York, NY

5,000 Brooklyn Music School, Brooklyn, NY

5,000 Studio in a School Association, New York, NY

International

10,000 International Radio and Television Society Foundation, New York, NY

Social Services

24,000 Jackie Robinson Foundation, New York, NY

5,000 Children's Art Carnival, New York, NY

DAIMLERCHRYSLER CORP.

 Number 39 of Top 100 Corporate Givers

Company Contact
1000 Chrysler Dr.
Auburn Hills, MI 48326-2766
Web: http://www.daimlerchrysler.com

Company Description

Former Name: Chrysler Corp.
Assets: US$130,397,000,000
Employees: 456,000
SIC(s): 3679 Electronic Components Nec, 3711 Motor Vehicles & Car Bodies, 3714 Motor Vehicle Parts & Accessories, 6141 Personal Credit Institutions.
Parent Company: DaimlerChrysler AG, Epplestrasese 225, Stuttgart, Germany

Operating Locations

AL: DaimlerChrysler, Huntsville, Mobile; AR: DaimlerChrysler, Little Rock; AZ: DaimlerChrysler, Phoenix; CA: DaimlerChrysler, Irvine, Long Beach, Los Angeles, Ontario, Rancho Cordova, San Diego, San Leandro; CO: DaimlerChrysler, Denver; CT: DaimlerChrysler, Cheshire, Danbury, Greenwich, Stamford; DE: DaimlerChrysler, Newark; FL: DaimlerChrysler, Lake Mary, Orlando, Tampa; IL: DaimlerChrysler, Arlington Heights, Belvidere, Midlothian, Oak Brook; IN: DaimlerChrysler, Kokomo, New Castle; KS: DaimlerChrysler, Shawnee Mission; MD: DaimlerChrysler, Bowie; MI: DaimlerChrysler, Center Line, Detroit, Highland Park, Marysville, Sterling Heights, Trenton, Troy, Warren; MN: DaimlerChrysler, Plymouth Village; MO: DaimlerChrysler, Fenton; NC: DaimlerChrysler, Charlotte; NY: DaimlerChrysler, East Syracuse; OH: DaimlerChrysler, Dayton, Perrysburg, Solon, Toledo; OK: DaimlerChrysler, Oklahoma City; OR: DaimlerChrysler, Beaverton; PA: DaimlerChrysler, Allentown; SC: DaimlerChrysler, Columbia; TX: DaimlerChrysler, Houston, Laredo, Richardson; VA: DaimlerChrysler, Dunn Loring; WI: DaimlerChrysler, Waukesha; WY: DaimlerChrysler, Green River

Nonmonetary Support

Value: $6,000,000 (1997); $6,000,000 (1996); $6,000,000 (1995)
Type: Donated Equipment; Donated Products
Note: Nonmonetary support is principally in the form of vehicles donated to educational institutions for use in training mechanics.

Corporate Sponsorship

Range: less than $1,000,000
Type: Arts & cultural events; Music & entertainment events
Contact: Jim Julow, Executive Director of Marketing Operations

DaimlerChrysler Corp. Fund

Giving Contact

Lynn A. Feldhouse, Vice President & Secretary
DaimlerChrysler Corp. Fund
CIMS: 485-02-46
1000 Chrysler Dr.
Auburn Hills, MI 48326-2766
Phone: (248)512-2502
Fax: (248)512-2503
Web: http://www.fund.daimlerchrysler.com
Note: Groups serving communities where Chrysler Corp. has a facility with a large number of employees should address materials to local DaimlerChrysler facility.

Description

Founded: 1953
EIN: 386087371
Organization Type: Corporate Foundation
Giving Locations: headquarters and operating communities and nationally.
Grant Types: Emergency, Employee Matching Gifts, General Support, Project.
Note: Employee matching gift ratio: 2 to 1 up to $5,000 per employee annually.

Giving Philosophy

'DaimlerChrysler Corp. is a Fortune 50 company that employs more than 400,000 talented people and has billions of dollars invested in plants and equipment in 54 countries around the world. These facts are reason enough for the company to take its corporate citizenship seriously. However, there are other equally compelling reasons.

'First, being socially responsible in every part of our business is not a requirement for success; it is a privilege that accompanies our right to conduct business in a free enterprise environment. Second, for DaimlerChrysler Corporation to continue to thrive and grow, we must be a part of building social conditions that help people and communities prosper.

'The purpose of our corporate citizenship is to improve the communities and business environments in which DaimlerChrysler Corporation conducts its business.

'Our mission is to be a leader and a catalyst in building a competitive, safe and productive society and to use our skills and resources to: develop a skilled workforce; support responsive, healthy and attractive communities; encourage employee participation and involvement; and respond to public policy and marketplace issues.' *DaimlerChrysler Corporation Fund 1998 Annual Report*

Financial Summary

Total Giving: $25,398,484 (1998); $25,372,261 (1997); $22,701,371 (1996). Note: Contributes through corporate direct giving program and foundation.
Giving Analysis: Giving for 1996 includes: foundation ($21,652,712); 1997: foundation ($25,372,261); 1998: foundation ($22,070,414); foundation grants to United Way ($3,328,070)
Assets: $66,952,995 (1998); $65,959,627 (1997); $67,300,997 (1996)
Gifts Received: $21,270,000 (1998); $18,360,000 (1997); $26,610,000 (1996). Note: Contributions were received from DaimlerChrysler Corp., formerly Chrysler Corp.

Typical Recipients

Arts & Humanities: Arts Associations & Councils, Arts Centers, Arts Funds, Arts Institutes, Community Arts, Ethnic & Folk Arts, Arts & Humanities-General, Historic Preservation, History & Archaeology, Libraries, Museums/Galleries, Music, Opera, Performing Arts, Public Broadcasting, Theater
Civic & Public Affairs: African American Affairs, Business/Free Enterprise, Chambers of Commerce, Community Foundations, Economic Development, Economic Policy, Employment/Job Training, Ethnic Organizations, Civic & Public Affairs-General, Housing, Minority Business, Municipalities/Towns, Nonprofit Management, Parades/Festivals, Professional & Trade Associations, Public Policy, Rural Affairs, Safety, Urban & Community Affairs, Women's Affairs, Zoos/Aquariums
Education: Agricultural Education, Arts/Humanities Education, Business Education, Colleges & Universities, Community & Junior Colleges, Continuing Education, Economic Education, Education Associations, Education Funds, Education Reform, Engineering/Technological Education, Faculty Development, Education-General, Health & Physical Education, Literacy, Minority Education, Private Education (Precollege), Public Education (Precollege), Science/Mathematics Education, Student Aid
Health: Cancer, Diabetes, Emergency/Ambulance Services, Health Organizations, Hospices, Hospitals, Speech & Hearing
Religion: Jewish Causes, Religious Welfare
Science: Scientific Centers & Institutes
Social Services: Animal Protection, Child Welfare, Community Centers, Community Service Organizations, Emergency Relief, Food/Clothing Distribution, People with Disabilities, Recreation & Athletics, Scouts, Senior Services, Substance Abuse, United Funds/United Ways, Volunteer Services, YMCA/YWCA/YMHA/YWHA, Youth Organizations

Contributions Analysis

Giving Priorities: Education, health and human service, culture and arts, and civics. Domestically, contributions for international purposes are rare.
Arts & Humanities: 10%. Supports local and national cultural organizations,with emphasis on the performing arts. Receipients include performing arts centers, historical societies, music groups, libraries, museums, and public broadcasting.
Civic & Public Affairs: 24%. Supports organizations that work for social welfare and the improvement of the economy and quality of life in operating communities. Other interests include economic research anddevelopment, resource study, safety, transportation, trade-related issues, and women's affairs.
Education: 41%. About one-half of education support reaches precollege education programs and institutions, K-12 education, and community colleges. The other half supports colleges and universities, with special emphasis on business, automotive design, and engineering programs; state associations of colleges and universities; minority education programs; and national educational organizations. Also provides scholarships for employees' children and matching gifts. The goal of the fund's educational spending is to prepare the future workforce.
Health: About 20%. Supports single-disease health organizations and medical research.
Social Services: 21%. Supports organizations serving youth and the disadvantaged, community centers, and the Salvation Army and United Way.
Note: Total contributions made by DaimlerChrysler Corp. Fund in 1998.

Application Procedures

Initial Contact: Send a two- to three-page proposal letter.
Application Requirements: The letter should include an outline of the proposal, and responses to the following questions: a. What issue or problem does your program or project address? b. How does this issue relate to DaimlerChrysler Corporation's goals, areas of focus and criteria? c. What are the credentials or special capabilities of your organization to address this issue? d. What is the scope of your program? e. Who are the clients, audience or people served by this program? f. What is the goal or expected outcome of the program for which you seek support? g. What specifically are you requesting of DaimlerChrysler Corporation? h. What is the rationale for this request and the amount requested of DaimlerChrysler Corporation? i. What are the key program or deadline dates? j. How will you measure results or success of this program? k. How will you sustain this program after DaimlerChrysler Corporation support ends? l. What will your organization expect of DaimlerChrysler Corporation in the future? Also include the following required attachments: a copy of your organizations's IRS tax exempt 501(c)(3) letter (or similar letter for educational institutions); most recent annual report or other available information about your organization, its volunteer board and leadership, and current programs; program and organization budget; financial statement; and a list of other current or proposed contributors.
Deadlines: None.
Evaluative Criteria: Supported programs demonstrate: leadership, innovation, a model of effective change, organizational self-sufficiency, empowered people, involved employees, teamwork, continuous improvement, and results; grants are increasingly made on the initiative of the company or through competitive grants.
Notes: The fund asks that organizations request guidelines prior to submitting a formal letter. Applications are accepted online.

Restrictions

The fund does not support organizations without 501(c)(3) status; individuals; discriminatory organizations; endowment funds; religious organizations for religious purposes; fraternal associations or athletic groups; veterans or labor organizations, social clubs, or similar associations; political organizations or campaigns; requests for loans or debt retirement programs; programs or projects involving the delivery of direct health care; disease-specific organizations; multi-year requests; capital campaigns; operating expenses of United Way local agencies; fund-raising activities related to individual sponsorship; the purchase of courtesy advertising; conferences, seminars, trips, or similar events; or seminaries, theological institutions, bible colleges and other religious schools that restrict entry to those students who profess a certain faith or belong to a specific denomination or sect or whose graduates (50% or more) are prepared for a religious profession.

No support is given to organizations that might in any way pose a conflict with Chrysler's mission, goals, programs, products or employees. Projects and organizations without connection to a major DaimlerChrysler Corp. plant community will not be consider. Neither the DaimlerChrysler Corp. Fund nor DaimlerChrysler Corp. donates vehicles for on-road use.

Additional Information

In May of 1998, Daimler-Benz of Stuttgart, Germany, and Chrysler Corp. of Auburn Hills, MI, merged to create DaimlerChrysler.

Publications: Community Involvement Guidelines

Corporate Officials

Thomas Patrick Capo: senior vice president, treasurer B Detroit, MI 1951. ED University of Detroit (1973); University of Detroit (1975). PRIM CORP EMPL senior vice president, treasurer: DaimlerChrysler. CORP AFFIL director: Chrysler Canada Ltd.; director: Chrysler Financial Corp.

Robert James Eaton: co-chairman, president, chief executive officer B Buena Vista, CO 1940. ED University of Kansas BSME (1963). CORP AFFIL chairman, director: Saab Automobile; director: International Paper Co.; director: Electronic Data Systems Corp.; director: Group Lotus. NONPR AFFIL director: United Way Southeast Michigan; member advisory council: University Michigan College Engineering; member: U.S.-Japan Business Council; fellow: Society Automotive Engineers; member industries advisory council: Stanford University College Engineering; member: National Academy Engineering; member: President Advisory Committee Trade Policy & Negotiations; director: Michigan Leaders Health Care Group; fellow: Engineering Society Detroit; member: Indus Technology Institute; director: Detroit Symphony Orchestra; director: Economic Alliance Michigan; chairman: Detroit Renaissance Inc.; member: Business Council; member: Business Roundtable; chairman, director: American Automobile Manufacturers Association.

W. Frank Fountain, Jr.: senior vice president government affairs B Brewton, AL 1944. ED Hampton Institute (1966); University of Pennsylvania (1973). PRIM CORP EMPL senior vice president government affairs: DaimlerChrysler Corp.

Arthur C. Liebler: vice president communications B Pittsburgh, PA 1942. ED Wayne State University; Marquette University AB (1964). PRIM CORP EMPL vice president communications: DaimlerChrysler. NONPR AFFIL director: American Advertising Federation; director: Public Relations Society America. CLUB AFFIL member: Detroit Adcraft Club; member: Detroit Golf Club.

Kathleen M. Oswald: vice president human resources PRIM CORP EMPL vice president human resources: DaimlerChrysler.

E. Thomas Pappert: vice president sales & service PRIM CORP EMPL vice president sales & service: DaimlerChrysler.

Dennis K. Pawley: executive vice president manufacturing B 1941. ED Oakland University BS (1982). PRIM CORP EMPL executive vice president manufacturing: DaimlerChrysler.

Jurgen E. Schrempp: chairman B Stuttgart, Germany 1944. PRIM CORP EMPL chairman: DaimlerChrysler.

Gary C. Valade: executive vice president, chief financial officer B Detroit, MI 1942. ED Michigan State University BS (1966); Michigan State University MBA (1968). PRIM CORP EMPL executive vice president, chief financial officer: Chrysler Corp. ADD CORP EMPL global procurement: Daimler Chrysler Corp. CORP AFFIL trustee: Henry Ford Health Systems; chairman: DaimlerChrysler Aviation Inc. NONPR AFFIL chairman: Michigan Colleges Foundation; member, director: Michigan State University Eli Broad College Business Alumni Association; trustee: Chrysler Corp. Fund; member corp. counsel: Interlochen Center Arts; trustee: Adrian College.

Foundation Officials

Lynn Alexandra Feldhouse: vice president, secretary B Detroit, MI 1951. ED Wayne State University BS (1981); Oakland University (1991). PRIM NONPR EMPL vice president, secretary: Chrysler Corp. Fund. NONPR AFFIL volunteer: United Way Southeast Michigan; volunteer: Wayne State University Alumni Association; member national corporate com: Philanthropic Adv SVC; volunteer: Michigan Corporate Volunteer Council; trustee, treasurer: Michigan Womens Foundation; trustee: Council Michigan Foundations; member executive committee: Detroit Funders Collaborative; trustee: Citizens Scholarship Foundation America; member national corporate com: Council BBBs.

W. Frank Fountain, Jr.: president (see above)

J. A. Kozlowski: assistant secretary PRIM CORP EMPL secretary: Chrysler Transport Inc.

Arthur C. Liebler: trustee (see above)

William J. O'Brien, III: trustee (see above)

Kathleen M. Oswald: trustee (see above)

E. Thomas Pappert: trustee (see above)

Ling J. Piedra: trustee

Gary C. Valade: trustee (see above)

Grants Analysis

Disclosure Period: calendar year ending 1998
Total Grants: $22,070,414*
Number of Grants: 1,200 (approx)
Average Grant: $18,392 (approx)
Highest Grant: $1,000,000
Typical Range: $1,000 to $50,000
***Note:** Giving excludes United Way.

Recent Grants

Note: Grants derived from 1998 Form 990.

Arts & Humanities

1,000,000	American Battle Monuments Commission, VA
350,000	Detroit Symphony Orchestra Hall, Detroit, MI
150,000	Michigan Opera Theatre, Detroit, MI
100,000	Detroit Educational Television Foundation WTVS, Detroit, MI
100,000	Friends of the Detroit Public Library, Inc., Detroit, MI

Civic & Public Affairs

1,000,000	Highland Park DEVCO, Inc., Highland Park, MI
380,500	Operation Outreach - USA, Inc., Natick, MA
150,000	Greater Downtown Partnership, Inc., Detroit, MI
100,000	Arab Community Center for Economic & Social Services, Dearborn, MI
100,000	Automotive Youth Educational Systems, Troy, MI
100,000	Automotive Youth Educational Systems, Troy, MI
100,000	Automotive Youth Educational Systems, Troy, MI
100,000	Community Foundation for Southeastern Michigan, Detroit, MI
100,000	Museum of African American History, Detroit, MI
100,000	National Association for the Advancement of Colored People Special Contribution Fund, Baltimore, MD
100,000	New Detroit, Inc., Detroit, MI

Education

800,000	Macomb County Intermediate School District, Clinton Township, MI
762,833	Citizens' Scholarship Foundation of America, St. Peter, MN
500,000	United Negro College Fund, Fairfax, VA
325,000	Reading Is Fundamental, Washington, DC
284,000	Michigan Colleges Foundation, Southfield, MI
250,000	Citizens For A Sound Economy Education Foundation, Washington, DC
250,000	First - For Inspiration and Recognition of Science and Technology, Manchester, NH
250,000	Wayne State University, Detroit, MI
200,000	Detroit Area Pre-College Engineering Program, Detroit, MI
200,000	Oakland University, Rochester, MI
189,000	United Negro College Fund, Fairfax, VA
172,500	Oakland Community College, Bloomfield Hills, MI
172,500	Oakland Schools, Waterford, MI
150,000	Marygrove College, Detroit, MI
125,000	Cornerstone Schools Association-Genesis Foundation, Detroit, MI
125,000	Junior Achievement of Southeastern Michigan, Detroit, MI
125,000	University Cultural Center Association, Detroit, MI
100,000	Duquesne University, Pittsburgh, PA
100,000	Junior Achievement of Southeastern Michigan, Detroit, MI
100,000	National Academy of Engineering, Washington, DC

Health

100,000	Rose Hill Center, Inc., Holly, MI

Religion

250,000	Society of St. Vincent De Paul, Detroit, MI

Science

600,000	Focus: Hope Center for Advanced Technologies, Detroit, MI

Social Services

800,000	United Way Community Services, Detroit, MI
275,000	United Way Community Services, Detroit, MI
275,000	United Way Community Services, Detroit, MI
275,000	United Way Community Services, Detroit, MI
275,000	United Way Community Services, Detroit, MI
250,000	The National Center On Addiction & Substance Abuse at Columbia University, New York, NY
200,000	The National Center On Addiction & Substance Abuse at Columbia University, New York, NY
150,000	United Way of Greater Toledo, Toledo, OH
129,600	United Way of Greater St. Louis, St. Louis, MO
120,000	Detroit Police Athletic League, Detroit, MI
100,000	Independence For Life Corporation, Southfield, MI

DAIN BOSWORTH INC.

Company Contact

Minneapolis, MN

Company Description

Assets: US$933,000,000
Employees: 1,500
SIC(s): 6211 Security Brokers & Dealers.
Parent Company: Inter-Regional Financial Group, Inc.

Corporate Sponsorship

Type: Arts & cultural events; Music & entertainment events
Contact: Martha Baumbach, Manager of Community Relations
Phone: (612)371-7753

Dain Bosworth Foundation

Giving Contact

Sherry Koster, Charitable Giving Specialist Senior
Dain Bosworth Foundation
Dain Bosworth Plz.
PO Box 1160
Minneapolis, MN 55440-1160
Phone: (612)371-2765
Fax: (612)371-7933
Web: http://www.dain.com

Description

Founded: 1961
EIN: 416030639
Organization Type: Corporate Foundation
Giving Locations: MN: Minneapolis, Saint Paul headquarters and operating communities.
Grant Types: Capital, Employee Matching Gifts, Matching, Operating Expenses, Project, Seed Money.
Note: Employee matching gift ratio: 1 to 1 for gifts to qualified non-profits and educational institutions, up to $500.

Giving Philosophy

'The Foundation's mission is to improve the quality of life in our communities by partnering with nonprofit organizations in an attempt to make a positive difference in the communities where we do business.' Guidelines for Giving

Financial Summary

Total Giving: $1,294,081 (1997); $1,035,000 (1996); $1,000,000 (1995). Note: Contributes through corporate direct giving program and foundation.
Giving Analysis: Giving for 1997 includes: foundation grants to United Way ($119,500)
Assets: $687,766 (1997); $650,939 (1996); $622,265 (1995)
Gifts Received: $1,300,000 (1997); $1,035,000 (1996); $1,005,853 (1995). Note: Contributions are received from Dain Bosworth Inc.

Typical Recipients

Arts & Humanities: Arts Associations & Councils, Arts Centers, Arts Funds, Arts Institutes, Ballet, Arts & Humanities-General, Museums/Galleries, Music, Opera, Performing Arts, Public Broadcasting, Theater
Civic & Public Affairs: Chambers of Commerce, Community Foundations, Economic Development, Employment/Job Training, Civic & Public Affairs-General, Housing, Municipalities/Towns, Native American Affairs, Nonprofit Management, Parades/Festivals, Public Policy, Urban & Community Affairs, Women's Affairs, Zoos/Aquariums
Education: Afterschool/Enrichment Programs, Business Education, Colleges & Universities, Community & Junior Colleges, Economic Education, Education Funds, Education-General, Leadership Training, Minority Education, Preschool Education, Private Education (Precollege), Public Education (Precollege), Secondary Education (Private), Secondary Education (Public), Special Education, Student Aid, Vocational & Technical Education
Environment: Environment-General
Health: AIDS/HIV, Cancer, Children's Health/Hospitals, Clinics/Medical Centers, Diabetes, Emergency/Ambulance Services, Health Organizations, Heart, Hospices, Hospitals, Kidney, Medical Rehabilitation, Medical Research, Prenatal Health Issues, Public Health, Research/Studies Institutes, Single-Disease Health Associations
International: International Organizations, International Peace & Security Issues
Religion: Religious Welfare
Social Services: At-Risk Youth, Big Brother/Big Sister, Child Welfare, Community Service Organizations, Day Care, Domestic Violence, Family Planning, Family Services, Food/Clothing Distribution, People with Disabilities, Recreation & Athletics, Scouts, Senior Services, Sexual Abuse, Shelters/Homelessness, Special Olympics, Substance Abuse, United Funds/United Ways, Veterans, YMCA/YWCA/YMHA/YWHA, Youth Organizations

Contributions Analysis

Arts & Humanities: About 25%. Interests include art institutes, associations, and centers; public broadcasting; theater; music; and programs that generate an appreciation of diverse cultures.
Civic & Public Affairs: 13%. Supports community youth organizations and foundations.
Education: About 21%. Emphasizes helping young people understand our country's economic system and helping disadvantaged youth. Supports K-12 programs that impact students of color or the economically disadvantaged.
Health: 9%. Supports the Courage Center and children's hospitals.
Social Services: 32%. Supports the United Way. Special Olympics, family services, family planning, domestic violence concerns, and food distribution. Focuses on fostering economic independence, self-sufficiency, breaking the cycle of poverty, and strengthening the family.

Application Procedures

Initial Contact: Call for guidelines, then written proposal.
Application Requirements: Include either a completed Minnesota Common Grant Application Form, or the following: description of project, including how it fits within Foundation's priorities, amount requested and explanation of use, expected results and evaluation plan, information about how Dain Bosworth or Interra employees are involved; and enclose a current operating budget with income and expenses, product budget, list of current and projected financial support, list of board of directors, most recent audited financial statements, and proof of tax-exempt status.
Deadlines: February 27 and July 31 for Twin Cities requests; anytime for local requests, but by November 15 for consideration in current calendar year.
Evaluative Criteria: Favors programs where employees play an active role and programs benefiting youth development and education; awards based on organization's impact and contributions to community.
Decision Notification: Foundation board meets in February, March, August, and September, applicants are notified in late May and September, local branches decide monthly.
Notes: Proposals should be sent to the Foundation office for Twin Cities requests, or to the nearest Dain Bosworth branch.

Restrictions

Low priority projects are capital or endowment campaigns, multi-year commitments, and start up organizations.
Foundation will not support fund-raising events; non-501(c)(3) requests; projects that benefit religious, political, fraternal or veterans organizations; travel, tours or conferences; individuals; academic or scientific research; national or international organizations; or athletic teams.
In youth education, areas not funded include: program support for schools, higher education, environmental education, and child safety. In social services, areas not funded include: developmental disabilities, health or mental health services, disease-specific organizations, emergency or disaster relief, senior citizens, housing, or day care.
An organization may only submit one request per year.

Additional Information

Charitable requests in Dain's major markets (Chicago, Denver, and Seattle) are reviewed and approved by Regional Advisory Boards. Contact foundation for Community Involvement Report, which contains contact information.
Publications: Annual Report (including Application Guidelines)

Corporate Officials

John C. Appel: vice chairman, president fixed income group B 1948. PRIM CORP EMPL vice chairman, president fixed income group: Dain Rauscher Corp. ADD CORP EMPL chairman, president, chief executive officer: Clayton Brown & Associates; president: Dain Rauscher Inc.
Irving Weiser: chairman, president, chief executive officer B Munich, Germany 1947. ED State University of New York Buffalo BA (1969); Brooklyn Law School JD (1973). PRIM CORP EMPL chairman, president, chief executive officer: Inter-Regional Financial Group Inc. CORP AFFIL director: Dain Bosworth; director: Rauscher Pierce Refinances Inc. NONPR AFFIL director: Temple Israel; member: Young President Organization; member: American Management Association; director: Childrens Home Society Minnesota. CLUB AFFIL Minneapolis Club.

Foundation Officials

John C. Appel: director (see above)
Nelson D. Civello: director B Buffalo, NY 1945. ED Canisius College (1967); Bowling Green State University (1969). PRIM CORP EMPL executive vice president: Dain Bosworth Inc. CORP AFFIL vice president: Dain Rauscher Corp.; executive vice president: Dain Rauscher Inc. NONPR AFFIL member executive committee: PSA Municipal Securities Division; treasurer, member executive committee: Public Securities Association; treasurer: Bond Market Association.
Sherry Koster: board member, grants coordinator
John Tschetter: director
Kenneth J. Wessels: director PRIM CORP EMPL senior vice president: Dain Rauscher Corp.

Grants Analysis

Disclosure Period: calendar year ending 1997
Total Grants: $1,294,081
Number of Grants: 626 (approx)
Average Grant: $2,067
Typical Range: $1,000 to $5,000

Recent Grants

Note: Grants derived from 1997 Form 990.

Arts & Humanities

25,000	Seattle Symphony, Seattle, WA
20,000	Minnesota Orchestral Association, Minneapolis, MN
20,000	Penumbra Theatre Company, Minneapolis, MN

20,000	Seattle Symphony, Seattle, WA
12,000	The Children's Theatre Company, Minneapolis, MN
12,000	Minneapolis Institute of Arts, Minneapolis, MN
10,000	The Guthrie Theater, Minneapolis, MN
10,000	Minnesota Orchestral Association, Minneapolis, MN
8,000	Penumbra Theatre Company, Saint Paul, MN
7,500	Lake Superior Big Top Chautauqua, Washburn, WI
7,000	Theatre De La Jeune Lune, Minneapolis, MN
6,000	Saint Paul Chamber Orchestra, Saint Paul, MN
5,000	Minnesota Children's Museum, Minneapolis, MN
5,000	Plymouth Music Series of Minnesota, Minneapolis, MN
5,000	Walker Art Center, Minneapolis, MN

Civic & Public Affairs

30,000	Minnesota Zoo Foundation, Apple Valley, MN
10,000	Project for Pride in Living, Inc., Minneapolis, MN
10,000	University of Oregon, Eugene, OR -- Oregon Bach Festival
8,500	Twin Cities Habitat for Humanity, Minneapolis, MN
8,000	Habitat for Humanity -- Greater Fox Cities Area
6,000	Youth Trust, Minneapolis, MN
5,000	Chicanos Latinos Unidos En Servicio (CLUES), Minneapolis, MN
5,000	Community Foundation Serving N. Colorado Disaster Relief, Fort Collins, CO
5,000	The Minneapolis Foundation, Minneapolis, MN -- support Minnesota Futures Fund
5,000	Minnesota Zoo Foundation, Apple Valley, MN

Education

25,000	The Jeremiah Program, Minneapolis, MN
22,000	Junior Achievement of the Upper Midwest, Inc., Bemidji, MN
13,200	Business Economics Education Foundation, Minneapolis, MN
10,500	Harvest Preparatory School, Minneapolis, MN
10,000	Community Youth Program
10,000	Confidence Learning Center, Crosby, MN
10,000	Page Education Foundation, Minneapolis, MN
6,000	Minnesota Private College Fund, Minneapolis, MN
5,500	Assistance League of Minneapolis and Saint Paul, Minneapolis, MN
5,000	Dunwoody Institute, Minneapolis, MN
5,000	Little Earth Residents Association, Minneapolis, MN
5,000	Minnesota Independent School Fund, Inc., Minneapolis, MN
5,000	North Career Center, Minneapolis, MN -- North Community High School
5,000	Oak Grove Lutheran High School
5,000	United Negro College Fund, Inc., Minneapolis, MN
5,000	University of St. Thomas, Minneapolis, MN -- support Bridge for Success

Health

25,000	Courage Center, Golden Valley, MN
10,000	Courage Center, Golden Valley, MN
10,000	Doernbecher Children's Hospital, Portland, OR
5,000	Doernbecher Children's Hospital Foundation, Portland, OR
5,000	St. Jude Children's Research Hospital, Memphis, TN

Religion

5,000	Salvation Army Disaster Relief Fund, Oklahoma City, OK

Social Services

115,500	United Way of Minneapolis Area, Minneapolis, MN
25,000	Colorado Children's Campaign, Denver, CO
10,000	Boys & Girls Club of Minneapolis
10,000	Boys Town Nebraska, Omaha, NE
7,500	Family Hope Services, Minneapolis, MN
6,000	Cornerstone Advocacy Service, Bloomington, MN
5,000	Big Brothers & Big Sisters of Dane County, Madison, WI
5,000	Boys & Girls Club of Minneapolis, Minneapolis, MN
5,000	Children's Home Society of Minnesota, Minneapolis, MN
5,000	Children's Law Center, Minneapolis, MN
5,000	Family & Children's Service, Minneapolis, MN
5,000	Harriet Tubman Center, Inc., Minneapolis, MN
5,000	Minneapolis Crisis Nursery, Minneapolis, MN
5,000	Minneapolis Crisis Nursery, Minneapolis, MN
5,000	Phillips Community Initiatives for Children (PCIC), Minneapolis, MN
5,000	Resources for Child Caring, Saint Paul, MN
5,000	United Way of King County, Seattle, WA

DANA CORP.

Company Contact

Toledo, OH
Web: http://www.dana.com

Company Description

Acquired: Echlin Inc. (1998).
Revenue: US$13,159,000,000 (1999)
Profit: US$534,100,000
Employees: 86,400 (1999)
Fortune Rank: 131, per FORTUNE Magazine's list of 500 Largest U.S. Corporations (1999).
FF 131
SIC(s): 3566 Speed Changers, Drives & Gears, 3568 Power Transmission Equipment Nec, 3592 Carburetors, Pistons, Rings & Valves, 3714 Motor Vehicle Parts & Accessories.

Operating Locations

Operates internationally in the Asian Basin, Canada, Europe, and South America.

Nonmonetary Support

Type: Donated Equipment; In-kind Services; Loaned Employees; Loaned Executives
Note: Nonmonetary support is provided by the foundation and the company.

Corporate Sponsorship

Type: Arts & cultural events; Music & entertainment events; Festivals/fairs
Contact: Gary Corrigan

Dana Corp. Foundation

Giving Contact

Mr. Don M. Decker, Administrator
Dana Corp. Foundation
PO Box 1000
Toledo, OH 43697
Phone: (419)535-4601
Fax: (419)535-4896

Description

EIN: 346544909
Organization Type: Corporate Foundation
Giving Locations: principally near operating locations and to national organizations.
Grant Types: Award, Capital, Challenge, Emergency, General Support, Matching, Multiyear/Continuing Support.

Giving Philosophy

"People Finding a Better Way' reflects the principles and priorities of the Dana style. People are our most important asset, and we are committed to improving the communities in which they live and work. Indeed, we 'help' by focusing financial support through grants from the Dana Corporation Foundation to the communities where Dana plants and facilities are located and to the causes to which our employees, friends and neighbors are committed.' *Guidelines for Giving*

Financial Summary

Total Giving: $2,184,205 (fiscal year ending March 31, 1998); $2,276,844 (fiscal 1996); $2,000,000 (fiscal 1995). Note: Contributes through corporate direct giving program and foundation. Giving includes foundation only.
Giving Analysis: Giving for fiscal 1995 includes: foundation ($1,275,103); foundation matching gifts ($235,325); foundation scholarships ($3,000); fiscal 1996: foundation ($1,201,488); foundation grants to United Way ($638,094); foundation matching gifts ($427,262); foundation scholarships ($10,000); fiscal 1998: foundation ($1,054,724); foundation grants to United Way ($696,958); foundation matching gifts ($416,523); foundation scholarships ($16,000)
Assets: $11,251,907 (fiscal 1998); $8,066,618 (fiscal 1996); $10,205,450 (fiscal 1995)
Gifts Received: $2,000,000 (fiscal 1998); $2,250,000 (fiscal 1995); $2,000,000 (fiscal 1994)

Typical Recipients

Arts & Humanities: Arts Associations & Councils, Arts Centers, Arts Institutes, Ballet, Historic Preservation, Museums/Galleries, Music, Opera, Public Broadcasting
Civic & Public Affairs: Botanical Gardens/Parks, Business/Free Enterprise, Chambers of Commerce, Civil Rights, Community Foundations, Economic Development, Housing, Municipalities/Towns, Professional & Trade Associations, Public Policy, Urban & Community Affairs, Women's Affairs, Zoos/Aquariums
Education: Agricultural Education, Business Education, Colleges & Universities, Community & Junior Colleges, Economic Education, Education Funds, Engineering/Technological Education, Health & Physical Education, Medical Education, Minority Education, Private Education (Precollege), Public Education (Precollege), Science/Mathematics Education, Secondary Education (Public), Special Education, Student Aid
Environment: Air/Water Quality, Environment-General
Health: AIDS/HIV, Alzheimers Disease, Emergency/Ambulance Services, Health Organizations, Hospices, Hospitals, Preventive Medicine/Wellness Organizations, Single-Disease Health Associations
Religion: Religious Organizations, Religious Welfare
Science: Scientific Centers & Institutes
Social Services: Camps, Child Welfare, Community Centers, Community Service Organizations, Delinquency & Criminal Rehabilitation, Emergency Relief, Family Planning, Family Services, Food/Clothing Distribution, Homes, People with Disabilities, Recreation & Athletics, Scouts, Shelters/Homelessness, Substance Abuse, United Funds/United Ways, Volunteer Services, YMCA/YWCA/YMHA/YWHA, Youth Organizations

Contributions Analysis

Giving Priorities: Social services, education, arts, public affairs.

Arts & Humanities: 17%. Emphasis on public broadcasting, arts associations, museums, and music.

Civic & Public Affairs: 8%. Interests include business and free enterprise, public policy, and zoos and botanical gardens. Other areas of concern include civil rights, environmental affairs, and urban and community affairs.

Education: 10%. Funding primarily supports colleges and universities. Also supports private, public, and precollege education, and medical and technical education.

Health: 1%. Supports hospitals, hospices, health organizations, pediatric health, and medical research.

Religion: 2%.

Social Services: 62%. Majority of funding supports united funds. Other interests include youth organizations, child welfare, community centers, community service organizations, drug and alcohol programs, and emergency relief.

Note: Total contributions in fiscal 1998.

Application Procedures

Initial Contact: Send a letter or proposal; requests from local organizations should be sent to headquarters of the nearest Dana Corp. facility.

Application Requirements: Include the overall objectives of the organization, purpose of project, an organizational chart, the most recent financial statement and tax return, and any supplemental information which would be beneficial.

Deadlines: None.

Review Process: Seven regional screening committees review requests.

Evaluative Criteria: Clear articulation of objectives and plans; incorporation of active volunteer boards, respected leadership, competent administrations and a broad base of support; demonstration of a measurable and potentially lasting impact through the projects/services provided; 501(c)3 status under the Internal Revenue Code.

Decision Notification: Board meets quarterly.

Restrictions

Foundation does not make grants to individuals, organizations that practice discrimination, religious organizations for programs exclusively denominational or sectarian in purpose, political organizations or campaigns, or United Way affiliated organizations that are applying for operating expense support.

Additional Information

In July 1998, Echlin Inc. merged with Dana Corp.

Corporate Officials

Bob Fesenmyer: general manager, vice president PRIM CORP EMPL general manager, vice president: Dana Corp., Spicer Driveshaft Division.

Joseph M. Magliochetti: president, chief executive officer, director B 1942. ED University of Illinois. PRIM CORP EMPL president, chief executive officer, director: Dana Corp. CORP AFFIL director: Danaven; director: Spicer SA; director: AMP Inc. NONPR AFFIL member: Equipment Manufacturers Institute; director: Motor Equipment Manufacturers Association; member: Automotive Original Equipment Manufacturers Association; member: Automotive Service Indiana Association.

John Shaner: vice president corporate relations PRIM CORP EMPL vice president corporate relations: Dana Corp.

Foundation Officials

Faith Curry: director

Don M. Decker: administrator PRIM CORP EMPL vice president corporate services: Dana Corp.

Bob Fesenmyer: director (see above)

Cheryl Kline: assistant treasurer, director

Joseph M. Magliochetti: president, director (see above)

Ann Marie Riley: director

Joe Stancaxi: director

Grants Analysis

Disclosure Period: fiscal year ending March 31, 1998

Total Grants: $1,054,724*

Number of Grants: 256

Average Grant: $3,803*

Highest Grant: $85,000

Typical Range: $1,000 to $5,000

***Note:** Giving excludes matching gifts, scholarship, and the United Way. Average grant figure excludes highest grant.

Recent Grants

Note: Grants derived from 1998 Form 990.

Arts & Humanities

85,000 Toledo Cultural Arts Center, Inc., Toledo, OH
35,000 Public Broadcasting of Northwest Ohio, Toledo, OH
20,000 Reading Public Museum Foundation, Reading, PA
17,500 Toledo Opera Association, Toledo, OH
15,000 Toledo Symphony, Toledo, OH
12,500 Arts Commission of Greater Toledo, Toledo, OH
10,000 Coca-Cola Memorabilia Museum of E-Town, Elizabethtown, KY
7,150 Paris-Henry County Arts Council, Paris, TN

Civic & Public Affairs

30,000 C.O.S.I., Toledo, OH
25,000 Focus Hope, Detroit, MI
10,000 Berks County Community Foundation, Reading, PA
10,000 Headwaters Park Commission, Ft. Wayne, IN
10,000 Local Initiatives Support Corporation, Toledo, OH
10,000 Victory Center, Toledo, OH

Education

30,000 Hopkinsville Community College, Hopkinsville, KY
25,000 Cornerstone Schools, Detroit, MI
25,000 Junior Achievement of Northwestern Ohio, Inc., Toledo, OH
12,000 Kutztown University, Kutztown, PA
11,000 University of Tennessee at Martin School of Engineering, Martin, TN
8,500 Junior Achievement of Northeast Indiana, Ft. Wayne, IN
7,800 Kentucky Tech, Elizabethtown, KY

Health

10,000 Wellness Community of Northwest Ohio, Toledo, OH

Religion

20,000 St. Anthony Vilia, Toledo, OH

Science

14,000 Tennessee Technology Center at Paris, Paris, TN

Social Services

252,500 United Way of Greater Toledo, Toledo, OH
63,000 United Way of Allen County, Ft. Wayne, IN
50,000 YMCA of Greater Toledo, Toledo, OH
40,000 United Way of Berks County, Reading, PA
35,000 United Way of Gaston County, Gastonia, NC
28,500 United Way of Muskegon, Muskegon, MI
20,000 Salvation Army Family Shelter, Gastonia, NC
18,000 United Way of Minneapolis, Minneapolis, MN
17,500 Stateline United Way, Beloit, WI
17,000 Gaston Family YMCA, Gastonia, NC
16,000 United Way of Grant County, Marion, IN
15,700 United Way of Pottstown, Pottstown, PA
15,000 Metro United Way of Hardin County, Elizabethtown, KY
15,000 United Way of Whitewater Valley, Richmond, IN
15,000 YMCA of Dekalb County, Auburn, IN
14,400 United Way of Bristol, Bristol, CT
12,150 United Way of Greater Lima, Lima, OH
10,500 United Way of Hopkinsville/Chirstian County, Hopkinsville, KY
10,000 Aid to Adoption of Special Kids, Maumee, OH
10,000 Boys and Girls Clubs of Ft. Wayne, Fort Wayne, IN
10,000 New Connecting Point, Toledo, OH
10,000 United Way of Fulton County, Rochester, IN
10,000 YMCA of Dyer County, Dyersburg, TN
9,000 United Way of Central/Metro Oklahoma, Oklahoma City, OK
8,000 Burke County United Way, Morganton, NC
8,000 United Way of Dillon, Dillon, SC

DANIS COMPANIES

Company Contact

Dayton, OH

Company Description

Employees: 1,500

SIC(s): 1541 Industrial Buildings & Warehouses, 1542 Nonresidential Construction Nec.

Danis Foundation

Giving Contact

John Danis, President
Danis Foundation
Two River Place
PO Box 725
Dayton, OH 45401
Phone: (937)228-1225

Description

Founded: 1957

EIN: 316041012

Organization Type: Corporate Foundation

Giving Locations: OH

Grant Types: Capital, Endowment, General Support, Scholarship.

Financial Summary

Total Giving: $333,134 (1995); $170,283 (1994); $163,139 (1993)

Assets: $732,798 (1995); $862,618 (1994); $1,001,134 (1993)

Gifts Received: $75,000 (1995); $125,000 (1993); $225,000 (1992). Note: In 1995, contributions were received from Danis Building Construction ($25,000) and Danis Heavy Construction ($50,000).

Typical Recipients

Arts & Humanities: Arts Associations & Councils, Arts Centers, Arts Funds, Arts Institutes, Community Arts, Dance, Museums/Galleries, Music, Performing Arts, Public Broadcasting, Theater

Civic & Public Affairs: African American Affairs, Community Foundations, Economic Development, Civic & Public Affairs-General, Parades/Festivals, Safety, Urban & Community Affairs, Women's Affairs

Education: Business Education, Colleges & Universities, Education Funds, Engineering/Technological

Education, Leadership Training, Legal Education, Literacy, Private Education (Precollege), Religious Education, Science/Mathematics Education, Secondary Education (Private), Secondary Education (Public), Student Aid
Environment: Environment-General
Health: Alzheimers Disease, Arthritis, Cancer, Children's Health/Hospitals, Clinics/Medical Centers, Health Funds, Health Organizations, Heart, Hospices, Hospitals, Medical Research, Public Health, Single-Disease Health Associations
Religion: Churches, Religious Organizations, Religious Welfare, Social/Policy Issues
Science: Science Museums
Social Services: At-Risk Youth, Big Brother/Big Sister, Child Welfare, Community Service Organizations, Crime Prevention, People with Disabilities, Scouts, United Funds/United Ways, YMCA/YWCA/YMHA/YWHA, Youth Organizations

Application Procedures

Initial Contact: Return completed application form along with transcripts and a short explanation of field of study, why it was chosen, and future goals.
Deadlines: May 31.

Additional Information

The foundation makes a limited number of grants or loans to sons, daughters, and grandchildren of employees of the Danis Companies and its affiliates and subsidiaries. Employees and their spouses are ineligible.
Publications: Application Form; Guidelines

Corporate Officials

Jim Fuller: chief financial officer, vice president finance PRIM CORP EMPL chief financial officer, vice president finance: Danis Industries.
Richard C. Russell: president, chief operating officer, director PRIM CORP EMPL president, chief operating officer, director: Danis Companies.
Glenn P. Schimpf: chairman PRIM CORP EMPL chairman: Danis Industries.

Foundation Officials

Darrell Hammond: treasurer
Gregory L. McCann: assistant secretary
Richard C. Russell: vice president (see above)
Glenn P. Schimpf: vice president (see above)

Grants Analysis

Disclosure Period: calendar year ending 1995
Number of Grants: 77
Highest Grant: $155,000
Typical Range: $100 to $20,000

Recent Grants

Note: Grants derived from 1997 Form 990.

Arts & Humanities

19,500 Dayton Art Institute, Dayton, OH
3,950 Victoria Theater Association, Dayton, OH

Civic & Public Affairs

4,050 Womanline, Dayton, OH
3,000 Cityfolk, Dayton, OH
2,000 Sinclair Foundation, Dayton, OH
1,000 Dayton Holiday Festival, Dayton, OH
750 Martin Luther King Holiday, Dayton, OH
500 Law Enforcement Foundation, Dublin, OH

Education

75,000 Alter High School, Kettering, OH
37,500 Chaminade Julienne High School, Dayton, OH
25,000 Construction Education Foundation, Washington, DC
5,000 Cedarville College, Cedarville, OH
4,800 University of Cincinnati Foundation, Cincinnati, OH
2,500 Carroll High School, Dayton, OH
2,000 Ohio Foundation of Independent Colleges, Columbus, OH
2,000 University of Cincinnati, Cincinnati, OH
1,000 Auburn University, Auburn, AL
1,000 Marquette University, Milwaukee, WI
1,000 Miami University, Middletown, OH
1,000 Miami University, Oxford, OH
1,000 Miami Valley Catholic Education Council, Dayton, OH
1,000 University of Kentucky, Lexington, KY
1,000 Wright State University, Dayton, OH
1,000 Wright State University, Dayton, OH
500 Miami Valley Literacy Council, Dayton, OH
500 University of Rio Grande, Rio Grand, OH

Environment

3,200 Clark County Solid Waste Management District, Springfield, OH -- Earth Day Community Clean Up

Health

15,600 Kettering Medical Center Foundation, Dayton, OH
8,000 St. Joseph Children's Treatment Center, Dayton, OH
5,300 Samaritan Health Foundation, Dayton, OH
5,028 Hipple Cancer Research, Dayton, OH
5,000 Alzheimer's Association, Dayton, OH
4,750 Auxiliary of Bethesda Hospitals, Cincinnati, OH
3,960 Mount Carmel Heath Foundation, Columbus, OH
1,590 American Heart Association, Dayton, OH
1,500 Community Hospital Endowment Fund, Springfield, OH
1,360 Miami Valley Health Foundation, Dayton, OH
690 American Cancer Society, Dayton, OH
500 Otterbein Lebanon Benevolent Care Fund, Lebanon, OH

Religion

4,000 Catholic Social Services, Dayton, OH
1,050 Franciscan Sisters of the Poor, Dayton, OH
500 National Conference of Christians and Jews, Dayton, OH
500 Salvation Army, Dayton, OH

Social Services

21,000 United Way, Dayton, OH
5,500 YMCA, Dayton, OH
5,000 YMCA, Dayton, OH
3,500 Boy Scouts of America, Dayton, OH
1,500 Kids Voting, Dayton, OH
550 Rotary Foundation, Dayton, OH
500 Teen Works, Dayton, OH

DAYTON HUDSON

★ Number 15 of Top 100 Corporate Givers

Company Contact

Minneapolis, MN
Web: http://www.dhc.com

Company Description

Revenue: US$30,951,000,000
Profit: US$935,000,000
Employees: 244,000 (1999)
SIC(s): 5311 Department Stores, 5331 Variety Stores.
Parent Company: Target Corp., 777 Nicollet Mall, Minneapolis, MN, United States

Operating Locations

Operates in 33 states.

Nonmonetary Support

Type: Cause-related Marketing & Promotion; Workplace Solicitation
Volunteer Programs: Each division of the company has its own volunteer program. Company-wide, Target Corp. jointly sponsors 'Day of Giving' in the spring/summer.
Note: Nonmonetary support is provided by local operating divisions. Nonmonetary Support Contact: General Managers at local stores. Nonmonetary support is valued at more than $5,000,000 annually.

Corporate Sponsorship

Type: Arts & cultural events; Festivals/fairs; Music & entertainment events
Contact: Gail Dorn
Note: Sponsors events which fit their giving focus.

Target Foundation

Giving Contact

Dee Henry Williams, Grants Program Assistant
Target Foundation
777 Nicollet Mall
Minneapolis, MN 55402
Phone: (612)370-6553
Fax: (612)370-5542
Email: dee.henrywilliams@dhcmail.com
Web: http://www.targetcorp.com/community/target-foundation.asp

Description

Founded: 1918
EIN: 416017088
Organization Type: Corporate Foundation
Former Name: Dayton Hudson Corporate.
Giving Locations: MN: Minneapolis, Saint Paul headquarters and operating communities.
Grant Types: Employee Matching Gifts, General Support, Multiyear/Continuing Support, Project, Scholarship.
Note: Capital grants and endowments are only provided to existing partners of the foundation.

Giving Philosophy

'The Target Corporation family of companies, including Target have been giving back to the community since we opened our first Dayton's store 53 years ago. We give $57 million back to the communities we serve each year. That's over 1 million every single week. This money goes for worthwhile projects that benefit families, education, children and the arts. Target is proud of the communities we are in. And we have each been giving back to them on every purchase since we opened in 1962.'

Financial Summary

Total Giving: $66,465,600 (fiscal year ending January 31, 1999 approx); $57,000,000 (fiscal 1998 approx); $45,831,462 (fiscal 1997). Note: Contributes through corporate direct giving program and foundation.
Giving Analysis: Giving for fiscal 1997 includes: corporate direct giving ($38,333,392); foundation ($7,498,070); fiscal 1998: corporate direct giving (approx $50,210,000); foundation (approx $7,300,000); fiscal 1999: corporate direct giving (approx $57,510,000); foundation ($7,900,600); foundation grants to United Way ($1,055,000)
Assets: $32,544,554 (fiscal 1999); $29,000,000 (fiscal 1996 approx); $21,982,456 (fiscal 1995). Note: Assets exist as a reserve fund.
Gifts Received: $2,704,571 (fiscal 1999); $7,069,611 (fiscal 1995); $10,195,142 (fiscal 1993). Note: Contributions are received from Dayton Hudson Corp.

Typical Recipients

Arts & Humanities: Arts Appreciation, Arts Associations & Councils, Arts Centers, Arts Funds, Arts Institutes, Arts Outreach, Community Arts, Dance, Ethnic & Folk Arts, Film & Video, Arts & Humanities-General, History & Archaeology, Libraries, Literary Arts, Museums/Galleries, Music, Opera, Performing Arts, Public Broadcasting, Theater, Visual Arts
Civic & Public Affairs: African American Affairs, Botanical Gardens/Parks, Business/Free Enterprise, Civil Rights, Clubs, Community Foundations, Economic Development, Employment/Job Training, Hispanic Affairs, Housing, Legal Aid, Minority Business, Native American Affairs, Nonprofit Management, Professional & Trade Associations, Public Policy, Urban & Community Affairs, Women's Affairs
Education: Arts/Humanities Education, Colleges & Universities, Education Reform, Engineering/Technological Education, International Exchange, Literacy, Private Education (Precollege), Public Education (Precollege), School Volunteerism, Special Education
Health: AIDS/HIV, Health Organizations, Research/Studies Institutes
International: Trade
Religion: Religious Welfare
Social Services: At-Risk Youth, Child Welfare, Community Centers, Community Service Organizations, Family Planning, Family Services, People with Disabilities, Refugee Assistance, Shelters/Homelessness, United Funds/United Ways, YMCA/YWCA/YMHA/YWHA, Youth Organizations

Contributions Analysis

Giving Priorities: The arts, human services, health, civics, and education.
Arts & Humanities: 40%. Supports professional nonprofit arts organizations in all disciplines. Highest priorities are large arts institutions that achieve a place of national importance within their respective disciplines, provide a variety of employment opportunities for local artists and administrators, and interact with a larger pool of national artists whose presence in the Twin Cities enriches the local art scene; arts institutions that spring from communities that may be under-represented or under-served by other arts groups; arts institutions whose primary mission is the creation of new works by living artists; and service organizations whose primary mission is to support professional nonprofit arts institutions and/or individual artists, and whose services are integral to the continued well-being of the arts fields they serve.
Social Services: 40%. Supports programs and projects which assist low-income individuals to prepare for work in order to leave or avoid welfare, or which develop neighborhood strategies that retain or create jobs for local residents.
Note: Target stores (Mervyn's California, Target, Dayton's, Hudson's, and Marshall Field's) also support giving programs. See separate entries for more information. Total contributions made in 1998.

Application Procedures

Initial Contact: Minnesota organizations that fit the foundation's guidelines should contact the foundation; organizations in other store communities should contact appropriate operating company as explained in Grant Application Guidelines available from individual stores; initial inquiries by letter or telephone are encouraged.
Application Requirements: For proposals to the foundation: description of proposed program and need, people to be served, and time period to be covered by grant; results to be accomplished and how results will be evaluated; a description of organization, its mission, and program objectives; names and qualifications of those who would manage the project or program; copy of most recent IRS tax-exempt certification; organization's officers and directors with their affiliations; recent financial statement (preferably audited); organization and program budget for the last and current years, showing anticipated expenses and income sources; and representative list of donors who contributed to organization/program for past 12 months and amounts received. received.
Deadlines: None, for the foundation, although preferred submission times are February through November; operating divisions may have deadlines.
Review Process: Reviews are conducted by foundation staff or staff of operating divisions.
Evaluative Criteria: Whether group is focused within key areas of interest for foundation or operating divisions, and whether they can realistically accomplish their objective.
Decision Notification: Usually within 90 days of receipt of proposal.

Restrictions

Funding is only given to organizations with IRS tax-exempt status.
Funding is rarely given to organizations during their first year of operation.
Support is usually not provided for health, recreation, therapeutic or residential programs, housing and living subsidies, care of people with disabilities, or emergency care.
Support is not provided for religious groups for religious purposes, individuals, fund-raising events, fraternal organizations, goodwill advertising, or political or lobbying groups.
Giving to national programs is not a priority for the foundation. Foundation only supports national programs that complement local arts programs or the promotion of philanthropy.

Additional Information

Dayton Hudson Corporation changed its name to Target Corporation effective January 30, 2000. In conjunction with the corporation's name change, Dayton Hudson Foundation changed its name to Target Foundation. The foundation announced a new emphasis on involving company staff in grantmaking decisions. New guidelines are anticipated, but the foundation will remain committed to giving in the arts and social action as well as to giving focused on Minnesota and the Twin Cities.
Target Corporation's philanthropic contributions policy calls for the company to donate 5% of its federal taxable income annually to charitable organizations. Target's operating divisions include the Department Store Division (which includes Dayton's, Hudson's, and Marshall Field's), Mervyn's, and Target Stores; operating companies manage contributions in communities where they have stores. The Target Foundation manages contributions in the Minneapolis/Saint Paul metropolitan area and a small program of national giving.
Publications: Summary of Community Involvement; Grant Application Guidelines

Corporate Officials

Linda Ahlers: president, department store division PRIM CORP EMPL president, department store division: Dayton Hudson Corp. CORP AFFIL director: United States Bancorp.
Gail Dorn: vice president, communications PRIM CORP EMPL vice president, communications: Dayton Hudson Corp.
James Thomas Hale: senior vice president, general counsel, secretary B Minneapolis, MN 1940. ED Dartmouth College BA (1962); University of Minnesota LLB (1965). PRIM CORP EMPL senior vice president, general counsel, secretary: Dayton Hudson Corp. CORP AFFIL director: North Atlantic Life Insurance Co. NONPR AFFIL member: Order Coif; member: Phi Beta Kappa; director: Minnesota Continuing Legal Education; member executive committee: Fund Legal Aid Society; member: Hennepin County Bar Association.
Gerald L. Storch: senior vice president strategic business B 1957. ED Harvard University JD; Harvard University MBA; Harvard University BA. PRIM CORP EMPL senior vice president strategic business: Dayton Hudson Corp.
Robert J. Ulrich: chairman, chief executive officer, director B Minneapolis, MN 1944. ED University of Minnesota (1967); Stanford University Executive Program (1978). PRIM CORP EMPL chairman, chief executive officer, director: Dayton Hudson Corp. PRIM NONPR EMPL chairman, chief executive officer, director: Target Stores. CORP AFFIL director: Tricon Global Restaurants Inc.

Giving Program Officials

Polly M. Talen: senior program officer, social action
Geol L. Weirs: arts senior program officer

Foundation Officials

Linda Ahlers: trustee (see above)
Timothy Baer: secretary
Gail Dorn: trustee (see above)
Larry Gilpin: trustee B Benton, IL 1943. ED Louisiana State University; Western Kentucky University BS (1965); University of Kentucky MBA (1971). PRIM CORP EMPL executive vice president: Dayton Hudson Corp.
James Thomas Hale: trustee (see above)
Dee Henry-Williams: grants program assistant
Stephen C. Kowalke: treasurer PRIM CORP EMPL vice president, treasurer: Dayton Hudson Corp.
Christine Park: director, trustee
Robert J. Ulrich: chairman, trustee (see above)
Michael J. Wahlig: assistant secretary PRIM CORP EMPL assistant secretary: Dayton's Travel Service Inc.

Grants Analysis

Disclosure Period: fiscal year ending January 31, 1999
Total Grants: $6,845,600*
Number of Grants: 255
Average Grant: $21,213*
Highest Grant: $600,000
Typical Range: $5,000 to $30,000
***Note:** Grants analysis includes foundation. Giving excludes United Way. Average grant excludes three highest grants ($1,500,000).

Recent Grants

Note: Grants derived from 1999 Form 990.

Arts & Humanities

250,000	Minnesota Orchestral Association, Minneapolis, MN -- support of general operations
176,800	The Minneapolis Institute of Arts, Minneapolis, MN -- support of general operations
150,000	Twin Cities Public Television, St. Paul, MN -- support of 1998 arts and cultural programming
147,000	The Guthrie Theater, Minneapolis, MN -- support of general operations
121,300	Saint Paul Chamber Orchestra, Saint Paul, MN -- support of general operations
100,000	Minnesota Public Radio, St. Paul, MN -- support of arts and culture programming
100,000	Walker Art Center, Minneapolis, MN -- support of general operations
80,000	The Children's Theatre Company, Minneapolis, MN -- support of general operations
80,000	Jerome Foundation, St. Paul, MN -- support of the Travel and Study Grant Program
80,000	The Minnesota Opera, Minneapolis, MN -- support of general operations
50,000	Artspace Projects, Inc., Minneapolis, MN -- support of capital campaign for the Calhoun Building
50,000	The Metropolitan Museum of Art, New

York, NY -- support of Museum's Corporate Patron Program (DHF/Masterworks)
50,000 SPRC, Inc., St. Paul, MN -- support of 50th Anniversary Campaign's Employment Services Components
45,000 Illusion Theater, Minneapolis, MN -- support of the 25th Anniversary Capital Campaign
40,000 The Playwrights' Center, Minneapolis, MN -- support of capital campaign
30,000 Resources and Counseling for the Arts, St. Paul, MN -- support for the Dayton Hudson Artist Loan Fund
30,000 Walker Art Center, Minneapolis, MN -- support of Common Time project
27,500 Resources and Counseling for the Arts, St. Paul, MN -- support of general operations
25,000 Penumbra Theatre Company, St. Paul, MN -- support of general operations

Civic & Public Affairs

600,000 St. Paul Riverfront Corporation, St. Paul, MN
500,000 The Minneapolis Foundation, Minneapolis, MN -- support for the Capital Challenge Grant
400,000 Saint Paul Riverfront Corporation, St. Paul, MN -- support of the restoration of Harriet Island Regional Park, Saint Paul
60,000 WomenVenture, St. Paul, MN -- support of general operations
55,000 Chicanos Latinos Unidos En Servicio, Minneapolis, MN -- support of education and employment programs in St. Paul and Minneapolis
55,000 Metropolitan Economic Development Association, Minneapolis, MN -- support of general operations
50,000 African American Family Services, Minneapolis, MN -- capital campaign
50,000 American Indian Business Development Corporation, Minneapolis, MN -- support of capital campaign for Ancient Traders Market project
50,000 Greater Minneapolis Chamber Development Foundation, Minneapolis, MN -- support the marketing program of the Minnesota Keystone Program
50,000 Minnesota Diversified Industries, Inc., Saint Paul, MN -- support of capital improvements for the Phillips Jobs Initiative
50,000 Rebuild Resources, Inc., Minneapolis, MN -- support of capital campaign and equipment expenses for Rebuild Academy
50,000 St. Paul Urban League, St. Paul, MN -- support of the Neighborlink employment collaborative
35,000 Minneapolis Urban League, Minneapolis, MN -- support of adult employment and training and youth work readiness programs
30,000 American Indian OIC, Minneapolis, MN -- support of employment training and placement
30,000 Urban Coalition, St. Paul, MN -- support of general operations

Education

50,000 University of Minnesota Foundation, Minneapolis, MN -- support of the Discover Series
45,000 Metropolitan Federation of Alternative Schools, Inc., Minneapolis, MN -- one-time support of Unlimited Possibilities campaign
30,000 COMPAS, St. Paul, MN -- support of Arts Leadership Initiative (sabbatical)
30,000 University of St. Thomas, St. Paul, MN -- support of the pilot Institute for Executive Directors program
29,000 Summit Academy, OIC, Minneapolis, MN -- support of general operations for training and placement

Health

50,000 Minnesota AIDS Project, Minneapolis, MN -- support of the nonprofit cultural community's participation in the 1998 AIDS walk

Religion

60,000 Episcopal Community Services, Inc., Minneapolis, MN -- support of Families Working Together

Social Services

850,000 United Way of Minneapolis Area, Minneapolis, MN -- support of the corporate contribution for the 1998 campaign
205,000 United Way of the Saint Paul Area, St. Paul, MN -- support of the corporate contribution for the 1998 campaign
125,000 YWCA of Minneapolis, Minneapolis, MN
125,000 YWCA of Minneapolis, Minneapolis, MN -- support of the capital campaign for the Community and Urban Sports Center (first payment on total commitment of $250,000)
100,000 East Side Neighborhood Service, Inc., Minneapolis, MN -- support of capital campaign
55,000 Project for Pride in Living, Minneapolis, MN -- support of adult and youth employment programs
55,000 Project for Pride in Living, Minneapolis, MN
50,000 Loring Nicollet-Bethlehem Community Centers, Minneapolis, MN -- support of employment and education programs
33,000 Children's Home Society of Minnesota, St. Paul, MN -- one-time support of strategic planning

DAYTON POWER AND LIGHT CO.

Company Contact

Dayton, OH

Company Description

Employees: 2,908
SIC(s): 4911 Electric Services, 4924 Natural Gas Distribution, 4961 Steam & Air-Conditioning Supply.
Parent Company: DPL Inc.

Nonmonetary Support

Range: $30,000 - $50,000
Type: Donated Equipment; In-kind Services
Note: Fund goodwill advertising, and dinner/benefit tickets. Requests for nonmonetary support are handled directly by area managers.

Corporate Sponsorship

Type: Festivals/fairs
Note: Sponsors health services and fund raisers.

Dayton Power and Light Co. Foundation

Giving Contact

Vicki Shortal, Foundation Administrator
Dayton Power and Light Co. Foundation
Courthouse Plaza Southwest
PO Box 1247
Dayton, OH 45401
Phone: (937)259-7131
Fax: (937)259-7245

Description

EIN: 311138883
Organization Type: Corporate Foundation
Giving Locations: headquarters and operating communities.
Grant Types: Capital, General Support, Multiyear/Continuing Support, Project, Scholarship.

Giving Philosophy

'The Dayton Power and Light Company established The Dayton Power and Light Foundation in 1985 as the major giving vehicle for the corporation. The company believes that healthy communities are important to the success of the company. The community provides essential social, educational and cultural advantages for the company and its employees. Working with other corporations, private and community foundations, local government agencies, and numerous community organizations ensures that the places where we live and work enrich our lives and support those in need.

'The foundation makes contributions to charitable and educational organizations that greatly impact the well-being and general welfare of our communities. The majority of the Foundation's contributions are made to programs in support of education and charitable activities in communities where DP&L people live. This support is generally made through community funds such as United Way or Community Chests. Direct donations may also be made to qualified civic, cultural, or health and welfare organizations that do not participate in community funds, but serve a real need. The remaining funds are contributed to organizations that provide additional educational or charitable support in our 24 county service area.' Foundation Guidelines

Financial Summary

Total Giving: $1,473,577 (1998); $1,163,927 (1997); $1,049,245 (1996). Note: Contributes through corporate direct giving program and foundation.
Giving Analysis: Giving for 1997 includes: foundation ($945,039); foundation grants to United Way ($218,888); 1998: foundation ($1,263,526); foundation grants to United Way ($210,051)
Assets: $30,820,179 (1998); $26,351,857 (1997); $22,214,769 (1996)
Gifts Received: $3,000,000 (1990)

Typical Recipients

Arts & Humanities: Arts Associations & Councils, Arts Funds, Arts Institutes, Arts Outreach, Ballet, Dance, Ethnic & Folk Arts, Historic Preservation, History & Archaeology, Libraries, Museums/Galleries, Music, Opera, Performing Arts, Public Broadcasting, Theater, Visual Arts
Civic & Public Affairs: African American Affairs, Community Foundations, Economic Development, Economic Policy, Employment/Job Training, Housing, Municipalities/Towns, Parades/Festivals, Philanthropic Organizations, Public Policy, Urban & Community Affairs, Women's Affairs
Education: Business Education, Colleges & Universities, Community & Junior Colleges, Education Reform, Engineering/Technological Education, Faculty Development, Public Education (Precollege), Science/Mathematics Education, Student Aid
Environment: Energy, Resource Conservation
Health: Cancer, Children's Health/Hospitals, Transplant Networks/Donor Banks
Religion: Churches, Social/Policy Issues
Science: Science Exhibits & Fairs, Science Museums
Social Services: Big Brother/Big Sister, Child Welfare, Community Service Organizations, Domestic Violence, Food/Clothing Distribution, People with Disabilities, Scouts, Senior Services, Substance Abuse, United Funds/United Ways, YMCA/YWCA/YMHA/YWHA, Youth Organizations

Contributions Analysis

Giving Priorities: The arts, human services, education, civics, and health organizations.

Arts & Humanities: 10%. Supports arts centers, opera, dance, theater, and orchestras.

Civic & Public Affairs: 45%. Supports ecomonic development efforts, community improvement, historical societies, and crime prevention.

Education: 11%. Support includes colleges and universities, public schools, and scholarships.

Health: 2%. Supports medical centers; single disease causes, such as the Multiple Sclerosis Society.

Science: 11%. Funds a science museum.

Social Services: 20%. Supports united funds and other health related organizations; youth organizations, including a large amount of support to YMCA's.

Note: Total foundation contributions in 1998.

Application Procedures

Initial Contact: Send a proposal letter with financial attachments.

Application Requirements: Include description of the history, structure, purpose and program of the organization; amount requested, and purpose of funds sought; detailed financial information on the organization (such as an independent financial audit, budget, sources of income, breakdown of expenditures by program, administration and fundraising); a list of other corporate donors and level of support; proof of tax-exempt status; and copy of the most recent IRS Form 990.

Deadlines: None.

Decision Notification: Distribution committee normally meets quarterly.

Restrictions

Does not support individuals; individual members of federated campaigns; fraternal, labor, or veterans organizations; political or lobbying groups; religious organizations; conduit organizations; college fundraising associations; capital campaigns; endowment or development funds; hospital operating budgets; sports leagues; telephone or mass-mail solicitations; or national organizations outside the DP&L service territory.

Corporate Officials

Peter Hans Forster: chairman, director B Berlin, Germany 1942. ED University of Wisconsin BS (1964); Brooklyn Law School JD (1972). PRIM CORP EMPL chairman, director: Dayton Power & Light Co. CORP AFFIL director: Comair Inc.; chairman, chief executive officer, president, director: DPL Inc.; director: Comair Holdings Inc.; director: Amcast Industries Corp.; director: Bank One Dayton NA. NONPR AFFIL trustee: Medical American Health Systems; member: Ohio Bar Association; director: Dayton Business Committee; member: American Bar Association; member: Dayton Bar Association.

Allen M. Hill: president, chief executive officer B Dayton, OH 1945. ED University of Dayton BS (1967); University of Dayton MBA (1972). PRIM CORP EMPL president, chief executive officer: Dayton Power & Light Co. NONPR AFFIL president, chief executive officer, director: DPL Inc.

Foundation Officials

Thomas A. Jenkins: treasurer, trustee B Cleveland, OH 1942. ED Purdue University (1965); Indiana University (1968). PRIM CORP EMPL vice president, senior trustee counsel: Bank One Indianapolis NA.

Stephen F. Koziar, Jr.: president, trustee B Webster, MA 1944. ED University of Dayton BSIE (1967); Salmon P. Chase College of Law JD (1971). PRIM CORP EMPL group vice president, secretary: Dayton Power & Light Co. CORP AFFIL president: Miami Valley Development Co.; president: Miami Valley Resources Inc.; secretary: DPL Inc.

Judy W. Lansaw: secretary, trustee B Dayton, OH 1951. ED Wright State University BA (1988). PRIM CORP EMPL group vice president: Dayton Power & Light Co. CORP AFFIL group vice president: DPL Inc.

Vicki Shortal: foundation administrator

Grants Analysis

Disclosure Period: calendar year ending 1998
Total Grants: $1,263,526*
Number of Grants: 53
Average Grant: $23,840
Highest Grant: $200,000
Typical Range: $1,000 to $50,000
*Note: Giving excludes United Way.

Recent Grants

Note: Grants derived from 1997 Form 990.

Arts & Humanities

150,000	Carlton Historical Park, Dayton, OH
75,000	Dayton Art Institute, Dayton, OH
30,000	Dayton Art Institute Art Ball, Dayton, OH
16,200	Muse Machine, Dayton, OH
10,000	Carlton Historical Park, Dayton, OH
10,000	Dayton Ballet, Dayton, OH
10,000	Dayton Contemporary Dance Company, Dayton, OH
10,000	Dayton Opera Association, Dayton, OH
10,000	Dayton Philharmonic Orchestra Association, Dayton, OH
10,000	Sponsor National Folk Festival, Dayton, OH
10,000	Victoria Theater Association, Dayton, OH
8,200	Culture Works, Dayton, OH
5,000	Champaign County Library Theater, Urbana, OH
5,000	Human Race Theater Company, Dayton, OH

Civic & Public Affairs

20,000	2003 Committee, Dayton, OH
10,800	Kids Voting Founders Region, Dayton, OH
10,000	Jobs for Graduates of the Miami Valley, Dayton, OH
10,000	West Area Renovations, Dayton, OH
8,500	Committee for Economic Development, New York, NY
5,260	Dayton Urban League, Dayton, OH
5,000	American Enterprise Institute for Public Policy Research, Washington, DC
5,000	Engineers Club Foundation, Dayton, OH
5,000	McPherson Town Neighborhood Development Corp, Dayton, OH
3,000	Christmas in April, Dayton, OH
3,000	Marion Community Development Organization, Marion Stein, OH

Education

25,000	University of Dayton, Dayton, OH
15,000	Sugarcreek Local Schools, Bellbrook, OH
12,000	Cedarville College, Cedarville, OH
12,000	Maria University, Oxford, OH
12,000	Ohio State University, Columbus, OH
12,000	University of Cincinnati, Cincinnati, OH
12,000	Wilberforce University, Wilberforce, OH
12,000	Wilmington College, Wilmington, OH
12,000	Wright State University, Fairborn, OH
9,000	Dayton Public Schools, Dayton, OH
7,500	Alliance for Education, Dayton, OH
6,000	Edison Community College, Piquay, OH
6,000	Maysville Community College, Maysville, KY
6,000	Sinclair Community College Foundation, Dayton, OH

Environment

50,000	Consumer Energy Council of America Research Foundation, Washington, DC
25,000	Energy Policy Forum
20,000	Nature Conservancy, Arlington, VA
10,000	Ohio Energy Project, Columbus, OH

Health

50,000	St. Joseph Children's Treatment Center, Dayton, OH
11,608	Hippia Cancer Research Center, Dayton, OH
5,000	Community Blood Center, Dayton, OH

Social Services

200,000	United Way, Dayton, OH
50,000	Arternes Center for Alternatives to Domestic Violence, Dayton, OH
3,000	Reach Out of Montgomery County, Dayton, OH
2,500	University Support Services, St. Peter, MN

DEERE &CO.

★ Number 83 of Top 100 Corporate Givers

Company Contact

Moline, IL
Web: http://www.deere.com

Company Description

Revenue: US$13,821,500,000
Profit: US$1,021,400,000
Employees: 33,900
Fortune Rank: 149, per FORTUNE Magazine's list of 500 Largest U.S. Corporations (1999).
FF 149
SIC(s): 3519 Internal Combustion Engines Nec, 3523 Farm Machinery & Equipment, 3524 Lawn & Garden Equipment, 3531 Construction Machinery.

Operating Locations

Argentina: Industrias John Deere Argentina SA, Granadero Baigorria, Santa Fe; Canada: John Deere Finance Ltd., Burlington; John Deere Insurance Co. of Canada, Grimsby; John Deere Ltd., Grimsby; Homelite Canada Ltd., Lachine; Phoenix Piston Hydraulics, Nisku; France: John Deere SA, Ormes; Homelite Atlantic, St. Ouen L'Aumone, Val d'Oise; Textron TSM SARL, St. Ouen L'Aumone, Val d'Oise; Germany: John Deere European Parts Distribution Center, Bruchsal, Baden-Wuerttemberg; John Deere Werke Bruchsal Zweigniederlassung der Deere & Co. European Office Mannheim, Bruchsal, Baden-Wuerttemberg; SABO Maschinenfabrik GmbH, Gummersbach; Deere & Co. Europeen Office Mannheim Zweigniederlassung der Deere & Co. Molineillinois/USA, Mannheim, Baden-Wuerttemberg; Eurag Holding AG, Mannheim, Baden-Wuerttemberg; John Deere Capital Services GmbH, Mannheim, Baden-Wuerttemberg; John Deere Export-A Div. of Deere & Co. in Mannheim Zweigniederlassung der Firma Deere & Co., Mannheim, Baden-Wuerttemberg; John Deere Handels GmbH, Mannheim, Baden-Wuerttemberg; John Deere Intercontinental GmbH, Mannheim, Baden-Wuerttemberg; John Deere Lanz Verwaltungsaktiengesellschaft, Mannheim, Baden-Wuerttemberg; John Deere Vertrieb Deutschland, Mannheim, Baden-Wuerttemberg; John Deere Werke Mannheim Zweigniederlassung der Deere & Co. Mannheim Sitz Wilmington, Mannheim, Baden-Wuerttemberg; Maschinenfabrik Kemper GmbH & Co. KG, Stadtlohn, Nordrhein-Westfalen; John Deere Werke Zweibruecken Zweigniederlassung der Deere & Co., Zweibruecken, Rheinland-Pfalz; Italy: John Deere Italiana, Vignate, Lombardia; Mexico: Industrias John Deere SA de CV, Garza Garcia; John Deere SA de CV, Garza Garcia; Netherlands: Roberine BV, Enschede, Overijssel; Douven Beheer BV, Horst, Limburg; Douven Onroerend Goed BV, Horst, Limburg; Machinefabriek Gebr Douven BV, Horst, Limburg; Homelite Netherlands BV, Nieuw Vennep, Noord-Holland; Spain: John Deere Iberica SA, Getafe, Madrid; Sweden: Svenska John Deere AB

Nonmonetary Support

Value: $250,000 (1995); $375,000 (1994); $433,000 (1993)
Type: In-kind Services; Loaned Employees; Loaned Executives
Note: Nonmonetary support is provided by the company.

Corporate Sponsorship

Value: $256,091 (1995)
Contact: Donald Morganthaler, President of John Deere Foundation
Note: Sponsors programs that support business and marketing activities important to John Deere; supports National 4-H Council and Outstanding Young Farmer Program.

John Deere Foundation

Giving Contact

Darlene Ellis, Contributions Representative
John Deere Foundation
John Deere Rd.
Moline, IL 61265-8098
Phone: (309)765-4137
Fax: (309)765-9855
Email: DP51104@deere.com

Description

EIN: 366051024
Organization Type: Corporate Foundation
Giving Locations: principally near operating locations and to national organizations.
Grant Types: Capital, Department, General Support, Project.

Giving Philosophy

'The John Deere Foundation was organized in 1948 and is funded by Deere & Company. The primary objective of the foundation is to support programs and activities that meet one or more of the following guidelines: projects that address specific community needs and suggest solutions designed to meet these challenges; programs that offer opportunities for enriched life and that provide members of a community with skills, knowledge, and assistance to accomplish positive social goals; projects seeking self-support or broad-based community support as their ultimate goal.

'The Contributions Committee, which is the other active grant-making organization of Deere & Company, supports organizations that impact our business. Contributions Committee grants will be judged on their business merits.

'Currently, the John Deere contributions program calls for priority funding in these areas: health and human services organizations; education, including K-12 efforts and universities and two-year colleges that are important to our recruiting, research, and training efforts; community revitalization efforts; and cultural organizations.' 1996 Report of Contributions

Financial Summary

Total Giving: $10,000,000 (fiscal year ending October 31, 2000 approx); $9,300,000 (fiscal 1999 approx); $9,152,871 (fiscal 1998). Note: Contributes through corporate direct giving program and foundation.
Giving Analysis: Giving for fiscal 1997 includes: foundation ($6,655,788); domestic and international subsidiaries ($1,223,978); corporate direct giving ($1,018,688); fiscal 1998: foundation ($6,843,843); domestic and international subsidiaries ($1,566,046); corporate direct giving ($742,982)
Assets: $22,000,000 (fiscal 1999 approx); $23,940,678 (fiscal 1998); $28,443,155 (fiscal 1997)
Gifts Received: $210,000 (fiscal 1998); $6,740,000 (fiscal 1997); $7,166,637 (fiscal 1996). Note: Foundation received contributions from Deere & Co., John Deere Insurance Company, Deere & Company - Kansas City Branch, Heritage National Healthplan Services, Inc.

Typical Recipients

Arts & Humanities: Arts Centers, Community Arts, Arts & Humanities-General, Historic Preservation, History & Archaeology, Libraries, Museums/Galleries, Music, Opera, Public Broadcasting, Theater
Civic & Public Affairs: Botanical Gardens/Parks, Business/Free Enterprise, Chambers of Commerce, Community Foundations, Economic Development, Civic & Public Affairs-General, Municipalities/Towns, Parades/Festivals, Professional & Trade Associations, Public Policy, Rural Affairs, Urban & Community Affairs, Zoos/Aquariums
Education: Afterschool/Enrichment Programs, Agricultural Education, Arts/Humanities Education, Business Education, Colleges & Universities, Community & Junior Colleges, Economic Education, Engineering/Technological Education, Education-General, Minority Education, Private Education (Precollege), Public Education (Precollege), Science/Mathematics Education, Secondary Education (Private), Vocational & Technical Education
Environment: Environment-General, Research, Resource Conservation
Health: Emergency/Ambulance Services, Health Policy/Cost Containment, Health Organizations, Hospices, Outpatient Health Care, Public Health, Transplant Networks/Donor Banks
International: Foreign Educational Institutions
Religion: Religious Welfare
Science: Science Museums
Social Services: Child Welfare, Community Centers, Community Service Organizations, Day Care, Family Services, Homes, People with Disabilities, Recreation & Athletics, Scouts, Senior Services, Substance Abuse, United Funds/United Ways, YMCA/YWCA/YMHA/YWHA, Youth Organizations

Contributions Analysis

Giving Priorities: Health, social welfare, safety, education, the arts, civics, and nonprofit international organizations. Foundation interests include support for Third World development through U.S.-based nonprofits with international interests. Deere's foreign subsidiaries act independently and give directly to organizations in their locale. Corporate headquarters records the total amount given by all foreign subsidiaries, but does not disclose the figure.
Arts & Humanities: About 7%. Supports historical societies and museums, cultural centers, orchestras, and other cultural activities.
Civic & Public Affairs: About 13%. Supports organizations concerned with public policy, business and free enterprise, civil rights, law and justice, and economic development.
Education: Around 50%. Supports higher education, K-12 programs, minority education associations, and economic, science, and technical education. Emphasis on recruiting, research, and retraining programs.
Health: About 27%. Majority supports united funds. Other interests include health and youth organizations, programs for drug and alcohol abuse, child welfare, and the handicapped.
Note: Above percentages reflect corporate and foundation giving in fiscal 1998.

Application Procedures

Initial Contact: Request guidelines, then send written proposal.
Application Requirements: Applications should include a description of organization and statement of objectives and goal; description of benefits and geographic area to be served; program budget; amount requested and complete explanation of activity; goals of program and deadlines for result; and verification of tax-exempt status.
Deadlines: None.
Review Process: Requests are reviewed in order of receipt, board meets as needed; initial response can be expected in four to six weeks.
Evaluative Criteria: 'The John Deere Foundation considers requests only from tax-exempt, nonprofit organizations, located in the U.S. or its possessions.' 'Priority funding centers upon programs in this order: health and human services; education, including K-12, university, and college efforts that are important to our employee recruiting, research, and training; community revitalization efforts; and cultural organizations.' *Deere & Company Corporate Contributions Program 1998 Report of Contributions***Notes:** Organizations located in Moline, IL area or which are national in scope should direct requests to the foundation; other organizations should send requests to the manager of operating unit in community.

Restrictions

John Deere Foundation will not provide support for individuals; dinners or special events; fraternal organizations; goodwill advertising; or political or lobbying groups.

Additional Information

Publications: Annual Contributions Report

Corporate Officials

Hans Walter Becherer: chairman, chief executive officer, director B Detroit, MI 1935. ED Trinity College BA (1957); Munich University (1958); Harvard University MBA (1962). PRIM CORP EMPL chairman, chief executive officer, director: Deere & Co. CORP AFFIL director: Schering-Plough Corp.; president: John Deere Industries Equipment Co.; president: Deere Marketing Services Inc.; chairman: John Deere Credit Co.; director: Deere Credit Inc.; director: John Deere Capital Corp.; director: Chase Manhattan Bank; director: Chase Manhattan Corp.; director: AlliedSignal Inc. NONPR AFFIL member: Equipment Manufacturer Institute; vice president, trustee: Saint Katherines-Saint Marks School; member: Council Foreign Relations; trustee: Committee for Economic Development; member: Conference Board; member: Business Council; member: Business Roundtable. CLUB AFFIL Rock Island Club; Arsenal Golf Club; Chicago Club.
Wade Clark: vice president government affairs PRIM CORP EMPL vice president government affairs: John Deere & Co.
John K. Lawson: senior vice president B Moline, IL 1940. ED Iowa State University BA (1962). PRIM CORP EMPL senior vice president: John Deere & Co. ADD CORP EMPL vice president: John Deere Commercial Products. CORP AFFIL director: Deere Marketing Services Inc. NONPR AFFIL director: Iowa State University Foundation; director: Research Board; governor: Iowa College Foundation; director: Arrowhead Ranch.

Giving Program Officials

Donald R. Margenthaler: president, director PRIM CORP EMPL director community relations: Deere Co.

Foundation Officials

Hans Walter Becherer: director (see above)
Barron W. Curtis: assistant treasurer
Darlene S. Ellis: assistant secretary
Joseph Walker England: chairman, director B Moline, IL 1940. ED University of Illinois BS (1962). PRIM CORP EMPL senior vice president worldwide parts & corporate administration: John Deere & Co. CORP AFFIL director: Deere Credit Inc.; director: First Midwest Bank Corp. Inc.; vice president, director: John Deere Capital Corp.
John K. Lawson: director (see above)
Donald R. Margenthaler: president, director (see above)
Sonja J. Sterling: secretary

Grants Analysis

Disclosure Period: fiscal year ending October 31, 1997
Total Grants: $6,599,173*
Number of Grants: 295
Average Grant: $22,234
Highest Grant: $728,000
Typical Range: $1,000 to $25,000
***Note:** Giving excludes corporate direct giving; domestic and international subsidiaries.

Recent Grants

Note: Grants derived from 1998 Form 990.

Arts & Humanities

150,000	Terrace Hill Society, Des Moines, IA
150,000	World War II Memorial, Washington, DC -- Civic/ Community Development
100,000	Harry S. Truman Library Institute, Independence, MO
35,000	Quad City Arts, Rock Island, IL
25,000	Playcrafters Barn Theatre, Inc., Moline, IL
20,000	Hudson Public Library, Hudson, IA

Civic & Public Affairs

100,000	Quad City Botanical Center Foundation, Rock Island, IL
100,000	Renew Moline, Inc., Moline, IL
50,000	Redeem, Inc., East Moline, IL
50,000	Society of Automotive Engineers, Warrendale, PA
25,000	Ided Foundation/Iowa Summit, Des Moines, IA
25,000	Rock Island Economic Growth Corporation, Rock Island, IL

Education

250,000	University of Northern Iowa, Cedar Falls, IA
250,000	University of Wisconsin-Platteville Foundation, Platteville, WI
55,000	Junior Achievement of the Quad Cities, Inc., Moline, IL
50,000	Carl Sandburg College, Galesburg, IL
50,000	St. Katharine's/St. Mark's School, Bettendorf, IA
32,500	Bradley University, Peoria, IL
30,000	Central College, Pella, IA
30,000	Moline High School, Moline, IL
30,000	St. Katharine's/St. Mark's School, Bettendorf, IA
30,000	York Technical College, Rock Hill, SC
25,000	Junior Achievement of Black Hawk Land, Inc., Cedar Falls, IA
25,000	University of Illinois Foundation, Urbana, IL
20,000	Colorado School of Mines, Golden, CO
20,000	Greenville Technical College, Greenville, SC

Environment

225,000	The Nature Conservancy of Illinois, Chicago, IL
25,000	The PLCAA Educational and Research Foundation, Inc., Marietta, GA

Health

50,000	911 Communication Centre Board, Moline, IL
50,000	Cedar Valley Hospice, Waterloo, IA
30,000	American Red Cross, Rock Island, IL
20,000	Family Health Foundation of Iowa, Des Moines, IA
20,000	Mississippi Valley Regional Blood Center, Davenport, IA

Social Services

796,000	United Way of the Quad Cities Area, Davenport, IA
320,000	Cedar Valley United Way, Waterloo, IA
104,800	The Moline YMCA, Moline, IL
103,060	Scott County Family Y, Davenport, IA
100,000	United Way Services, Inc., Dubuque, IA
100,000	YMCA/YWCA of Dubuque, Dubuque, IA
95,000	United Way of Central Iowa, Des Moines, IA
75,000	Skip-A-Long Daycare Center, Moline, IL
34,000	United Way of Wapello County, Ottumwa, IA
25,000	Boy Scouts of America, Bay Lakes Council, Menasha, WI
25,000	Boys and Girls Club of Waterloo, Waterloo, IA
25,000	Coffeyville United Fund, Coffeyville, KS
25,000	Quad Cities Sports Commission, Moline, IL
25,000	United Way of Dodge County, Beaver Dam, WI
25,000	United Way of the Quad Cities Area, Davenport, IA
20,000	United Way International, Alexandria, VA
19,600	United Way of Gaston County, Gastonia, NC

DEKALB GENETICS CORP.

Company Contact

DeKalb, IL
Web: http://www.dekalb.com

Company Description

Revenue: US$314,400,000
Employees: 2,200
SIC(s): 0115 Corn, 0116 Soybeans, 0213 Hogs, 8731 Commercial Physical Research.

Nonmonetary Support

Type: In-kind Services

DeKalb Genetics Foundation

Giving Contact

Dave Wagley, Treasurer & Vice President, Finance
3100 Sycamore Rd.
DeKalb, IL 60115
Phone: (815)758-3461

Description

Founded: 1964
EIN: 366117737
Organization Type: Corporate Foundation
Giving Locations: headquarters and operating communities.
Grant Types: Award, Capital, Employee Matching Gifts, Endowment, Multiyear/Continuing Support, Scholarship.

Financial Summary

Total Giving: $395,868 (fiscal year ending August 31, 1998); $325,312 (fiscal 1997); $179,530 (fiscal 1996)
Giving Analysis: Giving for fiscal 1997 includes: foundation ($177,268); foundation grants to United Way ($91,791); foundation matching gifts ($56,253); fiscal 1998: foundation ($243,047); foundation grants to United Way ($98,753); foundation matching gifts ($54,069)
Assets: $776,695 (fiscal 1998); $17,870 (fiscal 1997); $299,947 (fiscal 1996)
Gifts Received: $1,185,000 (fiscal 1998); $299,946 (fiscal 1997); $452,400 (fiscal 1996). Note: Contributions are received from Dekalb Genetics Corporation.

Typical Recipients

Arts & Humanities: Libraries, Museums/Galleries, Public Broadcasting
Civic & Public Affairs: Botanical Gardens/Parks, Community Foundations, Economic Development, Civic & Public Affairs-General, Municipalities/Towns, Professional & Trade Associations, Public Policy, Rural Affairs, Urban & Community Affairs, Zoos/Aquariums
Education: Agricultural Education, Business Education, Colleges & Universities, Community & Junior Colleges, Economic Education, Education Associations, Elementary Education (Private), Elementary Education (Public), Engineering/Technological Education, Education-General, International Studies, Public Education (Precollege), Science/Mathematics Education, Secondary Education (Private), Secondary Education (Public), Special Education
Environment: Resource Conservation
Health: Cancer, Clinics/Medical Centers, Emergency/Ambulance Services, Health-General, Health Policy/Cost Containment, Hospices, Hospitals, Mental Health, Preventive Medicine/Wellness Organizations
Science: Scientific Centers & Institutes, Scientific Labs, Scientific Organizations
Social Services: Community Centers, Day Care, Family Services, Food/Clothing Distribution, Recreation & Athletics, Substance Abuse, United Funds/ United Ways, YMCA/YWCA/YMHA/YWHA

Contributions Analysis

Giving Priorities: Civic organizations, agricultural foundations, and the United Way.
Civic & Public Affairs: 35%. Supports civic improvements.
Education: 7%. Funds colleges and universities and agricultural education programs.
Environment: 18%. Supports agricultural foundations.
Health: 1%. Supports hospitals and medical centers.
Social Services: 38%. Supports the United Way.
Note: Total contributions made in fiscal 1998.

Application Procedures

Initial Contact: Send a brief letter of inquiry.
Application Requirements: Include a description of organization, amount requested, and purpose of funds sought.
Deadlines: None. Telephone requests are not accepted.

Restrictions

The foundation funds the following general categories: united funds, higher education, health and welfare, agricultural and/or natural resource agencies, and economic education. Does not support individuals, religious organizations for sectarian purposes, political or lobbying groups, or organizations outside operating areas.

Additional Information

Company also donates equipment.
Publications: Annual Report; Application Guidelines

Corporate Officials

Bruce P. Bickner: chairman, chief executive officer, director B Chicago, IL 1943. ED DePauw University (1965); University of Michigan Law School (1968). PRIM CORP EMPL chairman, chief executive officer, director: DeKalb Genetics Corp. CORP AFFIL director: Pride Petroleum Services Inc.; chairman: DeKalb Energy Co. NONPR AFFIL member: American Bar Association.
Thomas R. Rauman: chief financial officer B DeKalb, IL 1948. ED Western Illinois University (1970); University of Illinois (1973). PRIM CORP EMPL chief financial officer: DeKalb Genetics Corp.
Richard O. Ryan: president, director PRIM CORP EMPL president, director: DeKalb Genetics Corp.

Foundation Officials

Thomas R. Rauman: treasurer, director (see above)
Richard O. Ryan: president, chief operating officer (see above)
Dave Wagley: secretary, director PRIM CORP EMPL treasurer, vice president finance: DeKalb Genetics Corp.

Grants Analysis

Disclosure Period: fiscal year ending August 31, 1998
Total Grants: $161,899*
Number of Grants: 60
Average Grant: $2,698
Highest Grant: $50,249
Typical Range: $250 to $9,500
***Note:** Giving excludes matching gifts; United Way.

Recent Grants

Note: Grants derived from 1997 Form 990.

Civic & Public Affairs

10,000	DeKalb County Economic Development, Sycamore, IL -- civic improvements

Education

25,000	University of Minnesota Department of Agronomy and Plant Genetics, St. Paul, MN
20,000	Iowa State University Foundation, Ames, IA
10,000	National Future Farmers of America Foundation, Madison, WI
5,000	DeKalb School System, DeKalb, IL -- civic improvements
5,000	Depauw University, Greencastle, IN
5,000	Texas A&M Foundation, College Station, TX
5,000	University of Minnesota Department of Agronomy and Plant Genetics, St. Paul, MN
4,150	University of Illinois Foundation, Champaign, IL
2,700	University of Illinois College of Agriculture, Urbana, IL

Health

50,000	Kishwaukee Community Hospital, DeKalb, IL -- civic improvements
17,025	Kishwaukee Community Hospital, DeKalb, IL

Social Services

11,835	DeKalb United Way, DeKalb, IL
11,665	DeKalb United Way, DeKalb, IL
10,000	YMCA, DeKalb, IL -- civic improvements
9,813	Sycamore United Way, Sycamore, IL
9,687	Sycamore United Way, Sycamore, IL
8,100	YMCA, DeKalb, IL
5,731	Seward County United Way, Liberal, KS
5,731	Seward County United Way, Liberal, KS

DELOITTE &TOUCHE

Company Contact

Wilton, CT
Web: http://www.dhus.com

Company Description

Former Name: Deloitte, Haskins & Sells.
Revenue: US$2,925,000,000
Employees: 26,889 (1999)
SIC(s): 8721 Accounting, Auditing & Bookkeeping, 8742 Management Consulting Services.

Deloitte & Touche Foundation

Giving Contact

Kathy Shoztic, Foundation Administrator
Deloitte & Touche Foundation
10 Westport Rd.
PO Box 820
Wilton, CT 06897-0820
Phone: (203)761-3248
Fax: (203)834-2294

Description

Founded: 1928
EIN: 136400341
Organization Type: Corporate Foundation
Giving Locations: nationally.
Grant Types: Conference/Seminar, Employee Matching Gifts, Fellowship.
Note: Foundation matches employee gifts to academic programs at degree-granting institutions in the U.S. and Puerto Rico.

Financial Summary

Total Giving: $3,200,000 (fiscal year ending May 31, 1999 approx); $2,223,818 (fiscal 1998); $2,200,000 (fiscal 1997 approx). Note: Contributes through corporate direct giving program and foundation.
Giving Analysis: Giving for fiscal 1998 includes: foundation matching gifts ($1,389,673); foundation ($632,770); foundation fellowships ($180,000); foundation scholarships ($21,375)
Assets: $3,477,111 (fiscal 1998); $203,854 (fiscal 1996); $343,442 (fiscal 1995)
Gifts Received: $5,225,702 (fiscal 1998); $2,158,025 (fiscal 1996); $2,239,519 (fiscal 1994). Note: In fiscal 1998, contributions were received from Deloitte & Touche ($2,200,000); the Arthur Schwertfeger Estate ($2,850,000); and individual gifts under $10,000.

Typical Recipients

Civic & Public Affairs: Nonprofit Management, Professional & Trade Associations
Education: Business Education, Colleges & Universities, Continuing Education, Education Associations, Education Funds, Education Reform, Engineering/Technological Education, Faculty Development, Education-General, Minority Education, Science/Mathematics Education, Student Aid

Contributions Analysis

Giving Priorities: Higher education; provides matching gifts and doctoral fellowships.
Education: 100%. Foundation supports excellence in the teaching of students who plan a career in the practice, research, or teaching of accounting and business; improvements in pedagogy and curricula; cooperation among practicing professionals, teachers, researchers, and students; research that improves the practice of accounting and business; and efforts to integrate practice with research and teaching. Major support is awarded to the foundation's Doctoral Fellowship Program, which supports students working toward their doctorates in accounting. The foundation also provides direct financial support to many colleges, universities, funds, various conferences, seminars, and symposia for projects, and other activities with educators.

Application Procedures

Initial Contact: Send a a brief letter of inquiry and proposal; application form required for doctoral fellowship program.
Application Requirements: Include a description of organization, amount requested, purpose of funds sought, recently audited financial statement, and proof of tax-exempt status.
Deadlines: October 16 for doctoral fellowship program; apply for other programs at any time.
Decision Notification: Decisions are made in December for the fellowship program; throughout the year for other programs.

Restrictions

No grants are given for general support or publications. The foundation does not make loans.

Corporate Officials

Carl Burton: director marketing communication department PRIM CORP EMPL director marketing communication department: Deloitte & Touche.
J. Michael Cook: chairman, chief executive officer B New York, NY 1942. ED University of Florida BS (1964). PRIM CORP EMPL chairman, chief executive officer: Deloitte & Touche. NONPR AFFIL board governors: United Way America; advisory committee: University Florida School Business; member: U.S.-Japan Business Council; executive committee: Securities Regulation Institute; trustee: U.S. Council International Business; advisory counsel: International Accounting Standards Committee; member: New York City Partnership; vice chairman: Drugs Dont Work Leadership Council; trustee, chairman oversight committee: Fin Accounting Foundation; member: Conference Board; member, board overseers: Cornell University Medicine College; director: Catalyst; member deans advisory council: Columbia University Business School; member: American Institute CPAs. CLUB AFFIL Greenwich Country Club; Blind Brook Club; Economic Club.
James E. Copeland: managing partner PRIM CORP EMPL managing partner: Deloitte & Touche.
William A. Fowler: chief financial officer, national managing director finance PRIM CORP EMPL chief financial officer, national managing director finance: Deloitte Touche Tohmatsu.
Edward A. Kangas: chairman, chief executive officer B 1944. ED University of Kansas (1967). PRIM CORP EMPL chairman, chief executive officer: Deloitte & Touche Tohmatsu International. NONPR AFFIL board advisors: University Kansas Business School; board overseers: University Pennsylvania Wharton School Business; trustee: Committee for Economic Development; chairman fund raising committee, member finance committee: National Multiple Sclerosis Society.

Foundation Officials

John Bava: director-at-large
Mike Burton: director-at-large
Mark Chain: president
J. Michael Cook: chairman (see above)
Mary Hadley-Devine: director-at-large
Jack Robinson: director
Manoj Singh: director-at-large
Jim Wall: treasurer, secretary

Grants Analysis

Disclosure Period: fiscal year ending May 31, 1998
Total Grants: $632,770*
Number of Grants: 13
Average Grant: $48,675
Highest Grant: $184,770
Typical Range: $5,000 to $50,000
***Note:** Giving excludes matching gifts, scholarship, fellowships.

Recent Grants

Note: Grants derived from 1998 Form 990.

Education

74,496	University of Notre Dame, Notre Dame, IN -- matching gift
59,322	University of Southern California, Los Angeles, CA -- matching gift

57,547	University of Southern California, Los Angeles, CA
47,106	University of Pennsylvania, Pittsburgh, PA -- matching gift
39,400	University of California, Berkeley, CA -- matching gift
37,663	University of North Carolina, Chapel Hill, NC -- matching gift
36,127	Michigan State University, Detroit, MI -- matching gift
33,500	University of Kansas, Lawrence, KS -- Symposium on Auditing Problems
30,450	University of Tennessee, Knoxville, TN -- matching gift
30,200	University of Washington, Seattle, WA -- matching gift
29,852	Michigan State University, Detroit, MI
28,600	Miami University of Ohio, Miami, OH -- matching gift
26,363	University of North Carolina, Chapel Hill, NC
25,575	Xavier University, Cincinnati, OH -- matching gift
24,340	North Carolina A&T State University Foundation, Greensboro, NC -- matching gift
24,130	University of California, Los Angeles, CA -- matching gift
22,999	The Ohio State University, Columbus, OH -- matching gift
22,504	Harvard University, Cambridge, MA -- matching gift
21,375	North Carolina A&T State University, Greensboro, NC -- scholarships
21,005	University of Michigan, Ann Arbor, MI -- matching gift
20,750	Lehigh University, Lehigh, PA -- Matching gift
20,163	Duke University, Durham, NC -- Matching gift
19,288	University of Illinois, Bloomington, IL -- matching gift
18,905	University of Florida, Miami, FL -- Matching gift
18,510	Columbia University, New York, NY -- Matching gift
17,750	University of Texas, Austin, TX -- matching gift
15,000	Miami University of Ohio, Miami, OH
14,800	Fordham University, New York, NY -- Matching gift
14,527	University of Georgia, Athens, GA -- matching gift
14,000	Rice University, Houston, TX -- matching gift
13,009	Dartmouth College, Dartmouth, MA -- Matching gift
12,950	University of Kansas, Lawrence, KS -- Matching gift
12,450	Carnegie Mellon University, Pittsburgh, PA -- Matching gift
12,325	University of Wisconsin - Madison Foundation, Madison, WI -- matching gift
12,105	University of Minnesota Foundation, Minneapolis, MN -- matching gift
11,900	University of Chicago, Chicago, IL -- Matching gift
11,500	Georgia State University Foundation, Atlanta, GA -- Matching gift
10,632	University of Nebraska Foundation, Lincoln, NE -- matching gift
10,598	John Carroll University, Cleveland, OH -- Matching gift
9,740	Villanova University, Villanova, PA -- matching gift
9,350	Cornell University, Ithaca, NY -- Matching gift
9,350	Saint John's University, New York, NY -- Matching gift
9,335	University of Akron Foundation, Akron, OH -- Matching gift

DELTA AIR LINES, INC.

Company Contact

Atlanta, GA
Web: http://www.delta-air.com

Company Description

Revenue: US$14,138,000,000
Profit: US$1,001,000,000
Employees: 63,441
Fortune Rank: 116, per FORTUNE Magazine's list of 500 Largest U.S. Corporations (1999). FF 116
SIC(s): 4512 Air Transportation--Scheduled.

Operating Locations

Operates from 153 other cities in the U.S.

Nonmonetary Support

Type: Donated Products

Corporate Sponsorship

Type: Arts & cultural events

Delta Air Lines Foundation

Giving Contact

Michael M. Young, Vice President, Community Affairs
Delta Air Lines Foundation
Hartsfield Atlanta International Airport
Department 979
Atlanta, GA 30320-6001
Phone: (404)715-7922
Fax: (404)715-5876
Email: mike.young-air@deltaair.com

Description

EIN: 586073119
Organization Type: Corporate Foundation
Giving Locations: headquarters and operating communities.
Grant Types: Capital, Employee Matching Gifts.

Giving Philosophy

'The foundation has strengthened its commitment to the people who live in communities where Delta Air Lines has a presence. Community investment is one of the core values of Delta Air Lines. We know that our success is linked closely to the quality of life in the communities of our customers, stockholders, and Delta people. And we feel that an investment in our comminutes benefits not just the recipient organizations, but all of the people who live and work in cities served by Delta Air Lines. We will concentrate our community investments strategically in three focus areas: building communities, strengthening families with young children, and increasing cultural understanding.' *The Delta Air Lines Foundation Perspective*

Financial Summary

Total Giving: $2,159,932 (fiscal year ending June 30, 1998); $1,511,382 (fiscal 1997); $1,358,656 (fiscal 1996). Note: Contributes through foundation only. Fiscal 1998 Giving includes $3,397 in refunds and voided contributions checks.
Giving Analysis: Giving for fiscal 1996 includes: foundation ($656,000); foundation matching gifts ($384,344); foundation grants to United Way ($318,312); fiscal 1997: foundation matching gifts ($416,535); foundation grants to United Way ($291,812); fiscal 1998: foundation ($1,439,291); foundation grants to United Way ($370,275); foundation matching gifts ($353,763)
Assets: $33,140,169 (fiscal 1998); $24,411,436 (fiscal 1997); $18,407,378 (fiscal 1996)
Gifts Received: $5,000,000 (fiscal 1998); $2,500,000 (fiscal 1997). Note: Contributions are received from Delta Air Lines, Inc.

Typical Recipients

Arts & Humanities: Arts Appreciation, Arts Centers, Arts Funds, Arts Outreach, Ballet, Music, Opera, Performing Arts, Theater
Civic & Public Affairs: Community Foundations, Economic Development, Employment/Job Training, Civic & Public Affairs-General, Hispanic Affairs, Municipalities/Towns, Nonprofit Management, Professional & Trade Associations, Urban & Community Affairs
Education: Afterschool/Enrichment Programs, Colleges & Universities, Education Funds, Education Reform, Elementary Education (Public), Engineering/Technological Education, Gifted & Talented Programs, International Exchange, Legal Education, Literacy, Medical Education, Minority Education, Preschool Education, Religious Education, Science/Mathematics Education, Special Education, Vocational & Technical Education
Environment: Watershed
Health: AIDS/HIV, Children's Health/Hospitals, Clinics/Medical Centers, Emergency/Ambulance Services, Health Organizations
International: Health Care/Hospitals, International Affairs, Missionary/Religious Activities
Religion: Jewish Causes, Religious Organizations, Religious Welfare
Science: Scientific Centers & Institutes
Social Services: At-Risk Youth, Camps, Child Welfare, Community Service Organizations, Counseling, Family Services, People with Disabilities, Shelters/Homelessness, United Funds/United Ways, Youth Organizations

Contributions Analysis

Giving Priorities: Education.
Arts & Humanities: 25%. Supports theater, performing arts, music and art.
Civic & Public Affairs: 18%. Supports community affairs, and neighborhood development.
Education: 43%. Funds educational programs, colleges and universities.
Health: About 3%.
Religion: 2%. Funds religious causes.
Science: 1%.
Social Services: 8%. Supports homeless, youth and social services, and the United Way.
Note: Total contributions in fiscal 1998.

Application Procedures

Initial Contact: Send a letter requesting application form.
Application Requirements: Include a description of the project for which funds are sought, amount requested, IRS 501 (c)(3) determination letter, annotated Board of Directors list, latest annual report, last two audited financial statements, budget and cash flow statements, and a list of current funding sources.
Deadlines: March 31, June 30, September 30, and December 31.
Review Process: Initial review by director, followed by board of trustees reviews.
Evaluative Criteria: Need of community served; clear, reasonable goals and measurable outcomes; collaboration or cooperation with other nonprofit organizations; and opportunities for Delta employee involvement.
Decision Notification: Board meets quarterly to evaluate proposals.

Restrictions

Does not support individuals, religious activities, political organizations or campaigns, specialized single-issue health organizations, endowment campaigns, capital campaigns (except in focus area of Community

Building), operating expenses, fraternal organizations, professional associations, membership groups, or fundraising events.

Additional Information

Priority will also be given to projects where the foundation's involvement will leave a legacy.

Corporate Officials

Malcolm Armstrong: executive vice president operations B Bastrop, LA. ED Auburn University MBA; Louisiana State University BS. PRIM CORP EMPL executive vice president operations: Delta Air Lines, Inc.

Robert L. Colman: executive vice president human resources ED Bates College BS; University of Pennsylvania Wharton School MBA; Vanderbilt University JD. PRIM CORP EMPL executive vice president human resources: Delta Air Lines Inc.

Vicki Escarra: executive vice president customer service ED Columbia University Executive Management Program; Georgia State University BA. PRIM CORP EMPL executive vice president customer service: Delta Air Lines Inc. NONPR AFFIL director: Atlanta Opera.

Robert Shelton Harkey: senior vice president, general counsel, secretary B Charlotte, NC 1940. ED Emory University BA (1963); Emory University LLB (1965). PRIM CORP EMPL senior vice president, general counsel, secretary: Delta Air Lines, Inc. NONPR AFFIL member: Georgia Bar Association; trustee: Woodruff Arts Center; member: Corporate Council Association Greater Atlanta; board visitors: Emory University; member: American Bar Association; member: Atlanta Bar Association; chairman, law council: Air Transport Association. CLUB AFFIL Commerce Club.

Leo Francis Mullin: chairman, president, chief executive officer B Concord, MA 1943. ED Harvard University AB (1964); Harvard University MS (1965); Harvard University Graduate School of Business Administration MBA (1967). PRIM CORP EMPL chairman, president, chief executive officer: Delta Air Lines Inc. CORP AFFIL director: Johnson & Johnson; director: BellSouth Corp. NONPR AFFIL member: President's Export Council; director: Robert W. Woodruff Arts Center; trustee: Georgia Research Alliance; chairman: International Air Transport Association; director: Atlanta Chamber of Commerce.

Frederick W. Reid: executive vice president, chief marketing officer ED University of California at Berkeley BA (1973). PRIM CORP EMPL executive vice president, chief marketing officer: Delta Air Lines Inc.

Edward H. West: chief financial officer ED Emory University BA. PRIM CORP EMPL chief financial officer: Delta Air Lines Inc.

Foundation Officials

W. Martin Braham: trustee B Chicago, IL 1945. ED North Texas State University; University of Dallas (1968). PRIM CORP EMPL vice president global services: Delta Air Lines, Inc.

Robert Shelton Harkey: trustee (see above)

Mike Young: vice president community affairs

Grants Analysis

Disclosure Period: fiscal year ending June 30, 1998
Total Grants: $1,439,291*
Number of Grants: 47
Average Grant: $30,623
Highest Grant: $178,000
Typical Range: $10,000 to $50,000
*Note: Giving excludes matching gifts; United Way.

Recent Grants

Note: Grants derived from fiscal 1997 Form 990.

Arts & Humanities

75,000	Atlanta Symphony Orchestra, Atlanta, GA
50,000	Woodruff Arts Center, Atlanta, GA
50,000	Woodruff Arts Center, Atlanta, GA
20,000	Cincinnati Association for Performing Arts, Cincinnati, OH
20,000	Woodruff Arts Center, Atlanta, GA
10,000	Atlanta Theater Coalition, Atlanta, GA
5,000	Young Audiences, Atlanta, GA
3,000	Theater Gael, Atlanta, GA
2,500	Atlanta Opera, Atlanta, GA

Civic & Public Affairs

100,000	Atlanta Neighborhood Development, Atlanta, GA
50,000	Corporation for Olympic Development, Atlanta, GA
50,000	East Lake Community Foundation, Atlanta, GA
22,500	GFIC
10,000	Latin American Association
10,000	Rich Brown Foundation
6,000	National Center for Nonprofit Boards, Washington, DC

Education

25,000	Georgia State University Foundation, GA
25,000	University of Georgia, Athens, GA
10,000	Adaptive Learning Center, Atlanta, GA
10,000	Dr. Ronald E. McNair Foundation, Atlanta, GA
10,000	Early Years, Fayetteville, GA
7,500	Emory University Child Advocacy Project, Atlanta, GA
7,500	Mount St. Mary's College, Los Angeles, CA
6,000	Literacy Action, Atlanta, GA
4,508	Blaney Elementary School, Elgin, SC

Environment

5,000	Watershed Project Governors Office Disaster Relief

Health

20,000	Egleston Children's Hospital, Atlanta, GA
5,000	American Red Cross Relief Fund, Atlanta, GA

International

100,000	Carter Center, Atlanta, GA
15,000	Friends of the Israel Defense Forces, New York, NY
5,000	Global Health Action, Atlanta, GA

Religion

13,000	Atlanta Union Mission, Atlanta, GA
10,000	Genesis Shelters, Atlanta, GA

Science

6,000	Scitrek Foundation, Atlanta, GA

Social Services

180,000	United Way, Atlanta, GA
25,000	United Way, Cincinnati, OH
24,000	United Way, Dallas, TX
15,750	United Way, New York, NY
15,000	Project Open Hand, Atlanta, GA
10,000	Homeless Children's Foundation, Salt Lake City, UT
7,875	United Way, Miami, FL
6,150	United Way, Detroit, MI
6,000	United Way, Fort Lauderdale, FL
5,625	United Way, Seattle, WA
5,625	United Way Texas Gulf Coast, Houston, TX
5,000	Braille Institute, Los Angeles, CA
5,000	Helping Youth Pursue Excellence, Atlanta, GA
2,250	United Way, Portland, OR
1,875	United Way Palm Beach County, Boynton Beach, FL
1,500	Don't Just Sit There

DELUXE CORP.

Company Contact

St. Paul, MN
Web: http://www.deluxe.com

Company Description

Employees: 15,100 (1999)
SIC(s): 2754 Commercial Printing--Gravure, 2782 Blankbooks & Looseleaf Binders.

Nonmonetary Support

Value: $504,600 (1993); $242,891 (1992); $161,735 (1991)
Type: Donated Products

Corporate Sponsorship

Contact: Carolyn Werlein, Community Affairs Coordinator

Deluxe Corp. Foundation

Giving Contact

Jennifer A. Anderson, Director of Foundations
Deluxe Corp. Foundation
PO Box 64235
St. Paul, MN 55164-0235
Phone: (612)483-7842
Fax: (612)481-4371
Email: jennyanderson.@deluxe.com

Alternate Contact

Pam Bridger
3680 Victoria Street North
Shoreview, MN 55126-2966
Phone: (651)787-5124

Description

Founded: 1952
EIN: 416034786
Organization Type: Corporate Foundation
Giving Locations: headquarters and operating communities.
Grant Types: Capital, Employee Matching Gifts, General Support, Operating Expenses, Project.
Note: Employee matching gift ratio: 2 to 1 for the first $500; 1 to 1 for the second $500. Company matches employee gifts to accredited schools, historic preservation organisation, wildlife preserves, professional performing arts organisation, public broadcasting, and museums.

Giving Philosophy

'We have always felt a strong commitment to corporate citizenship, and we are pleased that the financial success of the Company has allowed us to respond to the many social needs of the communities where our employees live and work.' *Corporate Responsibility Report*

Financial Summary

Total Giving: $2,599,962 (1998); $3,099,999 (1997); $3,200,000 (1996 approx). Note: Contributes through corporate direct giving program and foundation.
Giving Analysis: Giving for 1996 includes: foundation (approx $3,200,000); 1997: foundation ($2,445,674); foundation matching gifts ($356,432); foundation scholarships ($297,893); 1998: foundation ($2,233,624); foundation matching gifts ($366,338)
Assets: $31,397,593 (1998); $31,111,770 (1997); $26,814,789 (1995)
Gifts Received: $600 (1998); $1,000,000 (1995); $600,000 (1993)

Typical Recipients

Arts & Humanities: Arts Appreciation, Arts Associations & Councils, Arts Centers, Arts Institutes, Dance, Arts & Humanities-General, Historic Preservation, History & Archaeology, Literary Arts, Museums/Galleries, Music, Opera, Performing Arts, Public Broadcasting, Theater
Civic & Public Affairs: African American Affairs, Community Foundations, Economic Development, Employment/Job Training, Civic & Public Affairs-General, Hispanic Affairs, Native American Affairs, Nonprofit Management, Urban & Community Affairs, Women's Affairs
Education: Arts/Humanities Education, Business Education, Colleges & Universities, Economic Education, Education Associations, Education Funds, Elementary Education (Private), Education-General, Minority Education, Minority Education, Private Education (Precollege), Religious Education, Special Education, Student Aid, Vocational & Technical Education
Environment: Environment-General
Health: AIDS/HIV, Cancer, Children's Health/Hospitals, Clinics/Medical Centers, Emergency/Ambulance Services, Eyes/Blindness, Health Organizations, Medical Rehabilitation, Single-Disease Health Associations
Religion: Churches, Religious Welfare
Science: Science Museums
Social Services: At-Risk Youth, Camps, Child Welfare, Community Service Organizations, Counseling, Day Care, Domestic Violence, Emergency Relief, Family Services, Food/Clothing Distribution, Homes, People with Disabilities, Scouts, Senior Services, Shelters/Homelessness, Substance Abuse, United Funds/United Ways, Volunteer Services, YMCA/YWCA/YMHA/YWHA, Youth Organizations

Contributions Analysis

Giving Priorities: Human services, education, and the arts.
Arts & Humanities: 22%. Supports public broadcasting, museums, theater, arts associations and centers, music, dance, and arts appreciation.
Civic & Public Affairs: 6%. Funds rebuild resources, and community services.
Education: 45%. Funding supports colleges and universities, student aid, education funds, and scholarships that are administered through the National Merit Scholarship Corporation, National Hispanic Scholarship Fund, the United Negro College Fund, and public television.
Health: 14%. Funds women's cancer research, American Red Cross, and health centers.
Religion: 6%. Funds religious causes.
Science: 2%. Majority of support is given to science museums.
Social Services: 6%. Supports youth programs, with emphasis on at-risk youth; programs that serve the mentally challenged people, special focus on employment programs; programs that serve people who are physically challenged; programs for senior citizens e.g., home delivered meals, companionship, chore services and other programs that enable seniors to remain in their homes; programs for victims of domestic abuse; transitional housing programs; programs that provide emergency needs, e.g., clothing, food, housing; programs that assist financially disadvantaged people; and programs that serve people of color.
Note: Total contributions in 1998.

Application Procedures

Initial Contact: Send a letter of inquiry and full proposal.
Application Requirements: Include organization's mission, geographical focus, and type of grant sought; complete proposal will include background, description, and purpose of organization and grant request; amount requested and total needed for project; other sources of support; copy of IRS letter of determination; budget and recently audited financial statement; list of directors and officers; staff and organizational chart; persons or groups served; list of others being solicited; and copy of Form 990-PF.
Deadlines: None.
Review Process: If organization meets guidelines, the foundation will send an application to contact person.
Evaluative Criteria: Tax-exempt status; operation for at least two years; support secured from other corporations; serve communities where Deluxe facilities are located.
Decision Notification: Response to initial inquiry within 6 to 8 weeks; board does not review grants in December, January or February.

Restrictions

Foundation generally will not make grants to individuals, conferences/seminars, primary and secondary schools, religious organizations, lobbying causes, athletic events, start-up organizations, public funded colleges and universities, national organization, tours and travel expenses, sponsorships, long-term housing, community theater and music groups, civic organizations, libraries, zoos, research projects or endowments, or nontax-exempt organizations. No grants are made outside Deluxe communities, for publicly funded colleges and universities, for tours or travel expenses, or sponsorships. Foundation rarely considers requests for multiyear commitments. publicly funded colleges and universities, for tours or travel expenses, or sponsorships. Foundation rarely considers requests for multiyear commitments.

Additional Information

The foundation reports that the contributions budget has been significantly reduced in recent years.
Publications: Foundation Annual Report

Corporate Officials

J. A. Blanchard, III: president, chief executive officer, director B 1942. ED Princeton University BA (1965); Massachusetts Institute of Technology MS (1978). PRIM CORP EMPL president, chief executive officer, director: Deluxe Corp. CORP AFFIL director: Saville System; director: Wells Fargo; director: Norwest Corp.
Lois Martin: vice president, controller ED Augustana College (1985). PRIM CORP EMPL vice president, controller: Deluxe Corp.

Foundation Officials

Stuart Alexander: president, director B Indianapolis, IN 1949. PRIM CORP EMPL vice president corporate communications: Deluxe Corp.
Jennifer A. Anderson: director
Morris Goodwin, Jr.: director PRIM CORP EMPL vice president, treasurer: Deluxe Corp.
John H. Lefevre: director
Lois Martin: director (see above)
Lawrence Mosner: director
Thomas Van Himbergen: director ED University of Wisconsin BA (1971). PRIM CORP EMPL executive vice president, chief financial officer: Deluxe Corp.

Grants Analysis

Disclosure Period: calendar year ending 1998
Total Grants: $2,233,624*
Number of Grants: 304
Average Grant: $7,347
Highest Grant: $75,000
Typical Range: $1,000 to $10,000
*Note: Giving excludes matching gifts.

Recent Grants

Note: Grants derived from 1998 Form 990.

Arts & Humanities

50,000 Ordway Music Theatre, St. Paul, MN -- Capital
28,000 Guthrie Theater Foundation, Minneapolis, MN
28,000 Minnesota Orchestral Association The Minneapolis Symphony, Minneapolis, MN
27,000 Children's Theatre Company and School, Minneapolis, MN
25,000 Minneapolis Society of Fine Arts, Minneapolis, MN
23,000 St. Paul Chamber Orchestra Society, St. Paul, MN
18,000 Minnesota Opera Company, Minneapolis, MN
15,000 St. Paul Chamber Orchestra Society, St. Paul, MN
15,000 Walker Art Center, Minneapolis, MN
10,000 Childrens Museum Inc. (The) Minnesota Children's Museum, St. Paul, MN
10,000 Lyric Opera of Kansas City, Kansas City, MO -- Renovation Support
10,000 Minnesota Public Radio, St. Paul, MN
10,000 Ordway Music Theatre, St. Paul, MN

Civic & Public Affairs

25,000 Katahdin, Inc., Minneapolis, MN -- Capital
15,000 Centro Cultural Chicano, Minneapolis, MN -- Equipment Support
12,000 Chicanos Latinos Unidos en Servicios CLUES, St. Paul, MN
10,000 MIGIZI Communications, Minneapolis, MN -- Equipment Support
10,000 National Black MBA Association, Inc., Chicago, IL -- Scholarship

Education

60,000 Minnesota Private College Fund, St. Paul, MN -- College Support
51,520 National Merit Scholarship Corporation, Evanston, IL -- Scholarship
50,000 Colorado Springs School District Eleven Tesla Alternative School, Colorado Springs, CO
50,000 Gustavus Adolphus College, St. Peter, MN -- Capital
50,000 Marva Collins Preparatory School of Wisconsin, Milwaukee, WI
50,000 Mississippi Creative Art Magnet School, St. Paul, MN
50,000 Westview Elementary, Olathe, KS
30,000 University of Texas at Austin (The), Austin, TX -- Renovation Support
25,000 A Chance To Grow Inc., Minneapolis, MN -- Capital
25,000 Learning Center, Minneapolis, MN -- Capital
17,000 United Negro College Fund, Inc., Minneapolis, MN -- Scholarship
13,336 Groveland Park Elementary School, St. Paul, MN
13,000 A Chance To Grow Inc., Minneapolis, MN
12,000 Learning Disabilities Association, Inc., Minneapolis, MN
12,000 National Hispanic Scholarship Fund, Inc., San Francisco, CA -- Scholarship
10,000 King's College, Wilkes-Barre, PA -- Equipment Support
10,000 Marquette University, Milwaukee, WI
10,000 Minneapolis College of Art and Design, Minneapolis, MN -- Capital
10,000 Northwestern University, Evanston, IL
10,000 A & T State University Foundation, Inc., Greensboro, NC -- Scholarship

Health

75,000 St. Paul Rehabilitation Center Inc., St. Paul, MN -- Capital
50,000 Children's Health Care, Minneapolis, MN -- Capital
20,000 Courage Center, Golden Valley, MN
15,000 Vision Loss Resources Inc., Minneapolis, MN -- Capital

10,000 American National Red Cross - St. Paul Chapter, St. Paul, MN -- Disaster Relief

Religion

75,000 Union Gospel Mission of St. Paul, St. Paul, MN -- Capital

Science

23,000 Science Museum of Minnesota, St. Paul, MN

Social Services

25,000 Hennepin County Emergency Food Shelves, Minneapolis, MN -- Capital

14,000 Children's Home Society of Minnesota, St. Paul, MN

12,000 Family Service Inc., St. Paul, MN

10,000 Little Brothers-Friends of the Elderly, Minneapolis, MN

10,000 Minneapolis Youth Diversion Program, Minneapolis, MN -- capital

DEMOULAS SUPERMARKETS INC.

Company Contact

Tewksbury, MA

Company Description

Employees: 7,000
SIC(s): 5411 Grocery Stores.

Demoulas Foundation

Giving Contact

T.A. Demoulas
Demoulas Foundation
875 East Street
Tewksbury, MA 01876
Phone: (978)851-8000
Fax: (978)640-8392

Description

Founded: 1964
EIN: 042723441
Organization Type: Corporate Foundation
Giving Locations: primarily New England.
Grant Types: Endowment, General Support.

Financial Summary

Total Giving: $1,448,470 (1998); $1,323,930 (1997); $875,265 (1996). Note: Contributes through foundation only.
Assets: $37,753,882 (1998); $36,226,968 (1996); $33,903,855 (1995)
Gifts Received: $600,000 (1989). Note: Contributions are received from Demoulas Supermarkets Inc., and the Demoulas family.

Typical Recipients

Arts & Humanities: Arts Associations & Councils, Arts Centers, Ballet, Dance, Arts & Humanities-General, Historic Preservation, History & Archaeology, Libraries, Literary Arts, Museums/Galleries, Music, Opera
Civic & Public Affairs: Botanical Gardens/Parks, Clubs, Civic & Public Affairs-General, Housing, Municipalities/Towns, Parades/Festivals, Philanthropic Organizations, Safety, Urban & Community Affairs, Women's Affairs
Education: Business Education, Colleges & Universities, Education Funds, Education-General, International Studies, Leadership Training, Medical Education, Private Education (Precollege), Religious Education, Secondary Education (Private), Special Education, Student Aid
Environment: Environment-General
Health: Cancer, Children's Health/Hospitals, Diabetes, Health Organizations, Hospices, Hospitals, Long-Term Care, Medical Rehabilitation, Medical Research, Respiratory, Single-Disease Health Associations, Trauma Treatment
Religion: Churches, Religious Organizations, Religious Welfare
Science: Science Museums
Social Services: Camps, Community Centers, Community Service Organizations, Food/Clothing Distribution, Homes, People with Disabilities, Recreation & Athletics, Scouts, Senior Services, Substance Abuse, Veterans, YMCA/YWCA/YMHA/YWHA, Youth Organizations

Contributions Analysis

Arts & Humanities: 20%. Supports a variety of arts organizations, including ballet and operas, music, arts centers, and museums.
Civic & Public Affairs: 15%. A majority of funding supports urban affairs and revitalization projects. Also supports philanthropic organizations.
Education: 35%. Majority of funding supports colleges and universities in the New England area. Also supports religious education and private secondary education.
Health: 15%. The majority of support funds hospitals. Also supports medical rehabilitation for burn victims, pediatric health, and single-disease health associations.
Religion: 8%. Majority of contributions for religion support Greek Orthodox and Catholic churches in the Massachusetts area. Also funds religious organizations.
Social Services: 7%. Funds community centers, recreation, and youth organizations. Community service organizations, the disabled, food and clothing distribution, and housing also receive funds.
Note: Total contributions in 1998.

Application Procedures

Initial Contact: Send a brief letter of inquiry.
Application Requirements: Include a brief history of organization and description of need.
Deadlines: None.

Corporate Officials

Telemachus A. Demoulas: president, chief executive officer, treasurer director B 1923. PRIM CORP EMPL president, chief executive officer, treasurer: Demoulas Supermarkets Inc.
D. Harold Sullivan: vice president finance, treasurer, director B 1923. PRIM CORP EMPL vice president finance, treasurer, director: Demoulas Supermarkets Inc.

Foundation Officials

Arthur T. Demoulas: trustee B 1955. ED Bentley College (1976). PRIM CORP EMPL vice president, director: Demoulas Supermarkets Inc. ADD CORP EMPL president, chief executive officer, treasurer: Market Basket Inc.
Telemachus A. Demoulas: trustee (see above)

Grants Analysis

Disclosure Period: calendar year ending 1998
Total Grants: $1,448,470
Number of Grants: 161
Average Grant: $8,997
Highest Grant: $260,000
Typical Range: $5,000 to $25,000

Recent Grants

Note: Grants derived from 1997 Form 990.

Arts & Humanities

23,000 Whistler House
19,430 Metropolitan Opera Association, New York, NY
5,000 Celebrity Selves
5,000 Maliotis Cultural Center
5,000 Sun Coast Symphony Orchestra, Clearwater, FL

Civic & Public Affairs

325,000 Lowell Plan, Lowell, MA
5,000 Lyngblomsten Foundation, St. Paul, MN
5,000 Rotary Club of Tewksbury

Education

200,000 Pike School, Andover, MA
25,000 Massachusetts General Roman DeSanclis Scholarship, MA
25,000 Notre Dame School, New York, NY
20,000 Central Catholic High School, Toledo, OH
10,000 Hellenic College
10,000 Merrimack College, North Andover, MA
10,000 Pingree School, Hamilton, MA
10,000 St. Anselms College
5,000 Bradford College, Bradford, MA
5,000 Immaculate Conception School
5,000 Lowell Catholic High School, Lowell, MA
5,000 Paul Center for Learning, Chelmsford, MA
5,000 Perkins School for the Blind, Watertown, MA
5,000 University of New Hampshire, Durham, NH

Health

25,000 Lowell General Hospital, Lowell, MA
20,000 Dana Farber Cancer Institute, Boston, MA
10,000 Beth Israel Hospital, Boston, MA
10,000 Holy Family Hospital, New Richmond, WI
10,000 Lawrence General Hospital, Lawrence, MA
10,000 Nosenid Nursing Home
6,000 Saints Memorial Hospital
5,000 Anna Jacques Hospital, Newburyport, MA
5,000 Joslin Diabetes Center, Boston, MA

Religion

100,000 Greek Orthodox Archdiocese of America, New York, NY
50,000 Holy Trinity Orthodox Church
25,000 Holy Apostles Orthodox Church
10,000 Annunciation Greek Orthodox Cathedral
6,500 Annunciation Greek Orthodox Church
5,000 Assumption of the Virgin Mary
5,000 Holy Trinity Church, Poughkeepsie, NY
5,000 Immaculate Conception Church, Chicago, IL
5,000 St. Georges Church
5,000 St. Patrick's Church, Cleveland, OH
5,000 St. Philip Hellenic Orthodox Church
5,000 Transfiguration Church, Lowell, MA

Social Services

25,000 Lowell Boys Club, Lowell, MA
10,000 Lawrence Boys Club, Lawrence, MA
5,000 Human Services Corporation, Lowell, MA
5,000 Lowell Association for the Blind, Lowell, MA
5,000 New England Food Foundation, West Roxbury, MA
5,000 Noburn Boys Club
5,000 YMCA of Taunton

DEPOSIT GUARANTY NATIONAL BANK

Company Contact

Jackson, MS

Company Description

Income: US$39,040,000
Employees: 1,686
SIC(s): 6021 National Commercial Banks.
Parent Company: Deposit Guaranty Corp.

Nonmonetary Support

Type: Cause-related Marketing & Promotion
Note: Nonmonetary support is handled by various departments, including marketing and retail divisions.

Corporate Sponsorship

Type: Arts & cultural events; Music & entertainment events; Pledge-a-thon

Deposit Guaranty Foundation

Giving Contact

James L. Moore, Senior Vice President, Public Affairs
Deposit Guaranty Foundation
1 Deposit Guaranty Plz.
Jackson, MS 39215
Phone: (601)354-8571
Fax: (601)354-8192

Description

EIN: 646026793
Organization Type: Corporate Foundation
Giving Locations: MS
Grant Types: Employee Matching Gifts, General Support.
Note: Employee matching gift ratio: 1 to 1 for education only, up to a maximum of $1,000 annually.

Financial Summary

Total Giving: $847,364 (fiscal year ending January 31, 1999); $895,638 (fiscal 1997); $800,000 (fiscal 1996 approx). Note: Contributes through corporate direct giving program and foundation.
Giving Analysis: Giving for fiscal 1997 includes: foundation ($694,275); foundation grants to United Way ($201,363); fiscal 1999: foundation ($640,916); foundation grants to United Way ($185,320); foundation matching gifts ($21,128)
Assets: $15,751,865 (fiscal 1999); $1,096,630 (fiscal 1997); $2,091,559 (fiscal 1994)
Gifts Received: $15,670,200 (fiscal 1999); $750,000 (fiscal 1997); $2,525,000 (fiscal 1994). Note: The foundation receives contributions from Deposit Guaranty National Bank.

Typical Recipients

Arts & Humanities: Arts Appreciation, Arts Associations & Councils, Arts Centers, Arts Festivals, Ballet, Community Arts, Historic Preservation, Museums/Galleries, Music, Opera, Performing Arts, Public Broadcasting, Theater, Visual Arts
Civic & Public Affairs: African American Affairs, Business/Free Enterprise, Civil Rights, Community Foundations, Civic & Public Affairs-General, Housing, Law & Justice, Nonprofit Management, Philanthropic Organizations, Public Policy, Urban & Community Affairs, Zoos/Aquariums
Education: Business Education, Colleges & Universities, Community & Junior Colleges, Economic Education, Education Funds, Elementary Education (Public), Faculty Development, Leadership Training, Literacy, Private Education (Precollege), Public Education (Precollege), Religious Education, School Volunteerism, Science/Mathematics Education, Special Education
Environment: Environment-General
Health: Children's Health/Hospitals, Diabetes, Health Organizations, Hospitals, Single-Disease Health Associations, Transplant Networks/Donor Banks
International: Foreign Arts Organizations, Foreign Educational Institutions
Religion: Religious Welfare, Seminaries
Science: Observatories & Planetariums, Scientific Organizations
Social Services: Child Welfare, Community Centers, Delinquency & Criminal Rehabilitation, Family Services, Food/Clothing Distribution, Homes, People with Disabilities, Recreation & Athletics, Scouts, Senior Services, Shelters/Homelessness, Substance Abuse, United Funds/United Ways, Volunteer Services, Youth Organizations

Contributions Analysis

Giving Priorities: Education, housing, community development, social services, and the arts.
Arts & Humanities: 5% to 10%. Supports arts associations, dance, museums, music, theater, opera, community and performing arts, and symphonies.
Civic & Public Affairs: Less than 5%. Funding supports housing, community development, and youth organizations.
Education: 50% to 55%. Majority supports Mississippi colleges and universities. Other interests include public education, education funds, international studies, and private education.
Health: Less than 5%. Supports medical centers and single-disease associations.
Religion: 5% to 10%. Funds religious causes.
Social Services: 25% to 30%. Supports family services, food banks, youth services, and the United Way.
Note: Total contributions in fiscal 1999.

Application Procedures

Initial Contact: Send brief letter.
Application Requirements: Include a description of organization, amount requested, purpose of funds sought, recently audited financial statement, proof of tax-exempt status.
Deadlines: Proposals must be mailed by November 1.
Review Process: Decisions are made by three-person committee after research and report from requesting organization.
Evaluative Criteria: Organizations must be in DGNB operating area, have potential for widespread benefit, involve bank customers and/or employees.
Decision Notification: Usually monthly.

Restrictions

Foundation does not support individuals.

Additional Information

Foundation grants are basically restricted to civic, charitable, and educational organizations in the local banking area. The bank does not give out of the state or out of the counties in which it operates.

Corporate Officials

Howard Lamar McMillan, Jr.: president, chief operating officer, director B Jackson, MS 1939. ED University of Mississippi BA (1960); Louisiana State University School of Banking (1966); Harvard University Advanced Management Program (1979). PRIM CORP EMPL president, chief operating officer, director: Deposit Guaranty National Bank. CORP AFFIL president, chief executive officer: Deposit Guaranty Corp. NONPR AFFIL general chairman: United Way Jackson; member: University Mississippi Alumni Association; director: Jackson Chamber of Commerce; member: Mississippi Bankers Association; director: American Bankers Association. CLUB AFFIL 100 Club Jackson.
E. B. Robinson, Jr.: chairman, chief executive officer, director B Centreville, MS 1941. ED Davidson College BS (1963); Harvard University MBA (1967). PRIM CORP EMPL chairman, chief executive officer, director: Deposit Guaranty National Bank. CORP AFFIL member: Miscellaneous Hospitality Development Corp.; director: Federal Reserve Bank Atlanta; chairman, chief executive officer, director: Deposit Guaranty Corp. NONPR AFFIL member: Phi Beta Kappa; member: Young President Organization; member: Jackson Chamber of Commerce; chairman finance committee: Millsaps College; treasurer: Council Support Higher Education; member: Dealer Bank Association; director: Columbia Seminary; member: Association Reserve City Bankers. CLUB AFFIL Jackson Country Club; Harvard Club.

Foundation Officials

James L. Moore: senior vice president public affairs

Grants Analysis

Disclosure Period: fiscal year ending January 31, 1998
Total Grants: $640,916*
Number of Grants: 38
Average Grant: $16,866
Highest Grant: $60,000
Typical Range: $100 to $20,000
***Note:** Giving excludes United Way and matching gifts.

Recent Grants

Note: Grants derived from 1999 Form 990.

Arts & Humanities

10,000	Mississippi Opera, Jackson, MS -- 1998 sponsorship
5,000	Mississippi Opera, Jackson, MS -- Glorious Sounds of Wagner

Civic & Public Affairs

37,400	Habitat for Humanity, Jackson, MS
20,000	Metro Jackson Housing Project, Jackson, MS
15,000	Foundation for the Mid South, Jackson, MS
10,000	Greater Jackson Foundation, Jackson, MS
10,000	Mississippi Center for Non Profits, Jackson, MS
2,400	Oakes African-American Cultural Center, Yazoo City, MS -- 1998 pledge payment

Education

50,000	Millsaps College, Jackson, MS
50,000	Mississippi College, Clinton, MS
44,750	Belhaven College, Jackson, MS
30,000	Caddo Public Education Foundation, Shreveport, LA
30,000	Public Education Forum-MS, Jackson, MS
25,000	Mississippi State University, Mississippi State, MS
25,000	University of Mississippi, Jackson, MS -- Conner Hall renovation
20,000	Parents for Public Schools, Jackson, MS -- 1998 pledge
20,000	Parents for Public Schools/Jackson, Jackson, MS -- 1998 pledge
20,000	Phi Theta Kappa, Jackson, MS -- Key Opportunity Campaign Pledge
20,000	Piney Woods Country Life School, Piney Woods, MS
19,600	Junior Achievement of Jackson, Jackson, MS -- Operating Fund pledge payment
12,500	CEO America, Houston, TX
11,025	Mississippi State University, Mississippi State, MS
10,000	Magnolia Speech School, Jackson, MS -- 1998 pledge payment
5,000	Meridian Community College, Meridian, MS -- Renewal of regular support
3,997	University of Mississippi, Jackson, MS
1,550	Mississippi College, Clinton, MS
1,000	Delta State University, Cleveland, MS -- 1998 Deposit Guaranty Scholarship
1,000	Hinds Community College, Raymond, MS -- 1998 pledge payment
1,000	Ole Miss Alumni Club, Jackson, MS -- to sponsor scholarship

660	University of Southern Mississippi, Hattiesburg, MS
500	Delta State University, Cleveland, MS -- 1998 matching grant
500	Jackson State University, Jackson, MS -- 1998 matching grant
500	University of Miss., School of Dentistry, Jackson, MS -- Honors Day Awards
500	University of Miss., School of Medicine, Jackson, MS -- Honors Day Awards
300	Belhaven College, Jackson, MS -- 1998 matching grant
300	Meridian Community College, Meridian, MS -- 1998 matching grant
300	University of Miss., School of Health Related Sciences, Jackson, MS -- Honors Day Awards
300	University of Miss., School of Nursing, Jackson, MS -- Honors Day Awards
245	Millsaps College, Jackson, MS -- 1998 matching grant

Health

10,000	Mississippi Blood Services

International

20,000	USA IBC, Jackson, MS -- 1998 pledge

Religion

60,000	Salvation Army of Shreveport, Shreveport, LA
10,000	Mission Mississippi, Jackson, MS
1,000	Reformed Theological Seminary, Jackson, MS -- 1998 matching grant
250	Columbia Theological Seminary, Decatur, GA -- 1998 matching grant

Social Services

185,320	United Way of the Capital Area, Jackson, MS
25,000	Boys & Girls Clubs of Metropolitan -- 1998 pledge payment
16,666	Mississippi Food Network, Jackson, MS
2,500	Bottom Line for Kids Event, Boston, MA -- 1998 pledge
500	Desoto Sunrise Inc., Hernando, MS

DETROIT EDISON CO.

Company Contact

Detroit, MI
Web: http://www.detroitedison.com

Company Description

Assets: US$11,014,900,000
Employees: 8,423
SIC(s): 4911 Electric Services, 4931 Electric & Other Services Combined.

Nonmonetary Support

Type: Donated Equipment; In-kind Services; Loaned Executives; Workplace Solicitation

Corporate Sponsorship

Type: Arts & cultural events; Festivals/fairs
Note: Sponsors events in southeastern Michigan.

Detroit Edison Foundation

Giving Contact

Ms. Karla Hall, Secretary & Director
Detroit Edison Foundation
2000 Second Ave., 1046 WCB
Detroit, MI 48226
Phone: (313)235-9271
Fax: (313)235-0285
Email: hallk@detroitedison.com

Note: Ms. Hall is als Administrator, Corporate Contributions.

Description

EIN: 382708636
Organization Type: Corporate Foundation
Giving Locations: MI: Detroit including southeastern metropolitan area
Grant Types: Capital, Challenge, Conference/Seminar, Employee Matching Gifts, Endowment, General Support, Project.
Note: Foundation matches employee gifts to all educational and Michigan cultural institutions up to a limit of $5,000 per donor annually. Foundation also sponsors 'Holiday Season Matching Gifts' program between November 1 and December 31 annually, through which it matches employee gifts to agencies that provide emergency food and shelter services.

Giving Philosophy

'While serving millions of customers in hundreds of municipalities, we believe we have to give something back to those we serve. We understand and are anxious to meet our obligation to help improve the quality of life in our service area. Thus, we established the Detroit Edison Foundation (DEF) which, as (our) motto implies, is 'Giving Resources to Create Resources.' .. The goal of DEF is the same as those seeking assistance. Both want a better future.' *Detroit Edison Foundation Guidelines*

Financial Summary

Total Giving: $3,911,000 (1998); $3,626,000 (1997); $3,828,303 (1996). Note: Contributes through corporate direct giving program and foundation.
Giving Analysis: Giving for 1996 includes: corporate direct giving ($2,000,000); foundation ($1,828,303); 1997: foundation ($3,300,000); corporate direct giving ($326,000); 1998: foundation ($2,013,212); foundation grants to United Way ($1,053,250); corporate direct giving ($588,447); foundation matching gifts ($256,091)
Assets: $14,136,782 (1998); $13,390,127 (1997); $12,320,631 (1996)
Gifts Received: $3,000,000 (1998); $2,240,000 (1997); $2,250,000 (1996). Note: Gifts are received from the Detroit Edison Co.

Typical Recipients

Arts & Humanities: Arts Associations & Councils, Arts Centers, Arts Institutes, Historic Preservation, Libraries, Museums/Galleries, Music, Opera, Performing Arts, Public Broadcasting, Theater
Civic & Public Affairs: African American Affairs, Business/Free Enterprise, Chambers of Commerce, Civil Rights, Community Foundations, Economic Development, Economic Policy, Housing, Municipalities/ Towns, Parades/Festivals, Professional & Trade Associations, Public Policy, Safety, Urban & Community Affairs, Women's Affairs, Zoos/Aquariums
Education: Agricultural Education, Arts/Humanities Education, Business Education, Business-School Partnerships, Colleges & Universities, Community & Junior Colleges, Economic Education, Education Associations, Education Funds, Engineering/Technological Education, Environmental Education, Education-General, Literacy, Minority Education, Private Education (Precollege), Public Education (Precollege), School Volunteerism, Science/Mathematics Education, Student Aid
Environment: Environment-General, Wildlife Protection
Health: Children's Health/Hospitals, Emergency/Ambulance Services, Health Funds, Health Organizations, Hospitals, Mental Health, Public Health, Single-Disease Health Associations
Religion: Religious Welfare
Science: Scientific Centers & Institutes, Scientific Organizations
Social Services: Child Welfare, Community Centers, Community Service Organizations, Delinquency & Criminal Rehabilitation, Family Services, Food/Clothing Distribution, Recreation & Athletics, Substance Abuse, United Funds/United Ways, Youth Organizations

Contributions Analysis

Giving Priorities: United funds, social services, education, cultural institutions, and civic causes.
Arts & Humanities: (Culture) 18%. Primarily supports region's major cultural institutions. Interests include music, theater, arts centers and funds, libraries, museums, historical societies, and public broadcasting. Youth educational programs and event or project sponsorship are preferable to general operating support.
Civic & Public Affairs: 21%. Interests include economic development, crime prevention, race relations, public policy research, zoos, environmental programs, and neighborhood revitalization. Urban and community development coalitions are a high priority. Particular interest in local citizen and community self-help initiatives and projects where funds can complement support from the public sector.
Education: 23%. Funds school readiness (preschool), K-12 education improvement, vocational education, school-to-work and career awareness programs, citizenship education, environmental education, and higher education. In higher education, emphasis is placed on business and engineering and programs that increase student participation and retention, including pre-college math and science enrichment programs, and student tutoring and mentoring programs.
Social Services: (Health and Human Services) 38%. Funds the United Way, emergency food and shelter, teen pregnancy prevention and parenting skills.
Note: Total cash contributions made in 1998. Percentages provided by foundation.

Application Procedures

Initial Contact: Submit a written proposal.
Application Requirements: Include proof of tax-exempt status; summary of the organization's mission, goals, and major past accomplishments; a description of organization, including number of clients, attendance or usage statistics, or any other data regarding quantity of services performed annually; recently audited financial statement; amount of the current year's operating budget, and if applicable, line item project budget; list of members of the governing board and affiliations; the project or overall program evaluation plan; and donor recognition opportunities and key publicity-related dates. Attach a cover letter signed by the chief executive or senior development officers of the organization, or the chair of its volunteer board. The foundation suggestions including the following additional information: most recent annual report; description of the fund-raising plan, including the total goal, corporate goal, and projected fund-raising expenses; a list of other corporate and foundation funders, either during the past year (general operating requests), or to last year's special event (underwriting requests), or to this request date (if broad-based campaign request); a description of any cooperative actions with other similar organizations; an organization chart of paid staff positions; and a brief description of quantity and types of support given by non-board volunteers. For specific project requests, include the project's objectives, time frame, and, if for a continuing activity, possible sources of replacements funds after grant expires.
Deadlines: March 15, June 15, September 15, and December 15.
Review Process: Proposals are reviewed upon receipt and then referred to contributions committee for consideration.
Evaluative Criteria: Evidence of cooperative working arrangements among local organizations addressing same or similar goals.
Decision Notification: Quarterly, usually within 60-90 days after receipt of proposal.

Notes: Foundation encourages applicants to use the Council of Michigan Foundations' Common Grant Application. Faxes and videos are discouraged. Requests must be made in writing.

Restrictions

Support is not provided for individuals (including direct scholarships); political parties, organizations, or activities; religious organizations for sectarian purposes; organizations that cannot demonstrate a commitment to equality and diversity; student group trips; national or international organizations, unless providing benefits directly to Detroit Edison service-area residents; or projects which may result in undue personal benefit to a member of the Detroit Edison Foundation board or any Detroit Edison director or employee.

Additional Information

Prefers to fund specific projects rather than annual operating budgets or multi-purpose capital campaigns.

Publications: Guidelines; Application Form; Annual Report

Corporate Officials

James F. Connelly: manager regional relations PRIM CORP EMPL manager regional relations: Detroit Edison Co.

Anthony Francis Earley, Jr.: president, chief operating officer B Jamaica, NY 1949. ED University of Notre Dame BS (1971); University of Notre Dame JD (1979); University of Notre Dame MS (1979). PRIM CORP EMPL president, chief operating officer: Detroit Edison Co. ADD CORP EMPL president, chief operating officer, director: DTE Energy Co. CORP AFFIL director: Mutual America. NONPR AFFIL vice chairman: Michigan Chamber of Commerce; member advisory council: University Notre Dame College Engineering; member: American Bar Association.

Larry Gailbert Garberding: chief financial officer, executive vice president B Albert City, IA 1938. ED Iowa State University BS (1960). PRIM CORP EMPL chief financial officer, executive vice president: Detroit Edison Co. ADD CORP EMPL chief financial officer, executive vice president: DTE Energy Co.; president: Edison Development Corp.; vice president: Midwest Energy Resources Co. NONPR AFFIL member: American Institute CPAs.

Karla Hall: administrator corporate contributions PRIM CORP EMPL administrator corporate contributions: Detroit Edison Co.

Christopher C. Nern: vice president, general counsel B New York, NY 1944. ED Michigan State University (1967); Wayne State University (1972). PRIM CORP EMPL vice president, general counsel: DTE Energy Co. ADD CORP EMPL vice president, general counsel: Detroit Edison Co.

S. Martin Taylor: senior vice president PRIM CORP EMPL senior vice president: Detroit Edison Co. ADD CORP EMPL senior vice president: DTE Energy Co.

Foundation Officials

Susan M. Beale: director B Richmond, IN 1948. ED Michigan State University (1970); University of Michigan (1976). PRIM CORP EMPL vice president, secretary: Detroit Edison Co. CORP AFFIL director: Edison Illuminating Co. Detroit; director: Saint Clair Energy Corp.; vice president, corporate secretary: DTE Energy Co.

Robert J. Buckler: director B Flint, MI 1949. ED University of Michigan BSME (1971); University of Michigan MSME (1973). PRIM CORP EMPL executive vice president: Detroit Edison Co. ADD CORP EMPL president, chief operating officer: DTE Energy Distribution Inc.

James F. Connelly: director (see above)

Anthony Francis Earley, Jr.: director (see above)

Larry Gailbert Garberding: director (see above)

Karla Hall: secretary, director (see above)

Leslie Louis Loomans: treasurer, director B Greenville, MI 1943. ED University of Michigan BS (1966); University of Michigan MBA (1973). PRIM CORP EMPL vice president, treasurer: Detroit Edison Co. ADD CORP EMPL executive vice president, treasurer: DTE Energy Co. CORP AFFIL director: Energy Insurance Mutual. NONPR AFFIL director: NSF International.

Christopher C. Nern: director (see above)

S. Martin Taylor: president, director (see above)

Grants Analysis

Disclosure Period: calendar year ending 1998
Total Grants: $2,013,212*
Number of Grants: 295
Average Grant: $6,824
Highest Grant: $150,000
Typical Range: $500 to $20,000
***Note:** Giving excludes matching gifts; United Way.

Recent Grants

Note: Grants derived from 1996 Annual Report.

Arts & Humanities

160,000	Detroit Symphony Orchestra Hall, Detroit, MI -- operating support
100,000	Detroit Institute of Arts Founders Society, Detroit, MI -- for Partnership for Renewal Campaign
45,000	Michigan Opera Theater, Detroit, MI -- capital campaign
32,500	Detroit Educational Television Foundation, Detroit, MI -- for Sesame Street
25,000	Michigan Opera Theater, Detroit, MI -- for La Boheme sponsorship

Civic & Public Affairs

255,111	Detroit Renaissance Foundation, Detroit, MI -- for Woodward Corridor Revitalization Project
72,500	Detroit Renaissance Foundation, Detroit, MI -- for Detroit Compact Support
70,000	Detroit Renaissance Foundation, Detroit, MI -- operating support
56,925	Kids Voting Program, Detroit, MI -- operating support
35,000	Greater Detroit Chamber Foundation, Detroit, MI -- for Detroit Compact Endowment Support
30,000	Detroit Zoological Society, Detroit, MI -- for Wild Lights Holiday Display
30,000	Michigan Thanksgiving Parade Foundation, Detroit, MI -- parade sponsor
25,000	Detroit Economic Growth Association, Detroit, MI -- operating support
25,000	Warren/Conner Development Coalition -- operating support
18,000	Citizens Research Council of Michigan, Detroit, MI -- operating support
15,700	Michigan Thanksgiving Parade Foundation, Detroit, MI -- events support
15,000	Detroit Neighborhood Housing Services, Detroit, MI -- operating support
15,000	Economic Alliance for Michigan, Detroit, MI -- operating support
15,000	Greening of Detroit, Detroit, MI -- operating support

Education

143,234	Wayne County Regional Educational Service Agency, Wayne, MI -- for Parent Connector Program
100,000	University of Detroit Mercy, Detroit, MI -- operating support, capital campaign, endowment support
45,000	University of Michigan, Ann Arbor, MI -- Engineering Center capital campaign
30,240	Detroit Area Pre-College Engineering Program, Detroit, MI -- operating support, benefit support
25,000	University Cultural Center Association, Detroit, MI -- for Detroit Festival of the Arts sponsorship
25,000	University of Michigan, Ann Arbor, MI -- for Environmental Education Center
20,000	Cornerstone Schools Association, Detroit, MI -- for Partnership Program
20,000	Engineering Society of Detroit Development Fund, Detroit, MI -- endowment campaign
20,000	Michigan Technological University, Houghton, MI -- for Electrical Power Engineering Program support
20,000	Woodward Academy, College Park, GA -- capital support
18,230	Oakland Community College Foundation, Bloomfield Hills, MI -- for summer program for Pontiac High School students
16,694	High Scope Educational Research Foundation -- for Parent Connector Program evaluation
15,000	University of Michigan Dearborn, Dearborn, MI -- for Center for Engineering Education and Practice, capital campaign
15,000	Wayne State University, Detroit, MI -- for Arts Centered Education program
14,000	Michigan 4-H Foundation, MI -- for Vision 2001 Campaign
13,740	University of Detroit Mercy, Detroit, MI -- event sponsor, equipment donation
13,000	Junior Achievement of Southeastern Michigan, Detroit, MI -- program support

Environment

64,300	Wildlife Habitat Council, Silver Spring, MD -- for St. Clair River Project, donated office space

Health

20,000	American Red Cross Southeastern Michigan Chapter, MI -- event sponsor
20,000	Greater Detroit Area Health Council, Detroit, MI -- operating support
15,000	Children's Hospital of Michigan, Detroit, MI

Social Services

525,000	United Way Annual Campaign Support, Detroit, MI -- for community services
182,250	United Way Community Services, Detroit, MI -- for New Detroit Fund
112,000	United Way Community Services, Detroit, MI -- capital campaign
90,000	United Way Monroe County
60,500	United Way St. Clair County, Port Huron, MI
25,000	Life Directions, Detroit, MI -- for Peer Motivation at Taft Middle and Henry Ford High Schools
23,600	Washtenaw United Way, Ann Arbor, MI
17,600	Plymouth Community United Way, Plymouth, MI
15,000	Capuchin Charity Guild -- capital campaign
12,720	Capuchin Community Center, Detroit, MI -- holiday season food, shelter gifts

Deutsch Co.

Company Contact

Santa Monica, CA

Web: http://www.db.com

Company Description

Employees: 3,000

SIC(s): 3452 Bolts, Nuts, Rivets & Washers, 3625 Relays & Industrial Controls.

Deutsch Foundation

Giving Contact

Lester Deutsch, Executive Vice President
Deutsch Foundation
2444 Wilshire Blvd., Ste. 600
Santa Monica, CA 90403
Phone: (310)453-0055
Fax: (310)453-6467

Description

EIN: 956027369
Organization Type: Corporate Foundation
Giving Locations: CA: including southern California
Grant Types: General Support.

Financial Summary

Total Giving: $222,565 (fiscal year ending August 31, 1998); $228,755 (fiscal 1996); $200,075 (fiscal 1995). Note: Contributes through foundation only.
Giving Analysis: Giving for fiscal 1998 includes: foundation ($222,565)
Assets: $4,066,526 (fiscal 1998); $3,202,521 (fiscal 1996); $3,406,291 (fiscal 1995)

Typical Recipients

Arts & Humanities: Arts Associations & Councils, Arts Centers, Arts Institutes, Dance, Arts & Humanities-General, Museums/Galleries, Music, Public Broadcasting, Theater
Civic & Public Affairs: Botanical Gardens/Parks, Civil Rights, Civic & Public Affairs-General, Law & Justice, Legal Aid, Municipalities/Towns, Nonprofit Management, Philanthropic Organizations, Public Policy, Safety, Urban & Community Affairs, Women's Affairs, Zoos/Aquariums
Education: Arts/Humanities Education, Business Education, Colleges & Universities, Education Associations, Education Reform, Engineering/Technological Education, Environmental Education, Education-General, International Studies, Private Education (Precollege)
Environment: Environment-General, Resource Conservation
Health: Arthritis, Cancer, Children's Health/Hospitals, Clinics/Medical Centers, Eyes/Blindness, Geriatric Health, Health Organizations, Hospitals, Hospitals (University Affiliated), Medical Rehabilitation, Medical Research, Mental Health, Public Health, Research/Studies Institutes, Single-Disease Health Associations, Trauma Treatment
International: Foreign Arts Organizations, Foreign Educational Institutions, Health Care/Hospitals, International Relations, Missionary/Religious Activities
Religion: Jewish Causes, Religious Organizations, Religious Welfare, Social/Policy Issues, Synagogues/Temples
Science: Science Museums
Social Services: Animal Protection, Big Brother/Big Sister, Camps, Child Welfare, Community Centers, Community Service Organizations, Counseling, Crime Prevention, Day Care, Family Planning, Family Services, Food/Clothing Distribution, People with Disabilities, Recreation & Athletics, Senior Services, Sexual Abuse, Shelters/Homelessness, Substance Abuse, United Funds/United Ways, Volunteer Services, YMCA/YWCA/YMHA/YWHA, Youth Organizations

Contributions Analysis

Giving Priorities: Jewish organizations, synagogues, international organizations, social services, health, education, museums, and public broadcasting.
Arts & Humanities: About 2%. Interests include music centers, museums, dance societies, and public broadcasting.
Civic & Public Affairs: 16%. Supports women's affairs, gardens, community foundations, and environmental concerns.
Education: 3%. Supports colleges and universities, public and private precollege education, art schools, and education associations.
Health: 3%. Interests include single-disease health organizations, pediatric and geriatric medicine, and health centers.
International: 2%. Supports arts and athletic associations and universities, primarily in Israel.
Religion: 56%. Supports Jewish welfare funds, temples, and Jewish emergency funds.
Social Services: 18%. Youth organizations are major recipients. Other interests include sexual abuse issues, substance abuse prevention programs, aid for the homeless, athletics, and animal welfare.
Note: Total contributions in fiscal 1998.

Application Procedures

Initial Contact: Send a a brief letter.
Application Requirements: Include amount needed and purpose for which funds are sought.
Deadlines: None.
Review Process: Gifts are awarded at discretion of trustees after investigation as to purpose of gift.
Decision Notification: Decisions are made monthly.

Additional Information

Foundation strongly favors organizations engaged in scientific research, education, and social service.

Corporate Officials

William Holler: treasurer B Grand Rapids, MI 1931. PRIM CORP EMPL treasurer: Deutsch Co.

Foundation Officials

Carl Deutsch: president B 1937. ED University of Southern California (1959). PRIM CORP EMPL chairman: Deutsch Engineered Connecting Devices. CORP AFFIL director: Deutsch Fastener Corp.
Lester Deutsch: executive vice president B 1917. PRIM CORP EMPL partner, executive vice president: Deutsch Co.

Grants Analysis

Disclosure Period: fiscal year ending August 31, 1998
Total Grants: $222,565
Number of Grants: 40
Average Grant: $2,681*
Highest Grant: $118,000
Typical Range: $250 to $5,000
***Note:** Average grant excludes highest grant.

Recent Grants

Note: Grants derived from 1998 Form 990.

Arts & Humanities

4,500 Music Center of Los Angeles County, Los Angeles, CA -- Education
1,000 Bob Hope Cultural Center, Palm Desert, CA -- Welfare/Education

Civic & Public Affairs

10,000 Pacific Legal Foundation, Sacramento, CA -- Welfare
5,000 American Association for Science and Public Policy, Los Angeles, CA -- Education
5,000 City of Hope, Los Angeles, CA -- Health
5,000 New York Zoological Society, Bronx, NY -- Welfare
4,300 K C E T/Women's Council, Los Angeles, CA -- Education
2,500 City of Banning, Banning, CA -- Welfare
1,425 Westside Women's Health Center, Santa Monica, CA -- Welfare
1,000 Beverly Hills Police Foundation, Beverly Hills, CA -- Welfare
1,000 Mountains Recreation & Conservation Authority (MRCA), Beverly Hills, CA -- Welfare
500 Friends of Charlie Farrell, Palm Springs, CA -- Welfare
100 Santa Monica Firefighters, Santa Monica, CA -- Welfare

Education

5,000 University of California Riverside Foundation, Riverside, CA -- Education
1,000 Pepperdine University, Malibu, CA -- Education
1,000 Stanford University, Stanford, CA -- Education
500 University of Southern California, Los Angeles, CA -- Education

Health

1,000 Arthritis Foundation, Palm Desert, CA -- Health/Welfare
1,000 Jonsson Cancer Center/UCLA, Los Angeles, CA -- Health
1,000 Psychological Trauma Center, Los Angeles, CA -- Health
1,000 Scleroderma Research Foundation, Santa Barbara, CA -- Health
1,000 Venice Family Clinic, Venice, CA -- Health/Welfare
500 Friends of Julie Ann Singer, Los Angeles, CA -- Welfare
250 AMC Cancer Research Cntr, Rancho Mirage, CA -- Health/Welfare

International

5,000 American Society for Technion, Los Angeles, CA -- Education

Religion

118,000 Jewish Federation Council Greater Los Angeles, Los Angeles, CA -- Welfare
5,000 American Friends of the Israel Philharmonic Orchestra, New York, NY -- Education
1,000 Jewish Community Centers, Assoc, Los Angeles, CA -- Welfare
100 American Jewish Committee, Los Angeles, CA -- Education

Social Services

15,000 Hemet Youth Baseball, Inc, Hemet, CA -- Welfare
7,500 Seagaze, Inc, Oceanside, CA -- Welfare
5,000 Boys & Girls Club of Coachella, Palm Desert, CA -- Welfare
5,000 Humane Society of New York, New York, NY -- Health/Welfare
1,140 Vista Del Mar Assoc, Los Angeles, CA -- Welfare
1,000 Camp Ramah in Calif Inc., Los Angeles, CA -- Welfare
1,000 Helping Hand of Los Angeles, Los Angeles, CA -- Health/Welfare
1,000 Thalians, Beverly Hills, CA -- Health/Welfare
1,000 United Hostesses' Charities, Los Angeles, CA -- Health/Welfare
1,000 YMCA-Gardena/Carson, Gardena, CA -- Welfare
250 Pacific Southwest Youth Tennis Foundation, Los Angeles, CA -- Welfare

Dexter Corp.

Company Contact

Windsor Locks, CT

Company Description

Employees: 4,600
SIC(s): 2819 Industrial Inorganic Chemicals Nec, 2833 Medicinals & Botanicals, 2836 Biological Products Except Diagnostic, 2899 Chemical Preparations Nec.

Nonmonetary Support

Value: $100,000 (1989); $100,000 (1988)
Type: Loaned Employees; Loaned Executives

Note: Loaned employees and loaned executives are provided for local United Way drives.

Dexter Corp. Foundation

Giving Contact

Mrs. Lani Kretschmar, Coordinator
Dexter Corp. Foundation
1 Elm Street
Windsor Locks, CT 06096
Phone: (860)627-9051
Fax: (860)292-7669

Description

EIN: 061013754
Organization Type: Corporate Foundation
Giving Locations: CT: headquarters and operating communities, including Dexter, Hartford
Grant Types: Employee Matching Gifts, General Support, Project, Research.

Giving Philosophy

'The Dexter Corporation Foundation is committed to aiding the communities within which our employees live through a corporate giving program. Contributions have included programs for health, education, culture, history, conservation, environment, as well as youth-related activities.'

Financial Summary

Total Giving: $357,021 (1998); $411,581 (1997); $381,227 (1996). Note: Contributes through foundation only.
Giving Analysis: Giving for 1996 includes: foundation grants to United Way ($74,380); foundation matching gifts ($39,828); 1997: foundation grants to United Way ($72,713); foundation matching gifts ($49,346); 1998: foundation grants to United Way ($74,201); foundation matching gifts ($48,321)
Assets: $217,341 (1998); $110,554 (1997); $58,870 (1996)
Gifts Received: $450,000 (1998); $450,000 (1997); $450,000 (1996). Note: Contributions received from Dexter Corp.

Typical Recipients

Arts & Humanities: Arts Associations & Councils, Ballet, Dance, Historic Preservation, History & Archaeology, Libraries, Literary Arts, Museums/Galleries, Music, Opera, Public Broadcasting, Theater
Civic & Public Affairs: Economic Development, Employment/Job Training, Legal Aid, Minority Business, Municipalities/Towns, Urban & Community Affairs, Women's Affairs
Education: Arts/Humanities Education, Business Education, Colleges & Universities, Community & Junior Colleges, Continuing Education, Education Associations, Engineering/Technological Education, Education-General, Minority Education, Private Education (Precollege), Public Education (Precollege), Religious Education, Secondary Education (Public), Student Aid
Environment: Environment-General, Environment-General, Protection, Resource Conservation, Watershed
Health: Children's Health/Hospitals, Clinics/Medical Centers, Emergency/Ambulance Services, Health Funds, Health Organizations, Hospitals, Mental Health, Nursing Services, Public Health, Single-Disease Health Associations
Religion: Religious Organizations, Religious Welfare
Science: Science Museums, Scientific Centers & Institutes
Social Services: Child Welfare, Community Service Organizations, Delinquency & Criminal Rehabilitation, Domestic Violence, Food/Clothing Distribution, People with Disabilities, Scouts, Shelters/Homelessness, Substance Abuse, United Funds/United Ways, Youth Organizations

Contributions Analysis

Giving Priorities: Education, civic concerns, conservation, and the environment.
Arts & Humanities: 11%. Areas of interest include arts associations, historic preservation, museums, music, opera, public broadcasting, theater, dance, history, and libraries.
Civic & Public Affairs: 4%. Interests include economic development, public policy, safety, and urban and women's affairs organizations.
Education: 28%. Foundation primarily gives funds in the form of matching gifts. Direct support goes to education funds, colleges and universities, minority education organizations, public secondary schools, religious education, and community and junior colleges.
Environment: 5%. Funds nature conservancy and environmental concerns.
Health: 14%. Interests include hospitals, single-disease health associations, health funds, mental health organizations, pediatric health, and nursing services.
Religion: 5%. Fund religious causes.
Social Services: 33%. Most support goes to the United Way in the form of employee matching gifts; other interests include shelters for the homeless, organizations that help the abused, youth organizations, food and clothing distribution, and volunteer services.

Application Procedures

Initial Contact: Send a written proposal.
Application Requirements: Include a cover letter on organization letterhead, signed by board chairperson and executive director of organization; brief description of the organization including name, purpose, activities and programs, list of staff and members of the board of directors, name and phone number of the executive director or the current contact located at the local branch of a national organization; description of the social need which the proposal addresses; statement of goals and description of programs in place to achieve these goals; description of the population and location served by the organization; exact amount requested; budget and financial statements demostrating past and present sources and use of income, and recent annual report if available; fundraising strategy outlining potenital sources of income, both current and future; copy of IRS determination letter.
Deadlines: None.

Restrictions

Foundation will not fund organizations based overseas; central headquarters of a national organization that is remote from company operating locations; dinners or sporting events and similar activities designed as fundraising vehicles when a benefit is derived by the participation of a company employee; individuals; political organizations or campaigns; religious activities or organizations which are denominational or sectarian; requests for funding research or research projects; lobbying groups; discriminatory organizations; or organizations which received financial support through the United Way.

Corporate Officials

Kathleen Burdett: vice president, chief financial officer B 1955. ED Northwestern University MBA; Dartmouth College BA (1977). PRIM CORP EMPL vice president, chief financial officer: Dexter Corp. CORP AFFIL director: Life Technologies Inc.
Grahame Walker: chairman, chief executive officer B West Bridgford, England 1937. ED Britannia Royal Naval College (1957); Royal Naval Engineering College (1962). PRIM CORP EMPL chairman, chief executive officer: Dexter Corp. CORP AFFIL director, chairman: Life Techs Inc. NONPR AFFIL chairman: Connecticut Business & Industry Association. CLUB AFFIL Hartford Club.

Foundation Officials

Bruce H. Beatt: secretary B Minneapolis, MN 1952. ED Vassar College BA (1974); Temple University JD (1978). PRIM CORP EMPL vice president, general counsel, secretary: Dexter Corp. CORP AFFIL director: Life Techs Inc.
Kathleen Burdett: vice president (see above)
Lanie Kretschmar: coordinator
John D. Thompson: treasurer B 1949. ED Cleveland State University BA (1971). PRIM CORP EMPL senior vice president strategic & business development: Dexter Corp.
Grahame Walker: president (see above)

Grants Analysis

Disclosure Period: calendar year ending 1998
Total Grants: $234,499*
Number of Grants: 133
Average Grant: $1,763
Highest Grant: $18,000
Typical Range: $1,000 to $5,000
*Note: Giving excludes matching gifts; United Way.

Recent Grants

Note: Grants derived from 1998 Form 990.

Arts & Humanities

18,000 Greater Hartford Arts Council, Hartford, CT
5,000 Mark Twain House, Hannibal, MD
5,000 Old State House, Hartford, CT

Civic & Public Affairs

5,000 Metrohartford Growth Council Foundation, Hartford, CT
2,500 Concord Pavilion Association, Concord, MA
2,500 Waukegan Sunrise, Waukegan, IL

Education

10,000 Trinity College, Hartford, CT
7,000 Inroads/Greater Hartford, Hartford, CT
6,000 Trinity College, Hartford, CT
4,000 Princeton University, Princeton, NJ
4,000 Regis High School, New York, NY
4,000 University of Tennessee, Knoxville, TN
3,500 New England Board of Higher Education, Boston, MA
3,000 Boston College, Boston, MA
3,000 Connecticut College, New London, CT
3,000 Roger Williams College, Bristol, RI
3,000 University of Connecticut, Hartford, CT
3,000 University of Hartford, Hartford, CT
2,500 A Better Chance, Boston, MA
2,500 Junior Achievement of North Central Connecticut, Hartford, CT
2,500 University of Hartford, Hartford, CT
2,500 Western New England College, Springfield, MA
2,000 Colby College, Waterville, ME
2,000 Emory & Henry College, Emory, VA
2,000 Kingswood-Oxford School, Hartford, CT

Environment

5,000 American Fisheries Society, Bethesda, MD
3,500 Farmington River Watershed Association, Simsbury, CT
2,500 Connecticut River Watershed Council, East Hampton, CT

Health

8,333 Olean General Hospital, Olean, NY
6,000 VNA Fund, Boston, MA
5,000 Campaign for Saint Francis/Mount Sinai, New York, NY
5,000 Connecticut Children's Medical Center, Hartford, CT
4,000 Bickford Health Care Center, Windsor Locks, CT

2,500 American Red Cross, Hartford, CT
2,500 Visiting Nurse Association, Boston, MA
2,000 Johnson Memorial Hospital, Enfield, CT

Religion
5,000 Salvation Army, Hartford, CT
4,000 Arstanda Christian Youth Alliance
4,000 Arstanda Christian Youth Alliance

Social Services
10,000 United Way/Combined Health Appeal, Hartford, CT
10,000 United Way/Combined Health Appeal, Hartford, CT
10,000 United Way/Combined Health Appeal, Hartford, CT
10,000 United Way/Combined Health Appeal, Hartford, CT
10,000 United Way of Lake County, Waukegan, IL
8,015 United Way/Region II, Boston, MA
8,000 United Way of Lake County, Waukegan, IL
4,000 United Way of Central Alabama, Birmingham, AL
3,644 United Way, Hartford, CT
3,500 Boy Scouts of America - Mt. Diablo Council, Pleasant Hill, CA
2,500 Hartford Guides, Hartford, CT

DIAL CORP.

Company Contact
Scottsdale, AZ
Web: http://www.dialcorp.com

Company Description
Employees: 2,800
SIC(s): 2841 Soap & Other Detergents, 5912 Drug Stores & Proprietary Stores, 5947 Gift, Novelty & Souvenir Shops, 5994 News Dealers & Newsstands.

Viad Corp. Fund

Giving Contact
Diane Tierney, Manager, Corp. Contributions
Dial Corp.
15501 North Dial Boulevard
Scottsdale, AZ 85260-1619
Phone: (602)754-5028
Fax: (602)754-1098

Description
Founded: 1987
EIN: 742499884
Organization Type: Corporate Foundation. Supports preselected organizations only.
Giving Locations: AZ: statewide, Phoenix
Grant Types: General Support.

Financial Summary
Total Giving: $238,580 (1998); $236,603 (1997); $301,560 (1996). Note: Contributes through foundation only.
Assets: $3,339,073 (1998); $4,155,928 (1997); $4,071,078 (1996)
Gifts Received: $256,942 (1994); $116,000 (1993). Note: In 1994, contributions were received from Dial Corp.

Typical Recipients
Arts & Humanities: Arts Associations & Councils, Arts Centers, Arts Funds, Ballet, Dance, Libraries, Museums/Galleries, Music, Opera, Performing Arts, Public Broadcasting, Theater
Civic & Public Affairs: African American Affairs, Business/Free Enterprise, Chambers of Commerce, Civil Rights, Economic Development, Economic Policy, Civic & Public Affairs-General, Housing, Law & Justice, Native American Affairs, Public Policy, Safety, Urban & Community Affairs, Zoos/Aquariums
Education: Business Education, Business-School Partnerships, Colleges & Universities, Community & Junior Colleges, Faculty Development, Education-General, International Studies, Literacy, Minority Education, Preschool Education, Private Education (Precollege), Public Education (Precollege)
Environment: Environment-General
Health: Alzheimers Disease, Arthritis, Cancer, Children's Health/Hospitals, Diabetes, Emergency/Ambulance Services, Eyes/Blindness, Health Funds, Health Organizations, Heart, Hospices, Hospitals, Kidney, Medical Rehabilitation, Prenatal Health Issues, Preventive Medicine/Wellness Organizations, Respiratory, Single-Disease Health Associations
International: Human Rights, International Relations
Religion: Jewish Causes, Ministries, Religious Organizations, Religious Welfare, Social/Policy Issues
Social Services: Animal Protection, Child Abuse, Child Welfare, Community Service Organizations, Crime Prevention, Day Care, Delinquency & Criminal Rehabilitation, Domestic Violence, Family Planning, Family Services, Food/Clothing Distribution, Homes, People with Disabilities, Recreation & Athletics, Scouts, Sexual Abuse, Shelters/Homelessness, Substance Abuse, YMCA/YWCA/YMHA/YWHA, Youth Organizations

Contributions Analysis
Arts & Humanities: 32%. Supports performing arts, museums and galleries. Recipients include the Heard Museum, Phoenix Symphony, and Scottsdale Cultural Council.
Civic & Public Affairs: 5%. Supports economic development, urban and community affairs, and public policy.
Health: 8%. Supports the American Lung Association, the March of Dimes, and single-disease associations.
Social Services: 29%. Supports youth organizations, family services, and community service organizations.
Note: Total contributions in 1998.

Restrictions
Company does not support individuals.

Additional Information
The Dial Corp. has split into two companies. The Dial Corp. now handles consumer products, and the Viad Corp. is service-based. The Dial Corp. gives through the Viad Corp. Fund.

Corporate Officials
John William Teets: B Elgin, IL 1933. ED University of Illinois. CORP AFFIL chairman, chief executive officer: J. W. Teets Enterprise LLC; chairman emeritus: Viad Corp.; director: Greycas Inc.; director: Greyhound Transportation Leasing Co.; director: Armour International Co.; officer: Finova Group Inc. NONPR AFFIL member: Christian Businessmens Association; trustee: National Institute Foodservice Industry; member: American Management Association.

Giving Program Officials
Diane Tierney: manager corporate contributions PRIM CORP EMPL manager community relations: The Dial Corp.

Foundation Officials
Frederick George Emerson: vice president, secretary, director B Quincy, MA 1933. ED University of Virginia BA (1955); University of Virginia JD (1960). PRIM CORP EMPL vice president, secretary: Viad Corp. CORP AFFIL vice president, section: Viad Corp. Subsidiaries; treasurer: Glacier Park Inc.; section: Greyhound Transportation Leasing Co. NONPR AFFIL secretary, director, member executive committee: American Society of Corporate Secretaries.
Armen Ervanian: vice president B Chicago, IL 1937. ED Wilson Junior College (1960); LaSalle University (1969). PRIM CORP EMPL vice president: Dial Corp. CORP AFFIL vice president: Greyhound Transportation Leasing Co.; vice president: Viad Corp. NONPR AFFIL membership: International Association Corp. Real Estate; membership: International Development Research Council.
Richard C. Stephan: vice president, controller, director B Effingham, IL 1940. ED Quincy University (1961). PRIM CORP EMPL vice president, controller: Dial Corp. CORP AFFIL vice president: Greyhound Transportation Leasing Co.; vice president: Viad Corp. NONPR AFFIL member: American Institute CPAs; member: Financial Executives Institute.
John William Teets: president, chief executive officer, director (see above)

Grants Analysis
Disclosure Period: calendar year ending 1998
Total Grants: $238,580
Number of Grants: 73
Average Grant: $3,268
Highest Grant: $20,000
Typical Range: $500 to $10,000

Recent Grants
Note: Grants derived from 1998 Form 990.

Arts & Humanities
20,000 Phoenix Symphony, Phoenix, AZ
15,000 The Heard Museum, Phoenix, AZ
15,000 Phoenix Art Museum, Phoenix, AZ
15,000 The Phoenix Symphony, Phoenix, AZ
5,000 Scottsdale Cultural Council, Scottsdale, AZ
2,000 Phoenix Public Library, Phoenix, AZ
2,000 Tullywinney Arts & Education Fund, Helena, MT

Civic & Public Affairs
5,000 Phoenix Chamber of Commerce Economic Development, Phoenix, AZ
3,000 Christmas in April - Phoenix, Tempe, AZ
1,500 The National Conference for Community & Justice, Phoenix, AZ
1,000 Greater Phoenix Urban League, Phoenix, AZ
1,000 Maricopoa County Sheriff's Office Memorial Plaza, Phoenix, AZ

Education
10,000 Grand Canyon University, Phoenix, AZ
5,000 A Better Chance, Chicago, IL
5,000 Southwest Human Development, Phoenix, AZ
4,000 ASU Alumni Association, Tempe, AZ
4,000 Junior Achievement of Central Arizona, Inc., Phoenix, AZ

Health
4,000 American Red Cross-Central AZ Chapter, Phoenix, AZ
2,500 American Lung Association of AZ, Phoenix, AZ
2,500 Scottsdale Memorial Health Foundation, Scottsdale, AZ
2,000 March of Dimes Birth Defects Foundation, Phoenix, AZ
1,000 Alzheimer's Association, Phoenix, AZ
1,000 American Cancer Society, Phoenix, AZ
1,000 American Red Cross, Washington, DC
1,000 Arizona Coalition for Tomorrow, Phoenix, AZ
1,000 Foundation for Blind Children, Phoenix, AZ
1,000 The Wellness Community - Central AZ, Phoenix, AZ

Religion
15,000 St. Vincent de Paul, Phoenix, AZ
15,000 Salvation Army, Phoenix, AZ
2,000 Beatitudes Center D.O.A.R., Phoenix, AZ

1,000 Tri-City Jewish Community Center, Tempe, AZ

Social Services

15,000 St. Mary's Food Bank, Phoenix, AZ
10,000 Arizona Voice for Crime Victims, Phoenix, AZ
5,000 Aid to Adoption of Special Kids, Phoenix, AZ
5,000 Drugs Don't Work in Arizona, Phoenix, AZ
4,000 Westside Food Bank, Sun City, AZ
3,500 Child Improvement Through Therapy, Scottsdale, AZ
3,000 Sojourner Center, Phoenix, AZ
2,500 Aid to Adoption of Special Kids, Phoenix, AZ
2,500 HomeBase Youth Services, Phoenix, AZ
2,000 Boys Hope Girls Hope of Arizona, Phoenix, AZ
2,000 Goodwill of Central Arizona, Phoenix, AZ
2,000 Sun Sounds Radio Reading Service, Phoenix, AZ
1,500 Children's Angel Foundation, Phoenix, AZ
1,500 Grand Canyon Boy Scout Council, Phoenix, AZ
1,000 Boys & Girls Club of the East Valley, Tempe, AZ
1,000 Camp Fire Council of Great Arizona, Phoenix, AZ
1,000 Central Arizona Shelter Services, Inc., Phoenix, AZ
1,000 Children's Angel Foundation, Phoenix, AZ
1,000 Crisis Nursery, Phoenix, AZ
1,000 Gompers Center for the Handicapped, Phoenix, AZ

DIEBOLD, INC.

Company Contact

North Canton, OH
Web: http://www.diebold.com

Company Description

Employees: 5,980
SIC(s): 3499 Fabricated Metal Products Nec, 3578 Calculating & Accounting Equipment, 3579 Office Machines Nec, 3699 Electrical Equipment & Supplies Nec.

Nonmonetary Support

Type: Donated Equipment; Donated Products; Loaned Employees; Loaned Executives; Workplace Solicitation

Giving Contact

Charles B. Scheurer, Vice President, Human Resources
Diebold, Inc.
PO Box 3077
Canton, OH 44720-8077
Phone: (330)490-4000
Fax: (330)490-4549

Description

Founded: 1993
Organization Type: Corporate Giving Program
Giving Locations: headquarters and operating communities.
Grant Types: Capital, General Support.

Financial Summary

Total Giving: $300,000 (1997 approx); $250,000 (1996 approx); $200,000 (1995 approx). Note: Contributes through corporate direct giving program only.

Typical Recipients

Arts & Humanities: Arts & Humanities-General
Civic & Public Affairs: Civic & Public Affairs-General
Education: Education-General
Health: Health-General
Social Services: Social Services-General

Application Procedures

Initial Contact: brief letter and proposal (all requests must be in writing)
Application Requirements: a description of organization, amount requested, purpose of funds sought, recently audited financial statement, and proof of tax-exempt status

Restrictions

Company does not support individuals, religious organizations, or political or lobbying groups.

Corporate Officials

Donald Eason: vice president, president, chief executive officer, director PRIM CORP EMPL vice president: Diebold, Inc.
Robert W. Mahoney: chairman, president, chief executive officer, director B New York, NY 1936. ED Villanova University BS (1958); Roosevelt University MBA (1961). PRIM CORP EMPL chairman, president, chief executive officer, director: Diebold, Inc. CORP AFFIL director: Timken Co.; director: Sherwin-Williams Co. NONPR AFFIL trustee: Mt Union College.

Giving Program Officials

Charles B. Scheurer: director B Canton, OH 1941. ED University of Akron (1968). PRIM CORP EMPL vice president human resources: Diebold, Inc.

Grants Analysis

Disclosure Period: calendar year ending 1997
Total Grants: $300,000 (approx)

Recent Grants

Note: Grants derived from 1994 Form 990.

Arts & Humanities

Cultural Center for Arts, Canton, OH

Education

Ohio Foundation for Independent Colleges, Columbus, OH

Social Services

United Way, Canton, OH

WALT DISNEY CO.

Company Contact

Burbank, CA
Web: http://www.disney.com

Company Description

Revenue: US$22,976,000,000
Profit: US$1,850,000,000
Employees: 71,000
Fortune Rank: 66, per FORTUNE Magazine's list of 500 Largest U.S. Corporations (1999).
FF 66
SIC(s): 6531 Real Estate Agents & Managers, 7812 Motion Picture & Video Production, 7996 Amusement Parks.

Operating Locations

Canada: Walt Disney Co. (Canada), Etobicoke; France: Walt Disney Co. (France), Paris; Germany: Walt Disney Co. (Germany) GmbH, Frankfurt am Main; Italy: Walt Disney Co. (Italia), Milan; Japan: Walt Disney Enterprises of Japan Ltd., Tokyo; United Kingdom: Walt Disney Co. Ltd., London

Walt Disney Co. Foundation

Giving Contact

Tillie J. Baptie, Executive Director
Walt Disney Co. Foundation
500 S. Buena Vista St.
Burbank, CA 91521-0987
Phone: (818)560-1006

Description

EIN: 956037079
Organization Type: Corporate Foundation
Giving Locations: CA: Los Angeles County, Orange County; FL: Orange County, Osceola County headquarters and operating communities.
Grant Types: Capital, Challenge, General Support, Operating Expenses, Project, Research, Scholarship.

Giving Philosophy

'The Walt Disney Company Foundation was established in 1951 as a non-profit corporation dedicated exclusively to the support of charitable, educational and scientific activities. Contributions from the Walt Disney Company and its associated companies make it possible to have a planned program of substantial giving to these endeavors. In addition to the active support of numerous health, community, educational and youth organizations throughout the United States, the Foundation, from time to time, sponsors its own activities, of which the College Scholarship Program is an example.' *Walt Disney Company Foundation*

Financial Summary

Total Giving: $4,832,441 (fiscal year ending September 30, 1998); $4,151,513 (fiscal 1997); $4,027,863 (fiscal 1996). Note: Contributes through corporate direct giving program and foundation.
Giving Analysis: Giving for fiscal 1994 includes: foundation ($1,760,265); foundation scholarships ($246,256); fiscal 1995: foundation ($2,354,151); foundation scholarships ($300,300); foundation grants to United Way ($33,000); fiscal 1996: foundation ($3,613,970); foundation scholarships ($380,889); foundation grants to United Way ($33,000);
Assets: $1,789,359 (fiscal 1998); $1,705,076 (fiscal 1997); $921,757 (fiscal 1996)
Gifts Received: $4,925,000 (fiscal 1998); $4,950,000 (fiscal 1997); $3,606,215 (fiscal 1996). Note: Contributions are received from the Walt Disney Company.

Typical Recipients

Arts & Humanities: Arts Associations & Councils, Arts Centers, Arts Festivals, Arts Funds, Arts Institutes, Ethnic & Folk Arts, Film & Video, Arts & Humanities-General, Libraries, Museums/Galleries, Music, Performing Arts, Public Broadcasting
Civic & Public Affairs: African American Affairs, Business/Free Enterprise, Community Foundations, Economic Development, Civic & Public Affairs-General, Hispanic Affairs, Law & Justice, Legal Aid, Native American Affairs, Philanthropic Organizations, Public Policy, Urban & Community Affairs, Zoos/Aquariums
Education: Arts/Humanities Education, Business Education, Colleges & Universities, Education Funds, Education Reform, Engineering/Technological Education, Education-General, Health & Physical Education, Legal Education, Medical Education, Minority Education, Science/Mathematics Education, Special Education
Environment: Environment-General, Resource Conservation, Wildlife Protection
Health: Cancer, Children's Health/Hospitals, Clinics/Medical Centers, Diabetes, Eyes/Blindness, Health-General, Health Organizations, Hospitals, Medical Rehabilitation, Mental Health, Public Health, Single-Disease Health Associations

International: International Environmental Issues, International Relations
Religion: Missionary Activities (Domestic), Religious Welfare
Science: Scientific Centers & Institutes, Scientific Labs
Social Services: Animal Protection, Camps, Child Welfare, Community Centers, Community Service Organizations, Domestic Violence, Family Services, Food/Clothing Distribution, People with Disabilities, Recreation & Athletics, Scouts, United Funds/United Ways, Volunteer Services, YMCA/YWCA/YMHA/YWHA, Youth Organizations

Contributions Analysis

Giving Priorities: Education, college scholarships, community funds, hospitals, human service, the arts.
Arts & Humanities: 49%. Recipients include the California Institute of the Arts, colleges, art funds and art institutes.
Civic & Public Affairs: 5%. Supports minority affairs and special funds.
Education: 17%. Supports minority education and college funds.
Environment: 13%. Interest include Wildlife Conservation, Audubon Society, and the Atlanta Zoo.
Health: 6%. Grants support single-disease health funds, hospitals and other facilities in company operating areas. Supports Children's hospitals and health care centers.
Social Services: 7%. Supported programs include Junior Achievement and various Boys and Girls Clubs of America.

Application Procedures

Initial Contact: Send brief letter or proposal.
Application Requirements: Include financial statements, preferably audited; list of major contributors, sources of income, and board members, including their affiliations; history of the organization; and proof of tax exemption.
Deadlines: proposals should be submitted by December 31 to be evaluated the following spring; scholarship applications due October 1 to be issued the following summer.
Review Process: Applications reviewed by foundation staff as received, then passed on to the donations committee.
Evaluative Criteria: Recipients must be tax-exempt, must have been in operation for at least three years, and must make significant use of volunteers.
Decision Notification: Donations committee makes its final decision at its annual spring meeting

Restrictions

Foundation does not support public agencies, educational institutions, or other nonprofit organizations supported predominantly by tax dollars; agencies receiving funds from United Way, Permanent Charities Committee, or other similar consolidated giving programs to which the foundation contributes; sectarian, religious, or political organizations; agency building campaigns; agency start-up campaigns or for seed money purposes; research programs, loans, conferences, general fund drives or annual charitable appeals, conduct organizations or individuals. individuals.

Additional Information

In past years, most grants have gone to repeat recipients.
Scholarship applicant qualifications include: must be a high school senior or academic equivalent with the expectation of graduating within the 12-month period following October 1 of that year; must be in upper one-third of high school graduating class; must be qualified, upon graduation, to enroll at an accredited four-year college or university; must be a child, stepchild or adopted child of a qualified employee (a full time regular employee who has completed at least one year of continuous service and is a resident or citizen of the United States); must file an official application form which must be received no later than October 1 of the year in which the candidate is eligible to apply.
Publications: Guidelines

Corporate Officials

Roy Edward Disney: vice chairman, directorvice president, chief corporate operations, director B Los Angeles, CA 1930. ED Pomona College BA (1951). PRIM CORP EMPL vice chairman, director: Walt Disney Co. Inc. CORP AFFIL vice chairman: Disney Enterprises Inc.; chairman, director, founder: Shamrock Holdings Inc. NONPR AFFIL fellow: University Kentucky; member: Writers Guild America; member advisory board: Saint Joseph Medical Center; member: U.S. Naval Academy Sailing Squadron; director: Big Brothers Greater Los Angeles; member: Directors Guild American West. CLUB AFFIL San Diego Yacht Club; Transpacific Yacht Club; Los Angeles Yacht Club; Saint Francis Yacht Club; California Yacht Club; Confrerie des Chevaliers du Tastevin Club; 100 Club.
Michael Dammann Eisner: chairman, chief executive officer, director B Mount Kisco, NY 1942. ED Denison University BA (1964). PRIM CORP EMPL chairman, chief executive officer, director: Walt Disney Co. Inc. ADD CORP EMPL president: Buena Vista International; president: WCO Parent Corp. CORP AFFIL principal: Disneyland International; chairman: Hollywood Records Inc.; chairman: Anaheim Sports Inc.; chairman: Disney Enterprises Inc. NONPR AFFIL trustee: Denison University; director: University California Los Angeles Board Medicine Science; director: Conservative International; director: American Hospital of Paris Foundation; trustee: California Institute Arts.
Sanford M. Litvack: senior executive vice president, chief corporate operations, director B Brooklyn, NY 1936. ED University of Connecticut BA (1956); Georgetown University LLB (1959). PRIM CORP EMPL senior executive vice president, chief corporate operations, director: Walt Disney Co. CORP AFFIL president: Disney Inc.; director: Disney International; director: Buena Vista Home Entertainment; senior executive vice president: Disney Enterprises Inc.

Foundation Officials

Tilly J. Baptie: executive director
Roy Edward Disney: trustee (see above)
Michael Dammann Eisner: president, trustee (see above)

Grants Analysis

Disclosure Period: fiscal year ending September 30, 1996
Total Grants: $3,597,545*
Number of Grants: 99
Average Grant: $21,346*
Highest Grant: $613,295
Typical Range: $1,000 to $50,000
***Note:** Giving excludes scholarship; United Way. Average grant figure excludes three highest grants totaling ($1,548,295).

Recent Grants

Note: Grants derived from fiscal 1997 Form 990.

Arts & Humanities

613,295	California Institute of the Arts, Valencia, CA
500,000	California Institute of the Arts, Valencia, CA
435,000	Matched Ticket Sales Benefit Premier "Hercules"
200,000	Music Center United Fund, Los Angeles, CA
100,000	Southern California Conservatory of Music, Sun Valley, CA
50,000	Library Foundation of Los Angeles, Los Angeles
50,000	Matched Ticket Sales Benefit Premier "Hercules"
25,000	Inner City Arts, Los Angeles, CA

Civic & Public Affairs

100,000	American Zoo & Aquarium Assoc.
25,000	Anaheim Community Foundation, Anaheim, CA
25,000	Zoo Atlanta, Atlanta, GA
10,000	CASA of Orange County, Orange, CA
10,000	Mexican American Opportunity Foundation, Montebello, CA
10,000	Native American Indian Cultural Center, Santa Ana, CA
10,000	Thursday's Of Old, West Hills, CA

Education

100,000	California Science Center, Los Angeles, CA
82,175	Junior Achievement Scholarship Program, Ntl. Award
10,000	Ringling School of Art and Design, Sarasota, FL
10,000	Ryman Carroll Foundation, Los Angeles, CA
10,000	School of Visual Arts, New York, NY
10,000	Shendan College, Canada
10,000	United Negro College Fund, New York, NY

Environment

250,000	Wildlife Conservation Society, Washington, DC
75,000	International Rhino Foundation, Columbus, OH
75,000	Peregrine Fund, Atlanta, GA
50,000	African Wildlife Foundation, Washington, DC
50,000	World Wildlife Fund, Washington, DC
10,000	Defenders of Wildlife, Washington, DC

Health

50,000	Children's Hospital of Los Angeles, Los Angeles, CA
50,000	Saint Joseph Medical Center Foundation, Burbank, CA
25,000	White Memorial Medical Center, Los Angeles
20,000	AltaMed, Los Angeles, CA
20,000	Verdugo Hills Hospital, Glendale, CA
10,000	Citrus Valley Health Foundation, Covina, CA
10,000	Doheny Eye Institute, Los Angeles, CA
10,000	Julia Singer Center, Los Angeles, CA
10,000	Martin Luther Hospital, Anaheim, CA
10,000	Orangewood Children's Foundation, Garden Grove, CA
10,000	Saint John's Hospital and Health Center, Santa Monica, CA

International

20,000	Jane Goodall Institute, Ridgefield, CT

Religion

10,000	Salvation Army-Orange County, Tustin

Science

100,000	Orlando Science Center, Orlando, FL

Social Services

75,000	Permanent Charities Committee, Los Angeles, CA
25,000	ASPCA, New York, NY
25,000	Phoenix Houses of California, Lake View Terrace, CA
20,000	Boy and Girls Club of Burbank, Burbank, CA
15,000	Brotherhood Crusade Black United Fund, Los Angeles, CA
15,000	United Way, Heart of Orange, Osceola and Seminole Co., FL
15,000	United Way of Orange County, CA
10,000	Forstig Center, Pasadena, CA
10,000	New Horizons, (SFVAR), North Hill

THE DIXIE GROUP, INC.

Company Contact

Chattanooga, TN
Web: http://www.thedixiegroup.com

Company Description

Former Name: Dixie Yarns, Inc.
Employees: 5,953
SIC(s): 2211 Broadwoven Fabric Mills--Cotton, 2241 Narrow Fabric Mills, 2257 Weft Knit Fabric Mills, 2281 Yarn Spinning Mills.

Nonmonetary Support

Contact: W. Derek Davis, Vice President Human Resources
Note: Company provides nonmonetary support.

Dixie Yarns Foundation, Inc.

Giving Contact

Ms. Starr T. Klein, Secretary, Treasurer & Trustee
Dixie Yarns Foundation
PO Box 751
Chattanooga, TN 37401
Phone: (423)698-2501
Fax: (423)493-7450

Alternate Contact

W. Derek Davis, Vice President of Human Resources
Phone: (423)493-7255

Description

EIN: 620645090
Organization Type: Corporate Foundation
Giving Locations: TN: Chattanooga
Grant Types: Capital, Emergency, Endowment, General Support, Scholarship.

Financial Summary

Total Giving: $178,975 (1997); $153,725 (1996); $283,540 (1994). Note: Contributes through corporate direct giving program and foundation.
Giving Analysis: Giving for 1996 includes: foundation ($129,425); foundation scholarships ($22,500); foundation gifts to individuals ($1,800); 1997: foundation ($91,175); foundation grants to United Way ($66,700); foundation scholarships ($18,500); foundation gifts to individuals ($2,600)
Assets: $861,998 (1997); $792,262 (1996); $591,694 (1994)
Gifts Received: $120,000 (1997); $200,000 (1996); $250,000 (1994). Note: Foundation receives contributions from Dixie Yarns, Inc.

Typical Recipients

Arts & Humanities: Arts Appreciation, Arts Associations & Councils, Arts Funds, Community Arts, Historic Preservation, History & Archaeology, Museums/Galleries, Music, Public Broadcasting
Civic & Public Affairs: African American Affairs, Chambers of Commerce, Community Foundations, Economic Development, Civic & Public Affairs-General, Housing, Philanthropic Organizations, Public Policy, Zoos/Aquariums
Education: Agricultural Education, Arts/Humanities Education, Business Education, Colleges & Universities, Community & Junior Colleges, Education Associations, Education Funds, Engineering/Technological Education, Education-General, International Studies, Minority Education, Private Education (Precollege), Public Education (Precollege), Secondary Education (Private), Student Aid
Environment: Environment-General, Resource Conservation
Health: Children's Health/Hospitals, Clinics/Medical Centers, Health Organizations, Hospitals, Medical Research, Mental Health
International: Foreign Educational Institutions, International Organizations
Religion: Religious Welfare, Social/Policy Issues
Science: Scientific Centers & Institutes
Social Services: Child Welfare, Community Centers, Community Service Organizations, Food/Clothing Distribution, Recreation & Athletics, Scouts, Shelters/Homelessness, Substance Abuse, United Funds/United Ways, YMCA/YWCA/YMHA/YWHA, Youth Organizations

Contributions Analysis

Arts & Humanities: 10%. Gives to art councils and funds libraries, museums,and public broadcasting.
Civic & Public Affairs: 4%. Supports parks and aquariums, philanthropic organizations, and economic development. Also provides assistance and aid to employees of Dixie Yarns, Inc.
Education: 30%. Gives to variety of educational organizations, including colleges and universities, education funds, education associations, private precollege education, and Junior Achievement.
Health: 1%. Recipients include a variety of health organizations and medical centers.
Social Services: 54%. Majority of contributions support United Way chapters near company's headquarters and operating locations. Also gives to youth organizations, YMCAs, and community service organizations.

Application Procedures

Initial Contact: Send a brief letter of inquiry.
Application Requirements: Include a description of organization, purpose for funds sought, and tax-exempt status.
Deadlines: None.

Restrictions

Does not support individuals, religious organizations for sectarian purposes, political or lobbying groups, or organizations outside operating areas.

Additional Information

Foundation emphasizes organizations near operating locations and those in which employees are involved.

Corporate Officials

Daniel K. Frierson: chairman, chief executive officer B 1942. ED University of Virginia BA (1964); University of Virginia MBA (1966). PRIM CORP EMPL chairman, chief executive officer: The Dixie Group, Inc. CORP AFFIL chairman, president, chief executive officer, director: Dixie Group Inc.; director: SunTrust Bank, Chattanooga, NA; director: Carriage Industries Inc.; director: Astec Industries Inc.; director: Bretlin Inc.

Foundation Officials

W. Derek Davis: trustee B 1951. ED Auburn University BSTM (1972). PRIM CORP EMPL vice president human resources: The Dixie Group, Inc.
Daniel K. Frierson: president, trustee (see above)
Starr T. Klein: secretary, treasurer, trustee B 1943. PRIM CORP EMPL secretary: The Dixie Group, Inc. CORP AFFIL secretary: Carriage Industries Inc.; corporate secretary: The Dixie Group Inc.; secretary: Bretlin Inc.

Grants Analysis

Disclosure Period: calendar year ending 1997
Total Grants: $91,175*
Number of Grants: 48
Average Grant: $1,674*
Highest Grant: $12,500
Typical Range: $1,000 to $10,000
***Note:** Giving excludes scholarship, United Way and gifts to individuals. Average grant figure excludes highest grant.

Recent Grants

Note: Grants derived from 1997 Form 990.

Arts & Humanities

12,500 Allied Arts Fund, Chattanooga, TN
2,200 WTCV-TV/Channel 45
1,000 Georgia Public Television, Atlanta, GA
1,000 WTCV-TV/Channel 45
250 Creative Arts Guild, Dalton, GA

Civic & Public Affairs

1,000 Blue Ridge Assembly, Black Mountain, NC
1,000 Blue Ridge Conference on Leadership
1,000 Chattanooga Area Urban League, Chattanooga, TN
1,000 Community Foundation, Chattanooga, TN
1,000 Dismas House
1,000 Habitat for Humanity
500 Cheer Haven Schools, Dalton, GA

Education

6,000 Baylor School, Chattanooga, TN
6,000 Girls Preparatory School, Chattanooga, TN
4,000 McCallie School, Chattanooga, TN
2,000 North Carolina Textile Foundation, Raleigh, NC
2,000 University of Tennessee Chattanooga Student Athlete Scholarship Fund, Chattanooga, TN
1,500 Junior Achievement, Chattanooga, TN
1,500 University of Virginia Miller Center, VA
1,500 University of Virginia Miller Center, VA
1,000 College Fund/UNCF
1,000 Joint Tech Georgia Development Fund, GA
1,000 University of Chattanooga Foundation, Chattanooga, TN
500 Georgia Foundation of Independent Colleges, Atlanta, GA
400 Catoosa County Schools
400 Junior Achievement of Northwest Georgia, Dalton, GA
375 Independent College Fund, Little Rock, AR
300 Alamance Community College Foundation

Environment

1,000 Tennessee River Gorge Trust, Chattanooga, TN
400 Chattanooga Nature Center, Chattanooga, TN

Health

1,000 AIM Center, Chattanooga, TN
1,000 Alamance Regional Medical Center

International

10,000 International Honors Program

Religion

1,000 Public School Bible Study Committee, Chattanooga, TN
500 Salvation Army, Chattanooga, TN
500 Salvation Army of Dalton

Social Services

60,000 United Way, Chattanooga, TN
10,000 Chattanooga Community Kitchen, Chattanooga, TN
4,000 United Way of Edgecombe County
3,000 United Way of Gaston County, Gastonia, NC
3,000 United Way of Randolph County
2,700 United Way of Jefferson
2,000 Stadium Fund
2,000 United Way of Northwest Georgia, GA
1,000 Boys Club, Chattanooga, TN
1,000 Chattanooga Youth Corps, Chattanooga, TN
1,000 United Way of Alamance County, Burlington, NC

500 Boy Scouts of America Cherokee Council
500 Boy Scouts of America Northwest Georgia Council, GA
500 Children's Home Chambliss Emergency Shelter

DOLLAR GENERAL CORP.

Company Contact
Nashville, TN
Web: http://www.dollargeneral.com

Company Description
Revenue: US$3,221,000,000
Employees: 25,400
Fortune Rank: 415, per FORTUNE Magazine's list of 500 Largest U.S. Corporations (1999).
FF 415
SIC(s): 5399 Miscellaneous General Merchandise Store.

Nonmonetary Support
Type: Donated Products; Loaned Employees

Giving Contact
Denine Brown, Corporate Contributions Committee
Dollar General Corp.
100 Mission Ridge
Goodlettsville, TN 37072
Phone: (615)263-6816

Description
Organization Type: Corporate Giving Program
Giving Locations: headquarters and operating communities.
Grant Types: Capital, General Support, Multiyear/Continuing Support, Operating Expenses, Seed Money.

Giving Philosophy
'Our (Dollar General Corp.) mission is 'Serving Others' and we are committed to providing financial support for organization's that promote literacy and youth development within our 24 states.'

Financial Summary
Total Giving: $800,000 (1998 approx); $800,000 (1997 approx); $500,000 (1996 approx). Note: Contributes through corporate direct giving program only.

Typical Recipients
Education: Colleges & Universities, Continuing Education, Education-General, Literacy

Application Procedures
Initial Contact: specific --typewritten-- proposal on organization's letterhead
Application Requirements: contact name, phone number and address, specific amount of funds for direct services, organization's 501c3 or non-profit status, background information on the history and mission of organization, and expected impact of contribution six months and one year after receiving funding.
Deadlines: None.
Notes: contributions committee meets monthly, allow 4 weeks for review.

Restrictions
Company does not support political or lobbying groups.

Corporate Officials
Cal Turner, Jr.: chairman, chief executive officer, director B Scottsville, KY 1940. ED Vanderbilt University BA (1962). PRIM CORP EMPL chairman, chief executive officer, director: Dollar General Corp. CORP AFFIL director: Thomas Nelson Publs; officer: Thomas Nelson Inc.; director: Shoneys Inc.; director: First America National Bank Nashville; director: First American Corp.; president: Dolgencorp of Texas Inc.; president: Dade Lease Management Inc.; president: Dolgencorp Inc. NONPR AFFIL chairman: Lindsey Wilson College; trustee: Vanderbilt University Medical Center.

Giving Program Officials
Cabot Pyle: PRIM CORP EMPL director corporate communications: Dollar General Corp.

Foundation Officials
Cal Turner, Jr.: trustee (see above)

Grants Analysis
Disclosure Period: calendar year ending
Typical Range: $1,000 to $2,500

DOMINION RESOURCES, INC.

Company Contact
120 Tredegar Street
Richmond, VA 23219
Phone: (804)819-2000
Email: dominion_resources@domres.com
Web: http://www.domres.com

Company Description
Revenue: US$5,520,000,000 (1999)
Profit: US$296,000,000 (1999)
Fortune Rank: 303, per FORTUNE Magazine's list of 500 Largest U.S. Corporations (1999).
FF 303

SUBSIDIARY COMPANIES
PA: Consolidated Natural Gas Co., Pittsburgh; OH: East Ohio Gas Co., Cleveland

Nonmonetary Support
Value: $200,000 (1996); $245,000 (1993); $325,500 (1991)
Type: Donated Equipment; In-kind Services; Loaned Employees; Loaned Executives

Giving Contact
Renee Johnson, Contributions Coordinator
Dominion Resources, Inc.
PO Box 26532
Richmond, VA 23261
Phone: (804)819-2580
Fax: (804)819-2217
Email: rjohnson@domres.com
Web: http://www.vapower.com/community/contributions.html

Description
Organization Type: Corporate Giving Program
Giving Locations: operating locations.
Grant Types: Capital, Employee Matching Gifts, General Support.
Note: Employee matching gift ratio: 0.5 to 1. The company matches gifts from $25 to $1,000 per employee annually.

Giving Philosophy
'As a public service company committed to improving the quality of life for its customers and employees, we award grants and donate surplus equipment to eligible nonprofit organizations serving the geographic areas where we operate. The company makes grants in four broad areas: human services, education, arts and humanities and the environment.'
'Human and social service organizations fill basic needs and answer fundamental social and economic problems in the communities we serve. The company gives priority to health care for underserved groups; housing, homelessness and hunger; youth and adult literacy, neighborhood improvement; and equal opportunity efforts.'
'Quality education is critical to a healthy society. Our support of education is targeted toward ensuring consistent standards of educational quality among the communities we serve, as well as preparing the future work force to function well within the company and contribute to the well-being of the community. The company gives priority to programs and scholarships in mathematics, science and technology; early childhood and precollege basics; programs and scholarships promoting cultural diversity in energy-related fields; and job training programs.'
'A rich cultural background enhances the social and economic climate of an area. Grants to cultural organizations are intended to broaden the availability of arts and cultural experience within the communities we serve. The company gives priority to arts enrichment and education, especially for underserved groups; programs that encourage arts volunteerism; and multicultural arts organizations.'
'The company supports organizations that approach environmental issues responsibly and understand the balance between the need for environmental improvement and the need for sustained economic growth. The company gives priority to organizations that enhance conservation of energy and natural resources and environmental education efforts.'
'United Way is supported extensively by the company and its employees through annual campaigns.' 1997 Corporate Giving Program brochure

Financial Summary
Total Giving: $2,150,000 (2000 approx); $2,154,610 (1999); $1,670,000 (1997 approx). Note: Contributes through corporate direct giving program only.

Typical Recipients
Arts & Humanities: Arts Associations & Councils, Arts Centers, Arts Festivals, Community Arts, Dance, Libraries, Literary Arts, Museums/Galleries, Music, Opera, Performing Arts, Public Broadcasting, Theater, Visual Arts
Civic & Public Affairs: Employment/Job Training, Housing, Safety, Urban & Community Affairs, Women's Affairs
Education: Colleges & Universities, Education Funds, Engineering/Technological Education
Environment: Environment-General
Health: Emergency/Ambulance Services, Health Organizations, Hospices, Hospitals, Mental Health
Social Services: Child Welfare, Food/Clothing Distribution, Homes, People with Disabilities, Senior Services, Shelters/Homelessness, Substance Abuse

Contributions Analysis
Giving Priorities: Human and social services, education, arts and humanities, and the environment.
Arts & Humanities: 10% to 15%. Supports theater, ballet, symphonic and choral music, opera, art councils, museums, multicultural arts associations, and public broadcasting.
Education: 15% to 20%. Supports early childhood and precollege basics programs, accredited private colleges and universities, independent college funds, job creation and training programs.
Environment: Less than 5%. Supports environmental education groups, wildlife conservation and endangered species protection programs, recycling programs, groups advocating responsible land use and wise use ofnatural resources.
Health: 40% to 50%. Supports United Way, health care groups, volunteer fire and rescue squads, Red Cross, civic groups, neighborhood improvement, cultural diversity groups, shelters, programs for older Americans, literacy programs, and programs for the homeless.

Application Procedures
Initial Contact: Submit a letter or proposal.
Application Requirements: Include organization's purpose and goals, most recent financial statement,

proof of tax-exempt status, amount of grant requested and total goal for contributions from individuals and corp.s, and a description of intended use of requested funds.
Deadlines: None.
Evaluative Criteria: Priority is given to organizations that address issues critical to the company's objectives; organizations that promote research and coalition-building rather than duplicating efforts; organizations that are tax-exempt; and organizations that operate within the northeastern quadrant of the United States.
Decision Notification: Statewide requests are reviewed quarterly and notices are sent in April, July, October, and December; other organizations receive notice within approximately 45 days.

Restrictions

Support is not given to organizations benefiting an individual or family; religious, political, fraternal, veteran, professional or membership organization; operating grants to organizations supported by the United Way; historic restoration; individual Scout troops, except area scouting councils that are not supported by the United Way; organizations that discriminate on the basis of race, creed, color, sex or national origin; or elementary and secondary schools.
In the area of human and social services the company does not make grants to national health organizations; for medical equipment or research; tax-supported hospitals or hospitals operated for-profit; or campaigns for sponsorship through program advertising.
In the area of education the company does not support private foundations benefiting from tax-supported education institutions; individual research or scholarship; operating support for individual universities; or athletic and extracurricular activities.
In the area of arts and humanities the company does not support film or video projects; endowment programs; or individual high school or college performing arts groups.
In the area of the environment the company does not make grants to groups whose objectives are inconsistent with the company's best interests; political or lobbying groups; or research or issues for which significant information is already available.

Additional Information

In January 2000, Dominion Resources merged with Consolidated Natural Gas Co. Under the terms of the merger agreement, Consolidated Natural Gas Co. became a direct subsidiary of Dominion.
Local community organizations should apply to nearest company offices. Addresses and phone numbers are listed in the Corporate Giving Program brochure, available upon request from the contributions administrator.
Grants for economic development are administered as a separate program by the Economic Development section of the company's Customer Service and Marketing Department.
Organizations that receive a capital grant must wait two years after receiving final payment to apply for another grant.
Publications: Corporate Giving Program Brochure

Corporate Officials

John B. Adams, Junior: chairman, president, chief executive officer B 1935. ED Virginia Military Institute; Washington & Lee University Law School (1969). PRIM CORP EMPL chairman, president, chief executive officer: Bowman Companies. CORP AFFIL director: Loudoun Mutual Industry Co.; director: Virginia Electric & Power Co.
Larry M. Girvin: senior vice president commercial operations PRIM CORP EMPL senior vice president commercial operations: Virginia Electric & Power Co.
James Thomas Rhodes: president, chief executive officer, director B Lincolnton, NC 1941. ED North Carolina State University BS (1963); Catholic University America MS (1968); Purdue University PhD (1972). PRIM CORP EMPL president, chief executive officer, director: Virginia Electric & Power Co. CORP AFFIL director: NationsBank Virginia NA.

Giving Program Officials

John B. Adams, Junior: member contributions committee B 1935. ED Virginia Military Institute; Washington & Lee University Law School (1969). PRIM CORP EMPL chairman, president, chief executive officer: Bowman Companies. CORP AFFIL director: Loudoun Mutual Industry Co.; director: Virginia Electric & Power Co.
Kathryn M. Fessler: PRIM CORP EMPL contributions administrator: Virginia Power Co.
Larry M. Girvin: member contributions committee PRIM CORP EMPL senior vice president commercial operations: Virginia Electric & Power Co.
James Thomas Rhodes: member contributions committee B Lincolnton, NC 1941. ED North Carolina State University BS (1963); Catholic University America MS (1968); Purdue University PhD (1972). PRIM CORP EMPL president, chief executive officer, director: Virginia Electric & Power Co. CORP AFFIL director: NationsBank Virginia NA.
Eva S. Teig: PRIM CORP EMPL senior vice president: Virginia Electric & Power Co. NONPR AFFIL director: Christian Childrens Fund Inc.

DOMINO'S PIZZA INC.

Company Contact

Ann Arbor, MI
Web: http://www.dominos.com

Company Description

Employees: 20,000
SIC(s): 5812 Eating Places, 6794 Patent Owners & Lessors.
Parent Company: Bain Capital Inc., 2 Copley Place, Boston, MA, United States

Nonmonetary Support

Type: Donated Equipment

Corporate Sponsorship

Type: Arts & cultural events; Festivals/fairs

Giving Contact

Barry Marshall, Public Affairs Director
Domino's Inc.
PO Box 997
Ann Arbor, MI 48106
Phone: (734)930-3030

Description

Organization Type: Corporate Giving Program. Supports preselected organizations only.
Giving Locations: MI: including southeast Michigan nationally for religion-oriented grants.
Grant Types: Project.

Financial Summary

Total Giving: $2,430,160 (1996); $879,801 (1995); $535,454 (1994). Note: Contributes through corporate direct giving program only.
Giving Analysis: Giving for 1994 includes: foundation ($535,454); 1995: foundation ($879,801)
Assets: $1,526,760 (1996); $92,095 (1995); $338,522 (1994)
Gifts Received: $3,861,500 (1996); $636,000 (1995); $600,000 (1994). Note: The foundation received contributions for Domino's Pizza, Inc.

Typical Recipients

Arts & Humanities: Libraries
Civic & Public Affairs: Nonprofit Management, Philanthropic Organizations, Public Policy
Education: Colleges & Universities, Private Education (Precollege), Religious Education, Secondary Education (Public), Student Aid
Health: Cancer
International: Foreign Educational Institutions, Missionary/Religious Activities
Religion: Churches, Ministries, Religious Organizations, Religious Welfare, Social/Policy Issues
Social Services: Family Services, People with Disabilities, Senior Services, Youth Organizations

Additional Information

In 1999, Domino's Pizza reported that the Thomas Stephen Monaghan Foundation no longer exists. All giving will be through the company.

Foundation Officials

Joseph E. Davis: program director
Betsy Kanitz: assistant secretary B 1964. PRIM CORP EMPL secretary: Domino's Pizza Inc. CORP AFFIL secretary: TISM Inc.

Grants Analysis

Disclosure Period: calendar year ending 1996
Total Grants: $2,430,160
Number of Grants: 21
Average Grant: $61,758*
Highest Grant: $1,195,000
Typical Range: $1,000 to $10,000 and $50,000 to $100,000
***Note:** Average grant figure excludes highest grant.

Recent Grants

Note: Grants derived from 1996 Form 990.

Arts & Humanities

60,000 University of Steubenville, Steubenville, OH -- library

Civic & Public Affairs

360 Council of Michigan Foundations, Grand Haven, MI -- operating support

Education

1,195,000 Spiritus Sanctus Academy, Ann Arbor, MI -- facility construction
200,000 University of Steubenville, Steubenville, OH -- for convention center
179,000 Spiritus Sanctus Academy, Ann Arbor, MI
73,500 Gabrill Richard High School, Ann Arbor, MI -- scholarship fund
30,000 Spiritus Sanctus Academy, Ann Arbor, MI -- convent construction
4,800 St. Thomas More High School, Rapid City, SD -- scholarship support
2,000 Trinity Education Center, Napa, CA

Health

30,000 Catherine McAuley Health Centers, Ann Arbor, MI -- for cancer care center

International

123,000 Catholic Church in Honduras, Zacapa, Honduras -- mission support
123,000 Catholic Church in Honduras, Zacapa, Honduras -- mission support

Religion

290,000 Legatus, Ann Arbor, MI -- operating support
100,000 Papal Foundation, Philadelphia, PA -- endowment fund
89,500 Credo, Ann Arbor, MI -- publication support
25,000 Catholic Campaign for America, Washington, DC -- operating support
5,000 Institute on Religious Life, Chicago, IL -- program support
2,000 Catholic Home Study Institute, Allentown, PA -- program development
1,000 Right to Life of Michigan, Grand Rapids, MI -- for Direct Connect Campaign

Social Services

10,000	Domino House Northeast Seniors, Ann Arbor, MI -- operating support
5,000	Ann Arbor Center for Independent Living, Ann Arbor, MI -- project support
5,000	Fund for the American Family, Scranton, PA -- operating support

DONALDSON CO., INC.

Company Contact

Minneapolis, MN
Web: http://www.donaldson.com

Company Description

Employees: 6,230
SIC(s): 3519 Internal Combustion Engines Nec.

Operating Locations

Operates plants in all locations.

Donaldson Foundation

Giving Contact

Mr. Jim Giertz, Trustee & Secretary
Donaldson Foundation
PO Box 1299 MS 100
Minneapolis, MN 55440
Phone: (612)703-4999
Fax: (612)887-3005
Email: donaldsonfoundation@mail.donaldson.com

Description

EIN: 416052950
Organization Type: Corporate Foundation
Giving Locations: headquarters and operating communities.
Grant Types: Award, Capital, General Support, Multiyear/Continuing Support, Scholarship.

Giving Philosophy

The Donaldson Foundation is established to support the needs and interests of Donaldson employees. Our belief is that this can best be done by directing our philanthropy to communities in which Donaldson Company, Inc., employees live and work, .. with an emphasis on the needs of education, conservation, social and human services, and the arts. The Foundation's focus is to increase assistance to social and human service, particularly United Way drives, early intervention programs and the preservation of the natural environment. The ratio for social services, particularly conservation, has increased each fiscal year.
Donaldson Foundation Application Guidelines and Annual Report

Financial Summary

Total Giving: $800,000 (fiscal year ending July 31, 1999 approx); $744,949 (fiscal 1998); $746,445 (fiscal 1996). Note: Contributes through corporate direct giving program and foundation.
Giving Analysis: Giving for fiscal 1998 includes: foundation ($384,636); foundation grants to United Way ($241,413); foundation scholarships ($114,400); foundation matching gifts ($4,500)
Assets: $3,992,732 (fiscal 1998); $1,950,000 (fiscal 1997 approx); $1,774,674 (fiscal 1996)
Gifts Received: $2,310,000 (fiscal 1998); $1,200,000 (fiscal 1996); $750,000 (fiscal 1994). Note: Contributions are received from Donaldson Company.

Typical Recipients

Arts & Humanities: Arts Centers, Arts Funds, Arts Institutes, Community Arts, Dance, Historic Preservation, History & Archaeology, Libraries, Museums/Galleries, Music, Opera, Performing Arts, Public Broadcasting, Theater
Civic & Public Affairs: Economic Development, Employment/Job Training, Environmental Affairs (Air/Water Quality), Environmental Affairs (Conservation), Housing, Nonprofit Management, Safety, Zoos/Aquariums
Education: Agricultural Education, Business Education, Colleges & Universities, Community & Junior Colleges, Economic Education, Education Funds, Education Reform, Elementary Education (Public), Engineering/Technological Education, Faculty Development, Health & Physical Education, Legal Education, Literacy, Minority Education, Private Education (Precollege), Public Education (Precollege), Science/Mathematics Education, Secondary Education (Public), Special Education, Student Aid, Vocational & Technical Education
Environment: Environment-General, Resource Conservation, Wildlife Protection
Health: Children's Health/Hospitals, Emergency/Ambulance Services, Health Funds, Health Organizations, Hospices, Hospitals, Medical Rehabilitation, Mental Health, Preventive Medicine/Wellness Organizations, Public Health
Religion: Religious Welfare
Science: Observatories & Planetariums, Science Museums
Social Services: Big Brother/Big Sister, Child Welfare, Community Centers, Community Service Organizations, Counseling, Day Care, Delinquency & Criminal Rehabilitation, Domestic Violence, Emergency Relief, Family Planning, Family Services, Food/Clothing Distribution, Homes, People with Disabilities, Senior Services, Shelters/Homelessness, Substance Abuse, United Funds/United Ways, Volunteer Services, YMCA/YWCA/YMHA/YWHA, Youth Organizations

Contributions Analysis

Arts & Humanities: 3%. Supports public broadcasting, arts centers, arts institutes, museums, theater, and historical preservation.
Civic & Public Affairs: 8%.
Education: 35%. Support goes to the foundation's scholarship program. Other interests include minority education funds, colleges and universities, engineering, law economics, and public education.
Environment: 10%.
Health: 5%.
Social Services: About 39%. Supports general charities, including United Way, health relief organizations, and community centers. Counseling and rehabilitation receive limited support; interests include opportunity workshops, homes, family planning, welfare transition, religious charity groups, and resources for women.

Application Procedures

Initial Contact: Send a brief letter of inquiry or proposal.
Application Requirements: Describe organization and its purpose, list of officers and directors, describe program or project needing assistance, discuss current progress toward goal, a budget and list of contributors, IRS tax exemption letter, and IRS letter stating organization is not a private foundation.
Deadlines: August, December, and April.
Decision Notification: Trustees review grants in September, January, and May; annual budget set at August meeting.

Restrictions

The foundation limits its support to local or regional drives in communities where Donaldson employees live. The foundation does not support individuals, religious purposes, groups that influence legislation, political campaigns, or national drives. Applicants must qualify for tax exemption under the IRS Code and cannot be a private foundation.

Additional Information

The foundation considers capital grants, but limits them to 30% of annual giving.
Applicants receiving grants are furnished with a Statement of Donee form, which must be returned to the foundation before payments can be made. The statement may be recalled for any future grant payments.
Publications: Application Guidelines; Annual Report

Corporate Officials

James R. Giertz: senior vice president, chief financial officero, director ED Iowa State University BS (1979); Harvard University MBA (1983). PRIM CORP EMPL senior vice president, chief financial officer: Donaldson Co., Inc.
Norman C. Linnell: general counsel, secretary B 1959. ED University of Minnesota (1981); University of Minnesota (1984). PRIM CORP EMPL general counsel, secretary: Donaldson Co., Inc.
William Grant Van Dyke: chairman, president, chief executive officer, director B Minneapolis, MN 1945. ED University of Minnesota BA (1967); University of Minnesota MBA (1972). PRIM CORP EMPL chairman, president, chief executive officer, director: Donaldson Co., Inc. ADD CORP EMPL president: Advanced Filtration Systems. CORP AFFIL director: Graco Inc. NONPR AFFIL member: Kappa Sigma Alumni Association.

Foundation Officials

Mary Barris: trustee
Becky Cahn: trustee
H. Young Chung: trustee
Patrick Fischer: trustee
James R. Giertz: chief financial officer, vice president (see above)
Tim Grafe: trustee
Dennis Grigal: trustee
Sandra Johnson: trustee
Norman C. Linnell: trustee (see above)
Jim Martin: trustee
Bonnie Schneider: trustee
Randy Thiele: trustee
Aileen Torgeson: trustee

Grants Analysis

Disclosure Period: fiscal year ending July 31, 1998
Total Grants: $384,636*
Number of Grants: 46
Average Grant: $4,396*
Highest Grant: $50,000
Typical Range: $1,000 to $5,000
***Note:** Giving excludes matching gifts, scholarship, and United Way. Average grant figure excludes four grants totaling $200,000.

Recent Grants

Note: Grants derived from 1997 Form 990.

Arts & Humanities

16,000	Twin Cities Public Television, St. Paul, MN -- educational programming
7,500	Minnesota Public Radio, St. Paul, MN -- educational radio programming
6,000	Minnesota Orchestral Association, Minneapolis, MN
5,000	Children's Museum, St. Paul, MN -- capital grant
5,000	Guthrie Theater Foundation, Minneapolis, MN
5,000	Minnesota Public Radio, St. Paul, MN -- capital grant
3,000	Minneapolis Institute of Arts, Minneapolis, MN
2,500	Elma Public Library, Cresco, IA
2,500	Elma Public Library, Cresco, IA

Civic & Public Affairs

3,500	Rebuild Resources, Minneapolis, MN -- rehabilitation
2,500	Minnesota Diversified Industry, St. Paul, MN -- rehabilitation
2,500	Opportunity Workshop, Minnetonka, MN -- rehabilitation

Education

101,190	Donaldson Scholarship Program, Minneapolis, MN -- scholarships
50,000	Harvard School of Public Health, Cambridge, MA -- capital grant
20,000	University of Minnesota Carlson School of Management, Minneapolis, MN -- capital grant
11,000	Minnesota Private College Fund, St. Paul, MN -- operations
8,500	Carlton College, Northfield, MN -- capital grant
8,000	Junior Achievement Upper Midwest, St. Paul, MN
7,000	Summit Academy, Minneapolis, MN -- trade school
5,000	Oelwein School District, Oelwein, IA -- capital grant
3,600	Bloomington Scholarship Fund, Minneapolis, MN -- scholarships
3,600	Normandale Community College, Bloomington, IN -- operations
3,400	Iowa College Fund, Des Moines, IA -- operations
3,100	Business Economics Education Fund, Minneapolis, MN -- operations
3,000	Chillicothe High School, Chillicothe, MO -- computers
3,000	Chillicothe R-II High School, Chillicothe, MO -- track and field
3,000	Wisconsin Independent College Fund, Milwaukee, WI -- operations
2,800	Missouri College Fund, Kansas City, MO -- operations
2,500	University of Minnesota Fund, Minneapolis, MN -- operations

Environment

3,500	Nature Conservancy -- capital grant
2,500	Central Wisconsin Wildlife, Stevens Point, WI -- conservation
2,500	Nature Conservancy Minnesota Chapter, MN -- conservation

Health

8,000	Wellness Center, Cresco, IA
4,000	Howard Community Hospital, Cresco, IA -- rehabilitation
3,500	Courage Center, Minneapolis, MN -- rehabilitation

Religion

8,350	Sister Kenny, Minneapolis, MN -- capital grant
5,448	Salvation Army, Minneapolis, MN

Social Services

145,101	Minneapolis United Way, Minneapolis, MN
12,000	Blue Grass United Way, Nicholasville, KY
11,000	Portage County United Way, Stevens Point, WI
10,000	Grinnell United Fund, Grinnell, IA
8,000	YMCA, Indianapolis, IN -- capital grant
7,153	Flood Relief
6,000	Clinton County United Way, Frankfort, KY
6,000	Oelwein United Fund, Oelwein, IA
5,000	Greater River YMCA, Chillicothe, MO
2,500	Friends of HOME, Bloomington, MN -- elderly aid
2,500	Prevention Alliance, Minneapolis, MN -- counseling services
2,480	Buck County United Way, Feasterville, PA
500	Dixon United Fund, Dixon, IL

R.R. DONNELLEY &SONS CO.

Company Contact

Chicago, IL

Web: http://www.rrdonnelley.com

Company Description

Revenue: US$5,183,000,000
Employees: 36,300 (1999)
Fortune Rank: 291, per FORTUNE Magazine's list of 500 Largest U.S. Corporations (1999).
FF 291
SIC(s): 2732 Book Printing, 2752 Commercial Printing--Lithographic, 2754 Commercial Printing--Gravure, 2759 Commercial Printing Nec.

Operating Locations

Barbados; France; Germany; Republic of Korea; Mexico: Mexico City Reynosa; Netherlands; Spain; United Kingdom

Nonmonetary Support

Type: Donated Equipment; Loaned Executives
Note: Company donates only used equipment. Company loans executives to the United Way only.

Giving Contact

Susan M. Levy, Director, Community Relations
R.R. Donnelley & Sons Co.
77 West Wacker Drive
Chicago, IL 60601-1696
Phone: (312)326-8102
Fax: (312)326-8262
Email: susan.levy@rrd.com

Description

Organization Type: Corporate Giving Program
Giving Locations: principally near operating locations and to national organizations.
Grant Types: Capital, Emergency, Employee Matching Gifts, General Support, Multiyear/Continuing Support, Scholarship, Seed Money.
Note: Employee matching gift ratio: 1 to 1 for educational and cultural gifts.

Giving Philosophy

'The Community Relations program meets three very important goals. First, it helps communities address issues that affect quality of life..Second, it helps strengthen and enliven the social, educational, and cultural fabric of these communities, thus ensuring that they remain good places to work and to live. Third, community involvement is an integral part of our approach to diversity, which also includes employment, education, workplace quality, financial and procurement initiatives.' 1996 Community Relations Annual Report

Financial Summary

Total Giving: $3,000,000 (2000 approx); $3,000,000 (1999 approx); $3,000,000 (1998 approx). Note: Contributes through corporate direct giving program only. Giving includes nonmonetary support.

Typical Recipients

Arts & Humanities: Arts Institutes, Historic Preservation, Libraries, Literary Arts, Museums/Galleries, Performing Arts, Theater
Civic & Public Affairs: Employment/Job Training, Public Policy, Urban & Community Affairs, Zoos/Aquariums
Education: Colleges & Universities, Education Associations, Literacy
Health: Hospitals, Mental Health
Social Services: Domestic Violence, Family Services, People with Disabilities, Shelters/Homelessness, United Funds/United Ways, Youth Organizations

Contributions Analysis

Giving Priorities: Human services, education, health, and social service.
Arts & Humanities: 10% to 15%. Interests include museums, libraries, and literary and performing arts. Matches employee gifts to cultural institutions.
Civic & Public Affairs: About 10%. Supports better government groups, and conservation and environmental projects. Other interests include civil rights and economic development. Main focus of national giving is public policy organizations.
Education: 20% to 25%. Emphasis is on higher education, especially independent college funds and educational institutions located in operating communities. Precollegiate education is also of interest. Matches employee gifts to higher and secondary education and provides scholarships to employees' children.
Social Services: 55% to 60%. Company contributes to organizations serving operating locations, including united funds and groups concerned with youth, the disabled, and minorities.
Note: Total contributions made in 1999. Donations are given either as special purpose grants, to support initiatives that require defined funds to launch or develop a major program, or as general operating grants, for ongoing assistance to local organizations. An overall company priority is organizations which promote the written word, including libraries and literary organizations.

Application Procedures

Initial Contact: Short written proposal.
Application Requirements: Include a description of organization, its activities, and its clients; amount requested, purpose of funds sought; recently audited financial statement, proof of tax-exempt status; list of board of directors; and other relevant supporting materials.
Deadlines: Proposals are accepted between January 1 and November 1.
Review Process: Requests evaluated by staff; decisions made at quarterly meetings of contributions committee.
Notes: Organizations located in operating communities should contact local manufacturing division.

Restrictions

Printing is provided only under exceptional circumstances.
Supports arts and cultural groups located within the city of Chicago only.
The company does not support individuals, religious or fraternal organizations, political or lobbying groups, or goodwill advertising, and seldom supports tax-supported organizations.
Funds are only provided to organizations in communities where employees live and work.
Scholarships are provided only to children of employees.
The company seldom participates in special-event fundraising.

Additional Information

Part of Donnelley's annual giving is administered by manufacturing divisions, although division grants tend to be smaller than those awarded by the corporate office. In general, manufacturing divisions award grants ranging from $25 to $15,000 each, while the corporate office awards grants ranging from $1,000 to $125,000 each.
Publications: Corporate Contributions Annual Report

Corporate Officials

Haven E. Cockerham: senior vice president human resources PRIM CORP EMPL senior vice president human resources: R.R. Donnelly & Sons Co.
William L. Davis: chairman, chief executive officer, director B 1943. ED Princeton University BA (1965). PRIM CORP EMPL chairman, chief executive officer, director: R.R. Donnelley & Sons Co. CORP AFFIL director: Mallinckrodt Inc.
James R. Donnelley: vice chairman B Chicago, IL 1935. ED Dartmouth College BA (1957); University of Chicago MBA (1962). PRIM CORP EMPL vice chairman: R.R. Donnelley & Sons Co. CORP AFFIL

director: Sierra Pacific Power Co.; director: Sierra Pacific Resources; director: Pacific Magazines & Printing Ltd.
Cheryl A. Francis: executive vice president, chief financial officer B Toledo, OH 1954. ED Cornell University BS (1976); University of Chicago MBA (1978). PRIM CORP EMPL executive vice president, chief financial officer: R.R. Donnelley & Sons Co. ADD CORP EMPL director investor relations: FMC Corp. NONPR AFFIL member: Financial Executives Institute; member: International Womens Forum.
Cheryl Malmloff: community relations administrator PRIM CORP EMPL community relations administrator: R.R. Donnelley & Sons Co.

Giving Program Officials

James R. Donnelley: B Chicago, IL 1935. ED Dartmouth College BA (1957); University of Chicago MBA (1962). PRIM CORP EMPL vice chairman: R.R. Donnelley & Sons Co. CORP AFFIL director: Sierra Pacific Power Co.; director: Sierra Pacific Resources; director: Pacific Magazines & Printing Ltd.
Cheryl A. Francis: B Toledo, OH 1954. ED Cornell University BS (1976); University of Chicago MBA (1978). PRIM CORP EMPL executive vice president, chief financial officer: R.R. Donnelley & Sons Co. ADD CORP EMPL director investor relations: FMC Corp. NONPR AFFIL member: Financial Executives Institute; member: International Womens Forum.
Susan M. Levy: secretary contributions committee PRIM CORP EMPL community relations manager, director: R.R. Donnelley & Sons Co.

Grants Analysis

Disclosure Period: calendar year ending
Typical Range: $1,000 to $10,000

Dow Chemical Co.

 Number 56 of Top 100 Corporate Givers

Company Contact

Midland, MI
Web: http://www.dow.com

Company Description

Revenue: US$18,441,000,000
Profit: US$1,310,000,000
Employees: 39,000
Fortune Rank: 89, per FORTUNE Magazine's list of 500 Largest U.S. Corporations (1999).
FF 89
SIC(s): 2819 Industrial Inorganic Chemicals Nec, 2821 Plastics Materials & Resins, 2869 Industrial Organic Chemicals Nec, 3089 Plastics Products Nec.

Operating Locations

Australia: Dow Chemical (Australia) Ltd., Frenchs Forest; Austria: Dow Austria GmbH, Vienna; Brazil: Dow Quimica SA, Sao Paulo; Canada: Essex Specialty Products Canada, London; Dowbrands Canada, Paris, Ville-de-Paris; Dow Chemical Canada, Sarnia; Dow Pipeline Ltd., Sarnia; Chile: Dow Quimica Chilena SA, San Antonio; Petroquimica Dow SA, Santiago; Colombia: Dow Quimica de Colombia SA, Bogota, Cundinamarco; Germany: BSL Pipeline Verwaltungsgesellschaft mbH Boehlen, Boehlen, De-Ost; Buna Sow Leuna Olefinverbund GmbH, Schkopau, De-Ost; Hong Kong: Dow Chemical (China) Ltd., Wan Chai; Dow Chemical (Hong Kong) Ltd., Wan Chai; Dow Chemical Pacific Ltd., Wan Chai; Ireland: Dow Chemical Co. Ltd., Dublin; Italy: Dow Italia SpA, Milano, Lombardia; Japan: Dow Chemical Japan Ltd., Tokyo; Dow Kakoh KK, Tokyo; Republic of Korea: Raychem Korea Ltd., Kangnam-Gu, Seoul; Ulsan Pacific Chemical Co. Ltd., Kyongsangnam, Seoul; Mexico: Dow Elanco Mexicana SA de CV, Ciudad de Mexico; Dow Quimica Mexicana SA de CV, Ciudad de Mexico; Netherlands: Dow Capital BV, Rotterdam, Zuid-Holland; New Zealand: Dow Chemical (New Zealand) Ltd., Auckland; Portugal: Dow Portugalprodutos Quimicos SA, Lisboa; Singapore: Dow Chemical (Singapore) Pte. Ltd., Singapore; Switzerland: Dow Europe SA, Horgen, Zurich; Thailand: Dow Chemical Thailand Ltd., Bangkok; Raychem Thai Ltd., Bangkok; Taiwan: Dow Chemical Taiwan Ltd., Taipei; United Kingdom: Dowchemco Pension Trust Ltd., Bath, Avon; Dow Chemical Co. Ltd., Uxbridge, Middlesex; Venezuela: Dow Venezuela CA, Caracas; Dowelanco Venezuela CA, Caracas

Nonmonetary Support

Value: $1,000,000 (1989)
Type: Donated Equipment; Donated Products; In-kind Services; Loaned Employees; Loaned Executives

Dow Chemical Co. Foundation

Giving Contact

Mr. Jerold E. Ring, Director of Global Contributions & Community Programs
Dow Chemical Co. Foundation
47 Building
Midland, MI 48667
Phone: (517)636-6891
Fax: (517)638-7238
Note: Inquiries about corporate contributions should be addressed to the nearest Dow Chemical location.

Description

EIN: 382314603
Organization Type: Corporate Foundation
Giving Locations: nationally.
Grant Types: Employee Matching Gifts, Fellowship, General Support, Project, Research, Scholarship.

Financial Summary

Total Giving: $15,494,464 (1998); $16,348,516 (1997); $12,328,981 (1996). Note: Contributes through corporate direct giving program and foundation. Giving includes foundation. Co. also administers an international contributions program, approximately $4,000,000 annually.
Giving Analysis: Giving for 1998 includes: foundation grants to United Way ($1,202,049)
Assets: $3,883,869 (1998); $9,267,447 (1997); $22,936,553 (1996)
Gifts Received: $10,000,000 (1998); $20,000,000 (1996); $15,000,000 (1995). Note: Foundation receives contributions from Dow Chemical Co.

Typical Recipients

Arts & Humanities: Arts Centers, History & Archaeology, Museums/Galleries, Music
Civic & Public Affairs: African American Affairs, Chambers of Commerce, Community Foundations, Employment/Job Training, Ethnic Organizations, Civic & Public Affairs-General, Parades/Festivals, Professional & Trade Associations, Public Policy
Education: Agricultural Education, Colleges & Universities, Continuing Education, Education Associations, Engineering/Technological Education, Education-General, International Studies, Minority Education, Public Education (Precollege), Science/Mathematics Education, Student Aid
Environment: Environment-General, Resource Conservation, Wildlife Protection
International: Foreign Educational Institutions, Health Care/Hospitals, International Development, International Organizations
Science: Scientific Centers & Institutes
Social Services: Camps, Community Centers, Day Care, Domestic Violence, United Funds/United Ways

Contributions Analysis

Giving Priorities: Education, health, community improvement, and the arts. Company's contributions program has been restructured in the past several years with a goal of establishing a global charitable giving program. Company has a program at some level currently active in its 113 operating locations in 30 countries. A global donations budget is established and approved by the company's board of directors. Company seeks to partner with in-country organizations on projects where their support will have an impact. Areas of support include improving the community, improving the environment, hands-on science, and university programs aligned with company's business interests. Company has established a 32-member global donations network. A seven-member corporate contributions committee, chaired by the company's chief executive, is responsible for global contributions strategy. In-country managers and site leaders are given the responsibility of identifying organizations to support through charitable contributions, as well as other community relations programs. Employee involvement is encouraged and support of programs in which employees are involved is a priority. Charitable contributions are viewed as a 'tool of community,' and this theme is echoed throughout the company's charitable and community programs.
Arts & Humanities: 10%. Funds children's museum, historical society, symphony orchestra, and arts centers.
Civic & Public Affairs: 12%. Supports science centers and engineering organizations.
Education: 49%. Highest priority of foundation. Chemical science education is main focus. Supports basic research and education in the physical and natural sciences at U.S. colleges and universities. Funding includes chemical engineering faculty support. A limited number of universities receive grants for undergraduate scholarships in the physical and natural sciences. Also supports science-based institutions and organizations such as the National Science Resource Center, American Chemical Society, Council for Chemical Research, and the Mathematical Association.
Environment: 2%. Funds parks and wildlife, conservation, and nature conservancy.
International: 2%. Supports international causes.
Social Services: 24%. Supports domestic violence and sexual abuse centers, community centers, youth and child services, and the United Way.
Note: Total foundation giving in 1998. Through direct giving programs, company and divisions disburse approximately 60% of support to Education, 30% to Health and Community Betterment, about 5% to Arts and Culture, and the remaining 5% to miscellaneous recipients. Company operating divisions administer independent contributions programs. Divisions support community projects (United Way and groups concerned with child welfare, health care, drug abuse prevention, etc.) and cultural activities in areas in which they are located.

Application Procedures

Initial Contact: Send a brief letter or proposal to foundation or manager of nearest Dow facility.
Application Requirements: Include a description of organization, amount requested, purpose for which funds are sought, recently audited financial statement, and proof of tax-exempt status.
Deadlines: None.
Review Process: Requests for funds are reviewed by grants committee, not the foundation's board of trustees.
Decision Notification: Grants committee meets four times per year; response usually follows within two to three months.

Restrictions

Generally does not support organizations or activities not related to chemical research or college scholarships; no grants to individuals, political or lobbying groups, health organizations or institutions, religious or fraternal organizations, goodwill advertising, dinners or special events.

Additional Information

Majority of foundation funds are committed to ongoing projects. Foundation prefers to initiate contact regarding the distribution of the remaining funds.

Corporate Officials

Anthony J. Carbone: vice chairman, director, director B 1940. ED Central Michigan University MS; Yale University BS. PRIM CORP EMPL vice chairman, director: Dow Chemical Co.

Enrique Crabb Falla: senior consult, director B Havana, Cuba 1939. ED University of Miami BBA (1965); University of Miami MS (1967). PRIM CORP EMPL senior consult, director: Dow Chemical Co. CORP AFFIL director: Guidant Corp.; director: K-Mart Corp.; director: Dow Corning Corp.

Barbara Hackman Franklin: director B Lancaster, PA 1940. ED Pennsylvania State University BA (1962); Harvard University MBA (1964). PRIM CORP EMPL director: Dow Chemical Co. CORP AFFIL director: Milacron Inc.; director: J.A. Jones Inc.; director: MedImmune Inc.; director: Guest Services Inc.; director: AMP Inc.; president, chief executive officer: Barbara Franklin Enterprises; director: Aetna Inc. NONPR AFFIL director: United States-China Business Council; member: Women's Forum Washington; member, board governors: National Women's Economic Alliance Foundation; member: NACD; member, Atlantic council director: National Committee on U.S.-China Relations; founding member: International Womens Forum; member, U.S.-China Business Council: Council Foreign Relations; member, chair international trade advisory council: Heritage Foundation; member: Bretton Woods Committee; member: Alumni Council of Pennsylvania State University; member: Asia Society. CLUB AFFIL Union League Club New York; Womens National Republican Club; Economic Club Washington; board of governors: 1925 F Street Club; Economic Club New York.

Michael D. Parker: president, chief executive officer, director PRIM CORP EMPL president, chief executive officer, director: Dow Chemical Co.

J. Pedro Reinhard: executive vice president, chief financial officer, director B Sao Paulo, SP Brazil 1945. ED Escola de Administration de Empresas de Fundacao Vargas; Stanford University; University of Cologne. PRIM CORP EMPL executive vice president, chief financial officer, director: Dow Chemical Co. CORP AFFIL chairman: Liana Ltd.; treasurer: Rofan Services Inc.; president: Hydrocarbons Dow Resources; director: Dorinco Reinsurance Co.; director: Dow Elanco; director: Destec Energy Inc.

William S. Stavropoulos: president, chief executive officer, director B Bridgehampton, NY 1939. ED Fordham University BA (1961); University of Washington PhD (1966). PRIM CORP EMPL president, chief executive officer, director: Dow Chemical Co. ADD CORP EMPL president: Dow Chemical USA. CORP AFFIL director: Marion Merrell Dow Inc.; director: NCR Corp.; director: Dow Corning Corp.; director: Chemical Bank & Trust Co.; director: Chemical Finance Corp.; director: BellSouth Corp.

Giving Program Officials

Andrew J. Butler: trustee B United Kingdom 1934. ED Cambridge University MA (1957). PRIM CORP EMPL senior vice president: Dow Chemical Co. CORP AFFIL president: Dow Chemical Europe SA. NONPR AFFIL director: European Center Chemical Manufacturing Federation.

Joseph L. Downey: trustee B 1936. ED Kansas State University BS (1959). CORP AFFIL chairman: Dow Elanco.

Enrique Crabb Falla: treasurer, trustee B Havana, Cuba 1939. ED University of Miami BBA (1965); University of Miami MS (1967). PRIM CORP EMPL senior consult, director: Dow Chemical Co. CORP AFFIL director: Guidant Corp.; director: K-Mart Corp.; director: Dow Corning Corp.

William S. Stavropoulos: trustee (see above)

Foundation Officials

A. H. Jenkins: secretary

Jan Larson: program manager

Enrique J. Sosa: trustee B 1939. PRIM CORP EMPL executive vice president: Amoco Corp. CORP AFFIL president: Amoco Chemical Holding Co.; director: Electronic Data Systems Corp.; executive vice president: Amoco Chemical Co.

Grants Analysis

Disclosure Period: calendar year ending 1998
Total Grants: $14,292,415*
Number of Grants: 1,050 (approx)
Average Grant: $12,449*
Highest Grant: $1,233,000
Typical Range: $1,000 to $22,000
***Note:** Giving excludes United Way. Average grant figure excludes highest grant.

Recent Grants

Note: Grants derived from 1997 Form 990.

Arts & Humanities

284,724	Midland Center for the Arts, Midland, MI
100,000	Children's Museum, Indianapolis, IN
100,000	Midland Historical Society, Midland, MI
74,000	Midland Symphony Orchestra, Midland, MI

Civic & Public Affairs

112,500	Matrix Midland Festival, Midland, MI
92,000	Bay Area Chamber Foundation Baysail, Bay City, MI
75,000	Mackinac Center for Public Policy, Midland, MI
65,700	Opportunities Industrialization Center, Saginaw, MI

Education

787,690	University of Michigan Ann Arbor, Ann Arbor, MI
372,404	Saginaw Valley State University Foundation, University Center, MI
343,918	Michigan Technological University, Houghton, MI
279,750	Michigan State University, East Lansing, MI
261,000	Purdue University, West Lafayette, IN
191,614	University of Texas Austin, Austin, TX
187,643	Northwood University, Midland, MI
183,477	Texas A&M University Development Foundation, College Station, TX
131,350	University of California, Oakland, CA
131,346	Central Michigan University, Mount Pleasant, MI
127,670	University of Minnesota Foundation, Minneapolis, MN
102,184	University of Florida Foundation, Gainesville, FL
102,000	University of Wisconsin System, Madison, WI
92,000	Texas A&M University, College Station, TX
91,800	California Institute of Technology, Pasadena, CA
90,000	Michigan 4-H Foundation, East Lansing, MI
90,000	National Science Teachers Association, Arlington, VA
88,900	South Dakota School of Mines and Technology, Rapid City, SD
88,410	University of Washington, Seattle, WA
82,925	Delta College, University Center, MI
80,000	Pennsylvania State University, University Park, PA
79,800	Pennsylvania State University, University Park, PA
76,226	Hillsdale College, Hillsdale, MI
76,000	National Consortium for Graduate Degrees, Notre Dame, IN
75,125	Carleton College, Northfield, MN
75,000	Mathcounts Foundation, Alexandria, VA
73,836	Northwestern University, Evanston, IL
67,020	Michigan State University Foundation, Lansing, MI

Environment

200,000	Ducks Unlimited, Memphis, TN
124,000	Conservation Fund, Arlington, VA
105,000	Nature Conservancy, East Lansing, MI
90,000	Parks and Wildlife Foundation, Austin, TX

International

234,000	Gemeente Terneuzen
234,000	Gemeente Terneuzen
72,860	Canadian Network of Toxicology Centers, Canada
72,860	Canadian Network of Toxicology Centers, Canada

Science

200,000	American Institute of Chemical Engineering, New York, NY

Social Services

615,600	Midland Community Center, Midland, MI
548,600	United Way of Midland County, Midland, MI
305,000	United Way of Brazoria County, Angleton, TX
126,700	United Way of the Capital Area, Baton Rouge, LA
120,000	Hayo Went Ha Camps
100,000	Council on Domestic Violence and Sexual Assault, Midland, MI
69,730	Child Care Concepts, Midland, MI

DOW CORNING CORP.

Company Contact

Midland, MI
Web: http://www.dowcorning.com

Company Description

Employees: 6,000
SIC(s): 2821 Plastics Materials & Resins, 2869 Industrial Organic Chemicals Nec.
Parent Company: Dow Chemical Co. & Corning Inc. (50/50 joint venture)

Operating Locations

Australia; Belgium; Brazil; France; Germany; Japan; Republic of Korea; Mexico; United Kingdom

Nonmonetary Support

Value: $100,000 (1988); $200,000 (1987); $149,500 (1986)

Dow Corning Foundation

Giving Contact

Anne M. DeBoer, Executive Director
Dow Corning Foundation
Midland, MI 48686-0994
Phone: (517)496-6290
Fax: (517)496-4393
Email: a.m.deboer@dowcorning.com

Description

EIN: 382376485
Organization Type: Corporate Foundation

Giving Locations: headquarters and operating communities.
Grant Types: Capital, Multiyear/Continuing Support, Project.

Giving Philosophy

'Dow Corning's vision recognizes that enduring success requires sensitivity to the public interest, not only through products and services that improve the quality of life but also through our responsiveness to priority social issues. We recognize that there are many social issues worthy of our attention and many organizations addressing these issues. We cannot attempt to support them all, so we have invested our time and effort to focus on issues we consider to be of vital concern to Dow Corning employees, neighbors, and to society.' *Contributions: To Improve the Quality of Life, Dow Corning Corp.*

Financial Summary

Total Giving: $758,000 (2000 approx); $702,000 (1999); $632,500 (1998). Note: Contributions through foundation.
Assets: $16,695,000 (2000 approx); $15,459,000 (1999 approx); $14,313,282 (1998)
Gifts Received: $1,262 (1994); $350 (1993). Note: In 1994, foundation received funds from Dow Corning Corp.

Typical Recipients

Arts & Humanities: Arts Associations & Councils, Arts Centers, Arts Festivals, Arts Institutes, Community Arts, Dance, Historic Preservation, Libraries, Museums/Galleries, Music, Performing Arts, Public Broadcasting, Theater, Visual Arts
Civic & Public Affairs: Chambers of Commerce, Community Foundations, Economic Development, Employment/Job Training, Municipalities/Towns, Philanthropic Organizations, Professional & Trade Associations, Urban & Community Affairs, Zoos/Aquariums
Education: Arts/Humanities Education, Colleges & Universities, Community & Junior Colleges, Engineering/Technological Education, Faculty Development, Minority Education, Science/Mathematics Education
Environment: Environment-General
Health: Medical Research
Science: Science Exhibits & Fairs, Scientific Centers & Institutes
Social Services: Community Centers, Community Service Organizations, Scouts, United Funds/United Ways, YMCA/YWCA/YMHA/YWHA, Youth Organizations

Contributions Analysis

Giving Priorities: Education, community development, United Way, the arts, and the environment.
Civic & Public Affairs: About 30%. Supports organizations in site communities.
Education: 55% to 60%. Supports both privately endowed and tax-supported colleges and universities. The majority of aid to education is directed toward institutions that have been sources of new employees, have strong, effective minority programs, or provide science and math improvements in K-12 education.
Environment: About 15%. Supports organizations that impact state/community where company has an operating location.

Application Procedures

Initial Contact: Letter or phone call.
Application Requirements: Scope and purpose of the project.
Deadlines: None; requests reviewed continuously.
Review Process: Applications reviewed by executive director; applications meeting criteria may be researched further and recommended to board of trustees for consideration.
Evaluative Criteria: Location of potential recipient within vicinity of plant operation, breadth of support, effectiveness of program.
Decision Notification: Board of trustees meets quarterly.

Restrictions

Does not support individuals; fraternal organizations; political, religious, or veterans organizations; athletic activity at the college/university level; scholarships; dinners or fund-raising events or ongoing operational support.

Additional Information

Contributions of Dow Corning products, material, or equipment are not provided; promotional items and samples are distributed when appropriate.
Dow Corning also sponsors a speakers' bureau.
Publications: Guidelines

Corporate Officials

Burnett S. Kelly: vice president PRIM CORP EMPL vice president: Dow Corning Corp. ADD CORP EMPL president: Dow Corning USA. CORP AFFIL director: Nalco Chemical Co.
Endvar Rossi: vice president PRIM CORP EMPL vice president: Dow Corning Corp.

Foundation Officials

Paula M. Albertson: trustee
Barbara S. Carmichael: trustee PRIM CORP EMPL vice president: Dow Corning Corp.
Anne M. DeBoer: executive director
Marie N. Eckstein: trustee B New York, NY 1917. ED Pace University BA. PRIM CORP EMPL secretary, treasurer: Fred Heinzelman & Sons, Inc.
Janet L. Elias: trustee
James Robert Jenkins: trustee B Waukegan, IL 1945. ED University of Michigan AB (1967); University of Michigan JD (1973).
Thomas H. Lane: trustee
Paul A. Marcela: secretary
Jere D. Marciniak: trustee
Joseph T. Rinaldi: treasurer
Endvar Rossi: trustee (see above)
James G. Sharpe: trustee

Grants Analysis

Disclosure Period: calendar year ending 1998
Total Grants: $632,500*
Number of Grants: 14
Average Grant: $45,179
Highest Grant: $125,000
Typical Range: $50,000 to $100,000
***Note:** Analysis provided by foundation.

Recent Grants

Note: Grants derived from 1996 Form 990.

Arts & Humanities

50,000 Hoyt Trust, Saginaw, MI -- for Hoyt Public Library

Civic & Public Affairs

120,000 Opportunity Education Center, Saginaw, MI -- for fund drive
50,000 Bay Area Community Foundation, Bay City, MI -- for Civic Arena
50,000 Midland Area Chamber Foundation, Midland, MI -- for fund drive
5,000 Midland Foundation, Midland, MI -- for Gerstacker Sculpture

Education

100,000 Alma College, Alma, MI -- for Gazmarian Chair
75,000 Delta College, University Center, MI -- capital campaign
50,000 Michigan Tech University, Houghton, MI -- for Chair in Chemical Process Safety

Social Services

125,000 Midland Community Center, Midland, MI -- for heat plant

Dow Jones &Co., Inc.

Company Contact

New York, NY
Web: http://www.dowjones.com

Company Description

Employees: 8,300
SIC(s): 2711 Newspapers.

Operating Locations

Operates internationally.

Dow Jones Foundation

Giving Contact

Mr. Leonard E. Doherty, Administrative Officer
Dow Jones Foundation
PO Box 300
Princeton, NJ 08543
Phone: (609)520-5143
Fax: (609)520-5180
Email: len.doherty@dowjones.com

Description

EIN: 136070158
Organization Type: Corporate Foundation
Giving Locations: principally near operating locations and to national organizations.
Grant Types: General Support.

Financial Summary

Total Giving: $1,472,320 (1998); $2,581,425 (1997); $2,580,186 (1996). Note: Contributes through corporate direct giving program and foundation.
Giving Analysis: Giving for 1996 includes: foundation ($1,470,750); domestic subsidiaries ($1,096,036); 1997: foundation ($1,469,448); domestic subsidiaries ($644,594); corporate direct giving ($467,383); 1998: foundation ($828,550); foundation scholarships ($342,770); foundation grants to United Way ($301,000)
Assets: $1,553,750 (1998); $1,891,568 (1997); $1,922,783 (1996)
Gifts Received: $1,000,000 (1998); $1,125,000 (1997); $1,250,000 (1996). Note: In 1998, contributions were received from Dow Jones and Co.

Typical Recipients

Arts & Humanities: History & Archaeology, Libraries, Museums/Galleries, Music, Theater
Civic & Public Affairs: African American Affairs, Asian American Affairs, Economic Policy, First Amendment Issues, Gay/Lesbian Issues, Civic & Public Affairs-General, Hispanic Affairs, Native American Affairs, Professional & Trade Associations, Public Policy, Urban & Community Affairs, Women's Affairs
Education: Arts/Humanities Education, Colleges & Universities, Education Associations, Journalism/Media Education, Minority Education, Private Education (Precollege), Student Aid
Health: Clinics/Medical Centers, Hospitals
International: Human Rights, International Organizations, International Relations
Social Services: Child Welfare, Community Service Organizations, Family Services, People with Disabilities, United Funds/United Ways, Volunteer Services

Contributions Analysis

Giving Priorities: Education, civic concerns, social welfare, the arts, and hospitals.

Arts & Humanities: Less than 5%. Museums, libraries, and musical organizations receive limited support.
Civic & Public Affairs: 40% to 50%. Majority of giving supports the Dow Jones Newspaper Fund in a single grant. Professional and trade associations, primarily in journalism, also receive significant support. Other interests include organizations concerned with First Amendment issues and civil rights.
Education: 30% to 35%. Donations to colleges and universities receive highest priority. Journalism education is also of significant interest. Other support goes to minority education and independent college funds.
Social Services: 20% to 30%. Primarily supports united funds. Child welfare also receives a substantial portion of social services funds. Other interests include youth groups and community service organizations.

Application Procedures

Initial Contact: Send brief letter or proposal.
Application Requirements: Include outline of proposed purpose of grant and proof of tax-exempt status.
Deadlines: September.
Decision Notification: Annual meeting in November.

Restrictions

Does not currently support medical and scientific research or cultural activities.

Additional Information

Foundation has policy of considering contributions to institutions and causes where there has been a history of active participation and support by company employees.
Foundation reports U.S. Trust Co. of New York as corporate trustee.
The Dow Jones Foundation routinely makes its largest grant to the Dow Jones Newspaper Fund, a program which supports journalism education for minority high school and college students. The fund also provides internships and fellowships. internships and fellowships.

Corporate Officials

Kenneth L. Burenga: president, chief operating officer, director B Somerville, NJ 1944. ED Rider College BS (1970). PRIM CORP EMPL president, chief operating officer, director: Dow Jones & Co., Inc. CORP AFFIL general manager: Wall Saint Journal; director: Telerate Holdings Inc.; chief executive officer: Dow Jones Telerate Inc.; director: Ottaway Newspapers Inc. NONPR AFFIL chairman: Better Business Bureau New York Inc.
William Coburn Cox, Jr.: director B 1931. PRIM CORP EMPL director: Dow Jones & Co., Inc.
Peter Robert Kann: chairman, chief executive officer, publisher, director B New York, NY 1942. ED Harvard University BA (1964). PRIM CORP EMPL chairman, chief executive officer, publisher, director: Dow Jones & Co., Inc. ADD CORP EMPL publisher: Wall Street Journal. NONPR AFFIL trustee: Aspen Institute; trustee: Institute Advanced Study. CLUB AFFIL Spee Club.
James Haller Ottaway, Jr.: senior vice president, director B Binghamton, NY 1938. ED Phillips Exeter Academy (1955); Yale University BA (1960). PRIM CORP EMPL senior vice president, director: Dow Jones & Co., Inc. CORP AFFIL chairman, director, chief executive officer: Ottaway Newspapers Inc.; chairman: Inquirer & Mirror Inc. NONPR AFFIL chairman: World Press Freedom Comm; trustee: World Wildlife Foundation USA; trustee: Storm King Art Center; member: Newspaper Association America; trustee: Phillip Exeter Academy; president: Magazine Group; member: American Socіety Newspaper Editors; director: Arden Hill Hospital Foundation; trustee: American School Classical Studies Athens; member: American Newspaper Publishers Association.

Foundation Officials

Nicole Bourgois: member advisory committee
Jane Bancroft Cook: chairman emeritus B 1912. CORP AFFIL director: Dow Jones & Co. Inc.
Leonard Edward Doherty: member advisory committee, admin officer B Lowell, MA 1940. ED Merrimack College BBA (1962). PRIM CORP EMPL treasurer, assistant secretary: Dow Jones & Co., Inc. ADD CORP EMPL assistant treasurer: National Delivery Service Inc.; treasurer, director: Dow Jones TeLerate Inc. NONPR AFFIL member: International Newspaper Fin Executives; member: New Jersey Society CPAs; member: American Institute CPAs; member: Institute Newspaper Contrs & Fin Offs.
Peter Robert Kann: member advisory committee (see above)
Jane Cox MacElree: member advisory committee B 1929. ED University of Pennsylvania (1949). CORP AFFIL director: Dow Jones & Co. Inc.
James Haller Ottaway, Jr.: member advisory committee (see above)
Elizabeth R. Steele: member advisory committee

Grants Analysis

Disclosure Period: calendar year ending 1998
Total Grants: $828,550*
Number of Grants: 88
Average Grant: $4,302*
Highest Grant: $450,000
Typical Range: $1,000 to $20,000
***Note:** Giving excludes United Way, scholarships. Average grant figure excludes highest grant.

Recent Grants

Note: Grants derived from 1996 Form 990.

Arts & Humanities

7,500	McCarter Theater Capital Fund, Princeton, NJ

Civic & Public Affairs

10,000	Center for Communications, New York, NY
10,000	Jamestown Foundation, Washington, DC
10,000	World Press Freedom Committee, Washington, DC
5,000	Asian American Journalists Association, San Francisco, CA
5,000	Asian American Journalists Association, San Francisco, CA
5,000	Asian American Journalists Association, San Francisco, CA
5,000	Aspen Institute, Queenstown, MD
5,000	Committee to Protect Journalists, New York, NY
5,000	In-Touch Networks, New York, NY
5,000	International Women's Media Foundation, Alexandria, VA
5,000	Los Angeles Gay and Lesbian Community Service Center, Los Angeles, CA
5,000	Manhattan Institute, New York, NY
5,000	National Urban League, New York, NY
5,000	Reporters Committee for Freedom of the Press, Arlington, VA
5,000	United Neighborhood Centers of America, Cleveland, OH

Education

310,000	National Merit Scholarship Corporation, Evanston, IL
35,000	Brooklyn Academy of Music, Brooklyn, NY
20,000	Oakwood School, North Hollywood, CA
10,000	Bard College, Annandale-on-Hudson, NY
10,000	Inner-City Scholarship Fund, Brighton, MA
8,000	University of Missouri, Columbia, MD
5,000	Independent Journalism Foundation, New York, NY
5,000	United Negro College Fund, New York, NY

Health

12,500	New York Downtown Hospital, New York, NY
10,000	Princeton University Medical Center, Princeton, NJ
5,000	Baystate Medical Center, Springfield, MA
5,000	Jersey City Medical Center, Jersey City, NJ

International

10,000	American Friends of Bilderberg, New York, NY
10,000	Council on Foreign Relations, New York, NY
5,000	Asia Society, New York, NY
5,000	Center for Foreign Journalists, Reston, VA
5,000	International Press Institute, Allentown, PA
5,000	Lawyers Committee for Human Rights, New York, NY

Social Services

55,000	United Way Pioneer Valley, Springfield, MA
55,000	United Way Tri-State Area, New York, NY
43,000	United Way Mercer County, Lawrenceville, NJ
20,000	United Way Central Jersey, Milltown, NJ
20,000	United Way Hudson County, Jersey City, NJ
11,200	United Way, Washington, DC
10,000	Children's Home Society, Trenton, NJ
10,000	Dreams Into Action, New York, NY
10,000	United Way, Dallas, TX
9,000	United Way, Naperville, IL
6,900	United Way, Chicago, IL
6,500	United Way Santa Clara County, Santa Clara, CA
5,900	United Way Orange County, Orlando, FL
5,800	United Way, Los Angeles, CA
5,200	United Way Texas Gulf Coast, Houston, TX
5,000	United Way, Riverside, CA

Dreyer's Grand Ice Cream

Company Contact

Oakland, CA

Company Description

Former Name: Dreyer's & Edy's Grand Ice Cream.
Employees: 2,500
SIC(s): 2024 Ice Cream & Frozen Desserts.

Nonmonetary Support

Type: Donated Products
Volunteer Programs: The company has a business-school partnership with a middle school and provides teachers for Junior Achievement.

Dreyer's Grand Ice Cream Charitable Foundation

Giving Contact

Kelly Su'a, Section-Treasurer
Dreyer's Grand Ice Cream Charitable Foundation
5929 College Ave.
Oakland, CA 94618
Phone: (510)652-8187

Description

EIN: 943006987
Organization Type: Corporate Foundation
Giving Locations: CA: Oakland
Grant Types: General Support, Operating Expenses, Project.

Financial Summary

Total Giving: $200,000 (1999); $230,000 (1998); $450,000 (1997). Note: Company gives directly and through the foundation.
Assets: $136,150 (1995); $137,303 (1994); $110,281 (1990)
Gifts Received: $186,000 (1995); $356,000 (1994); $190,000 (1990). Note: In 1995, contributions were received from Dreyer's Grand Ice Cream.

Typical Recipients

Arts & Humanities: Arts & Humanities-General
Education: Afterschool/Enrichment Programs, Arts/Humanities Education, Business Education, Colleges & Universities, Economic Education, Education Reform, Education-General, Private Education (Precollege), Public Education (Precollege), School Volunteerism, Secondary Education (Private), Secondary Education (Public), Student Aid
Environment: Environment-General
Health: Cancer, Emergency/Ambulance Services, Health Organizations
Religion: Religious Welfare
Science: Observatories & Planetariums
Social Services: At-Risk Youth, Big Brother/Big Sister, Child Abuse, Community Service Organizations, Family Services, Food/Clothing Distribution, People with Disabilities, Recreation & Athletics, Scouts, Shelters/Homelessness, Special Olympics, Youth Organizations

Contributions Analysis

Giving Priorities: Large Grants: Focuses on K-12 education programs that assist students in succeeding in their core academic subjects and graduate to post-secondary education or vocational training.
Small Grants: Offers product donations to arts and civic groups.

Application Procedures

Initial Contact: Send a full proposal.
Application Requirements: Include a a description of organization, amount requested, purpose of funds, audited financial statement, tax-exempt status, list of board members with affiliations, and recent operating and project budget.
Deadlines: October 15 and April 15 for large grants and monthly for small grants.

Restrictions

Does not support individuals, religious organizations for sectarian purposes, political or lobbying groups, or organizations outside operating areas.
The foundation also does not support video production or one day or one-time events or fundraisers.

Additional Information

The foundation's small grants program ($25-$999 and product donations). Support arts and humanities, civic and public affairs, education, environment, health, religion, science, and social services. The foundation's large grant program ($2,500-$50,000) focuses on K-12 education programs that assist students in succeeding in their core academic subjects and graduate to post-secondary education or vocational training.

Corporate Officials

William F. Cronk, III: president, director, director B 1942. ED University of California at Berkeley (1965). PRIM CORP EMPL president, director: Dreyer's Grand Ice Cream. CORP AFFIL director: Civic Bancorp. NONPR AFFIL chairman: Splash Club; member: University California Berkeley Alumni Council; director: Dairy Institute California; president: Boy Scouts America Mount Diablo Council.
T. Gary Rogers: chairman, chief executive officer, director B 1942. ED University of California at Berkeley BS (1963); Harvard University MBA (1967). PRIM CORP EMPL chairman, chief executive officer, director: Dreyer's Grand Ice Cream. CORP AFFIL partner: Montgomery Capital Assoc.

Foundation Officials

Margaret Ann Harrington: director
Diane McIntyre: president
Nancy Reed: director

Grants Analysis

Disclosure Period: calendar year ending 1995
Number of Grants: 89
Highest Grant: $5,000
Typical Range: $50 to $2,500

Recent Grants

Note: Grants derived from 1996 Form 990.

Arts & Humanities

25,000 Oakland Museum, Oakland, CA
5,000 Center for the Arts, Escondido, CA -- Youth Ambassador Program

Civic & Public Affairs

20,000 Oakland Zoo, Oakland, CA

Education

15,000 Teach for America, New York, NY
14,500 Junior Achievement, South San Francisco, CA
10,000 Junior Achievement, Oakland, CA
10,000 Junior Achievement, Oakland, CA
10,000 Northern Light School -- expansion of performing arts program
10,000 St. Elizabeth High School, Wilmington, DE -- support for Great Expectations-Great Results program
6,000 Junior Achievement, South San Francisco, CA
5,000 Chabot Parent-Teacher Association
5,000 Claremont Middle School, Claremont, CA
5,000 Junior Achievement, South San Francisco, CA
2,500 Harambee Preparatory School -- to sponsor Celebrity Basketball Game benefit

Science

15,000 Chabot Observatory, Oakland, CA

Social Services

10,000 Boy Scouts of America, Oakland, CA
10,000 Center for Living Skills, San Francisco, CA -- youth development project
10,000 City of Oakland, Oakland, CA -- Tomorrow's Answer Youth Development Program
10,000 Girls, Incorporated -- support for school-based SMART program
3,000 Boy Scouts of America San Francisco Bay Area Council, Oakland, CA

DSM Copolymer

Company Contact

Baton Rouge, LA
Web: http://www.dsm.nl

Company Description

Employees: 680
SIC(s): 2822 Synthetic Rubber.
Parent Company: DSM NV, Het Overloon 1, Heerlen, Netherlands

Operating Locations

GA: DSM Chemicals North America, Atlanta; DSM Melamine Americas, Atlanta; DSM Resins US, Augusta; IL: DSM Desotech, Elgin; IN: DSM Engineering Plastics, Evansville; LA: American Melamine Industries, Avondale; DSM Copolymer, Baton Rouge; MA: DSM Thermoplastic Elastomers, Leominster; DSM Sheffield Plastics, Sheffield; NJ: DSM Fine Chemicals USA, Saddle Brook; OH: DSM RIM Nylon, Westlake; PA: DSM Engineering Plastic Products, Reading; TX: DSM Hydrocarbons Americas, Houston; VA: Polymer Corp., Wytheville

Copolymer Foundation

Giving Contact

Larry R. Powell, Chairman, President & Chief Executive Officer
PO Box 2591
Baton Rouge, LA 70821
Phone: (225)267-3400
Fax: (225)267-3623

Description

EIN: 726021091
Organization Type: Corporate Foundation
Giving Locations: LA
Grant Types: Employee Matching Gifts, General Support, Scholarship.

Financial Summary

Total Giving: $86,838 (fiscal year ending September 30, 1998); $103,553 (fiscal 1997); $104,475 (fiscal 1996)
Giving Analysis: Giving for fiscal 1998 includes: foundation grants to United Way ($44,000); foundation ($41,693); foundation matching gifts ($1,145)
Assets: $21,333 (fiscal 1998); $8,384 (fiscal 1997); $11,937 (fiscal 1996)
Gifts Received: $100,000 (fiscal 1998); $100,000 (fiscal 1997); $100,000 (fiscal 1996). Note: Contributions received from DSM Copolymer.

Typical Recipients

Arts & Humanities: Arts Funds, Community Arts, Music, Public Broadcasting
Civic & Public Affairs: Botanical Gardens/Parks, Community Foundations, Civic & Public Affairs-General, Parades/Festivals, Philanthropic Organizations, Safety, Urban & Community Affairs
Education: Business Education, Colleges & Universities, Economic Education, Education Funds, Engineering/Technological Education, Literacy, Science/Mathematics Education, Student Aid
Environment: Environment-General, Resource Conservation
Health: Arthritis, Cancer, Hospices, Medical Research, Single-Disease Health Associations
Religion: Religious Welfare
Science: Science Exhibits & Fairs, Scientific Research
Social Services: Child Abuse, Community Service Organizations, Crime Prevention, Domestic Violence, Food/Clothing Distribution, United Funds/United Ways, Volunteer Services, Youth Organizations

Contributions Analysis

Arts & Humanities: 8%. Primarily for arts funds, symphonies, and public broadcasting.
Civic & Public Affairs: 4%. Community foundations.
Education: 37%. Colleges, universities, and scholarship funds.
Social Services: 51%. Focus on United Way.
Note: Total contributions in fiscal 1998.

Application Procedures

Initial Contact: Send brief letter describing program.
Deadlines: None.
Notes: Request application form for scholarships.

Restrictions

Provides scholarships to children of Copolymer employees who plan to attend a four-year accredited college or university.

Additional Information

Publications: Application Form

Corporate Officials

F. G. Anderson: treasurer, president, chief executive officer PRIM CORP EMPL treasurer: DSM Copolymer Inc.

Mike Davis: chief financial officer PRIM CORP EMPL chief financial officer: DSM Copolymer.

Larry R. Powell: chairman, president, chief executive officer B 1949. PRIM CORP EMPL chairman, president, chief executive officer: DSM Copolymer ADD CORP EMPL president: Copolymer Holding Co. Inc.

Foundation Officials

F. G. Anderson: assistant secretary-treasurer (see above)

Larry R. Powell: president (see above)

J. C. Tusa: secretary, treasurer

F. E. Woods: assistant secretary-treasurer

Grants Analysis

Disclosure Period: fiscal year ending September 30, 1998

Total Grants: $41,693*

Number of Grants: 23

Average Grant: $1,813

Highest Grant: $6,750

Typical Range: $500 to $3,000

***Note:** Giving excludes matching gifts, United Way.

Recent Grants

Note: Grants derived from fiscal 1998 Form 990.

Arts & Humanities

4,800 Community Fund for the Arts, Baton Rouge, LA

1,500 Louisiana Public Broadcasting, Baton Rouge, LA

1,000 Baton Rouge Symphony, Baton Rouge, LA

Civic & Public Affairs

1,750 Karnival Krewe de Louisiane, Baton Rouge, LA

1,000 Baton Rouge Area Foundation, Baton Rouge, LA

500 Keep America Beautiful Baton Rouge, Baton Rouge, LA

25 Foundation Assisting Zachary Education, Zachary, LA

Education

6,750 Copolymer Merit Scholarship, Baton Rouge, LA

3,300 Junior Achievement, Baton Rouge, LA

3,000 LSU Foundation, Baton Rouge, LA

3,000 University of Southern Mississippi, Hattiesburg, MS

2,500 Louisiana Independent College Fund, Baton Rouge, LA

2,500 Louisiana Tech University Chemical Engineering, Ruston, LA

2,500 LSU Foundation Center of Excellence, Baton Rouge, LA

2,500 Mississippi State University, Starkville, MS

2,000 LSU Foundation Scholarship, Baton Rouge, LA

720 Louisiana State University, Baton Rouge, LA

490 Stanford University, Stanford, CA

350 Louisiana Tech University, Ruston, LA

332 University of Southern Mississippi, Hattiesburg, MS

250 Babson College, Babson Park, MA

250 Iowa State University, Ames, IA

250 Western Illinois University, McComb, IL

E.I. Du Pont De Nemours &Co.

 Number 35 of Top 100 Corporate Givers

Company Contact

Wilmington, DE

Web: http://www.dupont.com

Company Description

Founded: 1802

Acquired: Pioneer Hi-Bred (1999).

Revenue: US$27,892,000,000 (1999)

Profit: US$7,690,000,000 (1999)

Employees: 101,000

Fortune Rank: 42, per FORTUNE Magazine's list of 500 Largest U.S. Corporations (1999).
FF 42

SIC(s): 1222 Bituminous Coal--Underground, 1311 Crude Petroleum & Natural Gas, 1321 Natural Gas Liquids, 2822 Synthetic Rubber.

Operating Locations

Argentina: Du Pont, Berazategui, Buenos Aires; Australia: Du Pont (Australia) Ltd., North Sydney; Austria: Du Pont Handels GmbH, Vienna; Belgium: Du Pont de Nemours International SA, Antwerpen, Anvers; Petrex SA, Brussels, Brabant; Du Pont Engineered Parts NV, Mechelen, Anvers; Du Pont de Nemours (Belgium) NV, Mechelen, Anvers; IDAC Belgium NV, Mechelen, Anvers; SECA, Uccle, Brabant; Enertech NV, Vilvoorde, Brabant; SECQ NV, Vilvoorde, Brabant; Societe Europeenne de Carburants NV, Vilvoorde, Brabant; Brazil: Du Pont Equipamentos de Precisao Ltda., Pinhais Muc de Piraquara; Canada: Du Pont Canada, Mississauga; Ontario Ltd., Mississauga; People's Republic of China: Du Pont China Holding Co. Ltd. Beijing Office, Beijing; Du Pont (China) Ltd., Tsim Sha Tsui, Kowloon; Colombia: Du Pont de Colombia SA, Bogota, Cundinamarco; Denmark: Du Pont Jet Danmark A/S, Albertslund, Copenhagen; Du Pont de Nemours (Agro) A/S, Albertslund, Copenhagen; England: Continental Oil Co. Ltd., London; Du Pont-Howson Pension Trust Ltd., London; Glen Petroleum Ltd., London; Warwick Technology Park Management Co. Ltd., London; France: Du Pont de Nemours Packaging, Le Trait, Seine-Maritime; Du Pont De Nemours Flandre, Loon Plage, Nord; Du Pont de Nemours France SA, Paris, Ville-de-Paris; Du Pont de Nemours Investissements, Paris, Ville-de-Paris; IDAC France SA, Paris, Ville-de-Paris; Du Pont Photomasks (France) SA, Rousset; Germany: Du Pont de Nemours (Deutschland) GmbH, Bad Homburg, Hessen; Du Pont Automotive Coatings GmbH & Co. KG, Bonn, Nordrhein-Westfalen; IDAC Automobillacke Verwaltungs GmbH, Bonn, Nordrhein-Westfalen; Du Pont Photomask GmbH, Hamburg; GKG Handelsgesellschaft Fuer Kraftstoffe und Energie GmbH, Hamburg; Interkraft Handel GmbH, Hamburg; Jettankstellenbetriebs GmbH, Hamburg; Du Pont de Nemours GmbH, Oestringen, Baden-Wuerttemberg; Hong Kong: Du Pont Orient Operations Ltd., Tsim Sha Tsui, Kowloon; Hungary: Du Pont-Conoco Hungary Kereskedelmi Korlatolt Felelossegut Tarsasag, Budapest; Indonesia: Continental Oil Co. of Indonesia, Jakarta, Jakarta Raya; Du Pont Far East (Indonesia), Jakarta, Jakarta Raya; India: Du Pont South Asia Ltd., Madurai; Du Pont India Ltd., New Delhi; Ireland: Newwater Insurance Ltd., Dublin; Italy: Protein Technologies Intl Italia Srl, Agrate Brianza, Lombardia; Du Pont de Nemours Italiana SpA, Cologno Monzese, Lombardia; Japan: Du Pont KK, Tokyo; Du Pont Toray Kevlar Ltd., Tokyo; Petco Enterprises Ltd., Tokyo; Republic of Korea: Du Pont Korea Inc., Kangnam-Gu, Seoul; Du Pont Korea Ltd., Kyonggi-Do; Luxembourg: Du Pont Engineering Products SA, Luxembourg; Mexico: Protein Technologies International SA de CV, Ciudad de Mexico; Du Pont SA de CV, Mexico; Malaysia: Du Pont Far East, Kuala Lumpur, Selangor; Netherlands: Baanhoekweg Energie Project I BV, Dordrecht, Zuid-Holland; Dordrecht Energy Supply Co. (Desco) BV, Dordrecht, Zuid-Holland; Du Pont de Nemours (Nederland) BV, Dordrecht, Zuid-Holland; Continental Netherlands Oil Co., Leidschendam, Zuid-Holland; Du Pont E&P BV, Leidschendam, Zuid-Holland; Du Pont Services BV, Leidschendam, Zuid-Holland; Du Pont Printing & Publishing BV, Soest, Utrecht; New Zealand: Du Pont (New Zealand) Ltd., Manukau City, Auckland; Du Pont Peroxide Ltd., Morrinsville; Poland: Du Pont Conoco Poland Sp Zoo, Warsaw, Warszawa; Portugal: Du Pont Howson (Portugal) Produtos Para A Industria Grafica Lda., Perafita, Matosinhos; Singapore: Du Pont (Singapore) Electronics Pte. Ltd., Singapore; Singapore Du Pont Pte. Ltd., Singapore; Spain: Du Pont Automotive Coatings Iberica SA, Barcelona, Cataluna; Du Pont Iberica SA, Barcelona, Cataluna; Protein Technologies Intl Iberica SA, Barcelona, Cataluna; Sweden: Du Pont Conoco Nordic AB, Stockholm; Switzerland: Du Pont de Nemours International SA, Le Grand-Saconnex, Geneva; Thailand: Du Pont (Thailand) Ltd., Bangkok; Taiwan: Du Pont Taiwan Ltd., Taipei; United Kingdom: Du Pont Investments Ltd., Cardiff, South Glamorgan; Vortoil Separation Systems Ltd., Gloucester, Gloucestershire; Du Pont Automotive Coatings (UK) Ltd., Hemel Hempstead, Hertfordshire; Du Pont Treasury Ltd., London; Jiffy Ltd., London; Du Pont (UK) Trustees Ltd., Stevenage, Hertfordshire; Du Pont (United Kingdom) Ltd., Stevenage, Hertfordshire; Jet Petroleum Ltd., Warwick, Warwickshire; Camtex Fabrics Ltd., Workington, Cumbria; Venezuela: Du Pont de Venezuela CA, Caracas

SUBSIDIARY COMPANIES

IA: Pioneer Hi-Bred International, Inc., Des Moines

Nonmonetary Support

Value: $9,300,000 (1995); $1,400,000 (1994); $860,000 (1993)

Type: Donated Equipment

Note: Company also donates property. For nonmonetary support contact nearest company site.

Corporate Sponsorship

Type: Arts & cultural events; Festivals/fairs

Note: Sponsors cause-related fundraising events.

Giving Contact

Pat Eggert, Contributions Coordinator
E. I. du Pont de Nemours & Co.
1007 Market St.
Wilmington, DE 19898
Phone: (302)774-2036
Fax: (302)773-2919
Web: http://www.dupont.com/corp/community.html

Alternate Contact

Dr. Claibourne D. Smith, Vice President of Technology
Phone: (302)774-5025
Note: Contact for the company's educational program.

Description

Organization Type: Corporate Giving Program

Giving Locations: headquarters and operating communities.

Grant Types: Capital, Conference/Seminar, Emergency, Fellowship, General Support, Multiyear/Continuing Support.

Giving Philosophy

'Healthy businesses need healthy communities to thrive. DuPont is committed to improving the quality

of life and enhancing the vitality of the communities in which we operate throughout the world by supporting community sustainability efforts.

'Sustainable communities recognize the interdependence of social progress, economic success and environmental excellence. Through financial contributions and the active volunteer participation of employees, DuPont provides support to programs and organizations that address one or more components of community sustainability.' *DuPont Community Involvement: Global Mission and Operating Philosophy*

Financial Summary

Total Giving: $28,000,000 (1999 approx); $28,000,000 (1998 approx); $28,000,000 (1997 approx). Note: Contributes through corporate direct giving program only. Giving includes domestic subsidiaries ($24,000,000); international subsidiaries ($4,000,000); nonmonetary support.

Typical Recipients

Arts & Humanities: Arts Appreciation, Arts Associations & Councils, Arts Centers, Arts Festivals, Arts Funds, Arts Institutes, Community Arts, Dance, Ethnic & Folk Arts, Historic Preservation, Libraries, Literary Arts, Museums/Galleries, Music, Opera, Performing Arts, Public Broadcasting, Theater, Visual Arts

Civic & Public Affairs: Business/Free Enterprise, Civil Rights, Economic Development, Economic Policy, Employment/Job Training, Housing, Law & Justice, Legal Aid, Municipalities/Towns, Nonprofit Management, Philanthropic Organizations, Professional & Trade Associations, Public Policy, Safety, Urban & Community Affairs, Women's Affairs, Zoos/Aquariums

Education: Agricultural Education, Business Education, Colleges & Universities, Community & Junior Colleges, Economic Education, Education Associations, Education Funds, Engineering/Technological Education, Faculty Development, International Exchange, International Studies, Journalism/Media Education, Legal Education, Literacy, Minority Education, Preschool Education, Private Education (Precollege), Public Education (Precollege), Science/Mathematics Education, Social Sciences Education, Student Aid

Environment: Environment-General

Health: Emergency/Ambulance Services, Geriatric Health, Health Policy/Cost Containment, Health Organizations, Hospices, Hospitals, Medical Rehabilitation, Medical Research, Medical Training, Mental Health, Single-Disease Health Associations

International: Foreign Educational Institutions, Health Care/Hospitals, International Peace & Security Issues, International Relations

Science: Science Exhibits & Fairs, Scientific Centers & Institutes, Scientific Organizations

Social Services: Animal Protection, Child Welfare, Community Centers, Community Service Organizations, Counseling, Day Care, Delinquency & Criminal Rehabilitation, Domestic Violence, Emergency Relief, Family Services, Food/Clothing Distribution, Homes, People with Disabilities, Recreation & Athletics, Senior Services, Shelters/Homelessness, Substance Abuse, United Funds/United Ways, Volunteer Services, Youth Organizations

Contributions Analysis

Giving Priorities: Education, scientific research, human services, hospitals, civics, the environment, international grants, and the arts. International grantmaking at Du Pont is administered by overseas subsidiaries to organizations outside the United States. Budgets are established independently in conjunction with corporate headquarters. Priorities vary depending on needs of operating community, but are disbursed across all categories of giving. About 5% of contributions support U.S.-based organizations with an international focus.

Arts & Humanities: 5% to 10%. Supports local museums, libraries, and other cultural organizations. A limited number of high visibility nationalorganizations also receive funding.

Civic & Public Affairs: Secondary areas of support disbursed as follows:

Education: About 45%. Almost all grants are made at the initiative of the Committee on Educational Aid, not in response to proposals or requests. Most support falls within six main categories: University Science and Engineering Grants, supporting undergraduate business, science, and engineering departments and interdisciplinary programs in such areas as occupational and environmental health; Minority Education Grants, to colleges and universities for scholarships and programs to advance the science and engineering education of minorities and to K-12 programs to help prepare minority students for engineering and technical careers; Young Faculty Grants, for research assistants;College Science Grants, to liberal arts colleges producing significant numbers of graduates who go on to advanced studies in science; Business and Economic Grants, supporting training and research at business schools; and Secondary School Grants, emphasizing improvement of teaching in science and economics. The bulk of funding is awarded in the first two categories listed above. The educational program emphasizes physical and life sciences, with grants awarded on the basis of scope, quality of institution's teaching and research, and company's research and recruitment needs.The goals of the program include the following: stimulating applied and basic research; improving higher, secondary, and special educational support programs for minorities in science, engineering, and business management; increasing the number of top graduates, minority scholars, and prospective employees in the fields of company enterprise; and promoting programs to improve the national science policy. Additional areas funded in recent years include energy policy, materials science, and computer-based science applications. Other educational support activities include sponsorship of visiting and adjunct professorships and postdoctoral appointments in DuPontresearch labs. Does not award direct grants to individuals; endowment and capital grants do not fall within preferred areas of giving.

Environment: About 5%. Conservation, public policy, research and education, and environmental management.

Health: 15% to 20%. Primarily supports United Way programs. Strong support is also given to hospital capital campaigns and health projects in operating locations. Other contributions go toward occupational medicine, employment training, youth organizations, minorities, the elderly, and the disabled.

International: Grants are issued outside the United States by overseas subsidiaries. Includes contributions in all of the above categories, although priorities vary depending on specific needs at a given location.

Application Procedures

Initial Contact: Submit a written proposal.

Application Requirements: Provide a one-to two-page a description of organization and program to be funded and an explanation of how it relates to the mission, operating philosophy, and areas of support of the DuPont Community Involvement Program.

Requests should be sent to the above address to the attention of the appropriate committee:

The Committee on Contributions and Memberships reviews all requests for non-education financial contributions.

The Committee on Educational Aid reviews requests for financial contributions to educational institutions.

Deadlines: None.

Review Process: The Committee on Contributions and Memberships generally reviews requests in May and September.

Evaluative Criteria: For Community Social Progress and Economic Success requests, DuPont prefers programs that both address a community need and reflect positively on the reputation and image of DuPont; programs that have extensive DuPont employee volunteer involvement; proposals that have well-defined goals and objectives and a method for evaluating results; and programs designed with long-lasting results in mind.

In the area of Environmental Excellence, DuPont has a preference for organizations that can provide evidence of demonstrated, credible environmental performance; proposals that leverage non-cash resources; proposals that involve partnerships and collaboration between industry, governmental, and community-based organizations; programs which involve DuPont employees; and programs that reflect favorably on DuPont's reputation and image.

DuPont focuses its funding in the Education program area on learning readiness, hands-on science, discovery math, work force readiness, and teacher preparation.

Decision Notification: Applicants are notified in writing.

Restrictions

DuPont does not support individuals other than through certain scholarship and fellowship programs; member agencies of united funds, except for capital needs; charitable organizations not eligible for support under the Internal Revenue Code; sectarian organizations whose programs are limited to members of one religious group; fraternal and veterans' groups; advertising or sponsorship opportunities; conferences or seminars; disease-specific organizations; endowments; or political organizations or campaigns. Endowment or capital campaigns for educational institutions are not supported. Most corporate grants involve programs in DuPont's headquarters community and communities where the company has a major presence.

Additional Information

The company awards between 5,000 and 6,000 grants annually.

DuPont contributions are focused on three areas of support:

Community Social Progress and Economic Success, particularly those programs that provide access to opportunity to people for whom that access does not currently adequately exist; help children, youth and families; foster understanding and respect between community members; revitalize neighborhoods; and help people achieve self-sufficiency.

Environmental Excellence, through support of initiatives that produce significant, measurable results in four major areas of environmental quality: conservation, public policy, research and education, and environmental management.

Education, by funding programs that support improvements in pre-school to grade 12 education. At the college/university level, DuPont opens access to leading-edge research and introduces talented students to the company.

Publications: Brochure

Corporate Officials

Charles O. Holliday, Jr.: chairman, chief executive officer, director B March 09, 1948. ED University of Tennessee BS. PRIM CORP EMPL chairman, chief executive officer, director: E.I. du Pont de Nemours & Co.

Robert E. McKee, III: executive vice president corporate strategy & development ED Colorado School of Mines; Massachusetts Institute of Technology. PRIM CORP EMPL executive vice president corporate strategy & development: Conoco, Inc. CORP AFFIL senior vice president corporate strategy & development: EI du Pont de Nemours & Co. NONPR AFFIL director: American Petroleum Institute; member: Society Petroleum Engineers.

Edgar Smith Woolard, Jr.: director B Washington, NC 1934. ED North Carolina State University BS (1956). PRIM CORP EMPL director: E.I. du Pont de

Nemours & Co. CORP AFFIL director: Citicorp; officer: EV International Inc.; director: Apple Computer Inc. NONPR AFFIL director: North Carolina Textile Foundation; trustee: Winterthur Museum Gardens; trustee: Medical Center DEast; trustee: North Carolina State University.

Giving Program Officials

Scott F. Nelson: manager
Dr. Claibourne D. Smith: PRIM CORP EMPL vice president technology & professional development: E.I. du Pont de Nemours & Co.

Grants Analysis

Disclosure Period: calendar year ending
Typical Range: $5,000 to $10,000

Recent Grants

Note: Grants derived from 1993 grants list.

Civic & Public Affairs

2,000,000 Business/Public Education Council, Wilmington, DE

Education

2,000,000 University of Delaware
105,000 Drexel University, Philadelphia, PA -- undergraduate engineering
32,000 Manhattan College, Riverdale, NY -- environmental science program
15,000 Spelman College, Atlanta, GA

DUCHOSSOIS INDUSTRIES INC.

Company Contact

Elmhurst, IL

Company Description

Employees: 6,500
SIC(s): 3483 Ammunition Except for Small Arms, 3484 Small Arms, 3699 Electrical Equipment & Supplies Nec, 7948 Racing Including Track Operations.

Duchossois Foundation

Giving Contact

Kimberly T. Duchossois, President
Duchossois Foundation
845 Larch Ave.
Elmhurst, IL 60126-1196
Phone: (847)381-6278
Fax: (847)381-4102

Description

EIN: 363327987
Organization Type: Corporate Foundation
Giving Locations: IL: Chicago
Grant Types: General Support, Multiyear/Continuing Support.

Giving Philosophy

The Foundation's purpose 'is to make grants to nonprofit organizations that serve as catalysts enabling community systems and residents to function productively and effectively. Family members have chosen to focus the efforts of the Foundation among their roots, generally within the Chicago metropolitan area. Primary consideration usually is given to those organizations that contribute to the family's specific interests in Health, Youth, and the Cultural Arts.' Foundation Guidelines

Financial Summary

Total Giving: $996,600 (1998); $689,600 (1997); $2,060,700 (1996). Note: Contributes through foundation only.
Giving Analysis: Giving for 1996 includes: foundation grants to United Way ($3,500); 1997: foundation grants to United Way ($3,500); 1998: foundation grants to United Way ($3,500)
Assets: $6,152,703 (1998); $231,911 (1997); $2,114,846 (1996)
Gifts Received: $2,500,000 (1998); $2,000,000 (1997); $3,900,000 (1996). Note: Contributions are received from Duchossois Industries.

Typical Recipients

Arts & Humanities: Arts Associations & Councils, Arts Funds, Arts Institutes, Arts Outreach, Ballet, Community Arts, Dance, Ethnic & Folk Arts, Arts & Humanities-General, History & Archaeology, Libraries, Literary Arts, Museums/Galleries, Music, Opera, Performing Arts, Public Broadcasting, Theater, Visual Arts
Civic & Public Affairs: Business/Free Enterprise, Chambers of Commerce, Clubs, Community Foundations, Economic Development, Civic & Public Affairs-General, Hispanic Affairs, Housing, Parades/Festivals, Philanthropic Organizations, Public Policy, Safety, Urban & Community Affairs, Women's Affairs, Zoos/Aquariums, Zoos/Aquariums
Education: Arts/Humanities Education, Business Education, Colleges & Universities, Education Funds, Education Reform, Elementary Education (Private), Engineering/Technological Education, Faculty Development, Education-General, Minority Education, Private Education (Precollege), Public Education (Precollege), Secondary Education (Public), Special Education, Student Aid
Environment: Forestry, Environment-General, Resource Conservation
Health: AIDS/HIV, Cancer, Children's Health/Hospitals, Clinics/Medical Centers, Health Funds, Health Organizations, Hospices, Hospitals, Hospitals (University Affiliated), Medical Rehabilitation, Medical Research, Mental Health, Prenatal Health Issues, Research/Studies Institutes, Single-Disease Health Associations, Speech & Hearing
International: Health Care/Hospitals, International Affairs, International Environmental Issues, Missionary/Religious Activities
Religion: Churches, Jewish Causes, Religious Organizations, Religious Welfare
Science: Scientific Organizations
Social Services: At-Risk Youth, Child Welfare, Community Service Organizations, Family Services, Homes, People with Disabilities, Recreation & Athletics, Scouts, Shelters/Homelessness, Substance Abuse, United Funds/United Ways, Volunteer Services, Youth Organizations

Contributions Analysis

Giving Priorities: Education, health, youth, and culture/arts.
Arts & Humanities: 11%. Supports the development and enrichment fine arts, cultural and educational museums, theater, music, and dance.
Civic & Public Affairs: 13%. Supports public policy, Habitat for Humanity, zoos, and community services.
Education: 32%. Funds colleges and universities.
Environment: 2%. Funds the Brandywine Conservancy.
Health: 21%. Supports research, education, and advocacy in three primary areas: AIDS, cancer, and mental health. Major support is for cancer research at the University of Chicago.
International: 1%. International aid.
Religion: 1%. Supports religious causes.
Social Services: 19%. Supports programs that seek to enhance the emotional growth and development of children and youth.
Note: Total contribution in 1998.

Application Procedures

Initial Contact: Send a one-page summary-request letter.
Application Requirements: Include a description of organization; its specific needs and purposes; the amount of support requested; list of board of directors and their business or professional affiliations.
Deadlines: None.
Review Process: Foundation will either reject initial inquiry or request a full proposal.
Decision Notification: Board meets semi-annually or as needed; major funding commitments are made at the January meeting.

Restrictions

The foundation does not support individuals, including scholarships or fellowships; lobbying groups; religious organizations for sectarian purposes; or organizations that are not tax-exempt.

Additional Information

Publications: Guidelines

Corporate Officials

Craig J. Duchossois: president, director B 1944. ED Southern Methodist University MBA (1968). PRIM CORP EMPL president, director: Duchossois Industries Inc. CORP AFFIL chairman: Saco Defense Inc.; chairman, chief executive officer, director: Thrall Car Manufacturing Co.; chairman: Chamberlain Group Inc.; director: Hill n Dale Farms Inc.
Richard Louis Duchossois: chairman, chief executive officer, director B Chicago, IL 1921. ED Washington & Lee University. PRIM CORP EMPL chairman, chief executive officer, director: Duchossois Industries Inc. CORP AFFIL chairman: Transportation Corp. Am; vice chairman: Thrall Car Manufacturing Co.; chairman: Duchossois Communication Co.; director: Hill n Dale Farms Inc.; director: Chamberlain Manufacturing Corp.; chairman: Arlington Management Services; director: Chamberlain Group Inc.; chairman: Arlington International Racecourse Ltd. NONPR AFFIL member: Chief Executives Organization. CLUB AFFIL Executive Club; Jockey Club; Economic Club.

Foundation Officials

Craig J. Duchossois: director (see above)
Dayle Paige Duchossois: director
Kimberly Duchossois: president
R. Bruce Duchossois: director
Richard Louis Duchossois: secretary (see above)

Grants Analysis

Disclosure Period: calendar year ending 1998
Total Grants: $993,100*
Number of Grants: 109
Average Grant: $6,881*
Highest Grant: $250,000
Typical Range: $1,000 to $20,000
***Note:** Giving excludes United Way. Average grant excludes highest grant.

Recent Grants

Note: Grants derived from 1998 Form 990.

Arts & Humanities

25,000 The Joffrey Ballet of Chicago, Chicago, IL -- Pledge commitment
15,000 Barrington Youth Dance Ensemble, Barrington, IL -- Annual support
13,500 The Joffrey Ballet of Chicago, Chicago, IL -- Gala/benefit support
10,000 Chicago Symphony Orchestra, Chicago, IL -- annual support
5,000 Barrington Youth Dance Ensemble, Barrington, IL -- operating support
5,000 Facing History and Ourselves, Chicago, IL
5,000 Facing History and Ourselves, Chicago, IL -- fund-raiser

Civic & Public Affairs

20,000 Chicago Zoological Society, Brookfield, IL -- pledge commitment

17,500 Ingalls Development Foundation, Harvey, IL -- Benefit support
13,000 Shoemaker Foundation, Inglewood, CA -- benefit gala
6,000 Ravinia Festival, Highland Park, IL -- gala
5,000 Advocate Charitable Foundation, Barrington, IL -- Support
5,000 American Enterprise Institute, Washington, DC -- Annual support
5,000 Barrington Area Community Foundation, Barrington, IL -- start-up funds
5,000 Barrington Fire Department, Barrington, IL -- Centennial Celebration
5,000 Chicago Commons, Chicago, IL -- Program Support
5,000 Chicago Foundation for Women, Chicago, IL -- Endowment for program funding
5,000 El Valor, Chicago, IL -- Tocar el Futuro program
5,000 John Templeton Foundation, Radnor, PA -- student essay contest
5,000 Lincoln Park Zoo, Chicago, IL -- Facility renovation support

Education
250,000 Culver Educational Foundation, Culver, IN -- Pledge Commitment
16,000 Illinois Institute of Technology, Chicago, IL -- Pledge
15,000 Illinois Institute of Technology, Chicago, IL -- Pledge
7,500 Governors State University, University Park, IL -- Center. for the Performing Arts
5,000 Culver Educational Foundation, Culver, IN
5,000 Glenwood School for Boys, Glenwood, IL -- Pro-American '98

Environment
12,000 Brandywine Conservancy, Chadds Ford, PA -- annual support

Health
100,000 Core Endowment-Virology Research, Chicago, IL -- Research support
33,000 CORE Foundation (The), Chicago, IL -- Pledge commitment
15,000 Beverly E. Duchossois Cancer Research Fund, Chicago, IL -- annual commitment
10,000 AIDS Foundation of Chicago, Chicago, IL -- operating support
10,000 The Billings Society, Chicago, IL -- annual support
10,000 Brain Research Foundation, Chicago, IL -- Benefit/Raffle
7,000 American Cancer Society, Palatine, IL -- Benefit underwriting
5,000 American Cancer Society, Palatine, IL -- Program sponsorship
5,000 Elks Childrens Hospital, Umatilla, FL -- Memorial
5,000 Mental Health Association in Illinois, Chicago, IL -- Fund-raising support (gala)

International
15,000 CARE Chicago (Guatemala), Chicago, IL -- Project support
6,500 Conservation International, Washington, DC -- annual support

Religion
5,000 Catholic Charities NW Suburban Services, Rolling Meadows, IL -- Operating support
5,000 Chicago Province of the Society of Jesus, Chicago, IL -- operating support

Social Services
100,000 United States Equestrian Team, Gladstone, NJ -- National Endowment Campaign
15,000 Barrington Youth Services, Barrington, IL -- Program Support
5,000 Boys & Girls Clubs of Chicago, Chicago, IL -- Visionary Awards Dinner
5,000 Bridge Youth & Family Services, Palatine, IL -- Annual Support
5,000 Cathedral Shelter of Chicago, Chicago, IL -- support
5,000 Girl Scouts, IL Crossroads Council, Elk Grove Village, IL -- Special fund-raising appeal
5,000 Gladstone Equestrian Association, Gladstone, NJ -- Event Support
5,000 Housing Options for the Mentally-Ill in Evanston (H.O.M.E.), Evanston, IL -- Annual support
5,000 McCormick Boys & Girls Club of Chicago, Chicago, IL -- Benefit support (Women's Auxiliary)

DUKE ENERGY

 Number 69 of Top 100 Corporate Givers

Company Contact
Charlotte, NC
Web: http://www.duke-energy.com

Company Description
Former Name: Duke Power Co.
Revenue: US$17,610,000,000
Profit: US$1,252,000,000
Employees: 17,726
Fortune Rank: 69, per FORTUNE Magazine's list of 500 Largest U.S. Corporations (1999).
FF 69
SIC(s): 4911 Electric Services.

Nonmonetary Support
Value: $30,000 (1997); $50,000 (1996)
Type: Donated Equipment; In-kind Services
Note: Co. provides nonmonetary support.

Duke Energy Foundation

Giving Contact
Christopher Carter, Jr., Director
Duke Energy Foundation
PO Box 1009
Charlotte, NC 28201-1009
Phone: (704)382-7200
Fax: (704)382-7600
Email: cecarter@duke-energy.com

Description
EIN: 581586283
Organization Type: Corporate Foundation
Former Name: Duke Power Co. Foundation.
Giving Locations: NC; SC headquarters and operating communities.
Grant Types: Award, Capital, Challenge, Conference/Seminar, Employee Matching Gifts, General Support, Multiyear/Continuing Support, Project, Scholarship.
Note: Employee matching gift ratio: 1 to 1 up to $12,000 per employee annually, for gifts to education.

Financial Summary
Total Giving: $12,000,000 (2000 approx); $12,000,000 (1999 approx); $12,000,000 (1998 approx). Note: Contributes through corporate direct giving program and foundation.
Giving Analysis: Giving for 1998 includes: foundation (approx $12,000,000)
Assets: $13,881,941 (1996); $17,199,978 (1994); $920,028 (1993)
Gifts Received: $7,434,793 (1996); $20,678,510 (1994); $1,028,747 (1993)

Typical Recipients
Arts & Humanities: Arts Associations & Councils, Arts Centers, Arts Festivals, Arts Funds, Community Arts, Dance, Ethnic & Folk Arts, Historic Preservation, Libraries, Museums/Galleries, Music, Opera, Performing Arts, Theater
Civic & Public Affairs: Business/Free Enterprise, Chambers of Commerce, Civil Rights, Economic Development, Housing, Legal Aid, Municipalities/Towns, Professional & Trade Associations, Public Policy, Rural Affairs, Safety, Urban & Community Affairs, Women's Affairs, Zoos/Aquariums
Education: Agricultural Education, Arts/Humanities Education, Business Education, Colleges & Universities, Economic Education, Education Associations, Education Funds, Elementary Education (Private), Engineering/Technological Education, Education-General, Literacy, Medical Education, Minority Education, Private Education (Precollege), Public Education (Precollege), Religious Education, Science/Mathematics Education, Social Sciences Education, Student Aid
Environment: Environment-General
Health: Emergency/Ambulance Services, Health Policy/Cost Containment, Health Organizations, Hospices, Hospitals, Mental Health, Nutrition, Single-Disease Health Associations
International: International Development, International Peace & Security Issues, International Relations
Religion: Churches, Jewish Causes, Ministries, Religious Welfare
Science: Science Exhibits & Fairs, Science Museums, Scientific Centers & Institutes, Scientific Organizations
Social Services: Animal Protection, Child Welfare, Community Centers, Community Service Organizations, Counseling, Emergency Relief, Family Planning, Family Services, Food/Clothing Distribution, People with Disabilities, Recreation & Athletics, Scouts, Senior Services, Substance Abuse, United Funds/United Ways, YMCA/YWCA/YMHA/YWHA, Youth Organizations

Contributions Analysis
Giving Priorities: Social service, hospitals, single disease health associations, education, civic concerns, and the arts.
Arts & Humanities: 15% to 20%. Primarily focuses on museums, art associations, galleries, and art funds.
Civic & Public Affairs: 5%. Focus on business and free enterprise. Interests include economic development, zoos and botanical gardens.
Education: About 40%. Supports colleges and universities, public schools, and educational funds and foundations.
Social Services: 20% to 25%. Primarily supports United Way chapters. Other interests include youth organizations, food and clothing distribution, and community service organizations.
Note: Total contributions made in 1999.

Application Procedures
Initial Contact: Call or write for application form, then submit written proposal.
Application Requirements: Completed application form; proposal including a description of organization, amount requested, purpose of funds sought; proof of tax-exempt status; list of board members with affiliations; current budget.
Deadlines: None.
Evaluative Criteria: Broad base of support, affects company service area, annual budget approved by board, board is active and responsible, clear statement of purpose, nonduplication of services.

Restrictions

Foundation does not support individuals (except within scholarship programs); political organizations, campaigns, or candidates; hospitals; single sectarian or denominational religious, veterans', or fraternal organizations; civic clubs; or projects, institutions, or organizations where the foundation would be the only donor. Does not support member agencies of united funds, or athletics. Foundation generally does not support organizations primarily supported through tax revenues or foundations whose contributions programs duplicate Duke Energy Foundation contributions. Energy Foundation contributions.

Additional Information

In June of 1997, Duke Power Company and PanEnergy Corporation merged to create Duke Energy Corporation.
Publications: Application Form

Corporate Officials

Phyllis T. Simpson: secretary PRIM CORP EMPL secretary: Duke Energy Corp.

Foundation Officials

S. Dock Kornegay: director, secretary
Sherwood L. Love: assistant treasurer PRIM CORP EMPL assistant treasurer - cash management: Duke Energy Corp.
Phyllis T. Simpson: assistant secretary (see above)

Grants Analysis

Disclosure Period: calendar year ending 1996
Total Grants: $5,375,211*
Number of Grants: 1,602
Average Grant: $3,355
Highest Grant: $217,282
Typical Range: $100 to $5,000
***Note:** Giving excludes scholarship and the United Way.

Recent Grants

Note: Grants derived from 1996 Form 990.

Arts & Humanities

125,000 Arts and Science Council, Charlotte, NC
28,325 Arts and Science Council, Charlotte, NC
28,325 Arts and Science Council, Charlotte, NC
28,325 Arts and Science Council, Charlotte, NC
27,500 Arts and Science Council, Charlotte, NC
25,000 Newberry Opera House Foundation, Newberry, SC
21,500 United Arts Council, Greensboro, NC

Education

217,282 University of North Carolina Charlotte, Charlotte, NC
133,502 Duke University, Durham, NC
122,400 Independent College Fund of North Carolina, Raleigh, NC
100,000 Johnson C. Smith University, Charlotte, NC
100,000 Medical University of South Carolina, Charleston, SC
90,045 Duke University, Durham, NC
60,000 University of North Carolina Chapel Hill, Chapel Hill, NC
50,000 Charlotte Mecklenburg Education Foundation, Charlotte, NC
50,000 Clemson University, Clemson, SC
50,000 Davidson College, Davidson, NC
50,000 Duke University, Durham, NC
50,000 North Carolina State University, Raleigh, NC
50,000 Queens College, Charlotte, NC
50,000 University of Tennessee, Knoxville, TN
35,858 North Carolina State University, Raleigh, NC
33,000 North Carolina Central University, Durham, NC
33,000 North Carolina State University, Raleigh, NC
30,000 North Carolina School of Science and Mathematics Foundation, Durham, NC
29,000 Junior Achievement, Charlotte, NC
25,085 Furman University, Greenville, NC
25,000 Clemson University Research Foundation, Clemson, SC
25,000 Governor's School for the Arts Foundation, Greenville, SC
20,800 Duke University, Durham, NC

Health

50,000 Presbyterian Hospital Foundation, Charlotte, NC
25,000 American Red Cross, Charlotte, NC

International

25,000 World Center Foundation, Raleigh, NC

Religion

85,464 Crisis Control Ministry, Winston-Salem, NC
66,200 Crisis Assistance Ministry, Charlotte, NC
65,520 Crisis Assistance Ministry, Charlotte, NC
43,687 Crisis Control Ministry, Winston-Salem, NC
34,103 Greensboro Urban Ministry, Greensboro, NC
28,488 Moravian Church American Southern Province, Winston-Salem, NC
25,216 Interfaith Assistance Ministry, Charlotte, NC

Science

30,000 North Carolina Museum of Life and Science, Durham, NC

Social Services

61,027 United Way Central Carolinas, Charlotte, NC
50,000 YMCA, Charlotte, NC
49,000 Charlotte Mecklenburg Senior Center, Charlotte, NC
34,000 Boy Scouts of America Mecklenburg County Council, Charlotte, NC
31,028 United Way Central Carolinas, Charlotte, NC
28,093 County of Durham Department of Social Services, Durham, NC
21,000 United Way Greenville County, Greenville, SC
21,000 United Way Greenville County, Greenville, SC
21,000 United Way Greenville County, Greenville, SC

DUN &BRADSTREET CORP.

Company Contact

Murray Hill, NJ
Web: http://www.dnb.com

Company Description

Revenue: US$2,159,200,000
Profit: US$320,800,000
Employees: 15,400
SIC(s): 2731 Book Publishing, 2741 Miscellaneous Publishing, 7319 Advertising Nec, 7323 Credit Reporting Services.

Corporate Sponsorship

Range: less than $1,000,000
Type: Arts & cultural events; Music & entertainment events; Sports events
Contact: William Doescher, Sr., Vice President, Chief Communications Officer

Dun & Bradstreet Corp. Foundation, Inc.

Giving Contact

Lisa Gale, Executive Administrator
Dun & Bradstreet Corp. Foundation, Inc.
1 Diamond Hill Road
Murray Hill, NJ 07974
Phone: (908)665-8052
Fax: (908)665-5022

Description

EIN: 136148188
Organization Type: Corporate Foundation
Giving Locations: nationally.
Grant Types: Employee Matching Gifts, General Support.

Financial Summary

Total Giving: $1,230,514 (1998); $803,958 (1997); $4,846,825 (1996). Note: Contributes through foundation only.
Giving Analysis: Giving for 1996 includes: foundation matching gifts ($3,659,840); foundation grants to United Way ($385,450); 1997: foundation ($516,996); foundation matching gifts ($286,962); 1998: foundation ($669,363); foundation matching gifts ($561,151)
Assets: $487,147 (1998); $1,353,891 (1997); $1,740,689 (1996)
Gifts Received: $1,210,000 (1998); $425,000 (1997); $4,550,000 (1996)

Typical Recipients

Arts & Humanities: Arts Associations & Councils, Arts Centers, Dance, Arts & Humanities-General, Historic Preservation, Libraries, Museums/Galleries, Performing Arts, Public Broadcasting, Theater
Civic & Public Affairs: African American Affairs, Business/Free Enterprise, Civil Rights, Clubs, Economic Development, Economic Policy, Law & Justice, Municipalities/Towns, Professional & Trade Associations, Public Policy, Urban & Community Affairs
Education: Business Education, Colleges & Universities, Community & Junior Colleges, Education Associations, Education Funds, Education-General, International Studies, Literacy, Minority Education, Student Aid
Health: AIDS/HIV, Cancer, Emergency/Ambulance Services, Health Organizations, Hospitals, Mental Health, Single-Disease Health Associations, Speech & Hearing
Religion: Religious Welfare
Science: Scientific Centers & Institutes
Social Services: At-Risk Youth, Child Welfare, Community Centers, Community Service Organizations, Family Services, Food/Clothing Distribution, People with Disabilities, Recreation & Athletics, Special Olympics, Substance Abuse, United Funds/United Ways, YMCA/YWCA/YMHA/YWHA, Youth Organizations

Contributions Analysis

Giving Priorities: Education, social services, civics, the arts, and health organizations.
Arts & Humanities: Areas of interest include music, art centers, libraries, museums, and the performing arts.
Civic & Public Affairs: Areas of interest include business, economics, civil rights, law and justice, and public policy.
Education: Interests include independent and minority college funds, higher education associations, and business education.
Health: Supports the American Red Cross, AIDS research, and single-disease health associations.
Social Services: Majority of funding supports United Way campaigns. Other areas of interest include child welfare, youth groups, and community service organizations.

Application Procedures

Initial Contact: Send brief letter or proposal.
Application Requirements: Include a description of organization, amount requested, purpose of funds sought, recently audited financial statement, and copy of IRS Code Section 501(c)(3) tax-exempt status.
Deadlines: October for grants to be made in following year.

Restrictions

Foundation does not make grants for dinners or special events, fraternal organizations, political or lobbying groups, religious organizations for sectarian purposes, goodwill advertising, or individuals.
Foundation will not consider organizations without an IRS 501(c)(3) tax exempt status.

Additional Information

In 1997 the foundation restructured its giving guidelines and priorities.

Corporate Officials

Daniel S. Miller: vice president tax financial planning PRIM CORP EMPL vice president tax financial planning: Dun & Bradstreet Corp.
Charles Worthington Moritz: chairman, director B Washington, DC 1936. ED Yale University BA (1958). PRIM CORP EMPL chairman, director: Dun & Bradstreet Corp. NONPR AFFIL member: Direct Marketing Association; Zeta Psi; member: Business Roundtable; member: American Management Association. CLUB AFFIL Wee Burn Country Club; Pine Valley Country Club; The Links Club; National Golf The Links America Club; Johns Island Club; Blind Brook Country Club; Economic Club.

Foundation Officials

Edwin A. Bescherer, Jr.: trustee B Brooklyn, NY 1933. ED Purdue University BS (1955). NONPR AFFIL member: Financial Executives Institute.
William Hobart Buchanan, Jr.: assistant secretary B Summit, NJ 1937. ED Princeton University AB (1959); Harvard University LLB (1963). PRIM CORP EMPL vice president law, secretary, director: Dun & Bradstreet Corp. CORP AFFIL president: Duns Investing Corp.; president: Dun & Bradstreet Software Services Inc.; president: Dun & Bradstreet Holdings Inc.; secretary, director: Dun & Bradstreet Plan Services Inc.; senior vice president, chief legal counsel, secretary: RH Donnelley Corp. NONPR AFFIL member: Association Bar New York City; member: New York State Bar Association; member: American Society of Corporate Secretaries; member: American Bar Association. CLUB AFFIL New Canaan Field Club; Princeton Club.
Philip C. Danford: treasurer B Columbus, OH 1944. ED Villanova University BS (1967); Harvard University (1969). PRIM CORP EMPL vice president, treasurer: Dun & Bradstreet Corp. ADD CORP EMPL treasurer: Duns Investing Corp.; chief financial officer: Reuben H Donnelley Corp.
William O. Frohlich: vice president
Juliann Gill: administrator
Daniel S. Miller: assistant treasurer (see above)
Dennis N. Pidherny: assistant treasurer PRIM CORP EMPL assistant treasurer: Dun & Bradstreet Corp.
Virginia Simone: secretary

Grants Analysis

Disclosure Period: calendar year ending 1997
Total Grants: $516,996*
Number of Grants: 175*
Average Grant: $2,954
Highest Grant: $200,000
Typical Range: $500 to $5,000
***Note:** Giving excludes matching gifts.

Recent Grants

Note: Grants derived from 1996 Form 990.

Arts & Humanities

25,000	John F. Kennedy Center for Performing Arts, Washington, DC
20,000	Dance Theater, New York, NY
3,500	Paper Mill Playhouse, Millburn, NJ
3,000	Union County Arts, Rahway, NJ

Civic & Public Affairs

30,000	Fairfield County Commission, Norwalk, CT
20,000	Conference Bureau, New York, NY
8,000	Better Business Bureau, Newark, NJ
5,000	New York Urban League, New York, NY
3,500	Urban League, New York, NY
2,600	New York Urban Commission, New York, NY
2,500	Direct Marketing Exchange, New York, NY

Education

200,000	University of Connecticut, Stamford, CT
60,558	National Merit Scholarship Fund, Evanston, IL
50,000	Norwalk Community College, Norwalk, CT
41,567	National Merit Scholarship Fund, Evanston, IL
10,000	A Better Chance, Wilton, CT
5,000	Inner-City Scholarship Fund, New York, NY
2,600	New Jersey Seeds, Hightstown, NJ
2,500	New York University, New York, NY
2,500	University of Notre Dame, Notre Dame, IN
2,000	Junior Achievement, Elizabeth, NJ

Health

5,000	Cerebral Palsy of New Jersey, Wanamassa, NJ
5,000	Valerie Fund, Maplewood, NJ
3,000	American Cancer Society, Elizabeth, NJ
3,000	Summit Speech Society, New Providence, NJ
2,700	Cystic Fibrosis Foundation, Philadelphia, PA
2,500	Cystic Fibrosis Foundation, Bethesda, MD

Religion

20,000	Salvation Army, New York, NY

Science

3,000	Center for Molecular Science, Newark, NY

Social Services

250,000	United Way Tri-State Area, New York, NY
60,000	Wilton Family Y, Wilton, CT
55,000	United Way, New York, NY
36,000	Jackie Robinson Foundation, New York, NY
30,000	Wilton Family Y, Wilton, CT
25,000	United Way Tri-State Area, New York, NY
15,000	United Way, Bethlehem, PA
12,000	United Way, Terre Haute, IN
10,000	Wabash Valley Community Center, Terre Haute, IN
5,000	New York Cares, New York, NY
5,000	United Way Southeast Pennsylvania, Wayne, PA
3,500	United Appeal, Cincinnati, OH
3,200	Search for Change, White Plains, NY
3,000	New Jersey Center, Summit, NJ
3,000	New Jersey Special Olympics, Piscataway, NJ
3,000	YMCA, Metuchen, NJ
2,750	YWCA, Plainfield, NJ
2,600	United Way, Albany, NY
2,500	City Harvest, New York, NY
2,500	Kids In Crisis, Cos Cob, CT
2,000	Shake-A-Leg, Newport, RI

DUQUESNE LIGHT CO.

Company Contact

Pittsburgh, PA
Web: http://www.dqe.com

Company Description

Revenue: US$1,180,284,000
Employees: 3,656
SIC(s): 4911 Electric Services.
Parent Company: DQE, Inc.

Nonmonetary Support

Type: Donated Equipment; In-kind Services; Loaned Employees; Loaned Executives

Giving Contact

Christine Beattie, Manager, Community Relations
Duquesne Light Co.
411 7th Ave.
Pittsburgh, PA 15230-1930
Phone: (412)393-6480
Fax: (412)393-6065

Description

Organization Type: Corporate Giving Program
Giving Locations: PA: Allegheny County, Beaver County
Grant Types: Employee Matching Gifts, General Support.

Financial Summary

Total Giving: Contributes through corporate direct giving program only.

Typical Recipients

Education: Education-General
Health: Health-General, Hospitals
Social Services: Social Services-General, United Funds/United Ways, Youth Organizations

Application Procedures

Initial Contact: written proposal
Application Requirements: a description of organization, amount requested, purpose of funds sought, recently audited financial statement, and proof of tax-exempt status
Deadlines: None.

Restrictions

Company is reluctant to give to church-related functions or government agencies.

Additional Information

The largest seven or eight grants awarded each year are to western Pennsylvania United Way agencies from corporate contributions and employee matching gifts.

Foundation Officials

Dr. Estella W. Smith: manager community relations PRIM CORP EMPL general manager public affairs: Duquesne Light Co.

DURACELL INTERNATIONAL

Company Contact

Bethel, CT

Web: http://www.duracell.com

Company Description

Employees: 9,600
SIC(s): 3691 Storage Batteries.
Parent Company: Gillette Co., Boston, MA, United States

Nonmonetary Support

Value: $50,000 (1997 approx)
Type: Donated Equipment; Donated Products; In-kind Services; Loaned Executives
Note: Also supports service award dinners, volunteer luncheons, a mentoring day, and Back-to-School day.

Corporate Sponsorship

Value: $1,000,000
Type: Arts & cultural events; Festivals/fairs; Music & entertainment events; Pledge-a-thon; Sports events
Contact: Susan Murphy, Contributions Administrator
Note: Sponsors school events and United Way.

Giving Contact

Deborah Pueschel
Duracell International
Research Drive
Berkshire Corporate Park
Bethel, CT 06801
Phone: (203)796-4000
Fax: (203)791-3039

Alternate Contact

Debbie Ferber
Duracell International

Description

Organization Type: Corporate Giving Program
Giving Locations: principally near operating locations and to national organizations.
Grant Types: Employee Matching Gifts, Matching, Multiyear/Continuing Support.
Note: Employee matching gift ratio: 1 to 1 up to $5,000. Matching gifts to educational institutions will only be made to: accredited public secondary schools, junior colleges, community colleges, four-year colleges, and universities, graduate and professional schools.

Financial Summary

Total Giving: $1,500,000 (1999 approx); $2,490,000 (1997 approx); $2,500,000 (1996). Note: Contributes through corporate direct giving program only. 1997 Giving includes nonmonetary support.

Typical Recipients

Arts & Humanities: Arts & Humanities-General
Civic & Public Affairs: Civic & Public Affairs-General
Education: Education-General
Health: Health-General
Science: Science-General
Social Services: Social Services-General

Application Procedures

Initial Contact: a brief letter of inquiry and full proposal
Application Requirements: a description of organization, amount requested, purpose of funds sought, recently audited financial statement, and proof of tax-exempt status

Restrictions

Does not support individuals, religious organizations for sectarian purposes, or political or lobbying groups.

Additional Information

In 1996, Gillette Co. purchased Duracell. Gillette Co. operates its own giving program (see separate entry).

Corporate Officials

Edward F. DeGraan: president PRIM CORP EMPL president: Duracell International Inc. CORP AFFIL executive vice president: Gillette Co.

Grants Analysis

Disclosure Period: calendar year ending
Typical Range: $2,500 to $5,000

Recent Grants

Note: Grants derived from 1996 grants list.

Arts & Humanities
Charles Ives Center for Arts, Danbury, CT
Connecticut Public Television, New Britain, CT

Civic & Public Affairs
DATAHR, Brookfield, CT
Housatonk Valey Association, Cornwall Bridge, CT
National Urban League, New York, NY

Environment
World Wildlife Fund, Washington, DC

Health
Danbury Hospital, Danbury, CT

Science
Science Center of Connecticut, Hartford, CT

Social Services
Boys and Girls Club of America, New York, NY
United Way Northern Fairfield County, Danbury, CT

DURIRON CO., INC.

Company Contact

Dayton, OH

Company Description

Revenue: US$532,730,000
Employees: 3,900
SIC(s): 3491 Industrial Valves, 3492 Fluid Power Valves & Hose Fittings, 3561 Pumps & Pumping Equipment, 3569 General Industrial Machinery Nec.

Nonmonetary Support

Type: Loaned Employees; Workplace Solicitation

Duriron Foundation

Giving Contact

Janet E. Hicks, Administrative Assistant
PO Box 8820
Dayton, OH 45401
Phone: (937)476-6150

Description

Founded: 1983
EIN: 311080064
Organization Type: Corporate Foundation
Giving Locations: headquarters and operating communities.
Grant Types: Award, Capital, Challenge, General Support, Professorship, Research, Scholarship.

Financial Summary

Total Giving: $409,638 (1997); $151,623 (1996); $140,910 (1995)
Assets: $256,677 (1996); $125,385 (1995); $75,938 (1994)
Gifts Received: $339,347 (1996); $205,848 (1994); $228,608 (1993). Note: In 1993, contributions were received from Duriron Co.

Typical Recipients

Arts & Humanities: Arts Associations & Councils, Arts Institutes, Ballet, Community Arts, Arts & Humanities-General, Music, Public Broadcasting, Theater
Civic & Public Affairs: African American Affairs, Botanical Gardens/Parks, Business/Free Enterprise, Clubs, Community Foundations, Employment/Job Training, Civic & Public Affairs-General, Housing, Safety, Urban & Community Affairs, Women's Affairs
Education: Business Education, Colleges & Universities, Education Funds, Education Reform, Engineering/Technological Education, Education-General, Minority Education, Public Education (Precollege), Student Aid, Vocational & Technical Education
Health: Children's Health/Hospitals, Emergency/Ambulance Services, Health-General, Health Funds, Health Organizations
International: Foreign Educational Institutions, International Affairs
Religion: Churches
Science: Science Museums
Social Services: Big Brother/Big Sister, Community Service Organizations, Family Services, Homes, People with Disabilities, Scouts, Senior Services, Social Services-General, Special Olympics, United Funds/United Ways, YMCA/YWCA/YMHA/YWHA, Youth Organizations

Application Procedures

Initial Contact: All requests must be in writing and include a description of organization, its history, purpose of funds sought, and how the program relates to the needs of the community, amount requested, project budget indicating projected sources and uses of funds, and proof of tax-exempt status.
Deadlines: None.

Restrictions

Does not support individuals, religious organizations for sectarian purposes, political or lobbying groups, or organizations outside operating areas. Grants are seldom made for medical research, to organizations already receiving major support from the United Way, to organizations outside of the communities where the Duriron Co. has facilities, and to sponsor social events.

Corporate Officials

William M. Jordan: president, chief executive officer, chairman, director B Los Angeles, CA 1944. ED University of Houston (1967); Stanford University (1986). PRIM CORP EMPL president, chief executive officer, chairman, director: Duriron Co.
Gregory L. Smith: chief financial officer, treasurer PRIM CORP EMPL chief financial officer, treasurer: Duriron Co.

Foundation Officials

B. E. Hines: secretary B Dayton, OH 1943. ED Miami University. PRIM CORP EMPL senior vice president, chief administrative officer: Durivon Co.
William M. Jordan: president (see above)
Gregory L. Smith: treasurer (see above)

Grants Analysis

Disclosure Period: calendar year ending 1997
Total Grants: $409,638
Number of Grants: 33
Highest Grant: $122,325
Typical Range: $100 to $10,000

Recent Grants

Note: Grants derived from 1997 Form 990.

Civic & Public Affairs

5,000	CEO Council, Dayton, OH -- educational
4,000	Kalamazoo Foundation, Kalamazoo, MI -- for youth and elderly
1,500	Affordable Housing Fund, Dayton, OH -- social services

Education

5,000	Dayton-Montgomery County Scholars, Dayton, OH -- educational

5,000	Ohio Foundation of Independent Colleges, Dayton, OH

Social Services

40,500	United Way, Kalamazoo, MI -- for youth and elderly
6,000	Family and Children Services, Dayton, OH -- for youth and elderly
1,000	Daybreak, Dayton, OH -- for youth and elderly
600	United Way, Buffalo, NY -- social services

DYNAMET, INC.

Company Contact

Washington, PA
Web: http://www.dynamet.com

Company Description

Employees: 280
SIC(s): 3356 Nonferrous Rolling & Drawing Nec, 3463 Nonferrous Forgings, 3599 Industrial Machinery Nec.

Giving Contact

Barbra Savarno, Treasurer & Executive Secretary
195 Museum Rd.
Washington, PA 15301
Phone: (412)228-1000
Fax: (412)228-2087

Description

Organization Type: Corporate Giving Program
Giving Locations: PA: Pittsburgh
Grant Types: General Support.

Financial Summary

Total Giving: $785,640 (1998); $767,620 (1997); $503,640 (1996). Note: Contributes through corporate direct giving program only. Foundation dissolved in 1997.
Giving Analysis: Giving for 1998 includes: foundation ($775,640); foundation grants to United Way ($10,000)
Assets: $21,446,952 (1998); $18,455,525 (1997); $10,375,126 (1996)
Gifts Received: $7,304,979 (1997); $1,172,500 (1996); $500,000 (1993). Note: Contributions received from Dynamet, Inc.

Typical Recipients

Arts & Humanities: Arts Centers, Arts Funds, Arts Institutes, Ballet, Film & Video, Historic Preservation, History & Archaeology, Libraries, Museums/Galleries, Music, Opera, Performing Arts, Public Broadcasting, Theater
Civic & Public Affairs: Economic Development, Employment/Job Training, Housing, Parades/Festivals, Philanthropic Organizations, Public Policy, Urban & Community Affairs, Zoos/Aquariums
Education: Colleges & Universities, Economic Education, Education Reform, Engineering/Technological Education, Education-General, Preschool Education, Religious Education, Science/Mathematics Education, Secondary Education (Public), Special Education
Environment: Resource Conservation
Health: Cancer, Children's Health/Hospitals, Clinics/Medical Centers, Diabetes, Emergency/Ambulance Services, Eyes/Blindness, Health Organizations, Hospices, Hospitals, Kidney, Medical Rehabilitation, Medical Research, Mental Health, Single-Disease Health Associations
International: Health Care/Hospitals, International Affairs, International Organizations, International Relations
Religion: Religious Organizations, Religious Welfare, Seminaries
Science: Scientific Centers & Institutes, Scientific Organizations, Scientific Research
Social Services: Camps, Child Welfare, Community Centers, Community Service Organizations, Food/Clothing Distribution, Homes, People with Disabilities, Recreation & Athletics, Scouts, Senior Services, Shelters/Homelessness, Special Olympics, Substance Abuse, United Funds/United Ways, Volunteer Services, YMCA/YWCA/YMHA/YWHA, Youth Organizations

Contributions Analysis

Giving Priorities: Focus on education, community services, and religious welfare.
Arts & Humanities: 3%. Supports museums, cultural resources, performing arts, music, and theater.
Education: 52%. Funds educational programs, and colleges and universities.
Health: 5%. Supports hospitals, rehabilitation centers, and single-disease concerns.
Religion: 35%. Funds religious welfare causes.
Science: 1%. Funds the Carnegie Institute, for scientific research.
Social Services: 3%. Supports handicapped services, volunteer services, senior care, people with mental disabilities, YM/YWCA, and youth services.
Note: Total contributions in 1998.

Application Procedures

Initial Contact: Contact co.

Additional Information

Foundation has recently dissolved; contact company for direct giving.

Corporate Officials

Alan Rossin: materials director PRIM CORP EMPL materials director: Dynamet Inc.
Bob Torcolini: president PRIM CORP EMPL president: Dynamet Inc.

Grants Analysis

Disclosure Period: calendar year ending 1998
Total Grants: $775,640*
Number of Grants: 50
Average Grant: $15,513
Highest Grant: $250,000
Typical Range: $1,000 to $50,000
***Note:** Giving excludes United Way.

Recent Grants

Note: Grants derived from 1998 Form 990.

Arts & Humanities

10,000	Carnegie Institute, Pittsburgh, PA -- Scientific research
10,000	Pittsburgh Trust for Cultural Resources, Pittsburgh, PA -- Recreational cultural organization
3,000	Pittsburgh Symphony Association, Pittsburgh, PA -- Recreational Programs
2,000	Civic Light Opera Association, Pittsburgh, PA -- Non-profit recreational programs
1,000	Carnegie Institute, Pittsburgh, PA -- Powdermill Natural Program
1,000	Meadowcraft Foundation, Avella, PA -- Recreational organization
1,000	Pittsburgh Ballet Theatre, Pittsburgh, PA -- Recreational programs
1,000	River City Brass Band, Pittsburgh, PA -- Non-profit recreational programs
1,000	WQED Pittsburgh, Pittsburgh, PA -- Recreational programs
500	Saltworks Theatre Company, Pittsburgh, PA -- Educational programs for youth
250	Pittsburgh Children's Museum, Pittsburgh, PA -- Child educational programs
250	Pittsburgh History & Landmarks Foundation, Pittsburgh, PA -- Recreational Programs
250	Pittsburgh Public Theater Corporation, Pittsburgh, PA -- Non-profit recreational programs

Civic & Public Affairs

2,000	Vocational Rehabiliation Center of Allegheny Co, Pittsburgh, PA -- Recreational programs
1,500	Zoological Society of Pittsburgh, Pittsburgh, PA -- Educational programs
1,000	Bob Prince Chartities, Pittsburgh, PA -- Handicapped children foundation
1,000	Canonsburg July Fourth Celebration, Inc, Canonsburg, PA -- Recreational programs
1,000	Try Again Homes, Inc., Pittsburgh, PA -- Housing program
500	National Flag Foundation, Pittsburgh, PA -- Educational programs

Education

250,000	Washington and Jefferson College, Washington, PA -- Educational assistance
125,000	Carnegie Mellon University, Pittsburgh, PA -- Educational programs
25,000	South Dakota School of Mines and Technology, Rapid City, SD -- Educational assitance
3,500	Alfred University, Alfred, NY -- Educational programs
2,500	Curtis High School Foundation, Pittsburgh, PA -- Educational assistance
1,000	Economic Education Foundation, Coal Center, PA -- Private Enterprise Market System
450	Washington and Jefferson College, Washington, PA -- Scientific research

Environment

300	Western Pennsylvania Conservancy, Pittsburgh, PA -- Agricultural organization

Health

25,000	Washington Hospital Foundation, Inc., Washington, PA -- Scientific charity
5,000	Childrens Hospital of Pittsburgh, Pittsburgh, PA -- Scientific research
2,500	Epilepsy Foundation of Western Pa, Pittsburgh, PA -- Epilesy research
2,440	Washington Hospital Foundation, Inc., Washington, PA -- Scientific charity
1,500	Morton Plant Mease Health Care, Inc., Clearwater, FL -- Scientific research
1,000	Family House, Inc., Pittsburgh, PA -- Terminally ill charitable organization
500	Southwinds, Inc., Carnegie, PA -- Assistance with aging adults with multiple di

International

1,000	World Affairs Council of Pittsburgh, Pittsburgh, PA -- International educational programs

Religion

250,000	Pittsburgh Theological Seminary, Pittsburgh, PA -- Educational assistance
20,000	Coalition for Christian Outreach, Pittsburgh, PA -- Ministry on college campus
5,000	St. Vincent Archabbey, Latrobe, PA -- Church related renovations
2,500	Cecil Christian Mission, Pittsburgh, PA -- Church building fund

Science

1,000	American Society for Mentals Foundation, Materials Park, OH -- Education and research programs

Social Services

10,000	The United Way of Southwest Pennsylvania, Pittsburgh, PA -- United Way
5,000	Wesley Institute, Pittsburgh, PA -- Educational assistance
1,000	Association for Retarded Citzens, Meadow Lands, PA -- Program for employment opportunities to

1,000 Give Kids the World, Kissimmee, FL -- Childrens leukemia society
1,000 Pittsburgh Special Olympics Organization, Pittsburgh, PA -- Children's recreation
1,000 Washington-Greene County Branch, Washington, PA -- Scientific research
1,000 Young Men's Christian Association of Pittsburgh, Pittsburgh, PA -- Young mens christian programs
1,000 Young Women's Christian Association of Pittsburgh, Pittsburgh, PA -- Young women's christian programs
500 Mom's House of Pittsburgh, Inc., Pittsburgh, PA -- Educational assistance to young mothers
500 National Child Safety Council, Coraopolos, PA -- Educational programs

EASTERN BANK

Company Contact

Salem, MA
Web: http://www.easternbank.com

Company Description

Assets: US$2,020,800,000
Employees: 731

Corporate Sponsorship

Type: Arts & cultural events; Music & entertainment events; Pledge-a-thon; Sports events

Eastern Bank Charitable Foundation

Giving Contact

Sumner W. Jones, Executive Vice President
Eastern Bank
217 Essex Street
Salem, MA 01970
Phone: (978)740-6319
Fax: (978)740-6329

Description

Founded: 1985
EIN: 223317340
Organization Type: Corporate Foundation
Giving Locations: MA: market area
Grant Types: Capital, General Support, Scholarship.

Financial Summary

Total Giving: $475,000 (fiscal year ending October 31, 1999 approx); $448,657 (fiscal 1998); $367,295 (fiscal 1997). Note: Contributes through foundation only.
Giving Analysis: Giving for fiscal 1998 includes: foundation grants to United Way ($45,175)
Assets: $11,008,666 (fiscal 1998); $3,090,593 (fiscal 1996); $2,277,413 (fiscal 1995)
Gifts Received: $202,396 (fiscal 1995); $105 (fiscal 1993). Note: Foundation receives contributions from Eastern Bank.

Typical Recipients

Arts & Humanities: Arts Centers, Community Arts, Arts & Humanities-General, Historic Preservation, History & Archaeology, Libraries, Museums/Galleries, Performing Arts
Civic & Public Affairs: African American Affairs, Asian American Affairs, Civil Rights, Clubs, Community Foundations, Economic Development, Employment/Job Training, Ethnic Organizations, Civic & Public Affairs-General, Hispanic Affairs, Housing, Native American Affairs, Nonprofit Management, Parades/Festivals, Safety, Urban & Community Affairs, Women's Affairs
Education: Afterschool/Enrichment Programs, Arts/Humanities Education, Business-School Partnerships, Colleges & Universities, Community & Junior Colleges, Education-General, Medical Education, Private Education (Precollege), Science/Mathematics Education, Student Aid
Health: AIDS/HIV, Children's Health/Hospitals, Clinics/Medical Centers, Health-General, Health Organizations, Heart, Hospices, Hospitals, Preventive Medicine/Wellness Organizations
Religion: Jewish Causes, Religious Welfare
Social Services: Camps, Child Welfare, Community Centers, Community Service Organizations, Delinquency & Criminal Rehabilitation, Domestic Violence, Family Services, Food/Clothing Distribution, People with Disabilities, Recreation & Athletics, Shelters/Homelessness, Social Services-General, United Funds/United Ways, YMCA/YWCA/YMHA/YWHA, Youth Organizations

Contributions Analysis

Giving Priorities: Primary support for health organizations and social services.
Arts & Humanities: 6%. Funds public broadcasting, libraries, museums, theaters, and community centers.
Civic & Public Affairs: 7%. Supports housing and community and economic development.
Education: 9%. Supports scholarship funds, colleges and universities, public and private elementary and secondary schools, and public libraries.
Health: 67%. Single-disease organizations, the Red Cross, United Way, shelters and services for the elderly, the abused, and the disadvantaged. Supports youth concerns, such as YMCAs, Boys and Girls Clubs, Junior Achievement, and local youth groups.
International: 2%.
Religion: 9%.
Note: Total contributions in 1998.

Application Procedures

Initial Contact: Contact foundation for guidelines, then letter or full proposal.
Application Requirements: For grants under $10,000: brief letter describing background of organization, amount requested and purpose of funds sought, and proof of tax-exempt status; grants of $10,000 or more must be requested using Associated Grantmakers of Massachusetts application form.
Deadlines: For grants $10,000 to $25,000: the 15th of May or November; for grants of less than $10,000: None.
Decision Notification: Major gifts ($10,000 to $25,000) are considered in June and December.

Restrictions

Recipients of major gifts may not reapply for funding for three years.
Does not support individuals or political or lobbying groups.

Additional Information

Foundation divides its annual giving budget, with half of contributions going to a few major gifts ($10,000 to $25,000), and half distributed broadly with smaller grants.
Publications: Annual Report

Corporate Officials

Sumner Jones: executive vice president PRIM CORP EMPL executive vice president: Eastern Bank.
Stanley J. Lukowski: president PRIM CORP EMPL president: Eastern Bank ADD CORP EMPL chairman: Eastern Bank Corp.; chairman: Eastern Bank and Trust Co. Inc.; chairman: Eastern Securities Corp. NONPR AFFIL chairman: Massachusetts Bankers Association.

Foundation Officials

James C. Callahan, Jr.: trustee
William F. Collins, Jr.: trustee
Fredrick England, Junior: trustee
Daryl A. Hellman: trustee
Andre C. Jasse, Jr.: trustee ED Georgia Institute of Technology BS (1963); Boston College LLB (1966). PRIM CORP EMPL chairman: Brown Rudnick Freed Gesmer. CORP AFFIL secretary: WNA Carthage Inc.; clerk: WNA Comet East Inc.; director: Waddington North America; vice president: Filemark Corp.; clerk: Pericomp Corp.
Joseph A. Jones: trustee
Wendell J. Knox: trustee
Laurence B. Leonard, Jr.: trustee
Nills Peterson: trustee
John A. Shane: trustee

Grants Analysis

Disclosure Period: fiscal year ending October 31, 1998
Total Grants: $403,482*
Number of Grants: 200
Average Grant: $2,017
Highest Grant: $25,000
Typical Range: $100 to $6,000
***Note:** Giving excludes United Way.

Recent Grants

Note: Grants derived from 1997 Form 990.

Arts & Humanities

10,000 Lynn Arts, Lynn, MA
3,000 Community Minority Cultural Center, Lynn, MA
2,500 Peabody Essex Museum
1,000 Listening Play
1,000 Salem Heritage Days, Salem, MA

Civic & Public Affairs

15,000 SCC Foundation
10,000 Women's Friend Society
3,000 Lynn Rotary Club, Lynn, MA
3,000 Salem Housing Authority, Salem, MA
2,500 Christmas in April
2,500 Essex County Community Organization, Peabody, MA
2,500 Salem Harbor Community Development Corporation, Salem, MA
2,300 Eastern Bank Charity Classic
2,280 Triangle
2,000 Maiden St. Patrick's Day Road Race
1,200 Older Workers Changing Job Market Committee
1,000 Richard Driscoll Testimonial
1,000 Yankee Clipper Council

Education

10,000 Marion Court College
10,000 North Shore Community College Foundation, Danvers, MA
5,500 Agganis Scholarship Foundation, Salem, MA
3,900 St. John's Preparatory School
3,124 Salem State College, Salem, MA
3,000 Biomedical Science Careers Project, Boston, MA
2,250 Steppingstone Foundation
2,000 Northeastern University, Boston, MA
1,100 Hellenic College Holy Cross

Health

20,000 North Shore Medical Center Foundation
5,250 Maiden Hospital
2,500 Health and Education Services, Beverly, MA
2,050 St. Elizabeth Medical Center, Granite City, IL
2,000 Salem Community Wellness
1,850 Winchester Hospital, Winchester, MA

Religion

15,968 Catholic Charities North
2,350 Anti-Defamation League of New England

Social Services

50,000 United Way of Massachusetts Bay, Boston, MA

20,000	Saugus Family YMCA
15,000	YMCA, Lynn, MA
10,000	New England Home for the Deaf, Danvers, MA
10,000	Supportive Living
6,000	Friends of Friendship
5,000	Children's and Family Service of North Shore
5,000	YWCA
3,980	Boys and Girls Club, Lynn, MA
3,725	Family and Children's Service of Greater Lynn
1,857	Hannah Charity Golf Classic
1,500	Fred Berry Charity Open
1,160	My Brother's Table, Lynn, MA
1,000	Project Playground
1,000	Tri-City Council on Youth and Family Services

Eastern Enterprises

Company Contact

9 Riverside Rd.
Weston, MA 02493
Phone: (781)647-2300
Fax: (781)647-2398
Web: http://www.efu.com

Company Description

Assets: US$1,421,600,000
Employees: 2,955
SIC(s): 4449 Water Transportation of Freight Nec, 4924 Natural Gas Distribution, 6719 Holding Companies Nec.

Nonmonetary Support

Type: Loaned Employees
Volunteer Programs: Eastern Enterprises promotes volunteerism by making available to employees booklets and brochures of organizations in need of service.

Eastern Enterprises Foundation

Giving Contact

Susan E. Carlson, Manager, Eastern Enterprises Foundation
Eastern Enterprises
Email: scarlson@efu.com
Web: http://www.efu.com/foundation.html

Description

EIN: 046109087
Organization Type: Corporate Foundation
Giving Locations: company's service territory.
Grant Types: Matching, Multiyear/Continuing Support, Project.
Note: Employee matching gift ratio: 2 to 1; 3 to 1 to organizations with which employees are actively involved.

Financial Summary

Total Giving: $1,050,000 (1999 approx); $1,016,800 (1998 approx); $806,821 (1997). Note: Contributes through corporate direct giving program and foundation.
Giving Analysis: Giving for 1996 includes: foundation ($717,795); foundation matching gifts ($248,591); 1998: foundation ($757,738); corporate direct giving ($259,062)
Gifts Received: $625,076 (1992); $547,336 (1991); $166,906 (1990). Note: The foundation receives gifts from Eastern Enterprises and its subsidiaries.

Typical Recipients

Arts & Humanities: Museums/Galleries, Public Broadcasting, Theater
Civic & Public Affairs: Zoos/Aquariums
Education: Colleges & Universities, Elementary Education (Private)
Social Services: Youth Organizations

Contributions Analysis

Giving Priorities: Primary focus is on programs that have long-term potential to improve the quality of life for young people.
Arts & Humanities: About 30%. Giving primarily goes to local art and science museums, symphony orchestras, and aquariums. Matching gift program also supports arts and humanties organizations.
Education: 25% to 30%. Focuses on educational programs for youth and higher education. Matching gift program also supports educational programs and institutions.
Health: 40% to 45%. Supports the United Way. Funds a limited range of health and human service organizations, primarily supporting youth programs which offer lasting solutions to problems. Administers the Eastern Enterprises Neighborhood Matching Fund, which matches neighborhood dollars to entrepreneurial programs for youth, based on the recommendations of an employee review committee. Matching gift program (in response to giving by employees, retirees, and trustees) supports a wide range of health and human service organizations.

Application Procedures

Initial Contact: Request guidelines.
Application Requirements: The foundation encourages use of the Associated Grantmakers of Massachusetts Common Proposal Format. In unavailable, a completed application should include proposal signed by authorized nonprofit officer describing history of organization, amount requested, purpose of funds sought, other sources of funding, current audited financial statement, copy of IRS 501 (c)(3) certificate and letter, latest Form 990 and a list of the board of directors. Proposals must be signed or approved in writing by the chief executive officer or development director of the organization.
Deadlines: Deadlines fluctuate; contact foundation for exact dates.
Review Process: After preliminary review, foundation may request additional information about organization or program; the foundation does not typically conduct personal interviews; applicants will receive written notice of decision. Applicants are limited to one proposal per year, additional proposals may be submitted one year from the date funding was provided or funding was denied.
Decision Notification: Within four months of proposal receipt.
Notes: Application materials should be kept to a minimum to avoid wasting charitable funds. Therefore, videos and other elaborate presentations are discouraged.

Restrictions

Does not support individuals, religious organizations for sectarian purposes, political or lobbying groups, awards, events, dinners, sponsorships, or advertisements.

Additional Information

The Eastern Enterprises Foundation represents the interests of Eastern Enterprises (Weston, MA), Boston Gas Company (Boston, MA), Midland Enterprises (Cincinnati, OH), WaterPro Supplies Corp. (Eden Prairie, MN). Each company administers its own giving program and the total figure represents contributions made by all entities.
In September 1998, Essex Gas Co. became a wholly-owned subsidiary of Eastern Enterprises. Eastern entered into an agreement to acquire EnergyNorth, Inc. in July 1999, with an expected outcome in mid-2000. In August 1999, Colonial Gas Company became a wholly-owned subsidiary of Eastern.
In November 1999, Eastern Enterprise entered into an agreement to be acquired by Keyspan Corporation. This transaction in expected to close within the next year.
Publications: Grant Application Guidelines

Corporate Officials

Michael J. Cawley: vice president risk management B Boston, MA 1950. ED Babson College; College of the Holy Cross. PRIM CORP EMPL vice president risk management: Eastern Enterprises. CORP AFFIL instructor: Bentley College; vice president: Eastern Enterprises Vol Associates. NONPR AFFIL director: Massachusetts Risk Insurance Management Society; president: Massachusetts Self Insurance Association.
Walter J. Flaherty: chief financial officer, senior vice president B 1948. ED Providence College BS (1970); Babson College MBA (1973); Bentley College MS (1981). PRIM CORP EMPL chief financial officer, senior vice president: Eastern Enterprises. CORP AFFIL officer: Boston Gas Co. NONPR AFFIL overseer: Boston Museum Science.
James J. Harper: vice president, controller PRIM CORP EMPL vice president, controller: Eastern Enterprises. CORP AFFIL member: Tax Executives Institute; member: American Gas Association; member: Financial Executive Institute. NONPR AFFIL member: American Institute CPAs.
J. Atwood Ives: chairman, chief executive officer, trustee B Atlanta, GA 1936. ED Yale University BA (1959); Stanford University Graduate School of Business Administration MBA (1961); Harvard University Advanced Management Program AMP (1975). PRIM CORP EMPL chairman, chief executive officer, trustee: Eastern Enterprises. CORP AFFIL director: Neiman Marcus Group Inc.; trustee Mutual Funds, director: Massachusetts Finance Services Co. NONPR AFFIL corporate advisory board: Stanford University Graduate School Business; director: United Way Massachusetts Bay; director: Massachusetts Business Roundtable; trustee: Museum Fine Arts; corporate advisory board: Boston College School of Management.
L. William Law, Jr.: senior vice president, general counsel, secretary B Clovis, NM 1945. ED Harvard University AB (1967); Harvard University JD (1970). PRIM CORP EMPL senior vice president, general counsel, secretary: Eastern Enterprises.
Jane W. McCahon: vice president corporate relations ED Bentley College (1982); Suffolk University (1988). PRIM CORP EMPL vice president corporate relations: Eastern Enterprises.
Fred C. Raskin: president, chief operating officer B New York, NY 1948. ED Syracuse University BS (1970); New York University JD (1973). PRIM CORP EMPL president, chief operating officer: Eastern Enterprises. CORP AFFIL president: River Fleets Inc.; president: Red Circle Transport Co.; president: Minnesota Harbor Service Inc.; president: Ohio River Co.; president: Hartle Marine Corp.; president: Midland Enterprise Inc.; president: Capital Marine Supply Inc.; president: Federation Barge Lines Inc. NONPR AFFIL member: Finance Executive Institute.
Terry D. Ray: vice president business development B Elmira, NY 1945. ED Marietta College (1967). PRIM CORP EMPL vice president business development: Eastern Enterprises.
Jean A. Scholtens: vice president, treasurer B Milwaukee, WI 1949. ED Luther College (1971); Dartmouth College MBA (1979). PRIM CORP EMPL vice president, treasurer: Eastern Enterprises ADD CORP EMPL vice president treasurer: Eastern Enterprises Vol Associates.

Foundation Officials

Susan E. Carlson: manager PRIM CORP EMPL senior: Eastern Enterprises.
Walter J. Flaherty: trustee (see above)
J. Atwood Ives: trustee (see above)
Chester R. Messer: trustee B Concord, NH 1942. ED Harvard University Advanced Management Program;

Northeastern University; University of New Hampshire BA (1963). PRIM CORP EMPL president, chief operating officer: Boston Gas Co. ADD CORP EMPL senior vice president: Establishmentern Enterprises. NONPR AFFIL director: Institute Gas Technology; director: New England Gas Association; director: American Gas Association.

Fred C. Raskin: trustee (see above)

Grants Analysis

Disclosure Period: calendar year ending 1998
Total Grants: $757,738*
Number of Grants: 280
Average Grant: $2,706
Highest Grant: $15,000
Typical Range: $1,000 to $5,000
***Note:** Analysis is provided by foundation; giving excludes corporate donations.

Recent Grants

Note: Grants derived from 1993 Form 990.

Arts & Humanities

18,100	Museum of Fine Arts, Boston, MA
18,050	Boston Symphony Orchestra, Boston, MA
17,500	Concord Museum, Concord, MA
11,900	Boston Ballet, Boston, MA
8,750	Huntington Theater Company, Huntington, NY
6,300	Wang Center for Performing Arts, Boston, MA
5,700	WGBH Educational Foundation, Springfield, MA
4,000	Handel and Haydn Society, Boston, MA

Civic & Public Affairs

13,000	New England Aquarium, Boston, MA
10,000	Jane Doe Safety Fund
10,000	Partnership, Boston, MA
8,500	Massachusetts Association, Boston, MA
8,000	City of Boston Department, Boston, MA
7,500	Main Street Point Pleasant, Point Pleasant, NJ
7,000	Associated Grantmakers, Boston, MA
5,200	First Night, Boston, MA

Education

38,951	Northeastern University, Boston, MA
13,300	Harvard College, Cambridge, MA
11,370	Harvard University, Cambridge, MA
7,780	Cornell University, Ithaca, NY
7,500	Thompson Island Outward Bound, Boston, MA
5,610	Paducah Junior College, Paducah, KY
5,000	Buckingham Browne and Nichols School, Cambridge, MA
5,000	Stanford University, Stanford, CA
4,700	Dartmouth College, Hanover, NH
4,400	Boston College, Chestnut Hill, MA
3,520	University of Massachusetts, Amherst, MA
3,100	Wentworth Institute of Technology, Boston, MA

Environment

5,520	Massachusetts Audubon Society, Lincoln, MA

Health

10,749	C. Eileen Tangvik Memorial Cancer Foundation
7,500	Illinois Elks Crippled Children's Corp, Chatman, IL
5,000	Emerson Health System, Concord, MA
4,144	American Cancer Society, Boston, MA
3,830	Children's Medical Center Corp, Boston, MA
3,340	Schepens Eye Research Institute, Boston, MA

Religion

5,000	Catholic Charities, Boston, MA

Science

4,860	Museum of Science, Boston, MA

Social Services

14,675	United Way, Boston, MA
14,500	Project Bread/Walk for Hunger, Boston, MA
10,000	Lowell Humane Society, Lowell, MA
8,225	United Way Massachusetts Bay, Boston, MA
6,620	Bridge Over Troubled Waters, Boston, MA
6,000	Greater Boston Food Bank, Boston, MA
5,000	Judge Baker Children's Center, Boston, MA
5,000	Massachusetts YMCA Youth and Govern, Boston, MA
5,000	Parents and Children's Services, Boston, MA
5,000	Shelter, Boston, MA
4,000	Share New England, Boston, MA
3,650	Rosie's Place, Boston, MA
3,250	Northeast Home for Little Wanderers, Boston, MA

EASTMAN CHEMICAL CO.

Company Contact

Kingsport, TN
Web: http://www.eastman.com

Company Description

Revenue: US$4,481,000,000
Employees: 17,500
Fortune Rank: 349, per FORTUNE Magazine's list of 500 Largest U.S. Corporations (1999).
FF 349
SIC(s): 2819 Industrial Inorganic Chemicals Nec, 2821 Plastics Materials & Resins, 2823 Cellulosic Manmade Fibers, 2865 Cyclic Crudes & Intermediates.

Corporate Sponsorship

Type: Arts & cultural events; Music & entertainment events; Festivals/fairs

Giving Contact

Paul W. Montgomery, Manager, Community Relations
Eastman Chemical Co.
PO Box 431
Kingsport, TN 37662
Phone: (423)229-1413
Fax: (423)229-8280

Description

Organization Type: Corporate Giving Program
Giving Locations: headquarters and operating communities.
Grant Types: General Support.

Financial Summary

Total Giving: $2,900,000 (2000 approx); $2,400,000 (1999 approx); $2,400,000 (1998 approx). Note: Contributes through corporate direct giving program only.

Typical Recipients

Arts & Humanities: Arts & Humanities-General
Civic & Public Affairs: Civic & Public Affairs-General
Education: Education-General
Health: Health-General
International: International-General
Science: Science-General
Social Services: Social Services-General

Contributions Analysis

Giving Priorities: Supports local educational institutions and programs, human services, and health care. Additional interests include the arts, the sciences, and civic organizations.

Application Procedures

Initial Contact: Letter or full proposal.
Application Requirements: A description of the organization, amount requested, purpose of funds sought, and proof of tax-exempt status.

Restrictions

The company does not support organizations without 501(c)(3) status.

Corporate Officials

Earnest W. Deavenport, Jr.: chairman, chief executive officer, director B Macon, MS 1938. ED Missisippi State University BS (1960); Massachusetts Institute of Technology MS (1985). PRIM CORP EMPL chairman, chief executive officer, director: Eastman Chemical Co. CORP AFFIL director: First American Corp. NONPR AFFIL member, director: Chemical Manufacturers Association; member executive committee: Society Chemical Industry; chairman: American Plastics Council.

Giving Program Officials

Paul Montgomery: senior public affairs representative PRIM CORP EMPL public affairs representative: Eastman Chemical Co.

Foundation Officials

Paul Montgomery: senior public affairs representative (see above)

EASTMAN KODAK CO.

 Number 78 of Top 100 Corporate Givers

Company Contact

Rochester, NY
Web: http://www.kodak.com

Company Description

Revenue: US$13,410,000,000
Profit: US$1,390,000,000
Employees: 86,200
Fortune Rank: 124, per FORTUNE Magazine's list of 500 Largest U.S. Corporations (1999).
FF 124
SIC(s): 2843 Surface Active Agents, 2865 Cyclic Crudes & Intermediates, 3081 Unsupported Plastics Film & Sheet, 3861 Photographic Equipment & Supplies.

Operating Locations

Australia: KLIKK Ltd., Carlton; Bondpark Pty. Ltd., Carlton; Mafano Pty. Ltd., Carlton; Kodak (Australasia) Pty. Ltd., Coburg; Pacific Film Superannuation Fund Nominees Pty. Ltd., Coburg; Replace-A-Film Laboratories Pty. Ltd., Coburg; Hermes Precisa Pty. Ltd., Erskineville; Intercraft Pty. Ltd., Kingsgrove; Dependable Mailing Services P/L, Milton; National Photographic Marketing Pty. Ltd., Southport; Austria: Fotokarussell Filmentwicklungs GmbH, Vienna; Fotoservice Grobhandelsgesmbh, Vienna; Kodak Fotoservice GmbH, Vienna; Kodak GmbH, Vienna; Kodak Imaging Services GmbH, Vienna; Belgium: Color Star Benelux SPRL, Brussels, Brabant; Litto-Color NV, Oostende, Flandre-Orientale; Kodak NV, Vilvoorde, Brabant; Brazil: Curt e Alex Associados Laboratorio Cinematografico Ltda., Sao Paulo; Eastman Chemical Brasileira Ltda., Sao Paulo; Canada: Colortron Photo Services Ltd., Burlington; Kodak Canada Inc., Toronto; Chile: Full Color Ltda., Santiago; Kodak Chilena SA Fotografica, Santiago; Muebles Sur Ltda., Santiago; Denmark: Sanofi Winthrop AS, Glostrup, Copenhagen; Kodak & H-Color de Forenede Fotolaboratorier A/S, Risskov, Arhus; Kodak A/S, Tastrup,

Arhus; Dominican Republic: Kodak Dominicana C por A; Finland: Kodak OY, Vantaa, Uusimaa; France: Kodak Villiot, Chalon Sur Saone; Eastman Software SA, Charenton Le Pont; Sterling Organics Sari, Clichy-la-Garenne; Kodak (Laboratoires et Services), Creteil, Val-de-Marne; Difim SA, Haubourdin, Nord; Union Chimique pour le Marche Commun, Longvic, Cote D'Or; Copylab SA, Lutry, Vaud; Agence Ernoult Features, Paris, Ville-de-Paris; Image Bank France, Paris, Ville-de-Paris; Kodak Pathe SA, Paris, Ville-de-Paris; Kodak SA, Paris, Ville-de-Paris; SCI et Fonciere Paris Province, Paris, Ville-de-Paris; Kodak Photo Service SA, Renens, Vaud; Litto Color, Roncq, Nord; Kodak Images Services, Tremblay en France; Germany: Colarvit Fotolabor GmbH, Freiburg, Baden-Wuerttemberg; Sterling Pharma GmbH, Norderstedt, Hamburg; Elon Informationssysteme GmbH, Ostfildern, Baden-Wuerttemberg; Kodak Dentalprodukte (Europa) GmbH, Ostfildern, Baden-Wuerttemberg; Kodak Rapidcolor Fotogrosslabor GmbH, Schloss Holte-Stukenbrok; Kodak AG, Stuttgart, Baden-Wuerttemberg; Kodak Fotoservice Nord GmbH, Stuttgart, Baden-Wuerttemberg; Kodak Unterstuetzungs GmbH, Stuttgart, Baden-Wuerttemberg; Kodak Verwaltung Und Serviceleistungen GmbH, Stuttgart, Baden-Wuerttemberg; Kontas Werbeagentur GmbH, Stuttgart, Baden-Wuerttemberg; Greece: Kodak (Near East) Inc., Amaroussion; Sterling Health LLC, Athens, Attiki; Hong Kong: TIB (Hong Kong) Ltd., Causeway Bay; Eastman Kodak Asia Pacific Ltd., North Point; Kodak (China) Ltd., North Point; Kodak (Export Sales) Ltd., North Point; Kodak (Far East) Ltd., North Point; Honduras: Sterling Products International SA, Tegucigalpa; Hungary: Kodak KFT, Budapest; India: Kodak India Ltd., Mumbai; Italy: Kodak SpA, Cinisello Balsamo, Lombardia; Japan: Marutan KK (Yokohama Sales Office), Fujisawa, Kanagawa; East West Sigma, Tokyo; Eastman Kodak (Japan) Ltd., Tokyo; Kodak Engineering Service Ltd., Tokyo; Kodak Far East Purchasing Co. Japan Branch, Tokyo; Kodak Imagica KK, Tokyo; Kodak Japan Ltd., Tokyo; Kodak Lab Tokyo KK, Tokyo; Kodak Japan Industries Ltd., Yokohama, Kanagawa; Republic of Korea: Kodak Korea Ltd., Seoul; Luxembourg: Photolux SARL, Luxembourg; Mexico: American Photo SA de CV, Ciudad de Mexico; Kodak Mexicana SA de CV, Ciudad de Mexico; Kodak de Mexico SA de CV, Guadalajara; Industria Mexicana de Fotocopiadoras SA de CV, Tijuana; Mauritius: Sterling Products International SARL, Port Louis; Malaysia: Kodak (Malaysia) Sdn. Bhd., Petaling Jaya, Selangor; Komal Sdn. Bhd., Petaling Jaya, Selangor; Nicaragua: Laboratorios Farmaceuticos de Nicaragua SA, Managua; Norway: Kodak Fotoservice AS, Kolbotn, Akershus; Kodak Image Center AS, Kolbotn, Akershus; Kodak Norge AS, Kolbotn, Akershus; Sanofi Winthrop AS, Osteras, Akershus; New Zealand: Kodak New Zealand Ltd., Auckland; Panama: Kodak Panama Ltd., Panama City; Sterling Products International SA, Panama City; Peru: Kodak Peruana Ltda., Lima; Philippines: Kodak Phils Ltd., Makati City, Manila; Portugal: Kodak Portuguesa Lda., Linda-a-Velha, Oeiras; Laboratorios Kodak Lda., Linda-a-Velha, Oeiras; Russia: Kodak AO, Moscow; Singapore: Eastman Chemical Asia Pacific Pte Ltd., Singapore; Fotoplus (Singapore) PTE Ltd., Singapore; Kodak (Singapore) Pte. Ltd., Singapore; Sanofi (Singapore), Singapore; Spain: Kodak SA, Las Rozas de Madrid, Madrid; Laboratorios Kodak SA, Madrid; Sweden: Hasselblads Fotografiska AB; Kodak AB; Sanofi Winthrop AB, Solna, Stockholm; Switzerland: Kodak SA, Lausanne, Vaud; Winthrop AG, Muenchenstein; Thailand: Kodak Thailand Ltd., Bangkok; Kodak Dealer Services (Thailand) Ltd., Samsennai Phyathai; Turkey: Kodak East (Merkezi New York Turikye Istanbul Subesi), Istanbul; Taiwan: Kodak Taiwan Ltd., Taipei; BASO Precision Optics Ltd., Tan-tzu; United Kingdom: Miller Brothers Hall & Co. Ltd., Aberdeen, Grampian; Scientific Imaging Systems Ltd., Cambridge, Cambridgeshire; Sanofi Winthrop (Overseas) Ltd., Guildford, Surrey; Winpharm Ltd., Guildford, Surrey; Eastman Kodak Co., Hemel Hempstead, Hertfordshire; Hedley Taylor Ltd., Hemel Hempstead, Hertfordshire; Imaging Services Ltd., Hemel Hempstead, Hertfordshire; Kodak (Eastern Europe) Ltd., Hemel Hempstead, Hertfordshire; Kodak Export Ltd., Hemel Hempstead, Hertfordshire; Kodak Finance Ltd., Hemel Hempstead, Hertfordshire; Kodak Leasing (United Kingdom) Ltd., Hemel Hempstead, Hertfordshire; Kodak Ltd., Hemel Hempstead, Hertfordshire; Kodak Manufacturing Ltd., Hemel Hempstead, Hertfordshire; Kodak Processing Companies Ltd., Hemel Hempstead, Hertfordshire; Kodak Research & Development Ltd., Hemel Hempstead, Hertfordshire; Kodak Service Solutions Ltd., Hemel Hempstead, Hertfordshire; Kodak UK Ltd., Hemel Hempstead, Hertfordshire; United Photofinishers Ltd., Hemel Hempstead, Hertfordshire; Bee Hive Hotel Ltd., London; Venezuela: Kodak de Venezuela SA, Caracas; Laboratorios Sterling de Venezuela SA, Caracas

Nonmonetary Support

Value: $100,000 (1996); $1,100,000 (1995); $16,500,000 (1994)
Type: Donated Equipment; Donated Products
Note: Co. donates property. Nonmonetary support budget is separate from the corporate giving budget.

Corporate Sponsorship

Type: Sports events
Contact: Ron Dickson, Corporate Marketing

Eastman Kodak Charitable Trust

Giving Contact

Essie L. Calhoun, President
Eastman Kodak Charitable Trust
343 State Street
Rochester, NY 14650-0517
Phone: (716)724-1376
Fax: (716)724-1376

Description

EIN: 166015274
Organization Type: Corporate Foundation
Giving Locations: nationally, especially in operating locations.
Grant Types: Award, Capital, Department, Emergency, Endowment, Fellowship, General Support, Matching, Multiyear/Continuing Support, Research, Scholarship.

Giving Philosophy

'Since its founding days, Eastman Kodak has recognized that the success of its business depends upon the vitality of the society in which the company lives. .. In our view, doing well financially as a business and doing good in the social sense are not separate concerns. The one is dependent upon the other, and both are important to the health of the company and the well-being of the communities in which Kodak has made sizable commitments. .. Like any other business activity, these investments are managed and administered in a way that increases the probability of substantial returns. .. for the company, for the communities where it operates, and for the people who live and work in those communities.' *Sound Investments, Eastman Kodak Co.*

Financial Summary

Total Giving: $9,958,451 (1998); $11,300,000 (1996 approx); $12,279,750 (1995). Note: Contributes through corporate direct giving program and foundation.
Giving Analysis: Giving for 1995 includes: corporate direct giving ($9,500,000); international subsidiaries ($1,300,000); foundation ($300,000); 1996: corporate direct giving (approx $9,703,000); foundation (approx $1,597,000); 1998: foundation ($7,713,151); foundation grants to United Way ($2,245,300)
Assets: $4,696,556 (1998); $23,152,135 (1996); $4,000,000 (1995)
Gifts Received: $21,000,000 (1996); $15,590 (1993); $20,075,000 (1990)

Typical Recipients

Arts & Humanities: Arts Associations & Councils, Arts Funds, History & Archaeology, Libraries, Museums/Galleries, Music, Performing Arts
Civic & Public Affairs: African American Affairs, Botanical Gardens/Parks, Business/Free Enterprise, Clubs, Economic Development, Economic Policy, Employment/Job Training, Ethnic Organizations, Civic & Public Affairs-General, Housing, Parades/Festivals, Professional & Trade Associations, Public Policy, Safety, Urban & Community Affairs
Education: Business Education, Colleges & Universities, Community & Junior Colleges, Education Funds, Education Reform, Elementary Education (Public), Engineering/Technological Education, Education-General, Health & Physical Education, Minority Education, Preschool Education, Private Education (Precollege), Public Education (Precollege), Religious Education, School Volunteerism, Science/Mathematics Education, Secondary Education (Private), Secondary Education (Public), Special Education, Student Aid
Environment: Environment-General, Resource Conservation
Health: Clinics/Medical Centers, Emergency/Ambulance Services, Health Organizations, Medical Rehabilitation, Mental Health, Nursing Services, Single-Disease Health Associations
International: Foreign Arts Organizations, Foreign Educational Institutions, Health Care/Hospitals, International Environmental Issues, International Organizations, International Relations, Missionary/Religious Activities
Religion: Jewish Causes, Religious Welfare
Science: Science Museums, Scientific Centers & Institutes, Scientific Organizations
Social Services: Child Welfare, Community Service Organizations, Day Care, Family Services, Homes, People with Disabilities, Recreation & Athletics, Scouts, United Funds/United Ways, Youth Organizations

Contributions Analysis

Giving Priorities: Colleges, universities, and educational programs that emphasize science and engineering; United Way; arts and cultural organizations; and civic organizations. Foreign subsidiaries administer autonomous contributions to address needs in communities. U.S.-based recipients include International Executive Service Corps, Africares, World Wildlife Fund, Direct Relief International, and Project Hope.
Civic & Public Affairs: 25%. Civic interests include youth programs, community centers, zoos, environmental conservation, economic development, home and neighborhood rehabilitation, employment programs, promotion of equal opportunities, and examination of key social issues. Also supports culture and the arts.
Education: 33%. Supports colleges, universities, preschool, and K-12 educational programs nationwide, with emphasis on science and engineering education. University funding includes seed money or start-up grants for research in the areas of U.S. manufacturing competitiveness, optics, imaging science, biotechnology, electronics, and material processing. Also provides scholarships. Kodak Fellows program provides grants to graduate students and specific departments of science and engineering. Educational organizations supported include minority and independent college funds, economics, and minority engineering associations. On the precollege level, focuses on academic opportunities in scientific, mathematics, and technical disciplines. Sponsors partnerships between the company and precollege educational institutions in local Kodak communities to improve science and mathematics achievement for all students. Also

funds school-based initiatives that aim at acquainting students with opportunities in manufacturing.
Health: 28%. Principally supports the United Way. Youth groups, local and national health organizations, job training, homes and shelters, child welfare, and services for the aged and the handicapped are also supported.
International: Foreign subsidiaries maintain autonomous giving programs. Supports projects revelant to manufacturing research, marketing, scientific, or community interests.
Note: Total contributions in 1998.

Application Procedures

Initial Contact: Send a written proposal.
Application Requirements: Cover letter should include legal name organization, mission statement, grant amount requested, purpose of grant; proposal (not to exceed five pages) should include proposal summary (one or two pages), mission and history of the organization, need for the project (in view of related work by others), project description, audience served, goals, objectives, action plan, expected quantifiable outcomes or results, method of evaluation, other sources of support, plan for continuing beyond company support; attachments should include most recent organizational financial statement and income and expense budget, list of other current and projected sources of funding, most recent Form 990, and list of board members and affiliations.
Deadlines: Proposals accepted January 1 through April 30.
Review Process: Kodak board of directors approves budget based on recommendation of company's corporate contributions council.
Decision Notification: Within 45 days of receipt.

Restrictions

Kodak does not support special events, fraternal organizations, goodwill advertising, member agencies of united funds, political or lobbying groups, religious organizations for sectarian purposes, individuals, commitments beyond three years; endowed chairs, or university capital campaigns.

Additional Information

Charitable trust generally does not solicit funding requests.
Kodak recycles more than a half billion pounds of material a year and supports a World Wildlife Fund program to increase the environmental literacy of students. Copies of Kodak's annual environmental report are available by writing: Principles and Progress, Coordinator of Environmental Communications, Eastman Kodak Company, Rochester, NY 14650-0518.
Publications: Contributions Program Brochure

Corporate Officials

Daniel A. Carp: president, chief operating officer, directorchief operating officer B 1948. ED Massachusetts Institute of Technology MS; Ohio University BBA; Rhode Island Institute of Technology MBA. PRIM CORP EMPL president, chief operating officer, director: Eastman Kodak Co. CORP AFFIL director: Texas Instruments Inc.
George Myles Cordell Fisher: chairman, president, chief executive officer, director B Anna, IL 1940. ED University of Illinois BS (1962); Brown University MS (1964); Brown University PhD (1966). PRIM CORP EMPL chairman, president, chief executive officer, director: Eastman Kodak Co. CORP AFFIL director: General Motors Corp.; director: AT&T Corp.; director: Delta Air Lines. NONPR AFFIL member: Institute Electrical & Electronics Engineers; director: National Merit Scholarship Board.
Harry L. Kavetas: chief financial officer, executive vice president, director B 1937. PRIM CORP EMPL chief financial officer, executive vice president, director: Eastman Kodak Co. CORP AFFIL director: Lincoln National Corp.
Carl F. Kohet: executive vice president, assistant chief operating officer PRIM CORP EMPL executive vice president, assistant chief operating officer: Eastman Kodak Co.

Giving Program Officials

Michael P. Benard: ED John Carroll University BA; Temple University MEd. PRIM CORP EMPL vice president, director communications & public affairs: Eastman Kodak Co.

Foundation Officials

Essie L. Calhoun: president PRIM CORP EMPL director community relations & contributions: Eastman Kodak Co.

Grants Analysis

Disclosure Period: calendar year ending 1998
Total Grants: $7,713,151*
Number of Grants: 430 (approx)
Average Grant: $17,938
Highest Grant: $400,000
Typical Range: $1,000 to $15,000 and $100,000 to $400,000
***Note:** Giving excludes United Way.

Recent Grants

Note: Grants derived from 1997 Form 990.

Arts & Humanities

200,000	Library of Congress, Washington, DC
130,000	Rochester Museum and Science Center, Rochester, NY
125,000	George Eastman House, Rochester, NY
125,000	George Eastman House, Rochester, NY
125,000	George Eastman House, Rochester, NY
125,000	George Eastman House, Rochester, NY
125,000	National Women's Hall of Fame, Seneca Falls, NY
125,000	Women in Military Service to American Memorial Foundation
100,000	George Eastman House, Rochester, NY
100,000	Rochester Science Museum, Rochester, NY
50,000	Rochester Philharmonic Orchestra, Rochester, NY
50,000	Susan B. Anthony House
50,000	Susan B. Anthony House

Civic & Public Affairs

100,000	American Chemical Society, Detroit, MI
50,000	Center for Governmental Research, Rochester, NY
50,000	Frederick Douglass Development Corporation
50,000	Ibero-American Action League, Rochester, NY

Education

664,000	University of Birmingham School of Electronic and Electric Engineering, Birmingham, AL
664,000	University of Birmingham School of Electronic and Electric Engineering, Birmingham, AL
664,000	University of Birmingham School of Electronic and Electric Engineering, Birmingham, AL
200,000	Massachusetts Institute of Technology, Cambridge, MA
150,000	Clarkson University, Potsdam, NY
150,000	Rensselaer Polytechnic Institute, Troy, NY
100,000	Howard University, Washington, DC
100,000	Howard University, Washington, DC
100,000	Rochester Institute of Technology, Rochester, NY
100,000	Spelman College, Atlanta, GA
75,000	North Carolina A&T State University, Greensboro, NC
75,000	North Carolina A&T State University, Greensboro, NC
75,000	Purdue University, West Lafa
75,000	Rochester Institute of Technol ester, NY
65,000	University of Birmingham Scho tronic and Electric Engineering, mingham, AL
55,000	Pennsylvania State University, Uni sity Park, PA
50,000	Junior Achievement, Rochester, NY
50,000	National Action Council for Minorities Engineering, New York, NY
50,000	Rochester Institute of Technology, Roc ester, NY
50,000	United Negro College Fund, New York, NY

International

340,000	World Wildlife Fund, Washington, DC
340,000	World Wildlife Fund, Washington, DC
50,000	Joint Center for Political and Economic Studies, Washington, DC
50,000	Joint Center for Political and Economic Studies, Washington, DC
50,000	Mercy Flight Central, Canandaigua, NY
50,000	Mercy Flight Central, Canandaigua, NY
50,000	Project Hope, Chevy Chase, MD
50,000	Project Hope, Chevy Chase, MD

Social Services

650,000	United Way, Rochester, NY
650,000	United Way, Rochester, NY
605,000	United Way, Rochester, NY
100,000	Achieve
65,000	Wilson Commencement Park, Rochester, NY
50,000	Association for the Blind and Visually Impaired, Rochester, NY
50,000	Boys and Girls Club
50,000	Boys and Girls Club
50,000	Rochester Children's Nursery, Rochester, NY

EATON CORP.

Company Contact

Eaton Center
Cleveland, OH 44114-2584
Phone: (216)523-5000
Fax: (216)523-4787
Web: http://www.eaton.com

Company Description

Acquired: Aeroquip-Vickers (1999).
Revenue: US$8,402,000,000 (1999)
Profit: US$617,000,000 (1999)
Employees: 63,000 (1999)
Fortune Rank: 213, per FORTUNE Magazine's list of 500 Largest U.S. Corporations (1999).
FF 213
SIC(s): 3452 Bolts, Nuts, Rivets & Washers, 3559 Special Industry Machinery Nec, 3561 Pumps & Pumping Equipment, 3714 Motor Vehicle Parts & Accessories.

Operating Locations

Argentina: Cutler-Hammer de Argentina S.A.; Eaton S.A.; Australia: Cutler-Hammer Controls Pty.Ltd; Eaton Finance G.P.; Eaton Finance Pty.Ltd.; Eaton Pty.Ltd.; Eaton Specialty Controls Pty.Ltd.; Austria: Eaton Holding GmbH; Bermuda: Saturn Insurance Company Ltd.; Barbados: Eaton Foreign Sales Corporation; Eaton Holding Limited; Eaton Services Limited; Brazil: Eaton Ltda.; Eaton Truck Components Ltda.; TGM Industria Electrometalurgica Ltda.; Canada: Eaton ETN Offshore Ltd.; Electrotechnique GFTL, Inc.; Tycor International Corporation, Calgary; Eaton Yale Ltd., Chatham; People's Republic of China: Eaton China Investments Co., Ltd.; Eaton Hydraulics (Shanghai) Co.,Ltd.; Eaton-Shenglong Automobile Components (Ningbo) Co., Ltd.; Eaton Truck & Bus Components Company (Shanghai) Ltd.; Jining

...hanghai Eaton En- ...d.; Suzhou Cutler- ... Rica: Eaton Con- ... Islands: Eaton Hold- ... Limited; Dominican ...; France: Eaton Auto- ...A.; Eaton Technologies ...otive GmbH; Eaton Con- ...rtnership); Eaton GmbH; ...ologies Limited; Italy: Eaton ...Srl; Fusion Italia Srl; Japan: ..., Fusion Semiconductor Japan ...ompany Limited; Sumitomo Ea- ...,Ltd.; Sumitomo Eaton Nova Cor- ...lic of Korea: Eaton Automotive Con- ... Eaton Limited; Eaton Semiconductor ...sion Pacific, Ltd.; Monaco: Eaton s.a.m.; ...ondura S. de R.L. de C.V.; Eaton Molded ... S. de R.L. de C.V.; Eaton Truck Compo- ... S.A. de C.V.; Operaciones de Maquila de Ju- ...z S de R.L. de C.V.; Malaysia: Cutler-Hammer ...ontrols Sdn.Bhd.; Netherlands: Eaton Automotive B.V.; Eaton B.V.; Eaton C.V. (Partnership); Eaton Finance B.V.; Eaton Holding B.V.; Eaton Holding International I B.V.; IKU Holding Montfoort B.V.; Technisch Bureau Hoevelaken B.V.; Philippines: Cutler-Hammer Asia Corporation; Poland: Eaton Controls Spolka z.o.o.; Eaton Truck Components S.A.; Republic of South Africa: Eaton Truck Components (Pty) Limited; Singapore: Cutler-Hammer Pte.Ltd.; Eaton Services Pte.Ltd.; Spain: Eaton Ros S.A.; Productos Eaton Livia S.A.; Switzerland: Eaton SA; Eaton Technologies SA; Thailand: Eaton Technologies Limited; Rubberon Technology Corporation Limited; Taiwan: Eaton Limited; Modern Molded Products Limited; United Kingdom: Cutler-Hammer Europa Pension Trustees Ltd.; Eaton Financial Services Limited; Eaton Holding Limited; Eaton Limited; Eaton Shared Services Limited; Fusion Europe Ltd.; Venezuela: Cutler-Hammer de Venezuela S.A.

Nonmonetary Support

Value: $4,600,000 (2000 approx); $23,264 (1990); $50,000 (1989)
Type: Donated Products
Volunteer Programs: Volunteer Services of all types are encouraged. Volunteers support many causes including teaching reading to the illiterate, coaching little league softball, organizing school aid programs, serving food at hunger centers, building houses for the needy, and chairing United Way campaigns.

Eaton Charitable Fund

Giving Contact

Mr. James L. Mason, Director, Public & Community Affairs
Eaton Corp.
1111 Superior Avenue, N.E.
Cleveland, OH 44114
Phone: (216)523-4452
Fax: (216)479-7013

Alternate Contact

Phone: (216)523-4944

Description

Founded: 1953
EIN: 346501856
Organization Type: Corporate Foundation
Giving Locations: corporate operating locations.
Grant Types: Award, Capital, Conference/Seminar, Emergency, Employee Matching Gifts, Fellowship, General Support, Matching, Multiyear/Continuing Support, Project.
Note: Employee matching gift ratio: 1 to 1 to educational arts and cultural institutions, Red Cross disaster relief funds and Habitat for Humanity.

Giving Philosophy

'The thread that runs through Eaton's approach to corporate responsibility is the belief that business has an obligation not only to produce, but to speak out; that it has the right to be heard, but not necessarily prevail; that to society we owe time as well as money, and judgment along with generosity.' *Eaton Charitable Fund*

Financial Summary

Total Giving: $4,864,359 (1999 approx); $4,600,000 (1998); $4,491,814 (1997). Note: Contributes through corporate direct giving program and foundation.
Giving Analysis: Giving for 1998 includes: corporate direct giving ($3,108,889); corporate grants to United Way ($1,285,455); corporate matching gifts ($470,015)
Assets: $4,444,827 (1997); $15,856,939 (1996); $17,609,161 (1995)
Gifts Received: $400,000 (1995); $3,110,000 (1994). Note: Contributions are received from Eaton Corporation.

Typical Recipients

Arts & Humanities: Arts Associations & Councils, Arts Centers, Arts Festivals, Arts Funds, Ballet, Community Arts, Dance, Historic Preservation, Libraries, Museums/Galleries, Music, Opera, Performing Arts, Public Broadcasting, Theater, Visual Arts
Civic & Public Affairs: Business/Free Enterprise, Community Foundations, Economic Development, Economic Policy, Employment/Job Training, Civic & Public Affairs-General, Housing, Law & Justice, Legal Aid, Municipalities/Towns, Parades/Festivals, Professional & Trade Associations, Public Policy, Rural Affairs, Safety, Urban & Community Affairs
Education: Business Education, Colleges & Universities, Community & Junior Colleges, Economic Education, Education Associations, Education Funds, Education Reform, Engineering/Technological Education, Education-General, Minority Education, Private Education (Precollege), Public Education (Precollege), Religious Education, Science/Mathematics Education, Secondary Education (Public), Student Aid
Environment: Environment-General
Health: Cancer, Clinics/Medical Centers, Emergency/Ambulance Services, Health Policy/Cost Containment, Health Funds, Health Organizations, Hospices, Hospitals, Hospitals (University Affiliated), Nursing Services, Public Health, Single-Disease Health Associations
International: International Relations
Religion: Religious Welfare
Science: Science Museums, Scientific Centers & Institutes
Social Services: Child Welfare, Community Centers, Community Service Organizations, Counseling, Delinquency & Criminal Rehabilitation, Emergency Relief, Family Services, Food/Clothing Distribution, Homes, People with Disabilities, Recreation & Athletics, Senior Services, Shelters/Homelessness, United Funds/United Ways, Volunteer Services, YMCA/YWCA/YMHA/YWHA, Youth Organizations

Contributions Analysis

Giving Priorities: Hospitals, united funds, single disease health associations, education, civic concerns, and the arts. Company supports international development and public policy organizations. Contributions are also made to hospitals and health-related activities. Outside the U.S., contributions are less than $50,000 annually and are targeted to Canada.
Civic & Public Affairs: 62%. Contributes to organizations that help people become self-sufficient, strengthen families, encourage neighborhood and economic development, and enhance the qualify of life through civic, cultural and arts programs. Major support for the United Way. Contributes to housing, shelters and social services, youth activities, health care facilities, and visual and performing arts institutions, public radio and television, civic improvements, and humanitarian efforts.
Education: 38%. Gifts go to educational institutions for programs that help students prepare for careers in business and industry, particularly in engineering. Supports programs that attract students at all grade levels to the study of math, science, and technology. Contributes to programs that help students overcome barriers to academic achievement and complete their education. Awards scholarships for minority engineering students.
Note: Contributions made in 1998.

Application Procedures

Initial Contact: Contact the company for guidelines; then submit a written proposal.
Application Requirements: Include a description of the organization's history and purpose; explanation of what will be accomplished during the period of the grant; how program's effectiveness will be measured; identification of other organizations involved in project; copies of most recent financial statements and current budget; roster of officers and directors; listing of corporate donors and amounts; employee involvement with organization (if applicable); and copy of IRS determination letter.
Deadlines: None.
Review Process: Eaton managers submit requests to the Corporate Contributions Committee, which meets regularly to review requests; written notification of decisions is sent.
Evaluative Criteria: The evaluative process takes into account the importance of the project to Eaton Corporation employees and their families; importance to the community with significant Eaton Corporation employment; contributions from other companies similar to Eaton Corporation; participation of Eaton Corporation employees in direction of the institution; and recommendation by an Eaton manager. Projects supported are aimed at prevention rather than reaction, have clearly defined objectives, measurable results and benchmarks to evaluate progress, efficient administration, ethical fundraising methods, and adequate budgetary controls.
Notes: Requests should be made through local Eaton manager.

Restrictions

Grants not awarded to religious, fraternal, or labor organizations; to individuals or individual endeavors; to annual operating budgets of United Way agencies or hospitals; for endowment funds; for fundraising benefits and sponsorships; or debt retirement.

Additional Information

Branch facilities may make grants up to $1,000 without headquarters approval.
Eaton limits funding to specific projects or programs which address their priorities or to capital campaigns which meet their criteria. The priorities are education and community improvement.
In April 1999, Eaton Corp. acquired Aeroquip-Vickers, Inc.
Publications: Contributions Guidelines

Corporate Officials

Brian R. Bachman: senior vice president semiconductor & specialty **** PRIM CORP EMPL senior vice president semiconductor & specialty systems: Eaton Corp. CORP AFFIL director: Keithley Instruments Inc.
Susan J. Cook: vice president human resources PRIM CORP EMPL vice president human resources: Eaton Corp.
Adrian T. Dillon: executive vice president, chief financial officer, planning officer ED Amherst College (1979). PRIM CORP EMPL executive vice president, chief financial officer, planning officer: Eaton Corp. CORP AFFIL chief financial officer: Fusion Systems Corp.

Stephen Roger Hardis: chairman, chief executive officer, director B New York, NY 1935. ED Cornell University BA (1956); Princeton University Woodrow Wilson School of International Public Affairs MA (1960). PRIM CORP EMPL chairman, chief executive officer, director: Eaton Corp. CORP AFFIL treasurer: Sybron Corp.; director: Progressive Companies; director: Progressive Corp.; director: Lexmark International Inc.; director: Nordson Corp.; director: Key Corp.; director: Lexmark International Group; director: Fision Systems Corp.; director: Key Bank Corp. NONPR AFFIL member: Phi Beta Kappa; trustee: Playhouse Square Foundation; member: Leadership Cleveland; trustee: Musical Arts Association; member: Cleveland Tomorrow; trustee: Greater Cleveland Growth Association; trustee: Cleveland Clinic Inc.

Giving Program Officials

Kristen Bihary: vice president corporate affairs
Veronica Runcis: administrator corporate contributions

Foundation Officials

Brian R. Bachman: senior vice president, member contributions committee (see above)
Susan J. Cook: vice president, member contributions committee (see above)
Gerald Lee Gherlein: member contributions committee B Warren, OH 1938. ED Ohio Wesleyan University (1956-1958); Ohio State University BS (1960); University of Michigan JD (1963). PRIM CORP EMPL executive vice president, general counsel: Eaton Corp. NONPR AFFIL member: Ohio Bar Association; trustee: WVIZ Public Television; member: Greater Cleveland Bar Association; member: American Bar Association; member: American Society of Corporate Secretaries. CLUB AFFIL Pepper Pike Country Club.
Carol S. Markey: manager community involvement
James L. Mason: director public affairs, member contributions committee B Joliet, IL 1938. ED John Carroll University (1960); Case Western Reserve University (1967).

Grants Analysis

Disclosure Period: calendar year ending 1998
Total Grants: $3,108,889*
Number of Grants: 207
Average Grant: $15,019
Highest Grant: $61,500
Typical Range: $1,000 to $25,000
***Note:** Giving excludes matching gifts and United Way.

Recent Grants

Note: Grants derived from 1996 Form 990.

Arts & Humanities

125,000	Musical Arts Association, Cleveland, OH
80,000	Cleveland Play House, Cleveland, OH
50,000	Playhouse Square Foundation, Cleveland, OH
20,000	Cleveland Ballet, Cleveland, OH
20,000	Rock and Roll Hall of Fame Museum, Cleveland, OH
20,000	Rock and Roll Hall of Fame Museum, Cleveland, OH

Civic & Public Affairs

259,325	Eaton Corporation Charitable Foundation
259,325	Eaton Corporation Charitable Foundation
91,082	Eaton Corporation Charitable Foundation
73,500	Eaton Corporation Charitable Foundation
50,283	Eaton Corporation Charitable Foundation
50,000	Cleveland Tomorrow, Cleveland, OH
41,600	Eaton Corporation Charitable Foundation
40,000	Habitat for Humanity, Cleveland, OH
38,000	Eaton Corporation Charitable Foundation
38,000	Greater Cleveland Roundtable, Cleveland, OH
38,000	Greater Cleveland Roundtable, Cleveland, OH
25,000	Cleveland Bicentennial Commission, Cleveland, OH
25,000	Cleveland Development Foundation, Cleveland, OH
25,000	Cooperative Housing Foundation, Silver Spring, MD
25,000	Society of Automotive Engineers, Warrendale, PA

Education

82,500	Eaton Other for Minority Engineering
62,500	Cleveland Initiative for Education, Cleveland, OH
50,000	John Carroll University, University Heights, OH
25,000	Baldwin Wallace College, Berea, OH
20,000	GMI Engineering and Management, Flint, MI
20,000	Kalamazoo Valley Community College, Kalamazoo, MI
20,000	Person County Education Foundation, Roxboro, NC
20,000	Person County Education Foundation, Roxboro, NC

Health

100,000	Cleveland Clinic Foundation, Cleveland, OH
35,000	American Red Cross, Cleveland, OH
35,000	American Red Cross, Cleveland, OH
25,000	Fairview General Hospital, Cleveland, OH
25,000	University Hospitals, Cleveland, OH
20,000	Healthcare Foundation
20,000	Sponsor Regional Healthcare Foundation

Science

50,000	Great Lakes Museum of Science, Cleveland, OH
25,000	Cleveland Museum of Natural History, Cleveland, OH
20,000	Great Lakes Museum of Science, Cleveland, OH
20,000	National Invention Center, Akron, OH

Social Services

250,000	YMCA, Cleveland, OH
72,500	United Way, Milwaukee, WI
72,500	United Way Services, Cleveland, OH
72,500	United Way Services, Cleveland, OH
50,000	YMCA Kearney Family
50,000	YMCA Kearney Family
34,000	United Way Services, Cleveland, OH
33,000	United Way, Detroit, MI
30,000	Harbor, Cleveland, OH
30,000	Harbor, Cleveland, OH

EBSCO INDUSTRIES, INC.

Company Contact

Birmingham, AL
Web: http://www.ebsco.com

Company Description

Revenue: US$1,530,000,000
Employees: 4,000
SIC(s): 2542 Partitions & Fixtures Except Wood, 2721 Periodicals, 2752 Commercial Printing--Lithographic, 2759 Commercial Printing Nec.

Nonmonetary Support

Type: Donated Products; Workplace So.

Corporate Sponsorship

Contact: James Stephens, President & Dir
Note: Provides sponsorship.

Giving Contact

Elton Bryson Stephens, Chairman
Ebsco Industries, Inc.
PO Box 1943
Birmingham, AL 35201
Phone: (205)991-1197
Fax: (205)995-1517

Description

Organization Type: Corporate Giving Program
Giving Locations: AL
Grant Types: General Support.

Financial Summary

Total Giving: Contributes through corporate direct giving program only.

Typical Recipients

Arts & Humanities: Arts & Humanities-General, Libraries
Civic & Public Affairs: Civic & Public Affairs-General
Education: Education-General
Health: Health-General
Social Services: Social Services-General

Application Procedures

Initial Contact: Send a brief letter of inquiry.
Deadlines: None.
Notes: The company is not currently accepting proposals.

Additional Information

In 1993 the company reported that two substantial long-term commitments have put the giving program over budget for the next four years.
The directors of the giving program report that the office is overwhelmed with requests that they do not have the time to read or the funds to support. Funding to new programs or organizations has ceased.
The company gives approximately 5% of pre-tax earnings.

Corporate Officials

Elton Bryson Stephens: founder, chairman B Clio, AL 1911. ED Birmingham-Southern College BA (1932); University of Alabama Law School LLB (1936). PRIM CORP EMPL founder, chairman: Ebsco Industries, Inc. CORP AFFIL chairman: Highland Bank; chairman, secretary: Ebsco Investment Services Inc.; chairman, vice president: Franklin Square Agency Overseas Inc.; chairman: CANEBSCO Subscription Services Ltd.; trustee, founder: Ebsco Employee Savings & Profit Sharing Trust; director: RA Brown Agency Ltd.; trustee: AlabamaBancorp Savings & Profit Sharing Trust; chairman: Bennett-Ebsco Subscription Services; chairman, founder: AlabamaBancorp. NONPR AFFIL chairman: TN-Tombigbee Waterway Authority Economic Pension Comm; member, don: Un Arts Fund/Metropolitan Arts Council; member: Phi Alpha Delta; chairman: Birmingham-Southern College Executive Comm; member: Omicron Delta Kappa; trustee: Birmingham Metropolitan YMCA; member: Alpha Tau Omega; director: Birmingham Chamber of Commerce. CLUB AFFIL Shades Valley Rotary Club; Summit Club; Mountain Brook Country Club; Birmingham Press Club; The Club.
James T. Stephens: president, director B 1939. ED Yale University BA (1961); Harvard University MBA (1964). PRIM CORP EMPL president, director: Ebsco Industries, Inc. CORP AFFIL president: Plastic Research & Development Corp.

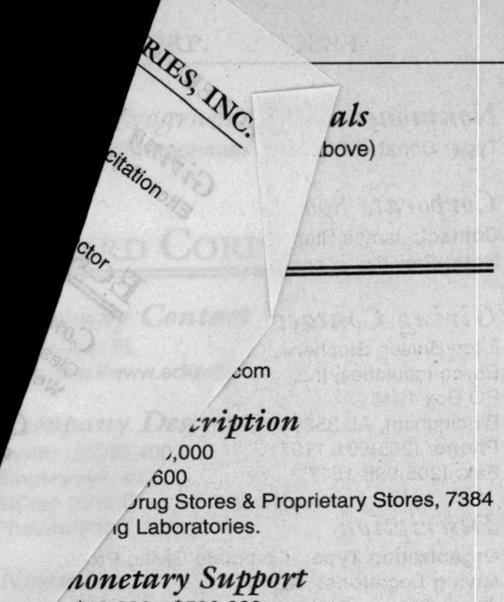

...als

...bove)

...com

...ription

...,000

...,600

...rug Stores & Proprietary Stores, 7384 ...g Laboratories.

...onetary Support

...: $10,000 - $500,000

...: Loaned Employees; Loaned Executives

...ote: Loaned executives are provided to United Way only.

Corporate Sponsorship

Contact: Bob Dyer, Directory, Advertising Services

Eckerd Corp. Foundation

Giving Contact

Tami Alderman, Foundation Administrator
Eckerd Corp. Foundation
PO Box 4689
Clearwater, FL 33758
Phone: (727)395-6289
Fax: (727)395-7934
Email: webmaster@eckerd.com

Description

EIN: 237322099
Organization Type: Corporate Foundation
Giving Locations: CT; DE; FL; GA; KS; LA; MD; MS; MO; NJ; NY; NC; OH; OK; PA; SC; TN; TX; VA; WV
Grant Types: Award, Capital, Employee Matching Gifts, Fellowship, Scholarship.
Note: Employee matching gift ratio: 1 to 1 up to $2,000 per employee annually.

Giving Philosophy

The foundation reports that it focuses its giving on education, health, and nonprofit organizations benefiting children and women.

Financial Summary

Total Giving: $2,000,000 (fiscal year ending February 01, 2000 approx); $2,000,000 (fiscal 1999 approx); $1,275,766 (fiscal 1998 approx). Note: Contributes through foundation only. Fiscal 1997 Giving includes matching gifts ($53,331); United Way ($260,454).
Assets: $3,368 (fiscal 1997); $9,410 (fiscal 1991); $596,000 (fiscal 1990)
Gifts Received: $824,600 (fiscal 1997)

Typical Recipients

Arts & Humanities: Community Arts, History & Archaeology, Museums/Galleries, Music, Performing Arts, Theater
Civic & Public Affairs: African American Affairs, Professional & Trade Associations, Public Policy, Urban & Community Affairs
Education: Business Education, Colleges & Universities, Economic Education, Education Funds, Engineering/Technological Education, Education-General, Medical Education, Minority Education, Public Education (Precollege)
Health: Cancer, Clinics/Medical Centers, Diabetes, Health Funds, Health Organizations, Hospices, Hospitals, Multiple Sclerosis, Public Health
Religion: Jewish Causes, Ministries, Religious Welfare
Social Services: Child Welfare, Community Service Organizations, People with Disabilities, Recreation & Athletics, United Funds/United Ways, Youth Organizations

Contributions Analysis

Giving Priorities: United funds, education, health, community improvement, and the arts.

Application Procedures

Initial Contact: Send a written request.
Application Requirements: Include a description of organization, amount requested, purpose of funds sought, and proof of tax-exempt status.
Deadlines: None.
Decision Notification: Three to six weeks after receipt of request; large request over $5,000 reviewed quarterly.

Restrictions

Does not support individuals, goodwill advertising, fraternal or political organizations, or religious organizations for sectarian purposes. Only accepts application from states where foundation concentrates giving.

Additional Information

Eckerd Corp. recently acquired Fay's Inc.

Foundation Officials

Dan Dero: chairman
Edward W. Kelly: trustee B 1946.
Curtis Dean Neel, Jr.: trustee B St. Louis, MO 1946. ED Purdue University (1968); Florida Institute of Technology (1978). PRIM CORP EMPL senior vice president logistics: Eckerd Corp. NONPR AFFIL member: International Material Management Society; district committee: National Association Chain Drug Stores; member: American Institute Industrial Engineer.
Richard R. Powis: trustee
Samuel G. Wright: trustee B 1950. ED University of West Florida BA.

Grants Analysis

Disclosure Period: fiscal year ending February 01, 1997
Total Grants: $510,916*
Number of Grants: 139
Average Grant: $3,676
Highest Grant: $253,504
Typical Range: $500 to $10,000
***Note:** Giving excludes matching gifts; United Way.

Recent Grants

Note: Grants derived from fiscal 1997 Form 990.

Arts & Humanities

5,000	Mahaffey Theater Foundation, St. Petersburg, FL
3,000	Tampa Bay History Center, Tampa, FL
2,500	Ringling Museum of Art Foundation, Sarasota, FL

Civic & Public Affairs

10,000	National Taxpayers Union Foundation, Washington, DC
5,000	Heritage Foundation, Washington, DC
5,000	Morton Plant Foundation, Clearwater, FL -- for Bush Dinner
5,000	NAACP -- annual support
2,500	James Madison Institute for Public Policy Studies, Tallahassee, FL

Education

60,000	United Negro College Fund, New York, NY
50,000	Eckerd College, St. Petersburg, FL
25,000	Eckerd College, St. Petersburg, FL
20,000	University of Texas Austin, Austin, TX -- third payment of five on pledge
10,000	University of Houston, Houston, TX -- third payment of five on pledge
7,936	Liberty City Charter School
7,500	Florida Council on Economic Education, Tampa, FL
6,500	Arnold and Marie Schwartz College of Pharmacy
6,500	Junior Achievement Suncoast, FL
5,000	Operation PAR, St. Petersburg, FL
5,000	Southwest Oklahoma State University, OK
5,000	Texas Technical University Foundation, Lubbock, TX
5,000	University of Florida Center for Retailing Education and Research, Gainesville, FL
5,000	University of Georgia College of Pharmacy, Athens, GA
5,000	University of Oklahoma, Norman, OK
3,500	Florida Independent College Fund, Lakeland, FL
3,000	Texas A&M Center for Retailing Studies, College Station, TX -- annual support
2,000	University of Texas Austin, Austin, TX -- conference sponsor

Health

10,000	Morton Plant Mease Foundation, Clearwater, FL -- first payment of five-year pledge
10,000	Tampa General Hospital Foundation, Tampa, FL
7,500	Skin Cancer Foundation, New York, NY
5,000	St. Petersburg Free Clinic, St. Petersburg, FL
5,000	Tallahassee Memorial Regional Medical Center, Tallahassee, FL
2,000	Juvenile Diabetes Foundation, New York, NY
2,000	National Breast Cancer Coalition, Washington, DC
1,750	National Multiple Sclerosis Society of the Florida Suncoast, FL
1,750	National Multiple Sclerosis Society of the Florida Suncoast, FL

Religion

5,000	American Jewish Committee, New York, NY
5,000	Metropolitan Ministries, Tampa, FL
5,000	Religious Community Services, Clearwater, FL
2,500	United Jewish Appeal Federation, New York, NY
2,000	Jewish National Fund, Baltimore, MD

Social Services

253,504	United Way -- for 1996 campaign
50,000	Take Stock in Children
35,000	Eckerd Family Youth Alternatives, Clearwater, FL
10,000	Abilities of Florida, Clearwater, FL -- fourth payment of five on pledge
10,000	Gulf Coast Community Care, FL
10,000	US Ski Team Foundation
5,000	United Way Pinellas County, St. Petersburg, FL -- to help meet 1995 goal
4,000	Abilities of Florida, Clearwater, FL
2,500	Tampa Lighthouse for the Blind, Tampa, FL
2,000	Florida House

Ecolab Inc.

Company Contact

St. Paul, MN

Web: http://www.ecolab.com

Company Description

Employees: 9,500

SIC(s): 2841 Soap & Other Detergents, 2879 Agricultural Chemicals Nec, 2899 Chemical Preparations Nec, 7342 Disinfecting & Pest Control Services.

Parent Company: Henkel KGAA, Henkelstrasse 67, Dusseldorf, Germany

Operating Locations

AL: Ecolab Inc., Birmingham, Mobile; CA: Ecolab Inc., Carlsbad, Roseville, San Jose, Simi Valley, Tulare; CO: Ecolab Inc., Denver; CT: Ecolab Inc., Tolland; DC: Ecolab Inc., Washington; FL: Ecolab Inc., Fort Myers, Altamonte Springs, Tampa; GA: Ecolab Inc., McDonough; HI: Ecolab Inc., Honolulu; IA: Ecolab Inc., West Des Moines; IL: Ecolab Inc., Glen Ellyn, Joliet, Lombard, Peoria; IN: Ecolab Inc., Granger, Huntington, Indianapolis; KS: Ecolab Inc., Lenexa; LA: Ecolab Inc., Saint Rose, Shreveport; MA: Ecolab Inc., Norwood, Wilmington; MD: Ecolab Inc., Gaithersburg, Ocean City; ME: Ecolab Inc., Brewer; MI: Ecolab Inc., Farmington Hills, Traverse City; MN: Ecolab Inc., Eagan, Mendota Heights, Minnetonka; Ecolab, Saint Paul; MO: Ecolab Inc., Kansas City, Springfield; NC: Ecolab Inc., Burlington, Charlotte, Winston Salem; NE: Ecolab Inc., Omaha; NH: Ecolab Inc., Amherst, Lebanon; NM: Ecolab Inc., Albuquerque; NV: Ecolab Inc., North Las Vegas, Reno; NY: Ecolab Inc., East Syracuse, New Hyde Park, New York, Rochester; OH: Ecolab Inc., Cleveland, Hebron, Pickerington; OK: Ecolab Inc., Oklahoma City, Tulsa; PA: Ecolab Inc., Allentown, Erie, Harrisburg, Lancaster, Plumsteadville; PR: Ecolab Inc., Dorado; SC: Ecolab Inc., North Charleston, Columbia; TN: Ecolab Inc., Brentwood, Knoxville, Memphis, Murfeesboro; TX: Ecolab Inc., Garland, Grand Prairie, Houston; UT: Ecolab Inc., Midvale; VA: Ecolab Inc., Roanoke, Virginia Beach; WA: Ecolab Inc., Gig Harbor, Renton; WI: Ecolab Inc., Janesville, Milwaukee, Sun Prairie

Nonmonetary Support

Value: $211,127 (1997 approx); $42,805 (1993)

Type: In-kind Services

Contact: James Dietz, Distribution

Note: Co. provides nonmonetary support.

Ecolab Foundation

Giving Contact

Lois West Duffy, Director, Community & Public Relations
Ecolab Inc.
370 North Wabasha Street
St. Paul, MN 55102
Phone: (651)293-2259
Fax: (651)225-3123

Description

EIN: 411372157

Organization Type: Corporate Foundation

Giving Locations: MN: emphasis on the Twin Cities areas where company has a major presence, and large numbers of employees live and work.

Grant Types: Capital, Employee Matching Gifts, General Support.

Giving Philosophy

'Recognizing the responsibility of the corporation to its host communities, Ecolab recognizes its responsibility to be a good corporate citizen. Over the years, strategic planning for community relations has focused on targeting dollar contributions to areas of specific interest to the company while leveraging funds with the time and expertise of employee volunteers.' *Ecolab Community Relations Report*

Financial Summary

Total Giving: $2,100,000 (1999 approx); $2,000,000 (1998 approx); $1,703,633 (1997). Note: Contributes through corporate direct giving program and foundation. 1996 Giving includes foundation.

Giving Analysis: Giving for 1997 includes: foundation ($1,454,870); foundation grants to United Way ($221,941); foundation scholarships ($26,822)

Assets: $4,945,609 (1997); $400,000 (1996 approx)

Gifts Received: $2,261,100 (1997). Note: In 1997, contributions were received from Ecolab Associates, Ecolab match of Associates, and Ecolab, Inc.

Typical Recipients

Arts & Humanities: Arts Associations & Councils, Arts Funds, Arts Outreach, History & Archaeology, Museums/Galleries, Music, Opera, Performing Arts, Public Broadcasting, Theater

Civic & Public Affairs: Business/Free Enterprise, Economic Development, Employment/Job Training, Ethnic Organizations, Civic & Public Affairs-General, Hispanic Affairs, Housing, Law & Justice, Nonprofit Management, Parades/Festivals, Urban & Community Affairs, Women's Affairs, Zoos/Aquariums

Education: Business Education, Business-School Partnerships, Colleges & Universities, Continuing Education, Economic Education, Education Associations, Education Funds, Education Reform, Environmental Education, Faculty Development, International Exchange, Minority Education, Public Education (Precollege), School Volunteerism, Science/Mathematics Education, Secondary Education (Public), Special Education, Student Aid

Environment: Environment-General

Health: AIDS/HIV, Cancer, Children's Health/Hospitals, Clinics/Medical Centers, Emergency/Ambulance Services, Long-Term Care, Medical Rehabilitation, Nutrition, Public Health, Speech & Hearing

International: International Environmental Issues

Religion: Religious Welfare

Science: Science Museums

Social Services: At-Risk Youth, Big Brother/Big Sister, Child Welfare, Community Service Organizations, Day Care, Delinquency & Criminal Rehabilitation, Emergency Relief, Family Planning, Family Services, Food/Clothing Distribution, People with Disabilities, Senior Services, Shelters/Homelessness, Substance Abuse, United Funds/United Ways, Volunteer Services, YMCA/YWCA/YMHA/YWHA, Youth Organizations

Contributions Analysis

Giving Priorities: Education, health and human services, community development, arts and culture and enviroment.

Arts & Humanities: About 37%. Supports major performing arts groups, mid-size arts organizations, museums, and theaters.

Civic & Public Affairs: 5%. Contributions are set aside to fund community relations task forces and contingencies. Community service organizations and child welfare and youth programs received support. Ecolab also donates products in cases of national disaster through disaster relief organizations, such as Red Cross. The company reports that it does not make cash gifts in this category.

Education: 30%. Interests include business and economic education, secondary education and colleges and universities. Also administers matching gift program.

Health: About 1%. Primarily supports united funds in St. Paul and other plant communities. Programs assisting children at risk and families to overcome problems of self-sufficiency are a primary concern. Includes preventive health care organizations and employment services that encourage self-sufficiency.

Science: 10%. Supporting the Science Museum.

Social Services: 16%. Emphasis mainly on United Way.

Application Procedures

Initial Contact: Letter of request.

Application Requirements: Brief descripti[...] ect including need, target group served, t[...] and geographic area served; specific dollar [...] requested with description of how the funds [...] used; a description of organization, historical [...] ground and goals, the name and qualifications [...] person responsible for administering the grant; [...] an indication of Ecolab Inc. employee involveme[...]

Deadlines: July 31

Evaluative Criteria: Priority given to programs [...] company operating areas that leverage corporate dol[...]lars with volunteer time and technical expertise; encourage self-sufficiency among disadvantaged groups in the community; encompass creative programs that are not duplicated through existing community organizations and resources; involve a significant number of employees; and have a direct impact on the end user.

Restrictions

Grants are made for general operations and specific projects; capital campaigns are occasionally supported. The company does not award grants for individuals; fundraisers or advertisements; religious organizations for sectarian or denominational programs; disease-specific organizations; sports or athletic programs; industry, trade, political, professional, or business associations; or loans or investments.

Additional Information

Company sponsors an Employee Volunteer Bonus Program (to provide grants to nonprofits in recognition of significant employee volunteer commitments), a Community Involvement Program (to recognize employees who serve on the boards of nonprofits), and a matching gifts program.

The company allocates 1% of pretax U.S. profits to charitable contributions each year.

Ecolab is a U.S. affiliate of Henkel KGAA, which has a 25% investment in the company. Other U.S. affiliates are Loctite Corp. (29%) and Clorox Co. (28%).

Publications: Annual Giving Report; Application Guidelines

Corporate Officials

Lawrence T. Bell: vice president law, general counsel, assistant secretaryon B 1947. PRIM CORP EMPL vice president law, general counsel, assistant secretary: Ecolab Inc.

William G. Crawford: vice president PRIM CORP EMPL vice president: Ecolab Inc.

Peter D'Almada: senior vice president PRIM CORP EMPL senior vice president: Ecolab Inc.

Dean deBuhr: vice president, general manager professional products PRIM CORP EMPL vice president, general manager professional products: Ecolab Inc.

John G. Forsythe: vice president tax and public affairs B Chicago, IL 1947. ED Loyola University (1969); Northwestern University (1973). PRIM CORP EMPL vice president tax and public affairs: Ecolab Inc. NONPR AFFIL chairman: Chemical Specialties Manufacturing Association.

Steven L. Fritze: vice president, treasurer B Saint Paul, MN 1954. ED University of Minnesota (1975); University of Minnesota (1977). PRIM CORP EMPL vice president, treasurer: Ecolab Inc. NONPR AFFIL member: Financial Executives Institute.

Arthur E. Henningsen, Jr.: senior vice president, controller PRIM CORP EMPL senior vice president, controller: Ecolab Inc.

Kenneth A. Iverson: vice president, corporate secretary B 1945. ED College of Saint Thomas BA (1967); University of Notre Dame JD (1970). PRIM CORP EMPL vice president, corporate secretary: Ecolab Inc.

Diana D. Lewis: vice president human resources PRIM CORP EMPL vice president human resources: Ecolab Inc.

e president indus-
e president indus-

utive vice president
utive vice president:

dent marketing PRIM
narketing: Ecolab Inc.
president external rela-
ce president external rela-

r vice president global opera-
MPL senior vice president global
Inc.

acher: vice president, chief technical
CORP EMPL vice president, chief tech-
Ecolab Inc.

chuman: president, chief executive officer,
, chairman B Sheridan, WY 1934. ED New
University BS (1955). PRIM CORP EMPL presi-
t, chief executive officer, director, chairman: Eco-
o Inc. CORP AFFIL director: Northern Studies Power Co.; director: Northern Studies Power Co. Minnesota; chairman: Industrial Maintenance Corp.

Michael E. Shannon: chairman, chief financial officer, chief administration officer, director B Evanston, IL 1936. ED University of Notre Dame BA (1958); Stanford University MBA (1960). PRIM CORP EMPL chairman, chief financial officer, chief administration officer, director: Ecolab Inc. NONPR AFFIL director: Minnesota Orchestra Association; director: National Association Manufacturer; member: Financial Executives Institute. CLUB AFFIL University Club; Minnesota Club; Rolling Rock Club; Minikahda Club; Minneapolis Club.

William Snedeker: vice president, general manager pest elimination PRIM CORP EMPL vice president, general manager pest elimination: Ecolab Inc.

John P. Spooner: senior vice president international PRIM CORP EMPL senior vice president international: Ecolab Inc.

William Tuominen: senior vice president, chief technology & environment ****B Floodwood, MN 1943. ED University of Minnesota BS (1965); University of Minnesota MS (1968); University of Minnesota PhD (1970). PRIM CORP EMPL senior vice president, chief technology & environment officer: Ecolab Inc.

Giving Program Officials

Lawrence T. Bell: member, corporate contributions committee (see above)

Lois West Duffy: B Forest City, IA 1939. ED Mankato State University BS (1976); Harvard University MPA (1986). PRIM CORP EMPL vice president corporate contributions committee: Ecolab Inc. NONPR AFFIL director: Tentmakers; director: Union Gospel Mission; commissioner: Saint Paul Civic Center Authority; president, chairman board: Saint Paul Cultural Dist; director: Nepal (Kathmandu) Social Service Agency; member: Saint Paul Area Chamber of Commerce; chairman: ECOPAC; director: Minnesota State Arts Board.

John G. Forsythe: member corporate contributions committee (see above)

Diana D. Lewis: member corporate contributions committee (see above)

William A. Mathison: member corporate contributions committee (see above)

Michael J. Monahan: president corporate contributions committee (see above)

Grants Analysis

Disclosure Period: calendar year ending 1997
Total Grants: $1,978,766
Number of Grants: 170
Average Grant: $11,640
Highest Grant: $150,000
Typical Range: $1,500 to $15,000
Note: Grants analysis supplied by foundation.

Recent Grants

Note: Grants derived from 1997 Form 990.

Arts & Humanities

150,000	Ordway Music Theater, St. Paul, MN
100,000	Ordway Music Theater, St. Paul, MN
100,000	Ordway Music Theater, St. Paul, MN
75,000	Minnesota Orchestral Association, Minneapolis, MN
25,000	Minnesota Opera Company, Minneapolis, MN
20,000	Minnesota Public Radio, St. Paul, MN
15,000	Minnesota Museum of American Art, St. Paul, MN
15,000	Minnesota Public Radio, St. Paul, MN
15,000	St. Paul Chamber Orchestra, St. Paul, MN
12,000	Guthrie Theater, Minneapolis, MN
12,000	Minnesota Children's Museum, St. Paul, MN
10,500	Twin Cities Public Television, St. Paul, MN
10,000	Minnesota Children's Museum, St. Paul, MN
10,000	Minnesota Children's Museum, St. Paul, MN
10,000	Minnesota Museum of American Art, St. Paul, MN
10,000	Minnesota Opera Company, Minneapolis, MN
10,000	WAMSO, Minneapolis, MN

Civic & Public Affairs

20,000	Minnesota Zoo, Apple Valley, MN
15,000	Grand Forks Foundation for America, Grand Forks, ND
12,500	Twin Cities Neighborhood Housing Services, St. Paul, MN
10,000	Ordway Circle of Stars
10,000	Twin Cities Neighborhood Housing Services, St. Paul, MN
10,000	WomenVenture

Education

200,000	University of Minnesota Foundation, Minneapolis, MN
100,000	Culinary Institute of America, Hyde Park, NY
75,000	University of Minnesota Carlson School of Management, Minneapolis, MN
43,814	St. Paul Public School District 625, St. Paul, MN
24,387	St. Paul Independent School District 625, St. Paul, MN
16,800	Business Economics Education Foundation, Minneapolis, MN
10,000	Business Economics Education Foundation, Minneapolis, MN
10,000	Metropolitan State University, St. Paul, MN
10,000	Minnesota Private College Fund, St. Paul, MN
10,000	University of Wisconsin, WI

Health

20,000	American Dietetic Association Foundation, Chicago, IL

International

20,000	Project EarthSense

Science

70,000	Science Museum, St. Paul, MN
70,000	Science Museum, St. Paul, MN
22,000	Science Museum, St. Paul, MN

Social Services

27,250	United Way, St. Paul, MN
26,750	United Way, St. Paul, MN
26,750	United Way, St. Paul, MN
26,750	United Way, St. Paul, MN
26,000	United Way of Will County, Joliet, IL
22,655	United Way of Will County, Joliet, IL
20,000	Hazelden Foundation, Center City, MN
20,000	Hospitality 2000 Campaign
20,000	United Way of Greater Greensboro, Greensboro, NC
15,120	United Way, Beloit, WI
13,000	Naomi Family Center
10,000	Boys and Girls Club -- gala

EDISON BROTHERS STORES, INC.

Company Contact

St. Louis, MO
Web: http://www.edisonbrothers.com

Company Description

Employees: 24,600
SIC(s): 5661 Shoe Stores, 5699 Miscellaneous Apparel & Accessory Stores.

Edison Family Foundation

Giving Contact

Andrew E. Newman, President
Edison Family Foundation
PO Box 16940
St. Louis, MO 63105
Phone: (314)727-6400
Fax: (314)727-1030

Description

Founded: 1956
EIN: 436047207
Organization Type: Corporate Foundation
Giving Locations: MO: primarily St. Louis
Grant Types: General Support.

Financial Summary

Total Giving: $200,000 (fiscal year ending May 31, 2000 approx); $200,000 (fiscal 1999 approx); $300,000 (fiscal 1997 approx). Note: Contributes through foundation only.
Assets: $2,403,414 (fiscal 1996); $2,336,371 (fiscal 1994); $3,458,098 (fiscal 1991)

Typical Recipients

Arts & Humanities: History & Archaeology, Libraries
Civic & Public Affairs: Clubs, Minority Business
Education: Business Education, Education Funds
Health: Public Health
Religion: Jewish Causes
Social Services: Community Service Organizations, Substance Abuse, United Funds/United Ways

Contributions Analysis

Civic & Public Affairs: About 90%. Supports a wide range of local programs across varying categories. Grantee recipients include Jewish United Funds, the St. Louis Mercantile Library Association, and the United Way.
Education: About 10%. Supports business schools, graduate studies, and local university foundations.

Restrictions

Company does not support individuals.

Foundation Officials

Bernard Alan Edison: member B Atlanta, GA 1928. ED Harvard University BA (1949); Harvard University MBA (1951). CORP AFFIL director: General America Life Insurance Co.; director: Reinsurance Group America Inc.; director: Anheuser-Busch Companies Inc.

Andrew E. Newman: member B Saint Louis, MO 1944. ED Harvard University BA (1966); Harvard University MBA (1968). PRIM CORP EMPL chairman,

chief executive officer, director: Race Rock International. CORP AFFIL director: Sigma-Aldrich Corp.; chairman: Race Rock Holdings; chairman, director: Edison Brothers Apparel Stores; director: Lee Enterprises Inc. NONPR AFFIL trustee: Washington University.

Grants Analysis

Disclosure Period: fiscal year ending May 31, 1996
Total Grants: $52,404
Number of Grants: 16
Average Grant: $3,275
Highest Grant: $27,000
Typical Range: $500 to $5,000

Recent Grants

Note: Grants derived from 1996 Form 990.

Arts & Humanities

1,000	Missouri Historical Society, St. Louis, MO
500	St. Louis Mercantile Library Association, St. Louis, MO

Civic & Public Affairs

2,000	St. Louis Minority Business Council, St. Louis, MO
2,000	Variety Club, St. Louis, MO

Education

5,635	Junior Achievement Mississippi Valley, Hazelwood, MO
1,000	Missouri Colleges Fund, Jefferson City, MO

Health

2,500	Business Health Coalition

Religion

27,000	Jewish Federation, St. Louis, MO
1,000	Iowa Jewish Senior Life Center, Des Moines, IA
200	Jewish United Fund, Chicago, IL

Social Services

4,469	United Way, St. Louis, MO
2,400	United Fund, Washington, MO
1,000	Boy Scouts of America, St. Louis, MO
1,000	Two/Ten Charity Trust
350	National Council of Alcoholism and Drugs, St. Louis, MO

EDISON INTERNATIONAL

 Number 88 of Top 100 Corporate Givers

Company Contact

2244 Walnut Grove Ave.
Rosemead, CA 91770
Phone: (626)302-1212
Fax: (626)302-2517
Web: http://www.edison.com

Company Description

Also Known As: Southern California Edison.
Revenue: US$9,670,000,000 (1999)
Profit: US$623,000,000 (1999)
Employees: 19,570 (1999)
Fortune Rank: 178, per FORTUNE Magazine's list of 500 Largest U.S. Corporations (1999).
FF 178
SIC(s): 4911 Electric Services.

Nonmonetary Support

Value: $254,000 (1996); $200,000 (1994); $80,000 (1989)
Type: Donated Equipment; In-kind Services; Loaned Executives
Contact: Marilyn Kalenda, Corp. Contributions Budget Analyst

Corporate Sponsorship

Value: $1,000
Type: Arts & cultural events
Note: Sponsors educational cultural/diversity events, arts, and health and human services programs.

Giving Contact

Lucia Galindo, Manager, Corporate Contributions
Southern California Edison Co.
Edison International
2244 Walnut Grove Ave.
PO Box 800
Rosemead, CA 91770
Phone: (626)302-9853
Fax: (626)302-8114
Email: galindle@SCE.com

Description

Organization Type: Corporate Giving Program
Giving Locations: CA: primarily in company's Southern CA service area; strategic giving outside traditional service territory
Grant Types: Employee Matching Gifts, General Support.
Note: Also awards special initative grants.

Financial Summary

Total Giving: $8,305,000 (1998); $8,125,000 (1997); $6,698,000 (1996). Note: Contributes through corporate direct giving program and foundation.
Giving Analysis: Giving for 1998 includes: corporate direct giving ($7,290,000); foundation ($1,015,000)

Typical Recipients

Arts & Humanities: Arts Associations & Councils, Arts Centers, Arts Institutes, Community Arts, Dance, Ethnic & Folk Arts, Historic Preservation, Libraries, Museums/Galleries, Music, Opera, Performing Arts, Public Broadcasting, Theater
Civic & Public Affairs: Business/Free Enterprise, Civil Rights, Economic Development, Economic Policy, Housing, Law & Justice, Professional & Trade Associations, Public Policy, Safety, Urban & Community Affairs, Women's Affairs, Zoos/Aquariums
Education: Business Education, Colleges & Universities, Economic Education, Engineering/Technological Education, Faculty Development, Education-General, Literacy, Minority Education, Private Education (Precollege), Science/Mathematics Education, Special Education
Environment: Environment-General
Health: Geriatric Health, Health Organizations, Hospices, Hospitals, Nursing Services
Science: Science Exhibits & Fairs, Scientific Centers & Institutes, Scientific Organizations
Social Services: Child Welfare, Community Centers, Community Service Organizations, Counseling, Emergency Relief, Family Services, People with Disabilities, Recreation & Athletics, Senior Services, Substance Abuse, United Funds/United Ways, Volunteer Services, Youth Organizations

Contributions Analysis

Giving Priorities: Minorities, social services, education, civic and public affairs, community centers, education, and the arts.

Application Procedures

Initial Contact: brief letter or proposal
Application Requirements: a description of organization, amount requested, purpose of funds sought, recently audited financial statement, and proof of tax-exempt status
Deadlines: None.

Restrictions

Company does not support fraternal, political, veterans, religious organizations, or public agencies.

Additional Information

Edison International is the parent compan ern California Edison and handles all re charitable contributions.
Publications: Guidelines

Corporate Officials

John E. Bryson: chairman, chief executive o contributions B New York, NY 1943. ED Stanford versity BA (1965); Freie University Berlin (19 1966); Yale University JD (1969). PRIM CORP EM chairman, chief executive officer: Edison Intern tional. CORP AFFIL chairman, chief executive office Southern California Edison Co.; director: Times Mirror Co.; director: Mission Group Inc.; director: Pacific America Income Shares Inc.; director: Boeing Corp.; chairman: Edison Mission Energy. NONPR AFFIL director: World Resources Institute; member, board editors, associate editor: Yale University Law Journal; member: Phi Beta Kappa; member: Stanford University Alumni Association; member: DC Bar Association; member: Oregon Bar Association; member: California Water Rights Law Review Committee; trustee: Claremont University Center; member: California Bar Association; member: California Pollution Control Financing Authority.
Stephen E. Frank: president, chief operating officer, director B 1938. PRIM CORP EMPL president, chief operating officer, director: Southern California Edison Co. CORP AFFIL director: Edison International; director: Arkwright Insurance Co. NONPR AFFIL director: University Virginia.
Thomas Higgins: vice president corporate contributions CORP AFFIL vice president: Southern California Edison Co.

Giving Program Officials

Thomas Higgins: vice president corporate contributions (see above)

Grants Analysis

Disclosure Period: calendar year ending 1998
Total Grants: $8,305,000
Typical Range: $500 to $10,000

Recent Grants

Note: Grants derived from 1994 grants list.

Education

100,000	East Los Angeles Community Union Education Foundation, Los Angeles, CA

EDS CORP.

Company Contact

Plano, TX
Web: http://www.eds.com

Company Description

Revenue: US$16,900,000,000
Profit: US$1,743,400,000
Employees: 20,000
Fortune Rank: 91, per FORTUNE Magazine's list of 500 Largest U.S. Corporations (1999).
FF 91
SIC(s): 7372 Prepackaged Software, 7373 Computer Integrated Systems Design, 7374 Data Processing & Preparation, 7379 Computer Related Services Nec.

Operating Locations

Belgium: AT Kearney Inc., Brussels, Brabant; Brazil: EDS do Brasil Ltda., Sao Paulo; Canada: Insurance Software Solutions Corp., Mississauga; AT Kearney Ltd., Toronto; EDS Canada Leasing Ltd., Toronto; EDS of Canada Ltd., Toronto; Denmark: AT Kearney A/S, Copenhagen; Electronic Data Systems Danmark A/S, Soborg, Frederiksborg; EDS-FLS Data A/S, Valby, Copenhagen; France: Progical SA, Freyming Merlebach, Moselle; EDS Exploitation SNC, Le Blanc

…s-de-Seine; EDS …-Seine; AT Kear… …uilly-sur-Seine; Eu… …eine; Europe Assur… …ille-de-Paris; STE …ion, Puteaux, Hauts… …om Clinical Research … Nordrhein-Westfalen; …mbH, Bonn, Nordrhein… …mbH, Duesseldorf; Fides … Frankfurt, Hessen; EDS Kauf… …nformatik GmbH, Leuna, De… …GmbH, Ruesselsheim, Hessen; …dustrie (Deutschland) GmbH, …essen; EDS Industrien (Deutsch… …uesselsheim, Hessen; EDS Informa… …gie und Service (Deutschland) GmbH, …eim, Hessen; EDS Hotline Telefon Service …iesbaden, Hessen; Hong Kong: EDS (Hong …td., Admiralty; Hungary: EDS Elektronikus Ad… …dszer Korlatolt Feleossego Tarsasag, Budapest; …and: EDS (Ireland) Ltd., Dublin; Neodata Services …td., Limerick; Sarsfield Systems Ltd., Limerick; Italy: AT Kearney SpA, Milano, Lombardia; EDS Italia SpA, Torino, Piemonte; Japan: AT Kearney International, Tokyo; EDS Japan Ltd., Tokyo; Mexico: EDS de Mexico SA de CV, Ciudad de Mexico; Netherlands: AT Kearney BV, Amsterdam, Noord-Holland; Electronic Data Systems (EDS) Intl BV, Leidschendam, Zuid-Holland; Electronic Data Systems (EDS) CVI NV, Utrecht; Centrum Voor Agri-Informatisering BV, Veenendaal, Utrecht; Norway: AT Kearney AS, Oslo, Akershus; AT Kearney Intl AS, Oslo, Akershus; Electronic Data Systems (EDS) AS, Oslo, Akershus; Haberstad Consulting AS, Oslo, Akershus; New Zealand: EDS (New Zealand) Holdings Ltd., Wellington; Poland: EDS Poland Sp Zoo, Warsaw, Warszawa; Portugal: EDS de Portugal Processamento de Dados Informaticos Lda., Lisboa; Singapore: EDS International (Singapore) Pte. Ltd., Singapore; Spain: Centro de Trabajos Bancarios y Organizacion de Servicos SA, Alcobendas, Madrid; EDS Espana SA, Alcobendas, Madrid; AT Kearney GmbH (Sucursal en Espana), Madrid; IGR Ingenieria y Gestion de Redes SA, Madrid; EDS Barcelona SA, Sant Cugat del Valles, Catalun; Sweden: EDS Forsvars Service AB, Stockholm; EDS Sweden AB, Stockholm; Switzerland: EDS (Schweiz) AG, Biel, Bern; Fides Informatik, Zurich; Taiwan: China Management Systems Corp., Taipei; United Kingdom: Insurance Software Solutions Corp., Crawley, West Sussex; AT Kearney Ltd., London; Venezuela: EDS de Venezuela, Caracas
Note: Operates throughout the USA.

Nonmonetary Support

Type: Cause-related Marketing & Promotion; Donated Equipment; Donated Products; In-kind Services; Loaned Employees; Loaned Executives; Workplace Solicitation
Volunteer Programs: Each year, the company sponsors a 'Global Volunteer Day,' an annual day of celebration for ongoing volunteerism and giving back. As the volunteerism movement has grown worldwide, EDS' program has grown in interest and participation.

Corporate Sponsorship

Type: Arts & cultural events; Music & entertainment events; Festivals/fairs
Note: Sponsors March of Dimes Walk America, Junior Achievement, United Way events, and blood, food, and clothing drives.

Giving Contact

Kym Webster, Director, Community Affairs
EDS Corp.
5400 Legacy Drive, H3-6F-47
Plano, TX 75024
Phone: (972)605-6825
Fax: (972)605-8625
Email: kym.webster@exsc01.exch.www.eds
Web: http://www.eds.com/community_affairs

Alternate Contact

Phone: (972)605-6824

Description

Organization Type: Corporate Giving Program
Giving Locations: headquarters and operating communities.
Grant Types: Award, Conference/Seminar, Emergency, General Support, Loan, Matching.

Giving Philosophy

'Increasingly, educators and business leaders are reaching the conclusion that education is the essential component of success for future generations. The success of many companies, including EDS, depends on a qualified workforce that can successfully compete in the information age.
'EDS' Community Affairs mission is to support educational initiatives that prepare individuals to lead productive and fulfilling lives in the global economy.
'Our contribution philosophy mirrors this mission in that we will give special consideration to programs advancing education. We will contribute to organizations who operate in locations where our employees live and work and those with which our employees are involved.
'In addition, all EDS contributions must meet the general policies set out in the guidelines.' *EDS Giving Guidelines*

Financial Summary

Total Giving: Contributes through corporate direct giving program only.

Typical Recipients

Arts & Humanities: Arts & Humanities-General
Civic & Public Affairs: Employment/Job Training, Civic & Public Affairs-General, Urban & Community Affairs
Education: Education-General
Social Services: Community Centers, Community Service Organizations, Counseling, Family Services, Homes, People with Disabilities, Recreation & Athletics, Shelters/Homelessness, Social Services-General, Substance Abuse, Volunteer Services, Youth Organizations

Contributions Analysis

Giving Priorities: EDS' philanthropy program extends worldwide and is based on its belief that the company has a responsibility to the communities in which it does business and where its employees work. In general, the company supports a wide variety of programs by supporting valuable ideas and building on community strengths. The company delivers not only dollars, but in-kind services as well.

Application Procedures

Initial Contact: Brief letter requesting copy of EDS Grant Application.
Application Requirements: Completed application form; names and affiliations of board members; list of current and potential donors, including amounts; proof of tax-exempt status and Form 990; copy of most recent CPA Audit Report; and annual report and any other support materials.
Deadlines: None, but proposals should be submitted two months prior to the date funding is needed.
Review Process: Requests are screened and reviewed by staff only when they comply with EDS grant criteria; most contributions are granted for one year; additional funding requires a new request in order to be considered.
Evaluative Criteria: Supports organizations where EDS support is vital or catalytic to success; programs which show strong, measurable success and contribute to organizations in locations where the company is a corporate citizen. Special consideration is given to nonprofit organizations in which EDS employees participate.
Decision Notification: Requests are evaluated quarterly, each February, May, August and November, by the EDS corporate contributions committee; applicants are informed in writing of the committee's funding decision.
Notes: Completed applications should be sent to a local EDS account.

Restrictions

Does not support individuals; endowment campaigns; grant-making foundations; fraternal, social or labor organizations; organizations discriminating by race, religion, color, sex or national origin; religious organizations for sectarian purposes; political or partisan organizations; trips or tours; or organizations receiving United Way funding, except for specific program requests not funded by the umbrella organization.
No grants are made for operating deficits, single-disease organizations, for sponsorship of athletic teams or events, or for journal or program advertising. Capital and multiyear grants are rarely made.
Requests that are not made in writing will not be considered for funding.

Additional Information

EDS grant recipients must submit a report within one year of the grant. The report should contain the following information: projected versus actual expenditures by expense category; whether project's or organization's objectives were met; new developments associated with the program; and any other supplementary information.
One-time grant requests receive the strongest consideration. Requests for multiyear and/or capital campaigns may be considered on a limited basis for exceptional projects. limited basis for exceptional projects.
Publications: Eds Guidelines for Grant Applications

Corporate Officials

Richard Harris Brown: chairman, chief executive officer, director B New Brunswick, NJ 1947. ED Ohio University BS (1969). PRIM CORP EMPL chairman, chief executive officer, director: EDS Corp. CORP AFFIL director: Seagram Co. Ltd.; director: Pharmacia and Upjohn Inc.; director: Cable & Wireless PLC; director: Hong Kong Telecom. NONPR AFFIL member: Sigma Chi.

Giving Program Officials

Diane Spradlin: PRIM CORP EMPL director community affairs: EDS Corp.

J.D. Edwards Enterprise Software

Company Contact

Denver, CO

Company Description

Former Name: J.D. Edwards World Solutions Co.
Employees: 3,996 (1999)
SIC(s): 7372 Prepackaged Software.

Nonmonetary Support

Type: Cause-related Marketing & Promotion; Donated Equipment
Volunteer Programs: Company provides employee volunteers for the Habitat for Humanity Summer Build Program.

J.D. Edwards Foundation

Giving Contact

Leslie Testa, Foundation Assistant
J.D. Edwards Foundation
1 Technology Way
Denver, CO 80237
Phone: (303)334-4807
Fax: (303)799-1705
Email: leslie_testa@jdedwards.com

Description

Founded: 1991
EIN: 841168312
Organization Type: Corporate Foundation
Giving Locations: CO: Denver
Grant Types: Emergency, General Support.

Giving Philosophy

'Founded in 1991, the Foundation has chosen to focus its financial support on organizations that touch the lives of people who face adversity. This would include, but not be limited to, the homeless, the hungry, the abused or forgotten child, and the teenager looking for assistance.'

Financial Summary

Total Giving: $596,727 (1998); $539,279 (1997); $454,900 (1996). Note: Contributes through foundation only.
Giving Analysis: Giving for 1997 includes: foundation ($539,279); 1998: foundation ($596,727)
Assets: $677,055 (1997); $1,067,378 (1996); $936,330 (1995)
Gifts Received: $300,000 (1996); $250,000 (1995); $252,000 (1994). Note: Contributions are received from J.D. Edwards & Co.

Typical Recipients

Arts & Humanities: Arts Outreach
Civic & Public Affairs: Economic Development, Employment/Job Training, Civic & Public Affairs-General, Housing, Native American Affairs, Nonprofit Management, Public Policy, Safety, Urban & Community Affairs
Education: Afterschool/Enrichment Programs, Colleges & Universities, Economic Education, Education Funds, Private Education (Precollege), Public Education (Precollege), School Volunteerism, Secondary Education (Private), Special Education
Health: Cancer, Children's Health/Hospitals, Clinics/Medical Centers, Prenatal Health Issues
International: International Organizations, Missionary/Religious Activities
Religion: Churches, Ministries, Religious Organizations, Religious Welfare
Social Services: At-Risk Youth, Child Welfare, Community Service Organizations, Counseling, Family Planning, Family Planning, Food/Clothing Distribution, People with Disabilities, Recreation & Athletics, Scouts, Shelters/Homelessness, Substance Abuse, Volunteer Services, Youth Organizations

Contributions Analysis

Giving Priorities: The foundation supports organizations that provide for the physical needs of underprivileged groups of people in the city of Denver.
Civic & Public Affairs: 26%. Supports housing and employment initiatives and urban affairs.
Education: 23%. Funds private education, tutoring, and economic education.
Health: 3%.
International: 4%.
Religion: 23%. Supports Christian ministries.
Social Services: 21%. Funds youth programs.
Note: Total contributions in 1997.

Application Procedures

Initial Contact: contact the foundation to receive funding guidelines
Application Requirements: One page cover letter tailored to address the interests and specific priorities of the funding source and amount requested; organization summary form provided by the foundation; a narrative, not to exceed three pages, including mission statement, goals, accomplishments, and current programs; purpose of funds sought; and the evaluation process. Also attach a list of board members, names and qualifications of key staff members, recently audited financial statement, agency budget, project budget, proof of tax-exempt status, list of other major contributors, and a list of volunteer involvements and in-kind contributions.
Deadlines: None.
Review Process: the board meets on a bi-monthly basis to review and approve/disapprove requests
Decision Notification: notification will be sent to requestors within thirty days of the Board's decisions
Notes: Requests will be considered wihin a six-month time frame from the time of receipt.

Restrictions

The foundation does not fund endowment funds; political campaigns; trips or tours; national health agencies or their local affiliates; general operating budgets or tax-supported educational institutions; religious organziations that are purely denominational or sectarian in purpose; brick and mortor projects; individuals; organizations that discriminate; fraternal organizations, clubs, school organizations, and school athletic funds; medical reseach and development funds; general operating budgets of organizations that receive more that 40% of their budget from the United Way; foundations that give grants; conferences, symposiums or workshops; annual memberships or affiliation campaigns, dinners or special events; travel or vehicle purchases; organizations relying on government funding (public tax dollars) for greater that 65% of annual operating revenue, except for pilot or demonstration projects for which government funding is not available; and general operating expenses, except in cases where continuity justifies grant support.

Corporate Officials

Richard E. Allen: vice president finance, chief financial officer PRIM CORP EMPL vice president finance, chief financial officer: J.D. Edwards Enterprise Software. CORP AFFIL chief financial officer: J.D. Edwards & Co.
C. Edward McVaney: founder, president B Omaha, NE 1941. PRIM CORP EMPL founder, president: J.D. Edwards Enterprise Software.

Foundation Officials

Mary E. Collison: vice chairman
Greg A. Dixon: chairman
Gary Fox: board member
Howard C. Kast: board member
Idella Kercher: treasurer
Kenneth London: board member
Jim Parish: board member

Grants Analysis

Disclosure Period: calendar year ending 1998
Total Grants: $596,727
Number of Grants: 33
Average Grant: $18,083
Highest Grant: $40,000
Typical Range: $10,000 to $20,000
Note: Grants analysis provided by foundation.

Recent Grants

Note: Grants derived from 1998 Form 990.

Arts & Humanities

10,000 Gathering Place, Denver, CO -- General Funds

Civic & Public Affairs

40,000 Habitat for Humanity, Denve[r, CO --] General Funds
20,000 Denver Works, Denver, CO -- [General] Funds
10,000 Damen House, Denver, CO -- G[eneral] Funds
10,000 Hope Communities, Denver, CO -- [Gen]eral Funds
5,000 Tailored Transitions, Denver, CO -- [Gen]eral Funds
250 Colorado Association of Foundations, Denver, CO -- General Funds

Education

50,447 Denver Street School, Denver, CO -- General Funds
33,280 Colorado Christian University, Lakewood, CO -- General Funds
30,000 Inner City Christian School Partnership, Barnhart, MO -- General Funds
25,000 Whiz Kids Tutoring, Denver, CO -- General Funds
10,000 Colorado Uplift, Denver, CO -- General Funds
5,000 Foundation for Students and Athletes, Logan, OH -- General Funds

Health

15,000 Inner City Health Center, Denver, CO -- General Funds

International

12,000 MOPS International, Denver, CO -- General Funds

Religion

40,000 COMPA Food Ministry, Denver, CO -- General Funds
28,000 Doulos Ministries, Denver, CO -- General Funds
25,000 Neighborhood Ministries, Denver, CO -- General Funds
20,000 Christian Corps International, Denver, CO -- General Funds
20,000 Network Ministries, Denver, CO -- General Funds
15,000 Denver Urban Ministries, Denver, CO -- General Funds
12,500 Fellowship of Christian Athletes, Englewood, CO -- General Funds
10,000 Colorado Christian Home, Denver, CO -- General Funds
5,000 Mile High Ministries, Denver, CO -- General Funds

Social Services

50,000 Executive Network/Prov. Homes, Denver, CO -- General Funds
25,000 Friends in Transition, Denver, CO -- General Funds
15,000 Genesis Jobs, Denver, CO -- General Funds
15,000 Save Our Youth, Denver, CO -- General Funds
10,000 Alternative Pregnancy Center, Denver, CO -- General Funds
10,000 Northwest Denver Young Life, Denver, CO -- General Funds
10,000 Urban Peak, Denver, CO -- General Funds
5,000 Warren Village, Denver, CO -- General Funds
3,500 Family Homestead, Denver, CO -- General Funds
2,000 Boy Scouts of America, Denver, CO -- General Funds

El Paso Energy Co.

Company Contact

Houston, TX

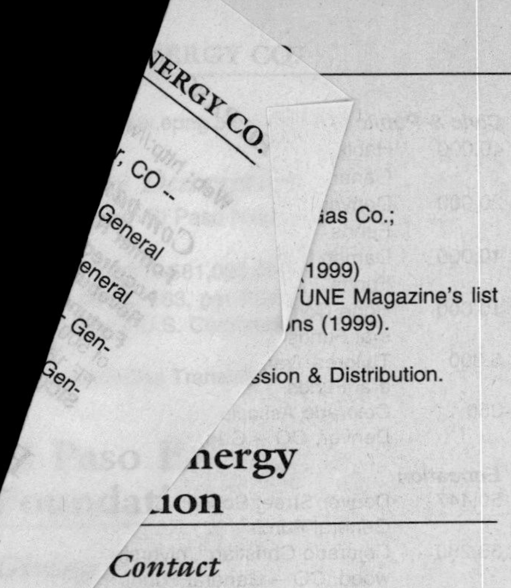

...as Co.;

...(1999)

...UNE Magazine's list ...ns (1999).

...ssion & Distribution.

...nergy ...ion

Contact

...unn, President
...Energy Foundation
... Louisiana Street
...uston, TX 77002
...hone: (713)420-3750
Fax: (713)420-4993

Description

Founded: 1992
EIN: 742638185
Organization Type: Corporate Foundation
Giving Locations: AZ; CA; CO; NM; TX: western area nationally.
Grant Types: Award, Challenge, Department, Employee Matching Gifts, General Support, Matching, Multiyear/Continuing Support.

Financial Summary

Total Giving: $2,404,773 (1997); $1,505,999 (1996); $1,500,000 (1995). Note: Contributes through foundation only. 1996 Giving includes United Way. 1995 Giving includes foundation and United Way.
Giving Analysis: Giving for 1996 includes: foundation ($1,426,989); foundation grants to United Way ($79,010); 1997: foundation ($2,226,482); foundation grants to United Way ($157,181); foundation scholarships ($21,110)
Assets: $5,092,168 (1997); $4,232,381 (1996); $4,238,184 (1995)
Gifts Received: $2,800,000 (1997); $1,180,000 (1996); $1,322,519 (1995). Note: Contributions were received from El Paso Natural Gas Co.

Typical Recipients

Arts & Humanities: Arts Centers, Ballet, History & Archaeology, Libraries, Museums/Galleries, Music, Opera, Performing Arts, Public Broadcasting, Theater
Civic & Public Affairs: Chambers of Commerce, Clubs, Community Foundations, Economic Development, Economic Policy, Civic & Public Affairs-General, Hispanic Affairs, Native American Affairs, Nonprofit Management, Urban & Community Affairs, Women's Affairs, Zoos/Aquariums
Education: Afterschool/Enrichment Programs, Agricultural Education, Arts/Humanities Education, Colleges & Universities, Community & Junior Colleges, Education Reform, Engineering/Technological Education, Education-General, International Studies, Legal Education, Public Education (Precollege), School Volunteerism, Science/Mathematics Education, Student Aid
Environment: Protection, Resource Conservation
Health: Alzheimers Disease, Cancer, Hospices, Hospitals (University Affiliated), Medical Rehabilitation, Medical Research, Nursing Services, Public Health
International: Foreign Arts Organizations, International Development, International Organizations
Religion: Ministries, Religious Welfare
Science: Scientific Centers & Institutes
Social Services: Animal Protection, At-Risk Youth, Child Abuse, Child Welfare, Community Service Organizations, Day Care, Domestic Violence, Family Services, Food/Clothing Distribution, People with Disabilities, Recreation & Athletics, Scouts, Senior Services, United Funds/United Ways, YMCA/YWCA/YMHA/YWHA, Youth Organizations

Contributions Analysis

Arts & Humanities: About 15%. Cultural support includes the performing arts, visual arts, historical centers, public and educational broadcasting, and other related activities.
Civic & Public Affairs: About 22%. Supports economic and community development and ethnic affairs organizations. Other interests include organizations that are government-related, community-based organizations concerned with crime prevention, and parks and recreation facilities.
Education: About 25% of funding. Supports public and private colleges and universities throughout its service region. Also provides major support for a summer school for the arts. Generally, contributions are directed toward the improvement of the quality of education. Ordinarily, the foundation does not support requests to finance the expansion of a student body or the payment of scholarships.
Health: About 4%. Supports hospitals and medical facilities and programs such as hospital building and equipment, and improvement campaigns. Operating expenses are not covered.
Social Services: About 31%. Major support for the United Way. Also supports traditional youth organizations and programs assisting runaway youth, chemical dependency prevention, senior citizens, spouse and child abuse prevention, offender programs, and women's programs.

Application Procedures

Initial Contact: Send letter requesting an application form.
Application Requirements: Organization name and contact information, project title and description, geographic area to be served, client group to be served, size of group, anticipated project period, type of request, total project cost, amount requested from the foundation, amount and source of pledges/commitments to date, other funding sources applied to for this project (including amount requested), purpose for project, statement of need, relevance to foundation, approach for implementing project, local support for the project, coordination with other groups in the community working on similar problems, how project will be evaluated, specific use of foundation's funds, future support, competence of organization to implement the project, and information on the use of outside consultants.
Deadlines: None.

Restrictions

Does not support religious organizations for religious purposes; war veterans and fraternal service organizations; endowment funds; national health organizations and programs, including their local chapters; grants or loans to individuals; fundraising events, including tickets, dinners, and telethons; corporate memberships or contributions to chambers of commerce, taxpayer associations, and other bodies whose activities are expected to directly benefit the company; political organizations, campaigns, and candidates; computers or computer-related projects. computers or computer-related projects.

Additional Information

Foundation emphasizes that incomplete applications or applications incorrectly completed will be returned. Foundation requests that applicants not call the foundation during the four-month review process. All applicants receive written notification of a funding decision when it has been reached.
Company was formerly known as the El Paso Natural Gas Company.

Corporate Officials

H. Brent Austin: executive vice president, chief financial officero, director B 1954. ED University of Texas BA (1975); University of Texas MBA (1978). PRIM CORP EMPL executive vice president, chief financial officer: El Paso Energy Co.
Norma F. Dunn: vice president investor & public relations PRIM CORP EMPL vice president investor & public relations: El Paso Energy Co.
William Allen Wise: chairman, president, chief executive officer, director B Davenport, IA 1945. ED Vanderbilt University BA (1967); University of Colorado JD (1970). PRIM CORP EMPL chairman, president, chief executive officer, director: El Paso Energy Co. CORP AFFIL director: Texas Commerce Bank; chairman: Tennessee Gas Pipeline Co.; director: Texas Commerce Bancshares Inc.; member: New York Mercantile Exchange; president: El Paso Gas Marketing Co.; chairman: El Paso Natural Gas Co.; chairman: Channel Industries Gas Co.; chairman: Altamont Gas Transmission; director: Battle Mountain Gold Co. NONPR AFFIL director: University Colorado Foundation; member business advisory council: University Texas; member: Tri-Regional Com.; director: Natural Gas Council; director: Texas Gov's Business Council; member: National Petroleum Council; director: Gas Industry Studies; director: Interstate Natural Gas Association America; member: Colorado Bar Association; director: American Gas Association; board visitors: M.D. Anderson Cancer Center. CLUB AFFIL River Oaks Country Club; Georgetown Club; Old Baldy Club; El Paso Country Club.

Foundation Officials

H. Brent Austin: vice president, treasurer, director (see above)
Richard Owen Baish: senior vice president, director B Fort Worth, TX 1946. ED Southwest Texas State University (1969); University of Texas (1972). PRIM CORP EMPL president: El Paso Natural Gas Co. CORP AFFIL president: El Paso Energy Corp.; president: Mojave Pipeline Co.
Norma F. Dunn: prs (see above)
Norbert R. Grijalva: tax officer
Stacy J. James: secretary PRIM CORP EMPL secretary: El Paso Energy Co.
Eldon J. Mitrisin: assistant secretary
Joel Richards, III: vice president B Salt Lake City, UT 1946. ED Brigham Young University BA (1969); Brigham Young University MA (1971). PRIM CORP EMPL executive vice president human resources administration: El Paso Energy Co. CORP AFFIL executive vice president: El Paso Tennessee Pipeline Co.; executive vice president: El Paso Natural Gas Co. NONPR AFFIL member: Pacific Coast Gas Association; member: Southern Gas Association; member: National Gas Transmission Employee Relations Group; member: Labor Policy Association.
Britton White, Jr.: vice president B 1944. ED Colorado College BA (1966); University of Colorado JD (1970). PRIM CORP EMPL executive vice president, general counsel, director government affairs: El Paso Energy Co. CORP AFFIL executive vice president: El Paso Natural Gas Co.; executive vice president: El Paso Tennessee Pipeline Co.
William Allen Wise: chairman, director (see above)

Grants Analysis

Disclosure Period: calendar year ending 1997
Total Grants: $2,226,482*
Number of Grants: 164
Average Grant: $12,304*
Highest Grant: $221,000
Typical Range: $7,500 to $15,000
***Note:** Giving excludes scholarship and United Way. Average grant figure excludes highest grant.

Recent Grants

Note: Grants derived from 1997 Form 990.

Arts & Humanities

55,000 The Santa Fe Opera, Santa Fe, NM
50,000 El Paso Museum of Art, El Paso, TX
50,000 Houston Grand Opera, Houston, TX
25,000 Georgia O'Keefe Museum, Santa Fe, NM
25,000 Houston Symphony Society, Houston, TX
15,000 El Paso Community Television Found, El Paso, TX
15,000 El Paso Symphony Orchestra Association, El Paso, TX

Civic & Public Affairs

2,800,000 El Paso Natural Gas Company, Houston, TX
150,000 Greater El Paso Chamber of Commerce Found, El Paso, TX
50,000 Greater El Paso Chamber of Commerce, El Paso, TX
25,000 El Paso Zoological Society, El Paso, TX
25,000 Women's Resource Center of El Paso, El Paso, TX
20,000 Urban Affairs Corp, Houston, TX
1,730 Council on Foundations, Washington, DC
1,250 Conference of Southwest Foundations, Dallas, TX

Education

221,205 University of Texas/El Paso, El Paso, TX
85,700 California State Summer School for the Arts, Los Angeles, CA
30,000 University of Colorado Foundation, Boulder, CO
27,046 Colorado School of Mines, Golden, CO
27,000 San Juan College, Farmington, NM
25,000 Foundation for Advancement of Science in Education, Los Angeles, CA
21,110 National Merit Scholarship Corp, Evanston, IN
20,000 Southwestern University, Georgetown, TX
15,000 Oncology Services of Texas Inc, Houston, TX
12,550 University of Oklahoma, Norman, OK

Environment

20,000 Nature Conservancy Inc, Santa Fe, NM

Health

50,000 MD Anderson Cancer Center, Houston, TX
Susan G Komen Breast Cancer Found, Houston, TX

International

25,000 The FEMAP Foundation, El Paso, TX

Religion

25,000 NW Assistance Ministers, Houston, TX

Social Services

151,000 Womens Resource Center of El Paso, El Paso, TX
106,395 United Way of El Paso County, El Paso, TX
50,000 Boys & Girls Club of El Paso, El Paso, TX
50,000 Chicano Family Center, Houston, TX
50,000 Young Women's Christian Association/El Paso, El Paso, TX
35,000 Young Womens Christian Association/Houston, Houston, TX
25,000 The Childrens Assessment Center Found, Houston, TX
25,000 Serve Houston Youth Corp, Houston, TX
25,000 Sun Bowl Association, El Paso, TX
20,000 Assistance League of El Paso, El Paso, TX
15,828 Junior Achievement, Houston, TX
15,000 Boy Scouts of America/Sam Houston, Houston, TX
15,000 Child Advocates Inc, Houston, TX
15,000 Initiatives for Children, Houston, TX
15,000 Junior Achievement Inc, Houston, TX

ELF ATOCHEM NORTH AMERICA, INC.

Company Contact

Philadelphia, PA

Company Description

Employees: 3,600
SIC(s): 1479 Chemical & Fertilizer Mining Nec, 2812 Alkalies & Chlorine, 2813 Industrial Gases, 2819 Industrial Inorganic Chemicals Nec.
Parent Company: Enterprise de Recherches et d'Activites Petrolieres
Parent Revenue: US$36,340,000,000

Operating Locations

AL: Elf Atochem North America, Inc., Mobile; CA: Turco Products Division, Long Beach; Elf Atochem North America, Inc., Los Angeles; Decco Division, Monrovia; Elf Atochem North America, Inc., Monrovia; Turco Products Division, Westminster; GA: Elf Atochem North America, Inc.; IA: Sanofi, Ft. Dodge; KY: Elf Atochem North America, Inc., Calvert City, Carrollton; MA: Pharmasol Corp., South Easton; MI: Atochem, Wyandotte; Elf Atochem North America, Inc., Wyandotte; MN: Atochem, Blooming Prairie; Sanofi Diagnostias Pasteur, Chaska; MO: Elf Aquitaine Asphalt, Saint Louis; NY: Elf Atochem North America, Inc., Buffalo; Elf Atochem Organic Peroxides Plant, Buffalo; Elf Atochem North America, Inc., Homer; Accecones Ricci USA, New York; Elf Aquitaine, New York; Elf Sanofi, New York; Parfums Van Cleef & Arpels, New York; Sanofi Beaute, New York; Sanofi Pharmaceuticals, New York; Sanofi Research, New York; Stendhal, New York; OH: Elf Atochem North America, Inc., Delaware; Turco Products Division, Marion; OK: Atochem, Pryor; Elf Atochem North America, Inc., Pryor, Tulsa; PA: Elf Atochem North America, Inc., Cornwells Heights, King of Prussia; Sanofi Research Division, Malvern; Aviation & Performance Chemicals Division, Philadelphia; Elf Atochem North America, Philadelphia; Elf Atochem North America, Agrichemicals Division, Philadelphia; Elf Atochem North America Basic Chemicals Division, Philadelphia; Elf Atochem North America, Fluorochemical Division, Philadelphia; Elf Atochem North America, Inc., Philadelphia; Specialty Chemicals, Philadelphia; Atochem Services, Valley Forge; SC: Atochem, Andrews; TX: Elf Atochem North America, Inc., Beaumont; Elf Exploration, Houston; Elf Trading, Houston; Elf Atochem North America, Inc., Seagraves; WA: Genetic Systems Corp., Seattle; Elf Atochem North America, Inc., Tacoma; WI: Ato-Findley, Wauwatosa

Elf Atochem North America Foundation

Giving Contact

Mr. George L. Hagar, Executive Secretary
Elf Atochem North America Foundation
2000 Market St.
Philadelphia, PA 19103
Phone: (215)419-7653
Fax: (215)419-5494

Description

Founded: 1957
EIN: 236256818
Organization Type: Corporate Foundation
Giving Locations: nationally; op communities.
Grant Types: Capital, Employee M General Support.
Note: Employee matching gift ratio: 1 to makes tuition payments for children of e

Financial Summary

Total Giving: $634,070 (1998); $486,503 $600,000 (1996 approx). Note: Contributes corporate direct giving program and foundatio
Giving Analysis: Giving for 1996 includes: fo tion ($366,985); foundation grants to United ($89,193); foundation matching gifts ($30,213); 19 foundation ($519,462); foundation grants to Unit Way ($86,143); foundation matching gifts ($28,462
Assets: $107,982 (1998); $232,978 (1997) $357,143 (1995)
Gifts Received: $527,143 (1998); $467,149 (1997); $800,008 (1995). Note: Contributions are received from the Elf Atochem North American, Inc.

Typical Recipients

Arts & Humanities: Arts Centers, Ballet, Community Arts, Dance, Historic Preservation, History & Archaeology, Libraries, Museums/Galleries, Music, Opera, Performing Arts, Public Broadcasting, Theater
Civic & Public Affairs: Business/Free Enterprise, Chambers of Commerce, Economic Development, Economic Policy, Employment/Job Training, Civic & Public Affairs-General, Law & Justice, Municipalities/Towns, Philanthropic Organizations, Professional & Trade Associations, Public Policy, Safety, Urban & Community Affairs, Zoos/Aquariums
Education: Arts/Humanities Education, Business Education, Colleges & Universities, Community & Junior Colleges, Economic Education, Education Reform, Engineering/Technological Education, Education-General, Minority Education, Private Education (Precollege), Science/Mathematics Education, Student Aid
Environment: Environment-General
Health: Clinics/Medical Centers, Emergency/Ambulance Services, Hospitals, Medical Rehabilitation, Medical Research
International: Foreign Educational Institutions
Science: Science Museums, Scientific Centers & Institutes, Scientific Organizations
Social Services: Big Brother/Big Sister, Community Service Organizations, People with Disabilities, United Funds/United Ways, Volunteer Services, YMCA/YWCA/YMHA/YWHA, Youth Organizations

Contributions Analysis

Giving Priorities: United Ways in Pennsylvaia and New Jersey, colleges and universities, and various civic and cultural organizations.
Arts & Humanities: 1%.
Civic & Public Affairs: 62%. Civic support goes to better government, economic development, the environment, and community affairs.
Education: 24%. Supports employee matching gifts to colleges and universities and other educational institutions, and tuition payments for children of employees. Also supports individual schools, Junior Achievement, education funds, and higher education associations.
Social Services: 13%. Funds United Ways.
Note: Total contributions in 1998.

Application Procedures

Initial Contact: Send a brief letter or proposal.
Application Requirements: Include a description of organization, amount requested, purpose of funds sought, recently audited financial statement, proof of tax-exempt status.
Deadlines: None.

Restrictions

The foundation generally does not support political or lobbying groups or member agencies of united funds.

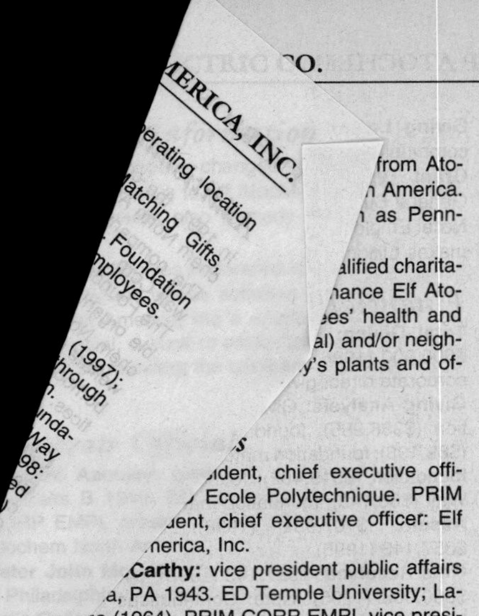

from Ato-
n America.
n as Penn-

alified charita-
nance Elf Ato-
ees' health and
al) and/or neigh-
y's plants and of-

s

ident, chief executive offi-
Ecole Polytechnique. PRIM
ident, chief executive officer: Elf
erica, Inc.
Carthy: vice president public affairs
a, PA 1943. ED Temple University; La-
ge (1964). PRIM CORP EMPL vice presi-
lic affairs: Elf Atochem North America, Inc.

undation Officials

eorge L. Hagar: executive secretary PRIM CORP EMPL executive secretary: Elf Atochem North America, Inc.

F. H. Lauchert: trustee

Peter John McCarthy: trustee (see above)

Grants Analysis

Disclosure Period: calendar year ending 1998
Total Grants: $519,462*
Number of Grants: 75
Average Grant: $6,926
Highest Grant: $200,000
Typical Range: $50 to $7,500
***Note:** Giving excludes matching gifts; United Way.

Recent Grants

Note: Grants derived from 1998 Form 990.

Arts & Humanities

200,000 Avenue of the Arts, Philadelphia, PA -- CIVIC
100,000 Philadelphia Museum, Philadelphia, PA -- CIVIC
12,000 Philadelphia Museum.., Philadelphia, PA -- CIVIC
10,000 Opera Company of Philadelphia, Philadelphia, PA -- CIVIC
5,000 Arden Theater Company, Philadelphia, PA -- CIVIC
5,000 WHYY-TV, Philadelphia, PA -- CIVIC
1,000 Afro-American Historical and Cultural Museum, Philadelphia, PA -- CIVIC
500 River Heritage Center, Paducah, KY -- Museum
350 WHYY-TV, Philadelphia, PA -- Broadcasting
325 WHYY-TV, Philadelphia, PA -- Broadcasting
324 WHYY-TV, Philadelphia, PA -- Broadcasting

Civic & Public Affairs

22,337 ELF Atochem, Philadelphia, PA -- CIVIC
5,000 Philadelphia Zoo, Philadelphia, PA -- CIVIC

Education

5,000 Academy of Music, Philadelphia, PA -- CIVIC
2,050 University of Pennsylvania, Philadelphia, PA -- Matching
1,500 Cornell University, Ithaca, NY -- Matching
1,400 Columbia University, New York, NY -- Matching
1,020 Lehigh University, Bethlehem, PA -- Matching
1,000 Elmira College, Elmira, NY -- Matching
1,000 Mississippi State University, Mississippi State, MS -- Matching
1,000 Mount Holyoke College, South Hadley, MA -- Matching
1,000 University of Florida, Gainesville, FL -- Matching
1,000 Villanova University, Villanova, PA -- Matching
925 St. Joseph's University, Philadelphia, PA -- Matching
550 Drexel University, Philadelphia, PA -- Matching
500 University of Pennsylvania, Philadelphia, PA -- Matching
500 University of Richmond, Richmond, VA -- Matching
500 Villanova University, Villanova, PA -- Matching
435 Rutgers University, New Brunswick, NJ -- Matching
425 Seton Hall University, South Orange, NJ -- Matching
350 University of Tulsa, Tulsa, OK -- Matching

International

1,000 Maharishi International University, Fairfield, IA -- Matching

Science

7,500 Franklin Institute, Philadelphia, PA -- CIVIC
6,500 Academy of Natural Science, Philadelphia, PA -- CIVIC

Social Services

41,143 United Way of Southeastern Pennsylvania, Philadelphia, PA -- United Way
22,000 United Way, Calvert City, KY -- United Way
10,000 United Way of Southwest Alabama, Axis, AL -- United Way
5,000 YMCA of Philadelphia, Philadelphia, PA -- CIVIC
3,200 United Way of Berks County, PA -- United Way
2,600 United Way of Livingston County, Rochester, NY -- United Way
2,000 United Way, MI -- United Way
1,400 United Way of Columbia Willamette, Houston, TX -- United Way
1,000 United Way, Plains, GA -- United Way
800 United Way of Cortland County -- United Way
800 United Way of Delaware County, Muncie, IN -- United Way
500 United Way, Beaumont, TX -- United Way
400 United Way of Georgetown County, Georgetown, SC -- United Way
300 United Way of Pierce County, Tacoma, WA -- United Way

Emerson Electric Co.

 Number 59 of Top 100 Corporate Givers

Company Contact

St. Louis, MO
Web: http://www.emersonelectric.com

Company Description

Revenue: US$14,270,000 (1999)
Profit: US$1,228,600,000
Employees: 116,900 (1999)
Fortune Rank: 121, per FORTUNE Magazine's list of 500 Largest U.S. Corporations (1999).
FF 121

SIC(s): 3423 Hand & Edge Tools Nec, 3491 Industrial Valves, 3546 Power-Driven Handtools, 3621 Motors & Generators.

Operating Locations

Australia: Fisher Rosemount Pty. Ltd., Bayswater; Ridge Tool (Australia) Pty. Ltd., Campbellfield; Leroy Somer Pty. Ltd., Deewhy; Ascomation Pty. Ltd., Frenchs Forest; Atlas Air Australia Pty. Ltd., Regents Park; Liebert Corp. Australia Pty. Ltd., Regents Park; Control Techniques Australia Pty. Ltd., Seven Hills; Fisher Controls Pty. Ltd., Wetherill Park; Sunvic Pty. Ltd., Wetherill Park; Austria: Buehlermet Handels GmbH, Modling, Niederosterreich; Leroy Somer Elektroantriebe GmbH, Vienna; Belgium: Bogerd NV, Antwerpen, Anvers; SA Joucomatic NV, Brussels, Brabant; Lipe-Rollway NV, Kontich, Anvers; Computational Systems, Leuven, Brabant; Computational Systems Inc. Europe NV, Leuven, Brabant; Ridge Tool Europe NV, Leuven, Brabant; Leroy Somer NV, Mechelen, Anvers; Fisher Rosemount NV, Mechelen, Brabant; Copeland GmbH Societe de Droit Allemand, Welkenraedt, Liege; Copeland Refrigeration Europe SA, Welkenraedt, Liege; Copeland SA, Welkenraedt, Liege; Control Techniques NV, Zaventem, Brabant; Brazil: Ridgid Ferramentas e Maquinas Ltda., Carapicuiba; Canada: Ascolectric Ltd., Brantford; Rosemount Instruments Ltd., Calgary; Appleton Electric Ltd., Cambridge, Cambridgeshire; Emerson Electric Canada Ltd., Markham; Metropolitan Wire (Canada) Ltd., Mississauga; Therm-O-Disc (Canada) Ltd., St. Thomas; Xomox Canada Ltd., Toronto; Computational Systems, Waterford; Fisher Controls, Woodstock; Denmark: Control Techniques A/S, Greve, Roskilde; Branson Ultrasonic Scandinavia, Kastrup, Copenhagen; Leroy Somer Denmark A/S, Odense, Fyn; Fisher Rosemount A/S, Porsgrunn, Telemark; France: Leroy Somer SA (Moteurs), Angouleme, Charente; Branson Ultrasons, Annemasse, Haute Savoie; Belzon et Richardot (Etablissements), Bavilliers; Constructions Electriques de Beaucourt, Beaucourt; Silvain (Societe Nouvelle), Beziers, Herault; Navarre Services, Billere, Pyrenees-Atlantiques; Michel (Societe Etablissment), Brie Comte Robert; Xomox France, Brunstatt, Haut Rhin; Silvain SA, Catillon Sur Sambre, Nord; Krautkramer France SA, Champagne Au Mont D'Or, Rhone; Bertrand Polico, Chateauneuf sur Charente; Metallurgie (Ste Confolentaise de), Confolens, Charente; Mezieres SARL, Cormontreuil, Marne; Ouest Electro Service, Coueron, Loire-Atlantique; Viet Services, Coulommiers, Seine-St.-Marne; Cocard Andre SA (A), Dijon, Cote-d'Or; Copeland France, Ecully, Rhone; Francel, Gallardon, Eure-et-Loir; Maintenance Industrie Service Rhone Alpes, Genas, Rhone; Mecanique et D'Electrothermie des Pays de L'Adour (SOC), Hasparren; Motadour SA, Hasparren; MIS Poitouraine, Joue les Tours, Indre-et-Loire; Electronique du Sud Ouest, La Couronne, Charente; Samov, Lalouvesc, Ardeche; Maintenance Industrie Services Rennes, Le Rheu, Ille et Vilaine; Girard Transmissions, Lons Pyrenees-Atlantiques; Patay (Moteurs), Lyon, Rhone; Etablissements Trepeau, Marennes; Reparation Electro Mecanique, Marly; Sevenier (ETS), Meyzieu, Rhone; Crouzet Appliance Controls, Montelier, Drome; Ridgid France, Morangis; Etirex SA, Noyant et Aconin, Aisne; J Michel (Establissements), Ponte Ste. Marie, Aube; Paillet Services (Ste Nouvelle), Rollot, Somme; MIS Spire, Rouen, Seine-Maritime; Asco Joucomatic SA, Rueil Malmaison; Emerson Europe, Rueil Malmaison; Maintenance Industrie Service, Soyaux, Charente; Marcel Oury (STE), St. Jean de la Ruelle, Loiret; Radiel Bobinage, Thyez, Haute Savoie; MIS Provence SA, Toulon; Maintenance Industrie Service Toulouse, Toulouse, Haute Garonne; Intellution SA, Tremblay en France; Maintenance Industrielle de Vierzon, Vierzon, Cher; Manutention (Francaise De), Vierzon, Cher; Constructions Electriques du Nord, Wasquehal, Nord; Germany: Emerson Electric (US) Holding Corp. Niederlassung Deutschland; Copeland GmbH, Berlin; Asco Joucomatic GmbH, Dietzenbach, Hessen; Emerson Electric GmbH, Dietzenbach, Hessen; Fisher

Rosemount GmbH, Dietzenbach, Hessen; Krautkraemer GmbH, Dietzenbach, Hessen; Xomox International GmbH, Dietzenbach, Hessen; INAG Electronic-U Motorenbau GmbH, Ditzingen, Baden-Wuerttemberg; Reglerwerk Dresden GmbH, Dresden, De-Ost; Fisher Controls GmbH, Duesseldorf; Wirtz Buehler GmbH, Duesseldorf; Leroy Somer Elektromotoren GmbH, Frankfurt, Hessen; Ridge Tool GmbH & Co. (OHG), Gevelsberg; Control Techniques GmbH, Hennef, Nordrhein-Westfalen; Liebert GmbH, Kirchheim, Bayern; Heraeus Sensor GmbH, Klein Ostheim, Bayern; Fisher Gulde Regelarmaturen GmbH & Co. KG, Ludwigshafen, Rheinland-Pfalz; Asco GmbH & Co., Ratingen, Nordrhein-Westfalen; Reta-Elektronik GmbH, Siegburg, Nordrhein-Westfalen; Lippe-Rollway Deutschland GmbH, Stolberg, Nordrhein-Westfalen; Emerson Electric GmbH & Co., Waiblingen, Baden-Wuerttemberg; Elomatic GmbH, Willich, Nordrhein-Westfalen; Hong Kong: Liebert Asia Ltd., Causeway Bay; Emerson Electric (Asia), Central District; Branson Ultrasonics (Asia Pacific) Co. Ltd., Kwun Tong, Kowloon; Fisher Controls Hong Kong Ltd., Wan Chai; Rosemount China (Hong Kong), Wan Chai; Hungary: Asco Magnesszelep Korlatolt Felelossegu Tarsasag, Budapest; IMI Elektromos Gepeket Gyarto KFT, Iklad, Pest; Ireland: Electric Drives Manufacturing Ltd., Dublin; Electric Drives Ltd., Newbridge; Italy: Crouzet Appliance Controls SpA, Bollate, Lombardia; Leroy Somer SpA, Lainate, Lombardia; Asco Joucomatic SpA, Milano, Lombardia; Sotrac SRL, Milano, Lombardia; Xomox Italia SRL, Opera, Lombardia; Control Techniques SpA, Rozzano, Lombardia; Japan: Asco (Japan) Co. Ltd., Nishinomiya, Hyogo; Emerson Japan Ltd., Tokyo; Nippon Fisher Co. Ltd., Tokyo; Mexico: Motores US de Mexico SA de CV, Apodaca; Usem de Mexico SA de CV, Apodaca; Ascomatica SA de CV, Ciudad de Mexico; Emerson Electric de Mexico SA de CV, Ciudad de Mexico; Transmisiones de Potencia Emerson SA de CV, El Salto; Asco Tech SA de CV, Mexicali; Fisher Controles de Mexico SA de CV, Toluca de Lerdo; Malaysia: Control Techniques Drives (Malaysia) Sdn. Bhd., Petaling Jaya, Selangor; Netherlands: Fusite BV, Almelo, Overijssel; Control Techniques Worldwide BV, Amsterdam, Noord-Holland; Intermetro Industries Corp., Breda, Noord-Brabant; Electrische Apparatenfabriek Capax BV, Eindhoven, Noord-Brabant; Elomatic BV, Hengelo, Overijssel; Newtech Cuikl BV, Hengelo, Overijssel; Fisher Rosemount BV, Rijswijk, Zuid-Holland; Asco Controls BV, Scherpenzeel, Gelderland; Asco Joucomatic ZA BV, Scherpenzeel, Gelderland; Asco Mideast BV, Scherpenzeel, Gelderland; Control Techniques Automation BV, Sliedrecht, Zuid-Holland; Control Techniques BV, Sliedrecht, Zuid-Holland; Branson Ultrasonics BV, Soest, Utrecht; Emerson Electric Nederland BV, Soest, Utrecht; Leroy Somer BV, Soesterberg, Utrecht; Emerson Computer Power BV, Swalmen, Limburg; Brooks Instrument BV, Veenendaal, Utrecht; Norway: Leroy Somer Norge AS, Asker, Akershus; ASI Control Techniques A/S, Drammen, Buskerud; New Zealand: Fisher Rosemount Ltd., Auckland; Ascomation (New Zealand) Ltd., Penrose; Portugal: Leroy Somer Motores e Sistemas Electrome Canicos Lda., Lisboa; Singapore: Control Techniques Asia Pacific Pte. Ltd., Singapore; Control Techniques Singapore Pte. Ltd., Singapore; Digital Appliance Controls Manufacturing Pte. Ltd., Singapore; Emerson Electric (South Asia/Pacific) Pte. Ltd., Singapore; Fisher Rosemount Singapore Private Ltd., Singapore; Leroy Somer (South East Asia) Pte. Ltd., Singapore; Liebert Far East Pte. Ltd., Singapore; Pacific Asia Control Techniques Mfg. Pte. Ltd. (Euro Control Techniques Pte. Ltd.), Singapore; Rosemount Singapore Pte. Ltd., Singapore; Spain: Fluidocontrol SA, Castro Urdiales, Cantabria; Leroy Somer Iberica SA, Irun, Navarra; Fisher Rosemount SA, Madrid; Branson Ultrasonidos SAE, Rubi, Cataluna; Sweden: Leroy Somer Norden AB; Asco AB, Boras, Alvsborg; Fisher Rosemount AB, Karlstad, Varmland; Switzerland: Fisher Rosemount AG, Baar, Zug; Ridgid Werkzeug AG, Rotkreuz, Zug; United Kingdom: Control Techniques Dynamics Ltd., Andover, Hampshire; Evershed Powerotor Ltd., Andover, Hampshire; Moore Reed & Co. Ltd., Andover, Hampshire; Metallurgical Services Laboratories Ltd., Betchworth, Surrey; Bannerscientific Ltd., Coventry, West Midlands; Buehler Europe Ltd., Coventry, West Midlands; Buehler Kraut Kramer, Coventry, West Midlands; Metaserv Ltd., Coventry, West Midlands; Computational Systems, Deeside, Clwyd; Leroy Somer Ltd., Hayes, Middlesex; Liebert Europe Ltd., Marlow, Buckinghamshire; Copeland Corp. Ltd., Newbury, Berkshire; Control Techniques Drives Ltd., Newtown, Powys; Control Techniques Precision Systems Ltd., Northampton, Northamptonshire; Computer Power Systems Ltd., Pulborough, West Sussex; Technodrives Ltd., Telford, Shropshire

Nonmonetary Support

Value: $10,000 (1993)

Corporate Sponsorship

Type: Arts & cultural events; Music & entertainment events; Sports events

Emerson Charitable Trust

Giving Contact

Ms. Jo Ann Harmon, Senior Vice President
Emerson ElectricCo.
8000 W. Florissant Ave.
Mail Station 3621
St. Louis, MO 63136
Phone: (314)553-3722
Fax: (314)553-1605

Description

EIN: 526200123
Organization Type: Corporate Foundation
Giving Locations: nationally, emphasizing operating locations.
Grant Types: Employee Matching Gifts, General Support, Project.

Giving Philosophy

'As a major manufacturer of some of the world's most technologically advanced products and systems, Emerson is constantly seeking ways to improve performance. The same holds true for our efforts to improve the quality of life in the communities where we operate. The objectives of the Emerson Electric Co. Charitable Trust are to encourage sound, innovative programs that enrich human lives, promote volunteerism, provide services directly to those in need, and increase the overall impact of contributed funds.' *Charitable Trust Guidelines*

Financial Summary

Total Giving: $14,410,121 (fiscal year ending September 30, 1998); $12,700,000 (fiscal 1997 approx); $12,500,000 (fiscal 1996). Note: Contributes through corporate direct giving program and foundation.
Giving Analysis: Giving for fiscal 1996 includes: foundation ($10,829,275); corporate direct giving ($1,841,725); fiscal 1998: foundation ($14,410,121)
Assets: $18,551,440 (fiscal 1998); $25,464,267 (fiscal 1996); $25,328,136 (fiscal 1994)
Gifts Received: $28,125 (fiscal 1996); $9,349,738 (fiscal 1994). Note: Foundation receives contributions from Emerson Electric.

Typical Recipients

Arts & Humanities: Arts Appreciation, Arts Associations & Councils, Arts Centers, Arts Funds, Arts Institutes, Ballet, Community Arts, Dance, Historic Preservation, History & Archaeology, Museums/Galleries, Music, Opera, Performing Arts, Public Broadcasting, Theater
Civic & Public Affairs: African Ame[illegible] tanical Gardens/Parks, Business/F[illegible] Civil Rights, Clubs, Community Fou[illegible] nomic Development, Economic Policy, [illegible] Job Training, Civic & Public Affairs-Ge[illegible] Justice, Parades/Festivals, Professional [illegible] sociations, Public Policy, Urban & Commu[illegible] Zoos/Aquariums
Education: Arts/Humanities Education, Bus[illegible] ucation, Business-School Partnerships, Co[illegible] Universities, Community & Junior Colleges[illegible] nomic Education, Education Associations, Edu[illegible] Funds, Engineering/Technological Education, Ed[illegible] tion-General, International Exchange, Leader[illegible] Training, Legal Education, Literacy, Medical Edu[illegible] tion, Minority Education, Private Education (Prec[illegible] lege), Public Education (Precollege), Science/Mathe[illegible] matics Education, Student Aid, Vocational & Technical Education
Environment: Environment-General, Protection
Health: AIDS/HIV, Alzheimers Disease, Children's Health/Hospitals, Health Organizations, Hospitals, Medical Research, Single-Disease Health Associations
International: International Relations
Religion: Religious Organizations
Science: Scientific Centers & Institutes
Social Services: Animal Protection, At-Risk Youth, Big Brother/Big Sister, Child Welfare, Community Centers, Community Service Organizations, Family Services, Homes, People with Disabilities, Recreation & Athletics, Scouts, Senior Services, Substance Abuse, United Funds/United Ways, YMCA/YWCA/YMHA/YWHA, Youth Organizations

Contributions Analysis

Giving Priorities: Social services, education, the arts, civics, and hospitals. The trust is restricted from making contributions overseas. Information on affiliates abroad is not tracked. Has supported U.S.-based organizations concerned with international relations such as the World Affairs Council, St. Louis, MO; Center for Stategic and Ineternational Studies, Washington, DC; and the Minnesota International Center, Minneapolis, MN.
Arts & Humanities: 10% to 15%. Almost all awards support organizations in the St. Louis area. Areas of interest are symphonies, arts centers, dance, historical societies, museums, and opera. Administers small matching gifts program in the arts.
Civic & Public Affairs: 10% to 15%. Areas of interest include minority representation in professional organizations, zoos and botanical gardens, business and free enterprise, public policy, and urban affairs.
Education: 30% to 35%. The majority is awarded to colleges and universities. Emphasis is on business, engineering, and technical education, with some interest in legal and medical education and public school systems. The majority of grants in this category are awarded in communities near company operating locations. Company administers employee matching grants program in education, and sponsors an educational scholarship program for children of employees.
Health: About 30%. Emphasis on united funds and youth organizations near company operating locations. Other areas of interest include community centers, homes, animal welfare, recreation and athletics, and substance abuse prevention and treatment.
Social Services: 25% to 30%. Supports youth development through mentoring, scouting, and related organizations.
Note: Foundation giving accounts for 80% of contributions; direct giving, 20%. Above priorities reflect foundation giving.

Application Procedures

Initial Contact: Send a written proposal.
Application Requirements: Include a brief description and history of the organization; statement of purpose and objectives of project, expected results, project budget, amount requested, statement of how funds will be used, and timetable; statement of the

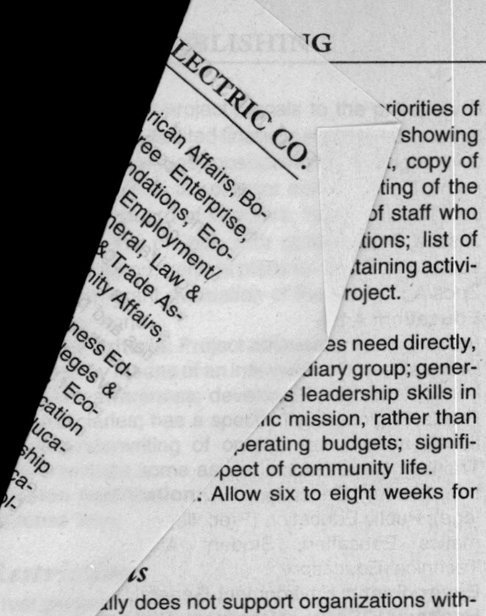

…riorities of … showing … , copy of … ting of the … of staff who … tions; list of … taining activi- … roject.

…es need directly, … diary group; gener- … s leadership skills in … ic mission, rather than … operating budgets; signifi- … pect of community life. … Allow six to eight weeks for

…s

…ally does not support organizations with- … 01(c)(3) tax-exempt status; organizations … ctice discrimination by race, color, creed, sex, … r national origin; religious or politically partisan … anizations; projects requiring funding directly to an … ganization located outside the United States or its territories; loans or investment funds; fraternal, veterans', or labor groups, unless they furnish services benefiting the general public; individuals; or underwriting of deficits or post-event funding.

Additional Information

Grantees must file a report on expenditures and results of funded project within one year of grant payment.

Publications: Charitable Trust Guidelines; Emerson Electric Co. Charitable Report

Corporate Officials

Laurance LeWright Browning, Jr.: director B Maysville, KY 1929. ED Cornell University BME (1952). PRIM CORP EMPL director: Emerson Electric Co. CORP AFFIL director: Star Banc Corp.; director: Star Bank NA.

Jo Ann Harmon: senior vice president administration PRIM CORP EMPL senior vice president administration: Emerson Electric Co.

Charles Field Knight: chairman, chief executive officer B Lake Forest, IL 1936. ED Cornell University BS (1958); Cornell University MBA (1959). PRIM CORP EMPL chairman, chief executive officer: Emerson Electric Co. ADD CORP EMPL chairman, director: Emerson Electric Holdings Inc.; chairman, director: Emerson Electric US Holdings Corp.; chairman: Emerson Puerto Rico Inc. CORP AFFIL director: Southwest Bell Corp.; director: Morgan Stanley Dean Witter Co.; director: SBC Communications Inc.; director: Caterpillar Inc.; director: IBM Corp.; director: Baxter International Inc.; director: BP Amoco Corp.; director: Anheuser-Busch Companies Inc. NONPR AFFIL member: Sigma Phi Epsilon; director, trustee: Washington University; director: Arts & Education Council. CLUB AFFIL Saint Louis Country Club; Glen View Golf Club; Log Cabin Club; Chicago Club; Crystal Downs Club.

Robert Wayne Staley: vice chairman Asia Pacific B Moline, IL 1935. ED Cornell University (1958); Cornell University (1959). PRIM CORP EMPL vice chairman Asia Pacific: Emerson Electric Co. CORP AFFIL director: Ace Ltd.

Albert E. Suter: senior vice chairman, chief administrative officer, director B East Orange, NJ 1935. ED Cornell University BME (1957); Cornell University MBA (1959). PRIM CORP EMPL senior vice chairman, chief administrative officer, director: Emerson Electric Co. CORP AFFIL director: Furniture Brands International Inc.; director: Nations Bank Corp. NONPR AFFIL director: Junior Achievement National Board; director: Saint Louis Science Center; director: Junior Achievement Mississippi Valley. CLUB AFFIL Old Warson Country Club; Saint Louis Club; member: Glenview Country Club; Log Cabin Club.

George W. Tamke: president, chief operating officer, director B 1948. PRIM CORP EMPL president, chief operating officer, director: Emerson Electric Co. CORP AFFIL president: Emerson Electric Overseas Finance Corp.

William Moore Van Cleve: partner B 1929. ED Princeton University AB (1950); Washington University JD (1953). PRIM CORP EMPL partner: Bryan Cave. CORP AFFIL director: Emerson Electric Co. NONPR AFFIL commissioner: Saint Louis Science Center; trustee, member executive committee: Washington University; vice chairman, trustee: Saint Louis Childrens Hospital; member: Saint Louis County Bar Association; member: Mound City Bar Association; vice president, director: Parents As Teachers National Center; member: Bar Association Metropolitan Saint Louis; member: American Bar Association. CLUB AFFIL Round Table Club; Saint Louis Country Club; Noonday Club; Princeton Club; Bogey Club.

Foundation Officials

Laurance LeWright Browning, Jr.: member public policy committee (see above)

Jo Ann Harmon: senior vice president (see above)

William Moore Van Cleve: member public policy committee (see above)

Eugene Flewellyn Williams, Jr.: member public policy committee B Saint Louis, MO 1923. ED Yale University BA (1945). CORP AFFIL director: Pitchfork Land & Cattle Co.; director: Saint Louis Refrigerator Car Co.; director: Manufacturers Railway Co.; director: America Airlines Inc.; director: Emerson Electric Co.

Grants Analysis

Disclosure Period: fiscal year ending September 30, 1996

Total Grants: $10,829,275

Number of Grants: 2,220

Average Grant: $4,466*

Highest Grant: $920,000

Typical Range: $25 to $10,000

***Note:** Average grant figure excludes highest grant.

Recent Grants

Note: Grants derived from fiscal 1997 Form 990.

Arts & Humanities

224,700 Interlochen Center for the Arts, Interlochen, MI
200,000 St. Louis Symphony Orchestra, St. Louis, MO
150,000 Municipal Theater Association, St. Louis, MO
100,000 Magic House, St. Louis, MO
100,000 Sheldon Arts Foundation, St. Louis, MO
97,500 Sheldon Arts Foundation, St. Louis, MO
49,500 Missouri Historical Society, St. Louis, MO

Civic & Public Affairs

600,000 St. Louis Zoo, St. Louis, MO
500,000 Forest Park Forever, St. Louis, MO
200,000 Missouri Botanical Gardens, St. Louis, MO
178,000 Civic Progress, St. Louis, MO
98,830 YP Fair Foundation
90,000 Variety Club, St. Louis, MO
75,000 Employment Policy Foundation, Washington, DC
65,000 Laumeier Sculpture Park, St. Louis, MO
53,000 Urban League, Jacksonville, FL
50,000 Urban League, St. Louis, MO

Education

200,000 St. Louis Regional Education, St. Louis, MO
200,000 University of Missouri Rolla, Rolla, MO
100,000 David Ranken Jr. Technical College, St. Louis, MO
100,000 Junior Achievement, St. Louis, MO
100,000 Today and Tomorrow Educational Foundation, St. Louis, MO
99,500 Webster University, Webster Groves, MO
90,000 University of Missouri St. Louis, St. Louis, MO
80,000 Junior Achievement, St. Louis, MO
80,000 St. Louis University, St. Louis, MO
50,000 Personal Responsibility Education Program
50,000 University of Kentucky, Lexington, KY
50,000 University of Minnesota, Minneapolis, MN
50,000 Valparaiso University, Valparaiso, IN
49,000 Personal Responsibility Education Program
45,000 Academy Research and Development Institute, Colorado Springs, CO

Health

100,000 Alzheimer's Association, St. Louis, MO
96,000 Oasis Institute Center for Attitudinal Healing, Knoxville, TN
54,650 City of Hope, Duarte, CA
53,000 City of Hope, Duarte, CA
50,000 St. Louis Children's Hospital, St. Louis, MO
50,000 St. Louis Children's Hospital, St. Louis, MO

Religion

50,000 St. Joseph Institute

Social Services

965,000 United Way, St. Louis, MO
100,000 Girl Scouts of America, St. Louis, MO
100,000 YWCA, St. Louis, MO
87,000 United Way Franklin County, Columbus, OH
85,000 United Way, Marshalltown, IA
80,000 Big Brothers and Big Sisters, St. Louis, MO
75,000 Boone Valley Classic Foundation, St. Louis, MO
75,000 United Way, Minneapolis, MN
70,000 United Way, Minneapolis, MN
63,801 United Way, Racine, WI
50,000 American Youth Foundation, St. Louis, MO

EMI MUSIC PUBLISHING

Company Contact

Hollywood, CA

Web: http://www.emimusicpub.com

Company Description

Former Name: Capital Industries-EMI Inc.

Employees: 2,000

SIC(s): 2741 Miscellaneous Publishing, 3652 Prerecorded Records & Tapes, 6719 Holding Companies Nec.

Parent Company: EMI Group Plc, 4 Tenterden St., Hanover Sq., London, England

Operating Locations

CA: Virgin Records America, Beverly Hills; C & L Marketing, Hollywood; Capitol Industries-EMI, Hollywood; Capitol Records, Hollywood; EMI Music Publishing, Hollywood; DE: Thorn EMI Inc., Wilmington; KS: Remco America, Inc., Wichita; MI: EMI Music Publishing; NY: EMI Music, New York; EMI Music Publishing, New York; TN: EMI Music Publishing

Note: Also operates in Canada.

Nonmonetary Support

Type: Donated Products

Corporate Sponsorship

Type: Arts & cultural events; Music & entertainment events

Giving Contact
Martin Bandier, Chief Executive Officer
EMI Music Publishing
1290 Avenue of the Americas
New York, NY 10104
Phone: (212)492-1208
Fax: (212)492-1750

Description
Organization Type: Corporate Giving Program
Giving Locations: nationally.
Grant Types: General Support.

Financial Summary
Total Giving: Contributes through corporate direct giving program only.

Typical Recipients
Arts & Humanities: Music, Performing Arts
Civic & Public Affairs: Civic & Public Affairs-General
Education: Private Education (Precollege), Public Education (Precollege)
Health: Medical Research
Social Services: Domestic Violence, People with Disabilities, Senior Services, Substance Abuse, United Funds/United Ways, Youth Organizations

Application Procedures
Initial Contact: letter
Application Requirements: a description of organization, the amount requested, and the purpose of funds sought
Deadlines: None.

Additional Information
The company sponsors a program in which some of the proceeds from the sales of certain artists' music are contributed to Ronald McDonald Charities.

Corporate Officials
Gary Gersh: president, chief executive officer PRIM CORP EMPL president, chief executive officer: EMI Music Publishing. CORP AFFIL officer: EMI America; president: Geffen Records Inc.

Grants Analysis
Disclosure Period: fiscal year ending March 31,
Typical Range: $1,000 to $3,000

Employers Insurance Of Wausau, Amutual Co.

Company Contact
Wausau, WI
Web: http://www.wausau.com

Company Description
Employees: 6,300
SIC(s): 6311 Life Insurance, 6321 Accident & Health Insurance, 6331 Fire, Marine & Casualty Insurance.
Parent Company: Liberty Mutual Insurance Group, 175 Berkeley St., Boston, MA, United States

Corporate Sponsorship
Range: less than $200,000
Type: Other
Note: Sponsors voting activities (Kids Voting - USA), educational conventions and export seminars (Wisconsin Worldwide).

Giving Contact
Brad Zweck, Senior Public Relations Coordinator
Employers Insurance of Wausau
2000 Westwood Dr.
PO Box 8017
Wausau, WI 54402-8017
Phone: (715)845-5211
Fax: (715)843-3690

Alternate Contact
Phone: 800-826-9781

Description
Organization Type: Corporate Giving Program
Giving Locations: primarily at headquarters and operating communities.
Grant Types: General Support.

Financial Summary
Total Giving: $600,000 (2000 approx); $600,000 (1999 approx); $830,000 (1997 approx). Note: Contributes through corporate direct giving program only.

Typical Recipients
Arts & Humanities: Arts & Humanities-General
Civic & Public Affairs: Civic & Public Affairs-General
Education: Education-General
Health: Health-General
Social Services: Social Services-General, United Funds/United Ways

Contributions Analysis
Giving Priorities: Company contributes on a case-by-case basis. The company reports contributions support education, civic and community, arts and humanities, health and human services. Other support includes United Way contributions.

Application Procedures
Initial Contact: Written proposal.
Application Requirements: Name, address, and telephone number of organization and contact person; a description of organization; description of program; names of directors and officers; financial condition; certificate of tax-exempt status; certification of request, such as board resolution; purpose of project; project budget; need; other sources of funding; people involved in project; evaluation techniques; and future funding.
Deadlines: None.

Restrictions
Company does not support individuals, religious organizations, political organizations, labor organizations, or agencies supported by the United Way.
Only organizations with a tax-exempt status will be considered.

Additional Information
In 1994, the company formed a partnership with the Nationwide Insurance Enterprise Foundation.
Preference is given to organizations seeking multiple sources of support.
Publications: Corporate Contributions Program Guidelines

Corporate Officials
David O. Miller: chairman PRIM CORP EMPL chairman: Wausau Insurance Companies. CORP AFFIL director: Scottsdale Insurance Co.; chairman: Wausau Preferred Health Insurance Co.; director: Nationwide Mutual Insurance Co.; director: Nationwide Life Insurance Co.; director: Nationwide Mutual Fire Insurance Co.; director: Nationwide Financial Services; director: Nationwide General Insurance Co.; director: Nationwide Advisory Services; director: Allied Life Financial Corp.; director: Colonial Insurance Co. California.

Giving Program Officials
Lynn Kordus: coordinator PRIM CORP EMPL senior public relations coordinator: Wausau Insurance Companies.

Foundation Officials
Dwight D. Davis: president, chief [illegible] ED Michigan State University MA; Univ[illegible] PhD; University of Wisconsin, Stout BA [illegible] EMPL president: Employers Life Industr[illegible] CORP AFFIL president: Wausau Preferr[illegible] dustry Co.

Grants Analysis
Disclosure Period: calendar year ending
Typical Range: $2,500 to $5,000

Employers Mutual Casualty Co.

Company Contact
Des Moines, IA
Web: http://www.emcinsurance.com

Company Description
Employees: 1,795
SIC(s): 6311 Life Insurance, 6321 Accident & Health Insurance, 6331 Fire, Marine & Casualty Insurance.
Parent Company: Employers Mutual Companies

Operating Locations
Operates branch offices in 17 states.

Nonmonetary Support
Type: Donated Equipment; Loaned Executives

Employers Mutual Charitable Foundation

Giving Contact
Joe Smith, Manager, Executive Director
Employers Mutual Charitable Foundation
PO Box 712
Des Moines, IA 50303
Phone: (515)280-2171

Description
EIN: 421343474
Organization Type: Corporate Foundation
Giving Locations: IA
Grant Types: General Support.

Financial Summary
Total Giving: $665,975 (1998); $490,427 (1997); $312,701 (1996). Note: Contributes through foundation only.
Giving Analysis: Giving for 1996 includes: foundation grants to United Way ($12,107); 1997: foundation grants to United Way ($116,992); 1998: foundation grants to United Way ($129,402)
Assets: $3,942,075 (1998); $4,351,932 (1997); $2,439,224 (1996)
Gifts Received: $94,756 (1998); $2,050,986 (1997); $583,455 (1996). Note: Contributions are received from Employers Mutual Charitable Trust and Employers Mutual Casualty Company.

Typical Recipients
Arts & Humanities: Arts Associations & Councils, Arts Centers, Ballet, Arts & Humanities-General, Historic Preservation, History & Archaeology, Libraries, Museums/Galleries, Music, Opera, Performing Arts, Public Broadcasting
Civic & Public Affairs: Botanical Gardens/Parks, Business/Free Enterprise, Clubs, Community Foundations, Civic & Public Affairs-General, Housing, Municipalities/Towns, Parades/Festivals, Public Policy, Safety, Urban & Community Affairs, Women's Affairs, Zoos/Aquariums

& Univer-
ies, Mi-
c Educa-
ource Con-
ergency/Am-
th Policy/Cost
tiple Sclerosis
s Welfare
stitutes
, Community Centers,
ations, Family Services,
Recreation & Athletics,
es, Shelters/Homelessness,
eral, Special Olympics, United
s, Volunteer Services, YMCA/
WHA, Youth Organizations

ations Analysis

iorities: Company supports civic and public education, the arts, and health and welfare.
& Humanities: 30%. Funds art centers, music, d historic preservation.
Civic & Public Affairs: 8%. Supports community foundations and a zoo.
Education: 29%. Focus on higher education.
Health: 2%.
Religion: 1%.
Science: 1%.
Social Services: 29%. Funds United Ways, YMCAs, and youth organzations.

Application Procedures

Initial Contact: Send a letter of inquiry.
Application Requirements: Include intended use of funds, verification of tax-exempt status, and a list of major donors.
Deadlines: None.

Corporate Officials

Richard W. Hoffmann: general counsel, chief operating officer B Des Moines, IA 1953. ED Dartmouth College (1976); University of Colorado (1979). PRIM CORP EMPL general counsel: Employers Mutual Casualty Co. ADD CORP EMPL general counsel: American Liberty Insurance Co.; general counsel: Illinois EMCASCO Insurance Co.; general counsel: Dakota Fire Insurance Co.; general counsel: EMC Insurance Group Inc.; general counsel: EMC Reinsurance Co.; general counsel: EMCASSCO Insurance Co.; general counsel: Employers Modern Life Co.; general counsel: Farm and City Insurance Co.; general counsel: Union Insurance Co. of Providence ADD NONPR EMPL member legal committee: Alliance of American Insurers. NONPR AFFIL member: American Corp. Counsel Association; member: American Council Life Insurers; member: American Bar Association.
Fredrick A. Schiek: executive vice president, chief operating officer B Readlyn, IA 1934. ED Drake University (1959). PRIM CORP EMPL executive vice president, chief operating officer: EMC Insurance Group Co. CORP AFFIL director: Mutual Reinsurance Bureau. NONPR AFFIL director: Employers Mutual; vice chairman: Union Insurance Co. of Providence; director: CCIC; director: Alliance of American Insurers.

Foundation Officials

Bruce Gunn Kelley: vice president, director B Philadelphia, PA 1954. ED Dartmouth College AB (1976); University of Iowa Law School JD (1979). PRIM CORP EMPL president, chief executive officer, director: Employers Mutual Casualty Co. ADD CORP EMPL president, chief executive officer: EMC Insurance Group Inc.; treasurer: EMC Underwriters Ltd. Inc. CORP AFFIL chairman: Illinois Emcasco Insurance Co.; chief executive officer: Employers Modern Life Co.; chairman: Farm City Insurance Co.; director: Alliance America Insurance Co.; chairman: American Liberty Insurance Co. NONPR AFFIL president: Midl-owa Council Boy Scouts America; trustee: National Committee Drunk Drivers; member: Iowa Bar Association; member advisory board: Iowa Public Employees Retirement Systems; director: Des Moines Arts Center; director: Greater Des Moines Sports Authority. CLUB AFFIL Masons Club; Rotary Club; Des Moines Club.

Grants Analysis

Disclosure Period: calendar year ending 1998
Total Grants: $536,573*
Number of Grants: 85
Average Grant: $4,623*
Highest Grant: $148,200
Typical Range: $500 to $10,000
*Note: Giving excludes United Way. Average grant figure excludes highest grant.

Recent Grants

Note: Grants derived from 1998 Form 990.

Arts & Humanities

110,000	Salisbury House Foundation, Des Moines, IA
40,000	Living History Farms, Des Moines, IA
14,000	Civic Center of Greater Des Moines, Des Moines, IA
7,800	Des Moines Playhouse, Des Moines, IA
6,400	Civic Music Association, Des Moines, IA
5,000	Des Moines Arts Center, Des Moines, IA
3,125	Des Moines Symphony, Des Moines, IA
2,500	Des Moines Opera, Des Moines, IA
2,500	West Des Moines Historical Society, West Des Moines, IA
2,000	Des Moines Children's Chorus Inc., Des Moines, IA

Civic & Public Affairs

16,815	Wisconsin Sesquicentennial Commission, Madison, WI
10,000	FINE Foundation, Des Moines, IA
7,500	Tax Education Foundation, Muscatine, IA
5,750	Variety Club of Iowa, Des Moines, IA
5,000	Blank Park Zoo, Des Moines, IA
5,000	Oakridge Neighborhood Services, Des Moines, IA
2,500	National Commission Against Drunk Driving, Washington, DC

Education

148,200	Drake University, Des Moines, IA
8,000	Iowa College Foundation, Des Moines, IA
7,500	Grand View College, Des Moines, IA
5,000	Morris Scholarship Fund, Des Moines, IA
3,560	Iowa State University, Ames, IA
3,200	Iowa Scholarship Fund, Iowa City, IA
3,000	Iowa Council for International Understanding, Des Moines, IA
2,500	Appalachian State University, Boone, NC
2,500	Washington Center for Internships, Washington, DC
2,000	Ripon College, Ripon, WI

Health

5,000	Health Policy Corporation of Iowa, Des Moines, IA
4,035	Dowling/St. Joseph Foundation, Des Moines, IA
2,500	John Ruan/MS Charity, Des Moines, IA

Religion

5,000	Jewish Federation of Greater Des Moines, Des Moines, IA

Science

5,000	Science Center of Iowa, Des Moines, IA

Social Services

88,732	United Way of Central Iowa, Des Moines, IA
16,000	University of Wisconsin, Madison, WI
12,368	United Way - Wichita, Wichita, KS
8,000	YWCA of Greater Des Moines, Des Moines, IA
7,849	United Way - Omaha, Omaha, NE
5,000	Goodwill Industries, Des Moines, IA
5,000	Luther Care Services, Des Moines, IA
4,719	United Way - Missouri Slope, Bismarck, ND
4,505	United Way - Milwaukee, Milwaukee, WI
4,209	John R. Grubb YMCA, Des Moines, IA
4,000	YMCA of Greater Des Moines, Des Moines, IA
3,658	EMC Explorer Post - Boy Scout Program, Des Moines, IA
3,605	United Way - Providence, Providence, RI
3,000	Foundation for Children & Families of Iowa, Des Moines, IA
3,000	Iowa Summit on Volunteerism, Des Moines, IA
2,972	United Way - Dallas, Dallas, TX
2,500	Camp Fire Boys & Girls - Heart of the Hawkeye, Des Moines, IA
2,176	United Way - Lansing, Lansing, MI

ENSIGN-BICKFORD INDUSTRIES

Company Contact

Simsbury, CT
Web: http://www.ensign-bickford.com

Company Description

Employees: 153
SIC(s): 2672 Coated & Laminated Paper Nec, 2823 Cellulosic Manmade Fibers.

Nonmonetary Support

Type: Donated Equipment

Ensign-Bickford Foundation

Giving Contact

Linda Angelastro, Executive Director, Corporate Communications
Ensign-Bickford Foundation
10 Mill Pond Ln.
Simsbury, CT 06070
Phone: (860)658-4411

Description

Founded: 1952
EIN: 066041097
Organization Type: Corporate Foundation
Giving Locations: CT: Avon, Simsbury primarily in areas of company operations.
Grant Types: Capital, Conference/Seminar, Employee Matching Gifts, General Support, Multiyear/Continuing Support, Project, Research, Scholarship, Seed Money.

Financial Summary

Total Giving: $215,337 (1998); $217,634 (1997); $312,000 (1996 approx). Note: Contributes through corporate direct giving program and foundation.
Giving Analysis: Giving for 1995 includes: foundation ($94,710); foundation scholarships ($9,000); 1997: foundation ($201,634); foundation scholarships ($16,000)
Assets: $45,542 (1998); $41,952 (1997); $129,517 (1995)

Gifts Received: $220,000 (1998); $152,250 (1997); $158,000 (1995). Note: Contributions are received from Ensign-Bickford Industries.

Typical Recipients

Arts & Humanities: Arts Associations & Councils, Arts Centers, Arts & Humanities-General, Historic Preservation, History & Archaeology, Libraries, Museums/Galleries, Music, Opera, Performing Arts, Theater
Civic & Public Affairs: Botanical Gardens/Parks, Clubs, Economic Development, Employment/Job Training, Civic & Public Affairs-General, Legal Aid, Municipalities/Towns, Parades/Festivals, Professional & Trade Associations, Public Policy, Safety, Urban & Community Affairs, Women's Affairs
Education: Arts/Humanities Education, Business Education, Colleges & Universities, Engineering/Technological Education, Medical Education, Private Education (Precollege), Public Education (Precollege), Secondary Education (Public), Student Aid
Environment: Environment-General, Sanitary Systems
Health: Cancer, Children's Health/Hospitals, Health Organizations, Hospitals, Multiple Sclerosis, Nursing Services, Single-Disease Health Associations
International: Health Care/Hospitals
Religion: Churches, Religious Organizations, Religious Welfare
Science: Scientific Organizations
Social Services: Camps, Child Welfare, Community Centers, Community Service Organizations, Crime Prevention, People with Disabilities, Recreation & Athletics, Scouts, Senior Services, United Funds/ United Ways, Volunteer Services, Youth Organizations

Contributions Analysis

Arts & Humanities: 30%. Supports history and archaeological issues, arts associations and councils.
Civic & Public Affairs: 40%. Supports municipalities and towns, safety issues, civic affairs, and employment and job training.
Education: 11%. Supports public and private schools.
Health: 7%.
Social Services: 6%. Supports united funds.

Application Procedures

Initial Contact: Send brief letter.
Application Requirements: Include purpose of request, annual budget, other funding, and geographic areas in which proceeds will be distributed.
Deadlines: None.

Corporate Officials

Herman J. Fonteyne: president, chief executive officer, director B Ghent, Belgium 1939. ED University of Louvain (1961); University of Ghent (1963). PRIM CORP EMPL president, chief executive officer, director: Ensign-Bickford Industries Inc. CORP AFFIL officer: Ensign-Bickford Haz-Pros Inc.; chairman: Ensign-Bickford Realty Corp.; director: CT Natural Gas Corp.; chairman, chief executive officer, director: Ensign-Bickford Co.
Joseph Ensign Lovejoy: chairman, director B Boston, MA 1940. ED Nichols College (1963). PRIM CORP EMPL chairman, director: Ensign-Bickford Industries Inc. ADD CORP EMPL director: Ensign-Bickford Co.

Foundation Officials

Linda W. Angelastro: executive director PRIM CORP EMPL director corporate communications: Ensign-Bickford Industries.
Robert Edward Darling, Jr.: chairman B Oakland, CA 1937. ED San Francisco State University BA (1959); Yale University School of Drama MFA (1963). PRIM CORP EMPL artistic producer: Acorn Theatre. CORP AFFIL manager: MG Taylor Corp.; manager: Darling Associates Garden Design; director: Ensign-Bickford Industries; vice president: Bushnell Horace Memorial Hall Corp. NONPR AFFIL member: Un Scenic Artists; member: Washington Daffodil Society; member, panelist: Opera America; panelist: National Institute Music Theater; panelist: National Opera Institute; member: Logan Circle Association; member: Actors Equity - Canada; member: American Guild Musical Artists.
Janet DeLissio: treasurer
Michael Thomas Long: director B Hartford, CT 1942. ED University of Notre Dame BA (1964); University of Connecticut JD (1967). PRIM CORP EMPL vice president, general counsel, secretary: Ensign-Bickford Industries Inc. CORP AFFIL director: Windsor Locks; president, director: Ensign-Bickford Haz-Pros Inc.; secretary, director: Ensign-Bickford Realty Corp.; administration, director: Ensign-Bickford Co. NONPR AFFIL member: International Society Explosive Engineers; scholarship chairman: University Notre Dame Alumni Clubs Greater Hartford; member: Hartford County Bar Association; board governors: Institute Makers Explosives; member: Connecticut Bar Association; member: Greater Hartford Chamber of Commerce; director: American Corporate Counsel Association; chairman: Bradley International Airport Committee; member: American Bar Association. CLUB AFFIL Simsbury Farms Men's Club; Hop Meadow Country Club.

Grants Analysis

Disclosure Period: calendar year ending 1997
Total Grants: $201,634*
Number of Grants: 30
Average Grant: $5,229*
Highest Grant: $50,000
***Note:** Giving excludes scholarship; average grant excludes highest grant.

Recent Grants

Note: Grants derived from 1997 Form 990.

Arts & Humanities

45,000	Hartford Symphony, Hartford, CT
18,000	Simsbury Friends for Music, Simsbury, CT
8,250	Simsbury Free Library, Simsbury, CT
6,493	Simsbury Historical Society, Simsbury, CT
2,500	Bushnell
1,000	Simsbury Arts Council, Simsbury, CT
150	Farmington Valley Arts Center, Avon, CT

Civic & Public Affairs

28,000	Campaign for Madisonville
1,000	Simsbury Culture Parks and Recreation, Simsbury, CT
800	GHCC Gold Classic
500	Show Me Mules
500	Town of Simsbury, Simsbury, CT
100	Simsbury American Legion, Simsbury, CT
50	Massacoh Plantation Pillory

Education

50,000	Montana Tech Foundation, Butte, MT
4,500	Junior Achievement
4,000	Shawnee High School
1,500	Payson High School
1,500	Spanish Fork High School
1,500	Springville High School

Health

5,500	St. Francis Hospital, Tulsa, OK
5,000	American Cancer Society
5,000	Hartford Hospital, Hartford, CT
190	National Multiple Sclerosis Society, New York, NY

Social Services

5,000	Country Camp
2,500	Kevin Hanley Men's Golf
1,000	McLean Golf Tournament
1,000	Simsbury Police Benevolen bury, CT
500	Revitalization Corps, Hartford
100	Hartford Camp Courant

ENTERGY CORP.

Company Contact

New Orleans, LA
Web: http://www.entergy.com

Company Description

Revenue: US$11,494,800,000
Employees: 13,363
Fortune Rank: 198, per FORTUNE Magazine's list of 500 Largest U.S. Corporations (1999).
FF 198
SIC(s): 4911 Electric Services.

Operating Locations

Company operates in 3 states.

Nonmonetary Support

Volunteer Programs: Entergy sponsors Community Connectors, an employee volunteer program. Employees and retirees who volunteer as Connectors can earn grants through their volunteer hours (up to $250 on an individual basis and $500 per team) and designate those grants to a qualified organization of their choice.

Corporate Sponsorship

Contact: DeAnne Rodriguez, Vice President, Corporate Contributions
Entergy Corp.

Giving Contact

Angela Gallagher, Corporate Contributions Representative
Entergy Corp.
PO Box 6100
New Orleans, LA 70161
Phone: (504)576-5785
Fax: (504)576-2190
Email: agallag@entergy.com
Web: http://www.entergy.com/contributions

Description

Organization Type: Corporate Giving Program
Giving Locations: AR; LA; MS; TX company's service area.
Grant Types: General Support, Matching.
Note: Employee matching gift ratio: 1 to 1 for contributions between $25 and $1,000 annually to secondary schools, and between $25 and $2,000 annually to colleges and universities.

Giving Philosophy

'The mission and focus of Entergy's grant program is to improve (our) communities as a whole. Thus we look for giving opportunities in the areas of education and literacy, economic and environmental development; arts and culture; and health and social services. Since the inception of our program, more than 1,500 non-profit organizations have received our support.' *Entergy Corporation Grant Programs: Building Better Communities Through the Power of People*

Financial Summary

Total Giving: $8,000,000 (2000 approx); $8,000,000 (1999 approx); $7,500,000 (1998 approx). Note: Contributes through corporate direct giving program only.

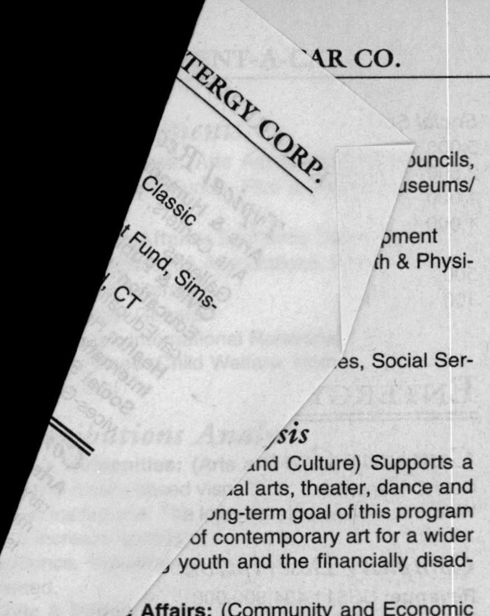

...ouncils,
...useums/
...pment
...th & Physi-

...es, Social Ser-

...sis

...(Arts and Culture) Supports a ...al arts, theater, dance and ...ong-term goal of this program ... of contemporary art for a wider ... youth and the financially disad-

... **Affairs:** (Community and Economic ...) Supports community-based projects ...ams that focus on workforce and economic ...ment.

...**ation:** (Education and Literacy) Supports proj-...s that impact education enhancement, student de-...elopment, and community enrichment, including adult literacy, mobile automated learning laboratories, a student athlete program, school-business partnerships, and public, private, and parochial schools.

Environment: (Environmental Improvement) Funds environmental causes that support enhancements, innovative approaches, and meaningful solutions to resolve environmental issues, including tree planting, habitat restoration, and park improvement.

Social Services: (Health and Social Services) Funds programs in the company's service area that support children's educational and emotional, including recreational or academic after-school activities, and mentoring programs. Family programs and other social services are also supported.

Note: Dollar for dollar matching funds must be secured for the requested grant amount.

Application Procedures

Initial Contact: Request guidelines and application form from community relations coordinator of local operating unit; applications are also available on Web site.

Application Requirements: Submit completed application, a copy of 501(c)(3) status letter, and any supporting documents.

Deadlines: April 15.

Review Process: An advisory board of educators and community representatives makes decisions.

Evaluative Criteria: Thorough approach in working toward a solution to the need or issue; clearly defined and realistic goals and objectives, with measurable results; outline of benefits to the public; evidence of community involvement.

Decision Notification: Applicants receive notification in August.

Restrictions

Entergy does not fund groupgs without 501(c)(3) status; political candidates or groups; religious organizations; service organizations; individuals; amateur sporting groups or events; fraternities or sororities; or social clubs.

Additional Information

Operating companies of Entergy Corp. include Entergy Arkansas, Inc., Entergy Gulf States, Inc., Entergy Louisiana, Inc., Entergy Mississippi, Inc., and Entergy New Orleans, Inc.

Entergy gives charitably through its Corporate Giving Program, a Community Partnership Grants program, which awards matching money for education and community enhancement initiatives, and through a Volunteer Assistance Program. Applicants for the Corporate Giving Program should request an application and follow the general submission guidelines. Community Partnership Grants of up to $1,000 are available for projects that effectively impact education enhancement, student development and community enrichment. Dollar-for-dollar matching funds must be secured. Applicants for partnership grants should specifically request guidelines and an application for the Community Partnership Grants program.

Corporate Officials

Wayne Lervett: chief executive officer

Giving Program Officials

Carol A. Clawson: B New York, NY 1946. ED Ohio Wesleyan University BA (1967). PRIM CORP EMPL director corporate communications: Entergy Corp.

Enterprise Rent-A-car Co.

Company Contact

St. Louis, MO
Web: http://www.pickenterprise.com

Company Description

Former Name: Enterprise Leasing.
Revenue: US$2,470,000,000
Employees: 22,000
SIC(s): 7514 Passenger Car Rental, 7515 Passenger Car Leasing.

Operating Locations

Operates throughout the USA.

Enterprise Rent-A-Car Foundation

Giving Contact

JoAnn T. Kindle, President
Enterprise Rent-A-Car Foundation
600 Corporate Park Drive
St. Louis, MO 63105
Phone: (314)512-2754
Fax: (314)512-4754

Description

EIN: 431262762
Organization Type: Corporate Foundation
Grant Types: General Support, Multiyear/Continuing Support, Operating Expenses, Project.

Financial Summary

Total Giving: $3,490,543 (fiscal year ending July 31, 1998); $3,490,543 (fiscal 1997); $2,605,807 (fiscal 1996). Note: Contributes through foundation only.

Giving Analysis: Giving for fiscal 1996 includes: foundation grants to United Way ($986,672); fiscal 1997: foundation grants to United Way (approx $1,200,000); fiscal 1998: foundation matching gifts ($1,171,026); foundation grants to United Way ($25,000)

Assets: $19,536,708 (fiscal 1998); $19,536,708 (fiscal 1997); $13,004,943 (fiscal 1996)

Gifts Received: $7,278,453 (fiscal 1998); $7,278,435 (fiscal 1997); $6,024,691 (fiscal 1996). Note: Foundation receives contributions from Enterprise Rent-A-Car Company on behalf of its subsidiaries and affiliates.

Typical Recipients

Arts & Humanities: Arts Associations & Councils, Arts Centers, Arts Festivals, Dance, Arts & Humanities-General, History & Archaeology, Museums/Galleries, Music, Public Broadcasting, Theater

Civic & Public Affairs: Botanical Gardens/Parks, Business/Free Enterprise, Clubs, Community Foundations, Economic Development, Civic & Public Affairs-General, Housing, Parades/Festivals, Rural Affairs, Urban & Community Affairs, Zoos/Aquariums

Education: Arts/Humanities Education, Colleges & Universities, Education Funds, Minority Education, Private Education (Precollege), Special Education, Vocational & Technical Education

Health: Alzheimers Disease, Cancer, Children's Health/Hospitals, Clinics/Medical Centers, Diabetes, Emergency/Ambulance Services, Health Organizations, Hospitals, Mental Health, Preventive Medicine/Wellness Organizations, Single-Disease Health Associations

Religion: Churches, Jewish Causes, Religious Welfare

Science: Science Museums, Scientific Centers & Institutes

Social Services: Child Welfare, Community Service Organizations, Domestic Violence, Family Planning, Food/Clothing Distribution, Recreation & Athletics, Scouts, Special Olympics, United Funds/United Ways, YMCA/YWCA/YMHA/YWHA, Youth Organizations

Contributions Analysis

Giving Priorities: Emphasis on human services, United Way, civic concerns and education.

Arts & Humanities: 5%. Gives to symphonies, orchestras, and operas. Also supports public museums, historical societies, and public broadcasting. Generally, giving for the arts has been limited to the St. Louis, MO, area.

Civic & Public Affairs: 19%. Areas of interest include urban renewal, housing, botanical gardens, zoos, and conservation.

Education: 12%. Primarily supports colleges and universities within Missouri. Also supports junior achievement programs.

Health: 5%. Supports single-disease health associations, children's hospitals, and health organizations.

Religion: 1%.

Social Services: 56%. Supports United Ways, religious welfare, projects designed to aid children, family planning, and Special Olympics.

Note: Total contributions in 1998.

Application Procedures

Initial Contact: Send brief letter of inquiry.

Application Requirements: Include a description of organization, amount requested, purpose of funds sought, recently audited financial statement, and proof of tax-exempt status.

Deadlines: None.

Decision Notification: Notification of approval, rejection, or request for more information within approximately three months.

Restrictions

Does not support individuals, political groups, or lobbying groups.

Emphasis on organizations where Enterprise employees are volunteers or board members, and organizations where customers are volunteers.

Additional Information

Priority is given to charitable and educational organizations.

Board looks for employee or other involvement before approving any grant requests.

Corporate Officials

William Holkemp: executive vice presidento, director PRIM CORP EMPL executive vice president: Enterprise Rent-A-Car Co.

JoAnn Taylor Kindle: executive vice president public relations PRIM CORP EMPL executive vice president public relations: Enterprise Rent-A-Car Co.

John T. O'Connell: chief financial officer PRIM CORP EMPL chief financial officer: Enterprise Rent-A-Car Co.
Andrew C. Taylor: president, chief executive officer, director B 1947. ED Denver University (1970). PRIM CORP EMPL president, chief executive officer, director: Enterprise Rent-A-Car Co. ADD CORP EMPL president: Enterprise Leasing Co. West; president: Camrac Inc.; executive vice president, treasurer: Crawford Corp. Inc.; treasurer: Elco Chevrolet Inc. CORP AFFIL president: Enterprise Rent-a-Car Co. Texas; chairman: Snorac Inc.; president: Enterprise Rent-a-Car Co. Sacramento; president: Enterprise Rent-a-Car Co. Pittsburgh; president: Enterprise Rent-a-Car Co. Rhode Island; treasurer: Enterprise Rent-a-Car Co. Los Angeles; president: Enterprise Rent-a-Car Co. Oregon; president: Enterprise Rent-a-Car Co. Kentucky; vice president: Enterprise Leasing Co. Southeast; president: Enterprise Leasing Co. Southwest; president: Enterprise Leasing Co. Minnesota; president: Enterprise Leasing Co. Philadelphia; president: Enterprise Leasing Co. Kansas; vice president: Enterprise Leasing Co. Houston; president: Enterprise Leasing Co. Indianapolis; president: Enterprise Leasing Co. Denver; president: Enterprise Leasing Co. Detroit; director: Anheuser-Busch Companies Inc.; chairman: Enterprise Coffee & Supply Co.

Giving Program Officials

Donald L. Ross: PRIM CORP EMPL senior vice president: Enterprise Rent-A-Car Co.

Foundation Officials

Dianne Huber: assistant secretary
JoAnn Taylor Kindle: president (see above)
Marianne Knaup: director
John T. O'Connell: vice president, treasurer (see above)

Grants Analysis

Disclosure Period: fiscal year ending July 31, 1998
Total Grants: $2,294,517*
Number of Grants: 336
Average Grant: $6,829
Highest Grant: $130,000
Typical Range: $1,000 to $25,000
***Note:** Giving excludes United Way; matching gifts.

Recent Grants

Note: Grants derived from 1997 Form 990.

Arts & Humanities

50,000	Missouri Historical Society, St. Louis, MO
50,000	Missouri Historical Society, St. Louis, MO
37,500	KETC Channel 9, St. Louis, MO
37,500	KETC/Channel 9, St. Louis, MO
25,000	Magic House, St. Louis, MO
25,000	The Magic House, St. Louis, MO
25,000	St. Louis Symphony, St. Louis, MO
25,000	St. Louis Symphony Orchestra, St. Louis, MO

Civic & Public Affairs

100,000	MICDS
100,000	St. Louis 2004, St. Louis, MO
100,000	St. Louis 2004, St. Louis, MO
100,000	St. Louis Zoo, St. Louis, MO
100,000	St. Louis Zoo, St. Louis, MO
60,000	Fair St. Louis, St. Louis, MO
60,000	Fair St. Louis, St. Louis, MO
50,000	Forest Park Forever, Chicago, IL
50,000	Forest Park Forever, St. Louis, MO
20,000	Nashville Zoo, Nashville, TN
20,000	Nashville Zoo, Nashville, TN
16,500	Beaumont Foundation, Chicago, IL
15,000	Better Business Bureau, St. Louis, MO
15,000	Better Business Bureau, St. Louis, MO
15,000	Corporate Alliance, St. Louis, MO
15,000	St. Louis Regional Commerce & Growth, St. Louis, MO
15,000	St. Louis Regional Commerce and Growth Association, St. Louis, MO
15,000	State of St. Louis Foundation, St. Louis, MO

Education

100,000	MICDS, St. Louis, MO
50,000	Washington University
50,000	Washington University, St. Louis, MO
25,000	Harris Stowe State College, St. Louis, MO
25,000	School Sisters of Notre Dame
25,000	School Sisters of Notre Dame, St. Louis, MO
23,000	Harris Stowe State College, St. Louis, MO
15,000	James Madison University, Harrisburg, VA
15,000	James Madison University, Harrisonburg, VA
15,000	St. Louis University, St. Louis, MO
15,000	University of Missouri St. Louis, St. Louis, MO
15,000	University of Missouri St. Louis, St. Louis, MO
13,000	Missouri Colleges Fund, Jefferson City, MO
12,000	Arts and Education Council, St. Louis, MO

Health

30,000	St. Louis Children's Hospital, St. Louis, MO
30,000	St. Louis Children's Hospital, St. Louis, MO
25,000	United Cerebral Palsy St. Louis, St. Louis, MO
21,500	Juvenile Diabetes Foundation, New York, NY
21,500	Juvenile Diabetes Foundation, St. Louis, MO
15,000	Wellness Community, Philadelphia, PA
15,000	The Wellness Community of Philadelphia, Philadelphia, PA
14,500	Life with Cancer
14,000	Life With Cancer, St. Louis, MO

Religion

25,100	Salvation Army, St. Louis, MO
25,100	Salvation Army, St. Louis, MO

Science

15,000	The Science Place Museum
15,000	Science Place Museum

Social Services

368,470	United Way, St. Louis, MO
368,470	United Way of Greater St. Louis, St. Louis, MO
175,486	United Way of Los Angeles, Los Angeles, CA
175,485	United Way, Los Angeles, CA
130,000	Boone Valley Classic Foundation, St. Louis, MO
130,000	Boone Valley Classic Foundation, St. Louis, MO
33,421	United Way San Francisco, San Francisco, CA
33,420	United Way, San Francisco, CA
32,500	United Way of Broward County, Fort Lauderdale, FL
32,500	United Way Broward County, Fort Lauderdale, FL
26,987	United Way of the National Capi, Washington, DC
26,924	United Way Southeastern Pennsylvania, Philadelphia, PA
26,923	United Way Southeastern Pennsylvania, Philadelphia, PA
25,518	United Way of Central Alabama, Birmingham, AL
25,517	United Way Central Alabama, Birmingham, AL
25,514	United Way of Massach ton, MA
25,513	United Way Massachuset ton, MA
24,987	United Way National Capita Washington, DC
21,134	United Way Detroit, Detroit, M
21,124	United Way, Detroit, MI
20,550	United Way Greater New Orlea Orleans, LA
20,549	United Way, New Orleans, LA
20,000	Our Little Haven, St. Louis, MO
20,000	Our Little Haven, St. Louis, MO
19,577	United Way of Elmhurst, Elmhurst, I
19,576	United Way Elmhurst
19,112	United Way of the Columbia-Will
19,111	United Way Columbia-Williamette, Port land, OR
17,500	Mathews Dickey Boys Club, St. Louis, MO
17,500	Matthews Dickey Boys Club
16,964	United Way Services Northeast Ohio, Cleveland, OH
16,603	United Way Southwestern Pennsylvania, Pittsburgh, PA
16,602	United Way Southwestern Pennsylvania, Pittsburgh, PA
16,363	United Way, Dallas, TX
16,363	United Way of Metropolitan Dallas, Dallas, TX
16,031	United Way of Hillsborough County, Tampa, FL
16,031	United Way Hillsborough County, Tampa, FL
15,427	United Way Central Maryland, Baltimore, MD
15,425	United Way Central Maryland, Baltimore, MD
15,000	Cororate Alliance to End Partner Violence, Bloomington, IL
14,104	United Way Texas Gulf Coast, Houston, TX
14,103	United Way Texas Gulf Coast, Houston, TX
13,930	United Way Kentucky, Louisville, KY
13,930	United Way of Kentucky, Louisville, KY
13,918	United Way Valley of the Sun, Phoenix, AZ
13,771	United Way Mile High, Denver, CO
12,750	United Way Heart of Florida, Orlando, FL

EQUIFAX INC.

Company Contact

Atlanta, GA
Web: http://www.equifax.com

Company Description

Revenue: US$1,811,200,000
Employees: 14,100
SIC(s): 6411 Insurance Agents, Brokers & Service, 7323 Credit Reporting Services, 7374 Data Processing & Preparation, 7389 Business Services Nec.

Operating Locations

Canada: Equifax Canada, Anjou; United Kingdom: Equifax Europe, London
Note: Operates throughout the USA; locations above include affiliate operations.

Nonmonetary Support

Value: $100,000 (1993)
Type: Loaned Employees; Loaned Executives

Corporate Sponsorship

Type: Arts & cultural events; Festivals/fairs; Sports events

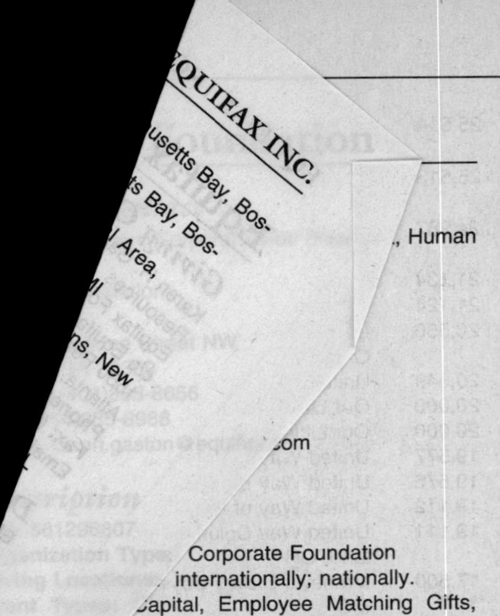

..., Human

...om

Corporate Foundation
...internationally; nationally.
...Capital, Employee Matching Gifts, ...port, Matching, Multiyear/Continuing

...ncial Summary

...Giving: $1,000,000 (1999 approx); $1,000,000 (1998 approx); $1,000,000 (1997 approx). Note: Contributes through corporate direct giving program and foundation. Giving includes corporate direct giving; foundation; domestic and international subsidiaries. 1996 Giving includes foundation ($696,470); matching gifts ($25,075); United Way ($355,000).
Assets: $2,086,623 (1996); $912,183 (1993); $1,259,509 (1990)
Gifts Received: $600,000 (1996); $380,100 (1993); $750,000 (1990). Note: In 1996, contributions received from Equifax Inc.

Typical Recipients

Arts & Humanities: Arts Associations & Councils, Arts Centers, Arts Funds, Ethnic & Folk Arts, Historic Preservation, Performing Arts
Civic & Public Affairs: Botanical Gardens/Parks, Business/Free Enterprise, Chambers of Commerce, Civil Rights, Economic Development, Economic Policy, Employment/Job Training, Housing, Legal Aid, Municipalities/Towns, Urban & Community Affairs, Women's Affairs, Zoos/Aquariums
Education: Arts/Humanities Education, Business Education, Colleges & Universities, Economic Education, Education Associations, Education Funds, Literacy, Medical Education, Minority Education, Preschool Education, Special Education
Health: Children's Health/Hospitals, Health Organizations, Hospices, Kidney, Medical Rehabilitation, Nursing Services, Prenatal Health Issues, Public Health, Research/Studies Institutes, Single-Disease Health Associations
International: Foreign Arts Organizations, International Development, International Organizations, International Peace & Security Issues, International Relations, Missionary/Religious Activities
Religion: Jewish Causes, Religious Welfare
Science: Observatories & Planetariums, Science Museums
Social Services: Camps, Child Welfare, Community Centers, Community Service Organizations, Day Care, Delinquency & Criminal Rehabilitation, Emergency Relief, Family Services, Food/Clothing Distribution, People with Disabilities, Senior Services, Shelters/Homelessness, Special Olympics, Substance Abuse, United Funds/United Ways, Youth Organizations

Contributions Analysis

Giving Priorities: Social welfare, single disease health associations, education, civic concerns, community improvement, and the arts.
Arts & Humanities: About 15%. Funding goes to Museums, art centers, art funds, and choirs.
Civic & Public Affairs: 15% to 20%. Supports economic developement programs, chamber of commerce, Habitat for Humanity, zoos and botanical gardens, and business associations.
Education: 10% to 15%. Supports universities, Junior Achievement, United Negro College Fund, literacy programs and K-12 education.
Health: 50% to 55%. Suport goes to youth groups, including children shelters, YMCA, and the Boys and Girls Club; medical institutions such as, the American Kidney Fund and Blind & Low Vision Services. Also funds The United Way, Salvation Army, rehabilitaion services and leadership programs for children.

Application Procedures

Initial Contact: written proposal
Application Requirements: a description of organization and project, proof of tax-exempt status
Review Process: proposals reviewed by foundation vice president prior to consideration by donations committee, then submitted to foundation committee for approval; committee consists of four executives

Restrictions

Foundation primarily supports organizations with which it has an established relationship.
Does not support fraternal organizations, goodwill advertising, individuals, political or lobbying groups, member agencies of united funds, or religious organizations for sectarian purposes.
In general, will not give grants for memorials, to cover operating deficits, to projects that are primarily fundraising events, or to local or regional chapters of national organizations. deficits, to projects that are primarily fundraising events, or to local or regional chapters of national organizations.

Additional Information

Grants are not renewed automatically. Organizations must re-apply for funding each year unless multi-year campaigns have been approved by the Donations Committee.
The Donations Committee, the panel which directs Equifax's contributions program, is made up of executive officers.
Trust Company Bank, Atlanta, GA, is also listed as the foundation's corporate trustee. corporate trustee.

Corporate Officials

John T. Chandler: corporate vice president, chief administrative officer B 1948. PRIM CORP EMPL corporate vice president, chief administrative officer: Equifax Inc. ADD CORP EMPL vice president: Equifax Payment Service Inc.
Karen H. Gaston: vice president corporate affairs PRIM CORP EMPL vice president corporate affairs: Equifax Inc.
David A. Post: corporate vice president, chief financial officer B Canfield, OH 1953. ED Ohio University BBA (1975). PRIM CORP EMPL corporate vice president, chief financial officer: Equifax Inc. ADD CORP EMPL chief financial officer: Equifax Credit Information Service.
C. B. Rogers, Jr.: chairman, director B Birmingham, AL 1930. ED Gettysburg College BA (1951); George Washington University MBA (1962). PRIM CORP EMPL chairman, director: Equifax Inc. CORP AFFIL director: Oxford Industries Inc.; director: Sears, Roebuck & Co.; chairman, chief executive officer, director: First Bankcard Systems Inc.; chairman, chief executive officer, director: Equifax Marketing Decision Systems; director: Equifax Payment Services Inc.; director: Equifax Canada; chairman, director: Equifax Credit Information Services; director: Briggs & Stratton Corp.; director: Dean Witter, Discover & Co.

Foundation Officials

John T. Chandler: trustee (see above)
David A. Post: vice president (see above)
C. B. Rogers, Jr.: chairman (see above)

Grants Analysis

Disclosure Period: calendar year ending 1996
Total Grants: $696,470*
Number of Grants: 63
Average Grant: $9,620*
Highest Grant: $100,000
Typical Range: $500 to $10,000
***Note:** Giving excludes matching gifts; United Way. Average grant excludes highest grant.

Recent Grants

Note: Grants derived from 1996 Form 990.

Arts & Humanities

50,000 Robert W. Woodruff Arts Center, Atlanta, GA
50,000 Robert W. Woodruff Arts Center, Atlanta, GA
20,000 Robert W. Woodruff Arts Center, Atlanta, GA
5,000 Metropolitan Atlanta Arts Fund, Atlanta, GA
2,000 Center for Puppetry Arts, Atlanta, GA

Civic & Public Affairs

100,000 REACH, Atlanta, GA
25,000 Atlanta Botanical Gardens, Atlanta, GA
25,000 Greater Atlanta Chamber of Commerce, Atlanta, GA
17,500 Habitat for Humanity, Atlanta, GA
15,000 Zoo Atlanta, Atlanta, GA
8,300 Corporation for Olympic Development in Atlanta, Atlanta, GA
5,000 National Alliance of Business, Washington, DC
2,500 Yes Atlanta, Atlanta, GA
1,000 Habitat for Humanity, Atlanta, GA

Education

20,000 Future Business Leaders of America, Mathews, VA
18,000 United Negro College Fund, Atlanta, GA
10,000 Georgia Foundation for Independent Colleges, Atlanta, GA
10,000 Literacy Action, Atlanta, GA
5,000 Georgia State University, Atlanta, GA
2,500 Georgia Foundation for Independent Colleges, Atlanta, GA
2,500 Junior Achievement of Georgia, Atlanta, GA
2,500 Morehouse School of Medicine, Atlanta, GA
1,000 Ben Hill UMC Preschool Academy, Atlanta, GA

Health

50,000 Cystic Fibrosis Foundation, Atlanta, GA
12,500 Visiting Nurse Health Systems, Atlanta, GA
7,500 Roosevelt Warm Springs Rehabilitation, Warm Springs, GA
7,500 Sheltering Arms Child Development Center, Atlanta, GA
5,000 St. Jude's Recovery Center, Atlanta, GA
3,000 Atlanta Respite Services, Atlanta, GA
1,000 American Kidney Fund, Dunwoody Park, GA
1,000 Atlanta Children's Shelter, Atlanta, GA
1,000 March of Dimes, Atlanta, GA

International

20,000 Carter Center Atlanta Project, Atlanta, GA
8,765 Equifax for Equifax Canada, Toronto, ON, Canada
5,000 Exodus, Atlanta, GA
2,500 Harmony International Youth Chorus, Atlanta, GA
1,500 US Committee for UNICEF, Atlanta, GA

Religion

5,000 Jerusalem House, Atlanta, GA
3,000 Salvation Army, Atlanta, GA

Science

25,000 Fernbank Museum of Natural History, Atlanta, GA
10,000 Fernbank Museum of Natural History, Atlanta, GA

Social Services

345,000 United Way, Atlanta, GA
10,000 Boys and Girls Clubs of America, Atlanta, GA
10,000 Success by Six United Way, Atlanta, GA
5,000 APOC Atlanta Paralympic Games, Atlanta, GA
5,000 APOC Atlanta Paralympic Games, Atlanta, GA
5,000 Empty Stocking Fund, Atlanta, GA
5,000 Mission New Hope United Way, Atlanta, GA
1,000 Blind and Low Vision Services, Smyrna, GA
1,000 Camp Best Friends Foundation, Atlanta, GA

Equitable Resources, Inc.

Company Contact

Pittsburgh, PA
Web: http://www.eriservices.com

Company Description

Assets: US$2,096,300,000
Employees: 2,100
SIC(s): 1311 Crude Petroleum & Natural Gas, 4923 Gas Transmission & Distribution, 6719 Holding Companies Nec.

Nonmonetary Support

Type: Donated Equipment; In-kind Services

Corporate Sponsorship

Contact: Murry Gerber, President & CEO
Equitable Resources, Inc.

Giving Contact

Estelle Christian, Executive Assistant to CEO
Equitable Resources, Inc.
One Oxford Center 3300
301 Grant Street
Pittsburgh, PA 15219
Phone: (412)553-7739
Fax: (412)553-5757

Description

Organization Type: Corporate Giving Program
Giving Locations: headquarters area only.
Grant Types: Capital, Employee Matching Gifts, Endowment, Fellowship, Project, Scholarship.

Financial Summary

Total Giving: $125,000 (2000 approx); $125,000 (1999 approx); $320,000 (1997 approx). Note: Contributes through corporate direct giving program and foundation. Giving includes foundation.

Typical Recipients

Arts & Humanities: Arts Institutes, Arts & Humanities-General, Music, Theater
Civic & Public Affairs: African American Affairs, Community Foundations, Economic Development, Civic & Public Affairs-General, Housing, Inner-City Development, Municipalities/Towns, Parades/Festivals, Safety, Women's Affairs
Education: Afterschool/Enrichment Programs, Arts/Humanities Education, Business-School Partnerships, Colleges & Universities, Community & Junior Colleges, Education-General, Legal Education, Medical Education, Science/Mathematics Education, Special Education, Vocational & Technical Education
Health: Arthritis, Children's Health/Hospitals, Health-General, Hospitals, Hospitals (University Affiliated)
Science: Science Exhibits & Fairs, Scientific Centers & Institutes, Scientific Organizations
Social Services: Community Service Organizations, Domestic Violence, People with Disabilities, Senior Services, Social Services-General, United Funds/United Ways, Volunteer Services, Youth Organizations

Contributions Analysis

Education: Focuses support on education.
Social Services: Primary support to United Way.

Application Procedures

Initial Contact: brief letter or inquiry and full proposal
Application Requirements: description of organization, amount requested, purpose of funds sought, recently audited financial statement, and proof of tax-exempt status
Deadlines: None.

Restrictions

Does not support individuals, religious organizations for sectarian purposes, or political or lobbying groups.

Additional Information

Giving program is still in operation, but grantmaking is currently suspended.

Corporate Officials

Frederick H. Abrew: chairman, president, chief executive officer, director PRIM CORP EMPL chairman, president, chief executive officer, director: ERI Services. CLUB AFFIL director: Duquesne Club.

Grants Analysis

Disclosure Period: calendar year ending
Typical Range: $2,500 to $5,000

Recent Grants

Note: Grants derived from 1996 grants list.

Arts & Humanities

Jenny Wiley Theater, KY
PBGH Cultural Trust, Pittsburgh, PA
Pittsburgh Symphony, Pittsburgh, PA

Civic & Public Affairs

UCP, Pittsburgh, PA

Education

Allegheny Valley School, Pittsburgh, PA
Big Sandy College, KY
Extra Mile Foundation, Pittsburgh, PA
Reading Is Fundamental Central Northside, Pittsburgh, PA
West Virginia Independent Colleges Foundation, WV
West Virginia University, Morgantown, WV

Erb Lumber Co.

Company Contact

Birmingham, MI

Company Description

Employees: 2,000
SIC(s): 5211 Lumber & Other Building Materials, 6513 Apartment Building Operators.

Erb Foundation

Giving Contact

Gary Robinette, President
PO Box 3013
Birmingham, MI 48012-3013
Phone: (248)644-5300

Alternate Contact

PO Box 458
Bloomfield Hills, MI 48303

Description

EIN: 386083275
Organization Type: Corporate Foundatio[n sup-]ports preselected organizations only.
Giving Locations: MI
Grant Types: General Support.

Financial Summary

Total Giving: $166,164 (1998); $208,558 (1996) $41,405 (1995). Note: In 1998, contributions were received from Microsoft Corp. ($1,033,125) and Yahoo, Inc. ($581,942). In 1994, contributions were received from Fred A. Erb.
Giving Analysis: Giving for 1998 includes: foundation ($164,757); foundation grants to United Way ($1,407)
Assets: $5,034,227 (1998); $2,662,413 (1996); $2,004,210 (1995)
Gifts Received: $1,615,067 (1998); $595,000 (1996); $1,015,315 (1994). Note: In 1994, contributions were received from Fred A. Erb. In 1998, contributions were received from Microsoft corp. ($1,053,125) and Yahoo, Inc. ($581,942).

Typical Recipients

Arts & Humanities: Arts Centers, Arts Institutes, Community Arts, History & Archaeology, Museums/Galleries, Music, Performing Arts, Public Broadcasting, Visual Arts
Civic & Public Affairs: Botanical Gardens/Parks, Clubs, Community Foundations, Civic & Public Affairs-General, Housing, Municipalities/Towns, Philanthropic Organizations, Public Policy, Safety, Urban & Community Affairs, Women's Affairs, Zoos/Aquariums
Education: Arts/Humanities Education, Business Education, Business-School Partnerships, Colleges & Universities, Economic Education, Engineering/Technological Education, Education-General, International Exchange, Minority Education, Private Education (Precollege), Science/Mathematics Education
Environment: Research, Resource Conservation
Health: Cancer, Eyes/Blindness, Hospices, Hospitals, Medical Research, Mental Health
International: Health Care/Hospitals, International Environmental Issues, International Organizations, International Relief Efforts, Missionary/Religious Activities
Religion: Churches, Jewish Causes, Religious Organizations, Religious Welfare
Science: Scientific Centers & Institutes
Social Services: At-Risk Youth, Camps, Child Welfare, Community Service Organizations, Delinquency & Criminal Rehabilitation, Family Planning, Family Services, Food/Clothing Distribution, Homes, People with Disabilities, Senior Services, Substance Abuse, United Funds/United Ways, YMCA/YWCA/YMHA/YWHA, Youth Organizations

Contributions Analysis

Giving Priorities: Science education, art, and social service and civic organizations.
Arts & Humanities: 8%. Supports art museums, the performing arts, and public broadcasting.
Civic & Public Affairs: 2%. Supports community foundations.
Education: 34%. Supports colleges and universities and private educational institutions.
Health: 1%. Supports hospitals, single-disease health orgs, and hospice programs.
Religion: 2%. Funds religious welfare organizations.
Science: 49%. Funds the Cranbrook Institute of Science.

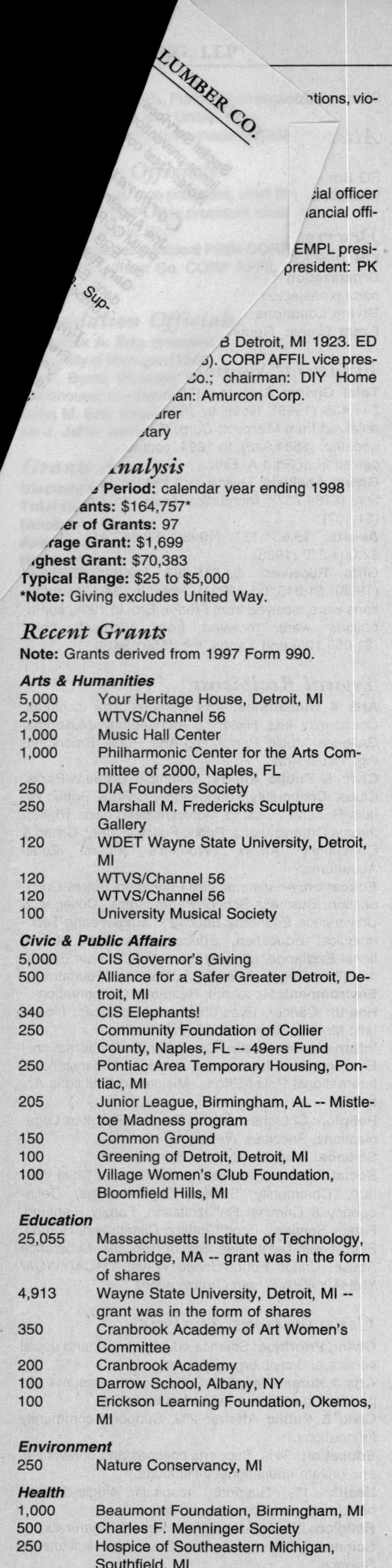

...tions, vio-

...cial officer
...nancial offi-

...EMPL presi-
...president: PK

...Sup-

...B Detroit, MI 1923. ED
...). CORP AFFIL vice pres-
...Co.; chairman: DIY Home
...an: Amurcon Corp.
...urer
...tary

...nalysis

...Period: calendar year ending 1998
...ants: $164,757*
...er of Grants: 97
...rage Grant: $1,699
...ghest Grant: $70,383
Typical Range: $25 to $5,000
*Note: Giving excludes United Way.

Recent Grants

Note: Grants derived from 1997 Form 990.

Arts & Humanities

5,000	Your Heritage House, Detroit, MI
2,500	WTVS/Channel 56
1,000	Music Hall Center
1,000	Philharmonic Center for the Arts Committee of 2000, Naples, FL
250	DIA Founders Society
250	Marshall M. Fredericks Sculpture Gallery
120	WDET Wayne State University, Detroit, MI
120	WTVS/Channel 56
120	WTVS/Channel 56
100	University Musical Society

Civic & Public Affairs

5,000	CIS Governor's Giving
500	Alliance for a Safer Greater Detroit, Detroit, MI
340	CIS Elephants!
250	Community Foundation of Collier County, Naples, FL -- 49ers Fund
250	Pontiac Area Temporary Housing, Pontiac, MI
205	Junior League, Birmingham, AL -- Mistletoe Madness program
150	Common Ground
100	Greening of Detroit, Detroit, MI
100	Village Women's Club Foundation, Bloomfield Hills, MI

Education

25,055	Massachusetts Institute of Technology, Cambridge, MA -- grant was in the form of shares
4,913	Wayne State University, Detroit, MI -- grant was in the form of shares
350	Cranbrook Academy of Art Women's Committee
200	Cranbrook Academy
100	Darrow School, Albany, NY
100	Erickson Learning Foundation, Okemos, MI

Environment

250	Nature Conservancy, MI

Health

1,000	Beaumont Foundation, Birmingham, MI
500	Charles F. Menninger Society
250	Hospice of Southeastern Michigan, Southfield, MI
100	Lighthouse of Oakland County, Pontiac, MI

International

250	African Wildlife Foundation, Washington, DC
200	CARE, New York, NY
188	Detroit Rescue Mission Ministries, Detroit, MI
100	Project Hope, Chevy Chase, MD

Religion

12,700	Christ Church of Cranbrook
500	Salvation Army
150	St. Peter's Home for Boys, Detroit, MI
100	St. Anne's Mead
100	United Jewish Foundation

Social Services

250	Mariner's Inn, Detroit, MI
250	Planned Parenthood Federation of America, New York, NY
250	Planned Parenthood Federation of America, New York, NY
250	YMCA, Birmingham, AL -- Invest in Youth program
230	Community House, Birmingham, MI -- Our Town program
210	United Way
200	Cass Corridor Youth Advocates, Detroit, MI
150	Alan Guttmacher Institute, New York, NY
100	Goodwill Industries, Detroit, MI
100	Oakland Family Services, Pontiac, MI
100	Orchards Children's Services, Southfield, MI

ERNST & YOUNG, LLP

Company Contact

New York, NY
Web: http://www.ey.com

Company Description

Revenue: US$2,540,000,000
Employees: 33,538 (1999)
SIC(s): 8721 Accounting, Auditing & Bookkeeping, 8742 Management Consulting Services.

Operating Locations

Operates nationally and internationally.

Nonmonetary Support

Value: $500,000 (1994)
Type: Cause-related Marketing & Promotion; Donated Equipment; Donated Products

Corporate Sponsorship

Note: Annual average for corporate sponsorship is $4,000,000.

Ernst & Young Foundation

Giving Contact

Ms. Ellen J. Glazerman, Director
Ernst & Young Foundation
1285 6th Avenue, 8th Floor
New York, NY 10019
Phone: (212)773-5686
Fax: (212)773-6504
Email: ellen.glazerman@ey.com
Note: Alternate fax: (212)773-2277.

Alternate Contact

Betty Owens, Matching Gifts Coordinator
Phone: (212)773-5740

Description

EIN: 346524211
Organization Type: Corporate Foundation
Giving Locations: nationally.
Grant Types: Conference/Seminar, Employee Matching Gifts, Matching, Multiyear/Continuing Support.
Note: Employee matching gift ratio: 1 to 1. The foundation reports that it also funds a Strategic Planning Partnership.

Financial Summary

Total Giving: $4,000,000 (2000 approx); $4,000,000 (1999 approx); $4,000,000 (1997 approx). Note: Contributes through corporate direct giving program and foundation. Giving includes foundation. Co.
Assets: $4,400,000 (1992 approx); $6,500,000 (1991 approx); $6,467,309 (1989)

Typical Recipients

Education: Business Education, Colleges & Universities, Education Associations, Minority Education

Contributions Analysis

Giving Priorities: Higher education.
Education: 95%. Generally limited to colleges and universities in the subject matter areas of tax, accounting, and other business areas. Matching gifts go to colleges and universities. Also supports higher education nationally, including support for professorships and doctoral fellowships. Interests include business education, graduate management studies, accounting-related education associations, and minority college funds. Grants also awarded to educational institutions through the foundation's Donor Individualized Giving Program.

Application Procedures

Initial Contact: brief letter or proposal to director of human resources at local company office
Application Requirements: a description of organization, amount requested, purpose for which funds are sought, recently audited financial statement, proof of tax-exempt status
Deadlines: None.

Corporate Officials

Philip A. Laskawy: chairman, chief executive officer, director B 1941. PRIM CORP EMPL chairman, chief executive officer, director: Ernst & Young, LLP.
David Tierno: vice president PRIM CORP EMPL vice president: Ernst & Young, LLP.

Giving Program Officials

Richard Lemeiux: treasurer PRIM CORP EMPL treasurer: Ernst & Young, LLP.

Foundation Officials

Ellen J. Glazerman: director
G. Thomas Hough: president
David Tierno: vice president (see above)

Grants Analysis

Disclosure Period: calendar year ending
Typical Range: $15,000 to $25,000

ERVING INDUSTRIES

Company Contact

Erving, MA

Company Description

Former Name: Erving Paper Mills.
Employees: 500
SIC(s): 2621 Paper Mills, 6719 Holding Companies Nec.

Housen Foundation

Giving Contact

Denis L. Emmett, Chief Financial Officer
120 E. Main St.
Erving, MA 01344
Phone: (978)544-3215
Fax: (978)544-2865

Description

Founded: 1968
EIN: 046183673
Organization Type: Corporate Foundation
Giving Locations: MA
Grant Types: Award, Capital, Emergency, Employee Matching Gifts, Endowment, Fellowship, General Support, Multiyear/Continuing Support, Operating Expenses, Project, Scholarship.

Financial Summary

Total Giving: $151,729 (1998); $145,450 (1997); $271,482 (1996)
Giving Analysis: Giving for 1997 includes: foundation ($147,150); foundation scholarships ($1,300); 1998: foundation ($149,929); foundation scholarships ($1,800)
Assets: $424,680 (1998); $514,719 (1997); $449,563 (1996)
Gifts Received: $40,000 (1998); $200,000 (1997); $300,000 (1996). Note: Contributions are received from Erving Paper Mills.

Typical Recipients

Arts & Humanities: Arts Associations & Councils, Arts Funds, Arts & Humanities-General, Libraries, Music, Performing Arts
Civic & Public Affairs: Clubs, Community Foundations, Ethnic Organizations, Civic & Public Affairs-General, Housing, Municipalities/Towns, Philanthropic Organizations
Education: Business-School Partnerships, Colleges & Universities, Community & Junior Colleges, Education Funds, Elementary Education (Public), Engineering/Technological Education, Education-General, Health & Physical Education, Literacy, Medical Education, Private Education (Precollege), Public Education (Precollege), Science/Mathematics Education, Secondary Education (Public), Social Sciences Education, Student Aid, Vocational & Technical Education
Health: Cancer, Clinics/Medical Centers, Emergency/Ambulance Services, Health-General, Heart, Home-Care Services, Hospices, Hospitals, Hospitals (University Affiliated), Preventive Medicine/Wellness Organizations
International: International Peace & Security Issues, Missionary/Religious Activities
Religion: Churches, Religion-General, Jewish Causes, Synagogues/Temples
Science: Science Museums
Social Services: At-Risk Youth, Child Abuse, Child Welfare, Crime Prevention, Domestic Violence, Food/Clothing Distribution, Recreation & Athletics, Scouts, Shelters/Homelessness, Social Services-General, United Funds/United Ways, Veterans, YMCA/YWCA/YMHA/YWHA, Youth Organizations

Contributions Analysis

Giving Priorities: The arts; foundations; universities, colleges and schools; medical centers; religious organizations; children's organizations, and community YMCA's
Arts & Humanities: 3%. In support of the performing arts.
Civic & Public Affairs: Less than 1%.
Education: 30%. Primary interest in Brandeis University.
Health: 2%. Supports the American Cancer Society, Franklin Medical Center, and Friends of Beth Israel Hospital.
International: 2%.
Religion: 53%. Benefitting Jewish Organizations.
Science: About 3%. to the Museum of Science.
Social Services: 6%. In support of YMCA's, Boy Scouts, and a Houston Food Bank.

Application Procedures

Initial Contact: Application forms are available upon request from the personnel administrator.
Deadlines: February 28.

Restrictions

Does not support individuals (except employee-related scholarships).

Additional Information

Provides scholarships to children of employees of Erving Industries and its subsidiaries.

Corporate Officials

Denis L. Emmett: chief financial officer, president, chief executive officer, director B 1954. ED University of Massachusetts BA (1976). PRIM CORP EMPL treasurer: Industries Inc. ADD CORP EMPL treasurer: Erving Paper Products Inc.; treasurer: Erving Paper Mills Inc.
Charles B. Housen: chairman, president, chief executive officer, director B 1932. PRIM CORP EMPL chairman, president, chief executive officer, director: Erving Industries Inc. ADD CORP EMPL chairman: Erving Paper Miles Inc.; president: Erving Paper Products Inc.; president: Flamingo Products Inc. CORP AFFIL director: Massachusetts Electric Co.

Foundation Officials

Charles B. Housen: president, director (see above)
Morris Housen: secretary, director PRIM CORP EMPL treasurer: Erving Industries Inc. ADD CORP EMPL assistant treasurer: Erving Paper Products Inc.
Morton A. Slavin: clerk, director

Grants Analysis

Disclosure Period: calendar year ending 1997
Total Grants: $147,150*
Number of Grants: 38
Average Grant: $2,626*
Highest Grant: $50,000
Typical Range: $1,000 to $50,000
***Note:** Giving excludes scholarships. Average grant figure excludes highest grant.

Recent Grants

Note: Grants derived from 1997 Form 990.

Arts & Humanities

2,000	Athol Performing Arts Association
2,000	Business Fund for the Arts, Greenfield, MA

Civic & Public Affairs

100	Elvira Svenningsen Fund
100	John A. Quadrino Foundation

Education

10,000	Brandeis University, Waltham, MA -- Class of 1956 Reunion
10,000	Brandeis University, Waltham, MA
10,000	Tufts University, Medford, MA
6,860	Erving Elementary School -- read-a-thon
5,000	Greenfield Community College Foundation, Greenfield, MA
2,500	American Physicians Fellowship
400	Mary Lyon Education Fund, Shelburne Falls, MA
50	Turners Falls High School, Turners Falls, MA

Health

1,000	American Cancer Society
1,000	Franklin Medical Center, Greenfield, MA
1,000	Friends of Beth Israel Hospital

International

2,000	Our Lady of Czestochow
1,000	Seeds of Peace, Washin

Religion

50,000	American Society of Techn
15,000	Hadassah, Palm Beach, FL
5,000	Combined Jewish Philanthrop ton, MA -- Shabtal Levi Childre
5,000	Combined Jewish Philanthropie ton, MA
1,000	Lubavitcher Yeshiva Academy
1,000	Temple Israel, Athol, MA
200	St. Mary's Church, Manhasset, MA
100	Blessed Sacrament Church, Jamaica Plains, MA
100	First Congregational Church of Turner Falls
100	First Congregational United Church of Christ, Sarasota, FL
35	Sisterhood Rodphey Sholom

Science

5,000	Museum of Science, Boston, MA

Social Services

5,000	YMCA, Athol, MA
1,000	Boy Scouts of America Great Trails Council
1,000	Greenfield Community YMCA, Greenfield, MA
1,000	Greenfield Community YMCA, Greenfield, MA
795	Northfield-Gill Police Association
300	Vietnam Veterans of America
250	Food Bank, Houston, TX
105	Franklin County Babe Ruth
100	Athol-Mahar Pop Warner Football, Athol, MA

Ethyl Corp.

Company Contact

Richmond, VA
Web: http://www.ethyl.com

Company Description

Employees: 1,500 (1999)
SIC(s): 2869 Industrial Organic Chemicals Nec, 5169 Chemicals & Allied Products Nec.

Nonmonetary Support

Type: Donated Equipment; Loaned Employees

Corporate Sponsorship

Type: Arts & cultural events; Festivals/fairs; Music & entertainment events; Sports events

Giving Contact

Henry C. Page, Jr., Vice President, Human Resources & External Affairs
Ethyl Corp.
330 S. 4th St.
Richmond, VA 23219
Phone: (804)788-5720
Fax: (804)788-5636
Note: Also contact nearest field location.

Description

Organization Type: Corporate Giving Program. Supports preselected organizations only.
Giving Locations: headquarters and operating communities.
Grant Types: Capital, Challenge, Employee Matching Gifts, Endowment, General Support, Professorship, Scholarship.
Note: Employee matching gift ratio: 1 to 1.

Giving Philosophy

'Ethyl believes in demonstrating responsible corporate citizenship by its active participation in local,

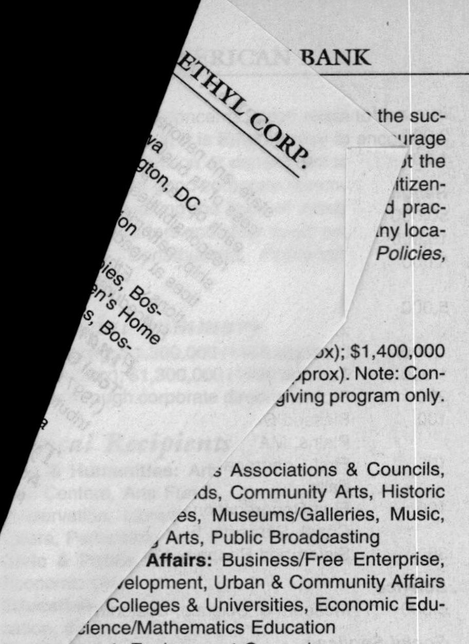

the suc- urage the itizen- d prac- ny loca- *Policies,*

x); $1,400,000 prox). Note: Con- giving program only.

s Associations & Councils, ds, Community Arts, Historic es, Museums/Galleries, Music, Arts, Public Broadcasting
Affairs: Business/Free Enterprise, velopment, Urban & Community Affairs
Colleges & Universities, Economic Education, cience/Mathematics Education
nment: Environment-General
th: Emergency/Ambulance Services, Health Organizations, Hospitals
Science: Observatories & Planetariums, Science Exhibits & Fairs, Scientific Centers & Institutes, Scientific Organizations
Social Services: Community Service Organizations, Shelters/Homelessness, United Funds/United Ways, Youth Organizations

Contributions Analysis

Giving Priorities: Higher education, health, social servic, the arts, economic education, government improvement, and international organizations. Company reports it does not makes contributions to U.S.-based nonprofit organizations with an international focus. Foreign subsidiaries do contribute to international organizations (financial information not available). Contributions program administered from headquarters; community relations committees determine involvement on local level, with vice president, corporate communications acting as liaison. Top management official at each field location is responsible for budgeting annual support.
Arts & Humanities: About 25%. Supports programs to improve the quality of life, particularly those designed to make a community more attractive to prospective employees.
Civic & Public Affairs: 5% to 10%. Emphasis is on economic education and better government organizations.
Education: 40% to 45%. Supports public and private institutions, with emphasis on those that serve as a potential source of employees or those which are of significance to employee family members. Administers matching gifts program and scholarship program for employee family members. Supports secondary, undergraduate, and graduate level study.
Health: About 25%. Emphasizes programs of direct benefit to employees in the areas of health, social services,recreation, and physical fitness. Includes support for United Way.
International: Company gives an unspecified amount to U.S.-based organizations with an international focus. Also gives to international organizations through foreign subsidiaries.

Application Procedures

Review Process: The program is administered from headquarters; community relations committees (plant manager, office manager, department head, deputy) determine involvement on local level, with vice president of external affairs acting as liaison; top management official at each field location responsible for budgeting annual support.
Evaluative Criteria: Evaluations are dependant upon the merits of the organization; benefit to company, shareholders, employees, customers, and operating community; extent to which amount contributed compares favorably with other companies in community (by such measures as number of employees, volume of business, and payrolls).
Decision Notification: The annual budget is presented and approved in late fall; contributions on an unbudgeted basis are extremely limited.

Restrictions

Contributions are not made to religious organizations for religious purposes, individuals in support of a personal project for profit, fraternal groups, local organizations in communities where company does not have significant operations, or in response to telephone or mass mail solicitations.
The corporation does not directly support political contributions. However, limited contributions are made through Ethyl Corporation Political Action Committee, which consists of funds contributed by Ethyl employees. Political Action Committee, which consists of funds contributed by Ethyl employees.

Additional Information

Company annually budgets a limited amount to support charitable organizations with small advertisements in printed programs aimed at raising funds.

Corporate Officials

Bruce Cobb Gottwald: chairman, chief executive officer, director B Richmond, VA 1933. ED University of Richmond; University of Virginia; Virginia Military Institute BS (1954). PRIM CORP EMPL chairman, chief executive officer, director: Ethyl Corp. CORP AFFIL director: Tredegar Industries; director: First Colony Corp.; director: James River Corp. Virginia; director: CSX Corp. NONPR AFFIL board governors: Virginia Council Economic Education; board visitors: Virginia Military Institute; vice president: Lewis Gintor Botanical Garden.
Thomas E. Gottwald: president, chief operating officer, director B 1962. ED Virginia Military Institute BS (1983); Harvard University MBA (1984). PRIM CORP EMPL president, chief operating officer, director: Ethyl Corp. ADD CORP EMPL president, director: Ethyl Petroleum Additives Inc.; president: Ethyl Additives Corp.
J. Robert Mooney: senior vice president, chief financial officer ED College of William and Mary (1967). PRIM CORP EMPL senior vice president, chief financial officer: Ethyl Corp.

Giving Program Officials

Bruce Cobb Gottwald: chief executive officer, member contributions management committee B Richmond, VA 1933. ED University of Richmond; University of Virginia; Virginia Military Institute BS (1954). PRIM CORP EMPL chairman, chief executive officer, director: Ethyl Corp. CORP AFFIL director: Tredegar Industries; director: First Colony Corp.; director: James River Corp. Virginia; director: CSX Corp. NONPR AFFIL board governors: Virginia Council Economic Education; board visitors: Virginia Military Institute; vice president: Lewis Gintor Botanical Garden.
Thomas E. Gottwald: B 1962. ED Virginia Military Institute BS (1983); Harvard University MBA (1984). PRIM CORP EMPL president, chief operating officer, director: Ethyl Corp. ADD CORP EMPL president, director: Ethyl Petroleum Additives Inc.; president: Ethyl Additives Corp.
J. Robert Mooney: ED College of William and Mary (1967). PRIM CORP EMPL senior vice president, chief financial officer: Ethyl Corp.
Henry C. Page, Jr.: PRIM CORP EMPL vice president human resources & external affairs: Ethyl Corp.

Grants Analysis

Disclosure Period: calendar year ending
Typical Range: $1,000 to $5,000

EUROPEAN AMERICAN BANK

Company Contact

Uniondale, NY
Web: http://www.eab.com

Company Description

Assets: US$6,843,500,000
Employees: 1,716
SIC(s): 6022 State Commercial Banks.
Parent Company: ABN AMRO Bank NV
Parent Income: US$27,510,000,000

Operating Locations

CA: ABN AMRO Bank NV, Los Angeles, San Francisco; FL: ABN AMRO Bank NV, Miami; GA: ABN AMRO Bank NV, Atlanta; IL: ABN AMRO Chicago Corp., Chicago; ABN AMRO North America, Chicago; ABN/LaSalle North America Inc., Chicago; American Real Estate Investment & Development Co., Chicago; LaSalle Cragin Bank, Chicago; LaSalle National Bank, Chicago; LaSalle-Talman Bank, Chicago; MA: ABN AMRO Bank NV, Boston; MI: Standard Federal Bank, Troy; NY: ABN AMRO Bank NV, New York; ABN AMRO Securities (USA) Inc., New York; Amsterdam-Rotterdam Bank NV New York, New York; European American Bank, Uniondale; European American Bank, Uniondale; European American Bank & Trust, Uniondale; PA: ABN AMRO Bank NV, Pittsburgh; AEL Leasing Co., Reading; American Commercial Credit, Reading; Business Outlet, Reading; Horrigan American, Reading; TX: ABN AMRO Bank NV, Houston; WA: ABN AMRO Bank NV, Seattle

Nonmonetary Support

Type: Donated Equipment; In-kind Services

Corporate Sponsorship

Type: Sports events
Note: Supports Walk-America.

Giving Contact

Linda Strongin, Vice President, Public Relations
European American Bank
1 EAB Plaza
Uniondale, NY 11555-2728
Phone: (516)296-5000
Fax: (516)296-6504

Description

Organization Type: Corporate Giving Program
Giving Locations: NY: emphasis on metropolitan New York City primarily headquarters and operating communities.
Grant Types: Employee Matching Gifts, General Support.

Financial Summary

Total Giving: Contributes through corporate direct giving program only.

Typical Recipients

Civic & Public Affairs: Business/Free Enterprise, Civil Rights, Economic Development, Public Policy, Urban & Community Affairs
Education: Colleges & Universities, Minority Education
Health: Hospitals, Single-Disease Health Associations
Social Services: Child Welfare, Senior Services, Substance Abuse, United Funds/United Ways, Youth Organizations

Contributions Analysis

Civic & Public Affairs: Priorities include organizations working in the areas of business/free enterprise, civil rights, economic development, public policy, and urban and community affairs.

Education: Funding favors colleges, universities, and minority education. Company also provides scholarship awards to local high school student athletes.
Health: Recipients include hospitals and single-disease health associations.
Social Services: Company supports united funds, volunteer services, youth organizations, groups working on behalf of the aged and child welfare, and programs addressing substance abuse.

Application Procedures

Initial Contact: Letter.
Application Requirements: A description of organization, amount requested, purpose for which funds are sought, a recently audited financial statement, proof of tax-exempt status, a list of the organization's board of directors, and a brief history of the program.
Deadlines: None.
Decision Notification: Contributions committee meets once a month.

Restrictions

Does not support individuals, religious organizations for sectarian purposes, political or lobbying groups, or organizations outside operating area.

Additional Information

European American Bank is a U.S. affiliate (20% investment) of Algemene Bank Nederland NV.

Corporate Officials

Mark Bo Anderson: senior vice presidento B Washington, DC 1955. ED University of Rochester BA (1977); University of Rochester MBA (1978). PRIM CORP EMPL senior vice president: European American Bank.
Brendan J. Dugan: president ED Saint Francis College BS. PRIM CORP EMPL president: European American Bank ADD CORP EMPL president: EAB Mortgage Co. Inc. NONPR AFFIL director: Good Shepherd Services.
Linda Strongin: vice president public relations PRIM CORP EMPL vice president public relations: European American Bank.
Edward Travaglianti: chairman, chief executive officer ED New York University Leonard N. Stern School of Business; Saint Francis College Economics. PRIM CORP EMPL chairman, chief executive officer: European American Bank New York.

Giving Program Officials

Mark Bo Anderson: (see above)

EVENING POST PUBLISHING CO.

Company Contact

Charleston, SC

Company Description

Employees: 650
SIC(s): 2711 Newspapers.

Post and Courier Foundation

Giving Contact

J. Douglas Donehue, Administrator
Post & Courier Foundation
134 Columbus Street
Charleston, SC 29403-4800
Phone: (803)722-0980

Description

EIN: 576020356
Organization Type: Corporate Foundation
Giving Locations: headquarters area only.
Grant Types: Award, Capital, Challenge, General Support.

Financial Summary

Total Giving: $965,040 (1998); $779,260 (1997); $703,191 (1996). Note: Contributes through foundation only.
Giving Analysis: Giving for 1997 includes: foundation grants to United Way ($39,819); 1998: foundation grants to United Way ($49,765); foundation scholarships ($4,850)
Assets: $8,207,299 (1998); $7,973,055 (1997); $6,994,651 (1996)
Gifts Received: $579,133 (1998); $631,092 (1997); $551,391 (1996). Note: Contributions are received from the Evening Post Publishing Company.

Typical Recipients

Arts & Humanities: Arts Associations & Councils, Arts Centers, Arts Festivals, Arts & Humanities-General, Historic Preservation, History & Archaeology, Libraries, Museums/Galleries, Music, Performing Arts, Theater
Civic & Public Affairs: Business/Free Enterprise, Chambers of Commerce, Economic Development, Civic & Public Affairs-General, Parades/Festivals, Professional & Trade Associations, Urban & Community Affairs, Women's Affairs, Zoos/Aquariums
Education: Arts/Humanities Education, Business Education, Colleges & Universities, Education Funds, Education Reform, Education-General, Health & Physical Education, Literacy, Private Education (Precollege), Public Education (Precollege), Secondary Education (Private)
Environment: Environment-General, Resource Conservation, Wildlife Protection
Health: Cancer, Health-General, Hospices, Preventive Medicine/Wellness Organizations
International: Trade
Religion: Jewish Causes, Religious Welfare
Social Services: Animal Protection, Community Service Organizations, People with Disabilities, Recreation & Athletics, Social Services-General, United Funds/United Ways, YMCA/YWCA/YMHA/YWHA, Youth Organizations

Contributions Analysis

Arts & Humanities: 23%. Museums, historic foundations, music, ballet, and art associations receive support.
Civic & Public Affairs: 10%. Primary support goes to ethnic affairs, trade associations, and community affairs.
Education: 8%. Recipients include South Carolina colleges, secondary schools, and educational organizations.
Environment: 5%. Funds conservation.
Health: 14%. Supports health care centers and single-disease associations.
Religion: 24%. Funds religious welfare organizations.
Social Services: 16%. Majority of funding supports Carolina Youth Development Center and the United Way.

Application Procedures

Initial Contact: Send a brief letter.
Application Requirements: Include program description, amount, and purpose of grant sought.
Deadlines: None.

Restrictions

Does not support individuals, religious organizations for sectarian purposes, political or lobbying groups, or organizations outside operating areas.

Corporate Officials

Ivan Verner Anderson, Jr.: president, chief executive officer B Columbus, OH 1939. ED University of North Carolina BA (1961); Univers lina MBA (1970). PRIM CORP EMP executive officer: Evening Post Publ AFFIL publisher: The Post & Courier, ber city board: Wachovia Bank South president: KXLF Communications Inc.; KRTV Communications Inc.; vice pres Communications Inc.; vice president: KPA nications Inc.; vice president: KCTZ Comm Inc.; secretary: KIVI; vice president: Ge Communications Inc. NONPR AFFIL visito University North Carolina Chapel Hill; memb versity Southern California College Business istration Business Partnership Foundation; dir Trident United Way; member: South Carolina P Association; member: Southern Newspaper Publ ers Association; director: South Carolina Histori Society; trustee: Nature Conservancy; membe Newspaper Association America; director: Indepen dent Colleges & Universities; director: Enston Home; director: ETV Endowment Board; director: Charleston Symphony Orchestra; director: Associated Press; member: Beta Gamma Sigma; director: Ashley Hall.
Peter Manigault: chairman B Charleston, SC 1927. ED Princeton University AB (1950). PRIM CORP EMPL chairman: Evening Post Publishing Co. NONPR AFFIL member: Audubon Society.
Travis O. Rockey: vice president, director B 1950. ED University of Florida BS (1973); Winthrop College MA (1979); Indiana University MA (1987). PRIM CORP EMPL vice president, director: Evening Post Publishing Co. CORP AFFIL secretary: KXLF Communications Inc.; treasurer: Sawtooth Communications Inc.; secretary, director: KTVQ Communications Inc.; secretary, director: Cordillera Communications Inc.; secretary: KETZ Communications Inc.

Giving Program Officials

James W. Martin: B 1943. ED Western Michigan University (1965). PRIM CORP EMPL treasurer, chief financial officer, director: Evening Post Publishing Co.

Foundation Officials

Ivan Verner Anderson, Jr.: vice president (see above)
J. Douglas Donehue: managing director B Cramerton, NC 1928. ED Columbia University (1964). PRIM CORP EMPL vice president corporate communications: Evening Post Publishing Co. CLUB AFFIL Rotary International Club.
Peter Manigault: president (see above)

Grants Analysis

Disclosure Period: calendar year ending 1998
Total Grants: $910,425*
Number of Grants: 79
Average Grant: $11,524
Highest Grant: $67,938
Typical Range: $500 to $10,000
***Note:** Giving excludes United Way, scholarships.

Recent Grants

Note: Grants derived from 1997 Form 990.

Arts & Humanities

50,000	Spoleto Festival
20,000	Charleston Symphony Orchestra, Charleston, SC
10,000	South Carolina Historical Society, Charleston, SC
6,500	Charleston Library Foundation, Charleston, SC
3,000	South Carolina Arts Commission
2,500	Carolina Art Association, Charleston, SC
2,500	National Trust for Historic Preservation, Washington, DC
2,000	Amazing Stage Company
2,000	Berkeley County Museum
2,000	Friends of Courthouse, Charleston, SC
2,000	North Charleston Cultural Arts Program, Charleston, SC

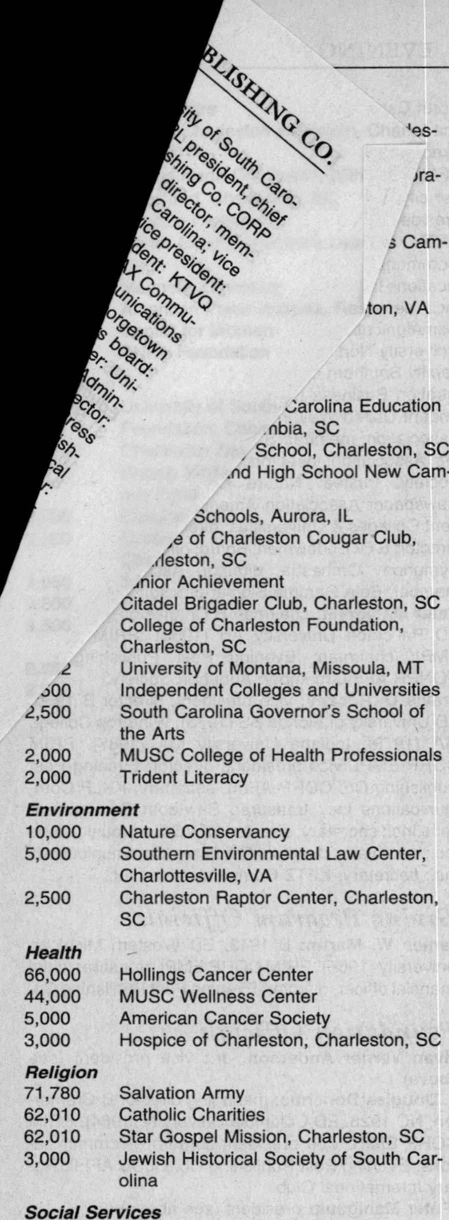

ton, VA

Carolina Education
nbia, SC
School, Charleston, SC
nd High School New Cam-

Schools, Aurora, IL
e of Charleston Cougar Club,
rleston, SC
nior Achievement
Citadel Brigadier Club, Charleston, SC
College of Charleston Foundation, Charleston, SC
2 University of Montana, Missoula, MT
500 Independent Colleges and Universities
2,500 South Carolina Governor's School of the Arts
2,000 MUSC College of Health Professionals
2,000 Trident Literacy

Environment

10,000 Nature Conservancy
5,000 Southern Environmental Law Center, Charlottesville, VA
2,500 Charleston Raptor Center, Charleston, SC

Health

66,000 Hollings Cancer Center
44,000 MUSC Wellness Center
5,000 American Cancer Society
3,000 Hospice of Charleston, Charleston, SC

Religion

71,780 Salvation Army
62,010 Catholic Charities
62,010 Star Gospel Mission, Charleston, SC
3,000 Jewish Historical Society of South Carolina

Social Services

39,819 Trident United Way, Charleston, SC
36,850 Carolina Youth Development Center
23,850 Association for the Blind
10,000 Carolina Cup Racing Association
10,000 Christian Family Y, Charleston, SC
8,334 Happy Days and Special Times, Charleston, SC
2,000 John Ancrum Society for Prevnetion of Cruelty to Animals

EXCEL CORP.

Company Contact
Wichita, KS

Company Description
Employees: 14,220
SIC(s): 2000 Food & Kindred Products.
Parent Company: Cargill Inc., Minneapolis, MN, United States

Nonmonetary Support
Type: Donated Products

Corporate Sponsorship
Range: less than $10,000
Type: Arts & cultural events; Pledge-a-thon
Note: Sponsors United Ways.

Giving Contact
Jackie Wendt, Director, Employee Publications
151 North Main Street
Wichita, KS 67202
Phone: (316)291-2500
Fax: (316)291-3499

Description
Organization Type: Corporate Giving Program
Giving Locations: headquarters and operating communities.
Grant Types: Employee Matching Gifts, Multiyear/Continuing Support, Scholarship.

Financial Summary
Total Giving: $260,000 (1998 approx); $220,000 (1997 approx); $170,000 (1996 approx). Note: Contributes through corporate direct giving program only.

Typical Recipients
Arts & Humanities: Libraries, Literary Arts, Public Broadcasting
Civic & Public Affairs: Chambers of Commerce, Community Foundations, Environmental Affairs (General), Civic & Public Affairs-General, Zoos/Aquariums
Education: Agricultural Education, Colleges & Universities, Elementary Education (Public), Education-General, Literacy
Health: Health-General, Medical Rehabilitation
Social Services: At-Risk Youth, Emergency Relief, Social Services-General, United Funds/United Ways

Corporate Officials
George Kwasniak: chief financial officer PRIM CORP EMPL chief financial officer: Excel Corp.
Gregory R. Page: president, chief executive officer PRIM CORP EMPL president, chief executive officer: Excel Corp. CORP AFFIL director: Viskase Companies Inc.
Warren R. Staley: chairman ED Kansas State University BA (1965); Cornell University MBA (1967). PRIM CORP EMPL president, chief executive officer: Cargill Inc.

Grants Analysis
Disclosure Period: calendar year ending
Typical Range: $10 to $1,000

EXTENDICARE HEALTH SERVICES

Company Contact
Milwaukee, WI

Company Description
Former Name: Unicare Health Facilities.
Employees: 20,000
SIC(s): 8051 Skilled Nursing Care Facilities, 8059 Nursing & Personal Care Nec.

Extendicare Foundation

Giving Contact
Ronald E. Retzke, PhD, Vice President, Community Relations
Extendicare Health Services
111 W. Michigan Street
Milwaukee, WI 53203
Phone: (414)908-8411

Description
Founded: 1985
EIN: 391549381
Organization Type: Corporate Foundation. Supports preselected organizations only.
Giving Locations: headquarters and operating communities.
Grant Types: Research.

Financial Summary
Total Giving: $280,000 (1999 approx); $279,933 (1998); $350,775 (1997)
Assets: $504,584 (1998); $433,618 (1996); $279,500 (1994)
Gifts Received: $247,718 (1998); $237,447 (1996); $140,857 (1994)

Typical Recipients
Arts & Humanities: Arts Associations & Councils, Arts Outreach
Civic & Public Affairs: Civic & Public Affairs-General, Professional & Trade Associations, Urban & Community Affairs, Zoos/Aquariums
Education: Colleges & Universities, Social Sciences Education
Health: Alzheimers Disease, Geriatric Health, Health Policy/Cost Containment, Health Organizations, Mental Health, Public Health
Religion: Religious Welfare
Social Services: Child Welfare, Community Centers, Family Services, Senior Services, Veterans

Contributions Analysis
Giving Priorities: All foundation grants are in the area of Health and Human Services.
Health: 100%. Funds education and research on Alzheimer's disease, caregiver education and quality of life initiatives.

Application Procedures
Initial Contact: Submit a brief letter ofinquiry.
Application Requirements: Include a description of organization, amount requested, and purpose of funds.

Restrictions
Grants are not made to individuals.

Additional Information
Company is a sponsor of the National Symposium on the Quality of Life in Nursing Homes.
Publications: Annual Report; Application Guidelines; Information Brochure

Corporate Officials
Dr. Joy Cal Kin: president, chief executive officer PRIM CORP EMPL president, chief executive officer: Extendicare Health Svcs.
J. Wesley Carter: chief operating officer PRIM CORP EMPL chief operating officer: Extendicare Health Services.
Steve Dineley: vice president, chief financial officer PRIM CORP EMPL vice president, chief financial officer: Extendicare Health Svcs.

Foundation Officials
Charles Bell: director
Gerard Bodalski: treasurer
Betty Brunner: director
J. Wesley Carter: chief executive officer (see above)
Mark Cowan: director
Lisa Felch: director
Holly Gould: director
Dr. David Lindeman: director
Stuart Lindeman: director
Robin Bieger Mayrl: director
Ronald E. Retzke, PhD: president, director PRIM CORP EMPL vice president marketing: Extendicare Health Services.
Jennifer Rittler: director
Dr Mark Sager: director
Joan Stebbins: director
Jim Wahner: director

Grants Analysis

Disclosure Period: calendar year ending 1998
Total Grants: $279,933
Number of Grants: 21
Average Grant: $13,330
Highest Grant: $62,500
Typical Range: $1,000 to $10,000

Recent Grants

Note: Grants derived from 1997 Form 990.

Education

4,000 Wisconsin School of Professional Psychology, Milwaukee, WI

Health

25,000 University of Wisconsin Center for Health Systems Research Analysis, Madison, WI
22,500 French Foundation for Alzheimer Research, Los Angeles, CA
9,500 Alzheimer's Association Tampa Bay Chapter, Pinellas Park, FL
6,500 Alzheimer's Treatment and Research Center, Saint Paul, MN
5,000 Alzheimer's Association West Central Texas Chapter, Abilene, TX
5,000 National Alzheimer's Association, Chicago, IL
4,000 Alzheimer's Association Chapter Network, Madison, WI
2,000 Alzheimer's Association Indianhead Chapter, Eau Claire, WI
2,000 Alzheimer's Association Northeastern Florida Chapter, Jacksonville, FL
2,000 Alzheimer's Association Southeastern Wisconsin Chapter, Milwaukee, WI

Religion

3,500 Catholic Charities of the Archdiocese of Milwaukee, Milwaukee, WI

Social Services

25,000 Commission on Aging with Dignity, Tallahassee, FL
15,000 Southeast Florida Center of Aging, North Miami, FL
9,000 Children of Aging Parents, Levittown, PA
5,000 United Community Center, Milwaukee, WI
3,775 Senior Services of South Sound, Olympia, WA

EXXON MOBIL CORP.

 Number 13 of Top 100 Corporate Givers

Company Contact

Irving, TX
Web: http://www.exxon.mobil.com

Company Description

Formed by Merger of: Mobil Corp. (1999).
Revenue: US$163,881,000,000 (1999)
Employees: 80,000
Fortune Rank: 3, per FORTUNE Magazine's list of 500 Largest U.S. Corporations (1999).
FF 3
SIC(s): 1311 Crude Petroleum & Natural Gas, 2911 Petroleum Refining.

Operating Locations

Australia: Associated Oil Co. Pty. Ltd., Bendigo; Exoil Ltd., Melbourne; Rundle Queensland Ltd., Melbourne; Exxon Coal & Minerals Australia Ltd., North Sydney; Owljura Pty. Ltd., North Sydney; UCM Finance Pty. Ltd., North Sydney; Wolfang Coal Mines Pty. Ltd., North Sydney; Lemington Coal Mines Ltd., Singleton; Esso Australia Ltd., Southbank; Esso Australia Resources Ltd., Southbank; Esso Employees Accumulation Plan Pty. Ltd., Sydney; Esso Standard Oil Pty. Ltd., Sydney; Exxon Ltd., Sydney; Austria: Esso Austria AG, Vienna; Exxon Handels GmbH, Vienna; Osterreichische Fernwarmegesellschaft mbH, Vienna; Belgium: Esso NV/SA, Antwerpen, Anvers; European Card Service NV, Antwerpen, Anvers; Servicar NV, Antwerpen, Anvers; Esso Coordination Center NV, Brussels, Brabant; Van Sande BVBA in Vereffening, Laarne, Flandre-Orientale; Brazil: Esso Brasileira de Petroleo Ltda., Rio de Janeiro; Sociedade Tecnica e Industrial de Lubrificantes Solutec SA, Rio de Janeiro; Canada: Canada Ltd., Calgary; Imperial Oil Resources Ltd., Calgary; Imperial Oil Resources Ventures Ltd., Calgary; Oslo Alberta Ltd., Calgary; Canada Imperical Oil Ltd., Toronto; Canada Ltd., Toronto; Devon Estates Ltd., Toronto; ESF Ltd., Toronto; Exxon Canada, Toronto; Imperial Oil Ltd., Toronto; McColl-Frontenac Petroleum, Toronto; Chile: Esso Chile Petrolera Ltda., Santiago; People's Republic of China: Exxon Chemical China Beijing, Beijing; Shanghao Yuelong NFM Ltd., Shanghai, Chiba; Colombia: International Columbia Resources Corp., Barranquilla; Czech Republic: Esso Spol SRO, Prague; Denmark: Exxon Chemical Danmark AS, Copenhagen; El Salvador: Esso Standard Oil SA Ltd., San Salvador; France: Exploitation et Developpement Operation Commerciale, Aubervilliers, Seine-St.-Denis; Liants Routiers Gard Esso Via France (GPT), Courbevoie, Hauts-de-Seine; Office Prive Assurances Courtage, Courbevoie, Hauts-de-Seine; Paris Niel (Ste. Immobiliere), Courbevoie, Hauts-de-Seine; Emulsions de Feyzin, Feyzin, Rhone; Noroxo SA, Harnes, Pas de Calais; Esso Lub'Services, La Plaine St. Denis; Worex SNC, Le Pecq, Yvelines; Expertises Technologies Services ETS, Mont St. Aignan; Exxon Chemical Polymeres SNC, Notre Dame de Gravenchon; Cloarec (ETS), Pleyben, Finistere; Butyl (Ste du Caoutchouc), Rueil Malmaison; Esso France SA, Rueil Malmaison; Esso Raffinage (Societe Anonyme Francaise), Rueil Malmaison; Esso Recherches Exploitation Petrolieres (Societe), Rueil Malmaison; Esso Societe Anonyme Francaise, Rueil Malmaison; Exxon Chemical France, Rueil Malmaison; Exxon Chemical SA, Rueil Malmaison; Exxon Chemical (Societe Francaise), Rueil Malmaison; Groupement Petrolier de Finistere, Rueil Malmaison; Germany: Esso Berlin GmbH, Berlin; Esso Tankdienst GmbH, Bremen; Kropp & Julius Mineraloelvertrieb GmbH, Bremerhaven, Bremen; Esso Sachsen Mineraloelvertrieb GmbH, Chemnitz, De-Ost; Deutsche Exxon Chemical GmbH, Cologne, Nordrhein-Westfalen; Esso Thueringen Mineraloelvertrieb GmbH, Erfurt, De-Ost; Esso Rhein Ruhr Mineraloelvertrieb GmbH, Gelsenkirchen; Esso AG, Hamburg; Esso Bunker GmbH, Hamburg; Esso Versicherungsvermittlung GmbH, Hamburg; Exxon Handelsund Dienstleistungs GmbH, Hamburg; Favorit-Unternehmens Verwaltung GmbH, Hamburg; Hans D. Schumacher GmbH, Hamburg; Esso Hannover Mineraloelvertrieb GmbH, Hannover, Niedersachsen; Esso Suedwest Mineraloelvertrieb GmbH, Karlsruhe, Baden-Wuerttemberg; Heinrich Schneider Spedition GmbH, Karlsruhe, Baden-Wuerttemberg; Esso Donau Mineraloelvertrieb GmbH, Koesching, Bayern; Tiba Speditions GmbH, Koesching, Bayern; Gebrueder Kaes Brennstoffhandel GmbH, Munich, Bavaria; TBN Tanklagerbetriebsges, Nuernberg, Bayern; Willy Eberlein Mineraloelvertrieb GmbH, Oberschleissheim, Bayern; TLS Tanklager Stuttgart GmbH, Stuttgart, Baden-Wuerttemberg; Guam: Esso Eastern, Tamuning; Hong Kong: Exxon Energy Ltd., Central District; Castle Peak Power Co. Ltd., Mongkok, Kowloon; Exxon Chemical International Services Ltd., Wan Chai; Hungary: Esso Hungaria Kereskedelmi Korlatolt Felelossegu Tarsasag, Budapest; Ireland: Esso Ireland Ltd., Blackrock; Esso Ireland Manufacturing Co. Ltd., Blackrock; Esso (Ireland) Pension Trust Ltd., Blackrock; Esso AG, Cork; Artane Service Station Ltd., Dublin; Exxon Ltd., Dublin; Italy: Mediterranea Iciom SRL, Catania, Sicilia; Toscana Lavorazione Petroli SRL, Firenze, Toscana; Kuen
Falca SRL, Merano, Trentino-A
Chemical Mediterranea Societe
Limitata, Milano, Lombardia; Aclam A
nti Lubrificanti Affini Milano SRL, Pe
Engycalor Energia Calore SRL, Roma
Italiana SpA, Roma, Lazio; Japan: Ess
Tokyo; Exxon Chemical Japan, Tokyo; M
Mexicana SA de CV, Ciudad de Mexico;
Maritimas SA de CV, Ciudad de Mexico;
Esso Borneo Sdn. Bhd., Kuching, Sarawa
lands: Esso Benelux Trading BV, Breda, No
bant; Exxon Funding BV, Breda, Noord-Braba
Aardgas BV, S'Gravenhage, Zuid-Holland; Es
nelux BV, S'Gravenhage, Zuid-Holland; Esso O
BV, S'Gravenhage, Zuid-Holland; Esso Holding
S'Gravenhage, Zuid-Holland; Esso Nederland
S'Gravenhage, Zuid-Holland; Exxon BV, S'Grave
hage, Zuid-Holland; Comma Oil & Chemicals Ltd
Weert, Limburg; Norway: Esso Exploration & Produc
tion Norway, Oslo, Akershus; Esso Norge AS, Oslo, Akershus; Progas AS, Oslo, Akershus; Tiger AS, Oslo, Akershus; Portugal: Esso Gas Lda., Lisboa; Esso Portuguesa SA, Lisboa; Exxon Portuguesa (Petroleos)-Productos Quimicos Comercio Geral e Turismo Lda., Lisboa; Singapore: Esso Singapore Private Ltd., Singapore; Switzerland: Esso (Schweiz) AG, Zurich; Thailand: Esso Standard Thailand Co. Ltd., Bangkok; Exxon Chemical Thailand Ltd., Bangkok; United Kingdom: Exxon Chemical Ltd., Abingdon, Oxfordshire; Comma Oil & Chemicals Ltd., Gravesend, Kent; Redline Oil Services Ltd., Hounslow, Greater London; Dart Oil Co. Ltd., Leatherhead, Surrey; Esso Holding Co. UK, Leatherhead, Surrey; Esso Petroleum Co. Ltd., Leatherhead, Surrey; Armley Road Services Ltd., Leeds, West Yorkshire; Lincolnshire Service Station Ltd., Lincoln, Lincolnshire; Ancon Insurance Co. (United Kingdom) Ltd., London; Esso Exploration & Production UK Ltd., London; Esso Marine UK Ltd., London; Esso Property Management Co. Ltd., London; Esso UK Plc, London; Retail Petroleum Services Ltd., London; Masters South London Ltd., Morden, Surrey

Corporate Sponsorship

Type: Arts & cultural events

Exxon Mobil Education Foundation

Giving Contact

Edward F. Ahnert, Manager, Contributions
ExxonMobil Corp. Contributions
5959 Las Colinas Blvd.
Irving, TX 75037-2298
Phone: (972)444-1000
Fax: (972)444-1405
Web: http://www.exxon.mobil.com

Alternate Contact

Exxon Mobil Education Foundation
5959 Las Colinas Boulevard
Irving, TX 75035-2298

Description

EIN: 136082357
Organization Type: Corporate Foundation
Former Name: Exxon Education Foundation (1999).
Giving Locations: internationally; nationally.
Grant Types: Employee Matching Gifts, General Support, Matching, Multiyear/Continuing Support.
Note: Employee matching gift ratio: 3 to 1 up to $5,000 per employee per year to colleges and universities, and to the United Negro College Fund, the American Indian College Fund, and the Hispanic Association of Colleges & Universities. Educational matching gifts are handled through the foundation. Employee matching gift ratio: 1 to 1 up to $1,000 per employee annually

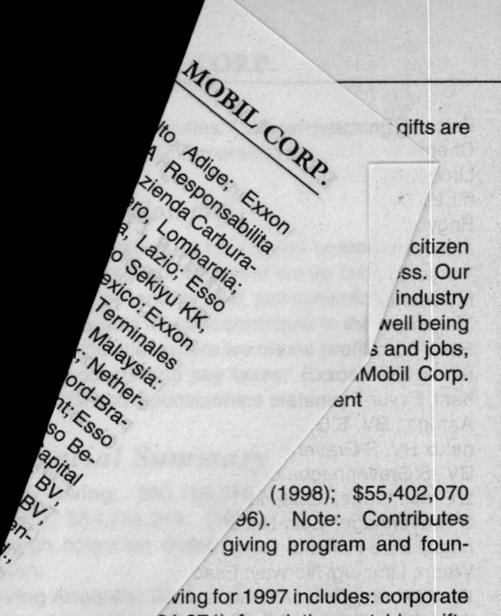

gifts are

citizen ss. Our industry well being s and jobs, Mobil Corp. ent

(1998); $55,402,070 96). Note: Contributes giving program and foun-

ving for 1997 includes: corporate 81,974); foundation matching gifts domestic and international subsidiar- 228); foundation ($6,361,639); corpo- to United Way ($3,512,275); foundation dividuals ($107,000); 1998: corporate direct ($23,387,582); foundation matching gifts ,973,743); domestic and international subsidiar- s ($13,137,160); foundation ($5,914,617); corporate grants to United Way ($3,618,216); corporate fellowships ($50,000); foundation fellowships ($45,000)

Assets: $11,870,405 (1998); $9,628,803 (1995); $32,763,000 (1990)

Gifts Received: $21,483,238 (1998); $22,229,370 (1995). Note: In 1998, contributions were received from Exxon Corporation.

Typical Recipients

Arts & Humanities: Arts Associations & Councils, Arts Centers, Arts Festivals, Arts Institutes, Community Arts, Dance, Ethnic & Folk Arts, Historic Preservation, Libraries, Museums/Galleries, Music, Opera, Performing Arts, Public Broadcasting, Theater

Civic & Public Affairs: African American Affairs, Botanical Gardens/Parks, Community Foundations, Economic Development, Economic Policy, Employment/Job Training, Hispanic Affairs, Housing, Law & Justice, Minority Business, Nonprofit Management, Professional & Trade Associations, Public Policy, Safety, Urban & Community Affairs, Women's Affairs, Zoos/Aquariums

Education: Business Education, Business-School Partnerships, Colleges & Universities, Economic Education, Education Associations, Education Funds, Education Reform, Engineering/Technological Education, Environmental Education, Faculty Development, Education-General, Health & Physical Education, Leadership Training, Medical Education, Minority Education, Public Education (Precollege), Science/Mathematics Education, Secondary Education (Public), Special Education, Student Aid

Environment: Air/Water Quality, Energy, Environment-General, Resource Conservation, Wildlife Protection

Health: Cancer, Clinics/Medical Centers, Emergency/Ambulance Services, Health Organizations, Hospitals, Medical Rehabilitation, Medical Research, Medical Training, Nursing Services, Public Health

International: Health Care/Hospitals, International Affairs, International Environmental Issues, International Peace & Security Issues, International Relations

Science: Science Museums, Scientific Centers & Institutes, Scientific Labs, Scientific Research

Social Services: Child Welfare, Community Service Organizations, Counseling, Day Care, Delinquency & Criminal Rehabilitation, Family Services, Scouts, Shelters/Homelessness, Substance Abuse, United Funds/United Ways, Volunteer Services, YMCA/YWCA/YMHA/YWHA, Youth Organizations

Contributions Analysis

Giving Priorities: Recipient areas include Environment; Public Information and Policy Research; Education; Health, Welfare and Community Services; and Arts, Museums, and Historical Associations.

Arts & Humanities: 5%. Supports programs that strengthen the community-building power of the arts. Special emphasis is placed on supporting organizations and programs that reach out to nontraditional audiences, provide greater access to arts and cultural institutions and programs, and incorporate the arts and culture into local schools.

Civic & Public Affairs: 7%. Supports organizations dealing with public policy alternatives with direct bearing on the company's business operations and interests, as well as legal policy research and education, environmental policy, and regulation. Also supports community foundations and local civic organizations.

Education: 42%. Supports pre-college and higher education through grants to colleges and universities, junior achievement, local schools, and minority education.

Environment: 12%. Supports environmental policy and research, and tiger conservation.

Health: 2%. Supports research projects on topics related to the company's business operations; occupational health education, especially for traditionally underrepresented populations; outreach to local institutions in ExxonMobil communities; and health matters affecting the workforce.

International: 23%. Funds a broad range of international organizations, including those dealing with international affairs and policy, social services, and environmental issues. International giving includes corporate direct contributions outside the United States.

Social Services: 9%. Supports community service organizations, community centers, and minority and women-oriented service organizations.

Note: Total contributions made in 1998.

Application Procedures

Initial Contact: For corporate direct giving request, send a proposal not exceeding five pages. For foundation requests, send a brief letter of inquiry (no longer than two pages).

Application Requirements: For corporate direct giving proposals: contact person and background information on the individuals responsible for administering the organization's programs; history and a description of the organization's work, and an explanation of the significance of that work; general operating budget; list of board of directors; list of current public and private contributors and level of support; audited financial statement; and proof of tax-exempt status. If support is requested for a specific project, also provide: a project description and an explanation of its significance; background information on individuals who will be carrying out the project; the total project budget; the amount requested; and if appropriate, a list of others who are or will be providing funds for the project.

For foundation letters of inquiry, describe: the problem or need your project is intended to address; the contemplated work, its expected outcomes, and the significance of those outcomes; the qualifications of those who will be carrying out the project; the total estimated project cost, and the amount requested; the project timetable; plans for evaluating the project; and plans for disseminating the outcomes of the work and/or the outcomes of its evaluation.

Deadlines: None.

Evaluative Criteria: The corporate direct giving programs favors grants that related to the conduct of U.S. business in general and the conduct of the petroleum and chemical industries in particular, as well as grants which improve the quality of life in communities where Exxon has a significant presence.

The foundation prefers projects that are concerned with a major educational issue and address only certain aspects of that issue; require funds for the early stages of innovate activities; and have a national impact.

Decision Notification: Review process is continuous.

Restrictions

Exxon Mobil's Direct Contributions Program does not make grants to individuals, local organizations or activities (unless they are geographically located in an area where Exxon Mobil has significant facilities or numbers of employees), or for political or religious causes. The corporation does not generally contribute to endowments or provide operating support to agencies funded by the United Way. Grants are made only to tax-exempt organizations.

The foundation does not make grants to individuals, does not provide funds for equipment acquisition, and does not award scholarship. The foundation rarely contributes to endowments or makes grants for construction or remodeling of facilities. Grants are made only to tax-exempt organizations.

Does not accept video tapes or books.

Additional Information

The Exxon Education Foundation's name was changed to Exxon Mobil Education Foundation as a result of the merger of Exxon Corp. and Mobil Corp. in 1999. The Exxon Mobil Education Foundation gives to education only and is separate from the corporate direct giving program.

The National Fish and Wildlife Foundation and Exxon Corp. established the Save the Tiger Fund in 1995 to help fund tiger conservation projects in Asia and research at universities and zoos. The funds also supports education programs to make the public aware that the tiger is near extinction in the wilderness.

Corporate Officials

Rene Dahan: senior vice president B Fez, Morocco 1941. ED Ecole Nationale D'Officiers De Marine (1959); Ecole d'Hydrographie (1961). PRIM CORP EMPL senior vice president: ExxonMobil Corp. ADD CORP EMPL president: Exxon International Services.

Harry J. Longwell: senior vice president B Bunkie, LA 1941. ED Louisiana State University (1963). PRIM CORP EMPL senior vice president: ExxonMobil Corp.

Lee R. Raymond: chairman, president, chief executive officer B Watertown, SD 1938. ED University of Wisconsin BSChE (1960); University of Minnesota PhD (1963). PRIM CORP EMPL chairman, chief executive officer: ExxonMobil Corp. ADD CORP EMPL senior vice president, director: Esso International-AM Inc. CORP AFFIL director: Morgan Guaranty Trust Co.; director: JP Morgan & Co. Inc. NONPR AFFIL member: University Wisconsin Foundation; trustee: Wisconsin Alumni Research Foundation; director: United Negro College Fund; member, board governors: United Way America; trustee: Southern Methodist University; member: Trilateral Commission; director: Project Shelter Pro-Am; member: Singapore-U.S. Business Council; partner emeritus: New York City Partnership; member: Occupl Physicians Scholarship Fund; member: National Petroleum Council; director: New American Schools Development Corp.; director: Jason Foundation for Education; member, director: National Academy Engineering; member: Emergency Committee American Trade; director: Dallas Citizens Council; member: Dallas Committee Foreign Relations; member: College Board; member: Council Foreign Relations; director: Business Council International Understanding Inc.; member: Business Roundtable; member: Business Council; member: American Society Engineering Educators; member, founder: American Society Royal Botanical Garden; director: American Petroleum Institute; member national advisory council: American Society Engineering; member: American Council Germany.

Robert E. Wilhelm: senior vice president PRIM CORP EMPL senior vice president: ExxonMobil Corp.

Foundation Officials

Edward F. Ahnert: president
Anthony W. Atkiss: chairman, trustee PRIM CORP EMPL vice president public affairs: Exxon Corp.

Grants Analysis

Disclosure Period: calendar year ending 1998
Total Grants: $5,914,617*
Number of Grants: 115
Average Grant: $39,389*
Highest Grant: $500,000
Typical Range: $1,000 to $50,000
***Note:** Giving excludes corporte giving, domestic and international subsidiaries, matching gifts, gifts to individuals, and United Way. Average grant figure excludes four highest grants ($1,542,400).

Recent Grants

Note: Grants derived from 1997 Form 990.

Arts & Humanities

38,934 Texas Christian University, Fort Worth, TX -- museum learning laboratory

Civic & Public Affairs

50,000 Hispanic Association of Colleges and Universities, San Antonio, TX

Education

436,588 National Science Teachers Association, Arlington, VA -- Building a Presence for Science-A Book in Every Building
275,000 National Action Council for Minorities in Engineering, New York, NY
275,000 National Science Teachers Association, Arlington, VA -- Building a Presence for Science supplement
250,000 University of Washington, Seattle, WA -- Education of Educators Phase Three
213,947 Southern University A&M College, Baton Rouge, LA -- lab school math and science program
212,186 Mathematical Association of America, Washington, DC -- New Experiences in Teaching continuation grant
200,100 Project Kaleidoscope, Washington, DC -- faculty for the 21st century
166,033 Paul Quinn College, Dallas, TX -- capital campaign
156,400 University of California Berkeley, Berkeley, CA -- preparing elementary teachers to teach science
125,000 University of Houston University Park, Houston, TX -- scholars community project
110,000 Iowa State University, Ames, IA -- Model Teacher Preparation
100,000 United Negro College Fund, Fairfax, VA -- Campaign 2000
90,000 Massachusetts Institute of Technology, Cambridge, MA -- Science and Policy of Global Change program
90,000 Stanford University, Stanford, CA -- Energy Research Program/Center for Economic Policy Research
82,500 Tucson Unified School District, Tucson, AZ -- K-3 mathematics specialist program continuation grant
77,602 University of Wisconsin Madison, Madison, WI -- Coalition for Education in the Life Sciences
75,000 Association of American Colleges, Washington, DC -- general education in the natural sciences
63,000 Conference Board of the Mathematical Sciences, Washington, DC -- education partnership
61,303 New Jersey Business/Industry/Science/Education Consortium, Hoboken, NJ -- disseminate environment-based science teaching modules
60,000 Georgia State University, Atlanta, GA -- research in undergraduate math education
59,600 National Council of Teachers of Mathematics, Reston, VA -- project facilitator
56,200 National Council of Teachers of Mathematics, Reston, VA -- K-3 Math Specialists and Project Directors Annual Conference
55,000 National Action Council for Minorities in Engineering, New York, NY -- alumni survey
52,679 Rice University, Houston, TX -- Greater Houston Essential Schools Cluster Project
52,300 San Francisco Unified School District, San Francisco, CA -- K-3 mathematics specialist continuation grant
50,000 Auburn University, Auburn, AL -- minority engineering program
50,000 Charter School Resource Center, Houston, TX -- developmental support
50,000 College Board, New York, NY -- national task force on minority high achievement
50,000 Engineers of Dreams, Keller, TX -- Technology Today
50,000 Lesley College, Cambridge, MA -- K-3 Evaluation, Disseminating, and Documenting continuation grant
50,000 National Hispanic Scholarship Fund, San Francisco, CA
50,000 Stanford University, Stanford, CA -- National Center for Accelerated Schools project
50,000 University of Texas Austin, Austin, TX -- support Texas Satellite Center for Accelerated Schools
49,400 Mathematical Association of America, Washington, DC -- enhancing educational activities and effective post-secondary math faculty
49,400 Texas Southern University, Houston, TX -- college algebra reform project
49,368 City University of New York City College, New York, NY -- Summermath in the City
48,123 Montana State University Billings, Billings, MT -- Partnership for Reform in Mathematical Education
45,000 American Society for Engineering Education, Washington, DC -- support for the 'Journal of Engineering Education'
44,000 Lesley College, Cambridge, MA -- K-3 Evaluation, Disseminating, and Documenting continuation grant
40,000 Massachusetts Institute of Technology, Cambridge, MA -- Exxon fellowship
40,000 National Alliance of State Science and Mathematics Coalitions, Washington, DC -- sustaining Standards-Based Reform Initiatives project and general support
35,000 Ex-Students Association of the University of Texas, Austin, TX -- Texas Excellence Awards for Outstanding High School Teachers

Environment

100,000 Harris County Education Foundation, Houston, TX -- education for the Energy Industry Program
75,000 Enterprise for Education, Santa Monica, CA -- Clean Air Challenge Program supplemental grant

Science

200,000 American Geological Institute Foundation, Houston, TX -- teacher education for earth science
100,000 American Geological Institute Foundation, Houston, TX -- teacher education for earth science
49,500 Chemical Heritage Foundation, Philadelphia, PA -- support and development of an information kiosk

Social Services

50,000 Salesmanship Club, Dallas, TX -- research, development, and service for at-risk children at the J. Erik Jonsson School

FABRI-KAL CORP.

Company Contact

Kalamazoo, MI

Company Description

SIC(s): 3089 Plastics Products Nec, 3993 Signs & Advertising Displays.

Nonmonetary Support

Type: Loaned Executives

Fabri-Kal Foundation

Giving Contact

Robert P. Kittredge, Chairman & Chief Executive Officer
Fabri-Kal Corp.
Plastics Pl.
Kalamazoo, MI 49001-4880
Phone: (616)385-5050
Fax: (616)385-0197

Description

EIN: 237003366
Organization Type: Corporate Foundation
Giving Locations: MI: Kalamazoo; PA: Hazleton; SC: Greenville
Grant Types: Capital, Endowment.

Financial Summary

Total Giving: $288,018 (1998); $297,342 (1997); $206,997 (1996)
Giving Analysis: Giving for 1997 includes: foundation ($271,651); foundation grants to United Way ($25,691); 1998: foundation gifts to individuals ($172,417); foundation ($84,335); foundation grants to United Way ($31,266)
Assets: $153 (1998); $77 (1997); $118 (1996)
Gifts Received: $288,144 (1998); $297,352 (1997); $202,042 (1996). Note: Contributions were received from the Fabri-Kal Corp.

Typical Recipients

Arts & Humanities: Arts Institutes, Arts & Humanities-General, History & Archaeology, Museums/Galleries, Music
Civic & Public Affairs: Botanical Gardens/Parks, Chambers of Commerce, Employment/Job Training, Civic & Public Affairs-General, Women's Affairs
Education: Education Reform, Education-General, Medical Education, Public Education (Precollege)
Environment: Environment-General
Health: Health-General, Nursing Services
Religion: Religious Organizations, Religious Welfare
Social Services: Big Brother/Big Sister, Camps, Child Welfare, Community Service Organizations, Family Services, Food/Clothing Distribution, People with Disabilities, Senior Services, Social Services-General, Substance Abuse, United Funds/United Ways, Volunteer Services, YMCA/YWCA/YMHA/YWHA, Youth Organizations

Contributions Analysis
Giving Priorities: Education, capital campaigns, and the United Way.
Education: 60%. Education grants for benefit of company's employees.
Social Services: 10%. Funds United Way.
Note: Total contributions made in 1998.

Application Procedures
Initial Contact: Submit a brief letter of inquiry.
Application Requirements: Include a description of organization, amount requested, purpose of funds sought, and proof of tax-exempt status.
Deadlines: None. Contributions are awarded once a year.

Restrictions
Does not support individuals, religious organizations for sectarian purposes, political or lobbying groups, or organizations outside operating areas.

Additional Information
In addition to providing general charitable contributions, the foundation provides educational grants for higher education to children of Fabri-Kal Corp. employees.

Corporate Officials
Gary C. Galia: vice president finance, treasurer PRIM CORP EMPL vice president finance, treasurer: Fabri-Kal Corp.
Robert P. Kittredge: chairman, chief executive officer, director B Bellevue, PA 1925. ED University of Michigan (1948). PRIM CORP EMPL chairman, chief executive officer, director: Fabri-Kal Corp.
John D. Michael: president, director PRIM CORP EMPL president, director: Fabri-Kal Corp.

Foundation Officials
Gary C. Galia: vice president finance (see above)
Robert P. Kittredge: president (see above)
R. L. Weyhing, III: secretary

Grants Analysis
Disclosure Period: calendar year ending 1998
Total Grants: $84,335*
Number of Grants: 20
Average Grant: $4,217
Highest Grant: $11,667
Typical Range: $500 to $10,000
***Note:** Giving excludes United Way; gifts to individuals.

Recent Grants
Note: Grants derived from 1997 Form 990.

Arts & Humanities

10,000	Heritage Community, Kalamazoo, MI
10,000	Kalamazoo Institute of Arts, Kalamazoo, MI
10,000	Kalamazoo Symphony Orchestra, Kalamazoo, MI

Civic & Public Affairs

3,333	Women's Education Coalition, Kalamazoo, MI
1,300	Parks Foundation of Kalamazoo County, Kalamazoo, MI

Environment

5,000	Kalamazoo Nature Center, Kalamazoo, MI -- support renovations

Religion

5,000	Kalamazoo Gospel Mission, Kalamazoo, MI

Social Services

11,407	United Way, Hazleton, PA -- campaign support
11,407	United Way Greenville County, Greenville, SC -- campaign support
10,000	Family and Children Services, Kalamazoo, MI
7,000	Goodwill Industries, Kalamazoo, MI
6,000	Senior Services, Kalamazoo, MI
5,000	Big Brothers and Big Sisters, Kalamazoo, MI
3,400	YMCA, Kalamazoo, MI -- capital campaign
3,300	Pretty Lake Vacation Camp, Kalamazoo, MI
2,877	United Way, Kalamazoo, MI -- campaign support
2,500	Voluntary Action, Kalamazoo, MI
2,000	Second Harvest Food Bank, Battle Creek, MI
1,700	Michigan Chamber of Commerce, Kalamazoo, MI -- support Drugs Don't Work Campaign
1,500	Pretty Lake Vacation Camp, Kalamazoo, MI

FANNIE MAE

★ Number 25 of Top 100 Corporate Givers

Company Contact
Washington, DC

Company Description
Former Name: Federal National Mortgage Association.
Revenue: US$31,498,800,000
Profit: US$3,418,100,000
Employees: 3,400
Fortune Rank: 26, per FORTUNE Magazine's list of 500 Largest U.S. Corporations (1999).
FF 26
SIC(s): 6111 Federal & Federally-Sponsored Credit.

Operating Locations
Operates nationally, through headquarters and 5 regional offices.

Nonmonetary Support
Type: Loaned Employees

Corporate Sponsorship
Range: less than $1,300,000
Type: Arts & cultural events; Festivals/fairs; Music & entertainment events; Pledge-a-thon; Sports events
Contact: Eilene Lefsey-Towns, Manager, Community Events

Fannie Mae Foundation

Giving Contact
Ann M. Wheelock, President and Chief Executive Officer
Fannie Mae Foundation
North Tower, Suite One
4000 Wisconsin Avenue, NW
Washington, DC 20016-2804
Phone: (202)274-8000
Fax: (202)274-8111
Web: http://www.fanniemaefoundation.org

Description
Founded: 1979
EIN: 521172718
Organization Type: Corporate Foundation
Giving Locations: DC: Washington national organizations; operating locations.
Grant Types: Award, Capital, Conference/Seminar, Emergency, Employee Matching Gifts, Endowment, General Support, Loan, Matching, Multiyear/Continuing Support.

Note: Employee matching gift ratio: 2 to 1 up to $500 annually. Employee matching gift ratio: 1 to 1 for gifts over $500.

Giving Philosophy
'The Fannie Mae Foundation-the leading foundation in the country devoted to affordable housing issues and largest giver in Greater Washington, D.C.-transforms communities through innovative partnerships and initiatives that revitalize neighborhoods and create affordable homeownership and housing opportunities across America.' *Fannie Mae Foundation Factsheet*

Financial Summary
Total Giving: $29,200,000 (1999 approx); $33,000,000 (1998 approx); $26,104,649 (1997). Note: Contributes through foundation only. 1996 Giving includes foundation ($16,323,314); matching gifts ($794,510); United Way ($408,000). 1995 Giving includes foundation ($13,705,024); matching gifts ($724,189).
Assets: $402,437,562 (1997); $373,458,648 (1996); $378,130,998 (1995)
Gifts Received: $123,300 (1997); $869,856 (1996); $17,000,000 (1995). Note: Contributions received from Fannie Mae.

Typical Recipients
Arts & Humanities: Dance, Museums/Galleries, Music, Opera, Performing Arts, Public Broadcasting, Theater
Civic & Public Affairs: Asian American Affairs, Community Foundations, Economic Development, Employment/Job Training, Hispanic Affairs, Housing, Professional & Trade Associations, Public Policy, Urban & Community Affairs, Women's Affairs
Education: Afterschool/Enrichment Programs, Minority Education, Student Aid, Vocational & Technical Education
Health: Single-Disease Health Associations
Religion: Jewish Causes, Religious Welfare
Social Services: Emergency Relief, Shelters/Homelessness, United Funds/United Ways, Youth Organizations

Contributions Analysis
Giving Priorities: The foundation's national grantmaking programs focus on supporting affordable homeownership and rental housing opportunities and community development. Within the Washington, D.C. area, the foundation supports housing, human development, community service, arts and humanities, and civic engagement and renewal activities of D.C. organizations.
Civic & Public Affairs: (Housing & Neighborhood Revitalization) 60% to 65%. Reflecting the corporation's role as a national provider of mortgages, the foundation's grantmaking is focused on identifying and properly preparing the next generation of homeowners; reaching out to lower-income families, individuals, and communities to revitalize the neighborhoods and create affordable housing opportunities; and preparing the next generation of leaders in the affordable housing industry in communities acros America. The foundation sponsors the Maxwell Awards of Excellence Program, a national grants program to acknowledge and reward outstanding examples of the work of nonprofit organizations in providing quality housing for low-income families and individuals. Sponsors the New Americans Initiative, designed to help immigrants break down the information barrier to become homeowners. Also participates in a partnership with the National Basketball Association to support community development, and funds a fellowship program at the John F. Kennedy School of Government. The foundation's Research Grant Program funds policy analysis and empirical or theoretical research that contributes to the state of knowledge on

housing policy, housing finance, and community development issues related to the Foundation's focus areas.

Application Procedures

Initial Contact: Call or write for guidelines.
Application Requirements: Submit two complete applications, with two copies of the following attachments: most recently audited financial statements or, if not available, most recent Form 990 (grant requests for $250,000 or more must submit both); existing or pending sources of support; current operating budget and most recent balance sheet, statement of activities, and statement of cash flow; list of board of directors with affiliations; roster of staff, with credentials; and job description of key staff and/or volunteers responsible for the project; and itemized project budget, including income and expenses and an explanation of how each expense item was calculated. Requirements differ for research grants and Capital City grants; refer to foundation guidelines.
Deadlines: January 17, May 1, August 15 for notification by May 1, August 15, and November 30, respectively, for community-based organizations and programs operating outside of the District of Columbia; March 30, July 27, and November 30 for notification by July 27, November 30, and March 30, respectively, for Capital City Initiatives Grant Program applications.
Review Process: Requests undergo a two-step review process; if they make it to the second step, a program officer is assigned to work directly with the applicant.
Decision Notification: The foundation acknowledges receipt of proposal within 15 days.
Notes: The foundation frequently makes Requests For Applications; these initiatives may have specific deadlines.

Restrictions

Does not support endowments; religious organizations for sectarian purposes; organizations located outside the United States; or multi-year funding requests.

Additional Information

Applications should be sent to regional offices; contact information is included in application guidelines.
Publications: Application Form; Foundation Annual Report; Application Guidelines

Corporate Officials

Kenneth J. Bacon: senior vice president B Houston, TX 1954. ED Stanford University (1976); Harvard University (1982). PRIM CORP EMPL senior vice president: Fannie Mae.
Jamie Shona Gorelick: vice chairman B New York, NY 1950. PRIM CORP EMPL vice chairman: Fannie Mae. CORP AFFIL member: Local Initiatives Support Corp. NONPR AFFIL member: Washington Legal Clinic for Homeless; member: Womens Bar Association; member: National Park Foundation; member: National Womens Law Center; member: National Community Support Law Enforcement; member: National Legal Center Public Interest; member: DC College Access; member: Carnegie Endowment; member: Council Foreign Relations; member: American Promise - Alliance for Youth; member: Bazelon Center Mental Health Law; follow: American Bar Foundation; member: American Law Institute.
James A. Johnson: chairman, chief executive officer, director B Benson, MN 1943. ED University of Minnesota BA (1965); Princeton University MA (1968). PRIM NONPR EMPL chairman, chief executive officer, director: Fannie Mae. CORP AFFIL director: Target Corp.; director: United HealthCare Corp.; director: Cummins Engine Co. Inc.; director: Kaufman & Broad Home Corp.
William R. Maloni: senior vice president policy & public affairs B Pittsburgh, PA 1944. ED Duquesne University (1968). PRIM CORP EMPL senior vice president policy & public affairs: Fannie Mae.
Franklin Delano Raines: chairman, chief executive officer B Seattle, WA 1949. ED Harvard University BA (1971); Oxford University (1971-1973); Harvard University JD (1976). PRIM CORP EMPL chairman, chief executive officer: Fannie Mae. CORP AFFIL director: Pfizer Inc.; director: PepsiCo; director: America Online Inc.; chairman: Federation National Mortgage Association. NONPR AFFIL member: White House Conference Children Youth.
Lawrence Malcolm Small: president, chief operating officer B 1941. ED Brown University BS (1963). PRIM CORP EMPL president, chief operating officer: Fannie Mae. CORP AFFIL director: Marriott International Inc.; director: Chubb Corp.; officer: Federation Insurance Co. NONPR AFFIL director: Spanish Repertory Theatre; member: U.S. Holocaust Memorial Council; trustee: New York University Medical Center; trustee: Morehouse College; trustee: National Building Museum; trustee emeritus: Brown University.
Barry Zigas: senior vice president B New York, NY 1951. ED Grinnell College (1973). PRIM CORP EMPL senior vice president: Federal National Mortgage Association. NONPR AFFIL director: National Housing Trust; director: Yachad Inc.; director: Mercy Housing Inc.; trustee: Enterprise Foundation; secretary, treasurer, director: Hands Net Inc.

Giving Program Officials

Michelle Greanias: PRIM CORP EMPL director grants administration: Fannie Mae.

Foundation Officials

Kenneth J. Bacon: director (see above)
Peter Beard: vice president national & neighborhood initiatives
John Buckley: director
James Carr: senior vice president
Floyd Harold Flake: director B Los Angeles, CA 1945. ED Northeastern University; Wilberforce University BA (1967); United Theology Seminary Din Ministry (1995). PRIM CORP EMPL pastor: Allen AME Church. NONPR AFFIL senior fellow: Manhattan Institute.
Colleen Hernandez: director
James A. Johnson: chairman (see above)
Anastasia Kelly: secretary
William R. Maloni: director (see above)
Ann D. McLaughlin: director
Tom Nides: treasurer
Franklin Delano Raines: director (see above)
John Sasso: director
Lawrence Malcolm Small: director (see above)
Ann Marie Wheelock: president, chief executive officer
Karen Hastie Williams: director B Washington, DC 1944. ED University of Neuchatel (Switzerland) (1965); Bates College BA (1966); Tufts University MA (1967); Catholic University America JD (1973). PRIM CORP EMPL partner: Crowell & Moring. CORP AFFIL director: SunAmerica Inc.; director: Washington Gas Light Co.; director: Gannett Co. Inc.; director: Crestar Financial Services Corp.; director: Federal National Mortgage Association; director: Continental Airlines Inc. NONPR AFFIL member: National Contract Management Association; member: Washington Bar Association; member: National Bar Association; chairman, trustee: Greater Washington Research Center; member, director legal defense fund: NAACP; member: American Bar Association.
Barry Zigas: director (see above)

Grants Analysis

Disclosure Period: calendar year ending 1997
Total Grants: $26,104,649*
Number of Grants: 1,262
Average Grant: $20,685
Highest Grant: $750,000
Typical Range: $5,000 to $25,000
***Note:** Giving excludes matching gifts.

Recent Grants

Note: Grants derived from 1996 Annual Report.

Civic & Public Affairs

500,000 Homesign, Seattle, WA -- construction financing for 28-unit single family housing for first-time buyers in Seattle
500,000 Marshall Heights Community Development Organization, Washington, DC -- capital reserve fund
500,000 National Rural Development and Finance Corporation, San Antonio, TX -- loan fund for community development low-income housing
450,000 Development Corporation of Columbia Heights, Washington, DC -- for capital reserve fund
375,000 North Capitol Neighborhood Development, Washington, DC -- support of capital reserve fund for low-income housing
335,000 Enterprise Foundation, Columbia, MD -- for five-year program expansion campaign
300,000 Jubilee Enterprise, Washington, DC -- construction line of credit for low- and moderate-income people
300,000 McAuley Institute, Silver Spring, MD -- loan fund for community development building low-income housing
250,000 Manna, Washington, DC -- construction line of credit for low-income housing
250,000 Self-Help Ventures Fund, Durham, NC -- for North Carolina Community Facilities Fund
250,000 Southern California Housing Development Corporation, Rancho Cucamonga, CA -- predevelopment, acquisition of two rental low-income properties
225,000 Washington Regional Association of Grantmakers, Washington, DC -- support Washington Community Development Support Collaborative
200,000 Cleveland Action to Support Housing, Cleveland, OH -- establish linked-deposit compensating balance pool
200,000 Cleveland Housing Network, Cleveland, OH -- support construction line of credit for development of low-income housing
200,000 Community Building Group, Baltimore, MD -- support Smart Home Community
200,000 Local Initiatives Support Corporation, New York, NY -- phase two of Homestart Program, support National Rural Program, operating support of programs
200,000 Michigan Housing Trust Fund, Lansing, MI -- loan fund for community development of low-income housing
200,000 Neighborhood Housing Services, Chicago, IL -- for Chicago Family Housing Fund
200,000 Northwest Corridor Community Development Corporation, Charlotte, NC -- acquisition, construction financing for 23 single family homes for first-time buyers
200,000 Rio Valle Rainbow, El Paso, TX -- predevelopment, construction financing for Socorro Homeownership Project
199,205 Foundation for the National Capital Region, Washington, DC -- support 1996 Help the Homeless program
185,000 East Bay Asian Local Development Corporation, Oakland, CA -- acquisition, development of 13 single family homes for low-income first-time buyers
175,000 Atlanta Neighborhood Development Partnership, Atlanta, GA -- operating support, community development organizations for technical support
175,000 Housing Partnership Development Corporation, New York, NY -- acquisition, rehabilitation of two buildings in Harlem for moderate-income housing

150,000 Atlanta Neighborhood Development Partnership, Atlanta, GA -- support community development corporations building low-income housing

150,000 Delaware Valley Community Reinvestment Fund, Philadelphia, PA -- support community development for low-income housing

150,000 Greater Miami Neighborhoods, Miami, FL -- predevelopment expenses, construction financing for single family homes for low-income and moderate-income homeowners

150,000 National Center for Lead-Safe Housing, Columbia, MD -- for development of public awareness programs

150,000 Southfair Community Development Corporation, Dallas, TX -- for development costs of 146-unit multifamily rehabilitation project in Dallas

150,000 Washington Area Community Investment Fund, Washington, DC -- for Revolving Loan Fund

125,000 Neighborhood of Affordable Housing, East Boston, MA -- renovation of four buildings for low-income first time buyers

100,000 Cornerstone, Washington, DC -- for special needs housing loan

100,000 Del Norte Neighborhood Development Corporation, Denver, CO -- for capital reserve fund

100,000 East of the River Community Development Corporation, Washington, DC -- for predevelopment costs for development of low-income housing

100,000 Greater Minneapolis Metropolitan Housing Corporation, Minneapolis, MN -- to build low-income housing

100,000 Hannah House, Washington, DC -- to bridge loan between grant and HUD funding

100,000 Help Homeless Service Corporation, New York, NY -- for predevelopment fund for housing for homeless

100,000 N Street Village, Washington, DC -- predevelopment, construction financing for low-income housing

100,000 Neighborhood Reinvestment Corporation, Washington, DC -- for NeighborWorks Campaign for Homeownership

100,000 Northeast Denver Housing Center, Denver, CO -- capital reserve fund for low-income housing

100,000 Resurrection Project, Chicago, IL -- acquisition, predevelopment, construction of rental housing for low-income families

100,000 Southern Mutual Help Association, New Iberia, LA -- capital reserve revolving loan fund

Education

250,000 East Lake Community Foundation, Atlanta, GA -- support Charles R. Drew New Discoveries After School Program

250,000 Harvard University John F. Kennedy School of Government, Cambridge, MA -- development of case studies, community forums, scholarships

150,000 Home Builders Institute, Washington, DC -- development of high school construction trades academy

Religion

250,000 Mercy Housing, Denver, CO -- loan fund for community development of low-income housing

200,000 Salvation Army, Washington, DC -- predevelopment, construction financing of Harbor Light Center

200,000 US Holocaust Memorial Council, Washington, DC -- support Bringing the Lessons Home program

125,000 Manna, Washington, DC -- renovate five single family homes and two condos for sale to low-income first time buyers

Social Services

137,500 United Way National Capital Area, Washington, DC

FARMERS GROUP, INC.

Company Contact

Los Angeles, CA
Web: http://www.armersinsurance.com

Company Description

Revenue: US$1,200,000,000
Employees: 18,000
SIC(s): 6311 Life Insurance, 6321 Accident & Health Insurance, 6331 Fire, Marine & Casualty Insurance.
Parent Company: Southwest Nominees Ltd.
Parent Revenue: US$40,733,644,000

Operating Locations

CA: Farmers Insurance Group, Fresno; Farmers Group, Inc., Los Angeles; Fire Underwriters Association, Los Angeles; Truck Underwriters Association, Los Angeles; Farmers Insurance Group, Rancho Mirage; Genstar Development Co., San Diego; Farmers Insurance Group, Santa Barbara; DE: Imasco Finance LLC, Wilmington; MN: Farmers Insurance Group, Mendota Heights; MO: Farmers Insurance Group, Lees Summit; NV: Farmers Insurance Group, Reno; NY: Imasco Holdings, Pearl River; OH: High State/Investors Guaranty, Columbus; Ohio State Life Insurance Co., Columbus; Farmers Insurance Group, Dayton; OR: Farmers Insurance Group, McMinnville, Portland; TX: Farmers Insurance Group, Fort Worth, Houston; WA: Farmers Group, Inc., Mercer Island; Farmers New World Life Insurance Co., Mercer Island

Farmers Group Safety Foundation

Giving Contact

Angela L. Easton, Community Relations Manager
Farmers Group
4680 Wilshire Blvd.
Los Angeles, CA 90010
Phone: (323)932-3200

Description

EIN: 956016633
Organization Type: Corporate Foundation
Giving Locations: headquarters and operating communities.
Grant Types: General Support, Project, Scholarship.
Note: Employee matching gift ratio: 1 to 1 for gifts to higher education.

Financial Summary

Total Giving: $87,900 (1998); $2,700,000 (1996); $2,600,000 (1995 approx). Note: Contributes through corporate direct giving program and foundation.
Giving Analysis: Giving for 1995 includes: foundation ($68,528); 1996: foundation ($70,737); 1998: foundation ($87,900)
Assets: $34,833 (1998); $41,781 (1995); $7,199 (1994)
Gifts Received: $84,055 (1998); $108,155 (1995); $30,515 (1994). Note: Contributions are received from Farmers Group.

Typical Recipients

Arts & Humanities: Arts & Humanities-General
Civic & Public Affairs: Civic & Public Affairs-General, Safety, Urban & Community Affairs
Education: Colleges & Universities, Education-General, Public Education (Precollege), Social Sciences Education
Health: Children's Health/Hospitals, Emergency/Ambulance Services, Health-General
Social Services: Community Service Organizations, Emergency Relief, Social Services-General, Substance Abuse

Contributions Analysis

Giving Priorities: Youth, education, health and safety, the arts, civic organizations.
Civic & Public Affairs: 80%. Funding supports organizations that enhance the overall quality of life in operating communities.
Education: 3%. Emphasis is on higher education, precollege education programs, and insurance education at select universities; the company also supports a scholarship program, and makes gifts to employees' Alma maters.
Health: 17%. Supports medical research and treatment, youth programs, and social services.

Application Procedures

Initial Contact: Send a brief letter of inquiry.
Application Requirements: Include a description of organization or program, amount requested and purpose of funds sought, audited financial statement, budget, annual report or list of sources of support, roster of board members, and proof of tax-exempt status.
Deadlines: None, but at least two months prior to date funds are desired.
Review Process: Decisions are made by Corporate Contributions Committee.

Restrictions

Does not support individuals, religious organizations for sectarian purposes, sporting events, or political or lobbying groups. Company does not take part in fundraising advertising programs or fund construction projects.
Contributions restricted to organizations in states in which company does business; no grants are made internationally.

Additional Information

Company has operating locations in nearly all 50 states.
The Thomas and Dorothy Leavey Foundation (Los Angeles, CA) provides scholarships to children of employees or agents of Farmers Group, Inc. and its subsidiaries.
All of Farmers' 17 regional offices and two life company offices, located primarily in the West and Midwestern United States, have their own contributions programs that support local charitable organizations and civic undertakings. Requests for regional and local company contributions funding should meet the same criteria as the headquarters area. Address requests to the regional manager or local company president for the office from which funds are being sought.
Company provides most of the funding.
Company offers Agents' Community Sponsorship Fund in which agents and district managers make recommendations to support community and civic activities.
Publications: Statement of Principle (including Application Guidelines)

Corporate Officials

Leo Edward Denlea, Jr.: retired chairman, president, chief executive officer, director B Brooklyn, NY 1932. ED Villanova University BS (1954); University of Pennsylvania MBA (1959). PRIM CORP EMPL retired chairman, president, chief executive officer, director:

Farmers Group, Inc. CORP AFFIL director: Matson Navigation Co. Inc.; director: Mid-Century Insurance Co.; director: Farmers Insurance Group Companies; director: BAT Industries PLC; director: Farmer Insurance Co. Oregon; director: Alexander & Baldwin Inc.
Martin D. Feinstein: chairman, chief executive officer B 1948. ED California State University BS. PRIM CORP EMPL chairman, chief executive officer: Farmers Group, Inc. CORP AFFIL chief executive officer: Farmers Insurance Exchange Farmers Group.
Anthony F. Gasich: vice president administration B Saint Louis, MO 1949. ED Temple University; University of Arkansas (1985). PRIM CORP EMPL vice president administration: Farmers Group, Inc. CORP AFFIL vice president: Fire Insurance Exchange.
James Stovall: vice president, director PRIM CORP EMPL vice president, director: Truck Insurance Exchange.
Diane Tasaka: director corporate communications PRIM CORP EMPL director corporate communications: Farmers Group, Inc.

Foundation Officials

Jeffrey C. Beyer: president B Sheboygan, WI 1954. ED Macalester College (1978). PRIM CORP EMPL vice president: Farmers Group, Inc. NONPR AFFIL director: National Commission Against Drunk Driving; director: Western Insurance Information Service; publ: Friendly Exchange; treasurer, director: Insurance Ed Foundation.
Leo Edward Denlea, Jr.: vice president (see above)
Lawrence Donald DeWolfe: vice president PRIM CORP EMPL vice president, director: Mid-Century Insurance Co.
Anthony F. Gasich: contributions officer (see above)
Maryanne Seltzer: secretary
Diane Tasaka: vice president (see above)

Grants Analysis

Disclosure Period: calendar year ending 1998
Total Grants: $87,900
Number of Grants: 9
Average Grant: $9,767
Highest Grant: $30,000
Typical Range: $1,000 to $10,000

Recent Grants

Note: Grants derived from 1998 Form 990.

Civic & Public Affairs

30,000 National Commission Against Drunk Driving, Washington, DC -- Fight for safer cars, better Highways, and changing public attitudes about drinking
25,000 Recording Artists Against Drunk Driving, Studio City, CA -- Fight for abstinence from drinking and driving.
5,000 Mothers Against Drunk Driving, Houston, TX -- Fight for abstinence from drinking and driving.
4,400 National Safety Council Greater Los Angeles Chapter, Los Angeles, CA -- Safety in the community
2,500 Livesavers 15, Arlington, VA -- Issues on contemporary highway safety
2,500 National Association of Governor' Highway Safety, Washington, DC -- Support for highway safety
1,000 Nevada Driver's Education, Carson City, NV -- Support for Nevada Driver's Education Assembly Bill

Education

2,500 OTS Summit/CSUF Foundation, Los Angeles, CA -- Support for 1997 Traffic Safety Summit

Social Services

15,000 American Red Cross - LA Ch., Los Angeles, CA -- Support for training the Rapid Response Corps. in disaster relief

FEDERAL-MOGUL CORP.

Company Contact

Southfield, MI
Web: http://www.federal-mogul.com

Company Description

Revenue: US$6,488,000 (1999)
Employees: 54,350 (1999)
Fortune Rank: 264, per FORTUNE Magazine's list of 500 Largest U.S. Corporations (1999).
FF 264
SIC(s): 3053 Gaskets, Packing & Sealing Devices, 3494 Valves & Pipe Fittings Nec, 3562 Ball & Roller Bearings, 3646 Commercial Lighting Fixtures.

Operating Locations

Argentina: Federal-Mogul Powertrain Systems, Buenos Aires; Czech Republic: Federal-Mogul Friction Products, Kostelec nad Orlici; England: Federal-Mogul Powertrain Systems, Bradford, Bridgwater, Buxton; Federal-Mogul General Products, Chapel-en-le Frith; Federal-Mogul General Production, Coventry; Federal-Mogul Camshafts Ltd., Elstead; Federal-Mogul General Products, Lydney, Rochdale; France: Federal-Mogul Powertrain Systems, Chasseneuil Du Poitou; Federal-Mogul General Products, Crepy-en-Valois; Federal-Mogul Powertrain Systems, Garennes sur Eure, Lesmureax; Federal-Mogul General Products, Noyon cedex; Federal-Mogul Powertrain Systems, Orleans; Federal-Mogul Sealing Systems, Saint-Priest; Germany: Federal-Mogul Powertrain Systems, Burscheid, Dresden; Federal-Mogul Sealing Systems, Herdorf; Federal-Mogul General Products, Marienheide; Federal-Mogul Powertrain Systems, Stadtallendorf; India: Federal-Mogul General Products, Gurgaon; Italy: Federal-Mogul Powertrain Systems, Alpignano, Cuirhne, Desenzana del Garda; Federal-Mogul General Products, Mondovi; Federal-Mogul Sealing Systems, Torino; Republic of Korea: Federal-Mogul Powertrain Systems, Chungnam; Mexico: Federal-Mogul Sealing Systems, Naucalpan; Federal-Mogul Powertrain Systems, Puebla; Federal-Mogul Sealing Systems, Tepotzlotlan; Republic of South Africa: Federal-Mogul General Products, Durban, Johannesburg; Federal-Mogul Sealing Systems, Port Elizabeth; Federal-Mogul Powertrain Systems, Roodepoort; Scotland:, Glasgow; Federal-Mogul General Products, Hurlford, Kilmarnock; Spain:, Badalona; Swaziland:, Ngwenya; Wales: Federal-Mogul Sealing Systems, Cardiff; Zimbabwe: Federal-Mogul General Products, Harare

Corporate Sponsorship

Note: Sponsors a variety of events and causes. Contact foundation for more information.

Giving Contact

Kim Welch, Vice President Corporate Affairs
Federal-Mogul Corp.
Corporate Communications
PO Box 1966
Detroit, MI 48235
Phone: (248)354-1916
Fax: (248)354-8103

Description

Organization Type: Corporate Giving Program. Supports preselected organizations only.
Former Name: Federal-Mogul Corp. Charitable Trust Fund (1999).
Giving Locations: headquarters and operating communities; nationally.
Grant Types: General Support.

Giving Philosophy

'The management of Federal-Mogul Corporation has long recognized that certain social responsibilities are fundamental to the operation of the business. That recognition has resulted in a policy which returns a portion of the Company's profits to worthwhile charitable, educational, civic and other activities, generally but not exclusively to programs in those communities or areas where major Federal-Mogul facilities are located. This policy reflects the management attitude that the Company has a self-imposed obligation to contribute to the improvement of those communities or areas for the benefit of its employees and other residents, which also improves the climate in which its facilities must operate.' *Corporate Contributions Guidelines, Federal-Mogul Corporation*

Financial Summary

Total Giving: $240,784 (1997); $600,000 (1996 approx); $407,795 (1995). Note: Contributes through corporate direct giving program only.
Giving Analysis: Giving for 1996 includes: foundation ($298,581); foundation grants to United Way ($115,000); 1997: foundation ($155,784); foundation grants to United Way ($85,000)
Assets: $47,417 (1997); $61,123 (1996); $22,212 (1995)
Gifts Received: $225,000 (1997); $450,000 (1996); $425,000 (1995). Note: Contributions are received from Federal-Mogul Corporation.

Typical Recipients

Arts & Humanities: Arts Associations & Councils, Arts Centers, Arts Festivals, Arts Funds, Arts Institutes, Community Arts, Historic Preservation, History & Archaeology, Libraries, Museums/Galleries, Music, Opera, Performing Arts, Public Broadcasting, Theater
Civic & Public Affairs: African American Affairs, Business/Free Enterprise, Civil Rights, Community Foundations, Economic Development, Economic Policy, Employment/Job Training, Housing, Law & Justice, Professional & Trade Associations, Public Policy, Rural Affairs, Safety, Urban & Community Affairs, Women's Affairs, Zoos/Aquariums
Education: Business Education, Business-School Partnerships, Colleges & Universities, Economic Education, Education Associations, Education Funds, Education Reform, Elementary Education (Private), Engineering/Technological Education, Education-General, Legal Education, Minority Education, Private Education (Precollege), Public Education (Precollege), Religious Education, Science/Mathematics Education, Student Aid
Health: Cancer, Children's Health/Hospitals, Clinics/Medical Centers, Diabetes, Health Funds, Health Organizations, Hospices, Hospitals, Medical Research, Prenatal Health Issues, Single-Disease Health Associations
International: Health Care/Hospitals, International Peace & Security Issues
Religion: Religious Welfare, Seminaries
Science: Science Exhibits & Fairs, Scientific Centers & Institutes
Social Services: Animal Protection, Child Welfare, Community Centers, Community Service Organizations, Delinquency & Criminal Rehabilitation, Family Services, Food/Clothing Distribution, People with Disabilities, Recreation & Athletics, Scouts, Substance Abuse, United Funds/United Ways, Volunteer Services, Youth Organizations

Contributions Analysis

Giving Priorities: United funds, youth organizations, and cancer research and treatment.
Arts & Humanities: About 15%. Supports bands and orchestras in Detroit, public broadcasting, arts centers and institutes, libraries, and dramatic arts groups.
Civic & Public Affairs: 20% to 25%. Recipients include business/free enterprise, zoological parks, community development, public policy, civil rights, safety, and urban affairs organizations.
Education: About 15%. A large portion goes to colleges and universities. Other interests include education funds; business, technical, and minority education; and education associations. Also administers employee matching gifts program.

Health: 10% to 15%. Recipients include medical research, single-disease health organizations, hospitals, and pediatric health.
Social Services: 30% to 35%. Majority of funding supports united funds. Organizations concerned with the disabled and youth also are supported.
Note: Above priorities are for the foundation only. The company now gives directly, and solely supports three charities: Big Brothers and Big Sisters, the Karmanos Institute, and the United Way.

Additional Information

Co. purchased Cooper Automotive in October of 1998.
Publications: Guidelines

Corporate Officials

Diane L. Kaye: vice president, secretary, general counsel ED University of Michigan JD; University of Michigan BA (1972). PRIM CORP EMPL vice president, secretary, general counsel: Federal-Mogul Corp.
Richard Snell: chairman, president, chief executive officer, director B Phoenix, AZ 1930. ED Stanford University BA (1952); Stanford University JD (1954). PRIM CORP EMPL chairman, president, chief executive officer, director: Pinnacle West Capital Corp. CORP AFFIL chairman: Suncor Development Co.; director: Suncor Homes Inc.; chairman: El Dorado Investment Co.; director: Bank One Arizona NA; director: Central Newspapers Inc.; director: Aztar Corp.; chairman: AR Public Service Co. NONPR AFFIL member: Arizona Bar Association; trustee: YMCA Metropolitan Phoenix & Sun Valley; member: American Bar Association; trustee: American Graduate School International Management. CLUB AFFIL Phoenix Country Club; Paradise Valley Country Club.
Kim Welch: vice president corporate affairs PRIM CORP EMPL vice president corporate affairs: Federal-Mogul Corp.

Grants Analysis

Disclosure Period: calendar year ending 1997
Total Grants: $155,784*
Number of Grants: 149
Average Grant: $1,045
Highest Grant: $65,000
Typical Range: $50 to $5,000
***Note:** Giving excludes United Way. Sample grants are representative of past foundation giving.

Recent Grants

Note: Grants derived from 1997 Form 990.

Arts & Humanities

20,000 Detroit Educational Television Foundation, Detroit, MI
5,000 Detroit Institute of Arts Founders Society, Detroit, MI
850 WTVS Channel 56/Detroit Educational Television Foundation, Detroit, MI
590 WTVS Channel 56/Detroit Educational Television Foundation, Detroit, MI
460 WTVS Channel 56/Detroit Educational Television Foundation, Detroit, MI
285 WTVS Channel 56/Detroit Educational Television Foundation, Detroit, MI

Civic & Public Affairs

31,300 Detroit Renaissance Foundation, Detroit, MI
5,000 New Detroit, Detroit, MI
400 Cadillac Area Community Foundation, Cadillac, MI

Education

25,000 Awda University Foundation, Kansas City, MO
3,350 University of Notre Dame, South Bend, IN
2,300 Emmaus Bible College, Dubuque, IA
2,000 Junior Achievement, Detroit, MI
2,000 St. Mary's College, Winona, MN
1,725 University of Michigan, Ann Arbor, MI
1,500 Michigan State University, East Lansing, MI
1,400 University of Michigan, Ann Arbor, MI
1,150 Allegheny College, Meadville, PA
1,150 Michigan State University, East Lansing, MI
1,100 Marygrove College, Detroit, MI
1,034 Bethany College, Lindsborg, KS
1,000 College of New Rochelle, New Rochelle, NY
1,000 St. Mary's College, Winona, MN
1,000 University of Detroit Mercy, Detroit, MI
1,000 Walsh College, North Canton, OH
760 University of Michigan, Ann Arbor, MI
600 Albion College, Albion, MI
600 University of Detroit Mercy, Detroit, MI
500 Christendom Educational Corporation, Front Royal, VA
500 Radford University Foundation, Radford, VA
500 University of Detroit Mercy, Detroit, MI
500 University of Michigan, Ann Arbor, MI
500 Washington State University, Pullman, WA
400 Greatlakes Bible College
400 Thomas Aquinas College, Santa Paula, CA
360 Hope College, Holland, MI
350 Capital University, Bexley, OH
300 Adrian College, Adrian, MI
300 GMI Engineering and Management Institute, Flint, MI
300 GMI Engineering and Management Institute, Flint, MI
300 Northwestern University, Evanston, IL
300 US Military Academy Association of Graduates, West Point, NY
300 Wayne State University, Detroit, MI

Health

10,000 Detroit Medical Center, Detroit, MI

Religion

3,000 Concordia Seminary, Detroit, MI
600 Winebrenner Theological Seminary, Findlay, OH

Social Services

65,000 United Way, Detroit, MI
20,000 United Way, Detroit, MI
275 Community House, Birmingham, MI
250 Boy Scouts of America

FEDERATED DEPARTMENT STORES, INC.

 Number 63 of Top 100 Corporate Givers

Company Contact

Cincinnati, OH
Web: http://www.federated-fds.com

Company Description

Revenue: US$15,833,000,000
Profit: US$662,000,000
Employees: 117,100
Fortune Rank: 97, per FORTUNE Magazine's list of 500 Largest U.S. Corporations (1999).
FF 97
SIC(s): 5311 Department Stores.

Nonmonetary Support

Type: Donated Equipment; In-kind Services; Loaned Employees
Volunteer Programs: Partners in Time program established in 1989 as a vehicle to organize and stimulate volunteerism activities. Multi divisional projects involve employees from divisions in the same city working together on a unified project.
Note: Nonmonetary support is provided by the company.

Corporate Sponsorship

Value: $500
Type: Arts & cultural events; Festivals/fairs; Music & entertainment events; Pledge-a-thon; Sports events
Note: Sponsors fundraising events for civic causes, the arts, health, and education.

Federated Department Stores Foundation

Giving Contact

Dixie Barker, Manager, Corporate Contributions
Federated Department Stores
7 West Seventh Street
Cincinnati, OH 45202
Phone: (513)579-7569
Fax: (513)579-7185

Alternate Contact

Carol Sanger, Vice President

Description

EIN: 311427325
Organization Type: Corporate Foundation
Former Name: Robert Campeau Family Foundation (U.S.).
Former Name: Ilse and Robert Campeau Family Foundation.
Giving Locations: headquarters and operating communities.
Grant Types: Capital, Conference/Seminar, Employee Matching Gifts, Endowment, General Support, Matching, Multiyear/Continuing Support.
Note: Employee matching gift ratio: 1 to 1 to eligible education, arts or cultural, women's affairs, or AIDS organisation.

Giving Philosophy

'Federated Department Stores, Inc. is a company that takes it civic and philanthropic responsibility seriously. We believe that stronger, healthier and more vibrant communities provide better environments for our stores to do business, and for our employees and customers to live and work. Federated translates its commitment to action by sharing its Resources, stimulating personal involvement, encouraging diversity and adhering to responsible, ethical business practices. Report to the Community.

Financial Summary

Total Giving: $15,000,000 (fiscal year ending January 01, 2000 approx); $14,000,000 (fiscal 1999 approx); $13,202,729 (fiscal 1998). Note: Contributes through corporate direct giving program and foundation.
Giving Analysis: Giving for fiscal 1997 includes: foundation ($5,880,239); corporate matching gifts ($2,491,350); corporate direct giving ($1,496,108); fiscal 1998: foundation ($8,373,155); corporate direct giving ($3,226,995); corporate matching gifts ($1,602,579)
Assets: $24,454,029 (fiscal 1998); $24,205,374 (fiscal 1997); $21,500,000 (fiscal 1996 approx)
Gifts Received: $5,000,000 (fiscal 1997). Note: Foundation receives contributions from Federated Department Stores, Inc.

Typical Recipients

Arts & Humanities: Arts Centers, Arts Funds, Arts Institutes, Ethnic & Folk Arts, Museums/Galleries, Music, Opera, Performing Arts, Public Broadcasting

Civic & Public Affairs: Business/Free Enterprise, Civil Rights, Economic Development, Employment/Job Training, Urban & Community Affairs, Women's Affairs
Education: Arts/Humanities Education, Business Education, Colleges & Universities, Continuing Education, Economic Education, Education Associations, Education Funds, Faculty Development, Literacy, Medical Education, Minority Education, Private Education (Precollege), Public Education (Precollege), Religious Education, Science/Mathematics Education, Special Education, Student Aid
Health: Eyes/Blindness, Health Funds, Hospices, Single-Disease Health Associations
International: Foreign Arts Organizations, Missionary/Religious Activities
Religion: Religious Welfare
Science: Scientific Centers & Institutes
Social Services: At-Risk Youth, Child Welfare, Community Service Organizations, Domestic Violence, Family Planning, Family Services, Food/Clothing Distribution, People with Disabilities, Recreation & Athletics, Senior Services, Shelters/Homelessness, Substance Abuse, United Funds/United Ways, Volunteer Services, Youth Organizations

Contributions Analysis

Giving Priorities: Social welfare, single disease health organizations, the arts, education, and civic concerns.
Arts & Humanities: About 20%.
Civic & Public Affairs: Less then 5%.
Education: 25% to 30%. Funds elementary, secondary, and higher education.
Health: About 50%. Priorities are the United Way, people with disabilities, minority affairs, and youth.

Application Procedures

Initial Contact: Call or write for an application form.
Application Requirements: Include completed application, with name, address, phone number, and type of organization; copy of IRS 501(c)(3) certification; list of organization's trustees and officers; list of other major supporters; previous year's financial statements, including balance sheet; operating budget or annual report; approximate amount requested; brief background history, including number of years in service, clientele serviced, location, and general description of service; and any documents filed with state regulatory agency.
Deadlines: None.

Restrictions

Does not support individuals or religious organizations for sectarian purposes.

For the most part, contributions are recommended by divisions and corporate offices, supporting organizations in communities where they operate. Sponsoring divisions include Macy's East (New York, NY), Macy's West (San Francisco, CA), Bloomingdale's (New York, NY), The Bon Marche (Seattle, WA), Burdine's (Miami, FL), Rich's/Lazarus/Goldsmith's (Atlanta, GA), and Stern's (Paramus, NJ). While approval authority remains decentralized within divisions, guidelines, priorities, and fiscal policy are determined by the foundation. The following are not eligible ofr matching gifts: contributions of less than $50; tuition fees, or dues; college fraternal organizations, including scholarship for such groups; tickets, dinners or performances; festivals, civic health/welfare organizations, United Way; religious purposes; international organizations that collect money for distribution to other organizations; gifts that are the result of a collection taken up by employees.

Additional Information

In 1995, the company reported that it has merged with its parent company, R.H. Macy & Co. Inc. At the time of publication, Federated Department Stores planned to maintain its name and separate giving program. Company is no longer connected to the Robert Campeau Family Foundation.

Corporate Officials

Thomas Gerald Cody: executive vice president legal & human resources B New York, NY 1941. ED Maryknoll College BA (1963); Saint John's University JD (1967). PRIM CORP EMPL executive vice president legal & human resources: Federated Department Stores, Inc. NONPR AFFIL member: Underground Railroad Freedom Center; trustee: Xavier University; chairman: Jesuit Secondary Education Association; trustee: Childrens Hospital; trustee: Childrens Hospital Medical Center; member: American Bar Association. CLUB AFFIL Queen City Club; Hyde Park Country Club; Bankers Club; Commonwealth Cinicinnati Club.
Ronald W. Tysoe: vice chairman, director B 1953. ED University of British Columbia (1978). PRIM CORP EMPL vice chairman, director: Federated Department Stores, Inc. CORP AFFIL director: E.W. Scripps Co.
James M. Zimmerman: chairman, chief executive officer, director B 1944. ED Rice University BA (1966). PRIM CORP EMPL chairman, chief executive officer, director: Federated Department Stores, Inc. CORP AFFIL director: Chubb Corp.; director: HJ Heinz Co.

Giving Program Officials

Dixie Barker: executive director, administrator (see above)
Thomas Gerald Cody: executive vice president (see above)
Carol A. Sanger: (see above)
Ronald W. Tysoe: (see above)

Foundation Officials

Dixie Barker: executive director, administrator (see above)

Grants Analysis

Disclosure Period: fiscal year ending January 01, 1998
Total Grants: $13,202,729*
Number of Grants: 2,736
Average Grant: $4,825
Highest Grant: $333,334
Typical Range: $1,000 to $20,000
***Note:** Giving includes foundation and non-foundation giving. Grants analysis provided by foundation.

Recent Grants

Note: Grants derived from fiscal 1997 Form 990.

Arts & Humanities

167,180	Cincinnati Institute of Fine Arts, Cincinnati, OH
50,000	Robert W. Woodruff Arts Center, Atlanta, GA
25,000	Boise Art Museum, Boise, ID

Civic & Public Affairs

25,000	Patrons of Northwest Civic, Cultural, and Charitable Organizations, Seattle, WA
17,000	Center for Career Alternatives, Seattle, WA

Education

103,000	Florida Education Foundation, Tallahassee, FL
22,000	Northwestern University, Evanston, IL
20,000	Art Academy of Cincinnati, Cincinnati, OH

International

25,000	Exodus, Atlanta, GA

Science

25,000	Buehler Challenger and Science Center, Paramus, NJ

Social Services

298,000	United Way, Atlanta, GA
250,000	United Way Tri-State, New York, NY
240,000	United Way Dade County, Miami, FL
240,000	United Way Dade County, Miami, FL
140,000	United Way King County, Seattle, WA
135,000	United Way Franklin County, Columbus, OH
125,000	United Way Bay Area, San Francisco, CA
94,000	United Way, Los Angeles, CA
94,000	United Way, Los Angeles, CA
80,000	United Way, Memphis, TN
80,000	United Way Eastern New England, Boston, MA
73,000	United Way, Dayton, OH
60,000	United Way, Atlanta, GA
60,000	United Way Allegheny County and Southwestern Pennsylvania, Pittsburgh, PA
59,250	United Way Allegheny County and Southwestern Pennsylvania, Pittsburgh, PA
48,000	United Way Central Indiana, Indianapolis, IN
30,000	United Way Hillsborough County, Tampa, FL
30,000	United Way Hillsborough County, Tampa, FL
25,500	United Way Santa Clara, San Jose, CA
25,000	United Way Central Alabama, Birmingham, AL
25,000	United Way Santa Clara, San Jose, CA
24,000	United Way Orange County, Irvine, CA
24,000	United Way Orange County, Irvine, CA
23,500	United Way Texas Gulf Coast, Houston, TX
23,000	United Way Texas Gulf Coast, Houston, TX
20,000	Jelani House, San Francisco, CA
18,000	Metro United Way, Louisville, KY
17,000	United Fund of Broward County, Fort Lauderdale, FL
15,000	United Crusade Sacramento Area, Sacramento, CA
15,000	United Fund of Broward County, Fort Lauderdale, FL
15,000	United Way, Sacramento, CA
15,000	United Way Bergen County, Oradell, NJ
13,000	United Way Snohomish County, Everett, WA
12,500	United Way Palm Beach County, Boynton Beach, FL
12,500	United Way Palm Beach County, Boynton Beach, FL
12,000	United Fund, Minneapolis, MN
12,000	United Way Pierce County, Tacoma, WA
11,000	United Community Services of San Diego County, San Diego, CA
11,000	United Way Central Savannah River, Augusta, GA
10,400	United Way Ada County, Boise, ID

FEDERATED MUTUAL INSURANCE CO.

Company Contact

Owatonna, MN

Company Description

Premiums: US$830,000,000
Employees: 2,700
SIC(s): 6321 Accident & Health Insurance, 6331 Fire, Marine & Casualty Insurance.

Federated Mutual Insurance Foundation

Giving Contact

Richard J. Kraus, Director, Human Resources
Federal Mutual Insurance Co.
121 E. Park Sq.
Owatonna, MN 55060
Phone: (507)455-5200

Description

EIN: 237173646
Organization Type: Corporate Foundation
Giving Locations: operating locations.
Grant Types: General Support, Project.

Financial Summary

Total Giving: $215,000 (1999 approx); $640,092 (1998); $184,438 (1997)
Giving Analysis: Giving for 1998 includes: foundation ($577,302); foundation grants to United Way ($62,790)
Assets: $124,447 (1998); $224,043 (1997); $13,850 (1996)
Gifts Received: $45,789 (1998); $18,814 (1997); $3,766 (1996)

Typical Recipients

Arts & Humanities: Arts Centers, Arts Festivals, Arts Institutes, Community Arts, Libraries, Music, Performing Arts, Theater
Civic & Public Affairs: Chambers of Commerce, Clubs, Community Foundations, Environmental Affairs (General), Environmental Affairs (Air/Water Quality), Environmental Affairs (Wildlife Protection), Civic & Public Affairs-General, Housing, Municipalities/Towns, Parades/Festivals, Professional & Trade Associations, Safety, Urban & Community Affairs, Zoos/Aquariums
Education: Afterschool/Enrichment Programs, Business Education, Business-School Partnerships, Colleges & Universities, Public Education (Precollege)
Environment: Environment-General, Wildlife Protection
Health: Cancer, Children's Health/Hospitals, Emergency/Ambulance Services, Health-General, Geriatric Health, Health Policy/Cost Containment, Health Organizations, Heart, Home-Care Services, Medical Research
Religion: Religious Welfare
Social Services: At-Risk Youth, Big Brother/Big Sister, Camps, Community Service Organizations, Emergency Relief, Family Services, Food/Clothing Distribution, People with Disabilities, Scouts, Senior Services, Shelters/Homelessness, Social Services-General, Special Olympics, Substance Abuse, United Funds/United Ways

Contributions Analysis

Giving Priorities: Social services, education, civics, and the arts.
Arts & Humanities: 6%. Funds community arts, performing arts, and arts centers and institutes.
Civic & Public Affairs: 5%. Supports community foundations and professional trade organizations.
Education: 23%. Supports colleges and universities and afterschool enrichment programs.
Environment: 1%. Funds general environment and wildlife protection organizations.
Health: 2%. Funds health and wellness organizations.
Social Services: 63%. Supports causes under the foundation's Human Services (54%) and Youth (9%) programs.
Note: Contributions Analysis provided by foundation. Total contributions made in 1999.

Application Procedures

Initial Contact: Send a brief letter of inquiry.
Deadlines: None.
Notes: The foundation has no formal grant application procedure or application form.

Restrictions

Does not support individuals, religious organizations, political or lobbying groups, or organizations outside operating areas.

Corporate Officials

Charles Ingraham Buxton, II: chairman B Owatonna, MN 1924. ED Carleton College (1942-1943); United States Naval Academy BS (1946); University of Pennsylvania postgrad (1950). PRIM CORP EMPL chairman: Federated Mutual Insurance Co. CORP AFFIL chairman, chief executive officer: Federal Service Insurance Co.; chairman, president, chief executive officer, director: Federal Life Insurance Co. NONPR AFFIL director: Minnesota Insurance Federation; director: Minnesota Insurance Information Service; board governors: American Institute Property & Liability Underwriters; trustee: Associate Churches Owatonna; director: Alliance American Insurers. CLUB AFFIL mem: Veterans Foreign Wars; mem: Rotary Club; mem: Shriners Club; mem: Minneapolis Athletic Club; Owatonna Country Club; mem: Masons Club; mem: Milwaukee Order of World Wars; mem: American Legion Club.
Kirk N. Nelson: president, chief executive officer PRIM CORP EMPL president, chief executive officer: Federated Mutual Insurance Co.
Raymond R. Stawarz: chief financial officer PRIM CORP EMPL chief financial officer: Federated Mutual Insurance Co.

Foundation Officials

Charles Ingraham Buxton, II: president (see above)
Rick Kraus: administrator NONPR AFFIL council member: City of Owatonna.
J. E. Meilahn: secretary
Kirk N. Nelson: vice president (see above)
Raymond R. Stawarz: treasurer (see above)

Grants Analysis

Disclosure Period: calendar year ending 1998
Total Grants: $577,302*
Number of Grants: 136
Average Grant: $938*
Highest Grant: $252,591
Typical Range: $100 to $35,000
***Note:** Giving excludes United Way. Average grant figure excludes three highest grants (totaling $452,591).

Recent Grants

Note: Grants derived from 1998 Form 990.

Arts & Humanities

4,000	Owatonna Arts Center, Owatonna, MN -- Arts & Humanities
3,600	Owatonna Public Library, Owatonna, MN -- Education

Civic & Public Affairs

252,591	City of Owatonna, Owatonna, MN -- Civic & Community - Buxton Trail
100,000	City of Owatonna, Owatonna, MN -- Civic & Community - Buxton Trail
100,000	City of Owatonna-Buxton Trail, Owatonna, MN -- Civic & Community - Buxton Trail
20,000	Alano Society of Owatonna, Owatonna, MN -- Human Services
5,000	City of Owatonna, Owatonna, MN -- Civic & Community

Education

7,500	Minnesota Private College Fund, St. Paul, MN -- Education
5,535	Owatonna Public Schools, Owatonna, MN -- Education
3,300	Owatonna High School, Owatonna, MN -- Youth
2,500	Mankato State University, Mankato, MN -- Education

Health

4,000	Steele County Red Cross, Owatonna, MN -- Human Services
2,400	Courage Center, Golden Valley, MN -- Human Services

Religion

4,000	Salvation Army-Tornado Relief, Minneapolis, MN -- Human Services

Social Services

38,480	United Way of Steele County, Owatonna, MN -- Human Services
5,616	United Way of Metro Atlanta, Atlanta, GA -- Human Services
4,472	Valley of the Sun United Way, Phoenix, AZ -- Human Services
3,500	Steele County Family to Family, Owatonna, MN -- Human Services
3,042	United Way of Minneapolis, Minneapolis, MN -- Human Services
3,000	Crossroads of Owatonna, Owatonna, MN -- Youth
2,210	Heart of America United Way, Kansas City, MO -- Human Services

FEDEX CORP.

Company Contact

6075 Poplar Avenue, Suite 300
Memphis, TN 38119
Phone: (901)369-3600
Fax: (901)395-2000
Web: http://www.fedexcorp.com

Company Description

Former Name: Federal Express Corp.; FDX Corp. (2000).
Revenue: US$16,773,500,000 (1999)
Profit: US$631,300,000 (1999)
Employees: 141,000 (1999)
Fortune Rank: 104, per FORTUNE Magazine's list of 500 Largest U.S. Corporations (1999).
FF 104
SIC(s): 4513 Air Courier Services, 4731 Freight Transportation Arrangement.

Operating Locations

Antigua-Barbuda: Federal Express (Antigua) Ltd., St. John; Australia: Federal Express (Australia) Pty. Ltd., Mascot; Belgium: Federal Express Europe & Co. VOF, Steenokkerzeel, Brabant; Federal Express European Services Inc. Vennootschap Naar Het Recht Van Staat Delaware, Steenokkerzeel, Brabant; Bahamas: Federal Express (Bahamas) Ltd., Nassau, New Providence; Bermuda: Federal Express (Bermuda) Ltd., Hamilton; Canada: Federal Express Canada Ltd., Mississauga; Cayman Islands: Federal Express (Cayman) Ltd., George Town, Grand Cayman; France: Federal Express International France, Gennevilliers, Hauts-de-Seine; Germany: Federal Express Europe Niederlassung Deutschland, Kelsterbach, Hessen; Grenada: Federal Express (Grenada) Ltd., St. George's; Hong Kong: Federal Express Pacific, Tsim Sha Tsui, Kowloon; Ireland: Federal Express Europe Inc., Dublin; Italy: Federal Express Corp., Segrate, Lombardia; Federal Express Europe, Segrate, Lombardia; Jamaica: Federal Express (Jamaica) Ltd., Kingston; Japan: Federal Express Japan KK, Tokyo; Mexico: Federal Express Holdings Mexico y Compaina SNC de CV, Ciudad de Mexico; Netherlands: Federal Express Europe, Eindhoven, Noord-Brabant; Federal Express (St. Maarten) NV, Philipsburg; Singapore: Federal Express (Singapore)

Pte. Ltd., Singapore; St. Kitts and Nevis: Federal Express (St. Kitts) Ltd., Basseterre; St. Lucia: Federal Express (St. Lucia) Ltd., Castries; Turks and Caicos Islands: Federal Express (Turks & Caicos) Ltd., Providenciales; Taiwan: Federal Express Corp. Taiwan Branch (USA), Taipei; United Kingdom: Fedex (NI) Ltd., Crumlin, Antrim

Nonmonetary Support

Value: $100,000 (1989); $100,000 (1988); $100,000 (1987)
Type: Cause-related Marketing & Promotion; Donated Equipment; Donated Products; In-kind Services; Loaned Employees; Loaned Executives
Volunteer Programs: Volunteer teams work with many organizations in various areas: Children and Youth; Adopt-a-School programs; Junior Achievement; Deaf United for the Community; Civic Affairs; and promotion of the arts.

Corporate Sponsorship

Type: Arts & cultural events
Note: Sponsors civic, humanitarian, and educational events.

Giving Contact

Patrick Melancon, Manager, Community Relations
FedEx Corp.
PO Box 727- Dept 1850
Memphis, TN 38194
Phone: (901)395-5006
Fax: (901)346-1013

Description

Organization Type: Corporate Giving Program
Giving Locations: headquarters; nationally.
Grant Types: Capital, Challenge, Employee Matching Gifts, General Support, Project, Seed Money.

Giving Philosophy

'At Federal Express, we accept an obligation to support, with our money and manpower, activities that are in the public interest. We pursue this corporate responsibility in the belief that our company and our employees will realize their fullest potential in a healthy and vital society. Just as we are committed to maintaining high standards of service in the communities we serve throughout the country, regardless of size, we are pledged to nondiscrimination when considering support of their community interests. Since our employees are essential producers of company resources, we give preference to projects with which they are associated.' *Community Affairs: Corporate Policy, Federal Express Corp.*

Financial Summary

Total Giving: Contributes through corporate direct giving program only.

Typical Recipients

Arts & Humanities: Arts Associations & Councils, Arts Centers, Arts Funds, Museums/Galleries, Public Broadcasting
Civic & Public Affairs: Business/Free Enterprise, Civil Rights, Urban & Community Affairs
Education: Colleges & Universities, Continuing Education, Minority Education
Environment: Environment-General
Health: Health Organizations, Single-Disease Health Associations
Social Services: Community Service Organizations, Delinquency & Criminal Rehabilitation, People with Disabilities, Senior Services, United Funds/United Ways, Youth Organizations

Contributions Analysis

Giving Priorities: Human services, hospitals, civics, education, and the arts.
The company has provided international shipping of emergency medical supplies. While types of support for international purposes are not restricted, they also have not been actively requested. With current economic conditions, any such support would be evaluated on a case-by-case basis.
Arts & Humanities: 10% to 15%. Supports organizations that foster the arts on a broad, nonexclusive basis. Support includes public broadcasting, arts councils, and museums.
Civic & Public Affairs: About 15%. Supports issue-oriented groups engaged in activities including civil rights, conservation, crime prevention, urban affairs, and community development. Also supports public policy organizations and business groups involved in matters such as transportation safety and business excellence, mostly in the company's headquarters area.
Education: 20% to 25%. Emphasizes higher education institutions in headquarters area. The company has taken an increasingly active role in supporting secondary school education in recent years. The Adopt-a-School Program is among the company's recipients in this area.
Health: 50% to 55%. Makes capital grants in support of community service organizations, with emphasis on people-to-people assistance programs that have broad, nonexclusive community impact. Makes capital grants to operating support (including building funds) in communities in which a significant number of employees are concentrated. Considers both capital and operating support of agencies that provide medical and health research materials. Areas of interest include united funds, youth organizations (including Junior Achievement), food banks, the handicapped, the elderly, the homeless, and hospitals.

Application Procedures

Initial Contact: contact the company directly for application procedures

Restrictions

Company generally does not make grants to individuals, political or lobbying groups, religious organizations for sectarian purposes, labor organizations, athletic groups, beauty contestants, public or private elementary or secondary schools, colleges, travel fund, United Way member organizations seeking additional support, special occasion advertising, additional funds to support organizations already receiving support, tax supported organizations, and requests for promotional merchandise.

Additional Information

FDX Corp. was formed by FedEx Corporation's acquisition of Caliber System, Inc. FDX Corp. consists of FedEx, RPS, Viking Freight, FDX Global Logistics, and Roberts Express.
FDX Corp. changed its name to FedEx Corp. in January 2000. The former RPS was renamed FedEx Ground, Roberts Express was renamed FedEx Custom Critical, and FDX Global Logistics became FedEx Global Logistics. Viking Freight has retained its name.

Corporate Officials

Alan B. Graf, Jr.: executive vice president, chief financial officero, director B Bloomington, IN 1954. ED Indiana University (1975); Indiana University MBA (1976). PRIM CORP EMPL executive vice president, chief financial officer: FDX Corp. CORP AFFIL director: Kimball International Inc.
Dennis H. Jones: chief information officer PRIM CORP EMPL chief information officer: FDX Corp.
Frederick Wallace Smith: chairman, president, chief executive officer, director B Marks, MS 1944. ED Yale University BA (1966). PRIM CORP EMPL chairman, president, chief executive officer, director: FDX Corp.

Giving Program Officials

Mr. Pat Melancon: manager community relations

Grants Analysis

Disclosure Period: calendar year ending
Typical Range: $1,000 to $5,000

FERRO CORP.

Company Contact

Cleveland, OH
Web: http://www.ferro.com

Company Description

Employees: 6,693 (1999)
SIC(s): 2816 Inorganic Pigments, 2819 Industrial Inorganic Chemicals Nec, 2821 Plastics Materials & Resins, 2851 Paints & Allied Products.

Operating Locations

Includes plant locations.

Nonmonetary Support

Type: Cause-related Marketing & Promotion; In-kind Services; Loaned Employees; Loaned Executives

Ferro Foundation

Giving Contact

James M. Hill, Secretary & Treasurer
Ferro Foundation
1000 Lakeside Avenue
Cleveland, OH 44114-1183
Phone: (216)641-8580
Fax: (216)696-5803

Description

Founded: 1959
EIN: 346554832
Organization Type: Corporate Foundation
Giving Locations: OH: Cleveland
Grant Types: Emergency, Employee Matching Gifts, General Support, Multiyear/Continuing Support, Operating Expenses.

Financial Summary

Total Giving: $477,642 (fiscal year ending April 30, 1999); $474,983 (fiscal 1998); $453,671 (fiscal 1997). Note: Contributes through foundation only.
Giving Analysis: Giving for fiscal 1998 includes: foundation ($297,170); foundation grants to United Way ($98,813); foundation scholarships ($79,000)
Assets: $31,984 (fiscal 1999); $497,033 (fiscal 1998); $934,274 (fiscal 1997)
Gifts Received: $1,250,000 (fiscal 1997); $550,000 (fiscal 1996); $300,000 (fiscal 1995). Note: Contributions are received from the Ferro Corp.

Typical Recipients

Arts & Humanities: Arts Outreach, Ballet, Arts & Humanities-General, Historic Preservation, History & Archaeology, Museums/Galleries, Music, Opera, Performing Arts, Public Broadcasting, Theater
Civic & Public Affairs: African American Affairs, Botanical Gardens/Parks, Economic Development, Employment/Job Training, Civic & Public Affairs-General, Hispanic Affairs, Municipalities/Towns, Parades/Festivals, Safety, Urban & Community Affairs, Zoos/Aquariums
Education: Arts/Humanities Education, Business Education, Colleges & Universities, Community & Junior Colleges, Education Funds, Education Reform, Education-General, Minority Education, Public Education (Precollege), Secondary Education (Private), Student Aid, Vocational & Technical Education
Environment: Environment-General
Health: Alzheimers Disease, Cancer, Children's Health/Hospitals, Clinics/Medical Centers, Diabetes, Emergency/Ambulance Services, Health-General, Hospitals, Hospitals (University Affiliated), Medical Rehabilitation, Mental Health, Multiple Sclerosis, Nursing Services
International: International Affairs
Religion: Churches, Religious Welfare

Science: Science Museums, Scientific Centers & Institutes
Social Services: Child Welfare, Community Centers, Community Service Organizations, Crime Prevention, People with Disabilities, Social Services-General, Substance Abuse, United Funds/United Ways, YMCA/YWCA/YMHA/YWHA

Contributions Analysis

Arts & Humanities: 22%. Supports performing arts, art history, and archaeology. Recipients include Musicial Arts Association, Playhouse Square Foundation and Western Reserve Historical Association.
Civic & Public Affairs: 16%. Supports employment and job training, towns and municipalities, and economic development. Recipients include Urban League of Northern Cleveland and Cleveland Technical Services Council.
Education: 11%. Supports private education, and college and universities. Recipients include Western Reserve University, Ohio Foundation of Independent Colleges, and Magnificat High School.
Health: 19%. Recipients include Visiting Nurses Association and Cleveland Clinic Foundation.
Science: 5%. Supports the Great Lakes Science Center.
Social Services: 28%. Supports united funds.
Note: Contributions made in 1998.

Application Procedures

Initial Contact: There is no application form. Send complete request.
Deadlines: None.

Restrictions

Does not support individuals, religious organizations for sectarian purposes, or political or lobbying groups.

Corporate Officials

Albert C. Bersticker: chairman, director, chief executive officer B Toledo, OH 1934. ED Miami University MS (1956); Miami University MS (1958). PRIM CORP EMPL chairman, director, chief executive officer: Ferro Corp. CORP AFFIL director: Oglebay Norton Co.; director: Ferro Southeast Asia PTE Ltd. Singapore; director: KeyCorp; director: Ferro Far East Ltd. Hong Kong; director: Centerior Energy Corp.; vice president, director: Ferro Enamel Espanola SA; director: Brush Wellman Inc. NONPR AFFIL member: Leadership Cleveland; director: University Health Care Systems; director: Greater Cleveland Growth Association; member: Chemical Manufacturers Association; director: Cleveland Tomorrow.
Hector R. Ortino: president, chief executive officer, director B Buenos Aires, Argentina 1942. ED Buenos Aires University (1971). PRIM CORP EMPL president, chief executive officer, director: Ferro Corp. CORP AFFIL director: Parker-Hannifin Corp. NONPR AFFIL member: Financial Executives Institute.

Foundation Officials

Albert C. Bersticker: president, trustee (see above)
James M. Hill: secretary, treasurer PRIM CORP EMPL risk manager: Ferro Corp.
Hector R. Ortino: vice president, trustee (see above)
G. G. Sislak: assistant treasurer, assistant secretary

Grants Analysis

Disclosure Period: fiscal year ending April 30, 1998
Total Grants: $297,170*
Number of Grants: 59
Average Grant: $4,469*
Highest Grant: $27,500
Typical Range: $1,000 to $20,000
***Note:** Giving excludes scholarship; United Way. Average grant figure excludes highest grant.

Recent Grants

Note: Grants derived from fiscal 1997 Form 990.

Arts & Humanities

13,000	Musical Arts Association Cleveland Orchestra, Cleveland, OH -- operating support
6,000	Cleveland Museum of Art, Cleveland, OH -- operating support
6,000	Cleveland Playhouse, Cleveland, OH -- operating support
5,000	Cleveland Ballet, Cleveland, OH -- operating support
5,000	Playhouse Square Foundation, Cleveland, OH -- operating support
5,000	Western Reserve Historical Society, Cleveland, OH -- operating support
2,500	Cleveland Opera, Cleveland, OH -- operating support
2,500	New Cleveland Opera Company, Cleveland, OH -- operating support
2,000	Cleveland Institute of Music, Cleveland, OH -- operating support
2,000	Great Lakes Theater Festival, Independence, OH -- operating support

Civic & Public Affairs

27,000	Cleveland Tomorrow, Cleveland, OH -- operating support
10,000	Greater Cleveland Roundtable, Cleveland, OH -- operating support
4,000	Work in Northeast Ohio Council, Independence, OH -- operating support
3,500	Urban League, Cleveland, OH -- operating support
2,500	Zoological Society, Cleveland, OH -- operating support

Education

10,000	Case Western Reserve University, Cleveland, OH -- operating support
10,000	Cleveland Scholarship Programs, Cleveland, OH -- operating support
9,350	National Merit Scholarship Corporation, Evanston, IL -- operating support
7,500	Cleveland Institute for Education, Cleveland, OH -- operating support
5,000	Ohio Foundation of Independent Colleges, Columbus, OH -- operating support
4,000	PM Foundation, Urban Community School, Cleveland, OH -- operating support
4,000	University Circle, Cleveland, OH -- operating support
3,500	National Technical Association, Philadelphia, PA -- operating support
3,000	Cleveland State University, Cleveland, OH -- operating support
3,000	Hiram College, Hiram, OH -- operating support
2,000	Cleveland Technical Societies Council, Cleveland, OH -- operating support
2,000	Cuyahoga Community College, Independence, OH -- operating support
2,000	David N. Myers College, Independence, OH -- operating support
2,000	Junior Achievement, Independence, OH -- operating support
2,000	Kent State University, Kent, OH -- operating support
2,000	United Negro College Fund, New York, NY -- operating support

Environment

3,000	Cleanland Ohio, Rapid Recovery, Cleveland, OH -- operating support

Health

27,500	American National Red Cross, Cleveland, OH -- operating support
20,500	University Hospitals, Cleveland, OH -- operating support
15,000	American Cancer Society, Cleveland, OH -- operating support
15,000	Cleveland Clinic Foundation, Cleveland, OH -- operating support
10,000	Visiting Nurses Association, Cleveland, OH -- operating support
5,000	Alzheimer's Association, Cleveland, OH -- operating support
4,000	Therapeutic Riding Center, Novelty, OH -- operating support
2,000	Health Hill Hospital, Independence, OH -- operating support

International

2,000	Cleveland Council on World Affairs, Cleveland, OH -- operating support

Religion

8,500	Salvation Army, Cleveland, OH -- operating support
6,000	Our Lady of the Wayside, Avon, OH -- operating support

Science

20,000	Great Lakes Museum of Science, Cleveland, OH -- operating support
8,000	Cleveland Museum of Natural History, Cleveland, OH -- operating support

Social Services

86,986	United Way Services, Cleveland, OH -- operating support
20,000	YMCA, Cleveland, OH -- operating support
4,000	Greater Cleveland Neighborhood Center Association, Cleveland, OH -- operating support
3,000	Alcoholism Services, Cleveland, OH -- operating support
2,500	Karamu House, Cleveland, OH -- operating support

FIDELITY INVESTMENTS

★ Number 66 of Top 100 Corporate Givers

Company Contact

Boston, MA
Web: http://www.fidelity.com

Company Description

Employees: 7,000
SIC(s): 6719 Holding Companies Nec, 6722 Management Investment--Open-End.
Parent Company: FMR Corp.

Corporate Sponsorship

Type: Arts & cultural events
Contact: Marcia Goodwin, Vice President Corporate Communications

Fidelity Foundation

Giving Contact

Margaret H. Morton, Program Director
Fidelity Foundation
82 Devonshire Street, S3
Boston, MA 02109
Phone: (617)563-6806
Fax: (617)476-4234

Description

EIN: 046131201
Organization Type: Corporate Foundation
Giving Locations: KY: Covington; MA: Marlborough; NH: Merrimack; NY: New York, New York; OH: Cincinnati, Cincinnati; RI: Smithfield, Smithfield; TX: Dallas; UT: Salt Lake City CAN: Toronto; Toronto, ON

Grant Types: Capital, Conference/Seminar, Employee Matching Gifts, Endowment, Fellowship, Matching.
Note: Employee matching gift ratio: 2 to 1, up to $1,000; 1 to 1 for $1,000 to $3,500.

Financial Summary

Total Giving: $12,540,809 (1998); $8,681,699 (1997); $6,061,059 (1996). Note: Contributes through foundation only.
Giving Analysis: Giving for 1996 includes: foundation matching gifts ($907,909); foundation grants to United Way ($7,500); 1997: foundation matching gifts ($1,858,484); 1998: foundation matching gifts ($1,551,869); foundation grants to United Way ($165,000)
Assets: $252,944,225 (1998); $229,279,674 (1997); $140,661,259 (1996)
Gifts Received: $5,125,877 (1996); $14,243,099 (1994); $18,121,469 (1993). Note: Contributions are received from the FMR Corporation and the Fidelity Charitable Gift Fund. In 1996 contributions were also received from Edward C. Johnson III in the form of $3,500,488 in stock.

Typical Recipients

Arts & Humanities: Art History, Arts Associations & Councils, Arts Centers, Arts Funds, Arts Outreach, Arts & Humanities-General, Historic Preservation, History & Archaeology, Libraries, Museums/Galleries, Music, Opera, Performing Arts
Civic & Public Affairs: African American Affairs, Community Foundations, Economic Development, Economic Policy, Employment/Job Training, Civic & Public Affairs-General, Housing, Legal Aid, Native American Affairs, Nonprofit Management, Parades/ Festivals, Philanthropic Organizations, Public Policy, Urban & Community Affairs, Women's Affairs, Zoos/ Aquariums
Education: Arts/Humanities Education, Business Education, Colleges & Universities, Education Reform, Education-General, Leadership Training, Literacy, Preschool Education, Private Education (Precollege)
Environment: Environment-General
Health: Cancer, Children's Health/Hospitals, Clinics/ Medical Centers, Health Organizations, Hospices, Hospitals, Medical Research, Mental Health
International: Foreign Arts Organizations, Foreign Educational Institutions, International Environmental Issues, International Relations, International Relief Efforts
Religion: Churches, Religious Organizations, Religious Welfare
Science: Scientific Centers & Institutes, Scientific Labs
Social Services: At-Risk Youth, Camps, Child Abuse, Child Welfare, Community Service Organizations, Family Services, Food/Clothing Distribution, People with Disabilities, Recreation & Athletics, Scouts, Senior Services, Shelters/Homelessness, United Funds/United Ways, Volunteer Services, YMCA/YWCA/YMHA/YWHA, Youth Organizations

Contributions Analysis

Giving Priorities: Community development, social services, the arts and culture, education, and medical research.
Arts & Humanities: 49%. Supports museums, music, theaters, dance, art institutes, and historic preservation.
Civic & Public Affairs: 22%. Community development interests include neighborhood housing services, economic development, environmental, nonprofit management, shelters family services, child welfare, the elderly, and the handicapped.
Education: 25%. Majority of support goes to matching gifts. Also supports universities, colleges and educational funds.
Environment: Less than 1%.
Health: 4%. Supports medical research in health organizations and hospitals. Also supports colleges and universities, generally through employee matching gifts program.
Note: Total contributions made in 1998.

Application Procedures

Initial Contact: Send a letter of request.
Application Requirements: Include foundation's project summary form, itemized project budget, recent audited financial statements, IRS 501(c)(3) determination letter, history of organization, including objectives and programs, list of officers and directors and their affiliations, list of other funders and status of requests, current operating budget, and description of request and rationale.
Deadlines: March 30 for a decision by August 1; or September 30 for a decision by February 1.
Notes: Contact the foundation to receive a project summary form. Applications should not be sent in folders, binders or packaging.

Restrictions

Foundation does not make multi-year grants or award grants to an organization in successive years.
Foundation does not make grants to individuals, religious organizations for sectarian purposes, start-up organizations, public school systems, disease-specific organizations, for operating support, scholarships, video or film projects, sponsorships, benefit events or for memberships.

Additional Information

Fidelity Investments created the foundation in 1965 in order to represent the company's philanthropic interests in the communities where it does business.

Corporate Officials

Edward Crosby Johnson, III: chairman, president, chief executive officer, director B Boston, MA 1930. ED Harvard University AB (1954). PRIM CORP EMPL chairman, president, chief executive officer, director: FMR Corp. ADD CORP EMPL president: Fidelity Government Securities Fund; chairman: Fidelity Management Research Co.; president: Fidelity Management Trust Co.; president: Fidelity Cash Reserve Fund; director: Fidelity Distributors Corp.; chairman: Fidelity Magellan Fund; president: Fidelity Trend Fund OCCUPATION Fidelity Intermediate Bond Fund. NONPR AFFIL director: Center Neurologic Diseases; member: Massachusetts Historical Society; fellow: American Academy of Arts & Sciences; honorary trustee: Boston Museum Fine Arts.

Foundation Officials

Edward Crosby Johnson, III: president (see above)
Margaret H. Morton: program officer
Ross E. Sherbrooke: trustee
Anne-Marie Soulliere: director

Grants Analysis

Disclosure Period: calendar year ending 1998
Total Grants: $10,823,940*
Number of Grants: 201
Average Grant: $32,045*
Highest Grant: $4,415,000
Typical Range: $5,000 to $50,000
***Note:** Giving excludes matching gifts; United Way. Average grant figure excludes highest grant.

Recent Grants

Note: Grants derived from 1997 Form 990.

Arts & Humanities

1,375,750	National Institute for the Conservation of Cultural Property, Washington, DC
125,000	Providence Performing Arts Center, Providence, RI
100,000	USS Constitution Museum Foundation, Boston, MA
50,000	Greater Boston Youth Symphony Orchestra, Boston, MA
40,000	Artspace
40,000	Young Audiences Foundation
30,000	Concord Antiquarian Society, Concord, MA
30,000	Historic Preservation League
30,000	New England Cultural Facilities Fund
30,000	Wenham Historical Association and Museum, Wenham, MA
25,000	Capital Center for the Arts
25,000	Central Massachusetts Symphony Orchestra, Worcester, MA
25,000	Cincinnati Opera Association, Cincinnati, OH
25,000	New England Conservatory of Music, Boston, MA
25,000	Salt Lake Acting Company, Salt Lake City, UT

Civic & Public Affairs

240,000	New England Aquarium, Boston, MA
75,000	Dallas Zoological Society, Dallas, TX
35,000	Commonwealth Zoological Corporation
30,000	Salt Lake Neighborhood Housing Service, Salt Lake City, UT
30,000	Trust for City Hall Plaza, Boston, MA
25,000	Peer Partnerships, Cambridge, MA
25,000	Women's Educational and Industrial Union, Boston, MA

Education

125,000	Wellesley College, Wellesley, MA
50,000	Bentley College, Waltham, MA
50,000	Stonehill College, North Easton, MA
35,000	Adopt-A-Student Foundation, Boston, MA
35,000	Johns Hopkins University, Baltimore, MD
25,000	Westminster College, Salt Lake City, UT

Environment

25,000	Audubon Society, Concord, NH

Health

75,000	Massachusetts General Hospital, Boston, MA
35,000	South Cove Community Health Center, Boston, MA
25,000	Irving Healthcare System Foundation, Irving, TX
25,000	Mental Health and Retardation Center of Cambridge and Somerville, Cambridge, MA
25,000	Roxbury Comprehensive Community Health Center, Roxbury, MA

International

35,000	International Charitable Fund of Bermuda, New York, NY
25,000	International Theatrical Arts Society, Dallas, TX
20,000	Japan Society, New York, NY

Religion

25,000	St. Francis House
25,000	Shelter Ministries, Dallas, TX

Science

2,274,998	Bermuda Underwater Exploration Institute

Social Services

100,000	Boys and Girls Clubs, Boston, MA
100,000	United Way of Massachusetts Bay, Boston, MA
50,000	Freestore Foodbank, Cincinnati, OH
50,000	YWCA, Salt Lake City, UT
30,000	South Valley Sanctuary, West Jordan, UT
25,000	Kids in Distressed Situations, Moorestown, NJ
25,000	Parish Kitchen
25,000	Southwestern Ohio Seniors Services, Cincinnati, OH
25,000	Swift Water Girl Scout Council, Manchester, NH
25,000	YWCA, Dallas, TX

Fifth Third Bancorp

Company Contact

Cincinnati, OH
Web: http://www.53.com

Company Description

Assets: US$41,589,000,000 (1999)
Profit: US$668,000,000
Employees: 6,549
Fortune Rank: 436, per FORTUNE Magazine's list of 500 Largest U.S. Corporations (1999).
FF 436
SIC(s): 6022 State Commercial Banks, 6712 Bank Holding Companies.

Corporate Sponsorship

Value: $45,400 (1998)
Type: Music & entertainment events

Fifth Third Foundation

Giving Contact

Lawra Baumann, Foundation Officer
Fifth Third Foundation
38 Fountain Square Plaza
Maildrop 1090D7
Cincinnati, OH 45263
Phone: (513)579-6034
Fax: (513)579-5461

Description

EIN: 316024135
Organization Type: Corporate Foundation
Giving Locations: OH: Cincinnati including metropolitan area
Grant Types: Capital, Conference/Seminar, Employee Matching Gifts, General Support, Project.
Note: Matches gifts to education.

Financial Summary

Total Giving: $1,881,808 (fiscal year ending September 30, 1998); $1,630,900 (fiscal 1997); $1,710,046 (fiscal 1996). Note: Contributes through foundation only.
Giving Analysis: Giving for fiscal 1997 includes: foundation grants to United Way ($412,211); foundation matching gifts ($40,661); fiscal 1998: foundation grants to United Way ($318,800); foundation matching gifts ($38,714)
Assets: $37,005,892 (fiscal 1998); $31,464,139 (fiscal 1997); $21,978,099 (fiscal 1996)
Gifts Received: $1,050,000 (fiscal 1996); $1,800,000 (fiscal 1995); $1,800,000 (fiscal 1994). Note: Contributions are received from Fifth Third Bank.

Typical Recipients

Arts & Humanities: Arts Associations & Councils, Arts Centers, Arts Funds, Community Arts, Historic Preservation, Museums/Galleries, Music, Performing Arts, Public Broadcasting, Theater
Civic & Public Affairs: African American Affairs, Business/Free Enterprise, Chambers of Commerce, Civil Rights, Clubs, Community Foundations, Economic Development, Employment/Job Training, Civic & Public Affairs-General, Housing, Law & Justice, Minority Business, Municipalities/Towns, Parades/Festivals, Urban & Community Affairs, Zoos/Aquariums
Education: Arts/Humanities Education, Business Education, Colleges & Universities, Education Funds, Engineering/Technological Education, Education-General, Medical Education, Public Education (Precollege), Religious Education, Secondary Education (Public), Special Education, Student Aid
Health: Children's Health/Hospitals, Emergency/Ambulance Services, Health Funds, Hospices, Hospitals, Medical Rehabilitation, Single-Disease Health Associations, Speech & Hearing
Religion: Jewish Causes, Religious Organizations, Religious Welfare
Social Services: Child Welfare, Community Centers, Community Service Organizations, Family Services, Food/Clothing Distribution, People with Disabilities, Recreation & Athletics, Scouts, Senior Services, United Funds/United Ways, YMCA/YWCA/YMHA/YWHA, Youth Organizations

Contributions Analysis

Giving Priorities: Focus on social services, civic causes, and the arts.
Arts & Humanities: 19%. Major support for music, arts funds, museums, and arts centers. Historic preservation, the performing arts, theater, and public broadcasting are also supported.
Civic & Public Affairs: 24%. Contributes to a variety of causes, including housing, law and justice, business, minority interests, and zoos.
Education: 9%. Majority of funding goes to colleges and universities, generally in grants of $5,000 or less. Other areas of interest include arts education, education funds, and youth, medical, precollege, and religious education.
Health: 5%.
Religion: 6%.
Science: 2%.
Social Services: 35%. Majority of funding supports United Way chapters. Major grants are also made to various youth organizations, especially those supporting scouting. Other interests include religious welfare, the aged, the disabled, and family services.
Note: Total contributions in fiscal 1998.

Application Procedures

Initial Contact: Send a brief letter.
Application Requirements: Include a description of program.
Deadlines: None.

Corporate Officials

Neil E. Arnold, Sr.: vice president, chief financial officer, treasurer PRIM CORP EMPL vice president, chief financial officer, treasurer: Fifth Third Bancorp.
Paul Michael Brumm: executive vice president, chief financial officer B Cincinnati, OH 1947. ED University of Cincinnati BA (1969); University of Cincinnati MBA (1976). PRIM CORP EMPL executive vice president, chief financial officer: Fifth Third Bancorp. NONPR AFFIL trustee: Mercury Health Systems; member: Salvation Army Business Advisor Board; member: Delta Mu Delta; member: Financial Executives Institute. CLUB AFFIL Coldstream Country Club; University Club; Athletic Club.
Roger W. Dean: controller, chief administrative officer B 1963. PRIM CORP EMPL controller, chief administrative officer: Fifth Third Bancorp.
Michael K. Keating: executive vice president, counsel, secretary B 1956. PRIM CORP EMPL executive vice president, counsel, secretary: Fifth Third Bancorp. CORP AFFIL secretary: Fifth Third Bank.
George A. Schaefer, Jr.: president B Cincinnati, OH 1945. ED United States Military Academy (1967); Xavier University (1974). PRIM CORP EMPL president: Fifth Third Bank. CORP AFFIL president, chief executive officer, chief operating officer, director: Fifth Third Bancorp. NONPR AFFIL vice chairman: Greater Cincinnati Chamber of Commerce.

Foundation Officials

Lawra Baumann: assistant vice president

Grants Analysis

Disclosure Period: fiscal year ending September 30, 1998
Total Grants: $1,478,894*
Number of Grants: 261
Average Grant: $5,666
Highest Grant: $85,000
Typical Range: $100 to $6,000
***Note:** Giving excludes United Way, matching gifts, and sponsorships.

Recent Grants

Note: Grants derived from fiscal 1997 Form 990.

Arts & Humanities

85,000	Fine Arts Fund, Cincinnati, OH
78,571	Cincinnati Arts Association, Cincinnati, OH -- grant support
50,000	USS Constitution Museum, Boston, MA
41,577	Cincinnati Arts Association, Cincinnati, OH
12,500	Enjoy Arts, Cincinnati, OH -- support underwriting for Corbett event
11,325	Playhouse in the Park, Cincinnati, OH -- capital campaign support
8,333	Broadcasting Foundation of Northwest Ohio, Toledo, OH
6,500	Fine Arts Fund, Cincinnati, OH

Civic & Public Affairs

50,000	2003 Fund, Dayton, OH -- support Bicentennial Celebration
35,000	Louisville Urban League, Louisville, KY -- support updating computer tracking systems
25,000	Downtown Cincinnati, Cincinnati, OH
18,000	Habitat for Humanity, Lexington, KY
12,835	Work and Rehabilitation Centers, Cincinnati, OH -- capital campaign support
12,500	Louisville Fund, Louisville, KY
10,000	City of Bellevue, Bellevue, KY
8,000	Louisville Olmsted Arks, Louisville, KY
7,700	Madisonville Community Urban and Business Redevelopment Corporation, Cincinnati, OH -- project support
7,500	Fair Housing Contact Service, Akron, OH
7,500	Fair Housing Contact Service, Akron, OH

Education

90,600	University of Cincinnati, Cincinnati, OH
50,000	University of Cincinnati, Cincinnati, OH -- support athletic facility campaign
25,000	Junior Achievement, Cincinnati, OH
21,998	Cincinnati Public Schools, Cincinnati, OH -- support capital campaign
18,332	Northern Kentucky University, Highland Heights, KY -- capital campaign support
10,000	Pontifical College Josephinum, Columbus, OH -- capital campaign support
9,437	St. Rita School for the Deaf, Cincinnati, OH
8,000	Junior Achievement, Cincinnati, OH
7,000	College of Mount St. Joseph, Cincinnati, OH
6,500	Northern Kentucky University, Highland Heights, KY
6,000	Tiffin University, Tiffin, OH

Health

10,000	American Red Cross, Louisville, KY
10,000	Columbus Speech and Hearing Center, Columbus, OH -- grant support
8,332	Children's Hospital Medical Center, Cincinnati, OH -- support capital campaign
7,294	American Red Cross, Cleveland, OH

Religion

15,000	Franciscan Foundation, Cincinnati, OH -- support delivery truck

Social Services

135,750	United Way, Cincinnati, OH
67,875	United Way, Cincinnati, OH
66,500	United Way, Cincinnati, OH
44,000	Metro United Way, Louisville, KY
25,375	United Way, Toledo, OH
15,000	United Way of Montgomery and Preble, Dayton, OH
14,500	United Way of Northern Kentucky, Cincinnati, OH

12,000	United Way of Central Indiana, Indianapolis, IN
10,557	United Way, Toledo, OH
9,500	United Way of Hancock County, Findlay, OH
9,500	United Way of Hancock County, Findlay, OH
8,250	Powell Crosley Junior Amateur, Edgewood, KY
7,869	Piquarea United Fund, Piqua, OH
7,500	United Way, Cincinnati, OH
6,667	YMCA, Columbus, OH -- capital campaign support

FINA

Company Contact
Dallas, TX

Company Description
Revenue: US$4,080,000,000
Employees: 2,693
SIC(s): 1311 Crude Petroleum & Natural Gas, 1381 Drilling Oil & Gas Wells, 2911 Petroleum Refining, 6719 Holding Companies Nec.
Parent Company: Petrofina SA, Rue de l'Industrie 52, Brussels, Belgium

Operating Locations
LA: FINA; Cos-Mar, Carville; Sigma Coatings, Harvey; TX: Fina Oil & Chemical Co. (Big Spring), Big Spring; American Petrofina Holding Co., Dallas; Fina, Dallas; FINA, Dallas; Fina Oil & Chemical Co. (Dallas), Dallas; Petrofina Delaware, Dallas; Fina Oil & Chemical Co. (Port Arthur), Port Arthur

Nonmonetary Support
Note: Foundation does not provide nonmonetary support.

FINA Foundation

Giving Contact
Ms. Jeanne Cullers, Director
FINA Foundation
PO Box 2159
Dallas, TX 75221
Fax: (214)890-1876

Description
Founded: 1974
EIN: 237391423
Organization Type: Corporate Foundation
Giving Locations: operating communities.
Grant Types: Employee Matching Gifts, General Support, Multiyear/Continuing Support.
Note: Employee matching gift ratio: 1 to 1 up to $5,000 annually.

Financial Summary
Total Giving: $363,597 (1998); $385,000 (1997 approx); $407,583 (1996). Note: Contributes through foundation only.
Giving Analysis: Giving for 1998 includes: foundation grants to United Way ($100,500)
Assets: $4,386,536 (1998); $4,592,200 (1996); $4,688,488 (1995)

Typical Recipients
Arts & Humanities: Museums/Galleries, Music, Opera, Public Broadcasting
Civic & Public Affairs: African American Affairs, Botanical Gardens/Parks, Business/Free Enterprise, Chambers of Commerce, Economic Development, Philanthropic Organizations, Urban & Community Affairs, Zoos/Aquariums
Education: Business Education, Colleges & Universities, Education Associations, Education Funds, Engineering/Technological Education, Education-General, Minority Education, Preschool Education, Private Education (Precollege), Public Education (Precollege), School Volunteerism, Student Aid
Environment: Environment-General
Health: Cancer, Clinics/Medical Centers, Health Organizations, Hospitals, Hospitals (University Affiliated), Public Health
International: International Relations
Religion: Religious Welfare
Science: Science Museums, Science Museums
Social Services: Child Welfare, Community Service Organizations, Recreation & Athletics, Scouts, United Funds/United Ways, YMCA/YWCA/YMHA/YWHA

Contributions Analysis
Giving Priorities: Focus on social services and the United Way, education, civic causes, and the arts.
Arts & Humanities: 10%. Recipients include opera, public broadcasting, and museums. Also supports dance and theater.
Civic & Public Affairs: 14%. Emphasis on philanthropic organizations, community development, and nonprofit management.
Education: 16%. Favors universities and minority education. Foundation operates matching gift program to accredited institutions of higher learning.
Health: 3%. Supports medical centers and cancer treatment and research.
Religion: 1%.
Science: 9%. Support includes science museums.
Social Services: 47%. Supports United Way in Texas. Also supports youth organizations, community service organizations, and community centers.
Note: Total contributions in 1998.

Application Procedures
Initial Contact: Send a letter of inquiry.
Application Requirements: Include history, purpose, and programs of the organization; a description of the use of the funds requested; current financial statement; copy of IRS ruling, classifying the organization as tax-exempt under Section 501(c)(3); a statement from a responsible officer or trustee that the ruling letter is still in effect; copy of most recent Form 990; a list of corporate and foundation donors and their level of support; and a list of the board of directors.
Deadlines: None.

Restrictions
Grants are not made to individuals or to organizations that do not have 501(c)(3) status. Institutions of higher education must be fully accredited.

Additional Information
Most contributions go to organizations located where FINA employees live and work, and to organizations that they support.
Publications: Annual Report (including Application Guidelines)

Corporate Officials
Ronald Wayne Haddock: president, chief executive officer, director B Saint Elmo, IL 1940. ED Purdue University BMechE (1963). PRIM CORP EMPL president, chief executive officer, director: FINA Inc. CORP AFFIL president, chief executive officer, director: FINA Oil & Chemical Co. NONPR AFFIL member: Public Comm Task Force; member: Round Table; member: National Petroleum Refiners Association; member: Long Range Strategy Task Force; member: National Petroleum Council; member: Indiana Producers Association; member: Dallas Un Board; member: Governor Business Council; member: Dallas Together Forum; member: Dallas Morning News Energy Board; director, executive committee: Dallas Opera; member: Dallas Chamber of Commerce; member: Dallas Citizens Council; chairman: Dallas Arboretum; member: American Petroleum Institute; member: American Plastics Council. CLUB AFFIL Petroleum Club; Dallas Petroleum Club; 25 Year Club; Brook Hollow Golf Club.

Foundation Officials
Jeanne E. Cullers: director
Cullen Michael Godfrey: vice president B Fort Worth, TX 1945. ED University of Texas BA (1968); University of Texas JD (1970). PRIM CORP EMPL senior vice president, secretary, general counsel: FINA. CORP AFFIL director: Trust Pipe Line Co.; vice president, general couns: Petrofina DE Inc.; director: River Pipeline Co.; director: FINA Oil & Chemical Co.; vice president, general couns: FINASERVE Inc.; vice president, general couns: FINA Natural Gas Co. NONPR AFFIL director: Texas Business Law Foundation; member: Texas State Bar Association; member: Southwest Legal Foundation; member: Texas Board Legal Specialization; trustee: Dallas Museum Art; president, director: Greater Dallas Crime Commission; member: Dallas Bar Association; fellow: Dallas Bar Foundation; member: American Bar Association.
Ronald Wayne Haddock: president (see above)

Grants Analysis
Disclosure Period: calendar year ending 1998
Total Grants: $252,597*
Number of Grants: 69
Average Grant: $3,661
Highest Grant: $30,700
Typical Range: $50 to $5,000
***Note:** Giving excludes United Way.

Recent Grants
Note: Grants derived from 1998 Form 990.

Arts & Humanities

25,000	Dallas Museum of Art, Dallas, TX
10,000	Art Museum of the Southeast, Beaumont, TX
10,000	Permian Basin Petroleum Museum, Midland, TX
2,500	New Conservatory of Dallas, Dallas, TX
460	KERA/KDTN, Dallas, TX
255	KVLU/Lamar University, Beaumont, TX

Civic & Public Affairs

10,000	Dallas Plan, Dallas, TX
10,000	Greater Dallas Chamber, Dallas, TX
10,000	Southwestern Ball, Dallas, TX
5,000	Dallas Urban League, Dallas, TX
5,000	Plano Futures Foundation, Plano, TX

Education

30,700	Southern Methodist University, Dallas, TX
10,000	Dallas Education Foundation, Dallas, TX
7,225	University of Texas at Austin, Austin, TX
5,000	Cary Maguire Oil & Gas Institute, Dallas, TX
5,000	Dallas Canl Academy, Dallas, TX
2,500	Communities in Schools, Dallas, TX
1,120	Association of Former Students TX A&M, College Station, TX
800	University of Nebraska, Lincoln, NE
650	Texas Tech Foundation, Lubbock, TX
618	Eastern College, St. Davids, PA
600	Long Island University, Brookville, NY
500	St. Louis University, St. Louis, MO
450	Oklahoma State University, Stillwater, OK
450	Virginia Military Institute, Lexington, VI
334	University of Oklahoma, Norman, OK
250	St. Olaf College, Northfield, MN
200	Pennsylvania State University, University Park, PA
200	Southern University, Baton Rouge, LA
200	Virginia Tech Foundation, Inc., Blacksburg, VA

175 University of South Florida, Tampa, FL
150 Arizona State University, Tempe, AZ
150 Colorado College, Colorado Springs, CO
100 University of Toledo, Toledo, OH

Health
10,000 Presbyterian Healthcare Foundation, Dallas, TX

Religion
5,000 Salvation Army, Dallas, TX

Science
20,000 The Science Place, Dallas, TX

Social Services
70,000 United Way of Metropolitan Dallas, Dallas, TX
29,000 United Community Services, Port Arthur, TX
17,300 Lone Star District Buffalo Trail Council BSA, Big Spring, TX
12,500 United Way of Gulf Coast (LA Porte), Houston, TX
9,000 United Way of Bigspring & Howard Co., Big Spring, TX
6,000 Capital Area United Way (Carville), Baton Rouge, LA
6,000 Crystal Charity Ball, Dallas, TX
6,000 United Way of Gulf Coast (Houston), Houston, TX
5,000 BSA (Inner City Scouting Program), Dallas, TX
4,500 Capital Area United Way (Cosmar), Baton Rouge, LA
2,500 United Way of Bayport, Houston, TX
500 United Way of Midland, Midland, TX
150 YWCA Metropolitan Dallas, Dallas, TX

FIREMAN'S FUND INSURANCE CO.

Company Contact
Novato, CA

Company Description
Employees: 9,000
SIC(s): 6331 Fire, Marine & Casualty Insurance, 6351 Surety Insurance.
Parent Company: Allianz of America, Inc.
Parent Revenue: US$25,879,000,000

Operating Locations
CA: Associated Indemnity Corp., Novato; FAMEX, Novato; Fireman's Fund Insurance Co., Novato; Fireman's Fund Insurance Co., Novato; Fireman's Fund Risk Management Services, Novato; San Francisco Reinsurance Co., Novato; GA: Fireman's Fund Insurance Co. of Georgia, Atlanta; HI: Fireman's Insurance Co. of Hawaii, Honolulu; IA: Fireman's Fund Insurance Co. of Iowa, Bettendorf; IL: Interstate National Corp., Chicago; National Surety Corp., Chicago; KS: Crop Growers Insurance, Overland Park; LA: Fireman's Fund Insurance Co. of Louisiana, Metairie; MO: American Automobile Insurance Co., Creve Coeur; NJ: Jefferson Insurance Co. of New York, Jersey City; Fireman's Fund Indemnity Corp., Parsippany; Fireman's Fund Insurance Co. of New Jesey, Parsippany; OH: Fireman's Fund Insurance Co. of Ohio, Cincinnati; TX: Fireman's Fund Insurance Co. of Texas, Dallas; WI: Fireman's Fund Insurance Co. of Wisconsin, Wauwatosa

Nonmonetary Support
Value: $100,000 (1995); $100,000 (1993); $100,000 (1992)
Type: Donated Equipment; In-kind Services

Fireman's Fund Foundation

Giving Contact
Barbara B. Friede, Secretary & Director
Fireman's Fund Foundation
777 San Marin Drive
Novato, CA 94998-1406
Phone: (415)899-2757
Fax: (415)899-2126

Description
Founded: 1953
EIN: 946078025
Organization Type: Corporate Foundation
Giving Locations: CA: Marin and Sonoma Counties
Grant Types: Employee Matching Gifts, Project.
Note: Employee matching gift ratio: 1 to 1.

Giving Philosophy
'The heart of the Fireman's Fund Foundation program is to be a good corporate citizen and through our grants to make the community a better place to live. We support a broad range of human services as well as cultural, civic, community and educational programs, concentrating in our headquarters location in Marin County, California.'

Financial Summary
Total Giving: $1,068,670 (1998); $950,561 (1997); $1,047,586 (1996). Note: Contributes through foundation only.
Giving Analysis: Giving for 1996 includes: foundation matching gifts ($152,447); foundation grants to United Way ($140,280); 1997: foundation matching gifts ($133,217); foundation grants to United Way ($132,710); 1998: foundation grants to United Way ($139,225); foundation matching gifts ($136,662)
Assets: $157,438 (1998); $167,258 (1997); $105,675 (1996)
Gifts Received: $1,045,690 (1998); $994,980 (1997); $1,000,000 (1996)

Typical Recipients
Arts & Humanities: Arts Centers, Arts Institutes, Arts Outreach, Ballet, Community Arts, Dance, Ethnic & Folk Arts, Historic Preservation, History & Archaeology, Libraries, Museums/Galleries, Music, Opera, Performing Arts, Public Broadcasting, Theater, Visual Arts
Civic & Public Affairs: Economic Development, Employment/Job Training, Gay/Lesbian Issues, Civic & Public Affairs-General, Housing, Legal Aid, Municipalities/Towns, Nonprofit Management, Parades/Festivals, Philanthropic Organizations, Safety, Urban & Community Affairs, Women's Affairs, Zoos/Aquariums
Education: Business Education, Colleges & Universities, Community & Junior Colleges, Continuing Education, Education Funds, Education-General, Literacy, Preschool Education, Private Education (Precollege), Public Education (Precollege), Religious Education, Science/Mathematics Education, Secondary Education (Public)
Environment: Environment-General, Resource Conservation
Health: AIDS/HIV, Alzheimers Disease, Health Organizations, Home-Care Services, Hospitals, Medical Rehabilitation, Mental Health, Preventive Medicine/Wellness Organizations
Religion: Ministries, Religious Organizations, Religious Welfare, Social/Policy Issues
Science: Observatories & Planetariums, Science Exhibits & Fairs, Science Museums
Social Services: At-Risk Youth, Big Brother/Big Sister, Child Welfare, Community Centers, Community Service Organizations, Day Care, Domestic Violence, Emergency Relief, Family Services, Food/Clothing Distribution, Homes, People with Disabilities, Senior Services, Shelters/Homelessness, Substance Abuse, United Funds/United Ways, Volunteer Services, YMCA/YWCA/YMHA/YWHA, Youth Organizations

Contributions Analysis
Giving Priorities: Human services, education, the arts, and community improvement.
Arts & Humanities: 23%. Supports the performing arts, projects, concerts, and exhibitions that make the arts accessible to youth, the low-income, the disabled, and senior citizens. Matches employee contributions to cultural groups.
Civic & Public Affairs: 13%. Interests include projects that improve the quality of community life.
Education: 25%. Funds match employee contributions to institutions of higher, secondary, and elementary learning.
Environment: 1%.
Health: 4%. Mental health, preventive medicine, and single-disease health associations.
Religion: 1%.
Science: 2%. Recipients include science museums and scientific institutes.
Social Services: 31%. Priorities include programs concerned with youth, the disabled, drugs and alcohol, the homeless, family services, mental health, and the aged.
Note: Total contributions in 1998.

Application Procedures
Initial Contact: Send a brief letter of not more than two pages, plus attachments.
Application Requirements: Include a description of organization; constituency served; statement of mission, objectives and goals; amount requested, and an explanation of how funds will be used to support a specific program or project; program budget showing expenses and income sources, list of current contributors and amounts, recently audited financial statement, proof of tax-exempt status; and list of board members, executive director and other key staff members.
Deadlines: None.
Review Process: Foundation director reviews proposals prior to consideration by distribution committee.
Evaluative Criteria: Broad community support and proven track record; demonstration of how sustainable, positive change will be achieved; project meets community needs and targets a wide audience; projects have demonstrated impact in the community.
Decision Notification: Distribution committee meets four times a year; grants usually made within 90 days.

Restrictions
Grants are not made to individuals; religious, veterans', labor, or fraternal organizations; capital campaigns, endowment funds or operating expenses; fund-raising or sporting events; subscription fees or admission tickets; insurance premiums; medical research and health organizations; political candidates; political or lobbying groups; dinners or special events; trips or tours; advertisements; public sector services; or videos, films, or television productions.

Additional Information
Publications: Guidelines

Corporate Officials
Gary E. Black: president claims division, director B 1945. PRIM CORP EMPL president claims division, director: Fireman's Fund Insurance Co. CORP AFFIL director: American Insurance Co. Inc.; director: Intertate National Corp.
Herbert F. Hansmeyer: chairman ED University of Bonn; University of Cologne. PRIM CORP EMPL chairman: Fireman's Fund Insurance Co. CORP AFFIL chairman: National Surety Corp.; director: San Francisco Reinsurance Co.; director: Monticello Insurance Co.; chairman: Firemans Fund Insurance Co. Ohio; director: Jefferson Insurance Co. of New York;

chairman: American Insurance Co. Inc.; chairman: Associated Indemnity Corp.; principal: American Automobile Insurance Co.; chairman: Allianz America Corp.; director: Allianz Life Insurance Co. North America.

David R. Pollard: officer PRIM CORP EMPL officer: Fireman's Fund Insurance Co. CORP AFFIL executive vice president: Associated Indemnity Corp.; officer: Interstate Fire & Casualty Co.

Jeffery H. Post: executive vice president, chief financial officer, chief actuary PRIM CORP EMPL executive vice president, chief financial officer, chief actuary: Fireman's Fund Insurance Co. ADD CORP EMPL chief financial officer: American Insurance Co. Inc.; vice president: Associated Indemnity Corp.

Thomas E. Rowe: director B 1950. ED Towson State University BA (1972). PRIM CORP EMPL director: Fireman's Fund Insurance Co. CORP AFFIL executive vice president, director: National Surety Corp.; director: San Francisco Reinsurance Co.; executive vice president, director: Associated Indemnity Corp.; executive vice president, director: American Automobile Insurance Co.; executive vice president: American Insurance Co. Inc.; director: Allianz Life Insurance Co. North America.

Joe L. Stinnette, Jr.: president, chief executive officer, director B 1937. ED East Tennessee State University BS (1959). PRIM CORP EMPL president, chief executive officer, director: Fireman's Fund Insurance Co. CORP AFFIL executive vice president: American Automobile Insurance Co.; president: Firemans Fund Insurance Co. Ohio; president: America Insurance Co. Inc.

Foundation Officials

Gary E. Black: president, director (see above)
Barbara Friede: secretary, operating director
Janet S. Kloenhammer: director
H. David Lundgren: director
Harold N. Marsh, III: treasurer B 1948. ED Mitchell College AA (1972). PRIM CORP EMPL senior vice president, treasurer: Fireman's Fund Insurance Co. ADD CORP EMPL treasurer: American Insurance Co. Inc.; treasurer: National Surety Corp.; treasurer: Firemans Fund Insurance Co. Ohio; treasurer: Parkway Insurance Co.
David R. Pollard: director (see above)
Thomas E. Rowe: chairman, director (see above)
Joe L. Stinnette, Jr.: director (see above)

Grants Analysis

Disclosure Period: calendar year ending 1998
Total Grants: $792,783*
Number of Grants: 89
Average Grant: $8,908
Highest Grant: $75,000
Typical Range: $100 to $10,000
***Note:** Giving excludes matching gifts; United Way.

Recent Grants

Note: Grants derived from 1998 Form 990.

Arts & Humanities

6,000,000 Vector Theater Company, San Francisco, CA
5,000,000 Youth in Arts, Inc., San Rafael, CA
1,200,000 The Mountain Play Association, Mill Valley, CA
1,000,000 Marin Shakespeare Company, San Rafael, CA
1,000,000 Marin Symphony, San Rafael, CA
800,000 KQED Inc., San Francisco, CA

Civic & Public Affairs

1,000,000 Buckelew Programs, San Rafael, CA
1,000,000 Family Law Center for Women and Children, San Rafael, CA
1,000,000 Homeward Bound of Marin, San Rafael, CA
1,000,000 Marin Abused Women's Services, Marin City, CA
1,000,000 The Marin Continuum Of Housing And Services, San Rafael, CA
1,000,000 San Francisco Zoological Society, San Francisco, CA
750,000 Lita, Inc., San Rafael, CA
750,000 Marin Concerned Citizens, Marin City, CA
600,000 Spectrum Center for Lesbian, Gay and Bisexual Concerns, San Anselmo, CA
500,000 Marin Services for Women, Inc., San Rafael, CA

Education

7,500,000 Marin County Office of Education, Marin County, CA
2,500,000 St. Mark's School, San Rafael, CA
2,000,000 North Bay Children's Center, Novato, CA
1,000,000 California Academy of Sciences, San Francisco, CA
1,000,000 Dominican College of San Rafael, San Rafael, CA
750,000 Marin Education Fund, Marin City, CA
700,000 Junior Achievement of the Bay Area, Inc., San Francisco, CA
650,000 Marin Literacy Program/LVA, Marin City, CA
600,000 Junior Achievement of the Redwood Empire, Santa Rosa, CA

Environment

750,000 Audubon Canyon Ranch, Inc., Novato, CA

Health

1,500,000 Community Institute for Psychotherapy, San Rafael, CA
1,000,000 Novato Human Needs Center, Novato, CA
500,000 Alzheimer's Disease & Related Disorders Association, San Rafael, CA

Religion

700,000 Ecumenical Community Services of Marin, San Rafael, CA

Science

1,000,000 Bay Area Discovery Museum, San Francisco, CA

Social Services

3,683,500 United Way of the Bay Area, San Rafael, CA
1,837,600 Volunteer Center of Sonoma County, Santa Rosa, CA
1,500,000 Volunteer Center of Marin, Inc., San Rafael, CA
1,200,000 Guide Dogs for the Blind, Inc., San Rafael, CA
1,200,000 Henry Ohlhoff House, San Francisco, CA
1,200,000 Marin Conservation Corps, Marin City, CA
1,000,000 Bay Area Community Resources, Larkspur, CA
1,000,000 Huckleberry Youth Programs, Inc., San Francisco, CA
1,000,000 Novato Youth Center, Novato, CA
918,200 Volunteer Center of Marin, Inc., San Rafael, CA
915,000 United Way/Crusade of Mercy, Chicago, IL
750,000 Bread & Roses, San Francisco, CA
750,000 Meals of Marin, San Rafael, CA
600,000 Orange County's United Way, Los Angeles, CA
600,000 Service Outreach Motivation Empowerment, Santa Rosa, CA
576,000 United Way of the Greater Lehigh Valley, Lehigh Valley, PA
561,000 United Way of Greater St. Louis, St. Louis, MO
555,000 United Way/Chad, Santa Clara, CA
550,000 Committee on the Shelterless, Petaluma, CA

First American Corp.

Company Contact

Nashville, TN

Company Description

Formed by Merger of: American Bank (1999).
Income: US$472,100,000
Employees: 3,500

First American Foundation

Giving Contact

Ashley Webster
First American Center
Nashville, TN 37237
Phone: (615)748-2000

Description

Founded: 1993
EIN: 582071018
Organization Type: Corporate Foundation
Giving Locations: headquarters and operating communities.

Financial Summary

Total Giving: $1,074,145 (1997)
Assets: $9,660,875 (1993)

Typical Recipients

Arts & Humanities: Ballet, Historic Preservation, Libraries, Literary Arts, Performing Arts
Civic & Public Affairs: Botanical Gardens/Parks, Chambers of Commerce, Economic Development, Civic & Public Affairs-General, Housing, Parades/Festivals, Urban & Community Affairs
Education: Arts/Humanities Education, Business Education, Colleges & Universities, Education-General, Preschool Education, Science/Mathematics Education, Student Aid
Health: Clinics/Medical Centers
Social Services: Community Centers, Community Service Organizations, Recreation & Athletics, Scouts, United Funds/United Ways, YMCA/YWCA/YMHA/YWHA, Youth Organizations

Application Procedures

Initial Contact: Send a brief letter of inquiry.
Application Requirements: a description of organization, amount requested, purpose of funds sought, recently audited financial statement, and proof of tax-exempt status.
Deadlines: None.

Restrictions

Does not support individuals, religious organizations for sectarian purposes, or political or lobbying groups.

Corporate Officials

Dennis C. Bottorff: chairman, president, chief executive officer, director B Clarksville, IN 1944. ED Vanderbilt University BE (1966); Northwestern University MBA (1968). PRIM CORP EMPL chairman, president, chief executive officer, director: First American Corp. CORP AFFIL director: Shoney's; president, chief operating officer: C&S/Sovran Corp.; director: Ingram Industries. NONPR AFFIL director: Tomorrow; trustee, member investment committee: Vanderbilt University; member: Nashville Chamber of Commerce; member: Bankers Association; director: INROADS. CLUB AFFIL Hundred Club; Belle Meade Country Club; Cumberland Club.

Grants Analysis

Disclosure Period: calendar year ending 1997
Total Grants: $1,074,145

Number of Grants: 122
Average Grant: $6,201*
Highest Grant: $215,929
Typical Range: $2,000 to $10,000 and $20,000 to $100,000
***Note:** Average grant figure excludes two highest grants.

Recent Grants

Note: Grants derived from 1997 Form 990.

Arts & Humanities

16,667 Tennessee Foxtrot Carousel, Antioch, TN -- to construct Wilma Rudolph figure
5,000 City Ballet, Knoxville, TN -- sponsor Partners in Art program
5,000 Downtown Kingsport Association, Kingsport, TN -- to renovate historic buildings
5,000 Johnson City Public Library, Johnson City, TN -- to purchase furnishings, equipment
5,000 Ladies' Hermitage Association, Hermitage, TN -- to restore Hermitage
5,000 National Storytelling Association, Jonesborough, TN -- to construct a new facility

Civic & Public Affairs

50,000 Partnership 2000, Nashville Area Chamber of Commerce, Nashville, TN -- for public relations and advertising activities
25,000 Bill Wilkerson Center, Nashville, TN -- to build a new facility
10,000 Clarksville Montgomery County, Clarksville, TN -- support Aspire 2000 program
10,000 Friends of Warner Parks, Nashville, TN -- for renovations to park entrance
10,000 Holston Habitat for Humanity, Kingsport, TN -- to construct houses for needy family
5,000 Affordable Housing, Nashville, TN -- sponsor mortgage counseling services
5,000 Stadium, Chattanooga, TN -- to renovate the stadium
5,000 Tennessee Network for Community Economic Development, Nashville, TN -- support Micro Enterprise Initiate Program
5,000 Woodbine Community Organization, Nashville, TN -- program support

Education

73,000 Vanderbilt University, Nashville, TN -- operating support
25,000 Success By Six, Nashville, TN -- operating support
15,000 Belmont University, Nashville, TN -- scholarships
15,000 David Lipscomb University, Nashville, TN -- scholarships
10,000 Carson Newman College, Jefferson City, TN -- to renovate student center
10,000 Fisk University, Nashville, TN -- for construction of running track
10,000 Pencil Foundation, Nashville, TN -- support Adopt-A-School program
10,000 Rosne State Foundation, Herrman, TN -- to construct Cumberland County Campus
9,500 Junior Achievement of Middle Tennessee, Nashville, TN -- support student programs
7,500 East Tennessee State University Foundation, Johnson City, TN -- sponsor Chair of Banking
6,000 Vanderbilt University Owen Graduate School of Management, Nashville, TN -- scholarships
5,000 Hands on Regional Museum, Johnson City, TN -- support Math-A-Mania
5,000 Vanderbilt University Blair School of Music, Nashville, TN -- scholarships

Health

5,000 Bristol Regional Medical Center Foundation, Bristol, TN -- operating support

Social Services

215,929 United Way Middle Tennessee, Nashville, TN -- to fund local allocations pool
114,500 United Way, Knoxville, TN -- to fund local allocations pool
50,000 United Way Middle Tennessee, Nashville, TN -- to fund local allocations pool
24,412 United Way Mid-South, Memphis, TN -- to fund local allocations pool
22,476 United Way Middle Tennessee, Nashville, TN -- to fund local allocations pool
11,500 United Way, Kingsport, TN -- to fund local allocations pool
11,000 United Way Bradley County, Cleveland, TN -- to fund local allocations pool
10,000 Cleveland Community Playground, Cleveland, TN -- playground support
8,600 United Way Roanoke Valley, Roanoke, VA -- to fund local allocations pool
8,137 United Way Mid-South, Memphis, TN -- to fund local allocations pool
7,200 YWCA Cable, Nashville, TN -- sponsor YWCA Academy for women achievers
7,000 United Way Anderson County, Oak Ridge, TN -- to fund local allocations pool
6,000 Johnson City Area United Way, Johnson City, TN -- to fund local allocations pool
5,100 United Way, Chattanooga, TN -- to fund local allocations pool
5,000 Boy Scouts of America Sequoyah Council 713, Bristol, TN -- support scouting activities
5,000 Boy Scouts of America Great Smoky Mountain Council, Knoxville, TN -- to renovate facility
5,000 Boys and Girls Club, Knoxville, TN -- operating support
5,000 Clarksville-Fort Campbell YMCA, Claksville, TN -- to construct a new facility
5,000 Helen Ross McNabb Foundation, Knoxville, TN -- to build supported apartment housing
5,000 Overlook Center, Knoxville, TN -- sponsor Run for Home event
5,000 YMCA, Chattanooga, TN -- to construct a new facility

FIRST FINANCIAL BANK

Company Contact

Stevens Point, WI

Company Description

Employees: 1,283
SIC(s): 6035 Federal Savings Institutions.
Parent Company: First Financial Corp.

First Financial Foundation

Giving Contact

Wanda Lay, Assistant Secretary
First Financial Foundation
1305 Main St.
Stevens Point, WI 54481
Phone: (715)341-0400

Description

Founded: 1977
EIN: 391277461
Organization Type: Corporate Foundation
Giving Locations: IL: areas of business; WI: areas of business
Grant Types: Capital, Employee Matching Gifts, General Support.

Financial Summary

Total Giving: $303,049 (1998); $224,383 (1997); $244,404 (1996)
Giving Analysis: Giving for 1997 includes: foundation ($146,775); foundation grants to United Way ($77,608); 1998: foundation ($174,200); foundation grants to United Way ($128,849)
Assets: $894,147 (1998); $1,153,175 (1997); $962,817 (1996)
Gifts Received: $360,000 (1997); $90,000 (1996); $300,000 (1994). Note: In 1996, contributions were received from First Financial Bank.

Typical Recipients

Arts & Humanities: Arts & Humanities-General, Libraries, Museums/Galleries, Music, Performing Arts, Public Broadcasting, Theater
Civic & Public Affairs: Botanical Gardens/Parks, Chambers of Commerce, Clubs, Community Foundations, Economic Development, Civic & Public Affairs-General, Housing, Municipalities/Towns, Urban & Community Affairs
Education: Agricultural Education, Colleges & Universities, Economic Education, Education Reform, Student Aid, Vocational & Technical Education
Environment: Environment-General
Health: AIDS/HIV, Children's Health/Hospitals, Clinics/Medical Centers, Health Funds, Hospitals, Medical Research, Public Health
Religion: Religious Organizations, Religious Welfare
Social Services: Community Centers, Community Service Organizations, People with Disabilities, Recreation & Athletics, Scouts, Senior Services, United Funds/United Ways, YMCA/YWCA/YMHA/YWHA, Youth Organizations

Contributions Analysis

Giving Priorities: United Way, social services, and education.
Arts & Humanities: 6%. Supports libraries, the performing arts, and arts councils.
Civic & Public Affairs: 8%. Funds housing and neighborhood development.
Education: 15%. Recipients include higher education and enrichment programs.
Health: 5%. Funds hospitals and health clinics.
Religion: 1%.
Social Services: 65%. Major support for United Ways; youth activities, including YMCA's are also funded.
Note: Total contributions in 1998.

Application Procedures

Initial Contact: Request a contribution request form.
Deadlines: September 1.

Restrictions

The foundation does not make contributions to individuals, political or lobbying groups, labor organizations, or veterans' organizations. Contributions to religious organizations are limited to those facilities that offer higher education or hospital care to the general public.

Additional Information

Publications: Application Form

Corporate Officials

Robert Sigfried Gaiswinkler: chairman, director, director B Chicago, IL 1932. ED University of Illinois BS (1953). PRIM CORP EMPL chairman, director: First Financial Bank. CORP AFFIL chairman: Venture Corp.; chairman: National Equity Securities; director review board: Saint Wisconsin Savings & Loan; chairman: National Equity Investments Corp.; chairman: National Equity Real Estate Corp.; chairman: National

Diversified Fin; chairman, director: First Fin Savings Association; chairman executive committee: Guaranty National Mortgage Corp.; director, member: Federal National Mortgage Association; chairman, director: First Fin Corp.; director review board: Drayton Co. NONPR AFFIL vice chairman: WMVS Education Television; director: WOSU Education Television; secretary: National Council Savings Institutions; director: KETC Education Television; trustee: Missouri Military Academy; member: Delta Upsilon; advisory board: Fed Savings & Loan Advisory Comm. CLUB AFFIL Blue Mound Country Club; Vantana Country Club.

Tom Newschaffer: executive vice president, chief financial officer PRIM CORP EMPL executive vice president, chief financial officer: First Financial Bank.

John C. Seramur: president, chief executive officer, director B 1943. PRIM CORP EMPL president, chief executive officer, director: First Financial Bank.

Foundation Officials

David W. Drought: treasurer

Robert Sigfried Gaiswinkler: director (see above)

James O. Heinecke: director

Wanda Lay: assistant secretary

Ignatius H. Robers: director

Robert M. Salinger: secretary B Milwaukee, WI 1950. ED University of Wisconsin BA (1972); University of Wisconsin JD (1976). CORP AFFIL general couns,secretary: First Fin Corp.; chairman: First Fin Political Action Committee; executive vice president: First Fin Bank. NONPR AFFIL member: Corp. Counsel Association; member: WI Bar Association; member: American Bar Association. CLUB AFFIL Stevens Point Country Club; Order Coif; Rotary Club.

Ralph R. Staven: chairman, president, mgr, director

Grants Analysis

Disclosure Period: calendar year ending 1998
Total Grants: $174,200*
Number of Grants: 85
Average Grant: $2,049
Highest Grant: $12,000
Typical Range: $300 to $11,000
***Note:** Giving excludes United Way, matching gifts.

Recent Grants

Note: Grants derived from 1997 Form 990.

Arts & Humanities

3,125 AMK Productions, Duluth, MN -- capital support
3,000 Corn Stalk Theater, Peoria, IL -- capital support

Civic & Public Affairs

5,000 Laird Center, Marshfield, WI -- building fund
5,000 Stevens Point Community Foundation, Stevens Point, WI -- capital support
5,000 Stevens Point, Plover Area Chamber Foundation, Stevens Point, WI -- capital support
3,500 Washington Heights Neighborhood Association, Milwaukee, WI -- capital support
3,000 Downtown Mainstreet, La Crosse, WI -- capital support
3,000 Regional Access and Mobilization Project, Rockford, IL -- capital support

Education

3,000 Carroll College, Waukesha, WI -- capital support

Health

11,000 St. Luke's Hospital, Milwaukee, WI -- building fund
5,000 Waukesha Memorial Hospital, Waukesha, WI -- capital support
3,000 Health Education Center of Wisconsin, Milwaukee, WI -- capital support

Religion

3,000 Salvation Army, Waukesha, WI -- capital support

Social Services

38,079 United Way Portage County, Stevens Point, WI -- health, welfare
12,000 YMCA Stevens Point, Stevens Point, WI -- capital support
10,863 United Way -- health, welfare
9,203 United Way, Milwaukee, WI -- health, welfare
9,199 United Way, Saint Louis, MO -- health, welfare
3,132 United Way Heart of Illinois, Peoria, IL -- health, welfare
3,000 L.E. Phillips Senior Center, Eau Claire, WI -- capital support

FIRST HAWAIIAN, INC.

Company Contact

Honolulu, HI

Company Description

Assets: US$8,002,200,000
Employees: 3,384
SIC(s): 6022 State Commercial Banks, 6159 Miscellaneous Business Credit Institutions, 6719 Holding Companies Nec.

Corporate Sponsorship

Type: Arts & cultural events; Music & entertainment events; Sports events
Contact: Brandt Farias, Senior Vice President, Marketing

First Hawaiian Foundation

Giving Contact

Lily K. Yao, President
First Hawaiian Foundation
PO Box 3200
Honolulu, HI 96847
Phone: (808)525-7766
Fax: (808)525-7750

Description

EIN: 237437822
Organization Type: Corporate Foundation
Giving Locations: HI
Grant Types: Capital, Employee Matching Gifts, General Support, Project.

Financial Summary

Total Giving: $1,500,000 (1999 approx); $1,296,939 (1998); $1,165,249 (1997). Note: Contributes through corporate direct giving program and foundation. 1996 Giving includes foundation, matching gifts, and United Way.

Giving Analysis: Giving for 1996 includes: foundation ($918,582); foundation grants to United Way ($300,000); foundation matching gifts ($10,350); 1997: foundation ($850,249); foundation grants to United Way ($305,000); foundation scholarships ($10,000)

Assets: $8,060,435 (1998); $7,460,551 (1997); $7,216,582 (1996)

Gifts Received: $4,504 (1998); $8,427 (1997); $8,649 (1996). Note: Contributions were received from First Hawaiian Credit Corp., First Hawaiian Bank, and First Hawaiian Leasing.

Typical Recipients

Arts & Humanities: Arts Associations & Councils, Arts Centers, Arts Funds, Film & Video, Historic Preservation, History & Archaeology, Libraries, Museums/Galleries, Music, Public Broadcasting, Theater, Visual Arts

Civic & Public Affairs: Asian American Affairs, Business/Free Enterprise, Community Foundations, Civic & Public Affairs-General, Housing, Law & Justice, Parades/Festivals, Philanthropic Organizations, Urban & Community Affairs

Education: Arts/Humanities Education, Business Education, Colleges & Universities, Continuing Education, Economic Education, Education Funds, Elementary Education (Public), Education-General, Gifted & Talented Programs, International Studies, Literacy, Preschool Education, Private Education (Precollege), Private Education (Precollege), Public Education (Precollege), Religious Education, Science/Mathematics Education, Secondary Education (Private), Secondary Education (Public), Social Sciences Education, Special Education, Student Aid

Environment: Environment-General, Resource Conservation

Health: Cancer, Children's Health/Hospitals, Clinics/Medical Centers, Emergency/Ambulance Services, Health Organizations, Hospitals, Medical Rehabilitation, Research/Studies Institutes, Single-Disease Health Associations

International: Foreign Educational Institutions, Health Care/Hospitals, Missionary/Religious Activities

Religion: Churches, Religious Welfare

Science: Science Museums, Scientific Centers & Institutes, Scientific Research

Social Services: Big Brother/Big Sister, Child Welfare, Community Centers, Community Service Organizations, Day Care, Domestic Violence, Family Services, Food/Clothing Distribution, Homes, People with Disabilities, Recreation & Athletics, Scouts, Senior Services, Shelters/Homelessness, Substance Abuse, United Funds/United Ways, Volunteer Services, YMCA/YWCA/YMHA/YWHA, Youth Organizations

Contributions Analysis

Giving Priorities: United funds, the visual arts, precollege education, health facilities, and the environment.

Arts & Humanities: 14%. Supports museums, arts centers, and music.

Civic & Public Affairs: 8%. Supports community services.

Education: 20%. Precollege education receives most support through capital campaigns and grants used to renovate or refurbish facilities. Grants are awarded to private and public schools.

Health: 20%. Supports health clinics, hospitals and health foundations.

Social Services: 35%. Majority of giving supports united funds. Funds also provided for services for youth and drug prevention.

Application Procedures

Initial Contact: Send letter of request.

Application Requirements: Include a description of organization, amount requested, project budget, purpose of funds sought, recently audited financial statement, proof of tax-exempt status, income level of service area, and list of board members and officers.

Deadlines: None.

Review Process: Board meets quarterly.

Restrictions

Company will only fund organizations with tax-exempt status.

Corporate Officials

Walter Arthur Dods, Jr.: chairman, chief executive officer, director B Honolulu, HI 1941. ED University of Hawaii BBA (1967). PRIM CORP EMPL chairman, chief executive officer, director: First Hawaiian, Inc. CORP AFFIL director: Suntory Resorts Inc.; director: Restaurant Suntory USA Inc.; director: RHP Inc.; chairman: Pacific One Dealer Center Inc.; chairman, chief executive officer: Real Estate Delivery Inc.;

chairman: Pacific One Bank; chairman: Pacific One Bank NA; director: Oceanic Cablevision; director: Pacific Guardian Life Insurance Co.; director: GTE Northwest Inc.; director: Matson Navigation Co. Inc.; director: GTE California Inc.; director: GTE Hawaiian Telephone Co. Inc.; director: First Insurance Co. Hawaii Ltd.; director: Grace Pacific Corp.; director: First Hawaiian Leasing Inc.; director: First Hawaiian Creditcorp Inc.; chairman, chief executive officer: First Hawaiian Insurance Inc.; chairman: FHL SPC One Inc.; chairman, chief executive officer, drc: First Hawaiian Bank; chairman, president: FHB Properties Inc.; director: FHL Lease Holding Co. Inc.; chairman, chief executive officer: FHB Mortgage Co. Inc.; trustee: Samuel Mills Damon Estate; chairman, president: FH Center Inc.; chairman: ANB Financial Corp.; director: A & B Hawaii Inc.; director: Alexander & Baldwin Inc. NONPR AFFIL trustee: Punahou School; treasurer: Rehabilitation Hospital Pacific; chairman, director: Pacific International Center High-Tech Research; member, board governors: Pacific Peace Foundation; member, board governors: Japanese Cultural Center Hawaii; trustee: Nature Conservancy Hawaii; trustee: Japan-American Institute of Management Science; Hawaii chairman: Japan-Hawaii Economic Council; director: Hawaii Visitors Bureau; member: Honolulu Press Club; trustee: Hawaii Maritime Center; executive committee: Hawaii Open; member: Hawaii Chamber of Commerce; board governors: Hawaii Employers Council; member: Hawaii Business Roundtable; member governors advisory board: Geothermal-Interisland Cable Project; director: Hawaii Bankers Association; member, director: Duty Free Shoppers Advisory Board; director: East-West Center Foundation; treasurer, director: Coalition Drug-Free Hawaii; trustee: Contemporary Museum; member executive board: Boy Scouts America; board governors, vice president finance: Center International Commercial Dispute Resolution; trustee: Blood Bank Hawaii; member governors advisory board: Blue Ribbon Panel Future Healthcare Hawaii; president, director: American Bankers Association; member: Bank Marketing Association; director: Ahahui Koa Anuenue; member executive board: Aloha Council. CLUB AFFIL member board of governors: Honolulu Country Club; treasurer: 200 Club.

Lily K. Yao: director PRIM CORP EMPL director: First Hawaiian, Inc. CORP AFFIL secretary: First Hawaiian Bank. NONPR AFFIL chairman board regents: University Hawaii.

Foundation Officials

Robert Alm: director CORP AFFIL trustee: Liliuokalani Trust.

Gary Caulfield: director

Walter Arthur Dods, Jr.: president, director (see above)

Anthony R. Guerrero, Jr.: director B Honolulu, HI 1945. ED University of Portland (1967). PRIM CORP EMPL executive vice president: First Hawaiian Bank. CORP AFFIL director: Oahu Transit Service Inc.

Donald G. Horner: vice president, director B Fayetteville, NC 1950. ED University of North Carolina (1972); University of Southern California (1977). PRIM CORP EMPL executive vice president: First Hawaiian, Inc. CORP AFFIL president, director: First Hawaiian Dealer Center Inc.; director: First Hawaiian Leasing Inc.; vice chairman: First Hawaiian Bank; chairman: First Hawaiian Creditcorp Inc.

Howard Henry Karr: treasurer, director B Honolulu, HI 1943. ED University of Hawaii (1966). PRIM CORP EMPL vice chairman, treasurer, chief financial officer: First Hawaiian, Inc. ADD CORP EMPL treasurer, director: Real Estate Delivery Inc.; executive vice president, chief financial officer: BancWest Corp.; vice president,treasurer, director: FHB Properties Inc.; vice president, director, secretary, treasurer: FHI International Inc.; vice president, treasurer, director: FHL Leasing Holding Co. Inc.; vice president, treasurer, director: First Hawaiian Creditcorp Inc.; vice president, treasurer, director: First Hawaiian Leasing Inc.; treasurer, director: Pacific One Dealer Center. CORP AFFIL vice president, treasurer, director: FH Center Inc.; vice chairman: First Hawaii Bank. NONPR AFFIL member: American Institute CPAs; member: Financial Executives Institute; treasurer, director: 1st Hawaiian Foundation.

Gerald M. Pang: director B Honolulu, HI 1948. ED University of Hawaii (1970). PRIM CORP EMPL executive vice president, chief credit officer: First Hawaiian Bank. NONPR AFFIL senior vice president, chief credit officer: 1st Hawaiian Inc.

Barbara Tomber: director

John K. Tsui: director B 1938. PRIM CORP EMPL president: First Hawaiian Bank. CORP AFFIL president: Bancwest Corp.; chief executive officer: First Hawaiian Leasing Inc.

Herbert Eric Wolff: secretary, director B Cologne, Germany 1925. ED Rutgers University BA (1953); University of Maryland BS (1957); George Washington University MA (1962); United States Army War College (1962); Harvard University (1979). PRIM CORP EMPL senior vice president, secretary: First Hawaiian, Inc. CORP AFFIL senior vice president, secretary: First Hawaiian Bank; section: First Hawaiian Leasing Inc. NONPR AFFIL member, trustee: U.S. Army Museum Society; director: USO; member: Phi Kappa Phi; member, vice president: Hawaii Comm Foreign Relations; president: Pacific Asian Affairs Council; director: Girl Scouts U.S.; president: Hawaii Army Museum Society; member: First Infantry Division Association; member executive board: Boy Scouts America Aloha Council; member: First Cavalry Division Association; member, trustee: Association U.S. Army; director: ASYMCA; member: American Society of Corporate Secretaries. CLUB AFFIL Rotary Club; Waialae Country Club; Honolulu Country Club; director: Plaza Club.

Grants Analysis

Disclosure Period: calendar year ending 1997
Total Grants: $850,249*
Number of Grants: 72
Average Grant: $10,637*
Highest Grant: $95,000
Typical Range: $5,000 to $20,000
***Note:** Giving excludes scholarship and United Way. Average grant figure excludes highest grant.

Recent Grants

Note: Grants derived from 1998 Form 990.

Arts & Humanities

50,000	Contemporary Museum, Honolulu, HI
45,000	Hawaii Labor Heritage Council, Honolulu, HI
25,000	Hawaii International Film Festival, Honolulu, HI
25,000	Lyman House Memorial Museum, Hilo, HI
16,667	USS Missouri Memorial Association, Honolulu, HI
15,000	Contemporary Museum, Honolulu, HI
10,000	The Hawaiian Legacy Series, Honolulu, HI
10,000	Prince Albert Foundation, Princeville, HI

Civic & Public Affairs

33,334	Bobby Benson Foundation, Honolulu, HI
16,667	Kuakini Foundation, Honolulu, HI
13,334	Self-Help Housing Corporation of Hawaii, Honolulu, HI
12,500	Hawaiian Language Resources Office, Honolulu, HI
10,000	National Japanese American Memorial Foundation, SanFrancisco, CA

Education

25,000	Damien High School, Honolulu, HI
25,000	Oceanic Institute, Honolulu, HI
25,000	Punahou School, Honolulu, HI
20,000	Augustine Educational Foundation, Kaneohe, HI
20,000	Brigham Young University - Hawaii, Laie, HI
20,000	Public Schools of Hawaii Foundation, Honolulu, HI
15,000	Island School, Honolulu, HI
13,500	Lewis and Clark College, Portland, OR
10,000	Chaminade University, Honolulu, HI
10,000	Iolani School, Honolulu, HI
10,000	Le Jardin Academy, Honolulu, HI
10,000	Nanaikapono Elementary School, Waianae, HI
10,000	Ready to Learn, Honolulu, HI

Environment

12,500	Nature Conservancy of Hawaii, Honolulu, HI
10,000	Hawaii Nature Center, Honolulu, HI

Health

20,000	Castle Medical Center Foundation, Honolulu, HI
20,000	Rehabilitation Hospital of the Pacific, Honolulu, HI
20,000	St. Francis Medical Center, Honolulu, HI
13,563	Waianae Coast Comprehensive Health Center, Honolulu, HI
10,000	Easter Seal Society of Hawaii, Honolulu, HI
10,000	North Hawaii Community Hospital, Inc., Honolulu, HI
10,000	Waikiki Health Center, Waikiki, HI

Religion

25,000	Episcopal Church, Honolulu, HI

Science

35,000	Pacific International Center for High Technology Research (PICHTR), Honolulu, HI
12,500	Pacific Tsunami Museum, Hilo, HI

Social Services

246,500	Aloha United Way, Oahu, Oahu, HI
25,500	Hawaii Island United Way, Honolulu, HI
21,500	Maui United Way, Maui, HI
16,667	Helping Hands Hawaii, Honolulu, HI
13,700	United Way of Kauai, Kauai, HI
13,333	Maui County Council of the Boy Scouts of America, Maui, HI
12,500	Independent Living, Inc., Honolulu, HI
12,203	Aloha United Way -- Additional Pledge, Honolulu, HI
10,000	Big Brothers/Big Sisters of Honolulu, Inc., Honolulu, HI
10,000	Goodwill Industries of Honolulu, Inc., Honolulu, HI
10,000	Honpa Hongwanji Hilo Betsuin, Honolulu, HI
10,000	Lunalilo Home, Honolulu, HI

FIRST MARYLAND BANCORP

Company Contact

Baltimore, MD
Web: http://www.aib.ie

Company Description

Assets: US$10,477,100,000
Employees: 4,824
SIC(s): 6021 National Commercial Banks.
Parent Company: AIB Group

Operating Locations

DE: First Maryland Bancorp, Millsboro; First Omni Bank, N.A., Millsboro; MD: First Maryland Annuities Agency Corp., Baltimore; First Maryland Bancorp, Baltimore; First Maryland Bancorp, Baltimore; First Maryland Brokerage Corp., Baltimore; First Maryland Credit Corp., Baltimore; First Maryland Leasecorp, Baltimore; First Maryland Life Insurance Co., Baltimore; First National Bank of Maryland, Baltimore; First Maryland Bancorp, Glen Burnie; First National

Mortgage Corp., Glen Burnie; NY: AIB Plc, New York; PA: Dauphin Deposit Bank & Trust Co., Harrisburg; Hopper Soliday & Co. Inc., Lancaster; First Maryland Bancorp, York; First Maryland International Banking Corp., York; York Bank and Trust Co., York

Nonmonetary Support

Value: $15,000 (1992); $15,000 (1991)
Type: Donated Equipment
Note: Company reports that it donates used furniture and equipment that is no longer needed.

Corporate Sponsorship

Value: $700,000
Type: Arts & cultural events; Festivals/fairs; Music & entertainment events; Sports events
Note: Sponsors civic community agencies and educational institutions.

First Maryland Foundation

Giving Contact

J. Michael Riley, Secretary
First Maryland Foundation
25 South Charles Street
Suite 1902
Baltimore, MD 21201
Phone: (410)244-3949
Fax: (410)545-2205

Description

Founded: 1967
EIN: 526077253
Organization Type: Corporate Foundation
Giving Locations: DE; DC: Washington; MD: Baltimore including metropolitan area headquarters and operating communities.
Grant Types: Capital, Employee Matching Gifts, Endowment, General Support, Multiyear/Continuing Support.
Note: Employee matching gift ratio: 1 to 1.

Financial Summary

Total Giving: $1,700,000 (1999 approx); $1,722,344 (1998); $1,881,118 (1997). Note: Contributes through foundation only.
Giving Analysis: Giving for 1997 includes: foundation ($1,567,312); foundation grants to United Way ($269,700); foundation matching gifts ($29,106); foundation scholarships ($15,000); 1998: foundation ($1,359,800); foundation grants to United Way ($330,625); foundation matching gifts ($81,909)
Assets: $1,400,000 (1999 approx); $1,683,180 (1998); $1,667,399 (1997)
Gifts Received: $751,761 (1998); $1,000,180 (1997); $1,000,300 (1996). Note: Foundation receives contributions from First National Bank of Maryland.

Typical Recipients

Arts & Humanities: Arts Centers, Arts Institutes, Dance, Historic Preservation, Libraries, Museums/Galleries, Music, Opera, Performing Arts, Theater, Visual Arts
Civic & Public Affairs: Botanical Gardens/Parks, Civil Rights, Community Foundations, Economic Development, Civic & Public Affairs-General, Housing, Philanthropic Organizations, Professional & Trade Associations, Women's Affairs, Zoos/Aquariums
Education: Arts/Humanities Education, Business Education, Colleges & Universities, Education Funds, Education Reform, Medical Education, Private Education (Precollege), Religious Education, Student Aid
Health: Clinics/Medical Centers, Hospices, Hospitals
Religion: Dioceses, Jewish Causes, Religious Welfare, Seminaries
Science: Scientific Centers & Institutes, Scientific Research
Social Services: Child Abuse, Community Service Organizations, Family Services, Recreation & Athletics, Scouts, United Funds/United Ways, YMCA/YWCA/YMHA/YWHA, Youth Organizations

Contributions Analysis

Giving Priorities: Higher education, social welfare, the arts, the civics, hospitals, single-disease health associations, religious organizations, and scientific organizations.
Arts & Humanities: 15%. Majority of support goes to museums, orchestras, and musical societies. Other priorities include performing arts, arts centers and associations, community arts groups, and libraries.
Civic & Public Affairs: 8%. Interests include zoos, civil rights, and philanthropic organizations.
Education: 24%. Most of educational funding is awarded in general support to colleges and universities. The foundation also supports arts and humanities education, and matches employee gifts to higher education.
Health: 8%. Supports medical centers.
Religion: Supports Jewish and Christian organizations.
Social Services: 26%. Funds primarily support the United Way. Other interests include youth, community, and family services, principally in the Baltimore area.
Note: Total contributions made in 1998.

Application Procedures

Initial Contact: Submit a brief letter.
Application Requirements: Include a reason for request and intended charitable purpose of funds disbursed, proof of tax-exempt status, budget, and recently audited financial statements.
Deadlines: None.
Review Process: Requests reviewed at least quarterly by board of trustees.
Evaluative Criteria: Whether project includes broad-based services, reaches a number of people, and exhibits evidence of volunteer support.

Restrictions

Does not support individuals.

Additional Information

Grantee organizations must be nonprofit with no political affiliation.

Corporate Officials

Frank P. Bramble: president, chief executive officer, director B 1948. PRIM CORP EMPL president, chief executive officer, director: First Maryland Bancorp ADD CORP EMPL president: Allfirst Financial Inc.; president: Allfirst Bank. CORP AFFIL chief executive officer, chief operating officer,president: MNC Finance Inc.
Jeremiah E. Casey: chairman B 1940. PRIM CORP EMPL chairman: First Maryland Bancorp ADD CORP EMPL chairman: First National Bank Maryland Inc. CORP AFFIL director: Rouse Co.; chief executive officer: United States of America Allied Irish Bank PLC.

Foundation Officials

Frank P. Bramble: president, trustee (see above)
Jeremiah E. Casey: chairman, trustee (see above)
Thomas D. Fitzsimmons: treasurer PRIM CORP EMPL senior vice president: First Maryland Bancorp. CORP AFFIL director: First Omni Bank NA.
J. Michael Riley: secretary PRIM CORP EMPL vice president external affairs: First Maryland Bancorp.

Grants Analysis

Disclosure Period: calendar year ending 1998
Total Grants: $1,359,800*
Number of Grants: 113
Average Grant: $12,034
Highest Grant: $100,000
Typical Range: $500 to $10,000
***Note:** Giving excludes matching gifts; United Way.

Recent Grants

Note: Grants derived from 1997 Form 990.

Arts & Humanities

105,000	Baltimore Symphony Orchestra, Baltimore, MD
83,000	Baltimore Center for the Performing Arts, Baltimore, MD
50,000	Baltimore City Life Museum, Baltimore, MD
50,000	Walters Art Gallery, Baltimore, MD
40,000	Maryland Institute College of Art, Baltimore, MD
30,000	Baltimore Museum of Art, Baltimore, MD
20,000	American Visionary Art Museum, Baltimore, MD
15,000	Baltimore Museum of Industry, Baltimore, MD
15,000	Baltimore and Ohio Railroad Museum, Baltimore, MD
10,000	Baltimore Opera Company, Baltimore, MD

Civic & Public Affairs

40,000	York Foundation, York, PA
25,000	Constellation Foundation, Baltimore, MD
25,000	St. Ambrose Housing Aid Center, Baltimore, MD
20,000	Enterprise Foundation, Columbia, MD
20,000	National Aquarium, Baltimore, MD
15,000	Association of Baltimore Area Grantmakers for Baltimore Neighborhood Collaborative, Baltimore, MD
10,000	Community Development Support Collaborative, Washington, DC
10,000	Women of Achievement in Maryland History, Silver Spring, MD

Education

100,000	Johns Hopkins University, Baltimore, MD
60,000	Morgan State University Foundation, Baltimore, MD
50,000	University of Maryland Medical System, Baltimore, MD
30,000	Goucher College, Towson, MD
20,000	Institute for Christian and Jewish Studies, Baltimore, MD
20,000	Loyola College, Baltimore, MD
20,000	University of Maryland College of Business and Management Foundation, Baltimore, MD
20,000	University of Maryland Foundation, Adelphi, MD
20,000	Western Maryland College, Westminster, MD
12,500	Independent College Fund, Baltimore, MD
10,000	St. Johns College, Annapolis, MD
10,000	University of Baltimore, Baltimore, MD
10,000	University of Maryland Baltimore County, Baltimore, MD

Health

65,000	Sinai Hospital, Baltimore, MD
30,000	Mercy Medical Center, Baltimore, MD
20,000	Greater Baltimore Medical Center/Henry and Jeanette Weinberg Community Health Center, Baltimore, MD
12,500	North Arundel Hospital Foundation, Glen Burnie, MD

Religion

75,000	Archdiocese of Baltimore, Baltimore, MD
50,000	Associated Catholic Charities-Cherry Hill, Baltimore, MD
20,000	St. Marys Seminary and University, Baltimore, MD
10,000	Associated Jewish Community Federation, Baltimore, MD
10,000	Franciscan Center, Baltimore, MD

Science

30,000	Columbus Center, Baltimore, MD
20,000	Maryland Academy of Science, Baltimore, MD

Social Services

225,000	United Way of Central Maryland, Baltimore, MD
20,000	United Way of Sussex County, Georgetown, DE
15,000	Caroline Center, Baltimore, MD
15,000	Family and Children's Services of Central Maryland, Baltimore, MD
12,500	Woodbourne Foundation, Baltimore, MD
11,500	United Way of Washington County, Hagerstown, MD
10,000	House of Ruth, Baltimore, MD
10,000	United Way of the National Capital Area, Washington, DC

First National Bank Of Evergreen Park

Company Contact
Evergreen Park, IL

Company Description
Assets: US$1,888,000,000
Employees: 645
SIC(s): 6021 National Commercial Banks.
Parent Company: First Evergreen Corp.

First Evergreen Foundation

Giving Contact
David Wagner, Chairman, President & Chief Executive Officer
111 Lyon Street Northwest
Grand Rapids, MI 49503
Phone: (616)771-5000
Fax: (616)771-4378

Description
Founded: 1985
EIN: 363456053
Organization Type: Corporate Foundation
Giving Locations: IL: Chicago southwest area
Grant Types: General Support.

Financial Summary
Total Giving: $370,000 (1997); $450,000 (1996); $303,500 (1994)
Assets: $6,629,236 (1997); $5,916,405 (1996); $5,041,463 (1994)
Gifts Received: $701,570 (1997); $500,000 (1996); $500,000 (1994). Note: In 1996 and 1997, contributions were received from the First National Bank of Evergreen Park.

Typical Recipients
Civic & Public Affairs: Civic & Public Affairs-General, Legal Aid, Urban & Community Affairs
Education: Colleges & Universities, Private Education (Precollege), Religious Education, Secondary Education (Private)
Health: Clinics/Medical Centers, Hospitals, Medical Rehabilitation, Mental Health
Religion: Bible Study/Translation, Ministries, Religious Organizations

Application Procedures
Initial Contact: The foundation has no formal grant application procedure or application form.
Deadlines: None.

Restrictions
Does not support individuals.

Corporate Officials
Kenneth J. Ozinga: chairman, president, chief executive officer, director PRIM CORP EMPL chairman, president, chief executive officer, director: First National Bank of Evergreen Park.
Robert C. Wall: executive vice president finance PRIM CORP EMPL executive vice president finance: First National Bank of Evergreen Park.

Foundation Officials
Alfred E. Bleeker: trustee
Jerome J. Cismoski: trustee
Stephen M. Hallenbeck: trustee
Kenneth J. Ozinga: principal mgr, trustee (see above)

Grants Analysis
Disclosure Period: calendar year ending 1997
Total Grants: $370,000
Number of Grants: 5
Highest Grant: $150,000
Typical Range: $5,000 to $50,000

Recent Grants
Note: Grants derived from 1996 Form 990.

Civic & Public Affairs

25,000	Center for Public Justice, Washington, DC

Education

25,000	Calvin College, Grand Rapids, MI
25,000	Southwest Chicago Christian Schools, Chicago, IL
20,000	St. Xavier University, Chicago, IL
10,000	Reformed Bible College, Grand Rapids, MI

Health

200,000	Christ Hospital and Medical Center, Oak Lawn, IL
75,000	Little Company of Mary Hospital, Evergreen Park, IL
50,000	Christ Hospital and Medical Center, Oak Lawn, IL
5,000	Calvary Rehabilitation Center, Phoenix, AZ

Religion

15,000	Roseland Christian Health Ministries, Chicago, IL

First Security Bank Of Idaho Na

Company Contact
Boise, ID

Company Description
Employees: 7,530
SIC(s): 6021 National Commercial Banks.
Parent Company: First Security Corp., Salt Lake City, UT, United States

Nonmonetary Support
Type: Donated Equipment; In-kind Services; Loaned Employees; Loaned Executives

Corporate Sponsorship
Range: less than $1,500,000
Type: Arts & cultural events; Sports events; Music & entertainment events
Contact: Amy McDevitt, Vice President
Note: Sponsors First Security Summer and Winter Games.

Giving Contact
Celeste Keller, Vice President
First Security Bank of Idaho, NA
PO Box 7069
Boise, ID 83730
Phone: (208)393-2079
Fax: (208)393-2187

Description
Organization Type: Corporate Giving Program
Giving Locations: ID
Grant Types: Capital, Endowment, General Support.

Financial Summary
Total Giving: $430,000 (fiscal year ending , 1998 approx); $395,000 (fiscal 1997 approx). Note: Contributes through corporate direct giving program only.

Typical Recipients
Arts & Humanities: Arts & Humanities-General
Civic & Public Affairs: Civic & Public Affairs-General
Education: Education-General
Social Services: Social Services-General

Application Procedures
Initial Contact: a brief letter of inquiry
Application Requirements: a description of organization, amount requested, purpose of funds sought, recently audited financial statement, list of board members, and proof of tax-exempt status
Deadlines: September 1

Corporate Officials
Spencer Fox Eccles: chairman, chief executive officer, director B Ogden, UT 1934. ED University of Utah BS (1956); Columbia University MA (1959). PRIM CORP EMPL chairman, chief executive officer, director, president: First Security Corp. CORP AFFIL director: Zions Corp.; director: Zions Corp. Mercantile Institute; director: Union Pacific Corp.; director: First Security Insurance Inc.; director: Merc Institute; director: Anderson Lumber Co. NONPR AFFIL member: Bankers Roundtable; member advisory council: University Utah Business College; member: American Bankers Association. CLUB AFFIL mem: Alta Club; mem: Salt Lake Country Club.
Amy McDevitt: vice president PRIM CORP EMPL vice president: First Security Bank of Idaho NA.
J. Patrick McMurray: president PRIM CORP EMPL president: First Security Bank NA.

Giving Program Officials
Celeste Keller: manager PRIM CORP EMPL vice president: First Security Bank of Idaho NA.

Grants Analysis
Total Grants: $430,000 (approx)

First Source Corp.

Company Contact
South Bend, IN

Company Description
Assets: US$1,987,100,000
Employees: 802
SIC(s): 6022 State Commercial Banks.

First Source Foundation

Giving Contact
Mary Sonneborn Hugus, Trust Officer
Care of First Source Bank
PO Box 1602
South Bend, IN 46601
Phone: (219)235-2000
Fax: (219)235-2771

Description

Founded: 1952
EIN: 356034211
Organization Type: Corporate Foundation
Giving Locations: IN
Grant Types: General Support.

Financial Summary

Total Giving: $1,055,066 (1998); $140,080 (1997); $97,000 (1996)
Giving Analysis: Giving for 1997 includes: foundation ($88,451); foundation grants to United Way ($51,629); 1998: foundation ($1,055,066)
Assets: $12,184,556 (1998); $12,511,195 (1997); $7,281,096 (1996)
Gifts Received: $951,907 (1998); $2,338,732 (1994); $258,445 (1993). Note: Contributions are received from First Source Corp.

Typical Recipients

Arts & Humanities: Arts Centers, Historic Preservation, History & Archaeology, Libraries, Museums/Galleries, Music, Public Broadcasting
Civic & Public Affairs: Botanical Gardens/Parks, Business/Free Enterprise, Community Foundations, Economic Development, Economic Policy, Civic & Public Affairs-General, Housing, Minority Business, Municipalities/Towns, Parades/Festivals, Urban & Community Affairs
Education: Arts/Humanities Education, Business Education, Colleges & Universities, Economic Education, Education Associations, Education Funds, Elementary Education (Private), Engineering/Technological Education, Education-General, International Exchange, Medical Education, Private Education (Precollege), Public Education (Precollege), Secondary Education (Private), Secondary Education (Public), Student Aid
Health: Health Funds, Health Organizations, Hospices, Hospitals, Mental Health, Preventive Medicine/Wellness Organizations, Public Health
Religion: Bible Study/Translation, Religious Organizations, Religious Welfare
Social Services: Animal Protection, Big Brother/Big Sister, Child Abuse, Community Service Organizations, Crime Prevention, Delinquency & Criminal Rehabilitation, Family Services, Food/Clothing Distribution, Homes, People with Disabilities, Recreation & Athletics, Shelters/Homelessness, Substance Abuse, United Funds/United Ways, YMCA/YWCA/YMHA/YWHA, Youth Organizations

Contributions Analysis

Note: Total contributions in 1998.

Application Procedures

Application Requirements: Send a written statement of purpose concerning grant request.
Deadlines: None.

Corporate Officials

Christopher J. Murphy, III: president, chief executive officer, director B Washington, DC 1946. ED University of Notre Dame BA (1968); University of Virginia JD (1971); Harvard University Graduate School of Business Administration MBA (1973). PRIM CORP EMPL president, chief executive officer, director: First Source Corp. CORP AFFIL director: Trust Corp. Mortgage Inc.; director: Quality Dining Inc.; director: Titan Holding; director: Comair Inc.; director: Omega Health System; chairman: 1st Source Industry Inc.; chairman, chief executive officer: 1st Source Bank; chairman: 1st Source Capital Corp. NONPR AFFIL member: Virginia Bar Association; international board director, member: Young President Organization; member: Saint Joseph County Bar Association; advisory council: Notre Dame College Arts and Letters; member: Robert Morris Associates; director, chairman: National Association Publically Traded Companies; member: National Association Securities Dealers; member: National Association Business Economists; member: Indiana Bar Association; chairman: Medical Education Foundation; member: American Bankers Association; member: American Bar Association.
Ernestine Morris Raclin: chairman emeritus, director B South Bend, IN 1927. ED Saint Mary's College (1947). PRIM CORP EMPL chairman emeritus, director: First Source Corp. CORP AFFIL chairman emeritus: 1st Source Bank.

Foundation Officials

Harry Gerber: director
Christopher J. Murphy, III: director (see above)
Ernestine Morris Raclin: chairman, director (see above)

Grants Analysis

Disclosure Period: calendar year ending 1998
Total Grants: $1,055,066
Number of Grants: 24
Average Grant: $2,394*
Highest Grant: $1,000,000
Typical Range: $500 to $3,000
***Note:** Average grant figure excludes highest grant.

Recent Grants

Note: Grants derived from 1998 Form 990.

Arts & Humanities

500	Mishawaka-Penn Library, Mishawaka, IN -- Charitable

Civic & Public Affairs

25,000	Northern Indiana Community Foundation, South Bend, IN -- Charitable
2,000	Walkerton Economic Development Foundation, Walkerton, IN -- Charitable
1,000	Fernwood Botanic Garden, Niles, MI -- Charitable
1,000	Pulaski County Community Development, Winimac, IN -- Charitable
500	Starke County Community Foundation, Logansport, IN -- Charitable

Education

1,000,000	University of Notre Dame, Notre Dame, IN -- Charitable
6,066	Bethel College, Mishawka, IN -- Charitable
2,000	Hebrew Day School, South Bend, IN -- Charitable
1,500	Indiana University Foundation, South Bend, IN -- Charitable
500	Ancilla College, Donaldson, IN -- Charitable
500	Junior Achievement, Elkhart, IN -- Charitable
500	Stanley Clark School, South Bend, IN -- Charitable

Health

500	Mental Health Association, South Bend, IN -- Charitable
500	St. Joseph's Care Foundation, South Bend, IN -- Charitable

Social Services

3,000	Bashor Home, Goshen, IN -- Charitable
2,000	Goodwill Industries of Michiana, Inc, South Bend, IN -- Charitable
1,500	Ymca-Ywca Foundation, South Bend, IN -- Charitable
1,000	Crime Stoppers, South Bend, IN -- Charitable
1,000	Humane Society, Mishawaka, IN -- Charitable
500	Boys & Girls Club of Marshall City, Plymouth, IN -- Charitable
500	Child Abuse Prevention Service, Elkhart, IN -- Charitable
500	Manitou Mountain, Rochester, IN -- Charitable

First Tennessee National Corp.

Company Contact

Memphis, TN
Web: http://www.ftb.com

Company Description

Former Name: First Tennessee Bank.
Assets: US$18,400,000,000 (1999)
Employees: 7,585 (1999)
SIC(s): 6021 National Commercial Banks, 6712 Bank Holding Companies.

Nonmonetary Support

Range: $5,000 - $15,000
Type: Donated Equipment; Donated Products; In-kind Services; Loaned Employees; Loaned Executives; Workplace Solicitation
Contact: Sue Jacks, Corporate Communications

Corporate Sponsorship

Type: Arts & cultural events; Sports events; Festivals/fairs
Contact: Terry Lee, Contact
Note: Also sponsors educational causes and marketing promotions.

First Tennessee Foundation

Giving Contact

J. Terrence Lee, Senior Vice President, Corporate Communications
First Tennessee National Corp.
PO Box 84
Memphis, TN 38101
Phone: (901)523-4352
Fax: (901)523-4354
Email: jth@ixlmemphis.com

Description

Organization Type: Corporate Foundation
Giving Locations: TN: headquarters and operating communities
Grant Types: Capital, Challenge, Endowment, General Support, Professorship, Project.

Giving Philosophy

'First Tennessee is eager to be a partner with other community-spirited organizations in the development of our city and its people. .. We invite community organizations to tell us about themselves, to get to know us and to let us get to know them and the work they do. We are especially interested in hearing about projects with a development purpose--that is, projects that, if conducted successfully, hold the promise of providing wealth and promoting self-sufficiency.'
Contributions: Program Guidelines and Application Procedures

Financial Summary

Total Giving: $4,400,000 (fiscal year ending , 1999 approx); $4,000,000 (fiscal 1998 approx); $1,100,000 (fiscal 1996 approx). Note: Contributes through corporate direct giving program and foundation.

Typical Recipients

Arts & Humanities: Arts Associations & Councils, Arts Centers, Arts Festivals, Arts Funds, Arts Institutes, Community Arts, Dance, Ethnic & Folk Arts, Historic Preservation, Libraries, Museums/Galleries, Music, Opera, Performing Arts, Public Broadcasting, Theater, Visual Arts
Civic & Public Affairs: Business/Free Enterprise, Civil Rights, Economic Development, Professional &

Trade Associations, Public Policy, Urban & Community Affairs, Zoos/Aquariums
Education: Colleges & Universities, Economic Education, Elementary Education (Private), Faculty Development, Preschool Education, Public Education (Precollege)
Environment: Environment-General
Health: Hospitals
Social Services: Community Service Organizations, United Funds/United Ways, Volunteer Services, Youth Organizations

Contributions Analysis

Giving Priorities: Arts, civic affairs, education, health, and social service.
Note: Focus of priorities is shifting toward emphasis on education and parental involvement in education.

Application Procedures

Initial Contact: a brief letter of inquiry to determine interest; proposal will be invited
Application Requirements: (after interest has been shown by First Tennessee Bank) a proposal that includes: name, address, telephone number and contact person of organization; brief a description of organization's history, accomplishments, and goals; objectives of program to be funded; amount sought in relation to total need; expected project outcomes; proposed evaluation method; geographic area and number of people served; current operating budget, expected project costs, and most recently audited financial statement; other funding sources, including government, individuals, foundations, corporations, and united funds; list of officers, board of directors, and other principles of the organization; involvement of volunteers in the organization; and proof of tax-exempt status volunteers in the organization; and proof of tax-exempt status
Deadlines: by the October prior to the year for which funding is requested
Review Process: after initial inquiry, notification within four weeks if written proposal is sought; complete review may take up to two months
Evaluative Criteria: relation to contributions policy objectives; extent to which project will prevent community problems or develop financial resources to respond to such problems; extent to which funding will promote self-sufficiency; community's need for program and lack of duplication of existing services; organization's record of accomplishment; community support; financial condition, management, and administrative costs of organization
Decision Notification: ongoing basis, with review process taking as long as two months; applicants notified in February of status of requests for that year
Notes: The program is decentralized; apply to Memphis office for proposals with a statewide or Memphis area focus; apply to local bank president for proposals of a local or regional focus. Very few unsolicited requests are accepted.

Restrictions

Grants are not made to individuals; charities sponsored solely by a single civic organization; charities that redistribute funds to other organizations, except recognized united funds and arts funds; member agencies of the United Way or united arts funds; bank 'clearinghouse' organizations; religious, veterans, social, athletic, or fraternal organizations; political organizations or other groups promoting a specific ideological point of view; trips or tours; operating budget deficits; multiyear commitments of four years or more; endowments; tickets to fund-raising benefits; goodwill advertising; or member agencies of united funds. tickets to fund-raising benefits; goodwill advertising; or member agencies of united funds.

Corporate Officials

John C. Kelley, Jr.: president Memphis Banking Group B 1943. ED Memphis State University (1966). PRIM NONPR EMPL president: First Tennessee Bank National Association.

Grants Analysis

Total Grants: $4,400,000 (approx)

First Union Bank

Company Contact

1500 Market Street, 42nd Floor
Philadelphia, PA 19101-7618
Phone: (215)973-8059

Company Description

Former Name: CoreStates Bank; CoreStates New Jersey National Bank.
Revenue: US$4,197,300,000
Profit: US$649,100,000
Employees: 19,114
SIC(s): 6000 Depository Institutions, 6700 Holding & Other Investment Offices.
Parent Company: First Union Corp., One First Union Center, Charlotte, NC, United States

Nonmonetary Support

Type: In-kind Services

Corporate Sponsorship

Type: Arts & cultural events

First Union Regional Foundation

Giving Contact

Ms. Bronal Z. Harris, Vice President, Community Development & Contributions
First Union Regional Foundation
1339 Chestnut Street
Philadelphia, PA 19107
Phone: (215)973-8022
Email: bronal.harris@firstunion.com

Description

Founded: 1985
EIN: 222625990
Organization Type: Corporate Foundation
Giving Locations: PA
Grant Types: Employee Matching Gifts, General Support, Multiyear/Continuing Support, Project.

Financial Summary

Total Giving: $9,663,363 (1997); $205,000 (1996); $277,500 (1995)
Giving Analysis: Giving for 1997 includes: foundation ($9,663,363)
Assets: $32,908,876 (1997); $4,781,145 (1996); $3,281,428 (1995)
Gifts Received: $36,499,168 (1997); $969,193 (1992); $504,553 (1990)

Typical Recipients

Arts & Humanities: Community Arts, Dance, Historic Preservation, History & Archaeology, Museums/Galleries, Music, Opera, Public Broadcasting, Theater
Civic & Public Affairs: Asian American Affairs, Business/Free Enterprise, Chambers of Commerce, Economic Development, Economic Policy, Employment/Job Training, Civic & Public Affairs-General, Hispanic Affairs, Housing, Law & Justice, Legal Aid, Minority Business, Municipalities/Towns, Public Policy, Urban & Community Affairs, Women's Affairs, Zoos/Aquariums
Education: Colleges & Universities, Education Associations, Education Funds, Education-General, International Exchange, Leadership Training, Private Education (Precollege), Science/Mathematics Education, Special Education
Health: AIDS/HIV, Cancer, Children's Health/Hospitals, Clinics/Medical Centers, Emergency/Ambulance Services, Hospitals, Hospitals (University Affiliated), Medical Rehabilitation, Medical Research, Single-Disease Health Associations
International: Health Care/Hospitals, International Affairs, International Organizations, International Relations
Religion: Churches, Religious Welfare
Social Services: At-Risk Youth, Big Brother/Big Sister, Child Welfare, Community Service Organizations, Emergency Relief, People with Disabilities, Substance Abuse, United Funds/United Ways, YMCA/YWCA/YMHA/YWHA, Youth Organizations

Contributions Analysis

Giving Priorities: Priorities include civic concerns, health organizations, education, and the arts.
Arts & Humanities: 5% to 10%. Funds music organizations that promote minorities through education and music performances.
Civic & Public Affairs: About 60%. Major support goes to the community, including neighborhood preservation, building and developing low-income housing, and stabilizing the community. Also funds mentoring programs, programs that develop leadership skills in minorities, and economic development and growth.
Education: 10% to 15%. Funding goes to programs that assist children with severe learning disabilities, and educational organizations and institutes.
Health: 10% to 15%. Supports medical centers, AIDS awareness programs, and research institutes.
Social Services: About 10%. Supports organizations that provide runaway and homeless young people with assistance, YMCA, American Red Cross fordisaster relief, and Big Brothers and Big Sisters.

Application Procedures

Initial Contact: The foundation has no formal grant application procedure or application form.
Deadlines: None.

Additional Information

Publications: Foundation Annual Report

Corporate Officials

Terrence A. Larsen: chairman, chief executive officer B Chicago, IL 1946. ED University of Dallas BA (1968); Texas A&M University PhD (1971). PRIM CORP EMPL chairman, chief executive officer: First Union Bank. CORP AFFIL director: CoreStates Bank NA; vice chairman: First Union Corp. NONPR AFFIL chairman: Greater Philadelphia Chamber of Commerce; Urban Affairs Coalition.

Foundation Officials

Joseph C. Bono: vice president
Noreen Casey: senior vice president
Charles L. Coltman, III: vice chairman PRIM CORP EMPL president: First Union Bank International. CORP AFFIL director: Congress Financial Corp.; director: CoreStates Bank NA.
Bronal Z. Harris: secretary, treasurer
Terrence A. Larsen: chairman (see above)
Thomas J. Patterson, Jr.: senior vice president

Grants Analysis

Disclosure Period: calendar year ending 1996
Total Grants: $205,000
Number of Grants: 7
Average Grant: $29,286
Highest Grant: $50,000
Typical Range: $10,000 to $50,000

Recent Grants

Note: Grants derived from 1996 Form 990.

Civic & Public Affairs

50,000 Latin American Economic Development

	Association, Camden, NJ -- to develop adult skills training center
50,000	Philadelphia Commercial Development Corporation, Philadelphia, PA -- support startup of One Stop Capital Shop
25,000	PICPA Foundation for Education and Research, Philadelphia, PA -- first of two payments on pledge for Pennsylvania Tax Blueprint Project
10,000	Southwest-Belmont Community Association, Philadelphia, PA -- support to purchase buildings for programs

Education

10,000	Stratford Friends School, Havertown, PA -- support for 21st Century Campaign

Health

10,000	University of Pennsylvania Medical Center, Philadelphia, PA -- support Philadelphia Community Health Internship Program

Social Services

50,000	United Way of Greater Lehigh Valley, Bethlehem, PA -- support of matching challenge grant effort

First Union Corp.

 Number 21 of Top 100 Corporate Givers

Company Contact

One First Union Center
Charlotte, NC 28288-0570
Web: http://www.firstunion.com

Company Description

Revenue: US$21,543,000,000
Profit: US$2,891,000,000
Employees: 44,333
Fortune Rank: 67, per FORTUNE Magazine's list of 500 Largest U.S. Corporations (1999).
FF 67
SIC(s): 6162 Mortgage Bankers & Correspondents, 6719 Holding Companies Nec.

First Union Foundation

Giving Contact

Judy Allison, Senior Vice President, Corp. Contributions & Community Involvement
First Union Corp.
301 S. College St.
Charlotte, NC 28288-0143
Phone: (704)374-6649
Fax: (704)374-2484

Description

Founded: 1987
EIN: 566288589
Organization Type: Corporate Foundation
Giving Locations: headquarters and operating communities.
Grant Types: Capital, Emergency, Employee Matching Gifts, Endowment, Fellowship, General Support, Matching, Multiyear/Continuing Support.
Note: Employee matching gift ratio: 1 to 1 for education only.

Giving Philosophy

'As a leader in the financial services industry, First Union is committed to serving the needs of our communities through focused investments of company resources and employee talents.
'First Union will strategically focus on innovative programs that have a measurable impact and: expand the availability of educational resources; improve the quality of education; help children and youth reach their full potential; enable individuals in our communities to overcome barriers to self-sufficiency; and support community development and revitalization efforts.
'In allocating our resources, First Union will give special consideration to programs that: have a high level of First Union employee involvement; and are collaborative efforts that leverage our investment in our communities. First Union is committed to providing unparalleled service and responsiveness to our communities, employees, customers, and shareholders.'*First Union Corporate Contributions*

Financial Summary

Total Giving: $38,194,000 (1998); $11,702,000 (1997); $11,107,300 (1996). Note: Contributes through corporate direct giving program and foundation. See separate listing for First Union Regional Foundation contributions. 1997 Giving excludes employee support ($11,697,000) and employee volunteer support ($16,373,000).
Giving Analysis: Giving for 1997 includes: foundation ($11,702,000); 1998: foundation ($29,974,000); corporate direct giving ($7,211,000); corporate matching gifts ($1,009,000)
Assets: $2,252,724 (1997); $1,986,568 (1996); $465,816 (1993)
Gifts Received: $10,712,381 (1997); $10,524,930 (1996); $7,238,220 (1993). Note: Contributions were received from First Union Corp, Dominion Charitable Trust, estate of York Cress, Savannah Charitable Trust, and miscellaneous contributors.

Typical Recipients

Arts & Humanities: Arts Associations & Councils, Arts Centers, Arts Festivals, Arts Funds, Arts Institutes, Community Arts, Dance, Ethnic & Folk Arts, Historic Preservation, Libraries, Literary Arts, Museums/Galleries, Music, Opera, Performing Arts, Public Broadcasting, Theater, Visual Arts
Civic & Public Affairs: Business/Free Enterprise, Chambers of Commerce, Clubs, Economic Development, Economic Policy, Employment/Job Training, Hispanic Affairs, Housing, Municipalities/Towns, Philanthropic Organizations, Safety, Urban & Community Affairs, Women's Affairs, Zoos/Aquariums
Education: Agricultural Education, Arts/Humanities Education, Business Education, Colleges & Universities, Community & Junior Colleges, Continuing Education, Economic Education, Education Associations, Education Funds, Education Reform, Engineering/Technological Education, Faculty Development, Legal Education, Literacy, Medical Education, Minority Education, Preschool Education, Private Education (Precollege), Public Education (Precollege), Science/Mathematics Education, Social Sciences Education, Special Education
Environment: Environment-General
Health: Children's Health/Hospitals, Emergency/Ambulance Services, Geriatric Health, Health Funds, Health Organizations, Hospices, Hospitals, Medical Rehabilitation, Mental Health, Research/Studies Institutes, Single-Disease Health Associations
Religion: Churches
Science: Observatories & Planetariums, Science Exhibits & Fairs, Science Museums, Scientific Centers & Institutes, Scientific Organizations
Social Services: Child Welfare, Community Centers, Community Service Organizations, Counseling, Day Care, Delinquency & Criminal Rehabilitation, Domestic Violence, Emergency Relief, Family Planning, Family Services, Food/Clothing Distribution, Homes, People with Disabilities, Senior Services, Shelters/Homelessness, Substance Abuse, United Funds/United Ways, Volunteer Services, YMCA/YWCA/YMHA/YWHA, Youth Organizations

Contributions Analysis

Giving Priorities: Social welfare, hospitals, health organizations, education, the arts, and civics.
Arts & Humanities: 19%. Supports arts funds and councils, museums, cultural centers, visual and performing arts organizations, and public libraries.
Civic & Public Affairs: 22%. Supports affordable housing, leadership development, environmental protection and conservation, and economic development.
Education: 27%. Supports special programs for public elementary and secondary schools (preK-12), public education funds and other programs that effect positive, systemic change in education, education-related programs such as Junior Achievement and drop-out prevention programs, and private and public institutions of higher education.
Health: 13%. Includes support for hospitals and medical centers, youth organizations, and local affiliates of national health and human services organizations.
Social Services: 19%. Supports youth organizations, community centers, homeless shelters and causes, and United Way.
Note: Total contributions made in 1998.

Application Procedures

Initial Contact: Submit a written request to the contributions office in the state in which the proposed program is located.
Application Requirements: Include a cover letter of not more than two pages with the following information about the project: objectives and background, budget and sources of funding, demonstration of need, specific plans and timetable, description of current and long term funding plans, and qualifications of organization and personnel involved. Also include current operating budget, list of board members and key management, proof of tax-exempt status, copy of the most recent audit, contact information for project, and First Union's relationship with organization, including contributions and employee volunteers.
Deadlines: None.
Evaluative Criteria: Geographic location; involvement of company employees; quality of management and effectiveness of organization; objectives well-stated and supported by community; sources of support; financial condition, based on annual reports and budgets; record of achievement and potential for success; amount spent on fund raising and administration; project's benefit to community; number of people served; compatibility with company's giving priorities; nonduplication of services now being provided; probability of success and for ongoing funding; collaboration and effective use of existing resources; innovative approach to achieve positive, measurable outcomes; incorporation of accountability and evaluation measures; contribution to long-term improvement of community.

Restrictions

The foundation does not make grants to support the following: individuals; political causes, candidates, or organizations whose primary purpose is to influence legislation; religious, veteran, or fraternal organizations or private clubs; travel or conferences; pre-college level private schools, except through the Educational Matching Gifts Program; organizations that already receive First Union support through United Way or united arts drives, except for approved capital campaigns; international organizations; intermediary organizations or agents that pass funds through to other organizations; or capital projects, unless they are part of a community-wide capital campaign. The foundation also does not make rants to support special events, fund-raising activities, sports competitions, or other projects for which First Union receives benefits or privileges. Grants are only provided to organizations recognized as tax-exempt under Section 501(c)(3) of the Internal Revenue Code, or to units of government.

Additional Information

Requests are handled regionally. Direct requests for funding to the contributions/community involvement contact in your region:

Connecticut, New York, & New Jersey: Fran Durst, 370 Scotch Road, Trenton, NJ 08628 (609)530-7347
Florida: Debbie Clark, P.O. Box 44250, Jacksonville, FL 32231 (904)361-3147
Georgia: Gwen Adams, 999 Peachtree Street NE, Atlanta, GA 30309 (404)225-4329
Pennsylvania & Delaware: Kevin Dow, 1339 Chestnut Street, 13th Fl., Philadelphia, PA 19107 (215)973-4181
Tennessee: Chris McComish, 150 4th Avenue N, 23rd Fl., Nashville, TN 37219 (615)251-0746
North Carolina, South Carolina, Virginia, Maryland, & Washington, DC: Robby Russell, 301 South College Street, Charlotte, NC 28288 (704)374-4912
First Union Securities: 10700 Wheat First Drive, Glen Allen, VA 23060 (804)965-2415
Publications: Corporate Contributions Pamphlet

Corporate Officials

Robert T. Atwood: executive vice president, chief financial officer counsel B 1940. ED University of North Carolina BS (1958); University of North Carolina Law School LLB (1964). PRIM CORP EMPL executive vice president, chief financial officer: First Union Corp. NONPR AFFIL treasurer: North Carolina Performing Arts Center.
Benjamin P. Jenkins, III: vice chairman general bank PRIM CORP EMPL vice chairman general bank: First Union Corp. ADD CORP EMPL president, chief operating officer: First Union - Florida.
G. Kennedy Thompson: president, chief operating officer ED University of North Carolina BS; Wake Forest University MS. PRIM CORP EMPL president, chief operating officer: First Union Corp.
Mark C. Treanor: senior vice president, general counsel PRIM CORP EMPL senior vice president, general counsel: First Union Corp.

Foundation Officials

Judith N. Allison: senior vice president, director corporate contributions
Robert T. Atwood: director (see above)
Malcolm E. Everett, III: director B 1946. ED University of Georgia. PRIM CORP EMPL president: First Union National Bank.
Benjamin P. Jenkins, III: member (see above)
Don R. Johnson: director PRIM CORP EMPL executive vice president: First Union Corp.
G. Kennedy Thompson: member (see above)
Mark C. Treanor: member (see above)

Grants Analysis

Disclosure Period: calendar year ending 1997
Total Grants: $11,702,000
Number of Grants: 2,000 (approx)
Average Grant: $5,851 (approx)
Highest Grant: $500,000
Typical Range: $500 to $10,000

Recent Grants

Note: Grants derived from 1997 Form 990.

Arts & Humanities

200,000	United Arts Council, Greensboro, NC
180,000	Avenue of the Arts, Philadelphia, PA
117,000	Arts and Science Council Charlotte Mecklenburg, Charlotte, NC
100,000	Jacksonville Symphony Association, Jacksonville, FL -- support combined campaign
83,333	South Florida Performing Arts Center Foundation, Miami, FL
50,000	New Jersey Performing Arts Center Corporation, Newark, NJ
50,000	United Arts Council of Central Florida, Orlando, FL
50,000	United Arts Council of Central Florida, Orlando, FL
41,667	South Florida Performing Arts Center Foundation, Miami, FL
41,667	South Florida Performing Arts Center Foundation, Miami, FL

Civic & Public Affairs

500,000	Chamber of Commerce Tax Credit -- civic
250,000	Lynnwood Foundation -- civic
250,000	Women's Community Revitalization Project, Philadelphia, PA -- civic
100,000	Metropolitan Business Foundation, Richmond, VA -- civic
70,000	Greater Philadelphia First Foundation, Philadelphia, PA -- civic
50,000	Florida Chamber of Commerce Educational Foundation, Tallahassee, FL -- educational
50,000	Foundation for the Carolinas, Charlotte, NC -- support Community Building Task Force
50,000	Global Transpark Foundation, Kinston, NC

Education

364,000	University of Connecticut Foundation, Storrs, CT -- educational
200,000	Children's Literacy Initiative, Philadelphia, PA -- educational
200,000	Cities in Schools, Ardmore, OK -- educational
50,000	New Jersey Academy for Aquatic Sciences, Camden, NJ
50,000	School District of Philadelphia, Philadelphia, PA -- support Children Achieving
50,000	University of North Carolina Chapel Hill, Chapel Hill, NC -- educational
50,000	University of Virginia, Charlottesville, VA -- educational
50,000	VCU Engineering and Seigal Center -- educational
40,000	Florida State University College of Business, Tallahassee, FL -- educational
40,000	Florida State University College of Business, Tallahassee, FL -- educational
40,000	North Carolina State University Foundation, Raleigh, NC -- educational
40,000	United Negro College Fund, New York, NY -- educational

Health

50,000	American Red Cross Northeast Florida Chapter, FL -- health and welfare
50,000	Charlotte-Mecklenburg Hospital Authority Foundation, Charlotte, NC -- support Carolinas ALS Center
50,000	Danbury Hospital Development Fund, Danbury, CT -- health and welfare
50,000	Deborah Hospital Foundation, Browns Mills, NJ -- health and welfare
50,000	Mayo Foundation, Rochester, MN -- health and welfare

Science

40,000	Exploris, Raleigh, NC

Social Services

339,100	United Way of Central Carolinas, Charlotte, NC
200,000	North Carolina Partnership for Children, Raleigh, NC -- educational
200,000	United Way of Dade County, Miami, FL
182,700	United Way of Southeast Pennsylvania, Wayne, PA
170,000	United Way of Northeast Florida, Jacksonville, FL
140,000	United Way of Essex and West Hudson, Newark, NJ
130,000	United Way, Atlanta, GA
100,000	North Ward Center, Newark, NJ -- educational
90,000	United Way of Roanoke Valley, Roanoke, VA
60,000	Heart of Florida United Way, Orlando, FL
60,000	United Way of Broward County, Fort Lauderdale, FL
55,500	United Way of the Greater Lehigh Valley, Bethlehem, PA
50,000	YMCA, Charlotte, NC -- health and welfare
41,000	United Way of Wilkes County, North Wilkesboro, NC

First Union National Bank, NA

Company Contact

Charlotte, NC
Web: http://www.firstunion.com

Company Description

Former Name: First Fidelity Bank.
SIC(s): 6021 National Commercial Banks, 6162 Mortgage Bankers & Correspondents, 6211 Security Brokers & Dealers, 6712 Bank Holding Companies.
Parent Company: First Fidelity Bancorp

Nonmonetary Support

Type: Donated Equipment; In-kind Services
Note: Co. provides nonmonetary support.

Giving Contact

Kevin Dow, Vice President, Contributions
First Union National Bank, NA
Widener Building
PA 1252
1339 Chestnut
Philadelphia, PA 19107
Phone: (215)973-4278
Fax: (215)973-8850
Web: http://www.firstunion.com/involve/

Alternate Contact

Susan Johnson
Phone: (215)973-4181

Description

Organization Type: Corporate Giving Program
Giving Locations: PA operating locations.
Grant Types: Capital, Employee Matching Gifts, General Support, Multiyear/Continuing Support, Operating Expenses, Project.
Note: Employee matching gift ratio: 2 to 1 for gifts to four-year, degree-granting colleges, universities, graduate schools, and federated campaigns up to $500, and on a 1 to 1 basis up to $1,500 annually. The bank matches gifts by retirees up to $250 annually.

Financial Summary

Total Giving: Contributes through corporate direct giving program only.

Typical Recipients

Arts & Humanities: Arts Appreciation, Arts Associations & Councils, Arts Centers, Arts Institutes, Community Arts, Dance, Ethnic & Folk Arts, Libraries, Literary Arts, Museums/Galleries, Music, Opera, Performing Arts, Public Broadcasting, Theater
Civic & Public Affairs: Business/Free Enterprise, Civil Rights, Economic Development, Employment/Job Training, Housing, Law & Justice, Legal Aid, Urban & Community Affairs, Women's Affairs, Zoos/Aquariums
Education: Arts/Humanities Education, Business Education, Colleges & Universities, Community & Junior Colleges, Economic Education, International Exchange, Literacy, Minority Education
Health: Geriatric Health, Hospices
International: International Relations
Social Services: Child Welfare, Community Centers, Community Service Organizations, Delinquency & Criminal Rehabilitation, Domestic Violence, Emergency Relief, Family Planning, Family Services, Food/Clothing Distribution, Homes, Recreation & Athletics, Senior Services, Shelters/Homelessness, Substance

Abuse, United Funds/United Ways, Volunteer Services, Youth Organizations

Contributions Analysis

Arts & Humanities: Interests include arts institutions which promote the Philadelphia area as a business location, and cultural institutions with a broad audience appeal. Recipients include arts centers, ethnic arts, libraries, museums, performing arts, and public broadcasting.
Civic & Public Affairs: Prefers to support organizations that enhance the business and economic climate of the area it serves. Recipients include better government, economics, housing, and the environment.
Education: Company reports that education is its top giving priority. Supports local four-year colleges and universities, an employee matching gift program, and economic education.
Health: Recipients include hospitals that are able to make a strong documented case of service to First Fidelity employees, their families, and customers, or that serve a special need in the community not adequately met by others. Youth agencies serving inner-city youth, children, or customers in more than one area of First Union's market are also funded.

Application Procedures

Initial Contact: Letter and full proposal.
Application Requirements: A description of organization, record as a viable organization for at least three years, information about governing board serving without compensation and holding regular meetings, amount requested, purpose of funds sought, detailed annual budget translating program plans into financial terms, audited financial statement, and proof of 501(c)(3) status.
Deadlines: September 1.
Notes: Applicants should keep grant requests to a single-page letter.

Restrictions

The company does not support individuals, religious organizations for sectarian purposes, political or lobbying groups, veterans or fraternal organizations other than projects which directly benefit the community, missionary activities abroad, organizations receiving government support, organizations that do not meet the Better Business Bureau's standard for charitable solicitations, organizations in violation of state or local government regulations, multi-year capital drive commitments, national philanthropies or organizations, or endowments.
The company also does not support human service agencies already receiving support from the United Way, annual operating budgets of hospitals, medical research, annual operating campaigns of individual four-year degree-granting colleges and universities and related graduate schools, or private or public secondary and elementary schools.

Additional Information

Special attention is given to proposals which advance and promote the economic life of the primary market area, and those that offer the broadest benefit to the community.
Contributions that support specific neighborhoods or localities are made through local branch offices. Usually the amount is less than $100.
Publications: Application Guidelines

Corporate Officials

Peter C. Palmieri: vice chairman, chief credit officer B Newark, NJ 1934. ED Harvard University; University of Dayton (1963). PRIM CORP EMPL vice chairman, chief credit officer: First Union National Bank, Northern Division. CORP AFFIL vice chairman, cheif credit officer, director: First Fidelity Bancorp.

Giving Program Officials

Jean Konrad: manager PRIM CORP EMPL vice president public affairs: First Union National Bank, NA.
David Newell: PRIM CORP EMPL senior vice president public affairs: First Union National Bank, NA. CORP AFFIL vice president public affairs & government: First Fidelity Bank NA New Jersey.

Grants Analysis

Disclosure Period: calendar year ending
Typical Range: $1,000 to $2,500

First Union Securities, Inc.

Company Contact

Riverfront Plaza
901 East Byrd Street
Richmond, VA 23219
Web: http://www.firstunionsec.com

Company Description

Acquired: Wheat First Union (1999).
Parent Company: First Union Corp., One First Union Center, Charlotte, NC, United States

Nonmonetary Support

Type: Donated Equipment
Note: Nonmonetary support is provided by the company.

Corporate Sponsorship

Type: Arts & cultural events; Festivals/fairs; Music & entertainment events; Pledge-a-thon

Wheat Foundation

Giving Contact

Robin Schilling, Associate Manager
First Union Securities, Inc.
PO Box 1357
Richmond, VA 23218-1357
Phone: (804)649-2311
Fax: (804)782-6698
Web: http://www.firstunionsec.com

Alternate Contact

Wheat First Union,
Riverfront Plaza
901 East Byrd Street
Richmond, VA 23219
Phone: 800-627-8625

Description

EIN: 546047119
Organization Type: Corporate Giving Program
Former Name: Wheat Foundation.
Former Name: Wheat, First Securities/Butcher & Singer Foundation.
Giving Locations: VA: Richmond change in giving area due to merger headquarters and operating communities.
Grant Types: Capital, Employee Matching Gifts, General Support.

Financial Summary

Total Giving: $2,660,366 (fiscal year ending March 31, 1998); $730,565 (fiscal 1997); $992,190 (fiscal 1996). Note: Contributes through corporate direct giving program only.
Giving Analysis: Giving for fiscal 1996 includes: corporate direct giving ($456,486); foundation ($408,503); foundation matching gifts ($127,201); fiscal 1997: foundation ($533,034); foundation matching gifts ($152,106); foundation grants to United Way ($41,425); foundation scholarships ($4,000); fiscal 1998: foundation ($2,265,540); foundation matching gifts ($337,326); foundation grants to United Way ($57,500)
Assets: $3,559,310 (fiscal 1997); $2,921,016 (fiscal 1996); $2,643,386 (fiscal 1994)
Gifts Received: $900,000 (fiscal 1998); $977,527 (fiscal 1997); $1,593,960 (fiscal 1994). Note: Contributions were received from Wheat First Securities, Inc.

Typical Recipients

Arts & Humanities: Arts Associations & Councils, Arts Centers, Arts Funds, Ballet, Ethnic & Folk Arts, Historic Preservation, History & Archaeology, Libraries, Museums/Galleries, Music, Opera, Performing Arts, Public Broadcasting, Theater
Civic & Public Affairs: Business/Free Enterprise, Community Foundations, Economic Development, Economic Policy, Civic & Public Affairs-General, Housing, Municipalities/Towns, Public Policy, Urban & Community Affairs, Women's Affairs
Education: Arts/Humanities Education, Business Education, Colleges & Universities, Community & Junior Colleges, Education Associations, Education Funds, Education Reform, Engineering/Technological Education, Faculty Development, Education-General, Legal Education, Medical Education, Minority Education, Private Education (Precollege), Religious Education, Student Aid
Environment: Air/Water Quality, Environment-General
Health: Cancer, Children's Health/Hospitals, Clinics/Medical Centers, Emergency/Ambulance Services, Eyes/Blindness, Health Organizations, Heart, Hospitals, Long-Term Care, Medical Research, Prenatal Health Issues, Single-Disease Health Associations
Religion: Jewish Causes, Religious Organizations, Religious Welfare
Science: Science Museums, Scientific Research
Social Services: Big Brother/Big Sister, Child Welfare, Community Centers, Community Service Organizations, Food/Clothing Distribution, People with Disabilities, Recreation & Athletics, Senior Services, Shelters/Homelessness, United Funds/United Ways, Youth Organizations

Contributions Analysis

Arts & Humanities: 12%. Funds symphony, performing arts, educational television, theater, and historic preservation.
Civic & Public Affairs: 23%. Supports municipalities, environmental concerns, and a business council.
Education: 40%. Funds are distributed to colleges and universities, primarily in Virginia, Pennsylvania, Maryland, and North Carolina. Also supports scholarship funds and higher education organizations.
Religion: 10%. Funds religious welfare.
Social Services: 15%. Supports the United Way and youth organizations.
Note: Total foundation contributions in 1998.

Application Procedures

Initial Contact: Send a letter of inquiry.
Application Requirements: Include a description of organization, amount requested, purpose of funds sought, recently audited financial statement, and proof of tax-exempt status.
Deadlines: None.
Review Process: Board meets quarterly.

Restrictions

Does not support individuals, religious organizations for sectarian purposes, political or lobbying groups, or organizations outside operating areas. Company does not support annual funds.

Additional Information

In February 1998, Wheat First Butcher Singer, Inc. merged with First Union Corp. to become Wheat First Union.

Wheat First Union Foundation has dissolved and reassembled as First Union Foundation.

Grants Analysis

Disclosure Period: fiscal year ending March 31, 1998
Total Grants: $2,265,400*
Number of Grants: 500 (approx)
Average Grant: $4,531
Highest Grant: $15,000
Typical Range: $500 to $5,000
***Note:** Giving excludes matching gifts; United Way.

Recent Grants

Note: Grants derived from 1998 Form 990.

Arts & Humanities

10,000	Center for the Arts & Sciences of West Virginia, Charleston, WV
10,000	Center for the Arts & Sciences of West Virginia, Charleston, WV
5,000	Philadelphia Museum of Art, Philadelphia, PA
5,000	Philadelphia Museum of Art, Philadelphia, PA
5,000	Philadelphia Museum of Art, Philadelphia, PA
5,000	Philadelphia Museum of Art, Philadelphia, PA
5,000	Philadelphia Museum of Art, Philadelphia, PA

Civic & Public Affairs

10,000	Richmond Metropolitan Habitat for Humanity, Richmond, VA
10,000	Richmond Metropolitan Habitat for Humanity, Richmond, VA
10,000	Richmond Metropolitan Habitat for Humanity, Richmond, VA
10,000	Richmond Metropolitan Habitat for Humanity, Richmond, VA
10,000	Richmond Metropolitan Habitat for Humanity, Richmond, VA
10,000	Richmond Metropolitan Habitat for Humanity, Richmond, VA
9,670	Richmond Forum, Richmond, VA
5,000	Community Foundation, Richmond, VA -- Leadership Metro Richmond Fund
5,000	George C. Marshall Foundation, Lexington, VA
5,000	George C. Marshall Foundation, Lexington, VA
5,000	Habitat for Humanity - Lancaster/Northumberland, Lancaster, PA

Education

15,000	Virginia Foundation for Independent Colleges, Richmond, VA
10,000	Center for the Arts & Sciences of West Virginia, Charleston, WV
10,000	Center for the Arts & Sciences of West Virginia, Charleston, WV
10,000	Pennsylvania Academy of Fine Arts, Philadelphia, PA -- Centennial Exhibition
10,000	Pennsylvania Academy of Fine Arts, Philadelphia, PA -- Centennial Exhibition
10,000	Pennsylvania Academy of Fine Arts, Philadelphia, PA -- Centennial Exhibition
10,000	Pennsylvania Academy of Fine Arts, Philadelphia, PA -- Centennial Exhibition
9,200	Virginia Commonwealth University, Richmond, VA
6,000	Howard University, Washington, DC
6,000	Howard University, Washington, DC
6,000	Randolph-Macon College, Lynchburg, VA
6,000	Randolph-Macon College, Lynchburg, VA
5,000	Allentown College of Saint Francis De Sales, Center Valley, PA -- Building Program
5,000	Allentown College of Saint Francis De Sales, Center Valley, PA -- Building Program
5,000	College of William & Mary, Williamsburg, VA -- Lectureship in International Finance
5,000	College of William & Mary, Williamsburg, VA -- Lectureship in International Finance
5,000	College of William & Mary, Williamsburg, VA -- Lectureship in International Finance
5,000	College of William & Mary, Williamsburg, VA -- Lectureship in International Finance
5,000	Trinity Episcopal School, Richmond, VA
5,000	Wake Forest University - Babcock Graduate School of Management, Winston-Salem, NC
5,000	Wake Forest University Babcock Graduate School of Management, Winston-Salem, NC

Religion

10,000	Sacred Heart Center, Richmond, VA -- Endowment
10,000	Sacred Heart Center, Richmond, VA -- Endowment
10,000	Sacred Heart Center, Richmond, VA -- Endowment
10,000	Sacred Heart Center, Richmond, VA -- Endowment

Social Services

25,000	United Way Services, Richmond, VA
6,000	Slam Dunk, Camden, DE
5,000	Meals on Wheels, Lynchburg, VA
5,000	Richmond Goodwill Industries, Inc., Richmond, VA
5,000	United Way of South Hampton Roads, Norfolk, VA
5,000	United Way of South Hampton Roads, Norfolk, VA
5,000	United Way of South Hampton Roads, Norfolk, VA

Firstar Bank Milwaukee NA

Company Contact

Milwaukee, WI

Company Description

Former Name: First Wisconsin National Bank of Milwaukee.
Employees: 3,000
SIC(s): 6021 National Commercial Banks.
Parent Company: Firstar Corp., 777 East Wisconsin Avenue, Milwaukee, WI, United States

Nonmonetary Support

Volunteer Programs: The Company has an active employee volunteer program.

Corporate Sponsorship

Type: Music & entertainment events
Note: Sponsors dinners.

Firstar Milwaukee Foundation

Giving Contact

Mr. Dennis Fredrickson, Secretary & Treasurer
Firstar Milwaukee Foundation
777 E. Wisconsin Ave.
Milwaukee, WI 53202
Phone: (414)765-4579
Fax: (414)765-6667

Description

EIN: 396042050
Organization Type: Corporate Foundation
Giving Locations: WI: Milwaukee
Grant Types: Capital, General Support, Multiyear/Continuing Support, Operating Expenses.

Financial Summary

Total Giving: $1,500,000 (1999 approx); $2,369,098 (1998); $1,508,603 (1997). Note: Contributes through corporate direct giving program and foundation.
Giving Analysis: Giving for 1996 includes: foundation ($970,377); foundation grants to United Way ($371,000); 1997: foundation ($1,098,218); foundation grants to United Way ($383,900); foundation scholarships ($26,485); 1998: foundation ($1,658,998); foundation grants to United Way ($710,100)
Assets: $26,581,413 (1998); $7,979,330 (1997); $7,820,831 (1996)
Gifts Received: $20,010,186 (1998); $500,000 (1997); $1,200,000 (1996). Note: Gifts were received from Firstar Bank Milwaukee, N.A.

Typical Recipients

Arts & Humanities: Arts Centers, Arts Institutes, Ballet, Dance, Historic Preservation, History & Archaeology, Libraries, Museums/Galleries, Music, Opera, Performing Arts, Theater
Civic & Public Affairs: African American Affairs, Business/Free Enterprise, Civil Rights, Economic Development, Employment/Job Training, Hispanic Affairs, Housing, Nonprofit Management, Parades/Festivals, Urban & Community Affairs, Women's Affairs, Zoos/Aquariums
Education: Business Education, Colleges & Universities, Economic Education, Education Funds, Education Reform, Engineering/Technological Education, Education-General, Health & Physical Education, Leadership Training, Literacy, Medical Education, Minority Education, Secondary Education (Public), Social Sciences Education, Student Aid
Health: Children's Health/Hospitals, Clinics/Medical Centers, Emergency/Ambulance Services, Health-General, Health Organizations, Heart, Hospices, Hospitals, Nursing Services, Single-Disease Health Associations, Transplant Networks/Donor Banks
Religion: Jewish Causes, Religious Welfare
Social Services: Child Welfare, Community Centers, Community Service Organizations, Delinquency & Criminal Rehabilitation, Family Services, People with Disabilities, Recreation & Athletics, Senior Services, Shelters/Homelessness, Substance Abuse, United Funds/United Ways, Volunteer Services, YMCA/YWCA/YMHA/YWHA, Youth Organizations

Contributions Analysis

Giving Priorities: Health, human services, higher education, the arts, and civic concerns.
Arts & Humanities: 30%. Primarily supports a performing arts fund. Also gives to museums, ballet, historic preservation, opera, symphonies, and libraries.
Civic & Public Affairs: 5%. About one-half supports economic and community development in Milwaukee. The remainder supports a variety of interests, including civil rights, professional organizations, public policy, nonprofit management, and zoos.
Education: 14%. Supports colleges and universities, exclusively in the state of Wisconsin.
Health: 3%. Supports single-disease health associations, medical research, nursing services, and health funds.
Religion: 1%.
Social Services: 47%. Recipients include youth organizations, religious welfare groups, community centers, child welfare, and programs for the aged.
Note: Total contributions made in 1998.

Application Procedures

Initial Contact: Send a letter of request.

Application Requirements: Include a description of organization; outline of project; amount requested; purpose of funds sought; recently audited financial statement; proof of tax-exempt status; budget for both project and organization; sources of funds received; names of officers and directors; statement of purpose; history of achievement; description of program activities and goals; other pertinent material.

Deadlines: None.

Restrictions

Foundation does give contributions to religious, charitable, scientific etc. organizations which were organized in the USA.

Corporate Officials

John A. Becker: president, chief operating officer, director B Kenosha, WI 1942. ED Marquette University BS (1963); Marquette University MBA (1965). PRIM CORP EMPL president, chief operating officer, director: Firstar Corp. CORP AFFIL director: Giddings & Lewis Corp.; chairman, executive vice president: First Wisconsin National Bank Milwaukee. NONPR AFFIL trustee: Marquette University.

Foundation Officials

Chris Michael Bauer: president B Milwaukee, WI 1948. ED University of Wisconsin BBA (1970); Marquette University MBA (1976). PRIM CORP EMPL chairman, chief executive officer, director: Firstar Bank of Milwaukee NA. CORP AFFIL director: American Automobile Association Michigan. NONPR AFFIL director: Saint Luke's Medical Center; director: University Wisconsin - Milwaukee Foundation; director: Next Door Foundation; director: Milwaukee Public Library Foundation; director: Milwaukee World Festival Inc.; member: Greater Milwaukee Committee; member: Bankers Roundtable. CLUB AFFIL Westmoor Country Club; Milwaukee Country Club; University Club.

Ned W. Bechtold: director CORP AFFIL director: Opus United States Corp.; director: Aurora Health Care Inc.; shareholder: Northeast Asphalt Inc. NONPR AFFIL director: Saint Luke's Medical Center.

John A. Becker: vice chairman (see above)

Roger Leon Fitzsimonds: chairman B Milwaukee, WI 1938. ED University of Wisconsin, Milwaukee BBA (1960); University of Wisconsin, Milwaukee MBA (1971). PRIM CORP EMPL chairman, chief executive officer, director: Firstar Corp. CORP AFFIL board directors: Firstar Bank Milwaukee NA; director: Firstar Trust Co. NONPR AFFIL member, director: Wisconsin Association Manufacturing & Commerce; director: Wisconsin Policy Research Institute; chairman advisory council: University Wisconsin School Business; director: Metropolitan Milwaukee Association Commerce; director: Milwaukee Boys & Girls Club; director: Medical College Wisconsin; director: Columbia Health System Inc.; director: Competitive Wisconsin Inc.; vice president, director: Bankers Roundtable. CLUB AFFIL Milwaukee Country Club.

Dennis Fredrickson: secretary, treasurer PRIM CORP EMPL senior vice president: Firstar Corp.

Sheldon B. Lubar: director B Milwaukee, WI 1929. ED University of Wisconsin BA (1951); University of Wisconsin LLB (1953); University of Wisconsin DSc (1988). PRIM CORP EMPL chairman: Christiana Companies, Inc. CORP AFFIL director: MGIC Investment Corp.; director: Weatherford International Inc.; chairman: Lubar & Co.; director: Massachusetts Mutual Life Insurance Co.; director: EVI Weatherford Inc.; director: Firstar Bank Corp.; director: Ameritech Corp.

Robert Joseph O'Toole: director B Chicago, IL 1941. ED Loyola University BS (1961). PRIM CORP EMPL chairman, president, chief executive officer, director: A.O. Smith Corp. CORP AFFIL director: Protection Mutual Insurance Co.; director: Smith Fiberglass Products Inc.; director: FM Global Insurance; director: Firstar Bank NA; director: Firstar Corp.; director: Briggs & Stratton Corp.

Grants Analysis

Disclosure Period: calendar year ending 1998
Total Grants: $1,658,998*
Number of Grants: 257
Average Grant: $6,455
Highest Grant: $110,000
Typical Range: $500 to $5,000
***Note:** Giving excludes United Way.

Recent Grants

Note: Grants derived from 1997 Form 990.

Arts & Humanities

110,000	United Performing Arts Fund, Milwaukee, WI
105,000	United Performing Arts Fund, Milwaukee, WI
60,000	Milw. Art Museum/Capital Camp., Milwaukee, WI
60,000	Milwaukee Art Museum/Capital Camp, Milwaukee, WI
50,000	Marcus Center for the Performing Arts, Milwaukee, WI
50,000	Marcus Center for the Performing Arts, Milwaukee, WI
50,000	Milw. Symphony Orch, Milwaukee, WI
50,000	Milw. Symphony Orchestra, Milwaukee, WI
20,000	Milw. Public Library Fdn., Milwaukee, WI
15,000	Captain Frederick Theatre, Milwaukee, WI
12,500	Milw. Public Museum, Milwaukee, WI
12,500	Milwaukee Public Museum, Milwaukee, WI
12,000	Florentine Opera Company, Milwaukee, WI
12,000	Florentine Opera Company, Milwaukee, WI
10,000	Betty Brinn Children's Museum, Milwaukee, WI

Civic & Public Affairs

25,000	The Great Circus Parade, Milwaukee, WI
25,000	The Great Circus Parade, Milwaukee, WI

Education

43,000	UW Foundation-Madison, Madison, WI
43,000	UW Foundation-Madison, Madison, WI
30,000	Marquette University, Milwaukee, WI
30,000	Marquette University, Milwaukee, WI
25,000	Marquette University, Milwaukee, WI
25,000	Marquette University, Milwaukee, WI
25,000	UW Foundation/Sesquicentennial Exh, Madison, WI
20,000	Medical College of Wisc., Milwaukee, WI
20,000	Medical College of Wisc., Milwaukee, WI
20,000	UW-Extension/The Pyle Center, Madison, WI
14,000	Inroad/Wisconsin, Inc., Milwaukee, WI
14,000	Inroads Wisconsin Inc., Milwaukee, WI

Health

20,000	Children's Hospital of Wisc., Milwaukee, WI
15,000	Blood Center of Southeastern WI, Milwaukee, WI
15,000	Blood Center of Southeastern Wisconsin, Milwaukee, WI
10,000	Community Memorial Hospital - Men. Falls, Menomonee Falls, WI
2,750	Children's Hospital of Wisc., Milwaukee, WI

Religion

10,000	Catholic Steward, Appeal, Milwaukee, WI

Social Services

391,800	United Way of Greater Milw. & Surr. Ctys., Milwaukee, WI
380,000	United Way of Greater Milw. & Surr. Ctys., Milwaukee, WI
27,000	Milw. Boys & Girls Club, Milwaukee, WI
27,000	Milw. Boys & Girls Club, Milwaukee, WI
25,000	Y.M.C.A. of Metropolitan Milwaukee, Milwaukee, WI
25,000	Y.W.C.A. King Heights Project, Milwaukee, WI
25,000	Y.W.C.A. of Metropolitan Milwaukee, Milwaukee, WI
20,000	Goodwill Industries, Milwaukee, WI
16,000	Y.W.C.A. of Greater Milwaukee, Milwaukee, WI
15,000	Family Service of Milwaukee, Milwaukee, WI
15,000	Family Service of Milwaukee, Milwaukee, WI
12,000	Junior Achievement, Milwaukee, WI
12,000	Junior Achievement, Milwaukee, WI

FIRSTENERGY CORP.

Company Contact

Akron, OH

Company Description

Former Name: Ohio Edison Co.
Revenue: US$6,320,000 (1999)
Employees: 1,944 (1999)
Fortune Rank: 274, per FORTUNE Magazine's list of 500 Largest U.S. Corporations (1999).
FF 274
SIC(s): 4911 Electric Services.

Nonmonetary Support

Type: Donated Equipment; In-kind Services
Contact: Delores Jones, Manager, Community Support
Note: on location basis only

Corporate Sponsorship

Type: Arts & cultural events; Music & entertainment events

Giving Contact

Mary Beth Carroll, Vice President
FirstEnergy Corp.
76 South Main Street
Akron, OH 44308
Phone: (330)761-4112
Fax: (330)384-3788
Email: carrollm@firstenergycorp.com

Alternate Contact

Email: tadams@firstenergycorp.com

Description

Organization Type: Corporate Giving Program
Giving Locations: headquarters and operating communities.
Grant Types: Capital, Employee Matching Gifts, General Support.

Giving Philosophy

The corporation is committed to helping improve the economic and social conditions in the communities where its customers and employees work and live.

Financial Summary

Total Giving: $3,158,800 (fiscal year ending , 1999); $2,468,590 (fiscal 1998); $2,526,747 (fiscal 1997). Note: Contributes through corporate direct giving program only.

Giving Analysis: Giving for fiscal 1998 includes: foundation (approx $2,758,000); corporate direct giving (approx $400,800)

Typical Recipients

Arts & Humanities: Arts & Humanities-General
Civic & Public Affairs: Civic & Public Affairs-General
Education: Education-General
Health: Health-General
Social Services: Social Services-General

Application Procedures

Initial Contact: a brief letter of inquiry
Application Requirements: a description of organization, amount requested, purpose of funds sought, audited financial statement, and proof of tax-exempt status
Deadlines: None.

Additional Information

In November 1997, Ohio Edison Co. merged with Centerior Energy Corp. under the new holding company called FirstEnergy Corp.

Corporate Officials

Anthony J. Alexander: executive vice president, general counsel PRIM CORP EMPL executive vice president, general counsel: FirstEnergy Corp.
H. Peter Burg: president, chief operating officer B 1946. ED Akron University MBA; Akron University BS; Harvard University. PRIM CORP EMPL president, chief operating officer: FirstEnergy Corp. ADD CORP EMPL president: Firstenergy Service Corp.; president: Ohio Edison Co.; president: The Cleveland Elc Illuminating; president: Toledo Edison Co. ADD NONPR EMPL director: Summit County Chapter ARC. CORP AFFIL director: Key Bank; director: Centerior Service Co.; director: Energy Insurance Mutual. NONPR AFFIL Edison Electric Institute.
John A. Gill: senior vice president B Clearfield, PA 1938. ED North Carolina State University (1962). PRIM CORP EMPL senior vice president: FirstEnergy Corp.
Willard R. Holland: chairman, chief executive officer B Springfield, TN 1936. ED Rose-Hulman Institute Technology BSEE (1965); Rose-Hulman Institute Technology MSEE (1966). PRIM CORP EMPL chairman, chief executive officer: FirstEnergy Corp. CORP AFFIL director: A Schulman Inc.; chairman: Ohio Edison Co.; chairman: Pennsylvania Power Co.; director: Cleveland Electric Illuminating; chief executive officer: FirstEnergy Services Corp. NONPR AFFIL director: Ohio Electric Utility Institute; board managers: Rose-Hulman Institute Technology; trustee: Ohio Business Roundtable; trustee: Leadership Akron; director: Nuclear Energy Institute; director: Greater Cleveland Growth Association; trustee: Cleveland Tomorrow; director: Edison Electric Institute; trustee: Childrens Hospital Medical Center Akron; trustee: Akron Tomorrow; director: Association of Edison Illuminating Companies; trustee: Akron Art Museum; trustee: Akron Roundtable. CLUB AFFIL Portage Country Club; Akron City Club; Firestone Country Club.

Giving Program Officials

Mary Beth Carol: PRIM CORP EMPL vice president: FirstEnergy Corp.

Grants Analysis

Total Grants: $3,158,800

FISHER BROTHERS CLEANING SERVICES

Company Contact

New York, NY

Company Description

Employees: 400
SIC(s): 7349 Building Maintenance Services Nec.

Fisher Brothers Foundation, Inc.

Giving Contact

Mr. Richard Fisher, Director
Fisher Brothers Foundation, Inc.
299 Park Ave.
New York, NY 10171
Phone: (212)752-5000
Fax: (212)940-6207

Alternate Contact

Kam Wong

Description

Founded: 1981
EIN: 133118286
Organization Type: Corporate Foundation. Supports preselected organizations only.
Giving Locations: NY: New York metropolitan area
Grant Types: General Support.

Financial Summary

Total Giving: $3,200,000 (1999 approx); $3,200,000 (1998 approx); $3,200,000 (1997 approx). Note: Contributes through foundation only.
Assets: $22,487 (1995); $36,238 (1994); $15,379 (1993)
Gifts Received: $725,000 (1995); $835,000 (1994); $842,000 (1993)

Typical Recipients

Arts & Humanities: Arts Associations & Councils, Arts Centers, Arts Festivals, Dance, Historic Preservation, Libraries, Museums/Galleries, Opera, Performing Arts, Theater
Civic & Public Affairs: African American Affairs, Botanical Gardens/Parks, Business/Free Enterprise, Civil Rights, Economic Development, Employment/ Job Training, Ethnic Organizations, Civic & Public Affairs-General, Hispanic Affairs, Housing, Municipalities/Towns, Professional & Trade Associations, Safety, Urban & Community Affairs
Education: Business Education, Colleges & Universities, Education Reform, Education-General, Medical Education, Minority Education, Private Education (Precollege), Public Education (Precollege), Student Aid
Environment: Air/Water Quality, Environment-General, Sanitary Systems
Health: AIDS/HIV, Cancer, Children's Health/Hospitals, Diabetes, Geriatric Health, Hospitals, Single-Disease Health Associations, Transplant Networks/Donor Banks
International: Health Care/Hospitals, International Peace & Security Issues
Religion: Jewish Causes, Religious Welfare, Synagogues/Temples
Science: Science Museums
Social Services: Big Brother/Big Sister, Community Service Organizations, Crime Prevention, People with Disabilities, Recreation & Athletics, Scouts, Senior Services, Shelters/Homelessness, Social Services-General, United Funds/United Ways, Volunteer Services, Youth Organizations

Contributions Analysis

Giving Priorities: Jewish philanthropy, social welfare, and civic interests. Generally limited international interests. Company has supported international development and relief efforts.
Arts & Humanities: 10% to 15%. Primarily supports performing arts, museums, art associations, libraries, and historic preservation.
Civic & Public Affairs: Less than 5%. Emphasis is on various ethnic organizations, urban affairs, minority business, safety issues, and housing.
Education: About 5%. Provides grants for colleges anduniversities, minority education, and private secondary education.
Health: Less than 5%. Focuses on hospitals and single-disease health organizations. Also interested in medical rehabilitation and research.
Religion: 60% to 65%. Funding supports the United Jewish Appeal and other Jewish welfare programs.
Social Services: 10% and 15%. The Police Athletic League and the New York City Partnership receive major support. Other recipients include people with disabilities, the United Way, the elderly, youth organizations, and family services.

Corporate Officials

Lawrence Fisher: partner B 1909. PRIM CORP EMPL partner: Fisher Brothers Cleaning Services. CORP AFFIL owner: 299 Cleaning Service Co.
Zachary Fisher: partner B 1910. PRIM CORP EMPL partner: Fisher Brothers Cleaning Service ADD CORP EMPL partner: 299 Cleaning Service Co.; partner: 400 Park avenue Co.; partner: Fisher Brothers Management Co.; partner: Fisher Sixth Avenue Co.; partner: Lane-Fisher Park Co.

Foundation Officials

Arnold Fisher: director PRIM CORP EMPL partner: 299 Cleaning Service Co.
Lawrence Fisher: director (see above)
M. Anthony Fisher: director PRIM CORP EMPL partner: 299 Cleaning Service Co.
Richard Fisher: director PRIM CORP EMPL partner: 299 Cleaning Service Co.
Zachary Fisher: director (see above)

Grants Analysis

Disclosure Period: calendar year ending 1995
Total Grants: $731,175
Number of Grants: 39
Average Grant: $8,452*
Highest Grant: $410,000
Typical Range: $1,000 to $10,000
***Note:** Average grant excludes highest grant.

Recent Grants

Note: Grants derived from 1995 Form 990.

Arts & Humanities

5,000 Metropolitan Museum of Art, New York, NY
5,000 Metropolitan Museum of Art R.E. Council, New York, NY
5,000 New York Landmarks Conservancy, New York, NY
3,500 Children's Museum, New York, NY
3,000 Circle in the Square, New York, NY
2,500 City Center, New York, NY
2,500 New York Public Library, New York, NY
2,500 Norton Museum of Art, New York, NY

Civic & Public Affairs

5,000 National Urban League, New York, NY
5,000 New York City Public-Private Initiatives, New York, NY
1,000 Congress of Racial Equality, New York, NY

Education

5,000 Brandeis University, Waltham, MA
5,000 Harlem Education Activities Fund, New York, NY
5,000 Prep for Prep, New York, NY
1,000 Realty Foundation, New York, NY
1,000 Yale Parents Fund, New Haven, CT
175 Jackie Robinson Foundation, New York, NY

Environment

1,000 Big Hole River Foundation, Butte, MT

Health

10,000 Cap Cure, Santa Monica, CA
5,000 National Breast Cancer Coalition Fund, New York, NY

3,000 American Italian Cancer Foundation, New York, NY
2,500 New York Blood Center, New York, NY
1,500 United Hebrew Geriatric Center, New Rochelle, NY

Religion
410,000 United Jewish Appeal, New York, NY
100,000 Jewish Federation of Palm Beach County, West Palm Beach, FL
25,000 Temple Israel, New York, NY
10,000 Congregation Emanu-El of New York, New York, NY
1,000 Catholic Charities, San Diego, CA

Social Services
50,000 Police Athletic League, New York, NY
15,000 New York City Police Foundation, New York, NY
10,000 United Way, New York, NY
10,000 United Way Northern Westchester, Mount Kisco, NY
5,000 Association to Help Retarded Children, New York, NY
5,000 HELP, New York, NY
5,000 New York Finest Foundation, New York, NY
2,500 Council of Senior Center Services, New York, NY
2,500 United Way Santa Fe County, Santa Fe, NM

FISHER SCIENTIFIC

Company Contact

Hampton, NH

Company Description

Former Name: Chatam Inc.; Winthrop Inc.
SIC(s): 3728 Aircraft Parts & Equipment Nec, 5084 Industrial Machinery & Equipment, 5085 Industrial Supplies.

Winthrop Foundation

Giving Contact

Spencer Stokes, President
Winthrop Inc.
1 Liberty Lane
Hampton, NH 03842
Phone: (603)926-5911
Fax: (603)929-2248

Description

EIN: 330240692
Organization Type: Corporate Foundation
Giving Locations: headquarters and operating communities.
Grant Types: Capital, Emergency, General Support.

Financial Summary

Total Giving: $1,087,611 (fiscal year ending May 31, 1994); $1,412,047 (fiscal 1993); $2,379,103 (fiscal 1992). Note: Contributes through foundation only.
Assets: $3,608,166 (fiscal 1994); $4,593,218 (fiscal 1993); $5,206,902 (fiscal 1992)
Gifts Received: $42,000 (fiscal 1994); $42,304 (fiscal 1989)

Typical Recipients

Arts & Humanities: Arts Associations & Councils, Arts Centers, Arts Funds, Community Arts, Ethnic & Folk Arts, History & Archaeology, Museums/Galleries, Music, Opera, Performing Arts, Public Broadcasting, Theater
Civic & Public Affairs: Botanical Gardens/Parks, Economic Policy, Employment/Job Training, Housing, Law & Justice, Philanthropic Organizations, Professional & Trade Associations, Public Policy, Zoos/Aquariums
Education: Business Education, Colleges & Universities, Education Reform, Faculty Development, Education-General, Medical Education, Minority Education, Private Education (Precollege), Secondary Education (Private)
Environment: Environment-General, Resource Conservation
Health: Cancer, Clinics/Medical Centers, Diabetes, Emergency/Ambulance Services, Health Organizations, Hospices, Hospitals, Medical Research, Research/Studies Institutes, Single-Disease Health Associations, Speech & Hearing, Transplant Networks/Donor Banks
International: Health Care/Hospitals, International Organizations, Missionary/Religious Activities
Religion: Religious Organizations
Science: Science Museums
Social Services: Community Service Organizations, Family Services, People with Disabilities, Scouts, Shelters/Homelessness, Social Services-General, United Funds/United Ways, YMCA/YWCA/YMHA/YWHA, Youth Organizations

Contributions Analysis

Arts & Humanities: 10% to 15%. Supports the performing arts and music. A variety of museums also receive substantial support, including those which focus on automobiles, modern art, and American art.
Civic & Public Affairs: 10% to 15%. Recipients include philanthropic organizations, civil rights, and law and justice.
Education: 20% to 25%. Supports colleges, universities and private precollege education.
Health: 20% to 25%. Interests include medical foundations, single-disease health associations, medical centers, and hospitals. Also funds disabled veterans.
International: 20% to 25%. Supports various organizations in Nassau, Bahamas.
Science: Less than 5%. Supports the American Museum of Natural History.
Social Services: 5% to 10%. Primarily supports united funds and youth organizations. Foundation also funds family counseling, daycare, and hospices.

Application Procedures

Initial Contact: brief letter
Application Requirements: purpose of grant and proof of tax exempt status

Additional Information

In 1997 Chatam Inc. became Winthrop Inc.

Foundation Officials

Mary D. Damas: assistant secretary
Michael David Dingman: partner, director B New Haven, CT 1931. ED University of Maryland. PRIM CORP EMPL president, chief executive officer: Shipston Group Ltd. CORP AFFIL director: Ford Motor Co.; director: Fisher Scientific International Inc. NONPR AFFIL member: Institute Electrical & Electronics Engineers. CLUB AFFIL San Diego Yacht Club; Union Club; New York Yacht Club; The Links Club; Lyford Cay Club; La Jolla Country Club; Bohemian Club; Cruising Club American.
Paul M. Meister: vice president, treasurer B Kalamazoo, MI 1952. ED University of Michigan BA (1974); Northwestern University MBA (1976). PRIM CORP EMPL chief financial officer, senior vice president finance: Fisher Science International Inc. ADD CORP EMPL managinging director: Latona Associate. CORP AFFIL director: Minerals Technologies Inc.; director: Power Control Technologies; director: MF Worldwide; vice chairman: General Chemical Group Inc.; vice chairman: Gentek Inc.
Paul Michael Montrone: vice president, partner B Scranton, PA 1941. ED University of Scranton BS (1962); Columbia University PhD (1965). PRIM CORP EMPL chief executive officer, chairman: Fisher Science International Inc. ADD CORP EMPL president: Henley Holdings Two Inc. CORP AFFIL advisory board: Zeneca Inc.; advisory board: Sintokagio Ltd.; director: Waste Management Inc.; chairman: Latona Associates; director: Prestolite Wire Corp.; director: Henley Group Inc.; advisory board: ICI Inc.; chairman: General Chemical Group Inc.; member board overseers: Consumer Protection Quality Healthcare Industry; chairman: Gen Tek Inc. NONPR AFFIL member dean's advisory council: Columbia University Business School; managing director: Metropolitan Opera Association; member board overseers: Business School Columbia University; member board overseers: Business Roundtable. CLUB AFFIL Lyford Cay Club; University Club; Bald Peak Colony Club; Brook Club.
Allison G. Pellegrino: secretary
Spencer Stokes: president

Grants Analysis

Disclosure Period: fiscal year ending May 31, 1994
Total Grants: $1,087,611
Number of Grants: 267
Average Grant: $4,073
Highest Grant: $60,000
Typical Range: $200 to $10,000

Recent Grants

Note: Grants derived from 1994 Form 990.

Arts & Humanities
12,500 Currier Gallery of Art, Manchester, NH -- pledge payment number one
12,500 Museum of Fine Arts, Boston, MA -- general operating support
10,000 Owl Head Transportation Museum, Owls Head, ME -- general operating support
6,000 John F. Kennedy Center for Performing Arts, New York, NY -- general operating support
5,250 New Hampshire Public Television Channel 11, Durham, NH -- general operating support
5,000 American Craft Museum, New York, NY -- general operating support
5,000 Business Committee for Arts, New York, NY -- general operating support
5,000 Metropolitan Museum of Art, New York, NY -- general operating support
5,000 Museum of Modern Art, New York, NY -- general operating support
5,000 Museum of Modern Art, New York, NY -- general operating support
5,000 New Hampshire Historical Society, Concord, NH -- general operating support
2,500 American Museum of Moving Images, New York, NY -- general operating support

Civic & Public Affairs
16,000 New England Aquarium, Boston, MA -- pledge payment final
15,000 National Tax Limitation Foundation, Roseville, CA -- general operating support
12,500 New Hampshire Charitable Foundation, Concord, NH -- pledge payment number two
10,000 American Agriculture Economic Association Foundation, Ames, IA -- CRW Appreciation Club -- general operating support
10,000 Central Park Conservancy, New York, NY -- general operating support
5,000 Christmas in April USA, Washington, DC -- general operating support
2,500 ACCF Center for Policy Research, Washington, DC -- general operating support

2,500	Washington Legal Foundation, Washington, DC -- general operating support
2,500	Winnacunnet High School Career Paths Program, Hampton, NH -- general operating support
Education	
60,000	Berwick Academy, South Berwick, ME -- pledge payment number three
33,333	New American Schools Development Corp, Arlington, VA -- pledge payment final
20,000	Bishop's School, La Jolla, CA -- pledge payment number four
5,000	Prep for Prep/Lilac Ball, New York, NY -- fundraiser
Health	
35,000	Brigham and Women's Hospital, Boston, MA -- general operating support
20,000	Brigham and Women's Hospital, Boston, MA -- pledge payment final
20,000	Dana Farber Cancer Institute, Boston, MA -- pledge payment number four
10,000	Juvenile Diabetes Foundation/San Diego Chapter, San Diego, CA -- fundraiser
10,000	National Marrow Donor Program, Minneapolis, MN -- pledge payment final
7,000	Salk Institute, San Diego, CA -- general operating support
5,000	American Red Cross of Greater New York, New York, NY -- general operating support
5,000	Animal Medical Center, New York, NY -- general operating support
5,000	Cap Cure, Santa Monica, CA -- fundraiser
5,000	Elizabeth Hospice, Escondido, CA -- general operating support
2,000	American Lung Association of New Hampshire, Manchester, NH -- general operating support
International	
50,000	Lyford Cay/Bahamas Heart Institute, Nassau, Bahamas -- general operating support
50,000	Lyford Cay Foundation, Nassau, Bahamas -- general operating support
9,000	Assemblies of Brethren in the Bahamas, Nassau, Bahamas -- general operating support
5,000	American Red Cross, Nassau, Bahamas -- general operating support
5,000	One Family Junkanoo Group, Nassau, Bahamas -- general operating support
Science	
5,000	American Museum of Natural History, New York, NY -- fundraiser
3,500	American Museum of Natural History, New York, NY -- general operating support
3,500	American Museum of Natural History, New York, NY -- general operating support
Social Services	
15,000	United Way, Greater Seacoast, Portsmouth, NH -- general operating support
6,500	Dole Foundation, Washington, DC -- general operating support
5,000	Hole in the Wall Gang Fund, New Haven, CT -- pledge payment final
3,333	YMCA, Camp Dudley, Westport, NY -- pledge payment number one
2,500	Boy Scouts of America, New York, NY -- general operating support
2,500	Project Turn-Around, Nacogdoches, TX -- general operating support

FLEETBOSTON FINANCIAL CORP.

Company Contact

100 Hundred Federal St.
Boston, MA 02110
Phone: (617)434-2629
Fax: (617)434-6072
Web: http://www.fleetbankbostonmerger.com

Company Description

Former Name: Shawmut National Corp.; Fleet Bank of New York (1999); Fleet Financial Group (1999);
Formed by Merger of:.
Assets: US$190,692,000,000 (1999)
Profit: US$2,038,000,000 (1999)
Employees: 36,000
Fortune Rank: 80, per FORTUNE Magazine's list of 500 Largest U.S. Corporations (1999).
FF 80
SIC(s): 6021 National Commercial Banks, 6712 Bank Holding Companies.

Corporate Sponsorship

Type: Arts & cultural events; Music & entertainment events; Pledge-a-thon; Sports events

FleetBoston Financial Foundation

Giving Contact

Michelle Courton-Brown, President
FleetBoston Financial Foundation
100 Hundred Federal Street
Boston, MA 02110
Phone: (617)434-2629
Fax: (617)434-6072

Description

Organization Type: Corporate Foundation
Giving Locations: CT; FL: in limited areas; ME; MA; NH; NJ; NY; RI
Grant Types: Capital, Employee Matching Gifts, General Support, Operating Expenses.
Note: Matching gifts are restricted to higher education. Company also provides program support.

Giving Philosophy

'FleetBoston Financial Foundation represents a significant coming together of two dynamic financial institutions, each having earned national recognition for their records in strategic philanthropy and strong civic leadership in the region. We enter this new century with a deep commitment to maintaining the leadership we have achieved in initiating societal change, supporting social entrepreneurs, improving the quality of life in our region, and encouraging the involvement of our employees and partners in civic and community service. We believe that it is our corporate responsibility to help shape the future of our community and operate under the guiding principle that good citizenship is also good business.'*FleetBoston Financial Foundation Grantmaking Guidelines*FleetBoston Financial Foundation seeks to be a catalyst for positive, systemic, social change that will have a lasting effect on its communities. It provides seed funding for new and innovative programs that can be sustained over the long term. Where possible, the Foundation seeks to leverage the effect of its grants by supporting model programs, which can then be replicated in other communities.'*FleetBoston Financial Foundation Grantmaking Strategy & Priorities*

Financial Summary

Total Giving: $25,000,000 (2000 approx)

Typical Recipients

Arts & Humanities: Arts Associations & Councils, Arts Centers, Arts Funds, Arts Institutes, Community Arts, Dance, Ethnic & Folk Arts, Historic Preservation, History & Archaeology, Libraries, Museums/Galleries, Music, Opera, Performing Arts, Public Broadcasting, Theater, Visual Arts
Civic & Public Affairs: African American Affairs, Asian American Affairs, Business/Free Enterprise, Chambers of Commerce, Civil Rights, Economic Development, Economic Policy, Employment/Job Training, Civic & Public Affairs-General, Hispanic Affairs, Housing, Law & Justice, Native American Affairs, Nonprofit Management, Philanthropic Organizations, Public Policy, Safety, Urban & Community Affairs, Women's Affairs, Zoos/Aquariums
Education: Arts/Humanities Education, Business Education, Colleges & Universities, Community & Junior Colleges, Continuing Education, Economic Education, Education Associations, Engineering/Technological Education, Education-General, Health & Physical Education, Literacy, Minority Education, Preschool Education, Public Education (Precollege), Social Sciences Education
Environment: Environment-General
Health: AIDS/HIV, Children's Health/Hospitals, Clinics/Medical Centers, Emergency/Ambulance Services, Heart, Hospices, Hospitals, Hospitals (University Affiliated), Medical Research, Nutrition, Prenatal Health Issues
Social Services: At-Risk Youth, Child Welfare, Community Centers, Community Service Organizations, Counseling, Day Care, Delinquency & Criminal Rehabilitation, Domestic Violence, Family Planning, Family Services, Food/Clothing Distribution, Homes, People with Disabilities, Recreation & Athletics, Refugee Assistance, Senior Services, Shelters/Homelessness, Substance Abuse, United Funds/United Ways, Volunteer Services, YMCA/YWCA/YMHA/YWHA, Youth Organizations

Contributions Analysis

Giving Priorities: Economic opportunity, youth development, public education, and arts and culture.
Arts & Humanities: Funding in this area includes sponsorship of initiatives from major exhibits to community and grassroots performances; educational outreach to low- and moderate-income youth; and projects that promote increased access to the arts.
Civic & Public Affairs: Funding in civic and public affairs focuses on economic opportunity, with a particular focus on community development programs; microenterprise, entrepreneurial, and small business development; job creation and employment training; affordable housing initiatives and homebuyer seminars; and selected programs that serve low- and moderate-income individuals.
Education: Funds public education programs, emphasizing programs that support literacy programs, business and finance education, transition from school to career, and long-term education reform efforts.
Social Services: Supports youth development, including programs that promote healthy development, adult mentoring support, job readiness and skill building, and leadership skills through community service.
Note: Contribution priorities were derived from the foundation's Grantmaking Guidelines.

Application Procedures

Initial Contact: Submit a grant request in writing.
Application Requirements: Include a cover letter on the requesting organization's stationery that states the amount requested and the purpose of the grant, and clearly indicate the name and telephone number of the contact person; brief descriptions of the organization's purpose, history, and accomplishments; financial statements (audited if available) for the most

recently completed fiscal year; most recent Form 990 (the combined federal and state charitable report); the current year's operating budget and next year's proposed budget for the organization and the specific project to be funded; a list of corporations and foundations that support the organization and the most recent amounts given; IRS determination letter of 501(c)(3) status and proof that the organization is not a private foundation under section 509(a) of the IRS Code; written agreement with the fiscal agent and a copy of its 501(c)(3), if a fiscal agent is to be used; names and affiliations of the board of directors; and a report on the last grant received from FleetBoston Financial Foundation or any of its legacy institutions, Fleet Financial Group or BankBoston.
Deadlines: None; proposals are accepted throughout the calendar year.
Review Process: Requests are reviewed quarterly by review committees.
Evaluative Criteria: The foundation prefers to fund new and innovative programs that promote positive, enduring social change and seek long-term solutions to economic and social problems.
Notes: The foundation accepts the Associated Grantmakers of Massachusetts Common Proposal Format.

Restrictions

Does not support individuals, national medical foundations, or political, religious, or fraternal organizations.

Additional Information

In October 1999, Fleet Financial Group, Inc. and BankBoston Corp. merged. The resulting company, FleetBoston Financial Corp., established the FleetBoston Financial Foundation.
Requests for grants and event support in Massachusetts should be sent to:
Grants Administrator, FleetBoston Financial Foundation, Mailstop: MA BOS 01-28-05, PO Box 2016, Boston, MA 02106 (617) 434-2804
Requests for all other regions should be addressed to: Community Relations Manager, FleetBoston Financial
Connecticut: Mailstop CT/MO/0395, 777 Main Street, Hartford, CT, 06115, (860) 986-5322
Rhode Island: Mailstop RI/MO/M18B, 111 Westminster Street, Providence, RI, 02903, (401) 278-6240
New Hampshire: Mailstop NH/NA/EO3A, 1155 Elm Street, Manchester, NH 03101 (603) 647,7611
Maine: Mailstop ME/PM/PO5B, 2 Portland Square, Portland, ME 04104, (207) 874-5102
NY - New York City/Westchester County: Mailstop NY/NY/A39B, 1133 Avenue of the Americas, 39th Floor, New York, NY 10036 (212) 703-1663
NY - Long Island: Mailstop NY/LI/MO3A, 300 Broad Hollow Road, Melville, NY 11747 (631) 547-7489
NY - Albany/Hudson Valley: Mailstop NY/KP/0302, Peter D. Kiernan Plaza, Albany, NY 12207 (518) 447-6145
NY - Buffalo/Rochester: Mailstop NY/FP/1000, 10 Fountain Plaza, 9th Floor, Buffalo, NY 14202 (716) 847-7245
NY Syracuse/Utica: Mailstop NY/SY/0495, One Clinton Square, Syracuse, NY 13202 (315) 426-4184
New Jersey: Mailstop NJ/SP/W03G, 1125 Route 22W, Bridgewater, NJ 08807 (908) 253-4570
Pennsylvania: Mailstop PA/SC/SO4G, One Fleet Way, Scranton, PA 18507 (570) 330-3708

Recent Grants

Civic & Public Affairs

2,345 Fleet Charitable Trust

FLORIDA POWER CORP.

Company Contact

St. Petersburg, FL

Company Description

Employees: 4,629
SIC(s): 4911 Electric Services.
Parent Company: Florida Progress Corp., St. Petersburg, FL, United States

Nonmonetary Support

Value: $45,000 (1993); $8,400 (1992); $100,000 (1991)
Type: Donated Equipment; Loaned Executives

Giving Contact

Karin S. Griffin, Manager, Contributions Program
Florida Power Corp.
PO Box 33042
St. Petersburg, FL 33733
Phone: (727)824-6424

Alternate Contact

Suzy Miller
Phone: (727)824-6444

Description

Organization Type: Corporate Giving Program
Giving Locations: FL
Grant Types: Capital, General Support.

Giving Philosophy

'Florida Power Corporation is a progressive electric utility company serving 1.3 million customers in one of the country's fastest growing geographic regions. We are committed to providing reliable energy, outstanding service and innovative products.
'Our corporate contributions program is designed to support the achievement of our primary business objective, which is to be a leading, customer-focused energy services company. One of the ways we work to achieve this goal is through investment in the economic and social vitality of the communities in which our customers and employees live and work. Florida Power's Corporate Contributions Program aims to foster education, promote economic development, support health and human services, and enhance cultural programs.' *Florida Power Corporation Corporate Contributions Program*

Financial Summary

Total Giving: $872,057 (1995 approx); $823,520 (1994); $880,887 (1993). Note: Contributes through corporate direct giving program only.

Typical Recipients

Arts & Humanities: Arts Associations & Councils, Arts Centers, History & Archaeology, Music, Public Broadcasting
Civic & Public Affairs: Economic Development, Housing, Legal Aid, Urban & Community Affairs
Education: Business Education, Colleges & Universities, Community & Junior Colleges, Medical Education, Minority Education
Environment: Environment-General
Health: Cancer, Clinics/Medical Centers, Emergency/Ambulance Services, Hospitals, Transplant Networks/Donor Banks
Science: Science Museums
Social Services: Community Service Organizations, Family Services, People with Disabilities, Recreation & Athletics, Senior Services, United Funds/United Ways, Youth Organizations

Contributions Analysis

Giving Priorities: Workforce readiness, social services, the enivronment, education, and community development.
Arts & Humanities: About 10%. Supports arts and cultural programs and institutions that cultivate tomorrow's creative leadership.
Civic & Public Affairs: About 15%. Supports work force and community infrastructure development, job creation and retention, job training, and job placement.
Education: About 50%. Supports programs that focus on preparing the younger generations to be productive in the work force.
Health: About 25%. Supports the United Way, targets special project and capital contributions to encourage resource sharing by agencies, and provides emergency relief to people experiencing temporary financial hardship by assisting with electricity, gas, oil, and firewood payments through company and customer contributions.

Application Procedures

Initial Contact: Submit a written request to the manager of the contributions program.
Application Requirements: A cover letter should state the mission of the organization, a description of the purpose of the request (including the community or target population served and quantifiable outcomes or results), the amount requested, and any previous Florida Power Corporation support, including dates and amounts. The request should be accompanied by the full legal name of the organization, address, phone number, and contact person; background/historical information of the organization; a copy of the organization's 501(c)(3) tax-exempt ruling; latest audited financial statement and current income-and-expense budget; list of officers and the board of directors or other principals of the organization; and a list of current funders, including the percentage of funding received by the organization's board of directors. Submit requests in duplicate.
Deadlines: None.
Decision Notification: Requests are generally processed within 30 days after receipt. The company will mail notification of its decision.

Restrictions

In general, the company does not consider requests for: individuals; organizations outside of the geographic area Florida Power Corporation serves; organizations that discriminate on the basis of race, gender, sexual orientation, age, disability, or religion; tickets for contests, raffles, or other activities with prizes; religious organizations; agencies that receive United Way funding; reducing debts or past operating deficits; political causes or candidates; trips or tours for individuals or groups; talent or beauty contests; athletic programs; disease-specific causes or health research programs and activities; courtesy or journal advertising campaigns; multi-year commitments; 501(c)(4) organizations; or in-kind contributions of equipment, materials, labor, or electricity service.

Additional Information

Publications: Application Form

Corporate Officials

George Leroy Campbell: vice president public affairs B Ray, AZ 1940. ED University of Arizona (1963); California State University, Long Beach (1966). PRIM CORP EMPL vice president public affairs: Florida Power Corp. CORP AFFIL member: Associated Industries Florida. NONPR AFFIL member: U.S. Chamber of Commerce; member: Utilities State Government Association; member: Public Affairs Council; director: Saint Petersburg Historical Society; member: Edison Electric Institute; member: National Association Manufacturer. CLUB AFFIL Capital Hill Club.

Giving Program Officials

Joseph H. Richardson: PRIM CORP EMPL president, chief executive officer: Florida Power Corp. CORP AFFIL president: Progress Energy Corp.; officer: Talguin Corp.; group vice president: Florida Progress Corp.

Grants Analysis

Disclosure Period: calendar year ending
Typical Range: $250 to $5,000

FLORIDA POWER &LIGHT Co.

Company Contact
West Palm Beach, FL
Web: http://www.fpl.com

Company Description
Employees: 11,243
SIC(s): 4911 Electric Services.
Parent Company: FPL Group, Inc.

FPL Group Foundation, Inc.

Giving Contact
John L. Kitchens, Contributions Administrator
9250 West Flagler Street
Miami, FL 33174
Phone: (305)552-4806
Fax: (305)552-4722
Email: John_Kitchens@fpl.com

Description
Founded: 1989
EIN: 650031452
Organization Type: Corporate Foundation
Giving Locations: co. service areas.
Grant Types: Capital, Employee Matching Gifts, Endowment, General Support, Multiyear/Continuing Support.

Financial Summary
Total Giving: $2,300,000 (1999 approx); $1,430,030 (1998); $1,445,483 (1997). Note: Contributes through corporate direct giving program and foundation.
Giving Analysis: Giving for 1998 includes: foundation grants to United Way ($629,800); foundation ($598,438); foundation matching gifts ($201,792)
Assets: $5,573,787 (1998); $5,335,541 (1997); $3,567,989 (1996)
Gifts Received: $1,500,161 (1998); $1,467,025 (1997); $2,444,255 (1996). Note: The foundation receives contributions from Florida Power & Light Co.

Typical Recipients
Arts & Humanities: Arts Centers, Arts Festivals, Ballet, Arts & Humanities-General, Museums/Galleries, Music, Performing Arts, Public Broadcasting
Civic & Public Affairs: African American Affairs, Botanical Gardens/Parks, Business/Free Enterprise, Chambers of Commerce, Community Foundations, Economic Development, Civic & Public Affairs-General, Municipalities/Towns, Public Policy, Urban & Community Affairs
Education: Colleges & Universities, Community & Junior Colleges, Education Reform, Engineering/ Technological Education, Education-General, Minority Education, Private Education (Precollege), Public Education (Precollege), Science/Mathematics Education, Student Aid, Vocational & Technical Education
Environment: Environment-General, Protection
Health: Cancer, Emergency/Ambulance Services, Geriatric Health, Geriatric Health, Health Organizations, Medical Rehabilitation
International: Foreign Arts Organizations
Religion: Religious Welfare
Social Services: Child Welfare, Community Service Organizations, Family Services, People with Disabilities, Scouts, Senior Services, Shelters/Homelessness, United Funds/United Ways, YMCA/YWCA/ YMHA/YWHA

Contributions Analysis
Giving Priorities: Major support for the United Way and social services; also supports education, civic causes, the arts, health, and environmental concerns.
Arts & Humanities: 5%. Performing arts centers, museums, and music receive support.
Civic & Public Affairs: 12%. Funds economic development, community affairs, and municipalities.
Education: 18%. Matching gifts program to schools and universities; funding also goes to community colleges, technology institutes, and nuclear education programs.
Environment: 2%. Environmental concerns are funded.
Social Services: 56%. United Way organizations and emergency relief, the aged, low-income family services, multi-cultural needs, and religious welfare foundations.
Note: Total contributions in 1998.

Application Procedures
Initial Contact: Write for application form.
Application Requirements: With complete application, include a description of organization, amount requested, purpose of funds sought, current annual budget, campaign budget, recently audited financial statement, and proof of tax-exempt status.
Deadlines: None.
Review Process: Applications are processed in two to four weeks.

Restrictions
The foundation does not support religious organizations, verbal requests, individuals, requests for operating support from United Way agencies, programs outside operating areas, political groups or candidates, hospital operating budgets, or requests related to trips or tours.

Additional Information
The foundation continually supports the United Way and its agencies.
Publications: Application Procedures; Application Form

Corporate Officials
James Lowell Broadhead: chairman, president, chief executive officer, director B New Rochelle, NY 1935. ED Cornell University BSME (1958); Columbia University LLB (1963). PRIM CORP EMPL chairman, president, chief executive officer, director: Florida Power & Light Co. ADD CORP EMPL officer: ESI Energy Inc.; chairman: FPL Group Inc. CORP AFFIL director: New York Life Insurance; director: Pittston Co.; director: Delta Air Lines.

Foundation Officials
James Lowell Broadhead: chief executive officer, director (see above)
Dennis Patrick Coyle: secretary, director B Detroit, MI 1938. ED Dartmouth College BA (1960); Columbia University JD (1964). PRIM CORP EMPL general counsel, secretary: Florida Power & Light Co. ADD CORP EMPL secretary: FPL Group Inc.; secretary: FPL Energy Services Inc. NONPR AFFIL member: American Bar Association; honorary lifetime trustee: Miami Beach Chamber of Commerce.
Paul John Evanson: president, treasurer, director B New York, NY 1941. ED Saint John's University BBA (1963); Columbia University JD (1966); New York University LLM (1970). PRIM CORP EMPL president: Florida Power & Light Co. CORP AFFIL vice president: Lynch Telephone Corp.; director: Southern Energy Homes; director: FPL Group Inc.
L. J. Kelleher: vice president B 1947. ED University of Miami MBA; University of Miami BS. PRIM CORP EMPL senior vice president human resources: Florida Power & Light Co. ADD CORP EMPL senior vice president human resources, corporate services: FPL Group Inc.
John L. Kitchens: administrator PRIM CORP EMPL corporate contributions administrator: Florida Power & Light Co.

Grants Analysis
Disclosure Period: calendar year ending 1998
Total Grants: $598,438*
Number of Grants: 76
Average Grant: $7,874
Highest Grant: $60,000
Typical Range: $500 to $10,000
*Note: Giving excludes United Way, matching gifts.

Recent Grants
Note: Grants derived from 1998 Form 990.

Arts & Humanities

25,000	Central Florida Cultural, Palm Beach, FL
10,000	Florida Philharmonic Orchestra, Fort Lauderdale, FL
10,000	Manatee County Agricultural Museum, Palmetto, SC
10,000	Norton Museum, West Palm Beach, FL

Civic & Public Affairs

60,000	Bayfront Park Management Trust, Miami, FL
19,678	Dade County Board of Commissioners, Miami, FL
15,000	Urban League, Jacksonville, FL
10,000	Brookings Institution, Washington, DC
10,000	Broward Community Foundation, Fort Lauderdale, FL
10,000	Florida Chamber of Commerce Foundation, Inc., Tallahassee, FL
10,000	Florida Counties Foundation, Tallahassee, FL

Education

50,000	South Florida Annenberg Challenge, Fort Lauderdale, FL
36,600	University of Florida Foundation, Gainesville, FL
22,500	College Assistance Program, Miami, FL
20,000	Stetson University, Miami, FL
11,250	Florida State University Foundation, Gainesville, FL
10,500	Auburn University Foundation, Auburn, AL
10,290	Benjamin School, North Palm Beach, FL
10,000	UNCF, Jacksonville, FL
10,000	Valley Forge Military Academy, Wayne, PA
9,000	Houghton Academy, Houghton, NY
7,000	Gator Boosters, Gainesville, FL
4,000	Georgia Institute of Technology Foundation, Atlanta, GA
4,000	Georgia Institute of Technology Foundation, Atlanta, GA
4,000	University Of Miami, Miami, FL
200	University of Miami, Miami, FL

Environment

20,000	Solutions to Avoid Red Tide Inc.,, Longboat Key, FL

Health

17,500	Komen Breast Cancer Foundation, Dallas, TX
9,530	American Red Cross, Jacksonville, FL
5,000	Florida Council On Aging, Tallahassee, FL
5,000	Women's Board of Genesis Rehab, Jacksonville, FL

Religion

25,000	Salvation Army, Tampa, FL
16,178	Salvation Army, Jacksonville, FL

Social Services

298,000	United Way of Dade County, Miami, FL
88,000	United Way of Broward County, Fort Lauderdale, FL
84,500	United Way of Palm Beach, Palm Beach, FL
21,000	United Way Of Volusia Flagler, Daytona Beach, FL

19,000	United Way of Martin County, Stuart, FL
17,500	United Way of Brevard County, Cocoa, FL
17,000	United Way of Manatee County, Bradenton, FL
15,400	United Way of Sarasota County, Sarasota, FL
15,200	United Way of St. Lucie County, Ft. Pierce, FL
13,900	United Way of Lee County, Fort Myers, FL
10,000	ARC (Association for Retarded Citizens), Tallahassee, FL
10,000	Boys Scouts Of America, Jacksonville, FL
7,878	Broward County Bureau of Children, Fort Lauderdale, FL
7,500	Charlotte County Family YMCA, Charlotte, NC
7,300	United Way of Charlotte County, Port Charlotte, FL
6,800	United Way of Collier County, Naples, FL
5,400	United Way of Indian River County, Vero Beach, FL

FLORIDA ROCK INDUSTRIES

Company Contact

Jacksonville, FL

Company Description

Employees: 2,385
SIC(s): 1442 Construction Sand & Gravel, 3271 Concrete Block & Brick, 3273 Ready-Mixed Concrete.

Florida Rock Industries Foundation

Giving Contact

H. B. Horner, Secretary
Florida Rock Industries Foundation
PO Box 4667
Jacksonville, FL 32201
Phone: (904)355-1781
Fax: (904)366-1866
Email: frih.b.horner@aol.com

Description

EIN: 592143326
Organization Type: Corporate Foundation
Giving Locations: FL; GA
Grant Types: General Support.

Financial Summary

Total Giving: $278,538 (fiscal year ending September 30, 1998); $239,375 (fiscal 1997); $228,640 (fiscal 1996)
Giving Analysis: Giving for fiscal 1998 includes: foundation ($234,938); foundation grants to United Way ($31,600); foundation scholarships ($12,000)
Assets: $2,429,155 (fiscal 1998); $2,353,205 (fiscal 1997); $1,931,918 (fiscal 1996)
Gifts Received: $250,000 (fiscal 1998); $144,000 (fiscal 1997); $125,000 (fiscal 1996). Note: Contributions are received from Florida Rock Industries.

Typical Recipients

Arts & Humanities: Arts Associations & Councils, Historic Preservation, History & Archaeology, Museums/Galleries, Music, Opera, Performing Arts, Public Broadcasting, Theater
Civic & Public Affairs: African American Affairs, Botanical Gardens/Parks, Employment/Job Training, Civic & Public Affairs-General, Urban & Community Affairs
Education: Business Education, Colleges & Universities, Continuing Education, Education-General, Minority Education, Student Aid, Vocational & Technical Education
Environment: Environment-General
Health: Alzheimers Disease, Cancer, Children's Health/Hospitals, Clinics/Medical Centers, Geriatric Health, Health Organizations, Medical Research, Single-Disease Health Associations
International: International Environmental Issues
Religion: Jewish Causes, Religious Organizations, Religious Welfare
Science: Science Museums
Social Services: Animal Protection, At-Risk Youth, Child Welfare, Community Centers, Community Service Organizations, Family Services, Homes, People with Disabilities, Recreation & Athletics, Scouts, Senior Services, Shelters/Homelessness, United Funds/United Ways, YMCA/YWCA/YMHA/YWHA, Youth Organizations

Contributions Analysis

Giving Priorities: Social service organizations, education, religious organizations, and health.
Arts & Humanities: 6%. Supports historical societies and performing arts.
Civic & Public Affairs: 3%. Supports urban leagues.
Education: 22%. Funds scholarships and universities.
Health: 11%. Supports single-disease health organizations.
Religion: 19%. Funds religious welfare and ministries.
Science: 6%. Supports a science museum.
Social Services: 33%. Supports the United Way, youth organizations, and homeless centers.
Note: Total contributions made in fiscal 1998.

Application Procedures

Initial Contact: Send brief letter describing program.
Application Requirements: Include recently audited financial statement, description of benefits or services provided, list of board members and leading contributors, whether activities qualify for 'Community Contributions Tax Credit' under the Florida Corporation Tax Act, whether contributions will be for capital or operating funds, and proof of tax-exempt status.
Deadlines: None.

Corporate Officials

Edward L. Baker: chairman, director, director B 1935. PRIM CORP EMPL chairman, director: Florida Rock Industries. CORP AFFIL generall partner: Baker Investments Ltd.; chairman, director: FRP Properties; chairman, director: Arundel Corp. CLUB AFFIL River Club.
John Daniel Baker, II: president, chief executive officer, director B Jacksonville, FL 1948. ED Princeton University BA (1970); University of Florida JD (1973). PRIM CORP EMPL president, chief executive officer, director: Florida Rock Industries. CORP AFFIL executive vice president, director: FRP Properties.

Foundation Officials

Edward L. Baker: president (see above)
John Daniel Baker, II: vice president (see above)
Ruggles B. Carlson: treasurer
H. B. Horner: secretary PRIM CORP EMPL treasurer: Florida Rock Industries.

Grants Analysis

Disclosure Period: fiscal year ending September 30, 1998
Total Grants: $234,938*
Number of Grants: 52
Average Grant: $4,518
Highest Grant: $31,327
Typical Range: $100 to $20,000
***Note:** Giving excludes scholarships; United Way.

Recent Grants

Note: Grants derived from fiscal 1997 Form 990.

Arts & Humanities

14,000	Performing Arts, Jacksonville, FL
3,400	Jacksonville Historical Society, Jacksonville, FL

Civic & Public Affairs

16,700	Jax Urban League, Jacksonville, FL
5,000	Quigley House of Clay County

Education

140,000	University of Florida Foundation, Gainesville, FL
90,000	University of North Florida, Jacksonville, FL
10,000	Berry College, Mount Berry, GA -- scholarship
6,000	United Negro College Fund, New York, NY

Health

60,000	Alzheimer's Care and Research Center, Jacksonville, FL

Religion

7,500	Young Life, Jacksonville, FL

Social Services

40,000	YWCA, Jacksonville, FL
15,000	Hubbard House
12,000	Guardian of Dreams
4,000	I.M. Sulzbacher Center for the Homeless

FLUOR CORP.

Company Contact

Irvine, CA
Web: http://www.fluor.com

Company Description

Revenue: US$12,417,000 (1999)
Profit: US$235,500,000
Employees: 53,561 (1999)
Fortune Rank: 144, per FORTUNE Magazine's list of 500 Largest U.S. Corporations (1999).
FF 144
SIC(s): 1221 Bituminous Coal & Lignite--Surface, 1241 Coal Mining Services, 1541 Industrial Buildings & Warehouses, 1629 Heavy Construction Nec.

Operating Locations

Argentina: AMECO SERVICES S.R.L., Buenos Aires, Tucuman; Australia: AMECO, Melbourne; Fluor Daniel, Melbourne, Perth; Brazil: Fluor Daniel Brazil, Sao Paulo; Canada: Fluor Daniel, Calgary; AMECO Services, Edmonton; Fluor Daniel, Vancouver; Chile: American Equipment, Alto Penuelas; AMECO - COLOSO, Antofagasta; AMECO, Santiago; Fluor Daniel, Santiago; People's Republic of China:, Beijing, Shanghai; Shanghai GE Construction Equipment Engineering Co., Ltd., Shanghai; England: Fluor Daniel, Camberley; Indonesia: PT. Fluor Daniel Indonesia Kawasan Industri Tanjung Uncang, Batam; PT. Ameco Servicindo, Jakarta; PT. Fluor Daniel Indonesia, Sumbawa; India: Fluor Daniel, New Dehli; Republic of Korea:, Seoul; Mexico: Maquinaria Panamericana S.A. de C.V., Guadalajara; Flour Daniels, Mexico City; Maquinaria Panamericana S.A. de C.V., Mexico City, Puebla; AMECO Services S.De R.L. de C.V., Santa Cantarina; Maquinaria Panamericana S.A. de C.V., Tlalnepantla; Netherlands: Fluor Daniel, Haarlem; Peru: American Construction Equipment Co., Lima, Moquegua; Philippines: Fluor Daniel, Jakarta; AMECO Services, Mandaue City; Fluor Daniel, Manila; AMECO Contractors, Metro Manila; AMECO Contractors Rentals, Inc., Quezon City; Poland: Fluor Daniel, Gliwice, Warsaw; Puerto Rico: American Equipment Company, Arecibo; Ameco Caribbean, Caguas; Fluor Daniel, San Juan; Russia:, Moscow;

Republic of South Africa:, Johannesburg; Saudi Arabia:, Dhahran; Singapore:; United Arab Emirates:, Dubai

Nonmonetary Support

Type: Donated Equipment; In-kind Services

Fluor Foundation

Giving Contact

Ms. Suzanne Huffmon Esber, Manager Community Relations
Fluor Foundation, 551Y
3353 Michelson Dr.
Irvine, CA 92698
Phone: (949)975-6797
Fax: (949)975-7175
Email: community.relations@fluordaniel.com

Description

EIN: 510196032
Organization Type: Corporate Foundation
Giving Locations: operating locations.
Grant Types: Capital, Employee Matching Gifts, Endowment, General Support, Matching, Operating Expenses, Project, Scholarship.
Note: Employee matching gift ratio: 1 to 1.

Giving Philosophy

'The Fluor Foundation serves as a philanthropic arm of the Fluor Corporation within the United States. Funded by contributions from the corporation, the Fluor Foundation responds to the needs, challenges and opportunities of our complex society by providing assistance to various responsible not-for-profit organizations. .. The Fluor Foundation has sought to identify activities in the communities where our employees live that provide meaningful service to their community.' *Fluor Foundation Publication*

Financial Summary

Total Giving: $3,272,912 (fiscal year ending October 31, 1998 approx); $4,806,825 (fiscal 1997); $4,194,270 (fiscal 1996). Note: Contributes through corporate direct giving program and foundation.
Giving Analysis: Giving for fiscal 1996 includes: foundation ($2,040,304); foundation matching gifts ($914,775); foundation scholarships ($720,080); foundation grants to United Way ($519,111); fiscal 1997: foundation ($3,683,716); domestic and international subsidiaries ($813,268); international subsidiaries ($272,371); corporate direct giving ($37,410); fiscal 1998: foundation ($3,272,912)
Assets: $5,191,302 (fiscal 1998); $5,624,285 (fiscal 1997); $4,834,612 (fiscal 1996)
Gifts Received: $2,391,873 (fiscal 1998); $3,881,432 (fiscal 1997); $4,725,797 (fiscal 1996). Note: 1996 contributions received from Fluor Corp.

Typical Recipients

Arts & Humanities: Arts Associations & Councils, Arts Centers, Arts Funds, Dance, History & Archaeology, Museums/Galleries, Music, Opera, Performing Arts, Public Broadcasting, Theater
Civic & Public Affairs: Botanical Gardens/Parks, Community Foundations, Economic Development, Employment/Job Training, Civic & Public Affairs-General, Hispanic Affairs, Housing, Nonprofit Management, Professional & Trade Associations, Public Policy, Safety, Urban & Community Affairs, Women's Affairs
Education: Business Education, Business-School Partnerships, Colleges & Universities, Education Associations, Education Funds, Education Reform, Engineering/Technological Education, Education-General, Medical Education, Minority Education, Public Education (Precollege), Science/Mathematics Education, Student Aid
Environment: Environment-General
Health: Cancer, Children's Health/Hospitals, Clinics/Medical Centers, Diabetes, Emergency/Ambulance Services, Hospitals
International: International Affairs, International Development
Religion: Religious Welfare
Science: Science Exhibits & Fairs, Scientific Centers & Institutes
Social Services: Child Welfare, Community Service Organizations, Scouts, Substance Abuse, United Funds/United Ways, Volunteer Services, YMCA/YWCA/YMHA/YWHA, Youth Organizations

Contributions Analysis

Giving Priorities: Education, social welfare, civic affairs, the arts, science, health, and international organizations. Contributions by overseas companies are independently administered. Organizations supported are identified in-country. Contributions overseas range form $250,000 to $300,000 annually.
Arts & Humanities: 5% to 10%. Focus is on performing arts, arts associations, opera, public broadcasting. Museums also receive support.
Civic & Public Affairs: 5% to 10%. Funding supports urban and community affairs, business and free enterprise groups, and public policy organizations.
Education: 55% to 60%. Majority of funding supports colleges and universities, with emphasis on science and technical education. Other interests include engineering education and minority education. Also sponsors employee matching gifts program.
Health: 10% to 15%. Supports emergency services, and some single-disease health organizations.
Social Services: 10% to 15%. Major priority is united funds, and significant support also funds youth organizations. The remainder is disbursed among child welfare, community service organizations and volunteer services.
Note: Above priorities based on foundation and direct giving. Total contributions were made in 1997.

Application Procedures

Initial Contact: Send a preliminary letter of request.
Application Requirements: Include full legal name of organization; mission statement and services provide total fundraising goal, amount raised to date. Include a description of organization, amount requested, purpose of funds sought, recently audited financial statement, and proof of tax-exempt status. List of governing board, list of other contributors, history of previous support by Fluor Daniel or A.T. Massey Coal, a description of organization of any volunteer involvement by Fluor Daniel or A.T. Massey Coal employees, and statement of why Fluor Daniel or A.T. Massey Coal might be appropriate donor.
Deadlines: None.
Review Process: After initial request is reviewed, additional information may be requested.
Decision Notification: Three to four months after receipt of request.

Restrictions

Does not provide funding directly to elementary or secondary schools, health initiatives or research, individual artists, film production, publishing activities, individuals, sports organizations, sports programs, veterans, fraternal, labor, religious organizations, lobbying organizations, or campaigns.

Corporate Officials

Philip Joseph Carroll: chairman, chief executive officer B New Orleans, LA 1937. ED Loyola University BS (1958); Tulane University MS (1961). PRIM CORP EMPL chairman, chief executive officer: Fluor Daniel Corp. CORP AFFIL director: Boise Cascade Corp. NONPR AFFIL director: Texas Medical Center; advisory council: Tulane University Center for Bioenvironmental Research; advisory board member: Salvation Army; member: National Petroleum Council; trustee: National Urban League; trustee: Museum Fine Arts; member: National Action Council Minorities Engineering; member: Government Business Council; director: Bretton Woods Committee; trustee: Committee for Economic Development; chairman: Botanic Garden; director: Boys & Girls Clubs of American; director: Baylor College Medicine; director: American Air Music; director: American Petroleum Institute. CLUB AFFIL Tchefuncta Country Club; River Oaks Country Club; 25 Year Petroleum Industries Club; Champions Golf Club.
James Ora Rollans: senior vice president, chief administrative officer, chief financial officer B Glendale, CA 1942. ED University of Southern California; California State University BS (1967). PRIM CORP EMPL senior vice president, chief administrative officer, chief financial officer: Fluor Corp. CORP AFFIL chairman: Lafayette Pharmaceutical Inc.; director: Plaza Communications Inc.; chief financial officer, director: Fluor Daniel Caribbean Inc.; officer, chief financial officer: Fluor Daniel Inc.; president: FD Engineers & Constructors; director: Flowserve Corp. NONPR AFFIL director: Irvine Medical Center; member: National Investor Relations Institute.
James C. Stein: president, chief operating officer B Columbus, OH 1943. ED Miami University (1964). PRIM CORP EMPL president, chief operating officer: Fluor Daniel Inc. CORP AFFIL director: Fluor Corp.

Giving Program Officials

John Robert Fluor, II: president, trustee B Orange, CA 1945. ED University of Southern California (1967). PRIM CORP EMPL vice president corporate relations: Fluor Corp.

Foundation Officials

Alan Boeckmann: trustee B 1948. ED University of Arizona. PRIM CORP EMPL group president: Fluor Daniel Inc.
Betty H. Bowers: trustee CORP AFFIL vice president government relations: Fluor Corp.
Philip Joseph Carroll: chairman, trustee (see above)
Suzanne Huffmon Esber: manager, community relationss
John Robert Fluor, II: president, trustee (see above)
James L. Gardner: trustee PRIM CORP EMPL senior vice president, general counsel: AT Masset Coal Co. Inc.
Charles R. Oliver: trustee B Nashville, TN 1943. ED Auburn University (1967); California State Polytechnic University, Pomona (1996). PRIM CORP EMPL group president global sales: Fluor Daniel, Inc.
James Ora Rollans: trustee (see above)
Andy Schwartz: treasurer
James C. Stein: trustee (see above)

Grants Analysis

Disclosure Period: fiscal year ending October 31, 1997
Total Grants: $1,429,658*
Number of Grants: 156
Average Grant: $4,595*
Highest Grant: $50,000
Typical Range: $100 to $20,000
***Note:** Giving excludes matching gifts, scholarship and United Way. Average grant excludes highest grant.

Recent Grants

Note: Grants derived from 1997 Form 990.

Arts & Humanities

50,000 CENTER FOR THE PERFORMING ARTS FOUNDATION, Greenville, SC

Education

486,989 CITIZENS' SCHOLARSHIP FOUNDATION OF AMERICA, Minneapolis, MN
212,520 CITIZENS' SCHOLARSHIP FOUNDATION OF AMERICA, Minneapolis, MN
100,000 CONSTRUCTION EDUCATION FOUNDATION, Rosslvn, VA

32,090	TEXAS A&M UNIVERSITY, College Station, TX
30,960	CITIZENS' SCHOLARSHIP FOUNDATION OF AMERICA, Minneapolis, MN
30,000	CAL POLY STATE UNIV, SAN LUIS OBISPO SCHOOL ENGINEERING, San Luis Obispo, CA
25,000	TEXAS A&M UNIVERSITY - COLLEGE STATION, College Station, TX
25,000	UNIVERSITY OF CALIFORNIA IRVINE - SCHOOL OF ENGINEERING, Irvine, CA
25,000	UNIVERSITY OF HOUSTON, Houston, TX
25,000	UNIVERSITY OF TEXAS AT AUSTIN, Austin, TX
21,000	UNIVERSITY OF NORTH CAROLINA AT CHAPEL HILL, Chapel Hill, NC
20,000	ARIZONA STATE UNIVERSITY, AZ
20,000	CALIFORNIA STATE POLYTECHNIC UNIVERSITY, POMONA, Pomona, CA
20,000	COLORADO SCHOOL OF MINES, Golden, CO
20,000	REGENTS OF THE UNIVERSITY OF CALIFORNIA, San Francisco, CA
20,000	UNIVERSITY OF CALIFORNIA, SAN DIEGO, La Jolla, CA
20,000	UNIVERSITY OF SOUTH CAROLINA, COLLEGE OF BUSINESS ADMIN., Columbia, SC
20,000	VIRGINIA POLYTECHNIC INSTITUTE AND STATE UNIVERSITY, VA
17,500	AUBURN UNIVERSITY, Auburn University, AL
17,500	GEORGIA INSTITUTE OF TECHNOLOGY - SCHOOL OF CHEMICAL, Atlanta, GA
17,500	NORTH CAROLINA STATE UNIVERSITY, Greensboro, NC
17,500	UNIVERSITY OF FLORIDA, Greensville, FL
15,000	CAL POLY STATE UNIV, SAN LUIS OBISOP - SCHOOL OF ENGINEERING, San Luis Obispo, CA
15,000	DREXEL UNIVERSITY, Philadelphia, PA
15,000	LOUISIANA STATE UNIVERSITY, Baton Rouge, LA
15,000	LOUISIANA STATE UNIVERSITY, Ruston, LA
15,000	MARSHALL UNIVERSITY FOUNDATION INC., Muntington, WV
15,000	NATIONAL SOCIETY OF PROFESSIONAL ENGINEERS, Alexandria, VA
15,000	NEW JERSEY INSTITUTE OF TECHNOLOGY, Newark, NJ
15,000	PURDUE UNIVERSITY, West Lafayette, IN
Health	
25,000	SUSAN G. KOMEN FOUNDATION, INC., McLean, VA
15,000	GREENVILLE MEDICAL CLINIC, Greenville, SC
10,000	ASSOC. FOR THE CURE OF CANCER OF THE PROSTATE (CAP CURE), Santa Monica, CA
AMERICAN NATIONAL RED CROSS, GREENWILLE COUNTY CHAPTER, Greenville, SC	
Science	
15,000	ROPER MOUNTAIN SCIENCE CENTER ASSOCIATION, Greenville, SC
Social Services	
178,906	UNITED WAY, WA
142,006	UNITED WAY OF ORANGE COUNTY, Irvine, CA
107,420	UNITED WAY OF ORANGE COUNTY, Irvine, CA
104,589	UNITED WAY OF ORANGE COUNTY, Irvine, CA
104,060	UNITED WAY OF ORANGE COUNTY, Irvine, CA
34,120	UNITED WAY OF ORANGE COUNTY, Irvine, CA
31,331	UNITED WAY OF RUTHERFORD COUNTY, Murfreesboro, IN
20,000	THUNDERBIRD, Glendale, AZ

FM GLOBAL

Company Contact

1301 Atwood Ave.
Johnston, RI 02919
Phone: (401)275-3000
Fax: (401)275-3029
Web: http://www.fmglobal.com

Company Description

Formed by Merger of: Allendale Insurance Co. (1999); Arkwright Mutual Insurance Co. (1999).
Assets: US$6,000,000,000 (1999)
Employees: 4,000 (1999)

Description

Organization Type: Corporate Giving Program

Giving Philosophy

FM Global is an insurance organization with a unique risk management focus. Our customers look to us to help them maintain continuity in their business operations, develop cost-effective insurance and risk financing solutions - and to minimize the overall financial impact if a loss does occur. We meet these needs with customized programs that draw upon our: State-of-the-art loss prevention engineering and research; Risk management skills and support services; Tailored risk transfer capabilities; and Superior financial strength.

We will ensure that our employees have the tools, resources and training they need to support our mission and to achieve personal success and career satisfaction. As we continue to evolve as a business and as an employer, we will be mindful that the strategies we pursue and decisions we make must ultimately be for the benefit of our mutual policyholders.

FMC CORP.

Company Contact

Chicago, IL
Web: http://www.fmc.com

Company Description

Revenue: US$4,378,400,000
Employees: 16,805
Fortune Rank: 386, per FORTUNE Magazine's list of 500 Largest U.S. Corporations (1999).
FF 386
SIC(s): 1041 Gold Ores, 1044 Silver Ores, 1479 Chemical & Fertilizer Mining Nec, 2819 Industrial Inorganic Chemicals Nec.

Operating Locations

Angola: FMC International AG; Argentina: Minera Del Altiplano S.A.; FMC Argentina SACI, Cordoba; Australia: FMC (Australia) Ltd., Noble Park; Austria: FMC Chemikalien Handels GmbH, Vienna; Belgium: FMC Europe NV, Sint-Niklaas, Oost-Vlaanderen; Bangladesh: FMC International AG; FMC International Sales Corporation; Brazil: FMC do Brasil Industria e Commercio Ltda.; Jetway Systems Equipmentos Aeroportuarios Ltda.; CBV Industria Mecanica SA, Rio de Janeiro; Canada: FMC Offshore Canada Company; FMC of Canada Ltd., Markham; Chile: FMC Corporation, Inc. Chile Ltda.; Neogel S.A.; People's Republic of China: FMC Asia Pacific Inc.; FMC Hong Kong Limited; Suzhou Fu Mei-Shi Crop Care Company, Ltd.; Colombia: FMC Latino America, S.A.; Czech Republic: F&N Agro Ceska Republica, S.r.o.; F&N Argo Slovensko. S.R.O.; Denmark: FMC A/S, Vallensbaek, Copenhagen; Equatorial Guinea: FMC Subsea Services, Inc.; Egypt: FMC International AG; France: Frigoscandia Equipment SA; FMC France SA, Montigny Le Bretonneux; FMC Food Machinery, Quimper, Finistere; FMC Europe (SA), Sens; FMC Overseas SA, Sens; Gabon: FMC Gabon S.A.R.L.; Germany: F.A. Sening GmbH; FMC GmbH; Frigoscandia Equipment GmbH; Smith Meter GmbH, Ellerbek, Schleswig-Holstein; Jetway GmbH, Frankfurt, Hessen; Greece: FMC Hellas, EPE; FMC International, AG; Guatemala: FMC Guatemala, S.A.; Hong Kong: FMC Hong Kong Ltd.; FMC Asia Pacific, Causeway Bay; Indonesia: FMC Hong Kong Limited; P.T. Bina Guna Kimia Indonesia; P.T. FMC Santana Petroleum Equipment Indonesia; India: FMC Asia Pacific, Inc.; FMC Sanmar Limited; Ireland: FMC International AG, Cork; Italy: FMC Italia SpA, Parma, Emilia-Romagna; Jordan: FMC International, AG; Japan: Asia Lithium Corporation; FMC K.K.; Honjo-FMC Energy Systems, Inc.; L.H. Company, Ltd.; Kenya: FMC International AG; Republic of Korea: FMC Korea Limited; Mexico: E.M.D., S.A. de C.V.; Fabricacion Maquinaria y Ceras S.A. de C.V.; FMC Equipo Petrolero S.A. de C.V.; FMC Ingredientes Alimenticios; Electro Quimica Mexicana SA de CV, Ciudad de Mexico; FMC de Mexico SA de CV, Ciudad de Mexico; FMC Agroquimica de Mexico de RL de CV, Zapopan; Malaysia: FMC Wellhead Equipment, Sdn. Bhd.; Jetway Systems Asia, Inc.; Netherlands: FMC Fluid Control (Nederland BV), Alphen Aan Den Rijn; FMC Industrial Chemicals (Netherlands) BV, Farmsum, Groningen; Norway: Kongsberg Offshore AS, Kongsberg, Buskerud; Oman: FMC ETEG & Partners LLC; Pakistan: FMC International S.A.; FMC United (Private) Ltd.; Panama: FMC Latino America S.A.; Philippines: FMC International S.A.; Marine Colloids (Philippines) Inc.; Poland: F&R Agro S.P. z.o.o.; FMC Corporation Poland; Puerto Rico: FMC International, AG; FMC Kongsberg International AG; Republic of South Africa: FMC (South Africa)(Proprietary)Ltd.; Singapore: FMC Singapore Pte.Ltd.; FMC Southeast Asia Pte.Ltd.; FMC Southeast Asia Pte. Ltd., Singapore; Spain: Frigoscandia Equipment Iberica, S.A.; Valentin Herraz, S.A.; FMC Airline Equipment Europe SA, Alcala de Henares; FMC Foret SA, Barcelona, Cataluna; Foraneto SL, Barcelona, Cataluna; Forel SL, Barcelona, Cataluna; Peroxidos Organicos SA, Barcelona, Cataluna; Sibelco Espanola SA, Barcelona, Cataluna; Forsean SL, Huelva; Sweden: Frigoscandia Equipment AB; Frigoscandia Equipment Holding AB; Frigoscandia Equipment International AB; Frigoscandia Equipment Norden AB; Frigoscandia Freezer AB; Potato Processing Machinery AB; Switzerland: FMC Kongsberg International AB; FMC International AG, Zug; Thailand: Thai Peroxide Company, Ltd.; FMC (Thailand) Ltd., Bangkok; United Arab Emirates: FMC International, S.A. (Dubai); United Kingdom: Sofec Ltd., Edinburgh, Lothian; FMC Corp. (United Kingdom) Ltd., Manchester, Greater Manchester; Ukraine: FMC Kiev; Uruguay: Lanfor Investment, S.A.; Venezuela: Tripoliven, C.A.

FMC Foundation

Giving Contact

Ms. Catherine Swigon, Executive Director
FMC Foundation
200 E. Randolph Dr.
Chicago, IL 60601
Phone: (312)861-6105
Fax: (312)861-6141
Email: fmcfoundation@fmc.com

Description

EIN: 946063032
Organization Type: Corporate Foundation
Giving Locations: nationally; operating locations.

Grant Types: Capital, Employee Matching Gifts, General Support.
Note: Employee matching gift ratio: 1 to 1 for higher education.

Giving Philosophy

'We believe that good corporate citizenship requires active involvement in our communities. We focus our giving in areas that most directly affect FMC, our employees and our public. We encourage our employees' voluntary participation in charitable activities both by matching a portion of their contributions to the United Way and by giving special consideration to organizations in which FMC people have been actively involved. We support only those organizations which have demonstrated their effectiveness and fiscal responsibility. We support organizations which promote individual liberty, favor limited government and strengthen private enterprise.' *FMC Foundation Annual Report*

Financial Summary

Total Giving: $2,000,000 (fiscal year ending November 30, 1999 approx); $1,716,280 (fiscal 1998 approx); $2,800,000 (fiscal 1997 approx). Note: Contributes through corporate direct giving program and foundation. 1995 Giving includes corporate direct giving; foundation ($949,970); matching gifts ($241,125); United Way ($317,765).
Assets: $121,413 (fiscal 1995); $761,951 (fiscal 1993); $861,863 (fiscal 1992)
Gifts Received: $5,500,000 (fiscal 1995)

Typical Recipients

Arts & Humanities: Arts Festivals, Arts Institutes, Community Arts, Museums/Galleries, Music, Opera
Civic & Public Affairs: African American Affairs, Business/Free Enterprise, Clubs, Economic Development, Economic Policy, Employment/Job Training, Law & Justice, Professional & Trade Associations, Public Policy, Rural Affairs, Urban & Community Affairs, Zoos/Aquariums
Education: Agricultural Education, Business Education, Colleges & Universities, Community & Junior Colleges, Economic Education, Education Funds, Engineering/Technological Education, International Exchange, Minority Education, Science/Mathematics Education, Student Aid
Environment: Air/Water Quality, Environment-General, Wildlife Protection
Health: Emergency/Ambulance Services, Health Policy/Cost Containment, Health Funds, Health Organizations, Hospitals, Medical Rehabilitation, Public Health
International: International Affairs, International Environmental Issues, International Peace & Security Issues
Science: Science Museums, Scientific Centers & Institutes, Scientific Organizations
Social Services: Child Welfare, Community Service Organizations, United Funds/United Ways, YMCA/YWCA/YMHA/YWHA, Youth Organizations

Contributions Analysis

Giving Priorities: Education, United Way, hospitals, community improvement, public issues, and urban affairs. Limited support for U.S.-based organizations with an international focus.
Civic & Public Affairs: 15% to 20%. Supports cultural organizations; youth groups that encourage initiative, independence, and self-reliance; and civic organizations that address recreational needs and environmental, urban, and governmental issues. Cultural recipients include museums, ballet, and music. Environmental interests promote policies that protect the environment yet encourage economic growth, job creation, and an abundant food supply. Priority is given to civic groups that raise the level of understanding of the competitive market economy. A small number of grants are made in plant communities for urban renewal, city planning, improved municipal services, and efficiencyin government. (Public Policy) 15% to 20%. Foundation supports local and national organizations that promote good government, economic opportunity, and a strong climate for free enterprise. Such programs include urban affairs organizations that benefit minorities, women, and the disabled in the fields of education and job training. Priority is given to organizations that encourage initiative, promote self-help, and foster economic self-reliance. In the field of public issues, support goes to programs that relate to the business community anddemonstrably affect public policy. Also supports organizations that promote a greater understanding of the U.S. economic system.
Education: 30% to 35%. Generally, almost half of foundation's education contributions are made through employee matching gifts program. In addition, supports student associations at 28 colleges and universities across the country that graduate a significant number of future employees. Sponsors children of employees through National Merit Scholarship Corporation and the Youth for Understanding exchange program. Grants are made to minority programs in fields relevant to company. Also supports free enterprise and economic education through colleges, universities, and other organizations for younger students.
Health: 30% to 35%. The majority of grants in this category support the United Way. Matches employee gifts to the United Way on a sliding scale. Foundation also funds hospitals and medical centers to ensure employees have access to stable, high-quality medical resources. Supports capital and major fund-raising campaigns. Emphasizes hospitals that engage in basic research, serve as teaching hospitals, and are affiliated with medical schools. Some support goes to human services in plant communities.
International: Makes contributions to U.S.-based nonprofit organizations with an international focus.

Application Procedures

Initial Contact: a brief (no more than two pages) typewritten letter
Application Requirements: a description of organization; statement of organization's activities and programs; specific amount of money requested; explanation of how funds will be used; project location; timetable; proof of tax-exempt status; and list of board of directors
Deadlines: None; budget determined in fall quarter
Review Process: if organization is local, request is forwarded for local management review and recommendation; if national, preliminary review by foundation committee, then review by foundation board
Evaluative Criteria: gives strong consideration to organizations which count a number of FMC employees among their active supporters; emphasizes groups that strive to improve communities in which employees live and work and to improve environment in which company does business; organization must have proven effectiveness and a broad base of community support; priority given to organizations and institutions promoting the free enterprise system
Decision Notification: foundation board meets at least twice a year
Notes: Foundation discourages submission of unsolicited and voluminous support materials. Based on application information listed above, if funding appears possible, foundation will request the following: audited financial report for most recently completed year of operation; organizational budget for current operating year, showing expenses and income by sources; copy of organization's IRS tax-exempt status ruling; and a sample donor's list showing corporate and foundation contributors to the organization for the past 12 months.

Restrictions

Foundation does not support individuals, state or regional associations of independent colleges, elementary or secondary schools, organizations that receive or qualify for United Way support, dinners or special events, fraternal organizations, goodwill advertising, political or lobbying groups, or religious organizations for sectarian purposes.
Foundation also does not support national health agencies or hospitals for operating expenses, or medical research.
Grants are not pledged for a period longer than one year.
The foundation usually only gives in plant communities.

Additional Information

Requests for special programs at hospitals (for example, outpatient alcoholism programs, drug addiction, or prenatal care) are not given high priority, but are considered individually as funds become available.
Publications: Foundation Annual Report

Corporate Officials

Patricia D. Brozowski: vice president communicationsaffairs PRIM CORP EMPL vice president communications: FMC Corp.
Robert Norcross Burt: chairman, chief executive officer, director B Lakewood, OH 1937. ED Princeton University BSChE (1959); Harvard University MBA (1964). PRIM CORP EMPL chairman, chief executive officer, director: FMC Corp. CORP AFFIL director: Warner-Lambert Co.; director: FMC Gold Co.; director: Phelps Dodge Corp. NONPR AFFIL director: Rehabilitation Institute Chicago; director: World Resources Institute; chairman leadership council: Princeton University School Engineering & Applied Science; member: Manufacturer Alliance Productivity & Innovation; director: Orchestra Association Chicago Symphony Orchestra; member: Illinois Business Roundtable; member: Business Roundtable; director: Evanston Hospital.
Robert Khristie: director public affairs PRIM CORP EMPL director public affairs: FMC Corp.

Foundation Officials

Patricia D. Brozowski: president, director (see above)
Robert Norcross Burt: director (see above)
William Joseph Kirby: vice president, director B Baltimore, MD 1937. ED Pennsylvania State University BA (1959); Cornell University MS (1961); Harvard University Advanced Management Program AMP (1981). PRIM CORP EMPL senior vice president: FMC Corp. NONPR AFFIL trustee: Roosevelt University; member director: University Wyoming Institute Environment & Natural Resources & Policy; fellow: National Academy Human Resources; member: Pers Roundtable; member: Labor Policy Association; director: Metropolitan Planning Council Chicago; member: Field Museum Natural History; member: Business Roundtable. CLUB AFFIL Mid-America Club; Harvard Club; Economic Club; Glen View Golf Club; Chicago Club.
James Allen McClung: vice president, director B Fostoria, OH 1937. ED College of Wooster BA (1959); University of Kansas MA (1962); Michigan State University PhD (1966). PRIM CORP EMPL vice president worldwide marketing: FMC Corp. CORP AFFIL director: FMC Canada Ltd.; director: FMC Nederland BV. NONPR AFFIL director: Japan-American Society; Manufacturer Alliance; director: American Graduate School International Management.
Daniel Norman Schuchardt: secretary, treasurer B Saint Louis, MO 1937. ED Washington University (1958); Northwestern University (1979). PRIM CORP EMPL assistant treasurer: FMC Corp. CORP AFFIL assistant treasurer: Frigoscandia Inc.; president: Mid-Atlantic Acceptance Co. Ltd.
Catherine Swigon: executive director

Grants Analysis

Disclosure Period: fiscal year ending November 30,
Total Grants: $949,970
Number of Grants: 162
Average Grant: $5,864

Highest Grant: $111,500
Typical Range: $1,000 to $10,000
Note: Analysis excludes United Way; matching gifts.

Recent Grants

Note: Grants derived from fiscal 1995 Form 990.

Arts & Humanities

24,685 Ravinia Festival Association, Highland Park, IL
15,000 University of Wyoming Foundation Art Museum, Laramie, WY
10,000 Chicago Symphony Orchestra, Chicago, IL
8,500 Lyric Opera, Chicago, IL

Civic & Public Affairs

50,000 Commercial Club Foundation, Chicago, IL
29,500 National Future Farmers of America, Madison, WI
17,500 Heritage Foundation, Washington, DC
15,000 American Enterprise Institute for Public Policy Research, Washington, DC
15,000 National Society of Black Engineers, Alexandria, VA
10,000 Employment Policy Foundation, Washington, DC
10,000 Lincoln Park Zoological Society, Chicago, IL
10,000 Product Liability Advisory Council Foundation, Detroit, MI
10,000 Resources for the Future, Washington, DC
9,000 Metropolitan Planning Council, Chicago, IL
7,500 Competitive Enterprise Institute, Washington, DC
7,500 Gateway Foundation, Chicago, IL
1,000 Western States Foundation, Annandale, VA

Education

36,269 National Merit Scholarship Corporation, Evanston, IL
34,000 University of Chicago, Chicago, IL
29,000 Academy of Natural Sciences, Philadelphia, PA
25,000 Youth for Understanding, Washington, DC
20,000 Roosevelt University, Chicago, IL
16,000 Princeton University, Princeton, NJ
11,000 Northwestern University, Chicago, IL
11,000 University of Pennsylvania Wharton School of Business, Philadelphia, PA
11,000 University of Virginia Darden Graduate School of Business Administration, Charlottesville, VA
9,500 Inroads, Chicago, IL
7,500 Julia R. Masterman Laboratory and Demonstration School, Philadelphia, PA
6,500 Junior Achievement, Chicago, IL
6,000 Saul School of Agricultural Sciences, Philadelphia, PA

Environment

15,000 Keystone Center, Keystone, CO
10,000 Green River Green Belt Task Force, Green River, WY

Health

10,000 American Council on Sciences and Health, New York, NY
10,000 Rehabilitation Institute, Chicago, IL

International

50,000 Center for Strategic and International Studies, Washington, DC
50,000 Center for Strategic and International Studies, Washington, DC
20,000 Hoover Institution on War, Revolution, and Peace, Stanford, CA
20,000 Hoover Institution on War, Revolution, and Peace, Stanford, CA
15,000 World Resources Institute, Washington, DC
15,000 World Resources Institute, Washington, DC

Science

15,000 Museum of Science and Industry, Chicago, IL

Social Services

111,500 United Way, Chicago, IL
60,155 United Way of Southeastern Pennsylvania, Philadelphia, PA
16,380 United Way Princeton Area Communities, Princeton Junction, NJ
14,475 United Campaigns, Pocatello, ID
12,500 Sweetwater County United Way, Rock Springs, WY
12,155 United Way Gaston County, Gastonia, NC
10,402 United Way Texas Gulf Coast, Houston, TX
10,000 Winners on Wheels, Fresno, CA
9,385 United Way, Stephenville, TX
7,745 United Way Faulkner County, Conway, AR
6,000 Heart of Florida United Way, Orlando, FL
5,635 United Way Delaware, Wilmington, DE

FORBES INC.

Company Contact

New York, NY

Company Description

Employees: 500
SIC(s): 2731 Book Publishing.

Corporate Sponsorship

Type: Arts & cultural events; Festivals/fairs; Music & entertainment events; Pledge-a-thon; Sports events

Forbes Foundation

Giving Contact

Mr. Leonard H. Yablon, Secretary & Treasurer
Forbes Foundation
Care of Forbes Inc.
60 5th Avenue
New York, NY 10011
Phone: (212)620-2248
Fax: (212)633-1958

Description

Founded: 1979
EIN: 237037319
Organization Type: Corporate Foundation. Supports preselected organizations only.
Giving Locations: NY: New York including metropolitan area
Grant Types: Capital, Endowment, General Support.

Financial Summary

Total Giving: $2,352,644 (1998); $1,273,185 (1997); $1,508,195 (1996). Note: Contributes through foundation only.
Giving Analysis: Giving for 1997 includes: foundation grants to United Way ($1,000); 1998: foundation grants to United Way ($2,000)
Assets: $5,455 (1998); $27,776 (1997); $25,641 (1996)
Gifts Received: $2,330,000 (1998); $1,275,000 (1997); $1,480,000 (1996). Note: The foundation receives contributions from Forbes Inc.

Typical Recipients

Arts & Humanities: Arts Associations & Councils, Arts Centers, Arts Funds, Arts Institutes, Dance, Ethnic & Folk Arts, Arts & Humanities-General, Historic Preservation, History & Archaeology, Libraries, Literary Arts, Museums/Galleries, Music, Opera, Performing Arts, Public Broadcasting, Theater
Civic & Public Affairs: African American Affairs, Botanical Gardens/Parks, Civil Rights, Community Foundations, Economic Development, Economic Policy, Employment/Job Training, Civic & Public Affairs-General, Housing, Legal Aid, Nonprofit Management, Philanthropic Organizations, Professional & Trade Associations, Public Policy, Safety, Urban & Community Affairs, Zoos/Aquariums
Education: Arts/Humanities Education, Colleges & Universities, Economic Education, Education Associations, Education Reform, Education-General, Leadership Training, Literacy, Medical Education, Minority Education, Private Education (Precollege), Public Education (Precollege), Science/Mathematics Education, Social Sciences Education, Special Education, Student Aid
Environment: Environment-General, Wildlife Protection
Health: AIDS/HIV, Arthritis, Cancer, Clinics/Medical Centers, Diabetes, Emergency/Ambulance Services, Health Funds, Health Organizations, Hospices, Hospitals, Medical Research, Mental Health, Nursing Services, Single-Disease Health Associations
International: Foreign Arts Organizations, Foreign Educational Institutions, Foreign Educational Institutions, Human Rights, International Affairs, International Organizations, International Peace & Security Issues, International Relations, International Relief Efforts
Religion: Churches, Jewish Causes, Religious Organizations, Religious Welfare
Science: Science Museums
Social Services: Child Welfare, Community Centers, Community Service Organizations, Family Planning, Family Services, Food/Clothing Distribution, Homes, Recreation & Athletics, Scouts, Senior Services, Substance Abuse, United Funds/United Ways, Volunteer Services, Youth Organizations

Contributions Analysis

Giving Priorities: Education, the arts, social welfare, religion, and civics.
Arts & Humanities: 6%. Funds arts associations, museums, libraries, and historical preservation.
Civic & Public Affairs: 5% to 10%. Business, public policy, and professional organizations receive support.
Education: 79%. Colleges, universities, and private precollege education are funded.
Health: 15%. Supports hospitals, medical education, and pediatric health.
Religion: 2%. Funds religious organizations.
Social Services: 3%. Supports child welfare and youth organizations.

Corporate Officials

Christopher 'Kip' Forbes: vice chairman, corporate secretary, director B Morristown, NJ 1950. ED Princeton University BA (1972). PRIM CORP EMPL vice chairman, corporate secretary, director: Forbes Inc. NONPR AFFIL board advisors: Princeton University Art Museum; director: Victorian Society America; director: New York Historical Society; director: Newark Museum; member president council: Museum City New York; member advisory committee: Museum Fine Arts; director: Friends New Jersey State Museum; national trustee: Baltimore Museum Art; director: Brooklyn Museum Art; member council: American Museum Britain. CLUB AFFIL Salmagundi Club; Grolier Club; National Arts Club; Century Club.
Malcolm Stevenson Forbes, Jr.: president B Morristown, NJ 1947. ED Princeton University BA (1970). PRIM CORP EMPL president: Forbes Inc.

Caspar Willard Weinberger: chairman B San Francisco, CA 1917. ED Harvard University AB (1938); Harvard University LLB (1941). PRIM CORP EMPL chairman: Forbes Magazine. NONPR AFFIL trustee: Winston Churchill Memorial Trust; member: Washington DC Court Appeals; member: American Bar Association; member: California Bar Association. CLUB AFFIL Harvard Club; Pacific-Union Club; Bohemian Club; Century Club.

Giving Program Officials

Caspar Willard Weinberger: chairman (see above)

Foundation Officials

Christopher 'Kip' Forbes: vice president (see above)

Malcolm Stevenson Forbes, Jr.: president (see above)

Leonard Harold Yablon: secretary-treasurer B New York, NY 1929. ED Long Island University BS (1950); City University of New York MBA (1969). PRIM CORP EMPL executive vice president, director, chief financial officer: Forbes Inc. CORP AFFIL director: SRJ Financial Group Inc.; director: United States Financial Group Inc.; vice president: Forbes Trinchera; president: Sangre de Cristo Ranches; president: Forbes Europe; vice president: Forbes Investors Advisory Institute; president: Fiji Forbes Inc.

Grants Analysis

Disclosure Period: calendar year ending 1998
Total Grants: $2,350,644*
Number of Grants: 330
Average Grant: $4,105*
Highest Grant: $1,000,000
Typical Range: $100 to $5,000
***Note:** Giving excludes United Way. Average grant figure excludes highest grant.

Recent Grants

Note: Grants derived from 1998 Form 990.

Arts & Humanities

25,000	New York Public Library, New York, NY
22,000	Business Committee for the Arts, New York, NY
15,000	New Jersey Historical Society, Newark, NJ
12,500	Historic House Trust of New York City, New York, NY
10,000	Association for Colonial Theater, Phoenixville, PA
10,000	Merchant's House Museum, New York, NY
10,000	Ronald Reagan Presidential Foundation, Simi Valley, CA
5,000	American Museum of Natural History, New York, NY
5,000	American Russian Youth Orchestra, New York, NY
5,000	Art Museum/Princeton University, Princeton, NJ

Civic & Public Affairs

50,000	Prince of Wales Foundation, Washington, DC
25,000	Community Coalition, New York, NY
25,000	Prince of Wales Foundation, Washington, DC
10,000	American Enterprise Foundation, Washington, DC
10,000	Center for Effective Compassion, Washington, DC
10,000	Frontiers of Freedom Institute, Arlington, VA
10,000	Old Westbury Gardens, Westbury, NY
5,000	Adopt A Bench Program, New York, NY
5,000	New York Botanical Garden, New York, NY

Education

1,000,000	Princeton University, Princeton, NJ
335,000	University of New Orleans Foundation, New Orleans, LA
75,000	St. Andrew's School, New York, NY
50,000	Far Hills Country Day School, Far Hills, NJ
30,000	Detroit Institute of Ophthalmology, Detroit, MI
25,000	Brown University - Annual Fund, Providence, RI
25,000	Purnell School, Pottersville, NJ
20,000	Drew University, Madison, NJ
20,000	New York Academy of Art, New York, NY
15,000	Jackie Robinson Foundation, New York, NY
14,830	Jackie Robinson Foundation, New York, NY
12,500	Friends of Grace Church School, New York, NY
10,000	Brooks School Annual Fund, North Andover, MA
10,000	CEO America, Bentonville, AR
10,000	Inner City Scholarship Fund, New York, NY
10,000	Tougaloo College, Tougaloo, MS
6,000	National Council on Economic Education, New York, NY
5,000	Brooklyn Academy of Music, Brooklyn, NY
5,000	Danny L. Davis Scholarship Fund, New York, NY
5,000	St. Mark's School, San Rafael, CA

Health

10,000	Presbyterian Hospital Gala, New York, NY
10,000	Providence Alaska Foundation, Anchorage, AK
5,000	Care Net, Falls Church, VA

International

5,000	American Academy in Rome, New York, NY

Religion

25,000	UJA-Federation of New York, New York, NY
9,000	Church of St. John on the Mountain, Bernardsville, NJ
5,000	Church of the Holy Spirit, Chicago, IL
5,000	Crisis Partnership, Atlanta, GA

Social Services

25,000	Police Athletic League, New York, NY
10,000	Boy's Club of New York, New York, NY
5,000	Citymeals-On-Wheels, New York, NY

FORD METER BOX CO.

Company Contact

775 Manchester Ave.
PO Box 443
Wabash, IN 46992-0443
Phone: (219)563-3171
Fax: (219)563-6781
Web: http://www.fordmeterbox.com

Company Description

Employees: 700
SIC(s): 3321 Gray & Ductile Iron Foundries, 3494 Valves & Pipe Fittings Nec, 3822 Environmental Controls, 3823 Process Control Instruments.

Ford Meter Box Foundation

Giving Contact

Marta D. Gidley, Secretary
Ford Meter Box Foundation

Description

Founded: 1988
EIN: 351253080
Organization Type: Corporate Foundation
Giving Locations: IN: Wabash County and surrounding area
Grant Types: General Support, Project.

Financial Summary

Total Giving: $296,542 (1998); $258,810 (1997); $348,043 (1996). Note: Contributes through foundation only.
Assets: $4,274,946 (1998); $3,731,578 (1997); $3,699,878 (1996)
Gifts Received: $500,000 (1998); $500,000 (1996); $1,000,000 (1995). Note: Contributions are received from Ford Meter Box Co.

Typical Recipients

Arts & Humanities: Arts Associations & Councils, Community Arts, Dance, Film & Video, Historic Preservation, History & Archaeology, Libraries, Museums/Galleries, Music, Opera, Performing Arts, Theater
Civic & Public Affairs: Botanical Gardens/Parks, Business/Free Enterprise, Clubs, Community Foundations, Economic Development, Economic Policy, Employment/Job Training, Civic & Public Affairs-General, Housing, Law & Justice, Municipalities/Towns, Nonprofit Management, Parades/Festivals, Philanthropic Organizations, Professional & Trade Associations, Public Policy, Safety, Urban & Community Affairs, Zoos/Aquariums
Education: Agricultural Education, Arts/Humanities Education, Business Education, Colleges & Universities, Education Associations, Education Funds, Elementary Education (Public), Education-General, International Studies, Leadership Training, Preschool Education, Private Education (Precollege), Public Education (Precollege), Religious Education, Science/Mathematics Education, Secondary Education (Public), Student Aid
Health: Cancer, Children's Health/Hospitals, Emergency/Ambulance Services, Eyes/Blindness, Geriatric Health, Health Organizations, Heart, Hospices, Hospitals, Medical Research, Mental Health, Outpatient Health Care, Prenatal Health Issues, Single-Disease Health Associations
International: Foreign Arts Organizations, Health Care/Hospitals, Missionary/Religious Activities
Religion: Churches, Religious Welfare
Social Services: Animal Protection, At-Risk Youth, Big Brother/Big Sister, Child Abuse, Child Welfare, Community Service Organizations, Crime Prevention, Domestic Violence, Emergency Relief, Family Services, Food/Clothing Distribution, Homes, Recreation & Athletics, Scouts, Senior Services, Substance Abuse, United Funds/United Ways, Youth Organizations

Contributions Analysis

Arts & Humanities: 2%. Museums, opera, music, and arts associations receive funding.
Civic & Public Affairs: 20%. Supports community-oriented philanthropic organizations and business and free enterprise.
Education: 12%. Focus on higher education, education funds, and public education.
Health: About 5%. Heart associations, pediatric medical research, and cancer agencies are funded.
Religion: 1%.
Social Services: 60%. Funds youth organizations and summer camps, animal shelters, homes, child welfare, and community service organizations.
Note: Total contributions in 1998.

Application Procedures

Initial Contact: Send written request.
Application Requirements: Include amount requested and purpose for which funds will be used.
Deadlines: None.

Corporate Officials

Terry D. Agness: president, director PRIM CORP EMPL president, director: Ford Meter Box Co. CORP AFFIL director: Uni-Flange Holdings Inc.

Steven R. Ford: secretary, treasurer PRIM CORP EMPL secretary, treasurer: Ford Meter Box Co.

David M. Kunkel: senior vice president, director PRIM CORP EMPL senior vice president, director: Ford Meter Box Co.

Henry A. Leander: chairman PRIM CORP EMPL chairman: Ford Meter Box Co.

Foundation Officials

Richard E. Ford: president

Steven R. Ford: treasurer (see above)

Marta D. Gidley: secretary

David M. Kunkel: vice president (see above)

Grants Analysis

Disclosure Period: calendar year ending 1998
Total Grants: $296,542
Number of Grants: 51
Average Grant: $5,815
Highest Grant: $60,000
Typical Range: $150 to $10,000

Recent Grants

Note: Grants derived from 1998 Form 990.

Arts & Humanities

2,000 Wabash Valley Dance Theater, Wabash, IN -- Christmas Festival
1,300 Paradise Spring, Inc., Wabash, IN -- Capital Improvement
1,100 Wabash Valley Music Association, Wabash, IN -- Program AD
1,000 Manchester Symphony Society, Manchester, IN -- General Fund
1,000 Wabash County Arts Council, Inc., Wabash, IN -- General Fund
500 Indianapolis Symphony Orchestra, Indianapolis, IN -- General Fund
250 Historic Landmarks Foundation of Indiana, Indianapolis, IN -- General Operating Fund
250 Indianapolis Museum of Art, Indianapolis, IN -- Operating Fund Campaign

Civic & Public Affairs

24,752 City of Wabash, Wabash, IN -- Iris Fire Helmets and Monitor
15,000 Community Foundation of Wabash County, Manchester, IN -- General Fund--2nd Pymt of 3 Year Pledge
6,500 City of Wabash, Wabash, IN -- Wabash City Park Master Plan
6,000 Wabash Marketplace, Wabash, IN -- Downtown Revitalization--Streetscape
2,500 Honeywell Foundation, The, Wabash, IN -- New Year's Eve Gala
2,400 Chester Township Volunteer Fire Department, North Manchester, IN -- Extrication Tools
700 Indiana Fiscal Policy Institute, Indianapolis, IN -- General Fund
500 Community Foundation of Wabash County, Manchester, IN -- Casey Sparling Memorial Athletic Scholarship
500 Hudson Institute, Indianapolis, IN -- General Fund
259 Indiana Donors Alliance, Indianapolis, IN -- General Fund
250 Community Foundation of Wabash County, Manchester, IN -- Manchester Garden Club-Eel River Project
250 Indianapolis Zoological Society, The, Indianapolis, IN -- General Operating Fund
225 Crime Stoppers Wabash County, Wabash, IN -- General Fund
200 National Fire Safety Council, Inc., Michigan Center, MI -- Fire Prevention Program
200 Wabash Kiwanis Club, Wabash, IN -- Pancake Day Contribution
156 Honeywell Foundation, The, Wabash, IN -- Pinocchio--Area Five Head Start
150 Honeywell Foundation, The, Wabash, IN -- Nine County Art Show

Education

30,000 Independent Colleges of Indiana Foundation, Indianapolis, IN -- Annual Contribution for Distribution
2,000 Junior Achievement of Wabash, Wabash, IN -- General Fund for 1997--1998 School Year
1,500 Tri State University, Coldwater, MI -- Equipment Modernization Fund
1,000 Indiana Wesleyan University, Marion, IN -- Wabash County Scholarship Program
525 Emmanuel Christian School, Wabash, IN -- Academic Banquet
300 Wedcor, Wabash, IN -- Wabash Co. Convention & Visitors Bureau Steeplechase
300 Wedcor, Wabash, IN -- Wabash Co. Convention & Visitors Bureau Steeplechase

Health

10,000 James Whitcomb Riley Memorial Association, Indianapolis, IN -- Riley Outpatient Center
2,600 Wabash County Council on Aging, Inc., Wabash, IN -- Matching Funds for Van
1,000 American Heart Association--In. Affiliate Region 4, Wabash, IN -- General Operating Fund
500 American Cancer Society--Wabash Co. Unit, Wabash, IN -- General Fund
500 Wabash County Hospital Foundation, Wabash, IN -- Quinton Telemetry Monitoring System
300 March of Dimes--Wabash County, Ft.Wayne, IN -- Walk America
250 Psiiota XI Mental Health Gift Lift, Manchester, IN -- Christmas Gifts for Nursing Homes

Religion

500 Manchester Church of the Brethren, Manchester, IN -- Building Fund
500 Roann Church of the Brethren, Roann, IN -- Start-Up for New Day Care--Tender Hearts Day Care Ministry

Social Services

60,000 Field of Dreams, Wabash, IN -- Sports Complex Project--3rd Pymt of 5 Year Pledge
60,000 White's Residential & Family Services, Wabash, IN -- Building and Renovation Project--3rd Pymt of 5 Yr Pledge
27,500 Wabash County United Fund, Wabash, IN -- Annual Fund Drive
25,000 White's Residential & Family Services, Wabash, IN -- Farm Shop
2,500 American Red Cross--Wabash Co. Chapter, Wabash, IN -- General Fund
750 Boy Scouts of America--Sagamore Council, Kokomo, IN -- General Fund
500 Big Brothers--Big Sisters, Wabash, IN -- Bowl for Kids Sake Fundraiser
250 Youthlinks Indiana, Indianapolis, IN -- Celebrity Golf Tournament
200 Family Service Society, Inc., Wabash, IN -- Court Appointed Special Advocate (CASA)

FORD MOTOR CO.

 Number 14 of Top 100 Corporate Givers

Company Contact

Dearborn, MI
Web: http://www.ford.com

Company Description

Revenue: US$162,558,000,000 (1999)
Profit: US$22,071,000,000
Employees: 363,892
Fortune Rank: 4, per FORTUNE Magazine's list of 500 Largest U.S. Corporations (1999).
FF 4
SIC(s): 3713 Truck & Bus Bodies, 3715 Truck Trailers.

Operating Locations

Belgium: Axus SA, Brussels, Brabant; Cegeac SA, Brussels, Brabant; Criee Automobile SA, Brussels, Brabant; Hertz Coordination Centre SA, Brussels, Brabant; Transports Servais & Fils SA, Brussels, Brabant; Fordwerke AG Genk Vennootschap Naar Duits Recht, Genk, Limbourg; Canada: Halla Climate Control Canada, Belleville; Jaguar Canada, Brampton; Freedom Ford Sales Ltd., Edmonton; Hertz Canada Ltd., Etobicoke; Stevens Lincoln Mercury Sales Ltd., Kitchener; Associates Capital Corp. of Canada, Markham; Ford Electronics Manufacturing Corp., Markham; Associates Commercial Corp. of Canada Ltd., Mississauga; Centre de Camion Signal Ford, Montreal; Corp. Financiere Teletech, Montreal; Montroyal Ford (1982), Montreal; Ovale Lincoln Mercury, Montreal; Avalon Ford Sales Ltd., Mount Pearl; American Road Insurance Co., Oakville; Ford Motor Co. of Canada Ltd., Oakville; Grand Trianon Automobile Ltee., Vanier; Ford Ensite International, Windsor; Czech Republic: Autopal SPO SRO, Novy Jicin; Denmark: First Rent-A-Car Danmark A/S, Copenhagen; Ford Motor Co A/S, Glostrup, Copenhagen; France: Ford Aquitaine Industries, Blanquefort; Ford Ardennes Industries SAS, Charleville Mezieres, Ardennes; Hertz Equipement Rental France, Gennevilliers, Hauts-de-Seine; Ford Credit Europe Plc, Rueil Malmaison; Ford Finance Automobiles SAS, Rueil Malmaison; Ford France SA, Rueil Malmaison; Hertz France, Trappes, Yvelines; Locaplan, Trappes, Yvelines; Germany: Fordforschungszentrum Aachen GmbH, Aachen, Nordrhein-Westfalen; Ford Bank AG, Cologne, Nordrhein-Westfalen; Ford of Europe Zweigniederlassung Koeln, Cologne, Nordrhein-Westfalen; Ford Investitions GmbH & Co. Offene Handelsgesellschaft, Cologne, Nordrhein-Westfalen; Fordwerke AG, Cologne, Nordrhein-Westfalen; Geometric Results (Deutschland) GmbH, Cologne, Nordrhein-Westfalen; XR Associates GmbH, Cologne, Nordrhein-Westfalen; Autohaus AM Messplatz GmbH, Darmstadt, Hessen; Autohaus Grotenburg GmbH, Detmold, Nordrhein-Westfalen; Hertz Autovermietung GmbH, Eschborn, Hessen; Jaguar Deutschland GmbH, Kronberg, Hessen; Mazda Bank GmbH (lgr.), Leverkusen; Ford-Werke AG und Co. Leasing KG, Lockstedt, Schleswig-Holstein; Ford Investitions GmbH, Magdeburg, De-Ost; Nutzfahrzeuge Am Autohof GmbH, Mannheim, Baden-Wuerttemberg; Hungary: Ford Hungaria Termelo es Ertekesito KFT, Szekesfehervar; India: Climate Systems (India) Ltd., New Delhi; Ireland: Henry Ford & Son Ltd., Cork; FCE Reinsurance Co. Ltd., Dublin; Henry Ford & Son (Finance) Ltd., Dublin; Hertz Intl RE Ltd., Dublin; Hertz Rent-A-Car Ltd., Dublin; YKP Ltd., Dublin; Italy: Geometric Results Iberia SA, Pomezia, Lazio; Axus Italiana SRL, Roma, Lazio; Ford Credit Europe Plc, Roma, Lazio; Ford Italia SpA, Roma, Lazio; Ford Leasing SpA, Roma, Lazio; Jaguar Italia SpA, Roma, Lazio; Ghia SpA, Torino, Piemonte; Japan: Japan Climate Systems Corp., Higashi Hiroshima, Hiroshima; AIC Corp., Tokyo; Autorama Inc., Tokyo; Ford

Motor Co. (Japan) Ltd., Tokyo; Republic of Korea: Halla Climate Control Corp., Daejeon, Seoul; Luxembourg: Hertz Luxembourg SA, Aeroport-Findel, Findel; Mexico: Carplastic SA de CV, Apodaca; Altec Electronica Chihuahua SA de CV, Chihuahua; Ford Motor Co. SA de CV, Chihuahua; Coclisa SA de CV, Ciudad Juarez; Ford Motor Co. SA de CV, Ciudad de Mexico; Hertz Latin America SA de CV, Ciudad de Mexico; Climate Systems Mexicana SA de CV, El Marquez; Lamosa SA de CV, Nuevo Laredo; Malaysia: FMS Audio Sdn. Bhd., Perai, Pulau Pinang; Netherlands: Acona BV, Amsterdam, Noord-Holland; Ford Capital BV, Amsterdam, Noord-Holland; Ford Credit Europe Plc, Amsterdam, Noord-Holland; Ford Export Services BV, Amsterdam, Noord-Holland; Ford Holding BV, Amsterdam, Noord-Holland; Ford Nederland BV, Amsterdam, Noord-Holland; Axus Nederland BV, Hoofddorp, Noord-Holland; Hertz Automobielen Nederland BV, Hoofddorp, Noord-Holland; Hertz Leasing BV, Hoofddorp, Noord-Holland; Stuurgroep Holland BV, Hoofddorp, Noord-Holland; Van Wijk Beheer BV, Hoofddorp, Noord-Holland; Van Wijk European Car Rental Service BV, Hoofddorp, Noord-Holland; Jaguar Nederland BV, Houten, Utrecht; Norway: Ford Motor Norge AS, Kolbotn, Akershus; First Rent-A-Car Norway AS, Osteras, Akershus; Finstad Autoco A/S, Sandvika, Akershus; New Zealand: Ford Motor Co. of New Zealand Ltd., Auckland; Ford Motor Credit Co. of New Zealand Ltd., Auckland; Vehicle Assemblers New Zealand Ltd., Auckland; Poland: Ford Poland SP ZOO, Warsaw, Warszawa; Portugal: Ford Lusitana SA, Lisboa; Ford Electronica Portuguesa Ltd. (Representacao), Palmela, Setubal; Halla Climate Control (Portugal)-AR Condicionado Lda., Palmela, Setubal; Hertz Portuguesa Automoveis de Aluguer Lda., Prior Velho, Loures; Singapore: Hertz Asia Pacific Pte. Ltd., Singapore; Spain: Cadiz Electronica SA, El Puerto de Santa Maria; Ford Espana SA, Madrid; Geometric Results Iberia SA, Madrid; Hertz Equipment Rental de Espana SA, Madrid; Hertz de Espana SA, Madrid; Jaguar Hispania SA, Pozuelo de Alarcon, Madrid; Sweden: Ford Motor Co. AB, Sollentuna, Stockholm; Switzerland: Ford Motor Co. (Switzerland) SA, Zurich; Taiwan: Ford Lio Ho Motor Co. Ltd., Chungli; Associates Finance Taiwan Inc., Taipei; United Kingdom: Project XJ 220 Ltd., Banbury, Oxfordshire; Hertz Claims & Risk Management Ltd., Bath, Avon; Heartlands Ltd., Birmingham, West Midlands; Automotive Finance Ltd., Brentwood, Essex; Ford Automotive Leasing Ltd., Brentwood, Essex; Ford Credit Europe Plc, Brentwood, Essex; Ford Credit Funding Plc, Brentwood, Essex; Ford of Europe, Brentwood, Essex; Ford Fleet Financing Ltd., Brentwood, Essex; Ford Motor Co. Ltd., Brentwood, Essex; Ford Pension Fund Investment Management Ltd., Brentwood, Essex; Ford Pension Fund Trustees Ltd., Brentwood, Essex; Ford Personal Import Export Ltd., Brentwood, Essex; Jaguar Financial Services Ltd., Brentwood, Essex; Primus Automotive Financial Services Ltd., Brentwood, Essex; US Leasing Ltd., Brentwood, Essex; USL Holdings Ltd., Brentwood, Essex; XR Associates Ltd., Brentwood, Essex; West Yorkshire Motors Ltd., Castleford, West Yorkshire; Geometric Results (Great Britain) Ltd., Colchester, Essex; Daimler Motor Co. Ltd., Coventry, West Midlands; Daimler Transport Vehicles Ltd., Coventry, West Midlands; Jaguar Cars Exports Ltd., Coventry, West Midlands; Jaguar Cars Ltd., Coventry, West Midlands; Jaguar Cars Overseas Holdings Ltd., Coventry, West Midlands; Jaguar Collection Ltd., Coventry, West Midlands; Jaguar Daimler Heritage Trust, Coventry, West Midlands; Jaguar Ltd., Coventry, West Midlands; Lanchester Motor Co. Ltd., Coventry, West Midlands; SS Cars Ltd., Coventry, West Midlands; Jaguar Insurance Ltd., Douglas, Isle of Man; Cumberland Life Assurance Co. Ltd., Edinburgh, Lothian; Dales of Falmouth Ltd., Falmouth, Cornwall; Johnsons of Gainsborough Ltd., Gainsborough, Lincolnshire; Strathford East Kilbride Ltd., Glasgow, Strathclyde; Associates Capital (Guernsey) Ltd., Guernsey, Channel Islands; Prestige Property Co. Ltd., Guernsey, Channel Islands; Hertz Europe Ltd., Hounslow, Greater London; SS Cars, Ilminster, Somerset; Associates Capital (Jersey) Ltd., Jersey, Channel Islands; Jaguar Holdings Ltd., Jersey, Channel Islands; Spellbound Holdings Ltd., Jersey, Channel Islands; Jaguar Intl Finance Ltd., Leamington Spa, Warwickshire; Aston Martin Sales Ltd., London; Daimler Hire Ltd., London; Hertz Car Sales Ltd., London; Hertz Rent-A-Car Ltd., London; Hertz (UK) Ltd., London; Lanka Drinks International Ltd., London; Aston Martin Lagonda Group Ltd., Newport Pagnell; Newton Abbot Motors Ltd., Newton Abbot, Devon; Associates Financial Corp. Ltd., Slough, Berkshire; Autoclub Intl Ltd., Slough, Berkshire; Cumberland Insurance Co. Ltd., Slough, Berkshire; Reid & Adams Ltd., Stranraer, Wigtownshire; Axus (United Kingdom) Ltd., Uxbridge, Middlesex; Associated Mortgage Corp. Ltd., Windsor, Berkshire; Associates Capital Corp. Ltd., Windsor, Berkshire; Medens Ltd., Windsor, Berkshire; Medens Trust Ltd., Windsor, Berkshire; Wessex Finance Corp. Ltd., Windsor, Berkshire; Venezuela: Talleres Rootes CA, Caracas; Productos Industriales CA, Punto Fijo, Falcon; Ford Motor de Venezuela SA, Valencia, Carabobo

Nonmonetary Support

Value: $534,800 (1996); $555,871 (1995); $300,000 (1994)
Type: Donated Equipment; Donated Products
Contact: Ray Byers, Manager, Contributions Programs
Phone: (313)248-4745
Note: Company also donates land.

Corporate Sponsorship

Type: Arts & cultural events; Sports events
Note: Sponsors banquets and dinners. Contact the manager for the Marketing Program and Special Events.

Ford Motor Co. Fund

Giving Contact

Gary L. Nielsen, Vice President and Executive Director
Ford Motor Co. Fund
The American Rd., Rm. 335
PO Box 1899
Dearborn, MI 48121-1899
Phone: (313)845-8711
Fax: (313)337-6680

Alternate Contact

Shirly Durham, Contributions Manager

Description

EIN: 381459376
Organization Type: Corporate Foundation
Giving Locations: headquarters and operating communities; national organizations.
Grant Types: Capital, Conference/Seminar, Department, Employee Matching Gifts, General Support, Multiyear/Continuing Support.
Note: Employee matching gift ratio: 1 to 1.

Giving Philosophy

'Ford Motor Company Fund, incorporated in 1949, is a non-profit corporation supported primarily by contributions from Ford Motor Company. It is in no way related to the Ford Foundation.. The Fund contributes to the betterment and improvement of mankind through grants to organizations operating exclusively for charitable, scientific, literary, or educational purposes.. A major segment of the Fund's activities concern grants in support of cultural organizations, United Funds, hospitals, urban affairs projects, educational institutions and selected national charities and associations.. ' *Ford Motor Company Fund Annual Report*

Financial Summary

Total Giving: $58,300,000 (1998); $33,025,152 (1997); $49,786,169 (1996). Note: Contributes through corporate direct giving program and foundation.
Giving Analysis: Giving for 1996 includes: foundation ($25,173,157); corporate direct giving ($9,351,500); international subsidiaries ($8,297,000); foundation matching gifts ($3,775,322); domestic subsidiaries ($2,653,000); 1997: foundation ($25,576,598); foundation grants to United Way ($4,228,587); foundation matching gifts ($3,219,967); 1998: foundation ($27,792,759); corporate direct giving (approx $22,462,510); foundation grants to United Way ($4,432,811); foundation matching gifts ($3,111,920); nonmonetary support (approx $500,000)
Assets: $100,817,419 (1998); $33,713,218 (1997); $25,129,121 (1996)
Gifts Received: $100,000,000 (1998); $39,742,321 (1997); $20,000,000 (1996). Note: Contributions are received from Ford Motor Company and Ford Holdings, Inc.

Typical Recipients

Arts & Humanities: Arts Associations & Councils, Arts Centers, Arts Festivals, Arts Institutes, Community Arts, Ethnic & Folk Arts, Arts & Humanities-General, Historic Preservation, History & Archaeology, Libraries, Museums/Galleries, Music, Opera, Performing Arts, Public Broadcasting, Theater
Civic & Public Affairs: African American Affairs, Botanical Gardens/Parks, Business/Free Enterprise, Chambers of Commerce, Civil Rights, Community Foundations, Economic Development, Economic Policy, Employment/Job Training, Civic & Public Affairs-General, Hispanic Affairs, Housing, Law & Justice, Philanthropic Organizations, Professional & Trade Associations, Public Policy, Safety, Urban & Community Affairs, Zoos/Aquariums
Education: Agricultural Education, Arts/Humanities Education, Business Education, Colleges & Universities, Economic Education, Education Associations, Education Reform, Engineering/Technological Education, Faculty Development, Education-General, Health & Physical Education, Journalism/Media Education, Minority Education, Public Education (Precollege), Science/Mathematics Education, Secondary Education (Public)
Environment: Environment-General
Health: Emergency/Ambulance Services, Health Policy/Cost Containment, Health Organizations, Hospices, Hospitals, Kidney, Prenatal Health Issues, Public Health
International: International Development, International Environmental Issues, International Organizations, International Peace & Security Issues, International Relations
Religion: Jewish Causes
Science: Science Museums, Scientific Centers & Institutes
Social Services: Camps, Child Welfare, Community Service Organizations, Delinquency & Criminal Rehabilitation, Recreation & Athletics, Substance Abuse, United Funds/United Ways, Volunteer Services, YMCA/YWCA/YMHA/YWHA, Youth Organizations

Contributions Analysis

Giving Priorities: Education, social welfare, health, the arts, community development, public policy, and international research. Domestic contributions to U.S.-based nonprofit organizations with an international focus amount to about 2% of contributions. Of international contributions, primarily supports domestic activities of organizations located in the U.S. whose principal objective is to conduct research concerning other countries or to solicit funds for aid and relief. Interest include U.S.-international relations, public policy, economic, development, foreign policy, and international management.

Arts & Humanities: 18%. Large part of this support goes to performing arts groups in areas such as music, opera, dance, and theater, mostly in the Detroit area. The remainder primarily supports museums, libraries, public broadcasting, and arts councils and centers.
Civic & Public Affairs: 12%. Emphasis on community improvement, which includes economic development, urban groups, and business associations. Other priorities are public policy research and youth groups. Employment training, traffic safety, housing, and education related to the free enterprise and economics also are of interest.
Education: 37%. Major support goes to engineering, scientific, and technical education. Other priorities include business education, education associations and funds, minority education, and general education (including, colleges and universities, public schools, and other organizations). Company also sponsors employee matching gifts program in this area, makes student loans to children of employees, and sponsors a program to promote scientific research.
Environment: 9%. Funds general environmental causes and research.
Health: 8%. Interests include hospitals, substance abuse programs, and other health organizations.
Social Services: 16%. Majority of support goes to United Way. The remainder supports social service groups such as food banks, shelters, recreation, programs, and organizations serving children, the elderly, and the disabled.
Note: Total contributions made in 1998. Above priorities are those of the Ford Motor Company Fund. Company also sponsors a direct giving program. Company reports that direct giving goes to a variety of organizations, but priorities are similar to those of the fund.

Application Procedures

Initial Contact: National organizations should submit a written proposal; organizations located in communities where Ford operates may submit requests to the fund or to the community relations committee at local plants.
Application Requirements: Include a description of the organization, proof of charitable organization, amount requested, proposed use of the funds, brief description of the specific project or program including goals and objectives, other sources of funds applicable to the proposal, detailed budget and financial information concerning the organization, status of other related projects previously supported by Ford Motor Company Fund, description of how Ford Motor Company fund would be recognized, and a summary of past performance, where applicable.
Deadlines: None.
Review Process: The fund will notify applicant by postcard if request does not fall within its scope.
Decision Notification: The fund will send a postcard notifying applicant that proposal has been received. No further notification will occur if there is no interest in the proposal. If there is an interest in the request, applicant will receive notification of the disposition within eight to ten weeks of receiving initial acknowledgment card.

Additional Information

Publications: Guidelines

Corporate Officials

William Clay Ford, Jr.: chairman, chief executive officer B 1958. ED Princeton University BA (1979); Michigan Institute of Technology MS (1984). PRIM CORP EMPL chairman: Ford Motor Co. CORP AFFIL treasurer: Detroit Lions Inc.; trustee: Henry Ford Health System. NONPR AFFIL trustee: Edison Institute; trustee: Michigan Nature Conservancy.
Jacques A. Nasser: president, chief executive officer PRIM CORP EMPL president, chief executive officer: Ford Motor Co.
Peter John Pestillo: executive chairman B Bristol, CT 1938. ED Fairfield University BSS (1960); Georgetown University LLB (1963). PRIM CORP EMPL executive chairman: Ford Motor Co. CORP AFFIL executive: UAW-Ford National Programs; director: Rouge Steel Co.; director: Hertz Corp.; director: Rouge Industries Inc. NONPR AFFIL director: National Association Manufacturer.
John M. Rintamaki: group vice president, chief of staff PRIM CORP EMPL group vice president, chief of staff: Ford Motor Co. ADD CORP EMPL assistant secretary: Ford Motor Credit Co.

Giving Program Officials

Raymond Lester Byers, Jr.: B Canton, OH 1943. ED Malone College BA (1967); University of Akron (1970-1974). PRIM CORP EMPL manager contributions programs: Ford Motor Co.

Foundation Officials

Leo Joseph Brennan, Jr.: vice president, executive director B Hancock, MI 1930. ED University of Notre Dame BA (1951); University of Notre Dame MA (1952); Georgetown University (1953). NONPR AFFIL director: Michigan Bach Festival; member: Michigan Historical Society; member: Detroit Zoological Society; trustee: Michigan 4-H Council; director: Brother Rice High School; member founders society: Detroit Institute Arts. CLUB AFFIL Bloomfield Open Hunt Club; Otsego Ski Club.
Shirley Durham: contributions manager
Alfred B. Ford: trustee B 1934.
Sheila F. Hamp: trustee PRIM CORP EMPL trustee: Edison International.
Peter John Pestillo: trustee (see above)
John M. Rintamaki: secretary (see above)
Dennis A. Tosh: assistant treasurer

Grants Analysis

Disclosure Period: calendar year ending 1998
Total Grants: $27,792,759*
Number of Grants: 1,292
Average Grant: $21,511*
Highest Grant: $1,250,000
Typical Range: $1,000 to $25,000
***Note:** Giving excludes matching gifts; United Way.

Recent Grants

Note: Grants derived from 1997 Form 990.

Arts & Humanities

350,000 Detroit Symphony Orchestra Hall, Detroit, MI
309,596 Michigan Opera Theater, Detroit, MI
255,000 Automotive Hall of Fame, Midland, MI
250,750 Philadelphia Museum of Art, Philadelphia, PA
250,000 Great Lakes Museum, Cleveland, OH
200,000 Museum of Contemporary Art, Los Angeles, CA
200,000 Museum of Modern Art, New York, NY

Civic & Public Affairs

200,000 American Society for Quality Control, Milwaukee, WI
100,500 Friends of the Zoo, Kansas City, MO
100,000 National Council of Negro Women, Washington, DC
100,000 New Community Corporation, Newark, NJ

Education

960,000 University of Michigan, Ann Arbor, MI
375,000 Ohio State University, Columbus, OH
375,000 United Negro College Fund, New York, NY
285,000 Duke University, Durham, NC
285,000 University of Michigan Dearborn, Dearborn, MI
255,000 Purdue University, West Lafayette, IN
250,000 Case Western Reserve University, Cleveland, OH
250,000 Michigan Tech University, Houghton, MI
250,000 Wayne State University, Detroit, MI
175,000 Tuskegee University, Tuskegee, AL
150,000 Detroit Area Pre-College Engineering Program, Detroit, MI
150,000 Engineering and Science Development Foundation, Detroit, MI
150,000 University of Illinois, Urbana, IL
137,200 University of Michigan, Ann Arbor, MI
125,000 Junior Achievement of Southeastern Michigan, Detroit, MI
125,000 Lawrence Technological University, Southfield, MI
115,100 Florida A&M University, Tallahassee, FL
106,000 National Action Council for Minorities in Engineering, New York, NY
100,000 Emory University, Atlanta, GA
100,000 Georgia Institute of Technology, Atlanta, GA
100,000 Yale University, New Haven, CT

Health

600,000 Henry Ford Hospital, Detroit, MI
600,000 Oakwood Health Services Corporation, Dearborn, MI
100,000 Hospice of Southeastern Michigan, Southfield, MI
100,000 March of Dimes Birth Defects Foundation, White Plains, NY

International

1,250,000 Conservation International Foundation, Arlington, VA
1,250,000 Conservation International Foundation, Arlington, VA
130,000 American Friends of Canada Committee, New York, NY
130,000 American Friends of Canada Committee, New York, NY
100,000 World Wildlife Fund, Washington, DC
100,000 World Wildlife Fund, Washington, DC

Science

1,200,000 Edison Institute, Dearborn, MI
275,000 Edison Institute, Dearborn, MI
125,000 Carnegie Institute, Pittsburgh, PA

Social Services

1,557,780 United Way Community Services, Detroit, MI
380,000 United Way Community Services, Detroit, MI
250,000 Genesis Foundation, Dearborn, MI
175,000 United Way Services, Cleveland, OH
125,000 Union Station Assistance Corporation, Kansas City, MO
100,000 Boys and Girls Clubs of America, Atlanta, GA
100,000 Hole in the Wall Camp Fund, Westport, CT
100,000 Metro United Way, Louisville, KY

FOREST CITY ENTERPRISES, INC.

Company Contact

Cleveland, OH

Company Description

Revenue: US$506,900,000
Employees: 3,287
SIC(s): 1521 Single-Family Housing Construction, 1522 Residential Construction Nec, 1531 Operative Builders, 6531 Real Estate Agents & Managers.

Operating Locations

Canada: Vancouver

Nonmonetary Support

Value: $25,000 (1988)
Type: Loaned Employees; Loaned Executives

Corporate Sponsorship

Type: Arts & cultural events; Festivals/fairs; Music & entertainment events; Pledge-a-thon; Sports events

Forest City Enterprises Charitable Foundation, Inc.

Giving Contact

Allan C. Krulak, Vice President
Forest City Enterprises
1100 Terminal Tower
50 Public Square, State 1100
Cleveland, OH 44113
Phone: (216)621-6060
Fax: (216)263-6208

Description

Founded: 1976
EIN: 341218895
Organization Type: Corporate Foundation
Giving Locations: NY: New York including metropolitan area; OH: Cleveland including metropolitan area operating locations.
Grant Types: General Support, Scholarship.

Financial Summary

Total Giving: $1,500,000 (fiscal year ending January 31, 1999 approx); $1,821,001 (fiscal 1998); $1,500,000 (fiscal 1997 approx). Note: Contributes through foundation only.
Giving Analysis: Giving for fiscal 1998 includes: foundation ($1,821,001)
Assets: $31,882 (fiscal 1998); $72,366 (fiscal 1996); $40,673 (fiscal 1995)
Gifts Received: $1,815,000 (fiscal 1998); $1,015,000 (fiscal 1996); $1,245,000 (fiscal 1995)

Typical Recipients

Arts & Humanities: Arts Associations & Councils, Arts Institutes, Ballet, Arts & Humanities-General, Museums/Galleries, Music, Opera, Performing Arts, Theater, Visual Arts
Civic & Public Affairs: African American Affairs, Business/Free Enterprise, Civil Rights, Clubs, Economic Development, Ethnic Organizations, Civic & Public Affairs-General, Housing, Municipalities/Towns, Parades/Festivals, Philanthropic Organizations, Public Policy, Safety, Urban & Community Affairs, Women's Affairs, Zoos/Aquariums
Education: Arts/Humanities Education, Colleges & Universities, Community & Junior Colleges, Education Funds, Education Reform, Engineering/Technological Education, Education-General, Private Education (Precollege), Religious Education, Student Aid
Environment: Forestry
Health: AIDS/HIV, Alzheimers Disease, Cancer, Children's Health/Hospitals, Clinics/Medical Centers, Diabetes, Emergency/Ambulance Services, Health Organizations, Hospices, Hospitals, Multiple Sclerosis, Prenatal Health Issues, Public Health, Single-Disease Health Associations
International: International Relations, International Relief Efforts, Missionary/Religious Activities
Religion: Churches, Dioceses, Jewish Causes, Religious Organizations, Religious Welfare, Seminaries, Social/Policy Issues
Science: Scientific Centers & Institutes
Social Services: Camps, Child Welfare, Community Service Organizations, Crime Prevention, Delinquency & Criminal Rehabilitation, Food/Clothing Distribution, Sexual Abuse, Substance Abuse, United Funds/United Ways, Volunteer Services, YMCA/YWCA/YMHA/YWHA, Youth Organizations

Contributions Analysis

Giving Priorities: Social service, health, education, civic concerns, the arts, religion, science, and international organizations.
Arts & Humanities: About 5%. Local arts groups, with interests including theater, music, dance, and museums.
Civic & Public Affairs: 5% to 10%. Organizations concerned with economic development, civil rights, youth, urban affairs, crime prevention, and employment.
Education: 20% to 25%. Majority supports scholarships. High priorities include science and technology education and religious education. Grants also support educational television.
Health: 20% to 25%. Primarily the United Way in Cleveland. Contributions also support a variety of other social service groups, including religious welfare organizations. Majority of health support focuses on hospitals. Interests also include medical research and single-disease health associations.
Religion: 35% to 40%. Primarily Jewish causes. Other recipients include Bible study groups, religious social policy groups, and religious welfare organizations.

Application Procedures

Initial Contact: Send a brief letter or proposal.
Application Requirements: Include a description of organization, amount requested, purpose of funds sought, and proof of tax-exempt status.
Deadlines: None; grants committee meets as needed.

Restrictions

Grants are not made to individuals.

Corporate Officials

Allan C. Krulak: vice president corporate & public affairs, director PRIM CORP EMPL vice president corporate & public affairs, director: Forest City Enterprises, Inc.
Albert Benjamin Ratner: co-chairman, director B Cleveland, OH 1927. ED Michigan State University BS (1951). PRIM CORP EMPL co-chairman, director: Forest City Enterprises, Inc. ADD CORP EMPL treasurer: Artus Inc.; president: Beachwood Place Inc.; vice president: Forest City Rental Properties Corp.; vice president: Forest City Residential Development Inc. CORP AFFIL managing partner: Southgate USA Management Co.; secretary: Sunrise Development Co.; director: F C Henderson Inc.; director: RPM Inc.; director: Forest City Management Inc.; director: Forest City Trading Group Inc.; member executive committee, director: America Greetings Corp.
Nathan P. Shafran: vice chairman, director B 1913. PRIM CORP EMPL vice chairman, director: Forest City Enterprises, Inc. ADD CORP EMPL vice president: Forest City Management Inc.; executive vice president: Forest City Rental Properties Corp.

Foundation Officials

Allan C. Krulak: vice president (see above)
Albert Benjamin Ratner: trustee (see above)

Grants Analysis

Disclosure Period: fiscal year ending January 31, 1996
Total Grants: $896,756*
Number of Grants: 171
Average Grant: $5,244
Highest Grant: $350,500
Typical Range: $500 to $10,000
***Note:** Giving excludes scholarship; United Way.

Recent Grants

Note: Grants derived from 1997 Form 990.

Arts & Humanities

18,000	Musical Arts Association Severance Hall, Cleveland, OH
13,000	Great Lakes Theater Festival, Cleveland, OH
5,000	National Building Museum, Washington, DC

Civic & Public Affairs

49,250	New Montefiore Campaign For All Our Tomorrows, Beachwood, OH
36,000	American Civil Liberties Union, Cleveland, OH
12,000	Greater Cleveland Roundtable, Cleveland, OH
10,000	Cleveland Bicentennial Commission, Cleveland, OH
10,000	Jennings Hall, Garfield Heights, OH
10,000	National Italian American Foundation, Washington, DC
7,000	Cleveland Tomorrow, Cleveland, OH
5,800	Black Professional Association Charitable Foundation, Cleveland, OH
5,000	Erickson Foundation, Chicago, IL
5,000	National Council for Urban Economic Development, Washington, DC
5,000	Stark County Foundation, Canton, OH

Education

54,500	Case Western Reserve University, Cleveland, OH
30,000	Cleveland Initiative for Education, Cleveland, OH
30,000	Hebrew Academy, Cleveland, OH
20,000	Ursuline College, Pepper Pike, OH
15,000	Agnon School, Beachwood, OH
10,000	Preterm, Cleveland, OH
10,000	Rabbinical College Telshe Yeshiva, Wickliffe, OH
6,500	Cleveland Scholarships Programs, Cleveland, OH
5,000	Cleveland Music School Settlement, Cleveland, OH
5,000	Illinois Institute of Technology, Chicago, IL
5,000	Ohio Foundation of Independent Colleges, Columbus, OH
5,000	Sacred Heart University, Fairfield, CT

Health

71,000	Cleveland Clinic Foundation, Cleveland, OH
5,500	American Red Cross, Cleveland, OH
5,200	Alzheimer's Association, Cleveland, OH

International

5,000	Endowment for Democracy in Eastern Europe, New York, NY

Religion

300,000	Jewish Community Federation, Cleveland, OH
25,000	Council for Initiatives in Jewish Studies, New York, NY
25,000	Wexner Center Foundation, Columbus, OH
20,000	Washington Jewish Community Center, Washington, DC
18,000	Jewish National Fund, Cleveland, OH
15,000	Jewish Family Service Association, Cleveland, OH
15,000	Jewish Theological Seminary, New York, NY
10,000	American Jewish Congress, Cleveland, OH
10,000	OFEQ Institute, Euclid, OH
8,250	Jewish Foundation for the Righteous, New York, NY
5,000	Mosdos Ohr Hatorah, Cleveland, OH
5,000	National Conference of Christians and Jews, Cleveland, OH
5,000	Union of American Hebrew Congregation, New York, NY

Science

10,500	Great Lakes Science Center, Cleveland, OH

Social Services

113,750	United Way Services, Cleveland, OH
6,000	Boys and Girls Clubs, Cleveland, OH
5,000	Business Volunteerism Council, Cleveland, OH
5,000	Karamu House, Cleveland, OH
5,000	Law Enforcement Foundation, Dublin, OH
5,000	Neighborhood Centers Association, Cleveland, OH

FORT JAMES CORP.

Company Contact

1650 Lake Cook Rd.
Deerfield, IL 60015-4753
Phone: (847)317-5000
Fax: (847)236-3755
Web: http://www.fortjames.com

Company Description

Former Name: James River Corp. of Virginia.
Revenue: US$7,157,900,000 (1999)
Profit: US$516,500,000 (1999)
Employees: 27,500 (1998)
Fortune Rank: 246, per FORTUNE Magazine's list of 500 Largest U.S. Corporations (1999).
FF 246
SIC(s): 2621 Paper Mills, 2656 Sanitary Food Containers, 2657 Folding Paperboard Boxes, 2676 Sanitary Paper Products.

Nonmonetary Support

Type: Donated Products
Note: Co. provides nonmonetary support. For nonmonetary support contact the plant Manager of the local facility that produces the particular product desired.

Corporate Sponsorship

Type: Arts & cultural events; Music & entertainment events
Contact: Chuck Wilson, Vice President, Public Affairs
Note: Sponsors tables/dinners.

The Fort James Foundation

Giving Contact

Christine W. Hale, Foundation Administrator
The Fort James Foundation
6802 Paragon Pl., Ste. 400
Richmond, VA 23230
Phone: (804)662-8385
Fax: (804)662-8846
Email: christine.hale@fortjamesmail.com

Description

Organization Type: Corporate Foundation
Giving Locations: communities where company employees live and work.
Grant Types: Capital, Employee Matching Gifts, General Support, Multiyear/Continuing Support.
Note: Employee matching gift ratio: 1 to 1 up to $5,000 per employee annually for all qualifying 501(c)(3) organizations.

Giving Philosophy

'The Foundation's contributions are directed to areas in which it has an immediate or long-range interest. The primary areas of interest are education; culture and the arts; civic activities; and health and human services.
'The Foundation generally gives preference to requests for one-time contributions and for programmatic and operating purposes. However, grants extending over a defined period of years or directed towards the support of specific building or other capital projects are considered as exceptions.
'Priority is given to organizations that serve communities in which James River has major operations or employee populations; to institutions that provide education or service to present or potential James River employees; and to organizations with activities directed toward the support of professions that directly or indirectly provide professionals and employees related to James River's primary areas of operation.'
Guidelines for Giving

Financial Summary

Total Giving: $4,500,000 (fiscal year ending , 1999 approx); $4,000,000 (fiscal 1998 approx); $2,000,000 (fiscal 1997 approx). Note: Contributions through foundation.

Typical Recipients

Arts & Humanities: Arts Associations & Councils, Arts Centers, Arts Funds, Community Arts, Libraries, Museums/Galleries, Performing Arts, Public Broadcasting, Theater, Visual Arts
Civic & Public Affairs: Business/Free Enterprise, Economic Development, Employment/Job Training, Housing, Professional & Trade Associations, Safety
Education: Colleges & Universities, Economic Education
Environment: Environment-General
Health: Emergency/Ambulance Services
Social Services: Delinquency & Criminal Rehabilitation, Shelters/Homelessness, Substance Abuse, United Funds/United Ways, Volunteer Services, Youth Organizations

Contributions Analysis

Giving Priorities: Education, health, social welfare, civic interests, and culture and the arts.
Civic & Public Affairs: 15% to 20%. Interested in programs that help improve the quality, and availability, of art and culture in local communities. Typical recipients include local arts funds or councils, libraries, and theaters. Recipient organizations address critical social concerns and ensure the betterment of company communities. Interests include administration of justice, public service, and social policy; crime and delinquency prevention; economic development; and conservation.
Education: 50% to 55%. Supports educational institutes, primarily at the college level, which provide educational opportunities to present or potential company employees. Chief interests are educational foundations, schools that develop human resource skills, economic education, and free enterprise.
Health: About 15%. Local United Way drives, youth organizations, hospitals, and volunteer fire and rescue squads receive top priority. Other interests include safety, family planning, drug abuse, and the homeless. Company also encourages employee volunteerism.

Application Procedures

Initial Contact: brief letter or proposal; no phone calls
Application Requirements: name, address, and telephone number of organization; contact person and title; amount of money or types of services requested; a description of organization or proposed project; brief statement citing the project's relevance to company, its employees, and local community; geographic area served; description of the organization's experience and ability to complete project; method of testing success of project; proof of tax-exempt status; audited financial statement; budget, salaries, and benefits of staff; organizational structure; annual report or other supporting materials
Deadlines: None.
Review Process: approval of local mill, plant or facility manager is required before funding is approved by the foundation; contributions committee meets annually; sometimes consults experts in specific fields
Decision Notification: grants generally approved in the fall for following year funding
Notes: Applications should be directed to the manager of the mill, plant, or facility in the area of the project or organization; in the Richmond, VA area, applications can be sent directly to the foundation.

Restrictions

Company does not make grants to individuals; organizations without tax-exempt status; purely social organizations; political organizations; religious, veteran, or fraternal organizations; advertising journals, booklets, etc.; social events or the purchase of tickets; symposiums or conferences; organizations not located within a company community; telephone or mass-mail solicitations; or organizations not approved by the Better Business Bureau.

Additional Information

James River Corp. merged with Fort Howard to become Fort James Corp.
For information regarding contributions to international organizations by the company's foreign subsidiaries, contact Ron Singer, Chief Executive Officer of the JA/MONT N.V. division at the company's headquarters in Richmond, VA.
For information about the James River Scholars Program, write or call James River Scholars Director, Human Resources Development Office, at the address listed under 'Contact,' or at (804)649-4436.
Contributions are considered one-time gifts, although some multiyear commitments are made in order to distribute payments evenly over several years.
Succeeding grants to the same organization generally are not considered until two years after the payment of the previous grant.
Pledges should compare favorably with other companies in the community as to total amount of employees, total payroll, or other measures of company's local obligation.
Foundation gives preference to requests for one-time contributions and for programmatic and operating purposes; multiyear and capital requests will be considered as exceptions.
Publications: Giving Guidelines

Corporate Officials

Norman Bush: vice president B New York, NY 1929. ED City University of New York BBA (1951); City University of New York MBA (1952); North Carolina State University PhD (1962). NONPR AFFIL member: American Statistical Association.
Clifford Armstrong Cutchins, IV: president B Norfolk, VA 1948. ED Princeton University BA (1971); University of Virginia MBA (1975); University of Virginia JD (1975). PRIM CORP EMPL president: Fort James Corp. CORP AFFIL director: Transmission Products; director: Jamont NV; director: Fort James Operating Co.; senior vice president, secretary, director: James River Paper Co. Inc.; director: Fort James Europe NV. NONPR AFFIL director: Henrico Doctors Hospital; member: Virginia Bar Association; director: Americas Utility Fund; member: American Bar Association. CLUB AFFIL Commonwealth Club; Virginia Country Club.
Daniel J. Girvan: senior vice president, director B 1948. PRIM CORP EMPL senior vice president, director: Fort James Corp. CORP AFFIL president: Fort James Operating Co.
Christine W. Hale: secretary PRIM CORP EMPL secretary: Fort James Corp.
Charles D. Wilson: vice president PRIM CORP EMPL vice president: Fort James Corp.

Foundation Officials

Etonya M. Beard: director B McPherson, KS 1952.
Kathleen M. Bennett: director
Clifford Armstrong Cutchins, IV: chairman, director (see above)
Daniel J. Girvan: director (see above)

Christine W. Hale: executive administrator (see above)
Charles D. Wilson: director (see above)

Grants Analysis

Total Grants: $4,500,000 (approx)

FORT WORTH STAR-TELEGRAM INC.

Company Contact

Fort Worth, TX
Web: http://www.star-telegram.com

Company Description

Employees: 1,303
SIC(s): 2711 Newspapers.
Parent Company: Capital Cities/ABC Inc.

Amon G. Carter Star Telegram Employees Fund

Giving Contact

Nenetta Carter Tatum, President
Amon G. Carter Star Telegram Employees Fund
PO Box 17480
Ft. Worth, TX 76102
Phone: (817)332-3535

Description

Founded: 1945
EIN: 756014850
Organization Type: Corporate Foundation
Giving Locations: TX
Grant Types: Capital, General Support, Scholarship.

Financial Summary

Total Giving: $1,306,253 (fiscal year ending April 30, 1997); $901,637 (fiscal 1996); $788,621 (fiscal 1995). Note: Contributes through foundation only.
Giving Analysis: Giving for fiscal 1997 includes: foundation ($1,013,850); foundation gifts to individuals ($189,403); foundation scholarships ($103,000)
Assets: $30,567,261 (fiscal 1997); $21,163,772 (fiscal 1996); $18,277,069 (fiscal 1995)
Gifts Received: $10,000 (fiscal 1997); $12,000 (fiscal 1996); $14,000 (fiscal 1995)

Typical Recipients

Arts & Humanities: Arts Associations & Councils, Arts Festivals, Ballet, Historic Preservation, History & Archaeology, Libraries, Museums/Galleries, Music, Opera, Performing Arts, Theater
Civic & Public Affairs: Business/Free Enterprise, Clubs, Housing, Law & Justice, Municipalities/Towns, Parades/Festivals, Safety, Urban & Community Affairs, Women's Affairs
Education: Afterschool/Enrichment Programs, Colleges & Universities, Education Reform, Education-General, Private Education (Precollege), Public Education (Precollege), Special Education
Environment: Environment-General
Health: AIDS/HIV, Cancer, Children's Health/Hospitals, Eyes/Blindness, Health Organizations, Hospitals, Medical Research, Nursing Services, Public Health, Research/Studies Institutes, Single-Disease Health Associations, Transplant Networks/Donor Banks
International: Foreign Arts Organizations, Missionary/Religious Activities
Religion: Jewish Causes, Religious Organizations, Religious Welfare
Science: Science Museums
Social Services: Big Brother/Big Sister, Child Welfare, Community Service Organizations, Counseling, Crime Prevention, Day Care, Domestic Violence, Family Planning, Food/Clothing Distribution, People with Disabilities, Recreation & Athletics, Scouts, Senior Services, Shelters/Homelessness, Substance Abuse, United Funds/United Ways, YMCA/YWCA/YMHA/YWHA, Youth Organizations

Contributions Analysis

Giving Priorities: Giving benefits. Tarrant County, Texas.
Arts & Humanities: 28%. Contributes to museums, arts councils, music, and community theater.
Civic & Public Affairs: 7%. Minor interests include community affairs, public safety associations, and community funds.
Education: 23%. Primarily supports universities in Texas. Also operates large scholarship program for the children of employees.
Health: 3%. Interests include children's hospitals and single-disease health associations.
Social Services: 21%. Includes community centers, community service organizations, counseling, and youth organizations.
Note: Total contributions made in 1997.

Application Procedures

Initial Contact: Send a brief letter of inquiry.
Application Requirements: One copy of proposal.
Deadlines: None.
Notes: The foundation may request additional information after reviewing initial letter.

Restrictions

Foundation limits its giving to Texas. No grants are given to individuals, except for employee-related scholarships and grants.

Additional Information

Giving is primarily for medical or hardship assistance and pension supplements for Star-Telegram employees. Scholarships are awarded to children of employees.

Corporate Officials

Richard L. Connor: president, publisher B Bangor, ME 1947. ED Hillsdale College BA (1970). PRIM CORP EMPL president, publisher: Fort Worth Star-Telegram Inc. NONPR AFFIL trustee: Tilton School; director: Wilkes-Barre Chamber of Commerce; trustee: Ft. Worth Academy; trustee: Misericordia College; member: American Society Newspaper Editors; director: Capital Cities Community Minorities Intern Program; member: American Newspaper Publishers Association.

Foundation Officials

George Carter: director
Mark L. Johnson: director
John H. Robinson: treasurer, secretary B 1923. CORP AFFIL director: Commercial Bank San Francisco; director: On-Point Tech Systems.
Nenetta Carter Tatum: president NONPR AFFIL director: Carter Amon Museum Western Art.

Grants Analysis

Disclosure Period: fiscal year ending April 30, 1997
Total Grants: $1,013,850*
Number of Grants: 66
Average Grant: $15,361
Highest Grant: $250,000
Typical Range: $1,000 to $25,000
***Note:** Giving excludes gifts to individuals; scholarship.

Recent Grants

Note: Grants derived from fiscal 1997 Form 990.

Arts & Humanities

250,000	Amon Carter Museum, Fort Worth, TX
250,000	Amon Carter Museum, Fort Worth, TX
50,000	Fort Worth Public Library Foundation, Fort Worth, TX
25,000	Casa Manana Theater, Fort Worth, TX
25,000	National Cowgirl Museum, Fort Worth, TX
25,000	Stage West, Fort Worth, TX
10,000	Circle Theatre, Fort Worth, TX
10,000	Fort Worth Opera Association, Fort Worth, TX
10,000	Fort Worth Theater, Fort Worth, TX
5,000	Arts Council, Fort Worth, TX
5,000	Circle Theater, Fort Worth, TX
5,000	Fort Worth Dallas Ballet, Fort Worth, TX
5,000	Fort Worth Opera Association, Fort Worth, TX
5,000	Jubilee Theatre, Fort Worth, TX
5,000	Shakespeare in the Park, Fort Worth, TX
5,000	Shakespeare in the Park, Fort Worth, TX
5,000	Tarrant County Cultural District, Fort Worth, TX
5,000	Texas Girls Choir, Fort Worth, TX
4,250	Arts Council of Fort Worth, Fort Worth, TX
3,000	Business Volunteers for the Arts, Fort Worth, TX
2,000	Van Cliburn Foundation, Fort Worth, TX
2,000	Youth Orchestra, Fort Worth, TX

Civic & Public Affairs

25,000	Downtown Fort Worth Initiatives, Fort Worth, TX
25,000	Women's Club of Fort Worth, Fort Worth, TX -- Historical Preservation
25,000	Women's Haven of Tarrant County, Fort Worth, TX
25,000	Women's Shelter, Fort Worth, TX
5,000	Jewel Charity Ball, Fort Worth, TX
5,000	Jewel Charity Ball, Fort Worth, TX
5,000	Liberation Community, Fort Worth, TX
5,000	Police Award Foundation, Fort Worth, TX
3,000	Housing Opportunities, Fort Worth, TX
3,000	Housing Opportunities of Fort Worth, Fort Worth, TX
2,500	City of Fort Worth, Fort Worth, TX

Education

100,000	Fort Worth Country Day School, Fort Worth, TX
100,000	Southwest Christian School, Fort Worth, TX
100,000	Trinity Valley School, Fort Worth, TX
50,000	Texas Wesleyan University, Fort Worth, TX
33,000	Summerbridge Fort Worth, Fort Worth, TX
7,500	Cassata Learning Center, Fort Worth, TX
6,200	Texas Christian University, Fort Worth, TX
3,000	Communities in Schools, Fort Worth, TX
2,500	Communities in Schools, Fort Worth, TX
2,000	Fort Worth Independent School District, Fort Worth, TX

Health

16,600	Cook Fort Worth Children's Medical Center, Fort Worth, TX
10,000	Baylor Health Care Foundation, Dallas, TX
10,000	J.L. West Presbyterian Special Care, TX
10,000	Tarrant County Cancer Care, Fort Worth, TX
10,000	Tarrant County Cancer Care, Fort Worth, TX
10,000	Visiting Nurses Association, Fort Worth, TX
8,750	Cook Fort Worth Children's Medical Center, Fort Worth, TX

7,500	Easter Seal Society, Fort Worth, TX
7,500	Easter Seal Society, Fort Worth, TX
5,000	American Cancer Society, Fort Worth, TX
5,000	National Jewish Medical Research, Dallas, TX
4,500	American Cancer Society, Fort Worth, TX
2,000	National Paraplegia Foundation, Fort Worth, TX
2,000	National Paraplegia Foundation, Fort Worth, TX

International

10,000	Challenge, Fort Worth, TX

Religion

16,000	J.L. West Presbyterian Special Care, Fort Worth, TX
10,000	Union Gospel Mission, Fort Worth, TX
5,000	Catholic Charities, Fort Worth, TX
5,000	National Jewish Medical Research, Dallas, TX
4,500	Fellowship of Christian Athletes, Fort Worth, TX
2,500	Fellowship of Christian Athletes, Fort Worth, TX
2,000	Trinity Youth Center, TX

Social Services

60,000	YWCA of Tarrant County, Fort Worth, TX
50,000	YMCA, Fort Worth, TX
50,000	YMCA Metropolitan Fort Worth, Fort Worth, TX
29,000	First Texas Council of Camp Fire, Fort Worth, TX
22,500	Star Telegram Charities, Inc., Fort Worth, TX -- Goodfellows
18,000	Metroplex Food Bank, Cleburne, TX
18,000	Star Telegram Charities, Fort Worth, TX
15,000	Boys and Girls Club, Fort Worth, TX
11,000	Boy Scouts of America--Longhorn Council, Fort Worth, TX
10,000	Senior Citizen Services of Tarrant Co., Fort Worth, TX
10,000	Senior Citizen Services of Tarrant County, Fort Worth, TX
10,000	United Way Metropolitan Tarrant County, Fort Worth, TX
10,000	WARM Place, Fort Worth, TX
10,000	Youth Sports, Fort Worth, TX
10,000	Youth Sports Council, Fort Worth, TX
10,000	YWCA Day Care, Fort Worth, TX
5,000	Big Brothers & Sisters of Tarrant Co., Fort Worth, TX
5,000	Challenge, Inc., Fort Worth, TX
5,000	Circle T Girl Scouts, Fort Worth, TX
5,000	Girl Scouts of America Circle T Council, Fort Worth, TX
5,000	Kids Who Care, TX
5,000	National Victim Center, Fort Worth, TX
5,000	Police Award Foundation, Fort Worth, TX
5,000	Stone Soup Connection, Fort Worth, TX
5,000	Tarrant Area Food Bank, Fort Worth, TX
5,000	Tarrant County Youth Collaboration, Fort Worth, TX
5,000	Youth as Resources, Fort Worth, TX
2,500	Big Brothers and Big Sisters, Fort Worth, TX
2,500	Bobby Bragan Youth Foundation, Fort Worth, TX
2,500	Gill Children's Services, Fort Worth, TX
2,500	Gill Children's Services, Fort Worth, TX
2,500	Meals on Wheels of Johnson County, Cleburne, TX
2,500	Tarrant County Youth Collaboration, Fort Worth, TX
2,500	Warm Place, TX
2,500	West Aid, TX

FORTIS, INC.

Company Contact

New York, NY
Web: http://www.us.fortis.com

Company Description

Former Name: Amev Holdings.
Revenue: US$3,400,000,000
Employees: 6,000
SIC(s): 6211 Security Brokers & Dealers, 6719 Holding Companies Nec.
Parent Company: Fortis AMEV
Parent Assets: US$51,342,001,000

Operating Locations

CA: ACSIA, Burlingame; FL: AdultCare, Deerfield Beach; GA: American Security Group, Atlanta; Auto Lenders Acceptance Corp., Atlanta; Fortis Inc., Atlanta; Remembrance Institute, Atlanta; United Family Life Insurance Co., Atlanta; Fortis Inc., Doraville; MN: Fortis Inc., Saint Paul; Fortis Financial Group, Woodbury; Fortis Inc., Woodbury; MO: Fortis Benefits Insurance Co., Kansas City; NY: Dental Health Alliance LLC, New York; Fortis, New York; Fortis Advisers, New York; WI: Fortis Inc., Milwaukee; Fortis Life, Milwaukee; Fortis Long Term Care, Milwaukee; Fortis Sales, Milwaukee; Time Insurance Co., Milwaukee

Fortis Foundation

Giving Contact

Allen Royal Freedman, Chief Executive Officer
1 Chase Manhattan Plaza, 41st Floor
New York, NY 10005
Phone: (212)859-7000
Fax: (212)859-7010

Description

Founded: 1982
EIN: 133156497
Organization Type: Corporate Foundation
Giving Locations: NY nationally health-related organizations.
Grant Types: Award, Employee Matching Gifts, Matching, Scholarship.

Financial Summary

Total Giving: $256,000 (fiscal year ending June 30, 1998 approx); $187,509 (fiscal 1997); $168,427 (fiscal 1996). Note: Contributes through foundation only.
Giving Analysis: Giving for fiscal 1996 includes: foundation ($139,534); foundation grants to United Way ($28,893)
Assets: $800,000 (fiscal 1999 approx); $728,956 (fiscal 1997); $864,615 (fiscal 1996)
Gifts Received: $10,000 (fiscal 1997); $1,800 (fiscal 1995); $1,200 (fiscal 1992). Note: In fiscal 1995, contributions were received from Fortis Inc.

Typical Recipients

Arts & Humanities: Museums/Galleries, Music
Civic & Public Affairs: Civic & Public Affairs-General
Education: Arts/Humanities Education, Business Education, Colleges & Universities, Education Funds, Engineering/Technological Education, Education-General, Legal Education, Student Aid
Health: AIDS/HIV, Cancer, Children's Health/Hospitals, Emergency/Ambulance Services, Multiple Sclerosis, Single-Disease Health Associations
International: Health Care/Hospitals
Social Services: Child Welfare, Community Service Organizations, Emergency Relief, Family Planning, Food/Clothing Distribution, Recreation & Athletics, Shelters/Homelessness, Social Services-General, Special Olympics, United Funds/United Ways, Youth Organizations

Contributions Analysis

Education: Matches employee gifts to education. About 10% of contributions go to scholarships for employees' children.

Application Procedures

Initial Contact: request application form for scholarships for employees' children only
Application Requirements: for other requests, send a brief letter of inquiry; include a description of organization, amount requested, purpose of funds sought, and proof of tax-exempt status
Deadlines: None.

Restrictions

Fortis Inc. does not consider the following for charitable contributions: individuals, goodwill advertising, political or lobbying groups, religious organizations for sectarian purposes, or organizations outside NY operating area.

Corporate Officials

Jon Kerry Clayton: executive vice presidento, president B Cincinnati, OH 1945. ED Georgia Institute of Technology BIE (1968); Harvard University MBA (1970). PRIM CORP EMPL executive vice president: Fortis Inc.
Allen Royal Freedman: chairman, chief executive officer, president B Suffern, NY 1940. ED Tufts University BA (1961); University of Virginia LLB (1964). PRIM CORP EMPL chairman, chief executive officer, president: Fortis Inc. CORP AFFIL chairman: Time Insurance Co.; director: United Family Life Insurance Co.; director: System & Computer Tech; director: Genesis Health Ventures Inc.; chairman: Interfinancial Inc.; director: Fortis Money Fund Inc.; director: Fortis Capital Fund Inc.; director: Fortis Income Portfolios Inc.; chairman: Fortis Capital Corp.; director: America Security Insurance Co.; president: First Fortis Life Insurance Co.

Foundation Officials

Jon Kerry Clayton: trustee (see above)
Allen Royal Freedman: trustee (see above)
Carroll Mackin: trustee
Grover Thomas: trustee PRIM CORP EMPL executive vice president: Fortis Inc.
J. G. Thomas: trustee

Grants Analysis

Disclosure Period: fiscal year ending June 30, 1998
Total Grants: $256,000*
Number of Grants: 200
Average Grant: $1,059
Highest Grant: $50,000
Typical Range: $500 to $5,000
***Note:** Grants analysis provided by the foundation.

Recent Grants

Note: Grants derived from fiscal 1997 Form 990.

Education

3,000	Dickenson School of Law, Carlisle, PA -- scholarships
1,500	Beloit College, Beloit, WI -- scholarships
1,500	Berry College, Mount Berry, GA -- scholarships
1,500	Brown University, Providence, RI -- scholarships
1,500	Cardinal Stritch College, Milwaukee, WI -- scholarships
1,500	College of St. Benedict, St. Joseph, MN -- scholarships
1,500	College of St. Catherine, Minneapolis, MN -- scholarships
1,500	College of William and Mary, Alexandria, VA -- scholarships
1,500	Cornell University, Ithaca, NY -- scholarships
1,500	Dickenson School of Law, Carlisle, PA -- scholarships

1,500	Drake University, Des Moines, IA -- scholarships
1,500	Florida State University, Tallahassee, FL -- scholarships
1,500	Florida State University, Tallahassee, FL -- scholarships
1,500	Georgia Tech University, Atlanta, GA -- scholarships
1,500	GMI Engineering and Manufacturing Institute, Flint, MI -- scholarships
1,500	Iowa State University, Ames, IA -- scholarships
1,500	Macalester College, St. Paul, MN -- scholarships
1,500	Marquette University, Milwaukee, WI -- scholarships
1,500	Marquette University, Milwaukee, WI -- scholarships
1,500	Messmer High School, Milwaukee, WI -- scholarships
1,500	Michigan Technological University, Houghton, MI -- scholarships
1,500	Milwaukee Institute of Art and Design, Milwaukee, WI -- scholarships
1,500	Mt. Holyoke College, South Hadley, MA -- scholarships
1,500	Ripon College, Ripon, WI -- scholarships
1,500	St. Cloud State University, St. Cloud, MN -- scholarships
1,500	Southwest Missouri State, Springfield, MO -- scholarships
1,500	Southwest Missouri State University, Springfield, MO -- scholarships
1,500	Syracuse University, Syracuse, NY -- scholarships
1,500	Teachers College, New York, NY -- scholarships
1,500	University of California San Diego, San Diego, CA -- scholarships
1,500	University of Georgia Student Financial Aid, Atlanta, GA -- scholarships
1,500	University of Miami, Miami, FL -- scholarships
1,500	University of Minnesota, Minneapolis, MN -- scholarships
1,500	University of Missouri Columbia, Columbia, MO -- scholarships
1,500	University of North Carolina, Chapel Hill, NC -- scholarships
1,500	University of North Texas, Denton, TX -- scholarships
1,500	University of Northern Colorado, Greeley, CO -- scholarships
1,500	University of St. Thomas, St. Paul, MN -- scholarships
1,500	University of Vermont, Burlington, VT -- scholarships
1,500	University of Wisconsin Eau Claire, Eau Claire, WI -- scholarships
1,500	University of Wisconsin Eau Claire, Eau Claire, WI -- scholarships
1,500	University of Wisconsin Eau Claire, Eau Claire, WI -- scholarships
1,500	University of Wisconsin Madison, Madison, WI -- scholarships
1,500	University of Wisconsin Madison, Madison, WI -- scholarships
1,500	University of Wisconsin Milwaukee, Milwaukee, WI -- scholarships
1,500	University of Wisconsin Oshkosh, Oshkosh, WI -- scholarships
1,500	University of Wisconsin Parkside, Kenosha, WI -- scholarships
1,500	Winona State University, Winona, NY -- scholarships
1,500	Young Harris College, Young Harris, GA -- scholarships
1,500	Young Harris College, Young Harris, GA -- scholarships

Fortis Insurance Co.

Company Contact

Milwaukee, WI

Company Description

Former Name: Time Insurance Co.
Employees: 2,000
SIC(s): 6311 Life Insurance, 6321 Accident & Health Insurance.
Parent Company: Fortis, Inc., New York, NY, United States

Operating Locations

WI: Fortis Insurance Co., Milwaukee; Time Insurance Co., Milwaukee

Nonmonetary Support

Value: $54,000 (1996); $25,000 (1992)
Type: Donated Equipment; In-kind Services; Loaned Employees; Loaned Executives; Workplace Solicitation

Corporate Sponsorship

Value: $50,000
Type: Arts & cultural events; Festivals/fairs; Pledge-a-thon; Sports events
Note: Sponsors Habitat for Humanity, blood drives, and corporate tables.

Fortis Insurance Foundation

Giving Contact

Jack Gochenaur, President
Fortis Insurance Foundation
501 West Michigan Avenue
PO Box 3050
Milwaukee, WI 53203-3050
Phone: (414)299-7702
Fax: (414)299-6900

Alternate Contact

Pat Cullen
Phone: (414)271-3011
Note: Pat Cullen may be reached at extension 6722.

Description

Founded: 1973
EIN: 237346436
Organization Type: Corporate Foundation
Former Name: Time Insurance Foundation.
Giving Locations: WI: Southeastern Wisconsin
Grant Types: Employee Matching Gifts, General Support.
Note: Employee matching gift ratio: 1 to 1 to social services, education, or cultural institutions, up to $500 annually. Also provides grants for specific organizational programs within the focus of the foundation.

Giving Philosophy

'Time Insurance Foundation grants are made to enhance and improve the quality of life in Southeastern Wisconsin through a range of health and human service organizations with priority given to efforts addressing epidemic health issues, substance abuse issues, and job creation and economic re-vitalization of our community.' *Reaching Out, Enhancing the Quality of Life in Southeastern Wisconsin,* Time Insurance Foundation Guidelines

Financial Summary

Total Giving: $285,086 (1998); $239,505 (1997); $250,000 (1996). Note: Contributes through foundation only.
Giving Analysis: Giving for 1997 includes: foundation grants to United Way ($50,000); foundation matching gifts ($30,302); 1998: foundation grants to United Way ($50,000); foundation matching gifts ($30,286)
Assets: $959,658 (1998); $889,942 (1997); $837,262 (1996)
Gifts Received: $277,565 (1998); $220,000 (1997); $134,370 (1996). Note: Contributions received from Fortis Insurance Co. (formerly known as the Times Industry Co.).

Typical Recipients

Arts & Humanities: Arts Associations & Councils, Arts Funds, Libraries, Museums/Galleries, Music, Performing Arts, Public Broadcasting
Civic & Public Affairs: African American Affairs, Economic Development, Employment/Job Training, Hispanic Affairs, Housing, Legal Aid, Nonprofit Management, Philanthropic Organizations, Public Policy, Safety, Urban & Community Affairs, Women's Affairs, Zoos/Aquariums
Education: Business Education, Economic Education, Health & Physical Education, Literacy, Minority Education, Public Education (Precollege), Science/Mathematics Education, Vocational & Technical Education
Environment: Environment-General
Health: AIDS/HIV, Alzheimers Disease, Children's Health/Hospitals, Clinics/Medical Centers, Geriatric Health, Health Policy/Cost Containment, Health Organizations, Hospitals, Medical Rehabilitation, Medical Research, Mental Health, Nutrition, Public Health, Respiratory, Single-Disease Health Associations
International: Health Care/Hospitals
Religion: Ministries, Religious Welfare
Social Services: Camps, Child Welfare, Community Centers, Community Service Organizations, Crime Prevention, Day Care, Domestic Violence, Family Planning, Family Services, Food/Clothing Distribution, People with Disabilities, Scouts, Substance Abuse, United Funds/United Ways, Veterans, Volunteer Services, YMCA/YWCA/YMHA/YWHA, Youth Organizations

Contributions Analysis

Giving Priorities: Primary support for the United Way and social service; also funds health organizations, education, civic affairs, and the arts.
Arts & Humanities: 3%. Funds museums, libraries, and art programs.
Civic & Public Affairs: 13%. Interests include community organizations in Wisconsin.
Education: 10%. Supports higher education, literacy services, and secondary schools in Wisconsin.
Health: 14%. Supports single-disease associations.
Religion: 2%.
Social Services: 48%. Supports United Way, caregivers' associations, and community centers.
Note: Total contributions in 1998.

Application Procedures

Initial Contact: Send a letter requesting grant application form.
Application Requirements: Application form requests information on organization's background, its mission, size, and history; description of proposed program, its purpose, budget and goals; description of beneficiaries, including the approximate number of people who will be helped; and information on personnel, including qualifications for those personnel who play a key role in carrying out the objectives of the organization; also include financial statements for the past fiscal year and a copy of the most recent IRS ruling under section 501(c)(3).
Deadlines: One month prior to bi-monthly meetings.
Review Process: The board of directors will evaluate the proposal on its merits, its consistency with the foundation's policies, and the availability of funds.
Evaluative Criteria: A preference will be given to proposals that improve the quality, accessibility, and efficiency of health-care services.

Decision Notification: The trustees meet bi-monthly to consider grant applications, in February, April, June, August, October, and December; applicants receive written notice regarding the board's decision within 21 days after the meeting.
Notes: Foundation uses the Common Application Form of the Donors Forum of Wisconsin.

Restrictions

Grants are generally not made to organizations that are primarily political, fraternal, municipal, religious, or labor-related.
Generally does not provide grants for fund-raising events or multiyear grants, nor does it provide endowment grants.
Foundation will not individually support operational grant requests from organizations that receive a substantial amount of their funding from United Way or United Performing Arts Fund. Will not support food and clothing drives, sporting teams, payment for school or tuition expenses, alumni or membership dues, fees for services, unpaid pledges, requests, subscription fees for publications, or insurance premium payments.

Additional Information

The foundation supports employee volunteer activities, with special consideration given to organizations where employees volunteer that fall within the foundation's focus areas. The foundation does consider grants to organizations where employees volunteer but are not within the foundation focus. However, grants of this nature are limited to $100 per organization, with priority given to programs providing education, training, and direct services.
The foundation's grant programs include a Discretionary Grant program, an Employee Community Involvement Program, a Community Cornerstone Grant program, and an Employee Matching Grant program. The Discretionary grant program awards grant monies to qualifying organizations addressing the priorities of the foundation: epidemic health issues, substance abuse issues, and job creation and economic revitalization of its operating community. Special consideration is given to organizations where company employees actively volunteer their services. Community Cornerstone grants are made for operational support to established community organizations providing equal and low-cost access to a variety of artistic, cultural, and scientific experiences. These grants are also made to support community-based fundraising initiatives such as the United Way and the United Performing Arts Fund. The Employee Matching Grant program provides for matching of personal employee contributions of $20 or more, to qualifying organizations, up to $500 per year per employee.
Publications: Community Annual Report; Application Guidelines; Application Form

Corporate Officials

Allen Royal Freedman: chairman, chief executive officer, president B Suffern, NY 1940. ED Tufts University BA (1961); University of Virginia LLB (1964). PRIM CORP EMPL chairman, chief executive officer, president: Fortis Inc. CORP AFFIL chairman: Time Insurance Co.; director: United Family Life Insurance Co.; director: System & Computer Tech; director: Genesis Health Ventures Inc.; chairman: Interfinancial Inc.; director: Fortis Money Fund Inc.; director: Fortis Capital Fund Inc.; director: Fortis Income Portfolios Inc.; chairman: Fortis Capital Corp.; director: America Security Insurance Co.; president: First Fortis Life Insurance Co.
Jack A. Gochenaur: senior vice president administration & services, chief financial officer B Sturgis, MI 1948. ED Manchester College BS (1970). PRIM CORP EMPL senior vice president administration & services, chief financial officer: Time Insurance Co. CORP AFFIL chief financial officer: Fortis Insurance Co.
Thomas M. Keller: president B 1948. ED Yale University BA (1970); University of California at Berkeley PhD (1971). PRIM CORP EMPL president: Time Insurance Co.

Foundation Officials

Kathy Clark: trustee
Pat Cullen: secretary
Jack A. Gochenaur: president, trustee (see above)
Wade Grove: trustee
Heidi Hansestein: treasurer, trustee
Steve Hart: trustee
Jackie Jeray: trustee
Gwen A. Johnson: trustee
Carrie Vorgard: vice president, trustee

Grants Analysis

Disclosure Period: calendar year ending 1998
Total Grants: $204,800*
Number of Grants: 39
Average Grant: $5,251
Highest Grant: $26,000
Typical Range: $1,000 to $6,000
***Note:** Giving excludes matching gifts; United Way.

Recent Grants

Note: Grants derived from 1997 Form 990.

Arts & Humanities

5,000	Milwaukee Public Museum, Milwaukee, WI
5,000	UPAF, Milwaukee, WI
2,000	Milwaukee Public Library, Milwaukee, WI
1,000	Artreach, Milwaukee, WI

Civic & Public Affairs

10,000	New Hope Project, Milwaukee, WI
7,000	Works for Wisconsin, WI
4,700	La Causa, Milwaukee, WI
3,000	Next Door Foundation, Milwaukee, WI
2,950	Zoological Society of Milwaukee County, Milwaukee, WI
2,500	Esperanza Unida, Milwaukee, WI
2,000	Greater Milwaukee Committee, Milwaukee, WI
1,000	Lisbon Avenue Neighborhood Development Corporation, Milwaukee, WI
1,000	MCADD

Education

11,701	Shotas Middle School
5,000	Office Technology Academy, Milwaukee, WI
1,500	Wisconsin Council on Economic Education, Milwaukee, WI
1,000	Literacy Services, Milwaukee, WI
100	Highland Community School, Milwaukee, WI

Health

7,500	AIDS Resource Center, Milwaukee, WI
5,000	American Lung Association
2,000	Alzheimer's Association, Philadelphia, PA
2,000	Easter Seal Foundation
1,000	Make-A-Wish Foundation
126	American Lung Association
126	American Lung Association

Religion

5,000	St. Camillus Ministries
3,500	Salvation Army

Social Services

50,000	United Way
15,000	United Community Center, Milwaukee, WI
7,500	Milwaukee Women's Center, Milwaukee, WI
5,000	Camp Heartland, Wauwatosa, WI
5,000	Milwaukee Police Athletic League, Milwaukee, WI
5,000	National Family Caregivers Association, Kensington, MD
5,000	Northcott Neighborhood House, Milwaukee, WI
5,000	Rosalie Manor, Milwaukee, WI
4,000	Hunger Task Force
2,500	16th Street Community Center
2,500	Boy Scouts of America Milwaukee County Council, Milwaukee, WI
2,000	Children's Services Society, West Allis, WI
2,000	Parenting Network
2,000	Second Harvest Food Bank
2,000	Walker's Point Youth and Family Center, Milwaukee, WI
1,500	Gathering
500	Boys and Girls Club

FORTUNE BRANDS, INC.

★ Number 94 of Top 100 Corporate Givers

Company Contact

Old Greenwich, CT
Web: http://www.fortunebrands.com

Company Description

Former Name: American Brands, Inc.
Revenue: US$4,797,200,000
Employees: 28,000
Fortune Rank: 321, per FORTUNE Magazine's list of 500 Largest U.S. Corporations (1999).
FF 321
SIC(s): 2085 Distilled & Blended Liquors, 2111 Cigarettes, 2121 Cigars, 6719 Holding Companies Nec.

Operating Locations

Australia: Torak Pty. Ltd., Busselton; Office Products International (Western Australia) Pty. Ltd., Morley; Prestige Group (Australia) Pty. Ltd., Northmead; Office Products International Ltd., Oakleigh; Marbig Rexel Pty. Ltd., Rosebery; Rexel Australia P/L, Rosebery; Belgium: ACCO-Rexel Belgium SA, Brussels, Brabant; Prestige Benelux SA, Brussels, Brabant; Canada: Alberta Distillers Ltd., Burnaby; Carrington Distillers Ltd., Burnaby; Carrington Imports Ltd., Burnaby; Featherstone & Co. Ltd., Burnaby; Windsor Distributors International Inc., Edmonton; Acme Systems Inc., Montreal; Societe Commerciale La Verendrye, Montreal; Day-Timers of Canada Ltd., Niagara Falls; Sandt Printing Co. Ltd., Niagara Falls; Moen Inc., Oakville; Plymouth Tool & Stamping Ltd., Scarborough; ACCO Canada Inc., Toronto; Acme Seeley Investments Canada Ltd., Toronto; Acme Visible Records of Canada Ltd., Toronto; Ameribrands Finance Canada Ltd., Toronto; Golden Belt Manufacturing (Canada) Ltd., Toronto; France: Silk Cut France SARL, Boulogne-Billancourt; Dacor SA, Paris, Ville-de-Paris; Master Lock Europe, Paris, Ville-de-Paris; Prestige France, Paris, Ville-de-Paris; Flavorpac SA, Roissy-en-France, Val-d'Oise; ACCO France SA, Savigny-le-Temple; Ateliers de Constructions Chaudronness de L'Ouest, Soudan, Loire-Atlantique; ACCO-Rexel France, Valreas, Vaucluse; Diffusion D'Articles de Classment et D'Organisation, Valreas, Vaucluse; Innova SA, Valreas, Vaucluse; Val Rex SA, Valreas, Vaucluse; ISS France, Villeurbanne, Rhone; Germany: Acushnet GmbH, Dietzenbach, Hessen; Flavorpac Deutschland GmbH, Dusseldorf; Prestige Haushaltswaren GmbH, Solingen, Nordrhein-Westfalen; ACCO International GmbH, Stuttgart, Baden-Wuerttemberg; Ireland: ACCO-Rexel Ltd., Dublin; Donal MacNally Opticians Ltd., Dublin; Gallaher (Dublin) Ltd., Dublin; Rexel (Ireland) Ltd., Dublin; Vendepac (Ireland) Ltd., Dublin; Italy: Prestige Italiana SPA, Locate Varesino, Lombardia; Filotechnica Salmoiraghi SPA, Milano, Lombardia; Istituto Ottico Vigano' SPA, Milano, Lombardia; King Mec SPA, Settimo Torinese, Piemonte; Jamaica: ACCO Jamaica Ltd., Kingston; Japan: Stanadyne Ltd., Tokyo; Titleist Japan Inc., Tokyo; Mexico: ACCO Mexicana SA de CV,

Lerma; Industrial de Carpetas Mexicanas SA de CV, Nogales; Netherlands: American Brands Finance Europe BV, Amsterdam, Noord-Holland; Prestige Housewares (New Zealand) Ltd., Avondale; International Business Controls BV, Cothen, Utrecht; New Zealand: ACCO International (New Zealand) Ltd., Granada North; Spain: General Optica SA, Barcelona, Cataluna; Sanmartin Inmuebles SA, Barcelona, Cataluna; Silk Cut SA, Barcelona, Cataluna; Gallaher Canarias SA, Canaria, Canarias; Fabricados Inoxidables SA, La Carolina, Andalucia; Gallaher Espana SA, Las Rozas de Madrid, Madrid; United Kingdom: Keeler Ltd., Berkshire, England; ACCO Europe plc, Buckingham; ACCO-Rexel Ltd., Buckingham; Acushnet Ltd., Cambridge, Cambridgeshire; Ofrex Office Supplies Ltd., Cheshire; Cumberland Pencil Co. Ltd., Cumbria; Dacor (United Kingdom) Ltd., East Sussex, England; Bonny Products Ltd., Hampshire; Mayfair Group Ltd., Hampshire, England; Marshell Group Ltd., Harrow, England; Rexel Business Machines Ltd., Hereford & Worcester, England; Bomefa Ltd., London; Designville Ltd., London; Ellams Duplicator Co. Ltd., London; Gresswell Don Ltd., London; Markplan Systems Ltd., London; Sobranie Ltd., London; Cotton John Ltd., Lothian, Scotland; Muir William Ltd., Lothian, Scotland; Scotch Whisky Heritage Centre Ltd., Lothian, Scotland; Eastlight Ltd., Manchester, Greater Manchester; Rexel Research & Development Ltd., Mid Glamorgan, Wales; Whyte & Mackay Group plc, Strathclyde, Scotland; Bendon & Hedges Ltd., Surrey; Cope Brothers & Co. Ltd., Surrey; Cope & Lloyd (Overseas) Ltd., Surrey; Forbuoys plc, Surrey, England; Freeman J R & Son Ltd., Surrey, England; Gallaher International Ltd., Surrey, England; Gallaher Ltd., Surrey, England; Karturs Vending Ltd., Surrey, England; Old Holborn Ltd., Surrey, England; Prestige Group plc, Surrey, England; Prestige Group United Kingdom plc, Surrey, England; Prestige Housewares Ltd., Surrey, England; Prestige Products Ltd., Surrey, England; T M Group plc, Surrey, England; ACCO-Rexel Group Services plc, West Drayton; Copy-King Ltd., West Drayton; Timbercrest Properties Ltd., West Drayton, England; Nileroy Ltd., West Drayton, Greater London; Dolland & Aitchison Group plc, West Midlands, England; Dollond & Aitchison Ltd., West Midlands, England; Dollond & Aitchison (Property) Ltd., West Midlands, England; Dollond & Aitchison Services Ltd., West Midlands, England; Venezuela: ACCO Manufacturing CA, Caracas, Distrito Federal

Note: Also has major operations in Weybridge, Surrey, England.

Nonmonetary Support

Value: $3,864,378 (1998); $514,387 (1997); $1,991,106 (1996)

Type: Donated Equipment; Donated Products; In-kind Services

Note: The company also reports that it donates the use of their facilities.

Giving Contact

Joan McGrath, Contributions Administrator
Fortune Brands, Inc. Contributions Program
1700 East Putnam Avenue
Old Greenwich, CT 06870
Phone: (203)698-5211
Fax: (203)698-5577
Email: jm@fortunebrands.com

Description

Organization Type: Corporate Giving Program

Giving Locations: headquarters and operating communities.

Grant Types: Employee Matching Gifts, General Support, Multiyear/Continuing Support, Scholarship.

Note: Employee matching gift ratio: 2 to 1.

Financial Summary

Total Giving: $7,428,618 (1998); $4,298,448 (1997); $8,050,525 (1996). Note: Contributes through corporate direct giving program only. Giving includes corporate direct giving; domestic and international subsidiaries; nonmonetary support.

Giving Analysis: Giving for 1996 includes: foundation ($7,416,789); foundation matching gifts ($180,912)

Typical Recipients

Arts & Humanities: Arts Centers, Community Arts, Historic Preservation, Libraries, Museums/Galleries, Music, Opera, Performing Arts, Public Broadcasting, Theater

Civic & Public Affairs: Civil Rights, Economic Development, Employment/Job Training, Legal Aid, Urban & Community Affairs, Women's Affairs, Zoos/Aquariums

Education: Arts/Humanities Education, Business Education, Colleges & Universities, Community & Junior Colleges, Continuing Education, Economic Education, Education Associations, Elementary Education (Private), Literacy, Minority Education, Private Education (Precollege), Public Education (Precollege), Special Education

Environment: Environment-General

Health: Emergency/Ambulance Services, Health Organizations, Hospitals, Medical Research, Public Health, Single-Disease Health Associations

International: Health Care/Hospitals, International Peace & Security Issues, International Relations

Social Services: Child Welfare, Community Centers, Community Service Organizations, Day Care, Food/Clothing Distribution, People with Disabilities, Recreation & Athletics, Shelters/Homelessness, Substance Abuse, United Funds/United Ways, Volunteer Services, Youth Organizations

Contributions Analysis

Giving Priorities: Education and community programs emphasizing women and minorities in business. Contributions program is highly decentralized, with substantial contributions made by foreign subsidiaries. Operating companies administer local programs. American Brands sets internal policy and approves contributions budgets. Contributions by foreign subsidiaries are channeled through the company's holding company in England. Recipients must be registered as charitable in England. Headquarters does not receive a breakdown of foreign contributions. Donations to U.S.-based nonprofits with an international focus primarily include international affairs organizations and public policy. Company's Gallaher's unit in the U.K. is active in Queen Elizabeth's Foundation for the Disabled, providing students with career training and work experience.

Application Procedures

Initial Contact: Send a brief letter of inquiry.

Application Requirements: Include organization's purpose, detailed description of project and amount of funding requested; list of other corporate contributors; and proof of tax-exempt status.

Deadlines: None.

Review Process: All requests are screened and approved by the corporate responsibility committee; operating companies administer local contributions programs.

Evaluative Criteria: Preference given to organizations close to company locations.

Decision Notification: Decisions are made as applications are received; final notification within one month.

Notes: The company reports that requests should be sent to the nearest company facility. The company's contributions program is highly decentralized.

Restrictions

Generally does not support individuals, political parties or candidates, fraternal organizations, member agencies of united funds, or religious organizations for sectarian purposes.

Additional Information

In 1997, American Brands, Inc. divided into two companies--Fortune Brands and Gallaher. Gallaher is based in the United Kingdom.

Corporate Officials

Thomas Chandler Hays: chairman, chief executive officer, director B Chicago, IL 1935. ED California Institute of Technology BS (1957); California Institute of Technology MS (1958); Harvard University Graduate School of Business Administration MBA (1963). PRIM CORP EMPL chairman, chief executive officer, director: Fortune Brands, Inc. CORP AFFIL director: Master Lock Co.; director: Gallaher Ltd.; director: AC Nielsen Corp.; director: Acushnet Co. NONPR AFFIL member: Conference Board & Economic; director: Southwest Area Commerce & Industry Association; member: Business Roundtable; director: Community Foundations Fairfield County; member: Ambassador Roundtable. CLUB AFFIL Economic Club; Tokeneke Club; Cincinnati Country Club; Darien Country Club; Bel-Air Bay Club.

Robert James Rukeyser: senior vice president corporate affairs B New Rochelle, NY 1942. ED Cornell University BA (1964); New York University MBA (1969). PRIM CORP EMPL senior vice president corporate affairs: Fortune Brands, Inc. CORP AFFIL director: MasterBrand Industries Inc.; director: Fortune Brands International Corp.; director: JBB Worldwide Inc.; director: ACCO World Corp.; director: Acushnet Co. NONPR AFFIL director, member finance & development committee: Hole in the Wall Gang Camp; director: Stamford Center Arts; member: Business Products Industry Association.

Norman H. Wesley: president, chief operating officer PRIM CORP EMPL president, chief operating officer: Fortune Brands, Inc. ADD CORP EMPL chairman: ACCO World Corp.

Giving Program Officials

Joan S. McGrath: contributions administrator

Grants Analysis

Disclosure Period: calendar year ending

Typical Range: $500 to $5,000

FOX ENTERTAINMENT GROUP

Company Contact

New York, NY
Web: http://www.newscorp.com

Company Description

Employees: 3,200

SIC(s): 4833 Television Broadcasting Stations, 7812 Motion Picture & Video Production.

Parent Company: News Corp. Ltd., 2 Holt Street, Sydney, NW, Australia

Operating Locations

CA: Fox Broadcasting Co., Beverly Hills; Fox Inc., Beverly Hills, Hollywood; Fox, Los Angeles; Fox Inc., Los Angeles; Fox Television Stations, Los Angeles; KTTV, Los Angeles; New World Entertainment, Los Angeles; Twentieth Century Fox Film Corp., Los Angeles; Twentieth Century Fox Home Entertainment, Los Angeles; DC: Fox Inc., Washington; WTTG, Washington; HI: KITV, Honolulu; IL: Fox Inc., Chicago; WFLD, Chicago; MA: WFXT-TV, Needham; WNAC, Rehobeth; MI: WZZM, Grand Rapids; Fox Video Co., Livonia; MO: KTVI-TV, Saint Louis; MS: WAPT, Jackson; NY: WGRV, Buffalo; Fox Inc., New York; WNYW, New York; TX: KTBC, Austin; Fox Inc.,

Dallas; KDAF, Dallas; KDFW, Dallas; Fox Inc., Houston; KRIV, Houston

Nonmonetary Support

Type: Donated Equipment; Donated Products
Volunteer Programs: The company sponsors an employee volunteer program that supports various activities, including an adopt-a-school relationship with Locke High School in South Central Los Angeles and events organized by the Permanent Charities Committee of the Entertainment Industries.

Giving Contact

Ms. Robin Corley, Director, Corporate Communications
Fox, Inc.
PO Box 900
Beverly Hills, CA 90213
Phone: (310)369-3029

Description

Founded: 1984
Organization Type: Corporate Giving Program
Giving Locations: headquarters area only.
Grant Types: Employee Matching Gifts, General Support.
Note: Employee matching gift ratio: 1 to 1 for education only.

Financial Summary

Total Giving: Contributes through corporate direct giving program only.

Typical Recipients

Arts & Humanities: Community Arts
Civic & Public Affairs: Civil Rights, Professional & Trade Associations
Education: Colleges & Universities
Health: Health-General, Hospitals
Social Services: Child Welfare, Senior Services, Youth Organizations

Application Procedures

Initial Contact: Send a brief letter of inquiry.
Application Requirements: Include a description of organization, amount requested, purpose of funds sought, recently audited financial statement, and proof of tax-exempt status.
Deadlines: None.

Corporate Officials

Chase Carey: chief executive officer, chairman PRIM CORP EMPL chief executive officer, chairman: Fox TV. CORP AFFIL director: Gateway Inc.; director: ICS CommunicationsS.
Peter Chernin: chairman, chief executive officer PRIM CORP EMPL chairman, chief executive officer: Fox Inc.
Rupert P. Murdoch: chairman B Melbourne, NW Australia 1931. ED Worcester College MA (1953). PRIM CORP EMPL chairman, chief executive officer: News Corp. Ltd. CORP AFFIL chairman: NYP Holdings Inc.; director: Philip Morris Companies Inc.; director: B Sky B.

Giving Program Officials

Robin Corley: PRIM CORP EMPL director corporate communications: Fox Inc.
Gloria Dickey: PRIM CORP EMPL giving officer: Fox Inc.

Franklin Electric Co.

Company Contact

Bluffton, IN

Company Description

Employees: 1,285
SIC(s): 3561 Pumps & Pumping Equipment, 3586 Measuring & Dispensing Pumps, 3621 Motors & Generators, 3625 Relays & Industrial Controls.

Nonmonetary Support

Type: Donated Equipment; Donated Products

Franklin Electric, Edward J. Schaefer, and T. W. KehoeCharitable and Educational Foundation

Giving Contact

Gary Merritt, Finance Manager
400 E. Spring St.
Bluffton, IN 46714
Phone: (219)824-2900
Fax: (219)827-5530

Description

EIN: 237399324
Organization Type: Corporate Foundation
Giving Locations: IN: Bluffton including surrounding area
Grant Types: Research.
Note: Scholarships are awarded to employees only.

Financial Summary

Total Giving: $202,647 (1998); $282,185 (1997); $290,035 (1996)
Giving Analysis: Giving for 1997 includes: foundation ($239,685); foundation grants to United Way ($30,000); foundation scholarships ($12,500); 1998: foundation ($136,847); foundation scholarships ($35,800); foundation grants to United Way ($30,000)
Assets: $435,916 (1998); $457,656 (1997); $205,353 (1996)
Gifts Received: $170,200 (1998); $523,799 (1997); $195,200 (1996). Note: In 1998, contributions were received from Franklin Electric Company, Inc.

Typical Recipients

Arts & Humanities: Arts Associations & Councils, Arts Centers
Civic & Public Affairs: Botanical Gardens/Parks, Chambers of Commerce, Safety, Urban & Community Affairs
Education: Business Education, Colleges & Universities, Engineering/Technological Education, Education-General, Private Education (Precollege), Student Aid, Vocational & Technical Education
Environment: Air/Water Quality
Health: Children's Health/Hospitals, Hospitals
Science: Scientific Centers & Institutes
Social Services: Child Welfare, Community Centers, Recreation & Athletics, Scouts, United Funds/United Ways, YMCA/YWCA/YMHA/YWHA

Contributions Analysis

Giving Priorities: Social service, education, civic organizations and arts organizations.
Arts & Humanities: 7%. Funds arts councils and museums.
Civic & Public Affairs: 11%. Supports a park, chamber of commerce, and festivals.
Education: 26%. Provides scholarships.
Environment: 1%. Funds a trail project.
Health: 2%. Supports health centers and single-disease health organizations.
Science: 1%. Supports a science center.
Social Services: 52%. Supports community centers, youth organizations, and the United Way.
Note: Total contributions made in 1998.

Application Procedures

Initial Contact: Request a scholarship application.
Deadlines: During the senior year of high school.

Additional Information

Provides scholarships to qualified students who are children of employees of Franklin Electric Co.

Corporate Officials

Jess B. Ford: chief financial officer, vice president PRIM CORP EMPL chief financial officer, vice president: Franklin Electric Co.
William Hogan Lawson, III: chairman, chief executive officer, director B Lexington, KY 1937. ED Purdue University BS (1959); Harvard University MBA (1961). PRIM CORP EMPL chairman, chief executive officer, director: Franklin Electric Co. CORP AFFIL director: Sentry Insurance; director: Skyline Corp.; director: JSJ Corp.; chairman: Oil Dynamics. NONPR AFFIL member: Harvard University Business School Association; trustee: Indiana Institute Technology; trustee: American Ground Water Trust. CLUB AFFIL Summit Fort Wayne Club; Fort Wayne Country Club; Harvard Club.
John B. Lindsay: president PRIM CORP EMPL president: Franklin Electric Co.

Foundation Officials

R. W. Cantwell: secretary
William Hogan Lawson, III: president (see above)

Grants Analysis

Disclosure Period: calendar year ending 1998
Total Grants: $136,847*
Number of Grants: 30
Average Grant: $4,562
Highest Grant: $25,000
Typical Range: $200 to $20,000
*Note: Giving excludes United Way and scholarship.

Recent Grants

Note: Grants derived from 1997 Form 990.

Arts & Humanities

3,000 Arts United, Fort Wayne, IN
2,275 Bager Creek Arts Center, Siloam Springs, AR

Civic & Public Affairs

20,000 Headwaters Park Campaign, Fort Wayne, IN
12,500 Pennville Volunteer Fire Department, Pennville, IN
1,300 Northwest Arkansas Council, Fayetteville, AR

Education

75,000 Southern Well Scholarships, Montpelier, IN
25,000 Indiana Institute of Technology, Fort Wayne, IN
15,000 Foundation Scholarship Fund EOSC, Wilburton, OK
10,000 Siloam Springs Scholarships, Siloam Springs, AR
5,000 Canterbury School, Fort Wayne, IN
5,000 Kiamichi Vo-Tech Foundation, Wilburton, OK
2,000 Bluffton, South Wells Dollars for Scholars, Bluffton, IN
1,500 St. Francis College, Fort Wayne, IN

Health

2,000 Siloam Springs Memorial Hospital Campaign, Siloam Springs, AR

Social Services

25,000 Wells County Community Center, Bluffton, IN
20,000 Fort Wayne YMCA, Fort Wayne, IN
15,000 United Way Siloam Springs, Bnt. County, Siloam Springs, AR

15,000	United Way Wells County, Bluffton, IN
5,000	Boy Scouts of America Anthony Wayne Area Council, Fort Wayne, IN
2,000	Siloam Springs American Legion Baseball, Siloam Springs, AR

THE FRANKLIN MINT

Company Contact
Franklin Center, PA

Company Description
Employees: 4,700
SIC(s): 2732 Book Printing, 3231 Products of Purchased Glass, 3911 Jewelry & Precious Metal, 3942 Dolls & Stuffed Toys.

Nonmonetary Support
Type: Donated Products
Note: Nonmonetary support is provided by the co. and the foundation.

Corporate Sponsorship
Type: Arts & cultural events

The Franklin Mint Foundation for the Arts

Giving Contact
Peter Gurney, Director
The Franklin Mint Foundation for the Arts
PO Box 64713
Los Angeles, CA 90064
Phone: (310)966-3622
Fax: (310)966-5798

Description
Organization Type: Corporate Foundation
Giving Locations: operating areas.
Grant Types: Award, Capital, General Support, Multiyear/Continuing Support.

Financial Summary
Total Giving: Contributes through corporate direct giving program and foundation.

Typical Recipients
Arts & Humanities: Arts Appreciation, Arts Associations & Councils, Arts Centers, Arts Festivals, Community Arts, Museums/Galleries, Music, Visual Arts
Civic & Public Affairs: Philanthropic Organizations, Professional & Trade Associations
Education: Arts/Humanities Education, Literacy
Environment: Environment-General
Health: Hospitals, Mental Health, Single-Disease Health Associations
Social Services: Animal Protection, Child Welfare, Food/Clothing Distribution, People with Disabilities, United Funds/United Ways

Contributions Analysis
Arts & Humanities: About 70%. The foundation's primary focus is national visual arts organizations.
Civic & Public Affairs: About 10%. Support goes to community activities in operating areas.
Health: About 20%. Supports facilities and programs within operating areas.

Application Procedures
Initial Contact: a brief letter of inquiry
Application Requirements: a description of organization, amount requested, purpose of funds sought, audited financial statement, and proof of tax-exempt status
Deadlines: None.

Restrictions
Does not support individuals, religious organizations for sectarian purposes, or political or lobbying groups.

Corporate Officials
Lynda Rae Resnick: vice chairman, co-owner B 1940. PRIM CORP EMPL vice chairman, co-owner: The Franklin Mint. CORP AFFIL American Protection Industries; chairman, president: Tele-Flora. NONPR AFFIL trustee: Philadelphia Museum Art; member board overseers: University Pennsylvania; director: Milken Family Foundation; trustee, member executive committee: Los Angeles County Museum Art; member sculpture deco arts committee: Metropolitan Museum Art; member director, chairman marketing committee: Conservative International; chairman: Acquisitions Exhibition Committee; director: CaP Cure; member: Acquisition Committee National Gallery Art.
Stewart A. Resnick: chairman, chief executive officer B Jersey City, NJ 1936. ED University of California, Los Angeles BS (1959); University of California, Los Angeles LLB (1962). PRIM CORP EMPL chairman, chief executive officer: The Franklin Mint ADD CORP EMPL chairman, owner: Paramount Citrus Co.; chairman, owner: Paramount Farms Inc.; chairman, owner: Roll International Corp.; chairman, owner: Tele-Flora. CORP AFFIL director: Warnaco Group Inc. NONPR AFFIL acquisitions committee: National Gallery; member, advisory board: University Pennsylvania Wharton School Business; member advisory board: Management Education Council; board trustees: Bard College.

Foundation Officials
Peter Gurney: executive director

Grants Analysis
Disclosure Period: calendar year ending
Typical Range: $1,000 to $2,500

FREDDIE MAC

 Number 64 of Top 100 Corporate Givers

Company Contact
McLean, VA

Company Description
Former Name: Federal Home Loan Mortgage Corp.
Revenue: US$18,048,000,000
Profit: US$1,700,000,000
Employees: 3,285
Fortune Rank: 62, per FORTUNE Magazine's list of 500 Largest U.S. Corporations (1999).
FF 62
SIC(s): 6111 Federal & Federally-Sponsored Credit.

Nonmonetary Support
Value: $250,000 (1992)
Type: Donated Equipment

Corporate Sponsorship
Type: Sports events
Contact: Barbara Butler, Manager Community Relations

Freddie Mac Foundation

Giving Contact
Shane Falter, Director of Foundation Giving
Freddie Mac Foundation
Mailstop A-40
8250 Jones Branch Dr.
McLean, VA 22102
Phone: (703)918-5788
Fax: (703)903-3585

Alternate Contact
Kelly Sumego, Administration Corporate
Phone: 800-424-5401
Note: Contact for employee matching gifts program, nonmonetary support, and the 'Reach Out to a Child' campaign

Description
Founded: 1990
EIN: 541573760
Organization Type: Corporate Foundation
Giving Locations: DC: Washington including metropolitan area; MD: Frederick County, Howard County, Montgomery County, Prince Georges County; VA: Loudoun and Prince William Counties, Alexandria, Arlington, Fairfax nationally organizations.
Grant Types: Capital, Conference/Seminar, Employee Matching Gifts, General Support, Matching, Multiyear/Continuing Support.
Note: The employee matching gift program is funded through the Foundation.

Giving Philosophy
'The Freddie Mac Foundation is dedicated to brightening the future of children, youth and families at risk. It fulfills this mission by providing funds to organizations working to strengthen the health, education and welfare of children and youth and to provide family support services. The Foundation provides funds for a variety of nonprofit organizations serving children and their families which are located in metropolitan Washington, DC as well as statewide initiatives in Maryland and Virginia. The Foundation also provides funding to organizations which provide services on a national scope. In addition to funding, the Foundation is a strong advocate for children, youth and families, supporting policies and programs that focus attention on their needs and foster positive solutions.' *Freddie Mac Foundation grant guidelines*

Financial Summary
Total Giving: $13,000,000 (1999 approx); $13,000,000 (1998 approx); $6,955,382 (1997). Note: Contributes through corporate direct giving program and foundation. 1998 Giving includes corporate direct giving ($6,500,000); foundation ($6,500,000). 1997 Giving includes foundation.
Assets: $18,436,468 (1996); $19,990,651 (1995); $13,700,365 (1994)
Gifts Received: $5,723,240 (1996); $11,986,935 (1995); $2,000,000 (1990)

Typical Recipients
Arts & Humanities: Arts Outreach, Public Broadcasting
Civic & Public Affairs: Business/Free Enterprise, Economic Development, Hispanic Affairs, Housing, Law & Justice, Legal Aid, Minority Business, Urban & Community Affairs, Women's Affairs
Education: Afterschool/Enrichment Programs, Business-School Partnerships, Education Associations, Education Reform, Elementary Education (Public), Leadership Training, Legal Education, Preschool Education, School Volunteerism, Science/Mathematics Education, Secondary Education (Public), Special Education, Student Aid
Environment: Protection
Health: AIDS/HIV, Children's Health/Hospitals, Health Organizations, Heart, Hospices, Mental Health, Prenatal Health Issues
International: Health Care/Hospitals
Religion: Churches, Jewish Causes, Ministries, Religious Welfare
Social Services: At-Risk Youth, Camps, Child Abuse, Child Welfare, Community Service Organizations, Counseling, Day Care, Delinquency & Criminal Rehabilitation, Domestic Violence, Family Planning,

Family Services, People with Disabilities, Recreation & Athletics, Senior Services, Shelters/Homelessness, Substance Abuse, YMCA/YWCA/YMHA/YWHA, Youth Organizations

Contributions Analysis

Education: Focus on early childhood education programs that address the developmental needs of children ages 0-6 and prepare them for learning. Includes early intervention services, strengthening day care and home day care systems; efforts to stimulate parental involvement in their child's educational development; school-based services for families, particularly pregnant or parenting teens; programs that enhance academic performance; initiatives to reform public education systems and advocate for stronger schools, including professional development opportunities and training for teachers; and programs that help children envision a successful future by providing teachers; and programs that help children envision a successful future by providing training and/or exposure to career opportunities.

Social Services: Focus on prevention of abuse (physical, sexual, emotional) and neglect. Targets factors leading to child abuse, including poor parenting skills, young inexperienced parents, stressful living situations and financial hardship, domestic violence, and substance abuse. Encourages grant requests in the following areas: parent training, eduation and support groups, home visitor programs, public awareness campaigns, comprehensive family support services, mental health services, teenage pregnancy prevention, services to parentsand children who are victims of domestic violence, father involvement programs, support services to parents who are substance abusers, treatment programs that enable families to stay together during the treatment period, and advocacy and system reform initiatives related to preventing child abuse through the strengthening of families and communities, as well as professional development opportunities for social workers.

Application Procedures

Initial Contact: preliminary telephone call prior to full proposal

Application Requirements: follow WRAG Common grant application and use the attached grant application summary; include copy of IRS 501(c)(3) CAP certificate, annual report or other information detailing program activities, audited financial statement, operating budget for preceding and current years, and any other pertinent information about organization (e.g. press articles or brochures)

Deadlines: contact the foundation for new deadlines

Review Process: within 30 days of submitting proposals, nonprofits will be informed of next step

Evaluative Criteria: organization's goal or impact; whether funds directly benefit children, especially young children; efficiency of nonprofit organization; level of community involvement, whether program is prevention-oriented, program's potential to build awareness; severity of need; and whether other programs duplicate services

Decision Notification: within three months of deadline date

Notes: Organizations seeking grants should not contact members of the Foundation board of directors.

Restrictions

Does not support organizations which discriminate in the hiring of staff on the basis of race, religion, sex, or disabilities. Applicants must be exempt from income taxes under Section 501(c)(3) of the Internal Revenue Code and be defined as a public charity. No grants are made to individuals, for training in or promotion of religions doctrine, or to fund debts.

Additional Information

The maximum grant awarded is $50,000. Concept papers must be submitted for requests greater than $50,000. After approval of concept paper, a full proposal will then need to be submitted to the foundation. 1997 was a transitional year for the foundation, in which a new five-year plan of giving was developed. No new grants were funded in 1997, but those which had already been committed to were honored. At the time of publication, the new guidelines for giving were not available; the information in this entry is historically accurate, but there may be changes in future giving focus and procedure. publication, the new guidelines for giving were not available; the information in this entry is historically accurate, but there may be changes in future giving focus and procedure.

Publications: Foundation Annual Report; Grant Guidelines

Corporate Officials

Leland C. Brendsel: chairman, chief executive officer, director B Sioux Falls, SD 1942. ED University of Colorado BA (1967); Northwestern University MBA (1974). PRIM CORP EMPL chairman, chief executive officer, director: Federal Home Loan Mortgage Corp. NONPR AFFIL director: Local Initiatives Support Corp.; director: Northwestern University Kellogg Graduate School Business Management.

Giving Program Officials

Donald John Schuenke: director B Milwaukee, WI 1929. ED Marquette University PhB (1950); Marquette University LLB (1958). PRIM CORP EMPL director: Northwest Mutual Life Insurance Co. CORP AFFIL chairman: Northern Telecom Ltd.; director: AO Smith Corp.; chairman: Nortel (Northern Telecom); director: Federal Home Loan Mortgage Corp.; director: Mortgage Guaranty Insurance Corp.; director: Badger Meter Inc.

Foundation Officials

Maxine Baker-Stokes: executive director

Leland C. Brendsel: director (see above)

Kathy Whelpley: associates director

Grants Analysis

Disclosure Period: calendar year ending 1997

Total Grants: $6,955,382

Number of Grants: 145

Average Grant: $47,968

Highest Grant: $500,000

Typical Range: $5,000 to $50,000

Recent Grants

Note: Grants derived from 1996 Annual Report.

Civic & Public Affairs

50,000 Chicago Park District, Chicago, IL -- provide basic summer activities to families in Chicago Housing Authority developments

50,000 DC Agenda, Washington, DC -- to create process to accomplish needed social changes in DC

45,000 Latin American Youth Center, Washington, DC -- establish foster care program serving Latino youth

Education

50,000 Sidwell Friends School, Washington, DC -- for academic enrichment program

49,700 Prince George's County Public Schools, Adelphi, MD -- to establish Even Start program at Bladensburg High School for 25 teen parents

47,300 Early Childhood Facilities Fund, Pennington, NJ -- provide technical assistance to Early Childhood New Jersey Collaborative of Washington, DC

40,000 Campagna Center, Alexandria, VA -- support Head Start program

40,000 Foundation for Educational Innovation, Washington, DC -- for technology-based education reform program at Seaton Elementary School

40,000 Knowledge Network, Arlington, VA -- support education campaign regarding school reform strategies for parents

40,000 Prince George's Community College Children's Development Clinic, Largo, MD -- support low-income developmentally disabled infant and toddler preschool program

Environment

250,000 National Center for Lead-Safe Housing, Columbia, MD -- support initiative to prevent lead's debilitating impact on children's early development

Health

600,000 Mary's Center for Maternal and Child Care, Washington, DC -- five-year support for Healthy Families America program

528,477 Zero to Three National Center for Clinical Infant Programs, Washington, DC -- support three-year initiative for infant and toddler child development, family support services

97,908 DC Public Schools, Washington, DC -- provide mental health to underserved children and youth

90,000 Reginald S. Lourie Center for Infants and Young Children, Rockville, MD -- improve life changes of young children with emotional/developmental problems, preserve families

50,000 Mary's Center for Maternal and Child Care, Washington, DC -- support adolescent pregnancy prevention program, parenting program

50,000 National Heart Start Association, Alexandria, VA -- operating support, advocacy, training, professional development, research

50,000 St. Ann's Infant and Maternity Home, Hyattsville, MD -- support children's residential program

49,500 Pregnancy AIDS Center, College Park, MD -- support Adolescent Outreach Program

38,970 Northern Virginia Urban League, Alexandria, VA -- support comprehensive service delivery model for City of Alexandria's pregnant and parenting teen population

Religion

50,000 Johenning Baptist Community Center, Washington, DC -- to establish a model comprehensive early childhood development center for at-risk infants and toddlers

50,000 National Council of Jewish Women, Baltimore, MD -- support school project in Prince George's County, MD

40,000 Sojourner Truth Foster Family Service Agency, San Francisco, CA -- support Intensive Family Reunification program

Social Services

2,500,000 National Committee to Prevent Child Abuse, Chicago, IL -- support Healthy Families America capital campaign

700,000 Action Alliance for Virginia's Children and Youth, Richmond, VA -- operating support

495,000 Northern Virginia Family Service, Washington, DC -- support Healthy Families America program in Prince William County, VA

300,000 Alexandria Community Network Preschool, Alexandria, VA -- to establish satellite family child care system

295,419 Northern Virginia Family Services, Falls Church, VA -- two-year support for capacity building project

225,000 DC Action for Children, Washington,

DC -- three-year grant to build organizational capacity

100,000 DC Children's Advocacy Center, Washington, DC -- salary support

100,000 Illinois Facilities Fund, Chicago, IL -- support Child and Family Resource Center

100,000 Virginia Poverty Law Center, Richmond, VA -- to support Children's Legal Rights project

75,000 Maryville Academy, Des Plaines, IL -- support Treatment Foster Care Program

65,000 Larkin Street Youth Center, San Francisco, CA -- support Foster Family Program

55,000 Illinois Action for Children, Chicago, IL -- support Guardianship Project

52,000 Children's Aid Society, New York, NY -- to find permanent homes for 30-40 children in foster care within one year

50,000 Advocates for Children and Youth, Baltimore, MD -- operating support

50,000 BBF Family Services, Chicago, IL -- support Teen Parenting Initiative program

50,000 Center for Family Life in Sunset Park, Brooklyn, NY -- support Neighborhood Foster Family Program

50,000 Child Welfare League of America, Washington, DC -- to increase number and quality of child welfare professionals

50,000 Dallas CASA, Dallas, TX -- support Home at Last Program

50,000 Fairfax County YMCA Metropolitan Washington, Oakton, VA -- support Resource Mothers program, Family Support Center

50,000 Family Place, Washington, DC -- operating support for two family centers

50,000 Governor's Office of Children, Youth and Families, Baltimore, MD -- develop statewide plan for prevention of child abuse and neglect

50,000 National Child Day Care Association, Washington, DC -- health screening, mental health services, services for children with disabilities, health education, safety education for low-income families

50,000 San Francisco Court-Appointed Special Advocates, San Francisco, CA -- for 50 new CASA program volunteers

46,312 Child Welfare League of America, Washington, DC -- beginning phase of four-year implementation and evaluation project

45,054 Northern Virginia Family Service, Falls Church, VA -- salary support for project manager of Healthy Families America

40,000 Black Adoption Placement and Research Center, Oakland, CA -- support Family and Children Service Enhancement Project

40,000 Stand for Children, Washington, DC -- support Stand For Children Day

FREEPORT-MCMORAN INC.

Company Contact

New Orleans, LA

Company Description

Employees: 504

SIC(s): 1094 Uranium, Radium & Vanadium Ores, 1311 Crude Petroleum & Natural Gas, 1475 Phosphate Rock, 1479 Chemical & Fertilizer Mining Nec.

Nonmonetary Support

Value: $500,000 (1996); $1,000,000 (1988)

Type: Cause-related Marketing & Promotion; Donated Equipment; In-kind Services; Loaned Employees; Loaned Executives

Corporate Sponsorship

Value: $400,000

Type: Arts & cultural events; Pledge-a-thon

Contact: Nancy Adkerson, Executive Director

Freeport-McMoRan Foundation

Giving Contact

Ursula Joseph, Administrative Assistant
Freeport-McMoRan Inc.
1615 Poydras St.
New Orleans, LA 70112
Phone: (504)582-4000
Fax: (504)582-4028

Alternate Contact

PO Box 61119
New Orleans, LA 70161

Description

Organization Type: Corporate Foundation

Giving Locations: principally near operating locations and to national organizations.

Grant Types: Capital, Conference/Seminar, Department, Employee Matching Gifts, Endowment, Fellowship, General Support.

Note: Employee matching gift ratio: 2 to 1 up to $500; 1 to 1 after $500 and up to $20,000 per employee annually.

Giving Philosophy

'The purpose of the Freeport-McMoran contributions program is to help improve the quality of life in the areas where our employees live and work. We also contribute to national health, cultural and environmental institutions. We also encourage and match employee gifts and in this way our giving program reflects the interests of our employees. .. (We believe we) can contribute to the community with more than just monetary donations. We can provide leadership from our wealth of very talented employees. We can work with community leaders to help devise programs that will serve the needs of the people. We believe there are no limits to the ways in which we, or any other company, can contribute to the well being of the community. The imagination, energy and vision that it takes to operate a worldwide company can also be applied to working with community leaders to build A Better Way Of Life For Everyone.' *Corporate Giving Program*

Financial Summary

Total Giving: $3,500,000 (2000 approx); $3,500,000 (1999 approx); $5,700,000 (1998 approx). Note: Contributes through corporate direct giving program and foundation.

Giving Analysis: Giving for 1997 includes: foundation ($5,900,000); 1998: foundation ($5,700,000); 1999: foundation ($3,500,000)

Typical Recipients

Arts & Humanities: Arts Appreciation, Arts Associations & Councils, Arts Centers, Arts Festivals, Arts Funds, Arts Institutes, Ballet, Community Arts, Dance, Ethnic & Folk Arts, Historic Preservation, History & Archaeology, Libraries, Museums/Galleries, Music, Opera, Performing Arts, Public Broadcasting, Theater

Civic & Public Affairs: African American Affairs, Botanical Gardens/Parks, Business/Free Enterprise, Clubs, Economic Development, Employment/Job Training, Housing, Legal Aid, Minority Business, Municipalities/Towns, Public Policy, Rural Affairs, Safety, Urban & Community Affairs, Women's Affairs, Zoos/Aquariums

Education: Agricultural Education, Business Education, Colleges & Universities, Community & Junior Colleges, Economic Education, Education Associations, Education Reform, Elementary Education (Private), Elementary Education (Public), Engineering/Technological Education, Education-General, Leadership Training, Legal Education, Literacy, Minority Education, Preschool Education, Private Education (Precollege), Public Education (Precollege), Science/Mathematics Education, Special Education, Student Aid

Environment: Environment-General, Resource Conservation, Wildlife Protection

Health: AIDS/HIV, Cancer, Children's Health/Hospitals, Clinics/Medical Centers, Emergency/Ambulance Services, Eyes/Blindness, Health Organizations, Heart, Hospitals, Medical Research, Mental Health, Prenatal Health Issues, Single-Disease Health Associations

International: International Affairs, International Relief Efforts

Science: Science Exhibits & Fairs, Science Museums, Scientific Centers & Institutes, Scientific Organizations

Social Services: At-Risk Youth, Big Brother/Big Sister, Camps, Child Welfare, Community Service Organizations, Counseling, Crime Prevention, Delinquency & Criminal Rehabilitation, Domestic Violence, Emergency Relief, Family Services, Food/Clothing Distribution, People with Disabilities, Recreation & Athletics, Scouts, Senior Services, Substance Abuse, United Funds/United Ways, Volunteer Services, YMCA/YWCA/YMHA/YWHA, Youth Organizations

Contributions Analysis

Giving Priorities: Higher education, social services, hospitals, medical research, the arts, civic concerns, and environmental affairs.

Arts & Humanities: 10% to 15%. Supports historical societies, museums, community arts funds, and music. Recipients include the New Orleans Museum of Art, the Acadiana Symphony, and Young Aspirations/Young Artists, Inc.

Civic & Public Affairs: 15% to 20%. Supports community revitaization, housing, and anti-crime activities. Supports Louisiana Executive Corp and the Greater New Orleans Foundation.

Education: 40% to 45%. Focus on science, math, and economic education in elementary, secondary and higher education.

Health: About 30%. Major support to the United Way. Recipients include organizations providing health care, shelter, food, and clothing. Also supports innovative environmental programs and recreation.

Note: Above priorities are for the foundation's 1999 contributions. Company also gives directly, through subsidiaries, and through the newly-created Research, Environmental, and Corporate Fund.

Application Procedures

Initial Contact: Call or write foundation to ascertain foundation interest and request application form.

Application Requirements: Proposals should include: summary statement, with history, mission, and goals; description of project and organization; amount and specific purpose of request; need for the project in community; detailed report of how money will be spent; detailed annual operating budget; method of evaluation; list of board members; any collaborative efforts; list of other sources of support; financial statements; and proof of tax-exempt status.

Deadlines: November 30.

Review Process: The executive director and vice president of community relations make recommendations to the board of trustees.

Evaluative Criteria: Efficiency of management and employee participation through contributions and volunteerism are considered when evaluating requests.

Decision Notification: A preliminary budget is drawn up in October and finalized in December; grants are announced by the end of February.

Restrictions

Does not support individuals; distributing foundations; national disease agencies; or religious, political, fraternal, labor, veterans, or tax-supported organizations (with the exception of public schools, colleges, and universities). The foundation also does not support sporting events, trips or festivals, organizations supported by the United Way, or discriminatory organizations.

Additional Information

Since 1996, the company has operated the Freeport-McMoRan Foundation and the Research, Environmental, and Corporate Fund.
Giving is based on 1% of pre-tax earnings; therefore the contributions budget varies from year to year.
All contributions are suspended for 1999.
Publications: Giving Annual Report; Application Form

Foundation Officials

David B. Lowry: executive director PRIM CORP EMPL vice president social & development programs: Freeport-McMoRan Copper & Gold Inc.

Grants Analysis

Disclosure Period: calendar year ending 1996
Total Grants: $6,479,650*
Number of Grants: 256
Average Grant: $25,311
Typical Range: $2,500 to $30,000
***Note:** Giving excludes matching gifts; nonmonetary support.

Recent Grants

Note: Grants derived from 1995 Annual Report.

Arts & Humanities
American Council for Arts, New York, NY
Austin Business Committee for Arts, Austin, TX
New Orleans Ballet Association, New Orleans, LA

Civic & Public Affairs
Austin Area Garden Center, Austin, TX -- Zilker Garden
Habitat for Humanity of New Haven, New Haven, CT
Junior League of New Orleans, New Orleans, LA
Texas Association of Minority Business Enterprises, TX

Education
Junior Achievement, TX
Loyola University, New Orleans, LA
National Action Council for Minorities in Engineering, New York, NY
New Orleans Public Schools, New Orleans, LA
Our Lady of Holy Cross College, New Orleans, LA
Southeastern Louisiana University, LA
Travis County 4-H, TX
United Negro College Fund, New York, NY
Xavier University, Cincinnati, OH
Youth Leadership Council

Environment
Baton Rouge Earth Day Committee, Baton Rouge, LA
Fish and Wildlife Department, Austin, TX
Gulf Coast Conservation Association, TX
Louisiana Nature and Science Center, New Orleans, LA
National Wildlife Research Center, TX

Health
AIDS Services of Austin, Austin, TX
American Heart Association
Austin Area Candlelighters Childhood Cancer Foundation, Austin, TX
Cancer Research Institute, New York, NY
Cancer Society of Greater Baton Rouge, Baton Rouge, LA
City of New Orleans, New Orleans, LA -- Healthy Baby Day
March of Dimes, Maiden, MA
New Orleans Ronald McDonald House, New Orleans, LA
Prevent Blindness, TX
United Cerebral Palsy of New York, New York, NY

International
Operation Smile, Norfolk, VA
Save the Children, Nashville, TN

Religion
Jewish Family Service Teen Life Counts Program
Jewish National Fund, Baltimore, MD
Little Sisters of the Poor, Chicago, IL

Science
Greater New Orleans Science and Engineering Fair, New Orleans, LA

Social Services
Austin Child Guidance Center, Austin, TX -- Festival of Trees
Austin Sunshine Camps, Austin, TX
Boy Scouts of America Capital Area, Austin, TX
Boys and Girls Clubs of Galveston, Galveston, TX
Boys Town of New Orleans, New Orleans, LA
Capital Area United Way, Austin, TX
Childhelp USA, Woodland Hills, CA
Children's Advocacy Center, Austin, TX
Family Crisis Center, Austin, TX
Girl Scouts of Louisiana, LA
Lighthouse for Blind, New York, NY
New Orleans Police Department, New Orleans, LA

FREIGHTLINER CORP.

Company Contact

4747 N. Channel
Portland, OR 97217
Phone: (503)735-8000
Fax: (503)735-8921
Web: http://www.freightliner.com

Company Description

Employees: 10,700
SIC(s): 3711 Motor Vehicles & Car Bodies, 3714 Motor Vehicle Parts & Accessories.
Parent Company: DaimlerChrysler Corp., 1000 Chrysler Dr., Auburn Hills, MI, United States
Parent Revenue: US$154,615,000,000

Operating Locations

AZ: Acoustic Imaging Technologies, Phoenix; CA: Freightliner Corp.; Mercedes-Benz Advanced Design of North America, Irvine; Siliconix, Santa Clara; CT: Mercedes-Benz Credit Corp., Norwalk; DE: Daimler-Benz Capital, Wilmington; FL: Adtranz Miami, Miami; GA: Dornier Medical Systems, Kennesaw; ME: Kassbohrer North America, Gray; NC: Freightliner Truck Mfg. Plant, Mount Holly; NJ: Freightliner Corp.; Mercedes-Benz of North America, Montvale; NV: Kassbohrer North America, Sparks; NY: Freightliner Corp.; Daimler-Benz North America Corp., New York; OR: Freightliner Corp., Portland; Freightliner Corp., Portland; PA: Adtrans Pittsburgh, Pittsburgh

Nonmonetary Support

Type: Cause-related Marketing & Promotion; Donated Equipment; Donated Products; In-kind Services; Loaned Employees

Giving Contact

Debi Nicholson, Corporate Relations and Communications
Freightliner Corp.
4747 North Channel Avenue
PO Box 3849
Portland, OR 97217-7699
Phone: (503)735-8535
Fax: (503)735-8006
Email: debinicholson@freightliner.com

Description

Organization Type: Corporate Giving Program
Giving Locations: headquarters and operating communities.
Grant Types: General Support, Matching, Project, Research, Seed Money.

Financial Summary

Total Giving: Contributes through corporate direct giving program only.

Typical Recipients

Arts & Humanities: Community Arts
Civic & Public Affairs: Urban & Community Affairs
Education: Education Associations
Science: Scientific Organizations
Social Services: Community Service Organizations, United Funds/United Ways, Youth Organizations

Application Procedures

Initial Contact: letter of inquiry
Application Requirements: a description of organization, amount requested, purpose of funds sought, recently audited financial statement, and proof of tax-exempt status
Deadlines: None.

Corporate Officials

James L. Hebe: chairman, president, chief executive officer PRIM CORP EMPL chairman, president, chief executive officer: Freightliner Corp. CORP AFFIL chairman: Kesi INC; director: Oshkosh Truck Corporation; chairman: Houston Freightliner Inc.; chairman: Atlanta Freightliner Truck Sales Service; president: Freightliner Market Development Corp.

Giving Program Officials

Debi Nicholson: manager PRIM CORP EMPL general manager: Freightliner Corp.

FRITO-LAY, INC.

Company Contact

Plano, TX
Web: http://www.fritolay.com

Company Description

Employees: 30,000
SIC(s): 2052 Cookies & Crackers, 2096 Potato Chips & Similar Snacks, 2099 Food Preparations Nec.
Parent Company: PepsiCo, Inc., Purchase, NY, United States

Nonmonetary Support

Type: Donated Products; Loaned Executives
Note: Frito-Lay executives serve on boards in the Metropolitan Dallas, TX area.

Giving Contact

Lynn Markley, Senior Vice President, Public Affairs
Frito-Lay, Inc.
7701 Legacy Dr.
Plano, TX 75024
Phone: (972)334-2404
Fax: (972)334-2045

Description

Organization Type: Corporate Giving Program
Giving Locations: TX: Dallas, Fort Worth
Grant Types: Employee Matching Gifts, General Support.
Note: Employee matching gift ratio: 1 to 1; 2 to 1 for employee volunteers.

Giving Philosophy

'Our philosophy for giving has always been a direct reflection of our own principle for operating a successful business. Our corporate contributions target programs and organizations with results-oriented approaches and direct community benefits. We are especially interested in worthwhile causes that further the education of our youth, the economic development of our communities, and improved interracial relations.

'Our community service includes direct program funding as well as active involvement by employees and expert counsel provided by executives serving on community boards in volunteer roles.

'We are happy to join the efforts of those nonprofit organizations serving the Dallas/Ft. Worth metroplex area who are working to empower the community in which we live and work.' Contributions Guidelines

Financial Summary

Total Giving: Contributes through corporate direct giving program only.

Typical Recipients

Arts & Humanities: Arts & Humanities-General
Civic & Public Affairs: Civic & Public Affairs-General
Education: Education-General
Health: Health-General
Social Services: Social Services-General

Contributions Analysis

Giving Priorities: Focus is on education, economic development, and employee involvement.

Application Procedures

Initial Contact: Send a brief letter of inquiry.
Application Requirements: Include a description of organization, amount requested, purpose of funds sought, audited financial statement, and proof of tax-exempt status.
Deadlines: August or September for the following year.
Review Process: Written notice of decision usually arrives after four weeks.

Restrictions

The company only supports nonprofit organizations. Contributions will not be made to religious or political organizations, campaigns or candidates for public office, lobbying groups, operating expenses of United Way agencies, veteran or fraternal organizations, sponsorship advertising in programs or brochures, or for tickets or tables at gala events.

Additional Information

Regional proposals should be sent directly to the nearest division office.
Giving program currently under review.

Corporate Officials

Steve S. Reinemund: chairman, chief executive officer B Queens, NY 1948. ED United States Naval Academy BS (1970); University of Virginia MBA (1978). PRIM CORP EMPL chairman, chief executive officer: Frito-Lay Co. CORP AFFIL director: ServiceMaster Co.; director: PepsiCo; director: Provident Life Insurance. NONPR AFFIL chairman: National Council of Laraza.

Giving Program Officials

Tod MacKenzie: PRIM CORP EMPL vice president public affairs: Frito-Lay, Inc.

FRONTIER CORP.

Company Contact

Rochester, NY
Web: http://www.frontiercorp.com

Company Description

Former Name: Rochester Telephone Corp.
Revenue: US$2,575,500,000
Employees: 7,900
SIC(s): 4812 Radiotelephone Communications, 4813 Telephone Communications Except Radiotelephone, 6719 Holding Companies Nec.

Nonmonetary Support

Value: $440,400 (1995)
Type: In-kind Services
Volunteer Programs: Company supports the Genesee Chapter of the Telephone Pioneers.
Note: In-kind services includes gifts to human services, arts and culture, and public broadcasting.

Frontier Corp. Educational Fund

Giving Contact

Pat Grover
Frontier Corp. Community Partnerships
3441 W. Henrietta Rd.
Rochester, NY 14623
Phone: (716)777-7702
Fax: (716)546-7898
Email: pgrover@frontiercorp.com

Description

EIN: 237167280
Organization Type: Corporate Foundation
Giving Locations: company's service areas.
Grant Types: General Support, Scholarship.

Financial Summary

Total Giving: $52,500 (1998); $1,500,000 (1997 approx); $1,500,000 (1996 approx). Note: Contributes through corporate direct giving program and foundation. 1996 Giving includes scholarship ($46,400).
Giving Analysis: Giving for 1998 includes: foundation scholarships ($52,500)
Assets: $536,683 (1998); $543,975 (1996); $561,955 (1995)
Gifts Received: $1,016 (1995)

Typical Recipients

Arts & Humanities: Arts & Humanities-General
Civic & Public Affairs: Economic Development, Civic & Public Affairs-General
Education: Colleges & Universities, Elementary Education (Private), Education-General, Minority Education, Public Education (Precollege), Science/Mathematics Education
Social Services: People with Disabilities, Senior Services, Social Services-General, Volunteer Services

Contributions Analysis

Arts & Humanities: 5% to 10%. Local arts centers and organizations.
Education: About 60%. Supports improvement of the quality of education and scholarships.
Social Services: About 30%. Primarily United Way and solutions to economic and societal problems, including programs that improve the quality of telecommunications service to the handicapped, elderly, and economically less advantaged.

Restrictions

Does not support individuals, religious organizations for sectarian purposes, political causes or candidates, organizations that discriminate, goodwill advertising, operating expenses of organizations during the life of a capital program pledge, operating expenses of United Way-supported organizations, organizations involved in medical research or patient care (except for building campaigns), organizations outside operating territories, organizations that serve a small segment or draw support from a very limited base, or mass mailing requests.

Fund only provides scholarships to employees. limited base, or mass mailing requests.
Fund only provides scholarships to employees.

Additional Information

The fund is still in operation, but grant making is suspended.
Publications: Annual Report; Corporate Contributions Brochure

Corporate Officials

Joseph P. Clayton: president, chief executive officer, director B 1949. ED Bellarmine College BA; Indiana University MBA. PRIM CORP EMPL president, chief executive officer, director: Frontier Corp. ADD CORP EMPL chief executive officer: Frontier Communications International; chief executive officer: Frontier Communications Services; chief executive officer: Frontier Communications Rochester. CORP AFFIL director: Frontier Information Technology; director: Frontier Network Systems Corp.

Grants Analysis

Disclosure Period: calendar year ending 1995
Total Grants: $1,576,050
Number of Grants: 124
Average Grant: $4,592*
Highest Grant: $500,000
Typical Range: $1,000 to $25,000
***Note:** Average grant excludes all grants over $100,000.

FROST NATIONAL BANK

Company Contact

San Antonio, TX
Web: http://www.frostbank.com

Company Description

Former Name: Cullen/Frost Bankers.
Employees: 1,700
SIC(s): 6021 National Commercial Banks.

Nonmonetary Support

Type: Donated Equipment; Donated Products; In-kind Services; Loaned Employees; Loaned Executives

The Charitable Foundation of Frost National Bank

Giving Contact

Melissa J. Adams, Assistant Vice President, Corporate Donations
Frost Bank
PO Box 1600
San Antonio, TX 78296
Phone: (210)220-4353
Fax: (210)220-5144

Description

Founded: 1981
Organization Type: Corporate Foundation
Giving Locations: headquarters and operating communities.
Grant Types: Capital, General Support, Matching, Multiyear/Continuing Support.

Financial Summary

Total Giving: $1,900,000 (2000 approx); $1,300,000 (1999 approx); $1,300,000 (1998 approx). Note: Contributes through foundation only.
Giving Analysis: Giving for 1998 includes: corporate direct giving (approx $650,000); foundation (approx $650,000)

Typical Recipients

Arts & Humanities: Arts Appreciation, Arts Associations & Councils, Arts Festivals, Arts Funds, Arts Institutes, Community Arts, Ethnic & Folk Arts, Historic Preservation, Libraries, Museums/Galleries, Music, Performing Arts, Public Broadcasting, Theater
Civic & Public Affairs: Business/Free Enterprise, Economic Development, Employment/Job Training, Professional & Trade Associations, Zoos/Aquariums
Education: Agricultural Education, Arts/Humanities Education, Business Education, Colleges & Universities, Education Funds, Engineering/Technological Education, Faculty Development, Health & Physical Education, International Exchange, Literacy, Medical Education, Preschool Education, Private Education (Precollege), Public Education (Precollege), Science/Mathematics Education
Environment: Environment-General
Health: Hospices, Hospitals, Medical Rehabilitation, Medical Research, Mental Health, Public Health, Single-Disease Health Associations
International: International Relations
Religion: Churches, Religious Organizations
Science: Scientific Organizations
Social Services: Child Welfare, Community Centers, Community Service Organizations, Counseling, Delinquency & Criminal Rehabilitation, Domestic Violence, Emergency Relief, Family Services, Food/Clothing Distribution, People with Disabilities, Recreation & Athletics, Senior Services, Substance Abuse, Volunteer Services, Youth Organizations

Application Procedures

Initial Contact: Send a brief letter of inquiry.
Application Requirements: Provide a description of organization, amount requested, purpose of funds sought, recently audited financial statements, proof of tax-exempt status, deadline for project approval, and signature of authorization by organization's highest ranking officer.
Deadlines: At least three weeks before funds are needed.
Decision Notification: Committee meets weekly.

Corporate Officials

Richard W. Evans, Jr.: chairman, chief executive officer B 1946. ED Southwest Texas Junior College (1965-1966); University of Texas BA (1968). PRIM CORP EMPL chairman, chief executive officer: Frost National Bank.
Thomas C. Frost, Senior: chairman B San Antonio, TX 1927. ED Austin University LLD; Washington & Lee University BS (1950). PRIM CORP EMPL chairman: Frost National Bank. CORP AFFIL chairman: Cullen/Frost Bankers Inc.

Giving Program Officials

Melissa J. Adams: PRIM CORP EMPL corporate donations officer: Frost National Bank.

Grants Analysis

Disclosure Period: calendar year ending
Typical Range: $1,000 to $2,500

Fuji Bank & Trust Co.

Company Contact

New York, NY

Company Description

Gross Operating Earnings: US$149,840,000,000
Employees: 134
SIC(s): 6081 Foreign Banks--Branches & Agencies.
Parent Company: Fuji Bank, Ltd., 5-5 Otemachi 1-chome, Chiyoda-ku, Tokyo, Japan

Operating Locations

NY: Fuji Bank & Trust Co., New York

Nonmonetary Support

Type: Donated Equipment; In-kind Services

Giving Contact

Ms. Akiko Mitsui, Vice President & CRA Officer
2 World Trade Center, 79th Fl.
New York, NY 10048
Phone: (212)898-2000

Description

Organization Type: Corporate Giving Program
Giving Locations: NY: New York within the five boroughs of Manhattan
Grant Types: Capital, Employee Matching Gifts, General Support, Loan, Operating Expenses.

Financial Summary

Total Giving: $200,000 (1997 approx); $200,000 (1996); $200,000 (1995)

Typical Recipients

Civic & Public Affairs: Civic & Public Affairs-General, Housing, Inner-City Development, Urban & Community Affairs

Restrictions

Does not support dinners or special events, fraternal organizations, political or lobbying groups, organizations outside operating areas, goodwill advertising, individuals, or religious organizations for sectarian purposes.

Corporate Officials

Hidetake Nakamura: president, chief executive officer PRIM CORP EMPL president, chief executive officer: Fuji Bank & Trust Co.
Takeshi Tanabe: chief financial officer PRIM CORP EMPL chief financial officer: Fuji Bank & Trust Co.

Grants Analysis

Disclosure Period: calendar year ending 1995
Typical Range: $2,500 to $5,000

Recent Grants

Note: Grants derived from 1995 grants list.

Civic & Public Affairs

Greater Jamaica Development Corp, Jamaica, NY
Lawyers Alliance for New York, New York, NY
Local Initiatives Support Corp, New York, NY
Low-Income Housing Fund, New York, NY
Neighborhood Housing Services, New York, NY
Nonprofit Facilities Fund, New York, NY
South Bronx Overall Economic Development Corp, Bronx, NY

Education

Junior Achievement, New York, NY

Health

Veritas Therapeutic Community, New York, NY

Social Services

Partnership for a Drug-Free America, New York, NY

H.B. Fuller Co.

Company Contact

St. Paul, MN
Web: http://www.hbfuller.com

Company Description

Employees: 6,000
SIC(s): 2842 Polishes & Sanitation Goods, 2851 Paints & Allied Products, 2891 Adhesives & Sealants.

Operating Locations

Argentina: HB Fuller Argentina, Pilar, Buenos Aires; Austria: HB Fuller Austria GmbH, Wels, Oberosterreich; Belgium: HB Fuller Belgium NV, Aartselaar, Anvers; Brazil: HB Fuller Brasil Ltda., Sorocaba; Canada: HB Fuller Canada, Mississauga; Chile: HB Fuller Chile SA, Santiago; Colombia: HB Fuller Colombia Ltda., Itagui; Costa Rica: HB Fuller de Costa Rica SA, Alajuela; Alfombras Canon SA, Barreal Heredia, Heredia; Deco Tintas SA, Cartago; Reca Quimica SA, Cartago; HB Fuller de Costa Rica SA, San Jose; Kativo Chemical Industries SA, San Jose; Pinturas Centroamericanas de Costa Rica SA, San Jose; Dominican Republic: HB Fuller Dominicana SA, Haina, San Cristo; Ecuador: HB Fuller Ecuador SA, Guayaquil, Guayas; Pinturas Ecuatorianas SA, Guayaquil, Guayas; France: HB Fuller France, Le Trait, Seine-Maritime; Germany: HB Fuller GmbH, Lueneburg, Niedersachsen; Isarrakoll Chemie GmbH, Lueneburg, Niedersachsen; HB Fuller GmbH, Munich, Bavaria; Guatemala: Kativo Comercial de Guatemala SA, Guatemala City; Honduras: Kativo de Honduras SA, San Pedro Sula, Cortes; Servicios e Inversiones SA de CV, Tegucigalpa; Italy: HB Fuller Italia SRL, Borgolavezzaro, Piemonte; Mexico: HB Fuller Mexico SA de CV, Ciudad de Mexico; Netherlands: HB Fuller Metherland BV, Amerongen, Utrecht; New Zealand: HB Fuller Powder Coatings (New Zealand) Ltd., Auckland; HB Fuller Co. (New Zealand) Ltd., Mangere Bridge; Panama: Fabrica de Pinturas Glidden SA, Panama City; Glidden Avenida Nacional SA, Panama City; Glidden Panama SA, Panama City; HB Fuller Panama SA, Panama City; Kativo de Panama SA, Panama City; Peru: Chemical Supply Peruana SA, Lima; HB Fuller Peru SA, Lima; Philippines: HB Fuller (Philippines), Manila; Spain: Prakol Prager Isar Rakoll Quimica SA, Alicante, Murcia; Sweden: HB Fuller Sverige AB, Vastra, Frolunda; Taiwan: HB Fuller Taiwan Co. Ltd., Hsin-chu; United Kingdom: HB Fuller Holdings Ltd., Alfreton, Derbyshire; HB Fuller UK Ltd., Alfreton, Derbyshire; HB Fuller Coatings Ltd., Birmingham, West Midlands; Hytak Ltd., Derby, Derbyshire; Uruguay: HB Fuller Uruguay Sociedad Anonima, Montevideo

Nonmonetary Support

Value: $15,000 (1993); $15,000 (1989); $15,000 (1988)
Type: Donated Equipment; Donated Products; In-kind Services

H.B. Fuller Co. Foundation

Giving Contact

Ms. Karen P. Muller, Executive Director
H.B. Fuller Co. Foundation
PO Box 64683
St. Paul, MN 55164-0683
Phone: (612)415-5217
Fax: (612)415-5165

Alternate Contact

1200 Willow Lake Boulevard
St. Paul, MN 55110-5132

Description

EIN: 363500811
Organization Type: Corporate Foundation
Giving Locations: headquarters and operating communities; internationally; nationally.
Grant Types: Employee Matching Gifts, General Support, Operating Expenses, Project.
Note: Employee matching gift ratio: 1 to 1 to education, .5 to 1 to the United Way. Company also has a matching gift program for employees serving on boards of community agencies.

Giving Philosophy

'We are a global company which values community involvement by employees. We endorse those efforts by returning a portion of company earnings back to society. Fuller's values about community involvement apply worldwide. This year we have taken significant steps to increase our financial and human resources contributions to our local communities around the globe. We're proud to be the first company to adopt a worldwide equation for charitable contributions.' *H.B. Fuller Co. Community Affairs Annual Summary*

Financial Summary

Total Giving: $1,750,437 (1998); $714,114 (1997); $1,385,170 (1996). Note: Contributes through corporate direct giving program and foundation.

Giving Analysis: Giving for 1997 includes: foundation ($526,100); foundation grants to United Way ($138,072); foundation matching gifts ($49,942); 1998: foundation ($1,085,645); corporate direct giving ($664,792)

Assets: $1,203,010 (1997); $1,037,844 (1995); $738,456 (1990)

Gifts Received: $1,127,321 (1998); $804,937 (1997); $709,549 (1996). Note: Contributions received from H.B. Fuller Company.

Typical Recipients

Arts & Humanities: Arts Centers, Arts Funds, Arts Outreach, Dance, Libraries, Literary Arts, Museums/Galleries, Music, Opera, Performing Arts, Public Broadcasting, Theater

Civic & Public Affairs: African American Affairs, Asian American Affairs, Economic Development, Employment/Job Training, Civic & Public Affairs-General, Housing, Legal Aid, Nonprofit Management, Public Policy, Urban & Community Affairs

Education: Afterschool/Enrichment Programs, Arts/Humanities Education, Colleges & Universities, Economic Education, Education Funds, Education Reform, Elementary Education (Private), Education-General, Minority Education, Preschool Education, Religious Education, Secondary Education (Public), Social Sciences Education, Special Education

Environment: Air/Water Quality, Forestry, Environment-General

Health: Emergency/Ambulance Services, Health Organizations, Mental Health, Research/Studies Institutes

International: Foreign Educational Institutions, Health Care/Hospitals, Human Rights, International Environmental Issues, International Organizations, International Relief Efforts

Religion: Religious Organizations, Religious Welfare

Science: Science Museums

Social Services: Big Brother/Big Sister, Camps, Child Abuse, Child Welfare, Community Centers, Community Service Organizations, Domestic Violence, Family Services, People with Disabilities, Recreation & Athletics, Refugee Assistance, Scouts, Shelters/Homelessness, Social Services-General, Special Olympics, Substance Abuse, United Funds/United Ways, Volunteer Services, YMCA/YWCA/YMHA/YWHA, Youth Organizations

Contributions Analysis

Giving Priorities: Higher education, international grants, united funds, and public broadcasting. Company has a long history of contributions overseas and has incorporated international contributions into its philanthropic mission. Business conditions have caused a reduction in domestic and international budgets. Generally, grants are made by local country operations to local projects only. Employee-managed Community Affairs Councils make decisions for all requests from local organizations.

Arts & Humanities: 20% to 25%. Focus on youth and creativity. Also supports arts institutions in headquarters area.

Civic & Public Affairs: (Public Policy) Less than 5%. Supports nonprofit resources and urban affairs.

Education: 15% to 20%. Supports programs for economically disadvantaged youth which provide the basics in literary and vocational training.

Health: 55% to 60%. Funds programs which provide activities and health care for disadvantaged youth, with the dual purpose of involving community adults and the development of local youth.

Note: Company gives through facilities, which respond to community needs. Above priorities are for foundation giving only.

Application Procedures

Initial Contact: Call or send a brief letter of inquiry

Application Requirements: Include a description of organization, amount requested, current budget information, and proof of tax-exempt status.

Deadlines: February, June, and October.

Review Process: Decisions are made by local employee committees and by foundation contributions committee.

Evaluative Criteria: Includes organization's intention to address underlying causes of problems, not merely resulting problems; proximity of organization to company facilities; employee involvement with agency; effectiveness and impact of organization; urgency and need for organization, its leverage, and organizational strength; and multi-level approach to issue or problem.

Decision Notification: Local councils meet monthly and review proposals as they are received; foundation reviews applications three times a year.

Notes: Both foundation and company accept the Minnesota Common Grant Application.

Restrictions

Foundation does not make grants to religious, political, fraternal, or veterans organizations except for programs that are of direct benefit to the community. Does not support individuals, lobbying or research organizations, fundraisers, or travel. Does not give to national organizations, organizations outside operating areas, educational organizations (except through matching gift program), scholarships, disease-specific organizations, courtesy/public service advertising, or capital or endowment drives.

Additional Information

Since 1987, H.B. Fuller's focus issue has been youth development. The company is committed to building strong communities which create economic and educational support for children and their families.

The foundation's primary areas of interest are social services organizations and organizations in which company employees are volunteers. Employees are encouraged to convey the needs of such organizations to the community affairs council for their location. Recipients of grants are required to submit complete financial reports.

H.B. Fuller allocates 3.5% of pre-tax profits to community affairs activities in the U.S.

In addition to company's community affairs budget, Community Affairs Councils operate in 33 communities in the United States, 23 in Latin America, and 11 in Europe. These councils contribute to over 270 local agencies and also provide nonmonetary support. A list of council chairpersons is available from the foundation.

Publications: Community Affairs Annual Report

Corporate Officials

Anthony Lee Andersen: chairman, director B 1935. ED Macalester College BS (1957). PRIM CORP EMPL chairman, director: H.B. Fuller Co.

Sarah R. Coffin: vice president specialty group ED DePauw University BA; Indiana University MBA. PRIM CORP EMPL vice president: B.F. Goodrich Co. CORP AFFIL director: SPX Corp.

Diane Helland: senior legal counsel PRIM CORP EMPL senior legal counsel: H.B. Fuller Co.

Walter Kissling: director B Limon, Costa Rica 1931. PRIM CORP EMPL director: H.B. Fuller Co. CORP AFFIL director: Pentair, Inc.

Gerhard Koosmann: division controller PRIM CORP EMPL division controller: H.B. Fuller Co.

David J. Maki: vice president, corporate controller PRIM CORP EMPL vice president, corporate controller: H.B. Fuller Co.

Lee Upton McGrath: vice president, treasurer B Roslyn, NY 1956. ED University Catolica del Ecuador (1977); Georgetown University BSBA (1978); University of Chicago MBA (1984). PRIM CORP EMPL vice president, treasurer: Jostens, Inc.

Mario Perez: vice president PRIM CORP EMPL vice president: H.B. Fuller Co.

Foundation Officials

Anthony Lee Andersen: director (see above)

Richard C. Baker: secretary PRIM CORP EMPL vice president, general counsel, secretary: H. B. Fuller Co.

Bob Blamer: director PRIM CORP EMPL customer representative: H.B. Fuller Co.

Evelyn M Borsheim: secretary PRIM CORP EMPL assistant corporate secretary: H.B. Fuller Co.

Sarah R. Coffin: director (see above)

Paul Huot: director B 1957. PRIM CORP EMPL vice president production, director: Huot Manufacturing Co.

Reatha Clark King: director ED Clark College BS (1958); University of Chicago PhD (1960). PRIM CORP EMPL vice president: General Mills, Inc. CORP AFFIL director: HB Fuller Co.; director: Exxon-Mobil Corp. NONPR AFFIL member: NAA; director: Saint Paul Corp. National and Community Service; board overseers: Clark Atlanta University; member: Delta Sigma Theta; chairman advisory council: ARC.

Naida Kissner: program assistant

David J. Maki: treasurer (see above)

Lee Upton McGrath: treasurer (see above)

James A. Metts: director PRIM CORP EMPL vice president: H.B. Fuller Co.

Karen P. Muller: executive director PRIM CORP EMPL director community affairs: H.B. Fuller Co.

Mario Perez: director (see above)

John Thomas Ray, Jr.: president, director B Shaw, MS 1937. ED Millsaps College BS (1960). PRIM CORP EMPL senior vice president, general manager adhesives division: H.B. Fuller Co. CORP AFFIL director: Sensormatic Electronics Corp.; vice president, director: HB Fuller Co. International Inc.; vice president, director: HB Fuller Co. PR; chairman, chief executive officer: Fiber-Resin Corp.; chairman, chief executive officer: HB Fuller Automotive Products Inc.; executive vice president, director: F A I Trading Co. Inc.; director: Adhesive & Sealant Council; chairman: EFTEC North America LLC. NONPR AFFIL treasurer, director: Adhesive Manufacturer Association; director: Packaging Education Foundation.

Rolf B. Schubert: director B Leipzig, Germany 1938. ED University of Minnesota (1962). PRIM CORP EMPL vice president corp. research & development, director, technology office: H.B. Fuller Co.

Jean M. West: vice president, director PRIM CORP EMPL shareholder representative: West Premium Corp.

Ann Wynia: director B Fort Worth, TX 1943. ED University of Texas BA (1965); University of Wisconsin MA (1968). NONPR AFFIL commissioner: Minnesota Department Human Services; instructor: North Hennepin Community College.

Grants Analysis

Disclosure Period: calendar year ending 1997

Total Grants: $526,100*

Number of Grants: 98

Average Grant: $5,368

Highest Grant: $25,000

Typical Range: $1,000 to $10,000

***Note:** Giving excludes matching gifts; United Way.

Recent Grants

Note: Grants derived from 1997 Form 990.

Arts & Humanities

80,000 Minnesota Public Radio, St. Paul, MN -- national and regional broadcasts of the Minnesota Orchestra and the St. Paul Chamber Orchestra
5,000 Friends of the St. Paul Public Library, St. Paul, MN -- summer reading program
5,000 Minnesota Children's Museum, St. Paul, MN -- school services program
5,000 Sounds of Hope, St. Paul, MN -- Songs of Hope
4,000 Ethnic Dance Theater, Minneapolis, MN -- Groveland Park Elementary School residency

Civic & Public Affairs

25,000 Family Housing Fund of Minneapolis and St. Paul, Minneapolis, MN -- technical assistance fund for providers of services and shelter for youth
11,000 Twin Cities Tree Trust, St. Louis Park, MN -- summer youth employment and training program
10,000 Ain Dah Yung, St. Paul, MN
9,000 Community Design Center, St. Paul, MN -- Dayton's Bluff/East Side Children's Project
8,000 University of Minnesota Foundation Center for Democracy and Citizenship, Minneapolis, MN -- public achievement
6,500 HIRED, Minneapolis, MN -- St. Paul youth employment enhancement
5,000 Infinity Systems for Nonprofits, Minneapolis, MN -- Esteem Academy
5,000 MELD, Minneapolis, MN -- MELD for Young Partners

Education

10,000 Institute for Education and Advocacy, Minneapolis, MN -- study connections
10,000 W. Harry Davis Leadership Institute, Minneapolis, MN -- Full Circle Initiative-African American youth leadership training and social action on environmental quality
8,000 Lauj Youth Society, St. Paul, MN -- tutoring program

Environment

5,000 Minnesota Environmental Fund, Minneapolis, MN

Health

11,000 Face to Face Health and Counseling Service, St. Paul, MN
7,500 Auburn Children's Psychological Clinic, Auburn, CA
6,000 Santa Teresita Child Development Center, Palatine, IL -- Santa Teresita Tot Lot

International

20,000 FUNDAR, Tegucigalpa, Honduras
20,000 FUNDAR, Tegucigalpa, Honduras

Religion

15,000 Salvation Army, St. Paul, MN -- preschool program

Science

5,000 Science Museum, St. Paul, MN -- field partners

Social Services

93,009 United Way, St. Paul, MN
20,000 Northwest Youth and Family Services, Shoreview, MN
20,000 Paducah Basketball Association, Paducah, KY -- Noble Park Basketball Court project
14,100 People, St. Paul, MN -- Families United in Need groups
10,000 Big Brothers and Big Sisters, St. Paul, MN
10,000 Family Service, Stillwater, MN -- youth development program
10,000 Minnesota Thunder Youth Development Organization, Elaine, MN
10,000 Ramsey County Parks and Recreation Department, Maplewood, MN
10,000 Sierra Adoption Services, Sacramento, CA -- Placer County Kids are Waiting
8,500 YMCA, Covington, GA -- Partners with Youth
7,500 SMART Kids, Sacramento, CA
7,000 Save Our Sons, St. Paul, MN
6,898 United Way Crusade of Mercy, Palatine, IL
6,700 Children Are People Support Groups, St. Paul, MN
6,315 United Way of the Columbia-Willamette, Portland, OR
6,000 Boy Scouts of America Indianhead Council, St. Paul, MN -- campership program
5,600 Family Support Network, St. Paul, MN
5,000 Bridge Youth and Family Services, Palatine, IL -- family violence prevention project
5,000 Farley Elementary School, Paducah, KY -- Camp Farley
5,000 Hands on Atlanta, Atlanta, GA -- Discovery Program
5,000 Harbour, Park Ridge, IL
5,000 Inner-City Youth League, St. Paul, MN
5,000 Rainbow House, Jonesboro, GA
5,000 Shelter, Arlington, IL
5,000 West Seventh Community Center, St. Paul, MN -- KidsPlus Program
4,567 United Way, Paducah, KY
4,000 Children's Home and Aid Society, Palatine, IL -- photography equipment and supplies

FURNITURE BRANDS INTERNATIONAL, INC.

★ Number 20 of Top 100 Corporate Givers

Company Contact

101 S. Hanley Rd.
St. Louis, MO 63105
Phone: (314)863-1100
Fax: (314)863-5306
Web: http://www.furniturebrands.com

Interco Inc. Charitable Trust

Giving Contact

Mr. Robert T. Hensley, Jr., Treasurer
Interco Inc. Charitable Trust
c/o Furniture Brands International, Inc.
101 S. Hanley Rd.
St. Louis, MO 63105
Phone: (314)863-1100 ext 108
Fax: (314)863-5306

Description

EIN: 436020530
Organization Type: Corporate Foundation
Giving Locations: MO: St. Louis principally near operating locations and to national organizations.
Grant Types: Capital, General Support.

Financial Summary

Total Giving: $40,455,365 (1998); $1,742,753 (1997); $1,839,564 (1996). Note: Contributes through foundation only.
Giving Analysis: Giving for 1996 includes: foundation grants to United Way ($175,250); 1997: foundation grants to United Way ($97,750)
Assets: $44,399,908 (1997); $39,001,342 (1996); $30,638,926 (1994)

Typical Recipients

Arts & Humanities: Arts Associations & Councils, Arts Centers, Arts Festivals, Arts Funds, Dance, Arts & Humanities-General, Historic Preservation, History & Archaeology, Museums/Galleries, Music, Opera, Performing Arts, Theater
Civic & Public Affairs: African American Affairs, Botanical Gardens/Parks, Business/Free Enterprise, Civil Rights, Clubs, Economic Development, Employment/Job Training, Civic & Public Affairs-General, Housing, Municipalities/Towns, Parades/Festivals, Philanthropic Organizations, Professional & Trade Associations, Public Policy, Urban & Community Affairs, Women's Affairs, Zoos/Aquariums
Education: Arts/Humanities Education, Business Education, Colleges & Universities, Community & Junior Colleges, Economic Education, Education Associations, Education Funds, Education Reform, Education-General, International Studies, Legal Education, Minority Education, Private Education (Precollege), Public Education (Precollege), School Volunteerism, Science/Mathematics Education, Special Education, Student Aid, Vocational & Technical Education
Environment: Forestry
Health: AIDS/HIV, Children's Health/Hospitals, Emergency/Ambulance Services, Hospices, Hospitals, Medical Research, Mental Health, Single-Disease Health Associations, Speech & Hearing
Religion: Churches, Jewish Causes, Religious Organizations, Religious Welfare
Science: Scientific Centers & Institutes
Social Services: Child Welfare, Community Centers, Community Service Organizations, Delinquency & Criminal Rehabilitation, Domestic Violence, Emergency Relief, Food/Clothing Distribution, Homes, People with Disabilities, Recreation & Athletics, Scouts, Senior Services, United Funds/United Ways, YMCA/YWCA/YMHA/YWHA, Youth Organizations

Contributions Analysis

Giving Priorities: Social welfare, education, and civic interests.
Arts & Humanities: 7%. Supports museums, symphonies and art associations.
Civic & Public Affairs: 14%. Giving focuses on zoos and botanical gardens and philanthropic organizations. Women's affairs and community development are also priorities.
Education: 33%. Interests include colleges and universities, technical, special, and economic education, and private secondary schools.
Health: 2%. Majority supports children's hospitals, with the remainder going to single-disease health associations and medical education.
Religion: 3% Supports Jewish causes.
Social Services: 41%. Supports local united funds and YMCAs. Also gives to Boy Scouts, crime prevention programs, and recreation and athletics.
Note: Total contributions in 1997.

Application Procedures

Initial Contact: Send brief letter of inquiry.
Application Requirements: Include a description of organization, amount requested and purpose of funds sought, recently audited financial statement, and proof of tax-exempt status.
Deadlines: None.

Corporate Officials

J. Thomas Foy: president, chief executive officer PRIM CORP EMPL president, chief executive officer: Action Industries, Inc.

Wilbert G. 'Mickey' Holliman: chairman, president, chief executive officer, director ED Mississippi State University BS (1960). PRIM CORP EMPL chairman, president, chief executive officer, director: Furniture Brands International, Inc. ADD CORP EMPL director: Broyhill Furniture Industries Inc.; president, chief executive officer, director: Lane Furniture Industries Inc.

David P. Howard: vice president, chief financial officer, treasurer B Wood River, IL 1950. ED Southern Illinois University BBA (1972). PRIM CORP EMPL vice president, chief financial officer, treasurer: Furniture Brands International, Inc. ADD CORP EMPL vice president: Lane Co. Inc.; director: Thomasville Furniture Industries.

Brent B. Kincaid: president, chief executive officer B 1933. PRIM CORP EMPL president, chief executive officer: Broyhill Furniture Industries. CORP AFFIL director: Furniture Brands International Inc.

Kenneth Scott Tyler, Jr.: president, chief executive officer B Lee County, VA 1940. ED University of Virginia (1962); University of Virginia (1964). PRIM CORP EMPL president, chief executive officer: Lane Co. Inc. CORP AFFIL director: Centra Health Inc.; director: First National Bank Altavista.

Grants Analysis

Disclosure Period: calendar year ending 1997
Total Grants: $1,645,003*
Number of Grants: 306 (approx)
Average Grant: $5,376 (approx)
Highest Grant: $100,000
Typical Range: $1,000 to $7,000
***Note:** Giving excludes United Way.

Recent Grants

Note: Grants derived from 1998 Form 990.

Arts & Humanities

20,000	Missouri Historical Society, St. Louis, MO
10,000	Grand Center, St. Louis, MO
10,000	Greensbord Children's Museum, Greensboro, NC
5,000	Reynolda House, Winston-Salem, NC
5,000	Union County Historical Society, Clayton, NM

Civic & Public Affairs

50,000	Cornell Foundation, New York, NY
10,000	Coro Midwestern Center, St. Louis, MO
5,000	City of Hickory, Hickory, NC
5,000	St Louis Kite Festival, St. Louis, MO
5,000	St Louis Variety Club, St. Louis, MO

Education

26,027	University of Missouri-St Louis, St Louis, MO -- Scholarship Award
20,000	Junior Achievement of Mississippi Valley, St. Louis, MO
15,000	Lee County Schools, Fort Myers, FL
10,000	High Point University, High Point, NC
10,000	Ursuline Academy, St. Louis, MO
10,000	Washington University School of Law, St. Louis, MO
7,500	United Negro College Fund, St. Louis, MO
7,000	University of Missouri-St Louis, St Louis, MO -- Scholarship Award
7,000	University of Missouri-St Louis, St Louis, MO -- Scholarship Award
5,150	Ursuline Academy, St. Louis, MO
5,000	DCCC Endowment, Media, PA
5,000	North Carolina Independent College Fund, Winston-Salem, NC
5,000	Thomasville Communities-In Schools, Thomasville, NC
5,000	Thomasville City School/Drama & Arts, Thomasville, NC
1,000	Virginia Foundation for Independent Colleges, Richmond, VA

Environment

40,000	Forest Park Forever, Chicago, IL

Health

50,000	Caldwell Memorial Hospital Foundation, Inc., Lenair, NC
20,000	St. Joseph's Institute for the Deaf, St. Louis, MO
12,500	Cystic Fibrosis Foundation, St. Louis, MO
10,000	United Cerebal Palsy, St. Louis, MO
6,000	American Red Cross-High Point, High Point, NC
6,000	Zink the Zebra Foundation, St. Louis, MO
5,000	Caldwell Memorial Hospital Foundation, Inc., Lenoir, NC
5,000	Community General Hospital Foundation, Thomasville, NC

Religion

20,000	Jewish Federation of St Louis, St. Louis, MO
10,000	The Salvation Army, St. Louis, MO
7,450	Anti-Defamation League, St. Louis, MO

Science

5,000	Catawba Science Center, Hickory, NC

Social Services

100,000	Mathews-Dickey Boys Club, St. Louis, MO
62,500	United Way of Greater St. Louis, St. Louis, MO
50,000	Altavista Area YMCA, Altavista, VA
25,000	Edgewood Children's Center, St. Louis, MO
15,000	Life Crisis Services, St. Louis, MO
6,000	Franklin County YMCA, Rocky Mount, VA
5,000	Echo (Emergency Children's Home), St. Louis, MO
5,000	Gardner-Simmons Home for Girls, Tupelo, MS
5,000	Greater St Louis Area Council Boy Scouts of America, St. Louis, MO
5,000	Saint Louis Association for Retarded Citizens, St. Louis, MO
5,000	Yocona Area Council, Tupelo, MS

E&J Gallo Winery, Inc.

Company Contact

Modesto, CA

Company Description

Employees: 2,500
SIC(s): 0172 Grapes, 2084 Wines, Brandy & Brandy Spirits, 3221 Glass Containers.

Corporate Sponsorship

Type: Arts & cultural events

Gallo Foundation

Giving Contact

Mrs. Ouida McCullough, Secretary
Gallo Foundation
PO Box 1130
Modesto, CA 95353
Phone: (209)341-3111
Fax: (209)341-3324

Description

EIN: 946061538
Organization Type: Corporate Foundation
Giving Locations: CA nationally.
Grant Types: General Support, Matching, Research, Scholarship.

Financial Summary

Total Giving: $486,903 (fiscal year ending May 31, 1998); $732,947 (fiscal 1997); $563,643 (fiscal 1996). Note: Contributes through corporate direct giving program and foundation.

Giving Analysis: Giving for fiscal 1996 includes: foundation ($550,950); foundation matching gifts ($12,693); fiscal 1997: foundation ($715,350); foundation matching gifts ($17,597); fiscal 1998: foundation ($469,350); foundation matching gifts ($17,553)

Assets: $107,185 (fiscal 1998); $40,730 (fiscal 1997); $69,271 (fiscal 1996)

Gifts Received: $552,332 (fiscal 1998); $702,853 (fiscal 1997); $600,000 (fiscal 1996). Note: Contributions are received from the E & J Gallo Winery.

Typical Recipients

Arts & Humanities: History & Archaeology, Libraries, Museums/Galleries, Music, Opera, Public Broadcasting, Theater

Civic & Public Affairs: African American Affairs, Business/Free Enterprise, Chambers of Commerce, Civil Rights, Clubs, Economic Development, Employment/Job Training, Ethnic Organizations, Civic & Public Affairs-General, Hispanic Affairs, Municipalities/Towns, Parades/Festivals, Professional & Trade Associations, Public Policy, Urban & Community Affairs, Women's Affairs

Education: Afterschool/Enrichment Programs, Agricultural Education, Business Education, Colleges & Universities, Community & Junior Colleges, Education Associations, Education Funds, Education Reform, Education-General, Legal Education, Minority Education, Minority Education, Private Education (Precollege), Public Education (Precollege), Religious Education, Secondary Education (Private), Secondary Education (Public), Student Aid

Environment: Resource Conservation, Wildlife Protection

Health: Alzheimers Disease, Cancer, Children's Health/Hospitals, Clinics/Medical Centers, Diabetes, Emergency/Ambulance Services, Geriatric Health, Health Organizations, Heart, Hospices, Hospitals, Medical Research, Multiple Sclerosis, Prenatal Health Issues, Public Health, Single-Disease Health Associations, Transplant Networks/Donor Banks

International: International Organizations, International Relief Efforts

Religion: Churches, Dioceses, Jewish Causes, Religious Organizations, Religious Welfare, Social/Policy Issues

Science: Scientific Organizations

Social Services: Animal Protection, At-Risk Youth, Big Brother/Big Sister, Child Abuse, Child Welfare, Community Service Organizations, Crime Prevention, Domestic Violence, Emergency Relief, Family Services, Food/Clothing Distribution, Homes, People with Disabilities, Recreation & Athletics, Scouts, Senior Services, Substance Abuse, United Funds/United Ways, YMCA/YWCA/YMHA/YWHA, Youth Organizations

Contributions Analysis

Civic & Public Affairs: 3%.

Education: 29%. Majority of funds support educational foundations and minority education. Other recipients include education funds and public education.

Health: 14%. Primarily supports hospitals and medical centers. Other interests include single-disease health associations and medical research.

International: Less than 1%. Supports the American Himalayan Foundation.

Religion: 2%. Supports religious causes.

Social Services: 52%. Interests include youth organizations, child welfare, and food banks.

Note: Total contributions in 1998.

Application Procedures

Initial Contact: Send a brief letter to one of the directors of the Gallo Foundation.
Application Requirements: Include duration of project, how funds will be used, and proof of tax-exempt status.
Deadlines: None.
Decision Notification: Throughout the year, although more grants are given toward end of year.

Restrictions

Grants are not made to individuals.
The company only funds qualified public charities.

Corporate Officials

Ernest Gallo: co-founder, chairmanen counsel B Jackson, CA 1909. PRIM CORP EMPL co-founder, chairman: E&J Gallo Winery, Inc. PRIM NONPR EMPL president, secretary: Ernest Gallo Clinic & Research Center.
Robert J. Gallo: co-president B 1934. PRIM CORP EMPL co-president: E&J Gallo Winery, Inc. ADD CORP EMPL president: Gallo Glass Co.
Jack Byron Owens: executive vice president, general counsel B Orange, CA 1944. ED Stanford University AB (1966); Stanford University JD (1969). PRIM CORP EMPL executive vice president, general counsel: E&J Gallo Winery, Inc. NONPR AFFIL member: Order Coif; member: Phi Beta Kappa; adj professor: Georgetown University Law School; member: American Bar Association; member: American Law Institute.

Foundation Officials

Louis Friedman: treasurer PRIM CORP EMPL executive vice president finance, treasurer: E&J Gallo Winery.
Ernest Gallo: director (see above)
Joseph E. Gallo: co-president B 1941. PRIM CORP EMPL co-president: E&J Gallo Winery, Inc. ADD CORP EMPL president: Gallo International Service; president: Gallo Sales Co. Inc.; owner: Joseph Gallo Farms. CORP AFFIL president: Pacific Coast Beverage Distribution; secretary: Valley Vinters Inc.; director: Fairbanks Trucking Inc.; partner: Midcal.
Robert J. Gallo: co-president (see above)
Ouida McCullough: secretary

Grants Analysis

Disclosure Period: fiscal year ending May 31, 1998
Total Grants: $469,350*
Number of Grants: 57
Average Grant: $4,810*
Highest Grant: $200,000
Typical Range: $100 to $5,000
*Note: Giving excludes matching gifts. Average grant figures excludes highest grant.

Recent Grants

Note: Grants derived from 1998 Form 990.

Arts & Humanities

250	Cloverdale Historical Society, Cloverdale, CA
250	Modesto Civic Theater, Modesto, CA

Civic & Public Affairs

5,000	American Institute of Wine & Food, San Francisco, CA
5,000	National Italian American Foundation, Washington, DC
2,750	Modesto Rotary Club Foundation, Modesto, CA

Education

100,000	Albertson College of Idaho, Caldwell, ID
10,000	University of California - Berkeley Foundation, Berkeley, CA
5,000	Stanislaus Partner in Education, Modesto, CA
5,000	University of Chicago, Chicago, IL
4,000	California Foundation for Agriculture in the Classroom, Sacramento, CA
3,500	Modesto Junior College Foundation, Modesto, CA
2,000	United Negro College Fund, Newark, NJ
1,000	Christ the King Educational Trust, Omaha, NE
1,000	Stanislaus County Dept. of Education, Modesto, CA
500	CA State University - Northridge, Northridge, CA
500	St Anne's School, Lodi, CA
250	Beyer High School, Modesto, CA
250	Davis High School, Modesto, CA
250	Denair High School, Denair, CA
250	Downey High School, Modesto, CA
250	Hughson High School, Hughson, CA

Health

50,000	Valley Children's Hospital Foundation, Fresno, CA
5,000	American Diabetes Association, Modesto, CA
5,000	Dana Farber Cancer Institute, Boston, MA
2,750	American Heart Association, Modesto, CA
2,250	American Cancer Society, Belle Haven, VA
1,000	Stanislaus County Health Services Agency, Modesto, CA
500	Community Hospice, Modesto, CA
500	Lodi Memorial Hospital Foundation, Lodi, CA

International

3,000	World Vision International, Monrovia, CA

Religion

4,000	Anti-Defamation League / B'Nai / Brith, New York, NY
3,500	Second Baptist Church, Modesto, CA
1,000	Salvation Army, Modesto, CA
500	St Patrick's Catholic Church, Meridian, MS
250	Our Lady of Fatima Church, Modesto, CA

Science

500	Histochemical Society, Inc., Seattle, WA

Social Services

200,000	Dole Foundation, Washington, DC
10,500	American Red Cross - Stanislaus Co, Modesto, CA
10,000	Children's Inn at National Institute of Health, Bethesda, MD
10,000	Parent Resource Center, Modesto, CA
5,000	YMCA of Stanislaus County, Modesto, CA
1,500	Kids Works, Inc, Modesto, CA
1,000	American Red Cross - Sonoma, Santa Rosa, CA
1,000	Girl Scouts Muir Trail Council, Modesto, CA
500	Children's Crisis Center, Modesto, CA
500	Oakdale Senior Housing Corp., Oakdale, CA
250	Big Brothers/Big Sisters, Santa Rosa, CA
250	Senior Opportunity Service Program, Modesto, CA
250	SPCA of Monterey County, Monterey, CA
250	United States Equestrian Team, Gladstone, NJ

GALTER CORP.

Company Contact

Chicago, IL

Galter Foundation

Giving Contact

Dollie Galter, Director
Galter Foundation
215 E. Chicago Ave.
Chicago, IL 60611
Phone: (312)664-5370

Description

Founded: 1943
EIN: 366082419
Organization Type: Corporate Foundation
Giving Locations: IL: Chicago
Grant Types: General Support.

Financial Summary

Total Giving: $3,000,000 (2000 approx); $3,000,000 (1999 approx); $1,952,394 (1996)
Assets: $13,003,305 (1996); $14,374,490 (1995); $12,404,859 (1994)
Gifts Received: $60,000 (1995); $600 (1994); $1,709,352 (1993). Note: In 1995, contributions were received from Dollie Galter.

Typical Recipients

Arts & Humanities: Libraries, Music, Public Broadcasting, Theater
Civic & Public Affairs: Clubs, Civic & Public Affairs-General
Education: Colleges & Universities, Medical Education, Private Education (Precollege), Religious Education
Health: AIDS/HIV, Arthritis, Cancer, Children's Health/Hospitals, Clinics/Medical Centers, Diabetes, Health Organizations, Heart, Home-Care Services, Hospitals, Hospitals (University Affiliated), Kidney, Medical Rehabilitation, Medical Research, Multiple Sclerosis, Prenatal Health Issues, Public Health, Respiratory, Single-Disease Health Associations
International: Missionary/Religious Activities
Religion: Churches, Jewish Causes, Missionary Activities (Domestic), Religious Organizations, Religious Welfare, Seminaries, Synagogues/Temples
Science: Scientific Centers & Institutes
Social Services: Animal Protection, Child Welfare, Community Service Organizations, People with Disabilities, Scouts, Senior Services, Special Olympics, United Funds/United Ways, Veterans, Youth Organizations

Contributions Analysis

Giving Priorities: Primary focus on health organizations and issues.

Additional Information

The company reported that all funds are committed until 2004. No applications will be accepted in the interim.

Corporate Officials

Dollie Galter: president, chief executive officer PRIM CORP EMPL president, chief executive officer: Galter Corp.

Foundation Officials

Charles Edwards: director
Dollie Galter: director (see above)
William Galter: director
Theodore Netzky: director

Grants Analysis

Disclosure Period: calendar year ending 1996
Total Grants: $1,952,394
Number of Grants: 19
Average Grant: $102,758
Highest Grant: $750,000
Typical Range: $5 to $500

Recent Grants

Note: Grants derived from 1997 Form 990.

Education

2,000	Cumberland College, Williamsburg, KY -- support services

Health

200,000	Rehabilitation Institute, Chicago, IL -- support services
5,000	Multiple Sclerosis, Chicago, IL -- support services
500	Juvenile Diabetes Foundation, Chicago, IL -- support services
25	United Cerebral Palsy Association, Chicago, IL -- support services
12	American Kidney Fund, Rockville, MD -- support services
5	Easter Seal Society, Chicago, IL -- support services

Science

1,000	Weizmann Institute of Science, New York, NY -- support services

Social Services

100	National Wheelchair Tournament, Park Ridge, IL -- support services

Gannett Co., Inc.

Company Contact

Arlington, VA
Web: http://www.gannett.com

Company Description

Revenue: US$5,121,300,000
Employees: 37,200
Fortune Rank: 304, per FORTUNE Magazine's list of 500 Largest U.S. Corporations (1999).
FF 304
SIC(s): 2711 Newspapers, 4832 Radio Broadcasting Stations, 4833 Television Broadcasting Stations, 5063 Electrical Apparatus & Equipment.

Operating Locations

Canada; Guam; Virgin Islands of the United States
Note: Application guidelines come with a complete listing of operating cities for the states listed above.

Nonmonetary Support

Value: $39,600,000 (1993); $32,800,000 (1992); $32,400,000 (1991)
Type: In-kind Services
Note: Co. provides nonmonetary support in the form of public service announcements and in-kind advertising for nonprofits. This support is handled locally, contact local office.

Gannett Foundation

Giving Contact

Irma E. Simpson, Manager
Gannett Foundation
1100 Wilson Blvd.
Arlington, VA 22234
Phone: (703)284-6000
Fax: (703)558-3819
Email: isimpson@gci1.gannett.com
Note: Grant requests should be made to the local CEOs in communities where Gannett has newspapers and broadcast stations.

Description

Organization Type: Corporate Foundation
Giving Locations: operating locations.
Grant Types: Capital, Employee Matching Gifts, General Support, Project.
Note: Employee matching gift ratio: 1 to 1.

Giving Philosophy

'The Gannett Communities Fund is a corporate giving program designed to serve those communities in which Gannett Co., Inc., has operations. The program makes contributions to qualified nonprofit organizations to improve the education, health and advancement of the people who live in Gannett communities. The contributions are our way of helping improve the quality of life and addressing the most pressing community problems.'

'We value projects which take a creative approach to such fundamental issues as education and neighborhood improvement, economic development, youth development, community problem-solving, assistance to people who are disadvantaged, environmental conservation, journalism education and cultural enrichment.' *Gannett Communities Fund Guidelines*

Financial Summary

Total Giving: $8,300,000 (2000 approx); $8,300,000 (1999 approx); $7,628,000 (1997). Note: Contributes through corporate direct giving program and foundation.
Giving Analysis: Giving for 1997 includes: foundation ($5,603,000); foundation grants to United Way ($1,197,000); foundation matching gifts ($828,000)
Assets: $27,500,000 (1997 approx); $7,620,000 (1996 approx); $12,935,000 (1995 approx)

Typical Recipients

Arts & Humanities: Arts Associations & Councils, Performing Arts, Visual Arts
Civic & Public Affairs: Economic Development, Employment/Job Training
Education: Literacy
Health: Mental Health
Social Services: Community Service Organizations, Counseling, People with Disabilities, Recreation & Athletics, Senior Services, Shelters/Homelessness, Youth Organizations

Contributions Analysis

Giving Priorities: Education and neighborhood improvement, economic development, the disadvantaged, the environment, and cultural enrichment.
Arts & Humanities: 10% to 15%. Supports arts organizations; also supports journalism (5% to 10%).
Civic & Public Affairs: 15% to 20%.
Education: 10% to 15%.
Health: About 10%.
Social Services: About 30%.
Note: Total contributions made in 1999.

Application Procedures

Initial Contact: Write or e-mail foundation manager, or call local CEO to request application form.
Application Requirements: Completed application form; proposal of no more than 5 pages, including: needs statement, objectives of the project to be funded, organization's qualifications to carry out the project, whether project is new or ongoing, constituency to be served, community and volunteer involvement, how project will be evaluated, plans for continued funding of project (if applicable), one-page project budget, organizational budget, list of other funding sources (committed and applied for), any pertinent publications, and IRS letter of 501(c)(3) determination.
Deadlines: None.
Review Process: Management Contributions Committee meets four times per year from February through November; local CEOs will notify applicants of decisions and distribute funds.
Decision Notification: Decisions generally take between 60 and 90 days.
Notes: If the organization has not been determined a tax-exempt organization under 501(c)(3), send a copy of the application for exempt status.

Restrictions

Fund will not make grants to individuals; organizations without IRS section 501 (c)(3) tax-exempt status; national or regional organizations, unless programs address specific local community needs; programs for religious purposes; elementary or secondary schools (except to provide special initiatives or programs not provided by regular school budgets); political action or legislative advocacy groups; endowment funds; multiple-year pledge campaigns; medical or other research organizations; organizations located in or benefiting nations other than the United States and its territories; fraternal groups; athletic teams; bands; veterans' organizations; volunteer firefighters or similar organizations; or organizations outside operating areas. nations other than the United States and its territories; fraternal groups; athletic teams; bands; veterans' organizations; volunteer firefighters or similar organizations; or organizations outside operating areas.

Additional Information

Publications: Foundation Annual Report

Corporate Officials

Thomas Leslie Chapple: senior vice president, general counsel, secretary B Canandaigua, NY 1947. ED Cornell University BA (1970); Albany Law School JD (1973). PRIM CORP EMPL senior vice president, general counsel, secretary: Gannett Co., Inc. CORP AFFIL secretary, director: Times Herald Co. Inc.; secretary, director: Pensacola News-Journal Inc.; secretary, director: KPNX Broadcasting Co.; secretary, director: KVUE-TV Inc.; secretary, general counsel: Gannett Co. Inc. DE; secretary, director: Detroit News Inc.; secretary: Florida Gannett Broadcasting; secretary, director: Des Moines Register & Tribune Co. NONPR AFFIL member: New York State Bar Association; member: Sigma Pi Phi; member: Association of Corporate Counsel; member: American Bar Association.

John J. Curley: chairman, chief executive officer, director B Easton, PA 1938. ED Dickinson College BA (1960); Columbia University MS (1963). PRIM CORP EMPL chairman, chief executive officer, director: Gannett Co., Inc. DC. CORP AFFIL chairman: Speidel Newspapers Inc.; director: Multimedia Inc.; director: Garnett Direct Marketing Service; director: KVUE-TV Inc.; director: Detroit News Inc.; director: Gannett Satellite Information Network; president: Binghampton Press Co. Inc.; director: Des Moines Register & Tribune Co. NONPR AFFIL chairman, emeritus: Newspaper Association America.

Mimi A. Feller: senior vice president public affairs & government relations B Omaha, NE. ED Creighton University BA (1970); Georgetown University JD (1981). PRIM CORP EMPL senior vice president public affairs & government relations: Gannett Co., Inc. NONPR AFFIL director: Creighton University; trustee: Marymount University.

Gracia C. Martore: vice president investor relations, treasurer B Somerville, MA 1951. ED George Washington University; Wellesley College (1973). PRIM CORP EMPL vice president investor relations, treasurer: Gannett Co., Inc.

Douglas H. McCorkindale: vice chairman, president B New York, NY 1939. ED Columbia University BA (1961); Columbia University LLB (1964). PRIM CORP EMPL vice chairman, president: Gannett Co., Inc. CORP AFFIL director: WFMY Television Corp.; director: USA Weekend Inc.; director: Visalia Newspapers Inc.; director: USA Today International Corp.; director: United States of America Today; director: United States of America Today Information Network; director: Times Herald Co. Inc.; director: Sun Co. San Bernardino California; director: Television 12 Jacksonville Inc.; director: Statesman-Journal Co.; director: Stockton Newspapers Inc.; director: Speidel Newspapers Inc.; director: Sioux Falls Newspapers

Inc.; director: Southland Publishing Co.; vice president, director: Shelter Media Communication Inc.; director: Salinas Newspapers Inc.; vice president, director: Shelter Media Arizona Inc.; director: Salem County Sampler Inc.; director: Reno Newspapers Inc.; director: Saint Cloud Newspapers Inc.; director, trustee: Prudential Mutual Group; director: Prudential Natural Resources Fund Inc.; trustee: Prudential Municipal Bond Fund; director: Prudential Global Genesis Fund; director: Prudential Multi-Sector Fund Inc.; trustee: Prudential Equity Income Fund; director: Pensacola News-Journal Inc.; trustee: Prudential Allocation Fund; vice president, director: Pacific & Southern Co. Inc.; director: Oklahoma Press Publishing Co.; director: Pacific Media Inc.; vice president, director: New York Subways Advertising Co. Inc.; director: News-Press Publishing Co.; trustee: Mutual Insurance Co. Ltd.; director: Lend-A-Hand Inc.; president, director: McClure Newspapers Inc.; director: KPNX Broadcasting Co.; director: KVUE-TV Inc.; director: Louis Harris International Inc.; director: Guam Publications Inc.; director: Louis Harris & Assoc Inc.; vice chairman, chief financial officer, chief administration off, director: Gannett TG Subsidiary Inc.; director: Global Government Plus Fund Inc.; director: Gannett Texas Broadcasting Inc.; director: Gannett Telemktg Inc.; director: Gannett Television; director: Gannett Supply Corp.; director: Gannett River Saint Publishing Corp.; president, director: Gannett Satellite Information Network; director: Gannett Retail Advertising Group; director: Gannett Outdoor Co. Texas; vice president, director: Gannett Pacific Corp.; director: Gannett News Service; director: Gannett Newspaper Division; director: Gannett News Media; director: Gannett Media Technologies International; director: Gannett National Newspaper Sales Inc.; director: Gannett Massachusetts Broadcasting Inc.; director: Gannett International; president, director: Gannett International Communication Inc.; director: Gannett Direct Marketing Services Inc.; director: Frontier Corp.; director: Gannett Broadcasting Division; director: Federal Publishing Inc.; director: Fort Collins Newspapers Inc.; director: Eleven-Fifty Corp.; director: Detroit News Inc.; director: El Paso Times; director: Desert Sun Publishing Co. Inc.; director: Daily News Publishing Co. Inc.; director: Des Moines Register & Tribune Co.; director: Courier-Journal & Louisville Times Co.; director: Continental Airlines Inc.; director: Courier Broadway Corp.; president, director: Combined Communications Corp.; director: Combined Communications Corp. Oklahoma Inc.; director: Citizen Publishing Co.; director: Cape Publishing Inc.; director: Children's Edition Inc.; director: California Newspapers Inc. NONPR AFFIL member: American Bar Association; member: Newspaper Association America. CLUB AFFIL Pine Valley Golf Club; Oak Hills Country Club; Burning Tree Club; Mid-Ocean Club.

Foundation Officials

Christopher Baldwin: treasurer
Thomas Leslie Chapple: secretary (see above)
John J. Curley: chairman (see above)
Mimi A. Feller: vice president (see above)
Gracia C. Martore: assistant treasurer (see above)
Douglas H. McCorkindale: president (see above)
Irma E. Simpson: manager

Grants Analysis

Disclosure Period: calendar year ending 1997
Total Grants: $5,603,000*
Number of Grants: 1,208
Average Grant: $4,638
Typical Range: $1,500 to $5,000
***Note:** Giving excludes matching gifts; United Way.

GAP, INC.

 Number 93 of Top 100 Corporate Givers

Company Contact

San Francisco, CA
Web: http://www.gap.com

Company Description

Former Name: Gap Foundation.
Revenue: US$9,054,500,000
Employees: 81,000
Fortune Rank: 152, per FORTUNE Magazine's list of 500 Largest U.S. Corporations (1999).
FF 152
SIC(s): 5651 Family Clothing Stores.

Operating Locations

Australia: Banana Republic Stores Pty. Ltd.; Bermuda: GPS (Bermuda) Insurance Services Ltd.; GPS (Bermuda) Ltd.; Canada: Gap (Canada) Inc.; England: Gap (ESO) Ltd.; The Gap Ltd.; GPS (Great Britain) Ltd.; France: Gap (France) SAS, Paris; Germany: Gap (Deutschland) GmbH, Dusseldorf; Hong Kong: Banana Republic (H.K.) Ltd.; Gap (Hong Kong) Ltd.; Gap International Sourcing (Holdings) Ltd.; Gap International Sourcing Ltd.; Ireland: Gap (Ireland) Ltd., Dublin; Japan: Gap (Japan) K.K., Tokyo; Mexico: Gap International Sourcing (Mexico) S.A. de CV; Netherlands: Gap (Netherlands) B.V., Amsterdam; Gap (RHC) B.V., Amsterdam; Goldhawk B.V., Amsterdam; GPS (International Investments) B.V., Amsterdam; Puerto Rico: Banana Republic (Puerto Rico) Inc.; Gap (Puerto Rico), Inc.; Old Navy (Puerto Rico) Inc.; Singapore: Gap International Sourcing Pte. Ltd.; Wales: Gap (ESO) Ltd.; The Gap Ltd.; GPS (Great Britain) Ltd.
Note: Operates throughout the USA.

Nonmonetary Support

Value: $1,240,000 (1999 approx); $1,681,059 (1995); $1,170,000 (1994)
Type: Donated Equipment; Donated Products; In-kind Services
Contact: Molly White, Senior Director
Note: Co. awards merchandise, office equipment (computers), and gift certificates.

Gap Foundation/Gap Inc. Community Relations

Giving Contact

Ms. Dotti Hatcher, Senior DRC
Gap Inc. Community Relations
1 Harrison Street
San Francisco, CA 94105
Phone: (415)427-2757
Fax: (415)427-2504
Web: http://www.gapinc.com/community/community.htm

Description

Founded: 1969
EIN: 942474426
Organization Type: Corporate Foundation
Giving Locations: CA: Los Angeles, San Francisco; IL: Chicago; NY: New York headquarters and operating locations.
Grant Types: Employee Matching Gifts, General Support.
Note: Employee matching gift ratio: 1 to 1 up to $2,000 per employee annually, including monies raised by employees via pledges collected for official fundraising events carried on by charitable organizations.

Giving Philosophy

Gap Inc. is committed to helping youth and supporting HIV/AIDS prevention programs.
'One of the primary way we help young people is by supporting youth learning programs that help kids develop self-esteem, stay in school, become inspired by dynamic teachers and visionary leaders, and succeed academically so they can grow up to lead rewarding and fulfilling lives.'
'Our long-standing commitment to help eradicate HIV/AIDS primarily focuses on prevention programs that work to reduce the risk of HIV infection among young people in under-served communities. We're particularly concerned about young people whose behavior or life circumstances-such as substance abuse or homelessness-may increase their risk of infection.'
'Our community relations program leverages committed employee volunteers in offices, distribution centers and stores around the world. Employees are linked to volunteer opportunities and board memberships through volunteermatch.org administered by Impact Online.
'Gap Foundation, the charitable arm of our program, provides funding to a few national and local organizations we've identified as meeting our community relations' mission.' Gap Community Relations and Gap Foundation website.

Financial Summary

Total Giving: $9,500,000 (fiscal year ending January 31, 1999 approx); $7,500,000 (fiscal 1998 approx); $2,114,514 (fiscal 1997). Note: Contributes through corporate direct giving program only.
Giving Analysis: Giving for fiscal 1998 includes: foundation ($1,961,033); foundation matching gifts ($1,112,095); fiscal 1999: corporate direct giving (approx $4,000,000); foundation (approx $3,500,000)
Assets: $12,850,812 (fiscal 1999); $9,100,000 (fiscal 1998 approx); $9,416,396 (fiscal 1997)
Gifts Received: $7,622,293 (fiscal 1997); $2,750,000 (fiscal 1996); $3,375,000 (fiscal 1995). Note: Contributions are received from The Gap, Inc.

Typical Recipients

Arts & Humanities: Arts Associations & Councils, Arts Centers, Arts Outreach, Dance, Arts & Humanities-General, Historic Preservation, Libraries, Museums/Galleries, Music, Opera, Performing Arts, Public Broadcasting, Theater, Visual Arts
Civic & Public Affairs: African American Affairs, Asian American Affairs, Botanical Gardens/Parks, Business/Free Enterprise, Civil Rights, Community Foundations, Economic Development, Employment/Job Training, Gay/Lesbian Issues, Civic & Public Affairs-General, Hispanic Affairs, Housing, Legal Aid, Municipalities/Towns, Nonprofit Management, Philanthropic Organizations, Urban & Community Affairs, Zoos/Aquariums
Education: Afterschool/Enrichment Programs, Arts/Humanities Education, Business Education, Colleges & Universities, Community & Junior Colleges, Education Funds, Leadership Training, Minority Education, Private Education (Precollege), Public Education (Precollege), Religious Education, School Volunteerism, Science/Mathematics Education
Environment: Air/Water Quality, Forestry, Environment-General, Protection, Resource Conservation, Watershed, Wildlife Protection
Health: AIDS/HIV, Cancer, Clinics/Medical Centers, Emergency/Ambulance Services, Health Funds, Health Organizations, Hospices, Hospitals, Medical Research, Prenatal Health Issues, Preventive Medicine/Wellness Organizations, Public Health, Research/Studies Institutes, Single-Disease Health Associations, Transplant Networks/Donor Banks, Trauma Treatment
International: International Relief Efforts, Missionary/Religious Activities
Religion: Churches, Religious Welfare
Science: Science-General, Science Museums, Scientific Centers & Institutes
Social Services: Camps, Child Welfare, Community Centers, Community Service Organizations, Day Care, Delinquency & Criminal Rehabilitation, Domestic Violence, Family Services, Food/Clothing Distribution, Recreation & Athletics, Senior Services, Shelters/Homelessness, United Funds/United Ways,

Volunteer Services, YMCA/YWCA/YMHA/YWHA, Youth Organizations

Contributions Analysis

Giving Priorities: Foundation has two primary focus areas: Youth and Business and HIV/AIDS Education and Prevention.

Youth and Business is a new program area created to help low-income youth ages 14-21 define their future and learn about the world of business. The programs has two components--enterprise education and business exploration--giving young people hands-on experience starting and running a business, and gain the skills they need to make informed decisions about their future professional lives. The foundation targets programs that introduce young people to careers in business, and provide opportunities for in-depth, on-the-job education that builds know-how from experience.

HIV/AIDS related programs will target underserved and at-risk youth ages 14-21.

Note: Gap divisional programs will initiate community activities by individual Gap, Inc. brands, with an emphasis on the metropolitan areas of Chicago, Los Angeles, New York, and San Francisco. Gap's Sourcing pilot program will focus giving on garment workers and the communities in which they live, especially overseas.

Application Procedures

Initial Contact: Gap, Inc. has revised application procedures for the Community Relations Program; not currently accepting applications.

Deadlines: None.

Restrictions

Does not donate to individuals, fund scholarships, political candidates, religious organizations for sectarian purposes, travel, films, conferences, videos, promotional tie-ins or sponsorships, or fundraising benefits.

Additional Information

The company reports that it will continue to donate 1% of its pre-tax earnings to charitable giving.

The Gap's divisions include Banana Republic, Gap Stores, GapKids, BabyGap, Gap Shoes, Gap Warehouses, and Old Navy.

The Gap reports that it donates cash, gift certificates, and limited contributions of merchandise.

Publications: Annual Report; Funding Guidelines

Corporate Officials

Millard S. Drexler: president, chief executive officer, director B New York, NY 1944. ED State University of New York Buffalo BS; Boston University MBA (1968). PRIM CORP EMPL president, chief executive officer, director: Gap, Inc. CORP AFFIL president: Banana Republic Inc.; director: Williams-Sonoma Inc.; president, chief executive officer, director: Ann Taylor Stores.

Donald George Fisher: founder, chairman, director B 1928. ED University of California BS (1950). PRIM CORP EMPL founder, chairman, director: Gap Inc. CORP AFFIL chairman: Banana Republic Inc.; director: Charles Schwab Corp.

Anne Gust: executive vice president human resources, legal, administration PRIM CORP EMPL executive vice president human resources, legal, administration: Gap Inc.

Anne B. Gust: executive vice president, chief administrative officer ED Stanford University (1980); University of Michigan JD (1983). PRIM CORP EMPL executive vice president, chief administrative officer: Gap Inc.

Heidi Kunz: executive vice president, chief financial officer PRIM CORP EMPL executive vice president, chief financial officer: Gap Inc.

Kenneth S. Pilot: president Gap brand PRIM CORP EMPL president Gap brand: Gap Inc.

Giving Program Officials

Dynell Garron: director

Foundation Officials

Myra Chow: director

Millard S. Drexler: trustee (see above)

Donald George Fisher: president (see above)

Doris F. Fisher: treasurer B 1931. CORP AFFIL director: The Gap Inc.

Robert J. Fisher: vice president (see above)

Dottie Hatcher: senior director

Grants Analysis

Disclosure Period: fiscal year ending January 31, 1999

Total Grants: $1,961,033*

Number of Grants: 147

Average Grant: $13,340

Highest Grant: $137,000

Typical Range: $5,000 to $15,000

*Note: Giving excludes matching gifts.

Recent Grants

Note: Grants derived from 1999 Form 990.

Arts & Humanities

250,000 Old Globe Theatre, San Diego, CA
200,000 San Diego Natural History Museum, San Diego, CA
125,000 La Jolla Playhouse, La Jolla, CA
100,000 KPBS, San Diego, CA
100,000 Museum of Contemporary Art, San Diego, CA
100,000 Museum of Photographic Art, San Diego, CA
33,000 Elijah Iles House Foundation, Springfield, IL
25,000 Iris & B. Gerald Canter Center for Visual Arts, Stanford, CA
19,000 San Diego Model Railroad Museum, San Diego, CA
15,000 New Conservatory Theater, San Francisco, CA
15,000 Under One Roof, San Francisco, CA
10,000 Joliet American Legion Band, Joliet, IL
10,000 Oceanside Museum of Art, Oceanside, CA
10,000 San Diego Museum of Man, San Diego, CA
10,000 San Diego Opera, San Diego, CA
10,000 San Francisco Community Music Center, San Francisco, CA
10,000 Sledgehammer Theatre, San Diego, CA
5,000 La Jolla Chamber Music Society, SummerFest, La Jolla, CA

Civic & Public Affairs

137,000 Delancey St. Foundation, San Francisco, CA
125,000 Global Education Partnership, Oakland, CA
75,000 Global Education Partneship, Oakland, CA
35,000 Citizens Committee for New York City, New York, NY
35,000 Northern California Grantmakers, San Francisco, CA
25,000 Eureka San Diego, San Diego
25,000 San Francisco Foundation Community Initiatives Fund, San Francisco, CA
20,000 NY Citywide School-to-Work Alliance, New York, NY
15,000 Entrepreneurial Development Institute, Washington, DC
15,000 San Francisco Foundation, San Francisco, CA
14,000 New York Community Trust, New York, NY
10,000 California Tomorrow, San Francisco
10,000 Committee to Protect Journalists, New York, NY
10,000 Joliet/Will County Project--Police Memorial Fund, Joliet, IL
10,000 Mutual Ground Inc., Aurora, IL
5,000 San Diego Organizing Project, San Diego, CA
5,000 Skill Centers of America, San Diego, CA

Education

43,509 Bradley University, Peoria, IL
40,000 United Negro College Fund, Fairfax, VA
35,000 National Foundation for Teaching Entrepreneurs
20,000 National Retail Institute, Washington, DC
16,000 Independent Colleges of Southern California, Los Angeles, CA
15,000 San Francisco Education Fund, San Francisco, CA
12,000 Bishop's School, The, La Jolla, CA
10,000 Fresno Public Education Fund, Fresno, CA
10,000 San Diego State University, San Diego, CA -- Border Voices
5,000 Julian Educational Foundation, Julian, CA

Environment

25,000 NRDC, San Francisco, CA
15,000 Certitied Forest Products Council, Beaverton, OR
15,000 Tree People Inc., Beverly Hills, CA
15,000 World Wildlife Fund, Washington, DC
10,000 Adopt-A-Watershed, San Francisco, CA
10,000 Yosemite National Institute, Sausallito, CA

Health

100,000 Scripps Foundation for Medicine, La Jolla, CA
50,000 American Red Cross, Washington, DC
30,000 Mission Neighborhood Health Center, San Francisco, CA
30,000 Wellness Center, Pasadena, CA
20,000 Black Coalition on AIDS, San Francisco, CA
16,666 Silver Cross Hospital Foundation, Joliet, IL
15,000 Alliance Healthcare Foundation/AIDS Collaboration, San Diego, CA
15,000 Black Coalition on AIDS, San Francisco, CA
10,000 Burn Institute, San Diego, CA
10,000 Hospice - San Diego, San Diego, CA
10,000 San Diego Blood Bank Foundation, San Diego, CA
5,000 Little Company of Mary Hospital Foundation, Torrance, CA
5,000 North County Health Services, Lompoc, CA
5,000 Wellness Community San Diego, San Diego, CA

International

20,000 South American Missionary Society, Ambridge, PA

Religion

60,000 St. Vincent DePaul Village, San Diego, CA
5,000 Saint Clare's Home, San Diego, CA

Science

50,000 San Diego Space & Science Foundation, San Diego, CA
15,000 Exploratorium, San Francisco, CA
10,000 Elementary Institute of Science, San Diego, CA
10,000 Marine Science Institute, Redwood, CA

Social Services

130,000 The Door 121 Avenue of the Americas, New York, NY
100,000 San Diego Hall of Champions, San Diego, CA

100,000	Youth Industries, San Francisco, CA
75,000	Columbia Park Boys & Girls Club, San Francisco, CA
45,000	San Francisco Works-The United Way, San Francisco, CA
35,000	KidsWay, Inc., Riverdale, NY
33,639	San Diego Union-Tribune Shoe Fund, San Diego, CA
25,000	Community Center Project, San Francisco, CA
25,000	For All Kids, New York, NY
25,000	Project Open Hand, San Francisco, CA
25,000	San Diego Crew Classic, San Diego, CA
20,000	Boys & Girls Clubs Fresno County, Fresno, CA
20,000	Noah Homes, Spring Valley, CA
20,000	Volunteer Center of San Francisco, San Francisco, CA
17,000	Victim Services, Inc., New York, NY
15,000	YMCA - Copley Family, La Jolla, CA
10,000	Children Now, Oakland, CA
10,000	Family Violence Prevention Fund, San Francisco, CA
10,000	Huckleberry Youth Program, San Francisco, CA
10,000	Incarnation Children's Center, New York, NY
10,000	Matthews-Dickey Boys' Club, St. Louis, MO
10,000	Meals-On-Wheels, Inc., San Diego, CA
10,000	Project Open Hand, San Francisco, CA
6,500	Help Them to Hope, San Diego, CA
5,000	Hugh O'Brian Youth Leadership, Los Angeles, CA
5,000	Senior Community Centers of San Diego, San Diego, CA
5,000	YMCA - San Diego County, San Diego, CA

GATES RUBBER CORP.

Company Contact
Denver, CO

Company Description
Former Name: Gates Corp.
Employees: 14,000
SIC(s): 3069 Fabricated Rubber Products Nec, 3714 Motor Vehicle Parts & Accessories.

Nonmonetary Support
Type: In-kind Services

Corporate Sponsorship
Note: Corporate sponsorship is coordinated by a committee.

Giving Contact
Anita Boone, Administrative Assistant
Gates Rubber Corp.
990 S. Broadway
50-1-2-A1
Denver, CO 80209
Phone: (303)744-4488
Fax: (303)744-4000

Description
Organization Type: Corporate Giving Program
Giving Locations: CO: Denver including immediate metropolitan area
Grant Types: Employee Matching Gifts, General Support.

Financial Summary
Total Giving: Contributes through corporate direct giving program only.

Typical Recipients
Arts & Humanities: Arts & Humanities-General
Civic & Public Affairs: Civic & Public Affairs-General
Education: Education-General
Health: Health-General
Social Services: Social Services-General

Application Procedures
Initial Contact: written proposal
Application Requirements: a description of organization, amount requested, purpose of funds sought, recently audited financial statements, and proof of tax-exempt status
Deadlines: None.
Decision Notification: contributions committee meets once a month

Restrictions
Does not support political or lobbying groups or tax-supported institutions.

Corporate Officials
John M. Riess: chairman B 1942. PRIM CORP EMPL chairman: Gates Corp. ADD CORP EMPL vice president: Formed-Fibre Gates Products; president: Gates Export Corp.

Foundation Officials
Irene McKay: admin assistant

GATX CORP.

Company Contact
Chicago, IL
Web: http://www.gatx.com

Company Description
Income: US$1,858,900,000 (1999)
Employees: 6,000 (1999)
SIC(s): 4432 Freight Transportation on the Great Lakes, 4613 Refined Petroleum Pipelines, 4741 Rental of Railroad Cars, 6159 Miscellaneous Business Credit Institutions.

Operating Locations
Australia: Australasian Asset Residual Management, Sydney; GATX Financial Services (Australia) Pty. Ltd., Sydney; Belgium: Gamatex N.V., Antwerp; General Dynamics International Corporation, Brussels; Computer Systems and Communications Overseas Office, Chievres; Canada: CGTX Calgary Office, Calgary; Computing Devices Canada Calgary Operation, Calgary; CGTX, Inc., Montreal; Computing Devices Canada, Nepean; GATX National Leasing, Ltd., Toronto; Egypt: General Dynamics Services Company, Cairo; England: Computing Devices Company Ltd., St. Leonards-on-Sea, E. Sussex; Computing Devices Company Ltd. Churchfields Site, St. Leonards-on-Sea, E. Sussex; France: GATX International Ltd.; CD Plus S.A., Paris; Germany: GATX Financial Services GmbH, Frankfurt, Hessen; Japan: Kawasaki Terminal, Kawasaki; Kobe Terminal, Kobe; GATX Capital Corporation Japanese Liason Office, Tokyo; Nippon Chemical Handling, Tokyo; Nippon GATX Co., Ltd., Tokyo; Showa GATX Company, Ltd., Tokyo; Yokohama Terminal, Yokohama; Mexico: GATX Logistics de Mexico, S.A. de C.V., Cuautitlan Izcalli; Gulfstream Aerospace, Mexicali; Netherlands: Continental European Representative Office, Rotterdam; Saudi Arabia: General Dynamics International Corporation, Riyadh; Mansour General Dynamics Ltd., Riyadh; Singapore: GATX Leasing (Pacific) Ltd.; GATX Private Ltd., Jurong; GATX Terminals (Pte.) Ltd., Jurong; Asia Representative Office, Singapore; Tankstore Pte. Ltd., Singapore; Spain: Produimica, S.A., Barcelona; Terminals Portuarias, S.A., Barcelona; Barcelona Terminal, Barcelona, Cataluna; Tarragona Terminal, Tarragona; Valencia Terminal, Valencia; Bilbao Terminal, Vizcaya, Ciervana; United Kingdom: Avonmouth Terminal, Avonmouth, Bristol; Belfast Terminal, Belfast; Edinburgh Terminal, Edinburgh; United Kingdom Lombard Network Services Ltd., Elstree, Hertfordshire; Glasgow Terminal, Glasgow; Gradys Terminal, Grays, Essex; GATX Finance (UK) Ltd., Kingston upon Thames, Surrey; GATX Terminals Ltd., Maidenhead, Berks; Unipen Ltd., Maidenhead, Berkshire; Unitank Storage Co. Ltd., Maidenhead, Berkshire; Tees Storage Company Ltd., Middlesbrough, Cleveland; Runcorn Terminal, Runcorn, Cheshire; GATX Asset Residual Management P.L.C., Woking, Surrey; Wymondham Oil Storage Company Ltd., Wymondham, Norfolk

Nonmonetary Support
Value: $100,000 (1999 approx); $106,000 (1996); $60,000 (1994)
Type: Donated Equipment; In-kind Services; Workplace Solicitation
Volunteer Programs: GATX employees nationwide are recognized for volunteer efforts from tutoring students to building playgrounds. GATX presents its Spirit of Volunteerism Award twice a year to honor those whose best exemplify principles of community service, teamwork, and good corporate citizenship.
Contact: Jessie Kane, Program Coordinator

Giving Contact
Christiane S. Wilczura, Manager, Community Affairs
GATX Corp.
500 West Monroe Street
Chicago, IL 60661-3676
Phone: (312)621-6221
Fax: (312)621-6677
Email: cswilzura@gatx.com

Description
Organization Type: Corporate Giving Program
Giving Locations: IL: Chicago operating locations.
Grant Types: Challenge, Employee Matching Gifts, General Support, Matching, Multiyear/Continuing Support, Operating Expenses, Project, Seed Money.

Giving Philosophy
'GATX's highest priority is to support programs which address underlying conditions that cause or contribute to our community's social and economic problems by strengthening the individual's ability to function..-priorities also include the cultural, civic, health care, and educational initiatives that strive to fill the needs of Chicago's economically disadvantaged population.' *GATX Corporation, Contributions Program Policy and Guidelines*

Financial Summary
Total Giving: $1,600,000 (2000 approx); $1,600,000 (1999 approx); $1,500,000 (1997 approx). Note: Contributes through corporate direct giving program only. Giving includes corporate direct giving; domestic subsidiaries. 1997 Giving includes corporate direct giving. 1996 Giving includes corporate direct giving; nonmonetary support.

Typical Recipients
Arts & Humanities: Arts Associations & Councils, Arts Institutes, Arts Outreach, Community Arts, Dance, Ethnic & Folk Arts, Historic Preservation, Libraries, Museums/Galleries, Music, Opera, Performing Arts, Public Broadcasting, Theater, Visual Arts
Civic & Public Affairs: Botanical Gardens/Parks, Civil Rights, Economic Development, Employment/Job Training, Housing, Public Policy, Urban & Community Affairs, Women's Affairs, Zoos/Aquariums
Education: Afterschool/Enrichment Programs, Arts/Humanities Education, Colleges & Universities, Education Associations, Education Reform, Elementary Education (Private), Faculty Development, Education-General, Literacy, Minority Education, Preschool Education, Private Education (Precollege), Science/

Mathematics Education, Special Education, Student Aid
Health: AIDS/HIV, Cancer, Clinics/Medical Centers, Geriatric Health, Health Organizations, Hospices, Hospitals, Medical Rehabilitation, Mental Health, Nutrition, Public Health, Single-Disease Health Associations
International: Human Rights
Religion: Religious Welfare
Science: Science Museums
Social Services: At-Risk Youth, Child Abuse, Child Welfare, Community Centers, Community Service Organizations, Counseling, Delinquency & Criminal Rehabilitation, Domestic Violence, Family Services, Food/Clothing Distribution, People with Disabilities, Senior Services, Shelters/Homelessness, Substance Abuse, United Funds/United Ways, Youth Organizations

Contributions Analysis

Giving Priorities: Social welfare, education, and the environment.
Education: Supports a variety of educational programs for economically disadvantaged children and youth. Progrmas focus on: intellectual and emotional development, academic and social preparation for high school and college; academic support to youth in higher education; arts education; and adult literacy education.
Environment: Funds programs that: address air and water pollution; water or land preservation; beautification; and preservation.
Social Services: Supports programs that: provide adults with skills training and placement services; prevent domestic and community violence; provide families with access to quality health care; enhance family communications and improve parenting capabilities; and work to provide affordable housing to families.

Application Procedures

Initial Contact: Call or write for an application form; then submit a written proposal.
Application Requirements: Proposal should include: statement of purpose and history of organization; current program activities and goals, specifics regarding particular project to be funded; itemized budget for the organization, with both projected revenues and expenses for the current fiscal year; current program budget; current sources of revenue; audited financial statement or Form 990 for the most recently completed fiscal year; grantee report using GATX form, if funded in the previous year; annual report; list of board members and affiliations; proof of tax-exempt status; it funded in prior year, grantee report using the Chicago Area Common Report Form.
Deadlines: By the 15th day of January, April, July, or October.
Review Process: The initial review is done by the manager; further review and decision is made by the contributions committee on a quarterly basis.
Evaluative Criteria: Evaluation is based on the involvement of company employees in organization; geographical area served; efficiency of structure and management; cost of fund-raising activities; existence or level of government funding; evidence of broad community support; proven effectiveness of organization in meeting community needs; potential of program to become self-sustaining; and the impact on the community.
Decision Notification: Completed applications will be acknowledge in writing; final decisions at meetings in February, May, August, and November, and as necessary.

Restrictions

Corporation does not support individuals; political organizations; religious organizations for sectarian purposes; trips, conferences, or tours; courtesy advertising; tickets for testimonials or similar benefit events for which only a fraction of the ticket price goes to the designated nonprofit sponsor; organizations which lack status as a 501(c) (3) organization or equivalent; capital campaigns; endowment funds; national organizations; land acquisition; deficit financing; member organizations of united funds for general operating support; organizations or programs which pose a potential conflict of interest; social, fraternal, athletic, labor, or veterans' groups serving a limited constituency. organizations or programs which pose a potential conflict of interest; social, fraternal, athletic, labor, or veterans' groups serving a limited constituency.

Additional Information

Recipients must submit progress reports as a condition of funding.
Grant renewals are not automatic.
Publications: Guidelines; Grants List; Application Form

Corporate Officials

David M. Edwards: vice president finance, chief financial officero, chief operating officer B Berkeley, CA 1951. ED University of California, Davis AB (1973); University of California, Davis MA (1975). PRIM CORP EMPL vice president finance, chief financial officer: GATX Corp. CORP AFFIL director: GATX Terminals Corp.; director: General American Transportation Corp.; member: Finance Executive Institute; director: GATX Capital Corp.
Ronald H. Zech: chairman, president, chief executive officer, chief operating officer B Reedsburg, WI 1943. ED Valparaiso University BSEE (1965); University of Wisconsin MBA (1967). PRIM CORP EMPL chairman, president, chief executive officer, chief operating officer: GATX Corp. CORP AFFIL president, chief executive officer: GATX Capital Corp.; director: McGrath Rentcorp.

Giving Program Officials

Debbie Dobson: vice president
Todd Emro: director
John Klyczek: director
Donald J. Schaffer: member contributions committee B Des Moines, IA 1956. ED Illinois State University (1978); Northwestern University (1988). PRIM CORP EMPL vice president finance, chief financial officer: General American Transportation Corp. NONPR AFFIL member: American Institute CPAs; member: Financial Executives Institute.
Paul Sholty: director
Don Spooner: vice president business development
Christiane S. Wilczura: manager community affairs

Grants Analysis

Disclosure Period: calendar year ending 1998
Total Grants: $1,200,000*
Number of Grants: 80
Average Grant: $10,000
Highest Grant: $67,000
Typical Range: $10,000 to $15,000
***Note:** Grants analysis provided by the corporation. Giving excludes nonmonetary support.

Recent Grants

Note: Grants derived from 1996 grants list.

Arts & Humanities

50,000	Music and Dance Theater -- capital campaign
50,000	Music and Dance Theater -- capital campaign
15,000	Hubbard Street Dance Company -- for outreach coordinator, program support
10,000	Museum of Contemporary Art, Los Angeles, CA -- support event
10,000	Shakespeare Repertory, Chicago, IL -- for Team Shakespeare
10,000	Steppenwolf Theater Company, Chicago, IL -- educational outreach
7,500	Chicago Children's Museum, Chicago, IL -- for Teen Initiative
7,500	Pegasus Players, Chicago, IL -- for Young Playwrights Festival
6,500	Chicago Youth Symphony Orchestra, Chicago, IL
6,000	Chicago Symphony Orchestra, Chicago, IL -- cultural enrichment program

Civic & Public Affairs

25,000	Chicago Botanic Garden, Chicago, IL -- for Green Chicago Program
9,000	Lakefront Single Room Occupancy, Chicago, IL -- for on-site social services
8,000	Jobs for Youth, Chicago, IL
7,500	Midwest Women's Center, Chicago, IL -- for Working Knowledge Program
7,500	Public Allies the National Center for Careers in Public Life, Washington, DC -- for Apprenticeship Program
7,000	Constitutional Rights Foundation, Los Angeles, CA -- for Law in My Life
6,000	John G. Shedd Aquarium, Chicago, IL -- educational, outreach programs

Education

20,000	Associated Colleges of Illinois, Chicago, IL -- for North Central College's Inner-City Tutoring Program, Rosary College's Tutoring Program with Farren School
14,442	Waterford Institute, Provo, UT -- for Early Reading Program at Farren School
12,500	National Lekotek Center, Evanston, IL -- for Lekotek of West Humboldt Park
10,000	Art Institute, Chicago, IL -- for Art Volunteers in the Classroom Program
10,000	Cabrini Connections, Chicago, IL -- tutor/mentor programs
10,000	Chicago Youth Centers, Chicago, IL -- for Lower North Center After School Program
10,000	Suzuki-Off School for Young Musicians -- for Project Image
10,000	Target Hope, Chicago, IL -- for Academic Achievement Program
8,500	Golden Apple Foundation, Chicago, IL -- for Golden Apple Scholars
7,500	Christopher House, Chicago, IL -- for CLASS Program
7,500	Lincoln Park Zoological Society, Chicago, IL -- for Summer Science Program
7,500	Pace Institute, Chicago, IL -- Literacy Program at Cook County Jail
7,036	Ada S. McKinley Community Service, Chicago, IL -- Early Intervention Tutoring Program
7,000	Hug-A-Book, Chicago, IL
7,000	Midtown Educational Foundation, Chicago, IL -- for Metro Achievement Center College Program

Health

10,000	Northwestern Memorial Hospital, Chicago, IL -- support event
10,000	Rehabilitation Institute, Chicago, IL -- for Free Care Program
8,500	Family Institute, San Diego, CA -- for Mental Health Program at Byrd Academy
8,000	Mental Health Association, Chicago, IL -- for Site Visitation Program
7,500	Uptown Community Learning Center, Chicago, IL -- for Year III of Campaign for Basic Health

International

45,000	Heartland Alliance for Human Needs and Human Rights, Chicago, IL -- for Neon Street Programs
45,000	Heartland Alliance for Human Needs and Human Rights, Chicago, IL -- for Neon Street Programs

Religion

15,000	Bonaventure House, Chicago, IL -- for housing services, support services
10,000	St. Martin de Porres House of Hope, Chicago, IL

Science

7,500	Museum of Science and Industry, Chicago, IL -- for Role Models and Leaders Project

Social Services

23,600	Robert Crown Center for Health Education, Hinsdale, IL -- for Farren School Family Life
20,000	Rainbow House/Arco Iris, Chicago, IL -- for Adolescent Services
20,000	Teen Living Programs, Chicago, IL -- for Belfort House
17,500	Big Shoulders Fund, Chicago, IL -- counseling services
15,000	Voices of Illinois Children, IL
12,500	Greater Chicago Food Depository, Chicago, IL -- for Food Rescue Program
12,500	Illinois Action for Children, Chicago, IL -- for Court-Appointed Special Advocates Program
10,000	Lawrence Hall Youth Services, Lawrence, IL -- for Independent Living Program
10,000	National Committee for the Prevention of Child Abuse, Chicago, IL -- for Healthy Families America North Lawndale

GEICO CORP.

Company Contact

Washington, DC
Web: http://www.directnet.geico.com

Company Description

Revenue: US$2,720,000,000
Profit: US$247,600,000
Employees: 8,151
SIC(s): 6311 Life Insurance, 6321 Accident & Health Insurance, 6331 Fire, Marine & Casualty Insurance, 6719 Holding Companies Nec.

Nonmonetary Support

Type: Donated Equipment; In-kind Services
Note: Annual nonmonetary support $20,000.

GEICO Philanthropic Foundation

Giving Contact

Karen Watson, Administrator
GEICO Philanthropic Foundation
c/o GEICO Corp.
1 Geico Plz.
Washington, DC 20076
Phone: (301)986-2387
Fax: (301)718-5239

Description

EIN: 521202740
Organization Type: Corporate Foundation
Giving Locations: organizations serving operating locations.
Grant Types: Employee Matching Gifts, General Support, Project, Research, Scholarship.

Giving Philosophy

'The philanthropic foundation makes contributions.. in five major areas: civic initiatives; educational enrichment; artistic and cultural endeavors; health and human services; and insurance-related programs.'

Financial Summary

Total Giving: $2,423,107 (1998); $1,912,843 (1997); $1,751,079 (1996). Note: Contributes through corporate direct giving program and foundation.
Giving Analysis: Giving for 1997 includes: foundation ($1,249,176); foundation grants to United Way ($546,674); foundation scholarships ($116,993); 1998: foundation ($2,423,107)
Assets: $26,356,847 (1998); $17,447,268 (1997); $13,665,694 (1996)
Gifts Received: $7,855,000 (1998); $2,655,000 (1997); $2,050,000 (1996). Note: Contributions were received from the Government Employees Insurance Company, Leo Goodwin Foundation, and The Byrne Foundation.

Typical Recipients

Arts & Humanities: Arts Associations & Councils, Community Arts, Arts & Humanities-General, Historic Preservation, Museums/Galleries, Music, Opera, Performing Arts, Public Broadcasting, Theater
Civic & Public Affairs: African American Affairs, Business/Free Enterprise, Economic Development, Employment/Job Training, Civic & Public Affairs-General, Housing, Law & Justice, Nonprofit Management, Parades/Festivals, Philanthropic Organizations, Professional & Trade Associations, Public Policy, Safety, Urban & Community Affairs
Education: Business Education, Colleges & Universities, Community & Junior Colleges, Education Associations, Education Funds, Education-General, Minority Education, Religious Education, Science/Mathematics Education, Secondary Education (Public), Special Education, Student Aid
Environment: Environment-General
Health: Cancer, Children's Health/Hospitals, Emergency/Ambulance Services, Heart, Hospices, Hospitals, Medical Rehabilitation, Medical Research, Mental Health, Public Health, Single-Disease Health Associations
International: International Relief Efforts
Religion: Social/Policy Issues
Science: Scientific Centers & Institutes
Social Services: Animal Protection, Child Welfare, Community Centers, Community Service Organizations, Counseling, Emergency Relief, Family Services, Food/Clothing Distribution, Homes, People with Disabilities, Recreation & Athletics, Scouts, Senior Services, Special Olympics, Substance Abuse, United Funds/United Ways, Veterans, Youth Organizations

Contributions Analysis

Giving Priorities: Social welfare, civic projects, higher education, hospital facilities, and performing arts.
Arts & Humanities: Less than 5%. Grants focus on performing arts, including symphonies and theaters, museums, historical societies, and others.
Civic & Public Affairs: 35% to 40%. Majority of funding supports the National Safety Association and other safety programs. Other grants support environmental projects, professional organizations, and groups promoting better government.
Education: 10% to 15%. Supports colleges and universities, with emphasis on business education. Also matches employee gifts to higher education. Other recipients include educational fund-raising organizations and scholarship foundations.
Health: About 5%. Funds go primarily to hospitals and single-disease research organizations. Some support is to hospices and other facilities.
Social Services: About 45% of contributions. Primarily supports united funds. Other major recipients include child welfare and recreation groups, programs for the mentally retarded and disabled, and family services.

Application Procedures

Initial Contact: Send a brief letter or proposal.
Application Requirements: Include a description and purpose of organization, statement on organization's management, amount of request, purpose of funds sought, other sources of income, operating budget, recently audited financial statement, proof of tax-exempt status.
Deadlines: None.
Review Process: All requests reviewed by company's Social Responsibility Task Force.

Restrictions

Foundation does not give to political or religious groups.
GEICO Philanthropic Foundation only contributes to 501(c)(3) organizations.

Corporate Officials

Charles Gerard Schara: treasurer, president B Rockville Centre, NY 1952. ED College of the Holy Cross BA (1974). PRIM CORP EMPL treasurer: GEICO Corp. ADD CORP EMPL treasurer: Government Employees Insurance Co.; treasurer, director: GEICO Casualty Co.; treasurer: GEICO Indemnity Co. NONPR AFFIL member: American Institute CPAs; member: Institute Internal Auditors.
Louis Allen Simpson: president, chief executive officer capital operations, director B Chicago, IL 1936. ED Northwestern University (1954-1955); Ohio Wesleyan University BA (1958); Princeton University AM (1960). PRIM CORP EMPL president, chief executive officer capital operations, director: GEICO Corp. CORP AFFIL director: Potomac Electric Power Co.; director: SAIC; director: Pacific America Income Shares Inc.; director: Potomac Capital Investment Corp.; director: LM Institutional Fund Advisors 1 Inc.; director: Media One Group Inc.; director: Cohr Inc. NONPR AFFIL member: San Diego Society Financial Analysts; trustee: Woodrow Wilson National Fellowship Foundation; member endowment committee: Ohio Wesleyan University; trustee: Cate School; regent: Loyola Marymount University. CLUB AFFIL Metropolitan Club; Chevy Chase Club; Los Angeles Country Club; Arts Chicago Club; California Club.
Donald Kaye Smith: senior vice president, general counsel, director B Berea, OH 1932. ED University of Maryland BA (1954); George Washington University JD (1957). PRIM CORP EMPL senior vice president, general counsel, director: GEICO Corp. CORP AFFIL director: Resolute Reins Co.; secretary: Southern Heritage Insurance Co.; secretary: Merastar Insurance Co.; chairman: GEICO Washington Properties Inc.; director: Government Employees Fin Corp.; chairman: GEICO Properties Inc.; director: Garden Saint Life Insurance Co.; general coun, director: GEICO General Insurance Co.; general coun, director: Criterion Casualty Insurance Co. NONPR AFFIL member: Sigma Phi Epsilon; trustee: Washington Opera; member: Phi Alpha Delta; member, board governors: Republic National Lawyers Association; trustee: Greater Washington Board Trade Legislative Bureau; trustee, treasurer: Maryland Board Trade; trustee: Fed City Council; member, director: American Corporate Counsel Association; director: DC Bar Association; director: American Bar Association. CLUB AFFIL Scottish Rite Club; Terrapin Club; Rotary Club; Johns Island Club; Masons Club; Columbia Country Club.
Edward Harold Utley: vice chairman, president B 1929. ED University of Colorado BS (1951). PRIM CORP EMPL vice chairman, president: GEICO Corp. ADD CORP EMPL senior vice president: Government Employees Insurance Co. CORP AFFIL director: Safe Driver Motor Club Inc.

Foundation Officials

August Paul Alegi: director B Yonkers, NY 1943. ED Pace University (1968); American University (1972). PRIM CORP EMPL group vice president: GEICO Indemnity Co. CORP AFFIL partner: Mirel & Alegi.

Charles R. Davies: president, general counsel, director B Pittsburgh, PA 1940. ED Duquesne University BS (1964); Georgetown University Law Center JD (1967). PRIM CORP EMPL vice president, general counsel: GEICO Corp. ADD CORP EMPL vice president, general counsel, director: Government Employees Insurance Co.
Carroll R. Franklin: director PRIM CORP EMPL vice president: GEICO Casualty Co.
Merrill Donaldson Knight, III: director B Lynchburg, VA 1930. ED George Washington University (1951); George Washington University Law School (1957). PRIM CORP EMPL vice president human resources: GEICO Corp. NONPR AFFIL member: International Association Insurance Council.
John J. Krieger: director PRIM CORP EMPL chairman emeritus: Interstate Johnson Lane Space Smith & Co.
Rosalind Ann Phillips: secretary B Columbia, MO 1941. ED University of Missouri (1962); University of Missouri (1969). PRIM CORP EMPL secretary: GEICO Corp. ADD CORP EMPL secretary: Government Employees Fin Corp.; secretary: GEICO Financial Services Inc.; secretary: GEICO General Insurance Co.; secretary: GEICO Products Inc.; secretary: GEICO Casualty Co.; secretary: GEICO Indemnity Co. CORP AFFIL secretary: Safe Driver Motor Club Inc.; secretary: Plaza Fin Services Co.; secretary: Plaza Resources Co.; secretary: Insurance Counselors Inc.; secretary: MD Ventures Inc.; secretary: Government Employees Insurance Co. NONPR AFFIL member: American Society of Corporate Secretaries.
Myrtle N. Pitsenbarger: assistant secretary
Charles Gerard Schara: assistant treasurer, director (see above)
Walter Alvon Sparks, Jr.: director B Newark, DE 1935. ED University of Delaware BS (1958). PRIM CORP EMPL executive vice president, chief financial officer, director: GEICO Corp. NONPR AFFIL member: American Institute CPAs; member: Financial Executives Institute.
Edward Harold Utley: chairman, director (see above)
Karen Watson: administrator

Grants Analysis

Disclosure Period: calendar year ending 1997
Total Grants: $1,249,176*
Number of Grants: 757
Average Grant: $1,152*
Highest Grant: $189,809
Typical Range: $500 to $5,000
***Note:** Giving excludes scholarship and United Way. Average grant figure excludes two highest grants totaling $379,559.

Recent Grants

Note: Grants derived from 1997 Form 990.

Arts & Humanities

10,000	Strathmore Hall Foundation, North Bethesda, MD
5,000	Kennedy Center for the Performing Arts, Washington, DC

Civic & Public Affairs

189,810	NAII Safety Association, Des Plaines, IL
189,750	NAII Safety Association, Des Plaines, IL
22,178	Council for Court Excellence, Washington, DC
20,000	District Curators, Washington, DC
20,000	Maryland ACT Committee, Washington, DC
15,000	Jubilee Jobs, Washington, DC
10,000	First Night Montgomery, Silver Spring, MD
10,000	Greater Washington Urban League, Washington, DC
10,000	Montgomery County Private Industry Council, Rockville, MD
10,000	National Commission Against Drunk Driving, Washington, DC
7,500	Network of Employers for Traffic Safety, Washington, DC
5,870	Davidson Foundation, Washington, DC
5,000	Council for Excellence in Government, Washington, DC
5,000	Drive Smart, Glen Allen, VA

Education

10,000	American Institute for Chartered PC, Malvern, PA
10,000	Harvard University, Cambridge, MA
10,000	Mentors, Washington, DC
10,000	Ohio Wesleyan University, Delaware, OH
10,000	Woodrow Wilson National Fellowship Foundation, Princeton, NJ
6,250	Federal Employee Education and Assistance Fund, Littleton, CO
6,250	Federal Employee Education and Assistance Fund, Littleton, CO
6,250	Federal Employee Education and Assistance Fund, Littleton, CO
6,250	Federal Employee Education and Assistance Fund, Littleton, CO
5,000	Insurance Education Foundation, Indianapolis, IN

Health

50,000	National Rehabilitation Hospital, Washington, DC
25,000	National Rehabilitation Hospital, Washington, DC
15,000	Children's Hospital, Washington, DC
12,157	Susan G. Komen Breast Cancer Foundation, Dallas, TX
10,000	American Cancer Society, Macon, GA
5,000	Loudon Healthcare, Leesburg, VA
5,000	Susan G. Komen Breast Cancer Foundation, La Jolla, CA

Social Services

196,119	United Way of Central Georgia, Macon, GA
96,194	United Way, Dallas, TX
84,311	United Way of Long Island, Deer Park, NY
79,631	United Way, Washington, DC
38,650	United Way Chad Campaign, San Diego, CA
25,418	United Way of Central Florida, Highland City, FL
15,881	United Way of South Hampton Roads, Virginia Beach, VA
12,000	United Service Organization, Fort Myer, VA
10,000	Boys and Girls Clubs, Silver Spring, MD
10,000	Kennedy Krieger Institute, Baltimore, MD
10,000	United Service Organization, Fort Myer, VA
5,870	Washington Regional Alcohol Program, Vienna, VA
5,602	Washington Regional Alcohol Program, Vienna, VA
5,500	Special Olympics, Dallas, TX
5,213	Washington Regional Alcohol Program, Vienna, VA
5,000	Greater DC Cares, Washington, DC
5,000	Youth for Tomorrow, Bristow, VA

GENAMERICA CORP.

Company Contact

700 Market St.
St. Louis, MO 63101
Phone: (314)231-1700
Fax: (314)525-6444
Web: http://www.genamerica.com

Company Description

Assets: US$23,594,300,000 (1999)
Fortune Rank: 411, per FORTUNE Magazine's list of 500 Largest U.S. Corporations (1999).
FF 411
SIC(s): 6311 Life Insurance, 6321 Accident & Health Insurance.
Parent Company: Metropolitan Life Insurance Co., 1 Madison Ave., New York, NY, United States

Nonmonetary Support

Volunteer Programs: Company executives and associates have assumed leadership roles in a variety of civic and charitable causes.

GenAmerican Foundation

Giving Contact

Cheryl Endicot, Community Relations Specialist
GenAmerica Foundation
700 Market Street
St. Louis, MO 63101
Phone: (314)444-0520
Fax: (314)444-0681

Description

EIN: 431401687
Organization Type: Corporate Foundation
Former Name: General American Corp. (1999).
Former Name: General American Foundation (1999).
Giving Locations: MO: St. Louis
Grant Types: Award, Capital, General Support, Multiyear/Continuing Support, Professorship, Project, Research, Scholarship.

Giving Philosophy

'It shall be the policy of the company to contribute to social, economic and cultural progress by accepting and discharging the obligations of good citizenship in products and services, in employment practices, in investment policies, in corporate contributions, and in the activities of associates.' *General American Corporate Contributions Policy*

Financial Summary

Total Giving: $900,000 (fiscal year ending November 30, 1996); $800,000 (fiscal 1995); $673,960 (fiscal 1994). Note: Contributes through foundation, direct/corporate giving, nonmonetary support, and domestic subsidiary giving.
Giving Analysis: Giving for fiscal 1995 includes: foundation ($440,870); foundation grants to United Way ($244,700); fiscal 1996: foundation ($512,323); foundation grants to United Way ($270,064)
Assets: $5,016,193 (fiscal 1996); $5,027,854 (fiscal 1995); $4,481,942 (fiscal 1994)
Gifts Received: $500,000 (fiscal 1996); $428,000 (fiscal 1995); $413,230 (fiscal 1994)

Typical Recipients

Arts & Humanities: Arts Centers, Arts Funds, Arts Outreach, Community Arts, Dance, History & Archaeology, Libraries, Museums/Galleries, Music, Opera, Performing Arts, Public Broadcasting, Theater
Civic & Public Affairs: African American Affairs, Botanical Gardens/Parks, Chambers of Commerce, Employment/Job Training, Civic & Public Affairs-General, Municipalities/Towns, Parades/Festivals, Philanthropic Organizations, Professional & Trade Associations, Public Policy, Urban & Community Affairs, Women's Affairs, Zoos/Aquariums
Education: Arts/Humanities Education, Business Education, Colleges & Universities, Economic Education, Education Associations, Education Funds, Medical Education, Minority Education, Public Education (Precollege), Science/Mathematics Education, Secondary Education (Public), Student Aid

Health: AIDS/HIV, Alzheimers Disease, Cancer, Children's Health/Hospitals, Clinics/Medical Centers, Diabetes, Emergency/Ambulance Services, Heart, Hospitals, Hospitals (University Affiliated), Medical Rehabilitation, Medical Research, Preventive Medicine/Wellness Organizations, Public Health, Single-Disease Health Associations
Religion: Churches, Jewish Causes, Ministries, Religious Organizations, Religious Welfare
Science: Scientific Centers & Institutes
Social Services: At-Risk Youth, Child Welfare, Community Centers, Community Service Organizations, Counseling, Domestic Violence, Emergency Relief, Family Planning, Food/Clothing Distribution, Homes, People with Disabilities, Recreation & Athletics, Scouts, Senior Services, Substance Abuse, United Funds/United Ways, Volunteer Services, YMCA/YWCA/YMHA/YWHA, Youth Organizations

Contributions Analysis

Giving Priorities: United Way, healthcare and medical research, education, arts, and community services.
Arts & Humanities: 10%. Support depends on the health-related dollar demands. Interests include orchestras, arts education funds, music, theater, arts associations, and the performing arts.
Civic & Public Affairs: 30%. A variety of causes are supported, including civil rights, public policy, philanthropic organizations, business associations, urban affairs organizations, and botanical gardens.
Education: 7%. Emphasis on colleges and universities. Interests include minority scholarships, medical education, and Junior Achievement programs.
Health: 17%. This is the foundation's highest priority. Percentage varies widely from year to year according to amount of solicitation. Gives primarily to cancer and AIDS research and support services in an effort to help cure disease. Also interested in wellness programs. Additional interests include single-disease health associations, medical education, hospitals, medical organizations, health centers, and mental health.
Social Services: 36%. Support depends on demand for health-related grants. Primarily supports United Way. Other interests include youth organizations, the aged, religious welfare, the disabled, and counseling.
Note: Total contributions made in 1999.

Application Procedures

Initial Contact: Send a brief letter or proposal and request for application form.
Application Requirements: Include a brief history of the organization, list of officers and board of directorys, including affiliations, a copy of the organization's most recent financial statement, and a copy of IRS Code Section 501(c)(3) tax-exempt letter.
Deadlines: October 1
Evaluative Criteria: Priority is given to health-related proposals, either research and support or wellness programs; for non-health-related proposals, those which impact on policy holders or employees directly or indirectly are given greater consideration.
Decision Notification: Grants are approved in December for the following year.

Restrictions

Does not contribute to individuals or any individual benefit, political organizations, candidates for political office, religious organizations for non-secular purposes, social clubs, or labor organizations for political or organizational purposes.

Additional Information

GenAmerica Corporation was formerly known as General America Corporation.

Corporate Officials

Charles L. Larance: vice president corporate relations, director B Ruston, LA 1938. ED Louisiana Tech University BA (1960); American University MS (1973). PRIM CORP EMPL vice president corporate relations: General American Life Insurance Co. NONPR AFFIL member: National Association Life Underwriters; member: Washington Board Trade; member: Life Insurance Advisory Association.
Richard A. Liddy: chairman, president, chief executive officer B 1935. ED Iowa State University BS (1957). PRIM CORP EMPL chairman, president, chief executive officer: General American Life Insurance Co. ADD CORP EMPL chairman: General American Corp.; chairman: Cova Corp.; chairman: Reins Group America Inc.; chairman: Security Mutual Life Insurance New York. CORP AFFIL director: Ralston Purina Co.; director: Security Equity Life Insurance Co.; director: Ameren Corp.; director: Brown Shoe Co. Inc.
Leonard Mark Rubenstein: executive vice president investment, director B New London, CT 1946. ED Washington University BA (1968); University of Missouri MBA (1972). PRIM CORP EMPL executive vice president investment, director: General American Life Insurance Co. CORP AFFIL president: General American Investment Management Co.

Foundation Officials

Cheryl Endicott: administrator
Charles L. Larance: president (see above)
Leonard Mark Rubenstein: vice president, director (see above)

Grants Analysis

Disclosure Period: fiscal year ending November 30, 1996
Total Grants: $782,387
Number of Grants: 138
Average Grant: $3,824
Highest Grant: $270,000
Typical Range: $500 to $5,000
Note: Average grant figure excludes highest grant.

Recent Grants

Note: Grants derived from fiscal 1997 Form 990.

Arts & Humanities

30,000	St. Louis Symphony Orchestra, Saint Louis, MO
20,000	St. Louis Symphony Orchestra, Saint Louis, MO
15,500	Missouri Historical Society, Saint Louis, MO
15,000	Missouri Historical Society, Saint Louis, MO
10,000	Opera Theater, Saint Louis, MO
10,000	Repertory Theater, Saint Louis, MO
5,000	St. Louis Art Museum, Saint Louis, MO
3,000	KETC/Channel 9, Saint Louis, MO

Civic & Public Affairs

43,000	St. Louis 2004, Saint Louis, MO
16,665	Operation Weed and Seed, Saint Louis, MO
15,000	RCGA, Saint Louis, MO
10,000	St. Louis Zoo Foundation, Saint Louis, MO
5,000	FOCUS, Saint Louis, MO
5,000	Missouri Botanical Garden, Saint Louis, MO
5,000	Urban League, Saint Louis, MO
5,000	Women's Self-Help Center, Saint Louis, MO

Education

12,500	University of Missouri St. Louis, Saint Louis, MO
10,000	Arts Education Council, Saint Louis, MO
10,000	Maryville University, Saint Louis, MO
10,000	Missouri Colleges Fund, Jefferson City, MO
10,000	St. Louis Public Schools, Saint Louis, MO
10,000	S.S. Huebner Foundation, Philadelphia, PA
10,000	Washington University School of Medicine, Saint Louis, MO
10,000	Webster University, Saint Louis, MO
5,000	Southern Illinois University, Edwardsville, IL
3,500	Logos High School, Saint Louis, MO
3,000	Inroads, Saint Louis, MO

Health

10,000	Institute of Molecular Virology, Saint Louis, MO
8,000	Life and Health Insurance Medical Research Fund, Washington, DC
7,500	American Red Cross, Saint Louis, MO
5,000	AMC Cancer Research Center, Saint Louis, MO
5,000	American Heart Association, Saint Louis, MO
5,000	St. Mary's Health Center, Richmond Heights, MO
3,000	Southwest Foundation for Biomedical Research, Saint Louis, MO

Religion

12,500	Jewish Community Centers, Saint Louis, MO
12,000	Salvation Army, Saint Louis, MO
3,000	Daughters of Charity of St. Vincent de Paul, Saint Louis, MO
3,000	St. Patrick Center, Saint Louis, MO

Science

5,000	St. Louis Science Center Foundation, Saint Louis, MO

Social Services

71,550	United Way, Saint Louis, MO
71,500	United Way, Saint Louis, MO
71,500	United Way, Saint Louis, MO
10,000	Boy Scouts of America, Saint Louis, MO
10,000	YMCA, Saint Louis, MO
5,000	Girl Scouts of America, Saint Louis, MO
5,000	Magic House, Saint Louis, MO
5,000	Matthews Dickey Boys and Girls Club, Saint Louis, MO
5,000	United Way Heart of America, Clayton, MO
3,000	Paraquad, Saint Louis, MO
2,500	Christmas in St. Louis, Saint Louis, MO

GENCORP

Company Contact

Fairlawn, OH

Company Description

Employees: 13,000
SIC(s): 2821 Plastics Materials & Resins, 2822 Synthetic Rubber, 3484 Small Arms, 3764 Space Propulsion Units & Parts.

Nonmonetary Support

Type: Donated Equipment; Donated Products; In-kind Services; Loaned Executives
Volunteer Programs: Company gives the Community Leadership Award to recognize employee volunteer efforts; award includes a cash grant to the organization where employee volunteers.
Note: Annual nonmonetary support $25,000.

Corporate Sponsorship

Value: $2,500 (1994); $10,000
Type: Arts & cultural events; Music & entertainment events; Other
Note: Sponsors concert events, museum exhibits, American Red Cross, Jobs for Ohio Graduation, and Junior Achievement.

GenCorp Foundation

Giving Contact

Theresa Carter, Director
GenCorp Foundation
175 Ghent Rd.
Fairlawn, OH 44333-3300
Phone: (330)869-4289
Fax: (330)869-4227
Email: tcarter@gencorp.com

Description

EIN: 346514223
Organization Type: Corporate Foundation
Giving Locations: nationally, with emphasis on corporate operating locations.
Grant Types: Employee Matching Gifts, Endowment, General Support, Multiyear/Continuing Support.
Note: Employee matching gift ratio: 1 to 1 for contributions to education only.

Giving Philosophy

'We believe our success as a Company depends on the strength of the people and communities that sustain us. That is why social responsibility is an ingrained and integral part of our business. The GenCorp Foundation serves as a powerful tool to put our beliefs into action, allowing us to support programs and services that improve education, economic development and quality of life.' GenCorp Foundation, Inc. Grant Guidelines

Financial Summary

Total Giving: $3,200,000 (fiscal year ending November 30, 1999 approx); $2,801,924 (fiscal 1998); $2,759,185 (fiscal 1997). Note: Contributes through corporate direct giving program and foundation.
Giving Analysis: Giving for fiscal 1997 includes: foundation ($2,759,185); fiscal 1998: foundation ($2,801,924); fiscal 1999: foundation (approx $3,200,000)
Assets: $57,935,410 (fiscal 1999); $56,134,381 (fiscal 1998); $53,942,828 (fiscal 1997)

Typical Recipients

Arts & Humanities: Arts Institutes, Ballet, Dance, Historic Preservation, Libraries, Museums/Galleries, Music, Performing Arts, Public Broadcasting, Theater
Civic & Public Affairs: Business/Free Enterprise, Community Foundations, Economic Development, Economic Policy, Employment/Job Training, Civic & Public Affairs-General, Housing, Legal Aid, Municipalities/Towns, Parades/Festivals, Professional & Trade Associations, Public Policy, Urban & Community Affairs, Women's Affairs, Zoos/Aquariums
Education: Business Education, Business-School Partnerships, Colleges & Universities, Community & Junior Colleges, Education Associations, Education Funds, Education Reform, Elementary Education (Private), Elementary Education (Public), Engineering/Technological Education, Education-General, Literacy, Minority Education, Private Education (Precollege), Public Education (Precollege), Science/Mathematics Education, Secondary Education (Public), Student Aid
Environment: Environment-General
Health: Cancer, Children's Health/Hospitals, Diabetes, Emergency/Ambulance Services, Hospitals, Hospitals (University Affiliated), Mental Health, Nursing Services
International: International Affairs
Science: Science Museums, Scientific Centers & Institutes, Scientific Organizations
Social Services: Community Centers, Family Services, Scouts, United Funds/United Ways, Volunteer Services, YMCA/YWCA/YMHA/YWHA, Youth Organizations

Contributions Analysis

Giving Priorities: Higher education, United Way, museums, performing arts, and civics.
Arts & Humanities: 3%. Supports organizations and programs rich in diversity that provide educational experiences, and performances and events that broaden awareness and appreciation for the arts.
Civic & Public Affairs: 17%. Supports projects that address important issues and are designed to improve the quality of life in operating communities, including select urban renewal projects, working collaboratively with community leaders and organizations; drug and crime prevention, and safety issues; and projects that promote community awareness of key issues and community educational opportunities.
Education: About 40%. Supports K-12 schools that address specific improvements and opportunities for academic excellence in areas such as: reading and economic literacy programs as basic educational needs, math and science, school-to-work readiness, initiatives that encourage professional development for teachers, parental involvement, and programs that advance state-of-the-art technologies. Also supports a select number of colleges and universities, elementary and secondary school programs, and state and local educational organizations whose activities support and encourage educational excellence in polymer science and engineering, and other endeavors related to GenCorp's core technology competencies. Supports adult literacy programs in communities where GenCorp employees take an active role as tutors and volunteers. Funds technology partnership grants, student achievement awards, scholarships, and internships.
Health: 15%. Funds hospitals, in limited, targeted, and pro-active ways.
Science: 5%.
Social Services: 20%. Funds United Way, disaster relief, and community needs.
Note: Total contributions in fiscal 1997.

Application Procedures

Initial Contact: Request guidelines, then written request.
Application Requirements: Include a description of organization, including legal name, activities, history, and purpose; budget information, including annual report or financial statement listing sources of support; proof of tax-exempt status; list of names and affiliations of board members and officers; statement of proposed project, including purpose, short- and long-term objectives, specific budget information, timeline, and evaluation procedures; list of company employee volunteers; and description of how foundation support will be recognized
Deadlines: None.
Review Process: Requests are reviewed by foundation trustees.
Evaluative Criteria: Preference is given to community projects that involve employee volunteers, and which are recommended by foundation coordinators at local facilities; specific projects rather than unrestricted funding; and organizations demonstrating competency and effectiveness, and focus on evaluating and reporting progress.
Decision Notification: Decisions are announced four to six weeks after receipt.

Restrictions

Foundation does not support: individuals; organizations which are not tax-exempt; private foundations; fraternal, social, labor, or veterans' organizations; discriminatory organizations, or those with limited beneficiaries; political parties, candidates, or lobbying activities; programs posing a conflict of interest to the company; local athletic or sports programs, or for purchase of sports equipment; travel funds for tours, expeditions, or trips; courtesy advertising, benefits, raffle tickets or other fundraising events involving purchases of tables, tickets, or advertisements; churches or religious organizations; organizations that offer direct benefit to trustees, employees, or directors of company or foundation; or research grants or conferences.

Additional Information

Publications: Guidelines

Corporate Officials

Edward R. Dye: assistant general counsel & secretaryuality PRIM CORP EMPL assistant general counsel & secretary: GenCorp Inc.
Sam W. Harmon: senior vice president human resources B Columbia, SC 1950. ED University of Central Florida BA (1974). PRIM CORP EMPL senior vice president human resources: GenCorp Inc.
Michael E. Hicks: trustee
James K. Lambert: senior vice president operations and quality
Nathaniel J. Mass: senior vice president strategic growth ED Austin Peay State College BS (1972). PRIM CORP EMPL senior vice president strategic growth: GenCorp Inc.
John B. Yasinsky: chairman, president, chief executive officer B Shenendoah, PA 1939. ED Wheeling Jesuit College BS (1961); University of Pittsburgh MS (1963); Carnegie Mellon University PhD (1966). PRIM CORP EMPL chairman, president, chief executive officer: GenCorp Inc. CORP AFFIL director: CMS Energy Corp.; director: Consumers Energy; chairman: Aerojet-General Corp.
Rosemary Younts: senior vice president communications B Dallas, TX 1955. ED California State University (1978). PRIM CORP EMPL senior vice president communications: GenCorp Inc. CORP AFFIL director: GAMA.

Foundation Officials

Theresa Carter: director
Edward R. Dye: financial secretary (see above)
Sam W. Harmon: trustee (see above)
Nathaniel J. Mass: trustee (see above)

Grants Analysis

Disclosure Period: fiscal year ending November 30, 1998
Total Grants: $2,801,924
Number of Grants: 563
Average Grant: $4,977
Highest Grant: $77,000
Typical Range: $1,000 to $10,000
Note: Grants analysis provided by foundation.

Recent Grants

Note: Grants derived from fiscal 1997 Form 990.

Arts & Humanities

20,000 KVIE/Channel 6, Sacramento, CA -- support for ongoing education experiences in science and nature
15,000 Northeastern Educational Television, Kent, OH -- continued support for 'Bill Nye the Science Guy' and sponsorship of 'NOVA'
10,000 Ohio Ballet, Akron, OH -- co-sponsorship of 'Jungle Book: The Adventures of Mowgli'

Civic & Public Affairs

56,000 Habitat for Humanity, Akron, OH -- to build a four-bedroom home
40,000 Akron Zoological Park, Akron, OH -- to support Tiger Valley educational stations
28,025 Accreditation Board for Engineering and Technology, New York, NY -- science screen reports sent to school districts in GenCorp communities
25,000 Society of Automotive Engineers, Warrendale, PA -- provide educational support for the community

22,500	Cuyahoga Valley Scenic Railroad -- upgrade GenCorp railcar and support school field trip education fund
20,000	Tri-County Jobs for Ohio Graduates, Akron, OH -- Community Service Impact Project-Habitat for Humanity Publication Awareness
11,000	Tri-County Jobs for Ohio Graduates, Akron, OH -- programming
10,000	Akron Zoological Park, Akron, OH -- Tiger Valley Project
10,000	Community Foundation of Grant County, Marion, IN
10,000	Downtown Akron Partnership, Akron, OH -- New Year's Eve celebration

Education

133,334	University of Akron, Akron, OH -- support for Science and Technology Endowed Fund
50,000	University of Akron E. J. Thomas Hall, Akron, OH -- support carpet replacement
50,000	Wheeling Jesuit College, Wheeling, WV -- Challenger Learning Center to train students and teachers
38,000	Akron Public Schools, Akron, OH -- fund the Schools as Multi-Service Centers and the Character Counts program
27,030	National Merit Scholarship Corporation, Evanston, IL
26,000	Penn State Schuylkill Campus, Schuylkill, PA -- scholarship endowment for all students in the area
25,000	University of Alabama Huntsville, Huntsville, AL -- Propulsion Research Center to create and equip the facility
21,000	Junior Achievement, Akron, OH -- continued support and title sponsorship of Bowl-A-Thon
20,000	Close-Up Foundation, Alexandria, VA -- support civic education programs in Arizona, California, and Indiana
17,500	University of Maine, Orono, ME -- paper surface science research to advance coating technology
15,000	Georgia Institute of Technology Polymer Program
15,000	Lehigh University, Lehigh, PA -- continued support for graduate research programs in emulsions
15,000	University of California Riverside Foundation College of Engineering, Riverside, CA -- discretionary fund for faculty support
12,500	Junior Achievement, Akron, OH
10,000	Akron Public Schools, Akron, OH -- funding to train administrators
10,000	California State Polytechnic University, Pomona, CA -- to purchase equipment for new labs
10,000	Carnegie Mellon University, Pittsburgh, PA -- financial aid program
10,000	Ferris State University, Big Rapids, MI -- support for National Elastomer Center
10,000	Lawrence Family Development and Education Fund, Lawrence, MA -- to expand the Lawrence Family Development Charter School for Hispanic students
10,000	Massachusetts Institute of Technology, Cambridge, MA -- to support a lab at the university
10,000	Rensselaer Polytechnic Institute, Troy, NY -- start-up grant to cover administration expenses and a small research program
10,000	Summit Education Initiative -- support community forums for education by television and the internet
10,000	University of Akron, Akron, OH -- Akron Knight Family Education Program to increase adult literacy levels

Health

150,000	Mental Health Association of Summit County, Cuyahoga Falls, OH -- funding for relocation of the facility
50,000	American Cancer Society Hope Lodge -- Residence for Recovery for cancer patients
10,000	American Diabetes Association, Phoenix, AZ -- walk sponsorship

Science

25,000	Inventure Place, Akron, OH -- Camp Invention
25,000	Inventure Place, Akron, OH -- Camp Invention
10,000	Inventure Place, Akron, OH -- sponsorship of Inventure Weekend

Social Services

73,500	United Way of Summit County, Akron, OH -- annual pledge
50,000	Open M, Akron, OH -- to support the construction of a neighborhood center in the heart of Akron
50,000	YMCA, Akron, OH -- fund partial renovations at downtown Y and the Phoenix School
30,000	United Way, Sacramento, CA
25,000	United Way of Summit County, Akron, OH
18,000	Boys and Girls Club of Shelby County -- renovate Boys Club and move Girls Club next door
15,000	United Way, Los Angeles, CA
12,000	United Way

GENENTECH INC.

Company Contact

San Francisco, CA
Web: http://www.gene.com

Company Description

Employees: 3,389 (1999)
SIC(s): 2834 Pharmaceutical Preparations, 8731 Commercial Physical Research.
Parent Company: Roche Holdings, AG

Operating Locations

CA: Genentech, San Francisco; Genentech Inc., San Francisco

Genentech Foundation for Biomedical Sciences

Giving Contact

Bunnie Jack, Foundation Coordinator
Genentech, Inc.
1 DNA Way
South San Francisco, CA 94080
Phone: (650)225-2487
Fax: (650)225-2414

Description

Founded: 1988
EIN: 943083018
Organization Type: Corporate Foundation
Giving Locations: CA: northern California
Grant Types: Research, Scholarship.

Financial Summary

Total Giving: $60,000 (fiscal year ending March 31, 1997); $645,000 (fiscal 1996 approx); $531,000 (fiscal 1995). Note: Contributes through corporate direct giving program and foundation.
Assets: $999,464 (fiscal 1997); $310,563 (fiscal 1995); $229,265 (fiscal 1994)
Gifts Received: $179,832 (fiscal 1997); $616,245 (fiscal 1995); $548,674 (fiscal 1994). Note: Foundation receives contributions from Genentech, Inc.

Typical Recipients

Civic & Public Affairs: Civic & Public Affairs-General
Education: Colleges & Universities, Community & Junior Colleges, Elementary Education (Private), Medical Education, Public Education (Precollege), Science/Mathematics Education, Student Aid
Health: Kidney
Science: Observatories & Planetariums, Science Exhibits & Fairs, Science Museums, Scientific Centers & Institutes

Contributions Analysis

Education: 65% to 70% of total contributions. Funds science and matches education programs in the San Francisco Bay area. Typical recipients include the University of California and Mills College. Also supports scholarship programs for math and science education.
Science: 25% to 30%. Support in this category includes grants to Stanford University School of Medicine for scientific scholarships; Science 2000 City School Service Fund in Redwood City, CA, for scientific educational kits; and to the University of California, San Francisco, Science and Health Educational Partnership for scientific educationalkits.

Application Procedures

Initial Contact: application for funding
Application Requirements: for proposed educational programs: a description of the educational program; the person(s) responsible for administering the program (including resumes); timetables for implementation of the program; if the program already is in existence, a discussion of the successes and failures of the program; for grants to students: a description of the criteria in selecting students, the type of research that will be encouraged; the amount of the proposed grants; any limits on the use of funds; proposed budget for the grant period; and or unaudited financial statements for the program (if available)
Deadlines: March 15
Evaluative Criteria: funds are to be used only for direct support of education and research in the biomedical sciences, programs and organizations fostering the participation of under-represented minorities and underprivileged groups in biomedical science; recipient organizations must be an educational or research organization located in or serving northern California; eligible institutions include primary, junior high, and high schools, school districts, colleges and universities, and charitable research or educational organizations; recipient must be a public charity; educational institutions above the high school level should be of high academic caliber and contribute in a substantial manner and on a regular basis to biomedical research; institution may apply for foundation funds for the purpose of making grants to students if the students demonstrate exemplary research or academic ability; the students study in an outstanding environment for biology education or are actively engaged in research in the biomedical sciences; and regarding student research grants, the research is of general interest to t he scientific community
Notes: Copies of IRS determination and classification letters confirming applicant's public charity status and non-private foundation status should be attached.

Restrictions

Does not support individuals except through scholarship programs or private foundations, nor indirect costs.

Additional Information

Genentech also funds the Genentech Endowment for Cystic Fibrosis, which is operated through an independent board of directors.

Genentech also funds the Genentech Foundation for Human Growth and Development, which is an independent, nonprofit organization geared towards encouraging physicians and nurses in their research efforts.

Genentech provides a Genentech Assistance Program for its other products.

Publications: Program Policy Statement; Application Guidelines

Corporate Officials

Herbert Wayne Boyer, PhD: co-founder, director B Pittsburgh, PA 1936. ED Saint Vincent College BA (1958); University of Pittsburgh MS (1960); University of Pittsburgh PhD (1963). PRIM CORP EMPL co-founder, director: Genentech Inc. CORP AFFIL director: Allergan Inc. NONPR AFFIL member: National Academy Sciences; fellow: Society Biological Chemical; fellow: American Academy Science.

Patricia M. Kaitz: chief financial officer, secretary PRIM CORP EMPL chief financial officer, secretary: Genentech Inc.

Louis J. Lavigne, Jr.: executive vice president, chief financial officer B Cheboygan, MI 1948. ED Babson College BBA (1969); Temple University MBA (1976). PRIM CORP EMPL executive vice president, chief financial officer: Genentech Inc. NONPR AFFIL member: Financial Executives Institute.

Dr. Arthur David Levinson: president, chief executive officer, director B Seattle, WA 1950. ED Princeton University; Education Institute BS (1972); University of Washington PhD (1977); University of San Francisco (1977-1980). PRIM CORP EMPL president, chief executive officer, director: Genentech Inc. NONPR AFFIL member: Society Microbiology; director: Telecommunication Network; member: Society Biochemistry & Molecular Biology; director: Bio Technology Industry Organization; director: Pharmacy Research Manufacturer America.

William D. Young: chief operating officer ED Purdue University BS (1966); Indiana University MBA (1971). PRIM CORP EMPL chief operating officer: Genentech Inc.

Foundation Officials

Bruce Michael Alberts, PhD: director B Chicago, IL 1938. ED Harvard College AB (1960); Harvard University PhD (1965). PRIM NONPR EMPL president: National Academy of Science. CORP AFFIL member advisory board: Bethesda Research Laboratories; member advisory board: Life Techs Inc. NONPR AFFIL member advisory board: National Science Resource Center Smithsonian Institute; member: Phi Beta Kappa; member: National Committee Science Education Standards Assesment; committee member department biology: Massachusetts Institute Technology; committee member: National Board Professional Teaching Standards; member science advisory committee: Marine Biology Laboratory; member: Markey Foundation; member science advisory board: Fred Hutchinson Cancer Research Center; director: Federal American Society Experimental Biology; member: Genetics Society America; member department embryology: Carnegie Institute; member: European Molecular Biology Organization; member: American Society Microbiology; member: American Society Biochemistry & Molecular Biology; member: American Society Cell Biology; member: American Chemical Society; member: American Philosophical Society; member: American Association Advancement Science.

Herbert Wayne Boyer, PhD: chairman, president, director (see above)

Goery Delacote, PhD: director B 1939. ED Ecole Normale Superieur PhD. PRIM NONPR EMPL executive director: Exploratorium.

Edward D. Harris, Jr.: director B Philadelphia, PA 1937. ED Dartmouth College AB (1958); Dartmouth College (1960); Harvard University MD (1962). PRIM NONPR EMPL chairman, professor: Stanford University School of Medicine. CORP AFFIL director: International MDL Service; officer: California Water Service Co. NONPR AFFIL member: New England Rheumatism Association; professor: Stanford University School Medicine; member: American Rheumatism Association; chief medical service: Middlesex General University Hospital; fellow: American College Physicians.

Robert A. Swanson: director B New York, NY 1947. ED Massachusetts Institute of Technology SM (1970); Massachusetts Institute of Technology SB (1970). CORP AFFIL president: Genentech Ltd. Japan. NONPR AFFIL director: San Francisco Museum Modern Art; director: Tech Center Silicon Valley; director: San Francisco Ballet Association; member corporate: Massachusetts Institute Technology; member: Royal Swedish Academy Engineering Science; member: American Chemical Society; member: American Society Microbiology; member: American Association Advancement Science.

Grants Analysis

Disclosure Period: fiscal year ending March 31, 1997
Total Grants: $60,000
Number of Grants: 2
Average Grant: $30,000
Highest Grant: $40,000
Typical Range: $20,000 to $70,000

Recent Grants

Note: Grants derived from 1997 Form 990.

Education

20,000	ARCS Foundation, San Francisco, CA -- scholarships

Science

40,000	Chabot Observatory and Science Center, Oakland, CA -- general support, equipment, supplies

GENERAL ATLANTIC PARTNERS II LP

Company Contact

New York, NY
Web: http://www.echoinggreen.org

Company Description

Employees: 35
SIC(s): 6799 Investors Nec.

Nonmonetary Support

Note: Nonmonetary support is provided by the foundation and the co. They report nonmonetary support is limited and offered only in the form of technical assistance.

Echoing Green Foundation

Giving Contact

Beth Manalo-Lamanna, Director of Search & Selection
Echoing Green Foundation
198 Madison Avenue 8th Floor
New York, NY 10016
Phone: (212)689-1165
Fax: (212)689-9010

Description

Founded: 1987
EIN: 133424419
Organization Type: Corporate Foundation
Giving Locations: NY: emphasis on New York
Grant Types: Fellowship, Seed Money.

Financial Summary

Total Giving: $1,521,597 (1998); $1,904,606 (1997); $912,708 (1996). Note: Contributes through foundation only.

Giving Analysis: Giving for 1996 includes: foundation gifts to individuals ($378,958); 1997: foundation fellowships ($1,904,606); 1998: foundation fellowships ($1,521,597)

Assets: $793,869 (1998); $1,139,622 (1997); $330,806 (1996)

Gifts Received: $2,944,288 (1998); $3,081,171 (1997); $5,002,333 (1995). Note: In 1998, the foundation received contributions from GAP II ($2,708,216); the Kellogg Foundation ($136,072); and the New York City Community Trust ($100,000).

Typical Recipients

Arts & Humanities: Arts Centers, Literary Arts, Theater

Civic & Public Affairs: African American Affairs, Asian American Affairs, Civil Rights, Community Foundations, Economic Development, Economic Policy, Employment/Job Training, Civic & Public Affairs-General, Law & Justice, Legal Aid, Municipalities/ Towns, Native American Affairs, Public Policy, Rural Affairs, Urban & Community Affairs, Women's Affairs

Education: Afterschool/Enrichment Programs, Colleges & Universities, Education Associations, Education Reform, Education-General, Legal Education, Medical Education, Preschool Education, Public Education (Precollege), Social Sciences Education, Student Aid

Environment: Environment-General, Resource Conservation

Health: Emergency/Ambulance Services, Health Organizations, Mental Health, Public Health

International: Foreign Educational Institutions, Human Rights, International Development, International Environmental Issues, International Organizations, International Relations, International Relief Efforts

Religion: Religious Welfare

Social Services: Child Welfare, Community Service Organizations, Domestic Violence, Family Services, Food/Clothing Distribution, Shelters/Homelessness, Substance Abuse, Youth Organizations

Contributions Analysis

Giving Priorities: Grants are in the form of fellowships to indivduals. Interests include environmental affairs, conservation, and international organizations.

Application Procedures

Initial Contact: Send a brief letter of inquiry.

Application Requirements: Include name and a description of organization, project's name, and financial information.

Deadlines: None.

Notes: The foundation generally does not accept unsolicited requests for funds, but will consider worthwhile proposals.

Additional Information

The foundation sponsors a fellowship program for graduate and undergraduate students who initiate independent public service projects.

The foundation was formerly known as the General Atlantic Partners Foundation and the Veronese Foundation.

Corporate Officials

Steven A. Denning: vice president B 1949. ED Stanford University (1976-1978). PRIM CORP EMPL vice president: General Atlantic Corp. CORP AFFIL director: Eclipsys Corp.; director: Great Interactive Software Corp.

Foundation Officials

Edwin C. Cohen: chairman
Beth Manalo: director search selection

Jim Pitofsky: vice president support & organizational development

Grants Analysis

Disclosure Period: calendar year ending 1998
Total Grants: $1,521,597*
Number of Grants: 103
Average Grant: $14,773
Highest Grant: $25,000
Typical Range: $7,500 to $15,000
***Note:** Giving includes fellowships.

Recent Grants

Note: Grants derived from 1996 Form 990.

Arts & Humanities

7,500 Community Arts Center, Cambridge, MA

Civic & Public Affairs

12,500 Asian Law Caucus, San Francisco, CA
12,500 Camden Center for Law, Camden, NJ
12,500 Center for Economic and Social Research, New York, NY
12,500 Collective Legal Services, Oakland, CA
12,500 Credit Where Credit is Due, New York, NY
12,500 Equal Rights Advocates, San Francisco, CA
12,500 Foundation for the Future, Altherton, CA
12,500 Lawyers Committee for Civil Rights of the San Francisco Bay Area, San Francisco, CA
12,500 Legal Action Center, Oakland, CA
12,500 Navaho Landowners Rights, Crownpoint, NM
12,500 Plugged In, Menlo Park, CA
12,500 Protection and Advocacy System, Albuquerque, NM
10,000 Rural Resources, Greeneville, TN
10,000 Workplace Project, Hempstead, NY
7,500 Berthrone in Calvin Mock, Jackson, MS
7,500 Collective Legal Services, Oakland, CA
7,500 Free At Last, East Palo Alto, CA
7,500 Justice Education and Action, Oakland, CA
7,500 Redefining Progress, San Francisco, CA
7,500 Women's Rights Network, Boston, MA
6,250 City on a Hill, Boston, MA

Education

30,000 Playing to Win, New York, NY
12,500 ACE Boston College Law School, Newton, MA
12,500 ACE Boston College Law School, Newton, MA
12,500 Bay Area School, San Francisco, CA
12,500 University of Miami School of Law, Miami, FL
10,000 College Kids, San Francisco, CA
10,000 National Association of Partners in Education, Alexandria, VA
7,500 Jumpstart for Young Children, Boston, MA
7,500 Jumpstart for Young Children, Boston, MA
7,500 Network of Educators, Washington, DC
5,000 Brown University, Providence, RI

Environment

12,500 Nature Conservancy, Boulder, CO
12,500 Outdoor Exploration, Cambridge, MA

Health

7,500 Partners in Health, Cambridge, MA

International

12,500 American University Center for Human Rights, Washington, DC
12,500 Resources International, Cumberland, RI
10,000 ISAR, Washington, DC
7,500 Earthrights International, Arlington, VA
7,500 International Youth Leadership, New York, NY

Religion

7,500 Porter Square Ecumenical, Cambridge, MA

Social Services

12,500 Community Youth Cooperative, Durham, NC
12,500 Family Van, Boston, MA
12,500 Food Project, Lincoln, NE
12,500 Homeless Advocacy Project, San Francisco, CA
12,500 Shakti for Children, Durham, NC
12,500 With Loving Care, Oakland, CA
7,500 Coalition on Homelessness, San Francisco, CA
7,500 United Services Agency, Palo Alto, CA

GENERAL DYNAMICS CORP.

Company Contact

3190 Fairview Park Dr.
Falls Church, VA 22042-4523
Phone: (703)876-3000
Fax: (703)876-3125
Web: http://www.gendyn.com

Company Description

Acquired: Gulfstream Aerospace Corp. (1999).
Revenue: US$8,959,000,000 (1999)
Profit: US$880,000,000 (1999)
Employees: 31,000 (1998)
Fortune Rank: 191, per FORTUNE Magazine's list of 500 Largest U.S. Corporations (1999).
FF 191
SIC(s): 1221 Bituminous Coal & Lignite--Surface, 1422 Crushed & Broken Limestone, 3272 Concrete Products Nec, 3731 Ship Building & Repairing.

Operating Locations

Canada: General Dynamics Manufacturing Ltd., Montreal

SUBSIDIARY COMPANIES

GA: Gulfstream Aerospace Corp., Savannah

Giving Contact

Diane Mossler, Director of Contributions and Government & Community Relations
General Dynamics Corp.
3190 Fairview Park Drive
Falls Church, VA 22042
Phone: (703)876-3000
Fax: (703)876-3600

Description

Organization Type: Corporate Giving Program. Supports preselected organizations only.
Giving Locations: nationally and in company operating areas.
Grant Types: Capital, Employee Matching Gifts, General Support, Operating Expenses.

Financial Summary

Total Giving: Contributes through corporate direct giving program only.

Typical Recipients

Arts & Humanities: Arts Associations & Councils, Performing Arts, Theater
Education: Colleges & Universities, Literacy, Medical Education
International: International Relations
Science: Scientific Centers & Institutes
Social Services: Child Welfare, Family Services, People with Disabilities, Shelters/Homelessness, Youth Organizations

Contributions Analysis

Giving Priorities: Higher education, United Way, museums, performing arts, and civics. Limited support for international development/relief. Overseas locations do not make charitable contributions.
Civic & Public Affairs: About 55%. Public policy and international exchange organizations.
Education: About 25%. Higher education, minority education, and education associations.
Health: About 10%. United Way, hospitals, drug abuse programs, family service organizations, and YWCA.

Additional Information

Material Service Corporation, a major subsidiary of General Dynamics Corp., operates its own giving program.

Corporate Officials

Nicholas D. Chabraja: chairman, chief executive officer, director B Gary, IN 1942. ED Northwestern University BA (1964); Northwestern University JD (1967). PRIM CORP EMPL chairman, chief executive officer, director: General Dynamics Corp. CORP AFFIL director: Ceridian Corp. NONPR AFFIL fellow: American College Trial Lawyers; member: Chicago Bar Association; member: American Bar Association.

Giving Program Officials

Kendall Pease: vice president communications PRIM CORP EMPL vice president communication: General Dynamics Corp.

Grants Analysis

Disclosure Period: calendar year ending
Typical Range: $25,000 to $50,000

GENERAL ELECTRIC CO.

 Number 23 of Top 100 Corporate Givers

Company Contact

Fairfield, CT
Web: http://www.ge.com

Company Description

Revenue: US$99,820,000,000
Profit: US$9,296,000,000
Employees: 293,000
Fortune Rank: 5, per FORTUNE Magazine's list of 500 Largest U.S. Corporations (1999).
FF 5
SIC(s): 3511 Turbines & Turbine Generator Sets, 3724 Aircraft Engines & Engine Parts, 3812 Search & Navigation Equipment.

Operating Locations

Australia: Nissan Finance Corporation Ltd., Melbourne, VIC; Brazil: General Electric do Brazil, S.A., Sao Paulo; Canada: G.E. Canada Power Systems, Lachine; GE Hydro, Lachine; Multilin, Markham; Camco Inc., Mississauga; G.E. Fanuc Automation Canada, Mississauga; G.E. Plastic Canada, Mississauga; General Electric Canada Inc., Mississauga; Transport International Pool of Canada Ltd., Mississauga; Camco Inc., Montreal; G.E. Canada, Peterborough, Peterborough; Germany: General Electric Plastics GmbH, Russelsheim; Hong Kong: General Electric (USA) China Company, Ltd., Hong Kong; Hungary: G.E. Tungstram Co., Vaciut; India: Fanuc GE Automation India Ltd., Bangalore; Ireland: G.E. Lighting (Ireland) Ltd., Dublin; Woodchester Investments plc, Dublin; Japan: GE Medical Systems Asia Ltd., Tokyo; Mexico: General Electric de Mexico, S.A. de C.V.; Netherlands: G.E. Plastics Europe, Bergen-op-Zoom; Philippines: General Electric Phillippines Inc., Makati; Saudi Arabia: Saudi American General Electric, Riyadh; Singapore: General Electric (USA)

Hermetic Motor Operation (Pte) Ltd., Jurong; Electric Component of PTE. Ltd., Singapore; Fanuc GE Automation Singapore Pte. Ltd., Singapore; Fuji/GE PTE Ltd., Singapore; G.E. Asia, Singapore; G.E. Plastics Pacific Ltd., Singapore; G.E. Technical Services, Singapore; G.E. (USA) Aviation Service Operation Pte. Ltd., Singapore; General Electric (USA) Asia Co., Singapore; General Electric (USA) Consumer Electronics (Pte) Ltd., Singapore; Thailand: B. Grimm, Bangkok; United Kingdom: G.E. Lighting Ltd., Enfield, Middlesex; G.E.-Thorn Lamps Presscaps, Enfield, Middlesex; G.E. Lighting Europe, London; General Electric International Operations, London; G.E. Lighting Ltd., Mitcham, Surrey

Nonmonetary Support

Value: $535,267 (1997); $2,123,004 (1996); $670,000 (1994)

Type: Donated Equipment; Donated Products

Volunteer Programs: GE supports the United Way and United Way-sponsored agencies where GE volunteers perform a variety of services, including agency clean-ups, refurbishing day care centers, and building houses through Habitat for Humanity. GE also supports Elfun, a global organization of GE employees and retirees who work to improve the company and communities through volunteerism, leadership, and camaraderie.

GE volunteer hours approach $500,000 in billable hours.

Note: For nonmonetary support contact nearest company office.

GE Fund

Giving Contact

Joyce Hergenhan, President
GE Fund
3135 Easton Turnpike
Fairfield, CT 06431
Phone: (203)373-3216
Fax: (203)373-3029
Email: edith.nelson@corporate.ge.com
Web: http://www.ge.com/fund

Alternate Contact

Gisele Hill, Secretary

Description

EIN: 222621967

Organization Type: Corporate Foundation. Supports preselected organizations only.

Former Name: GE Foundations.

Giving Locations: headquarters and operating communities; international organizations; national organizations.

Grant Types: Employee Matching Gifts, Fellowship, General Support, Multiyear/Continuing Support, Project, Research.

Note: Employee matching gift ratio: 1 to 1 for education and health and human services.

Giving Philosophy

'Programs are shaped by the issues that confront society today. .. Issues of such urgency that they make their way into our daily lives if not by actual experience then by newspaper headlines. .. In response, we believe that a capable workforce, a competitive economy and a compassionate society depend in large measure upon a well-educated citizenry. The key areas of Fund activity reflect the depth and diversity of this commitment.' *GE Fund Annual Report*

Financial Summary

Total Giving: $34,524,399 (1998); $50,674,423 (1997); $49,656,835 (1996). Note: Contributes through corporate direct giving program and foundation.

Giving Analysis: Giving for 1997 includes: foundation ($30,354,465); corporate direct giving ($12,927,561); domestic subsidiaries ($5,096,245); international subsidiaries ($1,760,885); 1998: foundation ($17,753,689); foundation matching gifts ($12,411,185); foundation grants to United Way ($4,359,525)

Assets: $22,262,000 (1996 approx); $19,000,787 (1995); $22,652,828 (1994)

Gifts Received: $28,108,781 (1995); $27,792,090 (1994). Note: Contributions are received from General Electric Company.

Typical Recipients

Arts & Humanities: Arts Associations & Councils, Arts Centers, Arts Funds, Dance, Ethnic & Folk Arts, Historic Preservation, Libraries, Music, Opera, Performing Arts, Public Broadcasting, Theater, Visual Arts

Civic & Public Affairs: African American Affairs, Business/Free Enterprise, Civil Rights, Community Foundations, Economic Development, Economic Policy, Employment/Job Training, Civic & Public Affairs-General, Housing, Law & Justice, Nonprofit Management, Professional & Trade Associations, Public Policy, Urban & Community Affairs, Women's Affairs, Zoos/Aquariums

Education: Arts/Humanities Education, Business Education, Colleges & Universities, Continuing Education, Economic Education, Education Associations, Education Reform, Engineering/Technological Education, Faculty Development, International Exchange, International Studies, Legal Education, Literacy, Medical Education, Minority Education, Public Education (Precollege), Science/Mathematics Education, Student Aid

Environment: Energy, Environment-General, Resource Conservation, Watershed, Wildlife Protection

Health: Clinics/Medical Centers, Emergency/Ambulance Services, Health Policy/Cost Containment, Health Organizations, Hospitals, Hospitals (University Affiliated)

International: Foreign Educational Institutions, Health Care/Hospitals, International Affairs, International Development, International Environmental Issues, International Organizations, International Peace & Security Issues, International Relations, International Relief Efforts, Missionary/Religious Activities, Trade

Religion: Ministries, Religious Welfare

Science: Scientific Centers & Institutes, Scientific Organizations

Social Services: Child Welfare, Community Centers, Community Service Organizations, Family Services, Food/Clothing Distribution, People with Disabilities, Senior Services, Shelters/Homelessness, Substance Abuse, United Funds/United Ways, Volunteer Services, Youth Organizations

Contributions Analysis

Giving Priorities: Education, human services, health, civics, arts education, U.S. -based nonprofit international organizations. The GE Fund supports U.S.-based nonprofits with interests in such critical global issues as the environment and international trade. The fund also makes grants to improve the quality of life for people from disadvantaged communities around the world. Fund priorities are training in management and engineering, improving children's health care, and strengthening community development projects. Awards to universities outside the United States are principally directed to engineering and business management schools. Health care grants are usually made in countries where GE has a presence. A community awards program supports local improvement efforts in selected locations overseas. Overseas subsidiaries administer contributions, though cash budgets for overseas businesses are relatively small. Individual subsidiaries make annual reports to the U.S. headquarters regarding general contributions activities.

Arts & Humanities: 5%. Fund's objective is to further arts education, particularly through partnerships of arts organizations with the public schools.

Civic & Public Affairs: 4%. Funding in this category is focused on public policy organizations promoting international business, economic development, and employment opportunities. Regional planning associations in operating locations are also supported. Minority groups are supported through job training and business education.

Education: 60%. Supports colleges and universities, and education associations and organizations. The Faculty for the Future Program is a decade-long program to help overcome the shortage of under-represented minority and women faculty in US schools of engineering, chemistry, physics, computer science, and business. The fund's graduate fellowship program awards grants to colleges and universities for support of first-year doctoral students which include stipends and departmental grants. The forgivable loan program supports doctoral candidates. Under this program, 25% of the loan is forgiven for each year the recipient serves as a faculty member at a college or university. Also makes direct grants to colleges, universities, and education associations for science and engineering program development and business curriculum development. Other initiatives include increased educational opportunities for women and minorities, with emphasis on engineering, management, and finance. Support includes sponsorship of a minority engineering scholarship program, funding for Hispanic scholarship programs, scholarships for first-year female engineering students, and aid for minority educational associations and institutions (including schools of engineering and faculty development). Grants on the precollege level emphasize improving math and science teaching and curricula and raising students' abilities in these subject areas. Also, the foundation supports school projects involving GE volunteers. Much support is in the form of matching gifts to colleges and universities. The GE Fund also supports international education.

International: 4%. Support includes healthcare for children in third world countries, including grants to Project Concern International to help establish volunteer teams trained in birthing, nutrition, and child health.

Social Services: 13%. Primarily supports United Way.

Application Procedures

Initial Contact: Send a brief written proposal.

Application Requirements: Include an executive summary, brief description of the organization (including legal name, primary purpose, and history), amount requested and how it will be used, clear statement of purpose of program and qualifications of program manager, budget information, work schedule and timetable, criteria for measuring success and plans for publicity, list of support from other donors, proof of tax-exempt status; for College Bound Program: school districts submit one to five pages that outline a clear, well-defined, workable plan to double number of college-bound students over a 3- to 5-year period, including demographics, current college-going rate, timetable, budget, explanation of how project will be managed; for Faculty for the Future Program: institutions submit letter, by invitation only, citing underrepresented minority and female enrollment and recent graduation statistics, which support record as developers of minority and female faculty talent.

Deadlines: None.

Review Process: Proposals are reviewed by managers and committees of the GE Fund; different committees handle specific areas of interest.

Evaluative Criteria: For College Bound Program: identifiable preconditions for a turnaround, such as potential for involvement by parents, volunteers, students, teachers, school officials, and civic groups; for Faculty for the Future Program: research universities with good track record in minority advancement, faculty development and undergraduate schools that have underrepresented minority and female students

in physical sciences, computer science, or engineering, and have histories as excellent sources for Ph.D. candidates.

Decision Notification: Quarterly, at meetings of GE Fund directors.

Restrictions

Fund does not make in-kind grants of GE equipment, award scholarships or research grants to individuals, or support religious or sectarian groups.

Fund generally does not support capital, endowment, or other special purpose campaigns, nor chairs or equipment purchases

Ability to review unsolicited proposals is extremely limited. Most proposals funded by the GE Fund are submitted upon invitation.

Additional Information

Company has operating locations in nearly all 50 states.

In 1994, GE combined its two charitable foundations, the GE Foundation, a trust established in 1952 to make grants in the US, and the GE Foundation, Inc., a corporation established in 1985 to make grants both domestically and internationally. The combined entity is known as the GE Fund and serves as the company's primary vehicle for philanthropic support.

Biographical information above covers the chairperson of each foundation committee. Complete list of committee members is available upon request from foundation office.

Publications: Annual Report

Corporate Officials

Dennis Dean Dammerman: vice chairman, director, director B Fairfield, IA 1945. ED University of Dubuque BS (1967). PRIM CORP EMPL vice chairman, director: General Electric Co. ADD CORP EMPL chairman,chief executive officer: Capital Services. CORP AFFIL vice president: Monogram General Agency Texas; director: Montgomery Ward Co. Inc.; officer: General Electric Capital Services; director: GE Fin Services Inc.; director: General Electric Capital Corp. NONPR AFFIL member: Officers Conference Group; director: University Dubuque; member: Financial Executives Institute; trustee: Fairfield University; trustee: Fin Accounting Foundation; member: Council Financial Executives.

William P. Driscoll, Junior: vice president, officer PRIM CORP EMPL vice president, officer: General Electric Co.

Steven Kerr: vice president corporate leadership development ED City University of New York PhD. PRIM CORP EMPL vice president corporate leadership development: General Electric Co.

John D. Opie: vice chairman, executive officer, director ED Michigan Technological Institute BS (1961). PRIM CORP EMPL vice chairman, executive officer, director: General Electric Co. CORP AFFIL director: National Broadcasting Co. Inc.

John Francis Welch, Jr.: chairman, chief executive officer, director B Peabody, MA 1935. ED University of Massachusetts BSChE (1957); University of Illinois MS (1958); University of Illinois PhD (1960). PRIM CORP EMPL chairman, chief executive officer, director: General Electric Co. CORP AFFIL director: General Electric Capital Services; chairman: National Broadcasting Co. Inc. NONPR AFFIL member: Business Roundtable; member: National Academy Engineering; member: Business Council.

Foundation Officials

William J. Conaty: director B Johnson City, NY 1945. ED Bryant College (1967). PRIM CORP EMPL senior vice president human resources: General Electric Co. NONPR AFFIL director: Labor Policy Association; fellow: National Academy Human Resources; director: Jobs for Americas Grads.

Michael J. Cosgrove: treasurer PRIM CORP EMPL executive vice president: General Electric Investment Corp. ADD CORP EMPL executive vice president: GE Investment Management Inc. CORP AFFIL trustee: General Electric S&S Long Term Fund; trustee: General Electric S&S Program.

Benjamin Walter Heineman, Jr.: director B Chicago, IL 1944. ED Harvard University BA (1965); Oxford University Balliol College (1967); Yale University JD (1971). PRIM CORP EMPL senior vice president, general counsel, secretary: General Electric Co. ADD CORP EMPL director: General Electric Capital Corp.; officer: General Electric Capital SVCs. NONPR AFFIL member: American Law Institute; member: Phi Beta Kappa; member: American Bar Association.

Joyce Hergenhan: director, president B Mount Kisco, NY 1941. ED Syracuse University BA (1963); Columbia University MBA (1978). PRIM CORP EMPL vice president corporate & public relations: General Electric Co.

Henry A. Hubschman: director B Newark, NJ 1947. ED Rutgers University BA (1969); Harvard University JD (1973). PRIM CORP EMPL president: GE Capital Aviation Service Inc.

Steven Kerr: director (see above)

Jane Louise Polin: manager, comptroller B New York, NY 1958. ED Wesleyan University BA (1980); Columbia University MBA (1988). NONPR AFFIL advisory board member: United Way America; advisory board member: Young Audiences; advisory board member: Institute International Economics; member: Ams for the Arts; advisory board member: ARC; member: Alpha Delta Phi.

Keith S. Sherin: director PRIM CORP EMPL senior vice president, finance, chief financial officer: General Electric Corp.

Lloyd G. Trotter: director PRIM CORP EMPL president, chief executive officer: GE Industrial Systems ADD CORP EMPL president: General Electric Co.

Grants Analysis

Disclosure Period: calendar year ending 1998
Total Grants: $17,753,689*
Number of Grants: 308
Average Grant: $57,642
Highest Grant: $406,855
Typical Range: $5,000 to $100,000
***Note:** Giving excludes United Way; matching gifts. Grants analysis derived from a 1998 grants list.

Recent Grants

Note: Grants derived from 1996 Annual Report.

Arts & Humanities

100,000	George Bush Presidential Library Foundation, College Station, TX -- special projects grant
100,000	New York Foundation for the Arts, New York, NY -- for the arts

Civic & Public Affairs

100,000	Committee for Economic Development, New York, NY -- public policy grants

Education

980,400	New England Board of Higher Education, Boston, MA -- science and engineering program educational grants
310,000	Cornell University, Ithaca, NY
292,793	Georgia Institute of Technology, Atlanta, GA -- educational
291,050	New Hanover County Schools, Wilmington, NC -- precollege grants
278,500	Rensselaer Polytechnic Institute, Troy, NY -- educational
250,000	NACM Educational Services, Phoenix, AZ -- science and engineering program educational grants
250,000	New American Schools Development Corporation, Arlington, VA
228,278	University of Massachusetts, Amherst, MA
220,000	Erie Public Schools, Erie, PA -- precollege grants
217,400	Durham Public Schools, Durham, NC -- precollege grants
216,579	Yale University, New Haven, CT -- corporation alumni program
200,000	Lynn Public Schools, Lynn, MA -- precollege grants
199,396	New England Medical Center, Boston, MA -- precollege grants
195,037	Schenectady City School District, Schenectady, NY -- precollege grants
185,000	Union College, Barbourville, KY
173,394	University of California Berkeley, Berkeley, CA
172,055	University of Pennsylvania, Philadelphia, PA -- corporation alumni program
167,000	University of Illinois, Urbana, IL
155,809	Pennsylvania State University, University Park, PA
153,476	Virginia Polytechnic Institute, Blacksburg, VA -- educational
150,000	Boston University, Boston, MA -- precollege grants
150,000	University of Wisconsin, Madison, WI
148,750	Rutgers University, New Brunswick, NJ -- management educational grants
145,000	Syracuse University, Syracuse, NY -- management educational grants
127,910	University of Connecticut, Storrs, CT
125,000	Columbia University, New York, NY -- management educational grants
125,000	Everybody Wins Foundation, New York, NY -- precollege grants
125,000	Florence Public Schools, Florence, SC -- precollege grants
122,000	Texas A&M University, College Station, TX
120,000	City University of New York, New York, NY
120,000	Massachusetts Institute of Technology, Cambridge, MA -- educational
119,000	University of Michigan, Ann Arbor, MI
118,537	University of Notre Dame, South Bend, IN -- corporation alumni program
112,550	Harvard University, Cambridge, MA -- corporation alumni program
110,000	Polytechnic University, Brooklyn, NY
110,000	Texas University El Paso, El Paso, TX -- science and engineering program educational grants
110,000	University of Iowa, Iowa City, IA
110,000	University of Texas El Paso, El Paso, TX
100,177	Boston College, Chestnut Hill, MA -- corporate alumni program
100,000	Ohio State University, Columbus, OH -- management educational grants
93,651	Northeastern University, Boston, MA -- science and engineering program educational grants
91,000	Wood County Public Schools -- precollege grants

Health

100,000	Massachusetts General Hospital, Boston, MA -- special projects grant

International

150,862	Institute for International Education, New York, NY -- international grants
150,862	Institute for International Education, New York, NY -- international grants
100,000	Center for Strategic and International Studies, Washington, DC -- public policy grant
100,000	Center for Strategic and International Studies, Washington, DC -- public policy grant
100,000	Project Hope, Chevy Chase, MD -- international grants
100,000	Project Hope, Chevy Chase, MD -- international grants

Religion

102,351	City Mission, Schenectady, NY

General Mills, Inc.

 Number 44 of Top 100 Corporate Givers

Company Contact
Minneapolis, MN
Web: http://www.generalmills.com

Company Description
Revenue: US$6,033,000,000
Employees: 10,035 (1999)
Fortune Rank: 279, per FORTUNE Magazine's list of 500 Largest U.S. Corporations (1999).
FF 279
SIC(s): 2026 Fluid Milk, 2034 Dehydrated Fruits, Vegetables & Soups, 2037 Frozen Fruits & Vegetables, 2043 Cereal Breakfast Foods.

Operating Locations
Canada: Toronto Macaroni & Imported Foods Ltd., Rexdale; France: Biscuiterie Nantaise-BN, SA, Nantes, Loire-Atlantique; Guatemala: Industria Harinera Guatemalteca, SA, Guatemala City; Netherlands: Smiths Food Group B.V., Maarssen, Utrecht; Panama: General Mills de Panama, SA, Panama City; Spain: Preparados y Congelados Alimenticios, SA, Madrid; United Kingdom: General Mills Europe Ltd., Berkshire

Nonmonetary Support
Value: $11,000,000 (1995); $5,300,000 (1992); $5,500,000 (1990)
Type: Donated Products; Loaned Employees; Loaned Executives
Volunteer Programs: General Mills' Volunteer Connection and Retirement PLUS programs promote employee volunteerism by matching volunteers with projects, and the Volunteer Advisory Board Steers Company involvement in volunteer endeavors.
Contact: David Nasby, Vice President
Phone: (612)540-4351
Note: Co. donates a substantial amount of food products primarily through Second Harvest food banks.

General Mills Foundation

Giving Contact
Reatha Clark King, President and Executive Director
General Mills Foundation
PO Box 1113
Minneapolis, MN 55440
Phone: (612)540-2579
Fax: (612)540-4114
Web: http://www.generalmills.com/explore/community/

Alternate Contact
Constance L. Schillings
General Mills Foundation
One General Mills Boulevard
Minneapolis, MN 55426
Note: Contact for volunteer questions and requests only.

Description
Founded: 1954
EIN: 416018495
Organization Type: Corporate Foundation
Giving Locations: nationally; operating locations.
Grant Types: Capital, Employee Matching Gifts, General Support, Multiyear/Continuing Support, Operating Expenses.
Note: Employee matching gift ratio: 1 to 1. Foundation makes a limited number of capital grants and only for special purposes that meet specific community needs within the foundation's funding focus.

Giving Philosophy
'In 1954, the General Mills Foundation was created to focus the philanthropic resources of General Mills on community needs. The Foundation's mission is to provide financial support to nonprofit organizations that make a distinctive contribution to the quality of life and that strengthen the capacity of communities to solve problems and create opportunities for all citizens..To more effectively address community needs, the Foundation works closely with other General Mills citizenship programs.'
'The Foundation's strategic objectives for fiscal years 2000-2003 are to: positively impact/strengthen the quality of life in engage/support personal involvement of employees and retirees in community service; communicate the contributions and impact of Foundation grants to employees and the public; and enhance General Mills' reputation as a top-decile corporate citizen.'*General Mills Grant Application Guidelines*

Financial Summary
Total Giving: $15,999,986 (fiscal year ending May 31, 1999); $21,600,038 (fiscal 1998); $16,000,000 (fiscal 1997 approx). Note: Contributes through corporate direct giving program and foundation.
Giving Analysis: Giving for fiscal 1998 includes: foundation ($16,000,038); corporate direct giving ($5,600,000); fiscal 1999: foundation ($12,142,039); foundation matching gifts ($3,857,948)
Assets: $46,929,735 (fiscal 1996); $54,310,223 (fiscal 1995); $58,199,306 (fiscal 1994)
Gifts Received: $7,500,000 (fiscal 1996); $9,000,000 (fiscal 1995); $15,000,000 (fiscal 1994). Note: The foundation receives contributions from General Mills and its subsidiaries.

Typical Recipients
Arts & Humanities: Arts Associations & Councils, Arts Centers, Arts Funds, Arts Institutes, Dance, Film & Video, Arts & Humanities-General, Historic Preservation, History & Archaeology, Libraries, Literary Arts, Museums/Galleries, Music, Opera, Performing Arts, Public Broadcasting, Theater
Civic & Public Affairs: African American Affairs, Asian American Affairs, Business/Free Enterprise, Civil Rights, Economic Development, Employment/Job Training, Civic & Public Affairs-General, Hispanic Affairs, Housing, Law & Justice, Legal Aid, Municipalities/Towns, Native American Affairs, Professional & Trade Associations, Public Policy, Urban & Community Affairs, Women's Affairs, Zoos/Aquariums
Education: Agricultural Education, Arts/Humanities Education, Business Education, Business-School Partnerships, Colleges & Universities, Community & Junior Colleges, Continuing Education, Economic Education, Education Associations, Education Funds, Education Reform, Elementary Education (Public), Engineering/Technological Education, Faculty Development, Education-General, Gifted & Talented Programs, International Exchange, International Studies, Legal Education, Literacy, Medical Education, Minority Education, Preschool Education, Private Education (Precollege), Public Education (Precollege), Religious Education, Science/Mathematics Education, Secondary Education (Public), Social Sciences Education, Special Education, Student Aid
Environment: Environment-General
Health: Cancer, Children's Health/Hospitals, Clinics/Medical Centers, Emergency/Ambulance Services, Geriatric Health, Health Policy/Cost Containment, Health Organizations, Hospitals, Medical Rehabilitation, Medical Research, Mental Health, Nutrition
Religion: Religious Welfare, Social/Policy Issues
Science: Science Museums
Social Services: At-Risk Youth, Big Brother/Big Sister, Child Welfare, Community Centers, Community Service Organizations, Counseling, Day Care, Delinquency & Criminal Rehabilitation, Domestic Violence, Emergency Relief, Family Planning, Family Services, Food/Clothing Distribution, Homes, People with Disabilities, Recreation & Athletics, Refugee Assistance, Scouts, Senior Services, Shelters/Homelessness, Substance Abuse, United Funds/United Ways, Volunteer Services, YMCA/YWCA/YMHA/YWHA, Youth Organizations

Contributions Analysis
Giving Priorities: Social service, education, civics, the arts, hospitals, and substance abuse programs.
Arts & Humanities: 24%. Foundation supports the performing and visual arts, public broadcasting, and cultural centers.
Civic & Public Affairs: 8%. Supports economic development, community foundations and housing.
Education: 28%. Supports Junior Achievement, literacy projects, pre-college programs, scholarship funds, colleges and universities. The foundation makes grants to programs which emphasize student academic achievement, particularly at the K-12 level, and on efforts to improve the quality and efficiency of educational services.
Health: 5%. The foundation supports programs that promote healthy lifestyles in underserved communities and educate individuals on self-care techniques.
Social Services: 33%. Foundation supports programs which strengthen families, nurture children, support youth development, address the needs of individuals with disabilities, and improve communities. Violence prevention initiatives will be favored. The foundation allocates grants to the United Way. Also supports the development and maintenance of domestic and international food distribution systems serving low-income families.
Note: Total contributions made in 1999.

Application Procedures
Initial Contact: Request grant application or download application from the foundation's web site.
Application Requirements: Completed application form; a description of organization and mission statement, with a list of its officers and board members, including affiliations; proof of tax-exempt status; a recently audited financial statement; objectives for the current fiscal year; the previous year's major accomplishments; and a major donor list.
Deadlines: None; board meets periodically throughout the year.
Review Process: If proposal meets foundation criteria, application is assigned to a program officer for review; officer analyzes proposal and makes recommendation to foundation's Grants Committee; officer will contact organization if additional information is required.
Evaluative Criteria: Priority is given to organizations whose mission is closely related to the foundation's priorities; programs focus on the needs of families, children, and youth; services are direct and of high quality; programs or activities are based in communities with General Mills facilities and employees; programs or activities involve General Mills employees and retirees.
Decision Notification: Four to six weeks after recommendation to Grants Committee.
Notes: Send proposals to the Community Partnership Council in applicant's region; see foundation guidelines for list of councils.

Restrictions
Foundation does not support organizations without 501(c)(3) and 509(a) status; individuals; travel by groups; social, labor, veterans, alumni or fraternal organizations serving a limited constituency; political causes, candidates, or legislative lobbying efforts; recreational, sporting events or athletic associations; religious organizations for religious purposes; or organizations seeking underwriting for advertising or program sponsorship. Generally, the foundation also does not support: conferences, seminars and workshops; underwriting for program sponsorship; campaigns to eliminate or control specific diseases; or

publications, films, or television programs. workshops; underwriting for program sponsorship; campaigns to eliminate or control specific diseases; or publications, films, or television programs.

Additional Information

Foundation funding takes four forms: grants to nonprofit organizations; gift-matching to education and arts and culture organizations; match of employee and retiree contributions to annual United Way campaign; and scholarships for children of employees.
Foundation grant amounts begin at $1,000 and can exceed $100,000 for a single project.
The foundation conducts both pre- and post-grant evaluations and seeks the participation of the nonprofit in this process. The foundation also keeps a confidential record of all grant requests that have been accepted in the past nine years. Records of grants requests that are declined are kept for three years.
Publications: Annual Report; Application Form

Corporate Officials

Stephen R. Demeritt: vice chairman PRIM CORP EMPL vice chairman: General Mills Inc.
James A. Lawrence: chief financial officer, executive vice president PRIM CORP EMPL chief financial officer, executive vice president: General Mills, Inc. CORP AFFIL director: Avnet Inc.
Siri M. Marshall: senior vice president, general counsel ED Harvard University BA (1970); Yale University JD (1974). PRIM CORP EMPL senior vice president, general counsel: General Mills Inc. CORP AFFIL director: Nova Care Inc. NONPR AFFIL member executive committee: Center Public; trustee: Minneapolis Institute Arts; American Arbitration Association.
Michael A. Peel: senior vice president human resources B 1950. PRIM CORP EMPL senior vice president human resources: General Mills, Inc.
Stephen W. Sanger: chairman, chief executive officer, director B 1946. ED DePauw University BA (1968); University of Michigan MBA (1970). PRIM CORP EMPL chairman, chief executive officer, director: General Mills, Inc. CORP AFFIL director: Dayton Hudson Corp.; director: Donaldson Co. Inc. NONPR AFFIL director: Conference Board Inc.; treasurer: Guthrie Theater Foundation.
Austin Padraic Sullivan, Junior: senior vice president corporate relations B Washington, DC 1940. ED Princeton University AB (1964). PRIM CORP EMPL senior vice president corporate relations: General Mills, Inc. NONPR AFFIL member: Grocery Manufacturer America; director: Minnesota Chamber of Commerce; member: Business Roundtable; board advisors: Democrat Leadership Council.
Raymond Viault: vice chairman, director B New York, NY 1944. ED Brown University (1967); Columbia University (1969). PRIM CORP EMPL vice chairman, director: General Mills, Inc. CORP AFFIL director: Willis Corroon Group LLC.

Foundation Officials

Reatha Clark King: president, executive director ED Clark College BS (1958); University of Chicago PhD (1960). PRIM CORP EMPL vice president: General Mills, Inc. CORP AFFIL director: HB Fuller Co.; director: ExxonMobil Corp. NONPR AFFIL member: NAA; director: Saint Paul Corp. National and Community Service; board overseers: Clark Atlanta University; member: Delta Sigma Theta; chairman advisory council: ARC.
Siri M. Marshall: trustee (see above)
Michael A. Peel: trustee (see above)
Stephen W. Sanger: chairman, trustee (see above)
Austin Padraic Sullivan, Junior: trustee (see above)
Cynthia A. Thelen: coordinator
David Van Benschoten: treasurer B 1955. ED University of Minnesota; Bethel College (1976). PRIM CORP EMPL vice president investment management: General Mills, Inc.

Grants Analysis

Disclosure Period: fiscal year ending May 31, 1999
Total Grants: $12,142,039*
Number of Grants: 631
Average Grant: $18,479*
Highest Grant: $500,000
Typical Range: $5,000 to $30,000
***Note:** Grants analysis derived from a 1999 foundation grants list. Giving excludes matching gifts. Average grant figure excludes highest grant.

Recent Grants

Note: Grants derived from 1994 Form 990.

Arts & Humanities

400,000	Minnesota Orchestral Association, Minneapolis, MN -- operating support
250,000	Minneapolis Society of Fine Arts, Minneapolis, MN -- operating support
250,000	Minneapolis Society of Fine Arts, Minneapolis, MN -- New Beginnings campaign
200,000	Twin Cities Public Television, Saint Paul, MN -- operating support
140,000	Twin Cities Public Television, Saint Paul, MN -- capital campaign
125,000	Community Communications, Orlando, FL -- development of remote television production unit
107,100	Minnesota Orchestral Association, Minneapolis, MN -- capital campaign
100,000	Minnesota Public Radio, Saint Paul, MN -- operating support
100,000	Minnesota Public Radio, Saint Paul, MN -- operating support
94,700	Guthrie Theater Foundation, Minneapolis, MN -- operating support
79,900	Walker Art Center, Minneapolis, MN -- operating support
63,600	Minneapolis Society of Fine Arts, Minneapolis, MN -- New Beginnings program
62,700	St. Paul Chamber Orchestra Society, Saint Paul, MN -- operating support
56,500	Public Broadcasting Foundation of Northwest Ohio, Toledo, OH -- Getting Ready to Learn project
50,700	Minnesota Public Radio, Saint Paul, MN -- St. Paul Sunday Morning
50,000	Hennepin Center for Arts, Minneapolis, MN -- capital campaign
50,000	Minnesota Public Radio, Saint Paul, MN -- capital campaign
50,000	St. Olaf College, Northfield, MN -- WCAL radio station, The Lives of the Children program
50,000	United Arts of Central Florida, Orlando, FL -- match of GMRI employee contributions
46,300	Children's Theater Company, Minneapolis, MN -- operating support
40,000	Illusion Theater and School, Minneapolis, MN -- operating support
40,000	Penumbra Theater Company, Saint Paul, MN -- operating support
35,000	Intermedia Arts Minnesota, Minneapolis, MN -- capital campaign
35,000	Plymouth Music Series of Minnesota, Minneapolis, MN -- witness program

Civic & Public Affairs

175,000	Greater Minneapolis Metropolitan Housing Corp, Minneapolis, MN -- develop low-cost housing for low-income families
135,000	The City, Incorporated, Minneapolis, MN -- operating support
90,000	National Center for Fathering, Shawnee Mission, KS -- African American Fatherhood Renaissance project
75,000	Albuquerque T-VI Foundation Incorporated, Albuquerque, NM -- Hispanics Advancing Via Education project
60,000	Division of Indian Work, Minneapolis, MN -- capital campaign
50,000	Legal Rights Center, Minneapolis, MN -- operating support
50,000	Minneapolis Urban League, Minneapolis, MN -- improve student programs and academic achievement project
40,000	The City, Incorporated, Minneapolis, MN -- operating support
40,000	Project for Pride in Living, Minneapolis, MN -- programs to assist individuals to become self sufficient

Education

352,500	Minneapolis Federation of Alternative Schools, Minneapolis, MN -- implement five-year plan for member schools
150,000	Carleton College, Northfield, MN -- Excellence in Science program
125,000	Advertising Educational Foundation, New York, NY -- film on advertising research
116,000	Wharton School of Business, Philadelphia, PA -- operating support
114,400	Citizens Scholarship Foundation of America, Saint Peter, MN -- post high school scholarships
101,525	Citizens Scholarship Foundation of America, Saint Peter, MN -- scholarship stipends
101,525	Citizens Scholarship Foundation of America, Saint Peter, MN -- scholarship stipends
100,000	Columbia Business School, New York, NY -- Faculty Diversity and Development program
100,000	Culinary Institute of America, Hyde Park, NY -- financial assistance to economically disadvantaged students
100,000	Orange County Public Schools, Orlando, FL -- alternative high school program
100,000	United Negro College Fund, New York, NY -- capital campaign for United Negro College Fund member institutions
100,000	University of Minnesota Foundation, Minneapolis, MN -- capital campaign
80,000	Augsburg College, Minneapolis, MN -- evaluation program
61,150	Maynard Evans High School, Orlando, FL -- school to work simulation program
60,000	Courage Center, Golden Valley, MN -- early childhood development program
50,000	Beloit College, Beloit, WI -- Beloit Academy program
50,000	Center School, Minneapolis, MN -- improve student progress and academic achievement project
50,000	Independent School District No. 281, Robbinsdale, MN -- Plymouth Middle School Drop-In Center
50,000	St. Xavier University, Chicago, IL -- Adelante program to increase number of Latino nurses
50,000	Smith College, Northampton, MA -- collaborative program between Smith College and the Springfield Public Schools
50,000	Teach for America, New York, NY -- operating support
50,000	University of Illinois Foundation, Chicago, IL -- Latino RFP
50,000	University of Minnesota Foundation, Minneapolis, MN -- Humphrey Institute of Public Affairs
47,000	Junior Achievement of the Upper Midwest, Minneapolis, MN -- operating support
45,350	University of Minnesota Foundation, Minneapolis, MN -- Patty Berg Development fund
45,000	Buffalo State College Alumni Foundation, Buffalo, NY -- Families United program

45,000 Lead Program in Business, New York, NY -- operating support
41,940 National Merit Scholarship Corp, Evanston, IL -- GMI scholarship program
40,000 College of Dupage, Glen Ellyn, IL -- Strong Education for Latinos' Future project
40,000 College of St. Catherine, Saint Paul, MN -- Adelante Latina program for junior and senior high school Latina students
39,000 Metropolitan State University Foundation, Saint Paul, MN -- improving communication skills of students
30,000 Case Western Reserve University, Cleveland, OH -- Diane Patterson Memorial scholarship fund
25,000 Bryn Mawr College, Bryn Mawr, PA -- presidential discretionary grant

Health
250,000 Children's Hospital Medical Center, Boston, MA -- Touchpoints project
75,000 Minnesota Medical Foundation, Minneapolis, MN -- capital for cancer center
50,000 American Red Cross National Headquarters, Washington, DC -- disaster relief assistance
50,000 Courage Center, Golden Valley, MN -- Courage Center racial and ethnic inclusiveness initiative
50,000 North Memorial Medical Center, Robbinsdale, MN -- New Vistas North program
50,000 South Chicago Health Care Foundation, Chicago, IL -- capital for Operation Lifeline
50,000 Susan G. Komen Foundation, Dallas, TX -- regional breast cancer summits

Religion
75,000 Plymouth Christian Youth Center, Minneapolis, MN -- operating support
50,000 University of St. Thomas, Saint Paul, MN -- program development
49,333 Catholic Charities of the Archdiocese of St. Paul and Minneapolis, Minneapolis, MN -- St. Joseph's Home for Children

Science
90,000 Science Museum of Minnesota, Saint Paul, MN -- operating support
75,000 New Mexico Museum of Natural History Foundation, Albuquerque, NM -- Latino RFP for 'Proyecto Futuro'

Social Services
528,076 United Way Minneapolis Area, Minneapolis, MN -- operating support
528,076 United Way Minneapolis Area, Minneapolis, MN -- match of employee and retiree contributions to United Way
212,500 YMCA Metropolitan Minneapolis, Minneapolis, MN -- capital campaign
150,000 Messiah Willard Day Care Center, Minneapolis, MN -- Northside Family Connection Way to Grow program
125,000 Harriet Tubman Women's Shelter, Minneapolis, MN -- relationship abuse prevention program
103,473 United Way East Central Iowa, Cedar Rapids, IA -- operating support
100,000 YMCA Metropolitan Atlanta, Covington, GA -- capital campaign
77,968 United Way San Joaquin County, Stockton, CA -- operating support
76,966 United Way Greater Toledo, Toledo, OH -- operating support
75,176 United Way Crusade of Mercy, Chicago, IL -- operating support
75,000 Sharing and Caring Hands, Minneapolis, MN -- capital campaign
55,000 East Side Neighborhood Service, Minneapolis, MN -- operating support
50,000 Coalition for the Homeless of Central Florida, Orlando, FL -- capital campaign
50,000 Greater Minneapolis Girl Scout Council, Minneapolis, MN -- operating support
50,000 Heart of Florida United Way, Orlando, FL -- central Florida capital funds campaign
50,000 United Way Buffalo and Erie County, Buffalo, NY -- operating support
40,000 Big Brothers and Big Sisters of Greater Tri-Cities, Johnson City, TN -- Intergenerational Mentoring program
40,000 Boys and Girls Clubs of Stockton, Stockton, CA -- operations of the St. Mark's Clubhouse
40,000 Loring Nicollet-Bethelem Community Centers, Minneapolis, MN -- improve student programs and academic achievement project
40,000 Partnership for a Drug-Free America, New York, NY -- educational anti-drug campaign
40,000 YMCA Canton Area, North Canton, OH -- integrated, physically challenged fitness program
32,000 Buffalo Public School 84, Buffalo, NY -- purchase and install a safe playground for health-impaired multiple-handicapped students

General Motors Corp.

 Number 9 of Top 100 Corporate Givers

Company Contact

Detroit, MI
Web: http://www.gm.com

Company Description

Revenue: US$189,058,000,000 (1999)
Employees: 388,000 (1999)
Fortune Rank: 1, per FORTUNE Magazine's list of 500 Largest U.S. Corporations (1999).
FF 1
SIC(s): 3663 Radio & T.V. Communications Equipment, 3711 Motor Vehicles & Car Bodies, 3743 Railroad Equipment, 3769 Space Vehicle Equipment Nec.

Operating Locations

Australia: Packard CTA Pty. Ltd., Arrat; Holden's Engine Products Overseas Corp., Melbourne; General Motors--Holden's Automotive Ltd., Melbourne; Isuzu-General Motors Australia, Melbourne; United Australian Automotive Industries Ltd., Saint Kilda; Austria: Packard Electric Burgenland GmbH, Grosspetersdorf; Packard Electric Europa GmbH, Grosspetersdorf; AC Rochester Products Austria, Vienna; General Motors Austria, Vienna; Belgium: General Motors Continental, Antwerp; Reinshagen Tournai S.A., Tournai; Brazil: DHB-Componentes Automotivos, S.A., Porto Alegre; Vanguarda Componentes Automotivos, S.A., Porto Alegre; General Motors do Brasil Ltda., Sao Caetano do Sul; Ericson Packard Electric Componentes S.A., Sao Jose de Campos; AC Rochester Division (Sao Paulo), Sao Paulo; Canada: General Motors Canada Ste. Therese Division, Boisbriand; CAMI Automotive, Inc., Ingersoll; General Motors Canada Diesel Division, London; General Motors of Canada Ltd., Oshawa; General Motors Canada Components Division, Saint Catharines; General Motors Canada Engine Division, Saint Catharines; General Motors Canada Foundry Division, Saint Catharines; General Motors Acceptance Corporation of Canada, Ltd., Toronto; Hughes Leitz Optical Technologies, Ltd., Vancouver; General Motors Canada Ste. Therese Division, Windsor; General Motors Canada Transmission Division, Windsor; Chile: General Motors Chile S.A., Industria Automotriz, Santiago; Congo: Genie Mechanique Zairose, S.A.R.L., Kinshasa; Colombia: General Motors Colmotores, S.A., Bogota; Denmark: Opel Danmark, Soeborg; Ecuador: General Motors Del Equador S.A., Quito; Omnibus BB Transportes, S.A., Quito; Egypt: General Motors Egypt S.A.E., Cairo; Finland: Opel Oy, Helsinki; France: General Motors France Automobiles S.A., Argenteuil; Harrison Radiator Division, Donchery; AC Rochester Division (Gennevilliers), Gennevilliers; General Motors France, Gennevilliers, Haute-de-Seine; Societe Francaise des Amortisseurs de Carbon S.A., La Garenne-Colombes; Hydra-matic Division, Strasbourg; Germany: Adam Opel AG, Russelsheim; Convesco Vehicle Sales GmbH, Russelsheim; General Motors Marketing Services Hellas AEE, Russelsheim; Kabelwerke Reinshagen GmbH, Wuppertal; Hungary: AC Bakony Kft., Budapest; General Motors Hungary, Budapest; General Motors Hungary (Distribution) Ltd., Budapest; General Motors Hungary (Manufacturing) Ltd., Szentgotthard; Packard Electric Vas Kft, Szombathely; Indonesia: P.T. Mesin Isuzu Indonesia, Bekasi; Ireland: General Motors Distribution Ireland Ltd., Dublin; Packard Electric Ireland Ltd., Dublin; Italy: Aura S.R.L., Bologna; General Motors Italia, S.p.A., Rome; Reinshagen Italia Srl., Turin; Japan: GM Allison Japan Ltd., Tokyo; GMOC Japan, Tokyo; Kenya: General Motors Kenya Ltd., Nairobi; Republic of Korea: Delkor Battery Company, Gumi; Shinsung Packard Company, Ltd., Kyonggi-Do; Daewoo Automotive Components, Ltd., Seoul; Sung San Company, Ltd., Taegu; Luxembourg: European Technical Center, Bascharage; General Motors Luxembourg Operations S.A., Bascharage; AC Rochester Luxembourg S.A., Luxembourg; Mexico: Aralmex, S.A. de C.V., Guadalajara; Cableados S.A. de C.V., Jaurez; Alambrados Automotrices, S.A. de C.V., Mexico; Alambrados y Circuitos Electricos, S.A. de C.V., Mexico; Compania Nacional de Direcciones Automotrices, S.A. de C.V., Mexico; Components Mecanicos de Matamoros S.A. de C.V., Mexico; Conductores Componentes Electricos de Juarez S.A. de C.V., Mexico; Ensamble de Cables y Componentes, S.A. de C.V., Mexico; General Motors de Mexico, S.A. de C.V., Mexico; Packard Electric Division Mexican Operations, Mexico; Promotora De Partes Electricas Automotrices, S.A. de C.V., Mexico; Rimir, S.A. de C.V., Mexico; Rio Bravo Electricos, S.A. de C.V., Mexico; Sistemas Electricos Y Conmutadores, S.A. de C.V., Mexico; Vestiduras Fronterizas, S.A. de C.V., Mexico; Delnosa, S.A. de C.V., Mexico, D.F.; Deltronicos de Matamoros S.A. de C.V., Mexico, D.F.; General Motors de Mexico, S.A. de C.V., Ramos Arizpe; Netherlands: OPEL Nederland B.V., Sliedrecht; Norway: Opel Norge AS, Skedsmokorset; New Zealand: General Motors New Zealand Ltd., Upper Hutt; Portugal: General Motors de Portugal, Sociedade Anonima, Lisbon; INLAN-Industria de Componentes Mecanicos, S.A., Ponte de Sor; Delco Remi-Componentes Electronicos, Lda., Seixal; CABLESA-Industria de Componentes Electricos Sociedade Anonima, Sintra; Spain: ACG Componentes, S.A., Agoncillo, Lagrono; Senalizacion y Accesorios Del Automovil Yorka, S.A., Barcelona; Hughes Microelectronics Europa Espana S.A., Correos, Malaga; GM Espana Fisher Guide, Logrono, Rioja; Conexionados Electricos Tarazona S.A., Pamplona; Unicables, S.A., Pamplona; Opel Espana, Zaragoza; Slovenia: Industrija Delova Automobila, Kikinda, Kikinda; Sweden: General Motors Nordiska AB, Haninge; Saab Automobile AB, Nykoping, Trollhattan; Switzerland: General Motors Suisse S.A., Bienne; General Motors (Europe) AG, Glattbrugg; Tunisia: Compagnie de Faisceaux Tunisian International S.A., Tunis; Industries Mecaniques Maghrebines, Tunis; Turkey: ITC Inland Teknik Oto Yan Sanayi Limited Sirketi, Bursa; Packard Elektrik Sistemleri Ltd. Sirketi, Istanbul; General Motors Turkiye Ltd. Sirketi, Izmir; Taiwan: General Motors Taiwan, Inc., Taipei; United Kingdom: Ilmor Engineering, Ltd., Brixworth; Reinshagen U.K., Coventry; General Motors Overseas Corp., Dunstable; Vauxhall, Luton, Bedfordshire; Vauxhall Motors Ltd., Luton, Bedfordshire; AC

Rochester Corporation, Southampton; AC Rochester Overseas Corporation, Southampton; Uruguay: General Motors Uruguay S.A., Montevideo; Venezuela: Componentes Delfa, C.A., Caracas; Constructora Venezolano de Vehiculos, C.A., Caracas; General Motors Venezolana, C.A., Caracas; General Motors de Venezuela C.A., Caracas

Nonmonetary Support

Value: $15,500,000 (1998); $17,900,000 (1996); $25,200,000 (1995)

Type: Donated Equipment; Donated Products; In-kind Services; Loaned Employees

Note: Co. also donates real estate. Co. will not donate products for on-highway use.

Corporate Sponsorship

Value: $1,500,000 (1995)

Type: Arts & cultural events; Festivals/fairs; Music & entertainment events; Pledge-a-thon; Sports events

Note: Events sponsored are in-line with contribution focus areas.

General Motors Foundation

Giving Contact

Lorna G. Utley, vice-chairperson
General Motors Foundation
600 Renaissance Center
Detroit, MI 48265-3000
Phone: (313)665-2992
Fax: (313)665-0746
Web: http://www.generalmotors.com/company/community_involvement

Alternate Contact

Phone: (313)556-4260

Note: Provides recorded messages with giving guidelines.

Description

EIN: 382132136
Organization Type: Corporate Foundation
Giving Locations: nationally; operating locations.
Grant Types: General Support, Project.

Giving Philosophy

'General Motors and the GM Foundation support a variety of activities in the communities where we operate and sell our products. Our philanthropic and community relations mission is to ensure that we maintain our leadership position as a valued, responsible corporate citizen by enhancing the quality of life and our corporate reputation, consistent with our business goals and objectives.' *1995 General Motors Philanthropic Report*

Financial Summary

Total Giving: $70,983,193 (1998); $73,200,000 (1997); $66,700,000 (1996). Note: Contributes through corporate direct giving program and foundation. Giving includes 1998 Giving includes charity events ($5,100,000). 1996 Giving includes sponsorships.

Giving Analysis: Giving for 1996 includes: foundation ($27,000,000); corporate direct giving ($18,100,000); 1997: corporate direct giving ($46,500,000); foundation ($26,700,000); 1998: foundation ($25,534,644); corporate direct giving ($22,700,000); nonmonetary support ($15,500,000); foundation matching gifts ($1,430,849); foundation scholarships ($542,700); foundation grants to United Way ($175,000)

Assets: $148,614,025 (1998); $115,000,000 (1996 approx); $112,180,108 (1995)

Gifts Received: $23,700,000 (1998); $14,350,000 (1995). Note: In 1998, contributions were received from General Motors Corp.

Typical Recipients

Arts & Humanities: Arts Associations & Councils, Arts Centers, Arts Festivals, Arts Funds, Arts Institutes, Dance, Historic Preservation, Libraries, Museums/Galleries, Music, Opera, Performing Arts, Public Broadcasting, Theater, Visual Arts

Civic & Public Affairs: African American Affairs, Business/Free Enterprise, Chambers of Commerce, Civil Rights, Community Foundations, Economic Development, Economic Policy, Employment/Job Training, Ethnic Organizations, First Amendment Issues, Civic & Public Affairs-General, Hispanic Affairs, Housing, Law & Justice, Minority Business, Municipalities/Towns, Nonprofit Management, Professional & Trade Associations, Public Policy, Rural Affairs, Safety, Urban & Community Affairs, Women's Affairs, Zoos/Aquariums

Education: Agricultural Education, Arts/Humanities Education, Business Education, Colleges & Universities, Community & Junior Colleges, Continuing Education, Economic Education, Education Associations, Education Funds, Education Reform, Elementary Education (Private), Engineering/Technological Education, Faculty Development, Education-General, Health & Physical Education, International Exchange, International Studies, Legal Education, Literacy, Minority Education, Public Education (Precollege), Science/Mathematics Education, Student Aid

Environment: Environment-General, Resource Conservation

Health: Alzheimers Disease, Cancer, Emergency/Ambulance Services, Health Organizations, Hospices, Hospitals, Medical Rehabilitation, Medical Training, Mental Health, Public Health, Single-Disease Health Associations

International: International Affairs, International Environmental Issues, International Peace & Security Issues, International Relations

Religion: Religious Welfare

Science: Science Exhibits & Fairs, Scientific Centers & Institutes, Scientific Organizations

Social Services: Child Welfare, Community Centers, Community Service Organizations, Family Services, Food/Clothing Distribution, Homes, People with Disabilities, Senior Services, Shelters/Homelessness, Substance Abuse, United Funds/United Ways, Volunteer Services, Youth Organizations

Contributions Analysis

Giving Priorities: Education, health, community relations, public policy, arts and culture, and environment and energy.

Arts & Humanities: 8%. Contributes to museums, art institutes and centers, public television, symphonies, and performing arts.

Civic & Public Affairs: 20%. Gives to disaster relief, and supports urban development and community action programs designed to improve communities in which the company operates. Responds to a variety of community needs. Interests include urban and community affairs, youth groups, and economic development. (Public Policy) 9% of total contributions. Giving specifically targets economic policies.

Education: 36%. The major objectives of GM's educational support programs are to assist the corporation in meeting its needs for talent, especially in engineering and business administration; to keep GM informed of technical and nontechnical research being carried out on the nation's campuses; to encourage research in areas of interest to the corporation; and to strengthen company's role as a responsible corporate citizen. More than half of annual educational cash contributions are given to colleges and universities on GM's Key Institutions list, selected primarily on the quality of their engineering and business-related educational programs. These are basically the schools from which GM recruits, and many are institutions with which GM has research and development contracts. Supports graduate, undergraduate, and precollege engineering, science, and business education. Precollege education supported through such organizations as MathCounts, Detroit Area Precollege Engineering Program, Summer Training and Education Programs, and The LEAD Program in business. At the higher education level, supports colleges and universities and provides scholarships in engineering, including major support to women and minorities. Promotes the participation of minorities in handling their legal affairs through special grants at six university law schools; and develops Hispanic student involvement in high-technology and business careers. Also matches employee contributions to higher education.

Environment: 5%. Focuses spending on environmental and energy causes.

Health: 30%. Supports health and human services. In the area of social services, company gives to anti-drug activities, mentoring, and community service organizations. Health giving emphasizes, cancer research, with a major annual grant to the GM Cancer Research Foundation.

Note: A high percentage of grants are awarded through domestic and international subsidiaries and divisions, which have decision-making autonomy for gifts of less than $5,000. Total contributions made 1998.

Application Procedures

Initial Contact: Send a one-page cover letter and concept summary.

Application Requirements: The cover letter should include the organization name; contact person; project purpose; specific funding, service, or in-kind request; time period; possible strategic link with GM; and total length of time GM support would be needed. The concept summary should include the following information, in bullet format and not exceeding two pages, using the following order and numeric identification: (1) date of application; (2) legal name of organization; (3) year founded; (4) current operating budget; (5) contact person, address, phone and fax; (6) project name; (7) purpose of grant (statement of requested support); (8) project time frame; (9) amount requested; (10) total project cost; (11)geographic area; (12) previous support and requests to GM or GM Foundation over the last five years; (13) other organizations to which requests are being submitted; (14) signature of chairperson/executive director; (15) latest IRS Form 990 and a copy of the IRS correspondence confirming the organization's tax-exempt status; indicate if organization has submitted this or other proposals to other GM units (e.g., marketing divisions) or subsidiaries (e.g. GMAC, Hughes Electronics Corp.)

Deadlines: GM and the GM Foundation accept and screen proposals for grants on a continuous basis; however, proposals must be received no less than 45 days prior to the month of the quarterly Contributions Planning Board (CPB) meeting in order to be included in the next review.

Review Process: The GM Contributions Planning Board (CPB) serves as the governing body for all contributions and memberships. Under the oversight of the CPB, various subcommittees -- centered on GM's identified program areas of education, health, public policy, environment/energy, and community relations -- set strategic direction within their scope as well as review and evaluate proposals prior to submitting recommendations to the CPB. The GM Corporate Relations staff refers regional and local proposals for consideration and handling to the appropriate local committee.

Evaluative Criteria: Primary consideration is given to requests that exhibit a clear purpose and defined need in one of GM's areas of focus; recognize innovative approaches in addressing the defined need; demonstrate an efficient organization and detail the organization's ability to follow through on proposal; explain clearly the benefits to GM and plant city communities; and have a strong commitment to diversity.

Decision Notification: Inappropriate applicants are informed on a timely basis; if recommended, application will be reviewed by the CPB, which meets quarterly in March, June, September and December.

Notes: Based on the outcome of the concept evaluation, GM may request submission of a comprehensive proposal for additional evaluation, including: expanded project description, goals, and objectives; description of persons or groups who will benefit; relevant experience of the project's principal staff; history of organization (most recent annual report); detailed workplan, time frame, and action plan for expected outcome; evaluation plan including criteria for measuring effectiveness of the proposed project; all current and projected sources of funding (list amount requested of other corporations, foundations, and funding sources); detailed budget and long-term funding strategy beyond the initial grant period; current financial statements; current Board of Directors with affiliations.

Restrictions

Does not support organizations that discriminate on the basis of race, religion, creed, gender, age, veteran status, physical challenge, or national origin. In addition, contributions are generally not provided to individuals; religious organizations; political parties or candidates; U.S. hospitals and health-care institutions (for general operating support); capital campaigns; United Way-sponsored organizations; endowment funds; or conferences, workshops, or seminars not directly related to GM's business interests. GM believes that giving to capital programs and endowment campaigns does not appropriately utilize the corporation's resources. Does not support multi-year grants; only the first year of multi-year requests will be considered and subsequent years will be evaluated annually for future support.

Additional Information

General Motors has established a nonprofit organization, the GM Cancer Research Foundation, which awards substantial prizes for outstanding individual achievement in cancer research. As an extension of the foundation's ongoing commitment in the fight against cancer, the foundation established an international science journalism awards program in 1989. This program recognizes excellence in reporting about biomedical research with application to cancer and cancer research. Three awards, one each for newspaper, magazine and book, and broadcast coverage, carry a $10,000 cash award and a limited-edition work of art.

In addition to its philanthropic activities, General Motors provides funding for numerous educational and public interest programs as a corporate sponsor (examples include the nationwide telecast of 'The Kennedy Center Honors: A Celebration of the Performing Arts' and a national concerto competition).

Company actively works to increase educational opportunities for minorities and women inside the corporation and in the business community.

Applications for general grants should be sent to the Director, GM Global Philanthropy, MC 482-111-134, 3044 West Grand Boulevard, Detroit, MI 48202; Education-related grants should be sent to Director, GM Education Relations MC 108-162, 3044 West Grand Boulevard, Detroit, MI 48202; and local grants requests should be directed to the local GM Community Relations Committee (contact the local GM Personnel Department for address).

Publications: Philanthropic Annual Report

Corporate Officials

Harry J. Pearce: vice chairman, chief executive officer, director ED United States Air Force Academy BS (1964); Northwestern University JD (1967). PRIM CORP EMPL vice chairman: General Motors Corp.

John Francis Smith, Jr.: chairman B Worcester, MA 1938. ED University of Massachusetts BBA (1960); Boston University MBA (1965). PRIM CORP EMPL chairman: General Motors Corp. CORP AFFIL director: Procter & Gamble Co.; trustee: Hughes Electronics Corp.; director: Electronic Data Systems Corp.; drc: General Motors Acceptance Corp. NONPR AFFIL business council: Memorial Sloan-Kettering Cancer Center; member: U.S.-Japan Business Council; member: Business Roundtable Policy Comm; member, board: Detroit Renaissance Inc.; member: Beta Gamma Sigma; director: Boards Global Business Management Council; member: American Society Corporate Executives; member, director: American Automobile Manufacturers Association. CLUB AFFIL director: Economic Club Detroit.

G. Richard Wagoner, Jr.: president, chief executive officer, director B Wilmington, DE 1953. ED Duke University BA (1975); Harvard University MBA (1977). PRIM CORP EMPL president, chief executive officer, director: General Motors Corp.

Foundation Officials

Wallace W. Creek: secretary B Kankakee, IL 1939. ED University of Illinois (1960); Michigan State University (1972). PRIM CORP EMPL comptroller: General Motors Corp.

Deborah I. Dingell: president

Grants Analysis

Disclosure Period: calendar year ending 1998
Total Grants: $25,534,644*
Number of Grants: 806 (approx)
Average Grant: $31,681 (approx)
Highest Grant: $1,500,000
Typical Range: $1,000 to $100,000
***Note:** Giving excludes matching gifts, scholarship, United Way. Grants analysis includes foundation giving only.

Recent Grants

Note: Grants derived from 1998 Form 990.

Arts & Humanities

300,000	Detroit Institute of Arts Founders Society, Detroit, MI
250,000	Detroit Symphony Orchestra Hall, Inc., Detroit, MI
200,000	Black Revolutionary War Patriots Foundation
125,000	Flint Cultural Center, Flint, MI

Civic & Public Affairs

500,000	FIRST Foundation -- operational costs
380,000	New Detroit, Inc., Detroit, MI
250,000	Society of Automotive Engineers, Warrendale, PA
200,000	Arab Community Center for Economic and Social Services, Dearborn, MI -- ACCESS Vision 2000
200,000	ESD Foundation, Southfield, MI
150,000	Greater Downtown Partnership, Inc., Detroit, MI -- continue the mission of accelerating economic development in downtown Detroit

Education

500,000	Automotive Youth Educational Systems, Inc., Troy, MI
330,000	Regents of the University of Michigan, Ann Arbor, MI
307,500	College Fund/UNCF, Fairfax, VA -- Campaign 2000
290,000	College Fund/UNCF, Fairfax, VA
278,000	Massachusetts Institute of Technology, Cambridge, MA
250,000	Wayne State University, Detroit, MI
200,000	Cornerstone Schools
200,000	Trustees of Princeton University, Princeton, NJ
175,000	Detroit Area Pre-College Engineering Program, Detroit, MI
166,000	Commission for Lansing Schools Success, Lansing, MI
165,000	Cornell University, Ithaca, NY
156,334	California Institute of Technology, Pasadena, CA
150,000	GALAXY Institute for Education
150,000	National Defense University Foundation, Inc., Washington, DC -- membership and contribution
150,000	National Defense University Foundation, Inc., Washington, DC
150,000	National Hispanic Scholarship Fund, Inc., San Francisco, CA
125,000	University of California Riverside Foundation, Riverside, CA
115,000	Detroit Area Pre-College Engineering Program, Detroit, MI
115,000	University of Illinois at Urbana-Champaign, Urbana, IL
110,000	Hispanic Association of Colleges and Universities, San Antonio, TX
110,000	National Action Council for Minorities in Engineering, Inc., New York, NY
110,000	National Consortium for Graduate Degrees for Minorities in Engineering and Science, Notre Dame, IN

Health

1,500,000	Karmanos Cancer Institute, Detroit, MI -- Campaign for Cancer Care and Cure
500,000	GM Cancer Research Foundation, Detroit, MI
250,000	GM Cancer Research Foundation, Detroit, MI
250,000	GM Cancer Research Foundation, Detroit, MI
222,793	GM Cancer Research Foundation, Detroit, MI
175,000	The Cleveland Clinic Foundation, Cleveland, OH -- genetic epidemiologic study of prostate cancer
175,000	The Cleveland Clinic Foundation, Cleveland, OH -- IMRT for localized prostate cancer research
150,000	GM Cancer Research Foundation, Detroit, MI
150,000	GM Cancer Research Foundation, Detroit, MI
150,000	GM Cancer Research Foundation, Detroit, MI -- cash grant to help cover annual expenses
142,857	Beaumont Foundation, Southfield, MI -- organization support

Social Services

1,345,000	Charities Funds Transfer, Alexandria, VA
350,000	FOCUS: Hope, Detroit, MI
150,000	FOCUS: Hope, Detroit, MI
117,364	Charities Funds Transfer, Alexandria, VA
113,575	Charities Funds Transfer, Alexandria, VA
100,480	Charities Funds Transfer, Alexandria, VA

GENERAL REINSURANCE CORP.

Company Contact

Stamford, CT
Web: http://www.genre.com

Company Description

SIC(s): 6321 Accident & Health Insurance, 6719 Holding Companies Nec.
Parent Company: General Re Corp.

Nonmonetary Support

Value: $5,000 (1987)
Type: Donated Equipment

Giving Contact

Richard W. Manz, Assistant Vice President
General Reinsurance Corp.
Financial Centre
PO Box 10351
Stamford, CT 06904
Phone: (203)328-5000
Fax: (203)328-5603

Description

Organization Type: Corporate Giving Program
Giving Locations: principally near operating locations and to national organizations.
Grant Types: Capital, Employee Matching Gifts, General Support.
Note: Employee matching gift ratio: 1 to 1.

Financial Summary

Total Giving: $4,000,000 (2000 approx); $4,000,000 (1999 approx); $3,700,000 (1995 approx). Note: Contributes through corporate direct giving program only.

Typical Recipients

Civic & Public Affairs: Economic Development, Employment/Job Training, Housing, Law & Justice, Public Policy, Safety, Women's Affairs
Education: Colleges & Universities, Community & Junior Colleges, International Studies, Literacy, Private Education (Precollege)
Environment: Environment-General
Health: Emergency/Ambulance Services, Health Policy/Cost Containment, Health Organizations, Hospices, Hospitals, Medical Rehabilitation, Medical Research, Medical Training, Mental Health, Public Health
Social Services: Community Service Organizations, Food/Clothing Distribution, People with Disabilities, Recreation & Athletics, Substance Abuse, United Funds/United Ways

Contributions Analysis

Giving Priorities: The arts, civics, higher education, and social service.
Civic & Public Affairs: 25% to 30%. Supports economic development through job training, environmental affairs, and women's affairs.
Education: 25% to 30%. Funds colleges and universities, especially those with interest in medical education or liberal arts education.
Health: 25% to 40%. Supports hospitals and hospices, medical research and training, and mental health.

Application Procedures

Initial Contact: Submit a full proposal.
Deadlines: August 31 to meet the budget cycle.
Review Process: A committee of seven employees prepares an annual contributions budget in late September, which is reviewed by management and approved by the board of directors.
Decision Notification: Applicants will be notified in December.

Restrictions

The foundation does not give to individuals, political or lobbying groups, sectarian purposes, dinners or special events, goodwill advertising, and will only give to a religious organization if its services are available to the public on a nondiscriminatory basis.

Corporate Officials

Ronald Eugene Ferguson: chairman, president, chief executive officer, director B Chicago, IL 1942. ED Blackburn College BA (1963); University of Michigan MA (1965). PRIM CORP EMPL chairman, president, chief executive officer, director: General Reinsurance Corp. CORP AFFIL director: Colgate-Palmolive Co.
Richard W. Manz: assistant vice president PRIM CORP EMPL assistant vice president: General Reinsurance Corp.

Grants Analysis

Disclosure Period: calendar year ending 1996
Typical Range: $500 to $2,500

GEORGIA-PACIFIC CORP.

Company Contact

Georgia-Pacific Center
133 Peachtree St. NE
Atlanta, GA 30303
Phone: (404)652-4000
Fax: (404)584-1470
Web: http://www.gp.com

Company Description

Acquired: Unisource Worldwide (1999).
Revenue: US$17,796,000,000 (1999)
Profit: US$716,000,000 (1999)
Employees: 47,500
Fortune Rank: 96, per FORTUNE Magazine's list of 500 Largest U.S. Corporations (1999).
FF 96
SIC(s): 2411 Logging, 2421 Sawmills & Planing Mills--General, 2431 Millwork, 5031 Lumber, Plywood & Millwork.

Operating Locations

Operates in Canada, Europe, and South and Central America.

Nonmonetary Support

Value: $500,000 (1996)
Type: Donated Equipment; Donated Products

Georgia-Pacific Foundation

Giving Contact

Curley M. Dossman, Jr., President
Georgia-Pacific Foundation
133 Peachtree Street Northeast
Atlanta, GA 30303
Phone: (404)652-4182
Fax: (404)584-1470

Description

EIN: 936023726
Organization Type: Corporate Foundation
Giving Locations: operating locations.
Grant Types: Capital, Employee Matching Gifts, Endowment, General Support, Scholarship.
Note: Employee matching gift ratio: 2 to 1.

Giving Philosophy

'Georgia-Pacific's vision is to be the best forest products company in the world and to be the best at everything we do. We believe success in achieving this vision is linked to the future of our communities.
'We know that putting resources back into our communities strengthens them and contributes to our own success as a company. That is why we created the Georgia-Pacific Foundation. The Foundation makes investments that improve the quality of life in communities where our employees live and work.
'To make a meaningful impact, the Foundation has chosen distinct investment areas (education, environment, community enrichment and employee involvement).. to support..' *Community Investment Program of the Georgia-Pacific Foundation*

Financial Summary

Total Giving: $3,845,408 (1997); $3,000,000 (1996); $2,828,798 (1995). Note: Contributes through corporate direct giving program and foundation.
Giving Analysis: Giving for 1995 includes: foundation ($2,284,819); corporate direct giving ($543,919); 1997: corporate direct giving (approx $2,782,208); foundation scholarships (approx $764,758); foundation grants to United Way (approx $251,130); foundation matching gifts (approx $47,312)
Assets: $1,107,815 (1997); $97,088 (1996); $701,341 (1992)
Gifts Received: $4,897,164 (1997); $4,300,215 (1996); $759,081 (1992)

Typical Recipients

Arts & Humanities: Arts Associations & Councils, Arts Centers, Arts Festivals, Dance, Ethnic & Folk Arts, Historic Preservation, Libraries, Museums/Galleries, Music, Opera, Public Broadcasting, Theater
Civic & Public Affairs: African American Affairs, Botanical Gardens/Parks, Business/Free Enterprise, Civil Rights, Community Foundations, Economic Development, Employment/Job Training, Civic & Public Affairs-General, Law & Justice, Municipalities/Towns, Public Policy, Safety, Urban & Community Affairs, Zoos/Aquariums
Education: Business Education, Colleges & Universities, Economic Education, Education Associations, Education Funds, Engineering/Technological Education, Environmental Education, Education-General, Leadership Training, Literacy, Minority Education, Private Education (Precollege), Science/Mathematics Education, Special Education, Student Aid
Environment: Air/Water Quality, Environment-General, Resource Conservation, Wildlife Protection
Health: Children's Health/Hospitals, Emergency/Ambulance Services, Eyes/Blindness, Health Funds, Health Organizations, Hospitals, Medical Rehabilitation, Medical Research, Single-Disease Health Associations
Religion: Jewish Causes, Religious Welfare
Science: Science Museums
Social Services: Big Brother/Big Sister, Camps, Child Welfare, Community Centers, Community Service Organizations, Family Services, Food/Clothing Distribution, People with Disabilities, Recreation & Athletics, Scouts, Substance Abuse, United Funds/United Ways, YMCA/YWCA/YMHA/YWHA, Youth Organizations

Contributions Analysis

Giving Priorities: Higher education, social service, the environment, the arts, and health.
Arts & Humanities: About 5%. Special interest in museums and music. Also supports arts associations, and historical groups.
Education: 30% to 35%. Most support goes to scholarships for students in areas where company has major operations. Also sponsors Georgia-Pacific Foundation Merit Scholarships. Other areas of interest include colleges and universities, literacy programs, school-to-work programs, higher education funds and associations, and technical education.
Environment: About 35%. Support goes to programs that promote environmental awareness. Interests include source reduction, recycling and environmental protection.
Health: Less than 5%. Support to hospitals, children's health organizations, and single-disease health associations.
Social Services: About 5%. Foundation generally emphasizes United Way chapters.Other recipients include religious welfare organizations, housing, programs for the handicapped, recreational activities and community service organizations

Application Procedures

Initial Contact: brief letter or proposal
Application Requirements: background information including name of organization and name of project, project's goal and objective, need project seeks to meet, priority area and company area project will affect, anticipated results, project budget, proof of tax-exempt status and list of board members and staff, including description of qualifications
Deadlines: October 31

Decision Notification: written notification within 45 days of receipt of proposal

Restrictions

Foundation does not support non-tax exempt organizations; organizations that discriminate on the basis of race, color, creed, nationality or gender; individuals; political causes; religious institutions or schools; social, labor, veterans, alumni or fraternal organizations; goodwill advertising or fundraising; sports; operating support for members of United Way; national groups whose local chapters already receive support; benefit tickets; operating support for colleges and universities; medical and nursing schools; academic chairs; organizations that channel funds; raffles, telethons, walk-a-thons and trips or tours. chairs; organizations that channel funds; raffles, telethons, walk-a-thons and trips or tours.

Corporate Officials

Alston Dayton 'Pete' Correll, Jr.: chairman, president, chief executive officer, director B Brunswick, GA 1941. ED University of Georgia BSBA (1963); University of Maine MS (1966); University of Maine MSChE (1967). PRIM CORP EMPL chairman, president, chief executive officer, director: Georgia-Pacific Corp. CORP AFFIL director: SunTrust Banks Inc.; director: Northwood Pulp & Timber Ltd.; director: Sears, Roebuck & Co.; president: Mead Timber Co.; president, chief executive officer, director: Great Northern Nekoosa Corp.; director: Kraft Co. Georgia; director: Brunswick Pulp & Paper Co.; director: British Columbia Forest Products Ltd. NONPR AFFIL trustee: University Georgia Foundation; trustee: Robert W. Woodruff Arts Center; chairman: United Negro College Fund; director: Miami Valley Ohio Boy Scouts; director: Nature Conservancy; director: Keep America Beautiful Inc.; member: Georgia Chamber of Commerce; director: Georgia Research Alliance; chairman: Central Atlanta Progress; director: Atlanta Symphony Orchestra; board counselor: Carter Center; vice chairman: Atlanta Action Forum; member: Atlanta Chamber of Commerce. CLUB AFFIL Commerce Club.

John Francis McGovern: chief financial officer, executive vice president B Port Chester, NY 1946. ED Fordham University BS (1968). PRIM CORP EMPL chief financial officer, executive vice president: Georgia-Pacific Corp. ADD CORP EMPL vice president, director: Great Northern Nekoosa Corp. NONPR AFFIL member: Financial Executives Institute. CLUB AFFIL Atlanta Country Club.

Foundation Officials

Gerard Brandt: director

Alston Dayton 'Pete' Correll, Jr.: director (see above)

Curley M. Dossman, Junior: president

Kenneth F. Khoury: secretary B New York, NY 1951. ED Rutgers University Stonier Graduate School of Banking BA (1972); Fordham University School of Law JD (1977). PRIM CORP EMPL vice president, secretary, deputy general counsel: Georgia-Pacific Corp.

John Francis McGovern: chairman (see above)

Kimberly Dyslin Roundtree: assistant secretary

Beth Clark Zoffmann: vice president, director B Atlanta, GA. ED Georgia State University BA. PRIM CORP EMPL vice president corporate communications: Georgia-Pacific Corp.

Grants Analysis

Disclosure Period: calendar year ending 1997
Total Grants: $2,782,208*
Highest Grant: $389,785
Typical Range: $1,000 to $10,000
***Note:** Giving excludes scholarship; matching gifts, United Way. Grants analysis is approximate.

Recent Grants

Note: Grants derived from 1997 Form 990.

Arts & Humanities

200,000	Robert W. Woodruff Art Center, Atlanta, GA
25,000	Arts Festival, Atlanta, GA
25,000	National Black Arts Festival, Atlanta, GA

Civic & Public Affairs

157,259	National Parks and Conservation, Washington, DC -- annual support
35,000	Zoo Atlanta, Atlanta, GA
27,200	100 Black Men of America, Atlanta, GA -- second payment on a two-year pledge
25,000	100 Black Men of America, Augusta, GA
25,000	Metropolitan Atlanta Community Foundation, Atlanta, GA -- first payment on a two-year pledge
25,000	NAACP, New York, NY -- annual support
25,000	Southeastern Firefighters Burn Foundation, Augusta, GA
25,000	SWOYA, Coos Bay, OR -- annual support
25,000	Zoo Atlanta, Atlanta, GA -- third payment on a three-year pledge
20,000	100 Black Men of America, Augusta, GA -- convention sponsorship
20,000	Jobs for America's Graduates, Alexandria, VA -- annual support
15,000	SERP Corporation
15,000	State Legislative Leaders Foundation, Centerville, MA -- annual membership

Education

406,065	National Merit Scholarship Corporation, Evanston, IL
50,000	College Fund
30,000	Virginia Polytechnic Institute, VA -- second payment on a five-year pledge
25,000	Oregon State University, Corvallis, OR -- funding for new forest research
20,000	Emory University, Atlanta, GA -- Haan Woods Project
20,000	Florida Education Foundation, Tallahassee, FL -- biodiversity project funding
20,000	Miami University Pulp and Paper Foundation, Miami, FL
15,000	Atlanta Outward Bound, Atlanta, GA -- environment
15,000	Georgia Tech Foundation, Atlanta, GA
15,000	Keystone Science School -- teaching program

Environment

66,667	Trees Atlanta, Atlanta, GA -- first payment on a three-year pledge
50,000	Piedmont Park Conservancy, Atlanta, GA -- improvements to the park
25,000	American Forests, Washington, DC -- sponsor Urban Forests conference
25,000	Charles Elliott Wildlife -- first payment on a two-year pledge
25,000	Georgia Conservancy, Atlanta, GA -- annual contribution
25,000	Path Foundation, Atlanta, GA -- third payment on a three-year pledge
15,000	Nature Conservancy

Health

50,000	Emory Eye Center, Atlanta, GA -- second payment on a three-year pledge
20,000	City of Hope, Duarte, CA

Social Services

47,500	United Way of South Wood, Wisconsin Rapids, WI
33,334	Boy Scouts of America -- third payment on a three-year pledge
25,463	United Way of Whatcom County, Bellingham, WA -- third and fourth quarter payments
25,000	Big Brothers and Big Sisters
25,000	Boys and Girls Club -- Hole-In-One Club
25,000	United Way of Columbia
25,000	YMCA, Atlanta, GA
20,000	Camp Twin Lakes, Atlanta, GA -- annual support
20,000	Lawrence County Civic Center -- building program
20,000	United Way of Lincoln County
17,664	United Way of Texarcana
15,826	Little River County United Way, Ashdown, AR
15,000	Camp Best Friends, Atlanta, GA
15,000	John E. Alexander YMCA -- faculty support
15,000	YWCA -- Beth Zoffman Honorary Chair

GEORGIA POWER CO.

Company Contact

Atlanta, GA
Web: http://www.georgiapowerco.com

Company Description

Assets: US$13,071,000,000
Employees: 11,000
SIC(s): 4911 Electric Services.
Parent Company: Southern Co., Atlanta, GA, United States

Nonmonetary Support

Type: Cause-related Marketing & Promotion; Donated Equipment; Donated Products; In-kind Services; Loaned Employees; Loaned Executives
Note: Annual Sponsorship Budget: $34,000 to $138,000.

Corporate Sponsorship

Type: Arts & cultural events; Festivals/fairs; Sports events

Georgia Power Foundation

Giving Contact

Judy M. Anderson, Vice President & Executive Director
Georgia Power Foundation
333 Piedmont Avenue Northeast
Bin 10230
Atlanta, GA 30308-3374
Phone: (404)506-6784
Fax: (404)526-2945

Alternate Contact

Don Martin, Manager of Charitable Giving
Phone: (404)506-1978

Description

Founded: 1930
EIN: 581709417
Organization Type: Corporate Foundation
Giving Locations: GA: operating locations and service area
Grant Types: Capital, Conference/Seminar, Emergency, Employee Matching Gifts, Endowment, General Support, Multiyear/Continuing Support, Professorship, Project, Research.

Giving Philosophy

'In 1986, the Georgia Power Foundation, Inc., was established to further its corporate citizenship efforts and to lend focus to its corporate contributions.. More than this, the Georgia Power Foundation represents one way in which Georgia Power lives up to its motto: 'A citizen wherever we serve.' .. The Georgia Power

Foundation endeavors to support the company's tradition of community involvement and to improve and enrich the communities in which it serves.' *Georgia Power Foundation*

Financial Summary

Total Giving: $9,500,000 (1999 approx); $4,707,852 (1998); $8,814,871 (1997). Note: Contributes through corporate direct giving program and foundation.

Giving Analysis: Giving for 1997 includes: foundation ($5,084,516); corporate direct giving ($3,730,355); 1998: foundation ($4,582,852); foundation grants to United Way ($125,000)

Assets: $105,422,551 (1998); $87,931,435 (1996); $60,000,000 (1995)

Gifts Received: $7,000,000 (1996); $2,566,083 (1993). Note: Foundation receives contributions from Georgia Power Co.

Typical Recipients

Arts & Humanities: Arts Associations & Councils, Arts Centers, Arts Festivals, Arts Funds, Arts Institutes, Community Arts, Dance, Ethnic & Folk Arts, Historic Preservation, Libraries, Museums/Galleries, Music, Performing Arts, Theater

Civic & Public Affairs: African American Affairs, Botanical Gardens/Parks, Chambers of Commerce, Civil Rights, Community Foundations, Economic Development, Economic Policy, Employment/Job Training, Civic & Public Affairs-General, Housing, Legal Aid, Municipalities/Towns, Philanthropic Organizations, Professional & Trade Associations, Rural Affairs, Urban & Community Affairs, Women's Affairs, Zoos/Aquariums

Education: Agricultural Education, Arts/Humanities Education, Business Education, Colleges & Universities, Community & Junior Colleges, Economic Education, Education Associations, Education Funds, Education Reform, Elementary Education (Private), Engineering/Technological Education, Faculty Development, Health & Physical Education, Journalism/Media Education, Leadership Training, Literacy, Medical Education, Minority Education, Private Education (Precollege), Public Education (Precollege), Science/Mathematics Education, Secondary Education (Public), Student Aid, Vocational & Technical Education

Environment: Environment-General, Resource Conservation, Wildlife Protection

Health: Cancer, Children's Health/Hospitals, Clinics/Medical Centers, Emergency/Ambulance Services, Geriatric Health, Health Organizations, Hospices, Hospitals, Medical Rehabilitation, Medical Research, Mental Health, Public Health, Single-Disease Health Associations

International: International Affairs, International Relations

Religion: Religious Welfare

Science: Science Museums, Scientific Centers & Institutes

Social Services: At-Risk Youth, Big Brother/Big Sister, Camps, Child Abuse, Child Welfare, Community Centers, Community Service Organizations, Day Care, Delinquency & Criminal Rehabilitation, Family Planning, Family Services, Food/Clothing Distribution, Homes, People with Disabilities, Recreation & Athletics, Scouts, Senior Services, Shelters/Homelessness, Special Olympics, Substance Abuse, United Funds/United Ways, YMCA/YWCA/YMHA/YWHA, Youth Organizations

Contributions Analysis

Giving Priorities: Social services, education, community affairs, art organizations, museums, and non-profit U.S.-based international organizations.

Arts & Humanities: 14%. Primarily supports arts organizations, historic preservation, and museums.

Civic & Public Affairs: 11%. Emphasis on chambers of commerce. Also funds a variety of activities including community affairs and development groups, trade associations, and civil rights organizations.

Education: 41%. Primarily supports colleges and universities, education funds, and secondary education. Interests include business, medical, engineering, technical, and legal education.

Environment: 8%. Funds conservation efforts.

Health: 25%. Focus on health and human services. Majority of funding supports the United Way. Interests also include traditional youth organizations, the YMCA and YWCA, hospitals and clinics, national health organizations, medical research, and the American Red Cross.

Science: 1%.

Note: Total contributions in 1998.

Application Procedures

Initial Contact: Send a brief letter or proposal.

Application Requirements: Include a brief a description of organization, list of officers and board members, amount requested, purpose for which funds are sought, sources of other support and the amounts assured or anticipated for the proposed project, and proof of tax-exempt status.

Deadlines: None.

Review Process: Each request is organized by category (education, health, etc.) and set up in files as well as on the philanthropy system.

Evaluative Criteria: Past contributions, survey data, tax status, and support of similar issues.

Decision Notification: Grants are made quarterly.

Restrictions

Does not give to individuals, political or lobbying groups, religious organizations, or private secondary schools.

Additional Information

The Georgia Power Foundation was established in December 1986 with a $10.5 million grant from Georgia Power Co., although the company also continues to give directly.

Southern Co., Georgia Power's parent company, does not administer a contributions program. However, several other subsidiaries administer direct giving programs: Alabama Power Co.; Gulf Power Company/Gulf Power Foundation, 500 Bayfront Parkway, PO Box 1151, Pensacola, FL 32520, 904-444-6325; and Mississippi Power Company/Mississippi Power Foundation. 32520, 904-444-6325; and Mississippi Power Company/Mississippi Power Foundation (see separate entry for details).

Publications: Brochure

Corporate Officials

Judy M. Anderson: vice president, corporate secretaryc B Jay, FL 1948. ED Troy State University (1971); Atlanta Law School (1979). PRIM CORP EMPL vice president, corporate secretary: Georgia Power Co. CORP AFFIL secretary: Piedmont-Forrest Corp. NONPR AFFIL member: American Bar Association.

W. C. Archer, III: senior vice president external affairs PRIM CORP EMPL senior vice president external affairs: Georgia Power Co.

James K. Davis: senior vice president corporate relations PRIM CORP EMPL senior vice president corporate relations: Georgia Power Co. NONPR AFFIL director: Georgia Department of Human Resources.

H. Allen Franklin: president, chief executive officer B 1945. ED University of Alabama BEE (1966). PRIM CORP EMPL president, chief executive officer: Georgia Power Co. CORP AFFIL director: Southern Energy Resources Inc.; director: SouthTrust Corp.; director: Southern Electric Generating Co.; director: SEI Holdings Inc.; executive vice president, director: Southern Co. Inc.

Warren Yancey Jobe: executive vice president B Burlington, NC 1940. ED University of North Carolina BS (1963); Emory University (1976); Harvard University (1981). PRIM CORP EMPL executive vice president: Georgia Power Co. CORP AFFIL director: Southern Electric Generating Co.; senior vice president corporate development: Southern Co. Inc. NONPR AFFIL member: American Institute of CPA's.

David M. Ratcliffe: chief financial officer, treasurer, director B Tifton, GA 1948. ED Valdosta State College (1970); Woodrow Wilson College (1975). PRIM CORP EMPL chief financial officer, treasurer, director: Georgia Power Co. ADD CORP EMPL senior vice president external affairs: Southern Co.

Foundation Officials

Judy M. Anderson: executive director, secretary, assistant treasurer (see above)

W. C. Archer, III: director (see above)

James K. Davis: director (see above)

Robert H. Haubein, Jr.: director B 1940. ED University of Missouri BSEE (1981). PRIM CORP EMPL senior vice president: Georgia Power Co.

Gene R. Hodges: director B 1938. ED Georgia State University BBA (1963). PRIM CORP EMPL executive vice president customer operations: Georgia Power Co.

Warren Yancey Jobe: president, director (see above)

Charles O. Rawlins: treasurer, assistant secretary

Grants Analysis

Disclosure Period: calendar year ending 1998

Total Grants: $4,582,852*

Number of Grants: 457

Average Grant: $10,028

Highest Grant: $250,000

Typical Range: $1,000 to $15,000

***Note:** Giving excludes United Way.

Recent Grants

Note: Grants derived from 1998 Form 990.

Arts & Humanities

250,000	Robert W. Woodruff Arts Center, Inc., Atlanta, GA -- operating
50,000	Sapelo Island Restoration Foundation, Inc., Atlanta, GA -- capital
25,000	Robert W. Woodruff Arts Center, Inc., Atlanta, GA -- capital

Civic & Public Affairs

80,000	Carter Center, Inc. (The), Atlanta, GA -- capital
50,000	Can't read Linear Park Alliance, Inc., Atlanta, GA -- capital
50,000	Carter Center, Inc. (The), Atlanta, GA -- operating
50,000	East Lake Community Foundation, Inc., Atlanta, GA -- operating
50,000	Techwood Park, Inc., Atlanta, GA -- Capital
25,000	City Of Plains, Atlanta, GA -- capital

Education

200,000	University System of Georgia Foundation, Inc., Atlanta, GA -- operating
125,000	Georgia State Department Of Education, Atlanta, GA -- operating
100,000	Georgia State University, Atlanta, GA -- operating
100,000	United Negro College Fund, Inc., New York, NY -- operating
80,000	Georgia Partnership For Excellence In Education, Inc., Atlanta, GA -- operating
50,000	Georgia Military College, GA -- capital
50,000	University Of Georgia, Athens, GA -- operating
45,000	Oglethorpe University, Atlanta, GA -- capital
33,334	Gwinnett Tech Foundation, Inc., Lawrenceville, GA -- capital
33,333	Berry College, Inc., Mount Berry, GA -- capital
33,333	Medical College Of Georgia Foundation, Inc., Augusta, GA -- operating
30,000	Brewton Parker College, Inc., Mount Vernon, GA -- Capital

30,000 University Of Georgia Foundation, Inc., Athens, GA -- operating
30,000 Valdosta State University Foundation, Inc., Valdosta, GA -- Operating
25,000 Georgia 4-H Club Foundation Cooperative Extension Service, Athens, GA -- capital
25,000 Junior Achievement of Greater Atlanta, Inc., Atlanta, GA -- operating

Environment

60,000 Georgia Department of Natural Resources, Atlanta, GA -- operating
33,334 Path Foundation, Inc., Atlanta, GA -- capital
30,000 Nature Conservancy, Inc., Atlanta, GA -- operating

Health

50,000 American Cancer Society, Inc.-Georgia Division, Atlanta, GA -- operating
50,000 George West Mental Health Foundation, Inc., Atlanta, GA -- capital
43,333 Scottish Rite Childrens Medical Center, Inc., Atlanta, GA -- capital
30,000 American Red Cross-Metropolitan Atlanta Chapter, Atlanta, GA -- operating
30,000 Georgia Baptist Health System, Inc., Atlanta, GA -- operating
25,000 Good Samaritan Health Center, Inc., (The), Atlanta, GA -- capital

Science

33,334 Fernbank, Inc., Atlanta, GA -- operating

Social Services

100,000 United Way Of Metropolitan Atlanta, Inc., Atlanta, GA -- capital
70,000 Georgia Golf Hall of Fame, Augusta, GA -- capital
50,000 Northwest Georgia Girl Scout Council, Inc., Atlanta, GA -- operating
50,000 YMCA Of Metropolitan Atlanta, Inc., Atlanta, GA -- operating
33,333 Boys & Girls Clubs Of Metro Atlanta, Inc., Atlanta, GA -- capital
30,000 Eagle Ranch, Inc., Chestnut Mountain, GA -- capital
28,920 Boy Scouts Of America National Council-Atlanta Area Council, Atlanta, GA -- capital
25,000 Big Brothers & Big Sisters of Metro Atlanta, Inc., Atlanta, GA -- capital

GERBER PRODUCTS CO.

Company Contact

Fremont, MI

Company Description

Employees: 9,200
SIC(s): 2032 Canned Specialties, 2033 Canned Fruits & Vegetables, 2043 Cereal Breakfast Foods, 2341 Women's/Children's Underwear.
Parent Company: Novartis U.S.A.

Operating Locations

AL: International Forest Seed Co., Odenville; AR: Gerber Products Co., Fort Smith; AZ: Sandoz Pharmaceutical Corp., Scottsdale; CA: Gerber Products Co., Anaheim; Biocine Co., Emeryville; Chiron Diagnostics, Emeryville; Gerber Products Co., Fremont; Ciba Corning Diagnostics Corp., Irvine; Biotrack, Mountain View; Ciba Corning Diagnostics Corp., Palo Alto; SyStemix, Palo Alto; CO: Geneva Pharmaceuticals, Broomfield; Gerber Products Co., Englewood; Hilleshog Mono-Hy, Inc., Longmont; DC: Sandoz Pharmaceutical Corp., Washington; FL: Maag Agrochemicals, Vero Beach; GA: CIBA Vision Corp., Duluth; Gerber Products Co., Norcross; HI: Gerber Products Co., Honolulu; ID: Rogers Brothers Seed Co., Boise; Rogers NK Seed Co., Boise; IL: Sandoz Agro, Inc., Des Plaines; Novartis Seeds, Downers Grove; Gerber Products Co., Schaumburg; IN: Gerber Products Co., Indianapolis; MA: Gerber Products Co., Chelmsford; Ciba Corning Diagnostics Corp., East Walpole; CIBA Corning Diagnostics Corp., Medfield; Ingold Electrodes, Wilmington; MD: Sandoz Consumer Pharmaceutical, Baltimore; Genetic Therapy, Gaithersburg; MI: Reed Plastics, Albion; Gerber Finance Co., Fremont; Gerber Products Co., Fremont; Gerber Products Co., Fremont; Gerber Products Overseas, Fremont; Gerber Products Co., Southfield; EMS-Togo, Taylor; MN: Fredonia Seed Co., Golden Valley; NK Lawn & Garden, Golden Valley; Northrup King Co., Golden Valley; Pedigree Seed Co., Golden Valley; Red Line Health Care Corp., Golden Valley; Sandoz Clinical and Nutrition Div., Minneapolis; Sandoz Food Service & Industrial Div., Minneapolis; Novartis Nutrition Corp., Saint Louis Park; Repligen Sandoz Research Corp., Saint Louis Park; NC: Gerber Products Co., Asheville; Sandoz Chemical Corp., Charlotte; CIBA Seeds, Greensboro; Gerber Products Co., Skyland; NJ: Gerber Products Co., Fort Lee; Novartis Pharmaceuticals, East Hanover; Sandoz Pharmaceutical Corp., East Hanover; Sandoz Research Institute, East Hanover; Sandoz Chemical Corp. Purchasing, Fair Lawn; Ohaus Corp., Florham Park; McHutchinson Div., Ridgefield Park; CIBA Self-Medication, Woodbridge; NY: Hi-Speed Checkweigher Co., Ithaca; Sandoz Corp., New York; CIBA-GEIGY Pharmaceutical Production, Suffern; Gerber Life Insurance Co., White Plains; OH: Gerber Products Co., Akron; Ciba Corning Diagnostics Corp., Oberlin; Summit Plastic Co., Tallmadge; PR: Gerber Products Co.; TN: Sandoz Consumer Pharmaceutical, Chattanooga; TX: Sandoz Argo Corp., Dallas; Reed Plastics, Grand Prairie; WI: CIBA-GEIGY Formulated Systems Group, Madison Heights; Gerber Products Co., Reedsburg; Gerber Products, Div.-Baby Care, Reedsburg
Note: Operates in Canada and Costa Rica.

Nonmonetary Support

Value: $1,500,000 (1989); $400,000 (1988); $400,000 (1987)
Type: Donated Products
Contact: Van Hinds, Director, Committee Affairs
Note: Company makes product donations to international relief organizations only.

Gerber Foundation

Giving Contact

Barbara Getz, Executive Director
Gerber Foundation
4747 W. 48th Street
Fremont, MI 49412
Phone: (231)924-3175
Fax: (231)924-3560

Description

EIN: 386068090
Organization Type: Corporate Foundation
Giving Locations: nationally.
Grant Types: Employee Matching Gifts, General Support, Multiyear/Continuing Support, Project, Scholarship.
Note: Matching gifts program supports educational institutions.

Giving Philosophy

'The Foundation's national grants program is categorized into three areas: programs offering Education and Training, particularly to parents and to care providers of very young children; Infant and Child-Related programs providing direct services to young children and their families; and Science and Research projects into infant nutrition, health, and development.' *The Gerber Foundation 1997-1998 Biennial Report*

Financial Summary

Total Giving: $3,900,000 (fiscal year ending May 31, 1999 approx); $3,300,000 (fiscal 1998 approx); $3,453,403 (fiscal 1997). Note: Contributes through corporate direct giving program and foundation.
Assets: $83,529,369 (fiscal 1998); $76,377,903 (fiscal 1997); $60,400,084 (fiscal 1995)
Gifts Received: $1,969 (fiscal 1997); $40,292 (fiscal 1996); $43,037 (fiscal 1995). Note: Foundation receives contributions from Gerber Companies.

Typical Recipients

Arts & Humanities: Public Broadcasting
Civic & Public Affairs: African American Affairs, Clubs, Community Foundations, Employment/Job Training, Civic & Public Affairs-General, Hispanic Affairs, Housing, Legal Aid, Parades/Festivals, Professional & Trade Associations, Public Policy, Safety, Zoos/Aquariums
Education: Agricultural Education, Arts/Humanities Education, Business Education, Colleges & Universities, Community & Junior Colleges, Education Funds, Engineering/Technological Education, Education-General, Medical Education, Minority Education, Private Education (Precollege), Public Education (Precollege), Science/Mathematics Education, Student Aid, Vocational & Technical Education
Environment: Environment-General
Health: AIDS/HIV, Cancer, Children's Health/Hospitals, Clinics/Medical Centers, Diabetes, Eyes/Blindness, Health-General, Health Policy/Cost Containment, Health Organizations, Heart, Hospices, Hospitals, Medical Rehabilitation, Medical Research, Medical Training, Nursing Services, Nutrition, Prenatal Health Issues, Preventive Medicine/Wellness Organizations, Public Health, Speech & Hearing
International: Health Care/Hospitals, International Relief Efforts
Religion: Religious Welfare
Science: Scientific Centers & Institutes, Scientific Organizations, Scientific Research
Social Services: At-Risk Youth, Child Abuse, Child Welfare, Community Service Organizations, Domestic Violence, Family Services, Food/Clothing Distribution, People with Disabilities, Recreation & Athletics, Special Olympics, United Funds/United Ways, Volunteer Services, YMCA/YWCA/YMHA/YWHA, Youth Organizations

Contributions Analysis

Giving Priorities: Education, social welfare, health, scientific institutions, and infant and child-related programs.
Education: 27%. Supports programs which promote responsible parenting, beginning at young ages and extending to adulthood. Supports formal and informal instruction in such areas as parenting skills, infant and young child care, nutrition and development training, child abuse prevention, school readiness and early school success, and avoidance of too-early child bearing. Scholarship grants are occasionally made to institutions to support students pursuing degrees for future careers in fields related to these areas.
Science: 23%. Supports accredited colleges and universities, teaching hospitals, and independent research institutions for research projects in the areas of nutrition, health, and development of infants and young children. Priority is given to projects which have the potential of resulting in publication of findings with broad applicability for the public good.
Note: Total contributions made in 1998.

Application Procedures

Initial Contact: Call or write for guidelines and application, then submit written proposal.
Application Requirements: Cover letter, signed by senior administrative official, which describes the applicant organization and endorses the proposed project; completed application form; proposal narrative, including: description of organization, current programs, services, and population served, description of

project, how it fits within organization, primary project audience, project schedule and anticipated outcomes, evaluation measures, description and status of any collaborations with other organizations, expected impact of the project nationally or regionally, potential for replication, plan of project funding, description of current or expected funding from other donors, plans for continuation of project after funding period; line-item project budget; most recent audited financial statement, or Form 990; board roster, including affiliations; proof of tax-exempt status; supporting information, such as: letters of support, news articles, annual report, newsletters, etc.
Deadlines: February 1 for Education & Training proposals; May 1 for Science & Research proposals; and August 1 for Infant & Child-Related Programs.
Review Process: Trustees review proposals in May, August, and November.
Evaluative Criteria: Specific projects with measurable national or regional impact.
Decision Notification: Up to three months after receipt.
Notes: Foundation staff is willing to discuss projects with applicants before a full proposal is submitted.

Restrictions

Grants are not made to agencies based outside of the United States.
Does not support dinners or special events, fraternal organizations, individuals, political or lobbying groups, religious organizations for sectarian purposes, or organizations not tax-exempt under the Internal Revenue Code.
Foundation does not generally support capital, endowment, or local projects.

Additional Information

Publications: Application Form; Guidelines

Corporate Officials

Richard E. Dunning: assistant treasurert, controller PRIM CORP EMPL assistant treasurer: Gerber Products Co.
Stan VanderRoest: vice president, comptroller, controller B Kalamazoo, MI 1961. ED Calvin College (1983); University of Pittsburgh (1984). PRIM CORP EMPL vice president, comptroller, controller: Gerber Products Co. NONPR AFFIL member: American Institute CPAs.

Foundation Officials

Reginald W. Baker: secretary, trustee PRIM CORP EMPL vice president: Market Strategies Inc.
Tracy A. Baker: trustee
K. Larry Beemer: trustee
Ted C. Davis: trustee
Richard E. Dunning: trustee (see above)
Michael G. Ebert: trustee
Barbara Getz: executive director
Barbara J. Ivens: president, trustee
John J. James: trustee
Jane Jeannero: trustee
David C. Joslin: trustee
Kaye A. McLeod: vice president, trustee
Carolyn R. Morby: trustee
Alfred A. Piergallini: trustee B Easton, PA 1946. ED Lafayette College BA (1968); University of Chicago MBA (1970).
Randy Puff: trustee
Stan VanderRoest: trustee, treasurer (see above)

Grants Analysis

Disclosure Period: fiscal year ending May 31, 1997
Total Grants: $3,453,403
Number of Grants: 582
Average Grant: $5,934
Highest Grant: $300,000
Typical Range: $500 to $10,000

Recent Grants

Note: Grants derived from 1997 Form 990.

Arts & Humanities

50,000 WGBH Educational Foundation, Boston, MA -- support education, training

Civic & Public Affairs

23,000 Gerald R. Ford Council, Grand Rapids, MI
20,000 Neighborhood House, Seattle, WA -- infant, child support
15,000 St. Louis Varsity Club, St. Louis, MO

Education

100,000 University of Texas Galveston Medical Branch, Galveston, TX -- support science, research
32,000 University of Iowa Foundation, Iowa City, IA -- support science, research
25,000 Harlem Educational Activities Fund, New York, NY -- support education, training
25,000 New York University, New York, NY -- support science, research
25,000 University of Miami School of Medicine, Miami, FL -- support science, research
25,000 University of Michigan Ann Arbor, Ann Arbor, MI -- support science, research
20,000 University of Arkansas, Fayetteville, AR
20,000 University of Iowa Foundation, Iowa City, IA -- infant, child support
15,000 EPIC Program, Ossining, NY -- support education, training
13,888 Freemont Christian School, Freemont, MI

Health

177,586 Butterworth Foundation, Grand Rapids, MI -- support Infant, Child programs
140,000 Elizabeth Glaser Pediatric AIDS Foundation, Santa Monica, CA -- support science, research
120,000 City of Hope, Scottsdale, AZ -- support spring fundraiser
91,000 Michigan State University Department of Pediatrics and Development, East Lansing, MI
50,000 Child Health Foundation, Columbia, MD -- support science and research
50,000 Deaf Family Clinic, Boston, MA
42,400 Research Foundation of State University of New York Binghamton, Binghamton, NY -- support science, research
40,000 American Nurses Foundation, Washington, DC -- support Infant, Child programs
33,000 Children's Research Institute, Washington, DC -- support science, research
30,000 Nurses for Newborns, St. Louis, MO -- support education, training
25,000 Children's Memorial Foundation, Chicago, IL
25,000 Mary Free Bed Hospital and Rehabilitation Center, Grand Rapids, MI -- support science, research
20,700 American Diabetic Association Foundation, Chicago, IL
20,000 National Black Child Development Institution, Washington, DC -- support infant, child programs
20,000 Pediatric AIDS Foundation, Santa Monica, CA -- support science, research
20,000 Pediatric AIDS Foundation, Santa Monica, CA -- support education, training
15,000 Children's Action Network, Los Angeles, CA -- support infant, children
15,000 National Coalition of Hispanic Health and Human Services Organization, Washington, DC -- support infant, child programs
14,200 Prevent Blindness, Raleigh, NC
12,500 Advertising Council, New York, NY -- support infant, child programs

Science

131,322 Moneli Chemical Senses Center, Philadelphia, PA -- support science, research
15,000 Institute of Food Technologists, Chicago, IL

Social Services

300,000 Food Research and Action Center, Washington, DC -- support infant, child programs
118,780 Children's Village, Dobbs Ferry, NY
80,000 Safe Sitter, Indianapolis, IN -- support infant, child programs
50,000 Childhelp USA, Hollywood, CA
45,000 Child and Family, PARTNERS, Knoxville, TN -- support education and training
32,200 Youth Services, Tulsa, OK -- support education, training
30,000 Children Now, Oakland, CA
30,000 Youth Services, Philadelphia, PA -- support infant, child
25,000 Project Open Hand, Atlanta, GA -- infant, child support
20,000 Kids in Distressed Situations, Moorestown, NJ
15,000 House of Ruth, Claremont, CA -- support infant, children
15,000 National Committee to Prevent Child Abuse, Chicago, IL -- support infant, child programs
15,000 National Court-Appointed Special Advocate Association, Seattle, WA -- support infant, children
15,000 National Fatherhood Initiative, Gaithersburg, MD -- support infant, children

GIANT EAGLE INC.

Company Contact

Pittsburgh, PA
Web: http://www.gianteagle.com

Company Description

Employees: 20,000
SIC(s): 2032 Canned Specialties, 2033 Canned Fruits & Vegetables, 2051 Bread, Cake & Related Products, 5411 Grocery Stores.

Giant Eagle Foundation

Giving Contact

Jody Clark, Administrator
Giant Eagle Foundation
101 Kappa Drive
Pittsburgh, PA 15238
Phone: (412)963-6200
Fax: (412)963-2540

Description

EIN: 256033905
Organization Type: Corporate Foundation
Giving Locations: PA: Pittsburgh
Grant Types: General Support, Research.

Financial Summary

Total Giving: $1,686,256 (fiscal year ending August 31, 1998); $1,572,449 (fiscal 1997); $1,138,766 (fiscal 1996). Note: Contributes through corporate direct giving program and foundation.
Giving Analysis: Giving for fiscal 1996 includes: foundation ($1,137,766); foundation grants to United Way ($1,000); fiscal 1997: foundation ($1,571,449); foundation grants to United Way ($1,000); fiscal 1998: foundation ($1,596,256); foundation grants to United Way ($73,000); foundation scholarships ($17,000)
Assets: $11,740,124 (fiscal 1998); $8,893,568 (fiscal 1997); $5,065,197 (fiscal 1995)

Gifts Received: $3,473,737 (fiscal 1998); $2,421,292 (fiscal 1997); $725,000 (fiscal 1995). Note: Contributions are received from Giant Eagle, Inc.

Typical Recipients

Arts & Humanities: Arts Associations & Councils, Arts Centers, Arts Institutes, Ballet, Community Arts, Dance, Arts & Humanities-General, History & Archaeology, Libraries, Museums/Galleries, Music, Opera, Performing Arts, Public Broadcasting, Theater
Civic & Public Affairs: African American Affairs, Civil Rights, Clubs, Economic Development, Economic Policy, Civic & Public Affairs-General, Law & Justice, Legal Aid, Municipalities/Towns, Philanthropic Organizations, Public Policy, Urban & Community Affairs, Women's Affairs, Zoos/Aquariums
Education: Business Education, Colleges & Universities, Education Funds, Elementary Education (Private), Faculty Development, Minority Education, Private Education (Precollege), Religious Education, Special Education, Student Aid
Environment: Environment-General, Resource Conservation, Wildlife Protection
Health: AIDS/HIV, Cancer, Children's Health/Hospitals, Diabetes, Emergency/Ambulance Services, Geriatric Health, Health Organizations, Heart, Hospitals, Kidney, Medical Rehabilitation, Medical Research, Mental Health, Prenatal Health Issues, Single-Disease Health Associations
International: Health Care/Hospitals, International Organizations, International Relief Efforts, Missionary/Religious Activities
Religion: Jewish Causes, Religious Organizations, Religious Welfare, Social/Policy Issues, Synagogues/Temples
Science: Scientific Centers & Institutes, Scientific Research
Social Services: At-Risk Youth, Big Brother/Big Sister, Child Welfare, Community Centers, Community Service Organizations, Counseling, Delinquency & Criminal Rehabilitation, Domestic Violence, Family Services, Food/Clothing Distribution, People with Disabilities, Recreation & Athletics, Scouts, Senior Services, Sexual Abuse, Shelters/Homelessness, Substance Abuse, United Funds/United Ways, YMCA/YWCA/YMHA/YWHA, Youth Organizations

Contributions Analysis

Arts & Humanities: 13%. Funding supports performing arts organizations, symphony, opera, ballet, theater, and dance.
Civic & Public Affairs: 6%. Supports community development, municipalities, and environmental affairs.
Education: 6%. Favors educational foundations and the University of Pittsburgh. Other recipients include private precollege education, Junior Achievement and minority education funds. Provides scholarships to children of employees.
Environment: 1%.
Health: 4%.Supports AIDS concerns, pediatric health-care facilities, medical rehabilitation, and medical research.
International: 1%. Supports international assistance and services.
Religion: 63%. Funding supports the United Jewish Federation in Pittsburgh, PA. Additional funding supports the Jewish National Fund and other Jewish organizations.
Social Services: 6%. Contributes to youth organizations including Big Brothers and Big Sisters and scouting, family services, and the United Way.
Note: Total contributions in 1998.

Application Procedures

Initial Contact: Send a written proposal.
Application Requirements: Include a description of organization, amount requested, purpose of funds sought, recently audited financial statement, and proof of tax-exempt status.
Deadlines: None.

Restrictions

Does not support individuals or non-501(c)(3) organizations.

Corporate Officials

David S. Shapira: chairman, chief executive officer, director B 1942. ED Oberlin College BA (1964); Stanford University MA (1966). PRIM CORP EMPL chairman, chief executive officer, director: Giant Eagle Inc. CORP AFFIL director: Mellon Bank NA; chairman, director: Phar-Mor Inc.; director: Equitable Resources Inc.; director: Mellon Bank Corp.

Foundation Officials

Gerald Chait: trustee CORP AFFIL director: Giant Eagle Inc.; director: Tamarkin Co. Inc.
Edward Moravitz: trustee B 1925. ED University of Pittsburgh (1948). CORP AFFIL director: Tamarkin Co. Inc.
Donald Plung: trustee
Charles W. Porter: trustee B 1912. CORP AFFIL officer: Tamarkin Co. Inc.
David S. Shapira: trustee (see above)
Norman Weizenbaum: trustee B 1933. ED University of Pennsylvania (1955). CORP AFFIL director: Giant Eagle Inc.; director: Tamarkin Co. Inc.

Grants Analysis

Disclosure Period: fiscal year ending August 31, 1998
Total Grants: $1,596,256*
Number of Grants: 138
Average Grant: $5,732*
Highest Grant: $811,000
Typical Range: $500 to $10,000
***Note:** Giving excludes United Way and scholarships. Average grant excludes highest grant.

Recent Grants

Note: Grants derived from 1998 Form 990.

Arts & Humanities

50,000 Cleveland Museum of Art, Cleveland, OH
20,000 The Pittsburgh Cultural Trust, Pittsburgh, PA
20,000 Pittsburgh Symphony Orchestra, Pittsburgh, PA
20,000 The Pittsburgh Symphony Society, Pittsburgh, PA
15,000 Pittsburgh Opera, Pittsburgh, PA
10,000 Carnegie Museum of Art, Pittsburgh, PA
10,000 Historical Society of Western Pennsylvania, Pittsburgh, PA
8,000 Pittsburgh Dance Council, Pittsburgh, PA
7,500 Carnegie Museums of Pittsburgh, Pittsburgh, PA
7,500 City Theatre Company, Pittsburgh, PA
7,500 Pittsburgh Ballet Theatre, Pittsburgh, PA
7,500 The Youngstown Symphony, Youngstown, OH
5,000 Civic Light Opera, Pittsburgh, PA
5,000 Pittsburgh Center for the Arts, Pittsburgh, PA
5,000 River City Brass Band, Pittsburgh, PA

Civic & Public Affairs

29,500 Allegheny Conference on Community Development, Pittsburgh, PA
25,000 Allegheny Policy Council, Pittsburgh, PA
7,500 Penn Southwest Association, Pittsburgh, PA
7,500 Pennsylvania Economy League, Pittsburgh, PA
7,500 Pittsburgh Zoo, Pittsburgh, PA
5,000 Pittsburgh Regional Alliance, Pittsburgh, PA

Education

40,000 Carnegie Mellon University, Pittsburgh, PA
30,000 Urban Community School, Cleveland, OH
20,000 Extra Mile Education Foundation, Pittsburgh, PA
5,000 Laroche College, Pittsburgh, PA

Environment

5,000 Audubon Society of Western Pennsylvania, Pittsburgh, PA
5,000 Conservation Consultants, Inc., Pittsburgh, PA
5,000 National Aviary, Pittsburgh, PA

Health

10,000 Crohn's and Colitis Foundation, Pittsburgh, PA
10,000 Persad Center, Pittsburgh, PA
10,000 Pittsburgh Aids Task Force, Pittsburgh, PA
10,000 To the CFIDS Association, Charlotte, NC
7,500 To Make-A-Wish Foundation, Pittsburgh, PA
5,000 American Heart Association, Pittsburgh, PA
5,000 D.T. Watson Rehabilitation Services, Sewickley, PA

International

10,000 Foundation for Developmentally Disabled Children in Israel, Ra'Anana, Israel

Religion

811,000 United Jewish Federation, Pittsburgh, PA
33,334 Adat Shalom, Pittsburgh, PA
15,000 Jewish Community Center, Pittsburgh, PA
13,000 Congregation Beth Shalom, Pittsburgh, PA
13,000 Congregation Beth Shalom, Pittsburgh, PA
10,000 The Jewish Community Federation of Cleveland, Cleveland, OH
10,000 Salvation Army, Pittsburgh, PA
10,000 Shaar Hitikvah-Gateway to Hope, Pittsburgh, PA
7,500 National Council of Jewish Women Race for the Cure, Pittsburgh, PA
5,000 Bnai Zion, Pittsburgh, PA

Social Services

72,000 United Way of Allegheny County, Pittsburgh, PA
10,000 YWCA of Greater Pittsburgh, Pittsburgh, PA
5,000 Pittsburgh Action Against Rape, Pittsburgh, PA
5,000 The Whale's Tale Foundation, Pittsburgh, PA

GIANT FOOD INC.

Company Contact

Landover, MD

Company Description

Revenue: US$4,230,600,000
Profit: US$94,200,000
Employees: 27,000
SIC(s): 5411 Grocery Stores, 5912 Drug Stores & Proprietary Stores.
Parent Company: Koninklijke Ahold NV, Albert Heijnweg 1, Zaandam, Netherlands

Operating Locations

CA: Giant Food Inc., Fresno; DC: Giant Food Inc., Washington; MD: Giant Food Inc., Baltimore, Burtonsville, Gaithersburg, Jessup, Joppa Heights; Giant Food, Landover; Giant Food Inc., Landover, Lutherville, Pikesville, Prince Frederick, Rockville, Silver

Spring, Upper Marlboro, Westminster; VA: Giant Food Inc., Annandale, Fredericksburg, Herndon, Lakeridge, McLean, Warrenton

Nonmonetary Support

Value: $50,000 (1991); $900,000 (1989); $900,000 (1988)
Type: Cause-related Marketing & Promotion; Donated Equipment; Donated Products; In-kind Services
Contact: Barry F. Scher, Vice President, Public Affairs

Giant Food Foundation

Giving Contact

Caron Sisson, Foundation Coordinator
Giant Food Foundation
PO Box 1804, D-599
Washington, DC 20013
Phone: (301)341-4561
Fax: (301)618-4972

Alternate Contact

Barry Scher, Vice President of Public Affairs
Note: Contact for sponsorship, direct giving and nonmonetary support.

Description

Founded: 1950
EIN: 526045041
Organization Type: Corporate Foundation
Giving Locations: DE; DC; MD; NJ; VA
Grant Types: General Support.

Financial Summary

Total Giving: $419,622 (fiscal year ending January 31, 2000); $410,817 (fiscal 1999); $514,067 (fiscal 1998). Note: Contributes through corporate direct giving program and foundation. Giving includes foundation.
Assets: $712,905 (fiscal 1998 approx); $712,905 (fiscal 1997 approx); $809,253 (fiscal 1996)
Gifts Received: $600,000 (fiscal 1996); $600,000 (fiscal 1995); $700,000 (fiscal 1993). Note: Contributions are received from Giant Food Inc.

Typical Recipients

Arts & Humanities: Arts Centers, Ballet, Community Arts, Dance, History & Archaeology, Libraries, Museums/Galleries, Music, Opera, Performing Arts, Public Broadcasting, Theater
Civic & Public Affairs: African American Affairs, Business/Free Enterprise, Chambers of Commerce, Employment/Job Training, Housing, Law & Justice, Urban & Community Affairs, Women's Affairs, Zoos/Aquariums
Education: Arts/Humanities Education, Colleges & Universities, Community & Junior Colleges, Education Funds, Medical Education, Minority Education, Religious Education, Science/Mathematics Education, Special Education, Student Aid
Health: Cancer, Children's Health/Hospitals, Geriatric Health, Heart, Hospices, Hospitals, Mental Health, Prenatal Health Issues, Single-Disease Health Associations
Religion: Jewish Causes, Religious Organizations, Religious Welfare, Social/Policy Issues
Social Services: Big Brother/Big Sister, Child Welfare, Community Centers, Community Service Organizations, Family Services, Food/Clothing Distribution, People with Disabilities, Recreation & Athletics, Scouts, Senior Services, Shelters/Homelessness, Substance Abuse, United Funds/United Ways, Youth Organizations

Contributions Analysis

Giving Priorities: Community service, the arts, health, medical research, and education.
Arts & Humanities: Less than 5%. Supports music and ballet, theater, museums, public broadcasting, arts festivals, and arts education.
Civic & Public Affairs: 85% to 90%. Majority of funding supports united funds and religious welfare projects. Other interests include urban affairs organizations and organizations aiding minorities, youth, the elderly, and the handicapped. Less than 5%. Includes grants to civil rights and public policy organizations.
Education: 5% to 10%. Interests include colleges and universities, private schools, medical and minority education, and education funds.
Health: About 5%. Primarily supports medical research for single diseases, hospitals, health and mental health organizations, andorganizations concerned with the handicapped.

Application Procedures

Initial Contact: brief letter or proposal
Application Requirements: a description of organization, amount requested, purpose of funds sought, recently audited financial statement, and proof of Internal Revenue Service Section 170(c) status
Deadlines: None.

Corporate Officials

Richard A. Baird: president, chief executive officer
Mark H. Berey: senior vice president, chief financial officer, treasurer B 1951. ED Indiana University BA (1974); Northwestern University MBA (1975). PRIM CORP EMPL senior vice president, chief financial officer, treasurer: Giant Food Inc.
Michael W. Broomfield: chief executive officer
Michael J. Bush: vice president real estate B Phoenix, AZ 1943. ED Stanford University (1965); Harvard University (1968). PRIM CORP EMPL vice president real estate: Giant Food Inc. CORP AFFIL vice president: GFS Realty Inc.; executive vice president, chief operating officer, director: Movado Group Inc.
Anthony Edward Dahm: controller B Evanston, IL 1948. ED Lewis University (1970); George Mason University (1978). PRIM CORP EMPL controller: Giant Food Inc. ADD CORP EMPL controller: Giant Maryland Inc.; controller: Giant Talbot County Inc. NONPR AFFIL member: American Institute CPAs.
Winston G. do Carmo: vice president human resources B Rio de Janeiro, RJ Brazil 1942. ED University of Maryland (1966). PRIM CORP EMPL vice president human resources: Giant Food Inc. ADD CORP EMPL vice president: Giant Maryland Inc.
Russell B. Fair: vice president pharmacy operations B Nashua, NH 1948. ED Northeastern University (1971). PRIM CORP EMPL vice president pharmacy operations: Giant Food Inc. ADD CORP EMPL vice president: Giant Maryland Inc.
Terry Alexander Gans: vice president, advertising B Washington, DC 1946. ED Miami University (1968); Loyola College (1982). PRIM CORP EMPL vice president, advertising: Giant Food Inc. ADD CORP EMPL director: GFS Financial; vice president: Giant maryland Inc.
M. Davis Herriman, Junior: senior vice president, chief merchandising officer B Washington, DC 1938. ED George Washington University (1961). PRIM CORP EMPL senior vice president, chief merchandising officer: Giant Food Inc. ADD CORP EMPL vice president: Giant of Maryland Inc.
Odonna Mathews: vice president consumer affairs B Washington, DC 1950. ED University of Maryland (1972); University of Maryland (1981). PRIM CORP EMPL vice president consumer affairs: Giant Food Inc. ADD CORP EMPL vice president: Giant Maryland Inc. NONPR AFFIL member consumer affairs committee: Food Marketing Institute; member: Society of Consumer Affairs Professionals.
Roger D. Olson: senior vice president human resources B 1944. PRIM CORP EMPL senior vice president human resources: Giant Food Inc. ADD CORP EMPL senior vice president: Giant Maryland Inc.
Stephen L. Oseroff: vice president real estate B Baltimore, MD 1941. ED University of Baltimore (1964). PRIM CORP EMPL vice president real estate: Giant Food Inc. CORP AFFIL vice president: Giant Maryland Inc.
David W. Rutstein: senior vice president, general counsel, chief administrative officer B New York, NY 1944. ED University of Pennsylvania BA (1966); George Washington University JD (1969). PRIM CORP EMPL senior vice president, general counsel, chief administrative officer: Giant Food Inc. ADD CORP EMPL senior vice president: Giant Maryland Inc. NONPR AFFIL member: Washington Metropolitan Area Corporate Counsel Association; treasurer, director: Washington Metropolitan Board Trade; trustee: Greater Washington Research Center; member: DC Bar Association; treasurer, director, member executive committee: Fed City Council.
Barry F. Scher: vice president public affairs B Richmond, VA 1942. ED College of William & Mary (1964); American University (1965). PRIM CORP EMPL vice president public affairs: Giant Food Inc. ADD CORP EMPL vice president: Giant Maryland Inc. NONPR AFFIL member: Public Relations Society America; director: Second Harvest; vice chairman: Maryland Retailers Association; member: Food Marketing Government Affairs & Communications Division; chairman food bank national task force: Food Marketing Institute.
Robert Walters Schoening: senior vice president information systems B Saint Louis, MO 1946. ED Washington University (1968); Washington University (1973). PRIM CORP EMPL senior vice president information systems: Giant Food Inc. ADD CORP EMPL senior vice president: Giant Maryland Inc.
Samuel E. Thurston: senior vice president distribution B New Haven, CT 1943. ED University of New Haven (1966). PRIM CORP EMPL senior vice president distribution: Giant Food Inc. CORP AFFIL senior vice president: Giant Maryland Inc.

Foundation Officials

David W. Rutstein: secretary (see above)

Grants Analysis

Disclosure Period: fiscal year ending January 31, 1997
Total Grants: $542,134
Number of Grants: 140
Average Grant: $3,872
Highest Grant: $160,000
Typical Range: $100 to $5,000
Note: Grants analysis provided by foundation.

Recent Grants

Note: Grants derived from 1996 Form 990.

Arts & Humanities

2,500	John F. Kennedy Center for Performing Arts, Washington, DC
2,500	WETA/Television 26 and Radio FM 91, Washington, DC
1,500	Fairfax Symphony, Annandale, VA
1,000	National Symphony Orchestra, Washington, DC
1,000	Washington Ballet, Washington, DC

Civic & Public Affairs

5,000	Jim Rouse Entrepreneurial Fund, Columbia, MD
5,000	National Aquarium in Baltimore, Schaefer Promenade, Baltimore, MD
1,000	Council for Court Excellence, Washington, DC
1,000	Montgomery Housing Partnership, Wheaton, MD
1,000	NAACP, Baltimore, MD
1,000	Thurgood Marshall Center for Service and Heritage, Washington, DC

Education

10,000	Shenandoah University School of Pharmacy, Leesburg, VA
10,000	University of Maryland Foundation, Adelphi, MD

5,000	University of Maryland School of Pharmacy, Baltimore, MD
2,500	Treatment and Learning Centers, Laurel, MD
2,500	United Negro College Fund, Washington, DC
2,500	University of Maryland Baltimore Campus Center of Marine Biotechnology, Baltimore, MD
1,500	University of Maryland School of Pharmacy Fund, Baltimore, MD
1,000	Gallaudet University Hall Memorial Building, Washington, DC

Health

2,500	Children's Cancer Foundation, Baltimore, MD
2,500	Hospice of Prince Georges County, Largo, MD
2,500	Suburban Hospital Capital Campaign, Washington, DC
2,500	Tourette Syndrome Association, Washington, DC
1,667	Potomac Hospital Foundation, Woodbridge, VA
1,666	Washington Hospital Center Deluxe Suite Pavilion, Washington, DC
1,500	American Heart Association Nations Capital Affiliate, Washington, DC
1,000	Mary Washington Hospital Foundation, Fredericksburg, VA
1,000	United Seniors Health Cooperative, Washington, DC
1,000	Washington Hospital Center, Washington, DC

Religion

100,000	United Jewish Appeal Federation of Greater Washington, Rockville, MD
100,000	United Jewish Appeal Federation of Greater Washington, Rockville, MD
5,000	Salvation Army Harbor Light and Turning Point Programs, Washington, DC
2,500	Anti-Defamation League of B'nai B'rith, New York, NY
2,500	Hebrew Home of Greater Washington, Washington, DC
2,000	Southern Christian Leadership Conference, Charlottesville, VA
1,000	American Jewish Committee, Chicago, IL
1,000	American Society of Technion, New York, NY
1,000	Jewish Family and Children's Service of Southern New Jersey, Cherry Hill, NJ
1,000	Jewish National Fund, Baltimore, MD

Social Services

160,000	United Way National Capital Area, Washington, DC
42,000	United Way Central Maryland, Baltimore, MD
2,000	Recording for Blind, Princeton, NJ
1,800	Rappahannock United Way, Fredericksburg, VA
1,800	United Way Frederick County, Frederick, MD
1,800	United Way Thomas Jefferson Area, Charlottesville, VA
1,600	United Way Lower Eastern Shore, Salisbury, MD
1,500	Second Genesis, Bethesda, MD
1,000	Big Brothers, Washington, DC
1,000	IONA Senior Services, Washington, DC
1,000	Thrift Shop Charities, Washington, DC

GIDDINGS &LEWIS

Company Contact
Fond du Lac, WI

Company Description
Employees: 3,967
SIC(s): 3541 Machine Tools--Metal Cutting Types, 3625 Relays & Industrial Controls, 3825 Instruments to Measure Electricity.

Corporate Sponsorship
Contact: Stephen Peterson, President, Chief Executive Officer
Giddings & Lewis

Giddings & Lewis Foundation

Giving Contact
Ms. Terry Lennop
Giddings & Lewis Foundation
PO Box 590
Fond du Lac, WI 54936-0590
Phone: (920)921-9400

Alternate Contact
142 Doty St.
Fond Du Lac, WI 54936

Description
Founded: 1952
EIN: 396061306
Organization Type: Corporate Foundation
Giving Locations: MI; OH; WI
Grant Types: General Support.

Financial Summary
Total Giving: $295,246 (1994); $292,730 (1993); $306,270 (1992)
Assets: $2,894,350 (1994); $3,190,295 (1993); $3,086,210 (1992)
Gifts Received: $250,000 (1993); $250,000 (1992)

Typical Recipients
Arts & Humanities: Arts Associations & Councils, Arts Centers, Community Arts, Libraries, Museums/Galleries, Music, Performing Arts, Theater
Civic & Public Affairs: Business/Free Enterprise, Clubs, Community Foundations, Economic Development, Civic & Public Affairs-General, Housing, Municipalities/Towns, Professional & Trade Associations, Safety, Urban & Community Affairs
Education: Business Education, Colleges & Universities, Education Funds, Engineering/Technological Education, Education-General, Private Education (Precollege), Public Education (Precollege), Secondary Education (Private), Secondary Education (Public), Student Aid
Health: Emergency/Ambulance Services, Heart, Hospices, Hospitals, Multiple Sclerosis, Nursing Services, Prenatal Health Issues, Single-Disease Health Associations, Transplant Networks/Donor Banks
Religion: Religious Organizations, Religious Welfare
Science: Science Museums
Social Services: Big Brother/Big Sister, Child Welfare, Community Service Organizations, People with Disabilities, Recreation & Athletics, Scouts, Substance Abuse, United Funds/United Ways, YMCA/YWCA/YMHA/YWHA, Youth Organizations

Application Procedures
Initial Contact: Send brief letter describing program. Include proof of tax-exempt status. There are no deadlines.

Additional Information
The majority of the foundation's giving is through a matching gift program.

Corporate Officials
Joseph R. Coppola: chairman, president, chief executive officer, director PRIM CORP EMPL chairman, president, chief executive officer, director: Giddings & Lewis.
Richard C. Kleinfeldt: vice president financial, chief financial officer, director B Fond du Lac, WI 1941. ED University of Wisconsin (1963); University of Wisconsin (1964). PRIM CORP EMPL vice president financial, chief financial officer, director: Giddings & Lewis. CORP AFFIL director: Giddings & Lewis Electronics Ltd.; secretary, treasurer, director: Marshall & Huschart Machinery Co. Indiana; secretary, treasurer, director: Basic Electronics Manufacturing Corp.

Foundation Officials
Robert D. Kamphuis: president PRIM CORP EMPL vice president, controller: Giddings & Lewis.

Grants Analysis
Disclosure Period: calendar year ending 1994
Number of Grants: 112*
Highest Grant: $30,000
Typical Range: $250 to $10,000*
***Note:** Number of grants and typical range do not include matching gifts.

Recent Grants
Note: Grants derived from 1997 Form 990.

Arts & Humanities

55,000	Fond Du Lac Arts Council, Fond Du Lac, WI
10,000	Arts Center, Fond Du Lac, WI
5,500	Fond Du Lac Community Theater, Fond Du Lac, WI
4,000	Fond Du Lac Symphonic Band, Fond Du Lac, WI
2,500	Henry Ford Museum, Dearborn, MI

Civic & Public Affairs

20,000	Building Janesville's Tomorrow
16,667	EAA Aviation Center, Oshkosh, WI
5,000	M&M Area Community Foundation
2,500	City of Fraser
2,500	WMC Foundation Business World
2,000	Habitat for Humanity
1,500	Fond Du Lac Fire Department, Fond Du Lac, WI

Education

103,000	Marian College -- educational
10,000	Wisconsin Foundation of Independent Colleges, Milwaukee, WI -- educational
9,000	UW Foundation -- educational
8,000	Marquette University, Milwaukee, WI -- educational
7,500	St. Mary's Springs High School -- educational
7,000	Milwaukee School of Engineering, Milwaukee, WI -- educational
4,000	Chatsworth High School -- educational
2,500	MPTC Foundation Scholarships -- educational
2,000	Blackhawk Tech Scholarships -- educational
2,000	Winnebago Lutheran Academy -- educational
1,500	Junior Achievement -- educational
1,500	START -- educational

Health

10,000	St. Agnes Hospital Foundation, Baltimore, MD
5,000	Tourette Syndrome Association
2,500	Hospice Home
1,250	Multiple Sclerosis Society
1,000	March of Dimes, MI

Religion

25,500	Fond Du Lac Lutheran Home, Fond Du Lac, WI
1,000	LA Mission

Social Services

35,000	YMCA Building Fund
30,000	Blue Line Hockey
30,000	United Way, Fond Du Lac, WI
25,100	FACES
24,000	United Way of North Rock County, Janesville, WI
22,000	United Way Foundation, Totowa, NJ
20,000	Beacon House, Pacific Grove, CA
17,000	Fond Du Lac Soccer Association, Fond Du Lac, WI
11,000	United Way, Dayton, OH
10,000	YMCA
5,000	United Way, Chatsworth, CA -- Fadal contribution
3,583	ARC of Fond du Lac County, Fond Du Lac, WI
3,000	United Way Capital Campaign -- support Building Hope
2,500	Bethany House
1,700	Tri-City Area United Way, Marinette, WI
1,500	Girl Scouts of America Badger Council
1,075	Boy Scouts of America Bay Lakes Council
1,000	Boy Scouts of America, Detroit, MI
1,000	Girl Scouts of America

GILLETTE CO.

Company Contact

Boston, MA
Web: http://www.gillette.com

Company Description

Revenue: US$10,056,000,000
Employees: 44,000
Fortune Rank: 172, per FORTUNE Magazine's list of 500 Largest U.S. Corporations (1999).
FF 172
SIC(s): 2844 Toilet Preparations, 3421 Cutlery, 3634 Electric Housewares & Fans, 3951 Pens & Mechanical Pencils.

Operating Locations

Argentina: Gillette Argentina SA, Buenos Aires; SylvaPen Distribuidora SACIYF, Panamericana (Garin); Australia: Oral-B Laboratories Pty. Ltd., North Sydney; Gillette (Australia) Pty. Ltd., Scoresby; Belgium: SA DuraCell Benelux NV, Aarchot; NV Duracell Batteries, SA, Aarschot; Brazil: Gillette do Brasil, Rio de Janeiro; Canada: Gillette Canada Inc., Kirkland; People's Republic of China: Shenmei Daily Use Products Ltd. Company, Shenyang; Egypt: Gillette Internile SAE, Cairo; Finland: Braun Finland Oy, Espoo; France: Braun France SA, Clicy; Gillette France, SA, Levallois-Perret; Waterman SA, Saint-Herblain; Germany: Gillette Deutschland GmbH, Berlin; Oral-B Laboratories GmbH, Frankfurt; Braun AG, Kronberg; Hong Kong: Gillette Far East Trading Ltd., Quarry Bay; India: Indian Shaving Products, Ltd., New Delhi; Ireland: Braun Ireland Ltd., Carlow; Italy: Braun Italia, Srl, Corsico; Gillette Group Italy Srl, Milan; Japan: Gillette (Japan) Inc., Tokyo; Braun Japan KK, Yokohama; Mexico: Braun de Mexico y Compania de CV, Mexico; Oral-B Laboratories SA de CV, Mexico; Gillette de Mexico SA de CV, Naucalpan de Jaurez, Mexico; Netherlands: Jraun Nederland BV, Rijswijk; Peru: Gillette de Peru SC, Lima; Philippines: Gillette (Philippines) Inc., Metro Manila; Republic of South Africa: Gillette South Africa Ltd., Bedfordview; Duracell South Africa (Proprietary) Ltd., Port Elizabeth; Spain: Braun Espanola, SA, Llobregat; Gillette Espanola, SA, Madrid; Switzerland: Gillette (Switzerland) AG, Schlieren; Turkey: Gillette Sanayi ve Ticaret AS, Istanbul; United Kingdom: DuraCell Batteries Ltd., Crawley; Gillette Products Division-Europe AMEE, Isleworth, Meddlesex; Gillette Europe, Isleworth, Middlesex; Gillette Industries, Ltd., Isleworth, Middlesex; Gillette UK Ltd., Isleworth, Middlesex; Parker Pen Company, New Haven, East Sussex; Braun (UK) Ltd., Sunbury, Middlesex

Nonmonetary Support

Value: $6,750,000 (1995); $6,740,000 (1992)
Type: Cause-related Marketing & Promotion; Donated Equipment; Donated Products; In-kind Services; Loaned Employees; Loaned Executives; Workplace Solicitation
Note: In-kind products given to in-need recipients in the locations where the company has a major presence.

Corporate Sponsorship

Type: Arts & cultural events; Festivals/fairs; Music & entertainment events; Sports events
Contact: Shawn Howell, Director, Marketing

Giving Contact

Mr. James P. Furlong, Director, Civic Affairs
The Gillette Co.
Prudential Tower Bldg.
Boston, MA 02199
Phone: (617)421-7722
Fax: (617)421-7874

Description

Organization Type: Corporate Giving Program
Giving Locations: MA: Boston operating locations.
Grant Types: Capital, General Support, Operating Expenses, Scholarship.
Note: Scholarships provided only through the National Merit Scholarship Program.

Financial Summary

Total Giving: $3,200,000 (2000 approx); $3,200,000 (1999 approx); $330,000 (1996). Note: Contributes through corporate direct giving program and foundation. 1996 Giving includes United Way ($330,000). 1995 Giving includes corporate direct giving ($3,148,500); foundation ($330,000); domestic subsidiaries ($9,875,500)
Assets: $4,016,893 (1996); $3,117,355 (1995); $2,283,905 (1992)
Gifts Received: $500,000 (1995)

Typical Recipients

Arts & Humanities: Arts Centers, Dance, Libraries, Museums/Galleries, Music, Public Broadcasting
Civic & Public Affairs: Employment/Job Training, Urban & Community Affairs
Education: Business Education, Colleges & Universities
Health: Clinics/Medical Centers, Emergency/Ambulance Services, Hospitals
Religion: Jewish Causes
Social Services: United Funds/United Ways, Youth Organizations

Contributions Analysis

Giving Priorities: Social welfare, higher education, civics, health, museums, and performing arts. In the Values portion of the Gillette Mission and Values statement, the company reaffirms its view of good citizenship: 'We will contribute to the communities in which we operate and address social issues responsibly.' The company fulfills this mission around the world. Gillette has adopted schools in several locations in the U.K.; renovated a school for kindergarten children in Santiago, Chile; sponsored literacy programs for young people in Johannesburg; supported a swimming club for the disabled in County Kildare, Ireland; and promoted preventive actions to fight the plague near New Delhi. The company seeks to support a wide range of organizationswith a goal of helping people help themselves. Education is a major focus of Gillette efforts around the world. Healthcare initiatives are geared to local needs and have included sponsoring clinics in South Africa that serve more than 10,000 families; underwriting chemotherapy treatments for impoverished children in Mexico City; and renovating the outpatient department of the city pediatric hospital in Buenos Aires, Argentina. The company also donates its products to assist in disaster relief efforts, and promotes employee volunteerism worldwide.
Arts & Humanities: About 10%. Support goes to museums, libraries, theater, dance, and music in the Boston area.
Civic & Public Affairs: 50% to 55%. Includes United Way grants. Many grants go to organizations in the Boston area focused on youth, women, the homeless, training assistance, housing and literacy.
Education: 25% to 30%. Support for colleges, universities, and education programs in the Boston area.
Health: 5% to 10%. Support for hospitals and neighborhood health centers.

Application Procedures

Initial Contact: brief proposal
Application Requirements: a description of organization or project; information on goals and objectives; who it serves; list of directors or trustees; budget information; and information on other sources of funding
Deadlines: None.
Decision Notification: within six to eight weeks
Notes: Many grant decisions are made within the first quarter of the year.

Restrictions

Contributions are made largely, but not exclusively, to the Boston area and other major plant locations.

Foundation Officials

James P. Furlong: director civic affairs PRIM CORP EMPL director civic affairs: Gillette Co.
John McGowan: director PRIM CORP EMPL vice president: Gillette Co.

Grants Analysis

Disclosure Period: calendar year ending 1996
Total Grants: $330,000
Number of Grants: 1
Typical Range: $300,000 to $500,000

Recent Grants

Note: Grants derived from 1997 Form 990.

Arts & Humanities

25,000	Boston Public Library, Boston, MA

Education

15,000	Babson College, Wellesley, MA

Health

30,000	American Red Cross

Religion

10,000	New England Holocaust Memorial Committee, Boston, MA

Social Services

350,000	United Way of New England

GLAXO WELLCOME INC.

 Number 92 of Top 100 Corporate Givers

Company Contact

Research Triangle Park, NC
Web: http://www.glaxowellcome.com

Company Description

Former Name: Glaxo Inc.
Employees: 8,900
SIC(s): 2834 Pharmaceutical Preparations.
Parent Company: Glaxo Holdings Plc

Operating Locations

NC: Allen & Hanburys, Research Triangle Park; Cerenex Pharmaceuticals, Research Triangle Park; Glaxo

Dermatology, Research Triangle Park; Glaxo Pharmaceuticals, Research Triangle Park; Glaxo Technical Operations, Research Triangle Park; Glaxo Wellcome, Research Triangle Park; Glaxo Wellcome Inc., Research Triangle Park; Glaxo Wellcome PLC, Research Triangle Park; Glaxo Wellcome, Zebulon; Glaxo Wellcome Inc., Zebulon

Nonmonetary Support

Value: $900,000 (1995); $1,360,000 (1993); $85,000 (1992)
Type: Donated Equipment; Donated Products; In-kind Services; Loaned Executives
Volunteer Programs: Glaxo's Investment in Volunteer Excellence (GIVE) matches employees' volunteer hours with monetary donations. GIVE grants are $500 for fifty or more hours volunteered during a 12 month period. The Glaxo Wellcome Foundation's primary interests are organizations and programs that fall within the fields of education, science, and health. Primary focus is seed funds for new and worthwhile educational programs. Supports Glaxo Wellcome Women in Science Scholars Program, which awards grants of $1,000 to women pursuing careers in science. Normally awards 3 or 4 grants annually.
Contact: Pat Pasteur, Corporate Contributions Coordinator

Corporate Sponsorship

Type: Arts & cultural events

Glaxo Wellcome Foundation

Giving Contact

Marilyn Foote-Hudson, Executive Director
Glaxo Wellcome Foundation
5 Moore Drive
Research Triangle Park, NC 27709
Phone: (919)483-2140
Fax: (919)483-8765

Alternate Contact

Mary Linda Andrews, Manager Corporate Contributions
Glaxo Wellcome Inc.
Phone: (919)483-2719
Fax: (919)315-3015

Description

Founded: 1986
EIN: 581698610
Organization Type: Corporate Foundation
Giving Locations: NC: Triangle Park area
Grant Types: Conference/Seminar, Employee Matching Gifts, Multiyear/Continuing Support, Project, Scholarship, Seed Money.
Note: Employee matching gift ratio: 1 to 1.

Giving Philosophy

'The Glaxo Foundation is a charitable trust dedicated to advancing education in the areas of science, mathematics and health. The Foundation is a natural outgrowth of Glaxo's corporate commitment to improving the quality of life through the research and discovery of medicines to benefit all people.
'We fund many initiatives which form a continuum of education -- providing opportunities for students from pre-school to professional levels.
'..The Glaxo Foundation endeavors to elevate human achievement and advance our quest for national and universal well-being. These are important components in the education continuum. From this base we can attract and retain students and professionals who are interested and involved in science as a profession. Only then can we prepare today's children to lead us into tomorrow.' Glaxo Wellcome Inc. Annual Report

Financial Summary

Total Giving: $7,633,842 (1998); $2,913,386 (1997); $2,457,409 (1996). Note: Contributes through corporate direct giving program and foundation.
Giving Analysis: Giving for 1996 includes: corporate direct giving ($11,500,000); foundation ($1,178,000); 1997: corporate direct giving ($2,913,386); 1998: corporate direct giving ($4,959,842); foundation ($2,674,000)
Assets: $65,834,352 (1998); $58,996,124 (1997); $50,976,609 (1996)
Gifts Received: $100,000 (1998); $300,000 (1997); $1,000,000 (1996). Note: Contributions are received from Glaxo Inc.

Typical Recipients

Arts & Humanities: Arts Associations & Councils, Arts Centers, Arts Funds, Community Arts, Historic Preservation, Museums/Galleries, Music, Performing Arts, Public Broadcasting, Theater, Visual Arts
Civic & Public Affairs: Business/Free Enterprise, Economic Development, Employment/Job Training, Safety, Urban & Community Affairs, Women's Affairs, Zoos/Aquariums
Education: Business Education, Colleges & Universities, Community & Junior Colleges, Education Associations, Elementary Education (Private), Faculty Development, Medical Education, Private Education (Precollege), Public Education (Precollege), Science/Mathematics Education
Health: Cancer, Clinics/Medical Centers, Eyes/Blindness, Health Policy/Cost Containment, Health Organizations, Hospitals, Medical Research, Preventive Medicine/Wellness Organizations, Research/Studies Institutes, Single-Disease Health Associations
International: Foreign Arts Organizations
Science: Science Exhibits & Fairs, Science Museums
Social Services: Child Welfare, Community Centers, Community Service Organizations, Day Care, Family Services, People with Disabilities, Senior Services, Substance Abuse, United Funds/United Ways, Youth Organizations

Contributions Analysis

Giving Priorities: Foundation grants support activities in North Carolina that help meet the education and health needs of today's society and future generations. The foundation focuses on programs that emphasize the understanding and application of health, science, and education at all academic and professional levels.

Application Procedures

Initial Contact: For the foundation: call for guidelines, then send written proposal; for direct corporate giving: call for guidelines, then send letter of request.
Application Requirements: For foundation proposals: 2-page executive summary, including the principal components of the project, and total amounts requested for each component and the entire project; narrative with objectives, overall strategy, rationale, and expected outcomes, staff information, resumes of key personnel, plans for collaboration and evaluation and dissemination of results, and plan for future funding; budget section, with information on the project and the entire organization, with other sources of funding and the percentage of funds requested from the foundation; and proof of tax-exempt status; for corporate donations requests: a description of organization, including name, statement of purpose, history, current and past sources of funding, and list of board members; objectives and current priorities; description of funding request, including project objective, background, timeframe, budget, staff, results expected, plans for evaluation; proof of tax-exempt status; and any supporting materials.
Deadlines: For the foundation: the first of January, April, July, or October; for corporate giving: None.
Decision Notification: Foundation board meets four times per year in March, June, September, and December, requests are processed within eight to twelve weeks, and notification is made by letter; corporate contributions committee meets bi-monthly, response within about 8 weeks.
Notes: Grant requests must be for at least $25,000. Only one application is accepted from each eligible institution per funding cycle. The grantee must submit a written report within 60 days of initial grant payment; interim and final reports are also required. If a grant is not used for approved purposes, the funds will be returned to the foundation. Grantees are required to supply written progress reports.

Restrictions

Does not support individuals; political, religious, or fraternal organizations; profit-making or discriminatory organizations; capital fund drives or general operating expenses; religious organizations for sectarian purposes; international programs; construction or restoration projects; film or video production; or organizations primarily supported by tax dollars.
Company ordinarily does not support programs that benefit only one city or county within North Carolina. Foundation does not ordinarily support programs benefiting a limited geographical region.
The corporate giving program is restricted to Durham, Orange, and Wake counties in North Carolina.

Additional Information

In 1995, Glaxo Inc. acquired Burroughs Wellcome Co. and changed its name to Glaxo Wellcome Inc. The giving program at Burroughs Wellcome Co. was rolled into the Glaxo giving program and foundation.
A merger between SmithKline Beecham and Glaxo Wellcome is expected to be finalized in summer 2000.
Publications: Contributions Report (including Application Form and Checklist); Foundation Annual Report; Application Guidelines

Corporate Officials

Margaret Dardess: senior vice presidento, director PRIM CORP EMPL senior vice president: Glaxo Wellcome Inc.
Robert A. Ingram: president, chief executive officer, director B 1942. PRIM CORP EMPL president, chief executive officer, director: Glaxo Wellcome Inc.

Foundation Officials

George Abercrombie: director
Walter Robert Connor: director B Worcester, MA 1934. ED Hamilton College BA (1956); Princeton University PhD (1961). PRIM NONPR EMPL president, director: National Humanities Center. NONPR AFFIL member: Century Association; member: Phi Beta Kappa; member: American Philosophical Society; member advisory board: Athens College; fellow: American Academy of Arts & Sciences; member: American Philosophical Association. CLUB AFFIL Princeton Club.
Margaret Dardess: president, director (see above)
Marilyn Foote-Hudson: executive director PRIM CORP EMPL contributions administrator: Glaxo Wellcome Inc.
Shirley T. Frye: director
Michael A. Gallucci, Jr.: assistant treasurer B 1948. PRIM CORP EMPL vice president, treasurer, director: Glaxo Wellcome Inc.
Thomas R. Haber: director PRIM CORP EMPL senior vice president finance, chief financial officer, director: Glaxo Wellcome Inc.
Adrian Hennah: treasurer
Paul A. Holcombe, Jr.: secretary
Robert A. Ingram: chairman, director (see above)
George J. Morrow: director PRIM CORP EMPL vice president: Glaxo Wellcome Inc.
Timothy D. Proctor: secretary, director PRIM CORP EMPL secretary, director: Glaxo Wellcome Inc.
Joseph J. Ruvane, Jr.: director PRIM CORP EMPL chairman: Systemix Inc. CORP AFFIL director: Connetics Corp.

Grants Analysis

Disclosure Period: calendar year ending 1998
Total Grants: $2,674,000*
Number of Grants: 14
Average Grant: $191,000
Highest Grant: $325,000
Typical Range: $25,000 to $500,000
***Note:** Giving excludes corporate direct giving.

Recent Grants

Note: Grants derived from 1997 Form 990.

Arts & Humanities

250,000 Children's Museum About the World -- to support exhibits and programs

Education

350,000 Guilford College, Greensboro, NC -- to endow a Glaxo Wellcome professorship in the natural sciences
350,000 North Carolina Central University, Durham, NC
313,050 North Carolina School of Science and Mathematics, Durham, NC -- to conduct a pilot project with the Durham city schools with the ultimate goal of restructuring science teaching throughout North Carolina
200,000 Hill Center -- to fully maximize the enormous potential of teacher training to improve school performance in North Carolina
200,000 University of North Carolina School of Pharmacy, Chapel Hill, NC -- to create a program of excellence in pharmaceutical care that will involve research concerning the optimum contribution of pharmacists and pharmaceut
150,000 Durham Technical Community College, Durham, NC -- to support the implementation of an information and communication technology plan
100,000 Appalachian State University, Boone, NC -- to further improve science education in North Carolina through the Alliance for Teaching Science
77,000 University of North Carolina Wilmington, Wilmington, NC -- to develop an innovative model for environmental education that will ultimately be used by middle school and high school teachers across the state as

Health

375,000 Duke University Medical Center, Durham, NC -- to support an endowed professorship in the Comprehensive Cancer Center
40,000 Southeastern Regional Vision -- to develop and evaluate an off-site component of the Hill Center project

Science

283,334 Museum of Life and Science -- for educational programming
125,000 North Carolina Museum of Natural Sciences, NC -- to support new exhibits that focus on aspects of North Carolina including natural habitats on land and water which provide an interactive learning ce

Social Services

100,000 North Carolina Center for Public Policy Research, Raleigh, NC -- to support a project for children with special needs in North Carolina

GLICKENHAUS &CO.

Company Contact

New York, NY

Company Description

Employees: 103
SIC(s): 6211 Security Brokers & Dealers, 6282 Investment Advice.

Glickenhaus Foundation

Giving Contact

Nancy G. Pier, President
Glickenhaus Foundation
6 East 43rd Street
New York, NY 10017
Phone: (212)953-7800
Fax: (212)983-8436

Description

Founded: 1960
EIN: 136160941
Organization Type: Corporate Foundation
Giving Locations: NY nationally.
Grant Types: Emergency, Endowment, Research.

Financial Summary

Total Giving: $925,000 (fiscal year ending November 30, 1998 approx); $650,000 (fiscal 1996); $920,286 (fiscal 1995). Note: Contributes through foundation only.
Assets: $1,926,166 (fiscal 1996); $2,051,021 (fiscal 1995); $1,890,548 (fiscal 1994)
Gifts Received: $506,179 (fiscal 1996); $634,030 (fiscal 1995); $324,268 (fiscal 1994). Note: Contributions are received from Seth and Sarah Glickenhaus.

Typical Recipients

Arts & Humanities: Arts Associations & Councils, Arts Centers, Ethnic & Folk Arts, Film & Video, Museums/Galleries, Music, Opera, Performing Arts, Public Broadcasting, Theater
Civic & Public Affairs: Botanical Gardens/Parks, Business/Free Enterprise, Economic Development, Employment/Job Training, Civic & Public Affairs-General, Housing, Law & Justice, Legal Aid, Municipalities/Towns, Professional & Trade Associations, Public Policy, Urban & Community Affairs, Women's Affairs
Education: Colleges & Universities, Education Associations, Education Funds, Education Reform, Education-General, Health & Physical Education, Legal Education, Literacy, Medical Education, Minority Education, Private Education (Precollege), Private Education (Precollege), Social Sciences Education, Special Education, Student Aid
Health: AIDS/HIV, Cancer, Children's Health/Hospitals, Clinics/Medical Centers, Emergency/Ambulance Services, Geriatric Health, Health Organizations, Hospitals, Kidney, Medical Research, Mental Health, Single-Disease Health Associations
International: Foreign Arts Organizations, Human Rights, International Affairs, International Peace & Security Issues, International Relations, International Relief Efforts, Missionary/Religious Activities
Religion: Churches, Jewish Causes, Religious Organizations, Religious Welfare
Social Services: Child Welfare, Community Service Organizations, Counseling, Day Care, Family Planning, Family Services, People with Disabilities, Senior Services, Shelters/Homelessness, United Funds/United Ways, YMCA/YWCA/YMHA/YWHA

Contributions Analysis

Arts & Humanities: 15% to 20%. Museums of ethnic and folk art in New York City.
Civic & Public Affairs: 10% to 15%. Legal awareness, community affairs, and botanical gardens.
Education: 35% to 40%. Primarily colleges and universities, as well as educational foundations and funds.
Health: About 20%. Single-disease health associations, medical research, and medical centers throughout New York.
International: Less than 5%. International healthcare, peace and security issues, and missionary activities.
Religion: 5% to 10%. Religious welfare, Jewish causes, and social policy organizations.
Social Services: 5% to 10%. Planned Parenthood and child care organizations.

Application Procedures

Initial Contact: send a full proposal
Deadlines: None.

Corporate Officials

Alfred Feinman: general partner B 1924. PRIM CORP EMPL general partner: Glickenhaus & Co.
James M. Glickenhaus: ltd. partner PRIM CORP EMPL ltd. partner: Glickenhaus & Co.
Seth M. Glickenhaus: general partner B 1916. ED Harvard University (1934); New York Law School (1938). PRIM CORP EMPL general partner: Glickenhaus & Co.

Foundation Officials

Alfred Feinman: secretary-treasurer (see above)
James M. Glickenhaus: vice president (see above)
Nancy G. Pier: president PRIM CORP EMPL ltd. partner: Glickenhaus Inc.

Grants Analysis

Disclosure Period: fiscal year ending November 30, 1996
Total Grants: $994,732*
Number of Grants: 230
Average Grant: $4,325
Highest Grant: $160,000
Typical Range: $250 to $5,000
***Note:** Grants analysis is approximate.

Recent Grants

Note: Grants derived from fiscal 1998 Form 990.

Arts & Humanities

25,000 American Craft Museum, New York, NY
25,000 American Craft Museum, New York, NY
10,000 Anderson Ranch Arts Center, Snowmass Village, CO
5,000 Friends of the Neuberger Museum, New York, NY
5,000 Friends of the Neuberger Museum, New York, NY
5,000 Metropolitan Opera Association, New York, NY
3,000 Friends of the Neuberger Museum, New York, NY
3,000 Lincoln Center - Film Society, New York, NY
2,500 Children's Museum of Manhattan, Manhattan, NY
2,500 Friends of Neuberger Museum, New York, NY
2,500 WNET - Channel 13, New York, NY

Civic & Public Affairs

10,000 World Federalist Association, Washington, DC
10,000 World Federalist Association - NY, New York, NY
7,503 Renaissance Project Foundation, New York, NY
7,503 Renaissance Project Foundation, New York, NY
7,503 Renaissance Project Foundation, New York, NY
5,000 New School for Social Research, New York, NY
5,000 Phipps Community Development Corp., New York, NY

Education

150,000 Rockefeller University, New York, NY
25,000 University of Pennsylvania, Philadelphia, PA

10,000	Ethical Culture Fieldston School, New York, NY
5,000	Catholic University of America, Washington, DC
5,000	East Harlem Tutorial Program, New York, NY
5,000	Jennifer Lynn Goldstein Memorial Art Scholarship, New York, NY
5,000	Manhattanville College, Purchase, NY
5,000	Reading Reform Foundation, Tacoma, WA
5,000	Student Advocacy, New York, NY

Health

15,000	Montefiore Medical Center, Bronx, NY
10,000	Sound Shore Medical Center of Westchester, Westchester, NY
5,000	Cystic Fibrosis Foundation, New York, NY
5,000	Montefiore Medical Center, Bronx, NY
5,000	National Center for Study of Wilson's Disease
5,000	PMI/Strang Cancer Prevention Center, New York, NY
5,000	Westchester Medical Center, Westchester, NY

International

11,800	Givat Haviva Educational Foundation, New York, NY
10,000	American Friends of the Israel Philharmonic, New York, NY
10,000	Israel Policy Forum, New York, NY
5,000	Givat Haviva Educational Foundation, New York, NY

Religion

10,000	Abraham Fund, New York, NY
5,000	Abraham Fund, New York, NY
5,000	American Ort, New York, NY
5,000	Women's American Ort, New York, NY
3,000	New York State Council of Churches, Syracuse, NY
2,500	Cathedral of St. John the Devine, New York, NY

Social Services

50,000	Fund for the Aged, New York, NY
25,000	Guidance Center, Bradford, PA
25,000	Planned Parenthood, New York, NY
10,000	Louise Wise Services, New York, NY
5,000	Union Settlement Association, New York, NY
5,000	YMCA, New York, NY

GLOBE CORP.

Company Contact

Scottsdale, AZ

Company Description

Employees: 17
SIC(s): 6799 Investors Nec.

Globe Foundation

Giving Contact

James L. Johnson, Treasurer & Assistant Secretary
Globe Foundation
6730 North Scottsdale Road, Suite 250
Scottsdale, AZ 85253-4416
Phone: (480)991-0500
Fax: (480)991-1912

Description

Founded: 1958
EIN: 366054050
Organization Type: Corporate Foundation. Supports preselected organizations only.
Giving Locations: AZ; IL
Grant Types: Capital, Employee Matching Gifts, Endowment, General Support.

Financial Summary

Total Giving: $1,352,520 (1998); $1,156,571 (1997); $939,184 (1996). Note: Contributes through foundation only.
Assets: $29,667,910 (1998); $25,243,688 (1997); $20,776,532 (1996)
Gifts Received: $636,160 (1994); $34,022 (1992); $511,950 (1991). Note: In 1994, contributions were received from the late George F. Getz, Jr.

Typical Recipients

Arts & Humanities: Arts Associations & Councils, Arts Institutes, Ballet, Dance, Arts & Humanities-General, History & Archaeology, Museums/Galleries, Music, Public Broadcasting
Civic & Public Affairs: Clubs, Community Foundations, Civic & Public Affairs-General, Housing, Philanthropic Organizations, Public Policy, Safety, Urban & Community Affairs, Women's Affairs, Zoos/Aquariums
Education: Business Education, Colleges & Universities, Environmental Education, Education-General, International Studies, Leadership Training, Legal Education, Literacy, Medical Education, Private Education (Precollege), Public Education (Precollege), Secondary Education (Private), Special Education, Student Aid
Environment: Air/Water Quality, Air/Water Quality, Environment-General, Resource Conservation, Wildlife Protection
Health: AIDS/HIV, Arthritis, Children's Health/Hospitals, Clinics/Medical Centers, Diabetes, Health Funds, Health Organizations, Heart, Hospices, Hospitals, Medical Research, Nursing Services, Public Health, Research/Studies Institutes, Single-Disease Health Associations
Religion: Churches, Religious Welfare
Science: Scientific Centers & Institutes
Social Services: Big Brother/Big Sister, Community Centers, Community Service Organizations, Day Care, Domestic Violence, Family Planning, Family Services, People with Disabilities, United Funds/United Ways, Volunteer Services, YMCA/YWCA/YMHA/YWHA, Youth Organizations

Contributions Analysis

Arts & Humanities: 2%. Support goes to historical preservation, art museums, ballet, and other performing arts.
Civic & Public Affairs: 30%. Gives to community and historical foundations.
Education: 6%. Support generally funds colleges and universities, religious education, and medical education.
Health: 56%. Funding goes to a variety of causes including health organizations, medical research, and education.
Social Services: 6%. YMCA and youth organizations receive the majority of support.
Note: Total contributions in 1998.

Restrictions

Does not support individuals.

Additional Information

Company offers a matching gifts program to its employees.

Corporate Officials

Bert A. Getz, Jr.: executive vice president B Chicago, IL 1937. ED University of Michigan (1959). PRIM CORP EMPL executive vice president: Globe Corp. CORP AFFIL director: Dean Foods Co.; director: Ameritas Life Insurance Corp.; director: Bank America Illinois. NONPR AFFIL president, director: Arthur R. Metz Foundation; vice president, director: National Historical Fire Foundation.
Bert A. Getz: chairman B Chicago, IL 1937. ED University of Michigan BBA (1959). PRIM CORP EMPL chairman: Globe Corp. ADD CORP EMPL chairman: Globe Illinois Inc. CORP AFFIL director: Dean Foods Co.; director: Ameritas Life Insurance Corp.; director: Bank America Illinois. NONPR AFFIL president, director: Arthur R Metz Foundation; vice president, director: National Historical Fire Foundation.
George F. Getz: president PRIM CORP EMPL president: Globe Corp. CORP AFFIL treasurer: Sedona Publishing Co.

Foundation Officials

James Wheeler Ashley: director B Chicago, IL 1923. ED Fordham University (1941-1943); Northwestern University JD (1948). PRIM NONPR EMPL of counsel: McDermott, Will & Emery. CORP AFFIL of couns: McDermott Will & Emery; director: Globe Corp.; director: Key Trust Co.; director: Chicago Tube & Iron Co. NONPR AFFIL member: Chicago Council Lawyers; member: Illinois Bar Association; member: Chicago Bar Association. CLUB AFFIL Monroe Club.
Bert A. Getz, Jr.: vice president (see above)
Bert A. Getz: president, director (see above)
George F. Getz: secretary, director (see above)
Sandra Lynn Getz: vice president, director PRIM CORP EMPL vice president: Globe Corp.
James L. Johnson: treasurer, assistant secretary PRIM CORP EMPL secretary, treasurer: Globe Corp.
Clifton L. Lux: director B Wadsworth, IL 1914. ED Northwestern University. CORP AFFIL director: Globe Corp. NONPR AFFIL treasurer, director: National Historical Fire Foundation.

Grants Analysis

Disclosure Period: calendar year ending 1998
Total Grants: $1,352,520
Number of Grants: 47
Average Grant: $10,098*
Highest Grant: $428,000
Typical Range: $1,000 to $12,000
***Note:** Average grant excludes 4 highest grants.

Recent Grants

Note: Grants derived from 1998 Form 990.

Arts & Humanities

10,000	Phoenix Boys Choir, Phoenix, AZ
5,000	Smithsonian Institution, Washington, DC
2,500	Holland Historical Trust, Holland, MI
1,000	Joffrey Ballet of Chicago, Chicago, IL
1,000	Solomon Guggenheim Foundation, New York, NY
500	Scottsdale Culture Council, Scottsdale, AZ

Civic & Public Affairs

290,300	National Historical Fire Foundation, Scottsdale, AZ -- Operating Needs
75,000	Arizona Zoo Society, Phoenix, AZ
35,000	Chicago Zoo Society, Brookfield, IL -- capital campaign
4,870	Globe Corporation, Scottsdale, AZ -- employee matching gifts
1,000	Heritage Foundation, Washington, DC
1,000	Scottsdale Charros Community Foundation, Scottsdale, AZ
250	Beta Theta Pi Foundation, Oxford, OH -- beta leadership fund

Education

26,000	University of Michigan Business School, Ann Arbor, MI
15,000	Desert Voices Oral Center, Phoenix, AZ
10,000	Avon Old Farms School, Inc., Avon, CT -- george m. trautman fund
10,000	Lawrenceville School, Lawrenceville, NJ
3,500	Evans Scholars Foundation, Chicago, IL
2,500	American Graduate School, Glendale, AZ
2,500	Centenary College, Hackettstown, NJ
2,150	ASU Foundation, Tempe, AZ -- dean's council

2,000	Junior Achievement of Arizona, Phoenix, AZ
1,000	Phoenix Country Day School, Phoenix, AZ
250	University of Pittsburgh, Pittsburgh, PA -- public semester at sea
Environment	
1,500	Santa Catalina Island, Avalon, CA
1,000	Arizona Nature Conservancy, Tucson, AZ
1,000	Lake Geneva Fresh Air, Williams Bay, WI -- holiday home camp
Health	
428,000	Mayo Foundation, Scottsdale, AZ -- property contribution
100,000	Children's Memorial Hospital, Chicago, IL
100,000	Mayo Foundation, Scottsdale, AZ -- Public R. Waller Endowment Fund
97,000	Mayo Foundation, Scottsdale, AZ -- concourse project
31,500	Columbus-Cabrini Medical Center, Chicago, IL -- public cinn research program
5,000	Scottsdale Memorial Health Foundation, Scottsdale, AZ
1,000	Hospice of the Valley, Phoenix, AZ
100	Juvenile Diabetes, Phoenix, AZ
Religion	
1,000	Prince of Peace Lutheran, Phoenix, AZ
Social Services	
50,000	Boys & Girls Clubs, Scottsdale, AZ -- capital campaign
10,000	United Way, Phoenix, AZ
5,000	Crisis Nursery Inc., Phoenix, AZ
5,000	Golden Gate Community Center, Phoenix, AZ
5,000	Youth Conservation Corps, Deerfield, IL
2,500	Boys & Girls Club of Phoenix, Phoenix, AZ
2,500	Planned Parenthood of Arizona, Phoenix, AZ
1,000	Chicago Child Care, Chicago, IL
1,000	Scottsdale/PV YMCA, Scottsdale, AZ
1,000	YMCA of Metro Chicago, Chicago, IL
100	Assistance League of YUMA, YUMA, AZ

GOLDMAN SACHS GROUP

Company Contact

New York, NY
Web: http://www.gs.com

Company Description

Revenue: US$25,363,000,000 (1999)
Employees: 8,664 (1999)
Fortune Rank: 54, per FORTUNE Magazine's list of 500 Largest U.S. Corporations (1999).
FF 54
SIC(s): 6211 Security Brokers & Dealers.

Operating Locations

Argentina: Goldman Sachs Argentina LLC, Buenos Aires; Australia: Goldman Sachs Australia LLC, Sydney; Brazil: Goldman Sachs & Companhia, Sao Paulo; Canada: Goldman Sachs Canada, Montreal, Toronto, Vancouver; People's Republic of China: Goldman Sachs (China) LLC, Beijing, Shanghai; Cayman Islands: Goldman Sachs (Cayman) Trust, Ltd., George Town; England: Goldman Sachs International, London; France: Goldman Sachs Paris Inc. et Cie, Paris; Germany: Goldman, Sachs & Co. oHG, Frankfurt am Main; Hong Kong: Goldman Sachs (Asia) LLC, Central District; India: Goldman Sachs (India) LLC, Mumbai; Italy: Goldman Sachs SIM SpA, Milan; Japan: Goldman Sachs (Japan) Ltd., Tokyo; Republic of Korea: Goldman, Sachs & Co., Seoul; Mexico: Goldman Sachs Mexico Casa de Bolsa, SA de CV, Mexico City; Russia: Goldman Sachs (AO) LLC, Moscow; Republic of South Africa: Goldman Sachs International, Johannesburg; Singapore: Goldman Sachs (Singapore) Pte., Singapore; Spain: Goldman Sachs International, Madrid; Sweden:, Stockholm; Switzerland: Goldman, Sachs & Co. Bank, Zurich; Thailand: Goldman Sachs (Asia) LLC, Bangkok; Taiwan: Goldman, Sachs & Co., Taipei

Nonmonetary Support

Volunteer Programs: The company encourages employee volunteerism through its Community TeamWorks program, which allows employees to spend a day working at a charitable organization of their choice while receiving full salary.

Goldman Sachs Foundation

Giving Contact

Stephanie Bell-Rose, President
Goldman Sachs Fund
275 Park Ave., Suite 1002
New York, NY 10152
Phone: (212)902-5402

Description

EIN: 237000346
Organization Type: Corporate Foundation. Supports preselected organizations only.
Giving Locations: nationally and internationally.
Grant Types: Employee Matching Gifts, Scholarship.

Giving Philosophy

The mission of the Goldman Sachs Foundation is, 'to promote innovation and excellence in education worldwide. Priorities include promoting academic performance, ecouraging the lifelong achievement of young people at the secondary school level, and encouraging education in business and entrepreneurship. The foundation represents an infusion of energy, focus, and resources devoted to societal contribution.'

Financial Summary

Total Giving: $10,000,000 (fiscal year ending June 30, 2000 approx). Note: Contributes through foundation only.

Typical Recipients

Arts & Humanities: Arts Centers, Arts Institutes, Literary Arts, Museums/Galleries, Music
Civic & Public Affairs: African American Affairs, Botanical Gardens/Parks, Business/Free Enterprise, Economic Development, Economic Policy, Civic & Public Affairs-General, Municipalities/Towns, Professional & Trade Associations, Public Policy, Urban & Community Affairs, Women's Affairs
Education: Business Education, Colleges & Universities, Continuing Education, Economic Education, Education Reform, Education-General, Medical Education, Minority Education, Private Education (Precollege), Public Education (Precollege), Secondary Education (Private), Social Sciences Education, Student Aid
Environment: Environment-General
Health: Emergency/Ambulance Services, Hospitals, Hospitals (University Affiliated)
International: Foreign Arts Organizations, Foreign Educational Institutions, Human Rights, International Affairs, International Organizations, International Peace & Security Issues, International Relations, International Relief Efforts, Missionary/Religious Activities
Religion: Jewish Causes
Social Services: At-Risk Youth, Child Welfare, Crime Prevention, United Funds/United Ways, Volunteer Services, YMCA/YWCA/YMHA/YWHA

Contributions Analysis

Giving Priorities: The Foundation focuses on excellence and innovation in education worldwide. According to a Goldman Sachs press release, an initial priority is 'improving academic performance and encouraging the lifelong achievement of young people at the middle and high school levels.'

Application Procedures

Initial Contact: Contact the foundation in writing.
Application Requirements: Include a description of the idea or proposal, a brief history of the organization, its mission, and its accomplishments.
Review Process: If the foundation is interested, it will request a full proposal.
Notes: The foundation will focus on funding organizations with which Goldman Sachs has cultivated relationships. The foundation will consider unsolicited requests in the manner described above.

Restrictions

Scholarships are limited to the spouses and children of Goldman Sachs & Co. employees.

Additional Information

The company formed the Goldman Sachs Foundation in 1999; the foundation will focus on education and youth programs.

Corporate Officials

David Dechman: managing director PRIM CORP EMPL managing director: Goldman Sachs Group Inc.
Stephen James Friedman: senior advisor B Brooklyn, NY 1938. ED Cornell University BA (1959); Columbia University LLB (1962). PRIM CORP EMPL senior advisor: Marsh & McLennan Risk Capital Corp. CORP AFFIL member: Federal National Mortgage Association; director: Walmart Stores Inc.
Henry M. Paulson, Jr.: chairman, chief executive officer PRIM CORP EMPL chairman, chief executive officer: Goldman Sachs Group Inc.
Esta Stecher: tax director, managing director PRIM CORP EMPL tax director, managing director: Goldman Sachs Group Inc.
John L. Thornton: president, chief operating officer PRIM CORP EMPL president, chief operating officer: Goldman Sachs Group Inc.

Foundation Officials

Stephanie Bell-Rose: president
Jonathan L. Cohen: secretary, director B New York, NY 1939. ED Dartmouth College AB (1960); Dartmouth College MBA (1961). PRIM CORP EMPL ltd. partner: Goldman Sachs Group. CORP AFFIL general partner: Goldman Sachs & Co. NONPR AFFIL member, board overseers: Dartmouth College Amos Tuck School Business Administration; member: Wildlife Conservation Society. CLUB AFFIL India House Club; Bond Club; Downtown Athletic Club; Bellport Bay Yacht Club.
Angelo DeCaro: treasurer, director B Brooklyn, NY 1943. ED Long Island University (1967); Long Island University (1975). PRIM CORP EMPL general partner: Goldman Sachs & Co.
Michael D. McCarthy: director CORP AFFIL general partner: Goldman Sachs & Co.
Thomas Payzant: member PRIM CORP EMPL superintendent: Boston Public Schools.
Esta Stecher: member (see above)
John L. Thornton: board member (see above)
John Livingston Weinberg: chairman, president, director (see above)
John Cunningham Whitehead: chairman board B Evanston, IL 1922. ED Haverford College BAA (1943); Harvard University MBA (1947). PRIM CORP EMPL chairman: AEA Investors Inc. NONPR AFFIL chairman: United Nations Association USA; chairman emeritus: Youth Understanding; trustee: Lincoln Center Theater; trustee: Rockefeller University; chairman: International House; chairman: International Rescue Committee; director: International Executive Service

Corps; member: Council Foreign Relations; trustee: Haverford College; chairman emeritus: Brookings Institute; co-chairman: Boy Scouts America New York Council. CLUB AFFIL University Club; The Links Club.

Grants Analysis

Disclosure Period: fiscal year ending June 30, 1998
Total Grants: $3,937,986*
Number of Grants: 825
Average Grant: $4,773
Highest Grant: $350,000
Typical Range: $50 to $5,000
***Note:** Giving excludes United Way. Grants analysis and recent grants are prior to the establishment of Goldman Sachs Foundation and reflect Goldman Sachs Fund giving.

Recent Grants

Note: Grants derived from fiscal 1998 Form 990.

Arts & Humanities

300,000 Charlotte Symphony Orchestra, Charlotte, NC
80,000 Chicago Symphony, Chicago, IL
30,000 Museum Illegible Text Fine Arts, Illegible Text, Houston, TX
25,000 Walker Art Center, Minneapolis, MN

Civic & Public Affairs

350,000 NYC Partnership Foundation, New York, NY
300,000 NYC Partnership Foundation, New York, NY
125,000 NAACP, New York, NY
50,000 Central Park Conservancy, New York, NY
50,000 NYC Partnership Foundation, New York, NY
25,000 Robert A. Toigo Foundation, Sacramento, CA
10,000 ACCF Center for Policy Research, Washington, DC
10,000 Brookings Institution, Washington, DC

Education

125,000 A Better Chance, Inc, New York, NY
125,000 Prep for Prep, New York, NY
100,000 Sponsors for Educational Opportunity, New York, NY
75,000 Sponsors for Educational Opportunity, New York, NY
50,050 United Negro College Fund, New York, NY
50,000 Columbia University, New York, NY
37,500 University of Chicago, Chicago, IL
32,500 University of Pennsylvania, Philadelphia, PA
25,000 A Better Chance, Inc, New York, NY
25,000 New York Academy of Medicine, New York, NY
25,000 Spelman College, Atlanta, GA
25,000 Western Reserve Academy, Richfield, OH
20,000 Dartmouth College, Hanover, NH
18,025 Student/Sponsor Partnership, Inc, New York, NY
15,000 University of Texas at Austin, Austin, TX
14,057 Harvard University, Cambridge, MA
12,365 University of Pennsylvania, Philadelphia, PA
10,811 Dartmouth College, Hanover, NH
10,000 Cornell University-Johnson Graduate School of Business, New York, NY
10,000 Duke University, Durham, NC
10,000 Howard University, Washington, DC
10,000 NYU Stern School of Business, New York, NY
10,000 UCLA Foundation, Los Angeles, CA
10,000 University of Michigan, Ann Arbor, MI
1,500 United Way, Short Hills, NJ
100 The Illegible Text Illegible Text, Banff, AB, Canada

Environment

25,000 The Nature Conservancy, Honolulu, HI
12,500 Illegible Text Trails New York, New York, NY

International

125,000 International Rescue Committee, New York, NY
125,000 United Nations Association of the USA, New York, NY
25,000 St. Paul's School, London, England
10,000 Ashinaga Ikueikai, Japan
10,000 The European Institute of Business Administration (INSEAD), Fontainebleau, France
10,000 Movimento De Apio a Integracao, Brazil
1,000 McGill University Graduate School, Toronto, ON, Canada
1,000 University of British Columbia, Vancouver, Canada
1,000 University of British Columbia, Vancouver, BC, Canada
1,000 The University of Western Ontario, London, ON, Canada
500 Oxford University, London, England
500 University of Western Ontario, London, ON, Canada
25 University of Toronto, Toronto, ON, Canada

Social Services

175,000 United Way, New York, NY
135,244 United Way, New York, NY
96,180 United Way, New York, NY
50,000 Illegible Text House, New York, NY
33,985 Covenant House, New York, NY
10,000 New York City Volunteer Program, New York, NY
5,000 Boundless Adventures, Toronto, ON, Canada

GOLUB CORP.

Company Contact

Schenectady, NY
Web: http://www.pricechopper.com

Company Description

Employees: 17,000
SIC(s): 5411 Grocery Stores.

Golub Foundation

Giving Contact

Melissa Pabis, Foundation Administrator
Golub Foundation
PO Box 1074
Schenectady, NY 12301
Phone: (518)356-9450

Alternate Contact

Phone: (518)356-9270
Note: Alternate phone number is for scholarship information only.

Description

Founded: 1981
EIN: 222341421
Organization Type: Corporate Foundation
Giving Locations: headquarters and operating communities.
Grant Types: Employee Matching Gifts, General Support, Scholarship.

Financial Summary

Total Giving: $500,000 (fiscal year ending March 31, 2000 approx); $500,000 (fiscal 1999 approx); $426,394 (fiscal 1997). Note: Contributes through foundation only.
Giving Analysis: Giving for fiscal 1997 includes: foundation (approx $347,864); foundation scholarships (approx $43,255); foundation grants to United Way (approx $32,300); foundation matching gifts (approx $2,975)
Assets: $717,065 (fiscal 1997); $690,828 (fiscal 1996); $40,780 (fiscal 1995)
Gifts Received: $445,000 (fiscal 1997); $1,028,350 (fiscal 1996); $1,834 (fiscal 1995). Note: Contributions are received from the Golub Corporation.

Typical Recipients

Arts & Humanities: Arts Institutes, Arts Outreach, Ethnic & Folk Arts, Historic Preservation, Literary Arts, Museums/Galleries, Music, Performing Arts, Theater
Civic & Public Affairs: African American Affairs, Civic & Public Affairs-General, Housing, Professional & Trade Associations, Public Policy, Urban & Community Affairs
Education: Business Education, Colleges & Universities, Community & Junior Colleges, Education-General, Literacy, Medical Education, Preschool Education, Public Education (Precollege), Science/Mathematics Education, Student Aid
Health: Arthritis, Cancer, Children's Health/Hospitals, Clinics/Medical Centers, Eyes/Blindness, Health Organizations, Hospices, Hospitals, Medical Rehabilitation, Prenatal Health Issues, Single-Disease Health Associations
Religion: Jewish Causes, Religious Organizations, Religious Welfare, Synagogues/Temples
Science: Science Museums
Social Services: Community Centers, Community Service Organizations, Counseling, Family Services, Food/Clothing Distribution, People with Disabilities, Recreation & Athletics, Scouts, Senior Services, United Funds/United Ways, YMCA/YWCA/YMHA/YWHA, Youth Organizations

Contributions Analysis

Arts & Humanities: 5% to 10%. Supports theaters, performing arts centers, and music.
Civic & Public Affairs: About 10%. Contributes to safety, community affairs, and public policy groups.
Education: 5% to 10%. Major interest in public education. Also supports colleges, literacy, and technology programs. Operates scholarship program for students attending colleges in New York, Massachusetts, Pennsylvania, Connecticut, and Vermont.
Health: 15% to 20%. Contributes to hospitals, medical centers, children's health, and single-disease health associations.
Religion: 30% to 40%. Support provided to synagogues and Jewish community centers.
Social Services: 10% to 15%. Favors community centers, united funds, community recreation and athletics, the disabled, and family services.

Application Procedures

Initial Contact: Brief letter for general proposals; letter requesting application form for scholarship awards.
Application Requirements: For grant proposals, a description of organization, amount requested, purpose of funds sought, recently audited financial statement, and proof of tax-exempt status.
Deadlines: for grant requests: None; for scholarship applications: March.

Additional Information

Publications: Informational Brochure

Corporate Officials

Lewis Golub: chairman, chief executive officer, director B 1931. ED Michigan State University BS (1953).

PRIM CORP EMPL chairman, chief executive officer, director: Golub Corp. CORP AFFIL director: Taylor Made Co.; chairman, chief executive officer: Price Chopper Oper Co. Massachusetts; chairman, chief executive officer: Price Chopper Oper Co. Pennsylvania; director: CIES; chairman, chief executive officer: Golub Service Stations Inc.; chairman: Central Distributors Inc.; member regional advisory board: Chase Bank; chairman: Cengo Construction Corp. NONPR AFFIL director: Saratoga Performing Arts Center; member advisory board: Union College; director: Proctor's Theater; advisor mba program: Russell Sage College; director: Food Marketing Institute; chairman: New York State Business Council; director: Empire State College Foundation.

Foundation Officials

Margaret Davenport: trustee
Mona Golub: trustee
Barbara B. Page: trustee B Borger, TX 1940. ED University of Oklahoma BS (1962). PRIM CORP EMPL secretary, treasurer, director: Stokes Canning Co. NONPR AFFIL member: National Food Processors Association; member: National Meat Canners.

Grants Analysis

Disclosure Period: fiscal year ending March 31, 1997
Total Grants: $347,864*
Number of Grants: 422
Highest Grant: $63,334
Typical Range: $50 to $2,500
***Note:** Giving excludes matching gifts; scholarship; United Way.

Recent Grants

Note: Grants derived from 1997 Form 990.

Arts & Humanities

5,000 Flynn Theater for Performing Arts, Burlington, VT -- pledge payment
1,500 Flynn Theater for Performing Arts, Burlington, VT -- annual support
1,250 Massachusetts Museum of Contemporary Art, North Adams, MA -- final payment on pledge
1,000 Irish American Heritage Museum, Albany, NY -- second and final payment on pledge

Civic & Public Affairs

5,000 Eddy, Troy, NY -- pledge payment
2,500 Muson Williams Procter Institute, Utica, NY -- 1996 pledge

Education

3,333 College of St. Rose, Albany, NY -- capital fund
2,500 Siena College, Albany, NY -- for M. Dean Potts Memorial Scholarship
2,000 Junior Achievement, Schenectady, NY -- for 1996 pledge
2,000 Utica Head Start Children and Families, Utica, NY -- final payment on pledge
1,667 Rensselaerville Institute, Rensselaerville, NY -- second payment on pledge
1,500 Schenectady County Community College, Schenectady, NY -- support Food for Thought Fundraiser
1,000 Junior Achievement Capital District New York, Schenectady, NY -- for annual bowl-a-thon
1,000 Marywood College, Scranton, PA -- annual donation
1,000 Sage Colleges, Troy, NY -- for annual business campaign
1,000 Siena College, Loudonville, NY -- for Cyprian Mensing, President's Circle
1,000 Union College, Schenectady, NY -- final payment on pledge
1,000 University at Albany Foundation, Albany, NY -- inaugural dinner for President Hitchcock

Health

10,000 Hospice, Schenectady, NY -- fourth payment on pledge
10,000 St. Claire's Hospital, Schenectady, NY -- first of five payments on pledge
5,000 St. Peter's Hospital, Albany, NY -- for five-year pledge
3,333 St. Francis Hospital, Schenectady, NY -- first of three payments on pledge
3,000 Samaritan Hospital, Troy, NY -- third payment on pledge
2,500 Columbia-Greene Community Hospital Foundation, Hudson, NY -- final payment on pledge
2,346 Seven Hills Occupational and Rehabilitation Services, Worcester, MA -- program pledge payment
2,000 Community General Hospital Foundation, Syracuse, NY -- pledge payment
1,666 Glens Falls Hospital Department of Institutional Advancement, Glens Falls, NY -- third and final payment on pledge
1,500 Muscular Dystrophy Association, Albany, NY -- for dinner auction
1,250 Brattleboro Memorial Hospital, Brattleboro, VT -- final pledge payment
1,250 Great Brook Valley Health Center, Worcester, MA -- first of two payments on pledge
1,200 St. Mary's Hospital, Troy, NY -- final payment on pledge
1,000 Arthritis Foundation, Albany, NY -- support Accolade for Community Dinner
1,000 Community Maternity Services, Albany, NY -- capital campaign for Farano Center
1,000 Foundation of St. Mary's Hospital, Amsterdam, NY -- pledge payment
1,000 Muscular Dystrophy Association, Albany, NY -- for golf star sponsorship

Religion

63,334 United Jewish Federation, Latham, NY -- second payment of three on $25,000 pledge
38,333 United Jewish Federation, Latham, NY -- pledge payment
38,333 United Jewish Federation, Latham, NY -- third and final payment on pledge
1,000 Jewish Community Center, Albany, NY -- pledge payment
1,000 Jewish Community Center, Albany, NY -- support Golf and Tennis Day

Social Services

5,000 Center for the Disabled, Albany, NY -- fourth payment on pledge
5,000 YMCA Capital District, Albany, NY -- pledge payment
3,000 Boy Scouts of America Twin Rivers Council, Albany, NY -- annual support
1,500 YMCA, Torrington, CT -- first of three payment for capital campaign
1,000 Boys and Girls Club, Burlington, VT -- final payment on pledge
1,000 Boys and Girls Club, Pittsfield, MA -- pledge payment
1,000 Double H Hole in the Woods Ranch, Glens Falls, NY -- for table at fund raiser
1,000 Food Bank of Central New York, East Syracuse, NY -- third payment on pledge
1,000 YMCA, Poughkeepsie, NY -- third and final payment on pledge
1,000 YWCA Dutchess County, Poughkeepsie, NY -- first of three payments on pledge

B.F. Goodrich Aerospace - Aerostructures Group

Company Contact

850 Lagoon Dr.
Chula Vista, CA 91910
Phone: (619)691-4111
Web: http://www.bfg-aerospace.com/aerostructures/

Company Description

Former Name: Rohr Industries; Rohr Inc.
Employees: 4,287
SIC(s): 3724 Aircraft Engines & Engine Parts, 3728 Aircraft Parts & Equipment Nec, 3829 Measuring & Controlling Devices Nec.
Parent Company: B.F. Goodrich Aerospace - Headquarters, 3 Coliseum Center, 2550 West Tyvola Road, Charlotte, NC, United States
Parent Revenue: US$3,950,800,000

Nonmonetary Support

Value: $5,000 (1992)
Type: Donated Equipment

Giving Contact

Bryan Broderick, Vice President Human Resources
BFGoodrich Aerospace/Aerostructures Group
850 Lagoon Dr.
Chula Vista, CA 91910
Phone: (619)691-3952
Fax: (619)691-4222
Email: bbroderick@aerostructures.bfg.com

Description

Organization Type: Corporate Giving Program
Giving Locations: headquarters and operating communities.
Grant Types: Employee Matching Gifts, General Support.

Financial Summary

Total Giving: $228,000 (1996 approx); $340,000 (1993 approx); $500,000 (1992 approx). Note: Contributes through corporate direct giving program only.

Typical Recipients

Arts & Humanities: Arts Associations & Councils, Music, Performing Arts, Public Broadcasting, Theater
Civic & Public Affairs: Economic Development, Economic Policy, Law & Justice, Zoos/Aquariums
Education: Business Education, Colleges & Universities, Community & Junior Colleges, Continuing Education, Elementary Education (Private), Engineering/Technological Education, Minority Education
Environment: Environment-General
Health: Health Organizations, Hospices, Hospitals, Single-Disease Health Associations
Science: Science Exhibits & Fairs
Social Services: Community Centers, Community Service Organizations, Counseling, Delinquency & Criminal Rehabilitation, Domestic Violence, Emergency Relief, Family Planning, Family Services, Food/Clothing Distribution, People with Disabilities, Senior Services, Substance Abuse, United Funds/United Ways, Youth Organizations

Contributions Analysis

Civic & Public Affairs: 5%.
Education: 10% to 15%.
Health: 75% to 80%.
Note: Company reports that contributions are primarily in the form of employee matching gifts.

Application Procedures

Initial Contact: a brief letter of inquiry
Application Requirements: a description of organization, amount requested, purpose of funds sought,

audited financial statement, and proof of tax-exempt status
Deadlines: None.

Giving Program Officials
Bryan Broderick: vice president human resources

GOSIGER, INC.

Company Contact
Dayton, OH

Company Description
Employees: 110

Gosiger Foundation

Giving Contact
Mrs. J. Haley, President
Gosiger Foundation
108 McDonough St.
Dayton, OH 45402
Phone: (937)228-5174
Fax: (937)463-7718

Description
Founded: 1992
EIN: 311365457
Organization Type: Corporate Foundation. Supports preselected organizations only.
Giving Locations: headquarters area only.

Financial Summary
Total Giving: $1,000,000 (1999 approx); $6,981 (1994); $3,699 (1993)
Assets: $29,110 (1994); $6,140 (1993)
Gifts Received: $30,000 (1994). Note: In 1994, contributions were received from Gosiger, Inc.

Typical Recipients
Arts & Humanities: Arts Associations & Councils, History & Archaeology, Music
Civic & Public Affairs: Botanical Gardens/Parks, Civic & Public Affairs-General
Education: Colleges & Universities, Education-General, Private Education (Precollege), Student Aid

Additional Information
Does not support individuals, religious organizations for sectarian purposes, or political or lobbying groups.

Corporate Officials
Jane Gosiger Haley: president PRIM CORP EMPL president: Gosiger.

Foundation Officials
Jerry Gecowets: executive vice president PRIM CORP EMPL executive vice president marketing: Gosiger.
Carrie L. Haley: treasurer
Jane Gosiger Haley: president (see above)
John Haley: vice president
Pete Haley: vice president
Hugh E. Wall, III: secretary

Grants Analysis
Disclosure Period: calendar year ending
Typical Range: $2,500 to $5,000

Recent Grants
Note: Grants derived from 1997 Form 990.

Arts & Humanities

5,000	Dayton Art Last, Dayton, OH
2,500	Society of National History
2,000	Dayton Philharmonic, Dayton, OH

Civic & Public Affairs

2,500	Artemis
1,000	Cox Arboretum Fund

Education

4,000	USMM Academy
2,500	Chaminade-Julienne
2,500	University of Dayton, Dayton, OH
1,000	University of Pittsburgh, Pittsburgh, PA
500	OFIC
340	WSU Foundation
340	WSU Foundation

GPU INC.

Company Contact
Morristown, NJ
Web: http://www.gpu.com

Company Description
Former Name: General Public Utilities Corp.
Revenue: US$459,000,000 (1999)
Employees: 8,957 (1999)
Fortune Rank: 338, per FORTUNE Magazine's list of 500 Largest U.S. Corporations (1999).
FF 338
SIC(s): 4911 Electric Services, 6719 Holding Companies Nec.

Nonmonetary Support
Type: Donated Equipment; In-kind Services
Note: Estimated value of nonmonetary support is $42,000 for 1998.

Corporate Sponsorship
Value: $750,000 (1998); $750,000
Type: Other; Festivals/fairs
Contact: Crystal Seitz, Manager, Community Initiatives
Note: Sponsors dances, dinners, and luncheons.

GPU Foundation

Giving Contact
Carole B. Snyder, Executive Vice President, Corporate Affairs
GPU, Inc.
300 Madison Avenue
PO Box 1911
Morristown, NJ 07962
Phone: (973)455-8200
Fax: (973)455-8777

Description
Organization Type: Corporate Foundation
Giving Locations: NJ: northern and central; PA: eastern and part of central and western
Note: Employee matching gift ratio: 1 to 1. Company matches gifts to accredited institutions of higher learning, recognized by the IRS as tax-exempt organisation.

Financial Summary
Total Giving: $1,900,000 (1998 approx); $1,800,000 (1997 approx); $1,689,000 (1996 approx). Note: Contributes through corporate direct giving program only. Giving includes corporate direct giving; domestic and international subsidiaries.

Typical Recipients
Civic & Public Affairs: Public Policy
Environment: Air/Water Quality, Environment-General, Resource Conservation

Contributions Analysis
Giving Priorities: Education and community development, prevention of substance abuse and facilitation for rehabilitation, youth development, assistance to people who are disadvantaged, and cultural enrichment.

Application Procedures
Initial Contact: Send a brief letter requesting application form.
Application Requirements: Federal tax exempt ID; 501(c)(3) IRS letter; summary of financial statement; board members and affiliations; name and address of the organization; executive directory name and telephone number; explanation as to how organization fit GPU's interest areas; capital campaign: project overview including cost, amount to be raised, other funding sources, timeline; explanation of the need the organization is filling in the community.
Deadlines: None.
Review Process: Grants are reviewed three times per year.
Decision Notification: Applicants should plan on about 90 days for processing and a decision.

Restrictions
The foundation does not support individuals, organizations for profit, national or regional organizations, the promotion of religious doctrines, schools, organizations providing support for specific health issues, political groups, endowment, fraternal groups, athletic teams, bands or veteran's organizations, hospitals, healthcare institutions, scholarships, campaigns, fundraising dinners, trips, tours, student exchange programs, documentaries and videos.

Additional Information
Publications: Annual Report

Corporate Officials
Fred Douglass Hafer: chairman, president, chief executive officer B West Reading, PA 1941. ED Drexel Institute of Technology (1959-1962); Alvernia College LHD (1993). PRIM CORP EMPL chairman, president, chief executive officer: GPU, Inc. CORP AFFIL director: Utilities Mutual Insurance Co.; president, chief executive officer, director: Pennsylvania Electric Co.; director: Meridian Bank; president, chief executive officer, director: Metro Edison Co.; director: GPU Service Corp.; director: Meridian Bancorp Inc.; director: GPU Nuclear Corp. NONPR AFFIL member executive committee: Pennsylvania Electric Association; board director: Reading Hospital & Medical Center; director: Manufacturer Association Berks County; director: Kutztown University Foundation; director: Leadership Pennsylvania; trustee: Caron Foundation; director: Foundation Drug-Free Pennsylvania; member: Berks County Chamber of Commerce; director: Berks Festivals; director: Berks Business Education Coalition. CLUB AFFIL Berkshire Country Club.

Giving Program Officials
Crystal A. Seitz: manager community initiatives
Carole B. Snyder: executive vice president corporate affairs

Foundation Officials
Carole B. Snyder: executive vice president corporate affairs (see above)

GPU ENERGY

Company Contact
Morristown, NJ
Web: http://www.gpu.com

Company Description
Employees: 3,077
SIC(s): 4911 Electric Services.
Parent Company: General Public Utilities Corp.

Corporate Sponsorship

Value: $838,400 (1999)
Type: Arts & cultural events; Festivals/fairs; Music & entertainment events; Sports events

GPU Foundation

Giving Contact

Maxi Shirey, Community Initiatives Manager
GPU Energy
2800 Pottsville Pike
PO Box 16001
Reading, PA 19640-0001
Phone: (610)929-3601
Fax: (610)921-6571

Description

Founded: 1999
EIN: 223624040
Organization Type: Corporate Giving Program
Giving Locations: headquarters and operating communities.
Grant Types: Employee Matching Gifts, General Support.
Note: Company matches employee gifts to accredited institutions of higher education.

Giving Philosophy

'GPU is committed to being a neighbor of choice throughout our service territories. Having a positive identity as a company that supports community concerns is of utmost importance to our business. We believe that helping make the communities we serve stronger makes good business sense for our company. That's why each year, GPU along with the GPU Foundation provides over $2 million in contributions to the communities where we do business.' *GPU Community Initiatives*

Financial Summary

Total Giving: $1,950,000 (2000 approx); $2,000,000 (1999 approx). Note: Contributes through corporate direct giving program and foundation.
Giving Analysis: Giving for 1999 includes: foundation (approx $1,250,000); corporate direct giving (approx $750,000); 2000: foundation (approx $1,280,000); corporate direct giving (approx $670,000)

Typical Recipients

Arts & Humanities: Arts & Humanities-General
Civic & Public Affairs: Civic & Public Affairs-General
Education: Education-General
Health: Hospitals
Social Services: United Funds/United Ways

Contributions Analysis

Giving Priorities: In 2000, GPU reported that it had, 'developed a strategic focus for charitable giving in alignment with GPU's business strategy. GPU's giving guidelines support organizations that address social issues surrounding youth at risk, outreach programs dealing with substance abuse intervention/prevention, with particular emphasis on educational programs for youth, organizations addressing the issue of essential needs of food, clothing and shelter, education, and cultural enrichment.' GPU Statement on Giving Priorities

Application Procedures

Initial Contact: Send a brief letter of inquiry.
Application Requirements: Include a description of organization, amount requested, purpose of funds sought, audited financial statement, and proof of tax-exempt status. GPU Foundation requires a list of the organization's board of directors.
Deadlines: None.

Restrictions

Does not support individuals, religious organizations for sectarian purposes, or political or lobbying groups. Support to arts and recreational programs is also restricted.

Additional Information

Organizations that fall within GPU's focus areas receive priority.
Publications: Program Guidelines

Corporate Officials

Dennis P. Baldassari: president, chief operating officer vice president B Pottstown, PA 1949. ED Drexel University BS (1972). PRIM CORP EMPL president, chief operating officer: GPU Energy ADD CORP EMPL director: GPU Energy Service Corp.; president: Jersey Central Power & Light Co. CORP AFFIL member: Pennsylvania Electric Association; director: First Morris Bank; director: New Jersey Utilities Association. NONPR AFFIL trustee: Liberty Science Center.
John Gourlay Graham: chief financial officer, senior vice president B Orange, NJ 1938. ED Upsala College AB (1960); Rutgers University JD (1963). PRIM CORP EMPL chief financial officer, senior vice president: GPU Energy Inc. PRIM NONPR EMPL adjunct professor: Seton Hall Law School ADD CORP EMPL director: GPU International Inc.; executive vice president, chief financial officer,director: GPU Service Corp.; vice president, chief financial officer: GPU Nuclear Corp. CORP AFFIL director: Viatel Inc.; chairman, director: Utilities Mutual Insurance Co.; chairman, director: Nuclear Electric Initiatives Ltd.; vice president, chief financial officer, director: Pennsylvania Electric Co.; vice president, chief financial officer: Metropolitan Edison Co.; director: Midlands Electricity PLC; director: Avon Energy Partners PLC; vice president, chief financial officer: Jersey Central Power & Light Co. NONPR AFFIL member: New Jersey Bar Association.

Grants Analysis

Disclosure Period: calendar year ending
Typical Range: $1,000 to $2,500

W.R. GRACE &CO.

Company Contact

Boca Raton, FL
Web: http://www.grace.com

Company Description

Employees: 6,300
SIC(s): 2064 Candy & Other Confectionery Products, 2066 Chocolate & Cocoa Products, 2819 Industrial Inorganic Chemicals Nec, 2869 Industrial Organic Chemicals Nec.

Operating Locations

Argentina: Grace Argentina SA, Buenos Aires; Australia: Grace Australia Pty. Ltd., Fawkner; Belgium: Grace NV, Antwerpen; Brazil: Grace Brasil SA, Sao Paulo; Chile: Grace Quimica Compania Limitada, Santiago; People's Republic of China: Grace China Ltd., Shanghai; Colombia: Grace Colombia SA, Bogota; Denmark: W.R. Grace A/S, Herlev; England: W.R. Grace Ltd., Slough, St. Neots; France: W.R. Grace SAS, Epernon; Germany: Grace GmbH, Norderstedt, Worms; Grenada: Grace Hellas EPE, Athens; Hong Kong: W.R. Grace (HK) Ltd., Quarry Bay; Indonesia: P.T. Grace Specialty Chemicals Indonesia, Cikarang, Bekasi 17530; India: W.R. Grace & Co., Bangalore; Ireland: Grace Construction Products (Ireland) Ltd., Western Industrial Estate, Naas Road; Italy: W.R. Grace Italiana SpA, Passirana di Rho (Milano); Japan: Grace Japan KK, Kaneda, Nagoya; Republic of Korea: Grace Korea Inc., Seoul; Mexico: W.R. Grace Holdings, SA de CV, Mexico City, Toluca; Malaysia: W.R. Grace Specialty Chemicals (Malaysia) Sdn. Bhd., Pahand Darul Makmur; W.R. Grace (Malaysia) Sdn. Bhd., Selangor Darul Ehsan; Netherlands: W.R. Grace BV, Rotterdam; New Zealand: Grace New Zealand Limited, Elsdon, Porirua; Peru: W.R. Grace & Co. -- Sucarsal, Lima; Philippines: W.R. Grace (Phillipines) Inc., Laguna; Poland: W.R. Grace Sp. zo.o., Warszawa; Russia: W.R. Grace LLC, Moscow; Republic of South Africa: W.R. Grace Africa (Pty) Ltd., Cape Town, Johannesburg; Singapore: W.R. Grace (Singapore) Pte. Ltd., Jurong Industrial Town, Singapore, Singapore; Spain: Grace SA, Barcleona; Sweden: Grace AB, Helsingborg; Thailand: W.R. Grace (Thailand) Limited, Aphur Muang, Samutprakan 10270, Samutprakan 10280; Taiwan: W.R. Grace Taiwan Inc., Taoyuan; Venezuela: Grace Venezuela SA, Valencia; Vietnam: W.R. Grace (HK) Ltd., Ho Chi Minh City

Nonmonetary Support

Type: Donated Equipment; Donated Products; In-kind Services; Loaned Employees; Loaned Executives
Contact: Susan Harris, Manager, Corporate Contributions
Note: Co. provides nonmonetary support.

Grace Foundation Inc.

Giving Contact

Mary Helen Johnson
Grace Foundation Inc.
7500 Grace Dr.
Columbia, MD 21044
Phone: (410)531-4000

Description

EIN: 136153305
Organization Type: Corporate Foundation
Giving Locations: corporate operating locations; nationally.
Grant Types: Capital, Employee Matching Gifts, General Support, Multiyear/Continuing Support, Scholarship.
Note: Employee matching gift ratio: 1 to 1. Company matches gifts to colleges, universities, and secondary schools in the U.S. and Canada.

Financial Summary

Total Giving: $1,250,000 (1999 approx); $1,500,000 (1998 approx); $2,300,000 (1997 approx). Note: Contributes through corporate direct giving program and foundation. Giving includes foundation.
Assets: $9,500,000 (1997 approx); $10,133,091 (1996); $10,398,997 (1995)

Typical Recipients

Arts & Humanities: Community Arts, Performing Arts, Theater
Civic & Public Affairs: Business/Free Enterprise, Civil Rights, Economic Development, Economic Policy, Employment/Job Training, Housing, Law & Justice, Public Policy, Urban & Community Affairs, Zoos/Aquariums
Education: Arts/Humanities Education, Business Education, Colleges & Universities, Economic Education, Education Funds, Engineering/Technological Education, Education-General, Medical Education, Minority Education, Private Education (Precollege), Public Education (Precollege), Science/Mathematics Education, Special Education, Student Aid
Environment: Air/Water Quality, Environment-General
Health: Health Funds, Health Organizations, Hospices, Hospitals, Medical Rehabilitation, Medical Research
International: International Peace & Security Issues
Religion: Religious Welfare
Science: Science Exhibits & Fairs, Scientific Organizations

Social Services: At-Risk Youth, Child Welfare, Community Centers, Community Service Organizations, Delinquency & Criminal Rehabilitation, Homes, People with Disabilities, Recreation & Athletics, Scouts, Senior Services, Substance Abuse, United Funds/United Ways, YMCA/YWCA/YMHA/YWHA, Youth Organizations

Contributions Analysis

Giving Priorities: Higher education, united funds, health care, social welfare, minority affairs, and culture. Domestically, company and foundation contributions for international purposes are rare. Has supported such relief organizations as CARE and AmeriCares. Overseas companies do make contributions; however, in-country managers are autonomous in choosing recipients for support and headquarters has no oversight of such activities.
Arts & Humanities: Less than 5%. Interest in major museums and similar institutions that perform a specialized function in the fields of art, history, or science.
Civic & Public Affairs: 20% to 25%. Interest in major national programs designed to improve the quality of life in cities and the general welfare of minorities, with emphasis on youth organizations. Also supports conservation programs and local zoos and parks. Company supportsunited funds nationwide with emphasis on employee communities.
Education: 55% to 60%. Supports colleges and universities with undergraduate and graduate schools of business and major departments of chemistry. Other priorities include special education, with emphasis on math and science. Sponsors employee matching gifts program for higher and secondary education institutions, which accounts for about 15% of contributions in this category. Scholarship program is available for children of company employees.
Social Services: 15% to 20%. Foundation interests include primary health-care facilities that serve the communities in which the company operates,hospitals whose activities are national in scope or unique in type of care delivered, major national medical research programs deemed vital to social welfare, major national organizations whose objective is the betterment of societal welfare, and a variety of community service organizations.
Note: Above priorities are for foundation giving. Company facilities also make grants in local communities; priorities may vary.

Application Procedures

Initial Contact: submit one copy of proposal to foundation; local organizations should submit proposals to local W.R. Grace division management
Application Requirements: a description of organization, amount requested, purpose for which funds are sought, recently audited financial statement, proof of tax-exempt status, list of current contributors indicating amounts contributed on annual basis
Deadlines: None; board meets as needed.
Decision Notification: three months after receipt of proposal

Restrictions

Does not support dinners or special events, fraternal organizations, goodwill advertising, individuals, political or lobbying groups, or religious organizations for sectarian purposes.

Additional Information

Company no longer sponsors events.

Corporate Officials

Robert J. Bettacchi: senior vice president, chief financial officer ED Villanova University BS. PRIM CORP EMPL senior vice president: W.R. Grace & Co. ADD CORP EMPL president: Grace Construction Products. CORP AFFIL director: Associated Industries Massachusetts; director: Cambridge Trust Co. NONPR AFFIL member: Conference Board; member: Massachusetts Governor's Council Economic Growth Technology; member: American Management Association.
Paul J. Norris: chairman, president, chief executive officer, director B 1947. ED Mount Saint Mary's College BA; University Maryland MBA. PRIM CORP EMPL chairman, president, chief executive officer, director: W.R. Grace & Co.
Robert M. Tarola: senior vice president, chief financial officer ED Temple University BA. PRIM CORP EMPL senior vice president, chief financial officer: W.R. Grace & Co. CORP AFFIL director: Legg Mason Institutional Fund Advisors II. NONPR AFFIL director: Saint Paul's School; board member: Temple University Accounting Advisory Board; member: American Institute CPAs.

Foundation Officials

Susan Harris: assistant treasurer
W. Brian McGowan: chairman ED Marist College BS (1972); Saint John's University MBA (1975). PRIM CORP EMPL senior vice president corporate administration: W.R. Grace & Co.
Paul J. Norris: director (see above)

Grants Analysis

Disclosure Period: calendar year ending 1996
Total Grants: $2,645,101
Number of Grants: 350 (approx)
Average Grant: $7,557 (approx)
Typical Range: $1,000 to $10,000

Recent Grants

Note: Grants derived from 1996 Form 990.

Arts & Humanities

10,000 Center for Performing Arts, Greenville, SC
10,000 National Theater Workshop of the Handicapped, New York, NY
10,000 Raymond F. Kravis Center for Performing Arts, West Palm Beach, FL

Civic & Public Affairs

10,000 American Concrete Institute, Detroit, MI
10,000 National Forum Foundation, Washington, DC

Education

205,000 Clemson University, Clemson, SC
175,000 Grace Institute, New York, NY
50,000 University of Wisconsin Foundation, Madison, WI
26,000 Keystone Science School, Keystone, CO
25,000 Fordham University, Bronx, NY
25,000 Hillsdale College, Hillsdale, MI
25,000 Inner-City Scholarship Fund, Brighton, MA
25,000 St. Andrew's School, Boca Raton, FL
20,000 Governor's School for Science and Mathematics Foundation, Hartsville, SC
20,000 Ohio State University, Columbus, OH
20,000 University of Missouri Rolla, Rolla, MO
15,000 Furman University, Greensville, SC
15,000 Georgia Tech Foundation, Atlanta, GA
12,500 Johns Hopkins University, Baltimore, MD
10,000 Barton's Boosters, Boca Raton, FL
10,000 Cambridge Partnership for Public Education, Cambridge, MA
10,000 Florida A&M University, Tallahassee, FL
10,000 Kenston Forest School, Blackstone, VA
10,000 Marquette University, Milwaukee, WI

Environment

10,000 Friends of Sandoway House Nature Center, Delray Beach, FL
10,000 Save Our Streams, Glen Burnie, MD

Health

10,000 Howard County General Hospital, Columbia, MD

International

20,000 Appeal of Conscience Foundation, New York, NY
20,000 Appeal of Conscience Foundation, New York, NY

Religion

50,000 Sisters of Charity, Bronx, NY
10,000 Salvation Army, Greensville, SC

Science

50,000 Massachusetts State Science Fair, Saugus, MA

Social Services

106,000 United Way Central Maryland, Baltimore, MD
100,000 Malta Human Services Foundation, New York, NY
71,662 United Way Greensville County, Greensville, SC
50,000 United Way New England, Boston, MA
38,202 United Way Piedmont, Spartanburg, SC
27,000 Calcasieu United Way, Lake Charles, LA
26,278 United Way East Central Iowa, Cedar Rapids, IA
26,012 United Way Central Maryland, Baltimore, MD
24,000 United Way, Wichita Falls, TX
20,000 United Way Palm Beach County, West Palm Beach, FL
15,500 United Way Crusade of Mercy, Chicago, IL
15,200 United Way Berks County, Reading, PA
12,000 United Way, Chattanooga, TN
12,000 United Way Brown County, Green Bay, WI
10,000 Boy Scouts of America Blue Ridge Council, Greensville, SC
10,000 Covenant House, New York, NY
10,000 Kennedy Krieger Institute, Baltimore, MD
10,000 Siouxland Soccer Foundation, Sioux City, IA
10,000 YMCA, Spartanburg, SC

Graco, Inc.

Company Contact

Minneapolis, MN
Web: http://www.graco.com

Company Description

Employees: 2,086
SIC(s): 3561 Pumps & Pumping Equipment.

Operating Locations

Belgium: Graco NV, Maasmechelen, Limburg; Canada: Graco Canada, Mississauga; People's Republic of China: Graco (HK) Limited, Shanghai; England: Graco UK Ltd., Wolverhampton; France: Graco SA, Rungis; Germany: Graco GmbH, Neuss, Nordrhein-Westfalen; Hong Kong: Graco Hong Kong Ltd., Causeway Bay; Italy: Graco Srl, Bologna; Japan: Graco KK, Yokohama; Republic of Korea: Graco Korea, Seoul; Norway: Graco Norge AS, Lommedalen; Spain: Graco SA Succursale Espagnole, Madrid; Taiwan: Graco Hong Kong Limited (Taiwan Liaison Office), Taipei

Nonmonetary Support

Value: $2,000 (1996); $20,000 (1993); $15,000 (1992)
Type: Donated Equipment
Note: Nonmonetary support is limited and contact is initiated through foundation.

Graco Foundation

Giving Contact

Robert M. Mattison, Vice President & Secretary
Graco Foundation
4050 Olson Memorial Highway
PO Box 1441
Minneapolis, MN 55440-1441
Phone: (612)623-6684
Fax: (612)623-6944
Email: Nancy_a_Skaalrud@Graco.com

Alternate Contact

Nancy Skaalrud, Legal Secretary, Foundation Administrator

Description

EIN: 416023537
Organization Type: Corporate Foundation
Giving Locations: MN; SD: Sioux Falls operating locations.
Grant Types: Capital, Employee Matching Gifts, General Support, Multiyear/Continuing Support.
Note: Employee matching gift ratio: 1 to 1. Contributions to education are matched to a maximum of $2,500 per year.

Giving Philosophy

'In 1996, Graco undertook a comprehensive review of the needs of the community and how the Graco Foundation could be most effective in addressing those needs. The following four areas were identified for focus of the Foundation's support in 1997 and beyond.'

'Building Capacity: Through grants specifically aimed at building capacity, including capital projects and program development, the Foundation's goal is to help organizations grow their capacity to serve community needs.'

'Productivity and Self Sufficiency: Priority will be given to organizations that have a proven track record in enabling people to be self-sufficient and more productive. Emphasis will be placed on educational programs, human service programs that promote self-sufficiency, and sports/youth development programs.'

'Business Awareness: Business depends on and thrives in healthy communities. Likewise, communities depend on and thrive around healthy businesses. Special consideration will be given to organizations that promote knowledge of business and the free enterprise system.'

'Civility and Respect: Community requires members that respect each other and conduct themselves with civility and in accordance with fundamental moral and ethical principles. Therefore, the Foundation will support organizations that promote morality, civility and ethical behavior.'

'In order to have the resources to address these focus areas and have a major impact on funded programs, the Foundation will no longer make a large number of smaller operation grants as it has in the past. It will continue to support the operations of many worthwhile programs through substantial United Way contributions.' *Graco Foundation 1996 Community Report*

Financial Summary

Total Giving: $1,500,000 (1999 approx); $1,604,667 (1998); $1,317,633 (1997). Note: Contributes through corporate direct giving program and foundation.
Giving Analysis: Giving for 1997 includes: foundation ($914,032); foundation grants to United Way ($381,238); foundation matching gifts ($22,363); 1998: foundation ($585,857); foundation grants to United Way ($456,784); foundation matching gifts ($22,026)
Assets: $4,956,291 (1998); $5,764,409 (1997); $4,338,277 (1996)
Gifts Received: $1,757,000 (1997); $1,411,000 (1996); $682,000 (1994). Note: Contributions are received from Graco, Inc.

Typical Recipients

Arts & Humanities: Arts Institutes, Arts & Humanities-General, History & Archaeology, Music, Public Broadcasting, Theater, Visual Arts
Civic & Public Affairs: Botanical Gardens/Parks, Business/Free Enterprise, Chambers of Commerce, Community Foundations, Economic Development, Employment/Job Training, Ethnic Organizations, Civic & Public Affairs-General, Housing, Native American Affairs, Nonprofit Management, Philanthropic Organizations, Public Policy, Urban & Community Affairs, Women's Affairs
Education: Afterschool/Enrichment Programs, Business Education, Colleges & Universities, Economic Education, Education Funds, Education Reform, Elementary Education (Private), Education-General, Literacy, Medical Education, Minority Education, Private Education (Precollege), Private Education (Precollege), Public Education (Precollege), Science/Mathematics Education, Secondary Education (Private), Secondary Education (Public), Special Education, Student Aid, Vocational & Technical Education
Environment: Forestry, Environment-General
Health: Cancer, Children's Health/Hospitals, Clinics/Medical Centers, Diabetes, Health Organizations, Hospitals, Medical Rehabilitation, Research/Studies Institutes
International: Foreign Educational Institutions, International Environmental Issues, International Relief Efforts
Religion: Religious Organizations, Religious Welfare
Science: Science Museums
Social Services: At-Risk Youth, Child Welfare, Community Centers, Community Service Organizations, Day Care, Domestic Violence, Emergency Relief, Family Services, Food/Clothing Distribution, People with Disabilities, Recreation & Athletics, Scouts, Senior Services, Shelters/Homelessness, Social Services-General, United Funds/United Ways, YMCA/YWCA/YMHA/YWHA, Youth Organizations

Contributions Analysis

Giving Priorities: Health associations, human services, education, community development, and the arts. Most overseas contributions are made through the Toronto office. Primary interests are small community service agencies. Canadian operations establish budgets independently, and figures are not included in totals above. Total contributions is estimated at less than $25,000 annually. Also has supported AFS International Scholarships.
Arts & Humanities: 2%.
Civic & Public Affairs: 20%.
Education: 25%.
Religion: 3%.
Social Services: 50%.
Note: Total contributions in 1998.

Application Procedures

Initial Contact: Send a brief letter.
Application Requirements: Letter should include a program description, and explain how it fits foundation's focus; if a full proposal is invited, include: mission statement, brief history and a description of organization, overview of community and population served, program objectives, method of program evaluation, brief information about staff members responsible for program, list of board of directors, copy of agency's overall budget and specific program budget if appropriate, list of other sources of program support, copy of 501(c)(3) form or other proof of tax-exempt status, and copy of IRS Form 990.
Deadlines: Full proposals are due June 1, September 1, and December 1.
Review Process: Foundation board of directors reviews requests quarterly.
Evaluative Criteria: Grant requests must address the Foundation's focus areas; emphasis will be on capacity building grants.

Restrictions

Grants are not awarded to individuals; political campaigns; fraternal organizations; national or local campaigns for disease research; for fundraising purposes, travel, special events, dinners, or courtesy advertising; or religious organizations for sectarian purposes. Grants are limited to Minnesota and communities where Graco Inc. has a significant number of employees.

Additional Information

The Foundation also sponsors a scholarship program for college age children of Graco employees. Graco makes 5% of its U.S. pretax earnings available each year for distribution to charitable organizations and community development programs.
Graco sponsors a scholarship program for children of employees.
Publications: Graco Foundation Community Report; Guidelines

Corporate Officials

George Aristides: president, chief executive officer, director B 1936. PRIM CORP EMPL president, chief executive officer, director: Graco, Inc.
Clayton R. Carter: vice president industrial equipment division PRIM CORP EMPL vice president industrial equipment division: Graco Inc.
James Graner: vice president, controller PRIM CORP EMPL vice president, controller: Graco Inc.
Clyde Hanson: vice president human resources PRIM CORP EMPL vice president human resources: Graco Inc.
John Heller: vice president Asia, Pacific, Latin America development **** PRIM CORP EMPL vice president Asia, Pacific, Latin America development marketing: Graco Inc.
Roger Leo King: vice president, officer B Blue Island, IL 1945. ED Colgate University AB (1967); University of Minnesota MA (1971). PRIM CORP EMPL vice president, officer: Graco, Inc.
David Andrew Koch: chairman, director B Boston, MA 1930. ED College of Notre Dame BA (1948-1951); College of Saint Thomas MBA (1952-1954). PRIM CORP EMPL chairman, director: Graco, Inc. CORP AFFIL director: ReliaStar Financial Corp.; director: BSI Inc.; director: FDL Reserve Bank. NONPR AFFIL trustee: College Saint Thomas.
David M. Lowe: vice president lubrication equip division B 1956. PRIM CORP EMPL vice president lubrication equip division: Graco Inc.
Robert Mayer Mattison: vice president, general counsel, secretary B Minneapolis, MN 1948. ED Saint John's University BA (1970); University of Minnesota JD (1973). PRIM CORP EMPL vice president, general counsel, secretary: Graco, Inc. NONPR AFFIL member: Minnesota Bar Association; member: Minnesota Corp. Counsel Association; member: Hennepin County Bar Association; member: American Corporate Counsel Association. CLUB AFFIL Golden Valley Country Club.
Kristen C. Nelson: assistant secretary PRIM CORP EMPL assistant secretary: Graco Inc.
Mark Sheahan: treasurer B Minneapolis, MN 1964. ED University of Minnesota (1986); William Mitchell College of Law (1990). PRIM CORP EMPL treasurer: Graco Inc. NONPR AFFIL member: American Bar Association.

Foundation Officials

Clayton R. Carter: director (see above)
David Andrew Koch: president (see above)
Robert Mayer Mattison: director (see above)
Charles L. Rescorla: director
Catherine Rohach: director
Mark Sheahan: treasurer (see above)

Grants Analysis

Disclosure Period: calendar year ending 1998
Total Grants: $585,857*
Number of Grants: 50

Average Grant: $9,915*
Highest Grant: $100,000
Typical Range: $5000 to $50,000
***Note:** Giving excludes matching gifts, United Way. Average grant figure excludes highest grant.

Recent Grants

Note: Grants derived from 1998 Form 990.

Arts & Humanities

25,000 Family Alternatives, Minneapolis, MN -- Grant

Civic & Public Affairs

100,000 East Side Neighborhood Services, Minneapolis, MN -- Grant - first installment of 3
50,000 Minnesota Diversified Industries (MDI) Phillips Initiative, Minneapolis, MN -- Grant
50,000 Rebuild Resources, Minneapolis, MN -- Grant - 2nd Installment
30,000 Genesis II for Women, Minneapolis, MN -- Grant
25,000 Urban Ventures, Minneapolis, MN -- Grant
18,900 Employment Action Center, Minneapolis, MN -- Grant
12,000 Employment Action Center, Minneapolis, MN -- Grant
7,500 Greater Minneapolis Metropolitan Housing Corp (GMMHC), Minneapolis, MN -- Grant
5,000 Harriet Tubman Center, Minneapolis, MN -- Grant - Discretionary
5,000 Hired, Minneapolis, MN -- Grant - Disc.
5,000 The Management Assistance Program for Nonprofits, St Paul, MN -- Grant - Disc.
5,000 Twin Cities One to One, Minneapolis, MN -- Grant - Discretionary
3,000 Neighborhood Employment Network (NET), Minneapolis, MN -- Grant - Disc.
1,200 Citizens Council, Minneapolis, MN -- Grant - Disc.

Education

75,000 University of St Thomas, St Paul, MN -- Grant - Third Installment (1997)
50,000 Seed Academy/Harvest Preparatory School, Minneapolis, MN -- Grant - 2nd Installment
48,250 Citizen's Scholarship Foundation of America, St. Peter, MN -- Payment of Scholarship awards (Grant)
33,800 Institute for Education and Advocacy, Minneapolis, MN -- Grant
25,000 Children's Scholarship Fund (Kids First Scholarship Program), Minneapolis, MN -- Grant
25,000 Junior Achievement of the Upper Midwest, Inc., Edina, MN -- Grant
25,000 Metropolitan Federation of Alternative Schools, Minneapolis, MN -- Grant - 1st Installment of 3
25,000 Minnesota Independent School Forum, St Paul, MN -- Grant
25,000 Minnesota Private College Fund, St Paul, MN -- Grant
25,000 Mona Moede Neighborhood Early Learning Center, Minneapolis, MN -- Grant - first installment of 2
5,000 Business Economic Education Foundation, Minneapolis, MN -- Grant
5,000 Page Educational Foundation, Minneapolis, MN -- Grant
5,000 UNCF - The College Fund, Fairfax, VA -- Grant
3,500 Dunwoody Institute, Minneapolis, MN -- Grant - Disc.

Environment

8,000 Project EarthSense/Minnesota Foundation, St Paul, MN -- Grant - Third Installment

Health

5,000 Courage Center/The Celebration of Courage, Golden Valley, MN -- Event Grant (Disc.) - Sponsorship of Golf Tournament
1,431 March of Dimes Birth Defects Foundation, Edina, MN -- Grant - Employee match for WalkAmerica 1998
1,000 American Cancer Society, Minneapolis, MN -- Grant - Quarter Century Club

Religion

27,000 Greater Minneapolis Council of Churches (Paint-A-Thon), Minneapolis, MN -- Grant - $6,500 Operating Support, balance Paint contribution
25,000 Catholic Charities, Minneapolis, MN -- Grant for St. Joseph's Home for Children

Science

50,000 Science Museum of Minnesota, St Paul, MN -- Grant

Social Services

426,842 United Way of Minneapolis Area, Minneapolis, MN -- Graco's contribution for 1998 (Grant)
100,000 Washburn Child Guidance Center, Minneapolis, MN -- Campaign for the New Generation of Children
50,000 Minneapolis Crisis Nursery, Minneapolis, MN -- Grant
50,000 Sabathani Community Center, Minneapolis, MN -- Grant
25,000 Girl Scout Council of Greater Minneapolis, Minneapolis, MN -- Grant
25,000 Tree Trust, St. Louis Park, MN -- Grant
17,742 Plymouth Community United Way, Plymouth, MI -- Graco's contribution for 1998 (Grant)
15,000 Youth Trust, Minneapolis, MN -- Grant
7,700 United Way - Loaned Executive Program, Minneapolis, MN -- Grant
7,000 Boy Scouts of America, Minneapolis, MN -- Grant - 2nd installment (1997)
5,000 Family Resource Center, Wyoming, MN -- Grant - Disc.
3,500 Sioux Empire United Way, Sioux Falls, SD -- Grant
3,000 Boys & Girls Clubs of Minneapolis, Minneapolis, MN -- Grant - Discretionary
3,000 North Community YMCA Branch, Minneapolis, MN -- Grant - Disc.

W.W. GRAINGER, INC.

Company Contact

Lincolnshire, IL
Web: http://www.grainger.com

Company Description

Revenue: US$4,341,300,000
Employees: 14,601
Fortune Rank: 355, per FORTUNE Magazine's list of 500 Largest U.S. Corporations (1999).
FF 355
SIC(s): 5063 Electrical Apparatus & Equipment, 5072 Hardware, 5074 Plumbing & Hydronic Heating Supplies, 5075 Warm Air Heating & Air-Conditioning.

Giving Contact

Diane Wilczenski, Coordinator, Charitable Contributions
W.W. Grainger, Inc.
100 Grainger Pkwy.
Lake Forest, IL 60045
Phone: (847)535-0540

Alternate Contact

Mike Murray, Vice President, Administrative Services
Phone: (847)535-0555
Fax: (847)535-9210

Description

Organization Type: Corporate Giving Program
Giving Locations: headquarters area only.
Grant Types: Employee Matching Gifts, General Support.
Note: Employee matching gift ratio: 3 to 1.

Financial Summary

Total Giving: Contributes through corporate direct giving program only. Company does not disclose contributions figures.

Typical Recipients

Arts & Humanities: Arts & Humanities-General
Civic & Public Affairs: Civic & Public Affairs-General
Education: Education-General
Social Services: Social Services-General

Application Procedures

Initial Contact: a brief letter of inquiry
Deadlines: None.

Additional Information

Company declined to release detailed information on charitable contributions.

Corporate Officials

Jere David Fluno: vice chairman, chief executive officer, president B Wisconsin Rapids, WI 1941. ED University of Wisconsin BBA (1963). PRIM CORP EMPL vice chairman: W.W. Grainger, Inc. CORP AFFIL director: Midwest Securities Trust Co.; director: Securities Trust Co. New Jersey; officer: Lab Safety Supply Inc.; director: Midwest Clearing Corp.; director: Grainger Caribe Inc.; director: Andrew Corp.; board governors: Chicago Stock Exchange. NONPR AFFIL trustee: Museum Science & Industry; chairman: University Wisconsin Foundation; member: American Institute CPAs.

David William Grainger: senior chairman B Chicago, IL 1927. ED University of Wisconsin BSEE (1950). PRIM CORP EMPL senior chairman: W.W. Grainger, Inc.

Richard Lee Keyser: chairman, chief executive officer, president B Harrisburg, PA 1942. ED United States Naval Academy BS (1964); Harvard University MBA (1971). PRIM CORP EMPL chairman, chief executive officer, president: W.W. Grainger, Inc. ADD CORP EMPL president: Grainger Caribe Inc. CORP AFFIL director: Morton International Inc.; director: Rohm & Haas Co.; director: Lab Safety Supply Inc. NONPR AFFIL director: Evanston Hospital Corp.; director: Lake Forest Graduate School Management; fellow: American Production & Inventory Control Society. CLUB AFFIL Harvard Business School Chicago Club; fellow: Commonwealth Club Chicago; Chicago Club; Commerical Club Chicago.

GRAND VICTORIA CASINO

Company Contact

Elgin, IL

Company Description

Parent Company: Hyatt Corp./Circus Circus Enterprises, Inc.

Grand Victoria Foundation

Giving Contact

Nancy Fishman, Executive Director
Grand Victoria Foundation
60 South Grove Avenue
Elgin, IL 60120
Phone: (847)289-8575
Fax: (847)289-8576

Description

Organization Type: Corporate Foundation
Giving Locations: IL: NE Illinois

Financial Summary

Total Giving: $3,677,980 (fiscal year ending , 1999); $3,478,017 (fiscal 1998); $11,000,000 (fiscal 1997 approx). Note: Contributions through foundation only.

Contributions Analysis

Civic & Public Affairs: Emphasis on economic development.
Education: Public and private-school programs serving very young children through adult learners.
Environment: Focus on land use, flood control, and public environmental education.
Note: Giving percentages vary depending upon applications received.

Application Procedures

Initial Contact: contact the foundation by phone to request guidelines

Additional Information

The foundation was established in mid-1996 and gave it's first round of grants in March 1997.
The foundation administers about two-thirds of total grants; the remaining one-third is given directly to Kane County, IL, which administers the funds in line with the foundation's giving priorities

Foundation Officials

Jana Fry: grant administration

Grants Analysis

Total Grants: $3,677,980

GREDE FOUNDRIES

Company Contact

Milwaukee, WI

Company Description

Employees: 4,000
SIC(s): 3321 Gray & Ductile Iron Foundries, 3325 Steel Foundries Nec.

Grede Foundation

Giving Contact

Loretta Tesch, Secretary to the Chairman
9898 West Bluemount
PO Box 26499
Milwaukee, WI 53226
Phone: (414)257-3600

Description

EIN: 396042977
Organization Type: Corporate Foundation
Giving Locations: WI
Grant Types: General Support, Scholarship.

Financial Summary

Total Giving: $402,230 (1998); $331,750 (1997); $203,350 (1996)
Giving Analysis: Giving for 1997 includes: foundation ($290,250); foundation grants to United Way ($25,500); foundation scholarships ($16,000); 1998: foundation ($335,730); foundation grants to United Way ($50,500); foundation scholarships ($16,000)
Assets: $583,422 (1998); $552,775 (1997); $438,807 (1996)
Gifts Received: $406,000 (1998); $429,000 (1997); $337,000 (1996). Note: Contributions received from Grede Foundries.

Typical Recipients

Arts & Humanities: Arts Associations & Councils, Libraries, Museums/Galleries, Performing Arts
Civic & Public Affairs: Community Foundations, Economic Development, Economic Policy, Civic & Public Affairs-General, Hispanic Affairs, Housing, Legal Aid, Professional & Trade Associations, Public Policy, Urban & Community Affairs
Education: Arts/Humanities Education, Colleges & Universities, Community & Junior Colleges, Education Funds, Engineering/Technological Education, Education-General, Medical Education, Private Education (Precollege), Public Education (Precollege), Science/Mathematics Education, Secondary Education (Public), Student Aid, Vocational & Technical Education
Health: Cancer, Clinics/Medical Centers, Hospitals, Medical Research, Single-Disease Health Associations, Speech & Hearing, Transplant Networks/Donor Banks, Transplant Networks/Donor Banks
Religion: Religious Welfare
Science: Scientific Centers & Institutes
Social Services: Child Welfare, Community Centers, Community Service Organizations, Family Services, People with Disabilities, Senior Services, United Funds/United Ways, YMCA/YWCA/YMHA/YWHA, Youth Organizations

Contributions Analysis

Giving Priorities: Emphasis on education, human services, the arts, and civic causes.
Arts & Humanities: 7%. Supports libraries, the performing arts, and museums.
Civic & Public Affairs: 7%. Funds public policy, legal issues, and economic education.
Education: 50%. Colleges, universities, and private pre-college education receive support.
Health: 3%. Supports hospitals, medical research, and single-disease health associations.
Religion: 1%.
Social Services: 32%. Primary support is for the United Way; also funds youth activities.
Note: Total contributions in 1998.

Application Procedures

Initial Contact: Send brief letter describing program. Request scholarship applications from Loretta Tisch by phone.
Deadlines: Scholarship applications are due December 31.

Additional Information

Provides scholarships to children of employees of Grede Foundries and its subsidiaries.
Publications: Application Form

Corporate Officials

Ron Burns: chief financial officer, director B Michigan City, IN 1937. ED Indiana University BS (1959). PRIM CORP EMPL chief financial officer: Grede Foundries.
Bruce E. Jacobs: president, director B Milwaukee, WI 1947. ED University of Wisconsin (1969). PRIM CORP EMPL president, director: Grede Foundries. CORP AFFIL owner: Watermark Press; owner: Watermark West Rare Books; owner: Watermark Books.
Burleigh Edmund Jacobs: chairman B Milwaukee, WI 1920. ED University of Wisconsin BA (1942). PRIM CORP EMPL chairman: Grede Foundries Inc. CORP AFFIL director: Marshall & Ilsley Bank; director: Marshall & Ilsley Corp.; director: Benz Oil Inc.

Foundation Officials

Betty G. Davis: director
Walter Stewart Davis: secretary, treasurer B Evanston, IL 1924. ED Northwestern University BS (1947); Northwestern University JD (1950). PRIM CORP EMPL vice president, general counsel, director: Grede Foundries. CORP AFFIL chairman: Thomas Industries Inc.; director: Grucon Corp.; director: Park Bank; senior partner: Davis & Kuelthau. NONPR AFFIL member: Milwaukee Bar Association; member: WI Bar Association; member: Intl Bar Association; member: Academy Basic Education. CLUB AFFIL Blue Mound Country Club; Milwaukee Club.
Bruce E. Jacobs: vice president, director (see above)
Burleigh Edmund Jacobs: president, director (see above)

Grants Analysis

Disclosure Period: calendar year ending 1998
Total Grants: $335,730*
Number of Grants: 74
Average Grant: $3,229*
Highest Grant: $100,000
Typical Range: $100 to $10,000
***Note:** Giving excludes scholarship; United Way. Average grant figure excludes highest grant.

Recent Grants

Note: Grants derived from 1998 Form 990.

Arts & Humanities

20,000	Reedsburg Public Library Fund, Reedsburg, WI
10,000	Milwaukee Public Library Foundation, Milwaukee, WI
5,000	United Performing Arts Fund, Milwaukee, WI
1,000	Miwaukee Public Museum, Milwaukee, WI
1,000	Pryor Area Arts & Humanities, Pryor, OK

Civic & Public Affairs

5,000	Wisconsin Forum, Milwaukee, WI
2,500	The Independent Institute, Oakland, CA
2,000	National Right to Work Legal Defense Foundation, Springfield, VA
1,000	Cynthiana-Harrison Community Fund, Cynthiana, KY
1,000	Neighborhood House, Milwaukee, WI

Education

100,000	Brookfield Academy, Brookfield, WI
15,000	Lakeland College, Sheboygan, WI
10,000	Bruce Guadalupe Community School, Milwaukee, WI
10,000	Maysville Community College, Maysville, KY
10,000	Pittsburg State University, Pittsburgh, PA
6,000	Wisconsin Lutheran College, Milwaukee, WI
5,000	Foundry Educational Foundation, Chicago, IL
5,000	Reedsburg Educational Foundation, Reedsburg, WI
5,000	University of Wisconsin Foundation, Milwaukee, WI
5,000	Wichita Collegiate School, Wichita, KS
2,500	Medical College of Wisconsin, Milwaukee, WI
2,000	American Communications Network, Hagerstown, IN
2,000	PAVE, Milwaukee, WI
1,000	Marva Collins Prep School of Wisconsin, Milwaukee, WI
1,000	Milwaukee School of Engineering, Milwaukee, WI

1,000	Piedmont Technical College, Greenwood, SC
1,000	String Academy of Wisconsin, Milwaukee, WI
1,000	Urban Day School, Milwaukee, WI
1,000	Wisconsin Foundation for Independent Colleges, Milwaukee, WI
1,000	Woodlands School, Milwaukee, WI

Health

5,000	Froedtert Cancer Center, Milwaukee, WI
2,500	Center for the Deaf, Milwaukee, WI
2,000	Self Memorial Hospital, Greenwood, SC
1,000	Blood Center Research Foundation, Milwaukee, WI
1,000	St. Mary's Hospital Foundation, Milwaukee, WI

Religion

1,500	Salvation Army, Milwaukee, WI
1,000	Milwaukee Rescue Mission, Milwaukee, WI

Social Services

55,000	YMCA - Milwaukee, Milwaukee, WI
36,000	United Way of Greater Milwaukee, Milwaukee, WI
6,000	United Way of Dickenson County, Lebanon, VA
5,000	Family Service America, Milwaukee, WI
5,000	YMCA Partners Campaign, La Crosse, WI
3,000	Partners with Youth, Brookfield, WI
3,000	Reedsburg Area United Fund, Reedsburg, WI
2,315	SCHCC Benefit Club Foundation, Reedsburg, WI
1,500	United Way of Greenwood County, Greenwood, SC
1,000	Harrison County United Fund, Clarksburg, WV
1,000	United Way of Mayes County, Pryor, OK
1,000	United Way of St. Cloud, St. Cloud, MN
1,000	YMCA - Black Achievers, Milwaukee, WI

GREEN BAY PACKAGING

Company Contact

Green Bay, WI

Company Description

Employees: 2,500
SIC(s): 2631 Paperboard Mills, 2653 Corrugated & Solid Fiber Boxes, 2657 Folding Paperboard Boxes, 2672 Coated & Laminated Paper Nec.

George Kress Foundation

Giving Contact

John Kress, Secretary & Treasurer
George Kress Foundation
c/o Green Bay Packaging
1700 North Webster Avenue
Green Bay, WI 54302
Phone: (920)433-5113

Description

Founded: 1953
EIN: 396050768
Organization Type: Corporate Foundation
Giving Locations: WI: primarily Green Bay occasionally to state aside from Wisconsin.
Grant Types: General Support, Scholarship.

Financial Summary

Total Giving: $1,444,141 (1998); $1,334,500 (1996); $775,735 (1995). Note: Foundation made grants to itself and its members in turn distributed funds to an organization of their choice. Total amount in 1998, ($66,215).
Giving Analysis: Giving for 1996 includes: foundation ($1,247,150); foundation grants to United Way ($86,350); foundation scholarships ($1,000); 1998: foundation ($1,289,476); foundation grants to United Way ($88,450); foundation program-related investments ($66,215)
Assets: $5,243,872 (1998); $5,700,324 (1996); $3,719,304 (1995)
Gifts Received: $3,000,000 (1996); $2,190,000 (1995); $900,000 (1994). Note: In 1995 and 1996, contributions were received from Green Bay Packaging, Inc.

Typical Recipients

Arts & Humanities: Arts Centers, Community Arts, History & Archaeology, Museums/Galleries, Music, Performing Arts, Theater
Civic & Public Affairs: Botanical Gardens/Parks, Community Foundations, Economic Development, Civic & Public Affairs-General, Professional & Trade Associations
Education: Colleges & Universities, Education-General, Medical Education, Religious Education, Science/Mathematics Education, Vocational & Technical Education
Environment: Environment-General, Wildlife Protection
Health: Children's Health/Hospitals, Emergency/Ambulance Services, Health Organizations, Hospitals, Hospitals (University Affiliated), Public Health, Single-Disease Health Associations
Religion: Churches, Religious Organizations, Religious Welfare
Science: Scientific Centers & Institutes
Social Services: Animal Protection, Big Brother/Big Sister, Camps, Child Welfare, Community Centers, Community Service Organizations, Day Care, Family Services, People with Disabilities, United Funds/United Ways, Volunteer Services, YMCA/YWCA/YMHA/YWHA, Youth Organizations

Contributions Analysis

Giving Priorities: Primary support to higher education. Also social services, civic causes, and health concerns.
Arts & Humanities: 3%. Funds symphonic and performing arts, creativity programs, and art and historical museums.
Civic & Public Affairs: 8%. Supports botanical gardens/parks, community foundations, economic development, and professional and trade associations.
Education: 63%. Significant grants were given to The Uiversity of Wisconsin and Saint Norbett College de Pere.
Environment: 1%. Supports environmental concerns and wildlife protection.
Health: 4%. Supports hospitals, single-disease health associations, and public health.
Religion: 3%. Funds churches, religious organizations, and religious welfare.
Science: 1%. Supports science museums.
Social Services: 16%. Animal protection, children's programs, volunteer services, family services, and united funds receive support.
Note: Total contributions made in 1998.

Application Procedures

Initial Contact: Send brief letter describing program.
Deadlines: None.

Corporate Officials

Walter J. Dauska: treasurer, director PRIM CORP EMPL treasurer: Green Bay Packaging.
George F. Kress: honorary chairman, director B Green Bay, WI 1903. ED University of Wisconsin BA (1925). PRIM CORP EMPL honorary chairman, director: Green Bay Packaging. NONPR AFFIL chairman, director: American Foundation Counsel Services. CLUB AFFIL Sun Valley Ski Club; Milwaukee Club; New York Yacht Club; Great Lakes Cruising Club; Mackinac Island Yacht Club; Elks Club.
James F. Kress: chairman, director B 1929. ED University of Wisconsin (1951). PRIM CORP EMPL chairman, director: Green Bay Packaging. CORP AFFIL director: HC Prange Co.; director: Shade Information System; director: Krueger International; director: Marshall & Ilsley Corp.
William F. Kress: president, director PRIM CORP EMPL president, director: Green Bay Packaging.

Foundation Officials

George F. Kress: president (see above)
John Kress: secretary, treasurer

Grants Analysis

Disclosure Period: calendar year ending 1998
Total Grants: $1,289,476*
Number of Grants: 250 (approx)
Average Grant: $2,358*
Highest Grant: $500,000
Typical Range: $50 to $40,000
***Note:** Giving excludes United Way and grants that were made to foundation to be distributed by members. Average grant figure excludes two highest grants ($500,000 and $200,000).

Recent Grants

Note: Grants derived from 1996 Form 990.

Arts & Humanities

20,000	Edward W. Weidner Center for Performing Arts, Green Bay, WI
10,000	Green Bay Symphony Orchestra, Green Bay, WI

Civic & Public Affairs

26,041	Green Bay Botanical Garden, Green Bay, WI
20,000	Greater Green Bay Community Foundation, Green Bay, WI
10,000	Heritage Hill Foundation, Green Bay, WI

Education

500,000	University of Wisconsin Madison, Madison, WI
25,000	University of Wisconsin Foundation, Madison, WI
20,000	St. Norbert College, De Pere, WI
16,667	Bellin College of Nursing, Green Bay, WI
10,000	Institutes of Religion and Health, New York, NY

Health

15,000	American Red Cross, Green Bay, WI
15,000	Cerebral Palsy Capital Campaign, Green Bay, WI

Social Services

100,000	YMCA, Green Bay, WI
100,000	YMCA Capital Campaign, Green Bay, WI
47,500	United Way Brown County, Green Bay, WI
25,000	Family Service Association, New York, NY
17,000	Brown County Association for Retarded Citizens, Green Bay, WI
12,000	Big Brothers and Big Sisters, Green Bay, WI
11,000	United Way, Kalamazoo, MI
10,000	Encompass Child Care, Green Bay, WI

Griffith Laboratories U.S.A.

Company Contact
Alsip, IL

Company Description
Employees: 1,600
SIC(s): 2035 Pickles, Sauces & Salad Dressings, 2099 Food Preparations Nec, 2834 Pharmaceutical Preparations, 2899 Chemical Preparations Nec.

Griffith Laboratories Foundation

Giving Contact
Joseph R. Maslick, Chief Financial Officer
Griffith Laboratories USA
1 Griffith Ctr.
Alsip, IL 60803
Phone: (708)371-0900
Fax: (708)371-4783

Description
EIN: 510195285
Organization Type: Corporate Foundation
Grant Types: General Support.

Financial Summary
Total Giving: $203,617 (fiscal year ending September 30, 1998); $380,440 (fiscal 1997); $131,664 (fiscal 1990)
Giving Analysis: Giving for fiscal 1998 includes: foundation ($203,617)
Assets: $197,922 (fiscal 1998); $803 (fiscal 1997); $47,752 (fiscal 1990)
Gifts Received: $400,826 (fiscal 1998); $208,500 (fiscal 1997); $147,258 (fiscal 1990). Note: Contributions are received from Griffith Labs Worldwide, Griffith Micro Science, Inc., and Griffith Laboratories USA, Inc.

Typical Recipients
Civic & Public Affairs: Civic & Public Affairs-General
Education: Student Aid
Environment: Environment-General
Health: Children's Health/Hospitals, Single-Disease Health Associations
International: Missionary/Religious Activities
Religion: Churches
Science: Science Exhibits & Fairs
Social Services: Special Olympics

Contributions Analysis
Giving Priorities: Religious organizations and international missionary activities.
International: 9%. Supports missionary activities.
Religion: 85%. Primarily supports churches and Christian groups.
Social Services: 3%. Children's groups and Special Olympics.
Note: Total contributions made in fiscal 1998.

Application Procedures
Initial Contact: Submit an application in letter form.
Application Requirements: Include attachments outlining the nature of the organization; the nature of the organization's work; and any specific projects for which contributions might be used.
Deadlines: July1.

Corporate Officials
Dean L. Griffith: chairman, president, chief executive officer, director PRIM CORP EMPL chairman, president, chief executive officer, director: Griffith Labs.
Joseph R. Maslick: executive vice president, secretary, chief financial officer PRIM CORP EMPL executive vice president, secretary, chief financial officer: Griffith.

Foundation Officials
Joseph R. Maslick: trustee (see above)

Grants Analysis
Disclosure Period: fiscal year ending September 30, 1998
Total Grants: $203,617
Number of Grants: 14
Average Grant: $8,442*
Highest Grant: $93,877
Typical Range: $1,000 to $6,000
***Note:** Average grant figure excludes highest grant.

Recent Grants
Note: Grants derived from fiscal 1997 Form 990.

Civic & Public Affairs
1,600 Executive Outreach, Farmersville, CA

Education
1,000 Evans Scholars Foundation, Golf, IL

Health
1,000 McDonald Children Charity, Oak Brook, IL
440 Lemont Serotoma, Lemont, IL

International
6,000 Christian Associates International, Thousand Oaks, CA

Religion
365,400 Chapel on the Hill, Lake Geneva, WI

Social Services
5,000 Illinois Special Olympics, Normal, IL

Group Health Plan

Company Contact
St. Louis, MO

Company Description
Assets: US$150,000,000
Employees: 900
SIC(s): 6300 Insurance Carriers.
Parent Company: Coventry Corp.

Group Health Foundation

Giving Contact
Robert M. Swanson, PhD, Secretary & Vice President
Group Health Foundation
3556 Caroline St.
St. Louis, MO 63104
Phone: (314)577-8105
Fax: (314)771-4544

Description
Founded: 1986
EIN: 431141117
Organization Type: Corporate Foundation
Giving Locations: headquarters and operating communities.
Grant Types: Award, General Support, Project, Scholarship, Seed Money.

Financial Summary
Total Giving: $350,000 (fiscal year ending October 31, 2000 approx); $350,000 (fiscal 1999 approx); $336,145 (fiscal 1998)
Assets: $4,000,000 (fiscal 1999 approx); $5,024,312 (fiscal 1997); $3,911,661 (fiscal 1994)

Typical Recipients
Civic & Public Affairs: Civic & Public Affairs-General, Women's Affairs
Education: Colleges & Universities, Education-General, Health & Physical Education, Medical Education, Private Education (Precollege)
Health: Adolescent Health Issues, AIDS/HIV, Alzheimers Disease, Arthritis, Cancer, Children's Health/Hospitals, Clinics/Medical Centers, Diabetes, Emergency/Ambulance Services, Eyes/Blindness, Health-General, Geriatric Health, Health Policy/Cost Containment, Health Organizations, Heart, Hospices, Hospitals, Hospitals (University Affiliated), Kidney, Long-Term Care, Medical Rehabilitation, Medical Research, Medical Training, Mental Health, Multiple Sclerosis, Nursing Services, Nutrition, Prenatal Health Issues, Preventive Medicine/Wellness Organizations, Public Health, Respiratory, Single-Disease Health Associations, Speech & Hearing, Transplant Networks/Donor Banks, Trauma Treatment
International: Health Care/Hospitals
Religion: Jewish Causes, Religious Organizations, Religious Welfare
Science: Science-General, Scientific Centers & Institutes, Scientific Research
Social Services: At-Risk Youth, Community Service Organizations, Day Care, Homes, People with Disabilities, Substance Abuse, Youth Organizations

Contributions Analysis
Giving Priorities: Health, medical research, community service organizations.
Education: 3%. Supports medical education.
Health: 74%. Supports hospitals and medical research.
Religion: 3%. Funds religious welfare organizations.
Social Services: 10%. Supports community service organizations.
Note: Total contributions made in 1997.

Application Procedures
Initial Contact: Send a brief letter of inquiry and a full proposal.
Application Requirements: Include a description of organization, amount requested, purpose of funds sought, proof of tax-exempt status, and a project budget.
Deadlines: None.

Restrictions
Does not support individuals, religious organizations for sectarian purposes, political or lobbying groups, or organizations outside operating areas.

Foundation Officials
Ralph L. Biddy, MD: director
Edward Edgerley, Jr,PhD: president, director
Richard P. Ellerbrake: director
Martin S. Greenberg, DDS: director
K. R. Guethle: director
Marvin A. Mueller: vice president, chairman of planning committee
Darwin W. Schlag, Jr.: director
Taylor C. Scott, CPA: treasurer, director
Robert M. Swanson, Ph.D.: secretary, director
Kenneth Worley: director

Grants Analysis
Disclosure Period: fiscal year ending October 31, 1998
Total Grants: $336,145
Number of Grants: 14
Average Grant: $24,010
Highest Grant: $61,500
Typical Range: $1,000 to $25,000

Recent Grants
Note: Grants derived from 1997 Form 990.

Civic & Public Affairs
25,890 Deaconess Foundation, Saint Louis, MO

Education

25,000	St. Louis University School of Nursing, Saint Louis, MO
12,500	Deaconess College of Nursing, Saint Louis, MO

Health

30,000	Washington University Department of Pediatrics, Saint Louis, MO
30,000	Washington University Department of Pediatrics, Saint Louis, MO
30,000	Washington University School of Medicine Department of Psychiatry, Saint Louis, MO
29,500	St. Louis University Geriatric Medicine Center, Saint Louis, MO
20,000	SSM Rehabilitation Institute
18,125	Practical Anatomy and Surgery Techniques Workshop, Saint Louis, MO
10,000	Unity Health Hospice Program

International

2,000	Care Partners

Religion

20,000	Barnes-Jewish Hospital Foundation, Saint Louis, MO
10,000	Catholic Community Services, Seattle, WA

Social Services

20,787	St. Louis Crisis Nursery, Saint Louis, MO
7,250	Places for People, Saint Louis, MO

GTE Corp.

 Number 38 of Top 100 Corporate Givers

Company Contact

1255 Corporate Drive
Irving, TX 75035
Phone: (972)507-5000
Web: http://www.gte.com

Company Description

Revenue: US$25,336,000,000 (1999)
Profit: US$2,172,000,000
Employees: 120,000 (1999)
Fortune Rank: 55, per FORTUNE Magazine's list of 500 Largest U.S. Corporations (1999).
FF 55
SIC(s): 2741 Miscellaneous Publishing, 3577 Computer Peripheral Equipment Nec, 3641 Electric Lamps, 3645 Residential Lighting Fixtures.

Operating Locations

Argentina: CTI Compania de Telefonos del Interior SA, Buenos Aires; CTI Norte Compania de Telefonos del Interior SA, Buenos Aires; Bermuda: GTE Reinsurance Co., Hamilton; Canada: Quebec-Telephone, Rimouski; Dominican Republic: Compania Domicana de Telefonos, C por A, Santo Domingo; Germany: GTE Internetworking GmbH, Munich; United Kingdom: GTE Internetworking UK Limited, West Drayton, Middlesex
Note: Operates throughout the USA.

Nonmonetary Support

Value: $1,000,000 (1994); $1,117,296 (1993); $1,295,220 (1992)
Type: Donated Equipment
Note: For nonmonetary support contact the Office of Committee Relations.

Corporate Sponsorship

Type: Arts & cultural events

GTE Foundation

Giving Contact

Maureen V. Gorman, Vice President
GTE Foundation
Phone: 888-GTE-3547
Fax: (972)507-5587
Web: http://www.gte.com/aboutgte/community

Alternate Contact

Sheila Reynolds
Phone: (972)507-5433
Note: matching gifts and special itiatives programs

Description

Founded: 1982
EIN: 136046680
Organization Type: Corporate Foundation
Giving Locations: operating locations.
Grant Types: Award, Capital, Emergency, Employee Matching Gifts, Fellowship, General Support, Matching, Multiyear/Continuing Support.
Note: Employee matching gift ratio: 3 to 1 for the first $200 annually; 2 to 1 up to $7,500.

Giving Philosophy

'The GTE Foundation is committed to investing corporate resources to improve education, health and human services and the local communities we serve. By dedicating resources to enhance the well-being of our local communities, we believe we are serving the interests of our customers, our employees and our shareholders. We support programs that are targeted, focused and strategic. We invest in programs that will provide us with the greatest yield, in terms of benefit to the communities. We focus our efforts on supporting programs which address causes of problems, not just symptoms. As a corporation, GTE is very concerned about America's ability to produce a well-educated, highly productive workforce. Thus, we have committed significant resources to improve education, with special emphasis on mathematics and science. Our programs support national goals on education, as expressed by the President of the United States and the nation's governors. We are especially proud of our employees who volunteer their time and make significant contributions. We realize that society's problems are complex and in many cases deeply embedded. Therefore, both financial and volunteer resources are required.' *GTE: Investing In Our Future*

Financial Summary

Total Giving: $32,000,000 (2000 approx); $30,000,000 (1999 approx); $26,252,923 (1998). Note: Contributes through corporate direct giving program and foundation. Giving includes foundation only.
Giving Analysis: Giving for 1998 includes: foundation ($19,381,279); foundation matching gifts ($3,632,655); foundation grants to United Way ($2,725,543); foundation scholarships ($513,446)
Assets: $54,000,000 (1999); $58,745,053 (1998); $47,000,000 (1997 approx)
Gifts Received: $23,890,922 (1998); $20,976,439 (1994); $20,221,119 (1993)

Typical Recipients

Arts & Humanities: Arts Associations & Councils, Arts Centers, Dance, History & Archaeology, Libraries, Museums/Galleries, Music, Opera, Performing Arts, Public Broadcasting, Theater, Visual Arts
Civic & Public Affairs: African American Affairs, Economic Development, Employment/Job Training, Civic & Public Affairs-General, Hispanic Affairs, Law & Justice, Professional & Trade Associations, Public Policy, Urban & Community Affairs, Zoos/Aquariums
Education: Business Education, Business-School Partnerships, Colleges & Universities, Community & Junior Colleges, Economic Education, Education Associations, Education Funds, Education Reform, Engineering/Technological Education, Faculty Development, Education-General, Gifted & Talented Programs, International Studies, Literacy, Minority Education, Private Education (Precollege), Science/Mathematics Education, Student Aid, Vocational & Technical Education
Environment: Air/Water Quality, Environment-General
Health: Emergency/Ambulance Services, Geriatric Health, Health Policy/Cost Containment, Hospitals
International: Foreign Educational Institutions
Science: Science Museums, Scientific Centers & Institutes
Social Services: Child Welfare, Community Centers, Community Service Organizations, Counseling, Domestic Violence, Emergency Relief, Family Services, People with Disabilities, Senior Services, Shelters/Homelessness, Substance Abuse, United Funds/United Ways, Volunteer Services, YMCA/YWCA/YMHA/YWHA, Youth Organizations

Contributions Analysis

Giving Priorities: Education, human services, hospitals, civic concerns, and the arts. Contributions to U.S.-based nonprofit organizations are made on a selected basis. Primary interests are disaster relief and refugee assistance. Information on contributions by foreign subsidiaries was not available.
Arts & Humanities: 7%. Supports cultural arts centers, funds, and councils; museums of art, science, and natural history; performing arts; theaters; and public television in major metropolitan cities such as Washington, DC, and corporate communities.
Civic & Public Affairs: 19%. Targets community centers; the environment; housing and urban renewal; justice and law; minority groups; the elderly, disabled, and women; public policy research; youth programs; and child care.
Education: 60%. Targets mathematics and science disciplines, with particular interest in under-represented minority groups. Objectives are to increase the general population's comfort with technology, to train future engineers and computer scientists, and to ensure an adequate number of mathematics and science teachers for the future. Objectives are accomplished at the secondary, undergraduate, and graduate levels through scholarships, fellowships, public lectures, curricula improvements, development of classroom-based programs, and specialized summer education programs. In addition, supports selected education programs such as academic excellence among amateur athletes, sponsors an employee matching gift program, and provides scholarships for employee children through established national programs. GTE also underwrites the PBS series 'Scientific American Frontiers,' providing free teaching material to 50,000 teachers of science at the elementary, junior high, and high school levels.
Health: 14%. Supports societal issues such as the homeless and alcohol and drug abuse that affect the environment of corporate communities. Also supports United Way and hospitals.
Note: Percentages provided by the foundation in 1999.

Application Procedures

Initial Contact: Send a brief letter or proposal.
Application Requirements: Include detailed objectives of the project, budget, sources of funding, evidence of 501(c)(3) tax-exempt status.
Deadlines: None.
Review Process: Applications are reviewed by foundation staff person; if appropriate, then by foundation president, vice president, and trustees.
Evaluative Criteria: Math/science education is primary focus; secondary focus, critical issues such as substance abuse prevention and literacy.

Decision Notification: Decisions are made quarterly.

Restrictions

Foundation does not support individuals; religious or sectarian groups; fraternal, athletic, social, or veterans organizations; mass mail appeals; political organizations; goodwill advertising; memberships in professional or trade organizations; organizations which do not have a Section 501(c)(3) public charity status; organizations primarily supported by tax dollars (some exceptions for education); international organizations which primarily support charitable programs outside of the U.S.; single disease organizations; or fundraising events, sponsorships, dinners, or conferences.

Additional Information

GTE is awaiting approval of a proposed merger with Bell Atlantic Corp. The merger's expected completion date is during the second quarter of 2000. The combined company will take the name Verizon.

Direct gifts usually account for 7% of GTE's total giving.

Publications: GTE: Investing in Our Future; Grant Application; Volunteer Initiatives Program

Corporate Officials

Kent B. Foster: president, directorhuman resources administration B 1943. ED North Carolina State University BSEE; University of Southern California MS. PRIM CORP EMPL president, director: GTE Corp. ADD CORP EMPL president: GTE West Inc.; president: GTE Media Ventures Inc. CORP AFFIL director: New York Life Insurance Co.; director: JC Penney Co. Inc.; director: Campbell Soup Co.; director: GTE Data Services Inc.

Glen S. Gilbert: vice president advertising & social responsibility B Hewlett, NY 1952. ED Hamilton College BA (1974). PRIM CORP EMPL vice president advertising & social responsibility: GTE Corp.

Charles Robert Lee: chairman, chief executive officer, director B Pittsburgh, PA 1940. ED Cornell University BS (1962); Harvard University MBA (1964). PRIM CORP EMPL chairman, chief executive officer, director: GTE Corp. ADD CORP EMPL chief executive officer: GTE Data Service International Inc.; chairman: GTE Service Corp. CORP AFFIL director: United Technologies Corp.; director: USX Corp.; director: Procter & Gamble Co. NONPR AFFIL member: President National Security Telecommunications Advisory Committee; director: Stamford Hospital Foundation; member committee American realities, trustee: National Planning Association; director: New American Schools Development Corp.; member: Financial Executives Institute; board director associates: Harvard University Business School; member: Business Roundtable; trustee: Cornell University. CLUB AFFIL Thunderbird Country Club; Laurel Valley Golf Club; Stanwich Club; Blind Brook Country Club.

J. Randall MacDonald: senior vice president human resources administration B Newburgh, NY 1948. ED Saint Francis College (1970); Saint Francis College (1971). CORP AFFIL officer: Covance Inc. NONPR AFFIL member: Labor Policy Association; member: National Alliance Business; member executive committee: Human Resources Policy Institute.

Michael Terry Masin: vice chairman, president international, director B Montreal, PQ Canada 1945. ED Dartmouth College BA (1966); University of California, Los Angeles JD (1969). PRIM CORP EMPL vice chairman, president international, director: GTE Corp. ADD CORP EMPL vice chairman: GTE Service Corp.; managing partner: O'Melveny & Myers. CORP AFFIL director: Trust Co. West; director: Compania Anonima Nacional Telefonos de Venezuela; director: Travelers Group Inc.; director: Citigroup Inc.; director: British Columbia Telecommunications. NONPR AFFIL member deans advisory committee: Dartmouth College; member business committee, board trustee: Museum Modern Art; board member: China American Society; member: Council Foreign Relations; member: American Bar Association; trustee: Carnegie Hall. CLUB AFFIL California Club; Brook Club.

Foundation Officials

Michael B. Esstman: trustee B 1947. PRIM CORP EMPL vice president: GTE Telecom International Systems ADD CORP EMPL senior vice president: GTE Corp. CORP AFFIL director: AG Communications Systems Corp.; director: GTE Data Services Inc.

Kent B. Foster: trustee (see above)

Glen S. Gilbert: vice president advertising & social responsibility (see above)

Maureen V. Gorman: vice president B Stamford, CT. ED Columbia University MA; Sacred Heart University BA. NONPR AFFIL member: New York Regional Association; member: Public Relations Society America; member: National Gallery Art; trustee: Long Wharf Theatre; member: National Alliance Business; member: Foundation Independent Higher Education; member: International Association of Business Communications; member: ARC; member: Conference Board.

Charles Robert Lee: chief executive officer, trustee (see above)

J. Randall MacDonald: trustee (see above)

Michael Terry Masin: trustee (see above)

Grants Analysis

Disclosure Period: calendar year ending 1998
Total Grants: $19,381,278*
Number of Grants: 1,430 (approx)
Average Grant: $13,553
Highest Grant: $720,000
Typical Range: $1,000 to $25,000
***Note:** Giving excludes United Way, matching gifts, scholarship.

Recent Grants

Note: Grants derived from 1996 Form 990.

Arts & Humanities

2,484,884	Connecticut Public Broadcasting, Hartford, CT
500,000	Metropolitan Museum of Art, New York, NY
400,000	Dallas Symphony Association, Dallas, TX
100,000	Carnegie Hall, New York, NY
100,000	Dallas Museum of Art, Dallas, TX
55,060	Metropolitan Museum of Art, New York, NY
50,000	Indiana State Symphony Society, Indianapolis, IN

Civic & Public Affairs

50,000	California Counties Foundation, Sacramento, CA
50,000	Center for the New West, Denver, CO
50,000	Committee for Economic Development, New York, NY
50,000	Florida Aquarium, Tampa, FL
50,000	Los Angeles Urban League, Los Angeles, CA

Education

207,000	United Negro College Fund, New York, NY
200,000	Cornell University, Ithaca, NY
200,000	New American Schools Development Corporation, Arlington, VA
190,625	University of South Florida Foundation, Tampa, FL
145,000	Literacy Volunteers of America, Los Angeles, CA
120,000	Dartmouth College, Hanover, NH
100,000	National Association of Secondary School Principals, Reston, VA
80,000	Rensselaer Polytechnic Institute, Troy, NY
75,000	University of Kentucky, Lexington, KY
70,000	University of California Los Angeles, Los Angeles, CA
50,000	Babson College, Wellesley, MA
50,000	California Institute of Technology, Pasadena, CA
50,000	California State University Long Beach, Long Beach, CA
50,000	National Hispanic Scholarship Fund, Baltimore, MD
50,000	Northeastern University Electromagnetics Center, Boston, MA
50,000	Northern Illinois University, DeKalb, IL
50,000	Pinellas County Education Foundation, Clearwater, FL
50,000	Purdue University, West Lafayette, IN
50,000	United Negro College Fund, New York, NY
45,000	National Action Council for Minorities in Engineering, New York, NY
45,000	Santa Monica College Foundation, Santa Monica, CA

Health

100,000	American Red Cross Disaster Relief Fund

Social Services

310,000	United Way Tri-State, New York, NY
240,000	United Way, Los Angeles, CA
180,000	Aloha United Way, Honolulu, HI
150,000	911 for Kids, Thousand Oaks, CA
138,268	United Way Hillsborough County, Tampa, FL
85,000	United Way Massachusetts Bay, Boston, MA
80,000	United Way Snohomish County, Everett, WA
60,000	La Miranda Volunteer Center, CA
60,000	Mount Baldy United Way, Los Angeles, CA
60,000	United Way, Durham, NC
60,000	United Way Allen County, Fort Wayne, IN
60,000	YMCA
58,000	United Way, Dallas, TX
51,211	United Way Pinellas County, Saint Petersburg, FL
51,066	United Way Bluegrass, Lexington, KY
50,000	United Combined Philanthropies, Dallas, TX

GUARDIAN LIFE INSURANCE CO. OF AMERICA

Company Contact

New York, NY
Web: http://www.theguardian.com

Company Description

Revenue: US$7,973,800,000
Employees: 5,046
Fortune Rank: 194, per FORTUNE Magazine's list of 500 Largest U.S. Corporations (1999).
FF 194
SIC(s): 6036 Savings Institutions Except Federal, 6311 Life Insurance, 6321 Accident & Health Insurance.

Giving Contact

Karen Olvany, Assistant Corporate Secretary
Guardian Life Insurance Co. of America
7 Hanover Square
New York, NY 10004
Phone: (212)598-7499
Fax: (212)919-2944

Description

Organization Type: Corporate Giving Program
Giving Locations: headquarters and operating communities.

Grant Types: Employee Matching Gifts, General Support.
Note: Employee matching gift ratio: 1 to 1 for gifts to higher education only.

Financial Summary

Total Giving: $850,000 (1999 approx); $800,000 (1998 approx); $653,400 (1997). Note: Contributes through corporate direct giving program only.

Typical Recipients

Arts & Humanities: Arts Centers, Community Arts, Historic Preservation, Libraries, Museums/Galleries, Music, Opera, Performing Arts, Public Broadcasting, Theater
Civic & Public Affairs: Business/Free Enterprise, Economic Development, Economic Policy, Law & Justice, Safety, Urban & Community Affairs, Zoos/Aquariums
Education: Arts/Humanities Education, Business Education, Colleges & Universities, Community & Junior Colleges, Economic Education, Education Funds, Literacy
Health: Health Policy/Cost Containment, Hospices, Medical Research, Single-Disease Health Associations
Social Services: Food/Clothing Distribution, Substance Abuse, United Funds/United Ways, Youth Organizations

Contributions Analysis

Arts & Humanities: About 10%. Funding supports historic preservation, libraries, museums, music, theater, and community arts.
Civic & Public Affairs: 10% to 15%. Supports economic development through free enterprise organizations, zoos and aquariums, and urban and community affairs.
Education: 25% to 30%. Primarily supports colleges, universities, education funds and literacy organizations.
Health: About 20%. Recipients include hospices, medical research, and single-disease health associations.
Social Services: 20% to 25%. Recipients include united funds, youth organizations, and substance abuse prevention centers.
Note: Total contributions made in 1999.

Application Procedures

Initial Contact: Submit a brief letter of inquiry.
Application Requirements: A description of organization, amount requested and purpose of funds sought, recently audited financial statement, and proof of tax-exempt status.
Deadlines: None.

Restrictions

Does not support individuals, religious organizations for sectarian purposes, or political or lobbying groups.

Additional Information

In 1992, the company began a direct giving program. The Guardian Life Charitable Trust was terminated in December 1993.

Corporate Officials

Peter Lounsbery Hutchings: president, chief executive officer, director B New York, NY 1943. ED Yale University BA (1964). PRIM CORP EMPL president: Guardian Life Insurance Co. of America ADD CORP EMPL director: Family Service Lifeline Co.; president, director: First International; director: Guardian Insurance & Annuity Co. Inc.; director: Guardian Investors Services Corp.; president, director: Park Avenue Life; president, director: Sentinel American Life Insurance. NONPR AFFIL member: American Academy of Actuaries; fellow: Society Actuaries; member: Actuarial Society Greater New York; director: 14th Street Business Improvement District; director: 14th Street Union Square Local Development Corp.

Joseph Dudley Sargent: president, chief executive officer, director B Philadelphia, PA 1937. ED Fairfield University AB (1959). PRIM CORP EMPL president, chief executive officer, director: Guardian Life Insurance Co. of America ADD CORP EMPL director: Family Service Life Insurance Co.; president, chief executive officer: Guardian Insurance & Annuity Co. Inc. NONPR AFFIL member: National Association Life Underwriters; director: United Way New York City; director: Life Office Management Association; director: Discovery Museum Bridgeport; director: Life Insurance Marketing & Research Institute.

Giving Program Officials

Karen Dickinson: PRIM CORP EMPL assistant corporate secretary: Guardian Life Insurance Co. of America.

Grants Analysis

Disclosure Period: calendar year ending
Typical Range: $1,000 to $2,500

GUCCI AMERICA INC.

Company Contact

Harmon Coves Outlet Center
50 Hartz Way
Secaucus, NJ 07094
Phone: (201)392-2670
Fax: (201)392-2679
Web: http://www.gucci.com

Company Description

Employees: 450
SIC(s): 5611 Men's & Boys' Clothing Stores, 5632 Women's Accessory & Specialty Stores, 5661 Shoe Stores, 5948 Luggage & Leather Goods Stores.
Parent Company: Gucci Group NV, Rembrandt Tower, Amstelplein 1, Amsterdam, Netherlands
Parent Assets: US$1,700,000,000

Operating Locations

GA: Burnham, Atlanta; Burnham Service Co., Atlanta; Simmons Co., Atlanta; Burnham General Partner, Columbus; Burnham World Forwarding, Columbus; NJ: Gucci America, Secaucus; Gucci America Inc., Secaucus; NY: Sun Dew Corp., Jamaica; Gucci America Inc., New York; Investcorp International, New York; TX: Color Tile, Fort Worth

Nonmonetary Support

Range: $500,000 - $1,000,000
Type: Donated Products
Note: Co. provides nonmonetary support.

Giving Contact

Lisa Schiek, Director, Public Relations
Gucci America, Inc.

Description

Organization Type: Corporate Giving Program
Giving Locations: primarily headquarters and operating communities.
Grant Types: General Support.

Financial Summary

Total Giving: Contributes through corporate direct giving program only.

Typical Recipients

Arts & Humanities: Arts Associations & Councils, Arts Centers, Arts Funds, Community Arts, Dance, Ethnic & Folk Arts, Museums/Galleries, Performing Arts, Public Broadcasting, Theater
Health: Hospitals, Medical Research, Single-Disease Health Associations
Religion: Religious Organizations
Social Services: Child Welfare, Senior Services, Substance Abuse, United Funds/United Ways, Youth Organizations

Contributions Analysis

Note: All of the donations are in the form of merchandise.

Application Procedures

Initial Contact: letter and full proposal
Application Requirements: a description of organizations, amount requested, purpose of funds, number of events attendees, and proof of tax-exempt status
Deadlines: between September 1 and October 1 for funding for the following year

Restrictions

Gucci does not support individuals, fraternal organizations, or political or lobbying groups.

Additional Information

All of Gucci's corporate donations are approved and made through the publicity department. Donations take the form of merchandise donations to raffles, door prizes, and special events benefits for designated charities. At this time, Gucci has no grants program.

Corporate Officials

Domenico DeSole: president, chief executive officer chief financial officer B 1944. PRIM CORP EMPL president, chief executive officer: Gucci America Inc. CORP AFFIL director: Bausch & Lomb Inc.
Arthur Leshin: senior vice president, chief financial officer B 1946. PRIM CORP EMPL senior vice president, chief financial officer: Gucci America Inc. CORP AFFIL vice president: GST Inc.; treasurer: Gucci Timepieces.

Giving Program Officials

Lisa Schiek: PRIM CORP EMPL director public relations: Gucci America Inc.

Grants Analysis

Disclosure Period: calendar year ending
Typical Range: $500 to $1,000*
***Note:** Typical grant range is for nonmonetary support.

GUESS?

Company Contact

Los Angeles, CA

Company Description

Employees: 2,600
SIC(s): 2325 Men's/Boys' Trousers & Slacks, 2339 Women's/Misses' Outerwear Nec, 2361 Girls'/Children's Dresses & Blouses, 3851 Ophthalmic Goods, 3873 Watches, Clocks, Watchcases & Parts.

Corporate Sponsorship

Contact: Paul Steele, Controller

Guess? Foundation

Giving Contact

Lena Chin, Accounting Manager
1444 South Alameda Street
Los Angeles, CA 90021
Phone: (213)765-3100
Fax: (213)765-5927

Description

Founded: 1995
EIN: 954500475
Organization Type: Corporate Foundation

Giving Locations: limited to headquarters area only.

Financial Summary

Total Giving: $900,000 (2000 approx); $900,000 (1999 approx); $2,867,315 (1995)
Assets: $1,311,048 (1996); $2,002,971 (1995); $2,002,971 (1994)
Gifts Received: $2,188,873 (1995); $2,820,467 (1994). Note: In 1995, contributions were received from Guess? ($1,888,873), Maurice Marciano ($447,800), Paul Marciano ($354,800), and Armand Marciano ($197,400).

Typical Recipients

Arts & Humanities: Arts Associations & Councils, Arts Institutes, Arts & Humanities-General, Music, Public Broadcasting
Civic & Public Affairs: Chambers of Commerce, Civil Rights, Civic & Public Affairs-General, Parades/ Festivals, Public Policy, Urban & Community Affairs
Education: Arts/Humanities Education, Colleges & Universities, Community & Junior Colleges, Education Funds, Education-General, Medical Education, Private Education (Precollege), Student Aid
Environment: Air/Water Quality, Forestry
Health: AIDS/HIV, Cancer, Clinics/Medical Centers, Diabetes, Health Organizations, Medical Research, Multiple Sclerosis, Prenatal Health Issues
International: Health Care/Hospitals, International Development, International Organizations, International Peace & Security Issues, Missionary/Religious Activities
Religion: Jewish Causes, Religious Welfare, Synagogues/Temples
Social Services: Child Welfare, Community Service Organizations, Crime Prevention, Food/Clothing Distribution, Scouts, Substance Abuse

Application Procedures

Initial Contact: The foundation has no formal grant application procedure or application form. You may contact any officer of the foundation.
Deadlines: None.

Corporate Officials

Maurice Marciano: chairman, chief executive officer PRIM CORP EMPL chairman, chief executive officer: Guess?.
Paul Marciano: president, director advtg PRIM CORP EMPL president, director advtg: Guess?.
Terrence Tsang: chief financial officer PRIM CORP EMPL chief financial officer: Guess?.

Foundation Officials

G. Nicholas Bires: cfo, secretary PRIM CORP EMPL director corporate tax: Guess?.
Bob Burkett: president
Armand Marciano: director
Maurice Marciano: director (see above)
Paul Marciano: director (see above)

Grants Analysis

Disclosure Period: calendar year ending 1995
Number of Grants: 89*
Highest Grant: $409,415
Typical Range: $1,000 to $40,000*
***Note:** Number of grants and typical range do not include miscellaneous grants totaling $1,138,873.

Recent Grants

Note: Grants derived from 1997 Form 990.

Civic & Public Affairs

60,000 US Fund
55,000 Mayors Alliance, Los Angeles, CA
40,000 TAJC
25,000 APLA Gucci, Los Angeles, CA
25,000 LACC
25,000 TCDF
11,000 Fabb
10,000 Devine Design, Los Angeles, CA
10,000 Fashion Association, New York, NY
10,000 TSWC

Education

100,000 Otis College of Art and Design, Los Angeles, CA
50,000 Maimonides Academy, Los Angeles, CA
10,000 Beverly Hills Education Foundation, Beverly Hills, CA
10,000 FIDM Scholarship Foundation, Los Angeles, CA

Environment

15,000 Fresh Air Fund, New York, NY

Health

25,000 City of Hope, New York, NY
15,000 Passport '97 AIDS Benefit, San Francisco, CA
11,000 National Multiple Sclerosis Society, Los Angeles, CA
10,000 Cedars-Sinai Medical Center, Los Angeles, CA
10,000 March of Dimes, Burbank, CA
10,000 Ovarian Cancer Research Fund
10,000 Race Multiple Sclerosis

International

10,000 American Committee for Tel Aviv, Marina Del Rey, CA
10,000 DARE America International, Inglewood, CA

Religion

50,000 United Jewish Fund, Los Angeles, CA
13,000 United Jewish Appeal Federation, New York, NY

Social Services

20,947 Do Something, New York, NY
10,000 Boy Scouts of America, New York, NY
10,000 Share, Beverly Hills, CA
10,000 We Can, New York, NY

GUIDEONE INSURANCE

Company Contact

West Des Moines, IA
Web: http://www.preferred-risk.com

Company Description

Former Name: Preferred Risk Mutual Insurance Co.
Premiums: US$305,000,000
Employees: 1,500
SIC(s): 6300 Insurance Carriers.

GuideOne Foundation

Giving Contact

Mark McDougal, Foundation Coordinator
1111 Ashworth Rd.
West Des Moines, IA 50265
Phone: (515)225-5156
Fax: (515)267-5588

Description

Organization Type: Corporate Foundation
Giving Locations: nationally.
Grant Types: Employee Matching Gifts.
Note: Matching gifts are given to colleges and universities.

Financial Summary

Total Giving: $325,000 (1999 approx); $325,000 (1998 approx)

Typical Recipients

Education: Colleges & Universities
Social Services: Substance Abuse, United Funds/ United Ways

Application Procedures

Initial Contact: send a brief letter of inquiry
Application Requirements: a description of organization, amount requested, purpose of funds sought, recently audited financial statements, and proof of tax-exempt status

Restrictions

Does not support individuals, religious organizations for sectarian purposes or political or lobbying groups.

Additional Information

100% of funds go toward eliminating drinking and driving, and underage drinking prevention programs.

Corporate Officials

Darryl Hansen: chairman, president, chief executive officer PRIM CORP EMPL chairman, president, chief executive officer: GuideOne Insurance.
Doug Howell: chief financial officer PRIM CORP EMPL chief financial officer: GuideOne Insurance.

Foundation Officials

Mark McDougal: foundation coordinator

Grants Analysis

Disclosure Period: calendar year ending
Typical Range: $10,000 to $25,000

GULF POWER CO.

Company Contact

Pensacola, FL

Company Description

Employees: 1,287
SIC(s): 4911 Electric Services.
Parent Company: Southern Co., Atlanta, GA, United States

Nonmonetary Support

Volunteer Programs: Company reports that it supports, 'Junior Achievement, (charity) runs and holiday shopping.'

Gulf Power Foundation

Giving Contact

Candy Klinglesmith, Administrator
Gulf Power Foundation
1 Energy Place
Pensacola, FL 32520
Phone: (850)444-6806

Description

Founded: 1987
EIN: 592817740
Organization Type: Corporate Foundation
Giving Locations: Northwest Florida.
Grant Types: Employee Matching Gifts, General Support, Scholarship.

Financial Summary

Total Giving: $225,000 (1999 approx); $191,539 (1998); $185,202 (1997)
Giving Analysis: Giving for 1998 includes: foundation ($116,500); foundation grants to United Way ($72,649); foundation matching gifts ($2,390)
Assets: $1,326,982 (1998); $1,364,243 (1997); $1,439,653 (1996)
Gifts Received: $200 (1997); $1,082,484 (1993); $1,000,000 (1992). Note: In 1997, contributions were received from J. Lewis Davidoson.

Typical Recipients

Arts & Humanities: Arts Associations & Councils, Arts & Humanities-General, Historic Preservation,

History & Archaeology, Libraries, Museums/Galleries, Music
Civic & Public Affairs: African American Affairs, Community Foundations, Civic & Public Affairs-General, Housing, Parades/Festivals, Safety, Urban & Community Affairs, Women's Affairs
Education: Agricultural Education, Business Education, Colleges & Universities, Community & Junior Colleges, Education Associations, Education Funds, Engineering/Technological Education, Education-General, Literacy, Student Aid
Environment: Environment-General, Wildlife Protection
Health: Cancer, Children's Health/Hospitals, Health Organizations, Hospices, Hospitals, Prenatal Health Issues, Single-Disease Health Associations
Religion: Ministries, Religious Organizations, Religious Welfare, Social/Policy Issues
Social Services: Child Welfare, Community Service Organizations, Counseling, Food/Clothing Distribution, Homes, People with Disabilities, Scouts, Senior Services, Shelters/Homelessness, United Funds/ United Ways, YMCA/YWCA/YMHA/YWHA, Youth Organizations

Contributions Analysis

Giving Priorities: Social services, education, and art organizations.
Arts & Humanities: 8%.
Civic & Public Affairs: 7%.
Education: 23%. Funds scholarships, colleges and universities, and education associations.
Environment: 2%.
Health: 3%. Supports single-disease health associations.
Religion: 2%.
Social Services: 55%. Primarily funds United Way and youth concerns.

Application Procedures

Initial Contact: Send a brief letter of inquiry.
Application Requirements: Include a description of organization, amount requested, and purpose of funds sought.
Deadlines: Quarterly.

Restrictions

The foundation does not support individuals or organizations outside service area.

Corporate Officials

Travis J. Bowden: chairman, president, chief executive officer, director B Greenville, AL 1938. ED University of Alabama (1960). PRIM CORP EMPL chairman, president, chief executive officer, director: Gulf Power Co.
Arlan Earl Scarbrough: vice president financial B Carnes, MS 1936. ED University of Southern Mississippi (1958); East Carolina University (1962). PRIM CORP EMPL vice president financial: Gulf Power Co. NONPR AFFIL member: American Institute CPAs.

Foundation Officials

Francis M. Fisher, Jr.: trustee
John E. Hodges, Jr.: chairman PRIM CORP EMPL vice president: Gulf Power Co.
Ronnie R. Labrato: secretary B Pensacola, FL 1953. ED University of West Florida (1974). PRIM CORP EMPL controller: Gulf Power Co.
Robert Moore: trustee
Arlan Earl Scarbrough: trustee (see above)
Warren E. Tate: treasurer

Grants Analysis

Disclosure Period: calendar year ending 1998
Total Grants: $116,500*
Number of Grants: 51
Average Grant: $2,284
Highest Grant: $10,000
Lowest Grant: $500
Typical Range: $200 to $10,000
***Note:** Giving excludes United Way; matching gifts.

Recent Grants

Note: Grants derived from 1997 Form 990.

Arts & Humanities

5,000	Arts Council of Northwest Florida, Pensacola, FL -- operating support
5,000	Historic Pensacola, Pensacola, FL -- capital funds
5,000	Pensacola Children's Chorus, Pensacola, FL -- operating support
3,000	Bay Arts Alliance, Panama City, FL -- operating support

Civic & Public Affairs

5,000	Pensacola Area Chamber Foundation, Pensacola, FL -- operating support
5,000	Santa Rosa Clean Community System, Milton, FL -- operating support
3,000	Lakeview Foundation, Pensacola, FL -- operating support
2,000	Florida House, Washington, DC -- operating support

Education

10,000	Okaloosa Walton Community College, Niceville, FL -- capital funds
5,500	Junior Achievement, Pensacola, FL -- operating support
2,500	University of West Florida, Pensacola, FL -- scholarships
2,000	Florida State University, Panama City, FL -- scholarships
2,000	Gulf Coast Community College, Panama City, FL -- capital funds
2,000	Okaloosa Public Schools Foundation, Fort Walton Beach, FL -- operating support

Social Services

39,512	United Way Escambia County, Pensacola, FL -- operating support
27,767	United Way Northwest Florida, Bay County, Panama City, FL -- operating support
10,000	YMCA Emerald Coast, Fort Walton Beach, FL -- capital funds
6,142	United Way Okaloosa/Walton County, Fort Walton Beach, FL -- operating support
3,847	United Way Santa Rosa County, Milton, FL -- operating support
3,700	Boy Scouts of America, Pensacola, FL -- operating support

Gulfstream Aerospace Corp.

Company Contact

500 Gulfstream Rd.
Savannah, GA 31408
Phone: (912)965-3000
Fax: (912)965-3011
Web: http://www.gulfstream.com

Company Description

Employees: 4,600
SIC(s): 3721 Aircraft.
Parent Company: General Dynamics Corp., 3190 Fairview Park Dr., Falls Church, VA, United States

Nonmonetary Support

Value: $50,000 (1995); $100,000 (1993)
Type: Donated Products; Loaned Employees; Loaned Executives

Corporate Sponsorship

Type: Arts & cultural events; Festivals/fairs; Pledge-a-thon

Giving Contact

Marsha Grovenstein, Director, Community Relations
Gulfstream Aerospace Corp.
PO Box 2206
Savannah, GA 31402
Phone: (912)965-3665
Fax: (912)965-3147

Description

Founded: 1990
Organization Type: Corporate Giving Program
Giving Locations: headquarters and operating communities; national organizations.
Grant Types: Award, Capital, Endowment, General Support, Loan.

Financial Summary

Total Giving: $700,000 (1997 approx); $600,000 (1996 approx); $600,000 (1995 approx). Note: Contributes through corporate direct giving program only.

Typical Recipients

Arts & Humanities: Arts Centers, Historic Preservation
Civic & Public Affairs: Philanthropic Organizations
Education: Colleges & Universities, Literacy, Public Education (Precollege), Science/Mathematics Education
Environment: Environment-General
Health: Hospices
Science: Science Exhibits & Fairs
Social Services: Child Welfare, Domestic Violence, Shelters/Homelessness, United Funds/United Ways

Contributions Analysis

Arts & Humanities: About 30%. Supports arts centers and historic preservation.
Civic & Public Affairs: About 20%. Contributes to environmental affairs and civic organizations.
Education: About 15%. Support goes to colleges and universities, science and mathematics education, public education, and literacy programs.
Health: About 10%. Contributions go to hospices and other health-care organizations.
Social Services: About 25%. Support for child welfare, prevention of domestic violence programs, help for the homeless, and united funds.

Application Procedures

Initial Contact: a brief letter of inquiry
Application Requirements: a description of organization, amount requested, purpose of funds sought, and proof of tax-exempt status
Deadlines: None.

Restrictions

Does not support religious organizations for sectarian purposes or political or lobbying groups.

Corporate Officials

Bill Boisture: president, chief executive officer
Theodore J. Forstmann: chairman B Greenwich, CT 1940. ED Yale University BA (1961); Columbia University JD (1965). PRIM CORP EMPL chairman: Gulfstream Aerospace Corp. PRIM NONPR EMPL general partner: Forstmann Little & Co.

Giving Program Officials

Patrick C. G. Coulter: senior vice president corporate communications B Seattle, WA 1941. ED California State University, Northridge BS (1975); University of Southern California MPA (1980). PRIM CORP EMPL senior vice president, corporate communications: Gulfstream Aerospace Corp. NONPR AFFIL member: Public Relations Society America; member: Society Professional Journalists.

Grants Analysis

Disclosure Period: calendar year ending
Typical Range: $1,000 to $2,500

Halliburton Co.

Company Contact

3600 Lincoln Plaza
500 N. Akard Street
Dallas, TX 75201-3391
Phone: (214)978-2600
Fax: (214)978-2611
Web: http://www.halliburton.com

Company Description

Revenue: US$14,898,000,000 (1999)
Profit: US$14,700,000
Employees: 107,800 (1999)
Fortune Rank: 115, per FORTUNE Magazine's list of 500 Largest U.S. Corporations (1999).
FF 115
SIC(s): 1389 Oil & Gas Field Services Nec, 1541 Industrial Buildings & Warehouses, 1629 Heavy Construction Nec, 1799 Special Trade Contractors Nec.

Operating Locations

; Azerbaijan: Halliburton International Inc., Azerbaijan; Algeria: Halliburton Limited, Alger; Halliburton Energy Services, Algiers; Halliburton, Hassi Messaoud; Halliburotn Limited, Ohanet, Le Bretonneux; Angola: Halliburton Overseas Limited, Cabinda, Luanda; Argentina: Halliburton Argentina SA, Buenos Aires, Chubut, Neuquen, Tartagal; Australia; Halliburton Australia Pty. Ltd., Adelaide Airport, S. Australia, Adelaide, South Australia, Berrimah, Brisbane, Canning Vale, W. Australia, Cheltenham; Halliburton Co., Melbourne; Halliburton Australia Pty Ltd/BRES, Perth, Western Australia; Halliburton Australia Pty. Ltd., Port Adelaide, South Australia, Roma, Southbank, Wurruck; Austria: Halliburton Co. Austria GmbH, Seyring; Halliburton Energy Services, Vienna; Bahrain: Halliburton Worldwide Ltd., Manama; Bolivia: Halliburton Latin America SA, Santa Cruz; Canada: Halliburton Canada Inc (Brown & Root), Edmonton; Halliburton Canada Inc., Esterhazy, Estevan, Fort Saint John, Fort Nelson, Grand Prairie, High Level, Lloydminster, Medicine Hat, Mount Pearl, Norman Wells, Rainbow Lake, Red Deer, Saint John's, Whitecourt; People's Republic of China: Halliburton Overseas Limited, Shekou, Shenzhen; Halliburton International Inc., Shenzhen; Cameroon: Halliburton SAS, Akwa-Douala; Congo: Halliburton Afrique SNC, Pointe Noire; Colombia: Halliburton Latin America SA, Bogota, Neiva, Sante Fe de Bogota, DC; Costa Rica: Halliburton Co., Trejas, Monte Alegre, Escazu; Croatia:, Zagreb; Denmark: Halliburton Co. Germany GmbH, Esbjerg; Ecuador: Halliburton Latin America SA, Quito; El Salvador:, La Libertad; France: Halliburton PAU, Billere; Halliburton SAS, Puteaux; Gabon:, Port Gentil; Germany: Halliburton Co. Germany GmbH, Celle, Vechta; Greece: Halliburton Co. GmbH, Kavala; Halliburton, Thessaloniki; Guatemala: Halliburton Energy Services, Ciudad de Guatemala; Indonesia: P.T. Halliburton Indonesia, Balikpapan, Batam Island; Halliburton Indonesia, Jakarta; Italy; Halliburton Italiana SpA, Cortemaggiore, Piacenza, San Giovanni Teatino, Chieti, San Gluliano, Milanese, Siracusa, Sicily; Japan: Halliburton Overseas Limited, Niigata-City, Niigata Perf., Tokyo; Kazakhstan: Halliburton International Inc., Tengiz; Kuwait: Halliburton Overseas Limited, East Ahmadi; Malta: Halliburton, Triq it-Tera, Ta' L-Ibrag; Mexico: Halliburton de Mexico SA de CV, Azul, Del Carmen; Halliburton de Mexico, SA de CV, Poza Rica, Reforma, Reynosa; Malaysia: Halliburton Services (M) Sdn Bhd, Miri, Sarawak; Nigeria: Halliburton Nigeria Limited, Port Harcourt, Rivers State, Victoria Island, Lagos; Netherlands: Halliburton BV, Leiderdorp; New Zealand: Halliburton Overseas Ltd, New Plymouth; Pakistan: Halliburton Limited, Islamabad; Papua New Guinea: Halliburton Australia Pty. Ltd., Moro, S. Highlands Provin; Qatar: Halliburton Limited, Doha; Russia: Halliburton International Inc., Moscow, Niznevartovsk, Yuzhno-Sakhalinsk; Saudi Arabia: Halliburton Co., Saudi Arabia Branch, Dhahran; Scotland: Halliburton Manufacturing & Services Ltd, Montrose, Angus; Singapore: Halliburton Manufacturing (Singapore) Pte. Ltd., Jurong; Suriname: Halliburton International Inc., Paramaribo; Thailand: Halliburton Co., Kamphaeng; Halliburton, Mattaput, Muang Rayong; Halliburton Co., Phitsanulok; Turkmenistan: Halliburton International Inc., Turkmenistan; Turkey: Halliburton Limited, Ankara; United Kingdom: Halliburton Manufacturing & Services Limited, Dyce, Aberdeen; Halliburton Manufacturing & Services Ltd, Kilwinning, Ayrshire; Vietnam: Halliburton Multinational Inc., Ho Chi Minh City

Nonmonetary Support

Type: Donated Equipment; Donated Products

Halliburton Foundation, Inc.

Giving Contact

Pat George, Community & Governmental Affairs Manager
Halliburton Foundation, Inc.
PO Box 3
Houston, TX 77001-0003
Email: pat.george@halliburton.com

Description

EIN: 751212458
Organization Type: Corporate Foundation
Giving Locations: TX Southwest U.S.
Grant Types: Employee Matching Gifts, Endowment, General Support.
Note: Employee matching gift ratio: 2 to 1.

Financial Summary

Total Giving: $1,435,592 (1998); $1,232,493 (1997); $1,579,798 (1996). Note: Contributes through foundation only.
Giving Analysis: Giving for 1999 includes: foundation (approx $1,200,000)
Assets: $12,000,000 (1999 approx); $20,425,526 (1998); $9,894,894 (1997)
Gifts Received: $823,986 (1998); $1,001,159 (1997); $957,971 (1996). Note: Gifts are received from Halliburton Energy Services and Brown & Root Companies.

Typical Recipients

Arts & Humanities: Arts Centers, History & Archaeology, Libraries, Museums/Galleries, Music, Opera, Performing Arts
Civic & Public Affairs: Business/Free Enterprise, Employment/Job Training, Civic & Public Affairs-General, Philanthropic Organizations, Public Policy, Urban & Community Affairs, Women's Affairs, Zoos/Aquariums
Education: Agricultural Education, Business Education, Business-School Partnerships, Colleges & Universities, Community & Junior Colleges, Elementary Education (Public), Engineering/Technological Education, Faculty Development, Education-General, Legal Education, Literacy, Medical Education, Minority Education, Religious Education, Science/Mathematics Education, Social Sciences Education
Environment: Energy, Environment-General
Health: Cancer, Hospitals
International: Foreign Educational Institutions
Religion: Religious Welfare, Seminaries
Science: Science Museums
Social Services: Scouts, Substance Abuse, YMCA/YWCA/YMHA/YWHA, Youth Organizations

Contributions Analysis

Giving Priorities: Grants are awarded to junior colleges, colleges, and universities located primarily in the Southwestern United States. Also funds health and welfare programs, civic organizations, and the arts.
Arts & Humanities: 2%. Supports historical center and the opera.
Education: 94%. Primarily support faculty, equipment acquisition, content development initiatives within engineering or technical departments. Limited unrestricted support.
Social Services: 4%. A small number of grants support youth organizations.
Note: Contributions made in 1998. These contributions made prior to the merger with Dresser Foundation.

Application Procedures

Initial Contact: Submit full proposal.
Application Requirements: Include description of organization to be funded, expected outcomes, program objectives with target dates, evaluation plan, and strategy to secure full funding for program. Also include 501(c)3 determination letter; list of board of directors and their business or other affiliations; audited financial statement; and current list of supporters.
Deadlines: None.
Review Process: Requests are reviewed throughout the year by the Corporate Contributions Committee. Decisions are based on available resources and eligibility of applying organization. Full review may take up to three months.

Restrictions

Support is not made for individuals, scholarships, advertising campaigns, travel expenses, or film and video projects. Also does not support religious organizations or organizations whose fundraising/administrative expenses exceed 15% of their annual budget.

Additional Information

Halliburton Co. merged with Dresser Industries effective September 1998.

Corporate Officials

William Edward Bradford: chairman, director B Dallas, TX 1935. ED Centenary College BS (1958); Texas A&M University (1975). PRIM CORP EMPL chairman, director: Halliburton Co. ADD CORP EMPL president: Wheatley TXT Corp. CORP AFFIL director: Ultramar Diamond Shamrock Corp.; director: Kerr-McGee Corp. NONPR AFFIL member: Society Petroleum Engineers; member: Texas Mid-Continent Oil & Gas Association; member: National Ocean Industry Association; member: Petroleum Equipment Suppliers Association; member: Association Oilwell Drilling Contractors; member: International Petroleum Association; member: American Association Petroleum Geologists; member: American Association Advancement Science. CLUB AFFIL University Houston Club; Petroleum Club; Raveneaux Country Club; Houston Club.
Richard B. Cheney: chief executive officer B Lincoln, NE 1941. ED University of Wyoming BA (1965); University of Wyoming MA (1966). PRIM CORP EMPL chief executive officer: Halliburton Co. ADD CORP EMPL chief executive officer: Halliburton Delaware Inc. CORP AFFIL director: Union Pacific Corp.; director: Union Pacific Railroad Co.; director: Procter & Gamble Co.; director: Electronic Data Systems Corp.; director: Landmark Graphics Corp.
David J. Lesar: president, chief operating officer B 1953. ED University of Wisconsin MBA; University of Wisconsin BS. PRIM CORP EMPL president, chief operating officer: Halliburton Co. ADD CORP EMPL chairman: Kellogg Brown & Root Inc. CORP AFFIL director: Highlands Insurance Co.; director: Southern Co. Inc.; director: Cordant Technology Inc.
Donald C. Vaughn: vice chairman ED Virginia Tech BS. PRIM CORP EMPL vice chairman: Halliburton Co.

Foundation Officials

Jerry Halbert Blurton: treasurer B 1944. PRIM CORP EMPL treasurer: Halliburton Co. CORP AFFIL director: Highlands Insurance Co.; director: Highlands Underwriters Insurance Co.

Richard B. Cheney: president (see above)

Celeste Colgan: vice president, secretary B Lander, WY 1939. ED University of Wyoming (1961); University of Maryland (1973). PRIM CORP EMPL vice president human resources: Halliburton Co. CORP AFFIL vice president human resources: Brown & Root Inc.

Susan Stewart Keith: assistant secretary, assistant treasurer B Austin, TX 1946. ED Baylor University BA (1968); Southern Methodist University JD (1975). PRIM CORP EMPL vice president, secretary, corporate counsel: Halliburton Co.

David J. Lesar: trustee (see above)

Grants Analysis

Disclosure Period: calendar year ending 1998
Total Grants: $1,435,592
Number of Grants: 254
Average Grant: $5,652
Highest Grant: $115,509
Typical Range: $2,000 to $20,000

Recent Grants

Note: Grants derived from 1997 Form 990.

Arts & Humanities

5,000 Buffalo Bill Memorial Association, Cody, WY -- support Buffalo Bill Historical Center
5,000 Dallas Opera, Dallas, TX -- support Arts Education Partnership

Civic & Public Affairs

50,000 American Enterprise Institute for Public Policy Research, Washington, DC
5,000 Dallas Zoological Society, Dallas, TX -- support capital campaign
500 Philanthropy Roundtable, Indianapolis, IN

Education

65,200 Oklahoma State University Foundation, Stillwater, OK -- support Advanced Polyester Technology Lab
27,500 Junior Achievement of Southeast Texas, Houston, TX
27,500 Texas A&M University, College Station, TX -- purchase equipment, curriculum development
25,000 Junior Achievement, Dallas, TX
23,000 Texas Alliance for Minorities in Engineering, Austin, TX -- support programs for minority students
20,000 Georgetown University, Washington, DC
20,000 Oklahoma State University Foundation, Stillwater, OK -- purchase equipment, curriculum development
20,000 Rice University, Houston, TX -- purchase equipment, curriculum development
20,000 Texas Tech University, Lubbock, TX -- purchase equipment, curriculum development
20,000 University of Oklahoma Foundation, Norman, OK -- purchase equipment, curriculum development
20,000 University of Texas Austin, Austin, TX -- purchase equipment, curriculum development
16,000 University of Missouri, Rolla, MO -- purchase equipment, curriculum development
15,000 Foundation for the National Capital Region, Washington, DC -- support Celebration of Reading benefit
15,000 University of Houston, Houston, TX -- purchase equipment, curriculum development
10,000 Louisiana State University Foundation, Baton Rouge, LA -- purchase equipment, curriculum development
10,000 Oklahoma State University Foundation, Stillwater, OK -- purchase equipment, curriculum development
7,500 Louisiana State University Foundation, Baton Rouge, LA -- purchase equipment, curriculum development
7,500 Texas A&M University, College Station, TX -- purchase equipment, curriculum development
7,500 Texas Tech University, Lubbock, TX -- purchase equipment, curriculum development
7,500 University of Florida Foundation, Gainesville, FL -- purchase equipment, curriculum development
7,500 University of Houston, Houston, TX -- purchase equipment, curriculum development
7,500 University of Oklahoma Foundation, Norman, OK -- purchase equipment, curriculum development
7,500 University of Texas Austin, Austin, TX -- support College of Business Administration
5,000 National Association of Elementary School Principals, Arlington, VA -- support Overseas Schools Advisory Council Program
3,000 Louisiana State University Foundation, Baton Rouge, LA -- support Internal Audit Pilot School Program
2,500 Georgia Institute of Technology, Atlanta, GA -- purchase equipment, curriculum development
1,000 Georgia Institute of Technology, Atlanta, GA
1,000 Oklahoma State University Foundation, Stillwater, OK
1,000 Texas A&M University, College Station, TX
1,000 Texas Tech University, Lubbock, TX
1,000 University of Missouri, Rolla, MO
1,000 University of Oklahoma Foundation, Norman, OK
1,000 University of Texas Austin, Austin, TX -- support Business Career Assistance Center
1,000 University of Texas Austin, Austin, TX -- support Engineering Career Assistance Center
750 Montana Tech of the University of Montana, Butte, MT
750 South Dakota School of Mines and Technology, Rapid City, SD
500 Michigan Technological University, Houghton, MI

Science

25,000 Manned Space Flight Education Foundation, Houston, TX -- support Kids Space Place at Space Center Houston
23,734 Offshore Rig Museum, Houston, TX -- support Offshore Energy Center Capital Campaign
10,000 Southwest Museum of Science and Technology Science Place, Dallas, TX -- support Science Place at Fair Park

Social Services

15,000 YWCA, Dallas, TX -- support math and science education programs
10,000 Boy Scouts of America National Council, Irving, TX -- support Circle Ten Council Friends of Scouting Campaign

HALLMARK CARDS INC.

★ Number 57 of Top 100 Corporate Givers

Company Contact

2501 McGee St.
Kansas City, MO 64108
Phone: (816)274-5111
Fax: (816)274-5061
Web: http://www.hallmark.com

Company Description

Employees: 20,945 (1998)
SIC(s): 2771 Greeting Cards, 5112 Stationery & Office Supplies.

Operating Locations

Co. operates nationwide.

Nonmonetary Support

Value: $15,300,000 (1993); $14,200,000 (1992); $6,600,000 (1991)
Type: Donated Equipment; Donated Products; In-kind Services; Loaned Employees
Volunteer Programs: Supports the Volunteer Involvement Pays Program, through which a $200 grant is contributed to a 501(c)3 organization that has benefitted from employee volunteers. Grant applications are employee initiated, and employees must volunteer at least 25 hours of service within a six-month period.
Note: For nonmonetary support contact the Charitable Contributions Manager-Product, Mail-Drop 297.

Hallmark Corporate Foundation

Giving Contact

Karen Bartz, Community Development Manager
Hallmark Cards Inc.
PO Box 419580
Dept. 323
Kansas City, MO 64141-6580
Phone: (816)274-8508
Fax: (816)274-8547

Description

EIN: 431303258
Organization Type: Corporate Foundation
Giving Locations: IL: Metamora; KS: Leavenworth, Topeka; MO: Kansas City, Liberty headquarters; principally near operating locations and to national organizations.
Grant Types: Capital, Challenge, Employee Matching Gifts, General Support, Project, Seed Money.
Note: Employee matching gift ratio: 1 to 1 to education, up to $6,000 per person annually, maximum $2,000 per institution.

Giving Philosophy

'As a matter of responsible corporate citizenship, Hallmark Cards Inc., is dedicated to taking an active role in improving the communities in which it operates through its support of causes which contribute to the community's economic and social development. .. In addition, the Company recognizes that its employees' best interests and its own long-term growth and prosperity are closely related to the environment in which it operates. Therefore, the Company both seeks out and responds to selected opportunities which enhance the business environment.' *Hallmark Cards Corporate Contribution Program Guidelines*

Financial Summary

Total Giving: $15,000,000 (1998 approx); $2,225,232 (1997); $2,793,553 (1996). Note: Contributes through corporate direct giving program and foundation.
Giving Analysis: Giving for 1997 includes: foundation ($1,582,975); foundation matching gifts ($441,007); foundation grants to United Way ($201,250); 1998: corporate direct giving (approx $8,046,586); foundation ($6,953,414)

Assets: $21,118,318 (1998); $29,251,506 (1997); $24,725,032 (1996)
Gifts Received: $789,700 (1997); $1,260,949 (1996)

Typical Recipients

Arts & Humanities: Arts Associations & Councils, Arts Centers, Arts Institutes, Arts Outreach, Ballet, Dance, Ethnic & Folk Arts, Film & Video, Arts & Humanities-General, Historic Preservation, History & Archaeology, Museums/Galleries, Music, Opera, Performing Arts, Public Broadcasting, Theater, Visual Arts
Civic & Public Affairs: African American Affairs, Botanical Gardens/Parks, Business/Free Enterprise, Community Foundations, Economic Development, Employment/Job Training, Civic & Public Affairs-General, Hispanic Affairs, Housing, Municipalities/Towns, Nonprofit Management, Public Policy, Rural Affairs, Safety, Urban & Community Affairs, Women's Affairs, Zoos/Aquariums
Education: Agricultural Education, Arts/Humanities Education, Business Education, Business-School Partnerships, Colleges & Universities, Continuing Education, Education Reform, Elementary Education (Private), Education-General, International Exchange, Literacy, Minority Education, Preschool Education, Private Education (Precollege), Public Education (Precollege), Science/Mathematics Education, Special Education, Student Aid
Environment: Environment-General
Health: AIDS/HIV, Cancer, Children's Health/Hospitals, Emergency/Ambulance Services, Health Organizations, Hospices, Hospitals, Long-Term Care, Mental Health, Public Health
Religion: Ministries, Religious Welfare
Social Services: Community Service Organizations, Crime Prevention, Day Care, Delinquency & Criminal Rehabilitation, Domestic Violence, Emergency Relief, Family Services, Food/Clothing Distribution, People with Disabilities, Recreation & Athletics, Scouts, Senior Services, Sexual Abuse, Shelters/Homelessness, Substance Abuse, United Funds/United Ways, Volunteer Services, YMCA/YWCA/YMHA/YWHA, Youth Organizations

Contributions Analysis

Giving Priorities: The arts, education, neighborhood development, business development, social services, disease prevention, and health care cost containment.
Arts & Humanities: 23%. The company expresses strong interest in the arts through the support of local professional arts organizations which have an impact on a broad segment of the community. Emphasis is on culturally diverse audiences and involving youth.
Civic & Public Affairs: 14%. Support for organizations which represent business interests or which promote community development, such as neighborhood preservation and redevelopment, especially neighborhoods adjacent to Hallmark facilities or in the urban core; business support groups/economic development; and social investments in support of housing or other redevelopment activities.
Education: 22%. Assistance is given to local schools, adult education, support of public television, and projects designed to improve teaching, and learning. Systemic educational reform efforts are of special interest. In addition, the company has a strong interest in the area of design education, initiating grants to art and design schools which are a source of talent for Hallmark Cards Inc.
Health: 37%. Support includes contributions to human service programs and/or agencies which serve minorities, low income, the homeless, disadvantaged youth, infant care, the disabled, AIDS patients, and others; primary support of such programs is through company contributions to local United Way campaigns. While the company does not make grants to governmental agencies, partnerships with the public sector in support of human service programs can be considered.
Note: Total foundation contributions in 1997. Company prefers to respond to requests on a case-by-case basis and has not established target levels for contribution categories.

Application Procedures

Initial Contact: Submit letter to Community Development Manager of Hallmark Cards in Kansas City, or to the local Contributions Committee in plant cities.
Application Requirements: Letter should include need, purpose, and general activities of requesting organization, as well as goals, objectives and amount requested.
Deadlines: None.
Review Process: Requests are initially reviewed and recommended by foundation staff; the Hallmark Executive Committee/Foundation Board of Directors sets program policy and reviews major grants.
Evaluative Criteria: Promotion of quality and excellence, responsiveness to community needs, enhancement of company's long-range interests, collaborative approach and nonduplication of services; preference given to innovative programs of fixed duration; programs should have plans for continued funding.
Decision Notification: Within four to six weeks, for initial inquiries.
Notes: If letter of inquiry falls within an area of interest, a full proposal will be requested.

Restrictions

The company and the foundation generally do not support individuals; religious, fraternal, international, or veterans' organizations; athletic or labor groups; endowment funds; social clubs; individual youth groups, troops, or clubs; disease specific organizations; or non tax-exempt organizations. Funding generally is not provided if the purpose is to cover past operating deficits, travel, conferences, scholarships, scholarly or health-related research, charitable advertisements, television or radio programs, political campaigns or causes, or fundraising campaigns such as walk-a-thons or telethons. campaigns or causes, or fundraising campaigns such as walk-a-thons or telethons.

Additional Information

The company and the foundation prefer to participate with others in funding programs.
Recipients of major grants must make periodic written reports and, at the expiration of funding, submit a written narrative report and an account of all disbursements. Recipients must ensure that grants are used for purposes stated in request. The company reserves the right to withdraw funding used for other than the purpose stated.
Company established the Hallmark Corporate Foundation in 1983, primarily to ensure a consistent level of giving in the event of a low-profit year. While foundation assets have grown, the program has not changed focus overall, and contributions levels will remain consistent with figures reported above.
Publications: Corporate Contributions Guidelines

Corporate Officials

Donald Joyce Hall: chairman board, director B Kansas City, MO 1928. ED Dartmouth College AB (1950). PRIM CORP EMPL chairman board, director: Hallmark Cards Inc. CORP AFFIL director: United Telecommunications Inc.; director: Mutual Benefit Life Insurance Co.; director: Target Corp.; director: Commerce Bank NA; director: William E Coutts Co. Ltd.; director: 1st National Bank Lawrence; director: Business Mens Assurance Co. NONPR AFFIL trustee: Midwest Research Institute; trustee: Nelson-Atkins Museum Art; director: Kansas City Minority Suppliers Development Council; director: Kansas City Symphony; director: Friends of Art; member: Kansas City Chamber of Commerce; director: American Royal Association; president: Civic Council Greater Kansas City; honorary member: American Institute Architects.
Irvine O. Hockaday, Jr.: president, chief executive officer, director B Ludington, MI 1936. ED Princeton University AB (1958); University of Michigan LLB (1961); University of Michigan JD (1961). PRIM CORP EMPL president, chief executive officer, director: Hallmark Cards Inc. ADD CORP EMPL president: Hallmark Entertainment Distribution Co.; director: Signboard Hill Productions Inc. CORP AFFIL director: UtiliCorp. United Inc.; director: Ford Motor Co.; director: Sprint Corp.; director: Dow Jones & Co. Inc. NONPR AFFIL trustee: Aspen Institute; member: Midwest Research Institute; director: 10th District Federal Reserve Bank.

Foundation Officials

Eleanor Anglebeck: assistant secretary
Jeanne M. Bates: vice president, secretary PRIM CORP EMPL manager community development: Hallmark Cards Inc.
Donald Joyce Hall: chairman (see above)
William Austin Hall: president B Kansas City, MO 1945. ED Southern Methodist University BBA (1967); Southern Methodist University MBA (1968). CORP AFFIL director: Somerville; director: Hugh M Woods; director: Mercantile Bancorp Inc.; director: Payless Cashways Inc.; director: Knox; director: Lumberjack; director: Furrow.
John A. MacDonald: treasurer
Terri R. Maybee: assistant treasurer
Danita Robinson: assistant secretary

Grants Analysis

Disclosure Period: calendar year ending 1997
Total Grants: $1,376,575*
Number of Grants: 350 (approx)
Average Grant: $3,944
Highest Grant: $99,485
Typical Range: $1,000 to $10,000 and $25,000 to $50,000
***Note:** Giving excludes United Way, matching gifts, and $206,400 in VIP grants.

Recent Grants

Note: Grants derived from 1997 Form 990.

Arts & Humanities

99,485	Nelson Gallery Foundation, Kansas City, MO
30,000	Kansas City Museum Association, Kansas City, MO
30,000	Kansas City Symphony, Kansas City, MO
15,000	Heart of America Shakespeare Festival, Kansas City, MO
15,000	Young Audiences, Kansas City, MO
11,500	Leavenworth County Historical Society, Leavenworth, KS -- capital improvements
10,000	Kansas City Public Television, Kansas City, MO -- auction underwriting
10,000	Midwest Museums Conference, St. Louis, MO
10,000	Topeka Civic Theater, Topeka, KS -- capital campaign

Civic & Public Affairs

30,000	Kansas City Consensus, Kansas City, MO
20,000	Greater Kansas City Community Foundation, Kansas City, MO -- neighborhood self-help fund
20,000	Kansas City Community Gardens, Kansas City, MO -- purchase of van
17,500	Main Street Corridor Development Corporation, Kansas City, MO
16,000	Seem to be Players, Lawrence, KS -- managing director support campaign
15,000	Kansas City Arson Task Force, Kansas City, MO -- fire safety house

10,000	Aspen Institute, Washington, DC
10,000	Project Neighbor-HOOD, Kansas City, MO

Education

58,000	Society of Illustrators, New York, NY -- student scholarship competition
35,000	College Fund/UNCF, Fairfax, VA
30,000	Art Center College of Design, Pasadena, CA -- art school support program
25,000	National 4-H Council, Chevy Chase, MD -- administrative expenses
15,000	University of Kansas Endowment Association, Lawrence, KS -- business school
13,000	Junior Achievement of Northeast Kansas, Topeka, KS
12,500	University of Kansas Endowment Association, Lawrence, KS -- symposium series
10,150	Pembroke Hill School, Kansas City, MO -- multicultural scholars program
10,000	National Hispanic Scholarship Fund, San Francisco, CA
10,000	University of Kansas Endowment Association, Lawrence, KS -- symposium series

Environment

12,000	Wildwood Outdoor Education Center, La-Cygne, KS -- summer program

Health

25,000	Heart of America United Way, Kansas City, MO -- National Community AIDS Partnership
10,000	Capper Foundation for Crippled Children, Topeka, KS -- capital campaign
10,000	Children's Mercy Hospital, Kansas City, MO -- Paul H. Henderson Endowment Fund
10,000	Susan G. Komen Breast Cancer Foundation, Kansas City, MO -- sponsorship

Religion

12,000	City Vision Ministries, Kansas City, KS -- urban homeowner improvement program
10,000	National Conference of Christians and Jews, Kansas City, MO -- The People Puzzle: A Children's Exhibition

Social Services

55,000	United Way of Douglas County, Lawrence, KS
45,000	United Way of Leavenworth County, Leavenworth, KS
30,750	United Way, Columbus, GA
25,000	United Way of Douglas County, Lawrence, KS -- capital improvement
20,000	Boy Scouts of America Jayhawk Area Council, Topeka, KS -- low-income and minority scout program
19,167	YMCA, Topeka, KS -- capital campaign
17,125	United Way, Topeka, KS
17,125	United Way, Topeka, KS
17,125	United Way, Topeka, KS
17,125	United Way, Topeka, KS
12,500	Girl Scouts of America Kaw Valley Council, Topeka, KS -- capital campaign
10,000	Foodchain, Kansas City, MO -- food donor development
10,000	Heart of America United Way, Kansas City, MO -- Outcome Measurement Initiative
10,000	Partnership for a Drug-Free America, New York, NY -- anti-drug media campaign
10,000	Westport Cooperative Services, Kansas City, MO -- senior companion program
10,000	YMCA, Kansas City, MO -- building extension

HAMILTON SUNDSTRAND CORP.

Company Contact

One Hamilton Rd.
Windsor Locks, CT 06096
Phone: (860)654-6000
Fax: (860)654-2399
Web: http://www.hamiltonsundstrandcorp.com

Company Description

Employees: 9,296
SIC(s): 3531 Construction Machinery, 3568 Power Transmission Equipment Nec, 3569 General Industrial Machinery Nec, 3728 Aircraft Parts & Equipment Nec.
Parent Company: United Technologies Corp., One Financial Plaza, Hartford, CT, United States

Sundstrand Corp. Foundation

Giving Contact

Kathryn L. Stokstad, Treasurer
Sundstrand Corp. Foundation
4949 Harrison Avenue
PO Box 7003
Rockford, IL 61125
Phone: (815)226-6594

Description

EIN: 366072477
Organization Type: Corporate Foundation
Giving Locations: IL: emphasis on the Rockford area headquarters and operating communities.
Grant Types: Capital, Employee Matching Gifts, General Support.

Financial Summary

Total Giving: $2,225,000 (fiscal year ending October 31, 1999 approx); $1,988,435 (fiscal 1998); $420,783 (fiscal 1997). Note: Contributes through foundation only.
Giving Analysis: Giving for fiscal 1998 includes: foundation ($846,979); foundation matching gifts ($815,456); foundation grants to United Way ($326,000)
Assets: $1,522,186 (fiscal 1998); $2,389,178 (fiscal 1997); $3,697,766 (fiscal 1996)
Gifts Received: $1,000,000 (fiscal 1998); $1,000,000 (fiscal 1996); $1,000,000 (fiscal 1994). Note: Foundation receives contributions from Sunstrand Corporation.

Typical Recipients

Arts & Humanities: Arts Associations & Councils, Arts Centers, Community Arts, Dance, Arts & Humanities-General, History & Archaeology, Libraries, Museums/Galleries, Music, Opera, Performing Arts, Public Broadcasting, Theater
Civic & Public Affairs: Botanical Gardens/Parks, Clubs, Community Foundations, Economic Policy, Employment/Job Training, Civic & Public Affairs-General, Hispanic Affairs, Housing, Parades/Festivals, Urban & Community Affairs
Education: Business Education, Colleges & Universities, Community & Junior Colleges, Economic Education, Engineering/Technological Education, International Studies, Literacy, Medical Education, Minority Education, Private Education (Precollege), Science/Mathematics Education, Student Aid, Vocational & Technical Education
Health: AIDS/HIV, Children's Health/Hospitals, Clinics/Medical Centers, Emergency/Ambulance Services, Hospices, Hospitals, Long-Term Care, Medical Research, Mental Health, Nursing Services, Transplant Networks/Donor Banks
International: Health Care/Hospitals
Religion: Religious Welfare
Science: Science Museums
Social Services: At-Risk Youth, Child Welfare, Community Centers, Day Care, Family Services, Food/Clothing Distribution, Homes, People with Disabilities, Recreation & Athletics, Scouts, Substance Abuse, United Funds/United Ways, YMCA/YWCA/YMHA/YWHA, Youth Organizations

Contributions Analysis

Giving Priorities: Social services, the arts and education.
Arts & Humanities: 28%. Supports history and fine arts organizations and the performing arts.
Civic & Public Affairs: 4%. Funds community foundations and minority issues.
Education: 12%. Funds colleges and universities, Junior Achievement and education funds.
Health: 3%. Supports health networks and accessibility for the disabled.
Religion: 2%. Funds religious welfare.
Science: 1%. Supports the National Aviation Hall of Fame.
Social Services: 50%. Supports the United Way, scouting and other youth activities, day care, and YMCAs.
Note: Total contributions made in 1998.

Application Procedures

Initial Contact: Send a brief letter; if interested, a full proposal will be requested.
Application Requirements: Include a description of organization, amount requested, purpose of funds sought, budget and recently audited financial statement, proof of tax-exempt status, and list of board of directors.
Deadlines: None.
Decision Notification: Final notification within two to three months following board meetings, held in March, June, September, and December.

Restrictions

Foundation generally will not support individuals, operating funds, projects of a religious or political nature, or organizations that receive funding from the United Way.

Corporate Officials

Maryanne Hynes: director PRIM CORP EMPL director: Sundstrand Corp.
Bob Jenkins: director PRIM CORP EMPL director: Sundstrand Corp.
Don R. O'Hare: director B Joliet, IL 1922. ED University of Minnesota BS (1943). PRIM CORP EMPL director: Sundstrand Corp. CORP AFFIL director: Marshall & Ilsley Corp.

Foundation Officials

James Gingrich: director
Marie Lynch: secretary
Don R. O'Hare: president, director (see above)
Kathryn L. Stokstad: treasurer
Pat Wynn: director

Grants Analysis

Disclosure Period: fiscal year ending October 31, 1998
Total Grants: $846,979*
Number of Grants: 106
Average Grant: $6,162*
Highest Grant: $200,000
Typical Range: $1,000 to $15,000
***Note:** Giving excludes matching gifts, United Way. Average grant figure excludes highest grant.

Recent Grants

Note: Grants derived from 1997 Form 990.

Arts & Humanities

17,000	New American Theater, Rockford, IL -- operating support

10,000 Artspace, Lima, OH -- operating support
8,000 United Performing Arts Fund, Milwaukee, WI -- operating support
5,500 Rockford Area Arts Council, Rockford, IL -- operating support
5,500 Rockford Symphony Orchestra, Rockford, IL -- operating support
5,500 Rockford Symphony Orchestra, Rockford, IL -- operating
5,000 Arvada Center for Arts and Humanities, Arvada, CO -- capital campaign
5,000 Lyric Opera, Dubuque, IA -- operating support
5,000 Marcus Center for Performing Arts, Milwaukee, WI -- operating support
3,000 Rockford Art Museum, Rockford, IL -- operating support
1,500 Michigan City Public Library, Michigan City, IN -- operating

Civic & Public Affairs

10,000 Opportunities Industrialization Center, Rockford, IL -- capital campaign
9,000 Esperanta Unida, Milwaukee, WI -- operating support
7,500 Northern Illinois Botanical Society, Rockford, IL -- operating support
5,000 Phantiva Regiment, Rockford, IL -- operating support
4,000 Grand Junction Air Show, Grand Junction, CO -- operating support
3,000 Mendelssohn Club, Rockford, IL -- operating
3,000 Mendelssohn Club, Rockford, IL -- operating
1,500 Habitat for Humanity, Rockford, IL -- operating

Education

40,000 Rockford College, Rockford, IL -- operating support
40,000 Rockford College, Rockford, IL -- capital
17,000 Junior Achievement Rock River Valley, Rockford, IL -- operating support
10,000 Illinois Mathematics and Science Academy, Aurora, IL -- operating support
8,400 YMCA Black Achievers, Milwaukee, WI -- operating support
6,100 Junior Achievement, Michigan City, IN -- operating support
5,000 Illinois Mathematics and Science Academy, IL
5,000 Lehigh University Milton Roy Sheehan Scholarship, Bethlehem, PA -- operating
5,000 Milwaukee Area Technical College, Milwaukee, WI -- operating support
5,000 Tinker Swiss College, Rockford, IL -- operating support
5,000 Tinker Swiss College, Rockford, IL -- capital
4,000 Medical College of Wisconsin, Milwaukee, WI -- operating support
1,000 Stateline Literacy Council, Rockford, IL -- operating

Health

68,000 Crusader Clinic, Rockford, IL -- capital campaign
15,000 Northern Illinois AIDS Resource Center, Rockford, IL -- operating support
15,000 Northern Illinois Hospice, Rockford, IL -- capital campaign
10,000 American Red Cross Rock River Chapter, Rockford, IL -- operating
9,000 Children's Hospital of Wisconsin, Milwaukee, WI -- capital campaign
7,500 American Red Cross Rock River Chapter, Rockford, IL -- operation support
2,000 Visiting Nurses Association, Michigan City, IN -- operating
1,000 Research Foundation, Michigan City, IN -- operating

Religion

20,000 Rockford Rescue Mission, Rockford, IL -- operating support
20,000 St. Elizabeth Community Center, Rockford, IL -- operations support

Science

17,000 Burpee Museum of Natural History, Rockford, IL -- capital campaign
5,000 Discovery Center, Rockford, IL -- capital campaign
5,000 Discovery Center, Rockford, IL -- capital

Social Services

203,525 United Way Rock River Valley, Rockford, IL -- operating support
42,200 United Way Michigan City, Michigan City, IN -- operating support
41,000 United Way, Milwaukee, WI -- operating support
26,500 YMCA Partners with Youth, Milwaukee, WI -- operating support
25,000 United Way San Diego County, San Diego, CA -- operating support
20,000 YMCA, Rockford, IL -- capital fund drive
18,000 Mile High United Way, Denver, CO -- operating support
17,500 United Way, Michigan City, IN -- operating
10,000 Family Advocate, Rockford, IL -- operating support
10,000 Harlem Community Center, Loves Park, IL -- operating support
8,000 Girl Scouts of America Rock River Valley, Rockford, IL -- capital campaign
8,000 Rockford Children's Home, Rockford, IL -- capital
6,000 United Way Chad County, San Diego, CA -- operating
5,500 United Way, York, NE -- operating support
5,000 Center for Sight and Hearing Impaired, Rockford, IL -- operating support
5,000 United Way Auburn and Lee County, Auburn, AL -- operating support
5,000 United Way Bucks County, Ivyland, PA -- operating support
5,000 United Way Mesa County, Grand Junction, CO -- operating support
5,000 YMCA, Milwaukee, WI -- operating support
5,000 YWCA, Rockford, IL -- capital campaign
4,000 Rocvale Children's Home, Rockford, IL -- capital campaign

JOHN HANCOCK FINANCIAL SERVICES

Company Contact

Boston, MA
Web: http://www.jhancock.com

Company Description

Former Name: John Hancock Mutual Life (2000).
Revenue: US$8,911,700,000
Employees: 19,000
Fortune Rank: 233, per FORTUNE Magazine's list of 500 Largest U.S. Corporations (1999).
FF 233
SIC(s): 6311 Life Insurance.

Operating Locations

Operates throughout the USA.

Nonmonetary Support

Type: Donated Products; In-kind Services; Loaned Employees; Loaned Executives
Note: Co. provides nonmonetary support in the form of meeting space, printing and graphic services, public relations assistance, photography, special events planning.

Corporate Sponsorship

Type: Sports events; Other
Note: Sponsors Special Olympics and U.S. Olympics teams. Also includes fundraising dinners.

Giving Contact

Carol Bolling, 2nd Vice President of Community Relations
John Hancock Mutual Life Insurance Co.
Box 111, T-58
Boston, MA 02117
Phone: (617)572-0451
Fax: (617)572-6290
Email: cbolling@jhancock.com

Description

Organization Type: Corporate Giving Program
Giving Locations: MA: Boston
Grant Types: Capital, Employee Matching Gifts, General Support, Project.
Note: Employee matching gift ratio: 1 to 1 for non-educational nonprofits and 0.5 to 1 for education institutions program allows employees to give to non-educational nonprofits through payroll deductions and have these gifts matched.

Giving Philosophy

'No company exists in a vacuum. Rather, it exists in, and draws its employees from, a number of communities with a variety of interests, problems and opportunities. John Hancock believes that supporting organizations which play a vital role in the social health of the community is a sound investment that pays tremendous human and business dividends. For this reason, the John Hancock companies have provided financial support to hundreds of local institutions for many years.' *A Continuing Commitment* - Contributions of the John Hancock Mutual Life Insurance Company

'As a matter of principle, John Hancock pledges to: allocate social, educational and charitable contributions to improve existing economic conditions and address social needs; encourage volunteerism and contribute in-kind resources for programs that support local communities; motivate employees and retirees to make financial contributions to foster education, health, cultural and community programs; assist in supporting and attracting high-quality sporting events that generate tourism revenue, create and maintain local jobs, and increase the reputation of Boston as a world-class city.' *John Hancock Community Involvement Philosophy*

Financial Summary

Total Giving: $3,700,000 (1999 approx); $3,600,000 (1998 approx); $3,500,000 (1997 approx). Note: Contributes through corporate direct giving program only. Giving includes nonmonetary support.
Giving Analysis: Giving for 1998 includes: corporate direct giving (approx $3,600,000)

Typical Recipients

Arts & Humanities: Arts Appreciation, Arts Associations & Councils, Arts Centers, Arts Institutes, Community Arts, Dance, Ethnic & Folk Arts, Historic Preservation, Libraries, Museums/Galleries, Music, Opera, Performing Arts, Public Broadcasting, Theater
Civic & Public Affairs: Business/Free Enterprise, Civil Rights, Economic Development, Economic Policy, Employment/Job Training, Law & Justice, Professional & Trade Associations, Public Policy, Urban & Community Affairs, Women's Affairs
Education: Business Education, Continuing Education, Economic Education, Education Funds, Medical Education, Minority Education, Science/Mathematics Education, Special Education

Environment: Environment-General
Health: Health Policy/Cost Containment, Hospitals, Medical Research, Nutrition, Public Health, Single-Disease Health Associations
Social Services: Child Welfare, Community Centers, Community Service Organizations, Counseling, Delinquency & Criminal Rehabilitation, Family Services, Food/Clothing Distribution, Homes, People with Disabilities, Recreation & Athletics, Senior Services, Shelters/Homelessness, Substance Abuse, United Funds/ United Ways, Volunteer Services, Youth Organizations

Contributions Analysis

Giving Priorities: United funds, civic interests, education, and health.
Arts & Humanities: 10% to 15%. In general, supports arts programs that have special initatives for inner-city residents. Music, dance, community arts, and performing arts are of interest.
Civic & Public Affairs: 50% to 55%. Primarily supports local United Ways in operating locations. Priority is given to programs that support affordable housing in Boston's neighborhoods.
Also sponsors economic education and economic opportunity support, minority/disadvantaged employment, motivational/self-help instruction, community service organizations, housing, emergency shelters, family services, youth organizations, volunteer services, economic development, job training, violence prevention, improving race relations, urban and community affairs, and women's affairs in the Boston, MA, area.
Education: 20%. Supports public schools through partnerships in Boston, MA. Emphasizes career/vocational training, and programs for the advancement of women, minorities, and the handicapped.
Health: 10% to 15%. Supports local hospitals, neighborhood health centers, and emergency services.
Note: Contributions analysis provided by the company.

Application Procedures

Initial Contact: brief letter or proposal
Application Requirements: objectives, services, program activities, and accomplishments of organization; purpose for which funds are sought; proof of tax-exempt status; names and affiliations of officers, trustees, and members of the board of directors; population served and their socioeconomic composition; annual budget for the project or program to be assisted agency budget audited financial statements, list of current and potential funds, and for program evaluation.
Deadlines: None.
Evaluative Criteria: provides innovative solutions to significant social needs; stimulates additional giving by other institutions and individuals.
Notes: All organizations receiving company grants are requested to submit periodic reports on how funds are used. All continuing grants are reviewed at least once in three years.

Restrictions

Does not support fraternal or political organizations, religious organizations for sectarian purposes, individuals, goodwill advertising, scholarships, conferences, or trips.

Corporate Officials

Stephen Lee Brown: chairman, chief executive officer, director B Providence, RI 1937. ED Middlebury College BA (1958). PRIM CORP EMPL chairman, chief executive officer, director: John Hancock Mutual Life Insurance Co. CORP AFFIL director: John Hancock Subsidiaries Inc.; director: Federal Reserve Bank Boston. NONPR AFFIL fellow: Society Actuaries; trustee: Wang Center Performing Arts; director: Jobs Massachusetts; director: Life Insurance Association America; member: Boston Life Underwriters Association; director: Committee for Economic Development; chairman: Boston Coordinating Committee; member: American Academy of Actuaries; member: American Council Life Insurance; member: Actuaries Club Boston. CLUB AFFIL Commercial Club; Algonquin Club.
David F. D'Alessandro: president, chief operating officer

Giving Program Officials

Carol Bolling: 2nd vice president, community relations

Grants Analysis

Disclosure Period: calendar year ending 1998
Total Grants: $3,600,000
Number of Grants: 2,200
Average Grant: $10,000
Typical Range: $5,000 to $20,000
Note: Grants analysis provided by the company.

M.A. HANNA CO.

Company Contact

Cleveland, OH
Web: http://www.mahanna.com

Company Description

Employees: 7,130 (1999)
SIC(s): 2821 Plastics Materials & Resins.

Nonmonetary Support

Note: Nonmonetary support is offered.

M.A. Hanna Co. Foundation

Giving Contact

John S. Pyke, Jr., Vice President, General Counsel & Secretary
M.A. Hanna Co.
200 Public Square, Ste. 36-5000
Cleveland, OH 44114-2304
Phone: (216)589-4000
Fax: (216)589-4034

Description

EIN: 237223605
Organization Type: Corporate Foundation
Giving Locations: headquarters and operating communities.
Grant Types: Employee Matching Gifts, General Support.

Financial Summary

Total Giving: $583,864 (1998); $455,930 (1997); $599,829 (1996). Note: Contributes through foundation only.
Giving Analysis: Giving for 1996 includes: foundation grants to United Way ($81,500); 1997: foundation grants to United Way ($79,000); 1998: foundation grants to United Way ($75,000)
Assets: $2,450 (1996); $20,373 (1995); $361,583 (1994)
Gifts Received: $566,500 (1998); $384,000 (1997); $667,500 (1996). Note: Contributions are received from the M.A. Hanna Co.

Typical Recipients

Arts & Humanities: Arts Centers, Arts Festivals, Arts Institutes, Ballet, Historic Preservation, History & Archaeology, Museums/Galleries, Music, Opera, Performing Arts, Public Broadcasting, Theater
Civic & Public Affairs: African American Affairs, Community Foundations, Economic Development, Employment/Job Training, Civic & Public Affairs-General, Law & Justice, Municipalities/Towns, Parades/ Festivals, Professional & Trade Associations, Safety, Urban & Community Affairs, Zoos/Aquariums
Education: Arts/Humanities Education, Business Education, Colleges & Universities, Community & Junior Colleges, Economic Education, Education Funds, Education Reform, Leadership Training, Legal Education, Minority Education, Private Education (Precollege), Science/Mathematics Education, Secondary Education (Private), Student Aid
Environment: Environment-General, Resource Conservation
Health: Alzheimers Disease, Cancer, Clinics/Medical Centers, Emergency/Ambulance Services, Eyes/ Blindness, Heart, Hospitals
Religion: Religious Organizations, Religious Welfare
Science: Science Museums, Scientific Centers & Institutes
Social Services: At-Risk Youth, Camps, Child Welfare, Community Centers, Community Service Organizations, Crime Prevention, Family Services, Food/ Clothing Distribution, People with Disabilities, Recreation & Athletics, Senior Services, Social Services-General, Substance Abuse, United Funds/United Ways, YMCA/YWCA/YMHA/YWHA, Youth Organizations

Contributions Analysis

Arts & Humanities: 25%. Supports cultural and fine arts organizations in the Cleveland area, including music and art institutes, and theater. Major recipients include the Musical Arts Association of the Cleveland Orchestra and the Cleveland Institute of Music.
Civic & Public Affairs: 2%. Priorities include job training, minority assistance, the Cleveland Zoological Society, and a scenic railroad.
Education: 15%. Funding supports colleges and universities, educational funds, and minority education.
Health: 19%. Supports American Cancer Society and health services.
Science: 19%. Supports the Great Lakes Science Center and Inventure Place.
Social Services: 18%. Primarily supports youth organizations, child welfare services, and the United Way.
Note: Total contributionss in 1998.

Application Procedures

Initial Contact: Send a brief letter of inquiry.
Application Requirements: Letter must include signature of officer of the organization, a description of organization, amount requested, purpose of funds sought, and proof of tax-exempt status.
Deadlines: None.
Notes: Recipient organizations must be listed in the IRS Cumulative List of Organizations.

Restrictions

Company does not support individuals, religious organizations for sectarian purposes, or political or lobbying groups.

Corporate Officials

Douglas J. McGregor: president, chief operating officer, director B Detroit, MI 1941. ED University of Michigan (1964); Eastern Michigan University (1970). PRIM CORP EMPL president, chief operating officer, director: M.A. Hanna Co. CORP AFFIL director: KeyCorp; president, chief executive officer, director: Vulcan Materials Co.
John Secrest Pyke, Jr.: vice president, secretary, general counsel B Lakewood, OH 1938. ED Haverford College (1956-1958); Columbia College BA (1960); Columbia College School Graduate Faculties (1960-1961); Columbia University School of Law JD (1964). PRIM CORP EMPL vice president, secretary, general counsel: M.A. Hanna Co. NONPR AFFIL member: Association Bar New York City; trustee: Case Western Reserve University; member: American Corporate Counsel Association; member: American Society

of Corporate Secretaries; member: American Bar Association. CLUB AFFIL Union Club; Cleveland Yacht Club; Clifton Club.
Martin Dean Walker: chairman, chief executive officer, director B Indianapolis, IN 1932. ED General Motors Institute BS (1954); Michigan State University MBA (1970). PRIM CORP EMPL chairman, chief executive officer, director: M.A. Hanna Co. CORP AFFIL director: Textron Inc.; director: Timken Co.; director: Reynolds & Reynolds Co.; director: Meritor Automotive Inc.; principal: Morwal Investments; director: Lexmark International Inc.; director: Comerica Inc.; director: Goodyear Tire & Rubber Co.; director: Comerica Bank; chairman: Chase Elastomer Midwest; vice president: Collins International Service Co.

Foundation Officials

Ped Wesley Phillips: vice president B Washington, PA 1943. ED Pennsylvania State University BS (1967); Golden Gate University MBA (1978). PRIM CORP EMPL vice president: Cadillac Plastic Group Inc.
John Secrest Pyke, Jr.: president, trustee (see above)
Frank G. Titas: secretary B 1949. PRIM CORP EMPL assistant general counsel: M.A. Hanna Co.

Grants Analysis

Disclosure Period: calendar year ending 1998
Total Grants: $508,864*
Number of Grants: 119
Average Grant: $4,276
Highest Grant: $100,000
Typical Range: $50 to $250 and $1000 to $5,000
*Note: Giving excludes United Way.

Recent Grants

Note: Grants derived from 1998 Form 990.

Arts & Humanities
75,000 Musical Arts Association, Cleveland, OH
35,000 Playhouse Square Foundation, Cleveland, OH
20,000 Cleveland Institute of Music, Cleveland, OH
5,000 The Cleveland Ballet, Cleveland, OH
5,000 The Old Stone Historical Preservation Society, Cleveland, OH
1,500 The Cleveland Museum of Art, Cleveland, OH
1,500 Cleveland Opera, Cleveland, OH
1,000 Cleveland Playhouse, Cleveland, OH

Civic & Public Affairs
2,000 Cuyahoga Valley Line Railroad, Cuyahoga Falls, OH
2,000 NAACP, Cleveland, OH
1,500 Urban League of Greater Cleveland, Cleveland, OH
1,200 Cleveland Zoological Society, Cleveland, OH
1,000 Cleveland Bar Foundation, Cleveland, OH
1,000 Law Enforcement foundation, Columbu, OH

Education
46,000 Kent State University, Kent, OH
5,000 Gordon College, Wenham, MA
5,000 The Ohio Foundation of Independent Colleges, Columbus, OH
3,625 University of Michigan, Detroit, MT
2,000 Cleveland Scholarship, Cleveland, OH
2,000 David N. Myers College, Cleveland, OH
2,000 Furman University, Greenville, NC
2,000 Santa Monica College Foundation, Santa Monica, CA
2,000 St Paul's School, Boston, MA
2,000 United Negro College Fund, Cleveland, OH
1,992 University of Tennessee, Memphis, TN
1,925 Western Reserve Academy, Cleveland, OH
1,700 The Cooper Union, New York, NY
1,500 Governor Dummer Academy, Worcester, MA
1,500 Hawken School, Cleveland, OH
1,500 Ohio University Foundation, Athens, OH
1,200 The King's Christian School, Cleveland, OH
1,000 Eastern Nazarene College, Wollaston, MA
1,000 Mount Vernon Nazarene College, Mount Vernon, OH

Environment
2,500 Clean-Land Ohio, Cleveland, OH

Health
100,000 American Cancer Society, Cleveland, OH
7,000 Alzheimer's Association, Cleveland, OH
1,000 Cleveland Sight Center, Cleveland, OH
1,000 Free Clinic of Greater Cleveland, Cleveland, OH

Religion
3,000 Fairview/Lutheran Foundation, Cleveland, OH
1,300 Young Life, Boston, MA
1,200 The Salvation Army, Cleveland, OH

Science
100,000 Great Lakes Science Center, Cleveland, OH
7,500 Inventure Place, Cleveland, OH

Social Services
75,000 United Way Services, Cleveland, OH
15,000 YMCA of Greater Cleveland, Cleveland, OH
5,300 Boys Hope, Cleveland, OH
3,000 The Benjamin Rose Institute, Cleveland, OH
3,000 Center for Families & Children, Cleveland, OH
3,000 Hunger Network of Greater Cleveland, Cleveland, OH
1,500 Saucon Valley Community Center, Hellertown, PA

HANNAFORD BROTHERS CO.

Company Contact

Scarborough, ME
Web: http://www.hannaford.com

Company Description

Revenue: US$3,323,600,000
Employees: 22,000
Fortune Rank: 445, per FORTUNE Magazine's list of 500 Largest U.S. Corporations (1999).
FF 445
SIC(s): 5411 Grocery Stores, 5912 Drug Stores & Proprietary Stores.
Parent Company: Sobey Inc., 115 King St., Stellarton, NS, Canada

Operating Locations

MA: Lowell; ME: Hannaford Brothers Co., Bangor, Portland; NC: Hannaford Brothers Co., Raleigh; NH: Manchester; NY: Albany; VA: Norfolk Richmond Virginia Beach; VT: Burlington

Nonmonetary Support

Type: Donated Products

Hannaford Charitable Foundation

Giving Contact

Donna Boyce, Secretary
Hannaford Charitable Foundation
PO Box 1000
Portland, ME 04104
Phone: (207)885-3834
Fax: (207)885-2859

Alternate Contact

Hannaford Scholarship Program
Scholarship Management Services, CSFA
PO Box 297
St. Peter, MN 56082
Phone: (507)931-1682
Note: For scholarship program information only.

Description

Founded: 1994
EIN: 010483892
Organization Type: Corporate Foundation
Giving Locations: headquarters and operating communities.
Grant Types: General Support, Scholarship.
Note: Scholarships are for employee children only.

Giving Philosophy

'Hannaford has long recognized that the company and our associates can play an important role in enhancing the quality of life in the communities in which we reside and do business. This philosophy has guided our charitable giving for many years. The Hannaford Charitable Foundation provides financial support for programs and organizations dedicated to improving the communities in which we operate and in which we live.'

Financial Summary

Total Giving: $931,501 (1998); $949,600 (1996); $682,434 (1995). Note: Contributes through corporate direct giving program and foundation. Giving includes foundation.
Giving Analysis: Giving for 1998 includes: foundation ($665,801); foundation grants to United Way ($265,700)
Assets: $1,682,820 (1998); $1,133,835 (1996); $1,250,063 (1995)
Gifts Received: $1,036,000 (1998); $785,000 (1996); $621,000 (1995). Note: Contributions are received from Hannaford Brothers Co.

Typical Recipients

Arts & Humanities: Arts Associations & Councils, Arts Centers, Arts Institutes, History & Archaeology, Libraries, Museums/Galleries, Music, Opera, Performing Arts, Theater
Civic & Public Affairs: Chambers of Commerce, Civic & Public Affairs-General, Nonprofit Management, Parades/Festivals, Urban & Community Affairs, Zoos/Aquariums
Education: Arts/Humanities Education, Business Education, Colleges & Universities, Environmental Education, Education-General, Leadership Training, Special Education, Student Aid
Environment: Environment-General, Resource Conservation
Health: AIDS/HIV, Alzheimers Disease, Cancer, Children's Health/Hospitals, Clinics/Medical Centers, Emergency/Ambulance Services, Health Organizations, Heart, Hospices, Hospitals, Hospitals (University Affiliated), Medical Research, Research/Studies Institutes
Religion: Religious Welfare
Science: Scientific Labs

Social Services: Animal Protection, Big Brother/Big Sister, Camps, Child Welfare, Day Care, Family Services, Food/Clothing Distribution, Scouts, Senior Services, Social Services-General, United Funds/United Ways, YMCA/YWCA/YMHA/YWHA, Youth Organizations

Contributions Analysis

Giving Priorities: Supports the arts, education, health concerns, and social programs including United Way.
Arts & Humanities: 9%. Funds support museums, libraries, art associations, and performing arts.
Education: 39%. Supports college education that focuses on food marketing, pharmacist, or other programs that meet Hannaford's needs for associates. Request for funding for tax-supported primary and secondary schools are not encouraged.
Health: 10%. Foundation will consider hospital building or capital funds, but not operating funds. Supports medical centers, hospice, and the American Red Cross.
Social Services: 42%. Primarily funds United Way or United Way supported agencies. Limited support to family services and youth organizations.
Note: Total contributions made in 1998.

Application Procedures

Initial Contact: submit a one- to two-page letter.
Application Requirements: Include name, address, and telephone number of organization; contact person and title; amount requested; population and geographic area served; a two- or three-sentence mission statement for your organization, with a brief description of its background; a two- or three-sentence description of the specific project or program for which you are seeking funding; a copy of your organization's tax-exemption letter indicating both Section 501(c)(3) and 509(a) status, and most recent Form 990 return, as well as a letter attesting that tax-exempt status is current; a list of current and potential funding sources; and a recent annual statement of revenues and expenses.
Deadlines: None.
Evaluative Criteria: Should have active and responsible boards of trustees, exhibit ethical publicity methods and solicitation of funds, provide for an appropriate audit to reveal income disbursements in reasonable detail, demonstrate long-term financial viability; preference given to programs that involve Hannaford associates and are located in Hannaford's marketing territory.
Notes: A member of the foundation may contact organization to request additional information.

Restrictions

The foundation will not contribute to institutions that, by virtue of their charters, programs, or policies, are open to a relatively small or restricted segment of the public; operations of veterans, fraternal, or religious organizations, except those that make their services fully available to the community on a nonsectarian basis; individuals; tax-supported institutions; or organizations that are not qualified as tax-exempt under IRS Section 501(c)(3).
The foundation will not give sales discounts or purchase advertisements in publications or programs.

Additional Information

Apart from its charitable foundation, Hannaford contributes to the community in many ways. Each Hannaford Store makes its own contributions to its local community through fundraising drives and sponsorships, as well as gift certificates and cash donations. All stores, distribution centers, and offices participate in the United Way's annual fund drive. Hannaford's promotions department sponsors nonprofit youth athletic leagues, school events, performing arts organizations, civic events, and environmental and health organizations. The company also is a major donor to local food banks, shelters, and soup kitchens.
Sobey Inc. has a 26% investment in Hannaford Brothers.
Publications: Guidelines Sheet

Corporate Officials

Hugh G. Farrington: president, chief executive officer, director B 1945. ED Dartmouth College BA (1967); University of New Hampshire MA (1968). PRIM CORP EMPL president, chief executive officer, director: Hannaford Brothers Co. CORP AFFIL president: Progressive Distributors Inc.; president: Shop'n Save Massachusetts Inc.; president: Boney Wilson Sons Inc.; president: Martins Foods of South Burlington Inc.

Giving Program Officials

Paul A. Fritzson: president, director B 1953. PRIM CORP EMPL executive vice president strategic development: Hannaford Brothers Co. CORP AFFIL director: Hannaford Trucking Co.

Foundation Officials

Richard A. Anicetti: director B 1957. PRIM CORP EMPL executive vice president: Hannaford Brothers Co.
Garrett D. Bowne, IV: treasurer PRIM CORP EMPL vice president, treasurer, controller: Hannaford Brothers Co. CORP AFFIL treasurer: Progressive Distributor Inc.; treasurer: Shop'n Save Massachusetts Inc.; treasurer: Martin's Food South Burlington Inc.; treasurer: Boney Wilson Sons Inc.; treasurer: Hannaford Trucking Co.
Donna J. Boyce: secretary
Paul A. Fritzson: president, director (see above)
Ronald C. Hodge: director B 1947. PRIM CORP EMPL executive vice president sales northeast operation: Hannaford Brothers Co. CORP AFFIL director: Hannaford Trucking Co.
Lisa R. Miller: director

Grants Analysis

Disclosure Period: calendar year ending 1998
Total Grants: $665,801*
Number of Grants: 66
Average Grant: $10,088
Highest Grant: $294,500
Typical Range: $2,000 to $12,000
***Note:** Giving excludes United Way.

Recent Grants

Note: Grants derived from 1998 Form 990.

Arts & Humanities

10,000	Albany Institute of History & Art, Albany, NY
10,000	Bangor Public Library, Bangor, ME
10,000	Portland Museum of Art, Portland, ME
7,500	Maine Humanities Council, Portland, ME
7,500	Portland Symphony--Magic of Christmas 1998, Portland, ME
5,000	Lewiston Public Library, Lewiston, ME
5,000	Lyric Theater Capital Campaign, Portland, ME
5,000	Portland Concert Association, Portland, ME
5,000	Skidompha Public Library Fund, Damariscotta, ME

Education

100,000	Citizens' Scholarship Foundation of America, Norway, ME
100,000	Citizens' Scholarship Foundation of America, Norway, ME
50,000	Bates College, Lewiston, ME
20,000	Colby College, Waterville, ME
10,000	Husson College, Bangor, ME
10,000	University of Albany, Albany, NY
5,000	Maine Coalition for Excellence in Education, Portland, ME

Health

30,000	Maine Medical Center, Portland, ME
10,000	American Red Cross, Richmond, VA
10,000	Jackson Laboratory, Bar Harbor, ME
7,500	Cancer Community Center, Portland, ME
6,250	Duke University--Children's Hospital, Durham, NC
5,000	The Community Hospice, Albany, NY
5,000	Northeast Health--Eddy Alzheimer's Center Campaign, Rockland, ME

Social Services

28,750	United Way of Greater Portland, Portland, ME
28,750	United Way of Greater Portland, Portland, ME
28,750	United Way of Greater Portland, Portland, ME
28,750	United Way of Greater Portland, Portland, ME
20,000	United Way of Eastern Maine, Bangor, ME
18,000	United Way of Northeastern New York, Albany, NY
15,000	Casco Bay Regional YMCA, Freeport, ME
13,333	Wilmington Family YMCA, Wilmington, NC
13,000	United Way of Kennebec Valley, Augusta, ME
12,000	United Way of York County, York, PA
10,000	Down East Family YMCA, Ellsworth, ME
10,000	Kennebec Girl Scout Council, South Portland, ME
10,000	United Way Services, Richmond, VA
10,000	YMCA of Greater Richmond, Richmond, VA
8,100	United Way of Greater Manchester, Manchester, NH
8,000	Cape Fear Area United Way, Wilmington, NC
8,000	Sweetser Children's Services, Saco, ME
7,050	Greater Seacoast United Way, Portsmouth, NH
6,100	United Way of Mid Coast Maine, Bath, ME
6,000	United Way of Mid Maine, Waterville, ME
5,800	Triangle United Way, Morrisville, NC
5,800	United Way of Androscoggin County, Lewiston, ME
5,400	Tri-County United Way, Queensbury, NY
5,000	Abnaki Girl Scout Council, Brewer, ME
5,000	Bangor-Brewer YMCA, Bangor, ME
5,000	Boothbay Region YMCA, Boothbay Harbor, ME
5,000	East End Children'sWorkshop, Portland, ME

HARCOURT GENERAL, INC.

Company Contact

Chestnut Hill, MA
Web: http://www.harcourtbrace.com

Company Description

Former Name: General Cinema Corp.
Revenue: US$4,235,300,000
Employees: 20,800
SIC(s): 2741 Miscellaneous Publishing, 5999 Miscellaneous Retail Stores Nec, 7389 Business Services Nec.

Nonmonetary Support

Type: Donated Products
Note: Company provides movie passes for raffles and auctions.

Harcourt General Charitable Foundation

Giving Contact

Kay M. Kilpatrick, Director of Corporate Giving
Harcourt General, Inc.
27 Boylston St.
Chestnut Hill, MA 02467
Phone: (617)232-8200
Fax: (617)731-2354

Description

Founded: 1990
EIN: 223026002
Organization Type: Corporate Foundation
Giving Locations: MA: Boston including metropolitan area
Grant Types: Capital, Challenge, Emergency, Employee Matching Gifts, Endowment, Fellowship, General Support, Multiyear/Continuing Support.
Note: Employee matching gift ratio: 2 to 1 from $25 to $2,000 per employee annually, for gifts to eligible educational, health, welfare, and cultural organizations.

Giving Philosophy

'Harcourt General has certain traditional strengths which we want to incorporate into the corporate giving program. One is its entrepreneurial spirit, its customary willingness to take measured risks and to innovate in the hope of achieving more significant results. Another is the priority we place on the involvement of our employees. The company takes pride in the activities and accomplishments of its employees. In turn, we want a corporate giving program of which they are proud, and which attracts their interest and enthusiasm. .. Our concern has been heightened in recent years because of the apparent sharp rise in the need for charitable funds throughout society. At the same time, because of Harcourt General's financial strength, we recognized that we could do more.'

Financial Summary

Total Giving: $2,290,390 (fiscal year ending October 31, 1996); $4,000,000 (fiscal 1995 approx); $1,474,305 (fiscal 1993). Note: Contributes through corporate direct giving program and foundation.
Giving Analysis: Giving for fiscal 1995 includes: corporate direct giving ($2,435,626); foundation ($1,546,374); nonmonetary support ($18,000); fiscal 1996: foundation ($2,290,390)
Assets: $35,617,999 (fiscal 1996); $32,112,590 (fiscal 1995); $28,771,877 (fiscal 1993)

Typical Recipients

Arts & Humanities: Arts Associations & Councils, Arts Centers, Ballet, Community Arts, Arts & Humanities-General, Historic Preservation, History & Archaeology, Libraries, Museums/Galleries, Music, Performing Arts, Theater
Civic & Public Affairs: African American Affairs, Business/Free Enterprise, Civil Rights, Economic Development, Economic Policy, Employment/Job Training, Ethnic Organizations, Civic & Public Affairs-General, Hispanic Affairs, Legal Aid, Municipalities/Towns, Philanthropic Organizations, Public Policy, Urban & Community Affairs, Zoos/Aquariums
Education: Business Education, Colleges & Universities, Continuing Education, Education Associations, Education Funds, Education Reform, Elementary Education (Public), Engineering/Technological Education, Education-General, Health & Physical Education, International Studies, Legal Education, Medical Education, Preschool Education, Public Education (Precollege), Special Education, Student Aid
Health: Cancer, Children's Health/Hospitals, Clinics/Medical Centers, Diabetes, Eyes/Blindness, Health Funds, Hospices, Hospitals, Hospitals (University Affiliated), Medical Research, Prenatal Health Issues, Research/Studies Institutes
Religion: Jewish Causes
Science: Science Museums, Scientific Centers & Institutes
Social Services: At-Risk Youth, Big Brother/Big Sister, Child Welfare, Community Service Organizations, Counseling, Crime Prevention, Domestic Violence, Family Services, People with Disabilities, Scouts, Shelters/Homelessness, Social Services-General, Volunteer Services, YMCA/YWCA/YMHA/YWHA, Youth Organizations

Application Procedures

Initial Contact: Send a brief letter, no more than three pages in length.
Application Requirements: Include an organizational history; project's goals and objectives, its impact, and its relation to Harcourt General's and applicant's priorities; amount requested; plans for evaluating project and for maintaining it after grant period; detailed operating budget, including list of other sources of funds; names and qualifications of project's personnel; audited financial statements for the most recent two years; breakdown of current financial support (i.e. corporate, foundation, government, etc.); list of major donors and board members; most recent tax return; proof of tax-exempt status.
Deadlines: January 1, April 1, July 1, and October 1; board meets in January, April, July and October.

Restrictions

Does not support sectarian religious activities, political or lobbying activities, projects usually supported by the general public, recent grantees, organizations whose applications have been denied in the past year, individuals, operating budgets, deficits, film, video, or television projects, or organizations where Harcourt General may become the predominant source of support.

Corporate Officials

John Rowland Cook: senior vice president, chief financial officerpresident B New York, NY 1941. ED Rutgers University BA (1963); Harvard University MBA (1969). PRIM CORP EMPL senior vice president, chief financial officer: Harcourt General, Inc.
Eric P. Geller: senior vice president, general counsel, secretary B 1947. ED Washington University BA (1969); Harvard University JD (1972). PRIM CORP EMPL senior vice president, general counsel, secretary: General Cinema Corp. CORP AFFIL corporate secretary: Neiman Marcus; senior vice president, general counsel: Harcourt General Inc. NONPR AFFIL member: Massachusetts Bar Association.
Richard Alan Smith: chairman, director, chief executive officer B Boston, MA 1924. ED Harvard University BS (1946). PRIM CORP EMPL chairman, director, chief executive officer: Harcourt General, Inc. CORP AFFIL chairman: GC Co. Inc.; chairman, chief executive officer: Neiman Marcus Group Inc.
Robert A. Smith: co-chief executive officer, director, president B 1959. ED Harvard University AB (1981); Harvard University MBA (1987). PRIM CORP EMPL co-chief executive officer, director, president: Harcourt General, Inc. ADD CORP EMPL co-chief executive officer: Harcourt Inc. CORP AFFIL chairman, chief executive officer group vice president: Neiman Marcus Group Inc.

Foundation Officials

John Rowland Cook: trustee (see above)
Eric P. Geller: trustee (see above)
Kay M. Kilpatrick: director of corporate giving PRIM CORP EMPL contributions administrator: Harcourt General, Inc.
Brian J. Knez: trustee B 1957. ED Arizona State University (1979); Boston College (1984). PRIM CORP EMPL president, co-chief executive officer, director: Harcourt General, Inc. ADD CORP EMPL chief executive officer: Harcourt Inc.; president, chief executive officer, director: Harcourt Brace & Co.
Robert A. Smith: trustee (see above)

Grants Analysis

Disclosure Period: fiscal year ending October 31, 1996
Total Grants: $2,290,390
Number of Grants: 105
Average Grant: $15,102*
Highest Grant: $250,000
Typical Range: $1,000 to $20,000
***Note:** Average grants excludes three highest grants ($750,000).

Recent Grants

Note: Grants derived from 1997 Form 990.

Arts & Humanities

25,000	Facing History and Ourselves, Boston, MA
20,000	Wang Center for Performing Arts, Boston, MA
18,000	Boston Symphony Orchestra
7,500	The Huntington, Theatre Co., Boston, MA
5,000	Boston Ballet, Boston, MA
3,000	Handel & Haydn, Boston, MA
3,000	New England Conservatory, Boston, MA

Civic & Public Affairs

125,000	City Year, Boston, MA
100,000	City Year, Boston, MA
25,000	AGM Summer Fund, Boston, MA
25,000	The Horizons Initiative, Boston, MA
25,000	Voices of Love & Freedom
8,000	Mass Taxpayers Assoc., Boston, MA
4,000	Boston Private Industry Council, Boston, MA
2,500	Associated Grantmakers of Mass., Boston, MA
2,500	N. E. Legal Foundation, Boston, MA
2,500	New England Aquarium, Boston, MA

Education

55,284	Boston Educational Development Foundation, Boston, MA
50,000	Boston Educational Development Foundation, Boston, MA
50,000	Boston Educational Development Foundation, Boston, MA
50,000	Boston Educational Development Foundation, Boston, MA
50,000	Brandeis University, Boston, MA
50,000	Harvard Medical School, Boston, MA
50,000	Harvard University, Boston, MA
50,000	Harvard University, Boston, MA
50,000	Jumpstart, Boston, MA
40,425	Boston Educational Development Foundation, Boston, MA
35,000	Boston Plan for Excellence - Annenberg, Boston, MA
25,000	Fletch School of Law & Diplomacy
22,650	Boston Educational Development Foundation, Boston, MA
15,000	Harvard Univ. Grad. School of Bus. Admin., Boston, MA
10,000	Adopt A School of Beaufort County
9,000	University of Connecticut, Storrs, CT
7,000	New England Colleges Fund, Boston, MA
2,500	Inner City Scholarship Fund, Boston, MA
2,500	Northeastern University, Boston, MA

Health

125,000	The Medical Foundation, Boston, MA
50,000	Boston Biomedical Research Institute, Boston, MA
50,000	Boston Medical Center, Boston, MA
50,000	Mass. General Hospital, Boston, MA
50,000	University of Mass. Medical Center, Amherst, MA

25,000	Dana Farber Cancer Institute, Boston, MA
20,000	United Cerebrial Palsy Research & Education Found, Washington, DC
2,500	Beth Isreal Deaconess Medical Center, Boston, MA
2,500	Perkins School for the Blind, Providence, RI

Science

250,000	Orlando Science Center, Orlando, FL
2,500	Museum of Science, Boston, MA

Social Services

25,000	Gang Peace, Boston, MA
5,550	Junior Achievement of Eastern Mass., Boston, MA
4,000	Big Brothers Association of Greater Boston, Boston, MA
4,000	Big Sister Assoc. of Greater Boston, Boston, MA
4,000	Boy Scouts of America, Boston Minuteman Council

JOHN H. HARLAND CO.

Company Contact

Atlanta, GA
Web: http://www.harland.net

Company Description

Revenue: US$702,500,000 (1999)
Employees: 5,393 (1999)
SIC(s): 2752 Commercial Printing--Lithographic.

Piedmont Charitable Foundation

Giving Contact

J. William Robinson, President
Piedmont Charitable Foundation
7 Piedmont Center, Suite 100
Atlanta, GA 30305
Phone: (404)816-5205
Fax: (404)816-3537

Description

Founded: 1957
EIN: 586035073
Organization Type: Corporate Foundation
Giving Locations: GA
Grant Types: General Support.

Financial Summary

Total Giving: $229,300 (1998); $283,600 (1997); $181,344 (1996)
Assets: $6,584,278 (1998); $5,780,743 (1997); $4,869,345 (1996)
Gifts Received: $145,000 (1991); $143,000 (1990); $78,000 (1989)

Typical Recipients

Arts & Humanities: Arts Centers, Historic Preservation, History & Archaeology, Museums/Galleries, Theater
Civic & Public Affairs: Botanical Gardens/Parks, Business/Free Enterprise, Civic & Public Affairs-General, Urban & Community Affairs
Education: Colleges & Universities, Continuing Education, Education Funds, Engineering/Technological Education, Leadership Training, Literacy, Private Education (Precollege)
Environment: Forestry, Resource Conservation
Health: Cancer, Clinics/Medical Centers, Geriatric Health, Hospitals, Single-Disease Health Associations
International: International Organizations
Religion: Churches, Religious Organizations, Religious Welfare
Social Services: Community Service Organizations, Homes, United Funds/United Ways, Youth Organizations

Contributions Analysis

Giving Priorities: Education is the major priority; social services health, and religious groups also receive support. The arts and civic organizations are lesser interests.
Arts & Humanities: 8%. Historic preservation and art centers are funded.
Education: 73%. Supports higher education, literacy, and educational enrichment.
Religion: 12%. Funds religious welfare.
Social Services: 7%. Supports services for youth.
Note: Total contributions in 1998.

Application Procedures

Initial Contact: Send a letter, including nature, backup material, and tax identification numbers of organization.
Deadlines: None.

Corporate Officials

William Michael Dollar: vice president, treasurer, chief financial officer B Lanett, AL 1948. ED Auburn University BS (1970). PRIM CORP EMPL vice president, treasurer, chief financial officer: John H. Harland Co. ADD CORP EMPL treasurer: Harland Dataprint. CORP AFFIL treasurer, chief financial officer, director: Scantron Corp.

Foundation Officials

Margaret R. Buker: vice president
J. William Robinson: president, director B 1917. ED University of Alabama.
John W. Robinson, IV: vice president
R. Lee Robinson: vice president
Sue S. Shore: secretary, treasurer

Grants Analysis

Disclosure Period: calendar year ending 1998
Total Grants: $229,300
Number of Grants: 20
Average Grant: $8,911*
Highest Grant: $60,000
Typical Range: $500 to $20,000
***Note:** Average grant figure excludes highest grant.

Recent Grants

Note: Grants derived from 1997 Form 990.

Arts & Humanities

5,000	Woodruff Arts Center, Atlanta, GA
2,500	Historic Oakland Foundation, Atlanta, GA
1,000	Custer Battlefield Preservation Committee, Hardin, MT

Civic & Public Affairs

12,500	Brookgreen Gardens, Murrells Inlet, SC
5,000	Georgia Business Forum, Atlanta, GA

Education

75,000	Young Harris College, Young Harris, GA
50,000	Emory University, Atlanta, GA
25,000	Schenck School, Atlanta, GA
10,000	Georgia Tech Alexander Tharpe Fund, Atlanta, GA
1,000	Robert H. Hull Leadership Development Fund, Atlanta, GA
500	Literacy Action, Atlanta, GA
300	Georgia Student Educational Fund, Athens, GA

Environment

10,000	Georgia Department of Resources, Covington, GA
10,000	Wesley Woods Foundation, Atlanta, GA

Health

10,000	American Cancer Society, Atlanta, GA
10,000	DeKalb Medical Center Foundation, Decatur, GA

International

5,000	International Teams, Prospect Heights, IL

Religion

10,000	Atlanta Union Mission, Atlanta, GA
5,000	Our Lady of Perpetual Help Home, Atlanta, GA
5,000	Salvation Army, Atlanta, GA

Social Services

30,000	Boys and Girls Clubs, Atlanta, GA
500	Rotary Foundation, Atlanta, GA
300	Youth Service Fund, Atlanta, GA

HARLEY-DAVIDSON CO.

Company Contact

Milwaukee, WI
Web: http://www.harley_davidson.com

Company Description

SIC(s): 2389 Apparel & Accessories Nec, 3519 Internal Combustion Engines Nec, 3714 Motor Vehicle Parts & Accessories, 3751 Motorcycles, Bicycles & Parts.

Nonmonetary Support

Type: Donated Products

Corporate Sponsorship

Contact: Joanne Bishman, Vice President Marketing

Harley-Davidson Foundation

Giving Contact

Mary Ann Martiny, Manager
Harley-Davidson Foundation
3700 West Juneau Avenue
Milwaukee, WI 53208
Phone: (414)342-4680

Description

Founded: 1993
EIN: 391769946
Organization Type: Corporate Foundation
Giving Locations: AL: headquarters and operating communities; PA: headquarters and operating communities; WI: headquarters and operating communities
Grant Types: Project.
Note: Foundation makes a small number of contributions for capital or operating support, but this is not the priority.

Financial Summary

Total Giving: $1,629,684 (1998); $1,800,000 (1997 approx); $1,334,861 (1996)
Giving Analysis: Giving for 1998 includes: foundation ($1,440,544); foundation grants to United Way ($189,140)
Assets: $5,241,291 (1998); $3,581,482 (1996); $2,652,940 (1995)
Gifts Received: $1,800,000 (1998); $1,825,000 (1996); $1,375,000 (1995). Note: In 1995, contributions were received from the Harley-Davidson Co.

Typical Recipients

Arts & Humanities: Arts Centers, Arts Institutes, History & Archaeology, Libraries, Museums/Galleries, Music, Opera, Performing Arts, Public Broadcasting, Theater

Civic & Public Affairs: African American Affairs, Business/Free Enterprise, Chambers of Commerce, Civil Rights, Community Foundations, Economic Development, Economic Policy, Employment/Job Training, Civic & Public Affairs-General, Hispanic Affairs, Housing, Inner-City Development, Urban & Community Affairs, Zoos/Aquariums
Education: Arts/Humanities Education, Business Education, Colleges & Universities, Education Reform, Engineering/Technological Education, Education-General, Health & Physical Education, Minority Education, Private Education (Precollege), Public Education (Precollege), Secondary Education (Public)
Environment: Environment-General
Health: Cancer, Children's Health/Hospitals, Clinics/Medical Centers, Diabetes, Emergency/Ambulance Services, Health Organizations, Mental Health, Public Health, Single-Disease Health Associations
Science: Science Museums, Scientific Centers & Institutes
Social Services: Child Welfare, Community Centers, Community Service Organizations, Crime Prevention, Family Planning, Family Services, Food/Clothing Distribution, Scouts, Substance Abuse, United Funds/United Ways, YMCA/YWCA/YMHA/YWHA, Youth Organizations

Contributions Analysis

Arts & Humanities: 29%. Support given to performing arts programs.
Civic & Public Affairs: 11%. Supports other foundations.
Education: 10%. Funds universities, colleges, and educational programs.
Environment: 1%. Funds an environmental center.
Health: 15%. Supports single-disease associations and hospital.
Science: 1%. Funds a science center.
Social Services: 33%. Primarily funds the United Way.

Application Procedures

Initial Contact: In Wisconsin, Milwaukee Area Funders submit common grant application form; in Pennsylvania and Alabama, request application form from foundation.
Application Requirements: For merchandise or table sponsorship, submit a letter describing the organization and how the event will benefit the community, including what percentage of the event's budget will result in a contribution to the organization; copy of 501(c)(3) letter and federal identification number.
Deadlines: April 15, July 15, and October 15.
Decision Notification: Bimonthly.
Notes: Call the foundation's information line for a list of current dates.

Restrictions

The foundation does not make grants to individuals, political causes or candidates, athletic events or teams, conferences, or religious causes unless for a major project that benefits the greater community.

Additional Information

The Harley-Davidson family of employees, dealers, and customers has raised approximately $20 million for the Muscular Dystrophy Association in the last 16 years.
The foundation's emphasis is community revitalization and education. However, other areas of interest are arts and culture, medicine, and the environment. Because of the number of requests the foundation receives, only one request per year from an organization is considered. considered.
Publications: Guidelines

Corporate Officials

Dr. Jeffrey L. Bleustein: president, chief executive officer, director B 1939. ED Columbia University MS; Columbia University PhD; Cornell University BS. PRIM CORP EMPL president, chief executive officer, director: Harley-Davidson Inc. CORP AFFIL president, chief executive officer, director: Harley-Davidson Motor Co.; director: Holiday Holding Corp.; president: Harley-Davidson Holding Co.; director: Brunswick Corp.; chief executive officer: Buell Motorcycle Co.

Foundation Officials

James M. Brostowitz: treasurer B Milwaukee, WI 1952. ED Marquette University (1974). PRIM CORP EMPL vice president, controller: Harley-Davidson Motor Co. CORP AFFIL vice president, treasurer, controller: Harley-Davidson Inc.; treasurer: Harley-Davidson Transportation Co.
C. William Gray: vice president PRIM CORP EMPL vice president: Harley-Davidson Inc.
Mr. Gail Lione: secretary
Mary Ann Martiny: assistant secretary
James L. Ziemer: president B 1950. ED University of Wisconsin BA (1975); University of Wisconsin MBA (1986). PRIM CORP EMPL vice president, chief financial officer: Harley-Davidson Inc. CORP AFFIL vice president: Harley-Davidson Transportation Co.

Grants Analysis

Disclosure Period: calendar year ending 1998
Total Grants: $1,440,544*
Number of Grants: 299
Average Grant: $4,818
Highest Grant: $122,575
Typical Range: $25 to $30,000
***Note:** Giving excludes United Way.

Recent Grants

Note: Grants derived from 1998 Form 990.

Arts & Humanities

122,575	Channel 10/36 Friends, Inc., Milwaukee, WI
50,000	Marcus Center for the Performing Arts, Milwaukee, WI
40,000	United Performing Arts Fund, Milwaukee, WI
25,000	Betty Brinn Children's Museum, Milwaukee, WI
25,000	Milwaukee Art Museum, Milwaukee, WI
25,000	Wisconsin History Foundation, Madison, WI
25,000	Wisconsin History Foundation, Madison, WI
20,000	Milwaukee Repertory Theater, Milwaukee, WI
10,000	First Stage Milwaukee, Milwaukee, WI
10,000	Milwaukee Children's Theater Company, Milwaukee, WI
10,000	York Little Theatre, York, PA
10,000	Milwaukee Institute of Art & Design, Milwaukee, WI

Civic & Public Affairs

25,000	The Greater Milwaukee Committee, Milwaukee, WI
25,000	Next Door Foundation, Milwaukee, WI
25,000	Spirit of Milwaukee, Milwaukee, WI
15,000	The Milwaukee Foundation, Milwaukee, WI
15,000	The Milwaukee Foundation, Milwaukee, WI
13,333	Inner City Redevelopment, Milwaukee, WI
10,000	The Milwaukee Foundation, Milwaukee, WI
10,000	Wauwatosa Economic Development, Wauwatosa, WI

Education

28,000	John Marshall High School, Los Angeles, CA
25,000	University of Wisconsin, Milwaukee, WI
20,000	Alverno College, Milwaukee, WI
20,000	Partners Advancing Values in Education, Milwaukee, WI
13,000	Urban Day School, Milwaukee, WI
10,000	Junior Achievement of Wisconsin, Milwaukee, WI

Environment

10,000	Friends of Schlitz Audubon Center, Bayside, WI

Health

100,000	York Health System, York, PA
30,000	American Cancer Society, Milwaukee, WI
20,000	Children's Hospital Guild Association, Palmdale, CA
10,000	Alliance for the Mentally Ill, Madison, WI
10,000	Sinai Samaritan Medical Center, Milwaukee, WI
10,000	Sinai Samaritan Medical Center, Milwaukee, WI

Science

10,000	Discovery World, Milwaukee, WI

Social Services

129,000	United Way of Greater Milwaukee, Milwaukee, WI
56,000	United Way of York County, York, PA
40,000	Hunger Task Force, Milwaukee, WI
28,000	Boys & Girls Club of Greater Milwaukee, Milwaukee, WI
20,000	YMCA of Metropolitan Milwaukee, Milwaukee, WI
17,500	Silver Spring Neighborhood Center, Milwaukee, WI
15,000	La Causa, Inc. Family Center, Milwaukee, WI
15,000	Second Harvest Food Bank, San Jose, CA
15,000	United Community Center, Milwaukee, WI
15,000	United Community Center, Milwaukee, WI
11,124	Milwaukee Community Service Corp, Milwaukee, WI
10,656	Planned Parenthood, Milwaukee, WI
10,000	Boy Scouts of America, Milwaukee, WI
10,000	Milwaukee Council of Alcoholism, Milwaukee, WI
10,000	Rosalie Manor, Milwaukee, WI

HARNISCHFEGER INDUSTRIES

Company Contact

Brookfield, WI

Company Description

Revenue: US$2,887,600,000
Profit: US$114,200,000
Employees: 17,100
SIC(s): 3532 Mining Machinery, 3536 Hoists, Cranes & Monorails, 3554 Paper Industries Machinery, 3599 Industrial Machinery Nec.

Harnischfeger Industries Foundation

Giving Contact

Sandy McKenzie, Executive Assistant
PO Box 554
Milwaukee, WI 53201-0554
Phone: (414)486-6855

Description

Founded: 1989
EIN: 391659070
Organization Type: Corporate Foundation. Supports preselected organizations only.
Giving Locations: AZ; DC; IL; MD; MI; MN; NY; PA; TX; VA; WI

Grant Types: General Support.

Financial Summary

Total Giving: $1,000,000 (fiscal year ending October 31, 1999 approx); $1,274,954 (fiscal 1998); $857,765 (fiscal 1997)
Giving Analysis: Giving for fiscal 1997 includes: foundation ($722,765); foundation grants to United Way ($135,000); fiscal 1998: foundation ($1,129,854); foundation grants to United Way ($145,100)
Assets: $10,196,512 (fiscal 1998); $11,045,572 (fiscal 1997); $10,344,852 (fiscal 1996)
Gifts Received: $2,256,024 (fiscal 1992); $1,847,000 (fiscal 1991). Note: In fiscal 1992, major contributions were received from Harnischfeger Fdn.

Typical Recipients

Arts & Humanities: Arts Associations & Councils, Libraries, Museums/Galleries, Music, Opera, Performing Arts
Civic & Public Affairs: Botanical Gardens/Parks, Chambers of Commerce, Clubs, Economic Development, Civic & Public Affairs-General, Housing, Municipalities/Towns, Nonprofit Management, Parades/Festivals, Philanthropic Organizations, Public Policy, Urban & Community Affairs, Women's Affairs, Zoos/Aquariums
Education: Arts/Humanities Education, Business Education, Colleges & Universities, Education Funds, Education Reform, Engineering/Technological Education, Education-General, Medical Education, Minority Education, Private Education (Precollege), Public Education (Precollege), Science/Mathematics Education, Secondary Education (Private)
Environment: Air/Water Quality, Energy
Health: AIDS/HIV, Cancer, Children's Health/Hospitals, Clinics/Medical Centers, Emergency/Ambulance Services, Heart, Medical Research, Mental Health, Prenatal Health Issues, Single-Disease Health Associations
Religion: Religious Organizations
Science: Science Museums, Scientific Centers & Institutes
Social Services: Camps, Child Welfare, Community Centers, Crime Prevention, Domestic Violence, People with Disabilities, Recreation & Athletics, United Funds/United Ways, YMCA/YWCA/YMHA/YWHA, Youth Organizations

Contributions Analysis

Giving Priorities: Primarily for social services, education, the arts, religious welfare, and civic causes.
Arts & Humanities: 19%. Supports museums, performing arts, libraries, the orchestra, and the theatre.
Civic & Public Affairs: 14%. Funds programs for ethnic and racial minorities, women's groups, foundations, and city offices.
Education: 20%. Supports education programs, colleges, and secondary schools.
Religion: 16%. Major grant to the United States Catholic Conference. Also supports religious philanthropic organizations.
Social Services: 23%. Major grant to the United Way. Funds programs for the blind, youth clubs, Special Olympics, and community athletic and social clubs.
Note: Total contributions made in fiscal 1998.

Application Procedures

Initial Contact: Send letter requesting guidelines for giving and grant request form.
Review Process: Most applications are processed within 90 days of receipt.

Restrictions

The foundation does not contribute to religious organizations or institutions primarily supported by taxes or public funds. Contributions are limited to organizations which are tax-exempt under IRC 501(c)(3). Contributions will not be made for use in foreign countries. The foundation typically does not accept unsolicited proposals.

Additional Information

Publications: Guidelines; Grant Request Form

Corporate Officials

Francis Michael Corby, Jr.: executive vice president finance & administration, chief financial officer B Chicago, IL 1944. ED Saint Mary Lake College BA (1966); Columbia University MBA (1969). PRIM CORP EMPL executive vice president finance & administration, chief financial officer: Harnischfeger Industries. CORP AFFIL director: Joy Tech; director: Industries Insurance Corp.; director: Harnischfeger Corp. NONPR AFFIL member: Financial Executives Institute. CLUB AFFIL Westmoor Country Club.
Jeffery T. Grade: chairman, chief executive officer, director B Chicago, IL 1943. ED Illinois Institute of Technology BS (1966); DePaul University MBA (1972). PRIM CORP EMPL chairman, chief executive officer, director: Harnischfeger Industries. CORP AFFIL director: Beloit Corp.; director: Harnischfeger International Corp.

Foundation Officials

David Brukardt: vice president
James A. Chokey: secretary
Francis Michael Corby, Jr.: treasurer (see above)
Eric Fonstad: assistant secretary
Jeffery T. Grade: president (see above)
John N. Hanson: vice president
John Spies: assistant treasurer
Kenneth Stark: assistant treasurer

Grants Analysis

Disclosure Period: fiscal year ending October 31, 1998
Total Grants: $1,129,854*
Number of Grants: 177
Average Grant: $5,601*
Highest Grant: $144,050
Typical Range: $50 to $1,000 and $5,000 to $20,000
***Note:** Giving excludes United Way. Average grant figure excludes highest grant.

Recent Grants

Note: Grants derived from 1997 Form 990.

Arts & Humanities

60,000 United Performing Arts Fund, Milwaukee, WI
37,030 Milwaukee Art Museum, Milwaukee, WI
10,000 Florentine Opera Company, Milwaukee, WI
10,000 Milwaukee Public Library Foundation, Milwaukee, WI

Civic & Public Affairs

25,000 Milwaukee Habitat for Humanity, Milwaukee, WI
20,000 Westown Association, Milwaukee, WI
10,150 Midtown Neighborhood Association, Milwaukee, WI
10,000 League of Martin, Milwaukee, WI
10,000 National Governors Association, Milwaukee, WI

Education

25,000 Beloit College, Beloit, WI
25,000 Partners Advancing Values in Education, Milwaukee, WI
10,000 Highland Community School, Milwaukee, WI
10,000 Material Handling Education Foundation, Charlotte, NC

Health

59,500 American Cancer Society, Wauwatosa, WI
17,750 Welfare Auxiliary of Children's Hospital of Wisconsin, Mequon, WI

Religion

67,500 US Catholic Conference, Washington, DC

Social Services

135,000 United Way, Milwaukee, WI
20,000 YWCA, Milwaukee, WI -- for Women's Enterprise Center
10,000 Milwaukee Police Athletic League, Milwaukee, WI
10,000 Milwaukee Women's Center, Milwaukee, WI

HARRAH'S ENTERTAINMENT INC.

Company Contact

Memphis, TN

Company Description

Revenue: US$1,588,100,000
Employees: 22,000

Operating Locations

Australia: Star City, Sydney

Nonmonetary Support

Type: Cause-related Marketing & Promotion; Donated Equipment; Donated Products

Corporate Sponsorship

Range: less than $1,000,000
Type: Other
Note: Sponsors Susan G. Komen Breast Cancer Foundation and the National Center for Responsible Gaming.

Giving Contact

Mary Jane Fuller, Director, Public Affairs
Harrah's Entertainment Inc.
1023 Cherry Road
Memphis, TN 38117
Phone: (901)762-8823
Fax: (901)762-8637

Description

Organization Type: Corporate Giving Program
Giving Locations: headquarters and operating communities.
Grant Types: Employee Matching Gifts, General Support, Scholarship.
Note: Employee matching gift ratio: 1 to 1. Company matches employee contributions to colleges and universities, public broadcasting, and the Susan G. Komen Breast Cancer Foundation.

Giving Philosophy

'Harrah's Entertainment will invest in programs and activities that build strong communities and advance causes important to our employees, customers, and areas where we conduct business. Our focus will be on programs that promote education and health and human services.'

Financial Summary

Total Giving: $3,000,000 (1999 approx); $3,100,000 (1998 approx); $3,100,000 (1997 approx). Note: Contributes through corporate direct giving program only.
Giving Analysis: Giving for 1998 includes: corporate direct giving ($3,100,000)

Contributions Analysis

Arts & Humanities: About 10%.
Civic & Public Affairs: About 10%. Recipients include National Center for Responsible Gaming and National Council on Problem Gambling.
Education: About 30%. Supports scholarship programs for employees and minorities.

Health: About 50%. Major support for Susan G. Komen Breast Cancer Foundation.

Application Procedures

Initial Contact: brief letter
Application Requirements: a description of organization, amount requested, purpose of funds sought, recently audited financial statement, and proof of tax-exempt status
Deadlines: None.
Review Process: requests are reviewed by staff
Evaluative Criteria: favors programs related to company business interests, that involve employees, and are national in scope
Notes: Company initiates majority of its funding.

Restrictions

Does not support dinners or special events, religious or veterans organizations, individuals, health agencies, or member agencies of the United Way.

Additional Information

Company donates 2% of annual net income to charitable organizations.

HARRIS CORP.

Company Contact

Melbourne, FL
Web: http://www.harris.com

Company Description

Revenue: US$3,939,100,000
Employees: 29,000
Fortune Rank: 427, per FORTUNE Magazine's list of 500 Largest U.S. Corporations (1999).
FF 427
SIC(s): 3669 Communications Equipment Nec, 3674 Semiconductors & Related Devices, 3679 Electronic Components Nec, 3861 Photographic Equipment & Supplies.

Operating Locations

Also operates in Canada, Europe, Latin America, and Asia.

Nonmonetary Support

Value: $817,000 (1991); $1,300,000 (1990); $1,636,874 (1989)
Type: Donated Equipment

Harris Foundation

Giving Contact

Richard L. Ballantyne, Secretary
Harris Foundation
1025 West NASA Boulevard
Melbourne, FL 32919
Phone: (407)727-9163
Fax: (407)727-9222

Alternate Contact

Vickie Boland
Phone: (404)727-9695

Description

EIN: 346520425
Organization Type: Corporate Foundation. Supports preselected organizations only.
Giving Locations: FL principally near operating locations and to national organizations.
Grant Types: Employee Matching Gifts, General Support.

Financial Summary

Total Giving: $784,657 (fiscal year ending June 30, 1998); $601,310 (fiscal 1997); $3,000,000 (fiscal 1996 approx). Note: Contributes through corporate direct giving program and foundation. Giving includes foundation only.
Giving Analysis: Giving for fiscal 1996 includes: corporate direct giving (approx $2,277,085); foundation ($622,915); foundation grants to United Way ($100,000); fiscal 1997: foundation ($501,310); foundation grants to United Way ($100,000); fiscal 1998: foundation ($412,160); foundation matching gifts ($272,497); foundation grants to United Way ($100,000)
Assets: $7,563,302 (fiscal 1998); $7,485,688 (fiscal 1997); $4,294,350 (fiscal 1996)
Gifts Received: $2,670,000 (fiscal 1997); $4,342,813 (fiscal 1994); $583,038 (fiscal 1993)

Typical Recipients

Arts & Humanities: Arts Associations & Councils, Arts Centers, Arts Funds, Community Arts, Museums/Galleries, Music, Performing Arts, Theater
Civic & Public Affairs: Business/Free Enterprise, Economic Development, Economic Policy, Civic & Public Affairs-General, Housing, Professional & Trade Associations, Urban & Community Affairs, Women's Affairs, Zoos/Aquariums
Education: Colleges & Universities, Community & Junior Colleges, Continuing Education, Education Funds, Engineering/Technological Education, Education-General, Minority Education, Public Education (Precollege), Secondary Education (Public)
Environment: Environment-General
Health: Cancer, Children's Health/Hospitals, Clinics/Medical Centers, Diabetes, Emergency/Ambulance Services, Health Organizations, Hospitals
Religion: Religious Welfare, Social/Policy Issues
Science: Science Museums, Scientific Centers & Institutes, Scientific Organizations
Social Services: Child Welfare, Community Service Organizations, Domestic Violence, Food/Clothing Distribution, Recreation & Athletics, Scouts, Substance Abuse, United Funds/United Ways, Youth Organizations

Contributions Analysis

Giving Priorities: Computer grants, community service, civics, united funds, the arts, and health.
Arts & Humanities: 21%. Museums, music, and arts associations.
Civic & Public Affairs: 4%. Housing, safety, and urban affairs.
Education: 44%. Matching gift program to secondary and higher education.
Health: 4%. Single-disease health associations, children's hospitals, and ambulance services.
Science: 2%.
Social Services: 25%. Child welfare, scouts, and food and clothing distribution.
Note: Above percentages reflect foundation giving in 1998 only. Company administers a direct giving program and a foundation. Both programs direct funds to eligible nonprofit organizations in Brevard County, FL, primarily through united funds, civic organizations, and various community serviceorganizations.

Application Procedures

Initial Contact: Send a letter of proposal.
Application Requirements: Include a description of organization, amount requested, purpose of funds sought, recently audited financial statement, published analysis report (if available), and proof of tax-exempt status.
Deadlines: None.

Corporate Officials

Richard Lee Ballantyne: vice president, general counsel, secretary B Evanston, IL 1939. ED University of Connecticut BS (1965); University of Connecticut MBA (1967); George Washington University JD (1969). PRIM CORP EMPL vice president, general counsel, secretary: Harris Corp. ADD CORP EMPL president: Harris Technical Service Corp.; secretary: Harris Data Service Corp. NONPR AFFIL member law council: Manufacturer Alliance Productivity & Innovation; member: Northeast Corporate Counsel Association Inc.; member: Licensing Executives Society; member: American Society of Corporate Secretaries; member: Computer Law Forum; member: American Bar Association.
Phillip W. Farmer: chairman, president, chief executive officer B Goldsboro, NC 1938. ED Duke University BA (1960). PRIM CORP EMPL chairman, president, chief executive officer: Harris Corp. ADD CORP EMPL president: Harris Technical Services Corp.; president: Harris Data Service Corp. CORP AFFIL chairman: Baseview Products Inc. NONPR AFFIL trustee: Florida Institute of Technology; director: Manufacturer Alliance; member: Electronic Industries Association; director: Aerospace Industries Association; member: Business Roundtable.
Nick E. Heldreth: vice president human resources corporate relations ED North Georgia College. PRIM CORP EMPL vice president human resources corporate relations: Harris Corp. NONPR AFFIL member: Society Human Resources Management; trustee: University Central Florida; member: Manufacturer Alliance; member: Organization Developmental Network; member: Human Resources Council; member: Labor Policy Association; overseer: Florida Institute Technology.
David Sherman Wasserman: vice president, treasurer B New York, NY 1942. ED University of Maryland (1965); University of Pennsylvania (1984). PRIM CORP EMPL vice president, treasurer: Harris Corp. CORP AFFIL president: Harris Technical Services Corp. NONPR AFFIL member: Financial Executives Institute; member: Tax Executives Institute; member: American Bar Association.

Foundation Officials

Richard Lee Ballantyne: secretary, treasurer (see above)
Phillip W. Farmer: president, trustee (see above)
Bryan Roger Roub: trustee B Berea, OH 1941. ED Ohio Wesleyan University (1959-1962); Ohio State University BS (1966); University of Pennsylvania Wharton School MBA (1978). PRIM CORP EMPL senior vice president finance, chief financial officer: Harris Corp. CORP AFFIL senior vice president finance: Harris Technical Services Corp. NONPR AFFIL chairman: Manufacturers Alliance Financial Council; member: Ohio Society CPA's; vice chairman: Machinery & Allied Products Institute; director: Financial Executives Institute; trustee: Financial Executives Research Foundation; member: American Institute CPAs; director: Easter Seal Society Brevard County. CLUB AFFIL La Cita Country Club; Westwood Country Club.
David Sherman Wasserman: trustee (see above)

Grants Analysis

Disclosure Period: fiscal year ending June 30, 1998
Total Grants: $412,160*
Number of Grants: 28
Average Grant: $4,486*
Highest Grant: $100,000
Typical Range: $1,000 to $10,000
***Note:** Giving excludes United Way and matching gifts. Average grant figure excludes three highest grants ($300,000).

Recent Grants

Note: Grants derived from fiscal 1998 Form 990.

Arts & Humanities

100,000 King Center for the Performing Arts, Cocoa, FL
5,596 Brevard Symphony Orchestra, Melbourne, FL
1,000 George Eastman House, Rochester, NY

Civic & Public Affairs

15,650 South Brevard Women's Center, Melbourne, FL

3,000	Financial Executive Research Foundation, Richmond, VA
3,000	Florida Council on Economics, Tampa, FL
40	Brevard Zoo, Melbourne, FL
Education	
100,000	Florida State University, Tallahassee, FL
100,000	University of Central Florida, Orlando, FL
20,000	Fund for Public Schools, New York, NY
3,000	Brevard Company Alliance of the SECME, Viera, FL
3,000	John Wood Community College, Quincy, IL
Health	
18,320	American Cancer Society, Tampa, FL
3,000	Easter Seal Society of East, Central Florida
590	Harbor City Volunteer Ambulance Squad, Melbourne, FL
225	American Diabetes Association, Los Angeles, CA
Science	
5,820	Brevard Museum of Art & Science, Melbourne, FL
2,386	Space Coast Marine Institute, Melbourne, FL
Social Services	
100,000	United Way of Brevard, Cocoa, FL
10,300	The Haven, Miami, FL
3,495	Central Florida Council - Boy Scouts, Orlando, FL
3,235	The Daily Bread, Miami, FL
3,000	San Carlos Youth Center, San Carlos, CA
2,000	Florida House on Capitol Hill, Washington, DC
1,826	Florida Children's Home, Lakeland, FL
1,595	Serene Harbor, Palm Bay, FL
1,382	South Brevard Sharing Center, Melbourne, FL
650	Genesis House, Chicago, IL
50	Boy Scouts of America, Orlando, FL

Harris Trust &Savings Bank

Company Contact

Chicago, IL

Company Description

Assets: US$14,206,600,000
Employees: 4,813
SIC(s): 6022 State Commercial Banks.
Parent Company: Harris Bankcorp, Inc.
Parent Assets: US$151,650,000,000

Operating Locations

AZ: Harris Trust Bank of Arizona, Scottsdale; Harris Trust & Savings Bank, Scottsdale; CA: Bank of Montreal - Los Angeles, Los Angeles; Harris Trust Co. of California, Los Angeles; Harris Trust & Savings Bank, Los Angeles, San Francisco; FL: Harris Trust Co. of Florida, West Palm Beach; Harris Trust & Savings Bank, West Palm Beach; IL: Harris Trust & Savings Bank, Batavia; Bank of Montreal - Chicago, Chicago; BMO Financial, Chicago; Harris Bank, Chicago; Harris Bankcorp, Inc., Chicago; Harris Futures Corp., Chicago; Harris-Nesbitt Thomson Securities, Chicago; Harris Trust & Savings Bank, Chicago; Harriscorp Finance, Inc., Chicago; Harriscorp Leasing, Inc., Chicago; HGC Bank, Chicago; Harris Bank Glencoe-Northbrook, N.A., Glencoe; Harris Trust & Savings Bank, Glencoe; Harris Bank Hinsdale N.A., Hinsdale; Harris Trust & Savings Bank, Hinsdale; Harris Bank Naperville, Naperville; Harris Bank Roselle, Roselle; Harris Trust & Savings Bank, Roselle, Summit; Harris Bank Argo, Summit Argo; Harris Trust & Savings Bank, West Chicago; Harris Bank Wilmette N.A., Wilmette; Harris Trust & Savings Bank, Wilmette; Harris Bank Winnetka N.A., Winnetka; MO: Harris Trust & Savings Bank; NY: Bank of Montreal - New York, New York; Bank of Montreal Trust Co., New York; Bankmont Financial Corp., New York; Harris Trust Co. of New York, New York; Harris Trust & Savings Bank, New York; TX: Bank of Montreal - Houston, Houston
Note: Also has facilities in Nassau, Bahamas.

Nonmonetary Support

Value: $77,262 (1994); $100,000 (1987)
Type: Donated Equipment; Donated Products; In-kind Services
Contact: Monica Sanguino, Community Affairs Officer
Note: Company also loans meeting space to area nonprofits.

Corporate Sponsorship

Range: less than $5,000
Type: Pledge-a-thon
Note: Sponsors three pledge-a-thons per year.

Harris Bank Foundation

Giving Contact

Donna Streibich Curtis, Secretary & Treasurer
Harris Trust & Savings Bank
200 W Monroe St.
PO Box 755
Chicago, IL 60690-0755
Phone: (312)461-5834
Fax: (312)987-4702

Description

Founded: 1953
EIN: 366033888
Organization Type: Corporate Foundation
Giving Locations: IL: Chicago
Grant Types: Award, Employee Matching Gifts, General Support, Loan, Multiyear/Continuing Support.
Note: Employee matching gift ratio: 2 to 1 to nonprofits where employee also volunteers; 1 to 1 for other gifts to educational and cultural institutions.

Giving Philosophy

'First, we believe that we should support Chicago's core institutions because grants made to major universities and cultural institutions help ensure the continuation of Chicago's reputation as a world class city. .. Secondly, (we seek) to discover not-for-profit neighborhood groups that provide direct one-to-one services to individuals in the areas of education, employment, economic development, and housing. Our intent is to stimulate the revitalization of Chicago's neighborhoods and enhance community stability. We believe it is critical to strengthen leadership and support local initiatives in a manner that encourages community pride and ownership.' Foundation Annual Report

Financial Summary

Total Giving: $2,250,000 (1998 approx); $2,152,361 (1997); $2,000,000 (1996). Note: Contributes through corporate direct giving program and foundation.
Giving Analysis: Giving for 1996 includes: corporate matching gifts (approx $1,007,250); foundation ($992,750); 1997: corporate direct giving (approx $997,639); foundation ($902,000); foundation matching gifts ($250,361); 1998: foundation ($1,086,250); corporate direct giving (approx $921,436); foundation matching gifts ($242,314)
Assets: $1,595,876 (1998); $1,408,388 (1997); $1,423,757 (1996). Note: Co. commits about 2% of yearly net profits to the foundation.
Gifts Received: $1,354,750 (1998); $1,058,000 (1997); $1,550,000 (1996). Note: Foundation receives contributions from Harris Bank.

Typical Recipients

Arts & Humanities: Arts Associations & Councils, Arts Festivals, Arts Funds, Arts Institutes, Dance, Ethnic & Folk Arts, Historic Preservation, History & Archaeology, Museums/Galleries, Music, Opera, Theater
Civic & Public Affairs: Asian American Affairs, Botanical Gardens/Parks, Economic Development, Employment/Job Training, Civic & Public Affairs-General, Hispanic Affairs, Housing, Municipalities/Towns, Native American Affairs, Nonprofit Management, Public Policy, Urban & Community Affairs, Women's Affairs, Zoos/Aquariums
Education: Afterschool/Enrichment Programs, Arts/Humanities Education, Business Education, Colleges & Universities, Education Reform, Engineering/Technological Education, Faculty Development, Literacy, Minority Education, Preschool Education, Private Education (Precollege), Public Education (Precollege), Science/Mathematics Education
Health: Clinics/Medical Centers, Health Organizations, Hospices, Medical Rehabilitation, Mental Health
Religion: Jewish Causes, Religious Organizations, Religious Welfare
Science: Observatories & Planetariums, Science Museums, Scientific Centers & Institutes
Social Services: Child Welfare, Community Service Organizations, Domestic Violence, Family Services, People with Disabilities, Scouts, Shelters/Homelessness, Social Services-General, United Funds/United Ways, Volunteer Services, YMCA/YWCA/YMHA/YWHA, Youth Organizations

Contributions Analysis

Giving Priorities: United funds, Education, civic affairs, youth, community service, social services, culture, and health care.
Arts & Humanities: 24%. Focus on promoting cultural diversity while providing access to the arts for underserved communities. Supports both the major cultural institutions and smaller art groups in Chicago. Museums, dance, theater, music, and zoos and parks receive support.
Civic & Public Affairs: 8%. Civic focus is on race relations, business and economic issues, infrastructure and environmental concerns, and strategic planning efforts. Community revitalization grants support programs which increase or improve housing for low/moderate income people in Chicago, and which promote commercial and industrial activity in low income neighborhoods.
Education: 10%. Supports higher education, particularly in Chicago. Also supports organizations advocating for training and/or public school reform; supports urban education and opportunities for inner-city youth. Provides scholarships for children of employees.
Health: 12%. Grants are designed to improve hospitals and health care delivery systems.
Social Services: 44%. Grants go to new projects or programs which provide direct services to underserved, financially disadvantaged populations. Includes grants to community revitalization organizations.
Note: Above priorities are for foundation giving in 1998. The company and its subsidiaries also make cash and nonmonetary donations; priorities vary according to community needs.

Application Procedures

Initial Contact: Send a brief proposal of no more than five pages.
Application Requirements: Preface proposal with cover letter, including a description of organization and project, amount requested, and purpose of funds sought; proposal should include detailed project description, including plans for implementation; project

budget, current organization budget; potential funding sources; recently audited financial statement, proof of tax-exempt status; names of officers and directors with affiliations; and list of current contributors with amounts.
Deadlines: None; requests must be received by the first day of the month preceding a board meeting.
Review Process: Screened by staff, placed on board agenda, voted on by board of directors.
Evaluative Criteria: Provision of a needed service to a measurable universe of people; realistic project description; community based, multi-racial, multi-ethnic board; evidence of advocacy for change.
Decision Notification: Grant approvals are made at quarterly meetings.
Notes: Colleges and universities are considered for operating support in the spring of each year for payment in following academic year.

Restrictions

Does not support individuals or fellowships, political activities, sectarian religious organizations, fraternal organizations, testimonials or benefits, advertising, hospitals or national health organizations, conferences or seminars, operating budgets of United Way members, private elementary or secondary schools, national or international organizations, foundations or grantmaking organizations, or tax-supported educational institutions or government agencies.

Additional Information

The bank is committed to making total contributions equal to 2% of net profits. Figures do not include contributions by other subsidiaries of Harris Bankcorp. The company reports that in the past several years it has focused about one-fourth of total grant making on community redevelopment programs. These programs focus on three areas: educating people, providing them with a safe and decent place to live, and trying to ensure that they have employment. In deciding which communities to target for funding, the company looks for neighborhoods with existing grassroots programs. grassroots programs.
Publications: Annual Report

Corporate Officials

Alan G. McNally: chairman, chief executive officer B Quebec, PQ Canada 1945. ED Cornell University BS; York University MBA; Cornell University MS (1967). PRIM CORP EMPL chairman, chief executive officer: Harris Bankcorp Inc. ADD CORP EMPL chief executive officer: Bankmont Financial Corp.; chairman, chief executive officer: Harris Bank; chief executive officer: Harris Bank Oakbrook Terr. CORP AFFIL chairman, chief executive officer: Harris Trust & Savings Bank; director: Walgreen Co. NONPR AFFIL treasurer: Queen Elizabeth Hospital Foundation; member board governors: York University; director: Kids Help Phone; advisory board member: Northwestern University Kellogg Graduate School Business Management; trustee: DePaul University; board member: Evenston Northwestern Healthcare; director: Canadian Council Aboriginal Business; director: Chicago Youth Centers. CLUB AFFIL member civic committee: Executives Club Chicago; member civic committee: Glen View Club; member civic committee: Commercial Club Chicago; director: Economic Club Chicago; director: Chicago Club.

Foundation Officials

Robin S. Coffey: director
Donna Streibich Curtis: secretary, treasurer
Robert Kato: director
Andrew Morua: director
JoLeen Spencer: director
Edward Joseph Williams: president, director B Chicago, IL 1942. ED Roosevelt University BBA (1973). PRIM CORP EMPL executive vice president: Harris Trust & Savings Bank. NONPR AFFIL member: Urban Bankers Forum; director: Voices Illinois Children; president: Neighborhood Housing Services America; member: Consumer Advisory Council; member: National Bankers Association; director: Chicago Council Urban Affairs. CLUB AFFIL Union League Club Chicago; Economic Club; Metro Club.

Grants Analysis

Disclosure Period: calendar year ending 1999
Total Grants: $1,086,250*
Number of Grants: 117
Average Grant: $9,284
Highest Grant: $100,000
Typical Range: $3,000 to $15,000
***Note:** Giving excludes matching gifts and corporate direct giving.

Recent Grants

Note: Grants derived from 1997 Form 990.

Arts & Humanities

100,000	Chicago Symphony/Lyric Opera, Chicago, IL
45,000	Goodman Theater, Chicago, IL
20,000	Art Institute, Chicago, IL
15,000	Chicago Music and Dance Theater, Chicago, IL
10,000	Museum of Contemporary Art, Chicago, IL
6,000	Ravinia Festival Association, Chicago, IL

Civic & Public Affairs

30,000	Neighborhood Housing Services, Chicago, IL
20,000	Brookfield Zoo, Chicago, IL
20,000	Chicago Community Loan Fund, Chicago, IL
20,000	National Training and Information Center, Chicago, IL
15,000	Lincoln Park Zoological Society, Chicago, IL
12,500	Chicago Association of Neighborhood Development Organizations, Chicago, IL
10,000	Chicago Foundation for Women, Chicago, IL
10,000	Chinese American Service League, Chicago, IL
10,000	Claretian Associates Neighborhood Development Office, Chicago, IL
10,000	Designs for Change, Chicago, IL
10,000	Peoples Reinvestment and Development Effort, Oak Park, IL
8,000	Antioch Foundation, Chicago, IL
7,500	Metropolitan Planning Council, Chicago, IL
7,500	Nonprofit Financial Center, Chicago, IL
6,000	DevCorp North, Chicago, IL
6,000	Illinois Facilities Fund, Chicago, IL
6,000	Jane Adams Resource Corporation, Chicago, IL
6,000	South Suburban Housing Center, Chicago, IL
5,000	Covenant Development Corporation, Chicago, IL
5,000	Fellowship Housing Corporation, Chicago, IL
5,000	Public Allies, Chicago, IL

Education

20,000	Roosevelt University, Chicago, IL
16,500	Harvard Business School, Chicago, IL
15,000	DePaul University, Chicago, IL
11,000	Institute of Technology, Chicago, IL
5,000	Christopher House, Chicago, IL
5,000	Cities in Schools, Chicago, IL
5,000	Community Youth Creative Learning Experiences, Chicago, IL
5,000	Junior Achievement, Chicago, IL

Health

100,000	Cook County/Rush Health Center, Chicago, IL
7,500	Erie Family Health Center, Chicago, IL

Religion

7,500	Lawndale Christian Development Corporation, Chicago, IL
5,000	Jewish Federation, Chicago, IL

Science

25,000	Field Museum of Natural History, Chicago, IL
15,000	Adler Planetarium, Chicago, IL

Social Services

30,000	YMCA, Chicago, IL
13,000	Chicago Youth Centers, Chicago, IL
10,000	Boys and Girls Club, Chicago, IL
7,500	Accion, Chicago, IL
7,500	Center for New Horizons, Chicago, IL
7,500	United Charities, Chicago, IL
6,500	Girl Scouts of America, Chicago, IL
5,000	Boy Scouts of America, Chicago, IL
5,000	Heartland Alliance for Human Needs and Rights, Chicago, IL

HARSCO CORP.

Company Contact

Camp Hill, PA

Company Description

Employees: 14,200
SIC(s): 2952 Asphalt Felts & Coatings, 3295 Minerals--Ground or Treated, 3494 Valves & Pipe Fittings Nec, 3743 Railroad Equipment.

Operating Locations

Also operates internationally.

Harsco Corp. Fund

Giving Contact

Mr. Robert G. Yocum, Chairman & Trustee
Harsco Corp. Fund
PO Box 8888
Camp Hill, PA 17001-8888
Phone: (717)763-7064

Description

EIN: 236278376
Organization Type: Corporate Foundation
Giving Locations: headquarters and operating communities.
Grant Types: Capital, Department, Employee Matching Gifts, General Support, Research, Scholarship.

Financial Summary

Total Giving: $1,008,231 (1998); $945,783 (1997); $898,095 (1996). Note: Contributes through foundation only.
Giving Analysis: Giving for 1995 includes: foundation grants to United Way ($94,420); foundation matching gifts ($24,331); 1996: foundation grants to United Way ($100,995); foundation matching gifts ($36,253); 1997: foundation ($833,847); foundation grants to United Way ($73,220); foundation matching gifts ($38,716);
Assets: $10,252,603 (1998); $11,549,957 (1997); $10,224,974 (1996)
Gifts Received: $210,000 (1997); $150,000 (1996); $150,000 (1995). Note: Fund receives contributions from the Harsco Corp and Sordoni Enterprises.

Typical Recipients

Arts & Humanities: Arts Associations & Councils, Arts Centers, Arts Festivals, Arts Funds, Community Arts, Dance, Historic Preservation, History & Archaeology, Libraries, Museums/Galleries, Music, Opera, Performing Arts, Public Broadcasting, Theater
Civic & Public Affairs: African American Affairs, Business/Free Enterprise, Chambers of Commerce,

Civil Rights, Economic Development, Economic Policy, Employment/Job Training, Ethnic Organizations, Civic & Public Affairs-General, Hispanic Affairs, Housing, Law & Justice, Legal Aid, Philanthropic Organizations, Professional & Trade Associations, Public Policy, Safety, Urban & Community Affairs
Education: Arts/Humanities Education, Business Education, Colleges & Universities, Community & Junior Colleges, Economic Education, Education Associations, Education Funds, Engineering/Technological Education, Education-General, International Exchange, Leadership Training, Medical Education, Minority Education, Public Education (Precollege), Religious Education, Science/Mathematics Education, Student Aid
Environment: Environment-General
Health: Cancer, Children's Health/Hospitals, Clinics/Medical Centers, Diabetes, Emergency/Ambulance Services, Health Organizations, Hospices, Hospitals, Medical Research, Mental Health, Public Health, Single-Disease Health Associations
International: Foreign Arts Organizations, International Relations
Religion: Religious Welfare, Social/Policy Issues
Science: Science Museums, Scientific Centers & Institutes
Social Services: Child Welfare, Community Centers, Community Service Organizations, Day Care, Emergency Relief, Family Planning, Food/Clothing Distribution, Homes, People with Disabilities, Recreation & Athletics, Scouts, Sexual Abuse, Shelters/Homelessness, Substance Abuse, United Funds/United Ways, Volunteer Services, YMCA/YWCA/YMHA/YWHA, Youth Organizations

Contributions Analysis

Giving Priorities: Social service organizations, higher education, health care, and the arts.
Arts & Humanities: 29%. Supports public broadcasting, the Harrisburg Symphony, libraries, arts centers and associations, and the performing arts.
Education: 47%. Includes colleges, universities, and other higher education organizations. Supports the National Merit Scholarship Corporation with a lagre grant for scholarships for employees's children.
Health: 23%. Includes social service organizations. Supports the United Way, boys and girls clubs, community service organization, planned parenthood, and single disease associations.
Note: Total contributions in 1998.

Application Procedures

Initial Contact: Send a brief letter or proposal; organizations in company operating locations should contact local divisions directly.
Application Requirements: Include a description of organization, amount requested, purpose of funds sought, recently audited financial statement, and proof of tax-exempt status.
Deadlines: None.
Evaluative Criteria: Organization must be in area where corporation has business operations.
Decision Notification: Annually, usually in January or February.

Restrictions

Does not support dinners or special events, fraternal organizations, goodwill advertising, political or lobbying groups, religious organizations for sectarian purposes, or individuals.
The fund seldom makes grants to organizations with limited purposes or for special projects that do not receive wide public support.

Corporate Officials

Derek C. Hathaway: chairman, chief executive officers, director B 1944. ED Aston University BS (1965). PRIM CORP EMPL chairman, chief executive officer: Harsco Corp.
Robert F. Nation: former president, director B 1926. ED Elizabethtown College (1947). PRIM CORP EMPL former president, director: Penn Harris Co. CORP AFFIL treasurer: Sun Enterprises Inc.; treasurer: Sun Motor Cars Inc.; director: Phico Insurance Co.; director: Phico Service Co.; treasurer: Mansun North Inc.; director: Phico Group Inc.; director: Harsco Corp.

Foundation Officials

Leonard A. Campanaro: treasurer B Philadelphia, PA 1948. ED Temple University BBA (1970). PRIM CORP EMPL president, chief operating officer director: Harsco Corp.
Malcolm W. Gambill: president, trustee B Crumpler, NC 1930. CORP AFFIL director: York International Corp.
Derek C. Hathaway: vice president, trustee (see above)
Robert F. Nation: trustee (see above)
Robert G. Yocum: secretary PRIM CORP EMPL treasurer, director: Harsco Corp.

Grants Analysis

Disclosure Period: calendar year ending 1998
Total Grants: $873,578*
Number of Grants: 126
Average Grant: $5,789*
Highest Grant: $150,000
Typical Range: $1,000 to $10,000
***Note:** Giving excludes matching gifts and United Way. Average grant figure excludes highest grant.

Recent Grants

Note: Grants derived from 1998 Form 990.

Arts & Humanities

56,600	Harrisburg Symphony Association, Harrisburg, PA
50,000	Capital Center for the Arts, Science & Education,, Harrisburg, PA
50,000	Susquehanna Museum of Art, Harrisburg, PA
37,420	WITF, Inc., Harrisburg, PA
22,000	Allied Arts Fund., Harrisburg, PA
15,000	Concertante Chamber Ensemble, Baltimore, MD
10,000	Harrisburg Opera Association., Harrisburg, PA
6,000	Harrisburg Community Theater., Harrisburg, PA
5,000	Open Stage of Harrisburg., Harrisburg, PA
3,000	Harrisburg Shakespeare Festival, Harrisburg, PA

Civic & Public Affairs

20,000	Project Leap Forward, Lancaster, PA
15,000	National Ethnic Coalition of Organizations Foundation, New York, NY
10,000	Hispanic American Organization, Harrisburg, PA
5,000	Finnegan Foundation, Reading, PA
4,000	Washington Legal Foundation, Washington, DC
3,000	National Legal Center for the Public Interest, Washington, DC
2,500	Capital Region Chamber of Commerce/Ace Foundation, Harrisburg, PA

Education

150,000	Messiah College, Grantham, PA
107,220	National Merit Scholarship Corporation, Chicago, IL
30,000	Eisenhower Exchange Fellowships, Inc., Philadelphia, PA
25,000	Council for Public Education, Harrisburg, PA
25,000	The Pennsylvania State University, University Park, PA
10,000	Penn State Harrisburg, Middletown, PA
5,000	Bucknell University, Lewisburg, PA
4,000	Dartmouth College, Hanover, NH
3,150	Harvard University, Cambridge, MA
2,000	Harrisburg Area Community College, Harrisburg, PA
50	University at Buffalo Foundation, Buffalo, NY

Health

26,000	United Cerebral Palsy of the Capital Area, Camp Hill, PA
15,020	American Red Cross PA Capital Region Chapter, Harrisburg, PA
11,500	Leukemia Society of America - Central PA Chapter, Harrisburg, PA
10,800	World Mission of Central Pennsylvania, Inc., Harrisburg, PA
10,000	Pennsylvania Breast Cancer Coalition, Ephrata, PA
5,000	Blytheville Emergency Squad, Blytheville, AR
5,000	Mental Health Association of Cumberland Dauphin & Perry Counties, Inc., Mechanicsburg, PA
2,700	Hospice of Central Pennsylvania, Enola, PA

International

2,500	Bretton Woods Committee, Washington, DC

Religion

6,500	Salvation Army, Harrisburg, PA

Social Services

35,333	YWCA, Harrisburg, PA
26,110	United Way of the Capital Region, Harrisburg, PA
12,500	YMCA, Butler, PA
7,500	United Way of Eastern Niagara, Lockport, NY
5,500	Goodwill Industries of Central PA, Inc., Harrisburg, PA
5,000	United Way of Franklin County, Columbus, OH
4,600	United Way of Fairmont, Minnesota, Fairmont, MN
4,500	United Way., Columbia, SC
3,650	South Central Pennsylvania Food Bank, Harrisburg, PA
3,500	United Way of Butler County, Butler, PA
3,370	United Way of Southwest Alabama, Mobile, AL
2,500	Keystone Council Boy Scout of America, Mechanicsburg, PA

HARTFORD STEAM BOILER INSPECTION &INSURANCE CO.

Company Contact

Hartford, CT
Web: http://www.hsb.com

Company Description

Assets: US$1,116,300,000
Employees: 2,027
SIC(s): 6331 Fire, Marine & Casualty Insurance, 8711 Engineering Services.

Giving Contact

Justine Long, Contact
Hartford Steam Boiler Inspection & Insurance Co.
1 State St.
PO Box 5024
Hartford, CT 06102-5024
Phone: (860)722-5040
Fax: (860)493-1038

Description

Organization Type: Corporate Giving Program
Giving Locations: headquarters area only.
Grant Types: Employee Matching Gifts, General Support.
Note: Employee matching gift ratio: 1 to 1.

Giving Philosophy

'The Hartford Steam Boiler Inspection and Insurance Company seeks: 'To take an active role in the social, political, cultural, and economic activities within the community in order to make a contribution to the quality of life in that area.' The objective relates to all the Company's resources, including financial contributions and the efforts of employees in community activities. In order to carry out this objective, the Company will encourage its employees to participate in community affairs and to be active, knowledgeable citizens. The Company recognizes that its health as a business enterprise is affected by the vitality of the communities in which its facilities and employees are located. Therefore, the Company will give financial support to certain health and welfare agencies, educational institutions, and civic and arts associations which enhance the quality of life in the Company's locations.' *Hartford Steam Boiler Contributions and Civic Affairs Plan*

Financial Summary

Total Giving: $600,000 (2000 approx); $600,000 (1999 approx); $600,000 (1997 approx). Note: Contributes through corporate direct giving program only.

Typical Recipients

Arts & Humanities: Arts Associations & Councils, Arts Centers, Ballet, Arts & Humanities-General, Literary Arts, Museums/Galleries, Music, Performing Arts, Public Broadcasting
Civic & Public Affairs: African American Affairs, Economic Development, Employment/Job Training, Civic & Public Affairs-General, Hispanic Affairs, Housing, Nonprofit Management, Urban & Community Affairs, Women's Affairs
Education: Business Education, Colleges & Universities, Education Funds, Elementary Education (Private), Education-General, Literacy, Minority Education, Private Education (Precollege), Special Education
Environment: Environment-General
Health: AIDS/HIV, Emergency/Ambulance Services, Health Organizations, Hospitals, Medical Rehabilitation
Religion: Religious Welfare
Social Services: People with Disabilities, Social Services-General, Substance Abuse, United Funds/United Ways, Volunteer Services, Youth Organizations

Contributions Analysis

Education: 100%. The company matches employee gifts to accredited colleges and independent secondary and elementary shools. Interests also include business education, literacy programs, and education funds.

Application Procedures

Initial Contact: letter of inquiry
Application Requirements: a concise cover letter summarizing the key points of the proposal; the amount of the request and how the money would be used; a brief a description of organization's history and mission; most recent annual report, including staff size and qualifications and a list of the Board of Directors; annual budget, including income and expense statement; funding sources; proof of 501(c)(3) status; and contact name, address and phone number
Deadlines: None.
Decision Notification: applicants will be notified of the company's decision in early January

Corporate Officials

Gordon W. Kreh: president, chief executive officer, director B Orangeville, ON Canada 1947. ED University of Western Ontario. PRIM CORP EMPL president, chief executive officer, director: Hartford Steam Boiler Inspection & Insurance Co. CORP AFFIL director: Boiler Inspection & Insurance Co. Canada; director: Radian Corp.

Grants Analysis

Disclosure Period: calendar year ending 1997
Total Grants: $600,000*
***Note:** Total grants figure is an estimate.

Recent Grants

Note: Grants derived from 1993 grants list.

Arts & Humanities
Charter Oak Cultural Center
CPTV
Florence Griswold Museum, Lyme, CT
Greater Hartford Arts Council, Hartford, CT
Hartford Stage Company, Hartford, CT
Hartford Symphony Orchestra, Hartford, CT
International Performing Arts Festival, Hartford, CT
Mark Twain Memorial, Hartford, CT
School of the Hartford Ballet, Hartford, CT
Summer Night Concert, Hartford, CT

Civic & Public Affairs
Community Renewal Team, Hartford, CT
Connecticut Housing Investment Fund, Hartford, CT
Coop-Initiatives, Hartford, CT
Coordinating Council for Foundations, Hartford, CT
El Hogar del Futuro, Hartford, CT
Hartford Area Habitat for Humanity, Hartford, CT
Hartford Consortium/Career Beginnings, Hartford, CT
Hartford Economic Development Corp, Hartford, CT
Hartford Vision Project, Hartford, CT
Local Initiatives Support Corp, Hartford, CT
Urban League, Hartford, CT
Women's League Day Care Center, Hartford, CT
Work Bank, Hartford, CT

Education
Achievement Unlimited, Hartford, CT
American School for the Deaf, West Hartford, CT
College of Insurance, New York, NY
Interracial Scholarship Fund, Hartford, CT
Junior Achievement of North Central Connecticut, New Britain, CT
Literacy Volunteers of Connecticut, New Haven, CT
Miss Porter's School, Farmington, CT
Reading is Fundamental, Hartford, CT
St. Joseph College
San Juan Tutorial Program, Hartford, CT
United Negro College Fund, Hartford, CT
University of Hartford, Hartford, CT
Wesleyan University, Middletown, CT

Environment
Farmington River Watershed Association, Simsbury, CT

Health
American Red Cross '93 Flood, Hartford, CT
Connecticut AIDS Services, Hartford, CT
Gaylord Hospital, Wallingford, CT
Greater Hartford HIV Action Initiative, Hartford, CT
Hartford Rehabilitation Center, Hartford, CT
Hospital for Special Care, Hartford, CT

Religion
St. Monica's Second Century Project, Hartford, CT

Social Services
Bellevue Square Youth Club, Glastonbury, CT
Boy Scouts Long River Council
Drugs Don't Work, Saint Petersburg, FL
Fidelco Guide Dog Foundation, Bloomfield, CT
Oakhill School for Blind
United Way Combined Health Appeal, Hartford, CT

THE HARTFORD

Company Contact

Hartford, CT
Web: http://www.thehartford.com

Company Description

Former Name: ITT Hartford Group, Inc.
SIC(s): 6331 Fire, Marine & Casualty Insurance.
Parent Company: Hartford Financial Services Group, Inc., Hartford, CT, United States

Operating Locations

Also operates in Canada and Western Europe.

Nonmonetary Support

Value: $400,000 (1990); $600,000 (1989); $3,000,000 (1987)
Type: Donated Equipment; In-kind Services; Loaned Executives

Corporate Sponsorship

Type: Arts & cultural events

Giving Contact

Edna Negron, Director, Community Affairs
The Hartford
Hartford Place
690 Asylum Avenue
Hartford, CT 06115
Phone: (860)547-5000
Fax: (860)547-3799
Email: EDNA.NEGRON@THEHARTFORD.com

Alternate Contact

Darlene Leak, corporate relations
Phone: (860)547-3133

Description

Organization Type: Corporate Giving Program
Giving Locations: CT: Hartford Greater Hartford area principally near operating locations and to national organizations, grant monies are allocated based on the size of the operation.
Grant Types: Capital, Challenge, Employee Matching Gifts, Endowment, General Support, Project, Research, Scholarship.
Note: Employee matching gift ratio: 1 to 1 up to $2,000 per employee annually for education.

Giving Philosophy

'Corporate contributions from the Hartford support efforts that enhance the quality of life in the community where the company maintains offices.'
Hartford's mission is to '1., Work to improve the quality of life in The Hartford's corporate headquarters region and in field office community, and 2., Increase awareness of The Hartford's programs to enhance its image among employees, shareholders, regulators, customers, and other key opinion leaders in the home office and in the field.

Financial Summary

Total Giving: $4,400,000 (2000 approx); $4,200,000 (1999 approx); $4,000,000 (1998 approx). Note: Contributes through corporate direct giving program only.
Assets: $562,532 (1995); $469,766 (1994); $76,033 (1993)
Gifts Received: $1,136,066 (1997); $2,500,000 (1995); $2,200,000 (1994). Note: Contributions are received from Hartford Fire Insurance Co.

Typical Recipients

Arts & Humanities: Arts Associations & Councils, Arts Centers, Arts Funds, Community Arts, Dance, Arts & Humanities-General, History & Archaeology, Libraries, Literary Arts, Museums/Galleries, Music, Opera, Performing Arts, Public Broadcasting, Theater

Civic & Public Affairs: African American Affairs, Botanical Gardens/Parks, Business/Free Enterprise, Civil Rights, Economic Development, Employment/Job Training, Civic & Public Affairs-General, Hispanic Affairs, Housing, Law & Justice, Nonprofit Management, Parades/Festivals, Professional & Trade Associations, Public Policy, Safety, Urban & Community Affairs, Women's Affairs
Education: Agricultural Education, Arts/Humanities Education, Business Education, Colleges & Universities, Community & Junior Colleges, Continuing Education, Education Associations, Education Funds, Education-General, Health & Physical Education, International Studies, Journalism/Media Education, Legal Education, Literacy, Medical Education, Minority Education, Private Education (Precollege), Public Education (Precollege), Religious Education, Science/Mathematics Education, Special Education, Student Aid, Vocational & Technical Education
Environment: Environment-General
Health: AIDS/HIV, Children's Health/Hospitals, Clinics/Medical Centers, Eyes/Blindness, Geriatric Health, Health Policy/Cost Containment, Health Organizations, Hospices, Hospitals, Medical Rehabilitation, Medical Research, Prenatal Health Issues, Preventive Medicine/Wellness Organizations, Public Health
Religion: Ministries, Religious Welfare
Social Services: Big Brother/Big Sister, Camps, Child Welfare, Community Service Organizations, Crime Prevention, Day Care, Delinquency & Criminal Rehabilitation, Domestic Violence, Emergency Relief, Family Services, Food/Clothing Distribution, Homes, People with Disabilities, Recreation & Athletics, Senior Services, Shelters/Homelessness, Social Services-General, Substance Abuse, United Funds/United Ways, YMCA/YWCA/YMHA/YWHA, Youth Organizations

Contributions Analysis

Giving Priorities: United Way, higher education, job placement, civic affairs, the arts, and elderly.
Arts & Humanities: 22%. Supports museums, public television, arts and the symphony orchestra.
Civic & Public Affairs: 10%. Funds organizations that provide programs to develop self-sufficiency to individualss with disabilities and to mature Americans. Also supports programs that provide employment training, job creation, housing, business development, transportation, neighborhood development, and law enforcement.
Education: 31%. Supports mostly colleges and universities, primarily for scholarships, development of academic programs, business education, and insurance education. Also supports job training and career advancement for minorities and the disadvantaged. Employee matching gifts to colleges and universities amount to nearly one third of all educational grants.

Application Procedures

Initial Contact: Organizations in Hartford should send a brief two-page letter requesting application form to headquarters; organizations near the company's regional offices should send requests to the local general manager for consideration, who may forward it to Hartford depending on the size of the grant requested. Individual applications for scholarships are not accepted.
Application Requirements: Send a brief a description of organization and project, including legal name, history, activities, and constituency served; summary of project for which funds are sought, including verification of need; goals and means for accomplishing them, including how many people will be affected; other organizations providing similar programs (if any) and how they differ; budget for organization and project; amount requested; actual and potential sources and amounts of funding; proof of tax-exempt and nonprivate foundation status; list of officers, directors, executive director, and other key people.
Deadlines: January 15, April 1, July 1, and September 15.
Review Process: Committee meets in March, June, September, and November for grant considerations. Decisions are generally based on written proposals, however, a periodic site visit by Hartford or a personal interview may be required.
Evaluative Criteria: Degree to which proposal meets company's guidelines, efficient management of program funds, human service value and practicality of objectives, nonduplication of existing programs, number of individuals served, fundraising stability of organization and range of support of program, organization's track record.
Decision Notification: Quarterly.

Restrictions

Excluded from consideration are endowments, health care issues or organizations, individualss, conferences and seminars, courtesy advertising, private foundations, religious purposes, athletic outings, reduing or eliminating a pre-existing debt, one-time events including testimonial and fund-raising dinners, environmental issues/organizations, or activities such as scouting band, and little league, etc. if they are not a part of programs that fall under the specified funding categories.
Capital support is generally limited to agencies in Greater Hartford. Organizations accepted for a capital grant may not also receive operating support in the same year.
Funding is generally not provided to agencies that receive United Way funding. Special programs can be an exception, but the agency must have the permission of the United Way before it solicits funding.

Additional Information

In 1997, the foundation was integrated into the corporate giving program.
Generally seeks to support organizations that enable individuals to help themselves and that are supported by creative and ultimately self-supporting funding initiatives.
Where possible, the Hartford will try to leverage its funds through matching and challenge grants and consider awarding multiple-year grants if appropriate and where desirable. matching and challenge grants and consider awarding multiple-year grants if appropriate and where desirable.

Corporate Officials

Ramani Ayer: chairman, president, chief executive officer B Kerala, KE India 1947. ED Indian Institute of Technology BS (1969); Drexel University MS (1973). PRIM CORP EMPL chairman, president, chief executive officer: The Hartford. CORP AFFIL president: Twin City Fire Insurance Co.; director: New York Stock Exchange Inc.; president: Hartford Insurance Midwest; president: Hartford Insurance Southeast; president, chief operating officer: Hartford Fire Insurance Co.; president: Hartford Casualty Insurance Co.; chairman, president, chief executive officer: Hartford Financial Services Group Inc.; president: Hartford Accident Indemnity Co. NONPR AFFIL trustee: Mark Twain House; trustee: Mark Twain House; trustee: Insurance Institute America; director: American Insurance Association.
Joseph H. Gareau: executive vice president, chief investment officer B Westfield, MA 1947. ED University of Massachusetts BBA (1973); University of Hartford MBA (1978). PRIM CORP EMPL executive vice president, chief investment officer: The Hartford Insurance Co. ADD CORP EMPL executive vice president: Hartford Financial Services Group Inc.; senior vice president, chief investment officer, director: Hartford Insurance Midwest; executive vice president: Hartford Insurance of the Southeast; executive vice president: Hartford Accident Indemnity Co.; executive vice president, director: Hartford Casualty Insurance Co.; president, chief invest officer: Hartford Investment Management Co.; vice president,chief investment officer: Pacific Industry Co. Inc. CORP AFFIL vice president, chief investment officer: Pacific Industry Co. Inc.
Edward L. Morgan: group senior vice president B Scranton, PA 1943. ED Gettysburg College (1965). PRIM CORP EMPL group senior vice president: The Hartford ADD CORP EMPL senior vice president: Hartford Financial Services Group Inc.; senior vice president: Hartford Fire Insurance Co.

Giving Program Officials

Ann D. De Raismes: member PRIM CORP EMPL senior vice president: Hartford Life Annuity Insurance Co.
Joseph H. Gareau: investment officer B Westfield, MA 1947. ED University of Massachusetts BBA (1973); University of Hartford MBA (1978). PRIM CORP EMPL executive vice president, chief investment officer: The Hartford Insurance Co. ADD CORP EMPL executive vice president: Hartford Financial Services Group Inc.; senior vice president, chief investment officer, director: Hartford Insurance Midwest; executive vice president: Hartford Insurance of the Southeast; executive vice president: Hartford Accident Indemnity Co.; executive vice president, director: Hartford Casualty Insurance Co.; president, chief invest officer: Hartford Investment Management Co.; vice president,chief investment officer: Pacific Industry Co. Inc. CORP AFFIL vice president, chief investment officer: Pacific Industry Co. Inc.
Helen G. Goodman: senior vice president B Bridgeport, CT 1941. ED Barnard College (1964); Columbia University (1979). PRIM CORP EMPL senior vice president: The Hartford. CORP AFFIL treasurer, director: Hartford Action Plan Infant Health; senior vice president: Hartford Financial Services Group Inc.
David M. Klein: vice president B Brooklyn, NY 1946. ED University of Rhode Island (1968); Temple University (1970). PRIM CORP EMPL senior vice president: The Hartford ADD CORP EMPL senior vice president: Hardford Insurance Group; executive vice president: Hartford Financial Service Group; senior vice president: Hartford Insurance Midwest.
Edward L. Morgan: member contributions committee B Scranton, PA 1943. ED Gettysburg College (1965). PRIM CORP EMPL group senior vice president: The Hartford ADD CORP EMPL senior vice president: Hartford Financial Services Group Inc.; senior vice president: Hartford Fire Insurance Co.
Edna Negron: PRIM CORP EMPL director community affairs: The Hartford.
Michael Stephen Wilder: B New Haven, CT 1941. ED Yale University BA (1963); Harvard University JD (1966). PRIM CORP EMPL senior vice president, general counsel: The Hartford Financial Services Group Inc. CORP AFFIL senior vice president: Twin City Fire Insurance Co.; vice president: ITT Hartford Insurance Group; vice president: Property Casualty Insurance; secretary: Hartford Insurance Southeast; officer: Hartford Fire Insurance Co.; officer: Hartford Insurance Midwest; secretary: Hartford Equity Sales Co.; officer: Hartford Accident Indemnity Co.; secretary: Hartford Casualty Insurance Co. NONPR AFFIL director: American Arbitration Association; member: American Bar Association.

Grants Analysis

Disclosure Period: calendar year ending 1997
Total Grants: $1,006,472*
Number of Grants: 250
Average Grant: $4,026
Highest Grant: $383,333
Typical Range: $50 to $5,000
***Note:** Giving excludes United Way.

Recent Grants

Note: Grants derived from 1997 Form 990.

Arts & Humanities

110,000	Greater Hartford Arts Council, Hartford, CT

88,000 Wadsworth Athenaeum, Hartford, CT
40,000 Mark Twain House
20,000 Mark Twain House
9,500 Hartford Stage Company, Hartford, CT
7,500 Amistad Foundation, Hartford, CT
5,000 Orange Firefighters Museum
2,500 KCET Community Television of Southern California, Los Angeles, CA
1,500 Baltimore Symphony Orchestra, Baltimore, MD

Civic & Public Affairs

15,000 National Safety Council, Chicago, IL
15,000 Neighborhood Housing Services, Hartford, CT
12,500 Hartford Areas Rally Together, Hartford, CT
10,000 Broad Park Development Corporation
10,000 Neighborhood Housing Services, Baltimore, MD
10,000 San Diego Neighborhood Housing Services, San Diego, CA
8,000 Hartford Guides, Hartford, CT
7,500 Asylum Hill Organizing Project, Hartford, CT
7,500 Revitalization Corps, Hartford, CT
6,000 West Indian Foundation, Hartford, CT
5,000 Bushnell Park Foundation, Hartford, CT
5,000 Neighborhood Housing Services, Saint Louis, MO
3,500 Los Angeles Works, Los Angeles, CA
3,000 San Diego Urban League, San Diego, CA
2,500 Daniel Molinaro Foundation
2,500 San Diego Urban League, San Diego, CA

Education

25,000 West Middle School Committee, Hartford, CT
15,380 National Merit Scholarship Corporation, Evanston, IL
12,500 Junior Achievement North Central Connecticut, Hartford, CT
10,000 Central Connecticut State University, New Britain, CT
10,000 Greater Hartford Consortium for Higher Education, Hartford, CT
6,000 University of Connecticut Department of English, Storrs, CT
5,000 San Juan Tutorial Program, Hartford, CT

Health

100,000 Connecticut Children's Medical Center, Hartford, CT
100,000 St. Francis Hospital and Medical Center
25,000 Hartford Action Plan on Infant Health, Hartford, CT
20,000 Hartford Foundation for Public Giving, Hartford, CT
10,000 St. Francis Hospital and Medical Center

Religion

40,000 Salvation Army, Hartford, CT
5,000 Family Life Ministry, Hartford, CT
5,000 Samaritans, Boston, MA

Social Services

383,333 United Way Capital Area
40,000 Disabled Sports USA, Rockville, MD
20,000 Child Council, Hartford, CT
12,000 Camp Courant, Hartford, CT
10,000 Foodshare, Hartford, CT
8,500 Nutmeg Big Brothers and Big Sisters, Hartford, CT
5,000 South Park Inn, Hartford, CT
2,500 Hartford Food System, Hartford, CT
2,500 Parson Child and Family Center, Albany, NY
1,500 Glens Falls Independent Living Center, Glens Falls, NY

Hartmarx Corp.

Company Contact

Chicago, IL

Company Description

Employees: 8,600
SIC(s): 2311 Men's/Boys' Suits & Coats, 2325 Men's/Boys' Trousers & Slacks, 2329 Men's/Boys' Clothing Nec, 6719 Holding Companies Nec.

Nonmonetary Support

Value: $10,000 (1989); $10,000 (1988)

Hartmarx Charitable Foundation

Giving Contact

Kay C. Nalbach, President
Hartmarx Charitable Foundation
101 North Wacker Drive
Chicago, IL 60606
Phone: (312)372-6300
Fax: (312)444-2710
Web: http://www.hartmarx.com
Note: Foundation is currently in the process of restructuring its giving program.

Description

EIN: 366152745
Organization Type: Corporate Foundation
Giving Locations: headquarters and operating communities.
Grant Types: Capital, Employee Matching Gifts, General Support, Research, Scholarship.
Note: Employee matching gift ratio: 1 to 1 up to $1,500 for each individual annually. Foundation will not match bequests, dues, tuitition fees, subscription fees, loan payment, or contributions not made as direct donations.

Financial Summary

Total Giving: $341,123 (fiscal year ending November 30, 1998); $231,483 (fiscal 1996); $288,858 (fiscal 1995). Note: Contributes through corporate direct giving program and foundation. 1996 Giving includes foundation ($124,258); matching gifts ($20,425); United Way ($86,800). 1993 Giving includes matching gifts ($16,155).
Giving Analysis: Giving for fiscal 1998 includes: foundation ($181,348); foundation grants to United Way ($134,200); foundation matching gifts ($25,575)
Assets: $113,919 (fiscal 1998); $50,933 (fiscal 1996); $22,865 (fiscal 1995)
Gifts Received: $3,315,000 (fiscal 1998)

Typical Recipients

Arts & Humanities: Arts Festivals, Arts Institutes, Dance, Arts & Humanities-General, Historic Preservation, History & Archaeology, Libraries, Museums/Galleries, Music, Opera, Performing Arts, Public Broadcasting, Theater
Civic & Public Affairs: African American Affairs, Botanical Gardens/Parks, Business/Free Enterprise, Clubs, Community Foundations, Economic Development, Civic & Public Affairs-General, Housing, Law & Justice, Legal Aid, Nonprofit Management, Professional & Trade Associations, Public Policy, Safety, Urban & Community Affairs, Women's Affairs, Zoos/Aquariums
Education: Arts/Humanities Education, Business Education, Colleges & Universities, Community & Junior Colleges, Economic Education, Education Associations, Education Funds, Education Reform, Engineering/Technological Education, Faculty Development, Literacy, Minority Education, Private Education (Precollege), Public Education (Precollege), Science/Mathematics Education, Student Aid, Vocational & Technical Education
Environment: Wildlife Protection
Health: AIDS/HIV, Cancer, Children's Health/Hospitals, Clinics/Medical Centers, Diabetes, Health Organizations, Hospitals, Nursing Services, Prenatal Health Issues, Public Health, Respiratory, Single-Disease Health Associations
International: Foreign Arts Organizations
Religion: Jewish Causes, Religious Organizations, Religious Welfare
Science: Science Museums
Social Services: Animal Protection, At-Risk Youth, Camps, Child Welfare, Community Centers, Community Service Organizations, Crime Prevention, Domestic Violence, Family Planning, Family Services, Food/Clothing Distribution, People with Disabilities, Recreation & Athletics, Scouts, Senior Services, Sexual Abuse, Shelters/Homelessness, United Funds/United Ways, Volunteer Services, YMCA/YWCA/YMHA/YWHA, Youth Organizations

Contributions Analysis

Giving Priorities: Social welfare, higher education, civic organiztions, the arts, and health care.
Arts & Humanities: 13%. Music, museums, opera, public broadcasting, and theater.
Civic & Public Affairs: 5%. Business organizations, community development, housing, professional associations, public policy, and women's affairs.
Education: 14%. Colleges and universities, education associations,minority education, and education funds. Sponsors educational matching gifts program.
Environment: 1%.
Health: 5%.
Religion: 2%. Jewish and Christian organizations, including united and federated funds.
Social Services: 60%. Primary support is awarded to united funds in or near company operating locations. Other areas of support are youth organizations, legal aid, recreation and athletics, child welfare, and religious welfare.
Note: About 60% of contributions are made from corporate headquarters; 40% is allocated and disbursed through operating companies. Total contributions made in 1998.

Application Procedures

Initial Contact: Submit a brief letter or proposal.
Application Requirements: Include legal name of organization, summary of specific project to be supported, amount requested, latest financial statements, and proof of tax-exempt status.
Deadlines: none .
Review Process: Foundation president and contributions committee review requests over $2,500, which are then submitted to board of directors for approval; grants of less than $2,500 must be approved by foundation president and the subsidiary's chief executive officer before processing.
Decision Notification: Quarterly, for contributions over $2,500.

Restrictions

Does not support goodwill advertising, political or lobbying groups, individuals, or religious organizations for sectarian purposes.

Corporate Officials

James Edward Condon: vice president, treasurer, director B Chicago, IL 1950. ED Illinois Institute of Technology BS (1972); Illinois Institute of Technology MS (1973); University of Chicago MBA (1976). PRIM CORP EMPL vice president, treasurer: Hartmarx Corp. CORP AFFIL treasurer: International Women's Apparel; treasurer, director: Hart Schaffner & Marx. NONPR AFFIL member: Association Investment Management & Research.
Elbert O. Hand: chairman, chief executive officer, director B 1939. ED Hamilton College BA (1961). PRIM CORP EMPL chairman, chief executive officer,

director: Hartmarx Corp. CORP AFFIL director: Jaymar-Ruby Inc.

Glenn R. Morgan: executive vice president, chief financial officer B Chicago, IL 1947. ED Northwestern University BS (1968); Northwestern University MBA (1970). PRIM CORP EMPL executive vice president, chief financial officer: Hartmarx Corp. CORP AFFIL vice president: Hart Schaffner & Marx. NONPR AFFIL chairman financial managing committee: American Apparel Manufacturer Association; member: Financial Executives Institute.

Homi Burjor Patel: president, chief operating officer, director B Bombay, MH India 1949. ED University of Bombay BS (1973); Columbia University MBA (1975). PRIM CORP EMPL president, chief operating officer, director: Hartmarx Corp. CORP AFFIL chairman, director: M Wile & Co.; treasurer, director: Textile Clothing Tech Corp.; director: Jaymar-Ruby Inc.; chairman: Plaid Clothing Co. Inc.; vice president: Hart Schaffner & Marx; president: Hart Services Inc. DEL. NONPR AFFIL executive vice president, member, director: Clothing Manufacturer Association America. CLUB AFFIL Chicago Club; University Club New York.

Foundation Officials

James Edward Condon: treasurer (see above)

Kay C. Nalbach: president B Moweaqua, IL. ED University of Illinois (1959). PRIM CORP EMPL assistant section: Hartmarx Corp. NONPR AFFIL member: American Society of Corporate Secretaries; member: Executive Women International.

Grants Analysis

Disclosure Period: fiscal year ending November 30, 1998

Total Grants: $181,348*

Number of Grants: 130

Average Grant: $1,395

Highest Grant: $25,000

Typical Range: $500 to $5,500

*Note: Giving excludes matching gifts, United Way.

Recent Grants

Note: Grants derived from fiscal 1998 Form 990.

Arts & Humanities

15,000	Music of the Baroque, Chicago, IL
5,000	Chicago Symphony Orchestra, Chicago, IL
5,000	Lyric Opera of Chicago, Chicago, IL
4,620	Ravinia Festival Association, Highland Park, IL
3,500	Hubbard Street Dance Club, Chicago, IL
2,000	The Field Museum, Chicago, IL
1,500	Shea's Performing Arts, Buffalo, NY

Civic & Public Affairs

10,000	Unity Foundation of LaPorte County, Michigan City, IN
2,500	Chicago Zoological Society, Brokfield, IL
1,500	Donors Forum of Chicago, Chicago, IL

Education

5,000	Center for Excellence in Education, McLean, VA
5,000	Fashion Institute of Technology, New York, NY
5,000	Philadelphia College of Textiles and Science, Philadelphia, PA
3,600	Northwestern University, Evanston, IL
3,500	Northwestern University, Evanston, IL
3,000	Hamilton College, Clinton, NY
3,000	Philadelphia College of Textiles & Sciences, Philadelphia, PA
2,000	Illinois Institute of Technology, Chicago, IL
2,000	St. John Fisher College, Rochester, NY
2,000	United Negro College Fund, Chicago, IL
1,500	Southeastern Community College, Whiteville, NY
1,500	University of Illinois College of Commerce & Business Administration, Champaign, IL
1,330	The School of the Art Institute of Chicago, Chicago, IL
1,100	Junior Achievement of Michigan City, Michigan City, IN
1,000	Literacy Chicago, Chicago, IL

Environment

2,500	Trout Unlimited Coldwater Conservation Fund, Arlington, VA

Health

6,000	American Cancer Society Illinois Division, Inc., Chicago, IL
4,000	St. Jude Children's Research, Chicago, IL
3,000	Rush-Presbyterian-St. Lukes Medical Center, Chicago, IL
2,500	The Children's Memorial Medical Center, Chicago, IL

Religion

4,000	Jewish United Fund, Chicago, IL
2,000	American Jewish Committee, Chicago, IL

Social Services

60,000	United Way/Crusade of Mercy, Chicago, IL
25,000	Rosie's Place, Boston, MA
22,000	United Way of Michigan City / Michiana Area, Inc., Michigan City, IN
15,000	United Way of Buffalo and Erie County, Buffalo, NY
13,500	United Way of Greater Rochester, Rochester, NY
6,000	United Way of Calhoun County, Anniston, AL
5,000	Metro United Way, Louisville, KY
5,000	National Committee to Prevent Child Abuse, New Brunswick, NJ
3,500	Boys & Girls Clubs of Chicago, Chicago, IL
3,500	United Way of South Central Kentucky, Somerset, KY
3,000	United Way of Fulton County, Rochester, IN
2,500	YMCA, Chicago, IL
2,000	Area Wide United Way, Cape Girardeau, MO
2,000	United Way of the Quad Cities Area, Davenport, IA
1,500	Thresholds, Chicago, IL
1,400	United Way of Greater St. Louis, St. Louis, MO
1,000	Infant Welfare Society, Lake Forest, IL
1,000	Operation Christmas, Arlington Heights, IL

HASBRO, INC.

Company Contact

1027 Neport Ave.
Pawtucket, RI 02861
Phone: (401)431-8697
Web: http://www.hasbro.com

Company Description

Revenue: US$3,304,500,000

Employees: 12,000

Fortune Rank: 376, per FORTUNE Magazine's list of 500 Largest U.S. Corporations (1999). FF 376

SIC(s): 3944 Games, Toys & Children's Vehicles.

Operating Locations

Australia: Tonka Corp. Pty. Ltd., Rhodes; Milton Bradley Australia Pty. Ltd., Rydalmere; Kenner Parker Australia Ltd., Rydalmere; Austria: Hasbro Osterreich GmbH, Vienna; Belgium: Hasbro MB SA, Brussels, Brabant; Canada: Hasbro Canada, Longueuil; Hasbro Sales, Mississauga; Kenner Products (Canada), Toronto; Denmark: Hasbro Scandinavia A/S, Glostrup, Copenhagen; France: Kenner Parker Toys, Paris; Hasbro SA, Paris Nord, Immeuble Ampere; Germany: Hasbro Deutschland GmbH, Dietzenbach, Hessen; Milton Bradley Gmbh, Furth; Kenner Parker Toys International, Rodgan; Greece: Hasbro Hellas SA, Athens, Attiki; Hong Kong: Tonka Far East Ltd., Kowloon; Hasbro Asia Pacific Marketing Ltd., Tsim Sha Tsui, Kowloon; Hasbro Bradley Far East Ltd., Tsim Sha Tsui, Kowloon; Kenner Parker (H.K.) Ltd., Tsim Sha Tsui, Kowloon; Kid Dimension Far East Ltd., Tsim Sha Tsui, Kowloon; Hungary: Hasbro Magyarorszag KFT, Budapest; Ireland: Hasbro Ireland Ltd., Waterford; MB Ireland, Waterford; Italy: MB Italy S.r.l., Milan; Tonka Italia Spa, Milan; Hasbro Italy SRL, Rozzano, Lombardia; Promotoys SRL, Rozzano, Lombardia; Japan: Hasbro Japan KK, Tokyo; Mexico: Hasbro de Mexico SA de CV, Ciudad de Mexico; Tonka Corp., Juarez; Juguetrenes SA de CV, Tijuana; Netherlands: Kenner Parker Toys, Amsterdam; MB International BV, Ter Apel, Groningen; Hasbro BV, Utrecht; Norway: Impra AS, Oslo, Akershus; New Zealand: Hasbro New Zealand Ltd., Auckland; Kenner Parker (N.Z.) Lt., Auckland; Portugal: Hasbro Importacao e Exportacao de Jogos e Brinquedos Lda., Estoril, Cascais; Hasbro, Marinha Grande; Spain: MB Espana SA, Quart de Poblet, Valencia; Switzerland: MB (Switzerland) AG, Aargau; Hasbro (Schweiz) AG, Berikon, Argovie; United Kingdom: Tonka Europe Ltd., Henley-on-Thames, Oxford; Kenner Parker Europe, Maidenhead; Hasbro Bradley UK Ltd., Uxbridge, Middlesex; Hasbro Consumer Services Ltd., Uxbridge, Middlesex; Hasbro Europe UK Ltd., Uxbridge, Middlesex; Hasbro Interactive Ltd., Uxbridge, Middlesex; Hasbro International, Uxbridge, Middlesex; Milton Bradley Ltd., Uxbridge, Middlesex; Milton Bradley Storage Ltd., Uxbridge, Middlesex

Nonmonetary Support

Value: $750,000 (1996); $500,000 (1992); $250,000 (1990)

Type: Donated Products

Note: Company donates toys nationally to direct service organizations that provide services around the clock for children (see 'Other Things You Should Know')

Hasbro Charitable Trust Inc.

Giving Contact

Ms. Karen Davis, Director
Hasbro Charitable Trust Inc.
1027 Newport Avenue
Pawtucket, RI 02862
Phone: (401)727-5429
Fax: (401)721-7275

Description

EIN: 222538470

Organization Type: Corporate Foundation

Giving Locations: headquarters and operating communities.

Grant Types: Employee Matching Gifts, Project.

Note: Employee matching gift ratio: 1 to 1 for higher education.

Financial Summary

Total Giving: $1,046,334 (1998); $907,873 (1997); $1,153,317 (1996). Note: Contributes through corporate direct giving program and foundation.

Giving Analysis: Giving for 1996 includes: foundation ($1,120,411); foundation matching gifts ($32,906); 1997: foundation ($705,930); foundation grants to United Way ($177,500); foundation matching gifts ($24,443); 1998: foundation ($860,000);

foundation grants to United Way ($170,000); foundation matching gifts ($16,634)
Assets: $1,518,944 (1998); $1,566,891 (1997); $1,498,023 (1996)
Gifts Received: $1,000,000 (1998); $1,000,000 (1997); $1,003,700 (1996). Note: The trust receives contributions from Hasbro Inc.

Typical Recipients

Arts & Humanities: Arts Centers, Arts Funds, Arts Institutes, Libraries, Museums/Galleries, Music, Performing Arts
Civic & Public Affairs: African American Affairs, Business/Free Enterprise, Community Foundations, Economic Development, Ethnic Organizations, Civic & Public Affairs-General, Housing, Law & Justice, Legal Aid, Minority Business, Municipalities/Towns, Public Policy, Urban & Community Affairs, Women's Affairs, Zoos/Aquariums
Education: Arts/Humanities Education, Business Education, Colleges & Universities, Economic Education, Education Funds, Education Reform, Elementary Education (Public), Education-General, Literacy, Preschool Education, Private Education (Precollege), Public Education (Precollege), School Volunteerism
Environment: Air/Water Quality, Forestry, Environment-General
Health: AIDS/HIV, Alzheimers Disease, Cancer, Children's Health/Hospitals, Clinics/Medical Centers, Diabetes, Emergency/Ambulance Services, Geriatric Health, Heart, Hospices, Hospitals, Hospitals (University Affiliated), Kidney, Medical Rehabilitation, Medical Research, Prenatal Health Issues, Public Health, Research/Studies Institutes, Single-Disease Health Associations
International: Health Care/Hospitals, Human Rights, International Affairs, International Organizations, International Peace & Security Issues, International Relations, International Relief Efforts
Religion: Jewish Causes, Religious Organizations, Religious Welfare
Science: Science Museums
Social Services: Big Brother/Big Sister, Child Welfare, Community Centers, Community Service Organizations, Day Care, Emergency Relief, Family Planning, Family Services, Food/Clothing Distribution, People with Disabilities, Recreation & Athletics, Refugee Assistance, Scouts, Senior Services, Sexual Abuse, Shelters/Homelessness, Special Olympics, United Funds/United Ways, Volunteer Services, YMCA/YWCA/YMHA/YWHA, Youth Organizations

Contributions Analysis

Giving Priorities: Hasbro reviews requests on a case-by-case basis. Highest priority is funding organizations concerned with the health and welfare of children. Support generally is project oriented. Also supports other human service organizations. Arts and civic organizations are lesser priorities. Contributions outside the U.S. are minimal and are handled on a case by case basis. In 1994, such support was estimated at $20,000. Domestically, limited support goes to local organizations with an international focus.
Arts & Humanities: 1%. Funds museums and libraries.
Civic & Public Affairs: 12%. Supports community and neighborhood associations, urban, minority, and legal affairs.
Education: 11%. Focus on higher education in Rhode Island.
Health: 14%. Funds children's health, the Red Cross, and single-disease health associations.
Social Services: 44%. Funds United Way, scouting, and children's services.
Note: Total foundation giving in 1997.

Application Procedures

Initial Contact: Request guidelines and application by phone.
Application Requirements: Include statement of purpose and objectives; history of organization's programs; list of board and staff, as well as record of financial commitment by board for proposed project; annual operating budget for organization and for year in which grant will occur; recently audited financial statement; description of program for which funds are requested, including its budget; amount requested; copy of tax-exempt determination letter; list of other corporations and foundations approached and level of financial support requested or received.
Deadlines: Prior to July 1 for consideration in current year.
Notes: Foundation only reviews requests in communities where company has operations.

Restrictions

From time to time, unusual or special projects will alter the grant review process.
Cash contributions are limited to operating locations. Does not support religious organizations, individuals, political organizations, scholarships, loans, endowments, goodwill advertising, fund raisers, sponsorship of recreational activities, or research.

Additional Information

Hasbro also sponsors the Hasbro Children's Foundation, which contributes about $2,000,000 annually to health, social services, and educational programs for children under the age of 12. Contact is Eve Weiss, Executive Director, Hasbro Children's Foundation, 32 W 23rd Street, New York, NY 10010, (212) 645-2400. Toy requests should be submitted by October 1. If an organization receives toys for two consecutive years, company follows with a two year hiatus. No participation in fundraisers, give-a-ways, or incentives. Toys go to supervised playrooms in organizations which provide direct services to children, especially shelters and child life departments of hospitals. Donates only to 501(c)(3) organizations within the U.S. Policy holds for Hasbro and its subsidiaries: Milton Bradley, Playskool, Tonka, Kenner, and Parker.

Corporate Officials

Alan Geoffrey Hassenfeld: chairman, chief executive officer B Providence, RI 1948. ED University of Pennsylvania BA (1970). PRIM CORP EMPL chairman, chief executive officer: Hasbro Inc. NONPR AFFIL trustee: Miriam Hospital; overseer: University Pennsylvania School Arts & Sciences; director: Foster Parents Plan; director: Jerusalem Foundation; trustee: Bryant College; trustee: Deerfield Academy Alumni Association; director: Association Government Boards, Colleges & Universities.
Cynthia Reed: senior vice president, general counsel ED Wellesley College AB (1977); Northeastern University JD (1980). PRIM CORP EMPL senior vice president, general counsel: Hasbro Inc.
Alfred J. Verrecchia: executive, director B Providence, RI 1943. ED University of Rhode Island BS (1967); University of Rhode Island MBA (1972). PRIM CORP EMPL executive, director: Hasbro Inc. CORP AFFIL president, director: Hasbro Global operations. NONPR AFFIL director: Bradley Hospital.

Foundation Officials

Karen Davis: director
Alan Geoffrey Hassenfeld: president (see above)
Cynthia Reed: assistant secretary (see above)
Alfred J. Verrecchia: treasurer, trustee (see above)

Grants Analysis

Disclosure Period: calendar year ending 1998
Total Grants: $806,000*
Number of Grants: 80
Average Grant: $10,750
Highest Grant: $77,500
Typical Range: $1,000 to $10,000
*Note: Giving excludes United Way, matching gifts.

Recent Grants

Note: Grants derived from 1997 Form 990.

Arts & Humanities

50,000	Springfield Libraries & Museums
5,000	Cincinnati Institute of Fine Arts, Cincinnati, OH

Civic & Public Affairs

25,000	Northern Rhode Island Collaborative, Cumberland, RI
25,000	Urban Collaborative, Providence, RI
15,000	Walking Shield American Indian Society
10,000	Beth Israel Medical Center, New York, NY
5,000	AVANCE, Houston, TX
5,000	Fund for Community Progress, Providence, RI
5,000	Rhode Island Foundation, Providence, RI
2,850	City of Pawtucket, Pawtucket, RI
2,500	Barton Street Neighborhood Association
2,500	New England Legal Foundation, Boston, MA

Education

50,000	University of Rhode island, Providence, RI
50,000	University of Rhode Island, Providence, RI
50,000	University of Rhode Island, Providence, RI
50,000	University of Rhode Island, Providence, RI
20,000	Rhode Island School of Design, Providence, RI
10,000	Bryant College, Providence, RI
5,000	BSR Education Fund, Inc., Washington, DC
3,000	Education Foundation for the Fashion Industries, New York, NY
2,500	Rhode Island Academic Decathlon

Environment

2,500	American Forestry Association, Washington, DC

Health

42,000	United Appeal Community Chest - Red Cross of the Cincinnati Area, Cincinnati, OH
42,000	United Appeal Community Chest - Red Cross of the Cincinnati Area, Cincinnati, OH
25,000	Children's Hospital Medical Center, Boston, MA
14,300	Genetic Disease Foundation
10,000	Memorial Hospital
9,250	Muscular Dystrophy Association
2,500	American Foundation for AIDS Research, New York, NY
2,500	Children Affected by AIDS Foundation, El Segundo, CA
2,500	National Kidney Foundation
2,500	Providence Ambulatory Health Care Foundation, Providence, RI
2,500	Rhode Island Project AIDS, Inc., Providence, RI

International

50,000	Institute for International Sport, Kingston, RI
15,000	Refugees International, Washington, DC
2,500	The Asia Society, New York, NY
2,500	Plan International, Inc., Warwick, RI

Religion

5,000	National Conference of Christians and Jews, Inc., New York, NY
5,000	National Jewish Center, New York, NY

Science

10,000	Arthur Ashe Foundation, New York, NY
2,500	American Museum of Natural History, New York, NY

Social Services

160,000	United Way of Southeastern New England
160,000	United Way of Southeastern New England
47,560	Children's Benefit Fund, Inc., New York, NY
25,000	Operation Smile, Inc.
25,000	Rhode Island Meals on Wheels, Inc.
25,000	YWCA of Cincinnati, Cincinnati, OH
20,000	Narragansett Council of Boy Scouts, Providence, RI
20,000	Narragansett Council of Boy Scouts, Providence, RI
20,000	Narragansett Council of Boy Scouts, Providence, RI
17,500	United Way of El Paso County, El Paso, TX
7,000	Junior Achievement of Rhode Island, Providence, RI
5,000	Institute for Childhood Resources
5,000	Ocean State Adoption Resource Exchange, Providence, RI
5,000	Police Athletic League, Inc - New York, New York, NY
5,000	Sojourner House, Inc., Providence, RI
3,500	Volunteers in Providence Schools, Providence, RI
3,000	Houchen Community Center, El Paso, TX
2,500	Big Brothers of Rhode Island, Pawtucket, RI
2,500	Collin County Children's Advocacy Center, Inc.
2,500	Pawtucket Police Athletic League, Inc., Pawtucket, RI

HASBRO, INC.

Company Contact

1027 Neport Ave.
Pawtucket, RI 02861
Phone: (401)431-8697
Web: http://www.hasbro.com

Company Description

Revenue: US$3,304,500,000
Employees: 12,000
Fortune Rank: 376, per FORTUNE Magazine's list of 500 Largest U.S. Corporations (1999).
FF 376
SIC(s): 3944 Games, Toys & Children's Vehicles.

Operating Locations

Australia: Tonka Corp. Pty. Ltd., Rhodes; Milton Bradley Australia Pty. Ltd., Rydalmere; Kenner Parker Australia Ltd., Rydalmere; Austria: Hasbro Osterreich GmbH, Vienna; Belgium: Hasbro MB SA, Brussels, Brabant; Canada: Hasbro Canada, Longueuil; Hasbro Sales, Mississauga; Kenner Products (Canada), Toronto; Denmark: Hasbro Scandinavia A/S, Glostrup, Copenhagen; France: Kenner Parker Toys, Paris; Hasbro SA, Paris Nord, Immeuble Ampere; Germany: Hasbro Deutschland GmbH, Dietzenbach, Hessen; Milton Bradley Gmbh, Furth; Kenner Parker Toys International, Rodgan; Greece: Hasbro Hellas SA, Athens, Attiki; Hong Kong: Tonka Far East Ltd., Kowloon; Hasbro Asia Pacific Marketing Ltd., Tsim Sha Tsui, Kowloon; Hasbro Bradley Far East Ltd., Tsim Sha Tsui, Kowloon; Kenner Parker (H.K.) Ltd., Tsim Sha Tsui, Kowloon; Kid Dimension Far East Ltd., Tsim Sha Tsui, Kowloon; Hungary: Hasbro Magyarorszag KFT, Budapest; Ireland: Hasbro Ireland Ltd., Waterford; MB Ireland, Waterford; Italy: MB Italy S.r.l., Milan; Tonka Italia Spa, Milan; Hasbro Italy SRL, Rozzano, Lombardia; Promotoys SRL, Rozzano, Lombardia; Japan: Hasbro Japan KK, Tokyo; Mexico: Hasbro de Mexico SA de CV, Ciudad de Mexico; Tonka Corp., Juarez; Juguetrenes SA de CV, Tijuana; Netherlands: Kenner Parker Toys, Amsterdam; MB International BV, Ter Apel, Groningen; Hasbro BV, Utrecht; Norway: Impra AS, Oslo, Akershus; New Zealand: Hasbro New Zealand Ltd., Auckland; Kenner Parker (N.Z.) Lt., Auckland; Portugal: Hasbro Importacao e Exportacao de Jogos e Brinquedos Lda., Estoril, Cascais; Hasbro, Marinha Grande; Spain: MB Espana SA, Quart de Poblet, Valencia; Switzerland: MB (Switzerland) AG, Aargau; Hasbro (Schweiz) AG, Berikon, Argovie; United Kingdom: Tonka Europe Ltd., Henley-on-Thames, Oxford; Kenner Parker Europe, Maidenhead; Hasbro Bradley UK Ltd., Uxbridge, Middlesex; Hasbro Consumer Services Ltd., Uxbridge, Middlesex; Hasbro Europe UK Ltd., Uxbridge, Middlesex; Hasbro Interactive Ltd., Uxbridge, Middlesex; Hasbro International, Uxbridge, Middlesex; Milton Bradley Ltd., Uxbridge, Middlesex; Milton Bradley Storage Ltd., Uxbridge, Middlesex

Nonmonetary Support

Type: Donated Products
Contact: Karen Davis, Hasbro Charitable Trust
Note: Annual Sponsorship Budget: $25,000 to $50,000.

Hasbro Children's Foundation

Giving Contact

Jane S. Englebardt, Executive Director
Hasbro Children's Foundation
32 West 23rd Street
New York, NY 10010
Phone: (212)645-2400
Fax: (917)606-6264

Description

Organization Type: Corporate Foundation
Giving Locations: nationally.
Grant Types: Project, Seed Money.

Giving Philosophy

'Imagine, for a moment, how the world looks to a child whose life is in pieces due to poverty, disability, or illness. It is this image that has inspired the Hasbro Children's Foundation over the past twelve years to find a way to help children, their families and their communities to pick up the pieces and create lives for themselves that include joy, health and a sense of well-being.'
'By identifying and supporting the development and expansion of innovative programs across the country that improve the quality of life for disadvantaged children, we attempt to fit together the essential pieces of the puzzle - education, family support, health, shelter, food and play - community by community.' *Expanding Children's Programs Community by Community*

Financial Summary

Total Giving: $2,500,000 (2000 approx); $2,500,000 (1999 approx). Note: Contributes through foundation only.

Typical Recipients

Arts & Humanities: Theater
Education: Colleges & Universities, Literacy, Minority Education, Special Education
Health: Hospitals, Mental Health, Nutrition
International: International Peace & Security Issues
Social Services: Child Welfare, Family Services, People with Disabilities

Application Procedures

Initial Contact: brief letter requesting guidelines
Deadlines: None.
Decision Notification: board meets three times a year

Restrictions

Grants are not made to individuals; for capital or operating expenses; overhead; equipment; research; scholarships; events; annual giving campaigns; capital support; or for general support.

Additional Information

Although recipient organizations may fall within several areas, all grants are directed to innovative projects of direct service to children under 12 years of age in the areas of health; special education, with a focus on the handicapped; and societal needs, including abuse and neglect, literacy, and the impact of homelessness on children.

Corporate Officials

Alan Geoffrey Hassenfeld: chairman, chief executive officer B Providence, RI 1948. ED University of Pennsylvania BA (1970). PRIM CORP EMPL chairman, chief executive officer: Hasbro Inc. NONPR AFFIL trustee: Miriam Hospital; overseer: University Pennsylvania School Arts & Sciences; director: Foster Parents Plan; director: Jerusalem Foundation; trustee: Bryant College; trustee: Deerfield Academy Alumni Association; director: Association Government Boards, Colleges & Universities.

Foundation Officials

Theresa Acquaviva: foundation administrator

HAWAIIAN ELECTRIC CO., INC.

Company Contact

Honolulu, HI
Web: http://www.hei.com

Company Description

SIC(s): 4449 Water Transportation of Freight Nec, 4911 Electric Services, 4939 Combination Utility Nec, 6719 Holding Companies Nec.
Parent Company: Hawaiian Electric Industries, Inc.

Operating Locations

Operates throughout Hawaii.

Nonmonetary Support

Value: $300,000 (1990); $300,000 (1989); $250,000 (1988)
Type: Loaned Employees; Loaned Executives; Workplace Solicitation
Volunteer Programs: Company sponsors an employee volunteerism program, including the Great Aloha Run, and the Special Olympics; small grants are awarded to nonprofits where employees volunteer through the Volunteer Recognition Program.

Hawaiian Electric Industries Charitable Foundation

Giving Contact

Scott Shirai, Director, Community Relations
Hawaiian Electric Industries Charitable Foundation
PO Box 730
Honolulu, HI 96808
Phone: (808)532-5867
Fax: (808)532-5869
Email: sshirai@hei.com
Web: http://www.heicf/heicf.html

Alternate Contact

Phone: (808)532-5862

Description

EIN: 990230697
Organization Type: Corporate Foundation
Giving Locations: HI
Grant Types: Capital, Emergency, Employee Matching Gifts, General Support, Multiyear/Continuing Support, Scholarship.
Note: Employee matching gift ratio: 1 to 1. Foundation matches personal gifts of employees to accredited higher education. Also offers employee matching gifts to health and human service agencies, and qualifying pre-college and higher education. Gifts matched range from $50 to $500.

Giving Philosophy

'For over a century, HEI companies have participated in and contributed to the growth and prosperity of Hawaii. We are committed not only to providing essential services in the state of Hawaii, but also to supporting the needs of its people. The HEI Charitable Foundation plays a major role in demonstrating this corporate commitment. .. The Foundation actively supports the work of a wide variety of community-focused social welfare, health, youth, cultural, educational, and environmental organizations here in Hawaii.' *HEI Charitable Foundation Annual Report*

Financial Summary

Total Giving: $1,193,000 (1999 approx); $1,161,000 (1998); $1,030,000 (1997). Note: Contributes through foundation only.
Giving Analysis: Giving for 1997 includes: foundation grants to United Way ($340,000); foundation matching gifts ($10,160); 1998: foundation grants to United Way ($350,000)
Assets: $2,000,000 (1999 approx); $2,500,000 (1998 approx); $2,164,775 (1997)
Gifts Received: $900,000 (1997); $5,942 (1994); $68,729 (1993). Note: Foundation receives contributions from Hawaiian Electric Industries, Inc. and subsidiaries.

Typical Recipients

Arts & Humanities: Arts Centers, Community Arts, Historic Preservation, History & Archaeology, Museums/Galleries, Music, Performing Arts, Public Broadcasting, Theater
Civic & Public Affairs: Botanical Gardens/Parks, Business/Free Enterprise, Clubs, Community Foundations, Civic & Public Affairs-General, Housing, Legal Aid, Parades/Festivals, Urban & Community Affairs, Women's Affairs
Education: Arts/Humanities Education, Colleges & Universities, Private Education (Precollege), Public Education (Precollege), Science/Mathematics Education, Secondary Education (Private), Student Aid, Vocational & Technical Education
Environment: Environment-General, Resource Conservation, Wildlife Protection
Health: Cancer, Children's Health/Hospitals, Clinics/Medical Centers, Emergency/Ambulance Services, Health Organizations, Heart, Hospices, Hospitals, Medical Rehabilitation, Mental Health, Public Health, Single-Disease Health Associations
International: Foreign Arts Organizations, Health Care/Hospitals, International Environmental Issues, International Relations
Religion: Religious Welfare
Science: Science Museums
Social Services: Big Brother/Big Sister, Community Centers, Community Service Organizations, Counseling, Family Services, Food/Clothing Distribution, People with Disabilities, Recreation & Athletics, Scouts, Special Olympics, United Funds/United Ways, YMCA/YWCA/YMHA/YWHA, Youth Organizations

Contributions Analysis

Giving Priorities: United Way, community development, education, environment, and family services.
Civic & Public Affairs: 7%. Supports community development, including working with the U.S.S. Missouri Association to complete community-requested projects.
Education: 39%. Education funds are directed to programs at Hawaiian colleges and universities, and secondary schools.
Environment: 6%. Supports organizations such as Hawaii Audubon Society, Hawaii Nature Center, and the Nature Conservancy of Hawaii.
Social Services: 48%. Majority of giving in this category goes to statewide United Way. Also supports youth organizations, drug abuse prevention, food and clothing distribution, child welfare, community centers, community development, family services, and other service organizations.
Note: Total giving in 1998.

Application Procedures

Initial Contact: Call for guidelines, then send written request.
Application Requirements: Include the nature, scope, and purpose of organization; copy of mission statement; proposed objective of project, information on need or problem, how project will be administered, how it fills a need not met by others, how it will improve community in which company operates, population served, and plans for evaluation; amount requested and purpose of funds; proposed project budget; organizational budget; other sources of funding, including contributions received, outstanding requests, and support from officers and board members; breakdown of monies spent on your major programs; percentage of total support represented by request; latest management audit or other outline of cost-effectiveness; list of directors; list of HEI employees involved with organization; copy of IRS 501(c)(3) determination letter and Form 990; CEO's compensation and benefits; number of paid staff and volunteers; outline of plans for acknowledging HEI's contribution.
Deadlines: June 30.
Review Process: Proposals are reviewed by operating companies then working with the community relations director, recommendations are submitted to the executive committee and board of directors; requests up to $10,000 are presented throughout the year to the committee, amounts over $10,000 are acted upon by the board.
Evaluative Criteria: Foundation considers cost-effectiveness, operation in communities where company operates, programs provide recognition and goodwill for the company, further the well-being of company employees, enhance company's business development opportunities, and support by company volunteers.
Decision Notification: Board of directors meets twice each year.

Restrictions

Grants are not made to: individuals; tax-supported activities; programs outside of HEI operating area; veterans' groups, fraternal, or labor organizations, unless activity will benefit entire community; political funds, religious activities of a particular denomination, program advertising, activities where management costs exceed 25% of income generated, golf tournaments, dinners, or luncheons.
Multiyear and capital pledges are very limited.
Multiyear and capital pledges are very limited.

Corporate Officials

Robert F. Clarke: chairman, president, chief executive officer, director B Oakland, CA 1942. ED University of California at Berkeley BA (1965); University of California at Berkeley MBA (1966). PRIM CORP EMPL chairman, president, chief executive officer, director: Hawaiian Electric Industries, Inc. CORP AFFIL president, chief executive officer: HEI Diversified Inc.; director: Young Brothers Ltd.; director: Hawaii Electric Light Co.; director: Dames & Moore Group; chairman: Hawaii Electric Co. Inc.
T. Michael May: president B 1947. ED Mississippi State University BA (1969); College of William & Mary MBA (1973). PRIM CORP EMPL president: Hawaiian Electric Co., Inc. ADD CORP EMPL senior vice president, director: Hawaiian Electric Industries Inc. CORP AFFIL chairman: Hawaiian Electric Light Co.

Foundation Officials

Robert F. Clarke: president, director (see above)
Peter C. Lewis: secretary
Dr. Victor Hao Li: director PRIM CORP EMPL co-chairman: Asia Pacific Consulting Group. CORP AFFIL vice president: General Reinsurance Corp.; director: Hawaii Electric Industries Inc.
T. Michael May: director (see above)
Wayne K. Minami: director B 1942. ED Yale University BA (1964); Stanford University LLB (1967). PRIM CORP EMPL president, director: American Savings Bank FSB.
Oswald K. Stender: director CORP AFFIL director: Kamehamela Investment Corp.; trustee: Kamehamela Schools/Bishop Estate; director: Hawaiian Electric Industries Inc.
Jeffrey N. Watanabe: director B Wailuku, HI 1943. ED University of California BA (1965); George Washington University JD (1968). PRIM CORP EMPL senior partner: Watanbe, Ing & Kawashima. CORP AFFIL secretary, director: Rehabilitation Hospital Pacific; director: Suntory Resort Inc.; controller: PC Service Inc.; director: Grace Pacific Corp.; director: Hawaiian Electric Industries Inc.

Grants Analysis

Disclosure Period: calendar year ending 1998
Total Grants: $811,000*
Number of Grants: 64
Average Grant: $12,672
Highest Grant: $350,000
Typical Range: $500 to $30,000
***Note:** Giving excludes United Way.

Recent Grants

Note: Grants derived from 1997 Form 990.

Arts & Humanities

50,000	Bishop Museum, Honolulu, HI
38,000	Hawaii Public Television, Honolulu, HI
12,500	Lyman House Memorial Museum
8,000	Dorothy J. Esser Theater Foundation, Kailua, HI
7,500	Hawaii Public Radio, Honolulu, HI
7,500	Polynesian Cultural Center, Laie, HI
2,000	Honolulu Theater for Youth, Honolulu, HI

Civic & Public Affairs

15,000	Malama Kai, HI
10,000	Aiea Lions Club, Aiea, HI
10,000	Fund for the Pacific Century, Honolulu, HI
10,000	Moanalua Gardens Foundation, Honolulu, HI
10,000	Pearl City Lions Club, Pearl City, HI
10,000	Pearl Harbor Lions Club, Pearl Harbor, HI
5,000	Matsunaga Charitable Foundation, Honolulu, HI
2,500	Hei O Wa'a Kaulua, HI
1,000	First Night Maui, HI
1,000	Hawaii Leeward Planning Conference, Kailua Kona, HI
1,000	Lana'i Community Association, Lanai City, HI

Education

140,000	Public Schools of Hawaii Foundation, Honolulu, HI -- Creativity Conference, Invention Convention, Kidscience, and Electric Marathon

25,000	Leeward School-to-Work Consortium
24,000	Citizens Scholarship Foundation, Lancaster, PA
16,628	Hawaii Pacific University, Honolulu, HI
11,250	Public Schools of Hawaii Challenger Center, Honolulu, HI
5,000	St. Anthony School
5,000	Seagulls School, Kailua, HI
3,000	University of Hawaii Foundation, Honolulu, HI
1,000	Brigham Young University, Provo, UT
1,000	Chaminade University, Honolulu, HI
Environment	
25,000	Hawaii Nature Center, Honolulu, HI
20,000	Hawaii Audubon Society, Honolulu, HI
15,000	Student Conservation Council
10,000	Nature Conservancy, HI
5,000	Garden Island Resource Conservation and Development, Lihue, HI
Health	
15,500	American Heart Association
12,500	St. Francis Healthcare Foundation, Honolulu, HI
10,000	American Cancer Society
10,000	Hospice, Hilo, HI
2,045	Easter Seal Society, Philadelphia, PA
International	
12,500	Asian-Pacific Foundation, Honolulu, HI
10,000	Aloha Medical Missions, Honolulu, HI
Science	
25,000	Children's Discovery Center
Social Services	
12,000	Great Aloha Run
10,000	Adult Friends for Youth, Honolulu, HI
10,000	Boys and Girls Club, Honolulu, HI
10,000	YMCA -- Cities in Schools
9,000	Kokua Kalihi Valley, Honolulu, HI -- late night basketball league
8,000	Special Olympics, HI
4,622	Hina Mauka, Honolulu, HI
2,000	YMCA, HI
1,309	Angel Network Charities, Honolulu, HI

Heilig-meyers Co.

Company Contact

Richmond, VA

Company Description

Revenue: US$2,500,000,000
Employees: 20,000
SIC(s): 5712 Furniture Stores, 5713 Floor Covering Stores, 5722 Household Appliance Stores, 5731 Radio, Television & Electronics Stores.

Heilig-Meyers Foundation

Giving Contact

Ron Ragland, Senior Vice President, Human Resources & Training
12360 West Creek Parkway
Richmond, VA 23238
Phone: (804)359-9171

Description

EIN: 541349045
Organization Type: Corporate Foundation. Supports preselected organizations only.
Giving Locations: headquarters and operating communities.

Financial Summary

Total Giving: $273,873 (1997). Note: Fiscal 1997 Giving includes scholarship ($273,873).
Assets: $222,861 (1997)
Gifts Received: $200,000 (1997)

Contributions Analysis

Giving Priorities: Company reported in 1998 that 41% of contributions support education; 31%, health and human services; 21%, capital programs/other; 4%, arts and humanities; and 3%, civic and public affairs.

Corporate Officials

James F. Cerza, Jr.: executive vice president operationsandising PRIM CORP EMPL executive vice president operations: Heilig-Meyers Co.
William Charles DeRusha: chairman, chief executive officer B Norfolk, VA 1950. ED Virginia Commonwealth University (1974). PRIM CORP EMPL chairman, chief executive officer: Heilig-Meyers Co.
Roy Goodman: executive vice president, chief financial officer PRIM CORP EMPL executive vice president, chief financial officer: Heilig-Meyers Co.
William E. Helms: executive vice president, Puerto Rico PRIM CORP EMPL executive vice president, Puerto Rico: Heilig-Meyers Co.
Curtis C. Kimbrell: executive vice president merchandising PRIM CORP EMPL executive vice president merchandising: Heilig-Meyers Co.
Donald S. Shaffer: president, chief operating officer PRIM CORP EMPL president, chief operating officer: Heilig-Meyers Co.

Grants Analysis

Disclosure Period: calendar year ending 1997
Total Grants: $273,873*
Number of Grants: 255
Typical Range: $1,000 to $2,500
*Note: Giving includes scholarship.

H.J. Heinz Co.

Company Contact

Pittsburgh, PA
Web: http://www.heinz.com

Company Description

Revenue: US$9,209,300,000
Employees: 44,700
Fortune Rank: 183, per FORTUNE Magazine's list of 500 Largest U.S. Corporations (1999).
FF 183
SIC(s): 2032 Canned Specialties, 2033 Canned Fruits & Vegetables, 2038 Frozen Specialties Nec, 2099 Food Preparations Nec.

Operating Locations

Australia: Fortuity Pty. Ltd., Dandenong; HJ Heinz Co. Australia Ltd., Doveton; Gutbusters Pty. Ltd., North Sydney; Belgium: HJ Heinz Belgium NV, Brussels, Brabant; HJ Heinz Societe de Droit Hollandais, Brussels, Brabant; Botswana: HJ Heinz (Botswana)(Proprietary) Ltd., Gaborone; Kgalagadi Soap Industries (Pty.) Ltd., Gaborone; Refined Oil Products (Proprietary) Ltd., Gaborone; Canada: Weight Watchers of British Columbia Ltd., Burnaby; Shady Maple Farm Ltd., La Guadeloupe; Pro Pastries, Mississauga; Fitness Institute Ltd., Toronto; HJ Heinz Co. of Canada Ltd., Toronto; Omstead Foods Ltd., Wheatley; Omstead Refrigerated Transportation Ltd., Wheatley; People's Republic of China: Heinz-UFE Ltd., Guangzhou, Chiba; Czech Republic: Heinz-PMV a.s., Zabreh; Egypt: Cairo Foods Industries SAE, Cairo; Cairo Foods Industries, Cairo, Al Qahirah; France: Paulet (Ets Paul), Douarnenez, Finistere; Weight Watchers France, Fontenay Le Fleury, Yvelines; HJ Heinz SARL, Paris, Ville-de-Paris; Weight Watchers Foods Central Europe BV, Paris, Ville-de-Paris; Germany: HJ Heinz GmbH, Cologne, Nordrhein-Westfalen; Weight Watchers (Deutschland) GmbH, Duesseldorf; Ghana: Pioneer Food Cannery Ltd., Tema, Greater Accra; Greece: Copais Food & Beverage SA, Athens, Attiki; Hungary: HJ Heinz Central Eastern Europe, Budapest; India: Heinz India (Private) Ltd., Mumbai; Ireland: HJ Heinz European Frozen & Chilled Foods Ltd., Dublin; Noble Insurance Co. Ltd., Dublin; Japan: Heinz Japan Ltd., Tokyo; Republic of Korea: Seoul-Heinz Ltd., Seoul; Mauritius: Indian Ocean Tuna Ltd., Port Louis; Netherlands: HJ Heinz BV, Elst, Gelderland; HJ Heinz Finance BV, Elst, Gelderland; Weight Watchers Foods Central Europe BV, Elst, Gelderland; New Zealand: Heinz-Wattie Holdings Ltd., Auckland; HJ Heinz Pacific Rim, Auckland; Poland: Pudliszki, S.A., Pudliszki; Heinz Polska Sp. Z.O.O., Warsaw; Russia: Heinz C.I.S., Moscow; Heinz Georgievsk., Oktyabraskaya; Republic of South Africa: Pets Products (Pty.) Ltd., Cape Town; Heinz South Africa (Pty.) Ltd., Johannesburg; HJ Heinz Southern Africa (Proprietary) Ltd., Johannesburg; Heinz Frozen Foods (Pty.) Ltd., Klerksdorp; Spain: Heinz Iberica SA, Madrid; Seychelles: Indian Ocean Tuna Ltd., Mahe; Thailand: Heinz Win Change Ltd., Samutprakan; United Kingdom: John West Foods Ltd., Liverpool; Heinz Europe, Ltd., Middlesex; Frank Cooper Ltd., Redditich; Single Service Ltd., Telford; Venezuela: Alimentos Heinz CA, Valencia, Carabobo; Zimbabwe: Chegutu Canners (Pvt.) Ltd., Chegutu; Olivine Industries (Private) Ltd., Harare

H.J. Heinz Co. Foundation

Giving Contact

Ms. Loretta M. Oken, Program Director
H.J. Heinz Co. Foundation
PO Box 57
Pittsburgh, PA 15230
Phone: (412)456-5772
Fax: (412)456-7868

Description

Founded: 1951
EIN: 256018924
Organization Type: Corporate Foundation
Giving Locations: principally near operating locations and to national organizations.
Grant Types: Capital, Challenge, Conference/Seminar, Employee Matching Gifts, Endowment, Fellowship, General Support, Project, Scholarship.
Note: Foundation gives to scholarship funds only and does not give individual scholarships.

Giving Philosophy

'No matter the pace of modern life, time and resources must be set aside to serve good causes and great needs.' Annual Report

Financial Summary

Total Giving: $6,200,000 (1999 approx); $6,690,018 (1998); $6,773,549 (1997). Note: Contributes through foundation only. Giving includes foundation; matching gifts.
Giving Analysis: Giving for 1998 includes: foundation ($6,690,018)
Assets: $1,236,850 (1998); $1,783,029 (1997); $2,396,212 (1996)
Gifts Received: $6,000,000 (1998); $6,000,000 (1997); $5,000,000 (1996). Note: Foundation receives contributions from the H.J. Heinz Company and various individuals.

Typical Recipients

Arts & Humanities: Arts Associations & Councils, Arts Centers, Arts Festivals, Arts Funds, Arts Outreach, Ballet, Dance, Film & Video, Arts & Humanities-General, Historic Preservation, History & Archaeology, Libraries, Literary Arts, Museums/Galleries, Music, Opera, Performing Arts, Public Broadcasting, Theater

Civic & Public Affairs: African American Affairs, Botanical Gardens/Parks, Business/Free Enterprise, Civil Rights, Community Foundations, Economic Development, Economic Policy, Employment/Job Training, Civic & Public Affairs-General, Housing, Law & Justice, Legal Aid, Philanthropic Organizations, Professional & Trade Associations, Public Policy, Rural Affairs, Safety, Urban & Community Affairs, Women's Affairs, Zoos/Aquariums
Education: Agricultural Education, Arts/Humanities Education, Business Education, Colleges & Universities, Community & Junior Colleges, Continuing Education, Economic Education, Education Associations, Education Funds, Elementary Education (Private), Environmental Education, Education-General, Health & Physical Education, International Exchange, International Studies, Journalism/Media Education, Legal Education, Literacy, Medical Education, Minority Education, Private Education (Precollege), Public Education (Precollege), Religious Education, Science/Mathematics Education, Secondary Education (Private), Special Education, Student Aid
Environment: Environment-General
Health: AIDS/HIV, Cancer, Children's Health/Hospitals, Clinics/Medical Centers, Health Organizations, Home-Care Services, Hospices, Hospitals, Medical Rehabilitation, Medical Research, Nutrition, Public Health, Single-Disease Health Associations
International: Foreign Educational Institutions, Health Care/Hospitals, Human Rights, International Affairs, International Development, International Organizations, International Peace & Security Issues, International Relations, International Relief Efforts
Religion: Religious Organizations, Religious Welfare
Science: Scientific Centers & Institutes, Scientific Organizations
Social Services: Animal Protection, Child Welfare, Community Centers, Community Service Organizations, Counseling, Delinquency & Criminal Rehabilitation, Family Planning, Family Services, Food/Clothing Distribution, Homes, People with Disabilities, Recreation & Athletics, Senior Services, Substance Abuse, United Funds/United Ways, Volunteer Services, YMCA/YWCA/YMHA/YWHA, Youth Organizations

Contributions Analysis

Giving Priorities: Higher education, social services, health, the arts, civic concerns, youth, international organizations, religion, and science. The foundation supports the American Ireland Fund. Other interests include international business training, youth development, international transplantation support groups, and poetry. All foundation contributions are made to 501(c)(3) organizations. International operating companies make contributions from their own operating budgets without reporting activities to headquarters.
Education: 42%. Includes support to pre-college and college education, educational foundations.
Health: 8%. Supports hospital foundations, children's health concerns, medical centers, hospice, community health centers.
Note: Total contributions made in 1998. Analysis based on partial grants list.

Application Procedures

Initial Contact: Submit a brief letter requesting guidelines.
Application Requirements: Include a formal proposal should include a description of organization, specific project description, amount requested, purpose of funds sought; to whom and where program will be offered, how objectives will be accomplished, whether request is for one-time or ongoing project, and how program evaluation will be made; list of board of directors, annual and project budgets, description of recent policy decisions; and proof of tax-exempt status.
Deadlines: None; board meets quarterly.
Evaluative Criteria: Priority to United Ways, scholarship programs in food-related courses of study, grants for health-related facilities in geographic areas served by the company, and organizations receiving matching gifts.

Restrictions

The foundation does not support individuals; general scholarships, fellowships, or travel grants; political campaigns; or sectarian religious purposes. No multiyear grants are made, except for capital campaigns.

Additional Information

Publications: Grant Application Information

Corporate Officials

William R. Johnson: president, chief executive officer CORP AFFIL director: Amerada Hess Corp.
Dr. F. Anthony John O'Reilly: chairman, director B Dublin, Ireland 1936. ED University College of Dublin BA (1965); University of Bradford PhD (1980). PRIM CORP EMPL chairman, director: H.J. Heinz Co. CORP AFFIL director: Washington Post Co.; director: Star-Kist Foods; director: New York Stock Exchange Inc.; director: Ore-Ida Foods Inc.; chairman: Fitzwilton PLC; chairman: Independent Newspapers PLC; partner: Cawley Sheerin Wynne & Co.; chairman: Atlantic Resources; director: Bankers Trust New York Corp. NONPR AFFIL trustee: University Pittsburgh; member national committee: Whitney Museum American Art; fellow: Royal Society Arts; board governors: Hugh O'Brian Youth Foundation; member council: Rockefeller University; treasurer: Law Society Ireland; chairman, chief executive officer council: International Life Science Institute Nutrition Foundation; council: Irish Management Institute; member: Institute Directors Inc.; secretary, director: Grocery Manufacturer America; director: Harvard University Graduate School Business Administration Associates; director: Executive Council Foreign Diplomats; director: Georgetown University; senior board directors: Conference Board; fellow: British Institute Management; trustee: Committee for Economic Development; chairman: American Irish Foundation. CLUB AFFIL University Club Dublin; Saint Stephen's Green Club; Union League Club; Rolling Rock Club; Pittsburgh Golf Club; Pittsburgh Press Club; Lyford Cay Club; Marks London Club; The Links Club; Kildare Street Club; Les Ambassadeurs Club; Duquesne Club; Fox Chapel Golf Club; Board Room New York City Club; Allegheny Club; Annabels Club.
David R. Williams: executive vice president, director B London, England 1943. ED Exeter University BA (1964). PRIM CORP EMPL executive vice president, director: H.J. Heinz Co. CORP AFFIL chief executive officer: StarKist Foods Inc. NONPR AFFIL member: Association Chartered Accts U.S.; member: Financial Executives Institute; member: Association Chartered Accts UK.

Foundation Officials

Karyll A. Davis: trustee
Dr. F. Anthony John O'Reilly: chairman, trustee (see above)
Loretta M. Oken: program manager
S. Donald Wiley: vice chairman, trustee B Pittsburgh, PA 1926. ED West Minster College BA (1950); University of Pennsylvania School of Law LLB (1953). CORP AFFIL director: HJ Heinz Co.
David R. Williams: trustee (see above)

Grants Analysis

Disclosure Period: calendar year ending 1998
Total Grants: $6,690,018
Number of Grants: 850 (approx)
Average Grant: $7,871 (approx)
Highest Grant: $465,000
Typical Range: $50 to $10,000 and $5,000 to $20,000

Recent Grants

Note: Grants derived from 1998 Form 990.

Arts & Humanities

100,000	The Pittsburgh Cultural Trust, Pittsburgh, PA
75,000	National Endowment for the Arts, Washington, DC
30,000	Pittsburgh Ballet Theatre, Inc., Pittsburgh, PA
4,200	Mt. Harrison Heritage Foundation, Burley, ID
3,680	Boise Art Museum, Boise, ID

Civic & Public Affairs

25,000	Manchester Craftsmen's Guild, Pittsburgh, PA
25,000	Vocational Rehabilitation Center of Allegheny County, Inc., Pittsburgh, PA
20,000	Colles-Graves Foundation, Incorporated, Westbury, NY
12,500	Committee for Economic Development, New York, NY

Education

50,000	Duquesne University, Pittsburgh, PA
50,000	The Education Foundation of the National Restaurant Association, Chicago, IL
50,000	Inner-City Scholarship Fund, New York, NY
25,000	Robert Morris College, Pittsburgh, PA
15,000	Business-Higher Education Forum American Council on Education, Washington, DC
12,000	The Foundation for California University of Pennsylvania, California, PA
10,050	Carnegie Mellon University, Pittsburgh, PA
10,000	Beauvoir School, Washington, DC
10,000	Foothills School of Arts & Sciences, Boise, ID
10,000	Roanoke College, Salem, VA
10,000	Shimer College, Des Plaines, IL
9,200	Westminster College, New Wilmington, PA
9,000	St. Luke's Christian School, Westminster, CA
5,000	Colgate University, Hamilton, NY
5,000	Denison University, Granville, OH
5,000	Michigan State University, East Lansing, MI
5,000	Sewickley Academy, Sewickley, PA
4,200	The Master's College, Santa Clarita, CA
4,000	Albertson College of Idaho, Caldwell, ID
3,300	Boise Public Schools Education Foundation, Boise, ID
3,214	University of Idaho Foundation Inc., Moscow, ID
3,090	St. Mary's College of California, Moraga, CA
3,000	Central Catholic High School, Portland, OR
3,000	Michigan State University Foundation, East Lansing, MI
3,000	St. John's EV Lutheran School, Jefferson, WI
3,000	St. Patrick School, Dallas, TX
3,000	University of Michigan - Ann Arbor, Ann Arbor, MI
2,500	Bloomsburg University, Bloomsburg, PA
2,400	Boise Public Schools Education Foundation, Boise, ID
2,400	St. Patrick Elementary School-Malvern PA, Malvern, PA

Health

50,000	Allegheny General Hospital, Pittsburgh, PA
33,335	The Rehabilitation Institute, Pittsburgh, PA
30,000	Magee-Women's Health Foundation, Pittsburgh, PA

5,000 North Side Christian Health Center, Pittsburgh, PA

International

50,000 The Brother's Brother Foundation, Pittsburgh, PA

50,000 Robert F. Kennedy Memorial, Washington, DC

Science

20,000 Institute of Food Technologists, Greenwich, CT

Social Services

56,877 American Humane Association, Englewood, CO

25,000 Girls Hope of Pittsburgh, Inc., Baden, PA

10,000 Boys & Girls Clubs of America, New York, NY

5,000 Idaho Foodbank Warehouse, Boise, ID

5,000 The Travelers Aid Society of Pittsburgh, Pittsburgh, PA

3,000 YWCA of Greater Pittsburgh, Pittsburgh, PA

HELLER FINANCIAL, INC.

Company Contact

500 West Monroe Street
Chicago, IL 60661
Web: http://www.hellerfin.com

Company Description

Revenue: US$8,000,000,000
Employees: 1,250
SIC(s): 6141 Personal Credit Institutions, 6153 Short-Term Business Credit.
Parent Company: Fuji Bank, Ltd., 5-5 Otemachi 1-chome, Chiyoda-ku, Tokyo, Japan

Operating Locations

CA: Heller Financial, Inc.; Fuji Bank Los Angeles, Los Angeles; Fuji Bank International, San Francisco; Fuji Bank San Francisco, San Francisco; DC: Washington, D.C. Representative Office, Washington; DE: FWI Holdings, Wilmington; FL: Miami Representative Office, Miami; GA: Heller Financial, Inc.; Fuji Bank Atlanta, Atlanta; IL: Heller Financial, Inc.; Fuji Bank Chicago Branch, Chicago; Fuji Securities - Chicago, Chicago; Heller Financial, Chicago; Heller Financial, Inc., Chicago; Heller International Corp., Chicago; NY: Fuji Bank New York Branch, New York; Fuji Bank & Trust Co., New York; Fuji Capital Holdings, New York; Fuji Capital Markets Corp., New York; Fuji Securities - New York, New York; Fuji-Wolfensohn International, New York; Fujilease Corp., New York; TX: Heller Financial, Inc.; Fuji Bank Houston, Houston; WA: Seattle Representative Office, Seattle

Nonmonetary Support

Type: Donated Equipment
Volunteer Programs: The company has a volunteer committee, an incentive program, and has adopted a public school.

Corporate Sponsorship

Type: Pledge-a-thon; Other
Note: The company sponsors events for corporate volunteers in connection with Goodwill agencies, education Associations, disadvantaged youth concerns, and Health Services.

Giving Contact

Judy Korba, Contributions Manager
Heller Financial Inc.
Phone: (312)441-6748
Fax: (312)441-6728

Description

Organization Type: Corporate Giving Program
Giving Locations: headquarters and operating communities.
Grant Types: Employee Matching Gifts, General Support.
Note: Matching gifts are for academic purposes only.

Financial Summary

Total Giving: $1,300,000 (2000 approx); $1,200,000 (1999 approx); $860,000 (1998 approx). Note: Contributes through corporate direct giving program only. Giving includes corporate direct giving; nonmonetary support.
Giving Analysis: Giving for 1998 includes: corporate direct giving (approx $1,200,000)

Typical Recipients

Arts & Humanities: Libraries, Music, Public Broadcasting
Civic & Public Affairs: Business/Free Enterprise, Professional & Trade Associations, Public Policy
Education: Colleges & Universities, Elementary Education (Private), Literacy, Minority Education, Private Education (Precollege), Public Education (Precollege)
Health: Mental Health
Social Services: United Funds/United Ways, Youth Organizations

Application Procedures

Initial Contact: brief letter of inquiry, then a full proposal
Application Requirements: a description of the organization, amount requested, purpose of funds sought, list of board of trustees or directors, percentage of budget used for administration and overhead, evidence of 501(c)(3) status, outcomes expected, method of evaluation, and list of funding from other organizations or government agencies
Deadlines: None.

Restrictions

Does not support individuals, organizations outside operating areas, political or lobbying groups, United Way-supported organizations, or religious organizations for sectarian purposes.

Additional Information

The majority of Heller Financial, Inc.'s charitable contributions is distributed by the corporate headquarters office in Chicago, IL, but a small percentage of funding is distributed through various regional offices.

Corporate Officials

Richard Almeida: chairman, chief executive officer B New York, NY 1942. ED George Washington University BA (1963); Syracuse University MA (1965). PRIM CORP EMPL chairman, chief executive officer: Heller Financial Inc. CORP AFFIL president: Heller Investments Inc.; director: Fuji Securities Inc.; chairman, chief executive officer: Heller International Inc.; chairman: Fuji America Holdings Inc.; director: Fuji Bank Trust New York. NONPR AFFIL director: Chicago Youth Programs; treasurer, trustee: Latin School of Chicago. CLUB AFFIL member: The Casino; member: Chicago Club.
Lauralee Martin: chief financial officer B Minneapolis, MN 1950. ED Oregon State University (1972); University of Connecticut (1979). PRIM CORP EMPL chief financial officer: Heller Financial. CORP AFFIL director: Gables Residental Trust.
Rick Wolfert: president, chief operating officer PRIM CORP EMPL president, chief operating officer: Heller Financial.

Giving Program Officials

Judy Korba: PRIM CORP EMPL contributions manager: Heller Financial.

Grants Analysis

Disclosure Period: calendar year ending
Typical Range: $1,000 to $25,000

HENSEL PHELPS CONSTRUCTION CO.

Company Contact

Greeley, CO
Web: http://www.henselphelps.com

Company Description

Revenue: US$540,000,000
Employees: 1,800
SIC(s): 1542 Nonresidential Construction Nec, 1611 Highway & Street Construction.

Nonmonetary Support

Type: In-kind Services; Loaned Employees; Loaned Executives

Hensel Phelps Foundation

Giving Contact

Eric Wilson, Vice President
Hensel Phelps Construction Co.
Phone: (970)352-6565

Description

EIN: 840715416
Organization Type: Corporate Foundation
Giving Locations: CO: CO some giving nationally.
Grant Types: General Support.

Financial Summary

Total Giving: $109,170 (fiscal year ending May 31, 1998); $224,443 (fiscal 1996); $218,556 (fiscal 1995). Note: Contributes through foundation only.
Giving Analysis: Giving for fiscal 1998 includes: foundation ($109,750)
Assets: $333,180 (fiscal 1998); $459,744 (fiscal 1996); $536,287 (fiscal 1995)
Gifts Received: $100,000 (fiscal 1996); $200,000 (fiscal 1995); $200,000 (fiscal 1994). Note: In fiscal 1996, contributions were received from Hensel Phelps Construction Co.

Typical Recipients

Arts & Humanities: Arts Institutes, Historic Preservation, Museums/Galleries, Theater
Civic & Public Affairs: Employment/Job Training, Civic & Public Affairs-General, Housing, Law & Justice, Legal Aid
Education: Colleges & Universities, Community & Junior Colleges, Economic Education, Education Associations, Engineering/Technological Education, Education-General, Gifted & Talented Programs, Literacy, Medical Education, Private Education (Precollege), Religious Education, Science/Mathematics Education, Student Aid
Health: Arthritis, Cancer, Clinics/Medical Centers, Heart, Hospitals, Respiratory, Speech & Hearing
Social Services: Camps, Community Centers, Community Service Organizations, People with Disabilities, Recreation & Athletics, United Funds/United Ways, Volunteer Services, YMCA/YWCA/YMHA/YWHA, Youth Organizations

Application Procedures

Initial Contact: Send a brief letter.
Application Requirements: Include a description of the program and purpose of funds sought.
Deadlines: None.

Restrictions

The foundation only makes contributions to organizations or programs in which company personnel have a direct interest or are personally involved.

Corporate Officials

Jerry L. Morgensen: president, chief executive officer, director B Lubbock, TX 1942. ED Texas Technology University BCE (1965). PRIM CORP EMPL president, chief executive officer, director: Hensel Phelps Construction Co. CORP AFFIL president: H.P. Environmental Service LLC.

Foundation Officials

Stephen J. Carrico: director B 1954. PRIM CORP EMPL vice president finance, chief financial officer: Hensel Phelps Construction Co. CORP AFFIL treasurer: Hensel Phelps Environmental Services; treasurer: Phelps Program Management.

Jerry L. Morgensen: director (see above)

Eric L. Wilson: director B 1955. ED Tufts University (1977). PRIM CORP EMPL vice president: Hensel Phelps Construction Co. CORP AFFIL secretary: H. P. Environmental Service LLC; secretary: Phelps Program Management LLC.

Grants Analysis

Disclosure Period: fiscal year ending May 31, 1998
Total Grants: $109,750
Number of Grants: 44
Average Grant: $2,087
Highest Grant: $20,000*
Typical Range: $25 to $20,000
***Note:** Average grant figure excludes highest grant.

Recent Grants

Note: Grants derived from 1996 Form 990.

Arts & Humanities

5,000	California Archives Foundation, Sacramento, CA
4,223	Colorado Institute of Art, Denver, CO
2,500	Austin Children's Museum, Austin, TX

Civic & Public Affairs

1,833	Institute of Business and Medical Careers, Fort Collins, CO
200	CENIKOR, Lakewood, CO
100	Mountain States Legal Foundation, Denver, CO

Education

25,000	University of Colorado Foundation, Boulder, CO
23,477	University of Northern Colorado, Greeley, CO
16,875	Colorado State University, Fort Collins, CO
9,815	University of Colorado Boulder and Denver, Boulder, CO
9,625	University of Arkansas, Little Rock, AR
7,476	University of California Regents, Davis, CA
5,500	Texas Tech University, Lubbock, TX
5,000	Kansas State University Department of Construction Science, Manhattan, KS
4,408	Aims Community College, Greeley, CO
4,100	Union College, Lincoln, NE
4,000	Montana State University Foundation, CET Development Fund, Bozeman, MT
3,375	Metropolitan State College, Denver, CO
3,000	Aims Community College Foundation, Greeley, CO
2,750	Albany Medical College, Albany, NY
2,750	California Polytechnic State University, San Luis Obispo, CA
2,750	California State University, Chico, CA
2,750	Eastern Washington University, Spokane, WA
2,750	Mesa State College, Grand Junction, CO
2,750	Regis University, Denver, CO
2,386	Const Engineering Iowa State University, Ames, IA
1,375	Laramie County Community College, Laramie, WY
1,375	Larimer County Community College, Fort Collins, CO
1,375	Sacramento State University, Sacramento, CA
1,375	Tarleton State University, Stephenville, TX
1,061	Arapahoe State College, Littleton, CO
867	Florida Community College, Jacksonville, FL
850	Front Range Community College, Fort Collins, CO
672	Jones Real Estate College, Denver, CO
500	North Colorado Math Counts, Greeley, CO
500	Rocky Mountain Junior Achievement, Fort Collins, CO
100	CACI Educational Foundation, Denver, CO
100	Fort Lewis College Football Program, Durango, CO

Health

20,000	North Colorado Medical Center Foundation, Greeley, CO
20,000	Poudre Valley Hospital Foundation, Fort Collins, CO
5,000	Caritas, Austin, TX
4,000	American Heart Association, Greeley, CO
2,500	American Lung Association of Alameda County, Oakland, CA

Social Services

5,000	Oakland Youth Policy Initiative, Oakland, CA
1,500	Austin Sunshine Camps, Austin, TX
750	Greeley American Legion Baseball, Greeley, CO
500	Greeley-Evans Youth League, Greeley, CO
500	Intermountain Tennis Association, Denver, CO
100	Conditioning Spa, Greeley, CO
100	Greeley Gymnastic Center, Greeley, CO

HERCULES INC.

Company Contact

Hercules Plaza
1313 N. Market Street
Wilmington, DE 19894-0001
Phone: (302)594-5000
Fax: (302)594-5400
Web: http://www.herc.com

Company Description

Profit: US$168,000,000 (1999)
Employees: 12,357 (1999)
Fortune Rank: 472, per FORTUNE Magazine's list of 500 Largest U.S. Corporations (1999).
FF 472
SIC(s): 2284 Thread Mills, 2672 Coated & Laminated Paper Nec, 2821 Plastics Materials & Resins, 2823 Cellulosic Manmade Fibers.

Nonmonetary Support

Type: Donated Equipment
Note: The company also sponsors mentoring programs at local elementary schools, Meals-on-Wheels, and United Way 'Days of Caring.'

Corporate Sponsorship

Type: Arts & cultural events; Festivals/fairs; Music & entertainment events

Giving Contact

Judith Morton, Community Relations Representative
Hercules Incorporated
Phone: (302)594-5251
Fax: (302)594-6909
Email: jmorton1@herc.com

Description

Organization Type: Corporate Giving Program
Giving Locations: DE principally near operating locations and to national organizations.
Grant Types: Capital, General Support, Multiyear/Continuing Support.

Financial Summary

Total Giving: $2,700,000 (2000); $3,000,000 (1999 approx); $3,200,000 (1998). Note: Contributes through corporate direct giving program only.
Giving Analysis: Giving for 1998 includes: corporate direct giving ($3,200,000)

Typical Recipients

Arts & Humanities: Arts & Humanities-General
Civic & Public Affairs: Civic & Public Affairs-General
Education: Education-General
Health: Health-General
Social Services: Social Services-General

Contributions Analysis

Giving Priorities: Primary interests include local education, social services, and cultural organizations. Support includes donations to the United Way of Delaware.

Application Procedures

Initial Contact: Send a brief letter of inquiry.
Application Requirements: Include a description of organization, amount requested, purpose of funds sought, audited financial statement, and proof of tax-exempt status.
Deadlines: September 1

Restrictions

Company does not support individuals or religious organizations.

Corporate Officials

Vincent J. Corbo: president, chief executive officer, directorlt, public affairs B 1943. ED Manhattan College BS (1965); Princeton University PhD (1969). PRIM CORP EMPL president, chief executive officer, director: Hercules Inc.

R. Keith Elliott: chief executive officer, president B Abbeville, SC 1942. ED University of South Carolina BS (1964); University of South Carolina MBA (1965). PRIM CORP EMPL chief executive officer, president: Hercules Inc. CORP AFFIL director: Computer Task Group Inc.; director: PECO Energy Co. NONPR AFFIL member: American Management Association; director: Chemical Manufacturers Association.

Robert E. Gallant: vice president investor relations, public affairs

Giving Program Officials

Thomas Ciconte: vice president external affairs & international PRIM CORP EMPL vice president external affairs & international: Hercules Inc.

Robert E. Gallant: vice president

Judith Morton: PRIM CORP EMPL community relations representative: Hercules Inc.

Grants Analysis

Disclosure Period: calendar year ending 1997
Total Grants: $2,157,000 (approx)

HERSHEY FOODS CORP.

Company Contact

Hershey, PA

Web: http://www.hersheys.com

Company Description

Revenue: US$4,435,600,000
Employees: 16,200
Fortune Rank: 403, per FORTUNE Magazine's list of 500 Largest U.S. Corporations (1999).
FF 403
SIC(s): 2064 Candy & Other Confectionery Products, 2066 Chocolate & Cocoa Products, 2098 Macaroni & Spaghetti.

Operating Locations

Canada: Hershey Canada, Mississauga; Leaf Canada, Scarborough; Italy: Sperlari S.R.L., Milan; Japan: Hershey Japan Co. Ltd., Tokyo; Mexico: Hershey's Mexico SA de CV, El Salto; Netherlands: Overspecht, B.V., Oosterhout

Nonmonetary Support

Value: $11,000,000 (1995); $8,244,281 (1993); $4,563,456 (1991)
Type: Cause-related Marketing & Promotion; Donated Products; Loaned Executives
Contact: Harold Miller, Senior Account Representative, Customer Service
Note: Loaned executives are for United Way only.

Corporate Sponsorship

Type: Arts & cultural events; Festivals/fairs; Music & entertainment events; Pledge-a-thon; Sports events
Contact: Robert Shelton, Director, Marketing

Giving Contact

John Long, Directory Corporate Communications
Hershey Foods Corp.
100 Crystal A Dr.
Hershey, PA 17033-0810
Phone: (717)534-7880
Fax: (717)534-7015

Description

Organization Type: Corporate Giving Program
Giving Locations: principally near operating locations and to national organizations.
Grant Types: Capital, Employee Matching Gifts, Endowment, General Support, Operating Expenses, Project, Research.
Note: Employee matching gift ratio: 2 to 1 to colleges only.

Giving Philosophy

'The Corporation recognizes that it has an inherent responsibility to be a good neighbor and responsible corporate citizen. It is corporate policy to make voluntary contributions in support of worthy educational, human service, civic and cultural organizations. Employees also are encouraged to take an active part in improving the quality of community life.' *Report on Contributions, Hershey Foods Corp.*

Financial Summary

Total Giving: $2,300,000 (1999 approx); $2,300,000 (1998 approx); $2,358,534 (1995). Note: Contributes through corporate direct giving program only. 1995 Giving includes foundation ($149,049).
Assets: $244,447 (1993); $139,702 (1992); $1,061,925 (1991)
Gifts Received: $2,400,000 (1993)

Typical Recipients

Arts & Humanities: Arts Associations & Councils, Libraries, Museums/Galleries, Theater
Civic & Public Affairs: Business/Free Enterprise, Community Foundations, Economic Development, Employment/Job Training, Civic & Public Affairs-General
Education: Colleges & Universities, Community & Junior Colleges, Economic Education, Engineering/Technological Education, Literacy, Science/Mathematics Education
Environment: Resource Conservation
Health: Clinics/Medical Centers, Hospitals, Nutrition
Science: Scientific Centers & Institutes, Scientific Organizations
Social Services: Community Service Organizations, Food/Clothing Distribution, People with Disabilities, Substance Abuse, United Funds/United Ways, Volunteer Services

Contributions Analysis

Giving Priorities: Education, community development, civic concerns, health, human services, and culture. The company has supported international organizations affiliated with the food industry, environmental affairs organizations, and international management.
Arts & Humanities: 10%. Supports museums, public broadcasting, symphonies, and art education and associations.
Civic & Public Affairs: About 15%. Emphasis is on economicdevelopment, safety organizations, research programs, and organizations that promote economic freedom and the protection of private and individual enterprise.
Education: About 40%. Approximately one-third of educational giving represents matched employee gifts. Supports education funds, with emphasis on nutrition, economic, science and business administration programs, and programs that promote a better understanding of the competitive economic system.
Health: 15% to 20%. Emphasis is on local United Way campaigns and food bank donations. Also supports youth groups, community service centers, and organizations serving minority and disadvantaged groups.

Application Procedures

Initial Contact: brief letter or proposal; organizations situated outside the Hershey, PA area should direct requests to management of facility in their area
Application Requirements: a description of organization and its purpose, including specific project for which funding is requested; need for the project and/or organization and the population (number, type, area) served; past and expected sources of support; fundraising activities/plans, project cost, and campaign goal; amount requested; list of board of directors and affiliations; any special state or federal tax credits that may accrue to donors; how organization relates to company interests; IRS determination letter
Deadlines: None; decisions generally made monthly; 60-day lead time needed.

Restrictions

Does not support fraternal, veterans, or labor organizations, or religious organizations or denominations for sectarian purposes.
Generally does not provide operating support to United Way-supported agencies or grants or scholarships to individuals.

Additional Information

The Hershey Fund is defunct; giving is now done at the discretion of the corporation.
Publications: Biennial Report

Corporate Officials

Michael Pasquale: chief operating officer PRIM CORP EMPL chief operating officer: Hershey Foods Corp.
Joseph P. Viviano: president, court B Louisville, KY 1938. ED Xavier University (1959). PRIM CORP EMPL president, court: Hershey Foods Corp. CORP AFFIL director: Huffy Corp.; director: RJ Reynolds Tobacco Holdings Inc.; director: Chesapeake Corp.; director: Harsco Corp. NONPR AFFIL member ind productivity council: Grocery Manufacturer Association; director: Xavier University; director: Chocolate Manufacturer Association; member ind productivity council: Grocery Manufacturer America.
Kenneth L. Wolfe: chairman, chief executive officer, director B 1939. ED Yale University BA (1961); University of Pennsylvania MBA (1967). PRIM CORP EMPL chairman, chief executive officer, director: Hershey Foods Corp. CORP AFFIL chairman: Henry Heide Inc.; director: Hershey Trust Co.; director: Bausch & Lomb Inc.; director: Carpenter Technology Corp.

Giving Program Officials

Joseph P. Viviano: trustee (see above)
Kenneth L. Wolfe: trustee (see above)

Grants Analysis

Disclosure Period: calendar year ending 1995
Total Grants: $2,358,534
Number of Grants: 250
Average Grant: $9,434
Highest Grant: $125,000
Lowest Grant: $1,000
Typical Range: $5,000 to $20,000

Recent Grants

Note: Grants derived from 1993 Form 990.

Arts & Humanities

36,500 Allied Arts Fund, Harrisburg, PA
25,000 Hershey Museum of American Life, Hershey, PA
19,600 Mid-Atlantic Chamber Orchestra, Waynesboro, VA
19,600 Waterbury Symphony Orchestra, Waterbury, CT
17,500 Savannah Symphony Orchestra Society, Savannah, GA
15,600 WITF-TV/FM Channel 33 Sesame Street, Harrisburg, PA
10,000 Capital Cultural Campaign, Harrisburg, PA
10,000 Fresno Philharmonic Orchestra, Fresno, CA
7,500 Reading Symphony Orchestra, Reading, PA

Civic & Public Affairs

10,350 National Minority Supplier Development Council, New York, NY
9,500 Pennsylvania Economy League, Harrisburg, PA
8,500 Institute for Research on the Economics of Taxation, Washington, DC
8,000 Financial Accounting Foundation, Norwalk, CT
8,000 Food and Drug Law Institute, Washington, DC
7,500 Americans for Competitive Enterprise System, Harrisburg, PA

Education

96,500 Hershey Foods Corp Scholarship Program, Minneapolis, MN
60,000 Pennsylvania State University School of Education, University Park, PA
60,000 Pennsylvania State University School of Education, University Park, PA
60,000 Pennsylvania State University School of Education, University Park, PA
60,000 Pennsylvania State University School of Education, University Park, PA
60,000 Pennsylvania State University School of Education, University Park, PA
25,000 Lebanon Valley College, Annville, PA -- capital
20,000 Elizabethtown College, Elizabethtown, PA -- capital
12,500 Elizabethtown College, Elizabethtown, PA
10,000 American Graduate School of International Management, Glendale, AZ
10,000 Harrisburg Area Community College, Harrisburg, PA
10,000 Harrisburg Area Community College, Harrisburg, PA

10,000 Lebanon Valley College, Annville, PA
10,000 University of Georgia NESPAL, Tifton, GA
9,600 Inroads, Philadelphia, PA

Environment
25,000 Pennsylvania Association of Conservation Districts State Envirothon, Harrisburg, PA
25,000 Pennsylvania Association of Conservation Districts State Envirothon, Harrisburg, PA
10,000 Chesapeake Bay Foundation, Annapolis, MD

Health
50,000 M.S. Hershey Medical Center Biomedical Research Building, Hershey, PA
50,000 M.S. Hershey Medical Center Biomedical Research Building, Hershey, PA
41,500 M.S. Hershey Foundation, Hershey, PA
20,000 Oak Valley District Hospital Foundation, Oakdale, CA

International
42,000 International Life Sciences Institute Nutrition Foundation, Washington, DC
42,000 International Life Sciences Institute Nutrition Foundation, Washington, DC
18,000 International Life Sciences Institute A&I Institute, Washington, DC
18,000 International Life Sciences Institute A&I Institute, Washington, DC
18,000 International Life Sciences Institute Risk Science Institute, Washington, DC
18,000 International Life Sciences Institute Risk Science Institute, Washington, DC
14,000 International Life Sciences Institute HNI, Washington, DC
14,000 International Life Sciences Institute HNI, Washington, DC

Religion
20,000 United Theological Seminary, New Brighton, MN

Science
10,000 American Council on Science and Earth, New York, NY

Social Services
125,000 Pennsylvania Association for Blind, Harrisburg, PA
75,000 Lady Keystone Open, Harrisburg, PA
57,000 United Way Lebanon County, Lebanon, PA
18,000 International Food Information Council, Washington, DC
10,000 Contact USA, Harrisburg, PA
10,000 Food Industry Crusade Against Hunger, Washington, DC
7,800 Volunteer Recognition Program

HEWLETT-PACKARD CO.

Number 11 of Top 100 Corporate Givers

Company Contact

Palo Alto, CA
Web: http://www.hp.com

Company Description

Revenue: US$48,253,000,000 (1999)
Employees: 83,200 (1999)
Fortune Rank: 13, per FORTUNE Magazine's list of 500 Largest U.S. Corporations (1999).
FF 13
SIC(s): 3571 Electronic Computers, 3577 Computer Peripheral Equipment Nec, 3823 Process Control Instruments, 3824 Fluid Meters & Counting Devices.

Operating Locations

Australia: Hewlett-Packard Australia, Ltd., Abbotsford; Hewlett-Packard Australia Finance Ltd., Blackburn; Hewlett-Packard Australia Ltd., Blackburn; Telstra Hewlett-Packard (R&D) Pty. Ltd., Blackburn North; Hewlett-Packard Australia, Ltd., Brisbane, Bruce, Osborne Park; Verifone Australia Pty. Ltd., North Sydney; Hewlett-Packard Australia Ltd., Parkside; Hewlett-Packard Australia, Ltd., Sydney, Milton, Dulwich; Austria: Hewlett-Packard GmbH, Vienna; Belgium: Hewlett-Packard Belgium SA, Brussels, Brabant; Brazil: Hewlett Packard Participaces S/A, Barueri; Canada: Hewlett-Packard (Canada) Ltd., Burlington, London, Sudbury, Calgary, Edmonton, Ft.McMurry, Dartmouth, Kirkland, Quebec, Mississauga, Ottawa, Markham, Kingston, Richmond, Nanaimo, Victoria, Saint Johns, Saskatoon, Regina; Verifone Ltd., Toronto; Hewlett-Packard (Canada) Ltd., Winnepeg, Moncton, Yellowknife; People's Republic of China: China Hewlett-Packard Co. Ltd., Shenzhen; Czech Republic: Hewlett-Packard Czechoslovakia SPOL SRO, Prague; Denmark: Hewlett-Packard A/S, Birkerod, Frederiksborg; France: Hewlett-Packard France, Courcouronnes, Essonne; Technologies et Paticipations, Courcouronnes, Essonne; Verifone SA, Paris, Ville-de-Paris; Leasametric, Velizy Villacoublay, Yvelines; Germany: Hewlett-Packard GmbH, Boeblingen, Baden-Wuerttemberg; Idacom Electronics GmbH, Boeblingen, Baden-Wuerttemberg; Cocreate Software GmbH, Sindelfingen; Leasametric GmbH, Sindelfingen; Verifone GmbH, Wiesbaden, Hessen; Greece: Hewlett-Packard Hellas, Amaroussion; Hong Kong: Yokogawa Hewlett-Packard, Admiralty; Hewlett-Packard Asia Pacific Ltd., Causeway Bay; Hewlett-Packard Hong Kong Ltd., Causeway Bay; VFI (Hong Kong) Ltd., Central District; India: Hewlett-Packard (India) Software Operation Private Ltd., Bangalore; Verifone India Ltd., Bangalore; Hewlett-Packard India Ltd., New Delhi; Ireland: Hewlett-Packard Ireland Ltd., Blackrock; Hewlett-Packard (HP) Re Ltd., Dublin; Italy: Hewlett-Packard Italiana SpA, Cernusco Sul Naviglio; Verifone SRL, Cinisello Balsamo, Lombardia; Japan: Hewlett-Packard Laboratories Japan Inc., Kawasaki, Kanagawa; Hewlett-Packard Japan Ltd., Tokyo; Mexico: Hewlett-Packard de Mexico SA de CV, Ciudad de Mexico; Hewlett Packard Regin Latinoamericana, Ciudad de Mexico; Verifone SA de CV, Ciudad de Mexico; Hewlett-Packard SA de CV, Garza Garcia; Malaysia: Hewlett-Packard (Malaysia) Sdn. Bhd., Bayan Lepas, Pulau Pinang; Hewlett-Packard Sales (Malaysia) Sdn. Bhd., Kuala Lumpur, Selangor; Netherlands: Hewlett-Packard Caribe BV, Amstelveen, Noord-Holland; Hewlett-Packard Europe BV, Amstelveen, Noord-Holland; Hewlett-Packard Holding BV, Amstelveen, Noord-Holland; Hewlett-Packard International Sales Corp. BV, Amstelveen, Noord-Holland; Hewlett-Packard Nederland BV, Amstelveen, Noord-Holland; Hewlett-Packard Start BV, Amstelveen, Noord-Holland; Hewlett-Packard (Technical) BV, Amstelveen, Noord-Holland; Prolin Automation BV, Amsterdam, Noord-Holland; Verifone BV, Amsterdam, Noord-Holland; Norway: Hewlett-Packard Norge AS, Oslo, Akershus; New Zealand: Hewlett-Packard (New Zealand) Ltd., Wellington; Portugal: Hewlett-Packard Portugal Sistemas de Informatica e de Medida SA, Oeiras, Lisboa; Russia: Hewlett-Packard Co. Representative Office, Moscow; Singapore: Applied Optoelectronic Technology (Asia) Pte. Ltd., Singapore; Hewlett-Packard Singapore Sales Pte. Ltd., Singapore; Verifone Pte. Ltd., Singapore; Verifone Technology Pte. Ltd., Singapore; Spain: Verifone Espana SA, Barcelona, Cataluna; Hewlett-Packard Espanola SA, Las Rozas de Madrid, Madrid; Sweden: Hewlett-Packard Sverige AB, Kisa, Ostergotland; Switzerland: Hewlett-Packard SA, Meyrin, Geneva; Hewlett-Packard (Schweiz) AG, Urdorf, Zurich; Turkey: Hewlett-Packard Biigisayar Ve Olcum Sistemleri AS, Istanbul; Taiwan: Verifone Taiwan Ltd.; Hewlett-Packard Taiwan Ltd., Taipei; United Kingdom: Apollo Computer (UK) Ltd., Bracknell, Berkshire; Hewlett-Packard Finance Ltd., Bracknell, Berkshire; Hewlett-Packard Ltd., Bracknell, Berkshire; Hewlett-Packard Product Leasing Ltd., Bracknell, Berkshire; BT&D Technologies Ltd., Ipswich, Suffolk; Verifone (UK) Ltd., Uxbridge, Middlesex

Nonmonetary Support

Value: $3,300,000 (1999); $50,701,000 (1998); $48,087,000 (1997)
Type: Donated Equipment; Donated Products
Contact: Nancy Thomas, National Grants Contact
Note: Totals for product donations are computed using list price values. Nonmonetary support is provided by the company. Contact Tony Napolitan for university grants.

Hewlett-Packard Co. Foundation

Giving Contact

Mr. Roy Verley, Director, Corporate Philanthropy
Hewlett-Packard Co.
PO Box 10301
Palo Alto, CA 94304-1185
Phone: (650)857-3053
Email: tony_napolitan@hp.com
Web: http://www.hp.com/go/grants

Description

EIN: 942618409
Organization Type: Corporate Foundation
Giving Locations: international principally near operating locations and to national organizations; nationally; U.S. principally near operating locations and to national organizations.
Grant Types: Employee Matching Gifts, Project.
Note: Employee matching gift ratio: 1 to 1 for employee cash gifts to colleges and universities only, minimum grant of $25 to a maximum of $5,000 per employee per year. Co. matches product donations 3 to 1 for gifts to education, from kindergarten to graduate school.

Giving Philosophy

'There are two major thrusts to HP philanthropy: 'Investment in higher education through gifts of state-of-the-art HP equipment, integrating it into laboratories where students are trained or research is conducted in science, engineering, medicine and business.
'Contributions of cash and equipment to selected nonprofit organizations that address intellectual and societal needs in math and science education, health and human services, culture and the arts, and civic areas where HP employees and customers are located.' Annual Report

Financial Summary

Total Giving: $57,900,000 (fiscal year ending October 31, 1999 approx); $64,811,000 (fiscal 1998 approx); $63,193,690 (fiscal 1997). Note: Contributes through corporate direct giving program and foundation.
Giving Analysis: Giving for fiscal 1996 includes: corporate direct giving ($14,434,000); foundation ($997,000); fiscal 1997: nonmonetary support ($48,087,000); corporate direct giving ($13,273,000); foundation ($1,833,690); fiscal 1998: nonmonetary support ($50,701,000); corporate direct giving ($14,110,000); foundation ($1,845,000);
Assets: $3,917,107 (fiscal 1998); $4,566,205 (fiscal 1997); $6,129,595 (fiscal 1996)
Gifts Received: $1,000,000 (fiscal 1998)

Typical Recipients

Arts & Humanities: Arts Associations & Councils, Arts Centers, Arts Funds, History & Archaeology, Museums/Galleries, Music

Civic & Public Affairs: Business/Free Enterprise, Clubs, Community Foundations, Economic Development, Employment/Job Training, Law & Justice, Municipalities/Towns, Nonprofit Management, Professional & Trade Associations, Zoos/Aquariums
Education: Business Education, Colleges & Universities, Education Reform, Elementary Education (Private), Elementary Education (Public), Engineering/Technological Education, Education-General, Medical Education, Minority Education, Public Education (Precollege), Science/Mathematics Education, Secondary Education (Public)
Environment: Environment-General
Health: Emergency/Ambulance Services, Eyes/Blindness, Health-General, Hospitals, Public Health
International: Foreign Arts Organizations, Foreign Educational Institutions, Health Care/Hospitals, International Affairs, International Organizations, International Relations, International Relief Efforts, Missionary/Religious Activities
Science: Science Museums, Scientific Organizations
Social Services: Community Service Organizations, Emergency Relief, Substance Abuse, Volunteer Services, YMCA/YWCA/YMHA/YWHA, Youth Organizations

Contributions Analysis

Giving Priorities: Education, international organizations, the arts, and human services. Major priorities are education and programs that advance the understanding of science and enhance human environment through health, human services, and the arts. Hewlett Packard donates equipment to foreign educational institutions and to disaster relief programs worldwide. Equipment grants are made only in countries where support is available. H.P. equipment installation, repair, and maintenance grant requests outside the U.S. should be made to H.P. subsidiaries in the country of origin. In 1999, approximately $6.1 million in support of site-based community-action plans was authorized for local giving. Local grants are decided by employee committees and are based on the budget limit of $40 per employee. In addition to local country grants, the European Grants Committee, which includes HPSA and country representatives, allocates budgets for donations and support K-12 education. In addition, the committee budgets and decides on some Pan European projects that operate in many countries. The grants budgeted by the committee are included in the surcharge billed the countries. HP's Pan European Initiatives include a Distance Learing Intiative; Global Information Infrastructure, High Speed Network & Security project; and Conceptual Learning of Science. The company's grants activities in these countries are guided by local management teams. Decisions about which specific programs to support in these regions are made by representative employee committees in the countries. These local committees investigate requests, decide which programs to support, fund the grants, and provide ongoing support for these efforts. The committees are made up of HP people from all parts of the business operations. The equipment grants often are supplemented by HP employees who volunteer their time to help the grant recipient.
Arts & Humanities: 2%. Supports the arts.
Civic & Public Affairs: 2%. Funds community foundations and civic institutions.
Education: 70%. The majority of this support takes the form of equipment grants to more than 100 colleges and universities, supporting science, engineering, business, and medical education. Focus is on science and mathematics in primary and secondary schools; and science, engineering, medicine, and business in colleges and universities.
Environment: 2%. Supports conservation efforts.
Health: 20%. Support goes to health organizations.
International: Co. reported that one-third of it's giving went to recipients outside of the United States. Donates cash and equipment, where permitted, in overseas operating locations where Hewlett-Packard subsidiaries operate.
Social Services: 4%. Supports the United Way, the Red Cross and substance abuse prevention.
Note: Overall priorities for both cash and equipment grants are programs that advance understanding of science and enhance the human environment through health, human services, and the arts. Total contributions made in 1999.

Application Procedures

Initial Contact: Visit the website for guidelines and forms.
Application Requirements: Include a description of the organization, history, and purpose; amount requested; purpose of grant; statement of need; sources and status of other funding; key personnel and qualifications of staff; recently audited financial statement; and proof of tax-exempt status.
Deadlines: For national grants: October, January, April, and July.
Review Process: Community contributions committees decide on local requests; grants review board makes decisions on nonacademic product donations and nationally oriented cash donations; University Grants Board makes decisions on equipment grants for higher education.
Evaluative Criteria: Clearly stated mission; specific, measurable goals and education criteria; organization's ability to develop and implement program effectively and efficiently; budgetary controls; percentage of funds spent on administration and fundraising; current funding sources; employee participation in, or knowledge of, organization; potential of project to duplicate or counteract efforts of others; board membership and their participation in fundraising.
Decision Notification: Local committees meet monthly or quarterly; national contribution decisions are made quarterly, higher education requests are considered three times per year.
Notes: University requests require a Hewlett-Packard employee sponsor. Proposals for local organizations should be directed to nearest major facility; national requests should be submitted to Nancy Thomas, Contributions Manager.

Restrictions

Equipment is donated only to organizations that have the staff and budget capacity to manage the new technology and must be used on the school's premises for educational purposes.
Hewlett-Packard does not support general fund drives or annual appeals, fundraising events or dinners, conferences, memberships, capital campaigns, endowments, faculty chairs, scholarships, grants to individuals, grants from Hewlett-Packard in the U.S. to organizations outside the U.S., organizations that are not tax-exempt, or religious or sectarian groups.
Contributions are made only in countries where company is located. Community grants are awarded only in the vicinity of company facilities.

Additional Information

Grant seekers should develop a knowledgeable, supportive Hewlett-Packard employee constituency prior to submitting a formal application. Company places strong emphasis on programs in which employees volunteer.
Publications: Guidelines

Corporate Officials

S.T. Jack Brigham, III: senior vice president corporate affairs, general counsel PRIM CORP EMPL senior vice president corporate affairs, general counsel: Hewlett-Packard Co.
Carleton S. Fiorina: president, chief executive officer, director B September 06, 1954. ED Stanford University BA (1976); Massachusetts Institute of Technology MBA (1980); Massachusetts Institute of Technology MS (1989). PRIM CORP EMPL president, chief executive officer, director: Hewlett-Packard Co. CORP AFFIL director: Kellogg Co.; director: Merck & Co. Inc.
Richard A. Hackborn: chairman PRIM CORP EMPL chairman: Hewlett-Packard Co.
Lewis Emmett Platt: chairman B Johnson City, NY 1941. ED Cornell University BSME (1964); University of Pennsylvania MBA (1966). CORP AFFIL director: Boeing Co. NONPR AFFIL chairman: World Trade Organization Task Force Member; board counsel: YMCA United States of America; member: Science Apparatus Manufacturing Association; member: Mid-Peninsula Young Men's Christian Association; vice chairman: Morehouse School of Medicine; co-chairman: Joint Venture Silicon Valley Network Board; director: Cornell University; member: Institute Electrical & Electronics Engineers; member: Computer Systems Policy Project; member: Business Roundtable.
Robert P. Wayman: executive vice president finance & administration, chief financial officer ED Northwestern University MBA; Northwestern University BS. PRIM CORP EMPL executive vice president finance & administration, chief financial officer: Hewlett-Packard Co.

Giving Program Officials

Tony Napolitan: PRIM CORP EMPL university grants manager: Hewlett-Packard Co.
Nancy Thomas: PRIM CORP EMPL national contributions manager: Hewlett-Packard Co.
Roy Verley: director corporate philanthropy PRIM CORP EMPL director corporate philanthropy: Hewlett-Packard Co.

Foundation Officials

Roy Verley: executive director (see above)

Grants Analysis

Disclosure Period: fiscal year ending October 31, 1998
Total Grants: $1,845,000*
Number of Grants: 27
Average Grant: $68,333
Highest Grant: $400,000
Typical Range: $2,500 to $200,000
***Note:** Giving includes foundation only.

Recent Grants

Note: Grants derived from 1999 Form 990.

Civic & Public Affairs

400,000	Monterey Bay Aquarium -- Environmental
400,000	Monterey Bay Aquarium, Monterey, CA -- Environmental
112,500	Peninsula Community Foundation, Palo Alto, CA
10,000	Commonwealth Club, San Francisco, CA

Education

1,830,000	Diversity in Education -- Education Related
600,000	Stanford University Graduate Fellowships -- Education Related
300,000	Stanford University Graduate Fellowship, Stanford, CA -- Education
150,000	San Jose State University School of Business, San Jose, CA -- Education
65,000	Boston Public Schools, Boston, MA -- Education
65,000	El Paso Independent District, El Paso, TX -- Education
65,000	Los Angeles Unified School District, Los Angeles, CA -- Education
50,000	American Physical Society, New York, NY
50,000	Northeastern University, Boston, MA -- Education
50,000	San Jose State University, San Jose, CA -- Education
50,000	University of California at Los Angeles, Los Angeles, CA -- Education

50,000	University of Texas El Paso, El Paso, TX -- Education
45,000	Alum Rock District, San Jose, CA -- Education
25,000	National Technology University, Fort Collins, CO -- Education
20,000	Eastside Union High School District, San Jose, CA -- Education
10,000	Green Mountain College, Poultney, VT

Health

50,000	American Physical Society

International

8,500	International Rescue Committee, New York, NY
5,000	International Diplomacy Council, San Francisco, CA

Science

200,000	Tech Museum of Innovation, San Jose, CA -- Museum
25,000	The Computer Museum, Boston, MA -- Museum
25,000	Tech Museum, San Jose, CA -- Museum

Social Services

20,000	American Red Cross, San Jose, CA
15,000	Just Say No, Oakland, CA
10,000	Puerto Rico Red Cross, San Juan, Puerto Rico
9,000	Canadian Red Cross, Gloucester, ON, Canada

HICKORY TECH CORP.

Company Contact

Mankato, MN
Web: http://www.hickorytech.com

Company Description

Employees: 479 (1999)
SIC(s): 4813 Telephone Communications Except Radiotelephone, 4841 Cable & Other Pay Television Services.

Corporate Sponsorship

Range: less than $4,000
Type: Music & entertainment events

Hickory Tech Corp. Foundation

Giving Contact

Jane L. Rush, Administrator
Hickory Tech Corp. Foundation
221 E. Hickory St.
PO Box 3248
Mankato, MN 56002-3248
Phone: (507)387-1866
Fax: (507)625-9191
Email: janerush@hickorytech.com

Description

Founded: 1963
EIN: 416034001
Organization Type: Corporate Foundation
Giving Locations: MN: Mankato
Grant Types: Capital, Employee Matching Gifts, General Support, Multiyear/Continuing Support, Scholarship.

Financial Summary

Total Giving: $200,000 (fiscal year ending February 28, 1999 approx); $200,375 (fiscal 1998); $208,132 (fiscal 1997). Note: Contributes through foundation only.
Assets: $3,200,000 (fiscal 1999 approx); $3,100,000 (fiscal 1998 approx); $3,458,881 (fiscal 1997)
Gifts Received: $10,000 (fiscal 1996); $70,000 (fiscal 1994); $450,000 (fiscal 1993). Note: Gifts are received from Mankato Citizens Telephone Co.

Typical Recipients

Arts & Humanities: Arts Outreach, Arts & Humanities-General, Historic Preservation, Libraries, Music, Performing Arts, Public Broadcasting, Theater
Civic & Public Affairs: Botanical Gardens/Parks, Business/Free Enterprise, Chambers of Commerce, Clubs, Community Foundations, Economic Development, Economic Policy, Civic & Public Affairs-General, Housing, Parades/Festivals, Urban & Community Affairs, Women's Affairs
Education: Arts/Humanities Education, Business Education, Business-School Partnerships, Colleges & Universities, Community & Junior Colleges, Economic Education, Education Funds, Engineering/Technological Education, Faculty Development, Education-General, International Studies, Leadership Training, Minority Education, Private Education (Precollege), Public Education (Precollege), Religious Education, Science/Mathematics Education, Secondary Education (Private), Secondary Education (Public), Social Sciences Education, Student Aid, Vocational & Technical Education
Environment: Environment-General, Resource Conservation, Wildlife Protection
Health: Hospitals, Medical Rehabilitation, Multiple Sclerosis, Trauma Treatment
Religion: Religious Welfare
Science: Observatories & Planetariums, Science Exhibits & Fairs
Social Services: At-Risk Youth, Camps, Community Service Organizations, Food/Clothing Distribution, Recreation & Athletics, Scouts, Senior Services, Social Services-General, United Funds/United Ways, Volunteer Services, YMCA/YWCA/YMHA/YWHA, Youth Organizations

Contributions Analysis

Arts & Humanities: About 5%. Supports local music and theater groups.
Civic & Public Affairs: Less than 5%. Supports the chamber of commerce and community-school partnerships.
Education: 45% to 50%. Supports public and private colleges and universities in company's headquarters area. The foundation also provides scholarships for children of employees, accounting for approximately one-third of education support, and has established scholarship programs at local universities.
Social Services: 30% to 35%. Primarily supports the United Way. Also supports youth organizations, shelters, clothes distribution and food distribution.

Application Procedures

Initial Contact: by telephone, to request guidelines
Application Requirements: if project meets foundation's mission: a description of project, including specific goals and completion dates; amount requested and percentage of budget it represents; current budget; audited financial statement; list of other contributors, and funding levels; a list of board of directors with affiliations; letter of tax-exempt status; description of how support will be recognized; a plan to evaluate the project's success; and any descriptive brochures or materials
Deadlines: November 10

Restrictions

Does not support individuals; political activities or organizations; religious organizations for sectarian purposes; fraternal, veteran or labor groups; special occasion or goodwill advertising; general operating purposes, except United Way; loans; sports programs or events; cause-related marketing; organizations that discriminate; hospital operating funds or capital funds; and organizations without 501(c)(3) status.

Corporate Officials

Robert D. Alton, Jr.: chairman, president, chief executive officer B 1948. ED Lindenwood University MBA; Iowa State University (1970). PRIM CORP EMPL chairman, president, chief executive officer: Hickory Tech Corp. CORP AFFIL chairman, director: Mankato Citizens Tel Co.; president: Network Horizons Inc.
Lyle T. Bosacker: director PRIM CORP EMPL director: Hickory Tech Corp.
Robert K. Else: director B 1935. ED University of Illinois MBA (1958); University of Chicago MBA (1959). PRIM CORP EMPL president: El Microcircuits Inc. CORP AFFIL director: Hickory Technology Corp.; director: Mankato Citizens Tel Co.
James H. Holdrege: director PRIM CORP EMPL director: Hickory Tech Corp. CORP AFFIL director: Mankato Citizens Tel Co.
R. Wynn Kearney, Jr.: director PRIM CORP EMPL director: Hickory Tech Corp. CORP AFFIL director: Hickory Technology Corp.
Starr J. Kirklin: director PRIM CORP EMPL director: Hickory Tech Corp. CORP AFFIL director: Mankato Citizens Tel Co.
Brett M. Taylor, Junior: director PRIM CORP EMPL director: Hickory Technology Corp. CORP AFFIL director: Mankato Citizens Tel Co.

Foundation Officials

Robert D. Alton, Jr.: trustee (see above)
Lyle T. Bosacker: trustee (see above)
Robert K. Else: secretary (see above)
James H. Holdrege: trustee (see above)
Lyle Gordon Jacobson: treasurer B Duluth, MN 1941. ED University of Minnesota (1963); University of Minnesota MS (1965). PRIM CORP EMPL president, chief executive officer: Katolight Corp. ADD CORP EMPL vice president: Jones Metal Products Inc.; treasurer: Winnebago Manufacturing Co. CORP AFFIL director: Mankato Citizens Tel Co.; director: Hickory Technology Corp.; director, owner: JKW Management Corp. NONPR AFFIL Kiwanis International.
R. Wynn Kearney, Jr.: trustee (see above)
Starr J. Kirklin: trustee (see above)
Brett M. Taylor, Junior: president (see above)

Grants Analysis

Disclosure Period: fiscal year ending February 28, 1997
Total Grants: $208,132
Number of Grants: 74
Average Grant: $2,358*
Highest Grant: $36,000
Typical Range: $100 to $3,500
***Note:** Average grant excludes highest grant.

Recent Grants

Note: Grants derived from fiscal 1997 Form 990.

Arts & Humanities

4,000	Mankato Symphony Orchestra, Mankato, MN
1,500	Mankato Area Lancer Marching Band, Mankato, MN
1,500	Minnesota Valley Regional Library, Mankato, MN
1,000	Mankato Youth Symphony, Mankato, MN
850	Mankato Symphony Orchestra, Mankato, MN
500	Mankato State University, Mankato, MN -- for KSMU Public Radio
500	Merely Players Community, Mankato, MN
250	Minnesota Public Radio, Saint Paul, MN
200	Merely Players Community, Mankato, MN

Civic & Public Affairs

1,000	MACS 21st Century, Mankato, MN
400	Women of Today, Anoka, MN
200	Martin Luther King Community Celebration, Mankato, MN

Education

36,000	Citizens Scholarship Foundation, Saint Peter, MN -- scholarships
26,500	Mankato State University, Mankato, MN -- scholarships
25,000	Bethany College, Mankato, MN -- capital campaign
6,000	Citizens Scholarship Foundation, Saint Peter, MN -- Employee Child Scholarship Program
5,000	Educare, Mankato, MN
5,000	Gustavus Adolphus College, Saint Peter, MN -- for Nobel Hall renovations
4,500	Gustavus Adolphus College, Saint Peter, MN -- scholarship program
4,000	Independent School District 77 Leadership Institute, Mankato, MN
4,000	Mankato State University, Mankato, MN -- for production of one play
3,000	South Central Technical College, North Mankato, MN
2,000	MACS Scholarship Foundation, Mankato, MN
1,200	Close-Up Foundation, Alexandria, VA -- scholarships
1,000	Gustavus Adolphus College, Saint Peter, MN
1,000	Knox College, Galesburg, IL
1,000	Mankato State University, Mankato, MN -- for solar care project
600	Independent School District 77, Mankato, MN -- for Graduation Night Party
500	Junior Achievement, Mankato, MN
500	Mankato Area Foundation, Mankato, MN -- for Academic Decathlon
225	Mankato State University Foundation, Mankato, MN

Environment

225	Delta Waterfowl Foundation, Bismarck, ND
200	Nicollet Conservation Club, Nicollet, MN

Health

500	Courage Center, Mankato, MN
250	Mankato Head Injury Support Group, Saint Paul, MN

Religion

25,000	Salvation Army, Mankato, MN -- Renovation Campaign
600	Salvation Army, Mankato, MN

Science

1,000	South Central Minnesota Science and Engineering Fair, Mankato, MN

Social Services

27,000	United Way, Mankato, MN
5,000	YWCA, Mankato, MN -- renovation campaign
3,000	ECHO Food Shelf, Mankato, MN
1,000	Overcoming Poverty Together, Mankato, MN
1,000	Youth in Government Program, Mankato, MN
750	Boy Scouts of America Twin Valley Council, Mankato, MN -- for Explorer Program
400	Mankato Area Girls Fastpitch Association, Mankato, MN
250	Mankato Area Hockey Association, Eagle Lake, MN
200	Boy Scouts of America Twin Valley Council, Mankato, MN
200	Covenant House, New York, NY
200	MRCI Thrift Shop, Mankato, MN
200	Volunteer Center, Mankato, MN

Hitachi America Ltd.

Company Contact

Tarrytown, NY

Web: http://www.hitachi.com

Company Description

Employees: 4,484

SIC(s): 2899 Chemical Preparations Nec, 3321 Gray & Ductile Iron Foundries, 3322 Malleable Iron Foundries, 3569 General Industrial Machinery Nec.

Parent Company: Hitachi Ltd., 6, Kanda-Surugadai 4-chome, Chiyoda-ku, Tokyo, Japan

Operating Locations

CA: Hitachi Consumer Products of America, Anaheim; Hitachi America Ltd., Brisbane, Fremont, Irvine, Long Beach, San Jose; Hitachi Instruments, San Jose; Hitachi Chemical Co. America Ltd., Santa Clara; Hitachi Data Systems Corp., Santa Clara; Hitachi America Ltd., Torrance; CO: Hitachi America Ltd., Denver; FL: Hitachi America Ltd., Fort Lauderdale; GA: Maxell Corp. of America, Conyers; GE-Hitachi HVB, Norcross; Hitachi Home Electronics, Norcross; Hitachi Home Electronics (America), Norcross; IL: Hitachi America Ltd., Buffalo Grove, Chicago, Itasca, Rolling Meadows; MA: Hitachi America Ltd., Burlington, Waltham; MI: Hitachi America Ltd., Dearborn, Farmington; NC: Hitachi America Ltd., Raleigh; NJ: Battery Products Division, Fair Lawn; Computer Products Division, Fair Lawn; Consumer Audio & Video Sales, Fair Lawn; Maxell Corp. of America, Fair Lawn; Professional Industrial Sales, Fair Lawn; Hitachi America Ltd., Florham Park, Montvale, Princeton; NY: Hitachi America Ltd., New York, Port Chester, Tarrytown; Hitachi America, Ltd., Tarrytown; OH: Euclid Hitachi, Cleveland; TN: Hitachi America Ltd., Nashville; TX: Hitachi America Ltd., Carrollton, Dallas; Hitachi Semiconductor (America), Irving

Note: Hitachi, Ltd. operates in 22 communities throughout the United States; Hitachi America, Ltd., a subsidiary, is headquartered in Tarrytown, NY.

Nonmonetary Support

Type: Donated Equipment; In-kind Services

Contact:
Hitachi America, Ltd.
Phone: (914)332-5800

Hitachi Foundation

Giving Contact

Laurie Regelbrugge, Vice President
Hitachi Foundation
1509 22nd Street, NW
Washington, DC 20037
Phone: (202)457-0588
Fax: (202)296-1098

Description

Founded: 1985

EIN: 521429292

Organization Type: Corporate Foundation. Supports preselected organizations only.

Giving Locations: continental United States; parent company gives internationally.

Grant Types: Award, Employee Matching Gifts, Multiyear/Continuing Support, Project, Seed Money.

Note: Employee matching gift ratio: 1 to 1, upon recommendation of local Community Action Committee of Hitachi employees. Matching gifts are based on team contributions rather than individual employee donations. United fund and college athletic program contributions are ineligible for foundation matching support.

Giving Philosophy

'As a result of its 1993-1994 long-range planning exercise, the Foundation Board and staff have adopted a highly focused program strategy that seeks to leverage the Foundation's ten years of experience and build upon its strategic advantage as a private and corporate foundation. While continuing to advance its mission of assisting people, institutions, and communities to participate effectively in a global society, the Foundation has several overriding goals for 1995 and beyond.

'To identify and pursue strategic interventions in education and community development that will build capacity to participate effectively in a rapidly changing global society.

'To promote understanding of the nature of a global society and the opportunities, challenges, and responsibilities it presents both to individuals and communities.

'To work collaboratively with key public and private institutions, grantee organizations, and other funders to develop and disseminate fresh insights and to replicate proven programs.

'To integrate efforts so they reinforce each other and place specific community concerns and action within their larger global context.

'To collaborate with Hitachi corporate units in furthering their community action strategies.

'To provide leadership within the field and an example of innovative, strategic philanthropy through Foundation operations and program decisions.' *The Hitachi Foundation Ten Year Retrospective*

Financial Summary

Total Giving: $2,700,000 (fiscal year ending March 31, 1998 approx); $2,492,567 (fiscal 1997); $1,682,938 (fiscal 1996). Note: Contributes through corporate direct giving program and foundation. Giving includes foundation.

Assets: $36,000,000 (fiscal 1998 approx); $38,318,161 (fiscal 1997); $35,591,740 (fiscal 1996)

Gifts Received: $247,081 (fiscal 1997); $4,460,340 (fiscal 1996); $1,175,000 (fiscal 1995). Note: Contributions are received from Hitachi, Ltd. and its subsidiaries.

Typical Recipients

Arts & Humanities: Arts Centers, Arts Outreach, Arts & Humanities-General, Historic Preservation, History & Archaeology, Literary Arts, Museums/Galleries, Music

Civic & Public Affairs: African American Affairs, Asian American Affairs, Business/Free Enterprise, Community Foundations, Economic Development, Employment/Job Training, Civic & Public Affairs-General, Hispanic Affairs, Housing, Law & Justice, Municipalities/Towns, Native American Affairs, Nonprofit Management, Public Policy, Rural Affairs, Urban & Community Affairs, Women's Affairs

Education: Arts/Humanities Education, Colleges & Universities, Community & Junior Colleges, Education Associations, Education Reform, Elementary Education (Private), Faculty Development, Education-General, International Exchange, International Studies, Leadership Training, Literacy, Medical Education, Minority Education, Public Education (Precollege), Science/Mathematics Education, Social Sciences Education, Special Education

Environment: Forestry, Environment-General, Resource Conservation

International: Foreign Educational Institutions, Human Rights, International Affairs, International Environmental Issues, International Organizations, International Peace & Security Issues, International Relations, International Relief Efforts

Religion: Churches

Science: Science Museums, Scientific Centers & Institutes

Social Services: Child Welfare, Community Centers, Community Service Organizations, Crime Prevention, Shelters/Homelessness, Volunteer Services, Youth Organizations

Contributions Analysis

Giving Priorities: Community development, economic development, education, and technology.

Civic & Public Affairs: 35% to 40%. Foundation is interested in helping to develop a wider definition of

and vision for communities and community development. Supports projects that enable people and organizations to identify their collective needs and then develop strategies for addressing those needs. Also seeks to support projects that develop and engage community leadership; bring a variety of community actors to the table; facilitate the building of strong and accountable community institutions; actively seek to explore innovative strategies, creative use of resources, and new organizational roles or institutional mechanisms to build community capacity, particularly at the local level in an integrative way; and make more effective use of existing resources while mobilizing new financial, material, and human resources for community development. In this area, the foundation does not support single-issue community development approaches such as small business development, commercial revitalization, and neighborhood beautification; housing development or housing specific programming in isolation from other community development efforts; leadership development programs disconnected from specific problem identification and solving efforts; or social service provision in isolation from larger community building strategies. The company sponsors the Yoshiyama Award to individuals for exemplary service to community. 5% to 10%. Foundation seeks to improve understanding of the roles and relationship of the United States and Japan as leaders in a rapidly changing world. Foundation believes global citizenship must incorporate tenets of inclusiveness, particularly of those groups that are most at-risk and underserved, and broad participation in decision-making, collaborative problem-solving, and recognition of the wider implications of local action and policy. Funding in this area is for projects focusing on the roles and responsibilities that must be adopted by global corporations and organizations, governments, public and private institutions, communities, and individuals.

Education: 35% to 40%. Foundation encourages projects that support children, youth, adults, and educators as they learn to participate in an increasingly pluralistic and complex society. Projects that further these goals include those that foster an understanding of diversity and global issues across disciplines, explore the role of museums and the arts in effective education, connect learning objectives with community service, and work force development. The majority of the foundation's education dollars are targeted toward the precollegiate level, with support at the post-secondary level directed mainly toward assisting institutions to build collaborative and cooperative programs with communities or the K-12 schools. Education projects that receive support reflect the necessity to prepare individuals to participate more fully as citizens and productive members of society; recognize that schools can play a significant role in building and stabilizing communities; improve and develop the connections between schools, parents, and communities; recognize the diversity of learning styles and pedagogical approaches needed to educate all of America's students; incorporate the arts or museums as an educator and provider of increased opportunities for creativity and problem solving; link education to economic opportunity; and utilize community resources, such as arts organizations, corporations, churches and synagogues, and community service organizations. In the area of education, the foundation does not support math and science programs that are not interdisciplinary and do not build upon emerging and existing research on teaching and learning; projects that focus on schools, teachers, and students in a vacuum, seeing them as separate from the community; or efforts to 'internationalize' curricula, programs, or institutions at the post-secondary level.

Science: 5% to 10%. Foundation makes grants to organizations for support programs that address technology-related issues in education and community development. Grants are not solely for acquisition or use of technology, nor for equipment purchase.

Application Procedures

Deadlines: April 1 for the Yoshiyama Award for Exemplary Community Service.

Review Process: The foundation issues requests for proposals, develops collaborative projects, convenes grantees, and undertakes related investments.

Evaluative Criteria: Foundation announcements specify the eligible organizations and submission criteria.

Notes: Interested organizations may respond to foundation requests for proposals, which are issued once or twice per year. The foundation maintains a 'Fax-on-Demand System' which provides current information on requests for proposals, recent grants, publications, and other initiatives. The system can be reached by telephone by dialin (202) 457-0588, ext. 551.

Restrictions

Grants are not made for medical research, publication of studies or reports, or general operating support. The Foundation does not fund individuals.

Additional Information

The Yoshiyama Award for Exemplary Community Service, initiated in 1987, recognizes and supports eight to ten high school seniors who have performed outstanding service to their communities. Seniors cannot nominate themselves; deadline is April 1.

The Matching Funds Program (MFP) is a partnership program between the Hitachi Foundation and Hitachi corporate facilities. Aiming to promote social responsibility at Hitachi corporate facilities, this program involves local employees and managers in sustained efforts to improve their communities and encourages employee volunteerism in community problem-solving efforts. The MFP is implemented through Community Action Committees, which determine funding priorities, identify community needs, and make recommendations to the foundation for matching grants. Matching funds are provided by the foundation for CAC-approved corporate grants and contributions, and, in some cases, for equipment donations, employee release time for volunteer service, and employee fundraising for charitable purposes.

Publications: Guidelines; Foundation Annual Report

Corporate Officials

Tomoharu Shimayama: president PRIM CORP EMPL president: Hitachi America Ltd.

Foundation Officials

Clara Apodaca: trustee B Las Cruces, NM 1934. ED New Mexico State University BA (1955). PRIM CORP EMPL director protocol: Overseas Private Investment Corp. NONPR AFFIL chairwoman national advisory board: Cornerstones; director: Hispanics in Philanthropy.

Sherry Salway Black: trustee B 1953. ED University of Pennsylvania Wharton School MBA (1982). PRIM NONPR EMPL vice president: First Nations Development Institute.

Takashi Chiba: treasurer

Lofton Durham: executive & program assistant

Patricia Albjerg Graham, PhD: trustee B Lafayette, IN 1935. ED Purdue University BS (1955); Purdue University MS (1957); Columbia University PhD (1964). CORP AFFIL trustee: Northwestern Mutual Life Insurance Co. NONPR AFFIL member: Phi Beta Kappa; member: Science Research Associatess; member: National Academy Education; council: American Association Advancement Science; member: American Historical Association.

Katrinka Hall: program assistant

Jo Ann Haltiwanter: program assistant

Renata D. Hron: program officer

Tsutomu Kanai: president B 1929. ED Tokyo University (1958). PRIM CORP EMPL president: Hitachi Ltd. CORP AFFIL managing director: Hitachi Seisakujo Co. Ltd.

Joseph Edward Kasputys: chairman, trustee B Jamaica, NY 1936. ED City University of New York Brooklyn College BA (1959); Harvard University MBA (1967); Harvard University DBA (1972). PRIM CORP EMPL chairman, president, chief executive officer: Primark Corp. CORP AFFIL director: Yankee Group Research Inc.; chairman: Primark Holding Corp.; director: Triad International Maint Corp.; director: Lifeline Systems Inc.; director: New Era of Networks; chairman: Baseline Financial Service. NONPR AFFIL member: Committee for Economic Development; member: Phi Beta Kappa. CLUB AFFIL Capital Hill Club; Harvard Business School Club.

Scott Lippman: secretary, treasurer

Ann L. Matikan: executive secretary

Katsushige Mita: honorary chairman B Tokyo, Japan 1924.

Roger H. Nozaki: senior program officer

Percy A. Pierre: trustee B Donaldsville, LA 1939. ED University of Notre Dame BSEE (1961); University of Notre Dame MSEE (1963); Johns Hopkins University PhD (1967); University of Michigan (1968). PRIM NONPR EMPL professor electricctrical engineering: Michigan State University. CORP AFFIL director: Old Kent Financial Corp.; member advisory panel: Office Exptl Research Development Incentives; officer: Old Kent Bank; director: Dual Inc.; trustee: Aerospace Corp.; director: CMS Energy Corp. NONPR AFFIL member: Sigma Xi; member: Tau Beta Pi; member advisory board: Lincoln Laboratories, MIT; director: Association Texas Colleges Universitys; member: Institute Electrical & Electronics Engineers.

Laurie A. Regelbrugge: vice president

Sidney Dillon Ripley, II: director emeritus B New York, NY 1913. ED Yale University BA (1936); Harvard University PhD (1943); Yale University MA (1961). NONPR AFFIL member U.S. board directors: World Wildlife Fund; fellow: Zoological Society India; director: White Memorial Foundation; member: Society Study Evolution; member: Society Systematic Zoology; member: National Academy Sciences; secretary emeritus: Smithsonian Institute; member: International Council of Museum Foundations; member: International Wild Waterfowl Association; member: Council Foreign Relations; member: French Institute; member: British Ornithologists Union; member: American Philosophical Society; member: Bombay Natural History Society; member: American Naturalists Society; fellow: American Ornithologists Union; member: American Academy Arts & Letters; fellow: American Association Advancement Science.

Peter William Stanley: trustee B Bronxville, NY 1940. ED Harvard University BA (1962); Harvard University MA (1964); Harvard University PhD (1970). PRIM NONPR EMPL president: Pomona College. NONPR AFFIL member: Phi Beta Kappa; humanities & science council: Stanford University; national advisory council: National Foreign Language Center; member: Council Foreign Relations; director: National Association Latino Elected Off Education Fund; member executive committee: Consortium Financing Higher Education; member: Association Asian Studies; vice chairman, trustee: College Board; member: American Historical Association; member: American Association University Professors; committee international education: American Council Education.

Soji Teramura: secretary, director B 1937. PRIM CORP EMPL president: Teramura International Inc.

Hirokichi Yoshiyama: chairman emeritus

Grants Analysis

Disclosure Period: fiscal year ending March 31, 1997

Total Grants: $2,492,567

Number of Grants: 54

Average Grant: $46,159

Highest Grant: $350,000

Typical Range: $10,000 to $250,000

Recent Grants

Note: Grants derived from 1997 Form 990.

Arts & Humanities

44,100	New Press, Rego Park, NY

Civic & Public Affairs

350,000	MFP-Foundation Administered Project
100,000	MDC, Chapel Hill, NC
98,000	Cornerstone Community Partnerships, Santa Fe, NM
77,855	Aspira Association, Washington, DC
67,525	Chugachmiut, Anchorage, AK
67,000	One-to-One, Detroit, MI
66,931	South Bronx Community Coalition, Bronx, NY
65,251	Hopi Foundation, Hoteville, AZ
62,500	Boggs Rural Life Center, Keysville, GA
60,300	Council for Excellence in Government, Washington, DC
57,500	Forward in the Fifth, Berea, KY
57,000	Greater Washington Urban League, Washington, DC
55,000	Puente Project, Oakland, CA
50,000	Rural Development Leadership Network, New York, NY
41,300	Newton County Resource Council, Jasper, AR
40,600	One-to-One, Philadelphia, PA
40,000	Penn Center
39,500	Highlander Research and Education Center, New Market, TN
25,000	Community Economic Development Center
20,000	Asia Pacific Philanthropy Consortium
20,000	Aspen Institute, Washington, DC
15,150	Coalition of Neighborhood Developers, Los Angeles, CA
15,000	Council on Foundations, Washington, DC
13,900	Community Women's Education Project, Philadelphia, PA
5,000	Ms. Foundation for Women, New York, NY

Education

87,840	Association of Science Technology Centers, Washington, DC
87,560	University of Virginia, Charlottesville, VA
42,250	Salish Kootenai College, Pablo, MT
32,700	University of Florida Department of Psychology, Gainesville, FL
30,000	Leadership Development in Interethnic Relations, Los Angeles, CA
29,000	Japan Center for International Exchange, New York, NY
25,400	Illinois Math and Science Academy, Aurora, IL
19,175	Winston-Salem State University, Winston-Salem, NC
7,500	National Society for Experiential Education, Raleigh, NC
5,000	Heartwood Institute, Pittsburgh, PA

Environment

40,000	Rogue Institute for Ecology and Economy, Ashland, OR
30,000	Chesapeake Bay Foundation, Annapolis, MD
10,000	Georgia Environmental Organization, Atlanta, GA

International

80,000	World Game Institute, Philadelphia, PA

Social Services

109,497	Volunteer Center, San Francisco, CA
78,460	Impact Services Corporation, Philadelphia, PA
70,000	Southend Community Services, Hartford, CT
64,556	Girls, Incorporated, San Leandro, CA
50,000	Conflict Management Group, Cambridge, MA
37,980	Greater DC Cares, Washington, DC
28,900	Points of Light Foundation, Washington, DC
25,000	Futures for Children, Albuquerque, NM
20,150	Youth Development Advisory Committee, Greenville, WV
10,000	Reach Center, Marietta, GA

Hoechst Marion Roussel, Inc.

Company Contact

Kansas City, MO
Web: http://www.hmri.com

Company Description

Employees: 9,421
SIC(s): 2834 Pharmaceutical Preparations.
Parent Company: Aventis S.A., Frankfurt am Main, Germany

Operating Locations

MO: Hoechst Marion Roussel, Kansas City

Nonmonetary Support

Type: Donated Products; In-kind Services
Note: Company will consider lending technical assistance for projects.

Giving Contact

Susan Wiggle, Jr., Administration Assistant
399 Interpace Parkway
Box 633
Parsippany, NJ 07054
Phone: (973)394-6000

Description

Organization Type: Corporate Giving Program
Grant Types: General Support, Research.

Financial Summary

Total Giving: $11,000,000 (1996 approx); $9,287,037 (1995). Note: Contributes through corporate direct giving program only. Giving includes nonmonetary support. 1995 Giving includes corporate direct giving ($2,316,203); Hoechst Marion Roussel Health Care Foundation for the Ill ($6,970,834); Marion Merrell Dow Foundation ($6,989,967); nonmonetary support.
Assets: $16,238,078 (1994)

Contributions Analysis

Arts & Humanities: Less than 5%.
Civic & Public Affairs: 15% to 20%.
Education: About 5%. Funds support math and science programs in K-12 education. A secondary focus is on economic education to promote free enterprise. Also supports higher education in local communities.
Health: About 45%. The company provides direct gifts and nonmonetary support. The main focus of giving is to provide access to medical care for the medically indigent.
Science: 40% to 45%. Company supports scientific research and training through partnerships and collaborative efforts with universities in company communities.

Application Procedures

Initial Contact: brief letter
Application Requirements: name, address, and telephone number of requesting organization; description of the need for the requested grant, amount, and its specific purpose; description of the program or project for which the grant is requested; detailed analysis of the amount of funding requested, how the funds would be applied, and when the funds would be needed; a current financial statement of requesting entity; a list of current trustees or board of directors; and a photocopy of the IRS letter stating that the applicant is tax-exempt, pursuant to Section 501(c)(3) and is not classified as a private foundation within the meaning of Section 509 of the IRS code
Deadlines: None.
Evaluative Criteria: applicant should have clearly defined and achievable objectives and a plan of action that can be monitored and audited; be an equal opportunity employer and operate programs in a manner supporting equal opportunity objectives; and have a worthy legal purpose fulfilling a clear societal need without unduly duplicating services already in the community
Decision Notification: twenty-one working days after proposal is received

Restrictions

Does not support individual scholarships; capital drives to construct or remodel facilities; partisan, political, or cultural organizations; sectarian organizations whose services relate to a single religious group; or courtesy advertising.

Additional Information

Hoechst Marion Roussel, Inc. was formed through a partnership between Hoechst, Marion Merrell Dow, Inc. (formed in 1989 by the merger of Marion Laboratories, Inc and Merrell Dow Pharmaceuticals, Inc.) and Roussel Uclaf (part of the Hoechst Group since 1974). Co. no longer operates a foundation, but instead, gives directly.

Giving Program Officials

Edward M. Connolly, Jr.: president

Hoffer Plastics Corp.

Company Contact

South Elgin, IL

Company Description

Employees: 700
SIC(s): 3082 Unsupported Plastics Profile Shapes, 3089 Plastics Products Nec.

Hoffer Foundation

Giving Contact

Robert A. Hoffer, Chairman, President & Chief Executive Officer
Hoffer Foundation
500 Collins St.
South Elgin, IL 60177
Phone: (847)741-5841
Email: hofferpl@inil.com

Alternate Contact

Linda Refchke

Description

Founded: 1966
EIN: 366160991
Organization Type: Corporate Foundation
Giving Locations: IL
Grant Types: General Support.

Financial Summary

Total Giving: $532,462 (fiscal year ending November 30, 1998); $1,053,797 (fiscal 1997); $437,820 (fiscal 1995). Note: Contributes through foundation only.
Giving Analysis: Giving for fiscal 1996 includes: foundation ($534,161); foundation grants to United Way ($59,000); fiscal 1997: foundation ($992,297); foundation grants to United Way ($61,500); fiscal 1998: foundation ($467,462); foundation grants to United Way ($65,000)
Assets: $4,677,291 (fiscal 1998); $4,818,353 (fiscal 1997); $4,458,946 (fiscal 1996)

Gifts Received: $156,526 (fiscal 1997); $25,000 (fiscal 1996); $400,000 (fiscal 1994). Note: Contributions are received from Robert A. Hoffer.

Typical Recipients

Arts & Humanities: Arts & Humanities-General, Historic Preservation, History & Archaeology, Museums/Galleries, Music, Performing Arts, Public Broadcasting
Civic & Public Affairs: Clubs, Civic & Public Affairs-General, Housing, Municipalities/Towns, Philanthropic Organizations
Education: Afterschool/Enrichment Programs, Business Education, Colleges & Universities, Education Reform, Elementary Education (Public), Education-General, Private Education (Precollege), Public Education (Precollege), Science/Mathematics Education, Secondary Education (Public)
Environment: Environment-General, Wildlife Protection
Health: Children's Health/Hospitals, Hospitals
Religion: Churches
Science: Science Museums
Social Services: Community Centers, Community Service Organizations, Counseling, Family Services, Recreation & Athletics, Scouts, United Funds/United Ways, YMCA/YWCA/YMHA/YWHA, Youth Organizations

Contributions Analysis

Giving Priorities: Supports museums, musical programs, historical societies, public broadcasting, education, housing services, Junior Achievement, wildlife preservation, science, churches and youth organizations.
Arts & Humanities: 21%.
Civic & Public Affairs: 1%.
Education: 49%.
Environment: 1%.
Health: 5%.
Religion: 5%.
Social Services: 18%.
Note: Total contributions made in 1998.

Application Procedures

Initial Contact: Send a brief letter.
Deadlines: None.

Corporate Officials

Robert A. Hoffer: president B 1919. PRIM CORP EMPL president: Hoffer Plastics Corp.
Robert A. Hoffer, Jr.: vice president B 1945. ED Purdue University BS (1967). PRIM CORP EMPL vice president: Hoffer Plastics Corp.

Foundation Officials

Helen C. Hoffer: trustee B 1918. PRIM CORP EMPL secretary: Hoffer Plastics Corp.
Robert A. Hoffer, Jr.: trustee (see above)
Robert A. Hoffer: trustee (see above)

Grants Analysis

Disclosure Period: fiscal year ending November 30, 1998
Total Grants: $457,632*
Number of Grants: 16
Average Grant: $28,602
Highest Grant: $156,310
Typical Range: $2,500 to $100,000
***Note:** Giving excludes miscellaneous contributions of less than $1,000 each totalling ($9,830); United Way.

Recent Grants

Note: Grants derived from fiscal 1998 Form 990.

Arts & Humanities
100,000 National Plastics Museum, Leominster, MA -- Education
4,500 Elgin Symphony Orchestra, Elgin, IL -- Education
2,000 WTTW Channel 11, Chicago, IL -- Education
1,500 Elgin Enrichment Series, Elgin, IL -- Education

Civic & Public Affairs
1,750 Neighborhood Housing Services, Elgin, IL -- Charity
1,200 Village of South Elgin, South Elgin, IL -- Education

Education
156,310 Purdue University, West Lafayette, IN -- Education
99,239 Judson College, Elgin, IL -- Education
2,500 Junior Achievement, Elgin, IL -- Education

Environment
4,150 Max McGraw Wildlife Foundation, Dundee, IL -- Scientific

Health
20,400 St. Joseph Hospital, Elgin, IL -- Scientific
6,217 Jayne Shover Easter Seals, Elgin, IL -- Scientific

Religion
28,070 Episcopal Church, Elgin, IL -- Charity

Social Services
65,000 United Way of Elgin, Elgin, IL -- Charity
24,796 Elgin YMCA, Elgin, IL -- Education
3,000 YWCA, Elgin, IL -- Education
2,000 Family Service Association, Elgin, IL -- Education

HOFFMANN-LA ROCHE INC.

Company Contact

Nutley, NJ
Web: http://www.roche.com

Company Description

Employees: 17,000
SIC(s): 2833 Medicinals & Botanicals, 2834 Pharmaceutical Preparations, 8071 Medical Laboratories.
Parent Company: Roche Holdings, AG

Operating Locations

CA: Syntex, Palo Alto; Syntex Agribusiness, Palo Alto; Genentech, San Francisco; CO: Syntex Chemicals, Boulder; NC: Hoffmann-La Roche Inc., Burlington; Roche Biomedical Laboratories, Burlington; NJ: Hoffmann-La Roche Inc., Belleville, Belvidere; American Roche Intl., Clifton; Givaudan-Roure Corp., Clifton; Givaudan-Roure Corp. Flavors Div., Clifton; Hoffmann-La Roche Inc., Montclair; Hoffmann-La Roche, Nutley; Hoffmann-La Roche Inc., Paramus; Roche Professional Service Centers, Paramus; Hoffmann-La Roche Inc., Raritan; Roche Diagnostic Systems, Somerville; Roche Molecular Systems, Somerville; Givaudan-Roure Corp. Fragrances Div., Teaneck; Hoffmann-La Roche Inc., Totowa

Nonmonetary Support

Type: In-kind Services

Hoffmann-La Roche Foundation

Giving Contact

Ms. Vivian Beetle, Director Community Affairs/Public Affairs
Hoffmann-La Roche Inc.
340 Kingsland St.
Nutley, NJ 07110-1199
Phone: (973)235-2055
Fax: (973)562-2999

Description

Founded: 1945
EIN: 226063790
Organization Type: Corporate Foundation
Giving Locations: NJ
Grant Types: Employee Matching Gifts, Fellowship, Research, Seed Money.

Giving Philosophy

'Hoffmann-La Roche, Inc. is one of the world's leading health care companies. Widely known for original research and development, Roche has produced numerous important pharmaceutical and medical products and is a leader in biotechnology. .. Beyond its professional responsibility to customers in the health care community, Roche is equally committed to social responsibility. The Roche Department of Community Affairs devotes considerable effort and resources to the support of programs in the communities of its sites and employees. .. Charitable contributions have been a vital element in the structure and development of our free society. Such support is a continuing responsibility of both individuals and corporations. Recognizing its obligation as a corporate citizen, Hoffmann-La Roche Inc. has established a program in corporate giving. Contributions will be made to domestic, nonprofit organizations engaged in programs in the areas of health, education and community social service activities in those communitites where Roche has a site or significant employee population.' *Hoffmann-La Roche Corporate Contributions Policies and Procedures*

Financial Summary

Total Giving: $1,000,000 (fiscal year ending July 31, 1999 approx); $1,000,000 (fiscal 1998 approx); $904,982 (fiscal 1997). Note: Contributes through corporate direct giving program and foundation.
Assets: $122 (fiscal 1997); $22,678 (fiscal 1996); $28 (fiscal 1994)
Gifts Received: $866,202 (fiscal 1997); $1,037,479 (fiscal 1996); $896,426 (fiscal 1994). Note: In 1994, the foundation received funds from Hoffmann-La Roche.

Typical Recipients

Arts & Humanities: Libraries, Museums/Galleries, Music, Opera, Performing Arts
Civic & Public Affairs: Community Foundations, Employment/Job Training, Civic & Public Affairs-General, Philanthropic Organizations, Professional & Trade Associations, Urban & Community Affairs, Zoos/Aquariums
Education: Colleges & Universities, Economic Education, Education Funds, Education-General, International Exchange, Medical Education, Minority Education, Private Education (Precollege), Science/Mathematics Education, Secondary Education (Public), Vocational & Technical Education
Environment: Environment-General, Wildlife Protection
Health: AIDS/HIV, Cancer, Children's Health/Hospitals, Emergency/Ambulance Services, Health Organizations, Hospices, Hospitals, Medical Research, Medical Training, Mental Health, Public Health, Single-Disease Health Associations, Transplant Networks/Donor Banks
International: Health Care/Hospitals, Human Rights, International Affairs, International Environmental Issues, International Relations
Religion: Churches, Religious Organizations
Science: Science Museums, Scientific Centers & Institutes, Scientific Labs, Scientific Organizations, Scientific Research
Social Services: Animal Protection, Community Service Organizations, People with Disabilities, Substance Abuse, United Funds/United Ways, YMCA/YWCA/YMHA/YWHA

Contributions Analysis

Giving Priorities: Higher education, health, science, civic concerns, and social service.
Arts & Humanities: 2%. Funds performing arts, libraries, and museums.
Civic & Public Affairs: 1%. Supports zoos and wildlife, community foundations, professional associations, and others.
Education: 52%. Primarily gives to universities, with priority placed on scientific research in medicine and biology. Supports education funds, including the Independent College Fund of New Jersey. Also funds educational programs that encourage math and science literacy.
Environment: 5%.
Health: 2%. Grants emphasize medical research and training. Supports hospitals, health organizations, and similar groups. Does not support medical delivery of services.
Religion: 1%.
Social Services: 37%. Funds substance abuse organizations, youth organizations, and animal welfare.
Note: Above priorities are based on foundation giving only. Company also sponsors a direct giving program, which is considerably larger than the foundation program. Financial data for the direct giving program is not available; interests include community development, human services, and arts organizations, with emphasis on plant communities.

Application Procedures

Initial Contact: Send a letter of inquiry of not more than three pages.
Application Requirements: Include basic background on the organization including contact information, purpose, and mission; and a description of the program for which support is requested including proposed purpose, current status, professional personnel, anticipated length of program, and final results, and program budget information.
Deadlines: None.
Decision Notification: Applicants are notified of decisions within six to eight weeks of receipt of letter.

Restrictions

The foundation will not consider requests for: gifts to individuals, endowment or scholarship funds; international organizations or projects; political organizations, parties, candidates, or office holders; the purchase, construction, expansion or modification of facilities; equipment or other capital expenditures; goodwill advertising; sectarian groups, except for education and health programs which serve the general population without regard to religious affiliation; or labor or veterans' organizations, unless the project in question is for the general welfare of an entire community in which Roche is present.

Additional Information

Preference is given to organizations located within the state of New Jersey and sites of Hoffmann-La Roche. Preference is also given to local chapters of national health organizations. National headquarters of health organizations are rarely funded.
Publications: Guidelines

Corporate Officials

Frederick C. Kentz, III: vice president, secretary, general counsel B Summit, NJ 1952. ED Georgetown University (1974); Fordham University (1977). PRIM CORP EMPL vice president, secretary, general counsel: Hoffmann-La Roche Inc. CORP AFFIL officer: Roche Diagnostics System; officer: Roche Molecular System Inc.; officer: Roche Carolina Inc.
Patrick J. Zenner: president, chief executive officer, director B 1948. ED Creighton University BSBA; Fairleigh Dickinson University MBA (1969). PRIM CORP EMPL president, chief executive officer, director: Hoffmann-La Roche Inc. CORP AFFIL officer: Roche Carolina Inc.; officer: Roche Molecular System Inc.; president: HLR Service Corp.

Foundation Officials

Vivian Beetle: admin director PRIM CORP EMPL director community affairs: Hoffmann-La Roche Inc.
Frederick C. Kentz, III: trustee (see above)
Patrick J. Zenner: trustee (see above)

Grants Analysis

Disclosure Period: fiscal year ending July 31, 1998
Total Grants: $1,282,290
Number of Grants: 111
Average Grant: $11,552
Highest Grant: $250,000
Typical Range: $10,000 to $50,000

Recent Grants

Note: Grants derived from 1998 Form 990.

Civic & Public Affairs

100,000	PhRMA Foundation, Washington, DC
25,000	Princeton Area Community Foundation, Inc., Princeton, NJ
15,000	Technical Training Project, Inc., Newark, NJ

Education

207,434	Foundation of the University of Medicine & Dentistry of New Jersey, Newark, NJ
75,000	Independent College Fund of New Jersey, Summit, NJ
50,000	The College Fund/UNCF Campaign 2000, Fairfax, VA
50,000	The Project Hope Health Sciences Education Center, Millwood, VA
50,000	The University of Wisconsin Foundation, Madison, WI
35,000	American College of Neuropsychopharmacology, Nashville, TN
35,000	Creighton University, Omaha, NE
17,500	American Foundation for Pharmaceutical Education, Rockville, MD

Health

50,000	Hollings Cancer Center, Charleston, SC
42,500	Sharp HealthCare Foundation, San Diego, CA
25,000	American Society of Health-System Pharmacists Research & Education Foundation, Bethesda, MD
2,500	American Society of Hospital Pharmacists Research & Education Foundation, Bethesda, MD

Science

50,000	I.L.S.I. Research Foundation, Washington, DC

Social Services

5,000	The Governors Council for a Drug Free Workplace, Newark, NJ

HOFMANN CO.

Company Contact

Concord, CA

Company Description

Revenue: US$19,000,000 (1999)
Employees: 150 (1999)
SIC(s): 6552 Subdividers & Developers Nec.

Hofmann Foundation

Giving Contact

Nick Rossi, General Counsel
Hofmann Foundation
PO Box 907
Concord, CA 94520-4912
Phone: (925)682-4830
Fax: (925)682-0126

Description

Founded: 1963
EIN: 946108897
Organization Type: Corporate Foundation
Giving Locations: CA: Bay Area organizations only
Grant Types: Capital, Emergency, Project, Research.

Financial Summary

Total Giving: $1,000,000 (fiscal year ending July 31, 2000 approx); $1,000,000 (fiscal 1999 approx); $1,000,000 (fiscal 1998 approx). Note: Contributes through foundation only.
Assets: $16,191,026 (fiscal 1996); $15,803,352 (fiscal 1995); $16,318,303 (fiscal 1994)
Gifts Received: $50,500 (fiscal 1996); $53,355 (fiscal 1995); $446,900 (fiscal 1994). Note: Contributions were received from the Hofmann Construction Co. and New Discovery.

Typical Recipients

Arts & Humanities: Arts Centers, Ballet, Museums/Galleries, Music, Public Broadcasting, Theater
Civic & Public Affairs: Botanical Gardens/Parks, Civil Rights, Clubs, Community Foundations, Civic & Public Affairs-General, Law & Justice, Legal Aid, Minority Business, Municipalities/Towns, Urban & Community Affairs
Education: Colleges & Universities, Education-General, Medical Education, Private Education (Precollege), Religious Education, Secondary Education (Private), Secondary Education (Public), Student Aid
Environment: Environment-General, Wildlife Protection
Health: AIDS/HIV, Cancer, Children's Health/Hospitals, Clinics/Medical Centers, Diabetes, Emergency/Ambulance Services, Health Organizations, Heart, Hospices, Hospitals, Medical Research, Preventive Medicine/Wellness Organizations, Public Health, Respiratory, Single-Disease Health Associations
International: International Environmental Issues, International Organizations, Missionary/Religious Activities
Religion: Churches, Jewish Causes, Religious Organizations, Religious Welfare, Seminaries, Synagogues/Temples
Science: Science Museums, Scientific Centers & Institutes
Social Services: Animal Protection, At-Risk Youth, Camps, Child Welfare, Community Service Organizations, Counseling, Day Care, Domestic Violence, Emergency Relief, Family Services, Food/Clothing Distribution, People with Disabilities, Recreation & Athletics, Scouts, Senior Services, Shelters/Homelessness, Special Olympics, United Funds/United Ways, Volunteer Services, Youth Organizations

Contributions Analysis

Arts & Humanities: Less than 5%. Most funding supports theatre, public broadcasting, symphonies, and museums.
Civic & Public Affairs: About 5%. Funding includes support for juveniles, crisis centers, food banks, animal rescue, and legal issues. Religious welfare also receives support.
Education: About 50%. Supports a variety of institutions, ranging from high schools and elementary schools to colleges and universities, that demonstrate a profound desire to challenge and improve the hearts and minds of their students.
Environment: About 20%. Majority of funding supports acquisition, preservation and conservation of wildlife lands; specifically, those wetlands and marshlands that provide sanctuary to waterfowl, and other related wildlife justice concerns. Funding supports the National Fish & Wildlife Foundation and other organizations.
Health: About 10%. Supports the local medical and health community aswell as single health associations including cancer, AIDS, paralysis and heart disease.

Religion: Less than 5%. Funding goes to Jewish as well as Christian organizations/churches.
Social Services: About 10%. Support includes Boys and Girls Clubs, Little Leagues and the Make-A-Wish Foundation.

Application Procedures

Initial Contact: all inquiries in writing, letter of no more than two pages requesting guidelines and foundation's annual report
Application Requirements: description of the organization, amount requested, purpose of funds sought, recently audited financial statement, proof of tax-exempt status, and names of officers and directors
Deadlines: None; board meets quarterly.

Restrictions

Does not provide general support, capital funding, operating expenses, or repayment of debts.

Additional Information

Publications: Annual Report (including Application Guidelines)

Corporate Officials

Kenneth H. Hofmann: president, director B 1934. ED United States Maritime Academy. PRIM CORP EMPL president, director: Hofmann Co. CORP AFFIL president, director: New Discovery Inc.
Albert T. Shaw: president B 1931. PRIM CORP EMPL president: Hofmann Construction Co. CORP AFFIL vice president: New Discovery Inc.

Foundation Officials

Kenneth H. Hofmann: president (see above)
Vita Lori Hofmann: director
Lisa Ann Hofmann-Seeno: director
Nick Rossi: general counsel
Albert T. Shaw: director (see above)

Grants Analysis

Disclosure Period: fiscal year ending July 31, 1996
Total Grants: $1,033,045
Number of Grants: 105
Average Grant: $9,839
Highest Grant: $250,000
Typical Range: $1,000 to $15,000

Recent Grants

Note: Grants derived from 1997 Form 990.

Arts & Humanities

6,000	California Symphony, Orinda, CA
5,000	Town Hall Theater, Quincy, CA
3,000	Baseball Sports Hall of Fame
3,000	Napa Valley Museum, Napa, CA
2,000	California Symphony, Orinda, CA
1,500	KQED, San Francisco, CA

Civic & Public Affairs

10,000	Criminal Justice Legal
10,000	Rotary District
5,000	EB Community Foundation
5,000	Pacific Legal Foundation, Sacramento, CA

Education

100,000	De La Salle High School, New Orleans, LA
52,847	St. Mary's College, Moraga, CA
33,285	St. Mary's College, Moraga, CA
27,509	St. Mary's College, Moraga, CA
25,000	American Academy of Achievement, Malibu, CA
25,000	St. Isidore's School
22,305	St. Mary's College, Moraga, CA
10,783	St. Mary's College, Moraga, CA
10,000	Micki Rainey Scholarship, Martinez, CA
10,000	St. Mary's College, Moraga, CA
5,000	Kennedy King Memorial Scholarship, Lafayette, CA
5,000	Samuel Merrit College, Oakland, CA
4,000	St. Mary's College, Moraga, CA
2,500	St. Mary's College, Moraga, CA

Environment

200,000	Ducks Unlimited, Memphis, TN
10,000	Ducks Unlimited, Memphis, TN

Health

100,000	American Red Cross, Concord, CA
5,000	American Cancer Society, Concord, CA
5,000	American Cancer Society, Concord, CA
5,000	American Heart Association, Concord, CA
5,000	Napa Emergency Women's Services, Napa, CA
3,000	John Muir Hospital Wawona Guild
2,500	St. Luke's Hospital
1,200	Queen of Valley Hospital Foundation, Napa, CA

Religion

2,500	LAF Orinda Presbyterian Church, Orinda, CA
2,500	LAF Orinda Presbyterian Church, Orinda, CA
2,000	LAF Orinda Presbyterian Church, Orinda, CA
2,000	LAF Orinda Presbyterian Church, Orinda, CA

Science

3,000	Palm Springs Air Museum, Palm Springs, CA

Social Services

100,000	United Way
35,000	Concord Youth Center, Concord, CA
30,000	Concord Youth Center, Concord, CA
30,000	Concord Youth Center, Concord, CA
30,000	Concord Youth Center, Concord, CA
30,000	Concord Youth Center, Concord, CA
20,000	Oakland Athletic Community Funds, Oakland, CA
10,000	Animal Rescue Fund, New York, NY
5,000	Contact Care Center
3,000	Heart to Heart
2,000	Guide Dogs for the Blind, San Rafael, CA

HOME DEPOT, INC.

 Number 67 of Top 100 Corporate Givers

Company Contact

Atlanta, GA
Web: http://www.homedepot.com

Company Description

Revenue: US$30,219,000,000
Profit: US$1,614,000,000
Employees: 80,800
Fortune Rank: 21, per FORTUNE Magazine's list of 500 Largest U.S. Corporations (1999).
FF 21
SIC(s): 5211 Lumber & Other Building Materials.

Operating Locations

Canada

Nonmonetary Support

Type: Cause-related Marketing & Promotion; Donated Equipment; Donated Products; In-kind Services

Corporate Sponsorship

Note: Sponsors the Centennial Olympic Games and Paralympic Games.

Giving Contact

Suzanne Apple, Director, Community Affairs
The Home Depot, Inc.
2455 Paces Ferry Road, NW
Atlanta, GA 30339-4024
Phone: (770)433-8211
Fax: (770)384-2345

Description

Organization Type: Corporate Giving Program
Giving Locations: principally near operating locations and to national organizations.
Grant Types: Award, Employee Matching Gifts, General Support.
Note: Employee matching gift ratio: 1 to 1 from $25 to $500; 0.5 to 1 for gifts from part-time employees.

Giving Philosophy

'Our first priority is to use the company's resources to encourage the development and rehabilitation of affordable housing in Home Depot communities. In addition, we like to use The Home Depot's unique resources of materials, volunteers and training in home improvement to projects to support our commitment to affordable housing.
'We also use contributions: to support programs and organizations that help meet the needs of troubled and at-risk youth in The Home Depot communities; to support environmental programs, particularly those related to building and home improvement; to promote economic development in The Home Depot communities; to support associate participation in the community through Team Depot volunteer projects.' Community Investment Guidelines

Financial Summary

Total Giving: $12,500,000 (1998 approx); $10,300,000 (1997 approx); $8,000,000 (1996 approx). Note: Contributes through corporate direct giving program only.
Giving Analysis: Giving for 1998 includes: corporate direct giving (approx $12,500,000)

Typical Recipients

Arts & Humanities: Museums/Galleries
Civic & Public Affairs: Employment/Job Training, Housing, Urban & Community Affairs
Education: Preschool Education
Environment: Environment-General
Social Services: Child Welfare, Community Centers, Counseling, Day Care, Emergency Relief, Homes, Shelters/Homelessness, Youth Organizations

Contributions Analysis

Civic & Public Affairs: (Housing & Neighborhood Revitalization) 40%. Supports organizations that develop and sustain affordable housing in low income neighborhoods in company markets, community development corporations, neighborhood housing service organizatios, neighborhood revitalization groups, Habitat for Humanity, and Christmas in April affiliates.
Environment: 7%. Supports organizations that promote environmental health and safety, sustainable development, and environmentally responsible building practices.
Social Services: 33%. Supports programs which increase self-esteem and self-sufficiency of children and young adults through focus on job readiness or skills related to the construction trade. Addresses problems such as drugs, violence, gangs, teen pregnancy, and dropping out of school. In 1998, the company started to fund disaster preparedness, responses, and relief.

Application Procedures

Initial Contact: letter of request, sent to the district manager in the organization's community
Application Requirements: organization's name, address, phone number, contact person; brief a description of organization's history, accomplishments, mission, and goals; evidence of tax-exempt status;

description of proposed project, whom it will serve, total budget, other project supporters, when it will take place, and how the company can help
Deadlines: None, for affordable housing and at-risk youth endeavors; January 1 through March 1 for environmental proposals.
Decision Notification: six weeks after receipt of proposal

Restrictions

Does not support individuals; religious, fraternal, political, labor, athletic, social, or veterans groups; fundraising benefits, dinners, exhibits, conferences, or sports events; charities sponsored solely by a single civic organization; courtesy or journal advertising campaigns; or multiyear commitments of four years or more.

Additional Information

Publications: Social Responsibility Report; Community Investment Guidelines; Matching Gift Application

Corporate Officials

Arthur M. Blank: president, chief executive officer, director director B Queens, NY 1942. ED Babson College BS (1963). PRIM CORP EMPL president, chief executive officer, director: The Home Depot, Inc. CORP AFFIL president: Home Depot United States of America Inc.; director: Post Properties Inc.; director: Canyon Ranch; director: Cox Enterprises Inc.
Ronald M. Brill: executive vice president, chief administrative officer, director ED Fairleigh Dickinson University BS (1966). PRIM CORP EMPL executive vice president, chief administrative officer, director: The Home Depot, Inc.
Bernard Marcus: chairman, director B Newark, NJ 1929. ED Rutgers University BS (1954). PRIM CORP EMPL chairman, director: The Home Depot, Inc. CORP AFFIL director: National Service Industries Inc.

Giving Program Officials

Suzanne H. Apple: PRIM CORP EMPL vice president community affairs: The Home Depot, Inc.

Foundation Officials

Carolyn Smillie: manager community affairs

Grants Analysis

Disclosure Period: calendar year ending

Recent Grants

Note: Grants derived from 1994 grants list.

Arts & Humanities

50,000	National Building Museum, Washington, DC -- for youth education program

Civic & Public Affairs

127,000	Housing Rehabilitation Fund

Environment

10,000	Nature Conservancy -- for land maintenance

HON INDUSTRIES INC.

Company Contact

Muscatine, IA
Web: http://www.honi.com

Company Description

Also Known As: Home-O-Nize.
Employees: 9,800 (1999)
SIC(s): 2521 Wood Office Furniture, 2522 Office Furniture Except Wood, 2678 Stationery Products, 3433 Heating Equipment Except Electric.

HON Industries Charitable Foundation

Giving Contact

Susan Cradick, Secretary-Treasurer
HON Industries Charitable Foundation
414 East Third Street
PO Box 1109
Muscatine, IA 52761-7109
Phone: (319)264-7400
Fax: (319)264-7217

Description

Founded: 1985
EIN: 421246787
Organization Type: Corporate Foundation. Supports preselected organizations only.
Giving Locations: IA: Muscatine headquarters and operating communities.
Grant Types: Capital, General Support, Scholarship.

Financial Summary

Total Giving: $1,200,000 (fiscal year ending June 30, 2000 approx); $1,200,000 (fiscal 1999 approx); $663,122 (fiscal 1997). Note: Contributes through corporate direct giving program and foundation. Giving includes foundation. Fiscal 1997 Giving includes foundation ($575,405); United Way ($87,717).
Assets: $7,000,000 (fiscal 1999 approx); $2,122,014 (fiscal 1997); $1,223,734 (fiscal 1994)
Gifts Received: $1,900,000 (fiscal 1997); $800,000 (fiscal 1994); $400,000 (fiscal 1993). Note: Contributions are received from HON Industries Inc.

Typical Recipients

Arts & Humanities: Arts Associations & Councils, Arts Centers, Arts Outreach, Arts & Humanities-General, Libraries, Museums/Galleries, Music
Civic & Public Affairs: Business/Free Enterprise, Chambers of Commerce, Community Foundations, Economic Development, Economic Policy, Civic & Public Affairs-General, Legal Aid, Minority Business, Municipalities/Towns, Public Policy, Urban & Community Affairs
Education: Afterschool/Enrichment Programs, Agricultural Education, Business Education, Colleges & Universities, Community & Junior Colleges, Education Reform, Engineering/Technological Education, Science/Mathematics Education, Secondary Education (Public), Student Aid
Environment: Environment-General, Resource Conservation
Health: Children's Health/Hospitals, Hospitals, Speech & Hearing
Religion: Churches, Religious Organizations, Religious Welfare
Science: Science Exhibits & Fairs, Scientific Centers & Institutes, Scientific Research
Social Services: Animal Protection, Community Centers, Community Service Organizations, Family Services, Recreation & Athletics, Scouts, United Funds/United Ways, Volunteer Services, YMCA/YWCA/YMHA/YWHA, Youth Organizations

Contributions Analysis

Civic & Public Affairs: 55% to 60% of total contributions. Donations are given mainly to organizations that benefit the business community. Emphasis on the city of Muscatine, IA.
Education: About 20%. Interests include colleges and universities, Junior Achievement, and secondary schools.
Social Services: About 20%. Support goes to YMCA, Boy Scouts, United Way and other youth-orientated organizations.

Corporate Officials

A. Mosby Harvey, Jr.: vice president, secretary, general counselc B Memphis, TN 1943. ED Dartmouth College (1965); University of Texas (1969). PRIM CORP EMPL vice president, secretary, general counsel: HON Industries Inc.
Stanley M. Howe: chairman emeritus, director B Muscatine, IA 1924. ED Iowa State University (1946); Harvard University Graduate School of Business Administration (1948). PRIM CORP EMPL chairman emeritus, director: HON Industries Inc. CORP AFFIL director: Pella Corp. NONPR AFFIL trustee: Iowa Wesleyan College; member: National Association Manufacturer; member: Benevolent Protectorate Elks; member: Bus Institutional Furniture Manufacturer Association. CLUB AFFIL Rotary Club; 33 Club; Elks Club.
Jack D. Michaels: chairman, president, chief executive officer, director B 1937. ED University of Cincinnati BA. PRIM CORP EMPL chairman, president, chief executive officer, director: HON Industries Inc. CORP AFFIL president, director: Holga Inc.; director: Snap-On Inc.

Giving Program Officials

Raymond E. Lasell: secretary, director B Des Moines, IA 1935. ED Iowa State University (1957). PRIM CORP EMPL secretary corporate gift committee: HON Industries.

Foundation Officials

R. Michael Derry: vice president B Owosso, MI 1937. ED Western Michigan University BBA (1960). PRIM CORP EMPL senior vice president administration: HON Industries Inc.
A. Mosby Harvey, Jr.: secretary (see above)
Stanley M. Howe: president (see above)
Raymond E. Lasell: secretary, director (see above)
Jack D. Michaels: secretary (see above)

Grants Analysis

Disclosure Period: fiscal year ending June 30, 1997
Total Grants: $575,405*
Number of Grants: 63
Average Grant: $9,133
Highest Grant: $197,400
Typical Range: $200 to $15,000
***Note:** Giving excludes United Way.

Recent Grants

Note: Grants derived from fiscal 1997 Form 990.

Arts & Humanities

1,000	Quad City Arts Visiting Artist, Davenport, IA

Civic & Public Affairs

30,600	MCSA, Muscatine, IA
15,000	Tax Education Foundation, Muscatine, IA
13,000	Muscatine Development Corporation, Muscatine, IA
5,000	MFG Institute, Washington, DC
5,000	Public Interest Institute, Mount Pleasant, IA
2,000	National Legal Center for the Public Interest, Washington, DC
2,000	PROTEUS, Muscatine, IA
600	Leadership, Muscatine, IA
500	Area Community Foundation, Muscatine, IA
500	Business Horizons, Des Moines, IA

Education

197,400	Iowa State University Foundation, Ames, IA
125,000	University of Iowa Foundation, Iowa City, IA
35,000	Iowa College Foundation, Des Moines, IA
25,000	Iowa Wesleyan College, Mount Pleasant, IA
10,705	Muscatine Community College, Muscatine, IA

9,750	St. Ambrose University, Davenport, IA
9,000	Southgate High School, Southgate, CA
7,500	Future Farmers of America, Muscatine, IA
6,750	Iowa Wesleyan College, Mount Pleasant, IA
3,000	Augustana College, Rock Island, IL
3,000	Junior Achievement, Muscatine, IA
2,500	Muscatine Community College, Muscatine, IA
1,500	Iowa State University, Ames, IA
1,500	Macalester College, Saint Paul, MN
1,500	Stanford University, Palo Alto, CA
1,500	University of Iowa, Iowa City, IA
1,000	Pennsylvania College of Technology, Williamsport, PA
1,000	Rockridge High School, Taylor Ridge, IL
1,000	University of Iowa Foundation, Iowa City, IA
1,000	University of Northern Iowa, Cedar Falls, IA
500	East Texas State University, Commerce, TX
500	Georgia Institute of Technology, Atlanta, GA
500	Panola College, Carthage, TX

Environment

6,000	Muscatine County Conservation Board, Muscatine, IA

Health

1,100	Muscatine County Parents Association for Hearing Impaired, Muscatine, IA

Religion

15,000	Muscatine Mobilization Church, Muscatine, IA

Science

1,500	Quad Cities Astronomical Society, Davenport, IA

Social Services

79,442	United Way, Muscatine, IA
8,000	Muscatine Community Y, Muscatine, IA
7,500	United Way, Mount Pleasant, IA
4,825	United Way, Owensboro, KY
4,000	YWCA, Muscatine, IA
2,500	Boy Scouts of America, Davenport, IA
2,450	United Way, Owensboro, KY
2,000	Voluntary Action Center, Muscatine, IA
1,000	Lycoming United Way, Williamsport, PA
1,000	Mercer County Family YMCA, Aledo, IL
1,000	Spay Neuter Association, Muscatine, IA
500	Sports World, New Tazwell, IA

HONEYWELL INTERNATIONAL INC.

 Number 74 of Top 100 Corporate Givers

Company Contact

Morristown, NJ
Web: http://www.honeywell.com

Company Description

Acquired: AlliedSignal Inc. (1999).
Revenue: US$23,735,000,000 (1999)
Profit: US$1,541,000,000 (1999)
Employees: 57,000
Fortune Rank: 65, per FORTUNE Magazine's list of 500 Largest U.S. Corporations (1999).
FF 65
SIC(s): 1711 Plumbing, Heating & Air-Conditioning, 3491 Industrial Valves, 3492 Fluid Power Valves & Hose Fittings, 3812 Search & Navigation Equipment.

Operating Locations

Argentina: Honeywell S.A.I.C., Buenos Aires; Australia: Honeywell-Measurex Pty.Ltd., Boronia; Honeywell Ltd., North Ryde; Austria: Honeywell Austria Gmbh, Vienna; Honeywell-Measurex International Gmbh, Voesendorf; Belgium: Honeywell sa/nv, Brussels; Brazil: Honeywell-Measurex do Brazil, Sao Paulo; Honeywell Do Brasil & Cia, Sao Paulo SP; Bulgaria: Honeywell EOOD, Sofia; Canada: Honeywell Ltd., North York; Honeywell-Measurex Devron, Vancouver; Chile: Honeywell Chile, Santiago; People's Republic of China: Honeywell (Tianjin) Ltd., Beijing, Shanghai; Honeywell China Inc., Shanghai; Colombia: Honeywell Columbia, Santa Fe de Bogota; Czech Republic: Honeywell s.r.o., Bratislava; Honeywell spol sr.o., Prague; Denmark: Honeywell A/S, Soeborg; Ecuador: Honeywell S.A., Quito; Egypt: Honeywell, Cairo; England: Honeywell-Measurex International Systems Ltd., Datchet; Finland: Honeywell-Measurex Oy, Espoo; Honeywell OY, Espoo; Roibox Oy, Kuopio; France: Honeywell-Measurex S.A.R.L., Rungis; Honeywell SA, Saint Aubin; Germany: Honeywell AG, Offenbach; Homeywell-Measurex Gmbh, Sulzbach; Greece: Honeywell E.P.E., Athens; Hong Kong: Honeywell China Inc., Kowloon Bay; Hungary: Honeywell Kft., Budapest; Indonesia: PT Honeywell Indonesia, Jakarta; India: Honeywell Europe Inc., Bombay; Tata Honeywell Ltd., Pune; Italy: Honeywell-Measurex Italia S.R.L., Milan; Honeywell S.p.A., Milan; Japan: Honeywell Asia Pacific Inc., Tokyo; Honeywell-Measurex Japan, Ltd., Tokyo; Yamatake-Honeywell Company Ltd., Tokyo; Kazakhstan: Honeywell Automation Controls LLP, Almaty; Republic of Korea: LG-Honeywell Co., Ltd., Seoul; Kuwait: Honeywell KSC; Mexico: Honeywell-Measurex S.A. de C.V., Colonia Condesa; Honeywell S.A. de C.V., Mexico City; Malaysia: Honeywell Engineering Sdn. Bhd., Selangor Darulehsan; Netherlands: Honeywell B.V., Amsterdam; Honeywell-Measurex B.V., Tiel; Norway: Honeywell A/S, Asker; Honeywell-Measurex Norway A/S, Oslo; New Zealand: Honeywell Ltd., Mt. Eden; Honeywell-Measurex Systems N.Z. Ltd., Roturua; Oman: Homeywell & Co., Mina Al-Fahal; Pakistan: Honeywell Pvt Ltd, Karachi; Peru: Honeywell Peru, Miraflores; Philippines: Honeywell Systems (Philippines) Inc., Pasig City; Poland: Honeywell Sp z o.o, Warsaw; Puerto Rico: Honeywell Inc., Caparra Heights; Portugal: Honeywell, Lda., Carnaxide; Honeywell-Measurex (Portugal) Sistemeas de Controle Ltda., Setubal; Romania: Honeywell, Bucharest; Russia: Honneywell Inc., Moscow; Republic of South Africa: Honeywell Southern Africa Ltd., Johannesburg; Honeywell (Pty) Ltd., Midrand; Saudi Arabia: Honeywell Turki Arabia Ltd., Dammam; Singapore: Honeywell Pte. Ltd., Chai Chee Industrial Park; Spain: Honeywell S.A., Madrid; Sweden: Honeywell AB, Stockholm; Switzerland: Honeywell-Measurex AG, Baar; Honeywell AG, Wallisellen; Thailand: Honeywell Systems (Thailand) Ltd., Bangkok; Trinidad and Tobago: Honeywell Trinidad, Port of Spain; Turkey: Honeywell A.S., Istanbul; Taiwan: Honeywell Taiwan Ltd., Chung Ho City; United Arab Emirates: Honeywell Sharjah, Sharjah; United Kingdom: Honeywell Limited, Bracknell; Ukraine: Honeywell Ltd., Kiev; Uzbekistan: Honeywell Technical Center, Tashkent; Venezuela: Honeywell CA, Caracas
Note: Operates throughout the USA.

Nonmonetary Support

Value: $1,129,589 (1996); $616,515 (1995); $130,828 (1993)
Type: Donated Equipment; Donated Products; In-kind Services
Note: Both the company and the foundation provide nonmonetary support. Product donations at retail value.

Honeywell Foundation

Giving Contact

Andre Lewis, Executive Director
Honeywell Foundation
PO Box 524
Minneapolis, MN 55440-0524
Phone: (612)951-2368
Fax: (612)951-0433

Description

EIN: 416023933
Organization Type: Corporate Foundation
Giving Locations: MN: organizations in Minnesota receive about 50% of total contributions major principally near operating locations and to national organizations.
Grant Types: Capital, Employee Matching Gifts, Endowment, General Support.
Note: Employee matching gift ratio: 0.5 to 1 for gifts to higher education and public broadcasting.

Giving Philosophy

'Since 1957, the Honeywell Foundation has strived to be a successful, caring and responsible citizen. The Foundation is based on a time-honored philosophy of providing community support on several levels. From fostering an extensive Honeywell volunteer program, to funding grants, to initiating collaborations with other partners to provide greater resources, Honeywell continues to invest in the future of its communities.
'The Honeywell Foundation is funded by a corporate contribution of 1.6% of Honeywell Inc.'s worldwide pre-tax profits..
'To fulfill our mission, the Honeywell Foundation effectively leverages the resources of the company to support: our children: helping children from birth to age 18 be successful students and become productive citizens of our neighborhoods; assisting communities with their safety, housing and economic development needs; our environment: promoting environmental awareness and the efficient use of natural resources.'
Our Community Commitment

Financial Summary

Total Giving: $10,700,000 (1998 approx); $7,941,845 (1997); $9,184,033 (1996). Note: Contributes through corporate direct giving program and foundation. 1997 Giving includes foundation ($6,023,990); domestic subsidiaries ($800,000); matching gifts ($278,269); United Way ($1,639,586); nonmonetary support.
Assets: $13,311,499 (1997); $16,998,504 (1992); $19,063,520 (1991)
Gifts Received: $12,870,810 (1997). Note: In 1997, contributions were received from Honeywell Inc.

Typical Recipients

Arts & Humanities: Arts Associations & Councils, Arts Centers, Arts Institutes, Arts Outreach, Community Arts, Dance, Ethnic & Folk Arts, History & Archaeology, Literary Arts, Museums/Galleries, Music, Opera, Performing Arts, Public Broadcasting, Theater
Civic & Public Affairs: African American Affairs, Business/Free Enterprise, Economic Development, Employment/Job Training, Civic & Public Affairs-General, Hispanic Affairs, Housing, Native American Affairs, Nonprofit Management, Philanthropic Organizations, Public Policy, Urban & Community Affairs, Women's Affairs, Zoos/Aquariums
Education: Business Education, Business-School Partnerships, Colleges & Universities, Community & Junior Colleges, Economic Education, Education Associations, Education Funds, Education Reform, Elementary Education (Private), Elementary Education (Public), Engineering/Technological Education, Environmental Education, Faculty Development, Education-General, International Exchange, Literacy, Minority Education, Preschool Education, Private

Education (Precollege), Public Education (Precollege), Science/Mathematics Education, Secondary Education (Public), Special Education, Student Aid, Vocational & Technical Education
Environment: Energy, Environment-General, Resource Conservation
Health: Adolescent Health Issues, Cancer, Children's Health/Hospitals, Health Organizations, Hospitals, Hospitals (University Affiliated), Mental Health, Prenatal Health Issues, Public Health, Research/Studies Institutes
International: International Organizations
Religion: Religious Welfare
Science: Science Museums
Social Services: At-Risk Youth, Big Brother/Big Sister, Child Welfare, Community Centers, Community Service Organizations, Crime Prevention, Delinquency & Criminal Rehabilitation, Domestic Violence, Emergency Relief, Family Planning, Family Services, Food/Clothing Distribution, People with Disabilities, Refugee Assistance, Scouts, Senior Services, Shelters/Homelessness, Substance Abuse, United Funds/ United Ways, YMCA/YWCA/YMHA/YWHA, Youth Organizations

Contributions Analysis

Giving Priorities: Education, health, human services, public broadcasting, and civic concerns. Company makes limited contributions to U.S.-based nonprofit organizations with an international focus.
Arts & Humanities: 10% to 15%. Provides capital grants, general support, and employee matching gifts to public radio and television. Other interests include theaters, arts centers and associations, and music and dance groups. Focuses on major arts organizations and aselect group of new and emerging arts programs.
Civic & Public Affairs: About 5%. The foundation's contributions support affordable housing, crime prevention in theneighborhood, and training and employment preparedness. Disbursements outside of Minneapolis are determined by the individual community needs. (United Funds & United Way) 15% to 20%. Foundation supports United Ways in operating areas.
Education: About 25%. Emphasis on early childhood development and elementary and secondary education programs in major Honeywell locations. Other interests include business, engineering, and increased educational opportunities for women and minorities in technical disciplines. Grant types include scholarship funds (to institutions, not individuals), general support, endowment, and employee matching gifts. Also supports independent college and minority education funds, education associations, and precollegiate programs in technological sciences.
Health: Less than 5%.

Application Procedures

Initial Contact: call or write requesting application form, then written application
Application Requirements: brief a description of organization, including its mission and goals; description of current programs, activities, service statistics, and strengths and accomplishments; description of the organization's relationship with other organizations working to meet the same needs or providing similar services, and how the organization differs from these agencies; list of board members, number of fulland part-time paid staff and volunteers; why organization is uniquely qualified; description of the need and the community the proposal addresses, and how the focus was determined and who was involved; specific activities for which funding is sought and who will carry out those activities; how the objectives will be met, and the time frame for meeting them; a long-term strategy for sustaining the proposed effort; and method for determining success; financial statements from the most recently completed fiscal year and an organizational and/or project budget; list of names of corporations and foundations that were solicited for funding, with dollar amount and indication of which sources are committed, pending, or anticipated; and a copy of current IRS determination letter indicating tax-exempt status
Deadlines: None.
Review Process: a board of directors comprised of Honeywell executives guides the Honeywell Foundation by setting giving policies and procedures, and committees approve the distribution of funds
Evaluative Criteria: Foundation gives priority to organizations where Honeywell facilities and employees are located and which involve Honeywell employee volunteers; priority is also given to programs which fit within the giving categories which the foundation has established, especially in education, community support, and energy and the environment
Decision Notification: foundation committees meet periodically to act on funding requests, board meets semi-annually; applicants are informed in writing about the foundation's funding decisions
Notes: Company operating facilities make local community grants; contact facility manager for procedures.

Restrictions

Foundation does not fund dinners, benefits, or conferences; recognition or testimonial events; single-disease associations; goodwill advertising; travel costs; individual scholarships or requests; fraternal, veterans', or professional associations; athletic scholarships; publication of books or annual reports, or production of films or videos; endowment campaigns; churches or religious organizations for denominational causes; or political activities or causes.

Additional Information

Company annually contributes 1.6% of worldwide profits.
Company allocates funds to Honeywell divisions based on number of employees, employee involvement in volunteer activities, and the location's community relations plans and projects. Many locations supplement these allocations with additional contributions from their operating budgets.
If awarded a grant, recipients must agree to provide information on the expenditures and results of project upon request by foundation staff or evaluators.
Publications: Application Guidelines

Corporate Officials

Michael Robert Bonsignore: chairman, chief executive officer, director B Plattsburg, NY 1941. ED Texas A&M University; United States Naval Academy BS (1963). PRIM CORP EMPL chairman, chief executive officer, director: Honeywell Inc. CORP AFFIL chairman: Honeywell Electronics Corp.; director: Saint Paul Companies Inc.; director: Cargill Inc.; director: Donaldson Co. Inc. NONPR AFFIL member devel board: University Michigan Global Leadership; member: US-USSR Trade Economic Council; member: U.S. Naval Academy Alumni Association; member advisory council: U.S. Trade Report; member advisory council: Office Technology Assessment; member: Sea-Space Symposium; National Association Underwater Inst: National Association Underwater Instituteructors; director: Hugh O'Brian Youth Foundation; director: Minnesota Orchestra Association; member advisory board: Minnesota Trade Office; vice president: American Chamber of Commerce Brussels; director: Metropolitan Economic Development Association.
Giannantonio A. Ferrari: president, chief operating officer, director ED Catholic University of Milan. PRIM CORP EMPL president, chief operating officer, director: Honeywell Inc. CORP AFFIL director: Northern Studies Power Co. NONPR AFFIL director: National Association Manufacturer; government: National Electrical Manufacturers Association.
James T. Porter: vice president, chief administrative officer ED Northwest Missouri State University (1974). PRIM CORP EMPL vice president, chief administrative officer: Honeywell International Inc. NONPR AFFIL director: Greater Minneapolis Metropolitan Housing Corp.
Larry W. Stranghoener: chief financial officer, vice president PRIM CORP EMPL chief financial officer, vice president: Honeywell Inc.

Foundation Officials

Terry D. Agness: director PRIM CORP EMPL president, director: Ford Meter Box Co. CORP AFFIL director: Uni-Flange Holdings Inc.
Ramon A. Alvarez: director PRIM CORP EMPL vice president, group executive: Honeywell Inc. Sensing & Control.
Michael Robert Bonsignore: director (see above)
John Richard Dewane: director B Cooperstown, WI 1934. ED University of Wisconsin BSME (1957); University of Minnesota MBA (1973). NONPR AFFIL national board advisors: University Arizona Keller Business School; member: University Wisconsin Alumni Advisory Council; member strategy council: United Way of Phoenix; member technical advisory committee on transportation eq: U.S. Department Commerce; member: U.S. Navy League; director: Success by Six; member: NASA Aeronautics Advisory Comm; member: State of Arizona Governor's Technical Commission; member: Minneapolis Chamber of Commerce; member: General Aviation Manufacturers Association; chairman: Habitat Humanity Endowment Committee; member: Association U.S. Army; chairman: Embry Riddle Aero University Curriculum Committee; director: Asia Pacific Economic Council; chairman: Arizona Cities in Schools Inc.; member, dean's 100 board: Arizona State University; member: American Defense Preparedness Association; member: APEC Satellite Communication Committee; member: Aircraft Owners & Pilots Association; member: Air Force Association. CLUB AFFIL Provost Club.
Giannantonio A. Ferrari: director (see above)
William M. Hjerpe: director ED University of Massachusetts BA (1973); Northeastern University MBA (1975). PRIM CORP EMPL president: Honeywell Inc. ADD CORP EMPL president: Honeywell Europe.
M. Patricia Hoven: president
Andre Lewis: executive director
James T. Porter: director (see above)
G. J. Skovholt: director
Larry W. Stranghoener: director (see above)
Markos I. Tambakeras: director B Ismailia, Egypt 1950. ED University of Witwatersrand (1975); Loyola Marymount University (1978). PRIM CORP EMPL president industrial & control: Honeywell Inc. CORP AFFIL vice chairman, director: Tata Honeywell, INC; director: USA South African Business Council; director: Pacific Basin Economic Council.
Gerald C. Vandevoort: director PRIM CORP EMPL vice president, general manager: Honeywell Inc.

Grants Analysis

Disclosure Period: calendar year ending 1997
Total Grants: $6,023,990*
Number of Grants: 800 (approx)
Average Grant: $8,606
Highest Grant: $300,000
Typical Range: $1,000 to $25,000
***Note:** Giving excludes matching gifts; United Way.

Recent Grants

Note: Grants derived from 1997 Form 990.

Arts & Humanities

200,000	Minnesota Orchestral Association, Minneapolis, MN -- capital campaign, operating support
60,000	KTCA-KTCI Twin Cities Public Television, St. Paul, MN -- capital support, general support
50,000	Guthrie Theater, Minneapolis, MN
50,000	Minnesota Opera Company, Minneapolis, MN
50,000	St. Paul Chamber Orchestra, St. Paul, MN
40,000	A Contemporary Theater, Seattle, WA -- capital campaign

40,000 Walker Art Center, Minneapolis, MN
35,000 Children's Theater Company, Minneapolis, MN

Civic & Public Affairs

103,000 Twin Cities Habitat for Humanity, Minneapolis, MN -- support CEO Blitz Build
100,000 Central Community Housing Trust, Minneapolis, MN -- support housing redesign for Portland Gardens
75,000 Summit Academy Opportunity Industry Center, Minneapolis, MN -- support Phillips Clean Sweep Program
50,000 Habitat for Humanity, Phoenix, AZ
50,000 Metropolitan Economic Development Association, Minneapolis, MN
50,000 National Alliance of Business, Washington, DC -- support Baldrige Initiative
50,000 Urban Ventures Leadership Foundation, Minneapolis, MN -- support Homefield
45,000 Project for Pride in Living, Minneapolis, MN -- support Train to Work Program
30,000 Stairstep Foundation, Minneapolis, MN

Education

300,000 United Negro College Fund, Fairfax, VA -- support Campaign 2000
100,000 University of Arizona, Tucson, AZ -- support technological upgrade
75,000 University of Wisconsin Foundation, Madison, WI -- support Center for Quality and Productivity
50,025 City of Glendale, Glendale, AZ -- support Computer Technology Center for Adults
50,000 Albuquerque Community Foundation, Albuquerque, NM -- to strengthen quality in schools
50,000 Friends of Minnesota Academic Excellence Foundation, St. Paul, MN -- support Partners for Quality Education Initiative
50,000 Malcolm Baldrige National Quality Award Foundation, New York, NY -- support Baldrige Education Endowment
50,000 Pinellas County Education Foundation, Clearwater, FL -- support Quality Initiative
50,000 Pinellas County Education Foundation, Clearwater, FL -- support Doorway Program
50,000 Pinellas County Education Foundation, Clearwater, FL -- support Quality Academy
40,000 Minnesota Windstar Connection, Findley, MN -- support Eco-Assemblies Program
40,000 National Association of Partners in Education, Alexandria, VA -- support Business Education Partnership
35,000 Friends of Minnesota Academic Excellence Foundation, St. Paul, MN -- support Classroom Quality Program
30,000 Phoenix Union Partnership of Business and Education, Phoenix, AZ

Health

75,000 Flinn Foundation, Phoenix, AZ -- support school-based health center

Science

125,000 Science Museum, St. Paul, MN -- capital support

Social Services

300,000 United Way, Minneapolis, MN
272,400 United Way, Minneapolis, MN -- partial payment of 1996-97 pledge
211,000 Valley of the Sun United Way, Phoenix, AZ
148,601 United Way of Pinellas County, St. Petersburg, FL
100,000 United Way, Minneapolis, MN
95,000 United Way of Northwest Illinois, Freeport, IL
91,699 United Way of Southeast Pennsylvania, Wayne, PA
75,000 Way to Grow, Minneapolis, MN -- support Phillips TLC Program
52,500 United Way of Central New Mexico, Albuquerque, NM
50,000 Police Executives Research Forum, Washington, DC -- support Minneapolis Crime Initiative
45,000 United Way of St. Paul Area, St. Paul, MN
40,000 City, Minneapolis, MN -- support Growth Cluster Project
40,000 Sabathani Community Center, Minneapolis, MN -- leadership grant
39,434 United Way, Minneapolis, MN
39,345 YWCA of Tampa Bay, USF Family Village, St. Petersburg, FL -- capital campaign
38,000 United Way, Minneapolis, MN
35,000 Family and Children's Service, Minneapolis, MN -- support Violence Intervention Program

HOUGHTON MIFFLIN CO.

Company Contact

Boston, MA
Web: http://www.hmco.com

Company Description

Employees: 2,420
SIC(s): 2731 Book Publishing, 2741 Miscellaneous Publishing.

Nonmonetary Support

Value: $1,750,000 (1994); $1,247,000 (1993); $1,764,000 (1991)
Type: Donated Products

Giving Contact

Ms. Ellen O' Leary, Manager, Corporate Contributions
Houghton Mifflin Co.
222 Berkeley Street
Boston, MA 02116-3764
Phone: (617)351-5000
Fax: (617)351-5014

Description

Organization Type: Corporate Giving Program
Giving Locations: principally near operating locations and to national organizations.
Grant Types: Capital, Employee Matching Gifts, Endowment, General Support, Operating Expenses.
Note: Employee matching gift ratio: 1 to 1 up to $1,500 annually.

Giving Philosophy

'For more than 160 years, Houghton Mifflin has shaped ideas, information, and instructional methods into a variety of useful forms. We have joined forces with leading authors and educators to create publications that satisfy the lifelong needs of individuals to learn, gain proficiency, and be entertained. .. We recognize that we share a social responsibility with.. other corporations, and foundations.'

Financial Summary

Total Giving: $620,000 (1998 approx); $560,000 (1996 approx); $550,000 (1995). Note: Contributes through corporate direct giving program only.

Typical Recipients

Education: Education Funds
Social Services: United Funds/United Ways

Contributions Analysis

Arts & Humanities: Funds a limited number of major cultural institutions near operating locations. Also matches employees gifts to cultural institutions.
Education: Umbrella organizations which support groups of colleges, such as United Negro College Fund. Also matches gifts by employees, directors, and retirees to educational institutions up to $1,500 annually. Does not give to individual colleges and universities.
Social Services: (United Funds & United Way) Large grant supports the United Way of Massachusetts Bay, which serves area near corporate headquarters. Local offices also support United Way chapters. Company also encourages employees to contribute individually. Considers requests on a case-by-case basis. Emphasizes organizations which have historically been disadvantaged, including racial and ethnic minorities, women, and the disabled.

Application Procedures

Initial Contact: Send a brief letter or proposal.
Application Requirements: Include historical background; list of directors, officers, and executive staff; most recently audited financial statement; current operating budget; proof of tax-exempt status; and statement relating program objectives to requested funds.
Deadlines: None.

Restrictions

Does not give to political organizations, lobbying groups, candidates for public office, national health organizations, religious groups for sectarian or denominational activities, veterans' organizations (except for purposes that benefit the entire community), individual foundations, and organizations with discriminatory practices.

Additional Information

Company's contributions committee administers a two-part program: corporate grantmaking, primarily in Boston area and on a limited basis to other communities where it has operating locations; and the matching gift program which responds to donations given by employees, directors, and retirees, to eligible educational and cultural institutions.

Corporate Officials

Nader Farhang Darehshori: chairman, president, chief executive officer B Shriraz, Iran 1936. ED University of Wisconsin BA (1966). PRIM CORP EMPL chairman, president, chief executive officer: Houghton Mifflin Co. CORP AFFIL director: State Street Corp.; director: Commercial Union Corp. NONPR AFFIL trustee: Wellesley College.

Giving Program Officials

Ellen O'Leary: PRIM CORP EMPL manager corporate contributions: Houghton Mifflin Co.

Grants Analysis

Disclosure Period: calendar year ending
Typical Range: $250 to $2,000

HOUSATONIC CURTAIN CO.

Company Contact

Stockbridge, MA

Company Description

Employees: 90

Giving Contact

Contributions Coordinator
Housatonic Curtain Co.
c/o Country Curtains
PO Box 954, Red Lion Inn
Stockbridge, MA 01262

Phone: (413)298-1605
Fax: (413)243-1067

Description

Founded: 1984
Organization Type: Corporate Giving Program
Giving Locations: MA: Western part of state
Grant Types: General Support, Scholarship.

Financial Summary

Total Giving: $1,237,896 (1995); $934,696 (1992)
Assets: $1,243,078 (1996); $1,243,078 (1995); $932,903 (1992)

Typical Recipients

Arts & Humanities: Arts & Humanities-General, Historic Preservation, History & Archaeology, Libraries, Museums/Galleries, Music, Opera, Performing Arts, Theater
Civic & Public Affairs: Employment/Job Training, Ethnic Organizations, Civic & Public Affairs-General, Native American Affairs, Parades/Festivals, Public Policy
Education: Arts/Humanities Education, Colleges & Universities, Community & Junior Colleges, Education-General, Private Education (Precollege)
Environment: Environment-General, Resource Conservation
Health: Hospitals, Prenatal Health Issues
Religion: Churches
Social Services: Child Welfare, Community Service Organizations, People with Disabilities, United Funds/ United Ways, Youth Organizations

Contributions Analysis

Arts & Humanities: About 90%. Support goes for historic preservation, museums, the performing arts, libraries and archaeology.
Civic & Public Affairs: Funding supports job training programs, ethnic groups, parades and festivals and public policy.
Education: Supports art education, colleges and univerisities, and community colleges.
Health: Funds hospitals and prenatal health issues.
Social Services: Support goes to child welfare issues, community service organizations, to assist people with disabilities, the United Way and youth groups.

Application Procedures

Initial Contact: a brief letter of inquiry
Deadlines: None.

Additional Information

For more information see Country Curtains.

Corporate Officials

John H. Fitzpatrick: president, director B 1925. PRIM CORP EMPL president, director: Housatonic Curtain Co. Inc. CORP AFFIL vice chairman: Country Curtains Inc.; director: Fitzpatrick Retail & Realty Co. Inc.
Nancy J. Fitzpatrick: president, director B 1946. PRIM CORP EMPL president, director: Country Curtains, Inc. ADD CORP EMPL treasurer: Berkshire Collections Inc.; vice president, director: Country Curtains Mail Order Inc.; president: Country Curtains Retail Inc.; executive vice president: Fitzpatrick Companies Inc.; treasurer, director: Fitzpatrick Retail & Realty Co. Inc.; vice president,director: Housatonic Curtain Co. Inc.; president,director: Red Lion Inc.

Foundation Officials

JoAnn Fitzpatrick Brown: director PRIM CORP EMPL vice president: Country Curtains, Inc. CORP AFFIL vice president: Housatonic Curtain Co. Inc.
Jane P. Fitzpatrick: chairman, treasurer B 1925. PRIM CORP EMPL chairman, chief executive officer, treasurer: Country Curtains, Inc. CORP AFFIL treasurer: Housatonic Curtain Co. Inc.; treasurer: Red Lion Inc.; chairman: Country Curtains Mail Order Inc.; chairman: Fitzpatrick Companies Inc.
John H. Fitzpatrick: president (see above)
Robert B. Trask: clerk B Springfield, MA 1946. ED Western New England College (1971). PRIM CORP EMPL president, chief operating officer, director: The Fitzpatrick Companies Inc. ADD CORP EMPL vice president, clearing houserk, director: Red Lion Inc. CORP AFFIL director: More Window Ways Inc.; member: New England Mail Order Association; director: Housatonic Curtain Co. Inc.; vice president: Lee Community Development Corp.; director: Fitzpatrick Retail & Realty Co. Inc.; clerk, director: Country Curtains Retail Inc.; member: Direct Marketing Association; trustee: City Savings Bank; president, chief operating officer, director: Country Curtains Mail Order Inc.; director: Berkshire Gas Co., Inc.; corporator: Berkshire Health Systems. NONPR AFFIL member: Knights of Columbus; corporator: North Adams State College Foundation; member: Institute of Management Accountants; trustee: Berkshire Theatre Festival; secretary, treasurer: High Meadow Foundation Inc.; member: American Institute CPAs; trustee: Berkshire Community College.

Grants Analysis

Disclosure Period: calendar year ending 1995
Total Grants: $1,237,896
Number of Grants: 382
Average Grant: $3,241
Highest Grant: $195,845
Typical Range: $200 to $20,000

Recent Grants

Note: Grants derived from 1995 Form 990.

Arts & Humanities

195,845	Berkshire Theater Festival, Stockbridge, MA
50,000	Berkshire Theater Festival, Stockbridge, MA -- Unicorn Pledges
35,500	Boston Symphony Orchestra, Boston, MA -- for Tanglewood
28,000	Edith Wharton Restoration, Lenox, MA
27,000	Lenox Library Association, Lenox, MA
23,000	Norman Rockwell Museum, Stockbridge, MA
22,500	Boston Symphony Orchestra, Boston, MA -- for Tanglewood
21,890	Boston Symphony Orchestra, Boston, MA
20,000	Berkshire Museum 21 Campaign, Stockbridge, MA
20,000	Hancock Shaker Village, Pittsfield, MA
15,150	Massachusetts Historical Society, Boston, MA
12,672	Berkshire Theater Festival, Stockbridge, MA -- for Red Lion Inn Rooms
10,000	Boston Symphony Orchestra, Boston, MA -- for Tanglewood
8,100	New York Center for Visual History, New York, NY
8,000	Shakespeare and Company, Lenox, MA

Civic & Public Affairs

30,000	Massachusetts Moca Foundation, MA
25,000	Trustees of Reservations, Beverly, MA
10,000	Your Hometown American Parade July 4th Parade
9,750	Trustees of Reservations, Beverly, MA
9,000	Chesterwood

Education

50,000	Green Mountain Junior College, Poultney, VT
50,000	North Adams State College, North Adams, MA
25,000	Williams College, Williamstown, MA
20,000	Emma Willard School, Troy, NY -- capital campaign
13,000	Berkshire Country Day School, Stockbridge, MA
10,800	Interlochen School of Art, Interlochen, MI
10,000	Berkshire Theater Festival, Stockbridge, MA -- scholarship for apprentice program
10,000	Conte Education Foundation

Environment

10,100	Nature Conservancy, MA

Health

35,000	Berkshire Medical Center for Special Care Nursery, Stockbridge, MA
10,000	Fairview Hospital

Religion

15,250	First Congregational Church, Stockbridge, MA

Social Services

37,000	Berkshire United Way, Stockbridge, MA
33,333	Boys and Girls Club of Pittsfield, Pittsfield, MA
10,000	Jacobs Pillow, Lee, MA

HOUSEHOLD INTERNATIONAL INC.

★ Number 53 of Top 100 Corporate Givers

Company Contact

Prospect Heights, IL
Web: http://www.household.com

Company Description

Revenue: US$9,499,100,000 (1999)
Profit: US$1,486,400,000 (1999)
Employees: 14,900
Fortune Rank: 179, per FORTUNE Magazine's list of 500 Largest U.S. Corporations (1999).
FF 179
SIC(s): 6141 Personal Credit Institutions.

Operating Locations

Operates 453 Household Financial Corp. offices and 119 Household Bank branches nationwide.

Nonmonetary Support

Value: $151,607 (1998); $44,106 (1997); $56,494 (1996)
Type: Donated Equipment
Note: Co. also supports a Volunteer Incentive Plan, United for Hope Campaign, and Junior Achievement Program.

Corporate Sponsorship

Value: $10,000
Type: Other
Note: Corporate sponsorship is provided on an exception basis only. Type of program likely to be sponspored is a Consumer Education Program.

Giving Contact

Donna M. Funk, Director, Employee & Philanthropic Services
Household International, Inc.
2700 Sanders Road
Prospect Heights, IL 60070
Phone: (847)564-6010
Fax: (847)564-7094
Web: http://www.household.com

Alternate Contact

Sharon Jacobs, program co-ordinator
Phone: (847)564-7973

Description

Organization Type: Corporate Giving Program
Giving Locations: headquarters area only.
Grant Types: Capital, Employee Matching Gifts, Endowment, General Support, Matching, Multiyear/Continuing Support, Project.

Note: Employee matching gift ratio: 2 to 1 up to $500 to eligible institutions of higher education; 1 to 1 thereafter.

Giving Philosophy

'Household International and its subsidiaries believe in good corporate citizenship. Each business group goes beyond a basic commitment for efficient and responsive consumer financial services through their support of a variety of community-oriented activities including: making cash and in-kind contributions to local nonprofit organizations that serve the communities in which they are located and best respond to the issues and needs of our shareholders, customers, and employees; encouraging employee volunteerism; and initiating or supporting responsive projects and programs to enhance the quality of life in their neighborhoods.' *Household International Philanthropic Guidelines*

Financial Summary

Total Giving: $4,200,000 (2000 approx); $4,073,686 (1999); $16,102,455 (1998)
Giving Analysis: Giving for 1996 includes: corporate direct giving ($1,667,667); domestic subsidiaries ($1,183,039); international subsidiaries ($137,196); 1997: corporate direct giving ($2,031,984); domestic subsidiaries ($998,880); international subsidiaries ($158,541); 1998: corporate direct giving ($15,013,143); domestic subsidiaries ($933,505); nonmonetary support ($151,697); international subsidiaries ($125,206);

Typical Recipients

Arts & Humanities: Museums/Galleries, Music, Opera
Civic & Public Affairs: Business/Free Enterprise, Civil Rights, Economic Development, Employment/Job Training, Housing, Nonprofit Management, Philanthropic Organizations, Public Policy, Urban & Community Affairs, Women's Affairs
Education: Business Education, Colleges & Universities, Economic Education, Education Associations, Literacy, Minority Education
Health: Health Organizations, Medical Rehabilitation, Mental Health
Social Services: Child Welfare, Community Centers, Community Service Organizations, Counseling, Delinquency & Criminal Rehabilitation, Family Services, Food/Clothing Distribution, Homes, People with Disabilities, Senior Services, Shelters/Homelessness, Substance Abuse, United Funds/United Ways, Volunteer Services, Youth Organizations

Contributions Analysis

Giving Priorities: Domestically, contributions to organizations with an international focus are separately tracked. Overseas, operating companies make contributions, with interests in education, social services, and health and hospitals.
Arts & Humanities: 5% to 10%. Only a small portion of the company's budget is allocated to cultural organizations. Nonprofit groups in this category must demonstrate how their organization and its programming efforts enhance the quality of life, educational readiness, or economic vitality of the community.
Civic & Public Affairs: 15% to 20%. Company takes particular interest in the economic vitality and physical rehabilitation of key communities around the nation where its customers and employees live and work. Programs that focus on strengthening consumer credit education; help those who need assistance in basic skills and job training; provide economic education programs which may enhance credit-worthiness; stabilize or improve housing, and revitalize neighborhoods, will take priority. It may also consider program grants to qualified agencies that encourage volunteerism or promote human relations.
Education: 20% to 25%. Company's emphasis is on programs thatsupport and enhance the efforts of our local school systems and work to impove the quality of education in its operating communities. It does not provide direct operating grants to secondary or elementary schools. The company also allocates a portion of its company-wide education budget for grants to select colleges and universities from which it recruits its employees, and for institutions that maintain outstanding research departments in topics of relevance to its industry. Such contribuitons are budgeted by its Support of Higher Education Program which is coordinated by staff in its headquarters. Unsolicited proposals from post-secondary institutions are not accepted.
Health: 20%. Company takes interest in the direct delivery of health care and human services and may make grants to community-based agencies which address the diverse needs of children and their families.
International: 9%. In 1999, the company's foreign business units contributed $350,703 to international organizations.
Social Services: 20%. Company may support the needs of senior citizens, the physically disabled, and providers of crisis and shelter care services. Company makes analysis contributions to the United Ways in its operating locations communities.

Application Procedures

Initial Contact: call or write for guidelines and an application
Application Requirements: a description of the organization's mission, history, and geographic area served; amount requested; description of program or project for which support is requested, the program's goals, and how the program relates to mission statement; how this program benefits the community; method of program evaluation; list of company's employees that volunteer at the organization; list of any cash or in-kind support from Household International within the last three years; copy of IRS 501(c)(3) determination letter; current operating budget; list of key staff; list of sources of income; latest audited financial statement; list of board of directors, including affiliations; latest annual report; and statement of administrative and fund-raising costs.
Deadlines: None.
Review Process: Proposals are reviewed by the contributions administrator of each business unit.
Evaluative Criteria: Priority given to programs that actively involve employees in volunteer leadership roles, address issues related to youth and education, enhance economic education, strengthen consumer credit education, and serve company operating communities.
Decision Notification: Review process takes up to three months; notification will be made in writing.
Notes: Guidelines contain a list of contacts for company's subsidiaries in the U.S. and abroad.

Restrictions

Does not support individuals, religious organizations serving a limited constituency, political groups, lobbying groups, fraternal organizations, veterans organizations, athletic clubs, athletic events, independent student aid, scholarships to individuals, travel, events, advertising, sponsorships, or organizations without 501(c)(3) tax status.
Support is not provided to hospitals or single-disease organizations.
Unsolicited requests from secondary and elementary schools are not accepted. organizations.
Unsolicited requests from secondary and elementary schools are not accepted.

Additional Information

Company reports that its contributions program operates on three levels: company-wide programs, such as the United Way, selected colleges and universities, and employee matching gifts program; headquarters community programs, which make grants to nonprofits where company's major business units are based; and local branch office community programs, which support organizations near branch communities and where employees volunteer. Grants to higher education are made through the Support of Higher Education Program; unsolicited requests from colleges or universities will not be accepted.
Besides its employee matching gifts program and VIP program, the company also sponsors the Household International Scholarship program, the Communities Need You program, and the Help for Community program.
Publications: Household International Philanthropic Guidelines

Corporate Officials

William F. Aldinger, III: chairman, chief executive officer, director B Brooklyn, NY 1947. ED City University of New York Bernard M. Baruch College BA (1969); Brooklyn Law School (1975). PRIM CORP EMPL chairman, chief executive officer, director: Household International Inc. CORP AFFIL executive vice president: Wells Fargo Bank NA; director: Stone Container Corp.; director: Sun America Inc.; president: Household Commercial Financial Services; president: Household Finance Corp.; chief executive officer: Beneficial California Inc.; chief executive officer: Beneficial Corp. NONPR AFFIL member: Consumer Bankers Association.
Lawrence N. Bangs: group executive B Springfield, MO 1936. ED Roosevelt University. PRIM CORP EMPL group executive: Household International Inc. ADD CORP EMPL chairman, director: Household Bank FSB.
Gary D. Gilmer: group executive B 1949. PRIM CORP EMPL group executive: Household International Inc. ADD CORP EMPL president: Household Finance Corp.
Colin P. Kelly: senior vice president human resources B 1943. ED California State University BA (1965). PRIM CORP EMPL senior vice president human resources: Household International Inc. ADD CORP EMPL senior vice president human resources: Household Finance Corp. CORP AFFIL director: Household Bank FSB.
Kenneth H. Robin: senior vice president, general counsel B Phildephia, PA 1947. ED Pennsylvania State University (1968); Temple University (1972). PRIM CORP EMPL senior vice president, general counsel: Household International Inc. ADD CORP EMPL vice president: Beneficial California Inc.; secretary: Housebold Finance Corp. NONPR AFFIL member: American Bar Association.
David A. Schoenholz: executive vice president, chief financial officer B Chicago, IL 1952. ED Harvard University; Duke University (1973). PRIM CORP EMPL executive vice president, chief financial officer: Household International Inc. CORP AFFIL chief financial officer: Household Finance Corp.; member: Financial Executive Institute. NONPR AFFIL member: American Institute CPAs.

Giving Program Officials

Donna M. Funk: director, philanthropic & employee services

Grants Analysis

Disclosure Period: calendar year ending 1999
Total Grants: $4,073,686
Typical Range: $500 to $5,000

HSBC BANK USA

Company Contact

New York, NY
Web: http://www.banking.us.hsbc.com

Company Description

Former Name: Marine Midland Bank (2000);
Acquired:.
Assets: US$28,300,000,000
Employees: 9,600

SIC(s): 6022 State Commercial Banks.
Parent Company: HSBC Holdings Plc, 10 Lower Thames St., London, United Kingdom

Operating Locations

AZ: Marmid Life Insurance Co., Tempe; CT: Marine Midland Bank; Equator Holdings Limited, Glastonbury; Marine Midland Business Loans, Norwalk; GA: Marine Midland Business Loans, Atlanta; NC: Marine Midland Mortgage Servicing Corp., Charlotte; NY: HSBC Americas, Buffalo; Marine Midland Bank, Buffalo; Marine Midland Banks, Buffalo; Marine Midland Leasing Corp., Buffalo; Marine Midland Mortgage Corp., Buffalo; Marine Midland Mortgage (USA), Buffalo; Marine Midland Realty Credit Corp., Buffalo; Marine Midland Securities, Buffalo; HSBC Asset Management Americas, New York; HSBC Futures, New York; HSBC Holdings, New York; HSBC Securities, New York; Marine Midland Bank, New York; Marine Midland Capital Markets, New York; Midland International Trade Services (USA) Corp., New York; Samuel Montagu, New York

Corporate Sponsorship

Type: Arts & cultural events; Festivals/fairs
Contact: Anne Nelson, Executive Vice President

Giving Contact

Linda Stryker, Senior Vice President, Public Affairs
HSBC Bank USA
140 Broadway
New York, NY 10005
Phone: (716)841-5003
Fax: (212)658-1460

Alternate Contact

Kristen Alvanson
Phone: (212)525-7974

Description

Organization Type: Corporate Giving Program
Giving Locations: headquarters and operating communities.
Grant Types: Employee Matching Gifts, General Support.

Financial Summary

Total Giving: Contributes through corporate direct giving program only.

Typical Recipients

Arts & Humanities: Arts & Humanities-General, Public Broadcasting
Civic & Public Affairs: Civic & Public Affairs-General, Public Policy
Education: Colleges & Universities, Education Associations, Education-General, Private Education (Precollege), Public Education (Precollege)
Environment: Environment-General
Health: Health-General
Social Services: Social Services-General, United Funds/United Ways, Youth Organizations

Contributions Analysis

Giving Priorities: Education, health and welfare, and housing.

Application Procedures

Initial Contact: Call to request application form.
Application Requirements: Include completed form and proposal of no more than 5 pages; a statement of need; proof of tax-exempt status; objectives of project, and projected outcomes; whether project is new or ongoing; organization's qualifications to carry out project; constituency served; community and volunteer involvement; list of board members; methods of evaluation; plans for continued funding; one-page project budget and organizational budget; list of other funding sources, committed and applied for; and pertinent publications.
Deadlines: None.
Review Process: Administrative officers review requests monthly.
Decision Notification: Officer will notify applicants of decisions and forward contributions, if applicable.
Notes: Application should either be sent to the headquarters or to the local office.

Restrictions

Does not support individuals; organizations which are not tax-exempt; organizations outside operating areas, or national or regional organizations unless they address a specific local need; political or lobbying groups, elementary or secondary schools, except for special projects not provided by school budgets; political or lobbying groups; endowment funds; multiyear pledges; religious organizations for sectarian purposes; or fraternal groups, athletic teams, bands, or similar groups.

Additional Information

HSBC Bank USA is the main subsidiary of the HSBC Group, which also includes HSBC Americas, Inc.; HSBC Asset Management Americas, Inc.; HSBC Corporate Banking; HSBC Futures, Inc.; HSBC Markets, Inc.; HSBC Securities, Inc.; HSBC James Capel; HSBC Washington Analysis; and Regional Treasury Center. All the entities in the HSBC Group have the same giving guidelines.
Publications: Guidelines; Application

Corporate Officials

Robert M. Butcher: chief financial officer vice president B 1944. PRIM CORP EMPL chief financial officer: Marine Midland Bank NA.
Linda Stryker: senior vice president

Grants Analysis

Disclosure Period: calendar year ending
Typical Range: $1,000 to $2,500

HUBBARD BROADCASTING, INC.

Company Contact

St. Paul, MN

Company Description

Revenue: US$330,000,000
Employees: 1,200
SIC(s): 4832 Radio Broadcasting Stations, 4833 Television Broadcasting Stations, 7812 Motion Picture & Video Production.

Hubbard Foundation

Giving Contact

Mr. Gerald D. Deeney, Secretary
Hubbard Foundation
3415 University Avenue
St. Paul, MN 55114
Phone: (612)642-4300
Fax: (612)642-4103

Description

EIN: 416022291
Organization Type: Corporate Foundation. Supports preselected organizations only.
Giving Locations: nationally; principally near operating locations and to national organizations.
Grant Types: Capital, Operating Expenses.

Financial Summary

Total Giving: $921,600 (fiscal year ending November 30, 1998); $933,610 (fiscal 1997); $1,377,491 (fiscal 1996)
Giving Analysis: Giving for fiscal 1996 includes: foundation ($1,364,241); foundation grants to United Way ($13,250); fiscal 1997: foundation ($916,360); foundation grants to United Way ($17,250); fiscal 1998: foundation ($914,600); foundation grants to United Way ($7,000)
Assets: $22,213,687 (fiscal 1998); $20,145,287 (fiscal 1997); $19,922,042 (fiscal 1996)

Typical Recipients

Arts & Humanities: Arts Associations & Councils, Arts Centers, Arts Funds, Arts Institutes, Arts Outreach, Ballet, Community Arts, Historic Preservation, History & Archaeology, Libraries, Museums/Galleries, Music, Opera, Performing Arts, Public Broadcasting, Theater, Visual Arts
Civic & Public Affairs: African American Affairs, Clubs, Economic Development, Civic & Public Affairs-General, Housing, Municipalities/Towns, Nonprofit Management, Philanthropic Organizations, Professional & Trade Associations, Public Policy, Safety, Zoos/Aquariums
Education: Arts/Humanities Education, Business Education, Colleges & Universities, Economic Education, Education Funds, Engineering/Technological Education, Education-General, Journalism/Media Education, Medical Education, Minority Education, Private Education (Precollege), Public Education (Precollege), Secondary Education (Private), Secondary Education (Public), Special Education, Student Aid, Vocational & Technical Education
Environment: Air/Water Quality, Environment-General, Research
Health: Arthritis, Cancer, Children's Health/Hospitals, Health Funds, Health Organizations, Hospitals, Kidney, Medical Rehabilitation, Medical Research, Mental Health, Preventive Medicine/Wellness Organizations, Research/Studies Institutes, Single-Disease Health Associations, Speech & Hearing
International: International Environmental Issues, International Organizations
Religion: Churches, Jewish Causes, Religious Welfare
Science: Science Museums
Social Services: Camps, Child Welfare, Community Service Organizations, Counseling, Day Care, Emergency Relief, Family Planning, Family Services, Food/Clothing Distribution, Homes, People with Disabilities, Recreation & Athletics, Scouts, Social Services-General, Substance Abuse, United Funds/United Ways, Volunteer Services, YMCA/YWCA/YMHA/YWHA, Youth Organizations

Contributions Analysis

Giving Priorities: The arts, youth organizations, social welfare, education, hospitals, health organizations, and the environment.
Arts & Humanities: 5%. Supports symphonic music, arts centers, theaters, historic preservation and arts associations.
Civic & Public Affairs: 23%. Funds neighborhood housing services, community services, and zoology.
Education: 24%. Colleges and universities receive primary support. Other priorities include Junior Achievement and education funds.
Environment: 2%. Funds community environmental programs.
Health: 11%. Primarily supports hospitals. Grants are also made to single-disease health associations, health organizations, and medical education and research.
Religion: 1%. Supports religious causes and churches.
Science: 27%. Major support to the Science Museum of Minnesota.
Social Services: 7%. Youth organizations are primary concern. United funds and child welfare organizations also received significant support.
Note: Total contributions made in fiscal 1998.

Application Procedures

Application Requirements: Send a summary and a description of organization, cooy of IRC sectin

501(c)(3) status letter, purpose of funds sought, and whether funds are intended to be used for operating or non-operating expenses.
Deadlines: November 30.

Restrictions

The foundation typically does not accept unsolicited proposals.

Corporate Officials

Gerald D. Deeney: vice president, chief financial officer PRIM CORP EMPL vice president, chief financial officer: Conus Communications Ltd. Partner.
Stanley S. Hubbard: chairman, president, chief executive officer B Saint Paul, MN 1933. ED University of Minnesota BA (1955). PRIM CORP EMPL chairman, president, chief executive officer: Hubbard Broadcasting, Inc. ADD CORP EMPL vice president: F & F Productions LLC. CORP AFFIL director: Fingerhut Co. Inc.; chairman, president, chief executive officer, director: US Satellite Broadcasting Co. Inc. NONPR AFFIL director: University Saint Thomas; member: World Business Council; director: University Minnesota Foundation; member: Society Professional Journalists; member: Society Satellite Professionals International; member: Royal Television Society London; chairman: Saint Croix Valley Youth Center; director: Ramsey County Ice Arena Committee; chairman, president, chief executive officer: Minnesota Business Partnership; member: Minnesota Executives Organization; member: Metropolitan Airports Public Foundation Advisory Board; director: Minneapolis American Friends Jamaica; member: International Radio & Television Society; director: Broadcast Pioneers Library; member: Broadcasters Foundation; director: Baptist Hospital Fund Sponsor Board; member: Broadcast Pioneers; director: Association Maximum Service Telecasters.
Kathryn Hubbard Rominski: corporate secretary PRIM CORP EMPL corporate secretary: Hubbard Broadcasting, Inc. ADD CORP EMPL secretary: F & F Productions LLC. CORP AFFIL secretary: D Diamond Sports Inc.

Foundation Officials

Gerald D. Deeney: secretary (see above)
Constance L. Eckert: assistant secretary
Karen H. Hubbard: trustee PRIM CORP EMPL Hubbard Broadcasting, Inc. CORP AFFIL secretary: United States Satellite Broadcasting Co.
Stanley S. Hubbard: president (see above)
Kathryn Hubbard Rominski: director (see above)

Grants Analysis

Disclosure Period: fiscal year ending November 30, 1998
Total Grants: $914,600*
Number of Grants: 215
Average Grant: $3,323*
Highest Grant: $203,500
Typical Range: $500 to $10,000
*Note: Giving excludes United Way. Average grant figure excludes highest grant.

Recent Grants

Note: Grants derived from fiscal 1997 Form 990.

Arts & Humanities

25,000 Minnesota Orchestral Association, Minneapolis, MN
5,000 Minneapolis Institute of Arts, Minneapolis, MN
3,000 Guthrie Theater, Minneapolis, MN
3,000 Minnesota Children's Museum, Saint Paul, MN

Civic & Public Affairs

5,000 Twin Cities Neighborhood Housing Services, Minneapolis, MN
3,000 Charities Review Council of Minnesota, Saint Paul, MN
3,000 Minnesota Zoo Beastly Ball, MN

Education

55,500 University of Minnesota Foundation Men's Athletic Department, Minneapolis, MN
35,000 University of Minnesota Department of Surgery, Minneapolis, MN
35,000 University of St. Thomas, Saint Paul, MN
30,000 Gustavus Adolphus College, Saint Peter, MN
15,000 Stillwater Area Schools Partnership Plan, Stillwater, OK
10,000 Mounds Park Academy, Saint Paul, MN
10,000 University of Minnesota Medical Foundation, Minneapolis, MN
10,000 University of Minnesota Sports Facility, Minneapolis, MN
8,000 Junior Achievement Upper Midwest, Minneapolis, MN
5,000 Working Classroom, Albuquerque, NM
3,500 Minneapolis College of Art and Design, Minneapolis, MN
3,000 Minnesota Private College Fund, Minneapolis, MN

Health

13,500 Gillette Children's Hospital Foundation, Saint Paul, MN
10,000 Arthritis Foundation, Boston, MA
10,000 Mayo Foundation for Medical Education and Research, Rochester, MN
10,000 University of Minnesota Children's Cancer Research, Minneapolis, MN
3,500 Listening Ear Crisis Center
3,000 Association of Children's Health Care, Minneapolis, MN
3,000 Children's Health Care Foundation, Saint Paul, MN

International

5,000 Project EarthSense, Saint Paul, MN

Religion

5,000 Basilica of St. Mary, Saint Paul, MN
5,000 Salvation Army, Saint Paul, MN
5,000 Salvation Army, Saint Paul, MN
3,000 Memorial Lutheran Church

Social Services

85,000 St. Croix Valley Youth Center, Saint Croix, MN
10,000 United Way, Saint Paul, MN
7,500 RecoverSource
6,000 Minnesota DARE, Minneapolis, MN
5,000 Edison Youth Hockey Association, New Brighton, MN
5,000 Edison Youth Hockey Association, New Brighton, MN
5,000 Hazelden Center for Youth and Families, Minneapolis, MN
5,000 Midwest Special Services, Saint Paul, MN
5,000 Minneapolis Crisis Nursery, Minneapolis, MN
5,000 Minneapolis Crisis Nursery, Minneapolis, MN
5,000 Ramsey Action Programs, Saint Paul, MN
5,000 Ramsey Action Programs, Saint Paul, MN
5,000 Rochester Family Resource Network, Rochester, NY
5,000 Sugarloaf Interpretive Center Association, Duluth, MN
5,000 Wildwood Programs, Schenectady, NY
3,500 Boy Scouts of America Indianhead Council, Saint Paul, MN
3,500 Boys and Girls Club, Saint Paul, MN
3,500 Boys and Girls Club, Minneapolis, MN
3,000 Minneapolis Crisis Nursery, Minneapolis, MN

Hubbell Inc.

Company Contact

Orange, CT

Company Description

Employees: 7,700
SIC(s): 3052 Rubber & Plastics Hose & Belting, 3089 Plastics Products Nec, 3357 Nonferrous Wiredrawing & Insulating, 3643 Current-Carrying Wiring Devices.

Corporate Sponsorship

Type: Arts & cultural events

Harvey Hubbell Foundation

Giving Contact

Harry B. Rowell, Trustee
Harvey Hubbell Foundation
PO Box 549
584 Derby-Milford Rd.
Orange, CT 06477-4024
Phone: (203)799-4100
Fax: (203)799-4333

Description

Founded: 1959
EIN: 066078177
Organization Type: Corporate Foundation
Giving Locations: principally near operating locations and to national organizations.
Grant Types: Capital, Employee Matching Gifts, General Support.

Financial Summary

Total Giving: $274,645 (1998); $245,880 (1997); $302,040 (1996). Note: Contributes through foundation only.
Giving Analysis: Giving for 1995 includes: foundation ($234,923); foundation matching gifts ($35,610); 1996: foundation ($251,925); foundation matching gifts ($50,115); 1997: foundation ($146,550); foundation grants to United Way ($64,350); foundation matching gifts ($34,980);
Assets: $5,185,816 (1998); $6,440,933 (1997); $5,252,290 (1996)
Gifts Received: $150,000 (1998); $100,000 (1997); $140,000 (1996). Note: Contributions are received from Hubbell Inc.

Typical Recipients

Arts & Humanities: Historic Preservation, History & Archaeology, Museums/Galleries, Music, Performing Arts
Civic & Public Affairs: Botanical Gardens/Parks, Business/Free Enterprise, Clubs, Economic Development, Economic Policy, Civic & Public Affairs-General, Housing, Parades/Festivals, Philanthropic Organizations, Professional & Trade Associations, Public Policy, Safety, Urban & Community Affairs
Education: Business Education, Colleges & Universities, Continuing Education, Education Associations, Education Funds, Elementary Education (Private), Engineering/Technological Education, Education-General, Medical Education, Preschool Education, Private Education (Precollege), Public Education (Precollege), Secondary Education (Private), Secondary Education (Public), Student Aid, Vocational & Technical Education, Vocational & Technical Education
Environment: Environment-General
Health: Cancer, Children's Health/Hospitals, Emergency/Ambulance Services, Health Organizations, Hospices, Hospitals, Hospitals (University Affiliated),

Medical Rehabilitation, Mental Health, Nursing Services, Public Health, Respiratory, Single-Disease Health Associations
International: International Organizations, International Relief Efforts
Religion: Religious Organizations, Religious Welfare
Science: Science Museums, Scientific Centers & Institutes
Social Services: At-Risk Youth, Child Welfare, Community Centers, Community Service Organizations, Domestic Violence, Emergency Relief, Family Services, Food/Clothing Distribution, People with Disabilities, Recreation & Athletics, Scouts, Social Services-General, Special Olympics, Special Olympics, United Funds/United Ways, Youth Organizations

Contributions Analysis

Arts & Humanities: 1%. Funds youth symphony assocation and the arts.
Civic & Public Affairs: 21%. Supports parks and recreational facilities, festivals.
Education: 32%. Contributes to several universities, and also supports medical education and scholarship programs.
Health: 22%. Interests include hospitals, emergency services, medical rehabilitation, and single disease organizations.
Social Services: 24%. Majority supports various United Way agencies in Connecticut. Other recipients include boys clubs and homes, scouting programs, community centers, and food and clothing distribution.
Note: Total contributions made in 1998.

Application Procedures

Initial Contact: Send a letter or proposal.
Application Requirements: Include a description of organization, amount requested, purpose of funds, recently audited financial statement, proof of 501(c)(3), list of officers and directors.

Restrictions

Does not support individuals.

Corporate Officials

George Jackson Ratcliffe, Jr.: chairman, president, chief executive officer B Charleston, WV 1936. ED Duke University AB (1958); University of Virginia JD (1961). PRIM CORP EMPL chairman, president, chief executive officer: Hubbell Inc. CORP AFFIL director: Olin Corp.; director: Praxair Inc.; director: Aquarian Co.

Foundation Officials

Richard Warren Davies: trustee B Lynn, MA 1946. ED Salem State College BA (1967); Purdue University (1968); Boston University JD (1971). PRIM CORP EMPL secretary, general counsel, vice president: Hubbell Inc. CORP AFFIL secretary: Hubbell Lighting Inc.; secretary: Pulse Communications Inc.; secretary: Gleason Reel Corp.; secretary: Hipotronics Inc.
George Jackson Ratcliffe, Jr.: trustee (see above)
Harry Brown Rowell, Jr.: trustee B Roberta, GA 1941. ED University of Georgia BA (1963); University of Georgia MA (1964). PRIM CORP EMPL executive vice president, chief operating officer: Hubbell Inc. CORP AFFIL executive vice president: Gleason Reel Corp.; chief executive officer: Pulse Communications Inc.; president: Fargo Manufacturing Co. Inc.

Grants Analysis

Disclosure Period: calendar year ending 1998
Total Grants: $190,675*
Number of Grants: 78
Average Grant: $2,445
Highest Grant: $34,400
Typical Range: $100 to $3,500
***Note:** Giving excludes matching gifts, United Way.

Recent Grants

Note: Grants derived from 1998 Form 990.

Arts & Humanities

2,000 The Kennedy Center, Inc., Bridgeport, CT -- Corporate

Civic & Public Affairs

25,000 Emergency Fund Harvey Hubbell, Orange, CT -- Corporate
15,000 Frontiers of Freedom, Arlington, VA -- Corporate
5,000 Frontiers of Freedom Institute, Arlington, VA -- Corporate
2,000 Friends of Martin Parks & Recreation -- Lighting
1,600 Orange Fire Marshall, Orange, CT -- Corporate
1,000 Centralia Anchor Festival, Centralia, IL -- A.B. Chance
1,000 Christmas in April - Dutchess County, Paughkeepsie, NY -- Fargo

Education

34,400 National Merit Scholarship, Evanston, IL -- Corporate
10,000 NAED Education Foundation, Bridgeport, CT -- Corporate
4,000 University of Connecticut, Hartford, CT -- Corporate
4,000 Virginia Tech Foundation, Blacksburg, VA -- Corporate
3,000 Yale University, New Haven, CT -- Corporate
2,000 Cheshire Education Foundation, Cheshire, CT -- Corporate
2,000 University of Missouri, St. Louis, MO -- A.B. Chance
2,000 West Virginia University, Morgantown, WV -- Corporate
1,861 University of Connecticut, Hartford, CT -- Corporate
1,750 St. Margaret's-McTernana School, Waterbury, CT -- Corporate
1,500 Jefferson County School System, Louisville, KY -- Anderson
1,250 Duke University, Durham, NC -- Corporate
1,000 Giles County School System, Pearisburg, VA -- Anderson
1,000 Harvard University, Boston, MA -- Corporate
1,000 Leeds High School, Leeds, AL -- Anderson
1,000 Martin Methodist College, Palaski, IN -- Anderson
1,000 University of Akron, Akron, OH -- Ohio Brass
1,000 University of Missouri, Columbia, MO -- A.B. Chance
1,000 University of South Carolina, Columbia, SC -- Ohio Brass
1,000 West Virginia University Foundation, Morgantown, WV -- Corporate

Health

25,000 Memorial Sloan Kettering Cancer Institute, New York, NY -- Corporate
20,000 Datahr Rehabilitation Institute, Brookfield, CT -- Corporate
5,000 Yale-New Haven Hospital, New Haven, CT -- Corporate
1,000 Children's Miracle Network, Peoria, IL -- A.B. Chance
1,000 The Cystic Fibrosis Foundation, Atlanta, GA -- Raco

Social Services

12,000 United Way of Dutchess County, Poughkeepsie, NY -- Fargo
6,250 United Way - Valley, Phoenix, AZ -- Kerite
6,000 United Way of St. Joseph's County, South Bend, IN -- Raco
5,000 United Way, Bridgeport, CT -- Corporate
3,500 Centralia Area United Way, Centralia, IL -- A.B. Chance
3,500 United Way of Northern Fairfield, Fairfield, CT -- Wiring Device
3,300 United Way, Bridgeport, CT -- Lighting
2,900 Connecticut Yankee Council, Milford, CT -- Corporate
2,500 Nutmeg Games, Hartford, CT -- Corporate
2,500 United Way of Aiken County, Aiken, SC -- Ohio Brass
2,500 United Way of Wadsworth, Wadsworth, OH -- Ohio Brass
2,000 Christiansburg Receation Center, Christiansburg, VA -- Lighting
1,500 United Way of Greater St. Louis, St. Louis, MO -- Killark
1,250 United Way of Jefferson & Shel by Counties, Leeds, AL -- Anderson
1,000 Connecticut Special Olympics, Hartford, CT -- Corporate
1,000 Farifield County Shehan Wildcats, Fairfield, CT -- Corporate
1,000 United Way of Colquitt County, GA -- Lighting

HUFFY CORP.

Company Contact

Dayton, OH

Company Description

Employees: 5,753 (1999)
SIC(s): 3423 Hand & Edge Tools Nec, 3524 Lawn & Garden Equipment, 3751 Motorcycles, Bicycles & Parts, 3944 Games, Toys & Children's Vehicles.

Nonmonetary Support

Value: $10,000 (1994)
Type: Donated Products

Huffy Foundation, Inc.

Giving Contact

Pamela K. Booher, Secretary
Huffy Foundation
225 Byers Road
Miamisburg, OH 45342
Phone: (937)865-2820
Fax: (937)865-5484

Description

EIN: 316023716
Organization Type: Corporate Foundation
Giving Locations: OH: Dayton headquarters; principally near operating locations and to national organizations.
Grant Types: Employee Matching Gifts, General Support, Scholarship.
Note: Employee matching gift ratio: 1 to 1 for gifts to education.

Financial Summary

Total Giving: $220,000 (fiscal year ending June 30, 1998 approx); $275,000 (fiscal 1997 approx); $275,000 (fiscal 1996). Note: Contributes through corporate direct giving program and foundation. Giving includes foundation.
Assets: $225,000 (fiscal 1997); $382,760 (fiscal 1996); $572,097 (fiscal 1995)
Gifts Received: $400,000 (fiscal 1995); $400,000 (fiscal 1994); $50,000 (fiscal 1992). Note: Foundation receives contributions from Huffy Corporation.

Typical Recipients

Arts & Humanities: Arts Associations & Councils, Arts Centers, Arts Funds, Arts Institutes, Ballet, Community Arts, Dance, Arts & Humanities-General, Historic Preservation, History & Archaeology, Museums/Galleries, Music, Opera, Public Broadcasting, Theater, Visual Arts

Civic & Public Affairs: African American Affairs, Botanical Gardens/Parks, Business/Free Enterprise, Community Foundations, Economic Development, Civic & Public Affairs-General, Housing, Municipalities/Towns, Parades/Festivals, Professional & Trade Associations, Safety, Urban & Community Affairs, Women's Affairs

Education: Arts/Humanities Education, Business Education, Colleges & Universities, Community & Junior Colleges, Education Funds, Education Reform, Engineering/Technological Education, Education-General, Legal Education, Minority Education, Private Education (Precollege), Public Education (Precollege), Secondary Education (Public), Student Aid

Environment: Environment-General, Resource Conservation

Health: Alzheimers Disease, Cancer, Children's Health/Hospitals, Health-General, Health Funds, Health Organizations, Hospices, Hospitals, Medical Research, Single-Disease Health Associations

International: International Affairs, International Development

Science: Science Museums

Social Services: Big Brother/Big Sister, Child Welfare, Community Service Organizations, Crime Prevention, Day Care, Family Planning, Family Services, People with Disabilities, Recreation & Athletics, Scouts, Social Services-General, Substance Abuse, United Funds/United Ways, YMCA/YWCA/YMHA/YWHA, Youth Organizations

Contributions Analysis

Arts & Humanities: About 15%. Supports art institutes, dance, classical music, and theater.

Civic & Public Affairs: About 30%. Supports local community affairs, historical societies, parks, housing, and women's and minority affairs. Also supports public policy, the Red Cross, and public broadcasting.

Education: 25% to 30%. Supports colleges and universities. Minor support for secondary education. Provides scholarships to children of employees.

Health: Less than 5%. Supports hospitals, research, hospices, community health, and single-disease health associations.

Social Services: 20% to 25%. Supports the United Way, combined charities, and United Cerebral Palsy. Less than 5%. Supports sports, Boys and GirlsClubs, scouting, and junior achievement.

Application Procedures

Initial Contact: letter of inquiry and full proposal

Application Requirements: a description of organization, amount requested, purpose of funds sought, recently audited financial statement, and proof of tax-exempt status

Deadlines: None.

Restrictions

Does not support individuals, religious organizations for sectarian purposes, political or lobbying groups, or organizations outside operating areas.

Additional Information

The foundation reports that scholarships are available to the families of employees. The scholarships will be given out once a year, and will amount to $1,500 a year for four years. Employees should contact headquarters or their local facilities for an application form.

Publications: General Information; Grant Application Procedures

Corporate Officials

Don R. Graber: chairman, president, chief executive officer, director B Warren, OH. ED Ohio State University BS (1966); Ohio State University MBA (1968). PRIM CORP EMPL chairman, president, chief executive officer, director: Huffy Corp. CORP AFFIL director: Precision Castparts Corp.

Richard L. Molen: chairman, chief executive officer, director B Cincinnati, OH 1940. ED University of Cincinnati BBA (1962); Xavier University (1965). PRIM CORP EMPL chairman, chief executive officer, director: Huffy Corp. CORP AFFIL director: Durco International Inc.; director: Huntington National Bank; director: Alltrista Corp.

Foundation Officials

Pamela K. Booher: secretary PRIM CORP EMPL executive assistant: Huffy Corp.

Don R. Graber: trustee (see above)

Richard L. Molen: trustee (see above)

Frederick C. Smith: chairman, trustee B Ridgewood, NJ 1916. ED Cornell University BS (1938); Harvard University MBA (1940). NONPR AFFIL trustee, chairman: Sinclair Community College Foundation; trustee: United Way Ohio; chairman policy committee: Governments Human Investment Council; trustee emeritus: Alan Guttmacher Institute.

Grants Analysis

Disclosure Period: fiscal year ending June 30, 1996
Total Grants: $208,160
Number of Grants: 107
Average Grant: $1,752*
Highest Grant: $22,400
Typical Range: $100 to $2,500
***Note:** Average grant figure excludes highest grant.

Recent Grants

Note: Grants derived from fiscal 1996 Form 990.

Arts & Humanities

22,400	Dayton Art Institute, Dayton, OH
8,000	Carillon Historical Park, Dayton, OH
6,667	Fraze Pavilion, Kettering, OH
5,500	Carillon Historical Park, Dayton, OH
3,000	Cultureworks, Philadelphia, PA
2,000	Dayton Philharmonic Orchestra, Dayton, OH
2,000	Huffman Historic Society
1,200	San Diego Symphony, San Diego, CA
1,000	Dayton Contemporary Dance Company, Dayton, OH

Civic & Public Affairs

6,667	Fraze Pavilion
6,500	Dayton Foundation, Dayton, OH
5,000	2003 Committee
2,500	Cox Arboretum Associates, Dayton, OH
2,500	Focus on Farmington Foundation
2,500	Ohio Manufacturer's Association, OH
2,100	Dayton Foundation, Dayton, OH
1,500	City of Thornton, Thornton, OH -- community and civic
1,500	Cox Arboretum, Dayton, OH
1,000	Dayton Foundation, Dayton, OH
1,000	Dayton Montgomery County Housing, Dayton, OH
750	Martin Luther King Celebration
500	Dayton Fund for Home Rehabilitation, Dayton, OH
500	Party 2000

Education

5,607	University of Dayton Law School, Dayton, OH
5,000	Wright State University Athletic Department, Dayton, OH
4,600	Miami University, Miami, FL
4,500	Wright State University, Dayton, OH
4,450	Miami University, Oxford, OH
3,000	Ohio Northern University, Ada, OH
3,000	Ohio Northern University, Ada, OH -- scholarships
2,993	University of Dayton, Dayton, OH
2,500	Ohio Manufacturer's Association, OH
2,500	University of Dayton Guardian, Dayton, OH
2,500	University of Dayton Guardian, Dayton, OH
2,000	Goshen College, Goshen, IN
2,000	Lake Forest College, Lake Forest, IL
2,000	Lake Forest College, Lake Forest, IL
2,000	Ridgeville Christian Schools, Springboro, OH
2,000	Suring/Gillet High School Scholarship
2,000	Xavier University, Cincinnati, OH
1,569	Colby College, Waterville, ME
1,500	Bluffton College, Bluffton, OH
1,500	Case Western Reserve University, Cleveland, OH
1,500	Case Western Reserve University, Cleveland, OH -- scholarships
1,500	Holy Apostles School
1,500	Lebanon Valley College, Annville, PA
1,500	Miami University, Miami, FL -- scholarships
1,500	Ohio State University, Columbus, OH -- scholarships
1,500	Ohio State University, Columbus, OH
1,500	University of Akron, Akron, OH -- scholarships
1,500	University of Arkansas, Fayetteville, AR -- scholarships
1,500	University of Dayton, Dayton, OH
1,500	University of Minnesota, Minneapolis, MN
1,500	University of Missouri, Columbia, MO -- scholarships
1,500	University of Missouri, Columbia, MO
1,500	University of San Diego, San Diego, CA -- scholarships
1,500	University of San Diego, San Diego, CA
1,500	University of Wisconsin, Madison, WI -- scholarships
1,500	University of Wisconsin, Milwaukee, WI
1,050	University of Dayton, Dayton, OH
1,000	Cedarville College, Cedarville, OH
1,000	Centerville High School, Centerville, OH
1,000	Granite Hills High School, Spring Valley, CA
1,000	Sinclair Community College, Dayton, OH
1,000	Wisconsin Foundation of Independent Colleges, Milwaukee, WI
600	University of Dayton Law School, Dayton, OH
500	Alliance for Education, Worcester, MA
500	Troy High School

Environment

2,500	US Top of Michigan Trail
2,500	US Top of Michigan Trail, MI

Health

1,500	Ronald McDonald House -- community and civic
1,000	City of Hope, Duarte, CA
600	United Cerebral Palsy, New York, NY

International

2,500	Dayton Council on World Affairs, Dayton, OH
2,500	Global Village Community
1,000	Executive Women International

Social Services

20,000	United Way, Dayton, OH -- public welfare
15,000	Celina Combined Services Appeal, Celina, OH
10,000	Celina Combined Services Appeal, Celina, OH -- public welfare
6,667	United Way, Dayton, OH
6,000	Mile High United Way, Denver, CO -- public welfare
5,000	United Way Appeal Waukesha County, Waukesha, WI

5,000	United Way Appeal Waukesha County, Waukesha, WI -- public welfare
4,000	Farmington's Children Home
4,000	Farmington's Children Home
4,000	Miami Valley Regional Bicycle Council, Dayton, OH
3,500	Miami Valley Regional Bike Council, OH
3,000	Bike-A-Thon, Dayton, OH
2,500	Naga Waukee Park Ice Arena
2,500	Naga-Waukee Park Ice Arena -- youth activities
2,500	United Way, San Diego, CA -- public welfare
2,100	Dayton Boys and Girls Club, Dayton, OH -- youth activities
2,000	Dayton Cycling Club, Dayton, OH
2,000	Gateway Outreach Center
1,500	United Way Capital Region, Harrisburg, PA -- public welfare
1,500	United Way Capital Region, Harrisburg, PA
1,500	YMCA Youth Basketball
1,200	Big Brothers and Big Sisters, Dayton, OH
1,000	Wisconsin Foundation for Independence, WI
500	Girl Scouts of America, Dayton, OH

HUGHES ELECTRONICS CORP.

Company Contact

200 N. Sepulveda Blvd.
El Segundo, CA 90245
Phone: (310)364-6000
Fax: (310)568-6390
Web: http://www.hughes.com

Company Description

Former Name: Hughes Aircraft Co.
Employees: 86,000
SIC(s): 3357 Nonferrous Wiredrawing & Insulating, 3441 Fabricated Structural Metal, 3489 Ordnance & Accessories Nec, 3761 Guided Missiles & Space Vehicles.
Parent Company: General Motors Corp., Detroit, MI, United States

Nonmonetary Support

Type: Donated Equipment

Corporate Sponsorship

Note: The company sponsors local fundraising events.

Giving Contact

Maria A. Zumbrun, Manager, Philanthropy & Memberships
Hughes Electronics Corp.
PO Box 956
ES, 001, A121
200 N. Sepulveda Blvd.
El Segundo, CA 90245-0956
Phone: (310)662-9648
Fax: (310)640-3464
Email: maria.zumbrun@hughes.com

Description

Organization Type: Corporate Giving Program
Giving Locations: CA: Southern California
Grant Types: Award, Emergency, Employee Matching Gifts, General Support.
Note: Employee Matching Gifts applied to education only.

Giving Philosophy

'H.E. (Hughes Electronics) sponsors many kinds of organizations serving the needs of a diverse population. Special emphasis is placed on multi-ethnic collaboration opportunities, inner-city revitalization, and job training. Organizations are selected for grants because they provide life-enhancing opportunities to the underserved, and strengthen the community-at-large by their presence. Also, recognizing that successful technical education and scientific research programs greatly influence U.S. competitiveness, H.E. solidly supports colleges and universities across the nation. In aiding California in the nineties, major disaster relief has been extended to victims of fires, floods, and earthquakes.' *Hughes Electronics: A Resource to the Community*

Financial Summary

Total Giving: Company does not disclose contributions figures.

Typical Recipients

Civic & Public Affairs: Economic Development
Education: Colleges & Universities, Education Reform, Elementary Education (Public), Engineering/Technological Education, Faculty Development, Science/Mathematics Education
Environment: Air/Water Quality
International: International Relations
Social Services: Community Service Organizations, Emergency Relief, United Funds/United Ways, Youth Organizations

Contributions Analysis

Giving Priorities: Education, civic affairs, and community services.

Application Procedures

Initial Contact: For general inquiries, send a brief letter or call the corporation.
Application Requirements: General program requests should include a description of organization, summary of services provided, purpose of funds sought, list of board of directors, copy of 501(c)(3) tax-exempt certificate, audited financial statement or copy of most current income-tax return.
Deadlines: None.

Corporate Officials

Jo-Ann G. Costa: director public affairs & administration PRIM CORP EMPL director public affairs & administration: Hughes Electronics Corp.
Sandra L. Harrison: senior vice president PRIM CORP EMPL senior vice president: Hughes Electronics Corp.

Giving Program Officials

Maria Zumbrun: manager philanthropy & membership

Grants Analysis

Disclosure Period: calendar year ending

HUMANA, INC.

 Number 80 of Top 100 Corporate Givers

Company Contact

Louisville, KY
Web: http://www.hamana.com

Company Description

Revenue: US$10,113,000,000 (1999)
Employees: 16,800
Fortune Rank: 168, per FORTUNE Magazine's list of 500 Largest U.S. Corporations (1999).
FF 168
SIC(s): 6321 Accident & Health Insurance, 6324 Hospital & Medical Service Plans, 6411 Insurance Agents, Brokers & Service, 8062 General Medical & Surgical Hospitals.

Operating Locations

Bermuda: Insurance Resources Co., Ltd., Hamilton; Switzerland: Hospital de la Tour, Geneva; United Kingdom: Humana Hospital-Wellington I, London; Humana Hospital-Wellington II, London

Humana Foundation

Giving Contact

Virginia Kelly-Judd, Executive Director
Humana Foundation
500 West Main Street
PO Box 1438
Louisville, KY 40201
Phone: (502)580-3041
Fax: (502)580-1256

Description

EIN: 611004763
Organization Type: Corporate Foundation
Giving Locations: KY: Louisville principally near operating locations and to national organizations.
Grant Types: Capital, Conference/Seminar, Department, Employee Matching Gifts, Endowment, General Support, Research, Scholarship.
Note: Employee matching gift ratio: 1 to 1 for contributions made by officers and board of directors members only.

Financial Summary

Total Giving: $9,298,267 (1998); $6,427,952 (1997); $7,191,128 (1996). Note: Contributes through corporate direct giving program and foundation. Giving includes foundation.
Giving Analysis: Giving for 1997 includes: foundation ($6,125,058); foundation grants to United Way ($302,894); 1998: foundation ($8,990,267); foundation grants to United Way ($308,000)
Assets: $55,762,060 (1998); $63,221,190 (1997); $66,711,115 (1996)
Gifts Received: $6,746,773 (1994); $1,804,184 (1993); $6,599,870 (1991). Note: Gifts received from Humana Inc.

Typical Recipients

Arts & Humanities: Arts Associations & Councils, Arts Centers, Arts Festivals, Arts Funds, Ballet, Community Arts, Dance, Historic Preservation, History & Archaeology, Libraries, Museums/Galleries, Music, Opera, Performing Arts, Public Broadcasting, Theater
Civic & Public Affairs: African American Affairs, Asian American Affairs, Botanical Gardens/Parks, Business/Free Enterprise, Civil Rights, Community Foundations, Economic Development, Civic & Public Affairs-General, Hispanic Affairs, Housing, Legal Aid, Nonprofit Management, Philanthropic Organizations, Professional & Trade Associations, Urban & Community Affairs, Women's Affairs, Zoos/Aquariums
Education: Business Education, Colleges & Universities, Community & Junior Colleges, Continuing Education, Education Associations, Education Funds, Education Reform, Elementary Education (Private), Education-General, Leadership Training, Literacy, Medical Education, Minority Education, Preschool Education, Private Education (Precollege), Public Education (Precollege), Secondary Education (Private), Special Education, Student Aid
Environment: Environment-General, Resource Conservation
Health: Cancer, Children's Health/Hospitals, Clinics/Medical Centers, Emergency/Ambulance Services, Health Organizations, Heart, Hospitals, Medical Research, Mental Health, Nursing Services, Public Health, Single-Disease Health Associations

International: Foreign Educational Institutions, Human Rights
Religion: Churches, Dioceses, Religious Organizations, Religious Welfare
Science: Science Museums, Scientific Centers & Institutes, Scientific Organizations
Social Services: Animal Protection, Child Welfare, Community Centers, Community Service Organizations, Emergency Relief, Family Planning, Family Services, Food/Clothing Distribution, Homes, People with Disabilities, Recreation & Athletics, Scouts, Senior Services, United Funds/United Ways, YMCA/YWCA/YMHA/YWHA, Youth Organizations

Contributions Analysis

Giving Priorities: Education, the arts, civic affairs, and social welfare. International interests are limited; has supported foreign educational institutions and international studies at U.S.-based universities.
Arts & Humanities: 13%. Almost exclusively gives major grants to arts groups in Louisville, KY, such as the Actors Theatre of Louisville, Louisville Orchestra, and the Greater Louisville Fund for the Arts.
Civic & Public Affairs: 19%. Supports economic development, business and free enterprise, philanthropic organizations, and urban and community affairs.
Education: 42%. Major support goes to colleges and universities, including medical education programs. Other interests include public and private precollege education, education funds and associations, and business and economic education.
Health: 16%. Recipients include hospitals, single-disease health associations, and mental health organizations.
Social Services: 6%. Major support goes to the Metro United Way of Louisville, KY. Other recipients include youth organizations, recreation and athletics, child welfare, the aged, and community services.
Note: Total contributions in 1998.

Application Procedures

Initial Contact: Send written request application.
Application Requirements: Include a description of organization amount requested, purpose of funds sought, other funding commitments to date, and copy of IRS tax-exemption letter. Scholarship applications are available from the foundation.
Deadlines: None.
Decision Notification: Foundation responds promptly to applications, either rejecting them or requesting full proposals; final decisions are made by the contributions committee within about three months.

Restrictions

Company does not give to fraternal organizations, political or lobbying groups, religious organizations for sectarian purposes, or individuals.
Recipient organizations must be 501(c)3 according to IRS regulations.

Additional Information

Scholarships are awarded to children of full-time Humana employees.
Publications: Application Form

Corporate Officials

David Allen Jones: co-founder, chairman, director B Louisville, KY 1931. ED University of Louisville BS (1954); Yale University JD (1960). PRIM CORP EMPL co-founder, chairman, director: Humana, Inc. CORP AFFIL director: Abbott Laboratories. NONPR AFFIL member: Louisville Area Chamber of Commerce.
Gregory H. Wolf: president, chief operating officer, director ED Pennsylvania State University BS (1977); Central Michigan University MS (1988). PRIM CORP EMPL president, chief operating officer, director: Humana, Inc. CORP AFFIL president: Humana Health Plan Texas; president: Humana Kansas City Inc.

Foundation Officials

George G. Bauernfeind: vice president PRIM CORP EMPL vice president tax: Humana, Inc. CORP AFFIL vice president: Humana Health Plan Inc.; vice president: Humana Health Plan Texas.
James Willard Doucette: vice president, treasurer B Louisville, KY 1951. ED University of Louisville (1972); University of Pennsylvania Wharton School (1976). PRIM CORP EMPL vice president investment management, treasurer: Humana, Inc. CORP AFFIL treasurer: Humana Health Plan Inc.; treasurer: Humana Health Plan Texas; treasurer: Humana Health Insurance Co. NV. NONPR AFFIL member: National Association HMO Regulators; member: Treasury Management Association; member: American Philatelic Society; member: Association Investment Management & Research.
David Allen Jones: chairman, chief executive officer, director (see above)
Virginia Kelly-Judd: executive director
James E. Murray: chief operating officer, senior vice president ED Dayton BS (1975). PRIM CORP EMPL vice president, chief financial officer: Humana, Inc. CORP AFFIL vice president, controller, director: Humana Health Plan Inc.
Walter Emerson Neely: vice president B Springfield, MA 1944. ED Lehigh University (1965); Columbia University (1968). PRIM CORP EMPL secretary, director: HMPK Inc. CORP AFFIL secretary: Humana Health Plan Texas; vice president, assistant secretary, associate, general counsel: Humana Inc.; secretary, director: Humana Health Plan Ohio Inc.; secretary: Humana Health Insurance NV Inc.; secretary: Humana Health Plan Inc.; secretary: H Plan Inc.

Grants Analysis

Disclosure Period: calendar year ending 1998
Total Grants: $8,990,267*
Number of Grants: 97
Average Grant: $79,065*
Highest Grant: $1,400,000
Typical Range: $1,000 to $100,000
***Note:** Giving excludes United Way. Average grant excludes highest grant.

Recent Grants

Note: Grants derived from 1998 Form 990.

Arts & Humanities

563,500	Actors Theatre of Louisville Inc., Louisville, KY -- Festival of New American Plays
200,000	J. B. Speed Art Museum, Louisville, KY
195,600	Greater Louisville Fund for the Arts, Louisville, KY
100,000	Kentucky Historical Society Foundation, Inc., Frankfort, KY
50,000	Library Foundation, Louisville, KY
28,000	Kentucky Center for the Arts, Louisville, KY
15,000	John F. Kennedy Center Corporate Board Fund, New York, NY

Civic & Public Affairs

1,400,000	Louisville Waterfront Development Corp., Louisville, KY
60,000	Triangle Foundation, Lexington, KY
50,000	Downtown Development Corp., Louisville, KY
50,000	Greater Louisville Foundation, Inc., Louisville, KY
50,000	Neighborhood House, Louisville, KY
24,750	Louisville Urban League, Louisville, KY
20,999	Black Achievers, Louisville, KY -- Chestnut Street YMCA
15,000	Green Bay Botanical Garden, Inc., Green Bay, WI
15,000	Institute for Intercultural Understanding Inc., Louisville, KY
15,000	Lincoln Foundation, Louisville, KY
15,000	Louisville Community Foundation, Louisville, KY

Education

800,000	Middlebury College, Middlebury, VT
650,000	University of Louisville Foundation, Inc., Louisville, KY
507,817	Educational Testing Service, Princeton, NJ -- Humana Foundation Scholarships
440,000	Spalding University, Louisville, KY
300,000	University of Louisville Foundation, Inc., Louisville, KY
275,000	Partnership for Kentucky Schools, Lexington, KY
250,000	Berea College, Berea, KY
200,000	Yale University, New Haven, CT
125,000	City University of New York Graduate Center Foundation, New York, NY
110,000	Sacred Heart Academy, Louisville, KY
100,000	Kentucky Country Day School Incorporated, Louisville, KY
100,000	Trinity High School, Louisville, KY
75,000	Jefferson Community College, Lexington, KY
60,000	Male Traditional High School, Louisville, KY
50,000	St. Xavier High School, Louisville, KY
44,000	University of Kentucky, Lexington, KY -- Endowment funds
25,000	Transylvania University, Lexington, KY

Health

951,543	American Lung Association, New York, NY
376,814	University Pediatrics Foundation, Inc., Louisville, KY
60,000	Jefferson County Medical Society, Louisville, KY
50,000	CORE Foundation, Chicago, IL

International

15,000	Robert F. Kennedy Memorial, Washington, DC

Religion

250,000	Archdiocese of Louisville, Louisville, KY -- Endocument for Excellence campaign
100,000	St. Stephen's Baptist Church, Louisville, KY
50,000	Presbyterian Community Center, Louisville, KY

Social Services

182,000	Metro United Way, Louisville, KY
150,000	American Red Cross, Washington, DC
105,000	United Way of Brown County, Green Bay, WI
21,000	United Way of Dane County, Green Bay, WI
20,000	YMCA of Greater Louisville, Louisville, KY
15,000	Boy Scouts of America, Louisville, KY
15,000	Greater Green Bay YMCA, Green Bay, WI

Hunt Manufacturing Co.

Company Contact

Philadelphia, PA
Web: http://www.hunt-corp.com

Company Description

Employees: 2,056
SIC(s): 2522 Office Furniture Except Wood, 2679 Converted Paper Products Nec, 2893 Printing Ink, 3579 Office Machines Nec.

Nonmonetary Support

Value: $5,000 (1998)
Type: Donated Products

Giving Contact

Cheryl M. Walmsley, Grant Administrator
Hunt Manufacturing Co.
1 Commerce Sq.
2005 Market St.
Philadelphia, PA 19103-7085
Phone: (215)841-2403
Fax: (215)656-3714
Email: cheryl_walmsley@Hunt-Corp.com

Description

Organization Type: Corporate Giving Program
Giving Locations: headquarters.
Grant Types: Capital, Employee Matching Gifts, General Support, Project, Seed Money.

Giving Philosophy

'Hunt Manufacturing Co. believes that businesses have an obligation to the communities in which they are located. This obligation extends not only to promoting the general quality of life in those communities, but also to solving the pressing social and economic problems they face. In 1955, the Hunt Manufacturing Co. Contributions Program was formed as a vehicle to enhance the impact of the charitable dollars the corporation wished to reinvest in the communities in which it had a presence. Recognizing that the existing needs of these communities far exceeds any one corporation's capacity to give, the Contributions Program will impact preferential treatment to grant applications which most closely fit our areas of concentration. The mission of the Hunt Manufacturing Co. Contributions Program is to shape better communities for future generations by encouraging and supporting initiatives that primarily involve the visual arts and children, especially children in need. A secondary area of concentration is direct services to children.' Guidelines for Applicants, Hunt Manufacturing Co.

Financial Summary

Total Giving: $200,000 (fiscal year ending November 30, 2000 approx); $200,000 (fiscal 1999 approx); $379,185 (fiscal 1995). Note: Contributes through corporate direct giving program only. Foundation became defunct as of 1997. 1995 Giving includes foundation($302,525); matching gifts ($70,660).
Assets: $444 (fiscal 1995); $4,451 (fiscal 1991); $3,116 (fiscal 1989)

Typical Recipients

Arts & Humanities: Arts Appreciation, Arts Associations & Councils, Arts Centers, Ballet, Community Arts, Dance, Arts & Humanities-General, Libraries, Museums/Galleries, Music, Opera, Performing Arts, Public Broadcasting, Theater, Visual Arts
Civic & Public Affairs: Clubs, Economic Development, Economic Policy, Employment/Job Training, Legal Aid, Safety, Urban & Community Affairs
Education: Afterschool/Enrichment Programs, Arts/Humanities Education, Business-School Partnerships, Colleges & Universities, Community & Junior Colleges, Elementary Education (Private), Literacy, Public Education (Precollege), Secondary Education (Public), Student Aid, Vocational & Technical Education
Health: AIDS/HIV, Children's Health/Hospitals
International: International Affairs
Religion: Ministries
Science: Scientific Centers & Institutes
Social Services: Big Brother/Big Sister, Child Abuse, Child Welfare, Counseling, Domestic Violence, Family Services, Food/Clothing Distribution, Senior Services, United Funds/United Ways, YMCA/YWCA/YMHA/YWHA, Youth Organizations

Contributions Analysis

Giving Priorities: Art and culture, civic and public affairs, and education.
Arts & Humanities: 25%. Supports programs which enable young people in low-income neighborhoods t participate in creative activities in their respective neighbothoods so far as such opportunities are either inadequate or non-existent.
Civic & Public Affairs: 50%. Supports selected civic organizations which provide leadership on issues of importance to Philadelphians. Also contributes to programs where significant Hunt employee involvement has been demonstrated. Unusual approaches to problems outside of the above priority areas such as research projects or public policy forums are also considered.
Education: 25%. Foundation places special emphasis on educational inititiatives which provide art-related educational programs to lower-income and/or educationally disadvantaged populations at the elementary and secondary levels, promote literacy, or contribute to curriculum development, specific skills training and/or educational innovation.
Note: Total contributions made in 1998.

Application Procedures

Initial Contact: brief letter or proposal
Application Requirements: name of organization and contact person; a description of organization and its programs; copy of current year budget and most recently audited financial statements; copy of IRS determination letter; NAA number, if organization has received designation as a Neighborhood Assistance Act organization; and if requesting project support, include description of project including objectives, methodology, budget, key staff, sources of funding, and expected results
Deadlines: March 15 and September 15
Decision Notification: at Contributions Committee meetings held twice a year, usually during April and October
Notes: Does not make contributions in response to telephone solicitations. Grantees are required to submit applications on an annual basis.

Restrictions

Company generally does not provide general support, endowment funds or building funds to schools, colleges or universities. However, grants may be made to both educational institutions and non-profit educational organizations for specific educational programs.
Support for national appeals is minimal. Contributions to fund-raising dinners, testimonials, and courtesy advertising strictly limited. Grants are not made to individuals or for religious, social, or political purposes. Grants for building and capital campaigns, general support for education and health care institutions, and endowments are made only in exceptional cases.
No telephone or fax solicitations.

Additional Information

Company's goal is to donate 3% of pretax profits to charitable organizations.
Favors applications that leverage company funds with monies from other sources. Encourages proposals for specific projects instead of general operating support.
In 1998, the company reported that the foundation is inactive.
The company only funds a project for three consecutive years. Organization must wait one year before reapplying for grants.

Corporate Officials

William Everett Chandler: senior vice president finance, secretary, chief financial officer B Chattanooga, TN 1943. ED University of Florida BSBA (1965); University of Florida (1966). PRIM CORP EMPL senior vice president finance, secretary, chief financial officer: Hunt Co. CORP AFFIL treasurer: Hunt Holdings Inc.; secretary: Hunt Graphics America Corp. NONPR AFFIL member: Financial Executives Institute.
Kathleen Essex: vice president-human resources PRIM CORP EMPL vice president-human resources: Hunt Manufacturing Co.
Donald L. Thompson: chairman, chief executive officer B 1941. ED University of Vermont (1962); State University of New Jersey (1971). PRIM CORP EMPL chairman, chief executive officer, president: Hunt Corp.

Giving Program Officials

William Everett Chandler: secretary B Chattanooga, TN 1943. ED University of Florida BSBA (1965); University of Florida (1966). PRIM CORP EMPL senior vice president finance, secretary, chief financial officer: Hunt Co. CORP AFFIL treasurer: Hunt Holdings Inc.; secretary: Hunt Graphics America Corp. NONPR AFFIL member: Financial Executives Institute.
Kathleen Essex: PRIM CORP EMPL vice president-human resources: Hunt Manufacturing Co.
Donald L. Thompson: B 1941. ED University of Vermont (1962); State University of New Jersey (1971). PRIM CORP EMPL chairman, chief executive officer, president: Hunt Corp.
Cheryl M. Walmsley: grant administrator

Grants Analysis

Disclosure Period: fiscal year ending November 30, 1999
Total Grants: $300,000
Number of Grants: 30
Average Grant: $2,000
Highest Grant: $20,000
Typical Range: $1,000 to $5,000
Note: Grants analysis provided by the co.

Recent Grants

Note: Grants derived from fiscal 1996 Form 990.

Arts & Humanities

4,000	Village of Arts and Humanities, Philadelphia, PA

Civic & Public Affairs

3,000	Philadelphia Futures, Philadelphia, PA
2,000	Brandywine Workshop, Philadelphia, PA
2,000	Print Club, Philadelphia, PA

Education

2,000	Settlement Music School, Philadelphia, PA

Health

2,000	AIDS Law Project, Philadelphia, PA

Social Services

9,000	United Way Southeastern Pennsylvania, Philadelphia, PA
4,000	Family Services, Philadelphia, PA

HUNT OIL CO.

Company Contact

Dallas, TX

Company Description

Employees: 1,900
SIC(s): 1311 Crude Petroleum & Natural Gas, 2911 Petroleum Refining.
Parent Company: Hunt Consolidated Inc.

Nonmonetary Support

Type: Donated Equipment; In-kind Services
Contact: Jim Oberwetter, Vice President Governmental and Public Affairs

Giving Contact

Jim Oberwetter, Vice President, Governmental & Public Affairs
Hunt Oil Co.
1445 Ross Ave.
Dallas, TX 75202-2785
Phone: (214)978-8000
Fax: (214)978-8888

Description
Organization Type: Corporate Giving Program
Giving Locations: headquarters area only.
Grant Types: General Support.

Financial Summary
Total Giving: Contributes through corporate direct giving program only.

Typical Recipients
Arts & Humanities: Arts & Humanities-General
Civic & Public Affairs: Civic & Public Affairs-General
Education: Education-General
Health: Health-General
Social Services: Social Services-General

Application Procedures
Initial Contact: letter of inquiry
Application Requirements: a description of organization, amount requested, purpose of funds sought, recently audited financial statement, and proof of tax-exempt status
Deadlines: None.

Corporate Officials
Ray Lee Hunt: chairman, chief executive officer, director B New York, NY 1943. ED Southern Methodist University BBA (1965). PRIM CORP EMPL chairman, chief executive officer, director: Hunt Oil Co. ADD CORP EMPL chairman, president, chief executive officer: Hunt Consolidated Inc. CORP AFFIL chairman, director: Yemen Hunt Oil Co.; director: PepsiCo; chairman, president, chief executive officer, director: RRH Corp.; director: Ergo Science Corp.; director: Halliburton Co.; director: Electronic Data Systems Corp. NONPR AFFIL director: American Petroleum Institute.
Gary Thomas Hurford: president, director B Woodson, TX 1936. ED University of Texas BS (1959). PRIM CORP EMPL president, director: Hunt Oil Co. ADD CORP EMPL president: Hunt Overseas Oil Inc.; president, chief executive officer, director: Yemen Hunt Oil Co. CORP AFFIL director: Nabors Industries Inc.
James Burnett Jennings: president B Temple, TX 1940. ED Del Mar College AA (1961); Trinity University BS (1963); Purdue University MS (1965); Cornell University (1967). PRIM CORP EMPL president: Hunt Oil Co. NONPR AFFIL member: Association International Petroleum Negotiators; member: Society Exploration Geophysicists; member: American Association Petroleum Geologists.
Thomas E. Meurer: senior vice president administration B 1941. ED University of Washington BA (1963). PRIM CORP EMPL senior vice president administration: Hunt Oil Co. ADD CORP EMPL vice president: Hunt Investment Corp. CORP AFFIL director: Hunt Overseas Oil Inc.; director: Yemen Hunt Oil Co.

Giving Program Officials
Jim Oberwetter: PRIM CORP EMPL vice president public & government affairs: Hunt Oil Co.

Huntington Bancshares Inc.

Company Contact
Huntington Center
41 South High Street, 34th Floor
Columbus, OH 43287
Web: http://www.huntington.com

Company Description
Assets: US$20,254,600,000
Employees: 7,551
SIC(s): 6021 National Commercial Banks, 6022 State Commercial Banks, 6035 Federal Savings Institutions, 6712 Bank Holding Companies.

Nonmonetary Support
Type: Cause-related Marketing & Promotion; Donated Equipment; In-kind Services; Loaned Employees; Loaned Executives

Corporate Sponsorship
Type: Arts & cultural events; Other

Giving Contact
Dorothy Brownley, Executive Vice President, Director of Corporate & Government Relations
Phone: (614)480-4531

Description
Organization Type: Corporate Giving Program
Giving Locations: headquarters area only; States where company has business locations.
Grant Types: Award, Capital, Challenge, Emergency, Endowment, Multiyear/Continuing Support, Operating Expenses, Professorship, Project, Research, Scholarship, Seed Money.

Financial Summary
Total Giving: $3,500,000 (1997). Note: Contributes through corporate direct giving program only. Total giving is approximately 2% of Huntington's annual pre-tax earnings.

Typical Recipients
Arts & Humanities: Arts Associations & Councils, Arts Institutes, Ballet, Ethnic & Folk Arts, Arts & Humanities-General, Libraries, Museums/Galleries, Opera, Performing Arts, Theater, Visual Arts
Civic & Public Affairs: African American Affairs, Asian American Affairs, Business/Free Enterprise, Chambers of Commerce, Community Foundations, Economic Development, Employment/Job Training, Environmental Affairs (Conservation), Ethnic Organizations, Civic & Public Affairs-General, Housing, Inner-City Development, Minority Business, Nonprofit Management, Parades/Festivals, Philanthropic Organizations, Urban & Community Affairs, Women's Affairs, Zoos/Aquariums
Education: Agricultural Education, Business Education, Business-School Partnerships, Colleges & Universities, Community & Junior Colleges, Economic Education, Elementary Education (Private), Education-General, Health & Physical Education, International Exchange, International Studies, Minority Education, Science/Mathematics Education, Student Aid, Vocational & Technical Education
Health: Alzheimers Disease, Arthritis, Cancer, Children's Health/Hospitals, Eyes/Blindness, Health-General, Geriatric Health, Heart, Hospices, Hospitals, Hospitals (University Affiliated), Long-Term Care, Medical Research, Multiple Sclerosis, Respiratory, Speech & Hearing
International: International Affairs, International Development, Trade
Religion: Jewish Causes
Science: Science-General, Science Museums
Social Services: Animal Protection, Camps, Homes, Shelters/Homelessness, Social Services-General, United Funds/United Ways, Volunteer Services, Youth Organizations

Application Procedures
Initial Contact: Send a brief letter of inquiry.
Application Requirements: Include a description of organization, amount requested, purpose of funds sought, recently audited financial statement, and proof of tax-exempt status.
Deadlines: None. Company prefers to receive requests in summer for fall consideration of the following year's budget.

Restrictions
Does not support individuals, religious organizations for sectarian purposes, political or lobbying groups, or organizations outside operating areas.

Corporate Officials
Peter E. Geier: vice chairman, chief executive officer, director B Richmond, IN 1957. ED Purdue University (1979); Butler University (1983). PRIM CORP EMPL vice chairman: Huntington Bankcshares ADD CORP EMPL president: The Huntington National Bank. CORP AFFIL director: Cyber Mark LLC. NONPR AFFIL director: Childrens Hospital Inc.
Ron J. Seiffert: vice chairman B Akron, OH 1957. ED Washington University (1979). PRIM CORP EMPL vice chairman: Huntington Bancshares. CORP AFFIL chief executive officer: Huntington Leasing Co.; vice chairman: Huntington National Bank. NONPR AFFIL trustee: Columbus Museum Art; trustee: Ohio Dominican College; trustee: Cleveland State University.
Frank Wobst: chairman, chief executive officer, director B Dresden, Germany 1933. ED University of Erlangen (1956); University of Goettingen (1958); Rutgers University (1964). PRIM CORP EMPL chairman, chief executive officer, director: Huntington Bancshares. CORP AFFIL director: Midland Mutual Life Insurance Co.; member: Robert Morris Associates; chairman: Huntington Trust Co. NONPR AFFIL member: Greater Columbus Chamber of Commerce; member: Newcomen Society; member: American Institute Banking; member: Association Reserve City Bankers. CLUB AFFIL Sciotto Country Club.

Grants Analysis
Disclosure Period: calendar year ending

IBP

Company Contact
Dakota City, NE
Web: http://www.ibpinc.com

Company Description
Revenue: US$12,848,600,000
Employees: 30,000
Fortune Rank: 125, per FORTUNE Magazine's list of 500 Largest U.S. Corporations (1999).
FF 125
SIC(s): 2011 Meat Packing Plants.

Nonmonetary Support
Type: Donated Equipment; Donated Products; Loaned Executives

IBP Foundation

Giving Contact
Don Willoughby, Manager, Government, Community; Executive Director Foundation
PO Box 515
Dakota City, NE 68731
Phone: (402)494-2061
Fax: (402)241-2969

Description
Founded: 1979
EIN: 476014039
Organization Type: Corporate Foundation
Giving Locations: ID: Boise; IL: Joslin; IN: Logansport; IA: Columbus Junction; KS: Emporia; MN: Luverne; NE: Dakota City; TX: Amarillo; WA: Pasco
Grant Types: Award, Capital, Challenge, General Support.

Financial Summary
Total Giving: $256,035 (1999 approx); $380,807 (1998); $243,360 (1996)
Giving Analysis: Giving for 1998 includes: foundation ($283,307); foundation grants to United Way ($97,500)

Assets: $3,462,324 (1998); $3,423,717 (1996); $3,557,298 (1995)
Gifts Received: $1,000,000 (1994). Note: In 1994, substantial contributions were received from IBP.

Typical Recipients

Arts & Humanities: Libraries, Public Broadcasting
Civic & Public Affairs: Native American Affairs, Philanthropic Organizations, Professional & Trade Associations, Rural Affairs, Safety, Urban & Community Affairs
Education: Community & Junior Colleges, Elementary Education (Public), Education-General, Preschool Education, Public Education (Precollege), Secondary Education (Public)
Health: Clinics/Medical Centers, Emergency/Ambulance Services, Hospitals, Prenatal Health Issues
Religion: Churches, Religious Welfare
Social Services: Community Service Organizations, Recreation & Athletics, United Funds/United Ways, Youth Organizations

Contributions Analysis

Giving Priorities: Primary support for the United Way, community services, and health organizations.
Arts & Humanities: 9%. Supports libraries and museums.
Civic & Public Affairs: 10%. Supports foundations, community groups, and fire departments.
Education: 5%. Funds colleges, a school district, and educational activities.
Health: 21%. Major support to a health clinic and a hospital.
Social Services: 55%. Majority of support to United Ways in various communities and to the Crittendon Center in Iowa, which is a social services center supporting adoption, pregnancy counseling and family and child counseling.
Note: Total contributions made in 1998.

Application Procedures

Initial Contact: Send a full proposal. Include a description of organization, amount requested, purpose of funds sought, recently audited financial statement, and proof of tax-exempt status.
Deadlines: None.

Additional Information

Publications: Application Form

Corporate Officials

Robert L. Peterson: chairman, chief executive officer, director B NE 1932. ED University of Nebraska. PRIM CORP EMPL chairman, chief executive officer, director: IBP. CLUB AFFIL Sioux City Country Club.
Larry Shipley: chief financial officer PRIM CORP EMPL chief financial officer: IBP.

Foundation Officials

Donald E. Willoughby: executive director PRIM CORP EMPL manager government & industry affairs: IBP.

Grants Analysis

Disclosure Period: calendar year ending 1998
Total Grants: $283,307*
Number of Grants: 28
Average Grant: $6,789*
Highest Grant: $100,000
Typical Range: $1,000 to $10,000
***Note:** Giving excludes United Way. Average grant figure excludes two highest grantss.

Recent Grants

Note: Grants derived from 1997 Form 990.

Arts & Humanities

1,200	Finney County Public Library, Garden City, KS
1,000	KWIT Radio Station, Sioux City, IA
500	Friends of Sioux City Public Library, Sioux City, IA

Civic & Public Affairs

7,000	American Meat Association
2,000	Safer Foundation, Joslin, IL
2,000	Siouxland Diversity Workshop, Sioux City, IA
1,000	Emmerson Volunteer Fire Department, Emmerson, NE
1,000	Madison County Agricultural Society, Madison, NE
1,000	Vision 2000 Group, Perry, IA

Education

30,000	Success by Six
5,000	United National Collegiate Meat Animal Evaluation Contest
2,000	Des Moines Area Community College, Ankeny, IA
1,500	Lewis and Clark Elementary, South Sioux City, NE
1,500	South Sioux City Community Schools, South Sioux City, NE
1,000	Hawkeye Community College
1,000	Iowa Central Community College, Fort Dodge, IA
1,000	Schribner-Snyder High schools, Schribner, NE
1,000	Western Iowa Tech Community College, Sioux City, IA

Health

5,000	Homer Fire and Rescue, Homer, NE
1,000	Hospital Foundation of Crawford County, Denison, IA
1,000	Perry Free Medical Clinic, Perry, IA
500	Stork's Nest of Siouxland

Religion

10,000	Emmaus Mission Center, Logansport, IN
500	St. Thomas Episcopal Church, Sioux City, IA

Social Services

250,000	Boys and Girls Home, Sioux City, IA
86,500	United Way
21,000	Lexington Recreation Center, Lexington, NE
2,000	Cardinal Little League, South Sioux City, NE
1,000	Boyer Fields, Denison, IA
500	Central Plains Center for Services, Broken Bow, NE

IDAHO POWER CO.

Company Contact

Boise, ID

Company Description

Employees: 1,626
SIC(s): 4911 Electric Services.

Nonmonetary Support

Type: Donated Equipment
Volunteer Programs: Co. supports employee volunteerism and notifies employees of community events and projects.

Giving Contact

Fran Martin, Executive Assistant
Idaho Power Corporate Contributions Committee
1221 Idaho Street
PO Box 70
Boise, ID 83707
Phone: (208)388-2530

Description

Organization Type: Corporate Giving Program
Giving Locations: ID: Southern Idaho; OR: Eastern Oregon headquarters and operating communities.
Grant Types: Capital, General Support, Multiyear/Continuing Support, Operating Expenses.

Financial Summary

Total Giving: $600,000 (2000 approx); $600,000 (1999 approx); $562,000 (1998)

Typical Recipients

Arts & Humanities: Community Arts, Arts & Humanities-General, Music, Performing Arts, Public Broadcasting
Civic & Public Affairs: Chambers of Commerce, Employment/Job Training, Civic & Public Affairs-General, Public Policy
Education: Colleges & Universities, Education-General
Environment: Wildlife Protection
Health: Health-General
Social Services: Animal Protection, Child Welfare, Community Service Organizations, Scouts, Social Services-General, United Funds/United Ways, YMCA/YWCA/YMHA/YWHA, Youth Organizations

Contributions Analysis

Giving Priorities: Arts, public affairs, education, and social services.
Arts & Humanities: Funds historic preservation and cultural centers.
Civic & Public Affairs: Supports housing, animal welfare, and community recreation.
Social Services: The Idaho Ronald McDonald House and social services organizations receive funding.

Application Procedures

Initial Contact: send a brief letter of inquiry and a full proposal
Application Requirements: a description of organization, amount requested, purpose of funds sought, recently audited financial statement, and proof of tax-exempt status
Deadlines: None.

Restrictions

Does not support individuals, religious organizations for sectarian purposes, political or lobbying groups, or organizations outside operating areas.

Additional Information

Publications: Application; Informational Brochure

Corporate Officials

J. LaMont Keen: vice president, chief financial officer B Burley, ID 1952. ED College of Idaho (1974). PRIM CORP EMPL vice president, chief financial officer: Idaho Power Co. CORP AFFIL member finance committee: Northwest Electric Light & Power Association; director: Security Offshore Insurance Ltd.; vice president, treasurer, director: ID Energy Research Co.
Joseph W. Marshall: chairman, chief executive officer B Twin Falls, ID 1938. ED United States Naval Academy (1961). PRIM CORP EMPL chairman, chief executive officer: Idaho Power Co. NONPR AFFIL trustee: Albertson College Idaho; trustee: Saint Alphonsus Regional Medical Center.
Jan Packwood: president, chief operating officer PRIM CORP EMPL president, chief operating officer: Idaho Power Co.

Grants Analysis

Disclosure Period: calendar year ending
Typical Range: $1,000 to $2,500

Recent Grants

Note: Grants derived from 1998 Form 990.

Arts & Humanities

Boise Philharmonic, Boise, ID
IDA Public Television, Boise, ID

Civic & Public Affairs

IDA Association for Affirmative Action, Boise, ID

Education

IDA and Eastern Oregon Colleges and University, OR

Environment

Peregrine Fund, Boise, ID

Social Services

Boy Scouts of America, Boise, ID
Girl Scouts of America, Boise, ID
IDA Humane Society, Boise, ID
United Way, Boise, ID
YMCA, Boise, ID

IKON OFFICE SOLUTIONS, INC.

Company Contact

Malvern, PA
Web: http://www.ikon.com

Company Description

Former Name: Alco Standard Corp.
Revenue: US$5,522,000,000 (1999)
Employees: 39,400 (1999)
Fortune Rank: 302, per FORTUNE Magazine's list of 500 Largest U.S. Corporations (1999).
FF 302
SIC(s): 5044 Office Equipment, 7359 Equipment Rental & Leasing Nec.

Operating Locations

Includes plant and division locations.

Corporate Sponsorship

Type: Arts & cultural events; Music & entertainment events
Contact: Beth Sexton, Vice President Human Resources

IKON Office Solutions Foundation, Inc.

Giving Contact

Carol Halpin, Executive Assistant
IKON Office Solutions, Inc.
Valley Forge, PA

Description

EIN: 237378726
Organization Type: Corporate Foundation
Giving Locations: PA: Philadelphia including greater metropolitan area nationally.
Grant Types: Employee Matching Gifts, General Support.
Note: Employee matching gift ratio: 1 to 1 to higher education, schools, public broadcasting, and the AMR Red Cross Disaster Relief Fund; the foundation does not otherwise make contributions to higher education and schools.

Giving Philosophy

'The Foundation makes contributions to charitable, educational, scientific and other similar non-profit organizations which have been recognized as tax exempt organizations under Section 501(c)(3) of the Internal Revenue Code. All of the financial support of IKON Office Solutions Foundation is provided by IKON Office Solutions, Inc., and the Foundation makes contributions consistent with IKON Office Solution, Inc.'s views of its responsibilities.
'Since IKON Office Solutions, Inc. operates in a very large number of communities and geographical locations, the Foundation provides support to IKON Office Solutions marketplaces by making contributions to qualified organizations in their communities which have been identified by the senior management of the marketplace region.
'The Foundation also acts in support of the IKON Office Solutions, Inc.'s matching gift program, making contributions (subject to certain limits) equal to the contributions of IKON Office Solution's employees to universities, colleges, schools, public broadcasting, and the American Red Cross Disaster Relief Fund. Because of the matching gift program, the Foundation does not otherwise make contributions to universities, colleges and schools.' *IKON Office Solutions Foundation, Inc. Contribution Guidelines*

Financial Summary

Total Giving: $500,000 (1999 approx); $500,000 (1998 approx); $500,000 (1996). Note: Contributes through corporate direct giving program and foundation.
Assets: $4,365,320 (1996); $3,251,938 (1994); $3,514,942 (1993)
Gifts Received: $450,000 (1996); $300,000 (1994). Note: Foundation receives contributions from IKON Office Solutions, Inc.

Typical Recipients

Arts & Humanities: Arts Associations & Councils, Arts Institutes, Museums/Galleries, Music, Opera, Public Broadcasting, Theater
Civic & Public Affairs: African American Affairs, Chambers of Commerce, Civil Rights, Community Foundations, Economic Development, Employment/Job Training, Municipalities/Towns, Native American Affairs, Philanthropic Organizations, Professional & Trade Associations, Public Policy, Urban & Community Affairs, Women's Affairs, Zoos/Aquariums
Education: Arts/Humanities Education, Colleges & Universities, Education Funds, Environmental Education, Education-General, Private Education (Precollege), Public Education (Precollege), Special Education, Student Aid
Environment: Environment-General, Resource Conservation
Health: AIDS/HIV, Alzheimers Disease, Cancer, Children's Health/Hospitals, Emergency/Ambulance Services, Health Funds, Health Organizations, Heart, Hospitals, Multiple Sclerosis, Nursing Services, Prenatal Health Issues, Single-Disease Health Associations
International: International Affairs, International Peace & Security Issues
Religion: Churches, Jewish Causes, Religious Organizations, Religious Welfare
Science: Science Museums, Scientific Centers & Institutes, Scientific Organizations
Social Services: Animal Protection, Big Brother/Big Sister, Camps, Community Centers, Community Service Organizations, Crime Prevention, Emergency Relief, Recreation & Athletics, Scouts, Special Olympics, Substance Abuse, United Funds/United Ways, YMCA/YWCA/YMHA/YWHA, Youth Organizations

Contributions Analysis

Giving Priorities: Colleges and universities, single disease health associations, private education and United Way chapters.
Arts & Humanities: 5% to 10%. Supports museums, theaters, arts institutes, and arts associations in the Philadelphia area.
Civic & Public Affairs: About 10%. Support goes to zoological societies, other philanthropic organizations, women's issues, and civil rights.
Education: 20% to 25%. Majority of support goes to matching gifts to universities and colleges. The remainder goes directly to private schools and education funds.
Health: 10% to 15%. Support includes single-disease organizations, nurses associations, Easter Seals, and hospitals.
Social Services: About 45% of total contributions. Primarily supports United Way chapters across the country. The remainder supports youth organizations and community service groups.

Application Procedures

Initial Contact: written proposal
Application Requirements: a description of organization, amount requested, purpose of funds sought, recently audited financial statement, and proof of tax-exempt status
Deadlines: None.

Additional Information

The company was originally known as Alco Standard Corp.
The foundation only contributes to colleges, universities, schools, and public broadcasting through their matching fund program.

Foundation Officials

Oliver Gordon Brewer, Jr.: vice president finance, treasurer B Winston-Salem, NC 1936. ED Guilford College BA (1960); Harvard University Graduate School of Business Administration AMP (1983). PRIM CORP EMPL vice president finance, treasurer: IKON Office Solutions, Inc. CORP AFFIL director: Corp. Insurance & Reinsurance Co. Ltd.; director: Sunsource LP.

Grants Analysis

Disclosure Period: calendar year ending 1996
Total Grants: $522,684
Number of Grants: 1,161
Average Grant: $450
Highest Grant: $35,679
Typical Range: $25 to $1,000

Recent Grants

Note: Grants derived from 1998 Form 990.

Arts & Humanities

7,500	Peoples Light & Theatre C, Malvern, PA
1,000	WQED Pittsburgh, Pittsburgh, PA
500	Philadelphia Singers, Philadelphia, PA

Civic & Public Affairs

12,500	Zoological Society of Philadelphia, Philadelphia, PA
3,000	Zoological Society of Philadelphia, Philadelphia, PA
2,500	Arapahoe House, Thornton, CO
1,500	Human Resource Development, Kansas City, MO
1,000	City of Hurricane, Hurricane, WV
1,000	Community Involvement Programs, Minneapolis, MN

Education

26,340	National Merit Scholarship, Evanston, IL
8,000	University of Nebraska, Lincoln, NE
3,000	Case Western Reserve, Cleveland, OH
2,720	The Rhode Island School for the Deaf, Providence, RI
1,000	Grand View College, Des Moines, IA

Health

5,500	American Cancer Society, Valley Forge, PA
5,000	March of Dimes Birth Defects, Valley Forge, PA
3,136	American Cancer Society, Valley Forge, PA
3,000	Miami Valley Health Foundation, Dayton, OH
3,000	Missouri Easter Seal Society, St. Louis, MO

2,785	AIDS Cycle, Inc., Jefferson City, MO
2,000	American Cancer Society, Valley Forge, PA
2,000	Children's Health Care, St. Paul, MN
1,846	March of Dimes Birth Defects, Valley Forge, PA
1,000	Missouri Easter Seal Society, St. Louis, MO
1,000	National Multiple Scleros, Kansas City, MO
500	Leukemia Society of America, Valley Forge, PA
500	National Hemophilia Foundation, Pittsburgh, PA
Social Services	
29,226	United Way of Southeastern Pennsylvania, Philadelphia, PA
10,000	Police Athletic League, San Francisco, CA
6,535	United Way of the Capital Area, Hartford, CT
6,410	United Way of Massachusetts, Boston, MA
5,000	Police Athletic League, San Francisco, CA
4,500	Boy Scouts of America, Kansas City, MO
3,400	Boy Scouts of America, Philadelphia, PA
2,905	United Way of Central Massachusettss, Worcester, MA
2,575	United Way of Milford, Milford, CT
2,000	United Way of Greater St. Louis, St. Louis, MO
1,500	United Way Inc., Portland, OR
1,350	United Way of Greater St. Louis, St. Louis, MO
1,140	United Way of Buffalo & Erie County, Buffalo, NY
1,070	United Way of the Central Massachusetts, Worcester, MA
1,000	John West Hereford Boys Club
1,000	Opportunities, Chicago, IL
1,000	Philadelphia Tennis Patrons, Philadelphia, PA
1,000	Young Men's Christian, Charleston, WV
500	Big Brothers Big Sisters, Kansas City, MO

ILLINOIS POWER CO.

Company Contact

Decatur, IL
Web: http://www.illinova.com

Company Description

Assets: US$5,712,800,000
Employees: 3,635
SIC(s): 4911 Electric Services, 4923 Gas Transmission & Distribution.
Parent Company: Illinova Corp.

Nonmonetary Support

Value: $100,000 (1996); $100,000 (1994); $150,000 (1993)
Type: Donated Equipment; In-kind Services; Loaned Employees

Corporate Sponsorship

Type: Festivals/fairs

Giving Contact

Tom Mollet, Community Relations Specialist
Illinois Power Co.
500 South 27th Street
PO Box 511
Decatur, IL 62525
Phone: (217)424-6600
Fax: (217)424-7390

Description

Organization Type: Corporate Giving Program
Giving Locations: locally only.
Grant Types: Award, General Support, Multiyear/Continuing Support, Operating Expenses, Scholarship.

Giving Philosophy

'The company is dedicated to supporting organizations and programs which improve the overall quality of life, both in the communities IP serves and in society at large. Because funds are limited, Illinois Power must carefully evaluate each request to determine eligibility and compliance with company guidelines and available funds. Even if we can't say yes to your request for financial aid, sometimes we can find other ways to help promote or assist your programs. Illinois Power is strongly committed to providing quality service to its customers. That includes helping a broad variety of community service agencies.' Illinois Power Company Contributions Policy and Grant Guidelines

Financial Summary

Total Giving: $800,000 (2000 approx); $800,000 (1999 approx); $700,000 (1998 approx). Note: Contributes through corporate direct giving program only.

Typical Recipients

Arts & Humanities: Performing Arts, Public Broadcasting
Civic & Public Affairs: Economic Development, Urban & Community Affairs
Education: Colleges & Universities, Faculty Development, Education-General, Minority Education, Public Education (Precollege), Science/Mathematics Education, Secondary Education (Public)
Environment: Environment-General
Social Services: Community Service Organizations, United Funds/United Ways, Volunteer Services

Contributions Analysis

Civic & Public Affairs: 35% to 40%. Emphasis on minority affairs, environmental concerns, and economic development organizations.
Education: 20% to 25%. Priorities are precollegiate education.
Social Services: 35% to 40%. Primarily supports united funds and community services.

Application Procedures

Initial Contact: request guidelines
Application Requirements: goals, objectives, and brief historical a description of organization; total budget or project cost and the planned use of the sum requested; list of current contributors, particularly companies and foundations; explanation of relationships to united fund organizations or government agencies; list of officers and board members; proof of tax-exempt status; most recent audited financial statement; suggestions on how company employees can participate as volunteers; and anticipated recognition of company as a result of contribution
Deadlines: None.
Evaluative Criteria: presence in service territory, program measurable in some degree so that impact can be assessed, and opportunities for employees to volunteer time and talent to enhance the effort

Restrictions

The company does not offer support to individuals; organizations not classified as 501(c)(3); political organizations or campaigns; religious organizations for sectarian purposes; operating expenses of organizations supported by United Funds, other than through United Funds; government-supported agencies or organizations; single-disease research programs; labor organizations; fraternal organizations, social clubs, athletic teams, veterans organizations, or similar groups; organizations that limit participation by race, color, creed, religion, or nationality; organizations, projects, or programs whose activities are mainly international; courtesy or goodwill advertising; or telephone solicitation. or nationality; organizations, projects, or programs whose activities are mainly international; courtesy or goodwill advertising; or telephone solicitation.

Additional Information

Company reports that giving is decentralized as much as possible, and decisions are made by local offices.
Publications: Contributions Policy; Grants Guidelines

Corporate Officials

Larry F. Altenbaumer: senior vice president, chief financial officer, corporate secretary B Centralia, IL 1948. ED University of Illinois BSEE (1970). PRIM CORP EMPL senior vice president, chief financial officer: Illinois Power Co. CORP AFFIL treasurer, chief financial officer, controller: Illinova Corp.
Charles Edward Bayless: chairman, president, chief executive officer, director B Dunbar, WV 1942. ED West Virginia Institute of Technology BSEE (1968); West Virginia University MSEE (1971); West Virginia University JD (1972); University of Michigan MBA (1977). PRIM CORP EMPL chairman, president, chief executive officer, director: Illinova Corp. CORP AFFIL chairman, director: Illinova Generating Co.; chairman: Illinois Energy Partners; chairman, president, chief executive officer: Illinois Power Co. NONPR AFFIL member: American Bar Association; member finance committee: Edison Electric Institute.
David Wayne Butts: senior vice president B Decatur, IL 1955. ED General Motors Institute BSEE (1978); University of Illinois MBA (1986). PRIM CORP EMPL senior vice president: Illinois Power Co. ADD CORP EMPL president: Illinova Energy Partners. CORP AFFIL director: First American Bank.
Paul Louis Lang: vice president B Pittsburgh, PA 1940. ED Carnegie Mellon University BSEE (1962); Indiana University MSBA (1973). PRIM CORP EMPL vice president: Illinois Power Co. NONPR AFFIL member: American Gas Association.
Leah Manning Setzner: vice president, general counsel, corporate secretary B Hettinger, ND 1948. ED University of North Dakota (1970); University of Minnesota JD (1977). PRIM CORP EMPL vice president, general counsel, corporate secretary: Illinois Power Co. CORP AFFIL secretary, general couns: Illinova Corp.

Grants Analysis

Disclosure Period: calendar year ending
Typical Range: $100 to $2,500

ILLINOIS TOOL WORKS, INC.

Company Contact

3600 W. Lake Ave.
Glenview, IL 60025-5811
Phone: (847)724-7500
Fax: (847)657-4392
Web: http://www.itwinc.com

Company Description

Acquired: Premark International (1999).
Revenue: US$9,333,200,000 (1999)
Profit: US$841,100,000 (1999)
Employees: 52,800 (1999)
Fortune Rank: 181, per FORTUNE Magazine's list of 500 Largest U.S. Corporations (1999).
FF 181
SIC(s): 2899 Chemical Preparations Nec, 3082 Unsupported Plastics Profile Shapes, 3089 Plastics Products Nec, 3429 Hardware Nec.

SUBSIDIARY COMPANIES

IL: Premark International Inc., Deerfield

Nonmonetary Support

Type: Donated Equipment; In-kind Services

Corporate Sponsorship

Value: $500,000
Type: Arts & cultural events

Illinois Tool Works Foundation

Giving Contact

Mary Ann Mallahan, Manager, Community Relations
Illinois Tool Works Foundation
3600 West Lake Avenue
Glenview, IL 60025
Phone: (847)657-4092
Fax: (847)657-4505

Description

EIN: 366087160
Organization Type: Corporate Foundation
Giving Locations: IL principally near operating locations and to national organizations.
Grant Types: Capital, Employee Matching Gifts, General Support, Multiyear/Continuing Support, Scholarship.
Note: Employee matching gift ratio: 3 to 1 for donations to nonprofit charitable organisation not already sponsored by company.

Financial Summary

Total Giving: $4,500,000 (fiscal year ending February 28, 2000 approx); $4,048,316 (fiscal 1999); $4,000,000 (fiscal 1998 approx)
Giving Analysis: Giving for fiscal 1999 includes: foundation matching gifts ($2,153,608); foundation ($1,324,253); foundation grants to United Way ($570,455)
Assets: $13,465,701 (fiscal 1999); $14,000,000 (fiscal 1996 approx); $12,000,000 (fiscal 1995 approx)

Typical Recipients

Arts & Humanities: Arts Associations & Councils, Arts Festivals, Arts Institutes, Dance, Historic Preservation, History & Archaeology, Libraries, Museums/Galleries, Music, Opera, Performing Arts, Public Broadcasting, Theater
Civic & Public Affairs: Business/Free Enterprise, Civil Rights, Clubs, Economic Development, Employment/Job Training, Housing, Law & Justice, Legal Aid, Nonprofit Management, Professional & Trade Associations, Public Policy, Urban & Community Affairs, Women's Affairs, Zoos/Aquariums
Education: Business Education, Colleges & Universities, Community & Junior Colleges, Economic Education, Education Associations, Education Funds, Engineering/Technological Education, Education-General, Literacy, Minority Education, Private Education (Precollege), Science/Mathematics Education, Student Aid
Health: Children's Health/Hospitals, Clinics/Medical Centers, Heart, Hospitals, Medical Rehabilitation, Medical Research, Mental Health, Nursing Services
Religion: Religious Welfare
Science: Observatories & Planetariums, Science Exhibits & Fairs, Science Museums, Scientific Centers & Institutes
Social Services: Child Welfare, Family Planning, Family Services, Homes, People with Disabilities, Scouts, Senior Services, Substance Abuse, United Funds/United Ways, Volunteer Services, YMCA/YWCA/YMHA/YWHA, Youth Organizations

Contributions Analysis

Giving Priorities: Social welfare, education, civic interests, and the arts.
Arts & Humanities: 5% to 10%. Primarily supports the Chicago Symphony Orchestra, Newberry Library, and the Shedd Aquarium. Museums, theater, music, dance, and public broadcasting also receive funding.
Civic & Public Affairs: 10% to 15%. Supports the Commerical Club of Chicago Civic Committee. Also makes matching grants to various civic organizations. Other interests include economic development, government improvement, professional and business organizations, and zoos.
Education: 20% to 25%. Colleges and universities receive the majority of funds, largely in the form of matching grants. Other interests include education associations and funds and student aid.
Health: 5% to 10%. Supports hospitals and medical centers.
Religion: 25% to 30%. Supports the Crusade of Mercy.
Science: Less than 5%. Supports museums.
Social Services: 20% to 25%. Primarily supports united funds; youth organizations also receive substantial support. Other interests include child welfare, volunteer services, and employment services.
Note: Total contributions made in 1999.

Application Procedures

Initial Contact: Send a brief letter or proposal.
Application Requirements: Provide a description of organization; amount requested and purpose of funds sought; recently audited financial statement; and proof of tax-exempt status.
Deadlines: None.

Corporate Officials

W. James Farrell: chairman, chief executive officer B New York, NY 1942. ED University of Detroit BA (1965). PRIM CORP EMPL chairman, chief executive officer: IL Tool Works Inc. CORP AFFIL director: Quaker Oats Co.; director: Sears, Roebuck & Co.; director: Morton International Inc.; director: Premark International Inc.

Foundation Officials

John Carpin: director
Stewart Skinner Hudnut: director B Cincinnati, OH 1939. ED Princeton University AB (1961); Oxford University JD (1962); Harvard University JD (1965); Pace University (1991). PRIM CORP EMPL senior vice president, general counsel, secretary: Illinois Tool Works, Inc. NONPR AFFIL member: Illinois Bar Association; member: Phi Beta Kappa; member: American Bar Association; director: Guild Lyric Opera Chicago.
Michael Lynch: director

Grants Analysis

Disclosure Period: fiscal year ending February 28, 1999
Total Grants: $1,324,253*
Number of Grants: 91
Average Grant: $14,552
Highest Grant: $200,000
Typical Range: $5,000 to $20,000
***Note:** Giving excludes United Way and matching gifts.

Recent Grants

Note: Grants derived from fiscal 1997 Form 990.

Arts & Humanities

33,334	Chicago Children's Museum, Chicago, IL
25,000	Chicago Symphony Orchestra, Chicago, IL
25,000	Lyric Opera, Chicago, IL
20,000	Art Institute, Chicago, IL
15,000	Art Institute, Chicago, IL
15,000	Chicago Symphony Orchestra, Chicago, IL
10,000	Hubbard Street Dance Company, Chicago, IL
10,000	Ravinia Festival, Highland Park, IL
5,000	Chicago Historical Society, Chicago, IL
5,000	Lyric Opera, Chicago, IL
5,000	Newberry Library, Chicago, IL
5,000	North Shore Center for the Performing Arts in Skokie, Chicago, IL

Civic & Public Affairs

50,000	Civic Committee of the Commercial Club, Chicago, IL
10,000	Lincoln Park Zoological Society, Chicago, IL
6,000	Metropolitan Planning Council, Chicago, IL
5,000	Brookfield Zoo, Brookfield, IL

Education

96,400	Citizens Scholarship Foundation of America, Saint Peter, MN
20,000	Northwestern University, Evanston, IL
20,000	United Negro College Fund, New York, NY
19,587	National Merit Scholarship Corporation, Evanston, IL
15,000	Harvard School, Chicago, IL
15,000	Junior Achievement, Chicago, IL
10,000	Citizens Scholarship Foundation of America, Saint Peter, MN
5,000	DePaul University, Chicago, IL
5,000	Midtown Educational Foundation, Chicago, IL
5,000	Midtown Educational Foundation, Chicago, IL
5,000	Roosevelt University, Chicago, IL
5,000	University of Illinois Champaign, Champaign, IL

Health

20,000	Northwestern Memorial Foundation, Chicago, IL
20,000	Rush Presbyterian-St. Luke's Medical Center, Chicago, IL
10,000	Evanston Hospital Corporation, Evanston, IL
5,000	American Heart Association, Chicago, IL
5,000	Lutheran General Children's Hospital, Chicago, IL

Science

200,000	Museum of Science and Industry, Chicago, IL
20,000	Field Museum of Natural History, Chicago, IL
15,000	Center for Science and Industry, Toledo, OH
5,000	Adler Planetarium, Chicago, IL
5,000	Field Museum of Natural History, Chicago, IL
5,000	Museum of Science and Industry, Chicago, IL

Social Services

265,000	United Way Crusade of Mercy, Chicago, IL
31,000	United Way Fox Cities
22,000	Chicago Youth Centers, Chicago, IL
20,000	United Way, Elgin, IL
20,000	United Way, Troy, OH
15,000	Metropolitan Family Services, Chicago, IL
11,000	United Way Central Naugatuck Valley, Waterbury, CT
10,000	Chicago Youth Centers, Chicago, IL
5,000	Boys and Girls Clubs of America, Chicago, IL
5,000	Girl Scouts of America, Chicago, IL
5,000	United Way Will County, Joliet, IL

Independent Stave Co.

Company Contact

Lebanon, MO

Web: http://cooperage.com

Company Description

Employees: 500
SIC(s): 2429 Special Product Sawmills Nec, 2449 Wood Containers Nec, 2499 Wood Products Nec.

Corporate Sponsorship

Type: Music & entertainment events

Boswell Foundation, Inc.

Giving Contact

Paul Walker, Secretary
Boswell Foundation, Inc.
PO Box 104
Lebanon, MO 65536
Phone: (417)588-4151
Fax: (417)588-3344

Description

Founded: 1985
EIN: 431409051
Organization Type: Corporate Foundation
Giving Locations: FL: Palm Beach; MO: Lebanon nationally.
Grant Types: Capital, General Support, Research.

Financial Summary

Total Giving: $863,656 (fiscal year ending November 30, 1997); $1,220,551 (fiscal 1996); $470,919 (fiscal 1995). Note: Contributes through foundation only.
Assets: $82,043 (fiscal 1997); $33,572 (fiscal 1996); $116,565 (fiscal 1995)
Gifts Received: $822,500 (fiscal 1997); $1,070,780 (fiscal 1996); $499,970 (fiscal 1995). Note: Contributions are received from Independent Stave Co., Amie Boswell Foundation, Johnathan Boswell Foundation, Lois K. Boswell Charitable Lead Trust, Joe Boswell Foundation, and Julie Boswell Foundation.

Typical Recipients

Arts & Humanities: Film & Video, Arts & Humanities-General, Music
Civic & Public Affairs: Community Foundations, Civic & Public Affairs-General, Housing, Zoos/ Aquariums
Education: Business Education, Education-General, Medical Education, Private Education (Precollege), Public Education (Precollege)
Environment: Wildlife Protection
Health: Arthritis, Cancer, Public Health, Single-Disease Health Associations
International: International Environmental Issues
Religion: Churches, Jewish Causes, Ministries, Religious Welfare, Social/Policy Issues
Science: Science Museums
Social Services: Animal Protection, Child Welfare, Community Service Organizations, Family Planning, Family Services, Recreation & Athletics, Scouts, Special Olympics, Youth Organizations

Application Procedures

Initial Contact: letter of request
Application Requirements: background of organization, 501(c)(3) exemption letter, and purpose of grant
Deadlines: None.
Evaluative Criteria: preference is given to charitable and educational organizations
Decision Notification: notices of approval or rejection or request for more information within three months

Restrictions

Grants are not made to individuals.

Corporate Officials

John Joseph Boswell: chairman, secretary, treasurer B Granite City, IL 1947. ED University of Missouri, Columbia (1969). PRIM CORP EMPL chairman: Independent Stave Co. Inc. CORP AFFIL president: Isco Holding Co. Inc.; president: Missouri Cooperage Co. Inc.
W. Paul Walker: chief financial officer, secretary, treasurer B 1947. ED Draughons Business College (1973). PRIM CORP EMPL chief financial officer, secretary, treasurer: Independent Stave Co. Inc.

Foundation Officials

John Joseph Boswell: president (see above)
Tiffany R. Boswell: vice president
W. Paul Walker: secretary (see above)

Grants Analysis

Disclosure Period: fiscal year ending November 30, 1997
Total Grants: $863,656
Number of Grants: 41
Average Grant: $21,065
Highest Grant: $186,905
Typical Range: $500 to $50,000

Recent Grants

Note: Grants derived from fiscal 1997 Form 990.

Arts & Humanities

1,025	Music Works WPB
300	Video Projections

Civic & Public Affairs

11,000	CRBIS
10,500	Lebanon Area Foundation, Lebanon, MO
10,351	Silver SAC
7,500	Brad Boswell Foundation
3,180	Mayors Jewelers
500	Frozen Assets
250	Edith and Robert Callahan Endowment

Education

100,200	Benjamin School, North Palm Beach, FL
79,000	Meredith-Dunn Learning Center, Louisville, KY
45,000	Lebanon School System, Lebanon, MO
10,000	University of Southern California School of Medicine, Los Angeles, CA
3,000	Landmark Schools
100	Junior Achievement, Omaha, NE

Environment

3,500	Roar Foundation, Acton, CA

Health

11,500	Lupus Foundation
5,000	Intracoastal Health Foundation
2,000	Arthritis Foundation, Boston, MA
1,000	Melanoma Task Force
750	Cystic Fibrosis Foundation, Philadelphia, PA
500	Leukemia Society
500	Muscular Dystrophy Association

International

65,000	Orangutang Foundation International, Los Angeles, CA
20,000	Orangutang Foundation International, Los Angeles, CA
175	Valed Park International

Religion

186,905	Palm Beach Community Church, West Palm Beach, FL
100,650	Chapel Haven, New Haven, CT
50,000	National Right to Life, Washington, DC
10,000	Simon Wiesenthal Center, Los Angeles, CA

Social Services

50,000	City of Lebanon, Lebanon, KY
50,000	Sky Ranch Foundation, Fredericksburg, VA
10,750	HomeSafe, Ashtabula, OH
8,000	Parent Resource Center, Orlando, FL
3,170	Women's Pregnancy Center
1,000	Boy Scouts of America
1,000	Haven of the Ozarks
250	North City Humane Society
100	Special Olympics

INDIANA MILLS & MANUFACTURING

Company Contact

Westfield, IN

Company Description

Employees: 300
SIC(s): 2399 Fabricated Textile Products Nec, 3429 Hardware Nec.

IMMI Word and Deed Foundation

Giving Contact

Donald C. Boyle, Director
IMMI Word and Deed Foundation, Inc.
PO Box 408
Westfield, IN 46074
Phone: (317)896-9531
Fax: (317)867-0311

Description

Founded: 1991
EIN: 351859427
Organization Type: Corporate Foundation
Grant Types: Fellowship, General Support.

Financial Summary

Total Giving: $1,025,135 (fiscal year ending November 30, 1998); $772,900 (fiscal 1997); $661,800 (fiscal 1996)
Assets: $0 (fiscal 1998); $669,608 (fiscal 1997); $470,907 (fiscal 1996)
Gifts Received: $1,341,000 (fiscal 1998); $942,000 (fiscal 1997); $897,924 (fiscal 1996). Note: In fiscal 1998, contributions were received from Indiana Mills & Manufacturing, Inc. ($1,227,000), and James R. and Beverly S. Anthony ($114,000).

Typical Recipients

Civic & Public Affairs: Civic & Public Affairs-General
Health: Long-Term Care
International: International Affairs, International Organizations, International Relief Efforts, Missionary/ Religious Activities
Religion: Churches, Jewish Causes, Ministries, Missionary Activities (Domestic), Religious Welfare
Social Services: Community Service Organizations, Family Services

Contributions Analysis

Religion: 100%. All grants are to religious organization's. Organizations range from campus ministries, relief support, public broadcasting, sports programs, and to organization's that are international in scope.
Note: Total contributions in fiscal 1998.

Application Procedures

Initial Contact: Request application form.
Deadlines: None.

Restrictions

Grants are not made to individuals.

Additional Information

Contributions are made to religious organizations for the purpose of assisting them in spreading the gospel of Jesus Christ in Word & Deed.

Corporate Officials

Beverly S. Anthony: secretary PRIM CORP EMPL secretary: Indiana Mills & Manufacturing.
James R. Anthony: chairman PRIM CORP EMPL chairman: Indiana Mills & Manufacturing.

Foundation Officials

James R. Anthony: president (see above)
James T. Anthony: director
Donald C. Boyle: director
Suzanne Anthony Wilhelm: director

Grants Analysis

Disclosure Period: fiscal year ending November 30, 1998
Total Grants: $1,025,135
Number of Grants: 64
Average Grant: $14,653*
Highest Grant: $102,000
Typical Range: $100 to $200,000
***Note:** Average grant figures excludes highest grant.

Recent Grants

Note: Grants derived from fiscal 1996 Form 990.

Civic & Public Affairs

12,100	TEAM Development, Barrington, IL
5,500	High Five America, San Diego, CA

International

8,100	Peter Deyneka Russian Ministries, Wheaton, IL
4,700	African Leadership Henderson Support, Greenwood, IN
3,700	BPO International, New York, NY
3,700	Operation Mobilization, Tyrone, GA

Religion

243,800	Campus Crusade for Christ Ministry Support, Orlando, FL
195,100	River Oaks Community Church, Carmel, IN
12,000	Lighthouse Mission, Indianapolis, IN
12,000	Samaritan's Purse, Boone, NC
6,100	Grace Fellowship, Carmel, IN
6,000	Indiana Sports Outreach Ministry Support, Indianapolis, IN
6,000	Promise Keepers, Boulder, CO
6,000	Wheeler Ministries, Indianapolis, IN
4,300	Hephzibah House, New York, NY
3,100	Artists in Christian Testimony, Franklin, TN
3,100	Christian Lay Ministries, Lake Junaluska, NC
2,850	Great Commission Ministry, Worthington, OH

Social Services

12,000	Insight for Living, Anaheim, CA
6,000	Indiana Family Institute, Indianapolis, IN

INDUSTRIAL BANK OF JAPAN TRUST CO. (NEW YORK)

Company Contact

New York, NY

Company Description

Employees: 450
SIC(s): 6021 National Commercial Banks.
Parent Company: Industrial Bank of Japan, Ltd., 3-3, Marunouchi 1-chome, Chiyoda-ku, Tokyo, Japan

Operating Locations

CA: Industrial Bank of Japan, Ltd. (Los Angeles Agency), Los Angeles; Industrial Bank of Japan Trust Co. (New York), Los Angeles; Industrial Bank of Japan, Ltd. (San Francisco), San Francisco; Industrial Bank of Japan Trust Co. (New York), San Francisco; DC: Industrial Bank of Japan, Ltd. (Washington), Washington; Industrial Bank of Japan Trust Co. (New York), Washington; GA: Industrial Bank of Japan Trust Co. (Atlanta Agency), Atlanta; Industrial Bank of Japan Trust Co. (New York), Atlanta; IL: Industrial Bank of Japan Ltd. (Chicago Branch), Chicago; NY: Aubrey G. Lanston & Co., New York; Bridgeford Group, New York; Execution Services, New York; IBJ Schroder Bank & Trust Co., New York; IBJ Schroder Banking Corp., New York; IBJ Schroder International Bank, New York; IBJ Schroder Leasing Corp., New York; Industrial Bank of Japan, Ltd. (New York Branch), New York; Industrial Bank of Japan Trust Co., New York; Industrial Bank of Japan Trust Co. (New York), New York; TX: Industrial Bank of Japan, Ltd. (Houston), Houston; Industrial Bank of Japan Trust Co. (New York), Houston

Nonmonetary Support

Type: Donated Equipment; In-kind Services; Loaned Employees; Loaned Executives
Note: Co. provides nonmonetary support. Co. donates used computer equipment and used office furniture.

IBJ Foundation

Giving Contact

Lesley Harris Palmer, Executive Director
IBJ Foundation
1251 Avenue of the Americas
New York, NY 10020-1104
Phone: (212)282-4190
Fax: (212)354-7355

Description

EIN: 133550008
Organization Type: Corporate Foundation
Giving Locations: CA: Los Angeles, San Francisco; GA: Atlanta; IL: Chicago; NY: New York; TX: Houston principally near operating locations and to national organizations.
Grant Types: Employee Matching Gifts, Project.
Note: Employee matching gift ratio: 1 to 1 to education, arts and culture, and community affairs Organizations.

Giving Philosophy

'The goal of the IBJ Foundation is to serve as a catalyst for innovative programs in the United States that promote the education of global citizens and strengthen urban communities. These grantmaking themes reflect the Bank's identity as a global financial institution, its history of helping to build society's infrastructure, and desire to address critical needs in American communities.'

'Education of Global Citizens: The IBJ Foundation supports educational programs that cultivate greater awareness and understanding of the profound issues affecting our evolving global society. The goal of these programs is to initiate responsible and informed participation in global concerns. IBJ aims to improve learning among all age groups, with a focus on K-12 public education. The Foundation is interested in innovative programs that enhance students' professional development for educators.'

'Stregthening Urban Communities: The IBJ Foundation funds programs intended to improve the quality of life in urban neighborhoods. The Foundation supports programs that address community needs such as low-income housing renovation and management, job training and generation, and neighborhood reinvestment. The Foundation is interested in integrated approaches to community revitalization that link the provision of affordable housing with support services and/or economic development.' *The IBJ Foundation Guidelines*

Financial Summary

Total Giving: $500,000 (2000 approx); $500,000 (1999 approx); $437,000 (1998 approx). Note: Contributes through corporate direct giving program and foundation. Giving includes foundation.
Assets: $12,000,000 (1999 approx); $12,000,000 (1998 approx); $11,500,000 (1997 approx)
Gifts Received: $500,000 (1995); $2,000,000 (1993); $2,000,000 (1992). Note: Contributions received from Industrial Bank of Japan Trust Co.

Typical Recipients

Arts & Humanities: Museums/Galleries
Civic & Public Affairs: Economic Development, Employment/Job Training, Civic & Public Affairs-General, Housing, Nonprofit Management, Urban & Community Affairs, Women's Affairs
Education: Colleges & Universities, Education Funds, Education Reform, Elementary Education (Public), Environmental Education, Education-General, International Studies, Public Education (Precollege), Science/Mathematics Education, Secondary Education (Public), Social Sciences Education
Health: Home-Care Services
International: Foreign Educational Institutions, International Affairs, International Relations
Science: Science Museums, Scientific Organizations
Social Services: Day Care

Contributions Analysis

Giving Priorities: Civic causes and education.
Civic & Public Affairs: 40%. The foundation supports programs designed to improve and enhance the quality of life in urban neighborhoods, focusing on housing, childcare, and economic development.
Education: 60%. The foundation supports educational programs that foster among Americans a deeper understanding of the profound changes now occurring in an evolving global society. This focus includes programs from elementary school through adult education, universities, and museums.
Note: Total contributions made in 1998.

Application Procedures

Initial Contact: Request and review guidelines, then send a brief (maximum of 3 pages) concept paper outlining proposal.
Application Requirements: Include name and address of organization; contact person, title, and phone number; list of board of directors or similar governing body; organization's history, mission and goals; outline and time frame of proposal; expected outcome and evaluation methods; amount requested and purpose; budget; latest financial statement and annual report; proof of 501(c)(3) status; and geographic area and population served.
Deadlines: July 1 for concept papers.
Review Process: Foundation staff reviews concept papers, and either declines or requests full proposals within six to eight weeks; board of directors make final decisions in the fall.
Evaluative Criteria: The foundation considers the following criteria when reviewing proposals: an organization must satisfy one of the two grantmaking priorities; meet the needs of the communities where company employees live and work; present innovative initiatives that can serve as a model for future projects; collaborate efforts between public, private, and nonprofit sectors; the foundation's contribution must make a considerable difference to the project; provide volunteer opportunities to company employees; serve the community without discrimination on the basis of race, sex, or religion; keep its books available for regular independent outside audit, and make results

available to all potential contributors; and comply with applicable laws regarding registration and financial reporting.

Restrictions

Foundation does not give general operating support, nor does it make grants to individuals; religious, sectarian, fraternal, veterans' or labor groups; political organizations or candidates; organizations whose primary purpose is to influence legislation; fundraising activities; journal advertisements or purchase of tickets; or capital campaigns or any building and/or construction costs. Supported organizations must be tax-exempt and non-discriminatory.

Additional Information

Publications: Guidelines

Corporate Officials

Akio Kariya: senior vice president PRIM CORP EMPL senior vice president: Industrial Bank of Japan Trust Co.
Hajime Nakai: president PRIM CORP EMPL president: Industrial Bank of Japan Trust Co.
Shoji Noguchi: general manager

Foundation Officials

Jennifer Barnes: program officer
Hilary Finkelstein: senior program officer
Lesley Harris Palmer: executive director
John H. Higgs: director B Baltimore, MD 1934. ED Dartmouth College AB (1956); University of Pennsylvania LLB (1960). PRIM CORP EMPL partner: Morgan, Lewis & Bockius. CORP AFFIL director: Industries Bank Japan Trust Co.; partner: Skyport Industrial Park.
Akio Kariya: treasurer (see above)
Hajime Nakai: president (see above)
Merlin Edward Nelson: chairman, director B Fargo, ND 1922. ED University of Oregon BS (1943); Fordham University (1943-1944); Yale University JD (1948). PRIM CORP EMPL consultant: AMF Inc. CORP AFFIL director: Exeter International Corp.; director: Industrial Bank Japan Trust Co.; member: Avon International Advisory Council; director: Derby International Corp. NONPR AFFIL chairman advisory council: Trust Public Land; president: Tuckernuck Land Trust; member: Phi Beta Kappa; member: Council Foreign Relations; member: Overseas Development Council.
Shoji Noguchi: director (see above)
Eric Tarlow: secretary

Grants Analysis

Disclosure Period: calendar year ending 1998
Total Grants: $437,000
Number of Grants: 11
Average Grant: $40,000
Highest Grant: $125,000
Typical Range: $25,000 to $50,000
Note: Grants analysis provided by the foundation.

Recent Grants

Note: Grants derived from 1996 Form 990.

Arts & Humanities

75,000 Brooklyn Children's Museum, Brooklyn, NY -- educational of global citizens

Civic & Public Affairs

65,000 Neighborhood Housing Services, New York, NY -- to strengthen urban communities
50,000 Local Initiatives Support Corporation, New York, NY -- to strengthen urban communities
30,000 Nonprofit Facilities Fund, New York, NY -- to strengthen urban communities
25,000 Enterprise Foundation, New York, NY -- to strengthen urban communities
15,000 Community Preservation Corporation, New York, NY -- to strengthen urban communities

Education

62,000 Stanford University California International Studies Project, Stanford, CA -- educational of global citizens
45,000 University Settlement Society, New York, NY -- to strengthen urban communities
24,500 International House at University of California at Berkeley, Berkeley, CA -- educational of global citizens

Health

50,000 Home Care Associates Training Institute, New York, NY -- to strengthen urban communities

International

72,500 World Game Institute, New York, NY -- educational of global citizens
25,000 United Nations Association, New York, NY -- educational of global citizens

Science

75,000 American Museum of Natural History, New York, NY -- educational of global citizens
30,000 National Geographic Society Education Foundation, Washington, DC -- educational of global citizens

Social Services

50,000 Child Care, New York, NY -- to strengthen urban communities

INFORMIX SOFTWARE, INC.

 Number 77 of Top 100 Corporate Givers

Company Contact

Menlo Park, CA
Web: http://www.informix.com/informix/grants/

Company Description

Gross Operating Earnings: US$662,000,000
Profit: US$356,900,000
Employees: 3,489

Nonmonetary Support

Value: $10,000,000 (1997 approx)
Type: Donated Products; In-kind Services

Giving Contact

Denise T. Taylor, Grants Program Coordinator
Informix Grants Program Informix Software, Inc.
300 Lakeside Drive
Suite 2700
Oakland, CA 94612
Phone: (510)628-3932
Fax: (510)628-3951
Email: grants@informix.com

Alternate Contact

4100 Bohannon Drive
Menlo Park, CA 94025
Phone: (415)926-6300

Description

Organization Type: Corporate Giving Program
Giving Locations: internationally; nationally.

Giving Philosophy

'The Informix for Innovation Software Grant Program enables educational and philanthropic organizations to benefit from the use of Informix software technology -- in the classroom to accelerate learning, in research situations to advance the state of the art, and as a business tool to operate at maximum efficiency. The goal of the program is to encourage innovation now and in the future. By contributing to the success of educational and philanthropic organizations, Informix is taking an active role in maintaining the health of the community and environment in which we all live.'

'Informix for Innovation Educational Grant Program: Educational institutions play a critical role in our future. The Informix for Innovation Educational Grant Program is designed to offer educators around the world opportunity to use leading technology as a teaching tool in the classroom and as an engine for academic research. The software provided through this program will encourage research breakthroughs and give students the opportunity to prepare for their future using the latest technology available. Software grants will be awarded to educational institutions for use only as teaching tools or in research settings.'

'The Informix for Innovation Philanthropic Grant Program: Informix recognizes that our success depends on the well being of the environments and communities in which we operate -- and places a high value on the nonprofit organizations that help sustain or enhance our society and experiences. The goal of the Informix for Innovation Philanthropic Grant Program is to support nonprofit organizations in the United States by providing them with the world's leading database technology to further their causes.' 1997 Informix for Innovation Software Program brochure

Financial Summary

Total Giving: $10,000,000 (2000 approx); $10,000,000 (1999 approx); $10,000,000 (1998 approx). Note: Contributes through corporate direct giving program only. Giving includes nonmonetary support.

Application Procedures

Initial Contact: request an application
Deadlines: None.
Evaluative Criteria: projects or organizations that are highly visible in the community; project or organization should be located in institution's operating community; project must have projected time span, specific goals, and measurable results; applicants will be judged on technical and resource feasibility and impact on company's technical support

Restrictions

Awards are not made to individuals; special interest groups; or political, labor, religious, or fraternal organizations.

Additional Information

Recipients receive a one-year product license, which includes software, documentation, support, updates, and training. If the license if renewed, support and training is available for subsequent years at a discount rate.

INGRAM INDUSTRIES INC.

Company Contact

Nashville, TN

Company Description

Employees: 5,000
SIC(s): 4491 Marine Cargo Handling, 6411 Insurance Agents, Brokers & Service.

Nonmonetary Support

Type: Cause-related Marketing & Promotion

Giving Contact

Martha R. Ingram, Chairman
Ingram Industries Inc.
4400 Harding Rd.
Nashville, TN 37205
Phone: (615)298-8200

Fax: (615)298-7579

Description

Organization Type: Corporate Giving Program
Giving Locations: headquarters area only.
Grant Types: General Support.

Financial Summary

Total Giving: Contributes through corporate direct giving program only.

Typical Recipients

Arts & Humanities: Arts & Humanities-General
Civic & Public Affairs: Civic & Public Affairs-General
Education: Education-General
Environment: Environment-General
Health: Health-General
Religion: Religion-General
Social Services: Social Services-General

Application Procedures

Initial Contact: letter of inquiry
Application Requirements: proof of tax-exempt status
Deadlines: None.
Review Process: proposals are reviewed as time permits; committee decides based on current budget

Corporate Officials

Martha R. Ingram: chairman, director B Charleston, SC. ED Vassar College BA (1957). PRIM CORP EMPL chairman, director: Ingram Industries Inc. CORP AFFIL director: Weyerhaeuser Co.; chairman: Ingram Customer Systems Inc.; director: Ingram Micro Inc.; director: Baxter International Inc.; director: First American Corp. NONPR AFFIL trustee: Vanderbilt University; director: Vassar College; founder, director: Tennessee Repertory Theater; director: Nashville Symphony; director: Tennessee Performing Arts Center; director: Nashville Institute for Arts; director: Nashville Opera; director: Nashville Ballet; director: Nashville Community Foundation; member advisory board: Kennedy Center for Performing Arts; member: Nashville Area Chamber of Commerce; director: Harpeth Hall School; director: Ashley Hall.

Giving Program Officials

Martha R. Ingram: director (see above)

INLAND CONTAINER CORP.

Company Contact

Indianapolis, IN

Company Description

Revenue: US$1,250,000,000
Employees: 7,500
SIC(s): 2653 Corrugated & Solid Fiber Boxes.
Parent Company: Temple-Inland Inc., Diboll, TX, United States

Inland Foundation, Inc.

Giving Contact

Vicki Perkins, Director
Inland Foundation, Inc.
4030 Vincennes Rd.
Indianapolis, IN 46268-0937
Phone: (317)879-4220
Fax: (317)337-8865
Email: vperkin@iccnet.com

Description

EIN: 356014640
Organization Type: Corporate Foundation
Giving Locations: IN: Indianapolis headquarters and operating communities.
Grant Types: General Support, Multiyear/Continuing Support.

Giving Philosophy

'The Inland Foundation recognizes that the people within our communities--our employees, their families, our neighbors, our customers, and those who promote the health of our industry--are key to Inland's success. Every effort of the Inland Foundation will support our vision of being a contributing citizen and leader in our communities and industry.' Inland Foundation Guidelines

Financial Summary

Total Giving: $1,900,000 (1999 approx); $1,930,000 (1998); $1,750,000 (1997 approx). Note: Contributes through corporate direct giving program and foundation. Giving includes foundation.
Assets: $13,000,000 (1999 approx); $12,627,130 (1996); $12,920,954 (1995)

Typical Recipients

Arts & Humanities: Arts Associations & Councils, Arts Centers, Arts Festivals, Arts Funds, Historic Preservation, Libraries, Museums/Galleries, Music, Performing Arts, Public Broadcasting, Theater
Civic & Public Affairs: Botanical Gardens/Parks, Business/Free Enterprise, Chambers of Commerce, Civil Rights, Economic Development, Public Policy, Urban & Community Affairs, Zoos/Aquariums
Education: Business Education, Colleges & Universities, Education Associations, Education Funds, Elementary Education (Public), Engineering/Technological Education, Education-General, International Exchange, Minority Education, Private Education (Precollege), Public Education (Precollege), Science/Mathematics Education, Student Aid
Environment: Environment-General
Health: Children's Health/Hospitals, Health Organizations, Hospitals, Single-Disease Health Associations
International: International Organizations, International Relief Efforts
Religion: Ministries, Religious Welfare
Social Services: Child Welfare, Community Centers, Emergency Relief, People with Disabilities, Scouts, Senior Services, Shelters/Homelessness, Substance Abuse, United Funds/United Ways, Youth Organizations

Contributions Analysis

Giving Priorities: Health, social welfare, and education.
Arts & Humanities: About 5%. Particular interest in projects with strong educational components, which promote access to cultural opportunities for young people or the economically disadvantaged, and which advocate community involvement.
Civic & Public Affairs: About 5%. Of particular interest are programs that address environmental issues, leadership development, job creation, community safety, and economic development in depressed neighborhoods.
Education: 35% to 40%. Emphasis is placed on improving educational opportunities at public schools; in particular, those public schools that have established a partnership with Inland and with which company employees actively volunteer. Grants are designed to strengthen basic educational programs in reading, math, and science, as well as for the professional development of teachers, with primary emphasis on elementary schools. Colleges that provide specialized education in the fields of pulp, paper, packaging, and graphics are supported. Other targeted activities are those aligned to company's interests and the specialized educational needs of local plant communities, including literacy programs and programs designed to benefit minorities and at-risk young people.
Health: 50% to 55%. Major support to the United Way. Supports initiatives that emphasize quality health care, particularly for the benefit of the disadvantaged, disabled, minority populations, children, and families. Supports youth organizations which improve the quality of life for young people, particularly those most at risk.

Application Procedures

Initial Contact: Call or write for guidelines, then send brief written proposal.
Application Requirements: Include the mandatory Inland Foundation Grant Proposal Cover Page; description of organization, including history and purpose; description of community need addressed; information about other organizations working on problem, and cooperative activities; summary budget for project, with anticipated expenses and sources of income; plan for funding, including anticipated foundation and corporate support; amount requested; plan for communicating project and its supporters to community; list of board members with affiliations; proof of tax-exempt status.
Deadlines: October 15, for funding in the following year.
Review Process: Local facilities screen applications, then send to foundation staff for review; board members make final decisions at meetings in June and December.
Evaluative Criteria: Projected impact and usefulness to community, feasibility, and prospects for sound financing; preference given to organizations in which employees volunteer.
Notes: For projects outside of Indianapolis, address application to the manager of local Inland facility.

Restrictions

Foundation does not support grants to individuals; organizations which are not tax-exempt, or which are discriminatory; political, fraternal, labor, or veterans' organizations; political candidates or groups which influence legislation; denominational religious causes; endowments or memorials; fundraising events: tickets for dinners, golf outings, sporting events, etc.; diseases, disorders, or medical research; second-party giving, including service organizations raising money for charitable purposes; nursing or retirement homes.
The following are given low priority: national health organizations, except the United Way; building capital campaigns; hospitals; medical research; local athletic or sports programs (except Special and U.S. Olympics); travel funds for tours, expeditions, or trips by individuals or groups; organizations that receive a large portion of their budget from local, state, or federal funds.

Additional Information

Publications: Application Guidelines

Corporate Officials

Patricia A. Foley: assistant secretarys, controller B Buffalo, NY 1942. ED Indiana University (1971); Indiana University MBA (1977). PRIM CORP EMPL assistant secretary: Inland Container Corp.
Steven L. Householder: vice president, assistant secretary, general counsel PRIM CORP EMPL vice president, assistant secretary, general counsel: Inland Container Corp.; vice president, assistant secretary, general counsel: Inland Paperboard and Packaging Inc.
William B. Howes: chairman, chief executive officer B Washington, DC 1937. ED Furman University BA (1959); Harvard University Advanced Management Program (1977). PRIM CORP EMPL director, executive vice president: Temple-Inland Inc. ADD CORP EMPL chairman, chief executive officer: Inland Paperboard & Packaging Inc.
Donna L. Reynolds: vice president communications PRIM CORP EMPL vice president communications: Inland Container Corp.

Joseph Ernest Tomlinson: vice president, treasurer, controller B Sycamore, IL 1939. ED University of Illinois BS (1962). PRIM CORP EMPL vice president, treasurer, controller: Inland Container Corp. ADD CORP EMPL treasurer: Inland Paper Co. Inc.; vice president, trustee, controller: Inland Paperboard Packaging Inc.; assistant treasurer: Temple-Inland Inc. CORP AFFIL treasurer, assistant secretary, director: El Morro Corrugated Box Corp. NONPR AFFIL member: Financial Executives Institute. CLUB AFFIL Crooked Stick Golf Club.

Foundation Officials

Patricia A. Foley: secretary, treasurer, director (see above)
Steven L. Householder: vice president, director (see above)
William B. Howes: vice president, director (see above)
Donna L. Reynolds: vice president, director (see above)
Joseph Ernest Tomlinson: vice president, director (see above)

Grants Analysis

Disclosure Period: calendar year ending 1998
Total Grants: $1,930,000
Number of Grants: 608
Average Grant: $3,174
Highest Grant: $91,703
Typical Range: $500 to $10,000
Note: Grants analysis provided by the foundation.

Recent Grants

Note: Grants derived from 1996 Form 990.

Arts & Humanities

10,000 Indianapolis Art Center, Indianapolis, IN

Civic & Public Affairs

10,000 Hudson Institute, Indianapolis, IN
10,000 Indianapolis Chamber of Commerce Corporate Community Council, Indianapolis, IN
10,000 White River State Park Commission, Indianapolis, IN

Education

10,000 Independent Colleges of Indiana Foundation, Indianapolis, IN
10,000 Indiana University Foundation, Bloomington, IN
10,000 IPS Education Foundation, Indianapolis, IN
9,780 McKinley Elementary Tracy, Tracy, CA
8,800 Jefferson County Public Schools Vanderhoff, Wheat Ridge, CO
8,000 Midwest Academy, Indianapolis, IN
6,761 Petersburg Public School Foundation, Petersburg, VA
6,540 Fishburn Avenue School, Maywood, CA
6,000 Pulp and Paper Foundation, Raleigh, NC
5,080 Morrison Elementary, Fort Smith, AR

Health

6,000 Geisinger Children's Pavilion, Hazleton, PA

Social Services

91,703 United Givers Fund of Rome and Floyd County, Rome, GA
87,841 United Way Central Indiana, Indianapolis, IN
75,724 United Fund, Orange, TX
21,519 United Fund Humphreys County, Waverly, TN
14,299 United Way Crusade of Mercy, Chicago, IL
14,160 United Way, El Morro, CA
13,633 United Way San Joaquin County, Stockton, CA
12,354 United Way Hidalgo County, McAllen, TX
11,942 United Way Ontario, Ontario, CA
11,363 United Way, Hazleton, PA
11,300 United Way Southeast Region, Santa Fe Springs, NM
10,920 United Way, Ontario, CA
10,129 United Way Maysville, Maysville, KY
9,000 Pleasant Run Children's Home, Indianapolis, IN
9,000 United Way North Central Massachusetts, Fitchburg, MA
8,964 United Way, Lexington, KY
8,957 Mile High United Way, Wheat Ridge, CO
8,735 Heart of Florida United Way, Orlando, FL
7,560 United Way, Newark, NJ
7,554 Montgomery County United Way, Crawfordsville, IN
7,485 United Way, Saint Louis, MO
7,405 United Way Southside Virginia, Petersburg, VA
7,350 United Way, Los Angeles, CA
7,146 United Way, Rock Hill, SC
6,928 United Givers Fund, Hattiesburg, MS
6,760 United Fund Adams County, Biglerville, PA
6,368 United Way, Minneapolis, MN
6,300 United Way Wabash Valley, Newport, IN
6,244 United Fund, Milwaukee, WI
6,200 United Way, Wilmington, DE
6,133 United Way, Fort Smith, AR
6,000 Commission on Child and Youth, Rome, GA
5,906 United Way Erie County, Sandusky, OH
5,520 United Way, Middletown, OH
5,080 United Way, Kansas City, MO

INMAN MILLS

Company Contact

Inman, SC

Company Description

Employees: 1,259
SIC(s): 2211 Broadwoven Fabric Mills--Cotton.

Nonmonetary Support

Note: The co. and the foundation provides nonmonetary support.

Corporate Sponsorship

Type: Arts & cultural events; Music & entertainment events; Sports events
Contact: Patricia Robbins, Secretary

Inman-Riverdale Foundation

Giving Contact

Patricia Robbins, contact
Inman-Riverdale Foundation
Inman Mills
Inman, SC 29349
Phone: (864)472-2121

Description

EIN: 576019736
Organization Type: Corporate Foundation. Supports preselected organizations only.
Giving Locations: SC
Grant Types: General Support.

Financial Summary

Total Giving: $5,000,000 (fiscal year ending November 30, 2000 approx); $5,000,000 (fiscal 1999 approx); $601,949 (fiscal 1996). Note: Contributes through foundation only. 1996 Giving includes scholarship ($97,425).
Assets: $5,000,000 (fiscal 1999 approx); $5,000,000 (fiscal 1998 approx); $6,466,967 (fiscal 1996)
Gifts Received: $50,000 (fiscal 1991)

Typical Recipients

Arts & Humanities: Arts Associations & Councils, Arts Festivals, Arts Funds, Community Arts, Libraries, Music
Civic & Public Affairs: Business/Free Enterprise, Clubs, Community Foundations, Employment/Job Training, Civic & Public Affairs-General, Professional & Trade Associations, Urban & Community Affairs
Education: Business Education, Colleges & Universities, Continuing Education, Education Funds, Engineering/Technological Education, Education-General, Private Education (Precollege), Public Education (Precollege), Student Aid, Vocational & Technical Education
Health: Clinics/Medical Centers, Health Organizations, Heart, Hospices, Medical Research, Research/Studies Institutes, Single-Disease Health Associations
Religion: Churches, Religious Organizations, Religious Welfare
Social Services: Community Centers, Community Service Organizations, Food/Clothing Distribution, People with Disabilities, Recreation & Athletics, Scouts, United Funds/United Ways, YMCA/YWCA/YMHA/YWHA, Youth Organizations

Contributions Analysis

Arts & Humanities: 15%. Interests include arts associations, arts festivals, community arts, and music.
Civic & Public Affairs: 5% to 10%. Funding supports civic institutes, professional associations, recreation centers, and playground facilities.
Education: 30% to 35%. A majority of support goes to scholarship programs for nursing schools and undergraduate degrees at universities.
Health: 10%. Supports Red Cross and single-disease health associations.
Religion: 5% to 10%. Recipients include churches and religious organizations.
Social Services: 25% to 30%. Favors food banks, youth organizations, scouting programs, and the disabled.

Additional Information

Publications: Guidelines

Corporate Officials

Robert H. Chapman, III: president B 1951. PRIM CORP EMPL president: Inman Mills ADD CORP EMPL president: Inman Holding Co.
James C. Pace, Jr.: controller PRIM CORP EMPL controller: Inman Mills ADD CORP EMPL controller: Inman Holding Co.
John F. Renfro, Jr.: vice president B 1937. PRIM CORP EMPL vice president: Inman Mills.
Patricia H. Robbins: secretary PRIM CORP EMPL secretary: Inman Holding Co.

Foundation Officials

Norman H. Chapman: trustee PRIM CORP EMPL vice president: Inman Holding Co. ADD CORP EMPL executive vice president: Inman Mills.
Robert H. Chapman, III: chairman (see above)
James C. Pace, Jr.: trustee (see above)
John F. Renfro, Jr.: treasurer, trustee (see above)
Patricia H. Robbins: secretary (see above)

Grants Analysis

Disclosure Period: fiscal year ending November 30, 1996
Total Grants: $504,524*
Number of Grants: 75
Average Grant: $4,729*
Highest Grant: $60,000

Typical Range: $500 to $5,000
***Note:** Giving excludes scholarship. The average grant figure excludes three highest grants ($150,000).

Recent Grants

Note: Grants derived from fiscal 1996 Form 990.

Arts & Humanities

50,000 Spartanburg County Library, Spartanburg, SC
25,000 Arts Partnership, Spartanburg, SC

Civic & Public Affairs

17,900 Spartanburg County Foundation, Spartanburg, SC
6,000 Spartanburg Community Events, Spartanburg, SC
5,000 LSCHH
2,500 New Beginnings Foundation, Spartanburg, SC
1,500 Foundation for Professional Development, Columbia, SC
1,000 Junior League, Spartanburg, SC

Education

60,000 Independent Colleges and Universities
25,000 District One Schools
25,000 Spartanburg Methodist College, Spartanburg, SC
11,000 Independent Colleges and Universities
8,333 Spartanburg Day School, Spartanburg, SC
5,000 South Carolina Governor's School for Science and Math, Hartsville, SC
5,000 Spartanburg Technical College, Spartanburg, SC
4,000 ITT Graduate Fellowship Program
4,000 Junior Achievement, Spartanburg, SC
3,000 Adult Learning Center, Spartanburg, SC
3,000 Institute of Textile Technology, Charlottesville, VA
2,000 Spartanburg Day School, Spartanburg, SC
1,500 Converse College, Spartanburg, SC
1,000 USIC Educational Foundation

Health

40,000 Spartanburg Regional Medical Center, Petersburg, VA
5,000 Greenwood Genetic Center, Greenwood, SC
1,150 American Heart Association
1,000 Duke Center for Living, Durham, NC
1,000 Hospice

Religion

12,500 First Presbyterian Church, Spartanburg, SC
5,000 Potter's House Church of God
2,400 Inman Pentecostal Holiness Church, Inman, SC
2,400 Inman United Christian Church, Inman, SC
2,100 First Baptist Church
2,000 Fellowship of Christian Athletes
2,000 Mount Zion AME Church Cross Anchor
2,000 Salvation Army, Spartanburg, SC
1,000 Inman Presbyterian Church, Inman, SC
1,000 Mabry's Temple Bible Way Church

Social Services

33,000 YMCA, Spartanburg, SC
25,000 Mobile Meal Service, Spartanburg, SC
18,670 United Way, Spartanburg, SC
17,000 Foundation for Multihandicapped, Blind, and Deaf of South Carolina, Spartanburg, SC
10,000 Rocky Bottom Camp for Blind, Columbia, SC
8,500 Boy Scouts of America Palmetto Council
6,480 Inman Youth Association, Inman, SC
5,000 Bethlehem Community Center, Columbia, SC
4,500 IPTAY
4,000 Boys and Girls Clubs
2,000 Spartanburg Boys Home, Spartanburg, SC
1,500 Boy Scouts of America Palmetto Council
1,000 Girl Scout Council

INTEL CORP.

 Number 6 of Top 100 Corporate Givers

Company Contact

Santa Clara, CA
Web: http://www.intel.com

Company Description

Revenue: US$29,389,000,000 (1999)
Employees: 38,377 (1999)
Fortune Rank: 39, per FORTUNE Magazine's list of 500 Largest U.S. Corporations (1999).
FF 39
SIC(s): 3577 Computer Peripheral Equipment Nec, 3674 Semiconductors & Related Devices, 3679 Electronic Components Nec.

Operating Locations

Australia: Intel Australia Pty. Ltd., Crows Nest; Brazil: Intel Semicondutores do Brazil, Sao Paulo-SP; Denmark: Intel Denmark, Copenhagen; Finland: Intel Finland OY, Hensinki; France: Intel Corporation S.A.R.L., Saint Quentin; Intel Europe, Saint Quentin; Germany: Intel Gmbh, Munich; Intel Semiconductor Gmbh, Munich; Hong Kong: Intel Semiconductor Ltd., Hong Kong, Queensway Central; Israel:, Tel Aviv; Italy: Intel Corporation Italia Spa, Milan; Japan: Intel Kabushiki Kaisha, Ibaraki-Ken; Intel Japan, Tokyo; Intel Japan K.K., Tsukuba; Republic of Korea: Intel Semiconductor Asia Ltd., Seoul; Netherlands: Intel Semiconductor B.V., Rotterdam; Norway: Intel Norway, Skjetten; Singapore: Intel Singapore Ltd., Singapore; Spain: Intel Iberia S.A., Madrid; Sweden: Intel Sweden, Soina; Switzerland: Intel Switzerland, Zurich; Taiwan: Intel Technology Far East Ltd., Taipei; United Kingdom: Intel Corporation (UK) Ltd., Swindon, Wiltshire

Nonmonetary Support

Value: $67,730,366 (1998); $39,104,624 (1996); $18,058,124 (1995)
Type: Donated Equipment
Volunteer Programs: $268,900 was paid to schools through Intel's Employee Matching Gift program.
Contact: Jeanne Maixher, Academic Relations
Note: Nonmonetary support is fair market value.

Corporate Sponsorship

Value: $3,201,066 (1998)
Type: Other
Note: Sponsors engineering and science events through a decentralized program.

Intel Foundation

Giving Contact

Alisa Hampton, Program Officer
Intel Foundation
5200 NE Elam Young Pkwy., F15-63
Hillsboro, OR 97124-6497
Phone: (503)696-8080
Fax: (503)696-8179
Email: alisa_hampton@ccm.hf.intel.com
Web: http://www.intel.com/intel/community

Alternate Contact

Peter Broffman, Executive Director
Phone: (503)696-8072

Note: Contact foundation for list of contacts for local organizations.

Description

Founded: 1988
EIN: 943092928
Organization Type: Corporate Foundation
Giving Locations: AZ; CA; MA; NM; OR; TX; WA headquarters and operating communities; nationally; operating locations.
Grant Types: Award, Employee Matching Gifts, Fellowship, Scholarship.
Note: Fellowship and scholarship grants are awarded to schools, not directly to individuals. The foundation and company provide program support.

Giving Philosophy

'Intel established the Intel Foundation in 1989 for the purpose of developing and funding educational and charitable contribution programs. Our four areas of interest are: Improving the quality of life in communities where Intel has a major presence; a special emphasis is given to basic literacy, mathematics and science skills training for elementary and secondary school students. Advancing science and engineering education. Promoting public understanding of electronics technologies and their impact on contemporary life. Promoting the entrance of women and minorities into science and engineering careers.'

Financial Summary

Total Giving: $109,162,282 (1998); $96,301,152 (1997 approx); $55,613,575 (1996). Note: Contributes through corporate direct giving program and foundation.
Giving Analysis: Giving for 1997 includes: foundation ($3,037,823); foundation scholarships ($2,627,129); foundation matching gifts ($443,543); foundation grants to United Way ($310,000); 1998: corporate gifts to individuals ($18,102,607); corporate direct giving ($12,008,959); foundation ($7,223,340); corporate scholarships ($4,245,214); foundation grants to United Way ($440,000); corporate matching gifts ($365,818); foundation matching gifts ($365,817); corporate fellowships ($355,500); foundation gifts to individuals ($109,999)
Assets: $42,908,364 (1998); $31,169,427 (1996); $16,947,784 (1995)
Gifts Received: $14,676,500 (1998); $20,000,210 (1996); $13,013,080 (1995). Note: Contributions are received from Intel Corp.

Typical Recipients

Arts & Humanities: Arts Centers, Community Arts, Film & Video, Museums/Galleries, Music, Public Broadcasting
Civic & Public Affairs: Chambers of Commerce, Native American Affairs, Women's Affairs, Zoos/Aquariums
Education: Afterschool/Enrichment Programs, Business Education, Business-School Partnerships, Colleges & Universities, Community & Junior Colleges, Continuing Education, Elementary Education (Private), Engineering/Technological Education, Education-General, Minority Education, Preschool Education, Private Education (Precollege), Public Education (Precollege), Science/Mathematics Education, Student Aid
International: Foreign Educational Institutions, International-General
Religion: Religious Welfare
Science: Science Exhibits & Fairs, Science Museums, Scientific Centers & Institutes, Scientific Organizations
Social Services: Community Centers, Community Service Organizations, Counseling, United Funds/United Ways, Youth Organizations

Contributions Analysis

Giving Priorities: Foundation makes two types of grants, national grants and community grants where

Intel has a major facility. Company makes contributions through foreign operating companies as part of its community grants program. Intel sites around the world contribute funding and employee time to local nonprofit organizations. Contributions are channeled through both the Intel Foundation and through local public affairs offices. Most contributions support higher education, and programs are underway in China, the UK, Ireland, Israel, Malaysia, the Philippines, and Russia.

Arts & Humanities: 1%. Funds a major art exhibit.

Education: 91%. Of the total, 62% went to higher education. 29% to K-12 education. Supports colleges and universities through equipment donations, research grants, a visiting faculty program, Distinguished Lectures in Technology Series, and employee matching gifts. Goals are to enhance education in math and science, increase the use of technology in community schools, and develop a future work force that represents the diversity of operating communities. Grants support curriculum development, teacher training, and the administration of literacy programs that involve math, science, and technology.

Environment: 5%. Supports clean-up projects in communities where employees live and work, through cash, equipment, cash, and volunteers.

Social Services: 3%. Supports local community needs, disaster relief programs, and the United Way.

Application Procedures

Initial Contact: For foundation grants, call for application form; for community grants, contact local Intel Public Affairs Office.

Application Requirements: For foundation grants: Grant Application Cover Sheet and full proposal, including: organizational information, with mission, need for problem addressed, description of current programs, and population served; project description, with statement of primary purpose, population to benefit, how they will benefit, strategies used to implement project, and anticipated timetable; results anticipated and methods of evaluation; most recent audited financial statement, organization budget for current year, and project budget; list of board of directors; one-paragraph resumes of key staff; and proof of tax-exempt status.

Deadlines: None.

Review Process: On a continuous basis.

Decision Notification: Usually within three months.

Notes: Community grants applications should be directed to nearest Public Affairs office. Corporate and Foundation applications may be directed to address above.

Restrictions

Does not make grants solely for general operating expenses. Does not support private foundations, as defined under section 509(a) of the Internal Revenue Code; political organizations; organizations that practice or promote discrimination or illegal acts; luncheons, dinners or auctions; goodwill advertising; grants to individuals, analysis fund drives, endowment or capital improvement campaigns, or projects that influence elections or legislation. Generally does not support health sciences, environmental sciences, television/radio production costs, religious or fraternal organizations, or the creation of personal or organization web sites. fraternal organizations, or the creation of personal or organization web sites.

Additional Information

Publications: Corporate Citizenship Report (Includes Foundation Annual Report); Application Form; Guidelines

Corporate Officials

Craig R. Barrett: president, chief operating officer, director B San Francisco, CA 1939. ED Stanford University BS (1961); Stanford University MS (1963); Stanford University PhD (1964). PRIM CORP EMPL president, chief operating officer, director: Intel Corp. CORP AFFIL director: United States West Inc.; director: Pandesic LLC; director: Sematech; director: Komag Inc. NONPR AFFIL member: National Academy of Engineering; director: United States Semiconductor Industry Association.

Andy D. Bryant: senior vice president, chief financial & enterprise services officer PRIM CORP EMPL senior vice president, chief financial & enterprise services officer: Intel Corp.

Dr. Andrew S. Grove: chairman B Budapest, Hungary 1936. ED City College of New York BS (1960); University of California at Berkeley PhD (1963). PRIM CORP EMPL chairman: Intel Corp. NONPR AFFIL fellow: Institute Electrical & Electronics Engineers; member: National Academy Engineering; fellow: Academy Arts & Sciences.

Gordon E. Moore, PhD: co-founder, chairman emeritus, director B San Francisco, CA 1929. ED University of California BS (1950); California Institute of Technology PhD (1954). PRIM CORP EMPL co-founder, chairman emeritus, director: Intel Corp. CORP AFFIL director: TransAmerica Corp.; director: Varian Associates Inc.; director: Gilead Sciences Inc.; chairman: Intel Puerto Rico Ltd. NONPR AFFIL fellow: Institute Electrical & Electronics Engineers; member: National Academy Engineering; member: American Physics Society; trustee: California Institute Technology.

Patricia Murray: vice president, director human resources PRIM CORP EMPL vice president, director human resources: Intel Corp.

Arthur Rock: co-founder, chairman executive committee, director B Rochester, NY 1926. ED Syracuse University BS (1948); Harvard University MBA (1951). PRIM CORP EMPL co-founder, chairman executive committee, director: Intel Corp. CORP AFFIL director: Echelon Corp.; principal: Arthur Rock & Co.; director: Argonaut Group Inc.; director: Argonaut Insurance Co.; director: AirTouch Communications Inc. NONPR AFFIL trustee: California Institute Technology; director: San Francisco Museum Modern Art.

Arvind Sodhani: corp. vice president, treasurer B 1954. ED University of London; University of Michigan (1978). PRIM CORP EMPL corp. vice president, treasurer: Intel Corp.

Leslie L. Vadasz: executive vice president, director PRIM CORP EMPL executive vice president, director: Intel Corp.

Foundation Officials

Peter Broffman: executive director CORP AFFIL administration social policy: Rainier Bancorp.

F. Thomas Dunlap, Jr.: secretary, director B Pittsburgh, PA 1951. ED University of Cincinnati BSEE (1974); University of Santa Clara JD (1979). PRIM CORP EMPL vice president, secretary, general counsel: Intel Corp.

Alisa Hampton: program officer

Paige Kuni: program officer

Gordon E. Moore, PhD: trustee (see above)

Patricia Murray: chairman (see above)

Arvind Sodhani: treasurer (see above)

Grants Analysis

Disclosure Period: calendar year ending 1998

Total Grants: $7,223,340*

Number of Grants: 314

Average Grant: $21,480*

Highest Grant: $500,000

Typical Range: $10,000 to $50,000

***Note:** Giving excludes corporate direct giving; matching gifts; individuals; United Way. Average gratn excludes highest grant.

Recent Grants

Note: Grants derived from 1997 Form 990.

Civic & Public Affairs

81,800	American Indian Science and Engineering Society, Boulder, CO
55,000	Albuquerque Hispanic Chamber of Commerce, Albuquerque, NM
51,600	American Indian Science and Engineering Society, Boulder, CO
46,200	American Indian Science and Engineering Society, Boulder, CO

Education

100,000	Wepan Women in Engineering Programs and Advocates Network Mentornet
91,000	Maricopa County Community College District Foundation, Tempe, AZ
75,000	Puget Sound Works, WA
60,000	Northwest Regional Education Service District
60,000	Puyallup School
57,000	Pacific Lutheran University, Tacoma, WA
56,000	International Society for Technology in Education, Eugene, OR
51,500	Eastern New Mexico University, NM
50,000	Capitol Center Mesa, Mesa, AZ
50,000	Folsom Cordova Unified School District, Folsom, CA
49,000	University of New Mexico Minority Engineering Programs, Albuquerque, NM
48,700	Princeton University, Princeton, NJ
45,000	Folsom High School, Folsom, CA
40,000	Computer Research Association
40,000	Northwest Regional Education Service District
38,400	Carnegie Mellon University, Pittsburgh, PA
38,400	Carnegie Mellon University, Pittsburgh, PA
38,300	Rensselaer Polytechnic Institute, Troy, NY
38,300	University of Michigan, Ann Arbor, MI
37,000	University of Michigan, Ann Arbor, MI
35,800	Massachusetts Institute of Technology, Cambridge, MA
35,800	Stanford University, Stanford, CA
34,700	California Institute of Technology, Pasadena, CA
34,500	Georgia Institute of Technology, Atlanta, GA
34,500	Georgia Institute of Technology, Atlanta, GA
34,100	California Institute of Technology, Pasadena, CA
34,100	California Institute of Technology, Pasadena, CA
32,700	Carnegie Mellon University, Pittsburgh, PA
32,600	University of Wisconsin, Madison, WI
32,000	Purdue University, West Lafayette, IN
30,000	Carnegie Mellon University, Pittsburgh, PA
30,000	Tacoma Pierce County Mesa, Tacoma, WA
28,800	University of North Carolina Chapel Hill, Chapel Hill, NC
25,000	Tucson Unified School District, Tucson, AZ

International

250,000	Science Service, Washington, DC
250,000	Science Service, Washington, DC

Religion

60,000	Salvation Army

Science

148,000	American Association for the Advancement of Science, Washington, DC
75,000	New Mexico Technet, Albuquerque, NM
43,500	Pacific Science Center, Seattle, WA
40,000	Oregon Museum of Science and Industry, Portland, OR

Social Services

65,000	United Way Valley of the Sun, Phoenix, AZ
60,000	United Way Santa Clara County, Santa Clara, CA

60,000 University Park Community Center
50,000 United Way Central New Mexico, Albuquerque, NM
50,000 United Way Columbia Willamette
40,000 United Way, Sacramento, CA

INTERNATIONAL BUSINESS MACHINES CORP.

 Number 5 of Top 100 Corporate Givers

Company Contact

Armonk, NY
Web: http://www.ibm.com

Company Description

Foreign Name: IBM
Also Known As: IBM Corp.
Revenue: US$87,548,000,000 (1999)
Profit: US$6,328,000,000
Employees: 291,067 (1999)
Fortune Rank: 6, per FORTUNE Magazine's list of 500 Largest U.S. Corporations (1999).
FF 6
SIC(s): 3572 Computer Storage Devices, 3577 Computer Peripheral Equipment Nec, 3661 Telephone & Telegraph Apparatus, 3955 Carbon Paper & Inked Ribbons.

Operating Locations

Argentina: IBM Argentina Sociedad Anonima, Martinez, Buenos Aires; Australia: Energy Information Technology Co. Pty. Ltd., Melbourne; IBM Australia Credit Ltd., Pennant Hills; IBM Australia Leasing Pty. Ltd., Pennant Hills; IBM Global Services Australia Ltd., Sydney; Wangaratta Manufacturing Services Pty. Ltd., Wangaratta; IBM Australia Finance Pty. Ltd., West Pennant Hills; IBM Australia Ltd., West Pennant Hills; Austria: IBM Central Europe & Russia, Vienna; IBM Oesterreich Internationale Buromaschinen GmbH, Vienna; IBM Pensionskasse AG, Vienna; Infoservice Informations-Systeme Betriebs GmbH, Vienna; OCS Computer Service GmbH, Vienna; Belgium: Cimad Consultants NV, Bornem, Anvers; CGI Systems SA, Brussels, Brabant; IBM Belgium Financial Services Co. SA, Brussels, Brabant; IBM Belgium SA, Brussels, Brabant; IBM European International Services Co. SA, Brussels, Brabant; Logon Solution Integrator SA, Brussels, Brabant; Bolivia: IBM de Bolivia SA, La Paz; Brazil: GSI Servicos de Informatica Ltda., Hortolandia; IBM Brasil Industria Maquinas e Servicos Ltda., Rio de Janeiro; IBM Brasil Leasing Arrendamento Mercantil SA, Rio de Janeiro; IBM Empresa Brasileira de Exporta AO SA, Rio de Janeiro; Canada: Nulogix Technical Services, Concord; Expercomp Services Ltd., Markham; IBM Canada Ltd., Markham; IBM Global Services Corp., Markham; STS Microscan, Markham; ISM Societe de Gestion Systemes d'Information, Montreal; Logiciel Sirc, Montreal; ISM Information Systems Management Corp., Regina; Footprint Software, Toronto; ISM Information Systems Management Manitoba Corp., Winnipeg; ISM Library Information Services Ltd., Winnipeg; Polar Bear Software Corp., Winnipeg; Chile: IBM de Chile SA, Santiago; People's Republic of China: IBM China Co., Beijing; Colombia: IBM de Colombia SA, Bogota, Cundinamarco; Czech Republic: IBM Ceska Republika Spol Sro, Prague; Denmark: Parkegaard Partners A/S, Arhus; SDC-Finanssystem AS, Ballerup, Frederiksborg; IBM Denmark A/S, Lyngby, Frederiksborg; Nordic Software Co. APS, Lyngby, Frederiksborg; Ecuador: IBM del Ecuador CA, Quito, Pichincha; El Salvador: IBM World Trade Corp., San Salvador; France: Informatique (Pyrenees), Biarritz, Pyrenees-Atlantiques; Intexis SA, Charbonnieres Les Bains, Rhone; Advanced Memories France SNC, Courbevoie, Hauts-de-Seine; Cimad Conseil France, Courbevoie, Hauts-de-Seine; CR2A-DI, Courbevoie, Hauts-de-Seine; IBM Eurocoordination SA, Courbevoie, Hauts-de-Seine; IBM Europe Middle East Africa, Courbevoie, Hauts-de-Seine; IBM France (Compagnie), Courbevoie, Hauts-de-Seine; IBM France Financement, Courbevoie, Hauts-de-Seine; IBM France Location SNC, Courbevoie, Hauts-de-Seine; Montics SA, Courbevoie, Hauts-de-Seine; Progipart SA, Ecully, Rhone; Logic Line Operations, Evry, Essonne; Sedit Marianne, Metz, Moselle; Technologies (Montpellier), Montpellier, Herault; Eurequip SA, Nanterre, Hauts-de-Seine; Axone SA, Noisy Le Grand; LY-D Informatique, Noisy Le Grand; Seprim SA, Noisy Le Grand; Ardal SCI, Paris, Ville-de-Paris; CR2A Holding, Paris, Ville-de-Paris; GMV Conseil, Paris, Ville-de-Paris; Informatique (Compagnie Generale D'), Paris, Ville-de-Paris; Sigeo, Paris, Ville-de-Paris; Anelia, Pau, Pyrenees-Atlantiques; Partitiel SA, St. Germain en Laye, Yvelines; Worldwide Chain Store Systems, St. Germain en Laye, Yvelines; Aurea, Toulouse, Haute Garonne; Perfelec SA, Tours; Groupe Eurequip Europe, Vaucresson, Hauts-de-Seine; Germany: CSG Computer Service GmbH, Berlin; IBM Deutschland GmbH, Berlin; IBM Deutschland Entwicklung GmbH, Boeblingen, Baden-Wuerttemberg; Sercon Servicekonzepte Fuer Informations Systeme GmbH, Boeblingen, Baden-Wuerttemberg; IDG Informations Verarbeitung und Dienstleistung GmbH, Cologne, Nordrhein-Westfalen; IBM Unternehmensberatung GmbH, Hamburg; ICA Informations Systeme Consulting und Anwendungs GmbH, Hannover, Niedersachsen; IBM Deutschland Bildungs GmbH, Herrenberg, Baden-Wuerttemberg; IBM Deutschland Direktvertrieb GmbH, Herrenberg, Baden-Wuerttemberg; CGI Informatik GmbH, Langenfeld; IBM Deutschland Speichersysteme GmbH, Mainz, Rheinland-Pfalz; DVO-Datenverarbeitungs-Service Oberhausen GmbH, Oberhausen; IBM Deutschland Kreditbank GmbH, Sindelfingen; IBB Informations Systeme, Stuttgart, Baden-Wuerttemberg; IBM Anwendungssysteme GmbH, Stuttgart, Baden-Wuerttemberg; IBM Beteiligungs GmbH, Stuttgart, Baden-Wuerttemberg; IBM Deutschland Informations Systeme GmbH, Stuttgart, Baden-Wuerttemberg; Italy: ABMCG Architecture & Business Models Consulting Group SpA, Milano, Lombardia; CGI Consulting SpA, Milano, Lombardia; CGI Informatica SRL, Milano, Lombardia; IBM Semea SpA, Milano, Lombardia; Sistemi Informativi SpA, Roma, Lazio; IBM Italia SpA, Segrate, Lombardia; Solution Team SpA, Torino, Piemonte; Servizi Informatici Nord est Spain Forma Abbreviata-Sinest SpA, Venezia, Veneto; Japan: IBM Asia Pacific Service Corp., Tokyo; IBM Japan Ltd., Tokyo; Encyclo Soft Engineering & Services Co. Ltd., Yamato, Kagawa; Republic of Korea: IBM Korea, Seoul; IBM Korea Systems Corp., Seoul; Luxembourg: IBM Belgium Financial Services Co., Luxembourg; Madagascar: IBM Madagascar, Madagascar; Mexico: Aplicaciones de Alta Tecnologa SA de CV, Zapopan; Netherlands: IBM International Centre for Asset Management NV, Amsterdam, Noord-Holland; IBM International Finance NV, Amsterdam, Noord-Holland; IBM International Holdings BV, Amsterdam, Noord-Holland; IBM Nederland Financieringen BV, Amsterdam, Noord-Holland; IBM Nederland NV, Amsterdam, Noord-Holland; Information Systems Management Plus BV, Amsterdam, Noord-Holland; International Logistics & Services BV, Amsterdam, Noord-Holland; International Sales & Services BV, Amsterdam, Noord-Holland; CGI Systems, Delft, Zuid-Holland; IBM Nederland Automotive Services BV, Leusden, Utrecht; ICG Informationssysteme Consulting Und Betriebs GmbH, Salzgitter, Niedersachsen; Viamet BV, Uithoorn, Noord-Holland; Cimad Consultants BV, Utrecht; IBM Nederland Systems Facilities Services BV, Utrecht; Central Service Group BV, Veenendaal, Utrecht; CGI Informatica Holding BV, Woerden, Utrecht; CGI Systems BV, Woerden, Utrecht; Computerij Opleidingen BV, Zwolle, Overijssel; Norway: Concrea AS, Kolbotn, Akershus; International Business Machines A/S, Kolbotn, Akershus; New Zealand: Centurion Ltd., Wellington; IBM New Zealand Ltd., Wellington; Peru: IBM del Peru SA, Lima; Philippines: IBM Philippines, Makati, Rizal; Russia: IBM Corp. Moscow Representative Office, Moscow; IBM Corp. Representative Office, Moscow; Singapore: IBM Product Distribution Co. (Singapore) Pte. Ltd., Singapore; IBM Singapore Pte. Ltd., Singapore; Informational Application Solutions Pte. Ltd., Singapore; Spain: CGI Informatica SA, Madrid; Corporacion IBM Espana SA, Madrid; Hisusa Holding de Infraestructuras y Servicios Urbanos SA, Madrid; IBM Financiacion EFC SA, Madrid; International Business Machines SA, Madrid; Redes de Ordenadores y Servicios SA, Madrid; IBM Global Services Espana SA, San Fernando de Henares; Sweden: IBM Nordic AB; IBM Svenska AB, Stockholm; Package Consulting & Management Nordic AS, Stockholm; Switzerland: CGI Informatique SA, Meyrin, Geneva; Itserv AG, Winterthur, Zurich; Datamind Data Information Services Ltd., Zurich; Datamind Services AG, Zurich; IBM (Schweiz), Zurich; IBM Switzerland, Zurich; Thailand: IBM Thailand Co. Ltd., Bangkok; Thai Systems Corp. Ltd., Bangkok; Tunisia: IBM, Tunis; Tunisian Business Machines SARL, Tunis; Taiwan: IBM Taiwan Corp., Taipei; United Kingdom: Data Sciences Ltd., Farnborough, Hampshire; Datasolve Ltd., Farnborough, Hampshire; CGI Corp. Ltd., Leamington Spa, Warwickshire; CGI (Great Britain) Ltd., Leamington Spa, Warwickshire; CGI LS3 Ltd., Leamington Spa, Warwickshire; LS3 Ltd., Leamington Spa, Warwickshire; MAS (Management Application Support) UK Ltd., London; Bedfont Property Investmetns Ltd., Portsmouth, Hampshire; IBM Service Plus Ltd., Portsmouth, Hampshire; IBM United Kingdom Asset Finance Ltd., Portsmouth, Hampshire; IBM United Kingdom Credit Ltd., Portsmouth, Hampshire; IBM United Kingdom Financial Services Ltd., Portsmouth, Hampshire; IBM United Kingdom Holdings Ltd., Portsmouth, Hampshire; IBM United Kingdom Leasing Ltd., Portsmouth, Hampshire; IBM United Kingdom Ltd., Portsmouth, Hampshire; IBM United Kingdom Pensions Trust Ltd., Portsmouth, Hampshire; IBM United Kingdom Rentals, Portsmouth, Hampshire; Individual Computer Products International Ltd., Portsmouth, Hampshire; Integrated Systems Solutions Co. Ltd., Portsmouth, Hampshire; Early Cloud & Co. (Software) Ltd., Reading, Berkshire; Worldwide Chain Store Systems International Ltd., Reading, Berkshire; Tivoli Systems (UK) Ltd., Slough, Berkshire; Softswitch Ltd., Staines, Surrey; Data Sciences Management Ltd., Sunbury-On-Thames, Middlesex; LA Computer Services Ltd., Sunbury-On-Thames, Middlesex; CGI Systems Ltd., Sutton, Surrey; IBM Services Ltd., Swindon, Wiltshire; IBM United Kingdom Laboratories Ltd., Winchester, Hampshire; Uruguay: IBM del Uruguay SA, Montevideo; Venezuela: IBM de Venezuela SA, Caracas; Vietnam: IBM Vietnam, Hanoi; Zimbabwe: Bedford Investments (PVT) Ltd., Bulawaya

Nonmonetary Support

Value: $79,000,000 (1998 approx); $70,200,000 (1997); $62,500,000 (1996)
Type: Donated Equipment; Donated Products; In-kind Services; Loaned Employees; Loaned Executives
Note: Figures are calculated at retail value.

IBM International Foundation

Giving Contact

Paula Blaker
IBM Corp.
New Orchard Road
Armonk, NY 10504
Phone: (914)499-6420
Fax: (914)499-7624

Alternate Contact

Note: For local projects, contact the Corporate Relations Manager at the local IBM office.

Description

Founded: 1985
EIN: 133267906
Organization Type: Corporate Foundation
Former Name: IBM South Africa Project Fund.
Giving Locations: principally near operating locations and to national organizations.
Grant Types: Capital, Employee Matching Gifts, Fellowship, General Support, Matching, Multiyear/Continuing Support, Project, Research.
Note: Employee matching gift ratio: 1 to 1. There is a maximum of $5,000 cash per donor per institution, up to $10,000 in gifts annually. Matching for retired employees on a 0.5 to 1 ratio. An equipment match option is available on a 2 to 1 or 3 to basis for activeemployees and .75 to 1 for retirees. Gifts are matched for colleges and universities after $5,000, and hospitals after $2,500. Gifts are also matched for hospices, nursing homes, cultural and environmental organisation, and K-12 education.

Giving Philosophy

'IBM is guided by a new corporate strategy that states that IBM will combine its technology and its people in effective partnerships to bring solutions to the systemic problems that impact society, business, and our quality of life. In corporate contributions, we have resolved to make that same planning, support and care that we provide to our customers available to our grantees. As we see it, technology is as valuable in education or job training as it is in business.

'There are four key elements in all new IBM contributions:

'IBM technology & service: Grant programs offer IBM's state-of-the-art technology and solutions, including hardware, software, and services, with a target of 50 percent of all IBM contributions to be in equipment. Support includes IBM technical consultation, where required, to assure the technology is appropriate, manageable, fully utilized, and helps the recipient to achieve measurable improvements and plan for the future. Technology-supported programs cut costs, increase productivity and carry projects and their lessons around the country and world.

'IBM expertise: IBM's employees offer their talent and expertise in conjunction with technology to multiply the impact of IBM's contributions. Both in the U.S. and around the world, IBMers play a variety of supportive roles--convening meetings, brokering collaborations, and networking among leaders in many different fields.

'IBM partnerships: Grant recipients can look to IBM as a full partner in planning and implementation efforts. They can expect IBM to encourage and act in partnership with other businesses, foundations, and decision-makers to provide broad-based support for their efforts.

'Rigorous measurements: Beyond receiving benefits from its corporate citizenship, such as enhanced public image, stakeholder value, and employee pride, IBM insists on one thing from its investments -measurable results for society.' IBM Philanthropy Report.

Financial Summary

Total Giving: $70,000,000 (1999 approx); $116,100,000 (1998); $96,800,000 (1997)
Giving Analysis: Giving for 1997 includes: corporate direct giving ($26,300,000); foundation ($300,000); 1998: corporate direct giving (approx $30,631,068); foundation matching gifts ($5,425,052); foundation ($1,144,880)
Assets: $122,381,647 (1998)
Gifts Received: $20,331,500 (1998); $20,255,000 (1994); $3,450,435 (1993). Note: Contributions are received from IBM Corp.

Typical Recipients

Arts & Humanities: Arts Associations & Councils, Arts Centers, Arts Funds, Arts Institutes, Community Arts, Dance, Ethnic & Folk Arts, Historic Preservation, Libraries, Museums/Galleries, Music, Opera, Performing Arts, Public Broadcasting, Theater, Visual Arts
Civic & Public Affairs: Civil Rights, Employment/Job Training, Public Policy, Urban & Community Affairs, Women's Affairs, Zoos/Aquariums
Education: Colleges & Universities, Community & Junior Colleges, Education Associations, Engineering/Technological Education, Faculty Development, Literacy, Minority Education, Private Education (Precollege), Public Education (Precollege), Science/Mathematics Education, Special Education
Environment: Environment-General
Health: Health Policy/Cost Containment, Health Organizations, Hospitals, Mental Health, Single-Disease Health Associations
International: Foreign Educational Institutions, Health Care/Hospitals, International Peace & Security Issues
Science: Science Exhibits & Fairs, Scientific Organizations
Social Services: Child Welfare, Community Service Organizations, Delinquency & Criminal Rehabilitation, Emergency Relief, Family Services, People with Disabilities, Senior Services, Substance Abuse, United Funds/United Ways, Volunteer Services, Youth Organizations

Contributions Analysis

Giving Priorities: Education, social welfare, civic concerns, and the arts. International grant making is an integral part of IBM's worldwide corporate social responsibility. IBM has a network of staff responsible for corporate social responsibility throughout 152 countries in which it does business. World Trade units have independent budgets for corporate social responsibility to fund projects within operating communities. U.S.-based nonprofit organizations with an international focus are the responsibility of domestic corporate support programs. Program includes cash, equipment, and a strong focus on employee volunteerism. Regional managers worldwide (U.S., Canada, Latin America, Europe, the MiddleEast, Africa, and Asia/Pacific) are kept abreast of each other's projects via a central database. Support goes across all categories of giving. The company's giving categories include education, the environment, health, persons with disabilities, the disadvantaged, the arts, and employee involvement. In partnership with IBM in individual countries, the company will be launching 'global initiatives.' A global initiative addresses a societal issue that is of interest to multiple IBM locations worldwide, an initiative that would be considered a world class solution to a problem and supports IBM's business objectives. The IBM International Foundation wasestablished in 1985 to support philanthropic initiatives in South Africa. The Foundation's charter was expanded in 1992 to encompass a wide array of worldwide iniatives, including enviromental research in Australia, Belgium, and Chile; job training in countries such as Spain and South Africa, and various other programs in Nigeria, Zambia, Tanzania, parts of Europe, the United States and the Asian Pacific. In 1995, the IBM International Foundation was expanded again to provide organizational structure to encompass the company's major new initiatives in the U.S. and worldwide. According to company materials, the IBM International Foundation will over time become a'flagship' or 'signature' focus representing 'the good deeds IBM does worldwide.'
Arts & Humanities: 10%. IBM makes grants to major performing and visual arts organizations, sponsors museum exhibits, programming for public television, and funds world-class libraries, including the Library of Congress and the New York Public Library. Supports museum restoration, children's and science museums, community performing arts organizations, orchestras, and a variety of artistic endeavors.
Civic & Public Affairs: 4%.
Education: 69%. Through the Reinventing Education Program, the company's K-12 education focus, IBM promotes fundamental school restructuring and broad-based systemic change to improve student performance. Program motivates and enables districts to use technology to teach as well as restructure. Also promotes adult education, job training, literacy and helping disadvantaged youth acquire education and skill with technology. Contributions take place within context of large-scale, district-wide reform efforts initiated locally. The program offers equipment, technical and consultant services, and volunteer support. The Environmental Research Program provides support for research into environmental problems.
Environment: 1%. Supports several research programs at universities that search for solutions to environmental problems such as groundwater pollution and depletion of the ozone layer. Enables such schools to receive additional aid from various foundations and agencies such as the National Science Foundation and the United States Environmental Protection Agency.
Health: 4%.
International: Giving overlaps other categories of contributions. Gives through foundation and international subsidiaries to Global initiatives in environmental research, total quality management, job training, management development, support programs for the disabled, and education reform.
Science: 1%.
Social Services: 7%.
Note: Total contributions made in 1998.

Application Procedures

Initial Contact: Send a two-page letter.
Application Requirements: Send a brief statement fully describing the mission of the organization, the amount requested, and purpose of contribution; description of problem to be addressed, proposed solution and how IBM technology and volunteers will be incorporated (if appropriate); name, address, and telephone number of the project contact; project budget with anticipated sources of income; and a plan to measure results.
Deadlines: None.
Review Process: Unsolicited proposals are reviewed on an ongoing basis, but funding is limited. Notification is usually sent within one month.
Evaluative Criteria: Priority given to requests involving IBM technology or employee volunteers; consideration is also given to organizations currently receiving other types of company support.
Notes: Majority of funding is initiated by IBM and does not stem from unsolicited proposals. Videotapes and supplemental materials are strongly discouraged at initial stage.

Restrictions

Does not support individuals; political, labor, religious, or fraternal organizations; sports groups; organizations without tax-exempt status; operating cost requests from United Way member organizations; raffles or telethons; auctions; capital campaigns; chairs; construction and renovation; endowments; scholarships; and company generally does not underwrite conferences, sports competitions, or symposia.

Additional Information

Publications: Corporate Support Programs Guidelines; Reinventing Education Guidelines

Corporate Officials

Nicholas M. Donofrio: senior vice president technology manufacturing PRIM CORP EMPL senior vice president technology manufacturing: International Business Machines Corp.
Louis Vincent Gerstner, Jr.: chairman, chief executive officer, director B Mineola, NY 1942. ED Dartmouth College BA (1963); Harvard University MBA (1965). PRIM CORP EMPL chairman, chief executive officer, director: International Business Machines Corp. CORP AFFIL director: Bristol-Myers Squibb Co. NONPR AFFIL member: Next Century Schools Foundation; director: Sloan-Kettering Cancer Center;

member: New York City Partnership; trustee: New York Public Library; director: Lincoln Center Performing Arts; director: New American Schools Development Corp.; director: Japan Society; member: Council Foreign Relations; member: Grocery Manufacturer America; trustee, advisory board: Center Strategic & International Studies; director: America China Society; member: Business Roundtable.
David B. Kalis: vice president communications PRIM CORP EMPL vice president communications: International Business Machines Corp.

Giving Program Officials

Carol Cromwell: program manager
Robin Willner: PRIM CORP EMPL director corporate social policy & programs: International Business Machines Corp.

Foundation Officials

Paula W. Baker: vice president PRIM CORP EMPL director corporate support plans & programs: International Business Machines Corp.
Cliff Clifford: manager
Stanley S. Litow: president PRIM CORP EMPL vice president corporate & community relations: International Business Machines Corp.

Grants Analysis

Disclosure Period: calendar year ending

International Flavors &Fragrances Inc.

Company Contact

New York, NY
Web: http://www.iff.com

Company Description

Profit: US$249,000,000
Employees: 4,670
SIC(s): 2087 Flavoring Extracts & Syrups Nec, 2844 Toilet Preparations, 2869 Industrial Organic Chemicals Nec.

Operating Locations

Argentina: International Flavors & Fragrances SACI, Buenos Aires; Australia: International Flavors & Fragrances (Australia) Pty.Ltd., Deewhy; Brazil: I.F.F. Essencias e Fragancias Ltda., Avenida; Canada: International Flavors & Fragrances, Concord; Chile:, Santiago; People's Republic of China:, Beijing, Shanghai, Xinjiang, Guangzhou; Colombia: Saboresy Fragancias S.A., Bogota; France: International Flavors & Fragrances I.F.F. (France) S.A.R.L., Bois-Columbes, Dijon; Germany: International Flavors & Fragrances I.F.F. (Deutschland) GmbH, Emmerich; Hong Kong: International Flavors & Fragrances (Hong Kong) Ltd., Hong Kong; Hungary: International Flavors & Fragrances, Budapest; Indonesia: P.T. Essence Indonesia, Jakarta; Ireland: Irish Flavors & Fragrances Limited, Dublin, Drogheda; Italy: International Flavors & Fragrances I.F.F. (Italia) S.r.l., Milan; Japan: International Flavors & Fragrances, Gotemba, Osaka; International FLavors & Fragrances (Japan) Ltd., Tokyo; Kenya: International Flavors & Fragrances I.F.F. (East Africa) Ltd., Nairobi; Republic of Korea: International Flavors & Fragrances (Korea) Inc., Seoul; Mexico: International Flavors & Fragrances (Mexico) S.A. de C.V., Tlainepantia; Netherlands: International Flavors & Fragrances I.F.F. (Nederland) B.V., Hilversum; I.F.F. (Nederland) B.V., Saint Maartensdijk; International Flavors & Fragrances, Tilburg; Norway:, Oslo; Philippines: International Flavors & Fragrances (Philippines) Inc., Manilla; Portugal: International Flavors & Fragrances I.F.F. (Portugal) Lda., Lisbon; Republic of South Africa: International Flavors & Fragrances, Rhodepoort; Singapore: International Flavors & Fragrances (Singapore) Pte. Ltd., Singapore; Spain: International Flavors & Fragrances, Barcelona, Colmenar; International Flavors & Fragrances (Espana) S.A., Madrid; Sweden: International Flavors & Fragrances, Stockholm; Switzerland: International Flavors & Fragrances I.F.F. (Switzerland) A.G., Reinach; Thailand: International Flavors & Fragrances (Thailand) Ltd., Bangkok; Turkey: International Flavors & Fragrances, Istanbul; United Kingdom: I.F.F. (Great Britian) Ltd., Haverhill; International Flavours & Fragrances I.F.F. (Great Britian) Ltd., London; Venezuela: International Flavors & Fragrances de Venezuela C.A., Caracas

IFF Foundation Inc.

Giving Contact

Douglas Wetmore, Treasurer
IFF Foundation Inc.
Phone: (212)765-5500
Fax: (212)708-7144

Description

EIN: 136159094
Organization Type: Corporate Foundation. Supports preselected organizations only.
Giving Locations: NY: New York
Grant Types: Employee Matching Gifts, General Support, Project.
Note: Employee gifts to educational institutions are matched up to $2,000 per employee annually.

Financial Summary

Total Giving: $500,000 (2000 approx); $500,000 (1999 approx); $530,261 (1998). Note: Contributes through corporate direct giving program and foundation. Giving includes foundation.
Giving Analysis: Giving for 1997 includes: foundation ($443,579); foundation matching gifts ($31,627); 1998: foundation ($502,751); foundation matching gifts ($27,510)
Assets: $295,247 (1998); $392,621 (1996); $215,910 (1995). Note: Figures are for foundation giving.
Gifts Received: $200,000 (1998); $626,268 (1996); $516,256 (1995). Note: The foundation receives contributions from International Flavors & Fragrances Inc.

Typical Recipients

Arts & Humanities: Ballet, Dance, Libraries, Museums/Galleries, Music, Opera, Performing Arts, Public Broadcasting, Theater
Civic & Public Affairs: Botanical Gardens/Parks, Clubs, Employment/Job Training, Ethnic Organizations, Civic & Public Affairs-General, Philanthropic Organizations, Professional & Trade Associations, Rural Affairs, Safety, Women's Affairs, Zoos/Aquariums
Education: Arts/Humanities Education, Business Education, Colleges & Universities, Education Associations, Education Reform, Engineering/Technological Education, Education-General, International Studies, Public Education (Precollege), School Volunteerism, Science/Mathematics Education, Student Aid
Environment: Environment-General
Health: Cancer, Clinics/Medical Centers, Diabetes, Emergency/Ambulance Services, Eyes/Blindness, Health Policy/Cost Containment, Heart, Hospitals, Medical Research, Mental Health, Single-Disease Health Associations, Trauma Treatment
International: Foreign Arts Organizations, International-General, Health Care/Hospitals, International Development, International Relations, International Relief Efforts
Religion: Jewish Causes
Science: Scientific Centers & Institutes, Scientific Organizations, Scientific Research
Social Services: Child Abuse, Child Welfare, Community Service Organizations, Day Care, Domestic Violence, Family Planning, Family Services, Food/Clothing Distribution, People with Disabilities, Recreation & Athletics, Scouts, Senior Services, Substance Abuse, United Funds/United Ways, Youth Organizations

Contributions Analysis

Arts & Humanities: 42%. Majority of funds support the performing arts including ballet and opera. Also funds museums and libraries.
Civic & Public Affairs: 12%. Majority of contributions support the New York Botanical Garden. Also gives to women's affairs, environmental affairs, and urban safety.
Education: 6%. Colleges and universities, private precollege education, education associations, and international studies.
Health: 23%. Primarily supports cancer research; also funds hospitals, medical centers, and single-disease health associations. The foundation is an ongoing sponsor of Monell Chemical Senses Center for research on mechanisms of taste and smell.
International: 11%. An international hospital foundation and the NationalCommittee on United States-China Relations.
Religion: 1%.
Science: 1%.
Social Services: 4%. Most of the funding supports the United Way of Tri-State, NY. Also gives to child welfare and youth organizations,the disabled, and the aged.
Note: Figures exclude the foundation-administered employee matching gifts program. Total contributions made in 1998.

Corporate Officials

Richard Mortimer Furlaud: interim chief executive officer B New York, NY 1923. ED Princeton University AB (1944); Harvard University LLB (1947). PRIM CORP EMPL interim chief executive officer: International Flavors & Fragrances Inc. CORP AFFIL director, honorary chairman: America Express Co.; director: Shearson Lehman Brothers Holdings Inc. NONPR AFFIL chairman: Rockefeller Archives Center; chairman board trustees: Rockefeller University; chairman: Millbrook Research Field Center; member: Association Bar New York City; member: Council Foreign Relations. CLUB AFFIL The Links Club; River Club.

Foundation Officials

Stephen A. Block: secretary B Philadelphia, PA 1945. ED Yale University BA (1966); Harvard University JD (1969). PRIM CORP EMPL vice president, secretary, general counsel: International Flavors & Fragrances Inc.

Grants Analysis

Disclosure Period: calendar year ending 1998
Total Grants: $502,751*
Number of Grants: 85
Average Grant: $5,915
Highest Grant: $50,000
Typical Range: $500 to $10,000
***Note:** Giving excludes matching gifts.

Recent Grants

Note: Grants derived from 1996 Form 990.

Arts & Humanities

50,600	New York City Ballet, New York, NY -- Guild Table for Gala Opening night
50,000	Whitney Museum of American Art, New York, NY -- annual fund drive
35,670	Metropolitan Opera, New York, NY -- 1996-97 season subscription, annual fund
10,000	Metropolitan Museum of Art, New York, NY -- for Corporate Patron Educational Programs
7,500	Lincoln Center Consolidated Corporate Fund, New York, NY -- annual appeal, support educational programs

6,000 Carnegie Hall Corporate Fund, New York, NY -- fundraising
2,500 John F. Kennedy Center for Performing Arts, New York, NY -- annual fund drive

Civic & Public Affairs

25,000 New York Botanical Garden, Bronx, NY -- for Rose Garden Dinner Dance
15,000 National Ethnic Coalition of Organizations, New York, NY -- annual fund drive
4,000 Union Beach Fire Department, Union Beach, NJ -- annual fund drive
2,000 Versailles Foundation, New York, NY -- contribution for benefit
1,200 Monmouth Junction Volunteer Fire Department, Monmouth Junction, NJ -- fund drive
1,000 Epiphany House, Long Branch, NJ -- annual appeal

Education

10,000 Colbert Foundation, New York, NY -- for 1996 Gala Benefit Dinner fundraiser
5,000 Augusta Technical Institute, Augusta, GA -- fund drive
5,000 Monmouth University, West Long Beach, NJ -- fund drive
5,000 Ohio State University Wexner, Columbus, OH -- fund drive for educational programs in the arts
2,000 School of American Ballet, New York, NY -- for Workshop Benefit
750 DeWitt Clinton Alumni, Bronx, NY -- fundraising for student scholarships

Health

15,750 American Cancer Society, New York, NY -- annual appeal, Dreamball patron pledge
12,500 Breast Cancer Research Foundation, New York, NY -- annual fund drive
10,000 Fountain House, New York, NY -- second payment on three-year pledge for model program of psychiatric rehabilitation for men and women
10,000 Olfactory Research Fund, New York, NY -- fundraising Medal of Honor
10,000 Riverview Foundation, Red Bank, NJ -- second payment on three-year pledge for fund drive
3,000 American Red Cross, Hazlet, NJ -- annual fund drive for needy families
2,000 Medical Center Princeton Foundation, Princeton, NJ -- annual fundraiser
1,250 American Heart Association, North Brunswick, NJ -- annual appeal
1,200 Hazlet First Aid and Rescue Squad, Hazlet, NJ -- annual fund drive
1,000 Juvenile Diabetes Foundation, Farmingdale, NJ -- Walk for a Cure annual fundraising event
1,000 Monmouth Junction First Aid Squad, South Brunswick, NJ -- fund drive
1,000 United Cerebral Palsy, New York, NY -- for 1996 Beauty Industry Breakfast

International

25,000 American Friends of Paris Opera and Ballet, New York, NY -- for fundraising benefit
25,000 American Hospital of Paris, Paris, France -- second payment on $50,000 pledge for 1995 French Designer Showhouse
3,000 Accion International, Somerville, MA -- annual appeal

Science

25,000 Monell Chemical Senses Center, Philadelphia, PA -- sponsor's fee, Research Mechanisms of Taste
4,684 Agricultural and Food Chemistry Division, Washington, DC -- annual award for Advancement of Agriculture
2,500 Society of Cosmetic Chemists, New York, NY -- 1996 fund drive sponsorship

Social Services

25,000 Lighthouse for Blind, New York, NY -- support Winternight 1996
5,000 Bayshore Senior Day Care Center, Keansburg, NJ -- fourth payment on five-year pledge for fund drive
5,000 MMC/Monte Carlo Benefit -- corporate sponsor for Children in Need for 1996
2,000 Bayshore Youth and Family Services, Matawan, NJ -- annual appeal
1,250 National Council on Alcoholism and Drug Dependency, East Brunswick, NJ -- annual fundraising appeal
1,250 National Council on Alcoholism and Drug Dependency, Red Bank, NJ -- annual fundraising appeal
1,250 New Jersey Council on Alcoholism and Drug Abuse, Trenton, NJ -- programs to benefit IFF employees, certification of alcohol counselors
1,000 Bayshore Youth Athletic Association, Leonardo, NJ -- annual fund drive
1,000 Boy Scouts of America Monmouth Council, Edison, NJ -- annual fund drive
1,000 Boy Scouts of America Thomas A. Edison Council -- annual fund drive
1,000 Girl Scout Council, Farmingdale, NJ -- annual fundraiser
700 Hazlet Youth Athletic League, Hazlet, NJ -- annual fund drive
700 Union Beach Little League, Union Beach, NJ -- annual fund drive

INTERNATIONAL MULTIFOODS CORP.

Company Contact

Minneapolis, MN
Web: http://www.multifoods.com

Company Description

Revenue: US$2,290,000,000
Employees: 6,807
SIC(s): 2045 Prepared Flour Mixes & Doughs, 5145 Confectionery, 5149 Groceries & Related Products Nec.

Operating Locations

Canada: Multifoods, Markham; Robin Hood Multifoods, Markham; Bick's Pickles & Relishes, Scarborough; Mexico: La Hacienda S.A. de C.V., Los Morales Polanco; Venezuela: Molinos Nacionales CA, Caracas

Nonmonetary Support

Value: $106,000 (1990); $130,000 (1989)
Type: Donated Products
Note: Products are donated through the Second Harvest Food Bank network. Annual nonmonetary support approximately $100,000.

International Multifoods Charitable Foundation

Giving Contact

Ms. Karen Anderson, Foundation Administrator
International Multifoods Charitable Foundation
200 E. Lake Street
Wayzata, MN 55391-1662
Phone: (612)594-3568
Fax: (612)594-3304

Description

EIN: 237064628
Organization Type: Corporate Foundation
Giving Locations: MN: Minneapolis, St. Paul Major principally near operating locations and to national organizations.
Grant Types: Capital, Employee Matching Gifts, General Support, Multiyear/Continuing Support.
Note: Employee matching gift ratio: 1 to 1 for higher education only.

Giving Philosophy

'International Multifoods, as a responsible corporate citizen, is committed to working in partnership with communities to maintain a vital, high quality of life where Multifoods employees live and work.'

'As its community investment, the company annually contributes to nonprofit organizations that complement its business and reflect the needs of its local communities.'

'Leveraging contributions with employee volunteer time and expertise, giving is focused on programs in which Multifoods can make an impact.'

'The company currently allocates two percent of its U.S. pretax earnings for charitable giving. Nonprofit organizations must qualify for tax-exempt status according to IRS code 501(c)(3) and comply with state charities laws.' *Multifoods Community Connection*

Financial Summary

Total Giving: $250,000 (fiscal year ending February 28, 2000 approx); $219,687 (fiscal 1999 approx); $204,318 (fiscal 1998)
Giving Analysis: Giving for fiscal 1998 includes: foundation ($204,318); fiscal 1999: foundation ($202,587); corporate direct giving ($17,100)
Assets: $312,000 (fiscal 1999 approx); $221,147 (fiscal 1998); $130,054 (fiscal 1997 approx)
Gifts Received: $200,000 (fiscal 1998); $100,000 (fiscal 1997); $302,000 (fiscal 1993). Note: Foundation receives contributions from International Multifoods Corporation.

Typical Recipients

Arts & Humanities: Arts Institutes, Community Arts, Ethnic & Folk Arts, Libraries, Museums/Galleries, Music, Opera, Theater
Civic & Public Affairs: Botanical Gardens/Parks, Clubs, Civic & Public Affairs-General, Hispanic Affairs, Municipalities/Towns
Education: Agricultural Education, Business Education, Colleges & Universities, Economic Education, Education Funds, Elementary Education (Public), Education-General, Minority Education, Private Education (Precollege), Public Education (Precollege), Religious Education, Science/Mathematics Education, Special Education
Environment: Environment-General
Health: Diabetes
Religion: Churches
Science: Science Museums
Social Services: At-Risk Youth, Big Brother/Big Sister, Child Welfare, Community Service Organizations, Crime Prevention, Family Services, Food/Clothing Distribution, People with Disabilities, Recreation & Athletics, Scouts, Substance Abuse, United Funds/United Ways, Volunteer Services, YMCA/YWCA/YMHA/YWHA, Youth Organizations

Contributions Analysis

Giving Priorities: Health, social welfare, education, and civic interests. Contributions outside the United States constitute approximately 20% to 30% of contributions. International contributions follow the same general guidelines as domestic philanthropic program: Multifoods supports organizations and programs in the areas of education (emphasis on higher education programs which complement interests and business such as agriculture, business management, food chemistry, and foodservice); human service programs assisting the hungry, and providing education

and training in the area of nutrition; economic development; and, organizations offering cultural programs and touring shows to company's rural and field communities. Only a smallnumber of initiatives can be supported each year. All charitable contributions are administered through the headquarters corporate communications deparment.
Arts & Humanities: Less than 5%. Supports art groups with touring companies and educational outreach in company communities.
Civic & Public Affairs: Less than 5%. Funds programs involving youth leadership, community involvement, and urban affairs.
Education: 30% to 35%. Recipients include educational institutions and associations that prepare youth to become responsible adults. Alsosponsors an employee matching gift program and science museums.
Social Services: 35% to 40%. Funding supports the United Way and independent programs throughout the country. Also funds organizations that target the problems of hunger and nutrition among youth. 15% to 20%. Focus on organizations that meet the needs of youth in selected operating locations. Employee committees solicit proposals from local nonprofits, and financial contributions are leveraged with employee volunteers.

Application Procedures

Initial Contact: Request guidelines and application form from the foundation.
Application Requirements: Include name, history, and purpose of organization; proof of tax-exempt status, copy of IRS Form 990; statement of current objectives, priorities, how organization fits Multifoods' priorities, and summary of past two years' accomplishments; list of board of directors; copy of recent annual report; and current year's operating budget.
Deadlines: None.
Review Process: Applications are screened by community affairs staff and reviewed by contributions committee.
Evaluative Criteria: Proximity of service area to company operating locations.
Decision Notification: Contributions committee meets biannually; notification usually within 90 days of receipt.
Notes: Requests for funding a specific project must include description of project and objectives, problems addressed, timetable, and expected results; budget and sources of income; evaluative criteria; and plans for sustaining project support.

Restrictions

The company does not support religious groups for sectarian purposes; political campaigns or organizations; individuals; dinners or social functions; sports fund-raising activities; advertising; loans or investments; special events; industry, trade or professional association memberships; organizations receiving 25% of their support from the United Way; or medical research treatment or equipment.
The company does not consider requests for support through telephone solicitation or form letters.

Additional Information

Grantees are required to provide periodic progress reports; site visits by company staff also may be requested. Company gives 2% of its pretax profits for charitable activities. No more than 10% to 12% of annual contributions budget will be designated to capital grants.
Publications: Multifoods Community Connection

Corporate Officials

Frank W. Bonvino: vice president, secretary, general counsel B Mount Vernon, NY 1941. ED Coe College BA (1963); William Mitchell College of Law JD (1968). PRIM CORP EMPL vice president, secretary, general counsel: International Multifoods Corp. CORP AFFIL secretary: Multifoods Distribution Group Inc. NONPR AFFIL member: American Bar Association; member: Minnesota State Bar Association.
Gary E. Costley: chairman, president, chief executive officer, director B 1943. ED Oregon State University PhD; Oregon State University MS (1970). PRIM CORP EMPL chairman, president, chief executive officer, director: International Multifoods Corp. CORP AFFIL director: Bush Brothers; chairman: Multifoods Distribution Group Inc.
Jill W. Schmidt: vice president communications B 1958. PRIM CORP EMPL vice president communications: International Multifoods Corp.

Grants Analysis

Disclosure Period: fiscal year ending February 28, 1998
Total Grants: $196,286*
Number of Grants: 46
Average Grant: $3,375
Highest Grant: $10,000
Typical Range: $500 to $5,000
***Note:** Grants analysis provided by foundation. Giving excludes corporate direct giving; matching gifts.

Recent Grants

Note: Grants derived from fiscal 1998 Form 990.

Arts & Humanities

1,000 Kansas City Art Institute, Kansas City, MO
1,000 Lansing Community Library, Bonner Springs, KS

Civic & Public Affairs

3,000 Mi Casa, Denver, CO
1,000 Edwardsville Jaycees, Bonner Springs, KS

Education

10,000 Denver Street School, Denver, CO
10,000 Duncanville Education Foundation, Dallas, TX
5,000 Junior Achievement of Orange County, Anaheim, CA
5,000 Los Alisos Middle School, La Mirada, CA
2,500 John Foster Dulles Elementary School, La Mirada, CA
1,983 Washington Elementary School, Sedalia, MO
1,100 St. John's University
1,056 DeSales Catholic School, Lockport, NY
700 Antioch College, Yellow Springs, OH
500 Delaware Valley College, Doylestown, PA
500 Reno Bobwhite 4-H Club, Bonner Springs, KS
500 Tiblow 4-H Club, Bonner Springs, KS

Environment

500 Adventure Woods, Kansas City, KS

Social Services

42,944 United Way, Minneapolis, MN
24,596 Mile High United Way, Denver, CO
11,402 United Way, St. Cloud, MN
10,000 Hands On Atlanta, Atlanta, GA
9,177 Sedalia-Pettis County United Way, Sedalia, MO
5,000 Denver Kids, Denver, CO
5,000 Girls Count, Denver, CO
5,000 Hope House, Independence, MO
4,128 Boys and Girls Club, Sedalia, MO
3,739 Wyndham Lawn Home for Children, Lockport, NY
3,229 Heart of Florida United Way, Orlando, FL
3,000 Colorado Sports for the Physically Challenged, Highlands Ranch, CO
2,000 Boy Scouts of America Troop 13, Pewaukee, WI
2,000 DARE, Aurora, CO
1,728 United Way of Central Illinois, Springfield, IL
1,456 Valley of the Sun United Way, Tempe, AZ
1,388 DARE, Sedalia, MO
1,356 Eastern Niagara United Way, Lockport, NY
1,339 United Way, Atlanta, GA
1,258 United Way of the Columbia-Willamette, Portland, OR
1,205 Girl Scouts of America Niagara County Council, NY
1,196 United Way Western Region, Anaheim, CA
1,000 Bonner Springs Youth Wrestling Club
1,000 Boy Scouts of America Iroquois Trail Council, Lockport, NY
1,000 DARE, Bonner Springs, KS
1,000 Kaw Valley Center, Bonner Springs, KS
883 United Way of Gloucester County, Woodbury, NJ
742 Heart of America United Way, Kansas City, MO
628 United Way
530 United Way of Central Indiana, Indianapolis, IN
500 Boy Scouts of America Troop 50, Kansas City, MO
500 Boy Scouts of America Troop 150, Kansas City, KS
500 YMCA, Lockport, NY

International Paper Co.

Company Contact

2 Manhatanville Rd.
Purchase, NY 10577
Phone: (914)397-1500
Fax: (914)397-1596
Web: http://www.ipaper.com

Company Description

Acquired: Union Camp (1999).
Revenue: US$24,573,000,000 (1999)
Profit: US$183,000,000 (1999)
Fortune Rank: 61, per FORTUNE Magazine's list of 500 Largest U.S. Corporations (1999).
FF 61
SIC(s): 1499 Miscellaneous Nonmetallic Minerals, 2493 Reconstituted Wood Products, 2499 Wood Products Nec, 2631 Paperboard Mills.

Operating Locations

Australia: Tate Access Floors, Enfield; International Paper Company Pty. Limited, Sydney; Belgium: International Paper (Europe) S.A., Brussels; Anitec Image International B.V., Leiden; Canada: International Paper Canada, Inc, Toronto; Chile: Envases Modernos (CHH) S.A., Santiago; Colombia: Productora de Papeles S.A., Cali; France: Societe Martiniquaise de Carton Ondule, Lementin, Martinique; Societe Mediterraneenne d'Emballages, Saint Cloud; Societe Normande de Carton Ondule, Saint Cloud; Germany: Hammermill Paper GmbH, Aachen; Bergvik Chemie GmbH, Hamburg; Guadeloupe: Societe Guadeloupeene de Carton Ondule, Basse Terre; Hong Kong: International Paper (Asia) Limited, WanChai; Israel: International Paper USA Ltd., Haifa; Japan: International Paper Company (Japan) Ltd., Tokyo; IPI Corporation, Tokyo; Republic of Korea: International Paper korea Ltd., Seoul; Netherlands: Akrosil Europe B.V., Heerlen; Bergvik Chemie B.V., Huizen; New Zealand: Best-Wood Limited, Auckland; B.J. (N.Z.) Limited, Auckland; Carter Holt Harvey Limited, Auckland; Carter Holt Harvey Timber, Auckland; Caxton Forests Limited, Auckland; The Caxton Group of Companies, Auckland; Cemac Commercail Interiors Ltd., Auckland; Comalco-CHH Aluminum, Auckland; Dominion Paper Products, Auckland; International

Business Forms Limited, Auckland; Multiwall Packagin Limited, Auckland; New Zealand Fibre Glass, Auckland; New Zealand Forest Products Limited, Auckland; Packagin House NZFP Limited, Auckland; Printpac-UEB Carton Group, Auckland; Propak, Auckland; Smith & Smith Glass Ltd., Auckland; Te Papapa Paper Mill, Auckland; Tradcor International Industries, Auckland; Transport Fuel Systems (NZ) Limited, Auckland; Wood Export New Zealand (1986) Limited, Auckland; ANI Roll-A-Door, East Tamaki; Aakronite New Zealand, Glenfield; Carter Holt Harvey Plastic Products Group Ltd., Hamilton; South Pacific Aluminum, Hamilton; Plix Packaging Limited, Hastings; Caxton Paper Limited, Kawerau; Mataura Paper Mill, Mataura; Baigent Forest Industries Limited, Nelson; Canterbury Timber Products Limited, Rangiora; Caxton Products Limited, Seaview; Danbrand Products Australasis, Te Papapa; Kinleith Mill, Tokoroa; Precision Office Industries, Wellington; Shatham Industries, Wellington; Whakatane Board Mill, Whakatane; Spain: Industrias De Tablerod Y Derivados De La Madera S.A., Barcelona; International Paper (Espana) S.L., Barcelona; Cartonajes Internacional S.A., Madrid; Switzerland: International Paper Company (Europe) Limited, Zurich; Taiwan: International Paper Taiwan Ltd., Taipei; United Kingdom: Bergvik Sales Limited, Leatherhead; Venezuela: Envases Internacional S.A., Caracas

Nonmonetary Support

Type: Donated Products; In-kind Services

Note: For nonmonetary support contact the local facility.

International Paper Co. Foundation

Giving Contact

Dennis Thomas, Vice President, Corporate Communications
International Paper Co. Foundation
2 Manhattanville Road
Purchase, NY 10577
Phone: (914)397-1500
Fax: (914)397-1684

Note: In communities where company maintains facilities, contact mill or plant manager, or communications, human resources, or public affairs manager.

Description

EIN: 136155080

Organization Type: Corporate Foundation

Giving Locations: nationally; principally near operating locations and to national organizations.

Grant Types: Employee Matching Gifts, General Support.

Note: Employee matching gift ratio: 2 to 1 for employee gifts up to $200 each year; 1 to 1 for gifts over $200. Minimum gift foundation will match is $25, the maximum amount is $6,000 per employee annually. The foundation also supports specific educational and environmental programs.

Giving Philosophy

'Since its incorporation in 1953, International Paper Company Foundation has sought out and funded programs which address social and civic needs in communities where the company operates. This commitment to improving life in areas where International Paper employees live and work continues today and is illustrated by the foundation's support of community initiatives. With a growing demand for support, the foundation has taken steps to assure that its resources are utilized as effectively as possible. To this end, we direct our grantmaking to four broad giving categories, and continue to make contributions for programmatic, rather than general, support. While the great majority of funds are allocated to projects in our local communities, national programs which address specific concerns identified by the foundation's board of directors are also eligible for support. At both the local and national levels, the foundation provides support for programs in education, community and civic development, health and welfare, and culture and the arts.' *International Paper Co. Foundation*

Financial Summary

Total Giving: $8,000,000 (1998 approx); $3,256,656 (1997); $2,848,173 (1996). Note: Contributes through corporate direct giving program and foundation.

Giving Analysis: Giving for 1997 includes: foundation ($2,504,340); foundation matching gifts ($458,316); foundation fellowships ($294,000); 1998: foundation ($4,500,000); corporate direct giving ($3,500,000)

Assets: $55,826,133 (1997); $48,992,318 (1996); $40,000,000 (1995 approx)

Gifts Received: $272,566 (1997); $139,625 (1996); $158,390 (1993)

Typical Recipients

Arts & Humanities: Arts Associations & Councils, Arts Centers, Arts Festivals, Arts Funds, Dance, Historic Preservation, Libraries, Museums/Galleries, Music, Opera, Public Broadcasting, Theater

Civic & Public Affairs: Botanical Gardens/Parks, Civic & Public Affairs-General, Municipalities/Towns, Professional & Trade Associations, Urban & Community Affairs, Zoos/Aquariums

Education: Agricultural Education, Business Education, Colleges & Universities, Economic Education, Education Reform, Elementary Education (Private), Elementary Education (Public), Engineering/Technological Education, Education-General, Literacy, Minority Education, Private Education (Precollege), Public Education (Precollege), Science/Mathematics Education, Secondary Education (Public)

Environment: Environment-General, Resource Conservation

Health: Clinics/Medical Centers, Emergency/Ambulance Services, Health Organizations, Hospitals

Religion: Dioceses, Religious Organizations, Religious Welfare

Science: Scientific Labs

Social Services: Child Welfare, Community Centers, Community Service Organizations, Day Care, Family Services, Food/Clothing Distribution, Homes, Senior Services, Shelters/Homelessness, Social Services-General, Substance Abuse, Volunteer Services, Youth Organizations

Contributions Analysis

Giving Priorities: Education, environment, civic interests, and arts and culture. Foundation guidelines exclude contributions to foreign organizations or for use outside the United States. Foreign operating companies do not make contributions in-country except for the Masonite Foundation in South Africa. This foundation is independently administered, and headquarters does not track information on priorities or level of support.

Arts & Humanities: 4%. Supports a variety of local arts groups, museums, and libraries, with a special interest in the visual arts.

Civic & Public Affairs: 5%. Supports local groups concerned with literacy, community and economic development, and volunteerism. Donations of $100 to $500 are available to organizations that have a significant number of International Paper Company volunteers. Also contributes to environmental groups and zoos, and provides substantial support to the National 4-H Council.

Education: 87%. For precollege education, focus is on improving the quality of teaching and learning in operating communities. Most contributions support the foundation's Education and Community Resources Program (EDCORE), which assists selected public school districts in areas where company employees are concentrated. Also gives to other precollege programs and institutions. The bulk of funding for higher education is disbursed through an employee matching gifts program. Also sponsors fellowship programs at selected institutions. Minority education receives between 5% and 10% of total annual contributions, including programs, funds, and institutions, with an emphasis onincreasing career opportunities for minorities in the fields of science and engineering. Economic education also receives between 5% and 10% of total annual contributions.

Note: Percentages reflect 1997 foundation giving only. Company direct giving is about the same amount as foundation giving. Priorities are educational institutions, professional and trade associations relating to company's business interests, local youth and community organizations, hospitals, civic organizations, and arts groups.

Application Procedures

Initial Contact: Request application form from local facility; send to manager of local International Paper Co. facility, or to International Paper Co. Foundation.

Application Requirements: Include a brief background of organization, including board of directors; concise description of program and objectives; audited financial statement; IRS tax-exemption letter; current funding sources and specific amounts; current annual report; and program budget, including amount requested.

Deadlines: Check with local facilities for local deadlines; if submitting directly to foundation, applications are accepted from January 1 through March 1.

Decision Notification: Board meets in June.

Restrictions

Does not support individuals; programs for gifted students; general operating expenses; endowments; capital expenses for cultural, civic, or educational institutions; veterans or labor groups; athletic organizations; religious, political, or lobbying groups; organizations located outside or whose contributed funds are distributed outside the United States and its territories; tables at charitable functions or courtesy advertising; organizations which discriminate on the basis of sex, race, or creed; or groups that do not have 501(c)(3) tax-exempt status. status.

Corporate Officials

Michael Amick: executive vice president forest products & industrial packaging ED North Carolina State University (1963). PRIM CORP EMPL executive vice president forest products & industrial packaging: International Paper Co.

John T. Dillon: chairman, chief executive officer, director B Schroon Lake, NY 1938. ED University of Hartford (1965); Columbia University (1971). PRIM CORP EMPL chairman, chief executive officer, director: International Paper Co. CORP AFFIL director: Caterpillar Inc.; director: Capital Formation Inc.; director: Carter Holt Harvey Ltd. NONPR AFFIL trustee: Economic Education.

John A. Georges: director B El Paso, TX 1931. ED University of Illinois BS (1951); Drexel University MS (1958). PRIM CORP EMPL director: International Paper Co. CORP AFFIL director: Warner-Lambert Co.; senior managing director: Windward Capital Partner LP; director: Ryder System Inc.; director: AK Steel Corp.; director: AK Steel Holding Corp.

Phillip S. Giaramita: vice president corporate communications B Brooklyn, NY 1947. ED New York University. PRIM CORP EMPL vice president corporate communications: International Paper Co.

James Patrick Melican, Jr.: executive vice president legal & external affairs B Worcester, MA 1940. ED Fordham University BA (1962); Harvard University JD (1965); Michigan State University MBA (1971). PRIM CORP EMPL executive vice president legal & external affairs: International Paper Co. CORP AFFIL director: Scitex Corp. Ltd. NONPR AFFIL member: Industries Sector Advisory Comm Paper Products for Trade Policy Matters; chairman finance & management policy

committee: National Association Manufacturer; member: Association General Counsel; trustee: Fordham Prep School; member: American Law Institute; member: Association Bar New York City; member: American Bar Association.
Marianne M. Parrs: executive vice president B 1944. ED Brown University (1965). PRIM CORP EMPL executive vice president: International Paper Co.

Giving Program Officials

Phillip S. Giaramita: president, director (see above)

Foundation Officials

John A. Georges: director (see above)
Phillip S. Giaramita: president, director (see above)
James Walter Guedry: president B Morgan City, LA 1941. ED Georgetown University AB (1962); University of Brussels (1962-1963); University of Virginia LLB (1966). PRIM CORP EMPL corporate secretary, vice president: International Paper Co. CORP AFFIL vice president, section: IP Timberlands Ltd.; section: International Paper Realty Corp. NONPR AFFIL member: Association Bar New York City.
Marianne Larsen: manager contributions program
James Patrick Melican, Jr.: director (see above)
Joyce Nelson: treasurer
Ken Reeves: vice president, administrator, director
Ann Marie Ryan: secretary
Sandra C. Wilson: vice president administration, director B 1949.

Grants Analysis

Disclosure Period: calendar year ending 1997
Total Grants: $3,256,656*
Number of Grants: 1650 (approx)
Average Grant: $1,974
Highest Grant: $250,000
Typical Range: $1,000 to $5,000
***Note:** Giving includes matching gifts, fellowships.

Recent Grants

Note: Grants derived from 1997 Form 990.

Arts & Humanities

18,000	Memphis Arts Council, Memphis, TN
10,000	Arts Council, Erie, NY
10,000	Very Special Arts, Muncie, IN

Civic & Public Affairs

33,749	Marriotts Bay Point Resort
10,000	Cypress Valley Alliance
9,800	Parks and People Foundation, Baltimore, MD

Education

250,000	University of Illinois Foundation, Urbana, IL
117,500	National Council on Economic Education, New York, NY
75,000	Marymount College, Tarrytown, NY
50,000	Paper Technology Foundation, Kalamazoo, MI
46,800	Foundation for Excellent Schools, Middlebury, VT
34,500	Foundation for Excellent Schools, Middlebury, VT
25,000	Southeastern Consortium for Minorities in Engineering, Atlanta, GA
15,000	Mississippi 4-H Club Foundation
15,000	National Council on Economic Education, New York, NY
14,979	Mobile County Public School System, Mobile, AL
11,500	Columbus County Schools
11,500	Jay School Department
11,500	Ukiah Unified School District
11,500	Watson Chapel Schools
11,000	Bay County School District
11,000	Pine Bluff School District
10,995	Hamilton City School District
10,946	Texarkana Independent School District
10,000	Georgia Tech Foundation, Atlanta, GA
10,000	Gurdon Public Schools, Gurdon, AR
10,000	Natchitoches Parish School Board, Natchitoches, LA
10,000	Rockwall Independent School District
10,000	Shelbyville Community Unit School District
10,000	Stephen F. Austin State University, Nacogdoches, TX
10,000	Taylor Public Schools, Taylor, MI
9,999	Webster Parish School
9,998	Moriah Central School District
9,995	Jay School Department
9,969	Beaufort County School District, Washington, NC
9,500	Gurdon Public Schools, Gurdon, AR
9,500	Ukiah Unified School District
9,401	Mobile County Public School System, Mobile, AL
9,000	Trinity Christian School
8,865	Pine Bluff School District
8,580	North Carolina State University, Raleigh, NC
8,265	University of Mobile, Mobile, AL
8,000	Center Independent School District
8,000	Georgetown University, Washington, DC
8,000	Spring Valley Elementary School

Environment

8,000	Coalition for Natural Resources

Religion

11,000	Morehouse Parish School Board, Bastrop, LA
9,705	Morehouse Parish School Board, Bastrop, LA

Science

8,000	Gulf Coast Research Laboratory, Ocean Springs, MS

Social Services

10,000	Boys Home, Covington, VA

INTERPUBLIC GROUP OF COMPANIES, INC.

Company Contact

New York, NY

Company Description

Revenue: US$3,968,700,000
Employees: 21,700
Fortune Rank: 351, per FORTUNE Magazine's list of 500 Largest U.S. Corporations (1999).
FF 351
SIC(s): 7311 Advertising Agencies.

Giving Contact

Linda Sindoni, Administrative Assistant, Human Resources
Interpublic Group of Companies, Inc.
1271 Avenue of the Americas
New York, NY 10020
Phone: (212)399-8058
Fax: (212)399-8130

Alternate Contact

C. Kent Kroeber, Senior Vice President of Human Resources, Chairman of the

Description

Organization Type: Corporate Giving Program
Giving Locations: headquarters area only.
Grant Types: General Support.

Financial Summary

Total Giving: Contributes through corporate direct giving program only.

Typical Recipients

Arts & Humanities: Arts & Humanities-General
Civic & Public Affairs: Civic & Public Affairs-General
Education: Education-General
Health: Health-General
Social Services: Social Services-General

Contributions Analysis

Arts & Humanities: 50%. Supports the arts.
Civic & Public Affairs: 10%.
Education: 25%.
Health: Supports cancer research.

Application Procedures

Initial Contact: a brief letter of inquiry
Application Requirements: a description of organization, amount requested, purpose of funds sought, recently audited financial statement, and proof of tax-exempt status
Deadlines: None.

Corporate Officials

Philip Henry Geier, Jr.: chairman, president, chief executive officer B Pontiac, MI 1935. ED Colgate University BA (1957); Columbia University MS (1958). PRIM CORP EMPL chairman, president, chief executive officer: Interpublic Group of Companies, Inc. CORP AFFIL director: Venator Group Inc.; director: Fiduciary Trust Corp.; executive: Newspaper Services America Inc.; director: Fiduciary Trust Co. International. NONPR AFFIL director: School American Ballet; trustee: Whitney Museum American Art; board overseers, manager: Memorial Sloan-Kettering Cancer Center; trustee: Museum Delta Kappa Epsilon Foundation; board overseers: Columbia University Business School; director: International Tennis Hall of Fame. CLUB AFFIL Sloane Club; Hurlingham Club; River Club; Doubles Club.

Giving Program Officials

C. Kent Kroeber: chairman contributions committee B Pelham, NY 1939. ED New York University BS (1962). PRIM CORP EMPL senior vice president human resources: Interpublic Group of Companies, Inc.
Linda Sindoni: contact corp. contributions PRIM CORP EMPL administration assistant human resources: Interpublic Group of Companies, Inc.

INTRUST FINANCIAL CORP.

Company Contact

Wichita, KS

Company Description

Income: US$40,250,000
Employees: 800
SIC(s): 6712 Bank Holding Companies.

Nonmonetary Support

Type: Donated Equipment; Loaned Executives
Volunteer Programs: INTRUST recruits employees to volunteer in school classrooms during regular work hours.

Corporate Sponsorship

Range: $150,000 - $200,000
Type: Arts & cultural events; Festivals/fairs

INTRUST Bank Charitable Trust

Giving Contact

Diane M. Iseman, marketing officer
INTRUST Bank, NA
PO Box One
Wichita, KS 67201

Phone: (316)383-1236
Fax: (316)383-5879
Email: dmiseman@intrustbank.com
Web: http://www.intrustbank.com

Description

EIN: 486102412
Organization Type: Corporate Foundation
Giving Locations: operating locations.
Grant Types: Award, Capital, General Support, Loan, Matching, Scholarship.

Financial Summary

Total Giving: $300,000 (2000 approx); $315,000 (1999 approx); $341,500 (1998)
Giving Analysis: Giving for 1996 includes: foundation ($182,750); foundation grants to United Way ($111,930); 1997: foundation ($190,450); foundation grants to United Way ($108,000); 1998: foundation ($218,500); foundation grants to United Way ($123,000)
Assets: $54,355 (1998); $96,441 (1997); $151,476 (1996)
Gifts Received: $300,000 (1998); $244,000 (1997); $216,000 (1996). Note: Contributions are received from INTRUST Bank.

Typical Recipients

Arts & Humanities: Arts Centers, Arts & Humanities-General, Historic Preservation, History & Archaeology, Museums/Galleries, Music, Performing Arts, Theater, Visual Arts
Civic & Public Affairs: Botanical Gardens/Parks, Economic Development, Employment/Job Training, Civic & Public Affairs-General, Hispanic Affairs, Housing, Urban & Community Affairs, Zoos/Aquariums
Education: Business Education, Colleges & Universities, Community & Junior Colleges, Education Funds, Faculty Development, Education-General, Public Education (Precollege), Student Aid
Health: Cancer, Children's Health/Hospitals, Health-General, Health Organizations, Hospices, Hospitals, Mental Health, Preventive Medicine/Wellness Organizations, Single-Disease Health Associations, Single-Disease Health Associations
Religion: Ministries, Religious Organizations, Religious Welfare
Social Services: Big Brother/Big Sister, Child Welfare, Community Centers, Community Service Organizations, Family Services, Homes, People with Disabilities, Recreation & Athletics, Scouts, Social Services-General, United Funds/United Ways, YMCA/YWCA/YMHA/YWHA, Youth Organizations

Contributions Analysis

Arts & Humanities: 6%. Supports arts centers, museums and galleries, and music and operas.
Education: 14%. Supports public education and colleges and universities.
Health: 15%. Supports health and wellness concerns and Cerebal Palsy research.
Religion: 13%. Funds a ministry and religious philanthropy.
Social Services: 52%. Supports child welfare, youth organizations, family services, community services, neighborhood revitalization, and the United Way.
Note: Total contributions made in 1998.

Application Procedures

Initial Contact: Send a brief letter of inquiry.
Deadlines: March 15; June 15; September 15.

Additional Information

Publications: Analysis report (annually)

Corporate Officials

Charles Q. Chandler: chairman, director B Wichita, KS 1926. ED Kansas State University (1949). PRIM CORP EMPL chairman: Intrust Financial Corp. CORP AFFIL director: Western Resources Inc.
Charles Quarles Chandler, IV: president, director B Wichita, KS 1953. ED Kansas State University (1975); Northwestern University (1976). PRIM CORP EMPL president, director: INTRUST Financial Corp. CORP AFFIL director: Western Resources Inc.; director: Will Rogers Bank; director: First National Bank Pratt.

Foundation Officials

Ron Baldwin: vice chairman
Charles Q. Chandler: co-trustee (see above)
Charles Quarles Chandler, IV: co-trustee (see above)
J. V. Lintell: vice chairman
Rod Pitts: senior vice president
G. E. Proffitt: co-trustee

Grants Analysis

Disclosure Period: calendar year ending 1998
Total Grants: $218,500*
Number of Grants: 21
Average Grant: $10,404
Highest Grant: $40,000
Typical Range: $2,000 to $40,000
***Note:** Giving excludes United Way.

Recent Grants

Note: Grants derived from 1998 Form 990.

Arts & Humanities

10,000	Music Theater of Wichita, Wichita, KS -- 5 Yr Pledge, 2nd of Five Payments
5,000	Wichita Center for the Arts, Wichita, KS -- Lighting System-Last of Five Payments
3,500	Wichita Symphony Society, Inc., Wichita, KS -- Maintenance Fund
2,500	Stage One Productions, Wichita, KS -- Payment of Pledge

Education

20,000	Friends University, Wichita, KS -- 1st Pymt on 3 Year Pledge, Davis Admin Building
12,500	Wichita State University, Wichita, KS -- 1st Installment, 5 Year Pledge, FBO University Library
5,000	Kansas Independent College Fund, Topeka, KS -- Various Colleges
5,000	Wichita State University Endowment Association, Wichita, KS -- Pymt for Upward Bound Prgm Bridge Student
4,000	Junior Achievement, Wichita, KS -- 1998 Donation
1,000	Wichita State Univerisyt Endowment Association, Wichita, KS -- Pymt for Trio Scholarship

Health

30,000	Cerebral Palsey Research Found. of KS, Wichita, KS -- Five Year Pledge-4th of Five Payments
10,000	Center for Health & Wellness, Wichita, KS -- 5yr Pledge-2nd Payment
10,000	Heartspring, Wichita, KS -- Annual Contribution

Religion

40,000	Salvation Army, Wichita, KS -- Capital Fund Campaign-4th of Five Payments
5,000	Inter-Faith Ministries, Wichita, KS -- 2nd Payment of 3 Year Pledge

Social Services

115,000	United Way, Wichita, KS -- Various Charities
20,000	Y.M.C.A., Wichita, KS -- 1st Installment on 5 Year Pledge
10,000	Kansas Masonic Home, Wichita, KS -- Cost of Refurbishing Two Rooms in Medical
10,000	Quality of Life Center, Wichita, KS -- Payment of Pledge
8,000	United Way of the Plains, Wichita, KS -- Third Annual Installment for Purchase of Wat
7,500	Wichita Area Girl Scout Council, Wellington, KS -- Final Installment of 2yr Pledge
4,000	Midtown Community Resource Center, Wichita, KS -- First Payment of $10,000 Pledge
3,500	Wichita Child Guidance Center, Wichita, KS -- Three Year Pledge-3rd of Three Payments

INVACARE CORP.

Company Contact

One Invacare Way
PO Box 4028
Elyria, OH 44036-2125
Email: info@invacare.com
Web: http://www.invacare.com

Company Description

Employees: 4,889 (1999)
SIC(s): 2599 Furniture & Fixtures Nec, 3842 Surgical Appliances & Supplies.

Nonmonetary Support

Type: Donated Equipment; Donated Products; In-kind Services
Note: Nonmonetary support is provided by the company.
Volunteer Programs: Company participates in the United Way Day of Sharing.

Invacare Foundation

Giving Contact

David T. Williams, Vice President
The Invacare Foundation
Phone: (216)329-6000
Fax: (440)365-4558
Email: dtwilliams@invacare.com

Description

Founded: 1994
EIN: 341726060
Organization Type: Corporate Foundation
Giving Locations: headquarters and operating communities.
Grant Types: Award, General Support, Multiyear/Continuing Support.

Giving Philosophy

'As the company continues its steady growth, Invacare realizes the importance of enhancing the lives of people with disabilities, not only through the innovative products which we design and manufacture, but through our continued support of worthy philanthropic and charitable causes.' Invacare 1997 Annual Report

Financial Summary

Total Giving: $307,875 (fiscal year ending June 30, 1998); $368,958 (fiscal 1997); $196,325 (fiscal 1996). Note: Company gives through foundation only.
Assets: $2,150,000 (fiscal 1997); $2,013,537 (fiscal 1996); $1,939,719 (fiscal 1995)
Gifts Received: $82,800 (fiscal 1994)

Typical Recipients

Arts & Humanities: Arts Associations & Councils, History & Archaeology, Music, Opera, Theater
Civic & Public Affairs: Botanical Gardens/Parks, Business/Free Enterprise, Clubs, Community Foundations, Economic Development, Employment/Job Training, Civic & Public Affairs-General, Hispanic Affairs, Municipalities/Towns, Native American Affairs, Safety, Urban & Community Affairs

Education: Arts/Humanities Education, Community & Junior Colleges, Economic Education, Education Funds, Education Reform, Elementary Education (Public), Medical Education, Public Education (Precollege), Secondary Education (Private), Secondary Education (Public), Student Aid
Health: Alzheimers Disease, Arthritis, Cancer, Children's Health/Hospitals, Clinics/Medical Centers, Diabetes, Health-General, Health Funds, Heart, Hospices, Hospitals, Medical Rehabilitation, Multiple Sclerosis, Nursing Services, Prenatal Health Issues, Respiratory, Single-Disease Health Associations
Religion: Religious Welfare
Science: Science Museums
Social Services: Animal Protection, Camps, Child Welfare, Community Service Organizations, Crime Prevention, Day Care, People with Disabilities, Recreation & Athletics, Scouts, Senior Services, Special Olympics, United Funds/United Ways, YMCA/YWCA/YMHA/YWHA, Youth Organizations

Contributions Analysis

Giving Priorities: Primary support for social services, health organizations, and civic causes.
Arts & Humanities: 4%. Music and theater.
Civic & Public Affairs: 11%. Job training, municipalities, and parks.
Education: 8%. Colleges and private secondary schools.
Health: 30%. Primarily for single-disease health associations.
Social Services: 47%. United funds, the aged, youth organizations, and people with disabilities.
Note: Total contributions made in 1997.

Application Procedures

Initial Contact: Send a brief letter of inquiry.
Application Requirements: Include a description of organization, amount requested, purpose of funds sought, and proof of tax-exempt status.
Deadlines: None.

Restrictions

Grants are awarded to improve the lives of people with disabilities or to benefit the communities where Invacare employees live and work.

Additional Information

Company reports that 80% of contributions go to programs, projects, and organizations in support of people with disabilities.

Corporate Officials

Gerald B. Blouch: president, chief operating officer B 1946. ED Bowling Green State University BA; Ohio State University MA. PRIM CORP EMPL president, chief operating officer: Invacare Corp. ADD CORP EMPL president: Florida Invacare Corp.; president: Mobilite Corp.
A. Malachi Mixon, III: chairman, chief executive officer B Spiro, OK 1940. ED Harvard University (1962); Harvard University (1968). PRIM CORP EMPL chairman, chief executive officer: Invacare Corp. director: Lamson Sessions Co.; director: NCS Healthcare CORP AFFIL director: Sherwin-Williams Co. NONPR AFFIL director: Primus Capital Fund.

Foundation Officials

Gerald B. Blouch: trustee (see above)
Jerome E. Fox, Jr.: secretary, treasurer
A. Malachi Mixon, III: trustee (see above)
Larry Steward: president, trustee
Debra Warden: assistant secretary
David T. Williams: vice president

Grants Analysis

Disclosure Period: fiscal year ending June 30, 1998
Total Grants: $307,875
Number of Grants: 50
Average Grant: $2,158*
Highest Grant: $200,000
Typical Range: $200 to $5,000
***Note:** Average grant excludes highest grant.

Recent Grants

Note: Grants derived from fiscal 1997 Form 990.

Arts & Humanities

5,000 Cleveland Institute of Music, Cleveland, OH -- operations support
2,500 Cleveland Sign Stage Theater, Cleveland, OH -- operations support

Civic & Public Affairs

5,000 Vocational Guidance Services, Cleveland, OH -- operations support
4,000 Law Enforcement Foundation, Dublin, OH -- operations support
3,000 Hattie Larlham League, Hudson, OH -- operations support
2,500 Lorain County Metro Parks, LaGrange, OH -- operations support
2,000 City of Elyria, Elyria, OH -- business development project
2,000 Hattie Larlham League, Hudson, OH -- operations support

Education

5,000 Lorain County Community College, Elyria, OH -- operations support
5,000 Ohio Federation of Independent Colleges, Columbus, OH -- operations support
3,500 Magnificat High School, Rocky River, OH -- operations support

Health

13,800 Juvenile Diabetes Foundation, Independence, OH -- operations support
10,000 Muscular Dystrophy Association, Nashville, TN -- capital construction project
10,000 National Multiple Sclerosis Society, Cleveland, OH -- operations support
5,000 Alzheimers Association, Cleveland, OH -- operating support
3,333 American Cancer Society and Hope Lodge, Cleveland, OH -- operating support
3,250 Rainbow Babies and Children's Hospital, Cleveland, OH -- operations support
3,200 March of Dimes Birth Defects Foundation, Cleveland, OH -- operations support
2,000 American Lung Association of Northeast Ohio, Cleveland, OH -- operations support
2,000 Arthritis Foundation Northeast Ohio Chapter, Cleveland, OH -- operations support

Social Services

44,500 United Way of Greater Lorain County, Lorain, OH -- operations support
13,000 Golden Age Centers, Cleveland, OH -- operations support
6,000 Boy Scouts of America, Cleveland, OH -- operations support
5,000 YES, Cleveland, OH -- operations support
3,500 Achievement Center for Children, Cleveland, OH -- operating support
3,000 Christ Child Society, Lakewood, OH -- operations support
2,500 Disability Network, Columbus, OH -- operations support
2,100 Youth Challenge, Fairview Park, OH -- operations support
2,000 Boy Scouts of America Heart of Ohio Council, Mansfield, OH -- operations support
1,500 YMCA, Cleveland, OH -- operations support

ISE AMERICA

Company Contact

Galena, MD

Company Description

Employees: 1,000
SIC(s): 2015 Poultry Slaughtering & Processing.
Parent Company: Ise Inc., 181 Fukuoka Shin Fukuoka, Nishi Tonami-Gun, Toyama, Japan

Operating Locations

MD: Ise America, Galena

Corporate Sponsorship

Type: Arts & cultural events

Ise Cultural Foundation

Giving Contact

Mr. Shigano Ichimura, Director
555 Broadway
New York, NY 10012
Phone: (212)925-1649
Fax: (212)226-9362

Description

EIN: 222530466
Organization Type: Corporate Foundation
Giving Locations: NY: New York
Grant Types: Project.

Financial Summary

Total Giving: $112,211 (1998); $98,357 (1997); $67,500 (1996). Note: Contributes through foundation only.
Giving Analysis: Giving for 1995 includes: foundation ($263,520); foundation gifts to individuals ($4,500); 1996: foundation ($64,500); foundation gifts to individuals ($3,000); 1997: foundation ($93,857); foundation gifts to individuals ($4,500);
Assets: $23,642 (1998); $5,390 (1997); $1,260 (1996)
Gifts Received: $132,741 (1998); $104,647 (1997); $68,400 (1996)

Typical Recipients

Arts & Humanities: Arts Appreciation, Arts Associations & Councils, Arts Funds, Dance, Ethnic & Folk Arts, Arts & Humanities-General, Museums/Galleries, Visual Arts
Civic & Public Affairs: Asian American Affairs, Civic & Public Affairs-General
Education: Arts/Humanities Education, Colleges & Universities, Education-General, Secondary Education (Public)
International: Foreign Arts Organizations, International Organizations

Application Procedures

Initial Contact: Request guidelines from foundation.

Additional Information

The foundation is funded by 10% of the annual profits of Ise America, the U.S. subsidiary of Japan's largest egg corporation.

Foundation Officials

Hikonobu Ise: president, trustee
Donald Keene: vice president, trustee
Yoshio Morito: treasurer
Michio Nagai: vice president, trustee
Isaac Shapiro: chairman, secretary, trustee B Tokyo, Japan 1931. ED Institute de Droit Compare; Columbia University AB (1954); Columbia University LLB (1956); University of Paris (1956-1957). PRIM CORP EMPL partner: Skadden, Arps, Slate, Meagher &

Flom. CORP AFFIL director: Printing Group Inc.; adjunct professor, director Russian Legal Studies: Columbia Law School; director: Bank Tokyo Mitsubishi Trust Co.; director: Carl Zeiss Inc. NONPR AFFIL member: New York State Bar Association; president, trustee: Isamu Noguchi Federation; member: Japan Society; member: Association Bar New York City; Council Foreign Relations; member: American Bar Association.

Senji Tsutsumi: vice president, trustee B Japan 1927. ED University of Tokyo (1951). CORP AFFIL founder: Saison Group.

Grants Analysis

Disclosure Period: calendar year ending 1998
Total Grants: $108,211*
Number of Grants: 5
Average Grant: $21,642
Highest Grant: $86,030
Typical Range: $200 to $70,000
***Note:** Giving excludes gifts to individuals.

Recent Grants

Note: Grants derived from 1998 Form 990.

Arts & Humanities

2,000 Empire Within-Group Exhibition, New York, NY -- Art Exhibition
2,000 Shigeno Ichimura, New York, NY -- Art Exhibition
2,000 Summer show-Group Exhibition, New York, NY -- Art Exhibition
2,000 Tomoko Nomura, New York, NY -- Art Exhibition

International

86,030 ISE Cultural Foundation Gallery, New York, NY -- Operating Costs
13,636 7th Artistic Movement in Toyama, Toyama, Japan -- Dance Performance
4,545 Shanghai Museum, Shanghai, People's Republic of China -- Sur Everyday Life Exhibition Art Exhibition

JACOBS ENGINEERING GROUP

Company Contact

Pasadena, CA

Company Description

Employees: 7,350
SIC(s): 7349 Building Maintenance Services Nec, 8711 Engineering Services, 8741 Management Services.

Jacobs Engineering Foundation

Giving Contact

John W. Prosser, Jr., Senior Vice President, Finance & Administration
Jacobs Engineering Group
1111 South Arroyo Parkway
Pasadena, CA 91105
Phone: (626)449-2171
Fax: (626)578-6837

Description

EIN: 953195445
Organization Type: Corporate Foundation. Supports preselected organizations only.
Giving Locations: headquarters area only.
Grant Types: Capital, General Support.

Financial Summary

Total Giving: $200,000 (1999 approx); $473,023 (1998); $553,946 (1997). Note: Contributes through foundation only.
Giving Analysis: Giving for 1997 includes: foundation ($343,618); foundation grants to United Way ($68,250); 1998: foundation ($397,323); foundation grants to United Way ($75,750)
Gifts Received: $473,073 (1998); $553,991 (1997); $431,158 (1996). Note: Contributions are received from Jacobs Engineering Group.

Typical Recipients

Arts & Humanities: Arts Centers, Arts & Humanities-General, Historic Preservation, History & Archaeology, Museums/Galleries, Music, Public Broadcasting, Theater, Visual Arts
Civic & Public Affairs: African American Affairs, Business/Free Enterprise, Chambers of Commerce, Civil Rights, Clubs, Community Foundations, Economic Development, Economic Policy, Civic & Public Affairs-General, Hispanic Affairs, Housing, Philanthropic Organizations, Public Policy, Safety, Urban & Community Affairs, Women's Affairs
Education: Agricultural Education, Arts/Humanities Education, Business Education, Colleges & Universities, Education Reform, Elementary Education (Public), Engineering/Technological Education, Education-General, Social Sciences Education, Student Aid
Environment: Environment-General, Wildlife Protection
Health: Alzheimers Disease, Cancer, Children's Health/Hospitals, Clinics/Medical Centers, Health-General, Health Organizations, Heart, Hospices, Hospitals, Medical Research, Multiple Sclerosis, Preventive Medicine/Wellness Organizations, Public Health, Research/Studies Institutes, Single-Disease Health Associations
International: International Affairs, International Relations
Religion: Churches, Jewish Causes, Religious Welfare
Social Services: Big Brother/Big Sister, Camps, Child Welfare, Community Centers, Community Service Organizations, Counseling, Family Services, Recreation & Athletics, Scouts, Senior Services, Shelters/Homelessness, Social Services-General, Substance Abuse, United Funds/United Ways, Volunteer Services, YMCA/YWCA/YMHA/YWHA, Youth Organizations

Contributions Analysis

Arts & Humanities: 1%. Supports public broadcasting.
Civic & Public Affairs: 25%. Supports community foundations and public policy.
Education: 35%. Educational programs, educational funds, and universities.
Health: 6%. Funding goes primarily to hospitals.
International: 1%. Funds international programs.
Social Services: 32%. Funding is awarded to the United Way, senior centers, and youth programs.
Note: Total contributions in 1998.

Corporate Officials

Dr. Joseph J. Jacobs: chairman, director, director B New York, NY 1916. ED Polytechnic Institute BS (1937); Polytechnic Institute MS (1939); Polytechnic Institute PhD (1942). PRIM CORP EMPL chairman, director: Jacobs Engineering Group PRIM NONPR EMPL treasurer, director: Jacobs Family Foundation. CORP AFFIL director: Digital Gene Techs; director, chairman: Cedars Bank. NONPR AFFIL director: California Economic Development Corp.

John Warren Prosser, Jr.: senior vice president finance & administration, treasurer B Glendale, CA 1945. ED California State University, Northridge (1969). PRIM CORP EMPL senior vice president finance & administration, treasurer: Jacobs Engineering Group Inc. NONPR AFFIL contact: Jacobs Engineering Foundation; treasurer: Jacobs Engineering Group Ohio; treasurer: Jacobs Constructors California; member: Financial Executives Institute; treasurer: Jacobs Applied Technology Inc.; member: American Institute CPAs.

Noel G. Watson: president, chief executive officer, director ED North Dakota State University BS (1958). PRIM CORP EMPL president, chief executive officer, director: Jacobs Engineering Group Inc. CORP AFFIL director: Jacobs Applied Technology Inc.; president: Jacobs Engineering Group Ohio; director: CRSS Constructors Inc.

Foundation Officials

Dr. Joseph J. Jacobs: president, director (see above)

William C. Markley, III: secretary, director B 1945. PRIM CORP EMPL vice president: Jacobs Engineering Group Inc. ADD CORP EMPL secretary: JE Remediation Technology; secretary: Jacobs Engineering Group of Ohio; secretary: Jacobs Applied Technology Inc.; director, secretary: Merit, JE Constructors Inc. CORP AFFIL secretary: Jacobs Applied Technology Inc.

John Warren Prosser, Jr.: treasurer, director (see above)

Nazim G. Thawerbhoy: controller B Bombay, MH India 1947. ED Chittagong University (1970); Tulane University (1974). PRIM CORP EMPL senior vice president, controller: Jacobs Engineering Group. NONPR AFFIL member: Financial Executives Institute.

Noel G. Watson: vice president, director (see above)

Grants Analysis

Disclosure Period: calendar year ending 1998
Total Grants: $397,273*
Number of Grants: 143
Average Grant: $2,778
Highest Grant: $50,000
Typical Range: $100 to $5,000
***Note:** Giving excludes United Way.

Recent Grants

Note: Grants derived from 1998 Form 990.

Arts & Humanities

3,500 KCET, Los Angeles, CA

Civic & Public Affairs

30,000 Reason Foundation, Los Angeles, CA
27,500 American Enterprise Institute, Washington, DC
10,000 CATO, Washington, DC
10,000 The Cato Institute, Washington, DC
6,000 Minority Economic Resources Corps, Chicago, IL
5,000 Accion, New Mexico, Albuquerque, NM
3,000 Iberville Foundation, Plaquemine, LA
3,000 Jacobs Engineering Group, Pasadena, CA
3,000 Women's Transportation Coalition, Spokane, WA
2,500 Greater Dallas Chamber of Commerce, Dallas, TX

Education

50,000 The Center for the Study of Popular Culture, Los Angeles, CA
36,000 University of Texas, Houston, TX
10,000 ASU Foundation/ACE, Tempe, AZ
10,000 Polytechnic University, Brooklyn, NY
5,200 Junior Achievement of Arizona, Inc., Phoenix, AZ
5,000 The David S. Dodge Endowment Scholarship
5,000 The Institute for Contemporary Studies, San Francisco, CA
5,000 University of California Regents, Los Angeles, CA
3,000 Auburn Pulp & Paper Foundation, Auburn, AL

3,000	Junior Achievement of Southeast Texas, Inc., Houston, TX
2,500	Miami University Paper, Science and Engineering Foundation, Oxford, OH
2,500	Miami University Pulp & Paper Foundation, Oxford, OH
Health	
5,000	American. Heart Association/Western States Affiliate, Burlinghame, CA
5,000	Huntington Memorial Research Institute, Pasadena, CA
5,000	National Osteoporosis Foundation, Toledo, OH
3,000	Driscoll Children's Hospital, Corpus Christi, TX
2,500	Driscoll Children's Hospital, Corpus Christi, TX
2,500	Huntington Memorial Hospital, Pasadena, CA
International	
3,000	The Asia Society, Houston, TX
Social Services	
17,500	Capital Area United Way Campaign, Houston, TX
15,000	United Way, Los Angeles, CA
15,000	United Way of Greenville County, Greenville, SC
11,500	United Way, Houston, TX
10,000	United Way, Los Angeles, CA
8,000	United Way of Greater Los Angeles, Los Angeles, CA
6,000	Boy Scouts of America, Hartford, CT
5,000	Audubon Girl Scout Council, Baton Rouge, LA
5,000	Boy Scouts of America, Pasadena, CA
5,000	Hugh O'Brian Youth Leadership, Los Angeles, CA
5,000	J.J. Jacobs United Way Contribution
5,000	SGVC Boy Scouts of America, San Gabriel, CA
5,000	SGVC Boy Scouts of America, San Gabriel, CA
3,000	United Way, Cincinnati, OH
3,000	United Way of Morgan County, Decatur, AL
2,700	Hugh O'Brian Youth Foundation, Los Angeles, CA
2,500	Boy Scouts of America, Los Angeles, CA

BENJAMIN JACOBSON & SONS

Company Contact

New York, NY
Web: http://www.bjsons.com

Company Description

Revenue: US$17,000,000
Employees: 55
SIC(s): 6200 Security & Commodity Brokers.

Benjamin Jacobson & Sons Foundation

Giving Contact

Robert J. Jacobson, Sr., President
Benjamin Jacobson & Sons Foundation
40 Wall Street, 45th Floor
New York, NY 10005
Phone: (212)952-1012
Fax: (212)952-0920

Description

EIN: 132630862
Organization Type: Corporate Foundation. Supports preselected organizations only.
Giving Locations: NY: New York nationally.
Grant Types: General Support.

Financial Summary

Total Giving: $360,000 (fiscal year ending June 30, 2000); $360,000 (fiscal 1999); $355,857 (fiscal 1997). Note: Contributes through foundation only. Fiscal 1997 Giving includes United Way ($1,300).
Assets: $268,236 (fiscal 1997); $366,824 (fiscal 1996); $183,454 (fiscal 1995)
Gifts Received: $250,000 (fiscal 1997); $560,000 (fiscal 1996); $350,000 (fiscal 1995). Note: In fiscal 1997, contributions were received from Robert J. Jacobson, Jr. ($100,000), James A. Jacobson ($100,000), and Earl E. Ellis (50,000). In fiscal 1996, contributions were received from Benjamin Jacobson & Sons ($310,000), Robert J. Jacobson, Jr. ($100,000), Earl E. Ellis ($50,000) and James Jacobson ($100,000).

Typical Recipients

Arts & Humanities: Museums/Galleries, Music, Opera, Performing Arts, Public Broadcasting
Civic & Public Affairs: Botanical Gardens/Parks, Clubs, Community Foundations, Ethnic Organizations, Civic & Public Affairs-General, Housing, Municipalities/Towns, Parades/Festivals, Philanthropic Organizations, Urban & Community Affairs, Zoos/Aquariums
Education: Colleges & Universities, Education Associations, Medical Education, Private Education (Precollege), Public Education (Precollege), Religious Education, Secondary Education (Private), Student Aid
Environment: Resource Conservation
Health: Arthritis, Cancer, Children's Health/Hospitals, Clinics/Medical Centers, Diabetes, Emergency/Ambulance Services, Health Organizations, Hospitals, Medical Research, Single-Disease Health Associations
International: International Relief Efforts, Missionary/Religious Activities
Religion: Churches, Jewish Causes, Religious Organizations, Religious Welfare, Social/Policy Issues, Synagogues/Temples
Science: Scientific Research
Social Services: Camps, Child Welfare, Community Service Organizations, Counseling, Family Services, Food/Clothing Distribution, People with Disabilities, Recreation & Athletics, Scouts, Substance Abuse, United Funds/United Ways, YMCA/YWCA/YMHA/YWHA, Youth Organizations

Contributions Analysis

Arts & Humanities: 10% to 15%. Funds museums, performing arts centers, music, and public broadcasting.
Civic & Public Affairs: Less than 5%. Supports philanthropic organizations, researchfunds, and community affairs.
Education: 5% to 10%. Funds colleges and universities, student aid, and private education.
Environment: Less than 5%. Supports conservation.
Health: 25% to 30%. Supports cancer research, hospitals, single-disease health associations, and health organizations.
Religion: 30% to 35%. Supports Jewish organizations, temples, and churches.
Social Services: 15% to 20%. Favors youth organizations, the needy, child welfare, family services, and community services organizations.

Corporate Officials

Robert J. Jacobson, Jr.: partner PRIM CORP EMPL partner: Benjamin Jacobson & Sons.

Foundation Officials

Arthur L. Jacobson: treasurer, director PRIM CORP EMPL partner: Benjamin Jacobson & Sons.
James A. Jacobson: director PRIM CORP EMPL owner: Benjamin Jacobson & Sons.
Robert J. Jacobson, Jr.: secretary, director (see above)
Robert J. Jacobson, Sr.: president, director

Grants Analysis

Disclosure Period: fiscal year ending June 30, 1997
Total Grants: $354,557*
Number of Grants: 316
Average Grant: $1,122
Highest Grant: $30,000
Typical Range: $100 to $3,500
***Note:** Giving excludes United Way.

Recent Grants

Note: Grants derived from fiscal 1997 Form 990.

Arts & Humanities	
12,500	Lower Eastside Tenement Museum, New York, NY
10,000	WLIW/Channel 21
5,000	Raymond F. Kravis Center for Performing Arts, West Palm Beach, FL
3,000	Tilles Center for Performing Arts
2,500	Museum of Television and Radio, New York, NY
1,800	WLEW/Channel 21
1,200	Richard Tucker Music Foundation, New York, NY
1,000	WLUW/Channel 21
Civic & Public Affairs	
6,000	Liu Gala XVI
2,500	National Italian American Foundation
1,000	Variety Club Foundation, New York, NY
Education	
10,000	CCL Inner-City Schools Archdiocese of New York, New York, NY
3,000	Taft School, Watertown, CT
2,500	Dowling College, Oakdale, NY
2,000	Dartmouth Alumni Fund, Hanover, NH
1,500	University of Southern California, Los Angeles, CA
Environment	
5,000	Central Park Conservancy, New York, NY
Health	
25,000	Cancer Research Center, Columbia, MO
12,500	Werther Research Foundation
10,000	Juvenile Diabetes Foundation, New York, NY
10,000	St. Jude's Children's Research Hospital, Memphis, TN
5,000	Floating Hospital, New York, NY
3,500	Make-A-Wish Foundation, New York, NY
2,500	Mount Sinai Hospital, New York, NY
1,500	Joslyn Diabetes Center
Religion	
30,000	United Jewish Appeal Federation, New York, NY
10,000	American Jewish Committee, New York, NY
10,000	American Jewish Committee, New York, NY
10,000	Reformed Church of Locust Valley
7,500	Anti-Defamation League, New York, NY
5,000	National Conference of Christian and Jews, New York, NY
5,000	Seton Foundation, Staten Island, IL
3,500	Jewish Foundation, Palm Beach, FL
2,091	Larchmont Temple, Larchmont, NY
2,000	Catholic Big Brothers, New York, NY
2,000	Fountain Baptist Church, Hampton, VA
2,000	Our Lady of Victory
1,000	Temple Beth Miriam

Social Services

12,550	Food for the Poor, Pompano Beach, FL
10,000	Boy Scouts of America, New York, NY
10,000	YMCA, New York, NY
5,000	Exchange Christmas Dinner Fund, New York, NY
3,000	United Combined Philanthropies of Suffolk, NY
2,500	Members Handicapped Children's Fund, New York, NY
2,000	United Combined Philanthropies of Suffolk, NY
1,500	Clear Pool Camp, New York, NY
1,110	Hackers for Hope, Danbury, CT
1,000	Skating Club, Bridgewater, VA
1,000	United Way
1,000	Youth and Family Counseling Agency

JELD-WEN, INC.

Company Contact

Klamath Falls, OR

Company Description

Employees: 9000
SIC(s): 2431 Millwork.

Jeld-wen Foundation

Giving Contact

Roderick C. Wendt, President & Director
JELD-WEN Foundation
PO Box 1329
Klamath Falls, OR 97601
Phone: (541)882-3451
Fax: (541)885-7454

Description

EIN: 936054272
Organization Type: Corporate Foundation
Giving Locations: major principally near operating locations and to national organizations.
Grant Types: Capital, Challenge, General Support, Project, Scholarship, Seed Money.

Giving Philosophy

'The JELD-WEN Foundation was established in 1969 with the expressed purpose of 'helping worthy endeavors' in communities where company plant or business operations exist. The foundation prioritizes requests on the basis of demonstrated impact toward making our communities better places to live. An assessment is also made as to how many company employees and families will use the services. Generally stated, top priorities of the foundation include: education activities, social welfare, health care, youth activities, arts and cultural activities, and free market, free enterprise oriented projects. Requests not falling in these areas may occasionally be accepted for consideration, if they provide significant community impact or involve sizeable numbers of our employees.' *Criteria for Evaluation of Donation Requests, JELD-WEN Foundation*

Financial Summary

Total Giving: $3,551,301 (1997); $1,664,085 (1996); $2,103,269 (1995). Note: Contributes through foundation only. 1996 Giving includes scholarship ($117,600); United Way ($371,519).
Assets: $40,299,202 (1997); $30,566,158 (1996); $27,056,079 (1995)
Gifts Received: $5,085,000 (1997); $2,136,000 (1996); $3,328,000 (1995). Note: Contributions are received from JELD-WEN Inc.

Typical Recipients

Arts & Humanities: Arts Associations & Councils, Arts Centers, Arts Festivals, History & Archaeology, Libraries, Museums/Galleries, Music, Opera
Civic & Public Affairs: Botanical Gardens/Parks, Business/Free Enterprise, Chambers of Commerce, Economic Development, Employment/Job Training, Housing, Municipalities/Towns, Public Policy, Safety, Urban & Community Affairs, Women's Affairs
Education: Colleges & Universities, Community & Junior Colleges, Education Reform, Elementary Education (Public), Engineering/Technological Education, Education-General, Preschool Education, Private Education (Precollege), Public Education (Precollege), Science/Mathematics Education, Student Aid, Vocational & Technical Education
Environment: Environment-General, Wildlife Protection
Health: Emergency/Ambulance Services, Health Policy/Cost Containment, Health Organizations, Hospices, Hospitals, Public Health
Religion: Ministries
Science: Science Museums
Social Services: Animal Protection, Child Welfare, Community Centers, Crime Prevention, People with Disabilities, Recreation & Athletics, Scouts, Senior Services, United Funds/United Ways, Volunteer Services, YMCA/YWCA/YMHA/YWHA, Youth Organizations

Contributions Analysis

Arts & Humanities: Less than 5%. Recipients include museums and libraries. Additional funding supports arts festivals and associations.
Civic & Public Affairs: 10% to 15%. Grants support community organizations, firedepartments, business associations, and housing organizations.
Education: About 15%. Most grants support higher education, including community colleges and universities. Some funding supports secondary institutions, such as preparatory schools.
Health: 5% to 10%. Recipients include family and child medical centers and national health organizations such as the Red Cross.
Science: 5% to 10%. Supports scientific museums.
Social Services: About 45%. United Way contributions account for the majority of grants in this category. Funds also support children's organizations, community centers such as YMCAs, and recreational and athletic groups.

Application Procedures

Initial Contact: request application; submit completed form to the foundation
Application Requirements: as indicated in the application
Deadlines: write in to request deadline dates
Review Process: foundation board generally meets on a quarterly basis; receipt is acknowledged, and proposal may be accepted, rejected, or referred for modification within two weeks; proposals accepted for consideration are then reviewed at trustees' meeting in March, June, September, or December; proposal contact persons are notified within two weeks after meeting
Evaluative Criteria: location of organization relative to company operating areas, value of project to company employees and families, involvement of employees in organization and project proposed
Decision Notification: at quarterly trustees' meetings
Notes: Foundation meeting dates vary due to requests received and scheduling logistics of foundation trustees.

Restrictions

Foundation does not fund projects related to religious purposes; proposals which duplicate government or private agency programs; projects which serve a very narrow segment of the community; proposals that the foundation feels are not clearly defined, not feasible, not cost effective, or inappropriate to meet existing needs.
Foundation generally discourages requests for annual support outside of United Way giving.
Rejected proposals may not be resubmitted during the same calendar year.

Additional Information

The foundation may fund an outstanding organization more than once in a short period of time, but is cautious not to let organizations become dependent on regular giving.
The foundation requests that organizations refrain from calling unless it is imperative to the project.

Corporate Officials

William Bernard Early: senior vice president, assistant secretary, director B Mexico, MO 1936. ED Stanford University (1958); Harvard University (1964). PRIM CORP EMPL senior vice president, assistant secretary, director: Jeld-Wen, Inc. CORP AFFIL vice president: Bend Millwork System Inc.
Richard L. Wendt: chief executive officer, chairman B 1931. PRIM CORP EMPL chief executive officer, chairman: Jeld-Wen, Inc. CORP AFFIL director: Columbia Forest Products Inc.; director: Windmill Inns America Inc.; chairman: Avanti Industries Inc.; chairman: Bend Millwork System Inc.
Roderick C. Wendt: president, director B 1954. ED Willamette University Law School JD (1980). PRIM CORP EMPL president, director: Jeld-Wen, Inc. CORP AFFIL president: Bend Millwork System Inc.; treasurer: Windmill Inns America Inc.; president: 3D Industries Inc.
Larry V. Wetter: vice chairman, director B Rockwell City, IA 1933. ED Iowa State University of Science & Technology (1955). PRIM CORP EMPL vice chairman, director: Jeld-Wen, Inc. CORP AFFIL executive vice president: Bend Millwork System Inc.

Foundation Officials

William Bernard Early: trustee (see above)
Nancy Wendt: trustee
Richard L. Wendt: trustee (see above)
Roderick C. Wendt: trustee (see above)
Larry V. Wetter: trustee (see above)

Grants Analysis

Disclosure Period: calendar year ending 1997
Total Grants: $3,555,901*
Number of Grants: 276
Average Grant: $12,884
Highest Grant: $200,000
Typical Range: $1,000 to $20,000
***Note:** Giving includes scholarship; United Way.

Recent Grants

Note: Grants derived from 1996 Form 990.

Arts & Humanities

50,000	High Desert Museum, Bend, OR
25,000	Oregon Symphony Association, Portland, OR
15,000	Deschutes County Historical Society, Bend, OR
13,200	Cultural Activities Center, Temple, TX
12,212	Grand Opera House, Dubuque, IA

Civic & Public Affairs

40,000	Opportunity Center of Central Oregon, Redmond, OR
38,134	Knox County Airport, Mount Vernon, OH
25,000	City of Stayton, Stayton, OR
20,000	Yakima Valley Partners, Yakima, WA
15,000	Selah Parks Foundation, Selah, WA
12,500	Mecklenburg County Council, Charlotte, NC
10,000	Housing Hope, Everett, WA

Education

50,000	OMSI, Portland, OR
34,000	Smart, Klamath Falls, OR
25,000	Mount Vernon Nazarene College, Mount Vernon, OH
14,000	Oregon Tech Foundation, Klamath Falls, OR
14,000	Seven Peaks Foundation, Bend, OR
13,700	Klamath Falls City Schools, Klamath Falls, OR
10,200	Oregon Institute of Technology, Klamath Falls, OR
10,000	Bend-Lapine School District, Bend, OR
9,600	Central Oregon Community College, Bend, OR
7,750	Stride Learning Center, Cheyenne, WY

Environment

15,000	Oregon Outback Visitor Association, Klamath Falls, OR
10,500	Wilderness Trails, Medford, OR

Health

35,000	National Center for Policy Analysis, Dallas, TX
15,000	Mount Ascutney Hospital, Windsor, VT
12,000	American Institute of Medical Preventics, Albany, CA

Religion

25,000	Kleos Ministries, Chiloquin, OR

Social Services

200,000	Boy Scouts of America Crater Lake Council, Central Point, OR
70,500	United Way Klamath Basin, Klamath Falls, OR
50,000	Children's Family House of Oregon, Bend, OR
30,000	Ringtown Area Recreation, Ringtown, PA
29,200	United Community Fund of Knox County, Mount Vernon, OH
27,500	Deschutes United Way, Bend, OR
25,000	Boys and Girls Club, Plymouth, IN
23,500	United Way King County, Seattle, WA
20,000	YMCA, Yakima, WA
19,500	YMCA, Mount Vernon, OH
15,000	Boys and Girls Club, Corvallis, OR
15,000	Senior Citizens Services, Sioux Falls, SD
13,861	Humane Society, Redmond, OR
12,500	Klamath County Sheriff Department, Klamath Falls, OR
10,000	Champ Racis Family YMCA, Shenandoah, PA
10,000	Dubuque Soccer Alliance, Dubuque, WA
10,000	Kids and Company, Gresham, OR
10,000	Redcap Boys and Girls Club, Redmond, OR
10,000	Senior Citizens of Sweet Home, Sweet Home, OR
10,000	Yakima Family YMCA, Yakima, WA
8,000	Girl Scouts of America Little Cloud Council, Dubuque, IA
7,800	Sparta-White Counties United Givers Fund, Sparta, TN

JOHNSON CONTROLS INC.

Company Contact

Milwaukee, WI
Web: http://www.johnsoncontrols.com

Company Description

Revenue: US$12,586,800,000
Profit: US$337,700,000
Employees: 65,800
Fortune Rank: 108, per FORTUNE Magazine's list of 500 Largest U.S. Corporations (1999).
FF 108
SIC(s): 2531 Public Building & Related Furniture, 3081 Unsupported Plastics Film & Sheet, 3085 Plastics Bottles, 3822 Environmental Controls.

Operating Locations

Australia: Johnson Controls Australia Pty. Ltd., Silverwater; Johnson Controls Australia Pty. Ltd. (Automotive Div.), Thomastown; Austria: Johnson Controls Austria GmbH, Mandling, Steiermark; JCI Regelungstechnik GmbH, Vienna; Belgium: Johnson Controls Automotive NV, Geel, Anvers; Johnson Controls, Kraainem, Brabant; Johnson Controls International SA, Kraainem, Brabant; Johnson Controls Plastics Holding NV, Kraainem, Brabant; Canada: Cunningham Refrigeration & Heating Ltd., Camrose; Academy Technical Services Ltd., Edmonton; Johnson Controls Ltd., Markham; Johnson Controls World Services Ltd., Markham; Canadian Fabricated Products Ltd., Stratford; France: Johnson Controls Cemis, Aubervilliers, Seine-St.-Denis; Uniloy France, Bron, Rhone; Johnson Controls France, Colombes, Hauts-de-Seine; Johnson Control Roth SA, Strasbourg, Bas-Rhin; Johnson Controls Automotive France, Strasbourg, Bas-Rhin; Johnson Controls Roth (Manufacture Pour L'Automoblile), Strasbourg, Bas-Rhin; Roth Johnson Technologie, Strasbourg, Bas-Rhin; Soc. Industrielle Johnson Controls Roth, Strasbourg, Bas-Rhin; Germany: B&W Kunststoffmaschinenbau & Handels GmbH, Berlin; Johnson Controls Objekt Bog=chum GmbH & Co. KG, Bochum, Nordrhein-Westfalen; JCI Beteilsgung GmbH, Burscheid, Nordrhein-Westfalen; Johnson Controls GmbH, Burscheid, Nordrhein-Westfalen; Johnson Controls/ Naue Engineering GmbH, Burscheid, Nordrhein-Westfalen; Johnson Controls Lahnwerk GmbH & Co. KG, Dautphetal, Hessen; Johnson Controls Beteiligungs GmbH, Espelkamp, Nordrhein-Westfalen; KTL Kunststoff Technik GmbH & Co., Espelkamp, Nordrhein-Westfalen; Johnson Controls Integrated Facility Management GmbH & Co. KG, Essen; Johnson Controls Schwalbach GmbH, Schwalbach, Saarland; Greece: Johnson Controls Plastic CI SA, Athens, Attiki; Hungary: Johnson Controls International Gyarto Es Kereskedelmi KFT, Budapest; Italy: Schmalbach Lubeca PET Containers Italia SpA, Bologna, Emilia-Romagna; Uniloy SRL, Calenzano, Toscana; Johnson Control SpA, Lomagna, Lecco; Schmalbach Lubeca PET Containers Sim Italia SpA, Loreto, Marche; Johnson Controls SpA, Milano, Lombardia; Mexico: Johnson Controls de Mexico SA de CV, Ciudad de Mexico; Johnson Control Automotriz Mexico SA de CV, San Luis Teolocholco; Malaysia: Johnson Controls (M) Sdn. Bhd., Petaling Jaya, Selangor; Netherlands: Johnson Controls Integrated Facility Management BV, Amsterdam, Zuidoost; Johnson Controls Automation Systems BV, Gorinchem, Zuid-Holland; Johnson Controls Nederland BV, Leeuwarden, Friesland; Johnson Controls International BV, Rotterdam, Zuid-Holland; Johnson Controls Nederland Holding BV, Rotterdam, Zuid-Holland; Norway: Johnson Controls Norden AS, Oslo, Akershus; Singapore: Johnson Controls (S) Pte. Ltd., Singapore; Spain: Johnson Controls Alagon SA, Alagon, Zaragoza; Johnson Controls Espana SL, Madrid; Novel Lahnwerk Espanola SA, Sant Joan Despi, Cataluna; Slovenia: Johnson Controls, Slovenj Gradec; United Kingdom: Uniloy (UK) Ltd., Banbury, Oxfordshire; Haydon Distribution Ltd., Bournemouth, Dorset; Kentair (Wholesale) Ltd., Bournemouth, Dorset; Prince APG Ltd., Coventry, West Midlands; Paul Carter (Environmental Services) Ltd., Horsham, West Sussex; Johnson Control Systems Ltd., Leatherhead, Surrey; Johnson Controls Ltd., London; Haydon Management Services Ltd., Manchester, Greater Manchester; Johnson Controls Automotive (UK) Ltd., Mansfield, Nottingham; Johnson Controls Battery (UK) Ltd., Romsey, Hampshire; Johnson Control Systems Pension Ltd., Swindon, Wiltshire; Jphnson Controls (UK) Ltd., Swindon, Wiltshire; AJC Johnson Controls Ltd., Warwick, Warwickshire; Procord Ltd., Waterlooville, Hampshire; Procord Pension Trustees Ltd., Waterlooville, Hampshire; Haydon Air Conditioning Ltd., Wimborne, Dorset; Haydon & Co. Ltd., Wimborne, Dorset; Haydon Group Ltd., Wimborne, Dorset

Nonmonetary Support

Type: Donated Equipment; In-kind Services
Note: Co. provides nonmonetary support.

Corporate Sponsorship

Type: Pledge-a-thon

Johnson Controls Foundation

Giving Contact

Valerie Adisek, Administrative Secretary
Johnson Controls Foundation
PO Box 591, M/S x-46
Milwaukee, WI 53201-0591
Phone: (414)228-2296
Fax: (414)228-3200

Description

EIN: 396036639
Organization Type: Corporate Foundation
Giving Locations: in areas where company has a significant presence.
Grant Types: Capital, Department, Employee Matching Gifts, General Support, Multiyear/Continuing Support, Scholarship.

Giving Philosophy

'The corporate purpose of Johnson Controls, Inc., includes recognition of the fact that its success as a business enterprise is related to the economic and social climate, not only in the communities in which it operates, but in society at large. Therefore, a corporate contributions program, designed to advance the general welfare and to respond to the broader needs of society, was established.' *Policies and Guidelines for Making Contributions, Johnson Controls Foundation*

Financial Summary

Total Giving: $4,000,000 (1999 approx); $4,233,049 (1998); $3,858,043 (1997). Note: Contributes through corporate direct giving program and foundation. 1997 Giving includes foundation (1,860,471); scholarship ($112,825); United Way ($1,884,747).
Assets: $36,439,406 (1998); $30,878,201 (1997); $28,183,155 (1996)
Gifts Received: $3,500,000 (1998); $3,500,000 (1997); $3,500,000 (1996). Note: Contributions are from Johnson Control, Inc.

Typical Recipients

Arts & Humanities: Arts Associations & Councils, Arts Centers, Arts Festivals, Arts Funds, Arts Institutes, Ballet, Dance, Historic Preservation, Libraries, Museums/Galleries, Music, Opera, Performing Arts, Public Broadcasting, Theater
Civic & Public Affairs: Business/Free Enterprise, Civil Rights, Economic Development, Employment/ Job Training, Civic & Public Affairs-General, Housing, Nonprofit Management, Parades/Festivals, Professional & Trade Associations, Urban & Community Affairs, Women's Affairs, Zoos/Aquariums
Education: Agricultural Education, Arts/Humanities Education, Business Education, Colleges & Universities, Community & Junior Colleges, Continuing Education, Economic Education, Education Associations, Education Funds, Education Reform, Elementary Education (Private), Engineering/Technological Education, Education-General, Literacy, Medical Education, Minority Education, Private Education (Precollege), Public Education (Precollege), Science/Mathematics Education, Student Aid

Environment: Energy, Environment-General, Resource Conservation
Health: Cancer, Children's Health/Hospitals, Clinics/Medical Centers, Health Organizations, Hospitals, Medical Research, Public Health, Single-Disease Health Associations, Transplant Networks/Donor Banks
International: International Relations
Religion: Religious Welfare
Science: Science Museums, Scientific Centers & Institutes
Social Services: Child Welfare, Community Centers, Community Service Organizations, Counseling, Family Services, Food/Clothing Distribution, People with Disabilities, Recreation & Athletics, Senior Services, Substance Abuse, United Funds/United Ways, YMCA/YWCA/YMHA/YWHA, Youth Organizations

Contributions Analysis

Giving Priorities: Social welfare, education, and the arts.
Arts & Humanities: About 40%. Primarily to Milwaukee-based arts organizations. Priorities include public broadcasting, museums, ballet, and visual, performing, and literary arts organizations and funds. Sponsors matching gifts program.
Civic & Public Affairs: Less than 5%. Mainly supports community and neighborhood development, justice and law, civil rights and equal opportunity, citizenship, safety, and environmental affairs.
Education: 10% to 15%. Primarily supports public and private colleges and universities. Other interests include adult education, education associations, and programs that seek to increase public knowledge of economics. Scholarships to employees' children and a matching gifts program.
Health: Less than 5%. Primarily supporting hospitals and single-disease healthassociations. Will consider grants to capital fund programs supporting hospitals only if programs have been approved by appropriate health planning agencies.
Science: Less than 5%. Science museums.
Social Services: 40% to 45%. Major support to the United Way. Youth organizations are also a primary concern. Other interests include child welfare, the disabled, homes, the aged, and family and community centers. Also matches employee gifts to United Ways.

Application Procedures

Initial Contact: clear, concise letter on organization letterhead
Application Requirements: description of the organization's structure, purpose, history, and programs; a list of current officers and governing board members, including their outside affiliations; summary of need for support and its intended use; geographic area served; current income and expense budget, and copy of most recent audited financial statement; statement of other funding sources, community support and involvement; copy of 501 (c)(3) status letter
Deadlines: None.
Evaluative Criteria: organization's general structure, objectives, management capacity, relationship to community, population to be served, position relative to other organizations performing similar functions
Decision Notification: advisory board meets approximately three times per year in March, September, and November; allow up to 120 days for decision
Notes: In preliminary stage, personal visits, phone calls to the foundation, and video tapes are discouraged.

Restrictions

Foundation does not support organizations which are not tax-exempt; individuals; private foundations or endowment funds; political or lobbying groups; goodwill advertising; fraternal, veterans', or labor groups; or organizations based or located outside the United States. The foundation does not generally support precollege education; medical or scientific research; Religious groups for sectarian purposes; testimonials, fundraising events, tickets to benefits, or shows; or travel, tours, seminars, conferences, or publications.

Additional Information

Grants are not automatically renewed.
Publications: Giving Guidelines

Corporate Officials

James Henry Keyes: president B LaCrosse, WI 1940. ED Marquette University BS (1962); Northwestern University MBA (1963). PRIM CORP EMPL president: Johnson Controls Inc. ADD CORP EMPL president: Johnson Controls International; president: Johnson Controls Battery Group; president: Johnson Controls Interiors Inc.; vice president: Johnson Controls World Services Inc.; president: Prince Holding Corp. CORP AFFIL director: Universal Foods Corp.; director: LSI Logic Corp.; director: Pitney Bowes Inc.; director: Federation Reserve Bank Chicago. NONPR AFFIL member: Manufacturers Alliance; member: National Association Manufacturers; member: American Institute CPAs.

Foundation Officials

Valerie Adisek: admin secretary
James Henry Keyes: advisor (see above)
R. Douglas Ziegler: advisor B Milwaukee, WI 1927. ED Northwestern University (1949). PRIM CORP EMPL chairman: Ziegler Companies Inc. CORP AFFIL president: Prin Preservation Portfolios; vice president: Ziegler Asset Management Co.; director: Johnson Controls Inc.
Denise M. Zutz: member advisory board B Milwaukee, WI 1951. ED University of Wisconsin (1973). PRIM CORP EMPL vice president corporate communications: Johnson Controls Inc.

Grants Analysis

Disclosure Period: calendar year ending 1998
Total Grants: $4,233,049*
Number of Grants: 1,000 (approx)
Average Grant: $4,233
Highest Grant: $500,000
Typical Range: $1,000 to $10,000
***Note:** Giving includes scholarship; United Way.

Recent Grants

Note: Grants derived from 1998 Form 990.

Arts & Humanities

275,000	United Performing Arts Fund, Milwaukee, WI
100,000	Milwaukee Art Museum, Milwaukee, WI
75,000	Milwaukee Symphony Orchestra, Milwaukee, WI
59,197	United Performing Arts Fund, Milwaukee, WI
50,000	Milwaukee Ballet, Milwaukee, WI
50,000	Milwaukee Performing Arts Center, Milwaukee, WI
50,000	Milwaukee Performing Arts Center, Milwaukee, WI
30,000	Milwaukee Art Museum, Milwaukee, WI
25,000	Channel 10/36 Friends, Inc., Milwaukee, WI
25,000	Milwaukee Repertory Theater, Milwaukee, WI
25,000	Pabst Theater (Friends of the), Milwaukee, WI
20,000	Ko-Thi Dance Company, Inc., Milwaukee, WI
20,000	Milwaukee Public Library Foundation, Milwaukee, WI
20,000	Wisconsin Conservatory of Music, Milwaukee, WI

Civic & Public Affairs

100,000	Focus Hope, Detroit, MI
50,000	New Hope Project, Inc., Milwaukee, WI
25,000	Great Circus Parade, Milwaukee, WI
20,000	Wisconsin Sesquicentennial Committee, Milwaukee, WI

Education

100,000	Pave/Partners Advancing Values in Education, Milwaukee, WI
50,000	New Orleans Public Schools, New Orleans, LA
29,000	Junior Achievement of Wisconsin, Racine, WI
20,000	Cornerstone Schools, Detroit, MI

Health

30,000	Blood Center of Southeastern Wisconsin, Milwaukee, WI
25,000	Ashrae Foundation, Spokane, WA
25,000	Elmbrook Memorial Hospital, Brookfield, WI
20,000	Children's Hospital of Wisconsin, Milwaukee, WI
20,000	Froedtert Memorial Luthern Hospital, Milwaukee, WI
20,000	Karmanos Cancer Institute, Milwaukee, WI
20,000	Our Lady of Mercy Medical Center, Milwaukee, WI
17,000	Sinai Samaritan Medical Center, Milwaukee, WI

Science

50,000	Discovery World Museum, Milwaukee, WI

Social Services

181,492	Plymouth Community United Way, Plymouth, MN
136,325	United Way of Greater Milwaukee, Milwaukee, WI
126,530	United Way of Greater Milwaukee, Milwaukee, WI
126,529	United Way of Greater Milwaukee, Milwaukee, WI
126,529	United Way of Greater Milwaukee, Milwaukee, WI
97,734	United Way of West Tennessee, Jackson, TN
78,063	United Way of Greater St. Joseph, St. Joseph, MO
38,355	United Way of Greater Toledo, Toledo, OH
33,000	Safe & Sound, Pittsburgh, PA
30,000	YMCA of Metropolitan Milwaukee, Milwaukee, WI
27,139	United Way of Kitsap County, Bremerton, WA
26,988	United Way of Mcminn County, Athens, TN
26,078	United Way of Mason County, Shelton, WA
25,000	American Red Cross, Milwaukee, WI
24,810	United Way of Brevard County, Cocoa, FL
24,066	United Way of Orange County, Garden Grove, CA
22,745	United Way of South Mississippi, Osceola, AR
17,000	Family Service of Milwaukee, Milwaukee, WI

JOHNSON &JOHNSON

★ Number 2 of Top 100 Corporate Givers

Company Contact

New Brunswick, NJ
Web: http://www.jnj.com

Company Description

Revenue: US$27,471,000,000 (1999)
Employees: 37,991 (1999)
Fortune Rank: 43, per FORTUNE Magazine's list of 500 Largest U.S. Corporations (1999).
FF 43

SIC(s): 2676 Sanitary Paper Products, 2834 Pharmaceutical Preparations, 2844 Toilet Preparations, 3842 Surgical Appliances & Supplies.

Operating Locations

Argentina: Janssen-Cilag Farmaceutica, Buenos Aires; Johnson & Johnson de Argentina S.A. C.e.I., Buenos Aires; Johnson & Johnson Medical S.A., Buenos Aires; Australia: Johnson & Johnson Medical Pty.Ltd., North Ryde; Janssen-Cilag Pty.Ltd., Lane Cove; Ortho-Clinical Diagnostics, Melbourne; DePuy Australia Pty.Ltd, Nottinghill; Johnson & Johnson Pacific Pty.Limited, Sydney; Tasmanian Alkaloids Pty.Ltd., Westbury; Austria: Johnson & Johnson GmbH, Hallein; Janssen-Cilag Gmbh, Vienna; Belgium: Janssen-Cilag N.V., Antwerp; Janssen Pharmaceutica N.V., Beerse; Janssen Research Foundation, Beerse; LifeScan Benelux, Beerse; Cordis N.V., Zaventem; Brazil: Janssen-Cilag Farmaceutica Ltda., Sao Paula; Johnson & Johnson Professional Products Ltda., Sao Paulo; Canada: LifeScan Canada, Ltd., Burnaby; McNeil Consumer, Guelph; Depuy Canada Ltd., Mississauga; Ortho-Clinical Diagnostics, Mississaugo; Johnson & Johnson Inc., Montreal; Janssen-Ortho Inc., North York; Johnson & Johnson Medical Products Inc., Peterborough; Chile: Janssen-Cilag Farmaceutica S.A., Bogota; Johnson & Johnson Medical Colombia, Bogota; Johnson & Johnson de Chile S.A., Santiago; People's Republic of China: Johnson & Johnson China Ltd., Shanghai; Johnson & Johnson Medical Ltd., Shanghai; Shanghai Johnson & Johnson, Shanghai; Xian-Janssen Pharmaceutical Ltd., Xian; Egypt: Johnson & Johnson (Egypt) S.A.E., Cairo; France: Johnson & Johnson S.A., Issy-Les-Molineaux; LifeScan, Issy-Les-Molineaux; Neutrogena France, Issy-Les-Molineaux; Ortho-Clinical Diagnostics S.A., Issy-Les-Molineaux; Cordis S.A., Issy-Les-Moulineaux; Ethicon Endo-Surgery S.A., Issy-Les-Moulineaux; Ethicon S.A., Issy-Les-Moulineaux; DePuy France, Villeurbanne; Germany: Johnson & Johnson GmbH, Dusseldorf; Cordis GmbH, Haan; LifeScan GmbH, Neckargemund; Ethicon Endo-Surgery (Europe) GmbH, Norderstedt; Ethicon GmbH, Norderstedt; Johnson & Johnson Medical GmbH, Norderstedt; Janssen-Cilag GmbH, Rosellen; DePuy Orthopadie GmbH, Sulzbach; Greece: Janssen-Cilag Pharmaceutical S.A.C.I., Athens; Johnson & Johnson Hellas S.A., Athens; Johnson & Johnson Medical Products S.A., Athens; Hong Kong: Janssen-Cilag, Hong Kong; Johnson & Johnson (Hong Kong) Limited, Hong Kong; Johnson & Johnson Medical Hong Kong, Hong Kong; Hungary: Johnson & Johnson Kft., Budapest; Indonesia: Janssen-Cilag Pharmaceutica, Jakarta; P.T. Johnson & Johnson Indonesia, Jakarta; India: Janssen-Cilag, Mumbai; Johnson & Johnson Limited, Mumbai; Johnson & Johnson Professional, Mumbai; Ireland: Janssen-Cilag Pharmaceutical Limited, Cork; Johnson & Johnson (Ireland) Limited, Tallaght; Israel: Biosense Europe, Haifa; J-C Healthcare, Ltd., Kibbutz Shefayim; Italy: Cordis SpA, Milan; Janssen-Cilag SpA, Milan; Ortho-Clinical Diagnostics SpA, Milan; Ethicon Endo-Surgery SpA, Rome; Johnson & Johnson SpA, Rome; LifeScan SpA, Rome; Japan: DePuy Japan, Inc., Tokyo; Janssen-Kyowa Co., Tokyo; Johnson & Johnson Medical K.K., Tokyo; Ortho-Clinical Diagnostics K.K., Tokyo; Vistakon Japan, Tokyo; Kenya: Johnson & Johnson (Kenya) Limited, Nairobi; Republic of Korea: Janssen-Cilag Korea, Ltd., Seoul; Johnson & Johnson Korea, Ltd., Seoul; Johnson & Johnson Medical Korea Ltd., Seoul; Mexico: Janssen-Cilag Farmaceutica, S.A. de C.V., Mexico City; Johnson & Johnson de Mexico, S.A. de C.V., Mexico City; Morocco: Johnson & Johnson Morocco S.A., Casablanca; Malaysia: Johnson & Johnson Medical Mfg. Sdn. Bhd., Selangor Darul Ehsan; Johnson & Johnson Sdn. Bhd., Selangor Darul Ehsan; Netherlands: Johnson & Johnson/Gaba B.V., Almere; Johnson & Johnson Medical B.V., Amersfoort; Janssen-Cilag B.V., Tilburg; Pakistan: Johnson & Johnson Pakistan (Private) Limited, Karachi; Panama: Johnson & Johnson, Panama City; Peru: Johnson & Johnson del Peru S.A., Lima; Philippines: Janssen-Cilag Philippines, Metro Manila; Johnson & Johnson Medical Philippines, Metro Manila; Johnson & Johnson (Philippines), Inc., Metro Manila; Poland: Johnson & Johnson Poland, Sp.z.o.o., Warsaw; Puerto Rico: Johnson & Johnson (Caribbean), Caguas; Portugal: Johnson & Johnson Professional Products, Limitada, Quelaz; Janssen-Cilag Farmaceutica Ltda., Queluz; Johnson & Johnson Limitada, Queluz; Russia: Johnson & Johnson Health Care Ltd., Moscow; Johnson & Johnson Ltd., Moscow; Republic of South Africa: Johnson & Johnson (Pty.) Limited, East London; Johnson & Johnson Professional Products (Pty) Ltd., Halfway House; Janssen-Cilag (Pty.) Ltd., Sandton; Scotland: Ethicon Limited, Edinburgh; Singapore: Janssen-Cilag Singapore/Malaysia, Singapore; Johnson & Johnson Medical S.I.M., Singapore; Johnson & Johnson Pte. Ltd., Singapore; Ortho-Clinical Diagnostics, Singapore; Spain: Janssen-Cilag S.A., Madrid; Johnson & Johnson S.A., Madrid; LifeScan, Madrid; Ortho-Clinical Diagnostics, Madrid; Vistakon, Madrid; Slovenia: Johnson & Johnson S.E., Ljubljana; Sweden: Janssen-Cilag AB, Sollentuna; Johnson & Johnson AB, Sollentuna; Johnson & Johnson Consumer Products, Sollentuna; Switzerland: Greiter AG, Baar; Janssen-Cilag AG, Baar; Cilag AG, Schaffhausen; Johnson & Johnson AG, Spreitenbach; Johnson & Johnson AG Medical, Spreitenbach; Janssen-Cilag, Zug; Thailand: Janssen-Cilag Pharmaceutica Limited, Bangkok; Johnson & Johnson Medical Thailand, Bangkok; Johnson & Johnson (Thailand) Limited, Bangkok; Turkey: Johnson & Johnson Limited, Istanbul; Taiwan: Janssen-Cilag Taiwan, Taipei; Johnson & Johnson Medical Taiwan, Taipei; Johnson & Johnson Taiwan, Ltd., Taipei; United Arab Emirates: Johnson & Johnson (Middle East) Inc., Dubai; United Kingdom: Ortho-Clinical Diagnostics, Amersham; Johnson & Johnson Medical Limited, Ascot; Ethicon Endo-Surgery U.K., Bracknell; Johnson & Johnson Professional Europe, Bracknell; Vistakon Europe, Bracknell; Janssen-Cilag Limited, High Wycombe; DePuy International Limited, Leeds; Johnson & Johnson Limited, Maidenhead; Venezuela: Janssen-Cilag Farmaceutia C.A., Caracas; Johnson & Johnson de Venezuala, S.A., Caracas; Zimbabwe: Johnson & Johnson (Private) Limited, Harare

Nonmonetary Support

Value: $125,400,000 (1998); $96,900,000 (1997); $44,000,000 (1996)
Type: Cause-related Marketing & Promotion; Donated Products
Note: Product donations at retail value. Co. provides products for medical aid in underdeveloped countries and emergency disaster relief. Co. donates real estate.

Corporate Sponsorship

Type: Arts & cultural events; Festivals/fairs; Music & entertainment events; Sports events
Note: Sponsors the Johnson & Johnson Live for Life program, and hospital, museum, and library events.

Johnson & Johnson Family of Companies Contribution Fund

Giving Contact

Helen M. Hughes, Director, Corporate Contributions
Johnson & Johnson
One Johnson & Johnson Plz.
New Brunswick, NJ 08933
Phone: (732)524-3255
Fax: (732)524-3300

Alternate Contact

Conrad Person, Manager of International Programs
Note: Contact for arts, volunteerism, and K-12 education.

Description

EIN: 226062811
Organization Type: Corporate Foundation
Giving Locations: internationally; nationally; principally near operating locations and to national organizations.
Grant Types: Emergency, Employee Matching Gifts, General Support, Project.
Note: Employee matching gift ratio: 2 to 1 to education, libraries, and cultural organisation. Maximum $12,500 per employee annually.

Giving Philosophy

'We are responsible to the communities in which we live and work and to the world community as well. We must be good citizens -- support good works and charities and bear our fair share of taxes. We must encourage civic improvements and better health and education.' *Johnson & Johnson*

Financial Summary

Total Giving: $176,200,000 (1998); $146,300,000 (1997); $92,981,201 (1996). Note: Contributes through corporate direct giving program and foundation.
Giving Analysis: Giving for 1998 includes: corporate direct giving (approx $45,800,000); foundation matching gifts (approx $6,000,000); international subsidiaries (approx $5,000,000)
Assets: $209,572 (1997); $152,917 (1996); $252,000 (1995)
Gifts Received: $5,170,636 (1997); $4,367,233 (1996)

Typical Recipients

Arts & Humanities: Arts Centers, Community Arts, Dance, Museums/Galleries, Music, Performing Arts, Public Broadcasting
Civic & Public Affairs: Employment/Job Training, Safety, Women's Affairs
Education: Business Education, Colleges & Universities, Minority Education
Health: Cancer, Geriatric Health, Health Organizations, Hospitals, Medical Research, Single-Disease Health Associations
Social Services: People with Disabilities, Shelters/Homelessness, Substance Abuse, United Funds/United Ways, Youth Organizations

Contributions Analysis

Giving Priorities: Health, education, and civic interests. Company supports international organizations based in the U.S. through the Contributions Fund and a separate corporate contributions pool. Johnson & Johnson companies located outside the United States provide support to organizations in their operating communities. Overseas contributions decisions are shaped by local affiliates, giving consideration to the community's needs and the company's overall philanthropic guidelines, with emphasis on health care and education. Johnson & Johnson directs product donations through a small group of nonprofit organizations and does not encourage unsolicited requests for funding in this area. Also includes Johnson & Johnson Worldwide Child Survival Program conducted in partnership with UNICEF. The Worldwide Child Survival Program is designed to help reduce the high mortality rate of children under age five in developing countries by improving opportunities for children and parents to access necessary health services; promoting wider acceptance and use of oral rehydration, breast feeding, immunization, and growth monitoring; and carrying out projects and activities in which Johnson & Johnson's local management has strong interest. Funds for the Worldwide Child Survival Program are generated through products supplied to UNICEF by Johnson & Johnson operating companies in the United States. The system begins with Johnson & Johnson companies, primarily McNeil Consumer Products Co. and Ethicon, Inc., producing products

that are donated to UNICEF for distribution to developing countries around the world. UNICEF, in turn, credits Johnson & Johnson with funds that can be used exclusively for the Worldwide Child Survival Program. Quantities of product donations and overall levels of funding for program activities are approved and monitored by the corporate contributions committee. In Guatemala, program funding has helped to supply rehydration packets to thousands of children who suffer from chronic diarrhea and dehydration. The packets contained illustrated instructions to help illiterate parents understand how to use them. Funds also have been designated for a comprehensive breast feeding program for young mothers and for the development and testing of growth monitoring charts that alert physicians and parents to any growth irregularities in children. Program activities have extended to Zimbabwe, Zambia, Ecuador, Kenya, and the Philippines.

Arts & Humanities: Less than 5%. Supports the arts worldwide, with an emphasis on operating locations.

Civic & Public Affairs: 10% to 15%. Supports urban, women's, and minority affairs and public policy. Also supports law and justice, public safety, and economic development.

Education: 10% to 15%. Supports higher education, particularly medical and minority education. Also supports early learning programs and math and science education.

Environment: Less than 5%. Major support goes to conservation of ecosystems and wildlife, public health, and disease prevention.

Health: About 47%. Supports health and medical research.

International: Less than 1%.

Application Procedures

Initial Contact: brief preliminary letter; organizations in communities where affiliate companies have a presence should direct requests to companies in those locations

Application Requirements: amount requested; statement of purpose for request; organization's mission statement; demonstration that request meets company's guidelines and giving priorities; tax-exempt status; description of purposes and goals; budget for proposed project; and acknowledgment of other forms of support

Deadlines: None.

Review Process: staff responds to initial letter, either declining request or requesting full proposal; contributions committee at headquarters determines how most cash donations are allocated and monitors non-cash donations; each affiliate company also makes independent judgments about cash support within corporate guidelines (most product and equipment gifts are made at affiliate company level)

Evaluative Criteria: 501(c)(3) status, effect on company's operating communities, method of evaluating project results, competency of organization's management

Notes: Guidelines are for corporate program. Company cannot return supplemental materials sent with requests.

Restrictions

The company does not consider funding individuals; requests for unrestricted funds; loans; trips or tours; endowments of any kind; advertising for benefit purposes; sectarian and religious organizations that do not serve the general public on a nondenominational basis; capital requests; or political, fraternal, or athletic groups.

Additional Information

Donates up to 5% of worldwide pre-tax income annually.

Requests for specific projects or program support generally receive more favorable attention than proposals for unrestricted funding. Giving program also seeks to be proactive in meeting objectives and priorities.

Most Johnson & Johnson operating companies conduct separate cash giving programs and use these contributions program guidelines to make their funding decisions. make their funding decisions.

Publications: Annual Report; Giving Guidelines

Corporate Officials

Aldrage B. Cooper: vice president community relations PRIM CORP EMPL vice president community relations: Johnson & Johnson.

Robert W. Croce: group chairman PRIM CORP EMPL group chairman: Johnson & Johnson.

William D. Dearstyne, Jr.: group chairman PRIM CORP EMPL group chairman: Johnson & Johnson.

Ruth C. Edelson: director special projects PRIM CORP EMPL director special projects: Johnson & Johnson.

Roger Seth Fine: vice president, general counsel B Brooklyn, NY 1942. ED Columbia College BA (1963); New York University LLB (1966). PRIM CORP EMPL vice president, general counsel: Johnson & Johnson. NONPR AFFIL director: Robert Wood Johnson University Hospital; trustee: University Medicine Dentistry New Jersey; member: National Center State Courts; member: American Arbitration Association; member: American Bar Association.

Ronald G. Gelbman: chairman diagnostics group PRIM CORP EMPL chairman diagnostics group: Johnson & Johnson.

Robert Zalmon Gussin, PhD: vice president science & technology B Pittsburgh, PA 1938. ED Duquesne University BS (1959); Duquesne University MS (1961); University of Michigan PhD (1965). PRIM CORP EMPL vice president science & technology: Johnson & Johnson. NONPR AFFIL member: American Society Nephrology; member: American Society Pharmacology & Experimental Therapeutics; member: American Society Clinical Pharmacology & Therapeutics; member: American Federation Clinical Research; member: American Heart Association; member: American Academy of Arts & Sciences.

JoAnn Heffernan Heisen: vice president, chief information officer B Washington, DC 1950. ED Syracuse University BA (1972); New York University MBA (1978). PRIM CORP EMPL vice president, chief information officer: Johnson & Johnson. NONPR AFFIL director: Women's First Healthcare; director: Women's Research Education Institute; trustee: Princeton Medical Center; director: Recordings for Blind; director visitors committee: Massachusetts Institute Technology Sloan School Management; director: Maxwell School Citizenship Public Affairs; member: Financial Womens Association. CLUB AFFIL Economic Club New York.

Ralph Stanley Larsen: chairman, president, chief executive officer, director B Brooklyn, NY 1938. ED Hofstra University BS (1962). PRIM CORP EMPL chairman, president, chief executive officer, director: Johnson & Johnson. CORP AFFIL director: Xerox Corp.; chairman: Johnson & Johnson International; director: New York Stock Exchange Inc.; director: AT& T Corp. NONPR AFFIL member: Business Council; member: Business Roundtable.

Willard D. Nielsen: vice president public affairs PRIM CORP EMPL vice president public affairs: Johnson & Johnson.

Foundation Officials

Michael J. Bzdak: director corporate contributions

Aldrage B. Cooper: member corporate contributions committee (see above)

Paulo F. Costa: member corporate contributions committee B 1950. PRIM CORP EMPL president, director: Janssen Pharmaceutica Inc.

William D. Dearstyne, Jr.: member corporate contributions committee (see above)

Ruth C. Edelson: member corporate contributions committee (see above)

Roger Seth Fine: president (see above)

Ronald G. Gelbman: member corporate contributions committee (see above)

Robert Zalmon Gussin, PhD: member corporate contributions committee (see above)

JoAnn Heffernan Heisen: treasurer (see above)

Helen M. Hughes: director corporate contributions B 1951. PRIM CORP EMPL senior administrator corp. contributions: Johnson & Johnson.

Wendy B. Logan: member corporate contributions committee

Alfred T. Mays: member corporate contributions committee PRIM CORP EMPL chairman: McNeil Specialty Products Co.

Willard D. Nielsen: member corporate contributions committee (see above)

Gerlad M. Ostrov: member corporate contributions committee

Conrad Person: manager international programs & product giving

Grants Analysis

Disclosure Period: calendar year ending

Recent Grants

Note: Grants derived from 1994 grants list.

Education

1,700,000 Wharton School, University of Pennsylvania, Philadelphia, PA

Health

179,500 Cancer Institute of New Jersey, New Brunswick, NJ

50,000 Alliance for Aging Research, Washington, DC

Social Services

35,000 National Alliance to End Homelessness, Washington, DC

S.C. JOHNSON &SON

Company Contact

Racine, WI

Web: http://www.scjohnsonwax.com

Company Description

Employees: 13,200

SIC(s): 2841 Soap & Other Detergents, 2842 Polishes & Sanitation Goods, 2844 Toilet Preparations, 2879 Agricultural Chemicals Nec.

Operating Locations

Australia: SC Johnson & Son Pty. Ltd., Lane Cove; Chile: Johnson SC de Centro-America SA, San Jose; People's Republic of China: Shanghi Johnson, Ltd., Shanghai; Egypt: Johnson Wax Egypt Co., Cairo; Ghana: SC Johnson Wax, Ltd., Accra; Hong Kong: Johnson SC Ltd., Wan Chai; Indonesia: PTSC Johnson & Son, Jakarta; India: Lever-Johnson PVT, LTD., Pune; Japan: Johnson Co., Ltd., Yokohama; Kenya: Johnson Wax (East Africa) Ltd., Nairobi; Republic of Korea: Korea Johnson Co. Ltd., Seoul; Mexico: Johnson SC & Son SA de CV, Mexico City; Malaysia: Scientific-Chem Jobs Sdn.Bhd., Selangor Derul Ehsan; Nigeria: Johnson Wax Nigeria Limited, Isolo, Lagos; New Zealand: Johnson Wax New Zealand Limited, Auckland; Philippines: SC Johnson & Son, Inc., Makati City; Puerto Rico: SC Johnson de Puerto Rico, Inc., Hata Rey; Republic of South Africa: SC Johnson & Son of South Africa, Fairland; Saudi Arabia: Saudi Johnson Co., Ltd., Jeddah; Singapore: SC Johnson & Son Pte. Limited, Singapore; Thailand: Johnson SC & Son Ltd., Bangkok; Turkey:, Istanbul; Taiwan: SC Johnson & Son Taiwan Ltd., Taipei; United Kingdom: SC Johnson Wax, Surrey; Vietnam: SC Johnson & Son, Inc., Thuan An

Nonmonetary Support

Type: Donated Equipment; Donated Products; In-kind Services; Loaned Executives

Contact: Kari Iselin, Community Relations Administrator

S.C. Johnson Wax Fund

Giving Contact

Tom Porter, Vice President & Executive Director
S.C. Johnson Wax Fund, Inc.
1525 Howe St., Mail Station 066
Racine, WI 53403
Phone: (262)260-3894
Fax: (262)260-2652

Description

EIN: 396052089
Organization Type: Corporate Foundation
Giving Locations: WI: Racine nationally.
Grant Types: Employee Matching Gifts, Fellowship, General Support, Project, Scholarship, Seed Money.
Note: Employee matching gift ratio: 1 to 1 for gifts to education and the United Way.

Giving Philosophy

'Philanthropy is a marketplace where demand always seems to outpace supply. Organizations expand or arise to deal with growing or new problems, and as they do, pressure increases on all of us for support. As a civic-minded corporation, we are continuously striving to help meet those needs. Our challenge, given finite resources, is to find ways to make our philanthropy more effective. We have two important assets we can employ: money and people. SC Johnson Wax has always supported worthy endeavors to the maximum extent possible and targeted that funding in the communities where it operates to produce the greatest impact. .. We have entered into and supported partnerships with other businesses, educational institutions, local government and community organizations. .. We also have encouraged philanthropy and volunteerism among our employees.' *Contributions Program of SC Johnson Wax and the Johnson's Wax Fund, Inc.*

Financial Summary

Total Giving: $2,647,873 (fiscal year ending June 30, 1997); $2,420,829 (fiscal 1996); $3,000,000 (fiscal 1995 approx). Note: Contributes through corporate direct giving program and foundation. Giving includes foundation. Corporate Annual Giving Range: $500,000 to $1,000,000.
Giving Analysis: Giving for fiscal 1997 includes: foundation ($1,147,929); foundation matching gifts ($974,307); foundation scholarships ($525,637)
Assets: $5,165,000 (fiscal 1998 approx); $2,663,464 (fiscal 1997); $2,790,252 (fiscal 1996)
Gifts Received: $2,476,464 (fiscal 1997). Note: Foundation received contributions from S.C. Johnson & Son.

Typical Recipients

Arts & Humanities: Arts Associations & Councils, Arts Centers, Arts Funds, Arts Institutes, Community Arts, Ethnic & Folk Arts, Historic Preservation, History & Archaeology, Libraries, Museums/Galleries, Music, Performing Arts, Public Broadcasting, Theater
Civic & Public Affairs: Business/Free Enterprise, Civil Rights, Economic Development, Employment/Job Training, Hispanic Affairs, Housing, Law & Justice, Municipalities/Towns, Professional & Trade Associations, Public Policy, Safety, Urban & Community Affairs, Women's Affairs, Zoos/Aquariums
Education: Arts/Humanities Education, Business Education, Colleges & Universities, Economic Education, Education Funds, Engineering/Technological Education, Education-General, Health & Physical Education, International Exchange, Leadership Training, Literacy, Medical Education, Minority Education, Private Education (Precollege), Public Education (Precollege), Religious Education, Science/Mathematics Education, Secondary Education (Private), Social Sciences Education, Special Education, Student Aid
Environment: Air/Water Quality, Environment-General, Resource Conservation, Wildlife Protection
Health: Cancer, Children's Health/Hospitals, Clinics/Medical Centers, Health Organizations, Hospitals, Medical Research, Medical Training, Nutrition, Single-Disease Health Associations
International: International Environmental Issues, International Relations
Religion: Religious Welfare
Social Services: Animal Protection, Child Welfare, Community Service Organizations, Crime Prevention, Day Care, Delinquency & Criminal Rehabilitation, Emergency Relief, Family Services, Homes, Recreation & Athletics, Scouts, Substance Abuse, United Funds/United Ways, Veterans, YMCA/YWCA/YMHA/YWHA, Youth Organizations

Contributions Analysis

Giving Priorities: Education, social welfare, and community concerns. Company's overseas operations are active in their communities, and good corporate citizenship worldwide is incorporated into the company's statement of principles. In recent years, the company has supported efforts in Mexico to assist senior citizens and homeless youth, providing food and medicine, as well as cleaning products; in Thailand to construct a new well, water-holding tanks, and water lines leading to vegetable fields in order to reverse the effects of a devastating drought; in the Philippines to combat Dengue disease; and in Argentina to support several educational programs. The company also recognizes environmental stewardship and volunteerism byemployees and retirees through several awards programs that incorporate overseas operating companies.
Civic & Public Affairs: 35% to 40%. Majority of funding is disbursed as matching gifts to the Racine Area United Way and other united funds. Other interests include the needy, the elderly, and youth organizations, such asRacine's Taylor Home, for a program to help at-risk youth ages 13 to 15. Supports museums, arts funds, theater, and other arts organizations.
Education: 35% to 45%. Majority of funding supports scholarships and fellowships for employee children, and minority students in a variety of fields. Matches employee gifts to education. Also supports capital campaigns and specific programs at local colleges and universities. Education funds, associations, high schools, and INROADS/Wisconsin's Racine Youth Leadership Academy receive funding as well.
Note: Priorities based on contributions made by S.C. Johnson Wax Fund only. Corporation also sponsors the Johnson Foundation, a private operating foundation. The Johnson Foundation hosts conferences (known as Wingspread conferences) devoted to the improvement of society in several key areas: international understanding, educational excellence, improvement of the human environment, and intellectual and cultural growth. The foundation carries out program extension activities and publications through which it shares with a wideraudience the information generated in these conferences. The corporation also offers limited direct contributions. Direct contributions are made to worthy causes for education, social welfare, culture and the arts, youth activities, health and medical concerns, preservation of the environment, emergency and disaster relief, and the disadvantaged.

Application Procedures

Initial Contact: call or write for application form
Application Requirements: completed application, with following attachments: itemized annual and project budgets, list of corporate and foundation donors, copy of most recent Form 990, most recent audited financial statements, current list of board members, and proof of tax-exempt status
Deadlines: March 1, July 1, and November 1
Review Process: process involves four advisory committees in program areas, who make recommendations to the trustees; proposals are acknowledged upon receipt; if within guidelines and interest of fund, follow-up contact is made; trustees meet three times a year to review advisory committee recommendations
Evaluative Criteria: project reflects favorably on company's public image; employee involvement; nonduplication or overlap of services and programs provided by organizations already receiving funds or corporate support, either directly or indirectly through united funds; broad support within community; impacts a community where employees live and work; for requests for seed money, future funding plan must be spelled out
Decision Notification: committees review proposals in June, October, and February prior to each board meeting

Restrictions

The fund does not support individuals; social, athletic, veterans', labor, or fraternal organizations, or religious institutions. (A program may be considered if it is not restricted to organization members and is available to the community as a whole.) The fund also does not support political actions or lobbying efforts; national health fund drives or national health organizations; or salary or wage support. Fund does not make individual grants to United Way agencies for operating expenses, but will consider major capital requests. The Wax Fund should not be the only funding source for an organization. (Sole source funding may be given for special, one time projects.) Grants are given for one year to discourage dependence of the recipient on this source. Private foundations are not funded.
The Johnson Foundation, Inc., an entirely separate institution, operates the Wingspread Conference Center and also receives contributions from S.C. Johnson & Son, Inc. Therefore, the fund generally does not support conferences, workshops, or seminars.

Additional Information

Guidelines may change due to strategic planning efforts by the Fund in 1997.
Preference is given to agencies and programs in the communities in which company employees live and work and to organizations and projects not primarily or normally financed by public tax funds. Grants outside the United States are rare.
Corporation contributes at least 5% of pre-tax profit to nonprofit organizations.
Corporation contributes at least 5% of pre-tax profit to nonprofit organizations.
Publications: Social Responsibility Report; Application Form; Contributions Policy and Guidelines (Pamphlet)

Corporate Officials

James F. DiMarco: senior vice president, advisor B 1935. ED University of Minnesota BS (1959); University of Minnesota MA (1964). PRIM CORP EMPL senior vice president: S.C. Johnson & Son.
Samuel Curtis Johnson: chairman, director, president B Racine, WI 1928. ED Cornell University BA (1950); Harvard University MBA (1952). PRIM CORP EMPL chairman, director, president: S.C. Johnson & Son. CORP AFFIL chairman: Johnson Wax Fund; chairman: Johnson Worldwide Associates Inc.; director: Johnson Bank; chairman: Johnson International Inc.; director: HJ Heinz Co.; director: John Deere & Co.; director: ExxonMobil Corp.; director: Cargill Inc. NONPR AFFIL founder, chairman emeritus: Prairie School; regent emeritus: Smithsonian Institute; member national board governors: Nature Conservatory; chairman advisory council: Cornell University Johnson Graduate School Management; trustee emeritus: Mayo Foundation; trustee emeritus: Cornell University; honorary member: Business Council; member: Chi Psi; trustee: American Museum Natural History. CLUB AFFIL University Club; Racine Country Club; America Club; Cornell Club.
John M. Schroeder: senior vice president, advisor PRIM CORP EMPL senior vice president, advisor: S.C. Johnson & Son Inc.

Foundation Officials

Patricia L. Barlament: trustee
Reva A. Holmes: vice president, executive director, trustee
Samuel Curtis Johnson: chairman, trustee (see above)
John M. Schroeder: treasurer (see above)

Grants Analysis

Disclosure Period: fiscal year ending June 30, 1997
Total Grants: $1,147,929*
Number of Grants: 46
Average Grant: $24,954
Highest Grant: $150,000
Typical Range: $1,000 to $30,000
***Note:** Giving excludes matching gifts; scholarships.

Recent Grants

Note: Grants derived from fiscal 1997 Form 990.

Arts & Humanities

105,000 Milwaukee Art Museum, Milwaukee, WI
30,000 Racine United Arts Fund, Racine, WI
30,000 United Performing Arts Fund, Milwaukee, WI
25,000 Racine Fire Bell Museum Association, Racine, WI
10,000 Wisconsin Public Broadcasting Foundation, Madison, WI

Civic & Public Affairs

150,000 Downtown Racine Corporation, Racine, WI
20,000 Opportunities Industrialization Corp of Racine County, Racine, WI
18,500 City of Racine, Racine, WI
16,000 Center for Community Concerns, Racine, WI
15,000 Hispanic Education and Support Outreach Services, Racine, WI
10,000 City of Racine, Racine, WI
10,000 Habitat for Humanity, Racine, WI

Education

53,500 Reading is Fundamental, Washington, DC
45,000 Eisenhower Exchange Fellowships, Philadelphia, PA
27,500 University of Wisconsin Parkside Benevolent Foundation, Kenosha, WI
26,000 Milwaukee School of Engineering, Milwaukee, WI
25,000 Racine Unified School District, Racine, WI
25,000 Youth Leadership Academy, Milwaukee, WI
20,000 University of Wisconsin Parkside Benevolent Foundation, Kenosha, WI
15,000 Mount Senario College, Ladysmith, WI
15,000 Racine Montessori Society, Racine, WI
12,000 Racine Society for Christian Instruction, Racine, WI
10,000 Carroll College, Waukesha, WI
10,000 Carthage College, Kenosha, WI
10,000 CESA Foundation, Madison, WI
10,000 Cornell College, Ithaca, NY
10,000 Cornell University, Ithaca, NY
10,000 Illinois Wesleyan University, Bloomington, IL
10,000 Lac du Flambeau Public School District, Lac du Flambeau, WI
10,000 Luther College, Decorah, IA
9,000 Bennett College, Greensboro, NC
9,000 Fisk University, Nashville, TN
9,000 Oakwood College, Huntsville, AL
9,000 Philander Smith College, Little Rock, AR
9,000 Spelman College, Atlanta, GA
9,000 Talladega College, Talladega, AL
9,000 Xavier University of Louisiana, New Orleans, LA
7,500 University of Wisconsin Milwaukee Foundation, Milwaukee, WI

Environment

100,000 Nature Conservancy, Arlington, VA
20,000 Zink the Zebra Foundation, Milwaukee, WI
15,000 Zink the Zebra Foundation, Milwaukee, WI
15,000 Zink the Zebra Foundation, Milwaukee, WI

Health

25,000 Children's Hospital, Boston, MA

International

20,000 Earthwatch Expeditions, Watertown, MA
20,000 Earthwatch Expeditions, Watertown, MA
9,000 International Crane Foundation, Baraboo, WI
9,000 International Crane Foundation, Baraboo, WI

Social Services

87,000 Boy Scouts of America Southwest Wisconsin Council, Racine, WI
12,500 Homeward Bound of Racine County, Racine, WI
10,000 Boys Club, Wilmington, CA
10,000 Milwaukee County War Memorial Center, Milwaukee, WI
7,500 Racine County Sheriff's Department, Racine, WI

EDWARD D. JONES &CO.

Company Contact

Maryland Heights, MO
Web: http://www.edwardjones.com

Company Description

Employees: 18,187 (1999)
SIC(s): 6211 Security Brokers & Dealers.

Edward D. Jones & Co. Foundation

Giving Contact

John Bachmann, Chairman
Edward D. Jones & Co. Foundation
12555 Manchester Rd.
St. Louis, MO 63131
Phone: (314)515-2000
Fax: (314)515-3269

Description

Founded: 1992
EIN: 431595600
Organization Type: Corporate Foundation. Supports preselected organizations only.
Giving Locations: CA: Claremont; MO: St. Louis
Grant Types: General Support.

Financial Summary

Total Giving: $420,000 (1998); $340,000 (1997); $320,000 (1996). Note: Giving includes foundation.
Assets: $12,904,758 (1998); $10,363,895 (1997); $8,678,966 (1996)
Gifts Received: $600,049 (1998); $1,169,761 (1997); $1,095,408 (1996). Note: Contributions are received from Edward D. Jones and Co.

Typical Recipients

Arts & Humanities: Arts Associations & Councils, Museums/Galleries, Music, Opera
Civic & Public Affairs: Business/Free Enterprise, Housing, Urban & Community Affairs, Zoos/Aquariums
Education: Business Education, Colleges & Universities
Environment: Environment-General
Health: Emergency/Ambulance Services
Religion: Religious Welfare
Social Services: Animal Protection, United Funds/United Ways, YMCA/YWCA/YMHA/YWHA

Contributions Analysis

Giving Priorities: Funds given in support of education, opera theater, orchestras, zoos, Habitat for Humanity, universities, and YMCAs.
Arts & Humanities: 5%.
Civic & Public Affairs: 24%.
Education: 71%.

Corporate Officials

John W. Bachmann: managing partner B Centralia, IL 1938. ED Wabash College AB (1960); Northwestern University MBA (1962). PRIM CORP EMPL managing partner: Edward D. Jones & Co. CORP AFFIL managing partner: Jones Financial Co. LTD; director: TWA; managing partner: EDI Leasing Co. LP. NONPR AFFIL member: Securities Industry Association; trustee: Wabash College; chairman: Saint Louis Symphony Society; chairman board visitors: Drucker Center Claremont Graduate School; member: National Association Securities Dealers; director: Arts & Education Council Greater Saint Louis. CLUB AFFIL Bogey Club; Saint Louis Club.

Foundation Officials

John W. Bachmann: chairman (see above)

Grants Analysis

Disclosure Period: calendar year ending 1998
Total Grants: $420,000
Number of Grants: 4
Highest Grant: $200,000
Typical Range: $10,000 to $100,000

Recent Grants

Note: Grants derived from 1997 Form 990.

Arts & Humanities

100,000 St. Louis Symphony Orchestra, St. Louis, MO
80,000 Magic House, St. Louis, MO
25,000 St. Louis Arts and Education Council, St. Louis, MO

Civic & Public Affairs

25,000 St. Louis 2004, St. Louis, MO

Education

10,000 William Woods University

Environment

100,000 Gateway Trailnet, St. Louis, MO

JOSTENS, INC.

Company Contact

Minneapolis, MN
Web: http://www.jostens.com

Company Description

Employees: 6,800 (1999)
SIC(s): 2389 Apparel & Accessories Nec, 2741 Miscellaneous Publishing, 2752 Commercial Printing--Lithographic, 3911 Jewelry & Precious Metal.

Operating Locations

Canada: Manitoba Montreal Sherbrooke Toronto Winnipeg

Nonmonetary Support

Value: $50,000 (1992); $228,000 (1989)
Type: Donated Products; In-kind Services; Loaned Employees; Loaned Executives
Note: Co. provides nonmonetary support.

The Jostens Foundation Inc.

Giving Contact

John Bleskatcheck, Foundation Administrator
The Jostens Foundation, Inc.
5501 Norman Center Dr.
Minneapolis, MN 55437
Phone: (612)830-3235
Fax: (612)897-4116
Note: Contact for school officials interested in information on Jost en's Renaissance program for education.

Description

EIN: 411280587
Organization Type: Corporate Foundation
Giving Locations: principally near operating locations and to national organizations.
Grant Types: Emergency, Employee Matching Gifts, General Support, Multiyear/Continuing Support, Project.

Giving Philosophy

'The Jostens Foundation is committed to supporting educational and human service programs that help children and young people become healthy, productive adults. Priority consideration is given to requests that strengthen families and increase the capacity of schools and nonprofit organizations to serve children and youth.' 1994 Annual Report of the Jostens Foundation Inc.

Financial Summary

Total Giving: $500,000 (fiscal year ending June 30, 2000 approx); $500,000 (fiscal 1999 approx); $500,000 (fiscal 1998 approx). Note: Contributes through corporate direct giving program and foundation. Fiscal 1997 Giving includes corporate direct giving ($293,795); foundation ($37,000); matching gifts ($91,576). Fiscal 1996 Giving includes foundation ($337,966); matching gifts ($172,839); scholarship ($20,500).
Assets: $63,197 (fiscal 1997); $74,626 (fiscal 1995); $952,183 (fiscal 1989)
Gifts Received: $628,189 (fiscal 1994). Note: Contributions made by Jostens, Inc.

Typical Recipients

Arts & Humanities: Arts Associations & Councils, Arts Centers, Arts Institutes, Ethnic & Folk Arts, Arts & Humanities-General, Libraries, Museums/Galleries, Music, Opera, Performing Arts, Public Broadcasting, Theater
Civic & Public Affairs: Economic Development, Employment/Job Training, Civic & Public Affairs-General, Housing, Legal Aid, Nonprofit Management, Public Policy, Women's Affairs, Zoos/Aquariums
Education: Business Education, Colleges & Universities, Economic Education, Education Associations, Education Funds, Education Reform, Education-General, Gifted & Talented Programs, Literacy, Minority Education, Public Education (Precollege)
Environment: Environment-General
Health: Arthritis, Cancer, Children's Health/Hospitals, Emergency/Ambulance Services, Eyes/Blindness, Hospices, Hospitals, Prenatal Health Issues, Public Health, Trauma Treatment
Science: Science Museums
Social Services: At-Risk Youth, Big Brother/Big Sister, Camps, Child Abuse, Child Welfare, Community Centers, Community Service Organizations, Day Care, Family Services, People with Disabilities, Scouts, Senior Services, Special Olympics, Substance Abuse, United Funds/United Ways, YMCA/YWCA/YMHA/YWHA, Youth Organizations

Contributions Analysis

Giving Priorities: Education, health, social welfare, the arts, and civic interests.
Arts & Humanities: Less than 5%. Interests include arts associations and centers, music, and theater. Emphasis is on programs for youth.
Education: 35%. Funds economic and business education. Supports education funds, public education, and minority grants. Also supports the Junior Achievement and Reading Is Fundamental programs. Sponsors the Jostens Scholars and Holt Memorial Programs for dependents of employees and sales agents.
Health: About 30%. Supports youth organizations, disability centers, pediatric health clinics, single-disease health associations, and drug and substance abuse services.
Note: Above priorities reflect foundation giving. The company also supports regional giving, directed by employees on Plant Contribution Committees. The company supports Jostens Renaissance Program, designed to recognize academic achievement through a business approach to education.

Restrictions

In general, does not make grants directly to schools, school districts, scholarship funds or educational foundations established on behalf of an individual or institution; fundraising or special event sponsorship, including ticket purchases; churches or religious groups; endowment funds, general operating support, or capital campaigns; organizations involved in highly political or controversial issues; or organizations providing services located outside of Jostens' operating area.
Foundation gives grants only to 501(c)(3) organizations.
Foundation gives grants only to 501(c)(3) organizations.

Additional Information

Program grants generally made during the current year and not in installments for future years.
In 1987, Jostens organized employee contributions committees in several operating locations across the country. These committees make charitable grants within employees' local communities from dollars allocated by the foundation.
Publications: Annual Report; Application Form; Guidelines

Corporate Officials

Robert C. Buhrmaster: president, chief executive officer, director, chairman B Schenectady, NY 1947. ED Rensselaer Polytechnic Institute BS (1969); Dartmouth College MBA (1974). PRIM CORP EMPL president, chief executive officer, director, chairman: Jostens, Inc. CORP AFFIL president, director: Jostens Photography Inc.; director: Toro Co.; president: American Yearbook Co.; president: Jostens Direct Inc.

Foundation Officials

Lee Upton McGrath: treasurer B Roslyn, NY 1956. ED Georgetown University BA (1978); University of Chicago MBA (1984). PRIM CORP EMPL vice president, treasurer: Jostens, Inc. ADD CORP EMPL treasurer: American Yearbook Co.; senior financial analyst: General Motors Corp.; international banker: First National Bank Chicago; assistant treasurer: HB Fuller Co.; treasurer: Jostens Direct Inc.
Kevin Whalen: director PRIM CORP EMPL vice president corporate communications & investor relations: Jostens, Inc.

Grants Analysis

Disclosure Period: fiscal year ending June 30, 1997
Total Grants: $37,000*
Number of Grants: 3
Typical Range: $1,000 to $5,000
***Note:** Giving excludes matching gifts.

Recent Grants

Note: Grants derived from fiscal 1997 Form 990.

Arts & Humanities

2,000 Child's Play Theater Company, Hopkins, MN

Civic & Public Affairs

30,000 Minnesota Zoo Foundation, Apple Valley, MN
30,000 Minnesota Zoo Foundation, Apple Valley, MN
2,700 Shelby Residential and Vocational Services, Memphis, TN
2,610 Everywoman's Resource Center, Topeka, KS
2,500 HIRED, Minneapolis, MN
2,500 Rebuild Resources, Minneapolis, MN
2,000 Alano Society, Owatonna, MN
2,000 Red Wings Area Coalition for Transitional Housing, Red Wing, MN
2,000 Sprout Ranch, Lancaster, CA

Education

15,000 Minnesota Private College Fund, Saint Paul, MN
5,000 United Negro College Fund, Fairfax, VA
5,000 United Negro College Fund, Fairfax, VA
4,000 Junior Achievement Upper Midwest, Minneapolis, MN
3,500 Minnesota Independent School Fund, Saint Paul, MN
3,000 Friends for Academic Excellence Foundation, Saint Paul, MN
2,500 Presbyterian College, Clinton, SC
2,000 Business Economics Education Foundation, Minneapolis, MN
2,000 Compas, Saint Paul, MN
2,000 Education Ventures, Minneapolis, MN
2,000 Minnesota Institute for Talented Youth, Saint Paul, MN
1,500 Anderson Center for Interdisciplinary Studies, Red Wing, MN

Environment

2,500 Massachusetts Audubon Society, Attleboro, MN

Health

10,000 American National Red Cross, Minneapolis, MN
2,600 Community Health Systems, Attleboro, MA
2,600 Cure Childhood Cancer Association, Rochester, NY
2,500 American Cancer Society, Memphis, TN
2,500 Hospice of Laurens County, Clinton, SC
2,500 Kaweah Delta Hospital Foundation, Visalia, CA
2,000 Perry Memorial Hospital Foundation, Princeton, IL

Social Services

5,000 Kids N Kinship, Apple Valley, MN
3,800 Children's Bureau, Memphis, TN
3,000 Minneapolis Crisis Nursery, Minneapolis, MN
2,650 Owatonna Montessori Children's Home, Owatonna, MN
2,500 Bridge for Runaway Youth, Minneapolis, MN
2,500 Children Safety Centers Network, Saint Paul, MN
2,500 Laurens County Safe Homes Network, Laurens, SC
2,500 Senior Options, Clinton, SC
2,400 Camp Smile, Webster, NY
2,000 Boys and Girls Club, Minneapolis, MN
2,000 Bridging, Bloomington, MN
2,000 Family and Children's Service, Minneapolis, MN
2,000 Inner-City Youth League, Saint Paul, MN

2,000	Minnesota DARE, Saint Paul, MN
2,000	PACER Center, Minneapolis, MN
2,000	Visalia Citizens for Drug Abuse Resistance Education, Visalia, CA
2,000	YMCA, Red Wing, MN
1,950	Big Brothers and Big Sisters, Owatonna, MN
1,800	Self-Help for Hard of Hearing People, Attleboro, MA
1,665	Community Day Care Center, Shelbyville, TN
1,300	Centre County Youth Service Bureau, State College, PA
1,300	Huntington Community Center, Huntington, PA
1,300	YMCA, State College, PA

Journal Communications, Inc.

Company Contact

Milwaukee, WI
Web: http://www.jc.com

Company Description

Employees: 7,400
SIC(s): 2711 Newspapers, 4813 Telephone Communications Except Radiotelephone, 4832 Radio Broadcasting Stations.

Nonmonetary Support

Type: Donated Equipment; In-kind Services; Loaned Employees; Loaned Executives

Giving Contact

Mr. Robert Dye, Vice President, Corporate Communications
Journal Communications, Inc.
PO Box 661
Milwaukee, WI 53201
Phone: (414)224-2725
Fax: (414)224-2469

Description

Organization Type: Corporate Giving Program
Giving Locations: headquarters.
Grant Types: General Support.

Financial Summary

Total Giving: Contributes through corporate direct giving program only.

Typical Recipients

Arts & Humanities: Arts & Humanities-General
Civic & Public Affairs: Civic & Public Affairs-General
Education: Education-General
Social Services: Social Services-General

Application Procedures

Initial Contact: a brief letter of inquiry
Application Requirements: a description of organization, amount requested, purpose of funds sought, recently audited financial statements, and proof of tax-exempt status
Deadlines: None.

Restrictions

Does not support individuals, religious organizations for sectarian purposes, or political or lobbying groups.

Giving Program Officials

Robert M. Dye: B Saint Charles, MO 1947. ED Baylor University BA (1969). PRIM CORP EMPL vice president corporate communications, director: Journal Communications, Inc. ADD CORP EMPL vice president: Journal/Sentinel Inc.

Grants Analysis

Disclosure Period: calendar year ending
Typical Range: $1,000 to $2,500

Journal-Gazette Co.

Company Contact

Fort Wayne, IN

Company Description

Employees: 600
SIC(s): 2711 Newspapers.

Journal-Gazette Foundation, Inc.

Giving Contact

Richard G. Inskeep, President
Journal-Gazette Foundation, Inc.
701 South Clinton Street
Ft. Wayne, IN 46802
Phone: (219)424-5257
Fax: (219)426-0949

Description

Founded: 1985
EIN: 311134237
Organization Type: Corporate Foundation
Giving Locations: IN: Northeast Indiana
Grant Types: Capital, Operating Expenses.

Financial Summary

Total Giving: $500,000 (1999 approx); $643,505 (1998); $490,113 (1997). Note: Contributes through foundation only.
Giving Analysis: Giving for 1997 includes: foundation ($402,837); foundation grants to United Way ($87,276); 1998: foundation ($560,905); foundation grants to United Way ($82,600)
Assets: $8,887,846 (1998); $8,435,942 (1997); $5,649,655 (1996)
Gifts Received: $11,250 (1998); $92,173 (1997); $92,342 (1996). Note: Contributions are received from Richard G. Inskeep and Harriett J. Inskeep.

Typical Recipients

Arts & Humanities: Arts Appreciation, Arts Associations & Councils, Arts Funds, Arts Outreach, Historic Preservation, History & Archaeology, Libraries, Museums/Galleries, Music, Performing Arts, Public Broadcasting, Theater
Civic & Public Affairs: African American Affairs, Botanical Gardens/Parks, Chambers of Commerce, Clubs, Community Foundations, Employment/Job Training, Civic & Public Affairs-General, Hispanic Affairs, Municipalities/Towns, Parades/Festivals, Public Policy, Rural Affairs, Urban & Community Affairs, Women's Affairs, Zoos/Aquariums
Education: Agricultural Education, Business Education, Colleges & Universities, Continuing Education, Education Associations, Education Funds, Education-General, Education-General, Journalism/Media Education, Literacy, Medical Education, Private Education (Precollege), Public Education (Precollege), Secondary Education (Private), Secondary Education (Public), Special Education, Student Aid
Environment: Air/Water Quality, Resource Conservation
Health: AIDS/HIV, Cancer, Children's Health/Hospitals, Clinics/Medical Centers, Emergency/Ambulance Services, Geriatric Health, Health Organizations, Hospitals, Mental Health, Research/Studies Institutes, Single-Disease Health Associations
Religion: Churches, Jewish Causes, Ministries, Religious Organizations, Religious Welfare
Science: Science Museums, Scientific Centers & Institutes
Social Services: At-Risk Youth, Camps, Child Abuse, Child Welfare, Community Service Organizations, Crime Prevention, Day Care, Family Planning, Family Services, Food/Clothing Distribution, People with Disabilities, Recreation & Athletics, Scouts, Senior Services, Shelters/Homelessness, Substance Abuse, United Funds/United Ways, Volunteer Services, YMCA/YWCA/YMHA/YWHA, Youth Organizations

Contributions Analysis

Arts & Humanities: 21%. Supports arts organizations and public broadcasting in Ft. Wayne, IN.
Civic & Public Affairs: 13%. Supports fairgrounds, community foundations, and minority organizations.
Education: 25%. Major support goes to the Indiana University Foundation. Also contributes to Junior Achievement, secondary and higher education, and literacy programs.
Environment: Supports local parks.
Health: 6%. Primarily supports hospitals and the American Red Cross. Also supports health services and an AIDS task force.
Religion: 3%. Supports local churches.
Science: Supports science initiatives.
Social Services: 32%. Support goes to the YMCA, the United Way, food banks, Planned Parenthood, and a Lutheran social services organization.
Note: Total contributions made in 1998.

Application Procedures

Initial Contact: Send a brief letter.
Application Requirements: Include the need for financial assistance and timeframe.
Deadlines: None.
Decision Notification: Committee meets quarterly.

Restrictions

Recipient organization must be in the general geographic area of northeast Indiana and qualify under the IRS code as a 501(c)(3) organization.

Corporate Officials

Richard G. Inskeep: ownerr B 1925. PRIM CORP EMPL owner: Journal-Gazette Co.
Craig Klugman: editor B Fargo, ND 1945. PRIM CORP EMPL editor: Journal-Gazette Co. NONPR AFFIL member: American Newspaper Editors.

Foundation Officials

Jerry D. Fox: secretary, treasurer, director B 1952. PRIM CORP EMPL secretary, treasurer, director: Journal-Gazette Co.
Harriet J. Inskeep: director
Richard G. Inskeep: president, director (see above)
Julie Inskeep Walda: director PRIM CORP EMPL vice president, director: Journal-Gazette Co.

Grants Analysis

Disclosure Period: calendar year ending 1998
Total Grants: $560,905*
Number of Grants: 108
Average Grant: $5,194
Highest Grant: $50,500
Typical Range: $500 to $6,000
***Note:** Giving excludes United Way.

Recent Grants

Note: Grants derived from 1998 Form 990.

Arts & Humanities

50,500	Allen County Courthouse Preservation Trust, Fort Wayne, IN -- capital
30,000	Embassy Theatre Foundation, Fort Wayne, IN -- capital
14,000	Arts United of Greater Fort Wayne, Fort Wayne, IN
9,860	The Lincoln Museum, Fort Wayne, IN
5,000	Peabody Public Library, Columbia City, IN -- capital

5,000	Vietnam Memorial Committee of Allen County, Inc, Fort Wayne, IN -- capital
4,000	WFWA-TV39 PBS Television, Fort Wayne, IN
2,840	WBNI FM 89.1 Public Radio, Fort Wayne, IN
2,500	Fort Wayne Philharmonic, Fort Wayne, IN

Civic & Public Affairs

30,000	Headwaters Park Campaign, Fort Wayne, IN -- capital
10,100	IPFW Foundation - Helmke Library, Fort Wayne, IN -- capital
10,000	Auburn Parks & Recreation Department, Auburn, IN -- capital
9,375	Friends of Fort Wayne, Fort Wayne, IN
5,000	Wells County Foundation--Museum Project, Bluffion, IN -- capital
4,700	The Mad Anthonys, Inc, Fort Wayne, IN
2,500	Greater Ft Wayne Chamber of Commerce, Fort Wayne, IN
2,000	Steuben County Community Playground Project, Angola, IN -- capital

Education

50,000	Alumni Center Campaign - Library, Bloomington, IN -- capital
25,000	University of Texas MD Anderson Cancer Research Center, Houston, TX
20,000	Indiana University Foundation Class Campaigns, Bloomington, IN -- capital
10,000	Bishop Dwenger/Bishop Luers Improvements, Fort Wayne, IN -- capital
10,000	Concordia Lutheran High School, Fort Wayne, IN -- capital
5,000	Indiana University Foundation School of Journalism, Bloomington, IN
5,000	Indiana University Foundation School of Law, Bloomington, IN
5,000	University of Saint Francis, Fort Wayne, IN -- capital
4,500	Indiana University Foundation, Bloomington, IN
3,500	Junior Achievement of NE Indiana, Fort Wayne, IN
3,000	Martin Luther King Montessori School, Fort Wayne, IN -- capital
2,895	Three Rivers Literacy Alliance, Fort Wayne, IN
2,000	Indiana University Foundation DASA, Bloomington, IN

Health

20,000	Alliance for the Mentally Ill, Indianapolis, IN -- capital
5,600	American Cancer Society-Vera Bradley Classic, Indianapolis, IN
4,000	Allen County Council on Aging, Fort Wayne, IN
3,000	Ft Wayne Community Schools Community Programs, Fort Wayne, IN

Religion

10,000	Love Church, Fort Wayne, IN -- capital
5,500	First Presbyterian Church, Fort Wayne, IN
5,000	Faith Methodist Church, Bloomington, IN

Social Services

82,500	United Way of Allen County, Inc, Fort Wayne, IN -- Operations
30,000	Ft Wayne Parks & Recreation Foundation, Fort Wayne, IN -- Capital
20,000	YWCA of Fort Wayne, Fort Wayne, IN -- capital
10,100	Turnstone Center for Disabled Children & Adults, Fort Wayne, IN
10,000	Family & Children's Services, Fort Wayne, IN -- capital
10,000	LifeLine Youth & Family Services, Inc, Elkhart, IN
6,525	Police Athletic League-PAL Youth Center, Indianapolis, IN
6,500	Community Harvest Food Bank, Fort Wayne, IN -- Operations
5,000	The Cedars-Homeless Task Force of Ft Wayne, Inc, Fort Wayne, IN
5,000	YMCA/Old Fort Branch--Fine Arts Program, Fort Wayne, IN
4,000	YMCA/Old Fort Brance--Partner With Youth, Fort Wayne, IN
3,000	Villages & Pathways Youth Program, Fort Wayne, IN

JSJ CORP.

Company Contact

Grand Haven, MI

Company Description

Employees: 2,000
SIC(s): 2522 Office Furniture Except Wood, 3089 Plastics Products Nec, 3364 Nonferrous Die-Castings Except Aluminum, 3469 Metal Stampings Nec.

Nonmonetary Support

Type: Donated Equipment

JSJ Foundation

Giving Contact

Lynne Sherwood, Secretary & Trustee
JSJ Foundation
700 Robbins Road
Grand Haven, MI 49417-2651
Phone: (616)842-6350
Fax: (616)847-3112

Description

EIN: 382421508
Organization Type: Corporate Foundation
Giving Locations: CA: southern; FL; MI; TX; WI
Grant Types: Capital, Employee Matching Gifts, General Support, Multiyear/Continuing Support.

Financial Summary

Total Giving: $275,000 (2000 approx); $364,600 (1999 approx); $283,311 (1998). Note: Contributes through Corporate and Foundation.
Giving Analysis: Giving for 1998 includes: foundation ($254,976); foundation grants to United Way ($28,335)
Assets: $601,445 (1998); $698,000 (1997); $630,623 (1996)
Gifts Received: $250,000 (1998); $250,000 (1995); $500,000 (1994). Note: In 1998, contributions were received from JSJ Corp.

Typical Recipients

Arts & Humanities: Arts Associations & Councils, Arts Centers, Arts Funds, Arts Institutes, Community Arts, Arts & Humanities-General, Museums/Galleries, Music, Opera, Performing Arts, Public Broadcasting, Theater
Civic & Public Affairs: Community Foundations, Civic & Public Affairs-General, Municipalities/Towns, Public Policy, Urban & Community Affairs, Women's Affairs, Zoos/Aquariums
Education: Afterschool/Enrichment Programs, Arts/Humanities Education, Business Education, Colleges & Universities, Community & Junior Colleges, Continuing Education, Economic Education, Education Associations, Education Funds, Engineering/Technological Education, Education-General, Minority Education, Private Education (Precollege)
Health: Health Policy/Cost Containment, Health Organizations, Hospices
Religion: Ministries, Religious Organizations, Religious Welfare
Social Services: Community Service Organizations, Counseling, Day Care, Family Services, Homes, Recreation & Athletics, Scouts, Shelters/Homelessness, Social Services-General, Substance Abuse, United Funds/United Ways, Volunteer Services, YMCA/YWCA/YMHA/YWHA, Youth Organizations

Contributions Analysis

Giving Priorities: Youth services, community development, education, and religious organizations.
Arts & Humanities: 7%. Supports arts, museums and music.
Civic & Public Affairs: 8%. Supports women's causes, Habitat for Humanity, and community development.
Education: 19%. Supports higher education.
Health: 5%. Supports hospice, and healthcare.
Religion: 20%. Supports YMCA, and religious organizations and causes.
Social Services: 41%. Supports humane society, united funds and United Way, and youth services.
Note: Total contributions made in 1998.

Application Procedures

Initial Contact: The foundation has no formal grant application procedure or application form. Send a brief letter of inquiry. Include a description of organization, amount requested, purpose of funds sought, recently audited financial statement, and proof of tax-exempt status. Also indicate total goal.
Deadlines: Late October.

Restrictions

Education, the humanities, and the arts receive special emphasis. Does not support individuals, religious organizations for sectarian purposes, political or lobbying groups, or organizations outside operating areas.

Corporate Officials

F. Martin Johnson: chairman, chief executive officer, director PRIM CORP EMPL chairman, chief executive officer, director: JSJ Corp.
Michael D. Metzger: vice president, chief financial officer B Buchanan, MI 1947. ED Western Michigan University (1969); Seidman Graduate School MBA (1977). PRIM CORP EMPL vice president, chief financial officer: JSJ Corp. NONPR AFFIL member: Financial Executives Institute.
Philip E. Taylor: president ED Ball State University BS (1968); University of Wisconsin MBA (1980). PRIM CORP EMPL president: JSJ Corp.

Foundation Officials

Donald A. Johnson: chairman, secretary
F. Martin Johnson: trustee (see above)
Edward L. Ozark: trustee B Buffalo, NY 1944. ED Canisius College (1967); Aquinas College (1994). PRIM CORP EMPL vice president, treasurer, assistant secretary: JSJ Corp. NONPR AFFIL director: Priority Health; member: Risk & Insurance Management Society.
John P. Richardson: trust CORP AFFIL director: JSJ Corp.
Lynne Sherwood: secretary, trustee PRIM CORP EMPL secretary: JSJ Corp.

Grants Analysis

Disclosure Period: calendar year ending 1998
Total Grants: $254,976*
Number of Grants: 48
Average Grant: $5,312
Highest Grant: $55,000
Typical Range: $500 to $10,000
***Note:** Giving excludes United Way.

Recent Grants

Note: Grants derived from 1997 Form 990.

Arts & Humanities

7,500	Grand Rapids Symphony, Grand Rapids, MI -- operations support

4,000 Muskegon Museum of Art, Muskegon, MI -- operations support
3,000 West Shore Symphony Orchestra, Muskegon, MI -- operations support
2,000 Grand Rapids Art Museum, Grand Rapids, MI -- operations support

Civic & Public Affairs
5,000 City of Grand Haven, Grand Haven, MI -- Tank Farm Project
3,000 La Crosse Community Foundation, La Crosse, WI -- operations support
2,000 Citizens Research Council, Farmington Hills, MI -- operations support

Education
20,000 Grand Valley University Foundation Grand Rapids Campus, Grand Rapids, MI
9,500 Alma College, Alma, MI -- operating support
8,000 St. Mary's School, Spring Lake, MI -- capital campaign
6,000 St. John's Lutheran School, Grand Haven, MI -- capital campaign
4,400 Junior Achievement West Michigan Lake Shore, Grand Haven, MI -- operations support for Project Business
3,300 Grand Valley University Foundation, Grand Rapids, MI -- President's Fund

Health
8,000 Alliance for Health, Grand Rapids, MI -- operations support
6,000 Hospice of North Ottawa Community, Grand Haven, MI -- special grant
2,300 Hospice of North Ottawa Community, Grand Haven, MI -- operations support

Religion
5,200 Tri-Cities Ministries, Grand Haven, MI -- operations support
4,000 OAR, Holland, MI -- capital campaign
2,000 OAR, Holland, MI -- operations support

Social Services
55,000 Tri-Cities Area United Fund, Grand Haven, MI -- operations support
25,000 Tri-Cities Family YMCA, Grand Haven, MI -- capital campaign
20,000 Spring Lake Junior Sailing Association, Spring Lake, MI -- capital campaign
7,000 United Way of Central Texas, Temple, TX -- operations support
7,000 United Way of Volusia County, Daytona Beach, FL -- operations support
6,500 United Way, La Crosse, WI -- operations support
6,000 Tri-Cities Family YMCA, Grand Haven, MI -- operations support
3,000 Boy Scouts of America Gerald R. Ford Council, Grand Rapids, MI -- capital campaign
3,000 Heart of West Michigan United Way, Grand Rapids, MI -- operations support
2,500 United Way of Oceana County -- operations support
2,000 Michigan Organizing Project, Muskegon, MI -- operations support

KAMAN CORP.

Company Contact
Bloomfield, CT
Web: http://www.kaman.com

Company Description
Employees: 5,476
SIC(s): 3721 Aircraft, 3724 Aircraft Engines & Engine Parts, 3728 Aircraft Parts & Equipment Nec, 3764 Space Propulsion Units & Parts.

Giving Contact
Russell H. Jones, Vice President
Kaman Corp.
PO Box 1
Bloomfield, CT 06002
Phone: (860)243-8311
Fax: (860)243-6365

Description
Organization Type: Corporate Giving Program
Giving Locations: headquarters and operating communities.
Grant Types: Capital, General Support, Operating Expenses.

Financial Summary
Total Giving: Contributes through corporate direct giving program only.

Typical Recipients
Arts & Humanities: Arts & Humanities-General
Civic & Public Affairs: Civic & Public Affairs-General
Education: Education-General
Health: Health-General
Social Services: People with Disabilities, Social Services-General

Contributions Analysis
Note: Company reports that 55% of all contributions target organizations and activities serving the disabled and the disadvantaged.

Application Procedures
Initial Contact: a brief letter of inquiry
Application Requirements: a description of organization; a description of (and budget for) the project to funded, a listing of the organization's board of directors and key staff; amount requested; purpose of funds sought; recently audited financial statements; proof of tax-exempt status; and contact information for further information.
Deadlines: None.
Decision Notification: Budgeting is done between November and March.

Restrictions
Does not support individuals, recipients of state grants, organizations with taxing authority or receiving funds from a taxing authority, religious organizations for sectarian purposes, political or lobbying groups, advertising in program booklets, galas and events, endowment funds, and agencies receiving funds from the United Way/Combined Health Appeal.

Corporate Officials
Charles Huron Kaman: chairman, president, chief executive officer, director B Washington, DC 1919. ED Catholic University America BS (1940). PRIM CORP EMPL chairman, president, chief executive officer, director: Kaman Corp. CORP AFFIL chairman: Kaman X Corp.; chairman: Kamatics Corp.; chairman: Kaman Instrumentation Corp.; chairman: Kaman Music Corp.; chairman: Kaman Electro Magnetics Corp.; chairman: Kaman Industries Tech; chairman: Kaman Aerospace International Corp.; chairman: Kaman Diversified Tech Corp.; director: ITT Systems & Sciences Corp.; chairman: Kaman Aerospace Corp.; director: AirKaman Jacksonville Inc. NONPR AFFIL member: Royal Aeronautical Society; founder: University Hartford American Leadership Forum; member: Newcomen Society; member: Pi Tau Sigma; member: Naval Helicopter Association; member national advisory council: Navy League U.S.; member: National Academy Engineering; member: National Museum of Naval Aviation; member: Helicopter Association International; director: Institute Living; member: Connecticut Society Professional Engineers; president, director: Fidelco Guide Dog Foundation Inc.; member: Connecticut Aeronautics Historical Association; member: Connecticut Business & Industry Association; board governors: Catholic University America; member: Connecticut Academy Science & Engineering; member: Aviation Hall of Fame; member: Beta Gamma Sigma; member: American Helicopter Society; member: American Institute Aeronautics & Astronautics.

Giving Program Officials
Robert M. Garneau: chief financial officer B Windsor, VT 1944. ED American International University BS (1967). PRIM CORP EMPL executive vice president, chief financial officer: Kaman Corp. CORP AFFIL treasurer: Kaman Aerospace Corp.; chief financial officer: Kaman Diversified Technical Corp. NONPR AFFIL treasurer, director: Fidelco Guide Dog Foundation Inc.; director: New England Air Museum.
Russell H. Jones: officer B Hartford, CT 1944. ED University of Connecticut (1966); Hartford Seminary (1994). PRIM CORP EMPL vice president, treasurer: Kaman Corp. CORP AFFIL vice president: Kaman Industrial Technology Corp.; vice president: Kaman Music Corp.; director: CIGNA Mutual Funds; vice president: Kaman Aerospace Corp.

Grants Analysis
Disclosure Period: calendar year ending
Typical Range: $500 to $5,000

KATTEN, MUCHIN & ZAVIS

Company Contact
Chicago, IL

Company Description
Revenue: US$93,000,000
Employees: 981
SIC(s): 8111 Legal Services.

Katten, Muchin & Zavis Foundation

Giving Contact
Marylou Rack, Contributions
Katten, Muchin & Zavis Foundation
525 West Monroe Street, Suite 1600
Chicago, IL 60661-3693
Phone: (312)902-5410
Fax: (312)902-1061

Description
Founded: 1982
EIN: 363165216
Organization Type: Corporate Foundation
Giving Locations: IL: Chicago nationally and internationally.
Grant Types: General Support.

Financial Summary
Total Giving: $629,790 (1997); $582,766 (1996); $526,914 (1995). Note: Contributes through foundation only.
Assets: $68,739 (1997); $85,484 (1996); $46,369 (1995)
Gifts Received: $612,810 (1997); $621,724 (1996); $566,504 (1995). Note: Contributions are received fromm Katten Muchin & Zavis, and from individuals.

Typical Recipients
Arts & Humanities: Arts Centers, Arts Festivals, Arts Funds, Ballet, Dance, Museums/Galleries, Music, Opera, Public Broadcasting, Theater
Civic & Public Affairs: African American Affairs, Business/Free Enterprise, Civil Rights, Economic Development, Civic & Public Affairs-General, Law & Justice, Legal Aid, Public Policy, Urban & Community Affairs, Women's Affairs, Zoos/Aquariums
Education: Business Education, Colleges & Universities, Education Reform, Engineering/Technological

Education, Education-General, Legal Education, Literacy, Private Education (Precollege), Secondary Education (Private)
Health: AIDS/HIV, Alzheimers Disease, Cancer, Children's Health/Hospitals, Clinics/Medical Centers, Diabetes, Emergency/Ambulance Services, Health Organizations, Hospitals, Medical Research, Mental Health, Multiple Sclerosis, Public Health, Single-Disease Health Associations
International: Foreign Educational Institutions, International Organizations, International Relief Efforts, Missionary/Religious Activities
Religion: Churches, Jewish Causes, Religious Organizations, Social/Policy Issues
Social Services: At-Risk Youth, Big Brother/Big Sister, Child Abuse, Child Welfare, Community Service Organizations, Emergency Relief, Family Services, Food/Clothing Distribution, People with Disabilities, Scouts, Senior Services, Substance Abuse, United Funds/United Ways, YMCA/YWCA/YMHA/YWHA, Youth Organizations

Contributions Analysis

Arts & Humanities: 9%. Supports museums, opera, theater, and local arts organizations.
Civic & Public Affairs: 17%. Contributions support organizations affiliated with company's business interests, including the Lawyers Committee for Civil Rights and other legal affairs groups.
Education: 7%. Supports business education and colleges and universities.
Health: 9%. Primarily supports hospitals, health care, and local chapters of single-disease health associations.
International: 1%. Supports international organizations with ties to Israel, higher education, and children.
Religion: 52%. Supports Jewish organizations and activities, with major support for the Jewish United Fund.
Social Services: 10% to 15%. Supports youth organizations, the United Way, and numerous community service organizations.
Note: Total contributions in 1997.

Application Procedures

Initial Contact: Send brief letter outlining request.
Application Requirements: Include purpose for which grant will be used, amount requested, a description of organization, and proof of tax-exempt status.
Deadlines: None.

Corporate Officials

Allan B. Muchin: chairman partner B Manitowoc, WI 1936. ED University of Wisconsin, Manitowoc BBA (1958); University of Wisconsin, Manitowoc JD (1961). PRIM CORP EMPL chairman: Katten, Muchin & Zavis. CORP AFFIL director: Alberto-Culver Co.; director: Nationwide Beef Inc.
Michael W. Zavis: managing partner B Chicago, IL 1937. ED University of Pennsylvania BS (1958); University of Chicago JD (1961). PRIM CORP EMPL managing partner: Katten, Muchin & Zavis. NONPR AFFIL director: Illinois Development Fin Authority; member advisory committee: University Chicago School Social Services; fellow: Chicago Bar Association; fellow: Illinois Bar Association; fellow: American Bar Association. CLUB AFFIL Standard Club; Boca Rio Country Club; Bryn Mawr Country Club.

Foundation Officials

Alan D. Croll: director
Nina B. Matis: director B New York, NY 1947. ED Smith College AB (1969); New York University JD (1972). PRIM CORP EMPL partner: Katten, Muchin & Zavis. CORP AFFIL partner: Katten Muchin & Zavis. NONPR AFFIL member: American College Lawyers; member: Urban Land Institute.
Allan B. Muchin: director (see above)
Melvin E. Pearl: treasurer, director B Chicago, IL 1936. ED University of Wisconsin BBA (1957); Northwestern University LLB (1960). PRIM CORP EMPL partner: Katten, Muchin & Zavis. CORP AFFIL officer: Guarantee Reserve Life Insurance Co.
David R. Schulman: director CORP AFFIL director: Edward Don & Co.
Vincent A. F. Sergi: director
Norman Steinberg: secretary
Herbert S. Wander: secretary, director B Cincinnati, OH 1935. ED University of Michigan AB (1957); Yale University LLB (1960). PRIM CORP EMPL partner: Katten, Muchin & Zavis. CORP AFFIL director: Telephone & Data System. NONPR AFFIL trustee: Michael Reese Foundation; member: Yale University Law School Association; director: Jewish United Fund; member: Phi Beta Kappa; member: Illinois Bar Association; director: Jewish Federation Metropolitan Chicago; director: Council Jewish Federations; member, chairman-elect: American Bar Association; member: Chicago Bar Association. CLUB AFFIL Northmoor Country Club; Standard Club; Economic Club.
Michael W. Zavis: president, director (see above)

Grants Analysis

Disclosure Period: calendar year ending 1997
Total Grants: $623,927*
Number of Grants: 161
Average Grant: $2,289*
Highest Grant: $257,709
Typical Range: $100 to $5,000
*Note: Giving excludes United Way. Average grant figure excludes highest grant.

Recent Grants

Note: Grants derived from 1996 Form 990.

Arts & Humanities

11,000	Lyric Opera, Chicago, IL
9,500	Chicago Cultural Center Foundation, Chicago, IL
6,500	National Foundation for Advancement in the Arts, Miami, FL
5,500	Museum of Contemporary Art, Los Angeles, CA
4,500	Ravinia Festival Association, Highland Park, IL
3,600	Joffrey Ballet, Chicago, IL

Civic & Public Affairs

35,000	CBA Partnership for Future
27,170	Chicago Liberties Committee for Civil Rights, Chicago, IL
25,295	NAACP Legal Defense Fund, New York, NY
5,920	Legal Assistance Foundation, Chicago, IL
4,550	Business and Professional People for the Public Interest, Chicago, IL
3,950	California Women's Law Center, Los Angeles, CA
3,450	Public Counsel, Los Angeles, CA
3,400	Constitutional Rights Foundation, Los Angeles, CA
3,250	House of Justice
3,000	Pro Bono Advocates, Chicago, IL
2,725	Chicago Volunteer Legal Services Foundation, Chicago, IL
2,500	Cabrini-Green Legal Aid Clinic, Chicago, IL
2,265	Public Interest Law Initiative, Chicago, IL

Education

5,000	CFA Education Foundation
5,000	Francis Xavier Warde School
4,500	Providence-St. Mel High School, Chicago, IL
2,500	Junior Achievement
2,500	Roosevelt University, Chicago, IL

Health

10,630	AIDS Project, Los Angeles, CA
6,100	Juvenile Diabetes Foundation, New York, NY
5,000	Multiple Sclerosis Society
3,333	American Red Cross Orange County, CA
3,061	American Cancer Society, Chicago, IL
2,250	David A. Winston Health Policy Fellowship, Washington, DC
2,250	Highland Park Hospital Foundation, Chicago, IL
2,250	Sheepish Convent Hospital
2,040	Cystic Fibrosis Foundation, Philadelphia, PA
2,000	Ronald McDonald House Charities, Chicago, IL
1,900	MCHC Chicago Hospital Council, Chicago, IL

Religion

240,212	Jewish United Fund, Chicago, IL
5,475	Anti-Defamation League of B'nai B'rith, New York, NY
4,970	Holy Trinity Cathedral
4,000	American Jewish Congress Legal Clinic
2,500	American Jewish Committee, Chicago, IL

Social Services

5,400	BBF Family Services
4,250	Big Sisters, Los Angeles, CA
4,200	MRIC Children's Memorial Foundation
4,150	James Jordon Boys and Girls Club and Family Life
2,500	Emergency Fund for Needy People, Chicago, IL
2,500	Sarah's Circle, Washington, DC
2,500	Share Our Strength
2,450	Alliance for Children's Rights, Los Angeles, CA
2,000	Chicago Anti-Hunger Federation, Chicago, IL
2,000	Legal Clinic for the Disabled, Philadelphia, PA

KELLOGG CO.

 Number 90 of Top 100 Corporate Givers

Company Contact

Battle Creek, MI
Web: http://www.kelloggs.com

Company Description

Revenue: US$6,984,200,000 (1999)
Employees: 15,000 (1999)
Fortune Rank: 250, per FORTUNE Magazine's list of 500 Largest U.S. Corporations (1999).
FF 250
SIC(s): 2038 Frozen Specialties Nec, 2043 Cereal Breakfast Foods, 2053 Frozen Bakery Products Except Bread.

Corporate Sponsorship

Type: Arts & cultural events
Contact: David Stevenson, Director, Corporate Contributions

Kellogg Co. Twenty-Five Year Employees' Fund Inc.

Giving Contact

Timothy Knowlton, Director
Kellogg Co. Twenty-Five Year Employees' Fund Inc.
One Kellogg Square
Battle Creek, MI 49016-3599

Phone: (616)961-3125
Fax: (616)961-3494

Alternate Contact

Dawn Rich, Corporate Center Coordinator
Phone: (616)961-2867

Description

EIN: 386039770
Organization Type: Corporate Foundation
Giving Locations: MI
Grant Types: Employee Matching Gifts, General Support.

Financial Summary

Total Giving: $8,000,000 (1999 approx); $8,000,000 (1998 approx); $7,277,361 (1997). Note: Contributes through corporate direct giving program and foundation.
Giving Analysis: Giving for 1997 includes: foundation ($5,950,225); foundation gifts to individuals ($1,327,136)
Assets: $2,879,189 (1997); $69,981,930 (1996); $84,038,416 (1995)

Typical Recipients

Arts & Humanities: Arts Associations & Councils, History & Archaeology
Civic & Public Affairs: Botanical Gardens/Parks, Community Foundations, Municipalities/Towns, Nonprofit Management, Philanthropic Organizations, Public Policy, Urban & Community Affairs, Zoos/Aquariums
Health: Clinics/Medical Centers, Emergency/Ambulance Services, Health Organizations, Hospices, Hospitals
Religion: Religious Organizations
Social Services: At-Risk Youth, Big Brother/Big Sister, Community Service Organizations, Food/Clothing Distribution, People with Disabilities, Senior Services, Substance Abuse, Volunteer Services, YMCA/YWCA/YMHA/YWHA, Youth Organizations

Application Procedures

Initial Contact: For monthly supplemental living grants, send written request for the Application for Assistance Form; for charitable contributions, send a brief letter of inquiry.
Application Requirements: Include a description of organization, amount requested, purpose of funds sought, recently audited financial statement, and proof of tax-exempt status.
Deadlines: None.

Restrictions

To qualify for monthly supplemental living expense grants, applicants must: have been employed by Kellogg Company or one of its subsidiaries for 25 or more years, or be a spouse of such a person; complete the Application for Assistance Form (copy available from the Fund); meet minimum financial-need requirements as determined by Fund Trustees; and be approved by Fund Trustees.
To qualify for charitable contributions, organizations must submit request in writing to Trustees and prove ability to provide benefits to 25-Year Club members as deemed by Trustees. request in writing to Trustees and prove ability to provide benefits to 25-Year Club members as deemed by Trustees.

Additional Information

The Twenty-Five Year Employees' Fund Inc. is a company-run giving program, and a separate entity from the W.K. Kellogg Foundation. The W.K. Kellogg Foundation was established in 1930 with contributions from the company, and is one of the largest grant-making institutions in the world.

Corporate Officials

Richard McCourt Clark: senior vice president, general counsel, secretary B Bridgewater, MA 1937. ED College of the Holy Cross AB (1959); Cornell University LLB (1962). PRIM CORP EMPL senior vice president, general counsel, secretary: Kellogg Co. CORP AFFIL secretary: Kellogg Sales Co. NONPR AFFIL member: Michigan General Counsel Association; member: New York State Bar Association; member: Michigan Bar Association; trustee: Michigan Colleges Foundation; director: Food & Drug Law Institute; director: Gilmore International Keyboard Festival; member: Connecticut Bar Association; member: Association Bar New York City; member president council: College Holy Cross; member: American Society of Corporate Secretaries; member: American Bar Association; member: American Corporate Counsel Association.
John R. Hinton: executive vice president administration, chief financial officer B 1946. ED Michigan State University MBA; University of Wisconsin BBA. PRIM CORP EMPL executive vice president administration, chief financial officer: Kellogg Co. CORP AFFIL senior vice president: Kellogg Sales Co.; director: Kellogg United States of America Inc.; vice president: Kellogg Caribbean Corp.
Janet L. Kelly: executive vice president corporate development, general counsel, secretary B 1957. ED Grinnell College BA (1979); Yale University JD (1983). PRIM CORP EMPL executive vice president corporate development, general counsel, secretary: Kellogg Co. ADD CORP EMPL senior vice president, secretary, general counsel: Sara Lee Corp. CORP AFFIL trustee: Stein Roe Farnham; director: Evanston Hospital Corp. NONPR AFFIL trustee: Grinnell College.
Arnold Gordon Langbo: chairman, chief executive officer, director B Richmond, BC Canada 1937. ED University of British Columbia. PRIM CORP EMPL chairman, chief executive officer, director: Kellogg Co. CORP AFFIL chairman, chief executive officer: Mrs. Smith's Frozen Foods Co.; director: Whirlpool Corp.; president, chief operating officer: Kellogg International; director: Kellogg U.S.A. Inc.; director: Atlantic Richfield Co.; director: Johnson & Johnson. NONPR AFFIL member advisory board: Northwestern University Kellogg Graduate School Business Management; director: Tea Council Canada; director: Grocery Products Manufacturer Canada; vice president: Hockey International; director: Gilmore International Keyboard Festival; director: Grocery Manufacturer America; member: British Columbia Premier's Advisory Council; member: Canadian-American Committee; trustee: Albion College; member: American Frozen Food Institute.
Joseph Melvin Stewart: senior vice president corporate affairs B Maringouin, LA 1942. ED Southern University BS (1965). PRIM CORP EMPL senior vice president corporate affairs: Kellogg Co. NONPR AFFIL director: Battle Creek Health Systems; director: Second Harvest National Food Bank Network; director: American School Foodsvc Association Foundation.
Donald W. Thomason: executive vice president service & technology B 1943. PRIM CORP EMPL executive vice president service & technology: Kellogg Co. CORP AFFIL director: Kellogg United States of America Inc.

Foundation Officials

Arthur A. Byrd: trustee PRIM CORP EMPL executive vice president: Kellogg United States of America Inc.
Richard McCourt Clark: vice president, trustee (see above)
John R. Hinton: president, trustee (see above)
S. A. Karibjanian: trustee
J. W. Misner: trustee
Joseph Melvin Stewart: trustee (see above)
Donald W. Thomason: trustee (see above)

Grants Analysis

Disclosure Period: calendar year ending 1997
Total Grants: $5,950,225*
Number of Grants: 5
Average Grant: $10,944*
Highest Grant: $5,906,250
Typical Range: $1,500 to $15,000
***Note:** Giving excludes employee assistance. Average grant figure excludes highest grant.

Recent Grants

Note: Grants derived from 1997 Form 990.

Arts & Humanities

5,906,250	Heritage Center Foundation, Battle Creek, MI

Civic & Public Affairs

3,600	Council of Michigan Foundation, Grand Haven, MI

Social Services

14,500	Battle Creek Kellogg Retirees Association, Battle Creek, MI
10,000	Memphis Retiree Association, Cordova, TN
2,000	San Leandro Retiree Association, Pleasant Hill, CA

KELLWOOD CO.

Company Contact

Chesterfield, MO

Company Description

Employees: 17,000
SIC(s): 2321 Men's/Boys' Shirts, 2325 Men's/Boys' Trousers & Slacks, 2331 Women's/Misses' Blouses & Shirts, 2335 Women's/Misses' Dresses.

Kellwood Foundation

Giving Contact

Terri Wise, Secretary, Treasurer & Director
Kellwood Foundation
600 Kellwood Parkway
Chesterfield, MO 63017
Phone: (314)576-3431
Fax: (314)576-3439

Alternate Contact

PO Box 14374
St. Louis, MO 63178

Description

Founded: 1965
EIN: 366141441
Organization Type: Corporate Foundation
Giving Locations: MO: St. Louis including greater metropolitan area
Grant Types: Capital, Employee Matching Gifts, General Support.

Financial Summary

Total Giving: $260,000 (fiscal year ending April 30, 2000 approx); $260,000 (fiscal 1999 approx); $250,000 (fiscal 1998 approx). Note: Contributes through corporate direct giving program and foundation. Fiscal 1997 Giving includes foundation ($121,602); matching gifts ($23,112); United Way ($50,000). 1996 Giving includes foundation ($157,875); United Way ($58,182); matching gifts ($27,730).
Assets: $672,550 (fiscal 1997); $572,560 (fiscal 1996); $558,408 (fiscal 1995)
Gifts Received: $258,389 (fiscal 1997); $246,720 (fiscal 1996); $366,710 (fiscal 1995). Note: In fiscal 1996, contributions were received from the Kellwood Company.

Typical Recipients

Arts & Humanities: Arts Associations & Councils, Arts & Humanities-General, Museums/Galleries, Performing Arts, Theater
Civic & Public Affairs: Botanical Gardens/Parks, Business/Free Enterprise, Civic & Public Affairs-General, Nonprofit Management, Professional & Trade Associations, Urban & Community Affairs, Women's Affairs, Zoos/Aquariums
Education: Business Education, Colleges & Universities, Education Funds, Education-General, International Studies, Minority Education, Private Education (Precollege), Public Education (Precollege), Special Education
Environment: Forestry
Health: Cancer, Children's Health/Hospitals, Diabetes, Emergency/Ambulance Services, Eyes/Blindness, Health-General, Single-Disease Health Associations, Transplant Networks/Donor Banks
International: International Affairs
Religion: Dioceses, Religious Organizations, Religious Welfare, Seminaries
Science: Observatories & Planetariums
Social Services: Animal Protection, At-Risk Youth, Camps, Child Welfare, Community Service Organizations, Day Care, Family Services, Food/Clothing Distribution, People with Disabilities, Scouts, Social Services-General, Substance Abuse, United Funds/United Ways, YMCA/YWCA/YMHA/YWHA, Youth Organizations

Application Procedures

Initial Contact: written request
Application Requirements: proof of tax-exempt 501(c)(3) status
Deadlines: November 15
Decision Notification: foundation board meets quarterly

Restrictions

Does not support individuals.

Corporate Officials

James C. Jacobsen: vice chairman emeritus B Highland Park, IL 1935. ED Lake Forest College BA (1957); University of Illinois MS (1962). PRIM CORP EMPL vice chairman: Kellwood Co. CORP AFFIL senior vice president fin: Tri-W Corp.; director: Utex Textiles; director: Smart Shirts Manufacturer Ltd.; director: South Asia Garments Ltd.; director: Smart Shirts Lanka Ltd.; director: Smart Shirts Ltd.; senior vice president: Sierra Designs Acquisition Corp.; director: Lee Ming & Co. Ltd.; senior vice president finance, director: Robert Scott David Brooks Outlet Stores Inc.; director: Kellwood Honduras; chairman, senior vice president fin: KWD Holdings; vice president, treasurer, director: Kellwood Asia Ltd.; treasurer: Kellwood Haiti; senior vice president Finance: Kellwood Acquisitions Co.; director: Ivy International Ltd.; director: JW Confecciones; director: Greenland Garments Ltd.; senior vice president finance, director: Halmode Apparel Inc.; director: Diplom Ltd.; senior vice president finance: Force One Inc.; senior vice president finance: David Dart Inc.; senior vice president fin, director: Canadian Recreation Products; vice president, treasurer, director: Cen-Tex Holdings Inc.; director: Arden Fabrics Ltd.; director: Bluet Investment Co. Ltd.; director: Altair International; senior vice president fin, director: America Recreation Products Inc.; senior vice president fin, director: 2426-4152 Quebec Inc.
William John McKenna: director, chairman B New York, NY 1926. ED Iona College BBA (1949); New York University MA (1950). PRIM CORP EMPL director, chairman: Kellwood Co. CORP AFFIL director: United Missouri Bank Saint Louis; chairman: Halmode Apparel Inc.; director: UMB Fin Corp.; director: Genovese Drug Stores Inc. NONPR AFFIL trustee: Saint Louis University; member: Sovereign Military Order Malta; director: Cardinal Ritter Institute; permanent deacon: Archdiocese Saint Louis; trustee: Boys Hope. CLUB AFFIL Bellerive Country Club; Saint Louis Club.
Hal Jay Upbin: president, chief executive officer, director B Bronx, NY 1939. ED Pace University BBA (1961). PRIM CORP EMPL president, chief executive officer, director: Kellwood Co. CORP AFFIL chairman: America Recreation Products Inc. NONPR AFFIL alumni advisory board trustee: Pace University; member: State SOC CPAs; member: Jaycees Franklin; member: American Institute CPAs.
Fred William Wenzel: chairman emeritus B Saint Louis, MO 1916. ED University of Wisconsin (1937). PRIM CORP EMPL chairman emeritus: Kellwood Co.

Foundation Officials

James C. Jacobsen: vice president, director (see above)
William John McKenna: chairman, president, director (see above)
Terri Wise: secretary, treasurer, director

Grants Analysis

Disclosure Period: fiscal year ending April 30, 1997
Total Grants: $121,602*
Number of Grants: 133
Average Grant: $914
Highest Grant: $10,000
Typical Range: $100 to $25,000
*Note: Giving excludes matching gifts; United Way.

Recent Grants

Note: Grants derived from fiscal 1997 Form 990.

Arts & Humanities

2,500	Arts and Education Council, Saint Louis, MO
750	St. Louis Art Museum Foundation, Saint Louis, MO

Civic & Public Affairs

1,500	Metropolitan Association for Philanthropy, Saint Louis, MO
750	Metropolitan Association for Philanthropy, Saint Louis, MO
750	Missouri Botanical Garden, Saint Louis, MO
400	St. Louis Association of Community Organizations, Saint Louis, MO
300	Beverly Farm Foundation, Godfrey, IL

Education

10,000	Maryville University Accelerated Development Program, Saint Louis, MO
10,000	St. Louis University, Saint Louis, MO
10,000	St. Louis University, Saint Louis, MO
5,510	St. Louis University, Saint Louis, MO
5,490	St. Louis University, Saint Louis, MO
5,000	Washington University, Saint Louis, MO
3,220	St. Louis University, Saint Louis, MO
1,750	Junior Achievement Mississippi Valley, Saint Louis, MO
1,570	St. Louis University, Saint Louis, MO
1,560	St. Louis University, Saint Louis, MO
1,550	St. Louis University, Saint Louis, MO
1,200	Good Shepherd School for Children, Saint Louis, MO
1,000	American Apparel Education Foundation, Arlington, VA
1,000	Maryville University, Saint Louis, MO
600	Vanderschmidt School, Saint Louis, MO
500	Metropolitan School
300	Logos School

Health

2,000	American Red Cross, Saint Louis, MO
1,000	Delta Gamma Center for Children with Visual Impairments, Saint Louis, MO
781	AMC Cancer Research Center, Aurora, CO
500	Ronald McDonald House, Saint Louis, MO
481	Leukemia Society of America, Saint Louis, MO

Social Services

6,000	Boys Hope, Girls Hope, Bridgeton, MO
4,000	Boy Scouts of America, Saint Louis, MO
3,000	Central Institute for the Deaf, Saint Louis, MO
2,000	West County YMCA
1,000	Girl Scouts of America, Saint Louis, MO
1,000	Girl Scouts of America, Saint Louis, MO
1,000	Girl Scouts of America, Saint Louis, MO
1,000	Girl Scouts of America, Saint Louis, MO
750	Partnership for a Drug-Free America, Saint Louis, MO
700	Operation Food Search, Saint Louis, MO
600	YWCA, Saint Louis, MO
500	St. Louis Area Food Bank, Saint Louis, MO
400	Children's Foundation of Mid-America, Saint Louis, MO
400	ECHO Emergency Children's Home
400	Edgewood Children's Center, Saint Louis, MO
400	Epworth Children's Home, Webster Groves, MO
350	St. Louis Association for Retarded Citizens, Saint Louis, MO
350	St. Louis Society for Children and Adults with Physical Disabilities Awareness Program, Saint Louis, MO
300	Hosea House, Saint Louis, MO
300	Paraquad, Saint Louis, MO
300	Support Dogs, Saint Louis, MO

Kelly Services

Company Contact

Troy, MI

Company Description

Revenue: US$4,029,300,000
Employees: 61,000
Fortune Rank: 374, per FORTUNE Magazine's list of 500 Largest U.S. Corporations (1999).
FF 374
SIC(s): 7363 Help Supply Services.

Nonmonetary Support

Type: Donated Equipment; Donated Products; In-kind Services

Corporate Sponsorship

Value: $59,288 (1998)

Kelly Services Foundation

Giving Contact

Lori Beirne-Kennedy, Foundation Administrator
999 W. Big Beaver
Troy, MI 48084
Phone: (248)813-3945

Description

Founded: 1994
EIN: 383207679
Organization Type: Corporate Foundation
Giving Locations: MI
Grant Types: General Support, Multiyear/Continuing Support, Operating Expenses.

Financial Summary

Total Giving: $251,048 (1998); $396,156 (1996); $234,850 (1995)
Giving Analysis: Giving for 1998 includes: foundation ($229,548); foundation grants to United Way ($21,500)

Assets: $322,604 (1998); $364,466 (1996); $772,867 (1995)
Gifts Received: $250,050 (1998); $1,000,000 (1994). Note: In 1998, contributions were received from Kelly Services Inc. ($250,000) and miscellaneous sources ($50).

Typical Recipients

Arts & Humanities: Arts Festivals, Arts Institutes, Arts & Humanities-General, Museums/Galleries, Music, Opera
Civic & Public Affairs: Employment/Job Training, Parades/Festivals, Public Policy, Urban & Community Affairs, Women's Affairs, Zoos/Aquariums
Education: Business Education, Colleges & Universities, Community & Junior Colleges, Education Funds, Education-General, Literacy, Minority Education
Health: Alzheimers Disease, Cancer, Children's Health/Hospitals, Clinics/Medical Centers, Eyes/ Blindness, Health-General, Heart, Home-Care Services, Hospitals, Long-Term Care
Social Services: Child Welfare, Community Centers, Community Service Organizations, People with Disabilities, Scouts, Senior Services, Social Services-General, United Funds/United Ways, YMCA/YWCA/ YMHA/YWHA, Youth Organizations

Contributions Analysis

Giving Priorities: Primary support for hospitals, social services, and civic concerns.
Arts & Humanities: 4%. Funds festivals, performing arts, and cultural centers.
Civic & Public Affairs: 20%. Funds foundations, professional associations, and a zoological institute.
Education: 9%. Supports schools, academies, and the United Negro College Fund.
Health: 43%. Supports hospitals and single-disease associations.
Religion: 1%. Funds religious social services and a congregation.
Social Services: 23%. Supports child abuse prevention, Boys & Girls Clubs, Ronald McDonald House, Make-A-Wish Foundation, and various other organizations.
Note: Total contributions made in 1998.

Application Procedures

Initial Contact: Send a brief letter of inquiry.
Application Requirements: Send a description of organization, amount requested, purpose of funds sought, and proof of section 501(c)(3) status.
Deadlines: None.

Restrictions

Does not support individuals, religious organizations for sectarian purposes, or political or lobbying groups. Limited to organizations in the continental U.S.

Additional Information

In February 1993, the University of Michigan announced the establishment of the William Russell Kelly Professorship in Business Administration. The professorship was established as a result of a $1.2 million gift from Kelly Services, including William Russell Kelly, its founder and chairman.
In 1998, most grants above $250 were given as sponsorship gifts. The more common gifts $250 were for operational support.

Corporate Officials

Terence E. Adderley: chairman, president, chief executive officer, director B Detroit, MI 1933. ED University of Michigan BBA (1951); University of Michigan BMA (1956). PRIM CORP EMPL chairman, president, chief executive officer, director: Kelly Services. CORP AFFIL director: NBD Bank NA; director: Detroit Edison Co.; director: NBD Bancorp Inc. NONPR AFFIL director: Auburn-Cord-Duesenberg Museum.
William Gerber: executive vice president finance, chief financial officer PRIM CORP EMPL executive vice president finance, chief financial officer: Kelly Services.

Foundation Officials

Mary E. Adderley: vice president, director
Terence E. Adderley: president, director (see above)
Carl T. Camden: director
Tommi A. White: director

Grants Analysis

Disclosure Period: calendar year ending 1998
Total Grants: $229,548*
Number of Grants: 254
Average Grant: $614*
Highest Grant: $50,000
Typical Range: $250 to $1,000
***Note:** Giving excludes United Way. Average grant figure excludes two highest grants, to the American Red Cross ($50,000) and the Detroit Renaissance Foundation ($24,900).

Recent Grants

Note: Grants derived from 1996 Form 990.

Arts & Humanities

10,000	Detroit Symphony Orchestra Hall, Detroit, MI -- operating support
7,300	Detroit Institute of Arts Founders Society, Detroit, MI -- operating support
4,000	Michigan Opera Theater, Detroit, MI -- operating support
3,000	Detroit Festival of the Arts, Detroit, MI -- sponsor event

Civic & Public Affairs

41,000	Detroit Renaissance Foundation, Detroit, MI -- operating support
5,000	Detroit Zoological Society, Detroit, MI -- operating support
5,000	Financial Accounting Foundation, Norwalk, CT -- operating support
3,000	First Night Birmingham, Bingham Farms, MI -- sponsor event

Education

5,000	Consortium for Graduate Study in Management, Saint Louis, MO -- operating support
5,000	Michigan Colleges Foundation, Southfield, MI -- operating support
5,000	Walsh College, Troy, MI -- operating support
3,000	United Negro College Fund, Detroit, MI -- sponsor event

Health

100,000	Detroit Medical Center, Detroit, MI -- operating support
50,000	American Red Cross, Detroit, MI -- operating support
10,000	American Red Cross, Detroit, MI -- sponsor event
5,000	Arthritis Foundation Michigan Chapter, Southfield, MI -- operating support

Social Services

16,750	United Way Community Services, Detroit, MI -- operating support
10,350	Operation ABLE of Michigan, Southfield, MI -- operating support
4,000	Genesis Foundation, Detroit, MI -- operating support
3,000	Boys and Girls Club, Troy, MI -- sponsor event

Kemper National Insurance Companies

Company Contact

Long Grove, IL
Web: http://www.kemperinsurance.com

Company Description

Former Name: Kemper Corp.
Revenue: US$6,893,100,000
Employees: 9,000
SIC(s): 6331 Fire, Marine & Casualty Insurance.

Nonmonetary Support

Value: $50,000 (1991)
Type: In-kind Services
Note: Company contributes printing and creative support in the way of writing and design.

James S. Kemper Foundation

Giving Contact

James R. Connor, Executive Director
James S. Kemper Foundation
One Kemper Drive
Long Grove, IL 60049-0001
Phone: (847)320-2847
Fax: (847)320-7996

Alternate Contact

Charles W. Meinhardt, Corp. Contributions Coordinator
Note: Contact for direct giving program only.

Description

EIN: 366007812
Organization Type: Corporate Foundation
Giving Locations: IL: Chicago including metropolitan area nationally.
Grant Types: Award, Conference/Seminar, Fellowship, Multiyear/Continuing Support, Project, Scholarship.

Giving Philosophy

'In 1942, James Scott Kemper, founder of the Lumbermens Mutual Casualty Company and the related Kemper companies, established an independent private foundation chartered for general philanthropic purposes. The foundation has subsequently been supported by the Kemper companies, which have made substantial contributions to assets.'
'Within its broad mandate, the foundation has concentrated its resources on higher education. The initial activity of the foundation was to support the education of college students through a program combining summer experience in business with undergraduate financial aid. Over time, the foundation has expanded its activities to include other educational grants and grants for the educational programs of major cultural institutions. Additionally, the foundation makes grants for special purposes from time to time. It does not make grants for capital purposes.'
'Almost since its inception, the Kemper Foundation has interested itself in business education. For over 40 years, we have identified, through the Kemper Scholars grant program, unusually promising young people and helped them to prepare for careers in business. More recently, we have expanded our program to support undergraduate and graduate business schools for projects ranging from faculty research and curriculum development to business ethics.'
'The Kemper Scholars grant program is our largest and one of our most challenging activities. These grants provide summer work experience within the Kemper organization, and substantial scholarship support based on need. Although many aspects of the Scholars program are valuable, none is more central to the program's purpose than well-considered summer experiences in business. We continue to work with the various Kemper departments to maintain the quality and number of summer work experiences available to the program.'

'A further way in which we support the development of business people is by grants to the institutions that educate them. We have concentrated our funds upon support of undergraduate and graduate business programs, especially for projects, which strengthen the quality of the faculty and the curriculum. We will expand these activities as our resources permit.'
'Finally, we wish to retain the capacity to respond to specific and important projects in higher education, and to continue our support on a selective basis of the educational programs of major cultural institutions. Even though our resources for these areas are limited, our list of grants demonstrates our active interest.' *1995-96 Annual Report*

Financial Summary

Total Giving: $1,750,000 (fiscal year ending July 31, 1999 approx); $1,655,504 (fiscal 1998); $2,119,000 (fiscal 1997 approx). Note: Contributes through corporate direct giving program and foundation.
Giving Analysis: Giving for fiscal 1998 includes: foundation ($1,191,253); foundation scholarships ($439,255); foundation fellowships ($24,996)
Assets: $45,781,174 (fiscal 1998); $33,000,000 (fiscal 1997 approx); $30,000,000 (fiscal 1996)
Gifts Received: $6,256,515 (fiscal 1998); $7,705 (fiscal 1995). Note: Contributions are received from James S. Kemper, Jr.

Typical Recipients

Arts & Humanities: Arts Festivals, Arts Outreach, Libraries, Museums/Galleries, Music, Opera, Public Broadcasting, Theater
Civic & Public Affairs: Business/Free Enterprise, Public Policy
Education: Arts/Humanities Education, Business Education, Colleges & Universities, Community & Junior Colleges, Economic Education, Engineering/Technological Education, Faculty Development, Education-General, International Studies, Legal Education, Medical Education, Minority Education, Science/Mathematics Education, Student Aid
Health: Emergency/Ambulance Services, Hospitals, Medical Rehabilitation, Medical Research, Single-Disease Health Associations
Science: Science Museums
Social Services: People with Disabilities, Substance Abuse, Youth Organizations

Contributions Analysis

Giving Priorities: Nearly all to colleges and universities; also arts organizations.
Arts & Humanities: 2%. Arts institutes, museums, and opera.
Education: 91%. Grants are made to colleges and universities primarily for projects dealing with undergraduate or graduate business education. The Kemper Scholars grant program is offered in partnership with specific colleges and universities. The Foundation's Nursing Student grants are presently administered at Baylor University, Crouse-Irving Memorial Hospital School of Nursing, Massachusetts General Hospital Institute of Health Professions, and the University of Texas Austin. Fellowships are also supported at certain universities.
Note: Priorities reflect foundation giving in fiscal 1998. Direct giving supports youth, health and cultural activities.

Application Procedures

Initial Contact: Send a brief letter.
Application Requirements: Include a concise description of project, realistic time-frame, mission statement, detailed project budget, statement of how future funding needs will be met, amount needed to complete project, amount requested, information about personnel involved, and method of evaluation.
Deadlines: Applications must be received by November 1.
Decision Notification: Decisions are made annually, in late February or early March.
Notes: The foundation identifies colleges and universities and invites them to participate in the Kemper Scholars program. If they choose to do so, the institution conducts a selection process which leads to the identification of individuals from the freshman class who are the institutional nominees for the program. The foundation then selects one of the nominees as a Kemper Scholar.

Restrictions

Does not support dinners or special events, fraternal organizations, good-will advertising, member agencies of united funds, political or lobbying groups, or religious organizations for sectarian purposes.
The foundation rarely supports multi-year grants.

Additional Information

Publications: Foundation Annual Report

Corporate Officials

General John T. Chain, Junior: president PRIM CORP EMPL president: Quarterdeck Equity Partners Inc. CORP AFFIL director: RJR Nabisco Inc.; director: Thomas Group Inc.; director: RJR Nabisco Holdings Inc.; director: Nabisco Inc.; director: Northrop Grumman Corp.; director: American Motorists Insurance Co.
Roberta S. Karmel: partner B Chicago, IL 1937. ED Radcliffe College BA; New York University LLB (1962). PRIM CORP EMPL partner: Kelley, Drye & Warren. CORP AFFIL director: Kemper Insurance Companies; director: Mallinckrodt Inc. NONPR AFFIL member: Financial Womens Association; trustee: Practicing Law Institute; co-director: Center Study International Business Law; member: Association Bar New York City; professor: Brooklyn Law School; fellow: American Bar Foundation; member: American Law Institute; member: American Bar Association.
Gerald Leonard Maatman: director B Chicago, IL 1930. ED Illinois Institute of Technology BS (1951). CORP AFFIL chairman board trustees: Underwriters Laboratories; director: America Motorists Insurance Co. NONPR AFFIL director: National Down Syndrome Society; member: Tau Beta Pi; director: Advocates Highway & Auto Safety. CLUB AFFIL member: Springs Club; member: Knollwood Golf Club.
Kenneth A. Randall: CORP AFFIL director: Fidelity Life Association; director: Kemper Corp.

Foundation Officials

General John T. Chain, Junior: trustee (see above)
J. Reed Coleman: trustee CORP AFFIL director: Regal-Beloit Corp.
James Richard Connor: executive director B Indianapolis, IN 1928. ED University of Iowa BA (1951); University of Wisconsin MS (1954); University of Wisconsin PhD (1961). NONPR AFFIL member: Phi Kappa Phi; trustee: Woodrow Wilson National Fellowship Foundation; member: Phi Delta Kappa; member: Phi Eta Sigma; member: Phi Alpha Theta; member: Phi Beta Kappa; member: Organization American Historians; member: Golden Key; member: Order Omega; member: Delta Sigma Pi; director: Fairhaven Retirement Corp.; member: American Association University Professors; member: Beta Gamma Sigma. CLUB AFFIL member: Blue Key Club.
Peter Bannerman Hamilton: trustee B Philadelphia, PA 1946. ED Princeton University AB (1968); Yale University JD (1971). PRIM CORP EMPL senior vice president, chief financial officer: Brunswick Corp. CORP AFFIL director: Fidelity Life Association; director: Kemper National Insurance Co.; director: American Motorists Insurance Co.
Roberta S. Karmel: trustee (see above)
James Scott Kemper, Jr.: honorary chairman B Chicago, IL 1914. ED Harvard University LLB (1938); Yale University AB (1955). PRIM CORP EMPL chairman: Kemper Sports Management Inc. CORP AFFIL chairman: Kemper Sports Inc.
George Danner Kennedy: trustee B Pittsburgh, PA 1926. ED Williams College BA (1948). CORP AFFIL director: Scotsman Industries Inc.; director: Stone Container Corp.; director, chairman executive committee: IMCERA; director: Kemper National Insurance Companies; director: Brunswick Corp.; director: Illinois Tool Works Inc.; director: America National Canada Co. NONPR AFFIL director: Lyric Opera Chicago; trustee: National Commission Against Drunk Driving; director: Childrens Memorial Hospital & Medical Center; government member: Chicago Orchestral Association; trustee: Chicago Symphony Orchestra; regional trustee: Boys & Girls Clubs America; trustee: Center Workforce Preparation & Quality Education. CLUB AFFIL mem: Sleepy Hollow Country Club; Chicago Club; Indian Hill Club.
Dalton L. Knauss: trustee B Imboden, AK 1928. ED Illinois Institute of Technology; DeVry Institute of Technology (1951). CORP AFFIL director: American Motorists Insurance Co.; chairman, president, chief executive officer, director: Square D Co.
George Ralph Lewis: trustee B Burgess, VA 1941. ED Hampton University BS (1963); Iona College MBA (1966). PRIM CORP EMPL president, chief executive officer: Philip Morris Capital Corp. CORP AFFIL director: Ceridian Corp.
Katharine Culbert Lyall: trustee B Lancaster, PA 1941. ED Cornell University BA (1963); New York University MBA (1965); Cornell University PhD (1969). PRIM NONPR EMPL president: University of Wisconsin System. CORP AFFIL director: Marshall & Ilsley Corp.; director: Interstate Energy Corp.; director: Kemper Insurance Co.; member board: Carnegie Foundation Advancement Teaching; director: Heartland Development Corp. NONPR AFFIL member: Phi Beta Kappa; professor: University Wisconsin Madison; member: Association American Universities; member: American Economic Association.
Gerald Leonard Maatman: chairman, president, trustee (see above)
David B. Mathis: chairman B Atlanta, GA 1938. ED Lake Forest College BA (1960). PRIM CORP EMPL chairman, chief executive officer: Kemper Insurance Companies. CORP AFFIL director: TMC Global Inc.; chairman: Lumbermens Mutual Casualty Co.; chairman, chief executive officer: Kemper Corp.; director: Kemper Income Capital Prese; director: Fidelity Life Association; director: IMC Global Inc.; chief executive officer: American Manufacturer Mutual Insurance Co.; chairman: American Motorists Insurance Co. NONPR AFFIL director: Evanston Hospital Corp.
Kenneth A. Randall: trustee (see above)
Richard Nathaniel Rosett: trustee B Baltimore, MD 1928. ED Columbia University BA (1953); Yale University MA (1954); Yale University PhD (1957). PRIM CORP EMPL director quality cup programs: Rochester Institute of Technology. CORP AFFIL officer: ORMEC; director: Smith Corona Corp.; director: Lumbermens Mutual Insurance Co.; officer: American Motorists Insurance Co.; director: Hutchinson Techs Inc. NONPR AFFIL member: Phi Beta Kappa; president: United States Business School Prague; member: Mont Pelerin Society; member: Beta Gamma Sigma; trustee: Keuka College; member: American Economic Association. CLUB AFFIL Chicago Club.
William D. Smith: trustee
Daniel Roger Toll: trustee B Denver, CO 1927. ED Princeton University AB (1949); Harvard University MBA (1955). PRIM CORP EMPL chairman: Corona Corp. CORP AFFIL officer: Northern Illinois Gas Co.; director: Mallinckrodt Group Inc.; director: Nicor Inc.; director: Lincoln National Income Fund; director: Kemper National Insurance Companies; director: Lincoln National Convertible Securities Fund; director: AP Green Industries Inc.; director: Brown Group Inc.; director: American Motorists Insurance Co. NONPR AFFIL director: Northwestern Healthcare Network, Inc.; member: Phi Beta Kappa; director, executive committee, chairman finance committee & hospital ****vanston Hospital; president: Chicago Metropolitan Planning Commission. CLUB AFFIL Indian Hill Club; Union League Club; Economic Club; Harvard Business School Club; Chicago Club; Commercial Club.

Walter Lucas White: secretary, treasurer, trustee B Des Moines, IA 1940. ED Coe College (1962); Indiana University MBA (1964). PRIM CORP EMPL chief financial officer: Lumbermens Mutual Casualty Co. CORP AFFIL executive vice president: America Manufacturings Mutual Insurance Co.; senior vice president: America Motorists Insurance Co.

Grants Analysis

Disclosure Period: fiscal year ending July 31, 1998
Total Grants: $1,191,253*
Number of Grants: 51
Average Grant: $23,358
Highest Grant: $75,000
Typical Range: $10,000 to $25,000
*Note: Giving excludes fellowships and scholarships.

Recent Grants

Note: Grants derived from 1997 Form 990.

Arts & Humanities

15,000 Chicago Symphony Orchestra, Chicago, IL -- support outreach program for public and suburban schools
15,000 Lyric Opera, Chicago, IL -- support of the Young Singers Program
10,000 Goodman Theater, Chicago, IL -- support of matinee program for public schools

Civic & Public Affairs

25,000 American Risk and Insurance Association, Mount Vernon, VA -- support initiative of new journal
10,000 Griffith Foundation, Columbus, OH -- educational seminar for legislative chairs of insurance committees

Education

43,621 Brigham Young University, Provo, UT -- Kemper Scholar Grant
37,040 Northern Illinois University, DeKalb, IL -- Kemper Scholar Grant
35,845 University of the Pacific, Stockton, CA -- Kemper Scholar Grant
33,000 Howard University, Washington, DC -- Kemper Scholar Grant
29,925 Valparaiso University College of Business Administration, Valparaiso, IN -- Kemper Scholars National Conference
27,450 Beloit College, Beloit, WI -- Kemper Scholar Grant
26,100 Ripon College, Ripon, WI -- to improve software and hardware in the Kemper computer Laboratory for Business and Economics
25,700 Washington University, Saint Louis, MO -- Kemper Scholar Grant
25,000 Beloit College Department of Economics and Management, Beloit, WI -- support of Kemper Computer Center for Economics and Management
25,000 Carroll College Department of Business and Accounting, Waukesha, WI -- support for computer and video classroom
25,000 College of Insurance, New York, NY -- faculty development
25,000 College of St. Mary, Omaha, NE -- support of the Financial Management Program
25,000 Illinois State University, Normal, IL -- support undergraduate insurance program and insurance and Financial Services Endowed Professorship
25,000 Institute of International Education, Chicago, IL -- support for college business students at the Midwest conference of Fulbright Students
25,000 Insurance Education Foundation, Indianapolis, IN -- support educational workshops for high school teachers
25,000 Lake Forest College, Lake Forest, IL -- support of Chicago outreach program
25,000 Lycoming College Institute for Management Studies, Williamsport, PA -- endowment for Executive Seminary Series
25,000 Nebraska Wesleyan University Department of Business Administration, Lincoln, NE -- support for faculty development and upgrading microcomputers
25,000 Northern Illinois University College of Business, DeKalb, IL -- support of summer faculty development program
25,000 St. Augustine College, Chicago, IL -- support enhancement of computer technology for minority business students
25,000 University of Maryland College Park, College Park, MD -- support the Kemper Insurance Companies Endowed Undergraduate Grant in Fire Protection Engineering
25,000 University of Northern Iowa Department of Finance, Cedar Falls, IA -- funding to strengthen the Financial Services Program
25,000 University of the Pacific Eberhardt School of Business and Public Administration, Stockton, CA -- support upgrade and enhancement of computer resources
25,000 University of Wisconsin Whitewater College of Business and Economics, Whitewater, WI -- support endowed chair in marketing
25,000 Washington University John M. Olin School of Business, Saint Louis, MO -- support the Total Quality Schools Program
24,000 California State University Sacramento, Sacramento, CA -- support research in management and insurance programs
24,000 La Salle University, Philadelphia, PA -- Kemper Scholar Grant
24,000 Wake Forest University, Winston-Salem, NC -- Kemper Scholar Grant
23,500 Brigham Young University Marriott School of Management, Provo, UT -- support development of an Insurance Risk Management and Financial Services Program
23,200 University of Wisconsin Whitewater, Whitewater, WI -- Kemper Scholar Grant
22,484 Loyola University Chicago, Chicago, IL -- Kemper Scholar Grant
22,200 Lake Forest College, Lake Forest, IL -- Kemper Scholar Grant
21,000 Bradley University, Peoria, IL -- support development of business curriculum
20,000 North Central College, Naperville, IL -- support of internship component of the International Business Major
19,000 Wittenberg University Wittenberg Center for Applied Management, Springfield, OH -- support the WittCAM Program
18,906 Drake University, Des Moines, IA -- Kemper Scholar Grant
17,950 Washington and Lee University, Lexington, VA -- Kemper Scholar Grant
17,690 Valparaiso University, Valparaiso, IN -- Kemper Scholar Grant
14,700 Millikin University, Decatur, IL -- Kemper Scholar Grant
11,000 Greenville College, Greenville, IL -- support creation of a smart classroom for business students
10,000 College of St. Francis, Joliet, IL -- support of the Kemper Business Learning Program
10,000 United Negro College Fund, Fairfax, VA -- support Campaign 2000
10,000 United Negro College Fund, Fairfax, VA -- support Campaign 2000

Health

20,000 Cook County-Rush Health Center, Chicago, IL -- research on communicable diseases
20,000 Northwestern Memorial Hospital Foundation, Chicago, IL -- support of Kemper Emergency Laboratory

KENDALL INTERNATIONAL, INC.

Company Contact

Mansfield, MA
Web: http://www.kendallhq.com

Company Description

Former Name: Kendall Healthcare Products Co.
Employees: 8,800
SIC(s): 2891 Adhesives & Sealants, 3841 Surgical & Medical Instruments, 3842 Surgical Appliances & Supplies.
Parent Company: Tyco International Ltd.

Nonmonetary Support

Type: Donated Products

Giving Contact

Shay Studley-Toland, Interim Contributions Manager
Kendall International, Inc.
15 Hampshire Street
Mansfield, MA 02048
Phone: (508)261-8000
Fax: (508)261-8105

Description

Organization Type: Corporate Giving Program
Giving Locations: headquarters area only.
Grant Types: General Support.

Financial Summary

Total Giving: Contributes through corporate direct giving program only.

Typical Recipients

Arts & Humanities: Arts & Humanities-General
Civic & Public Affairs: Civic & Public Affairs-General
Education: Education-General
Health: Health-General
Social Services: Social Services-General

Application Procedures

Initial Contact: a brief letter of inquiry
Application Requirements: a description of organization, amount requested, purpose of funds sought, recently audited financial statement, and proof of tax-exempt status
Deadlines: None.

Restrictions

The company requests written correspondence. Phone calls are not accepted.

Additional Information

The company was formerly known as Kendall Healthcare Products.

Corporate Officials

Richard J. Meelia: president, chief executive officer B 1949. PRIM CORP EMPL president, chief executive officer: Kendall, Sherwood, Davis & Geck ADD CORP EMPL president, chief executive officer: Kendall International, INC; vice president: Tyco International Inc.

Giving Program Officials

Gina Spencer: PRIM CORP EMPL contributions manager: Kendall International, Inc.

Kennametal, Inc.

Company Contact

Latrobe, PA
Web: http://www.kennametal.com

Company Description

Employees: 7,500
SIC(s): 3313 Electrometallurgical Products, 3339 Primary Nonferrous Metals Nec, 3399 Primary Metal Products Nec, 3545 Machine Tool Accessories.

Operating Locations

Includes plant locations.

Kennametal Foundation

Giving Contact

Richard P. Gibson, Secretary & Treasurer
Kennametal Foundation
PO Box 231
Route 981 South
Latrobe, PA 15650
Phone: (724)539-5203
Fax: (724)539-5024

Description

EIN: 256036009
Organization Type: Corporate Foundation. Supports preselected organizations only.
Giving Locations: East coast.
Grant Types: Employee Matching Gifts, General Support.

Financial Summary

Total Giving: $600,000 (fiscal year ending June 30, 1999 approx); $600,000 (fiscal 1998 approx); $600,000 (fiscal 1997 approx). Note: Contributes through foundation only.
Assets: $1,548,022 (fiscal 1996); $1,459,273 (fiscal 1995); $1,190,382 (fiscal 1994)
Gifts Received: $600,000 (fiscal 1996); $600,000 (fiscal 1995); $400,000 (fiscal 1994)

Typical Recipients

Arts & Humanities: Arts Centers, Community Arts, Historic Preservation, History & Archaeology, Libraries, Museums/Galleries, Music, Public Broadcasting, Theater
Civic & Public Affairs: Business/Free Enterprise, Chambers of Commerce, Community Foundations, Economic Development, Economic Policy, Civic & Public Affairs-General, Philanthropic Organizations, Public Policy, Urban & Community Affairs, Women's Affairs
Education: Colleges & Universities, Community & Junior Colleges, Economic Education, Education Associations, Education Funds, Engineering/Technological Education, Education-General, Public Education (Precollege), Religious Education, Student Aid
Environment: Environment-General, Resource Conservation
Health: Cancer, Diabetes, Health Organizations, Heart, Hospitals, Medical Research, Mental Health, Single-Disease Health Associations
International: International Affairs, International Relations
Religion: Seminaries
Science: Scientific Centers & Institutes
Social Services: At-Risk Youth, Camps, Community Service Organizations, People with Disabilities, Recreation & Athletics, Scouts, United Funds/United Ways, YMCA/YWCA/YMHA/YWHA, Youth Organizations

Contributions Analysis

Arts & Humanities: 15% to 20%. Supports libraries, music, public broadcasting, and historic preservation.
Civic & Public Affairs: Less than 5%. Primarily supports community foundations and organizations for economic development. Other interests include free enterprise, minority affairs, taxation, and environmental affairs.
Education: 50% to 55%. Majority of funding supports the National Merit Scholarship Corporation and the Foundation of Independent Colleges of Pennsylvania. The remainder supports Eastern colleges and universities.
Health: Less than 5%.Major support to emergency services, hospitals, and single disease health organizations.
Social Services: 25%. Primarily supports the United Way. Family services, youth organizations, and people with disabilities also receive support.

Corporate Officials

James R. Breisinger: vice president, controller, chief financial officer B Pittsburgh, PA 1950. ED Duquesne University BA (1972). PRIM CORP EMPL vice president, controller, chief financial officer: Kennametal, Inc. ADD CORP EMPL chief operating officer: Greenfield Indiana Inc. NONPR AFFIL member: American Institute CPAs.
Timothy D. Hudson: vice president, director human resources B Altoona, PA 1946. PRIM CORP EMPL vice president, director human resources: Kennametal, Inc.

Foundation Officials

James R. Breisinger: vice president, controller (see above)
Richard P. Gibson: secretary, treasurer B 1935. PRIM CORP EMPL assistant treasurer, director: Kennametal, Inc.
Timothy D. Hudson: trustee (see above)
William Rankin Newlin: trustee B Pittsburgh, PA 1940. ED Princeton University AB (1962); University of Pittsburgh JD (1965). PRIM CORP EMPL partner, managing director, chief executive officer: Buchanan Ingersoll Professional Corp. CORP AFFIL director: Parker/Hunter; chairman: National City Bank Pennsylvania; chairman: JLK Direct Distribution; director, chairman: Kennametal Inc.; director: Integra National Bank; partner: Colker and Newlin Management Association; director: Greenfield Industries Inc.; managing partner: CEO Venture Fund; director: Black Box Corp.; director: Black Box Corp. of Pennsylvania. NONPR AFFIL secretary, director: Pittsburgh High Technology Council; director: Pittsburgh Regional Alliance; trustee: Pennsylvania Southwest Association; director: Pennsylvania Technology Council; director: Greater Pittsburgh Chamber of Commerce; member: Pennsylvania Bar Association; member: Association Bar New York City; fellow: American Bar Foundation; member: American Law Institute; member: American Bar Association; member: Allegheny County Bar Association. CLUB AFFIL director: Rivers Club; Duquesne Club; Laurel Valley Golf Club; director: Allegheny Country Club.

Grants Analysis

Disclosure Period: fiscal year ending June 30, 1996
Total Grants: $554,118
Number of Grants: 118
Average Grant: $3,685*
Highest Grant: $122,970
Typical Range: $100 to $5,000
***Note:** Average grant figure excludes highest grant.

Recent Grants

Note: Grants derived from fiscal 1997 Form 990.

Arts & Humanities

33,000 Palace Theater, Greensburg, PA
25,000 Greensburg Hempfield Area Library, Greensburg, PA
15,000 Adams Memorial Library, Latrobe, PA
5,000 Art Conservation Trust, Latrobe, PA
5,000 River City Brass Band, Pittsburgh, PA
2,447 Metropolitan Pittsburgh Public Broadcasting, Pittsburgh, PA
1,000 Old Brick Historical Society, Orwell, OH
715 Westmoreland County Museum of Art, Greensburg, PA

Civic & Public Affairs

50,000 Eastern Westmoreland Development Corp, Latrobe, PA
25,000 Community Foundation, Greensburg, PA
9,500 Pennsylvania Free Enterprise Week, Erie, PA
3,500 Latrobe Area Chamber of Commerce, Latrobe, PA
1,000 Q-Net, Pittsburgh, PA

Education

50,000 Westmoreland County Community College, Youngwood, PA
35,835 Seton Hill College, Greensburg, PA
29,741 St. Vincent College, Latrobe, PA
25,800 National Merit Scholarship Corporation, Evanston, IL
25,000 Foundation for Independent Colleges of Pennsylvania, Harrisburg, PA
17,940 University of Pittsburgh, Greensburg, PA
17,000 University of Pittsburgh, Pittsburgh, PA
9,000 Ohio Foundation of Independent Colleges, Columbus, OH
5,000 Tennessee Independent College Fund, Nashville, TN
5,000 Virginia Foundation for Independent Colleges, Richmond, VA
4,355 North Carolina State University Alumni Association, Raleigh, NC
3,375 Michigan State University, East Lansing, MI
2,500 Amherst College, Amherst, MA
2,500 Bedford County Regional Campus Everett, Everett, PA
2,500 SME Manufacturing Engineering Education Foundation, Dearborn, MI
2,275 Pennsylvania State University, University Park, PA
2,075 Duquesne University, Pittsburgh, PA
1,100 Virginia Tech Foundation, Blacksburg, VA
1,000 Milwaukee School of Engineering, Milwaukee, WI
800 University of North Carolina Chapel Hill, Chapel Hill, NC
500 Duke University, Durham, NC
500 University of Michigan, Ann Arbor, MI
500 Wayne State University, Detroit, MI

Environment

1,000 Western Pennsylvania Conservancy, Pittsburgh, PA

Health

5,000 American Heart Association Westmoreland County, Greensburg, PA
5,000 Latrobe Area Hospital, Latrobe, PA
1,200 American Diabetes Association, Greensburg, PA

International

2,200 World Affairs Council, Pittsburgh, PA
2,200 World Affairs Council, Pittsburgh, PA

Religion

3,600 Michigan Theological Seminary, Plymouth, MI

Science

27,845 Carnegie Institute, Pittsburgh, PA

Social Services

40,000 United Way Westmoreland County, Greensburg, PA

25,000	Adelphoi, Latrobe, PA
25,000	Westmoreland County Blind Association, Greensburg, PA
3,500	United Community Services, Ashtabula, OH
3,000	United Way, Roanoke Rapids, NC
1,500	Boy Scouts of America Westmoreland Fayette Council, Greensburg, PA

Kerr-mcgee Corp.

Company Contact

Oklahoma City, OK
Web: http://www.kerr-mcgee.com

Company Description

Employees: 3,367 (1999)
SIC(s): 1221 Bituminous Coal & Lignite--Surface, 1222 Bituminous Coal--Underground, 1311 Crude Petroleum & Natural Gas, 1321 Natural Gas Liquids.

Nonmonetary Support

Value: $80,000 (1995); $58,000 (1993); $113,000 (1989)
Type: Donated Equipment; In-kind Services

Corporate Sponsorship

Type: Arts & cultural events; Music & entertainment events; Festivals/fairs

Kerr-McGee Foundation

Giving Contact

Martha Brady, Administrator, Contributions
Kerr-McGee Corp.
PO Box 25861
Kerr McGee Center
Oklahoma City, OK 73125
Phone: (405)270-1313 ext 3924
Fax: (405)270-3940

Description

Organization Type: Corporate Foundation
Former Name: Kerr-McGee Foundation Corp.
Giving Locations: OK: Oklahoma City operating locations.
Grant Types: Employee Matching Gifts, General Support, Project, Scholarship.

Financial Summary

Total Giving: $1,200,000 (2000 approx); $1,200,000 (1999 approx); $1,200,000 (1998). Note: Contributes through corporate direct giving program and foundation. 1998 Giving includes corporate direct giving ($240,000); foundation ($960,000).

Typical Recipients

Arts & Humanities: Arts Associations & Councils, Arts Funds, Historic Preservation, Museums/Galleries, Music, Performing Arts, Theater
Civic & Public Affairs: Economic Development, Economic Policy, Law & Justice, Legal Aid, Professional & Trade Associations, Public Policy, Safety, Urban & Community Affairs, Zoos/Aquariums
Education: Colleges & Universities, Economic Education, Education Associations, Engineering/Technological Education, International Studies, Legal Education, Minority Education, Science/Mathematics Education, Student Aid
Health: Health Funds, Health Organizations, Hospices, Hospitals, Medical Research, Medical Training, Single-Disease Health Associations
International: International Relations
Religion: Religious Organizations, Religious Welfare
Social Services: Community Centers, Community Service Organizations, Emergency Relief, People with Disabilities, Recreation & Athletics, United Funds/United Ways, Youth Organizations

Contributions Analysis

Giving Priorities: Oklahoma state universtities and technical, mining, and engineering education; civic organizations; and arts organizations.
Arts & Humanities: 13%. Supports arts funds, museums, and performing artsorganizations. Major grants are awarded in Oklahoma City.
Civic & Public Affairs: 38%. Principal concerns include safety, economics, and professional organizations, as well as groups concerned with legal and public policy issues.
Education: 31%. Interests include state universities in Oklahoma; technical, mining, and engineering education; independent and minority college funds; and economic education associations.
Health: 18%. Interests include hospitals, health organizations, single-disease health associations, and health funds. Also supports united funds, legal aid organizations, youth agencies, and community services.

Application Procedures

Initial Contact: brief letter or proposal
Application Requirements: a description of organization, amount requested, purpose of funds sought, recently audited financial statement, proof of tax-exempt status
Deadlines: October.

Corporate Officials

Luke Corbitt: chairman, chief executive officer, director PRIM CORP EMPL chairman, chief executive officer, director: Kerr-McGee Corp.
Tom J. McDaniel: vice chairman, director B Muskogee, OK 1938. ED Oklahoma State University BA (1960); University of Oklahoma JD (1963). PRIM CORP EMPL vice chairman, director: Kerr-McGee Corp. CORP AFFIL director: UMB Bank; director: UMB Financial Services. NONPR AFFIL director: American Petroleum Institute; director: National Association Manufacturers; member: American Bar Association.

Giving Program Officials

Martha Brady: administrator public affairs (see above)
John Charles Linehan: (see above)
Tom J. McDaniel: vice chairman (see above)

Foundation Officials

Martha Brady: administrator public affairs (see above)

Grants Analysis

Disclosure Period: calendar year ending
Typical Range: $200 to $5,000

Key Bank Of Cleveland

 Number 50 of Top 100 Corporate Givers

Company Contact

Cleveland, OH

Company Description

Former Name: Society National Bank.
Employees: 26,963
SIC(s): 6021 National Commercial Banks.
Parent Company: KeyCorp

Nonmonetary Support

Type: In-kind Services
Volunteer Programs: Company employees volunteer at Neighbors Make The Difference Day, a program where key closes its office for one afternoon and send its employees to perform volunteer services.

Key Foundation

Giving Contact

Bruce H. Akers, Senior Vice President, Public Affairs
KeyBank of Cleveland
127 Public Square
Cleveland, OH 44114
Phone: (216)689-7598
Fax: (216)689-3865
Email: bruce_akers@keybank.com

Description

Organization Type: Corporate Foundation
Giving Locations: primarily service area.
Grant Types: Capital, Conference/Seminar, Employee Matching Gifts, General Support, Matching, Multiyear/Continuing Support, Operating Expenses.

Giving Philosophy

'As a corporate citizen that cares, KeyBank shares the hopes and dreams of the communities it serves, and joins in partnership with others trying to make those communities better places in which to live and work. KeyBank offers three basic contributions to this partnership. First, in our role as a bank, we strive to provide the financial services our customers need within the community. Second, in our role as an employer, we strive to encourage and assist our employees to volunteer their time and talents within their individual communities. Third, in our role as a corporate citizen, we provide charitable support to organizations who serve the public interest and address critical needs within the community. KeyBank firmly believes that by working together, we can improve the quality of life and create positive change.'
'In KeyBank's role as a corporate citizen, the primary mission of our charitable giving program is to support a wide range of organizations whose programs and activities give maximum benefit to KeyBank customers and employees in the communities we serve.' Guidelines for Giving.

Financial Summary

Total Giving: $19,500,000 (2000 approx); $19,500,000 (1999 approx); $16,724,000 (1998). Note: Contributes through corporate direct giving program and foundation.

Typical Recipients

Arts & Humanities: Performing Arts
Civic & Public Affairs: Business/Free Enterprise, Economic Development, Civic & Public Affairs-General, Urban & Community Affairs
Education: Business Education, Colleges & Universities
Health: Hospitals
Social Services: Community Centers, United Funds/United Ways

Contributions Analysis

Giving Priorities: Health and human services, education, arts and culture, and civic and community.

Application Procedures

Initial Contact: Submit a written proposal.
Application Requirements: Include history and purpose of the organization; amount requested and purpose of funds sought; budget information; list of officers, directors, or trustees; last annual financial statement; and proof of tax-exempt status.
Deadlines: None.
Review Process: Local contributions committees review requests throughout the year; annual budget is approved in December.
Evaluative Criteria: Programs and objectives must benefit communities served by the company. The organization should enhance the civic, cultural, or educational goals of the community, or provide for the health and welfare of its citizens. The organization

must demonstrate sound fiscal management, nonduplication of services, and evidence of broad community support.
Decision Notification: Decisions are made locally.
Notes: Requests should be directed to the nearest KeyBank office.

Restrictions

Company does not support United Way member agencies; individuals; private foundations, endowments, or athletic activities; requests which are political, sensitive, controversial, or harmful, or those which pose a potential conflict of interest; pre-college education; churches or religious programs; fraternal, social, labor, or veterans' groups; or national or international organizations.

Additional Information

In 1994, Society Corp. merged with KeyCorp and changed its name to Society National Bank
Society National Bank changed its name to Key Bank of Cleveland in 1995.
Publications: Guidelines for Giving

Foundation Officials

Bruce H. Akers: chairman PRIM CORP EMPL senior vice president corporate affairs: KeyBank of Cleveland.

Peter Kiewit Sons' Inc.

Company Contact

1000 Kiewit Plaza
Omaha, NE 68131-3374
Email: miscellaneous@kiewit.com
Web: http://www.kiewit.com

Company Description

Revenue: US$4,012,600,000 (1999)
Employees: 20,000
Fortune Rank: 396, per FORTUNE Magazine's list of 500 Largest U.S. Corporations (1999).
FF 396
SIC(s): 6719 Holding Companies Nec.

Nonmonetary Support

Type: Loaned Employees; Loaned Executives; Workplace Solicitation
Note: Co. provides nonmonetary support.

Kiewit Companies Foundation

Giving Contact

Michael L. Faust, Foundation Administrator
Kiewit Companies Foundation
Phone: (402)271-2950
Fax: (402)943-1302
Email: mike.faust@kiewit.com

Description

EIN: 476098282
Organization Type: Corporate Foundation
Giving Locations: NE: Omaha operating locations.
Grant Types: Capital, General Support, Multiyear/Continuing Support, Project.

Financial Summary

Total Giving: $4,000,000 (2000 approx); $3,240,000 (1999); $4,937,159 (1998). Note: Contributes through foundation only.
Assets: $15,900,000 (1998); $17,100,000 (1996 approx); $19,300,000 (1995 approx)

Typical Recipients

Arts & Humanities: Arts Associations & Councils, Dance, Historic Preservation, Museums/Galleries, Music, Opera, Theater
Civic & Public Affairs: Business/Free Enterprise, Economic Development, Zoos/Aquariums
Education: Colleges & Universities, Economic Education, Engineering/Technological Education, Minority Education
Social Services: Community Service Organizations, Homes, People with Disabilities, Recreation & Athletics, United Funds/United Ways, Youth Organizations

Contributions Analysis

Giving Priorities: Local arts groups, colleges and universities, united funds, hospitals, and some civic organizations.
Arts & Humanities: 20% to 25%. The United Arts of Omaha, Omaha Children's Museum, theater, and operas.
Civic & Public Affairs: About 30%. Business and free enterprise, housing and community development, civil rights, and women's affairs.
Education: About 40%. Majority to colleges and universities. Other interests include private precollege education, education funds, economic education, university athletic programs, and higher education in engineering.
Social Services: About 20%. Primarily supports united funds in operating areas. Also supports youth organizations, religious welfare, and family planning.
Note: In 1998, 92% of foundation funding went to Omaha organizations.

Application Procedures

Initial Contact: Send brief letter or proposal.
Application Requirements: Include a description of organization, amount requested, purpose of funds sought, recently audited financial statement, proof of tax-exempt status.
Deadlines: None.

Restrictions

The foundation generally does not support endowment funds, elementary schools, individual churches and religious groups, or tax-supported public institutions. The foundation never makes grants to individuals or private profit-making businesses.

Additional Information

The majority of funding is repeat grants to local organizations in Omaha, NE. Limited funding is available to new grant seekers.

Corporate Officials

Kenneth E. Stinson: chairman, chief executive officer, director B 1942. ED University of Notre Dame BS (1964); Stanford University MS (1970). PRIM CORP EMPL chairman, chief executive officer, director: Peter Kiewit Sons' Inc. CORP AFFIL director: MFS Communications Co.; director: United Metro Materials Inc.; director: Kiewit Western Co.; director: Kiewit Industrial Co.; executive vice president: Peter Kiewit Sons De Corp.; chairman, chief executive officer, director: Kiewit Construction Group Inc.; director: Kiewit Diversified Group Inc.; director: Kiewit Construction Co.; director: ConAgra Inc.; director: Global Surety & Insurance Co.

Foundation Officials

Michael L. Faust: administrator PRIM CORP EMPL assistant to chairman: Peter Kiewit Sons' Inc.
Walter Scott, Jr.: member contributions committee B Omaha, NE 1931. ED Colorado State University BS (1953). PRIM CORP EMPL director: Peter Kiewit Sons' Inc. CORP AFFIL director: MidAmerica Holdings Co.; director: Level 3 Telecommunications Holdings Inc.; director: MidAmerica Energy Holdings Co.; chairman: Level 3 Communications Inc.; president: Kiewit Coal Properties Inc.; director: Kiewit Mining Group Inc.; director: ConAgra Inc.; director: Burlington Resources Inc.; director: CalEnergy Co. Inc.; director: Berkshire Hathaway Inc. NONPR AFFIL director: Hastings College Foundation; president: Joslyn Art Museum; chairman: Creighton University.
Kenneth E. Stinson: member contributions committee (see above)

Grants Analysis

Disclosure Period: calendar year ending 1998
Total Grants: $4,937,159
Number of Grants: 193
Average Grant: $25,581
Highest Grant: $1,000,000
Typical Range: $1,000 to $10,000
Note: Grant analysis was provided by the foundation.

Kimball International, Inc.

Company Contact

1600 Royal Street
Jasper, IN 47549-1001
Phone: 800-842-1616
Web: http://www.kimball.com

Company Description

Employees: 8,949
SIC(s): 2421 Sawmills & Planing Mills--General, 2426 Hardwood Dimension & Flooring Mills, 2435 Hardwood Veneer & Plywood, 2521 Wood Office Furniture.

Habig Foundation

Giving Contact

Douglas A. Habig, Chairman & Chief Executive Officer
Habig Foundation
Phone: (812)482-1600
Fax: (812)482-8166

Description

Founded: 1951
EIN: 356022535
Organization Type: Corporate Foundation
Giving Locations: headquarters and operating communities.
Grant Types: Capital, General Support, Scholarship.
Note: Scholarships for children of company employees only.

Financial Summary

Total Giving: $600,000 (fiscal year ending June 30, 2000); $550,000 (fiscal 1999); $535,264 (fiscal 1998). Note: Contributes through foundation only.
Giving Analysis: Giving for fiscal 1996 includes: foundation ($326,484); foundation scholarships ($88,233); fiscal 1997: foundation ($306,864); foundation scholarships ($110,050); fiscal 1998: foundation ($398,164); foundation scholarships ($137,100)
Assets: $1,716,792 (fiscal 1997); $416,117 (fiscal 1996); $1,600,000 (fiscal 1995 approx)
Gifts Received: $400,000 (fiscal 1996); $262,000 (fiscal 1990). Note: In fiscal 1996, contributions were received from Kimball International, Inc.

Typical Recipients

Arts & Humanities: Arts Appreciation, Community Arts, Arts & Humanities-General, Museums/Galleries, Music, Public Broadcasting, Theater
Civic & Public Affairs: African American Affairs, Business/Free Enterprise, Chambers of Commerce, Community Foundations, Economic Development, Economic Policy, Housing, Legal Aid, Parades/Festivals, Safety, Urban & Community Affairs, Women's Affairs

Education: Agricultural Education, Arts/Humanities Education, Business Education, Colleges & Universities, Education Funds, Elementary Education (Public), Education-General, Medical Education, Minority Education, Private Education (Precollege), Public Education (Precollege), Religious Education, Science/Mathematics Education, Secondary Education (Public)
Environment: Resource Conservation
Health: Hospices, Hospitals, Mental Health
International: Foreign Arts Organizations, International Development
Religion: Churches, Ministries, Religious Organizations, Religious Welfare, Seminaries
Social Services: Community Service Organizations, Emergency Relief, Scouts, Senior Services, United Funds/United Ways, Volunteer Services, Youth Organizations

Contributions Analysis

Giving Priorities: Supports community organizations, fire departments, civic groups, social service organizations, United Way, the arts, wildlife organizations, foundations, hospitals and health organizations, and single-disease health associations.
Arts & Humanities: 3%. Supports arts programs.
Civic & Public Affairs: 30%.
Education: 48%. Supports colleges, elementary and secondary schools, and organizations promoting education.
Health: 2%. Funds hospitals and health organisations.
Religion: 15%. Supports churches and ministries.
Social Services: 2%.
Note: Total contributions made in fiscal 1997.

Application Procedures

Initial Contact: Submit full proposal.
Application Requirements: Include a description of organization, amount requested, purpose of funds sought, and proof of tax-exempt status.
Deadlines: None, for grants; April 1 for scholarships.
Review Process: Three independent members of a selection committee review scholarship applications.
Evaluative Criteria: Decisions for grants are based on merit, availability of funds, and benefit to company operating communities.
Notes: Applications for scholarships (to children of company employees only) are available by contacting the foundation.

Restrictions

Does not support individuals (except through scholarship program) or political or lobbying groups.

Corporate Officials

Gary P. Critser: senior executive vice president, secretary, treasurer, directorc B 1936. ED Evansville College BS (1958). PRIM CORP EMPL senior executive vice president, secretary, treasurer, director: Kimball International, Inc.
Douglas A. Habig: chairman, chief executive officer, director B Louisville, KY 1946. ED Saint Louis University BS (1968); Indiana University MBA (1972). PRIM CORP EMPL chairman, chief executive officer, director: Kimball International, Inc. ADD CORP EMPL chairman, chief executive officer: Kimball Electronics Inc.; president: Kimball Hospital Furniture; president, chief executive officer, director: Kimball Inc.; president, chief executive officer, director: Kimball International Manufacturing Inc.; president, director: Kimball International Mktg; president, director: Kimball International Transit Inc. CORP AFFIL director: Indiana Business Modernization & Technology Corp.; director: Springs Valley Bank & Trust Co.; director: INB National Bank.
Thomas L. Habig: vice chairman, director B Jasper, IN 1928. ED Tulane University BBA (1950). PRIM CORP EMPL vice chairman, director: Kimball International, Inc. ADD CORP EMPL chairman: National Office Furniture Co.; chairman: Artec; chairman: Batesville America Manufacturing Co.; chairman: Dale-Wood Manufacturing Co.; chairman: Evansville Veneer & Lumber Co.; chairman: Greensburg Manufacturing Co.; chairman: Hapers; chairman: Heritage Hills; chairman: IN Hardwoods; chairman: IN Hardwoods Cloverport Mill; chairman: Jasper Corp.; chairman: Jasper Laminates; chairman: Jasper Plastics; chairman: Kimball Electronics Inc.; chairman: Kimball Inc.; chairman: Kimball International Manufacturing Inc.; chairman: Kimball International Mktg; chairman: Kimball International Transit Inc.; chairman: Kimball Office Furniture Co.; chairman: Kimball World Inc.; chairman: Kimball Exports Inc.; chairman: Kimball Furniture Reproductions Inc.; chairman: Kimball Hospitality Furniture; chairman: Kimball Upholstered Products; chairman: Lafayette Manufacturing Co.; chairman: McAllen-America Corp.; chairman: Spring Valley Manufacturing; chairman: Tool Pro. CORP AFFIL secretary, director: SVB & T Corp. NONPR AFFIL member: Knights of Columbus.
Robert F. Schneider: executive vice president, chief financial officer, assistant treasurer PRIM CORP EMPL executive vice president, chief financial officer, assistant treasurer: Kimball International, Inc. CORP AFFIL chief financial officer: Kimball Inc.
James C. Thyen: president, director B Jasper, IN 1943. ED Xavier University BS (1965); Indiana University MBA (1967). PRIM CORP EMPL president, director: Kimball International, Inc. ADD CORP EMPL president: Kimball Electronics Inc.; president: Kimball Inc.; president: Kimball International Inc.; president: Kimball International Manufacturing Inc.; chief financial officer: Kimball International Mktg; chief financial officer: Kimball Hospitality Furniture. NONPR AFFIL member: Kiwanis International.
John T. Thyen: senior executive vice president marketing & sales, director B 1938. PRIM CORP EMPL senior executive vice president marketing & sales, director: Kimball International, Inc. ADD CORP EMPL senior executive vice president marketing sales: National Office Furniture Sales; senior executive vice president marketing sales: Harpers Sales; senior executive vice president: Kimball Electronics Inc.; senior executive vice president: Kimball Inc.; senior executive vice president: Kimball International Manufacturing Inc.; senior executive vice president: Kimball International Mktg; senior executive vice president marketing sales: Kimball Office Furniture Sales; senior executive vice president: Kimball Home Furnishings; senior executive vice president: Kimball Hospitality Furniture; senior executive vice president, director: Kimball U.K. Inc.
Ronald J. Thyen: senior executive vice president, chief operating officer director B New Albany, IN 1937. ED University of Notre Dame BS (1959). PRIM CORP EMPL senior executive vice president, chief operating officer director: Kimball International, Inc. ADD CORP EMPL senior executive vice president, director: Kimball Electronics Inc.; senior executive vice president: Kimball Inc.; director: Kimball International Manufacturing Inc.; vice president, director: Kimball International mktg; senior executive vice president: Kimball Hospitality Furniture. CORP AFFIL senior executive vice president, director: Facilities/Tech Support Group; director: Springs Valley Bank & Trust Co.

Foundation Officials

Gary P. Critser: senior executive vice president, secretary, treasurer, director (see above)
Brian K. Habig: director B 1957. ED Indiana University BA (1979). PRIM CORP EMPL executive vice president sales & marketing group: Kimball International, Inc. ADD CORP EMPL director: Kimball International Manufacturing Inc.; director: Kimball Electronics Inc.
Douglas A. Habig: chairman, chief executive officer, director (see above)
Thomas L. Habig: vice chairman, director (see above)
Robert F. Schneider: officer (see above)
James C. Thyen: president, director (see above)
John T. Thyen: senior executive vice president, director (see above)
Ronald J. Thyen: senior executive vice president, director (see above)
Christine M. Vujovich: director B 1951. ED University of Illinois BS (1974); University of Illinois MS (1978). PRIM CORP EMPL vice president: Cummins Engine Co. Inc. CORP AFFIL director: Kimball Inc.; director: Kimball International Inc.; director: Kimball Electronics Inc.
Dr. Jack Roberts Wentworth, Ph.D.: director B Elgin, IL 1928. ED Carleton College (1946-1948); Indiana University BS (1950); Indiana University MBA (1954); Indiana University DBA (1959). PRIM NONPR EMPL professor emeritus: Indiana University. CORP AFFIL director: Lone Star Industries Inc.; director: Market Facts Inc.; director: Jasper Corp.; director: Kimball International Inc. NONPR AFFIL national president, board governors: Beta Gamma Sigma; member: Graduate Management Admissions Council; member: American Marketing Association. CLUB AFFIL Masons Club; University Club.

Grants Analysis

Disclosure Period: fiscal year ending June 30, 1998
Total Grants: $398,164*
Number of Grants: 227
Average Grant: $1,754
Highest Grant: $50,000
Typical Range: $100 to $5,000
***Note:** Grants analysis provided by foundation. Giving excludes scholarships.

Recent Grants

Note: Grants derived from fiscal 1997 Form 990.

Arts & Humanities

3,000	Indiana Baseball Hall of Fame, Jasper, IN
500	Jasper Band Parents, Jasper, IN

Civic & Public Affairs

10,000	Network of Executive Women, Shawamo, WI
1,000	Hoosier Uplands, Mitchell, IN
1,000	Urban League, Louisville, KY

Education

20,000	St. Mary of the Woods College, Terre Haute, IN
15,000	Indiana University of Business, Bloomington, IN
15,000	Indiana University of Medicine, Bloomington, IN
6,000	Vincennes University Jasper Foundation, Jasper, IN
5,000	Brescia College, Owensboro, KY
5,000	University of Southern Indiana School of Business, Evansville, IN
4,000	Independent Colleges of Indiana Foundation, Indianapolis, IN
2,500	University of Evansville Computer Science, Evansville, IN
1,500	Gibault Foundation, Terre Haute, IN
1,500	United Negro College Fund, Columbus, IN
1,000	Indiana University Foundation, Bloomington, IN
1,000	Jasper High School Academic Decathlon, Jasper, IN
1,000	Jasper Middle School, Jasper, IN
1,000	North IDA College Foundation, Post Falls, ID
1,000	University of Evansville, Evansville, IN
750	Jasper High School Parent-Teacher's Organization Post Prom, Jasper, IN
500	Holy Family Catholic School, Coeur d'Alene, ID
500	Kappa Alpha Psi Fraternity, Evansville, IN

250	Spencer County 4-H, Rockport, IN
200	Holy Family School, Jasper, IN
170	Jasper Elementary Schools, Jasper, IN
150	Northeast Dubois High School Post Prom, Dubois, IN
100	Barr Reeve High School Post Prom, Montgomery, IN
100	Heritage Hills High School, Lincoln City, IN
100	Holy Family School, Jasper, IN
100	Loogootee High School Post Prom, Loogootee, IN
100	Perry Central High School Post Prom, Tell City, IN
100	Shoals High School Post Prom, Shoals, IN
Health	
3,500	Memorial Hospital Foundation, Jasper, IN
International	
4,200	National Ballet of Canada, ON, Canada
Religion	
20,000	Precious Blood Church, Jasper, IN
20,000	St. Nicholas Church, Santa Claus, IN
10,000	Precious Blood Church, Jasper, IN
6,500	Indiana Office of Campus Ministries, Indianapolis, IN
3,000	Shiloh United Methodist Church, Jasper, IN
2,500	Sisters of St. Benedict, Ferdinand, IN
1,000	Trinity United Church of Christ, Jasper, IN
500	Lemmind Church Association, Jasper, IN
500	St. Nicholas Church, Santa Claus, IN
100	Mary Help Christian Church, Siberia, IN
50	CACD, Saint Meinrad, IN
50	St. Henry Church, Saint Henry, IN
50	St. Martin of Tours Parish, Siberia, IN
25	St. Boniface Church, Fulda, IN
Social Services	
4,000	WFIE Flood of 97 Telethon, Evansville, IN

KIMBERLY-CLARK CORP.

 Number 76 of Top 100 Corporate Givers

Company Contact

Dallas, TX
Web: http://www.kimberly-clark.com

Company Description

Revenue: US$13,007,000,000 (1999)
Employees: 54,700 (1999)
Fortune Rank: 138, per FORTUNE Magazine's list of 500 Largest U.S. Corporations (1999).
FF 138
SIC(s): 2621 Paper Mills, 2676 Sanitary Paper Products.

Operating Locations

Argentina: Kimberly-Clark Argentina Holdings SA, Buenos Aires; Austria: Scott Paper Vertriesgesellschaft mbH, Linz, Oberosterreich; Belgium: Kimberly-Clark NV, Duffel, Anvers; Scott Continental NV, Duffel, Anvers; Scott Paper Coordination Center NV, Duffel, Anvers; Scott Paper International Trade Venture (Europe) NV, Duffel, Anvers; Brazil: Kimberly-Clark Kenko Industria e Commercio Ltda., Sao Paulo; Canada: Kimberly-Clark, Mississauga; Scott Paper Ltd., Mississauga; Cape Chignecto Lands Ltd., New Glasgow; Kimberly-Clark Nova Scotia, New Glasgow; Kimberly-Clark Forest Products, Terrace Bay; Omega Products Ltd., Vancouver; Chile: Kimberly-Clark Chile SA, Santiago; People's Republic of China: Kimberly-Clark Personal Hygienic Products Co. Ltd., Beijing; Kimberly-Clark CBG Hygienic Products Co. Ltd., Chengdu; Kimberly-Clark Paper (Guangzhou) Co. Ltd., Guangzhou, Chiba; Kimberly-Clark CBG Hygienic Products Co. Ltd, Handan, Kunming, Nanjing; Kimberly-Clark Paper (Shanghai) Ltd., Shanghai, Chiba; Costa Rica: Scott Paper Co. De Costa Rica SA, San Antonio de Belen, Heredia; Kimberly-Clark Costa Rica SA, San Jose; Czech Republic: Kimberly-Clark Inova AS; Ecuador: MIMO SA, Guayaquil, Guayas; El Salvador: Kimberly-Clark de Centro America SA, Sitio del Nino; France: Scott SA, Le Pecq, Yvelines; Kimberly-Clark Entreprise, Paris, Ville-de-Paris; Mauduit (Papeteries De), Quimper, Finistere; PDM Industries, Quimper, Finistere; Schweitzer Mauduit France, Quimper, Finistere; Papeteries De Malaucene, Vaucluse; Germany: Scott Paper Beteiligungs GmbH, Duesseldorf; Scott Paper GmbH, Duesseldorf; Intercargo Internationale Spedition GmbH, Koblenz, Rheinland-Pfalz; Kimberly-Clark GmbH, Koblenz, Rheinland-Pfalz; Scott GmbH, Neunkirchen, Saarland; Guatemala: Papeles Absorbentes SA, Guatemala City; Hong Kong: Kimberly-Clark (Hong Kong) Ltd., Kowloon; Scott Paper (Hong Kong) Ltd., To Kwa Wan, Kowloon; Scott Worldwide Pacific Operations (Wan Chai), Wan Chai; Honduras: Scott Paper Co. Honduras SA de CV, San Pedro Sula, Cortes; Indonesia: PT Scott Paper Indonesia, Jakarta Utara; India: Kimberly-Clark Pudumjee Ltd., Pune; Italy: Kimberly-Clark Italiana SRL, Agrate Brianza, Lombardia; Cartiera Scott Sud SpA, Verzuolo, Piemonte; Scott SpA, Verzuolo, Piemonte; Japan: Kimberly-Clark Japan Ltd., Tokyo; Scott Japan Ltd., Tokyo; Republic of Korea: YuHan Kimberly Ltd., Seoul; Malaysia: Kimberly-Clark Products (Malaysia) Sdn. Bhd., Kluang; Scott Paper (Malaysia) Sdn. Bhd., Kluang, Johor; Kimberly-Clark Malaysia Sdn. Bhd., Petaling Jaya, Selangor; Nicaragua: KIMNICA SA, Managua; Netherlands: Scott Paper International Finance (Netherlands) BV, Amsterdam, Noord-Holland; Kimberly-Clark Benelux Operations BV, Ede, Noord-Brabant; Scott Page BV, Geenep, Gelderland; Kimberly-Clark Canada European Finance BV, Veenendaal, Utrecht; Kimberly-Clark Sales Corp., Veenendaal, Utrecht; Panama: Kimberly-Clark International SA, Panama City; Paraguay: Kimberly-Clark Paraguay SA, Asuncion; Peru: Kimberly-Clark Peru SA, Lima; Philippines: Kimberly-Clark Philippines, Manila; Poland: Kimberly-Clark Poland SP Zoo, Warsaw, Warszawa; Portugal: Scott Madeiras Lda., Abrantes, Santarem; Kimberly-Clark Lda., Lisboa; Scott Paper Portugal Lda., Monumenta, Lisboa; Russia: Kimberly-Clark, Moscow; Republic of South Africa: Kimberly-Clark Southern Africa (Holdings) Pty. Ltd., Johannesburg; Singapore: Kimberly-Clark Far East Pte. Ltd., Singapore; Scott Paper (Singapore) Pte. Ltd., Singapore; Spain: Kimberly-Clark SA, Madrid; Scott Iberica SA, Madrid; Scott Miranda SA, Madrid; Scott Miranda Forestal SA, Miranda de Ebro; Thailand: Kimberley-Clark Thailand Ltd., Pathum Thani; Taiwan: Taiwan Scott Paper Corp., Taipei; United Kingdom: Kimberly-Clark Pension Trusts Ltd., Aylesford, Kent; Scott Paper (United Kingdom) Ltd., Gravesend, Kent; Kimberly-Clark Ltd., Maidstone, Kent; Scott Ltd., Reigate, Surrey; Uruguay: Kimberly-Clark Uruguay SA, Montevideo; Venezuela: Venekim CA, Caracas; Papelera Guaicaipuro CA, Maracay; Vietnam: K-C Vinathai Co. Ltd., Hanoi

Nonmonetary Support

Type: Donated Products
Note: Co. provides nonmonetary support in the form of donated products for disaster relief only.

Kimberly-Clark Foundation

Giving Contact

Carolyn Mentesana, Vice President
Kimberly-Clark Foundation
PO Box 619100
Dallas, TX 75261-9100
Phone: (972)281-1200
Fax: (972)281-1490
Note: Contact local plant manager for information on corporate direct giving.

Description

EIN: 396044304
Organization Type: Corporate Foundation
Giving Locations: national organizations; operating locations.
Grant Types: Capital, Employee Matching Gifts, General Support, Operating Expenses, Project.
Note: Employee matching gift ratio: 1 to 1.

Financial Summary

Total Giving: $10,500,000 (1998 approx); $6,408,988 (1997); $7,600,000 (1996). Note: Contributes through corporate direct giving program and foundation.
Giving Analysis: Giving for 1996 includes: foundation ($4,201,500); foundation matching gifts ($284,579); foundation grants to United Way ($68,175); 1997: foundation ($6,053,450); foundation matching gifts ($240,800); foundation grants to United Way ($114,738); 1998: foundation ($5,881,456); corporate direct giving ($3,929,290); foundation matching gifts ($529,023); foundation grants to United Way ($160,231)
Assets: $3,735,852 (1998); $5,918,828 (1997); $5,352,238 (1996). Note: Assets pertain to Foundation only.
Gifts Received: $8,757,209 (1997); $6,041,531 (1996); $4,104,080 (1994). Note: The foundation receives contributions from Kimberly Clark Corporation.

Typical Recipients

Arts & Humanities: Arts Appreciation, Arts Associations & Councils, Arts Centers, Arts Funds, Community Arts, Dance, Arts & Humanities-General, Historic Preservation, History & Archaeology, Libraries, Museums/Galleries, Music, Opera, Performing Arts, Public Broadcasting, Theater
Civic & Public Affairs: African American Affairs, Botanical Gardens/Parks, Business/Free Enterprise, Chambers of Commerce, Civil Rights, Clubs, Community Foundations, Economic Development, Economic Policy, Civic & Public Affairs-General, Law & Justice, Legal Aid, Municipalities/Towns, Parades/Festivals, Philanthropic Organizations, Public Policy, Safety, Urban & Community Affairs, Urban & Community Affairs, Women's Affairs, Zoos/Aquariums
Education: Arts/Humanities Education, Business Education, Colleges & Universities, Community & Junior Colleges, Economic Education, Education Associations, Education Funds, Engineering/Technological Education, Faculty Development, Education-General, International Studies, Literacy, Medical Education, Minority Education, Private Education (Precollege), School Volunteerism, Science/Mathematics Education, Special Education, Student Aid
Environment: Air/Water Quality, Environment-General, Resource Conservation
Health: Adolescent Health Issues, Cancer, Children's Health/Hospitals, Clinics/Medical Centers, Diabetes, Emergency/Ambulance Services, Health-General, Geriatric Health, Health Funds, Health Organizations, Hospitals, Hospitals (University Affiliated), Medical Research, Multiple Sclerosis, Nursing Services, Public Health, Single-Disease Health Associations
International: International Relations, International Relief Efforts
Religion: Religious Welfare
Science: Scientific Research
Social Services: Child Welfare, Community Centers, Community Service Organizations, Counseling, Delinquency & Criminal Rehabilitation, Domestic Violence, Family Services, Food/Clothing Distribution, People with Disabilities, Recreation & Athletics, Senior Services, Shelters/Homelessness, Substance

Abuse, United Funds/United Ways, Volunteer Services, YMCA/YWCA/YMHA/YWHA, Youth Organizations

Contributions Analysis

Giving Priorities: United Ways in operating communities, capital and operating support to colleges and universities, hospitals, municipalities, and arts organizations. Company does not release information regarding contributions policies. The foundation provides limited support to international sports federations. While overseas companies contribute in-country, the dollar amount or nature of these contributions is not tracked.
Arts & Humanities: 9%. Supports symphony associations, museums, the theater, and programs for writers.
Civic & Public Affairs: 9%. Interests include municipalities, legal affairs, women's causes, and foundations.
Education: 34%. Major support to colleges and universities as capital and operating grants, and to minority education programs.
Health: 18%. Support includes hospitals and health agencies, such as single-disease health associations.
Social Services: 20%. Emphasis on United Ways in operating communities. Other recipients include youth and the aged, services for the handicapped, and programs for the treatment and prevention of alchohol and drug abuse.
Note: Total contributions made in 1998.

Application Procedures

Initial Contact: Send a written proposal.
Application Requirements: Include amount requested, purpose of grant, and proof of tax-exempt 501(c)(3) status.
Deadlines: None; proposals reviewed as received.

Restrictions

The foundation does not make grants to sports or athletic activities; dinners or special events; individuals; fraternal organizations; state or secondary schools (except through matching gifts); religious organizations; goodwill advertising; member agencies of united funds; or political parties or candidates.

Additional Information

Kimberly-Clark Corp. annually budgets 1% of pretax domestic income averaged from preceding three years for charitable contributions, which may be given directly to qualified recipients or to the Kimberly-Clark Foundation for distribution. Since 1952, the foundation has served as the principal means through which the corporation supports tax-exempt charitable organizations.
In 1995, Kimberly-Clark Corp. acquired Scott Paper Co. All requests for contributions from Scott Paper are currently being considered by the Kimberly-Clark Foundation. for contributions from Scott Paper are currently being considered by the Kimberly-Clark Foundation.
Publications: Annual Report

Corporate Officials

Wayne R. Sanders: chairman, chief executive officer, director B Chicago, IL 1947. ED Illinois Institute of Technology BS (1969); Marquette University MBA (1972). PRIM CORP EMPL chairman, chief executive officer, director: Kimberly-Clark Corp. CORP AFFIL director: Chase Bank Texas; director: Adolph Coors Co. NONPR AFFIL trustee: Marquette University.

Foundation Officials

Tina S. Barry: president, director PRIM CORP EMPL vice president corporate communications: Kimberly-Clark Corp.
Donald Martin Crook: secretary B Wichita, KS 1947. ED University of Kansas BA (1970); University of Chicago Law School JD (1973). PRIM CORP EMPL vice president, secretary, chief counsel corporate affairs: Kimberly-Clark Corp. ADD CORP EMPL secretary: Kimberly-Clark Tissue Co. NONPR AFFIL member: American Society of Corporate Secretaries; member: Dallas Bar Association; member: American Bar Association.
W. Anthony Gamron: treasurer, director B Seymour, IN 1948. ED Indiana State University BS (1971); Indiana University MBA (1976). PRIM CORP EMPL vice president, treasurer: Kimberly-Clark Corp. ADD CORP EMPL treasurer: Kimberly Clark Tissue Co. CORP AFFIL treasurer: Avent Inc.
Carolyn Mentesana: vice president

Grants Analysis

Disclosure Period: calendar year ending 1998
Total Grants: $5,881,456*
Number of Grants: 80
Average Grant: $53,657*
Highest Grant: $1,642,500
Typical Range: $10,000 to $80,000
***Note:** Giving excludes matching gifts; United Way. Average grant excludes highest grant (given to the Bridget Futures Scholarship Program).

Recent Grants

Note: Grants derived from 1998 Form 990.

Arts & Humanities

50,000 Dallas Museum of Art, Dallas, TX
15,000 Irving Symphony Association, Irving, TX

Civic & Public Affairs

743,500 Community Partners, Houston, TX
250,000 Wausau Area Community Foundation, Inc., Wausau, WI
200,000 Dallas Zoological Society, Dallas, TX
100,000 Mid-State Economic Development Corporation, Fairfield, ME
75,000 Dallas Urban League, Inc., Dallas, TX
25,000 Dallas Arboretum and Botanical Society, Inc., Dallas, TX
15,000 Cato Institute, Washington, DC

Education

1,642,500 Bridget Futures Scholarship Program, Dallas, TX
250,000 University of Wisconsin Foundation, Madison, WI
125,000 Texan's Can, Dallas, TX
100,000 Michigan Technological University, Houghton, MI
100,000 Spelman College, Atlanta, GA
50,000 Marquette University, Milwaukee, WI
50,000 Paul Quinn College, Dallas, TX
25,000 Aiken Technical College Foundation, Inc., Aiken, SC
25,000 Lawrence University, Appleton, WI
25,000 Students in Free Enterprise, Springfield, MO
25,000 United Negro College Fund, Inc., Dallas, TX
20,000 Florida A & M University Foundation, Inc., Tallahassee, FL
15,000 The University of Texas at Dallas, Dallas, TX

Health

530,000 The June Allyson Foundation, Chicago, IL
200,000 Southwestern Medical Foundation, Dallas, TX
50,000 American Red Cross, Dallas, TX
50,000 American Red Cross, Dallas, TX
50,000 American Red Cross, Dallas, TX
50,000 American Red Cross in Eastern Maine, Bangor, ME
50,000 Juvenile Diabetes Foundation, Dallas, TX
50,000 National Health Council, Inc., Washington, DC
50,000 The Visiting Nurse Association of Texas, Dallas, TX
30,000 American Red Cross - Disaster Relief, Dallas, TX
30,000 American Uro-Gynecologic Society, Chicago, IL
24,571 Children's Memorial Foundation, Chicago, IL
15,000 Susan G. Komen Foundation, Inc., Dallas, TX

International

100,000 American Red Cross International Response Fund, Washington, DC

Religion

20,000 The Salvation Army, Dallas, TX

Science

100,000 Institute for in Vitro Sciences, Inc., Gaithersburg, MD

Social Services

100,000 Rawhide, Inc., New London, WI
100,000 United Way of Metropolitan Dallas, Dallas, TX
66,000 Paper Valley Youth Soccer Club, Inc., Neenah, WI
50,000 Boys & Girls Clubs of America, Dallas, TX
38,000 Mobile Area United Way - Mobile & Wash. Counties, Mobile, AL
34,000 Boys & Girls Clubs of Greater Dallas, Inc., Dallas, TX
25,000 The Betty Ford Center at Eisenhower, Rancho Mirage, CA
25,000 Partnership for a Drug Free America, Inc., New York, NY
25,000 YWCA, Dallas, TX
20,000 Family Gateway, Inc., Dallas, TX
20,000 Outagamie County Youth Service, Inc., Appleton, WI
13,919 United Way of Metropolitan Tarrant County, Fort Worth, TX

KINDER MORGN

Company Contact

1301 McKinney, Ste. 3400
Houston, TX 77010
Phone: (713)844-9500
Web: http://www.kindermorgan.com

Company Description

Former Name: KN Energy Co. (1999).
Revenue: US$5,927,200,000 (1999)
Employees: 3,308 (1998)
Fortune Rank: 290, per FORTUNE Magazine's list of 500 Largest U.S. Corporations (1999).
FF 290
SIC(s): 4900 Electric, Gas & Sanitary Services, 4923 Gas Transmission & Distribution, 5172 Petroleum Products Nec, 5983 Fuel Oil Dealers.

KN Energy Foundation

Giving Contact

Becky Jensen, Public Relations Coordinator
370 Van Gordon Street
Lakewood, CO 80228-8304
Phone: (303)989-1740
Fax: (303)914-4757

Description

Founded: 1990
EIN: 841148161
Organization Type: Corporate Foundation
Giving Locations: AR; CO; IA; KS; LA; MO; MT; NE; NM; OK; TX; UT; WY
Grant Types: Employee Matching Gifts, General Support.

Financial Summary

Total Giving: $296,714 (1997); $195,756 (1996); $163,405 (1995)
Assets: $5,167,102 (1998); $4,343,748 (1996); $3,899,429 (1995)

Typical Recipients

Arts & Humanities: Arts Associations & Councils, Arts Centers, Arts Funds, Arts & Humanities-General, Historic Preservation, History & Archaeology, Libraries, Museums/Galleries, Music, Performing Arts, Theater
Civic & Public Affairs: Business/Free Enterprise, Chambers of Commerce, Clubs, Community Foundations, Economic Development, Civic & Public Affairs-General, Municipalities/Towns, Parades/Festivals, Rural Affairs, Urban & Community Affairs
Education: Agricultural Education, Business Education, Colleges & Universities, Community & Junior Colleges, Engineering/Technological Education, Education-General, Leadership Training, Private Education (Precollege), Secondary Education (Private), Secondary Education (Public)
Environment: Air/Water Quality, Environment-General
Health: Children's Health/Hospitals, Emergency/Ambulance Services, Health-General, Health Organizations, Hospitals, Public Health
Religion: Religious Welfare
Science: Science Museums
Social Services: Child Welfare, Community Centers, Delinquency & Criminal Rehabilitation, Family Planning, Family Services, People with Disabilities, Recreation & Athletics, Senior Services, Social Services-General, YMCA/YWCA/YMHA/YWHA, Youth Organizations

Contributions Analysis

Giving Priorities: Focus on economic development, education, youth, and arts and culture.
Arts & Humanities: 10%. Funds arts associatins, museums, libraries, and the performing arts.
Civic & Public Affairs: 31%. Supports community and economic development.
Education: 26%. Higher education, including community colleges, is a priority; also funds preschoo1, K-12, and enrichment programs
Health: 6%. Funds health services.
International: 9%. Contributed to the G-7 Host Committee in Denver, Co.
Social Services: 13%. Supports youth activities and the U.S. Olympic Committee.
Note: Total contributions in 1997.

Application Procedures

Initial Contact: Send a brief letter of inquiry, not more than three pages.
Application Requirements: Include a description of organization, amount requested and total amount sought in campaign, and purpose of funds sought; statement of rationale for proposal including an indication of its goal, the need for such a program, any unique element, and population benefitted; what portion of the total goal is targeted for corporate support and from what source will remaining funds be solicited; an indication of broad-based community and corporate support; project evaluation plans and method of reporting results; itemized budget for the program or project; list of officers and directors, with affiliations; detailed organizational budget for the current year, with income and expenses; recently audited financial statement, and proof of tax-exempt status.
Deadlines: None.

Restrictions

Foundation will not fund individuals; political causes, candidates, or lobbying efforts; programs or organizations outside of the U.S.; advertising or sales.

Corporate Officials

Morton C. Aaronson: vice president, president, chief executive officer, director PRIM CORP EMPL vice president: KN Energy Inc. CORP AFFIL member: En. Able LLC.
John G. L. Cabot: vice chairman B Rio de Janeiro, RJ Brazil 1934. ED Harvard University BS (1956); Harvard University Graduate School of Business Administration MBA (1960). PRIM CORP EMPL vice chairman: KN Energy. CORP AFFIL director: Hollingsworth & Voge Co.; director: Eaton Vance Corp.; director: Cabot Corp.; director: Distrigas Massachusetts Corp. NONPR AFFIL president: New England Historic Genealogical Society.
Larry D. Hall: chairman, president, chief executive officer, director B Hastings, NE 1942. ED University of Nebraska BA (1964); University of Nebraska JD (1967). PRIM CORP EMPL chairman, president, chief executive officer, director: KN Energy ADD CORP EMPL president: KN Natural Gas Inc.; chairman: Natural Gas Pipeline of America; president: Northern Gas Co. ADD NONPR EMPL director: Rocky Mountain Oil & Gas Association. NONPR AFFIL member: Nebraska Bar Association; member: Press Association; director: Modern Language Association; member executive committee, director: Interstate Natural Gas Association America; chairman, director: Midwest Gas Association; member: Free Accepted Masons; director: Gas Research Institute; member: Colorado Bar Association; director: Federal Energy Bar Association; director: Colorado Alliance Business; director: Colorado Association Commerce & Industry; member: American Bar Association; member: Benevolent Protectorate Elks. CLUB AFFIL Elks Club; Hiwan Country Club; Club 30; Desert Mountain Club.

Foundation Officials

Morton C. Aaronson: director (see above)
Larry D. Hall: president, director (see above)
E. Wayne Lundhagen: treasurer B 1937. ED Concordia College (1960); University of California MBA (1971). PRIM CORP EMPL vice president: KN Natural Gas Inc. ADD CORP EMPL treasurer: Interenergy Corp.; treasurer: Northern Gas Co.
Martha B. Wyrsch: vice president, general counsel, secretary

Grants Analysis

Disclosure Period: calendar year ending 1997
Total Grants: $296,714
Number of Grants: 112
Average Grant: $2,649
Highest Grant: $26,100
Typical Range: $25 to $10,000

Recent Grants

Note: Grants derived from 1996 Form 990.

Arts & Humanities

10,000 Denver Art Museum, Denver, CO
7,500 Buffalo Bill Historical Center, Cody, WY
6,000 Nebraska Art Collection Foundation, Kearney, NE
5,000 High Plains Art Council, Sidney, NE
3,000 Denver Young Artists Orchestra, Denver, CO
3,000 Glenwood Springs Arts Council, Glenwood Springs, CO

Civic & Public Affairs

5,000 Colorado Small Business Development, Denver, CO
5,000 Colorado Springs Chamber Foundation, Colorado Springs, CO
2,554 Cambridge Development Foundation, Cambridge, NE

Education

25,100 Hastings College Foundation, Omaha, NE
17,250 Heartland Center for Leadership Development, Lincoln, NE
5,000 Red Rocks Community College, Lakewood, CO
3,500 Pikes Peak Community College Foundation, Colorado Springs, CO
3,000 University of Wyoming Foundation, Laramie, WY
2,500 Texas 4-H Youth Development Foundation, College Station, TX

Health

5,000 Children's Hospital Foundation, Denver, CO
2,500 Thayer County Health Services, Hebron, NE

Science

5,000 Houston Museum of Natural Sciences, Houston, TX

Social Services

5,000 Colorado Children's Campaign, Denver, CO
5,000 YMCA, Scottsbluff, NE

KINGSBURY CORP.

Company Contact

Keene, NH

Company Description

Employees: 225
SIC(s): 3541 Machine Tools--Metal Cutting Types, 3542 Machine Tools--Metal Forming Types.

Nonmonetary Support

Type: Donated Equipment; Donated Products; In-kind Services; Loaned Employees

Corporate Sponsorship

Type: Arts & cultural events; Festivals/fairs; Music & entertainment events; Pledge-a-thon; Sports events

Kingsbury Fund

Giving Contact

James E. O'Neil, Vice President, Technology
Kingsbury Corp.
80 Laurel Street
Keene, NH 03431-4207
Phone: (603)352-5212
Fax: (603)357-7419

Description

Founded: 1952
EIN: 026004465
Organization Type: Corporate Foundation
Giving Locations: NH: Cheshire county
Grant Types: Employee Matching Gifts, General Support, Multiyear/Continuing Support, Operating Expenses, Project, Scholarship, Seed Money.
Note: Matches gifts to educational institutions.

Financial Summary

Total Giving: $160,000 (1999 approx); $160,000 (1998 approx); $189,135 (1997). Note: Contributes through foundation only. 1996, 1995 Giving includes matching gifts; scholarship.
Giving Analysis: Giving for 1997 includes: foundation ($111,875); foundation matching gifts ($28,744); foundation grants to United Way ($27,191); foundation scholarships ($21,325)
Assets: $4,058,017 (1997); $3,570,917 (1996); $3,311,652 (1995)
Gifts Received: $88,105 (1997); $20,000 (1996); $40,000 (1994). Note: In 1997, contributions were received from Kingsbury Corp.

Typical Recipients

Arts & Humanities: Arts Appreciation, Arts Associations & Councils, Arts Centers, Arts Festivals, Arts Funds, Ballet, Community Arts, Dance, Ethnic & Folk Arts, Arts & Humanities-General, Historic Preservation, History & Archaeology, Libraries, Museums/Galleries, Music, Opera, Performing Arts, Public Broadcasting, Theater, Visual Arts

Civic & Public Affairs: Botanical Gardens/Parks, Chambers of Commerce, Clubs, Economic Development, Civic & Public Affairs-General, Parades/Festivals, Safety, Urban & Community Affairs, Women's Affairs

Education: Arts/Humanities Education, Business Education, Colleges & Universities, Community & Junior Colleges, Continuing Education, Education Funds, Elementary Education (Public), Engineering/Technological Education, Education-General, International Studies, Private Education (Precollege), Public Education (Precollege), School Volunteerism, Science/Mathematics Education, Student Aid, Vocational & Technical Education

Environment: Air/Water Quality, Environment-General, Resource Conservation

Health: Cancer, Children's Health/Hospitals, Clinics/Medical Centers, Health Organizations, Heart, Hospices, Medical Research

Religion: Religious Welfare

Science: Observatories & Planetariums

Social Services: Animal Protection, Camps, Community Centers, Community Service Organizations, Crime Prevention, Day Care, Emergency Relief, Family Services, Food/Clothing Distribution, Homes, Recreation & Athletics, Scouts, Senior Services, Social Services-General, Special Olympics, Substance Abuse, United Funds/United Ways, Volunteer Services, YMCA/YWCA/YMHA/YWHA, Youth Organizations

Contributions Analysis

Arts & Humanities: About 45%. Historic preservation, public broadcasting, art centers, and visual and performing arts.

Civic & Public Affairs: Less than 5%. Urban and community affairs and urban safety programs.

Education: 10% to 15%. Colleges and universities, scholarship funds, and secondary education.

Health: Less than 5%. Cancer centers and health care facilities.

Social Services: 35% to 40%. United Ways, YMCAs, youth organizations, and athletic programs.

Note: Total contributions made in 1997.

Application Procedures

Initial Contact: Request application guidelines for scholarship grants.

Deadlines: April 28.

Notes: There are no formal application procedures or deadlines for other grants.

Additional Information

Provides scholarships for higher education to the children of Kingsbury Machine employees.

Corporate Officials

John Simmons Cookson: vice president finance, treasurer, assistant secretary B New Haven, CT 1944. ED Colby College (1966); Babson College (1968). PRIM CORP EMPL vice president finance, treasurer, assistant secretary: Kingsbury Corp. CORP AFFIL vice president: Kingsbury Industries Inc.

James L. Koontz: president, chief executive officer, director B Dayton, OH 1934. PRIM CORP EMPL president, chief executive officer, director: Kingsbury Corp. CORP AFFIL president: Kingsbury Industries Inc.

Iris Mitropoulis: chairman B 1953. ED Rensselaer Polytechnic Institute MS (1975); University of Lowell BS (1975). PRIM CORP EMPL chairman: Kingsbury Corp. CORP AFFIL chief executive officer: Fellows Corp.; president: Ventura Industries.

James E. O'Neil: vice president technology PRIM CORP EMPL vice president technology: Kingsbury Corp.

Foundation Officials

John Simmons Cookson: trustee (see above)

Michael Hanrahan: trustee

James L. Koontz: trustee (see above)

Priscilla K. Maynard: trustee

James E. O'Neil: executive trustee (see above)

Jeffrey M. Toner: trustee B 1953. ED University of New Hampshire MBA; Pennsylvania State University (1974). PRIM CORP EMPL vice president: Kingsburg Corp. CORP AFFIL vice president: Kingsburg Industries Inc.

Grants Analysis

Disclosure Period: calendar year ending 1997

Total Grants: $111,875*

Number of Grants: 149

Average Grant: $751

Highest Grant: $25,000

Typical Range: $25 to $20,000

*Note: Giving excludes matching gifts; scholarship.; United Way.

Recent Grants

Note: Grants derived from 1997 Form 990.

Arts & Humanities

82,000	Colonial Theater
25,000	Colonial Theater
20,000	Historical Society of Cheshire County, NH
16,000	Colonial Theater
5,800	Grand Monadnock Arts Council
2,500	New Hampshire Symphony Orchestra, NH
2,000	WEVO Public Radio
1,000	Center Stage County
1,000	Currier Gallery of Art
1,000	Redfern Arts Center
1,000	Sullivan Public Library

Civic & Public Affairs

8,558	Monadnock United Way
1,000	Friends of Pisgah -- Visitor's Center fundraiser
1,000	Pathways for Keene, Keene, NH -- A2 phase fundraiser

Education

10,000	Keene State College, Keene, NH
2,000	Bob Jones University, Greenville, SC
2,000	Keene State College, Keene, NH
1,000	Boston College, Chestnut Hill, MA
1,000	Bucknell University, Lewisburg, PA
1,000	Bucknell University, Lewisburg, PA
1,000	Elementary School Project Playground
1,000	Keene State College, Keene, NH
1,000	Keene State College, Keene, NH
1,000	New Hampshire College, Manchester, NH
1,000	New Hampshire College, Manchester, NH
1,000	Plymouth State College, Plymouth, NH
1,000	Plymouth State College, Plymouth, NH
1,000	University of New England, Biddeford, ME
1,000	University of New England, Biddeford, ME
1,000	University of New Hampshire, Durham, NH
1,000	University of New Hampshire, Durham, NH
1,000	University of New Hampshire, Durham, NH
1,000	University of New Hampshire, Durham, NH
1,000	University of Rhode Island, Kingston, RI
1,000	University of Rhode Island, Kingston, RI

Health

2,200	Dartmouth-Hitchcock Annual Fund, Hanover, NH
2,200	Dartmouth-Hitchcock Fund, Hanover, NH

Social Services

8,558,025	Monadowood County Area Fire Department
855,825	Monadnock United Way
80,000	Cheshire County YMCA, NH
20,000	Cheshire County YMCA, NH
8,558	United Way -- corporate employee match
2,500	Westmoreland Community Gym
1,462	Kingsbury Employees Federal Credit Union
1,250	Cheshire County YMCA, NH
1,000	Boy Scouts of America
1,000	City of Keene State Park, Keene, NH
1,000	Swift Water Girl Scout Council

KIRKLAND &ELLIS

Company Contact

200 E. Randolph Drive
Chicago, IL 60601
Phone: (312)861-2000
Fax: (312)861-2200
Web: http://www.kirkland.com

Company Description

Revenue: US$205,000,000

Employees: 1,155

SIC(s): 8111 Legal Services.

Kirkland & Ellis Foundation

Giving Contact

Willard Fraumann, President
Kirkland & Ellis Foundation
Phone: (312)861-2038
Fax: (312)861-2200

Description

Founded: 1981

EIN: 363160355

Organization Type: Corporate Foundation. Supports preselected organizations only.

Giving Locations: headquarters and operating communities.

Grant Types: Employee Matching Gifts.

Financial Summary

Total Giving: $1,500,000 (2000); $1,500,000 (1999 approx); $1,000,000 (1998). Note: Contributes through foundation only.

Assets: $557,174 (1993); $622,855 (1992); $370,546 (1990)

Gifts Received: $902,072 (1993); $1,078,374 (1992); $649,941 (1990)

Typical Recipients

Arts & Humanities: Museums/Galleries, Music, Opera

Civic & Public Affairs: Civil Rights, Law & Justice

Education: Legal Education

Religion: Religious Organizations

Social Services: Substance Abuse, United Funds/United Ways

Contributions Analysis

Giving Priorities: Primarily education; also supports civic affairs, the arts, and health organizations.

Arts & Humanities: 7%. Opera, museums, and theater.

Civic & Public Affairs: 23%. Legal aid, civil rights, public policy, and minority affairs.
Education: 63%. Majority of funding supports legal education. Also supports minority education and colleges.
Health: 4%. Single-disease health organizations.

Additional Information

Total support goes through the employee matching gift program.
Information on the employee matching gift program is available in the company's employee handbook.

Corporate Officials

Willard George Fraumann: president, director, partner B San Francisco, CA 1948. ED University of Michigan AB (1970); Harvard University JD (1973). PRIM CORP EMPL president, director, partner: Kirkland & Ellis.

Foundation Officials

Willard George Fraumann: president (see above)
Vickie Hood: director
Marjorie P. Lindblom: director
Walter H. Lohmann: director
Stephen R. Patton: director
Jack Zackrison: director

Grants Analysis

Disclosure Period: calendar year ending 1999
Total Grants: $1,500,000 (approx)
Typical Range: $1,000 to $10,000

Recent Grants

Note: Grants derived from 1993 Form 990.

Arts & Humanities

21,700	Central City Opera House Association, Denver, CO
10,000	Museum of Contemporary Art, Los Angeles, CA
4,500	International Theater Festival of Chicago, Chicago, IL
3,334	Second Stage Theater, New York, NY
3,333	Chicago Sinfonietta Orchestra, Chicago, IL
2,667	Chicago Symphony Orchestra, Chicago, IL
2,334	National Symphony Orchestra, Washington, DC
2,000	Theater for a New Audience, New York, NY

Civic & Public Affairs

28,125	Legal Aid Society, New York, NY
26,580	Chicago Lawyers Committee/Civil Rights Under Law, Chicago, IL
12,000	Chicago Volunteer Legal Service Foundation, Chicago, IL
7,500	National Institute for Trial Advocacy, Notre Dame, IL
7,400	Public Interest Law Initiative
5,000	Chicago Bar Association, Chicago, IL
5,000	CPR Legal Program
5,000	National Legal Center for the Public Interest, Washington, DC
4,000	Legal Assistance Foundation of Chicago, Chicago, IL
4,000	Protection and Advocacy
3,625	Legal Aid Foundation of Colorado, CO
3,500	Colorado Lawyers Committee, CO
3,190	Public Counsel, Los Angeles, CA
3,000	American Enterprise Institute for Public Policy Research, Washington, DC
2,500	Association of the Bar/City of New York Fund, New York, NY
2,500	Legal Aid Society of the District of Columbia, Washington, DC
2,500	Pro Bono Advocates, Chicago, IL
2,000	Mexican American Legal Defense and Educational Fund, Commerce, CA
1,680	Legal Aid Bureau of Chicago, Chicago, IL
1,333	El Valor, Chicago, IL
1,000	National Association for Public Interest Law, Washington, DC
1,000	National Center for State Courts, Washington, DC

Education

201,250	Harvard Law School Fund, Cambridge, MA
150,000	Northwestern University School of Law, Evanston, IL
10,000	Chicago Kent College of Law, Chicago, IL
8,500	University of Chicago Law School, Chicago, IL
2,667	Chicago Board of Trade Educational Research Fund, Chicago, IL
2,150	I Have A Dream Foundation, New York, NY
1,956	Amherst College, Amherst, MA

Environment

2,000	Environmental Law Institute, Washington, DC

Health

8,000	Dana Farber Cancer Institute, Boston, MA
3,300	Rose Medical Center
2,000	Juvenile Diabetes Foundation, New York, NY
1,800	Leukemia Society of America, New York, NY

International

5,000	Weizmann Institute of Science, Washington, DC

Religion

4,000	United Jewish Appeal Federation, New York, NY
3,250	Jewish United Fund of Metropolitan Chicago, Chicago, IL
2,000	Anti-Defamation League, New York, NY

Social Services

5,667	Corp Against Drug Abuse, Washington, DC
2,667	Boy Scouts of America
1,300	United Charities
1,010	Neighbors in Need Fund

KMART CORP.

Company Contact

Troy, MI
Web: http://www.kmart.com

Company Description

Revenue: US$33,674,000,000
Profit: US$568,000,000
Employees: 265,000
Fortune Rank: 27, per FORTUNE Magazine's list of 500 Largest U.S. Corporations (1999).
FF 27
SIC(s): 5331 Variety Stores.

Operating Locations

Operates 2,147 stores in all 50 states and Puerto Rico.

Nonmonetary Support

Value: $9,000,000 (1996); $18,800,000 (1995); $11,000,000 (1993)
Type: Cause-related Marketing & Promotion; Donated Products; In-kind Services; Loaned Executives
Note: Nonmonetary support includes considerable international contributions.

Corporate Sponsorship

Type: Arts & cultural events; Festivals/fairs; Music & entertainment events; Sports events

Kmart Family Foundation

Giving Contact

Ms. Leslie Kota, Manager, Community Affairs
Kmart Corp.
3100 West Big Beaver Road
Troy, MI 48084-3163
Phone: (248)643-1776
Fax: (248)643-5513

Alternate Contact

Wendy Kemp

Description

Organization Type: Corporate Foundation
Giving Locations: national organizations; operating locations.
Grant Types: Emergency, Employee Matching Gifts, General Support.
Note: Employee matching gift ratio: 1 to 1 up to $1,000 per donor annually.

Giving Philosophy

'Through the company's Corporate Giving Programs, Kmart supports programs that positively impact children and families. Kmart believes that by responding to the community needs and working with other organizations, we can contribute toward making the communities where we do business better places to live and work. More than 2,100 Kmart Community Volunteer teams give their time and raise funds for local projects.'
'The Kmart Family Foundation is an extension of Kmart's direct giving programs. The Foundation will raise funds solely for the fight against drug abuse by children and youth.' *The Kmart Family Foundation Brochure* against drug abuse by children and youth.'
The Kmart Family Foundation Brochure

Financial Summary

Total Giving: $17,500,000 (1996 approx); $20,863,857 (1995); $21,000,000 (1993 approx).
Note: Contributes through corporate direct giving program and foundation. 1996 Giving includes corporate direct giving ($8,000,000); foundation ($500,000); nonmonetary support. 1995 Giving includes corporate direct giving ($2,063,857); nonmonetary support.

Typical Recipients

Arts & Humanities: Arts Institutes, Libraries, Museums/Galleries, Music, Opera, Performing Arts, Public Broadcasting, Theater
Civic & Public Affairs: Safety, Urban & Community Affairs, Women's Affairs, Zoos/Aquariums
Education: Colleges & Universities, Literacy, Minority Education
Social Services: Community Service Organizations, Family Services, Food/Clothing Distribution, United Funds/United Ways, Youth Organizations

Contributions Analysis

Giving Priorities: Organizations addressing drug abuse, youth organizations, and united funds; education curriculum development and business education; arts groups; and local health organizations. Overseas, companies support community organizations on a case by case basis, following general program guidelines. Corporation priorities include higher education, family-oriented programs, and universities where the company recruits.

Application Procedures

Initial Contact: phone for copy of guidelines and application

Application Requirements: completed application form; IRS letter of determination of 501(c)(3) tax exemption; cover letter signed by a senior official, outlining: whether it is a new or ongoing project; the extent of community and volunteer involvement; how Kmart associates may participate as volunteers in the program; and how the activity could take place at a Kmart facility; annual report; and roster of board of directors

Deadlines: None, for direct giving; December 31, March 31, June 30, and September 30 for foundation giving.

Review Process: letter of intent is reviewed and, if project is applicable, contributions committee reviews request; if request does not meet guidelines, the organization is notified

Evaluative Criteria: need for program, nonduplication of services, provision of appropriate recognition to corporation in community, impact on a particular need through support of specific project rather than general operations

Decision Notification: for the direct giving program; within 8 weeks of receipt; for the foundation, quarterly, at the end of February, May, June and September

Notes: For applications to the foundation, also include a written summary describing the purpose of the grant, including specifics on number of children served, evaluation procedures, etc. Applications to the foundation should be mailed to the Kmart Family Foundation at the above address. Kmart does not consider requests made by the phone.

Restrictions

Kmart does not make contributions to organizations devoted exclusively to research projects or to individuals.

Kmart also does not support the following: organizations not granted IRS 501(c)(3) status; local chapters of national organizations already supported; alumni associations; veterans', religious or political organizations; group travel expenses; school extra-curricular activities such as sports, band, etc.; organizations or programs outside the U.S.

The company does not provide individual scholarships.

The foundation does not support organizations that do not serve company communities or have an established drug prevention/educational program.

Additional Information

Contributions are usually made on an annual basis or for a limited, fixed term. Multiyear requests are not encouraged, nor does a contribution ensure future aid.

In 1996, Kmart formed the Kmart Family Foundation for the purpose of providing grants to charitable organizations which focus on the fight against and prevention of drug abuse among children, or which combat the effects that drug abuse by others can have on children and their families. their families.

Publications: Kmart Corporate Giving Programs Brochure

Corporate Officials

Floyd Hall: chairman, president, chief executive officer, director B Duncan, OK 1938. ED Bakersfield Junior College; Southern Methodist University; Harvard University Advanced Management Program (1977). PRIM CORP EMPL chairman, president, chief executive officer, director: Kmart Corp. CORP AFFIL director: Lynx Technologys; director: Mus Co. Inc.; director: Jundt Growth Fund; director: Kenwood Products; director: Grand Union Co. NONPR AFFIL trustee: Brooklyn Museum; director: Give Kids the World.

Giving Program Officials

Shawn M. Kahle: vice president PRIM CORP EMPL vice president corporate affairs: Kmart Corp.

Leslie Kota: manager PRIM CORP EMPL director corp. contributions: Kmart Corp.

Grants Analysis

Disclosure Period: calendar year ending

Recent Grants

Note: Grants derived from 1994 grants list.

Social Services

250,000 Share Our Strength, Washington, DC -- for hunger relief efforts

KNIGHT RIDDER

Company Contact

San Jose, CA
Web: http://www.kri.com

Company Description

Revenue: US$3,099,600,000
Employees: 20,263
Fortune Rank: 474, per FORTUNE Magazine's list of 500 Largest U.S. Corporations (1999).
FF 474
SIC(s): 2711 Newspapers.

Operating Locations

Australia: Sydney; England: London; Hong Kong; Japan: Tokyo; Singapore; Switzerland: Bern

Nonmonetary Support

Type: Loaned Executives

Corporate Sponsorship

Type: Arts & cultural events

Knight Ridder Fund

Giving Contact

Polk Laffon, Vice President & Corporate Secretary
Knight Ridder Fund
50 West San Fernando Street, Suite 1200
San Jose, CA 95113
Phone: (408)938-7838
Fax: (408)938-7766

Alternate Contact

Sara Rosado
Phone: (408)938-7881

Description

Organization Type: Corporate Foundation
Giving Locations: headquarters and operating communities.
Grant Types: Employee Matching Gifts, General Support.

Giving Philosophy

'We promise to be good citizens, to contribute to the quality of life and civic betterment of the communities that sustain us. We will do that through searching and sensitive journalism that fully meets our public-service obligations, through ethical and enlightened business practices, through civic participation, and financial support.' Knight Ridder

Financial Summary

Total Giving: Contributes through foundation only.

Typical Recipients

Civic & Public Affairs: First Amendment Issues, Professional & Trade Associations
Education: Education-General
Social Services: United Funds/United Ways, Volunteer Services

Contributions Analysis

Social Services: In a combined contribution with the Miami Herald, $2.5 million was pledged over five years for the rebuilding of South Dade County after Hurricane Andrew. Supports homeless shelters in Miami, FL, and the United Way.

Note: Specifically supports programs that improve the state of journalism.

Application Procedures

Initial Contact: call to request proposal coversheet and proposal checklist

Application Requirements: Proposal cover sheet; letter of application; project budget; organization's current operating budget; list of governing body/officers; audited financial statements; IRS documentation of current tax exempt status

Deadlines: None.

Decision Notification: contributions committee meets quarterly

Restrictions

Does not contribute to individuals or single-disease health organizations.

Additional Information

Knight Ridder's newspapers also have contributions programs to support activities in their individual markets.

Corporate Officials

Ross Jones: senior vice president, chief financial officer B New York, NY 1943. ED Brown University BA (1965); Columbia University MBA (1970). PRIM CORP EMPL senior vice president, chief financial officer: Knight Ridder Inc. CORP AFFIL chief financial officer: Pioneer Press Inc.; treasurer: Readers Digest Sales & Services Inc.; treasurer: Northwest Publications Inc.; secretary: Observer Transportation Co.; vice president: News Publishing Co. Inc.; vice president: Nittany Printing & Publishing Co. Inc.; vice president: Grand Forks Herald; treasurer: Mediastream Inc.

Polk Laffon, IV: vice president corporate relations, corporate secretary ED Pennsylvania State University MBA; Yale University (1967). PRIM CORP EMPL vice president corporate relations, corporate secretary: Knight Ridder.

Paul Anthony Ridder: chairman, chief executive officer, director B Duluth, MN 1940. ED University of Michigan BA (1962). PRIM CORP EMPL chairman, chief executive officer, director: Knight Ridder, Inc. CORP AFFIL director: Seattle Times Co.; director: Newspaper First. NONPR AFFIL director: United Way America; member president advisory board: University Michigan; member: Florida Chamber of Commerce; member advisory board: Center Economic Policy Development. CLUB AFFIL Pine Valley Golf Club; Cypress Point Club; Indian Creek Country Club.

Carol Weber: PRIM CORP EMPL director customer satisfaction/employee relations: Knight Ridder.

KOCH ENTERPRISES, INC.

Company Contact

Evansville, IN
Web: http://www.kochg.com

Company Description

Former Name: George Koch Sons.
Employees: 2,400
SIC(s): 2851 Paints & Allied Products, 3469 Metal Stampings Nec, 3559 Special Industry Machinery Nec, 3567 Industrial Furnaces & Ovens.

Koch Foundation

Giving Contact

Linda Wilson, Coordinator
Koch Foundation
10 South 11th Avenue
Evansville, IN 47744
Phone: (812)465-9600
Fax: (812)465-9613

Description

Founded: 1945
EIN: 356023372
Organization Type: Corporate Foundation
Former Name: George Koch Sons Foundation.
Giving Locations: IN; KY: especially western KY
Grant Types: Employee Matching Gifts, General Support, Scholarship.

Financial Summary

Total Giving: $500,000 (1998 approx); $400,000 (1997 approx); $717,207 (1996). Note: Contributes through foundation only.
Assets: $10,711,099 (1996); $9,171,510 (1995); $6,511,352 (1994)
Gifts Received: $600,000 (1996); $1,100,000 (1995); $100,000 (1994). Note: The foundation received contributions from George Koch Sons, Inc. and Gibbs Die Casting Aluminum Corp.

Typical Recipients

Arts & Humanities: Arts Associations & Councils, History & Archaeology, Museums/Galleries, Music, Public Broadcasting, Theater
Civic & Public Affairs: Botanical Gardens/Parks, Chambers of Commerce, Community Foundations, Economic Development, Civic & Public Affairs-General, Housing, Municipalities/Towns, Parades/Festivals, Public Policy, Safety, Urban & Community Affairs, Zoos/Aquariums
Education: Agricultural Education, Colleges & Universities, Community & Junior Colleges, Economic Education, Education Associations, Education Funds, Education Reform, Engineering/Technological Education, Education-General, Private Education (Precollege), Public Education (Precollege), Religious Education, Secondary Education (Private), Secondary Education (Public), Student Aid
Environment: Environment-General, Resource Conservation
Health: Cancer, Children's Health/Hospitals, Clinics/Medical Centers, Emergency/Ambulance Services, Hospitals, Medical Rehabilitation, Mental Health, Public Health, Single-Disease Health Associations
International: International Relief Efforts
Religion: Churches, Dioceses, Ministries, Religious Organizations, Religious Welfare, Social/Policy Issues
Science: Science Museums
Social Services: Community Service Organizations, Family Services, Food/Clothing Distribution, People with Disabilities, Scouts, Substance Abuse, United Funds/United Ways, YMCA/YWCA/YMHA/YWHA, Youth Organizations

Contributions Analysis

Arts & Humanities: About 5%. Supports Evansville area arts organizations, with interests in theater, music, and public broadcasting.
Civic & Public Affairs: 30%. Supports housing and economic development, organizations that promote civic pride, and local parks and zoos.
Education: 40%. Supports public education, independent college funds, and colleges and universities. Provides scholarships at several local higher education institutions. Also sponsors a scholarship program for employees' children, totaling about one-quarter of education contributions. Co. matches gifts to educational and medical research organizations.
Health: About 5%. Primarily supports hospitals and medical centers.
Religion: About 10% to 15%. Supports Catholic institutions and religious welfare.
Social Services: About 5%. Supports youth organizations and the United Way.

Application Procedures

Initial Contact: letter of inquiry or proposal
Application Requirements: a description of organization and the purpose of funds sought, how money will be used, who will benefit from contribution, and proof of 501(c)(3) status; the foundation will request additional information if necessary
Deadlines: None.

Corporate Officials

Robert Louis Koch, II: president, chief executive officer, director B Evansville, IN 1939. ED University of Notre Dame BSME (1960); University of Pittsburgh School of Business Administration (1962). PRIM CORP EMPL president, chief executive officer, director: Koch Enterprises Inc. CORP AFFIL vice president, director: Uniseal Inc.; director: Southern Indiana Minerals, Inc.; director: Southern Indiana Properties, Inc.; director: Sigcorp Inc.; director: Southern Indiana Gas & Electric Co.; chairman: Marco Sales Inc.; director: North American Green Inc.; partner: Fesk; chairman, chief executive officer: Gibbs Aluminum Die Casting Corp.; director: CNB Bancshares; director: Comsource, Inc.; director: Bindley Western Industries Inc.; vice president, director: Brake Supply Co.; board manager: Audubon Metals LLC. NONPR AFFIL member: World President Organization; member: Young President Organization; trustee, vice chairman: Purdue University; president: Signature Learning Center Inc.; member: Indiana Chamber of Commerce; member: Indiana University President Advisory Council; director: Independent Colleges Indiana; chairman: Indiana Business Higher Education Forum; vice chairman board trustees: Evansville Museum Arts & Science; director: Hoosiers for Higher Education; director: Community Alliance Foundation; director, member: Evansville Chamber of Commerce; president: Catholic Foundation Southwestern Indiana; director: Commit, Inc. CLUB AFFIL Tri State Athletic Club; Evansville Country Club.
Susan E. Parsons: secretary, treasurer B Gary, IN 1955. ED Purdue University (1977). PRIM CORP EMPL secretary, treasurer: Koch Enterprises Inc. ADD CORP EMPL treasurer: Gibbs Die Casting Corp.; secretary: Uniseal Inc. CORP AFFIL treasurer: Automated Office Solutions. NONPR AFFIL member: Institute of Management Accountant.

Foundation Officials

Robert Louis Koch, II: president, director (see above)
James Herman Muehlbauer: vice president, director B Evansville, IN 1940. ED Purdue University BSME (1963); Purdue University MS (1964). PRIM CORP EMPL executive vice president, director: Koch Enterprises Inc. CORP AFFIL director: Union Federal Savings Bank; vice president, director: Uniseal Inc.; director: Red Spot Paint & Varnish Co. Inc.; director: Red Spot Westland Inc.; director: Page Koch Europe Ltd.; director: Citizens National Bank Evansville; vice president, director: Gibbs Aluminum Die Casting Corp.; vice president, director: Brake Supply Co. NONPR AFFIL director: United Way Southwest Indiana; director: University Southern Indiana Foundation; national chairman, member: Society Manufacturing Engineers; director: Evansville Industry Foundation Inc.; member: National Society Professional Engineers; director: Catholic Foundation Southwestern Indiana; director: Deaconess Hospital; member: American Society Mechanical Engineers. CLUB AFFIL Evansville Petroleum Club; Evansville Country Club; Evansville Kennel Club.
Susan E. Parsons: secretary, treasurer, director (see above)

Grants Analysis

Disclosure Period: calendar year ending 1996
Total Grants: $717,207
Number of Grants: 115
Average Grant: $6,237
Highest Grant: $252,500
Typical Range: $1,000 to $10,000

Recent Grants

Note: Grants derived from 1996 Form 990.

Arts & Humanities

7,000	Arts Council of Southwestern Indiana, Evansville, IN -- operations
6,000	Henderson Area Arts Alliance, Henderson, KY -- operations
4,000	Evansville Civic Theater, Evansville, IN -- operations
4,000	WNIN TV9 Southwest Indiana Public Broadcasting, Evansville, IN -- operations
3,000	Evansville Philharmonic Orchestra, Evansville, IN -- operations
2,500	Evansville Symphonic Bank, Evansville, IN -- operations

Civic & Public Affairs

252,500	Community Foundation Alliance, Evansville, IN -- operations
3,700	Hudson Institute, Indianapolis, IN -- operations
3,100	Operation City Beautiful, Evansville, IN -- operations
2,500	CHOICE, Evansville, IN -- operations
2,500	Leadership Evansville, Evansville, IN -- operations
2,500	Smith Mills Volunteer Fire Department, Waverly, KY -- operations
2,200	Habitat for Humanity, Lexington, KY -- operations
2,125	Evansville Parks Foundation, Evansville, IN -- operations
2,000	Evansville Downtown Development Corp, Evansville, IN -- operations
2,000	Indiana Chamber of Commerce Foundation, Indianapolis, IN -- operations

Education

60,000	Henderson Community College, Henderson, IN -- operations
50,000	Signature Learning Center, Evansville, IN -- operations
46,950	University of Evansville, Evansville, IN -- operations
10,000	Evanville Catholic High Schools, Evansville, IN -- operations
8,000	Heritage High School, Monroeville, IN -- operations
7,100	Independent Colleges of Indiana Foundation, Indianapolis, IN -- operations
5,000	COMMIT Foundation, Indianapolis, IN -- operations
5,000	Kentucky Tech Jefferson Campus, Louisville, KY -- operations
4,600	University of Southern Indiana, Evansville, IN -- scholarships
3,000	Hanover College, Hanover, IN -- operations
2,600	Catholic Education Foundation, Evansville, IN -- operations
2,600	University of Louisville, Louisville, KY -- operations
2,025	Washington University, Saint Louis, MO -- scholarships
2,000	Purdue University, West Lafayette, IN -- scholarships
2,000	University of Notre Dame, Notre Dame, IN -- operations
380	Clemson University, Clemson, SC -- scholarships

Health

10,000	Tri-State Business Group on Health, Evansville, IN -- operations
7,000	Deaconess Hospital Foundation, Evansville, IN -- operations
3,600	St. Mary's Medical Center Foundation, Evansville, IN -- operations
2,000	American Cancer Society, Indianapolis, IN -- operations
2,000	Southwestern Indiana Easter Seal Society, Evansville, IN -- operations

International

5,000	Civitan International Foundation, Evansville, IN -- operations

Religion

30,000	St. Nicholas Church, Santa Claus, IN -- operations
25,000	Catholic Foundation of Southwest Indiana, Evansville, IN -- operations
7,000	Trinity Horizons, Lafayette, IN -- operations
5,000	Evansville Christian Life Center, Evansville, IN -- operations
5,000	Indiana Citizens for Life, Indianapolis, IN -- operations
4,000	Galilean Home Ministries, Liberty, KY -- operations
2,300	Young Life, Evansville, IN -- operations
2,000	St. Anthony Catholic Church, Evansville, IN -- operations

Science

10,100	Evansville Museum of Arts and Science, Evansville, IN -- operations

Social Services

33,083	United Way Southwestern Indiana, Evansville, IN -- operations
2,500	Boy Scouts of America Buffalo Trace Council, Evansville, IN -- operations
2,000	Girl Scouts of America Raintree Council, Evansville, IN -- operations

KOCH INDUSTRIES, INC.

Company Contact

Wichita, KS

Web: http://www.kochind.com

Company Description

Employees: 13,000

SIC(s): 0212 Beef Cattle Except Feedlots, 1311 Crude Petroleum & Natural Gas, 1321 Natural Gas Liquids, 2911 Petroleum Refining.

Fred C. and Mary R. Koch Foundation, Inc.

Giving Contact

Roger Ramseyer, Directory
Fred C. and Mary R. Koch Foundation, Inc.
PO Box 2256
Wichita, KS 67201
Phone: (316)828-7483
Fax: (316)828-5739
Email: ramseyer@kochind.com
Web: http://www.kochind.com/community.asp
Note: Visit company website for further giving contact information.

Description

EIN: 486113560
Organization Type: Corporate Foundation
Giving Locations: KS; LA: Baton Rouge; MN: St. Paul; OK: Oklahoma City; TX: Corpus Christi, Houston CAN: Calgary, AB
Grant Types: Capital, Endowment, Project, Scholarship.
Note: Also provides grants for special needs.

Financial Summary

Total Giving: $876,000 (1998); $1,134,417 (1997); $511,501 (1996). Note: Contributes through foundation only.
Giving Analysis: Giving for 1995 includes: foundation ($876,252); foundation scholarships ($30,000); 1996: foundation ($483,501); foundation scholarships ($28,000); 1998: foundation ($846,000); foundation scholarships ($30,000)
Assets: $22,580,993 (1998); $22,890,426 (1997); $22,891,575 (1996)
Gifts Received: $30,000 (1998); $30,000 (1997); $28,000 (1996). Note: Contributions are received from Koch Industries, Inc.

Typical Recipients

Arts & Humanities: Arts Associations & Councils, Arts Centers, Ballet, Dance, Ethnic & Folk Arts, Historic Preservation, Music, Opera
Civic & Public Affairs: Clubs, Economic Development, Philanthropic Organizations
Education: Arts/Humanities Education, Colleges & Universities, Legal Education, Special Education, Student Aid
Health: Cancer, Children's Health/Hospitals, Hospices, Single-Disease Health Associations
Science: Science Museums
Social Services: Child Welfare, Community Service Organizations, Family Services, Food/Clothing Distribution, People with Disabilities, Senior Services, United Funds/United Ways, Youth Organizations

Contributions Analysis

Giving Priorities: The foundation is primarily interested in supporting education, environmental stewardship, and human services.
Arts & Humanities: 7%. Supports arts centers, and the arts and humanities council.
Education: 73%. Supports universities, colleges and scholarship funds in Kansas. Particularly funds programs involving economic and scientific problem solving.
Health: 1%.
Social Services: 7%. Funds youth organizations. Supports programs that promote self-sufficiency, responsibility, and tolerance for others.
Note: Total contributions made in 1998.

Application Procedures

Initial Contact: Send a brief letter describing project.
Application Requirements: Include a list of board of directors, tax status, project budget, annual report, or audited financial statements.
Deadlines: None.

Restrictions

Grants limited to tax-exempt organizations. Scholarships limited to children of Koch Industries employees. Does not support individuals, religious organizations for sectarian purposes, political or lobbying groups, or organizations outside operating areas.

Corporate Officials

William W. Hanna: president, chief operating officer, director, president B 1936. ED Texas A&M University BS. PRIM CORP EMPL president, chief operating officer, director: Koch Industries, Inc. CORP AFFIL director: Security Benefit Group Inc.; director: Security Benefit Life Insurance Co.
Charles de Ganahl Koch: chairman, chief executive officer, director, president B Wichita, KS 1935. ED Massachusetts Institute of Technology BSE (1957); Massachusetts Institute of Technology MSME (1958); Massachusetts Institute of Technology MSChE (1959). PRIM CORP EMPL chairman, chief executive officer, director, president: Koch Industries, Inc. ADD CORP EMPL chairman: Koch Microelectronic Service Co.; principal: Koch Pipelines Co. LP. CORP AFFIL chairman: Koch Industries Inc.; director: Intrust Financial Corp.; director: Intrust Bank NA; director: Intrust Finance Corp. NONPR AFFIL chairman: Institute Humane Studies.

Foundation Officials

Donald L. Cordes: secretary B 1934. ED Kansas State University BS (1955); University of Kansas LLB (1959). PRIM CORP EMPL executive vice president, chief legal officer, director: Koch Industries, Inc.
Richard H. Fink: director PRIM CORP EMPL executive vice president, director: Koch Industries, Inc.
Vonda Holliman: treasurer
Victoria Hughes: vice president
David Hamilton Koch: director B Wichita, KS 1940. ED Massachusetts Institute of Technology BS (1962); Massachusetts Institute of Technology MS (1963). PRIM CORP EMPL executive vice president: Koch Industries, Inc. ADD CORP EMPL executive vice president: Koch Industries Chemical Technology Group. CORP AFFIL overseers: WGBH Channel 2; director: Koch Engineering Company Inc. NONPR AFFIL trustee: New York University Hospital Medical Center Fund; member: Whitehead Institute; trustee: Memorial Sloan Kettering Hospital; governor, chairman development committee: New York University Hospital; trustee: Guggenheim Museum; director: Institute Human Origins; director: Citizens for Sound Economy; director: Earthwatch; director: Aspen Institute; director: Cato Institute; director: American Museum Natural History. CLUB AFFIL River Club; Explorers Club; Racquet & Tennis Club.
Elizabeth B. Koch: president, director
Wayne Leighton: executive vice president
Harry Najim: director
Larry D. Spurgeon: director

Grants Analysis

Disclosure Period: calendar year ending 1998
Total Grants: $846,000*
Number of Grants: 12
Average Grant: $34,364*
Highest Grant: $468,000
Typical Range: $10,000 to $50,000
***Note:** Giving excludes scholarship. Average grant figure excludes highest grant.

Recent Grants

Note: Grants derived from 1997 Form 990.

Arts & Humanities

16,360	Wichita Center for the Arts, Wichita, KS -- support art programs
15,000	Wichita-Sedgwick County Arts and Humanities Council, Wichita, KS -- support art program

Education

463,057	Kansas University Endowment Association, Lawrence, KS -- educational programs
22,000	Friends University, Wichita, KS -- educational programs
20,000	Kansas Newman College, Wichita, KS -- educational programs
13,000	Wichita State University, Wichita, KS -- educational programs

Health

5,000	Hospice, Wichita, KS -- program support

Science

500,000	Exploration Place, Wichita, KS -- educational programs

Social Services

50,000	Rainbows United, Wichita, KS -- operating support

Kohler Co.

Company Contact

444 Highland Drive
Kohler, WI 53044
Web: http://www.kohlerco.com

Company Description

Employees: 17,000
SIC(s): 2514 Metal Household Furniture, 3088 Plastics Plumbing Fixtures, 3261 Vitreous Plumbing Fixtures, 3431 Metal Sanitary Ware.

Nonmonetary Support

Value: $500,000 (1996)
Type: Donated Equipment; Donated Products; In-kind Services

Giving Contact

Peter J. Fetterer, Manager, Civic Services
Kohler Co.
Phone: (920)457-4441
Fax: (920)457-9064
Email: pete.fetterer@kohlerco.com

Description

Organization Type: Corporate Giving Program
Giving Locations: operating locations.
Grant Types: Capital, General Support.

Financial Summary

Total Giving: $1,600,000 (1999 approx); $1,600,000 (1998 approx); $1,600,000 (1997). Note: Contributes through corporate direct giving program only. Giving includes nonmonetary support.
Giving Analysis: Giving for 1998 includes: corporate direct giving ($1,600,000)

Typical Recipients

Arts & Humanities: Arts Associations & Councils, Arts Funds, Historic Preservation, Museums/Galleries, Music, Theater
Civic & Public Affairs: Philanthropic Organizations
Education: Colleges & Universities, Education-General

Contributions Analysis

Giving Priorities: Education, health and welfare, conservation and historic groups, and arts and culture organizations.
Arts & Humanities: About 30%. Supports performing arts and historical societies.
Education: About 35%. Supports colleges and universities near headquarters location, and scholarship funds.
Health: About 35%. Major support to community United Ways. Some support for housing initiatives, the YMCA, and youth activities.
Note: Most grants are community and employee oriented.

Application Procedures

Initial Contact: letter format
Application Requirements: background and budget of organization and project
Deadlines: None.
Decision Notification: within six to ten weeks

Corporate Officials

Natalie A. Black: group vice president interiors, general counsel, director B Bakersfield, CA 1949. ED Stanford University AB (1972); Marquette University JD (1978). PRIM CORP EMPL group vice president interiors, general counsel, director: Kohler Co. CORP AFFIL secretary, director: Sterling Plumbing Group Inc.; secretary, director, vice chairman: McGuire Furniture Co.; vice president: Kohler Ltd.; secretary, director: Kohler Sanimex; vice president, secretary, director: Kohler of France; president, director: Kohler Interiors Group Ltd.; vice chairman, chief executive officer, director, secretary: Baker, Knapp & Tubbs; president, secretary, director: Dapha Ltd. NONPR AFFIL member: American Bar Association.
Jeffrey P. Cheney: senior vice president, finance PRIM CORP EMPL senior vice president, finance: Kohler Co.
William J. Drew: corporate secretary PRIM CORP EMPL corporate secretary: Kohler Co.
Herbert Vollrath Kohler, Jr.: chairman, president, director B Sheboygan, WI 1939. ED Choate School (1957); Yale University BS (1965). PRIM CORP EMPL chairman, president, director: Kohler Co. CORP AFFIL director: Sterling Plumbing Group Inc.; director: Harnischfeger Corp. NONPR AFFIL member, director: National Association Manufacturer; member: Sheboygan Chamber of Commerce; trustee: Lawrence University; director: Kiddies Camp Corp.; member advisory board: John Michael Kohler Arts Center; director, vice president: Friendship House; member: American Horse Show Association; member: American Morgan Horse Association. CLUB AFFIL Sheboygan Economic Club.
Clyde W. Kometer: corporate controller PRIM CORP EMPL corporate controller: Kohler Co.
Dale E. Snyder: senior vice president, technical services ED General Motors Institute BS; Rensselaer Polytechnic Institute MS. PRIM CORP EMPL senior vice president, technical services: Kohler Co.
George R. Tiedens: group president power systems ED University of Iowa BS (1960). PRIM CORP EMPL group president power systems: Kohler Co.

Giving Program Officials

Peter Fetterer: PRIM CORP EMPL manager media & civic service: Kohler Co.

Grants Analysis

Disclosure Period: calendar year ending

KPMG Peat Marwick LLP

Company Contact

New York, NY
Web: http://www.kpmgcampus.com

Company Description

Revenue: US$5,504,000,000
Employees: 70,000
SIC(s): 8721 Accounting, Auditing & Bookkeeping, 8742 Management Consulting Services.

Nonmonetary Support

Type: Donated Equipment

Corporate Sponsorship

Contact: Mary Downes, Practice Development
Note: The company occasionally sponsors fund raising dinners, conferences and symposia.

KPMG Peat Marwick Foundation

Giving Contact

Tara Perino, Manager
KPMG Peat Marwick Foundation
3 Chestnut Ridge Rd.
Montvale, NJ 07645
Phone: (201)307-7662
Fax: (201)307-7093
Email: tnelligan@kpmg.com
Web: http://www.kpmgfoundation.com

Description

EIN: 136262199
Organization Type: Corporate Foundation
Giving Locations: nationally.
Grant Types: Employee Matching Gifts, Endowment, Fellowship, Multiyear/Continuing Support, Professorship, Research, Scholarship.
Note: Individual gifts of up to $5,000 are matched by the foundation to colleges or universities whose donors are alumni, or where KPMG Peat Marwick recruits.

Giving Philosophy

'The KPMG Peat Marwick Foundation's broad spectrum of activities reflects its ambitious mission: to enhance the quality of accounting education at all levels, ultimately drawing even greater talent and skills into our profession and all business disciplines. For maximum impact, we have channeled our resources into a carefully selected group of the most effective programs that exist. The Foundation aims to impact upon the full range of education--from pre-college to faculty enrichment. At some levels, we found, there simply were no programs working toward the goals we considered most important, so we created them. While there are scores of programs carrying on important work in the education arena every day, the Foundation supports those we believe will make the greatest difference at every level.' *KPMG Peat Marwick Foundation Annual Report*

Financial Summary

Total Giving: $6,000,000 (fiscal year ending June 30, 1999 approx); $5,909,118 (fiscal 1998); $5,036,990 (fiscal 1997). Note: Contributes through corporate direct giving program and foundation.
Giving Analysis: Giving for fiscal 1997 includes: foundation matching gifts ($3,498,900); foundation ($913,750); foundation scholarships ($427,000); foundation fellowships ($197,340); fiscal 1998: foundation matching gifts ($3,927,836); foundation ($1,076,395); foundation scholarships ($757,500); foundation fellowships ($147,387)
Assets: $465,692 (fiscal 1998); $1,216,567 (fiscal 1997); $1,273,332 (fiscal 1996)
Gifts Received: $7,051,646 (fiscal 1998); $6,611,930 (fiscal 1997); $6,354,588 (fiscal 1996). Note: Contributions are received from KPMG Peat Marwick and other corporate, foundation, and individual donors.

Typical Recipients

Civic & Public Affairs: African American Affairs, Clubs, Economic Policy, Hispanic Affairs, Professional & Trade Associations
Education: Business Education, Colleges & Universities, Continuing Education, Education Reform, Engineering/Technological Education, Faculty Development, Education-General, International Studies, Leadership Training, Legal Education, Minority Education, Science/Mathematics Education, Student Aid
International: International Development

Contributions Analysis

Giving Priorities: Education sole priority: matches employee gifts; supports scholarship programs, a lecture series, faculty travel, and other ongoing academic programs and activities; and provides research fellowships.
Education: 100%. Matches gifts to higher education. The foundation is an active partner with INROADS, the national organization that provides outstanding minority students with training, work experience, and guidance to help them enter the business world. The Minority and Information Systems Doctoral Scholarships Program (the PhD Project) is open to African-Americans, Hispanic-Americans, and Native Americans who will be in full-time accounting or information systems doctoral programs. The foundation supports the Golden Key National Honor Society, providing

funding for scholarships around the nation, and supports the society's national convention. The Beta Alpha PsiScholarship Program receives a $10,000 annual grant and funds two $500 scholarships for each of the chapters rated 'superior' through an internal evaluation of their program activities. The foundation sponsors and provides scholarship money to the Consortium for Graduate Study in Management; foundation is a leading sponsor of the National Association of Black Accountants and anchor supporter of its Center for Academic Research. Provides grant program that offers reimbursement for all fees, dues, and advisor expenses for Historically Black Colleges and Universities in the American Assembly of Collegiate Schools of Business accreditation process. Thefoundation also supports LEAD, a nationwide program that identifies, targets and supports minority high school students and encourages them to consider careers in business. Also sponsors professorships.

Application Procedures

Initial Contact: For doctoral scholarships, send vita to foundation executive director.
Application Requirements: Include past grades, recommendation letters, graduate admissions test scores, and endorsement by accounting program administrator.
Deadlines: April 1.
Decision Notification: Doctoral scholarships are announced April 15.

Restrictions

Support is generally restricted to educational activities.
Foundation does not support dinners or special events, fraternal organizations, goodwill advertising, member agencies of united funds, political or lobbying groups, or religious organizations.

Additional Information

KPMG Peat Marwick also has a foundation in Los Angeles that contributes $60,000 to $70,000 annually. Contributions are made in the areas of arts and humanities, civic and public affairs, health, social services, and education.
Publications: Foundation Annual Report

Corporate Officials

Bernard J. Milano: executive director PRIM CORP EMPL executive director: KPMG Peat Marwick LLP.

Foundation Officials

William Blaufuss, Jr.: trustee PRIM CORP EMPL partner: KPMG LLP.
A. P. Dolanski: trustee CORP AFFIL partner Los Angeles: KPMG Peat Marwick.
Walter Duer: trustee PRIM CORP EMPL partner: KPMG Peat Marwick LLP.
Robert Elliott: trustee
Timothy Flinn: trustee
Scot R. Guempel: trustee
Jerry Hilbrich: chairman
Bernard J. Milano: trustee (see above)
Ronald Oehm: trustee
Alice Richter: trustee
Frank K. Ross: trustee PRIM CORP EMPL partner: K PMG Peat Marwick.
Dennis Van Mieghem: trustee

Grants Analysis

Disclosure Period: fiscal year ending June 30, 1998
Total Grants: $1,076,395*
Number of Grants: 45
Average Grant: $23,920
Highest Grant: $250,000
Typical Range: $100 to $25,000
***Note:** Giving excludes matching gifts; scholarship; professorships.

Recent Grants

Note: Grants derived from fiscal 1997 Form 990.

Civic & Public Affairs	
30,000	Journal of Accounting Research, Chicago, IL
30,000	Journal of Accounting Research, Chicago, IL
17,464	American Accounting Association, Sarasota, FL
11,207	American Accounting Association, Sarasota, FL
10,000	Hispanic Association of Colleges and Universities, San Antonio, TX
10,000	National Association of Black Accountants, Greenbelt, MD
9,000	American Tax Association, Sarasota, FL
7,292	American Accounting Association, Sarasota, FL
5,000	Tax Research Opportunities
Education	
133,334	Faculty Fellows Program
85,000	Golden Key Honor Society, Atlanta, GA
75,000	Beta Alpha Psi, Sarasota, FL
55,000	University of Kansas, Lawrence, KS
40,000	Columbia University, New York, NY
40,000	University of Texas Austin, Austin, TX
30,000	Duke University, Durham, NC
30,000	University of Chicago, Chicago, IL
25,000	Duke University, Durham, NC
25,000	Florida A&M University, Sarasota, FL
25,000	George Washington University, Washington, DC
25,000	North Carolina A&T State University, Greensboro, NC
24,911	University of Illinois Urbana, Urbana, IL
24,584	University of Michigan Ann Arbor, Ann Arbor, MI
20,000	University of Michigan Ann Arbor, Ann Arbor, MI
20,000	University of Texas Austin, Austin, TX
19,220	Accreditation Assistance
17,960	Brigham Young University, Provo, UT
15,000	University of Georgia, Athens, GA
12,992	New York University, New York, NY
11,241	Duke University, Durham, NC
10,000	Golden Key Honor Society, Atlanta, GA
10,000	Providence College, Providence, RI
10,000	Temple University, Philadelphia, PA
10,000	University of Illinois Urbana, Urbana, IL
10,000	University of Pennsylvania, Philadelphia, PA
9,400	Research Opportunities in Auditing
7,580	Brigham Young University, Provo, UT
6,800	James Madison University, Harrisonburg, VA
5,915	Southwest Doctoral Consortium
5,800	Hampton University, Hampton, VA
5,000	Duke University, Durham, NC
5,000	Johnson C. Smith University, Charlotte, NC
5,000	Loyola College, Baltimore, MD
5,000	North Carolina State University, Raleigh, NC
5,000	San Diego State University, San Diego, CA
5,000	University of North Carolina Chapel Hill, Chapel Hill, NC
5,000	University of North Carolina Chapel Hill, Chapel Hill, NC
5,000	University of North Carolina Chapel Hill, Chapel Hill, NC
5,000	University of North Carolina Chapel Hill, Chapel Hill, NC
5,000	University of North Carolina Chapel Hill, Chapel Hill, NC

KRAFT FOODS, INC.

Company Contact

Northfield, IL

Company Description

Former Name: Kraft General Foods, Inc.
SIC(s): 2022 Cheese--Natural & Processed, 2026 Fluid Milk, 2035 Pickles, Sauces & Salad Dressings, 6719 Holding Companies Nec.
Parent Company: Philip Morris Companies Inc., New York, NY, United States

Operating Locations

Operates in over 250 communities in 48 states.

Nonmonetary Support

Range: $10,000 - $13,000
Type: Donated Products

Giving Contact

Wanda Goin, Manager, Community Affairs
Kraft Foods Corp. Contributions Program
Three Lakes Drive
Northfield, IL 60093-2753
Phone: (847)646-2000
Web: http://www.kraftfoods.com

Description

Organization Type: Corporate Giving Program
Former Name: Kraft General Foods Foundation.
Giving Locations: nationally and in operating communities.
Grant Types: Project.

Financial Summary

Total Giving: $11,000,000 (1996 approx); $13,000,000 (1995 approx); $24,000,000 (1994 approx). Note: Contributes through corporate direct giving program only. 1995 Giving includes corporate direct giving ($12,725,000); foundation ($275,000).
Assets: $138,177 (1996); $225,793 (1995); $298,266 (1994)
Gifts Received: $70,000 (1995); $275,000 (1994); $534,276 (1993). Note: Contributions are received from Phillip Morris Inc. and Kraft Foods, Inc.

Typical Recipients

Arts & Humanities: Arts Outreach, Dance, Music, Performing Arts, Theater, Visual Arts
Civic & Public Affairs: Civic & Public Affairs-General, Women's Affairs, Zoos/Aquariums
Education: Arts/Humanities Education, Minority Education, Public Education (Precollege)
Environment: Environment-General
Health: Health Organizations, Medical Research
Social Services: Child Welfare, Family Services, Shelters/Homelessness, United Funds/United Ways, Volunteer Services, Youth Organizations

Contributions Analysis

Giving Priorities: Strengthening education, hunger and nutrition, performing and visual arts, civic and community organizations, conservation and environment, and health and human services.

Application Procedures

Initial Contact: for general inquiries and national programs, and nonprofits operating in headquarters communities, send proposals to Manager, Community Affairs; programs operating in Kraft Foods communities should apply to the community contributions committee serving their city or region
Application Requirements: a brief (two-page maximum) summary statement of the organization's project or program need, including how proposal meets program objectives, focus areas, affirmative action priorities, funding period; any key program or deadline dates; organization name, address, phone number,

and the name of a contact person familiar with the proposal; budget for project, including all sources of financial support and amounts committed or pending; an audited financial statement for the previous year, or a letter of auditability; list of other donors to the organization, including a mounts contributed; and proof of tax-exempt status; proposals seeking support of $5,000 or more should also include a brief description of how the proposal addresses identified needs not met by other nonprofit organizations; why the applicant organization is qualified to get the job done; a clear statement of expected results; a plan for evaluation of the project; a timetable for project implementation, communication, and evaluation; a brief statement of history, purpose; and goals of the organization; information about the number of members it has, constituents served, geographic service are a, use of volunteers, and general accomplishments to date; copy of organization's operating budget for the past two years, indicating percentages used for program, administrative, fundraising, and general expenses; a list of officers and board members and their affiliations; copy of organization's most recent annual report; and a brief background statement on the executive director and key staff to be involved in the proposed project
Deadlines: None.

Restrictions

Generally does not provide support to individuals; organizations that discriminate on the basis of color, sex, religion, national origin, age, handicap, or veteran status; fraternal, veteran, labor, or religious organizations; political or lobbying organizations, or those supporting the candidacy of a particular individual; travel funds; support of endowments or certain capital campaigns; benefit tickets or courtesy advertising; or organizations that might pose a conflict with company's goals, programs, products, or employees.
Generally does not provide general operating support to United Way member agencies. However, requests for a special project may be considered with United Way authorization.

Additional Information

In 1997, Kraft Food Foundation reported that it is inactive and that contributions are made through Corporate Contributions, Kraft-Northfield.
In 1995, Kraft Foods, Inc. absorbed Oscar Mayer Foods Corp., which had previously operated its own direct giving program.
Philip Morris sponsors a direct giving program for its other subsidiaries. Kraft Foods Corporate Contributions Program maintains its own corporate contributions committee for making grant decisions.

Corporate Officials

Robert S. Morris: chief executive officer PRIM CORP EMPL chief executive officer: Kraft Foods, Inc.

Giving Program Officials

Wanda Goin: manager community affairs PRIM CORP EMPL assistant staff manager: Centel Corp.

Grants Analysis

Disclosure Period: calendar year ending 1995
Total Grants: $275,000
Number of Grants: 1

Recent Grants

Note: Grants derived from 1995 Form 990.

Health

275,000 American Health Foundation, New York, NY -- biomedical research

KROGER CO.

Company Contact

Cincinnati, OH

Company Description

Revenue: US$28,203,300,000
Profit: US$410,800,000
Employees: 212,000
Fortune Rank: 14, per FORTUNE Magazine's list of 500 Largest U.S. Corporations (1999).
FF 14
SIC(s): 2000 Food & Kindred Products, 5300 General Merchandise Stores, 5400 Food Stores, 5900 Miscellaneous Retail.

Nonmonetary Support

Type: Cause-related Marketing & Promotion; Donated Products; In-kind Services
Note: For nonmonetary support contact local store manager.

The Kroger Co. Foundation

Giving Contact

Janet Ausdenmoore, Administrator
The Kroger Co. Foundation
1014 Vine Street
Cincinnati, OH 45202-1100
Phone: (513)762-4000
Fax: (513)762-4370
Web: http://www.kroger.com

Description

EIN: 311192929
Organization Type: Corporate Foundation
Former Name: Kroger Co. Foundation.
Giving Locations: principally near operating locations and to national organizations.
Grant Types: Capital, General Support, Operating Expenses, Seed Money.

Giving Philosophy

'The Kroger Company's philanthropic objectives are to (1) enhance the general societal conditions favorable to the company's growth and profitability; and (2) enhance the quality of life in communities with a concentration of Kroger customers and employees. The Kroger Company Foundation was created to help the company meet these objectives.' Kroger Company Foundation

Financial Summary

Total Giving: $2,900,000 (1999 approx); $2,841,888 (1998); $2,764,776 (1997)
Giving Analysis: Giving for 1998 includes: foundation grants to United Way ($1,297,406)
Assets: $18,253,008 (1998); $18,771,051 (1997); $19,936,044 (1996)

Typical Recipients

Arts & Humanities: Arts Associations & Councils, Arts Centers, Arts Festivals, Arts Funds, Ballet, Dance, Historic Preservation, Libraries, Museums/Galleries, Music, Opera, Performing Arts, Public Broadcasting, Theater, Visual Arts
Civic & Public Affairs: Botanical Gardens/Parks, Business/Free Enterprise, Chambers of Commerce, Civil Rights, Community Foundations, Economic Development, Employment/Job Training, Housing, Municipalities/Towns, Parades/Festivals, Philanthropic Organizations, Professional & Trade Associations, Public Policy, Rural Affairs, Safety, Urban & Community Affairs, Women's Affairs, Zoos/Aquariums
Education: Agricultural Education, Agricultural Education, Business Education, Colleges & Universities, Community & Junior Colleges, Economic Education, Education Associations, Education Funds, Elementary Education (Private), Literacy, Medical Education, Minority Education, Private Education (Precollege), Public Education (Precollege), Science/Mathematics Education, Student Aid
Environment: Environment-General
Health: Arthritis, Cancer, Children's Health/Hospitals, Diabetes, Eyes/Blindness, Health Organizations, Hospices, Hospitals, Medical Rehabilitation, Medical Research, Nutrition, Prenatal Health Issues, Single-Disease Health Associations
International: Foreign Arts Organizations, International Relations
Religion: Churches, Religious Welfare
Science: Science Exhibits & Fairs
Social Services: Animal Protection, Big Brother/Big Sister, Child Welfare, Community Centers, Community Service Organizations, Day Care, Delinquency & Criminal Rehabilitation, Emergency Relief, Food/Clothing Distribution, Homes, People with Disabilities, Recreation & Athletics, Scouts, Senior Services, Shelters/Homelessness, Special Olympics, Substance Abuse, United Funds/United Ways, YMCA/YWCA/YMHA/YWHA, Youth Organizations

Contributions Analysis

Giving Priorities: Social services, with emphasis on local united funds; colleges and universities, with emphasis on nutrition and food-related education; and local arts organizations.
Arts & Humanities: 4%. Supports a broad spectrum of disciplines in operating locations.
Civic & Public Affairs: 12%. Funds community revitalization projects, parks, and employment projects.
Education: 11%. Interests include colleges and universities, with emphasis on nutrition and food-related education. Minority and independent college funds also supported.
Social Services: (United Funds & United Way) 73%. Most of this supports local united funds. Other interests include substance abuse programs, youth organizations, human services, food and clothing distribution, and crime prevention.
Note: Kroger targets its giving program to domesticproblems related to food and pharmaceuticals by donating products to emergency community services, food banks, soup kitchens, and shelters for the homeless; drug abuse prevention and education programs; and nutrition consumer education.

Application Procedures

Initial Contact: brief letter or proposal
Application Requirements: a description of organization, statement of goals and objectives, amount requested, purpose of funds sought, recently audited financial statement, proof of tax-exempt status, list of board of trustees
Deadlines: None.
Review Process: requests are reviewed by foundation trustees on a weekly basis
Evaluative Criteria: ability to address an identified need in the community; clearly defined goals and objectives; strong base of community support
Decision Notification: decisions usually made within one to two weeks

Restrictions

The foundation does not assist religious institutions or organizations for sectarian purposes; individuals; endowment campaigns; or program or journal advertisements.

Additional Information

Certain national and regional groups are supported, but an important part of evaluating grant requests is the extent to which agency provides services to areas where the company operates.
The foundation was created in 1987.

Foundation Officials

Lynn Marmer: president
Lawrence Turner: vice president, secretary

Grants Analysis

Disclosure Period: calendar year ending 1998
Total Grants: $1,544,482*
Number of Grants: 390 (approx)

Average Grant: $3,960
Highest Grant: $99,000
Typical Range: $500 to $5,000
***Note:** Giving excludes United Way.

Recent Grants

Note: Grants derived from 1998 Form 990.

Arts & Humanities

10,000 Lawrence Arts Center, Lawrence, KS -- General Support

Civic & Public Affairs

55,000 Habitat for Humanity - International, Indianapolis, IN -- Funds for Building Indianapolis Oprah House
20,000 The Denver Foundation, Denver, CO -- General Support

Education

12,000 Future Farmers of America, Madison, WI -- 1st yr. of 3yr. pledge
10,000 Ohio State University - Dept. Of Food Science, Columbus, OH -- Third installment on 4yr. $40,000 pledge
10,000 Tougaloo College, Tougaloo, MS -- Sponsor Kroger Athletics & Assembly Center

Health

50,000 March of Dimes - Dallas, Dallas, TX -- 1998 WalkAmerica Sponsorship
15,000 International Children's Heart Foundation, Memphis, TN -- Home for Re-hab of Children recovering from surgery
15,000 Muscular Dystrophy Association, Roanoke, VA -- Fund Raising Event Support
10,000 Roanoke Valley Juvenile Diabetes Foundation, Roanoke, VA -- Sponsorship of 1998 Walk to Cure Diabetes
10,000 St. Mary's Hospital Development Fund, Grand Junction, CO -- Final Installment of 5yr. $50,000 pledge

Religion

10,000 St. Clare of Assisi Parish Building Fund, Edwards, CO -- Building Costs for Family Learning Center

Social Services

199,000 United Way - Greater Cincinnati, Cincinnati, OH
199,000 United Way - Greater Cincinnati, Cincinnati, OH
55,000 United Way - Franklin County, Columbus, OH
39,700 United Way - Indianapolis, Indianapolis, IN
30,000 United Way - Atlanta, Atlanta, GA
30,000 United Way - Montgomery, Greene & Preble Counties, Dayton, OH
23,500 United Way - Metro Dallas, Dallas, TX
23,500 United Way - Metro Dallas, Dallas, TX
22,000 United Way - Gulf Coast, Houston, TX
20,000 Memphis Redbirds, Memphis, TN -- Sponsor Youth Baseball in the Inner City
19,125 United Way - Louisville, Louisville, KY
19,125 United Way - Metro, Louisville, KY
19,125 United Way - Metro Louisville, Louisville, KY
19,125 United Way - Metro - Louisville, Louisville, KY
18,500 United Way - Nacogdoches, Nacogdoches, TX
15,000 United Way - Coastal Empire, Savannah, GA
15,000 United Way - Rapid City, Rapid City, SD
15,000 United Way - Reno County, Hutchinson, KS
12,500 Hannah Neil, Columbus, OH -- World of Children Award Sponsor
12,500 United Way, Peoria, IL
12,500 United Way - Mile High, Denver, CO
12,500 United Way - Mile High, Denver, CO
12,500 United Way - Mile High, Denver, CO
12,500 University of CO School of Pharmacy, Denver, CO -- General Support
12,100 United Way of the Ozarks, Springfield, MO
12,050 United Way - Tarrant County, Fort Worth, TX
12,000 University of Colorado School of Pharmacy, Denver, CO -- Funds for Scholarships
11,000 United Way - Greater Cincinnati, Cincinnati, OH -- Community Chest Campaign
10,742 United Way - Mile High, Denver, CO
10,000 FreeStore/FoodBank, Cincinnati, OH -- Rubber Duck Regatta Support
10,000 Memphis Food Bank, Memphis, TN -- Feed the Hungry Program Support
10,000 S A.Y. Soccer USA, Cincinnati, OH
10,000 United Way - Bradley County, Cleveland, TN
10,000 United Way - Greater Tucson, Tucson, AZ
10,000 United Way - Plains, Wichita, KS
1,535 United Way - Upper Ohio Valley, Columbus, OH
600 United Way - The Virginias, Bluefield, WV

LA-Z-BOY INC.

Company Contact

1284 North Telegraph Rd.
Monroe, MI 48162-3390
Web: http://www.lazyboy.com

Company Description

Former Name: La-Z-Boy Chair Co.
Employees: 12,155
SIC(s): 2512 Upholstered Household Furniture, 2514 Metal Household Furniture, 2521 Wood Office Furniture, 2522 Office Furniture Except Wood.

La-Z-Boy Foundation

Giving Contact

Donald E. Blohm, Administrator
La-Z-Boy Foundation
Phone: (734)242-1444
Fax: (734)457-2005
Note: Mr. Blohm's extension is 3680.

Description

Founded: 1953
EIN: 386087673
Organization Type: Corporate Foundation
Giving Locations: AK: Siloam Springs; CA: Redlands; MI: Monroe; MS: Leland, Newton; MO: Neosho; NC: Lincolnton; SC: Florence; TN: Dayton; UT: Tremonton operating locations.
Grant Types: General Support.

Giving Philosophy

'The purpose of the Foundation is to receive and administer funds for charitable purposes with emphasis on United Ways, health and human service agencies, education, and governmental units solely for public purposes.' *1998 Annual Report*

Financial Summary

Total Giving: $1,050,000 (2000 approx); $1,046,000 (1999); $922,250 (1998). Note: Contributes through foundation only.
Giving Analysis: Giving for 1998 includes: foundation ($922,250)
Assets: $20,402,000 (1998); $18,933,000 (1997); $14,894,583 (1996)

Typical Recipients

Arts & Humanities: Arts Associations & Councils, Arts Centers, Community Arts, Historic Preservation, History & Archaeology, Libraries, Museums/Galleries, Music, Public Broadcasting, Theater
Civic & Public Affairs: Business/Free Enterprise, Community Foundations, Economic Development, Housing, Municipalities/Towns, Safety, Women's Affairs
Education: Colleges & Universities, Community & Junior Colleges, Education Funds, Elementary Education (Public), Education-General, Public Education (Precollege), Religious Education, Secondary Education (Public), Special Education
Health: Clinics/Medical Centers, Diabetes, Emergency/Ambulance Services, Hospices, Hospitals, Single-Disease Health Associations
Religion: Churches, Ministries, Religious Welfare
Social Services: Animal Protection, At-Risk Youth, Community Centers, Community Service Organizations, Crime Prevention, Family Services, Senior Services, United Funds/United Ways, Veterans, YMCA/YWCA/YMHA/YWHA, Youth Organizations

Contributions Analysis

Giving Priorities: United funds, youth groups, municipalities and local fire departments, colleges and universities, hospitals and single-disease health organizations, Lutheran churches, cultural centers and historical societies.
Arts & Humanities: 5%.
Education: 20%.
Health: 15%. Major grants benefit hospitals and the American Red Cross.
Religion: 7%. Primarily provides support to churches.
Social Services: 53%. United funds, YMCA's, and youth groups receive majority of funding. Also supported are community centers.

Application Procedures

Initial Contact: Brief letter or proposal.
Application Requirements: Include a description of organization, amount requested, purpose of funds sought, recently audited financial statement, the organization's budget, and list of directors, proof of 501(c)(3) tax-exempt status, how and by whom program is to be carried out, time span and estimated costs, and benefits of the project to the community.
Deadlines: February 15, May 15, August 15, November 15; board of trustees meets quarterly in March, June, September, and December.
Notes: Personal interviews are arranged upon the foundation's initiative only. Sufficient funding must be assured for successful completion of the project.

Restrictions

Foundation does not make direct grants to individuals; does not make loans; does not fund travel or conferences; and does not provide startup funds or seed money. The geographic areas for grant consideration are normally limited to the communities where La-Z-Boy Inc. production plants are located, and within a fifteen mile radius of corporate headquarters.

Corporate Officials

David K. Hehl: director B 1947. ED Michigan State University BA. PRIM CORP EMPL partner: Cooley, Hehl, Wohlgamuth & Carlton. CORP AFFIL director: La-Z-Boy Chair Co.; director: La-Z-Boy Inc.
Frederick H. Jackson: executive vice president finance, director B Cleveland, OH 1930. ED Bowling Green State University (1951); Case Western Reserve University (1960). PRIM CORP EMPL executive vice president finance, director: La-Z-Boy Inc.
James W. Johnston: director
Gerald L. Kiser: president, chief operating officer, director ED Western Carolina University BBA (1969).

PRIM CORP EMPL president, chief operating officer, director: La-Z-Boy Inc.
Dr. H. George Levy: director PRIM CORP EMPL director: La-Z-Boy Inc.
Patrick H. Norton: chairman, director B 1923. PRIM CORP EMPL chairman, director: La-Z-Boy Inc. CORP AFFIL director: Culp Inc.; director: England/Corsair Inc.
Lorne G. Stevens: director
John F. Weaver: director PRIM CORP EMPL vice chairman: Monroe Bank & Trust Co.

Foundation Officials

Donald E. Blohm: administrator
Gene M. Hardy: director B Selma, AL 1937. ED University of Alabama (1959). PRIM CORP EMPL secretary, treasurer, director: La-Z-Boy Inc. NONPR AFFIL member: Financial Executives Institute.

Grants Analysis

Disclosure Period: calendar year ending 1998
Total Grants: $922,250
Number of Grants: 189
Average Grant: $4,880
Highest Grant: $50,000
Typical Range: $250 to $5,000
Note: Grants analysis was provided by the foundation.

Recent Grants

Note: Grants derived from 1996 Form 990.

Arts & Humanities

35,000 Monroe County Historical Society, Monroe, MI -- humanities, arts, cultural
25,000 Monroe High School, Monroe, MI -- educational, libraries
15,000 River Raisin Centre Arts -- humanities, arts, cultural
10,000 Concordia College, Moorhead, MN -- educational, libraries
10,000 Mississippi State University, Jackson, MS -- educational, libraries
10,000 St. Mary Catholic Central High -- educational, libraries
9,000 Rhea County Department of Education -- educational, libraries
7,000 Tennessee Valley Theater, Spring City, TN -- humanities, arts, cultural
5,500 Monroe Public Cable Television, Monroe, MI -- humanities, arts, cultural
5,000 Bedford Community Foundation -- educational, libraries
5,000 High Point University, High Point, NC -- educational, libraries
5,000 Leland Public Library -- educational, libraries
5,000 Monroe County Community College, Monroe, MI -- educational, libraries
5,000 Newton Municipal School District -- education, libraries
5,000 Public Broadcasting Foundation -- educational, libraries
4,900 Riverside Elementary School, Coral Springs, FL -- educational, libraries

Civic & Public Affairs

14,000 Lincoln County, Crouse Fire Department -- human services
10,000 Monroe County Independent Development Company, Monroe, MI -- public benefit
10,000 Town of Decatur Fire Department, Decatur, GA -- human services
7,500 Community Foundation, Monroe, MI -- public benefit
5,000 Habitat for Humanity, Louisville, KY -- human services
5,000 Habitat for Humanity Monroe County, Monroe, MI -- human services

Health

40,000 Mercy Memorial Hospital Foundation, Monroe, MI
15,000 American Red Cross, Monroe, MI -- human service
10,000 Hospice, Monroe, MI -- health care
10,000 Rhea County Hospital
5,000 St. Vincent Medical Center Foundation

Religion

20,000 Trinity Lutheran Church
10,000 Grace Lutheran Church, Stratford, CT
10,000 Holy Ghost Lutheran Church
10,000 Zion Lutheran Church, Minneapolis, MN
5,000 Catholic Social Services -- human services
5,000 Salvation Army, Monroe, MI -- human services

Social Services

40,000 United Way Monroe County, Monroe, MI -- human services
30,200 Neosho United Fund -- public benefit
25,000 Monroe Family YMCA, Monroe, MI -- human services
20,200 Newton United Givers Fund -- public benefit
20,000 Southwest Family YMCA -- human services
15,000 Caldwell County United Way, Lenoir, NC -- public benefit
15,000 Rhea County United Way, Dayton, TN -- human services
10,000 Monroe County Sheriff's Department, Monroe, MI -- human services
6,500 Tremonton City Corp -- public benefit
5,000 A. Lesow Community Center -- human services
5,000 Boysville of Michigan, Clinton, MI -- human services
5,000 Humane Society, Monroe, MI -- environmental, zoos
5,000 Lincoln County United Way -- human services
5,000 Town of Decatur, Decatur, GA -- human services
5,000 United Way, Monroe, MI -- public benefit
5,000 United Way Washington County, Washington, PA -- human services
5,000 Vets, Southeast Michigan Service Center -- human services

LACLEDE GAS CO.

Company Contact

St. Louis, MO
Web: http://www.lacledegas.com

Company Description

Employees: 2,040 (1999)
SIC(s): 4924 Natural Gas Distribution.

Nonmonetary Support

Value: $2,000 (1999); $60,000 (1988); $50,000 (1987)
Type: Donated Equipment; Donated Products

Corporate Sponsorship

Type: Sports events; Arts & cultural events; Festivals/fairs
Note: Sponsors the Salvation Army.

Laclede Gas Charitable Trust

Giving Contact

Mary C. Kullman, Secretary, Charitable Contributions
Laclede Gas Charitable Trust
720 Olive Street, Room 1527
St. Louis, MO 63101
Phone: (314)342-0531
Fax: (314)421-1979

Description

EIN: 436068197
Organization Type: Corporate Foundation. Supports preselected organizations only.
Giving Locations: MO: St. Louis area
Grant Types: Award, Capital, Employee Matching Gifts, General Support, Matching, Multiyear/Continuing Support.
Note: Capital grants are now provided only by company.

Financial Summary

Total Giving: $1,000,000 (fiscal year ending September 30, 2000 approx); $975,000 (fiscal 1999 approx); $980,000 (fiscal 1998 approx). Note: Contributes through corporate direct giving program and foundation.
Giving Analysis: Giving for fiscal 1996 includes: corporate direct giving ($548,570); foundation ($364,500); foundation matching gifts ($53,703); fiscal 1998: corporate direct giving (approx $583,234); foundation grants to United Way ($297,000); foundation ($78,775); foundation matching gifts ($20,991); fiscal 1999: corporate direct giving (approx $575,000); foundation (approx $400,000)
Assets: $6,000,000 (fiscal 1999 approx); $6,174,421 (fiscal 1998); $6,200,284 (fiscal 1996)
Gifts Received: $517,000 (fiscal 1996). Note: The foundation receives donations from Laclede Gas Co.

Typical Recipients

Arts & Humanities: Arts Associations & Councils, Dance, Historic Preservation, Museums/Galleries, Music, Opera, Performing Arts
Civic & Public Affairs: Economic Development, Public Policy, Urban & Community Affairs, Zoos/Aquariums
Education: Business Education, Colleges & Universities, Economic Education, Private Education (Precollege), Student Aid, Vocational & Technical Education
Health: Children's Health/Hospitals, Hospitals, Mental Health
Religion: Jewish Causes, Seminaries
Science: Observatories & Planetariums
Social Services: Animal Protection, Child Welfare, Community Service Organizations, Counseling, People with Disabilities, Scouts, United Funds/United Ways, Youth Organizations

Contributions Analysis

Giving Priorities: Social service, with major support to United Way; colleges and universities; arts organizations; and some to hospitals and pediatric health organizations.
Arts & Humanities: 15%. Arts and Education Council of St. Louis, MO, and the St. Louis Symphony.
Education: 5%. Supports schools and education prgs.
Health: 2%. Funds a hospital.
Religion: 2%. Supports religious schools.
Social Services: 77%. United Way of St. Louis.
Note: Total contributions in fiscal 1998.

Restrictions

The trust does not support individuals, churches or sectarian organizations, political organizations, fraternal or veterans groups, dinners or special events, or goodwill advertising.

Corporate Officials

John Moten, Junior: vice president community relations B Saint Louis, MO 1941. ED Morehouse College BS (1962). PRIM CORP EMPL vice president community relations: Laclede Gas Co. CORP AFFIL director: Saint Louis Board Election Commission; director: Arts Education Council; director: College Fund Advisory. NONPR AFFIL member: Saint Louis Roundtable; director: Salvation Army Advisory; member: Association Energy Engineers; member: Civic Progress Dialogue; member: American Chemical Society.

Foundation Officials

Robert Christian Jaudes: chairman, trustee (see above)
Ronald L. Krutzman: treasurer PRIM CORP EMPL treasurer: Laclede Gas Co.
Mary C. Kullman: secretary, trustee
Jerald T. McNeive: trustee
Douglas H. Yaeger: chairman, trustee PRIM CORP EMPL executive vice president: Laclede Gas Co. CORP AFFIL vice president, director: Laclede Pipeline Co.; vice president, director: Laclede Venture Corp.; director: Laclede Investment Corp.; vice president, director: Laclede Energy Resources Inc.; director: Laclede Gas Family Service Inc.; director: Laclede Development Co.

Grants Analysis

Disclosure Period: fiscal year ending September 30, 1998
Total Grants: $78,775*
Number of Grants: 7
Average Grant: $11,254
Highest Grant: $35,000
Typical Range: $5000 to $25,000
***Note:** Giving excludes United Way, matching gifts, and corporate direct giving.

Recent Grants

Note: Grants derived from fiscal 1998 Form 990.

Arts & Humanities

40,000	St. Louis Symphony, St. Louis, MO -- operating expenses
35,000	St. Louis Symphony, St. Louis, MO -- operating expenses
25,000	Arts & Education Council, St. Louis, MO -- operating
25,000	Arts & Education Council, St. Louis, MO -- operating expenses

Education

2,000	Bradley University, Peoria, IL -- matching gift program
2,000	Christ Community Lutheran School, St. Louis, MO -- matching gift program
1,000	Christendom College, Front Royal, VA -- matching gift program
1,000	Holy Cross Lutheran School, St. Louis, MO -- matching gift program
900	Central Methodist College, Fayette, MO -- matching gift program
500	Brehm Prepatory School, Carbondale, IL -- matching gift program
500	DePauw University, Greencastle, IN -- matching gift program
356	Duschesne High School, St. Charles, MO -- matching gift program
320	Academy of the Sacred Heart, St. Charles, MO -- matching gift program
150	Bishop DuBourg High School, St. Louis, MO -- matching gift program
150	Chaminade College Prepatory, St. Louis, MO -- matching gift program
75	Fontbonne College, St. Louis, MO -- matching gift program
50	Harvard Business School, Cambridge, MA -- matching gift program
40	College of the Ozarks, Point Lookout, MO -- matching gift program
25	Cor Jesu Academy, St. Louis, MO -- matching gift program
25	Culver-Stockton College, Canton, MO -- matching gift program

Health

5,000	Barnes-Jewish Hospital Foundation, St. Louis, MO -- operating expenses

Religion

6,000	Jewish Federation, St. Louis, MO -- operating expenses
6,000	Jewish Federation, St. Louis, MO -- operating expenses
100	Concordia Seminary, St. Louis, MO -- matching gift program

Social Services

309,000	United Way, St. Louis, MO -- operating expenses
297,000	United Way, St. Louis, MO -- operating expenses
6,000	Boy Scouts, St. Louis, MO -- operating expenses
5,775	Boy Scouts of America, St. Louis, MO -- operating expenses
1,000	Hope House, St. Louis, MO -- operating expenses
1,000	Paraquad, St. Louis, MO -- operating expenses

LADISH CO., INC.

Company Contact

Cudahy, WI
Web: http://www.ladishco.com

Company Description

Employees: 1,800
SIC(s): 3462 Iron & Steel Forgings, 3463 Nonferrous Forgings, 3494 Valves & Pipe Fittings Nec.

Corporate Sponsorship

Contact: Wayne Larson, trustee

Ladish Co. Foundation

Giving Contact

Jim Miller, Trustee
Ladish Co. Foundation
5481 South Packard Avenue
Cudahy, WI 53110
Phone: (414)747-2863
Fax: (414)747-2915
Email: wlarson@ladishco.com

Description

EIN: 396040489
Organization Type: Corporate Foundation. Supports preselected organizations only.
Giving Locations: WI: Cudahy, Milwaukee
Grant Types: General Support.

Financial Summary

Total Giving: $1,000,000 (fiscal year ending November 30, 2000 approx); $1,000,000 (fiscal 1999 approx); $1,000,000 (fiscal 1998 approx). Note: Contributes through foundation only.
Assets: $24,976,185 (fiscal 1997 approx); $18,539,684 (fiscal 1996); $13,564,286 (fiscal 1994)

Typical Recipients

Arts & Humanities: Arts Funds, Libraries, Museums/Galleries, Performing Arts, Public Broadcasting
Civic & Public Affairs: Business/Free Enterprise, Hispanic Affairs, Housing, Professional & Trade Associations, Public Policy, Zoos/Aquariums
Education: Business Education, Business-School Partnerships, Colleges & Universities, Education Associations, Education Funds, Engineering/Technological Education, Education-General, Literacy, Private Education (Precollege), Science/Mathematics Education, Secondary Education (Public), Special Education, Student Aid, Vocational & Technical Education
Health: Alzheimers Disease, Arthritis, Cancer, Children's Health/Hospitals, Clinics/Medical Centers, Emergency/Ambulance Services, Eyes/Blindness, Health Organizations, Heart, Heart, Hospitals, Medical Research, Multiple Sclerosis, Nursing Services, Prenatal Health Issues, Respiratory, Single-Disease Health Associations, Speech & Hearing, Transplant Networks/Donor Banks
Religion: Religious Welfare
Social Services: Animal Protection, Child Welfare, Community Service Organizations, Day Care, Family Services, Food/Clothing Distribution, Homes, People with Disabilities, Recreation & Athletics, Senior Services, Shelters/Homelessness, Special Olympics, United Funds/United Ways, Volunteer Services, YMCA/YWCA/YMHA/YWHA, Youth Organizations

Contributions Analysis

Education: 25% to 30%. Majority of funding supports the Wisconsin Foundation of Independent Colleges and the Michigan Tech Fund. The remainder funds colleges, universities, and secondary schools in Wisconsin.
Health: 15% to 20%. Hospitals and health-care foundations in Milwaukee,WI, and organizations for blindness and disease prevention.
Social Services: 30% to 35%. Primarily supports the United Way of Milwaukee, WI. Also supports youth organizations, food distribution, child welfare, the disabled, and community service organizations.

Foundation Officials

John Ladish: trustee B Milwaukee, WI 1924. ED University of Wisconsin (1948). CORP AFFIL president, chief executive officer: Ladish Malting Co. NONPR AFFIL director: Columbia Health System Inc.
Wayne E. Larson: trustee B Indianapolis, IN 1954. ED Marquette University (1977); Marquette University Law School (1980). PRIM CORP EMPL vice president: Ladish Co., Inc. CORP AFFIL secretary, general couns: Landing Holdings Inc. NONPR AFFIL member: American Bar Association; member: American Corporate Counsel Association.
Ronald O. Wiese: trustee B 1934. PRIM CORP EMPL treasurer: Ladish Co., Inc.

Grants Analysis

Disclosure Period: fiscal year ending November 30, 1997
Total Grants: $753,105
Number of Grants: 128 (approx)
Average Grant: $5,884
Highest Grant: $70,000 (approx)
Typical Range: $2,000 to $12,000

Recent Grants

Note: Grants derived from fiscal 1998 Form 990.

Arts & Humanities

15,000	Milwaukee Public Museum, Friends of, Milwaukee, WI -- General Support
10,000	United Performing Arts Fund, Inc., Milwaukee, WI -- General Support

Civic & Public Affairs

25,000	Zoological Society of Milwaukee County -- Educational Programs
7,000	Next Door Foundation, Inc., Milwaukee, WI -- General Support
5,730	Wisconsin Taxpayers Alliance, Madison, WI -- General Support
5,000	Neighborhood House, Milwaukee, WI -- General Support

Education

150,000 Wisconsin Foundation of Independent Colleges, Inc., Milwaukee, WI -- Scholarships

21,000 Wisconsin Foundation of Independent Colleges, Inc., Milwaukee, WI -- General Support - "21 Club"

20,000 Cudahy High School, Cudahy, WI -- Scholarships

20,000 Milwaukee School of Engineering, Milwaukee, WI -- Scholarships

14,000 Marquette University, Milwaukee, WI -- Scholarships

12,000 Michigan Tech Fund, Houghton, MI -- Engineering Scholarships

10,000 Forging Industry Educational & Research Foundation, Cleveland, OH -- General Support

10,000 Wisconsin Lake Schooner Education Association, Inc., Milwaukee, WI -- General Support

8,000 Junior Achievement, Milwaukee, WI -- General Support

7,500 Pave - Partners Advancing Values in Education, Milwaukee, WI -- Scholarship Program

7,200 WMC Foundation, Madison, WI -- Business World Tuition

6,000 St. Coletta School, Jefferson, WI -- General Support

5,000 Ripon College, Ripon, WI -- Scholarships

Health

15,000 Center for Blind & Visually Impaired Children, Inc., Milwaukee, WI -- Training & Education for blind infants & preschool children

14,000 Children's Hospital of Wisconsin, Milwaukee, WI -- General Support

12,000 Penfield Children's Center, Milwaukee, WI -- Rehabilitation of Disabled Children

10,000 Center for Deaf - Blind Persons Inc, Milwaukee, WI -- Communication Learning Center

10,000 St. Luke's Medical Center/Aurora Foundation, Milwaukee, WI -- General Support

8,000 American Cancer Society, Milwaukee, WI -- Research & Education

8,000 Arthritis Foundation, Milwaukee, WI -- Education & Patient Services

8,000 Midwest Athletes Against Childhood Cancer, Milwaukee, WI -- Research for Childhood Cancer

8,000 National Multiple Sclerosis Society, Wis Chapter, Milwaukee, WI -- Research & Patient Care

8,000 Shriner's Hospitals for Crippled Children, Milwaukee, WI -- General Support

7,000 American Heart Assn, Milwaukee, WI -- Research & Education

7,000 Cystic Fibrosis Foundation, Wis. Chapter, Milwaukee, WI -- Research & Education

6,000 Easter Seal Society of Milwaukee County, Inc, Wis. -- Therapy, Recreation & Equipment

6,000 Leukemia Society of America, Milwaukee, WI -- Research

6,000 Prevent Blindness-Wisconsin, Inc., Milwaukee, WI -- General Support

6,000 Ronald McDonald House Charities, Wauwatosa, WI -- General Support

6,000 St. Mary's Hospital Foundation, Milwaukee, WI -- General Support

5,500 Muscular Dystrophy Association, Milwaukee, WI -- Patient Care & Public Education

Religion

10,000 Lss De Paul Foundtion, Milwaukee, WI -- Substance Abuse Rehab Program

10,000 St. Francis Foundation, Milwaukee, WI -- Outreach Medical Services for the Needy

10,000 Salvation Army, Milwaukee, WI -- General Support

9,000 Society of St. Vincent De Paul, Milwaukee, WI -- Meals Program

6,000 Sojourner Truth House, Milwaukee, WI -- General Support

Social Services

105,000 YMCA - South Shore Branch, Cudahy, WI -- Capital Campaign

50,000 United Way of Greater Milwaukee Inc., Milwaukee, WI -- General Support

16,000 YMCA - South Shore Branch, Cudahy, WI -- Partner of Youth Program

15,000 Cudahy/st. Francis Little Baseball Assn, Inc., Cudahy, WI -- Facilities Improvements

12,000 Hunger Task Force of Milwaukee, Inc., Milwaukee, WI -- Emergency Food Pantries

12,000 Milwaukee Rescue Mission, Milwaukee, WI -- Care & Support of Needy

10,000 Special Olympics, Greater Milwaukee Area, Mequon, WI -- General Support

6,000 Northcott Neighborhood House, Milwaukee, WI -- Youth Development Programs

LANCASTER LENS, INC.

Company Contact

Columbus, OH
Web: http://www.lancastercolony.com

Company Description

Employees: 4,275
SIC(s): 2000 Food & Kindred Products, 3000 Rubber & Miscellaneous Plastics Products, 3200 Stone, Clay & Glass Products, 3700 Transportation Equipment.

Lancaster Lens Foundation

Giving Contact

Clarence D. Clapham, Secretary
Lancaster Lens Foundation
37 West Broad Street
Columbus, OH 43215
Phone: (614)224-7141
Fax: (614)469-8219

Description

Founded: 1953
EIN: 316023927
Organization Type: Corporate Foundation. Supports preselected organizations only.
Giving Locations: OH
Grant Types: General Support.

Financial Summary

Total Giving: $294,800 (fiscal year ending July 31, 1998); $262,019 (fiscal 1996); $232,700 (fiscal 1995). Note: Contributes through foundation only.
Giving Analysis: Giving for fiscal 1996 includes: foundation grants to United Way ($39,250)
Assets: $8,339,537 (fiscal 1998); $5,373,369 (fiscal 1996); $5,804,487 (fiscal 1995)
Gifts Received: $500 (fiscal 1996); $1,000 (fiscal 1994)

Typical Recipients

Arts & Humanities: Arts Associations & Councils, Ballet, History & Archaeology, Museums/Galleries, Music
Civic & Public Affairs: African American Affairs, Civic & Public Affairs-General, Municipalities/Towns, Philanthropic Organizations, Professional & Trade Associations, Safety, Zoos/Aquariums
Education: Arts/Humanities Education, Business Education, Colleges & Universities, Education Funds, Journalism/Media Education, Minority Education, Private Education (Precollege)
Health: Cancer, Heart, Medical Research, Respiratory, Single-Disease Health Associations
Religion: Churches, Jewish Causes
Social Services: Child Welfare, Community Service Organizations, Crime Prevention, Homes, Recreation & Athletics, Shelters/Homelessness, Substance Abuse, United Funds/United Ways, YMCA/YWCA/YMHA/YWHA, Youth Organizations

Contributions Analysis

Arts & Humanities: 34%. Supports the Ohio Historical Society.
Civic & Public Affairs: 1%. Funds law enforcement.
Education: 45%. Funds higher education in Columbus, OH.
Social Services: 20%. Supports youth activities.
Note: Total contributions in fiscal 1998.

Restrictions

Grants are not made to individuals.

Corporate Officials

Jay Gerlach, Jr.: chairman, president, chief executive officer, chief operating officer, director PRIM CORP EMPL chairman, president, chief executive officer, chief operating officer, director: Lancaster Lens, Inc.

Foundation Officials

Clarence D. Clapham: secretary
Bruce L. Rosa: president PRIM CORP EMPL vice president: Lancaster Colony Corp.
Joseph E. Schmidhammer: treasurer

Grants Analysis

Disclosure Period: fiscal year ending July 31, 1998
Total Grants: $294,800
Number of Grants: 8
Average Grant: $36,250
Highest Grant: $100,800
Typical Range: $10,000 to $50,000

Recent Grants

Note: Grants derived from 1997 Form 990.

Arts & Humanities

63,300 Columbus Museum of Art, Columbus, OH

63,300 Greater Columbus Arts Council, Columbus, OH

58,025 Ohio Historical Society, Columbus, OH

Education

7,500 Students in Free Enterprise, Columbus, OH

2,000 Wellington School, Columbus, OH

Religion

450 Agudas Achim Brotherhood, Columbus, OH

Social Services

2,000 Law Enforcement Foundation, Lancaster, OH

LANCE, INC.

Company Contact

Charlotte, NC

Company Description

Employees: 5,000
SIC(s): 2052 Cookies & Crackers, 2064 Candy & Other Confectionery Products, 2096 Potato Chips & Similar Snacks, 2099 Food Preparations Nec.

Lance Foundation

Giving Contact

Mr. Zean Jamison, Jr., Director
Lance Foundation
PO Box 32368
Charlotte, NC 28232-2368
Phone: (704)554-5529
Fax: (704)556-5636

Description

EIN: 566039487
Organization Type: Corporate Foundation
Giving Locations: NC
Grant Types: General Support.

Financial Summary

Total Giving: $473,000 (fiscal year ending June 30, 1997 approx); $486,665 (fiscal 1996); $519,850 (fiscal 1994). Note: Contributes through corporate direct giving program and foundation. Giving includes foundation.
Assets: $4,876,028 (fiscal 1996); $4,843,243 (fiscal 1994); $5,075,386 (fiscal 1992)
Gifts Received: $166,824 (fiscal 1996); $176,507 (fiscal 1994); $197,302 (fiscal 1992). Note: Contributions were received from Lance, Inc.

Typical Recipients

Arts & Humanities: Arts Associations & Councils, Arts Centers, Museums/Galleries, Music, Performing Arts, Public Broadcasting
Civic & Public Affairs: Clubs, Economic Development, Economic Policy, Civic & Public Affairs-General, Housing, Municipalities/Towns, Nonprofit Management, Philanthropic Organizations, Professional & Trade Associations, Safety, Urban & Community Affairs, Women's Affairs, Zoos/Aquariums
Education: Agricultural Education, Business Education, Colleges & Universities, Community & Junior Colleges, Economic Education, Education Associations, Education Funds, Health & Physical Education, Minority Education, Public Education (Precollege), Religious Education, Secondary Education (Public), Social Sciences Education, Student Aid
Health: Adolescent Health Issues, Cancer, Emergency/Ambulance Services, Health Organizations, Medical Research, Nutrition, Single-Disease Health Associations, Trauma Treatment
International: Health Care/Hospitals, International Relations
Religion: Religious Organizations, Social/Policy Issues
Science: Science Museums
Social Services: Child Welfare, Community Service Organizations, Crime Prevention, Family Planning, Family Services, People with Disabilities, Recreation & Athletics, Scouts, Senior Services, Special Olympics, United Funds/United Ways, YMCA/YWCA/YMHA/YWHA, Youth Organizations

Contributions Analysis

Arts & Humanities: 5% to 10%. Arts associations, museums, public broadcasting, and arts centers are supported.
Civic & Public Affairs: 5% to 10%. Emphasis is on community affairs, housing, women's affairs, trade associations, and safety issues.
Education: 45% to 50%. Colleges and universities, education funds, business, minority, agricultural, economic, and public education receive support.
Health: About 15%. Supports medical research, trauma treatment, emergency services, and single-disease health organizations.
Social Services: 20% to 25%. Majority of funding supports the United Way. Senior services, youth organizations, crime prevention, family services, and community service organizations also receive support.

Application Procedures

Initial Contact: brief letter
Application Requirements: a description of organization and program; amount requested, and purpose of funds sought
Deadlines: None.

Corporate Officials

J. William Disher: chairman, chief executive officer, director B Charlotte, NC 1933. ED Wake Forest University (1959). PRIM CORP EMPL chairman: Lance, Inc. CORP AFFIL director: First Union National Bank Charlotte.
Zean Jamison, Jr.: director human resources B Gastonia, NC 1932. ED Belmont Abbey College (1959). PRIM CORP EMPL director human resources: Lance, Inc. CLUB AFFIL Masons Club.
William B. Meacham: vice president acquisitions & subsidiaries, director B 1943. ED Kings Business College (1964). PRIM CORP EMPL vice president acquisitions & subsidiaries, director: Lance, Inc.
John S. Moore: vice president, director PRIM CORP EMPL vice president, director: Lance, Inc.
Paul A. Stroup, III: president, chief executive officer, director PRIM CORP EMPL president, chief executive officer, director: Lance, Inc.

Foundation Officials

J. William Disher: director (see above)
Thomas Borland Horack: vice president, director B Durham, NC 1946. ED Atlantic Christian College BS (1969). PRIM CORP EMPL executive vice president finance, director: Lance, Inc.
Zean Jamison, Jr.: director (see above)
William B. Meacham: director (see above)
Albert Frazier Sloan: director B Charlotte, NC 1929. ED Presbyterian College (1955); University of North Carolina (1969). CORP AFFIL director: Bassett Upholstery Division; director: Photo Corp. of America; director: Bassett Tables; director: Bassett Furniture Co.; director: Bassett Furniture Industries Inc.; director: Bassett Bedding.
Paul A. Stroup, III: director (see above)

Grants Analysis

Disclosure Period: fiscal year ending June 30, 1996
Total Grants: $486,665
Typical Range: $1,000 to $15,000

Recent Grants

Note: Grants derived from fiscal 1997 Form 990.

Arts & Humanities

25,000 Arts and Science Council, Charlotte, NC
10,000 WTVI/Channel 42, Charlotte, NC
5,000 Mint Museum of Art, Charlotte, NC
5,000 Museum of York County, Rock Hill, SC
1,000 Spirit Square Arts Center, Charlotte, NC

Civic & Public Affairs

10,000 Foundation for the Carolinas, Charlotte, NC
10,000 North Carolina Zoological Society, Asheboro, NC
7,500 Save the Seed, Charlotte, NC
2,000 North Carolina Center for Nonprofits, Raleigh, NC
2,000 Women's Resource Center, Hickory, NC
1,500 Good Fellows Club, Charlotte, NC

Education

26,000 Independent Colleges and University of South Carolina, Taylors, SC
25,000 Independent College Fund of North Carolina, Raleigh, NC
25,000 Wake Forest University, Winston-Salem, NC
20,000 Central Piedmont Community College, Charlotte, NC
15,000 Junior Achievement, Charlotte, NC
12,500 United Negro College Fund, Fairfax, VA -- Johnson C. Smith University Program
10,500 University of North Carolina Charlotte Athletics Foundation, Charlotte, NC
4,000 Pembroke State University, Pembroke, NC
2,500 North Carolina 4-H Development Fund, Raleigh, NC
2,500 North Carolina Council on Economic Education, Greensboro, NC
1,000 Cumberland College, Williamsburg, KY
1,000 Iowa College Foundation, Des Moines, IA
1,000 North Carolina Agricultural Foundation, Raleigh, NC
1,000 Public School Forum of North Carolina, Raleigh, NC
1,000 Southeastern Community College, Whiteville, NC

Health

10,000 American Red Cross Greater Carolinas Chapter, Charlotte, NC
2,000 Community Health and Nutrition, Charlotte, NC
2,000 Teen Health Connection, Charlotte, NC

International

5,000 Juvenile Diabetes Foundation International, New York, NY

Religion

1,000 National Conference of Christians and Jews, Charlotte, NC
1,000 Society of St. Andrew, Big Island, VA

Science

5,000 Discovery Place, Charlotte, NC

Social Services

100,000 United Way Central Carolina, Charlotte, NC
25,000 YMCA, Charlotte, NC
20,000 Charlotte-Mecklenburg Senior Center, Charlotte, NC
10,000 Boy Scouts of America Mecklenburg County Council, Charlotte, NC
10,000 United Way Dent County, Greenville, IA
10,000 YMCA Blue Ridge Assembly, Black Mountain, NC
9,000 Burlington Young Men's and Young Women's Building Corporation, Burlington, IA
8,000 Burlington-West Burlington Area United Way, Burlington, IA
7,500 AAU Junior Olympic Games, Washington, DC
5,000 Rock Hill Community YMCA, Rock Hill, NC
4,000 YMCA, Charlotte, NC -- community outreach program
2,500 Mecklenburg Council on Adolescent Pregnancy, Charlotte, NC
2,500 North Carolina Special Olympics, Raleigh, NC
2,000 Heroes Program, Rock Hill, SC
2,000 North Carolina Amateur Sports, Research Triangle Park, NC
1,000 Girl Scouts of America Hornet's Nest Council, Charlotte, NC
1,000 Recording for the Blind and Dyslexic, Princeton, NJ

LAND O'LAKES, INC.

Company Contact

Arden Hills, MN
Web: http://www.landolakesinc.com

Company Description

Employees: 5,000
SIC(s): 2021 Creamery Butter, 5143 Dairy Products Except Dried or Canned, 5451 Dairy Products Stores.

Operating Locations

Mexico: Land O'Lakes, Celaya, Culican, Guadalajara, Huimanguillo, Lagos, Los Belenes, Mexico City, Monterrey, Multitec, Tlaxcala; Poland:, Grodzisk; Land O'Lakes, Kozmin; Land O'Lakes, Miescisko, Paslek, Tainan; Lol Agra International S P Zoo, Warsaw

Nonmonetary Support

Value: $450,000 (1998); $375,000 (1994); $250,000 (1993)
Type: Donated Products; Loaned Executives
Note: Food donations are made only through Second Harvest Foodbank Network. Company also participates in Dollars for Doers and Dreamcatchers programs.

Land O'Lakes Foundation

Giving Contact

Bonnie Neuenfeldt, Executive Director
Land O'Lakes Foundation
PO Box 64150
St. Paul, MN 55164-0150
Phone: (651)481-2212
Fax: (651)481-2000
Email: bneve@landolakes.com

Description

EIN: 411864977
Organization Type: Corporate Foundation
Giving Locations: CA; ID; IA; MN; MT; NE; ND; OR; PA; SD; WA; WI
Grant Types: Capital, Employee Matching Gifts, General Support, Matching, Multiyear/Continuing Support.
Note: Employee matching gift ratio: 1 to 1 for gifts to post-secondary education, ranging from $25 to $500 annually.Also offers a cooperative match program (for member cooperatives).

Giving Philosophy

The company's mission statement is: 'Land O'Lakes is an agricultural supply, dairy processing and food marketing cooperative serving 300,000 farmers and ranchers across the North Central and Northwestern regions of the United States. The company demonstrates a commitment to improving and enhancing the quality of life in communities where it has facilities, plants, members and employees through donations of cash, products and services. We encourage and support employee volunteerism. Land O'Lakes provides resources according to its budget, geographically and by focus areas.' *Contribution Program Guidelines, Land O'Lakes, Inc.* The foundation's mission statement is: 'Land O'Lakes Foundation is committed to improving the quality of life in communities where Land O'Lakes, Inc. has members, employees, plants and facilities. Land O'Lakes Foundation proactively helps rural communities prosper and prepare for tomorrow by donating resources that develop and strengthen organizations dedicated to human service, education, and youth, civic and art endeavors.' *Community Grants Program Guidelines*

Financial Summary

Total Giving: $1,000,000 (2000 approx); $1,000,000 (1999 approx); $1,036,530 (1998). Note: 1996 and 1995 Giving includes corporate direct giving.
Giving Analysis: Giving for 1997 includes: corporate direct giving ($889,233); foundation ($640,767)
Assets: $2,900,000 (1998); $2,633,153 (1997); $2,000,000 (1996 approx)
Gifts Received: $982,025 (1997); $2,000,000 (1996). Note: In 1996 and 1997, contributions were received from Land O'Lakes, Inc.

Typical Recipients

Arts & Humanities: Arts Associations & Councils, Arts Centers, Arts Institutes, Community Arts, Ethnic & Folk Arts, Performing Arts, Public Broadcasting, Theater
Civic & Public Affairs: Business/Free Enterprise, Clubs, Economic Policy, Employment/Job Training, Housing, Parades/Festivals, Professional & Trade Associations, Public Policy, Rural Affairs, Safety, Urban & Community Affairs, Zoos/Aquariums
Education: Agricultural Education, Business Education, Colleges & Universities, Continuing Education, Elementary Education (Public), Faculty Development, Minority Education, Private Education (Precollege), Public Education (Precollege), Secondary Education (Public), Student Aid
Environment: Environment-General, Wildlife Protection
Health: Children's Health/Hospitals, Emergency/Ambulance Services, Geriatric Health
International: International Development
Religion: Religious Welfare
Science: Science Museums, Scientific Centers & Institutes
Social Services: Child Welfare, Community Centers, Day Care, Domestic Violence, Family Services, Food/Clothing Distribution, People with Disabilities, Recreation & Athletics, Senior Services, Shelters/Homelessness, Special Olympics, United Funds/United Ways, Volunteer Services, YMCA/YWCA/YMHA/YWHA, Youth Organizations

Contributions Analysis

Giving Priorities: Agricultural inputs & services, dairy & food products. About $10,000 annually goes to the CARE program. Also supports organizations that work to support stewardship of soil and water resources while maintaining a positive balance between the environment, agriculture, and global food needs.
Arts & Humanities: 7%. Supports quality artistic endeavors that enhance the cultural environment in communities with significant numbers of employees or members.
Civic & Public Affairs: 17%. Supports organizations active in addressing and solving community problems, and programs that work toward the preservation and wise use of water and soil resources between the environment, agriculture, and global food needs. Rural and general agricultural programs also receive special consideration.
Education: 16%. Supports programs that reflect the business and membership interests of the company, such as agriculture, business, economic, and cooperative education programs, and programs designed to develop knowledge and leadership skills in rural and minority youth. Matches employee gifts to colleges and universities.
Health: 5%. Rural nursing services and the American Red Cross.
Science: 1%. Supports a science museum.
Social Services: 54%. Primarily supports the United Way and hunger relief organizations.
Note: Total contributions made in 1997.

Application Procedures

Initial Contact: For direct company grants toward programs of local interest, send a brief letter on organization's stationery to facility manager at nearest Land O'Lakes facility; for other corporate grants and for foundation grants, send a completed application form to Community Relations Director.
Application Requirements: Include a copy of the most recent annual report with financial information included, or a brief history and current activities of the organization; a current operating budget and proposed budget; a copy of the organization's tax-exempt ruling, or a description of organization's ownership and/or management.
Deadlines: None; arts grants will be considered at the spring board meeting only.
Review Process: For direct company giving: operating locations are responsible for budgeting contributions strictly benefiting their communities; requests with broad applications are submitted to headquarters; for foundation giving: requests will be reviewed by foundation board for grants of over $5,000, and by the foundation staff for grants of less than $5,000.
Evaluative Criteria: The foundation looks for quality delivery of a needed service; potential benefit to a substantial segment of community; results which are predictable and can be evaluated; broad-based community support; competent, qualified staff and board; fiscal and management capability to carry out program.
Decision Notification: The foundation board meets in May, August, October, and January.

Restrictions

Does not support individuals; national groups (except those related to agriculture); lobbying, political, or religious organizations; veteran, fraternal, or labor organizations; advertising; fund-raising events, dinners, or benefits; scholarships, or private colleges or universities; travel expenses; disease/medical research or treatment; or racing/sports sponsorships.

Additional Information

Because Land O'Lakes is a farmer-owned cooperative, rural- and agriculture-related programs receive special consideration. About 80% of donations are made to rural areas, and 20% to urban communities. Special consideration also is given to organizations in which company employees are involved.
In December 1996, 'Land O'Lakes, Inc., officially created and endowed the Land O'Lakes Foundation..with an initial donation of $2,000,000. The foundation continues Land O'Lakes' well-established corporate giving program and focuses on improving the quality of life in rural America.'
Land O'Lakes dedicates 2% of pre-tax earnings to charitable giving, with 1.5% going to the Foundation and .5% into direct corporate giving.
The company and the foundation continue to focus on the North Central, Northwest and Eastern United States, where most of their operating facilities are located; also on rural areas.
Publications: Community Grants Program Guidelines

Corporate Officials

Robert M. Dever: vice president public affairs
John E. Gherty: president, chief executive officer B New Richmond, WI 1944. ED University of Wisconsin BBA (1965); University of Wisconsin MA (1970); University of Wisconsin JD (1970). PRIM CORP EMPL president, chief executive officer: Land O'Lakes, Inc. CORP AFFIL member executive committee: CF Industries Inc.; director: Recovery Engineering Inc.; director: Alpine Lace Brands Inc.; director: Cenex/Land O Lakes Agronomy Co. NONPR AFFIL member, director: National Council Farmer Coops; director: National Parenting Association; director: Minnesota Business Partnership; member: American Bar Association; director: Graduate Institute Coop Leadership.
Stanley James Zylstra: chairman, director B Hull, IA 1943. ED Northwestern College BA (1965); University of South Dakota MA (1969). PRIM CORP EMPL chairman, director: Land O'Lakes, Inc. CLUB AFFIL Kiwanis Club.

Foundation Officials

Lydia Botham: vice chairman, secretary PRIM CORP EMPL director test kitchens: Land O'Lakes, Inc.
Judy Kahler: director PRIM CORP EMPL human resources & building services supervisor: Land O'Lakes, Inc.

George Koch: director PRIM CORP EMPL director: Land O'Lakes Inc.
Bonnie Neuenfeldt: executive director PRIM CORP EMPL director community relations: Land O'Lakes, Inc.
Larry Wojchik: chairman PRIM NONPR EMPL general manager: Equity Cooperative of Amery Lake Wisconsin. CORP AFFIL director: Land O'Lakes Inc.

Grants Analysis

Disclosure Period: calendar year ending 1998
Total Grants: $1,036,530
Average Grant: $3,750
Typical Range: $500 to $5,000
Note: Grants analysis provided by the company.

Recent Grants

Note: Grants derived from 1997 Form 990.

Arts & Humanities

10,000 Regional Public Television Stations, Vadnais Heights, MN -- general operating support
5,000 South Dakota Humanities Foundation, Brookings, SD -- establish endowment for Native American culture program
3,500 Minneapolis Institute of Arts, Minneapolis, MN -- general operating support
2,500 North Valley Arts Council, Grand Forks, ND

Civic & Public Affairs

10,000 Holstein Foundation, Brattleboro, VT -- Young Dairy Leaders Institute
10,000 Homestead Housing Center, Inver Grove Heights, MN -- general operating support
7,500 Spencer Area Fire Department and Ambulance Service, Spencer, WI -- replace ambulance
5,000 American Farm Bureau Foundation for Agriculture, Park Ridge, IL -- World Congress of Young Farmers
5,000 Impact Seven, Alameda, WI -- rural LISC program
5,000 Leadership Idaho Agriculture Foundation, Meridian, ID -- Washington, DC Experience
5,000 Opportunity Development Center, Marshfield, WI -- capital campaign to construct new facility
4,500 Management Assistance Project, St. Paul, MN -- general operating support

Education

10,000 Iowa State University, Fort Dodge, IA -- to purchase equipment
10,000 Resource Center of the Americas, Minneapolis, MN -- training workshops for educators
7,500 Imperial Grade School Foundation, Imperial, NE -- TASEL project
5,000 Minnesota 4-H Foundation, St. Paul, MN
5,000 University of Iowa, Iowa City, IA -- exhibition
5,000 University of Minnesota, Minneapolis, MN
5,000 Washington Agriculture and Forestry Education Foundation, Spokane, WA -- fellowship seat on leadership program
3,000 Minnesota Agriculture in the Classroom, St. Paul, MN -- general operating support

Health

10,000 Living at Home Block Nurse Program, St. Paul, MN -- rural component of Communications Link to Serve Seniors project
5,000 American Red Cross, Grand Forks, MN -- flood disaster relief efforts
2,000 American Red Cross, Worthington, MN -- youth volunteer programs

International

2,500 World Dairy Expo, Madison, WI -- children's programs
2,500 World Dairy Expo, Madison, WI -- children's programs

Science

2,500 Science Museum, St. Paul, MN -- general operating support

Social Services

41,200 United Way, St. Paul, MN
12,700 United Way, Fort Dodge, IA
12,045 Second Harvest North Central Food Bank, Grand Rapids, MN -- freezers
10,400 United Way, Sioux Falls, SD
10,000 Second Harvest Food Bank, Chicago, IL -- general operating support
7,500 Great Bear Recreation Park, Sioux Falls, SD -- capital campaign
7,500 Sandcastle Family Support Nursery, Walla Walla, WA -- crisis nursery facility lease
6,675 United Way, Ravenna, OH
6,000 Northland Foundation, Duluth, MN -- Helping Hands Summit: Connecting Kids and Community
6,000 YMCA, Minot, SD -- capital campaign
5,000 Food Research and Action Center, Washington, DC -- Building Blocks Project
5,000 United Way, Perham, MN
5,000 YMCA, Beatrice, NE -- two-year capital campaign grant
5,000 YWCA, Fargo, ND -- new community center
4,500 Pine Island United Fund, Pine Island, MN
3,780 United Way, Faribault, MN
3,500 Young Parents Network, Cedar Rapids, IA -- rural outreach program
3,000 Council on Abused Women's Services, Bismarck, ND -- general operating support
3,000 Minnesota Food Bank Network, Arden Hills, MN -- purchase computer upgrades
2,500 Hunger Task Force, Milwaukee, WI -- Transforming Anti-Hunger Leadership project
2,500 Northwest Youth and Family Services, Shoreview, MN -- general operating support
2,500 Project for Pride in Living, Minneapolis, MN -- general operating support
2,500 Roseau Area Senior Citizens Center, Roseau, MN -- construct new facility
2,500 Youth Frontiers, Minneapolis, MN -- general operating support
2,500 YWCA, Des Moines, IA -- general operating support

LandAmerica Financial Services

Company Contact

Richmond, VA
Web: http://www.landam.com

Company Description

Former Name: Lawyers Title Insurance Corp.
SIC(s): 6361 Title Insurance.
Parent Company: LandAmerica Financial Group, Inc.

Nonmonetary Support

Volunteer Programs: Co. encourage its employees to volunteer on a housing project with local colleges.

Corporate Sponsorship

Type: Other
Note: Tend to favor community development corporations that require substantial volunteer labor.

LandAmerica Foundation

Giving Contact

W. Riker Purcell, Trustee, Vice President and Regulatory Counsel
101 Gateway Center Parkway
Richmond, VA 23235
Phone: (804)267-8330
Fax: (804)282-5453

Alternate Contact

Jean Dickens
Note: matching gifts program

Description

EIN: 546031167
Organization Type: Corporate Foundation. Supports preselected organizations only.
Giving Locations: operating locations.
Grant Types: General Support, Matching.

Financial Summary

Total Giving: $200,000 (1999 approx); $273,630 (1998); $161,658 (1996)
Giving Analysis: Giving for 1998 includes: foundation ($225,040); foundation grants to United Way ($48,590)
Assets: $105,124 (1998); $236,054 (1996); $275,101 (1994)
Gifts Received: $242,269 (1996); $321,242 (1994); $65,727 (1993). Note: In 1996, contributions were received from Lawyers Title Insurance Corp.

Typical Recipients

Arts & Humanities: Historic Preservation
Civic & Public Affairs: African American Affairs, Business/Free Enterprise, Economic Development, Civic & Public Affairs-General, Housing, Municipalities/Towns, Women's Affairs
Education: Business Education, Colleges & Universities, Education Associations, Education Funds, Education-General, Legal Education, Minority Education, Private Education (Precollege), Secondary Education (Private), Student Aid
Health: Cancer, Diabetes, Emergency/Ambulance Services, Heart, Hospitals, Single-Disease Health Associations
International: International Organizations, International Peace & Security Issues, International Relief Efforts
Religion: Ministries, Religious Organizations, Religious Welfare, Synagogues/Temples
Social Services: At-Risk Youth, Community Service Organizations, Food/Clothing Distribution, Shelters/Homelessness, United Funds/United Ways, Youth Organizations

Contributions Analysis

Giving Priorities: Emphasis on higher education, social services, and civic causes.
Arts & Humanities: 1%. Supports public broadcasting and museums.
Civic & Public Affairs: 21%. Funds foundations, women's causes, gay and lesbian support programs, community activities, economic development, and housing.
Education: 45%. Funds private and public colleges, universities, and college educational foundations.
Health: 5%. Supports single-disease associations.
Religion: 3%. Supports churches, religious schools, and religious causes.
Social Services: 25%. Supports United Way, children's programs, and food banks.

Note: Total contributions made in 1998.

Application Procedures

Initial Contact: Request application form.
Deadlines: Meetings are held in April and October.
Notes: Company mostly funds preselected organizations.

Restrictions

Does not support religious organizations for sectarian purposes, individuals, or pol.

Additional Information

Contribution emphasis is on employee matching gifts program. Gifts range from a minimum of $50 to a cumulative maximum of $5,000 per year. Local analysis United Way program is matched by 50%. Retired employees may participate.
Requests for other contributions will be referred to the appropriate senior vice president for consideration as an operating expense.

Corporate Officials

Janet A. Alpert: president, chief operating officer, director B Peoria, IL 1946. ED University of California BA (1968); University of Connecticut MBA (1978). PRIM CORP EMPL president, chief operating officer, director: LandAmerica Financial Services. NONPR AFFIL member: Beta Gamma Sigma.
Charles H. Foster, Jr.: chairman, chief executive officer, director PRIM CORP EMPL chairman, chief executive officer, director: LandAmerica Financial Services.

Foundation Officials

Janet A. Alpert: trustee (see above)
Charles H. Foster, Jr.: trustee (see above)
W. Riker Purcell: trustee, secretary

Grants Analysis

Disclosure Period: calendar year ending 1998
Total Grants: $225,040*
Number of Grants: 503
Average Grant: $447
Highest Grant: $37,500
Typical Range: $100 to $1,000
***Note:** Giving excludes United Way.

Recent Grants

Note: Grants derived from 1996 Form 990.

Arts & Humanities

2,500	Historic Landmarks Foundation of Indiana, Indianapolis, IN

Civic & Public Affairs

5,000	Metropolitan Business Foundation, Richmond, VA
2,000	Richmond Habitat Women's Project, Richmond, VA
1,250	Christmas in April, Richmond, VA
700	Chesterfield County Black History Month Celebration, Chesterfield, VA

Education

4,876	University of Kentucky, Lexington, KY
2,500	Mount St. Mary's College, Emmitsburg, MD
2,500	Schreiner College, Kerrville, TX
2,500	University of Virginia Fund, Charlottesville, VA
2,000	Virginia State University, Parkersburg, VA
1,500	Georgia Student Education Fund, Athens, GA
1,500	St. Clement School, Lakewood, OH
1,500	St. Ignatius High School, Cleveland, OH
1,250	University of Virginia Darden Graduate School of Business, Charlottesville, VA
1,200	Dallas Christian College, Dallas, TX
1,000	Concordia College, Ann Arbor, MI
1,000	Frankenmuth School, Frankenmuth, MI
1,000	Junior Achievement Central Virginia, Richmond, VA
1,000	Marymount Foundation, Richmond, VA
1,000	North Central College, Naperville, IL
1,000	University of California Santa Barbara, Santa Barbara, CA
1,000	University of Connecticut Foundation, Hartford, CT
1,000	University of Georgia Law School, Athens, GA
1,000	Wake Forest University, Winston-Salem, NC
850	Virginia Student Aid Foundation, Charlottesville, VA
850	Virginia Student Aid Foundation, Charlottesville, VA
760	Christian Community School, Johnstown, OH
640	Columbus Academy, Gahanna, OH

Health

5,000	MCV-VCU Hospital Hospitality House, Richmond, VA -- capital campaign
760	Cystic Fibrosis Foundation, Chicago, IL
759	Muscular Dystrophy Association, Richmond, VA
750	American Heart Association Heart Walk, Richmond, VA

Religion

4,541	Sacred Heart Foundation, Cleveland, OH
1,055	United Methodist Senior Services of Mississippi, Tupelo, MS

Social Services

20,400	United Way, Richmond, VA
6,283	United Way El Paso County, El Paso, TX
3,000	AGAPE, Nashville, TN
2,855	United Way, Memphis, TN
2,825	United Way Columbia-Willamette, Portland, OR
1,785	United Way, Houston, TX
1,620	United Way, Memphis, TN
1,156	Army Distaff Foundation, Washington, DC
1,000	Daily Planet, Richmond, VA
1,000	Hill Country Youth Ranch, Ingram, TX
1,000	Meals on Wheels, Richmond, VA
920	United Way Camarillo, Camarillo, CA
888	United Way Erie County, Sandusky, OH
860	United Way, Medford, OR
825	United Way Central Carolinas, Charlotte, NC
756	United Way Tennessee, Nashville, TN

Landmark Communications Inc.

Company Contact

150 W. Brambleton Ave.
Norfolk, VA 23501

Company Description

Employees: 4,150
SIC(s): 2711 Newspapers, 2752 Commercial Printing--Lithographic, 2759 Commercial Printing Nec, 4833 Television Broadcasting Stations.

Nonmonetary Support

Type: Cause-related Marketing & Promotion; In-kind Services

Landmark Communications Foundation

Giving Contact

Linda Hyatt, Executive Director
Landmark Communications Foundation
Phone: (757)446-2011
Fax: (757)446-2489
Email: Lhyatt@Lcimedia.com

Description

EIN: 546038902
Organization Type: Corporate Foundation
Giving Locations: NV: Las Vegas; NC: Greensboro; TN: Nashville; VA: Norfolk, Roanoke
Grant Types: Capital, Conference/Seminar, Emergency, Endowment, Fellowship, Matching, Multiyear/Continuing Support.
Note: Also offers leadership gifts.

Giving Philosophy

'The Landmark Foundation was established in 1953 to help support selected organizations whose projects respond to specific needs within our communities. Primary areas of giving include education, human services, journalism/communications, and the arts.'
Landmark Charitable Foundation

Financial Summary

Total Giving: $2,500,000 (1999 approx); $1,986,850 (1998); $1,737,062 (1997). Note: Contributes through corporate direct giving program and foundation.
Giving Analysis: Giving for 1997 includes: foundation ($1,333,754); foundation grants to United Way ($403,308); 1998: foundation ($1,651,605); foundation grants to United Way ($335,245)
Assets: $51,813,107 (1998); $45,417,609 (1997); $36,668,592 (1996)
Gifts Received: $1,098,514 (1998); $940,000 (1997); $700,000 (1996). Note: Foundation receives contributions from Landmark Communications, Inc., and its subsidiaries.

Typical Recipients

Arts & Humanities: Arts Associations & Councils, Arts Centers, Arts Funds, Ethnic & Folk Arts, History & Archaeology, Museums/Galleries, Music, Opera, Theater
Civic & Public Affairs: African American Affairs, Asian American Affairs, Civic & Public Affairs-General, Housing, Nonprofit Management, Philanthropic Organizations, Professional & Trade Associations, Public Policy, Urban & Community Affairs, Zoos/Aquariums
Education: Business Education, Colleges & Universities, Community & Junior Colleges, Education Funds, Faculty Development, Education-General, Journalism/Media Education, Literacy, Minority Education, Public Education (Precollege), Science/Mathematics Education, Student Aid
Environment: Resource Conservation
Health: Emergency/Ambulance Services, Hospitals, Research/Studies Institutes
Religion: Ministries, Religious Welfare
Science: Science Museums, Scientific Centers & Institutes
Social Services: Child Welfare, Community Service Organizations, Food/Clothing Distribution, Shelters/Homelessness, United Funds/United Ways, YMCA/YWCA/YMHA/YWHA, Youth Organizations

Contributions Analysis

Giving Priorities: Social services, with majority to united funds; museums, arts centers and associations, and festivals; journalism programs at colleges and universities; professional journalism organizations; and some hospital building funds.

Arts & Humanities: 28%. The highest priorities are museums, arts centers and associations. Also supports performing arts, such as music and theater.
Civic & Public Affairs: 4%. Supports a wide variety of interests, including professional organizations (primarily journalistic), environmental projects, leadership programs and other community affairs organizations.
Education: 33%. Most grants support colleges and universities, often funding journalism programs. Business and minority education, literacy, and education funds also receive support.
Social Services: 35%. Majority of funds support the United Way. Other interests include youth organizations, athletic and recreational programs, and community service organizations.
Note: Contributions made in 1998.

Application Procedures

Initial Contact: Send one-page letter to the president of the nearest subsidiary.
Application Requirements: Include a description of organization, amount requested, purpose of funds sought, impact foundation funds would have on the program and community, evidence of other support, program timetable, expected sources of future revenue, program budget, and proof of tax-exempt status.
Deadlines: None.
Review Process: Applications are screened by local company and, if approved, forwarded to the foundation for further screening and possible inclusion in the foundation's annual budget.
Evaluative Criteria: Priority given to projects that reach a broad section of the community; yield substantial benefits to the community for costs involved; promote cooperation among agencies within their fields of interest; project seeks funds for new innovative programs, or to expand an innovative program to other parts of the community; is part of a capital campaign; demonstrates in-kind services; has not received foundation funding for a similar program.

Restrictions

Foundation does not make grants to organizations not tax-exempt under IRS standards, individuals, or any organization that has received a capital pledge from the foundation within the preceding two years. Foundation does not give for religious or political purposes; deficit financing; projects normally the responsibility of a government agency; health care; or medical education or research.

Additional Information

Individual budgets from participating Landmark companies are submitted to corporate headquarters in November each year, where they are reviewed and receive final approval during the month of January.
Capital pledges are made with the provision that a campaign meets its goal and that the project goes forward as proposed.
Programs supportive of the broadcasting and publishing industries on a national scale occasionally receive grants from corporate headquarters. headquarters.
Publications: Foundation Guidelines

Corporate Officials

Richard Francis Barry, III: vice chairman, chief executive officer B Norfolk, VA 1943. ED LaSalle College BA (1964); University of Virginia JD (1967). PRIM CORP EMPL vice chairman: Landmark Communications Inc. CORP AFFIL vice president: Trader Publishing Co. Landmark Television Inc.; director: Weather Channel; director: Times-World Corp.; director: Greensboro Daily News & Record; director: Infinet Co.; director: Capital Gazette Newspapers Inc. NONPR AFFIL director: United Way South Hampton; trustee: University Virginia Colgate Business School Foundation; trustee: Old Dominion University Education Foundation; trustee: Chrysler Museum; trustee: Norfolk Academy; trustee: Catholic High School.
Frank Batten, Junior: executive vice president B 1958. PRIM CORP EMPL executive vice president: Landmark Communications Inc. ADD CORP EMPL president: Commonwealth Printing Co.
Frank Batten, Sr.: chairman B Norfolk, VA 1927. ED University of Virginia AB (1950); Harvard University MBA (1952). PRIM CORP EMPL chairman: Landmark Communications Inc. CORP AFFIL chairman: Weather Channel; chairman: WTVF-Nashville; chairman: Roanoke Times & World-News; chairman: Travel Channel; chairman: KLAS-TV Las Vegas; chairman: Norfolk Virginian-Pilot & Ledger Star; chairman: Greensboro Daily News & Record. NONPR AFFIL trustee: U.S. Naval Academy Foundation; trustee: University Virginia Colgate Business School; member: Sigma Xi; trustee: Southern Newspaper Publishers Association Foundation; member: Newspaper Association America; member: Sigma Delta Chi; member, board visitors: College William & Mary; trustee: Culver Education Foundation.
John Oliver Wynne: president, chief executive officer B Norfolk, VA 1945. ED Princeton University BA (1967); University of Virginia JD (1971). PRIM CORP EMPL president, chief executive officer: Landmark Communications Inc. CORP AFFIL chairman: Weather Channel; chairman: Travel Channel. NONPR AFFIL member, director: National Cable Television Association; trustee: Norfolk Academy. CLUB AFFIL Harbor Club.

Foundation Officials

Richard Francis Barry, III: director (see above)
Frank Batten, Sr.: chairman, director (see above)
Linda S. Hyatt: vice president, executive director
John Oliver Wynne: president, director (see above)

Grants Analysis

Disclosure Period: calendar year ending 1998
Total Grants: $1,651,605*
Number of Grants: 175
Average Grant: $9,438
Highest Grant: $158,000
Typical Range: $1,000 to $10,000
***Note:** Giving excludes United Way.

Recent Grants

Note: Grants derived from 1997 Form 990.

Arts & Humanities

35,122 Business Consortium for Arts Support, Norfolk, VA -- support encouragement of wholesome community life
35,122 Business Consortium for Arts Support, Norfolk, VA -- support encouragement of wholesome community life
25,000 Chrysler Museum, Norfolk, VA -- support encouragement of wholesome community life
25,000 Norfolk Armed Forces Memorial, Norfolk, VA -- support encouragement of wholesome community life
10,000 General Douglas MacArthur Foundation, Norfolk, VA -- support encouragement of wholesome community life
10,000 National D-Day Memorial Foundation, Bedford, VA -- support encouragement of wholesome community life
10,000 Roanoke Symphony Society, Roanoke, VA -- support encouragement of wholesome community life

Civic & Public Affairs

50,000 American Press Institute, Reston, VA -- support encouragement of wholesome community life
30,000 Virginia Zoological Society, Norfolk, VA -- support encouragement of wholesome community life
25,000 CIVIC, Norfolk, VA -- support encouragement of wholesome community life
16,667 Virginia Institute of Political Leadership, Charlottesville, VA -- support encouragement of wholesome community life
10,000 Habitat for Humanity, Greensboro, NC -- support encouragement of wholesome community life
10,000 Nashville Zoo, Nashville, TN -- support encouragement of wholesome community life
10,000 Southeastern Council of Foundations, Atlanta, GA -- support encouragement of wholesome community life

Education

50,000 University of Virginia Darden Graduate Business School, Charlottesville, VA -- support encouragement of wholesome community life, capital campaign
50,000 Virginia Wesleyan College, Norfolk, VA -- support encouragement of wholesome community life, capital campaign
33,000 University of North Carolina School of Journalism and Mass Communications, Chapel Hill, NC -- support encouragement of wholesome community life
25,000 Nashville READ, Nashville, TN -- support encouragement of wholesome community life
25,000 University of North Carolina Greensboro, Greensboro, NC -- support encouragement of wholesome community life
25,000 Virginia Foundation for Independent Colleges, Richmond, VA -- support encouragement of wholesome community life
24,000 Ferrum College, Ferrum, VA -- support encouragement of wholesome community life
20,000 Hollins College, Roanoke, VA -- support encouragement of wholesome community life, capital campaign
16,666 Guilford College, Greensboro, NC -- support encouragement of wholesome community life
16,000 Greensboro Scholastic Achievement Scholars, Greensboro, NC -- support encouragement of wholesome community life
16,000 Nashville READ, Nashville, TN -- support encouragement of wholesome community life
10,000 Fisk University, Nashville, TN -- support encouragement of wholesome community life
10,000 Inroads, Nashville, TN -- support encouragement of wholesome community life
10,000 University of Virginia, Charlottesville, VA -- support encouragement of wholesome community life

Environment

18,900 Chesapeake Bay Foundation, Annapolis, MD -- support encouragement of wholesome community life

Religion

12,500 Rescue Mission, Roanoke, VA -- support encouragement of wholesome community life
10,000 Salvation Army, Greensboro, NC -- support encouragement of wholesome community life

Science

30,000 Virginia Marine Science Museum, Virginia Beach, VA -- support encouragement of wholesome community life, capital campaign

Social Services

152,000 United Way of South Hampton Roads, Norfolk, VA -- support encouragement of wholesome community life
80,000 United Way of South Hampton Roads, Norfolk, VA -- support encouragement of wholesome community life

51,000	United Way of Roanoke Valley, Roanoke, VA -- support encouragement of wholesome community life
44,348	United Way, Greensboro, NC -- support encouragement of wholesome community life
30,000	Southside Boys and Girls Club, Norfolk, VA -- support encouragement of wholesome community life
25,000	Foodbank of Southeastern Virginia, Norfolk, VA -- support encouragement of wholesome community life
25,000	Planning Council, Norfolk, VA -- support encouragement of wholesome community life
25,000	YMCA of Suffolk, Capital Project, Norfolk, VA -- support encouragement of wholesome community life
20,000	United Way of Middle Tennessee, Nashville, TN -- support encouragement of wholesome community life
15,810	United Way of Southern Nevada Service Link, Las Vegas, NV -- support encouragement of wholesome community life
15,000	Kids Voting, Nashville, TN -- support encouragement of wholesome community life
15,000	Kids Voting, Norfolk, VA -- support encouragement of wholesome community life
15,000	Kids Voting, Norfolk, VA -- support encouragement of wholesome community life
15,000	United Way of Southern Nevada Volunteer Center, Las Vegas, NV -- support encouragement of wholesome community life
12,000	United Way of Southern Nevada, Las Vegas, NV -- support encouragement of wholesome community life
10,000	Apple Ridge Farm, Jefferson Center, Roanoke, VA -- support encouragement of wholesome community life
10,000	Kids Voting, Norfolk, VA -- support encouragement of wholesome community life
10,000	Southside Boys and Girls Club, Norfolk, VA -- support encouragement of wholesome community life

LEE APPAREL CO.

Company Contact

Merriam, KS
Web: http://www.leejeans.com

Company Description

Employees: 11,000
SIC(s): 2300 Apparel & Other Textile Products.
Parent Company: VF Corp., Greensboro, NC, United States

Giving Contact

Carol Eubank, Manager, Employee Benefits
PO Box 2940
Shawnee Mission, KS 66201
Phone: (913)384-4000
Fax: (913)384-0190

Description

Organization Type: Corporate Giving Program

Financial Summary

Total Giving: $300,000 (2000 approx); $300,000 (1999 approx); $300,000 (1998 approx). Note: Contributes through corporate direct giving program only.

Application Procedures

Initial Contact: contact co. for guidelines

Corporate Officials

Terry Lay: president, Lee affairs B Greensboro, NC 1942. ED Wake Forest University (1964). PRIM CORP EMPL president, Lee: VF Jeanswear Inc. CORP AFFIL director: United Missouri Bank; president: VF Corp. NONPR AFFIL director: Kids in Distressed Situations; director: Waverly Children's Home.
Jamie Lockard: director community affairs PRIM CORP EMPL director community affairs: Lee Apparel Co.

Grants Analysis

Disclosure Period: calendar year ending

LEE ENTERPRISES

Company Contact

Davenport, IA
Web: http://www.lee.net

Company Description

Employees: 5,300
SIC(s): 2711 Newspapers, 4813 Telephone Communications Except Radiotelephone, 4833 Television Broadcasting Stations.

Lee Foundation

Giving Contact

Russel R. Kennel, Secretary & Director
Lee Foundation
215 North Main Street
Davenport, IA 52801
Phone: (319)383-2102
Fax: (319)326-2972

Description

Founded: 1962
EIN: 426057173
Organization Type: Corporate Foundation
Giving Locations: IL; IA; MT; ND; OR; WI
Grant Types: Capital, Endowment, General Support.

Financial Summary

Total Giving: $450,000 (fiscal year ending September 30, 1998 approx); $413,283 (fiscal 1997); $441,783 (fiscal 1996). Note: Contributes through foundation only.
Assets: $6,742,672 (fiscal 1997); $5,907,309 (fiscal 1996); $5,788,000 (fiscal 1995)
Gifts Received: $500,000 (fiscal 1992); $500,000 (fiscal 1989). Note: Contributions were received from Lee Enterprises, Inc.

Typical Recipients

Arts & Humanities: Arts Centers, Arts & Humanities-General, Historic Preservation, History & Archaeology, Libraries, Literary Arts, Museums/Galleries, Music, Public Broadcasting, Theater, Visual Arts
Civic & Public Affairs: Business/Free Enterprise, Community Foundations, Employment/Job Training, Civic & Public Affairs-General, Law & Justice, Municipalities/Towns, Parades/Festivals, Professional & Trade Associations, Public Policy, Rural Affairs, Urban & Community Affairs, Women's Affairs, Zoos/Aquariums
Education: Afterschool/Enrichment Programs, Business Education, Colleges & Universities, Community & Junior Colleges, Economic Education, Education Funds, Environmental Education, Education-General, International Studies, Journalism/Media Education, Medical Education, Minority Education, Private Education (Precollege), Public Education (Precollege), Science/Mathematics Education, Secondary Education (Public), Social Sciences Education, Vocational & Technical Education
Environment: Environment-General, Resource Conservation, Wildlife Protection
Health: Clinics/Medical Centers, Emergency/Ambulance Services, Geriatric Health, Hospitals, Public Health, Single-Disease Health Associations
International: Human Rights
Religion: Jewish Causes, Religious Welfare
Science: Science Museums
Social Services: Child Welfare, Community Centers, Community Service Organizations, Day Care, Emergency Relief, Family Planning, Family Services, Food/Clothing Distribution, Homes, Recreation & Athletics, Scouts, Senior Services, Special Olympics, United Funds/United Ways, YMCA/YWCA/YMHA/YWHA, Youth Organizations

Contributions Analysis

Arts & Humanities: 17%.
Civic & Public Affairs: 18%.
Education: 39%.
Environment: 1%.
Health: 4%.
Religion: 4%.
Science: 3%.
Social Services: 14%.
Note: Total contributions made in 1997.

Application Procedures

Initial Contact: Send a brief letter of inquiry.
Application Requirements: Include a description of organization and purpose of funds sought.
Deadlines: None.
Notes: The foundation has no formal grant application procedure or application form.

Restrictions

Foundation does not support individuals.

Corporate Officials

Larry L. Bloom: chief financial officer, director B 1949. ED DePaul University BS. PRIM CORP EMPL chief financial officer: Lee Enterprises Inc.
Richard Douglas Gottlieb: president, chief executive officer, director B Davenport, IA 1942. ED University of Arizona BS (1964). PRIM CORP EMPL president, chief executive officer, director: Lee Enterprises Inc. CORP AFFIL director: NAPP Systems Inc.; president: Consumer's Press; director: Madison Newspapers Inc. NONPR AFFIL director: Newspaper Advertising Bureau; treasurer: Newspaper Association America.
Lloyd G. Schermer: chairman, director B Saint Louis, MO 1927. ED Amherst College (1950); Harvard University Graduate School of Business Administration MBA (1952). PRIM CORP EMPL chairman, director: Lee Enterprises Inc. NONPR AFFIL chairman: Smithsonian Institute National Board.

Foundation Officials

Richard Douglas Gottlieb: president, chief executive officer, director (see above)
Russel R. Kennel: secretary, director
Ronald L. Rickman: vice president, director B 1939. PRIM CORP EMPL president newspapers, director: Lee Enterprises Inc.
Gary N. Schmedding: vice president, director
George C. Wahlig: treasurer, director PRIM CORP EMPL officer: Lee Enterprises Inc.

Grants Analysis

Disclosure Period: fiscal year ending September 30, 1997
Total Grants: $413,283
Number of Grants: 53
Average Grant: $7,798
Highest Grant: $40,000
Typical Range: $500 to $30,000

Recent Grants

Note: Grants derived from fiscal 1997 Form 990.

Arts & Humanities

20,000	Frank Lloyd Wright Convention Center, Madison, WI -- capital campaign
10,000	Miracle of America Museum, Polson, MT -- capital campaign
10,000	New Art Center Campaign, Billings, MT -- building fund
10,000	WVIK Radio Foundation, Moline, IL -- endowment fund
5,000	Family Museum of Arts and Sciences Foundation, Bettendorf, IA -- capital campaign
5,000	Lewis and Clark Interpretative Center, Washburn, ND -- capital campaign
3,000	Huntington Museum of Art, Huntington, WV -- capital campaign
3,000	Western Heritage Museum Business Hall of Fame, Omaha, NE -- renovation fund
2,500	Children's Museum of Illinois, Decatur, IL -- capital campaign
1,666	Winona County Historical Society, Winona, MN -- building fund

Civic & Public Affairs

20,000	Dakota Zoo Discovery, Bismarck, ND -- for 2000 Capital Campaign
18,000	Help Your Farm Neighbor, Bismarck, ND -- capital campaign
12,500	Renew Moline, Moline, IL -- capital campaign
10,000	American Women in Radio and Television, McLean, VA -- endowment fund
10,000	Zoo Montana, Billings, MT -- capital campaign
5,000	Bismarck Community Project, Bismarck, ND -- building fund

Education

40,000	St. Ambrose University, Davenport, IA -- building fund
30,000	Eastern Iowa Community College, Davenport, IA -- building fund
25,000	Rocky Mountain College, Billings, MT -- capital campaign
10,000	St. Ambrose College, Davenport, IA -- endowment fund
10,000	University of Wisconsin Foundation, Madison, WI -- endowment fund
5,000	Bettendorf Learning Campus, Bettendorf, IA -- capital campaign
5,000	Marshall University, Huntington, WV -- building fund
5,000	News Management Internship for Minority Students, Washington, DC -- endowment fund
5,000	Southern Illinois University Foundation, Carbondale, IL -- endowment fund
5,000	University of Mary, Bismarck, ND -- building fund
5,000	University of Wisconsin School of Hope, Madison, WI -- endowment fund
2,500	Iowa College Foundation, Des Moines, IA -- endowment fund
2,500	Muscatine High School, Muscatine, IA -- capital campaign
2,500	Self Enhancement, Portland, OR -- capital campaign
1,500	Oregon Independent College Foundation, Portland, OR -- endowment fund
1,000	United Negro College Fund, New York, NY -- endowment fund
1,000	University of Nebraska Foundation, Lincoln, NE -- endowment fund

Environment

5,000	Montana Wildlife Rehabilitation Center, Helena, MT -- building fund

Health

10,000	Community Health Care, Davenport, IA -- capital campaign
3,750	Wapello County Public Health Grant, Ottumwa, IA -- endowment fund
2,500	Genesis Health Services Foundation, Davenport, IA -- capital campaign

Religion

10,000	Salvation Army, Davenport, IA -- building fund
6,333	Wichita Salvation Army, Wichita, KS -- capital campaign

Science

12,500	Exploration Place, Wichita, KS -- capital campaign

Social Services

12,000	Center for Aging Services, Davenport, IA -- endowment fund
10,000	Quad City Sports Center Association, Davenport, IA -- capital campaign
8,334	Florence Children's Home, Helena, MT -- building fund
7,000	We Care Disaster Relief Fund, Bismarck, ND -- capital campaign
5,000	Mother Lode, Butte, MT -- building fund
5,000	Yellowstone Boys and Girls Ranch Foundation, Billings, MT -- building fund
3,200	Huntington YMCA, Huntington, WV -- capital campaign
3,000	Student Hunger Drive, Davenport, IA -- capital campaign
2,500	Special Olympics -- capital campaign
2,500	YMCA's Partner with Youth, Kids to Camp, Davenport, IA -- endowment fund

LEHIGH PORTLAND CEMENT CO.

Company Contact

Allentown, PA

Company Description

Employees: 2,300
SIC(s): 3241 Cement--Hydraulic, 3272 Concrete Products Nec.
Parent Company: Heidelberger Zement A.G., Berliner Strasse 6, Heidelberg, Germany

Operating Locations

AL: Birmingham; CA: Los Angeles; IN: Glastonbury; MN: Minnesota; PA: Lehigh Portland Cement Co., Allentown; VA: Mannassas Norfolk

Giving Contact

Corliss Hirst, communications co-ordinator
7660 Imperial Way
Allentown, PA 18195
Phone: (610)366-4764
Web: http://www.portlandcement.com

Description

Organization Type: Corporate Giving Program
Former Name: Lehigh Portland Cement Co. (1999).
Giving Locations: headquarters and operating communities.
Grant Types: Employee Matching Gifts, General Support, Scholarship.

Financial Summary

Total Giving: $700,000 (1999 approx); $21,176 (1997); $239,485 (1996). Note: The Co.'s corporate office location has a funding budget of approximately $200,000. Each economic base unit, or sales office location, has a funding budget of $50,000 to $100,000.
Giving Analysis: Giving for 1996 includes: foundation matching gifts ($90,000); 1999: corporate direct giving (approx $700,000)
Assets: $1,821 (1998); $737 (1997); $31,807 (1996)
Gifts Received: $225,000 (1995)

Typical Recipients

Arts & Humanities: Arts Funds, Historic Preservation, History & Archaeology, Libraries, Museums/Galleries, Music, Performing Arts, Public Broadcasting, Theater
Civic & Public Affairs: Business/Free Enterprise, Community Foundations, Employment/Job Training, Civic & Public Affairs-General, Municipalities/Towns, Native American Affairs, Professional & Trade Associations, Urban & Community Affairs, Zoos/Aquariums
Education: Business Education, Business-School Partnerships, Colleges & Universities, Community & Junior Colleges, Continuing Education, Economic Education, Education Associations, Education Funds, Elementary Education (Public), Engineering/Technological Education, Education-General, Literacy, Preschool Education, Private Education (Precollege), Public Education (Precollege), Science/Mathematics Education, Secondary Education (Public), Special Education, Student Aid, Vocational & Technical Education
Environment: Environment-General
Health: Cancer, Children's Health/Hospitals, Emergency/Ambulance Services, Health-General, Health Organizations, Heart, Hospices, Hospitals, Prenatal Health Issues, Transplant Networks/Donor Banks
Religion: Churches
Science: Scientific Organizations
Social Services: At-Risk Youth, Camps, Child Welfare, Community Service Organizations, Counseling, Day Care, Domestic Violence, Emergency Relief, Family Services, People with Disabilities, Recreation & Athletics, Scouts, Sexual Abuse, Shelters/Homelessness, Social Services-General, Substance Abuse, United Funds/United Ways, YMCA/YWCA/YMHA/YWHA, Youth Organizations

Contributions Analysis

Giving Priorities: Social service efforts such as food banks, Toys for Tots, and United Way; environmental concerns, including The Wildlife Conservancy; and a scholarship program to promote education.

Application Procedures

Initial Contact: Send a brief letter of inquiry.
Deadlines: None.

Restrictions

Funding is provided to organization's in operating locations only.

Additional Information

The Lehigh Portland Cement Co. Charitable Trust dissolved in 1999.

Corporate Officials

Richard Kline: president B 1941. ED Lafayette College (1961). PRIM CORP EMPL president: Lehigh Portland Cement Co. NONPR AFFIL director: American Portland Cement Association.
Peter Otto: president B Heilbronn, Germany 1938. ED Technology University Aachen (1965); Technology University Aachen (1968). PRIM CORP EMPL president: Heidelberg Cement Inc. CORP AFFIL director: Lehigh Portland Cement Co.

Foundation Officials

Jeffry H. Brozyna: trustee B Schenectady, NY 1952. ED Hubart College (1974); Albany Law School (1977). PRIM CORP EMPL vice president, general counsel: Lehigh Portland Cement Co. CORP AFFIL secretary: Addiment Inc. NONPR AFFIL director: American Portland Cement Alliance.
Helmut Leube: trustee B Salzburg, Austria 1941. ED University of Vienna (1968); University of Vienna

(1969). PRIM CORP EMPL vice president administration & coordination: Lehigh Portland Cement Co. CORP AFFIL vice president: Heidelberg Cement Co.
Linda M. Schulter: trustee PRIM CORP EMPL executive secretary: Lehigh Portland Cement Co.
Frank Ronald Snyder, II: trustee B Minersville, PA 1939. ED Lehigh University (1962); Lehigh University MBA (1970). PRIM CORP EMPL vice president, treasurer, controller: Lehigh Portland Cement Co. CORP AFFIL treasurer: Heidleberg Cement Inc. NONPR AFFIL member: Financial Executives Institute.
Peter B. Tait: trustee PRIM CORP EMPL vice president: Lehigh Portland Cement Co.

Grants Analysis

Disclosure Period: calendar year ending 1996
Total Grants: $149,485*
Number of Grants: 250 (approx)
Average Grant: $598
Highest Grant: $19,755
Typical Range: $50 to $1,000
***Note:** Giving excludes matching gifts.

Recent Grants

Note: Grants derived from 1996 Form 990.

Arts & Humanities

5,500	WLVT/Channel 39, Bethlehem, PA
3,500	Allentown Symphony, Allentown, PA
2,000	Bethlehem Musikfest Association, Bethlehem, PA
1,000	Children's Museum, Indianapolis, IN
1,000	Prince William Symphony Orchestra, Prince William, VA

Civic & Public Affairs

6,000	Center for Business and Industry, Waldorf, MD
5,000	Mason City Foundation, Mason City, IA
2,550	Upper Macungie Township, Breinigsville, PA
2,000	Bryan and Christine Vann Fund, Birmingham, AL
2,000	Mitchell on the Move, Mitchell, IN
1,800	Dabbs Area Vocational Center, Birmingham, AL
1,500	Americans for Native Americans, Doylestown, PA

Education

19,755	National Merit Scholarship Corporation, Evanston, IL
5,504	NIACC, Mason City, IA
5,130	NIACC, Mason City, IA
5,000	Western Maryland College, Westminster, MD
2,500	Mason City High School, Mason City, IA
2,500	Virginia Student Aid Foundation, Charlottesville, VA
2,500	York College of Pennsylvania, York, PA
2,000	LV Business and Education Partnership, Bethlehem, PA
1,800	Alabama Association of Independent Colleges and Universities, Birmingham, AL
1,200	Lehigh University, Bethlehem, PA
1,050	Kutztown University Foundation, Kutztown, PA
1,000	Allentown College of St. Francis de Sales, Center Valley, PA
1,000	Carroll Community College Foundation, Westminster, MD
1,000	Independent College Fund of Maryland, Baltimore, MD
1,000	Independent College Fund of Maryland, Westminster, MD
1,000	Junior Achievement, Hunt Valley, MD
1,000	Leeds Educational Assistance Program, Leeds, AL
1,000	Muhlenberg College, Allentown, PA

Environment

1,000	Iowa Natural Heritage Foundation, Des Moines, IA

Health

2,000	Frederick Memorial Hospital, Frederick, MD
2,000	March of Dimes Birth Defects Foundation, Baltimore, MD
1,000	American Red Cross, Bethlehem, PA
1,000	Children's Hospital of Alabama, Birmingham, AL

Social Services

14,681	United Way Greater Lehigh Valley, Bethlehem, PA
6,200	United Way Central Maryland, Baltimore, MD
4,000	United Way North Iowa, Mason City, IA
3,000	United Way McLennan County, Waco, TX
2,500	Boy Scouts of America Minsi Trails Council, Lehigh Valley, PA
2,000	Frederick County Family YMCA, Frederick, MD
2,000	Lake Area United Way, Griffith, IN
1,500	United Way Central Indiana, Indianapolis, IN
1,500	United Way Lawrence County, Beford, IN
1,350	United Way Central Alabama, Birmingham, AL
1,300	United Way York County, York, PA
1,200	United Way Frederick County, Frederick, MD
1,000	Camp ASCCA, Jackson Gap, AL
1,000	Crisis Intervention Service, Mason City, IA
1,000	US Olympic Committee, Charlottesville, VA

Leigh Fibers, Inc.

Company Contact

Wellford, SC

Company Description

Employees: 404

Corporate Sponsorship

Contact:
100 Ledgewood Place 103
Rockland, MA
Phone: (617)871-5860

Orchard Foundation

Giving Contact

Brigitte L. Kingsbury, Executive Director
Orchard Foundation
PO Box 2587
South Portland, ME 04116
Phone: (207)799-0686
Fax: (207)799-0686
Email: orchard@maine.rr.com
Web: http://www.orchardfoundation.org

Description

EIN: 046660214
Organization Type: Corporate Foundation. Supports preselected organizations only.
Giving Locations: NY New England area.
Grant Types: Award, General Support, Multiyear/Continuing Support, Operating Expenses, Seed Money.

Giving Philosophy

'Fields of interest: Environment: The foundation focuses primarily on natural resources, aquatic systems, and habitat and wildlife preservation. Children, youth, and family welfare: The foundation has a two-pronged approach for this area of giving. The first consists of support for programs that teach basic parenting skills and provide basic parenting support (along with family planning tools). Programs that lend support to new and at-risk families before and after birth will be considered. The second approach includes enrichment programs aimed at all age levels of children. These programs may include literacy projects for young children and their parents.' Proposal Guidelines, 1997

Financial Summary

Total Giving: $1,000,163 (1998); $419,900 (1997); $657,109 (1996). Note: Contributes through foundation only.
Assets: $10,948,933 (1998); $8,313,589 (1997); $5,512,164 (1996)
Gifts Received: $1,701,000 (1998); $1,585,088 (1997); $1,032,300 (1996). Note: In 1995, contributions were received from Leigh Fibers, In c. In 1996, contributions were received from the Moose Mountain Trust.

Typical Recipients

Arts & Humanities: Arts Associations & Councils, Arts Centers, Arts Festivals, Film & Video, Historic Preservation, History & Archaeology, Libraries, Museums/Galleries, Music, Public Broadcasting
Civic & Public Affairs: Community Foundations, Economic Development, Economic Policy, Employment/Job Training, Civic & Public Affairs-General, Hispanic Affairs, Native American Affairs, Philanthropic Organizations, Public Policy, Women's Affairs
Education: Arts/Humanities Education, Business Education, Colleges & Universities, Community & Junior Colleges, Education Funds, Engineering/Technological Education, Environmental Education, International Studies, Medical Education, Private Education (Precollege), Public Education (Precollege), Science/Mathematics Education, Secondary Education (Private), Vocational & Technical Education
Environment: Air/Water Quality, Forestry, Environment-General, Protection, Resource Conservation, Watershed, Wildlife Protection
Health: AIDS/HIV, Alzheimers Disease, Arthritis, Children's Health/Hospitals, Clinics/Medical Centers, Health Funds, Hospices, Hospitals, Medical Research, Multiple Sclerosis, Nursing Services, Outpatient Health Care
International: Health Care/Hospitals, International Development, International Environmental Issues, International Organizations, International Relief Efforts
Religion: Churches, Dioceses, Religious Organizations, Religious Welfare
Science: Scientific Centers & Institutes, Scientific Research
Social Services: Camps, Child Abuse, Child Welfare, Community Centers, Community Service Organizations, Counseling, Crime Prevention, Domestic Violence, Family Planning, Family Services, People with Disabilities, Senior Services, Shelters/Homelessness, Youth Organizations

Contributions Analysis

Giving Priorities: The foundation makes three kinds of grants. Board grants in response to unsolicited letters of inquiry are made in the following fields of interest: Environment, including legal advocacy. Children, youth, and families, with four program areas: child and family advocacy, supporting projects that promote child welfare at local, state and federal levels by addressing systemic issues, such a funding or rights, as opposed to direct service projects; enrichment, supporting projects that enlighten and empower children, including literacy programs; parenting skills and support, with the aim of targeting the specific subset of teen and/or at-risk new parents and teaching family planning along with parenting skills; and pregnancy prevention, supporting programs that encourage middle and high school students to delay childbearing. Invitation-only board grants are made for campaign finance reform at the state and federal

level. Discretionary grants are made in response to the initiatives of individual board members; no applications are accepted for these grants.
Arts & Humanities: 4%. Supports public radio, historic preservation organizations, and Boston area arts organizations.
Civic & Public Affairs: 18%. Interests include Native Americans and community affairs organizations.
Education: 51%. Major support for the Buckingham Browne and Nichols Schools. Also supports Boston area higher education institutions and private secondary schools. Focus is enrichment programs for children of all ages, and literacy projects.
Environment: 14%. Focus on natural resources, pollution prevention, aquatic systems, and habitat and wildlife protection and preservation.
Health: 4%. Supports a children's hospital and various health organizations.
Social Services: 7%. Interests include children, youth, and family welfare. Focus is on basic parenting skills and support.
Note: Total contributions in 1998.

Restrictions

Grants are not made to individuals, endowments, annual or capital campaigns, religious programs or religion-affiliated organizations, conference participation/travel unrelated to current foundation grant, scholarships, fellowships, animal hospitals/rehabilitation centers, single disease health associations, research efforts unrelated to advocacy interests of the foundation, for endowments, equipment needs, film and video projects, building projects, land acquisition, or loans.

Additional Information

Grantees must file progress reports with the foundation.
Publications: Proposal Guidelines

Corporate Officials

Carl P. Lehner: president, chief executive officer ED Amherst College. PRIM CORP EMPL president, chief executive officer: Leigh Fibers, Inc.
Philip Lehner: chairman B 1924. ED Harvard College. PRIM CORP EMPL chairman: Leigh Fibers, Inc.

Foundation Officials

M. Gordon Ehrlich: trustee B Springfield, MA 1930. ED Yale University BS (1951); Harvard University LLB (1954). PRIM CORP EMPL partner: Bingham, Dana. CORP AFFIL clerk: Ehrlich Manufacturing Co. Inc. NONPR AFFIL lectr: Harvard University Law School; member: Massachusetts Bar Association; member, chairman: Boston Estate Planning & Business Council; member, chairman: Boston Tax Forum; member: American Law Institute; trustee: Beth Israel Hospital; member: American Bar Association.
Brigitte L. Kingsbury: executive director, trustee
Carl P. Lehner: trustee (see above)
Heidi Lehner: trustee
Peter Lehner: trustee PRIM CORP EMPL officer: Leigh Fibers Inc.
Philip Lehner: trustee (see above)

Grants Analysis

Disclosure Period: calendar year ending 1998
Total Grants: $1,000,163
Number of Grants: 114
Average Grant: $8,773
Highest Grant: $125,000
Typical Range: $3,000 to $15,000

Recent Grants

Note: Grants derived from 1998 Form 990.

Arts & Humanities

15,000 The Catticus Corporation, Berkeley, CA -- General Operating Budget
9,000 Zumix, East Boston, MA -- Hands-On (Youth Outreach through Music) Program
5,000 Berkshire Museum, Pittsfield, MA -- Community Science

Civic & Public Affairs

100,000 The Spartanburg County Foundation, Spartanburg, SC -- The Lehner Family Fund
10,000 Maine Citizen Leadership Fund, Portland, ME -- Maine Citizens for Clean Elections
10,000 Portland West Neighborhood Planning Council, Portland, ME -- After School StoryCamp
10,000 Zamorano, Washington, DC -- Escuela Agricola Panamericana Zamorano
9,000 Concilio Hispano de Cambridge, Cambridge, MA -- AHORA: Youth Advocacy & Enrichment Program
7,000 The Center for Reproductive Law & Policy, New York, NY -- Corporate Responsibility Initiative

Education

125,000 Buckingham Browne & Nichols School, Cambridge, MA -- Campaign 2000
50,000 Harvard University, Cambridge, MA -- Capital Campaign
50,000 Massachusetts Institute of Technology, Cambridge, MA -- Mechanical Engineering Department
30,000 Middlebury College, Middlebury, VT -- Annual Fund
25,000 Buckingham Browne & Nichols School, Cambridge, MA -- Senior Class Gift
25,000 Christ Church Episcopal School, Greensville, SC -- Campaign for Excellence
25,000 Trustees of Hampshire College, Amherst, MA -- Lehner-Hewitt Endowed Writing Program
15,000 San Francisco School of Circus Arts, San Francisco, CA -- General Operating Support
15,000 Westchester Community College Foundation, Valhalla, NY -- Capital Campaign
10,000 Harvard University, Cambridge, MA -- Annual Fund Giving
10,000 Hudson River Sloop Clearwater, Poughkeepsie, NY -- PCB Response and Outreach Project
10,000 North Yarmouth Academy, Yarmouth, ME -- The Austin D. Higgins Music and Performing Arts Building
9,000 Maine School of Science and Mathematics Foundation, Limestone, ME -- Nurturing Nature and Numbers
7,000 Smith College Alumnae Fund, Northampton, MA -- Annual Fund
7,000 University of Maine Cooperative Extension, Belfast, ME -- Parents are Teachers Too Program
5,000 University of Southern Maine, Portland, ME -- The Economy & The Environment conference

Environment

15,000 Scenic Hudson, Poughkeepsie, NY -- PCB's in the Hudson River
13,000 Natural Resources Defense Council, New York, NY -- Dump Dirty Diesels Campaign
12,000 Appalachian Mountain Club, Boston, MA -- Wildlands Air Quality Policy Project
10,000 Public Employees for Environmental Responsibility, Washington, DC -- New England Environmental Protection Program
10,000 The Trustees of Reservations, Beverly, MA -- Charles Eliot Society
10,000 Vermont Natural Resources Council, Montpelier, VT -- Peterson Dam Removal on the Lamoille River
8,000 Neponset River Watershed Association, Canton, MA -- Managing the Cumulative Impact of Interbasin Transfers within the East Branch of the Neponset River
7,000 Center for Health, Environment & Justice, Falls Church, VA -- Stop Dioxin Exposure Campaign (New England)
7,000 Coast Alliance, Washington, DC -- Coastal Non-Point Pollution Prevention Project (NE Atlantic)
7,000 Natural Resources Council of Maine, Augusta, ME -- Capital Campaign
7,000 Natural Resources Council of Maine, Augusta, ME -- Reducing the Toxic's Load in Maine's Environment
7,000 World Wildlife Fund, Washington, DC -- Klamath-Siskiyou Living Communities Campaign (Community Outreach)

Health

20,000 The Lahey Clinic Foundation, Burlington, MA -- Institute of Urology
10,000 Inwood House, New York, NY -- Adolescent Parents in Training

Religion

10,000 Archdiocese of Boston, Brighton, MA -- Cardinal's Charity Fund
9,000 Casa Myrna Vasquez, Boston, MA -- S.T.A.R. - Sisters Teaching About Relationships

Science

7,000 The Woods Hole Research Center, Woods Hole, MA -- Climate Change and the Forests of New England

Social Services

10,000 Bridge Over Troubled Waters, Boston, MA -- Single Parent House
10,000 Center to Prevent Handgun Violence, Washington, DC -- General Operating Support
10,000 Children's Friend, Worchester, MA -- School Age Mothers Younger Sisters Program
10,000 The Elizabeth Stone House, Jamaica Plain, MA -- Parent/Child Center
10,000 Girls Incorporated of Holyoke, Holyoke, MA -- Operation S.M.A.R.T.
7,000 Vermont Youth Conservation Corps, Waterbury, VT -- General Support for Work & Study Expansion Program
5,000 Family Crisis Center, Portland, ME -- Young Adult Abuse Prevention Project

LENNOX INTERNATIONAL, INC.

Company Contact

Dallas, TX
Web: http://www.davelennox.com

Company Description

Employees: 8,000
SIC(s): 3433 Heating Equipment Except Electric, 3585 Refrigeration & Heating Equipment.

Operating Locations

Includes plant locations.

Lennox Foundation

Giving Contact

Dorothy Henson, Contact
Lennox Foundation
PO Box 799900
Dallas, TX 75379
Phone: (972)497-5000
Fax: (972)497-5268

Description

EIN: 426053380
Organization Type: Corporate Foundation. Supports preselected organizations only.
Giving Locations: nationally.
Grant Types: General Support, Scholarship.

Financial Summary

Total Giving: $1,097,867 (fiscal year ending November 30, 1997); $768,603 (fiscal 1996). Note: Contributes through foundation only.
Assets: $22,794,316 (fiscal 1997); $20,850,089 (fiscal 1996)
Gifts Received: $440,000 (fiscal 1997); $250,000 (fiscal 1996)

Typical Recipients

Civic & Public Affairs: Civic & Public Affairs-General, Housing, Municipalities/Towns, Zoos/Aquariums
Education: Colleges & Universities, Education Associations, Education Funds, Engineering/Technological Education, Education-General, Gifted & Talented Programs, Private Education (Precollege), Science/Mathematics Education, Student Aid
Environment: Environment-General, Resource Conservation
Health: Emergency/Ambulance Services, Health Funds, Health Organizations, Public Health, Single-Disease Health Associations
International: Foreign Educational Institutions, International Environmental Issues
Science: Science Museums
Social Services: Community Centers, Community Service Organizations, Counseling, Family Planning, Family Services, Recreation & Athletics, United Funds/United Ways, YMCA/YWCA/YMHA/YWHA

Contributions Analysis

Education: 28%. Majority goes to Grinnell College in Grinnell, IA. Other support goes to the US Academic Decathlon and the National Merit Scholarship Corporation.
Environment: 13%. Funds nature conservancy, and environmental concerns.
Health: 13%. Supports women's health, mitochondial disease foundation, and other health concerns.
International: 32%. Funds international concerns.
Social Services: 13%. Primarily to community service organizations and family planning.

Corporate Officials

Richard W. Booth: chairman PRIM CORP EMPL chairman: Lennox International, Inc.

Foundation Officials

David H. Anderson: vice chairman, trustee CORP AFFIL director: Lennox International Inc.
Richard W. Booth: chairman, treasurer, trustee (see above)
David V. Brown: secretary, trustee CORP AFFIL director: Lennox International Inc.

Grants Analysis

Disclosure Period: fiscal year ending November 30, 1997
Total Grants: $1,097,867
Number of Grants: 16
Average Grant: $68,617
Highest Grant: $356,000
Typical Range: $5,000 to $25,000

Recent Grants

Note: Grants derived from fiscal 1997 Form 990.

Education

150,000 Grinnell College, Grinnell, IA
88,740 Rudolf Steiner School, Great Barrington, MA
52,607 National Merit Scholarship Corporation, Evanston, IL
20,000 US Academic Decathalon, Costa Mesa, CA

Environment

100,000 Texas Nature Conservancy, San Antonio, TX
30,000 Landtrust Alliance, Washington, DC
10,000 Nature Conservancy, San Francisco, CA

Health

100,000 Mitochondial Disease Foundation, La Jolla, CA
30,000 Mercy Airlift, Fort Worth, TX
15,170 Womencare Age's Association, Dover Foxcroft, ME

International

356,000 Bat Conservation International, Austin, TX

Social Services

50,000 YMCA-YWCA, Marshalltown, IA
30,350 Central Nassau Services, Hicksville, NY
30,000 American Camping Association, Martinsville, IN
30,000 Planned Parenthood, Monterey, CA
5,000 Kara, Palo Alto, CA

LEVI STRAUSS &CO.

Company Contact

San Francisco, CA
Web: http://www.levistrauss.com

Company Description

Employees: 30,000
SIC(s): 2325 Men's/Boys' Trousers & Slacks, 2329 Men's/Boys' Clothing Nec, 2339 Women's/Misses' Outerwear Nec.
Parent Company: Levi Strauss Associates Inc.

Operating Locations

France: Dockers France, Paris, Ville-de-Paris; Germany: Dockers Germany Vertriebsgmbh, Duesseldorf; Italy: Dockers Italy SRL, Milano, Lombardia; Netherlands: Dockers Europe BV, Amsterdam, Noord-Holland; Dockers Nederland BV, Amsterdam, Noord-Holland; Levi Strauss Nederland BV, Amsterdam, Noord-Holland; Poland: Levi Strauss Poland Ltd., Warsaw, Warszawa; Spain: Dockers Hispania SA, Barcelona, Cataluna; United Kingdom: Dockers United Kingdom Ltd., London

Levi Strauss Foundation

Giving Contact

Richard Woo, Executive Director
Levi Strauss Foundation
1155 Battery St., 7th Fl.
San Francisco, CA 94111
Phone: (415)501-6579
Fax: (415)501-6575
Email: rwoo@levi.com

Description

Founded: 1952
EIN: 946064702
Organization Type: Corporate Foundation
Giving Locations: operating communities.
Grant Types: Employee Matching Gifts, General Support, Multiyear/Continuing Support.
Note: Employee matching gift ratio: 1 to 1 for qualified community organizations and educational programs, up to $1,200 per employee annually.

Giving Philosophy

The Foundation's policies and programs incorporate:
'A belief in each individual's capacity to make a difference: we believe that each person has the potential to grow, learn and advance. Therefore, the Foundation supports programs that remove barriers to full economic and social participation in society.'
'An appreciation for diversity: We value diversity and recognize each community's ability to craft programs that will best contribute to the success of its members..'
'A commitment to empower individuals: We support programs that enable individuals to play an active and responsible role in their communities. The Foundation targets community projects in which participants are also decision-makers.'
'A commitment to lead social change: We are committed to tackling difficult social issues identified as critical by the communities we serve. The Foundation seeks to support innovative economic development, AIDS services and social justice programs where our help can contribute to lasting social change.'
'An appreciation and support of the volunteer efforts of Levi Strauss & Co. employees: We are committed to promoting employee involvement in community service. Recognizing that Levi Strauss & Co. employees have a unique knowledge of their communities, we provide the opportunity to play a significant role in the design and implementation of Levi Strauss Foundation programs.' *Levi Strauss Foundation Report*

Financial Summary

Total Giving: $14,126,812 (1997); $19,700,000 (1996 approx); $12,000,000 (1995 approx). Note: Contributes through corporate direct giving program and foundation.
Giving Analysis: Giving for 1996 includes: foundation ($11,908,990); corporate direct giving ($7,516,010); foundation grants to United Way ($275,000); 1997: foundation ($12,341,802); foundation matching gifts ($1,235,510); foundation grants to United Way ($549,500)
Assets: $121,916,033 (1997); $114,914,449 (1996); $76,265,865 (1994)
Gifts Received: $7,650,000 (1996); $12,440,000 (1994). Note: Contributions are received from Levi Strauss Co.

Typical Recipients

Arts & Humanities: Arts Associations & Councils, Arts Outreach, Film & Video, Arts & Humanities-General, Museums/Galleries, Public Broadcasting, Theater
Civic & Public Affairs: African American Affairs, Asian American Affairs, Business/Free Enterprise, Civil Rights, Community Foundations, Economic Development, Economic Policy, Employment/Job Training, Gay/Lesbian Issues, Civic & Public Affairs-General, Hispanic Affairs, Housing, Legal Aid, Minority Business, Municipalities/Towns, Native American Affairs, Nonprofit Management, Professional & Trade Associations, Public Policy, Rural Affairs, Urban & Community Affairs, Women's Affairs
Education: Afterschool/Enrichment Programs, Colleges & Universities, Community & Junior Colleges, Education Funds, Faculty Development, Education-General, International Studies, Leadership Training, Literacy, Public Education (Precollege), School Volunteerism, Science/Mathematics Education, Social Sciences Education, Student Aid
Environment: Environment-General, Resource Conservation
Health: AIDS/HIV, Cancer, Clinics/Medical Centers, Emergency/Ambulance Services, Health Organizations, Long-Term Care, Public Health, Research/Studies Institutes, Respiratory
International: Foreign Educational Institutions, Health Care/Hospitals, International Affairs, International Development, International Environmental Issues, International Organizations, International Relief Efforts
Religion: Jewish Causes, Ministries, Religious Organizations, Religious Welfare, Social/Policy Issues

Social Services: At-Risk Youth, Child Welfare, Community Service Organizations, Day Care, Delinquency & Criminal Rehabilitation, Domestic Violence, Family Services, Food/Clothing Distribution, Homes, People with Disabilities, Refugee Assistance, Scouts, Senior Services, Sexual Abuse, Shelters/Homelessness, United Funds/United Ways, Volunteer Services, YMCA/YWCA/YMHA/YWHA, Youth Organizations

Contributions Analysis

Giving Priorities: Economic development, especially benefiting women, minorities, and teens; social services through employee involvement grants; and United Way. Levi Strauss & Co. administers one of the most structured and sophisticated international contributions programs through its Corporate Social Investment Program. International contributions committees follow guidelines similar to domestic philanthropy program. Company goal is to contribute to the well-being of the communities in which it operates by promoting volunteerism and community service among employees as individuals and as teams through training, consulting, and recognition of effort; contributing cash and products; providing technical assistance; and working in partnership with others. Contributions fall into the following categories: AIDS Prevention and Care, Economic Empowerment, Social Justice, and Youth Empowerment. Contributions programs are underway in Scotland, South Africa, Belgium, Denmark, England, Finland, France, Spain, Sweden, Portugal, Norway, Netherlands, Ireland, Italy, Poland, Turkey, Germany, Czech Republic, Greece, Hungary, Australia, Hong Kong, India, Indonesia, Japan, Malaysia, Canada, Argentina, Brazil, Chile, Colombia, and Mexico.

Arts & Humanities: 1%.

Civic & Public Affairs: 44%. Support is provided in four areas: Economic Development, AIDS and Disease Prevention, Social Justice, and Youth Empowerment. In economic development, the foundation seeks to enhance economic opportunities for low-income people, including the working poor. Priorities include job creation and community-based economic development; job training, placement, and access; leadership development; and micro-enterprise. In the category of AIDS and Disease Prevention, priorities include direct assistance to persons with AIDS and their caregivers; risk reduction education for those with high-risk behaviors. The Social Justice program seeks to break down barriers that prevent low-income and disenfranchised people from realizing their basic human rights. The Youth Empowerment initiative supports programs that challenge and involve youth in improving social and economic prospects, and which engage them as decision-makers. The company supports programs that seek to remove racial and other discriminatory barriers; ease tension between groups; promote diversity in community leadership; and prevent violent acts of racial and cultural prejudice.

Education: 16%. Supports educational programs and university scholarships.

Environment: 2%.

Health: 5%. Majority of support given to AIDS education organizations.

International: 15%. Foreign subsidiaries contribute directly in communities where company operates.

Religion: 6%. Primarily for religious conferences.

Social Services: 11%. More than half of social service contributions support the United Way in the Bay Area. Other funds support YWCA, and social services.

Note: Total contributions in 1997.

Application Procedures

Initial Contact: Contact foundation for guidelines, then send a brief letter of inquiry.

Application Requirements: Include a brief statement of organization's history, goals, and accomplishments; exact purpose of project, population to be served, amount requested and how funds will be used; time-frame for project; total project budget and total organization budget; and sources of committed and anticipated funds.

Deadlines: None.

Evaluative Criteria: Sound planning, follow-up initiatives, clear objectives, and proposed measures of success.

Decision Notification: Letters are responded to within 30 days; full proposals reviewed between 60 and 90 days.

Notes: Letter should be addressed to appropriate regional manager; list is included in guidelines.

Restrictions

Funding will not be considered for projects by individuals; for political, sectarian, or religious purposes; tickets for dinners or other special events; sponsorships, or courtesy advertising. Research and conferences are generally not considered for funding unless they are an integral part of a larger effort that the Foundation is funding.

Foundation will not make grants to discriminatory organizations.

Organizations must be tax exempt under IRS code 501(c)(3) or 509(a).

Additional Information

Publications: Levi Straus Foundation Report; Levi Strauss Foundation Grants List; Guidelines

Corporate Officials

Peter Edgar Haas, Sr.: chairman executive committee, director B San Francisco, CA 1918. ED University of California at Berkeley AB (1940); Harvard University MBA (1943). PRIM CORP EMPL chairman executive committee, director: Levi Strauss & Co. ADD CORP EMPL chairman executive committee, director: Levi Strauss Associates Inc. Holding Corp. CORP AFFIL director emeritus: AT&T Corp. NONPR AFFIL trustee: San Francisco Foundation; associate: Smithsonian Institute National Board; director: Northern California Grantmakers.

Robert Douglas Haas: chairman, chief executive officer, director B San Francisco, CA 1942. ED University of California at Berkeley BA (1964); Harvard University MBA (1968). PRIM CORP EMPL chairman, chief executive officer, director: Levi Strauss & Co. ADD CORP EMPL chairman: Levi Strauss Associates Inc. NONPR AFFIL honorary director: San Francisco AID South Foundation; member: Trilateral Commission; member: Phi Beta Kappa; member: Council Foreign Relations; director: Meyer Friedman Institute; member: Conference Board; trustee: Brookings Institution; member: California Business Roundtable; director: Bay Area Council; director: American Apparel Association; director: Bay Area Community.

Peter A. Jacobi: president B 1943. ED San Jose State University BS (1965). PRIM CORP EMPL president: Levi Strauss International. CORP AFFIL president, chief operating officer, director: Levi Strauss & Co.

George Barker James, II: senior vice president, chief financial officer B Haverhill, MA 1937. ED Harvard University AB (1959); Stanford University MBA (1962). PRIM CORP EMPL chairman, director: Crown Vantage Inc. CORP AFFIL director: Redem Corp.; director: Pacific Studies Industries, Inc.; director: Clayton Group Inc.; director: Fibreboard Corp.; director: Clayton Acquisition Co.; director: Basic Vegetable Products Inc. NONPR AFFIL chairman, director: Towle Trust Fund; vice chairman: World Affairs Council; trustee: Stern Grove Festival Association; member: Select Congressional Committee World Hunger; director: Stanford University Hospital; member: San Francisco Commission Foreign Relations; trustee: National Corp. Fund Dance; trustee: San Francisco Ballet Association; director: KQED; trustee: Cate School; trustee: Committee for Economic Development; member advisory council: California State Employees Pension Fund; director: California Pacific Medical Center. CLUB AFFIL Pacific-Union Club; New York Athletic Club; Harvard Club; Menlo Circus Club; Bohemian Club.

Foundation Officials

Judy Belk: vice president, secretary PRIM CORP EMPL vice president community affairs: Levi Strauss & Co. NONPR AFFIL director: Independent Sector.

Robert Douglas Haas: president (see above)

Peter A. Jacobi: vice president (see above)

Richard A. Woo: executive director

Grants Analysis

Disclosure Period: calendar year ending 1997

Total Grants: $12,249,902*

Number of Grants: 1,559 (approx)

Average Grant: $7,858

Highest Grant: $329,123

Typical Range: $1,000 to $50,000

***Note:** Giving excludes matching gifts, $91,900 in board service grants, and United Way.

Recent Grants

Note: Grants derived from 1997 Form 990.

Arts & Humanities

50,000	Connecticut Educational Telecommunications Corporation, Hartford, CT

Civic & Public Affairs

200,000	Women Making Movies, New York, NY
160,000	Corporation for Enterprise Development, Washington, DC
140,000	Accion, San Antonio, TX
107,000	First Nations Development Institute, Fredericksburg, VA
90,000	Valdosta Project Change, Valdosta, GA
77,000	East Tennessee Community Design Center, Knoxville, TN
75,000	Arkansas Development Finance Authority, Little Rock, AR
75,000	Enterprise Corporation of the Delta, Jackson, MS
75,000	Tennessee Network for Community Economic Development, Nashville, TN
70,000	Center for Entrepreneurship and Economic Development, Edinburg, TX
70,000	City Year, San Antonio, TX
68,000	East Tennessee Community Design Center, Knoxville, TN
57,250	Arkansas Human Development Corporation, Little Rock, AR
50,000	Arkansas Enterprise Group, Arkadelphia, AR
50,000	Center for Assessment and Policy Development, Bala Cynwyd, PA
50,000	City of Dallas, Dallas, TX
50,000	Knoxville Area Urban League, Knoxville, TN
50,000	Ms. Foundation for Women, New York, NY
50,000	National Council of Contractors Association, Little Rock, AR
50,000	Northern California Grantmakers, San Francisco, CA
50,000	Tomas Rivera Policy Institute, Claremont, CA
49,000	Women Making Movies, New York, NY
45,000	Centro del Obrero Fronterizo, El Paso, TX
42,000	Knoxville Women's Center, Knoxville, TN

Education

329,163	Citizens Scholarship Foundation of America, St. Peter, MN
122,660	Institute of International Education, San Francisco, CA
70,000	Valdosta State University Foundation, Valdosta, GA
50,000	NALEO Educational Fund, Los Angeles, CA

50,000	St. Mary's University, San Antonio, TX
45,000	El Paso County Community College, El Paso, TX

Environment

75,000	Tides Center, San Francisco, CA

Health

65,000	US-Mexico Border Health Association, El Paso, TX
60,000	San Antonio AIDS Foundation, San Antonio, TX
50,000	Northern California Grantmakers AIDS Task Force, San Francisco, CA
40,000	Valley AIDS Council, McAllen, TX

International

250,000	Fondation de France, Paris, France
250,000	Fondation de France, Paris, France
184,000	Japan Center for International Exchange, Tokyo, Japan
184,000	Japan Center for International Exchange, Tokyo, Japan
75,000	Fondation de France, Paris, France
75,000	Fondation de France, Paris, France
45,000	Leadership Education for Asian Pacifics, Los Angeles, CA
45,000	Leadership Education for Asian Pacifics, Los Angeles, CA
43,800	Canadian AIDS Society, Ottawa, ON, Canada
43,800	Canadian AIDS Society, Ottawa, ON, Canada

Religion

74,900	New Mexico Conference of Churches, Albuquerque, NM -- Albuquerque Project Change
52,000	New Mexico Conference of Churches, Albuquerque, NM -- Albuquerque Project Change
50,000	Valley Interfatih, Mercedes, TX
47,500	National Conference of Christians and Jews, Little Rock, AR

Social Services

225,000	United Way of the Bay Area, San Francisco, CA
72,000	YWCA Project Change, El Paso, TX
60,000	United Way of El Paso County, El Paso, TX
58,850	YWCA, El Paso, TX
50,000	Texas Immigration and Refugee Coalition, Dallas, TX

Leviton Manufacturing Co. Inc.

Company Contact

Little Neck, NY
Web: http://www.leviton.com

Company Description

Employees: 8,000
SIC(s): 3357 Nonferrous Wiredrawing & Insulating, 3613 Switchgear & Switchboard Apparatus, 3643 Current-Carrying Wiring Devices, 3674 Semiconductors & Related Devices.

Leviton Foundation New York

Giving Contact

Harold I. Leviton, President
Leviton Foundation New York
Phone: (718)229-4040
Fax: (718)631-6467
Email: hleviton@leviton.com

Description

Founded: 1952
EIN: 116006368
Organization Type: Corporate Foundation. Supports preselected organizations only.
Giving Locations: NY; RI
Grant Types: General Support.

Financial Summary

Total Giving: $298,675 (1998); $170,025 (1997); $229,650 (1996). Note: Contributes through foundation only.
Giving Analysis: Giving for 1998 includes: foundation ($272,425); foundation grants to United Way ($26,250)
Assets: $112,925 (1998); $106,715 (1997); $491 (1996)
Gifts Received: $305,000 (1998); $275,000 (1997); $225,000 (1996). Note: Contributions were recieved from Leviton Manufacturing Co., Inc.

Typical Recipients

Arts & Humanities: Arts Appreciation, Arts Associations & Councils, Dance, Museums/Galleries, Performing Arts, Theater
Civic & Public Affairs: Economic Development, Civic & Public Affairs-General, Parades/Festivals, Public Policy, Safety, Women's Affairs
Education: Arts/Humanities Education, Business Education, Colleges & Universities, Community & Junior Colleges, Elementary Education (Public), Engineering/Technological Education, Medical Education, Preschool Education, Public Education (Precollege), Science/Mathematics Education, Student Aid
Health: Cancer, Children's Health/Hospitals, Heart, Hospices, Hospitals, Kidney, Medical Research, Respiratory, Single-Disease Health Associations
International: Missionary/Religious Activities
Religion: Churches, Jewish Causes, Religious Organizations, Religious Welfare
Social Services: At-Risk Youth, Big Brother/Big Sister, Community Centers, Community Service Organizations, Emergency Relief, Family Services, Scouts, Senior Services, United Funds/United Ways, YMCA/YWCA/YMHA/YWHA, Youth Organizations

Contributions Analysis

Arts & Humanities: 1%.
Civic & Public Affairs: 4%.
Education: 3%. Supports colleges and universities.
Environment: 1%.
Health: 30%. Primarily supports hospitals, medical centers, and single-disease associations.
International: 1%.
Religion: 51%. Grants primarily support the United Jewish Appeal Federation and other Jewish causes. The Anti-Defamation League and St. Patrick's Cathedral also received support.
Social Services: 9%. Primarily supports United Way of Southeastern New England. Also supports youth organizations, family services, and at-risk youth.
Note: Total contributions made in 1998.

Restrictions

Does not support individuals.

Corporate Officials

Jack Amsterdam: chairman, treasurer, director B 1908. ED Saint John's University JD. PRIM CORP EMPL chairman, treasurer, director: Leviton Manufacturing Co. Inc. CORP AFFIL director: Pacific Electricord Co.
Harold Leviton: president, chief executive officer B 1917. ED University of Miami BS (1939). PRIM CORP EMPL president, chief executive officer: Leviton Manufacturing Co. Inc. CORP AFFIL director: Pacific Electricord Co.

Foundation Officials

Jack Amsterdam: secretary, treasurer (see above)
Donald Hendler: assistant treasurer B 1945. ED Franklin and Marshall College BA (1967). PRIM CORP EMPL vice president distribution: Leviton Manufacturing Co. Inc.
Harold Leviton: president (see above)
Shirley Leviton: treasurer CORP AFFIL director: Leviton Manufacturing Co. Inc.

Grants Analysis

Disclosure Period: calendar year ending 1998
Total Grants: $272,425
Number of Grants: 35
Average Grant: $7,784
Highest Grant: $100,625
Typical Range: $1,000 to $12,500
Note: Giving excludes United Way.

Recent Grants

Note: Grants derived from 1997 Form 990.

Arts & Humanities

1,000	Friends of the Arts, Englewood, NJ
500	LBJ Foundation for Arts and Sciences
250	United Service Organizations, Washington, DC

Civic & Public Affairs

5,000	National Electrical Safety Foundation, Rosslyn, VA
3,800	Western Piedmont Foundation, Morganton, NC
250	Little Neck-Douglaston Memorial Day Parade, Little Neck, NY
100	Motors and Armatures

Education

5,000	Beaver College, Beaver, PA
5,000	Massachusetts Institute of Technology Sloan School, Cambridge, MA
500	Center of University Design
500	Miami Student Aid Association
200	Junior Achievement, New York, NY

Health

50,000	City of Hope, Duarte, CA -- hardware for home improvements
1,000	Cystic Fibrosis Foundation, Philadelphia, PA
100	Easter Seal Society

Religion

10,875	United Jewish Federation, Pittsburgh, PA
10,000	National Council of Jewish Women, Greer, SC
6,000	Anti-Defamation League
1,000	Cardinal's Appeal
500	Dominican Mission Office

Social Services

55,000	United Way of Southeastern New England, Providence, RI
12,250	United Way of Burke County
350	Boys and Girls Club, Chicago, IL
250	Boy Scouts of America
200	Shake-A-Leg
200	United Way, Toledo, OH
100	Cross Island YMCA
100	Knights of Columbus

LG&E Energy Corp.

Company Contact

Louisville, KY
Web: http://www.lgeenergy.com

Company Description

Revenue: US$5,528,700,000
Employees: 5,000

Fortune Rank: 454, per FORTUNE Magazine's list of 500 Largest U.S. Corporations (1999).
FF 454
SIC(s): 4911 Electric Services, 4922 Natural Gas Transmission, 6719 Holding Companies Nec.

LG&E Energy Foundation

Giving Contact

Shauna Cole, Grants Administrator
PO Box 32010
Louisville, KY 40232
Phone: (502)627-2000

Description

Founded: 1994
EIN: 611257368
Organization Type: Corporate Foundation
Giving Locations: KY: Louisville headquarters and operating communities.
Grant Types: Capital, Employee Matching Gifts, General Support, Matching, Scholarship.

Financial Summary

Total Giving: $1,261,045 (1998); $1,175,572 (1997); $1,011,278 (1996)
Giving Analysis: Giving for 1997 includes: foundation ($769,004); foundation grants to United Way ($406,568); 1998: foundation ($744,230); foundation grants to United Way ($402,063); foundation matching gifts ($99,152); foundation scholarships ($15,600)
Assets: $21,158,682 (1998); $21,083,961 (1997); $19,160,991 (1996)
Gifts Received: $4,882 (1997); $15,000,000 (1994)

Typical Recipients

Arts & Humanities: Arts Associations & Councils, Arts Centers, Arts Funds, Ballet, Ethnic & Folk Arts, History & Archaeology, Libraries, Museums/Galleries, Music, Public Broadcasting
Civic & Public Affairs: African American Affairs, Economic Development, Housing, Law & Justice, Urban & Community Affairs, Women's Affairs
Education: Business Education, Colleges & Universities, Education Reform, Engineering/Technological Education, Environmental Education, Literacy, Minority Education, Science/Mathematics Education, Student Aid
Environment: Resource Conservation
Health: Children's Health/Hospitals, Emergency/Ambulance Services
Religion: Religious Organizations, Religious Welfare
Science: Science Exhibits & Fairs, Scientific Centers & Institutes
Social Services: At-Risk Youth, Child Welfare, Community Service Organizations, Day Care, Family Services, Food/Clothing Distribution, Scouts, United Funds/United Ways

Contributions Analysis

Giving Priorities: Emphasis on social services, education, and the arts.
Civic & Public Affairs: 4%. Funds youth and leadership programs, zoos, and a women's organization.
Education: 33%. Major grant to the University of Kentucky Athletics Association. Supports a variety of educational programs and colleges.
Environment: 2%. Grants were given to a nature conservancy and a park.
Health: 1%. Funds the Children's Hospital Foundation.
Social Services: 42%. Major support to the United Way through an Employee Matching gift program. Also funds social service programs for children.
Note: Total contributions in 1998.

Application Procedures

Initial Contact: Request a corporate contributions request form.
Application Requirements: Include a description of organization, amount requested, purpose of funds sought, recently audited financial statement, proof of tax-exempt status, and board of directors list.
Deadlines: January 31, April 30, July 31, October 31.

Restrictions

Does not support individuals, religious organizations for sectarian purposes, political or lobbying groups, or organizations outside operating areas. Applicant must be a 501(c)(3) organization.

Additional Information

Publications: Application Form; Guidelines

Corporate Officials

Roger W. Hale: chairman, chief executive officer, director B Baltimore, MD 1943. ED University of Maryland BA (1965); Massachusetts Institute of Technology MS (1979). PRIM CORP EMPL chairman, chief executive officer, director: LG&E Energy Corp. CORP AFFIL director: H & R Block; director: PNC Bank Corp.; director: Edison Electric Inst.
Charles A. Markel, III: vice president finance, treasurer PRIM CORP EMPL vice president finance, treasurer: LG&E Energy Corp.
Stephen R. Wood: president PRIM CORP EMPL president: LG&E Energy Corp.

Foundation Officials

Roger W. Hale: president (see above)
Charles A. Markel, III: vice president, treasurer (see above)
John McCall: vice president
Grant Ringel: vice president
Victor A. Staffieri: vice president
Stephen R. Wood: vice president (see above)

Grants Analysis

Disclosure Period: calendar year ending 1998
Total Grants: $744,230*
Number of Grants: 46
Average Grant: $13,427*
Highest Grant: $140,000*
Typical Range: $5,000 to $15,000
***Note:** Giving excludes United Way, scholarships, and matching gifts. Average grant figure excludes highest grant.

Recent Grants

Note: Grants derived from 1997 Form 990.

Arts & Humanities

66,150 Fund for the Arts, Louisville, KY -- program support
50,000 J.B. Speed Art Museum, Louisville, KY -- capital campaign
40,000 Mohammed Art Museum, Louisville, KY -- capital campaign
27,000 Louisville Ballet, Louisville, KY -- program support
20,000 Louisville Free Public Library, Louisville, KY -- support Library 2000 Campaign
20,000 WKPC/Channel 15, Louisville, KY -- for auction underwriting fee

Civic & Public Affairs

25,000 Southern Growth Policies Board, Research Triangle Park, NC -- support Commission of Future of South
15,000 Louisville Bar Association, Louisville, KY -- capital campaign

Education

40,000 LG&E College Relations -- support for college relations
33,333 Rose Hulman Institute of Technology, Terre Haute, KY -- support Vision to be the Best Campaign
32,000 University of Louisville, Louisville, KY -- scholarship endowment
30,000 Bellarmine College, Louisville, KY -- for 1997 corporate support
25,200 Junior Achievement, Louisville, KY -- program support
22,200 LG&E Foundation Scholarship Program -- support scholarships

Environment

25,000 Olmstead Parks Conservancy, Louisville, KY -- support Olmstead Parks Campaign

Religion

50,000 Cathedral Heritage, Louisville, KY

Science

33,333 Louisville Science Center, Louisville, KY -- support World We Create program
20,000 International Science and Engineering Fair, Louisville, KY -- support Science and Math Competition

Social Services

360,915 United Way, Louisville, KY -- building campaign, support 1995 campaign
16,433 Crusade for Children, Louisville, KY -- support special project

Liberty Corp.

Company Contact

Greenville, SC
Web: http://www.libertycorp.com

Company Description

Revenue: US$605,680,000
Employees: 3,157
SIC(s): 4833 Television Broadcasting Stations, 6311 Life Insurance, 6321 Accident & Health Insurance, 6552 Subdividers & Developers Nec.

Nonmonetary Support

Type: Donated Equipment; Loaned Executives

Liberty Corp. Foundation

Giving Contact

Sophia Vergas, Secretary
Liberty Corp. Foundation
PO Box 789
Greenville, SC 29602
Phone: (864)609-8398
Fax: (864)609-3176
Email: svergas@libertycorp.com

Description

EIN: 570468195
Organization Type: Corporate Foundation
Giving Locations: SC nationally.
Grant Types: Award, Capital, General Support, Multiyear/Continuing Support, Scholarship.

Financial Summary

Total Giving: $306,704 (fiscal year ending August 31, 1998); $563,747 (fiscal 1997); $287,611 (fiscal 1996). Note: Contributes through foundation only. 1997 Giving includes United Way ($118,467). 1996 Giving includes foundation ($188,563); matching gifts ($22,423); United Way ($76,625).
Giving Analysis: Giving for fiscal 1998 includes: foundation grants to United Way ($100,050); foundation matching gifts ($17,287)
Assets: $70,927 (fiscal 1998); $5,714 (fiscal 1997); $37,829 (fiscal 1996)

Gifts Received: $371,650 (fiscal 1998); $531,916 (fiscal 1997); $182,145 (fiscal 1996). Note: Contributions were received from Liberty Corporation; and Cosmos Broadcasting Corp.

Typical Recipients

Arts & Humanities: Arts Centers, Arts Festivals, Arts Funds, Community Arts, Arts & Humanities-General, Libraries, Museums/Galleries, Music, Performing Arts, Theater
Civic & Public Affairs: African American Affairs, Botanical Gardens/Parks, Business/Free Enterprise, Chambers of Commerce, Community Foundations, Economic Development, Employment/Job Training, Housing, Legal Aid, Municipalities/Towns, Philanthropic Organizations, Professional & Trade Associations, Urban & Community Affairs, Women's Affairs, Zoos/Aquariums
Education: Arts/Humanities Education, Business Education, Colleges & Universities, Education Associations, Education Funds, Education Reform, Engineering/Technological Education, Education-General, Private Education (Precollege), Private Education (Precollege), Public Education (Precollege), Science/Mathematics Education, Special Education, Student Aid
Environment: Environment-General, Resource Conservation, Wildlife Protection
Health: Cancer, Children's Health/Hospitals, Clinics/Medical Centers, Emergency/Ambulance Services, Health Organizations, Hospitals, Research/Studies Institutes, Single-Disease Health Associations
International: Foreign Educational Institutions, International Relations
Religion: Churches, Religious Welfare
Science: Scientific Centers & Institutes
Social Services: Child Welfare, Community Centers, Community Service Organizations, Emergency Relief, Family Services, People with Disabilities, Scouts, United Funds/United Ways, YMCA/YWCA/YMHA/YWHA, Youth Organizations

Contributions Analysis

Arts & Humanities: 3%. Support goes to performing arts, libraries, and visual arts.
Civic & Public Affairs: 11%. Primary support to economic development, urban affairs, and business concerns.
Education: 22%. Supports colleges, universities, and pre-college education.
Environment: 1%. Southern Environmental Law Center, nature conservancy, and wildlife.
Health: 4%. Emphasis on hospitals and single-disease organizations.
Social Services: 58%. Primarily supports United Ways, YMCA, and Boy Scouts.
Note: Total contributions in fiscal 1998.

Application Procedures

Initial Contact: Send a brief letter.
Application Requirements: Include proof of tax-exempt status of organization.
Deadlines: None.

Restrictions

Awards are not made to individuals.
Contributions are made only to organizations exempt from Federal income tax under 501(c)(3).

Additional Information

Matching gifts program discontinued in 1999.
Publications: Policies Fact Sheet

Corporate Officials

Mary Anne Bunton: vice president public relations PRIM CORP EMPL vice president: Liberty Corp. treasurer: Press Printing International.
William Hayne Hipp: president, chief executive officer, director B Greenville, SC 1940. ED Washington & Lee University BA (1962); University of Pennsylvania Wharton School MBA (1965). PRIM CORP EMPL president, chief executive officer, director: Liberty Corp. CORP AFFIL director: SCANA Corp.; director: Wachovia Corp.; director: American Council Life Insurance; chairman: Pierce National Life Insurance Co. NONPR AFFIL member: Greenville Chamber of Commerce; director: South Carolina Research Authority; chairman, trustee: Alliance for Quality Education; trustee: Communication Economic Development New York.
Kenneth W. Jones: controller PRIM CORP EMPL controller: Liberty Corp.
Carry Price: director public relations PRIM CORP EMPL director public relations: Liberty Corp.

Foundation Officials

Mary Anne Bunton: vice president (see above)
William Hayne Hipp: chairman, president, director (see above)
Kenneth W. Jones: controller, treasurer (see above)
Sophia Vergas: secretary, administrator
Martha G. Williams: director

Grants Analysis

Disclosure Period: fiscal year ending August 31, 1997
Total Grants: $189,367*
Number of Grants: 38*
Average Grant: $4,983
Highest Grant: $25,000
Typical Range: $1,000 to $15,000
***Note:** Giving excludes United Way and matching gifts. Number of grants is approximate.

Recent Grants

Note: Grants derived from 1998 Form 990.

Arts & Humanities

5,000 Columbia Museum of Art, Columbia, SC
2,500 The Museum Association, Inc., Greenville, SC
1,000 Alabama Shakespeare Festival, Birmingham, AL
1,000 Fund for the Arts, Louisville, KY

Civic & Public Affairs

10,000 Greenville Chamber Foundation, Greenville, SC
6,000 Emrys Foundation
5,000 Brookgreen Gardens, Murrells Inlet, SC
5,000 National Development Council, New York, NY
5,000 Urban League of the Upstate, Inc., Greenville, SC

Education

15,500 Independent Colleges and Universities of SC, Columbia, SC
12,500 SC Public Education Foundation, Columbia, SC
10,000 Alliance for Quality Education, Greenville, SC
10,000 Christ Church School, Christ Church, VA
5,000 Benedict College-Gressette Leadership Center, Columbia, SC
5,000 Erskine College - Science Building Campaign, Due West, SC
2,500 Life Education Fund
1,500 McNeese State University, Lake Charles, LA
1,000 USI Foundation, Evansville, IN

Environment

5,000 Palmetto Conservation Foundation, Columbia, SC
1,000 The Nature Conservancy of SC, Greenville, SC

Health

10,000 Health Sciences Foundation (Hollings Cancer Center), Greenville, SC

Social Services

80,000 United Way of Greenville County, Greenville, SC
25,000 Palmetto Family Council, Columbia, SC
21,667 American Red Cross, Greenville, SC
16,150 United Way, Louisville, KY
10,000 Palmetto Project, Charleston, SC
2,900 United Way, LA
2,500 YMCA - Youth in Government, Greenville, SC
1,000 Kids Voting-USA, Seattle, WA
1,000 North Toledo Community Center, Toledo, OH
1,000 United Way, Jonesboro, AR
850 Sunbelt Human Advancement Resources, Inc., Greenville, SC

LIBERTY DIVERSIFIED INDUSTRIES

Company Contact

Minneapolis, MN
Web: http://www.libertydiversified.com

Company Description

Employees: 1,300
SIC(s): 2631 Paperboard Mills, 2653 Corrugated & Solid Fiber Boxes, 3554 Paper Industries Machinery.

Jack and Bessie Fiterman Foundation

Giving Contact

David Lenzen, Executive Vice President
5600 N. Hwy. 169
Minneapolis, MN 55428
Phone: (612)536-6636
Fax: (612)536-6694
Email: davidlenzen@libertydiversified.com

Description

Founded: 1966
EIN: 416058465
Organization Type: Corporate Foundation
Giving Locations: MN
Grant Types: General Support.

Financial Summary

Total Giving: $241,200 (fiscal year ending May 31, 2000 approx); $291,575 (fiscal 1999); $275,650 (fiscal 1994)
Giving Analysis: Giving for fiscal 1999 includes: foundation ($241,575); foundation grants to United Way ($50,000)
Assets: $1,550,266 (fiscal 1999); $604,089 (fiscal 1994); $748,102 (fiscal 1993)
Gifts Received: $600,000 (fiscal 1999); $100,000 (fiscal 1994); $200,000 (fiscal 1993). Note: In fiscal 1999, contributions were received from Liberty Carton Co. ($320,000); Liberty Paper, Inc. ($150,000); Liberty Diversified Industries, Inc. ($50,000); Safco Product Co. ($40,000); Valley Craft, Inc. ($30,000); and Diversi Plast Products, Inc. ($10,000).

Typical Recipients

Arts & Humanities: Arts Centers, Arts Institutes, Music
Civic & Public Affairs: Business/Free Enterprise, Civil Rights, Civic & Public Affairs-General, Law & Justice, Municipalities/Towns, Zoos/Aquariums
Education: Agricultural Education, Business Education, Colleges & Universities, Economic Education, Science/Mathematics Education
Environment: Resource Conservation
Health: Alzheimers Disease, Children's Health/Hospitals, Diabetes, Long-Term Care, Medical Research
Religion: Jewish Causes, Religious Organizations, Religious Welfare, Social/Policy Issues
Science: Science Museums

Social Services: Child Welfare, Community Service Organizations, Food/Clothing Distribution, Homes, People with Disabilities, Recreation & Athletics, Substance Abuse, United Funds/United Ways, YMCA/YWCA/YMHA/YWHA, Youth Organizations

Contributions Analysis

Giving Priorities: Emphasis on Jewish welfare organizations and human services.
Arts & Humanities: 1%. Supports arts centers and historic preservation.
Civic & Public Affairs: 3%. Supports recreation, community organizations, and foundations.
Health: 2%. Funds single-disease associations.
Religion: 62%. Majority of support of the Minnesota Jewish Federation. Also supports religious welfare, and Jewish community programs.
Social Services: 32%. Funds children's clubs, United Way, and soc services organizations.
Note: Minor support given to the areas of science and education. Total contributions made in fiscal 1999.

Application Procedures

Initial Contact: Request an application form.
Deadlines: None.

Restrictions

Does not support individuals, or lobbying or advocacy groups.

Corporate Officials

Ben Fiterman: chairman PRIM CORP EMPL chairman: Liberty Diversified Industries.
Michael Fiterman: president, chief executive officer PRIM CORP EMPL president, chief executive officer: Liberty Diversified Industries.

Foundation Officials

Ben Fiterman: secretary, director (see above)
Linda Fiterman: treasurer, director
Michael Fiterman: president, director (see above)

Grants Analysis

Disclosure Period: fiscal year ending May 31, 1999
Total Grants: $241,575*
Number of Grants: 66
Average Grant: $1,363*
Highest Grant: $153,000
Typical Range: $75 to $100,000
***Note:** Giving excludes United Way. Average grant figure excludes highest grant.

Recent Grants

Note: Grants derived from 1997 Form 990.

Arts & Humanities
1,200 Hopkins Center for the Arts

Civic & Public Affairs
1,000 Civil Liberties Action League

Education
2,500 Life Lab Learning Institute
1,000 University of Minnesota Foundation, Minneapolis, MN

Health
500 Gillette Children's Hospital Foundation, Saint Paul, MN

Religion
120,600 Minneapolis Federation for Jewish Services, Minneapolis, MN
50,000 Adath Jeshurun
5,000 Jewish Family and Children's Services, San Francisco, CA
1,800 Basilica of St. Mary -- for Project Jeremiah
1,800 Jay Phillips Center for Jewish-Christian Learning
1,800 Jewish Community Center
1,500 Catholic Charities
600 Jewish Community Center

Social Services
30,000 United Way, Minneapolis, MN
5,000 Living Legacy
5,000 Sharing and Caring Hands, Minneapolis, MN
1,331 United Way Tarrant County, Fort Worth, TX
1,000 Washburn Child Guidance Center, Minneapolis, MN
500 Loaves and Fishes Too, Minneapolis, MN
500 Variety Children's Association

LIBERTY MUTUAL INSURANCE GROUP

Company Contact

175 Berkeley St.
Boston, MA 02117
Phone: (617)357-9500
Fax: (617)350-7648
Web: http://www.libertymutual.com

Company Description

Revenue: US$15,499,000,000 (1999)
Profit: US$501,000,000 (1999)
Fortune Rank: 111, per FORTUNE Magazine's list of 500 Largest U.S. Corporations (1999).
FF 111
SIC(s): 6331 Fire, Marine & Casualty Insurance.

SUBSIDIARY COMPANIES

WI: Employers Insurance of Wausau, A Mutual Co., Wausau

Nonmonetary Support

Value: $10,000 (1993)
Type: Donated Equipment; Loaned Employees; Workplace Solicitation
Note: Co. offers limited nonmonetary support by donating furniture, computers, and printing services. Workplace solicitation is for the United Way only.

Corporate Sponsorship

Type: Other; Sports events
Note: Primarily sponsors dinners and golf benefit tournaments. Interested parties should contact the co. at local and Regional level for sponsorship opportunities.

Giving Contact

David W. Hoffman, Assistant Vice President & Director of Corporate Public Affairs
Liberty Mutual Insurance Co.
175 Berkeley St.-10B
Boston, MA 02117
Phone: (617)357-9500 ext 41615
Fax: (617)574-6688
Email: David.Hoffman@LibertyMutual.com

Description

Organization Type: Corporate Giving Program
Giving Locations: headquarters and operating communities.
Grant Types: Capital, Emergency, Endowment, Fellowship, General Support, Multiyear/Continuing Support.

Giving Philosophy

'We contribute to a variety of non-profit organizations and attempt to achieve a giving pattern that is broad, balanced and maximizes the impact of our charitable contributions. In general, our contributions fall into three distinct categories:
Business Related Contributions. We recognize that our communities have serious and pressing needs today, and that corporate philanthropy can play a role in addressing those needs. However, we are also mindful that we are a business organization, and so we seek to direct our philanthropic resources, whenever possible, to those community needs that are related in some fashion to our business. In this way we maximize the return on our social investments by doing good for our communities while also doing well for our business.
The United Way. We favor the United Way as the vehicle for making charitable contributions in the communities where we do business. We do that because we believe the United Way is the most efficient system for delivering contributions to community services that need our support.
Other Worthy Causes. We also give serious consideration to responsible organizations and causes that seek to address the important social issues of the day.' Philanthropic Guidelines.

Financial Summary

Total Giving: $3,500,000 (1999 approx); $3,250,000 (1998 approx); $496,235 (1997). Note: Contributes through corporate direct giving program only.
Gifts Received: $235,424 (1997)

Typical Recipients

Arts & Humanities: Arts & Humanities-General
Civic & Public Affairs: Civic & Public Affairs-General
Education: Education-General
Health: Health-General
Social Services: Social Services-General

Contributions Analysis

Arts & Humanities: 9%. Supports the orchestra, museums, and arts institutes.
Civic & Public Affairs: 3%. Supports community and neighborhood service.
Education: 14%. Supports universities and colleges.
Environment: Less than 5%. Supports hospitals, medical centers, and single-disease concerns.
Social Services: 46%. Supports child and youth services, and the United Way.
Note: Contributions analysis provided by the company.

Application Procedures

Initial Contact: Send a brief letter of inquiry to the nearest Liberty Mutual office.
Application Requirements: Include a description of organization, amount requested, purpose of funds sought, recently audited financial statement, proof of tax-exempt status, list of trustees or directors, information on any other corporate support.
Deadlines: None.
Decision Notification: Proposals are reviewed throughout the year; organization will be notified as to the status of their proposal within 30 days.
Notes: Proposals not receiving funding may be held over until the next review.

Restrictions

Does not support religious organizations for sectarian purposes.

Corporate Officials

Gary Lee Countryman: chairman, chief executive officer B South Bend, WA 1939. ED University of Oregon BS (1961); University of Oregon MS (1963). PRIM CORP EMPL chairman: Liberty Mutual Insurance Co. CORP AFFIL president, director: Saint James Realty Corp.; director: Unisource Worldwide Inc.; director: Neiman Marcus Group Inc.; director: Saint James Holding Co. Bermuda Ltd.; chairman, chief executive officer: LM Insurance Corp.; director: Neiman Marcus Group Helmsman Management Services; director: Liberty Mutual Management Bermuda Ltd.; chairman: Liberty Northwest Corp.; chairman: Liberty Mutual Fire Insurance Co.; director: Liberty Mutual Insurance Group; chairman: Liberty Mutual Bermuda Ltd.; chairman: Liberty Mutual Capital Corp.; director: Liberty International Insurance Agency;

chairman, chief executive officer: Liberty Life Assurance Co. Boston; chairman, chief executive officer: Liberty Insurance Co.; director: Liberty Insurance Co. Massachusetts Ltd.; director: LEXCO Ltd.; director: Liberty Finance Corp.; director: Harcourt General Inc.; director: Helmsman Management Services Inc.; director: First National Bank Boston; director: FleetBoston Financial Corp.; director: Boston Edison Co.; chairman, chief executive officer: First Liberty Insurance Corp.; director: BEC Energy; president, director: Berkeley Management Corp.; director: Alliance America Insurance Co. NONPR AFFIL trustee: Northeastern University; trustee: University New England; board overseers: Massachusetts General Hospital; director: American Institute Property & Liability Underwriters; chairman: Dana Farber Cancer Institute. CLUB AFFIL Algonquin Club.

Barry S. Gilvar: secretary PRIM CORP EMPL secretary: Liberty Mutual Insurance Co. CORP AFFIL clerk: Liberty Mutual Equity Corp.; section: Liberty Mutual Fire Insurance Co.; secretary: Liberty Life Assurance Co. Boston; vice president, section: Liberty Insurance Co.; secretary: Liberty Insurance Corp.; clerk: Helmsman Insurance Agency Inc.

Edmund F. Kelly: president, chief executive officer B 1946. PRIM CORP EMPL president, chief executive officer: Liberty Mutual Insurance Co. ADD CORP EMPL president: Helmsman Management Services; president: LM Insurance Corp.; president: Liberty Insurance Corp.; president: Liberty Life Assurance Co. Boston; president: Liberty Mutual Equity Corp.; president: Liberty Mutual Fire Insurance Corp. CORP AFFIL president: First Liberty Insurance Corp.

Giving Program Officials

David W. Hoffman: director PRIM CORP EMPL assistant vice president, director corporate public affairs: Liberty Mutual Insurance Co.

Grants Analysis

Disclosure Period: calendar year ending 1997
Total Grants: $496,235
Number of Grants: 187
Average Grant: $2,654
Highest Grant: $50,000
Typical Range: $100 to $5,000

ELI LILLY &CO.

 Number 4 of Top 100 Corporate Givers

Company Contact

Indianapolis, IN
Web: http://www.lilly.com

Company Description

Revenue: US$10,002,900,000 (1999)
Employees: 14,951 (1999)
Fortune Rank: 170, per FORTUNE Magazine's list of 500 Largest U.S. Corporations (1999).
FF 170
SIC(s): 2833 Medicinals & Botanicals, 2834 Pharmaceutical Preparations.

Operating Locations

Argentina: Eli Lilly Interamerica, Inc. (Argentina Branch), Buenos Aires; Australia: Eli Lilly Australia Pty. Ltd., West Ryde; Austria: Eli Lilly Ges.m.b.h., Vienna; Belgium: Eli Lilly Benelux, Brussels; Lilly MSG Development Centre, SA, Mont Saint Guibert; Brazil: Eli Lilly do Brasil Limitada, Sao Paulo; Bulgaria: Eli Lilly (Suisse) S.A., Sofia; Chile: Carmencita 25, Santiago; People's Republic of China: Lilly Suzhou Pharmaceutical Co., Ltd., Jiang Su Province; Eli Lilly Asia Inc. (China Office), Shanghai; Eli Lilly Asia Inc. (Greater China), Shanghai; Colombia: Eli Lilly Interamerica Inc. (Colombian Branch), Cali; Cote d'Ivoire: Bureau d'Informations, Abidjan; Croatia: Eli Lilly (Suisse) S.A., Zagreb; Czech Republic: Eli Lilly s.r.o., Prague; Denmark: Eli Lilly Denmark A/S, Copenhagen; Egypt: Eli Lilly Egypt S.A.E., Cairo; Estonia: Eli Lilly (Suisse) S.A. Eesti filiaal, Tallinn; Finland: Oy Eli Lilly Finland Ab, Vantaa; France: Lilly France S.A., Fegersheim, St. Cloud; Germany: Lilly Deutschland GmbH, Bad Homburg, Giessen; Beiersdorf-Lilly GmbH, Hamburg; Greece: Pharmaserve-Lilly Saci, Athens; Hong Kong: Eli Lilly Asia, Inc. (Hong Kong Branch); Hungary: Lilly Hungaria KFT, Budapest; Indonesia: P.T. Tempo Scan Pacific, Rasuna; India: Eli Lilly Ranbaxy JV, New Dehli; Ireland: Eli Lilly and Company (Ireland) Ltd., Kinsale, Dublin; Israel: Eli Lilly Israel Operations, Tel-Aviv; Italy: Eli Lilly Italia S.p.A., Florence; Japan: Eli Lilly Japan K.K., Chuoku, Nishi-ku; Eli Lilly Japan K.K. MDD, Tokyo; Kazakhstan: Eli Lilly (Suisse) S.A., Almaty; Kenya:, Nairobi; Republic of Korea: Lilly Korea, Ltd., Seoul; Latvia: Eli Lilly (Suisse) S.A. Representative Office, Riga; Lebanon: Eli Lilly S.A., Beirut; Lithuania: Eli Lilly (Suisse) S.A. Representative Office, Rudninku; Morocco: Eli Lilly Maroc Sarl, Casablanca; Malaysia: Eli Lilly Malaysia SDN BHD, Selangor; Netherlands: El Lilly Nederland b.v., Nieuwegein; Norway: Eli Lilly Norge A.S., Etterstad; New Zealand: Eli Lilly and Company (N.Z.) Limited, South Auckland; Pakistan: Eli Lilly Scientific Office, Karachi; Peru: Eli Lilly Interamerica,Inc. (Sucursal Peruana), Lima; Philippines: Eli Lilly (Philippines), Incorporated, Quezon City; Poland: Lilly Polska Sp.Z.O.O., Warsaw; Portugal: Lilly Farma - Produtos Farmaceuticos, Lda., Arquiparque-Miraflores; Romania: Eli Lilly (Suisse) S.A., Bucharest; Russia: Eli Lilly Export S.A., Moscow; Republic of South Africa: Eli Lilly (S.A.) (PTY) Ltd., Isando; Southern Africa, Sub-Sahara, Isando; Saudi Arabia: Eli Lilly, Riyadh; Singapore: Eli Lilly Asia Pacific Pte Ltd, Forum; Spain: Apartado do Correcos 585, Madrid; Slovenia: Eli Lilly (Suisse) S.A., Bratislava, Ljubljana; Sweden: Eli Lilly Sweden AB, Stockholm; Switzerland: Eli Lilly (Suisse) S.A., Geneva; Thailand: Eli Lilly Asia, Inc. (Thailand Branch), Bangkok; Tunisia: Lilly Suisse S.A.; Turkey: Lilly Ilac Ticaret AS, Istanbul; Taiwan: Eli Lilly and Company (Taiwan),Inc., Taipei; United Arab Emirates: Eli Lilly (Suisse) S.A., Dubai; United Kingdom: Eli Lilly and Company Limited, Basingstoke, London, Windlesham Surrey; Ukraine: Eli Lilly (Suisse) S.A., Kiev; Uzbekistan: Eli Lilly, Tashkent; Vietnam: Eli Lilly Asia, Inc (Vietnam), Ho Chi Minh City; Yugoslavia: Eli Lilly (Suisse) S.A., Belgrade

Nonmonetary Support

Value: $90,000,000 (1998); $40,992,720 (1996); $47,678,308 (1995)
Type: Donated Products
Contact: Pat Gibson, Product Contributions Specialist
Note: Donations are in the form of pharmaceuticals (wholesale cost) to nonprofit organizations for disaster assistance.

Corporate Sponsorship

Type: Arts & cultural events; Other; Music & entertainment events; Sports events
Note: Sponsors health fairs and educational programs in schools, and the NCAA (National Collegiate Athletic Association).

Eli Lilly Foundation

Giving Contact

Thomas A. King, President
Eli Lilly & Co. Foundation
Lilly Corporate Center
Indianapolis, IN 46285
Phone: (317)276-3177
Fax: (317)277-6719

Alternate Contact

Kendy Smith, Senior Contributions Assistant

Description

EIN: 356202479
Organization Type: Corporate Foundation
Giving Locations: headquarters and operating communities; international organizations; national organizations.
Grant Types: Capital, Employee Matching Gifts, General Support, Multiyear/Continuing Support.
Note: Employee matching gift ratio: 1 to 1.

Giving Philosophy

'Eli Lilly and Co. recognizes, as a fundamental element of its corporate purpose, that the company's success as a business enterprise is affected by the vitality of the communities in which it operates. Corporate resources for the foundation's programs are invested with the same care and planning that govern other uses of corporate funds. Accordingly, the foundation applies the same professionalism and creative management process to its grant making that characterizes Lilly's other activities.

'As an innovator in scientific discovery and health care advances, Lilly is dedicated to saving lives and improving the health of people around the world. Consequently, in addition to a large employee-directed and plant-site giving program, the foundation is primarily interested in providing grants to organizations and programs concerned with health-care. Aligning its giving with its research objectives, Lilly is seeking positive change in areas of urgent, unmet medical needs where the company believes it has the knowledge and resources to create innovative solutions. Consequently, Lilly's program operates within a strategic framework that reflects its strengths and thus produces the greatest value for its charitable beneficiaries and for the company.

'Social needs align with business objectives, resulting in a powerful partnership between Lilly and nonprofit organizations whose efforts support programs for people affected by the diseases they're targeting. Special consideration is given to organizations and programs that improve the quality of and access to health-care and that undertake research and provide education on public policy issues related to the company's mission.' Report Corporate Citizenship, 1996

Financial Summary

Total Giving: $121,350,736 (1998); $102,800,752 (1997); $16,498,057 (1996)
Giving Analysis: Giving for 1997 includes: nonmonetary support (approx $42,420,730); foundation ($15,410,382); domestic subsidiaries ($10,072,182); international subsidiaries (approx $4,707,400); corporate direct giving ($610,788); 1998: foundation ($14,825,163)
Assets: $10,406,705 (1998); $3,423,048 (1997); $6,092,660 (1996)
Gifts Received: $23,750,000 (1998); $16,540,606 (1997); $13,722,596 (1996). Note: Gifts are received fron Eli Lilly & Co.

Typical Recipients

Arts & Humanities: Arts Associations & Councils, Arts Funds, Arts Outreach, Ballet, Community Arts, Dance, Ethnic & Folk Arts, Historic Preservation, History & Archaeology, Libraries, Museums/Galleries, Music, Opera, Performing Arts, Public Broadcasting, Theater
Civic & Public Affairs: African American Affairs, Botanical Gardens/Parks, Business/Free Enterprise, Chambers of Commerce, Civil Rights, Community Foundations, Economic Development, Economic Policy, Employment/Job Training, Civic & Public Affairs-General, Hispanic Affairs, Housing, Law & Justice, Municipalities/Towns, Parades/Festivals, Professional & Trade Associations, Public Policy, Urban & Community Affairs, Zoos/Aquariums

Education: Business Education, Business-School Partnerships, Colleges & Universities, Education Associations, Education Funds, Education Reform, Engineering/Technological Education, Faculty Development, Health & Physical Education, International Studies, Leadership Training, Medical Education, Minority Education, Private Education (Precollege), Public Education (Precollege), Religious Education, Science/Mathematics Education, Secondary Education (Private)
Environment: Environment-General
Health: AIDS/HIV, Cancer, Children's Health/Hospitals, Diabetes, Emergency/Ambulance Services, Health Policy/Cost Containment, Health Organizations, Heart, Medical Research, Mental Health, Prenatal Health Issues, Public Health, Single-Disease Health Associations, Trauma Treatment
International: Health Care/Hospitals, International Affairs
Religion: Ministries, Religious Welfare
Social Services: Camps, Child Welfare, Community Service Organizations, Homes, People with Disabilities, Recreation & Athletics, United Funds/United Ways, YMCA/YWCA/YMHA/YWHA, Youth Organizations

Contributions Analysis

Giving Priorities: Pharmaceutical and medical education, local united funds, a zoological society, and civic organizations. Company's philanthropic efforts for international purposes are primarily in the form of donated products and equipment. The company supports charitable and private voluntary agencies with established credentials in the developing world. Also has supported physicians and dentists serving abroad on medical missions sponsored by qualified organizations. Recipient organizations are required to have 501(c)(3) status. The foundation supports community funds in Puerto Rico, where the company has 1,300 employees, and some civic and educational programs with an international focus, including health-related charities. Eli Lilly International Corp. supports organizations in its operating communities. Mangers are autonomous in choosing recipients for support. While budgets are approved by headquarters, it has no oversight of programs abroad.
Arts & Humanities: About 15%. Priorities include Indianapolis music and theater groups. Also supports arts funds and associations, historic preservation, museums, children's museums and concerts, and dance. Focus is on plant-site communities.
Civic & Public Affairs: About 5%. Supports zoos and other interests such as public policy, local economic development, civil rights, and urban and community affairs.
Education: About 40%. Major support goes to pharmaceutical and medical education, colleges and universities, and higher education associations. Also funds minority education and precollege education. Focus is on science and technical education.
Health: About 40%. Primary support goes to united funds in corporate communities. Supports medical research, medical centers, and local health organizations, primarily in Indiana. Also funds national health organizations concerned with mental health and diabetes research, innovative programs that help inform patients about disease symptoms and potential treatments, and programs that support patients and their families affected by these diseases. Foundation provides matching gifts to the United Way.
Note: Percentages are based on cash grants only.

Application Procedures

Initial Contact: foundation reports that it is not accepting unsolicited proposals at this time; organizations may be approached as possible grant recipients; they are asked to provide the following information:
Application Requirements: project objectives, annual report or other budget information, sources and amounts of other funding, description and purpose of organization, amount requested, purpose of funds sought, plan for evaluation, recently audited financial statement, names and affiliations of board of directors, proof of tax-exempt status 501(c)(3), and how the organization will acknowledge Lilly support.
Deadlines: February; August
Review Process: initial review by staff and appropriate components within company

Restrictions

Does not support individuals; non-tax-exempt organizations; fraternal, labor, athletic, or veterans' organizations; political activities; construction of buildings; endowments or endowed chairs; religious organizations for sectarian purposes; nonaccredited educational institutions; or travel expenses for individuals or groups.
Also does not support debt reduction, political contributions, beauty contests, conferences and media productions, and memorials. beauty contests, conferences and media productions, and memorials.

Additional Information

Products, including insulin and anticancer agents, are donated throughout the developing world, to Eastern Europe, summer camp programs for children with diabetes, and emergency relief agencies.
Physician requests for the Lilly Cares--Indigent Patient Program should contact Lilly Cares Program Administrator, PO Box 9105, McLean, VA 22102-0105, (800)545-6962.
In March of 1997, the American Red Cross received a $1,000,000 grant from the foundation, which will be used to train nearly 11,000 mental health professionals over five years to help meet the emotional needs of victims, families, and relief workers during times of disaster.
Publications: Charitable Contributions Report

Corporate Officials

Charles E. Golden: executive vice president, chief financial officer PRIM CORP EMPL executive vice president, chief financial officer: Eli Lilly & Co.
Edwin W. Miller: vice president, treasurer PRIM CORP EMPL vice president, treasurer: Eli Lilly & Co.
Sidney Taurel: chairman, president, chief executive officer B February 09, 1949. ED Columbia University MBA (1971). PRIM CORP EMPL chairman, president, chief executive officer: Eli Lilly & Co.
Randall L. Tobias: chairman emeritus B Lafayette, IN 1942. ED Indiana University BS (1964). PRIM CORP EMPL chairman emeritus: Eli Lilly & Co. CORP AFFIL director: Phillips Petroleum Co.; director: Knight-Ridder Inc.; director: Northwest Publications Inc.; director: Kimberly-Clark Corp. NONPR AFFIL director: Indianapolis Symphony Orchestra; member: Theta Chi; board governors: Indianapolis Museum Art; director: Indiana University Foundation; member: Indianapolis Corp. Community Council; vice chairman: Colonial Williamsburg Foundation; trustee: Duke University; member: Business Council; member: Amwell Valley Conservancy. CLUB AFFIL University Club; Woodstock Club; Economic Club Indianapolis; Meridian Hills Country Club; Athletic Club; Columbia Club.

Foundation Officials

Mitchell E. Daniels, Jr.: chairman, treasurer PRIM CORP EMPL vice president: Eli Lilly & Co. CORP AFFIL director: Indianapolis Power & Light Co.; director: Ipalco Enterprises.
Thomas A. King: president
Kendra Smith: secretary

Grants Analysis

Disclosure Period: calendar year ending 1997
Total Grants: $15,437,179
Number of Grants: 153*
Average Grant: $40,533*
Highest Grant: $1,176,806
Typical Range: $10,000 to $50,000
***Note:** Number of grants and average grant excludes matching gifts. .

Recent Grants

Note: Grants derived from 1997 Form 990.

Arts & Humanities

299,067	Indiana State Symphony Society, Inc., Indianapolis, Indianapolis, IN
250,000	Indianapolis Symphony Orchestra Foundation
145,231	Indianapolis Museum of Art, Inc., Indianapolis, IN
127,826	Children's Museum of Indianapolis, Inc., Indianapolis, IN
100,000	Colonial Williamsburg Foundation
100,000	Colonial Williamsburg Foundation
100,000	Colonial Williamsburg Foundation
100,000	Colonial Williamsburg Foundation
100,000	Colonial Williamsburg Foundation

Civic & Public Affairs

129,836	Indianapolis Zoological Society, Inc., Indianapolis, IL

Education

469,292	Purdue University Foundation, West Lafayette, IN
433,540	Indiana University Foundation, Bloomington, IN
333,335	Indiana University Foundation
333,333	Indiana University Foundation
333,333	Indiana University Foundation
289,777	Our Lady of Mount Carmel Parochial School Trust, Carmel, IN
219,496	Park Tudor School / Indianapolis, Indianapolis, IN
149,532	Wabash College, Crawfordsville, IN
147,577	University of Illinois Foundation, Champaign, IL
131,014	University of North Carolina at Chapel Hill, Chapel Hill, NC
120,208	Butler University, Indianapolis, IN
115,430	Calvary Lutheran School / Indianapolis, Indianapolis, IN
115,081	DePauw University, Greencastle, IN
107,414	St. Mark Catholic School / Indianapolis, Indiana, Indianapolis, IN
102,853	Central Catholic High School / Lafayette, Lafayette, IN
102,615	Brebeuf Preparatory School / Indianapolis, Indianapolis, IN

Health

260,265	American Red Cross National Headquarters
226,275	American Red Cross National Headquarters
200,000	American Cancer Society Indiana Division
200,000	American Cancer Society Indiana Division
200,000	American Cancer Society Indiana Division
200,000	American Cancer Society Indiana Division
194,925	American Red Cross National Headquarters
188,775	American Red Cross National Headquarters
182,425	American Red Cross National Headquarters

International

500,000	World Health Organization
500,000	World Health Organization
500,000	World Health Organization
500,000	World Health Organization
500,000	World Health Organization

Social Services

1,176,806	United Way of Central Indiana
1,176,806	United Way of Central Indiana
500,000	Indiana Sports Corporation
500,000	Indiana Sports Corporation
500,000	Indiana Sports Corporation
500,000	Indiana Sports Corporation

223,790 United Way of Greater Lafayette
109,331 United Way of the Wabash Valley

Lincoln Electric Co.

Company Contact

Cleveland, OH
Web: http://www.lincolnelectric.com

Company Description

Employees: 5,693
SIC(s): 3548 Welding Apparatus, 3621 Motors & Generators.

Nonmonetary Support

Value: $250,000 (1997); $250,000 (1996)
Type: Donated Equipment; Donated Products

Corporate Sponsorship

Note: Sponsors Harvest for Hunger and Juvenile Diabetes Walk.

Lincoln Electric Foundation

Giving Contact

Paul J. Beddia, Vice President, Government & Community Affairs
Lincoln Electric Foundation Trust
22801 St. Clair Ave.
Cleveland, OH 44117
Phone: (216)383-2249
Fax: (216)486-6476

Description

EIN: 346518355
Organization Type: Corporate Foundation
Giving Locations: OH: Cleveland including metropolitan area
Grant Types: Award, Capital, Endowment, General Support, Multiyear/Continuing Support, Operating Expenses, Project, Seed Money.

Financial Summary

Total Giving: $828,571 (1998); $1,114,300 (1997); $804,450 (1996). Note: Contributes through corporate direct giving program and foundation.
Giving Analysis: Giving for 1996 includes: foundation ($554,450); nonmonetary support ($250,000); 1997: foundation ($725,150); nonmonetary support ($250,000); foundation grants to United Way ($139,150)
Assets: $1,788,631 (1998); $1,433,212 (1997); $1,020,221 (1996)
Gifts Received: $1,000,000 (1998); $1,200,000 (1997); $1,500,000 (1996). Note: The foundation receives gifts from Lincoln Electric Co.

Typical Recipients

Arts & Humanities: Ballet, Dance, Historic Preservation, History & Archaeology, Museums/Galleries, Music, Opera, Performing Arts, Theater
Civic & Public Affairs: Botanical Gardens/Parks, Business/Free Enterprise, Community Foundations, Economic Development, Employment/Job Training, Law & Justice, Municipalities/Towns, Parades/Festivals, Professional & Trade Associations, Safety, Zoos/Aquariums
Education: Arts/Humanities Education, Business Education, Colleges & Universities, Education Associations, Education Funds, Education Reform, Engineering/Technological Education, Public Education (Precollege), Student Aid, Vocational & Technical Education
Environment: Environment-General
Health: Cancer, Children's Health/Hospitals, Clinics/Medical Centers, Emergency/Ambulance Services, Health Organizations, Hospitals, Long-Term Care, Mental Health, Nursing Services, Preventive Medicine/Wellness Organizations, Public Health, Respiratory, Single-Disease Health Associations
International: International Affairs, International Relations
Religion: Religious Welfare
Science: Science Museums
Social Services: Camps, Child Welfare, Community Service Organizations, Crime Prevention, Family Planning, Food/Clothing Distribution, People with Disabilities, Scouts, Substance Abuse, United Funds/United Ways, Volunteer Services, Youth Organizations

Contributions Analysis

Giving Priorities: Local colleges and universities, United Way, hospitals, the arts, and environmental and nature organizations.
Arts & Humanities: 8%. Supports the Cleveland Orchestra, ballet, opera, theater, and fine arts museums.
Civic & Public Affairs: About 9%. Interests include environmental affairs, law enforcement, Cleveland civic associations, international organizations, and philanthropic organizations.
Education: 34%. Most funds support local colleges and universities. Education funds and Junior Achievement also receive support.
Health: 21%. Primarily assists area hospitals. Support also goes to single-disease health organizations.
Science: 6%. Funds the Great Lakes Museum.
Social Services: 21%. Majority of funds support the United Way. Remaining funds typically benefit youth organizations, recreation, and religious welfare.
Note: Total contributions in 1997.

Application Procedures

Initial Contact: Send a brief letter or proposal.
Application Requirements: Include a description of organization; amount requested and purpose of funds sought; recently audited financial statement; and proof of tax-exempt status.
Deadlines: September 20.
Decision Notification: Decisions are generally made at end of calendar year.

Restrictions

Gives to immediate geographical area serving employees in higher education, medical services, cultural and civic institutions and the United Way.

Additional Information

Society Bank of Cleveland, OH, acts as the foundation's corporate trustee.

Corporate Officials

Paul J. Beddia: vice president government & community affairso PRIM CORP EMPL vice president government & community affairs: Lincoln Electric Co.
Anthony A. Massaro: president, chief executive officer, chairman, chief operating officer B 1944. ED University of Pittsburgh BS (1967). PRIM CORP EMPL president, chief executive officer, chairman, chief operating officer: Lincoln Electric Co. CORP AFFIL chairman: Lincoln Electric Holdings; director: Thomas Industries Inc.; director: Commercial Metals Co.
Roy L. Morrow: director corporate relations PRIM CORP EMPL director corporate relations: Lincoln Electric Holding Inc.

Foundation Officials

Paul J. Beddia: vice president government & community affairs (see above)
Roy L. Morrow: vice president government & community affairs (see above)

Grants Analysis

Disclosure Period: calendar year ending 1997
Total Grants: $725,150*
Number of Grants: 82
Average Grant: $8,843
Highest Grant: $70,000*
Typical Range: $1,000 to $20,000
***Note:** Giving excludes nonmonetary support; United Way.

Recent Grants

Note: Grants derived from 1996 Form 990.

Civic & Public Affairs

1,000 Vocational Guidance Services, Cleveland, OH

Education

1,000 Cleveland Music School Settlement, Cleveland, OH

Social Services

2,500 Youth Opportunities Unlimited, Pittsburgh, PA

Lincoln Financial Group

★ Number 95 of Top 100 Corporate Givers

Company Contact

Fort Wayne, IN
Web: http://www.lfg.com

Company Description

Revenue: US$6,087,100,000
Employees: 10,320
SIC(s): 6311 Life Insurance, 6321 Accident & Health Insurance, 6331 Fire, Marine & Casualty Insurance, 6719 Holding Companies Nec.

Nonmonetary Support

Type: Donated Equipment; Loaned Employees; Loaned Executives

Corporate Sponsorship

Type: Arts & cultural events; Festivals/fairs; Music & entertainment events; Other
Contact: Debra Patterson, Program Officer
Note: Sponsors educational workshops and conferences; community events; and fundraising events.

Lincoln National Foundation

Giving Contact

Mary J. Johnson, Assistant Vice President
Lincoln National Corp.
1300 South Clinton Street
PO Box 7863
Ft. Wayne, IN 46801-7863
Phone: (219)455-3879
Fax: (219)455-4004
Email: mjohnson@lnc.com

Description

Organization Type: Corporate Foundation
Giving Locations: communities where their employees live and work.
Grant Types: Award, Capital, Conference/Seminar, Emergency, Employee Matching Gifts, General Support, Loan, Matching, Multiyear/Continuing Support.
Note: Employee matching gift ratio: 1 to 1, for gifts to colleges and universities only. Also match donations made by LFG career producers.

Giving Philosophy

'Lincoln National Foundation assists philanthropic programs which enhance the quality of life in communities where Lincoln National employees live and work. The Foundation has established three priority areas for funding: Arts and Culture, Education, and

Human Services. We believe the arts are a stabilizing influence, stimulating the development of creativity, understanding, responsibility and tolerance. We believe education opens the door to independence, fulfillment and progress. We believe what people do to or for others is a direct reflection on the state of humanity. We believe we are helping to build powerful connections with people, their communities, and future generations.' *Making Connections: Lincoln National Foundation Corporate Public Involvement 1995*

Financial Summary

Total Giving: $7,500,000 (2000 approx); $7,400,000 (1999 approx); $7,333,387 (1998). Note: Contributes through corporate direct giving program and foundation. Giving includes corporate direct giving ($302,816); foundation ($5,500,541); domestic subsidiaries ($1,200,000); international subsidiaries ($330,000).
Giving Analysis: Giving for 1998 includes: foundation ($5,500,541); international subsidiaries ($330,000); corporate direct giving ($302,816)
Assets: $15,200,000 (1998 approx); $14,000,000 (1997 approx); $12,666,071 (1996)

Typical Recipients

Arts & Humanities: Arts Associations & Councils, Arts Festivals, Arts Funds, Community Arts, Dance, Historic Preservation, Museums/Galleries, Music, Performing Arts, Public Broadcasting, Theater
Civic & Public Affairs: African American Affairs, Economic Development, Employment/Job Training, Ethnic Organizations, Housing, Municipalities/Towns, Parades/Festivals, Public Policy, Urban & Community Affairs, Women's Affairs, Zoos/Aquariums
Education: Arts/Humanities Education, Business Education, Colleges & Universities, Economic Education, Education Associations, Education Funds, Literacy, Minority Education, Preschool Education
Environment: Environment-General
Health: AIDS/HIV, Medical Research, Mental Health, Single-Disease Health Associations
Religion: Religious Welfare
Science: Science Exhibits & Fairs
Social Services: Child Welfare, Community Centers, Community Service Organizations, Day Care, Delinquency & Criminal Rehabilitation, Domestic Violence, Emergency Relief, Family Services, Food/Clothing Distribution, Recreation & Athletics, Senior Services, Shelters/Homelessness, Substance Abuse, United Funds/United Ways, Youth Organizations

Contributions Analysis

Giving Priorities: Social services, higher education, arts funds, and AIDS research.
Arts & Humanities: 30% to 35%. Support covers cultural spectrum: dance, museums, art exhibits, orchestras, theater, and historic preservation.
Education: 30% to 35%. Focus on higher education. Supports colleges and universities, higher education associations, and actuarial scholarships. Also gives to the Local Education Fund, Junior Achievement, and preschool education. Provides matching gifts to higher education.
Health: Less than 5%. Supports medical research, with focus on AIDS.
Social Services: 30% to 35%. Supports united funds, community services, the elderly, domestic violence, and youth programs. Also funds food banks, homeless shelters, drug treatment programs, and AIDS education programs.
Note: Lincoln Financial Group administers various community programs: Let Happiness Ring (annual free holiday telephoning program for senior citizens); Math Scholar Program (annual math enrichment course for high-achieving high school juniors); and the Ian M. Rolland Community Service Awards for home office and field employees, in recognition of their community service; for each award recipient, a $3,000 donation is made to a nonprofit that represents these volunteer efforts.

Application Procedures

Initial Contact: Call for application form., then submit written proposal.
Application Requirements: Summary of need for assistance: including background, amount, objective, time period, key staff, and budget; financial statements for last three years, if available; membership of governing board, including number of minority and non-minority males and females; list of other sources of support or sources to whom proposals are pending; 501 (c)(3) determination letter; number of people and geographical area served; amount of annual expenditures.
Deadlines: Varies; contact foundation for exact dates.
Review Process: Recommendations made by Corporate Public Involvement Foundation Committee.
Evaluative Criteria: Purpose and objective of proposal; relevance of problem addressed; qualifications of organization and its personnel; well-defined plan of action; evaluative criteria; adequate representation of women and minorities on governing board; quality of organization's financial management; involvement of company employees; long-term effects of project; and financial accounting.
Decision Notification: Quarterly.
Notes: Applications should be requested from and returned to Lincoln National affiliate offices. Fort Wayne-based programs may contact Corporate Public Involvement Program Officer.

Restrictions

Corporation makes grants only to 501(c)(3) organizations that fall under priority categories of Arts and Culture, Education, or Human Services and have nondiscriminatory policies.
Foundation guidelines prohibit gifts to public or private elementary or secondary schools; hospitals, hospital programs or foundations and nursing homes; posts or organizations of war veterans; service organizations including police and fire departments; fraternal organizations; churches; and individuals.
Foundation does not provide support for general operating budgets, deficits, or the continuation of an established service. Funding is focused on projects, pilot programs, and capital grants.
Funding is not provided for religious causes, political causes, sporting events, purchase of tickets or tables, or tournaments.
Support for endowments is seldom considered and multi-year funding is discouraged.

Additional Information

Lincoln National Corporation expects grant recipients to submit final reports.
Giving at the affiliate level is decentralized, with each affiliate having decision making power.
Low-income adults seeking entry or re-entry into the workforce are eligible for education grants and loans under a new program financed by Lincoln National Corporation and the Foellinger Foundation, and administered by the Ft. Wayne Education Foundation.
Lincoln Financial Group donates 2% of pre-tax earnings each year.
Publications: Corporate Public Involvement Annual Report

Giving Program Officials

Mary J. Johnson: manager PRIM CORP EMPL CPI officer: Lincoln National Corp.
Debra Patterson: PRIM CORP EMPL program officer: Lincoln National Corp.
C. Suzanne Womack: director B 1949. PRIM CORP EMPL secretary: Lincoln National Corp. CORP AFFIL secretary: Lincoln National (China) Inc.; secretary: Lincoln National Management Service.

Grants Analysis

Disclosure Period: calendar year ending 1998
Total Grants: $7,333,387
Number of Grants: 900*
Average Grant: $10,000
Highest Grant: $500,000
Typical Range: $5,000 to $40,000
***Note:** Grants analysis was provided by the company.

Recent Grants

Note: Grants derived from 1994 grants list.

Arts & Humanities

5,000	Fort Wayne Children's Choir
1,000	Indiana Humanities Council

Civic & Public Affairs

15,000	Fort Wayne Urban League, Fort Wayne, IN
5,000	National League of Cuban American Community-Based Centers
5,000	Sister Cities Program
4,500	Three Rivers Festival
2,500	Fort Wayne Women's Bureau, Fort Wayne, IN
2,500	Inroads/Indiana, Inc. -- for youth leadership training
2,500	Leadership Fort Wayne, Fort Wayne, IN
1,000	Scottish Cultural Society of Fort Wayne

Education

15,000	Junior Achievement, Fort Wayne, IN
5,000	Indiana-Purdue Foundation
2,500	Foundation for Art and Music in Elementary Education -- for teacher workshops

Health

5,000	National Leadership Coalition on AIDS

Religion

60,000	Youth for Christ, Fort Wayne, IN -- for youth outreach program
6,000	Lutheran Social Services

Social Services

100,000	Boys and Girls Club of Fort Wayne, Fort Wayne, IN
100,000	Community Harvest Food Bank, Fort Wayne, IN
20,000	Big Brothers/Big Sisters of Greater Fort Wayne, Fort Wayne, IN
11,000	YMCA Greater Fort Wayne
4,000	South Side Opportunity Services, Inc. -- for recreation equipment
2,352	L A Gear Future Stars Youth League
1,500	Boys and Girls Club -- annual dinner

Lipton Co.

Company Contact

Englewood Cliffs, NJ
Web: http://www.unilever.com

Company Description

Former Name: Thomas J. Lipton Co.
Employees: 7,400
SIC(s): 2034 Dehydrated Fruits, Vegetables & Soups, 2035 Pickles, Sauces & Salad Dressings, 2099 Food Preparations Nec.
Parent Company: Unilever House Victoria Embankment
Parent Revenue: US$45,180,000,000

Operating Locations

CA: Lipton Co., Los Angeles, Santa Cruz; FL: Lipton Co., Jacksonville; IA: Lipton Co., Sioux City; NJ: Lipton Co., Englewood Cliffs; Lipton Co., Fairfield, Flemington, Moonachie; PA: Lipton Co., Harrisburg; VA: Lipton Co., Suffolk

Lipton Foundation

Giving Contact

Suzanne Cuff, Contact
Lipton Foundation
800 Sylvan Avenue
Englewood Cliffs, NJ 07632
Phone: (201)894-7405
Fax: (201)871-8198

Description

Founded: 1952
EIN: 226063094
Organization Type: Corporate Foundation
Giving Locations: primarily near corporate headquarters and plant locations.
Grant Types: Employee Matching Gifts, General Support.

Giving Philosophy

'It is the policy of the Lipton Foundation to make contributions of cash to health and human service organizations, civic and community organizations, art and cultural organizations and to educational institutions of higher learning with particular reference to food science and nutrition. We concentrate our contributions to programs and activities that are geographically located in the proximity to Lipton headquarters and to our several facilities in the U.S. Only after these and several major assistance contributions are made do we consider other requests.' Lipton Foundation Guidelines

Financial Summary

Total Giving: $400,000 (1996); $346,986 (1995); $462,732 (1994). Note: Contributes through foundation only. 1995 Giving includes foundation ($300,135); matching gifts ($23,351); United Way ($23,500).
Assets: $167,710 (1995); $61,932 (1994); $73,175 (1992)
Gifts Received: $443,795 (1995); $402,296 (1994); $993,750 (1992). Note: In 1995, the foundation received contributions from value of Colgate stock ($351,006) and from Conopco Inc. ($92,789).

Typical Recipients

Arts & Humanities: Arts Associations & Councils, Arts Centers, Arts Festivals, Dance, Historic Preservation, Libraries, Museums/Galleries, Music, Performing Arts, Public Broadcasting, Theater
Civic & Public Affairs: Business/Free Enterprise, Civil Rights, Economic Development, Civic & Public Affairs-General, Law & Justice, Legal Aid, Philanthropic Organizations, Public Policy, Safety, Urban & Community Affairs, Women's Affairs, Zoos/Aquariums
Education: Business Education, Colleges & Universities, Community & Junior Colleges, Economic Education, Education Associations, Education Funds, Education Reform, Health & Physical Education, Legal Education, Literacy, Medical Education, Minority Education, Private Education (Precollege), Public Education (Precollege), Science/Mathematics Education, Student Aid
Environment: Environment-General
Health: Cancer, Children's Health/Hospitals, Clinics/Medical Centers, Diabetes, Health Funds, Health Organizations, Heart, Hospices, Hospitals, Medical Rehabilitation, Medical Research, Medical Training, Mental Health, Multiple Sclerosis, Nutrition, Prenatal Health Issues, Single-Disease Health Associations
International: International Organizations, International Relations
Religion: Missionary Activities (Domestic), Religious Organizations, Religious Welfare
Science: Scientific Organizations
Social Services: At-Risk Youth, Big Brother/Big Sister, Community Centers, Community Service Organizations, Emergency Relief, Family Planning, Food/Clothing Distribution, People with Disabilities, Recreation & Athletics, Scouts, Special Olympics, Substance Abuse, United Funds/United Ways, Volunteer Services, Youth Organizations

Contributions Analysis

Giving Priorities: Social services; health, with emphasis on nutrition; higher education; civic organizations; and arts groups.
Arts & Humanities: 5% to 10%. Arts centers and institutes, historic preservation, museums, libraries, public broadcasting, and the performing arts. Also matches employee contributions to arts organizations.
Civic & Public Affairs: About 30%. Community groups, environmental affairs, civil rightsorganizations, and others.
Education: About 30%. National scholarship programs, higher education institutions, food sciences and nutrition, and technology and business education. Also sponsors matching gifts program.
Health: About 30%. Nutrition programs, united funds, youth organizations, legal aid agencies, family planning, recreation and athletics, community service organizations, hospitals, single-disease health organizations, and medical research groups.
Note: Priorities remain flexible in an effort to respond to community needs.

Application Procedures

Initial Contact: write for guidelines; then a letter or proposal
Application Requirements: description of the organization and its purpose, amount requested, purpose of funds sought, recently audited financial statement, proof of tax-exempt status, list of current sponsors and amount each contributes, past record of support, description of programs offered and their geographical scope, annual report, name of agency executive and phone number, methods to be used for evaluating program or project
Deadlines: to be included in next year's budget, no later than December; some late applications are approved if proposal meets requirements and funds are available; many are held over to the next year
Notes: Currently funded organizations wishing continued support should send letter by end of year with updated information.

Restrictions

Does not support individuals, dinners, tours, or special events.
Restricted from supporting international giving where funds will be spent overseas.

Additional Information

Publications: Guidelines

Corporate Officials

Patrick Cescau: president, chief executive officer, director PRIM CORP EMPL president, chief executive officer: Lipton Co.
Richard A. Goldstein: president, chief executive officer, director B Boston, MA 1942. ED Boston University LLB; University of Massachusetts BBA (1963); Harvard University LLM (1968). PRIM CORP EMPL president, chief executive officer, director: Unilever US, Inc. ADD CORP EMPL chairman: Lipton Co.

Foundation Officials

Helen Siegle: administrator

Grants Analysis

Disclosure Period: calendar year ending 1995
Total Grants: $300,135*
Number of Grants: 65
Average Grant: $4,617
Highest Grant: $75,000
Typical Range: $100 to $5,000 and $10,000 to $20,000
***Note:** Giving excludes matching gifts; United Way.

Recent Grants

Note: Grants derived from 1995 Form 990.

Arts & Humanities

5,000	John Harms Concerts, Englewood, NJ
2,000	Cultural Council
750	Center for Modern Dance
750	Center for Modern Dance Education
500	Art Center
300	Theater IV

Civic & Public Affairs

5,000	Pascack Valley, Westwood, NJ
2,500	Livingston County
750	Jane Voorhees Fund
500	Flemington Fund
500	Riddick's Fund
500	Spectrum

Education

1,500	Virginia College Fund, Richmond, VA
1,000	Foundation for Independent Colleges
1,000	Foundation for Independent Colleges
1,000	Foundation for Independent Colleges
500	Cabrillo College, Aptos, CA
500	St. Joseph's School
500	Schools Plus, Santa Rosa, CA
500	University of Cincinnati, Cincinnati, OH
400	Virginia College Fund, Richmond, VA

Health

25,000	Juvenile Diabetes Foundation, New York, NY
15,000	Juvenile Diabetes Foundation, New York, NY
10,982	Juvenile Diabetes Foundation, New York, NY
4,000	Deborah Hospital, Browns Mills, NJ
3,044	March of Dimes
3,000	Holy Name Hospital
2,000	American Heart Association
1,655	Valerie Fund, Maplewood, NJ
1,000	Medical Center
1,000	National Multiple Sclerosis Society, New York, NY
684	March of Dimes
300	Children's Hospital

International

300	Operation Smile, Norfolk, VA

Religion

1,000	Crusade for Christ
200	Bethesda Mission, Harrisburg, PA

Social Services

9,000	United Way
6,000	Suffolk United, Suffolk, VA
4,500	United Way
3,000	Heart of America United Way, Kansas City, MO
2,000	Hope House, Santa Fe, NM
1,500	Boys and Girls Club
1,500	Independence Fund
1,000	Boy Scouts of America
1,000	Girl Scouts of America, Chicago, IL
1,000	Tri-County United
500	Boys Club
300	Independence Fund
200	Community Assistance Fund, Chicago, IL
200	Suffolk Youth, Suffolk, VA

Arthur D. Little, Inc.

Company Contact

Cambridge, MA
Web: http://www.arthurdlittle.com

Company Description

Revenue: US$589,000,000
Employees: 3,300

SIC(s): 8731 Commercial Physical Research, 8742 Management Consulting Services.

Operating Locations

Argentina: Arthur D. Little de Argentina S.A., Buenos Aires; Austria: Arthur D. Little International GmbH, Vienna; Belgium: Arthur D. Little International, Inc., Brussels; Brazil: Arthur D. Little Limitada, Sao Paulo; Canada: Arthur D. Little of Canada Limited, Toronto; Colombia: Arthur D. Little de Colombia, Ltda., Bogota; Czech Republic: Arthur D. Little International, Inc., Prague; France:, Paris; Germany:, Berlin, Dusseldorf, Munich, Wiesbaden; Hong Kong: Arthur D. Little Asia Pacific, Inc., Hong Kong; India: Arthur D. Little India Consultancy, Mumbai; Italy: Arthur D. Little International, Inc., Milan, Rome; Japan: Arthur D. Little (Japan) Inc., Tokyo; Republic of Korea: Arthur D. Little Korea, Inc., Seoul; Mexico: Arthur D. Little Latin America, S.A. de C.V., Mexico City; Arthur D. Little Mexicana, S.A. de C.V., Monterrey; Malaysia: Arthur D. Little (Malaysia) Sdn Bhd, Kuala Lumpur; Norway: Arthur D. Little International, Inc., Oslo; Portugal:, Lisbon; Russia:, Moscow; Saudi Arabia: Arthur D. Little International, Inc, Riyadh; Singapore: Arthur D. Little Southeast Asia Singapore, Singapore; Spain: Arthur D. Little S.L., Madrid; Sweden: Arthur D. Little AB, Gothenburg; Arthur D. Little AB., Stockholm; Switzerland: Arthur D. Little AG, Thalwil/Zurich; United Arab Emirates: Arthur D. Little International, Inc, Abu Dhabi, Dubai; United Kingdom: Arthur D. Little Limited, Cambridge, Harrogate, London; Venezuela: Arthur D. Little de Venezuela, C.A., Caracas

Nonmonetary Support

Type: In-kind Services
Note: In-kind services are in the form of printing.

Arthur D. Little Foundation

Giving Contact

Annemarie Gattuso, Secretary for the Trustees
Arthur D. Little Foundation
25 Acorn Park
Cambridge, MA 02140
Phone: (617)498-6035
Fax: (617)498-7119
Note: Giving program is being restructured.

Description

Founded: 1953
EIN: 046079132
Organization Type: Corporate Foundation
Giving Locations: MA: Cambridge operating locations.
Grant Types: Award, Fellowship, General Support, Multiyear/Continuing Support, Project.

Financial Summary

Total Giving: $342,300 (1997); $345,300 (1996); $347,300 (1995). Note: Contributes through foundation only.
Giving Analysis: Giving for 1995 includes: foundation grants to United Way ($44,250); 1996: foundation grants to United Way ($100,750); 1997: foundation grants to United Way ($39,350)
Assets: $7,536 (1997); $5,151 (1996); $6,868 (1995)
Gifts Received: $350,000 (1997); $350,000 (1996); $350,000 (1995). Note: Contributions are from Arthur D. Little, Inc.

Typical Recipients

Arts & Humanities: Arts Associations & Councils, Arts Outreach, Ballet, Libraries, Museums/Galleries, Music, Performing Arts, Public Broadcasting, Theater
Civic & Public Affairs: Business/Free Enterprise, Community Foundations, Economic Development, Employment/Job Training, Civic & Public Affairs-General, Hispanic Affairs, Housing, Legal Aid, Municipalities/Towns, Nonprofit Management, Philanthropic Organizations, Professional & Trade Associations, Urban & Community Affairs, Women's Affairs, Zoos/Aquariums
Education: Afterschool/Enrichment Programs, Arts/Humanities Education, Business Education, Business-School Partnerships, Colleges & Universities, Continuing Education, Education Funds, Engineering/Technological Education, Environmental Education, Faculty Development, Education-General, Leadership Training, Minority Education, Private Education (Precollege), Public Education (Precollege), School Volunteerism, Science/Mathematics Education, Special Education, Student Aid, Vocational & Technical Education
Environment: Environment-General, Resource Conservation
Health: Adolescent Health Issues, AIDS/HIV, Children's Health/Hospitals, Emergency/Ambulance Services, Hospices, Hospitals, Medical Research, Mental Health, Public Health
International: Foreign Educational Institutions, International Development, International Environmental Issues, International Relief Efforts
Science: Science Exhibits & Fairs, Science Museums, Scientific Centers & Institutes
Social Services: Camps, Child Abuse, Child Welfare, Community Centers, Community Service Organizations, Counseling, Delinquency & Criminal Rehabilitation, Emergency Relief, Family Services, Homes, People with Disabilities, Senior Services, Sexual Abuse, Shelters/Homelessness, United Funds/United Ways, Veterans, Volunteer Services, Youth Organizations

Contributions Analysis

Giving Priorities: Company supports organizations near business offices worldwide in keeping with its overall contributions guidelines. The foundation makes contributions in the areas of education, scientific research, health care, and community services.
Arts & Humanities: 9%. Funds libraries and orchestras.
Civic & Public Affairs: 26%. Supports minority and civic affairs.
Education: 33%. Foundation makes contributions to nonprofit organizations primarily aimed at improving education, at all levels and across a range of institutional settings. A particular emphasis is placed on improving learning and teaching in the areas of mathematics, science, and technology. In some cases, educational programs in human services, arts and environmental organizations which affect the quality of life in communities where Arthur D. Little employees live and work will be considered for funding.
Science: 9%. Funds research and science museums.
Social Services: 21%. Major support for the United Way.
Note: Total contributions made in 1997.

Application Procedures

Initial Contact: Send a written proposal or a preliminary inquiry.
Application Requirements: Include information on the operations of organization and a recent balance sheet.
Deadlines: None.

Restrictions

Does not support individuals; religious or political organizations; national health organizations; events such as dinners, lunches, galas, or marches; or individual scholarships or research.
Only gives to organizations operating in areas where the company has an office.

Additional Information

Foundation reported that it is in the process of establishing new guidelines; contact the foundation for details.

Publications: Application Guidelines

Corporate Officials

Judith C. Harris: vice president human resources PRIM CORP EMPL vice president: Arthur D. Little, Inc.
Charles Robert LaMantia: president, chief executive officer, director B New York, NY 1939. ED Columbia University BA (1960); Columbia University BS (1961); Columbia University MS (1962); Columbia University ScD (1965); Harvard University Graduate School of Business Administration (1979). PRIM CORP EMPL president, chief executive officer, director: Arthur D. Little, Inc. CORP AFFIL director: State Street Boston Corp.; director: State Street Bank & Trust Co. NONPR AFFIL member: Society Chemical Industry; member, board overseers: WGBH Public Broadcasting; trustee: Memorial Dr Trust; member: Massachusetts Business Roundtable; member: Massachusetts Governor's Council; member: Conference Board; director: Boston Public Library Foundation; member advisory council: Columbia University School Engineering; member advisory council: Boston College School of Management; member: American Institute Chemical Engineers.
John Francis Magee: chairman, director B Bangor, ME 1926. ED Bowdoin College AB (1946); Harvard University Graduate School of Business Administration MBA (1948); University of Maine MS (1952). PRIM CORP EMPL chairman, director: Arthur D. Little, Inc. CORP AFFIL director: John Hancock Mutual Life Insurance Co.; director: Houghton Mifflin Co. NONPR AFFIL chairman, trustee: Thompson Island Outward Bound Educational Center; honorary trustee: Woods Hole Oceanographic Institute; member: Phi Beta Kappa; member: Phi Kappa Psi; trustee: New England Aquarium; member: Operations Research America; trustee: Emerson Hospital; member: Institute for Management Sciences; trustee: Boston University Medical Center; trustee emeritus: Bowdoin College. CLUB AFFIL Country Club; Somerset Club; Concord Country Club.
P. Ranganath Nayak: senior vice president B New Delhi, DH India 1942. ED Victoria Jubilee Technology Institute Bombay BE (1963); Massachusetts Institute of Technology PhD (1968). PRIM CORP EMPL senior vice president: Arthur D. Little, Inc.
David C. Shanks: vice president human resources B Indianapolis, IN 1939. ED Cornell University (1962); University of Delaware (1968). PRIM CORP EMPL vice president human resources: Sunoco Inc. CORP AFFIL vice president: Sun Co. Inc.; director: Corion Corp. NONPR AFFIL director: Associate Industry MA.

Foundation Officials

Ann Farrington: secretary
Ann Gillespie: trustee
Judith C. Harris: trustee (see above)
Theodore Paul Heuchling: trustee B Chicago, IL 1925. ED Massachusetts Institute of Technology (1946-1948). PRIM CORP EMPL senior vice president: Arthur D. Little, Inc. CORP AFFIL senior vice president: Arthur D Little Inc.
P. Ranganath Nayak: trustee (see above)
David C. Shanks: trustee (see above)

Grants Analysis

Disclosure Period: calendar year ending 1997
Total Grants: $302,950*
Number of Grants: 26
Average Grant: $11,652
Highest Grant: $24,290
Typical Range: $1,000 to $15,000
***Note:** Giving excludes United Way.

Recent Grants

Note: Grants derived from 1996 Form 990.

Arts & Humanities

10,000 Boston Symphony Orchestra, Boston, MA

7,000	WGBH Educational Foundation, Boston, MA
5,000	Boston Ballet, Boston, MA
2,500	Children's Museum, Cambridge, MA
2,500	Children's Museum, Cambridge, MA
Civic & Public Affairs	
15,000	Arthur D. Little Foundation
10,000	Centro de Investigacion Familiar
5,000	American Institute of Chemical Engineers, New York, NY
5,000	Center for Law and Education, Cambridge, MA
3,500	Associated Grantmakers of Massachusetts, Boston, MA
1,500	Cambridge Foundation, Cambridge, MA
1,500	New England Aquarium, Boston, MA
Education	
25,000	Bowdoin College, Bowdoin, ME
12,000	Thompson Island Outward Bound Education Center, Boston, MA
10,000	Northeastern University Department of Chemistry, Boston, MA
7,000	United Negro College Fund, New York, NY
5,500	United Negro College Fund, Boston, MA
5,000	Cambridge Partnership for Public Education, Cambridge, MA
5,000	Thompson Island Outward Bound Education Center, Boston, MA
5,000	University of Rhode Island Graduate School of Oceanography, Narragansett, RI
3,000	Hardy School
2,000	Cambridge School Volunteers, Cambridge, MA
Environment	
5,000	Keystone Center, Keystone, CO
5,000	Keystone Center, Keystone, CO
Health	
2,500	Alliance for the Mentally Ill, MA
International	
15,500	American Friends of Cambridge University, Cambridge, England
15,500	American Friends of Cambridge University, Cambridge, England
12,000	International Management Education Foundation, Cedex, France
12,000	International Management Education Foundation, Cedex, France
5,000	Accion International, New York, NY
5,000	Accion International, New York, NY
2,000	United Way National Capital Area, Washington, DC
2,000	United Way National Capital Area, Washington, DC
Science	
2,500	Houston Museum of Natural Science, Houston, TX
2,500	Museum of Science, Boston, MA
1,000	Woods Hole Oceanographic Institute, Woods Hole, MA
Social Services	
35,000	United Way Massachusetts Bay, Boston, MA
34,000	United Way Massachusetts Bay, Boston, MA
33,000	Massachusetts Society for Prevention of Cruelty to Children, Boston, MA
25,000	CAST, Boston, MA
9,000	Just A Start Corporation, Cambridge, MA
3,500	United Way Bay Area, San Francisco, CA
3,500	United Way Texas Gulf Coast, Houston, TX
3,050	United Way Bay Area, San Francisco, CA
2,500	Shelter, Columbia, MO
2,500	Trident United Way, Charleston, SC
2,200	United Way Texas Gulf Coast, Houston, TX
2,000	Cambridge Community Services, Cambridge, MA
1,850	United Way National Capital Area, Washington, DC
1,500	Phillips Brooks House Associates, Cambridge, MA
1,500	United Way Crusade of Mercy, Chicago, IL
1,100	Trident United Way, Charleston, SC
1,000	United Way National Capital Area, Washington, DC
750	United Way Crusade of Mercy, Chicago, IL

LITTON INDUSTRIES, INC.

Company Contact

Woodland Hills, CA
Web: http://www.littoncorp.com

Company Description

Revenue: US$4,399,900,000
Employees: 31,500
Fortune Rank: 333, per FORTUNE Magazine's list of 500 Largest U.S. Corporations (1999).
FF 333
SIC(s): 3571 Electronic Computers, 3629 Electrical Industrial Apparatus Nec, 3663 Radio & T.V. Communications Equipment, 3679 Electronic Components Nec.

Foundation of the Litton Industries

Giving Contact

Janette Thomas, President
Foundation of the Litton Industries
21240 Burbank Blvd.
Woodland Hills, CA 91367-6675
Phone: (818)598-5423
Fax: (818)598-2068

Description

EIN: 956095343
Organization Type: Corporate Foundation
Giving Locations: CA: Los Angeles national and and regional appeals centered in metropolitan area nationally.
Grant Types: Endowment, General Support, Scholarship.
Note: Employee matching gift ratio: 1 to 1.

Financial Summary

Total Giving: $1,000,000 (fiscal year ending April 30, 2000); $1,000,000 (fiscal 1999); $1,082,927 (fiscal 1997). Note: Contributes through foundation only. Giving includes domestic subsidiaries. Fiscal 1997 Giving includes foundation ($743,665); matching gifts ($99,262); United Way ($240,000). 1996 Giving includes foundation ($682,279); matching gifts ($110,904); United Way ($240,000).
Assets: $16,988,183 (fiscal 1997); $16,990,768 (fiscal 1996); $15,941,754 (fiscal 1995)
Gifts Received: $110,000 (fiscal 1997); $441,950 (fiscal 1996); $120,000 (fiscal 1995). Note: Contributions are received from Litton Industries and its primary subsidiaries.

Typical Recipients

Arts & Humanities: Arts Associations & Councils, Ballet, Museums/Galleries, Music, Opera, Performing Arts, Public Broadcasting
Civic & Public Affairs: Civic & Public Affairs-General, Law & Justice, Legal Aid, Nonprofit Management, Professional & Trade Associations, Public Policy, Women's Affairs
Education: Business Education, Colleges & Universities, Education Associations, Education Funds, Education Reform, Elementary Education (Private), Elementary Education (Public), Engineering/Technological Education, Minority Education, Private Education (Precollege), Public Education (Precollege), Science/Mathematics Education, Secondary Education (Public), Social Sciences Education, Student Aid
International: Foreign Educational Institutions, Health Care/Hospitals, International Affairs
Religion: Religious Organizations, Religious Welfare
Science: Science Museums, Scientific Centers & Institutes, Scientific Organizations
Social Services: Child Welfare, Community Service Organizations, People with Disabilities, Recreation & Athletics, Scouts, United Funds/United Ways, Volunteer Services, YMCA/YWCA/YMHA/YWHA, Youth Organizations

Contributions Analysis

Giving Priorities: Scholarships and direct grants to colleges and universities; social services, with an emphasis on United Way; music and other arts groups; and civic organizations.
Arts & Humanities: 9%. Interests include community television, music, museums, and the performing arts.
Civic & Public Affairs: 1%. Interests include law, ethics, and minorities.
Education: 58%. Emphasis on math, engineering, and science. Supports universities and public and private schools at the elementary and secondary levels. Also supports minorities and students with military ties.
Religion: 1%. Supports religious causes.
Science: 2%. Funds the california Science center.
Social Services: 29%. Supports the United Way and organizations for children and youth.
Note: Above percentages reflect foundation priorities only. The company also operates a scholarship program for higher education.

Application Procedures

Initial Contact: brief letter or proposal
Application Requirements: a description of organization, amount requested, purpose of funds sought, recently audited financial statement, and proof of tax-exempt status
Deadlines: None; board meets as necessary.

Restrictions

Foundation does not support building or capital funding, nor does it make grants to individuals.

Corporate Officials

Michael Brown: president, chief operating officer B 1941. ED Ottawa University BS. PRIM CORP EMPL president, chief operating officer: Litton Industries, Inc.
Rudolph E. Lang, Jr.: senior vice president, chief financial officer B 1936. ED Brigham Young University BS (1959); University of San Francisco MBA (1984). PRIM CORP EMPL senior vice president, chief financial officer: Litton Industries, Inc. CORP AFFIL vice president: Litton System Inc.
John Michael Leonis: chairman, director B Whittier, CA 1933. ED University of Arizona BEE (1959). PRIM CORP EMPL chairman, director: Litton Industries, Inc. CORP AFFIL president: Litton Systems Inc. NONPR AFFIL member: Naval Helicopter Association; director: World Affairs Council Town Hall; member: Institute Navigation; member: Association Naval Aviation; member: Association U.S. Army; member: American Electronics Association; member: American Institute Aeronautics & Astronautics; member: Air Force Association; government: Aerospace Industries Association.

Foundation Officials

Michael Brown: president (see above)
Clarence L. Price: director
Ana R. Rodriguez: secretary
Carol A. Wiesner: treasurer, director B Meadville, PA 1939. ED Pennsylvania State University BS (1960). PRIM CORP EMPL vice president, controller: Litton Industries, Inc. CORP AFFIL vice president: Litton System Inc.

Grants Analysis

Disclosure Period: fiscal year ending April 30, 1997
Total Grants: $743,666*
Number of Grants: 117
Average Grant: $6,356
Highest Grant: $100,000
Typical Range: $1,000 to $6,000
***Note:** Giving excludes matching gifts; United Way.

Recent Grants

Note: Grants derived from fiscal 1997 Form 990.

Arts & Humanities

50,000	Music Center Unified Fund, Los Angeles, CA
20,000	Alliance for the Arts, Thousand Oaks, CA
5,000	John F. Kennedy Center for Performing Arts, Washington, DC
4,930	Los Angeles Music Center Opera, Los Angeles, CA

Civic & Public Affairs

5,000	Ethics Research Center, Washington, DC
3,000	Society of Women Engineers, Bellflower, CA
3,000	Washington Legal Foundation, Washington, DC
2,500	Manhattan Institute, New York, NY

Education

100,000	Carnegie Mellon University, Pittsburgh, PA
100,000	Stanford University, Stanford, CA
70,000	Iowa State University Foundation, Ames, IA
50,000	California State Polytechnic University, San Luis Obispo, CA
37,000	Regent University, Stanford, CA
20,000	University of Massachusetts, Amherst, MA
16,000	Independent Colleges of Southern California, Los Angeles, CA
10,500	Moss Point School District, Moss Point, MS
10,000	Carnegie Mellon University, Pittsburgh, PA
10,000	Gautier High School, Gautier, MS
10,000	Jackson County School District, Vancleave, MS
10,000	Regent University, Virginia Beach, VA
10,000	Stanford University School of Engineering, Stanford, CA
8,000	Ocean Springs School District, Ocean Springs, MS
7,500	University of Oregon, Eugene, OR
7,000	Claremont McKenna College, Claremont, CA
7,000	Don Bosco College, Rosemont, CA
6,000	United Negro College Fund, New York, NY
5,500	St. Peter the Apostle Catholic School, Pascagoula, MS
5,015	Virginia Tech Foundation, Blacksburg, VA
5,000	Brigham Young University, Provo, UT
5,000	Center for Excellence in Education, McLean, VA
5,000	Harvard University, Cambridge, MA
5,000	Harvey Mudd College, Claremont, CA
5,000	Stanford University, Stanford, CA
3,180	Fund for American Studies, Washington, DC
3,000	Aerospace Education Foundation, Arlington, VA
3,000	California State Polytechnic University, San Luis Obispo, CA
3,000	Kansas University Endowment Association, Lawrence, KS
3,000	Native American Scholarship Fund, Albuquerque, NM
2,000	Polytechnic University, Brooklyn, NY
2,000	University of Arizona, Tucson, AZ

Religion

6,000	Resurrection Catholic, Pascagoula, MS

Science

15,000	California Science Center, Los Angeles, CA
5,000	California Science Center, Los Angeles, CA

Social Services

240,000	United Way, Los Angeles, CA
16,000	Jimmy Stewart Relay Marathon, Santa Monica, CA
5,000	ARCS Foundation Los Angeles Chapter, Los Angeles, CA
4,000	League for Children, Los Angeles, CA
2,500	Boy Scouts of America, Van Nuys, CA
2,500	Girl Scouts of America Angeles Council, Los Angeles, CA
2,500	Hugh O'Brian Youth Leadership Foundation, Los Angeles, CA

LIZ CLAIBORNE, INC.

Company Contact

New York, NY
Web: http://www.lizclaiborne.com

Company Description

Employees: 7,100
SIC(s): 2331 Women's/Misses' Blouses & Shirts, 2335 Women's/Misses' Dresses, 2337 Women's/Misses' Suits & Coats, 2339 Women's/Misses' Outerwear Nec.

Nonmonetary Support

Type: Donated Products
Note: Support is very limited, and products are only donated in support of significant employee volunteer involvement.

Liz Claiborne Foundation

Giving Contact

Melanie Lyons, Director
Liz Claiborne Foundation
1441 Broadway Avenue
New York, NY 10018
Phone: (212)626-5767
Fax: (212)626-8060
Web: http://www.lizclaiborne.com/lizinc/foundation

Description

Founded: 1981
EIN: 133060673
Organization Type: Corporate Foundation
Giving Locations: AL: Montgomery; NJ: Hudson County; NY: New York
Grant Types: Challenge, Employee Matching Gifts, General Support, Project.

Giving Philosophy

In 1981 five years after Liz Claiborne Inc. was founded, the company's principals established the Liz Clairborne Foundation to serve as the company's center for charitable activities. The Foundation has grown since that time, through increasing levels of grant distributions, a developing scope of program initiatives and expanded support for employees' involvement in volunteer efforts.

The foundation works to meet the needs of the communities where the major facilities of Liz Claiborne Inc. are located. It provides active assistance to various nonprofit organizations, especially those which address issues of particular concern to women and their families. Projects focus primarily on helping disadvantaged women gain their self-sufficiency through job training and microenterprise development; serving the special needs of women who are HIV-positive or have AIDS; working toward prevention of family violence while assisting abused women and children in their recovery; and expanding educational opportunities and developmental activities for underserved children. In addition, the foundation provides ongoing support to many artistic and cultural institutions which enhance the livability of our communities.

The Liz Claiborne Foundation actively encourages employees to volunteer at local nonprofit organizations, and supports their charitable interests in the arts, human services, health, education and the environment through a wide-ranging Matching Gifts Program.

Financial Summary

Total Giving: $1,360,534 (1998); $1,302,270 (1997); $1,099,143 (1996). Note: Contributes through foundation only.
Assets: $22,118,279 (1998); $24,594,628 (1997); $22,508,785 (1996)
Gifts Received: $915,483 (1996); $1,171,218 (1995); $1,006,303 (1994). Note: In 1996, contributions were received from Liz Claiborne Inc.

Typical Recipients

Arts & Humanities: Arts Associations & Councils, Arts Centers, Community Arts, Ethnic & Folk Arts, History & Archaeology, Libraries, Museums/Galleries, Music, Opera, Public Broadcasting, Theater
Civic & Public Affairs: Asian American Affairs, Botanical Gardens/Parks, Employment/Job Training, Gay/Lesbian Issues, Civic & Public Affairs-General, Housing, Law & Justice, Urban & Community Affairs, Women's Affairs, Zoos/Aquariums
Education: Arts/Humanities Education, Colleges & Universities, Education Funds, Education Reform, Elementary Education (Public), Education-General, Literacy, Medical Education, Minority Education, Preschool Education, Private Education (Precollege), Public Education (Precollege), Science/Mathematics Education, Secondary Education (Private)
Environment: Air/Water Quality, Environment-General
Health: AIDS/HIV, Cancer, Clinics/Medical Centers, Eyes/Blindness, Health Organizations, Hospitals, Long-Term Care, Prenatal Health Issues, Public Health, Single-Disease Health Associations
International: Human Rights
Religion: Jewish Causes, Religious Welfare
Science: Science Museums
Social Services: Big Brother/Big Sister, Camps, Child Abuse, Child Welfare, Community Service Organizations, Crime Prevention, Day Care, Delinquency & Criminal Rehabilitation, Domestic Violence, Emergency Relief, Family Services, Food/Clothing Distribution, Recreation & Athletics, Senior Services, YMCA/YWCA/YMHA/YWHA, Youth Organizations

Contributions Analysis

Giving Priorities: AIDS education, outreach, and services; environmental broadcast programming and education; New York City museums and other arts groups; an adopted high school; and local hospitals.

Arts & Humanities: 14%.
Civic & Public Affairs: 25%. To help women and families in need gain their self-sufficiency through long-term, broad-based solutions to poverty; improve opportunities for women through multi-dimensional job readiness, adult education, vocational training, career advancement, and enterprise development programs.
Education: 11%.
Health: 8%. To enhance services to meet the special needs of HIV-positive women and their children; increase access to effective education and prevention programs targeting women and girls.
Social Services: 42%. Supports organizations that provide comprehensive services to aid abused women and children in their recovery; address the causes of violence and abuse against women and children, and work toward prevention. To expand opportunities for economically disadvantaged children and teens to meet their full potential through innovative child care and educational approaches, and through exceptional programs providing solid preparation for higher education and the world of work.

Application Procedures

Initial Contact: Call or write for guidelines, then full written proposal.
Application Requirements: Include a statement of goals, history, and accomplishments; statement of purpose or objective; description of how the program or project is to be implemented; plans to evaluate project's success; amount requested; current organization budget and proposed project budget, showing expenses and income, and following year's budgets if the proposal is submitted within three months of new fiscal year; most recent audited financial statements; list of funding sources and amounts contributed in current and previous year; funding pending approval for current year; amount of funding for project supplied by the organization's general budget; number of professional and support staff, with titles; list of board members, with affiliations; proof of tax-exempt status.
Deadlines: None.
Review Process: Initial staff review, final review, and funding decision by grant-making committee.
Evaluative Criteria: Preference given to direct services; relevance to foundation's priorities and geographic focus; strength of project or program; managerial, planning, and financial capability of organization; other funding sources; employee involvement.
Decision Notification: Board meets in April, July, October, and December.
Notes: The foundation does not accept unsolicited proposals for the arts or the environment.

Restrictions

Contributions are not made to programs and projects based and/or operating outside the United States; religious, fraternal, or veterans' organizations; individuals; research; professional meetings, conferences, or symposia; building funds or equipment; endowments; hospital-based programs or single-disease organizations; film, video, television, or radio projects; or for sponsorship of events, performances, or exhibits.

Corporate Officials

Robert Bernard: senior vice president international sales PRIM CORP EMPL senior vice president international sales: Liz Claiborne, Inc.
Jerome A. Chazen: co-founder, chairman, director B New York, NY 1927. ED University of Wisconsin BA (1948); Columbia University MBA (1950). PRIM CORP EMPL chairman emeritus: Liz Claiborne, Inc. ADD CORP EMPL chairman: Liz Claiborne Foreign Holdings Inc.
Harvey L. Falk: president, vice chairman B 1934. ED New York University (1955). PRIM CORP EMPL president, vice chairman: Liz Claiborne, Inc. CORP AFFIL vice chairman: Liz Claiborne Cosemetics Inc.; vice chairman: Liz Claiborne Foreign Holdings Inc.
Joseph Allen McNeary: senior vice president B New York, NY 1948. ED Georgetown University BA (1969). PRIM CORP EMPL senior vice president: Liz Claiborne, Inc. CORP AFFIL president: Liz Claiborne Retail Group. NONPR AFFIL director: Clearport School. CLUB AFFIL Heights Casino Club.

Foundation Officials

Robert Bernard: member grantmaking committee (see above)
Jerome A. Chazen: trustee (see above)
Harvey L. Falk: member grantmaking committee (see above)
Melanie Lyons: director, member grant committee
Jay M. Margolis: member grantmaking committee B New York, NY 1949. ED Queens College BA (1971). PRIM CORP EMPL vice chairman: Liz Claiborne, Inc. NONPR AFFIL member, board: Fathers Day/Mothers Day Council. CLUB AFFIL City Athletic Club.
Joseph Allen McNeary: member grantmaking committee (see above)
Nancy Rogers: member grantmaking committee

Grants Analysis

Disclosure Period: calendar year ending 1998
Total Grants: $1,335,534*
Number of Grants: 163
Average Grant: $8,182
Highest Grant: $153,350
Typical Range: $500 to $10,000
***Note:** Giving excludes United Way. Number of grants and average grant figure excludes contributions under $500.

Recent Grants

Note: Grants derived from 1997 Form 990.

Arts & Humanities

150,000 Educational Broadcasting Corps, New York, NY
17,000 American Crafts Museum, New York, NY
10,100 Carnegie Hall Society, New York, NY
8,000 Arts Connection, New York, NY

Civic & Public Affairs

50,000 Women's Housing and Economic Development, New York, NY
20,000 Carroll Gardens Neighborhood, Brooklyn, NY
20,000 Iris House Center for Women, New York, NY
15,000 Community IMPACT, Palo Alto, CA
15,000 Let's Celebrate
15,000 New York Asian Women's Center, New York, NY
15,000 Non-Traditional Employment, New York, NY
10,841 York Street Project, Jersey City, NJ
10,000 Committee for Lawyers
10,000 National Marfan Foundation, Port Washington, NY

Education

35,000 Educational Foundation, New York, NY
25,128 High School of Fashion Industry, New York, NY
20,000 Clearpool, New York, NY
20,000 Community Research Initiative
20,000 Student Sponsor Partnership, New York, NY
15,000 Albert O. Oliver Program, New York, NY
15,000 East Harlem School at Exodus, New York, NY
15,000 Entrenet
15,000 Learning Project, New York, NY
15,000 New York City Technical, New York, NY
15,000 Queens College Foundation, Queens, NY
10,000 Kenmare School, Jersey City, NJ
9,425 Multitasking Systems of New York, New York, NY

Health

20,000 Montgomery AIDS Outreach, Montgomery, AL
15,000 Hispanic AIDS Forum, New York, NY
15,000 HIV Law Project, New York, NY
15,000 New Jersey Women and AIDS Network, New Brunswick, NJ
15,000 Women Fighting AIDS

Religion

112,500 United Jewish Appeal Federation, New York, NY
15,000 Good Shepherd Services, New York, NY
15,000 Park Slope Christian Help, Brooklyn, NY
15,000 St. Matthew's and St. Timothy's Neighborhood Center, New York, NY
10,000 Faith Services, Greensburg, PA

Social Services

40,000 YWCA Hudson County, Bayonne, NJ
25,000 Maura Clarke Itaford Center
22,500 Steps to End Family Violence, New York, NY
20,000 Violence Intervention Program, New York, NY
15,000 Alonzo Daughtry Family Life, Brooklyn, NY
15,000 Asphalt Green, New York, NY
15,000 Center for Anti-Violence Education, Brooklyn, NY
15,000 Garment Industry Day Care, New York, NY
15,000 HELP Social Service Corp
15,000 Lower East Side Family Union, New York, NY
15,000 YWCA, New York, NY
10,000 Family Sunshine Center
10,000 Girls, Incorporated, New York, NY

Lockheed Martin Corp.

★ Number 49 of Top 100 Corporate Givers

Company Contact

Bethesda, MD
Web: http://www.lockheedmartin.com

Company Description

Revenue: US$26,266,000,000
Profit: US$1,001,000,000
Employees: 190,000
Fortune Rank: 52, per FORTUNE Magazine's list of 500 Largest U.S. Corporations (1999).
FF 52
SIC(s): 3721 Aircraft, 3728 Aircraft Parts & Equipment Nec, 3761 Guided Missiles & Space Vehicles, 3764 Space Propulsion Units & Parts.

Lockheed Martin Corp. Foundation

Giving Contact

David E. Phillips, Manager, Corporate Philanthropy
Lockheed Martin Corp.
6801 Rockledge Drive
Bethesda, MD 20817
Phone: (301)897-6292
Fax: (301)897-6252
Email: David_E_Phillips@ccmail.orl.mme.com

Description

Founded: 1995
Organization Type: Corporate Foundation
Giving Locations: in communities were employees live and work.

Giving Philosophy

'The Lockheed Martin Corporation is committed to a program of philanthropy that supports the Corporation's strategic business goals and invests in the quality of life in the communities where our employees work and live.' Lockheed Martin Corp. Philanthropy.

Financial Summary

Total Giving: $18,000,000 (2000 approx); $17,900,000 (1999 approx); $17,450,000 (1998 approx). Note: Contributes through corporate direct giving program and foundation. 1998 Giving includes corporate direct giving ($8,725,000); foundation ($8,725,000).
Gifts Received: In 1994, The Lockheed Leadership Fund received $1,624,900 in contributions from the Lockheed Corporation. In 1994, the Martin Marietta Corporation Foundation received $7,117,000 in contributions from the Martin Marietta Corporation.

Application Procedures

Application Requirements: Include a description of organization and its goals; amount requested and its specific purpose; statement as to how the contribution will benefit the community; copy of recent IRS Section 501(c)(3) tax exempt letter; list of board members and other funders, indicating stability of organization.
Deadlines: None.
Evaluative Criteria: Applicant should have active, diverse boards, effective leadership, continuity and efficiency of administration; specific programs are preferred over capital campaigns.
Decision Notification: Applications are evaluated quarterly.
Notes: Philanthropic activities are administered by the communications representatives at the corporation's operating locations around the country, and by the Manager of Corp. Philanthropy at the corporate headquarters. Contact information is included in guidelines.

Restrictions

Company does not support organizations that discriminate by race, creed, gender, sexual orientation, age, religion, or national origin.
Company does not fund home-based child care or educational services; individuals; religious organizations for religious purposes; professional associations, labor organizations, fraternal organizations, social clubs, or athletic groups.
Company does not sponsor social events organized by social clubs or purchase advertising in souvenir booklets, yearbooks, or journals unrelated to the company's business interests.
Each organization is limited to one grant per year, except in unusual circumstances.

Additional Information

The Lockheed Martin Corporation was formed by the merger of the Lockheed and Martin Marietta corporations in 1995. The philanthropic activities of the Lockheed Leadership Fund and the Martin Marietta Corporation Foundation have been combined to form the Lockheed Martin Corporation Foundation.
New requests are evaluated equally with previously funded organizations.
Publications: Guidelines

Corporate Officials

Dr. Vance Coffman: vice president
David E. Phillips

Giving Program Officials

David E. Phillips: manager corporate philanthropy (see above)

LOCTITE CORP.

Company Contact

Hartford, CT

Company Description

Employees: 4,242
SIC(s): 2821 Plastics Materials & Resins, 2891 Adhesives & Sealants, 5169 Chemicals & Allied Products Nec.
Parent Company: Henkel KGAA, Henkelstrasse 67, Dusseldorf, Germany

Operating Locations

CT: Loctite Corp., Hartford, Newington, Rocky Hill; Loctite Corp., Rocky Hill; Loctite Corp. North American Group, Rocky Hill; IL: Loctite Corp., Aurora; NY: Visolox Systems, Troy; OH: Loctite Corp., Cleveland, Solon, Warrensville Heights; PR: Loctite Corp., Sabana Grande

Corporate Sponsorship

Type: Arts & cultural events; Sports events; Pledge-a-thon

Giving Contact

Karin Cooley, Administrator, Corporate Contributions
Loctite Corp.
Hartford Sq. N.
10 Columbus Blvd.
Hartford, CT 06106
Phone: (860)571-5100
Fax: (860)520-5073
Email: karin.cooley@loctite.com
Note: Ms. Cooley's extension is 5438.

Description

Organization Type: Corporate Giving Program
Giving Locations: areas where the company has offices.
Grant Types: Employee Matching Gifts, Fellowship, General Support, Matching, Multiyear/Continuing Support.

Financial Summary

Total Giving: $700,000 (1997 approx); $584,000 (1996 approx); $500,000 (1995 approx). Note: Contributes through corporate direct giving program only. Giving includes corporate direct giving; domestic subsidiaries.

Typical Recipients

Arts & Humanities: Arts & Humanities-General
Civic & Public Affairs: Civic & Public Affairs-General
Education: Education-General
Health: Health-General

Contributions Analysis

Arts & Humanities: About 10%.
Civic & Public Affairs: Less than 5%.
Education: About 65%. About one-third of educational funding supports pre-high school education, including infant and pre-kindergarten programs.
Health: About 20%

Application Procedures

Initial Contact: call or write for Coordinating Council for Foundations Common Grant Application Form
Application Requirements: proposal narrative, including: a description of organization, amount requested, purpose of funds sought, plans for evaluation; recently audited financial statement, proof of tax-exempt status, board of directors, with affiliations; list of contributors to organization; most recent annual report; budget for grant request; organizational budget for this year and last; and organizational chart
Deadlines: None.

Restrictions

Does not support individuals, religious organizations for sectarian purposes, political or lobbying groups, or informational/educational videos or documentaries.

Corporate Officials

David Freeman: chairman, president, chief executive officer, director B 1944. ED Institute of Chartered Accountants of England & Wales (1965); University of Durham (England) (1965-1968). PRIM CORP EMPL chairman, president, chief executive officer, director: Loctite Corp. CORP AFFIL director: Sealed Air Corp.

Giving Program Officials

Karin Cooley: administrator corp. contributions

LOEWS CORP.

Company Contact

New York, NY

Company Description

Revenue: US$20,713,000,000
Profit: US$464,800,000
Employees: 34,300
Fortune Rank: 72, per FORTUNE Magazine's list of 500 Largest U.S. Corporations (1999).
FF 72
SIC(s): 2111 Cigarettes, 6311 Life Insurance, 6331 Fire, Marine & Casualty Insurance, 6719 Holding Companies Nec.

Operating Locations

Australia: Lombard Insurance Holdings Ltd., North Sydney; Diamond Offshore General Co., Perth; Belgium: Continental Insurance Co., Brussels, Brabant; Brazil: Ema Artefatos De Papeis Ltda., Sao Paulo; Canada: LGC Development Corp., Montreal; Bulova Watch Co. Ltd., Toronto; Marine Office of America Corp., Toronto; Germany: Continental Insurance Co. Niederlassung Fuer Deutschland, Frankfurt, Hessen; Monaco: Loews Hotel, Monaco; Netherlands: Diamond Offshore Netherlands BV, Haarlem, Noord-Holland; United Kingdom: Odeco Drilling (United Kingdom) Ltd., Aberdeen, Grampian; CNA International Reinsurance Co. Ltd., London; CNA Re Management Co. Ltd., London; Continental Insurance Co., London; Continental Management Services Ltd., London; Continental Reinsurance Management Co. Ltd., London; Fireman's Insurance Co. of Newark New Jersey, London; Market Insurance Services Ltd., London; Odeco Drilling Ltd., London

Nonmonetary Support

Type: Donated Products

Loews Foundation

Giving Contact

Peter Keegan, Senior Vice President & Chief Financial Officer
Loews Foundation
667 Madison Avenue
New York, NY 10021
Phone: (212)521-2950
Fax: (212)521-2329

Description

Founded: 1957
EIN: 136082817
Organization Type: Corporate Foundation
Giving Locations: NY operating locations.
Grant Types: Employee Matching Gifts, General Support, Matching, Scholarship.

Note: Scholarships are provided for children of Loews Corporation through the National Merit Scholarship Corp.

Financial Summary

Total Giving: $1,980,563 (1997); $2,081,410 (1996); $2,669,678 (1995). Note: Contributes through foundation only.
Giving Analysis: Giving for 1995 includes: foundation scholarships ($77,605); foundation matching gifts ($31,623); 1996: foundation scholarships ($79,630); foundation matching gifts ($44,264); foundation grants to United Way ($25,000); 1997: foundation matching gifts ($53,725); foundation grants to United Way ($25,000); foundation scholarships ($9,660)
Assets: $22,403 (1997); $3,051 (1996); $9,546 (1995)
Gifts Received: $2,000,000 (1997); $2,075,000 (1996); $2,655,000 (1995). Note: Foundation receives contributions from Loews Corporation and its subsidiaries.

Typical Recipients

Arts & Humanities: Arts Associations & Councils, Arts Festivals, Arts Funds, Arts Outreach, Dance, Historic Preservation, Libraries, Museums/Galleries, Music, Performing Arts, Public Broadcasting, Theater
Civic & Public Affairs: African American Affairs, Botanical Gardens/Parks, Business/Free Enterprise, Chambers of Commerce, Clubs, Economic Development, Employment/Job Training, Civic & Public Affairs-General, Legal Aid, Municipalities/Towns, Parades/Festivals, Philanthropic Organizations, Professional & Trade Associations, Public Policy, Safety, Urban & Community Affairs, Women's Affairs, Zoos/Aquariums
Education: Arts/Humanities Education, Business Education, Colleges & Universities, Education Funds, Education Reform, Education-General, International Studies, Legal Education, Literacy, Medical Education, Minority Education, Public Education (Precollege), Secondary Education (Private), Social Sciences Education, Student Aid
Environment: Forestry, Environment-General, Resource Conservation, Wildlife Protection
Health: AIDS/HIV, Cancer, Children's Health/Hospitals, Clinics/Medical Centers, Diabetes, Emergency/Ambulance Services, Geriatric Health, Health Organizations, Hospitals, Medical Rehabilitation, Medical Research, Multiple Sclerosis, Nutrition, Prenatal Health Issues, Public Health, Research/Studies Institutes, Single-Disease Health Associations, Speech & Hearing
International: Foreign Arts Organizations, Health Care/Hospitals, Human Rights, International Organizations, International Peace & Security Issues, International Relations, International Relief Efforts, Missionary/Religious Activities
Religion: Jewish Causes
Science: Science Museums
Social Services: Animal Protection, Camps, Child Welfare, Community Service Organizations, Family Planning, People with Disabilities, Recreation & Athletics, Scouts, United Funds/United Ways, Volunteer Services, YMCA/YWCA/YMHA/YWHA, Youth Organizations

Contributions Analysis

Giving Priorities: United Jewish Appeal and other social service organizations, colleges and universities, various arts groups, health organizations, and some civic organizations. Supports Jewish organizations in Israel. Also supports public policy, human rights, and international development.
Arts & Humanities: 6%. Support goes to museums; libraries; public broadcasting; arts organizations; and music, dance and performing arts groups.
Civic & Public Affairs: 17%. Interests include professional and trade associations, economic development groups, consumer affairs groups, and zoological societies.
Education: 21%. Support includes higher education, scholarships and matching gifts.
Health: 5%. Supports hospitals, single-disease associations, and medical research.
International: 3%. International relations and foreign aid.
Religion: 41%. Supports Jewish organizations, with the highest grant going to the United Jewish Appeal Federation.
Science: 1%. Supports American Museum of Natural History.
Social Services: 6%. Funds the United Way, family planning, and youth concerns.

Application Procedures

Initial Contact: Contact foundation by letter; no phone calls.
Application Requirements: Include a description of organization and project, budget, and proof of tax exemption.
Deadlines: None.
Notes: Applications for employee-related sponsorships are available from the foundation.

Restrictions

Foundation does not make grants to individuals.

Additional Information

All charitable giving is through the foundation. Subsidiaries do not make contributions independent of Loews Foundation, except for CNA Insurance Co., which is affiliated with CNA Financial Corp., a Loews Corp. joint venture.

Corporate Officials

John J. Kenny: treasurer, co-chief executive officer B Jersey City, NJ 1938. ED New York University (1965); Saint John's University School of Law (1972). PRIM CORP EMPL treasurer: Loews Corp. ADD CORP EMPL treasurer, director: 48th Street & 8th Avenue Corp.; treasurer: Lowes Hotels Inc. NONPR AFFIL trustee: Loews Foundation.
Laurence Alan Tisch: chairman, co-chief executive officer B New York, NY 1923. ED New York University BS (1942); University of Pennsylvania MA (1943); Harvard University Law School (1946). PRIM CORP EMPL chairman, co-chief executive officer: Loews Corp. ADD CORP EMPL chief executive officer: CNA Financial Corp.; chief executive officer: Continental Loss Adjusting Service. CORP AFFIL director: Petrie Stores Corp.; director: Transcontinental Insurance Co. New York; chairman: CNA Financial Corp.; director: Automatic Data Processing Inc.; director: Bulova Corp. NONPR AFFIL chairman board trustees: New York University; director: United Jewish Appeal Federation; trustee: New York Public Library; member: Council Foreign Relations; trustee: Metropolitan Museum Art.
Preston Robert Tisch: co-chairman, co-chief executive officer, director B Brooklyn, NY 1926. ED Bucknell University (1943-1944); University of Michigan BA (1948). PRIM CORP EMPL co-chairman, co-chief executive officer, director: Loews Corp. ADD CORP EMPL owner, chief executive officer, chairman: New York Football Giants Inc. CORP AFFIL director: Transcontinental Insurance Co. New York; director: Rite Aid Corp.; director: CNA Financial Corp.; director: Hasbro Inc.; director: Bulova Watch Corp.; director: Bulova Corp. NONPR AFFIL trustee: New York University; member: Sigma Alpha Mu; member: Governments Business Advisory Council New York; chairman emeritus: New York Convention & Visit Bureau; president: Citymeals Wheels. CLUB AFFIL Rye Racquet Club; Century Country Club.

Foundation Officials

Peter Keegan: senior vice president B Providence, RI 1944. ED Brown University BA (1966); Columbia University MBA (1970). PRIM CORP EMPL senior vice president, chief financial officer: Loews Corp.
John J. Kenny: secretary, treasurer, trustee (see above)
Laurence Alan Tisch: trustee (see above)
Preston Robert Tisch: trustee (see above)

Grants Analysis

Disclosure Period: calendar year ending 1997
Total Grants: $1,892,178*
Number of Grants: 87
Average Grant: $13,281*
Highest Grant: $750,000
Typical Range: $1,000 to $50,000
***Note:** Giving excludes matching gifts; scholarship; United Way. Average grant figure excludes highest grant.

Recent Grants

Note: Grants derived from 1997 Form 990.

Arts & Humanities

25,000	New York Shakespeare Festival, New York, NY
25,000	WNET/Educational Broadcasting Corporation
15,000	Lincoln Center for the Performing Arts, New York, NY
15,000	New York Theater Ballet, New York, NY
10,000	Elaine Kaufman Cultural Center, New York, NY
10,000	New York Foundation of the Arts, New York, NY
5,000	City Center 55th Street Theater Foundation, New York, NY
5,000	Museum of Television and Radio, New York, NY

Civic & Public Affairs

166,666	New York City Partnership, New York, NY
50,000	Central Park Conservancy, New York, NY
30,000	American Hotel Foundation, Palm Springs, CA
25,000	American Society of Associated Executives Foundation
25,000	Teamwork Foundation, New York, NY
10,000	National Urban League, New York, NY
10,000	New York Restoration Project, New York, NY
5,000	CATO Institute, Washington, DC

Education

150,000	Bennett College, Greensboro, NC
100,000	Cornell University School of Hotel Administration, Ithaca, NY
50,000	New York University Scholarship Fund, New York, NY
40,000	Yale Law School, New Haven, CT
12,500	University Settlement, New York, NY
10,000	Cardinal Hayes High School, Bronx, NY
10,000	Institute of International Education, New York, NY
7,500	Queens College Foundation, Queens, NY
5,000	Barnard-Columbia Center for Urban Policy
5,000	Bellmont Abbey College
5,000	School for Strings, New York, NY

Environment

5,000	Woodlands Campaign

Health

25,000	Buoniconti Fund to Cure Paralysis, Miami, FL
10,000	Capcure
10,000	Children's Hearing Institute, New York, NY
10,000	National Multiple Sclerosis Society, New York, NY
10,000	National Multiple Sclerosis Society, New York, NY

10,000	St. Jude Hospital Foundation
10,000	St. Vincent's Hospital
5,000	March of Dimes
International	
25,000	Council on Foreign Relations, New York, NY
25,000	Council on Foreign Relations, New York, NY
10,000	International Women's Forum-Leadership Foundation
10,000	International Women's Forum-Leadership Foundation
7,500	International Rescue Committee, New York, NY
7,500	International Rescue Committee, New York, NY
6,000	Meeting Planners International
6,000	Meeting Planners International
5,000	Boys Town Jerusalem Foundation of America, Washington, DC
5,000	Boys Town Jerusalem Foundation of America, Washington, DC
Religion	
750,000	United Jewish Appeal Federation, New York, NY
Science	
25,000	American Museum of Natural History, New York, NY
Social Services	
25,000	Camp Heartland, Wauwatosa, WI
25,000	United Way, New York, NY
25,000	YMCA
10,000	City Kids Foundation
7,500	Hole in the Wall Gang Camp, New Haven, CT
5,000	Achilles Track Club, New York, NY
5,000	Planned Parenthood, New York, NY

LOTUS DEVELOPMENT CORP.

Company Contact

Cambridge, MA
Web: http://www.lotus.com

Company Description

Employees: 4,400
SIC(s): 3577 Computer Peripheral Equipment Nec, 7372 Prepackaged Software, 7375 Information Retrieval Services.
Parent Company: International Business Machines Corp., Armonk, NY, United States

Operating Locations

Argentina: Lotus Development Argentina S.A., Buenos Aires; Australia: Lotus Brisbane, Brisbane; Lotus Development Australia, Melbourne, Sydney; Austria: Lotus Development Ges.m.b.H., Vienna; Brazil: Lotus Desenbolvimento de Software Ltda., Sao Paulo, Rio de Janeiro; Canada: Lotus Canada Limitee, Montreal; Lotus Development Canada Limited, Toronto, Ottawa; Chile: Lotus Development Corporation, Santiago; Colombia:, Santa Fe de Bogota; Costa Rica: Lotus Development Corporacion de Costa Rica, San Jose; Denmark: Lotus Development Danmark A/S, Horsholm; Finland: Lotus Development Finland Oy, Helsinki; Germany: Lotus Development GmbH, Ismaning; Hungary: Lotus Development Corporation, Budapest; New Zealand: Lotus Development New Zealand, Auckland, Wellington; Republic of South Africa: Lotus South Africa, Cape Town, Gauteng; Switzerland: Lotus Development (Schweiz) AG, Dietikon

Nonmonetary Support

Value: $2,975,000 (1996); $2,200,000 (1995)
Type: Donated Products; In-kind Services
Contact:
Lotus Philanthropy Software Donation Program
55 Cambridge Parkway
Cambridge, MA 02142
Note: Nonmonetary support is retail value of software. For Lotus Gifts-in-Kind support contact Virginia office.

Corporate Sponsorship

Type: Arts & cultural events; Other
Note: Supports Massachusetts NetDay, an annual program wherein volunteers wire schools for networks and Internet access. Supports auctions.

Lotus Development Philanthropy Program

Giving Contact

Patty Olan, Lotus Philanthropy Program
Lotus Development Corp.
55 Cambridge Parkway
Cambridge, MA 02142
Phone: (617)693-1667
Fax: (617)693-3728

Description

EIN: 043078090
Organization Type: Corporate Foundation
Giving Locations: headquarters and operating communities.
Grant Types: Employee Matching Gifts, Project, Seed Money.
Note: Employee matching gift ratio: 2 to 1, up to $200 per employee.

Giving Philosophy

'We believe that individuals and communities have the inherent capacity to provide the most effective solutions to the challenges facing them. A fundamental component of our overall business strategy is to partner with our communities in identifying those solutions. Our business is built around information, technology and the way people communicate and work together. We believe that the same innovative solutions our technology has brought to businesses can be effective in assisting nonprofit efforts to address social problems.
'We have taken a leadership position in global corporate citizenship by developing a strong commitment to socially responsible business practices, including efforts to enhance the quality of life and level of opportunity afforded individuals within our communities throughout the world.
'The Lotus Philanthropy Program is the focal point of our community-oriented initiatives. The program is based on the fundamental belief that employees should play a central role in defining and implementing those initiatives, and we are proud of their dedication. Hundreds of our employees sit on policy and grantmaking committees, provide technology training and technical assistance to nonprofit organizations and engage in volunteer efforts worldwide.' *Annual Report, The Lotus Development Corporation Philanthropy Program*

Financial Summary

Total Giving: $4,321,000 (1996); $1,354,000 (1995); $1,354,000 (1994 approx). Note: Contributes through corporate direct giving program only. 1996 Giving includes corporate direct giving ($3,903,000); domestic and international subsidiaries; matching gifts ($418,000); nonmonetary support. 1995 Giving includes corporate direct giving ($3,414,000); foundation ($10,294); domestic and international subsidiaries; matching gifts ($327,000); nonmonetary support.

Typical Recipients

Arts & Humanities: Arts Associations & Councils, Arts Centers, Arts Institutes, History & Archaeology, Museums/Galleries, Public Broadcasting, Theater
Civic & Public Affairs: African American Affairs, Asian American Affairs, Business/Free Enterprise, Civil Rights, Economic Development, Employment/Job Training, Ethnic Organizations, Hispanic Affairs, Housing, Nonprofit Management, Public Policy, Urban & Community Affairs, Women's Affairs
Education: Afterschool/Enrichment Programs, Education Reform, Elementary Education (Private), Engineering/Technological Education, Faculty Development, Education-General, Minority Education, Preschool Education, Science/Mathematics Education, Special Education
Environment: Environment-General, Protection
Health: AIDS/HIV, Health Organizations, Mental Health, Nutrition, Prenatal Health Issues, Public Health
International: Human Rights, International Peace & Security Issues
Religion: Jewish Causes, Religious Welfare
Science: Science Museums, Scientific Centers & Institutes
Social Services: At-Risk Youth, Camps, Child Welfare, Community Centers, Community Service Organizations, Day Care, Domestic Violence, Family Planning, Family Services, People with Disabilities, Refugee Assistance, Shelters/Homelessness, Social Services-General, YMCA/YWCA/YMHA/YWHA, Youth Organizations

Contributions Analysis

Giving Priorities: Education, training, and computer literacy; cross-cultural understanding and prejudice reduction; community empowerment, economic development, and leadership training; and pre- and post-natal care for at-risk mothers. Foreign subsidiaries support local, grassroots funding in countries where Lotus has larger locations. Currently, International Philanthropy Committees are in Dublin, Ireland; Staines, U.K.; Germany; Sweden; Italy; South Africa; Singapore; Canada; and Australia. Locally based committees set budgets and make funding decisions. Emphasis also is placed on employee involvement. Examples of funded projects include providing computer training, employment counseling, and social services to the children and adults of Ballymun, the largest low-income housing development in Dublin; to programs serving the disabled and terminally ill near companyheadquarters west of London; and to programs assisting young cancer patients in Scandinavia. Other programs include services to the blind in Canada, youth organizations in Australia, public school support in Puerto Rico, therapeutic programs for the mentally handicapped in Germany, environmental and agricultural education in the Guatemalan tropical rain forest, and community programs in Essex, England. Total contributions figures do not include giving by foreign subsidiaries.
Civic & Public Affairs: Supports projects with an action component which prevent or combat the development of biased and prejudicial attitudes regarding race, primarily, and class, secondarily. Focus on direct civic participation, public policy initiatives, or demonstrated leadership. Focus on efforts to educate and mobilize community residents to advocate, speak out, and takecontrol over a particular challenge; causes receiving support have been welfare rights, lead poisoning initiatives, housing, public safety, job creation, entrepreneurship, and economic development. Supports the rights of families and individuals to live violence-free and with adequate support, particularly in communities of color and inner-city neighborhoods.
Health: Addresses racial and class inequities of the health care environment, and increased access to public health services, such as pre- and post-natal education and treatment; AIDS advocacy, education, and treatment; and preventative health care.
Science: Supports the extension of computer-related skills and technologies to people and organizations otherwise not enjoying access to such technologies and training. Both individual skill development programs and technological enhancement and capacity-building projects are supported.

Application Procedures

Initial Contact: write for application
Application Requirements: completed application, copy of IRS Section 501(c)(3) tax-exempt letter, five copies of entire proposal
Deadlines: deadlines are January 1, May 1, and September 1
Review Process: the Cambridge-based Philanthropy Committee is employee-driven and makes recommendations concerning the distribution of funds to community organizations in Cambridge, Boston, Somerville, and surrounding areas
Evaluative Criteria: grants must be in one or both of the following categories: computer-related skill transfer (supporting dissemination of computer-related skills to minorities and low-income groups) and anti-racism (for efforts to eliminate causes and effects of racial discrimination)
Decision Notification: notification is generally May 15, September 15, or January 15

Restrictions

Does not support the following: organizations that promote religious faith or political nominees or candidates to political office; colleges and universities; or individuals.

Additional Information

For many years, Lotus has provided staff members of nonprofit organizations in Eastern New England with free standardized training in certain Lotus desktop products. More recently, a new program called Lotus Philanthropy Partners was launched in Cambridge, MA, to provide more customized technology training and assistance for specific nonprofit agencies. Organizations accepted as partners can receive training for staff as a group, for more consistent agency-wide impact, with solutions that meet specific needs and provide holistic support to nonprofit agencies. Agencies may apply for space in standardized training courses or to form a Partnership by completing an Agency Application Form. Forms are available by calling the Philanthropy Program at the above number.
In 1996, the company merged with IBM. The philanthropy program will continue to function, with a more narrow focus on company operating locations to complement IBM's giving to national and international organizations.
Publications: Annual Report

Corporate Officials

Edwin J. Gillis: president B 1948. ED Clark University (1970); Harvard University Graduate School of Business Administration (1976). PRIM CORP EMPL president: Computervision Corp. CORP AFFIL chief financial officer: Lotus Development Corp.; chief financial officer: Parametric Technology Corp.

Giving Program Officials

Edwin J. Gillis: treasurer, director B 1948. ED Clark University (1970); Harvard University Graduate School of Business Administration (1976). PRIM CORP EMPL president: Computervision Corp. CORP AFFIL chief financial officer: Lotus Development Corp.; chief financial officer: Parametric Technology Corp.
Thomas Michael Lemberg: clerk B Detroit, MI 1946. ED Princeton University BA (1966); Yale University LLB (1969). PRIM CORP EMPL vice president, secretary, general counsel: Lotus Development Corp. CORP AFFIL senior vice president, general counsel: Polaroid Corp. NONPR AFFIL member: Phi Beta Kappa; chairman government affairs committee: Software Pubs Association; member, director: Bus Software Alliance.
James Paul Manzi: president, director B New York, NY 1952. ED Colgate University BA (1973); Tufts University MALD (1979). PRIM CORP EMPL chairman: Lotus Development Corp.

Foundation Officials

Janet Axelrod: director
Michael Durney: director
Thomas Michael Lemberg: clerk (see above)
Patty Olan: manager philanthropy program

Grants Analysis

Disclosure Period: calendar year ending
Typical Range: $5,000 to $10,000

Recent Grants

Note: Grants derived from 1996 Annual Report.

Arts & Humanities

10,000	Cambridge Community Television, Cambridge, MA -- support community technology training center

Civic & Public Affairs

10,000	Chelsea Community Economic Development Alliance, Chelsea, MA -- organizing access to income jobs, affordable child care, job training, skills development
10,000	Cooperative Economics for Women -- program support
10,000	Neighborhood of Affordable Housing, Boston, MA -- support outreach to newly settled Latino residents
9,000	Boston Can, Boston, MA -- operating support
9,000	God Bless the Child Production -- support production The Dilemma of a Black Man
7,000	Boston Can, Boston, MA -- operating support
7,000	Hyde Square Task Force, Jamaica Plain, MA -- youth leadership, community activism
7,000	Hyde Square Task Force, Jamaica Plain, MA -- youth leadership, community activism
5,000	Dudley Street Neighborhood Initiative, Roxbury, MA -- support Nubian Roots Youth Advocacy Program
5,000	Homeowners Rehab, Cambridge, MA -- to train low-income tenants issues of acquisition of property ownership
5,000	Leadership, Education, and Employment Opportunities, Roxbury, MA -- program support
5,000	Massachusetts Human Services Coalition, Boston, MA -- support People of Color Task Force
5,000	National Foundation for Teaching Entrepreneurship -- to teach entrepreneurship to at risk inner city youth
5,000	Oficina Hispana, Boston, MA -- expansion of job training center
5,000	Social Justice for Women, Boston, MA -- support Multicultural Council, operating support for Women's Health and Learning Center
5,000	Somerville Haitian Coalition -- to advocate public policy improvements
5,000	Women's Institute for Housing and Economic Development, Boston, MA -- support WE CAN project

Education

15,000	Reaching Out to Chelsea Adolescents, Chelsea, MA -- to establish computer center
11,000	Mission Hill Community Center, Boston, MA -- purchase computer hardware for community computer center
10,000	Bridging Bridges, The Greater Boston Morehouse Alumni Association, Boston, MA -- support Audio Skills Training Course
10,000	La Alianza Hispana, Roxbury, MA -- to initiate Community Computer Advancement program
10,000	Massachusetts Institute of Technology Black Alumni, Cambridge, MA -- support for Robert R. Taylor Network
9,000	Summerbridge, Cambridge, MA -- support summer program for low-income bilingual youth
6,500	Malden Haitian Teachers -- to create afterschool program for Haitian immigrant children
5,000	Cambridge Algebra Project, Cambridge, MA -- to prepare middle school students for successful completion of college prep math sequence in high school
5,000	Centro Hispano de Chelsea, Chelsea, MA -- computer skills training program
5,000	Lowell Telecommunication Corporation, Lowell, MA -- training, computer equipment
5,000	Mary McLeod Bethune Institute -- educational enrichment program
5,000	Supplementary Program of Educational Skills -- support afterschool program for girls in Boston

Environment

5,000	Environmental Diversity Forum, Boston, MA -- support advocacy for environmental concerns
5,000	Lead Action Collaborative -- to reduce childhood lead poisoning

Health

9,000	Multicultural AIDS Coalition, Boston, MA -- for production of Positive Voices
6,500	Boston City Hospital Fund for Excellence, Boston, MA -- support Boston Health CREW
6,000	Allston-Brighton Health Boston Coalition, MA -- leadership training, community development program
5,000	WEATOC, Boston, MA -- develop peer educators and leaders

Religion

12,500	Black Church Capacity Building Project, Hyams Trusts -- for community revitalization
10,000	Anti-Defamation League A World of Difference, New York, NY -- support prejudice awareness/reduction campaign
7,500	Christian Economic Coalition, Dorchester, MA -- to create worker-owned businesses in Boston's poorest neighborhoods
5,000	East Boston Ecumenical Community Council, Boston, MA -- support Multicultural Youth Program
5,000	Mattapan-Dorchester Churches in Action -- to improve neighborhood life, build citizen participation

Science

7,000	Engineering and Scientific Resources for Advancement -- program support

Social Services

10,000	Federated Dorchester Neighborhood Houses, Dorchester, MA -- support for small business owners
7,000	Peace at Home, Boston, MA -- support Violence Against Women A Curriculum for Empowerment
6,500	Homes for Families -- support to break the cycle of homelessness
5,000	Asian Task Force Against Domestic Violence, Boston, MA -- for Asian women's shelter
5,000	Massachusetts Coalition for the Homeless, Boston, MA -- support Home-stretch Project
5,000	Project LIFE, New York, NY -- for parenting program, pregnancy program
5,000	Respond, Camden, NJ -- operating support

5,000 Shelter, Project CONNECT -- to make voicemail service available to homeless men and women

LOUISIANA LAND & EXPLORATION CO.

Company Contact

New Orleans, LA
Web: http://www.br-inc.com

Company Description

Employees: 745
SIC(s): 1311 Crude Petroleum & Natural Gas, 6792 Oil Royalty Traders.
Parent Company: Burlington Resources, Inc., Houston, TX, United States

Operating Locations

Canada; United Kingdom

Louisiana Land & Exploration Co. Foundation

Giving Contact

Dee McBride
Louisiana Land & Exploration Co. Foundation
PO Box 4239
Houston, TX 77210-3239
Phone: (713)624-9366
Fax: (713)624-9645

Description

EIN: 720866443
Organization Type: Corporate Foundation
Giving Locations: operating locations.
Grant Types: Capital, Employee Matching Gifts, Endowment, General Support, Multiyear/Continuing Support, Scholarship.
Note: Employee matching gift ratio: 1 to 1 to education. Capital grants are awarded only if a member of the board makes a special request or if the foundation is particularly interested in a certain organization.

Financial Summary

Total Giving: $799,027 (1997); $796,000 (1996); $796,000 (1995 approx). Note: Contributes through corporate direct giving program and foundation.
Giving Analysis: Giving for 1997 includes: foundation ($458,140); foundation matching gifts ($135,606); foundation scholarships ($121,981); foundation grants to United Way ($83,300)
Assets: $4,245,415 (1997); $4,491,185 (1993); $18,649 (1991)

Typical Recipients

Arts & Humanities: Arts Associations & Councils, Arts Centers, Ballet, Community Arts, Dance, Ethnic & Folk Arts, Historic Preservation, Museums/Galleries, Music, Opera, Public Broadcasting, Theater
Civic & Public Affairs: Botanical Gardens/Parks, Economic Policy, Law & Justice, Municipalities/Towns, Nonprofit Management, Professional & Trade Associations, Public Policy, Safety, Urban & Community Affairs, Zoos/Aquariums
Education: Afterschool/Enrichment Programs, Business Education, Colleges & Universities, Continuing Education, Economic Education, Education Funds, Engineering/Technological Education, Education-General, Leadership Training, Minority Education, Preschool Education, Private Education (Precollege), Religious Education, Science/Mathematics Education, Student Aid
Environment: Energy, Environment-General
Health: Diabetes, Emergency/Ambulance Services, Health Organizations, Hospices, Medical Research, Single-Disease Health Associations
Religion: Churches, Religious Organizations, Religious Welfare
Science: Science Exhibits & Fairs, Scientific Centers & Institutes
Social Services: Animal Protection, At-Risk Youth, Child Welfare, Community Service Organizations, Counseling, Crime Prevention, Day Care, Delinquency & Criminal Rehabilitation, Emergency Relief, Recreation & Athletics, Scouts, Substance Abuse, United Funds/United Ways, Youth Organizations

Contributions Analysis

Giving Priorities: Colleges and universities through unrestricted support, scholarships, and matching gifts; arts organizations; and health and welfare, with most supporting united funds.
Arts & Humanities: 4%. Majority of funding supports city of New Orleans, arts funds, historic preservation, and housing.
Civic & Public Affairs: 4%.
Education: 59%. Highest priority is colleges and universities, both in unrestricted support and through scholarships; also awards major grants through multiyear commitments to universities. Employee matching gifts account for a significant portion of education contributions (about one-third). Other interests include Junior Achievement and various education associations. Also sponsors scholarship programs for children of employees.
Environment: 9%. Major support for the Audubon Institute.
Health: 1%. Funds American Red Cross.
Science: 2%. Supports research and science centers.
Social Services: 21%. Majority of funding supports united funds. Youth organizations also receive significant support.
Note: Total foundation contributions in 1997.

Application Procedures

Initial Contact: Send a brief letter or proposal.
Application Requirements: Include a description of organization, amount requested, purpose of funds sought, one-page budget summary, proof of tax-exempt status.
Deadlines: None.
Review Process: If local organization meets guidelines, request is considered at contribution committee meeting for subsequent review at next year's budget meeting.
Decision Notification: Decisions are ongoing; some requests considered for following year's budget meeting early in the calendar year.

Restrictions

Generally does not accept applications from national groups, organizations located outside operating areas, or for capital grants. Usually does not support fraternal organizations, goodwill advertising, individuals, member agencies of united funds, political or lobbying groups, or religious organizations for sectarian purposes.

Corporate Officials

John Frederick Greene: executive vice president exploration & production, director B Muskegon, MI 1940. ED University of Michigan BS (1963); University of Michigan MS (1970). PRIM CORP EMPL executive vice president exploration & production, director: Louisiana Land & Exploration Co. CORP AFFIL director: World Trade Center New Orleans. NONPR AFFIL member: American Petroleum Institute; member: New Orleans Geological Society; member: American Association Petroleum Geologists. CLUB AFFIL Petroleum Club.
Louis A. Raspino, Jr.: senior vice president, chief financial officer B New Orleans, LA 1952. ED Louisiana State University (1973); Loyola University (1983). PRIM CORP EMPL senior vice president, chief financial officer: Louisiana Land & Exploration Co.
H. Leighton Steward: chairman, chief executive officer, president B Fairfield, TX 1934. ED Southern Methodist University BS (1958); Southern Methodist University MS (1960). PRIM CORP EMPL chairman, chief executive officer, president: Louisiana Land & Exploration Co. CORP AFFIL director: First Commerce Corp.; director: First National Bank Commerce; vice chairman: Burlington Resources Inc.; director: Banc One Corp. CLUB AFFIL New Orleans Country Club.
John A. Williams: president, chief executive officer B 1944. ED University of Wales BS (1966); University of Wales PhD (1970). PRIM CORP EMPL president, chief executive officer: Burlington Resources International. CORP AFFIL senior vice president: Burlington Resources Inc.; senior vice president: Louisiana Land Exploration Co.

Foundation Officials

Richard Arthur Bachmann: vice president, secretary, treasurer, director B Green Bay, WI 1944. ED Wisconsin State University BBA (1967); University of Wisconsin MBA (1968). PRIM CORP EMPL director: Louisiana Land & Exploration Co. NONPR AFFIL member advisory board: Summerbridge; director: University Health Care System Government Comm; director: Covenant House; board governors, director: Isadore Newman School; director: Audubon Park Zoological Garden; director, member executive committee: Boy Scouts America New Orleans Council; director, chairman financial oversight committee: Arts Fund; director: Audubon Institute Aquarium Americas.
Betty Hoag: contributions coordinator
Louis A. Raspino, Jr.: director (see above)
H. Leighton Steward: director (see above)
John A. Williams: director (see above)

Grants Analysis

Disclosure Period: calendar year ending 1997
Total Grants: $458,140*
Number of Grants: 87
Average Grant: $5,266
Highest Grant: $65,000
Typical Range: $1,000 to $10,000
***Note:** Giving excludes matching gifts; scholarships; United Way.

Recent Grants

Note: Grants derived from 1997 Form 990.

Arts & Humanities

10,000 New Orleans Museum of Art, New Orleans, LA
5,000 Louisiana Philharmonic Orchestra, Until 9507, New Orleans, LA
5,000 Louisiana State Museum Foundation, New Orleans, LA
5,000 The National D-Day Museum, New Orleans, LA
5,000 The National D-Day Museum, New Orleans, LA
5,000 New Orleans Ballet Association, New Orleans, LA

Civic & Public Affairs

10,000 Audubon Park & Zoological Garden, New Orleans, LA
10,000 Metrovision Partnership Foundation, New Orleans, LA
6,000 Friends of City Park, New Orleans, LA
5,000 Center for Effective Non-Profit, New Orleans, LA
5,000 Metrovision Partnership Foundation, New Orleans, LA

Education

69,000 University of New Orleans
65,000 Tulane University, New Orleans, LA
48,500 Louisiana State University
30,000 University of New Orleans Foundation, New Orleans, LA

25,000 Summerbridge of New Orleans
15,000 Texas A&M University, College Station, TX
12,850 Project New Orleans Foundation, New Orleans, LA
11,903 Louisiana State University, Baton Rouge, LA
11,663 University of Southwestern Louisiana, Lafayette, LA
9,700 University of Southern Mississippi, Hattiesburg, MS
8,580 University of Texas at Austin, Austin, TX
8,000 Southern University of Baton Rouge
7,725 Junior Achievement of Southeastern Louisiana, Metairie, LA
7,500 Auburn University, Auburn, AL
7,000 Southern University of New Orleans
6,500 University of Southwestern Louisiana
5,500 Northeastern University
5,000 Centenary College, Hackettstown, NJ
5,000 New Orleans Summerbridge, New Orleans, LA
5,000 Xavier University of Louisiana, New Orleans, LA
3,270 University of New Orleans Foundation, New Orleans, LA

Environment

500,000 Audubon Institute, Inc., New Orleans, LA
53,000 Audubon Institute, Inc., New Orleans, LA
20,000 UNO - Institute for Energy/Environmental Information, New Orleans, LA
5,000 Offshore Energy Center, Houston, TX

Health

10,000 American Red Cross, New Orleans, LA

Science

12,000 Louisiana Nature and Science Center, Inc., New Orleans, LA
10,000 American Geological Institute, FallsChurch
5,000 American Geological Institute Foundation, Houston, TX

Social Services

69,500 United Way for the Greater New Orleans Area, New Orleans, LA
63,500 Boy Scouts of America, New Orleans, LA
10,000 Kingsley House, New Orleans, LA
9,100 United Way of Texas Gulf Coast, Houston, TX
5,000 Covenant House, New Orleans, LA
5,000 Covenant House New Orleans, New Orleans, LA
5,000 Crimestoppers, Inc., New Orleans, LA
5,000 Crimestoppers, Inc., New Orleans, LA

LOUISIANA-PACIFIC CORP.

Company Contact

Portland, OR

Company Description

Employees: 12,000 (1999)
SIC(s): 2421 Sawmills & Planing Mills--General, 2431 Millwork, 2435 Hardwood Veneer & Plywood, 2436 Softwood Veneer & Plywood.

Nonmonetary Support

Value: $811,698 (1995)
Type: Donated Equipment; Donated Products
Note: Co. provides some nonmonetary support.

Louisiana-Pacific Foundation

Giving Contact

Kim Miller
Louisiana-Pacific Foundation
111 Southwest Fifth Avenue
Portland, OR 97204
Phone: (503)221-0800
Fax: (503)821-5322
Email: kim.miller@lpcorp.com

Alternate Contact

Phone: (503)821-5326

Description

EIN: 237268660
Organization Type: Corporate Foundation
Giving Locations: primarily headquarters and operating communities.
Grant Types: Capital, Emergency, General Support, Project, Scholarship.
Note: Scholarships are for dependents of employees.

Financial Summary

Total Giving: $173,275 (1998); $459,909 (1997); $1,622,780 (1996). Note: Contributes through corporate direct giving program and foundation. Giving includes foundation.
Assets: $13,951 (1998); $42,603 (1997); $27,644 (1996)
Gifts Received: $150,000 (1998); $475,000 (1997); $400,000 (1996). Note: In 1997, contributions were received from Louisiana-Pacific Corp. ($475,000). In 1994, the foundation received contributions from Louisiana-Pacific Corp. and Ketchikan Pulp Co.

Typical Recipients

Arts & Humanities: Arts Centers, Ballet, History & Archaeology, Libraries, Museums/Galleries, Music, Opera, Performing Arts, Theater
Civic & Public Affairs: Botanical Gardens/Parks, Business/Free Enterprise, Civic & Public Affairs-General, Housing, Municipalities/Towns, Public Policy, Urban & Community Affairs, Zoos/Aquariums
Education: Afterschool/Enrichment Programs, Business Education, Colleges & Universities, Community & Junior Colleges, Education Funds, Education-General, Leadership Training, Literacy, Private Education (Precollege), Public Education (Precollege), Religious Education, Science/Mathematics Education, Secondary Education (Public), Student Aid
Environment: Forestry, Environment-General, Wildlife Protection
Health: Cancer, Children's Health/Hospitals, Emergency/Ambulance Services, Health Organizations, Heart, Hospices, Hospitals, Medical Research, Prenatal Health Issues, Public Health, Single-Disease Health Associations
International: Foreign Educational Institutions, Health Care/Hospitals, International Development, International Environmental Issues, International Organizations, International Relief Efforts
Religion: Ministries, Religious Organizations, Religious Welfare
Science: Science Exhibits & Fairs, Science Museums
Social Services: At-Risk Youth, Child Welfare, Community Service Organizations, Emergency Relief, Family Services, Food/Clothing Distribution, Homes, People with Disabilities, Recreation & Athletics, Scouts, Shelters/Homelessness, Special Olympics, Substance Abuse, United Funds/United Ways, YMCA/YWCA/YMHA/YWHA, Youth Organizations

Contributions Analysis

Giving Priorities: Education through scholarships to employee dependants; Habitat for Humanity; arts associations; youth organizations, United Way, and recreation and athletics; civic organizations; and hospitals.
Civic & Public Affairs: About 20%. Environmental affairs, economic development, and community affairs organizations and Habitat for Humanity.
Education: About 80%. Virtually all funding supports a foundation-sponsored scholarship program for dependents of company employees. Limited support to public education and junior colleges, as well as to the Horatio Alger Association, a youth education and scholarship program.

Application Procedures

Initial Contact: Send a brief letter or proposal.
Application Requirements: Include a description of organization, amount requested, purpose of funds sought, recently audited financial statement, and proof of tax-exempt status.
Deadlines: None, for grants; March 1 for scholarships.
Review Process: Trustees review all applications at quarterly meetings.
Evaluative Criteria: For scholarships: academic achievement and potential; specific aptitudes, as indicated by special interests and as appraised by faculty members; desire to continue education; character and promise of future contribution to society; record of leadership in extracurricular and school affairs; use of spare time after school, on Saturday and during summer vacation periods; and financial need; applicant must be a dependent of an employee of Louisiana-Pacific, who has worked at the company for at least three years.
Decision Notification: Scholarship applications are reviewed in mid-March.

Corporate Officials

Anton Conrad Kirchhof: corporate secretary, general counsel B Portland, OR 1945. ED Portland State University (1967); Stanford University School of Law (1971). PRIM CORP EMPL corporate secretary, general counsel: Louisiana-Pacific Corp. NONPR AFFIL member: American Society of Corporate Secretaries; member: Western Pension Conference; member: American Corporate Counsel Association.

Foundation Officials

William L. Hebert: assistant secretary, treasurer B 1944. PRIM CORP EMPL secretary, treasurer, director: Hanco Inc. CORP AFFIL treasurer: Ketchikan Pulp Co.; treasurer: Cleret Inc. NONPR AFFIL purchasing manager: Cumberland Co. Training Resource Center.
Anton Conrad Kirchhof: secretary (see above)
Kimberly Ann Miller: vice president
Mark A. Suwyn: chairman, president B Denver, CO 1942. ED Hope College BS (1964); Washington State University PhD (1967). PRIM CORP EMPL chairman, chief executive officer, director: Louisiana - Pacific Corp. CORP AFFIL director: Scitex Corp. Ltd.; Shareholder Fitness Mania Inc.

Grants Analysis

Disclosure Period: calendar year ending 1998
Total Grants: $173,275
Number of Grants: 93
Average Grant: $1,699*
Highest Grant: $17,000
Typical Range: $500 to $15,000
***Note:** Average grant figure excludes highest grant.

Recent Grants

Note: Grants derived from 1997 Form 990.

Civic & Public Affairs

5,000 Portland Organizing Project, Portland, OR

Education

30,000	Junior Achievement
5,000	Bethune-DuBois Fund, Washington, DC
5,000	Junior Achievement
2,250	American College, Bryn Mawr, PA
2,250	Baylor University, Waco, TX
2,250	Brigham Young University, Provo, UT
2,250	David Lipscomb University, Nashville, TN
2,250	Linfield College, McMinnville, OR
2,250	Marquette University, Milwaukee, WI
2,250	Mount Holyoke College, South Hadley, MA
2,250	Northwestern College, Kirkland, WA
2,250	Ohio Northern University, Ada, OH
2,250	Philadelphia College of the Bible, Langhorne, PA
2,250	Ricks College, Rexburg, ID
2,250	University of Dayton, Dayton, OH
2,000	Barbour County Local Education Fund, Clayton, AL
2,000	University of California Berkeley, Berkeley, CA
1,540	Northeastern State University, Tahlequah, OK
1,500	Auburn University, Auburn, AL
1,500	Auburn University, Auburn, AL
1,500	Boise State University, Boise, ID
1,500	California Polytechnic State University, San Luis Obispo, CA
1,500	East Central Community College
1,500	Eastern Oregon State College, OR
1,500	Embry-Riddle Aeronautical University
1,500	Humboldt State University, Arcata, CA
1,500	Montana State University, Bozeman, MT
1,500	Northeast Louisiana University, Monroe, LA
1,500	Ohio State University, Columbus, OH
1,500	St. Cloud State University, St. Cloud, MN
1,500	Sam Houston State University, Huntsville, TX
1,500	Sam Houston State University, Huntsville, TX
1,500	Stephen F. Austin State University, Nacogdoches, TX
1,500	Texas Tech University, Lubbock, TX
1,500	University of Alabama, Tuscaloosa, AL
1,500	University of Idaho, Moscow, ID
1,500	University of Minnesota, Minneapolis, MN
1,500	University of Nevada, Reno, NV
1,500	University of Texas Austin, Austin, TX
1,500	University of Texas Dallas, Dallas, TX
1,500	University of Wisconsin, WI
1,500	University of Wisconsin Eau Claire, Eau Claire, WI
1,500	University of Wisconsin Madison, Madison, WI
1,500	Wallace Community College, Selma, AL

Environment

5,000	National Fish and Wildlife Foundation, Washington, DC

International

185,000	Northwest Medical Teams International
30,000	Junior Achievement International
15,000	Junior Achievement International

Social Services

17,565	United Way of the Columbia-Willamette, Portland, OR

LOWE'S COMPANIES

Company Contact

North Wilkesboro, NC
Web: http://www.lowes.com

Company Description

Revenue: US$12,244,900,000
Employees: 45,000
Fortune Rank: 109, per FORTUNE Magazine's list of 500 Largest U.S. Corporations (1999).
FF 109
SIC(s): 5211 Lumber & Other Building Materials, 5251 Hardware Stores.

Operating Locations

Company has 303 stores in 290 communities in 20 southeastern states.

Lowe's Charitable and Educational Foundation

Giving Contact

David Oliver, Director, Community Relations
PO Box 1111
North Wilkesboro, NC 28656
Phone: (336)658-4000

Description

EIN: 566061689
Organization Type: Corporate Foundation
Giving Locations: headquarters and operating communities.
Grant Types: General Support.

Financial Summary

Total Giving: $912,953 (1998); $565,400 (1997); $705,308 (1996). Note: Fiscal 1997 Giving includes United Way ($2,000).
Giving Analysis: Giving for 1998 includes: foundation ($910,952); foundation grants to United Way ($2,000)
Assets: $845,222 (1998); $1,087,302 (1997); $1,350,462 (1996)
Gifts Received: $639,162 (1998); $233,875 (1997); $429,125 (1996). Note: In fiscal 1998, contributions were received from Lowe's Companies and Thomas E. Whiddon.

Typical Recipients

Arts & Humanities: Arts & Humanities-General, Libraries
Civic & Public Affairs: Economic Development, Civic & Public Affairs-General, Philanthropic Organizations, Public Policy, Safety, Urban & Community Affairs, Women's Affairs
Education: Colleges & Universities, Engineering/Technological Education, Education-General, Medical Education, Secondary Education (Public)
Environment: Resource Conservation
Health: Health-General, Hospices, Hospitals
Religion: Religious Welfare
Social Services: Community Service Organizations, Social Services-General

Contributions Analysis

Giving Priorities: Major emphasis on youth programs and community services. Also supports education, civic concerns, the arts, and health.
Arts & Humanities: 4%. Supports libraries.
Civic & Public Affairs: 12%. Funds foundations, associations, and public offices.
Education: 13%. Supports colleges, universities, and secondary schools.
Health: 1%. Funds hospitals, hospices, and health services.
Social Services: 70%. Funds youth programs, community programs, and united funds.
Note: Total contributions made in fiscal 1998.

Application Procedures

Initial Contact: All applications must be in written form.
Deadlines: None.

Restrictions

Does not support individuals, religious organizations for sectarian purposes, political or lobbying groups, or organizations outside operating areas.

Corporate Officials

Robert L. Tillman: chairman, president, chief executive officer PRIM CORP EMPL chairman, president, chief executive officer: Lowes Companies.

Foundation Officials

Leonard Gray Herring: vice president B Snow Hill, NC 1927. ED University of North Carolina BS (1948). CORP AFFIL member: Lowe's Companies Employee Stock Ownership Plan; director: First Union Corp. NONPR AFFIL trustee: Pfeiffer College; member, board visitors: University North Carolina; member board visitors: Davidson College; member: Chi Psi.
Petro Kulynych: chairman, treasurer B Smithmills, PA 1921. ED United States Merchant Marine Academy (1943); Kings Business College (1946). PRIM CORP EMPL founding director: Lowes Companies. CORP AFFIL director: Wachovia Bank & Trust Co. CLUB AFFIL mem: Shriners Club; mem: Elks Club.
Robert Louis Strickland: vice president B Florence, SC 1931. ED University of North Carolina BA (1952); Harvard University MBA (1957). PRIM CORP EMPL director, chairman: Lowes Companies. CORP AFFIL director: Summit Communication; director: Hannaford Brothers; director: T Rowe Price Associates. NONPR AFFIL member: Scabbard & Blade; trustee: University North Carolina Chapel Hill; member: Republican Senatorial Inner Circle; member: Phi Beta Kappa; member: Pi Kappa Alpha; member: National Association Over-the-Counter Companies; member: Newcomen Society; member: Employee Stock Ownership Association. CLUB AFFIL Roaring Gap Club; Twin City Club; Hound Ears Club; Piedmont City Club; Elk River Club; Forsyth Club.
William C. Warden, Jr.: secretary B Winchester, VA 1952. ED Wake Forest University (1974); Wake Forest University (1976). PRIM CORP EMPL senior vice president, secretary, general counsel: Lowes Companies.

Grants Analysis

Disclosure Period: calendar year ending 1998
Total Grants: $910,952*
Number of Grants: 149
Average Grant: $2,776*
Highest Grant: $500,000
Typical Range: $100 to $5,000
***Note:** Giving excludes United Way. Average grant figure excludes highest grant.

Recent Grants

Note: Grants derived from 1997 Form 990.

Arts & Humanities

33,333	Wilkes County Library -- building fund
33,333	Wilkes County Library Capital Reserve Fund

Civic & Public Affairs

20,000	Global Transpark Foundation, Kinston, NC
20,000	Global Transpark Foundation, Kinston, NC
12,500	Old Hickory Council
8,333	North Carolina Center for Public Policy Research, Raleigh, NC
5,000	Junior Women's Club, Greensboro, NC
5,000	Lincoln Foundation, Louisville, KY
5,000	North Vernon Volunteer Fire Department, North Vernon, IN
5,000	Stanley County Economic Development

Education

50,000	Wake Forest University, Winston-Salem, NC
16,667	Bowman Gray School of Medicine, Winston-Salem, NC

10,000	Johnson C. Smith University, Charlotte, NC
5,000	Florida A&M University, Sarasota, FL
5,000	North Carolina High School Athletic Association, Chapel Hill, NC

Environment

10,000	Wild North Carolina Nature Conservancy, NC

Health

5,000	Hospice of Cleveland County, Shelby, NC
5,000	Jennings Community Hospital, North Vernon, IN

Religion

37,500	Memorial Mission Foundation

Social Services

8,333	Rainbow Center, North Wilkesboro, NC

LTV Corp.

Company Contact

Cleveland, OH
Web: http://www.ltvsteel.com

Company Description

Revenue: US$4,273,000,000
Employees: 14,400
Fortune Rank: 384, per FORTUNE Magazine's list of 500 Largest U.S. Corporations (1999).
FF 384
SIC(s): 3312 Blast Furnaces & Steel Mills.

Nonmonetary Support

Range: $100,000 - $150,000
Type: Donated Equipment; In-kind Services; Loaned Employees; Loaned Executives; Workplace Solicitation

Corporate Sponsorship

Note: Sponsors a wellness/health event for employees.

LTV Foundation

Giving Contact

Laura Stacko, Director
LTV Foundation
200 Public Square
Cleveland, OH 44114
Phone: (216)622-5000
Fax: (216)622-4578

Description

EIN: 346505330
Organization Type: Corporate Foundation
Giving Locations: principally near operating locations and to national organizations.
Grant Types: Capital, Challenge, General Support, Multiyear/Continuing Support, Operating Expenses, Research, Scholarship.

Financial Summary

Total Giving: $800,000 (1999 approx); $1,000,000 (1998 approx); $943,911 (1997). Note: Contributes through foundation only.
Giving Analysis: Giving for 1997 includes: foundation grants to United Way ($152,191)
Assets: $14,801,618 (1997); $13,182,872 (1996); $10,404,511 (1994)

Typical Recipients

Arts & Humanities: Arts Associations & Councils, Arts Centers, Arts Festivals, Arts Funds, Ballet, Community Arts, Dance, Arts & Humanities-General, Historic Preservation, History & Archaeology, Libraries, Museums/Galleries, Music, Opera, Performing Arts, Public Broadcasting, Theater
Civic & Public Affairs: African American Affairs, Business/Free Enterprise, Economic Development, Employment/Job Training, Law & Justice, Municipalities/Towns, Parades/Festivals, Safety, Urban & Community Affairs, Women's Affairs, Zoos/Aquariums
Education: Business Education, Colleges & Universities, Community & Junior Colleges, Economic Education, Education Funds, Education Reform, Elementary Education (Private), Engineering/Technological Education, Faculty Development, Education-General, Literacy, Minority Education, Private Education (Precollege), Public Education (Precollege), Science/Mathematics Education, Secondary Education (Public), Student Aid
Environment: Environment-General
Health: Alzheimers Disease, Cancer, Children's Health/Hospitals, Clinics/Medical Centers, Eyes/Blindness, Health Policy/Cost Containment, Health Funds, Health Organizations, Heart, Hospitals, Hospitals (University Affiliated), Kidney, Medical Research, Mental Health, Public Health, Single-Disease Health Associations
International: Health Care/Hospitals
Religion: Religious Organizations, Religious Welfare
Science: Science Museums, Scientific Centers & Institutes
Social Services: Child Welfare, Community Centers, Community Service Organizations, Counseling, Crime Prevention, Day Care, Delinquency & Criminal Rehabilitation, Domestic Violence, Emergency Relief, Family Services, Food/Clothing Distribution, People with Disabilities, Recreation & Athletics, Scouts, Senior Services, Shelters/Homelessness, Substance Abuse, United Funds/United Ways, Volunteer Services, YMCA/YWCA/YMHA/YWHA, Youth Organizations

Contributions Analysis

Giving Priorities: Community service, education, health care, and the arts.
Arts & Humanities: 11%. Funds historic preservation, theater, libraries, history & archaeology, music, performing arts, and museums.
Civic & Public Affairs: 11%. Supports employment/job training, minority business, economic development, urban/community affairs, law & justice, housing, women's affairs, professional/trade associations, and African American affairs.
Education: 23%. Supports minority education, public education (precollege), secondary education (public and private), science/mathematics education, student aid, and vocational/technical education.
Health: 1%. Recipients include clinics/medical centers, children's health/hospitals, health organizations, single-disease associations, kidney, speech & hearing, diabetes, arthritis, cancer, heart, and rehabilitation.
Religion: About 1%.
Science: 12%. Great Lakes Science Center.
Social Services: 41%. Recipients include food/clothing distribution, YMCA, scouts, child welfare, community service organizations, volunteer services, recreation/athletics, youth organizations, and the United Way.
Note: Total contributions in 1997.

Application Procedures

Initial Contact: Send a letter or brief proposal.
Application Requirements: Include a description of organization, including basic purpose and record of recent accomplishments; names and positions of governing board and staff; proof of tax-exempt status; list of principal corporate and foundation supporters; purpose for grant; copy of most recent financial statement; and the extent of LTV employee participation as volunteers.
Deadlines: None.
Review Process: Requests are reviewed by contributions advisory committee, which meets quarterly; recommendations are forwarded to the trust committee, which has final authority on foundation grants.
Evaluative Criteria: Organization's record of competence and effectiveness in providing stated service; active participation of board of directors or trustees; competent professional or volunteer staff headed by effective manager; effective financial control system; ethical fund-raising activities; community support; involvement of LTV employees and executives as volunteers.
Decision Notification: Applicants are notified within three to four months.
Notes: Foundation prefers that it not be contacted by phone.

Restrictions

The foundation does not support individuals; political, labor, fraternal, social, athletic, or veterans' groups; churches or religious organizations; international organizations; college athletic programs; government agencies; educational or cultural consortia; courtesy advertising; telephone solicitations; or member agencies of united funds.

Additional Information

The foundation seeks opportunities to make challenge grants to organizations. Multiyear pledges are made only in special cases where single-year grants are inappropriate.

Corporate Officials

David H. Hoag: chairman, president, chief executive officer, director B 1939. ED Allegheny College BA (1960). PRIM CORP EMPL chairman, president, chief executive officer, director: The LTV Corp. ADD CORP EMPL chairman, chief executive officer, president, director: LTV Steel Co. Inc.; chief executive officer: LTV-Trico Inc. CORP AFFIL director: Lubrizol Corp.; director: M.A. Hanna Co.; director: Chubb Corp.
J. Peter Kelly: president, chief operating officer, director B 1941. ED Harvard University AB (1963); Duquesne University JD (1972). PRIM CORP EMPL president, chief operating officer, director: The LTV Corp. ADD CORP EMPL president, chief operating officer: LTV Steel Co. Inc.; president, Director: LTV Steel Tubular Products Co.; president: LTV Trico Inc. CORP AFFIL director: Monongahela Connecting Railway Co.; director: River Terminal Railway Co.; director: Aliquippa Southern Railway Co.; director: Cuyahoga Valley Railway Co. Inc.
John C. Skurek: vice president, treasurer B Fort Worth, TX 1944. ED Baldwin-Wallace College BS (1966); Kent State University MBA (1970). PRIM CORP EMPL vice president, treasurer: The LTV Corp. ADD CORP EMPL treasurer: LTV Steel Co. Inc.; treasurer: LTV Trico Inc.

Foundation Officials

David H. Hoag: trustee (see above)
J. Peter Kelly: trustee (see above)
John C. Skurek: trustee (see above)
Laura Stacko: director

Grants Analysis

Disclosure Period: calendar year ending 1997
Total Grants: $791,720*
Number of Grants: 167
Average Grant: $4,741
Highest Grant: $100,000
Typical Range: $500 to $10,500
***Note:** Giving excludes United Way.

Recent Grants

Note: Grants derived from 1997 Form 990.

Arts & Humanities

20,000	Playhouse Square Foundation, Cleveland, OH
20,000	Rock and Roll Hall of Fame and Museum, Cleveland, OH

10,000	Cleveland Ballet, Cleveland, OH
10,000	Cleveland Museum of Natural History, Cleveland, OH
7,500	Cleveland Museum of Art, Cleveland, OH
7,500	Musical Arts Association, Cleveland, OH
5,250	Western Reserve Historical Society, Cleveland, OH
5,000	B.F. Jones Memorial Library
5,000	Carnegie Museum, Pittsburgh, PA
5,000	Musical Arts Association, Cleveland, OH

Civic & Public Affairs

80,000	Cleveland Tommorow, Cleveland, OH
5,000	Downtown Development Coordinators
5,000	Law Enforcement Foundation, Dublin, OH
5,000	Law Enforcement Foundation, Dublin, OH

Education

30,000	Allegheny College, Meadville, PA
25,000	Case Western Reserve University, Cleveland, OH
25,000	Cleveland Initiative for Education, Cleveland, OH
25,000	Notre Dame College, Cleveland, OH
24,510	National Merit Scholarship Corporation, Chicago, IL
15,000	South High School, Cleveland, OH -- LTV Steel/Huntington Bank Partnership
10,000	David N. Myers College, Cleveland, OH
7,500	Cleveland Education Fund, Cleveland, OH
6,000	Cleveland Community College Foundation, Cleveland, OH -- President's Scholarship Fund
5,000	Cleveland Scholarship Programs, Cleveland, OH
5,000	South High School, Cleveland, OH -- LTV Steel/Huntington Bank Partnership
5,000	University Circle, Cleveland, OH
5,000	Youngstown State University, Youngstown, OH

Health

5,000	Cleveland Sight Center, Cleveland, OH
3,500	Five Star Sensation, Cleveland, OH

Religion

10,000	Hope Lodge, Cleveland, OH

Science

100,000	Great Lakes Science Center, Cleveland, OH

Social Services

128,941	United Way Services, Cleveland, OH
28,941	United Way Services, Cleveland, OH
28,941	United Way Services, Cleveland, OH
28,940	United Way Services, Cleveland, OH
20,000	YMCA of Greater Cleveland, Cleveland, OH
12,500	Lake Area United Way, Criffin, IN
12,500	Lake Area United Way, Griffith, IN
12,500	Lake Area United Way, Griffith, IN
12,500	Lake Area United Way, Griffith, IN
10,000	Youth Opportunities Unlimited, Cleveland, OH
8,310	Key Services Corporation
5,000	1999 Cleveland Junior Olympics, Cleveland, OH
5,000	Harvest for Hunger, Cleveland, OH
5,000	Neighborhood Centers Association, Cleveland, OH
5,000	Southwest Airlines Employees Club
5,000	Southwest Airlines Employees Club
4,000	United Way of Beaver County, Monaca, PA
4,000	United Way of Northeast Minnesota, Chisholm, MN

THE LUBRIZOL CORP.

Company Contact

Wickliffe, OH
Web: http://www.lubrizol.com

Company Description

Employees: 4,358
SIC(s): 2869 Industrial Organic Chemicals Nec, 2899 Chemical Preparations Nec.

Nonmonetary Support

Type: Donated Equipment; Loaned Employees; Loaned Executives
Note: The company provides nonmonetary support.

Corporate Sponsorship

Value: $50,000 (1997)
Type: Arts & cultural events; Festivals/fairs; Music & entertainment events
Contact: Ginny Langill, Committee Relations Specialist

The Lubrizol Foundation

Giving Contact

Kenneth Iwashita, President & Chief Operating Officer
The Lubrizol Foundation
29400 Lakeland Boulevard
Drop 053A
Wickliffe, OH 44092-2298
Phone: (440)943-4200
Fax: (440)943-9076
Email: kmi@lubrizol.com
Web: http://www.lubrizol.com/aboutlubrizol/lz_foundation/index.html
Note: Mr. Iwashita's extension is 5080.

Description

EIN: 346500595
Organization Type: Corporate Foundation
Giving Locations: OH: metropolitan area; TX: Houston metropolitan area
Grant Types: Award, Capital, Employee Matching Gifts, Fellowship, General Support, Multiyear/Continuing Support, Scholarship.
Note: Employee matching gift ratio: 1 to 1. Gifts to educational institutions and other charitable organisation have a maximum match of $5,000 in no more than 10 gifts annually.

Giving Philosophy

'The Lubrizol Foundation makes grants in support of educational, youth, health, human service and civic and cultural activities of a tax-exempt, charitable nature. Contributions from The Lubrizol Corporation and the earnings on the Foundation's investments are its principal sources of funding. A private foundation established in 1952, The Lubrizol Foundation is a nonprofit Ohio corporation and exempt from Federal income tax under section 501(c)(3) of the Internal Revenue Code.' *The Lubrizol Foundation Annual Report*, 1995

Financial Summary

Total Giving: $2,200,000 (1999 approx); $1,834,668 (1998); $1,489,920 (1997). Note: Contributes through corporate direct giving program and foundation.
Giving Analysis: Giving for 1997 includes: foundation ($585,500); foundation matching gifts ($404,170); foundation scholarships ($295,000); foundation grants to United Way ($205,250); 1998: foundation ($870,600); foundation matching gifts ($438,318); foundation scholarships ($313,000); foundation grants to United Way ($212,750)
Assets: $21,636,083 (1998); $21,355,073 (1997); $19,008,750 (1996)
Gifts Received: $16,076,250 (1994); $151,928 (1991). Note: In 1994, the foundation received contributions in the form of stock from The Lubrizol Corporation.

Typical Recipients

Arts & Humanities: Arts Associations & Councils, Arts Funds, Arts Institutes, Dance, Historic Preservation, History & Archaeology, Museums/Galleries, Music, Opera, Performing Arts, Public Broadcasting, Theater
Civic & Public Affairs: African American Affairs, Botanical Gardens/Parks, Business/Free Enterprise, Economic Development, Employment/Job Training, Civic & Public Affairs-General, Parades/Festivals, Zoos/Aquariums
Education: Arts/Humanities Education, Business Education, Colleges & Universities, Community & Junior Colleges, Economic Education, Education Funds, Engineering/Technological Education, Education-General, Minority Education, Private Education (Precollege), Public Education (Precollege), Science/Mathematics Education, Student Aid
Environment: Environment-General
Health: Alzheimers Disease, Children's Health/Hospitals, Clinics/Medical Centers, Emergency/Ambulance Services, Eyes/Blindness, Geriatric Health, Health Organizations, Hospices, Hospitals, Long-Term Care, Medical Rehabilitation, Nursing Services, Public Health, Single-Disease Health Associations
International: International Affairs
Religion: Jewish Causes, Religious Welfare
Science: Science Exhibits & Fairs, Science Museums, Scientific Centers & Institutes
Social Services: Community Centers, Community Service Organizations, People with Disabilities, Recreation & Athletics, Scouts, Social Services-General, United Funds/United Ways, Youth Organizations

Contributions Analysis

Giving Priorities: Selected colleges and universities that emphasize chemistry and chemical and mechanical engineering, community service and health organizations, the arts, and civic organizations.
Arts & Humanities: 15%. Funds the arts, music, and public broadcasting.
Civic & Public Affairs: 2%. Supports parks and nature centers and special interest groups.
Education: 54%. Major support for higher education. Through the scholarship program, the foundation selects the colleges and universities and designates the fields of study. Emphasis is on chemistry, chemical engineering, and mechanical engineering. Also makes grants for capital and operating purposes to colleges and universities and private and secondary schools. Grants are also made to educational programs and combined educational funds.
Health: 6%. Provides direct capital and operating support for health organizations in its primary communities. Grants go to hospitals and specialized health care providers.
Religion: 1%.
Science: 1%. Funds science centers, and science causes.
Social Services: 21%. Supports united funds and human services groups providing basic human needs. Supports organizations which grant youth the opportunity to enjoy healthy recreation and experience leadership and responsible citizenship.

Application Procedures

Initial Contact: Send a proposal with cover letter summarizing purpose of the request, signed by the executive officer of the organization.
Application Requirements: Include a narrative of specific information related to the subject of the request; current audited financial statements and a specific project budget, if applicable; documentation of the organization's federal tax-exempt status; additional descriptive literature, such as an annual report.
Deadlines: None.

Notes: Upon review, further information may be requested including an interview or site visit. Only one proposal per organization should be submitted in any 12 month period.

Restrictions

Grants are not made for religious or political purposes, to individuals nor, generally, to endowments.

Additional Information

Publications: Annual Report

Corporate Officials

William G. Bares: chairman, president, chief executive officer B 1941. ED Purdue University BSChE (1963); Case Western Reserve University MBA (1969). PRIM CORP EMPL chairman, president, chief executive officer: The Lubrizol Corp. CORP AFFIL director: KeyCorp; director: Oglebay Norton Co.; director: Applied Industrial Technologies Inc.; director: Bearings Inc.

Stephen A. DiBiase: vice president research & development PRIM CORP EMPL vice president research & development: The Lubrizol Corp.

Joseph E. Hodge: vice president operations PRIM CORP EMPL vice president operations: The Lubrizol Corp.

Mark W. Meister: vice president PRIM CORP EMPL vice president: The Lubrizol Corp.

Foundation Officials

William G. Bares: trustee (see above)

William T. Beargie: trustee B Cleveland, OH 1930. ED University of Notre Dame (1952). PRIM CORP EMPL senior vice president: Rock Creek Aluminum Inc.

Stephen A. DiBiase: trustee (see above)

George Richard Hill: president, trustee B Ogden, UT 1941. ED Carnegie Mellon University BSChe (1963); Carnegie Mellon University MSChe (1964); Carnegie Mellon University PhD (1969). senior vice president: Lubrizol Corp. NONPR AFFIL member: Sigma Xi; professor: University Utah; member: Phi Kappa Phi; member: Sigma Pi Sigma; fellow: National Academy Engineering; member: National Coal Council; member fossil energy advisor commission: Department Energy; member: American Institute Chemical Engineers; fellow: American Institute Chemists; member: American Chemical Society; member: Alpha Phi Omega; member: American Association Advancement Science; member: AIME.

Joseph E. Hodge: trustee (see above)

Kenneth M. Iwashita: president

William Monroe LeSuer: trustee

K. J. Marr: trustee

Mark W. Meister: trustee (see above)

L. K. Naylor: trustee

Mary Salomon: trustee

Grants Analysis

Disclosure Period: calendar year ending 1998
Total Grants: $870,600*
Number of Grants: 161
Average Grant: $5,407
Highest Grant: $150,000
Typical Range: $1,000 to $10,000
***Note:** Giving excludes matching gifts; scholarship; United Way.

Recent Grants

Note: Grants derived from 1998 Form 990.

Arts & Humanities

75,000 Musical Arts Association, Cleveland, OH -- Toward the renovation of Severance Hall
45,000 The Cleveland Play House, Cleveland, OH -- Toward the purchase of sound and electrical equipment
25,000 Musical Arts Association, Cleveland, OH
5,000 Western Reserve Historical Society, Cleveland, OH -- Toward historical educational programs for youth

Civic & Public Affairs

10,000 Cuyahoga Valley Scenic Railroad, Peninsula, OH -- For capital/programming
5,000 Cleveland Zoological Society, Cleveland, OH -- Toward the $7 million capital campaign for the new children's zoo, the Australian Adventure
5,000 NAACP Special Contribution Fund, Baltimore, MD

Education

150,000 Case Western Reserve University, Cleveland, OH -- Toward the capital campaign for a $26 million science complex
30,000 John Carroll University, Cleveland, OH -- Toward the $30 million capital campaign for the sciences
28,500 The Ohio State University, Columbus, OH
25,000 The Pennsylvania State University, University Park, PA
22,000 Purdue University, West Lafayette, IN
21,000 Indiana University, Bloomington, IN
20,000 Baldwin-Wallace College, Berea, OH -- Toward the purchase and installation of a NMR Spectrometer
19,200 Carnegie Mellon University, Pittsburgh, PA
19,000 The University of Wisconsin, Madison, WI
18,750 University of Pittsburgh, Pittsburgh, PA
17,500 University of Illinois at Urbana, Champaign, IL
15,000 Beaumont School, Cleveland, OH -- Toward the enhancement of the chemistry and physics curriculum
15,000 Benedictine High School, Cleveland, OH -- Toward a computer laboratory
15,000 Defiance College, Defiance, OH -- Toward the campaign to upgrade its science programs
15,000 Mount Union College, Alliance, OH -- Toward support to replace the computer control system on their NMR
13,750 University of Cincinnati, Cincinnati, OH
12,000 Howard University, Washington, DC
10,000 Lake Erie College, Painesville, OH -- Toward the construction of the Arthur S. Holden Center
10,000 The Lakeland Foundation, Cleveland, OH -- Partners in Science Excellence Program
10,000 The University of Akron, Akron, OH
10,000 University of Notre Dame, Notre Dame, IN
8,000 SAE Foundation - Vision 2000, Warrendale, PA -- Science/Engineering Education
7,500 John Carroll University, Cleveland, OH
6,000 North Carolina A&T State University, Greensboro, NC
6,000 Texas A&M University, College Station, TX
5,600 San Jacinto College Central, Houston, TX
5,550 Cuyahoga Community College, Cleveland, OH
5,500 Lakeland Community College, Mentor, OH
5,500 The University of Michigan, Ann Arbor, MI
5,250 Lake Erie College, Painesville, OH
5,000 Cleveland State University, Cleveland, OH
5,000 Kent State University, Kent, OH -- Toward the Moulton Hall Learning Technologies Center

Health

30,000 The American Red Cross - Cleveland Chapter, Cleveland, OH -- Disaster planning for the elderly
25,000 Rainbow Babies and Children's Hospital, Cleveland, OH -- Toward the renovation of the pediatric operating rooms
5,000 Ronald McDonald House, Cleveland, OH -- Production of marketing film

Religion

15,000 The Salvation Army-Greater Cleveland, Cleveland, OH -- Toward safety improvements to Camp NEOSA

Science

5,000 Center of Science and Industry (COSI), Columbus, OH -- Toward outreach science programs
1,500 The Health Museum, Cleveland, OH

Social Services

89,000 United Way Services of Cleveland, Cleveland, OH
79,750 United Way of Lake County, Inc., Mentor, OH
43,000 United Way of the Texas Gulf Coast, Houston, TX
6,000 Greater Western Reserve Council, Warren, OH

LYONDELL CHEMICAL CO.

Company Contact

Houston, TX
Web: http://www.lyondell.com

Company Description

Former Name: Lyondell Petrochemical Co.
Revenue: US$3,693,000,000 (1999)
Employees: 2,732
Fortune Rank: 434, per FORTUNE Magazine's list of 500 Largest U.S. Corporations (1999).
FF 434
SIC(s): 2819 Industrial Inorganic Chemicals Nec, 2911 Petroleum Refining.

Giving Contact

David Williams, Gifts Co-ordinator
Lyondell Chemical Co.
1221 McKinney Street, Suite 700
Houston, TX 77010
Phone: (713)652-7200
Fax: (713)309-4816

Alternate Contact

David Harpol, Manager, Public Relations

Description

Organization Type: Corporate Giving Program
Acquired: ARCO Chemical Co. (1998).
Giving Locations: headquarters and operating communities.
Grant Types: Employee Matching Gifts, General Support.

Financial Summary

Total Giving: $200,000 (2000 approx); $200,000 (1999 approx); $500,000 (1997 approx)
Giving Analysis: Giving for 1995 includes: corporate direct giving ($500,000)

Typical Recipients

Arts & Humanities: Arts & Humanities-General
Education: Public Education (Precollege)
Social Services: United Funds/United Ways

Contributions Analysis

Education: Supports organizations and activities that benefit pre-college education either through support of schools, enrichment of the educational experience

for students, recognition and continuing education for educators or curriculum development.
Environment: Funds projects or organizations that promote conservation, environmental education and sustainable development.
Social Services: Supports activities and organizations that encourage community sustainability, which includes projects that further solutions to community problems.

Application Procedures
Initial Contact: Send a a brief letter of inquiry
Deadlines: None.

Restrictions
Foundation does not support individualss, political, religious, labor or fraternal organizations, donations to cover travel expenses for individualss or groups, organizations which discriminate based on age, race, religion, color, sex, disability, national origin, ancestry, marital status, sexual orientation, or veteran status. Generally does not support agencies that receive 50 percent of their financial support from United Way or organizations that not directly involved in the community in which Lyondell or Equistar have operations.

Additional Information
Lyondell Petrochemical Co. announced the acquisition of ARCO Chemical Co was completed on July 23, 1998. The acquisition of ARCO Chemical gives Lyondell a preeminent, global market position in propylene oxide and other intermediate and specialty chemicals, driven by advantaged technology positions.

Corporate Officials
Robert T. Blakely: executive vice president, chief financial officer PRIM CORP EMPL executive vice president, chief financial officer: Lyondell Chemical Co.
Morris Gelb: executive vice president, chief operating officer PRIM CORP EMPL executive vice president, chief operating officer: Lyondell Chemical Co.
Jeffrey R. Pendergraft: executive vice president, chief administrative officer PRIM CORP EMPL executive vice president, chief administrative officer: Lyondell Chemical Co.
Dan F. Smith: president, chief executive officer, director PRIM CORP EMPL president, chief executive officer, director: Lyondell Chemical Co.

Giving Program Officials
Jackie Wilson: PRIM CORP EMPL public affairs officer: Lyondell Chemical Co.

Grants Analysis
Disclosure Period: calendar year ending
Typical Range: $2,500 to $5,000

MACMILLAN BLOEDEL INC.

Company Contact
Montgomery, AL
Web: http://www.mbpi.com

Company Description
Employees: 2,500
SIC(s): 2631 Paperboard Mills.
Parent Company: MacMillan Bloedel, Ltd., 925 W. Georgia St., Vancouver, BC, Canada

Operating Locations
AL: MacMillan Bloedel Inc., Montgomery, Pine Hill; GA: MacMillan Bloedel, Alpharetta; ID: Trus Joist MacMillan, Boise; OH: MacMillan Bloedel Inc., Cleveland; WA: MB Paper, Seattle

Corporate Sponsorship
Range: less than $5,000
Type: Sports events
Contact: Rufus Craig, Vice President-Law & Government Affairs
Note: Co. sponsors a golf tournament: Children's Charity Classic.

MacMillan Bloedel Foundation

Giving Contact
Lynn Jonakin, President
MacMillan Bloedel Foundation
c/o MacMillan Bloedel Packaging Inc.
PO Box 336
Pine Hill, AL 36769
Phone: (334)963-4391
Fax: (334)963-2762
Email: rcraig@mbpi.com

Alternate Contact
MacMillan Bloedel Packaging Inc.,
1001 Carmichael Rd., Suite 300
Montgomery, AL 36106-3635
Phone: (334)213-6100

Description
Founded: 1989
EIN: 570901594
Organization Type: Corporate Foundation. Supports preselected organizations only.
Giving Locations: headquarters area only.
Grant Types: Capital, General Support.

Financial Summary
Total Giving: $194,718 (1998); $208,879 (1997); $185,490 (1996). Note: Contributes through corporate direct giving program and foundation. 1997 Giving includes corporate direct giving ($50,000); foundation (158,879).
Giving Analysis: Giving for 1998 includes: foundation ($194,718)
Assets: $1,411 (1998); $814 (1997); $3,142 (1996)
Gifts Received: $195,328 (1998); $156,564 (1997); $185,979 (1996). Note: Contributions are received from MacMillan Bloedel Inc.

Typical Recipients
Arts & Humanities: Arts Festivals, Arts Institutes, Libraries, Theater
Civic & Public Affairs: Botanical Gardens/Parks, Professional & Trade Associations, Safety
Education: Afterschool/Enrichment Programs, Arts/Humanities Education, Colleges & Universities, Community & Junior Colleges, Continuing Education, Elementary Education (Public), Education-General, Literacy, Public Education (Precollege), Science/Mathematics Education, Secondary Education (Public), Student Aid
Health: Emergency/Ambulance Services
Religion: Churches
Social Services: Child Welfare, Community Centers, Day Care, Family Services, Recreation & Athletics

Contributions Analysis
Arts & Humanities: 10%. Giving to the theater, library, and an arts institute.
Education: 88%. Supports literacy programs for children and adults, public education, and science and math education.
Social Services: 2%. Supports community programs.
Note: Total contributions made in 1998.

Restrictions
Grants are not made to individuals.

Corporate Officials
Fred V. Ernst: president, director B Cape Town, Republic of South Africa 1938. ED Harvard University. PRIM CORP EMPL president, director: MacMillan Bloedel Packaging Inc. CORP AFFIL director: MacMillan Bathurst; president: MacMillan Bloedel Timberlands.

Foundation Officials
Lynn Jonakin: president
Creola Moorer: secretary, treasurer
Jackie Walburn: vice president
Robert Williams: president

Grants Analysis
Disclosure Period: calendar year ending 1998
Total Grants: $194,718
Number of Grants: 24
Average Grant: $8,113
Highest Grant: $37,625
Typical Range: $5,000 to $50,000

Recent Grants
Note: Grants derived from 1998 Form 990.

Arts & Humanities
12,500 Alabama Shakespeare Festival, Montgomery, AL -- Donation
5,000 Wilcox County Library, Camden, AL -- Donation
1,500 Alabama Institute for the Arts, Montgomery, AL -- Educational Program

Civic & Public Affairs
1,337 Mobile Register, Mobile, AL -- News for Education

Education
37,625 Sylvan Learing Center, Decatur, AL -- Summer Enrichment Program
37,625 Sylvan Learing Center, Decatur, AL -- Summer Enrichment Program
28,000 Write to Read -- Reading & Writing Program
20,000 Sylvan Learing Center, Decatur, AL -- Summer Enrichment Program
13,172 Horions for Learning, Montgomery, AL -- Math Program
11,777 Horizons for Learning, Montgomery, AL -- Math Program
6,000 Scholarship Program, Birmingham, AL -- High School & College Students
5,000 Auburn Extension, Auburn, AL -- BEE Program
5,000 Sylvan Learning Center, Decatur, AL -- Software
2,669 Adult Learning Center, Pine Hill, AL -- Repairs
1,624 Adult Learning Center, Pine Hill, AL -- Repairs
1,500 Sylvan Learing Center, Decatur, AL -- Summer Enrichment Program
674 Adult Learning Center, Pine Hill, AL -- Repairs
644 CSAT/WA, Montgomery, AL -- Science Program
187 Adult Learning Center, Pine Hill, AL -- Repairs
104 Adult Learning Center, Pine Hill, AL -- Repairs

Religion
500 Oak Grove Baptist Church, Springville, AL -- Summer Enrichment Program

Social Services
1,000 Rosebud Community Center, Pine Apple, AL -- Donation
782 Freedom Quilting Bee, Alberta, AL -- Material Donation

500 Freedom Quilting Bee, Alberta, AL -- Supplies

MACY'S EAST INC.

Company Contact
New York, NY

Company Description
Employees: 37,100
SIC(s): 5311 Department Stores.
Parent Company: Federated Department Stores, Inc., Cincinnati, OH, United States

Giving Contact
Tom Zapf, Director, Consumer Affairs & Charitable Contributions
Macy's East
151 West 34th Street, Room 1825
New York, NY 10001
Phone: (212)494-5669

Alternate Contact
Phone: (212)494-4342
Note: For general information.

Description
Organization Type: Corporate Giving Program
Giving Locations: company operating locations.
Grant Types: Employee Matching Gifts, General Support, Project.

Financial Summary
Total Giving: Contributes through corporate direct giving program only.

Typical Recipients
Arts & Humanities: Arts Associations & Councils, Arts Centers, Arts Festivals, Arts Funds, Arts Institutes, Community Arts, Dance, Historic Preservation, Libraries, Literary Arts, Museums/Galleries, Music, Opera, Performing Arts, Public Broadcasting, Visual Arts
Civic & Public Affairs: Business/Free Enterprise, Civil Rights, Economic Policy, Employment/Job Training, Law & Justice, Legal Aid, Professional & Trade Associations, Public Policy, Safety, Urban & Community Affairs, Women's Affairs, Zoos/Aquariums
Education: Business Education, Colleges & Universities, Community & Junior Colleges, Continuing Education, Economic Education, Education Funds, Legal Education, Medical Education, Minority Education, Private Education (Precollege), Social Sciences Education, Special Education
Health: Emergency/Ambulance Services, Health Funds, Health Organizations, Hospitals, Medical Rehabilitation, Medical Research, Medical Training, Mental Health, Public Health
Social Services: Child Welfare, Community Centers, Community Service Organizations, Counseling, Delinquency & Criminal Rehabilitation, Emergency Relief, Homes, People with Disabilities, Recreation & Athletics, Senior Services, Substance Abuse, United Funds/United Ways, Volunteer Services, Youth Organizations

Contributions Analysis
Giving Priorities: Avariety of health and welfare organizations, civic organizations, the arts, and colleges and universities.
Arts & Humanities: 20% to 25%. Supports museums, the performing arts, publicbroadcasting, and other arts organizations. Cultural organizations are eligible for matching gifts.
Civic & Public Affairs: 20% to 25%. Urban and community affairs, civil rights, public policy, community development, and business and free enterprise organizations are among areas of interest.
Education: 10% to 15%. Supports colleges and universities with interests in economic, minority, vocational, business, and journalism education. Also supports education funds, community and junior colleges, and adult education programs.
Health: 35% to 40%. Areas of interest include united funds, community service organizations, youth and child welfare, employment, the aged, and the disabled. Also supports hospitals, local and national health organizations, medical research, and mental health. Health care institutions are eligible for matching gifts.

Application Procedures
Initial Contact: letter and proposal
Application Requirements: a description of organization, amount requested, purpose of funds sought, recently audited financial statement, last year's operating budget, list of major corporate contributors, copy of IRS determination letter
Deadlines: None.
Decision Notification: notification of funding decision will be made in writing
Notes: The company is unable to provide a status report on applications.

Additional Information
Although the company is now in Chapter 11, it is continuing its contributions. However, requests are being reviewed more carefully.
The company's objective is to donate 1% of pretax earnings to charitable activities.

Corporate Officials
James E. Gray: president, chief operating officer PRIM CORP EMPL president, chief operating officer: Macy's East Inc.

Giving Program Officials
Edward Jay Goldberg: PRIM CORP EMPL vice president consumer affairs: R.H. Macy & Co. Inc.
Tom Zapf: PRIM CORP EMPL director consumer affairs: Macy's East Inc.

MADISON GAS &ELECTRIC CO.

Company Contact
Madison, WI

Company Description
Revenue: US$248,590,000
Employees: 683
SIC(s): 4939 Combination Utility Nec.

Madison Gas & Electric Foundation

Giving Contact
Jim Boll, Grants Coordinator
Madison Gas & Electric Foundation
PO Box 1231
Madison, WI 53701-1231
Phone: (608)252-7279

Description
Founded: 1966
EIN: 396098118
Organization Type: Corporate Foundation
Giving Locations: WI
Grant Types: General Support.

Financial Summary
Total Giving: $251,197 (1997); $176,037 (1996); $180,296 (1995). Note: 1997 Giving includes United Way ($78,450).
Assets: $6,015,214 (1997); $5,116,497 (1996); $6,623,495 (1994)
Gifts Received: $140,550 (1997); $116,222 (1996); $59,000 (1994). Note: In 1996, contributions were received from Madison Gas & Electric Co.

Typical Recipients
Arts & Humanities: Arts Associations & Councils, Arts Centers, Community Arts, Arts & Humanities-General, History & Archaeology, Libraries, Museums/ Galleries, Music, Public Broadcasting, Theater
Civic & Public Affairs: African American Affairs, Asian American Affairs, Botanical Gardens/Parks, Business/Free Enterprise, Chambers of Commerce, Clubs, Community Foundations, Economic Development, Civic & Public Affairs-General, Housing, Parades/Festivals, Safety, Urban & Community Affairs, Women's Affairs, Zoos/Aquariums
Education: Business-School Partnerships, Colleges & Universities, Education Funds, Elementary Education (Public), Minority Education, Preschool Education, Public Education (Precollege), Secondary Education (Public), Special Education, Student Aid
Environment: Environment-General
Health: AIDS/HIV, Children's Health/Hospitals, Health Organizations, Heart, Hospitals, Medical Research, Public Health, Single-Disease Health Associations
Religion: Religious Organizations, Religious Welfare
Social Services: At-Risk Youth, Child Welfare, Community Centers, Community Service Organizations, Day Care, Domestic Violence, Family Services, Food/ Clothing Distribution, Homes, People with Disabilities, Recreation & Athletics, Scouts, Senior Services, Special Olympics, United Funds/United Ways, Veterans, YMCA/YWCA/YMHA/YWHA, Youth Organizations

Application Procedures
Initial Contact: Scholarship application forms and deadline information are published in company newsletter. For organization grants, send a brief letter of inquiry containing name, address, amount requested, and purpose of funds sought.
Deadlines: None.

Restrictions
Organizations must be located within Madison Gas & Electric Co.'s service territory in order to be considered.

Corporate Officials
Mr. Terry Hanson: chief financial officer vice president administration PRIM CORP EMPL chief financial officer: Madison Gas & Electric Co.
David Cummins Mebane: chairman, president, chief executive officer, director B Toledo, OH 1933. ED Arizona State University (1957); University of Wisconsin (1960). PRIM CORP EMPL chairman, president, chief executive officer, director: Madison Gas & Electric Co. CORP AFFIL director: First Federal Savings Bank Madison/LaCrosse; director: First Capital Investment Corp. Madison; director: First Federal Capital Corp. NONPR AFFIL director: Madison Gas & Electric Foundation Madison; trustee: University Wisconsin Research Park Corp.
Carol A. Wiskowski: assistant vice president administration PRIM CORP EMPL assistant vice president administration: Madison Gas & Electric Co.
Gary J. Wolter: senior vice president administration PRIM CORP EMPL senior vice president administration: Madison Gas & Electric Co.

Foundation Officials
Donald J. Helfrecht: chairman
Joseph T. Krzos: treasurer B Chicago, IL 1944. ED University of Wisconsin (1971).
David Cummins Mebane: vice president (see above)
Richard Henry Thies: assistant treasurer B Reedsburg, WI 1941. ED University of Wisconsin (1963). PRIM CORP EMPL vice president gas system

operation: Madison Gas & Electric Co. NONPR AFFIL secretary, director: Diggers Hotline; member: Midwest Gas Association; member: American Gas Association; member: American Public Works Association.

Frank Charles Vondrasek, Jr.: president B Omaha, NE 1928. ED Iowa State University of Science & Technology BSEE (1949); Creighton University MBA (1965). PRIM CORP EMPL vice chairman, director: Madison Gas & Electric Co. CORP AFFIL director: Firstar Bank. NONPR AFFIL member: Edison Electric Institute. CLUB AFFIL Shriners Club.

Carol A. Wiskowski: secretary (see above)

Gary J. Wolter: vice president (see above)

Grants Analysis

Disclosure Period: calendar year ending 1997
Total Grants: $172,747*
Number of Grants: 64
Highest Grant: $50,000
Typical Range: $25 to $10,000
*Note: Giving excludes United Way.

Recent Grants

Note: Grants derived from 1997 Form 990.

Arts & Humanities

2,000	Madison Symphony Orchestra, Madison, WI -- program support
1,000	Capitol City Band -- program support
1,000	Dane County Historical Society -- program support
1,000	Friends of Sun Prairie Public Library -- program support

Civic & Public Affairs

50,000	Monona Terrace Funding Corporation, Madison, MI -- program support
5,000	Habitat for Humanity of Dane County, Madison, WI -- program support
2,000	Northside Planning Council -- program support
1,600	Mendota Gridiron Club, Madison, WI -- program support
1,119	Tenney-Lapham Neighborhood -- program support
1,000	Wisconsin Sesquicentennial Commission, WI -- program support

Education

47,128	University of Wisconsin Foundation, Madison, WI -- program support
1,500	WMC Foundation -- program support
1,200	Business and Education Partnership, Madison, WI -- program support
1,100	Wisconsin Foundation for Independent Colleges, Milwaukee, WI -- program support

Health

10,000	Ronald McDonald House of Madison -- program support
7,500	South Madison Health and Family Center, Madison, WI -- program support

Religion

20,000	Salvation Army -- program support

Social Services

78,450	United Way Dane County, Madison, WI -- for various charities
7,500	City of Madison -- support Summer Youth Employment Program
1,000	Madison Area Youth Soccer Association -- program support

MALLINCKRODT CHEMICAL, INC.

Company Contact

Chesterfield, MO
Web: http://www.mallinckrodt.com

Company Description

Employees: 1,100
SIC(s): 2819 Industrial Inorganic Chemicals Nec.
Parent Company: Mallinckrodt Group Inc.

Nonmonetary Support

Type: Donated Equipment; In-kind Services

Giving Contact

Brenda Spencer, Corporate Communications Coordinator
Mallinckrodt Chemical, Inc.
675 McDonnel Blvd.
PO Box 5840
St. Louis, MO 63134
Phone: (314)654-5329
Fax: (314)654-5381

Description

Organization Type: Corporate Giving Program
Giving Locations: headquarters and operating communities.
Grant Types: Capital, Emergency, Endowment, Fellowship, General Support, Matching, Multiyear/Continuing Support, Scholarship.

Giving Philosophy

'The people of Mallinckrodt Chemical, Inc. recognize that the right to operate our plants in each of our locations derives from the community. Our goal is to develop and maintain in each operating locale a relationship with the community based on mutual respect and understanding by conducting our business as a responsible corporate citizen. We seek to achieve our goal by dealing openly, honestly and fairly with our employees, customers, suppliers and fellow citizens. As a part of our commitment to our communities, we strive to operate our plants so that they are safe and efficient and protect the environment.' *Community Partnership Program*

Financial Summary

Total Giving: $650,000 (1995 approx); $540,000 (1994 approx); $510,000 (1993 approx). Note: Contributes through corporate direct giving program only.

Typical Recipients

Arts & Humanities: Arts Appreciation, Historic Preservation, Music, Opera, Performing Arts, Theater
Civic & Public Affairs: Municipalities/Towns, Philanthropic Organizations, Safety, Urban & Community Affairs, Women's Affairs, Zoos/Aquariums
Education: Colleges & Universities, Engineering/Technological Education, Faculty Development, Minority Education, Science/Mathematics Education
Environment: Environment-General
Health: Hospitals
Science: Observatories & Planetariums, Scientific Centers & Institutes
Social Services: Community Centers, Community Service Organizations, Counseling, People with Disabilities, Shelters/Homelessness, Substance Abuse, United Funds/United Ways, Volunteer Services, Youth Organizations

Contributions Analysis

Civic & Public Affairs: 30% to 35%.
Education: 5% to 10%.
Environment: About 5%. Contributions support nonprofit organizations working toward protection, preservation, and enhancement of the environment, as well as those providing emergency response services in operating communities and those striving toward conservation of natural resources.
Note: Company reserves 10% of support for discretionaryfunding.

Application Procedures

Initial Contact: contact company for application guidelines and formal grant application
Application Requirements: completed application form; proof of tax-exempt status; governing board list, showing active board balanced with volunteers having no material conflict of interest, serving without compensation, and meeting regularly; current fiscal picture, including current operating budget and cash flow statement, demonstrating sound management practice, prudent asset investment, and reasonable compensation, program, and funding costs; most recent audited financial statements documenting program accomplishments, fiscal conditions, and fund-raising activities
Deadlines: by July 31 for review in August, October 31 for review in November, January 31 for review in February, and April 30 for review in May
Decision Notification: corporate contributions committee meets quarterly

Restrictions

The company does not make charitable contributions to political causes, candidates, or legislative or lobbying efforts; religious, veteran, or fraternal organizations; individuals seeking loans or financial aid; organizations soliciting goodwill advertising for fund-raising benefits and program books; organizations offering family planning; organizations whose activities involve trespassing, vandalizing, or damaging property; organizations located outside operating communities; athletic events or organizations unrelated to nonprofit organization; general operating funds for organizations receiving funding from United Way; purchase of tickets for testimonial and other special-event dinners; endowments; or capital campaigns. nonprofit organization; general operating funds for organizations receiving funding from United Way; purchase of tickets for testimonial and other special-event dinners; endowments; or capital campaigns.

Additional Information

Company donates approximately 1.2% to 1.5% of its pretax profits to nonprofit organizations.
Company reserves 10% of support for discretionary funding.
Publications: Application Guidelines; Application Form

Corporate Officials

Barbara A. Abbett: vice president communicationsgroup
Ashok Chawla: president global business group
Michael J. Collins: president pharmaceuticals group
Brad Fercho: president imaging group
June Fowler: director community affairs
Carl Ray Holman: chairman, chief executive officer, director B Fort Smith, AR 1942. ED University of Missouri BS (1964). PRIM CORP EMPL chairman, chief executive officer, director: Mallinckrodt Inc.
Roger A. Keller: vice president, secretary, general counsel
Mack G. Nichols: president, chief executive officer, director B Selma, AL 1938. ED Auburn University BS (1961). PRIM CORP EMPL president, chief executive officer, director: Mallinckrodt Specialty Chemicals. CORP AFFIL president: MSCH Co.; president: Nellcor Puritan Bennett Inc.; president: Mallinckrodt International Corp.; president: Mallinckrodt Medical Inc.; president, director: Mallinckrodt Chemical Inc.; director: Mallinckrodt Inc.; director: Great Lakes Corp.
Oye Olukotun: vice president medical affairs
Michael A. Rocca: senior vice president, chief financial officer

Giving Program Officials

Margie L. Schlinker: PRIM CORP EMPL manager communications: Mallinckrodt Chemical, Inc. CORP AFFIL senior community associate: Mallinckrodt Specialty Chemicals.

Grants Analysis

Disclosure Period: calendar year ending 1995
Total Grants: $650,000

Typical Range: $2,500 to $5,000

MAMIYE BROTHERS

Company Contact
Keasbeyk, NJ

Company Description
Employees: 280
SIC(s): 2361 Girls'/Children's Dresses & Blouses.

Mamiye Foundation

Giving Contact
David E. Mamiye, Secretary
Mamiye Foundation
300 Mac Lane
Keasbey, NJ 08832
Phone: (732)417-9400
Fax: (732)346-3694

Description
Founded: 1982
EIN: 222471712
Organization Type: Corporate Foundation
Giving Locations: NJ
Grant Types: General Support.

Financial Summary
Total Giving: $330,000 (1999 approx); $358,130 (1998); $390,614 (1997). Note: Contributes through foundation only.
Assets: $14,496 (1998); $10,685 (1997); $41,341 (1996)
Gifts Received: $363,000 (1998); $360,000 (1997); $360,500 (1996)

Typical Recipients
Arts & Humanities: Music
Civic & Public Affairs: Economic Policy, Employment/Job Training, Civic & Public Affairs-General, Professional & Trade Associations
Education: Education-General, Private Education (Precollege), Religious Education, Student Aid
Health: Children's Health/Hospitals, Geriatric Health, Health Organizations, Hospitals, Medical Research, Single-Disease Health Associations
International: Missionary/Religious Activities
Religion: Jewish Causes, Religious Organizations, Synagogues/Temples
Social Services: At-Risk Youth, Child Welfare, Community Service Organizations, United Funds/United Ways, YMCA/YWCA/YMHA/YWHA, Youth Organizations

Contributions Analysis
Civic & Public Affairs: 4%. Supports economic development and community foundations.
Health: 1%. Funds a youth treatment center.
Religion: 90%. Supports various Jewish causes.
Social Services: Less than 5%. Supports child welfare and family organizations.
Note: Total contributions in 1998.

Application Procedures
Initial Contact: Send a letter of inquiry.
Application Requirements: Include name and a description of organization; letter of tax exemption; purpose and amount of request.
Deadlines: None.

Corporate Officials
Jack C. Mamiye: chairman, president, chief executive officer, director B 1925. PRIM CORP EMPL chairman, president, chief executive officer, director: Mamiye Brothers.

Foundation Officials
Charles D. Mamiye: vice president B 1952. PRIM CORP EMPL secretary, treasurer, director: Mamiye Brothers Inc.
David Mamiye: secretary PRIM CORP EMPL executive: American Knitting Mills of Miami.
Jack C. Mamiye: president (see above)

Grants Analysis
Disclosure Period: calendar year ending 1998
Total Grants: $358,130
Number of Grants: 58
Average Grant: $6,175
Highest Grant: $22,000
Typical Range: $500 to $15,000

Recent Grants
Note: Grants derived from 1998 Form 990.

Civic & Public Affairs

5,000	Council on Economic Prioritization, New York, NY -- 1998 Corporation Conscience Award
5,000	Success Track, Brooklyn, NY -- 1998 Campaign
4,500	The Fashion Association, New York, NY -- American Image Awards
1,000	The Needlers Foundation Inc, New York, NY -- 2 sponsor tickets

Education

1,000	Educational Foundation for Fashion Industry, New York, NY -- Tribute Journal

Health

2,000	Vitam Youth Treatment Center, Norwalk, CT

Religion

22,000	Hillel Yeshiva, Ocean, NJ -- 97 Pledge
20,000	Hillel Yeshiva, Ocean, NJ -- Building Fund
20,000	Sephardic Bikur Holim, Brooklyn, NY -- Building Fund
19,250	Magen David Yeshiva, Brooklyn, NY -- 97 Pledge
18,000	Magen David Yeshiva, Brooklyn, NY -- 97 Pledge
14,750	Magen David Yeshiva, Brooklyn, NY -- 1997 Kippur Pledge
14,000	Hillel Yeshiva, Ocean, NJ -- 1997 Kippur Pledge
13,000	Hillel Yeshiva, Ocean, NJ -- 97 Pledge
13,000	Sephardic Bikur Holim, Brooklyn, NY -- 97 Pledge
13,000	UJA Federation of New York, New York, NY -- 97 Pledge
10,000	Hillel Yeshiva, Ocean, NJ -- Building Fund
10,000	Sephardic Bikur Holim, Brooklyn, NY -- Building Fund
8,500	UJA Federation of New York, New York, NY -- Table of 10 & Journal Ad
7,000	Hillel Yeshiva, Ocean, NJ -- 1997 Kippur Pledge
7,000	Magen David Yeshiva, Brooklyn, NY -- Special Need
6,500	Sephardic Bikur Holim, Brooklyn, NY -- 1997 Kippur Pledge
6,500	Sephardic Bikur Holim, Brooklyn, NY -- 97 Pledge (2 of 4)
6,500	UJA of New Jersey, Deal, NJ
6,500	UJA of New Jersey, Deal, NJ
6,000	Magen David Yeshiva, Brooklyn, NY -- Journal Sponsor
6,000	Yeshivat Shaare Torah, Brooklyn, NY -- Pledge paid in full
5,600	Hillel Yeshiva, Ocean, NJ -- 98 Scholarship Ad Journal
5,000	Gesher Yehuda, Brooklyn, NY -- 97 Pledge
5,000	Hillel Yeshiva, Ocean, NJ -- 98 Auction Sponsor
5,000	Merkaz Hatoral, New York, NY -- 1 of 2 Pledge
5,000	Merkaz Hatoral, New York, NY
5,000	Sephardic Studie Center, New York, NY
3,600	Sephardic Institute, Brooklyn, NY -- Building Renovation
3,600	Sephardic Institute, Brooklyn, NY -- 97-98 Annual Pledge
3,600	Sephardic Torah Center, Deal, NJ -- 1998 Annual Pledge
3,000	Shehaber Sephardic Center, New York, NY -- 1 of 2 1997 Pledge
3,000	Shehaber Sephardic Center, New York, NY -- 97 Pledge
2,600	Hatzolah, Brooklyn, NY
2,500	Ahi Ezer, Brooklyn, NY
2,500	Ahi Ezer, Brooklyn, NY
2,500	Yeshiva of Flatbush, Brooklyn, NY
2,500	Yeshiva of Flatbush, Brooklyn, NY -- 97 Pledge
2,000	Echo, Spring Valley, NY
1,000	Anti Defamation League, Boston, MA
1,000	Sephardic Community Center, Brooklyn, NY -- Gourmet Expo 1998
1,000	Yadihl Torah Publication, Oakhurst, NJ -- Book
1,000	Yeshiva of Kings Bay, Brooklyn, NY

Social Services

15,000	Children's Benefit Fund, New York, NY -- MB Kids Clothes Donation
1,500	Lubavitch Youth Organization, Brooklyn, NY -- Testimonial Dinner

MANOR CARE HEALTH SVS, INC.

Company Contact
Gaithersburg, MD

Company Description
Revenue: US$152,700,000
Employees: 36,000
SIC(s): 6719 Holding Companies Nec, 8051 Skilled Nursing Care Facilities, 8059 Nursing & Personal Care Nec.
Parent Company: Manor Care Inc.

Operating Locations
Operates in 29 states throughout the USA.

HCR ManorCare Foundation

Giving Contact
Jennifer Steiner, Executive Director
HCR ManorCare Foundation
333 North Summit Street
PO Box 10086
Toledo, OH 43604-0086
Phone: (419)252-5578

Description
EIN: 522031975
Organization Type: Corporate Foundation
Former Name: Manor Care Health SVS, Inc. (2000).
Giving Locations: states/service areas in which the co. operates.
Grant Types: General Support, Matching, Operating Expenses, Project, Research, Seed Money.

Financial Summary
Total Giving: $250,000 (2000 approx); $1,000,000 (1999 approx); $719,417 (1998). Note: Figures are for the foundation only. HCR ManorCare's direct corporate contributions range between $250,000 and $500,000 annually.

Typical Recipients

Civic & Public Affairs: Civic & Public Affairs-General
Education: Colleges & Universities, Medical Education
Health: Alzheimers Disease, Geriatric Health, Heart, Home-Care Services, Hospices, Long-Term Care, Nursing Services, Public Health, Research/Studies Institutes
Religion: Jewish Causes, Religious Welfare
Social Services: Senior Services

Application Procedures

Initial Contact: Send letter, or call (419) 252-5989, requesting foundation's application guidelines. The application process begins with a letter of inquiry; the format for this letter is specifically outlined in the guidelines. If applicant meets foundation's criteria and funding priorities, the organization will be asked to submit a formal proposal. Letters and applications are accepted on a rolling basis. The foundation's board meets up to three times a year to review requests.

Restrictions

The foundation does not accept requests for fundraising or political events, advertising, individuals, or multiyear commitments. It generally does not fund building, equipment, or capital campaigns.

Additional Information

Corporate support goes to local education, human services, and civic organizations. Foundation support focuses on community service and outreach to the elderly and their caregivers, as well as medical research and public education efforts on diseases and disorders affecting the elderly.
The same proposal will not be considered more than once in a 12-month period.
Publications: Guidelines

Corporate Officials

Stewart William Bainum, Jr.: chairman B Takoma Park, MD 1946. ED Andrews University; Pacific Union College BA (1968); University of California, Los Angeles MBA (1970). PRIM CORP EMPL chairman: HCR Manor Care Inc. CORP AFFIL chairman, chief executive officer: Manor Healthcare Corp.; vice chairman: Vitalink Pharmacy Services; chairman, chief executive officer: Four Seasons Nursing Centers.

Foundation Officials

J. Susan Hines: vice president medical programs
Jennifer Steiner: executive director

Grants Analysis

Disclosure Period: calendar year ending
Total Grants: $719,417
Typical Range: $10,000 to $25,000

Recent Grants

Note: Grants derived from 1998 Form 990.

Civic & Public Affairs
Life Steps Foundation, Culver City, CA

Education
Johns Hopkins University Foundation, Baltimore, MD
University of Pennsylvania Foundation Medical School, Philadelphia, PA

Health
Alzheimer's Association, Chicago, IL
Mayo Foundation for Medical Education and Research, Rochester, MN
National Citizen's Coalition for Nursing Home Reform, Washington, DC
National Stroke Association, Englewood, CO
Sinai Family Health Centers, Chicago, IL

Religion
Catholic Charities Collier County, Naples, FL
Jewish Family and Children's Services, Philadelphia, PA

Social Services
Iona Senior Services, Washington, DC
Senior Services, Seattle, WA

Manufacturers & Traders Trust Co.

Company Contact

Buffalo, NY

Company Description

Former Name: Central Trust Co.
Parent Company: First Empire State Corp., Buffalo, NY, United States

Nonmonetary Support

Type: Cause-related Marketing & Promotion; Donated Equipment; In-kind Services; Loaned Employees; Loaned Executives

Corporate Sponsorship

Type: Arts & cultural events; Festivals/fairs; Music & entertainment events; Sports events; Other
Note: Supports human Services, American Cancer Society, Golf Classic, Buffalo General Hospital, and Cancer Institute events.

M&T Charitable Foundation

Giving Contact

Debbie Pringle, Charitable Contributions Coordinator
M&T Charitable Foundation
1 M&T Center, 12th Floor
Buffalo, NY 14203-2301
Phone: (716)842-4618
Fax: (716)848-7318

Description

Founded: 1994
EIN: 161448017
Organization Type: Corporate Foundation
Giving Locations: headquarters and operating communities.
Grant Types: General Support.

Financial Summary

Total Giving: $5,500,000 (2000 approx); $5,500,000 (1999 approx); $3,200,000 (1997 approx). Note: Giving includes foundation ($2,097,802); United Way ($337,480).
Assets: $12,141,682 (1996); $18,654,697 (1995); $15,904,344 (1994)

Typical Recipients

Arts & Humanities: Music, Opera, Performing Arts, Theater
Civic & Public Affairs: Zoos/Aquariums
Education: Private Education (Precollege)
Religion: Jewish Causes, Religious Welfare
Social Services: United Funds/United Ways

Contributions Analysis

Arts & Humanities: 10% to 15%. Giving to the theater, orchestra, and performing arts.
Civic & Public Affairs: Less than 5%. Zoological Society.
Education: About 55%. Major grant to the Westminister Academy.
Religion: 5% to 10%. Jewish community center and Catholic charities.
Social Services: About 25%. Major grant to the United Way.

Application Procedures

Initial Contact: Contact the company for the application form they call Corporate Contributions Guidelines.
Application Requirements: The application form; a board member list and their affiliations; copy of IRS 501(c)(3) federal tax exemption letter of determination; 1-2 page proposal that includes the following: mission statement/purpose of your organization; detailed description of the need for funding; description of how the contribution will benefit the quality of life in our community; the nature and sources of permanent funding; and an annual budget and/or project budget.
Deadlines: None; committee evaluates proposals monthly.
Decision Notification: Meetings are held the third Tuesday of each month; requests must be received two weeks prior to the committee meetings to be considered for a particular month.

Restrictions

Grants are not made to individuals; organizations that lack a 501(c)(3) tax exempt status; political organizations, candidates or lobbying efforts; fraternal or veterans organizations; sports teams; national or international organizations unless their programs have significant local impact; or religious or sectarian organizations, except when they are conducting programs secular in nature and have wide public impact.

Corporate Officials

Michael P. Pinto: executive vice president, chief financial officero B New Delhi, DH India 1956. ED University of Delhi (1975); University of Pennsylvania (1985). PRIM CORP EMPL executive vice president, chief financial officer: MT Bank Corp. CORP AFFIL chief financial officer: Manufacturers & Traders Trust Co.
Robert E. Sadler, Jr.: executive vice president PRIM CORP EMPL executive vice president: M & T Bank Corp. CORP AFFIL executive vice president: Mfrs & Traders Trust Co.
Robert George Wilmers: chairman, president, chief executive officer B New York, NY 1934. ED Harvard College BA (1956); Harvard University (1958-1959). PRIM CORP EMPL chairman, president, chief executive officer: M & T Bank Corp. CORP AFFIL director: Federation Reserve Bank New York; chairman, chief executive officer, director: Mfrs & Traders Trust Co.; director: Buffalo Niagara Partnership. NONPR AFFIL member: Council Foreign Relations; member governors council: New York State Bankers Association; director: A/Knox Art Gallery; director: Business Council New York State.

Foundation Officials

Edward L. Beideck: vice president
Keith M. Belanger: vice president
John A. Carmichael: vice president, director
Shelley C. Drake: chairman, president
Edward Gajewski: vice president
Richard A. Lammert: secretary, director B 1949. PRIM CORP EMPL senior vice president: Manufacturers & Traders Trust Co. CORP AFFIL secretary: M & T Mortgage Corp.; secretary: M & T Securities Inc.; secretary: M & T Bank Corp.; director: M & T Financial Corp.
Timothy G. McEvoy: assistant secretary
Robert E. Sadler, Jr.: chief executive officer (see above)

Grants Analysis

Disclosure Period: calendar year ending 1996
Total Grants: $2,097,802*
Number of Grants: 9
Average Grant: $43,400*
Highest Grant: $764,023
Typical Range: $25,000 to $250,000
***Note:** Giving excludes United Way. Average grant excludes 2 highest grants and other miscellaneous grants ($1,029,979).

Recent Grants

Note: Grants derived from 1996 Form 990.

Arts & Humanities
85,000 Studio Arena Theater, Buffalo, NY
40,000 Buffalo Philharmonic Orchestra, Buffalo, NY
29,000 Sheas Performing Arts Center, Buffalo, NY
27,000 Greater Buffalo Opera Company, Buffalo, NY

Civic & Public Affairs
43,000 Zoological Society, Buffalo, NY

Education
764,023 Westminster Academy, Buffalo, NY -- supplemental funding for school

Religion
41,800 Jewish Community Center, Buffalo, NY
38,000 Catholic Charities, Buffalo, NY

Social Services
337,480 United Way, Buffalo, NY

MANULIFE FINANCIAL

Company Contact

200 Bloor St. E.
Toronto, ON, Canada M4W 1E5
Web: http://www.manulife.com

Company Description

Revenue: US$7,163,521,300
SIC(s): 6200 Security & Commodity Brokers, 6300 Insurance Carriers.

Nonmonetary Support

Value: $50,000 (1996)
Type: Donated Equipment; Loaned Employees
Contact: Sharon Cobban, Manager Corporate Citizenship
Note: Company also provides office space for event headquarters.

Corporate Sponsorship

Value: $1,000
Note: Co. sponsors health related issues and educational initiatives or programs.

Giving Contact

Alison Ricco, Manager, Corporate Giving Programs
Manulife Financial
73 Tremont Street, Suite 1300
Boston, MA 02108
Phone: (617)854-4345
Email: alison_ricco@.manulife.com

Alternate Contact

Sharon Cobban
Phone: (416)926-6151
Fax: (416)926-5410
Email: sharon_cobban@manulife.com

Description

Organization Type: Corporate Giving Program
Giving Locations: headquarters and operating communities.
Grant Types: Employee Matching Gifts, General Support.
Note: Corporation supports employee matching gifts to the United Way.

Giving Philosophy

'In these difficult economic times being felt around the world, Manulife Financial's philanthropic commitment has strengthened.. Being a good corporate citizen is part of the company's core values; it's an investment in the future for the company, for its employees and for the many communities in which the company operates.' *Manulife Financial Annual Review, 1993*

Financial Summary

Total Giving: $2,800,000 (1999); $2,300,000 (1998); $1,700,000 (1997). Note: Contributes through corporate direct giving program only. Giving includes foundation; international subsidiaries.

Typical Recipients

Arts & Humanities: Arts & Humanities-General, Public Broadcasting
Education: Colleges & Universities, Education-General
Health: Arthritis, Cancer, Health-General, Health Organizations, Heart, Hospitals, Medical Research, Public Health, Single-Disease Health Associations
International: Foreign Arts Organizations, Foreign Educational Institutions, Health Care/Hospitals, Human Rights, International Organizations
Religion: Religious Welfare
Social Services: Community Service Organizations, Food/Clothing Distribution, Social Services-General, United Funds/United Ways

Contributions Analysis

Arts & Humanities: Less than 5%.
Civic & Public Affairs: Less than 5%.
Education: 30% to 35%.
Health: 35% to 40%.
Social Services: 20% to 25%. United Way.

Application Procedures

Initial Contact: Submit a letter of intent and a full proposal.
Application Requirements: Provide a description of the organization, amount requested, purpose of funds sought, recently audited financial statement, and proof of tax-exempt status.
Deadlines: None.

Restrictions

Does not support individuals, religious organizations for sectarian purposes, political or lobbying groups, or organizations outside operating areas.

Additional Information

The company reports that it merged with North American Life Insurance Co. The company name remains the same, and the giving program is expected to continue.
The company does business as Manulife Financial. Its legal name is Manufacturers Life Insurance Co.

Corporate Officials

Dominic D'Alessandro: president, chief executive officer, director B Molise, Italy 1947. ED Loyola College Montreal (1967); McGill University (1971). PRIM CORP EMPL president, chief executive officer, director: Manulife Financial. CORP AFFIL director: Hudsons Bay Co. NONPR AFFIL cochairman: Capital Fund Breast Cancer Research; fellow: Institute Chartered Accountants; member: Business Council National Issues.
Arthur Sawchuck: chairman, director CORP AFFIL director: Trimac Corp.; director: Manitoba Telecom Services Inc.; director: Ontario Power Generation Inc. NONPR AFFIL director: Ontario Jobs and Investment Board.

Giving Program Officials

Sharon Cobban: PRIM CORP EMPL manager corporate citizenship: Manulife Financial.

Grants Analysis

Disclosure Period: calendar year ending 1998
Total Grants: $2,300,000*
Typical Range: $1,000 to $25,000
*Note: Grants analysis provided by foundation.

Recent Grants

Note: Grants derived from 1996 Annual Report.

Arts & Humanities
136,000 WGBH Educational Foundation, Springfield, MA
24,028 Foot and Mouth Painters

Education
149,600 American College, Bryn Mawr, PA
20,000 Wilfred Laurier University
15,000 Conestoga College Campaign
10,000 Learning Partnerships, Saint Paul, MN

Health
100,000 Corporate Fund for Breast Cancer Research
48,280 Arthritis Foundation Southern California Chapter, CA
40,000 John P. Robarts Institute
25,000 North York General Hospital
16,000 Arthritis Society
15,000 Center for Autism and Related Disorders
15,000 St. Joseph's Health Centre
14,550 Singapore Cancer Society
13,600 S.S. Huebner Foundation, Philadelphia, PA
11,000 Arthur Sommer Rotenberg Research Fund
10,200 American Heart Association
10,000 Foundation for Health
10,000 Homewood Foundation
10,000 Peterborough Civic Hospital, Peterborough, NH
10,000 Windsor Essex County Hospital

International
175,859 Greater Metro Toronto Fund, Toronto, ON, Canada
100,000 Canadian Institute for Advanced Research, ON, Canada
85,608 University of Waterloo, Waterloo, ON, Canada
80,040 Canadian International School, Canada
80,000 Kitchener Waterloo Hospital Foundation, Kitchener, ON, Canada
35,000 Skills Canada, Canada
33,000 Blood Donation Centre, Taiwan
25,000 British Columbia Children's Hospital, Vancouver, ON, Canada
25,000 Lakehead University, Thunder Bay, ON, Canada
25,000 Rotary Club, Toronto, ON, Canada -- for Health Business
20,000 Children's Health Centre at Surrey Memorial Hospital, Canada
20,000 University of Waterloo, Waterloo, ON, Canada
20,000 York University, Toronto, ON, Canada
18,000 Canadian Friends of the Hebrew University, ON, Canada -- for Rabin Scholarship Fund
15,000 Ontario Science Centre, ON, Canada
15,000 Oshawa General Hospital, Oshawa, ON, Canada
15,000 Royal Ontario Museum Foundation, Toronto, ON, Canada
13,600 Business Fund for Canadian Studies in the US, ON, Canada
13,203 China Scholars Coordinating Committee, Cambridge, MA
10,000 Canadian Women's Foundation, Canada
10,000 Carleton University, Ottawa, ON, Canada -- capital campaign
10,000 La Foundation de L'Universite du Quebec a Montreal, Montreal, PQ, Canada -- for l'UQAM
10,000 McGill University, Montreal, PQ, Canada
10,000 Queen Elizabeth Hospital, Montreal, PQ, Canada

10,000 University of Calgary, Calgary, AB, Canada
10,000 University of Manitoba, Winnipeg, MB, Canada

Religion
16,000 Genesis Foundation, Detroit, MI

Social Services
22,000 Hopespring, Charlotte, NC
15,000 New York Harvest Food Bank, New York, NY

MARCUS CORP.

Company Contact
Milwaukee, WI
Web: http://www.marcuscorp.com

Company Description
Revenue: US$303,400,000
Employees: 7,000
SIC(s): 5812 Eating Places, 7011 Hotels & Motels, 7832 Motion Picture Theaters Except Drive-In.

Marcus Corp. Foundation

Giving Contact
Charles W. Parker, Jr., General Manager
Marcus Corp. Foundation
250 East Wisconsin Avenue, Suite 1700
Milwaukee, WI 53202-4220
Phone: (414)905-1407
Fax: (414)905-2636

Description
EIN: 396046268
Organization Type: Corporate Foundation
Giving Locations: WI: Milwaukee
Grant Types: General Support.

Financial Summary
Total Giving: $599,964 (1997); $3,556,122 (1996); $484,817 (1995). Note: Contributes through foundation only. 1997 Giving includes foundation ($541,009); United Way ($58,955). 1996 Giving includes foundation ($3,506,847); United Way ($49,275).
Assets: $1,617,908 (1997); $981,533 (1996); $3,482,632 (1995)
Gifts Received: $1,173,168 (1997); $980,032 (1996); $2,823,419 (1995). Note: Contributions were received from the Marcus Corporation.

Typical Recipients
Arts & Humanities: Arts Centers, Arts Festivals, Arts Institutes, Community Arts, Dance, Film & Video, Historic Preservation, History & Archaeology, Libraries, Museums/Galleries, Music, Opera, Performing Arts, Theater
Civic & Public Affairs: African American Affairs, Clubs, Economic Development, Employment/Job Training, Civic & Public Affairs-General, Hispanic Affairs, Housing, Municipalities/Towns, Parades/Festivals, Philanthropic Organizations, Professional & Trade Associations, Public Policy, Urban & Community Affairs
Education: Business Education, Colleges & Universities, Education Associations, Education Funds, Engineering/Technological Education, Faculty Development, Education-General, Leadership Training, Medical Education
Environment: Wildlife Protection
Health: Alzheimers Disease, Arthritis, Cancer, Children's Health/Hospitals, Clinics/Medical Centers, Health Organizations, Heart, Hospitals, Medical Research, Prenatal Health Issues, Public Health, Single-Disease Health Associations, Trauma Treatment
International: Foreign Arts Organizations, Foreign Educational Institutions, International Development
Religion: Jewish Causes, Religious Organizations, Religious Welfare
Social Services: Child Abuse, Child Welfare, Community Centers, Community Service Organizations, Crime Prevention, Day Care, Domestic Violence, Family Services, Recreation & Athletics, Scouts, Shelters/Homelessness, United Funds/United Ways, Volunteer Services, YMCA/YWCA/YMHA/YWHA, Youth Organizations

Contributions Analysis
Arts & Humanities: 47%. Recipients include performing arts, music, film, and arts associations. Also funds public broadcasting and museums.
Civic & Public Affairs: 6%. Funding supports parades, festivals, and economic development in operating areas. Other recipients include African American affairs and community programs.
Education: 15%. Supports colleges, universities, and educational programs.
Health: 7%. Primarily supports hospitals and single-disease health organizations.
International: 6%.
Religion: About 2%. Primarily supports Jewish programs and organizations.
Social Services: 17%. Supports United Way, child welfare, youth organizations, and people with disabilities.

Application Procedures
Initial Contact: a brief letter of inquiry
Application Requirements: organization history, annual report, financial statements, specific objectives, requested amount, timing, proof of tax-exepmt status and explanation of specific area for which funds will be used
Deadlines: INone.
Decision Notification: in late May and late November

Corporate Officials
Stephen Howard Marcus: chairman, chief executive officer B Minneapolis, MN 1935. ED University of Wisconsin BBA (1957); University of Michigan LLB (1960). PRIM CORP EMPL chairman, chief executive officer: Marcus Corp. ADD CORP EMPL president: Centre Theatres Corp.; president: Marcus Restaurants Inc.; president: Marcus Cinemas Inc.; president: Vending Corp. CORP AFFIL chairman: Budgetel Inns Inc.; trustee: Marc Plz Corp.; chairman: Baymont Inns Suites.

Foundation Officials
Stephen Howard Marcus: president, director (see above)

Grants Analysis
Disclosure Period: calendar year ending 1997
Total Grants: $541,009*
Number of Grants: 165
Average Grant: $3,279
Highest Grant: $56,905
Typical Range: $1,000 to $5,000
***Note:** Giving excludes United Way.

Recent Grants
Note: Grants derived from 1997 Form 990.

Arts & Humanities
50,000 Great Circus Parade -- for community betterment
45,000 Marcus Center for the Performing Arts -- building fund
40,000 United Performing Arts Fund, Milwaukee, WI -- community betterment
20,250 Wisconsin History Foundation, Madison, WI -- program support
20,000 Milwaukee Repertory Theater, Milwaukee, WI -- program support
13,150 Milwaukee Symphony Orchestra League, Milwaukee, WI -- program support
10,000 Milwaukee Symphony Orchestra, Milwaukee, WI -- program support
6,250 Milwaukee Public Library Foundation, Milwaukee, WI -- program support
5,000 Captain Frederick Pabst Theater, Milwaukee, WI -- community betterment
5,000 Gerald A. Bartell Community Theater Foundation, Black Earth, WI -- community betterment
3,500 Milwaukee Art Center, Milwaukee, WI -- educational
3,000 Skylight Opera Company -- educational
2,750 Milwaukee Public Museum, Milwaukee, WI -- program support
2,500 American Film Institute, Los Angeles, CA -- building program
2,500 Betty Brinn Children's Museum, Milwaukee, WI -- educational
2,000 Waukesha Symphony Orchestra, Waukesha, WI -- community betterment

Civic & Public Affairs
5,000 American Hotel Foundation, Palm Springs, CA -- program support
5,000 Forward Wisconsin, Discover Wisconsin, Madison, WI -- program support
5,000 New Hope Project, Milwaukee, WI -- community betterment
5,000 Wisconsin Scottish Rite Foundation, Milwaukee, WI -- community betterment
4,000 Milwaukee Job Initiative, Milwaukee, WI -- community betterment
3,000 Milwaukee Urban League, Milwaukee, WI -- community betterment
2,500 Alliance for Future Transit, Milwaukee, WI -- program support, educational

Education
22,000 University of Wisconsin Milwaukee Business Administration, Milwaukee, WI
20,000 University of Wisconsin Madison Business Administration, Madison, WI -- building fund
10,000 Alverno College, Milwaukee, WI
8,500 Junior Achievement, Milwaukee, WI -- operating support
5,381 Youth Leadership Academy, Milwaukee, WI -- educational
5,000 Wisconsin Restaurant Association Education Fund, Madison, WI -- educational
4,000 University of Wisconsin Milwaukee Architecture School, Milwaukee, WI

Health
20,000 Sinai Samaritan, Milwaukee, WI -- community education
4,460 United Cerebral Palsy of Southeast Wisconsin, WI -- program support, learning programs
4,000 Vincent T. Lombardi Cancer Fund, Washington, DC -- community betterment
2,000 Ripon Memorial Hospital, Ripon, WI -- community betterment
2,000 Waukesha Memorial Hospital, Waukesha, WI
2,000 Will Rodgers Memorial Fund, White Plains, NY

International
25,000 Milwaukee World Festival, Milwaukee, WI -- program support
3,500 Wisconsin World Trade Center, WI -- program support

Religion
7,000 US Holocaust Memorial Museum, Washington, DC -- building fund
2,500 American Jewish Committee, New York, NY -- program support

Social Services

56,905	United Way, Milwaukee, WI -- community betterment
7,500	Boy Scouts of America, Milwaukee, WI -- program support
4,000	Family Service, Milwaukee, WI -- medical, community betterment
3,333	Ozaukee Ice Association, Mequon, WI -- program support
3,000	Children's Service Society of Wisconsin, Milwaukee, WI -- program support
2,500	Wisconsin State Police and Fire Games, WI -- program support
2,500	Wisconsin Volunteerism Foundation, WI -- program support
2,000	United Community Center, Milwaukee, WI -- program support
2,000	YMCA, Milwaukee, WI -- program support
2,000	YWCA, Milwaukee, WI -- program support

MARITZ INC.

Company Contact

Fenton, MO
Web: http://www.mpiconline.maritz.com

Company Description

Employees: 5,000
SIC(s): 8740 Management & Public Relations.

Nonmonetary Support

Value: $20,000 (1994); $150,000 (1993); $150,000 (1992)
Type: Donated Equipment; Donated Products; In-kind Services; Loaned Employees; Loaned Executives

Giving Contact

Norm Schwesig, Senior Vice President, Corporate Communications
Maritz Inc.
1375 North Highway Drive
Fenton, MO 63099
Phone: (314)827-4000
Fax: (314)827-3708

Description

Organization Type: Corporate Giving Program
Giving Locations: headquarters and operating communities.
Grant Types: Award, Capital, Conference/Seminar, Emergency, Employee Matching Gifts, General Support, Matching, Multiyear/Continuing Support.
Note: Employee matching gift ratio: 1 to 1. The company also awards one-time grants.

Financial Summary

Total Giving: $900,000 (1999 approx); $900,000 (1998 approx); $900,000 (1996 approx). Note: Contributes through corporate direct giving program and foundation. 1998 Giving includes foundation ($450,000); corporate direct giving ($450,000).

Typical Recipients

Arts & Humanities: Arts Associations & Councils, Arts Funds, Arts Institutes, Community Arts, Dance, Ethnic & Folk Arts, Historic Preservation, Libraries, Museums/Galleries, Music, Opera, Performing Arts, Public Broadcasting, Theater, Visual Arts
Civic & Public Affairs: Business/Free Enterprise, Civil Rights, Economic Development, Employment/ Job Training, Municipalities/Towns, Philanthropic Organizations, Public Policy, Women's Affairs, Zoos/ Aquariums
Education: Colleges & Universities, Community & Junior Colleges, Economic Education, Elementary Education (Private), Literacy, Minority Education, Preschool Education, Public Education (Precollege)
Environment: Environment-General
Health: Health-General, Hospitals, Mental Health
Social Services: Child Welfare, Delinquency & Criminal Rehabilitation, Domestic Violence, Emergency Relief, Food/Clothing Distribution, People with Disabilities, Shelters/Homelessness, Social Services-General, Substance Abuse, United Funds/United Ways, Youth Organizations

Contributions Analysis

Arts & Humanities: About 20%. Supports a broad spectrum of community arts organizations, including libraries, museums, the performing arts, theater, and public broadcasting.
Civic & Public Affairs: About 15%. Interests include economic development, business and free enterprise, civil rights, environmental affairs, public policy, and municipalities.
Education: 30% to 35%. Interests include colleges and universities, economic education, literacy, minority education, and precollege education at all levels.
Health: 25% to 30%. Major support to youth organizations. Also supports child welfare, drug and alcohol prevention, united funds, food and clothing distribution, and employment and job training.
Social Services: About 5% of contributions.

Application Procedures

Initial Contact: a brief letter of inquiry and a full proposal
Application Requirements: a description of organization, amount requested, purpose of funds sought, and recently audited financial statement
Deadlines: None.

Restrictions

Does not support individuals or religious organizations for sectarian purposes.

Corporate Officials

James Kienker: chief financial officer
W. Stephen Maritz: president, chief operating officer B 1958. PRIM CORP EMPL president, chief operating officer: Maritz Inc.
William Edward Maritz: chairman, chief executive officer, president B Saint Louis, MO 1928. ED Princeton University BA (1950). PRIM CORP EMPL chairman, chief executive officer, president: Maritz Inc. CORP AFFIL founder, chairman board: Laclede Landing Development Corp.; chairman: Maritz Corp. Services; director: Brown Group Inc. NONPR AFFIL chairman: VP Fair Foundation; director: Washington University; member: Regional Commerce Growth Association; director: Saint Lukes Hospital; director: Missouri Botanical Gardens; director: Princeton University; director: Cystic Fibrosis Foundation; director: KETC; director: Camping Education Foundation; director: Community School; director: American Youth Foundation; director: John Burroughs School.

Grants Analysis

Disclosure Period: calendar year ending
Typical Range: $500 to $2,000

MARK IV INDUSTRIES

Company Contact

Amherst, NY
Web: http://www.mark-iv.com

Company Description

Employees: 15,800
SIC(s): 3714 Motor Vehicle Parts & Accessories.

Operating Locations

Cetec Corp. and Dayco Products Inc. each operate 4 divisions in locations.

Corporate Sponsorship

Type: Arts & cultural events; Festivals/fairs; Music & entertainment events; Sports events

Mark IV Industries Foundation

Giving Contact

Joanne Eckert, Executive Assistant
Mark IV Industries Foundation
PO Box 810
Amherst, NY 14226-0810
Phone: (716)689-4972 ext 418
Fax: (716)689-6098

Description

Founded: 1976
EIN: 161082605
Organization Type: Corporate Foundation
Giving Locations: NY: Buffalo
Grant Types: Award, Capital, Employee Matching Gifts, General Support.

Financial Summary

Total Giving: $240,000 (fiscal year ending April 30, 1999); $282,061 (fiscal 1998); $272,976 (fiscal 1996). Note: Contributes through foundation only.
Giving Analysis: Giving for fiscal 1998 includes: foundation ($272,061); corporate grants to United Way ($10,000)
Assets: $1,500,000 (fiscal 1999 approx); $1,482,199 (fiscal 1998); $1,737,252 (fiscal 1996)
Gifts Received: $21,265 (fiscal 1989)

Typical Recipients

Arts & Humanities: Arts Funds, Museums/Galleries, Music, Public Broadcasting, Theater
Civic & Public Affairs: Botanical Gardens/Parks, Business/Free Enterprise, Clubs, Community Foundations, Economic Development, Civic & Public Affairs-General, Parades/Festivals, Philanthropic Organizations, Urban & Community Affairs, Women's Affairs, Zoos/Aquariums
Education: Arts/Humanities Education, Business Education, Colleges & Universities, Community & Junior Colleges, Leadership Training, Medical Education, Science/Mathematics Education, Student Aid
Health: Cancer, Children's Health/Hospitals, Diabetes, Emergency/Ambulance Services, Heart, Hospices, Hospitals, Multiple Sclerosis, Prenatal Health Issues, Single-Disease Health Associations
International: Foreign Educational Institutions, International Affairs, International Organizations
Religion: Jewish Causes, Religious Organizations, Religious Welfare, Social/Policy Issues
Social Services: Child Welfare, Community Service Organizations, Crime Prevention, Family Services, People with Disabilities, Recreation & Athletics, Special Olympics, Substance Abuse, United Funds/ United Ways, Veterans, YMCA/YWCA/YMHA/YWHA

Contributions Analysis

Arts & Humanities: 7%. Funds orchestra, ballet, and public broadcasting.
Civic & Public Affairs: 6%. Supports community activities and parks.
Education: 47%. Funds higher education.
Health: 30%. Hospitals and single-disease concerns.
Religion: 5%. Supports Jewish organizations and causes.
Social Services: 5%. Supports United Way and youth services.
Note: Total contributions made in fiscal 1998.

Application Procedures

Initial Contact: Send a letter of inquiry.
Application Requirements: Include a detailed description of purpose for which funds are to be used, and audited financial statements.

Deadlines: None.

Additional Information

Publications: Annual Report

Corporate Officials

Salvatore Harry Alfiero: founder, chairman, chief executive officer, director B Westerly, RI 1937. ED Rensselaer Polytechnic Institute BS (1964); Harvard University MBA (1966). PRIM CORP EMPL founder, chairman, chief executive officer, director: Mark IV Industries Inc. CORP AFFIL director: Phoenix Home Life Mutual Insurance Co.; director: Southwire Co.; director: Niagara Mohawk Power Corp.; director: Marine Midland Banks Inc.; director: National Health Care Affiliates Inc.

William Patrick Montague: president, chief operating officer, director B Wilkes-Barre, PA 1946. ED Wilkes University BS (1968); Wilkes University MBA (1977). PRIM CORP EMPL president, chief operating officer, director: Mark IV Industries Inc. CORP AFFIL director: Purolator Products Co.; president: NRD, LLC; vice president: Gulton Industries Inc.; director: International Imaging Materials Inc.; director: Gibraltar Steel Corp.; director: Gleason Corp.; director: Dayco Products Inc.; chief financial officer: F-P Technology Holding Corp. NONPR AFFIL member: American Institute CPAs.

Foundation Officials

Salvatore Harry Alfiero: chairman (see above)

Gerald Sanford Lippes: secretary B Buffalo, NY 1940. ED University of Michigan (1958-1961); University of Buffalo JD (1964). PRIM CORP EMPL senior partner: Lippes, Silverstein, Mathias & Wexler. CORP AFFIL director: Upgrade Corp. Am; secretary: Purolator Products Co.; director: Rights Exchange Inc.; secretary: NRD LLC; secretary: Gulton Industries Inc.; secretary, director, general couns: Mark IV Industries; director: Gibraltar Steel Corp.; secretary: Dayco Products Inc.; secretary: FP Technologies Holding Corp.; secretary: Dayco Distributing Inc. NONPR AFFIL chairman: University Buffalo Law School; chairman: University Buffalo Law School Foundation; chairman: University Buffalo Foundation; member: New York State Bar Association; chairman: University Buffalo Council; chairman: New York State Arts Council; chairman: Jewish Philanthropies, Inc.; director: National Heathcare Affil; member: Erie County Bar Association; director: Childrens Hospital Buffalo; director: Downtown Medical Center; director: CGF Health Care System; member: American Society of Corporate Secretaries; board director: Buffalo Fine Arts Academy.

William Patrick Montague: president (see above)

Grants Analysis

Disclosure Period: fiscal year ending April 30, 1999
Total Grants: $230,000*
Number of Grants: 52
Average Grant: $4,615
Highest Grant: $20,000
Typical Range: $25 to $12,500
***Note:** Giving excludes United Way. Grants analysis provided by the foundation.

Recent Grants

Note: Grants derived from fiscal 1997 Form 990.

Arts & Humanities

1,000 Irish Classical Theater, Buffalo, NY

Civic & Public Affairs

10,609 Greater Buffalo Partnership, Buffalo, NY
10,000 Festival of Trees, Spokane, WA
5,000 Buchanan Area Foundation, Buchanan, MI
5,000 Buchanan Area Foundation, Buchanan, MI
5,000 Buffalo Renaissance Foundation, Buffalo, NY
3,500 NCCJ
2,500 New York Junior League, New York, NY
2,500 Roswell Alliance Fund
2,500 Roswell Alliance Fund
199 Buffalo PBA, Buffalo, NY
195 Reunion Journal

Education

17,986 Buffalo State College, Buffalo, NY
15,000 St. Bonaventure University, NY
11,658 Buffalo State College, Buffalo, NY
5,250 State University of New York Buffalo, Buffalo, NY
5,000 Buffalo Fine Arts Academy, Buffalo, NY
3,585 Erie Community College, Erie, PA
3,500 State University of New York Buffalo, Buffalo, NY
3,477 State University of New York Buffalo, Buffalo, NY
3,166 Erie Community College, Erie, PA
3,000 Junior Achievement Western New York, Buffalo, NY
1,750 Buffalo State College, Buffalo, NY
1,750 Buffalo State College, Buffalo, NY
1,750 Buffalo State College, Buffalo, NY
1,750 Erie Community College, Erie, PA
1,750 State University of New York Buffalo, Buffalo, NY
1,750 State University of New York Buffalo, Buffalo, NY
1,145 Erie Community College, Erie, PA
1,145 Erie Community College, Erie, PA
1,077 Buffalo State College, Buffalo, NY
1,000 Outward Bound, Buffalo, NY
725 Junior Achievement Western New York, Buffalo, NY
450 Junior Achievement Western New York, Buffalo, NY
225 Pennsylvania State University, University Park, PA
100 Donald Polluck Scholarship Fund

Health

15,000 Children's Hospital Golf Tournament, Buffalo, NY
10,000 Children's Hospital Golf Tournament, Buffalo, NY
5,000 Juvenile Diabetes Foundation, Buffalo, NY
2,000 Sisters Hospital Foundation
1,000 Tourette Syndrome Association, Washington, DC
500 Leukemia Society, Buffalo, NY
500 March of Dimes, Buffalo, NY
500 National Multiple Sclerosis Society, Buffalo, NY
300 Buffalo General Hospital, Buffalo, NY
175 American Heart Association, Buffalo, NY

Religion

3,500 United Jewish Appeal, Buffalo, NY

Social Services

3,500 Healing the Children Foundation
500 Blind Association of Western New York, Buffalo, NY
500 YMCA, Buffalo, NY

MARRIOTT INTERNATIONAL INC.

Company Contact

Bethesda, MD
Web: http://www.marriott.com

Company Description

Former Name: Marriott Corp.
Revenue: US$8,739,000,000 (1999)
Employees: 121,932 (1999)
Fortune Rank: 200, per FORTUNE Magazine's list of 500 Largest U.S. Corporations (1999).
FF 200
SIC(s): 5812 Eating Places, 7011 Hotels & Motels.

Operating Locations

Operates throughout the USA.

Nonmonetary Support

Type: Donated Equipment; Donated Products; In-kind Services
Note: For nonmonetary support contact operating divisions or appropriate local company for more information.

Giving Contact

Judi A. Hadfield, Vice President Community Relations & Corporate Projects
Marriott International Inc.
1 Marriott Drive
Washington, DC 20058
Phone: (301)380-7430
Fax: (301)380-2843

Description

Organization Type: Corporate Giving Program
Giving Locations: organizations near headquarters and some national organizations.
Grant Types: General Support, Operating Expenses, Project.

Giving Philosophy

'The contributions program at Marriott emphasizes four areas: education--mostly at the university level; civic; health and human services--done mostly through United Way; and cultural arts. Most of the company's contributions are made in communities in which Marriott has operations. They are given to organizations which fill important community needs.'

Financial Summary

Total Giving: Contributes through corporate direct giving program only. Company does not disclose contributions figures.

Typical Recipients

Arts & Humanities: Arts Associations & Councils, Arts Institutes, Museums/Galleries, Performing Arts, Public Broadcasting, Theater
Civic & Public Affairs: Employment/Job Training, Urban & Community Affairs, Women's Affairs
Education: Colleges & Universities
Health: Health Funds, Health Organizations, Single-Disease Health Associations
Social Services: Community Service Organizations, People with Disabilities, Youth Organizations

Contributions Analysis

Giving Priorities: Health and human services, primarily through United Way; universities with an interest in the hospitality industry; civic organizations; and the arts.

Arts & Humanities: 5% to 10%. Supports the performing arts, arts organizations, public broadcasting, and historic preservation in headquarters area or programs which are national in scope.

Civic & Public Affairs: 10% to 15%. Grants disbursed primarily in headquarters area. Interests are professional and tradeorganizations, urban and community affairs, cultural diversity, and minority affairs.

Education: About 30%. Most contributions are made at the university level, supporting schools where company actively recruits, with interest in the hospitality industry. Contributions at the secondary level are national in scope and promote cultural diversity or serve minority or disadvantaged students.

Health: About 50%. Primarily supports the United Way in operating communities. The remaining funds support health and human service organizations in

headquarters community and select national organizations, with focus on people with disabilities and hunger relief.

Application Procedures

Initial Contact: brief letter

Application Requirements: a description of organization, specific financial needs, purpose of funds sought, current budget, recently audited financial statement, list of sources of past and current funds, proof of tax-exempt status, and latest annual report

Deadlines: None, preferably in fall; applications must be received at least six weeks prior to deadline

Decision Notification: within one month of receipt

Notes: Direct applications to Contributions Coordinator, Dept. 977.01, at above address. Telephone inquiries are strongly discouraged.

Restrictions

Does not support fraternal organizations, goodwill advertising, individuals, political or lobbying groups, or religious organizations for sectarian purposes.

Additional Information

Marriott also makes contributions of complimentary lodgings.

Corporate Officials

J. Willard Marriott, Jr.: chairman, chief executive officer B Washington, DC March 25, 1932. ED University of Utah BS (1954). PRIM CORP EMPL chairman, chief executive officer: Marriott International Inc. ADD CORP EMPL director: Host Marriott Corp.; director: Host Marriott Services Corp. CORP AFFIL director: Outboard Marine Corp.; director: General Motors Corp. NONPR AFFIL director: United States-Russia Business Council; member executive committee: World Travel Tourism Council; member: Sigma Chi; member conference board: U.S. Chamber of Commerce; trustee: National Geographic Society; director: Naval Academy Endowment Trust; member: Business Roundtable; member: Conference Board; member national advisory board: Boy Scouts America; member conference board: Business Council; member: Bald Peak Chamber of Commerce. CLUB AFFIL Metro Club; member: Avenel Golf Club; Burning Tree Club.

Joseph Ryan: executive vice president, general counsel PRIM CORP EMPL executive vice president, general counsel: Marriott International Inc.

William J. Shaw: president, chief operating officer PRIM CORP EMPL president, chief operating officer: Marriott International Inc.

Arne M. Sorenson: executive vice president, chief financial officer PRIM CORP EMPL executive vice president, chief financial officer: Marriott International Inc.

William R. Tiefel: vice chairman, director PRIM CORP EMPL vice chairman, director: Marriott International Inc.

Giving Program Officials

Judi A. Hadfield: vice president corporate relations

MARSHALL FIELD'S

Company Contact

Chicago, IL
Web: http://www.marshallfields.com

Company Description

Employees: 214,000
SIC(s): 5311 Department Stores.
Parent Company: Target Corp., 777 Nicollet Mall, Minneapolis, MN, United States

Giving Contact

Angelique Williams, Community Relations Specialist
Marshall Field's
111 North State Street
Chicago, IL 60602
Phone: (312)781-5460
Fax: (312)781-4604

Description

Founded: 1853
Organization Type: Corporate Giving Program
Giving Locations: IL: Chicago operating locations.
Grant Types: Award, General Support, Project.

Giving Philosophy

'We (Marshall Field's) contribute five percent of our pretax profits to support programs in the communities where we do business. It's not something we have to do. It's something we want to do. And in many ways, we gain as much as we give. The result of our involvement is healthier, more vital communities that help sustain our stores in return. .. We concentrate our giving on our most precious resource-children and youth-because that is what our guests and team members have told us is a priority for them. Our three focus areas are child abuse prevention, youth self-sufficiency and education through the arts.' *Community Giving Program Grant Application Guidelines 1998*

Financial Summary

Total Giving: $2,000,000 (fiscal year ending January 31, 2000 approx); $2,000,000 (fiscal 1999 approx); $2,000,000 (fiscal 1998 approx). Note: Contributes through corporate direct giving program only.

Typical Recipients

Arts & Humanities: Arts Associations & Councils, Arts Centers, Arts Festivals, Arts Funds, Arts Institutes, Arts Outreach, Community Arts, Dance, Ethnic & Folk Arts, Literary Arts, Museums/Galleries, Music, Opera, Performing Arts, Theater, Visual Arts

Civic & Public Affairs: Employment/Job Training, Hispanic Affairs, Urban & Community Affairs, Women's Affairs

Education: Arts/Humanities Education, Education Reform, Elementary Education (Public), Literacy, Student Aid

Health: AIDS/HIV

Social Services: At-Risk Youth, Community Service Organizations, People with Disabilities, United Funds/ United Ways, Youth Organizations

Contributions Analysis

Arts & Humanities: Funds programs forschool-age youth (K-12) that improve educational outcomes, encourage youth access and involvement in the arts, and educate children about different cultures.

Social Services: Supports child abuse prevention by funding programs that educate parents in parenting and coping skills, provide parent support and self-help groups, provide mentors for parents and caregivers, support crisis nurseries and hotlines, develop home visitor programs for at-risk families, and create general public awareness and education about child abuse prevention. A second priority is developing youth self-sufficiency; funds programs that provide opportunities for school-age children to gain employment leadership skills, increase awareness in career opportunities with caring adults, and engage young people in community service.

Note: Each Marshall Field's store has a small discretionary fund of $1,000 to $3,000 for contributions to local nonprofits. Contact local store manager for details.

Application Procedures

Initial Contact: call or write for application form

Application Requirements: a description of organization and project, amount requested (can not exceed $5,000), purpose of funds sought, methods of evaluation, recently audited financial statements, timetable, list of board and staff, other corporate funding sources, and proof of tax-exempt status

Deadlines: January 15 for the City of Chicago; March 13 for the suburbs of Chicago; May 15 for store communities in Illinois, Wisconsin, and Fort Wayne, Indiana; June 15 for store communities in South Bend Indiana and Ohio.

Review Process: applicants will receive acknowledgement and may receive request for further information; information will then be reviewed by Community Involvement Committee, which consists of employee representatives

Decision Notification: committees meet annually

Notes: Each store/market area has its own Community Involvement Committee. Each Chicago area store has representation on an employee arts and social action committee.

Restrictions

Does not support individuals; religious organizations for sectarian purposes; sheltered work projects; maintenance of food, clothing or shelters; educational institutions for instructional services; recreation; housing and residential programs; disability or emergency care; fund-raising events; sports teams or events; programs for medical or substance abuse; merchandise or gift certificate requests; or advertising in program books. Company generally does not make capital, endowment, or multiyear grants. Also, company does not sponsor programs outside of its operating area. outside of its operating area.

Additional Information

Publications: Grant Application Guidelines; Circle of Giving Brochures

Corporate Officials

Daniel Skoda: president B New York, NY 1946. PRIM CORP EMPL president: Marshall Field's. CORP AFFIL senior vice president: Neiman Marcus Group Inc.

Giving Program Officials

Katherine Davis: PRIM CORP EMPL director public affairs & communications: Marshall Field's.

Grants Analysis

Disclosure Period: fiscal year ending January 31, 1995
Total Grants: $1,236,000
Number of Grants: 150
Average Grant: $3,500
Highest Grant: $163,300
Typical Range: $2,500 to $5,000

Recent Grants

Note: Grants derived from 1994 grants list.

Arts & Humanities

37,500	Art Institute of Chicago, Chicago, IL -- Comprehensive Arts Support Program (CASP)
37,500	Chicago Symphony Orchestra, Chicago, IL -- Comprehensive Arts Support Program (CASP)
37,500	Goodman Theater, Chicago, IL -- Comprehensive Arts Support Program (CASP)
37,500	Lyric Opera of Chicago, Chicago, IL -- Comprehensive Arts Support Program (CASP)
37,500	Ravinia Festival, Highland Park, IL -- Comprehensive Arts Support Program (CASP)
18,750	Hubbard Street Dance Company, Chicago, IL -- Comprehensive Arts Support Program (CASP)
18,750	Museum of Contemporary Art, Chicago, IL -- Comprehensive Arts Support Program (CASP)

18,750	Steppenwolf Theater Company, Chicago, IL -- Comprehensive Arts Support Program (CASP)
17,900	Whirlwind Performance Company, Chicago, IL -- planning grant for Neighborhood Arts Partnership
10,000	Black Ensemble Theater Corp, Chicago, IL -- sponsorship of performance of PERFECT DUET in Chicago
5,000	Beacon Street Gallery and Theater, Chicago, IL -- multicultural/multi-arts community arts education program
5,000	Chicago Chamber Musicians, Chicago, IL -- model music development program at Sullivan High School
5,000	Chicago Children's Choir, Chicago, IL -- in-school and afterschool music education and choral performance program
5,000	Chicago City Theater Company, Chicago, IL -- technical assistance for Neighborhood Arts Partnership
5,000	City of Chicago Department of Cultural Affairs, Chicago, IL -- sponsorship of Gallery 37 for 1993
5,000	Lifeline Theater, Chicago, IL -- in-school residency program
5,000	Mexican Fine Arts Center Museum, Chicago, IL -- visiting artist's program for local schools
5,000	Milwaukee Repertory Theater, Milwaukee, WI -- community services program for youth
5,000	Milwaukee Symphony Orchestra, Milwaukee, WI -- arts in community education (ACE) program
5,000	Museum of Contemporary Art, Chicago, IL -- partnership with schools for arts education
5,000	Music/Theater Workshop, Chicago, IL -- Under Pressure program and 'Someone You Can Trust'
2,500	Chicago Neighborhood Artists, Chicago, IL -- arts and education program and Artist/Mentor project
2,500	Glen Ellyn Children's Chorus, Chicago, IL -- youth outreach program

Civic & Public Affairs

5,000	South Austin Job Referral Service, Austin, TX -- job counseling and placement
5,000	Travelers and Immigrants Aid, Chicago, IL -- the Learning Center at Neon Street Center
5,000	Women Employed Institute, Chicago, IL -- career links
5,000	Youth Service Project, Chicago, IL -- enrichment for Latinos Leading to Advancement (ELLA) program

Education

35,000	Robert Healy Elementary School, Chicago, IL -- planning grant and technical assistance for Neighborhood Arts Partnership
25,000	Illinois Alliance for Arts Education, Chicago, IL
5,000	Chicago Moving Company, Chicago, IL -- Chicago in-school residency program
5,000	ETA Creative Arts Foundation, Chicago, IL -- the Brownell and McCosh Elementary Schools playwriting/creative dramatics
5,000	Golden Apple, Chicago, IL -- Golden Apple Scholars of Illinois
5,000	Literacy Chicago, Chicago, IL -- ESL program
5,000	Whirlwind Performance Company, Chicago, IL -- talented teachers program
2,500	Erikson Institute, Chicago, IL -- assessments of children's development in the fine arts

Health

40,000	AIDS Foundation of Chicago, Chicago, IL -- general support for grant making program for AIDS service

Social Services

187,300	United Way Crusade of Mercy, Chicago, IL -- 1993 corporate gift
25,000	United Way Chicago, Chicago, IL -- for Family-to-Family Child Care initiative in Chicago area
18,400	United Way Greater Milwaukee, Milwaukee, WI -- 1993 corporate gift
8,200	United Way Texas Gulf coast, Houston, TX -- 1993 corporate gift
5,000	Access Living, Chicago, IL -- transitions to Independence Program
5,000	Ada S. McKinley Community Services, Chicago, IL -- early intervention program for 7th and 8th grade students
5,000	Aunt Martha's Youth Service Center, Matteson, IL -- Project New Chance comprehensive teen parent program
5,000	Boy Scouts of America, Chicago, IL -- law enforcement exploring program
5,000	Chicago Lighthouse, Chicago, IL -- youth transition program
5,000	United Way Crusade of Mercy, Chicago, IL -- pledged support of the 1992 Loaned Executive program
4,800	United Way Dane County, Chicago, IL -- 1993 corporate gift
4,500	United Way Lake County, Waukegan, IL -- 1993 corporate gift
4,400	United Way Franklin County, Columbus, OH -- 1993 corporate gift
3,800	United Way Metropolitan Dallas, Dallas, TX -- 1993 corporate gift

MARSHALL &ILSLEY CORP.

Company Contact

Milwaukee, WI
Web: http://www.micorp.com

Company Description

Also Known As: Marshall & Ilsley Bank.
Assets: US$13,655,600,000
Employees: 8,993
SIC(s): 6021 National Commercial Banks, 6712 Bank Holding Companies.

Marshall & Ilsley Foundation, Inc.

Giving Contact

Ms. Diane Sebion, Secretary
Marshall and Ilsley Foundation
770 North Water Street
Milwaukee, WI 53202
Phone: (414)765-7585
Fax: (414)765-7899

Description

Founded: 1958
EIN: 396043185
Organization Type: Corporate Foundation
Giving Locations: WI: emphasis on Milwaukee
Grant Types: Capital, General Support, Scholarship.

Financial Summary

Total Giving: $3,000,000 (1999 approx); $1,672,700 (1998); $1,753,750 (1996). Note: Contributes through foundation only.
Giving Analysis: Giving for 1996 includes: foundation ($1,694,750); foundation scholarships ($56,000); foundation grants to United Way ($3,000); 1998: foundation ($1,279,700); foundation grants to United Way ($345,000); foundation scholarships ($48,000)
Assets: $1,265,633 (1998); $1,184,197 (1996)
Gifts Received: $297,860 (1998). Note: In 1998, contributions were received from M&I corp, and M&I Bank.

Typical Recipients

Arts & Humanities: Arts Associations & Councils, Arts Festivals, Arts Funds, Arts Institutes, Film & Video, Historic Preservation, Libraries, Museums/Galleries, Music, Performing Arts, Public Broadcasting, Theater, Visual Arts
Civic & Public Affairs: Economic Development, Employment/Job Training, Hispanic Affairs, Housing, Professional & Trade Associations, Urban & Community Affairs, Women's Affairs, Zoos/Aquariums
Education: Arts/Humanities Education, Business Education, Colleges & Universities, Community & Junior Colleges, Education Associations, Education Funds, Education Reform, Elementary Education (Private), Engineering/Technological Education, Leadership Training, Literacy, Medical Education, Minority Education, Private Education (Precollege), Secondary Education (Private), Student Aid
Environment: Environment-General
Health: Cancer, Children's Health/Hospitals, Clinics/Medical Centers, Health Organizations, Hospitals, Long-Term Care, Medical Research, Medical Training, Mental Health, Nursing Services, Research/Studies Institutes, Single-Disease Health Associations, Transplant Networks/Donor Banks, Trauma Treatment
International: International Relations
Religion: Religious Organizations, Religious Welfare
Science: Science Museums
Social Services: Animal Protection, Child Welfare, Community Centers, Community Service Organizations, Day Care, Family Planning, Family Services, Food/Clothing Distribution, People with Disabilities, Recreation & Athletics, Shelters/Homelessness, United Funds/United Ways, Volunteer Services, YMCA/YWCA/YMHA/YWHA, Youth Organizations

Contributions Analysis

Giving Priorities: Youth organizations, united funds, and child welfare; urban and community and environmental affairs; colleges and universities; hospitals and health centers; and musical and theatrical organizations.
Arts & Humanities: 23%. Musical and theatrical organizations, arts funds, and history and arts associations.
Civic & Public Affairs: 6%. Urban and community affairs, environmental affairs, zoos and botanical gardens, housing, and professional and trade organizations.
Education: 21%. Largely to colleges and universities, and to scholarships and scholarship funds. Interests also include arts education, particularly in music, and business, elementary, and private precollege education.
Health: 15%. Hospitals and health centers, medical research, single-disease health organizations, and nursing services.
Religion: 1%. Religious groups and religious welfare organizations.
Social Services: 34%. Primarily youth organizations, united funds, and child welfare. Interests also include community services and centers, volunteer services, family services, and organizations concerned with the disabled.
Note: Total contributions made in 1998.

Application Procedures

Initial Contact: Send a brief letter or proposal.
Application Requirements: Include a a description of organization, amount requested, purpose of funds sought, recently audited financial statement, and proof of tax-exempt status.

Deadlines: None.

Corporate Officials

Dennis J. Kuester: president B 1942. ED University of Milwaukee BBA (1966). PRIM CORP EMPL president: Marshall & Ilsley Corp. CORP AFFIL director: Modine Manufacturing Co.; director: Super Steel Products Corp.; president: Marshall & Ilsley Bank; director: Krueger International Inc.; chairman, chief executive officer: M&I Data Services Inc.

James B. Wigdale: vice president B 1936. PRIM CORP EMPL vice president: Marshall & Ilsley Corp. CORP AFFIL chairman, chief executive officer: Marshall & Ilsley Bank; director: M&I First National Leasing; director: M&I Mortgage Corp.; chairman: M & I Marshall & Ilsley Bank; director: M&I Capital Markets Group; director: Columbia Health System Inc.; director: Green Bay Packaging Inc. NONPR AFFIL chairman: Medical College Wisconsin; vice chairman: Metropolitan Milwaukee Association.

Foundation Officials

Wendell Francis Bueche: director B Flushing, MI 1930. ED University of Notre Dame BSME (1952). PRIM CORP EMPL retired chairman, chief executive officer: IMC Fertilizer Inc. CORP AFFIL director: Wisconsin Gas Co.; director: Marshall & Ilsley Corp.; director: WICOR Inc.; Director: M & I Marshall & Ilsley Bank; director: IMC Global Inc.; chairman: IMC Global Operation Delaware. NONPR AFFIL member: Mid-Atlantic Committee for International Business; member: National Association Manufacturer; member: Council Medicine College Wisconsin. CLUB AFFIL Westmoor Country Club; Milwaukee Country Club; member: Mission Hills Country Club; member: Longboat Key Club.

Burleigh Edmund Jacobs: director B Milwaukee, WI 1920. ED University of Wisconsin BA (1942). PRIM CORP EMPL chairman: Grede Foundries Inc. CORP AFFIL director: Marshall & Ilsley Bank; director: Marshall & Ilsley Corp.; director: Benz Oil Inc.

Jack F. Kellner: director, board member B 1916. CORP AFFIL treasurer: MCP Co. Inc.; chairman: Western Industries Inc.; director: Marshall & Ilsley Corp.; director: Grede Foundries Inc.; director: M & I First National Leasing.

John A. Puelicher: president, director B Milwaukee, WI 1920. ED Harvard University Graduate School of Business Administration; University of Wisconsin BA (1943). CORP AFFIL director: Sentry Insurance Co.

Meg Surges: secretary

James B. Wigdale: vice president, director (see above)

James O. Wright: director B Milwaukee, WI 1921. ED Yale University BS (1944). PRIM CORP EMPL chairman, director: Badger Meter, Inc. CORP AFFIL director: Northwestern Mutual Life Insurance Co.; director: Wisconsin Natural Gas Co.; director: Marshall & Ilsley Corp.; director: Grede Foundries Inc.; director: Marshall & Ilsley Bank; director: Becor Western Inc.

Grants Analysis

Disclosure Period: calendar year ending 1998
Total Grants: $1,279,700*
Number of Grants: 119
Average Grant: $10,754
Highest Grant: $90,000
Typical Range: $1,000 to $25,000
***Note:** Giving excludes scholarship; United Way.

Recent Grants

Note: Grants derived from 1997 Form 990.

Arts & Humanities

125,000	Milwaukee Public Museum, Milwaukee, WI
80,000	United Performing Arts Fund, Milwaukee, WI
50,000	Milwaukee Art Museum, Milwaukee, WI
50,000	Milwaukee Public Library Foundation, Milwaukee, WI
50,000	Milwaukee Public Museum, Milwaukee, WI
50,000	Milwaukee Symphony Orchestra, Milwaukee, WI
50,000	Performing Arts Center
40,000	Milwaukee Repertory Theater, Milwaukee, WI
20,000	Milwaukee Public Museum, Milwaukee, WI
20,000	Performing Arts Center
17,000	Captain Frederick Pabst Theater
10,000	Milwaukee Art Museum, Milwaukee, WI

Civic & Public Affairs

25,000	Local Initiatives Support Corporation
20,000	Opportunity Development Centers, Wisconsin Rapids, WI
15,000	Neighborhood Housing Services, New York, NY
10,000	Council for the Spanish Speaking, Milwaukee, WI

Education

100,000	University of Wisconsin Foundation, Madison, WI
50,000	Alverno College, Milwaukee, WI
50,000	Brookfield Academy, Brookfield, WI
50,000	Medical College of Wisconsin, Milwaukee, WI
40,000	Wisconsin Conservatory of Music, Milwaukee, WI
33,000	University of Wisconsin Foundation, Madison, WI
30,000	Cardinal Stritch College, Milwaukee, WI
30,000	Partners Advancing Values in Education, Milwaukee, WI
30,000	UWM Foundation
25,000	Lawrence University, Appleton, WI
25,000	Milwaukee School of Engineering, Milwaukee, WI
20,000	Medical College of Wisconsin, Milwaukee, WI
20,000	Silver Lake College
11,000	Junior Achievement, Racine, WI
10,000	Marquette University, Milwaukee, WI

Health

50,000	Children's Hospital, Milwaukee, WI
50,000	Sinai Samaritan Medical Center, Milwaukee, WI
30,000	St. Luke's Medical Center, Phoenix, AZ
25,000	Marshfield Medical Research Foundation
25,000	Mayo Foundation for Medical Education and Research, Rochester, MN
20,000	East Valley Regional Cancer Center
16,500	Blood Center of Southeastern Wisconsin, Milwaukee, WI

Religion

40,000	St. Ann Center Intergenerational Care

Social Services

157,500	United Way, Milwaukee, WI
52,500	United Way, Milwaukee, WI
50,000	YMCA, Milwaukee, WI
30,000	Ozaukee Ice Association, Cedarburg, WI
25,000	Goodwill Industries of Southeastern Wisconsin, Milwaukee, WI
20,000	Boys and Girls Clubs, Milwaukee, WI
20,000	Boys and Girls Clubs, Milwaukee, WI
20,000	Second Harvest Food Bank, Milwaukee, WI
16,500	Family Service, Milwaukee, WI
15,000	Rosalie Manor, Milwaukee, WI
15,000	United Community Center, Milwaukee, WI

Masco Corp.

Company Contact

Taylor, MI

Web: http://www.masco.com

Company Description

Revenue: US$4,345,000,000
Employees: 20,500
Fortune Rank: 275, per FORTUNE Magazine's list of 500 Largest U.S. Corporations (1999).
FF 275
SIC(s): 2299 Textile Goods Nec, 2511 Wood Household Furniture, 2519 Household Furniture Nec, 3432 Plumbing Fixtures Fittings & Trim.

Operating Locations

Operates internationally.

Masco Corp. Charitable Trust

Giving Contact

Director, Corporate Contributions
Masco Corp. Charitable Trust
21001 Van Born Road
Taylor, MI 48180
Phone: (313)792-6757
Fax: (313)374-6135

Description

EIN: 386043605
Organization Type: Corporate Foundation
Giving Locations: nationally; communities with operating facilities.
Grant Types: Capital, General Support.

Financial Summary

Total Giving: $1,182,500 (1998); $673,000 (1997); $700,000 (1996). Note: Contributes through foundation only.
Giving Analysis: Giving for 1996 includes: foundation ($616,000); foundation grants to United Way ($84,000); 1997: foundation ($589,000); foundation grants to United Way ($84,000); 1998: foundation ($1,100,500); foundation grants to United Way ($82,000)
Assets: $13,654,678 (1998); $12,084,946 (1997); $12,205,158 (1996)
Gifts Received: $2,000,000 (1998); $2,000,000 (1996); $2,000,000 (1995). Note: Contributions received from Masco Corp.

Typical Recipients

Arts & Humanities: Art History, Arts Associations & Councils, Arts Centers, Arts Funds, Arts Institutes, Arts & Humanities-General, Historic Preservation, History & Archaeology, Museums/Galleries, Music, Opera, Performing Arts, Public Broadcasting
Civic & Public Affairs: Community Foundations, Economic Development, Ethnic Organizations, Civic & Public Affairs-General, Legal Aid, Philanthropic Organizations, Professional & Trade Associations, Zoos/Aquariums
Education: Arts/Humanities Education, Business-School Partnerships, Colleges & Universities, Education Associations, Education Funds, Faculty Development, Education-General, Medical Education, Minority Education, Public Education (Precollege), Religious Education, Science/Mathematics Education, Secondary Education (Public)
Environment: Environment-General
Health: Health Organizations, Hospitals, Hospitals (University Affiliated), Medical Research, Public Health
International: International Relief Efforts
Religion: Religious Organizations, Religious Welfare
Science: Scientific Centers & Institutes
Social Services: Community Service Organizations, Recreation & Athletics, Shelters/Homelessness, United Funds/United Ways, YMCA/YWCA/YMHA/YWHA, Youth Organizations

Contributions Analysis

Giving Priorities: Museums and other arts organizations, colleges and universities, and health and social service organizations.

Arts & Humanities: 34%. Supports museums, historical societies, opera, and arts organizations.

Civic & Public Affairs: 25%. Supports accounting aid and economic development.

Education: 13%. Funds private schools, colleges and universities, minority education and education foundations.

Health: 7%. Gives to health-care systems and a cancer institute.

International: 2%. Provides funding for Armenian aid.

Religion: 2%. Funds an interfaith center.

Science: 1%. Supports a science center.

Social Services: 16%. Supports youth organizations, food distribution, and the United Way.

Note: Total contributions made in 1998.

Application Procedures

Initial Contact: Send a brief letter of request.

Application Requirements: Include the history of organization, amount requested, specific purpose of funds sought, need met by request, federal identification number, recently audited financial statement, list of other funders, and proof of tax-exempt status.

Deadlines: None.

Review Process: Requests reviewed as received.

Notes: Because much of giving is predetermined, the trust has limited funds available for new programs.

Restrictions

The Trust does not support individuals, loans, endowments, or in-kind donations, and rarely supports religious organizations.

Additional Information

Company lists Comerica Bank of Detroit as a corporate trustee.

Corporate Officials

Dr. Lillian Bauder: vice president corporate affairsrc B 1939. ED Douglass College (1961); University of Michigan (1973). PRIM CORP EMPL vice president corporate affairs: Masco Corp. CORP AFFIL director: Detroit Edison Co.; director: DTE Energy Co.; director: Comerica Bank.

Wayne Barton Lyon: president, chief operating officer, director B Dayton, OH 1932. ED University of Cincinnati BSChE (1955); University of Chicago MBA (1968). PRIM CORP EMPL chairman: Lifestyle Furnishings International ADD CORP EMPL chairman: Amtex Fabrics Inc.; president: Aobert Allen Group; chairman: Berkline Corp.; chairman: Furnishings International; vice president, director: Henredon Furniture Industries. CORP AFFIL director: Payless Cashways Inc.; director: Sunbury Textile Mills Inc.; director: Emco Ltd. London & Canada; director: Formica Corp.; director: Comerica Inc.; director: Drexel Heritage Furnishings; vice president, director: Baldwin Hardware Corp.; director: Brass Craft Manufacturing Co.; director: Arrow Specicalty Co. NONPR AFFIL lecturer: American Medical Association; board governors, trustee: Cranbrook Kingswood Schools. CLUB AFFIL TPC of Michigan Club; Fairlane Club; Orchard Lake Country Club; Bloomfield Hills Country Club.

Richard Alexander Manoogian: chairman, chief executive officer, director B Long Branch, NJ 1936. ED Yale University BA (1958). PRIM CORP EMPL chairman, chief executive officer, director: Masco Corp. ADD CORP EMPL chairman, chief executive officer: Masco Industries; chairman, director: MascoTech Inc.; chairman, director: Trimas Corp. CORP AFFIL director: MSX International Inc.; chairman board: Norris Cylinder Co.; chairman board: Marvel Group Inc.; chairman, chief executive officer, director: MascoTech Forming Technologies; trustee: Henry Ford Hospital; chairman board: Lamons Metal Gasket Co.; chairman board: Baldwin Hardware Corp.; director: Bank One Corp. NONPR AFFIL member: Yale Alumni Association; director: Yale University Art Gallery; trustee: Smithsonian Institute; president: Detroit Institute Arts Founder Society; director: Detroit Renaissance Inc.; member: American Federation Arts; Community Foundation Southeastern Michigan; member: American Association Museums; director: American Business Conference.

Giving Program Officials

Sandy Banks: director corp. contributions

Grants Analysis

Disclosure Period: calendar year ending 1998
Total Grants: $1,100,500*
Number of Grants: 33
Average Grant: $20,983*
Highest Grant: $250,000
Typical Range: $10,000 to $30,000
***Note:** Giving excludes United Way. Average grant figure excludes 2 highest grants totaling $450,000.

Recent Grants

Note: Grants derived from 1997 Form 990.

Arts & Humanities

100,000	Detroit Institute of Arts Founders Society, Detroit, MI
35,000	WTVS Channel 56/Detroit Educational Television Foundation, Detroit, MI
30,000	Jackson Arts Council
25,000	Arts League of Michigan, Detroit, MI
25,000	Diplomatic Rooms Endowment Fund, Washington, DC
20,000	Automotive Hall of Fame, Dearborn, MI
10,000	Detroit Historical Society, Detroit, MI
10,000	Detroit Opera House, Detroit, MI

Civic & Public Affairs

20,000	Community Foundation for Southeast Michigan, Detroit, MI
13,000	Damon Keith Law Collection, Detroit, MI
12,500	Accounting Aid Society, Detroit, MI

Education

50,000	University of Detroit, Detroit, MI
25,000	Center for Mind Body Medicine
15,000	Cranbrook Educational Commission, Bloomfield, MI
15,000	Georgetown University, Washington, DC
10,000	Michigan Colleges Foundation, Southfield, MI
10,000	United Negro College Fund, Detroit, MI
10,000	University of Liggett School, Grosse Point Woods, MI
10,000	Yale University, New Haven, CT

Environment

11,500	Wild Foundation, Fort Collins, CO

Health

25,000	Merrill Palmer Institute, MI
20,000	Oakwood Health Care System
10,000	Henry Ford Health System, Detroit, MI

International

20,000	Agbu Armenian Aid, Saddle Brook, NJ

Science

10,000	Detroit Science Center, Detroit, MI

Social Services

84,000	United Way, Detroit, MI
25,000	Share Our Strength, Washington, DC
12,000	Boys and Girls Clubs, Detroit, MI
10,000	National Alliance to End Homelessness, Washington, DC

Massachusetts Mutual Life Insurance Co.

Company Contact

1295 State St.
Springfield, MA 01111

Web: http://www.massmutual.com

Company Description

Revenue: US$10,668,100,000
Employees: 9,993
Fortune Rank: 173, per FORTUNE Magazine's list of 500 Largest U.S. Corporations (1999).
FF 173
SIC(s): 6311 Life Insurance, 6321 Accident & Health Insurance.

Nonmonetary Support

Value: $50,000 (1996); $57,416 (1995); $25,532 (1993)

Type: Donated Equipment; In-kind Services; Loaned Executives

Volunteer Programs: Company sponsors volunteer activities, such as Junior Achievement, literacy, and tutor/mentor programs. Supports the volunteers in Action Program, which awards cash grants to organizations where employees actively volunteer.

Note: Company provides nonmonetary support.

Corporate Sponsorship

Type: Arts & cultural events; Music & entertainment events; Sports events; Other

Contact: Ronald Copes, Vice President
Hartford, CT

Note: Sponsors arts, cultural, educational, and health events. Springfield area contact: Jeanette Jez.

The MassMutual Foundation for Hartford, Inc.

Giving Contact

Ronald Copes, Vice President
Massachusetts Mutual Life Insurance Co.
140 Garden St.
Hartford, CT 06154
Phone: (860)987-6500
Fax: (860)987-6532
Email: rcopes@massmutual.com

Description

EIN: 510192500
Organization Type: Corporate Foundation
Giving Locations: CT: Hartford; MA: Springfield
Grant Types: Employee Matching Gifts, General Support, Matching, Multiyear/Continuing Support.
Note: Employee matching gift ratio: 1 to 1, up to $1,000 for employees and up to $2,500 for directors.

Giving Philosophy

'The MassMutual Contributions Program is intended to support the Company's business objectives, reflect the needs of our home office community, and operate within the framework of the Company's values, structure and budget parameters.'

'The Contributions Program is designed to make a significant difference in the Springfield and Hartford communities. Its overall objectives are to: sponsor and encourage community quality-of-life efforts that help retain existing businesses and attract new ones to Springfield and Hartford communities; serve as a good corporate citizen through partnerships with other businesses, city leadership and key community organizations; support and encourage efforts that are primarily preventive rather than remedial in nature and which, in effect, offer assistance on issues before they become problems; reflect the values of the corporation and the philosophy of the Chief Executive Officer; create a positive image of MassMutual in the community to assist in attracting new associates, retaining present associates and promoting a diverse work force; and support MassMutual's business strategies, including the corporate, political, social and lines of

business operating needs.' *MassMutual Contributions Program Guidelines*

Financial Summary

Total Giving: $3,600,000 (1998 approx); $1,253,874 (1997); $2,987,688 (1996). Note: Contributes through corporate direct giving program and foundation.
Giving Analysis: Giving for 1996 includes: corporate direct giving ($1,367,255); foundation ($1,115,690); foundation matching gifts ($454,743); 1997: foundation ($967,104); foundation grants to United Way ($255,000); foundation matching gifts ($31,770)
Assets: $12,197,705 (1997); $1,208,033 (1996)

Typical Recipients

Arts & Humanities: Arts & Humanities-General, Libraries, Museums/Galleries, Music, Public Broadcasting, Theater
Civic & Public Affairs: Civic & Public Affairs-General
Education: Colleges & Universities, Community & Junior Colleges, Education Funds, Public Education (Precollege)
Health: Medical Research
Social Services: At-Risk Youth

Contributions Analysis

Arts & Humanities: 15%. Supports music, libraries, theater, and fine arts institutions which educate, inspire, and enrich the lives of Springfield and Hartford residents.
Civic & Public Affairs: 8%. Emphasizes violence prevention, youth leadership development, clean streets, civic pride, ethnic and cultural diversity, youth activities, employment, and downtown events in Springfield and Hartford. Goal is to improve the economic and residental viability of neighborhoods. Promotes small business growth and first-time home ownership. Supports the Urban League, housing, and youth employment.
Education: 26%. Supports business and school partnerships, teacher and student training, incentives for academic achievement in Springfield and Hartford schools, and colleges through scholarships.Grants emphasize school improvement, including academic excellence, safety, and scholarship opportunities.
Health: 11%. Provides support for preventive health care programs in operating communities, and adequate and accessible health care and human services for residents. Also supports AIDS care.
Social Services: 40%. Support the United Way, Salvation Army, family services, child welfare, and shelters.
Note: Total contributions in 1997.

Application Procedures

Initial Contact: Request 2 copies of application and contribution guidelines, then submit a written proposal.
Application Requirements: Include pertinent organizational data, with name, address, phone number, date of incorporation, fiscal year, geographic area served, and number of staff and volunteers (identifying MassMutual employees by name); concise description of organization's mission; description of the program for which funding is requested, including the program budget; specific criteria to be used for measuring success of the program; list of other corporate and foundation sources approached for funding, noting commitments to date; current listing of officers and board of directors, with their professional affiliations; copy of the organization's most recent audited financial statement and annual report; and copy of IRS 501(c)(3) tax-exemption letter.
Deadlines: The last day of the month, to be given consideration for the next scheduled meeting.
Decision Notification: Funding decisions will generally be made during the eight-week period following receipt of the request and communicated to applicant in writing.
Notes: All requests for contributions must be submitted on a MassMutual application form. Springfield requests should be marked Attn: B308; Hartford requests should be addressed Attn: H356.

Restrictions

Contributions will not be made for: individuals; operating costs and expenses, such as transportation, refreshments and promotional items; deficit reduction campaigns; fraternal societies, labor organizations and veterans' groups; independent fundraising activities of United Way agencies, other than selected capital fund campaigns; organizations which are not tax-exempt; religious or political organizations; or fundraising activities such as golf tournaments, auctions, walkathons, etc.

Additional Information

Company has operating in nearly all 50 states.
Mass Mutual merged with Connecticut Mutual in 1996. The Connecticut Mutual Foundation became the MassMutual Foundation for Hartford; the Massachusetts Mutual Contributions Program continues its support for the Springfield, MA area.
Those organizations which receive support are required to provide a status report of the program funded at the end of the grant period, usually within six months of funding. A MassMutual report form will be provided for this purpose when the grant is awarded. Any future support will be contingent on MassMutual's receipt of this information in a timely manner.
Publications: Social Report; Guidelines; Application Form

Corporate Officials

John Joseph Pajak: president, chief operating officer chief investment officer B Chicopee, MA 1935. ED College of the Holy Cross (1956); Western New England College (1962). PRIM CORP EMPL president, chief operating officer: Massachusetts Mutual Life Insurance Co. CORP AFFIL president: MassMutual Corp. Investors Inc.
Gary Edward Wendlandt: executive vice president, chief investment officer B Milwaukee, WI 1950. ED Washington University BS (1972). PRIM CORP EMPL executive vice president, chief investment officer: Massachusetts Mutual Life Insurance Co. CORP AFFIL funds director: MML Series Investors Fund/ Institute; director: Oppenheimer Acquisition Corp.; chairman, trustee: MassMutual Participation Investors; director: Merrill Lynch Derivatives Products Inc.; president, director: MassMutual Holding Co.; president: MassMutual Holding Co. Two; director: David L. Babson Co., Inc.; chairman, trustee: MassMutual Corp. Investors Inc.
Thomas Beardsley Wheeler: chairman, chief executive officer B Buffalo, NY 1936. ED Yale University BA (1958). PRIM CORP EMPL chairman, chief executive officer: Massachusetts Mutual Life Insurance Co. CORP AFFIL director: Textron Inc.; director: FleetBoston Financial Corp.; chairman: Oppenheimer Acquisition Corp.; director: BankBoston NA; chairman: David L. Babson Acquisition Co., Inc. NONPR AFFIL member: Springfield Life Underwriters Association; trustee: Springfield Orchestral Association; trustee, chairman: Springfield College; member: Massachusetts Association Life Underwriters; member: Million Dollar Round Table; member: Boston Underwriters Association; member: Health Insurance Association America; trustee: Basketball Hall Fame; member: American Society Clubs. CLUB AFFIL Yale Club; Long Meadow Country Club; Port Royal Club; The Links Club; Chapoquoit Yacht Club; Colony Club.

Giving Program Officials

Ronald A. Copes: executive director PRIM CORP EMPL vice president Hartford, CT area: Massachusetts Mutual Life Insurance Co.

Foundation Officials

Ronald A. Copes: executive director (see above)

Grants Analysis

Disclosure Period: calendar year ending 1997
Total Grants: $967,104*
Number of Grants: 137
Average Grant: $7,059
Highest Grant: $133,333
Typical Range: $1,000 to $20,000
***Note:** Giving excludes matching gifts; United Way.

MATSUSHITA ELECTRIC CORP. OF AMERICA

Company Contact

Secaucus, NJ
Web: http://www.panasonic.com

Company Description

Employees: 16,000
SIC(s): 3631 Household Cooking Equipment, 3651 Household Audio & Video Equipment, 3661 Telephone & Telegraph Apparatus, 5064 Electrical Appliances--Television & Radio.
Parent Company: Matsushita Electric Industrial Co., Ltd., 1006 Oaza Kadoma, Kadoma, Osaka, Japan

Operating Locations

AL: JVC Disc America Co., Tuscaloosa; JVC Magnets America Co., Tuscaloosa; CA: Hughes-JVC Technology Corp., Carlsbad; JVC Information Products Co. of America, Santa Clara; JVC Laboratory of America, Santa Clara; HI: Matsushita Electric Corp. of America, Ewa Beach; IL: Matsushita Television Co., Elgin; Panasonic Factory Automation Co., Elgin; Matsushita Electric Corp. of America, Elk Grove Village, Franklin Park; NJ: JVC Co. of America, Elmwood Park; JVC Manufacturing Co., Elmwood Park; JVC Professional Products, Elmwood Park; JVC Service & Engineering Co. of America, Fairfield; Matsushita Electric Corp. of America, Secaucus; Matsushita Electric Corp. of America, Secaucus; Matsushita Services Co. Div., Secaucus; Panasonic Broadcast Systems Co., Secaucus; Panasonic Broadcast & Television Systems Co., Secaucus; Panasonic Consumer Electric Co., Secaucus; Panasonic Industrial Co., Secaucus; WA: Matsushita Avionics Systems, Bothell
Note: Operates 14 divisions, subsidiaries, and affiliated companies and a nationwide service and engineering organization. Parent company has 46 manufacturing and 34 sales companies overseas. For a complete list of operating locations, contact Marilyn Jones at (201) 392-4134.

Nonmonetary Support

Type: Donated Products; Loaned Employees

Panasonic Foundation

Giving Contact

Sophie Sa, Executive Director
Panasonic Foundation
1 Panasonic Way 1F5
Secaucus, NJ 07094
Phone: (201)392-4132
Fax: (201)392-4126
Email: info@foundation.panasonic.com
Web: http://www.panasonic.com/MECA/foundation/ foundation.html

Alternate Contact

Marilyn Joseph, Assistant General Manager, Government & Public Affairs
1 Panasonic Way
Secaucus, NJ 07094
Phone: (201)392-4134

Note: Contact for corporate contributions.

Description

Founded: 1984
EIN: 222548639
Organization Type: Corporate Foundation
Former Name: Matsushita Foundation.
Giving Locations: nationally.
Grant Types: Conference/Seminar, General Support.
Note: Foundation provides technical assistance to schools and school districts. Grants are made on related topics at foundation's initiation.

Giving Philosophy

'The ultimate goal of the Panasonic Foundation is to significantly increase learning for all students. To accomplish this, the Foundation believes it is important to restructure entire systems, rather than simply improve isolated classrooms or individual schools. The reason? Schools are not independent entities; they are parts of local school districts and state systems of education. Unless these systems transform themselves from bureaucracies that control and impede school-level efforts into organizations that nurture them, individual schools will not improve significantly or in large enough numbers.
'Accordingly, Panasonic has entered into partnerships with state departments of education and school districts to equip educators to rethink and reformulate their roles at each level--the state level, the district level, and the level of the school building.
'In an ideal system..schools would be held accountable for the success of their students, districts would be held accountable for the success of their schools, and states would be held accountable for a statewide system of education in which both high student learning standards and equity are achieved. It is the goal of the Foundation to create such systems.' *The Panasonic Foundation*

Financial Summary

Total Giving: $2,000,000 (1999 approx); $1,560,904 (1998); $1,662,996 (1997). Note: Contributes through corporate direct giving program and foundation. Giving includes foundation.
Assets: $24,540,941 (1998); $24,314,411 (1997); $23,614,900 (1996)
Gifts Received: $3,000,000 (1995); $3,000,000 (1994)

Typical Recipients

Civic & Public Affairs: Business/Free Enterprise, Nonprofit Management
Education: Elementary Education (Private), Elementary Education (Public), Education-General, Public Education (Precollege)

Contributions Analysis

Giving Priorities: Education sole priority; promotes excellence and equity in elementary and secondary schools through partnerships working toward systemic, whole-school reform.
Education: 100%. Foundation's sole concern is promoting equity and excellence in elementary and secondary schools through five- to ten-year partnerships with school districts to promote systemic, school-based, whole-school reform. These partnerships are initiated by the foundation. Also supports conferences, seminars and educational materials for partnership school districts.

Application Procedures

Initial Contact: Districts can submit a brief letter of interest to the foundation; for direct corporate gifts, send brief letter to corporate contributions contact.
Application Requirements: A brief history of organization, description of goals, and explanation of how funds will be used.
Deadlines: None.
Review Process: Funding decisions of the foundation are made by the board of directors.
Evaluative Criteria: The prospective school district must serve disadvantaged youth; commit time and resources to developing a restructuring agenda; commit to long-term improvement in policy, authority, and resource allocations to achieve agenda; and agree with foundation's beliefs about systemic, school-based, whole-school reform.
Notes: The foundation does not generally accept unsolicited requests for grants.

Restrictions

The foundation does not support individuals; endowments; capital and annual fund-raising campaigns; building construction; out-of-country organizations; cultural performances and exhibitions except as they relate to the defined program areas; journals, dinners or special events, or goodwill advertising; political or lobbying groups; fraternal organizations; religious organizations for sectarian purposes; or regular conferences of professional organizations.

Additional Information

The Foundation was established in 1984 as a private American philanthropic organization by an endowment from Matsushita Electric Corporation of America to celebrate its 25th anniversary.
The foundation supports elementary and secondary schools primarily by paying consulting fees for educational improvement programs. The foundation generally initiates such support.
In 1989, Matsushita's parent in Tokyo created the $32 million Matsushita International Foundation, which sponsors projects that emphasize international understanding. The company also has several other worldwide philanthropic activities, such as the Panasonic Trust in the United Kingdom, a Japan-based foundation for science and technology, as well as science research and training centers in Indonesia, Tanzania, Malaysia, and Thailand.
Publications: Foundation Guidelines; Newsletters

Corporate Officials

Charlie Churchill: vice president, North America industrial group PRIM CORP EMPL vice president, North America industrial group: Matsushita Electric Corp. of America.
Yoshinori Kobe: chairman, president, chief executive officer PRIM CORP EMPL chairman, president, chief executive officer: Matsushita Electric Corp. of America.
Ted Takahashi: vice president, finance PRIM CORP EMPL vice president, finance: Matsushita Electric Corp. of America. CORP AFFIL treasurer: Panasonic Technologies Inc.

Giving Program Officials

Marilyn Jones: manager PRIM CORP EMPL assistant general manager government & public affairs: Matsushita Electric Corp. of America.

Foundation Officials

Robert Stephen Ingersoll: chairman, director B Galesburg, IL 1914. ED Yale University BS (1937). CORP AFFIL partner, director: First Chicago Capital Markets, Asia, Ltd. NONPR AFFIL vice chairman advisory council: Un Techs Pacific; life trustee, deputy chairman, board trustees: University Chicago; chairman: Panasonic Foundation; member: Council Foreign Relations; member: Japan Society; member: Business Council; member: Chicago Council Foreign Relations. CLUB AFFIL Yale Club; Indian Hill Club; Old Elm Club; Desert Mountain Club; Economic Club; Commercial Club; Desert Forest Golf Club; Bohemian Club; Chicago Club.
Richard A. Kraft: president, director B 1928. ED Purdue University BSEE (1950). CORP AFFIL officer: Matsushita Electric Corp. America.
Lawrence E. Levine: secretary B New York, NY 1932. ED New York University (1953); Harvard University Law School (1956). PRIM CORP EMPL secretary, counsel: Panasonic Services Co. CORP AFFIL senior corporate attorney: Matsushita Electric Corp. America. CLUB AFFIL Masons Club.
Deborah Meier: director
Martin Meyerson: director B New York, NY 1922. ED Columbia University BA (1942); Harvard University MCP (1949); University of Pennsylvania LLD (1970). PRIM NONPR EMPL professor: University of Pennsylvania. CORP AFFIL director: Universal Health Services; director: Scott Paper Co.; director: St-Gobain Corp.; director: Penn Mutual Life Insurance Co.; director: First Fidelity Bancorp; director: Norton; director: CertainTeed Corp.; director: Avatar Holdings Inc. NONPR AFFIL chairman: University Pennsylvania Foundation; chairman: University Pennsylvania Press; president emeritus: University Pennsylvania; director: U.S. Commission Constellation System; trustee: United World College New Mexico; co-chairman, senior fellow: Salzburg Seminar Board; director: Philadelphia Museum Art; fellow: Royal Society Arts; chair international selection committee: Philadelphia Liberty Medal; director: Panasonic Foundation; member: Phi Beta Kappa; fellow: National Academy Education; co-chairman, chairman executive committee: Marconi International Fellowship Council; chairman: Monell Chemical Senses Center; director: Mahoney Institute Neuroscis; board overseers: Koc University; director: Lauder Institute of Management & International Studies; director: International Literacy Institute; member: International Association Universities; trustee: International House Center; chairman: Institute Research on Higher Education Fels Center; director: Hebrew University; director: Institute Contemporary Art; trustee: Foreign Policy Research Institute; president: Foundation for International Exchange of Science & Cultural Information; member: European Academy Arts Science & Letters; director: Center for Visual History; member: Council Foreign Relations; member: American Society of Planning Officials; fellow: American Philosophical Society; director: American Schools Oriental Research; member: American Institute Planners; fellow: American Academy of Arts & Sciences. CLUB AFFIL University Club Pennsylvania; Philadelphia Club; Century Club; Cosmos Club.
Ralph J. Pagano: treasurer
Ira Perlman: director PRIM CORP EMPL vice president general administration: Matsushita Electric Corp. of America.
Sophie Sa: executive director
Ted Takahashi: vice president (see above)

Grants Analysis

Disclosure Period: calendar year ending 1998
Total Grants: $29,520*
Number of Grants: 7
Average Grant: $14,217
Highest Grant: $20,000
Typical Range: $1,000 to $5,000
***Note:** Giving excludes program projects and developments.

Recent Grants

Note: Grants derived from 1997 Form 990.

Civic & Public Affairs

1,000 Conference Board, New York, NY -- for membership renewal
1,000 Foundation Center, New York, NY

Education

5,000 Philadelphia Area Labor Management Committee, Philadelphia, PA -- to support discussion between School District of Philadelphia and the Philadelphia Federation of Teachers
5,000 Philadelphia Area Labor Management Committee, Philadelphia, PA -- to support discussion between School District

of Philadelphia and the Philadelphia Federation of Teachers
1,000 Grantmakers for Education, Washington, DC -- for membership renewal

Mattel Inc.

Company Contact

333 Continental Ave.
El Segundo, CA 90245-3802
Web: http://www.mattel.com

Company Description

Revenue: US$4,781,900,000
Employees: 25,000
Fortune Rank: 305, per FORTUNE Magazine's list of 500 Largest U.S. Corporations (1999).
FF 305
SIC(s): 3942 Dolls & Stuffed Toys, 3944 Games, Toys & Children's Vehicles.

Operating Locations

Argentina: Mattel Argentina SA, Vincente Lopez, Buenos Aires; Australia: JW Spear & Sons Pty. Ltd., Moorabbin; Mattel Pty. Ltd., Port Melbourne; Austria: Tyco Toys GmbH, Vienna; Mattel GmbH, Wiener Neudorf; Belgium: Fisher-Price NV, Brussels, Brabant; Mattel BV Naar Nederlands Recht, Brussels, Brabant; Tyco Manufacturing (Europe), Sint-Niklaas, Oost-Vlaanderen; Tyco Toys Europe NV, Sint-Niklaas, Oost-Vlaanderen; Canada: Mattel Canada, Mississauga; Mattel Holdings Ltd., Mississauga; Tyco Toys (Canada), Mississauga; Denmark: Mattel Northern Europe AS, Brondby, Copenhagen; France: Corolle SA, Langeais, Indre-et-Loire; JW Spear SA, Orly, Val-de-Marne; Mattel France, Orly, Val-de-Marne; Germany: Fisher-Price Beteiligungs GmbH, Dreieich, Hessen; Mattel GmbH, Dreieich, Hessen; Hong Kong: Tyco (Far East) Ltd., Central District; TBL Ltd., Kwai Chung; Universal Associated Co. Ltd., Mongkok, Kowloon; Mattel (Hong Kong) Ltd., Shau Kei Wan; Matchbox Trading Co. Ltd., To Kwa Wan, Kowloon; Unitoys Co. Ltd., To Kwa Wan, Kowloon; Fisher-Price (Hong Kong) Ltd., Tsim Sha Tsui East, Kowloon; Arco Toys Ltd., Tsim Sha Tsui, Kowloon; Matchbox International Ltd., Tsim Sha Tsui, Kowloon; Mattel Asia Ltd., Tsim Sha Tsui, Kowloon; Mattel Toys Vendor Operations Ltd., Tsim Sha Tsui, Kowloon; Universal International (Holdings) Ltd., Tsim Sha Tsui, Kowloon; Indonesia: PT Mattel Indonesia, Bekasi, Wjv; India: Mattel Toys (India) Ltd., Mumbai; Italy: Matchbox Toys Ltd., Cesano Maderno, Lombardia; Mattel Manufacturing Europe SRL, Oleggio Castello, Piemonte; Mattel SRL, Oleggio Castello, Piemonte; Japan: Mattel KK, Tokyo; Macao: Macao Die-Casting Toys Ltd. Fabrica de Brinquedos Metalicos Macau Ida, Andar; Mexico: Montoi Sa de CV, Santa Catarina; Mabamex SA, Tijuana; Malaysia: Mattel (KL) Sdn. Bhd., Kelang, Selangor; Mattel (Malaysia) Sdn. Bhd., Perai, Pulau Pinang; Mattel Tools Sdn. Bhd., Wellesley, Pulau Pinang; Netherlands: Mattel BV, Amstelveen, Noord-Holland; Mattel Europa BV, Amstelveen, Noord-Holland; JW Spear & Sons Plc Assen Div., Assen, Drenthe; JW Spear, Harmelen, Utrecht; New Zealand: Mattel Toys New Zealand Ltd., Auckland; Singapore: Mattel Toys (Singapore) Pte. Ltd., Singapore; Spain: Mattel Espana SA, Barcelona, Cataluna; Switzerland: Mattel AG, Bern; United Kingdom: JW Spear & Sons Plc, Enfield, Greater London; Corgi Toys Ltd., Leicester, Leicestershire; Illco UK Ltd., Leicester, Leicestershire; Mattel Group Plc, Leicester, Leicestershire; Mattel United Kingdom Ltd., Leicester, Leicestershire; Matchbox Toys Ltd., Marlow, Buckinghamshire; Fisher-Price Toys Ltd., Peterlee, Durham; Kiddicraft Ltd., Peterlee, Durham; Matchbox Collectibles (Europe) Ltd., Rugby, Warwickshire; Kiddicraft (Group) Ltd., Southall, Middlesex

Nonmonetary Support

Value: $500,000 (1998); $560,167 (1996); $546,034 (1995)
Type: Donated Products
Volunteer Programs: Employees may apply for Employee Volunteer Grants. Grants amounts are linked to the lenght of service of requesting employee, and by number of other Mattel employees volunteering within the organization.
The Foundation coordinates more than 30 volunteer activities annually to encourage employee volunteerism.
Contact: Regina Rodman, Toy Donations Coordinator

Corporate Sponsorship

Contact: Glenn Bozarth, Senior Vice President Corporate Communication
Note: Sponsors events focused on children.

Mattel Foundation

Giving Contact

Paul R. Millman, Foundation Directory
Mattel Children's Foundation
333 Continental Blvd.
Mail Stop M1-1418
El Segundo, CA 90245-5012
Phone: (310)252-3802
Fax: (310)252-3802

Description

EIN: 953263647
Organization Type: Corporate Foundation
Giving Locations: CA: Los Angeles nationally.
Grant Types: Capital, Employee Matching Gifts, General Support, Matching, Scholarship.
Note: Employee matching gift ratio: 1 to 1 up to $5,000 per employee annually.

Giving Philosophy

'The Mattel Foundation was established to provide support to worthwhile charitable organizations that provide services to children and youth. The corporation believes that it has an ongoing obligation to the community and the nation.' *Mattel Foundation*

Financial Summary

Total Giving: $5,070,000 (1998 approx); $5,500,000 (1997 approx); $3,567,390 (1996). Note: Contributes through corporate direct giving program and foundation.
Giving Analysis: Giving for 1996 includes: foundation ($3,212,130); corporate grants to United Way ($211,000); corporate matching gifts ($144,260); 1998: foundation ($3,837,177); nonmonetary support (approx $500,000); corporate direct giving (approx $340,000); corporate matching gifts ($215,653); corporate grants to United Way ($177,000)
Assets: $971,876 (1996); $831,984 (1995); $758,323 (1994)
Gifts Received: $4,250,000 (1996); $3,165,300 (1995); $2,601,270 (1994). Note: Foundation receives contributions from Mattel, Inc.

Typical Recipients

Arts & Humanities: Arts Institutes, Ballet, Libraries, Music, Performing Arts, Theater
Civic & Public Affairs: African American Affairs, Botanical Gardens/Parks, Business/Free Enterprise, Civil Rights, Community Foundations, Economic Development, Economic Policy, Employment/Job Training, Civic & Public Affairs-General, Housing, Philanthropic Organizations, Public Policy, Urban & Community Affairs, Women's Affairs
Education: Business Education, Colleges & Universities, Economic Education, Education Funds, Education Reform, Elementary Education (Private), Elementary Education (Public), Engineering/Technological Education, Education-General, Leadership Training, Literacy, Medical Education, Minority Education, Private Education (Precollege), Public Education (Precollege), Science/Mathematics Education, Secondary Education (Public), Special Education, Student Aid
Environment: Air/Water Quality, Environment-General
Health: AIDS/HIV, Cancer, Children's Health/Hospitals, Clinics/Medical Centers, Diabetes, Health Organizations, Hospitals, Medical Rehabilitation, Multiple Sclerosis, Public Health, Single-Disease Health Associations
International: Health Care/Hospitals, International Development, International Relief Efforts
Religion: Religious Welfare
Science: Scientific Centers & Institutes, Scientific Organizations
Social Services: Animal Protection, Big Brother/Big Sister, Camps, Child Welfare, Community Centers, Community Service Organizations, Delinquency & Criminal Rehabilitation, Family Services, People with Disabilities, Recreation & Athletics, Substance Abuse, United Funds/United Ways, YMCA/YWCA/YMHA/YWHA, Youth Organizations

Contributions Analysis

Giving Priorities: Direct human care for children; United Way; education, largely through matching gifts; local health clinics; and some arts and civic organizations.
Arts & Humanities: Less than 5%. Supports orchestra groups, libraries, ballet, and performing arts.
Civic & Public Affairs: 5% to 10%. Primarily supports housing, philanthropic organizations, free enterprise, and community foundations.
Education: 45% to 50%. Interests include literacy, math education, private education, and colleges and universities.
Health: 15% to 20%. Majority of funds support single-disease health organizations, and clinics.
Social Services: 20% to 25%. Majority supports direct care services for youth and children. Other areas of interest include aid for the handicapped, family services, food banks, substance abuse prevention programs, and volunteer services.
Note: Above priorities are for foundation only. Foundation funding priorities include construction of Mattel Children's Hospital at UCLA, the Mattel Family Learing Program and Technology and Kids with Special Needs.

Application Procedures

Initial Contact: brief letter of application
Application Requirements: a description of organization, including legal name, history, activities, and board composition; description of program for which funds are sought; program budget and amount requested; list of other sources of support with amounts indicated; copy of most recently audited annual report and Form 990; and IRS determination letter
Deadlines: None.
Evaluative Criteria: ability of program to alleviate hardships, provide opportunities for better lives for children, or strengthen family life
Decision Notification: quarterly; meetings are in February, May, August, and November
Notes: Most grants are initiated by the foundation, and only a limited number of discretionary grants are made annually.

Restrictions

Foundation generally does not support capital facilities; religious activities; research activities; endowments; individuals; religious, fraternal, political, athletic, social, or veterans organizations; labor groups; programs receiving substantial financial support; federal, state, or local government agencies; or courtesy advertising.

Only gives to nonprofit organizations that benefit children.

Additional Information

Fischer-Price is now part of Mattel, Inc.

Corporate Officials

Jill Elikann Barad: chairman, chief executive officer, director B New York, NY 1951. ED Queens College BA (1973). PRIM CORP EMPL chairman, chief executive officer, director: Mattel Inc. CORP AFFIL director: BankAmerica NA; director: Microsoft Corp.; director: ARCO Toys. NONPR AFFIL trustee: Queens College; director: Town Hall California; board governor: Childrens Miracle Network; director: Claremont University Center.

N. Ned Mansour: president, director ED University of Southern California BS (1970); University of San Diego Law School JD (1973). PRIM CORP EMPL president, director: Mattel Inc.

Foundation Officials

Jill Elikann Barad: director (see above)

Harold Brown, PhD: chairman B New York, NY 1927. ED Columbia University AB (1945); Columbia University AM (1946); Columbia University PhD (1949). PRIM NONPR EMPL counsel: Center Strategic International Studies. CORP AFFIL director: Alumax Inc.

Joseph C. Gandolfo: director B 1942. PRIM CORP EMPL president operations, director: Mattel Inc.

Paul Millman: director

Grants Analysis

Disclosure Period: calendar year ending 1998
Total Grants: $3,837,177*
Number of Grants: 320
Average Grant: $8,894*
Highest Grant: $1,000,000
Typical Range: $1,000 to $10,000
***Note:** Grants analysis provided by Foundation. Giving excludes matching gifts and United Way and corporate giving. Average grant figure excludes highest grant.

Recent Grants

Note: Grants derived from 1996 Form 990.

Arts & Humanities

37,500 New World Symphony, Miami Beach, FL -- operating support
30,000 Buffalo Philharmonic Orchestra Society, Buffalo, NY -- operating support
20,000 Telluride Repertory Theater Company, Telluride, CO -- operating support

Civic & Public Affairs

70,000 California Community Foundation, Los Angeles, CA -- operating support
37,500 Fidelity Investments Charitable Gift Fund, Boston, MA -- operating support
25,000 Fort Wayne Park Foundation, Fort Wayne, IN -- operating support
20,000 New Economics for Women, Los Angeles, CA -- operating support

Education

500,000 Foundation for Technology Access, San Rafael, CA -- for Family Learning Centers
250,000 Institute for Educational Leadership, Washington, DC -- operating support
56,500 PUENTE Learning Center, Los Angeles, CA -- operating support
55,000 Chicago Public Schools, Chicago, IL -- operating support
40,000 Philadelphia Schools Collaborative, Philadelphia, PA -- operating support
37,500 Dartmouth College, Hanover, NH -- operating support
37,500 Prep for Prep, New York, NY -- operating support
31,000 Communities in Schools, San Antonio, TX -- operating support
30,000 Puente Learning Center, Los Angeles, CA -- for Family Learning Centers
25,000 Brunswick School, Greenwich, CT -- operating support
25,000 National Foundation for the Improvement of Education, Washington, DC -- operating support
25,000 New York Fund for Public Schools, Brooklyn, NY -- operating support
19,750 Columbia College Fund, New York, NY -- operating support
18,750 California Institute of Technology, Pasadena, CA -- operating support
15,000 Harrison Elementary School, Los Angeles, CA -- for Family Learning Centers
15,000 Junior Achievement of Western New York, Buffalo, NY -- operating support
13,250 University of California Riverside, Riverside, CA -- operating support
12,500 Greenwich Academy, Greenwich, CT -- operating support

Health

185,000 AttaMed Health Services, Los Angeles, CA -- for Health Care Initiative
50,000 Bethel Head Start, Buffalo, NY -- for Health Care Initiative
43,500 Children Affected by AIDS, El Segundo, CA -- operating support
30,000 Texas Women's University Foundation, Denton, TX -- for Health Care Initiative
29,000 Independent Health Foundation, Buffalo, NY -- operating support
27,000 Children Affected by AIDS Foundation, El Segundo, CA -- operating support
25,000 INMED, Compton, CA -- for Health Care Initiative
25,000 New City Health Center, Chicago, IL -- for Health Care Initiative
20,000 Barbara Sinatra Children's Center, Eisenhower Medical Center, Rancho Mirage, CA -- operating support
17,000 Lothlorien Therapeutic Riding Center, East Aurora, NY -- operating support

Religion

20,000 Catholic Charities, Los Angeles, CA -- operating support
16,000 Catholic Charities, Buffalo, NY -- operating support

Social Services

100,000 United Way, Los Angeles, CA -- operating support
66,000 United Fund of Buffalo and Erie County, Buffalo, NY -- operating support
50,000 Foundation for the Junior Blind, Los Angeles, CA -- operating support
50,000 Parents Anonymous of Buffalo and Erie County, Buffalo, NY -- operating support
50,000 Phoenix House of California, Lake View Terrace, CA -- operating support
50,000 United Way Buffalo and Erie County, Buffalo, NY -- operating support
47,400 United Fund for Western Orleans County, Medina, NY -- operating support
40,000 Boys and Girls Club, Tampa, FL -- operating support
33,000 Ackerman Institute of the Family, New York, NY -- operating support
25,000 Foundation for the Children of the Californias, San Diego, CA
20,000 Buffalo Evening News Charity Fund, Buffalo, NY -- operating support
18,500 Children First in Oregon, Portland, OR -- operating support
13,000 California State University, Carson, CA -- for Family Learning Centers

MAY DEPARTMENT STORES CO.

★ Number 58 of Top 100 Corporate Givers

Company Contact

St. Louis, MO
Web: http://www.maycompany.com

Company Description

Revenue: US$13,413,000,000
Profit: US$849,000,000
Employees: 111,000
Fortune Rank: 122, per FORTUNE Magazine's list of 500 Largest U.S. Corporations (1999).
FF 122
SIC(s): 5311 Department Stores, 5661 Shoe Stores.

Operating Locations

Operates approximately 325 department stores and approximately 3,000 Payless ShoeSource stores. Also operates in 14 offices overseas.

Nonmonetary Support

Type: Cause-related Marketing & Promotion

Corporate Sponsorship

Type: Arts & cultural events; Festivals/fairs; Sports events

The May Department Stores Computer Foundation

Giving Contact

Joni Sullivan Baker, Manager, Corporate Communications
The May Department Stores Co.
611 Olive St.
St. Louis, MO 63101
Phone: (314)342-6742
Fax: (314)342-4461

Description

Founded: 1945
EIN: 436028949
Organization Type: Corporate Foundation
Giving Locations: operating locations.
Grant Types: Capital, Employee Matching Gifts, Operating Expenses.
Note: Employee matching gift ratio: 1 to 1 to eligible schools, colleges, cultural organisation, and hospitals.

Financial Summary

Total Giving: $14,935,226 (1998 approx); $14,000,000 (1997 approx); $13,321,326 (1996). Note: Contributes through corporate direct giving program and foundation.
Giving Analysis: Giving for 1998 includes: foundation (approx $10,986,696); foundation grants to United Way (approx $3,948,530)
Assets: $21,245,574 (1996); $30,349,149 (1993); $13,204,430 (1992)
Gifts Received: $7,210,132 (1996); $26,258,807 (1993). Note: Contributions are received from the May Department Store Company.

Typical Recipients

Arts & Humanities: Arts Associations & Councils, Arts Centers, Arts Funds, Ballet, Community Arts, Ethnic & Folk Arts, Historic Preservation, Libraries, Museums/Galleries, Music, Performing Arts, Public Broadcasting, Theater

Civic & Public Affairs: African American Affairs, Botanical Gardens/Parks, Civil Rights, Clubs, Economic Development, Employment/Job Training, Civic & Public Affairs-General, Housing, Municipalities/Towns, Parades/Festivals, Public Policy, Safety, Urban & Community Affairs, Zoos/Aquariums
Education: Agricultural Education, Arts/Humanities Education, Business Education, Colleges & Universities, Continuing Education, Education Associations, Education Funds, Education Reform, Engineering/Technological Education, Education-General, Literacy, Medical Education, Minority Education, Public Education (Precollege), Science/Mathematics Education, Student Aid
Environment: Environment-General
Health: AIDS/HIV, Cancer, Children's Health/Hospitals, Emergency/Ambulance Services, Health Funds, Health Organizations, Heart, Hospitals, Multiple Sclerosis, Respiratory
Religion: Churches, Dioceses, Jewish Causes, Ministries, Religious Organizations, Religious Welfare, Synagogues/Temples
Science: Scientific Centers & Institutes
Social Services: Child Welfare, Community Centers, Community Service Organizations, Counseling, Food/Clothing Distribution, People with Disabilities, Scouts, Substance Abuse, United Funds/United Ways, YMCA/YWCA/YMHA/YWHA, Youth Organizations

Contributions Analysis

Giving Priorities: Health and welfare, higher education, the arts, and civic organizations.
Arts & Humanities: 15% to 20%. Supports major museums, music groups, dance, and dramatic arts organizations.
Civic & Public Affairs: (United Funds & United Way) 25% to 30%. Supports United Ways in company operating locations. 5% to 10%. Support includes improving downtowns and neighborhoods, local festivals, and civil rights.
Education: 20% to 25%. Contributes to higher education. Company is also the national sponsor for OASIS, the national health and wellness program for adults over 55. Members meet in paticipating May Department Stores and are involved in volunteer programs, including the OASIS Intergenerational Tutoring program to help grade school children in reading. Supports literacy efforts, scholarships,and internship programs.
Health: 25% to 30%. Supports hospitals, single-disease health associations, and federated organizations. Supports hunger relief, services for the homeless and victims of domestic abuse, AIDS and cancer efforts.
Note: Except for civic grants, employee matching gifts are included in all areas of giving.

Application Procedures

Initial Contact: Letter.
Application Requirements: Description of organization, including history, goals, and breadth of support it receives from constituents; amount requested, and purpose of funds sought; recently audited financial statement; proof of tax-exempt status.
Deadlines: None.

Restrictions

Foundation does not give to individuals.

Additional Information

Associated companies of May Department Stores are Lord & Taylor, Hecht's, Strawbridge's, Foley's, Robinsons-May, Kaufmann's, Filene's, Famous-Barr, L.S. Ayres, The Jones Store, and Meier & Frank. Some associated companies have their own giving programs.

Corporate Officials

Jan Rogers Kniffen: senior vice president, treasurer B Herrin, IL 1948. ED University of Illinois (1966-1968); Southern Illinois University BS (1968-1971); Lindenwood College MBA (1978); Saint Louis University (1985). PRIM CORP EMPL senior vice president, treasurer: The May Department Stores Co. ADD CORP EMPL treasurer director: Ma Department Stores International ADD NONPR EMPL adj professor, director: Lindenwood College. CLUB AFFIL Media Club; Noonday Club.
Jerome Thomas Loeb: chairman, director B Saint Louis, MO 1940. ED Tufts University BS (1962); Washington University MA (1964). PRIM CORP EMPL chairman, director: The May Department Stores Co. NONPR AFFIL member, board commissioner: Saint Louis Science Center; director: United Way Greater Saint Louis; director: National Retail Federation; chairman: Junior Achievement Michigan Valley; director: Junior Achievement National Board; vice chairman: Jewish Hospital Saint Louis; director: Barnes-Jewish Hospital; director: Barnes-Jewish Inc./Christian Health Services; member president's cabinet: American Jewish Committee. CLUB AFFIL Persimmon Woods Golf Club; Westwood Country Club; Boone Valley Golf Club.
Rhonda K. West: vice president corporate communications PRIM CORP EMPL vice president corporate communications: The May Department Stores Co.

Foundation Officials

Robert F. Cerulli: assistant treasurer, director
Jan Rogers Kniffen: vice president, secretary, treasurer, director (see above)
Jerome Thomas Loeb: president, director (see above)

Grants Analysis

Disclosure Period: calendar year ending 1998
Total Grants: $10,986,696 (approx)*
Number of Grants: 600 (approx)
Highest Grant: $900,500
Typical Range: $1,000 to $5,000
***Note:** Giving excludes United Way.

Recent Grants

Note: Grants derived from 1996 Form 990.

Arts & Humanities

125,000	Los Angeles County Museum, Los Angeles, CA
125,000	St. Louis Symphony, Saint Louis, MO
50,000	St. Louis Symphony, Saint Louis, MO

Civic & Public Affairs

200,000	Missouri Botanical Garden, Saint Louis, MO
75,000	VP Fair Foundation, Saint Louis, MO
50,000	David May Employees Trust Fund, Saint Louis, MO

Education

430,000	National Merit Scholarship Corporation, Evanston, IL
158,000	Inroads, Saint Louis, MO
125,000	Washington University, Saint Louis, MO
75,000	Wabash College, Crawfordsville, IN
68,000	Arts and Education Council, Saint Louis, MO
65,000	Arts and Education Council, Saint Louis, MO
60,000	Junior Achievement, Saint Louis, MO
50,000	St. Louis University, Saint Louis, MO
50,000	United Negro College Fund, Saint Louis, MO

Health

297,841	OASIS, Saint Louis, MO
196,625	OASIS, Saint Louis, MO
187,240	OASIS, Saint Louis, MO
184,125	OASIS, Saint Louis, MO
150,000	National Community AIDS
67,500	OASIS, Saint Louis, MO
67,500	OASIS, Saint Louis, MO
67,500	OASIS, Saint Louis, MO
67,500	OASIS, Saint Louis, MO
50,000	Memorial Sloan-Kettering Cancer Center, New York, NY

Religion

65,000	Jewish Federation, Saint Louis, MO

Social Services

885,000	United Way, Saint Louis, MO
430,500	United Way, Saint Louis, MO
209,250	United Way New England, Providence, RI
184,400	United Way Texas Gulf Coast, Houston, TX
171,000	United Way National
155,500	United Way, Saint Louis, MO
155,500	United Way, Saint Louis, MO
155,500	United Way, Saint Louis, MO
155,500	United Way, Saint Louis, MO
155,500	United Way, Saint Louis, MO
155,500	United Way, Saint Louis, MO
151,669	United Way Tri-State, New York, NY
129,000	United Way Southwestern Pennsylvania, Pittsburgh, PA
125,000	YMCA, Saint Louis, MO
117,929	United Way, Saint Louis, MO
100,000	United Way Southeastern
90,000	United Way Central Indiana, Indianapolis, IN
83,000	United Way, Saint Louis, MO
74,000	United Way, Columbia, MO
60,000	Girl Scouts of America, Saint Louis, MO
58,800	United Way, Saint Louis, MO
50,600	United Way Mile High, Denver, CO
50,000	Save Our Strength
50,000	Second Genesis, Bethesda, MD

MAYBELLINE, INC.

Company Contact

Memphis, TN

Company Description

Employees: 1,600
SIC(s): 2844 Toilet Preparations, 5122 Drugs, Proprietaries & Sundries.
Parent Company: L'Oreal SA, Haut de Seine, 41 Rue Martare, Clichy, Cedex, France

Operating Locations

AR: Maybelline, Inc., Little Rock; CA: Maybelline, Inc., Los Angeles; FL: Maybelline, Inc., Miami; NJ: Maybelline, Inc., Liberty Corner; TN: Maybelline, Memphis; Maybelline, Inc., Memphis

Nonmonetary Support

Type: Donated Products

Corporate Sponsorship

Type: Arts & cultural events
Contact: Kathryn Barrow, Communications Coordinator

Giving Contact

Tricia White, Assistant Vice President, Public Relations
Maybelline, Inc.
575 5th Avenue
New York, NY 10017
Phone: (212)984-4535
Fax: (212)984-5146

Description

Organization Type: Corporate Giving Program
Giving Locations: AR: Little Rock; TN: Memphis
Grant Types: General Support.

Typical Recipients
Civic & Public Affairs: Women's Affairs

Application Procedures
Initial Contact: written request
Application Requirements: amount requested, description of program, and copy of 501(c)(3) tax-exempt certificate
Deadlines: at least three months prior to request deadline
Review Process: a letter will be returned regarding the company's decision

Corporate Officials
Joseph Jaeger: vice president finance public relations PRIM CORP EMPL vice president finance: Maybelline, Inc.
John R. Wendt: president B 1942. ED Fairleigh Dickinson University BS; New York University MBA. PRIM CORP EMPL president: Maybelline, Inc.
Patricia White: assistant vice president public relations PRIM CORP EMPL assistant vice president public relations: Maybelline, Inc.

MAYTAG CORP.

Company Contact
Newton, IA
Web: http://www.maytagcorp.com

Company Description
Revenue: US$4,069,300,000
Employees: 20,464
Fortune Rank: 368, per FORTUNE Magazine's list of 500 Largest U.S. Corporations (1999).
FF 368
SIC(s): 3581 Automatic Vending Machines, 3582 Commercial Laundry Equipment, 3631 Household Cooking Equipment, 3633 Household Laundry Equipment.

Nonmonetary Support
Value: $20,000 (1994); $13,000 (1992); $102,000 (1991)
Type: Donated Products
Note: 1997 giving figures ($41,655). Support is offered by various Maytag divisions, including Magic Chef Co., Maytag Co., Jenn-Air, Hoover Co. & Admiral Co

Maytag Corp. Foundation

Giving Contact
Janis C. Cooper, Director, Foundation Programs
Maytag Corp. Foundation
403 W. 4th St. N.
PO Box 39
Newton, IA 50208
Phone: (515)787-6357
Fax: (515)787-8676

Description
EIN: 341502495
Organization Type: Corporate Foundation
Giving Locations: IL: Galesburg, Herrin; IA: Newton; MO: Clarence, Jefferson City; NH: Bow; OH: North Canton; PA: Quakertown; SC: Williston; TN: Cleveland, Jackson; TX: El Paso; VT: Burlington, Williston
Grant Types: Capital, Employee Matching Gifts, General Support, Multiyear/Continuing Support.

Giving Philosophy
'As a Fortune 500 company with major investments in facilities, technology, and employees in many locations, we view our commitment to being a responsible corporate citizen and a good neighbor as a natural extension of our strategic mission, and a good way to do business. Our mission for contributions is to improve the vitality of our communities, and address issues important to our employees, and to the future of the company and its customers.'
'We will focus our support on: education that builds a skilled work force; programs that enhance family life; activities that involve and recognize the value of our employees; and programs that enhance Maytag communities.'
'Our support focuses on four major areas: a competitive work force, targeting its support on educational programs that build a competitive work force for Maytag and the communities where the company operates, such as school-to-work training, technical skills, and higher education; strong families and early childhood, such as parenting skills and new families, early childhood development, and work and family; social, economic and cultural vitality, including funding for United Way, community-wide arts and culture, innovative community problem solving, and community development; and employee and Maytag involvement, through employee and company sponsored volunteer activities, including a matching gift program that supports higher education and cultural organizations.'

Financial Summary
Total Giving: $2,575,838 (1997); $2,447,391 (1996); $2,151,000 (1995). Note: Contributes through corporate direct giving program and foundation.
Giving Analysis: Giving for 1995 includes: foundation ($1,916,572); corporate direct giving ($236,546); 1996: foundation ($2,150,621); corporate direct giving ($296,770); 1997: foundation ($2,356,218); corporate direct giving ($177,965)
Assets: $11,007,193 (1996); $10,007,475 (1995); $9,648,171 (1994)

Typical Recipients
Arts & Humanities: Arts Centers, Dance, Museums/Galleries, Music, Opera, Public Broadcasting
Civic & Public Affairs: Business/Free Enterprise, Zoos/Aquariums
Education: Business Education, Colleges & Universities, Education Associations, Education Funds, Engineering/Technological Education, Minority Education, Public Education (Precollege)
Environment: Environment-General
Social Services: Family Services, People with Disabilities, Recreation & Athletics, United Funds/United Ways

Contributions Analysis
Giving Priorities: Education through scholarships, career education awards, and matching grants; United Way and youth groups; the arts; and civic organizations.
Arts & Humanities: 20%. Supports community-wide arts and culture. Grants go to historical organizations, music, museums, and public broadcasting.
Civic & Public Affairs: 15%. Supports organizations concerned with business and free enterprise. Interest is in community betterment and public service. Supports innovative community problem solving and community development.
Education: 40%. Major support is given to colleges through college fund and the foundation's gift-matching plan. Direct student aid is given through scholarships and career education awards to the children of U.S. employees. Supports school-to-work training and technical skills.
Environment: Less than 1%.
Health: 2%. Supports medical centers.
Social Services: 20%. Supports United Way and community centers.

Application Procedures
Initial Contact: Contact foundation for guidelines, which include a series of questions to be answered in a brief proposal letter.
Application Requirements: Include organization's purpose; description of program; organizational and project budgets; amount of aid sought; copy of most recent annual financial statement; proof of tax-exempt status; a list of other current or proposed contributions; and leadership and volunteer board.
Deadlines: None.
Evaluative Criteria: Programs that put people first as the beneficiary of support; provide innovative programs for addressing issues and solving problems; demonstrate and attract leadership; build linkages and partnerships with other groups and the community; demonstrate ownership from volunteers, staff and others committed to its success; have the capacity to achieve results.
Notes: Requests from organizations serving communities with Maytag operations must be reviewed and approved by the manager of the local operation prior to submission the foundation.

Restrictions
Foundation does not support individuals; business ventures, organizations without IRS 501(c)(3) tax-exempt status; organizations that limit membership and services based on race, religion, color, creed, sex, age or national origin; organizations or projects outside the U.S.; endowments; conferences, seminars, trips, tours or similar events; programs/projects involving the delivery of direct health care; advertising for benefit or courtesy purposes; requests for loans or debt retirements; operating expenses of organizations supported by United Way other than through United Way; religious or sectarian programs for religious purposes; national health organizations or their local affiliates; veterans, labor and political organizations or campaigns; fraternal, athletic, and social clubs; projects and organizations without connection to a major Maytag plant community; organizations that might in any way pose a conflict with Maytag's mission, goals, programs, products, or employees.

Corporate Officials
Leonard Anson Hadley: chairman, chief executive officer, director B Earlham, IA 1934. ED Drake University (1952-1953); University of Iowa BSc (1958). CORP AFFIL director: Snap-On Inc.; director: Norwest Bank; director: Deere & Co. NONPR AFFIL board visitors: University Iowa Foundation; board visitors: University Iowa School Business; member: Newton Chamber of Commerce; member: Newton First Un Methodist Church; member: Iowa Technological Transfer Council; member: National Association Manufacturer; member: Iowa College Foundation; member: Iowa Business Council. CLUB AFFIL Rotary International Club; Des Moines Club.
Gerald J. Pribanic: executive vice president, chief financial officer B 1943. ED Pennsylvania State University BS (1965); Fairleigh Dickinson University MBA (1970). PRIM CORP EMPL executive vice president, chief financial officer: Maytag Corp. NONPR AFFIL member: Institute Certified Management Accountants.

Foundation Officials
William M. Beer: trustee
James Bennet: secretary
Janis Campbell Cooper: vice president B Laurel, MS 1947. ED University of Southern Mississippi BS (1969). NONPR AFFIL member: American Association Family & Consumer Sciences; member: Public Relations Society America.
Lynne Dragomier: trustee
Leonard Anson Hadley: president, trustee (see above)
Jon O. Nicholas: vice president, trustee B Syracuse, NY 1939. ED University of Louisville (1965). PRIM CORP EMPL corporate vice president human resources: Maytag Corp. CORP AFFIL vice president: Maytag Appliances. NONPR AFFIL member: Society Human Resources Management; adjunct faculty member: Southern Illinois University; member: Rotary

International; adjunct faculty member: Carl Sandburg College; member: Human Resources Planning Society.

Gerald J. Pribanic: trustee (see above)
Cheryl Ritter: treasurer
Lloyd D. Ward: trustee

Grants Analysis

Disclosure Period: calendar year ending 1997
Total Grants: $2,575,838
Number of Grants: 206
Average Grant: $12,504
Typical Range: $5,000 to $30,000
Note: 1997 figures supplied by foundation.

Recent Grants

Note: Grants derived from 1993 grants list.

Arts & Humanities

50,000	Hoover Presidential Library, West Branch, IA
50,000	Newton Library, Newton, IA
34,500	Des Moines Symphony Association, Des Moines, IA
32,500	Ballet Iowa, West Des Moines, IA
30,000	Des Moines Metro Opera, Des Moines, IA
20,000	Edmundson Art Foundation, Edmundsen, IA -- Des Moines Art Center
20,000	Knox Galesburg Symphony, Galesburg, IL
12,000	Indianapolis Symphony Orchestra, Indianapolis, IN -- operating
10,000	Prairie Players Civic Theater, Galesburg, IL -- operating
6,600	Cultural Center United Arts Fund
6,500	Canton Symphony, Canton, NY

Civic & Public Affairs

37,839	Career Awards for 1993
15,000	Stark Development Board, Canton, OH
10,000	Newton, Iowa, City of Project AWAKE, Newton, IA

Education

206,183	Scholarships Funds 1993
100,000	University of Iowa, Iowa City, IA -- Writers Workshop
100,000	University of Iowa, Iowa City, IA -- College of Business
75,000	Iowa College Foundation, Des Moines, IA
70,000	FINE Education Research Foundation, Des Moines, IA
56,905	Drake University, Des Moines, IA
52,785	Grand View College, Des Moines, IA
51,000	Iowa State University, Ames, IA
50,000	Galesburg Public Schools Foundation, Galesburg, IL
32,000	Ohio Foundation of Independent Colleges, Columbus, OH
26,000	Newton Community School District, Newton, IA
15,000	Lee College, Baytown, TX
15,000	Malone College Capital Campaign, Canton, OH
14,110	University of Iowa Foundation, Iowa City, IA
12,001	Central College, Pella, IA
12,000	Junior Achievement of Bradley County
9,662	Iowa State University Foundation, Ames, IA
9,000	Associated Colleges of Indiana, Indianapolis, IN

Environment

25,000	America's Historic Forest

Health

75,000	Skiff Medical Center
25,000	Bradley Memorial Hospital Foundation, Southington, CT

International

10,000	Iowa Peace Institute, Grinnell, IA

Religion

24,247	Salvation Army

Social Services

140,000	United Way Stark County, Canton, OH
100,000	Wesley Retirement Services, Des Moines, IA -- Park Center Project
81,700	United Way
66,450	1993 United Way Grant
60,000	United Way Bradley County, Cleveland, OH
50,000	Knox County United Way, Galesburg, IL
15,000	Children and Families of Iowa, Des Moines, IA
12,500	Iowa Sports Foundation, Des Moines, IA -- Iowa Games
12,055	Iowa Cares, Des Moines, IA
12,000	YMCA North Canton, North Canton, OH
7,200	Bradley County United Way, Cleveland, TN
6,600	Community Christmas Committee
6,500	Stark Hunger Task Force, Canton, OH

Mazda North American Operations

Company Contact

Irvine, CA

Company Description

Employees: 275
SIC(s): 5012 Automobiles & Other Motor Vehicles, 6719 Holding Companies Nec.
Parent Company: Mazda Motor Corp., 3-1 Shinchi, Fuchu-cho, Aki-gun, Hiroshima, Japan

Operating Locations

CA: Mazda Motor of America, Irvine; Mazda Motor of America Western Region, Irvine; Mazda North American Operations, Irvine; Mazda R&D of North America, Irvine; MI: AutoAlliance International, Flat Rock; Mazda Systems of North America, Flat Rock; Mazda Distributors (Great Lakes), Grand Rapids; TX: Mazda Motor of America Gulf Region, Sugar Land

Nonmonetary Support

Type: Cause-related Marketing & Promotion; Donated Equipment; Donated Products

Mazda Foundation (USA), Inc.

Giving Contact

Barbara Nocera, Director, Government Affairs
1025 Connecticut Avenue, Suite 910
Washington, DC 20036
Phone: (202)467-5096
Fax: (202)233-6490

Alternate Contact

7755 Irvine Center Drive
Irvine, CA 92618
Phone: (714)727-1990

Description

EIN: 382952236
Organization Type: Corporate Foundation. Supports preselected organizations only.
Giving Locations: headquarters and operating communities.
Grant Types: General Support.

Financial Summary

Total Giving: $451,041 (fiscal year ending September 30, 1996); $230,250 (fiscal 1995); $261,250 (fiscal 1994). Note: Figures are for foundation only. Company also gives directly.
Assets: $8,519,627 (fiscal 1996); $8,376,309 (fiscal 1995); $7,990,830 (fiscal 1994)
Gifts Received: $1,000,000 (fiscal 1994); $3,000,000 (fiscal 1993). Note: In fiscal 1994, contributions were received from Mazda North America.

Typical Recipients

Arts & Humanities: Ethnic & Folk Arts, Performing Arts
Civic & Public Affairs: Civil Rights, Civic & Public Affairs-General
Education: Leadership Training, Literacy, Student Aid
Health: Medical Research
Social Services: Child Welfare, People with Disabilities, Senior Services, Substance Abuse, Youth Organizations

Restrictions

Mazda does not consider the following for charitable contributions: dinners or special events, good-will advertising, or religious organizations for sectarian purposes.

Corporate Officials

Richard Beatty: president, chief executive officer PRIM CORP EMPL president, chief executive officer: Mazda North American Operations.

Giving Program Officials

Julie Giles: PRIM CORP EMPL contact: Mazda North American Operations.

Foundation Officials

Yutaka Hirose: chairman, trustee
Hiroshi Hosaka: trustee
Hidetoshi Tanaka: president, secretary, treasurer, trustee
Yoji Toyama: trustee

Grants Analysis

Disclosure Period: fiscal year ending September 30, 1996
Number of Grants: 3
Highest Grant: $204,041
Typical Range: $100,000 to $200,000
Note: Figures are for foundation only.

Recent Grants

Note: Grants derived from fiscal 1997 Form 990.

Education

225,000	Outward Bound, Morgantown, NC -- provide scholarship
104,025	Citizens Scholarship Foundation of America, St. Peter, MN -- provide scholarship
47,012	Reading is Fundamental, Washington, DC -- distribute books to children

Health

50,000	Harvard Institute of Medicine, Boston, MA -- cancer and AIDS education program

MBIA Inc.

Company Contact

Armonk, NY
Web: http://www.mbia.com

Company Description

Assets: US$4,730,000,000
Employees: 551
SIC(s): 6399 Insurance Carriers Nec.

Nonmonetary Support

Value: $50,000 (1995)
Type: Donated Equipment; In-kind Services
Note: The company also offers the use of its auditorium.

Corporate Sponsorship

Type: Sports events; Pledge-a-thon
Note: Sponsors the MBIA Invitational (fundraiser for Westchester Association for Retarded Citizens), local Special Olympics, Walk for Justice, and Child Hospital Fund.

Giving Contact

Arlene Altomare, Vice President
MBIA Inc.
113 King Street
Armonk, NY 10504
Phone: (914)273-4545
Fax: (914)765-3163
Email: PAULEN@mbia.com

Description

Organization Type: Corporate Giving Program
Giving Locations: generally in tri-state area where employees live.
Grant Types: Emergency, Employee Matching Gifts, Endowment.
Note: Employee matching gift ratio: 2 to 1 up to $1,000; 1 to 1 from $1,001 to $1,500. Employee matching gifts are for higher education only.

Giving Philosophy

'MBIA Corporation is committed to its role as a good corporate citizen. To that end the Corporation supports charitable organizations, encourages and supports employee volunteerism and provides matching support to employee contributions to higher education.'
'The Corporation's Charitable Contributions Guidelines are as follows:
Support those groups whose goal is to effect long-term solutions to human and community needs, with particular emphasis on health, education and housing concerns;
to support those business, government and civic groups that provide a positive impact on the people served;
to support those programs that directly benefit the community via the arts, parks and recreation, cultural events; and
to support not-for-profit organizations with 501(c)(3) tax-exempt status(SIC).' *Municipal Bond Investors Assurance Corporation: Charitable Contributions Program*

Financial Summary

Total Giving: $800,000 (1999 approx); $775,000 (1998 approx); $775,000 (1997 approx). Note: Contributes through corporate direct giving program only.

Typical Recipients

Arts & Humanities: Arts Associations & Councils, Arts & Humanities-General, Historic Preservation, Libraries, Museums/Galleries, Performing Arts
Civic & Public Affairs: Employment/Job Training, Civic & Public Affairs-General, Housing, Municipalities/Towns, Women's Affairs
Education: Business Education, Colleges & Universities, Elementary Education (Private), Education-General, Legal Education
Health: Health-General, Geriatric Health, Health Organizations, Medical Research, Single-Disease Health Associations
Social Services: Community Centers, Community Service Organizations, Counseling, Day Care, Family Planning, Family Services, Food/Clothing Distribution, Homes, People with Disabilities, Recreation & Athletics, Senior Services, Shelters/Homelessness, Social Services-General, Substance Abuse, Volunteer Services, Youth Organizations

Contributions Analysis

Arts & Humanities: About 10%. Funds arts associations, historic preservation, libraries, museums, and the performing arts.
Civic & Public Affairs: About 20%. Recipients include ethnic and minority affairs, housing programs, municipalities, and women's affairs.
Education: About 30%. Supports business, elementary, and legal education. Also funds colleges and universities. Employee matching gift program supports institutions of higher education.
Health: About 40%. Interests include geriatric health, health organizations, medical research, single-disease associations, family services, community service organizations, volunteer services, youth organizations, and other social services.
Note: Primary focus is on programs for children, which receive half of all contributions.

Application Procedures

Initial Contact: Call or write for application, then full proposal
Application Requirements: a description of organization, program description, budget information, needs assessment, amount requested, purpose of funds sought, audited financial statements and Form 990's for past three years, and proof of tax-exempt status
Deadlines: None.
Review Process: requests reviewed by the Charitable Contributions Committee
Evaluative Criteria: employee volunteer involvement; impact on the trio-state area; focus on the cause of a problem; organization serves society's neediest; project improves quality of life; highest priority to organizations that will benefit most from contribution

Restrictions

The company does not support individuals, religious organizations for sectarian purposes, umbrella agencies, for general operating support, or for sponsorships or table purchases (unless there is a clear business reason).

Additional Information

Publications: Guidelines; Application Form

Corporate Officials

Joseph Warner Brown, Jr.: chairman, chief executive officer B Evanston, IL 1949. ED Northern Illinois University (1974). PRIM CORP EMPL chairman, chief executive officer: MBIA Inc. ADD CORP EMPL chairman: Industries Indemnity Holdings Inc.; chairman: Apprise Corp.; chairman: Constitution Re corp.; chairman: Coregis Group Inc.; chairman: Crum & Forster Holdings Inc.; chairman: Enuision Claims Management Corp.; chairman: Resolution Group Inc.; chairman, president, chief executive officer: Viking Insurance Holdings Inc.; chairman: Westchester SPLty Group Inc. CORP AFFIL director: First Quadrant Corp. NONPR AFFIL trustee: Ins Institute America; member: Society Chartered Property & Casualty Underwriters; trustee: American Institute Chartered Property & Casualty Underwriters; member: American Academy of Actuaries.
David Holland Elliott: consultant, chairman executive committee B Canaan, CT 1941. ED Yale University BA (1964); Boston University LLB (1967). PRIM CORP EMPL consultant, chairman executive committee: MBIA Inc. CORP AFFIL chief executive officer: Municipal Bond Insurance Association Corp.; director: National Legal Pub Interest; director: Gryphon Holdings Inc.; chairman: MBIA Inc.
Richard L. Weill: president B Lincoln, NE 1943. ED University of Nebraska BS (1964); New York University LLB (1967). PRIM CORP EMPL president: MBIA Inc. CORP AFFIL president: MBIA Insurance Corp.

Giving Program Officials

Arlene S. Altomare: PRIM CORP EMPL officer: MBIA Inc.

Grants Analysis

Disclosure Period: calendar year ending
Typical Range: $2,500 to $7,500

McClatchy Co.

Company Contact

2100 Q St.
Sacramento, CA 95816
Phone: (916)321-1846
Fax: (916)321-1964
Web: http://www.mcclatchy.com

Company Description

Former Name: Cowles Media Co.
Revenue: US$1,087,900,000 (1999)
Employees: 2,900
SIC(s): 2711 Newspapers, 2721 Periodicals.

SUBSIDIARY COMPANIES

MN: Star Tribune Co., Minneapolis

Star Tribune Foundation

Giving Contact

Sandra K. Fleitman, Foundation Coordinator
Star Tribune Foundation
Phone: (612)673-7314
Fax: (612)673-7020

Description

EIN: 416031373
Organization Type: Corporate Foundation
Former Name: Cowles Media Foundation.
Giving Locations: MN: Minneapolis-St. Paul
Grant Types: Capital, Employee Matching Gifts, Endowment, General Support.
Note: Employee matching gift ratio: 1 to 1 for schools, colleges and civic and cultural organisation.

Financial Summary

Total Giving: $3,000,000 (fiscal year ending March 31, 1999 approx); $3,049,701 (fiscal 1998); $2,497,303 (fiscal 1997). Note: Contributes through corporate direct giving program and foundation.
Giving Analysis: Giving for fiscal 1997 includes: foundation ($2,297,858); foundation matching gifts ($199,445); fiscal 1998: foundation ($3,049,701)
Assets: $25,288,230 (fiscal 1998); $11,952,683 (fiscal 1996); $8,155,864 (fiscal 1993)
Gifts Received: $10,089,651 (fiscal 1998); $1,359,500 (fiscal 1996). Note: In 1998, contributions were received from Cowles Media Co.

Typical Recipients

Arts & Humanities: Arts Associations & Councils, Arts Centers, Arts Festivals, Arts Funds, Arts Institutes, Arts Outreach, Community Arts, Dance, Ethnic & Folk Arts, Historic Preservation, Libraries, Literary Arts, Museums/Galleries, Music, Opera, Performing Arts, Public Broadcasting, Theater, Visual Arts
Civic & Public Affairs: Chambers of Commerce, Civil Rights, Community Foundations, Economic Development, Employment/Job Training, First Amendment Issues, Civic & Public Affairs-General, Housing, Native American Affairs, Nonprofit Management, Professional & Trade Associations, Public Policy, Urban & Community Affairs, Women's Affairs, Zoos/Aquariums
Education: Arts/Humanities Education, Business Education, Colleges & Universities, Community & Junior Colleges, Continuing Education, Economic Education, Education Associations, Education Funds, Education Reform, Elementary Education (Private), Engineering/Technological Education, Faculty

Development, Journalism/Media Education, Leadership Training, Literacy, Minority Education, Private Education (Precollege), Public Education (Precollege), Social Sciences Education, Vocational & Technical Education
Environment: Resource Conservation
Health: Medical Rehabilitation
International: Foreign Educational Institutions, Human Rights
Religion: Churches, Missionary Activities (Domestic), Religious Welfare
Science: Science Exhibits & Fairs, Science Museums
Social Services: At-Risk Youth, Child Welfare, Community Centers, Community Service Organizations, Crime Prevention, Day Care, Delinquency & Criminal Rehabilitation, Domestic Violence, Emergency Relief, Family Planning, Family Services, Food/Clothing Distribution, People with Disabilities, Recreation & Athletics, Refugee Assistance, Shelters/Homelessness, Substance Abuse, United Funds/United Ways, Volunteer Services, YMCA/YWCA/YMHA/YWHA, Youth Organizations

Contributions Analysis

Giving Priorities: The arts, human services, education, and media.
Arts & Humanities: 29%. Support goes to major organizations that form the core of the cultural community, primarily in the Twin Cities. Also funds smaller organizations that have demonstrated promise or community interest. Recipients include theaters, orchestral and music groups, the visual arts, and organizations concerned with literature and writing.
Civic & Public Affairs: 20%. Funds organizations concerned with neighborhood development, both socially and economically. Also supports programs that help people understand world issues and that encourage people to participate in important civc issues. Sponsors an employee matching gifts program for civic and cultural organizations that have a company employee on the governing board.
Education: 9%. Emphasis is on the preeminent institutions and on writing-related programs that also enlighten social consciousness. Support is directed to organizations concerned with the First Amendment and to policy issues in journalism and communications, and to professional education programs. Recipients include: journalism education programs, particularly for minorities; the Minnesota Newspaper Foundation, conferences concerned with newspapers, reports, and editors; and groups interested in Libel and freedom of the press.
Religion: 4%. Supports religious welfare organizations.
Science: 6%. Funds a science museum.
Social Services: 32%. A majority of giving supports social services. Funds organizations which assist people to move from dependence to self-reliance; in particular, those organizations which help create opportunities, aid self-reliance, assist people to meet basic needs, and respond to current and future needs. Supports local United Way chapter in the headquarters area; a portion of this funding is in matching gifts. Also supports organizations concerned with adolescents, youth groups, teen pregnancy and parenting. Aids emergency services such as food distribution and matches employee gifts to the Emergency Food Shelf.
Note: Total contributions in fiscal 1998.

Application Procedures

Initial Contact: Send a brief letter or proposal.
Application Requirements: Include purpose of funds being sought; total project budget; a description of organization, its objectives, and how program will be administered; information about organization's officers and directors, current finances, and current contributors; and copy of current IRS tax-exempt ruling.
Deadlines: For general grants, None; for annual operating grants, January.
Review Process: General support is committed at the beginning of the fiscal year (April); large grants and capital requests are considered at the quarterly meetings of the board of directors.
Evaluative Criteria: The proposal must meet company objectives in one of the funding categories.
Decision Notification: Applications are considered on a quarterly basis; a response is made generally within three months.
Notes: Preliminary inquiries by phone or fax may be useful in determining the extent to which a proposed project relates to guidelines and existing commitments. The foundation now accepts the Minnesota Common Grant Application Form.

Restrictions

Generally does not support organizations principally related to medicine and specific diseases, substance abuse, rehabilitation, and related research; religious or international programs; development of low-income housing; dinners or special events; publications or films; recreation, athletic groups and sporting events; individuals, including travel; conferences and writing or performing; fund raising events; or political or lobbying groups.

Additional Information

A stipulation of the 1998 merger between McClatchy and Cowles Media provided for an annual contribution of a least $3 million to Twin Cities community causes for at least 10 years.
Publications: Contributions Report

Corporate Officials

Randy Miller Lebedoff: vice president, general counsel B Washington, DC 1949. ED Smith College BA (1971); Indiana University JD (1975). PRIM CORP EMPL vice president, general counsel: Star Tribune. CORP AFFIL assistant secretary: Star Tribune Cowles Media Co. NONPR AFFIL director: Minnesota Newspapers Association; member: Newspaper Association America.
John R. Schueler: publisher, president PRIM CORP EMPL publisher, president: Star Tribune Co.
Robert J. Weil: vice president operations ED Indiana University. PRIM CORP EMPL vice president operations: The McClatchy Co. ADD CORP EMPL vice president operations: McClatchy Newspapers Inc.

Foundation Officials

Craig Eiter: member PRIM CORP EMPL vice president finance: Star Tribune Co. Inc.
Randy Miller Lebedoff: secretary (see above)
Franklin Joseph Parisi: chairman B Elmhurst, NY 1945. ED Ohio University BS (1968). PRIM CORP EMPL vice president corporate communications: Cray Research Inc. NONPR AFFIL member: National Journalism Society; member: Public Relations Seminar.
Evelyn Piano: president, vice president community affairs
Robert J. Weil: member (see above)

Grants Analysis

Disclosure Period: fiscal year ending March 31, 1998
Total Grants: $2,764,701*
Number of Grants: 386
Average Grant: $7,162
Highest Grant: $254,000
Typical Range: $1,000 to $15,000
***Note:** Giving excludes United Way.

Recent Grants

Note: Grants derived from 1998 Form 990.

Arts & Humanities

200,000	The Ordway Music Theatre, St. Paul, MN
70,000	Minnesota Museum of American Art, St. Paul, MN
63,000	St. Paul Chamber Orchestra, St. Paul, MN
48,000	COMPAS, Inc., St. Paul, MN
43,000	Walker Art Center, Minneapolis, MN
42,000	Stamford Center for the Arts, Inc., Stamford, CT
30,000	Minnesota Children's Museum, St. Paul, MN
25,000	Minnesota Opera, Minneapolis, MN
24,500	Minnesota Orchestra Association, Minneapolis, MN
22,000	Graywolf Press, St. Paul, MN
22,000	Guthrie Theater, Minneapolis, MN
18,000	Milkweed Editions, Minneapolis, MN
16,000	Minneapolis Institute of Arts, Minneapolis, MN

Civic & Public Affairs

57,500	American Press Institute, Reston, VA
50,000	St. Paul Riverfront Corporation, St. Paul, MN
50,000	Twin Cities RISE!, Minneapolis, MN
40,000	Lyndale Neighborhood Association, Minneapolis, MN
37,500	Minneapolis Foundation, Minneapolis, MN
25,000	Citizens League, Minneapolis, MN
25,000	Harrison Neighborhood Association, Chicago, IL
25,000	Northside Residents Redevelopment Council, Minneapolis, MN
25,000	Urban Ventures Leadership Foundation, Minneapolis, MN
25,000	Women of Nations, St. Paul, MN
20,000	The Access Fund, Boulder, CO
20,000	Eden Programs, Inc., Minneapolis, MN
20,000	Elliot Park Neighborhood, Inc., Minneapolis, MN

Education

51,018	University of Minnesota Foundation, Minneapolis, MN
50,000	University of Minnesota Humphrey Institute, Minneapolis, MN
30,000	Northwestern University / Medill School of Journalism, Evanston, IL
20,000	Minneapolis Public School Foundation, Minneapolis, MN
20,000	Minnesota Humanities Commission, St. Paul, MN
18,000	Summit Academy OIC, St. Paul, MN

Health

15,000	North American Riding for Handicapped Association, Denver, CO

Religion

30,000	Catholic Charities, Minneapolis, MN
25,000	St. Paul Area Council of Churches, St. Paul, MN
15,713	Salvation Army, Minneapolis, MN
15,000	The Cookie Cart/Mercy Missionaries, Minneapolis, MN

Science

118,875	Science Museum of Minnesota, St. Paul, MN

Social Services

254,000	United Way of Minneapolis Area, Minneapolis, MN
100,200	YWCA of Minneapolis, Minneapolis, MN
50,000	Little Earth Residents Association, Minneapolis, MN
44,426	Pillsbury Neighborhood Services, Inc., Minneapolis, MN
35,000	Boys & Girls Club of Minneapolis, Minneapolis, MN
27,500	Minneapolis Crisis Nursery, Minneapolis, MN
25,000	City, Inc., Minneapolis, MN
25,000	Plymouth Christian Youth Center, Minneapolis, MN
24,091	American Red Cross, St. Paul, MN -- Capital Campaign
22,500	Glenwood-Lyndale Community Center, Minneapolis, MN

21,000 United Way of St. Paul Area, St. Paul, MN
15,000 Phyllis Wheatley Community Center, Harrisburg, PA

MCCORMICK &CO. INC.

Company Contact

Sparks, MD
Web: http://www.mccormick.com

Company Description

Employees: 8,900
SIC(s): 2079 Edible Fats & Oils Nec, 2087 Flavoring Extracts & Syrups Nec, 2099 Food Preparations Nec, 3085 Plastics Bottles.

Nonmonetary Support

Type: Donated Products

Giving Contact

Allen M. Barrett, Jr., Vice President, Corporate Communications
McCormick & Co. Inc.
18 Loveton Circle
Sparks, MD 21152-6000
Phone: (410)771-7310
Fax: (410)527-8289

Description

Organization Type: Corporate Giving Program
Giving Locations: headquarters and operating communities.
Grant Types: Capital, Employee Matching Gifts, Scholarship.
Note: Employee matching gift ratio: 1 to 1 for education institutions and cultural organisation.

Financial Summary

Total Giving: $1,500,000 (2000 approx); $1,500,000 (1999 approx); $1,500,000 (1995 approx). Note: Company gives directly through the McCormick Fund.

Typical Recipients

Arts & Humanities: Historic Preservation, Libraries, Museums/Galleries, Music, Public Broadcasting, Theater
Civic & Public Affairs: Business/Free Enterprise, Economic Development, Law & Justice, Professional & Trade Associations, Urban & Community Affairs
Education: Business Education, Colleges & Universities, Economic Education, Minority Education, Science/Mathematics Education, Student Aid
Environment: Environment-General
Health: Health Organizations, Medical Research, Nutrition
Science: Scientific Organizations
Social Services: Community Service Organizations, Family Planning, Family Services, Food/Clothing Distribution, United Funds/United Ways, Volunteer Services, Youth Organizations

Contributions Analysis

Giving Priorities: Primarily education, including colleges and universities, with emphasis on business education. Also supports social services through united fund drives and volunteer services; civic organizations; and the arts.
Arts & Humanities: Limited support goes to museums, historic preservation, and public broadcasting.
Civic & Public Affairs: Supports professional and trade associations and programs promoting economic development and the free enterprise system.
Education: Primary support is given to colleges and universities, with an emphasis on business education programs. Supports scholarship programs.
Social Services: The highest priority, with an emphasis on united fund drives and volunteer service programs. Also supports family and community service organizations and youth activities.

Application Procedures

Initial Contact: call or write for guidelines, then written proposal
Application Requirements: a one-page, written summary statement, including: amount requested and funding periods, key deadline dates, program/project needs, organization's goals and objectives, mission statement, project fit with McComick's business operations; organization's name, address, phone number, and name of contact; current operating budget and project budget; sources of financial support; amounts committed or pending; statement of administrative, fundraising, and general expenses; audited financial statements; annual report; proof of tax-exempt status; and list of officers and board members, with affiliations
Deadlines: None.
Review Process: Charitable Donations Committee allocates donations from the fund and makes recommendations to the company; personal interviews are often requested
Evaluative Criteria: priority given to food-related causes, projects in communities with company operations, and McCormick representation on board of directors

Restrictions

Company does not support individuals; fraternal, veterans', or labor organizations; religious and sectarian organizations; political or lobbying groups; secondary schools; travel funds; organizations that might pose a conflict with company goals; or promotional activities, such as goodwill advertising or benefit events.

Additional Information

The McCormick Fund is a vehicle through which the company makes direct contributions.
Publications: Guidelines

Corporate Officials

Francis A. Contino: executive vice president, chief financial officero, chief operating officer, director B 1944. PRIM CORP EMPL executive vice president, chief financial officer: McCormick & Co. Inc.
Robert J. Lawless: chairman, president, chief executive officer, chief operating officer, director B Guelph, ON Canada 1946. ED University of Windsor. PRIM CORP EMPL chairman, president, chief executive officer, chief operating officer, director: McCormick & Co. Inc. CORP AFFIL director: Carpenter Technology Corp. NONPR AFFIL director: Grocery Manufacturers America Inc.; director: Kennedy Krieger Institute.

Giving Program Officials

Allen M. Barrett, Jr.: chairman B Baltimore, MD 1949. ED Dartmouth College (1971); Loyola College (1983). PRIM CORP EMPL vice president corporate communications: McCormick & Co. Inc. NONPR AFFIL member: Public Relations Society America.

Grants Analysis

Disclosure Period: calendar year ending
Typical Range: $5,000 to $10,000

MCDERMOTT INC.

Company Contact

New Orleans, LA
Web: http://www.mcdermott.com

Company Description

Employees: 14,600
SIC(s): 1389 Oil & Gas Field Services Nec, 1623 Water, Sewer & Utility Lines, 1629 Heavy Construction Nec, 1799 Special Trade Contractors Nec.
Parent Company: McDermott International Inc., Domiciliary Eificio Dallarino, 8V O P1SO, Caile 5ZY Elure,, Mendez Partado, Panama 6, Panama

Operating Locations

AR: Babcock & Wilcox ST Co., Little Rock; LA: Fabrication & Offshare Operations, Morgan City; McDermott Inc., Morgan City; McDermott, New Orleans; McDermott Inc., New Orleans; OH: McDermott Inc., Alliance; Babcock & Wilcox Co., Barberton; McDermott Inc., Barberton; Diamond Power Specialty Co., Lancaster; TX: Hudson Engineering & Project Management Services, Houston; Hudson Enginering Corp., Houston; McDermott Inc., Houston; VA: McDermott Inc., Lynchburg

Giving Contact

Don Washington, Manager, Communications & Investor Relations
McDermott Inc.
1450 Poydras St.
New Orleans, LA 70112-6058
Phone: (504)587-4080
Fax: (504)587-5677

Description

Organization Type: Corporate Giving Program
Giving Locations: national organizations; operating locations.
Grant Types: Capital, General Support.

Financial Summary

Total Giving: $750,000 (2000 approx); $750,000 (1999 approx); $750,000 (1998 approx). Note: Contributes through corporate direct giving program only.

Typical Recipients

Arts & Humanities: Public Broadcasting
Civic & Public Affairs: Business/Free Enterprise, Professional & Trade Associations, Safety
Education: Colleges & Universities
Health: Hospitals
Social Services: Community Service Organizations, United Funds/United Ways, Youth Organizations

Contributions Analysis

Giving Priorities: Civic organizations; colleges and universities; social services, including united funds and youth organizations; hospitals and medical research; and some arts. In 1991, company contributed $10,000 to U.S.-based nonprofit organizations with an international focus and $10,000 to local organizations by foreign subsidiaries.
Arts & Humanities: 5% to 10%. Supports community arts groups, museums, and public broadcasting.
Civic & Public Affairs: About 35%. Supports business and free enterprise, professional and trade associations, public policy and better government, safety organizations, and industrial liaison programs with scientific institutions.
Education: 25% to 30%. Emphasizes colleges and universities, education funds and associations, and minority education.
Health: 5% to 10%. Supports hospitals and medical research.
Social Services: 20% to 25%. Recipients include youth organizations, united funds, community service organizations, community centers,volunteer services, and emergency relief.

Application Procedures

Initial Contact: letter or proposal
Application Requirements: a description of organization, amount requested, purpose of funds sought,

recently audited financial statement, proof of tax-exempt status, list of contributors and amounts contributed, list of any supporters within company
Deadlines: None.
Decision Notification: quarterly, at contributions committee meetings

Additional Information

McDermott International (headquartered in Canada) is the parent company of the McDermott group of companies, which includes the marine construction services of J. Ray McDermott, SA and the power generation systems and equipment business of McDermott Inc. McDermott conducts its power generation business primarily through its subsidiary Babcock & Wilcox Co., supplying fossil-fuel and nuclear steam generating equipment to the electric power generation industry, and nuclear reactor components and nuclear fuel assemblies to the U.S. Navy.

Corporate Officials

Roger E. Tetrault: chairman, chief executive officer, director director corporate compliance B Hartford, CT 1941. PRIM CORP EMPL chairman, chief executive officer, director: McDermott International Inc. CORP AFFIL chairman, chief executive officer: McDermott Inc.; chairman: J. Ray McDermott S.A.; director: Handy & Harman; chairman: Babcock & Wilcox Co.; chairman: Babcock & Wilcox Investment Co.
Don Washington: director communications & investor relations PRIM CORP EMPL director communications & investor relations: McDermott International Inc.
J. R. Woolsey: executive vice president, chief administrative officer, director corporate compliance PRIM CORP EMPL executive vice president, chief administrative officer, director corporate compliance: McDermott International Inc.

Giving Program Officials

Don Washington: member contributions committee (see above)

Grants Analysis

Disclosure Period: calendar year ending
Typical Range: $500 to $5,000

MCDONALD &CO. SECURITIES, INC.

Company Contact

Cleveland, OH

Company Description

Revenue: US$200,000,000
Employees: 1,030
SIC(s): 6211 Security Brokers & Dealers.
Parent Company: McDonald & Co. Investments, Inc.

Nonmonetary Support

Type: Donated Equipment; Donated Products; Inkind Services; Loaned Employees; Loaned Executives
Note: Company provides nonmonetary support, but this is not the preferred method of giving.

Corporate Sponsorship

Type: Arts & cultural events; Festivals/fairs; Music & entertainment events; Pledge-a-thon; Sports events

McDonald & Co. Securities Foundation

Giving Contact

Thomas G. Clevidence, Senior Managing Director
McDonald & Co. Securities Foundation
McDonald Investment Center
800 Superior Ave.
Cleveland, OH 44114-2603
Phone: (216)443-2981
Fax: (216)443-3865

Alternate Contact

Phone: 800-553-2240

Description

EIN: 341386528
Organization Type: Corporate Foundation
Giving Locations: headquarters and operating communities.
Grant Types: Award, Capital, General Support, Matching, Multiyear/Continuing Support, Operating Expenses, Project, Scholarship.

Financial Summary

Total Giving: $800,000 (fiscal year ending March 31, 1999 approx); $991,970 (fiscal 1998); $700,000 (fiscal 1997 approx). Note: Contributes through corporate direct giving program and foundation.
Giving Analysis: Giving for fiscal 1998 includes: foundation ($961,131); foundation grants to United Way ($30,839)
Assets: $1,098,352 (fiscal 1998); $1,000,000 (fiscal 1996 approx); $1,005,016 (fiscal 1995)
Gifts Received: $528,000 (fiscal 1998); $181,338 (fiscal 1995); $463,000 (fiscal 1994). Note: Contributions were received from McDonald & Company Securities, Inc.

Typical Recipients

Arts & Humanities: Arts Associations & Councils, Arts Centers, Arts Festivals, Ballet, Community Arts, Ethnic & Folk Arts, Historic Preservation, Libraries, Museums/Galleries, Music, Opera, Performing Arts, Public Broadcasting, Theater, Visual Arts
Civic & Public Affairs: African American Affairs, Asian American Affairs, Business/Free Enterprise, Civil Rights, Community Foundations, Economic Development, Economic Policy, Employment/Job Training, Ethnic Organizations, Civic & Public Affairs-General, Hispanic Affairs, Inner-City Development, Law & Justice, Municipalities/Towns, Parades/Festivals, Philanthropic Organizations, Professional & Trade Associations, Public Policy, Urban & Community Affairs, Urban & Community Affairs, Women's Affairs, Zoos/Aquariums
Education: Afterschool/Enrichment Programs, Business Education, Colleges & Universities, Community & Junior Colleges, Economic Education, Education Funds, Education Reform, Elementary Education (Public), Education-General, Literacy, Minority Education, Public Education (Precollege), Student Aid
Environment: Environment-General, Wildlife Protection
Health: AIDS/HIV, Alzheimers Disease, Cancer, Children's Health/Hospitals, Diabetes, Emergency/Ambulance Services, Eyes/Blindness, Health-General, Health Organizations, Hospices, Hospitals, Medical Research, Mental Health, Multiple Sclerosis, Nursing Services, Single-Disease Health Associations, Speech & Hearing
International: Trade
Religion: Dioceses, Jewish Causes, Religious Organizations, Religious Welfare, Social/Policy Issues
Science: Science Museums, Scientific Centers & Institutes
Social Services: Animal Protection, At-Risk Youth, Camps, Child Welfare, Community Centers, Community Service Organizations, Counseling, Day Care, Delinquency & Criminal Rehabilitation, Domestic Violence, Emergency Relief, Family Planning, Family Services, Food/Clothing Distribution, People with Disabilities, Recreation & Athletics, Senior Services, Sexual Abuse, Shelters/Homelessness, Social Services-General, Substance Abuse, United Funds/United Ways, Volunteer Services, YMCA/YWCA/YMHA/YWHA, Youth Organizations

Contributions Analysis

Giving Priorities: Civic organizations, education, health care services, religious organizations, arts, international services, and social services.
Arts & Humanities: 13%. Supports musemus, theater, music, and art.
Civic & Public Affairs: 27%. Supports community and neighborhoods development, clubs, and community foundations.
Education: 13%. Funds higher education, education foundations, and education programs.
Health: 15%. Supports hospitals, medical centers, single-disease associations, and AIDS prevention.
International: 1%. Funs international causes.
Religion: 9%. Supports religious organizations and services.
Social Services: 22%. Supports youth services, the disabled, social services, and United Way.
Note: Total contributions made in 1998.

Application Procedures

Initial Contact: Send a brief letter of inquiry, followed by a brief proposal.
Application Requirements: Include a description of organization, amount requested, purpose of funds sought, and proof of tax-exempt status.
Deadlines: None.
Evaluative Criteria: Requests must conform to either the Greater Cleveland Growth Association or Better Business Bureau guidelines; organizations must be nonprofit and tax-exempt; preference is given to regional rather than national projects.
Notes: Requests from branch offices which follow guidelines will also be considered.

Restrictions

Does not support individuals; community attractions that draw primarily from their immediate area or are nature-related; religious organizations for sectarian purposes; political or lobbying groups; organizations outside operating areas; athletic and sport related civic or national events such as the Olympics; causes that use tickets/lunches for fundraising; any subcommittee or auxiliary group of an organization to which a donation has already been made; individual colleges or secondary schools, both for annual support and capital programs.
Higher education is supported only through contributions to the Ohio Foundation for Independent Colleges and colleges not affiliated with OFIC.
Religious and welfare grants will be restricted to local arms of United Way, United Jewish Welfare Fund, and Catholic Charities.

Additional Information

Publications: Guidelines

Corporate Officials

Richard Clark: manager corporate communicationrs PRIM CORP EMPL manager corporate communication: McDonald & Co. Securities, Inc.
Thomas G. Clevidence: executive PRIM CORP EMPL executive: McDonald & Co. Securities.
Robert T. Clutterbuck: president PRIM CORP EMPL president: McDonald & Co. Securities, Inc. CORP AFFIL treasurer: McDonald Co. Investments.
William B. Summers, Jr.: chairman, chief executive officer, president PRIM CORP EMPL chairman, chief executive officer, president: McDonald & Co. Securities, Inc. CORP AFFIL president: McDonald Co. Investments Delaware.

Foundation Officials

Pamela Burke: trustee
Thomas G. Clevidence: secretary (see above)
Fred Cummings: trustee
Lynn Ann Gries: trustee
Thomas McDonald: trustee
John F. O'Brien: trustee B Cleveland, OH 1936. ED Georgetown University BS (1958). PRIM CORP

EMPL senior managing partner: McDonald & Co. Investments. CORP AFFIL director: Viatro Corp.; director: McDonald & Co. Securities. NONPR AFFIL member: Leadership Cleveland; trustee: Saint Edward High School; member: Greater Cleveland Growth Association; member: Alcohol & Drug Addiction Services Cuyahoga. CLUB AFFIL Westwood Country Club; Catawba Island Club; Cleveland Yacht Club.

William B. Summers, Jr.: trustee (see above)

Grants Analysis

Disclosure Period: fiscal year ending March 31, 1998
Total Grants: $991,970
Number of Grants: 314
Average Grant: $3,159
Highest Grant: $17,312
Typical Range: $250 to $5,000

Recent Grants

Note: Grants derived from 1999 Form 990.

Arts & Humanities

15,000 Cultural Center for the Arts, Canton, OH -- General Fund
10,000 Musical Arts Association, The, Cleveland, OH -- General Fund
10,000 Playhouse Square Foundation, Cleveland, OH -- General Fund
8,750 Playhouse Square Foundation, Cleveland, OH -- General Fund
7,500 Cleveland Museum of Art, The, Cleveland, OH -- General Fund
7,500 Museum of American Financial History, New York, NY -- General Fund
6,500 Cleveland Playhouse, The, Cleveland, OH -- General Fund
5,000 Cleveland Opera, Cleveland, OH -- General Fund
5,000 Rock & Roll Hall of Fame and Museum, Inc., Cleveland, OH -- General Fund
5,000 Rock & Roll Hall of Fame and Museum, Inc., Cleveland, OH -- General Fund

Civic & Public Affairs

30,000 Cleveland Tomorrow, Cleveland, OH -- General Fund
30,000 Cleveland Tomorrow, Cleveland, OH -- General Fund
20,000 Cleveland Tomorrow, Cleveland, OH -- General Fund
12,500 City Year, Cleveland, OH -- General Fund
10,000 Law Enforcement Foundation, Inc., Dublin, OH -- General Fund
10,000 Law Enforcement Foundation, Inc., Dublin, OH -- General Fund
10,000 New Cleveland Campaign, Cleveland, OH -- General Fund
9,580 NAACP Cleveland Branch, Cleveland, OH -- General Fund
8,500 Urban League of Greater Cleveland, Cleveland, OH -- General Fund
7,000 National Conference for Community and Justice, New York, NY -- General Fund
5,000 Cleveland Development Foundation, Cleveland, OH -- General Fund
5,000 Indianapolis Urban League, Indianapolis, IN -- General Fund

Education

35,000 Cleveland Initiative for Education, Cleveland, OH -- General Fund
15,000 Cleveland Initiative for Education, Cleveland, OH -- General Fund
12,500 Ohio Foundation of Independent Colleges, Inc., The, Cleveland, OH -- General Fund
7,500 El Barrio, Cleveland, OH -- General Fund
5,815 Cuyahoga Community College Foundation, Cleveland, OH -- General Fund

Health

10,000 American Red Cross, Cleveland, OH -- General Fund
10,000 Riley Hospital for Children--RCA Championships, Indianapolis, IN -- General Fund
9,000 Juvenile Diabetes Foundation International-Northeast Ohio Chapter, Cleveland, OH -- General Fund
8,600 American Cancer Society - Cuyahoga County, Cleveland, OH -- General Fund
8,400 Aids Housing Council of Greater Cleveland, Cleveland, OH -- General Fund
5,000 American Cancer Society - Franklin County, Columbus, OH -- General Fund
5,000 Diabetes Association of Greater Cleveland, Cleveland, OH -- General Fund
5,000 Health Hill Hospital for Children, Cleveland, OH -- General Fund

Religion

20,000 Catholic Diocese of Cleveland, Cleveland, OH -- General Fund
12,500 Jewish Community Federation of Cleveland, The, Cleveland, OH -- General Fund
12,500 Jewish Community Federation of Cleveland, The, Cleveland, OH -- General Fund
10,000 Catholic Diocese of Cleveland, Cleveland, OH -- General Fund
7,500 Sisters of Notre Dame--School Funds, Cleveland, OH -- General Fund

Social Services

17,312 United Way of Greater Cleveland, Cleveland, OH -- General Fund
15,000 Junior Olympic Games--1999 AAU, Cleveland, OH -- General Fund
10,000 Achievement Centers For Children, Cleveland, OH -- General Fund
10,000 Center for Prevention of Domestic Violence, Cleveland, OH -- General Fund
10,000 Recovery Resources, Cleveland, OH -- General Fund
8,900 Major League Baseball Players Alumni, Colorado Springs, CO -- General Fund
7,500 U.S. Olympics Committee, Colorado Springs, CO -- General Fund
6,700 United Way Services, Cleveland, OH -- General Fund
5,000 Center for Families and Children, Cleveland, OH -- General Fund
3,000 Business Volunteerism Council, Cleveland, OH -- General Fund

MCDONALD'S CORP.

Company Contact

Oak Brook, IL
Web: http://www.rmhc.com

Company Description

Revenue: US$12,421,400,000
Employees: 267,000
Fortune Rank: 132, per FORTUNE Magazine's list of 500 Largest U.S. Corporations (1999).
FF 132
SIC(s): 5812 Eating Places, 6794 Patent Owners & Lessors.

Operating Locations

Operates throughout the USA.

Corporate Sponsorship

Type: Other
Note: The company supports fundraising dinners.

McDonald's Corp. Charitable Foundation

Giving Contact

Ken Barun, Executive Vice President & Managing Director
McDonald's Corp.
One Kroc Drive
Oak Brook, IL 60523
Phone: (630)623-7048
Fax: (630)623-7488

Description

Organization Type: Corporate Foundation
Giving Locations: nationally and in local operating areas.
Grant Types: Emergency, Employee Matching Gifts, General Support.
Note: Employee matching gift ratio: 1 to 1.

Giving Philosophy

'In today's world where everything seems to move faster, grow larger, and become more challenging, we still like to make the simple donations, but the greater emphasis of our contributions is on forming partnerships for our future. McDonald's is a 'hands-on' business, and we seek to work with those organizations who are developing hands-on projects to solve tough problems, push against the traditional barriers and open up the world of opportunity for the nation's young people -- our future. I'm proud to say that our local McDonald's restaurant licensees, managers and employees drive our giving because.. they are involved. We all live, work and benefit by the good health of their neighborhoods. And we give back to the communities where we do business because it is good business.' McDonald's Giving, *A Commitment to Our Communities*

Financial Summary

Total Giving: $2,000,000 (fiscal year ending March 28, 1997 approx); $2,000,000 (fiscal 1996 approx); $1,500,000 (fiscal 1995 approx). Note: Contributes through corporate direct giving program and foundation. Fiscal 1997 Giving includes corporate direct giving; foundation ($698,179); United Way ($7,905).
Assets: $1,005,806 (fiscal 1997)
Gifts Received: $464,000 (fiscal 1997)

Typical Recipients

Arts & Humanities: Museums/Galleries
Civic & Public Affairs: Employment/Job Training
Education: Arts/Humanities Education, Colleges & Universities, Health & Physical Education, Literacy, Minority Education, Special Education
Health: Hospitals, Nutrition, Single-Disease Health Associations
Social Services: Child Welfare, Community Centers, Family Services, Homes, People with Disabilities, Substance Abuse, Youth Organizations

Contributions Analysis

Giving Priorities: Educational programs for youth and disabled youth, and seed money for community projects that focus on and include young people. Company supports U.S.-based nonprofit organizations with an international focus.

Application Procedures

Initial Contact: request guidelines and application; submit proposal
Application Requirements: one- or two-page cover letter on organization stationary signed by senior management official; three- to four-page proposal detailing project's goals and objectives, target audiences, timetable, project evaluation component, and number of people involved or benefiting from project; one-page organizational summary; a donors list from

previous 12 months; detailed annual operating budget; recently audited financial statement; itemized project budget; list of other financial sources; names and affiliations of board members; proof of tax-exempt status; and if applicable a letter of endorsement from a McDonald's representative(s)
Deadlines: None.
Review Process: national and international grants are reviewed by trustees in headquarters; local proposals are reviewed by local committees.
Evaluative Criteria: clearly defined problems and proposed solutions; measurable results; consistent and effective management; programs directly benefit children; broad base of funding support
Decision Notification: proposals are acknowledged within 30 days; decisions may take up to 60 days

Restrictions

Does not make grants to individuals, general operating funds, endowments or capital campaigns; building, loan, or investment funds; or United Way campaigns outside metropolitan Chicago.
No support for salaries.
Does not award individual scholarships.

Additional Information

Contributions of over 11,200 McDonald's franchises total about three times that of corporation.
All grants made for one year with no implied renewals.
Company also provides general and operating support through Ronald McDonald Children's Charities.
Publications: Guidelines; Application Form

Corporate Officials

James R. Cantalupo: vice chairman vice president, corporate general counsel
Michael L. Conley: executive vice president, chief executive officer
Jack M. Greenberg: chairman, chief executive officer
Jeffrey B. Kindler: executive vice president, corporate general counsel
Michael Robert Quinlan: chairman executive committee B Chicago, IL 1944. ED Loyola University BS (1967); Loyola University MBA (1970). PRIM CORP EMPL chairman executive committee: McDonald's Corp. CORP AFFIL president: McDonald's Restaurants Missouri; president: McDonald's Restaurants New Jersey; chairman, director: McDonald's Restaurants Illinois; chief executive officer, director: McDonald's Restaurants Arizona; chairman: McDonald's Restaurants Colorado; director: May Department Stores Co.; chairman: McDonald's Restaurant Operations; director: Dun & Bradstreet Corp. CLUB AFFIL Butterfield Country Club; Oakbrook Handball-Racquetball Club.
Fred L. Turner: senior chairman, director B Des Moines, IA 1933. ED Drake University (1954). PRIM CORP EMPL senior chairman, director: McDonald's Corp. CORP AFFIL senior chairman: McDonald's Restaurants Colorado; chairman: McDonald's Restaurants New Jersey; senior chairman, director: McDonald's Restaurant Operations; director: Baxter International Inc.; director: WW Grainger Inc.; director: AON Corp.

Foundation Officials

Kenneth Lee Barun: president, director B New York, NY 1948. ED University of Houston BS (1980). PRIM NONPR EMPL executive director: Ronald McDonald Children's Charities.
Michael Robert Quinlan: director (see above)

Grants Analysis

Disclosure Period: fiscal year ending March 28, 1997
Total Grants: $698,179*
Number of Grants: 234
Average Grant: $2,984
Highest Grant: $50,000
Typical Range: $3,000 to $5,000
***Note:** Giving excludes United Way.

MCGRAW-HILL COMPANIES, INC.

Company Contact

New York, NY
Web: http://www.mcgraw-hill.com/philanthropy/index.html

Company Description

Revenue: US$3,729,100,000
Employees: 16,220
Fortune Rank: 401, per FORTUNE Magazine's list of 500 Largest U.S. Corporations (1999).
FF 401
SIC(s): 2711 Newspapers, 2721 Periodicals, 2731 Book Publishing, 2741 Miscellaneous Publishing.

Operating Locations

Australia: McGraw-Hill Book Co. Australia Pty. Ltd.; Belgium: DRI Europe, Inc., Brussels, Brabant; Standard & Poor's International SA, Brussels, Brabant; Canada: McGraw-Hill Information Systems Co. of Canada Ltd., Whitby; McGraw-Hill Ryerson, Ltd., Whitby; France: MEDSI/McGraw-Hill, Paris, Ville-de-Paris; Germany: McGraw-Hill Book Co. UK, Ltd., Hamburg; India: Tata McGraw-Hill Publishing Co., Private Ltd., New Delhi; Italy: McGraw-Hill Libri Italia, S.r.l., Milan; Japan: McGraw-Hill Book Kabushiki Kaisha, Tokyo; Mexico: McGraw-Hill/Interamericana de Mexico, Mexico City; Portugal: Editora McGraw-Hill de Portugal, Ltda, Lisbon, Lisboa; Spain: McGraw Hill Interamencana de Espana SA, Madrid; United Kingdom: McGraw-Hill Book Co. (U.K.) Ltd., Berks; Datapro Services, Berkshire; McGraw-Hill International Publications Co. Ltd., Berkshire; DRI Europe (U.K.) Ltd., London

Nonmonetary Support

Value: $4,362,000 (1993); $6,216,000 (1992); $3,200,000 (1991)
Type: Donated Products

Giving Contact

Susan A. Wallman, Manager, Corporate Contributions
McGraw-Hill Companies, Inc.
1221 Avenue of the Americas
New York, NY 10020-1095
Phone: (212)512-6480
Fax: (212)512-3611
Email: gabriele@mcgraw-hill.com

Description

Organization Type: Corporate Giving Program
Giving Locations: NY: New York national organizations; primarily headquarters and operating communities.
Grant Types: Employee Matching Gifts, General Support.
Note: Employee matching gift ratio: 2 to 1.

Giving Philosophy

'The McGraw-Hill Companies will support innovative programs that increase the abilities of people around the world to learn, to grow intellectually, to master new skills, and to maximize their individual talents for school, work and community.' Corporate Contributions and Community Relations Guidelines for Giving

Financial Summary

Total Giving: $3,200,000 (2000 approx); $3,200,000 (1999 approx); $2,440,094 (1996). Note: Contributes through corporate direct giving program only, as of 1997. 1996 Giving includes foundation ($761,749); matching gifts ($1,198,505); United Way ($479,840).
Assets: $893,426 (1996); $840,524 (1995); $596,638 (1994)
Gifts Received: $2,400,000 (1996); $2,300,000 (1995); $2,650,000 (1994)

Typical Recipients

Arts & Humanities: Arts Centers, Dance, Libraries, Museums/Galleries, Music, Performing Arts, Public Broadcasting
Civic & Public Affairs: African American Affairs, Business/Free Enterprise, Civil Rights, Economic Development, Employment/Job Training, First Amendment Issues, Hispanic Affairs, Housing, Law & Justice, Professional & Trade Associations, Public Policy, Women's Affairs
Education: Business Education, Colleges & Universities, Education Associations, Education Funds, Education Reform, Engineering/Technological Education, Education-General, Journalism/Media Education, Literacy, Minority Education, Private Education (Precollege), Student Aid
Environment: Air/Water Quality
Health: AIDS/HIV, Clinics/Medical Centers, Eyes/Blindness, Health Organizations, Hospitals, Hospitals (University Affiliated), Transplant Networks/Donor Banks
International: International Development
Religion: Religious Welfare
Social Services: Community Service Organizations, Family Services, People with Disabilities, Substance Abuse, United Funds/United Ways, Volunteer Services, YMCA/YWCA/YMHA/YWHA

Contributions Analysis

Giving Priorities: Colleges and universities, mainly through matching gifts; nationally prominent performing arts centers and other arts organizations; united funds; national and local health organizations; and civic groups; emphasis on economic literacy and entrepreneurship. Company provides $7,500 in support to US based nonprofits with an international focus.

Application Procedures

Initial Contact: Send preliminary proposal letter.
Application Requirements: Brief background of your organization, including its goals and objectives, staff, and board of directors; a concise description of the program and objectives for which funds are sought; a copy of most recent audited financial statement and annual report; current year's budget and the sources of funding; the budget for the program for which you support is sought, and the sum requested; and evidence of your public charity status under the U.S. Internal Revenue Code.
Deadlines: None.
Review Process: If request fits current priorities, meeting may be arranged and on-site visits conducted.
Evaluative Criteria: Organization staffed by people with demonstrated competence and experience in the field; project addresses problems affecting communities the company serves; contribution supports projects that can be evaluated and serve as models elsewhere; project extends reach globally, and utilizes unique applications of new and developing technologies.
Decision Notification: Corporate Contributions and Community Relations Committee meets quarterly.

Restrictions

Foundation does not support political activities or organizations established to influence legislation; individuals; publication of books, magazines, videos, or films; member organizations of United Way funds; sectarian or religious organizations; endowment funds; loans; or institutions and agencies clearly outside McGraw-Hill's primary geographic concerns and interests.
Foundation does not subscribe to tables or tickets for charitable events, sponsor courtesy advertisements,

or pledge support for walk-a-thons or similar activities. events, sponsor courtesy advertisements, or pledge support for walk-a-thons or similar activities.

Additional Information

Grants are not renewed automatically; new requests must be submitted each year.
Recipients are asked to submit periodic reports on, and evaluation of, progress and an annual financial report.
Foundation ceased operations in 1997; all contributions are now made through Corporate Contributions and Community Relations.
Publications: Giving Guidelines

Corporate Officials

Frank Joseph Kaufman: senior vice president taxes B New York, NY 1944. ED Hamilton College BA (1966); Harvard University JD (1972). PRIM CORP EMPL senior vice president taxes: McGraw-Hill Companies, Inc. CORP AFFIL vice president: Standard & Poors Compustat Services Inc.; vice president: Standard & Poors Corp.
Harold Whittlesey 'Terry' McGraw, III: chairman, president, chief executive officer B Summit, NJ 1948. ED Tufts University BA (1972); University of Pennsylvania Wharton School MBA (1976). PRIM CORP EMPL chairman, president, chief executive officer: McGraw-Hill Companies, Inc. CORP AFFIL chairman, director: Standard & Poors Securities Inc.; chairman: Tower Group International; president: McGraw-Hill Fin Services Co.; chairman: Standard & Poors Compustat Services Inc.; assistant vice president pension investment: GTE Management Corp. NONPR AFFIL director: Brunswick School; director: Hartley House.
Barbara A. Munder: senior vice president new initiatives B New York, NY 1945. ED Elmira College (1967); New York University Leonard N. Stern School of Business MBA (1980). PRIM CORP EMPL senior vice president new initiatives: McGraw-Hill Companies, Inc. NONPR AFFIL member: Information Industry Association; director: Lighthouse.
Louise Raymond: director corporate contributions
Donald S. Rubin: senior vice president investor relations B Chicago, IL 1934. ED Columbia University; University of Miami AB (1956). PRIM CORP EMPL senior vice president investor relations: McGraw-Hill Companies, Inc.
Susan A. Wallman: manager corporate contributions

Foundation Officials

Antonio Garcia-Maroto: PRIM CORP EMPL managing director: Editora McGraw-Hill de Portugal. CORP AFFIL managing director: McGraw-Hill Interamencana de Espana SA (Spain).
Frank Dennis Penglase: vice president, treasurer B Sherman, TX 1940. ED Stanford University BA (1962); Columbia University MBA (1966). PRIM CORP EMPL senior vice president treasury operation: McGraw-Hill Companies, Inc. CORP AFFIL director: Westminster Homeowners Inc.; treasurer: Standard & Poors Corp.; president: New York Treas Group; treasurer: Standard & Poors Compustat Services Inc.; treasurer: McGraw-Hill Publishing Overseas Corp. NONPR AFFIL member: Financial Executives Institute.
Thomas John Sullivan: vice president, director B Jersey City, NJ 1935. ED Saint Peter's College BS (1957); Seton Hall University JD (1969). PRIM CORP EMPL executive vice president administration: McGraw-Hill Companies, Inc. NONPR AFFIL member: National Association Accts; member: New Jersey Bar Association; member: Institute of Management Accountants; member: American Bar Association; member: Financial Executives Institute.

Grants Analysis

Disclosure Period: calendar year ending 1996
Total Grants: $761,749*
Number of Grants: 174
Average Grant: $4,378
Highest Grant: $109,710
Typical Range: $1,000 to $20,000
***Note:** Giving excludes matching gifts; United Way.

Recent Grants

Note: Grants derived from 1996 Form 990.

Arts & Humanities

25,000	Lincoln Center for Performing Arts, New York, NY
25,000	New York Public Library, New York, NY
10,000	Colorado Springs Symphony Orchestra Association, Colorado Springs, CO
10,000	Library Foundation, San Francisco, CA
10,000	Monterey County Symphony Association, Carmel, CA
5,000	New York Philharmonic, New York, NY

Civic & Public Affairs

10,000	Advertising Council, New York, NY
10,000	Five Points Media Center Corporation, Denver, CO
10,000	Jobs for Youth, New York, NY
5,000	American Woman's Economic Development Corporation, New York, NY

Education

109,710	National Merit Scholarship Corporation, Evanston, IL
30,000	Cornell University Knight-Baghot Fellowship, New York, NY
25,000	A Better Chance, New York, NY
15,000	Council for Aid to Education, New York, NY
11,000	United Negro College Fund, Fairfax, VA
10,000	Business Press Education Foundation, New York, NY
10,000	Literacy Volunteers of America, Syracuse, NY
10,000	Partnership for New Jersey, New Brunswick, NJ
10,000	Prep for Prep, New York, NY
8,000	Literacy Volunteers, New York, NY
7,500	Building With Books, Stamford, CT
6,000	Association Governing Board of Universities and Colleges, Washington, DC
5,305	Citizens Scholarship Foundation of America, Saint Peter, MN
5,000	Citizens Scholarship Foundation of America, Saint Peter, MN
5,000	Junior Achievement, New York, NY
5,000	National Book Foundation, New York, NY
5,000	Settlement College Readiness Program, New York, NY

Environment

10,000	Fresh Air Fund, New York, NY

Health

10,000	St. Joseph's Hospital, Paterson, NJ
6,500	University of Rochester Medical Center, Rochester, NY
5,000	American Foundation for AIDS Research, New York, NY
5,000	American Foundation for Blind, New York, NY

International

5,000	International Executive Service Corporation, Stamford, CT

Religion

50,000	Salvation Army, New York, NY

Social Services

361,680	United Way Tri-State Area, New York, NY
50,000	National Organization on Disability, Washington, DC
50,000	National Organization on Disability, Washington, DC
30,400	United Way Burlington County, Mount Holly, NJ
20,000	Hartley House, New York, NY
15,000	Lighthouse, New York, NY
12,000	United Way San Diego County, San Diego, CA
10,000	YWCA, New York, NY
8,000	Mile High United Way, Denver, CO
7,500	Pikes Peak United Way, Colorado Springs, CO
7,500	United Way Franklin County, Columbus, OH
6,244	United Way Buffalo and Erie Counties, Buffalo, NY
6,000	United Way Central Indiana, Indianapolis, IN
6,000	United Way Monterey Peninsula, Monterey, CA
6,000	YWCA, New York, NY
5,000	National Association on Drug Abuse, New York, NY

MCI WORLDCOM, INC.

Company Contact

Jackson, MS
Web: http://www.mciworldcom.com

Company Description

Former Name: MCI Communications Corp.
Revenue: US$37,120,000,000 (1999)
Profit: US$2,669,000,000
Employees: 55,285
Fortune Rank: 25, per FORTUNE Magazine's list of 500 Largest U.S. Corporations (1999).
FF 25
SIC(s): 4813 Telephone Communications Except Radiotelephone, 4899 Communications Services Nec.

Operating Locations

MCI WorldCom, Inc. subsidiaries are MCI Telecommunications Corp., MCI International, and Telecom USA.

Nonmonetary Support

Value: $2,000,000 (1995)
Type: Donated Equipment; Donated Products; In-kind Services
Note: MCI donates telecommunications equipment for educational purposes only. Value of nonmonetary support is an approximate. 1997 nonmonetary support $300,000.

Corporate Sponsorship

Type: Arts & cultural events; Festivals/fairs; Music & entertainment events; Pledge-a-thon; Sports events
Contact: Bob Speltz, Program Officer

MCI WorldCom Foundation

Giving Contact

Caleb M. Schutz, Director
MCI WorldCom Foundation
1200 Hays Street
Arlington, VA 22202
Phone: (703)415-6927
Fax: (703)415-7175

Description

Founded: 1986
EIN: 510294683
Organization Type: Corporate Foundation
Giving Locations: headquarters and operating communities.
Grant Types: Project.
Note: Funding is focused on integrating technology education.

Giving Philosophy

'The MCI Foundation has at its core a commitment to service: the conviction that companies have an important role in bringing economic opportunity and a better quality of life to communities. The Foundation has, as its mission, the spread of state-of-the-art information access to different parts of the country, especially isolated and underserved areas. In the 21st century, good jobs and a quality education will demand a level of technical literacy virtually unheard of even a decade ago. By supporting a variety of approaches, from elementary education, to public access through community institutions, the foundation is making tangible progress in the effort to bring Americans access to the information super highway. Our MCI Foundation efforts emphasize creativity and sustainability-our goal is to create programs that will continue to benefit communities long after grants are made.' *Friends of the Community/About MCI Website*

Financial Summary

Total Giving: $6,000,000 (1998 approx); $4,327,245 (1997); $5,000,000 (1996). Note: Contributes through corporate direct giving program and foundation. 1998 Giving includes foundation ($5,000,000); corporate direct giving ($1,000,000). 1996 Giving includes foundation ($3,910,848); scholarship ($200,000)
Assets: $7,086,266 (1997); $4,945,163 (1996); $5,292,081 (1993)
Gifts Received: $5,000,000 (1997); $6,200,000 (1996); $2,800,000 (1993). Note: In 1996, the foundation received $6,000,000 from MCI Communications Corp. and $200,000 from the William G. McGowan Charitable Fund. In 1997, the foundation received $5,000,000 form MCI Communications Corp.

Typical Recipients

Arts & Humanities: Arts Centers, Arts Outreach, Film & Video, Libraries, Museums/Galleries, Music, Performing Arts, Public Broadcasting
Civic & Public Affairs: African American Affairs, Business/Free Enterprise, Economic Development, Employment/Job Training, Civic & Public Affairs-General, Housing, Nonprofit Management, Professional & Trade Associations, Public Policy, Urban & Community Affairs
Education: Business Education, Colleges & Universities, Economic Education, Education Associations, Education Funds, Education Reform, Faculty Development, Education-General, International Studies, Legal Education, Medical Education, Private Education (Precollege), Public Education (Precollege), Science/Mathematics Education, Special Education, Student Aid
Environment: Environment-General
Health: Arthritis, Cancer, Emergency/Ambulance Services, Health Organizations, Hospitals, Medical Training, Single-Disease Health Associations
International: Human Rights
Science: Science Museums, Scientific Centers & Institutes
Social Services: Child Welfare, Emergency Relief, Family Planning, Homes, People with Disabilities, Recreation & Athletics, United Funds/United Ways, Youth Organizations

Contributions Analysis

Education: 95%. Emphasis on programs that promote technology and education, especially grades K-12.

Application Procedures

Initial Contact: a brief letter of inquiry or proposal
Application Requirements: name and address of organization, purpose of grant requested, copy of IRS 501 (c)(3) tax letter, and detailed description of how funds will be used
Deadlines: None.
Notes: The foundation is not receiving unsolicited proposals at this time.

Restrictions

The foundation does not support individuals, religious organizations for sectarian purposes, or political or lobbying groups. The foundation also does not buy advertising as a form of contribution.

Additional Information

Regional or local nonprofit organizations should submit written proposals to the public relations directors at the following MCI divisional headquarters offices:
MCI Eastern Division, 5 International Dr., Rye Brook, NY 10573 handles inquiries for Connecticut, Delaware, Maine, Massachusetts, Maryland, New Hampshire, New Jersey, New York, Pennsylvania, Rhode Island, Vermont, Virginia, and West Virginia.
MCI Central Division, 205 N. Michigan Ave., Ste. 3200, Chicago, IL 60601 handles inquiries for Illinois, Indiana, Iowa, Michigan, Minnesota, Nebraska, North Dakota, Ohio, South Dakota, and Wisconsin.
MCI West Division, 201 Spear St., 9th Fl., San Francisco, CA 94105 handles inquiries for Alaska, Arizona, California, Colorado, Hawaii, Idaho, Montana, Nevada, New Mexico, Oregon, Utah, Washington, and Wyoming.
MCI Southern Division, 400 Perimeter Ctr., Ste. 400, Atlanta, GA 30346 handles inquiries for Alabama, Arkansas, Florida, Georgia, Kansas, Kentucky, Louisiana, Mississippi, Missouri, North Carolina, South Carolina, Oklahoma, Tennessee, and Texas.
MCI WorldCom was formed from the merger of WorldCom and MCI Communications in 1998.

Corporate Officials

Bernard J. Ebbers: president, chief executive officer, director B Edmonton, AB Canada 1941. ED Mississippi College BA (1962). PRIM CORP EMPL president, chief executive officer, director: WorldCom, Inc. ADD CORP EMPL owner: Angelina Plantation; director: Biz Tel Corp.; president: Compuserve Corp.; president: EBBS; president: IDD WorldCom Services Inc.; president: Idb WorldCom Inc.; president: Ldds Kansas City Inc.; president: Lincoln Hospitality Inc.; president: Master Corp.; president: WorldCom Wireless Inc. CORP AFFIL director: Jitney Jungle America. NONPR AFFIL trustee: Mississippi College.
Timothy Price: president, chief executive officer, director B Boston, MA 1953. ED Tufts University (1975). PRIM CORP EMPL president, chief executive officer, director: MCI WorldCom Communications Corp. CORP AFFIL president: MCI Ventures Corp.; director: MCI WorldCom Inc.; president: MCI Research Inc.; president, chief operating officer: MCI Telecommunications Group.
Bert C. Roberts, Jr.: chairman B 1942. ED Johns Hopkins University BS (1965). PRIM CORP EMPL chairman: MCI WorldCom, Inc. CORP AFFIL chairman, chief executive officer: MCI Telecommunication Corp.; chairman: Teleconnect Co.
John W. Sidgmore: vice chairman

Grants Analysis

Disclosure Period: calendar year ending 1996
Total Grants: $3,910,848*
Number of Grants: 156*
Average Grant: $25,070
Highest Grant: $225,000
Typical Range: $5,000 to $25,000
***Note:** Giving excludes scholarship.

Recent Grants

Note: Grants derived from 1996 Form 990.

Arts & Humanities

135,000	Fund for AmericaN Libraries, Chicago, IL -- for library link
40,000	University of Maryland Foundation, Baltimore, MD -- medical library
35,000	Robert W. Woodruff Arts Center, Atlanta, GA -- for 1996 annual corporate campaign
30,000	Austin Public Library, Austin, TX -- for link between library and community
30,000	Cedar Falls Public Library, Cedar Falls, IA -- for link between library and community
30,000	Cedar Rapids Public Library, Cedar Rapids, IA -- for link between library and community
30,000	Dallas Public Library, Dallas, TX -- for link between library and community
30,000	Enoch Pratt Free Library, Baltimore, MD -- for link between library and community
30,000	Multnomah County Library, Portland, OR -- for link between library and community
30,000	Richmond Public Library, Richmond, VA -- for link between library and community
30,000	Springfield-Greene County Library District, Springfield, MO -- for link between library and community
30,000	Tampa-Hillsborough County Public Library System, Tampa, FL -- for link between library and community
25,000	National Symphony Orchestra Association, Washington, DC -- training for students

Civic & Public Affairs

80,000	Consumer Action, San Francisco, CA -- website
65,000	Consumer Action, San Francisco, CA -- for website
50,000	National Alliance of Business, Washington, DC -- for 1996 annual campaign
50,000	National Fraud Information Center, Washington, DC -- for internet
35,000	US Telecommunications Training Institute, Washington, DC -- training
35,000	US Telecommunications Training Institute, Washington, DC -- training

Education

225,000	Tech Corps, Sudbury, MA -- for Classroom on Wheels/Cybered
200,000	Tech Corps, Sudbury, MA -- for Classroom on Wheels/Cybered
200,000	Tech Corps, Sudbury, MA -- for Classroom on Wheels/Cybered
150,000	National Coalition for Consumer Education, Madison, NJ -- scholarships, competitions at high school level
150,000	National Coalition for Consumer Education, Madison, NJ -- scholarships, competitions for high schools
127,000	Washington Area Project for Youth, Washington, DC -- for Internet access
75,000	Leadership, Education, and Athletics in Partnership, New Haven, CT -- for Computer Learning Center
50,000	CompuMentor, San Francisco, CA -- for recruiting mentors
50,000	Heritage Classics Foundation, Hilton Head, SC -- for scholarship program
50,000	Tech Corps, Sudbury, MA -- for Classroom on Wheels/Cybered
45,000	Chicago Commons, Chicago, IL -- for technology learning center
41,000	St. Ambrose Catholic School, Baltimore, MD -- for Internet access
40,000	University of Maryland Foundation, Baltimore, MD -- for medical library
35,000	College of William and Mary, Williamsburg, VA -- for networking
35,000	Education Excellence Partnership, Washington, DC -- for Public Service Advent Campaign
30,000	Global School Net Foundation, Bonita, CA -- to educate youths with different cultures
28,500	Global School Net Foundation, Carlsbad, CA -- website

27,000 Gallaudet University, Washington, DC -- for deaf student's literacy in science
25,000 Bentonville 2000, Bentonville, AR -- for multimedia classroom
25,000 Concordia University System, Saint Louis, MO -- Hub for 10 universities
25,000 Fisher Center for Information Technology and Management, Berkeley, CA -- research of information technology
25,000 Foundation for Independent Colleges, Harrisburg, PA -- for Internet
25,000 Marshall McLuhan Center on Global Communications, San Francisco, CA -- for Teacher Award Program
25,000 Munei S. Snowden International School at Copely, Boston, MA -- to purchase hardware, software
25,000 North Harns Montgomery Community College District, Houston, TX -- for online learning environment
25,000 Points of Light Foundation, Washington, DC -- for NetDay USA Event for schools
25,000 University of Connecticut, Storrs, CT -- training, research center

International
100,000 Children's Institute International, Los Angeles, CA -- support Forum for Violence Against Children

Science
35,000 Computer Museum, Boston, MA -- for Internet
25,000 Museum of Science and Industry, Chicago, IL -- for four learning labs

Social Services
25,000 ASPIRA of Florida, Miami, FL -- for youth development program

MCKESSON-HBOC CORP.

Company Contact

San Francisco, CA
Web: http://www.mckhboc.com

Company Description

Revenue: US$30,382,300,000 (1999)
Profit: US$154,900,000
Employees: 13,350
Fortune Rank: 38, per FORTUNE Magazine's list of 500 Largest U.S. Corporations (1999).
FF 38
SIC(s): 2842 Polishes & Sanitation Goods, 3069 Fabricated Rubber Products Nec, 5047 Medical & Hospital Equipment, 5122 Drugs, Proprietaries & Sundries.

Nonmonetary Support

Value: $400,000 (1990); $250,000 (1989); $250,000 (1988)
Type: Donated Products
Note: Estimated value of nonmonetary support is about $250,000 annually.

McKesson Foundation

Giving Contact

Ms. Marcia M. Argyris, President
McKesson Foundation
1 Post St.
San Francisco, CA 94104
Phone: (415)983-9325
Fax: (415)983-7590

Description

EIN: 596144455
Organization Type: Corporate Foundation
Giving Locations: CA: San Francisco Bay area communities where company has a sizeable employee representation.
Grant Types: Capital, Employee Matching Gifts, General Support.
Note: Employee matching gift ratio: 1 to 1 for education only.

Giving Philosophy

'Playing an active role in the community is part of the way we do business at McKesson. It's more than good corporate citizenship. It's a matter of investing in each other--and in what we have in common. With more than $2,000,000 in annual grants, the McKesson Foundation supports health-related, social, educational, civic and cultural projects across the U.S. and Canada, especially for youth. We look at our role as that of a matchmaker, linking community needs with volunteers' interests and philanthropic support.'
McKesson in the Communtiy

Financial Summary

Total Giving: $2,600,000 (fiscal year ending March 31, 1998 approx); $2,234,245 (fiscal 1997); $2,313,000 (fiscal 1996). Note: Contributes through corporate direct giving program and foundation. 1998 Giving includes foundation.
Giving Analysis: Giving for fiscal 1996 includes: foundation ($1,977,460); corporate direct giving ($213,000); foundation matching gifts ($122,540); fiscal 1997: foundation ($1,862,427); foundation grants to United Way ($220,000); foundation matching gifts ($123,853); foundation scholarships ($27,965)
Assets: $24,000,000 (fiscal 1997 approx); $24,000,000 (fiscal 1996 approx); $21,000,000 (fiscal 1995 approx)

Typical Recipients

Arts & Humanities: Arts Appreciation, Dance, Museums/Galleries, Music, Opera, Performing Arts, Public Broadcasting, Theater
Civic & Public Affairs: Civic & Public Affairs-General, Legal Aid, Nonprofit Management, Public Policy, Urban & Community Affairs, Women's Affairs, Zoos/Aquariums
Education: Colleges & Universities, Education Funds, Education Reform, Private Education (Precollege), Secondary Education (Public), Special Education, Student Aid
Health: AIDS/HIV, Children's Health/Hospitals, Clinics/Medical Centers, Emergency/Ambulance Services, Hospitals, Public Health
Religion: Religious Welfare
Social Services: Camps, Child Welfare, Community Centers, Community Service Organizations, Counseling, Delinquency & Criminal Rehabilitation, Family Services, Food/Clothing Distribution, People with Disabilities, Shelters/Homelessness, Special Olympics, Substance Abuse, United Funds/United Ways, Volunteer Services, Youth Organizations

Contributions Analysis

Giving Priorities: Youth and human services; higher education, largely through matching gifts; and regional grants recommended by an employee committee to organizations in operating communities.
Arts & Humanities: 5% to 10%. Supports museums, symphonies, and the performing arts in theSan Francisco Bay Area.
Civic & Public Affairs: About 10%. Employee committees in operating communities evaluate and recommend grants. 5% to 10%. Supports volunteer centers and public broadcasting. Less than 5%. Primarily encourages and supports employee volunteers. The company has created special grant programs: the Community Action Team Fund Grant program, which supports nonprofit organizations in which fiveor more McKesson employees and retirees are involved on a volunteer basis (grants range from $500 to $5,000); the Community Action Fund Grant program, which funds nonprofits with grants for specific items or special programs (grants range up to $1,000 and are limited to organizations where employees, retirees, or their spouses volunteer); and the Neil Harlan Award for Community Service program, which awards grants to organizations appointed by chosen employees who are being honored for community service (grants to nonprofits range from $300 to $5,000 and employees must work for company for one year).
Education: About 20%. Contributions support colleges, universities, and other educational institutions, both in the form of grants and through the employee matching gifts program. Also supports scholarships.
Social Services: 60%. (Health programs for at-risk children) Priority is given to youth educational enrichment programs, especially those that deal with the prevention of substance abuse, development of decision-making skills, exploration of career directions, after-school community service projects, and K-12 public school education. The company's program is divided into three components: Learning Exchange (tutoring program), Work Experience Program, and Summer Youth Employment Program. Emphasis is on pre-teen and adolescent age groups. Other areas of interest include emergency services for families in crisis, including emergency food programs,services for runaway youth, and shelter for mothers and children in temporary crisis situations.

Application Procedures

Initial Contact: request guidelines, then letter of request (one to three pages)
Application Requirements: organization's mission and purpose; purpose and description of the program for which funding is requested; what the program is expected to accomplish, how results will meet community needs, and how results will be evaluated; amount requested; itemized program budget; description of any expected cooperation or collaboration with other community organizations; list of board of directors; organization's budget for prior and current funding year, including list of funding sources and amounts; proof of tax-exempt status
Deadlines: None.
Review Process: foundation directors meet quarterly
Evaluative Criteria: priority is given to projects that deal with youth or emergency concerns; have a strong volunteer base; address manageable problems; and provide McKesson with the opportunity to bring businesses, agencies, schools, and community leaders together to work toward a common goal
Decision Notification: 30 to 90 days after receipt

Restrictions

Grants are not made to endowment campaigns, individuals, religious organizations for sectarian purposes, advertising or charitable publications, political causes or campaigns, research studies, or health organizations concentrating on one disease.

Additional Information

The foundation recognizes the value of new programs created to respond to changing needs and considers grants to projects of an original or pioneering nature.
Publications: Foundation Annual Report

Corporate Officials

David L. Mahoney: co-chief executive officerceo, director, chairman B Brighton, MA 1954. ED Princeton University AB (1975); Harvard University MBA (1981). PRIM CORP EMPL co-chief executive officer: McKesson HBOC Inc. CORP AFFIL president: McKesson Corp. DE; president: McKesson Pharm International Services; director: Cytel Corp. CLUB AFFIL City Club.
Ivan D. Meyerson: vice president, general counsel ED University of California at Berkeley AB (1966); Stanford University JD (1969). PRIM CORP EMPL vice president, general counsel: McKesson Corp. ADD CORP EMPL vice president: McKesson HBOC Inc.
Mark A. Pulido: president, chief executive officer, director, chairman B 1952. ED University of Arizona BS (1976); University of Minnesota MS (1977). PRIM

CORP EMPL president, chief executive officer, director, chairman: McKesson Corp. CORP AFFIL chairman: Medimart Inc.; president: Medinet Inc.; director: Imation Enterprises Inc.

Foundation Officials

Marcia M. Argyris: president
Tom Capizzi: trustee
Jon W. d'Alessio: trustee B Ross, CA 1946. ED University of California at Berkeley (1968); Stanford University (1974). PRIM CORP EMPL treasurer: McKesson Corp. CORP AFFIL treasurer: Armar All Products Corp. NONPR AFFIL member: Financial Executives Institute; member: National Association of Corporate Treasurers; member: Association for Corporate Growth.
Donna Draher: trustee
Tom George: trustee
Larry Kurtz: trustee ED Princeton University AB. PRIM CORP EMPL vice president corp. communication: McKesson HBOC Inc.
Claudia Newbold: trustee
Kim Salley: trustee
Tim Warner: trustee

Grants Analysis

Disclosure Period: fiscal year ending March 31, 1997
Total Grants: $1,862,427*
Number of Grants: 146 (approx)
Average Grant: $12,756
Highest Grant: $92,000
Typical Range: $2,500 to $15,000
***Note:** Giving excludes matching gifts; scholarships; United Way.

Recent Grants

Note: Grants derived from 1996 Annual Report.

Arts & Humanities

25,000 American Conservatory Theater, San Francisco, CA
25,000 Committee to Restore the Opera House, San Francisco, CA
25,000 KQED, San Francisco, CA
17,000 San Francisco Symphony, San Francisco, CA
10,000 San Francisco Museum of Modern Art, San Francisco, CA

Civic & Public Affairs

25,000 San Francisco Zoological Society, San Francisco, CA
15,000 Central City Hospitality House, San Francisco, CA
12,000 Walden House, San Francisco, CA
10,000 San Francisco Urban Service Project, San Francisco, CA
10,000 Youth Law Center, San Francisco, CA

Education

138,500 Citizens Scholarship Foundation of America, Saint Peter, MN
92,292 National Merit Scholarship Corp, Evanston, IL
29,360 Thomas E. Drohan Scholarship Program
20,000 University of California Berkeley, Berkeley, CA -- Incentive Awards Program
15,000 Partners in School Innovation, San Francisco, CA
15,000 San Francisco Educational Services, San Francisco, CA
13,500 Enterprise for High School Students, San Francisco, CA
10,500 San Francisco Education Fund, San Francisco, CA
10,000 Audrey L. Smith Development Center and Freedom School, San Francisco, CA

Health

25,000 Asian Health Services, Oakland, CA
25,000 Lucile Salter Packard Children's Hospital at Stanford, Stanford, CA
20,900 San Francisco General Hospital Foundation, San Francisco, CA
12,000 Mission Neighborhood Health Center, San Francisco, CA
10,000 American Red Cross, Oklahoma City, OK
10,000 Northern California Grantmakers, San Francisco, CA -- AIDS Task Force
10,000 San Francisco Community Clinic Consortium, San Francisco, CA

Religion

32,600 Young Life, San Francisco, CA
10,000 Catholic Charities, San Rafael, CA
10,000 St. Mary's Center, Oakland, CA
10,000 Salvation Army, San Francisco, CA

Social Services

150,000 United Way Bay Area, San Francisco, CA
25,000 Girls, Incorporated Alameda County, CA
25,000 San Francisco Food Bank, San Francisco, CA
19,500 Columbia Park Boys and Girls Club, San Francisco, CA
15,000 Children Now, Oakland, CA
15,000 Hamilton Family Center, San Francisco, CA
15,000 Jubilee West, Oakland, CA
15,000 Northern California Grantmakers, San Francisco, CA -- AmeriCorps Program
15,000 Raphael House, San Francisco, CA
15,000 San Francisco Special Olympics, San Francisco, CA
14,500 Center for Living Skills, Lafayette, CA
12,900 San Francisco School Volunteers, San Francisco, CA
12,500 Aim High, San Francisco, CA
12,000 Bay Area Women's and Children's Center, San Francisco, CA
10,200 Coleman Advocates for Children and Youth, San Francisco, CA
10,000 Alameda County Community Food Bank, Oakland, CA
10,000 Alumni Resources, San Francisco, CA
10,000 Boys and Girls Clubs, Oakland, CA
10,000 Compass Community Services, San Francisco, CA
10,000 Utah Boys Ranch, West Jordan, UT

McWane Inc.

Company Contact

Birmingham, AL

Company Description

Employees: 4,200
SIC(s): 3321 Gray & Ductile Iron Foundries, 3491 Industrial Valves.

McWane Foundation

Giving Contact

Jeanette Sommers, Corporate Secretary
2900 Highway 280, Suite 300
Birmingham, AL 35223
Phone: (205)414-3100
Fax: (205)414-3180

Description

Founded: 1961
EIN: 636044384
Organization Type: Corporate Foundation
Giving Locations: AL
Grant Types: Capital, General Support, Scholarship.

Financial Summary

Total Giving: $2,004,066 (1997); $1,302,000 (1996); $320,100 (1993)
Assets: $813,693 (1997); $982,159 (1996); $1,270,414 (1993)
Gifts Received: $1,775,000 (1997); $1,300,000 (1996); $400,000 (1993). Note: In 1996 and 1997, contributions were received from McWane, Inc.

Typical Recipients

Arts & Humanities: Arts Associations & Councils, Arts Festivals, Arts Funds, Ballet, Dance, Museums/Galleries, Music, Performing Arts, Public Broadcasting
Civic & Public Affairs: Civil Rights, Clubs, Economic Development, Civic & Public Affairs-General, Law & Justice, Philanthropic Organizations, Safety, Urban & Community Affairs, Zoos/Aquariums
Education: Arts/Humanities Education, Business Education, Colleges & Universities, Education Reform, Engineering/Technological Education, Education-General, Literacy, Private Education (Precollege), Public Education (Precollege), Student Aid
Environment: Environment-General
Health: Cancer, Children's Health/Hospitals, Diabetes, Emergency/Ambulance Services, Heart, Hospitals, Mental Health, Multiple Sclerosis, Single-Disease Health Associations
Religion: Churches, Jewish Causes, Religious Welfare, Social/Policy Issues
Science: Science Museums
Social Services: Animal Protection, At-Risk Youth, Big Brother/Big Sister, Community Service Organizations, Crime Prevention, Family Services, Recreation & Athletics, Scouts, Substance Abuse, YMCA/YWCA/YMHA/YWHA, Youth Organizations

Application Procedures

Initial Contact: send written request
Deadlines: None.

Corporate Officials

Glenda Burson: vice president, treasurer, chief executive officer, treasurer PRIM CORP EMPL vice president, treasurer: McWane.
John J. McMahon, Jr.: chairman, president, chief executive officer, treasurer PRIM CORP EMPL chairman, president, chief executive officer, treasurer: McWane Inc. CORP AFFIL director: John H. Harland Co.; director: Protective Life Corp.; director: Birmingham Airport Authority; chief executive officer: Clow Corp.

Foundation Officials

John J. McMahon, Jr.: trustee (see above)

Grants Analysis

Disclosure Period: calendar year ending 1997
Total Grants: $2,004,066
Number of Grants: 35
Average Grant: $28,061*
Highest Grant: $1,050,000
Typical Range: $500 to $50,000
***Note:** Average grant figure excludes highest grant.

Recent Grants

Note: Grants derived from 1998 Form 990.

Arts & Humanities

1,000,000 Mcwane Center, Birmingham, AL
30,000 Alabama Symphony Orchestra, Birmingham, AL
10,000 Alabama Ballet, Birmingham, AL
10,000 Birmingham International Festival, Birmingham, AL
7,500 Robinson & Robinson Communications, Chicago, IL
5,000 Alabama Shakespeare Festival, Birmingham, AL
2,500 Alabama Humanities Foundation, Birmingham, AL

1,000 Metropolitan Arts Council, Birmingham, AL
1,000 Southern Playworks, Birmingham, AL
500 Jr. Patrons/Birmingham Museum of Art, Birmingham, AL

Civic & Public Affairs
60,000 Birmingham Civil Rights Institute, Birmingham, AL
33,333 Reading Alabama, Inc., Rye Brook, NY
15,000 Urban Development Group, Birmingham, AL
10,000 Region 2020, Birmingham, AL
2,500 Junior League of Birmingham, Birmingham, AL

Education
59,000 Birmingham Southern College, Birmingham, AL
50,000 University of Alabama, Birmingham, AL
50,000 Vanderbilt University, Evanston, IL
40,000 Mountain Brook City Schools Foundation, Birmingham, AL
24,000 Auburn University, Birmingham, AL
16,500 Bryant Jordan Scholarship, Birmingham, AL
15,000 A Research Foundation, Birmingham, AL
10,000 Robert T. Jones Scholarship, Atlanta, GA
9,000 Junior Achievement, Birmingham, AL
5,000 A Coalition for Better Education, Montgomery, AL
500 Bga/Lady Legacy Scholarship, Birmingham, AL

Health
10,000 Juvenile Diabetes Foundation, Atlanta, GA
1,500 Cystic Fibrosis Foundation, Birmingham, AL
1,000 American Heart Association, Birmingham, AL

Religion
10,000 Birmingham Jewish Foundation, Birmingham, AL
5,000 National Conference of Christians and Jews, Birmingham, AL
1,000 First Christian Church, Atlanta, GA -- memorial for mr. allison

Social Services
30,000 YWCA, Birmingham, AL
2,000 Birmingham Fop Lodge, Birmingham, AL
2,000 Service Guild of Birmingham, Birmingham, AL
1,500 Big Brothers/Big Sisters, Birmingham, AL
1,000 Birmingham Humane Society, Birmingham, AL
1,000 The King's Ranch, Birmingham, AL

MEAD CORP.

Company Contact
Dayton, OH
Web: http://www.mead.com

Company Description
Revenue: US$4,579,200,000
Employees: 16,100
Fortune Rank: 423, per FORTUNE Magazine's list of 500 Largest U.S. Corporations (1999).
FF 423
SIC(s): 2411 Logging, 2421 Sawmills & Planing Mills--General, 2426 Hardwood Dimension & Flooring Mills, 2621 Paper Mills.

Operating Locations
Operates internationally.

Nonmonetary Support
Range: $550,000 - $750,000
Type: Donated Equipment; Donated Products; In-kind Services
Note: Nonmonetary support is provided by the company.

Mead Corp. Foundation

Giving Contact
R.F. Budzik, Executive Director
Mead Corp. Foundation
Courthouse Plaza, Northeast
Dayton, OH 45463
Phone: (937)495-3849
Fax: (937)495-4103
Web: http://www.mead.com/corpcontributions/corpcontributions.cfm
Note: Submit requests for education grants to the foundation.

Description
Founded: 1957
EIN: 316040645
Organization Type: Corporate Foundation
Giving Locations: operating locations.
Grant Types: Capital, Employee Matching Gifts, General Support, Multiyear/Continuing Support, Project.
Note: Employee matching gift ratio: 1 to 1. Higher education is matched for $50 or more up to $5,000. Volunteer leader grants are matched of $25 or more up to $2,500.

Financial Summary
Total Giving: $3,379,175 (1997); $3,250,200 (1996); $2,776,338 (1995). Note: Contributes through corporate direct giving program and foundation. Giving includes foundation. 1996 Giving includes United Way ($618,748).
Assets: $36,425,443 (1997); $32,091,378 (1996); $25,494,130 (1995)
Gifts Received: $2,000,000 (1996); $2,000,200 (1995); $5,000,000 (1994). Note: Contributions are received from Mead Corp.

Typical Recipients
Arts & Humanities: Arts Associations & Councils, Arts Centers, Arts Festivals, Arts Institutes, Community Arts, Dance, Historic Preservation, History & Archaeology, Libraries, Museums/Galleries, Music, Opera, Performing Arts, Public Broadcasting, Theater
Civic & Public Affairs: African American Affairs, Botanical Gardens/Parks, Business/Free Enterprise, Chambers of Commerce, Community Foundations, Economic Development, Civic & Public Affairs-General, Municipalities/Towns, Native American Affairs, Philanthropic Organizations, Safety, Urban & Community Affairs, Women's Affairs, Zoos/Aquariums
Education: Arts/Humanities Education, Colleges & Universities, Community & Junior Colleges, Continuing Education, Economic Education, Education Associations, Education Funds, Education Reform, Engineering/Technological Education, Health & Physical Education, Literacy, Minority Education, Public Education (Precollege), Science/Mathematics Education, Secondary Education (Public), Vocational & Technical Education
Environment: Resource Conservation
Health: Diabetes, Emergency/Ambulance Services, Hospices, Public Health
International: International Development, International Organizations
Religion: Missionary Activities (Domestic), Religious Welfare
Science: Science Museums, Scientific Centers & Institutes
Social Services: Child Welfare, Community Service Organizations, Domestic Violence, Family Services, Food/Clothing Distribution, Scouts, Shelters/Homelessness, Special Olympics, United Funds/United Ways, YMCA/YWCA/YMHA/YWHA, Youth Organizations

Contributions Analysis
Giving Priorities: Health and human services, education, culture and civic.
Arts & Humanities: 15% to 20%. Priorities include arts funds and institutes, museums, and public broadcasting. Arts centers, historic preservation, and libraries are also of interest.
Civic & Public Affairs: Less than 5%. Main interests are environmental affairs and economic development. Also supports housing, business, safety, and public policy groups.
Education: 35% to 40%. Supports colleges and universities; emphasis on technical, precollege, and business education.
Health: 40% to 45%. Primary emphasis is on united fund drives. Other priorities include youth organizations and community service organizations.
Note: Company also offers a matching gift program for higher education and volunteer leaders.

Application Procedures
Initial Contact: Request guidelines; submit a written request to local Mead unit manager.
Application Requirements: a description of organization, including need, area of service, and population served; amount requested, purpose of funds and benefits provided; list of board of directors and officers; recently audited financial statement; proof of tax-exempt status; current budget; and statement decribing how success of project will be measured.
Deadlines: None.
Review Process: Initial review by local Mead unit manager or foundation staff, then referred to governing committee for decision.
Evaluative Criteria: Program provides greater efficiency and coordination of services, or use an integrated problem solving approach; encourage citizen involvement and volunteerism; and deal with root problems rather than secondary ones.
Decision Notification: Within six weeks of receipt.

Restrictions
Does not support individuals; national, fraternal, labor, or veterans' organizations, religious or denominational organizations for religious purposes; political parties or candidates; loans; organizations, including colleges and universities, outside operating areas; or tax-supported institutions, excluding schools. Also, does not support goodwill advertising, dinners, or tickets, grants for operating support, or organizations already supported by United Way.

Additional Information
Mead unit managers review local requests and are encouraged to adjust charitable priorities to meet local needs.
Publications: Guidelines

Corporate Officials
Jerome F. Tatar: chairman, chief executive officer, president

Foundation Officials
Ronald F. Budzik: executive director PRIM CORP EMPL vice president government affairs: The Mead Corp.
Kathryn Strawn: vice president, administrative officer

Grants Analysis
Disclosure Period: calendar year ending 1997
Total Grants: $3,379,175
Number of Grants: 700 (approx)
Average Grant: $4,827

Highest Grant: $250,000
Typical Range: $100 to $15,000

Recent Grants

Note: Grants derived from 1997 Form 990.

Arts & Humanities

100,000	Cultural Works
26,000	William Bonifas Fine Arts Center, Escanaba, MI
25,600	Dayton Opera Association, Dayton, OH -- educational
25,000	Pine Mountain Music Festival, Iron Mountain, MI
13,500	Dayton Art Institute, Dayton, OH

Civic & Public Affairs

150,000	Miami Valley Economic Development Research Corporation, Dayton, OH
100,000	Uptown Columbus, Columbus, OH -- educational
60,200	Dayton Urban League, Dayton, OH
35,000	Cincinnati Zoo and Botanical Garden, Cincinnati, OH -- educational
30,000	Phenix City-Russell Foundation, Phenix City, AL
25,000	BAWAC, Florence, KY -- educational

Education

100,375	Michigan Technological University, Houghton, MI -- educational
75,600	Florida A&M University, Sarasota, FL -- educational
59,000	Chillicothe City Schools -- health, human services
54,370	University of Dayton, Dayton, OH -- educational
43,400	Rapid River Public Schools, Rapid River, MI -- educational
42,297	Northern Michigan University Development Fund, Marquette, MI -- educational
34,200	Chillicothe High School, Chillicothe, OH -- educational
31,500	Ross County Public School -- educational
30,000	Alliance for Education, Worcester, MA -- educational
30,000	Dayton Area Graduate Studies Institute, Dayton, OH -- educational
30,000	Vinton County School Education Foundation, McArthur, OH -- educational
26,900	Delta Schoolcraft Intermediate School District -- educational
25,600	Troy State University Foundation, Troy State University, AL -- educational
25,000	Muscogee Educational Excellence Foundation, Columbus, GA -- educational
20,000	Ohio University Chillicothe, Chillicothe, OH -- educational
15,400	University of Cincinnati Foundation, Cincinnati, OH -- educational
13,525	Wright State University Foundation, Fairborn, OH -- educational
11,275	Auburn University Foundation, Auburn University, AL
10,874	Missouri Western College Foundation, St. Joseph, MO -- educational

Health

50,000	St. Joseph Residential Treatment and Child Care Center -- health, human services
20,000	Southern Healthcare -- health, human services
13,125	American National Red Cross, Dayton, OH -- health, human services

Science

250,000	Dayton Society of Natural History, Dayton Museum of Natural History, Dayton, OH -- educational

Social Services

170,000	Ross County Coalition Against Domestic Violence, Chillicothe, OH -- health, human services
84,050	United Way of Ross County, Chillicothe, OH -- health, human services
83,000	YMCA, Dayton, OH -- health, human services
80,000	United Way, Dayton, OH -- health, human services
50,500	United Way, Atlanta, GA -- health, human services
50,000	Rise -- health, human services
50,000	United Way of Delta County, Escanaba, MI -- health, human services
46,000	United Way, St. Joseph, MO -- health, human services
32,900	United Way of Huntingdon County Fund, Huntingdon, PA -- health, human services
31,000	United Way of Neenah-Menasha, WI -- health, human services
22,970	United Way of Columbus, Phenix City, and Fort Benning -- health, human services
20,439	Berkshire United Way, Pittsfield, MA -- health, human services
13,500	Orange County United Crusade/West -- health, human services
12,400	Greater Kalamazoo United Way, Kalamazoo, MI -- health, human services
11,025	United Way of the Bay Area, San Francisco, CA -- health, human services
10,200	United Way of the Columbia-Willamette, Portland, OR -- health, human services

MEDTRONIC, INC.

 Number 89 of Top 100 Corporate Givers

Company Contact

Minneapolis, MN
Web: http://www.medtronic.com

Company Description

Revenue: US$4,134,100,000 (1999)
Profit: US$468,400,000 (1999)
Employees: 12,466
Fortune Rank: 381, per FORTUNE Magazine's list of 500 Largest U.S. Corporations (1999).
FF 381
SIC(s): 3841 Surgical & Medical Instruments, 3845 Electromedical Equipment.

Operating Locations

Australia: Medtronic Australasia Pty. Ltd., Northbridge; Austria: Medtronic Osterreich GmbH, Vienna; Vitatron GmbH, Vienna; Belgium: Medtronic Belgium NV, Grimbergen, Brabant; Medtronic Europe NV, Grimbergen, Brabant; Vitatron Belgium NV, Leuven, Brabant; Brazil: Medtronic do Brasil Ltda., Barueri; Canada: Medtronic of Canada Ltd., Mississauga; France: Vitatron, Paris, Ville-de-Paris; Medtronic France, Rueil Malmaison; Germany: Vitatron GmbH, Cologne, Nordrhein-Westfalen; Medtronic GmbH, Duesseldorf; Cardiotron Medizintechnik GmbH, Halle, De-Ost; Hong Kong: Medtronic International Ltd., Wan Chai; Italy: Biotec International SRL, Bologna, Emilia-Romagna; Medtronic Italia SpA, Milano, Lombardia; Japan: Medtronic Japan Co. Ltd., Tokyo; Netherlands: Vitatron Beheersmaatschappij BV, Dieren, Gelderland; Vitatron Medical BV, Dieren, Gelderland; Vitatron NV, Dieren, Gelderland; BV Medtronic FSC, Kerkrade, Limburg; Medtronic BV, Kerkrade, Limburg; Bakken Research Center BV, Maastricht, Limburg; Vitatron Nederland BV, Veenendaal, Utrecht; Vitatron Scientific BV, Velp, Gelderland; Spain: Medtronic Iberica SA, Madrid; Vitatron Medical Espana SA, Madrid; Switzerland: Medtronic (Schweiz) AG, Duebendorf, Zurich; United Kingdom: Q R S Ltd., London; Vitatron United Kingdom Ltd., Marlow, Buckinghamshire; Medtronic Ltd., Watford, Hertfordshire; Venezuela: Medtronic de Venezuela SA, Caracas
Note: Operates in Canada, Europe, and Asia.

Nonmonetary Support

Value: $144,015 (1996); $4,700,000 (1994); $3,500,000 (1993)
Type: Donated Equipment; Donated Products
Note: Nonmonetary support is provided by the company. 1998 nonmonetary support ($1,300,000).

Corporate Sponsorship

Note: Support depends on the area and is very limited.

Medtronic Foundation

Giving Contact

Ms. Penny Hunt, Executive Director, Community Affairs
Medtronic Foundation
7000 Central Ave., NE
Minneapolis, MN 55432
Phone: (612)514-3024
Fax: (612)514-3464
Web: http://www.medtronic.com/foundation

Description

EIN: 411306950
Organization Type: Corporate Foundation
Giving Locations: MN: Minneapolis metropolitan area, St. Paul metropolitan area internationally in Medtronic plant communities; nationally in Medtronic plant communities.
Grant Types: Employee Matching Gifts, Project.
Note: The foundation matches gifts to educational institutions up to $4,000 per employee annually.

Giving Philosophy

'Since our company was founded in 1949, Medtronic has been dedicated to being a good corporate citizen. To maintain good citizenship as a company is part of the mission statement that has guided Metronic for more than 40 years. As a corporate citizen, we seek to share our success and make positive contributions to the communities in which we operate. For us, that includes employee volunteerism, a focused grant program, product donations and special corporate programs.' *Commitment To Our Communities*, Medtronic 1993 Corporate Citizenship Report

Financial Summary

Total Giving: $8,139,216 (fiscal year ending April 30, 1998); $7,175,000 (fiscal 1997); $4,860,000 (fiscal 1996). Note: Contributes through corporate direct giving program and foundation. Giving includes corporate direct giving; foundation; nonmonetary support. Fiscal 1997 Giving includes corporate direct giving ($600,000); foundation ($6,506,200); nonmonetary support.
Assets: $7,311,400 (fiscal 1997); $1,262,453 (fiscal 1996); $1,224,093 (fiscal 1995)
Gifts Received: $4,910,000 (fiscal 1996); $3,900,000 (fiscal 1995). Note: Contributions are received from Medtronic, Inc.

Typical Recipients

Arts & Humanities: Arts Centers, Arts Institutes, Arts Outreach, Arts & Humanities-General, Libraries, Museums/Galleries, Music, Opera, Performing Arts, Public Broadcasting, Theater, Visual Arts
Civic & Public Affairs: African American Affairs, Botanical Gardens/Parks, Community Foundations, Employment/Job Training, Hispanic Affairs, Housing, Municipalities/Towns, Safety, Urban & Community Affairs, Zoos/Aquariums

Education: Arts/Humanities Education, Business Education, Colleges & Universities, Community & Junior Colleges, Education Reform, Elementary Education (Private), Engineering/Technological Education, Faculty Development, Education-General, Health & Physical Education, Medical Education, Minority Education, Private Education (Precollege), Public Education (Precollege), Science/Mathematics Education, Student Aid
Health: Adolescent Health Issues, Cancer, Children's Health/Hospitals, Clinics/Medical Centers, Emergency/Ambulance Services, Geriatric Health, Health Policy/Cost Containment, Health Organizations, Heart, Hospitals, Long-Term Care, Nursing Services, Preventive Medicine/Wellness Organizations, Public Health, Trauma Treatment
International: Foreign Educational Institutions, International-General, Health Care/Hospitals, International Affairs, International Environmental Issues, International Relief Efforts
Religion: Religious Welfare
Science: Science Exhibits & Fairs, Science Museums, Scientific Centers & Institutes
Social Services: At-Risk Youth, Community Centers, Community Service Organizations, Family Services, Senior Services, United Funds/United Ways, Volunteer Services, YMCA/YWCA/YMHA/YWHA, Youth Organizations

Contributions Analysis

Giving Priorities: Programs that improve employment opportunities and life for noninstitutionalized elderly people, higher education for women and minorities in science and medicine, health programs, and Twin Cities performing arts groups. Medtronic works with U.S. nonprofit organizations to provide Medtronic products for the care of indigent patients around the world. In 1994, the foundation launched an international grant program, with guidelines similar to domestic interests. Interests include post-secondary education; art, human service, and civic programs; and health organizations. Company contributions are only a part of Medtronic's philanthropy. Employee volunteerism is encouraged and promoted worldwide.
Arts & Humanities: Less than 5%. Funds public television, orchestral association and the Institute of Arts.
Civic & Public Affairs: 5% to 10%. Grants are made to strengthen communities, and specifically to improve the lives of people who are socioeconomically disadvantaged, through grants to selected human service, arts and culture, and civic programs. United Ways are supported by Medtronic employees through employee campaigns; human service programs that benefit disadvantaged children and youth and their families; programs of arts organizations that increase access to the arts by people who are disadvantaged; civic organizations that address the needs of the disadvantaged; and cultural organizations that make significant contributions to the life of the community.
Education: 50% to 55%. Supports K-12 education, with focus on kindergarten through grade 12 science education programs under STAR (Science and Technology Are Rewarding), a grant initiative designed to stimulate and sustain the interest of young people in science. Limited funding is available for creative programs that have a lasting impact on children. Post-secondary education is supported with grants in programs that benefit those traditionally underrepresented in science, technology, engineering or health, socio-economically disadvantaged students and women.
Health: 5% to 10%. Grants are provided under the Medtronic Healthy Tomorrows Programs to programs and projects that directly impact the lives of community members who are most in need. Supports projects that: serve economically disadvantaged people, cultural communities, and those most vulnerable in operating communities; address the need to strengthen the capacity of communities, violence, access to health care, and developing and maintaining healthy lifestyles; involve the people most affected by the problem in defining and then delivering the solutions; emphasize prevention of health problems, includingoutreach efforts, support groups, health education, and supportive services; and include partnerships and collaborations in the sponsorship of programs. Special consideration is given to projects that focus on diseases or conditions that are addressed by Medtronic as a business, including: heart disease, neurological disorders, incontinence, sleep apnea, and chronic pain.
International: 5%. International affairs.
Science: 5% to 10%. Funds science education and science museums.
Social Services: 15% to 20%. Majority of funds support United Way. Other funds support YMCA, YWCA and social services.

Application Procedures

Initial Contact: call or write for application form and guidelines, then written proposal
Application Requirements: brief a description of organization; all previous Medtronic Foundation grants received by organization; current requested amount of funds and purpose for their use; project description, including constituents served, geographic area, use of volunteers, major accomplishments; implementation timetable; evaluation criteria; organization's current operating budget, including income (with top five donors and amounts given), and anticipated expenses; budget for proposed project, including income, expenses and grants pending; for requests for renewal of support provide brief but specific report on results of grant; copy of IRS 501(c)(3) nonprofit determination letter; list of officers and directors and their affiliations; latest annual report; most recent audited financial statement; any other information that aids in understanding how the organization or program operates
Deadlines: None, for grants of $10,000 or less; for $10,000 or more, the 15th of February, April, July, and October; arts requests in the Twin Cities must be received by April 15
Review Process: requests are reviewed by staff, then go to appropriate committee, and, if necessary, to the foundation board; the board is comprised of members of Medtronic's management; and foundation has four standing committees, comprised of company employees and the board members; employee committees in communities outside Minneapolis-St. Paul determine grants up to $20,000 in their communities
Evaluative Criteria: programs that receive funds usually; support a Medtronic focus area of emphasis; are innovative, yet simple in design; address factors causing problems in lives of people; are developed or implemented with assistance of Medtronic employees; and serve as a model that could be replicated in other communities
Decision Notification: September, December, April, and June, for grants of more than $10,000; within 90 days of receipt for requests of $10,000 or less
Notes: Foundation accepts the Minnesota Common Application Form.

Restrictions

The foundation does not support health treatment or scientific research; advertising; primarily social organizations or functions; fundraising events; lobbying, religious, or political activities; individuals; fraternal organizations; building endowments; general support for educational institutions; United Way funded agencies; or long-term counseling and personal development.
Only in special situations will foundation consider programs outside of operating communities, multiyear commitments, or capital and endowment grants requests. outside of operating communities, multiyear commitments, or capital and endowment grants requests.

Additional Information

Company is committed to contributing at least 2% of pretax profits to charitable organizations. Company sponsors employee volunteer programs and supports minority vendors whenever possible.
For direct gifts, a committee--comprised of the company's president and ceo, company's vice-chairman, and the foundation's chairman--considers grants request. Most contributions are for one-time projects or events and to organizations supported by employees in their communities. Some corporate contributions are leveraged with additional support from public relations, employee relations, or customer relations. Medtronic facilities also provide some contributions to projects and programs in their immediate vicinity and are generally less than $250.
Publications: Medtronic Community Affairs Annual Report; Application Form; Medtronic Foundation Matching Gifts to Education Program; Foundation Guidelines; Matching Gifts to Education Form

Corporate Officials

Arthur D. Collins: chief operating officer vice president human resources
Janet S. Fiola: senior vice president human resources PRIM CORP EMPL senior vice president human resources: Medtronic Inc.
William Wallace George: chief executive officer, chairman B Muskegon, MI 1942. ED Georgia Institute of Technology BS (1964); Harvard University MBA (1966). PRIM CORP EMPL chief executive officer, chairman: Medtronic, Inc. CORP AFFIL director: Toro Co.; director: Valspar Corp.; director: Medtronic Bio-Medicus Inc.; director: Imation Corp.; director: Imation Enterprises Inc.; director: Allina Health System Inc.; director: Dayton Hudson Corp.; trustee: Abbott-Northwestern Hospital. NONPR AFFIL chairman: Minnesota Thunder Pro Soccer; member: Sigma Chi; chairman: Health Industry Manufacturers Association; vice chairman: Minnesota Institute of the Arts. CLUB AFFIL Minnesota Club; Minikahda Club.
Glen David Nelson, MD: vice chairman ED Harvard University BA (1959); Minnesota University MD (1963). PRIM CORP EMPL vice chairman: Medtronic, Inc. CORP AFFIL director: Saint Paul Companies Inc.; director: ReliaStar Financial Corp.; director: Carlson Holdings Inc.; director: Medtronic Bio-Medicus Inc.; director: Carlson Co. Inc. NONPR AFFIL member: Jackson Hole Group; professor: University Minnesota; member: Hennepin County Medicine Association; member: American Medical Association; member: Greater Minneapolis Chamber of Commerce; member: American College Physician Executives; member: American Academy Medicine Directors.

Giving Program Officials

Penny Hunt: executive director staff PRIM CORP EMPL executive director community affairs: Medtronic, Inc.

Foundation Officials

Deborah Ashton: secretary
Carmen Diersen: treasurer
Penny Hunt: executive director staff (see above)
Lowell Jacobsen: chairman
Stanton D. Myrum: chairman communications committee PRIM CORP EMPL vice president technology & operations Medtronic Europe: Medtronic, Inc.
Bob Ryan: vice chairman

Grants Analysis

Disclosure Period: fiscal year ending April 30, 1997
Total Grants: $7,166,788*
Number of Grants: 375 (approx)
Average Grant: $19,111
Highest Grant: $1,000,000
Typical Range: $2,000 to $20,000
***Note:** Giving excludes matching gifts; volunteerism; United Way.

Recent Grants

Note: Grants derived from fiscal 1998 Form 990.

Arts & Humanities

150,000 Bakken Library and Museum of Electricity in Life, Minneapolis, MN -- Educational Programs
138,138 National Public Radio, Washington, DC -- Underwriting Support for Morning Edition
67,500 Minneapolis Institute of Arts, Minneapolis, MN -- Public Programs and Audio Tour Guide Program
66,000 Walker Art Center, Minneapolis, MN -- Free First Saturdays and Art Lab on Wheels
38,000 Twin Cities Public Television, Minneapolis, MN -- Underwrite Nova, New Explorers and the Body Electric
29,285 Time-n-Talent Fund, Minneapolis, MN

Civic & Public Affairs

120,000 Dallas, Dallas, TX
90,000 Maricopa County, Maricopa County, AZ
84,000 Appleton/Calumet County, Appleton, WI
82,000 Buffalo, Buffalo, NY
80,000 St. Louis, St. Louis, MO
80,000 Tampa, Tampa, FL
73,938 Indianapolis, Indianapolis, IN
68,000 Fayette County, Fayette County, GA
60,000 Bergen County, Bergen County, NJ
50,000 City of Fridley, Fridley, MN -- Fridley Community Center
50,000 Westmoreland County, Westmoreland County, PA
48,000 Houston, Houston, TX
32,250 Minnesota Zoo, Minneapolis, MN -- Zoo Mentor Program
20,000 East Hartford, East Hartford, CT
19,454 Minneapolis Suburbs, Minneapolis, MN

Education

87,000 Teacher and Instructional Services, Minneapolis, MN -- Science Center Revitalization
85,000 University of St. Thomas, Minneapolis, MN -- Support of Fellowship in Health Policy
50,000 Johns Hopkins University, Baltimore, MD -- Medtronic Fellowships
50,000 Massachusetts Institute of Technology, Boston, MA -- Medtronic Fellowships
50,000 Minnesota Private College Fund, Minneapolis, MN -- Medtronic Scholars
50,000 Morehouse School of Medicine, Atlanta, GA -- Scholarships
50,000 North Community High School, St. Paul, MN -- Narrowing the Gap in Science
49,864 Metropolitan Federation of Alternative Schools, Minneapolis, MN -- MFAS Science Curriculum Project
33,220 Western Michigan University Foundation, Kalamazoo, MI -- Pre-Service Science Teacher Course
30,000 Roosevelt High School, Minneapolis, MN -- Health/Careers Medical Magnet
30,000 Summit Academy, OIC, St. Paul, MN -- Career and Technology Center

Health

50,000 Allina Foundation, Minneapolis, MN -- Illegible Text House - AIDS Program
30,000 Regions Hospital Foundation, St. Paul, MN -- Bilingual Bicultural Partners in Health Education

International

80,000 Rotary International District 3060, India -- Heart Needs Your Attention, South & Central Gujarat, India
80,000 Styria Province, Styria Province, Austria
50,000 Children's HeartLink, Minneapolis, MN -- Building a Healthy Future, India
35,000 CARE, New York, NY -- Community Initiatives for Child Survival in Siaya, India
35,000 The Medtronic Southern Africa Institute of Cardiovascular Medicine Charitable Trust, Johannesburg, Republic of South Africa -- General Support
30,000 The Osaka Community Foundation, Osaka, Japan -- Training Centers for the Handicapped
30,000 Tokyo Goodwill Bank, Tokyo, Japan -- Training Centers for the Handicapped
25,000 Laubach Literacy International, Syracuse, NY -- China Health Literacy Project
18,000 Florence, Florence, Italy
10,000 Canadian Red Cross, Ottawa, ON, Canada -- Support for Ice Storm Relief
10,000 Foundation Project HOPE Suisse, Geneva, Switzerland -- Polish Health Care Management Course
3,269 The Year of Engineering Success, London, England -- Sponsorship of Health Week

Science

1,000,000 Bakken Library and Museum of Electricity in Life, Minneapolis, MN -- Capital Campaign
100,000 Science Museum of Minnesota, St. Paul, MN -- Capital Campaign

Social Services

824,960 United Way of Minneapolis Area, Minneapolis, MN -- General Support
80,148 Valley of the Sun United Way, Phoenix, AZ -- General Support
50,000 Minneapolis Youth Coordinating Board, Minneapolis, MN -- Camden's Future - Way to Grow
50,000 Minneapolis Youth Coordinating Board, Minneapolis, MN -- Camden's Future - Way to Grow
50,000 YWCA of Minneapolis, Minneapolis, MN -- Capital Campaign

MEIJER, INC.

Company Contact

Grand Rapids, MI
Web: http://www.meijer.com

Company Description

Employees: 45,000
SIC(s): 5399 Miscellaneous General Merchandise Store, 5411 Grocery Stores.

Nonmonetary Support

Type: Donated Products

Corporate Sponsorship

Type: Arts & cultural events; Festivals/fairs; Music & entertainment events; Pledge-a-thon; Sports events
Note: Sponsors the Children's Miracle Network and 'We Care about the Earth We Share'.

Meijer Foundation

Giving Contact

John Zimmerman, Director Public and Consumer Affairs
Meijer Foundation
2929 Walker Avenue, Northwest
Grand Rapids, MI 49544-9428
Phone: (616)453-6711
Fax: (616)791-5312

Alternate Contact

Pam Kleibusch, Executive Assistant

Description

Founded: 1991
EIN: 386575227
Organization Type: Corporate Foundation
Giving Locations: operating locations.
Grant Types: General Support.

Financial Summary

Total Giving: $373,498 (fiscal year ending September 30, 1998); $517,181 (fiscal 1997); $495,773 (fiscal 1996). Note: Contributes through foundation only.
Assets: $25,540,777 (fiscal 1998); $17,156,535 (fiscal 1997); $4,901,229 (fiscal 1996)
Gifts Received: $10,402,308 (fiscal 1998); $10,698,525 (fiscal 1997); $1,686,000 (fiscal 1996). Note: Contributions were received from Meijer, Inc., Meijer Companies Ltd., and Frederik G. H. Meijer.

Typical Recipients

Arts & Humanities: History & Archaeology
Civic & Public Affairs: Botanical Gardens/Parks, Clubs, Civic & Public Affairs-General, Municipalities/Towns, Parades/Festivals, Zoos/Aquariums
Environment: Environment-General

Contributions Analysis

Giving Priorities: Civic causes and the arts.
Arts & Humanities: 35%. Supports Friends of the Frederik Meijer Health Heartland Trail.
Civic & Public Affairs: 65%. Funds botanic gardens and horticultural societies.

Application Procedures

Initial Contact: Interested parties may apply at local Meijer stores.

Corporate Officials

James McLean: president PRIM CORP EMPL president: Meijer Inc.
Douglas Meijer: co-chairman, director, chief executive officer B 1954. ED University of Michigan. PRIM CORP EMPL co-chairman, director, chief executive officer: Meijer, Inc. CORP AFFIL vice president, treasurer, director: Meijer Companies Ltd.
Frederik G. H. Meijer: chairman executive committee, director B 1919. PRIM CORP EMPL chairman executive committee, director: Meijer, Inc.
Hendrik G. Meijer: co-chairman, director B 1952. PRIM CORP EMPL co-chairman, director: Meijer, Inc. CORP AFFIL secretary: Meijer Companies Ltd.; director: Old Kent Financial Corp.

Foundation Officials

Frederik G. H. Meijer: trustee (see above)

Grants Analysis

Disclosure Period: fiscal year ending September 30, 1998
Total Grants: $373,498
Number of Grants: 3
Average Grant: $124,499
Highest Grant: $188,600
Typical Range: $50,000 to $150,000

Recent Grants

Note: Grants derived from fiscal 1998 Form 990.

Arts & Humanities

132,000 Friends of the Frederik Meijer Heartland Trail, Greenville, MI

Civic & Public Affairs

188,600 West MI Horticultural Society, Grand Rapids, MI
52,898 Michigan Botanic Garden Foundation, Grand Rapids, MI

Mellon Financial Corp.

 Number 45 of Top 100 Corporate Givers

Company Contact

One Mellon Bank Center
500 Grant Street
Pittsburgh, PA 15258
Phone: (412)234-5000
Fax: (412)234-7525
Web: http://www.mellon.com

Company Description

Former Name: Mellon Bank Corp. (2000).
Revenue: US$5,814,000,000
Employees: 24,700
Fortune Rank: 288, per FORTUNE Magazine's list of 500 Largest U.S. Corporations (1999).
FF 288
SIC(s): 6021 National Commercial Banks, 6712 Bank Holding Companies.

Nonmonetary Support

Value: $7,957,300 (1997); $4,633,000 (1996); $4,594,500 (1995)
Type: Donated Equipment; In-kind Services; Loaned Employees; Loaned Executives
Volunteer Programs: Mellon Volunteer Professionals - a volunteer program that supports nonprofit initiatives.
Note: Company also provides below-market rate financing and technical assistance and advice.

Corporate Sponsorship

Value: $4,318,300 (1995); $3,500,000
Type: Arts & cultural events; Festivals/fairs; Music & entertainment events
Note: Sponsors Community Counts and Mellon Jazz Festival in Pittsburgh and Harrisburg Pennsylvania respectively.

Giving Contact

James P. McDonald, Vice President, Community Affairs
Mellon Bank Corp.
One Mellon Bank Ctr., Room 1830
Pittsburgh, PA 15258-0001
Phone: (412)234-2732
Fax: (412)236-1662

Description

Organization Type: Corporate Giving Program
Giving Locations: DE; MA: greater Boston; NJ: parts of; PA retail location areas.
Grant Types: Capital, Employee Matching Gifts, General Support.
Note: Employee matching gift ratio: 1 to 1. Company matches employee cash contributions to colleges, universities, secondary schools and cultural organisation up to a maximum of $1,000/year.

Giving Philosophy

'Economic, technological and social changes are transforming our communities, the way we live and the nature of our business. At Mellon, we have broadened our product and service offerings to remain strong and capable of meeting the evolving needs of our customers. We have, in fact, created a financial services company with a bank at its core which is both well balanced and well positioned for sustained leadership in a changing society.'
'As our communities face continuing challenges that shape our future, Mellon supports the development of resources and capabilities that promote economic health and stability today, while building foundations for a tomorrow that is even stronger. Through targeted lending and investing, charitable giving and the application of other Corporate resources, Mellon provides opportunities that build on the strengths of our communities and enable them and their residents to help themselves.' *Mellon Bank Corporation Community Report*

Financial Summary

Total Giving: $19,297,800 (1998); $17,730,300 (1997); $15,000,000 (1996). Note: Contributes through corporate direct giving program only.
Giving Analysis: Giving for 1997 includes: corporate direct giving ($9,773,000); nonmonetary support ($7,957,300); 1998: nonmonetary support ($10,003,000); corporate direct giving ($8,016,050); corporate grants to United Way ($1,278,750)
Assets: $39,000,000 (1994); $38,000,000 (1993); $6,301,549 (1990). Note: Above figures reflect corporate assets.

Typical Recipients

Arts & Humanities: Arts Associations & Councils, Arts Festivals, Community Arts, Dance, Museums/Galleries, Music, Opera, Performing Arts, Theater
Civic & Public Affairs: Business/Free Enterprise, Economic Development, Housing, Nonprofit Management, Urban & Community Affairs, Women's Affairs
Education: Business Education, Literacy, Minority Education
Health: Health Organizations
Social Services: Community Centers, Family Services, People with Disabilities, Shelters/Homelessness, United Funds/United Ways, Youth Organizations

Contributions Analysis

Giving Priorities: Neighborhood and economic development; education, stressing business, literacy, and minorities; health and human services; and arts and culture.
Arts & Humanities: 15%. Supports museums, arts centers and festivals, music groups, and programs concerned with historic preservation.
Civic & Public Affairs: 19%. Favors community initiatives that attract and develop business and jobs. Also supports efforts to promote affordable housing, homeownership, and economic development in low and moderate income areas.
Education: 12%. Interests include business education, literacy and minority education funds. Matches employee gifts to colleges and universities.
Health: 6%. Health grants given to hospitals, health centers, special care facilities, and health cost containment programs. Human service grants include organizations concerned with the disabled, drug and alcohol abuse, and food distribution.

Application Procedures

Initial Contact: Local organizations should submit grant requests directly to the Community Affairs Division of the Mellon Bank in their area, Mellon's Community Affairs office in Pittsburgh will consider proposals that have statewide impact in Pennsylvania.
Application Requirements: Send a brief description of the organization, including service area, mission, accomplishments and beneficiaries; current operating budget including other support and future funding; list of officers and directors; audited financial statement; copy of 501(c)(3) tax exempt form; amount requested; purpose of funds sought and how goal will be achieved; procedure and criteria for evaluating results.
Deadlines: None; requests considered upon receipt.
Evaluative Criteria: Proposals should support community development in one of the following ways: business and job development, affordable housing, literacy and education, art and culture, technical assistance for nonprofit organizations and fundraising and advertising to promote nonprofit groups as well as the company; also considers active board leadership, comprehensive resource development plan that includes in-kind support, income-generating activities, resource sharing with other nonprofit groups, support from individuals, and efficient and effective administration of funds and programs.
Notes: A list of Community Affairs divisions may be obtained from Mellon Bank in Pittsburgh, PA. Requests for less than $500 do not need to include all the information required in a full proposal. The Common Grant Application Format is accepted for requests submitted to Mellon's Community Affairs office in Pittsburgh. For grant requests submitted to Mellon Trust/The Boston Company, call (617)722-7340 for an application form.

Restrictions

Does not support individuals, religious or other sectarian groups, fraternal organizations like police or fire associations, scholarships, fellowships, travel grants, conferences and seminars, specialized health campaigns, endowments, national projects, international projects, political organizations, individual United Way agencies.

Additional Information

Mellon Bank Community Development Corporation, formed as a separate subsidiary in 1987, provides special bank loans and technical assistance for community development.
Copies of Mellon Community Affairs publications, Discover Total Resources: A Guide for Nonprofits and Neighbors Helping Neighbors: A Directory for Nonprofit Organizations, can be obtained by writing to Mellon Community Affairs, Room 1830, One Mellon Bank Center, Pittsburgh, PA 15258-0001.
Since consolidation of Mellon's Pennsylvania banks, proposals that have a statewide impact in priority areas should be sent to corporate headquarters in Pittsburgh. Proposals in priority areas that are region-specific should be sent to the nearest regional office.
Publications: Opportunities and Accomplishments; Mellon Bank Corp. Community Report

Corporate Officials

Steven G. Elliot: chief financial officer vice chairman, member corporate review committee, director B 1946. PRIM CORP EMPL chief financial officer: Mellon Bank Corp.
Jeffrey L. Leininger: vice chairman specialized commercial banking ED Pennsylvania State University (1967); Rutgers University (1982). PRIM CORP EMPL vice chairman specialized commercial banking: Mellon Bank Corp. ADD CORP EMPL director: Mellon Ventures Inc. CORP AFFIL director: Tuscarora Inc.
David R. Lovejoy: vice chairman-financial markets & corporate development PRIM CORP EMPL vice chairman-financial markets & corporate development: Mellon Bank Corp.
Martin Gregory McGuinn: chairman, chief executive officer B Philadelphia, PA 1942. ED Villanova University AB (1964); Villanova University JD (1967). PRIM CORP EMPL chairman, chief executive officer: Mellon Financial Corp. CORP AFFIL chairman, chief executive officer: Mellon Bank NA; director: Regl Industries Development Corp.; director: General Reinsurance Corp.; director: MasterCard International Inc. NONPR AFFIL director: University Pittsburgh Medical Center; director, consult: Villanova Law School; member: Pennsylvania Bar Association; director: Pennsylvania Chamber Business & Industry; trustee: Hist Society West Pennsylvania; member: New York State Bar Association; member: Bankers Roundtable; trustee: Carnegie Museum Art; member: American Law Institute; member: American Society of Corporate Secretaries; member: Allegheny County Bar Association; member: American Bar Association.
W. Keith Smith: senior vice chairman, member corporate review committee, director ED University of Saskatchewan BComm (1955); University of Western Ontario MBA (1960). PRIM CORP EMPL senior vice

chairman, member corporate review committee, director: Mellon Bank Corp. CORP AFFIL director: Dentsply International Inc.; chairman, chief executive officer: Boston Safe Deposit & Trust Co.; chairman: Boston Group Holdings Inc. NONPR AFFIL member: Financial Executives Institute. CLUB AFFIL Duquesne Club.

Giving Program Officials

Paul S. Beideman: PRIM CORP EMPL member corporate review committee: Mellon Bank Corp. NONPR AFFIL vice president: Boy Scouts America Philadelphia Council.

Walter R. Day, III: PRIM CORP EMPL member corporate review committee: Mellon Bank Corp.

Jeffrey L. Leininger: membership, corporate review committee ED Pennsylvania State University (1967); Rutgers University (1982). PRIM CORP EMPL vice chairman specialized commercial banking: Mellon Bank Corp. ADD CORP EMPL director: Mellon Ventures Inc. CORP AFFIL director: Tuscarora Inc.

David R. Lovejoy: membership corporate review committee PRIM CORP EMPL vice chairman-financial markets & corporate development: Mellon Bank Corp.

James P. McDonald: PRIM CORP EMPL member corporate review committee: Mellon Bank Corp.

Sandra J. McLaughlin: member corporate review commission PRIM CORP EMPL senior vice president: Mellon Bank Corp.

William J. Stallkamp: member corporate review committee B Quincy, MA 1939. ED Carnegie Mellon University; University of Pittsburgh; Miami University BSBA (1961). PRIM CORP EMPL chairman: Mellon PSFS. CORP AFFIL director: Matthews International Corp.; vice chairman: Mellon Bank Corp.

Grants Analysis

Disclosure Period: calendar year ending 1998
Total Grants: $19,297,800*
Typical Range: $2,500 to $10,000
***Note:** Giving excludes United Way; matching gifts; gifts to individuals; foundation.

Memphis Light Gas & water Division

Company Contact

Memphis, TN
Web: http://www.mlgw.com

Company Description

Employees: 2,634
SIC(s): 4911 Electric Services, 4924 Natural Gas Distribution, 4941 Water Supply.

Nonmonetary Support

Value: $50,000 (1996)
Type: Cause-related Marketing & Promotion; Donated Equipment; In-kind Services; Loaned Executives
Note: Nonmonetary Support Contact: Regina Allen, Coordinator, Employee Activities.

Corporate Sponsorship

Range: less than $50,000
Type: Arts & cultural events; Festivals/fairs; Pledge-a-thon; Sports events
Contact: Regina Allen, Coordinator

Giving Contact

Herman Morris, Jr., President & Chief Executive Officer
Memphis Light Gas & Water Division
PO Box 430
Memphis, TN 38101-0430
Phone: (901)528-4151
Fax: (901)528-4758

Description

Organization Type: Corporate Giving Program
Giving Locations: company service area.
Grant Types: General Support, Multiyear/Continuing Support, Project.

Giving Philosophy

'MLGW's objectives for community outreach and involvement shall be: to provide support for MLGW employees involved in specific community and civic organizations; and encourage volunteerism throughout the Division as a vehicle for further employee development; to enhance cultural and educational opportunities for the residents of Memphis and Shelby County; to promote economic growth and development in Memphis; to support organizations which promote the city of Memphis and contribute to the enhancement of the quality of life for the overall community.' Community Involvement & Guidelines

Financial Summary

Total Giving: $1,000,000 (2000 approx); $1,000,000 (1999 approx); $1,000,000 (1998 approx). Note: Contributes through corporate direct giving program only. Giving includes corporate direct giving; nonmonetary support.

Typical Recipients

Arts & Humanities: Arts Associations & Councils, Arts Festivals
Civic & Public Affairs: Chambers of Commerce, Civil Rights, Clubs, Community Foundations, Economic Development, Employment/Job Training, Civic & Public Affairs-General, Housing, Safety
Education: Business Education, Business-School Partnerships, Colleges & Universities, Education-General, Health & Physical Education, Minority Education, Student Aid
Environment: Air/Water Quality, Environment-General, Resource Conservation, Wildlife Protection
Health: Cancer, Children's Health/Hospitals, Health-General, Mental Health, Prenatal Health Issues, Transplant Networks/Donor Banks
Religion: Religious Welfare
Social Services: Food/Clothing Distribution, Social Services-General, United Funds/United Ways, Volunteer Services

Application Procedures

Initial Contact: letter of inquiry
Application Requirements: brief background of organization, most recent annual report, specific objectives of program, program budget, amount requested, current funding sources with amounts
Review Process: Community Involvement Allocation Committee meets annually to decide on grants over $1,000; president decides all other funding requests
Evaluative Criteria: how project relates to company guidelines, employee involvement, potential for self-support, community need, record of accomplishments, community support

Restrictions

Company does not support individuals; religious organizations for sectarian purposes; or political or lobbying groups.

Additional Information

Publications: Guidelines

Corporate Officials

Kenneth O. Cole: vice president customer service B Memphis, TN 1936. ED LeMoyne-Owen College (1958); Fisk University (1968). PRIM CORP EMPL vice president customer service: Memphis Light, Gas & Water Division.

Herman Morris, Jr.: president, chief executive officer B Memphis, TN 1951. ED Rhodes College BA (1973); Vanderbilt University JD (1977). PRIM CORP EMPL president, chief executive officer: Memphis Light, Gas & Water Division. NONPR AFFIL chairman: Board of Professional Responsibility; member, president Ben F. Jones chapter: National Bar Association; member: American Bar Association.

Grants Analysis

Disclosure Period: calendar year ending

Recent Grants

Note: Grants derived from 1996 grants list.

Arts & Humanities

2,495	Memphis Arts Council, Memphis, TN

Civic & Public Affairs

1,067	Memphis Light and Gas Works Law Explorers Post, Memphis, TN
300	Curve Optimist Club, Memphis, TN

Education

13,130	Junior Achievement, Memphis, TN
560	Junior Achievement, Memphis, TN -- for lane fees

Health

25,002	March of Dimes, Memphis, TN
13,300	St. Jude's Children's Research Hospital, Memphis, TN
3,040	LifeBlood, Memphis, TN
1,025	St. Jude's Children's Research Hospital, Memphis, TN
225	St. Jude's Children's Research Hospital, Memphis, TN

Religion

500	St. Peter's Home, Memphis, TN

Social Services

4,739	Operation Feed, Memphis, TN

Menasha Corp.

Company Contact

Neenah, WI
Web: http://www.menasha.com

Company Description

Employees: 5,500
SIC(s): 2421 Sawmills & Planing Mills--General, 2631 Paperboard Mills, 2653 Corrugated & Solid Fiber Boxes, 2759 Commercial Printing Nec.

Operating Locations

Includes plant locations.

Corporate Sponsorship

Type: Arts & cultural events; Festivals/fairs; Music & entertainment events; Sports events

Menasha Corp. Foundation

Giving Contact

Steve Kromholz, President
Menasha Corp. Foundation
PO Box 367
Neenah, WI 54957-0367
Phone: (920)751-1000
Fax: (920)751-1236

Alternate Contact

Phone: 800-558-5073

Description

EIN: 396047384
Organization Type: Corporate Foundation
Giving Locations: headquarters and operating communities.
Grant Types: Emergency, Employee Matching Gifts, General Support, Multiyear/Continuing Support, Project, Scholarship.

Note: Employee matching gift ratio: 2 to 1 up to $1,500 per employee annually.

Financial Summary

Total Giving: $1,277,961 (1997); $1,015,108 (1996); $730,000 (1995). Note: Contributes through corporate direct giving program and foundation. 1997 Giving includes foundation ($985,998); matching gifts ($80,602); scholarship ($74,546); United Way ($136,815).
Assets: $1,084,413 (1997); $999,250 (1996); $848,543 (1995)
Gifts Received: $1,140,750 (1997); $1,142,130 (1996); $742,819 (1995). Note: Foundation receives contributions from Menasha Corporation.

Typical Recipients

Arts & Humanities: Community Arts, Arts & Humanities-General, Historic Preservation, History & Archaeology, Museums/Galleries, Music, Performing Arts, Public Broadcasting, Theater
Civic & Public Affairs: Botanical Gardens/Parks, Economic Development, Hispanic Affairs, Housing, Professional & Trade Associations, Safety, Urban & Community Affairs, Women's Affairs, Zoos/Aquariums
Education: Arts/Humanities Education, Business Education, Colleges & Universities, Education Reform, Engineering/Technological Education, Education-General, Secondary Education (Private), Vocational & Technical Education
Environment: Environment-General, Research, Resource Conservation, Watershed, Wildlife Protection
Health: Children's Health/Hospitals, Clinics/Medical Centers, Emergency/Ambulance Services, Hospitals, Nursing Services, Public Health
Social Services: Animal Protection, Child Abuse, Child Welfare, Community Service Organizations, Domestic Violence, Food/Clothing Distribution, People with Disabilities, Recreation & Athletics, Senior Services, Shelters/Homelessness, Substance Abuse, United Funds/United Ways, Volunteer Services, YMCA/YWCA/YMHA/YWHA, Youth Organizations

Contributions Analysis

Arts & Humanities: 10% to 15%. Major support goes to Wisconsin public broadcasting, museums and galleries, music, opera, history, and archeology.
Civic & Public Affairs: About 10%. Interests include urban and community affairs and local clubs and chambers of commerce. Focus on community redevelopment.
Education: 30% to 35%. Funding is awarded to universities and colleges in Wisconsin, economic education, education funds, minority education, and literacy programs. Also supports youth education projects.
Environment: 5% to 10%. Primarily interested in wildlife protection and resource conservation.
Health: 35% to 40%. Major support goes to united funds, people with disabilities, and youth organizations.

Application Procedures

Initial Contact: brief written request (not more than 3 pages)
Application Requirements: description of the organization, including history and goals; amount requested; purpose of funds, including how problem will be solved and method of evaluation; other sources of support; approximate number and description of group of people to be helped by project; total project budget; total organization budget; percentage of organizational budget devoted to administration; percentage of organizational budget devoted to fundraising; names of company employees who are volunteers for the organization; list of present directors with affiliations, and senior staff members; and proof of 501(c)(3) status
Deadlines: January 15 for the February board meeting, April 15 for the May meeting, August 15 for the September meeting, and November 15 for the December meeting
Decision Notification: board meetings held quarterly in February, May, September and December

Restrictions

Does not support individuals, religious organizations for sectarian purposes, or political or lobbying groups.

Additional Information

Recipients of grants over $1,000 are subject to evaluation.
Grants to private colleges and universities are made under the foundation's matching gift program and the scholarship program, which is limited to employees' children.
Publications: Application Guidelines

Corporate Officials

Robert D. Bero: president, chief executive officer B 1941. ED Ohio State University BS (1967); Ohio State University MS (1969). PRIM CORP EMPL president, chief executive officer: Menasha Corp. CORP AFFIL chairman: Menasha Transport, Inc.; president: NJP Insertco Inc.; director: First National Bank Fox Valley.
Kenneth John Bonkoski: controller B Wausau, WI 1941. ED Mount Senario College (1985). PRIM CORP EMPL controller: Menasha Corp. CORP AFFIL treasurer, director: Wisconsin Paper Group.
Bernard John McCarragher: chairman, director B Waukesha, WI 1927. ED Marquette University BS (1951). PRIM CORP EMPL chairman, director: Menasha Corp. CORP AFFIL director: City Forest Corp. CLUB AFFIL Rotary International Club.

Foundation Officials

Kenneth John Bonkoski: treasurer (see above)
Steven S. Kromholz: president
Bernard John McCarragher: chairman (see above)
Kristi Pavletich: secretary
Oliver C. Smith: chairman PRIM CORP EMPL director: Menasha Corp. CORP AFFIL director: First National Bank Fox Valley.

Grants Analysis

Disclosure Period: calendar year ending 1997
Total Grants: $985,998*
Number of Grants: 350
Average Grant: $2,817
Highest Grant: $80,000
Typical Range: $150 to $10,000
***Note:** Giving excludes matching gifts, scholarship, and United Way.

Recent Grants

Note: Grants derived from 1997 Form 990.

Arts & Humanities

20,000	EAA Aviation Center, Oshkosh, WI -- support John Snyder Memorial
18,373	Menasha Historical Society, Menasha, WI -- support for Smith Park Gazebo
15,000	Bergstrom-Mahler Museum
10,000	WCATY -- educational
8,700	Wisconsin Public Broadcasting Foundation, Madison, WI -- educational
8,525	Wisconsin Public Broadcasting Foundation, Madison, WI -- second of two payments for Nova and American Explorer
7,500	American Player's Theater -- second of three payments for cultural purposes
5,000	Betty Brinn Children's Museum, Milwaukee, WI -- second of three payments on pledge for educational purposes
5,000	Fox Valley Symphony Orchestra, Menasha, WI -- support for 1997 Pops Concert
5,000	Madison Children's Museum, Madison, WI

Civic & Public Affairs

20,000	Future Neenah Development Corporation, Neenah, WI -- civic
20,000	Future Neenah Development Corporation, Neenah, WI
20,000	Future Neenah Development Corporation, Neenah, WI
20,000	Habitat for Humanity of the Greater Fox Cities Area -- support for house building
10,000	Future Neenah Development Corporation, Neenah, WI -- civic
5,500	Zoological Society of Milwaukee County, Milwaukee, WI -- environmental
5,000	City of Otsego -- second of five payments on pledge for civic purposes
5,000	Memorial Park Arboretum and Gardens -- second of five payments for environmental purposes

Education

80,000	St. Mary's Central High School, Menasha, WI -- support for tennis courts
40,000	Lawrence University, Appleton, WI
15,000	Fox Cities Alliance for Education, Appleton, WI -- second of two payments for educational purposes
15,000	Lakeland College, Sheboygan, WI -- educational
10,000	Lawrence University, Appleton, WI -- educational
8,000	Dieu Donne Papermill, New York, NY -- educational
5,000	FISC/CCCS -- second of three payments on pledge for educational purposes
5,000	Junior Achievement, Racine, WI -- educational
5,000	University of Wisconsin Fox Valley, Fox Valley, WI -- educational
5,000	WMC Foundation, Madison, WI -- remaining 1997 pledge payment

Environment

15,000	Nature Conservancy -- second of three payments for environmental purposes
10,000	Sigurd Olson Environmental Institute -- environmental

Health

15,000	American Red Cross -- health and welfare
15,000	American Red Cross -- health and welfare
12,500	Fox Cities Community Clinic, Appleton, WI -- health and welfare
10,000	Visiting Nurse Association -- fourth of five payments for health and welfare

Social Services

50,000	Champaign Family YMCA -- health and welfare
30,000	United Community Services, Orwell, OH -- final of three payments for health and welfare
25,000	CAP Services, Stevens Point, WI -- second of three payments for educational purposes
16,700	Emergency Shelters, Appleton, WI -- health and welfare
12,500	United Way of Fox Cities, Menasha, WI -- first of four payments on pledge for health and welfare
12,500	United Way of Fox Cities, Menasha, WI -- final of four payments for health and welfare
12,500	United Way of Fox Cities, Menasha, WI -- health and welfare
12,500	United Way of Fox Cities, Menasha, WI -- third of four payments for health and welfare
10,000	Goodwill Industries of North Central Wisconsin, Menasha, WI -- support Fox Cities Capital Campaign
10,000	Neenah-Menasha YMCA, Neenah, WI --

	final of five payments for capital campaign
10,000	Rawhide Boys Ranch, New London, WI -- health and welfare
10,000	Regional Domestic Abuse Services, Neenah, WI -- first of three payments for health and welfare purposes
8,000	YMCA -- support K-C Playground Project
5,000	Indiana-Purdue Foundation -- second of four payments for McKay Soccer Project pledge
5,000	Paper Valley Youth Soccer Club -- civic
5,000	Second Harvest Food Bank, Milwaukee, WI -- health and welfare

MERCANTILE BANK NA

Company Contact

St. Louis, MO

Company Description

Employees: 3,326
SIC(s): 6021 National Commercial Banks.
Parent Company: Firstar Corp., 777 East Wisconsin Avenue, Milwaukee, WI, United States

Operating Locations

Operates branches in at least 35 cities throughout Missouri and southern Illinois.

Nonmonetary Support

Value: $10,000 (1991); $10,000 (1990)
Type: Loaned Employees; Loaned Executives
Contact:
Contact Human Resources for nonmonetary support information.
Note: Company encourages employees to volunteer in such programs as United Way, Arts and Education Council, St. Louis Symphony, and the Neighborhood Assistance Program.

The Mercantile Foundation

Giving Contact

Edward D. Higgins, Chairman
The Mercantile Foundation
Mercantile Tower-Tram 15-4
PO Box 387
St. Louis, MO 63166
Phone: (314)418-1960
Fax: (314)418-3910

Description

EIN: 436020630
Organization Type: Corporate Foundation
Giving Locations: MO: St. Louis metrtopolitan area headquarters and operating communities only.
Grant Types: Capital, Challenge, Fellowship, Operating Expenses, Project, Scholarship.

Financial Summary

Total Giving: $1,901,930 (fiscal year ending February 28, 1997). Note: Contributes through corporate direct giving program and foundation. Fiscal Giving includes foundation.
Assets: $2,509,033 (fiscal 1997); $3,807,171 (fiscal 1994); $4,594,375 (fiscal 1993)
Gifts Received: $2,945,460 (fiscal 1997); $10,452 (fiscal 1994); $2,000,000 (fiscal 1993). Note: In fiscal 1997, gifts were received from Mercantile Bank ($2,939,790), and various employees ($5,670).

Typical Recipients

Arts & Humanities: Arts Associations & Councils, Arts Centers, Arts Outreach, Dance, Ethnic & Folk Arts, History & Archaeology, Museums/Galleries, Music, Performing Arts, Visual Arts
Civic & Public Affairs: African American Affairs, Botanical Gardens/Parks, Clubs, Community Foundations, Economic Development, Civic & Public Affairs-General, Municipalities/Towns, Professional & Trade Associations, Urban & Community Affairs, Zoos/Aquariums
Education: Afterschool/Enrichment Programs, Business Education, Colleges & Universities, Engineering/Technological Education, Medical Education, Science/Mathematics Education, Special Education, Vocational & Technical Education
Health: Cancer, Children's Health/Hospitals, Clinics/Medical Centers, Emergency/Ambulance Services, Hospitals, Medical Training
Religion: Dioceses, Jewish Causes, Religious Welfare
Science: Scientific Centers & Institutes
Social Services: At-Risk Youth, Child Welfare, Community Centers, Community Service Organizations, Emergency Relief, Family Services, People with Disabilities, Scouts, Special Olympics, United Funds/United Ways, YMCA/YWCA/YMHA/YWHA, Youth Organizations

Contributions Analysis

Giving Priorities: Youth organizations; hospitals and pediatric health; colleges, universities, and education programs in St. Louis; various arts organizations; and economic development.
Arts & Humanities: 18%. Main support to symphony, museums, and arts councils.
Civic & Public Affairs: 12%. Supports botanical gardens, clubs, jobs, and foundations.
Education: 15%. Colleges and universities mainly.
Health: 5%.
Religion: 5%.
Social Services: 45%. Main priority is United Way.
Note: Percentages above are for 1997 foundation giving only. Corporate direct grantmaking has been suspended.

Application Procedures

Initial Contact: Submit a brief letter or proposal.
Application Requirements: Description of organization, amount requested, purpose of funds sought, recently audited financial statement, proof of tax-exempt status, other financial support.
Deadlines: None.

Restrictions

Does not support dinners or special events, fraternal organizations, goodwill advertising, individuals, member agencies of United Way, political or lobbying groups, religious organizations for sectarian purposes, or sporting events.

Additional Information

The foundation reported in 1998 that their giving program is still in operation, but grant making is suspended.

Corporate Officials

Thomas Herbert Jacobsen: chairman, president, chief executive officer B Chicago, IL 1939. ED Lake Forest College BS (1963); University of Chicago MBA (1968); Harvard University Advanced Management Program (1979). PRIM CORP EMPL chairman, president, chief executive officer: Mercantile Bancorp Inc. CORP AFFIL director: Transworld Airlines Inc.; chairman, chief executive officer: Mercantile Acquisition Corp.; director: Mercantile Bank Saint Louis NA; chairman advisor to board directors: Ameribanc Inc.; director: Federation Reserve Bank Saint Louis. NONPR AFFIL director: National Boy Scouts America; life trustee: Saint Louis Symphony Society; treasurer: Civic Progress; chairman: Mercantile Bank National Association; executive board member: Boy Scouts America; chairman: Boy Scouts America Saint Louis Area Council; member: Bankers Roundtable. CLUB AFFIL Bob Olink Golf Club; Saint Louis Country Club; Bogey Club.

Grants Analysis

Disclosure Period: fiscal year ending February 28, 1997
Total Grants: $1,901,930
Number of Grants: 175 (approx)
Average Grant: $10,868
Highest Grant: $250,000
Typical Range: $500 to $20,000

Recent Grants

Note: Grants derived from fiscal 1997 Form 990.

Arts & Humanities	
250,000	St. Louis Symphony Orchestra, Saint Louis, MO
25,000	St. Louis Art Museum, Saint Louis, MO
9,500	Arts and Education Council, Saint Louis, MO
9,500	Arts and Education Council, Saint Louis, MO
9,500	Arts and Education Council, Saint Louis, MO
5,000	St. Louis Art Museum, Saint Louis, MO
Civic & Public Affairs	
75,000	Union Station Assistance Corporation, Kansas City, MO
38,000	Missouri Botanical Gardens, Saint Louis, MO
25,000	Sheldon
20,000	MUNY, Saint Louis, MO
15,000	Focus, Saint Louis, MO
10,000	St. Louis Variety Club, Saint Louis, MO
10,000	TRCC Foundation
5,000	Iowa Cattleman's Association, Ames, IA
5,000	Missouri Cattlemen Foundation, Columbia, MO
5,000	Urban League, Saint Louis, MO
Education	
100,000	St. Louis University, Saint Louis, MO
80,000	Washington University, Saint Louis, MO
25,000	Iowa College Foundation, Des Moines, IA
25,000	Iowa College Foundation, Des Moines, IA
16,000	Junior Achievement Mississippi, Hazelwood, MO
12,000	Logan College of Chiropractics, Chesterfield, MO
10,000	Ranken Technical College, Saint Louis, MO
10,000	Webster University, Webster Groves, MO
5,000	Fontbonne College, Saint Louis, MO
5,000	William Woods College, Fulton, MO
2,500	Drury College, Springfield, MO
1,500	Ranken Technical College, Saint Louis, MO
1,350	Greenville College, Greenville, IL
1,350	Greenville College, Greenville, IL
Health	
10,000	St. John's Mercy Medical Center, Saint Louis, MO
10,000	St. Louis Children's Hospital, Saint Louis, MO
2,149	American Red Cross, Saint Louis, MO
Religion	
24,000	Jewish Community Association
10,000	Salvation Army
2,000	Salvation Army, Kansas City, MO
Social Services	
138,000	United Way, Saint Louis, MO
138,000	United Way, Saint Louis, MO
138,000	United Way, Saint Louis, MO
138,000	United Way, Saint Louis, MO
50,000	Boy Scouts of America, Saint Louis, MO
50,000	Boy Scouts of America, Saint Louis, MO
50,000	Girl Scout Council, Saint Louis, MO

50,000	YMCA, Saint Louis, MO
28,000	Boy Scouts of America, Saint Louis, MO
20,000	Boys and Girls Hope
20,000	Herbert Hoover Boys and Girls Club, Saint Louis, MO
6,000	Paraquad, Saint Louis, MO
4,000	Silver Springs Community Center
3,000	Christmas in St. Louis, Saint Louis, MO

MERCK &CO.

Number 1 of Top 100 Corporate Givers

Company Contact

Whitehouse Station, NJ
Web: http://www.merck.com

Company Description

Revenue: US$32,714,000,000 (1999)
Employees: 35,956 (1999)
Fortune Rank: 34, per FORTUNE Magazine's list of 500 Largest U.S. Corporations (1999).
FF 34
SIC(s): 0254 Poultry Hatcheries, 2048 Prepared Feeds Nec, 2819 Industrial Inorganic Chemicals Nec, 2833 Medicinals & Botanicals.

Operating Locations

Australia: Merck Sharp & Dohme (Australia) Pty. Ltd., Granville; Austria: Merck Sharp & Dohme GmbH, Vienna; Belgium: Merck Sharp & Dohme Societe De Droit Hollandais, Brussels, Brabant; Hubbard Belgium International NV, Kortrijk, Flandre-Occidentale; Canada: Merck Frosst Canada, Montreal; Denmark: Chibret AS, Glostrup, Copenhagen; France: Merck Sharp & Dohme Idea, La Celle St. Cloud, Yvelines; Merck Sharp & Dohme Chibret (Laboratoires), Paris, Ville-de-Paris; Merck Sharp et Dohme (SA), Paris, Ville-de-Paris; MSD (Financiere), Paris, Ville-de-Paris; Germany: Chibret Pharmazeutische GmbH, Haan; Guam: Merck Foreign Sales Corp., Agana; Hong Kong: Merck Sharp & Dohme (Asia) Ltd., Wan Chai; Italy: Neo Abello SpA, Bollate, Lombardia; Merck Sharp & Dohme Italia SpA, Roma, Lazio; Neopharmed SpA, Roma, Lazio; Japan: MSD (Japan) Co. Ltd., Tokyo; Luxembourg: Merck Sharp & Dohme Overseas Finance SA, Luxembourg; Netherlands: Merck Sharp & Dohme BV, Haarlem, Noord-Holland; Hubbard Nederland BV, Oldebroek, Gelderland; Norway: MSD Norge AS, Drammen, Buskerud; New Zealand: Charles E. Frosst (New Zealand) Ltd., Auckland; Merck Sharp & Dohme (New Zealand) Ltd., Wiri, Auckland; Peru: Laboratorios Prosalud SA, Lima; Philippines: Merck Sharp & Dohme (Philippines), Makati, Rizal; Portugal: Frosst Portuguesa Productos Farmaceuticos Lda., Barcarena, Loures; Merck Sharp & Dohme Lda., Queluz; Spain: Fabrica de Productos Quimicos y Farmaceuticos Abello SA, Madrid; Frosst Iberica SA, Madrid; Merck Sharp & Dohme Espana SA, Madrid; Sweden: MSD Latkemedel (Scandinavia) AB; Switzerland: Merck Sharp & Dohme Chibret AG, Opfikon, Zurich; United Kingdom: Charles E. Frosst (United Kingdom) Ltd., Hoddesdon, Hertfordshire; Merck Sharp & Dohme (Holdings) Ltd., Hoddesdon, Hertfordshire; Merck Sharp & Dohme Ltd., Hoddesdon, Hertfordshire; Morsonthomas & Son Ltd., Hoddesdon, Hertfordshire; Venezuela: Merck Sharp & Dohme de Venezuela CA, Caracas

Nonmonetary Support

Value: $116,000,000 (1996); $100,000,000 (1995); $58,000,000 (1994)
Type: Donated Products
Note: Nonmonetary support through product donations (wholesale value) to international humanitarian relief and health in Eastern European & the Third World. 1997 nonmonetary support $157 million.

Corporate Sponsorship

Type: Festivals/fairs
Contact: Ellen Roehm, Manager, Employee Services
Note: Sponsors science fairs.

Merck Co. Foundation

Giving Contact

John R. Taylor, Executive Vice President
Merck Co. Foundation
One Merck Dr.
PO Box 100
Whitehouse Station, NJ 08889-0100
Phone: (908)423-2042
Fax: (908)423-1987

Description

EIN: 226028476
Organization Type: Corporate Foundation
Giving Locations: internationally; nationally; primarily headquarters and operating communities.
Grant Types: Department, Employee Matching Gifts, Fellowship, Project.

Giving Philosophy

'The Merck Company Foundation has long directed its efforts to the enhancement of education in medicine and science at the college and university level. These efforts are effective, but it must be recognized that a majority of students are ill-prepared and uninterested in the sciences before they reach college. Indeed, the decline of education in science in U.S. schools threatens the quality and quantity of research-based innovation on which the American standard of living and way of life depend. Therefore, the Foundation is now making a limited number of grants aimed at stimulating an interest in science at the elementary and secondary level.'

'Another important goal of our contributions program is to continue to support health and social services and civic and cultural activities in the communities where we operate. This helps ensure that our towns and cities can continue to offer employees and neighbors an environment with opportunities for a full and productive life.' Charitable Giving Report, The Merck Company Foundation

Financial Summary

Total Giving: $221,000,000 (1998 approx); $190,300,000 (1997); $140,500,000 (1996 approx). Note: Contributes through corporate direct giving program and foundation.
Giving Analysis: Giving for 1996 includes: foundation ($17,000,000); corporate direct giving ($4,700,000); domestic subsidiaries ($2,800,000); 1997: foundation ($19,000,000); corporate direct giving ($12,000,000); domestic subsidiaries ($2,300,000); 1998: foundation ($23,168,251)
Assets: $273,174,899 (1998); $189,069,896 (1995); $41,544,538 (1994)
Gifts Received: $70,000 (1998); $202,154,100 (1995); $13,200,000 (1994). Note: Foundation receives contributions from Merck & Co.

Typical Recipients

Arts & Humanities: Arts Centers, Libraries, Museums/Galleries, Music, Performing Arts, Public Broadcasting, Theater
Civic & Public Affairs: Botanical Gardens/Parks, Civic & Public Affairs-General, Hispanic Affairs, Professional & Trade Associations, Public Policy, Safety, Urban & Community Affairs, Women's Affairs
Education: Arts/Humanities Education, Business Education, Colleges & Universities, Community & Junior Colleges, Economic Education, Education Associations, Education Funds, Engineering/Technological Education, Faculty Development, Education-General, Health & Physical Education, International Exchange, Journalism/Media Education, Medical Education, Minority Education, Public Education (Precollege), Science/Mathematics Education
Environment: Environment-General, Resource Conservation
Health: Cancer, Children's Health/Hospitals, Clinics/Medical Centers, Emergency/Ambulance Services, Geriatric Health, Health Policy/Cost Containment, Health Organizations, Heart, Hospitals, Hospitals (University Affiliated), Medical Research, Medical Training, Public Health, Research/Studies Institutes, Single-Disease Health Associations
International: Foreign Educational Institutions, Health Care/Hospitals, Human Rights, International Affairs, International Relations
Religion: Religious Welfare
Science: Science Exhibits & Fairs, Scientific Centers & Institutes, Scientific Labs, Scientific Organizations
Social Services: Child Welfare, Community Service Organizations, Day Care, Family Services, Senior Services, Shelters/Homelessness, Substance Abuse, United Funds/United Ways, Youth Organizations

Contributions Analysis

Giving Priorities: Needy Third-World nations through donated health-related products; medical science; community programs, largely through United Way; and public policy. Foreign subsidiaries administer independent programs. Company sponsors international fellowship in clinical pharmacology with donations to foreign educational institutions and medical schools worldwide. Merck contributes its health-related products to U.S. organizations serving the needy in Third World nations and Eastern European countries, and for emergency disaster relief programs. Product donations include hepatitis B vaccines administered to children in Romania through Project HOPE; antiparasitic drugs that have treated more that 7 million people in 34 countries for victims of the tropical disease onochocerciasis or River blindness; and freemedical care and products fpr children in Russia through support of the Children's Health Fund. In 1994, product donations totaled $55.0 million. Established in the 1960s, Merck's Product Donation Program has provided more than $240 million in products to U.S.-based private voluntary relief organizations. Other interests include health care, especially prenatal care for mothers; economic development; and community affairs.
Civic & Public Affairs: About 30%. Funds social services through the United Way, and health interests such as hospitals, medical centers, children's health; the arts and the environment receive minor support. Some civic groups also receive funding. (Public Policy) About 10%. Mainly supports groups concerned with health policy issues. Also supports organizations dealing with the pharmaceutical business, economics, and health care cost containment.
Education: About 50%. Supports programs designed to increase knowledge of medicine and science. Also emphasizes the creation of education opportunities for minorities. Support tosecondary and primary science education in selected locations.
International: About 10%. Giving follows similar priorities as above.

Application Procedures

Initial Contact: written proposal
Application Requirements: summary of project, amount requested, planned objectives, background and significance; means for accomplishing the goal; project budget; sources of funding; proof of tax-exempt status
Deadlines: None.

Evaluative Criteria: evidence of a sound program; competent leadership; ability to accomplish objectives; relevance to interests of the company and its philanthropic priorities; clear success criteria and assessment system in place

Restrictions

Does not support individuals; political, labor, or fraternal or veterans' groups; sectarian groups; endowments; or publications. Except within established programs, grants are not given for scholarships or fellowships, elementary or secondary education, research, travel, or conferences.

Sufficient resources are not available to fund unsolicited requests from educational institutions or organizations with purposes of limited relationship to Merck's mission. relationship to Merck's mission.

Additional Information

Foundation sponsors numerous established programs. For this reason, many grants are made on the initiative of the foundation.

The company also makes gifts for activities such as continuing education programs in medicine and pharmacy, public education in health awareness, and memberships in professional and business organizations, which do not qualify as charitable under the Internal Revenue Code.

Publications: Contributions Report

Corporate Officials

Kenneth C. Frazier: vice president, deputy general counsel PRIM CORP EMPL vice president, deputy general counsel: Merck & Co.

Raymond V. Gilmartin: chairman, president, chief executive officer B Washington, DC 1941. ED Union College BS (1963); Harvard University MBA (1968). PRIM CORP EMPL chairman, president, chief executive officer: Merck & Co. Inc. CORP AFFIL director: Public Service Electric & Gas Co.; director: Public Service Enterprise Group Inc.; director: General Mills Inc.; director: Pharmaceutical Research & Management America. NONPR AFFIL chairman: Valley Health Systems Inc.; chairman: Valley Hospital; director: United Negro College Fund; director: Healthcare Leadership Council; director: Project Hope; director, board associates: Harvard Business School; advisory board: Harvard University; member: Conference Board Inc.; director: Ethics Resource Center; member: Business Roundtable; member: Committee for Economic Development; member: Alliance for Healthcare Reform; member: Business Council.

Christopher P. Lynch: assistant treasurer

Nicholas P. Procyk: assistant treasurer

John R. Taylor: senior director public construction PRIM CORP EMPL senior director public construction: Merck Co. Inc.

Foundation Officials

Horace Brewster Atwater, Jr.: trustee B Minneapolis, MN 1931. ED Princeton University AB (1952); Stanford University MBA (1954). CORP AFFIL director: National Broadcasting Co. Inc.; director: General Electric Co.; secretary: Morgan Guaranty Trust Co.; director: Darden Restaurants Inc. NONPR AFFIL trustee: Mayo Foundation; director: Walker Art Center.

William Gordon Bowen, PhD: trustee B Cincinnati, OH 1933. ED Denison University BA (1955); Princeton University PhD (1958). CORP AFFIL chairman, director: JST Oregon; director: Merck & Co. Inc. NONPR AFFIL regent emeritus: Smithsonian Institute; director: University Corp. for Advanced Internet Development; member: Phi Beta Kappa; trustee: Denison University; member: Industrial Relations Research Association; member: American Economic Association; member: Council Foreign Relations.

Brenda D. Colatrella: assistant secretary

Carolyne Kahle Davis, PhD: trustee B Penn Yan, NY 1932. ED Johns Hopkins University BS (1954); Syracuse University MS (1965); Syracuse University PhD (1972). CORP AFFIL director: Pharmaceutical Marketing Services Inc.; director: Prudential Insurance Co. America; director: Minimed Sylmar; director: Beverly Enterprises; director: Merck & Co. Inc.; director: Beckman Instruments. NONPR AFFIL vis com: University Michigan Medical Center; trustee: University Pennsylvania Medical Center; member: Phi Delta Kappa; member: Sigma Theta Tau; member: National Academy Sciences Institute Medicine; member: National League Nursing; vis com: Medical University South Carolina.

Lloyd Charles Elam, MD: trustee B Little Rock, AR 1928. ED Roosevelt University BS (1950); University of Washington MD (1957); University of Illinois (1957-1958); University of Chicago (1958-1961). CORP AFFIL director: Tupperware Corp. Inc.; director: Premark International Inc.; director: Merck & Co. Inc.; director: Phoenix Health System; director: EGT. NONPR AFFIL member: National Medicine Association; member: RF Boyd Medicine Society; member: Nashville Academy Medicine; member: Frontiers America; member: Institute Medicine; member: American Psychiatric Association; member: American Medical Association.

Charles Errol Exley, Jr.: trustee B Detroit, MI 1929. ED Wesleyan University BA (1952); Columbia University MBA (1954). CORP AFFIL director: Banc One Corp.; director: Merck & Co. Inc.

Raymond V. Gilmartin: chairman (see above)

Ruth E. Goldman: program officer

Shuang R. Huang: vice president

Susan J. Quass: fund administrator

John R. Taylor: executive vice president (see above)

Dennis Weatherstone: trustee B London, England 1930. ED Northwestern Polytechnic Institute (1946-1949). CORP AFFIL director: General Motors Corp.; director: Merck & Co. Inc.

Grants Analysis

Disclosure Period: calendar year ending 1995
Total Grants: $13,056,611*
Number of Grants: 251
Average Grant: $39,926*
Highest Grant: $2,114,982
Typical Range: $2,500 to $50,000
***Note:** Giving excludes matching gifts. Average grant excludes two highest grants ($3,114,982).

Recent Grants

Note: Grants derived from 1996 Form 990.

Arts & Humanities

462,500 WGBH, Boston, MA
462,500 WGBH, Boston, MA
462,500 WGBH, Boston, MA
250,000 WGBH, Boston, MA
100,000 Philadelphia Orchestra Association, Philadelphia, PA
50,000 Crossroads Theater Company, New Brunswick, NJ

Civic & Public Affairs

250,000 Ethics Resource Center, Washington, DC
100,000 Fondos Unidos de Puerto Rico, San Juan, PR
55,000 Women's Research and Education Institute, Washington, DC

Education

745,000 United Negro College Fund, New York, NY
500,000 University of Pennsylvania, Philadelphia, PA
480,000 United Negro College Fund, New York, NY
200,000 Cornell University, Ithaca, NY
150,000 University of Pennsylvania Leonard Davis Institute, Philadelphia, PA
100,000 Columbia University, New York, NY
100,000 Harvard University School of Public Health, Cambridge, MA
100,000 Johns Hopkins University School of Medicine, Baltimore, MD
100,000 University of Texas Southwestern Medical College, Dallas, TX
97,229 ESC Foundation of America, Washington, DC
80,000 Harvard School of Public Health, Cambridge, MA
75,000 Polytechnic University, Brooklyn, NY
70,000 American Medical Student Association Foundation, Reston, VA
67,000 Bowman Gray School of Medicine, Winston-Salem, NC
67,000 Research Foundation of the State University of New York, NY
65,000 University of California Los Angeles, Los Angeles, CA
60,000 Purdue University, West Lafayette, IN
60,000 University of Michigan College of Pharmacy, Ann Arbor, MI
55,000 United Negro College Fund, New York, NY
53,000 Raritan Valley Community College, Somerville, NJ
50,000 Association for Academic Minority Physicians, Bardonia, NY
40,000 American Foundation for Pharmaceutical Education, North Plainfield, NJ

Health

500,000 American Red Cross, New York, NY
212,114 American Federation for Aging Research, New York, NY
210,000 American College of Cardiology, Bethesda, MD
120,000 Association for Academic Minority Physicians, Bardonia, NY
60,000 Tufts Managed Care, Medford, MA
58,500 University of Pennsylvania Health System Institute on Aging, Philadelphia, PA
55,000 National Foundation for Infectious Diseases, Bethesda, MD
55,000 National Foundation for Infectious Diseases, Bethesda, MD
50,000 Beth Israel Hospital, Boston, MA
50,000 Columbia Health Law Project
50,000 Florida Public Health Association, FL
45,000 American Society of Health System Pharmacists Research and Education Foundation

International

400,000 Public Radio International, Minneapolis, MN
400,000 Public Radio International, Minneapolis, MN
250,000 University of Cape Town, Rondebosch, Republic of South Africa
250,000 University of Cape Town, Rondebosch, Republic of South Africa

Religion

50,000 First Baptist Community Development Corporation

Social Services

400,000 North Penn United Way, Lansdale, PA
275,000 United Way Union County, Elizabeth, NJ
110,000 Hunterdon United Way
100,000 Children's Inn, Bethesda, MD

MEREDITH CORP.

Company Contact

Des Moines, IA
Web: http://www.meredith.com

Company Description

SIC(s): 2721 Periodicals, 2731 Book Publishing, 4833 Television Broadcasting Stations, 6531 Real Estate Agents & Managers.

Meredith Corp. Foundation

Giving Contact

Gail Stilwill, APR, Manager, Community Relations
Meredith Corp. Contributions Program
1716 Locust St.
Des Moines, IA 50309-3023
Phone: (515)284-2656
Fax: (515)284-3153

Description

Organization Type: Corporate Foundation
Giving Locations: IA: Des Moines metropolitan area
Grant Types: Capital, Emergency, Employee Matching Gifts, General Support, Loan, Project.
Note: Employee matching gift ratio: 1 to 1 for contributions to nonprofit human service or arts organisation and to public educational institutions. Employee matching gift ratio: 2 to 1 for contributions to private secondary and post-secondary educational institutions.

Giving Philosophy

'At Meredith Corporation we have a continuing commitment to community support and social responsibility -- and to making a positive difference. support to a variety of community projects and programs. We search out and support those that offer the best solutions to identified community needs. Because dollars alone are not always the answer, we encourage our employees to be active community volunteers. Our goal is to help make our community stronger and to help ensure a better quality of life for all residents.' Corporate Contributions Program Policy Statement

Financial Summary

Total Giving: $1,200,000 (2000 approx); $1,200,000 (1999 approx); $1,200,000 (1998 approx). Note: Contributes through corporate direct giving program and foundation.

Typical Recipients

Arts & Humanities: Arts Centers, Historic Preservation, Museums/Galleries, Performing Arts, Visual Arts
Civic & Public Affairs: Housing
Education: Colleges & Universities, Journalism/Media Education, Preschool Education
Social Services: Community Service Organizations, Family Services, United Funds/United Ways, Youth Organizations

Contributions Analysis

Arts & Humanities: About 35%. Supports the performing and visual arts, museums, and similar activities and organizations. Emphasis is on projects and programs that help make the arts accessible to a more varied audience, including children, the elderly, persons with disabilities, and the disadvantaged.
Education: About 30%. Contributions primarily support two journalismschools, with an emphasis on magazine journalism. The corporation generally believes that the funding of public education is the responsibility of government and private groups. However, support may be considered for local programs that address specific needs such as children at risk or early childhood education. Also provides educational matching gifts.
Social Services: About 35%. Provides annual support to special projects, and operating support for human services agencies and programs that help meet the needs of under-served people, particularly families and children at risk.

Application Procedures

Initial Contact: written proposal
Application Requirements: name, address, and telephone number of the person submitting the application; copy of the 501(c)(3) tax-exempt letter given by the IRS; a summary of the organization's objectives, a statement of how the organization meets an identified community need, and an indication of the population served by the organization; the specific amount of money being requested and an explanation of how the funds would be used; a current year budget, clearly illustrating earnings and revenues; a list of the organization's board of directors, executive director, and number of staff employed; and an audited financial statement for the most recently completed year of operation
Deadlines: None.
Review Process: the manager of community relations reviews and researches all grant proposals, then makes recommendations to the corporate contributions committee, which is composed of corporate officers
Decision Notification: executives meet quarterly to make contribution decisions
Notes: If the request is for a capital drive or a specific project, a related budget should be included in the proposal, along with an explanation of the need for the drive and a timetable for the campaign.

Restrictions

Does not support individuals, religious organizations for sectarian purposes, organizations outside operating areas, or political or lobbying groups.

Additional Information

The corporation established The Meredith Corporation Foundation in September 1994. The foundation operates separately, but has policies and guidelines similar to the corporate giving program.
Publications: Guidelines Brochure

Corporate Officials

William T. Kerr: chairman, chief executive officer, director B Seattle, WA 1941. ED Oxford University BA (1962); University of Washington BA (1963); Oxford University MA (1965); Harvard University MBA (1967); Harvard University Graduate School of Business Administration MBA (1969). PRIM CORP EMPL chairman, chief executive officer, director: Meredith Corp. CORP AFFIL director: Storage Technology Corp.; director: Principal Financial Group; director: Principal Mutual Life Insurance Co.; chairman: Golf Digest/Tennis Inc.; director: Maytag Corp. NONPR AFFIL director: International Federation Periodical Press; member: Magazine Publishers American; member: Century Association. CLUB AFFIL Union Club; Wakonda Golf Club; Quogue Field Club; Reform Club; Des Moines Club; Litchfield Country Club; Brook Club.
Edwin Thomas Meredith, III: chairman executive committee B Chicago, IL 1933. ED University of Arizona (1953). PRIM CORP EMPL chairman executive committee: Meredith Corp.
Jack Daniel Rehm: chairman emeritus, director B Yonkers, NY 1932. ED College of the Holy Cross BSBA (1954). PRIM CORP EMPL chairman emeritus, director: Meredith Corp. CORP AFFIL director: Norwest Bank Iowa NA; director: Vernon Co.; director: Equitable of Iowa Companies; director: International Multifoods Corp. NONPR AFFIL member business committee: Museum Modern Art; member mag. & print committee: U.S. Information Agency; member: Iowa Business Council; director: Magazine Publishers Association; board governors: Drake University; member business committee: Greater Des Moines Committee; director: American Council Capital Formation; trustee: College Holy Cross. CLUB AFFIL Scarsdale Golf Club; Wakonda Golf Club; Pine Valley Golf Club.
Allen L. Sabbag: president B 1944. ED University of New Hampshire BA. PRIM CORP EMPL president: Meredith MA Corp. CORP AFFIL Director: Realtor Information Network.

Giving Program Officials

Leo R. Armatis: B Grand Island, NE 1937. ED Creighton University (1959). PRIM CORP EMPL vice president corp. relations: Meredith Corp.
William T. Kerr: vice president B Seattle, WA 1941. ED Oxford University BA (1962); University of Washington BA (1963); Oxford University MA (1965); Harvard University MBA (1967); Harvard University Graduate School of Business Administration MBA (1969). PRIM CORP EMPL chairman, chief executive officer, director: Meredith Corp. CORP AFFIL director: Storage Technology Corp.; director: Principal Financial Group; director: Principal Mutual Life Insurance Co.; chairman: Golf Digest/Tennis Inc.; director: Maytag Corp. NONPR AFFIL director: International Federation Periodical Press; member: Magazine Publishers American; member: Century Association. CLUB AFFIL Union Club; Wakonda Golf Club; Quogue Field Club; Reform Club; Des Moines Club; Litchfield Country Club; Brook Club.
Jack Daniel Rehm: president B Yonkers, NY 1932. ED College of the Holy Cross BSBA (1954). PRIM CORP EMPL chairman emeritus, director: Meredith Corp. CORP AFFIL director: Norwest Bank Iowa NA; director: Vernon Co.; director: Equitable of Iowa Companies; director: International Multifoods Corp. NONPR AFFIL member business committee: Museum Modern Art; member mag. & print committee: U.S. Information Agency; member: Iowa Business Council; director: Magazine Publishers Association; board governors: Drake University; member business committee: Greater Des Moines Committee; director: American Council Capital Formation; trustee: College Holy Cross. CLUB AFFIL Scarsdale Golf Club; Wakonda Golf Club; Pine Valley Golf Club.
Gail Stilwill: PRIM CORP EMPL manager community relations: Meredith Corp.

Grants Analysis

Disclosure Period: calendar year ending
Typical Range: $5,000 to $25,000

Merit Oil Corp.

Company Contact

Haverford, PA

Company Description

Employees: 150

Merit Gasoline Foundation

Giving Contact

Robert M. Harting, Executive Director
Merit Gasoline Foundation
551 West Lancaster Avenue
Haverford, PA 19041
Phone: (610)527-7900

Description

Founded: 1956
EIN: 236282846
Organization Type: Corporate Foundation
Giving Locations: cities in the Mid-Atlantic and New England states where company has operating gasoline stations.
Grant Types: Employee Matching Gifts, General Support, Operating Expenses.

Financial Summary

Total Giving: $224,431 (fiscal year ending August 31, 1998); $211,678 (fiscal 1997); $197,930 (fiscal 1996). Note: Contributes through corporate direct giving program and foundation.

Giving Analysis: Giving for fiscal 1997 includes: foundation grants to United Way ($40,520); fiscal 1998: foundation grants to United Way ($42,570)
Assets: $432,010 (fiscal 1998); $299,355 (fiscal 1997); $327,296 (fiscal 1996)
Gifts Received: $352,000 (fiscal 1998); $175,000 (fiscal 1997); $225,000 (fiscal 1996)

Typical Recipients

Arts & Humanities: Arts Centers, Ethnic & Folk Arts, Arts & Humanities-General, History & Archaeology, Libraries, Museums/Galleries, Music, Performing Arts
Civic & Public Affairs: Community Foundations, Employment/Job Training, Civic & Public Affairs-General, Urban & Community Affairs
Education: Arts/Humanities Education, Colleges & Universities, Community & Junior Colleges, Education-General, Medical Education, Private Education (Precollege), Vocational & Technical Education
Environment: Environment-General, Resource Conservation
Health: Arthritis, Children's Health/Hospitals, Clinics/Medical Centers, Emergency/Ambulance Services, Health-General, Health Organizations, Hospitals, Multiple Sclerosis, Public Health, Single-Disease Health Associations
Religion: Jewish Causes, Religious Organizations, Religious Welfare
Social Services: Child Welfare, Community Service Organizations, Domestic Violence, Family Services, Food/Clothing Distribution, Recreation & Athletics, Scouts, Shelters/Homelessness, Social Services-General, Substance Abuse, United Funds/United Ways, Youth Organizations

Contributions Analysis

Giving Priorities: Primary emphasis on Jewish welfare, social services, and education.
Arts & Humanities: 31%. Supports museums and art centers, orchestra, and the performing arts.
Civic & Public Affairs: 1%.
Education: 18%. Primarily funds universities and colleges.
Environment: About 1%. Supports nature conservancy.
Health: 8%. Supports medical services and single-disease causes.
Religion: 46%. Supports Jewish causes.
Social Services: 23%. Focus on the United Way and child welfare.
Note: Total contributions in fiscal 1998.

Application Procedures

Initial Contact: Send a full proposal.
Application Requirements: Include a statement of need; purpose and activities of organization; purpose of funds sought; problem being addressed, goals to be accomplished, and activities planned; organization name and address; evidence from the IRS indicating organization is not a private foundation and contributions are tax deductible; detailed project budget, amount requested, sources of additional funding, recent annual report and financial statement, including a list of current major donors; and a list of directors and officers, including affiliations.
Deadlines: None.

Restrictions

Does not support individuals, political or lobbying groups, or organizations outside operating areas.

Additional Information

The company reports that giving is very limited, and it does not generally welcome unsolicited requests for funding.

Corporate Officials

Ivan H. Gabel: president, chief executive officer B 1932. PRIM CORP EMPL president, chief executive officer: Merit Oil Corp. CORP AFFIL president: Merit Oil Connecticut Inc.; president: Merit Oil Maryland Inc.; president, chief executive officer: Meadville Corp.

Foundation Officials

Ivan H. Gabel: trustee (see above)
Leonard E. Gilmar: trustee PRIM CORP EMPL senior vice president: Merit Oil of Maryland Inc.
Robert M. Harting: executive director, trustee PRIM CORP EMPL vice president: Meadville Corp. CORP AFFIL vice president: Merit Oil Corp.; secretary: Merit Oil Maryland Inc.
Joseph M. Jerome: trustee
David A. Laubach: trustee PRIM CORP EMPL treasurer: Meadville Corp. CORP AFFIL treasurer: Merit Oil Connecticut Inc.; treasurer: Merit Oil Maryland Inc.; treasurer: Merit Oil Co.
Morton Sand: trustee
Lois B. Victor: chairman, trustee

Grants Analysis

Disclosure Period: fiscal year ending August 31, 1998
Total Grants: $181,861*
Number of Grants: 151
Average Grant: $1,204
Highest Grant: $66,000
Typical Range: $500 to $3,000
***Note:** Giving excludes United Way.

Recent Grants

Note: Grants derived from 1998 Form 990.

Arts & Humanities

2,000	Painted Bride Art Center, Philadelphia, PA
1,500	Curtis Institute of Music, Philadelphia, PA
1,000	Philadelphia Museum of Art, Philadelphia, PA
1,000	Philadelphia Orchestra, Philadelphia, PA
849	The Mann Center for the Performing Arts, Philadelphia, PA

Civic & Public Affairs

1,000	Fund for Philadelphia, Inc., Philadelphia, PA

Education

6,000	University of Connecticut, Storrs, CT
3,000	Dickinson College, Carlisle, PA
3,000	Fairleigh Dickinson University, Teneck, NJ
3,000	Hampton University, Hampton, VA
3,000	Johnson & Wales University, Providence, RI
3,000	Lasalle University, Philadelphia, PA
3,000	Rowan University, Glassboro, NJ
3,000	Salem State College, Salem, MA
2,000	Suffolk County Community College, Brentwood, NY
1,250	Settlement Music School, Philadelphia, PA
1,150	Mount Union College, Alliance, OH
1,000	Barnard College, New York, NY
1,000	Howard University, Cambridge, MA
1,000	Polytechnic Preparatory Country Day School, Brooklyn, NY
1,000	Rider University, Lawrenceville, NJ

Environment

1,000	The Wyck Association, Philadelphia, PA

Health

15,000	Albert Einstein Healthcare Network, Philadelphia, PA
1,000	Cystic Fibrosis Foundation, New York, NY
650	Arthritis Foundation, Philadelphia, PA

Religion

66,000	Jewish Federation of Greater Philadelphia, Philadelphia, PA
11,000	UJA-Federation, New York, NY
8,500	Combined Jewish Philanthropies of Greater Boston, Boston, MA
1,500	Allied Appeal of the Jewish Federation of Southern New Jersey, Cherry Hill, NJ
1,440	New Hampshire Catholic Charities, Inc./Future of Our Faith Campaign, Manchester, NH
1,300	Federation Allied Jewish Appeal, Philadelphia, PA
1,000	Jewish Family & Children's Service of Greater Philadelphia, Philadelphia, PA

Social Services

16,500	United Way of Southeastern Pennsylvania, Philadelphia, PA
6,435	United Way of New York City, New York, NY
2,640	United Way of Long Island, Deer Park, NY
2,500	Pal of Philadelphia, Philadelphia, PA
2,145	United Way of Massachusetts Bay, Inc., Boston, MA
2,000	Bethesada Project, Philadelphia, PA
2,000	Philabundance, Philadelphia, PA
2,000	Share a Night, Philadelphia, PA
1,320	United Way of Central Maryland, Inc., Baltimore, MD
1,320	United Way of Southeastern New England, Providence, RI
990	United Way of Essex & West Hudson, Newark, NJ
990	United Way of Greater New Haven, New Haven, CT
825	United Way of Bergen County, Oradell, NJ
825	United Way of Camden County, Camden, NJ
825	United Way of Hudson County, Jersey City, NJ
800	Corporate Alliance for Drug Education, Philadelphia, PA
660	United Way of Delaware, Inc., Wilmington, DE
660	United Way Services, Richmond, VA

MERRILL LYNCH &CO., INC.

Company Contact

New York, NY
Web: http://www.ml.com

Company Description

Revenue: US$34,879,000,000 (1999)
Profit: US$1,259,000,000
Employees: 56,600
Fortune Rank: 29, per FORTUNE Magazine's list of 500 Largest U.S. Corporations (1999).
FF 29
SIC(s): 6211 Security Brokers & Dealers, 6719 Holding Companies Nec.

Operating Locations

Netherlands: SNC Farringdon International (Holdings) BV, Amsterdam, Noord-Holland; Panama: Merrill Lynch International Bank, Panama City; Singapore: Merrill Lynch Pierce Fenner & Smith (Singapore) Pte. Ltd., Singapore; Smith New Court (Singapore) Pte. Ltd., Singapore; Spain: Merrill Lynch Capital Markets Espana SA SVB, Madrid; Sweden: Merrill Lynch NV; Switzerland: Rowe (Europe) SA, Geneva; United Kingdom: Merrill Lynch Trust CO. (Jersey) Ltd., Jersey, Channel Islands; Chetwynd Nominees Ltd., London; Crestgrove Finance Ltd., London; Farringdon Investments Ltd., London; Hackremco Ltd., London; Merrill Lynch Asset Management UK Ltd., London; Merrill Lynch Bank (Suisse) SA, London; Merrill Lynch Capital Markets Plc, London;

Merrill Lynch Equities Ltd., London; Merrill Lynch Europe Plc, London; Merrill Lynch Gilts Ltd., London; Merrill Lynch Global Asset Management Ltd., London; Merrill Lynch International, London; Merrill Lynch Money Markets London, London; Merrill Lynch Pierce Fenner & Smith (Brokers & Dealers) Ltd., London; New Court Securities Ltd., London; NY Nominees Ltd., London; Sealion Nominees Ltd., London; Smith Bros. Plc, London; Smith Bros. (Services & Leasing) Ltd., London; SNC Corporate Finance Ltd., London; SNC Financial Services Ltd., London; SNC International (Holdings) Ltd., London; SNC Securities Ltd., London; Trading Technology Ltd., London

Nonmonetary Support

Type: Donated Equipment; In-kind Services
Contact: Bettina Lauf, Assistant Vice President, Corporate Responsibility
Note: Company donates equipment when available.

Corporate Sponsorship

Type: Arts & cultural events; Festivals/fairs; Music & entertainment events; Pledge-a-thon
Contact: Linda Federici, Director, Executive Communications/Client Service

Merrill Lynch & Co. Foundation Inc.

Giving Contact

Ms. Westina L. Matthews, Corporate Responsibility
Merrill Lynch & Co.
World Financial Ctr., South Tower
New York, NY 10080-6106
Phone: (212)231-4519
Fax: (212)236-8007
Web: http://www.ml.com/woml/phil_prog/index.htm

Description

Founded: 1950
EIN: 136139556
Organization Type: Corporate Foundation
Giving Locations: NY: New York metropolitan area national organizations; primarily in areas where Merrill Lynch & Co. maintains offices.
Grant Types: Capital, Employee Matching Gifts, General Support, Multiyear/Continuing Support.
Note: Employee matching gift ratio: 1 to 1 up to $1,500 annually to educational institutions.

Giving Philosophy

'We believe that no conflict need exist between pursuing our interests as a corporation and furthering the interests of society as a whole. Across a wide variety of fields, Merrill Lynch employees and Merrill Lynch charitable contributions are at work promoting the interests of our communities, our clients, and our stockholders -- indeed, of everyone. We strive to address philanthropic opportunities with a maximum of flexibility and openness. We also believe that consistency is important, and so we give in ways that will create the most sustained benefits. These efforts are a practical expression of our belief in the values that have made us a success in business and a leader in responsible corporate citizenship.'

Financial Summary

Total Giving: $31,454,780 (1997); $21,059,659 (1996); $16,885,357 (1995). Note: Contributes through corporate direct giving program and foundation. 1997 Giving includes corporate direct giving ($12,513,426); foundation ($18,941,354); domestic subsidiaries.
Assets: $54,161,696 (1997); $55,009,956 (1996); $37,282,895 (1995)
Gifts Received: $11,691,271 (1994); $7,206,475 (1993); $6,603,422 (1992). Note: Gifts received from Merrill Lynch and Company, Inc.

Typical Recipients

Arts & Humanities: Arts Centers, Arts Outreach, Ethnic & Folk Arts, Historic Preservation, History & Archaeology, Libraries, Museums/Galleries, Music, Opera, Performing Arts, Public Broadcasting, Theater
Civic & Public Affairs: African American Affairs, Botanical Gardens/Parks, Business/Free Enterprise, Civil Rights, Community Foundations, Economic Development, Employment/Job Training, Civic & Public Affairs-General, Housing, Municipalities/Towns, Public Policy, Women's Affairs, Zoos/Aquariums
Education: Business Education, Business-School Partnerships, Colleges & Universities, Economic Education, Education Reform, Health & Physical Education, Journalism/Media Education, Legal Education, Literacy, Minority Education, Science/Mathematics Education, Special Education, Student Aid
Environment: Wildlife Protection
Health: AIDS/HIV, Cancer, Children's Health/Hospitals, Clinics/Medical Centers, Emergency/Ambulance Services, Geriatric Health, Health Organizations, Heart, Hospitals, Medical Research, Single-Disease Health Associations, Transplant Networks/Donor Banks
International: Foreign Educational Institutions, Health Care/Hospitals, International Affairs, International Development, International Peace & Security Issues, International Relations, International Relief Efforts
Religion: Jewish Causes, Religious Welfare
Science: Science Museums, Scientific Centers & Institutes, Scientific Labs
Social Services: At-Risk Youth, Child Welfare, Community Centers, Crime Prevention, Emergency Relief, Family Services, Food/Clothing Distribution, People with Disabilities, Recreation & Athletics, Scouts, Senior Services, Shelters/Homelessness, Substance Abuse, United Funds/United Ways, Veterans, YMCA/YWCA/YMHA/YWHA, Youth Organizations

Contributions Analysis

Giving Priorities: Colleges and universities; museums and arts centers and funds, primarily in New York City; public policy research; a variety of local and national social service organizations; and hospitals. Company supports public policy, international trade, and professional organizations. In 1995, contributions to domestic organizations with an international focus were more than $300,000.
Arts & Humanities: 20% to 25%. Major areas of support include music, ethnic and folk museums, arts centers and institutes and dance theaters. Includes Access to the Arts program in New York City.
Civic & Public Affairs: 10% to 15%. Interests include business, civil rights, jobtraining, urban and community affairs, and women's and minority affairs. (United Funds & United Way) 5% to 10%.
Education: 35% to 40%. Supports education reform, minority education, student aid, colleges and universities, and business and technical education. Additionally, awards scholarships to children of employees based both on merit and need.
Health: 10% to 15%. Donations fund single-disease health associations,hospitals and health organizations, clinics and medical centers, geriatric health groups, children's health concerns, and emergency services.
Social Services: 10% to 15%. Gives to a variety of local and national organizations, with emphasis on youth and community service organizations. Other interests include substance abuse programs, YMCAs, and people with disabilities.

Application Procedures

Initial Contact: brief letter of inquiry; if outside greater New York area, apply directly to local branch office
Application Requirements: description and background of organization, amount requested, purpose of funds sought, duration of project, plan to evaluate the use of the funds, copy of 501(c)(3) tax exemption letter, list of governing board members, most recent annual audited financial statement, current financial statement, and current operating budget
Deadlines: None.
Review Process: proposals reviewed by manager of corporate contributions and foundation president for recommendation to board of trustees; decision to decline request made immediately; trustees meet quarterly
Evaluative Criteria: priority given to organizations in greater New York metropolitan area
Decision Notification: decisions for direct gifts are generally made within two months of receipt

Restrictions

The company will not make grants to the following: individuals; fraternal, social or athletic organizations; religious organizations or government agencies (for operating support); political parties, groups, or candidates; local affiliates of national organizations; or organizations that serve a very limited geographic area. The company will not make grants for the reduction of an operating deficit or to liquidate a debt.

Additional Information

The company will consider support of capital needs when the specific project submitted has distinctive importance or the promise of a unique contribution to the field.
Since the company has a predetermined limit on multiyear commitments, grants usually are of a one-year duration. Requests for continuing support are considered using the company's priorities for the proposed grant year.
Publications: Responsible Citizenship Annual Report

Corporate Officials

Herbert Monroe Allison, Jr.: president, chief operating officer B Pittsburgh, PA 1943. ED Yale University BA (1965); Stanford University MBA (1971). PRIM CORP EMPL president, chief operating officer: Merrill Lynch & Co., Inc. CORP AFFIL president: Merrill Lynch International Financial Corp.; chief financial officer, executive vice president: Merrill Lynch Pierce Fenner & Smith.
Paul W. Critchlow: senior vice president marketing & communications PRIM CORP EMPL senior vice president marketing & communications: Merrill Lynch & Co., Inc.
Stephen Lawrence Hammerman: vice chairman, general counsel B Brooklyn, NY 1938. ED University of Pennsylvania BS (1959); New York University LLB (1962). PRIM CORP EMPL vice chairman, general counsel: Merrill Lynch & Co., Inc. ADD CORP EMPL general counsel: Merrill Lynch Pierce Fenner & Smith. NONPR AFFIL member: New York Stock Exchange Inc.; member: Securities Industry Association; member, investment committee chairman: Association Bar New York City.
David H. Komansky: chairman, chief executive officer B Mount Vernon, NY 1939. ED University of Miami. PRIM CORP EMPL chairman, chief executive officer: Merrill Lynch & Co., Inc. ADD CORP EMPL president: Merrill Lynch, Pierce, Fenner & Smith Inc. CORP AFFIL director: New York Stock Exchange Inc.
Westina Lomax Matthews: senior director, first vice president corporate respons B Chillicothe, OH 1948. ED University of Dayton BS (1970); University of Dayton MS (1974); University of Chicago PhD (1980). PRIM CORP EMPL senior director, first vice president corporate respons: Merrill Lynch & Co., Inc.
John Laundon Steffens: executive vice president B Cleveland, OH 1941. ED Dartmouth College (1963). PRIM CORP EMPL executive vice president: Merrill Lynch & Co., Inc. CORP AFFIL executive vice president: Merrill Lynch Pierce Fenner & Smith.

Foundation Officials

Herbert Monroe Allison, Jr.: vice president, trustee (see above)
Stanley Baumblatt: assistant secretary

William L. Burke: trustee
Paul W. Critchlow: president, trustee (see above)
Stephen Lawrence Hammerman: vice president, trustee (see above)
David H. Komansky: trustee, vice president (see above)
Thomas J. Lombardi: treasurer
Westina Lomax Matthews: secretary, trustee (see above)
Mary E. Taylor: vice president, trustee

Grants Analysis

Disclosure Period: calendar year ending 1997
Total Grants: $31,454,780
Number of Grants: 7,829
Average Grant: $4,018
Typical Range: $1,000 to $20,000
Note: Grants analysis provided by foundation.

Recent Grants

Note: Grants derived from 1995 Form 990.

Arts & Humanities

250,000 New York Public Library, New York, NY -- second of three payments on $665,000 grant, for business and industry library
175,000 New Jersey Performing Arts Center, Newark, NJ -- final of three payments on $500,000 grant, for first phase of building plan
55,000 Lincoln Center for Performing Arts Consolidated Corporate Fund, New York, NY
50,000 Jacksonville Symphony Orchestra, Jacksonville, FL -- capital campaign
50,000 National Museum of the American Indian, Washington, DC -- third of four payments on $250,000 grant, for capital campaign
50,000 Opera Company, Lincoln, MA -- final of two payments on $100,000 grant, for capital campaign
50,000 Whitney Museum of American Art, New York, NY -- capital campaign
30,000 Metropolitan Museum of Art, New York, NY -- corporate membership
25,000 A.A. Cunningham Air Museum Foundation, Havelock, NC -- second of three payments on $75,000 grant, for capital campaign

Civic & Public Affairs

150,000 Central Park Conservancy, New York, NY -- final of three payments on $500,000 grant, for capital campaign
50,000 Fund for the City of New York, New York, NY -- for short-term loan program
50,000 Jacksonville Zoological Gardens, Jacksonville, FL -- capital campaign
50,000 New York Botanical Garden, Bronx, NY -- first of three payments on $150,000 grant, for capital campaign
25,000 East Harlem Employment Services, New York, NY -- for Project Strive

Education

100,000 Cornell University, Ithaca, NY -- first of three payments on $250,000 grant, for Financial Engineering Program
75,000 United Negro College Fund, Fairfax, VA -- final of three payments on $250,000 grant, for Campaign 2000
75,000 University of Virginia Darden School of Business, Charlottesville, VA -- second of three payments on $200,000 grant, for capital campaign
50,000 Boston College, Chestnut Hill, MA -- first of three payments on $150,000 grant
50,000 Columbia University Graduate School of Business, New York, NY -- second of three payments on $150,000 grant, for capital improvements
50,000 Hofstra University Frank G. Zarb School of Business, Hempstead, NY
50,000 United Negro College Fund, New York, NY
50,000 University of Chicago Graduate School of Business, Chicago, IL -- for research projects
50,000 University of Chicago Graduate School of Management, Chicago, IL -- final of two payments on $100,000 grant, for Downtown Center
30,000 Jackie Robinson Foundation, New York, NY -- final of four payments on $120,000 grant, for scholarships
27,000 Knight-Bagehot Fellowship in Economics and Business, New York, NY -- scholarship program
26,000 Centenary College, Shreveport, LA -- for scholars program
25,000 Amherst College, Amherst, MA -- first of four payments on $100,000 grant, for Winthrop H. Smith Chair
25,000 Bradley University, Peoria, IL
25,000 Fairfield University, Fairfield, CT -- final of four payments on $100,000 grant
25,000 Howard University, Washington, DC -- second of four payments on $100,000 grant, for scholarships
25,000 Inner-City Scholarship Fund, New York, NY
25,000 New York University, New York, NY -- final of two payments on $50,000 grant, for Thurgood Marshall Scholarship Program
25,000 Providence College, Providence, RI -- final of two payments on $50,000 grant, for business diversity program
25,000 St. John's University, Jamaica, NY -- for scholarship program
25,000 Smith College, Northampton, MA -- final of three payments on $75,000 grant, for Community College Connections Program
25,000 University of Mississippi, University, MS -- first of two payments on $50,000 grant, for capital campaign
25,000 University of North Florida College of Business Administration, Jacksonville, FL -- for financial services classroom
25,000 University of Virginia, Charlottesville, FL -- final of two payments on $50,000 grant, for Charles Ross Fellowship

Environment

50,000 Wildlife Conservation Society, Bronx, NY -- first of three payments on $150,000 grant, for general education program

Health

250,000 Massachusetts General Hospital, Boston, MA -- third of four payments on $1 million grant, for Schreyer Cardiac Fellowship
75,000 New York Downtown Hospital, New York, NY -- final of three payments on $225,000 grant, for Campaign for Excellence
50,000 Dana-Farber Cancer Institute, Boston, MA -- capital campaign
25,000 Morehouse School of Medicine, Atlanta, GA -- for pediatric center

International

250,000 Center for Strategic and International Studies, Washington, DC
250,000 Center for Strategic and International Studies, Washington, DC

Religion

50,000 Museum of Jewish Heritage, New York, NY -- final of two payments on $100,000 grant, for capital campaign

Social Services

1,000,000 United Way Tri-State Area, New York, NY
35,000 National Center for Disability Services, Albertson, NY -- second of three payments on $100,000 grant, for capital campaign
30,000 Boys Club, New York, NY -- final of three payments on $100,000 grant, for Flushing Clubhouse renovations
30,000 YMCA, New York, NY -- final of three payments on $100,000 grant, for Campaign for Youth
25,000 Big Shoulders Fund, Chicago, IL -- first of two payments on $50,000 grant

MERVYN'S CALIFORNIA

Company Contact

22301 Foothill Boulevard
Hayward, CA 94541
Phone: (510)727-3000
Web: http://www.mervyns.com

Company Description

SIC(s): 5311 Department Stores.
Parent Company: Target Corp., 777 Nicollet Mall, Minneapolis, MN, United States

Nonmonetary Support

Type: Donated Products

Corporate Sponsorship

Type: Arts & cultural events; Music & entertainment events; Pledge-a-thon; Festivals/fairs
Contact: Shanin Sullivan, Community Relations Specialist
Note: Supports family-oriented arts programs, March of Dimes, AIDS walks, and events for disadvantaged children, the disabled, and seniors.

Giving Contact

Jeff Spiegel, Manager, Community Relations
Mervyn's California
Mail Stop 479
22301 Foothill Blvd.
Hayward, CA 94541
Phone: (510)727-5679
Fax: (510)727-5666

Alternate Contact

Phone: (510)727-5669

Description

Organization Type: Corporate Giving Program
Giving Locations: headquarters and operating communities, including stores and distribution centers.
Grant Types: Project.

Financial Summary

Total Giving: $6,200,000 (1998 approx); $5,300,000 (1997 approx); $1,530,000 (1996). Note: Contributes through corporate direct giving program only.

Typical Recipients

Arts & Humanities: Arts Associations & Councils, Arts Centers, Arts Festivals, Dance, Ethnic & Folk Arts, Museums/Galleries, Music, Opera, Performing Arts, Theater, Visual Arts
Social Services: Day Care, Family Services, United Funds/United Ways

Contributions Analysis

Arts & Humanities: Funds professional arts organizations that provide affordable and accessible arts programs for families and children. Supports family

arts programs which offer reduced ticket prices, making them accessible to diverse audiences.
Education: 30% to 35%. Supports family involvement in education by funding community-based nonprofit organizations that are in partnership with local schools and their parent organizations. Participates in the School Partnership Program, partnering with one school in each store community to strengthen and improve the education of children. Sponsors ChildSpree program, through which matching funds are provided up to $3,000 to local nonprofit agencies to help economically disadvantaged children get the clothes they need for school. Committed to providing scholarship to female graduating senoirs through the Women's Sports Foundation, one grant of $25,000 and one hundred$1,000 grants.
Social Services: 25% to 30%. Funds critical social action programs designed to serve the needs of disadvantaged women and children. Priority is given to comprehensive programs that prepare women for work and enable families to become self-sufficient. Focus on youth, especially self-esteem building activities.

Application Procedures

Initial Contact: letter of inquiry, or call the Community Giving Hotline (510)727-5669 for details on proposals
Deadlines: None.
Evaluative Criteria: priority is given to proposals which fall within established guidelines and respond to communities of color and/or promote cultural diversity, and which serve local store communities
Decision Notification: applicants are notified within 60 to 90 days
Notes: Guidelines are available at Mervyn's stores; applications can be directed to local stores, or mailed to above address. To locate your nearest Mervyn's California store, call (800) MERVYNS.

Restrictions

Does not support individuals, religious organizations for sectarian purposes, or political or lobbying groups.

Additional Information

Contributions from Mervyn's are included in parent company Dayton Hudson's giving totals.
Publications: Guidelines

Corporate Officials

Bart Butzer: president director PRIM CORP EMPL president: Mervyn's. CORP AFFIL president: Dayton Hudson Corp.
Jan O'Laughlin: headquarters director PRIM CORP EMPL headquarters director: Mervyn's.

Giving Program Officials

Bernard Boudreaux: senior community relations representative
Linda Kendrix Burroughs: senior communication relations representative
Jan O'Laughlin: senior community relations representative PRIM CORP EMPL headquarters director: Mervyn's.
Jeff Spiegel: community relations manager

Grants Analysis

Disclosure Period: calendar year ending
Typical Range: $500 to $5,000

METROPOLITAN LIFE INSURANCE CO.

 Number 51 of Top 100 Corporate Givers

Company Contact

1 Madison Ave.
New York, NY 10010-3690
Phone: (212)578-2211
Fax: (212)578-3320
Web: http://www.metlife.com

Company Description

Also Known As: MetLife.
Revenue: US$25,426,000,000 (1999)
Profit: US$617,000,000 (1999)
Employees: 42,300 (1999)
Fortune Rank: 53, per FORTUNE Magazine's list of 500 Largest U.S. Corporations (1999).
FF 53
SIC(s): 6311 Life Insurance, 6371 Pension, Health & Welfare Funds.

Operating Locations

Canada: Metropolitan Life Financial Management Ltd., Ottawa; Metropolitan Life Financial Services Ltd., Ottawa; Metropolitan Life Holdings Ltd., Ottawa; Morguard Investments Ltd., Toronto; Metropolitan Life Insurance Co., Windsor; Republic of Korea: Kolon Metlife Insurance Co., Iga Jung-Ku, Seoul; Taiwan: Metropolitan Life Insurance Co. Ltd. Taiwan Branch, Taipei; United Kingdom: Albany International Assurance Ltd., Castletown, Isle of Man; ACFC Home Loans Ltd., London; Albany Pension Managers & Trustees Ltd., London; GFM International Investors Ltd., London; GFM Investments Ltd., London; Metlife Investments Ltd., London; Metropolitan Reinsurance Co. (United Kingdom) Ltd., London; ACFC Corporate Finance Ltd., Potters Bar, Hertfordshire; Albany General Insurance Co. Ltd., Potters Bar, Hertfordshire; Albany Life Assurance Co. Ltd., Potters Bar, Hertfordshire; Metlife Group Services Ltd., Potters Bar, Hertfordshire; Metlife Independent Financial Services Ltd., Potters Bar, Hertfordshire; Metlife (United Kingdom) Ltd., Potters Bar, Hertfordshire; Metropolitan Home Loans Ltd., Potters Bar, Hertfordshire; Metropolitan Unit Trust Managers Ltd., Potters Bar, Hertfordshire

SUBSIDIARY COMPANIES

MO: GenAmerica Corp., St. Louis

Nonmonetary Support

Value: $128,694 (1987)
Type: Donated Equipment; In-kind Services; Loaned Employees; Loaned Executives
Volunteer Programs: Recognizes company volunteers with the MetLife Volunteer ServiceAwards; also sponsors an employee volunter program that helps employees find volunteer opportunities with nonprofits, schools, and other public agencies. There is a full-time volunteer coordinator at the headquarters location, and several branch offices have structured volunteer programs. Company makes small grants to organizations where employees actively volunteer, through the Volunteer Ventures program.
Contact: Dennis White, Vice President
Note: The company also offers select use of facilities by nonprofits.

Corporate Sponsorship

Type: Arts & cultural events; Festivals/fairs; Music & entertainment events; Pledge-a-thon; Sports events
Contact: Dennis White, Vice President

MetLife Foundation

Giving Contact

Sibyl C. Jacobson, President & Chief Executive Officer
MetLife Foundation
1 Madison Ave.
New York, NY 10010
Phone: (212)578-6272
Fax: (212)685-1435
Web: http://www.metlife.com/Companyinfo/Community/index.html

Description

EIN: 132878224
Organization Type: Corporate Foundation
Giving Locations: programs that are national in scope; special consideration to communities in which Metropolitan has a major presence.
Grant Types: Employee Matching Gifts, General Support, Loan, Multiyear/Continuing Support, Project, Research, Scholarship, Seed Money.
Note: Employee matching gift ratio: 1 to 1. Scholarships are for employees children only.

Giving Philosophy

'Metropolitan Life Foundation was created for the purpose of supporting various scientific, educational, health and welfare, and civic and cultural organizations. The primary objective of the Foundation is to assist tax-exempt organizations through a program of financial support, particularly in the communities in which Metropolitan has a major presence. The Foundation continues a tradition of corporate contributions and community involvement begun and carried forward by Metropolitan since 1909.' Metropolitan Life Foundation Policy and Guidelines for Grant Consideration

Financial Summary

Total Giving: $16,629,185 (1998); $13,605,413 (1997); $13,050,206 (1996). Note: Contributes through corporate direct giving program and foundation.
Giving Analysis: Giving for 1997 includes: foundation ($9,640,200); corporate direct giving ($2,539,551); foundation grants to United Way ($1,425,662); foundation scholarships ($253,730); 1998: foundation ($9,484,840); corporate direct giving ($4,857,780); foundation grants to United Way ($1,335,480); foundation matching gifts ($697,355)
Assets: $253,717,567 (1998); $108,969,353 (1995); $94,338,092 (1994)
Gifts Received: $53,000 (1998); $144,833,024 (1996); $1,625,000 (1994)

Typical Recipients

Arts & Humanities: Arts Associations & Councils, Arts Centers, Arts Institutes, Ballet, Dance, Ethnic & Folk Arts, Film & Video, Historic Preservation, Libraries, Museums/Galleries, Music, Opera, Performing Arts, Public Broadcasting, Theater, Visual Arts
Civic & Public Affairs: African American Affairs, Botanical Gardens/Parks, Business/Free Enterprise, Civil Rights, Economic Development, Economic Policy, Employment/Job Training, Civic & Public Affairs-General, Hispanic Affairs, Housing, Law & Justice, Municipalities/Towns, Professional & Trade Associations, Public Policy, Rural Affairs, Safety, Urban & Community Affairs, Women's Affairs, Zoos/Aquariums
Education: Agricultural Education, Arts/Humanities Education, Business Education, Colleges & Universities, Community & Junior Colleges, Economic Education, Education Associations, Education Reform, Engineering/Technological Education, Faculty Development, Education-General, Health & Physical Education, Literacy, Medical Education, Minority Education, Science/Mathematics Education, Student Aid
Environment: Environment-General
Health: AIDS/HIV, Cancer, Children's Health/Hospitals, Clinics/Medical Centers, Health Policy/Cost Containment, Health Funds, Health Organizations, Heart, Hospitals, Medical Research, Medical Training, Nursing Services, Nutrition, Prenatal Health Issues, Public Health, Research/Studies Institutes, Transplant Networks/Donor Banks
International: Foreign Arts Organizations, Foreign Educational Institutions, Health Care/Hospitals, International Organizations, International Peace & Security Issues, International Relief Efforts
Religion: Religious Welfare
Science: Science Museums, Scientific Centers & Institutes

Social Services: At-Risk Youth, Child Welfare, Community Service Organizations, Counseling, Crime Prevention, Delinquency & Criminal Rehabilitation, Family Services, Food/Clothing Distribution, Homes, Scouts, Shelters/Homelessness, Substance Abuse, United Funds/United Ways, Volunteer Services, YMCA/YWCA/YMHA/YWHA, Youth Organizations

Contributions Analysis

Giving Priorities: Public education improvement; health and safety, drug abuse prvention for youth, and wellness programs; public broadcasting; United Way; civic affairs; and cultural organizations.

Arts & Humanities: 26%. Foundation aims to bring enriching cultural experiences to diverse audiences across the country. Grants are made for arts education, as well as tours, traveling exhibitions, cultural broadcasts, public broadcasting, national arts centers, museums, journalism, and the written, performing and visual arts. Funding is also provided for creation of new work and initiatives that foster greater understanding and appreciation of diversity.

Civic & Public Affairs: 20%. The foundation awards civic affairs grants to help organizations meet the pressing economic and social needs of their communities. Targeted to low- and moderate-income areas, these grants are earmarked for affordable housing, economic development, family and youth programs, and business, economic and public policy research organizations. Volunteer activity, especially among young people and MetLife employees, is also supported.

Education: 15%. Foundation works primarily with national organizations to respond to the need to continue teacher training and update curricula to reflect the changing needs of employers. Grants are made in the areas of teacher preparation, school-to-work transition, and youth violence prevention, with support also given to business, insurance and economic education.

Health: 16%. Foundation funds public information campaigns to provide individuals and communities with the facts they need to preserve and enhance physical health. Grants fupport national health education andpromotion initiatives that reach large audiences, particularly youth, minorities and other at-risk populations. Areas of focus are addressing youth violence, promoting healthy lifestyles for youth, providing information to parents, Alzheimer's Disease research, and safety promotion, research, and education.

Social Services: 8%. Supports the United Way.

Note: Above priorities include 1998 foundation and direct giving.

Application Procedures

Initial Contact: Send a written request.

Application Requirements: Include a description of organization (legal name, history, activities, purpose, and governing board), purpose for which grant is requested, amount requested and list of other sources of financial support, most recently audited financial statement, copy of IRS determination letter indicating 501(c)(3) tax-exempt status, and Form 990; requests for funds to support a specific project or program should include fully defined need, objective, benefits, plans (including time frame and evaluative criteria), staff, and budget including sources of financial support committed and pending.

Deadlines: None; requests reviewed throughout year.

Evaluative Criteria: Considers organization's general structure, history, objectives, and management capability, relationship to community and population served, position and service relative to similar organizations, financial position and sources of income; projects are evaluated on goals and implementation plans, time frame, ultimate disposition of project, staff capabilities, benefits of the project, and sources of financial and other support.

Notes: If request falls under foundation guidelines and program priorities, organization may be asked to provide more complete information before a decision is made. Foundation occasionally issues requests for proposals.

Restrictions

Grants are not made to individuals; private foundations; hospital capital fund campaigns; organizations receiving support from United Way; organizations whose activities are mainly international; local chapters of national organizations; disease-specific organizations; organizations primarily engaged in patient care or direct treatment; drug treatment centers or community health clinics; elementary or secondary schools; endowments; courtesy advertising or festival participation; labor organizations; or religious, fraternal, political, athletic, social, or veterans' organizations. athletic, social, or veterans' organizations.

Additional Information

Occasionally, foundation establishes particular areas of interest for emphasis within a program area. When this is done, foundation actively seeks opportunities for providing grants and may issue requests for proposals.

Grant renewals are not automatic and cannot be guaranteed from year to year.

Publications: Contributions Report

Corporate Officials

James M. Benson: chief executive officer vice president, treasurer PRIM CORP EMPL chief executive officer: Metropolitan Life Insurance Co. ADD CORP EMPL chairman, chief executive officer: New England Life Insurance Co.

Harry Paul Kamen: chairman, president, chief executive officer B Montreal, PQ Canada 1933. ED University of Pennsylvania AB (1954); Harvard University LLB (1957). PRIM CORP EMPL chairman, president, chief executive officer: Metropolitan Life Insurance Co. CORP AFFIL director: Pfizer Inc.; director: Bethlehem Steel Corp.; director: New England Investment Companies LP; director: Banco Santander. NONPR AFFIL government: National Association Security Dealers; director: New England Financial; director: American Council Life Insurance.

Catherine Amelia Rein: vice president B Lebanon, PA 1943. ED Pennsylvania State University BA (1965); New York University JD (1968). PRIM CORP EMPL vice president: Metropolitan Life Insurance Co. ADD CORP EMPL president, chief executive officer: Metropolitan Property Casualty Insurance Co. CORP AFFIL director: Corning Inc.; director: GPU Inc.; director: Bank New York Co. Inc.; director: Broadmoor Housing Inc.

Arthur G. Typermass: senior vice president, treasurer B New York, NY 1937. ED Wesleyan University AB (1957); Columbia University MBA (1959). PRIM CORP EMPL senior vice president, treasurer: Metropolitan Life Insurance Co.

Foundation Officials

William Thomas Friedewald, MD: director B New York, NY 1939. ED University of Notre Dame BS (1960); Yale University MD (1963); Stanford University (1968-1969). PRIM CORP EMPL senior vice president, chief medical director: Metropolitan Life Insurance Co. NONPR AFFIL director: American Heart Association.

Sibyl C. Jacobson: president, chief executive officer, director PRIM CORP EMPL senior vice president external affairs: Metropolitan Life Insurance Co.

Catherine Amelia Rein: director (see above)

Vincent P. Reusing: director

Grants Analysis

Disclosure Period: calendar year ending 1998

Total Grants: $9,484,840*

Number of Grants: 256

Average Grant: $37,050

Highest Grant: $648,349

Typical Range: $5,000 to $30,000

***Note:** Grants analysis includes foundation giving. Giving excludes United Way, matching gifts, scholarship.

Recent Grants

Note: Grants derived from 1996 Form 990.

Arts & Humanities

1,250,000	Lincoln Center for Performing Arts, New York, NY
750,000	Educational Broadcasting Corps, New York, NY
75,000	Carnegie Hall, New York, NY
75,000	Lincoln Center for Performing Arts, New York, NY
75,000	Paul Taylor Dance Foundation, New York, NY

Civic & Public Affairs

150,000	Enterprise Foundation, Columbia, MD
100,000	Columbus Works, Columbus, OH
100,000	National Urban League, New York, NY
100,000	New York Botanical Garden Institute of Economic Botany, New York, NY
100,000	Salud Para la Gente, Watsonville, CA
75,000	El Museo del Barrio, Hamilton, NY
75,000	National Urban League, New York, NY
70,000	Local Initiatives Support Corp, New York, NY
70,000	New York City Partnership Foundation, New York, NY
60,000	Neighborhood Housing Services, New York, NY

Education

165,000	Reading Is Fundamental, Washington, DC
159,569	Citizens Scholarship Foundation of America, Saint Peter, MN
130,000	National Center for Health Education, New York, NY
110,000	Smith College, Northampton, MA
101,644	National Merit Scholarship Corporation, Evanston, IL
100,000	College of Insurance, New York, NY
100,000	National Association of Partners in Education, Alexandria, VA
100,000	United Negro College Fund, New York, NY
90,000	Impact II, New York, NY
85,000	Education Commission of the States, Denver, CO
80,000	Institute for Educational Leadership, Washington, DC
50,000	Brooklyn Academy of Music, Brooklyn, NY

Environment

125,000	Trust for Public Land, San Francisco, CA

Health

200,000	New York Academy of Medicine, New York, NY
130,000	Harvard School of Public Health Center for Health, Boston, MA
125,000	Memorial Sloan-Kettering Cancer Center, New York, NY
100,000	National AIDS Fund, Washington, DC
100,000	New York Blood Center, New York, NY
50,000	Healthy Mothers, Health Babies, Washington, DC
50,000	Life and Health Insurance Medical Research Fund, Washington, DC

International

200,000	Royal Institute for the Advancement of Learning-McGill University, Montreal, PQ, Canada
111,330	United Ways Canada, Canada
100,000	Wayne State University Center for Peace and Conflict Studies, Detroit, MI

Science

125,000	American Museum of Natural History, New York, NY

Social Services

700,000	United Way, New York, NY
571,500	United Way, New York, NY
140,000	Family Foundation of North America, Milwaukee, WI
140,000	Girl Scouts of America, New York, NY
111,330	United Way, New York, NY
100,000	Children's Home and Aid Society, Chicago, IL
100,000	Judge Baker Children's Center, Boston, MA
70,000	Boys and Girls Clubs of America, New York, NY
60,000	Girls, Incorporated, New York, NY
50,000	Boys and Girls Clubs of America, Atlanta, GA
50,000	Freedom From Hunger, Davis, CA

MFA INC.

Company Contact

Columbia, MO

Web: http://www.mfaincorporated.com

Company Description

Employees: 1,200

SIC(s): 2047 Dog & Cat Food, 2048 Prepared Feeds Nec, 2875 Fertilizers--Mixing Only, 5191 Farm Supplies.

Corporate Officials

Don Copenhaver: president, chief executive officer B 1943. ED Gem Business College (1962). PRIM CORP EMPL president, chief executive officer: MFA Inc. CORP AFFIL director: CF Industries Inc.; senior vice president: Morris Farm Center Inc.

G. David Jobe: senior vice president B California, MO 1943. ED Central Missouri State University (1965). PRIM CORP EMPL senior vice president: MFA Inc. CORP AFFIL senior vice president: Morris Farm Center Inc.

Bill Streeter: senior vice president

MFA Foundation

Giving Contact

Lois Meredith, Secretary & Treasurer
MFA Foundation
201 Ray Young Dr.
Columbia, MO 65201
Phone: (573)874-5111

Description

Founded: 1958

EIN: 436026877

Organization Type: Corporate Foundation

Giving Locations: MO: primarily in rural areas

Grant Types: Scholarship.

Financial Summary

Total Giving: $324,810 (fiscal year ending June 30, 1998); $309,950 (fiscal 1997); $320,709 (fiscal 1996). Note: Contributes through foundation only. 1998 Giving includes foundation($48,500); scholarship ($276,310). 1997 Giving includes foundation; scholarship ($264,050).

Assets: $9,245,385 (fiscal 1998); $7,756,369 (fiscal 1997); $6,648,103 (fiscal 1996)

Gifts Received: $114,597 (fiscal 1991); $143,901 (fiscal 1990). Note: In 1991, contributions over $5,000 were received from MFA ($28,675), MFA Oil Company ($12,750), and the Cooperative Buyers Association ($6,000).

Typical Recipients

Education: Agricultural Education, Colleges & Universities, Student Aid

Health: Health Organizations

Social Services: Youth Organizations

Contributions Analysis

Education: Foundation reports that most of its funds are given in the form of scholarships for high school seniors who live in the corporation's trade areas.

Application Procedures

Initial Contact: application form is required for scholarships, which may be obtained at the student's school counseling office during the month of February.

Deadlines: March 15.

Foundation Officials

Ken Caspall: director PRIM CORP EMPL senior vice president: MFA Petroleum Canada. CORP AFFIL vice president sales: MFA Oil Co.

Don Copenhaver: director (see above)

Dale H. Creach: vice president, director B 1941. ED Drury College (1964). CORP AFFIL president: MFA Oil Co.; president: MFA Petroleum Co.

Ormal C. Creach: director

James Cunningham: director

Burdette L. Frew: president, director B 1933. ED Bradley University BSME. PRIM CORP EMPL president, chief executive officer: MFA Inc. CORP AFFIL director: Mutual Service Co-Operative; director: Mutual Service Life Insurance Co.; director: Cornwall & Stevens Co. Inc.; director: Mutual Service Casualty Insurance Co.

J. Brian Griffith: director PRIM CORP EMPL secretary: MFA Inc.

G. David Jobe: director (see above)

Stacy Knight: director

Fred Koenig: director

Lois Meredith: secretary, treasurer

Phil Perkins: director

Grants Analysis

Disclosure Period: fiscal year ending June 30, 1998

Total Grants: $48,500*

Number of Grants: 19

Average Grant: $2,552

Typical Range: $1,000 to $5,000

***Note:** Giving excludes 284 scholarship ($276,310).

MGIC INVESTMENT CORP.

Company Contact

Milwaukee, WI

Web: http://www.mgic.com

Company Description

Assets: US$2,222,300,000

Employees: 1,026

SIC(s): 6159 Miscellaneous Business Credit Institutions.

Giving Contact

John Ludwick, Vice President Human Resources
MGIC Investment Corp.
PO Box 488
Milwaukee, WI 53202
Phone: (414)347-6361
Fax: (414)347-6959

Description

Organization Type: Corporate Giving Program

Giving Locations: WI: Milwaukee

Grant Types: General Support.

Financial Summary

Total Giving: $700,000 (1999); $600,000 (1998 approx); $500,000 (1997 approx). Note: Contributes through corporate direct giving program only.

Typical Recipients

Arts & Humanities: Performing Arts

Civic & Public Affairs: Employment/Job Training

Education: Colleges & Universities

Health: Hospitals, Single-Disease Health Associations

Social Services: Community Service Organizations, Domestic Violence, Family Services, Food/Clothing Distribution, Senior Services, Shelters/Homelessness, Substance Abuse, United Funds/United Ways, Volunteer Services, Youth Organizations

Application Procedures

Initial Contact: a brief letter of inquiry

Application Requirements: a description of organization, amount requested, purpose of funds sought, recently audited financial statement, and proof of tax-exempt status

Deadlines: None.

Restrictions

The company generally does not provide multiyear cash pledges or support dinners, banquets, festivals, parades, or national or statewide requests.

First-time grants to nonprofit organizations newly applying are limited to $2,000 or less.

Requests for support from colleges and universities must be for a specific program at a Wisconsin institution. specific program at a Wisconsin institution.

Corporate Officials

William Howard Lacy: president B Chicago, IL 1945. ED United States Air Force Academy; University of Wisconsin, Milwaukee BBA (1968). PRIM CORP EMPL president: MGIC Investment Corp. CORP AFFIL chairman, president: MGIC Reinsurance Corp.; president, chief executive officer, director: Mortgage Guaranty Insurance Corp.; director: MGIC Mortgage Securities Corp.; chairman, president: MGIC Real Estate Servicing Corp.; chairman, president: MGIC Mortgage Insurance Corp.; chairman, president: MGIC Mortgage Marketing Corp.; chairman, president: MGIC Mortgage Corp.; chairman, president: MGIC Insurance Services Corp.; chairman, president: MGIC Investor Services Corp.; chairman: MGIC Holdings Corp.; director: Firstar Corp.; director: Johnson Controls Inc.; director: Firstar Bank Milwaukee NA.

J. Michael Lauer: executive vice president, chief financial officer B 1944. PRIM CORP EMPL executive vice president, chief financial officer: MGIC Investment Corp. CORP AFFIL executive vice president, chief financial officer: Mortgage Guaranty Insurance Corp.; executive vice president, chief financial officer: Mortgage Guaranty Reinsurance Corp.; executive vice president, chief financial officer: MGIC Mortgage Insurance Corp.

Giving Program Officials

John D. Ludwick: vice president human resources B Springfield, OH 1941. ED Wittenberg University (1962); Indiana University (1964). PRIM CORP EMPL vice president human resources: Mortgage Guaranty Insurance Corp.

MICHIGAN CONSOLIDATED GAS CO.

Company Contact

Detroit, MI

Web: http://www.michcon.com

Company Description

Employees: 3,364

SIC(s): 4924 Natural Gas Distribution.

Parent Company: MCN Corp.

Nonmonetary Support

Type: Donated Equipment; In-kind Services; Loaned Employees

MichCon Foundation

Giving Contact

Ms. Mary E. Bradish, Secretary
MichCon Foundation
500 Griswold Street
Detroit, MI 48226
Phone: (313)256-5077

Description

EIN: 382570358
Organization Type: Corporate Foundation
Giving Locations: company's service area.
Grant Types: Capital, Employee Matching Gifts, General Support, Matching, Multiyear/Continuing Support.
Note: Also makes grants to promote employee volunteerism.

Giving Philosophy

'MichCon has a 130-year tradition of active involvement in the communities it serves. The Company recognizes that the economic vitality and quality of life in these communities are essential to the success of the people who live and work there, as well as to MichCon.. Contributions support efforts to stimulate confidence, pride and community involvement by residents and to assist recipient organizations in achieving their goals.' *Foundation Guidelines*

Financial Summary

Total Giving: $1,274,000 (1998 approx); $1,027,600 (1997); $1,200,000 (1996). Note: Contributes through corporate direct giving program and foundation. 1997 giving includes foundation. 1996 Giving includes corporate direct giving; United Way.
Giving Analysis: Giving for 1997 includes: corporate grants to United Way ($226,620)
Assets: $17,014,582 (1997); $15,895,016 (1996); $15,176,000 (1995 approx)
Gifts Received: $1,000,000 (1993)

Typical Recipients

Arts & Humanities: Arts Associations & Councils, Arts Institutes, History & Archaeology, Museums/Galleries, Music, Opera, Performing Arts, Public Broadcasting, Theater
Civic & Public Affairs: African American Affairs, Business/Free Enterprise, Chambers of Commerce, Community Foundations, Economic Development, Employment/Job Training, Civic & Public Affairs-General, Housing, Parades/Festivals, Philanthropic Organizations, Professional & Trade Associations, Public Policy, Urban & Community Affairs, Zoos/Aquariums
Education: Business Education, Business-School Partnerships, Colleges & Universities, Community & Junior Colleges, Education Associations, Education Funds, Engineering/Technological Education, Environmental Education, Education-General, Minority Education, Public Education (Precollege), Student Aid
Environment: Air/Water Quality, Environment-General
Health: Health Organizations, Hospitals, Mental Health, Nursing Services
Religion: Churches, Religious Organizations, Religious Welfare
Science: Science Museums, Scientific Centers & Institutes, Scientific Organizations
Social Services: Child Abuse, Community Centers, Community Service Organizations, Food/Clothing Distribution, People with Disabilities, Recreation & Athletics, Senior Services, Substance Abuse, United Funds/United Ways, Youth Organizations

Contributions Analysis

Giving Priorities: Community services, united funds, programs that strengthen higher education systems in operating communities, urban and economic development, and cultural institutions and graphic and performing arts programs.
Arts & Humanities: 19%. Focus on cultural institutions and active graphic and performing arts programs in service areas. Supports symphonies, arts associations, community theaters, and museums. Matches employee gifts to the arts.
Civic & Public Affairs: 43%. Concentrates on existing and new programs that serve community needs, improve neighborhoods, provide skills training, and develop local neighborhood and community leadership. Major recipients include youth employment programs and community organizations. Primarily supports local economic development organizations. Program emphasizes employment training, attracting new businesses, promoting growth in existing businesses, housing development, and neighborhood stabilization.
Education: 9%. Primary commitment is to teacher mini-grants to enhance classroom curriculum. Grants also are made to specific projects and programs such as 'Detroit Compact.' Also sponsors employee matching gifts program.
Health: About 1%.
Science: About 1%. Funds a museum.
Social Services: 27%. Supports United Way chapters.
Note: Total foundation contributions made in 1997.

Application Procedures

Initial Contact: In the Detroit area, send written request to Mary Bradish, Secretary, MichCon Foundation; outside the Detroit area, grant requests and correspondence should be sent to the MichCon public affairs office in Ann Arbor, Grand Rapids, Mt. Pleasant, or Traverse City.
Application Requirements: Send a a description of organization, its purpose and history; list of organization's officers and board members; copy of 501(c)(3) tax-exempt letter; copy of most recently audited financial statement; information about fund-raising activities; description of program or project including objectives and how they will be met; budget (with projected income and expenses for the current fiscal year); other possible sources of financial support; proposed project evaluation method; summary of why financial support is needed.
Deadlines: Applications accepted any time; deadline for funding requests for a calendar year is October 30.
Review Process: Board meets six times per year to review requests.
Evaluative Criteria: General eligibility and conformity with foundation guidelines, available funds, amount needed to achieve desired results, program priorities, geographic location, quality of management and accountability, ability to stimulate volunteerism.

Restrictions

Grants are not made to organizations outside company service areas; organizations devoted exclusively to research projects; organizations receiving support from united funds; individuals for scholarships or any other reason; political activities; or religious endeavors. Foundation does not provide money for loans, endowments, trips, tours, testimonial dinners, fund-raising events, or advertising for benefit auctions.

Funds nonprofits only in service area. Does not fund organizations outside of the state of Michigan.

Grants generally are limited to one year.

Foundation does not accept contribution formulas prepared by soliciting organizations.

Additional Information

Foundation asks recipient organizations for proof of the results of their programs or conducts its own audit of organization activities.

In 2000, DTE Energy Co. announced plans to acquire MCN Energy Group Inc., MichCon's parent co.

Corporate Officials

Anne R. Cooke: vice president marketing, sales PRIM CORP EMPL vice president marketing, sales: Michigan Consolidated Gas Co.
Howard L. Dow, III: senior vice president, chief financial officer, treasurer PRIM CORP EMPL senior vice president, chief financial officer, treasurer: Michigan Consolidated Gas Co. ADD CORP EMPL vice president, secretary, treasurer: Citizens Gas Fuel Co.; vice president, secretary, treasurer: CoEnergy Trading Co.; senior vice president, chief financial officer, treasurer: MCN Investment Corp.; treasurer: MCNIC Gas Storage; treasurer: MCNIC Oil Gas CPN; treasurer: MCNIC Pipeline Processing Co.; vice president, secretary: MCNIC Power Co.; treasurer: Michcon Pipeline Co.
Stephen E. Ewing: president, chief executive officer, director B 1944. ED DePauw University BA (1965); Michigan State University MBA (1971); Harvard University Graduate School of Business Administration AMP (1982). PRIM CORP EMPL president, chief executive officer, director: Michigan Consolidated Gas Co. CORP AFFIL chairman: Michcon Pipeline Co.; chairman: Saginaw Bay Lateral Co.; director: MCN Energy Group Inc.; director: Michcon Gathering Co.
Mary A. Findlay: vice president customer operations PRIM CORP EMPL vice president customer operations: Michigan Consolidated Gas Co.
Benson Manlove: vice president PRIM CORP EMPL vice president: Michigan Consolidated Gas Co.
David R. Nowakowski: vice president human resources PRIM CORP EMPL vice president human resources: Michigan Consolidated Gas Co.
Fred Shell: vice president public policy PRIM CORP EMPL vice president public policy: Michigan Consolidated Gas Co.

Giving Program Officials

Mary E. Bradish: secretary

Foundation Officials

Mary E. Bradish: secretary (see above)
Mary A. Findlay: vice president (see above)
David R. Nowakowski: treasurer, director (see above)

Grants Analysis

Disclosure Period: calendar year ending 1996
Total Grants: $800,980*
Number of Grants: 317
Average Grant: $2,527
Highest Grant: $66,230
Typical Range: $100 to $5,000
***Note:** Giving excludes corporate direct giving; United Way.

Recent Grants

Note: Grants derived from 1997 Form 990.

Arts & Humanities

66,230	Detroit Symphony Orchestra Hall, Detroit, MI -- general support
27,712	Founders Society Detroit Institute of Arts, Detroit, MI
25,000	Detroit Symphony Orchestra Hall, Detroit, MI -- capital
23,500	Detroit Educational Television Foundation, Detroit, MI -- program underwriting
10,000	State Theater Group, Traverse City, MI -- capital
6,040	Michigan Opera Theater, Detroit, MI
6,000	Music Hall Center for Performing Arts, Detroit, MI
5,000	Central Michigan University, Mount Pleasant, MI -- public broadcasting
5,000	Michigan Theater Foundation, Ann Arbor, MI -- capital

Civic & Public Affairs

62,000	New Detroit, Detroit, MI -- general support
50,000	Local Initiatives Support Corporation,

	Detroit, MI -- community development funders collaborative
48,000	Michigan First, Lansing, MI
25,000	Detroit Renaissance Foundation, Detroit, MI -- general support
25,000	Greater Detroit Chamber Foundation, Detroit, MI -- Detroit Regional Economic Partnership
25,000	Michigan Parade Foundation, Detroit, MI
20,000	Grand Rapids Chamber Foundation, Grand Rapids, MI -- the Right Place program
18,000	Accounting Aid Society, Detroit, MI
17,000	Greater Detroit Chamber Foundation, Detroit, MI -- capital
15,000	Detroit Economic Growth Association, Detroit, MI
15,000	Think Twice Foundation, Southfield, MI
12,500	Community Foundation for Southeastern Michigan, Detroit, MI -- Team 500 program
10,000	Black United Fund, Detroit, MI
10,000	Michigan Economic Developers Association, Lansing, MI
10,000	Motor City Blight Busters, Detroit, MI -- Detroit Blitz Build
7,000	Citizens Research Council, Detroit, MI
7,000	Detroit Zoological Society, Royal Oak, MI
6,300	Detroit Renaissance Foundation, Detroit, MI -- Detroit Strategic Plan
5,500	Metropolitan Affairs Corporation, Detroit, MI
5,000	Corporation for Supportive Housing, Plymouth, MI
5,000	Council for Excellence in Government, Washington, DC
5,000	Grand Action Foundation, Ada, MI -- capital

Education

35,000	Focus HOPE, Detroit, MI -- capital
8,800	Michigan Colleges Foundation, Southfield, MI
8,000	College Fund/UNCF, Detroit, MI
6,000	Detroit Area Pre-College Engineering Program, Detroit, MI
6,000	Junior Achievement of Southeastern Michigan, Detroit, MI
5,000	Business Education Training Alliance, Detroit, MI
5,000	Focus HOPE, Detroit, MI -- general support
5,000	Muskegon Community College, Muskegon, MI

Health

5,000	Greater Detroit Area Health Council, Detroit, MI -- Healthy Detroit program

Science

5,000	Ann Arbor Hands-On Museum, Ann Arbor, MI -- capital
5,000	Detroit Science Center, Detroit, MI

Social Services

172,000	United Way Community Services, Detroit, MI -- general support
24,000	United Way Community Services, Detroit, MI -- capital
21,000	Heart of West Michigan United Way, Grand Rapids, MI
10,000	Food Bank Council, Lansing, MI
5,495	Grand Traverse Area United Way, Traverse City, MI
5,400	Washtenaw United Way, Ann Arbor, MI
5,000	Growth Works, Plymouth, MI -- community youth initiative
5,000	Mercy Housing, Cadillac, MI -- Cadillac area program

MICROSOFT CORP.

 Number 7 of Top 100 Corporate Givers

Company Contact

Redmond, WA
Web: http://www.microsoft.com/giving/

Company Description

Revenue: US$19,747,000,000 (1999)
Employees: 22,222 (1999)
Fortune Rank: 84, per FORTUNE Magazine's list of 500 Largest U.S. Corporations (1999).
FF 84
SIC(s): 7371 Computer Programming Services, 7372 Prepackaged Software.

Operating Locations

Australia: Microsoft Pty. Ltd., Sydney; Austria: Microsoft GmbH, Vienna; Belgium: Microsoft NV, Brussels, Brabant; Brazil: Microsoft Informatica Ltda., Sao Paulo; Canada: Microsoft Canada, Mississauga; Chile: Microsoft Chile SA, Santiago; People's Republic of China: Microsoft Corp.-Beijing, Beijing; Colombia: Microsoft de Colombia, Bogota, Cundinamarco; Costa Rica: Microsoft de Centroamerica SA, San Jose; Czech Republic: Microsoft SRO, Prague; Denmark: Microsoft Danmark APS, Hedehusene; Ecuador: Corporacion Microsoft del Ecuador, Quito, Pichincha; Finland: Microsoft Oy, Helsinki; France: Microsoft Europe, Paris; Microsoft France, Paris; Germany: Microsoft GmbH, Munich, Unterschleissheim; Greece: Microsoft Hellas SA, Athens, Attiki; Hungary: Microsoft KFT, Budapest; India: Microsoft Corp. (India) Private Ltd., New Delhi; Ireland: Microsoft Manufacturiing BV, Dublin; Israel: Microsoft Israel Ltd., Tel Aviv; Italy: Microsoft SpA, Milan; Japan: Microsoft Co. Ltd., Tokyo; Republic of Korea: Microsoft CH, Seoul; Mexico: Microsoft Mexico SA de CV, Mexico City; Morocco: Microsoft Maroc SARL, Casablanca; Malaysia: Microsoft (Malaysia) Sdn. Bhd., Kuala Lumpur, Selangor; Netherlands: Microsoft BV, Hoofddorp, Noord-Holland; Norway: Microsoft Norge AS, Oslo, Akershus; New Zealand: Microsoft New Zealand Ltd., Auckland; Philippines: Microsoft Philippines, Manila; Poland: Microsoft sp z.o.o., Warsaw; Portugal: MSFT Software Para Microcomputadores Lda., Oeiras, Lisboa; Russia: Microsoft ZAO, Moscow; Republic of South Africa: Microsoft SA Pty Ltd., Johannesburg; Slovakia: Microsoft SRO, Bratislava; Spain: Microsoft Iberica SRL, Madrid; Slovenia: Microsoft, Ljubljana; Sweden: Micrsoft AB, Stockholm; Switzerland: Microsoft AG, Spreitenbach, Zurich; Thailand: Microsoft (Thailand) Ltd., Bangkok; Turkey: Microsoft Bilgisayar Yazilim Hizmetieri Ltd. Sirketi, Istanbul; Taiwan: Microsoft Taiwan Corp., Taipei; United Arab Emirates: Microsoft Corp. Dubai, Dubai; Venezuela: Corporation MS de Venezuela, Caracas
Note: Operates in 21 countries.

Nonmonetary Support

Value: $79,013,000 (1999); $89,639,000 (1998); $45,164,980 (1997)
Type: Donated Products
Note: Product donations at estimated retail value.

Corporate Sponsorship

Note: Sponsors local table sponsorships.

Giving Contact

Bruce Brooks, Director, Community Affairs
Microsoft Corp.
One Microsoft Way
Redmond, WA 98052-6399
Phone: (425)936-8185
Fax: (425)936-7329
Email: giving@microsoft.com

Description

Organization Type: Corporate Giving Program
Giving Locations: WA some national initiatives.
Grant Types: Capital, Employee Matching Gifts, Fellowship, General Support, Multiyear/Continuing Support, Scholarship.
Note: Employee matching gift ratio: 1 to 1 for contributions of cash, stock, or software up to $12,000 per employee annually.

Giving Philosophy

'At Microsoft, we make grants of cash, software, and technical support to nonprofit organizations around the world. Our giving is guided by three objectives: to help bring the benefits of information technology to underserved people and communities; to provide support to organizations in communities in which our employees live and work; and to support our employees taking an active role in their community through volunteer and matching gift programs.' Microsoft 1999 Annual Report

Financial Summary

Total Giving: $104,659,000 (fiscal year ending June 30, 1999); $107,122,000 (fiscal 1998); $59,166,294 (fiscal 1997). Note: Contributes through corporate direct giving program only. 1999 Giving includes corporate direct giving ($25,000,000); nonmonetary support. 1998 Giving includes corporate direct giving ($17,383,000); nonmonetary support.
Giving Analysis: Giving for fiscal 1999 includes: nonmonetary support ($79,013,000); corporate direct giving ($25,646,000)

Typical Recipients

Arts & Humanities: Arts Associations & Councils
Civic & Public Affairs: Civic & Public Affairs-General
Education: Colleges & Universities, Education Reform
Environment: Environment-General
Science: Scientific Centers & Institutes
Social Services: Community Service Organizations, Social Services-General

Contributions Analysis

Civic & Public Affairs: 13%. Supports community efforts including civic affairs, technology and the arts, and the environment.
Education: 60%. Donates cash and software to colleges and universities, educational funds, and awards programs. Also supports local elementary education, and provides scholarships to employees' children. Makes Access to Technology grants, and Instructional Grant software licenses to colleges and universities to support innovative uses of technology in academic areas such as computer science, business information technologies, engineering, and math.
International: 3%.
Social Services: 24%. Includes employee programs and matching gifts.

Application Procedures

Initial Contact: Call or write for guidelines, then submit written proposal.
Application Requirements: Include with the proposal narrative: a description of organization, including mission, major accomplishments, governance, area and population served; operating budget for the current fiscal year, including fund sources; list of current board members and key staff; copy of IRS tax-exempt determination letter.
Deadlines: For community support grants, tax-exempt organizations may submit requests throughout the year. However, internal grantmaking deadlines are the 15th of February, May, or October.
Decision Notification: Applicants will be notified approximately one month after the deadline.
Notes: Proposal materials cannot be returned. Company will request further information, if necessary.

Restrictions

The following are not eligible for Microsoft donations of cash or software: individuals; political, labor, religious or fraternal groups; amateur or professional sports groups, teams or events; conferences or symposia; hospitals or medical clinics; programs serving people and communities outside the United States (exceptions may be made for pilot programs initiated by a Microsoft subsidiary in another country); or unsolicited proposals for sponsorship of charitable fundraising events such as luncheons, dinners, walks, runs, and sports tournaments. Only tax-exempt organizations may be supported. runs, and sports tournaments. Only tax-exempt organizations may be supported.

Additional Information

Microsoft has enlisted the services of Gifts-in-Kind International at (703)836-2121, and CompuMentor at (800)659-3579, to assist in the distribution of Microsoft software outside of Washington.

Requests should be submitted to the appropriate person, according to category: arts, culture, civic or environmental requests, please address requests to Mary Pembroke, senior program manager. For human services or education requests, please address requests to Bruce M. Brooks, manager corporate contributions and community programs.

In 1997, contributions from Microsoft Corp. and the Gates family endowed the Gates Library Foundation. The Foundation is a private, nonprofit entity, separate from Microsoft Corp., and has its own giving program and guidelines. In 1999, the Gates Library Foundation merged with Technology Resource Institute, another private foundation.

Publications: Annual Report; Guidelines

Corporate Officials

Steven Anthony Ballmer: president, chief executive officer, directornd administration, chief financial officer B Detroit, MI March 24, 1956. ED Harvard University Graduate School of Business Administration; Stanford University Graduate School of Business Administration. PRIM CORP EMPL president, chief executive officer, director: Microsoft Corp.

Bruce M. Brooks: director community affairs PRIM CORP EMPL director community affairs: Microsoft Corp. ADD CORP EMPL senior vice president: MMW/Savit.

John Connors: senior vice president finance and administration, chief financial officer PRIM CORP EMPL senior vice president finance and administration, chief financial officer: Microsoft Corp.

William Henry Gates, III: co-founder, chairman, chief software architect B Seattle, WA 1955. ED Harvard University (1975). PRIM CORP EMPL co-founder, chairman, chief software architect: Microsoft Corp. ADD CORP EMPL chairman: Corbis Corp. CORP AFFIL director: ICO South Corp.; director: Teledesic Corp.

Robert J. Herbold: executive vice president, chief operating officer ED Case Western Reserve University PhD; Case Western Reserve University MS. PRIM CORP EMPL executive vice president, chief operating officer: Microsoft Corp.

Giving Program Officials

Emily Hine: program manager
Christopher Jones: senior program officer
Sarah Meyer: senior program officer
Jane Meseck Yeager: program analyst

Grants Analysis

Disclosure Period: fiscal year ending June 30, 1999
Total Grants: $104,659,000
Number of Grants: 820 (approx)
Average Grant: $127,633
Typical Range: $5,000 to $25,000

Recent Grants

Note: Grants derived from fiscal 1994 grants list.

Education

226,000	Illinois Alliance for Essential Schools, Urbana, IL

Science

300,000	Pacific Science Center, Seattle, WA

MID-AMERICA BANK OF LOUISVILLE

Company Contact

Louisville, KY

Company Description

Former Name: Bank of Louisville.
Employees: 820
SIC(s): 6712 Bank Holding Companies.
Parent Company: Mid-America Bancorp

Nonmonetary Support

Type: Cause-related Marketing & Promotion; Donated Equipment; Donated Products; Loaned Executives; Workplace Solicitation

Corporate Sponsorship

Type: Arts & cultural events; Festivals/fairs
Note: Also sponsors education events.

Bank of Louisville Charities

Giving Contact

Beth Paxton Klein, Senior Vice President, Community Relations
500 W Broadway
PO Box 1101
Louisville, KY 40201
Phone: (502)589-3351
Fax: (502)562-5403

Description

Founded: 1973
EIN: 237423454
Organization Type: Corporate Foundation
Giving Locations: KY: Jefferson County, Oldham
Grant Types: Capital, General Support, Matching, Multiyear/Continuing Support.

Financial Summary

Total Giving: $454,690 (1998); $367,709 (1996); $352,344 (1995). Note: Contributes through foundation only. 1996 Giving includes foundation ($296,909); United Way ($70,800).
Assets: $3,349,947 (1996); $3,474,617 (1995); $3,209,374 (1994)
Gifts Received: $147,462 (1996); $309,069 (1995); $440 (1994). Note: Contributions are received from the Bank of Louisville.

Typical Recipients

Arts & Humanities: Arts Associations & Councils, Arts Centers, Arts Festivals, Arts Funds, Ballet, Dance, Ethnic & Folk Arts, Arts & Humanities-General, History & Archaeology, Museums/Galleries, Music, Opera, Performing Arts, Public Broadcasting, Theater, Visual Arts
Civic & Public Affairs: African American Affairs, Botanical Gardens/Parks, Clubs, Community Foundations, Economic Development, Employment/Job Training, Civic & Public Affairs-General, Housing, Municipalities/Towns, Parades/Festivals, Philanthropic Organizations, Public Policy, Urban & Community Affairs, Women's Affairs, Zoos/Aquariums
Education: Business Education, Colleges & Universities, Education Associations, Education Funds, Education-General, Legal Education, Minority Education, Private Education (Precollege), Public Education (Precollege), Secondary Education (Private), Secondary Education (Public), Social Sciences Education
Health: Cancer, Children's Health/Hospitals, Emergency/Ambulance Services, Health-General, Heart, Hospitals, Medical Rehabilitation, Multiple Sclerosis, Nursing Services, Prenatal Health Issues
Religion: Churches, Dioceses, Jewish Causes, Religious Organizations, Religious Welfare, Social/Policy Issues
Science: Science Museums, Scientific Centers & Institutes
Social Services: Community Centers, Community Service Organizations, Domestic Violence, Family Services, People with Disabilities, Recreation & Athletics, Scouts, Sexual Abuse, Shelters/Homelessness, Social Services-General, Special Olympics, United Funds/United Ways, Volunteer Services, YMCA/YWCA/YMHA/YWHA, Youth Organizations

Contributions Analysis

Arts & Humanities: About 25%. Supports the Greater Louisville Fund for the Arts. Also supports ballet, visual and performing arts.
Civic & Public Affairs: 10% to 15%. Supports organizations working toward economic development and community improvement projects.
Education: About 25%. Primarily supports public education.
Health: Less than 5%.
Religion: Less than 5%.
Social Services: About 30%. Primarily supports the Metro United Way.

Application Procedures

Initial Contact: The foundation has no formal application procedures; inquiries must be submitted in writing.
Application Requirements: Description of organization, amount requested, proof of tax-exempt status, and how funds will be used.
Deadlines: None.

Restrictions

Funds are given only to organizations located in Jefferson and Oldham Counties.

Corporate Officials

Raymond Kendrick Guillaume: vice chairman, chief executive officer B Louisville, KY 1943. ED Western Kentucky University BS (1965). PRIM CORP EMPL vice chairman, chief executive officer: Mid-America Bank of Louisville ADD CORP EMPL vice chairman, chief executive officer: Bank of Louisville. CORP AFFIL chief executive officer, vice chairman: Mid-America Bank of Louisville. NONPR AFFIL chairman: Metropolitan United Way West Kentucky; member: Western Kentucky University National Alumni Association; treasurer, director: Metropolitan United Way Louisville; chairman: Kentucky Bar Association; member, director: Kentucky Center Arts Endowment Fund. CLUB AFFIL Pendennis Club; Louisville Boat Club; Jefferson Club; Kentuckians New York Club.

Bertram W. Klein: chairman, director B Louisville, KY 1930. ED University of Pennsylvania (1952). PRIM CORP EMPL chairman, director: Mid-America Bank of Louisville. CORP AFFIL chairman: Mid-America Bancorp/Bank Louisville.

Beth Paxton Klein: senior vice president community relations PRIM CORP EMPL senior vice president community relations: Mid-America Bank of Louisville.

Orson Oliver: president, director B Campton, KY 1943. ED Eastern Kentucky University BA (1965); University of Kentucky LLD (1968); Northwestern University National Graduate Trust School (1974). PRIM CORP EMPL president, director: Mid-America Bank of Louisville. CORP AFFIL president: Mid-America Bancorp.

Foundation Officials

Bertram W. Klein: chairman, director (see above)
Beth Paxton Klein: director (see above)
David Klein: director

Grants Analysis

Disclosure Period: calendar year ending 1996
Total Grants: $296,909*
Number of Grants: 195
Average Grant: $1,523
Highest Grant: $42,000
Typical Range: $100 to $5,000
***Note:** Giving excludes United Way.

Recent Grants

Note: Grants derived from 1998 Form 990.

Arts & Humanities

35,000	Greater Louisville Fund for the Arts, Louisville, KY
25,000	Louisville Orchestra, Louisville, KY
15,000	Louisville Ballet, Louisville, KY
12,000	Greater Louisville Fund for the Arts, Louisville, KY
10,000	Kentucky Public Radio, Louisville, KY
6,000	Kentucky Center for the Arts, Louisville, KY
5,000	Clifton Cultural Center, Louisville, KY
5,000	Louisville Ballet, Louisville, KY
5,000	Louisville Ballet, Louisville, KY
4,750	Music Theatre of Louisville, Louisville, KY
3,000	Kentucky Center for the Arts, Louisville, KY
2,600	Kentucky Art and Craft Foundation, Louisville, KY
2,500	Commonwealth Endowment for Kentucky Educational Television, Lexington, KY
2,500	Louisville Ballet, Louisville, KY
2,500	Louisville Orchestra, Louisville, KY
2,000	Actors Theater of Louisville, Louisville, KY
2,000	Kentucky Derby Museum, Louisville, KY
1,500	Actors Theater of Louisville, Louisville, KY
1,250	Kentucky Derby Museum, Louisville, KY

Civic & Public Affairs

25,000	Greater Louisville Foundation, Louisville, KY
10,000	Louisville Zoo, Louisville, KY
5,163	Louisville Zoo, Louisville, KY
4,250	Louisville Community Foundation, Louisville, KY
2,500	Louisville Olmsted Parks Conservancy, Louisville, KY
2,000	Habitat for Humanity - Louisville, Louisville, KY
2,000	Louisville Urban League, Louisville, KY
1,750	Leadership Louisville Foundation, Louisville, KY
1,500	Kentucky Fair & Exposition Center, Louisville, KY

Education

42,000	Jefferson County Public Education Foundation, Louisville, KY
17,000	University of Louisville - College of Business, Louisville, KY
10,000	St. Xavier High School, Louisville, KY
2,000	The College Fund / UNCF, Bowling Green, KY
2,000	Urban Montessori School, Louisville, KY
1,500	Junior Achievement of Kentuckiana, Inc., Louisville, KY

Health

3,750	Kosair Children's Hospital / Children's Hospital Foundation, Louisville, KY
2,000	American Heart Association, Louisville, KY
1,500	Leukemia Society of America, Louisville, KY
1,500	Multiple Sclerosis Society, Louisville, KY
1,250	Kosair Children's Hospital / Children's Hospital Foundation, Louisville, KY

Religion

10,000	Archdiocese of Louisville, Louisville, KY

Social Services

72,000	Metro United Way, Louisville, KY
5,000	Metro United Way, Louisville, KY
4,000	Family Life Center / St Stephen Baptist Church, Louisville, KY
2,800	The Cabbage Patch Settlement House, Louisville, KY
2,500	Family & Children's Agency, Louisville, KY
2,362	Family Place & Child Abuse Treatment Agency, Louisville, KY
2,100	The Healing Place, Hendersonville, NC
1,260	Volunteers of America, Louisville, KY
1,218	Pro-Power, Louisville, KY
1,110	H.O.S.T. Youth Shelter, La Grange, KY

MidAmerican Energy Holdings Co.

Company Contact

666 Grand Ave.
Des Moines, IA 50303-0657
Phone: (515)252-6400
Fax: (515)281-2389
Web: http://www.midamerican.com

Company Description

Former Name: Iowa-Illinois Gas & Electric Co.; CalEnergy (1999).
Revenue: US$4,398,800,000 (1999)
Profit: US$167,200,000 (1999)
Employees: 1,387
Fortune Rank: 367, per FORTUNE Magazine's list of 500 Largest U.S. Corporations (1999). FF 367
SIC(s): 4911 Electric Services, 4923 Gas Transmission & Distribution.
Parent Company: Berkshire Hathaway Inc., Omaha, NE, United States

Mid-American Foundation

Giving Contact

Paul J. Leighton, Vice President
Des Moines, IA

Description

EIN: 426101963
Organization Type: Corporate Foundation
Giving Locations: headquarters and operating communities.
Grant Types: Capital, General Support, Loan, Multiyear/Continuing Support, Operating Expenses.

Financial Summary

Total Giving: $512,721 (1997); $518,088 (1996). Note: Contributes through foundation only. 1996 Giving includes foundation ($482,368); United Way ($35,720).
Assets: $953,369 (1997); $1,073,325 (1996)
Gifts Received: $324,875 (1997); $800,000 (1996). Note: In 1996, contributions were received from MidAmerican Energy Co.

Typical Recipients

Arts & Humanities: Arts Centers, Arts Festivals, Ballet, History & Archaeology, Libraries, Music, Performing Arts
Civic & Public Affairs: Business/Free Enterprise, Clubs, Community Foundations, Civic & Public Affairs-General, Housing, Public Policy, Urban & Community Affairs, Zoos/Aquariums
Education: Business Education, Colleges & Universities, Education-General, Leadership Training, Preschool Education, Private Education (Precollege), Student Aid
Environment: Environment-General, Resource Conservation
Health: Cancer, Children's Health/Hospitals, Diabetes, Emergency/Ambulance Services, Heart, Multiple Sclerosis
International: Foreign Educational Institutions, International Organizations, Missionary/Religious Activities
Religion: Jewish Causes, Jewish Causes, Religious Organizations, Religious Welfare, Social/Policy Issues, Synagogues/Temples
Science: Scientific Labs
Social Services: Child Welfare, Community Service Organizations, Family Planning, Family Services, People with Disabilities, Recreation & Athletics, Scouts, Shelters/Homelessness, United Funds/ United Ways, YMCA/YWCA/YMHA/YWHA

Application Procedures

Initial Contact: send a letter to the closest company facility
Application Requirements: proof of tax-exempt status, list of board of directors, a description of organization, list of additional sources and amounts of funding, and recently audited financial statement
Deadlines: None.
Decision Notification: contributions committee meets in January, April, July, and October

Corporate Officials

Stanley J. Bright: chairman, president, chief executive officer, director B Rochester, NY 1940. ED George Washington University BBA (1963). PRIM CORP EMPL chairman, president, chief executive officer, director: Mid-American Energy Co. CORP AFFIL chairman: Midwest Capital Group Inc.; director: UTILX Corp.; chairman, president, chief executive officer: Mid-American Energy Holdings Co.; chairman: Midamerican Energy Corp.; director: Dakota Dunes Development Co.; chairman: Mid-American Capital Co. CLUB AFFIL Rotary Club.

Foundation Officials

David B. Hawkins: trustee PRIM CORP EMPL vice chairman: Mid-America Group Ltd. ADD CORP EMPL vice chairman: Mid-America Development Co. CORP AFFIL director: Gaylord Container Corp.
Marvin Alvin Pomerantz: trustee B Des Moines, IA 1930. ED University of Iowa BS (1952). PRIM CORP EMPL chairman, chief executive officer, director: Gaylord Container Corp. CORP AFFIL chairman, president, chief executive officer: Mid-America Group Ltd.; director: Norwest Bank Iowa NA; director: Berkley Co. NONPR AFFIL trustee: Drake University; member: Greater Des Moines Committee; director: American Forest & Paper Association.
Steve Zumbach: trustee

Grants Analysis

Disclosure Period: calendar year ending 1997
Total Grants: $512,721
Number of Grants: 120
Average Grant: $4,273
Highest Grant: $50,400
Typical Range: $5,000 to $15,000

Recent Grants

Note: Grants derived from 1998 Form 990.

Arts & Humanities

37,000	West Des Moines Library Friends Foundation, Des Moines, IA
20,000	Civic Music Endowment Foundation, Des Moines, IA

13,000 Civic Center of Greater Des Moines, Des Moines, IA
12,000 Living History Farms, Des Moines, IA
6,000 Des Moines Playhouse, Des Moines, IA
5,000 Des Moines Art Festival, Des Moines, IA
5,000 Des Moines Symphony Guild, Des Moines, IA

Civic & Public Affairs
31,000 Greater Des Moines Foundation, Des Moines, IA
20,100 Blank Park Zoo Foundation, Des Moines, IA
7,270 Governor's Charity Steer Show, Iowa City, IA -- Ronald McDonald House
5,307 Variety Club, Des Moines, IA
2,500 Habitat for Humanity, Des Moines, IA
2,500 Urban Dreams, Des Moines, IA
2,250 Minority and Women Business Expo & Conference, San Francisco, CA

Education
9,500 Iowa College Foundation, Des Moines, IA
4,000 Grand View College, Des Moines, IA
3,000 ISU Foundation, Des Moines, IA
2,880 Dowling/St. Joseph Adopt-A-Student Program, Des Moines, IA
2,543 Junior Achievement, Des Moines, IA

Environment
10,000 Iowa Natural Heritage Foundation, Des Moines, IA
2,500 The Nature Conservancy, Des Moines, IA

Health
15,500 American Diabetes Association, Des Moines, IA
10,000 American Heart Association, Des Moines, IA
5,200 Juvenile Diabetes Foundation, Des Moines, IA
4,000 American Red Cross, Des Moines, IA
4,000 Red Cross Capital Campaign, Des Moines, IA
2,650 American Cancer Society, Des Moines, IA
2,500 John Ruan MS/Charity, Des Moines, IA

International
3,500 MASORTI, Hyattsville, MD
2,000 Iowa Sister States, Des Moines, IA

Religion
42,360 Des Moines Jewish Academy, Des Moines, IA
35,825 Tifereth Israel Synagogue, Des Moines, IA
18,000 Jewish Federation of Greater Des Moines, Des Moines, IA
10,000 American Friends of the Hebrew University, New York, NY
3,021 Temple B'Nai Jeshurun, Des Moines, IA
2,300 National Conference of Christians & Jews, Des Moines, IA
2,250 Judaic Resource Center, Rockville, MD

Science
25,000 Friends of Lakeside Lab, Inc., Milford, IA

Social Services
30,000 United Way of Central Iowa, Des Moines, IA
27,400 Israel Tennis Centers, New York, NY
20,000 St. Joseph Emergency Family Shelter, St Joseph, MO
10,500 Moingoina Girl Scout Council, Des Moines, IA
10,150 Creative Visions, Des Moines, IA
10,000 Oakridge Neighborhood Service, Des Moines, IA
10,000 Planned Parenthood of Greater Iowa, Des Moines, IA
9,668 Foundation for Children & Families of Iowa, Des Moines, IA
9,590 Mid-Iowa Council Boy Scouts of America, Des Moines, IA
6,500 YMCA of Greater Des Moines, Des Moines, IA
5,000 YWCA, Des Moines, IA
4,000 Goodwill Industries of Central Iowa, Des Moines, IA

Milacron, Inc.

Company Contact

2090 Florence Avenue
PO Box 63716
Cincinnati, OH 45206-2425
Phone: (513)487-5000
Fax: (513)487-5057
Web: http://www.milacron.com

Company Description

Employees: 12,598
SIC(s): 3291 Abrasive Products, 3541 Machine Tools--Metal Cutting Types, 3542 Machine Tools--Metal Forming Types, 3545 Machine Tool Accessories.

Operating Locations

Austria; France; Germany; Netherlands; United Kingdom

Nonmonetary Support

Value: $50,000 (2000 approx); $10,000 (1990)
Type: Donated Equipment
Note: Co. provides nonmonetary support.

Corporate Sponsorship

Type: Arts & cultural events

Milacron Foundation

Giving Contact

John Francy, Assistant Secretary
Milacron Foundation
4701 Marburg Ave.
Cincinnati, OH 45209
Phone: (513)841-8321
Fax: (513)841-8008

Description

EIN: 316030682
Organization Type: Corporate Foundation
Former Name: Cincinnati Milacron Inc.
Giving Locations: principally near operating locations and to national organizations.
Grant Types: Capital, General Support, Multiyear/Continuing Support, Scholarship.

Financial Summary

Total Giving: $700,000 (2000 approx); $700,000 (1998 approx); $636,347 (1997). Note: Contributes through corporate direct giving program and foundation.
Assets: $261,517 (1997); $187,745 (1996); $239,260 (1995)
Gifts Received: $695,000 (1997); $430,000 (1996); $600,000 (1995). Note: Contributions were received from Cincinnati Milacron.

Typical Recipients

Arts & Humanities: Arts Centers, Arts Funds, History & Archaeology, Museums/Galleries, Music, Performing Arts, Public Broadcasting
Civic & Public Affairs: African American Affairs, Business/Free Enterprise, Community Foundations, Employment/Job Training, Civic & Public Affairs-General, Public Policy, Safety, Urban & Community Affairs, Zoos/Aquariums
Education: Arts/Humanities Education, Business Education, Colleges & Universities, Community & Junior Colleges, Education Funds, Engineering/Technological Education, Education-General, Private Education (Precollege), Science/Mathematics Education, Secondary Education (Public), Special Education, Student Aid, Vocational & Technical Education
Health: Cancer, Emergency/Ambulance Services, Health Organizations, Hospices
International: International Relief Efforts
Religion: Religious Organizations, Religious Welfare
Science: Science Museums, Scientific Organizations
Social Services: Child Welfare, Community Centers, Family Services, United Funds/United Ways, YMCA/YWCA/YMHA/YWHA, Youth Organizations

Contributions Analysis

Giving Priorities: Social service, education, civics, arts funds.
Arts & Humanities: About 15%. Primarily supports local arts funds. Also supports museums, public broadcasting, fine arts centers, and historic preservation.
Civic & Public Affairs: 30% to 35%. Supports business and free enterprise and youth employment services.
Education: About 10%. Supports university scholarships with emphasis on technical, engineering, and science education. Also contributes to college and university fund drives and special and economic education.
Social Services: 40% to 45%. Majority of funding supports United Way campaigns near operating locations. Other interests include youth and community service organizations and groups concerned with employment.
Note: Total contributions made in 1998.

Application Procedures

Initial Contact: brief letter or proposal
Application Requirements: a description of organization, amount requested, purpose of funds sought, recently audited financial statement, and proof of tax-exempt status
Deadlines: None.
Review Process: proposals are reviewed by a committee
Decision Notification: board meets quarterly

Restrictions

Foundation does not support individuals, endowments, or special projects.

Corporate Officials

Neil A. Armstrong: director, president, chief executive officer, director B Wapakoneta, OH 1930. ED University of Southern California MS; Purdue University BS (1955). PRIM CORP EMPL director: Cincinnati Milacron, Inc. CORP AFFIL director: Thiokol Corp.; director: USX Corp.; director: Eaton Corp.; director: RMI Titanium Co.; chairman: AIL Systems Inc.; director: Cinergy Corp. NONPR AFFIL member: National Academy Engineering; fellow: Society Explorational Test Pilots; member: International Astronautical Federation.
Barbara Glenn Kasting: vice president human resources PRIM CORP EMPL vice president human resources: Milacron, Inc. CORP AFFIL vice president: Cincinnati Milocron Marketing Co.
Daniel Joseph Meyer: chairman, president, chief executive officer, director B Flint, MI 1936. ED Purdue University BSEE (1958); Indiana University MBA (1963). PRIM CORP EMPL chairman, president, chief executive officer, director: Cincinnati Milacron, Inc. CORP AFFIL director: Valenite Inc.; director: Star Banc Corp.; director: Milacron Marketing Co.; director: E.W. Scripps Co.; director: Milacron International Marketing Co.; director: Hubbell Inc.; director: Milacron Inc.; chairman, director: Cincinnati Milacron Marketing Co.; director: Cincinnati Bell Inc. NONPR AFFIL member: American Institute CPAs. CLUB AFFIL Kenwood Country Club.

Foundation Officials

Neil A. Armstrong: trustee (see above)
Ronald D. Brown: assistant treasurer B Cincinnati, OH 1953. ED University of Cincinnati BBA (1975); University of Dayton JD (1978). PRIM CORP EMPL president, chief operating officer: Milacron Inc. ADD CORP EMPL vice president: Milacron Marketing Corp.; vice president: Valenite Inc. NONPR AFFIL director: Student Loan Funding Resource.
Lyle J. Everingham: trustee B Flint, MI 1926. ED University of Toledo. CORP AFFIL director: Kroger Co.; director: Providian Financial Corp.; director: Commonwealth General Corp.; director: Federated Department Stores Inc.
Barbara Glenn Kasting: assistant secretary (see above)
Daniel Joseph Meyer: president (see above)

Grants Analysis

Disclosure Period: calendar year ending 1998
Total Grants: $760,315
Number of Grants: 54
Average Grant: $14,080
Highest Grant: $255,000
Typical Range: $500 to $25,000

Recent Grants

Note: Grants derived from 1997 Form 990.

Arts & Humanities

50,000	Children's Museum, Cincinnati, OH
47,000	Fine Arts Fund, Cincinnati, OH
2,500	Cincinnati Historical Society, Cincinnati, OH
1,000	Cincinnati Arts Festival, Cincinnati, OH -- Sing Cincinnati

Civic & Public Affairs

20,000	Cincinnati Zoo and Botanical Gardens, Cincinnati, OH
15,000	Urban League, Cincinnati, OH
10,000	Blue Chip Campaign
5,000	Downtown Cincinnati, Cincinnati, OH
5,000	Youth Employment Services

Education

40,000	Xavier University, Cincinnati, OH -- capital fund
27,000	University of Cincinnati College of Engineering, Cincinnati, OH -- scholarship
10,000	College of Mount St. Joseph, Cincinnati, OH -- fund drive
10,000	Junior Achievement
10,000	Northern Kentucky University, Highland Heights, KY -- fund drive
6,500	Purdue University, West Lafayette, IN -- scholarship
5,500	University of Cincinnati, Cincinnati, OH -- corporate fund drive
3,000	Cincinnati State Technical and Community College, Cincinnati, OH -- scholarship
3,000	Cincinnati State University, Cincinnati, OH -- fund drive
3,000	Ohio State University, Columbus, OH -- scholarship
3,000	University of Cincinnati College of Applied Science, Cincinnati, OH -- scholarship
2,000	Miami University, Oxford, OH -- scholarship
2,000	Withrow High School -- scholarship
1,250	Ohio Foundation of Independent Colleges, Columbus, OH -- scholarship
1,250	Ohio Foundation of Independent Colleges, Columbus, OH -- scholarship
1,000	Chatfield College -- fund drive
1,000	College of Mount St. Joseph, Cincinnati, OH -- annual grant
1,000	Fund for Northern Kentucky University Foundation, KY -- annual grant
1,000	Northern Kentucky University, Highland Heights, KY -- scholarship
1,000	Ohio University, Athens, OH -- scholarship
1,000	Rensselaer Polytechnic Institute, Troy, NY -- scholarship
1,000	Society of Plastics Engineers -- scholarship
1,000	Southern State Community College, Hillsboro, OH -- scholarship
1,000	Thomas More Fund Drive
1,000	University of Cincinnati Clermont, Cincinnati, OH -- scholarship

Health

20,000	American Red Cross -- flood disaster
16,667	Hospice Capital Campaign
5,000	Hospice, Cincinnati, OH

International

1,640	United Way, Windsor, ON, Canada

Religion

5,000	St. Joseph's Home

Science

1,600	Science Screen Report, Aptos, CA

Social Services

242,000	United Way, Cincinnati, OH
16,666	YWCA
12,440	United Way of Oconee County, SC
11,000	United Way of Warren County
6,700	United Way, Madison Heights, MI
5,000	Cincinnati Youth Collaborative, Cincinnati, OH
4,000	United Way of Cooke County, TX
3,300	United Way, Detroit, MI
1,500	Family Service, Cincinnati, OH
1,000	Madisonville YMCA, Cincinnati, OH

MILLIKEN &CO.

Company Contact

Spartanburg, SC
Web: http://www.milliken.com

Company Description

Employees: 16,000
SIC(s): 2211 Broadwoven Fabric Mills--Cotton, 2221 Broadwoven Fabric Mills--Manmade, 2231 Broadwoven Fabric Mills--Wool.

Milliken Foundation

Giving Contact

Sid Nichols, Executive Director
Milliken Foundation
PO Box 1926
Spartanburg, SC 29304
Phone: (864)503-2540
Fax: (864)503-1830

Description

Founded: 1945
EIN: 136055062
Organization Type: Corporate Foundation. Supports preselected organizations only.
Giving Locations: headquarters and operating communities; nationally.
Grant Types: Capital, Employee Matching Gifts, General Support.

Financial Summary

Total Giving: $1,753,002 (1998); $1,515,037 (1997); $1,401,460 (1996). Note: Contributes through corporate direct giving program and foundation.
Giving Analysis: Giving for 1997 includes: foundation ($1,271,849); foundation grants to United Way ($243,188); 1998: foundation ($1,620,251); foundation grants to United Way ($132,751)
Assets: $7,015,060 (1998); $5,390,728 (1997); $5,487,894 (1996)
Gifts Received: $2,777,500 (1998); $1,042,027 (1997); $1,030,437 (1996). Note: In 1997, contributions were received from Milliken & Company ($1,000,000) and Minot K. Milliken ($42,027).

Typical Recipients

Arts & Humanities: Arts Associations & Councils, Arts Centers, Arts Funds, Arts & Humanities-General, History & Archaeology, Libraries, Museums/Galleries, Music, Performing Arts, Public Broadcasting, Theater
Civic & Public Affairs: Chambers of Commerce, Clubs, Community Foundations, Economic Development, Civic & Public Affairs-General, Law & Justice, Municipalities/Towns, Professional & Trade Associations, Public Policy, Safety, Urban & Community Affairs
Education: Arts/Humanities Education, Business Education, Colleges & Universities, Economic Education, Education Associations, Education Funds, Education Reform, Engineering/Technological Education, Education-General, Journalism/Media Education, Medical Education, Minority Education, Private Education (Precollege), Public Education (Precollege), Science/Mathematics Education, Special Education
Environment: Environment-General, Resource Conservation
Health: Children's Health/Hospitals, Clinics/Medical Centers, Emergency/Ambulance Services, Hospitals, Medical Rehabilitation, Prenatal Health Issues, Public Health, Single-Disease Health Associations
International: International Relations
Religion: Churches, Jewish Causes, Ministries, Religious Welfare, Social/Policy Issues
Science: Scientific Centers & Institutes, Scientific Research
Social Services: Child Welfare, Community Centers, Community Service Organizations, Family Planning, Food/Clothing Distribution, Homes, People with Disabilities, Recreation & Athletics, Scouts, Shelters/Homelessness, Special Olympics, Substance Abuse, United Funds/United Ways, YMCA/YWCA/YMHA/YWHA, Youth Organizations

Contributions Analysis

Giving Priorities: United funds and youth organizations; colleges and universities, especially those specializing in textile research; civic and political affairs; textile research institutes; and some arts institutions.
Arts & Humanities: 15%. Supports arts associations and councils, libraries, and the theater.
Civic & Public Affairs: 18%. Most goes to public policy and better government organizations; also supports business and free enterprise organizations and several local fire departments.
Education: 36%. Main interests are colleges and universities, and scientific and technical institutions, particularly schools for textile research. Other interests include private precollege, economic, and medical education.
Health: 12%. Supports the March of Dimes, rescue squads, and hospitals and clinics.
Religion: 4%. Limited support to churches.
Science: 3%. Major interests include scientific research and science institutes and centers.
Social Services: 12%. Most of social service giving went to united funds and youth organizations. Other interests include recreation, athletics, religious welfare, community service organizations, food and clothing distribution, and programs for the disabled.
Note: Total contributions made in 1998.

Corporate Officials

Thomas J. Malone: president, chief operating officer PRIM CORP EMPL president, chief operating officer: Milliken & Co.
Roger Milliken: chairman, chief executive officer B New York, NY 1915. ED Groton School (1929-1933); Yale University AB (1937). PRIM CORP EMPL chairman, chief executive officer: Milliken & Co. NONPR AFFIL member: Textile Institute; trustee: Wofford College; trustee: South Carolina Foundation Independent

Colleges; director: South Carolina Textile Manufacturer Association; chairman: Greenville-Spartanburg Airport Comm; chairman emeritus: Institute Textile Technology; member: Business Council; honorary member: AIA; director: American Textile Manufacturer Institute. CLUB AFFIL Yeamans Hall Club; The Links Club; Union League Club; Augusta National Golf Club.

Foundation Officials

Lawrence Heagney: member advisory committee, contact B 1937. ED Fairleigh Dickinson University BS; New York Law School LLB. PRIM CORP EMPL vice president, secretary, treasurer: Milliken & Co. ADD CORP EMPL secretary: Sylvan Chemical Co.

Thomas J. Malone: member advisory committee (see above)

Gerrish H. Milliken, Jr.: member advisory committee B New York, NY 1917. ED Yale University (1940).

Minot King Milliken: member advisory committee B New York, NY 1916. ED Princeton University (1937). PRIM CORP EMPL vice president, treasurer, director: Milliken & Co.

Roger Milliken: member advisory committee (see above)

Grants Analysis

Disclosure Period: calendar year ending 1998
Total Grants: $1,620,251*
Number of Grants: 104
Average Grant: $15,579
Highest Grant: $200,000
Typical Range: $200 to $25,000
***Note:** Giving excludes United Way.

Recent Grants

Note: Grants derived from 1997 Form 990.

Arts & Humanities

140,200	Arts Partnership, Spartanburg, SC
127,000	Spartanburg County Public Library, Spartanburg, SC
10,000	Agricultural Heritage Center
10,000	Automotive Hall of Fame, Midland, MI
7,500	Lincoln Center for Performing Arts, New York, NY
5,514	ETV Endowment, Spartanburg, SC
5,000	Greenville County Library, Greenville, SC
5,000	LaGrange Symphony Orchestra, LaGrange, GA
5,000	McCormick Arts Council, McCormick, SC

Civic & Public Affairs

50,000	Free Congress Research and Education Foundation, Washington, DC
50,000	National Development Council
25,000	Conservative Caucus Research Analysis and Education Foundation, Vienna, VA
20,500	Spartanburg County Foundation, Spartanburg, SC
20,000	Town of Johnston, Johnston, SC
12,500	Town of McCormick, McCormick, SC
10,000	Phyllis Wheatley Association, Steubenville, OH
9,500	Spartanburg Community Events, Spartanburg, SC

Education

100,000	LaGrange College, LaGrange, GA
50,000	Independent Colleges and Universities, Columbia, SC
35,000	Furman University, Greenville, SC
28,000	Long Cane Academy, McCormick, SC
28,000	Spartanburg Methodist College, Spartanburg, SC
26,000	Limestone College, Gaffney, SC
25,000	Erskine College, Due West, SC
25,000	Newberry College, Newberry, SC
15,000	National Science Foundation Trust Fund, Arlington, VA
15,000	Union Academy, Union, SC
12,400	Junior Achievement of Columbia, Greenville and Spartanburg, SC
10,000	South Carolina Governor's School for Arts Foundation, SC
10,000	South Carolina Policy Council Education Foundation, Columbia, SC
9,000	Adult Learning Center, Spartanburg, SC
8,000	Independent College Fund, Winston-Salem, NC
6,000	Foundation for Economic Education
6,000	St. George's School, Newport, RI
5,000	Intercollegiate Studies Institute, Bryn Mawr, PA

Health

28,536	March of Dimes National Foundation
6,000	Mount Desert Island Hospital, Bar Harbor, ME

Religion

25,500	Miracle Hill Ministries, Greenville, SC
8,000	Salvation Army
7,000	Christian Anti-Communism Crusade, Long Beach, CA
5,500	Anderson Interfaith Ministries, Anderson, SC

Science

27,500	Textile Research Institute, Princeton, NJ

Social Services

51,667	YMCA
21,950	Boy Scouts of America
20,000	Mobile Meal Service of Spartanburg County, Spartanburg, SC
15,000	LaGrange Sports Authority, LaGrange, GA
10,000	Rocky Bottom Camp of the Blind, Columbia, SC
10,000	South Carolina Special Olympics, Columbia, SC
6,000	Landrum Sports Association
5,580	Meals on Wheels

MILLIPORE CORP.

Company Contact

Bedford, MA
Web: http://www.millipore.com

Company Description

Employees: 4,289
SIC(s): 3081 Unsupported Plastics Film & Sheet, 3089 Plastics Products Nec, 3826 Analytical Instruments.

Operating Locations

Argentina: Biopore S.R.L., Buenos Aires; Australia: Millipore Australia Pty, Ltd., North Ryde; Austria: Millipore GmbH, Vienna, Wien; Belgium: Millipore SA/NV, Brussels, Brabant; Bangladesh: Sarban International, Dhaka; Brazil: Millipore Industria e Comercio Ltda., Sao Paulo; Bulgaria: Slavimex and D., Sofia; Canada: Millipore (Canada) Ltd., Etobicoke; Chile: Filterpore Ltda.td., Providencia, Santiago; People's Republic of China: Millipore China Ltd., Beijing, China-Singapore, Suzhou, Guangzhou, Shanghai, Shenyang; Colombia: Purificacion y Analisis de Fluidos Ltda., Bogota; Costa Rica: DEINSA, San Jose; Croatia: Labena, Ljubljana; Cyprus: Biotronics Ltd., Nicosia; Czech Republic: Millipore spol. s.r.o., Prague; Denmark: Millipore A/S, Glostrup; Ecuador: Purifluidos Ltda., Quito; Egypt: Etamco, Cairo; El Salvador: Coresa SA, San Salvador; England: Millipore, Watford; Estonia: BioExpert Ltd., Tallinn; Finland: Millipore Oy, Espoo, Uusimaa; France: Millipore SA, Yvelines Cedex; Germany: Millipore GmbH, Eschborn, Eschborn, Hessen; Greece: Malva Ltd., Kifissia; Guatemala: RECASA, Guatemala; Hong Kong: Millipore Asia Ltd./Millipore China Ltd., Wanchai; Hungary: Millipore Kft, Budapest; India: Millipre Pvt Ltd., Bangalore; Israel: Millitech Israel, Ness Ziona; Italy: Ziliale Millipore SpA, Rome, Vimodrone; Jamaica: Industrial and Technical Supplies, Kingston; Japan: Nihon Millipore Ltd., Tokyo; Republic of Korea: Millipore Korea Co. Ltd., Seoul; Latvia: Zinatniska komercfirma fanex, Riga; Lithuania: BIOMEDIKA UAB, Vilnius; Luxembourg: Millipore SA-NV, Brussels; Malta: Panta Marketing and Service Co., Msida; Mexico: Millipore SA de CV, Argentina Poniente; Morocco: Imatec, Casablanca; Malaysia: Millipore Asia Ltd., Selangor; Netherlands: Millipore BV, Etten-Leur; Norway: Millipore AS, Oslo; Nepal: Associated Enterprises, Kathmandu; New Zealand: BIOLAB, Auckland; Pakistan: The Scientific Corporation, LaShore; Paraguay: ALVOG SA, Asuncion; Peru: Cientifica Andina SA, Lima; Poland: Millipore Sp. z.o.o., Warsaw; Puerto Rico: Millipore Cidra Inc., Cidra; Romania: Teknolab Srl, Bucharest; Russia: Millipore, Moscow; Republic of South Africa: Microsep Pty Ltd., Johannesburg; Saudi Arabia: I.D.C.G., Jeddan; Singapore: Millipore Singapore Pte Ltd., TechLink; Spain: Millipore Iberica, SA, Madrid; Sri Lanka: Indosol Put. Ltd., Dehiwela; Slovenia: Labena, Ljubljana; Sweden: Millipore AB, Askim, Goteborg, Helsingborg, Sundbyberg, Stockholm; Switzerland: Millipore AG, Volketswil, Zurich, le Mont sur Lausanne; Trinidad and Tobago: Wesern Scientific Co. Ltd.; Turkey: Analytik AS, Ankara; Anamed, Istanbul; Kurteks, Istanbul; Taiwan: Millipore Asia Ltd. Taiwan Branch (USA), Taipei; United Arab Emirates: Gulf Scientific Corporate, Jebel Ali, Dubai; Uruguay: Poliuruaguay SRL, Montevideo; Venezuela: Corporacion Technipore SA, Caracus

Nonmonetary Support

Type: Donated Equipment; Donated Products
Note: Nonmonetary support is provided by both the company and the foundation.

The Millipore Foundation

Giving Contact

Ms. Charleen Johnson, Executive Director
The Millipore Foundation
80 Ashby Road
Bedford, MA 01730-2271
Phone: (781)533-2210
Fax: (781)533-3301
Email: Charleen_Johnson@millipore.com
Web: http://www.millipore.com/foundation

Description

EIN: 222583952
Organization Type: Corporate Foundation
Giving Locations: MA: cash grants made primarily in Massachusetts matching gifts awarded nationally.
Grant Types: Capital, Employee Matching Gifts, General Support, Matching, Multiyear/Continuing Support.
Note: Employee matching gift ratio: 2 to 1 up to $5,000 annually per employee.

Giving Philosophy

'The Foundation's mission is to support Millipore's interest in scientific and technological advancement; to support specific public policy issues that affect Millipore's stockholders, employees and customers; to help improve the quality of life in Millipore's communities; and to assist and encourage Millipore's employees in volunteer efforts.

'While Millipore's products and business pursuits often make significant contributions to society, we believe we have an additional commitment to serve the public interest more directly--through contributions to selected non-profit organizations and institutions.

'We believe those contributions directly benefit not only the causes, communities and organizations that

are the recipients of Millipore Foundation donations, but also Millipore's stockholders, employees and customers. Our contributions are part of our social responsibility, and they are also a part of our investment in the future--the future of our business and the future of the communities in which we do business.

'The Millipore Foundation recognizes that it cannot meet every request--since there are so many groups and organizations in need of assistance. We want to focus our activities and resources on those areas in which we can make a significant impact; we seek to give those organizations and institutions most closely connected to Millipore's goals and identity as a company, and to the Foundation's purpose. Toward that end, we have established some objectives and guidelines that serve as touchstones for our contributions. 'Through our contributions, we seek to accomplish the following objectives:

To foster advances in science and technology related to Millipore's business objectives;

To create a positive recognition and image of Millipore in those communities where the company resides;

To improve the quality of life in those communities in which Millipore employees live and work;

To stimulate volunteerism and active community involvement by Millipore employees.' The Millipore Foundation 1995 fiscal report

Financial Summary

Total Giving: $1,375,000 (fiscal year ending September 30, 1999 approx); $1,375,437 (fiscal 1998); $1,273,387 (fiscal 1997). Note: Contributes through foundation only.

Giving Analysis: Giving for fiscal 1996 includes: foundation matching gifts ($136,086); fiscal 1997: foundation matching gifts ($350,692); fiscal 1998: foundation matching gifts ($421,421)

Assets: $1,050,527 (fiscal 1998); $1,369,717 (fiscal 1997); $1,260,776 (fiscal 1996)

Gifts Received: $1,040,771 (fiscal 1998); $1,131,084 (fiscal 1997); $1,092,500 (fiscal 1996). Note: Contributions are received from Millipore Corp.

Typical Recipients

Arts & Humanities: Arts Associations & Councils, Arts Centers, Arts Funds, Ballet, Libraries, Museums/Galleries, Music, Performing Arts, Public Broadcasting

Civic & Public Affairs: African American Affairs, Clubs, Employment/Job Training, Hispanic Affairs, Legal Aid, Municipalities/Towns, Native American Affairs, Nonprofit Management, Philanthropic Organizations, Professional & Trade Associations, Public Policy, Urban & Community Affairs, Zoos/Aquariums

Education: Afterschool/Enrichment Programs, Business Education, Business-School Partnerships, Colleges & Universities, Community & Junior Colleges, Education Reform, Elementary Education (Public), Engineering/Technological Education, Education-General, Leadership Training, Literacy, Medical Education, Minority Education, Preschool Education, Private Education (Precollege), Public Education (Precollege), Religious Education, Science/Mathematics Education, Secondary Education (Private), Secondary Education (Public), Student Aid, Vocational & Technical Education

Environment: Environment-General, Wildlife Protection

Health: AIDS/HIV, Cancer, Children's Health/Hospitals, Clinics/Medical Centers, Diabetes, Emergency/Ambulance Services, Health Organizations, Home-Care Services, Hospitals, Medical Research, Medical Training, Mental Health, Public Health, Single-Disease Health Associations

International: Foreign Educational Institutions, International Relief Efforts

Science: Science Exhibits & Fairs, Science Museums, Scientific Centers & Institutes, Scientific Organizations, Scientific Research

Social Services: At-Risk Youth, Community Service Organizations, Delinquency & Criminal Rehabilitation, Family Services, Food/Clothing Distribution, Homes, People with Disabilities, Recreation & Athletics, Substance Abuse, United Funds/United Ways, Youth Organizations

Contributions Analysis

Giving Priorities: Universities and teaching hospitals involved in research and training in chemistry, biochemistry, and engineering; social service and health organizations; local arts groups; and public policy. The foundation has limited funds for contributions to U.S.-based nonprofit organizations with an international focus. Primarily supports the resolution of key industrial policy issues at the local, national, and international levels.

Arts & Humanities: 11%. Funds public library, performing arts, museums, and fine arts.

Civic & Public Affairs: 11%. (Public Policy) Support for the resolution of key industrial policy issues, at local, national and international levels. Support goes to selected cultural activities, social services, healthcare institutions, and other local funds and programs.

Education: 38%. Supports selected organizations, universities, institutions, and teaching hospitals engaged in research and training--primarily in the fields of chemistry, biochemistry and engineering.

Health: 22%. Funds hospitals, medical centers and biomedical research.

International: 1%.

Science: 6%. Supports science museums.

Social Services: 11%. Supports programs in minority education (national organizations that extend opportunities for minorities at all educational levels) and youth development (regional programs that provide employment and self-development--particularly for inner-city youth).

Application Procedures

Initial Contact: Send written inquiries and proposals.

Application Requirements: Application should include summary of proposed program or project, including specific goals and objectives; dollar amount or nature of request; purpose of requested funds; itemized budget for project; financial statements for most recently completed fiscal year; proof of tax-exempt status; history and accomplishments of requesting organization; list of staff and board of directors; and other sources of support; current contact name, address, and phone number.

Deadlines: None.

Decision Notification: The board meets quarterly to evaluate proposals.

Notes: Foundation accepts the Associated Grantmakers of Massachusetts Common Proposal format.

Restrictions

The foundation does not support religious or political programs.

Additional Information

The foundation will support new projects or new nonprofit organizations in certain cases.

The foundation conducts periodic evaluations and does not guarantee continuing support for a project or program.

Publications: Foundation Annual Report

Corporate Officials

Francis Lunger: chief financial officer, corporate vice presidento B Erie, PA 1945. ED Gannon University BS (1968). PRIM CORP EMPL chief financial officer, corporate vice president: Millipore Corp. CORP AFFIL director: Stormedia Inc.

Jeffrey Rudin: vice president, general counsel PRIM CORP EMPL vice president, general counsel: Millipore Corp.

C. William Zadel: chairman, president, chief executive officer B Chicago, IL 1943. ED United States Military Academy BS (1965); University of Chicago MBA (1974). PRIM CORP EMPL chairman, president, chief executive officer: Millipore Corp. CORP AFFIL director: Span Instruments Inc.; director: Zoll Medical; director: Kulicke Soffa Industries; director: Matritech.

Foundation Officials

Charleen Johnson: executive director

Joanne Nikka: trustee B Dublin, Ireland 1951. PRIM CORP EMPL vice president: Millipore Corp. NONPR AFFIL instructor: American Compensation Association.

Geoffrey Nunes: chairman B New York, NY 1930. ED Princeton University AB (1952); Harvard University LLB (1957). PRIM CORP EMPL senior vice president, general counsel: Millipore Corp. CORP AFFIL director: Reebok International Ltd.

Jeffrey Rudin: trustee (see above)

C. William Zadel: trustee (see above)

Grants Analysis

Disclosure Period: fiscal year ending September 30, 1998

Total Grants: $954,015*

Number of Grants: 119

Average Grant: $8,017

Highest Grant: $37,500

Typical Range: $1,000 to $10,000

***Note:** Giving excludes matching gifts.

Recent Grants

Note: Grants derived from fiscal 1998 Form 990.

Arts & Humanities

15,000	Museum of Fine Arts, Boston, MA
14,000	DeCordova Museum, Lincoln, MA
10,000	Boston Ballet, Boston, MA
10,000	Isabella Stewart Gardner Museum, Boston, MA
10,000	Wang Center for the Performing Arts, Boston, MA
10,000	ZUMIX, Boston, MA
9,000	American Textile History Museum, Lowell, MA

Civic & Public Affairs

35,750	City Year, Inc., Boston, MA
10,000	New England Aquarium, Boston, MA
10,000	STRIVE, Boston Employment Service, Dorchester, MA
9,800	Associated Grantmakers of Massachusettes, Boston, MA
9,436	Appalachian Mountain Club, Boston, MA

Education

30,000	Citizens Scholarship Foundation, St. Peter, MN
25,000	City on a Hill Charter School, Boston, MA
25,000	A Different September Foundation, Boston, MA
23,500	Bedford Public Schools, Bedford, MA -- education
20,000	Cary Christian School, Cary, NC
15,000	Boston Renaissance Charter School, Boston, MA
15,000	Concord Academy, Concord, MA
15,000	Marblehead Charter School, Marblehead, MA
15,000	Summerbridge Cambridge, Cambridge, MA -- education
15,000	United Negro College Fund, Boston, MA
15,000	University of Massachusetts, Amherst, MA
10,000	Hebrew College, Brookline, MA
10,000	Massachusettes Corporation for Educational Telecommunications, Boston, MA
10,000	Neighborhood House Charter School, Dorchester, MA
10,000	New England Colleges Fund, Woburn, MA
10,000	Plano International Preschool, Plano, TX

Health

37,500	Lahey Clinic, Burlington, MA
20,000	MA General Hospital, Boston, MA
20,000	New England Baptist Hospital, Boston, MA
15,000	American Medical Resources Foundation, Brockton, MA
10,000	Beth Israel Deaconess Medical Center, Boston, MA
10,000	Boston Biomedical Research Institute, Boston, MA
10,000	Deaconess-Waltham Hospital, Waltham, MA
10,000	Emerson Hospital, Concord, MA
10,000	Franciscan Children's Hospital, Boston, MA
10,000	Whitehead Institute, Boston, MA

International

10,000	AmeriCares, Inc., New Canaan, CT

Science

25,000	The Heard Natural Science Museum, McKinney, TX
15,800	Museum of Science, Boston, MA

Social Services

29,000	Allen Community Outreach, Allen, TX
16,500	One With One, Brighton, MA
15,000	Concord-Assabet Adolescent Services, Acton, MA
10,000	Adolescent Consultation Services, Inc., Cambridge, MA
10,000	Italian Home for Children, Jamaica Plain, MA

Mine Safety Appliances Co.

Company Contact

Pittsburgh, PA
Web: http://www.msanet.com

Company Description

Employees: 4,100 (1999)
SIC(s): 3823 Process Control Instruments, 3842 Surgical Appliances & Supplies.

Operating Locations

Operates internationally.

Mine Safety Appliances Co. Charitable Foundation

Giving Contact

James E. Herald, Secretary
Mine Safety Appliances Co. Charitable Foundation
PO Box 426
Pittsburgh, PA 15230
Phone: (412)967-3000
Fax: (412)967-3452

Description

EIN: 256023104
Organization Type: Corporate Foundation
Giving Locations: PA: Pittsburgh operating location communities.
Grant Types: Capital, Conference/Seminar, General Support, Project.

Financial Summary

Total Giving: $500,000 (1999 approx); $750,125 (1998); $500,000 (1997 approx). Note: Contributes through foundation only.
Giving Analysis: Giving for 1998 includes: foundation grants to United Way ($258,000)
Assets: $3,543,801 (1998); $4,272,900 (1990); $5,115,428 (1989)
Gifts Received: $13,209 (1998)

Typical Recipients

Arts & Humanities: Arts Centers, Arts Festivals, Ballet, Dance, Libraries, Museums/Galleries, Music, Opera, Performing Arts, Public Broadcasting, Theater
Civic & Public Affairs: Botanical Gardens/Parks, Economic Development, Professional & Trade Associations, Public Policy, Safety, Urban & Community Affairs, Zoos/Aquariums
Education: Business Education, Colleges & Universities, Community & Junior Colleges, Economic Education, Education Associations, Education Funds, Engineering/Technological Education, Minority Education, Preschool Education, Science/Mathematics Education, Special Education
Environment: Environment-General
Health: Children's Health/Hospitals, Emergency/Ambulance Services, Health Funds, Health Organizations, Health Organizations, Hospitals, Kidney, Medical Rehabilitation, Mental Health, Multiple Sclerosis, Single-Disease Health Associations
International: International Peace & Security Issues, International Relations
Religion: Dioceses, Religious Organizations, Religious Welfare
Science: Observatories & Planetariums, Scientific Centers & Institutes
Social Services: Child Welfare, Community Service Organizations, Emergency Relief, Family Services, People with Disabilities, Recreation & Athletics, Scouts, United Funds/United Ways, Youth Organizations

Contributions Analysis

Giving Priorities: The arts, united funds, Pittsburgh-area colleges and universities, economic development and public policy, and hospitals.
Arts & Humanities: 2%. The Pittsburgh Symphony receives substantial funding. Other interests include ballet, opera, the performing arts, museums, and libraries.
Civic & Public Affairs: 14%. Emphasis on economic development and public policy. Supports business, professional, and safety organizations in addition to those with an emphasis on urban and community affairs.
Education: 10%. Pittsburgh area colleges and universities receive funding. Also supports economic, engineering, and minority education and independent college funds.
Health: 12%. Hospitals, pediatric health, rehabilitation centers, and single-disease health associations.
Religion: Less than 5%.
Social Services: 39%. Primarily supports united funds. Also funds housing, youth organizations, emergency relief, child welfare, and the disabled.
Note: Total contributions made in 1998.

Application Procedures

Initial Contact: Send brief letter or proposal.
Application Requirements: a description of organization, amount requested, purpose of funds sought, recently audited financial statement, proof of tax-exempt status.
Deadlines: None.

Restrictions

Foundation does not award scholarships or provide grants to individuals.

Corporate Officials

James E. Herald: vice president financeo PRIM CORP EMPL vice president finance: Mine Safety Appliances Co.
John Thomas Ryan, III: chairman, chief executive officer B Pittsburgh, PA 1943. ED University of Notre Dame AB (1965); Harvard University MBA (1969). PRIM CORP EMPL chairman, chief executive officer: Mine Safety Appliances Co. CORP AFFIL director: Penns Southwest; director: Auergesellschaft GmbH; chairman: Federal Reserve Bank Cleveland/ Pittsburgh. NONPR AFFIL member: Council Foreign Relations; vice chairman, director: Industrial Safety Equipment Association.

Foundation Officials

James E. Herald: secretary (see above)

Grants Analysis

Disclosure Period: calendar year ending
Total Grants: $492,125*
Number of Grants: 109*
Average Grant: $4,515
Highest Grant: $220,000
Typical Range: $1,000 to $5,000
***Note:** Giving excludes United Way. Number of grants excludes United Way.

Recent Grants

Note: Grants derived from 1998 Form 990.

Arts & Humanities

103,000	Pittsburgh Oratory, Pittsburgh, PA
15,000	Pittsburgh Symphony Orchestra Society, Pittsburgh, PA
7,500	Civic Light Opera, Pittsburgh, PA
6,000	Carnegie Museums of Pittsburgh, Pittsburgh, PA
5,000	Opera Theater of Pittsburgh, Inc., Pittsburgh, PA
5,000	Pittsburgh Ballet Theatre, Pittsburgh, PA
5,000	Pittsburgh Opera, Pittsburgh, PA

Civic & Public Affairs

18,500	Allegheny Conference on Community Development, Pittsburgh, PA
15,000	Penn's Southwest Association, Pittsburgh, PA
8,400	Pennsylvania Economy League, Western Division, Pittsburgh, PA
6,500	National Safety Council Foundation for Safety and Health, Itasca, IL
6,000	American Society of Safety Engineers, Des Plaines, IL
6,000	Operation Better Block, Pittsburgh, PA
6,000	Pittsburgh Regional Alliance, Pittsburgh, PA
5,000	American Enterprise Institute for Public Policy Research, Washington, DC
4,000	Friends of the New Park, Cranberry Township, PA

Education

10,000	University of Pittsburgh Center for Latin American Studies, Pittsburgh, PA
7,500	Harvard Business School, Boston, MA
6,000	(The) Extra Mile Education Foundation, Pittsburgh, PA
5,000	ASSET, Incorporated, Pittsburgh, PA
5,000	DePaul Institute, Pittsburgh, PA
5,000	Seton Hill College, Greensburg, PA
5,000	University of Pittsburgh Health Policy Institute Graduate School of Public Health, Pittsburgh, PA
5,000	University of Pittsburgh University Center for International Studies, Pittsburgh, PA
4,000	Carlow College, Pittsburgh, PA
3,500	Junior Achievement of Southwest Pennsylvania, Pittsburgh, PA
3,000	Society of Women Engineers, Pittsburgh, PA
2,500	(The) College Fund/UNCF, Philadelphia, PA

Health

40,000	Children's Hospital of Pittsburgh, Pittsburgh, PA
10,000	American Industrial Hygiene Association Foundation, Fairfax, VA

8,500	National Kidney Foundation of Western Pennsylvania, Pittsburgh, PA
5,000	American Red Cross, Pittsburgh, PA
5,000	D. T. Watson Rehabilitation Services, Sewickley, PA -- Children's Care Campaign
5,000	Multiple Sclerosis Service Society, Clairton, PA
3,000	Ronald McDonald House Charities of Pittsburgh, Pittsburgh, PA

International

4,000	Trilateral Commission, New York, NY
4,000	World Affairs Council of Pittsburgh, Pittsburgh, PA

Religion

12,500	Holy Family Institute, Pittsburgh, PA
10,000	St. Barnabas Charitable Foundation, Gibsonia, PA
5,000	Catholic Charities, Diocese of Pittsburgh, Pittsburgh, PA
5,000	Diocese of Pittsburgh, Pittsburgh, PA -- Bishop's Education Fund

Social Services

220,000	United Way of Southwestern Pennsylvania, Pittsburgh, PA
20,000	United Way, Butler, PA
13,000	United Way of Westmoreland County, Greensburg, PA
5,000	ARC Allegheny, Pittsburgh, PA
5,000	Boys & Girls Clubs of Western Pennsylvania, Pittsburgh, PA
5,000	Girls Hope of Pittsburgh, Inc., Baden, PA
5,000	United Way - Mile High (Denver), Denver, CO
3,000	Girl Scouts of Southwestern Pennsylvania, Pittsburgh, PA
3,000	Mom's House, Pittsburgh, PA

MINNESOTA MINING & MANUFACTURING CO.

 Number 26 of Top 100 Corporate Givers

Company Contact

St. Paul, MN
Web: http://www.mmm.com

Company Description

Also Known As: 3M.
Revenue: US$15,021,000,000
Profit: US$1,175,000,000
Employees: 73,564
Fortune Rank: 110, per FORTUNE Magazine's list of 500 Largest U.S. Corporations (1999).
FF 110
SIC(s): 2672 Coated & Laminated Paper Nec, 2834 Pharmaceutical Preparations, 2891 Adhesives & Sealants, 2899 Chemical Preparations Nec.

Operating Locations

Argentina: 3M Argentina Pacifica, Hurlingham, Buenos Aires; Australia: 3M Australia Pty. Ltd., Pymble; Austria: 3M Osterreich GmbH, Perchtoldsdorf; Belgium: 3M Belgium NV, Mechelen, Brabant; Canada: 3M Canada, London; Chile: 3M Chile SA, Santiago; People's Republic of China: 3M China Ltd., Shanghai; Colombia: 3M Colombia SA, Bogota, Cundinamarco; Costa Rica: 3M Costa Rica, San Jose; Denmark: 3M A/S, Glostrup, Copenhagen; Dominican Republic: 3M Dominicana SA, Santo Domingo; Ecuador: 3M Ecudor CA, Guayaquil; Egypt: 3M Egypt Ltd., Cairo; El Salvador: 3M El Salvador SA de CV, San Salvador; Finland: Suomen 3M OY, Espoo; France: 3M France, Cergy Pontoise Cedex; Germany: 3M Deutschland GmbH, Neuss, Nordrhein-Westfalen; Greece: 3M Hellas Ltd., Maroussi; Guatemala: 3M Guatemala SA, Guatemala City; Guam: 3M Co., Tamining; Hong Kong: 3M Hong Kong Ltd., Causeway Bay; Honduras: 3M Honduras, San Pedro Sualockholm; Hungary: 3M Hungary KFT, Budapest; India: Birla 3M Ltd., Bangalore; Ireland: 3M Dublin Ltd., Dun Laoghaire; 3M (Ireland) Ltd., Dun Laoghaire; Italy: 3M Italia SpA, Milano; Jamaica: 3M Interamerica INC, Kingston; Japan: Sumitomo 3M Ltd., Tokyo; Kenya: 3M Kenya Ltd., Nairobi; Republic of Korea: 3M Korea Ltd., Seoul; Mexico: 3M Mexico SA de CV, Cuidad de Mexico; Malaysia: 3M Malaysia Sdn. Berhand, Pealing Jaya, Selangor; Nigeria: Minnesota Nigeria Ltd., Laaps; Netherlands: 3M Nederland B.V., Leiden; Norway: 3M Norway AS, Skjetten, Akershus; New Zealand: 3M New Zealand Ltd., Takapuna, Auckland; Pakistan: 3M Pakistan (Pvt) Ltd., Karachi; Panama: 3M Panama SA, Panama; Peru: 3M Peru SA, Lima; Philippines: 3M Philippines, Makati, Rizal; Poland: 3M Poland SP Z00, Warsaw; Puerto Rico: 3M Puerto Rico, Carolina; Portugal: Minnesota 3M de Portugal Lda., Lison, Codex; Russia: 3M Russia, Moscow; Republic of South Africa: 3M South Africa (Pty) Ltd., Johannesburg; Singapore: 3M Singapore Pte. Ltd., Singapore; Spain: 3M Espana SA, Madrid; Sri Lanka: Sri Lanka Private Ltd., Colombo; Sweden: 3M Svenska AB, Sollentuna, Stockholm; Switzerland: 3M (East) AG, Rot Kreuz; 3M (Schweiz), Rueschlikon; Thailand: 3M Thailand Ltd., Bangkok; Trinidad and Tobago: 3M Intramerica, Inc., Trinidad; Turkey: 3M Sanayii ve Ticaret AS, Istanbul; Taiwan: 3M Taiwan Ltd., Taipei; United Arab Emirates: 3M Gulf Ltd., Deira, Dubai; United Kingdom: 3M United Kingdom PLC, Bracknell; Mobil Gas Marketing (United Kingdom) Ltd., London; Uruguay: 3M Uraguay SA, Montevideo; Venezuela: 3M Manufacturing Venezuala SA, Caracas; Vietnam: 3M Vietnam Ltd., Ho Chi Minh City; Zimbabwe: 3M Zimbabwe (PTY) Ltd., Msaba, Haware

Nonmonetary Support

Value: $16,608,454 (1998); $18,921,376 (1997); $30,875,990 (1996)
Type: Donated Equipment; Donated Products; In-kind Services
Volunteer Programs: 3M supports two employee/retiree volunteer programs: CARES (Community Action Retired Employees Services) involving about 1,200 retirees, and CSEP (Community Service Executive Program) that has 10 participants. More than 150 employees serve on 20 advisory committees.
Contact: Richard E. Hanson, Director Community Affairs; Vice President
3M Foundation.
Note: Donated equipment at fair market value.

3M Foundation

Giving Contact

Cynthia F. Kleven, Manager Contributions
3M Community Affairs 3M Contributions Program
591-30-02 3M Ctr.
St. Paul, MN 55144-1000
Phone: (651)733-0144
Fax: (651)737-3061
Email: cfkleven@mmm.com

Alternate Contact

Richard E. Hanson, Contact
3M Foundation
St. Paul, MN 55144
Phone: (651)733-8335

Description

Founded: 1953
EIN: 416038262
Organization Type: Corporate Foundation
Giving Locations: headquarters and operating communities.
Grant Types: Challenge, Employee Matching Gifts, Fellowship, General Support, Operating Expenses, Project, Scholarship.
Note: Employee matching gift ratio: 1 to 1.

Giving Philosophy

'3M recognizes its responsibilities as a corporate citizen through the 3M contributions program which supports educational, cultural, community, health and human service activities in communities where 3M has a maj0r presence.' 3M contributions program.

Financial Summary

Total Giving: $32,000,000 (1999 approx); $32,426,000 (1998); $34,989,839 (1997). Note: Contributes through corporate direct giving program and foundation.
Giving Analysis: Giving for 1997 includes: foundation ($7,168,440); corporate direct giving ($5,659,599); foundation grants to United Way ($1,705,308); foundation matching gifts ($1,535,116); 1998: nonmonetary support ($16,608,454); foundation ($9,832,853); corporate direct giving ($5,984,564)
Assets: $8,851,862 (1998); $10,852,129 (1996); $9,769,998 (1993)
Gifts Received: $3,232,020 (1996)

Typical Recipients

Arts & Humanities: Arts Institutes, Arts Outreach, Ethnic & Folk Arts, Historic Preservation, Libraries, Museums/Galleries, Music, Opera, Performing Arts, Public Broadcasting, Theater
Civic & Public Affairs: African American Affairs, Business/Free Enterprise, Chambers of Commerce, Community Foundations, Economic Development, Employment/Job Training, Civic & Public Affairs-General, Hispanic Affairs, Legal Aid, Municipalities/Towns, Native American Affairs, Nonprofit Management, Parades/Festivals, Professional & Trade Associations, Safety, Urban & Community Affairs
Education: Business Education, Colleges & Universities, Economic Education, Education Associations, Education Funds, Engineering/Technological Education, International Exchange, Journalism/Media Education, Medical Education, Minority Education, Science/Mathematics Education, Social Sciences Education, Student Aid, Vocational & Technical Education
Environment: Environment-General
Health: Clinics/Medical Centers, Emergency/Ambulance Services, Geriatric Health, Health Policy/Cost Containment, Health Organizations, Hospices, Hospitals, Medical Rehabilitation, Mental Health, Transplant Networks/Donor Banks
International: Foreign Educational Institutions
Religion: Religious Welfare, Social/Policy Issues
Science: Science Museums, Scientific Research
Social Services: Child Welfare, Community Centers, Community Service Organizations, Counseling, Crime Prevention, Day Care, Delinquency & Criminal Rehabilitation, Domestic Violence, Emergency Relief, Family Services, Food/Clothing Distribution, Homes, People with Disabilities, Recreation & Athletics, Scouts, Senior Services, Shelters/Homelessness, Substance Abuse, United Funds/United Ways, Volunteer Services, YMCA/YWCA/YMHA/YWHA, Youth Organizations

Contributions Analysis

Giving Priorities: Three primary areas of focus: education, especially math, science, and economics; health and human services, with a focus on strenghtening families and youth development; and arts and culture, supporting the integration of arts into education.
Arts & Humanities: 55%. Supports arts organizations with emphasis on educational achievement and also community outreach programs.
Civic & Public Affairs: 8%. Supports local initiatives in 3M communities.

Education: 55%. Supports elementary through graduate education, where science, technology, and business are targeted educational area. K-12 programs focus on programs that stimulate student interest and achievement. Teacher training is also an area of support.
Health: 30%. Includes human service. Especially interested in programs that support families and have an emphasis on youth development, including parenting skills and employment training. Health care initiatives are supporting patient safety issues.

Application Procedures

Initial Contact: Send foundation brief letter of inquire. Telephone requests are not accepted.
Application Requirements: Include brief organizational history, project description, targeted group of people will be benefited, specific amount requested, and proof of tax-exempt status.
Deadlines: April 30, September 30, and January 31.
Review Process: If letter of inquiry demonstrates your organization meet 3M criteria, and geographic restrictions and funding priorities are met, you may be invited to submit a formal grant application.

Restrictions

Grants are not considered for advocacy; individual; religious, fraternal, social, veterans, or military organizations; lobbying efforts to influence legislation; travel; purchase of equipment not manufactured by 3M; for-profit organizations; or endowment funds.
Generally, grants are not made to organizations outside of 3M communities; conferences, seminars, or workshops; fund-raising testimonial and athletic events; emergency operating support; funding for more than 10 percent of an organization's annual budget; or funding programs beyond three years.

Additional Information

In countries where 3M has subsidiary operations, requests should be directed to that location. For more information regarding international giving, contact Richard Hanson, director, Community Affairs, and vice president, 3M Foundation.
Inquiries from the St. Paul, MN, area should be addressed to the designated staff person at the above address. The contact people include the following: Wendell J. Butler, health & human services at 612-736-3781; David E. Ginkel, civic/community and contribution of product and property at 612-733-1420; and Barbara W. Kaufmann, arts and education at612-733-1241. For locations outside of St. Paul where 3M has an operation, contact Cynthia Kleven at 613-733-1721 or your local 3M facility.
Publications: Giving Guidelines

Corporate Officials

J. Marc Adam: vice president marketing B Montreal, ON Canada 1938. ED University of Ottawa. PRIM CORP EMPL vice president marketing: Minnesota Mining & Manufacturing Co. CORP AFFIL directory: Clarcor Inc.
Harry C. Andrews: executive vice president PRIM CORP EMPL executive vice president: Minnesota Mining & Manufacturing Co.
Ronald O. Baukol: director, executive vice president B Chicago, IL 1937. ED Iowa State University (1959); Massachusetts Institute of Technology (1960). PRIM CORP EMPL director, executive vice president: Minnesota Mining & Manufacturing Co. CORP AFFIL director: Toro Co.; director: Graco Inc. NONPR AFFIL trustee: U.S. Council International Business.
John W. Benson: executive vice president health care B St. James, MN 1944. ED University of Minnesota (1966); University of Washington (1968). PRIM CORP EMPL executive vice president health care: Minnesota Mining & Manufacturing Co.
William E. Coyne: senior vice president B Toronto, ON Canada 1936. ED University of Toronto BS (1958); University of Toronto MS (1960); University of Virginia PhD (1963). PRIM CORP EMPL senior vice president: Minnesota Mining & Manufacturing Co. ADD CORP EMPL group vice president: 3 M Health Care Group. CORP AFFIL director: Life Imaging System; director: Dofasco Inc.; director: Health One. NONPR AFFIL Minnesota Medical Foundation; chairman: Science Museum Minnesota.
Livio Diego DeSimone: chairman, chief executive officer B Montreal, PQ Canada 1936. ED McGill University BS (1957). PRIM CORP EMPL chairman, chief executive officer: Minnesota Mining & Manufacturing Co. CORP AFFIL director: Vulcan Materials Co.; director: General Mills Inc.; executive vice president: Minnesota Mining & MFG Co. Canada; director: Dayton Hudson Corp.; director: Conference Board Inc.; director: Cray Research Inc.; director: Cargill Inc. NONPR AFFIL member: United States Chamber of Commerce; trustee: University Minnesota Foundation; department chairman: Prince Wales Business Leaders Forum; director: Conference Board Canada; National Legal Center Public Interest.
M. Kay Grenz: vice president human resources B Owatonna, MN 1946. ED University of North Dakota (1969). PRIM CORP EMPL vice president human resources: Minnesota Mining & Manufacturing Co. CORP AFFIL director: Eastern Heights Bank. NONPR AFFIL member: Human Resources Roundtable Group; director: INROADS; member: Human Resources Planning Society; director: Gillette Children's Specialty Healthcare.
Cynthia F. Kleven: director community affairs PRIM CORP EMPL director community affairs: Minnesota Mining & Manufacturing Co.
Mohamed S. Nozari: executive vice president PRIM CORP EMPL executive vice president: Minnesota Mining & Manufacturing Co.
Charles Reich: executive vice president PRIM CORP EMPL executive vice president: Minnesota Mining & Manufacturing Co.
Raymond C. Richelsen: executive vice president PRIM CORP EMPL executive vice president: Minnesota Mining & Manufacturing Co. CORP AFFIL director: Banta Corp.
John Joseph Ursu: general counsel, senior vice president legal affairs B Detroit, MI 1939. ED University of Michigan AB (1962); University of Michigan JD (1965). PRIM CORP EMPL general counsel, senior vice president legal affairs: Minnesota Mining & Manufacturing Co. NONPR AFFIL member: Association General Counsel; member: CLO Roundtable; member: America Bar Association.
Harold J. Wiens: executive vice president PRIM CORP EMPL executive vice president: Minnesota Mining & Manufacturing Co.

Giving Program Officials

J. Marc Adam: president, director (see above)
John W. Benson: director (see above)
William E. Coyne: director (see above)
Livio Diego DeSimone: director (see above)
Richard E. Hanson: vice president, director (see above)
Barbara W. Kaufmann: director (see above)
Raymond C. Richelsen: director PRIM CORP EMPL executive vice president: Minnesota Mining & Manufacturing Co. CORP AFFIL director: Banta Corp.
John Joseph Ursu: director B Detroit, MI 1939. ED University of Michigan AB (1962); University of Michigan JD (1965). PRIM CORP EMPL general counsel, senior vice president legal affairs: Minnesota Mining & Manufacturing Co. NONPR AFFIL member: Association General Counsel; member: CLO Roundtable; member: America Bar Association.
Janet L. Yeomans: treasurer, director B Washington, DC 1948. ED Connecticut College (1970); University of Chicago MBA (1979). PRIM CORP EMPL vice president, treasurer: Minnesota Mining & Manufacturing Co.

Foundation Officials

J. Marc Adam: president, director (see above)
M. Kay Grenz: director (see above)
Richard E. Hanson: vice president, director (see above)
Cynthia F. Kleven: secretary, director (see above)
Raymond C. Richelsen: director (see above)
John Joseph Ursu: director (see above)
Janet L. Yeomans: treasurer, director (see above)

Grants Analysis

Disclosure Period: calendar year ending 1998
Total Grants: $15,817,417*
Number of Grants: 527 (approx)
Average Grant: $30,000
Highest Grant: $1,284,000
Typical Range: $2,000 to $50,000
***Note:** Grants analysis provided by Foundation. Giving excludes nonmonetary support and international contributions.

Recent Grants

Note: Grants derived from 1996 Form 990.

Arts & Humanities

1,565,795	Twin Cities Public Television, Saint Paul, MN
100,000	Minnesota Orchestral Association, Minneapolis, MN
100,000	Ordway Music Theater, Saint Paul, MN
100,000	St. Paul Chamber Orchestra, Saint Paul, MN
55,000	Minnesota Opera, Minneapolis, MN
50,000	Minneapolis Institute of Arts, Minneapolis, MN
35,000	KSJN Minnesota Public Radio, Minneapolis, MN
25,000	Children's Theater Company, Saint Paul, MN
20,000	Guthrie Theater Foundation, Minneapolis, MN
20,000	Minnesota Children's Museum, Saint Paul, MN
20,000	Minnesota Museum of American Art, Saint Paul, MN

Civic & Public Affairs

100,000	City of St. Paul Department of Planning and Economic Development, Saint Paul, MN
50,000	American Indian Opportunities Industrialization Center, Minneapolis, MN
50,000	Ramsey County Opportunities Industrialization Center, Saint Paul, MN
50,000	Twin Cities Opportunities Industrialization Center, Minneapolis, MN
34,300	Metropolitan Economic Development Association, Minneapolis, MN
27,000	Ramsey County Opportunities Industrialization Center, Saint Paul, MN
25,000	Minnesota State Industrialization Council, MN
17,400	Management Assistance Project for Nonprofits, Saint Paul, MN
12,500	Anishinabe Opportunities Industrialization Center, Onamia, MN

Education

200,000	University of Minnesota, Minneapolis, MN
200,000	University of St. Thomas, Saint Paul, MN
93,010	Junior Achievement Upper Midwest, Minneapolis, MN
75,000	Mathcounts Foundation, Peterborough, NH
50,000	White House Fellowships
30,100	Concordia College, Moorhead, MN
30,000	Eisenhower Exchange Fellowships, Philadelphia, PA
25,070	University of Wisconsin, Stout, WI
25,000	St. Paul Technical School, Saint Paul, MN

Health

125,000	Courage Center, Golden Valley, MN
24,533	National Marrow Donor Program, Minneapolis, MN

Religion

121,760	Salvation Army, Saint Paul, MN
70,920	Union Gospel Mission

Science

620,000	Science Museum of Minnesota, Saint Paul, MN

Social Services

1,200,000	United Way, Saint Paul, MN
150,000	Boys and Girls Clubs, Saint Paul, MN
80,000	Human Services, Saint Paul, MN
60,000	United Way Capital Area, Minneapolis, MN
58,640	YMCA, Saint Paul, MN
50,000	Capital Area Food Bank, Austin, TX
50,000	Center for Battered Women, Austin, TX
50,000	Minnesota Citizens Council on Crime and Justice, Minneapolis, MN
37,734	YMCA, Saint Paul, MN
36,000	Merrick Community Services, Saint Paul, MN
30,000	Boy Scouts of America Indianhead Council, Saint Paul, MN
25,000	Harrison County Community Service Center, Corydon, IN
23,900	United Way Ventura County, Camarillo, CA
23,300	United Way Morgan County
22,095	United Way Crusade of Mercy, Chicago, IL
12,000	Boys and Girls Club, MN

MINNESOTA MUTUAL LIFE INSURANCE CO.

Company Contact

St. Paul, MN
Web: http://www.minnesotamutual.com

Company Description

Assets: US$10,000,000,000
Employees: 4,000
SIC(s): 6311 Life Insurance, 6321 Accident & Health Insurance.

Nonmonetary Support

Value: $150,000 (1996); $240,000 (1995); $230,000 (1994)
Type: In-kind Services; Loaned Employees; Loaned Executives; Workplace Solicitation

Minnesota Mutual Foundation

Giving Contact

Lori J. Koutsky, Manager
Minnesota Mutual Foundation
400 Robert St. North
St. Paul, MN 55101-2098
Phone: (612)665-3501
Fax: (612)665-3551

Description

EIN: 363608619
Organization Type: Corporate Foundation
Giving Locations: MN: Minneapolis metropolitan area, St. Paul metropolitan area
Grant Types: Capital, Employee Matching Gifts, General Support, Multiyear/Continuing Support.
Note: Employee matching gift ratio: 1 to 1 for gifts to higher education, cultural organisation, and hospitals.

Financial Summary

Total Giving: $1,400,000 (1999 approx); $1,143,300 (1998); $1,033,136 (1997). Note: Contributes through corporate direct giving program and foundation.
Giving Analysis: Giving for 1996 includes: foundation ($613,654); foundation grants to United Way ($242,800); corporate direct giving ($84,500); foundation matching gifts ($59,100); 1998: foundation ($777,075); foundation grants to United Way ($280,000); foundation matching gifts ($86,225)
Assets: $24,792,984 (1998); $24,574,425 (1997); $13,047,498 (1996)
Gifts Received: $11,701,000 (1998); $1,000 (1997); $3,940,409 (1996). Note: Contributions are received from the Minnesota Mutual Life Insurance Company.

Typical Recipients

Arts & Humanities: Arts Funds, Arts Institutes, Arts & Humanities-General, Historic Preservation, History & Archaeology, Libraries, Museums/Galleries, Music, Opera, Public Broadcasting, Theater
Civic & Public Affairs: Asian American Affairs, Clubs, Economic Development, Employment/Job Training, Housing, Legal Aid, Minority Business, Nonprofit Management, Parades/Festivals, Professional & Trade Associations, Public Policy, Urban & Community Affairs, Zoos/Aquariums
Education: Business Education, Business-School Partnerships, Colleges & Universities, Economic Education, Education Funds, Education Reform, Elementary Education (Private), Leadership Training, Literacy, Minority Education, Science/Mathematics Education
Health: AIDS/HIV, Emergency/Ambulance Services, Health Funds, Long-Term Care, Medical Rehabilitation, Medical Research, Nursing Services, Prenatal Health Issues, Public Health, Research/Studies Institutes
International: Human Rights, International Organizations
Religion: Religious Organizations, Religious Welfare
Science: Science Museums
Social Services: Child Abuse, Community Service Organizations, Crime Prevention, Domestic Violence, Emergency Relief, Family Services, Food/Clothing Distribution, People with Disabilities, Refugee Assistance, Scouts, Shelters/Homelessness, Substance Abuse, United Funds/United Ways, YMCA/YWCA/YMHA/YWHA, Youth Organizations

Contributions Analysis

Arts & Humanities: 28%. Supports chamber orchestras and united arts funds.
Civic & Public Affairs: 7%. Gives to civic groups in operating locations, particularly busines-related causes.
Education: 14%. Interests include colleges and universities, business and economic education, literacy, and science education. Supports college scholarship programs.
Health: Less than 5%. Supports health-care services for the disadvantaged, and medical research.
Religion: Less than 5%. Supports religious causes.
Social Services: 45%. Majority of funds support the United Way. Also supports family services and child welfare.
Note: Total contributions made in 1998.

Application Procedures

Initial Contact: Call or write for guidelines and applications, then written proposal.
Application Requirements: Completed Minnesota Common Grant Application, with the following attachments: financial statements from most recent fiscal year, organization and project budgets, list of funding sources with dollar amounts, list of board members with affiliations, description of key staff, proof of tax-exempt status.
Deadlines: February 15, May 15, August 15, or November 15.
Evaluative Criteria: Supports direct gifts rather than benefit activities; organizations must meet either requirements of Minnesota Charitable Solicitation Act of the National Information Bureau, meet guidelines of foundation, or meet an important need not otherwise met; program has reasonable chance of success; program is not a duplication of effort; substantial support from other sources.

Restrictions

Does not support organizations which are not tax-exempt, endowments, benefits, trips or tours, individuals, religious organizations for sectarian purposes, or political or lobbying groups.
Does not generally support member organizations of united or federated funds.

Additional Information

Publications: Corporate Contributions Policy

Corporate Officials

Dennis E. Prohofsky: senior vice president, general counsel, secretary B Saint Paul, MN 1940. ED University of Minnesota (1965); William Mitchell College of Law (1972). PRIM CORP EMPL senior vice president, general counsel, secretary: Minnesota Mutual Life Insurance Co. ADD CORP EMPL secretary: Mimlic Sales Corp. CORP AFFIL director: Sargasso Mutual.
Robert L. Senkler: chairman, president, chief executive officer B Saint Paul, MN 1952. ED University of Minnesota, Duluth (1974); Minnesota Deluth College BA (1979). PRIM CORP EMPL chairman, president, chief executive officer: Minnesota Mutual Life Insurance Co. NONPR AFFIL member, fellow: Society Actuaries.
Gregory S. Strong: vice president actuary B 1944. PRIM CORP EMPL vice president actuary: Minnesota Mutual Life Insurance Co.

Foundation Officials

Keith M. Campbell: vice president, director B 1945. PRIM CORP EMPL vice president: Minnesota Mutual Life Insurance Co.
Lori J. Koutsky: foundation manager
Dennis E. Prohofsky: secretary (see above)
Robert L. Senkler: president, director (see above)
Gregory S. Strong: treasurer (see above)

Grants Analysis

Disclosure Period: calendar year ending 1998
Total Grants: $770,075*
Number of Grants: 118
Average Grant: $6,526
Highest Grant: $280,000
Typical Range: $1,000 to $10,000
***Note:** Giving excludes matching gifts; United Way.

Recent Grants

Note: Grants derived from 1997 Form 990.

Arts & Humanities

75,000	Ordway Music Theater, St. Paul, MN -- support building campaign
34,500	St. Paul Chamber Orchestra, St. Paul, MN -- annual support
21,000	Minnesota Museum of American Art, St. Paul, MN -- support American Art
16,000	KTCA-TV/Channel 2, St. Paul, MN -- support educational television
12,000	Minnesota Centennial Showboat, St. Paul, MN -- support renovations of showboat
10,500	Minnesota Orchestral Association, Minneapolis, MN
10,000	A Capital New York-Culture, St. Paul, MN -- support showcase of downtown St. Paul
10,000	Minnesota History Center, St. Paul, MN -- support museum
6,500	Minnesota Opera Company, St. Paul, MN

Civic & Public Affairs

10,000 Frogtown Action Alliance, St. Paul, MN -- support jobs, support training center
7,000 Milestone Growth Fund, Minneapolis, MN -- support capital fund
6,000 Junior League, St. Paul, MN -- support project with homeless shelters for women and children
5,000 Common Bond Communities, St. Paul, MN -- to build houses, rent for low-income people
5,000 Habitat for Humanity, Minneapolis, MN -- support low-income for poor
5,000 Horatio Alger Association of Distinguished Americans, Alexandria, VA
5,000 Minnesota Futures Fund, Minneapolis, MN
5,000 Owobopte Industries, Eagan, MN -- building campaign
3,400 Ramsey County Opportunities Industries, St. Paul, MN -- support employment, training services
3,400 Twin Cities Neighborhood Housing, St. Paul, MN -- housing for low-income
3,000 Families Working Together, Minneapolis, MN -- support employment training for disadvantaged

Education

31,250 University of Minnesota Carlson School of Management, Minneapolis, MN -- building campaign
20,000 Metropolitan State University, St. Paul, MN -- support building campaign
10,000 A Chance to Grow, Minneapolis, MN -- support services
7,100 Junior Achievement, St. Paul, MN -- program support
5,000 AHEAD, Metro State University, St. Paul, MN -- to encourage young people of color to pursue higher education
5,000 American College, Bryn Mawr, PA
5,000 Carleton College, Northfield, MN -- building campaign
4,000 Bicultural Training Partnership, St. Paul, MN -- support leadership development
4,000 United Negro College Fund, Minneapolis, MN

Health

18,000 St. Paul Red Cross, St. Paul, MN -- support disaster services program
8,500 Life and Health Insurance Medical Research Fund, Washington, DC -- support for research
6,000 Health Fund, Minneapolis, MN
5,000 Hathe Q. Brown Community Center, St. Paul, MN -- support health services programs to disadvantaged
5,000 Healthier Communities Summit, Minneapolis, MN -- support community education forum
5,000 Minnesota Health Data Institute, St. Paul, MN -- to provide quality health care
4,000 Face-to-Face Health and Counseling, St. Paul, MN -- health education, counseling services
4,000 Living at Home/Block Nurse Program, St. Paul, MN -- to help residents in nursing home
3,500 Development Corporation for Children, Minneapolis, MN -- to develop child care facilities for low-income

Religion

16,500 Gospel Mission, St. Paul, MN -- program support
10,000 Presbyterian Homes, St. Paul, MN -- support housing for low-income seniors

Science

64,000 Science Museum, St. Paul, MN -- museum support

Social Services

255,000 United Way Campaign, St. Paul, MN -- support health, welfare
27,000 Boys and Girls Club, St. Paul, MN -- program support
10,000 Ramsey Action Programs, St. Paul, MN -- support building campaign
5,000 Human Services, Oakdale, MN
3,900 HRDADS, St. Paul, MN
3,500 Family Service, St. Paul, MN -- support assistance to abused children
3,000 Lifeworks Services, Eagan, MN -- support community services
3,000 MELD, Minneapolis, MN -- support educational programs for teenage parents
3,000 Southeast Asian Refugee Community, Minneapolis, MN -- program support

MITSUBISHI ELECTRIC AMERICA

Company Contact

1050 East Arques Ave.
Sunnyvale, CA 94086
Phone: (408)730-5900
Fax: (408)732-9382
Web: http://www.mitsubishichips.com

Company Description

Founded: 1980
Employees: 60
SIC(s): 3571 Electronic Computers, 3694 Engine Electrical Equipment.
Parent Company: Mitsubishi Electric Corp., Mitsubishi Denki Bldg., 2-3, Marunouchi 2-chome, Chiyoda-ku, Tokyo, Japan

Operating Locations

CA: Mitsubishi Electric America, Cypress; Mitsubishi Electric America, Cypress; Mitsubishi Electric Sales America, Cypress; Mitsubishi Electronics America, Cypress; Mitsubishi Electric America, Nevada City; Mitsubishi Consumer Electronics America, Santa Ana; Mitsubishi Electric America, Santa Ana, Sunnyvale; FL: Mitsubishi Electric America, Lake Mary; GA: Mitsubishi Electric America, Braselton, Norcross; IL: Mitsubishi Electric America; Mitsubishi Electric Industrial Control, Mount Prospect; MA: Mitsubishi Electric America, Cambridge, Waltham; MI: Mitsubishi Electric America, Plymouth; Optrex Glass, Plymouth; NC: Mitsubishi Electric America, Durham; Mitsubishi Semiconductor America, Durham; NY: Diamond Vision, New York; Mitsubishi Electric America, White Plains; OH: Mitsubishi Electric America, Mason; Mitsubishi Electric Manufacturing, Mason; PA: Mitsubishi Electric America, Warrendale; Powerex, Youngwood; TX: Mitsubishi Electric America, Irving

Nonmonetary Support

Value: $20,000 (1996); $100,000 (1994)
Type: Donated Equipment; Donated Products; In-kind Services; Loaned Executives
Volunteer Programs: To recognize growing interest in volunteerism among Mitsubishi Electric America employees, the Foundation administers the MEA Foundation Starfish Enterprise Award program.

Corporate Sponsorship

Type: Pledge-a-thon

Mitsubishi Electric America Foundation

Giving Contact

Rayna Aylward, Executive Director
Mitsubishi Electric America Foundation
1560 Wilson Boulevard, Suite 1150
Arlington, VA 22209
Phone: (703)276-8240
Email: rayna.aylward@hq.meaf.org
Web: http://www.meaf.org

Description

Founded: 1991
EIN: 521700855
Organization Type: Corporate Foundation
Giving Locations: nationally; operating locations.
Grant Types: Award, Employee Matching Gifts, General Support, Matching, Project.
Note: Employee matching gift ratio: 1 to 1. To match personal donations to organizations with the Foundation's mission.

Giving Philosophy

'The mission of the Mitsubishi Electric America Foundation is to contribute to the greater good of society by assisting young people with disabilities, through education and other means, to lead fuller and more productive lives.' *MEA Foundation Annual Report*

Financial Summary

Total Giving: $510,000 (2000 approx); $485,000 (1999); $435,000 (1998). Note: Contributes through foundation only.
Giving Analysis: Giving for 1998 includes: foundation ($485,000)
Assets: $19,000,000 (2000 approx); $19,000,000 (1999); $17,000,000 (1998 approx)
Gifts Received: $750,026 (1996); $814,248 (1995); $2,161,036 (1992). Note: In 1995, contributions were received from Mitsubishi Electronics Inc. ($345,300); Mitsubishi Consumer Electronics America, Inc. ($231,200); Mitsui Semiconductor America, Inc. Funds ($78,000); Mitsubishi Electric Manufacturing Cincinnati, Inc. ($41,700); Mitsubishi Electric Industrial Controls, Inc. ($21,100); Mitsubishi Electric Power Products, Inc. ($7,100); Mitsubishi Electric Research Laboratories, Inc. ($6,100); Astronet Corp. ($8,900); and other sources less than $5,000 each ($74,848).

Typical Recipients

Arts & Humanities: Arts Associations & Councils, Arts Funds, Film & Video
Civic & Public Affairs: Botanical Gardens/Parks, Employment/Job Training, Housing, Nonprofit Management
Education: Arts/Humanities Education, Education-General, International Studies, Legal Education, Preschool Education, Private Education (Precollege), School Volunteerism, Science/Mathematics Education, Social Sciences Education, Special Education, Student Aid
Environment: Environment-General, Resource Conservation
Health: Cancer, Children's Health/Hospitals, Diabetes, Medical Rehabilitation, Single-Disease Health Associations
Religion: Religious Welfare
Social Services: Child Welfare, Community Service Organizations, Family Services, People with Disabilities, Recreation & Athletics, Scouts, Special Olympics, United Funds/United Ways, Volunteer Services, YMCA/YWCA/YMHA/YWHA, Youth Organizations

Contributions Analysis

Giving Priorities: Currently, the MEA Foundation is exclusively focused on exploring technological approaches to serving the needs of youth with disabilities.

Social Services: 100%. Funding supports a range of projects addressing the needs of people with disabilities. Grants have supported interships ofr visually imparied students, online meeting places for children with disabilities, and training for teachers to improve their ability to assist disabled students.

Application Procedures

Initial Contact: Submit a short (not to exceed three pages) concept paper to the foundation.
Application Requirements: Concept paper should include explanation of the need and objectives for funds requested; project's national impact; plans for project evaluation; how this project will build on similar work being carried out in the field, and how this project is unique; how this project will make use of information technology; budget summary.
Deadlines: July 31. Concept proposals submitted after this date will be considered for the following year.
Review Process: Concept papers are reviewed throughout the year. Applicants whose concept papers pass preliminary review will be invited to submit a full proposal. New grants are announced in the fall, with funding to begin the following January.
Notes: Due to MEA Foundation's small staff size, phone calls are discouraged during the application process.

Restrictions

Does not support: individuals; intermediary organizations such as the United Way; organizations whose services are limited to a particular ethnic, fraternal, labor, or political constituency; organizations that discriminate by disability, race, color, creed, religion, veteran status, or national origin; religious organizations for religious purposes; organizations engaged exclusively in political activities or lobbying; organizations or programs connected with controversial social or political issues; loans of money for any purpose; endowments, capital campaigns, or annual fundraising drives; tickets; advertising or mass mailings; conference expenses; projects or events that are already completed; or projects exclusively benefiting individuals or groups outside the United States.
Grants are made only to nonprofit organizations that have been granted exemption from federal income tax under Section 501(c)(3) of the Internal Revenue Code.

Additional Information

Foundation grants are provided to national organizations and matching grants are given to organizations within the Foundation's mission for general operating support and project support.
In February 1991, the Mitsubishi Electric America (MEA) group of companies established the Mitsubishi Electric America Foundation.
Publications: Foundation Guidelines; Annual Report

Corporate Officials

Akira Katayama: chairman, chief executive officer PRIM CORP EMPL chairman, chief executive officer: Mitsubishi Electric of America.
Ichiro Taniguchi: president PRIM CORP EMPL president: Mitsubishi Electric America.

Foundation Officials

Rayna Aylward: executive director
Roger Barna: director B 1941. PRIM CORP EMPL president, director: Mitsubishi Electric Power.
Bruce R. Brenizer: director
David Chang: assistant treasurer PRIM CORP EMPL controller: Mitsubishi Electric America.
Yasul Iwamoto: director B 1939. CORP AFFIL president: Mitsubishi Electric Auto American.
Akira Katayama: director (see above)
William Lambert: director B 1948. PRIM CORP EMPL executive vice president: Mitsubishi Electric Information.
Helaine F. Lobman, Esq.: assistant secretary
Takao Nishimura: director
Alan P. Olschwang, Esq.: secretary B Chicago, IL 1942. ED University of Illinois BS (1963); University of Illinois JD (1966). PRIM CORP EMPL executive vice president, general counsel, director: Mitsubishi Electric of America. CORP AFFIL secretary, director: Astronet Corp.; secretary: Mitsubishi Consumer Electric America. NONPR AFFIL member: Illinois Bar Association; member: New York Bar Association; member: Chicago Bar Association; member: Association Bar New York City; member: California Bar Association; member: American Bar Association; member: American Corporate Counsel Association; member: American Arbitration Association.
Pete Salarantis: assistant secretary, assistant treasurer
John Savage: president, director CORP AFFIL vice president: Mitsubishi Electronics America.
Chris Schuneman: employee representative
Martha Stevens: employee representative
Ichiro Taniguchi: director (see above)
Hiroki Yoshimatsu: treasurer PRIM CORP EMPL president: Mitsubishi Electric Financial America.

Grants Analysis

Disclosure Period: calendar year ending 1999
Total Grants: $485,000*
Number of Grants: 105 (approx)
Average Grant: $4,619
Highest Grant: $95,688 (approx)
Typical Range: $2,500 to $20,000
***Note:** Giving excludes matching gifts.

Recent Grants

Note: Grants derived from 1996 Form 990.

Arts & Humanities

40,000	Washington Very Special Arts, Washington, DC -- national grant
2,000	Greater Durham United Arts Fund, Durham, NC -- operating support
1,000	Descriptive Video Services, Boston, MA -- operating support

Civic & Public Affairs

1,000	Christmas in April, Boston, MA -- for housing rehabilitation project

Education

95,688	University of Minnesota Institute on Community Integration, Minneapolis, MN -- national grant
21,600	University of California Berkeley Graduate School of Public Policy, Berkeley, CA -- support Mitsubishi Electric America Scholars program
10,000	Boston Educational Development Foundation, Boston, MA -- sponsor Class Link project
8,700	National Technical Institute for the Deaf, Rochester, NY -- national grant
5,000	Meredith College, Raleigh, NC -- for Meredith Autism Program
3,333	Northwest Suburban Special Education Organization, Bartlett, IL -- for picnic tables, slide audio view projector, video camera, sleeping bags
3,000	Early Learning Institute, Pittsburgh, PA -- to sponsor Fourth Annual Tour de Sewickley
3,000	Gainesville College, Gainesville, GA -- purchase two mobile lab stations
2,800	Irving Independent School District, Irving, TX -- purchase computer
2,220	Boston Educational Development Foundation, Boston, MA -- sponsor Class Link project
1,360	Early Learning Institute, Pittsburgh, PA -- to reimburse volunteer hours
1,000	Camp Fire, First Texas Council, Fort Worth, TX -- scholarships
1,000	St. Rita School for the Deaf, Cincinnati, OH -- operating support

Environment

1,000	Outdoor Explorations, Chestnut Hill, MA -- for Wild Work Project

Health

45,000	United Cerebral Palsy Associations, Washington, DC -- for Tech Tots Library project
9,000	Via Rehabilitation Services, Santa Clara, CA -- operating support
5,100	CURE Childhood Cancer and Leukemia, Atlanta, GA -- to reimburse volunteer hours
5,000	Duke Children's Classic Fitness Festival and Health Walk, Durham, NC -- support operations of pediatric hospital
5,000	Duke Children's Classic Fitness Festival and Health Walk, Durham, NC -- to sponsor event
4,000	American Cancer Society, Gainesville, GA -- for cancer research
4,000	Massachusetts Easter Seals Society, Boston, MA -- support Counselors in Training Program
3,950	CURE Childhood Cancer and Leukemia, Atlanta, GA -- to reimburse volunteer hours
2,664	Egleston Children's Hospital, Atlanta, GA -- support Festival of Trees
2,400	American Cancer Society, Gainesville, GA -- for annual Relay for Life fundraiser
2,000	United Cerebral Palsy Association of Orange County, Santa Ana, CA -- support Tech Tots Library
1,750	Lenox Baker Children's Hospital, Durham, NC -- operating support

Religion

6,667	Our Lady of Providence Center, Northville, MI -- employment preparation and training for disabled young adults
5,000	Our Lady of Providence Center, Northville, MI -- to reimburse volunteer hours
3,333	Our Lady of Providence Center, Northville, MI -- employment programs

Social Services

50,000	University of Wisconsin Madison, Madison, WI -- national grant for Family Village
39,472	Institute on Disability and Human Development, Chicago, IL -- support Opportunities for Children with Disabilities project
6,000	Timpany Center, San Jose, CA -- for aquatic rehabilitation and physical therapy for disabled youth
5,465	National Foundation of Wheelchair Tennis, San Clemente, CA -- to sponsor annual children's camp for disabled kids
5,000	Accelerated Habilitation Education and Development with Horses, Sun Valley, CA -- to reimburse for volunteer hours
5,000	Hillview Acres Children's Home, Chino, CA -- for 40 twin beds
5,000	LeRoy Hanes Center for Children and Family Services, La Verne, CA -- for Boy Scouts uniforms, comforters for beds, infant care supplies
5,000	Windrush Farm, Boxford, MA -- to sponsor equestrian therapy for disabled youth
4,000	Goodwill Industries of Orange County, Santa Ana, CA -- support employment training program
3,668	YMCA North Hills Area, Pittsburgh, PA -- provide transportation to Camp High Hopes
3,044	Seminole Family YMCA, Lake Mary, FL -- to purchase swim lift and door operator
2,500	Middletown City Schools, Middletown,

	OH -- to identify and treat disabled children in school system
2,200	Northwest Suburban Area Special Olympics, Rolling Meadows, IL -- sporting equipment for needy athletes
2,006	YMCA North Hills Area, Pittsburgh, PA -- to reimburse volunteer hours
2,000	Northwest Suburban Area Special Olympics, Rolling Meadows, IL -- operating support
1,920	Northwest Suburban Area Special Olympics, Rolling Meadows, IL -- to reimburse volunteer hours
1,000	Alexander Children's Home, Charlotte, NC -- operating support

MONARCH MACHINE TOOL CO.

Company Contact
Sidney, OH

Company Description
Revenue: US$85,000,000
Employees: 525
SIC(s): 3500 Industrial Machinery & Equipment.

Monarch Machine Tool Co. Foundation

Giving Contact
Robert B. Reithman, Treasurer
Suite 2600
Kettering Tower
Dayton, OH 45423
Phone: (937)910-9300

Description
Founded: 1952
EIN: 346556088
Organization Type: Corporate Foundation
Giving Locations: NY; OH
Grant Types: General Support.

Financial Summary
Total Giving: $500,000 (1997); $205,600 (1996); $186,500 (1995). Note: 1996 Giving includes scholarship ($2,000); United Way ($7,500).
Assets: $3,759,610 (1996); $3,329,979 (1995); $2,704,859 (1994)
Gifts Received: $63,204 (1996); $58,806 (1995); $115,598 (1994). Note: In 1995, contributions were received from the Monarch Machine Tool Co.

Typical Recipients
Arts & Humanities: Arts Associations & Councils, Dance, Libraries, Music, Public Broadcasting
Civic & Public Affairs: African American Affairs, Botanical Gardens/Parks, Chambers of Commerce, Civic & Public Affairs-General, Public Policy, Urban & Community Affairs
Education: Agricultural Education, Colleges & Universities, Community & Junior Colleges, Education Funds, Faculty Development, Education-General, Preschool Education, Private Education (Precollege), Religious Education, Student Aid
Health: Cancer, Children's Health/Hospitals, Clinics/Medical Centers, Hospitals, Long-Term Care
Religion: Religious Organizations, Religious Welfare
Science: Scientific Labs
Social Services: At-Risk Youth, Big Brother/Big Sister, Child Welfare, Community Centers, Community Service Organizations, Homes, People with Disabilities, Scouts, United Funds/United Ways, YMCA/YWCA/YMHA/YWHA, Youth Organizations

Application Procedures
Initial Contact: brief of inquiry and full proposal
Application Requirements: a description of organization, amount requested, purpose of funds sought, proof of tax-exempt status

Corporate Officials
Richard Clemens: president, chief executive officer PRIM CORP EMPL president, chief executive officer: Monarch Machine Tool Co.
Robert B. Riethman: chief financial officer B Sidney, OH 1947. ED Ohio State University (1973). PRIM CORP EMPL chief financial officer: Monarch Machine Tool Co. CLUB AFFIL Knights of Columbus.

Foundation Officials
Karl S. Frydryk: trustee B 1954. PRIM CORP EMPL chief financial officer, vice president: Monarch Machine Tool Co. CORP AFFIL vice president finance, secretary, director: Nord Resources Corp.
Tim Gibson: trustee
N. V. Gushing: trustee
Robert B. Riethman: treasurer, secretary (see above)

Grants Analysis
Disclosure Period: calendar year ending 1996
Total Grants: $196,100*
Number of Grants: 35
Average Grant: $5,603
Highest Grant: $37,500
Typical Range: $100 to $20,000
***Note:** Giving excludes scholarship, United Way.

Recent Grants
Note: Grants derived from 1997 Form 990.

Arts & Humanities

3,000	Gateway Arts Council, Sidney, OH
1,500	Amos Memorial Library
1,000	Greater Dayton Public Television, Dayton, OH
500	Sidney Dance Company, Sidney, OH
400	Sidney Music Boosters

Civic & Public Affairs

12,500	Monarch Foundation
10,000	Lock One Park
3,000	Main Street Sidney
500	Sidney-Shelby Black Achievers

Education

10,000	Holy Angels School
3,500	Alpha, Tucson, AZ
2,500	Lehman Scholarship Fund
2,000	4-H Clubs of Shelby County
2,000	Wright State College -- scholarship
750	Council of Religious Education
500	Shelby County Academia Scholarship
350	Sidney Christian School
200	Sidney Rotary Scholarship Fund

Health

15,000	Dorothy Love Retirement Living Care
3,000	Wilson Memorial Hospital, Wilson, NC
1,000	Cortland Hospital Foundation
1,000	Joint Township District Memorial Hospital, St. Marys, OH
1,000	Shrine Children's Hospital

Religion

7,500	Salvation Army
500	Shelby County Ministerial Association, Shelbyville, IN

Science

37,500	Lehman Science Laboratory

Social Services

200,000	City of Sidney Community Center Fund
20,000	Shelby County YMCA, Shelbyville, IN -- building fund
11,500	Boy Scouts of America Baden Powell Council
7,500	Cortland County United Way
7,500	Shelby County United Way, Sidney, OH
2,500	Auglaize Mercer Family YMCA, Celina, OH
2,000	Shelby County YMCA, Shelbyville, IN -- operations support
1,500	Boy Scouts of America Shelby County Council
1,000	Cortland YMCA -- operations support
1,000	Cortland Youth Bureau
500	Big Brothers and Big Sisters
500	Shelby County Association for Retarded Citizens, Shelbyville, IN
400	National Child Safety Council, Greenwood, SC

MONSANTO CO.

 Number 30 of Top 100 Corporate Givers

Company Contact
St. Louis, MO
Web: http://www.monsanto.com

Company Description
Revenue: US$8,648,000,000
Employees: 30,600
Fortune Rank: 167, per FORTUNE Magazine's list of 500 Largest U.S. Corporations (1999).
FF 167
SIC(s): 2099 Food Preparations Nec, 2282 Throwing & Winding Mills, 2299 Textile Goods Nec, 3089 Plastics Products Nec.

Operating Locations
Australia: Searle Australia, Fairfield, New South Wales; Monsanto Australia Ltd., Melbourne; Belgium: Monsanto European, Antwerp; Monsanto Europe SA, Brussels, Brabant, Louvain-la-Neuve; Brazil: Monsanto Do Brasil Ltda., Sao Paulo; Canada: Solutia Canada, Mississauga; England: Monsanto, Liverpool; Searle Pharmaceuticals, Morpeth; France: Searle Industrio, Evreux; Hong Kong: Monsanto Far East Ltd., Quarry Bay; Japan: Searle Yakuhin KK, Oita, Prefacture; Monsanto Japan Ltd., Tokyo; Republic of Korea: Searle Ciba-Geigy Korea, Kangwon-Do; Mexico: Searle de Mexico SA de CV, Coapa; Monsanto Comercial SA de CV, El Cerrillo; Puerto Rico: Monsanto Puerto Rico, Caguas; Searle Peurto Rico, San Juan; Scotland: Monsanto Co., Girvan, Ayshire; Singapore: Monsanto Singapore Co. (Pte.) Ltd., Singapore; Taiwan: Searle, u-Liang Ltd. Taiwan, Taoyuan; Venezuela: Searle de Venezuela CA, Guarenas; Wales: Monsanto, Ruabon

Nonmonetary Support
Value: $500,000 (1993); $500,000 (1992); $100,000 (1990)
Type: Donated Equipment; Donated Products
Contact: Lyn Barth, Director Corporate Contributions

Monsanto Fund

Giving Contact
John L. Mason, Chairman & President
Monsanto Fund
800 N. Lindbergh Blvd.
St. Louis, MO 63167
Phone: (314)694-4596
Fax: (314)694-7658

Description
EIN: 436044736
Organization Type: Corporate Foundation
Giving Locations: operating facilities.
Grant Types: Conference/Seminar, Employee Matching Gifts, Project.

Note: Employee matching gift ratio: 1 to 1.

Giving Philosophy

'Monsanto Company recognizes its responsibility to be a good corporate citizen by enhancing society's vitality and quality of life. In doing so, it seeks to earn acceptance and respect as an effective, caring corporate citizen everywhere it operates in the world..For over two decades, the Company has relied on the Monsanto Fund, the Company's philanthropic arm, to help enrich the communities of which Monsanto is a part and to help the Company earn its place in society.' *Monsanto Fund, Investing for Results*

Financial Summary

Total Giving: $22,000,000 (1999 approx); $29,396,646 (1998); $22,000,000 (1997 approx). Note: Contributes through corporate direct giving program and foundation.
Giving Analysis: Giving for 1996 includes: foundation ($9,923,398); foundation matching gifts ($1,000,000); 1997: foundation ($10,897,535); domestic subsidiaries ($7,000,000); corporate direct giving ($3,000,000); international subsidiaries ($1,000,000); 1998: foundation ($27,836,246); foundation grants to United Way ($1,560,400)
Assets: $10,633,857 (1998); $10,114,461 (1997); $11,890,025 (1996)
Gifts Received: $60,142 (1998); $376,456 (1997); $737,220 (1996). Note: Contributions were received from Monsanto Co.

Typical Recipients

Arts & Humanities: Arts Associations & Councils, Arts Centers, Dance, Ethnic & Folk Arts, Arts & Humanities-General, Historic Preservation, History & Archaeology, Libraries, Museums/Galleries, Music, Opera, Performing Arts, Public Broadcasting, Theater
Civic & Public Affairs: African American Affairs, Botanical Gardens/Parks, Clubs, Civic & Public Affairs-General, Housing, Municipalities/Towns, Nonprofit Management, Professional & Trade Associations, Public Policy, Safety, Urban & Community Affairs, Zoos/Aquariums
Education: Afterschool/Enrichment Programs, Arts/Humanities Education, Business Education, Colleges & Universities, Community & Junior Colleges, Education Reform, Engineering/Technological Education, Education-General, Journalism/Media Education, Minority Education, Private Education (Precollege), Public Education (Precollege), Science/Mathematics Education, Secondary Education (Public), Vocational & Technical Education
Environment: Resource Conservation
Health: AIDS/HIV, Alzheimers Disease, Cancer, Children's Health/Hospitals, Clinics/Medical Centers, Emergency/Ambulance Services, Health Policy/Cost Containment, Health Organizations, Hospitals, Medical Research, Research/Studies Institutes
International: International Organizations
Religion: Dioceses, Jewish Causes, Religious Welfare, Social/Policy Issues
Science: Science Museums, Scientific Centers & Institutes
Social Services: Child Welfare, Community Service Organizations, Crime Prevention, Day Care, Domestic Violence, Family Services, Food/Clothing Distribution, Scouts, Shelters/Homelessness, Substance Abuse, United Funds/United Ways, YMCA/YWCA/YMHA/YWHA, Youth Organizations

Contributions Analysis

Giving Priorities: Precolleges and higher education, with emphasis on science; United Way; municipalities and economic development; the arts; and health organizations. Company supports U.S. nonprofits with international focus and foreign subsidiaries make contributions in host country. Focus is on improving the quality of life in communities through support of education, with an emphasis on science education; community and civic affairs; and arts and culture. Contributions are made at the descretion of area managers in foreign countries. A contributions budget for each international operating company is approved by headquarters; however, foreign contributions are not monitored or tracked.
Arts & Humanities: 23%. Supports a broad spectrum of disciplines.
Civic & Public Affairs: 15%.
Education: 16%. Supports both precollege and higher educational institutions, with strong emphasis on science, agriculture, biotechnology, and sustainable development.
Environment: 11%.
Social Services: 30%. Supports youth services, health and human services, and the United Way.
Note: Contributions analysis reflects giving based on the fund's 1998 Grants by Category and does not include a grant to the Plant Science Institute of $21,010,250 or miscellaneous uncategorized grants totaling $2,023,700.

Application Procedures

Initial Contact: organizations near a Monsanto facility should contact local manager.
Application Requirements: Include the mission or purpose of the organization; statement of the need or problem, including summary of the background of the need or problem; amount requested; other sources of income; plans for permanent financial support; proof of 501(c)(3) tax-exempt status; copy of most recent financial statements; list of members of governing board; detailed description of proposed project and purpose, including why organization is involved and special qualifications; program budget; measurable goals and plan outlining how goals will be achieved; additional literature that further defines organization's goals and achievements.
Deadlines: None; board meets quarterly.
Decision Notification: Fund attempts to respond to written requests within three months; proposals that do not meet guidelines are turned down immediately.

Restrictions

Unsolicited proposals are rarely considered.
Long-term commitments are rarely made. Fund occasionally makes grants for two years at most. Organizations repeating a request in the same year are not considered for additional funding.
Fund does not support individuals, religious organizations, fraternal or political groups, member agencies of united funds, goodwill advertising, organizations that cannot provide adequate accounting records, tax-supported colleges and universities for operating purposes, consortia of universities, sporting events, or fundraising events.
Fund rarely supports capital expansion.

Additional Information

Decisions concerning organizations near a Monsanto facility are made by that particular facility; plant locations establish giving priorities autonomously.
Grant requests must be resubmitted on an annual basis unless otherwise stipulated.
In the 1990s, the fund continued to sharpen its focus on supporting programs with measurable results. It funded more 'catalyst' projects and fewer 'maintenance' programs; it looked for creative partnerships with nonprofit organizations; and awarded fewer but more sizable grants. In future years, the fund will play a greater role in supporting communities outside the United States, a reflection of the company's growing international identity.
Monsanto Co. merged with Pharmacia & Upjohn in January 2000.

Corporate Officials

Juanita H. Hinshaw: vice president, treasurer, chief executive officer, director B Asheboro, NC 1945. ED University of North Carolina (1973). PRIM CORP EMPL vice president, treasurer: Monsanto Co. NONPR AFFIL chairman: Bethesda Hospital; director: National Association of Corporate Treasurers; member finance council: American Management Association.
Robert B. Shapiro: chairman, president, chief executive officer, director B New York, NY 1938. ED Harvard University AB (1959); Columbia University LLB (1962). PRIM CORP EMPL chairman, president, chief executive officer, director: Monsanto Co. CORP AFFIL director: Rockwell International Corp.; director: Silicon Graphics; director: Northwestern Membership Hospital; director: NutraSweet Kelco Co. Inc.; director: Citicorp; director: Citigroup Inc.; director: Citibank NA.

Giving Program Officials

Lynn Barth: director corporate contributions

Foundation Officials

Sonya M. Davis: secretary
Juanita H. Hinshaw: treasurer (see above)
John L. Mason: chairman, president

Grants Analysis

Disclosure Period: calendar year ending 1998
Total Grants: $29,396,646*
Number of Grants: 165 (approx)
Average Grant: $39,276*
Highest Grant: $21,010,250
Typical Range: $500 to $50,000
***Note:** Average grant figure excludes three highest grants totaling $23,033,980.

Recent Grants

Note: Grants derived from 1997 Form 990.

Arts & Humanities

175,000 St. Louis Symphony Orchestra, St. Louis, MO
100,000 National Museum of American History, Washington, DC
100,000 Opera Theater, St. Louis, MO
65,000 Arts and Education Council, St. Louis, MO
60,000 Repertory Theater, St. Louis, MO
54,000 Springfield Library and Museums Association, Springfield, MA

Civic & Public Affairs

700,000 Forest Park Forever, St. Louis, MO
300,000 Ecumenical Housing Production Corporation, St. Louis, MO
250,000 National Urban League, New York, NY
250,000 St. Louis 2004, St. Louis, MO
200,000 Missouri Botanical Garden, St. Louis, MO
165,000 Media Institute, Washington, DC
48,931 City of Everett, Everett, MA
25,000 Foundation for American Communications, Los Angeles, CA
25,000 Metropolitan Association for Philanthropy, St. Louis, MO
25,000 Muscatine Island Levee District, Muscatine, IA

Education

254,000 Washington University, St. Louis, MO
250,000 Ranken Technical College, St. Louis, MO
150,000 Howard University College of Arts and Sciences, Washington, DC
149,167 St. Louis University, St. Louis, MO
100,000 Results Educational Fund, Washington, DC -- support Microcredit Summit
85,000 Junior Achievement of Mississippi Valley, Hazelwood, MO
75,000 University of Mississippi, St. Louis, MO -- support St. Louis Bridge Program
58,975 St. Louis Internship Program, St. Louis, MO

55,000	Council of Independent Colleges, Washington, DC
50,000	Occidental College, Los Angeles, CA
50,000	Vanderschmidt School, St. Louis, MO
38,500	Hartselle City Schools, Hartselle, AL
30,000	Lander University, Greenwood, SC
25,000	Augusta Technical Institute, Augusta, GA
Environment	
50,000	Conservation Fund, Shepherdstown, WV
Health	
50,000	Emory University, Atlanta, GA -- support Goizueta Cancer Research Fund
35,000	Greenwood Genetic Center, Greenwood, SC
Religion	
284,350	National Conference of Christians and Jews, New York, NY
200,000	Archdiocese of St. Louis, St. Louis, MO
Science	
245,615	St. Louis Science Center, St. Louis, MO
200,000	San Diego Natural History Museum, San Diego, CA
Social Services	
1,600,000	United Way, St. Louis, MO
250,000	Jackie Joyner-Kersee Youth Center Foundation, St. Louis, MO
178,000	United Way of Escambia County, Pensacola, FL -- support Forward Together Program
100,000	Girl Scouts of America, St. Louis, MO
80,000	United Way of Pioneer Valley, Springfield, MA
71,000	United Way of Brazoria County, Angleton, TX -- support Loaned Executive Program
68,000	United Way of Greenwood County, Greenwood, SC
52,086	United Way of Morgan County, Decatur, AL
50,000	Food Research and Action Center, Washington, DC
44,800	United Way, Muscatine, IA -- support Emergency Response Program
35,000	United Way of St. Charles, Hahnville, LA
32,300	Boy Scouts of America, St. Louis, MO
29,000	United Way, Detroit, MI -- support Account 1-000246

MONTANA POWER CO.

Company Contact

40 East Broadway
Butte, MT 59701-9394
Web: http://www.mtpower.com

Company Description

Former Name: Montana Power/Entech.
Assets: US$2,698,200,000
Employees: 2,949
SIC(s): 1221 Bituminous Coal & Lignite--Surface, 1222 Bituminous Coal--Underground, 1311 Crude Petroleum & Natural Gas, 4939 Combination Utility Nec.

Operating Locations

Canada: Canadian-Montana Gas Co. Inc., Calgary; Canadian-Montana Pipe Line Corp., Calgary; Intercontiental Energy Corp., Calgary; Roan Resources Ltd., Calgary; Canadian-Montana Gas Co. Ltd., Foremost

Nonmonetary Support

Type: Donated Equipment
Volunteer Programs: In 1998, Montana Power announced the launch of an official corporate volunteer program. The Montana Power Company Hearts and Hands Employee Volunteer Program will acknowledge employee volunteer efforts through the New Dollars for Doers program, by which donations will be made to non-profit organizations supported by employee volunteers.

Corporate Sponsorship

Type: Arts & cultural events; Festivals/fairs; Music & entertainment events; Pledge-a-thon; Sports events

Montana Power Foundation

Giving Contact

William D. Cain, Director Corporate Community Relations
Montana Power Foundation Inc.
Phone: (406)497-2602
Fax: (406)497-2451
Email: community@mtpower.com
Web: http://www.mtpower.com/community/foundation.htm

Description

Founded: 1985
EIN: 810432484
Organization Type: Corporate Foundation
Giving Locations: headquarters and operating communities.
Grant Types: Capital, Conference/Seminar, Employee Matching Gifts, General Support, Matching, Multiyear/Continuing Support.
Note: Employee matching gift ratio: 1 to 1.

Financial Summary

Total Giving: $500,000 (1999 approx); $963,653 (1998); $547,206 (1997). Note: Contributes through corporate direct giving program and foundation.
Giving Analysis: Giving for 1997 includes: foundation ($414,220); corporate grants to United Way ($76,569); corporate matching gifts ($35,767); corporate scholarships ($20,650); 1998: foundation ($535,916); corporate direct giving ($320,502); foundation grants to United Way ($89,235); corporate scholarships ($18,000)
Assets: $173,441 (1998); $162,741 (1997); $334,534 (1996)
Gifts Received: $647,868 (1998); $254,444 (1997); $254,444 (1996). Note: Contributions are received from Montana Power Co., Entech Inc., and Independent Power Group Inc.

Typical Recipients

Arts & Humanities: Arts Centers, Arts Funds, Historic Preservation, History & Archaeology, Libraries, Museums/Galleries, Music, Performing Arts, Public Broadcasting, Theater
Civic & Public Affairs: Business/Free Enterprise, Clubs, Employment/Job Training, Civic & Public Affairs-General, Housing, Professional & Trade Associations, Public Policy, Urban & Community Affairs
Education: Agricultural Education, Colleges & Universities, Community & Junior Colleges, Engineering/Technological Education, Education-General, Preschool Education, Private Education (Precollege), Public Education (Precollege), Science/Mathematics Education, Secondary Education (Private), Secondary Education (Public), Student Aid, Vocational & Technical Education
Environment: Environment-General, Resource Conservation, Wildlife Protection
Health: Cancer, Children's Health/Hospitals, Clinics/Medical Centers, Diabetes, Emergency/Ambulance Services, Health Organizations, Hospitals
International: Foreign Educational Institutions, International Affairs
Social Services: Big Brother/Big Sister, Child Welfare, Community Centers, Community Service Organizations, Domestic Violence, Family Planning, Food/Clothing Distribution, Recreation & Athletics, Scouts, United Funds/United Ways, YMCA/YWCA/YMHA/YWHA, Youth Organizations

Contributions Analysis

Giving Priorities: While the majority of support is at the state and local level, the foundation has provided limited support for U.S.-based nonprofit organizations with an international focus.
Arts & Humanities: 10%. Museums, historical societies, theatres, and music received support.
Civic & Public Affairs: 7%. Supports scouting, business organizations, youth clubs and ranches, employment initiatives, community activities, public radio, special events, civic improvement, and senior citizens organizations.
Education: 49%. Supports the University Excellence Program. Funds are applied to higher education at public and private colleges, universities, and vocational and technical programs within the state. Additional grants were made for capital programs, matching gifts, and scholarships to these same schools and additional primary and secondary schools in the state in the fields of math, science and youth leadership.
Environment: 3%. Supports resource conservation, including habitat preservation and fish and wildlife protection.
Health: 6%. Supports traditional youth organizations and family services, hospitals, andsingle-disease health associations.
Social Services: 25%. Majority of support is given to the United Way. Other funds go toward community services, Big Brothers and Big Sisters, and YMCA.
Note: Contributions analysis based on foundation giving only.

Application Procedures

Initial Contact: request guidelines and application form in writing
Deadlines: None.
Review Process: each application is reviewed by donations committee for merit; large grant requests are deferred to the board of directors, which meets three times a year
Evaluative Criteria: whether the activity impacts the utility service area, previous history of contributions, perceived effectiveness of the organization, need for the activity or facility relative to other organizations in area, number of people it will benefit, support from other sources
Decision Notification: initial response within six weeks

Restrictions

The foundation does not support non-tax-exempt organizations, United Way umbrella organizations (except for capital funds), or fraternal, veterans', service, social, athletic, or religious organizations. Prefers to support capital fund drives rather than operating funds (except for organizations such as the United Way). No support to individuals or political or lobbying groups. Foundation generally will not fund economic and commercial development projects, national health organizations, the purchase of medical equipment, or research projects.
The foundation prefers not to fund multiyear requests.
research projects.
The foundation prefers not to fund multiyear requests.

Additional Information

The foundation was formerly known as MPCo/Entech Foundation.
Publications: Annual Report (including Application Guidelines)

Corporate Officials

William D. Cain: director corporate & community relations PRIM CORP EMPL director corporate & community relations: Montana Power Co.

Richard F. Cromer: executive vice president, chief operating officer energy supply division ED Montana State University BS (1967). PRIM CORP EMPL executive vice president, chief operating officer energy supply division: Montana Power Co. CORP AFFIL president, chief operating officer, director: Continental Energy Services Inc.; chairman, president: Glacier Gas Co.

Robert P. Gannon: chairman, president, director, chief executive officer B 1944. ED University of Notre Dame BA (1966); University of Montana JD (1969). PRIM CORP EMPL chairman, president, director, chief executive officer: Montana Power Co. CORP AFFIL director: Entech Inc.; vice chairman: North American Resources Co.; president: Canadian-Montana Gas Co. Ltd.

Pamela K. Merrell: secretary B Panguitch, UT 1952. ED University of Utah (1974); University of Utah Law School (1997). PRIM CORP EMPL secretary: Montana Power Co. CORP AFFIL secretary: Continental Energy Services Inc. NONPR AFFIL member: American Bar Association; member: American Society of Corporate Secretaries.

Jerrold P. Pederson: vice president, chief financial officer, director B Billings, MT 1942. ED Gonzaga University BA (1964). PRIM CORP EMPL vice president, chief financial officer, director: Montana Power Co. CORP AFFIL chief financial officer: Western Energy Co.; vice president: Tetragenics Co.; chief financial officer: Touch America Inc.; chief financial officer: Entech Inc.; chief financial officer: North American Resources Co.; vice president, chief financial officer: Atlanta Exploration Co.; vice president: Canadian-Montana Gas Co. Ltd. NONPR AFFIL member finance committee: Edison Electric Institute.

Ellen M. Senechal: treasurer B 1949. PRIM CORP EMPL treasurer: Montana Power Co. CORP AFFIL vice president, treasurer, director: Touch America Inc.; treasurer: Western Energy Co.; treasurer, director: Northwestern Resources Co.; treasurer: Tetragenics Co.; vice president, treasurer: Entech Inc.; vice president, treasurer, director: North American Resources Co.; treasurer: Altana Exploration Co.; treasurer: Continental Energy Services Inc.

Michael E. Zimmerman: vice president, general counsel B 1949. ED Montana State University BA (1972); University of Montana JD (1980). PRIM CORP EMPL vice president, general counsel: Montana Power Co. CORP AFFIL vice president, general counsel: North American Resources Co.; vice president, general counsel: Touch America Inc.; vice president, general counsel: Entech Inc.

Foundation Officials

Alan F. Cain: director B 1939. ED University of Montana Law School (1969). PRIM CORP EMPL president, chief executive officer: Blue Cross & Blue Shield of Montana. CORP AFFIL director: Montana Power Co. NONPR AFFIL chairman: Vocational Resources Inc.

William D. Cain: executive director (see above)

Richard F. Cromer: director (see above)

Steve Dee: director

Robert P. Gannon: president, director (see above)

Jack Haffey: director

Judy K. Hursh: assistant secretary

Carl Lehrkind, III: director B 1939. PRIM CORP EMPL president, director: Lehrkind's Inc. CORP AFFIL director: Montana Power Co.; president, director, owner, operator: Yellowstone Country Food & Beverage.

Pamela K. Merrell: vice president, secretary (see above)

Jerrold P. Pederson: director (see above)

Ellen M. Senechal: treasurer (see above)

Grants Analysis

Disclosure Period: calendar year ending 1998
Total Grants: $496,061*
Number of Grants: 110
Average Grant: $4,510
Highest Grant: $50,000
Typical Range: $500 to $6,000
***Note:** Giving excludes matching gifts; scholarship; United Way.

Recent Grants

Note: Grants derived from 1998 Form 990.

Arts & Humanities

30,000	C. M. Russell Museum, Great Falls, MT
10,000	Museum of the Rockies, Bozeman, MT
6,000	Butte Center for Performing Arts, Butte, MT
5,000	Dillon City Library, Dillon, MT
5,000	Paris Gibson Square Museum, Great Falls, MT
2,500	Great Falls Symphony, Great Falls, MT

Civic & Public Affairs

15,500	Habitat for Humanity Southwest Montana, Butte, MT
10,000	Rocky Mountain Elk Foundation, Billings, MT
5,000	Governors Summit 1998, Billings, MT
4,000	Jobs for Montana Graduates, Helena, MT

Education

50,000	Montana State University, Billings, MT
45,000	Montana Tech Foundation, Butte, MT
30,000	Montana State University, Northern, Havre, MT
25,000	Carroll College, Helena, MT
20,000	University of Great Falls, Great Falls, MT
20,000	Western Montana College Education Foundation, Dillon, MT
15,000	Rocky Mountain College, Billings, MT
8,225	University of Montana Foundation, Missoula, MT
8,000	Butte Central Catholic Schools, Butte, MT
7,000	Billings College of Technology, Billings, MT
7,000	Butte College of Technology, Butte, MT
7,000	Great Falls College of Technology, Great Falls, MT
7,000	Helena College of Technology, Helena, MT
7,000	Missoula College of Technology, Missoula, MT
6,635	Montana State University Foundation, Bozeman, MT
5,680	Montana Tech Foundation, Butte, MT
5,000	Central Montana Head Start, Lewiston, MT
5,000	Lewis & Clark 4-H Leaders, Helena, MT
2,700	Montana State University, Bozeman, MT
2,700	University of Montana, Missoula, MT

Health

10,000	Ronald McDonald House, Billings, MT
5,000	Airlifeline, Statewide, Sacramento, CA
5,000	Butte Silver Bow Primary Health Care, Butte, MT
4,250	American Diabetes Association, Great Falls, MT

Social Services

45,686	United Way, Butte, MT
27,500	Butte Family YMCA, Butte, MT
10,268	United Way, Missoula, MT
10,216	United Way, Great Falls, MT
8,696	United Way, Billings, MT
7,500	Montana Food Bank Network Council, Missoula, MT
6,088	United Way, Bozeman, MT
6,000	Caring Program for Children, Helena, MT
5,000	Billings Food Bank, Billings, MT
5,000	Boys/Girls Club, Missoula, MT
5,000	Heisey Memorial Youth Center, Great Falls, MT
5,000	Whitefish Community Center, Whitefish, MT
4,188	United Way, Helena, MT
3,100	Big Brothers & Big Sisters, Butte, MT

Montgomery Ward & Co., Inc.

Company Contact

Chicago, IL
Web: http://www.mward.com

Company Description

Employees: 62,500
SIC(s): 5311 Department Stores.

Operating Locations

Operates in 39 states with more than 360 stores, 31 distribution centers, 131 product service centers and 23 liquidation stores.

Nonmonetary Support

Value: $32,000 (1995); $500,000 (1993)
Type: Cause-related Marketing & Promotion; Donated Equipment; Donated Products

Montgomery Ward Foundation

Giving Contact

Charles H. Knittle, Vice President, Governmental Affairs and Corporate Communications
Montgomery Ward Foundation
535 West Chicago Avenue
Chicago, IL 60671
Phone: (312)467-7642
Fax: (312)467-3975
Web: http://www.mward.com/HTML/communityservices.html

Description

EIN: 362670108
Organization Type: Corporate Foundation
Giving Locations: IL: Chicago headquarters and operating communities.
Grant Types: Award, Employee Matching Gifts, General Support, Multiyear/Continuing Support.
Note: Employee matching gift ratio: 1 to 1 to fully accredited two or four year colleges and universities, and to public television and radio stations.

Giving Philosophy

'Providing support to programs that improve the quality of life for people who live and work where Montgomery Ward does business is an important aspect of the company's enduring heritage of community service. The Montgomery Ward Charitable Funds offer a way to continue this proud tradition. Montgomery Ward giving centers on supporting the family and children in need and in crisis. We've focused on the family because it is the essential unit of our society, whatever its composition, and because our business is to serve the needs of families. We emphasize children because they are most vulnerable in our society, and because they hold the promise of our future, as a community and as a business. The Montgomery Ward Charitable Funds include: The Montgomery Ward

Foundation, which was established in 1969; a corporate giving fund; and gifts of merchandise sold by Montgomery Ward retail stores.' *Giving Guidelines*

Financial Summary

Total Giving: $100,000 (1998); $782,638 (1997); $1,454,220 (1996). Note: Contributes through corporate direct giving program and foundation. Giving includes foundation; matching gifts.
Assets: $66,190 (1998); $86,265 (1997); $18,611 (1996)
Gifts Received: $80,000 (1998); $850,000 (1997); $1,358,155 (1996). Note: Contributions are received from Montgomery Ward.

Typical Recipients

Arts & Humanities: Arts Centers, Arts Institutes, Museums/Galleries, Music, Public Broadcasting
Civic & Public Affairs: Botanical Gardens/Parks, Economic Development, Civic & Public Affairs-General, Hispanic Affairs, Housing, Legal Aid, Nonprofit Management, Philanthropic Organizations, Professional & Trade Associations, Urban & Community Affairs, Zoos/Aquariums
Education: Agricultural Education, Arts/Humanities Education, Colleges & Universities, Education Associations, Education Funds, Education-General, Preschool Education, Private Education (Precollege), Public Education (Precollege), School Volunteerism, Secondary Education (Private), Special Education, Student Aid
Health: AIDS/HIV, Cancer, Children's Health/Hospitals, Emergency/Ambulance Services
Religion: Bible Study/Translation, Jewish Causes, Religious Organizations, Religious Welfare, Seminaries
Social Services: Child Abuse, Child Welfare, Community Service Organizations, Emergency Relief, Family Services, Food/Clothing Distribution, People with Disabilities, Recreation & Athletics, Scouts, Shelters/Homelessness, United Funds/United Ways, Volunteer Services, YMCA/YWCA/YMHA/YWHA, Youth Organizations

Contributions Analysis

Giving Priorities: United Way, education through matching gifts, civic and welfare organizations, and public television through matching gifts.

Application Procedures

Initial Contact: Send a written proposal.
Application Requirements: information includes a short history of organization, statement of purpose, people and geographic area served; amount requested; proof of tax-exempt status; copy of most recent annual report and audited financial statement; list of other funding sources and amounts.
Deadlines: Last working day in February, May, August, or November.
Review Process: Monetary requests reviewed in March, June, September and December; requests for merchandise are reviewed weekly.
Evaluative Criteria: Organization is tax-exempt, provides direct services to families and children in extreme need or crisis, serves neighborhoods near stores or company buildings, organization is non-discriminatory and receives no United Way funding.
Decision Notification: Notification within 15 days of meeting.

Restrictions

The Montgomery Ward Foundation will not support individuals; religious or political organizations; advertising in special interest publications; educational funds; endowment funds; other foundations; programs of municipal, state, or federal agencies; organizations not tax-exempt under section 501(c)(3) of the Internal Revenue Code; or organizations with discriminatory policies.
The foundation does not give direct grants to individuals as scholarships, except through National Merit Scholarships for children of employees and the National Hispanic Scholarship Fund in key Hispanic markets. No grants are made for operating funds of public colleges or universities.

Additional Information

Montgomery Ward, a former Mobil Corp. operating company, is now a privately held company after a leveraged buyout in 1988.
Montgomery Ward has supported United Way or Community Funds since the earliest days of these organizations. Each year, the company conducts a United Way campaign to generate associate contributions in each work location. Additionally, the company makes a corporate grant to each local United Way in which the company has a work location. The Montgomery Ward Foundation Board determines the funding level for each year. The grants are provided through Charities Fund Transfer to each United Way in January. Local United Ways are asked not to apply directly.
Companyis reviewing giving programs and considering revising strategy and guidelines.
Publications: Guidelines

Corporate Officials

Don Civgin: vice president, treasurer PRIM CORP EMPL senior vice president: Montgomery Ward & Co. Inc. ADD CORP EMPL treasurer: Montgomery Ward Holding Corp.
Roger V. Goddu: chairman, chief executive officer, director B 1950. PRIM CORP EMPL chairman, chief executive officer, director: Montgomery Ward & Co. Inc. CORP AFFIL chief executive officer: Montgomery Ward Holding Corp. NONPR AFFIL director: Kids in Distressed Situations; director: Project Pride Living.
Carol J. Harms: vice president, treasurer B Aurora, IL 1953. ED Carroll College (1975); University of Connecticut (1977). PRIM CORP EMPL vice president, treasurer: Montgomery Ward & Co., Inc.
Spencer H. Heine: executive vice president, secretary B 1942. ED Columbia College BA (1963); Saint John's University JD (1969). PRIM CORP EMPL executive vice president, secretary: Montgomery Ward & Co., Inc. ADD CORP EMPL secretary: Montgomery Ward Holding Corp.; president: Montgomery Ward Properties.
Robert Albert Kasenter: executive vice president human resources B Pittsburgh, PA 1946. ED Grove City College BA (1968); University of Pittsburgh Law School JD (1974). PRIM CORP EMPL executive vice president human resources: Montgomery Ward & Co. Inc. ADD CORP EMPL executive vice president human resources: Montgomery Ward Holding Corp.
John L. Workman: executive vice president B 1951. ED Indiana University BS (1973); University of Chicago MBA (1985). PRIM CORP EMPL executive vice president: Montgomery Ward & Co., Inc. CORP AFFIL chief financial officer: Montgomery Ward Holding Corp.

Foundation Officials

James R. Butler: vice president
Don Civgin: vice president, treasurer (see above)
Judy Gustafson: vice president, corp. learning & human resources development PRIM CORP EMPL vice president, corp. learning & human resources: Montgomery Ward & Co. Inc.
Carol J. Harms: senior vice president (see above)
Spencer H. Heine: president (see above)
Robert Albert Kasenter: executive vice president (see above)
Charles H. Knittle: vice president PRIM CORP EMPL vice president governmental affairs corp. communications: Montgomery Ward Co. Inc.
John L. Workman: executive vice president, director (see above)

Grants Analysis

Disclosure Period: calendar year ending 1998
Total Grants: $100,000
Number of Grants: 3
Highest Grant: $40,000
Typical Range: $20,000 to $40,000

Recent Grants

Note: Grants derived from 1999 Form 990.

Education

40,000	Cabrini-Green Tutoring Program, Incorporated, Chicago, IL

Social Services

40,000	Cabrini Green Connections, Chicago, IL
20,000	Jesse White Tumbling Team, Chicago, IL

THE MONY GROUP

Company Contact

New York, NY
Web: http://www.mony.com

Company Description

Former Name: The Mutual Life Insurance Co. of New York.
Assets: US$11,519,800,000
Employees: 5,148
SIC(s): 6311 Life Insurance, 6321 Accident & Health Insurance.

Nonmonetary Support

Value: $280,000 (1999); $500,000 (1993); $500,000 (1992)
Type: Donated Equipment; In-kind Services; Workplace Solicitation

Corporate Sponsorship

Range: less than $20,000
Type: Sports events
Note: Sponsors the Harlem Junior Tennis program. Annual Sponsorship Budget: approx. $20,000.

The MONY Life Insurance of New York

Giving Contact

Ms. Lynn Stekas, President
The MONY Life Insurance Co. of New York
1740 Broadway
New York, NY 10019
Phone: (212)708-2136
Fax: (212)708-2001

Description

EIN: 133398852
Organization Type: Corporate Foundation
Giving Locations: headquarters and operating communities.
Grant Types: Award, Employee Matching Gifts, Project.
Note: Employee matching gift ratio: 1 to 1. Company matches gifts up to $1,000 in contributions made by eligible employees and sales representatives throughout the US. Matching gifts are open to all 501(c)(3) organization. Political, sectarian, religious, or United Way organization are not eligible for matching gifts.

Giving Philosophy

'As an insurer, investor, employer and corporate citizen, Mutual of New York believes that the health of the communities it serves is directly related to the health and profitability of the company. We are committed to actively participating in the growth and development of these communities through the investment of time, talent, financial and in-kind support.' *Mutual Of New York Giving Guidelines*

Financial Summary

Total Giving: $1,141,530 (1999); $1,150,000 (1998 approx); $942,186 (1997). Note: Contributes through corporate direct giving program and foundation. 1997 corporate direct giving ($180,595); Foundation ($942,186).
Giving Analysis: Giving for 1997 includes: corporate matching gifts ($290,950); corporate grants to United Way ($130,256)
Assets: $43,262 (1997); $52,707 (1995); $90,314 (1994)
Gifts Received: $943,736 (1997); $695,864 (1995); $700,000 (1994). Note: Foundation receives contributions from The Mutual Life Insurance Co. of New York.

Typical Recipients

Arts & Humanities: Arts Centers, Dance, Libraries, Literary Arts, Museums/Galleries, Opera, Performing Arts, Public Broadcasting
Civic & Public Affairs: African American Affairs, Business/Free Enterprise, Community Foundations, Economic Development, Employment/Job Training, Gay/Lesbian Issues, Civic & Public Affairs-General, Hispanic Affairs, Housing, Law & Justice, Nonprofit Management, Urban & Community Affairs, Women's Affairs
Education: Business Education, Colleges & Universities, Economic Education, Education-General, Leadership Training, Literacy, Private Education (Precollege), Public Education (Precollege), Social Sciences Education
Environment: Environment-General
Health: AIDS/HIV, Cancer, Emergency/Ambulance Services, Health Organizations, Hospices, Medical Research, Mental Health, Prenatal Health Issues, Public Health, Research/Studies Institutes, Single-Disease Health Associations
International: International Development
Religion: Churches, Religious Welfare
Social Services: Big Brother/Big Sister, Child Welfare, Community Centers, Community Service Organizations, Day Care, Family Planning, Family Services, Food/Clothing Distribution, People with Disabilities, Refugee Assistance, Scouts, Senior Services, Shelters/Homelessness, Substance Abuse, United Funds/United Ways, Volunteer Services, YMCA/YWCA/YMHA/YWHA, Youth Organizations

Contributions Analysis

Giving Priorities: Issues arising from the company-defined focus of 'The Changing American Family,' such as the aging population, dual-income and single-parent families, and dependant care.
Arts & Humanities: About 1%.
Civic & Public Affairs: 13%. Funds economic development.
Education: 34%. Supports higher education relevant to the insurance industry.
Environment: 2%.
Health: 4%. Interests include AIDS and cancer.
Religion: 2%.
Social Services: 44%. Funds United Way and services for youth and families.
Note: Total contributions in 1997.

Application Procedures

Initial Contact: Phone call.
Application Requirements: Send a brief description (one to two pages) of the program or organization to be funded, including a clear statement of goals and objectives, a proposed budget, a copy of the IRS 501(c)(3) determination letter, a recent Form 990, a list of the organization's board of directors, and an audited financial statement.
Deadlines: None.
Evaluative Criteria: Funding goes to well-defined programs that conform to the company's giving priorities; well-managed organizations, with ability to achieve specific objectives; organizations within company operating areas requesting reasonable amounts.
Decision Notification: Please call each site for timelines.
Notes: After reviewing the material, the foundation requests additional information if necessary. Contributions guidelines brochure should be reviewed before submitting request.

Restrictions

In general, MONY will not consider requests for the following: capital fund drives; private foundations; fully participating members of the United Way; religious, fraternal, political, athletic, social, or veterans organizations; endowments, memorials, or contingency funds; individuals; good will advertising; dinners or special events; or organizations with a financial deficit. Foundation gives to colleges and universities in the form of matching funds only. matching funds only.

Additional Information

In addition to direct grants given through the Corporate Social Policy Division in New York, NY, a portion of the contributions budget is disbursed through the Syracuse Operations Center, Syracuse, NY; and Glenpointe Marketing Center, Teaneck, NJ.

Corporate Officials

Thomas J. Conklin: senior vice president, secretaryc B Bronx, NY 1946. ED Saint Joseph's Seminary BA (1968); Saint Joseph's Seminary MDiv (1971); Western Connecticut State College (1971). PRIM CORP EMPL senior vice president, secretary: The Mutual Life Insurance Co. of New York. NONPR AFFIL member: American Society of Corporate Secretaries; member: New York Personnel Management Association.
Samuel J. Foti: president, chief operating officer, director B 1952. ED University of Pennsylvania Wharton School MA; University of Pennsylvania Wharton School BS. PRIM CORP EMPL president, chief operating officer, director: The Mutual Life Insurance Co. of New York Inc. CORP AFFIL president, director: Mony Life Insurance of America Arizona Corp.
Kenneth M. Levine: executive vice president, chief investment officer, director B Bronx, NY 1946. ED City University of New York (1968). PRIM CORP EMPL executive vice president, chief investment officer, director: The Mutual Life Insurance Co. of New York ADD CORP EMPL director: 1740 Advisors Inc.; president: 1740 Ventures Inc.; executive vice president: MONY Group Inc.; executive vice president: MONY Life Insurance Co.; executive vice president: MONY Life Insurance of American Arizona Corp.; president: MONY Realty Partners Inc. NONPR AFFIL member: Society Actuaries.
Michael I. Roth: chairman, chief executive officer, director B Brooklyn, NY 1945. ED City College of New York BS (1967); Boston University JD (1971); New York University LLM (1973). PRIM CORP EMPL chairman, chief executive officer, director: The Mutual Life Insurance Co. of New York. CORP AFFIL director: Promus Hotel Corp.; chairman: Mony Life Insurance of America Arizona Corp.; director: Pitney Bowes Inc. NONPR AFFIL director: Life Insurance Council; director: Metropolitan Development Association; director: Insurance Marketplace Standards Association; director: Enterprise Foundation; director: Enterprise Group; director: Committee for Economic Development; member: American Council Life Insurance; member: American Institute CPAs.

Foundation Officials

Thomas J. Conklin: director (see above)
Richard M. Daddario: chief financial officer B Hartford, CT 1947. ED University of Hartford BS (1969); University of Hartford MS (1975). PRIM CORP EMPL executive vice president, chief financial officer: The Mutual Life Insurance Co. of New York. CORP AFFIL vice president: 1740 Advisors Inc.; director finance: Mony Life Insurance American AZ Corp.
Samuel J. Foti: director (see above)
Kenneth M. Levine: director (see above)
Michael I. Roth: director (see above)
Lynn Stekas: president
Frederick Tedeschi: secretary
David V. Weigel: treasurer B Hartford, CT 1946. ED Gettysburg College (1969). PRIM CORP EMPL treasurer, director: MONY Life Insurance Co. of America. CORP AFFIL treasurer, director: 1740 Advisors Inc.; vice president, treasurer: Mutual Life Insurance Co. of New York.

Grants Analysis

Disclosure Period: calendar year ending 1997
Total Grants: $520,980*
Number of Grants: 60
Average Grant: $8,683
Highest Grant: $100,000
Typical Range: $1,000 to $10,000
***Note:** Giving excludes corporate matching gifts; United Way.

Recent Grants

Note: Grants derived from 1997 Form 990.

Arts & Humanities

5,000 Mattie Rhodes Counseling and Arts Center, Kansas City, MO

Civic & Public Affairs

15,000 Committee for Economic Development, New York, NY
15,000 Support Center, NY
10,000 Enterprise Foundation, Columbia, MD
10,000 Momentum Project, New York, NY
10,000 Townwide Fund of Huntington, Huntington, NY
5,000 Augusta-Richmond Opportunities Center
5,000 Lawyers Alliance for New York, New York, NY
5,000 Victory Gallop, Akron, OH
3,000 REACH, New York, NY

Education

100,000 Life and Health Insurance Foundation for Education
25,000 American College, Bryn Mawr, PA
25,000 American College, Bryn Mawr, PA
25,000 Bank Street College of Education, New York, NY
25,000 Florida A&M University School of Business and Industry, Tallahassee, FL
6,535 Danforth Magnet School, Syracuse, NY
5,000 Mercy Learning Center

Environment

10,000 Tides Center, San Francisco, CA

Health

8,000 AIDS Task Force, New York, NY
7,000 United Cerebral Palsy and Handicapped Children's Association, Syracuse, NY
5,000 AIDS Community Services of Western New York, Buffalo, NY
5,000 American Cancer Society, Corpus Christi, TX

Religion

10,000 Catholic Home Bureau
5,000 Salvation Army Boys and Girls Club, Oklahoma City, OK

Social Services

69,698 United Way of Central New York, Syracuse, NY
50,553 United Way of Tri-State, New York, NY
11,950 Consortium for Children's Services, Syracuse, NY
10,000 Association to Benefit Children, New York, NY
10,000 Center for Children and Families, New York, NY
10,000 Park Slope Project Reach Youth, Brooklyn, NY
10,000 United Way, New York, NY
6,200 Social Service Federation, Englewood, NJ

6,000	Contact, Syracuse, NY
5,000	Bergen County Council on Alcoholism and Drug Abuse, Paramus, NJ
5,000	Big Brothers and Big Sisters, Rochester, NY
5,000	Boy Scouts of America Cascade Pacific Council, Portland, OR
5,000	Boy Scouts of America Desert Pacific Council
5,000	Boy Scouts of America Montana Council, MT
5,000	Boys and Girls Club, Syracuse, NY
5,000	BRC Human Services Corporation, New York, NY
5,000	BRC Human Services Corporation, New York, NY
5,000	Camp Fire, Longview, TX
5,000	Camp Fire Boys and Girls Illinois Prairie Council
5,000	Children's Garden, CA
5,000	Coleman Adoption Services, Indianapolis, IN
5,000	Multi-Services of Central Florida, Orlando, FL
5,000	National Center for Missing and Exploited Children, New York, NY
5,000	Salesmanship Club Youth and Family Centers, Dallas, TX
5,000	Volunteer Center of Bergen County, Hackensack, NJ
5,000	Webster Avenue Family Resource Center, Rochester, NY

J.P. MORGAN &CO. INC.

★ Number 48 of Top 100 Corporate Givers

Company Contact

New York, NY
Web: http://www.jpmorgan.com

Company Description

Revenue: US$18,110,000,000 (1999)
Profit: US$963,000,000
Employees: 15,674 (1999)
Fortune Rank: 92, per FORTUNE Magazine's list of 500 Largest U.S. Corporations (1999).
FF 92
SIC(s): 6712 Bank Holding Companies.

Operating Locations

Argentina: J.P. Morgan Argentina Sociedad de Bolsa S.A., Buenos Aires; Australia: J.P. Morgan Australia Ltd., Melbourne, Sydney; Belgium: J. P. Morgan Benelux S.A., Brussels; Bahamas: Morgan Trust Co. of The Bahamas Ltd., Nassau; Brazil: Banco J.P. Morgan, S.A., Rio de Janeiro RJ, Brazil, Sao Paulo; Canada: J.P. Morgan Canada, Montreal, Toronto; Chile: J.P. Morgan Chile Ltda., Santiago; People's Republic of China: J.P. Morgan & Co. Inc., Beijing; J.P. Morgan and Co. Inc., Shanghai; Cayman Islands: J.P. Morgan Delaware banking office, Grand Cayman; Czech Republic: J.P. Morgan International Ltd., Prague; France: Societe de Bourse J.P. Morgan SA, Paris; Germany: J.P. Morgan GmbH, Frankfurt; Hong Kong: J.P. Morgan Futures Hong Kong Ltd., Hong Kong; Indonesia: Morgan Guaranty Trust Co., Jakarta; India:, Mumbai; Italy: J.P. Morgan SGR S.p.A., Milan; Morgan Guaranty Trust Co., Rome; Japan: J.P. Morgan Investment Management Inc., Minato-ku; Republic of Korea: J.P. Morgan Securities Asia Pte. Ltd., Seoul; Mexico: Banco J.P. Morgan, SA, Mexico City; Malaysia: J.P. Morgan Malaysia Ltd., Labuan; Peru: Morgan Guaranty Trust Co., Lima; Philippines:, Makati City; Poland: J.P. Morgan Polska Sp. z o.o., Warsaw; Russia: J.P. Morgan International Ltd., Moscow; Republic of South Africa: J.P. Morgan Securities South Africa Ltd., Johannesburg; Singapore: J.P. Morgan Futures Inc., Singapore; Spain: J.P. Morgan Espana S.A., Madrid; Switzerland: J.P. Morgan (Suisse) S.A., Geneva; J.P. Morgan Securities Ltd., Zurich; Thailand: J.P. Morgan Securities Asia Ltd., Bangkok; Taiwan: J.P. Morgan Securities Asia Pte. Ltd., Taipei; United Kingdom: J.P. Morgan Securities Ltd., London; Venezuela: Centro Professional Eurobuilding, Caracas

Nonmonetary Support

Type: Donated Equipment
Contact: Jeanne Collins, Associate
Note: Nonmonetary support is provided by the company.

Corporate Sponsorship

Type: Arts & cultural events
Contact: Cynthia Heusing, Vice President
Note: Some sponsorship is handled through regional offices.

J.P. Morgan Charitable Trust

Giving Contact

Hildy Simmons, Managing Director, Community Relations
J.P. Morgan & Co.
60 Wall St., 46th Floor
New York, NY 10260
Phone: (212)648-9673
Fax: (212)648-5082
Web: http://www.jpmorgan.com/communityinvolvement

Description

EIN: 136037931
Organization Type: Corporate Foundation
Giving Locations: NY: New York some funding internationally; some funding nationally.
Grant Types: Capital, Employee Matching Gifts, Endowment, General Support, Multiyear/Continuing Support, Project.
Note: Employee matching gift ratio: 1 to 1.

Giving Philosophy

'Our charitable giving is grounded in the belief that Morgan's success is closely related to the well-being of the communities in which we live and work. To that end, we are particularly interested in community and economic development programs. We focus our support on organizations with well-defined objectives, sound leadership, and a demonstrable record of achievement. We maintain a strong commitment to programs that provide access to affordable housing, primary health care, and quality child care-as well as to public education, the arts, adult literacy, job training, and employment programs. We also support programs that promote increased understanding among peoples of different cultures and ethnic background; that secure and maintain the rights of all citizens; and that safeguard the environment.' JP Morgan 1997 Annual Report.

Financial Summary

Total Giving: $17,000,000 (1999 approx); $17,510,195 (1998); $17,778,905 (1997). Note: Contributes through corporate direct giving program and foundation.
Giving Analysis: Giving for 1998 includes: foundation ($12,650,845); international subsidiaries ($3,101,133); corporate direct giving ($749,692); corporate matching gifts ($569,325); foundation grants to United Way ($439,200)
Assets: $12,393,668 (1998); $17,337,434 (1997); $29,741,557 (1996)
Gifts Received: $7,000,000 (1998); $6,413 (1996); $5,000,000 (1995). Note: Trust receives contributions from J.P. Morgan & Company.

Typical Recipients

Arts & Humanities: Arts Associations & Councils, Arts Centers, Arts Funds, Arts Outreach, Ballet, Dance, Arts & Humanities-General, History & Archaeology, Libraries, Museums/Galleries, Music, Opera, Performing Arts, Public Broadcasting, Theater, Visual Arts
Civic & Public Affairs: African American Affairs, Botanical Gardens/Parks, Business/Free Enterprise, Community Foundations, Economic Development, Employment/Job Training, Gay/Lesbian Issues, Hispanic Affairs, Housing, Law & Justice, Legal Aid, Municipalities/Towns, Nonprofit Management, Philanthropic Organizations, Rural Affairs, Urban & Community Affairs, Women's Affairs, Zoos/Aquariums
Education: Afterschool/Enrichment Programs, Arts/Humanities Education, Business Education, Colleges & Universities, Education Reform, Faculty Development, Education-General, Leadership Training, Literacy, Medical Education, Minority Education, Public Education (Precollege), Science/Mathematics Education, Social Sciences Education, Student Aid, Vocational & Technical Education
Environment: Air/Water Quality, Forestry, Environment-General
Health: Cancer, Clinics/Medical Centers, Emergency/Ambulance Services, Geriatric Health, Health Policy/Cost Containment, Health Organizations, Hospitals, Public Health, Transplant Networks/Donor Banks
International: Foreign Arts Organizations, Foreign Educational Institutions, Human Rights, International Affairs, International Development, International Peace & Security Issues, International Relations, International Relief Efforts
Religion: Religious Welfare
Science: Science Museums
Social Services: At-Risk Youth, Child Welfare, Community Centers, Community Service Organizations, Counseling, Crime Prevention, Day Care, Domestic Violence, Family Planning, Family Services, Food/Clothing Distribution, People with Disabilities, Recreation & Athletics, Senior Services, Sexual Abuse, Shelters/Homelessness, Social Services-General, Volunteer Services, YMCA/YWCA/YMHA/YWHA, Youth Organizations

Contributions Analysis

Giving Priorities: Colleges and universities from which company recruits workforce; urban affairs and housing, with emphasis on direct services for the poor; and major and less-established cultural organizations. Under its International Affairs contributions category, Morgan supports organizations that promote an improved quality of life in the devloping regions of the world where it does business. It targets support to organizations working in the fields of economic development, environment, population, primary health care, and disaster relief. Company is interested in supporting organizations that rely on the involvement of local groups in designing and operating programs. Most of the contributions assist organizations with programs in Asia, Latin America, and Africa, including several working to create better educational, social, and economicopportunities for black South Africans. Morgan additionally supports organizations whose research and other programs in the fields of international affairs promote increased understanding among countries and peoples of different cultural and ethical backgrounds. Company also supports U.S. nonprofit organizations based overseas. Overseas subsidiaries' contributions follow similar guidelines. Company also matches gifts to international organizations, totaling $170,617 in 1996.
Arts & Humanities: 10% to 15%. Supports both major cultural institutions and smaller, less established programs. Trust promotes groups which bring the arts to new audiences, particularly underserved populations and neighborhoods that lack cultural enrichment. Also supports those organizations that enrich

the quality of life in New York City and encourage cultural diversity. Funds theater, dance, music, film and visual arts groups. Other recipients include libraries, arts in education, and programs which provide assistance to artorganizations. Art organizations also receive matching gifts.
Civic & Public Affairs: 30% to 35%. Supports organizations that seek to improve the quality of life in New York City. Interests include the preservation and development of affordable housing, assisting the economic development of the community, and projects that strengthen the neighborhoods by creating and preserving jobs, work readiness and employment training programs. Other interests include organizations that build on the strength of New York's racial and ethnicdiversity, secure and maintain civil rights, and promote cooperation among diverse people. Also supports programs that provide training, strategic planning, and other technical assistance. (United Funds & United Way) Less than 5%. Supports United Way and the organizations that are a part of the network of funding.
Education: 20% to 25%. Supports colleges and universities from which company recruits its workforce, that provide educational opportunities for disadvantaged students, or that work collaboratively with the New York City public school system. Increasing attention paid to programs designed to improve public education, especially programs that can be replicated throughout the educational system. Promotes programs that develop student skills, teacher training and support, professional development, educational advocacy, and parental involvement. Also funds literacy programs and minority education programs that provide opportunity and access toindependent secondary and higher education. Foundation matches gifts to education organizations.
Health: Less than 5%. Major goal is to make health care available to everyone, particularly low-income families in New York. Supports community-based primary care programs, health education, disease prevention, and AIDS programs. Also promotes programs that provide self-sufficiency for low-income families, child care, and youth services. Funds organizations that fight against homelessness,hunger, and violence.
International: Strives to help organizations worldwide break down barriers between people by fostering study and exchange and by promoting economic and social development in less-developed countries. Interests include environment, population, primary health care, and disaster relief. Most grants are to U.S.-based nonprofits, particularly those groups that rely on the involvement of communities in designing and operating their programs. Includes matching gifts.
Religion: Less than 5%. Funds religious causes.
Social Services: 20% to 25%. Supports children and youth services, food centers, Planned Parenthood, YMCA, and social services.
Note: Subsidiaries and overseas offices also make contributions.

Application Procedures

Initial Contact: Request guidelines, then written proposal.
Application Requirements: Include goals of organization, need or problem to be addressed, and a statement on the segment of the population to which grant is to be directed; latest annual report, if available; brief history of organization; brief description of programs and accomplishments in last year; explanation of how success will be evaluated; list of directors or trustees and their affiliations; a list of senior staff members, number of full staff, part-time staff, and volunteers, including one-paragraph resumes on key personnel; recently audited financial statement; current budget, including sources of projected income; budget for next fiscal year, if available; list of foundation and corporate supporters and other sources of income; copy of 501(c)(3) letter; recent Form 990; an outline of any plans to enlarge base of support from potential sources; a brief description of the specific project for which funds are requested; include primary purpose and problem, population it will serve, individual who will direct it and their qualifications, how long it will take, budget, and when funds are needed; plan for measuring the effectiveness of project; and three examples of recent articles or evaluations of organization.
Deadlines: Anytime prior to September 15 to be considered in that calendar year.
Review Process: Contributions Committee meets six times a year, between February and November.
Decision Notification: Within three months of receipt of application information. Grants approved in the first half of the year are normally paid in June, those in the second half in December.
Notes: Also accepts the New York Common Application Form, as long as additional requested information is provided. Application must be complete within two months of trust acknowledgement.

Restrictions

Does not support individuals, religious organizations for sectarian purposes, chemical dependency programs, specific disability or single-disease health associations other than AIDS programs, scholarly research, scholarships, or fellowships.

Additional Information

J.P. Morgan & Co. matches contributions of its employees, retired employees, bank directors, and any eligible person's spouse dollar-for-dollar. Gifts of cash, securities, and real estate are matched in six categories of giving--culture, education, environmental concerns, health care, human services, and international affairs. Minimum gift matched is $25. Maximum combined giving total matched is $8,000 per calendar year.
The Trust rarely contributes outside of the New York area, except for higher education and international affairs. Grants made outside the New York area are usually to organizations that operate nationwide.
An applicant whose proposals denied may not apply again for one year.

Corporate Officials

Walter Gubert: vice chairman, president, chief executive officer, director B 1947. PRIM CORP EMPL vice chairman: J.P. Morgan & Co. Inc. ADD CORP EMPL director: Morgan Guaranty Trust Co. of New York.
Michael E. Patterson: vice chairman B New York, NY 1942. ED Harvard University AB (1964); Columbia University LLB (1967). PRIM CORP EMPL vice chairman: J.P. Morgan & Co. Inc. ADD CORP EMPL director: J.P. Morgan Investment Management Inc.; director: Morgan Guaranty Trust Co. of New York.
Douglas Alexander Warner, III: chairman, president, chief executive officer, director B Cincinnati, OH 1946. ED Yale University BA (1968). PRIM CORP EMPL chairman, president, chief executive officer, director: J.P. Morgan & Co. ADD CORP EMPL president, chief executive officer, chairman: Morgan Guaranty Trust Co. New York. CORP AFFIL board counselor: Bechtel Group Inc.; director: General Electric Co.; director: Anheuser-Busch Companies Inc. NONPR AFFIL director: New York Clearing House Association; trustee: Pierpont Morgan Library; member, board overseers: Memorial Sloan-Kettering Cancer Center; member: Business Council; trustee: Cold Spring Harbor Laboratory; member: Bankers Roundtable. CLUB AFFIL Meadow Brook Club; River Club; The Links Club.

Giving Program Officials

Karen A. Erdos: PRIM CORP EMPL vice president community relations: J.P. Morgan & Co.
Edward L. Jones: vice president
Monica Neal: vice president
Lisa Philp: vice president
Amy C. Tully: associate

Foundation Officials

Hildy J. Simmons: managing director

Grants Analysis

Disclosure Period: calendar year ending 1998
Total Grants: $8,267,500*
Number of Grants: 379
Average Grant: $21,814
Highest Grant: $375,000
Typical Range: $5,000 to $25,000
***Note:** Giving excludes matching gifts; international subsidiaries; United Way.

Recent Grants

Note: Grants derived from 1998 Form 990.

Arts & Humanities

125,000	New York Public Library, New York, NY
100,000	Lincoln Center for the Performing Arts Inc, New York, NY
90,000	Alliance of Resident Theatres/New York, New York, NY
85,000	Disney Hall, San Francisco, CA
55,000	Orchestral Association, Chicago, IL
50,000	Bronx Council on the Arts, Bronx, NY
50,000	New York City 100, New York, NY
42,000	Asian Art Museum, San Francisco, CA

Civic & Public Affairs

200,000	Local Initiatives Support Corp, New York, NY
165,000	Enterprise Foundation, New York, NY
125,000	New York City Partnership, New York, NY
125,000	New York Community Trust, New York, NY -- Neighborhood 2000
100,000	NAACP Legal Defense & Educational Fund, Inc., New York, NY
75,000	Community Resource Exchange, New York, NY
75,000	MBD Community Housing Corporation, Bronx, NY
75,000	Nonprofit Facilities Fund, New York, NY
65,000	Citizens Committee for New York City Inc, New York, NY
50,000	Fund for the City of New York, New York, NY
50,000	National Federation of Community Development Credit Unions, New York, NY
40,000	Neighborhood Housing Services of New York City Inc, New York, NY
40,000	Per Scholas, New York, NY
40,000	South Bronx Overall Economic Development Corp, Bronx, NY
40,000	United Neighborhood Houses of New York, New York, NY

Education

375,000	New York University, New York, NY
125,000	Columbia University-Graduate School of Business, New York, NY
100,000	The Center for Arts Education, New York, NY
100,000	Pace University, New York, NY
80,000	University of Delaware, Newark, DE
60,000	Educators for Social Responsibility Metroplitan Area, New York, NY
50,000	Bank Street College of Education, New York, NY
50,000	Classroom, Inc., New York, NY
50,000	Columbia University - Teachers College, New York, NY
50,000	Partnership for After School Education/Park Slope, New York, NY
50,000	United Negro College Fund Inc, New York, NY
40,000	Teachers Network Inc, New York, NY

Health

50,000	Saint Vincent's Hospital and Medical Center, New York, NY
40,000	Institute for Urban Family Health, New York, NY

40,000	Primary Care Development Corporation, New York, NY

Religion

100,000	Good Shepherd Services, New York, NY
50,000	St. Christopher Ottilie/Cntr Family Life Sunset Park, Brooklyn, NY

Social Services

75,000	Food for Survival Inc, Bronx, NY
65,000	Community Food Resource Center, Inc, New York, NY
50,000	Children's Defense Fund, Washington, DC
50,000	Citymeals-on-Wheels, New York, NY
50,000	Community Service Building Corporation, Wilmington, DE
50,000	Planned Parenthood of New York City, New York, NY
50,000	Rheedlen Centers For Children And Families, New York, NY
50,000	YMCA of Greater New York, New York, NY
40,000	Community Service Society of New York, New York, NY
35,000	Court Appointed Special Advocates, New York, NY

MORGAN STANLEY DEAN WITTER &CO.

Company Contact

New York, NY
Web: http://www.msdw.com

Company Description

Revenue: US$33,928,000,000 (1999)
Profit: US$4,791,000,000 (1999)
Employees: 45,712
Fortune Rank: 30, per FORTUNE Magazine's list of 500 Largest U.S. Corporations (1999).
FF 30
SIC(s): 6211 Security Brokers & Dealers, 6221 Commodity Contracts Brokers & Dealers, 6289 Security & Commodity Services Nec.

Operating Locations

Australia: Morgan Stanley Melbourne, Melbourne; Morgan Stanley Sydney, Sydeny; Canada: Morgan Stanley Montreal, Montreal; Morgan Stanley Canada, Toronto; People's Republic of China: Morgan Stanley Beijing, Beijing; Morgan Stanley Shanghai, Shanghai; France: Morgan Stanley Paris, Paris; Germany: Morgan Stanley Frankfurt, Frankfurt; Hong Kong: Morgan Stanley Hong Kong, Hong Kong; India: Morgan Stanley Bombay, Mumbai; Italy: Morgan Stanley Milan, Milan; Japan: Morgan Stanley Japan, Tokyo; Republic of Korea: Morgan Stanley Seoul, Seoul; Luxembourg: Morgan Stanley Luxembourg, Senningerberg; Russia: Morgan Stanley Moscow, Moscow; Republic of South Africa: Morgan Stanley Johannesburg, Johannesburg; Singapore: Morgan Stanley Singapore, Singapore; Spain: Morgan Stanley Madrid, Madrid; Switzerland: Morgan Stanley Zurich, Zurich; Taiwan: Morgan Stanley Taipei, Taipei; United Kingdom: Morgan Stanley International, London

Nonmonetary Support

Type: Donated Equipment

Morgan Stanley Foundation

Giving Contact

Katheline Tullhill, Chairman
Morgan Stanley Foundation
1585 Broadway
New York, NY 10036
Phone: (212)761-4000
Fax: (212)761-0094

Description

Founded: 1961
EIN: 136155650
Organization Type: Corporate Foundation
Giving Locations: CA: Los Angeles branch locations, San Francisco branch locations; IL: Chicago branch locations; NY: New York branch locations
Grant Types: Employee Matching Gifts, General Support.
Note: Employee matching gift ratio: 1 to 1 for secondary and higher education only, minimum $50.

Giving Philosophy

'Each year, Morgan Stanley supports a wide variety of civic and cultural organizations, hospitals, social service agencies and educational institutions. We do this as a way of demonstrating the Firm's commitment to the communities in which we operate.

'While Foundation and corporate grants have increased steadily over the years, the Firm has expanded its philanthropic mission to include more than the distribution of grant dollars. Indeed, our approach to philanthropy continues to evolve, going beyond the bounds of conventional funding.

'Increasingly, we are establishing productive partnerships with national and local organizations testing new ideas in education, employment training, health care and social services. These organizations are uniquely placed to understand and address the specific challenges facing our urban communities. They are also a vital channel through which we in the private sector can participate in the communities where our principal offices are located.' *Morgan Stanley Philanthropic Activities 1993*

Financial Summary

Total Giving: $4,000,000 (1999 approx); $3,000,000 (1998); $2,600,000 (1996 approx). Note: Contributes through corporate direct giving program and foundation. 1997 Giving includes corporate direct giving ($1,500,000); foundation ($1,500,000). 1996 Giving includes foundation ($2,341,370); matching gifts ($283,901).
Assets: $15,666,840 (1995); $13,083,007 (1994); $13,000,000 (1992)
Gifts Received: $2,051,390 (1995); $401,387 (1994). Note: Contributions received from Morgan Stanley & Co.

Typical Recipients

Arts & Humanities: Arts Institutes, Ballet, Community Arts, Dance, Historic Preservation, History & Archaeology, Libraries, Museums/Galleries, Music, Performing Arts, Public Broadcasting, Visual Arts
Civic & Public Affairs: Botanical Gardens/Parks, Community Foundations, Economic Development, Employment/Job Training, Hispanic Affairs, Housing, Women's Affairs, Zoos/Aquariums
Education: Arts/Humanities Education, Business Education, Colleges & Universities, Education Associations, Engineering/Technological Education, Education-General, Leadership Training, Literacy, Minority Education, Public Education (Precollege), School Volunteerism, Special Education
Environment: Air/Water Quality, Environment-General, Wildlife Protection
Health: AIDS/HIV, Cancer, Children's Health/Hospitals, Home-Care Services, Hospitals, Hospitals (University Affiliated), Medical Rehabilitation, Prenatal Health Issues
Religion: Religious Welfare
Science: Science Museums
Social Services: At-Risk Youth, Child Welfare, Community Service Organizations, Crime Prevention, Emergency Relief, Family Planning, Family Services, Food/Clothing Distribution, Homes, Recreation & Athletics, Scouts, Shelters/Homelessness, United Funds/United Ways, Volunteer Services, YMCA/YWCA/YMHA/YWHA, Youth Organizations

Contributions Analysis

Giving Priorities: Various social welfare organizations, college and postgraduate education, the arts in New York City, and hospitals and health-related facilities.
Arts & Humanities: 10% to 15%. Museums, libraries, and performing arts centers in New York City, libraries, and public broadcasting stations receivesupport.
Education: 15% to 20%. Interests include graduate schools of business, college counseling, public and private school drop-out prevention initiatives, and arts-in-education programs. Also includes matching gifts.
Health: 10% to 20%. Supports hospitals and other pediatric health-related services.
Social Services: 55% to 60%. Contributes to united funds. Funds are distributed across a broad spectrum of interests, including counseling, youth, employment, recreational, and community service organizations, food distribution, and housing initiatives.

Application Procedures

Initial Contact: contact the foundation for guidelines, then brief written proposal
Application Requirements: a description of organization, amount requested, purpose of funds sought, recently audited financial statement, last year's and current funders with amounts, operating budget for these years, proof of tax-exempt status, list of board members and their affiliations
Deadlines: None.
Review Process: trustees meet three times per year; proposals are considered according to the schedule below
Decision Notification: February 15 for grant renewals and new requests within the areas of higher education, health care, and the arts; June 1 for grant renewals within the area of social service; October 15 for new requests within the area of social service
Notes: Requests for arts-in-education programs fall within the area of social service.

Restrictions

Generally, does not make grants to individuals, national organizations, goodwill advertising, dinners or special events, political or fraternal organizations, member agencies of united funds, religious organizations, organizations concerned with specific disease research, capital or building campaigns, or public or private schools.
Foundation is not currently accepting new applications for arts or higher education funding.

Additional Information

Morgan Stanley Dean Witter is the result of the merger of Morgan Stanley and Dean Witter in 1998.
Publications: Program Guidelines; Grants Listing

Grants Analysis

Disclosure Period: calendar year ending 1994
Total Grants: $2,341,370*
Number of Grants: 224
Average Grant: $10,453
Highest Grant: $50,000
Typical Range: $10,000 to $15,000
***Note:** Giving excludes matching gifts.

Recent Grants

Note: Grants derived from 1995 Form 990.

Arts & Humanities

25,000	Boys Choir of Harlem, New York, NY
25,000	Carnegie Hall Endowment Campaign, New York, NY
25,000	Lincoln Center for Performing Arts, New York, NY
10,000	Bryant Park Restoration Corp, New York, NY
10,000	WNYC, New York, NY

Civic & Public Affairs
25,000 Local Initiatives Support Corp, New York, NY
25,000 Neighborhood Housing Program Grant, New York, NY
25,000 New York Community Trust, New York, NY
25,000 New York Women's Foundation, New York, NY
15,000 American Women's Economic Development Corp, Long Beach, CA
15,000 Central Park Conservancy, New York, NY
12,500 Neighborhood Housing Services, New York, NY
12,500 South Bronx Overall Economic Development Corp, New York, NY

Education
50,000 Sports in Schools Foundation, Long Island City, NY
25,000 A Better Chance, Boston, MA
20,000 Brooklyn Academy of Music, Brooklyn, NY
20,000 Harvard University Graduate School of Business Administration, Cambridge, MA
20,000 New York City School Volunteers Program, New York, NY
15,000 Cities in Schools National, New York, NY
15,000 Classroom, New York, NY
15,000 Sponsors for Educational Opportunity, New York, NY
15,000 Student Sponsor Partnership, New York, NY
12,500 Union Settlement Association, New York, NY
10,000 Brooklyn Academy of Music, Brooklyn, NY
10,000 Stanford University Graduate School of Business, Stanford, CA
10,000 University of Pennsylvania Wharton School, Philadelphia, PA

Environment
10,000 New York Zoological Society, Wildlife Conservation Society, New York, NY

Health
50,000 Memorial Sloan-Kettering Cancer Center, New York, NY
40,000 University Hospitals Foundation, Cleveland, OH
25,000 Associates of Babies Hospitals
15,000 American Italian Foundation for Cancer, New York, NY
15,000 Children's Health Fund, New York, NY
12,000 Bronx Lebanon Hospital, Bronx, NY
10,000 Columbia University, Harlem Hospital, New York, NY
10,000 Floating Hospital, New York, NY

Religion
20,000 Incarnation Children's Center, Minneapolis, MN
12,500 Good Shepherd Services, New York, NY

Science
20,000 American Museum of Natural History, New York, NY

Social Services
50,000 New York City Police Foundation, New York, NY
50,000 Strategic Alliance Fund
37,500 Catalog for Giving
30,000 Children's Storefront Program Grant, New York, NY
25,000 Covenant House, New York, NY
25,000 MicroSociety, New York, NY
25,000 Young Adult Institute, New York, NY
20,000 Daytop Capital Campaign, New York, NY
20,000 Heartshare
20,000 United Way Crusade of Mercy, Chicago, IL
12,500 Children's Storefront, New York, NY
12,500 Henry Street Settlement, New York, NY

MORRIS COMMUNICATIONS CORP.

Company Contact

825 Broad Street
Augusta, GA 30903
Phone: (706)724-0851
Web: http://www.morriscomm.com

Company Description

Former Name: Stauffer Communications.
Employees: 4,900
SIC(s): 2711 Newspapers, 2721 Periodicals.

Stauffer Communications Foundation

Giving Contact

Stan Stauffer, Chairman
Stauffer Communications Foundation
616 Southeast Jefferson
Topeka, KS 66607
Phone: (785)295-1111
Fax: (785)295-1144
Note: Mr. Stauffer's direct line is: (785)295-1118.

Description

EIN: 486212412
Organization Type: Corporate Foundation
Giving Locations: KS; OK
Grant Types: Employee Matching Gifts, General Support.

Financial Summary

Total Giving: $150,000 (1999 approx); $230,836 (1998); $160,084 (1996). Note: Contributes through foundation only. 1995 Giving includes scholarship ($6,760).
Assets: $1,157,206 (1998); $1,167,972 (1996); $1,198,361 (1995)
Gifts Received: $106,000 (1998); $100,000 (1995); $100,000 (1994). Note: Contributions were received from Morris Communications Corp.

Typical Recipients

Arts & Humanities: Community Arts, History & Archaeology, Libraries, Literary Arts, Public Broadcasting, Theater
Civic & Public Affairs: Botanical Gardens/Parks, Chambers of Commerce, Civil Rights, Community Foundations, Economic Development, Employment/Job Training, Civic & Public Affairs-General, Law & Justice, Legal Aid, Municipalities/Towns, Philanthropic Organizations, Professional & Trade Associations, Public Policy, Rural Affairs, Urban & Community Affairs
Education: Business Education, Colleges & Universities, Community & Junior Colleges, Education Associations, Education Funds, Engineering/Technological Education, Education-General, Journalism/Media Education, Legal Education, Medical Education, Private Education (Precollege), Religious Education, Science/Mathematics Education, Secondary Education (Public), Student Aid, Vocational & Technical Education
Environment: Resource Conservation
Health: Alzheimers Disease, Cancer, Children's Health/Hospitals, Clinics/Medical Centers, Emergency/Ambulance Services, Health Organizations, Hospitals
International: Foreign Arts Organizations, Human Rights
Religion: Religious Organizations, Religious Welfare
Social Services: Animal Protection, Child Abuse, Child Welfare, Community Centers, Community Service Organizations, People with Disabilities, Recreation & Athletics, Scouts, Shelters/Homelessness, United Funds/United Ways, YMCA/YWCA/YMHA/YWHA, Youth Organizations

Contributions Analysis

Giving Priorities: Supports education, including journalism education, community and civic organizations, leadership development programs, youth organizations, and capital campaigns.
Arts & Humanities: 7%. Primarily for the literary arts.
Civic & Public Affairs: 47%. Support for a community foundation, philanthropic organizations, public policy groups, and civil rights causes.
Education: 21%. Colleges and universities, medical education, public and private secondary education, and vocational education.
Environment: Less than 1%. Conservation causes.
Health: 4%. Supports children's health and emergency services.
Social Services: 21%. Community centers, YM/YWCAs, scouting, child welfare, and youth organizations.

Application Procedures

Initial Contact: There is no specific application form.
Deadlines: None.

Corporate Officials

William A. Herman, III: secretary, treasurer, director B Augusta, GA 1938. ED University of Georgia (1963). PRIM CORP EMPL secretary, treasurer, director: Morris Communications Corp. CORP AFFIL secretary, treasurer, director: Southeastern Newspaper Corp.; secretary, treasurer, director: Stauffer Communications Inc.; secretary, treasurer, director: Mill Haven Co. Inc.; secretary, treasurer, director: Shivers Trading Operating Co.; secretary, treasurer, director: Azalea Development Co.; treasurer: Broadcaster Press Inc.; secretary, treasurer, director: Athens Newspapers Inc. CLUB AFFIL Knights of Columbus.
William Shivers Morris, III: founder, chairman, chief executive officer, director B Augusta, GA 1934. ED University of Georgia AB (1956). PRIM CORP EMPL founder, chairman, chief executive officer, director: Morris Communications Corp. CORP AFFIL chairman, chief executive officer: Southwest Newspapers Corp.; chairman: Stauffer Communications Inc.; director: Southern Co. Inc.; chief executive officer: Shivers Trading & Operating Co.; chairman, chief executive officer: Southeastern Newspaper Corp.; director: Georgia Power Co.; chairman, chief executive officer: North America Publs Inc.; chairman, chief executive officer: Florida Publishing Co.; publ, chairman, chief executive officer: Augusta Chronicle; chairman: Broadcaster Press Inc.; chairman, chief executive officer: Athens Newspapers Co. NONPR AFFIL member: Southeastern Newspaper Publisher's Association; member: Southern Newspaper Publishers Association; member: International Press Institute; member: American Newspaper Publishers Association; trustee: Augusta College Foundation. CLUB AFFIL University Club; Pinnacle Club; Commerce Club; Oglethorpe Club.
William Shivers Morris, IV: president, director B 1938. PRIM CORP EMPL president, director: Morris Communications Corp. CORP AFFIL president: Southeastern Newspapers Corp.; president: Stauffer Communications Inc.; president: Shivers Trading & Operating Co.; president: Athens Newspapers Inc.; president: Broadcaster Press Inc.

Foundation Officials

Dawn Goossen: trustee

William Shivers Morris, IV: trustee (see above)

William Shivers Morris, III: trustee (see above)

John H. Stauffer: trustee B Arkansas City, KS 1928. ED University of Kansas BS (1949). PRIM CORP EMPL director: Morris Communications Corp. CORP AFFIL chairman: Topeka-Capital Journal; director: Mercantile Bank Topeka. NONPR AFFIL member: Top Tower; member: Topeka Chamber of Commerce; member: Phi Delta Theta; member: Kansas City Chamber of Commerce; member: Kansas Press Association; member: Inland Press Association. CLUB AFFIL Topeka Country Club.

Stanley Howard Stauffer: chairman B Peabody, KS 1920. ED University of Kansas AB (1942). PRIM CORP EMPL director: Topeka/Shawnee County Development Corp. NONPR AFFIL trustee: Washburn University Endowment Association; trustee: William Allen White Foundation; chairman: Stauffer Communications Foundation; member: Phi Delta Theta; member: Sigma Delta Chi; trustee: Menninger Foundation; trustee: Midwest Research Institute; member: Kansas University Alumni Association; member: Masons; member: Kansas Chamber of Commerce & Industry; member: Kansas Press Association; member: Inland Daily Press Association; member: Air Force Association; member: Defense Orientation Conference Association. CLUB AFFIL Top Tower Club; Topeka Country Club; Garden of Gods Club; La Quinta Country Club.

Grants Analysis

Disclosure Period: calendar year ending 1996
Total Grants: $160,084
Number of Grants: 40
Average Grant: $4,002
Highest Grant: $62,500
Typical Range: $300 to $10,000

Recent Grants

Note: Grants derived from 1996 Form 990.

Arts & Humanities

10,000	Inland Press Foundation, Park Ridge, IL
2,000	Mark Twain Sonnenburg Building

Civic & Public Affairs

62,500	Kansas City Community Foundation, Kansas City, MO
5,000	Kansas Newspaper Foundation, KS
2,000	Dodge City Community Foundation, Dodge City, KS
2,000	Pittsburg Chamber of Commerce, Pittsburg, KS
1,666	Mariucci Lodge
750	Advertising Council, New York, NY
750	Reporters Committee for Freedom of the Press, Arlington, VA

Education

10,000	Kansas University Campaign, Lawrence, KS
5,000	Pittsburg State Tech Center, Pittsburg, KS
2,500	Stormont Vail Foundation, Topeka, KS
2,500	Yankton High School Summit Center, Yankton, SD
2,500	Yankton Technical Education Program
2,000	Washburn Convocation Center, Topeka, KS
1,900	Kansas State University Foundation, Manhattan, KS
1,500	St. Gregory's College, Shawnee, OK
1,000	Junior Achievement
1,000	St. Lawrence Campus Center
1,000	Topeka High School, Topeka, KS
1,000	University of Kansas Audio Reader Network, Lawrence, KS
500	Sterling College, Sterling, KS
200	Kansas State University Foundation, Manhattan, KS
160	University of Oklahoma, Norman, OK
125	Hays State University
100	Central Missouri State University, Warrensburg, MO
100	Pomona College, Pomona, CA

Environment

1,250	Nature Conservancy

Health

5,000	Capper Foundation for Crippled Children, Topeka, KS
750	Clark County Emergency Medical Services

Social Services

5,000	Medal Arena
5,000	YMCA, Kansas City, MO
5,000	YMCA Grand Island
4,000	Girl Scouts of America Kaw Valley Council
3,500	Topeka Capitals Baseball Team, Topeka, KS
3,333	Boy Scouts of America Jayhawk Council, KS
3,000	Doorstep, Topeka, KS
2,500	Kids Voting, Tempe, AZ
1,000	Boys Club of Oak Ridge, Oak Ridge, TN
1,000	Hillsdale Youth Baseball Association

MORRISON KNUDSEN CORP.

Company Contact

Boise, ID
Web: http://www.mk.com

Company Description

Employees: 8,200
SIC(s): 1081 Metal Mining Services, 1241 Coal Mining Services, 1541 Industrial Buildings & Warehouses, 6719 Holding Companies Nec.

Operating Locations

Australia; Canada; Indonesia; New Zealand

Nonmonetary Support

Type: Donated Equipment; In-kind Services; Loaned Employees; Loaned Executives

Morrison Knudsen Corp. Foundation, Inc.

Giving Contact

Marlene Puckett, Administrator, Director, Secretary
Morrison Knudsen Corp. Foundation, Inc.
PO Box 73
Boise, ID 83729
Phone: (208)386-8100

Description

EIN: 826005410
Organization Type: Corporate Foundation
Giving Locations: ID nationally; operating locations.
Grant Types: Employee Matching Gifts.
Note: Employee matching gift ratio: .5 to 1 up to $1,000 annually for educational institutions.

Giving Philosophy

'In 1991, the Foundation expanded its mission to share MK's success not only with needy employees but also with the impoverished in communities where MK conducts business or has business opportunities.' Morrison Knudsen Corporation Foundation brochure

Financial Summary

Total Giving: $350,000 (1996); $426,488 (1995); $670,254 (1994). Note: Contributes through foundation only.
Assets: $6,259,355 (1996); $6,372,190 (1995); $6,701,568 (1994)
Gifts Received: $150 (1996); $100 (1991)

Typical Recipients

Arts & Humanities: Arts Centers, Arts Festivals, Arts Funds, Community Arts, Ethnic & Folk Arts, History & Archaeology, Libraries, Museums/Galleries, Music, Opera, Performing Arts, Public Broadcasting, Theater
Civic & Public Affairs: African American Affairs, Business/Free Enterprise, Civil Rights, Community Foundations, Economic Development, Civic & Public Affairs-General, Hispanic Affairs, Housing, Legal Aid, Native American Affairs, Parades/Festivals, Philanthropic Organizations, Professional & Trade Associations, Public Policy, Safety, Urban & Community Affairs, Women's Affairs, Zoos/Aquariums
Education: Arts/Humanities Education, Business Education, Colleges & Universities, Education Funds, Education Reform, Engineering/Technological Education, Education-General, Minority Education, Private Education (Precollege), Public Education (Precollege), Secondary Education (Private), Student Aid
Environment: Environment-General, Resource Conservation, Wildlife Protection
Health: Children's Health/Hospitals, Emergency/Ambulance Services, Health Organizations, Long-Term Care, Medical Rehabilitation, Multiple Sclerosis, Public Health, Single-Disease Health Associations
International: Foreign Educational Institutions, International Relations, International Relief Efforts
Religion: Jewish Causes, Religious Organizations, Religious Welfare
Science: Science Museums
Social Services: Animal Protection, At-Risk Youth, Child Welfare, Community Centers, Community Service Organizations, Day Care, Domestic Violence, Family Services, People with Disabilities, Recreation & Athletics, Scouts, United Funds/United Ways, YMCA/YWCA/YMHA/YWHA, Youth Organizations

Application Procedures

Initial Contact: written request no longer than four pages
Application Requirements: activities of the applying organization, specific amount requested, outline of how grant would be used, proof of 501(c)(3) status, and prescribed financial statement
Deadlines: None.
Review Process: proposals reviewed at regular board meetings
Evaluative Criteria: individuals and families requesting aid live in the city where company has presence, and are classified as needy individuals; organizations must have 501(c)(3) status; importance of organization to employees; participation of employees in organization; impact gift will have; and history of giving to organization by foundation and employees

Restrictions

The foundation is unable to provide grants for business purposes, education such as tuition, legal fees, income taxes, etc.

They are unable to duplicate any services that may be available within the community, and may suggest to applicants other services for which they are qualified.

Additional Information

When approved, limited assistance is distributed as a one-time gift, for which payments are made to service providers or vendors, not given directly to the applicant.

Foundation Officials

Stephen G. Hanks: president B 1951. ED Brigham Young University BS (1974); University of Utah MBA

(1975); University of Idaho JD (1978). PRIM CORP EMPL executive vice president, chief legal officer: Morrison-Knudsen Corp. CORP AFFIL officer: Morrison Knudsen Corp. Delaware Corp.; secretary: Morrison Knudsen Corp. Ohio Corp.; secretary: American Piping Boiler Co.
Marlene Puckett: administrator, secretary, director
John Zabala: treasurer

Grants Analysis

Disclosure Period: calendar year ending 1996
Total Grants: $396,375
Number of Grants: 461
Average Grant: $860
Highest Grant: $15,000
Typical Range: $50 to $4,100

Recent Grants

Note: Grants derived from 1996 Form 990.

Arts & Humanities

2,500 Boise Philharmonic, Boise, ID -- for Head Start Informances
2,500 Chicago Symphony Orchestra, Chicago, IL
2,500 IDA Shakespeare Festival, Boise, ID
1,003 Boise State University Radio Network, Boise, ID
1,000 Chicago Children's Museum, Chicago, IL
1,000 Colorado Business Committee for the Arts, Denver, CO

Civic & Public Affairs

5,000 Habitat for Humanity, Cleveland, OH
2,500 CEO Foundation, San Antonio, TX
2,000 Habitat for Humanity, Las Vegas, NV
1,500 Lincoln Park Zoological Society, Chicago, IL
1,274 IDA Women's Fitness, Boise, ID
1,100 IDA Business Week, Boise, ID
1,050 League of United Latin American Citizens, San Antonio, TX
1,000 American Indian Science and Engineering Society, Boulder, CO
1,000 IDA Zoological Society, Boise, ID

Education

15,000 Athens College, New York, NY
7,500 Boston College, Chestnut Hill, MA
3,000 Boise Public Schools Education Foundation, Boise, ID -- for Partners in Excellence program
2,000 United Negro College Fund, Cleveland, OH
2,000 University of Akron, Akron, OH
2,000 University of Pittsburgh, Pittsburgh, PA
1,500 Princeton University, Princeton, NJ
1,000 Colorado Scholarship Coalition, Denver, CO
1,000 Holy Family School, Tulsa, OK
1,000 Massachusetts Institute of Technology, Cambridge, MA
1,000 Mesa State College, Grand Junction, CO
1,000 Union College, Barbourville, KY
1,000 University of Pittsburgh, Pittsburgh, PA

Environment

1,000 Nature Conservancy, Boise, ID

Health

5,000 Terry Reilly Health Services, Boise, ID -- for Boise Homeless Clinic
3,300 Healthwise
1,750 American Sickle Cell Anemia Association, Cleveland, OH

International

2,500 American University in Cairo, Cairo, Egypt

Religion

3,800 Salvation Army, Boise, ID
3,000 Congregation Ahavath Beth Israel
2,816 St. Alphonsus Festival of Trees
1,200 Congregation Ahavath Beth Israel
1,000 St. Luke's RMC Tennis Challenge

Science

5,000 Discovery Center of IDA, Boise, ID

Social Services

6,712 United Way, Cleveland, OH
5,655 United Way Ada County, Boise, ID
5,334 Girl Scouts of America Silver Sage Chapter
5,000 Boy Scouts of America, Boise, ID
3,171 YWCA, Boise, ID -- for Women and Children's Crisis Center
3,000 Fundsy, Boise, ID
2,500 Homeward Bound -- for Boise Neighborhood Housing
2,000 Rocky Canyon Sailtoads -- support Race to Robie Creek
1,500 Off the Street Club, Chicago, IL
1,000 St. Louis ARC, Saint Louis, MO
1,000 YMCA, Boise, ID -- for Barber to Boise Run, Christmas Run

MORTON INTERNATIONAL INC.

Company Contact

Chicago, IL
Web: http://www.mortonintl.com/comm/overcomm.htm

Company Description

Profit: US$294,100,000
Employees: 14,100
SIC(s): 2891 Adhesives & Sealants, 2899 Chemical Preparations Nec, 3714 Motor Vehicle Parts & Accessories.
Parent Company: Rohm & Haas Co., 100 Independence Mall West, Philadelphia, PA, United States

Nonmonetary Support

Value: $30,000 (1996); $25,000 (1994); $95,000 (1992)
Type: Donated Equipment
Note: Co. donates office furniture.

Giving Contact

Judy E. Schaefer, Community Relations Manager
Morton International Inc.
100 N Riverside Plz.
Chicago, IL 60606-1596
Phone: (312)807-2103
Fax: (312)807-2039
Email: jschaefer@morton.com

Description

Organization Type: Corporate Giving Program
Giving Locations: IL: Chicago metropolitan area, near company's headquarters
Grant Types: Emergency, Employee Matching Gifts, General Support.

Giving Philosophy

'Morton International works to strengthen the community and business environment through its contributions program. The company supports a variety of organizations through financial grants and gifts-in-kind. The organizations receiving funding are very diverse, and address issues that fall in the broader categories of health and welfare, education, culture, and civic concerns.' *General Guidelines*

Financial Summary

Total Giving: $1,415,900 (fiscal year ending June 30, 1999); $1,220,043 (fiscal 1998); $1,600,000 (fiscal 1997). Note: Contributes through corporate direct giving program only.

Typical Recipients

Arts & Humanities: Arts Institutes, Museums/Galleries, Opera, Performing Arts, Public Broadcasting
Civic & Public Affairs: Women's Affairs, Zoos/Aquariums
Education: Colleges & Universities, Minority Education
Health: Clinics/Medical Centers, Hospitals
Social Services: Emergency Relief, People with Disabilities, United Funds/United Ways, Youth Organizations

Contributions Analysis

Giving Priorities: United Way in company operating areas, scientific research and education, and symphony orchestras and operas.
Arts & Humanities: About 20%. Symphony orchestras and operas receive most support. Interests also include public broadcasting, museums, and historic restoration. Much of arts funding is through employee matching gifts program.
Civic & Public Affairs: 5% to 10%. Supports the Executive Service Corps and other community organizations.
Education: About 20%. Majority of funds supports scientific research and education. Also sponsors an employee matching gifts program. Other interests include education funds, international exchange programs; and economic, special, and minority education. Also supports National Merit Scholarship Awards.
Health: About 50%. United Ways in operating locations generally receive the most support. Also funds hospitals, with emphasis on employee matching gifts program.

Application Procedures

Initial Contact: call or write for application, then full proposal
Application Requirements: organization's history, mission, and objectives; description of current programs, activities, and major achievements; description of formal and informal associations with other organizations; description of the purpose of the contribution request; proof of 501(c)(3) status; audited financial statement for the last fiscal year; itemization of use of requested funds; verification that the organization is not a private foundation under 509(a); current year's operating budget including both projected expenses and revenues; and a completed contributions application
Deadlines: None, but budget is determined by February 28 for fiscal year beginning July 1
Review Process: each business unit submits annual contributions budget to community relations department for approval; committee reviews all requests for compliance with guidelines and advises business unit of approval or disapproval of its requests
Evaluative Criteria: large proportion of support goes to company location communities
Notes: The company recommends sending these helpful, but optional, additions to the proposal: an annual report; a list of current board members with related employment affiliation; and a staff composition.

Restrictions

Does not support individuals, political organizations, hospitals for capital or operating funds, religious organizations unless for nonsectarian activities, or conferences or seminars. Grants generally are not made to United Way-supported organizations. Multiyear commitments are also generally not made.

Additional Information

Publications: Guidelines; Application

Corporate Officials

Nancy A. Hobor: vice president communications & investor relations B Chicago, IL 1946. ED University of Chicago (1968); Northwestern University (1977). PRIM CORP EMPL vice president communications & investor relations: Morton International Inc. NONPR AFFIL adjunct professor: Northwestern University Medill School Journalism; member: Public Relations Seminar; member: Arthur Page Society; director: National Investor Relations Institute.

William E. Johnston, Junior: president, chief operating officer, director B Gary, IN 1940. ED Saint Joseph's College BA (1963); University of Chicago MBA (1973). PRIM CORP EMPL president, chief operating officer, director: Morton International Inc. ADD CORP EMPL president: Morton International Ltd. (Canada); president, director: Morton International Ltd. (Japan). CORP AFFIL director: Morton Japan Ltd.; director: NV Morton International SA; vice president finance, treasurer, director: Morton International SA de CV; director: Morton International SPA; director: Morton International Ltd.; director: Morton International SA; director: Morton International GmbH; director: Inagua Transports Inc.; director: Morfecor California; director: Ecuatoriana de Sal Y Productos Quimicos California; chairman: Canadian Salt Co. Ltd.; director: CVD Inc.; director: Bee Chemical Co.

Christopher K. Julsrud: vice president human resources B Chicago, IL 1947. ED Loyola University (1969). PRIM CORP EMPL vice president human resources: Morton International Inc.

S. Jay Stewart: chairman, chief executive officer, director B Pineville, WV 1938. ED University of Cincinnati BSChE (1961); West Virginia University MBA (1966). PRIM CORP EMPL chairman, chief executive officer, director: Morton International Inc. CORP AFFIL member: Household International Inc. NONPR AFFIL trustee: Rush-Presbyterian-Saint Lukes Medical Center; member executive committee: Society Chemical Industry; trustee: Museum Science & Industry; member: Northwestern University Associates; director: Chemical Manufacturers Association; member: Commerical Development Association; member: Chem Marketing Association; member: American Chemical Society; member: American Institute Chemical Engineers. CLUB AFFIL Commercial Club Chicago; Economic Club Chicago; Chicago Country Club.

Giving Program Officials

Nancy A. Hobor: vice president communications B Chicago, IL 1946. ED University of Chicago (1968); Northwestern University (1977). PRIM CORP EMPL vice president communications & investor relations: Morton International Inc. NONPR AFFIL adjunct professor: Northwestern University Medill School Journalism; member: Public Relations Seminar; member: Arthur Page Society; director: National Investor Relations Institute.

Judy E. Schaefer: community relations manager

Grants Analysis

Disclosure Period: fiscal year ending June 30, 1998
Total Grants: $1,220,043
Number of Grants: 75
Average Grant: $16,267
Highest Grant: $200,000
Typical Range: $5,000 to $20,000

Recent Grants

Note: Grants derived from fiscal 1993 grants list.

Health

1,000,000	Rush Presbyterian St. Luke's Medical Center, Chicago, IL

Motorola Inc.

Company Contact

1303 E. Algonquin Rd.
Schaumburg, IL 60196
Phone: (847)576-5000
Fax: (847)576-5372
Web: http://www.mot.com

Company Description

Acquired: General Instrument Corp. (2000).
Revenue: US$30,931,000,000 (1999)
Profit: US$962,000,000
Employees: 133,000 (1999)
Fortune Rank: 37, per FORTUNE Magazine's list of 500 Largest U.S. Corporations (1999).
FF 37
SIC(s): 3661 Telephone & Telegraph Apparatus, 3663 Radio & T.V. Communications Equipment, 3669 Communications Equipment Nec, 3694 Engine Electrical Equipment.

Operating Locations

Argentina: Motorola Argentina SA, Buenos Aires; Australia: Motorola Australia Pty. Ltd., Scoresby; Austria: High-Tech Nachrichtentechnische Anlagen GmbH, Vienna; Motorola Center Computersysteme GmbH, Vienna; Motorola GmbH, Vienna; Belgium: Motorola NV, Zaventem, Brabant; Brazil: Motorola Industrial Ltda., Jaguariuna; INO Servicos Especializados de Telecomunicaces Ltda., Sao Paulo; MCS Radio & Telefonia Ltda., Sao Paulo; Motorola do Brasil Ltda., Sao Paulo; Canada: Motorola Canada Ltd., Toronto; Chile: Buenaventura SA, Santiago; Telecom Celular SA, Santiago; Costa Rica: Motorola de Centroamerica SA, San Jose; Denmark: MDI Scandanavia AS, Brondby, Copenhagen; France: Motorola Electronique Automobile, AngersMaine-et-Loire; Motorola SA, Paris, Ville-de-Paris; Motorola Semiconducteurs SA, Toulouse, Haute Garonne; Germany: Motorola Betriebsfunk Berlin GmbH, Berlin; Motorola Electronic GmbH, Flensburg, Schleswig-Holstein; Motorola GmbH, Taunusstein, Hessen; Hong Kong: Hutchison Information Services Ltd., Admiralty; Motorola Aircommunications Ltd., Causeway Bay; Motorola Asia Pacific Ltd., Causeway Bay; Motorola Asia Ltd., Tai Po; Motorola Semiconductors Hong Kong Ltd., Tai Po; India: Motorola India Electronics Ltd., Bangalore; Motorola India Ltd., Bangalore; Ireland: Four Phase Overseas Corp., Cork; Motorola Ireland Ltd., Cork; TCS Insurance Co. of Ireland Ltd., Dublin; Motorola BV, Swords; Israel: Motorola South Israel Ltd., Arad; Motorola Israel Semiconductor Products Ltd., Herzliyya; Motorola Semiconductor Israel Ltd., Herzliyya; Beeper Communications Israel Ltd., Ramat Gan; Motorola Israel Information Systems Ltd., Ramat Gan; Motorola Communications Israel Ltd., Tel Aviv; Motorola Israel Ltd., Tel Aviv; Pele-Phone Communication Ltd., Tel Aviv; Italy: Motorola SpA, Assago, Lombardia; Japan: Tohoku Semiconductor Corp., Sendai, Miyagi; Nippon Motorola Ltd., Tokyo; Nippon Motorola Micro Electronics KK, Tokyo; Republic of Korea: Motorola Electronics & Communications, Kangnam-Gu, Seoul; Motorola Korea Ltd., Songdong-Gu; Mexico: Motorola de Mexico SA Div. Comunicaciones, Leon; Soluciones Celulares SA de CV, Matamoros; Motorola de Mexico SA, Zapopan; Malaysia: Motorola Electronics Sdn. Bhd., Penang, Pulau Pinang; Motorola Malaysia Sdn. Bhd., Petaling Jaya, Selangor; Motorola Semiconductor Sdn. Bhd., Seremban, Negeri Sembilan; Semiconductor Miniature Products (M) Sdn. Bhd., Seremban, Negeri Sembilan; Netherlands: Motorola BV, Best, Noord-Brabant; Motorola Finance BV, Rotterdam, Zuid-Holland; Norway: Motorola Norway AS, Oslo, Akershus; New Zealand: Motorola New Zealand Ltd., Mt. Wellington, Auckland; Pakistan: Pakistan Mobile Communications Pvt. Ltd., Islamabad; Philippines: Motorola Philippines, Paranaque, Manila; Portugal: Motorola Portugal Comunicacoes Lda., Alges, Lisboa; Singapore: Motorola Electronics Pte. Ltd., Singapore; Motorola South Asia Pte. Ltd., Singapore; Spain: Motorola Espana SA, Madrid; Telcel SA, Madrid; Sweden: Motorola AB, Solna, Stockholm; Switzerland: Motorola (Suisse) SA, Le Grand-Saconnex, Geneva; Thailand: Motorola (Thailand) Ltd., Prakanong, Bangkok; Taiwan: Motorola Electronics Taiwan Ltd., Chungli; United Kingdom: Communicate Ltd., Basingstoke, Hampshire; Motorola Ltd., Crawley, West Sussex; Venezuela: Motorola de Los Andes y del Caribe CA, Caracas

Corporate Sponsorship

Type: Arts & cultural events; Music & entertainment events; Sports events
Contact: Carrie Worley, Manager, Corporate Advertising & Promotions

Motorola Foundation

Giving Contact

Judy Adkins, Program Administrator
Motorola Foundation
1303 E Algonquin Rd.
Schaumburg, IL 60196
Phone: (847)576-7895
Fax: (847)576-3997

Alternate Contact

Garth Milne
Phone: (847)576-6200

Description

EIN: 366109323
Organization Type: Corporate Foundation
Giving Locations: headquarters community, plant locations, and to select national organizations.
Grant Types: Capital, Employee Matching Gifts, General Support, Multiyear/Continuing Support, Project, Scholarship.

Giving Philosophy

'Recognizing that reasonable support of charitable institutions is a requirement of good industrial citizenship, Motorola does, through its Foundation, support such activities on a selective basis and within budgeted amounts.' *General Principles, Motorola Foundation*

Financial Summary

Total Giving: $6,500,000 (1999 approx); $6,500,000 (1998 approx); $6,602,943 (1997). Note: Contributes through corporate direct giving program and foundation. 1997 Giving includes foundation ($4,202,776); matching gifts ($1,340,267); United Way ($1,059,900).
Assets: $20,394,151 (1997); $25,750,291 (1996); $12,381,622 (1993)
Gifts Received: $10,293,125 (1993); $5,107,670 (1992). Note: Contributions are received from Motorola, Inc.

Typical Recipients

Arts & Humanities: Arts Associations & Councils, Arts Funds, Arts Institutes, Dance, Ethnic & Folk Arts, Museums/Galleries, Music, Opera, Performing Arts, Public Broadcasting, Theater
Civic & Public Affairs: African American Affairs, Business/Free Enterprise, Civil Rights, Clubs, Economic Development, Economic Policy, Employment/Job Training, Housing, Law & Justice, Legal Aid, Nonprofit Management, Philanthropic Organizations, Professional & Trade Associations, Public Policy, Safety, Urban & Community Affairs, Women's Affairs, Zoos/Aquariums
Education: Agricultural Education, Business Education, Colleges & Universities, Community & Junior Colleges, Continuing Education, Economic Education, Education Associations, Education Funds, Engineering/Technological Education, Education-General, Literacy, Minority Education, Private Education

(Precollege), Public Education (Precollege), Science/Mathematics Education, Student Aid
Environment: Environment-General
Health: Emergency/Ambulance Services, Hospices, Hospitals, Single-Disease Health Associations
International: Foreign Educational Institutions, Health Care/Hospitals, International Affairs, International Organizations, International Relief Efforts
Religion: Religious Welfare
Science: Observatories & Planetariums, Science Exhibits & Fairs, Science Museums, Scientific Centers & Institutes
Social Services: Child Welfare, Community Service Organizations, Counseling, Crime Prevention, Food/Clothing Distribution, People with Disabilities, Recreation & Athletics, Senior Services, Shelters/Homelessness, Substance Abuse, United Funds/United Ways, Volunteer Services, YMCA/YWCA/YMHA/YWHA, Youth Organizations

Contributions Analysis

Giving Priorities: Colleges and universities in the areas of technology, business and engineering; united funds, community chests, and youth groups; business, free enterprise, and economic development; and the arts. Recognizing its position as a global enterprise, the company has begun directing contributions overseas. In 1996, company gave almost $1 million to foreign educational organizations and other interests. Focus currently is supporting high-technology colleges and universities, keeping contributions tied to company business.
Education: Supports engineering, technology, and science programs at universities; historically minority colleges and universities, based upon emphasis in engineering and science; programs providing technical assistance, research, and statistical information on the state of science and engineering education; strengthening science and mathematics education at the pre-college level; programs reaching traditionally under-represented groups in the areas of math, science, engineering, and business; pre-K programs; parental involvement in education programs; and educational programs that promote and support preserving the environment.
Health: Emphasis is placed on assistinghealth and human services delivery systems, primarily through support to local United Way organizations.

Application Procedures

Initial Contact: call or write for guidelines, then 2-page proposal
Application Requirements: cover letter, including brief a description of organization and proposed program, amount requested, organization name and contact information; narrative, including history and mission of the organization, population served, description of program and objectives, collaborative opportunities with other community based organization, strategies and activities or achievements of the organization in the past year, evaluation plan; financial information, including program budget detail, other sources of funding, amount requested, overall organization budget detail, most recent audited financial statement; proof of tax-exempt status
Deadlines: September 15 for national programs only; local operating location may have specific deadlines
Notes: National requests should be sent to the foundation; regional request should be sent to operating facility in area. Contact information is included in guidelines.

Restrictions

Foundation does not contribute to individuals; fraternal, veterans', labor, ethnic, athletic, or sectarian religious organizations; political or lobbying groups; endowment funds; films, videotapes, or radio promotions; fundraising events, conferences, or benefits, sponsorships, dinners, tickets, or goodwill advertising; national health organizations; disease-specific organizations; hospitals for specific programming or capital; capital fund drives of colleges or universities; trade schools; private foundations; or United Way member agencies.
Does not donate Motorola products or equipment.
Way member agencies.
Does not donate Motorola products or equipment.

Additional Information

Grants are made on an annual basis only with no renewals implied.
Publications: Guidelines

Corporate Officials

Albert R. Brashear: corp. vice president, director corporate communications PRIM CORP EMPL corp. vice president, director corporate communications: Motorola Inc.
Christopher B. Galvin: president, chief executive officer, director B 1951. ED Northwestern University BA; Northwestern University Kellogg Graduate School of Management MBA (1977). PRIM CORP EMPL president, chief executive officer, director: Motorola Inc. CORP AFFIL chief executive officer: Indala Corp.; president: Motorola de Puerto Rico Inc.
Kenneth James Johnson: vice president, controller, director B Chicago, IL 1935. ED University of Illinois BS (1958); University of Chicago MBA (1970). PRIM CORP EMPL vice president, controller, director: Motorola Inc. CORP AFFIL controller: Motorola Communication International. NONPR AFFIL member: Financial Executives Institute; member: Institute of Management Accountants; member: American Management Association.
Carl F. Koenemann: chief financial officer, executive vice president ED DePaul University BS (1964); Loyola University Chicago MBA (1969). PRIM CORP EMPL chief financial officer, executive vice president: Motorola Inc. CORP AFFIL vice president: Motorola Cellular Service Inc.; chief financial officer, director: Motorola Communication & Electricity; chief financial officer: Indala Corp.
Garth Leroy Milne: senior vice president, treasurer B Saint George, UT 1942. ED University of Utah BS (1966); Harvard University MBA (1968). PRIM CORP EMPL senior vice president, treasurer: Motorola Inc.
John Francis Mitchell: vice chairman, director B Chicago, IL 1928. ED Illinois Institute of Technology BS (1950). PRIM CORP EMPL vice chairman, director: Motorola Inc.

Foundation Officials

Albert R. Brashear: director public affairs (see above)
Christopher B. Galvin: director (see above)
Roberta Gutman: program administrator

Grants Analysis

Disclosure Period: calendar year ending 1997
Total Grants: $4,202,776*
Number of Grants: 523
Average Grant: $8,036
Highest Grant: $193,440
Typical Range: $1,000 to $15,000
***Note:** Giving excludes matching gifts; United Way.

Recent Grants

Note: Grants derived from 1997 Form 990.

Arts & Humanities

66,000	Chicago Symphony Orchestra, Chicago, IL

Civic & Public Affairs

75,000	National Council on Radiation Protection and Measurements, Bethesda, MD
50,000	National Alliance of Business, Washington, DC
38,000	National Urban League, New York, NY
25,000	Chicago Manufacturing Center, Chicago, IL
25,000	Clearbrook Center Foundation, Rolling Meadows, IL
25,000	Neighborhood Longhorns Program, Austin, TX
20,768	League of Women Voters of Illinois, Chicago, IL

Education

193,440	National Merit Scholarship Corporation, Evanston, IL
100,000	Arizona State University Foundation, Tempe, AZ
60,000	National Consortium for Graduate Degrees for Minorities in Engineering, Notre Dame, IN
52,500	Junior Achievement, Chicago, IL
50,000	Gallaudet University, Washington, DC
40,000	Chicago Public Schools, Chicago, IL
35,000	Promat College
25,000	Northeastern University, Boston, MA
25,000	United Negro College Fund, Chicago, IL
25,000	University of Michigan, Ann Arbor, MI
25,000	William Rainey Harper Educational Foundation, Palatine, IL
22,000	University of Illinois Foundation, Urbana, IL
20,000	Junior Achievement, Chicago, IL
20,000	Junior Achievement, Chicago, IL
20,000	National Academy of Engineering, Washington, DC
20,000	Roosevelt University, Chicago, IL
20,000	University of California Berkeley, Berkeley, CA
20,000	University of Connecticut Foundation, Storrs, CT
20,000	University of Michigan Business School, Ann Arbor, MI

International

85,000	Universidad del Valle de Mexico, Naucalpan, ME, Mexico
85,000	Universidad del Valle de Mexico, Naucalpan, ME, Mexico
55,000	China Youth Development Foundation, Beijing, People's Republic of China
55,000	China Youth Development Foundation, Beijing, People's Republic of China
45,000	Fundacion Ninos de los Andes, Bogota, Colombia
45,000	Fundacion Ninos de los Andes, Bogota, Colombia
45,000	Hertfordshire Multiple Sclerosis Therapy Centre, Letchworth, England
45,000	Hertfordshire Multiple Sclerosis Therapy Centre, Letchworth, England
40,000	Rewrite School
40,000	Rewrite School
30,000	EEPG CEL Amancio Bueno T400, Jaguarinho, MI, Brazil
30,000	EEPG CEL Amancio Bueno T400, Jaguarinna, MI, Brazil
30,000	EEPSG Professor Celso Henrique Tozzi, Sao Paulo, SP, Brazil
30,000	EEPSG Professor Celso Henrique Tozzi, Sao Paulo, SP, Brazil
25,000	Universidad del Valle de Mexico, Naucalpan, ME, Mexico
25,000	Universidad del Valle de Mexico, Naucalpan, ME, Mexico
24,000	Universiti Teknologi Malaysia, Kuala Lumpur, Malaysia
24,000	Universiti Teknologi Malaysia, Kuala Lumpur, Malaysia
20,000	Czech Technical University, Czech Republic
20,000	Czech Technical University, Czech Republic
20,000	ISTEC Latin American Institute, Albuquerque, NM
20,000	ISTEC Latin American Institute, Albuquerque, NM

Science

50,000	Campaign for Physics, College Park, MD

30,000 Field Museum of Natural History, Chicago, IL

Social Services

425,000 United Way Crusade of Mercy, Chicago, IL
275,000 Valley of the Sun United Way, Phoenix, AZ
90,000 United Way Capital Area, Austin, TX
73,400 Volunteer Grants Program
55,000 United Way Lake County, Mentor, OH
50,000 United Way McHenry County, Crystal Lake, IL
50,000 United Way Palm Beach County, West Palm Beach, FL
25,000 National Crime Prevention Council, Washington, DC
25,000 United Way Broward County, Fort Lauderdale, FL
20,000 Valley of the Sun United Way, Phoenix, AZ

MTD PRODUCTS INC.

Company Contact

Cleveland, OH
Web: http://www.mtdproducts.com

Company Description

Employees: 5,500
SIC(s): 3469 Metal Stampings Nec, 3524 Lawn & Garden Equipment, 3544 Special Dies, Tools, Jigs & Fixtures, 6141 Personal Credit Institutions.

The Jochum-Moll Foundation

Giving Contact

Chris Proto, Executive Administrator
The Jochum-Moll Foundation
PO Box 368022
Cleveland, OH 44136-9722
Phone: (330)225-2600
Fax: (330)225-0896

Description

EIN: 346538304
Organization Type: Corporate Foundation. Supports preselected organizations only.
Giving Locations: OH
Grant Types: General Support.

Financial Summary

Total Giving: $1,533,000 (fiscal year ending July 31, 1998); $1,089,500 (fiscal 1997); $1,126,284 (fiscal 1996). Note: Contributes through foundation only.
Giving Analysis: Giving for fiscal 1996 includes: foundation grants to United Way ($55,000); fiscal 1997: foundation scholarships ($41,500); foundation grants to United Way ($5,000)
Assets: $37,887,266 (fiscal 1998); $36,583,946 (fiscal 1997); $29,435,730 (fiscal 1996)
Gifts Received: $106,503 (fiscal 1998); $15,927 (fiscal 1997); $192,978 (fiscal 1996). Note: Contributions are received from MTD Products Inc., AGRI-FAB, and E. P. Barrus, Ltd.

Typical Recipients

Arts & Humanities: Libraries, Literary Arts, Museums/Galleries, Music, Performing Arts, Theater
Civic & Public Affairs: Botanical Gardens/Parks, Community Foundations, Employment/Job Training, Housing, Law & Justice, Urban & Community Affairs, Zoos/Aquariums
Education: Agricultural Education, Business Education, Colleges & Universities, Education Associations, Education Funds, Engineering/Technological Education, Education-General, Minority Education, Preschool Education, Private Education (Precollege), Religious Education, Secondary Education (Private)
Environment: Environment-General
Health: Cancer, Clinics/Medical Centers, Diabetes, Health Organizations, Hospitals, Research/Studies Institutes
International: International Relief Efforts, Missionary/Religious Activities
Religion: Bible Study/Translation, Churches, Religious Organizations, Religious Welfare
Science: Science Museums, Scientific Centers & Institutes, Scientific Research
Social Services: Child Welfare, Community Service Organizations, Day Care, Food/Clothing Distribution, People with Disabilities, Recreation & Athletics, Scouts, Shelters/Homelessness, United Funds/United Ways, YMCA/YWCA/YMHA/YWHA, Youth Organizations

Contributions Analysis

Giving Priorities: Priorities include education, religious organizations, and science. Also supports social services, health, civic concerns, and the arts.
Arts & Humanities: 1%. Funds an art museum and music.
Civic & Public Affairs: 6%. Supports law enforcement and civic institutions.
Education: 46%. Supports colleges, religious education, secondary schools, education funds, minority and private education.
Health: 8%. Funding supports hosptials and medical centers.
Religion: 11%. Funds religious organizations and churches.
Science: 20%. Supports the Cleveland Camp Work Wear project.
Social Services: 8%. Funds youth activities and the United Way.
Note: Total contributions in fiscal 1998.

Corporate Officials

David J. Hessler: president, partner B 1943. ED Valparaiso University BA (1965); Valparaiso University JD (1968). PRIM CORP EMPL president, partner: Wegman, Hessler, Vanderburg. CORP AFFIL secretary: Shiloh Corp.; secretary: Valley City Steel Co.; secretary: Sectional Stamping Inc.; secretary: MTD Products Inc.; secretary: Sectional Die Co.; director: Carnegie Body Co.; secretary: EFCO Inc.; chairman: Bird Technologies Group Inc.; secretary: Arnold Distributors Inc.; chairman: Bird Electronic Corp.

Foundation Officials

David J. Hessler: secretary, trustee (see above)
Emil Jochum: trustee PRIM CORP EMPL vice president: MTD Products.
Curtis E. Moll: treasurer, trustee B 1939. ED Ohio Wesleyan University (1961); Southern Methodist University (1963). PRIM CORP EMPL chairman, chief executive officer, director: MTD Products Inc. CORP AFFIL director: Valley City Steel Co.; director: Society National Bank; director: Standard Products Co.; director: Key Bank NA; director: Sherwin-Williams Co.; chairman, director: Arnold Distributors Inc.; director: Cub Cadet Corp. NONPR AFFIL trustee: Goodwill Industries.
Darrell Moll: trustee
Chris Proto: executive administrator

Grants Analysis

Disclosure Period: fiscal year ending July 31, 1998
Total Grants: $1,459,000*
Number of Grants: 57
Average Grant: $18,911*
Highest Grant: $400,000
Typical Range: $2,500 to $20,000
***Note:** Giving excludes United Way. Average grant figure excludes highest grant.

Recent Grants

Note: Grants derived from 1998 Form 990.

Arts & Humanities

10,000 Cleveland Orchestra, Cleveland, OH -- General, Unrestricted
5,000 Cleveland Museum of Art, Cleveland, OH -- General, Unrestricted
5,000 Ohio Boy's Choir, Parma, OH -- General, Unrestricted

Civic & Public Affairs

50,000 Job and Workforce Initiative, Cleveland, OH -- Jobs & Workforce Initiative
10,000 City of Martin - Parks & Recreation, Martin, TN -- One-Time Event
10,000 Indianola Community Fund, Indianola, MS -- General, Unrestricted
7,500 Northeast Ohio Roundtable, Solon, OH -- General, Unrestricted
5,000 Law Enforcement Foundation, Dublin, OH -- D.A.R.E. Program
2,500 Work in Northern Ohio Council, Independence, OH -- General, Unrestricted
2,000 Cleveland Zoological Society, Cleveland, OH -- General, Unrestricted

Education

400,000 Valparaiso University, Valparaiso, IN -- General, Unrestricted
135,000 Baldwin-Wallace College, Berea, OH -- Neal Malicky Building
60,000 Lutheran High School Association, Rocky River, OH -- General, Non-Restricted
50,000 David N. Myers College, Cleveland, OH -- 5 Year - 250,000 Pledge
15,000 Moody Bible Institute W.C.R.F., Bayton Beach, FL -- General, Unrestricted
10,000 Methodist Theological School, Delaware, OH -- Operations
10,000 Ohio Weselyan, Delaware, OH -- Christian Coalition
6,000 Mississippi Foundation of Independent College, Jackson, MS -- General, Non-Restricted
6,000 University of Tennessee, Martin, TN -- 3,000 to Bus. School and 3,000 to Engineering
5,000 Cleveland State University, Cleveland, OH -- Society of Automotive Engineers Project
5,000 Middleburg Early Education, Cleveland, OH -- General, Unrestricted
3,000 Ohio Foundation of Independent Colleges, Columbus, OH -- General, Non-Restricted
3,000 United Negro College Fund, Cleveland, OH -- Christian Coalition
2,000 Association for Excellence in Education, Laurel, MS -- General, Unrestricted

Health

100,000 The Cleveland Clinic, Cleveland, OH -- Capital Campaign Fund
15,000 Fairview Health System, Cleveland, OH -- Parish Nurse Program
2,000 Alpha House, Tupelo, Tupelo, MS -- General, Unrestricted

Religion

100,000 City Mission, The, Cleveland, OH -- 50,000 Camps 50,000 Operations
20,000 Salvation Army, Cleveland, OH -- General, Unrestricted
10,000 Baddour Memorial Center, Memphis, TN -- General, Unrestricted
10,000 Lutheran Chaplaincy Service, Cleveland, OH -- General, Unrestricted
5,000 Concert of Prayer, Wheaton, IL -- General, Unrestricted
5,000 Fellowship of Christian Athletes, Cleveland, OH -- General, Unrestricted

5,000 Good Samaritan Health Service, Tupelo, MS -- General, Unrestricted
5,000 Intervarsity, Madison, WI -- General, Unrestricted
4,000 Youth for Christ, Berea, OH -- General, Unrestricted
3,000 St. Philip's Church, Cleveland, OH -- General, Unrestricted
2,500 Immaculate Conception Church of Indianola, Miss, Indianola, MS -- General, Unrestricted

Science
200,000 Camp - Work Wear Project, Cleveland, OH -- Work Wear Project
100,000 Cleveland Advanced Manufacturing Program, Cleveland, OH -- Camp Work Wear Project

Social Services
74,000 United Way Services, Cleveland, OH -- Cuyahoga County, Medina County, Tupelo, MS
20,000 Goodwill Industries, Cleveland, OH -- Operations
10,000 Kindernest Child Development Center, Williard, OH -- General, Unrestricted
5,000 Boy Scouts of America - Tupelo Chapter, Tupelo, MS -- General, Unrestricted
5,000 May Dugan West Side Multi-Service Center, Cleveland, OH -- General, Unrestricted
2,000 Boy Scouts of America, Cleveland, OH -- Cleveland Area
2,000 Boy Scouts of America - Indianola Chapter, Indianola, MS -- General, Unrestricted
2,000 Coats for Kids, Cleveland, OH -- General, Unrestricted
1,500 Ridgewood Y.M.C.A., Parma, OH -- General, Unrestricted
1,500 Y.M.C.A. Greater Cleveland, Cleveland, OH -- General, Unrestricted

MTS Systems Corp.

Company Contact
Eden Prairie, MN

Company Description
Employees: 1,725
SIC(s): 3625 Relays & Industrial Controls, 3823 Process Control Instruments, 3829 Measuring & Controlling Devices Nec.

Nonmonetary Support
Type: Donated Equipment

Giving Contact
Donna Barker, Contributions Coordinator
14000 Technology Dr.
Eden Prairie, MN 55344
Phone: (612)937-4000
Fax: (612)937-4101
Email: donna.barker@mts.com

Description
Organization Type: Corporate Giving Program. Supports preselected organizations only.
Giving Locations: MN: Minneapolis
Grant Types: Employee Matching Gifts, Fellowship, General Support, Multiyear/Continuing Support, Professorship, Project, Scholarship.

Financial Summary
Total Giving: $210,000 (1998); $200,000 (1997); $150,000 (1996)

Typical Recipients
Civic & Public Affairs: Civic & Public Affairs-General
Education: Business Education, Colleges & Universities, Economic Education, Education Associations, Engineering/Technological Education, Journalism/Media Education, Science/Mathematics Education, Vocational & Technical Education
Science: Science Exhibits & Fairs
Social Services: United Funds/United Ways

Restrictions
Does not support religious organizations for sectarian purposes or political or lobbying groups.

Corporate Officials
Marshall L. Carpenter: vice president, chief financial officer B Sycamore, IL 1937. ED Augustana College AB (1959); University of Denver MBA (1960). PRIM CORP EMPL vice president, chief financial officer: MTS System Corp. NONPR AFFIL member: Financial Executives Institute; member: Minnesota Society CPA's; member: American Institute of CPA's.
Sidney W. Emery, Jr.: president, chief executive officer PRIM CORP EMPL president, chief executive officer: MTS System Corp.
Donald M. Sullivan: chairman, director PRIM CORP EMPL chairman, director: MTS System Corp.

Grants Analysis
Disclosure Period: calendar year ending
Typical Range: $1,000 to $2,500

Recent Grants
Note: Grants derived from 1998 Form 990.

Civic & Public Affairs
Eden Prairie Foundation, Eden Prairie, MN

Education
Dunwoody Institute
Junior Achievement, Minneapolis, MN
Mathcounts, Minneapolis, MN
Minnesota Council on Economic Education, Minneapolis, MN
Minnesota High Tech Council, Minneapolis, MN
University of Minnesota Mechanical Building Fund, Minneapolis, MN
University of Minnesota Solar Vehicle Project, Minneapolis, MN

Science
Twin Cities Regional Science Fair, Minneapolis, MN

Social Services
United Way, Minneapolis, MN

Murphy Oil Corp.

Company Contact
El Dorado, AR
Web: http://www.murphyoilcorp.com

Company Description
Employees: 1,679
SIC(s): 0811 Timber Tracts, 1311 Crude Petroleum & Natural Gas, 2421 Sawmills & Planing Mills--General, 2911 Petroleum Refining.

Operating Locations
Operates in Southeastern and Upper Midwestern United States.

Nonmonetary Support
Type: Loaned Executives
Note: Company also offers board services to nonprofits.

Giving Contact
Betty LeBrescu, Manager, Community & Public Relations
Murphy Oil Corp.
200 Peach Street
El Dorado, AR 71730
Phone: (870)864-6222
Fax: (870)864-6480
Email: Betty_LeBrescu@murphyoilcorp.com

Description
Organization Type: Corporate Giving Program
Giving Locations: headquarters and operating communities.
Grant Types: Capital, Employee Matching Gifts, Project.

Financial Summary
Total Giving: $900,000 (1997 approx). Note: Contributes through corporate direct giving program only.

Typical Recipients
Arts & Humanities: Arts Centers
Education: Colleges & Universities
Health: Hospitals
Social Services: Animal Protection, Community Service Organizations

Application Procedures
Initial Contact: a brief letter of inquiry
Application Requirements: a description of organization, amount requested, purpose of funds sought, list of board of directors, audited financial statement, and proof of tax-exempt status
Deadlines: None.

Restrictions
Company does not support individuals, religious organizations for sectarian purposes, national organizations, or political or lobbying groups.

Corporate Officials
Steven Anthony Cosse: senior vice president, general counsel B New Orleans, LA 1947. ED Southeastern Louisiana University BS (1969); Loyola University JD (1974). PRIM CORP EMPL senior vice president, general counsel: Murphy Oil Corp. ADD CORP EMPL vice president: Murphy Exploration & Products Co. CORP AFFIL vice president, general counsel: Murphy Oil USA Inc. NONPR AFFIL member: Rotary International.
Claiborne P. Deming: president, chief executive officer, director B Alexandria, LA 1954. ED Tulane University BA (1976); Tulane University Law School JD (1979). PRIM CORP EMPL president, chief executive officer, director: Murphy Oil Corp.
R. Madison Murphy: chairman, director B 1957. ED Hendrix College BA (1980). PRIM CORP EMPL chairman, director: Murphy Oil Corp. CORP AFFIL director: Deltic Timber Co.; director: First United Bancshares Inc.

Giving Program Officials
Betty LeBrescu: PRIM CORP EMPL manager: Murphy Oil Corp.

Grants Analysis
Disclosure Period: calendar year ending
Typical Range: $5,000 to $25,000

Mutual Of Omaha Insurance Co.

Company Contact
Omaha, NE
Web: http://www.mutualofomaha.com/inside/community

Company Description

Former Name: Mutual of Omaha-United of Omaha Insurance Co.
Revenue: US$3,820,100,000
Employees: 7,384
Fortune Rank: 379, per FORTUNE Magazine's list of 500 Largest U.S. Corporations (1999).
FF 379
SIC(s): 6311 Life Insurance, 6321 Accident & Health Insurance.

Nonmonetary Support

Type: Donated Equipment; Loaned Employees

Corporate Sponsorship

Contact: Linda McKenzie, Manager, Community Affairs
Note: Sponsors Race for the Cure.

Giving Contact

M. Jane Huerter, Executive Vice President-Corporate Services, Corporate Secretary
Mutual of Omaha Insurance Co.
Mutual of Omaha Plz.
Omaha, NE 68175
Phone: (402)342-7600
Fax: (402)351-2407

Description

Organization Type: Corporate Giving Program
Giving Locations: major business locations.
Grant Types: General Support, Project.

Financial Summary

Total Giving: $1,450,000 (1997 approx); $1,450,000 (1996); $1,545,603 (1995). Note: Contributes through corporate direct giving program only.

Typical Recipients

Arts & Humanities: Community Arts, Arts & Humanities-General, Museums/Galleries, Opera, Performing Arts, Theater
Civic & Public Affairs: Chambers of Commerce, Economic Development, Civic & Public Affairs-General, Minority Business, Safety, Zoos/Aquariums
Education: Colleges & Universities, Community & Junior Colleges, Education-General, Private Education (Precollege), Public Education (Precollege)
Health: AIDS/HIV, Health-General, Heart, Hospices
Social Services: At-Risk Youth, Domestic Violence, Homes, People with Disabilities, Shelters/Homelessness, Social Services-General, United Funds/ United Ways, Youth Organizations

Contributions Analysis

Arts & Humanities: 20%.
Civic & Public Affairs: 20%. Distributed equally among the arts, health and human services, and civic organizations.
Education: 40%.
Health: 20%.

Application Procedures

Initial Contact: a full proposal
Application Requirements: a description of organization, amount requested, purpose of funds sought, board of directors, and other sources of support

Restrictions

Does not support individuals, or organizations outside operating areas.

Corporate Officials

M. Jane Huerter: executive vice president, corporate secretary B Omaha, NE 1950. ED Creighton University (1972); Creighton University (1976). PRIM CORP EMPL executive vice president, corporate secretary: Mutual of Omaha Insurance Co. ADD CORP EMPL executive vice president, corp. secretary: United of Omaha Life Insurance Co.; vice president, corp. secretary: Companion Life Insurance Co.; secretary: Innowave Inc.; vice president, corp. secretary: Omaha Property & Casualty Co.
John Sturgeon: president, chief operating officer B Alliance, NE 1940. ED Midland Lutheran College (1962). PRIM CORP EMPL president, chief operating officer: Mutual of Omaha Insurance Co. CORP AFFIL director: United Omaha Life Insurance Co.; director: United World Life Insurance Co.; director: Tele-Trip Co.; director: Mutual Omaha Marketing Corp.; director: Omaha Indemnity Co.; chairman: Innowave Inc.; director: Kirkpatrick Pettis Smith Polian Inc.; director: Adjustment Services Inc.; director: Companion Life Insurance Co.
John William Weekly: chairman, chief executive officer B Sioux City, IA 1931. PRIM CORP EMPL chairman, chief executive officer: Mutual of Omaha Insurance Co. CORP AFFIL director: United Omaha Life Insurance Co.; chairman: United World Life Insurance Co.; director: Omaha Property & Casualty Insurance Co.; chairman: Tele-Trip Inc.; director: Omaha Airport Authority; director: Midwest Express Airlines Inc.; chairman: Mutual Omaha Investor Services Inc.; partner: Kirkpatrick Pettis Inc.; director: Harbor Holdings Inc.; director: Innowave Inc.; director, vice chairman: Companion Life Insurance Co. NONPR AFFIL director: American Council Life Insurance; director: Bellevue University.

Grants Analysis

Disclosure Period: calendar year ending
Typical Range: $1,000 to $25,000

Recent Grants

Note: Grants derived from 1996 grants list.

Arts & Humanities
United Arts of Omaha, Omaha, NE

Civic & Public Affairs
Greater Omaha Chamber Foundation, Omaha, NE
James B. Wilson Jr. Foundatin, Omaha, NE
NAACP, New York, NY

Education
Bellevue University, Bellevue, NE
United Negro College Fund, Omaha, NE

Health
Hospice House, Omaha, NE
Wellness Council of the Midlands, Omaha, NE

Religion
Salvation Army, Omaha, NE

Social Services
Girls, Incorporated, Omaha, NE

NABISCO GROUP HOLDINGS

Company Contact

Parsippany, NJ
Web: http://www.nabisco.com

Company Description

Revenue: US$8,268,000,000 (1999)
Profit: US$2,968,000,000 (1999)
Fortune Rank: 219, per FORTUNE Magazine's list of 500 Largest U.S. Corporations (1999).
FF 219

Nonmonetary Support

Type: Donated Equipment; Donated Products; In-kind Services

Nabisco Foundation Trust

Giving Contact

Mr. Henry Sandbach, Vice President, Public Relations
Nabisco Foundation Trust
7 Campus Drive
Parsippany, NJ 07054
Phone: (973)682-7098
Fax: (973)682-6265

Alternate Contact

Rose Marie Andriola, Contributions Manager
Phone: (973)682-7175

Description

Founded: 1953
EIN: 136042595
Organization Type: Corporate Foundation
Giving Locations: Nabisco corporate facilities locations.
Grant Types: Capital, Emergency, Employee Matching Gifts, General Support, Matching.

Financial Summary

Total Giving: $1,500,000 (2000 approx); $1,500,000 (1999 approx); $849,730 (1998). Note: Contributes through corporate direct giving program and foundation. Giving includes foundation.
Giving Analysis: Giving for 1998 includes: foundation grants to United Way ($455,500); foundation ($394,230)
Assets: $3,629,121 (1998); $2,839,089 (1997); $4,618,828 (1995)
Gifts Received: $1,010,000 (1998). Note: In 1998, contributions were received from Nabisco Co.

Typical Recipients

Arts & Humanities: Arts Funds, Community Arts, Dance, Libraries, Museums/Galleries, Music, Performing Arts, Public Broadcasting, Theater
Civic & Public Affairs: Business/Free Enterprise, Clubs, Economic Development, Civic & Public Affairs-General, Nonprofit Management, Parades/Festivals, Professional & Trade Associations, Public Policy, Rural Affairs, Urban & Community Affairs
Education: Business Education, Business-School Partnerships, Colleges & Universities, Education Funds, Elementary Education (Private), Education-General, Medical Education, Private Education (Precollege), Public Education (Precollege), Special Education, Student Aid
Environment: Environment-General
Health: Clinics/Medical Centers, Health Organizations, Hospitals, Nutrition
International: Foreign Educational Institutions
Religion: Jewish Causes, Religious Welfare
Science: Scientific Centers & Institutes
Social Services: Child Welfare, Food/Clothing Distribution, People with Disabilities, Recreation & Athletics, United Funds/United Ways, YMCA/YWCA/ YMHA/YWHA, Youth Organizations

Contributions Analysis

Giving Priorities: Colleges and universities, especially medical education and programs related to food marketing; hospitals; food distribution; and limited support to the arts and civic organizations.
Arts & Humanities: 5%. Arts funds, community arts, public broadcasting, andmuseums.
Civic & Public Affairs: 2%. Civic and business organizations, as well as economic and agricultural development.
Education: 16%. Primarily matching gifts program. Focus on higher education associations and funds, as well as scholarships. Supports colleges and universities, particularly for medical education and programs related to food marketing. Company has increased its support of elementary and secondary education.

Health: 4%. Hospitals and health foundations.
Social Services: 69%. Majority supports the United Way. Other recipients include food distribution services and youth organizations.
Note: Total contributions made in 1998.

Application Procedures

Initial Contact: brief letter or proposal
Application Requirements: a description of organization, amount requested, purpose of funds sought, recently audited financial statement, proof of tax-exempt status
Deadlines: None.

Foundation Officials

Robert K. Devries: member administration committee ED George Washington University Law School (1969-1971). PRIM CORP EMPL assistant secretary, director: Nabisco International South America.
John Frederick Manfredi: member administration committee B New York, NY 1940. ED Yale University (1958-1961); Columbia University BA (1967). PRIM CORP EMPL executive vice president corporate affairs: Nabisco, Inc. ADD CORP EMPL executive vice president: Nabisco Group Holdings Corp.; executive vice president: RJR Nabisco Inc.
Henry A. Sandbach: member administration committee PRIM CORP EMPL vice president public relations: Nabisco, Inc.

Grants Analysis

Disclosure Period: calendar year ending 1995
Total Grants: $394,230*
Number of Grants: 30
Average Grant: $13,141
Highest Grant: $280,000
Typical Range: $2,500 to $25,000
***Note:** Grant analysis excludes United Way.

Recent Grants

Note: Grants derived from 1995 Form 990.

Arts & Humanities

59,350 San Francisco Symphony, San Francisco, CA
50,000 Educational Broadcasting Corp, New York, NY
50,000 Lincoln Center for Performing Arts, New York, NY
10,000 Educational Broadcasting Corp, New York, NY
7,000 Waterloo Foundation for the Arts, Stanhope, NJ
5,000 New Jersey Symphony Orchestra, Newark, NJ
5,000 South Street Theater Company, Parsippany, NJ

Civic & Public Affairs

35,000 Partnership in Philanthropy, Newark, NJ
25,000 Advertising Council, New York, NY
10,000 Foundation for American Communications, Los Angeles, CA
10,000 Kiwanis Club, Palm Springs, CA
10,000 Morris 2000, Morristown, NJ
7,500 First Night Morris County, Morristown, NJ

Education

45,940 National Merit Scholarship Corp, Evanston, IL
14,500 Students in Free Enterprise, Springfield, MO
10,000 Kings College, PA
10,000 New Jersey Seeds, Hightstown, NJ
7,500 National Center for Learning Disabilities, New York, NY
5,000 Yale University, New Haven, CT

Health

60,000 Desert Hospital Foundation, Palm Springs, CA
50,000 Morristown Memorial Hospital, Morristown, NJ
20,000 St. Clare's Riverside Medical Center, Denville, NJ
15,000 IFIC Food Education Foundation, Washington, DC
12,000 IFIC Food Education Foundation, Washington, DC
5,000 St. Clare's Riverside Medical Center, Denville, NJ
5,000 Stoughton Hospital, Stoughton, WI

International

50,000 Friends of McGill University, New York, NY

Social Services

220,000 United Way Morris County, Morristown, NJ
60,000 United Way Crusade of Mercy, Chicago, IL
50,000 Second Harvest, Chicago, IL
50,000 United Way Desert, Palm Springs, CA
37,500 United Way Wyoming Valley, Wilkes-Barre, PA
35,000 United Way Bergen County, Fair Lawn, NJ
29,650 United Way
25,000 Barbara Sinatra Children's Center, Rancho Mirage, CA
25,000 Boys and Girls Club, Palm Springs, CA
20,000 LPGA Foundation, Daytona Beach, FL
18,000 United Way Southwestern Pennsylvania, Pittsburgh, PA
15,000 Seeing Eye, Morristown, NJ
11,000 United Way, Atlanta, GA
11,000 United Way, Richmond, VA
10,000 Citymeals on Wheels, New York, NY
10,000 Morris Center YMCA, Cedar Knolls, NJ
10,000 United Way Southeastern Pennsylvania, Philadelphia, PA
8,000 United Way Texas Gulf Coast, Houston, TX
7,500 YMCA, Madison, NJ
7,000 United Way, Niagara Falls, NY
6,000 United Way Buffalo and Erie County, Buffalo, NY
6,000 United Way Columbia Willamette, Portland, OR
5,000 United Way Dane County, Stoughton, WI

NALCO CHEMICAL CO.

Company Contact

One Nalco Center
1601 W. Diehl Rd.
Naperville, IL 60563-1198
Phone: (630)305-1000
Fax: (630)305-2900
Web: http://www.nalco.com

Company Description

Employees: 7,000
SIC(s): 2819 Industrial Inorganic Chemicals Nec, 2843 Surface Active Agents, 2869 Industrial Organic Chemicals Nec, 2899 Chemical Preparations Nec.

Operating Locations

Australia: Nalco Australia, Sydney; Brazil: Nalco Brazil Ltda., Sao Paulo; Canada: Nalco Canada, Burlington; Chile: Nalco Productos Quimicos de Chile SA, Santiago; People's Republic of China: Nalco Chemical (Suzhou) Co. Ltd., Suzhou, Jiangsu; Colombia: Quimica Nalco De Colombia SA, Bogota; Ecuador: Nalco Ecuador SA, Quito; Hong Kong: Nalco Chemical (Hong Kong) Ltd., Kowloon; Indonesia: PT Nalco Perkasa, Jakarta, Jakarta Raya; India: Nalco Chemicals India Ltd., Calcutta; Italy: Nalco Italiana SpA, Roma, Lazio; Japan: Nalco Japan Co. Ltd., Tokyo; Republic of Korea: Nalco Korea Co. Ltd., Seoul; Mexico: Nalcomex SA de CV, Naucalpan de Juarez; Netherlands: Nalco Europe, Oegstgeest, Leiden; Deryshares BV, Oegstgeest, Zuid-Holland; Nalco Applied Services of Europe BV, Oegstgeest, Zuid-Holland; Nalco Europe BV, Oegstgeest, Zuid-Holland; Nalco Chemical BV, Tilburg, Noord-Brabant; Nalco Ltd. UK, Willemstad, Noord-Brabant; Norway: Nalco Norge AS, Oslo, Akershus; Philippines: Nalco Chemical Co. (Philippines), Makati, Rizal; Saudi Arabia: Nalco Saudi Co. Ltd., Dumman; Singapore: Nalco Pacific, Jurong; Thailand: Nalco Checmical Co. Thailand, Bangkok; Taiwan: Taiwan Nalco Chemical Co. Ltd., Taipei; Taiwan Nalco Chemical Co. Ltd., Taipei; Venezuela: Nalco de Venezuela Ca, Caracas

Nonmonetary Support

Value: $293,178 (1997)
Type: Donated Equipment; Loaned Executives
Note: Support is provided by the company.

Corporate Sponsorship

Type: Other
Note: Company conducts drives for food, blood, toys, clothing, and school supplies.

Nalco Foundation

Giving Contact

Suzanne J. Gioimo, President
The Nalco Foundation
1 Nalco Center
Naperville, IL 60563-1198
Phone: (630)305-1566
Fax: (630)305-2985
Email: foundation@nalco.com

Description

EIN: 366065864
Organization Type: Corporate Foundation
Giving Locations: CA: Carson; IL: DuPage County, Chicago metropolitan area; LA: Garyville; NJ: Paulsboro; TX: Freeport, Sugarland
Grant Types: Capital, General Support, Project.
Note: Employee matching gift ratio: 2 to 1 for contributions over $25 to colleges and universities, up to $2,000 annually; 1 to 1 for gifts to hospitals and cultural institutions, up to $500 annually.

Giving Philosophy

'Our mission is quite simple. The Nalco Foundation strives to improve the quality of life in the communities in which Nalco Chemical Company and Nalco/Exxon Energy Chemicals, L.P. operate. The more than 200 groups The Foundation supported in 1995 provide a broad range of services from housing to healthcare, entertainment to education. They serve all ages, from newborn babies to senior citizens.
'In its early years most of The Foundation's support went to non-profit organizations in Illinois, especially in the Chicago area. As the Company grew, though, the number of communities we touched grew as well. The Foundation's giving reflects this growth with more contributions being made in California, Georgia, Louisiana, New Jersey, and Texas. Since 1991, The Foundation has directed an average of 30 percent of its grant dollars to groups located in communities outside Illinois..
'The Nalco Foundation represents only a part of our philanthropic efforts. Other corporate giving programs.. include the Matching Gift Plan, United Way, cash contributions to local organizations made by the Company's corporate and operating divisions, and Nalco employees' participation in community involvement projects. Through these programs and the contributions of The Nalco Foundation, we continue to honor our commitment to improve the quality of life in the communities where we and our friends live and work.' *1995 Report of Contributions*

Financial Summary

Total Giving: $2,541,422 (1998); $2,741,359 (1997); $2,420,373 (1996). Note: Contributes through corporate direct giving program and foundation. 1997 Giving includes corporate direct giving ($848,260); foundation ($1,599,921); nonmonetary support. 1996 Giving includes corporate direct giving ($314,715); foundation ($1,602,860); matching gifts ($311,722); United Way ($191,076).
Giving Analysis: Giving for 1996 includes: foundation ($1,602,860); corporate direct giving ($314,715); foundation matching gifts ($311,722); foundation grants to United Way ($191,076); 1997: foundation ($1,599,921); corporate direct giving ($848,260); 1998: foundation ($1,646,220); corporate matching gifts ($338,211); corporate direct giving ($324,352); corporate grants to United Way ($232,639)
Assets: $4,614,226 (1998); $5,239,257 (1997); $6,673,465 (1996)
Gifts Received: $7,000,073 (1994). Note: Gifts were received from Nalco Chemical Company.

Typical Recipients

Arts & Humanities: Arts Associations & Councils, Arts Funds, Arts Institutes, Community Arts, Dance, Historic Preservation, History & Archaeology, Libraries, Museums/Galleries, Music, Opera, Performing Arts, Public Broadcasting
Civic & Public Affairs: Business/Free Enterprise, Employment/Job Training, Civic & Public Affairs-General, Housing, Law & Justice, Legal Aid, Nonprofit Management, Safety, Urban & Community Affairs, Women's Affairs, Zoos/Aquariums
Education: Business Education, Colleges & Universities, Economic Education, Education Associations, Engineering/Technological Education, Faculty Development, Education-General, Literacy, Medical Education, Minority Education, Public Education (Precollege), Science/Mathematics Education, Social Sciences Education, Special Education, Student Aid
Environment: Environment-General
Health: AIDS/HIV, Alzheimers Disease, Cancer, Children's Health/Hospitals, Clinics/Medical Centers, Emergency/Ambulance Services, Geriatric Health, Health Policy/Cost Containment, Health Organizations, Heart, Home-Care Services, Hospices, Hospitals, Hospitals (University Affiliated), Medical Rehabilitation, Medical Research, Mental Health, Prenatal Health Issues, Preventive Medicine/Wellness Organizations, Public Health, Single-Disease Health Associations, Trauma Treatment
International: Foreign Educational Institutions, International Development, International Environmental Issues
Religion: Ministries, Religious Welfare
Science: Observatories & Planetariums, Science Museums, Scientific Centers & Institutes
Social Services: At-Risk Youth, Child Welfare, Community Centers, Community Service Organizations, Counseling, Delinquency & Criminal Rehabilitation, Domestic Violence, Family Services, Food/Clothing Distribution, People with Disabilities, Substance Abuse, YMCA/YWCA/YMHA/YWHA, Youth Organizations

Contributions Analysis

Giving Priorities: Domestic violence and crime, substance abuse, and hunger are current issues. Other focus areas are education, community and civic affairs, health, and culture and the arts.
Arts & Humanities: 10%. Funds go to art institutes, community theatre, performing arts, the symphony, and public broadcasting.
Civic & Public Affairs: 30%. Supports boys and girls clubs, housing assistance, career training, and youth issues.
Education: 35%. Supports junior achievement, precollege and college education, arts education, training for disabled, and scholarship awards.
Health: 25%. Support goes to AIDs programs, single-disease research, equipment needs, substance abuse programs, care for the disabled, hospitals, and medical centers.

Application Procedures

Initial Contact: Request guidelines or submit proposal in writing.
Application Requirements: Provide legal name and history of organization, summary of specified project or need, intended use of funds, latest financial statement or budget, list of board of directors and their affiliations and addresses, list of corporate and foundation contributions, proof of tax-exempt status, copy of annual report (if available), breakdown of expenses (if not already included in other material) and IRS Form 990.
Deadlines: None.
Review Process: Proposals are acknowledged and are reviewed at next scheduled board meeting.
Decision Notification: Board meetings are held on a quarterly basis, generally March, June, September, and December; applicant notified as soon as possible after meeting.

Restrictions

The foundation generally does not support individuals, political activities or lobbying groups, churches or religious education, secondary or elementary schools, state-supported colleges or universities, endowment funds, advertising in charitable publications, or purchase of tickets for fund-raising activities.

Additional Information

The foundation limits its giving to nonprofit organizations that provide services in the areas of education, community & civic affairs, health, and culture & art. The company sponsors a 'Community Involvement' program, which is defined as the 'giving of time and effort by individuals to special causes, with the company participating as originator or organizer.' In addition, the program also includes the establishment of Community Advisory Groups at facilities around the country, facility tours for students, teachers and neighbors, and the hiring of college students in the Cooperative Education program.
Publications: Contributions Report

Corporate Officials

David R. Bertran: senior vice president manufacturing & logistics ED University of Waterloo BS; University of Waterloo MS (1967). PRIM CORP EMPL senior vice president manufacturing & logistics: Nalco Chemical Co. NONPR AFFIL trustee: Elmhurst College; member: Ontario Association Professional Engineering.
William E. Buchholz: vice president, chief financial officer B 1942. ED Michigan State University BS; Michigan State University MBA. PRIM CORP EMPL vice president, chief financial officer: Nalco Chemical Co. NONPR AFFIL director: Financial Executives Institute.
James F. Lambe: senior vice president human resources B 1945. ED University of Illinois BScE (1969); DePaul University JD (1972). PRIM CORP EMPL senior vice president human resources: Nalco Chemical Co. NONPR AFFIL member: American Bar Association; trustee: North Central College.
Edward J. Mooney, Jr.: chairman, president, chief executive officer, director B Omar, WV 1941. ED University of Texas BS (1964); University of Texas JD (1967). PRIM CORP EMPL chairman, president, chief executive officer, director: Nalco Chemical Co. CORP AFFIL director: Morton International Inc.; director: Northern Trust Corp.; director: FMC Corp. NONPR AFFIL member: National Petroleum Refiners Association; member: Society Petroleum Engineers; member: Business Roundtable; member: Chemical Manufacturers Association.
William E. Parry: vice president, general counsel B Massena, NY 1951. ED University of Notre Dame BA (1973); Duquesne University JD (1978). PRIM CORP EMPL vice president, general counsel: Nalco Chemical Co. NONPR AFFIL member: American Corporate Counsel Association.

Foundation Officials

David R. Bertran: director (see above)
Joanne C. Ford: president, director
Craig J. Holderness: assistant treasurer PRIM CORP EMPL assistant treasurer: Nalco Chemical Co.
James F. Lambe: director (see above)
Terrence J. Taylor: treasurer
Mary Jane Wilson: secretary

Grants Analysis

Disclosure Period: calendar year ending 1998
Total Grants: $1,646,220*
Number of Grants: 232
Average Grant: $7,096
Typical Range: $2,000 to $10,000
***Note:** Grants analysis provided by Foundation. Giving excludes corporate direct giving; nonmonetary support.

Recent Grants

Note: Grants derived from 1997 Form 990.

Arts & Humanities

25,000 Lyric Opera, Chicago, IL -- capital campaign
20,000 Lake Jackson Historical Association, Lake Jackson, TX -- development of museum exhibit
18,000 Window to the World Communications/ WFMT Radio, Chicago, IL -- radio broadcast of 'Rising Stars of Ravinia'
16,500 Museum of Fine Arts, Houston, TX -- capital campaign
15,000 Brazosport Fine Arts Council, Lake Jackson, TX -- outdoor signage for the center

Civic & Public Affairs

20,000 Mutual Ground, Aurora, IL -- capital campaign
16,500 Brookfield Zoo/Chicago Zoological Society, Brookfield, IL -- capital campaign
10,000 Little Friends, Naperville, IL -- spectrum sheltered workshop

Education

29,930 Associated Colleges, Chicago, IL -- science equipment awards
25,856 Elmhurst College, Elmhurst, IL -- infrared spectrometer and accessories
25,000 North Central College, Naperville, IL -- science scholarship awards
24,000 Benedictine University, Lisle, IL -- science lab equipment
17,000 Illinois Institute of Technology, Chicago, IL -- lab equipment and accessories
15,000 Roosevelt University, Chicago, IL -- renovation of downtown campus
12,500 Junior Achievement, Chicago, IL -- Cook and DuPage County programs

Environment

85,000 Window to the World Communications/ WTTW, Chicago, IL -- underwrite 'Nature' series
25,000 Association for Community Television, Houston, TX -- underwrite 'Nature' series
24,000 Greater New Orleans Educational Television Foundation, New Orleans, LA -- underwrite 'Nature' series

Health

50,000 Rush Presbyterian-St. Luke's Medical Center, Chicago, IL -- Therapy-Induced Malignancy Evaluation program
30,000 Rehabilitation Institute, Chicago, IL -- capital campaign
25,000 Loyola University Medical Center, Maywood, IL -- research support

20,000 Good Samaritan Hospital, Downers Grove, IL -- senior health outreach program
20,000 Little Company of Mary Hospital, Evergreen Park, IL -- cancer center renovation
20,000 Trinity Hospital, Chicago, IL -- capital campaign
15,000 Children's Hospital, New Orleans, LA -- pediatric intensive care renovation project
15,000 DuPage Easter Seal Treatment Center, Villa Park, IL -- capital campaign
15,000 Easter Seal Society, Chicago, IL -- programs and facility renovations
10,000 Alton Ochsner Medical Foundation, Metairie, LA -- biomedical research
10,000 Central DuPage Hospital Association, Winfield, IL -- homecare program
10,000 Children's Memorial Foundation, Chicago, IL -- indigent care expenses
10,000 Copley Memorial Hospital Health Care Foundation, Aurora, IL -- capital campaign
10,000 Dyslexia Association, Baton Rouge, LA -- computer equipment
10,000 Easter Seal Rehabilitation Center of Will-Grundy Counties, Joliet, IL -- support services
10,000 La Rabida Children's Hospital and Research Center, Chicago, IL -- general support

International

15,000 COUNT, Johannesburg, Republic of South Africa -- teacher training workshops
15,000 COUNT, Johannesburg, Republic of South Africa -- teacher training workshops
13,000 Natar Schools Project Trust, Durban, Republic of South Africa -- science lab at Sesifikile School
13,000 Natar Schools Project Trust, Durban, Republic of South Africa -- science lab at Sesifikile School

Religion

12,000 St. Vincent de Paul Society, Baton Rogue, LA -- construction of waiting area

Science

16,700 Adler Planetarium, Chicago, IL -- capital campaign
15,000 Science and Technology Interactive Center, Aurora, IL -- general support

Social Services

15,000 Bethlehem Center Food Bank, St. Charles, IL -- capital campaign
15,000 Boys and Girls County, Houston, TX -- general support
15,000 Metropolitan Family Services, Wheaton, IL -- capital campaign
15,000 Odyssey House, Houston, TX -- general support
12,500 Bensenville Home Society Lifelink, Bensenville, IL -- capital campaign
11,000 Glenwood School for Boys, Chicago, IL -- continuing education for science teachers
10,000 Briarwood-Brookwood, Brookshire, TX -- capital campaign
10,000 Fort Bend County Child Advocates, Richmond, TX -- family assistance program
10,000 Fort Bend Regional Council on Alcoholism and Drug Abuse, Stafford, TX -- expansion of program into K-12 school system
10,000 Lawrence Hall Youth Services, Chicago, IL -- renovation of the Lakewood House
10,000 Marklund Children's Home, Glendale Heights, IL -- purchase of Parker bathtub and lift

NASDAQ Stock Market

Company Contact

1735 K Street, NW
Washington, DC 20006
Phone: (202)496-2500
Web: http://www.nasdaq.com

NASDAQ Stock Market Educational Foundation

Giving Contact

Nasdaq Educational Foundation
9513 Key West Ave.
Rockville, MD 20850-3339
Phone: 800-842-0356

Description

Founded: 1993
EIN: 521864429
Organization Type: Corporate Foundation. Supports preselected organizations only.
Giving Locations: nationally.
Grant Types: General Support.

Financial Summary

Total Giving: $221,000 (1995)
Assets: $7,960,513 (1995); $3,000,000 (1993)
Gifts Received: $1,310,000 (1995); $3,000,000 (1993). Note: In 1995, contributions were received from the NASDAQ Stock Market.

Typical Recipients

Civic & Public Affairs: Employment/Job Training
Education: Business Education, Colleges & Universities, Economic Education

Restrictions

Grants are not made to individuals.

Foundation Officials

James R. Allen: treasurer
Anson McCook Beard, Jr.: director B New York, NY 1936. ED Yale University BA (1958). PRIM CORP EMPL managing director: Morgan Stanley & Co., Inc. CORP AFFIL chairman: MS Securities Services Inc.
Joseph R. Hardiman: director
Charles B. Johnson: director
Michael J. Kulczak: secretary
Douglas Parrillo: vice president
Charles Symington, Jr.: director
Victor R. Wright: chairman

Grants Analysis

Disclosure Period: calendar year ending 1995
Number of Grants: 8
Highest Grant: $140,000
Typical Range: $5,000 to $25,000

Recent Grants

Note: Grants derived from 1995 Form 990.

Civic & Public Affairs

15,000 National Academy Foundation, New York, NY -- educational

Education

140,000 Securities Industry Foundation for Economic Education, New York, NY
25,000 Georgetown University School of Business, Washington, DC
12,500 National Council on Economic Education, New York, NY
10,000 University of Memphis Fogelman College of Business and Economics Institute for the Study of Securities Markets, Memphis, TN
10,000 University of Pennsylvania, Philadelphia, PA
5,000 New York University, New York, NY
3,500 University of Chicago Center for Research in Security Prices, Chicago, IL

National Bank Of Commerce Trust & Savings

Company Contact

Lincoln, NE
Web: http://www.banknbc.com

Company Description

Assets: US$1,192,700,000
Employees: 643
SIC(s): 6021 National Commercial Banks.
Parent Company: First Commerce Bancshares

NBC Foundation

Giving Contact

Jim Stuart III, Secretary, Treasurer
NBC Center
1248 O Street
Lincoln, NE 68508
Phone: (402)434-4622
Fax: (402)434-4181
Email: jstuart@fcbcorpo.com

Description

Founded: 1989
EIN: 363630215
Organization Type: Corporate Foundation
Giving Locations: headquarters and operating communities.
Grant Types: General Support.

Financial Summary

Total Giving: $466,000 (1999 approx); $403,000 (1998); $264,000 (1997)
Assets: $9,487,418 (1997); $6,656,971 (1996); $4,711,312 (1994)
Gifts Received: $1,129,875 (1997); $1,000,000 (1993); $2,000,000 (1992). Note: In 1993, contributions were received from the National Bank of Commerce Trust & Savings.

Typical Recipients

Arts & Humanities: Arts Associations & Councils, Museums/Galleries, Music, Performing Arts
Civic & Public Affairs: Employment/Job Training, Civic & Public Affairs-General, Housing, Urban & Community Affairs, Zoos/Aquariums
Education: Colleges & Universities, Medical Education, Private Education (Precollege), Public Education (Precollege), Secondary Education (Private), Student Aid
Health: Health Organizations, Hospitals, Long-Term Care, Public Health
Religion: Bible Study/Translation, Religious Organizations, Religious Welfare
Social Services: Animal Protection, Homes, Recreation & Athletics, Scouts, United Funds/United Ways

Application Procedures

Initial Contact: Send a brief letter of inquiry
Application Requirements: a description of organization, amount requested, and purpose of funds sought
Deadlines: None.

Corporate Officials

Don Kinley: chief financial officer, chief executive officer PRIM CORP EMPL chief financial officer: National Bank Commerce Trust & Savings.
Brad Korell: president PRIM CORP EMPL president: National Bank Commerce Trust & Savings.
James Stuart, Jr.: chairman, chief executive officer PRIM CORP EMPL chairman, chief executive officer: National Bank Commerce Trust & Savings.

Foundation Officials

James Stuart, III: secretary-treasurer
James Stuart, Jr.: president (see above)
Scott Stuart: vice president

Grants Analysis

Disclosure Period: calendar year ending 1997
Total Grants: $264,000
Number of Grants: 27
Average Grant: $9,777
Highest Grant: $17,000
Typical Range: $2,500 to $25,000

Recent Grants

Note: Grants derived from 1997 Form 990.

Arts & Humanities

17,000 Lincoln Community Playhouse, Lincoln, NE
6,000 Lincoln Symphony, Lincoln, NE
5,000 Lied Center for Performing Arts, Lincoln, NE

Civic & Public Affairs

30,000 Folsom Children's Zoo, Lincoln, NE
3,000 Parrish of the North American Martyrs, Lincoln, NE

Education

59,500 University of Nebraska Foundation, Lincoln, NE
30,000 Nebraska Wesleyan University, Lincoln, NE
17,000 Lincoln Medical Education Foundation, Lincoln, NE
10,000 Lincoln Lutheran High School, Lincoln, NE
7,500 Lincoln Public Schools Foundation, Lincoln, NE

Religion

5,000 Pius X, Lincoln, NE

Social Services

22,000 Friendship Home, Lincoln, NE
17,000 Optimist Youth Sports Complex, Lincoln, NE
10,000 Capital Humane Society, Lincoln, NE
7,500 Homestead Girl Scout Council, Lincoln, NE
7,500 Nebraska Sports Council, Lincoln, NE
5,000 Capital Sports Foundation, Lincoln, NE
5,000 Capital Sports Foundation, Lincoln, NE

NATIONAL CITY BANK OF CLEVELAND

Company Contact

Indianapolis, IN

Company Description

Former Name: Merchants National Corp.
SIC(s): 6021 National Commercial Banks.
Parent Company: National City Corp., Cleveland, OH, United States

Nonmonetary Support

Type: In-kind Services; Loaned Employees

Corporate Sponsorship

Type: Arts & cultural events; Sports events

Giving Contact

Sidney Weedman, Vice President, Marketing & Affairs
National City Bank of Indiana
101 W. Washington Street, Suite 685 S.
Indianapolis, IN 46255
Phone: (317)267-6102

Description

Organization Type: Corporate Giving Program
Giving Locations: IN
Grant Types: General Support.

Financial Summary

Total Giving: Contributes through corporate direct giving program only. Giving includes corporate direct giving; nonmonetary support.

Typical Recipients

Arts & Humanities: Arts & Humanities-General
Civic & Public Affairs: Civic & Public Affairs-General
Education: Education-General
Health: Health-General
Social Services: Social Services-General

Application Procedures

Initial Contact: Send a brief letter of inquiry.
Application Requirements: Description of organization, amount requested, purpose of funds sought, audited financial statement, list of board members, and proof of tax-exempt status.
Deadlines: None.

Restrictions

Does not support individuals, religious organizations for sectarian purposes, fraternal organizations, trips or tours, or member agencies of the United Way.

Corporate Officials

Vincent A. DiGirolamo: executive vice president, vice chairman B 1937. ED Ohio University; Rutgers University Stonier Graduate School of Banking MBA (1973). PRIM CORP EMPL executive vice president, vice chairman: National City Corp. CORP AFFIL director: National City Bank Pennsylvania. NONPR AFFIL trustee: Hiram College; trustee: Playhouse Square Foundation.
Stephen A. Stitle: chairman B 1945. PRIM CORP EMPL chairman: National City Bank of Indiana. CORP AFFIL director: National City Corp.

Giving Program Officials

Sidney Weedman: PRIM CORP EMPL vice president marketing & government relations: National City Bank of Cleveland.

NATIONAL CITY BANK OF COLUMBUS

 Number 62 of Top 100 Corporate Givers

Company Contact

Columbus, OH

Company Description

Former Name: BancOhio National Bank.
Assets: US$28,963,500,000
Employees: 4,200
SIC(s): 6021 National Commercial Banks.
Parent Company: National City Corp., Cleveland, OH, United States

Operating Locations

Operates in central Ohio

Nonmonetary Support

Type: Donated Equipment; In-kind Services; Loaned Employees; Loaned Executives; Workplace Solicitation

Corporate Sponsorship

Type: Arts & cultural events; Festivals/fairs; Music & entertainment events; Pledge-a-thon; Sports events

Giving Contact

Joanna Clark, Assistant Vice President, Corporate Public Affairs
National City
1900 E. 9th St.
Cleveland, OH 44114
Phone: (216)575-2995
Fax: (216)575-2670

Alternate Contact

Mary Jo Luck, Vice President Public Affairs
National City Bank
155 East Broad
Columbus, OH 43251
Phone: (614)463-8728
Fax: (614)463-8312

Description

Organization Type: Corporate Giving Program
Giving Locations: operating community.
Grant Types: Award, Capital, Conference/Seminar, Emergency, Employee Matching Gifts, Endowment, General Support.

Financial Summary

Total Giving: $13,500,000 (1998 approx); $6,200,811 (1995); $1,300,000 (1993). Note: Contributes through corporate direct giving program and foundation.
Giving Analysis: Giving for 1995 includes: foundation ($4,835,811); corporate direct giving ($1,365,000); 1998: foundation ($13,500,000)
Assets: $74,985 (1995)
Gifts Received: $2,919,585 (1995). Note: Contributions are received from National City Bank.

Typical Recipients

Arts & Humanities: Arts & Humanities-General
Civic & Public Affairs: Civic & Public Affairs-General
Education: Education-General
Health: Health-General, Health Organizations, Hospitals
Social Services: Social Services-General

Application Procedures

Initial Contact: written proposal
Application Requirements: summary of program and objectives; purpose of donation, funding needs, and proposed use of funds; explanation of how future funding will be sustained; organization's projected budget, income, and expense statements; total campaign goal; list of other foundations or companies solicited and amounts contributed or expected; list of principal staff and board members; proof of 501(c)(3) status; whether organization is a member agency of United Way or services are duplicated; description of community interests and businesses participating; and list of National City Bank employees involved
Deadlines: None.

Restrictions

Does not support individuals, religious organizations for sectarian purposes, political or lobbying groups, or organizations outside operating areas.

Additional Information

Publications: Application Guidelines

Corporate Officials

Gary A. Glaser: president, chief executive officer B Cleveland, OH 1944. ED Baldwin-Wallace College (1966); Case Western Reserve University (1971). PRIM CORP EMPL president, chief executive officer: National City Bank of Columbus. CORP AFFIL executive vice president: National City Corp.; director: First National Bank Dayton; president: National City Banking Division. NONPR AFFIL director: Grant/Riverside Methodist Hospital Foundation; director: Recreation Unlimited; director: Franklin University; member: Association Reserve City Bankers; director: Columbus Museum Art; member: American Bankers Association; member: American Institute Banking.

Giving Program Officials

Mary Jo Luck: PRIM CORP EMPL vice president public affairs: National City Bank of Columbus.

Grants Analysis

Disclosure Period: calendar year ending 1995
Total Grants: $4,835,811*
Number of Grants: 1,110
Average Grant: $4,357
Highest Grant: $285,000
***Note:** Giving excludes corporate direct giving.

National City Bank Of Minneapolis

Company Contact

Minneapolis, MN

Company Description

Assets: US$600,000,000
Employees: 270
SIC(s): 6021 National Commercial Banks.
Parent Company: National City Bancorporation

Corporate Sponsorship

Contact: Amanda Heien, Public Affairs

National City Bank Foundation

Giving Contact

Gloria Noetzelman, Secretary
National City Bank Foundation
PO Box E1919
Minneapolis, MN 55480
Phone: (612)904-8503
Fax: (612)904-8016

Description

Founded: 1970
EIN: 237097439
Organization Type: Corporate Foundation
Giving Locations: MN: Minneapolis
Grant Types: General Support.

Financial Summary

Total Giving: $387,070 (1998); $250,175 (1997 approx); $142,075 (1996). Note: Contributes through foundation only.
Giving Analysis: Giving for 1996 includes: foundation grants to United Way ($48,750); 1997: foundation grants to United Way ($80,000); 1998: foundation grants to United Way ($88,657)
Assets: $325,509 (1998); $248,758 (1997); $167,783 (1996)
Gifts Received: $460,000 (1998); $328,450 (1997); $293,000 (1996). Note: Contributions are received from National City Bank of Minneapolis and Diversified Business Credit Inc.

Typical Recipients

Arts & Humanities: Arts Centers, Arts Institutes, Community Arts, Film & Video, Arts & Humanities-General, Museums/Galleries, Music, Opera, Public Broadcasting, Theater
Civic & Public Affairs: African American Affairs, Asian American Affairs, Business/Free Enterprise, Clubs, Economic Development, Employment/Job Training, Civic & Public Affairs-General, Housing, Law & Justice, Legal Aid, Municipalities/Towns, Native American Affairs, Nonprofit Management, Philanthropic Organizations, Professional & Trade Associations, Public Policy, Urban & Community Affairs, Women's Affairs, Zoos/Aquariums
Education: Arts/Humanities Education, Business Education, Colleges & Universities, Education Funds, Education-General, Education-General, Literacy, Minority Education, Preschool Education, Public Education (Precollege), School Volunteerism, Student Aid
Health: AIDS/HIV, Children's Health/Hospitals, Emergency/Ambulance Services, Health Organizations, Kidney, Medical Rehabilitation, Research/Studies Institutes
International: Human Rights
Religion: Jewish Causes, Religious Organizations, Religious Welfare
Science: Science Museums
Social Services: Animal Protection, At-Risk Youth, Child Welfare, Community Centers, Community Service Organizations, Counseling, Day Care, Family Planning, Family Services, Homes, Recreation & Athletics, Refugee Assistance, Scouts, Senior Services, Social Services-General, Substance Abuse, United Funds/United Ways, YMCA/YWCA/YMHA/YWHA, Youth Organizations

Contributions Analysis

Giving Priorities: Supports civic affairs, social services, the arts, health, and education.
Arts & Humanities: 15%. Supports arts centers, the performing arts, and film.
Civic & Public Affairs: 24%. Funds housing, women's concerns, and community groups.
Education: 6%. Supports arts education and ACORN.
Health: 2%. Funds children's health initiatives.
Religion: 8%. Supports religious welfare.
Social Services: 44%. Funds United Way and youth concerns.
Note: Total contributions in 1998.

Application Procedures

Initial Contact: Call for application form.
Deadlines: None.

Additional Information

Publications: Application Form

Corporate Officials

David Lowell Andreas: chairman, chief executive officer B Saint Paul, MN 1949. ED University of Denver BA (1971); Mankato State University MA (1976). PRIM CORP EMPL chairman, chief executive officer: National City Bancorporation. CORP AFFIL president, chief executive officer, director: National City Bank of Minneapolis. NONPR AFFIL member advisory board: Minneapolis Junior League; member executive committee, director: Minnesota Center for Corporate Responsibility; member executive committee, director: Mankato University College of Business Advisory Council; trustee: Minneapolis College of Art & Design; member executive committee, director: Children's Heart Link. CLUB AFFIL Minneapolis Club.
David Curtis Malmberg: director B New Ulm, MN 1943. ED Mankato State University (1965). PRIM CORP EMPL director: Advance Circuits Inc. CORP AFFIL chairman: National City Bank Minneapolis; director: Camax Systems Inc. NONPR AFFIL member: American Electronics Association.

Foundation Officials

David Lowell Andreas: chairman, director (see above)
Gloria Noetzelman: secretary, director
Connie Weinman: director

Grants Analysis

Disclosure Period: calendar year ending 1998
Total Grants: $298,413*
Number of Grants: 119
Average Grant: $2,508
Highest Grant: $20,000
Typical Range: $1,000 to $5,000
***Note:** Giving excludes United Way.

Recent Grants

Note: Grants derived from 1998 Form 990.

Arts & Humanities

7,500	Guthrie Theater, Minneapolis, MN
7,500	Guthrie Theater, Minneapolis, MN
7,500	Minneapolis Institute of Arts, Minneapolis, MN
7,500	Minneapolis Institute of Arts, Minneapolis, MN
5,000	Minnesota Film Board, Minneapolis, MN
5,000	Minnesota Film Board, Minneapolis, MN
5,000	Minnesota Opera, Minneapolis, MN
5,000	Minnesota Opera, Minneapolis, MN
5,000	Minnesota Orchestra, Minneapolis, MN
5,000	Minnesota Orchestra, Minneapolis, MN
5,000	Ordway Music Theatre, St. Paul, MN
5,000	Ordway Music Theatre, St. Paul, MN
3,000	Child's Play Theatre Company, Hopkins, MN
3,000	Child's Play Theatre Company, Hopkins, MN
2,500	Theatre de la Jeune Lune, Minneapolis, MN
2,500	Theatre de la Jeune Lune, Minneapolis, MN
2,000	Cheyenne Productions, Inc., St. Anthony, MN
2,000	Cheyenne Productions, Inc., St. Anthony, MN
2,000	Illusion Theater, Minneapolis, MN
2,000	Minnesota Children's Museum, St. Paul, MN

Civic & Public Affairs

20,000	Milestone Growth Fund, Minneapolis, MN
20,000	Milestone Growth Fund, Minneapolis, MN
7,500	Harriet Tubman Center, Minneapolis, MN
7,500	Harriet Tubman Center, Minneapolis, MN
7,500	Women Venture, St. Paul, MN
7,500	Women Venture, St. Paul, MN
6,000	Twin Cities Neighborhood Housing Services, Inc., St. Paul, MN
6,000	Twin Cities Neighborhood Housing Services, Inc., St. Paul, MN
5,000	American Indian Business Development Corporation, Minneapolis, MN
5,000	American Indian Business Development Corporation, Minneapolis, MN
5,000	Center for Victims of Torture, Minneapolis, MN
5,000	Center for Victims of Torture, Minneapolis, MN
5,000	Edina ABC Foundation, Edina, MN
5,000	Family Housing Fund, Minneapolis, MN
5,000	Family Housing Fund, Minneapolis, MN
5,000	MEDA, Minneapolis, MN
5,000	MEDA, Minneapolis, MN
5,000	Project for Pride in Living, Inc., Minneapolis, MN

3,000 Greater Minneapolis Metropolitan Housing Corporati, Minneapolis, MN
3,000 Greater Minneapolis Metropolitan Housing Corporation, Minneapolis, MN
3,000 Kinship of Greater Minneapolis, Minneapolis, MN
3,000 Tree Trust, St. Louis Park, MN
3,000 Working Opportunities for Women, St. Paul, MN
3,000 Working Opportunities for Women, St. Paul, MN
2,500 Hmong American Partnership, St. Paul, MN
2,500 Hmong American Partnership, St. Paul, MN
2,500 Metro Paint-A-Thon, Minneapolis, MN
2,500 Minnesota News Council, Minneapolis, MN
2,500 Minnesota News Council, Minneapolis, MN
2,000 Amicus, Inc., Minneapolis, MN
2,000 Bridging, Inc., Bloomington, MN
2,000 Logan Park Neighborhood Association, Minneapolis, MN
2,000 Neighborhood Involvement Program, Minneapolis, MN

Education

5,000 Edina ABC Foundation, Edina, MN
5,000 Page Education Foundation, Minneapolis, MN
5,000 Page Education Foundation, Minneapolis, MN
3,000 Tree Trust, St. Louis Park, MN
2,500 English Learning Center, Minneapolis, MN
2,500 English Learning Center, Minneapolis, MN
2,500 Minneapolis College of Art & Design, Minneapolis, MN
2,000 ACORN, St. Paul, MN
2,000 ACORN, St. Paul, MN

Health

3,500 Children's Heartlink, Minneapolis, MN
3,500 Children's Heartlink, Minneapolis, MN
2,000 Courage Center, Golden Valley, MN

International

3,000 Council to Monitor Human Rights In Iran, Minneapolis, MN
3,000 Council of Monitor Human Rights In Iran, Minneapolis, MN

Religion

10,000 Catholic Charities, Minneapolis, MN
10,000 Catholic Charities, Minneapolis, MN
5,000 Lutheran Social Service of Minnesota, Minneapolis, MN
5,000 Lutheran Social Service of Minnesota, Minneapolis, MN
3,000 The Zoom House, Minneapolis, MN
3,000 The Zoom House, Minneapolis, MN
2,500 Minneapolis Jewish Federation, Minneapolis, MN
2,500 Minneapolis Jewish Federation, Minneapolis, MN
2,000 Assembly of Deacons, Minneapolis, MN
2,000 Assembly of Deacons, Minneapolis, MN
2,000 Home of the Good Shepherd, St. Paul, MN

Social Services

88,657 United Way of Minneapolis Area, Minneapolis, MN
88,657 United Way of Minneapolis Area, Minneapolis, MN
10,000 Greater Minneapolis Crisis Nursery, Minneapolis, MN
10,000 Greater Minneapolis Crisis Nursery, Minneapolis, MN
5,000 People Serving People, Inc., Minneapolis, MN
5,000 People Serving People, Inc., Minneapolis, MN
5,000 Project for Pride in Living, Inc., Minneapolis, MN
3,000 Boys & Girls Club of Minneapolis, Minneapolis, MN
3,000 Boys & Girls Club of Minneapolis, Minneapolis, MN
3,000 CommonBond, St. Paul, MN
3,000 CommonBond, St. Paul, MN
3,000 Kinship of Greater Minneapolis, Minneapolis, MN
3,000 YMCA of Metro Minneapolis, Minneapolis, MN
3,000 YMCA of Metro Minneapolis, Minneapolis, MN
2,500 Project Foundation, Minneapolis, MN
2,500 Project Foundation Home Away Centers, Minneapolis, MN
2,500 Southdale Branch YMCA, Edina, MN
2,500 Southdale Branch YMCA, Edina, MN
2,000 American Refugee Committee, Minneapolis, MN
2,000 Children's Home Society, St. Paul, MN
2,000 Children's Home Society, St. Paul, MN
2,000 Washburn Child Guidance Center, Minneapolis, MN

National City Bank Of Pennsylvania

Company Contact

Pittsburgh, PA

Company Description

Former Name: Integra Bank.
Assets: US$1,080,000,000
Employees: 5,000
SIC(s): 6021 National Commercial Banks.
Parent Company: National City Bank Corp., United States

Nonmonetary Support

Type: Donated Equipment; In-kind Services

Giving Contact

Angie J. Longa, Vice President, Public Affairs
National City Bank of Pennsylvania
20 Stanwix, 25-146
Pittsburgh, PA 15222-4802
Phone: (412)644-8083
Fax: (412)644-8099
Web: http://www.national-city.com/natcity/otherdocs/about/community.html

Description

Organization Type: Corporate Giving Program
Giving Locations: PA: headquarters and operating communities in western PA
Grant Types: Employee Matching Gifts, General Support, Matching.

Financial Summary

Total Giving: $1,200,000 (1996 approx); $484,861 (1995). Note: Contributes through corporate direct giving program only.

Typical Recipients

Arts & Humanities: Arts & Humanities-General
Civic & Public Affairs: Civic & Public Affairs-General
Education: Education-General
Health: Health-General
Religion: Religion-General
Social Services: Social Services-General

Contributions Analysis

Giving Priorities: Civic affairs, education, the arts, community services, and health concerns.
Arts & Humanities: Supports local museums, theater, and arts festivals.
Civic & Public Affairs: Emphasis on revitalization of low-to-modrate-income housing and neighborhoods.
Education: Provides scholarships to children of employees. Matches employee contributions to secondary schools and colleges and universities.
Health: Priorities include children's health and health services for the indigent.
Social Services: Supports the United Way and a variety of community service programs.

Application Procedures

Application Requirements: There are no written application guidelines. All applicants should inquire at local branches.

Restrictions

Does not support individuals, religious organizations for sectarian purposes, or political or lobbying groups.

Corporate Officials

Thomas W. Golonski: president, chairman, chief executive officer PRIM CORP EMPL president, chairman, chief executive officer: National City Bank of Pennsylvania.
Angie J. Longa: vice president public affairs PRIM CORP EMPL vice president public affairs: National City Bank of Pennsylvania.

Grants Analysis

Disclosure Period: calendar year ending 1996
Typical Range: $1,000 to $1,250

National City Corp.

Company Contact

Cleveland, OH

Company Description

Revenue: US$8,070,800,000
Employees: 26,256
Fortune Rank: 218, per FORTUNE Magazine's list of 500 Largest U.S. Corporations (1999).
FF 218
SIC(s): 6021 National Commercial Banks, 6712 Bank Holding Companies.

Nonmonetary Support

Value: $5,116 (1991); $161,360 (1990)
Type: Donated Equipment
Note: Company reports that amount of nonmonetary support varies from year to year.

Corporate Sponsorship

Range: less than $4,000,000
Type: Arts & cultural events; Pledge-a-thon; Sports events
Note: Affiliates in each market area decide upon sponsorships.

National City Corp. Charitable Foundation

Giving Contact

Allen C. Waddle, Senior Vice President
National City Corp.
c/o Corporate Public Affairs Dept.
1900 E 9th St., LOC 2172
Cleveland, OH 44114-3484
Phone: (216)575-2000
Fax: (216)575-2670

Description

EIN: 346519189
Organization Type: Corporate Foundation

Giving Locations: IN; KY; OH; PA: Western Pennsylvania considers national organizations on an individual basis.
Grant Types: Capital, Employee Matching Gifts, General Support.
Note: Employee matching gift ratio: 1 to 1.

Giving Philosophy

'Being a member of a community confers both benefits and responsibilities to individuals and corporate citizens alike. The benefits of a healthy economic environment, first class cultural, educational and health care institutions, public and social services, must be balanced by the contributions of citizens to the constant advancement of human welfare by a relentless striving to change and improve, giving new hope where hope has faded, bringing substance to dreams, and widening our horizons by broadening our vision. National City Bank has a proud record of living up to its responsibilities as a corporate citizen of the many communities we serve in northeastern Ohio.' *Our Commitment to the Community, National City Bank*

Financial Summary

Total Giving: $7,700,000 (1997 approx); $6,200,000 (1996 approx); $6,200,000 (1995 approx). Note: Contributes through corporate direct giving program and foundation. Giving includes foundation.
Assets: $32,000,000 (1996 approx); $6,613 (1993); $7,720 (1992)
Gifts Received: $3,428,545 (1992)

Typical Recipients

Arts & Humanities: Arts Associations & Councils, Arts Funds, Arts Institutes, Ballet, Dance, History & Archaeology, Libraries, Museums/Galleries, Music, Opera, Performing Arts, Theater
Civic & Public Affairs: African American Affairs, Botanical Gardens/Parks, Business/Free Enterprise, Economic Development, Economic Policy, Civic & Public Affairs-General, Housing, Municipalities/Towns, Parades/Festivals, Safety, Urban & Community Affairs, Zoos/Aquariums
Education: Arts/Humanities Education, Business Education, Colleges & Universities, Economic Education, Education Reform, Faculty Development, Education-General, Literacy, Minority Education, Private Education (Precollege), Public Education (Precollege), Secondary Education (Private)
Health: Children's Health/Hospitals, Clinics/Medical Centers, Geriatric Health, Hospitals, Hospitals (University Affiliated), Mental Health, Public Health
International: International Relief Efforts
Religion: Dioceses, Jewish Causes, Ministries, Seminaries
Science: Science Museums, Scientific Centers & Institutes
Social Services: Animal Protection, At-Risk Youth, Community Centers, Community Service Organizations, Food/Clothing Distribution, Recreation & Athletics, Scouts, Senior Services, Substance Abuse, United Funds/United Ways, YMCA/YWCA/YMHA/YWHA, Youth Organizations

Contributions Analysis

Giving Priorities: Variety of social service organizations including united funds and community service and religious welfare organizations, Cleveland-area colleges and universities, local art institutions, and civic organizations.
Arts & Humanities: 10% to 15%. Supports art institutions, museums, galleries, festivals, music, theater, and dance.
Civic & Public Affairs: 5% to 10%. Supports a wide range of civic causes promoting financial cooperation among government, business, and community leaders. Major support goes to economic development concerns, including neighborhood revitalization, inner-city and community development, and public-private partnerships. Also supports publicpolicy organizations, parks, minority affairs, and organizations concerned with violent crime.
Education: 20% to 25%. Supportes universities and colleges, providing capital and operating support. Supports business education through Inroads and Junior Achievement. Also supports economic, arts, andminority education, and private precollege education. Bank matches employee contributions to education.
Health: 50% to 60%. Primarily supports united funds, community service and religious welfare organizations, community centers, food and clothing distribution, and a range of organizations that provide services for the elderly, families, youth, and children. Has supported groups devoted to researching diseases including cancer, arthritis, cystic fibrosis, and kidney ailments.

Application Procedures

Initial Contact: call requesting guidelines, then brief letter
Application Requirements: statement of purpose, history of the organization, and listing of its current board members; description of program activities and goals; budget for project or period; and proof of tax-exempt status.
Deadlines: None.
Review Process: Charitable Contributions Committee meets quarterly to review requests, following receipt of all necessary information
Evaluative Criteria: active and responsible governing body serving without compensation, holding regular meetings, and exercising administrative control; detailed budget translating program plans into financial terms and showing that current fund raising is directed to a wide base in the community; annual audit prepared by certified public accountant showing detailed revenues and expenditures
Decision Notification: quarterly
Notes: Requests should be submitted to local a local affiliate. Contact information is included in guidelines.

Restrictions

Company rarely supports national or regional causes outside its market area.
Company does not provide operating support; it does not support individuals.

Additional Information

Publications: Grant Request Guidelines

Corporate Officials

David A. Daberko: chairman, chief executive officer B Hudson, OH 1945. ED Denison University BA (1967); Case Western Reserve University MBA (1970). PRIM CORP EMPL chairman, chief executive officer: National City Corp. CORP AFFIL director: National City Bank Pennsylvania; director: National City Bank, Pittsburgh; director: National City Bank Kalamazoo; director: National City Bank Kentucky; director: National City Bank Fort Wayne; director: National City Bank Indiana; director: Federal Reserve Bank Cleveland; chairman, chief operating officer: National City Bank Cleveland. NONPR AFFIL trustee: University Hospital Cleveland; trustee: University Hospital Health System; trustee: University Circle Inc.; trustee: Hawken School; trustee: Neighborhood Progress; trustee: Cleveland Tomorrow; trustee: Greater Cleveland Growth Association; member: Bankers Roundtable; trustee: Case Western Reserve University.
Allen C. Waddle: senior vice president PRIM CORP EMPL senior vice president: National City Corp.

Foundation Officials

Allen C. Waddle: administrator (see above)

Grants Analysis

Disclosure Period: calendar year ending
Typical Range: $500 to $5,000

Recent Grants

Note: Grants derived from 1997 Form 990.

Arts & Humanities

60,000	Pittsburgh Symphony Society, Pittsburgh, PA
50,000	Columbus Museum of Art, Columbus, OH
40,000	Columbus Symphony Orchestra, Columbus, OH
33,333	Health Museum, Cleveland, OH
30,100	Pittsburgh Ballet Theater, Pittsburgh, PA
25,000	Indianapolis Museum of Art, Indianapolis, IN
25,000	Warner Theater Preservation Trust, Erie, PA
20,000	Pittsburgh Cultural Trust, Pittsburgh, PA
17,500	Indiana Repertory Theater, Indianapolis, IN
16,000	Opera Columbus, Columbus, OH
12,500	Ohio Historical Society, Columbus, OH

Civic & Public Affairs

75,000	Greater Louisville Economics, Louisville, KY
63,825	Pittsburgh Partnership for Neighborhood Development, Pittsburgh, PA
55,000	Pittsburgh Community Reinvestment, Pittsburgh, PA
44,610	Cleveland Tomorrow, Cleveland, OH
40,000	Martin Luther King Center, Columbus, OH
24,532	Famicos Foundation, Cleveland, OH
22,500	Allegheny Conference on Community, Pittsburgh, PA
21,000	Aliquippa Alliance for Unity and Development, Aliquippa, PA
20,000	Housing Opportunities, McKeesport, PA
20,000	Pennsylvania's Southwest Association, Pittsburgh, PA
19,043	Neighborhood Progress, Cleveland, OH
13,000	Mon Valley Initiative, Homestead, PA
10,000	Crawford County Development Corporation, Meadville, PA

Education

200,000	Weatherhead School of Management, Cleveland, OH
35,100	University of Toledo Foundation, Toledo, OH
25,000	Mon Valley Initiative Center, Homestead, PA
25,000	Point Park College, Pittsburgh, PA
21,100	Foundation for California University of Pennsylvania, California, PA
21,100	Negro Educational Emergency Drive, Pittsburgh, PA
20,075	University of Pittsburgh, Pittsburgh, PA
19,200	Ashland University, Ashland, OH
15,050	Pennsylvania State University, University Park, PA
15,000	Negro Educational Emergency Drive, Pittsburgh, PA

Health

142,857	Cleveland Clinic, Cleveland, OH
15,250	Clearfield Foundation for Health, Clearfield, PA

Religion

20,000	Jewish Community Center of Pittsburgh, Pittsburgh, PA
15,000	United Jewish Appeal Federation, Pittsburgh, PA

Social Services

249,000	United Way Southwestern Pennsylvania, Pittsburgh, PA
187,500	United Way Services, Cleveland, OH
80,250	United Way Franklin County, Columbus, OH
35,000	Community Lender Credit Program, Pittsburgh, PA

30,000	YMCA, Butler, PA
25,000	Choice, Indianapolis, IN
20,700	United Way Westmoreland County, Greensburg, PA
13,500	YMCA, Bigler, PA
12,750	Youngstown Mahoning Valley United Way, Youngstown, OH
12,500	United Way Summit County, Akron, OH
12,200	United Way Mercer County, Sharon, PA
10,000	Community Tech Assistance Center, Pittsburgh, PA

NATIONAL COMPUTER SYSTEMS, INC.

Company Contact

Eden Prairie, MN
Web: http://www.ncs.com

Company Description

Employees: 2,700
SIC(s): 3577 Computer Peripheral Equipment Nec, 7372 Prepackaged Software, 7374 Data Processing & Preparation.

Nonmonetary Support

Type: Donated Equipment; Donated Products; Loaned Employees; Loaned Executives; Workplace Solicitation

Giving Contact

Jorge Fischer, Corporate Contributions Program Manager
National Computer Systems Inc.
11000 Prairie Lakes Dr.
Eden Prairie, MN 55344
Phone: (612)829-3000

Alternate Contact

PO Box 9365
Minneapolis, MN 55440

Description

Organization Type: Corporate Giving Program
Giving Locations: headquarters and operating communities.
Grant Types: Award, Capital, Challenge, Employee Matching Gifts, Operating Expenses, Professorship, Project, Scholarship.

Financial Summary

Total Giving: $500,000 (1998 approx); $402,500 (1997). Note: Contributes through corporate direct giving program only. 1997 Giving includes corporate direct giving ($340,000); domestic subsidiaries ($62,500).

Typical Recipients

Arts & Humanities: Arts Appreciation, Arts Centers, Arts Institutes, Community Arts, Arts & Humanities-General, Historic Preservation, Museums/Galleries, Music, Opera, Performing Arts, Public Broadcasting, Theater, Visual Arts
Civic & Public Affairs: Economic Development, Economic Policy, Employment/Job Training, First Amendment Issues, Civic & Public Affairs-General, Law & Justice, Nonprofit Management, Philanthropic Organizations, Professional & Trade Associations, Public Policy, Urban & Community Affairs, Women's Affairs, Zoos/Aquariums
Education: Arts/Humanities Education, Business Education, Colleges & Universities, Community & Junior Colleges, Continuing Education, Economic Education, Education Associations, Education Funds, Elementary Education (Private), Engineering/Technological Education, Faculty Development, Education-General, Health & Physical Education, International Exchange, International Studies, Minority Education, Preschool Education, Private Education (Precollege), Public Education (Precollege), Science/Mathematics Education, Special Education, Student Aid
Environment: Environment-General
Health: Health-General, Health Policy/Cost Containment, Hospices, Hospitals, Nutrition, Public Health, Single-Disease Health Associations
Science: Science Exhibits & Fairs, Scientific Centers & Institutes, Scientific Organizations
Social Services: Child Welfare, Community Centers, Day Care, Delinquency & Criminal Rehabilitation, Domestic Violence, Emergency Relief, Family Planning, People with Disabilities, Recreation & Athletics, Shelters/Homelessness, Social Services-General, Substance Abuse, United Funds/United Ways, Volunteer Services, Youth Organizations

Contributions Analysis

Arts & Humanities: 15% to 20%.Supports arts and humanities, including art appreciation, art centers, and art institutes. Focus is on larger, established, highly-visible institutions.
Civic & Public Affairs: About 20%. Contributions fund economic development, professional associations, nonprofit management, public policy, environmental affairs, and urban affairs.
Education: 25% to 30%. Recipients include arts education, business education, career/vocational education, and colleges and universities.
Health: 35% to 40%. Supports public health, hospitals, health care cost containment, and health maintenance services. Additional funding goes to child welfare agencies, chemical abuse treatment centers, employment programs for the handicapped, community services, youth and family organizations, shelters, united funds, and volunteer action.

Application Procedures

Initial Contact: written request
Application Requirements: narrative of 3 pages or less, including: description and purpose of organization, amount requested, purpose of funds sought, and measurable objectives; recently audited financial statement or Form 990; and proof of tax-exempt status; names of company employee volunteers; organization's history and major accomplishments; any additional materials
Deadlines: None.
Evaluative Criteria: first priority given to requests from organizations with which an employee is involved, and organizations serving company operating communities
Decision Notification: committee meets quarterly and reviews all requests received during that quarter
Notes: If organization is primarily local, request should be sent to local contributions committee.

Restrictions

Does not support individuals or religious or fraternal groups. No grants are made to organizations without a reasonable fiscal agent, for travel or social clubs, political or lobbying groups, or professional or collegiate athletics. Generally does not support groups which receive funds from the United Way.
Organizations must have 501(c)(3) tax-exempt status.
Grants are not usually made to national or regional organizations, unless a chapter serves a company community.
Grants are not usually made to national or regional organizations, unless a chaper serves a company community.

Additional Information

Publications: Guidelines

Corporate Officials

Russell A. Gullotti: chairman, president, chief executive officer B Waltham, MA 1942. ED Boston University BS (1964); University of New Hampshire MBA (1980). PRIM CORP EMPL chairman, president, chief executive officer: National Computer Systems, Inc. CORP AFFIL director: GenRad Inc.; director: MTS Inc.

Giving Program Officials

Jorge Fischer: manager corporate contributions

Grants Analysis

Disclosure Period: calendar year ending
Typical Range: $1,000 to $2,500

NATIONAL FUEL GAS DISTRIBUTION CORP.

Company Contact

Buffalo, NY
Web: http://www.nfg.natfuel.com/spweb1/default.htm

Company Description

Employees: 2,925
SIC(s): 4925 Gas Production & Distribution Nec.
Parent Company: National Fuel Gas Co.

Nonmonetary Support

Type: Cause-related Marketing & Promotion; Donated Products; Loaned Employees; Loaned Executives; Workplace Solicitation

Giving Contact

Ms. P. J. Watkins, Supervisor, Corporate Communications
National Fuel Gas Distribution Corp.
10 Lafayette Square
Buffalo, NY 14203
Phone: (716)857-7000
Fax: (716)857-7856

Description

Organization Type: Corporate Giving Program
Giving Locations: headquarters and operating communities.
Grant Types: Capital.

Financial Summary

Total Giving: $396,000 (1994 approx); $429,000 (1993 approx). Note: Contributes through corporate direct giving program only.

Typical Recipients

Arts & Humanities: Arts Associations & Councils, Historic Preservation, Museums/Galleries, Music, Public Broadcasting, Theater
Civic & Public Affairs: Civil Rights, Employment/Job Training, Zoos/Aquariums
Education: Colleges & Universities, Elementary Education (Private)
Health: Hospices, Hospitals, Mental Health
Science: Scientific Centers & Institutes
Social Services: Animal Protection, Community Centers, People with Disabilities, Substance Abuse, United Funds/United Ways

Contributions Analysis

Arts & Humanities: Arts associations and centers, historic preservation, museums, music, public broadcasting, and theater.
Civic & Public Affairs: Interests include better government, civil rights, consumer affairs, the environment, housing, safety, and zoos.
Education: Colleges and universities; education associations; engineering, elementary, minority, and health education; and literacy.
Health: Geriatrics, cost containment, hospitals and hospices, mental health, and single-disease associations.

Social Services: Programs for the aged, animal protection, community centers, drug and alcohol programs, employment and job training, the disabled, youth organizations, and united funds.

Application Procedures

Initial Contact: company does not accept unsolicited proposals

Restrictions

Does not support individuals, religious organizations for sectarian purposes, political or lobbying groups, or organizations outside operating areas.

Additional Information

Grantmaking has been suspended until further notice.

Corporate Officials

Philip Charles Ackerman: senior vice president, directoro, director B Kenmore, NY 1944. ED State University of New York BS (1965); Harvard University LLB (1968). PRIM CORP EMPL senior vice president, director: National Fuel Gas Co. CORP AFFIL executive vice president: National Fuel Gas Supply Corp.; president: Horizon Energy Development Inc.; president: National Fuel Gas Distr Corp.; president: Highland Land & Minerals; member Buffalo Regional board: Chase Manhattan Bank NA Inc.; president: Data-Track Account Services Inc. NONPR AFFIL member: New York State Bar Association; member: Pennsylvania Gas Association; board managers, vice president: Buffalo Society Natural Sciences; member: New York Gas Group; member: American Gas Association; member: Audubon Society. CLUB AFFIL Sitzmarker Ski Club.

Bernard Joseph Kennedy: chairman, president, chief executive officer, director B Niagara Falls, NY 1931. ED Niagara University BA (1953); University of Michigan Law School JD (1958). PRIM CORP EMPL chairman, president, chief executive officer, director: National Fuel Gas Co. CORP AFFIL chairman: Utility Constructors Inc.; chairman: National Fuel Gas Supply Corp.; director: Merchants Mutual Insurance Co.; chairman: National Fuel Gas Distr Corp.; director: Marine Midland Banks Inc.; director: America Precision Industries Inc.; chairman: Assoc Electric & Gas Insurance Services Ltd. NONPR AFFIL trustee: Niagara University; director utilities public committee: Public Utility Reports Inc.; member: National Petroleum Council; member: New York State Bar Association; chairman emeritus: Institute Gas Technology; director: Interstate Natural Gas Association America; chairman: Greater Buffalo Partnership; director: Erie County Chapter ARC; member: Fed Energy Bar Association; member: Erie County Bar Association; director: Business Council New York State; board regents: Business School Canisius College; director: American Gas Association; vice chairman gas committee: American Bar Association. CLUB AFFIL Sitzmarker Ski Club; Buffalo Club; Country Club Buffalo; Buffalo Canoe Club.

NATIONAL LIFE OF VERMONT

Company Contact

Montpelier, VT

Company Description

Assets: US$5,412,900,000
Employees: 960
SIC(s): 6311 Life Insurance.

Nonmonetary Support

Type: Donated Equipment; In-kind Services; Loaned Employees

Giving Contact

Donna Fitch, Director, Corporate Communications
One National Life Dr.
Montpelier, VT 05604
Phone: (802)229-3602

Description

Organization Type: Corporate Giving Program
Giving Locations: VT: Central Vermont
Grant Types: Award, Capital, Challenge, Emergency, General Support, Multiyear/Continuing Support, Operating Expenses, Research.

Financial Summary

Total Giving: $300,000 (1994); $200,000 (1991); $200,000 (1990)

Typical Recipients

Arts & Humanities: Arts & Humanities-General
Civic & Public Affairs: Civic & Public Affairs-General
Education: Elementary Education (Public), Secondary Education (Public)
Health: Health-General, Medical Research, Mental Health, Single-Disease Health Associations
Social Services: Community Centers, Day Care, Domestic Violence, Recreation & Athletics, Shelters/Homelessness, Substance Abuse, United Funds/United Ways, Youth Organizations

Application Procedures

Initial Contact: Request grant guidelines and application.
Deadlines: None.

Restrictions

Does not support individuals, religious organizations for sectarian purposes, or political or lobbying groups.

Additional Information

Publications: Guidelines; Application Form

Corporate Officials

Martin Klein: chief financial officer, executive vice president PRIM CORP EMPL chief financial officer, executive vice president: National Life Vermont.

Thomas H. MacLeay: president, chief operating officer B Windsor, VT 1949. ED Denison University (1971); University of Denver (1972). PRIM CORP EMPL president, chief operating officer: National Life of Vermont. CORP AFFIL director: Medical Information Bureau; director: Sargasso Mutual.

Patrick Welch: chief executive officer PRIM CORP EMPL chief executive officer: National Life of Vermont.

Grants Analysis

Disclosure Period: calendar year ending
Typical Range: $1,000 to $2,500

NATIONAL MACHINERY CO.

Company Contact

Tiffin, OH

Company Description

Employees: 800
SIC(s): 3452 Bolts, Nuts, Rivets & Washers.

National Machinery Foundation, Inc.

Giving Contact

Don B. Bero, Assistant Secretary
National Machinery Foundation, Inc.
161 Greenfield Street
PO Box 747
Tiffin, OH 44883
Phone: (419)447-5211
Fax: (419)443-2380

Description

EIN: 346520191
Organization Type: Corporate Foundation
Giving Locations: OH: Seneca County
Grant Types: General Support.

Financial Summary

Total Giving: $628,193 (1997); $661,617 (1996); $518,030 (1995). Note: Contributes through foundation only. 1996 Giving includes foundation ($519,986); grants ($45,280); scholarship ($61,350); United Way ($35,000). 1995 Giving includes foundation ($389,471); gifts to individuals ($54,659); scholarship ($37,000); United Way ($36,900).
Assets: $15,160,931 (1997); $13,056,101 (1996); $11,817,129 (1995)
Gifts Received: $300 (1991)

Typical Recipients

Arts & Humanities: Arts Festivals, History & Archaeology, Libraries, Performing Arts, Public Broadcasting, Theater
Civic & Public Affairs: Botanical Gardens/Parks, Economic Development, Employment/Job Training, Housing, Law & Justice, Legal Aid, Municipalities/Towns, Parades/Festivals, Safety, Urban & Community Affairs
Education: Agricultural Education, Business Education, Colleges & Universities, Education Funds, Elementary Education (Public), Education-General, Minority Education, Preschool Education, Private Education (Precollege), Public Education (Precollege), Religious Education, School Volunteerism, Science/Mathematics Education, Secondary Education (Public)
Health: AIDS/HIV, Cancer, Children's Health/Hospitals, Clinics/Medical Centers, Emergency/Ambulance Services, Geriatric Health, Health Organizations, Heart, Hospices, Hospitals, Medical Rehabilitation, Nursing Services, Single-Disease Health Associations
Religion: Religious Welfare
Social Services: At-Risk Youth, Big Brother/Big Sister, Child Welfare, Community Centers, Community Service Organizations, Crime Prevention, Domestic Violence, Emergency Relief, Family Services, Homes, Scouts, Senior Services, Substance Abuse, United Funds/United Ways, YMCA/YWCA/YMHA/YWHA, Youth Organizations

Contributions Analysis

Arts & Humanities: 20% to 25%. Major funding to theater for the performing arts. Also contributes to public broadcasting.
Civic & Public Affairs: 5% to 10%. Organizations in the city of Tiffin and other community affairs.
Education: 20% to 25%. Primarily Heidelberg College. Also supports public high schools, private education, universities, and Junior Achievement.
Health: About 25%. Rehabilitation centers, hospitals, nursing homes, hospices, and single-disease health associations.
Religion: Less than 5%. Religious welfare organizations.
Social Services: 20% to 25%. Primarily the YMCA. Other interests include community service organizations, homes, youth organizations, and alcohol counseling.

Application Procedures

Initial Contact: letter
Application Requirements: specify financial need and purpose
Deadlines: None.

Additional Information

In addition to grant making, the foundation assists needy individuals, operates a scholarship program, and awards citizenship gifts.

Corporate Officials

Paul Nathaniel Aley: president, director B Cleveland, OH 1944. ED Ohio State University (1968); Northeastern University (1970). PRIM CORP EMPL president, director: National Machinery Co. CLUB AFFIL Rotary International Club.

Foundation Officials

Paul Nathaniel Aley: president (see above)
Larry Baker: secretary, treasurer, trustee PRIM CORP EMPL vice president employee relations: National Machinery Co.
Donald B. Bero: assistant secretary, treasurer
Patricia Hillmer: trustee
A. H. Kalnow: trustee
Carl F. Kalnow: trustee PRIM CORP EMPL ltd. polytechnic: Seasongood & Mayer OCCUPATION investment banker. CORP AFFIL director: The National Machinery Co.
D. E. King: trustee
Philip Ashworth Stevens: vice president, trustee B Toledo, OH 1934. ED Ohio State University (1956); Massachusetts Institute of Technology (1958). PRIM CORP EMPL president, certified financial planner: Stevens Consulting Group. CORP AFFIL chairman NE region, trustee: Vision Service Plan Ohio; director: Vision Service Plan California. NONPR AFFIL trustee: Heidelberg College.

Grants Analysis

Disclosure Period: calendar year ending 1996
Total Grants: $519,986*
Number of Grants: 103
Average Grant: $5,048
Highest Grant: $50,000
Typical Range: $100 to $5,000
***Note:** Giving excludes gifts to individuals; scholarship; United Way.

Recent Grants

Note: Grants derived from 1996 Form 990.

Arts & Humanities

50,000	Ritz Theater for Performing Arts, Tiffin, OH
24,000	Ritz Theater for Performing Arts, Tiffin, OH
12,500	Tiffin Seneca Public Library, Tiffin, OH -- educational
5,000	Tiffin-Seneca Public Library, Tiffin, OH

Civic & Public Affairs

9,750	Sentinel Vocational Center, Tiffin, OH -- educational
7,500	Meadowbrook Park, Bascom, OH
5,000	Habitat for Humanity, Tiffin, OH
2,650	Heritage Festival, Tiffin, OH
1,000	Tiffin Firefighters' Christmas Fund, Tiffin, OH

Education

30,000	Heidelberg College, Tiffin, OH
25,000	Heidelberg College, Tiffin, OH
20,239	Tiffin University, Tiffin, OH
20,000	St. Joseph School, Tiffin, OH
10,000	Old Fort High School, Old Fort, OH -- for Auditorium Renovation Program
10,000	Seneca-Wyandot Center, Tiffin, OH -- for technology equipment
4,350	St. Joseph School, Tiffin, OH
4,000	Junior Achievement Northwestern Ohio, Toledo, OH -- educational
3,500	McCutchenville Elementary Technology Initiative, McCutchenville, OH
3,300	Melmore Elementary Technology Program, Melmore, OH
3,000	St. Mary's, Tiffin, OH -- educational
2,700	Bettsville Technology Initiative, Bettsville, OH -- educational
1,000	Future Farmers of America Foundation, Columbus, OH -- educational
1,000	Ohio Foundation of Independent Colleges, Columbus, OH -- educational
1,000	Tiffin Junior High, Tiffin, OH

Health

50,000	Betty Jane Memorial Rehabilitation Center, Tiffin, OH
30,000	Betty Jane Memorial Rehabilitation Center, Tiffin, OH
20,000	Mercy Hospital, Tiffin, OH -- for Vision 2000 Capital Fund Campaign
5,000	American Red Cross, Tiffin, OH
2,500	Hospice Care, Tiffin, OH
2,000	American Heart Association, Toledo, OH
2,000	Easter Seal Society of Northwestern Ohio, Fremont, OH
1,000	Seneca County AIDS Council, Tiffin, OH

Religion

10,000	St. Francis Home Child Care Center, Tiffin, OH
5,000	St. Francis Home, Tiffin, OH -- for Friend to Friend Campaign
3,000	Salvation Army, Tiffin, OH

Social Services

50,000	YMCA Recreation Center, Tiffin, OH
35,000	United Way Tiffin-Seneca County, Tiffin, OH
20,000	Patchworks House, Tiffin, OH
10,000	Tiffin-Seneca Teen Center, Tiffin, OH
6,000	Seneca County Court-Appointed Special Advocates, Tiffin, OH
5,400	Camp Fire Boys and Girls, Findlay, OH
5,400	Flat Rock Homes, Flat Rock, OH
4,000	DARE Program, Tiffin, OH -- educational
3,000	DARE Program, Tiffin, OH -- educational
3,000	First Step, Sandusky Valley Domestic Violence Center, Fostoria, OH
2,000	Emergency Heating Fund, Tiffin, OH
1,000	Association for Children for Enforcement of Support, Toledo, OH
1,000	Big Brothers and Big Sisters, Tiffin, OH
1,000	Fostoria Alcohol-Drug Center, Fostoria, OH
1,000	Senior Community Services, Tiffin, OH

NATIONAL PRESTO INDUSTRIES, INC.

Company Contact

Eau Claire, WI
Web: http://www.presto-net.com

Company Description

Employees: 547
SIC(s): 3634 Electric Housewares & Fans, 5064 Electrical Appliances--Television & Radio.

Presto Foundation

Giving Contact

Norma Jaenke, Executive Director
The Presto Foundation
3925 North Hastings Way
Eau Claire, WI 54703
Phone: (715)839-2119
Fax: (715)839-2122

Description

EIN: 396045769
Organization Type: Corporate Foundation
Giving Locations: WI: Northwestern Wisconsin, especially Eau Claire and Chippewa Counties headquarters and operating communities.
Grant Types: General Support, Scholarship.
Note: Scholarships are for children of employees.

Financial Summary

Total Giving: $650,000 (fiscal year ending May 31, 1999 approx); $650,000 (fiscal 1998 approx); $532,383 (fiscal 1997). Note: Contributes through corporate direct giving program and foundation. 1997 Giving includes foundation ($381,225); scholarship ($126,558); United Way ($24,600).
Assets: $14,291,832 (fiscal 1997); $15,093,121 (fiscal 1996); $15,130,668 (fiscal 1995)

Typical Recipients

Arts & Humanities: Museums/Galleries, Performing Arts, Public Broadcasting
Civic & Public Affairs: Botanical Gardens/Parks, Community Foundations, Employment/Job Training, Housing, Municipalities/Towns, Philanthropic Organizations
Education: Colleges & Universities, Community & Junior Colleges, Engineering/Technological Education, Public Education (Precollege), Science/Mathematics Education, Secondary Education (Public), Student Aid, Vocational & Technical Education
Environment: Environment-General, Wildlife Protection
Health: Cancer, Children's Health/Hospitals, Emergency/Ambulance Services, Health Funds, Heart, Hospitals, Medical Research, Multiple Sclerosis, Single-Disease Health Associations
Religion: Churches, Religious Organizations, Religious Welfare, Synagogues/Temples
Social Services: Community Centers, Community Service Organizations, Food/Clothing Distribution, Homes, People with Disabilities, Recreation & Athletics, Shelters/Homelessness, United Funds/United Ways, Youth Organizations

Contributions Analysis

Giving Priorities: Social welfare, the arts, religion, and higher education.
Arts & Humanities: 38%. Primarily supports instructional and training activities for local television stations. Also supports historical museums, cultural centers and symphonies.
Civic & Public Affairs: Less than 5%. Funds environmental conservation, community and career development, advocacy issues.
Education: 27%. Supports colleges and universities, scholarships to employee's children, career/vocational education, and publicpre-college education.
Health: 7%. Supports single-disease research, hospitals and other health associations.
Religion: 22%. Funds religious welfare groups and temples
Social Services: 4%. Primarily supports organizations concerned with individual growth, such as, Junior Achievement and Goodwill Industries. Also supports the United Way, housing, youth and sports.
Note: 22%. Contributions were made in 1997.

Application Procedures

Initial Contact: brief letter
Application Requirements: a description of organization and project, amount requested, proposed budget, and proof of tax-exempt status
Deadlines: None.
Notes: Additional information may be requested by the foundation.

Restrictions

Company does not make contributions to organizations outside operating areas.

Additional Information

Publications: Annual Report

Corporate Officials

Maryjo Rose Cohen: president, chief executive officer, director B Eau Claire, WI 1952. ED University of Michigan (1973); University of Michigan JD (1976). PRIM CORP EMPL president, chief executive officer, director: National Presto Industries, Inc. CORP AFFIL secretary, treasurer, director: Presto Export Ltd.; secretary, treasurer, director: Presto Manufacturing Co.; vice president, director: National Pipeline Co.; secretary, treasurer, director: National Defense Corp.; secretary, assistant treasurer, director: National Holding Investment Co.; vice president, secretary, treasurer, director: Jackson Sales & Storage Co.; vice president, director: National Automatic Pipeline Oper Inc.; secretary, treasurer, director: Canton Sales & Storage Co.; secretary, treasurer, director: Century Leasing & Liquidating Inc.

Melvin Samuel Cohen: chairman B Minneapolis, MN 1918. ED University of Minnesota BS (1939); University of Minnesota JD (1941). PRIM CORP EMPL chairman: National Presto Industries, Inc. CORP AFFIL president: Presto Export Ltd.; chairman, president: Presto Manufacturing Co.; president: National Defense Corp.; president: National Holding Investment Co.; president: Century Leasing & Liquidating Inc.; president, director: Jackson Sales & Storage Co.; president: Canton Sales & Storage Co.

Foundation Officials

Dean Boehne: trustee
Eileen Phillips Cohen: trustee
Maryjo Rose Cohen: vice president, treasurer, trustee (see above)
Melvin Samuel Cohen: chairman, president, trustee (see above)
Johannes Dahle: vice president, trustee
Geraldine Eaton: secretary, trustee
Norma Jaenke: executive director
Richard Myhers: trustee
Arthur Petzoad: vice president, trustee

Grants Analysis

Disclosure Period: fiscal year ending May 31, 1997
Total Grants: $381,225*
Number of Grants: 102
Average Grant: $3,737
Highest Grant: $100,000
Typical Range: $500 to $10,000
***Note:** Giving excludes scholarship; United Way.

Recent Grants

Note: Grants derived from 1997 Form 990.

Arts & Humanities

20,000	Friends of WHA TV, Madison, WI
15,000	Channel 10/36 Friends, Milwaukee, WI
10,000	WPID Television Greater Dayton Public Television, Dayton, OH
10,000	WVIA Northeast Pennsylvania Education Television Association, Pittston, PA
10,000	WVIZ Education Television Association of Metro Cleveland, Cleveland, OH
7,500	KRMA/Channel 6 Council for Public Television, Denver, CO
7,500	WKNO Mid-South Community Foundation, Memphis, TN
7,500	WLVT Lehigh Valley Telecommunication Corporation, Bethlehem, PA
7,500	WQLM TV, Erie, PA
7,500	WTVS Detroit Education Television Foundation, Detroit, MI
5,000	KCPT/Channel 19, Kansas City, MO
5,000	KETC/Channel 9, Saint Louis, MO
5,000	KSMQ/Channel 15, Austin, MN
5,000	KVPT/Channel 18 Valley Public Television, Fresno, CA
5,000	Maine Public Broadcasting, Lewiston, ME
5,000	WCET Greater Cincinnati Television Education Foundation, Cincinnati, OH
5,000	WGTE Public Broadcasting Foundation of Northwest Ohio, Toledo, OH
5,000	WJCT/Channel 7, Jacksonville, FL
5,000	WMHT Educational Telecommunications, Schenectady, NY
5,000	WNIT Michiana Public Broadcasting Corporation, Elkhart, IN
5,000	WOSU TV 34, Columbus, OH
5,000	WYES Greater New Orleans Education Television Foundation, New Orleans, LA
4,000	KWCM West Central Minnesota Educational Television, Appleton, MN
4,000	WTVP Illinois Valley Public Telecommunications Corporation, Peoria, IL

Civic & Public Affairs

5,500	Career Development Center, Eau Claire, WI
5,000	Starlight Foundation, New York, NY

Education

12,000	Bemidji State University, Bemidji, MN
9,000	Colorado School of the Mines, Golden, CO
8,408	University of Wisconsin, Eau Claire, WI
7,652	University of Wisconsin, Milwaukee, WI
7,437	University of Wisconsin, Menomonie, WI
7,260	Duquesne University, Pittsburgh, PA
7,233	University of Wisconsin, Stevens Point, WI
7,140	University of Wisconsin, La Crosse, WI
7,067	University of Wisconsin, Menomonie, WI
6,998	Wayne State University, Detroit, MI
6,103	Mississippi College, Clinton, MS
6,091	Fort Lewis College, Durango, CO
5,948	University of Wisconsin, Eau Claire, WI
5,402	University of Wisconsin, Menomonie, WI
4,963	University of Wisconsin, Platteville, WI
4,208	New Mexico State University, Alapogodo, NM
4,113	New Mexico State University, Las Cruces, NM
4,029	University of Wisconsin, Eau Claire, WI

Health

20,700	American Cancer Society, Cincinnati, OH
11,500	American Cancer Society, Pewaukee, WI

Religion

100,000	Salvation Army, Des Plaines, IL

Social Services

8,500	United Way, Eau Claire, WI
7,000	United Way Capital Area, Jackson, MS
3,500	Goodwill Industries, Jackson, MS

NATIONAL SERVICE INDUSTRIES, INC.

Company Contact

Atlanta, GA
Web: http://www.nationalservice.com

Company Description

Employees: 19,700 (1999)
SIC(s): 2677 Envelopes, 2782 Blankbooks & Looseleaf Binders, 3646 Commercial Lighting Fixtures, 7213 Linen Supply.

National Service Foundation

Giving Contact

James Balloun, President, Chairman & Chief Executive Officer
National Service Street Foundation
1420 Peachtree Street, N.E.
Atlanta, GA 30309-3002
Phone: (404)853-1000
Fax: (404)858-1015

Description

Founded: 1969
EIN: 586051102
Organization Type: Corporate Foundation
Giving Locations: GA
Grant Types: General Support.

Financial Summary

Total Giving: $450,000 (fiscal year ending August 31, 1999 approx); $391,417 (fiscal 1998); $264,185 (fiscal 1995). Note: Contributes through foundation only.
Giving Analysis: Giving for fiscal 1996 includes: foundation grants to United Way ($70,000); fiscal 1998: foundation grants to United Way ($78,400)
Assets: $472,613 (fiscal 1998); $59,297 (fiscal 1996); $8,545 (fiscal 1994)
Gifts Received: $447,298 (fiscal 1998); $1,000,000 (fiscal 1989). Note: Contributions are received from National Service Industries, Inc.

Typical Recipients

Arts & Humanities: Arts Centers, Arts Festivals, Arts Outreach, Historic Preservation, History & Archaeology, Libraries, Museums/Galleries, Music, Opera, Theater
Civic & Public Affairs: Botanical Gardens/Parks, Business/Free Enterprise, Clubs, Community Foundations, Economic Development, Economic Policy, Civic & Public Affairs-General, Municipalities/Towns, Philanthropic Organizations, Public Policy, Women's Affairs, Zoos/Aquariums
Education: Afterschool/Enrichment Programs, Arts/Humanities Education, Business Education, Colleges & Universities, Economic Education, Education Funds, Engineering/Technological Education, Education-General, Leadership Training, Legal Education, Literacy, Medical Education, Medical Education, Minority Education, Private Education (Precollege), Vocational & Technical Education
Environment: Environment-General
Health: Arthritis, Cancer, Diabetes, Heart, Hospitals, Medical Rehabilitation, Medical Research, Multiple Sclerosis, Prenatal Health Issues
International: Health Care/Hospitals, International Affairs, International Organizations
Religion: Jewish Causes, Religious Organizations, Religious Welfare, Social/Policy Issues
Social Services: Animal Protection, Camps, Child Abuse, Child Welfare, Community Centers, Community Service Organizations, Domestic Violence, Emergency Relief, Food/Clothing Distribution, People with Disabilities, Recreation & Athletics, Scouts, United Funds/United Ways, United Funds/United Ways, Volunteer Services, YMCA/YWCA/YMHA/YWHA, Youth Organizations

Contributions Analysis

Giving Priorities: Focus on social services, Jewish welfare, education, and the arts.
Arts & Humanities: About 13%. Supports arts centers, the performing arts, and libraries.
Civic & Public Affairs: 8%. Funds economic development and civic organizations.
Education: 15%. Supports colleges and universities, mninority education, and Junior Achievement.
Environment: 1%.

Health: 6%. Funds hospitals and single-disease health associations.
Religion: 20%. Supports Jewish causes and religious welfare.
Social Services: 38%. Funds United Way and youth conerns.
Note: Total contributions in fiscal 1998.

Application Procedures

Initial Contact: Submit a written request.
Deadlines: None.

Corporate Officials

James S. Balloun: chairman, chief executive officer, president ED Iowa State University of Science & Technology BS (1960); Harvard University MBA (1965). PRIM CORP EMPL chairman, chief executive officer, president: National Service Industries, Inc. CORP AFFIL director: Radiant System Inc.; director: Wachovia Corp.
Brock Alan Hattox: executive vice president, chief financial officer B Ecru, MS 1948. ED University of Mississippi BCE (1969); Harvard University Graduate School of Business Administration MBA (1971). PRIM CORP EMPL executive vice president, chief financial officer: National Service Industries Inc.

Foundation Officials

Mark Bachman: director
Brock Alan Hattox: director (see above)
David Levy: trustee B Atlanta, GA 1937. ED Emory University BA (1959); Emory University School of Law LLB (1961); Georgetown University Law Center LLM (1964). PRIM CORP EMPL executive vice president administration, counsel, director: National Service Industries, Inc. NONPR AFFIL member: American Bar Association; member: American Society of Corporate Secretaries.
Carol Morgan: chairperson

Grants Analysis

Disclosure Period: fiscal year ending August 31, 1998
Total Grants: $313,017*
Number of Grants: 128
Average Grant: $2,445
Highest Grant: $51,725
Typical Range: $50 to $21,000
*Note: Giving excludes United Way.

Recent Grants

Note: Grants derived from 1998 Form 990.

Arts & Humanities

15,250 Woodruff Arts Center, Atlanta, GA
7,150 Atlanta Symphony Orchestra, Atlanta, GA
7,000 Atlanta Opera, Atlanta, GA
6,050 Young Audiences, Atlanta, GA
5,000 Woodruff Arts Ctr Special Campaign, Atlanta, GA
2,500 Marietta/Cobb Museum Of Art, Marietta, GA
1,500 Pendragon Theatre, Saranac Lake, NY

Civic & Public Affairs

10,000 Citizens For A Sound Economy, Washington, DC
5,000 Carter Center, Atlanta, GA
5,000 Prince Of Wales Foundation, Washington, DC
2,500 Atlanta Botanical Garden, Atlanta, GA
2,500 Atlanta Women's Fund, Atlanta, GA
2,500 Trees Atlanta, Atlanta, GA

Education

18,125 Junior Achievement, Atlanta, GA
10,000 Morehouse School Of Medicine, Atlanta, GA
5,000 Tuskegee University, Tuskegee, AL
3,000 Issa Foundation, Chicago, IL
2,500 Hickory Log Vocational School, White, GA
2,000 Literacy Action, Atlanta, GA
2,000 Middle Georgia College, Cochran, GA
2,000 Northwestern University, Chicago, IL
2,000 United Negro College Fund, Atlanta, GA
2,000 Young Harris College, Young Harris, GA
1,854 University Of Georgia Foundation, Athens, GA
1,450 Emory University, Atlanta, GA
1,450 University Of Mississippi, Jackson, MS

Environment

5,000 Path Foundation, Atlanta, GA

Health

5,600 Egleston Hospital, Atlanta, GA
5,000 Georgia Research Alliance, Atlanta, GA
3,060 Hot Springs Rehab-C. Zook Fund, Hot Springs, AR
2,650 Arthritis Foundation, Atlanta, GA
2,500 City Of Hope, Atlanta, GA
1,500 March Of Dimes, Atlanta, GA

Religion

51,725 Atlanta Jewish Federation, Atlanta, GA
8,780 Atlanta Jewish Community Center, Atlanta, GA
5,000 American Friends Of Hebrew University, New York, NY
2,500 Holocaust Museum, Washington, DC
1,750 Salvation Army, Atlanta, GA

Social Services

78,400 United Way, Atlanta, GA
20,250 Camp Twin Lakes, Atlanta, GA
7,250 Atlanta Humane Society, Atlanta, GA
5,250 Advocates For Bartow's Children, Cartersville, GA
5,150 American Red Cross, Atlanta, GA
5,000 Atlanta Community Food Bank, Atlanta, GA
3,000 Boys' And Girls Clubs Of Atlanta, Atlanta, GA
2,500 Georgia Council On Child Abuse, Atlanta, GA
2,450 Hands On Atlanta, Atlanta, GA
2,200 Gwinnett Ymca, Gwinnett, GA
2,000 Tri-Lakes Humane Society, Saranac Lake, NY
1,300 Boy Scouts Of America, Atlanta, GA

NATIONAL STARCH & CHEMICAL CO.

Company Contact

Bridgewater, NJ

Company Description

Employees: 8,000
SIC(s): 2046 Wet Corn Milling, 2821 Plastics Materials & Resins, 2891 Adhesives & Sealants, 2899 Chemical Preparations Nec.
Parent Company: Unilever Plc, PO Box 68, Blackfriars, London, England

Operating Locations

AR: National Starch & Chemical Co., North Little Rock; CA: National Starch & Chemical Co., Berkeley, City of Commerce; GA: National Starch & Chemical Co., Atlanta; IL: National Starch & Chemical Co., Lincolnshire, Meredosia; IN: National Starch & Chemical Co., Indianapolis; LA: National Starch & Chemical Co., New Orleans; ME: National Starch & Chemical Co., Island Falls, Portland; MI: National Starch & Chemical Co., Farmington Hills; MN: National Starch & Chemical Co., Eden Prairie; MO: National Starch & Chemical Co., Kansas City, North Kansas City; NC: National Starch & Chemical Co., Salisbury; NJ: National Starch & Chemical Co., Bloomfield; National Starch and Chemical Co., Bridgewater; National Starch & Chemical Co., Plainfield; NY: National Starch & Chemical Co., West Seneca; OH: National Starch & Chemical Co., Cincinnati, Delaware; TN: National Starch & Chemical Co., Memphis; TX: National Starch & Chemical Co., Grand Prairie; WI: National Starch & Chemical Co., Appleton, Milwaukee

Nonmonetary Support

Volunteer Programs: In the counties surrounding company headquarters in Bridgewater, NJ, National actively supports the Science Alliance Program. Senior staffers devote their time and expertise to help teach middle school and high school students about science in an interesting and hands-on fashion. In Woodruff, SC, employees help nurture the growth and aspirations of children by serving as positive role models, confidants and supporters. Volunteerism extends to international National Starch and Chemical employees in England, Italy, and South Africa.

National Starch & Chemical Foundation

Giving Contact

Donna Kmetz, Foundation Financial Specialist
National Starch & Chemical Foundation
10 Finderne Avenue
Bridgewater, NJ 08807
Phone: (908)685-5201
Fax: (908)685-5096

Description

Founded: 1968
EIN: 237010264
Organization Type: Corporate Foundation
Giving Locations: primarily in headquarters and operating communities.
Grant Types: Capital, Employee Matching Gifts, General Support, Multiyear/Continuing Support, Operating Expenses, Research, Scholarship.
Note: The company matches employee gifts to United Way.

Financial Summary

Total Giving: $1,889,648 (1998); $2,000,000 (1997 approx); $2,400,000 (1996 approx). Note: Contributes through corporate direct giving program and foundation.
Giving Analysis: Giving for 1998 includes: foundation ($1,446,363); foundation grants to United Way ($443,285)
Assets: $244,936 (1998); $196,124 (1995); $314,529 (1993)
Gifts Received: $2,000,383 (1998); $1,963,150 (1995); $1,900,165 (1993)

Typical Recipients

Arts & Humanities: Arts Centers, Dance, Museums/Galleries, Music, Opera, Performing Arts, Theater, Visual Arts
Civic & Public Affairs: African American Affairs, Business/Free Enterprise, Economic Development, Civic & Public Affairs-General, Housing, Nonprofit Management, Philanthropic Organizations, Professional & Trade Associations, Public Policy, Urban & Community Affairs
Education: Business Education, Community & Junior Colleges, Education Associations, Education Funds, Elementary Education (Private), Engineering/Technological Education, Education-General, Minority Education, Preschool Education, Private Education (Precollege), Science/Mathematics Education, Secondary Education (Private), Secondary Education (Public), Student Aid
Environment: Environment-General, Resource Conservation
Health: Clinics/Medical Centers, Emergency/Ambulance Services, Health Funds, Health Organizations, Hospitals, Medical Rehabilitation, Medical Training, Nursing Services, Public Health

Science: Scientific Centers & Institutes, Scientific Organizations
Social Services: Child Welfare, Community Centers, Community Service Organizations, Emergency Relief, Family Services, Food/Clothing Distribution, Recreation & Athletics, Scouts, Substance Abuse, United Funds/United Ways, YMCA/YWCA/YMHA/YWHA, Youth Organizations

Contributions Analysis

Giving Priorities: Elementary and secondary schools and colleges and universities, United Way and other social service agencies, fire and rescue squads, the arts, and hospitals.
Arts & Humanities: 4%. Theater and performing arts; musical groups such as symphonies; museums and historical societies; and arts associations and festivals.
Civic & Public Affairs: 7%. Professional associations, public policy, urban leagues, business groups, and environmental organizations.
Education: 28%. Elementary and secondary schools, colleges and universities, and junior achievement. Also supports math and scienceeducation programs for minorities. Matching gifts constitute a large number of grants to colleges.
Environment: 1%. Resource conservation and the Indiana Environmental Institute.
Health: 8%. Hospitals, research, foundations, and single-disease health organizations.
Science: 5%. Scientific organizations and research.
Social Services: 47%. United Way organizations in various company-operating communities, child welfare and recreational groups, volunteer organizations, food banks, services for the elderly and disabled, and others.
Note: Total contributions made in 1998.

Application Procedures

Initial Contact: Send a letter.
Application Requirements: Include proof of 501(c)(3) status; for employee scholarships: application form and SAT/National Merit Scholarship Qualifying Test record.
Deadlines: Generally October or November to be considered for following calendar year; deadline for employee scholarships is December 31.
Review Process: Amount of funds devoted to particular giving fields is decided by company conference board.

Restrictions

No grants are given to individuals or religious organizations for sectarian purposes.
Scholarship program participants must take the PSAT and their parents must be employees of National Starch & Chemical Co. or an affiliate.

Additional Information

Many grants go to repeat recipients, although the foundation does consider new applicants.

Corporate Officials

Leonard J. Berlik: vice president vice president B Chicago, IL 1947. ED University of Tennessee (1969); Xavier University (1975). PRIM CORP EMPL vice president: National Starch & Chemical Co.
Ray Buchan: chief executive officer PRIM CORP EMPL chief executive officer: National Starch & Chemical Co.
Walter F. Schlauch: group vice president B New York, NY 1941. ED City University of New York (1963); Stevens Institute of Technology (1967). PRIM CORP EMPL group vice president: National Starch & Chemical Co.

Foundation Officials

P. C. Malaff: secretary
Suzanne Prendergast: financial specialist
Martin Torbert: chairman

Grants Analysis

Disclosure Period: calendar year ending 1998
Total Grants: $1,446,363*
Number of Grants: 786 (approx)
Average Grant: $1,840 (approx)
Highest Grant: $100,000
Typical Range: $100 to $20,000
***Note:** Giving excludes United Way.

Recent Grants

Note: Grants derived from 1995 Form 990.

Arts & Humanities

15,000	New Jersey Symphony Orchestra, Newark, NJ
12,500	George Street Playhouse, New Brunswick, NJ
12,000	Metropolitan Opera Association, New York, NY
8,000	Waterworks Visual Arts Center, Salisbury, NC

Civic & Public Affairs

77,000	Flora, Christiansburg, VA
50,000	Adhesive and Sealant Council Education Foundation, Washington, DC
10,000	PRIDE Convention, Indianapolis, IN
10,000	Somerset County Coalition on Affordable Housing, Bound Brook, NJ
10,000	West Indianapolis Development Corp, Indianapolis, IN -- housing revolving fund

Education

61,190	National Merit Scholarship Corp, Chicago, IL
30,000	New Jersey Institute of Technology, University Heights, NJ -- Hazardous Substances Research Center
25,000	Flexible Packaging Education Foundation, Washington, DC
25,000	Manufacturing Institute, Washington, DC
20,000	Plainfield School-Based Youth Services Program, Plainfield, NJ
15,000	New Jersey Institute of Technology, Newark, NJ -- FEMME Program
10,000	New Jersey Institute of Technology, Newark, NJ -- Center for Pre-College Programs
10,000	Rowan-Cabarrus Community College Foundation, Salisbury, NC -- CIM Project
10,000	Rutgers University Foundation, New Brunswick, NJ -- Center for Advanced Food Technology
10,000	Rutgers University Foundation Chemistry Department, New Brunswick, NJ
8,000	Lehigh University, Bethlehem, PA -- for unit operations lab
7,500	Rutgers University Foundation, New Brunswick, NJ -- Math and Science Learning Center
7,150	Accreditation Board for Engineering and Technology, Boca Raton, FL
7,000	United Negro College Fund, Fairfax, VA
6,500	University of Michigan Macromolecular Research Center, Ann Arbor, MI

Environment

15,000	Annapolis Center for Environmental Quality, Annapolis, MD
10,000	Indiana Environmental Institute, Indianapolis, IN
10,000	White River Greenway Fund of the Indianapolis Clean City Committee, Indianapolis, IN

Health

25,000	Muhlenburg Foundation, Plainfield, NJ
25,000	Somerset Medical Center, Somerville, NJ
17,500	American Council on Science and Health, New York, NY
10,000	Enoree Fire and Rescue, Enoree, SC
10,000	Hunterdon Medical Center Auxiliary, Flemington, NJ
10,000	Morristown Memorial Hospital, Morristown, NJ
10,000	St. Peter's Foundation, New Brunswick, NJ -- medical center

Social Services

163,000	United Way Somerset County, Somerville, NJ
47,000	United Way Central Indiana, Indianapolis, IN
25,000	Somerset Alliance for the Future, Somerville, NJ
22,350	Heart of America United Way, Kansas City, MO
22,300	United Way, Chattanooga, TN
21,780	United Way Piedmont, Spartanburg, SC
12,520	United Way Rowan County, Salisbury, NC
11,600	United Way Union County, Elizabeth, NJ
10,000	Girl Scouts of America, North Branch, NJ
10,000	Resource Center for Women and Their Families, Bound Brook, NJ
10,000	United Family and Children's Society, Plainfield, NJ
9,850	United Way Greater Los Angeles, Harbor and Southeast Region, Los Angeles, CA
9,000	Somerset Council on Alcoholism and Drug Dependency, Somerville, NJ
8,000	PeopleCare Center, Bridgewater, NJ
7,300	Prairieland United Way, Jacksonville, IL
7,000	United Way Crusade of Mercy, Chicago, IL

NATIONWIDE INSURANCE CO.

 Number 71 of Top 100 Corporate Givers

Company Contact

Columbus, OH
Web: http://www.nationwide.com

Company Description

Revenue: US$13,554,900,000 (1999)
Profit: US$512,800,000 (1999)
Employees: 12,150
Fortune Rank: 128, per FORTUNE Magazine's list of 500 Largest U.S. Corporations (1999).
FF 128
SIC(s): 6331 Fire, Marine & Casualty Insurance.

Nonmonetary Support

Type: Donated Equipment; In-kind Services; Loaned Executives
Note: Co. donated $99,823 in nonmonetary support in 1997. Co. sponsors Fan Club: for each 25 volunteer hours done by an employee, that organization receives a $100 grant.

Corporate Sponsorship

Value: $215,000
Type: Arts & cultural events; Festivals/fairs; Music & entertainment events; Pledge-a-thon; Sports events
Contact: Charlotte Glen-Frey, Community Relations Manager
Note: Co. sponsors lunches and dinners.

Nationwide Insurance Enterprise Foundation

Giving Contact

Stephen A. Rish, President
Nationwide Insurance Enterprise Foundation
1 Nationwide Plaza
Mail Drop 1-36-13
Columbus, OH 43215-2220
Phone: (614)249-5095
Fax: (614)677-0320
Email: styped@nationwide.com

Alternate Contact

Deborah Stype, Community Services Manager
Phone: (614)249-4310

Description

Founded: 1959
EIN: 316022301
Organization Type: Corporate Foundation
Giving Locations: OH: Central Ohio and near state operating locations
Grant Types: Capital, Emergency, Employee Matching Gifts, Endowment, General Support, Matching, Multiyear/Continuing Support.

Giving Philosophy

'Nationwide Insurance Enterprise is committed--through its formalized corporate Vision--to investing in our communities and being a good corporate citizen. This is translated into the ethical conduct of business, a dedication to service excellence, and a conscientious attentiveness to social responsibility. Since 1959, the Nationwide Insurance Enterprise Foundation has worked in support of human service goals, and as a caring social outreach in the communities where the Nationwide Insurance Enterprise does business. The primary aim of the Foundation is to provide financial support for qualified tax-exempt organizations whose programs address basic human needs. The Foundation strives to maintain a contribution program that is objective and consistent, and is a positive response to the needs of a healthy society.'
Nationwide Insurance Foundation's guidelines brochure

Financial Summary

Total Giving: $11,600,000 (1999 approx); $11,542,819 (1998); $11,617,813 (1997). Note: Contributes through corporate direct giving program and foundation. 1997 Giving includes corporate direct giving ($840,615); foundation ($10,677,375); nonmonetary support.
Assets: $45,000,000 (1999 approx); $44,000,000 (1998 approx); $39,169,641 (1997)
Gifts Received: $8,160,922 (1996); $5,124,814 (1995); $9,261,240 (1993)

Typical Recipients

Arts & Humanities: Arts Associations & Councils, Arts Centers, Arts Funds, Ballet, Arts & Humanities-General, Historic Preservation, History & Archaeology, Museums/Galleries, Music, Opera, Performing Arts, Public Broadcasting, Theater
Civic & Public Affairs: African American Affairs, Botanical Gardens/Parks, Civil Rights, Economic Development, Economic Policy, Employment/Job Training, Ethnic Organizations, Civic & Public Affairs-General, Housing, Law & Justice, Nonprofit Management, Philanthropic Organizations, Professional & Trade Associations, Rural Affairs, Safety, Urban & Community Affairs, Zoos/Aquariums
Education: Agricultural Education, Arts/Humanities Education, Business Education, Colleges & Universities, Economic Education, Education Funds, Education Reform, Education-General, Legal Education, Literacy, Minority Education, Public Education (Precollege), Student Aid
Environment: Environment-General, Resource Conservation, Wildlife Protection
Health: AIDS/HIV, Alzheimers Disease, Cancer, Children's Health/Hospitals, Emergency/Ambulance Services, Eyes/Blindness, Health Organizations, Heart, Hospitals, Long-Term Care, Medical Research, Mental Health, Nursing Services, Single-Disease Health Associations, Speech & Hearing
International: Health Care/Hospitals, International Affairs, International Development, International Environmental Issues, International Organizations
Religion: Jewish Causes, Religious Organizations, Religious Welfare
Science: Science Museums, Scientific Centers & Institutes
Social Services: Animal Protection, Camps, Child Abuse, Child Welfare, Community Service Organizations, Counseling, Day Care, Emergency Relief, Family Planning, Family Services, Food/Clothing Distribution, Homes, People with Disabilities, Recreation & Athletics, Senior Services, Shelters/Homelessness, Substance Abuse, United Funds/United Ways, YMCA/YWCA/YMHA/YWHA, Youth Organizations

Contributions Analysis

Giving Priorities: United funds; colleges, universities, and independent college funds and associations; the arts; and civic organizations.
Arts & Humanities: 15% to 20%. Established and pioneering organizations and programs to support visual and performing artists and to broaden the cultural experiences of employees and the general public.
Civic & Public Affairs: Less than 5%. Supports economic development; improved quality of government and the legal system; business, economic, and public policy research; environmental conservation.
Education: 15% to 20%. Higher education, including colleges, universities and independent college funds and associations; business and economic education; equal opportunities for minorities and persons with disabilities. Preference is given to statewide associations of regionally-accredited colleges and universities.
Health: About 60%. Health, health understanding, and safety of the general public; availability and delivery of health care at reasonable cost; relief for the ill or rehabilitation of persons with disabilities; socially or economically disadvantaged individuals and groups; youth, the elderly, and persons with disabilities; job opportunities for the disadvantaged; family social services.

Application Procedures

Initial Contact: request an Applicant Information Sheet from foundation
Application Requirements: applicant information sheet must accompany a formal proposal narrative, no longer than five pages, details of which are outlined in the guidelines brochure containing the information sheet; also submit: a copy of the Treasury letter certifying 501(c)(3) tax-exempt status; documentation that the board of directors authorized the request; names and addresses of board of directors; and a copy of the organization's most recent IRS Form 990
Deadlines: September 1
Review Process: recommendations by contributions committee made to foundation trustees at the end of calendar year
Evaluative Criteria: organization's structure and assurance of successful completion of project; organization seeks multiple sources of support rather than relying on the foundation as a single funding source; project involves Nationwide employees in leadership positions; consistency of resources and programs; sources of financial or other support; benefit of programs to Nationwide employees and agents; convenience of monitoring organization's efforts; whether purpose addresses basic human needs, and applies the spirit of cooperation to help people to help themselves; whether the approach has been designed to meet objectives; evidence of broad community involvement, cooperative planning, and diversified funding; and project doesn't duplicate public or private sector interests
Decision Notification: final approval made by trustees at annual meeting in March of year in which contributions are made; response to recommended requests issued about three weeks after trustees' meeting

Restrictions

Contributions not made to individuals; political organizations; organizations that influence, promote, or attempt to initiate legislation; for research; fraternal or veterans organizations; or public elementary and secondary schools.

Additional Information

A brief report from the donee organization is required at the end of each grant period. Grant renewals are not automatic, and reports are an important factor in future funding decisions.

Corporate Officials

Dimon Richard McFerson: chairman, chief executive officer public involvement B Los Angeles, CA 1937. ED University of California, Los Angeles (1959); University of Southern California (1972). PRIM CORP EMPL chairman, chief executive officer: Nationwide Mutual Insurance Co. ADD CORP EMPL president: Nationwide General Insurance Co. NONPR AFFIL member: American Institute CPAs.
Stephen A. Rish: vice president, corporate public involvement B Columbus, OH 1946. ED Ohio Northern University (1968). PRIM CORP EMPL vice president, corporate public involvement: Nationwide Mutual Insurance Co.

Foundation Officials

Charles S. Bath: vice president
Duane M. Campbell: vice president, treasurer PRIM CORP EMPL vice president: Nationwide Mutual Insurance Co. ADD CORP EMPL treasurer: Aid Financial Service Inc.; treasurer: Nationwide General Industry Co.; treasurer: Nationwide Life Industry Co.
Dennis W. Click: vice president, assistant secretary B 1938. PRIM CORP EMPL vice president: Colonial Insurance Co. California ADD CORP EMPL secretary: Public Employees Benefit; secretary: Aid Finance Services Inc.; secretary: Allied Life Financial Corp.; secretary: Nationwide Financial Services; vice president: Nationwide General Insurance Co.; secretary: Nationwide Mutual Insurance Co.; secretary: Scottsdale Insurance Co.
W. Sidney Druen: director B Farmville, VA 1942. ED Hampden-Sydney College (1964); University of Virginia JD (1968). PRIM CORP EMPL co. senior vice president, general counsel, assistant secretary: Nationwide Life Insurance. CORP AFFIL senior vice president: Scottsdale Insurance Co.; senior vice president: Nationwide Mutual Insurance Co.; senior vice president: Public Employees Benefit Service; senior vice president, general counsel, assistant secretary: Nationwide Financial Services Inc.; senior vice president: Nationwide General Insurance Co.; senior vice president: Nationwide Advisory Services; senior vice president: Nationwide Corp.; senior vice president, general counsel, assistant, secretary: Employers Insurance of Wausau Mutual Co.; senior vice president: Gates McDonald Co.; senior partner: Druen Dietrich Reynolds & Koogler. NONPR AFFIL director: Ohio Chamber of Commerce; member: Virginia Bar Association; member: National Mutual Insurance Companies Board; member: Ohio Bar Association; member: Columbus Bar Association. CLUB AFFIL University Club.
Charles Louis Fuellgraf, Jr.: trustee B West Sunbury, PA 1931. ED Carnegie Mellon University (1953). PRIM CORP EMPL chief executive officer: Fuellgraf Electric Co. CORP AFFIL director: Wausau Insurance Companies; director: Nationwide Mutual Fire Insurance Co.; director: Nationwide Mutual Insurance Co.; director: Nationwide Insurance Companies; director:

Nationwide Life Insurance Co.; director: Nationwide General Insurance Co.; officer: Nationwide Advisory Services; director: Nationwide Financial Services. NONPR AFFIL Free Accepted Masons; president, director: National Electrical Contractors Association.

Edwin P. McCausland, Jr.: vice president fixed income securities PRIM CORP EMPL vice president: Nationwide General Insurance Co.

Dimon Richard McFerson: chairman, chief executive officer, trustee (see above)

David O. Miller: trustee PRIM CORP EMPL chairman: Wausau Insurance Companies. CORP AFFIL director: Scottsdale Insurance Co.; chairman: Wausau Preferred Health Insurance Co.; director: Nationwide Mutual Insurance Co.; director: Nationwide Life Insurance Co.; director: Nationwide Mutual Fire Insurance Co.; director: Nationwide Financial Services; director: Nationwide General Insurance Co.; director: Nationwide Advisory Services; director: Allied Life Financial Corp.; director: Colonial Insurance Co. California.

Robert Alan Oakley: executive vice president, chief financial officer B Columbus, OH 1946. ED Purdue University BS (1968); Ohio State University MBA (1969); Ohio State University PhD (1973). PRIM CORP EMPL executive vice president, chief financial officer: Nationwide Mutual Insurance Co. ADD CORP EMPL chief financial officer, executive vice president: Nationwide Life Insurance Co. NONPR AFFIL member: Financial Executives Institute; member: Society Chartered Property & Casualty Underwriters; member: Fin Management Association; member: American Finance Association; member: American Society Certified Life Underwriters.

James F. Patterson: trustee PRIM CORP EMPL chairman: Nationwide Financial Services ADD CORP EMPL director: Colonial Insurance Co. of California; officer: Nationwide Corp.; director: Nationwide General Insurance Co.; chairman: Nationwide Advisory Services; director: Nationwide Mutual Insurance Co.; director: Scottsdale Insurance Co.

Stephen A. Rish: president (see above)

Arden L. Shisler: trustee B 1941. PRIM CORP EMPL chairman, director: Nationwide Mutual Insurance Co. ADD CORP EMPL president, chief executive officer: K&B Transport; partner: Sweetwater Beef Farms. CORP AFFIL director: Nationwide Mutual Fire Insurance Co.; director: Scottsdale Insurance Co.; director: Nationwide General Insurance Co.; director: Nationwide Life Insurance Co.; director: Nationwide Corp.; director: Nationwide Financial Services; director: Colonial Insurance Co. California; director: Nationwide Advisory Services.

Robert J. Woodward, Jr.: executive vice president, chief investment officer B 1941. ED Capital University BA (1964); Capital University JD (1971). PRIM CORP EMPL vice president: Nationwide General Insurance Co. CORP AFFIL executive vice president: Nationwide Mutual Fire Insurance Co.; executive vice president: Nationwide Mutual Insurance Co.; officer: Nationwide Corp.; executive vice president: Nationwide Financial Services.

Grants Analysis

Disclosure Period: calendar year ending 1997
Total Grants: $10,676,063*
Number of Grants: 398
Average Grant: $22,306
Highest Grant: $1,285,924
Typical Range: $1,000 to $15,000
***Note:** Giving excludes corporate direct giving. Grants analysis is provided by foundation.

Recent Grants

Note: Grants derived from 1997 Form 990.

Arts & Humanities

900,000 Trilogy Fund, Columbus, OH -- support Campaign for the Arts
100,000 Columbus Association for the Performing Arts, Columbus, OH -- to renovate stage of Southern Theater
100,000 Columbus Museum of Art, Columbus, OH -- support capital improvements, educational programs
100,000 Columbus Symphony Orchestra, Columbus, OH -- operating support
70,000 Ballet Metropolitan, Columbus, OH -- support capital needs of 20th Anniversary Campaign
50,000 Ballet Metropolitan, Columbus, OH -- operating support
50,000 Ohio State University Fund, Columbus, OH -- support WOSU Endowment Campaign
50,000 Opera Association of Central Ohio, Columbus, OH -- operating support
30,000 Community Arts Project, King Arts Complex, Powell, OH -- operating support
25,000 Jazz Arts Group of Columbus, Powell, OH -- to sponsor performance, operating support
25,000 Performing Arts Foundation, Wausau, WI -- operating support
25,000 Wexner Center for the Arts, Powell, OH -- to develop core audience, increase community involvement

Civic & Public Affairs

60,000 Community Shelter Board, Columbus, OH -- support community needs assessment strategies
50,000 Cooperative Development Foundation, Washington, DC -- operating support for CLUSA Institute for Cooperative Development
40,000 Columbus Urban League, Columbus, OH -- support capital building campaign
40,000 Farm Safety 4 Just Kids, Earlham, IA -- operating support
30,000 Cooperative Development Foundation, Washington, DC -- support 1997 United Co-op Appeal
25,000 Columbus Zoo Association, Powell, OH -- support for educational materials

Education

500,000 Ohio State University Foundation Colleges of Business and Food, Agricultural, and Environmental Sciences, Columbus, OH -- support Affirm Thy Friendship Campaign
200,000 Otterbein College, Westerville, OH -- for renovations and repairs to Towers Hall
150,000 Capital University, Columbus, OH -- support Peter F. Frenzer Nationwide Insurance Enterprise Foundation Center for Dispute Resolution
140,000 Ohio Foundation of Independent Colleges, Columbus, OH -- operating support, support Plus 100 Campaign
100,000 Ohio Dominican College, Columbus, OH -- endowment funding
80,000 Derek Hughes-NAPSLO Educational Foundation, Kansas City, MO -- support Rolland L. Wiegers Educational Endowment
75,000 Franklin University, Columbus, OH -- support capital campaign for Student Services Center, renovation project
70,000 I Know I Can, Columbus, OH -- endowment support for scholarship program, operating support
46,342 National Merit Scholarship Corporation, Evanston, IL -- support 1997-98 scholarship program
45,000 Wisconsin Foundation of Independent Colleges, Milwaukee, WI -- operating support
25,000 Insurance Education Foundation, Indianapolis, IN -- support insurance education workshop
25,000 Ohio State University Foundation Department of Agricultural Economics, Powell, OH -- support Phase II of Director Development Program for Ohio Valley Region Cooperatives
25,000 Shawnee State University Development Foundation, Portsmouth, OH -- one month sponsorship of Reach for the Stars Campaign

Environment

40,000 Federation of Southern Cooperatives, Land Assistance Fund, East Point, GA -- operating support
25,000 Franklin Park Conservancy Joint Recreation District, Powell, OH -- support Grand Entrance and Boulevard Design Project

Health

400,000 Children's Hospital Foundation, Columbus, OH -- support For the Children Capital Campaign
100,000 American Red Cross National Headquarters, Washington, DC -- support Disaster Relief Fund
50,000 Children's Hospital Foundation, Columbus, OH -- support Center for Child Abuse Prevention
40,000 Riverside Methodist Hospital Foundation, Columbus, OH -- support campaign for McConnell Heart-Health Center at Riverside
34,027 Children's Hospital Foundation, Columbus, OH -- support HIV clinic program for families
25,000 Columbus Speech and Hearing Center, Columbus, OH -- capital campaign for Center for Communications Abilities

International

500,000 COSI-Columbus, Columbus, OH -- support Planet Ocean Exhibit
50,000 CARE Foundation, Chicago, IL -- seed money for economic opportunity fund

Social Services

100,000 Mid-Ohio Food Bank, Columbus, OH -- capital campaign
100,000 YWCA, Columbus, OH -- support Griswold Building Capital Campaign
53,960 United Way of Franklin County, Columbus, OH -- support 1997 campaign
50,000 Wausau YMCA Foundation, Wausau, WI -- support Woodson YMCA capital campaign
40,000 Goodwill Industries of Central Ohio, Columbus, OH -- support Invest in the Power of Work capital campaign
40,000 YMCA of Central Ohio, Columbus, OH -- support Restore the Glory capital campaign
35,028 United Way of Marathon County, Wausau, WI -- support 1997 campaign
33,000 LifeCare Alliance, Columbus, OH -- support Senior Wellness Center
25,000 Wausau Child Care Foundation, Wausau, WI -- support capital campaign

NAVCOM SYSTEMS

Company Contact

Manassas, VA

Company Description

Employees: 170
SIC(s): 3663 Radio & T.V. Communications Equipment.

Navcom Charities Foundation

Giving Contact

Liz Johnson, Administrative Assistant to the President
9815 Godwin Drive
Manassas, VA 20110-4156
Phone: (703)361-0884

Description

Founded: 1992
EIN: 521762240
Organization Type: Corporate Foundation
Giving Locations: headquarters area only.

Financial Summary

Total Giving: $378,944 (fiscal year ending June 30, 1996)
Assets: $43,190 (fiscal 1996)
Gifts Received: $30,000 (fiscal 1996). Note: In 1996, contributions were received from Navcom Systems.

Typical Recipients

Arts & Humanities: Music, Public Broadcasting
Civic & Public Affairs: Civic & Public Affairs-General
Education: Arts/Humanities Education, Colleges & Universities, Community & Junior Colleges, Education Associations, Engineering/Technological Education, Leadership Training
Health: AIDS/HIV
Religion: Churches, Missionary Activities (Domestic), Religious Organizations, Religious Welfare, Seminaries
Social Services: Recreation & Athletics

Application Procedures

Initial Contact: Send letter requesting application form.

Additional Information

Publications: Guidelines

Corporate Officials

William Gary: vice president operations PRIM CORP EMPL vice president operations: Navcom Systems.
Elijah Jackson: president, chief executive officer PRIM CORP EMPL president, chief executive officer: Navcom Systems.
Mary Jackson: executive vice president PRIM CORP EMPL executive vice president: Navcom Systems.
Carl J. Wallace: chief financial officer PRIM CORP EMPL chief financial officer: Navcom Systems.

Foundation Officials

Elijah Jackson: president (see above)
Mary Jackson: vice president (see above)

Grants Analysis

Disclosure Period: fiscal year ending June 30, 1996
Number of Grants: 20
Highest Grant: $201,700
Typical Range: $500 to $5,000

Recent Grants

Note: Grants derived from fiscal 1996 Form 990.

Arts & Humanities

5,125 Prince William Symphony, Prince William, VA -- community programs, welfare assistance programs
5,000 WDCU Radio, Washington, DC -- for Earnest White Show

Civic & Public Affairs

16,280 Gold Cross Foundation, Washington, DC -- air travel, lodging

Education

5,914 NVCCEF, Manassas, VA -- for Fund 0280
5,000 University of District of Columbia, Washington, DC -- for institutional advancement
3,500 Dassel Art Academy, Manassas, VA -- academy support
2,500 Prairie View A&M Foundation, Prairie View, TX -- sponsorship
500 American Association of University Women, Washington, DC -- for Leadership Summit

Health

3,500 African American Health Program, Washington, DC -- for Leadership Summit on AIDS

Religion

201,700 Mount Calvary Baptist Church, Manassas, VA -- missionary support
100,000 Richmond Virginia Seminary, Richmond, VA -- dormitory support
3,000 St. John Baptist Church, Luray, VA -- transportation support
945 Prince William Christian Coalition, Manassas, VA -- for conference

Social Services

5,000 Greater Manassas Football League, Manassas, VA -- sponsor team

NCR Corp.

Company Contact

Dayton, OH
Web: http://www.ncr.com

Company Description

Former Name: AT&T Global Information Solutions.
Revenue: US$6,505,000,000
Employees: 38,600
Fortune Rank: 283, per FORTUNE Magazine's list of 500 Largest U.S. Corporations (1999).
FF 283
SIC(s): 2761 Manifold Business Forms, 3575 Computer Terminals, 3577 Computer Peripheral Equipment Nec, 3578 Calculating & Accounting Equipment.
Parent Company: AT&T Corp., Basking Ridge, NJ, United States

Operating Locations

Argentina: Acceryval SRL, Buenos Aires; Australia: NCR Australia Pty. Ltd., North Sydney; NCR Productivity Savings Plan P/L, North Sydney; NCR Superannuation Nominees Ltd., North Sydney; Austria: NCR Osterreich GesmbH, Vienna; Canada: NCR Canada Ltd., Toronto; Denmark: NCR Danmark AS, Copenhagen; NCR Norden AS Likvidation, Copenhagen; Dominican Republic: NCR Dominicana C por A, Santo Domingo; Germany: NCR Central & Eastern Europe GmbH, Augsburg, Bayern; NCR GmbH, Augsburg, Bayern; NCR OEM Europe GmbH, Augsburg, Bayern; Hong Kong: NCR Asia-Pacific Ltd., Central District; NCR (China) Ltd., Central District; NCR (Hong Kong) Ltd., Wan Chai; NCR Parts Depot (Hong Kong) Ltd., Wan Chai; Italy: NCR Italia SpA, Milano, Lombardia; Lucent Technologies Italia SpA, Sesto San Giovanni, Lombardia; Malaysia: NCR (M) Sdn. Bhd., Kuala Lumpur, Selangor; Netherlands: NCR Emea Regional Care Center BV, Amsterdam, Zuidoost; NCR Nederland NV, Amsterdam, Zuidoost; NCR European Logistics Center BV, Heerlen, Limburg; Norway: NCR Norge AS, Oslo, Akershus; Singapore: AT&T Global Information Services Singapore Pte. Ltd., Singapore; Spain: NCR Espana SA, Madrid; Turkey: NCR Bilgi Islem Sistemleri AS, Istanbul; NCR Bilisim Sistemleri AS, Istanbul; United Kingdom: NCR Europe Ltd., London; NCR (Scotland) Pension Plan Trustees Ltd., London

Nonmonetary Support

Value: $1,000,000 (1994); $2,100,000 (1988); $2,300,000 (1987)
Type: In-kind Services
Note: The company is not currently providing nonmonetary support.

Corporate Sponsorship

Type: Arts & cultural events

NCR Foundation

Giving Contact

Mary W. Karr, Director
BCR Corp.
1700 S Patterson Blvd.
Dayton, OH 45479
Phone: (937)445-2577
Fax: (937)445-0636

Description

Founded: 1953
EIN: 316030860
Organization Type: Corporate Foundation
Giving Locations: OH: Dayton headquarters and operating communities.
Grant Types: Employee Matching Gifts.
Note: Employee matching gift ratio: 1 to 1 for gifts over $25.

Financial Summary

Total Giving: $1,497,385 (1997); $1,200,000 (1996); $1,211,808 (1995). Note: Contributes through corporate direct giving program and foundation. 1997 Giving includes foundation ($487,250); matching gifts ($449,907); United Way ($560,228). 1996 Giving includes foundation ($335,000); matching gifts ($799,728); scholarship ($48,500). 1995 Giving includes foundation (425,000); matching gifts ($691,852); scholarship ($94,956).
Assets: $4,246,058 (1997); $4,291,835 (1996); $1,702,830 (1995)
Gifts Received: $560,000 (1997); $3,595,000 (1996); $21,150 (1995). Note: Contributions are received from AT&T GIS Corp.

Typical Recipients

Arts & Humanities: Arts Funds, Arts Institutes, Ballet, Dance, Arts & Humanities-General, Performing Arts, Public Broadcasting
Civic & Public Affairs: Chambers of Commerce, Civic & Public Affairs-General
Education: Colleges & Universities, Continuing Education, Education-General, Minority Education, Student Aid
Health: Health Organizations
Science: Science Museums
Social Services: Community Service Organizations, United Funds/United Ways, YMCA/YWCA/YMHA/YWHA, Youth Organizations

Contributions Analysis

Giving Priorities: United funds; colleges and universities; museums and arts funds; and environmental, international, and economic organizations.

Application Procedures

Initial Contact: letter of request
Application Requirements: a description of organization, amount requested, purpose of funds sought, recently audited financial statement, proof of tax-exempt status
Deadlines: None.

Restrictions

Contributions are not made to individuals, nontarget communities, or national organizations.

Additional Information

NCR Corporation was formerly named AT&T Global Information Solutions

Corporate Officials

David Bearman: senior vice president, chief financial officer& administration, chief financial officer PRIM CORP EMPL senior vice president, chief financial officer: NCR Corp.
John L. Giering: senior vice president finance & administration, chief financial officer B Cleveland, OH 1944. ED Duke University BS (1966); Ohio State University MS (1968). PRIM CORP EMPL senior vice president finance & administration, chief financial officer: NCR Corp.

Giving Program Officials

Mary Karr: vice president PRIM CORP EMPL director, community relations: NCR Corp.

Foundation Officials

David Bearman: director (see above)
Bill Eisenman: trustee PRIM CORP EMPL senior vice president national accounts: NCR Corp.
Jon Hoak: trustee B Eugene, OR 1949. ED University of Colorado (1971); Drake University (1977). CORP AFFIL vice president, secretary, general counsel: NCR Corp. NONPR AFFIL member: American Bar Association; member: Fed Bar Association.
Mary Karr: vice president (see above)
L. K. Nyquist: secretary
Bo Sawyer: treasurer
Michael Tarpey: president PRIM CORP EMPL senior vice president: NCR Corp.

Grants Analysis

Disclosure Period: calendar year ending 1997
Total Grants: $487,250*
Number of Grants: 9
Average Grant: $54,139
Highest Grant: $449,907
Typical Range: $50,000 to $100,000
*Note: Giving excludes matching gifts; United Way.

Recent Grants

Note: Grants derived from 1997 Form 990.

Arts & Humanities

200,000	Dayton Art Institute, Dayton, OH
25,000	Dayton Ballet, Dayton, OH
21,500	Gwinnett Fine Arts, Gwinnett, GA
5,000	Wright State University Plays, Dayton, OH

Civic & Public Affairs

17,500	Metro Atlanta Chamber of Commerce, Atlanta, GA
5,000	SHPE Foundation

Education

150,000	Dayton Montgomery County Scholarship Program, Dayton, OH
33,250	Minority Scholarships

Social Services

449,907	United Way
30,000	YMCA, Dayton, OH

NEBCO EVANS

Company Contact

Greenwich, CT

Company Description

Revenue: US$7,421,000,000
Employees: 400
Fortune Rank: 199, per FORTUNE Magazine's list of 500 Largest U.S. Corporations (1999).
FF 199
SIC(s): 3273 Ready-Mixed Concrete.

Abel Foundation

Giving Contact

J. Ross McCown, Vice President
Abel Foundation
PO Box 80268
Lincoln, NE 68501
Phone: (402)434-1212
Fax: (402)434-1799

Description

Founded: 1951
EIN: 476041771
Organization Type: Corporate Foundation
Giving Locations: NE: Lincoln
Grant Types: General Support, Matching, Multiyear/Continuing Support.

Financial Summary

Total Giving: $400,000 (1999 approx); $398,745 (1998); $312,055 (1997). Note: Contributes through foundation only. 1997 Giving includes foundation ($277,000); United Way ($35,055).
Assets: $3,200,000 (1999 approx); $3,731,062 (1998); $2,477,747 (1997)
Gifts Received: $170,000 (1997); $169,000 (1996); $846,146 (1994). Note: In 1996, contributions were received from NEBSCO ($150,000); and Constructors Inc. ($19,000). In 1994, contributions were received from NEBCO ($830,921); and Constructors, Inc. ($14,500).

Typical Recipients

Arts & Humanities: Arts Associations & Councils, Arts Centers, Arts Festivals, Ballet, Arts & Humanities-General, History & Archaeology, Libraries, Literary Arts, Museums/Galleries, Music, Performing Arts, Public Broadcasting, Theater
Civic & Public Affairs: Botanical Gardens/Parks, Community Foundations, Economic Development, Economic Policy, Employment/Job Training, Civic & Public Affairs-General, Housing, Urban & Community Affairs, Zoos/Aquariums
Education: Agricultural Education, Arts/Humanities Education, Business Education, Colleges & Universities, Economic Education, Education Funds, Elementary Education (Public), Education-General, Health & Physical Education, Leadership Training, Literacy, Private Education (Precollege), Public Education (Precollege), Science/Mathematics Education, Secondary Education (Public), Student Aid
Environment: Environment-General, Resource Conservation
Health: Children's Health/Hospitals, Health Organizations, Heart, Hospitals, Mental Health, Research/Studies Institutes
Religion: Churches, Religion-General, Religious Organizations, Religious Welfare
Social Services: Animal Protection, Child Welfare, Community Centers, Community Service Organizations, Counseling, Domestic Violence, Family Planning, Family Services, Food/Clothing Distribution, Homes, People with Disabilities, Recreation & Athletics, Scouts, Senior Services, United Funds/United Ways, YMCA/YWCA/YMHA/YWHA, Youth Organizations

Contributions Analysis

Arts & Humanities: About 5%. Supports local arts organizations, the performing arts, and historical societies.
Education: 25% to 30%. More than half of education grants support Lincoln, NE, area colleges and universities. Also supports public education.
Religion: 35% to 40%. Support goes to First Plymouth Church, religious organizations, and social service agencies.
Social Services: About 20%. Supports the United Way and community and family services organizations.

Application Procedures

Initial Contact: Send a brief letter of inquiry.
Application Requirements: a description of organization, amount requested, purpose of funds sought, recently audited financial statement, and proof of tax-exempt status
Deadlines: None.

Corporate Officials

James P. Abel: president, director B 1950. PRIM CORP EMPL president, director: NEBCO. CORP AFFIL vice president: Concrete Industries Inc.; director: Constructors Inc.; director: Ameritas Life Insurance Corp.

Foundation Officials

Alice Abel: director
Elizabeth N. Abel: director
James P. Abel: president (see above)
John C. Abel: director CORP AFFIL officer: Constructors Inc.; officer: Kerford Limestone Inc.
Mary C. Abel: director
James Watt Hewitt: vice president, treasurer B Hastings, NE 1932. ED Hastings College (1950-1952); University of Nebraska BS (1954); University of Nebraska JD (1956); University of Nebraska MA (1994). PRIM CORP EMPL vice president, general counsel: NEBCO. CORP AFFIL community director: Norwest Bank. NONPR AFFIL member: Phi Delta Phi; trustee: University Nebraska Foundation; member: Newcomen Society; member: Nebraska Rose Society; executive vice president, director: Nebraska State Historical Society Foundation; director: Nature Conservancy Nebraska Saint Chapter; member: Nebraska Bar Association; member: Lincoln Rose Society; member: Fed Bar Association; member: Lincoln Bar Association; director: Bryan Memorial Hospital Foundation; member: Business Roundtable; member: Beta Theta Pi; fellow: American Bar Foundation; member: American Rose Society; member: American Bar Association. CLUB AFFIL Country Club Lincoln; Nebraska Club.
J. Ross McCown: vice president, secretary B 1946. ED University of Nebraska. PRIM CORP EMPL vice president: NEBCO.

Grants Analysis

Disclosure Period: calendar year ending 1997
Total Grants: $277,000*
Number of Grants: 98
Average Grant: $2,826
Highest Grant: $60,000
Typical Range: $100 to $3,000
*Note: Giving excludes United Way.

Recent Grants

Note: Grants derived from 1998 Form 990.

Arts & Humanities

60,000	Children's Museum, Lincoln, NE
5,000	Lincoln Children's Museum, Lincoln, NE
2,500	Stuhr Museum, Grand Island, NE
1,000	Lincoln Community Playhouse, Lincoln, NE
1,000	Nebraska Humanities Council, Lincoln, NE
1,000	Nebraska Shakespeare Festival, Omaha, NE
1,000	Wagon Train Project, Lincoln, NE

Civic & Public Affairs

60,000	Folsom Children's Zoo, Lincoln, NE
25,000	Nebraska Community Foundation, Lincoln, NE -- Governor's Residence
20,000	Madonna Foundation, Lincoln, NE
4,637	Parks & Recreation Foundation, Lincoln, NE
1,500	Habitat for Humanity, Lincoln, NE
1,500	Neighborhoods, Inc., Lincoln, NE
1,000	Lincoln Action Program, Lincoln, NE -- Gathering Place
1,000	Tabitha Foundation, Lincoln, NE

Education

23,000	Nebraska Wesleyan University, Lincoln, NE
10,000	Point Loma High School, Lincoln, NE
5,000	UNL Foundation, Lincoln, NE -- Directors Club
2,500	NICF, Lincoln, NE
2,000	Jr. Achievement, Lincoln, NE
1,500	Lincoln Literacy, Lincoln, NE
1,500	Lincoln Public Schools Foundation, Lincoln, NE
1,000	Bellevue University, Bellevue, NE
1,000	Nebraska Council on Economic Education, Lincoln, NE
1,000	UNL Foundation, Lincoln, NE -- Press Box Contribution

Environment

1,400	Nature Conservancy, Lincoln, NE
1,000	National Arbor Day Foundation, Lincoln, NE

Health

1,000	Heart Institute of the Desert, Rancho Mirage, CA

Religion

21,000	First Plymouth, Lincoln, NE -- Annual Pledge
12,500	First Plymouth, Lincoln, NE -- Organ Fund
2,000	Pius X Foundation, Lincoln, NE

Social Services

20,000	Homestead Girl Scout Council, Lincoln, NE
14,325	Lincoln/Lancaster United Way, Lincoln, NE
14,325	Lincoln/Lancaster United Way, Lincoln, NE
10,000	Friendship Home, Lincoln, NE
6,750	Food Bank of Lincoln, Lincoln, NE
5,000	Child Advocacy Center, Lincoln, NE
5,000	Lighthouse, Lincoln, NE
2,500	Bright Lights, Lincoln, NE
2,500	Family Resource Center, Lincoln, NE
2,500	Youth Leadership Lincoln, Lincoln, NE
2,000	Capital Humane Society, Lincoln, NE
1,750	Cornhusker Council - Boy Scouts, Lincoln, NE
1,500	Malone Community Center, Lincoln, NE
1,500	Rape/Spouse Abuse Crisis Center, Lincoln, NE
1,500	Young Life, Lincoln, NE
1,000	Beatrice YMCA, Beatrice, NE
1,000	Food Bank of Lincoln, Lincoln, NE
1,000	Planned Parenthood, Lincoln, NE
1,000	Samaritan Counseling Center, Lincoln, NE

NEC AMERICA, INC.

Company Contact

Melville, NY
Web: http://www.nec.com

Company Description

Employees: 2,400
SIC(s): 3661 Telephone & Telegraph Apparatus.
Parent Company: NEC Corp., 7-1, Shiba 5-chome, Minato-ku, Tokyo, Japan

Operating Locations

CA: NEC America, Inc., Bakersfield, Concord; NEC Business Communication Systems (West), Culver City; Packard Bell NEC, Mountain View; NEC America, Inc., Newport Beach, Rancho Dominguez; NEC Electronics (Manufacturing), Roseville; NEC Systems Laboratory, San Jose; NEC Electronics, Santa Clara; CO: NEC America, Inc., Englewood; FL: NEC America, Inc., Brandon, Pompano Beach, Tampa; IL: NEC America, Inc., Elk Grove Village, Itasca; MA: Packard Bell NEC, Boxborough; NHSX Supercomputers, Littleton; NEC America, Inc., Wakefield; MI: NEC America, Inc., Kentwood; NC: NEC America, Inc., Lincolnton; NJ: NEC America, Inc., Cherry Hill, Hackensack; NEC Research Institute, Princeton; NY: NEC Business Communication Systems (East), East Syracuse; NEC America, Melville; NEC America, Inc., Melville; NEC USA, Melville; NEC Industries, New York; OR: NEC America, Inc., Hillsboro; NEC America Manufacturing, Hillsboro; RI: NEC America, Inc., Cranston; TN: NEC America, Inc., Memphis; TX: NEC America, Inc., Dallas; NMI Corp., Dallas; NEC America, Inc., Irving, Richardson; VA: NEC America, Inc., Fairfax; NEC America, Herndon; NEC America, Inc., Herndon; WA: NEC America, Inc., Bothell; Packard Bell NEC, Fife

Nonmonetary Support

Type: In-kind Services

Corporate Sponsorship

Type: Arts & cultural events
Contact: Nancy Rasmussen, Manager, Special Events
Note: Company sponsors community events, fundraising events, and memberships.

NEC Foundation of America

Giving Contact

Ms. Sylvia Clark, Executive Director
NEC Foundation of America
8 Corporate Center Dr.
Melville, NY 11747-3112
Phone: (516)753-7021
Fax: (516)753-7096
Email: clarks@ccgate.ml.nec.com
Web: http://www.nec.com/company/foundation

Alternate Contact

Phone: (516)753-7904
Note: Alternate phone number is for TTY users.

Description

Founded: 1991
EIN: 113059554
Organization Type: Corporate Foundation
Giving Locations: nationally.
Grant Types: General Support, Project.

Giving Philosophy

'Technology is an equalizer. It enables each person to improve their abilities and to assert and fully develop their potential. We regard technology as essential to any effort to prepare individuals, regardless of physical condition, for the future. We are committed to helping to assure that individuals have the skills to continue to advance the boundaries of technology on both a personal and societal level. Today's high school students will lead society to overcome barriers to communication, be they barriers imposed by distance, time, language or physical condition. Today's investment in the scientific and technical education of young people represents an investment in the 21st century.'

'People with disabilities are challenged every day by barriers to communication. Their access to and interest in technology, in a sense, leads the way for all society to make significant progress toward improved global communication now and in the next century. Our funding interests are highly focused: we believe that this is the way for us to have the greatest impact. At the same time, possibilities within our interest areas are limited only by the creativity of grant applicants. We recognize that important initiatives are being made by a broad range of educational, social and scientific organizations, and welcome the opportunity to support a variety of organizations.' *Investing in Human Potential*

Financial Summary

Total Giving: $450,000 (fiscal year ending March 31, 1998); $6,500,000 (fiscal 1997); $7,300,000 (fiscal 1996). Note: Contributes through corporate direct giving program and foundation. Fiscal 1998 Giving includes foundation.
Assets: $14,510,753 (fiscal 1998); $11,874,075 (fiscal 1997); $11,282,637 (fiscal 1996)
Gifts Received: $200,000 (fiscal 1996); $200,000 (fiscal 1995); $100,000 (fiscal 1994). Note: Contributions were received from NEC Corp., Tokyo, Japan, and NEC USA.

Typical Recipients

Arts & Humanities: Theater
Civic & Public Affairs: Employment/Job Training
Education: Science/Mathematics Education, Special Education
Health: Children's Health/Hospitals, Eyes/Blindness, Medical Rehabilitation
Science: Science Museums, Scientific Centers & Institutes
Social Services: Community Service Organizations, People with Disabilities

Contributions Analysis

Giving Priorities: Scientific applications in education, health, and social services.
Arts & Humanities: 15% to 20%. Includes museums, public broadcasting, performing arts groups, and community arts centers.
Civic & Public Affairs: 5% to 10%.Includes local emergency rescue and fire departments, chambers of commerce, and a variety of community development activities.
Education: About 40%. Funding supports corporate associates programs, contributions, matching gifts, and tuition reimbursement for its employees. 20% to 25%. Focus is on K-12 education in NEC plant communities, science and technology at the secondary level, and professional membership associations.
Health: About 15%. Funding supports studies related to the educational and socio-psychological implications of technologies that are designed for people with disabilities, application of technology for the disabled, and organizations that serve youth.

Application Procedures

Initial Contact: request guidelines, then either a one-page preliminary proposal or full formal proposal
Application Requirements: formal proposals must include the following: 2- to 3-page proposal summary, with amount requested; purpose of grant; how proposal matches funding interests; statement of need; population served; expected outcomes; program milestones, with target dates; evaluation plan; and strategy to secure full funding for the project; also enclose an itemized budget of project, including income and expenses; annual report and organizational brochure; most recent audited financial statement; members of board of directors, including professional affiliations; list of other foundation and corporate donors to your organization and the proposed project; copy of IRS 501(c)(3) letter; and resume of project principals; employee volunteer opportunities; impact on community with a major company facility; opportunities for company recognition
Grant proposals should also include additional information on the actual or potential volunteer involvement of NEC employees; opportunities to further enhance the positive awareness and good-will of NEC and NEC Foundation of America; and impact of application organization in areas in which NEC has a major facility.
Deadlines: September 1 or March 1
Evaluative Criteria: national and broad-based efforts; collaboration among nonprofit organizations

from varied fields and perspectives; focus on self-determination and client involvement; and the potential to raise awareness among those who are not yet part of a conversation; actual or potential volunteer involvement of NEC employees; opportunities to further enhance the positive awareness and goodwill of NEC and NEC Foundation of America; and impact of organization in areas in which NEC has a major facility
Decision Notification: indication of foundation interest within 4 to 6 weeks of receipt; board meets in March and September, grants are awarded in April and October
Notes: Proposals received after a deadline will be held for the following cycle.

Restrictions

The foundation does not support individuals, including scholarships, stipends, or fellowships; capital campaigns/building funds; endowment campaigns; sports teams or athletic competitions; fundraising events or advertising; sectarian or religious activities; political campaigns or causes; individual elementary and secondary schools, or school districts; local chapters of national organizations; or organizations outside the United States.
The foundation also does not broker requests for product donations from NEC.
As a general rule, the foundation does not make multi-year grants and will not fund any organizations for more than two consecutive years.
Grants generally will not exceed $50,000 and will focus on national organizations.
Foundation requests one application for support per organization within an eighteen month period, applicable whether a proposal is funded or not.

Additional Information

Publications: Foundation Guidelines; Annual Report

Corporate Officials

Peter P. Cristallo: associate senior vice president human resources & administration B Brooklyn, NY 1940. ED Saint Francis College (1962). PRIM CORP EMPL associate senior vice president human resources & administration: NEC America, Inc.
Masahiro Kato: director PRIM CORP EMPL director: NEC America, Inc.
Larry Kremna: director human resources PRIM CORP EMPL director human resources: NEC America, Inc.

Giving Program Officials

Lourdes Cogswell: PRIM CORP EMPL assistant general manager corporate public relations division: NEC America, Inc.

Foundation Officials

Sylvia Clark: executive director PRIM CORP EMPL secretary, director: Empire-Orr.
Itsumi Iwasaki: treasurer PRIM CORP EMPL senior vice president, treasurer: NEC America, Inc.
Harumi Kato: general manager corporate planning PRIM CORP EMPL secretary: NEC Research Institute Inc.
Masahiro Kato: chairman, executive vice president (see above)
Shigeki Matsue: director PRIM CORP EMPL president: NEC Electronics, Inc.
H. Nakatogawa: assistant secretary PRIM CORP EMPL assistant corporate secretary: NEC America, Inc.
Dr. Mineo Sugiyama: chairman, president PRIM CORP EMPL president, chief executive officer, director: NEC America, Inc. CORP AFFIL executive vice president operations, director: NEC U.S.A. Inc.

Grants Analysis

Disclosure Period: fiscal year ending March 31, 1998
Total Grants: $415,000
Number of Grants: 14
Average Grant: $29,643
Highest Grant: $50,000
Typical Range: $6,500 to $30,000
Note: Grants analysis derived from partial grants list.

Recent Grants

Note: Grants derived from 1996 Form 990.

Arts & Humanities

25,000	Access Theater, Santa Barbara, CA -- for video production of international touring stage play based on the life of Neil Marus, a playwright/actor living with a neurological disorder

Education

30,300	Washington University at St. Louis School of Medicine, Saint Louis, MO
30,000	Girl Scouts of the USA, New York, NY -- expansion of the National Science Partnership to 10 additional sites across the country
26,000	Vanderbilt University, Peabody College, Nashville, TN
25,000	Center for Excellence in Education, McLean, VA
25,000	JASON Foundation for Education, New York, NY
25,000	Satellite Educational Resources Consortium, Columbia, SC
7,000	Communications Independence for the Neurologically Impaired, New York, NY
1,700	Talking Tapes for Blind, Saint Louis, MO -- to purchase recorders, microphones, and microphone stands to enable 10 additional volunteer readers to tape textbooks for student borrowers

Health

25,000	George Lucas Educational Foundation, San Rafael, CA -- toward major public awareness campaign related to a Edutopia: Vision of the Future Project
20,000	Adaptive Rehabilitation Technologies, Marblehead, MA
20,000	National Easter Seal Society, Chicago, IL

Science

30,000	Challenger Center for Space Science Education, Alexandria, VA
10,000	Long Island Museum of Science and Technology, Melville, NY -- toward planning phase of project to develop a new science and technological museum

NESTLE U.S.A. INC.

Company Contact

Glendale, CA

Company Description

Employees: 22,000
SIC(s): 8742 Management Consulting Services.
Parent Company: Nestle S.A., Avenue Nestle 55, Vevey, Switzerland

Operating Locations

AZ: Nestle Beverage Co., Casa Grande; Nestle U.S.A. Inc., Phoenix; CA: Maison Deutz Winery, Arroyo Grande; Calistoga Water Co., Calistoga; Carnation Grocery Products Div., Glendale; Carnation Products Div., Glendale; Contadina Fresh, Glendale; Culinary Foods Group, Glendale; Food Services Div., Glendale; Foreign Trade Div., Glendale; Friskies PetCare Div., Glendale; Nestle Beverage Co., Glendale; Nestle Chocolate & Confection, Glendale; Nestle USA, Glendale; Nestle U.S.A. Inc., Glendale; Pasta & Cheese, Glendale; Arrowhead Mountain Spring Water Co., Monterey Park; Nestle U.S.A. Inc., Pleasanton; Wine World Estates, Pleasanton; Nestle Beverage Co., Ripon; Chase & Sanborn Coffee, San Francisco; Wine World Estates Co., St. Helena; JJB Rice Co., Union City; Nestle Beverage Co., Union City; Wine World Estates, Yorba Linda; CO: Nestle U.S.A. Inc., Aurora; CT: Vanguard Div., Farmington; American Landmark Springs, Greenwich; Great Bear Spring Co., Greenwich; Great Waters of France, Greenwich; Perrier Group of America, Greenwich; Poland Spring Corp., Greenwich; FIDCO, New Milford; Nestle Capital Corp., Stamford; Nestle Holdings, Stamford; Wine World Estates, Stamford; FL: Zephyrhills Water Corp., Tampa; GA: Jim Dandy Co., Atlanta; Wine World Estates, Atlanta; IL: Nestle U.S.A. Inc., Naperville; Wine World Estates, Naperville; KS: Nestle U.S.A. Inc., Shawnee Mission; LA: Nestle Beverage Co., New Orleans; MA: Superior Brands, Quincy; MI: Nestle U.S.A. Inc., Northville; MO: Sunmark, Saint Louis; Contadina/Libby/Trenton Div., Trenton; NJ: Deer Park Spring Water, Carlstadt; Nestle Beverage Co., Freehold; NY: Jestle Beverage Co., Garden City; FIDCO, White Plains; OH: Nestle U.S.A. Inc., Cleveland; NDS, Columbus; Nestle Ice Cream, Columbus; Nestle U.S.A. Inc., Loveland; Food Div., Solon; L.J. Minor Corp., Solon; Nestle Frozen, Refrigerated, and Ice Cream Cos., Solon; Nestle Beverage Co., Sunbury; SC: Nestle Frozen/Refrigerated Food Co., Gaffney; TX: Wine World Estates, Addison; Galderma Laboratories, Fort Worth; Ozarka/Oasis Water Co., Fort Worth; Nestle U.S.A. Inc., Houston; UT: Nestle Frozen/Refrigerated Food Co., Springville; VA: Nestle Beverage Co., Norfolk

Nonmonetary Support

Value: $500,000 (1992)
Type: Donated Products

Giving Contact

Nestle U.S.A. Foundation
800 North Brand Boulevard
Glendale, CA 91203
Phone: (818)549-6000
Fax: (818)549-6952

Description

Founded: 1952
Organization Type: Corporate Giving Program. Supports preselected organizations only.
Giving Locations: manufacturing facility areas.
Grant Types: General Support.

Financial Summary

Total Giving: $900,000 (1996); $820,200 (1995); $745,230 (1994). Note: Contributes through corporate direct giving program only. Foundation dissolved in 1995. 1995 Giving includes foundation.
Assets: $18,302,956 (1996); $16,972,543 (1995); $5,864,425 (1994)
Gifts Received: $146,884 (1994). Note: Contributions made by Nestle USA and Nestle employees.

Typical Recipients

Arts & Humanities: Arts Centers, Arts Outreach, History & Archaeology, Libraries, Museums/Galleries, Music, Performing Arts, Theater
Civic & Public Affairs: Asian American Affairs, Botanical Gardens/Parks, Business/Free Enterprise, Economic Development, Employment/Job Training, Hispanic Affairs, Housing, Minority Business, Public Policy, Urban & Community Affairs, Women's Affairs, Zoos/Aquariums
Education: Agricultural Education, Arts/Humanities Education, Business Education, Colleges & Universities, Community & Junior Colleges, Education Reform, Engineering/Technological Education, Education-General, International Exchange, Literacy, Minority Education, Public Education (Precollege), Science/Mathematics Education, Secondary Education (Private), Student Aid
Environment: Resource Conservation, Wildlife Protection

Health: Clinics/Medical Centers, Emergency/Ambulance Services, Hospitals, Nutrition, Preventive Medicine/Wellness Organizations
Science: Science Museums, Scientific Organizations
Social Services: Child Welfare, Community Centers, Community Service Organizations, Food/Clothing Distribution, Homes, People with Disabilities, United Funds/United Ways, Youth Organizations

Contributions Analysis

Education: 100%. Volunteer activities in selected schools that promote academic excellence and build self-esteem.

Additional Information

As of 1995, funding is limited to the company's Adopt-A-School Program.

Corporate Officials

Peter Dominic Argentine: executive vice president, chief financial officer B Pittsburgh, PA 1948. ED University of Pittsburgh (1970); Duquesne University (1972). PRIM CORP EMPL executive vice president, chief financial officer: Nestle United States of America Inc. CORP AFFIL chief financial officer: Nestle United States of America Beverage Division.
James Herington Ball: senior vice president, general counsel, director B Kansas City, MO 1942. ED University of Missouri AB (1964); Saint Louis University JD (1973). PRIM CORP EMPL senior vice president, general counsel, director: Nestle U.S.A. Inc. CORP AFFIL senior vice president, general counsel, secretary: Nestle Holdings Inc.; secretary: Nestles Frozen Food Co. NONPR AFFIL director: American Swiss Foundation; member: Missouri Bar Association; director: Alliance for Childrens Rights.
Mario A. Corti: senior vice president, chief administrative officer PRIM CORP EMPL senior vice president, chief administrative officer: Nestle U.S.A. Inc. CORP AFFIL director: Credit Suisse First Boston Corp.; treasurer: Stouffer Corp.
Timm F. Crull: retired chairman B 1931. ED Michigan State University BA (1955). PRIM CORP EMPL retired chairman: Nestle U.S.A. Inc. CORP AFFIL chairman: TSC Holdings Inc.; president: Watermark Press; chairman: Nestle USA Inc.; director: Smart & Final Inc.; president, chief executive officer, vice chairman, director: Carnation Corp.; president: Nestle Holdings Inc.; director: BankAmerica Corp.
Cam Starrett: executive vice president human resources & corporate relations PRIM CORP EMPL executive vice president human resources & corporate relations: Nestle U.S.A. Inc. NONPR AFFIL director: Catalyst for Women Inc.
Joseph M. Weller: officer,director PRIM CORP EMPL officer,director: Nestle U.S.A. Inc.

Giving Program Officials

Betty A. Dumas: philanthropy & govt rels coordinator

Grants Analysis

Disclosure Period: calendar year ending 1996
Total Grants: $900,000
Number of Grants: 12
Average Grant: $75,000
Highest Grant: $202,000
Typical Range: $5,000 to $300,000

Recent Grants

Note: Grants derived from 1996 Form 990.

Arts & Humanities

100,000	Rock and Roll Hall of Fame and Museum, Cleveland, OH

Civic & Public Affairs

25,000	Advertising Council, New York, NY
20,000	Catalyst for Women, New York, NY
10,000	LEAD Program in Business, New York, NY

Education

175,000	Cornell University School of Hotel Administration, Ithaca, NY
120,000	Reading is Fundamental, Washington, DC
27,000	Youth for Understanding, Washington, DC

Environment

15,000	Wildlife on Wheels, Sunland, CA

Health

56,000	American Dietetic Association Foundation, Chicago, IL

Science

50,000	Great Lakes Museum of Science, Cleveland, OH

Social Services

202,000	United Way, Los Angeles, CA
100,000	Goodwill Industries, Los Angeles, CA

NEW CENTURY ENERGIES

Company Contact

Denver, CO
Web: http://www.ncenergies.com

Company Description

Revenue: US$3,610,900,000
Employees: 5160
Fortune Rank: 456, per FORTUNE Magazine's list of 500 Largest U.S. Corporations (1999).
FF 456
SIC(s): 4931 Electric & Other Services Combined, 4932 Gas & Other Services Combined.
Parent Company: Public Service Co. of Colorado

Nonmonetary Support

Range: $10,000 - $75,000
Type: Donated Equipment; In-kind Services
Note: Also provides technical support.

Corporate Sponsorship

Contact: Cynthia Evans, Secretary, Managing Director

New Century Energies Foundation

Giving Contact

Carol Shearon, Program Manager
New Century Energies Foundation
1225 17th Street, Suite 2000
Denver, CO 80202-5533
Phone: (303)294-2402
Fax: (303)294-8120

Alternate Contact

Phone: (303)294-2430

Description

Organization Type: Corporate Foundation
Giving Locations: CO: Denver headquarters and operating communities.
Grant Types: Capital, Employee Matching Gifts, Project.
Note: Employee matching gift ratio: 1 to 1.

Giving Philosophy

'Most of NEC's donations are made through the New Century Energies Foundation. Each year, there is a request for proposal (RFPs) in two areas of special interest to us: workforce readiness and affordable living.'
Workforce Readiness: '..Grants will be awarded by the NCE Foundation to qualified organizations for programs that support teachers and administrators in helping them get their students ready for the workforce. Grants of up to $50,000 will be awarded for collaborative efforts that improve the education system and provide students with the solid academic foundation that can enable them to go on to college or enter the workforce immediately.'
'As a part of our workforce readiness effort, New Century Energies developed the Classroom Connection Teacher Network. The program awards two types of grants to certified K-12 teachers through qualified schools. Dissemination grants go to teachers who have developed successful, innovative classroom programs and are willing to share their programs. Other teachers can then request curriculum materials for these classroom programs, and apply for Adapter grants to tailor programs for their own classroom.'
Affordable Living: 'Community profiles differ, but every healthy community has comfortable, safe and affordable neighborhoods and housing for its workforce and its families. An emphasis will be placed on serving low- to moderate-income working adults. Community-based partnerships between public, private and non-profit entities are encouraged as are matching grant opportunities.' 1997 *People Giving Community Solutions*

Financial Summary

Total Giving: $2,000,000 (1999 approx); $1,800,000 (1998 approx); $2,100,000 (1996 approx). Note: As of 1998, Contributes through foundation only. 1996, 1995, 1994 Giving includes corporate direct giving; foundation.

Typical Recipients

Arts & Humanities: Arts Associations & Councils, Arts Centers, Arts Festivals, Community Arts, Dance, Ethnic & Folk Arts, Historic Preservation, Museums/Galleries, Music, Opera, Performing Arts, Public Broadcasting
Civic & Public Affairs: Economic Development, Women's Affairs, Zoos/Aquariums
Education: Business Education, Colleges & Universities, Economic Education, Minority Education, Science/Mathematics Education
Environment: Environment-General
Social Services: Child Welfare, Community Service Organizations, Family Services, Senior Services, United Funds/United Ways, Volunteer Services, Youth Organizations

Contributions Analysis

Giving Priorities: Human service, health care, civic affairs, higher education, and the arts.
Civic & Public Affairs: Supports internships in local companies, strategic planning and goalsetting, team learning in classrooms, teacher training, and corporate and community volunteer programs. (Housing & Neighborhood Revitalization) Supports building, rehabilitating or operating affordable housing; revolving loan programs for rental or mortgage assistance; underwriting energy audits or check-ups, energy efficiency improvements or weatherization for existing or new affordable housing projects; affordable housing needs analysis, feasibility studies, planning and evaluation; home-related services for seniors including home repair and maintenance; transportation and services for working individuals whowork in and commute to communities where they cannot afford to live; clean-up efforts to revitalize and improve the appearance and safety of a community; home-related or budget counseling and education for aspiring or new homeowners; and projects for which employees can volunteer.

Application Procedures

Initial Contact: for general purpose grants submit a request in writing no more than four pages long; for workforce readiness or affordable living grants submit a self-addressed envelope addressed to the specific program area

Application Requirements: for general purpose grants only: organization name, contact's name, executive director's name, address, and phone number; organization's mission statement, goals and objectives, description of current programs, and activities and accomplishments; amount and purpose of request, include issues to be addressed, constituency served, target population and how they will benefit; how program and sponsors will be promoted or publicized; expected results and how success will be measured; an itemized project budget; a list of current board of directors; and proof of tax-exempt status
Deadlines: for general purpose grants March 1, June 1, September 1, and December 1; for work readiness grants March 15; for affordable living grants December 15
Decision Notification: notification is made about six weeks after deadline
Notes: To request a Classroom Connection catalog or application form call one of the NCE's Classroom Connection offices: Public Service Co. of Colorado (303)294-2430; Southwestern Public Service Co. (806)378-2714; and Cheyenne Light, Fuel and Power Co. (307)778-2136.

Restrictions

Does not make donations to individuals, political parties, school field trips, athletic or scholastic competitions, scholarship funds, video projects, endowment campaigns, evangelical missions, or multi-year campaigns.

Additional Information

Send request for general donations to the local NCE office to the attention of the Area Manager, Community and Economic Development, or directly to the foundation.
Workforce Readiness and Affordable Living Programs award grants of up to $50,000. General donations are made up to $1,000.

Corporate Officials

Wayne H. Brunetti: vice chairman, president, chief operating officer, director B Cleveland, OH 1942. ED University of Florida (1964); Harvard University (1974). PRIM CORP EMPL vice chairman, president, chief operating officer, director: New Century Energies Inc. CORP AFFIL chief executive officer: Public Service Co. Colorado.
Delwin D. Hock: chairman B Colorado Springs, CO 1935. ED University of Colorado BS (1956). PRIM CORP EMPL chairman: New Century Energies. CORP AFFIL chairman: PSR Investments Inc.; director: Hathaway Corp.; chairman: PS Colorado Credit Corp.; chairman: Fuel Resources Development Co.; chairman: Banncock Center Corp.; chairman: Cheyenne Light Fuel Power Co. NONPR AFFIL chairman: Western Gas Supply Co.; member: Western Regional Council; member: Western Energy Supply Transmission Associates; director: Nuclear Management Resources Council; director: Transit Construction Authority; director: National Natural Gas Vehicle Coalition; director: Greater Denver Corp.; director: INROADS; chairman: Greater Denver Chamber of Commerce; member: Colorado Society; member: Edison Electric Institute; director: Colorado Alliance Business; member: Colorado Forum; director: Association of Edison Illuminating Companies; member: American Gas Association; member: American Institute CPAs.
Richard C. Kelly: executive vice president, chief financial officer B 1946. ED University of Colorado; University of Michigan; Regis College BA (1968); Regis College MBA (1982). PRIM CORP EMPL executive vice president, chief financial officer: New Century Energies ADD CORP EMPL executive vice president: Public Service Co. Colorado. NONPR AFFIL director: Mercy Housing; member: Regis Accounting Advisory Committee; director: Colorado Public Expenditures Council.

Foundation Officials

Wayne H. Brunetti: president, chief executive officer (see above)
Cynthia Evans: manager director
Bill D. Helton: chairman B Wheeler, TX 1938. ED Texas Technology University BSEE (1964). PRIM CORP EMPL chairman, chief executive officer, director: New Century Energies Inc. CORP AFFIL chairman: SPS; chairman: Quixx Corp.; chairman: Southwestern Public Service Co.; chairman: PSCO; chairman: Public Service Co. Colorado; chairman: New Century Services Inc.; chairman: Cheyenne Light Fuel Power Co.; chairman: New Century Enterprises. NONPR AFFIL director: Association Electrical Companies Texas; member: Rotary International.
Richard C. Kelly: treasurer (see above)
David M. Wilks: vice president B Corpus Christi, TX 1946. ED Texas A&M University (1970); George Washington University (1974). PRIM CORP EMPL president, chief operating officer, director: Southwestern Public Service Co. CORP AFFIL president, retail services: New Century Services; executive vice president, director: Public Service Colorado; president: New Century Energies Inc.

Grants Analysis

Disclosure Period: calendar year ending
Typical Range: $1,000 to $5,000

New England Bio Labs

Company Contact

Beverly, MA

Company Description

Employees: 200
SIC(s): 2836 Biological Products Except Diagnostic.

Operating Locations

Canada: New England Biolabs Ltd., Mississauga; Germany: New England Biolabs GmbH, Schwalbach, Taunus; United Kingdom: New England Biolabs (UK) Ltd., Hitchin, Hertfordshire; Canada: New England Biolabs Ltd., Mississauga; Germany: New England Biolabs GmbH, Schwalbach, Taunus; United Kingdom: New England Biolabs (UK) Ltd., Hitchin, Hertfordshire; Canada: New England Biolabs Ltd., Mississauga; Germany: New England Biolabs GmbH, Schwalbach, Taunus; United Kingdom: New England Biolabs (UK) Ltd., Hitchin, Hertfordshire; Canada: New England Biolabs Ltd., Mississauga; Germany: New England Biolabs GmbH, Schwalbach, Taunus; United Kingdom: New England Biolabs (UK) Ltd., Hitchin, Hertfordshire; Canada: New England Biolabs Ltd., Mississauga; Germany: New England Biolabs GmbH, Schwalbach, Taunus; United Kingdom: New England Biolabs (UK) Ltd., Hitchin, Hertfordshire; Canada: New England Biolabs Ltd., Mississauga; Germany: New England Biolabs GmbH, Schwalbach, Taunus; United Kingdom: New England Biolabs (UK) Ltd., Hitchin, Hertfordshire; Canada: New England Biolabs Ltd., Mississauga; Germany: New England Biolabs GmbH, Schwalbach, Taunus; United Kingdom: New England Biolabs (UK) Ltd., Hitchin, Hertfordshire

Nonmonetary Support

Type: Donated Equipment

New England Bio Labs Foundation

Giving Contact

Martine Kellett, Executive Director
New England Bio Labs Foundation
32 Tozer Rd.
Beverly, MA 01915
Phone: (508)927-2404

Description

Founded: 1982
EIN: 042776213
Organization Type: Corporate Foundation
Giving Locations: MA internationally.
Grant Types: General Support, Operating Expenses, Project, Research, Seed Money.

Financial Summary

Total Giving: $289,042 (fiscal year ending November 30, 1997); $200,000 (fiscal 1996); $171,341 (fiscal 1995)
Assets: $6,093,354 (fiscal 1997); $4,025,730 (fiscal 1995); $3,850,910 (fiscal 1994)
Gifts Received: $100,000 (fiscal 1997); $239,447 (fiscal 1995); $108,190 (fiscal 1994). Note: In fiscal 1993, contributions were received from New England Bio Labs.

Typical Recipients

Arts & Humanities: Arts Associations & Councils, Arts Outreach, Ballet, Community Arts, Dance, Ethnic & Folk Arts, Arts & Humanities-General, Historic Preservation, History & Archaeology, Music, Performing Arts, Theater
Civic & Public Affairs: Botanical Gardens/Parks, Community Foundations, Economic Development, Environmental Affairs (General), Environmental Affairs (Air/Water Quality), Environmental Affairs (Conservation), Civic & Public Affairs-General, Inner-City Development, Legal Aid, Nonprofit Management, Rural Affairs, Urban & Community Affairs, Women's Affairs
Education: Afterschool/Enrichment Programs, Agricultural Education, Arts/Humanities Education, Colleges & Universities, Elementary Education (Public), Education-General, Preschool Education, School Volunteerism, Science/Mathematics Education, Vocational & Technical Education
Environment: Air/Water Quality, Forestry, Environment-General, Resource Conservation, Wildlife Protection
Health: Clinics/Medical Centers, Eyes/Blindness, Health-General, Health Organizations, Nutrition, Prenatal Health Issues, Preventive Medicine/Wellness Organizations, Public Health
International: Foreign Educational Institutions, International-General, Health Care/Hospitals, International Development, International Environmental Issues, International Relief Efforts
Science: Science-General, Scientific Centers & Institutes, Scientific Labs, Scientific Research
Social Services: Child Welfare, Community Centers, Community Service Organizations, Social Services-General, Youth Organizations

Application Procedures

Initial Contact: Send a brief letter of inquiry and a full proposal. Include a description of organization, amount requested, purpose of funds sought, recently audited financial statement, and proof of tax-exempt status.
Deadlines: March 1, September 1, and December 1.

Restrictions

Grants are not awarded for religious activities, capital endowments, hardship costs, species specific projects, or operating costs.

Additional Information

Publications: Informational Brochure (including Application Guidelines)

Corporate Officials

Dr. Donald G. Comb: president PRIM CORP EMPL president: New England Biological Laboratories.

Foundation Officials

Dr. Donald G. Comb: trustee (see above)
Douglas Foy: trustee
Martine Kellett: executive director
Dr. Henry P. Paulus: trustee

Grants Analysis

Disclosure Period: fiscal year ending November 30, 1997
Total Grants: $289,042
Number of Grants: 76
Average Grant: $3,803
Highest Grant: $15,000
Typical Range: $100 to $8,000

Recent Grants

Note: Grants derived from fiscal 1997 Form 990.

Arts & Humanities

7,500	Underground Railroad, Saginaw, MI

Civic & Public Affairs

8,000	Building Materials Resource Center, San Diego, CA
7,500	Pedals for Progress, High Bridge, NJ
7,000	Instituto Socorr
7,000	Salem Sound 2000, Salem, MA
5,000	Gloucester Fishermen's Wives, Gloucester, MA
5,000	Lesson One Foundation, Glendale, AZ

Education

7,000	ICSEE, Boston, MA

Environment

13,000	Ecologic Development
10,000	Ecological Enterprises
9,000	Ecological Development Fund, Cambridge, MA
8,000	Conservation Law Foundation, Boston, MA
7,000	Ecologic Development
7,000	Green Mountain Forest Watch, Brattleboro, VT
6,000	Environmental Foundation, Boston, MA
5,000	Natural Resources Council of Maine, Augusta, ME

Health

15,000	Art for Health, Boston, MA

International

10,000	World Wildlife Fund, Washington, DC
10,000	World Wildlife Fund, Washington, DC
7,000	Conservation International, Washington, DC
7,000	Conservation International, Washington, DC
7,000	E-Law, Boston, MA
7,000	E-Law, Boston, MA

NEW ENGLAND FINANCIAL

Company Contact

Boston, MA
Web: http://www.nefn.com

Company Description

Former Name: New England Life Insurance Co.; The New England.
Assets: US$16,580,000,000
Employees: 2,557
SIC(s): 6311 Life Insurance, 6321 Accident & Health Insurance.

Nonmonetary Support

Value: $21,000 (1993); $12,000 (1992)
Type: Donated Equipment; In-kind Services; Loaned Employees; Loaned Executives; Workplace Solicitation
Note: Workplace solicitation is for area nonprofits. Company holds blood drives with the American Red Cross. Company supports nonprofit by purchasing fundraising tickets.

Giving Contact

Bryan K. Spence, Director, Charitable Contributions
New England Financial
501 Boylston St., 5th Fl.
Boston, MA 02116-3700
Phone: (617)578-2119
Fax: (617)536-5566
Email: bspence@nefn.com

Description

Organization Type: Corporate Giving Program
Giving Locations: MA: Boston metropolitan area
Grant Types: Award, Capital, Employee Matching Gifts, Endowment, General Support, Multiyear/Continuing Support, Operating Expenses, Project, Research, Scholarship.
Note: Employee matching gift ratio: 1 to 1 for higher education.

Giving Philosophy

'The New England has a long and proud tradition of corporate social responsibility. Our charitable giving began with support for the United Way and the Red Cross in the 1930s and 1940s, expanded to . . . health care organizations in the 1950s and to the adoption of formal giving guidelines in the 1960s. Today our commitment to charitable contributions and other social responsibility programs is an integral part of our operations. .. The New England supports organizations that promote the general well-being of the Boston community. Grants are made in the areas of education, health care, social service, housing/community development, culture, and volunteerism.' 1996 Charitable Contributions Annual Report

Financial Summary

Total Giving: $1,450,000 (1999 approx); $1,400,000 (1998 approx); $1,250,000 (1997). Note: Contributes through corporate direct giving program only. 1997 Giving includes corporate direct giving ($781,000); matching gifts ($94,000); United Way ($375,000). 1996 Giving includes corporate direct giving ($705,000); United Way ($375,000).

Typical Recipients

Arts & Humanities: Arts Associations & Councils, Arts Centers, Arts Institutes, Ballet, Community Arts, Dance, Ethnic & Folk Arts, Historic Preservation, Literary Arts, Museums/Galleries, Music, Opera, Performing Arts, Theater, Visual Arts
Civic & Public Affairs: Civil Rights, Economic Development, Employment/Job Training, Hispanic Affairs, Housing, Nonprofit Management, Professional & Trade Associations, Urban & Community Affairs, Women's Affairs
Education: Arts/Humanities Education, Business Education, Business-School Partnerships, Colleges & Universities, Community & Junior Colleges, Continuing Education, Education Reform, Elementary Education (Private), Health & Physical Education, Literacy, Minority Education, Preschool Education, Public Education (Precollege), Secondary Education (Public), Special Education, Student Aid
Environment: Environment-General
Health: AIDS/HIV, Cancer, Children's Health/Hospitals, Clinics/Medical Centers, Geriatric Health, Health Organizations, Hospitals, Medical Rehabilitation, Medical Research, Mental Health, Nutrition, Prenatal Health Issues, Public Health
Religion: Churches, Religious Welfare
Social Services: Animal Protection, Big Brother/Big Sister, Camps, Community Centers, Community Service Organizations, Counseling, Day Care, Delinquency & Criminal Rehabilitation, Domestic Violence, Emergency Relief, Family Planning, Family Services, Food/Clothing Distribution, Homes, People with Disabilities, Recreation & Athletics, Refugee Assistance, Senior Services, Shelters/Homelessness, Substance Abuse, United Funds/United Ways, Volunteer Services, Youth Organizations

Contributions Analysis

Arts & Humanities: 5% to 10%. Supports art institutes that reach a large population and contribute to the community, art programs in the Boston Public schools, and organizations that make cultural events accesible to the community.
Civic & Public Affairs: (United Funds & United Way) Supports the United Way of Massachusetts Bay. (Housing & Neighborhood Revitalization) 10% to 15%. Provides grants to agencies that develop affordable, permanent, transitional, and shelter housing, and those that support community development initiatives.
Education: 25% to 30%. Supports Boston public schools, particularly in the area of basic skills that impact company's partnership schools, Jeremiah E. Burke High School and the Mather Elementary School. Also gives direct grants to Greater Boston area colleges and universities for special projects.
Health: 15% to 20%. Supports programs that are community-based, increase community access, targets under-served populations, and promote efficient care delivery.
Social Services: 25% to 30%. Supports organizations that focus on social and economic issues involving the community. Emphasis on youth programs, mentoring, jobtraining, women's issues, and other community-based programs.

Application Procedures

Initial Contact: short cover letter
Application Requirements: history organization and its mission, summary of intent and amount requested; program description, including budget; organization's current budget, recent financial statement, and list of other sources of support; list of board members and affiliations; and evidence of 501(c)(3) status
Deadlines: generally in February, May, August, and December; call for exact dates
Evaluative Criteria: effectiveness of management and service delivery, organization's financial stability and efficiency, size and type of population served, priority to groups located in Boston, and involvement of company associates
Decision Notification: quarterly
Notes: the Company accepts the Associated Grantmakers of Massachusetts Common Proposal Format.

Restrictions

Grants are restricted to 501(c)(3) organizations. The company does not support individuals; religious organizations for sectarian purposes; private foundations, veterans', fraternal, athletic, or social organizations; disease-specific organizations; or political or lobbying groups.

Additional Information

In 1996, The New England merged with Metropolitan Life Insurance Co. This merger has enabled the company to increase its charitable contributions.
Publications: Contributions Guidelines; Charitable Contributions Annual Report

Corporate Officials

James M. Benson: chairman, chief executive officer PRIM CORP EMPL chief executive officer: Metropolitan Life Insurance Co. ADD CORP EMPL chairman, chief executive officer: New England Life Insurance Co.
Kathryn F. Plazak: second vice president PRIM CORP EMPL second vice president: New England Life Insurance Co.

Bryan K. Spence: contributions administrator PRIM CORP EMPL contributions administrator: New England Life Insurance Co.

Grants Analysis

Disclosure Period: calendar year ending 1997
Total Grants: $900,000
Number of Grants: 160
Average Grant: $5,625
Typical Range: $2,500 to $15,000
Note: Analysis provided by company.

Recent Grants

Note: Grants derived from 1996 Annual Report.

Arts & Humanities
Boston Ballet, Boston, MA
Commonwealth Shakespeare Company, Boston, MA
Community Music Center, Boston, MA
Friends of Copley Square, Boston, MA

Civic & Public Affairs
Bay State Skills Corp, Boston, MA
Boston Employment Service, Boston, MA
Jobs for Youth, Boston, MA
La Alianza Hispana, Boston, MA
Neighborhood Development Support Collaborative, Boston, MA
Women's Educational and Industrial Union, Boston, MA
Women's Institute for Housing and Economic Development, Boston, MA

Education
Aquinas College, Grand Rapids, MI
Boston Adult Literacy Fund, Boston, MA
Boston College, Boston, MA
Boston Partners in Education, Boston, MA
Boston Schoolyard Initiative, Boston, MA
Citywide Education Coalition, Boston, MA
Committee for Boston Public Housing, Boston, MA
Jeremiah E. Burke High School Partnership, Boston, MA
Massachusetts Business Alliance for Education, Boston, MA
United Negro College Fund, Boston, MA
University of Massachusetts Boston Urban Scholars Program, Boston, MA

Health
AIDS Action Committee, Boston, MA
Boston Community AIDS Partnership, Boston, MA
Boston Medical Center Kids Fund, Boston, MA
Codman Square Health Center, Boston, MA
Dana-Farber Cancer Institute, Boston, MA
Failure to Thrive Growth Clinic, Boston, MA
Mobile Diagnostic Services, Boston, MA
Roxbury Comprehensive Community Health Center, Boston, MA
St. Mary's Women and Infants Center, Boston, MA

Religion
Samaritans, Boston, MA
South End Adults at Cathedral, Boston, MA

Social Services
Associated Grantmakers Summer Camp Fund, Boston, MA
Big Sister Association, Boston, MA
Boston Cares, Boston, MA
Boys and Girls Club, Boston, MA
Brookview House, Boston, MA
Child Care Resource Center, Boston, MA
Committee to End Elder Homelessness, Boston, MA
Crittenton Hastings House, Boston, MA
Family Van, Boston, MA
Greater Boston Food Bank, Boston, MA
Hale-Bernard Services for Older People, Boston, MA
Living Center, Boston, MA
Massachusetts Immigrant and Refugee Coalition, Boston, MA
Massachusetts Society for Prevention of Cruelty to Animals, Boston, MA
Pine Street Inn, Boston, MA
Project Parents, Boston, MA
WAITT House, Boston, MA

New Jersey Natural Gas Co.

Company Contact

Wall, NJ

Company Description

Revenue: US$426,660,000
Employees: 832
SIC(s): 4924 Natural Gas Distribution.
Parent Company: New Jersey Resources Corp.

Nonmonetary Support

Type: Donated Equipment; Loaned Employees

Corporate Sponsorship

Contact:
1415 Wyckoff Road
Wall, NJ 07719

New Jersey Natural Gas Foundation

Giving Contact

Tom Kononowitz, Senior Vice President
New Jersey Natural Gas Foundation
PO Box 1464
Wall, NJ 07719
Phone: (732)938-1134
Fax: (732)938-7183

Alternate Contact

Jim O'Keefe, community relations

Description

EIN: 222835065
Organization Type: Corporate Foundation
Former Name: New Jersey Resources Foundation, Inc. (1998).
Giving Locations: NJ: Monmouth County, Ocean County, portions of Morris County company's service area.
Grant Types: General Support, Matching.

Financial Summary

Total Giving: $250,000 (fiscal year ending September 30, 1999 approx); $250,000 (fiscal 1998 approx); $255,778 (fiscal 1997). Note: Contributes through foundation only. 1994 Giving includes foundation ($180,721); matching gifts ($65,400).
Assets: $37,007 (fiscal 1997); $64,785 (fiscal 1996); $71,796 (fiscal 1995)
Gifts Received: $229,751 (fiscal 1997); $247,081 (fiscal 1996); $236,519 (fiscal 1995). Note: Contributions are received from New Jersey Natural Gas Co.

Typical Recipients

Arts & Humanities: Arts & Humanities-General, Libraries
Civic & Public Affairs: African American Affairs, Botanical Gardens/Parks, Community Foundations, Economic Development, Civic & Public Affairs-General, Philanthropic Organizations, Public Policy, Safety, Urban & Community Affairs, Women's Affairs
Education: Colleges & Universities, Community & Junior Colleges, Education Funds, Education Reform, Education-General, Minority Education, Public Education (Precollege), Secondary Education (Public), Student Aid
Environment: Environment-General
Health: Cancer, Children's Health/Hospitals, Clinics/Medical Centers, Diabetes, Emergency/Ambulance Services, Health-General, Health Organizations, Hospitals, Prenatal Health Issues, Public Health, Single-Disease Health Associations
Religion: Jewish Causes, Religious Welfare, Social/Policy Issues
Social Services: Big Brother/Big Sister, Child Welfare, Community Centers, Community Service Organizations, Day Care, Family Services, Food/Clothing Distribution, People with Disabilities, Scouts, Social Services-General, Substance Abuse, United Funds/United Ways, YMCA/YWCA/YMHA/YWHA, Youth Organizations

Contributions Analysis

Civic & Public Affairs: About 10%. Civic organizations active in New Jersey.
Education: 25% to 30%. Colleges, universities, community colleges, and programs that assist minority students.
Environment: Less than 5%. Includes resource preservation.
Health: 30% to 35%. Medical centers and hospitals.
Religion: Less than 5%. Includes interfaith organizations.
Social Services: 30% to 35%. United Way, youth organizations, family services, and drug abuse prevention. Company also sponsors a 'Gift of Warmth' program.

Application Procedures

Initial Contact: letter of inquiry
Application Requirements: statement of purpose, amount requested, description of constituency served, and proof of tax-exempt status
Deadlines: None.
Review Process: inquiries are reviewed and evaluated weekly; foundation requests additional information as necessary
Decision Notification: the foundation board meets quarterly to review larger requests; small requests are decided upon within a shorter time frame

Additional Information

In 1998, Co. changed foundation name because New Jersey Natural Gas is a more recognized name. Foundation priorities did not change.

Corporate Officials

Laurence M. Downes: president, chief executive officer, director, chairman B Hackensack, NJ 1957. ED Iona College BA (1979); Iona College MBA (1981). PRIM CORP EMPL president, chief executive officer, director, chairman: New Jersey Resources Corp. CORP AFFIL president: New Jersey Natural Energy Co.; president, chief executive officer, chairman: New Jersey Natural Gas Co.; president: New Jersey Energy Co. NONPR AFFIL member: Financial Executives Institute; member: National Investor Relations Institute; chairman: American Gas Association.
Glenn C. Lockwood: senior vice president, chief financial officer B 1961. ED Saint Peter's College BS (1983). PRIM CORP EMPL senior vice president, chief financial officer: New Jersey Resources Corp. ADD CORP EMPL chief financial officer, treasurer: New Jersey Energy Co.

Foundation Officials

Laurence M. Downes: trustee (see above)
Oleta J. Harden: secretary ED University of California, Los Angeles JD (1979). PRIM CORP EMPL senior vice president, secretary, general counsel: New Jersey Resources Corp. CORP AFFIL secretary: New Jersey Natural Energy Co.; secretary: NJR Energy Corp.; secretary: Commercial Realty Resources Corp.
Thomas J. Kononowitz: vice president B 1942. PRIM CORP EMPL senior vice president marketing & consumer service: New Jersey Natural Gas Co.

CORP AFFIL senior vice president: New Jersey Resources Corp.
Glenn C. Lockwood: treasurer (see above)
Mary Ann Martin: trustee PRIM CORP EMPL vice president consumer & community relations: New Jersey Natural Gas Co.

Grants Analysis

Disclosure Period: fiscal year ending September 30, 1997
Total Grants: $232,728*
Number of Grants: 117
Average Grant: $1,989
Highest Grant: $39,350
Typical Range: $100 to $5,000
*Note: Giving excludes United Way.

Recent Grants

Note: Grants derived from fiscal 1997 Form 990.

Civic & Public Affairs

4,000	Community Foundation of New Jersey, Morristown, NJ
3,030	Monmouth County Urban League, Red Bank, NJ
1,700	CPC Foundation, Bethlehem, PA
1,500	New Jersey State Safety Council, Cranford, NJ
1,400	National Conference Monmouth-Ocean Counties Chapter, Monmouth, NJ
1,250	Women's Center of Monmouth County, Hazlet, NJ
1,000	CPC Foundation, Bethlehem, PA

Education

9,600	Monmouth University, Monmouth, NJ
8,600	Georgian Court College, Lakewood, NJ
5,360	Brookdale Community College, Brookdale, NJ
2,400	County College of Morris Foundation, Randolph, NJ
2,000	Ocean County College Foundation, Toms River, NJ
2,000	United Negro College Fund, New Brunswick, NJ
1,500	Independent College Fund of New Jersey, Summit, NJ
1,050	Monmouth University, West Long Beach, NJ

Health

9,850	Jersey Shore Medical Center Foundation, Neptune, NJ
4,800	Medical Center of Ocean County, Point Pleasant, NJ
4,385	Monmouth Health Care Foundation, Long Branch, NJ
4,300	American Red Cross
3,100	Riverview Foundation
3,000	SCAN, Fort Wayne, IN
2,800	Community Medical Center, Toms River, NJ
2,500	St. Clare Riverside Medical Center
2,300	Centrastate Medical Center, Freehold, NJ
2,250	American Cancer Society
2,200	Morristown Memorial Hospital, Morristown, NJ
2,125	Bayshore Community Hospital, Holmdel, NJ
1,850	Ronald McDonald House
1,570	Cerebral Palsy of Monmouth and Ocean Counties, Ocean, NJ
1,500	Kimball Medical Center Foundation, Lakewood, NJ
1,200	March of Dimes
1,050	Monmouth Medical Center Foundation, Long Branch, NJ
1,000	Deborah Hospital, Browns Mills, NJ
1,000	Northwest Covenant House Medical Center
1,000	Southern Ocean Hospital

Social Services

39,350	Gift of Warmth Fund
38,200	Gift of Warmth Fund
16,320	United Way Monmouth County
10,260	New Jersey Natural Gas Company Grills, NJ
5,585	United Way Ocean County, Toms River, NJ
3,400	Boy Scouts of America, Monmouth, NJ
2,570	Girl Scouts of America, Monmouth, NJ
2,160	Boys and Girls Club, Monmouth, NJ
1,800	Collier Services Foundation, Wickatunk, NJ
1,660	ARC, Monmouth, NJ
1,500	Substance Abuse Resources
1,335	Family and Children's Services
1,330	Community YMCA
1,300	United Way Morris County, Morristown, NJ
1,060	Big Brothers and Big Sisters, Monmouth, NJ

New United Motor Manufacturing Inc.

Company Contact

Fremont, CA
Web: http://www.toyota.co.jp

Company Description

Employees: 4,400
SIC(s): 3711 Motor Vehicles & Car Bodies.
Parent Company: Toyota Motor Corp., 1, Toyota-cho, Toyota, Aichi Pref., Japan

Operating Locations

CA: New United Motor Manufacturing, Fremont; New United Motor Manufacturing Inc., Fremont

Giving Contact

Michael Damer, Manager, Community Relations
45500 Fremont Blvd.
Fremont, CA 94538
Phone: (510)498-5763
Fax: (510)770-4010

Description

Organization Type: Corporate Giving Program
Giving Locations: headquarters community.
Grant Types: General Support.

Financial Summary

Total Giving: $300,000 (1997 approx); $300,000 (1996); $300,000 (1995)

Typical Recipients

Civic & Public Affairs: Civic & Public Affairs-General
Education: Education-General

Application Procedures

Initial Contact: a brief letter of inquiry
Application Requirements: a description of organization, amount requested, and purpose of funds sought
Deadlines: None.

Restrictions

Does not support individuals, religious organizations for sectarian purposes, or political or lobbying groups.

Corporate Officials

Iwao Itoh: chairman, president, chief executive officer ED Keio Gijyuka University BA. PRIM CORP EMPL chairman, president, chief executive officer: New United Motor Manufacturing Inc.

Giving Program Officials

Michael Damer: PRIM CORP EMPL manager community relations: New United Motor Manufacturing Inc.

Grants Analysis

Disclosure Period: calendar year ending
Typical Range: $100 to $1,000

New York Life Insurance Co.

Company Contact

New York, NY
Web: http://www.newyorklife.com

Company Description

Revenue: US$21,679,300,000 (1999)
Profit: US$752,900,000
Employees: 6,400
Fortune Rank: 70, per FORTUNE Magazine's list of 500 Largest U.S. Corporations (1999).
FF 70
SIC(s): 6311 Life Insurance.

Nonmonetary Support

Volunteer Programs: Provides grants to local grassroots organizations where employees volunteer.

New York Life Foundation

Giving Contact

Carol Reuter, Vice President & Executive Director
New York Life Foundation
51 Madison Avenue
New York, NY 10010-1655
Phone: (212)576-7341
Fax: (212)576-6220
Web: http://www.newyorklife.com/foundation

Description

EIN: 132989476
Organization Type: Corporate Foundation
Giving Locations: NY: New York nationally.
Grant Types: Capital, Employee Matching Gifts, General Support, Project, Scholarship.
Note: Employee matching gift ratio: 1 to 1 for higher education.

Financial Summary

Total Giving: $3,850,108 (1998); $2,494,862 (1996); $2,605,751 (1995). Note: Contributes through foundation only.
Giving Analysis: Giving for 1996 includes: foundation ($1,254,883); foundation grants to United Way ($928,600); foundation matching gifts ($248,879); foundation scholarships ($62,500); 1998: foundation ($2,208,357); foundation grants to United Way ($1,025,150); foundation matching gifts ($616,601)
Assets: $63,228,971 (1998); $48,240,340 (1996); $48,591,179 (1995)
Gifts Received: $4,420,313 (1998); $1,000,000 (1996); $1,000,000 (1995). Note: Contributions are received from the New York Life Insurance Company.

Typical Recipients

Arts & Humanities: Arts Associations & Councils, Arts Centers, Ballet, Historic Preservation, Libraries, Museums/Galleries, Music, Performing Arts, Public Broadcasting
Civic & Public Affairs: African American Affairs, Asian American Affairs, Business/Free Enterprise, Civil Rights, Economic Development, Economic Policy, Employment/Job Training, Law & Justice, Legal Aid, Municipalities/Towns, Nonprofit Management,

Philanthropic Organizations, Professional & Trade Associations, Public Policy, Urban & Community Affairs, Women's Affairs, Zoos/Aquariums
Education: Arts/Humanities Education, Business Education, Colleges & Universities, Community & Junior Colleges, Education Associations, Education Funds, Health & Physical Education, Legal Education, Literacy, Medical Education, Minority Education, Religious Education
Health: AIDS/HIV, Clinics/Medical Centers, Emergency/Ambulance Services, Geriatric Health, Health Organizations, Hospitals, Medical Rehabilitation, Medical Research, Medical Training, Mental Health, Nursing Services, Single-Disease Health Associations
Science: Science Museums, Scientific Organizations
Social Services: Child Welfare, Community Centers, Community Service Organizations, Counseling, Crime Prevention, Day Care, Domestic Violence, Family Services, Food/Clothing Distribution, People with Disabilities, Recreation & Athletics, Senior Services, Shelters/Homelessness, Substance Abuse, United Funds/United Ways, Volunteer Services, Youth Organizations

Contributions Analysis

Giving Priorities: United Way, colleges and universities, community development, AIDS research, and limited support to the arts.
Arts & Humanities: 3%. Recipients include performing arts centers, museums, arts foundations, libraries, and others.
Civic & Public Affairs: 17%. Supports community development programs, civil rights, women's groups, philanthropic organizations, and others.
Education: 13%. Supports scholarships for women in health professions, higher education, literacy, and arts education.
Environment: 7%. Supports the Trust for Public Land.
Social Services: 60%. Supports the United Way, child welfare, recreation organizations, community centers and volunteer groups.
Note: Total contributions made in 1998.

Application Procedures

Initial Contact: Send a brief letter and proposal.
Application Requirements: Include a list of officers and board members, brief background information on organization, description of current program, latest annual report and audited financial statement, concise description of program for which funds are sought, current budget and funding sources, proof of tax-exempt status, and list of corporate and foundation contributors during past 12 months.
Deadlines: None.
Decision Notification: Board meets in March, June, September, and December.

Restrictions

In general, the foundation does not make grants to individuals; public educational institutions; sectarian or religious organizations; fraternal, social, professional, athletic, or veterans' organizations; seminars, conferences or trips; preschool, primary, or secondary educational institutions; endowments, memorials, or capital campaigns; organizations that are members of United Way already supported by the foundation; or foundations that are themselves grant-making bodies.

Additional Information

The foundation requires periodic reports from all organizations that it supports.
Publications: Foundation Annual Report; Application Guidelines

Corporate Officials

George August William Bundschuh: vice president B Yonkers, NY 1933. ED Pace University BBA (1955); Columbia University School of Business Administration MS (1959). NONPR AFFIL trustee: Pace University.
Lee Morgan Gammill, Jr.: vice chairman, director B New York, NY 1934. ED Dartmouth College BA (1956). PRIM CORP EMPL vice chairman, director: New York Life Insurance Co. CORP AFFIL director: New York Life Realty Corp.; director: New York Life Securities Corp.; president, director: New York Life Insurance & Annuity Corp.; director: New York Life Equity Corp. NONPR AFFIL director, member executive committee: Life Underwriters Training Council; member: National Association Life Underwriters; chairman, trustee: American College; chairman: Life Insurance Marketing & Research Association International. CLUB AFFIL Pacific-Union Club; Lyford Cay Club; Mill Valley Tennis Club; Lagunitas Country Club; The Links Club; Bohemian Club.
Michael John McLaughlin: senior vice president, deputy general counsel B Cambridge, MA 1944. ED Boston College AB (1965); New York University School of Law JD (1968). PRIM CORP EMPL senior vice president, deputy general counsel: New York Life Insurance Co. NONPR AFFIL member: American Bar Association; member: New York State Bar Association.
Carol Joan Reuter: vice president B Brooklyn, NY 1941. ED Saint John's University BA (1962). PRIM CORP EMPL vice president: New York Life Insurance Co. NONPR AFFIL member corporate associates: United Way America.

Foundation Officials

George August William Bundschuh: director (see above)
Lee Morgan Gammill, Jr.: director (see above)
Harry George Hohn, Jr.: chairman, director B New York, NY 1932. ED New York University BS (1953); Fordham University JD (1956); New York University LLM (1959). CORP AFFIL director: Witco Corp.; director: New York Life Insurance Co. NONPR AFFIL vice chairman board trustees: National AID South Foundation; board governors: United Way Tri-State; chairman: Million Dollar Round Table Foundation; chairman: Life Insurance Council New York; trustee: Life Office Management Association; trustee: Foundation Independent Higher Education; trustee: Community Economic Development; member international advisory board: Credit Comml France; member: Association Life Insurance Council; trustee: American College.
Celia Holtzberg: treasurer
Michael John McLaughlin: secretary (see above)
Carol Joan Reuter: chief executive officer, director (see above)

Grants Analysis

Disclosure Period: calendar year ending 1998
Total Grants: $2,208,357*
Number of Grants: 154
Average Grant: $14,340
Highest Grant: $643,350
Typical Range: $100 to $20,000
***Note:** Giving excludes matching gifts; United Way.

Recent Grants

Note: Grants derived from 1996 Form 990.

Arts & Humanities

25,000	Lincoln Center for Performing Arts, New York, NY
12,000	Colonial Williamsburg Foundation, Williamsburg, VA
10,000	American Ballet Theater, New York, NY
10,000	John F. Kennedy Center for Performing Arts, Washington, DC
10,000	Metropolitan Museum of Art, New York, NY
10,000	Museum of Modern Art, New York, NY
10,000	New York Public Library, New York, NY
10,000	WNET/Channel 13, New York, NY

Civic & Public Affairs

62,500	Business and Professional Women's Foundation, Washington, DC
42,500	New York City Partnership Foundation, New York, NY
40,000	Mainstream, Bethesda, MD
27,500	Regional Plan Association, New York, NY
20,000	Committee for Economic Development, New York, NY
20,000	Volunteers of Legal Services, New York, NY
15,000	Public and Private Initiatives Yes Commission, New York, NY
10,000	Advertising Council, New York, NY
10,000	American Enterprise Institute for Public Policy Research, Washington, DC
10,000	Catalyst, New York, NY
10,000	National Center for Nonprofit Boards, Washington, DC
10,000	Support Center for Nonprofit Management, New York, NY

Education

110,000	Literacy Volunteers of America, Syracuse, NY
55,000	Literacy Volunteers, New York, NY
45,000	Literacy Assistance Center, New York, NY
35,000	Reading is Fundamental, Washington, DC
20,000	University of Pennsylvania S.S. Huebner Foundation, Philadelphia, PA
11,500	Independent College Fund, New York, NY
11,500	New England Colleges Fund, Boston, MA
11,000	Foundation for Independent Colleges, Harrisburg, PA
11,000	Foundation for Independent Colleges, Mechanicsburg, PA
10,000	Ohio Foundation of Independent Colleges, Columbus, OH

Health

100,000	Life and Health Insurance Medical Research Fund, Washington, DC
100,000	National AIDS Fund, Washington, DC
50,000	Black Leadership Commission on AIDS, New York, NY
47,595	Visiting Nurse Service, New York, NY
40,000	Hispanic AIDS Forum, New York, NY

Science

10,000	American Museum of Natural History, New York, NY

Social Services

500,000	United Way Tri-State Area, New York, NY
35,000	Park Slope Project Reach Youth, Brooklyn, NY
30,000	Children's Hope Foundation, New York, NY
24,600	United Way Services, Cleveland, OH
21,210	Bailey House, New York, NY
20,400	United Way, Minneapolis, MN
18,000	United Way, Atlanta, GA
17,250	United Way Bay Area, San Francisco, CA
16,000	United Way Crusade of Mercy, Chicago, IL
15,050	United Way, Dallas, TX
15,000	Citizens Crime Commission, New York, NY
13,500	United Way National Capital Area, Washington, DC
12,450	United Way, Los Angeles, CA
11,500	United Way Southeastern Pennsylvania, Philadelphia, PA

NEW YORK MERCANTILE EXCHANGE

Company Contact
New York, NY

Company Description
Employees: 375
SIC(s): 6231 Security & Commodity Exchanges.

Nonmonetary Support
Type: Donated Equipment

New York Mercantile Exchange Charitable Foundation

Giving Contact
Madeline Boyd, Chairman
New York Mercantile Exchange Charitable Foundation
1 North End Avenue, 15th Floor
New York, NY 10282-1101
Phone: (212)299-2770

Description
Founded: 1989
EIN: 133586378
Organization Type: Corporate Foundation
Giving Locations: principally near operating locations and to national organizations.
Grant Types: Emergency, General Support, Project, Research, Scholarship, Seed Money.

Financial Summary
Total Giving: $1,300,000 (1998 approx); $586,090 (1995); $360,750 (1994)
Assets: $140,000 (1995); $40,336 (1994); $315,879 (1993)
Gifts Received: $615,420 (1995); $100,725 (1994); $234,600 (1993). Note: In 1995, contributions were received from the New York Mercantile Exchange Corp. ($500,000), MBF Clearing Corp. ($11,440), Pioneer Futures ($15,270), Tudor Investment Corp. ($10,000), Richard Schaeffer ($7,000), and Philbro Energy ($5,000); miscellaneous contributions of less than $5,000 each also were received.

Typical Recipients
Arts & Humanities: Arts Associations & Councils, Arts Outreach, Community Arts, Arts & Humanities-General, Libraries, Museums/Galleries, Music, Public Broadcasting
Civic & Public Affairs: Asian American Affairs, Botanical Gardens/Parks, Community Foundations, Employment/Job Training, Ethnic Organizations, Civic & Public Affairs-General, Hispanic Affairs, Housing, Inner-City Development, Professional & Trade Associations, Public Policy, Urban & Community Affairs
Education: Afterschool/Enrichment Programs, Colleges & Universities, Education Reform, Elementary Education (Public), Faculty Development, Education-General, Medical Education, Private Education (Precollege), Public Education (Precollege), Special Education
Environment: Air/Water Quality, Environment-General, Resource Conservation
Health: AIDS/HIV, Cancer, Children's Health/Hospitals, Clinics/Medical Centers, Diabetes, Emergency/Ambulance Services, Health-General, Hospitals, Medical Rehabilitation, Multiple Sclerosis, Public Health, Research/Studies Institutes, Single-Disease Health Associations, Trauma Treatment
Religion: Churches, Religion-General, Jewish Causes, Religious Welfare, Synagogues/Temples
Social Services: Camps, Child Welfare, Community Centers, Community Service Organizations, Counseling, Crime Prevention, Day Care, Delinquency & Criminal Rehabilitation, Domestic Violence, Emergency Relief, Family Services, Food/Clothing Distribution, People with Disabilities, Recreation & Athletics, Senior Services, Shelters/Homelessness, Social Services-General, Substance Abuse, YMCA/YWCA/YMHA/YWHA, Youth Organizations

Contributions Analysis
Arts & Humanities: 10%.
Education: 10%.
Health: 10%.
Social Services: 70%. The foundation reports giving to disaster relief efforts and to summer camps.

Application Procedures
Initial Contact: Send a brief letter of inquiry.
Deadlines: None.

Restrictions
Does not support individuals.

Corporate Officials
Patrick F. Conroy: chief financial officer, director PRIM CORP EMPL chief financial officer: New York Mercantile Exchange.
Daniel Rappaport: chairman, director PRIM CORP EMPL chairman, director: New York Mercantile Exchange.
R. Patrick Thomson: president, director PRIM CORP EMPL president, director: New York Mercantile Exchange.

Foundation Officials
Madeline Boyd: chairman
Neil Citrone: director
Albert Helmig: director
Steven Karvellas: director
Daniel Rappaport: president, director (see above)
Richard Schaeffer: director
Mitchell Steinhause: vice president, director

Grants Analysis
Disclosure Period: calendar year ending 1995
Number of Grants: 99
Highest Grant: $60,000
Typical Range: $750 to $5,000

Recent Grants
Note: Grants derived from 1997 Form 990.

Arts & Humanities
10,000 WLIW/Channel 21

Civic & Public Affairs
10,000 Hitops
10,000 John Heuss Corporation
10,000 National Ethnic Coalition of Organizations, New York, NY
10,000 One to One, Philadelphia, PA
10,000 Russian Gift of Life, Sea Cliff, NY

Education
10,000 Eden II School for Autistic Children, Staten Island, NY
10,000 National Children's Educational Reform Foundation, New York, NY

Environment
10,000 Student Conservation Association, Charlestown, NH

Health
18,885 Ronald McDonald House
10,000 Leukemia Society of America
10,000 New York Downtown Hospital, New York, NY
10,000 Pediatric AIDS Foundation, Chicago, IL
10,000 St. Vincent Hospital
8,000 Xeroderma Pigmentosum Society, Poughkeepsie, NY

Religion
10,000 Holocaust Museum of Jewish Heritage
7,500 Chai Lifeline Camp Simcha

Social Services
70,000 American Camping Association, Martinsville, IN
15,000 Futures and Options for Kids, New York, NY
15,000 Happiness Is Camping, Bronx, NY
10,000 Camp Sussex, Forest Hills, NY
10,000 Herbert C. Birch Services
10,000 Ice Hockey in Harlem, New York, NY
10,000 New Jersey Association for the Deaf and Blind, Somerset, NJ
10,000 Police Athletic League
10,000 Robin Hood Foundation, New York, NY
10,000 Swim Across America, Darien, CT
7,500 Kindred Spirits Foundation, New York, NY
7,500 Morristown Neighborhood House, Morristown, NJ
7,500 Opportunities For a Better Tomorrow, Brooklyn, NY

NEW YORK STATE ELECTRIC &GAS CORP.

Company Contact
Binghamton, NY
Web: http://www.nyseg.com

Company Description
Revenue: US$2,010,000,000
Employees: 4,117
SIC(s): 4911 Electric Services, 4924 Natural Gas Distribution, 4931 Electric & Other Services Combined.

Nonmonetary Support
Type: Donated Equipment; In-kind Services

Giving Contact
Jim Jones, Director, Community Policy
New York State Electric& Gas Corp.
PO Box 5224
Binghamton, NY 13902
Phone: (607)729-2551
Fax: (607)762-8595

Description
Organization Type: Corporate Giving Program
Giving Locations: headquarters and operating communities.
Grant Types: Employee Matching Gifts, General Support.

Financial Summary
Total Giving: Contributes through corporate direct giving program only.

Typical Recipients
Arts & Humanities: Arts & Humanities-General
Civic & Public Affairs: Civic & Public Affairs-General
Education: Education-General
Health: Health-General
Social Services: Social Services-General

Contributions Analysis
Arts & Humanities: Less than 5%.
Civic & Public Affairs: 5%.
Education: 15%.
Health: 80%.
Note: Also makes employee matching gifts.

Application Procedures
Initial Contact: a brief letter of inquiry
Application Requirements: a description of organization, amount requested, purpose of funds sought,

recently audited financial statement, and proof of tax-exempt status
Deadlines: None.

Restrictions

Corporation only supports organizations within its service area.

NEW YORK STOCK EXCHANGE, INC.

Company Contact

New York, NY
Web: http://www.nyse.com

Company Description

Revenue: US$150,000,000
Employees: 1,440
SIC(s): 6231 Security & Commodity Exchanges.

New York Stock Exchange Foundation, Inc.

Giving Contact

James E. Buck, Secretary
New York Stock Exchange Foundation, Inc.
11 Wall Street, 6th Floor
New York, NY 10005
Phone: (212)656-2060
Fax: (212)656-5629

Description

EIN: 133203195
Organization Type: Corporate Foundation
Giving Locations: NY: New York
Grant Types: Employee Matching Gifts, General Support.

Financial Summary

Total Giving: $1,000,000 (2000 approx); $1,000,000 (1999 approx); $883,360 (1998). Note: Contributes through foundation only.
Giving Analysis: Giving for 1996 includes: foundation ($516,900); foundation matching gifts ($128,851); foundation grants to United Way ($95,000); 1998: foundation ($678,500); foundation matching gifts ($106,860); foundation grants to United Way ($98,000)
Assets: $23,167,757 (1998); $14,612,380 (1996); $11,717,994 (1995)
Gifts Received: $1,500,000 (1998); $2,000,000 (1996); $2,000,000 (1995). Note: Contributions are received from New York Stock Exchange, Inc.

Typical Recipients

Arts & Humanities: Arts Associations & Councils, Arts Centers, Community Arts, Libraries, Museums/Galleries, Music, Performing Arts, Public Broadcasting, Theater
Civic & Public Affairs: Botanical Gardens/Parks, Economic Development, Economic Policy, Civic & Public Affairs-General, Municipalities/Towns, Public Policy, Safety, Urban & Community Affairs
Education: Business Education, Business-School Partnerships, Colleges & Universities, Economic Education, Health & Physical Education, Legal Education, Medical Education, Private Education (Precollege), Student Aid
Environment: Environment-General
Health: Cancer, Hospitals
Religion: Religious Organizations, Religious Welfare
Social Services: At-Risk Youth, Camps, Child Welfare, Community Service Organizations, Crime Prevention, Day Care, Food/Clothing Distribution, People with Disabilities, Recreation & Athletics, Scouts, Shelters/Homelessness, United Funds/United Ways, Volunteer Services, YMCA/YWCA/YMHA/YWHA, Youth Organizations

Contributions Analysis

Arts & Humanities: 18%. Mainly supports public broadcasting, the performing arts, libraries, and museums in New York City.
Civic & Public Affairs: 12%. Activities supported include public policy, community affairs, and economic development.
Education: 18%. Supports Junior Achievement and other national educational programs and organizations.
Environment: 1%.
Health: 7%. Primarily supports hospitals and single-disease centers.
Social Services: 44%. Major support is awarded to the United Way. Other organizations supported include camps, youth organizations, and recreation programs.
Note: Total contributions made in 1998.

Application Procedures

Initial Contact: Send a brief letter.
Application Requirements: Include a description of the program.
Deadlines: None.

Corporate Officials

Richard A. Grasso: chairman, chief executive officer B 1946. ED Pace University BS; Harvard University Advanced Management Program (1985). PRIM CORP EMPL chairman, chief executive officer: New York Stock Exchange, Inc. CORP AFFIL director: Computer Associates International Inc. NONPR AFFIL advisory board: Yale University School Management; trustee: Young Men's Christian Association Greater New York; co-chairman: Project Smart School; director: New York City Police Foundation; director: New York City Public Private Initiatives; member: International Cap Markets Advisory Committee; director: National Italian American Foundation; honorary chairman: Friends of Statue of Liberty National Monument/Ellis Island; director: Centurion Foundation.
Leon Pannetta: director

Foundation Officials

Geoffrey Cyril Bible: director B Canberra, NW Australia 1937. ED Chartered Institute Management Accountants UK; Institute of Chartered Accountants Australia; Waverly College. PRIM CORP EMPL chairman, chief executive officer, director: Philip Morris Companies Inc. ADD CORP EMPL president: Kraft General Foods. NONPR AFFIL director: Lincoln Center Performing Arts; director: New York Stock Exchange Inc.; trustee: American Graduate School International Management.
James E. Buck: secretary PRIM CORP EMPL senior vice president, secretary: New York Stock Exchange, Inc.
Keith R. Helsby: treasurer B Scranton, PA 1944. ED Gettysburg College (1966). PRIM NONPR EMPL senior vice president, chief financial officer: New York Stock Exchange, Inc.
William R. Johnston: director PRIM CORP EMPL senior managing director: La Branche & Co. ADD CORP EMPL president: New York Stock Exchange Inc.
Deryck C. Maughan: director B Consett, England 1947. ED University of London Kings College BA (1969); Stanford University MBA (1978). PRIM CORP EMPL co-chairman, co-chief executive officer: Salomon Smith Barney ADD CORP EMPL president: Salomon Brothers Realty Corp. CORP AFFIL director: Salomon Brothers Inc.; chairman: Salomon Forex Inc.; vice chairman: Citigroup Inc.; officer: New York Stock Exchange Inc.

Grants Analysis

Disclosure Period: calendar year ending 1998
Total Grants: $678,500*
Number of Grants: 43
Average Grant: $15,779
Highest Grant: $100,000
Typical Range: $5,000 to $20,000
***Note:** Giving excludes matching gifts and United Way.

Recent Grants

Note: Grants derived from 1996 Form 990.

Arts & Humanities

50,000	Lincoln Center for Performing Arts, New York, NY
25,000	Metropolitan Museum of Art, New York, NY
15,000	WNET/Channel 13, New York, NY
10,000	New York Public Library, New York, NY
10,000	Pierpont Morgan Library, New York, NY
10,000	South Street Seaport Museum, New York, NY
5,000	John F. Kennedy Center for Performing Arts, Washington, DC

Civic & Public Affairs

50,000	Securities Industry Foundation for Economic Research, New York, NY
10,000	American Council for Capital Formation, Washington, DC
10,000	Centurion Foundation, New York, NY
10,000	Committee for Economic Development, New York, NY
10,000	New York City Partnership, New York, NY
10,000	Public Policy Institute of New York State, Albany, NY
5,000	Central Park Conservancy, New York, NY

Health

40,000	New York Infirmary Beekman Downtown Hospital, New York, NY
10,000	St. Vincent Hospital and Medical Center, New York, NY

Social Services

95,000	United Way Tri-State Area, New York, NY
25,000	YMCA, New York, NY
20,000	Buttonwood Foundation, New York, NY
15,000	Members Handicapped Children's Fund, New York, NY
15,000	Police Foundation, Washington, DC
10,000	Clear Pool Camp, New York, NY
10,000	Nassau County Crime Stoppers, Mineola, NY
10,000	Tomorrow's Children Fund, Hackensack, NJ
10,000	US Olympic Committee, New York, NY
5,000	City Harvest, New York, NY
5,000	George Junior Republic, New York, NY
5,000	Madison Square Boys and Girls Club, New York, NY
5,000	National Executive Service Corps, New York, NY
2,500	Boy Scouts of America Scouting for the Handicapped, New York, NY

NEW YORK TIMES CO.

Company Contact

229 West 43rd Street
New York, NY 10036
Phone: (212)556-1234
Web: http://www.nytco.com

Company Description

Revenue: US$3,130,600,000 (1999)
Employees: 12,300

Fortune Rank: 490, per FORTUNE Magazine's list of 500 Largest U.S. Corporations (1999).
FF 490
SIC(s): 2711 Newspapers, 2721 Periodicals, 4832 Radio Broadcasting Stations, 4833 Television Broadcasting Stations.

New York Times Co. Foundation

Giving Contact

Mr. Arthur Gelb, President
New York Times Co. Foundation
Phone: (212)556-1091
Fax: (212)556-4450

Description

EIN: 136066955
Organization Type: Corporate Foundation
Giving Locations: NY: New York metropolitan area localities served by company affiliates; some internationally; some nationally.
Grant Types: Employee Matching Gifts, General Support, Multiyear/Continuing Support, Scholarship.
Note: Employee matching gift ratio: 1.5 to 1 up to $3,000 annually.

Giving Philosophy

'In education, in the arts, in the professions--corporate philanthropy provides a model of responsible citizenship. The New York Times Company Foundation is dedicated to such service to American democracy.'
The New York Times Co. Foundation, Inc, Annual Report

Financial Summary

Total Giving: $5,153,643 (1997); $4,844,685 (1996); $4,794,824 (1995). Note: Contributes through corporate direct giving program and foundation.
Giving Analysis: Giving for 1996 includes: foundation ($3,742,450); foundation matching gifts ($1,006,770); foundation scholarships ($95,465); 1997: foundation matching gifts ($1,057,693)
Assets: $2,701,465 (1997); $1,311,868 (1996); $1,734,225 (1995)
Gifts Received: $5,000,000 (1997); $1,996,100 (1996); $1,728,000 (1995). Note: In 1997, contributions were received from The New York Times Company.

Typical Recipients

Arts & Humanities: Arts Centers, Arts Festivals, Arts Institutes, Arts Outreach, Ballet, Community Arts, Dance, Ethnic & Folk Arts, Film & Video, Historic Preservation, History & Archaeology, Libraries, Literary Arts, Museums/Galleries, Music, Opera, Performing Arts, Public Broadcasting, Theater
Civic & Public Affairs: Botanical Gardens/Parks, Economic Development, Employment/Job Training, First Amendment Issues, Housing, Law & Justice, Professional & Trade Associations, Safety, Urban & Community Affairs, Women's Affairs
Education: Arts/Humanities Education, Colleges & Universities, Community & Junior Colleges, Engineering/Technological Education, Faculty Development, Journalism/Media Education, Leadership Training, Legal Education, Literacy, Minority Education, Private Education (Precollege), Public Education (Precollege), School Volunteerism, Science/Mathematics Education, Special Education, Student Aid
Environment: Air/Water Quality, Environment-General, Wildlife Protection
International: Foreign Arts Organizations, Foreign Educational Institutions
Religion: Jewish Causes
Science: Science Museums
Social Services: Community Service Organizations, Crime Prevention, Delinquency & Criminal Rehabilitation, Food/Clothing Distribution, Homes, Recreation & Athletics, Senior Services, Shelters/Homelessness, Social Services-General, Substance Abuse, United Funds/United Ways, Volunteer Services, YMCA/YWCA/YMHA/YWHA, Youth Organizations

Contributions Analysis

Giving Priorities: Cultural affairs, education, community service, journalism and envioromental.
Arts & Humanities: 40% to 45%. Majority supports the performing arts, particularly the Metropolitan Museum of Art and Lincoln Center and its constituent institutions. Other interests include museums, libraries, public broadcasting, and literary arts. Journalism studies are a high priority, with support directed to foundations, institutes, and university programs. Also stresses support of minorities, maintenance of a free press, and management and production training.
Civic & Public Affairs: 10% to 15%. Contributes primarily to united funds and women's affairs organizations. Other interests include urban and economic development, employment programs, civil rights, and services for the elderly.
Education: 30% to 35%. Particular interest in minority education, arts and journalism programs, scholarships, and precollege education. Supports colleges and universities near operating locations, particularly NewYork.
Environment: About 10%. Environmental organizations with emphasis on New York City receive support.

Application Procedures

Initial Contact: Submit a brief letter.
Application Requirements: Include a description of organization, amount requested, purpose of funds sought, recently audited financial statement, proof of tax-exempt status, and other potential sources of support.
Deadlines: December 15 and July 15.
Decision Notification: The board of directors meets at least twice annually, within the first and third quarter of each calendar year, to review the president's recommendations and authorize grants to be disbursed.

Restrictions

Does not support individuals; sectarian religious organizations; health-, drug-, or alcohol-related programs; fraternal organizations; dinners or special events; goodwill advertising; or political or lobbying groups.
Grants are not usually made at the neighborhood level for urban affairs.

Additional Information

The company also administers the New York Times Neediest Cases Fund, which raises about $5 million annually for organizations that respond to urban needs such as hunger and homelessness.
Grantees must submit a post-grant report accounting for expenditures.
Publications: Foundation Annual Report

Corporate Officials

John Fellows Akers: director B Boston, MA 1934. ED Yale University BS (1956). PRIM CORP EMPL director: New York Times Co. CORP AFFIL director: PepsiCo; director: Springs Industries Inc.; director: Lehman Brothers Holdings Inc.
Russell T. Lewis: president, chief operating officer B 1947. PRIM CORP EMPL president, chief operating officer: New York Times Co. CORP AFFIL vice chairman: Affiliated Publications Inc.
Honorable Charles H. Price, II: B Kansas City, MO 1931. ED University of Missouri (1951-1953). CORP AFFIL director: US Industries Inc.; director: New York Times Co.; director: Texaco Inc.; director: Mercantile Bancorp Inc.; director: Mercantile Bank; director: Hanson PLC (London). NONPR AFFIL director: 360 Degree Committee Inc. CLUB AFFIL Swinley Forest Golf Club; White's Club; Eldorado Country Club; Kansas City Country Club; Castle Pines Golf Club; Cypress Point Club; Brook Club.
Arthur Ochs Sulzberger, Junior: director, chairman emeritus B Mount Kisco, NY 1951. ED Tufts University BA (1974); Harvard University Graduate School of Business Administration (1985). PRIM CORP EMPL director, chairman emeritus: New York Times Co. NONPR AFFIL member: Newspaper Association America; director: Times Square Business Improvement District.
Arthur Ochs Sulzberger, Sr.: director B New York, NY 1926. ED Columbia University BA (1951); Dartmouth College LLD (1964); Bard College LLD (1967). PRIM CORP EMPL director: New York Times Co. CORP AFFIL chairman: WQXR-FM; director: Times Printing Co.; chairman: WQEW-AM; chairman: Lakeland Ledger Publishing; chairman: Ledger; president, director: Gadsden Times Inc.; chairman: Interstate Broadcasting Co.; director: Affiliated Publishers Inc.; chairman, director: Chattanooga Times Co. NONPR AFFIL chairman, trustee: Metropolitan Museum Art; member: Sons American Revolution; trustee emeritus: Columbia University. CLUB AFFIL Metro Club; Overseas Press Club; Explorers Club.

Foundation Officials

John Fellows Akers: director (see above)
Laura J. Corwin: secretary B Cambridge, MA 1945. ED Brown University AB (1966); University of Pennsylvania MA (1967); University of Pennsylvania PhD (1970); Yale University JD (1975). PRIM CORP EMPL vice president, secretary: New York Times Co. ADD CORP EMPL secretary: Golf Digest/Tennis Inc.; secretary: Sarasota Herald-Tribune Co.
Richard Lee Gelb: director B New York, NY 1924. ED Yale University BA (1945); Harvard University MBA (1950). PRIM CORP EMPL chairman emeritus: Bristol-Myers Squib Co. CORP AFFIL director: New York Times Co. Inc.; director: SKI Realty Inc.; director: Federal Reserve Bank New York; director: New York Life Insurance Co.; director: Bessemer Securities Corp.; chairman: Bristol Caribbean Inc. NONPR AFFIL trustee: New York Racing Association; chairman: Sloan-Kettering Institute Cancer Research; partner: New York City Partnership Inc.; vice chairman, trustee: New York City Police Foundation; director: Lincoln Center Performing Arts; vice chairman board overseers: Memorial Sloan-Kettering Cancer Center; member: Conference Board; member: Council Foreign Relations; member: Business Council; trustee: Committee for Economic Development.
A. Leon Higginbotham, Jr.: director B Trenton, NJ 1928. ED Purdue University (1944-1946); Antioch College BA (1949); Yale University LLB (1952). PRIM CORP EMPL officer counsel: Paul, Weiss, Rifkind, Wharton & Garrison PRIM NONPR EMPL federal judge: U.S. Court of Appeals, Philadelphia. NONPR AFFIL professor: Harvard University John F Kennedy School Government; commissioner: United States Commn Civil Rights.
Robert Ashton Lawrence: director B Boston, MA 1926. ED Yale University (1947). PRIM CORP EMPL partner: Saltonstall Co. CORP AFFIL director: State Street Growth Fund Inc.; director: State Street Investment Trust; director: State Street Exchange Fund; director: Metropolitan Series Fund; director: New York Times Co.; director: Metropolitan Life Portfolios; director: Metropolitan Life State Street Mutual Funds; director: Fifty Associates; executive vice president: FMR Corp.
Honorable Charles H. Price, II: director (see above)
George Latimer Shinn: director B Newark, OH 1923. ED Amherst College AB (1948); Drew University MA (1990); Drew University PhD (1992). PRIM CORP EMPL director, consultant: Credit Suisse First Boston. CORP AFFIL director: Kelso & Co. NONPR AFFIL adj professor: Drew University; trustee: New Jersey Council Humanities; fellow: American Academy of Arts & Sciences; member: Century Association. CLUB AFFIL River Club; Morris County Golf Club.
Donald M. Stewart: director PRIM NONPR EMPL president, chief executive officer: College Board. CORP AFFIL director: Campbell Soup Co. NONPR

AFFIL advisor: Grinnell College; adj lect: John F. Kennedy School Government; president, director: College Entrance Examination Board.

Arthur Ochs Sulzberger, Sr.: chairman, director (see above)

Judith P. Sulzberger, MD: director PRIM NONPR EMPL attending physician: Columbia College, Physicians & Surgeons Genome Center. CORP AFFIL director: New York Times Co. Inc.

William Osgood Taylor: director B Boston, MA 1932. ED Harvard University BA (1954). PRIM CORP EMPL chairman, emeritus chief executive officer, director: Globe Newspaper Co. ADD CORP EMPL president: Affiliated Publishers Inc. CORP AFFIL director: New York Times Co.; chairman emeritus: Boston Globe Publishing; vice chairman: Federation Reserve Bank Boston. NONPR AFFIL member director: International Center Journalists; trustee: International Crisis Group; chairman: Freedom Trail Foundation; trustee: Boston Public Library; trustee: Boston Public Library Foundation; director: Boston Adult Literacy Fund.

Solomon Brown Watson, IV: vice president B Salem, NJ 1944. ED Howard University BA (1966); Harvard University JD (1971). PRIM CORP EMPL senior vice president, general counsel: New York Times Co. ADD CORP EMPL secretary, director: Cruising World Publishings. CORP AFFIL director: Affiliated Publications Inc. NONPR AFFIL member legal aff committee: Newspaper Association America; director: Veterans Advisor Board; member: Massachusetts Bar Association; member: Association Bar New York City; director: Legal Aid Society; member: American Bar Association; director: American Corporate Counsel Association; director: American Arbitration Association; director: Agent Orange Asst Fund.

Grants Analysis

Disclosure Period: calendar year ending 1997
Total Grants: $4,095,950*
Number of Grants: 440
Average Grant: $9,309
Highest Grant: $100,000
Typical Range: $2,000 to $25,000
***Note:** Giving excludes matching gifts.

Recent Grants

Note: Grants derived from 1996 Annual Report.

Arts & Humanities

100,000	Lincoln Center Consolidated Fund, New York, NY
70,000	New York Public Library, New York, NY -- research projects, general support
50,000	Lower East Side Tenement Museum, New York, NY -- for Heritage Resource Center
50,000	Metropolitan Museum of Art, New York, NY
50,000	New 42nd Street, New York, NY -- cultural programs for young audiences
40,000	Carnegie Hall, New York, NY -- music classroom for students at Adolph S. Ochs Public School
40,000	Lincoln Center-Beaumont Theater, New York, NY
35,000	Alliance for New American Musicals, New York, NY -- workshops by leading nonprofit theaters
35,000	Bryant Park Restoration, New York, NY -- free lunchtime concerts throughout spring and summer
30,000	Museum of Modern Art, New York, NY -- for New York Times centennial photographic exhibit
30,000	New York Public Library, New York, NY -- for transfer, maintenance of Times Morgue for use by public
30,000	WNET, South Bend, IN
25,000	Roundtable Theater -- new programs for experimental new second stage
20,000	Alvin Ailey Dance Theater, New York, NY -- for public school lecture demonstrations, classes for children
20,000	American Museum of the Moving Image, Astoria, NY -- for technology-based careers in the media
20,000	Brooklyn Museum, Brooklyn, NY -- support Saturday educational program for students and teachers
20,000	Chamber Music Society of Lincoln Center, New York, NY -- for new series by outstanding young artists
20,000	City Center, New York, NY -- concert versions of seldom-performed Broadway musicals
20,000	Eugene O'Neill Theater Center, New York, NY -- for playwright fellowship program
20,000	Film Society of Lincoln Center, New York, NY -- Saturday educational films for children
20,000	George Street Playhouse, New Brunswick, NJ -- anti-bias play and symposiums exploring Anne Frank's world for schools in New York and New Jersey
20,000	Manhattan Theater Club, New York, NY
20,000	Museum of the City of New York, New York, NY -- transfer historic photographs and other major collections into electronic database
20,000	New York City Ballet, New York, NY -- newsletter, educational projects
20,000	New York Historical Society, New York, NY -- for classical music series for distribution to public schools
20,000	New York Shakespeare Festival, New York, NY -- for Directors in Residence Program

Civic & Public Affairs

50,000	Central Park Conservancy, New York, NY -- operating support
40,000	American Press Institute, Reston, VA
40,000	New York Botanical Garden, New York, NY -- special programs for visiting school children
35,000	Parks Council, New York, NY -- for Urban Conservation Corps Program
25,000	Uptown Lexington, Lexington, NC -- to replace trees originally planted in 1982 at a gift from The Times
20,000	Prospect Park Alliance, Brooklyn, NY -- restoration programs for park's woodlands

Education

75,000	Columbia University Graduate School of Journalism, New York, NY -- for Columbia Journalism Review
50,000	City College, New York, NY -- for creative writing program, project for college's sesquicentennial
50,000	New York University, New York, NY -- creative writing fellowships
35,000	New York City Outward Bound Center, New York, NY
25,000	Columbia University, New York, NY -- for Knight-Bagehot Fellowships
25,000	Duke University, Durham, NC -- program solving, enrichment project for teachers
25,000	Princeton University, Princeton, NJ -- for Thomas Jefferson Papers
20,000	New York City School Volunteer Program, New York, NY -- tutorial assistance
20,000	Studio in a School, New York, NY -- art programs

Environment

75,000	Fresh Air Fund, New York, NY
60,000	Wildlife Conservation Society -- for free amphitheater show for students at Bronx Zoo
20,000	Council on Environment -- workshops in neighborhoods on environmental improvements

International

30,000	American Academy in Rome, Rome, Italy -- fellowships for writers and artists
20,000	British Museum, Metropolitan Museum of Art Partnership Project, New York, NY -- program for exchange of curators

Religion

22,000	Jewish Museum, New York, NY -- development of tolerance guide for teachers in public high schools

Science

80,000	American Museum of Natural History, New York, NY -- for Electronic Newspaper for fossil-dinosaur halls

Social Services

70,000	United Way Tri-State, New York, NY
25,000	Community Anti-Drug Coalitions of America, Alexandria, VA -- to create drug-free programs

NEWMAN'S OWN INC.

Company Contact

Westport, CT
Web: http://www.newmansown.com

Company Description

Employees: 12
SIC(s): 5149 Groceries & Related Products Nec.

Newman's Own Foundation

Giving Contact

Aaron E. Hotchner, Vice President & Director
Newman's Own Foundation
246 Post Road East
Westport, CT 06880-3615
Phone: (203)222-0136
Fax: (203)227-5630

Description

Founded: 1989
EIN: 061247230
Organization Type: Corporate Foundation
Giving Locations: internationally, where Newman's Own is sold;.
Grant Types: General Support.

Giving Philosophy

'Paul Newman donates 100% of his after-tax profits from Newman's Own to charitable and educational causes. Since he founded Newman's Own in 1982, over $75 million has been donated to charities both in the United States and abroad, in those countries where Newman's Own products are sold.' 1997 Brochure

Financial Summary

Total Giving: $362,040 (fiscal year ending August 31, 1998); $229,000 (fiscal 1997); $459,759 (fiscal 1996). Note: Contributes through corporate direct giving program and foundation.
Assets: $197,530 (fiscal 1998); $210,965 (fiscal 1997); $44,983 (fiscal 1996)
Gifts Received: $341,308 (fiscal 1998); $391,860 (fiscal 1997); $461,750 (fiscal 1996). Note: In 1998, the foundation received contributions from Meadowlea Foods. In 1996, contributions were received from Mauri Foods.

Typical Recipients

Arts & Humanities: Community Arts, Libraries, Museums/Galleries, Public Broadcasting, Theater
Civic & Public Affairs: Housing, Public Policy
Education: Literacy, Public Education (Precollege)
Environment: Environment-General
Health: Arthritis, Children's Health/Hospitals, Health Funds, Hospices, Hospitals, Medical Rehabilitation, Single-Disease Health Associations
International: Foreign Arts Organizations, Foreign Educational Institutions, Health Care/Hospitals, International Organizations, International Peace & Security Issues, International Relations, International Relief Efforts, Missionary/Religious Activities
Religion: Religious Welfare
Social Services: Camps, Child Abuse, Child Welfare, Community Centers, Community Service Organizations, Delinquency & Criminal Rehabilitation, Domestic Violence, Family Services, Family Services, Food/ Clothing Distribution, Homes, People with Disabilities, Senior Services, Shelters/Homelessness, Youth Organizations

Contributions Analysis

Giving Priorities: The foundation is primarily concerned with child welfare organizations, including hospitals, child abuse prevention, and pediatric health. Also supports the disabled, particularly the blind or deaf; single-disease health associations and donor programs; community centers; animal protection agencies; and other social service agencies in Australia and New Zealand. Other interests include women's affairs, farmer's aid, and universities.
Arts & Humanities: 2%. Funds museums.
Health: 38%. Supports hospitals and single-disease health associations.
Religion: Less than 1%. Religious welfare.
Social Services: 60%. Funds social services, especially those benefiting youth and the disabled.
Note: Total contributions in fiscal 1998.

Application Procedures

Initial Contact: Send a detailed written proposal including a cover sheet from the foundation.
Application Requirements: Include organization information including name and address, title and phone number of contact, geographic area served, any previous grants received from Salad King, Inc., or Newman's Own, percentage of income allocated to administrative overheads, and fundraising, percentage of income directly applied to program; grant request including amount requested, information on specific project, and detailed project budget; attachments including copy of IRS determination letter, most recently audited financial statement, copy of IRS Form 990, list of board of directors, latest annual report or mission statement, and funding sources; and any other pertinent supplementary information.
Deadlines: September 1.
Review Process: Proposals are acknowledged within 6-8 weeks of receipt.
Decision Notification: Awards are made by the end of December.
Notes: Only award recipients are notified.
Faxed proposals are not accepted.
Any materials submitted are nonreturnable.

Restrictions

Funds may not be used for propaganda purposes or to attempt to influence legislation.

Additional Information

Foundation requires regular reports of the progress of the project for which funds are granted. In addition to application information listed above, grant seekers must furnish specific certificates or other adequate proof that the organization is recognized as a bona fide charity under the laws of the country in which it operates.
Publications: Guidelines Sheet

Corporate Officials

Aaron Edward Hotchner: vice president, treasurer B Saint Louis, MO 1920. ED Washington University AB (1941). PRIM CORP EMPL vice president, treasurer: Newman's Own Inc. NONPR AFFIL member: PEN; member: Writers Guild America; vice president: Hole in the Wall Gang Camp; member: Missouri Bar Association; member: Authors Guild Foundation; member: Dramatists Guild; member: Authors Guild. CLUB AFFIL Century Club.
Paul L. Newman: B Cleveland, OH 1925. ED Lee Strasberg Actors Studio; Kenyon College BA (1949); Yale University School of Drama (1951).

Foundation Officials

Jamie K. Gerard: attorney CORP AFFIL secretary: Newmans Own Inc.
Aaron Edward Hotchner: vice president, director, executive (see above)
Paul L. Newman: president (see above)
Joanne Gignilliat Woodward: director B Thomasville, GA 1930. ED Neighborhood Playhouse Dramatic School; Louisiana State University (1947-1949).

Grants Analysis

Disclosure Period: fiscal year ending August 31, 1998
Total Grants: $362,040
Number of Grants: 37
Average Grant: $9,785
Highest Grant: $50,000
Typical Range: $2,500 to $15,000

Recent Grants

Note: Grants derived from 1998 Form 990.

Arts & Humanities

7,000	Museum of Contemporary Art, Australia

Health

50,000	Sydney Childrens Hospital, Australia
15,500	Balhannah Centre Inc., Australia -- for terminally ill people
10,540	Limbkids Support Association Inc., Australia -- services for children with missing limbs
10,540	Rett Syndrome Association of Australia, Australia
9,300	Queensland Muscular Dystrophy Association, Australia
6,200	Canteen, Australia -- teens with cancer
4,774	Osteogenesis Imperfecta Association of Victoria, Australia
4,340	Angleman Syndrome Association Inc., Australia -- neuro-genetic disorder support group
4,030	Marfan Association Australia Ltd., Australia -- support group for people with marfan syndrome
3,720	Australian CHARGE Association Inc., Australia -- children with rare developmental problems
3,100	Arthritis Foundation, Australia
3,100	Cystic Fibrosis Association of Tasmania, Australia
3,100	D.E.B.R.Association New Zealand, New Zealand
3,100	Muscular Dystrophy Association of New Zealand, New Zealand
1,240	Australian Leukodystrophy Support, Australia
1,240	Autistic Association of N.S.W., Australia -- for autistic children
1,240	Riding for the Disabled, Australia
1,116	Shwachman Syndrome Support Australia, Australia -- support for people with swachman-diamond disorder

Religion

3,100	Christchurch City Mission, New Zealand -- for poor and needy

Social Services

37,200	Camp Quality, Australia -- children with cancer
31,000	Child Abuse Prevention Service (CAPS), Australia
17,980	Shephert Centre, Australia -- deaf & hearing impaired children
16,120	Aunties & Uncles Co-operative Family Project Ltd., Australia -- adult mentors for socially & emotionally disadvantaged families
15,500	Lighthouse Foundation, Australia -- help disadvantaged youth
14,260	Carers Task Force Inc., Australia -- care for frail elderly and/or disabled
13,020	Peterborough Foundation, Australia -- school for severely handicapped children
12,400	Friendly Farms Association, Inc., Australia -- services/programs for homeless youth
12,400	Gawler & Barossa Youth Services, Inc., Australia -- for disenfranchised/disadvantaged youth
12,400	Tasmanian Association of People with Disabilities and their Advocates Inc., Australia
8,680	Wellington City Mission, Australia -- for poor & needy
7,440	Northcott Society, Australia -- handicapped youth and children
6,200	Geelong Regional Options for Individuals With a Disability Inc (G.R.I.D.), Australia
4,960	Sports & Leisure for the Handicapped Association Inc., Australia
3,100	Beverly Community Enterprises Inc., Australia -- help disabled/elderly
1,550	L'ARCHE, Australia Ltd., Australia -- for people with disability
1,550	Sanctuary 7 Association Inc., Australia -- women & children suffering from domestic abuse

NEWPORT NEWS SHIPBUILDING

Company Contact

Newport News, VA
Web: http://www.nns.com

Company Description

Former Name: Newport News Shipbuilding and Dry Dock Co.
Employees: 18,100
SIC(s): 3731 Ship Building & Repairing.

Nonmonetary Support

Type: Cause-related Marketing & Promotion; Donated Products; In-kind Services; Loaned Executives
Note: Company also donates the use of its facilities.

Giving Contact

Michael Hatfield, Vice President, Corporate Communications
4101 Washington Ave.
Newport News, VA 23607-2770
Phone: (757)380-3559

Description

Organization Type: Corporate Giving Program
Grant Types: Employee Matching Gifts, General Support.

Financial Summary

Total Giving: $825,012 (1996). Note: Figure is for company giving only. In addition, employees and retirees gave approximately $1.4 million to the United Way

and $265,000 to arts and education through matching gifts, bringing the total amount of support by Newport News and its employees to more than $2.5 million. Figure includes company matching gifts to arts and education totaling $284,950.

Application Procedures

Initial Contact: Send letter requesting appliation guidelines.

Additional Information

Publications: Application Form; Guidelines

Corporate Officials

David J. Anderson: senior vice president, chief financial officer PRIM CORP EMPL senior vice president, chief financial officer: Newport News Shipbuilding.
William Peavy Fricks: chairman, chief executive officer B Byron, GA 1944. ED Auburn University BS (1966); College of William & Mary MBA (1970). PRIM CORP EMPL chairman, chief executive officer: Newport News Shipbuilding, Inc.
Thomas C. Schievelbein: executive vice president B Fort Lewis, WA 1953. ED United States Naval Academy (1975); University of Virginia (1976). PRIM CORP EMPL executive vice president: Newport News Shipbuilding, Inc. NONPR AFFIL member: Association Naval Aviation; trustee: National Security Industry Association.

Grants Analysis

Disclosure Period: calendar year ending

NIAGARA MOHAWK HOLDINGS INC.

Company Contact

300 Erie Blvd. West
Syracuse, NY 13202
Phone: (315)474-1511
Fax: (315)460-1429
Web: http://www.nimo.com

Company Description

Revenue: US$3,827,340,000 (1999)
Employees: 8,400 (1999)
Fortune Rank: 389, per FORTUNE Magazine's list of 500 Largest U.S. Corporations (1999).
FF 389
SIC(s): 4911 Electric Services, 4925 Gas Production & Distribution Nec, 4931 Electric & Other Services Combined.

Nonmonetary Support

Type: Donated Equipment

Corporate Sponsorship

Range: less than $200,000
Type: Arts & cultural events; Festivals/fairs; Music & entertainment events
Note: Sponsors environmental events.

Niagara Mohawk Foundation

Giving Contact

Eileen V. Kelliher, Director, Public Affairs
300 Erie Blvd. W.
Syracuse, NY 13202
Phone: (315)428-6924
Fax: (315)428-5524
Email: KelliherE@nimo.com

Alternate Contact

Phone: (315)428-5691

Description

EIN: 223132237
Organization Type: Corporate Foundation
Giving Locations: NY: Upstate New York service areas.
Grant Types: Capital, Employee Matching Gifts, Matching, Multiyear/Continuing Support.
Note: Employee matching gift ratio: 1 to 1.

Financial Summary

Total Giving: $1,950,000 (1999 approx); $1,868,448 (1998); $1,285,782 (1997). Note: Contributes through corporate direct giving program and foundation.
Giving Analysis: Giving for 1998 includes: foundation ($1,573,057); corporate direct giving ($295,391)
Assets: $2,296,974 (1999 approx); $3,022,515 (1998); $2,776,004 (1997)
Gifts Received: $1,652,607 (1997); $800,115 (1996); $1,814,000 (1995)

Typical Recipients

Arts & Humanities: Arts Associations & Councils, Arts & Humanities-General, Historic Preservation, History & Archaeology, Libraries, Literary Arts, Museums/Galleries, Music, Performing Arts, Public Broadcasting, Theater
Civic & Public Affairs: Economic Development, Employment/Job Training, Civic & Public Affairs-General, Housing, Parades/Festivals, Rural Affairs, Safety, Urban & Community Affairs
Education: Agricultural Education, Business Education, Colleges & Universities, Community & Junior Colleges, Education-General, Minority Education, Preschool Education, Social Sciences Education
Environment: Environment-General, Resource Conservation, Wildlife Protection
Health: Cancer, Children's Health/Hospitals, Emergency/Ambulance Services, Health-General, Heart, Hospices, Hospitals, Prenatal Health Issues
Religion: Religious Welfare
Science: Science Museums
Social Services: Child Welfare, Community Service Organizations, Delinquency & Criminal Rehabilitation, Food/Clothing Distribution, People with Disabilities, Scouts, Social Services-General, Special Olympics, United Funds/United Ways, YMCA/YWCA/YMHA/YWHA, Youth Organizations

Contributions Analysis

Arts & Humanities: 10%. Support goes to public broadcasting, libraries, art museums, and the performing arts.
Civic & Public Affairs: 7%. Supports local initiatives and community services.
Education: 14%. Supports universities and colleges.
Environment: 1%. Funds parks, protection of the Adirondacks, an conservancy.
Health: 22%. Funds Hospice, hospitals, with majority of funds given to the American Redcross.
Religion: About 1%. Fund religious causes.
Science: 3%. Supports museums of science and technology.
Social Services: 42%. Funds child and youth services, and major support given to the United Way.
Note: Total contributions made in 1998.

Application Procedures

Initial Contact: Send a brief letter of inquiry.
Application Requirements: Description of organization, amount requested, purpose of funds sought, recently audited financial statements, and proof of tax-exempt status.
Deadlines: None.
Decision Notification: Requests are reviewed quarterly on a case-by-case basis.

Restrictions

The foundation does not support organizations outside of company service area, individuals, or religious organizations for sectarian purposes.

Corporate Officials

Albert J. Budney, Jr.: president, director ED Princeton University BS (1968); Harvard University MBA (1974). PRIM CORP EMPL president, director: Niagara Mohawk Power Corp.
William E. Davis: chairman, chief executive officer B Schenevus, NY 1942. ED United States Naval Academy (1964); George Washington University (1971). PRIM CORP EMPL chairman, chief executive officer: Niagara Mohawk Power Corp. CORP AFFIL director: Utilities Mutual Insurance Co.; director: Canadian Niagara Power; director: Opinac Energy. NONPR AFFIL director: Edison Electric Institute; director: Nuclear Energy Institute; director: Center for Clean Air Policy; director: Crouse-Irving Memorial Hospital; director: Association of Edison Illuminating Companies.

Giving Program Officials

Eileen V. Kelliher: director PRIM CORP EMPL director public affairs: Niagara Mohawk Power Corp.

Foundation Officials

David Dzwonkowski: treasurer
Eileen V. Kelliher: director (see above)
Tina Moran: secretary

Grants Analysis

Disclosure Period: calendar year ending 1998
Total Grants: $1,868,448*
Number of Grants: 1,092
Average Grant: $1,711
Highest Grant: $134,345
Typical Range: $25 to $20,000
***Note:** Grants Analysis provided by Foundation. Analysis includes corporate giving through Niagara Mohawk Power Corp. and Niagara Mohawk Foundation.

Recent Grants

Note: Grants derived from 1998 Form 990.

Arts & Humanities

52,931	Syracuse Symphony Orchestra, Syracuse, NY
21,275	Onondaga Historical Association, Syracuse, NY
15,000	Buffalo Philharmonic Orchestra, Buffalo, NY
10,000	Rosamond Gifford Lecture Series, Syracuse, NY
10,000	Shea's Performing Arts Center, Buffalo, NY
8,250	Syracuse Stage, Syracuse, NY
7,200	WCNY, New York, NY
6,985	Public Broadcasting Council CNY, New York, NY
5,000	Cazenovia College Theater, Cazenovia, NY
5,000	Lower Adirondack Regional Aris Council, Glens Falls, NY
5,000	WNY Public Broadcasting Association, New York, NY
3,594	Erie Canal Museum, Syracuse, NY

Civic & Public Affairs

11,235	Adirondack North Country Association, Saranac Lake, NY
10,000	Syracuse Economic Development Council, Syracuse, NY
5,000	Focus Greater Syracuse, Syracuse, NY
4,000	Olivet Employment Opportunity Program
4,000	Skaneateles Festival, Skaneateles, NY

Education

9,565 Clarkson University, Potsdam, NY
7,490 Canisius College, Buffalo, NY
6,500 Junior Achievement, Liverpool, NY
6,405 Syracuse University, Syracuse, NY
6,000 Sagamore Institute, Raquette Lake, NY
5,000 Holstein Foundation, Brattleboro, CT

Environment

5,000 Conservation Fund, St. James, NY
3,000 Nature Conservancy, New York, NY

Health

207,044 American Red Cross, Syracuse and Onondaga Counties, Syracuse, NY
5,300 Brooks Memorial Hospital, Dunkirk, NY
5,000 Bassett Hospital of Schoharie County, Cobleskill, NY
5,000 Columbia Memorial Hospital, Hudson, NY
5,000 March of Dimes, Bikers for Bable, New York, NY
5,000 North Country Children's Clinic, Watertown, NY

Religion

10,600 Salvation Army, Syracuse, NY
10,000 First Night Syracuse, Syracuse, NY
7,150 Catholic Charities Appeal, Buffalo, NY

Social Services

140,257 United Way of Central NY, Inc., Syracuse, NY
97,064 United Way of Buffalo/Erie/Niagara, Buffalo, NY
57,892 United Way of Northeastern NY, Albany, NY
52,760 United Way of Greater Oswego, Oswego, NY
15,610 United Way of Northern Chautauqua, Dunkirk, NY
14,162 United Way of Tri-County, Queensbury, NY
12,425 United Way of Schenectady, Schenectady, NY
10,000 Consolidated Industries of Greater Syracuse, Syracuse, NY
9,846 United Way of Northern New York, Watertown, NY
5,768 United Way of Rome, Rome, NY
5,654 United Way of Olean, Inc., Olean, NY
5,000 Dunbar Association, Syracuse, NY
5,000 Food Bank of Central New York, New York, NY
4,848 United Way of Genesee/LeRoy, Rochester, NY
4,246 United Way of Fulton County, Gloversville, NY
3,000 Greater NY Councils, Boy Scouts, New York, NY

NICOR GAS CO.

Company Contact

Aurora, IL

Company Description

Former Name: Northern Illinois Gas Co.
Revenue: US$1,480,000,000
Employees: 2,330
SIC(s): 1311 Crude Petroleum & Natural Gas, 6719 Holding Companies Nec.
Parent Company: NICOR Inc.

Nonmonetary Support

Type: Donated Equipment; In-kind Services; Loaned Employees; Loaned Executives; Workplace Solicitation

Giving Contact

Julian Brown, Director, Community Relations
PO Box 190
Aurora, IL 60507
Phone: (630)983-8676 ext 2763

Description

Organization Type: Corporate Giving Program
Grant Types: Employee Matching Gifts.

Financial Summary

Total Giving: $1,300,000 (1999 approx); $1,400,800 (1998); $1,196,000 (1997)

Application Procedures

Initial Contact: a brief letter of inquiry
Application Requirements: a description of organization, amount requested, purpose of funds sought, recently audited financial statement, proof of tax-exempt status

Giving Program Officials

Julian E. Brown: community relations director PRIM CORP EMPL community relations drc: Nicor Inc.

Grants Analysis

Disclosure Period: calendar year ending 1998
Total Grants: $1,400,800

NIKE, INC.

Company Contact

Beaverton, OR
Web: http://www.info.nike.com

Company Description

Revenue: US$8,776,900,000 (1999)
Employees: 218,000
Fortune Rank: 197, per FORTUNE Magazine's list of 500 Largest U.S. Corporations (1999).
FF 197
SIC(s): 2329 Men's/Boys' Clothing Nec, 2339 Women's/Misses' Outerwear Nec, 3149 Footwear Except Rubber Nec, 5139 Footwear.

Nonmonetary Support

Type: Donated Products; Workplace Solicitation
Note: 1997 nonmonetary support $1,587,606. NIKE donates shoes and apparel to children's homes, homeless shelters, and disaster relief efforts around the world.

Corporate Sponsorship

Type: Arts & cultural events; Sports events
Note: Sponsors youth sports and fitness programs. Supports annual 'Breaking the Glass Ceiling Awards' given by Women Executives in State Government to outstanding women.

Giving Contact

Barb Audiss, Manager, U.S. Community Affairs
Nike, Inc.
1 Bowerman Dr.
Beaverton, OR 97005
Phone: (503)532-0146
Fax: (503)532-0418

Alternate Contact

Gina Warren, Director Community Affairs
Fax: 800-352-6453

Description

Organization Type: Corporate Giving Program
Giving Locations: nationally; emphasis on headquarters and operating communities.
Grant Types: Employee Matching Gifts, General Support, Multiyear/Continuing Support, Scholarship.
Note: Employee matching gift ratio: 1 to 1 to nonprofits; 2 to 1 for P.L.A.Y. related programs.

Giving Philosophy

'NIKE's 'Just Do It' slogan is more than an inspiration to pursue physical excellence. It is a call to action at all levels. NIKE's Corporate Giving Programs are highly focused on three key Corporate Giving Objectives: providing more opportunities for America's children to enjoy the positive benefits of sports and fitness through an initiative called P.L.A.Y-Participate in the Lives of America's Youth; enriching the quality of life in NIKE's backyard communities where NIKE employees live and work; and supporting programs which address the special needs of minorities, women, children, and the environment. NIKE believes that the pursuit of these objectives serves the long-term interests of both our society, and our business.' *Corporate Contributions Guidelines*

Financial Summary

Total Giving: $10,549,010 (fiscal year ending June 30, 1997); $6,000,000 (fiscal 1996 approx); $6,000,000 (fiscal 1995 approx). Note: Contributes through corporate direct giving program only. Fiscal 1997 Giving includes corporate direct giving ($7,059,778); international subsidiaries ($1,901,626); nonmonetary support.

Typical Recipients

Arts & Humanities: Arts Associations & Councils, Arts & Humanities-General
Civic & Public Affairs: Civic & Public Affairs-General, Urban & Community Affairs
Education: Colleges & Universities, Education Funds, Minority Education
Environment: Environment-General
Social Services: Child Welfare, Food/Clothing Distribution, Recreation & Athletics, Shelters/Homelessness, United Funds/United Ways, Youth Organizations

Contributions Analysis

Arts & Humanities: Less than 5%. Supports arts institutions, mainly near headquarters area.
Civic & Public Affairs: 15% to 20%. Supports mainly minority affairs, including 100 Black Men of America and Hispanic associations. Also supports economic development and volunteerism. Less than 5%. Supports scholarship funds, leadership development, minority affairs, and higher education.
Education: 5% to 10%. Supports mentoring programs, scholarship funds, colleges and universities, and public education.
Environment: Less than 5%. Focus on West Coast conservation and environmental programs.
Health: Less than 5%. Supports research and single-disease organizations. Major focus is on AIDS.
International: 15% to 20%. Mainly supports fundraising sports events.
Social Services: 40% to 45%. Focus is on Nike's P.L.A.Y. (Participate in the Lives of America's Youth) initiative, which provides under-served kids access to inspirational coaches, organized activities, and safe places to play. Supports sports clinics, summer camps and community health and sports programs. Includes support to P.L.A.Y. CORPS, through which college students volunteer to coach disadvantaged children, and the Tiger Woods Foundation. Less than 5%. Supports United Ways, food banks, disaster relief, and social service agencies.

Application Procedures

Initial Contact: Submit a written proposal.
Application Requirements: Include purpose of organization; programs and goals; detailed explanation of dollar amount or type of support requested; copy of letter proving 501(c)(3) status; names of directors and their business affiliations; current budget; and names of contributors, including amount of funding provided by them.

Deadlines: None; processing takes approximately six weeks.

Restrictions

Company does not support individuals, political or religious organizations, hospitals and health organizations, capital campaigns, coverage of operating deficits, fraternal organizations, advertising in programs or brochures, research or study programs, organizations that discriminate against individuals on the basis of race, creed, color, sex, age, national origin, or veteran status, or any noncharitable purpose.

Additional Information

For printed or pre-recorded giving guidelines call (503) 671-3637. Applications may be completed and submitted at www.NikeBiz.com.
Publications: Nike Inc. Corporate Contributions Guidelines

Corporate Officials

Thomas E. Clarke: president, chief operating officer B Binghamton, NY 1951. ED University of Florida MS (1977); Pennsylvania State University PhD (1980). PRIM CORP EMPL president, chief operating officer: Nike, Inc. CORP AFFIL president: Nike International Ltd.
Richard King Donahue: vice chairman B Lowell, MA 1927. ED Dartmouth College AB (1948); Boston University JD (1951). PRIM CORP EMPL vice chairman: Nike, Inc. CORP AFFIL director: Epitope Inc.; director: Courier Corp. NONPR AFFIL member: Massachusetts Bar Association; member: New England Bar Association; member: American College Trial Lawyers; government house dels: American Bar Association; member: American Board Trial Advocates. CLUB AFFIL Yorick Club; Vesper Country Club; Federal City Club; Union League Club.
Philip Hampson Knight: chairman, chief executive officer B Portland, OR 1938. ED University of Oregon BBA (1959); Stanford University MBA (1962). PRIM CORP EMPL chairman, chief executive officer: Nike, Inc. ADD CORP EMPL president, director: Nike Retail Services Inc. CORP AFFIL chief executive officer, director: Nike International Ltd. NONPR AFFIL member: American Institute CPAs; director: U.S. Asian Business Council.

Giving Program Officials

Barbara Audiss: PRIM CORP EMPL U.S. community affairs manager: Nike, Inc.
Lisa Crawford: donations coordinator
Doug Stamm: PRIM CORP EMPL global community affairs manager: Nike, Inc.
David Strah: European communication affairs manager
Diana Tsui: Asian committee affairs manager

Grants Analysis

Disclosure Period: fiscal year ending June 30, 1997
Total Grants: $7,059,778*
Number of Grants: 185
Average Grant: $38,161
Typical Range: $5,000 to $50,000
***Note:** Giving excludes nonmonetary support.

Recent Grants

Note: Grants derived from fiscal 1994 partial grants list.

Civic & Public Affairs

29,000 American Indian College Fund, New York, NY -- to provide scholarships of $500 to two American Indian students, one man and one woman, at each of the 26 fund member colleges

Social Services

80,000 New York State Midnight Basketball League, New York, NY

Nissan North America, Inc.

Company Contact

Gardena, CA

Company Description

Former Name: Nissan Motor Corp. U.S.A.
Employees: 2,300
SIC(s): 5012 Automobiles & Other Motor Vehicles.
Parent Company: Nissan Motor Co., Ltd., 17-1, Ginza, 6-chome, Chuo-ku, Tokyo, Japan

Operating Locations

CA: Nissan Motor Corp. U.S.A., Gardena; Calsonic International, Irvine; Nissan Design International, San Diego; Nissan Motor Acceptance Corp., Torrance; Nissan North America, Torrance; HI: Nissan Motor Corp. Hawaii, Ltd., Honolulu; IL: Nissan Forklift Corp., North America, Marengo; MI: Nissan CR Corp., Farmington Hills; Nissan Research & Development Corp., Farmington Hills; Nissan Trading Corp. USA, Southfield; NC: Nissan Textile Machinery Corp. U.S.A., Charlotte; NY: Nissan Capital of America, New York; Nissan Finance of America, New York; TN: Nissan Forklift Corp. North America, Memphis; Nissan Motor Mfg. Corp., U.S.A., Smyrna

Nissan Foundation

Giving Contact

Dierdre Francis-Dickerson, Administrator
Nissan North America, Inc.
18501 South Figueroa Street
Carson, CA 90248-4504
Phone: (310)771-6461

Description

Founded: 1992
EIN: 954413799
Organization Type: Corporate Foundation
Giving Locations: CA: Los Angeles South Central LA
Grant Types: General Support, Multiyear/Continuing Support, Operating Expenses.

Financial Summary

Total Giving: $260,000 (fiscal year ending June 30, 1999 approx); $260,000 (fiscal 1998 approx); $260,000 (fiscal 1997)
Assets: $5,144,895 (fiscal 1997); $5,037,671 (fiscal 1996); $4,994,531 (fiscal 1995)
Gifts Received: $2,000,000 (fiscal 1994)

Typical Recipients

Civic & Public Affairs: African American Affairs, Asian American Affairs, Community Foundations, Economic Development, Employment/Job Training, Housing, Inner-City Development, Urban & Community Affairs
Education: Afterschool/Enrichment Programs, Business Education, Elementary Education (Public), Literacy, Minority Education, Public Education (Precollege), Science/Mathematics Education, Vocational & Technical Education
Health: Adolescent Health Issues, Children's Health/Hospitals, Clinics/Medical Centers, Health Funds, Health Organizations
Social Services: At-Risk Youth, Community Centers, Community Service Organizations, Food/Clothing Distribution

Application Procedures

Initial Contact: All requests must be submitted in writing. Telephone solicitations and unsigned letters are not considered. Send a full proposal. Include a description of organization as follows: brief history of the organization; copy of tax-exempt status; latest audited financial report; current operating budget and sources of income; listing of the organization's key management and board of directors; annual report or update of activities; and number of employees (paid and volunteer). Information regarding the particular program for which funding is being sought should include: purpose and objective of the program; needs to be addressed; population served; plan of action and time frame for proposed program; qualifications of program's administrators; total funding required and projected sources; amount of funds requested; methods of evaluation; and utilization of results.
Deadlines: April 15.

Restrictions

The following will not be considered for charitable contributions: fundraising activities of civic clubs; fraternal, veterans, or military organizations, individuals, political or lobbying groups; religious organizations for sectarian purposes; sponsorship of youth athletic teams or events; or sponsorship of trips or tours or promotional materials such as trophies and prizes. Nissan does not donate vehicles for promotional activities such as prizes, raffles, or trade of services, or as direct in-kind gifts for use by recipient organizations. Nissan does donate vehicles to automotive technician training programs in high schools, community colleges, or occupational centers.

Additional Information

Profile reflects Nissan Foundation priorities. The company also supports community-based organizations through direct corporate contributions. Specialist for Community Outreach at Nissan North America, Inc., is Maria Fernandez, PO Box 191, Gardena, CA 90248-0191.
Publications: Foundation Guidelines Brochure

Corporate Officials

Nobuo Araki: president, chief operating officer chief financial officer PRIM CORP EMPL president, chief operating officer: Nissan North America Inc.
Dierdre Francis-Dickerson: manager strategic relations PRIM CORP EMPL manager strategic relations: Nissan North American Inc.
Katsumi Ishii: vice president finance, chief financial officer PRIM CORP EMPL vice president finance, chief financial officer: Nissan North America Inc.

Foundation Officials

Dierdre Francis-Dickerson: foundation administrator (see above)
Koji Hijikata: president

Grants Analysis

Disclosure Period: fiscal year ending June 30, 1997
Total Grants: $260,000
Number of Grants: 6
Average Grant: $43,333
Highest Grant: $60,000
Typical Range: $10,000 to $60,000

Recent Grants

Note: Grants derived from fiscal 1997 Form 990.

Education

60,000 Accelerated School, Los Angeles, CA -- operating support, campus expansion
60,000 Youth Intervention Program, Los Angeles, CA -- support South Central Los Angeles Community Computer Center
40,000 Puente Learning Center, Los Angeles, CA -- literacy training at South Central Los Angeles schools
30,000 A Place Called Home, Los Angeles, CA -- for afterschool tutoring and mentoring program

Health

60,000 Para Los Ninos, Los Angeles, CA --

health services for low-income families, education for low-income families

Social Services

10,000 Food Bank of Southern California, Los Angeles, CA -- provide protein based foods for homeless and low-income people

NOMURA HOLDING AMERICA

Company Contact

New York, NY
Web: http://www.nomurany.com

Company Description

Former Name: Nomura Securities International.
Operating Revenue: US$280,000,000
Employees: 1,000
SIC(s): 6211 Security Brokers & Dealers, 6798 Real Estate Investment Trusts.
Parent Company: Nomura Securities Co. Ltd., 9-1, Nihonbashi 1-chome, Chuo-ku, Tokyo, Japan

Operating Locations

CA: Babcock & Brown, San Francisco; NJ: Nomura International Trust Co., Jersey City; NY: JAFCO America Ventures, New York; National Law Publishing Co., New York; New York Law Journal, New York; Nomura Asset Capital Corp., New York; Nomura Asset Management (U.S.A.), New York; Nomura Automation Management, New York; Nomura Capital Services, New York; Nomura Corporate Research & Asset Management Inc., New York; Nomura Holding America, New York; Nomura Holding America, New York; Nomura Mortgage Capital Corp., New York; Nomura Mortgage Fund Management Corp., New York; Nomura Real Estate U.S.A., New York; Nomura Realty Advisors, New York; Nomura Research Institute America, New York; Nomura Securities International, New York; Wasserstein Perella Group, New York

Nomura America Foundation

Giving Contact

P. J. Johnson, Director, Advertising & Public Relations
2 World Financial Center., Bldg. B, 17th Fl.
New York, NY 10281
Phone: (212)667-9300

Description

Founded: 1994
EIN: 133772961
Organization Type: Corporate Foundation
Giving Locations: headquarters and operating communities.
Grant Types: Project.

Financial Summary

Total Giving: $231,612 (1996); $357,200 (1995); $60,200 (1994)
Assets: $3,083,891 (1996); $1,302,325 (1995); $1,275,537 (1994)
Gifts Received: $1,700,000 (1996). Note: In 1996, contributions were received from Nomura Holding America.

Typical Recipients

Arts & Humanities: Arts & Humanities-General, Music, Opera, Performing Arts
Civic & Public Affairs: Botanical Gardens/Parks, Employment/Job Training, Civic & Public Affairs-General, Women's Affairs
Education: Arts/Humanities Education, Business Education, Colleges & Universities, Economic Education, Education Funds, Faculty Development, International Studies, Legal Education, Medical Education, Private Education (Precollege), Secondary Education (Private), Secondary Education (Public), Student Aid
Health: Arthritis, Cancer, Emergency/Ambulance Services, Health Funds, Multiple Sclerosis, Single-Disease Health Associations, Transplant Networks/Donor Banks
International: Health Care/Hospitals
Religion: Jewish Causes, Religious Organizations, Religious Welfare
Social Services: Scouts

Application Procedures

Initial Contact: Send letter of inquiry including a description of organization and project, amount requested, and proof of tax-exempt status. Request should explain specifically why support would be of interest to company and how it would benefit company.

Restrictions

Does not support individuals, religious organizations for sectarian purposes, political or lobbying groups, or organizations outside operating areas.

Corporate Officials

John E. Toffolon, Jr.: chief financial officer PRIM CORP EMPL chief financial officer: Nomura Holding America.
William Wraith: chief executive officer PRIM CORP EMPL chief executive officer: Nomura Holding America.

Giving Program Officials

P. J. Johnson: vice president PRIM CORP EMPL director advertising & public relations: Nomura Holding America.

Foundation Officials

Max Chapman, Jr.: chairman, chief executive officer, director
P. J. Johnson: vice president (see above)
William T. Maitland: secretary
John E. Toffolon, Jr.: treasurer, executive managing director, director (see above)

Grants Analysis

Disclosure Period: calendar year ending 1996
Number of Grants: 90
Highest Grant: $75,000
Typical Range: $50 to $5,000

Recent Grants

Note: Grants derived from 1997 Form 990.

Arts & Humanities

250 Harmonia Opera Company, New York, NY

Civic & Public Affairs

75,000 Central Park Conservancy, New York, NY -- restoration of Great Lawn
5,000 National Center for Disability Services, Albertson, NY
2,500 Starlight Foundation, New York, NY
1,000 Stanley M. Isaacs Park Association, New York, NY

Education

100,000 College of the Holy Cross, Worcester, MA
1,500 Regis High School, New York, NY
1,000 Colorado College, Colorado Springs, CO
1,000 Deerfield Academy, Deerfield, MA
1,000 Harvard College, Cambridge, MA
1,000 Stanford University, Stanford, CA
1,000 University of Tennessee, Knoxville, TN
1,000 Xavier High School, New York, NY
750 Brandeis University, Waltham, MA
500 Cornell University, Ithaca, NY
500 Dartmouth College, Hanover, NH
500 Deerfield Academy, Deerfield, MA
500 Gilman School, Baltimore, MD
500 Gilman School, Baltimore, MD
500 Morovian College, Bethlehem, PA
500 St. Bonaventure University, St. Bonaventure, NY
500 University of Rochester, Rochester, NY
500 University of Virginia, Charlottesville, VA
350 Washington University, St. Louis, MO

Health

10,000 Morristown Memorial Health Foundation, Morristown, NJ
5,000 American Red Cross of Geneva, New York, NY
2,500 Loch-Nylan Syndrome Children's Research Foundation, Lake Forest, IL
1,000 New York Blood Center, New York, NY

Religion

100,000 Simon Wiesenthal Center, Los Angeles, CA
450 Torah Umercrah, New York, NY

NORDSON CORP.

Company Contact

Westlake, OH

Company Description

Employees: 4,000 (1999)
SIC(s): 3569 General Industrial Machinery Nec, 5084 Industrial Machinery & Equipment.

Operating Locations

Germany: Lueneburg, Niedersachsen

Nonmonetary Support

Type: Donated Equipment; Donated Products; Loaned Employees

Nordson Corp. Foundation

Giving Contact

Constance Haqq, Executive Director
Nordson Corp. Foundation
28601 Clemens Road
Westlake, OH 44145-1148
Phone: (440)892-1580
Fax: (440)892-9507

Description

EIN: 341596194
Organization Type: Corporate Foundation
Giving Locations: GA: Atlanta; OH headquarters and operating communities.
Grant Types: Capital, Employee Matching Gifts, General Support, Project, Research.
Note: Employee matching gift ratio: 1 to 1 up to $5,000 annually per employee or retiree.

Financial Summary

Total Giving: $2,000,000 (fiscal year ending October 31, 1999 approx); $1,948,411 (fiscal 1998 approx); $1,882,735 (fiscal 1997). Note: Contributes through corporate direct giving program and foundation. 1997 Giving includes foundation giving. 1996 Giving includes corporate direct giving ($538,965); foundation ($1,799,318); matching gifts ($465,471). 1995 Giving

includes corporate direct giving ($630,532); foundation ($1,551,685); matching gifts ($474,846).
Assets: $6,188,844 (fiscal 1997); $5,848,651 (fiscal 1996); $5,561,672 (fiscal 1995)
Gifts Received: $1,000,000 (fiscal 1997); $1,500,000 (fiscal 1995). Note: Contributions are received from Nordson Corp.

Typical Recipients

Arts & Humanities: Arts Centers, Arts Festivals, Arts Institutes, Arts Outreach, Community Arts, Ethnic & Folk Arts, Arts & Humanities-General, Historic Preservation, History & Archaeology, Museums/Galleries, Music, Opera, Performing Arts, Public Broadcasting, Theater
Civic & Public Affairs: African American Affairs, Business/Free Enterprise, Civil Rights, Community Foundations, Economic Development, Employment/Job Training, Civic & Public Affairs-General, Hispanic Affairs, Housing, Legal Aid, Native American Affairs, Nonprofit Management, Professional & Trade Associations, Public Policy, Urban & Community Affairs, Zoos/Aquariums
Education: Arts/Humanities Education, Business Education, Colleges & Universities, Community & Junior Colleges, Education Associations, Education Funds, Education Reform, Education-General, International Studies, Leadership Training, Literacy, Medical Education, Minority Education, Preschool Education, Private Education (Precollege), Public Education (Precollege), Science/Mathematics Education, Secondary Education (Public), Social Sciences Education, Student Aid, Vocational & Technical Education
Environment: Environment-General
Health: Clinics/Medical Centers, Emergency/Ambulance Services, Hospices, Medical Research, Mental Health, Nursing Services, Single-Disease Health Associations, Speech & Hearing
International: International Relations
Religion: Churches, Ministries, Religious Welfare
Science: Science Museums, Scientific Centers & Institutes
Social Services: At-Risk Youth, Child Welfare, Community Centers, Community Service Organizations, Counseling, Day Care, Delinquency & Criminal Rehabilitation, Domestic Violence, Family Services, Food/Clothing Distribution, Homes, People with Disabilities, Recreation & Athletics, Scouts, Senior Services, Substance Abuse, United Funds/United Ways, Volunteer Services, YMCA/YWCA/YMHA/YWHA, Youth Organizations

Contributions Analysis

Giving Priorities: Family services and united funds, early childhood and elementary education, environmental and civic organizations, mental health, museums and other arts organizations.
Arts & Humanities: 11%. Funding is given to established arts organizations that actively seek to broaden their audience bases in Nordson communities. Supports museums, musical groups, art programs, public broadcasting, performing arts, and enhanced multicultural awareness.
Civic & Public Affairs: 28%. Supports environmental affairs, civil rights organizations, housing, and economic development. Efforts to involve citizens in community improvement are also a priority.
Education: 41%. Supports education reform, community colleges, minority education, student aid, education reform, and secondary public and private education.
Social Services: 20%. Funding supports organizations that promote prevention, crisis intervention, life transition opportunities, and systemic policy change. Also, supports family services and united funds. Other interests include services for the aged, youth organizations, and organizations concerned with employment. Each year, two or three organizations are chosen to receive intense assistance for one year in the form of grant money, emergency funding, equipment donations, and volunteer time.
Note: Total contributions made in fiscal 1997.

Application Procedures

Initial Contact: Write or call to request application from foundation staff in Westlake, OH, Atlanta, GA, or Monterey, CA.
Application Requirements: Send a copy of current 501(c)(3) form and a list of organization's officers and trustees, with affiliations.
Deadlines: The middle of the following months: November for review in January, February for review in April, May for July and August for review in October.
Evaluative Criteria: Geographic location and constituency served; special interest in disadvantaged persons, minorities, the handicapped, and projects which attack root causes of problems.
Decision Notification: Trustees meet in January, April, July, and October.

Additional Information

Approximately 5% of pretax profit is budgeted for charitable contributions.
On October 31, 1988, approximately $51 million in foundation assets were transferred to the Nord Family Foundation. The Nordson Foundation (EIN: 34-6539234) was liquidated and transferred $1.5 million to a newly established Nordson Corporation Foundation (EIN: 34-1596194) that continues to support charitable causes located in Nordson Corp. manufacturing cities. manufacturing cities.
Publications: Contributions Report to the Community

Corporate Officials

Christian C. Bernadotte: vice president law, assistant secretary B 1949. PRIM CORP EMPL vice president: Nordson Corp.
Edward Patrick Campbell: president, chief operating officer, drc B Longview, TX 1949. ED University of Notre Dame (1971); Harvard University Graduate School of Business Administration (1977). PRIM CORP EMPL president, chief operating officer, drc: Nordson Corp. CORP AFFIL trustee: Victory Funds Mutual Funds Group.
Thomas Leib Moorhead, Esq.: vice president law, assistant secretary B Senecaville, OH 1936. ED United States Military Academy BS (1959); George Washington University Law School JD (1967). PRIM CORP EMPL vice president law, assistant secretary: Nordson Corp.

Foundation Officials

Christian C. Bernadotte: vice president (see above)
Edward Patrick Campbell: trustee (see above)
Beverly J. Coen: assistant controller, director
Constance T. Haqq: executive director
John E. Jackson: trustee B Eagle Pass, TX 1945. ED United States Air Force Academy BS (1967); Harvard University Graduate School of Business Administration MBA (1973). PRIM CORP EMPL senior vice president: Nordson Corp.
Thomas Leib Moorhead, Esq.: trustee (see above)

Grants Analysis

Disclosure Period: fiscal year ending October 31, 1997
Total Grants: $1,882,735*
Number of Grants: 195
Average Grant: $9,655
Highest Grant: $250,000
Typical Range: $1,000 to $25,000
***Note:** Giving excludes corporate direct giving.

Recent Grants

Note: Grants derived from 1997 Form 990.

Arts & Humanities

120,000	Playhouse Square Foundation, Cleveland, OH
14,446	Oberlin Historical and Improvement Organization, Oberlin, OH
10,000	Cleveland Opera, Cleveland, OH
10,000	Harrison Cultural Community Center, Lorain, OH

Civic & Public Affairs

87,500	Workforce Institute of Lorain County
30,000	El Centro de Servicios Sociales, Lorain, OH
25,000	Lorain County 2020, Elyria, OH
25,000	Lorain County Community Alliance, Lorain, OH
10,892	National Conference
10,000	City of Elyria -- Envision Elyria
10,000	Cleveland Works, Cleveland, OH
10,000	Greater Cleveland Roundtable, Cleveland, OH
10,000	Mad Factory
10,000	Seventh Generation, Elyria, OH

Education

250,000	Center for Leadership in Education, Amherst, OH
150,000	Lorain County Community College, Lorain, OH
54,900	Baldwin-Wallace College, Berea, OH
25,750	Norcross High School
25,000	Ohio Foundation of Independent Colleges, Columbus, OH
20,000	Morehouse School of Medicine, Atlanta, GA
15,000	Community Youth Academy
15,000	Grassroots Leadership Development Program
10,000	Berry College, Rome, GA
10,000	David N. Myers College, Cleveland, OH
10,000	Morehouse College, Atlanta, GA
10,000	Northeast Ohio Council on Higher Education, Cleveland, OH
10,000	Project Read, Atlanta, GA
10,000	Urban Community School, Cleveland, OH

Health

50,000	Cleveland Clinic Foundation, Cleveland, OH
10,000	Shepard Spinal Center, Atlanta, GA

Religion

50,000	Salvation Army, Elyria, OH
36,215	Lilburn Cooperative Ministry, Lilburn, GA
15,000	Salvation Army Lorain Corps
10,000	Norcross Cooperative Ministry, Norcross, GA

Science

10,000	Great Lakes Science Center
10,000	Lake Erie Nature and Science Center, Bay Village, OH

Social Services

55,000	Karamu House, Cleveland, OH
25,000	YWCA, Lorain, OH
20,000	YMCA, Cleveland, OH
18,000	Access Program
15,000	W.G. Nord Community Mental Health Center, Lorain, OH
10,000	Alternate Life Paths, Atlanta, GA
10,000	Boy Scouts of America, Cleveland, OH
10,000	Cleveland Hearing and Speech Center, Cleveland, OH
10,000	Hunger Network, Cleveland, OH
10,000	Lorain Family YMCA, Lorain, OH
10,000	Lorain Opportunity Outreach Program, Lorain, OH
10,000	Northcoast Food Rescue, Rocky River, OH
10,000	Volunteer Action Center
10,000	Youth Service Learning

Norfolk Southern Corp.

Company Contact
Norfolk, VA
Web: http://www.nscorp.com

Company Description
Revenue: US$5,195,000,000 (1999)
Employees: 24,300 (1999)
Fortune Rank: 316, per FORTUNE Magazine's list of 500 Largest U.S. Corporations (1999).
FF 316
SIC(s): 6719 Holding Companies Nec.

Nonmonetary Support
Value: $250,000 (1999); $200,000 (1987)
Type: Donated Equipment; Donated Products
Note: Nonmonetary by the foundation.

Corporate Sponsorship
Note: Sponsors an educational event at the college level.

Norfolk Southern Foundation

Giving Contact
Ms. Deborah Wyld, Executive Director
Norfolk Southern Foundation
PO Box 3040
Norfolk, VA 23514-3040
Phone: (757)629-2366
Fax: (757)629-2798
Email: dhwyld@nscorp.com

Alternate Contact
Jessie A. Davis, Administrator

Description
EIN: 521328375
Organization Type: Corporate Foundation
Giving Locations: GA: Atlanta; VA: Hampton Roads, Roanoke operating areas.
Grant Types: Award, Capital, Challenge, Employee Matching Gifts, General Support.
Note: Employee matching gift ratio: 1 to 1 to higher education, arts/cultural organizations and certain environmental/conservation groups.

Financial Summary
Total Giving: $5,170,000 (2000 approx); $5,170,000 (1999); $5,200,000 (1998). Note: Contributes through corporate direct giving program and foundation.
Giving Analysis: Giving for 1997 includes: foundation ($1,289,715); foundation matching gifts ($1,064,089); foundation grants to United Way ($953,035); 1998: corporate direct giving ($1,390,000); foundation matching gifts ($1,247,396); foundation grants to United Way ($990,559); foundation ($842,148)
Assets: $7,580,314 (1998); $5,618,933 (1997); $8,030,911 (1996)
Gifts Received: $3,879,694 (1998); $5,000 (1997); $956,156 (1996). Note: The foundation receives contributions from Norfolk Southern Corporation.

Typical Recipients
Arts & Humanities: Arts Associations & Councils, Arts Centers, Arts Funds, Historic Preservation, History & Archaeology, Museums/Galleries, Music, Opera, Performing Arts, Public Broadcasting, Theater
Civic & Public Affairs: Botanical Gardens/Parks, Business/Free Enterprise, Civil Rights, Community Foundations, Economic Development, Civic & Public Affairs-General, Housing, Law & Justice, Parades/Festivals, Public Policy, Safety, Urban & Community Affairs, Zoos/Aquariums
Education: Arts/Humanities Education, Business Education, Colleges & Universities, Economic Education, Education Associations, Education Funds, Engineering/Technological Education, Faculty Development, Legal Education, Literacy, Medical Education, Minority Education, Private Education (Precollege), Science/Mathematics Education, Special Education, Student Aid
Environment: Air/Water Quality, Forestry, Environment-General, Resource Conservation
Health: Cancer, Children's Health/Hospitals, Emergency/Ambulance Services, Health Organizations, Heart, Hospitals, Medical Research, Research/Studies Institutes, Single-Disease Health Associations
Science: Science Museums, Scientific Centers & Institutes
Social Services: Child Welfare, United Funds/United Ways, YMCA/YWCA/YMHA/YWHA, Youth Organizations

Contributions Analysis
Giving Priorities: United funds; music, theater, and other performing arts organizations; education funds and associations and colleges and universities; urban and community affairs; and health organizations and hospitals.

Application Procedures
Initial Contact: letter
Application Requirements: outline and purpose of the organization, list of officers and board sources of funding, amount requested, purpose of funds sought, why foundation is being considered for funding, three years of audited financial statement, other sources of income, reasons for approaching foundation, proof of tax-exempt status, and a copy of IRS letter of determination
Deadlines: September 30.
Decision Notification: within ninety days

Restrictions
Grants are not made to individuals or health organizations.

Additional Information
Most grants are for collective fundraising organizations (such as United Way) and to accredited educational institutions through a matching gifts program for employees of Norfolk Southern Corporation.

Corporate Officials
David Ronald Goode: chairman, president, chief executive officer, director B Vinton, VA 1941. ED Duke University AB (1962); Harvard University Law School JD (1965). PRIM CORP EMPL chairman, president, chief executive officer, director: Norfolk Southern Corp. CORP AFFIL director: Trinova Corp.; director: Georgia-Pacific Corp.; director: Texas Instruments Inc.; director: Delta Air Lines; director: Caterpillar Inc.; vice president: Cincinnati, New Orleans, Texas Railway; director: Aeroquip-Vickers Inc. NONPR AFFIL member: Virginia Business Higher Education Council; trustee: Virginia Foundation Independent Colleges; member: Virginia Business Council; director: U.S. Chamber of Commerce; member: Virginia Bar Association; member: Transportation Research Board Executive Committee; business advisory council: Northwestern University; member: Roanoke Bar Association; member: Norfolk Military/Civilian Liaison Group; member: National Grain Car Council; member: Norfolk Bar Association; vice chairman: Kennedy Center Corp. Fund Board; member: National Freight Transportation Association; trustee: Hollins College; trustee: General Douglas MacArthur Memorial Foundation; member: Governments Advisory Council on Revenue Estimates; board visitors: Duke University; board visitors: Duke University Fuqua School Business; business advisory council: Coal Industries Advisory Board; director: Association American RRs; member: Business Roundtable; member: American Bar Association; member: American Society Corporate Executives. CLUB AFFIL Town Point Club; Virginia Golf Club; Princess Anne Country Club; Shenandoah Club; Norfolk Yacht Club & Country Club; The Links Club; Metro Club; Hunting Hills Country Club; Laurel Valley Golf Club; Harbor Club; Bayville Golf Club; East Lake Gulf Club.
Dezora M. Martin: corporate secretary B Bluefield, WV 1947. ED Concord College (1970). PRIM CORP EMPL corporate secretary: Norfolk Southern Corp. NONPR AFFIL member: American Society of Corporate Secretaries; member: National Association Stock Plan Professionals.
Kathryn B. McQuade: vice president financial planning PRIM CORP EMPL vice president financial planning: Norfolk Southern Corp.
L. I. Prillaman: vice chairman, chief marketing officer PRIM CORP EMPL vice president, chief marketing officer: Norfolk Southern Corp.
Steven C. Tobias: vice chairman, chief operating officer B Bogota, Colombia 1944. ED Citadel BA (1967); Harvard University (1986). PRIM CORP EMPL vice chairman, chief operating officer: Norfolk Southern Corp. CORP AFFIL management committee: Triple Crown Service; vice president, chief operating officer: Norfolk Southern Railway Co.; director: Terminal Railroad Association Saint Louis. NONPR AFFIL member: Association American RRs.
Henry C. Wolf: vice chairman, chief financial officer B 1942. ED College of William & Mary BA (1964); College of William & Mary JD (1966). PRIM CORP EMPL vice chairman, chief financial officer: Norfolk Southern Corp. CORP AFFIL director: Shenandoah Life Insurance Co.; director: Norfolk & Western RY Co.; vice president: Pocahontas Land Corp.; vice president: Norfolk Southern Properties; vice president, chief financial officer: Norfolk Southern Railway Co.; vice president: Cincinnati New Orleans Texas Railway; director: Greater Norfolk Corp. NONPR AFFIL director: Virginia Institute of Marine Science.

Foundation Officials
Dezora M. Martin: secretary (see above)
Kathryn B. McQuade: vice president, chief officer (see above)
Steven C. Tobias: director (see above)
Henry C. Wolf: vice president finance (see above)
Deborah Wyld: executive director

Grants Analysis
Disclosure Period: calendar year ending 1998
Total Grants: $842,148*
Number of Grants: 135*
Average Grant: $6,238
Highest Grant: $135,000
Typical Range: $500 to $25,000
***Note:** Giving excludes matching gifts; United Way.

Recent Grants
Note: Grants derived from 1997 Form 990.

Arts & Humanities

75,000	Virginia Opera, Norfolk, VA -- operating support
75,000	Virginia Stage Company, Norfolk, VA -- operating support
63,813	Business Consortium for Arts Support, Norfolk, VA -- operating support
37,000	Western Virginia Foundation for Arts, Roanoke, VA -- operating support
35,000	Hill Mountain Theater, Roanoke, VA -- operating support
25,000	Art Museum of Western Virginia, Roanoke, VA -- operating support
25,000	Roanoke Symphony, Roanoke, VA -- operating support
25,000	Virginia Symphony, Norfolk, VA -- operating support
20,000	Barter Theater, Abingdon, VA -- operating support

20,000 High Museum of Art, Atlanta, GA -- operating support

Civic & Public Affairs

50,000 East Lake Community Foundation, Atlanta, GA -- operating support

50,000 Zoological Society, Atlanta, GA -- operating support

30,000 Norfolk Botanical Garden Society, Norfolk, VA -- operating support

30,000 Virginia Zoological Society, Norfolk, VA -- operating support

25,000 Foundation for Roanoke Valley, Roanoke, VA -- operating support

Education

110,000 Virginia Foundation for Independent Colleges, Richmond, VA -- operating support

100,000 Virginia Wesleyan College, Norfolk, VA -- endowment support

81,563 National Merit Scholarship Corporation, Evanston, IL -- operating support

75,000 Virginia Tech Foundation, Blacksburg, VA -- operating support

50,000 Hollins College, Hollins, VA -- operating support

50,000 Northwestern University Transportation Center, Evanston, IL -- operating support

50,000 Pikeville College, Pikeville, VA -- operating support

50,000 Virginia Institute of Science, Gloucester Point, VA -- operating support

50,000 Virginia Wesleyan College, Norfolk, VA -- operating support

20,000 Medical University of South Carolina, Columbia, SC -- operating support

20,000 Mountain Mission School, Grundy, VA -- operating support

Environment

20,000 Nature Conservancy, Charlottesville, VA -- operating support

Health

25,000 Children's Hospital of King's Daughters, Norfolk, VA -- operating support

25,000 Old Dominion University, Norfolk, VA -- operating support

Science

75,000 Mouticus, National Maritime Center, Norfolk, VA -- operating support, capital campaign

20,000 Science Museum of Western Virginia, Roanoke, VA -- operating support

Social Services

147,253 United Way of Roanoke Valley, Roanoke, VA -- operating support

125,000 United Way, Atlanta, GA -- operating support

125,000 United Way of South Hampton Roads, Norfolk, VA -- operating support

80,000 United Way of South Hampton Roads, Norfolk, VA -- operating support

27,786 United Way, Chattanooga, TN -- operating support

26,202 United Way of Central Alabama, Birmingham, AL -- operating support

23,265 United Way of the Virginias, Bluefield, WV -- operating support

20,757 United Way of Southwest Virginia, Lebanon, VA -- operating support

19,041 United Way of Central Georgia, Macon, GA -- operating support

18,051 United Way, Knoxville, TN -- operating support

17,655 United Way of Decatur/Macon County, Decatur, IL -- operating support

14,982 Bellevue United Selective Fund, Bellevue, OH -- operating support

14,619 United Foundation, Williamson, WV -- operating support

13,332 United Way of Scioto County, Portsmouth, OH -- operating support

11,946 United Way of Alamance County, Burlington, NC -- operating support

11,847 United Way of Shoals Area, Sheffield, AL -- operating support

10,659 United Way of Central Virginia, Lynchburg, VA -- operating support

10,428 United Way, Cincinnati, OH -- operating support

10,065 United Way of Piedmont, Spartanburg, SC -- operating support

NORTEL

Company Contact

Nashville, TN
Web: http://www.nortelnetwork.com

Company Description

Also Known As: Northern Telecom Ltd.
Employees: 29,396 (1999)
SIC(s): 3572 Computer Storage Devices, 3661 Telephone & Telegraph Apparatus, 3663 Radio & T.V. Communications Equipment, 3672 Printed Circuit Boards.

Operating Locations

CA: Nortel; Nortel Communications, San Ramon; Meridian Communications Systems Div., Santa Clara; Nortel CALA, Sunrise; GA: Nortel; Northern Telecom-Transmission Div., Atlanta; IL: Nortel; MI: Nortel; NC: Northern Telecom Switching Networks, Morrisville; Digital Switching Div., Research Triangle Park; DMS-10 Div., Research Triangle Park; NH: Nortel; NJ: Nortel; TN: Nortel, Nashville; Northern Telecom, Nashville; Northern Telecom Finance Corp., Nashville; Northern Telecom-National Repair & Distribution Center, Nashville; TX: Data Communications & Networks, Richardson

Nonmonetary Support

Value: $500,000 (1995); $1,200,000 (1994); $1,500,000 (1993)
Type: Donated Equipment; In-kind Services; Loaned Executives
Note: Company supplied figure for 1995.

Corporate Sponsorship

Type: Arts & cultural events; Festivals/fairs; Music & entertainment events; Pledge-a-thon

Giving Contact

Francie Alter, Senior Manager Corporate Relations
Nortel
8200 Dixie Road
Brampton, ON, Canada L6T 5P6
Phone: (905)863-6490
Fax: (905)863-8263

Description

Organization Type: Corporate Giving Program
Giving Locations: principally near operating locations and to national organizations.
Grant Types: Award, Employee Matching Gifts, General Support, Matching, Project, Research.

Giving Philosophy

'Nortel (Northern Telecom) has demonstrated a long-term commitment to education at all levels, which has included numerous initiatives for the purpose of science, technology, engineering, and mathematics to young people across North America and beyond. The success of these programs is the result of dedicated staff and energetic volunteers, and a multi-level strategy which includes direct contact with students as well as broad community-based and national programs focused on educators. In each of these areas, Nortel has developed original initiatives and has played a critical supporting role in the development and maintenance of others.' Nortel Annual Report

Financial Summary

Total Giving: $1,500,000 (1996 approx); $2,000,000 (1995 approx); $3,500,000 (1994 approx). Note: Contributes through corporate direct giving program only. Giving includes nonmonetary support.

Typical Recipients

Arts & Humanities: Arts Centers, Community Arts, Museums/Galleries, Music, Opera, Performing Arts, Public Broadcasting, Theater, Visual Arts
Civic & Public Affairs: Civic & Public Affairs-General
Education: Colleges & Universities, Education Funds, Elementary Education (Private), Education-General, Minority Education, Public Education (Pre-college)
Science: Science Exhibits & Fairs
Social Services: United Funds/United Ways, Volunteer Services

Contributions Analysis

Giving Priorities: Company reports that contributions by Toronto company outside North America are about $1,000,000 annually. Contributions to host country organizations by overseas subsidiaries are approximately $2,000,000 annually.
International: Company reports that contributions by Toronto company outside North America are about $1,000,000 annually. Contributions by overseas subsidiaries to host country organizations are approximately $2,000,000 annually.

Application Procedures

Initial Contact: Send a letter of inquiry.
Application Requirements: Include a description of organization, amount and purpose of funds sought, a recently audited financial statement, proof of tax-exempt status, and a list of other support.
Deadlines: Early in the calendar year.

Restrictions

Program does not support individuals, political or lobbying groups, religious organizations, goodwill advertising, or agencies already receiving grants from united funds. Further, it rarely supports dinners or special events.

Corporate Officials

John Roth: president, chief executive officer, chief operating officer, director ED McGill University BE (1964); McGill University MEngg (1966). PRIM CORP EMPL president, chief executive officer, chief operating officer, director: Nortel. NONPR AFFIL member: Association Professional Engineers Ontario; member: National Advisor Board Science & Technology.

Giving Program Officials

Francie Alter: corp. relations manager

Grants Analysis

Disclosure Period: calendar year ending
Typical Range: $10,000 to $25,000

NORTH AMERICAN ROYALTIES

Company Contact

Chattanooga, TN

Company Description

Employees: 1,760
SIC(s): 1311 Crude Petroleum & Natural Gas.

North American Royalties Foundation

Giving Contact

Lorie Mallchok, Vice President, Corporate Affairs
200 E. 8th St.
Chattanooga, TN 37402
Phone: (423)265-3181

Description

EIN: 626052490
Organization Type: Corporate Foundation
Giving Locations: TN: Chattanooga
Grant Types: Award.

Financial Summary

Total Giving: $239,015 (1996); $179,260 (1994); $159,652 (1993)
Assets: $944,883 (1996); $656,867 (1994); $491,400 (1993)
Gifts Received: $327,479 (1996); $334,054 (1994); $312,013 (1993). Note: In 1996, contributions were received from North American Royalties.

Typical Recipients

Arts & Humanities: Historic Preservation, History & Archaeology, Libraries, Museums/Galleries, Public Broadcasting
Civic & Public Affairs: Business/Free Enterprise, Chambers of Commerce, Economic Development, Civic & Public Affairs-General, Parades/Festivals, Urban & Community Affairs, Zoos/Aquariums
Education: Colleges & Universities, Education Funds, Elementary Education (Public), Engineering/Technological Education, Education-General, Literacy, Private Education (Precollege), Public Education (Precollege), Science/Mathematics Education, Student Aid, Vocational & Technical Education
Environment: Air/Water Quality, Environment-General
Health: Clinics/Medical Centers
Social Services: Food/Clothing Distribution, People with Disabilities, United Funds/United Ways, YMCA/YWCA/YMHA/YWHA, Youth Organizations

Application Procedures

Initial Contact: Send a brief letter of inquiry. Scholarship application forms are available for employees. Deadline for scholarships is March 1.

Restrictions

Does not support individuals except for scholarships for dependents of employees.

Additional Information

Provides scholarships to dependents of current or deceased employees.

Corporate Officials

Gordon P. Street, Jr.: chairman, president, chief executive officer, director B Chattanooga, TN 1938. ED University of North Carolina (1960). PRIM CORP EMPL chairman, president, chief executive officer, director: North American Royalties. CORP AFFIL director: First Tennessee National Corp.; director: Provident Life & Accident Insurance Co.; director: CNO& TP Railroad; director: First Tennessee Bank NA Corp.
David Williams: chief financial officer PRIM CORP EMPL chief financial officer: North American Royalties.

Foundation Officials

Ronald W. Reese: trustee PRIM CORP EMPL vice president: North American Royalties.
Gordon L. Smith, Jr.: trustee PRIM CORP EMPL vice president planning: North American Royalties.
Gordon P. Street, Jr.: trustee (see above)

Grants Analysis

Disclosure Period: calendar year ending 1996
Number of Grants: 15*
Highest Grant: $50,000
Typical Range: $75 to $25,000*
***Note:** Number of grants and typical range do not include scholarships to individuals totaling $50,000.

Recent Grants

Note: Grants derived from 1997 Form 990.

Arts & Humanities

25,000	Creative Discovery Museum, Chattanooga, TN
12,400	WTCI-TV 45
2,500	Warren County Library

Civic & Public Affairs

50,000	Microcredit Development Fund
10,000	Chattanooga Downtown Partnership, Chattanooga, TN
3,000	READ
3,000	Tennessee Aquarium, Chattanooga, TN
2,700	Chattanooga Manufacturing Association, Chattanooga, TN
2,000	Tennessee 200, Nashville, TN
100	Warren County Chamber of Commerce

Education

9,996	Chattanooga State University, Chattanooga, TN
5,000	Foundry Educational Foundation, Des Plaines, IL
5,000	Warren Board of Education
2,500	University of the South, Sewanee, TN
1,500	Tennessee Business Week, TN

Environment

1,500	Chattanooga Nature Center, Chattanooga, TN

Social Services

60,000	Community Kitchen
40,500	United Way
5,000	Boys Club, Chattanooga, TN
1,000	Chattanooga YMCA, Chattanooga, TN

Northeast Utilities

Company Contact

Berlin, CT

Company Description

Revenue: US$4,471,300,000 (1999)
Employees: 9,077 (1999)
Fortune Rank: 360, per FORTUNE Magazine's list of 500 Largest U.S. Corporations (1999).
FF 360
SIC(s): 4911 Electric Services, 6719 Holding Companies Nec.

Nonmonetary Support

Value: $30,000 (1993); $30,000 (1989); $30,000 (1988)
Type: In-kind Services; Loaned Employees; Workplace Solicitation
Note: Loaned employees and in-kind services are provided only to the United Way.

Giving Contact

Sara Ellison, Secretary, Dues & Contributions Committee
Northeast Utilities
PO Box 270
Hartford, CT 06141-0270
Phone: (860)665-5000
Fax: (860)665-2796

Description

Organization Type: Corporate Giving Program
Giving Locations: company service areas.
Grant Types: Capital, Emergency, Employee Matching Gifts, General Support, Operating Expenses, Project.
Note: Employee matching gifts for education only.

Giving Philosophy

'While the first obligation of any business is to provide a return to its owners, business is not isolated from the society in which it functions. It is part of the community and shares in its collective strengths and weaknesses. A public utility has particularly close ties to the community it serves. .. The company not only intends to be responsive to people's needs, but also to be an initiator of action in the best tradition of good citizenship.' 1997 *Northeast Utilities* Corporate Contributions Policy

Financial Summary

Total Giving: $2,300,000 (1998 approx); $2,720,000 (1995 approx); $2,600,000 (1994 approx). Note: Contributes through corporate direct giving program only.

Typical Recipients

Arts & Humanities: Arts Funds
Civic & Public Affairs: Economic Development, Housing, Law & Justice, Legal Aid, Safety, Urban & Community Affairs
Education: Colleges & Universities, Community & Junior Colleges, Economic Education, Engineering/Technological Education, Literacy, Minority Education, Public Education (Precollege), Science/Mathematics Education
Environment: Environment-General
Health: Emergency/Ambulance Services, Hospitals, Mental Health, Nutrition
Social Services: Child Welfare, Community Centers, Community Service Organizations, Counseling, Delinquency & Criminal Rehabilitation, Domestic Violence, Family Services, Food/Clothing Distribution, Homes, People with Disabilities, Senior Services, Shelters/Homelessness, Substance Abuse, United Funds/United Ways, Volunteer Services, Youth Organizations

Contributions Analysis

Giving Priorities: Health and welfare; education, with emphasis on engineering; social and civic betterment; arts funds and symphonic music; and some environmental.
Arts & Humanities: Programs are funded which provide services to children and youth, the elderly, or other traditionally underserved groups.
Environment: Funds energy conservation with a focus on assisting low-and fixed-income residential customers or government to conserve energy, including alternate energy sources.
Health: Supports income assistance and energy assistance programs and efforts to maintain and improve basic prevention and rehabilitative health service.
Social Services: Supports education and training programs, including developing technically skilled people, develop basic budgeting skills and skills needed for entry-level jobs. Also funds economic development programs, social services and public safety issues, and services thatenable people to function independently.

Application Procedures

Initial Contact: brief letter requesting application form
Application Requirements: completed request form; a description of organization, services offered and beneficiaries of service, geographic area served, purpose of funds sought, recently audited financial statement, other sources of funding, list of board members, proof of tax-exempt status
Deadlines: by August 1 for following year
Review Process: requests reviewed by staff and presented to contributions committee

Evaluative Criteria: organization's areas of focus, community need, importance of company funding, availability of other funding, administrative effectiveness, efficiency of program
Decision Notification: primarily in November
Notes: Application forms are available from local managers.

Restrictions

Company generally will not make grants to permanent endowment funds or foundations. Capital grants normally are restricted to no more than 1% of private sector share of cost. Does not usually contribute to groups already receiving united fund support. Also does not give to fraternal, political or lobbying groups, or religious organizations for sectarian purposes.

Additional Information

The educational grants committee administers a separate contributions program for higher education. Grantees must submit a report of activities.
Publications: Guidelines; Application Form

Corporate Officials

John Forsgren: senior vice president, chief financial officers group B 1947. PRIM CORP EMPL senior vice president, chief financial officer: Northeast Utilities ADD CORP EMPL chief financial officer: Connecticut Light & Power Co. Inc.; chief financial officer: North Atlantic Energy Corp.; chief financial officer: Northeast Utilities Service Co.; chief financial officer: Northeast Utilities Volunteer Association; chief financial officer: Public Service Co. New Hampshire; chief financial officer: Western Massachusetts Electric Co.
Cheryl W. Grise: senior vice president, chief administrative officer B Madison, NC. ED University of North Carolina (1974); Western State University (1978). PRIM CORP EMPL senior vice president, chief administrative officer: Northeast Utilities ADD CORP EMPL senior vice president, chief administration officer: Community Light & Power Co.; vice president: North Atlantic Energy Corp.; senior vice president, chief administration officer: Northeast Nuclear Energy Co.; senior vice president, chief administration officer: Northeast Utilities Service Co.; senior vice president, chief administration officer: Western Massachusetts Electric Co.; senior vice president, chief administration officer: Holyoke Water Power Co. NONPR AFFIL director: Combined Health Appeal; overseer: University Connecticut School Business.
Hugh C. MacKenzie: president retail business group PRIM CORP EMPL president retail business group: Northeast Utilities Service Co. ADD CORP EMPL president: Holyoke Water Power Co.; president: Western Massachusetts Electric Co. CORP AFFIL officer: Public Service Co. New Hampshire.

Giving Program Officials

Sara Ellison: PRIM CORP EMPL secretary corporate dues & contributions committee: Northeast Utilities.
Cheryl W. Grise: B Madison, NC. ED University of North Carolina (1974); Western State University (1978). PRIM CORP EMPL senior vice president, chief administrative officer: Northeast Utilities ADD CORP EMPL senior vice president, chief administration officer: Community Light & Power Co.; vice president: North Atlantic Energy Corp.; senior vice president, chief administration officer: Northeast Nuclear Energy Co.; senior vice president, chief administration officer: Northeast Utilities Service Co.; senior vice president, chief administration officer: Western Massachusetts Electric Co.; senior vice president, chief administration officer: Holyoke Water Power Co. NONPR AFFIL director: Combined Health Appeal; overseer: University Connecticut School Business.
Ann Johnson-Bly: director PRIM CORP EMPL member education grant committee: Northeast Utilities.

Foundation Officials

John Keane: president
Dave McHale: treasurer

Grants Analysis

Disclosure Period: calendar year ending 1995
Total Grants: $2,720,000
Number of Grants: 800
Average Grant: $3,400
Typical Range: $50 to $5,000

NORTHERN INDIANA PUBLIC SERVICE CO.

Company Contact

Hammond, IN

Company Description

Assets: US$3,755,500,000
Employees: 3,562
SIC(s): 4931 Electric & Other Services Combined, 4932 Gas & Other Services Combined.
Parent Company: NiSource Inc., 801 E. 86th Ave., Merrillville, IN, United States

Nonmonetary Support

Range: $500 - $5,000
Type: In-kind Services; Loaned Employees; Loaned Executives

Corporate Sponsorship

Type: Arts & cultural events; Festivals/fairs; Music & entertainment events; Pledge-a-thon; Sports events

Giving Contact

Jan Lawrence-Stofer, Principal, Corporate Citizenship
Northern Indiana Public Service Co.
5265 Hohman Avenue
Hammond, IN 46320
Phone: (219)647-5089
Fax: (219)647-4010

Description

Organization Type: Corporate Giving Program
Giving Locations: IN: northern third of Indiana headquarters and operating communities.
Grant Types: Capital, Employee Matching Gifts, General Support, Matching, Multiyear/Continuing Support.
Note: Employee matching gift ratio: 1 to 1. The company also sponsors programs that match gifts at 0.7to 1.

Giving Philosophy

'Through its corporate contributions program, NI and its shareholders commit corporate earnings to support and fund charitable organizations which enhance the quality of life for NI customers and their families. By meeting the social, economic, educational, and cultural needs of our customers, we help develop strong business relationships, answer community needs, and create lasting commitments to the people and communities we serve.' Charitable Contributions Guidelines

Financial Summary

Total Giving: $2,000,000 (1998 approx); $2,400,000 (1997 approx); $2,400,000 (1996 approx). Note: Contributes through corporate direct giving program only.

Typical Recipients

Arts & Humanities: Arts Appreciation, Arts Associations & Councils, Arts Centers, Historic Preservation, Museums/Galleries, Music, Performing Arts, Public Broadcasting, Visual Arts
Civic & Public Affairs: Economic Development, Employment/Job Training
Education: Arts/Humanities Education, Business Education, Colleges & Universities, Education Funds, Engineering/Technological Education, Literacy
Health: Hospices, Hospitals, Nursing Services, Single-Disease Health Associations
Science: Science Exhibits & Fairs
Social Services: Animal Protection, Community Centers, Community Service Organizations, Counseling, Delinquency & Criminal Rehabilitation, Emergency Relief, Food/Clothing Distribution, People with Disabilities, Recreation & Athletics, Senior Services, Shelters/Homelessness, United Funds/United Ways, Volunteer Services, Youth Organizations

Contributions Analysis

Arts & Humanities: Less than 5%. Symphonies, united arts organizations, art centers, science exhibits and fairs, museums, performing arts, and historic preservation.
Civic & Public Affairs: 10% to 15%. Civic organization membership. Funds also supportnature preservation through assistance to wildlife organizations, and humane societies.
Education: 10% to 15%. Schools, colleges, and universities, including agricultural education, engineering, literacy, vocational education, liberal arts, science and technology, and student aid.
Health: 55% to 60%. Organizations promoting health and safety, as well as individuals and families confronted with various health issues, including cancer, arthritis, heart disease, and lung disease. Social Service funding supports services for the good of the community, including youth organizations, food and clothing distribution, community service organizations, civil rights advocacy, and community centers.

Application Procedures

Initial Contact: a brief letter of inquiry and full proposal
Application Requirements: a description of organization, amount requested, purpose of funds sought, audited financial statement, proof of tax-exempt status, and other sources of funding
Deadlines: None.
Review Process: contributions committee meets monthly and considers applications received three weeks in advance of the meeting.

Restrictions

Does not support individuals, religious organizations for sectarian purposes, or political or lobbying groups.

Additional Information

The contributions program also includes employee volunteer matching funds, in-kind contributions, an employee-driven environmental challenge fund, and community-based giving, which do not necessarily have the same restrictions as corporate contributions.
Publications: Contributions Fact Sheet; Guidelines

Corporate Officials

Owen C. Johnson, Jr.: vice president human resources, chief executive officer PRIM CORP EMPL vice president human resources: Northern Indiana Public Service Co. CORP AFFIL vice president human resources: NIPSCO Industries Management Services Co.
Gary L. Neale: chairman, president, chief executive officer B Lead, SD 1940. ED University of Washington BA (1962); University of Washington MBA (1965). PRIM CORP EMPL chairman, president, chief executive officer: Ni Source Inc. CORP AFFIL chairman: NIPSCO Energy Services Inc.; chairman: NIPSCO Development Co. Inc.; director: Mercantile National Bank Indiana; director: Modine Manufacturing Co.; director: Chicago Bridge Iron Co. NONPR AFFIL chairman, member government religious organizations for sectarian purposes committee: American Gas Association.

Foundation Officials

Janice Lawrence-Stofer: principal of corporate citizenship

Grants Analysis

Disclosure Period: calendar year ending
Typical Range: $1,000 to $2,500

NORTHERN STATES POWER CO.

Company Contact

414 Nicollet Mall
Minneapolis, MN 55401
Phone: 800-328-8226
Web: http://www.nspco.com

Company Description

Assets: US$6,636,900,000
Profit: US$275,800,000
Employees: 7,147
SIC(s): 4931 Electric & Other Services Combined, 4932 Gas & Other Services Combined.

Nonmonetary Support

Value: $550,000 (1995); $1,320,000 (1993); $485,000 (1991)
Type: Donated Equipment; In-kind Services; Loaned Executives

Giving Contact

Gaye D. Melton, Program Officer
Phone: (612)330-7701
Fax: (612)330-6947
Email: gaye.melton@nespco.com

Alternate Contact

Phone: (612)330-6933

Description

Organization Type: Corporate Giving Program
Giving Locations: near headquarters and service areas only.
Grant Types: Capital, Employee Matching Gifts, General Support, Project.
Note: Employee matching gift ratio: 1 to 1 to education, public broadcasting, and the Minnesota Foodshare Program.

Giving Philosophy

'In the past, we supported efforts that addressed the needs, problems, and deficiencies of people. We now believe that positive, long-term change is more likely to occur by focusing on the assets, skills and capabilities of individuals, families, and neighborhoods in order to build healthy, viable, strong communities. All individuals, regardless of their challenges, have capabilities and assets that can be mobilized to create ever-stronger communities.'
'We are interested in supporting efforts that recognize and build upon the existing strengths of people and communities. In a community whose assets are being fully recognized and mobilized, all of us can become contributors to the human capacity-building process.'
'NSP wants to support groups with the drive, energy, and vision to strive for and accomplish the betterment of our communities for this and future generations.'
'We are interested in projects that empower youth, adults, families, and neighborhoods to maximize their own skills and resources to address commonly-held problems or to build further on their current capabilities.' *Building Our Communities* Northern States Power Company's community report.

Financial Summary

Total Giving: $5,005,208 (1998); $4,898,627 (1997); $4,750,615 (1996). Note: Contributes through corporate direct giving program only. Giving includes corporate direct giving; domestic subsidiaries; matching gifts. 1997 Giving includes matching gifts ($160,007).
Giving Analysis: Giving for 1998 includes: corporate direct giving ($5,005,208)

Typical Recipients

Arts & Humanities: Arts Centers, Arts Funds, Arts Institutes, Community Arts, Ethnic & Folk Arts, History & Archaeology, Libraries, Museums/Galleries, Music, Opera, Performing Arts, Public Broadcasting, Theater
Civic & Public Affairs: Botanical Gardens/Parks, Employment/Job Training, Hispanic Affairs, Housing, Legal Aid, Municipalities/Towns, Native American Affairs, Nonprofit Management, Parades/Festivals, Safety, Urban & Community Affairs, Women's Affairs, Zoos/Aquariums
Education: Afterschool/Enrichment Programs, Business Education, Colleges & Universities, Community & Junior Colleges, Education Reform, Elementary Education (Public), Legal Education, Minority Education, Preschool Education, Student Aid
Environment: Environment-General, Wildlife Protection
Health: AIDS/HIV, Cancer, Clinics/Medical Centers, Health Organizations, Hospitals, Mental Health, Nursing Services, Single-Disease Health Associations
Religion: Religious Welfare
Social Services: Child Welfare, Community Centers, Community Service Organizations, Counseling, Day Care, Delinquency & Criminal Rehabilitation, Domestic Violence, Emergency Relief, Family Services, Food/Clothing Distribution, Homes, People with Disabilities, Refugee Assistance, Senior Services, Shelters/Homelessness, Substance Abuse, United Funds/ United Ways, Volunteer Services, Youth Organizations

Contributions Analysis

Giving Priorities: Supports programs that are committed to strengthening communities through service to individuals, families, and neighborhoods.
Arts & Humanities: 8%. Contributions provide opportunities for all individuals and families to learn and grow from the arts. Supports a broad spectrum of cultural activities, including theater, dance, music and arts organizations. Historic preservation and museums also supported. Emphasis on programs designed to increase accessibility to community performances for special populations.
Civic & Public Affairs: 35%. Contributions build stronger neighborhoods by providing opportunities for members of the community to rebuild their neighborhoods. Interests include urban and community affairs. 10% to 15%. Generally smaller grants made at the local level. Priorities will vary according to community needs.
Education: 14%. Contributes to education-focused programs to provide access to life-long learning, and opportunities for youth and adults to become contributing members of the workforce. Primarily supports post-secondary scholarship and financial assistance programs for low-income groups, minorities, and women. Emphasis onlearning-disabled children and adults. Capital grants awarded to higher education institutions. Also sponsors matching gifts program in education.
Social Services: 31%. Contributions focus on building the capacity of families and individuals of all ages to become stronger, more independent and self sufficient members in the community. Major support for programs that remove barriers for the economically or socially disadvantaged, including social services to special population groups; employment assistance; and short-term and crisis assistance programs such as food shelves, battered women's shelters, and crisis nurseries. Youth organizations, community centers, and organizations concerned with the elderly are also supported, as well as health care for under-served population groups.

Application Procedures

Initial Contact: brief letter of inquiry, and request for a grant application form
Application Requirements: NSP Grant application form or Minnesota Common Grant Application Form, a description of organization and its purpose, objectives of program to be funded, how objectives will be achieved, intended beneficiaries of program and how they will be involved, total amount needed, anticipated amount of request, method of evaluation, how project will strengthen organization, list of Board of Directors, letter from other groups working on project outlining how you will work together, audited financial report, organizational and project budgets, list of major donors including amounts pledged, proof of tax-exempt status
Deadlines: None.
Review Process: corporate contributions staff studies and evaluates proposals, then submits qualified grant requests to contributions committee
Evaluative Criteria: proposed program meets NSP's primary objective to provide access to opportunity for the disadvantaged, and programs that are involved in enhancing the quality of life for citizens within NSP's service area; how amount of funding requested relates to total need; organization's track record of success, stability, and sound management of human and financial resources; need for program or services; services target the cause of a problem or its effects; other organizations in same geographical area offering same services; community support and involvement; organization coordinates and works cooperatively with other agencies; organization's ability to evaluate and measure success of programs of programs
Decision Notification: applicants will be notified upon receipt of proposal, decisions generally take three to four months

Restrictions

Company does not support national organizations; research programs; endowments; multi-year pledges; religious, political, or fraternal organizations, except for programs for the direct benefit of the community; government agencies; individuals; travel, fund-raising activities, meetings, dinners, special events, conferences, or seminars; advertisements; agencies/programs receiving more than 50% of budget from United Way; disease-specific organizations; sports and athletic programs, capital projects of tax-supported institutions or bodies of government, or groups outside service area.
Applicants must be nonprofit, tax exempt organizations.

Additional Information

Within one year of receiving grant payment, recipient must submit report detailing the expenditures and results of project.
Addresses and names of the appropriate contact persons are contained in the company's funding guidelines.
First time grants are usually between $1,000 and $5,000.
Publications: Funding Guidelines; Application Form; Corporate Contributions Annual Report

Corporate Officials

James Joseph Howard, III: chairman, president, chief executive officer, director B Pittsburgh, PA 1935. ED University of Pittsburgh BBA (1957); Massachusetts Institute of Technology MS (1970). PRIM CORP EMPL chairman, president, chief executive officer, director: Northern States Power Co. CORP AFFIL director: Walgreen Co.; director: Honeywell Inc.; director: ReliaStar Financial Corp.; director: Federal Reserve Bank Minneapolis; director: Ameritech

Corp.; director: Ecolab Inc. NONPR AFFIL member: Nuclear Energy Institute; board trustee: University Saint Thomas; director: Electric Power Research Institute; member: Conference Board New York; director: Edison Electric Institute.

Tom Micheletti: vice president public & government affairs PRIM CORP EMPL vice president public & government affairs: Northern States Power Co.

Giving Program Officials

Linda J. Granoien: (see above)
James Joseph Howard, III: director (see above)
Tom Micheletti: (see above)

Grants Analysis

Disclosure Period: calendar year ending 1998
Total Grants: $5,005,208
Number of Grants: 1,007 (approx)
Average Grant: $4,970
Typical Range: $500 to $1,000 and $10,000 to $20,000

Recent Grants

Note: Grants derived from 1993 grants list.

Arts & Humanities

Augsburg College, Minneapolis, MN -- capital for library
Washington County Historic Courthouse, Stillwater, MN

Civic & Public Affairs

American Indian Opportunities Industrialization Center, Minneapolis, MN
Centro Legal, Minneapolis, MN
Crime Stoppers of Minnesota, Minneapolis, MN
Minnesota Council on Foundations, Minneapolis, MN
Native American Educational Services College, Minneapolis, MN
People for Parks, Minneapolis, MN
Pilot City Regional Center, Minneapolis, MN -- Juneteenth Celebration
Twin Cities Tree Trust, Saint Louis Park, MN

Education

Junior Achievement of the Upper Midwest, Minneapolis, MN
Learning Disabilities Association, Minneapolis, MN -- scholarship fund
Metropolitan State University, Saint Paul, MN -- student stipends program
Minneapolis Community College Foundation, Minneapolis, MN -- scholarships- Celebration of Diversity
Minnesota Academic Excellence Foundation, Saint Paul, MN
Minnesota Minority Education Partnership, Minneapolis, MN -- Full Circle
Minnesota Private College Fund, Saint Paul, MN -- need-based scholarships
A New Dimension Child Enrichment Center, Minneapolis, MN -- capital
Partners in Community Action, Minneapolis, MN -- capital grant for new Head Start facility in Brooklyn Park
St. Paul Public Schools, Saint Paul, MN -- Fresh Force Youth Community Service Learning and Leadership Program
William Mitchell College of Law, Saint Paul, MN -- minority scholarship program
YWCA of Minneapolis, Minneapolis, MN -- health and fitness scholarship program

Environment

Carpenter Nature Center, Hastings, MN -- wildlife rehabilitation program
Dodge Nature Center, West Saint Paul, MN -- environmental education program for K-6 students

Health

Alliance for the Mentally Ill of Minnesota, Saint Paul, MN
Alternatives for People with Autism, Brooklyn Park, MN
Archdiocesan AIDS Ministry Program, Minneapolis, MN -- emergency needs/relief fund
Community Clinic Consortium, Saint Paul, MN -- Community Health Fund
Hospitality House, Minneapolis, MN
Minnesota Medical Foundation Cancer Center, Minneapolis, MN
Southeast Seniors, Minneapolis, MN -- Living at Home/Block Nurse Program
Wayside House, Minneapolis, MN -- emergency medical assistance program

Religion

North Commons Day Shelter at St. Andrew's, Minneapolis, MN

Social Services

Alexandra House, Circle Pines, MN -- general operating/capital
Big Brothers and Big Sisters of Rice County, Faribault, MN
Boy Scouts of America Indianhead Council, Saint Paul, MN -- scouting for youth with special needs program
Capitol Community Services, Saint Paul, MN -- foodshelf
Care and Share Food Shelf, Minneapolis, MN
Children's Defense Fund, Saint Paul, MN
Committee Against Domestic Abuse, Mankato, MN -- Keep Me Safe Program
Community Action Council, Apple Valley, MN -- Emergency Services Program
Domestic Abuse Project, Minneapolis, MN -- legal and systems advocacy services
Emergency Foodshelf Network, Minneapolis, MN -- capital-equipment fund
FREE-Family Resource and Experience Exchange, Minneapolis, MN
Merrick Community Services, Saint Paul, MN -- foodshelf
Model Cities Family Development Center, Saint Paul, MN -- capital for expanded infant program
Neighbors, South Saint Paul, MN -- foodshelf
Stillwater Police Department, Stillwater, MN -- DARE (Drug Abuse Resistance Education)
YMCA Metropolitan Minneapolis, Minneapolis, MN -- youth development programs

NORTHERN TRUST CO.

Company Contact

Chicago, IL

Company Description

Income: US$200,390,000
Employees: 8,049 (1999)
SIC(s): 6022 State Commercial Banks.
Parent Company: Northern Trust Corp.

Operating Locations

Canada: Toronto; United Kingdom: London

Nonmonetary Support

Type: Cause-related Marketing & Promotion; Donated Equipment; In-kind Services; Loaned Executives

Corporate Sponsorship

Type: Arts & cultural events; Sports events
Contact: Susan Regan, Vice President, Corporate Affairs

Northern Trust Co. Charitable Trust

Giving Contact

Marjorie W. Lundy, Vice President, Community Affairs
Northern Trust Co. Charitable Trust
50 S. LaSalle Street, M-5
Chicago, IL 60675
Phone: (312)444-3538
Fax: (312)444-3108

Alternate Contact

Larry Wisniewski
Phone: (312)444-3533
Note: For information on the matching gift program.

Description

EIN: 366147253
Organization Type: Corporate Foundation
Giving Locations: IL: Chicago metropolitan area, with priority given to Cook County
Grant Types: Capital, Challenge, Employee Matching Gifts, General Support, Project, Seed Money.

Giving Philosophy

'Investing in Chicago is a tradition at The Northern Trust. This city has been good to us. Its prosperity has enabled us to grow and flourish. Accordingly, we feel a special responsibility to help improve the quality of life for all who live and work here.'
'Our giving program reflects a broad commitment to our community and a determination to maintain our reputation as a corporation that cares about people. Accordingly, our grantmaking is responsive to the needs of low and moderate income residents in Cook County, with particular attention to programs focused on early intervention and prevention, or designed to address systemic problems. Of equal priority are the major cultural, educational and health care institutions that help make Chicago a great city.' *Northern Trust Company Charitable Trust & Contributions Program*

Financial Summary

Total Giving: $2,500,000 (1998 approx); $2,117,712 (1997); $2,200,000 (1996). Note: Contributes through corporate direct giving program and foundation. 1997 Giving includes matching gifts ($574,039); United Way ($605,000). 1996 Giving includes foundation ($1,333,675); matching gifts ($506,251); United Way ($573,000).
Assets: $4,766 (1997); $34,835 (1996); $46,995 (1994)
Gifts Received: $2,079,258 (1997); $2,266,125 (1996); $2,240,025 (1994). Note: Contributions received from Northern Trust Bank.

Typical Recipients

Arts & Humanities: Arts Institutes, Dance, Museums/Galleries, Music, Opera, Performing Arts, Public Broadcasting, Theater
Civic & Public Affairs: African American Affairs, Business/Free Enterprise, Civil Rights, Economic Development, Employment/Job Training, Hispanic Affairs, Housing, Law & Justice, Public Policy, Urban & Community Affairs, Women's Affairs, Zoos/Aquariums
Education: Arts/Humanities Education, Colleges & Universities, Education Reform, Education-General, Literacy, Minority Education, Preschool Education, Private Education (Precollege), Public Education (Precollege), Special Education, Student Aid
Health: Adolescent Health Issues, AIDS/HIV, Children's Health/Hospitals, Clinics/Medical Centers, Health Organizations, Hospices, Hospitals, Medical Rehabilitation, Mental Health, Nutrition, Public Health, Research/Studies Institutes
Religion: Jewish Causes, Religious Welfare
Science: Observatories & Planetariums, Science Museums
Social Services: Child Welfare, Community Service Organizations, Day Care, Domestic Violence, Family Planning, Family Services, Food/Clothing Distribution, People with Disabilities, Recreation & Athletics, Sexual Abuse, Shelters/Homelessness, Substance Abuse, United Funds/United Ways, Volunteer Services, YMCA/YWCA/YMHA/YWHA, Youth Organizations

Contributions Analysis

Giving Priorities: United fund drives and Chicago youth organizations, Chicago colleges and universities, increased accessability to the arts, community revitalization, and health care cost containment.

Arts & Humanities: 4%. Giving is aimed at sustaining and enhancing well-established institutions and assisting smaller and newer groups. Priority is given to programs which reach out to the community, making cultural opportunities more accessible for hard-to-reach and disadvantaged populations.

Civic & Public Affairs: 19%. Supports projects designed to serve communities which have both limited local resources and the potential for significant development. Priority is given to programs which improve and increase affordable housing for low-income Cook County residents, and promote commercial and industrial development that creates and sustains jobs in low and moderate income neighborhoods.

Education: 4%. Contributes to higher education in the Chicago area, and nationally through the employee matching gifts program. Other priorities are groups which focus on prevention of school failure through early intervention, work to improve the Chicago public school system, and help the economically disadvantaged stay in school and further their education.

Health: 3%. Priority is given to programs which help the unemployed and underemployed break out of the cycle of poverty and public dependency; provide services to victims of domestic abuse; make primary health care services more accessible and affordable to low-income Cook County residents.

Social Services: 69%. Primary support for the United Way.

Note: Total contributions made in 1997.

Application Procedures

Initial Contact: Obtain application form by calling the trust.

Application Requirements: Completed application form; a 2-3 page proposal describing the program/project/activities to be funded, including purpose, timeline, expected outcomes and capacity to manage project (may omit if requesting general operating support); the agency's most recent annual report and informational brochure (include organizational history if new grantee); operating budget for current year, showing anticipated expenses and sources of income; project budget; financial statement; list of Chicago area corporate and foundation contributors and the amount each contributed in the last and current year; proof of 501 (c)(3) status; list of board members and their professional affiliations; list of management staff and their qualifications.

Deadlines: Proposals from major educational, health care and cultural institutions will be considered as received; all other contribution requests reviewed according to following schedule: community revitalization, December 1 and August 1; culture and arts, June 1; health and human services, February 1 and October 1; and education, April 1.

Decision Notification: Proposals are reviewed in the month following the deadlines.

Restrictions

Capital grants are not provided for universities or hospitals.

Does not support individuals, fraternal organizations, political activities, tickets or advertising for fundraising benefits, research, individual churches or sectarian organizations, or general operations of United Way agencies.

Trust does not make contributions to individual schools except for school-business partnerships. Grants are not made to single-disease health organizations. health organizations.

Corporate Officials

Perry R. Pero: senior executive vice president, chief financial officer B 1939. ED Clark University BA (1961); Harvard University MBA (1963). PRIM CORP EMPL senior executive vice president, chief financial officer: Northern Trust Co. ADD CORP EMPL officer: North Trust Global Advs.

Foundation Officials

Camille Fotopolous: member
John Fumagalli: member
Janet Gray: member
John Iwanicki: member
Steve Krause: member
Marjorie W. Lundy: secretary contributions committee PRIM CORP EMPL vice president: Northern Trust Co.
Loren Miller: member
William N. Setterstrom: chairman contributions committee B Brooklyn, NY 1942. ED Hobart College (1964). PRIM CORP EMPL senior vice president human resources: Northern Trust Co.

Grants Analysis

Disclosure Period: calendar year ending 1997
Total Grants: $1,439,273*
Number of Grants: 211
Average Grant: $6,822
Highest Grant: $25,000
Typical Range: $1,000 to $10,000
*Note: Giving excludes matching gifts; United Way.

Recent Grants

Note: Grants derived from 1997 Form 990.

Arts & Humanities

12,000 Orchestral Association, Chicago, IL -- first payment on a three-year, $36,000 grant for operating support
10,000 Art Institute, Chicago, IL -- second payment on a three-year, $30,000 grant for operating support
10,000 Lyric Opera, University Park, IL -- second payment on a three-year, $30,000 grant for operating support
7,500 WTTW/Chicago, Chicago, IL -- second payment on a three-year, $22,500 grant for operating support

Civic & Public Affairs

25,000 Neighborhood Housing Services, Chicago, IL -- second payment on a three-year, $75,000 grant for operating support
20,000 Local Initiatives Support Corporation, Highland Park, IL -- final payment on a three-year, $70,000 grant for community development projects
17,500 New Cities Community Development Corporation, Chicago, IL -- second payment on a three-year, $50,000 grant for operating support
15,000 National Training and Information Center, Chicago, IL -- second payment on a three-year, $45,000 grant for Chicago Neighborhood Revitalization project
15,000 Resurrection Project, Chicago, IL -- second payment on three-year, $45,000 grant in support of housing services
12,500 Chicago Association of Neighborhood Development Organizations, Chicago, IL -- second payment on a three-year, $37,500 grant for operating support
10,000 Dearborn Homes Community Development Corporation, Chicago, IL -- contribution for startup of micro-loan program
10,000 Designs for Change, Glenwood, IL -- operating support
10,000 Lakefront Single Room Occupancy Corporation, Chicago, IL -- second payment on a three-year, $30,000 grant for operating support
10,000 Roger Baldwin Foundation of American Civil Liberties Union, Chicago, IL -- children's and mental health initiatives
7,500 Chicago Roseland Coalition for Community Control, Chicago, IL -- housing initiatives
7,500 Greater North-Pulaski Development Corporation, Chicago, IL -- second payment on a three-year, $22,500 grant for operating support
7,500 Jobs for Youth, Chicago, IL -- final payment on a three-year, $22,500 grant for operating support
6,000 Chicago Urban League, Chicago, IL -- second payment on a three-year, $18,000 grant for operating support
5,000 Chicago Women in Trades, Chicago, IL -- FACT Program
5,000 Christmas in April, Chicago, IL -- operating support
5,000 Latino Institute, Chicago, IL -- education project

Education

10,000 Chicago Panel on School Policy, Chicago, IL -- operating support
6,125 Right Angle Educational Foundation, Chicago, IL -- Wells Academy scholarships
6,000 United Negro College Fund, Chicago, IL -- financial assistance for member schools
5,000 Chicago Communities in Schools, Chicago, IL -- second payment on a three-year, $15,000 grant for operating support
5,000 Hug-A-Book, Chicago, IL -- operating support
5,000 Scholarship and Guidance Association, Chicago, IL -- first payment on a three-year, $15,000 grant for school drop-out prevention program

Health

10,000 AIDS Foundation, Chicago, IL -- operating support
10,000 Erie Family Health Center, Chicago, IL -- second payment on a three-year, $30,000 grant for operating support
7,500 Larabida Children's Hospital, Chicago, IL -- first payment on a two-year, $15,000 grant for failure-to-thrive program

Religion

10,000 Lawndale Christian Development Corporation, Chicago, IL -- final payment on a three-year, $30,000 grant for operating support
8,000 Jewish United Fund, Chicago, IL -- operating support

Social Services

151,250 United Way Crusade of Mercy, Chicago, IL -- support of member agencies
151,250 United Way Crusade of Mercy, Chicago, IL -- support of member agencies
151,250 United Way Crusade of Mercy, Chicago, IL -- support of member agencies
151,250 United Way Crusade of Mercy, Des Plaines, IL -- support of member agencies
10,000 Erie Neighborhood House, Chicago, IL -- second payment on three-year, $30,000 grant for team tutoring program for Wells Academy students
10,000 Voices for Illinois Children, Westchester, IL -- final payment on a three-year, $30,000 grant for operating support
7,500 Chicago Rehabilitation Network, Chicago, IL -- housing initiatives
7,500 Rainbow House, Chicago, IL -- final payment on a three-year, $22,500 grant for operating support
7,500 Thresholds, Evanston, IL -- final payment on a three-year, $22,500 grant for operating support

6,000 Access Living, Chicago, IL -- final payment on a three-year, $18,000 grant for domestic violence and sexual assault program
5,000 Chicago Youth Success Foundation, Chicago, IL -- operating support
5,000 East Village Youth Program, Chicago, IL -- volunteer program
5,000 Esperanza Community Services, Chicago, IL -- first payment on a two-year, $10,000 grant for early intervention program adaptive playground
5,000 North Avenue Day Nursery, Chicago, IL -- early literacy project
5,000 Planned Parenthood Association, Chicago, IL -- linked services program in Englewood
5,000 Rape Victim Advocates, Chicago, IL -- operating support
5,000 Recording for the Blind and Dyslexic, Chicago, IL -- Chicago Public Schools project
5,000 Working in the Schools, Chicago, IL -- recruitment and training of volunteers

NORTHROP GRUMMAN CORP.

Company Contact

Los Angeles, CA
Web: http://www.northgrum.com

Company Description

Revenue: US$9,000,000,000 (1999)
Employees: 45,600 (1999)
Fortune Rank: 190, per FORTUNE Magazine's list of 500 Largest U.S. Corporations (1999).
FF 190
SIC(s): 3483 Ammunition Except for Small Arms, 3721 Aircraft, 3728 Aircraft Parts & Equipment Nec, 3812 Search & Navigation Equipment.

Nonmonetary Support

Type: Donated Equipment

Giving Contact

Cheryl Winn-Sanders, Community Relations
Northrop Grumman Corp.
1840 Century Park E
Los Angeles, CA 90067
Phone: (310)553-6262
Fax: (310)556-4510

Description

Organization Type: Corporate Giving Program
Giving Locations: emphasis on company plants and employee living areas.
Grant Types: Capital, General Support.

Financial Summary

Total Giving: $3,200,000 (1996 approx); $3,200,000 (1995 approx). Note: Contributes through corporate direct giving program only. Giving includes corporate direct giving; domestic subsidiaries.

Typical Recipients

Arts & Humanities: Arts & Humanities-General
Civic & Public Affairs: Civic & Public Affairs-General
Education: Education-General
Health: Health-General
Social Services: Social Services-General

Application Procedures

Initial Contact: a brief letter of inquiry
Application Requirements: a description of organization, amount requested, purpose of funds sought, scope of benefits of organization, sources of funding, audited financial statement, and proof of tax-exempt status
Deadlines: November 1 for consideration in the following year

Restrictions

Does not support individuals, religious organizations for sectarian purposes, or political or lobbying groups.

Additional Information

Publications: Program Guidelines

Corporate Officials

Kent Kresa: chairman, president, chief executive officer, director B New York, NY 1938. ED Massachusetts Institute of Technology BSAA (1959); Massachusetts Institute of Technology MSAA (1961); Massachusetts Institute of Technology EAA (1966). PRIM CORP EMPL chairman, president, chief executive officer, director: Northrop Grumman Corp. CORP AFFIL director: Atlantic Richfield Co.; director: Chrysler Corp. NONPR AFFIL member: Society Flight Test Engineers; director: John Tracy Clinic for the Hearing Impaired; member: Navy League; member (visiting committee): Massachusetts Institute Technology; member: Naval Aviation Museum Foundation; board governors: Los Angeles Music Center; member: Los Angeles World Affairs Council; member: DNA New Alternative Working Group; member: Defense Science Board; member: Department Aeronautics & Astronautics Corp.; member: Association U.S. Army; member: Chief Naval Operations Executive Panel Washington; fellow: American Institute Aeronautics & Astronautics; member: Aerospace Industries Association; member: American Defense Preparedness Association. CLUB AFFIL Los Angeles Country Club; National Space Club.

NORTHWEST AIRLINES, INC.

Company Contact

5101 Northwest Drive
St. Paul, MN 55111
Web: http://www.nwa.com

Company Description

Revenue: US$10,276,000,000 (1999)
Employees: 50,600
Fortune Rank: 165, per FORTUNE Magazine's list of 500 Largest U.S. Corporations (1999).
FF 165
SIC(s): 4512 Air Transportation--Scheduled, 6719 Holding Companies Nec.
Parent Company: NWA Inc.

Nonmonetary Support

Type: Cause-related Marketing & Promotion; Donated Products; In-kind Services
Note: Corporate giving is primarily in the form of airline tickets.

Corporate Sponsorship

Type: Arts & cultural events; Music & entertainment events; Sports events
Contact: Kevin Hoese, Manager, Sponsorship & Special Events

Giving Contact

Jane Eastlund, Manager, Community Relations
Northwest Airlines, Inc.
Dept. A1315
5101 Northwest Dr.
St. Paul, MN 55111-3034
Phone: (612)727-6797
Fax: (612)726-3942

Description

Organization Type: Corporate Giving Program
Note: The company awards trips.

Giving Philosophy

'During this time of unprecedented financial pressure on the airline industry, it is tempting to limit activities to only those that make an immediate and direct contribution to the bottom line.
'Northwest Airlines, Inc., however, refuses to take this short-sighted approach. We remain steadfastly committed to our goal of being 'an outstanding member of the communities we serve'. .. One example of this approach is the Northwest AirCares program, which taps Northwest resources in many areas to benefit a succession of worthwhile, charitable organizations.
'Through efforts such as these and many others, Northwest Airlines remains committed to becoming an industry leader in corporate citizenship and serving those less fortunate.'

Financial Summary

Total Giving: Contributes through corporate direct giving program only. Company does not disclose contributions figures.

Contributions Analysis

Giving Priorities: Company supports U.S. nonprofit organizations with an international focus, but does not publish information concerning activities. Generally, supports humanitarian activities in communities throughout its international routes. Company has supported International Special Olympics and Operation Smile International or World Plane, and Washington State/China Relations committee.

Application Procedures

Initial Contact: Contact co. for application information.

Additional Information

The AirCares program chooses one national or international nonprofit organization to assist through a major awareness, fund-raising and support campaign per quarter. To be considered as an AirCares Partner, nonprofits must be national or international in scope, not discriminate on the basis of gender, religion, race, or nationality, have 501(c)(3) status or the international equivalent, and operate within Northwest's route system. Organizations that focus on activities in regions of South America, India, Africa, or Eastern Europe are ineligible. Europe are ineligible.

Corporate Officials

Tom Bach: vice president revenue management and area marketing PRIM CORP EMPL vice president revenue management and area marketing: Northwest Airlines Inc. ADD CORP EMPL vice president: Northwest Airlines Corp.
James Cron: vice president planning & scheduling PRIM CORP EMPL vice president planning & scheduling: Northwest Airlines Inc.
John Parker: vice president information services PRIM CORP EMPL vice president information services: Northwest Airlines Inc.
Gary Lee Wilson: chairman, director B Alliance, OH 1940. ED Duke University BA (1962); University of Pennsylvania Wharton School MBA (1963). PRIM CORP EMPL chairman, director: Northwest Airlines, Inc. CORP AFFIL director: Walt Disney Co.; chairman: NWashington Inc.

Giving Program Officials

Christopher E. Clouser: B Saint Louis, MO 1952. ED University of Missouri (1972). PRIM CORP EMPL senior vice president administration: Northwest Airlines, Inc. CORP AFFIL director: Mesaba Holdings Inc. NONPR AFFIL member: International Association of Business Communications; member: Public Relations Society America; member: Advertising Council Inc.

Jane (Nachtigl) Eastlund: PRIM CORP EMPL manager community relations: Northwest Airlines, Inc.

NORTHWEST BANK NEBRASKA, NA

Company Contact

Omaha, NE

Company Description

Employees: 800
SIC(s): 6021 National Commercial Banks.
Parent Company: Norwest Corp., Minneapolis, MN, United States

Nonmonetary Support

Type: Cause-related Marketing & Promotion; Donated Equipment; In-kind Services; Loaned Employees; Loaned Executives

Corporate Sponsorship

Type: Arts & cultural events; Festivals/fairs
Note: Sponsors events and causes in Nebraska.

Giving Contact

Richard Schenck, Assistant Vice President & Director, Public Relations
Norwest Bank Nebraska, NA
1919 Douglas Street
PO Box 3408
Omaha, NE 68103
Phone: (402)536-2362

Description

Organization Type: Corporate Giving Program
Giving Locations: operating communities.
Grant Types: General Support.

Financial Summary

Total Giving: $650,000 (1998 approx); $600,000 (1996 approx); $625,000 (1995 approx). Note: Contributes through corporate direct giving program only.

Typical Recipients

Arts & Humanities: Arts Associations & Councils, Arts Festivals, Arts Funds, Community Arts, Dance, Libraries, Music, Performing Arts, Theater, Visual Arts
Civic & Public Affairs: Economic Development, Housing, Philanthropic Organizations, Zoos/Aquariums
Education: Agricultural Education, Colleges & Universities, Community & Junior Colleges, Education Funds, Elementary Education (Private), Public Education (Precollege), Religious Education
Health: Health Organizations, Mental Health, Public Health, Single-Disease Health Associations
Religion: Religious Welfare
Social Services: Child Welfare, Community Centers, Counseling, Family Planning, Food/Clothing Distribution, Homes, People with Disabilities, Recreation & Athletics, United Funds/United Ways, Youth Organizations

Contributions Analysis

Arts & Humanities: 10% to 15%. Contributes to theaters, arts festivals, ballet, symphonies, and arts centers.
Civic & Public Affairs: About 15%. Supports parades and community arts events. 5% to 10%. Primarily supports philanthropic associations and economic development.
Education: 20% to 25%. Supports colleges and universities, public high schools, education foundations, religious colleges, and Junior Achievement programs.
Social Services: 40% to 45%. Majority of funds support United Way agencies throughout Nebraska. Also supports religious organizations, community service organizations, scouting, and other youth organizations, Planned Parenthood, and community centers.

Application Procedures

Initial Contact: a brief letter of inquiry
Application Requirements: a description of organization; proof of tax-exempt status; list of officers and board members; statement outlining the purpose, including timeline and evaluation methods; complete budget for organization or project, including breakdown of programs and administrative expenses; list of contributors and amounts received in current and past year; and a financial statement
Deadlines: None.
Evaluative Criteria: organization's responsiveness to community, staff capability, financial management, commitment of board members and volunteers, performance against objectives, internal evaluation process, duplication with existing programs, and stability and range of funding sources
Decision Notification: board meets on the last Monday of each month; checks, requests for more information, or letters of refusal are sent within seven to 10 days after proposal is reviewed

Corporate Officials

Jane Braden: coordinator PRIM CORP EMPL coordinator: Norwest Bank of Nebraska.

Grants Analysis

Disclosure Period: calendar year ending

NORTHWEST NATURAL GAS CO.

Company Contact

Portland, OR
Web: http://www.nwnatural.com

Company Description

Assets: US$988,900,000
Employees: 1,304
SIC(s): 4924 Natural Gas Distribution.

Nonmonetary Support

Type: Donated Equipment; Donated Products; In-kind Services; Loaned Employees; Loaned Executives

Corporate Sponsorship

Type: Arts & cultural events; Music & entertainment events; Festivals/fairs
Contact: Don Graham, Director, Public Affairs

Giving Contact

Marie Krasnow, Administrative Assistant
Northwest Natural Gas Co.
220 Northwest 2nd Avenue
Portland, OR 97209
Phone: (503)226-4211
Fax: (503)220-2584

Description

Organization Type: Corporate Giving Program
Giving Locations: headquarters and operating communities.
Grant Types: Capital, Employee Matching Gifts, General Support, Multiyear/Continuing Support, Operating Expenses, Project, Research, Scholarship, Seed Money.
Note: Employee matching gifts support the United Way.

Financial Summary

Total Giving: $500,000 (2000 approx); $500,000 (1999 approx); $500,000 (1998 approx). Note: Contributes through corporate direct giving program only.

Typical Recipients

Arts & Humanities: Arts Appreciation, Arts Associations & Councils, Arts Centers, Arts Festivals, Arts Funds, Arts Institutes, Community Arts, Dance, Ethnic & Folk Arts, Arts & Humanities-General, Historic Preservation, Libraries, Museums/Galleries, Music, Opera, Performing Arts, Public Broadcasting, Theater, Visual Arts
Civic & Public Affairs: Economic Development, Civic & Public Affairs-General, Housing, Professional & Trade Associations, Urban & Community Affairs, Women's Affairs, Zoos/Aquariums
Education: Business Education, Colleges & Universities, Elementary Education (Private), Education-General, Minority Education
Health: Health-General, Health Organizations, Hospices, Hospitals, Medical Rehabilitation, Mental Health, Single-Disease Health Associations
Science: Science Exhibits & Fairs
Social Services: Animal Protection, Child Welfare, Community Centers, Counseling, Day Care, Delinquency & Criminal Rehabilitation, Food/Clothing Distribution, Homes, People with Disabilities, Senior Services, Shelters/Homelessness, Social Services-General, Substance Abuse, United Funds/United Ways, Volunteer Services, Youth Organizations

Contributions Analysis

Arts & Humanities: About 5%. Supports arts centers and funds, museums, music, performing arts, and visual arts.
Civic & Public Affairs: (United Funds & United Way) About 45% of total funding. Primary means for disbursement of funds. Also funded by employee matching gifts. 5% to 10%. Funding goes to economic development, housing, urban and community affairs, environmental concerns, and women's affairs. 5% to 10%. Supports community needs and concerns.
Education: 10% to 15%. Primary support goes to business education, colleges and universities, elementary education, and minority education.
Health: 10% to 15%. Supports hospices and hospitals, medical rehabilitation, mental health, the aged, child welfare, community centers, the disabled, food and clothing distribution, and traditional youth groups.

Application Procedures

Initial Contact: A brief letter of inquiry and a full proposal.
Application Requirements: Description of organization, amount requested, purpose of funds sought, and proof of tax-exempt status
Deadlines: None.

Restrictions

Does not support individuals, religious organizations for sectarian purposes, or political or lobbying groups. Company will not accept proposals from organizations outside of company service areas.

Additional Information

The company gives to the Oregon Community Foundation, who in turn re-grants to nonprofit organizations.

Corporate Officials

Gregg Kantor: vice president contributions PRIM CORP EMPL vice president: Northwest Natural Gas Co.
George E. Richardson, Jr.: chairman contributions PRIM CORP EMPL chairman contributions: Northwest Natural Gas Co.
Robert Louis Ridgley: chairman, director B Fort Wayne, IN 1934. ED Cornell University AB (1956); Harvard University JD (1959). PRIM CORP EMPL chairman, director: Northwest Natural Gas Co. CORP AFFIL director: Kaiser Permanente Inc.

Grants Analysis

Disclosure Period: calendar year ending 2000
Total Grants: $500,000 (approx)

Typical Range: $500 to $5,000

Norton Co.

Company Contact

Worcester, MA

Company Description

Employees: 12,058
SIC(s): 1389 Oil & Gas Field Services Nec, 2819 Industrial Inorganic Chemicals Nec, 3089 Plastics Products Nec, 3291 Abrasive Products.
Parent Company: Cie de Saint-Gobain SA

Operating Locations

AR: Norton-ALcoa Proppants, Fort Smith; Norton Co., Hot Springs; AZ: Norton Co., Scottsdale; CA: Penhall Diamond Products Co., Fullerton; Norton Performance Plastics Co., Quartz Hill; Norton Co., San Ramon; CT: Amplex/SGNIC, Bloomfield; Norton Co., Madison; IL: Halogen Insulator & Seal Corp., Elk Grove Village; IN: Norton Co., Indianapolis, Jasper; KY: Saint-Gobain Advanced Materials Corp., Louisville; LA: Norton Process Services, Baton Rouge; MA: Abrasives Marketing Group, Worcester; Advanced Ceramics, Worcester; Bonded Abrasives, Worcester; Consumer Products, Worcester; Norton Co., Worcester; Norton Co., Worcester; Norton Foreign Affiliates Holding Corp., Worcester; Norton International, Worcester; Norton Proppants, Worcester; Superabrasives and Construction Prods., Worcester; MI: Norton Co., Grand Rapids; NC: Norton Co., Arden, Greensboro; Carborundum Abrasives North America, High Point; NH: Norton Co., Littleton; Norton Pike Div., Littleton; Norton Co., Milford; NJ: CHEMPLAST, Wayne; Norton Performance Plastics, Wayne; NY: Norton Performance Plastics Co., Granville; Carborundum Corp., Niagara Falls; Clipper Abrasives, Niagara Falls; Coated Abrasives, Troy; Norton Co., Watervliet; OH: Norton Co., Akron, Hudson, Ravenna; Norton Performance Plastics Co., Ravenna; Norton Chemical Process Products Corp., Stow; PA: Pakco Industrial Ceramics, Latrobe; SC: Norton Co., Spartanburg; TN: Norton Co., Soddy Daisy; SCT B Inc., White House; TX: Norton Co., Brownsville, Bryan, Stephenville

Nonmonetary Support

Value: $10,500 (1988)
Type: Donated Products
Note: Company matches employee gifts 1 to 1 with a maximum of $2,000 annually for educational institutions, and $1,000 for charitable/cultural institutions.

Norton Co. Foundation

Giving Contact

Judith Cutts, Contributions Coordinator
Norton Co. Foundation
MS: 301-519
1 New Bond St.
PO Box 15138
Worcester, MA 01606
Phone: (508)795-2605
Fax: (508)795-2761

Description

Founded: 1953
EIN: 237423043
Organization Type: Corporate Foundation
Giving Locations: headquarters and operating communities.
Grant Types: Capital, Employee Matching Gifts, General Support, Multiyear/Continuing Support, Project.

Giving Philosophy

'Norton defines its mission as creating exceptional value for all its shareholders, including the people who live and work in the communities where Norton has plants. Norton's pledge to them is that the company will adhere to the highest ethical standards and be a responsible corporate citizen.. We believe that the health of the company and the health of our communities are intertwined. We encourage Norton people to be active, concerned participants in the life of the community, and we try to give something back to the people and places that have given us so much.' Norton Company Contributions Program

Financial Summary

Total Giving: $951,692 (1998); $1,046,202 (1997); $1,700,000 (1996). Note: Contributes through corporate direct giving program and foundation.
Giving Analysis: Giving for 1996 includes: foundation ($974,835); foundation matching gifts ($224,593); 1998: foundation ($449,531); foundation matching gifts ($257,501); foundation grants to United Way ($244,660)
Assets: $120 (1991)
Gifts Received: $951,692 (1998); $1,046,202 (1997); $1,148,372 (1995). Note: In 1998, contributions were received from Norton Company.

Typical Recipients

Arts & Humanities: Arts Appreciation, Arts Associations & Councils, Arts Centers, Arts Funds, Ballet, Community Arts, Dance, Ethnic & Folk Arts, Arts & Humanities-General, Historic Preservation, History & Archaeology, Libraries, Literary Arts, Museums/Galleries, Music, Opera, Performing Arts, Public Broadcasting, Theater, Visual Arts
Civic & Public Affairs: Botanical Gardens/Parks, Business/Free Enterprise, Civil Rights, Clubs, Community Foundations, Economic Development, Economic Policy, Employment/Job Training, Civic & Public Affairs-General, Hispanic Affairs, Legal Aid, Minority Business, Municipalities/Towns, Nonprofit Management, Parades/Festivals, Professional & Trade Associations, Public Policy, Rural Affairs, Safety, Urban & Community Affairs, Women's Affairs, Zoos/Aquariums
Education: Arts/Humanities Education, Business Education, Colleges & Universities, Community & Junior Colleges, Economic Education, Education Associations, Education Funds, Education Reform, Engineering/Technological Education, Faculty Development, Health & Physical Education, Literacy, Minority Education, Preschool Education, Private Education (Precollege), Public Education (Precollege), Science/Mathematics Education, Secondary Education (Private), Secondary Education (Public), Student Aid
Environment: Environment-General, Resource Conservation
Health: AIDS/HIV, Cancer, Children's Health/Hospitals, Clinics/Medical Centers, Clinics/Medical Centers, Emergency/Ambulance Services, Geriatric Health, Health Policy/Cost Containment, Health Organizations, Hospices, Hospitals, Medical Rehabilitation, Medical Research, Mental Health, Nursing Services, Nutrition, Prenatal Health Issues, Public Health, Single-Disease Health Associations
International: Foreign Arts Organizations, Foreign Educational Institutions, Health Care/Hospitals, International Development, International Organizations, International Relief Efforts
Religion: Churches, Religious Welfare
Science: Observatories & Planetariums, Science Exhibits & Fairs, Science Museums, Scientific Centers & Institutes, Scientific Organizations, Scientific Research
Social Services: Camps, Child Welfare, Community Centers, Community Service Organizations, Counseling, Delinquency & Criminal Rehabilitation, Domestic Violence, Emergency Relief, Family Planning, Family Services, Food/Clothing Distribution, Homes, People with Disabilities, Recreation & Athletics, Scouts, Senior Services, Sexual Abuse, Shelters/Homelessness, Social Services-General, Substance Abuse, United Funds/United Ways, Volunteer Services, YMCA/YWCA/YMHA/YWHA, Youth Organizations

Contributions Analysis

Giving Priorities: United funds; colleges and universities, mainly as matching gifts; various arts organizations through matching gifts; and civic and community activities.
Arts & Humanities: 8%. Recipients include historical preservation societies, arts centers, museums, public broadcasting stations, libraries, theaters, and community arts groups.
Civic & Public Affairs: 14%. Interests include safety, nonprofit management, providing housing to the homeless, and urban affairs. Also supports zoos and botanical gardens, job training, and community foundations.
Education: 17%. The majority of funds go to colleges and universities, and teaching programs for learning basic skills at primary and secondary levels. Other interests include arts, business, economic, public, religious, and secondary education.
Health: 1%. Supports various health interests, including hospices, emergency/ambulance services, and single-disease health organizations.
International: 3%.
Science: 2%. Supports science museums.
Social Services: 54%. Funds United Way and youth organizations.
Note: Contributions analysis reflects 1998 foundation excluding, matching gifts.

Application Procedures

Initial Contact: Submit a brief proposal letter to foundation.
Application Requirements: Include a description of organization and description of request, including evidence of the need to be met, implementation plan, and appropriateness of request; specific amount requested; timeline of project; list of other sources of support; copy of IRS letter indicating 501(c)(3) tax exemption; brief description of current operating budget for the requested project; copy of IRS Form 990; list of current corporate and foundation grants; and list of organization's board of directors and their affiliations.
Deadlines: None.
Review Process: Employee committees evaluate applicants and make recommendations to board of trustees.

Restrictions

Support is ordinarily restricted to communities where Norton has plant facilities and to programs that demonstrate ability to have a significant impact on the need being addressed over a significant period of time.
Foundation does not make contributions to individuals; political candidates; national organizations (including health agencies); a single sectarian or denominational religious, veteran, or fraternal organization (unless for a specific project that benefits the community); fund-raising dinners and events, or courtesy or journal advertising for nonprofit groups (unless there is a direct community relations benefit to Norton Company); large hospitals; capital/endowment drive unless an institution makes extraordinary contributions to Norton communities or to Norton Company; to any project for which Norton is the only donor; or programs receiving United Way support in locations where Norton makes an annual contribution to the United Way.

Additional Information

Each Norton location has a contributions budget and annually identifies one or two priorities in that community for special emphasis. You may approach local operations for contributions. Their priorities vary and may not be reflected in information listed above.

Publications: Guidelines

Corporate Officials

Gianpaolo Caccini: chairman, chief executive officer, directorbch ED University of Pavia PhD. PRIM CORP EMPL chairman, chief executive officer, director: CertainTeed Corp. CORP AFFIL chairman: Norton Co.; president: Saint-Gobain Corp.

Pierre-Andre de Chalendar: president abrasives branch PRIM CORP EMPL president abrasives branch: Saint-Gobain NA.

Foundation Officials

Lloyd Ambler: vice president, director PRIM CORP EMPL vice president, director: CertainTeed Corp.

Robert C. Ayotte: vice president, director B 1939. ED Harvard University Graduate School of Business Administration PMD; University of Rhode Island BS (1959). PRIM CORP EMPL executive vice president, director: CertainTeed Corp. CORP AFFIL president: Saint-Gobain Advanced Materials Corp.; president: Saint-Gobain Industrial Ceramics; president: Norton Performance Plastics; president: Carborundum Specialty Products; chairman: Norton Chemical Process Products Corp.

Dennis J. Baker: vice president, director PRIM CORP EMPL vice president, director: CertainTeed Corp.

Gianpaolo Caccini: president, director (see above)

Thomas Milton Landin: vice president B Bradford, PA 1937. ED Grove City College BS (1959); University of Denver JD (1967). PRIM CORP EMPL vice president, director: CertainTeed Corp. PRIM NONPR EMPL former vp (govt & pub aff): SmithKline Beecham. NONPR AFFIL member: Washington DC Bar Association; director: YMCA Greater Philadelphia; director: Manufacturer Association Delaware Valley; director: Public Affairs Council; trustee: Caribbean/Latin American Action; director: Citizens Crime Commission; director: American Music Theatre Festival; member: American Bar Association. CLUB AFFIL Vesper Club; Union League Club Philadelphia; Capital Hill Club; Georgetown Club; Army-Navy Country Club.

John P. Milulak: vice president, director

Thomas G. Rinisky: vice president, director

Dorothy C. Wackerman: secretary, clerk, director

Grants Analysis

Disclosure Period: calendar year ending 1997
Total Grants: $449,531*
Number of Grants: 323
Average Grant: $1,392
Highest Grant: $50,000
Typical Range: $100 to $5,000
***Note:** Giving excludes matching gifts; United Way.

Recent Grants

Note: Grants derived from 1998 Form 990.

Arts & Humanities

30,000	WPI, Worcester, MA
3,000	Mechanics Hall of Worcester, Worcester, MA
2,500	Music Worcester, Inc., Worcester, MA
2,500	Worcester Historical Museum, Worcester, MA
2,500	Worcester Historical Museum, Worcester, MA
2,000	Rio Grande Valley Ballet, McAllen, TX
1,800	East Granby Public Library, East Granby, CT

Civic & Public Affairs

50,000	Massachusetts Job Training, Worcester, MA
10,000	Massachusetts Job Training, Inc., Worcester, MA
2,500	Leprechaun Foundation, Inc., North Olmsted, OH
2,500	Seven Hills Foundation, Worcester, MA
2,000	Greater Louisville Economic Development Partnership, Louisville, KY
2,000	Junior League of Worcester, Worcester, MA
2,000	La Feria Economic Development Corporation, La Feria, TX
2,000	Roswell Park Alliance Foundation, Buffalo, NY
1,730	Watervliet Civic Chest, Watervliet, NY

Education

50,000	Rutgers University Foundation, New Brunswick, NJ
10,000	Alfred University, Alfred, NY
10,000	UMass Memorial Foundation, Worcester, MA
7,500	University of Texas at Brownsville, Brownsville, TX
4,000	The MLK, Jr. Business Empowerment Center, Worcester, MA
4,000	Upshur County Schools, Buckhannon, WV
3,000	Kent State University Foundation, Inc., Kent, OH
2,500	Abby Kelley Foster Regional Charter School, Worcester, MA
2,000	Memorial High School, McAllen, TX
2,000	Union Hill School, Worcester, MA

Health

2,500	Open Door Maternity Home, Inc., Wickliffe, OH
2,000	Mount St. Mary's Hospital, Lewiston, NY
2,000	Niagara Falls Memorial Medical Center, Niagara Falls, NY

International

10,000	The American Hospital of Paris Foundation, New York, NY
5,000	Institute for International Economics, Washington, DC

Religion

2,000	St. John's Episcopal Church, Worcester, MA

Science

9,000	Louisville Science Center, Louisville, KY
4,000	The Great Lakes Museum of Science, Environment and Technology, Cleveland, OH

Social Services

220,000	United Way of Central Massachusetts, Worcester, MA
25,000	YMCA of Greater Worcester, Worcester, MA
10,000	YMCA of Greater Worcester, Worcester, MA
8,000	Friendly House, Inc., Worcester, MA
7,830	Metro United Way, Louisville, KY
5,000	YouthNet, Worcester, MA
4,000	United Way of Niagara, Niagara Falls, NY
2,790	United Way of Asheville & Buncombe Cnty., Asheville, NC
2,500	Town Boys & Girls Club, Buffalo, NY
2,500	Youth Opportunities Upheld, Inc., Worcester, MA
2,340	Still Creek Boys Ranch, Bryan, TX
2,250	United Way of Hall County, Gainesville, GA
2,010	Food Bank of the Rio Grande Valley, Inc., McAllen, TX
2,010	Rio Grande Children's Home, Mission, TX
1,750	United Way of Westmoreland Country, Greensburg, PA
1,500	Youth Opportunities Upheld, Inc., Worcester, MA

NORWEST CORP.

Company Contact

Minneapolis, MN
Web: http://www.norwest.com

Company Description

Assets: US$80,175,400,000
Profit: US$956,000,000
Employees: 53,369
SIC(s): 6021 National Commercial Banks, 6022 State Commercial Banks, 6091 Nondeposit Trust Facilities, 6712 Bank Holding Companies.

Operating Locations

Argentina: Buenos Aires; Brazil: Sao Paulo; Chile: Santiago; Hong Kong; Mexico: Mexico City

Nonmonetary Support

Value: $400,000 (1987)

Corporate Sponsorship

Type: Arts & cultural events; Festivals/fairs; Music & entertainment events; Sports events
Contact: Michael Nolan, Director, Public Affairs & Special Events
Note: Sponsors events relating to the market.

Norwest Foundation

Giving Contact

Caroline Roby, Program Manager
Norwest Foundation
Norwest Ctr.
6th & Marquette
Minneapolis, MN 55479-1055
Phone: (612)667-7860
Fax: (612)667-8283

Description

EIN: 411367441
Organization Type: Corporate Foundation
Giving Locations: AZ; CO; IL; IN; IA; MN; MT; NE; NV; NM; ND; OH; SD; TX; WI; WY
Grant Types: Capital, Employee Matching Gifts, General Support, Multiyear/Continuing Support, Operating Expenses, Project.

Giving Philosophy

'The bank, as an independent, private, for-profit institution, has a symbiotic relationship with the community it serves in that the health of one affects the health of the other. The contributions program is part of a variety of services that the bank has established to ensure that the community remains in a state of good health. A strong community provides an environment that improves the quality of life for employees, attracts new businesses, and encourages the expansion of existing businesses. It is in the bank's self-interest to support the community, and one of the ways of doing that is through an enlightened corporate contributions program. Therefore, the first priority of the contributions program is to assist in enhancing the quality of life in the communities the bank serves.' Contributions Guidelines and Procedures, Norwest Corporation

Financial Summary

Total Giving: $13,354,884 (1996); $16,000,000 (1995 approx); $9,606,776 (1994). Note: Contributes through corporate direct giving program and foundation. 1996 Giving includes foundation ($9,825,849); matching gifts ($353,757); United Way ($3,175,278).
Assets: $81,484,084 (1996); $77,181,700 (1995); $83,163,326 (1994)
Gifts Received: $21,803,778 (1994); $69,838,480 (1993); $21,095,974 (1992). Note: Foundation received gifts from Norwest Equity Capital, Inc., and Norwest Growth Fund.

Typical Recipients

Arts & Humanities: Arts Associations & Councils, Arts Centers, Arts Funds, Arts Institutes, Ethnic & Folk Arts, Arts & Humanities-General, Historic Preservation, History & Archaeology, Libraries, Museums/Galleries, Music, Opera, Public Broadcasting, Theater
Civic & Public Affairs: African American Affairs, Asian American Affairs, Botanical Gardens/Parks, Chambers of Commerce, Economic Development, Employment/Job Training, Housing, Law & Justice, Legal Aid, Municipalities/Towns, Native American Affairs, Nonprofit Management, Philanthropic Organizations, Public Policy, Urban & Community Affairs, Women's Affairs, Zoos/Aquariums
Education: Agricultural Education, Business Education, Colleges & Universities, Community & Junior Colleges, Continuing Education, Education Funds, Engineering/Technological Education, Education-General, Minority Education, Public Education (Precollege), Student Aid
Environment: Air/Water Quality
Health: Cancer, Clinics/Medical Centers, Emergency/Ambulance Services, Hospitals, Medical Rehabilitation
Religion: Religious Welfare
Science: Science Museums, Scientific Research
Social Services: At-Risk Youth, Child Welfare, Community Centers, Community Service Organizations, People with Disabilities, Recreation & Athletics, Substance Abuse, United Funds/United Ways, YMCA/YWCA/YMHA/YWHA, Youth Organizations

Contributions Analysis

Giving Priorities: United Way and traditional youth organizations, higher education institutions and funds, major and recently established arts organizations, and neighborhood and commercial revitalization.
Arts & Humanities: About 10%. Interests include the performing arts, cultural centers, museums, historic sites, public broadcasting organizations, and arts funds.
Civic & Public Affairs: 15% to 20%. Neighborhood and commercial revitalization projects receive special consideration. Most grants are made for economic development purposes. Also supports recreation, environmental affairs, zoos, housing, and community foundations.
Education: 25% to 30%. Primarily supports higher education, education funds and associations, and student aid. The bank's primary interestsin this area are improving the educational process and expanding educational opportunities for low-income and minority students. Consideration is given to programs that provide adult basic education and that enhance business administration and economic or other programs related to the banking industry. Support of public institutions is limited to programs not funded by public sources. Support for private institutions generally is channeled through education funds. Also sponsors educational matching grants program. To be considered for long-term or capital support, colleges and universities must prove academic excellence, make a substantialimpact in the bank's trade area, and demonstrate concern for the education of women and minorities.
Health: About 40%. Majority of funding supports the United Way. Other social service interests include traditional youth organizations, nursing homes, community and senior centers, children's and family services, family planning agencies, and community services. The bank gives special consideration to programs that aid low-income people and neighborhoods, minorities, and women. Health interests include hospitals, single-disease health associations, and pediatric health.

Application Procedures

Initial Contact: organizations serving a specific neighborhood or city should apply directly to the nearest Norwest affiliate in that area; those serving the seven-county Minneapolis-St. Paul area should apply to Norwest Foundation-Metro; and those serving the state of Minnesota, the Upper Midwest region, should apply to Diane P. Lilly, President of the Norwest Foundation
Application Requirements: name of organization, including contact, address, and phone number; a description of organization, including any special population or geographic areas served; amount requested; statement outlining use of funds; budgets for organization and proposed project; list of officers and board members; list of contributors and amounts received; most recent audited financial statement; proof of tax-exempt status
Deadlines: None.
Review Process: staff of the foundation reviews and researches each request, then refers it to the appropriate committee for decision
Evaluative Criteria: program responsiveness to community, staff capability, sound fiscal management; board of directors with policy-making authority and reflecting organization's constituencies; commitment of board members and volunteers; performance against objectives; method to evaluate project results; lack of unnecessary duplication of similar projects; organization's plan for ongoing funding; geographic location of organization
Decision Notification: foundation decides at board meetings in March, June, September, and December; subsidiaries' schedules vary

Restrictions

The foundation does not award grants to organizations for greater than 10% of the contributions budget except to United Way.
The foundation generally does not support for religious organizations for religious purposes; political campaigns; organizations designed primarily for lobbying; or individuals.

Additional Information

Norwest Corporation and Norwest Foundation operate a highly decentralized giving program, in which the parent company, the foundation, and numerous banking subsidiaries throughout the country provide grants to qualified recipients in the communities in which the Norwest entities are located. Applicants are advised to target their inquiries to the nearest local Norwest bank for fastest turnaround. If you are unsure about which subsidiary to contact, call the foundation for assistance; the foundation will direct you to the appropriate subsidiary in your project's area.
The Norwest Foundation giving committee exercises control primarily over giving in the Twin Cities area of Minnesota. The foundation also acts as the repository of all contributions data for the parent company and its subsidiaries.
United Banks of Colorado merged into Norwest Corporation in April 1991, and, in April 1992, changed their name to Norwest Bank Colorado. The giving program for Norwest Bank Colorado and Norwest Bank Denver (formerly United Bank of Denver) are now contained within that of the parent company, Norwest Corporation and its foundation, Norwest Foundation.
Publications: Guidelines

Corporate Officials

Richard M. Kovacevich: chairman, president, chief executive officer B Tacoma, WA 1943. ED Stanford University BS (1965); Stanford University MBA (1967). PRIM CORP EMPL chairman, president, chief executive officer: Norwest Corp. ADD CORP EMPL president: Anfed Financial Inc.; president: Wells Fargo Bank NA. CORP AFFIL director: Northern Studies Power Co.; director: PetSmart Inc.; director: Cargill Inc.; director: Dayton Hudson Corp.
Diane P. Lilly: vice president PRIM CORP EMPL vice president: Norwest Corp.
Stanley Stephenson Stroup: executive vice president, general counsel B Los Angeles, CA 1944. ED University of Illinois BA (1966); University of Michigan JD (1969). PRIM CORP EMPL executive vice president, general counsel: Norwest Corp. CORP AFFIL director: Norwest Financial Service; executive vice president: Amfed Financial Inc.; vice president, director: GST Inc. NONPR AFFIL member adj faculty: William Mitchell of College Law; member: Regulatory Affairs Council; member: Minnesota Bar Association; member: California Bar Association; member: Illinois Bar Association; member: American Bar Association; member: Bank Administration Institute.
John T. Thornton: executive vice president, chief financial officer B New York, NY 1937. ED Saint John's University BBA (1959); Saint John's University JD (1972). PRIM CORP EMPL executive vice president, chief financial officer: Norwest Corp. CORP AFFIL chief executive officer, director: Norwest Nova Inc.; director: Norwest Venture Capital Management Inc.; director: Norwest Bank Minnesota NA; chief executive officer, director: Norwest Ltd. Inc.

Foundation Officials

Pat Donovan: director
Richard M. Kovacevich: director (see above)
Diane P. Lilly: president, director (see above)
Bruce Moland: secretary
Carolyn H. Roby: assistant secretary, assistant treasurer, program manager
John T. Thornton: treasurer (see above)

Grants Analysis

Disclosure Period: calendar year ending 1996
Total Grants: $9,825,849*
Number of Grants: 3,740
Average Grant: $2,627
Highest Grant: $178,995
Typical Range: $1,000 to $10,000
***Note:** Giving excludes matching gifts; United Way.

Recent Grants

Note: Grants derived from 1996 Form 990.

Arts & Humanities

110,667	Twin Citites Public Television, Saint Paul, MN
100,000	South Dakota Hall of Fame, Fort Pierre, SD
100,000	Twin Cities Public Television, Saint Paul, MN
100,000	Twin Citites Public Television, Saint Paul, MN
75,000	Twin Citites Public Television, Saint Paul, MN
75,000	Twin Citites Public Television, Saint Paul, MN
75,000	Twin Citites Public Television, Saint Paul, MN
51,785	Friends of the St. Paul Public Library, Saint Paul, MN

Civic & Public Affairs

75,000	Norwest Housing Foundation, Des Moines, IA
60,000	Ramsey Action Program, Saint Paul, MN
55,000	Home Ownership Center, Saint Paul, MN
50,000	Milestone Growth Fund, Minneapolis, MN
50,000	Minneapolis Foundation, Minneapolis, MN
50,000	Rejuvenate Davenport, Davenport, IA
41,450	Brush Up Iowa, Des Moines, IA
40,900	Minnesota Lawyer Trust Account Board, Minneapolis, MN
37,000	Twin Cities Neighborhood Housing Services, Saint Paul, MN

Education

178,995	Citizens Scholarship Foundation of America, Saint Peter, MN

100,000 Carleton College, Northfield, MN
100,000 Colorado State University Fort Collins, Fort Collins, CO
54,000 Augusta College Sioux Falls, Sioux Falls, SD
50,000 Colorado Scholarship Coalition, Denver, CO
50,000 St. Mary's University San Antonio, San Antonio, TX
50,000 University of Minnesota Carlson School of Management, Minneapolis, MN
41,750 Minnesota Private College Fund, Saint Paul, MN
40,000 United Negro College Fund, Minneapolis, MN
37,500 Drake University, Des Moines, IA
37,500 Minnesota Private College Fund, Saint Paul, MN
37,000 Montana State University Foundation, Bozeman, MT

Social Services
410,250 United Way, Minneapolis, MN
410,250 United Way, Minneapolis, MN
195,000 United Way, Des Moines, IA
160,417 United Way, Des Moines, IA
107,625 United Way, Denver, CO
107,625 United Way, Denver, CO
107,625 United Way, Des Moines, IA
100,000 United Way, Omaha, NE
96,000 United Way, Saint Paul, MN
92,000 United Way, Saint Paul, MN
72,975 United Way, Sioux Falls, IA
65,000 United Way Quad Cities, Rock Island, IL
61,000 United Way Valley Sun, Phoenix, AZ
61,000 United Way Valley Sun, Phoenix, AZ
60,000 YWCA, Minneapolis, MN
53,000 United Way, Albuquerque, NM
50,000 YMCA, Minneapolis, MN
45,000 United Way, Des Moines, IA
42,560 United Way, Sioux City, NM
40,000 Sabathani Community Center, Minneapolis, MN
37,000 Sharing Caring Hands, Minneapolis, MN

NOVARTIS CORPORATION

Company Contact
564 Morris Ave.
Summit, NJ 07901
Web: http://www.us.novartis.com

Company Description
Former Name: CIBA-GEIGY Corp.
Employees: 17,000
SIC(s): 2834 Pharmaceutical Preparations, 2861 Gum & Wood Chemicals, 2869 Industrial Organic Chemicals Nec, 2879 Agricultural Chemicals Nec.
Parent Company: Novartis International AG, Lichtstrasse 35, Basel, Switzerland

Operating Locations
AL: Novartis; CA: Novartis; Biocine Co., Emeryville; Chiron Diagnostics, Emeryville; Ciba Corning Diagnostics Corp., Irvine; Biotrack, Mountain View; Ciba Corning Diagnostics Corp., Palo Alto; CO: Novartis; Geneva Pharmaceuticals, Broomfield; DC: Novartis; FL: Novartis; GA: Novartis; CIBA Vision Corp., Duluth; CIBA Vision Group Management, Duluth; MA: Novartis; Ciba Corning Diagnostics Corp., East Walpole, Medfield; MD: Genetic Therapy, Gaithersburg; MI: Novartis; CIGA-GEIGY Corp. Formulated Systems Group (Automotive Center), Madison Heights; NC: Novartis; CIBA Seeds, Greensboro; NJ: Novartis; CIBA Self-Medication, Woodbridge; NY: Novartis, Ardsley; CIBA-GEIGY Pharmaceutical Production, Suffern; OH: Novartis; Ciba Corning Diagnostics Corp., Oberlin; WA: Novartis

Nonmonetary Support
Type: Donated Equipment; Donated Products; In-kind Services; Loaned Executives; Workplace Solicitation
Note: Contact: Office Operations Department for nonmonetary support.

Novartis US Foundation

Giving Contact
David French, Director
Novartis U.S. Foundation
564 Morris Avenue
A-2081
Summit, NJ 07901
Phone: (908)277-5850
Fax: (908)277-4680
Email: david.s1-french@pharma.novartis.com

Description
Organization Type: Corporate Foundation
Giving Locations: principally near operating locations and to national organizations.
Grant Types: Award, Employee Matching Gifts, General Support, Multiyear/Continuing Support.
Note: Employee matching gift ratio: 1 to 1.

Giving Philosophy
'The Novartis US foundation was established in 1997 as part of Novartis corporation's commitment to social investment. Its primary purpose is to support efforts among communities, businesses and nonprofit organizations on a range of social, health and educational issues related to Novartis' interests in the life sciences--healthcare, agribusiness and nutrition.'
'The Foundation's cornerstone is to encourage the advancement of the life sciences through effective education, and to help ensure that America's young people have the skills and support they need to lead healthy and productive lives, and to contribute to our shared future. Novartis firmly believes that these investments, to be truly effective, require coordinated and sustained action by private and public partnerships that are focused on common goals.'
'Generally, the Foundation's major initiative had two components. The first supports educational programs that advance the life sciences. The second seeks to assure that America's youth have access to the basic building blocks of development: caring adults, a healthy start, safe and structured learning activities during non-school hours, effective education for marketable skills, and opportunities to serve their communities.' Novartis Preliminary Grant Application

Financial Summary
Total Giving: $1,800,000 (fiscal year ending , 1999); $1,000,000 (fiscal 1998). Note: Contributes through foundation only.
Giving Analysis: Giving for fiscal 1998 includes: foundation ($625,000); foundation matching gifts ($375,000)

Typical Recipients
Education: Agricultural Education, Colleges & Universities, Engineering/Technological Education, Science/Mathematics Education, Vocational & Technical Education
Health: Nutrition

Contributions Analysis
Arts & Humanities: 20%. Provide funding for national and community based organizations such as the National Black Arts Festival, and community arts councils.
Civic & Public Affairs: 20%. Supports Chambers of Commerce.
Education: 20%. Supports the character Education Program, AgriScience computer laboratory, the Reading Connections Literacy program, the SEED Program, the South Louisiana School-to-Work Initiative, and scholarships and internships in the sciences.
Environment: 20%. Supports the Global Environmental Management Initiative, Renew America, Resources for the Future, and the World Environment Center.
Health: 20%.

Application Procedures
Initial Contact: request preliminary application form
Evaluative Criteria: Priority will be given to programs that target problems affecting large populations, or have potential for national replication.
Decision Notification: notification of request status within one month of receipt of application
Notes: Faxed applications are accepted.

Restrictions
The Foundation does not support religious organizations with a focus on religious programming/preference; individuals or political candidates; political organizations; social, labor, veterans, alumni or fraternal organizations; athletic organizations.

Additional Information
The Novartis US Foundation was formed in 1997 by the merger of the CIBA Educational Foundation and the Sandoz Foundation.

Corporate Officials
Jerry Putman: senior vice president

Giving Program Officials
David French: director
Sharon LeWinter: program officer

Foundation Officials
Douglas G. Watson: chairman PRIM CORP EMPL president, director: CIBA-GEIGY Corp. Pharmaceuticals Division. CORP AFFIL director: Engelhard Corp.; director: Geneva Pharmaceuticals Inc.

Grants Analysis
Total Grants: $625,000*
Number of Grants: 22
Average Grant: $28,409
Typical Range: $2,500 to $30,000
***Note:** Giving excludes matching gifts. Grants analysis derived from 1998 Annual Report.

NUCOR CORP.

Company Contact
Charlotte, NC
Web: http://www.nucor.com

Company Description
Revenue: US$4,009,300,000 (1999)
Employees: 6,600
Fortune Rank: 397, per FORTUNE Magazine's list of 500 Largest U.S. Corporations (1999).
FF 397
SIC(s): 3312 Blast Furnaces & Steel Mills, 3316 Cold-Finishing of Steel Shapes, 3441 Fabricated Structural Metal.

Operating Locations
Includes division locations

Nonmonetary Support
Type: Donated Equipment; Donated Products; In-kind Services; Loaned Executives

Nucor Foundation

Giving Contact

James M. Coblin, Manager, Personnel Service
2100 Rexford Rd.
Charlotte, NC 28211
Phone: (704)366-7000
Fax: (704)362-4208

Description

Founded: 1973
EIN: 237318064
Organization Type: Corporate Foundation
Giving Locations: NC
Grant Types: General Support, Scholarship.

Financial Summary

Total Giving: $537,120 (1997); $457,788 (1996); $338,682 (1993). Note: 1997 Giving includes gifts to individuals ($537,120).
Assets: $83,621 (1997); $167,538 (1996); $137,977 (1993)
Gifts Received: $475,000 (1997); $475,000 (1996); $275,000 (1993). Note: In 1996, contributions were received from Nucor Corporation.

Application Procedures

Initial Contact: Send brief letter requesting application.
Deadlines: March 1.

Additional Information

Provides scholarships to children of employees of Nucor Corp. to help finance undergraduate or vocational education.

Corporate Officials

John D. Correnti: president, chief executive officer, director, chief financial officer, director B Rochester, NY 1947. ED Clarkson University BCE (1969). PRIM CORP EMPL president, chief executive officer, director: Nucor Corp. CORP AFFIL director: Navistar International Corp.
Francis Kenneth Iverson: chairman, director B Downers Grove, IL 1925. ED Northwestern University (1943-1944); Cornell University BS (1946); Purdue University MS (1947). PRIM CORP EMPL chairman, director: Nucor Corp. CORP AFFIL director: Wachovia Corp.; director: Wal-Mart Stores; chairman, director: Nucor Bearing Products; director: Wachovia Bank & Trust Co.; director: First Wachovia Corp. NONPR AFFIL member: American Society Metals; member: National Association Manufacturer; member: American Institute Mining & Metallurgical Engineers. CLUB AFFIL Quail Hollow Country Club.
Samuel Siegel: vice chairman, secretary, treasurer, chief financial officer, director B Elizabeth, NJ 1930. ED City University of New York BBA (1952). PRIM CORP EMPL vice chairman, secretary, treasurer, chief financial officer, director: Nucor Corp. NONPR AFFIL member: American Society of Corporate Secretaries; member: Financial Executives Institute; member: American Institute CPA's.

Foundation Officials

Francis Kenneth Iverson: director (see above)
Samuel Siegel: director (see above)

Grants Analysis

Disclosure Period: calendar year ending 1997
Total Grants: $538,868*
Number of Grants: 288
Average Grant: $1,871
Typical Range: $1,100 to $3,300
***Note:** Giving includes gifts to individuals.

Occidental Oil And Gas

Company Contact

Bakersfield, CA
Web: http://www.oxy.com

Company Description

Former Name: Occidental Oil & Gas Corp.; Oxy U.S.A. Charitable Foundation.
SIC(s): 1311 Crude Petroleum & Natural Gas, 1321 Natural Gas Liquids.
Parent Company: Occidental Petroleum Corp., Los Angeles, CA, United States

Nonmonetary Support

Value: $50,000 (1995); $100,000 (1994); $200,000 (1993)
Type: Donated Equipment; In-kind Services
Volunteer Programs: Supports employee volunteerism with grants to nonprofit groups of $250 to $2,000 where employees volunteer.

Occidental Oil and Gas Foundation

Giving Contact

Jan Sieving, Manager Committee Public Affairs Division
Occidental Oil and Gas
PO Box 12021
Bakersfield, CA 93389
Phone: (805)321-6287
Fax: (805)321-6303

Description

EIN: 136081799
Organization Type: Corporate Foundation
Giving Locations: headquarters and operating communities.
Grant Types: Employee Matching Gifts, General Support, Scholarship.
Note: Employee matching gift ratio: 1 to 1 for gifts to educational institutions, up to $5,000.

Financial Summary

Total Giving: $527,471 (1998); $565,448 (1997); $600,000 (1996). Note: 1997 Giving includes foundation ($298,819); matching gifts ($99,609); United Way ($167,020). 1996 Giving includes foundation ($417,995); matching gifts ($107,519).
Giving Analysis: Giving for 1998 includes: foundation ($265,110); foundation grants to United Way ($165,225); foundation matching gifts ($97,136)
Assets: $10,183,022 (1998); $9,865,078 (1997); $9,755,298 (1996)

Typical Recipients

Arts & Humanities: Arts Associations & Councils, Arts Institutes, Ballet, Community Arts, Libraries, Museums/Galleries, Music, Opera, Theater
Civic & Public Affairs: Botanical Gardens/Parks, Chambers of Commerce, Economic Policy, Civic & Public Affairs-General, Housing, Legal Aid, Nonprofit Management, Public Policy, Rural Affairs, Urban & Community Affairs, Zoos/Aquariums
Education: Business Education, Colleges & Universities, Community & Junior Colleges, Education Funds, Elementary Education (Public), Engineering/Technological Education, Education-General, Literacy, Private Education (Precollege), Public Education (Precollege), Science/Mathematics Education, Secondary Education (Public), Student Aid
Environment: Air/Water Quality, Environment-General, Wildlife Protection
Health: Cancer, Children's Health/Hospitals, Clinics/Medical Centers, Diabetes, Emergency/Ambulance Services, Heart, Hospices, Hospitals, Medical Rehabilitation, Mental Health, Multiple Sclerosis, Single-Disease Health Associations, Speech & Hearing
International: International Affairs
Religion: Ministries, Religious Welfare
Science: Science Museums, Scientific Centers & Institutes, Scientific Organizations
Social Services: Big Brother/Big Sister, Camps, Child Welfare, Community Centers, Community Service Organizations, Crime Prevention, Delinquency & Criminal Rehabilitation, Domestic Violence, Emergency Relief, Family Services, Food/Clothing Distribution, People with Disabilities, Scouts, Scouts, Senior Services, Sexual Abuse, Shelters/Homelessness, Social Services-General, Special Olympics, Substance Abuse, United Funds/United Ways, Veterans, YMCA/YWCA/YMHA/YWHA, Youth Organizations

Contributions Analysis

Giving Priorities: Colleges and universities through matching gifts, domestic violence prevention and other social services, performing arts, single disease health organizations, and civic agencies.
Arts & Humanities: 5%. Emphasis on the performing arts. Other interests include museums, theaters, music, public broadcasting, arts funds, literary groups, and libraries.
Education: 39%. Contributions distributed primarily through matching gifts program to colleges and universities. Also supports secondary education and literacy programs.
Environment: 4%.
Health: 4%. Grants typically range from $500 to $5,000. Funds support United Way, youth organizations, and senior and family services. Health interests include support to single-disease health associations, hospitals, and handicapped services.
Social Services: 48%. Supports family, child, and youth services, and United Way.

Application Procedures

Initial Contact: brief letter or proposal
Application Requirements: a description of organization, amount requested and projected sources, operating budget and sources of income, geographic area and population served, percentage of income used for programs, list of key personnel and qualifications, plan of action, purpose of funds sought, recently audited financial statement, proof of tax-exempt status.
Deadlines: June through September.

Restrictions

Does not support dinners or special events, fraternal organizations, goodwill advertising, individuals, political or lobbying groups, labor organizations or religious organizations for sectarian purposes.

Additional Information

Occidental Oil and Gas was formerly known as Oxy USA, Inc.

Corporate Officials

Tommy Lynn Nowell: vice president finance, controller B Wichita Falls, TX 1947. ED East Central University BS (1974); University of Tulsa MBA (1980). PRIM CORP EMPL vice president finance, controller: Occidental Oil and Gas Corp. NONPR AFFIL member: Petroleum Accts Society; trustee: Union Public Schools Education Foundation; trustee: American Heart Association Tulsa Metropolitan Division; member: American Petroleum Institute.

Foundation Officials

Larry Meriage: president
Tommy Lynn Nowell: treasurer (see above)
Peter Vencent: director

Grants Analysis

Disclosure Period: calendar year ending 1998
Total Grants: $265,110*
Number of Grants: 226
Average Grant: $1,173
Highest Grant: $76,973
Typical Range: $500 to $5,000
***Note:** Giving excludes matching gifts and United Way.

Recent Grants

Note: Grants derived from 1998 Form 990.

Arts & Humanities

10,000	Oklahoma Arts Institute, OK City, OK -- (3rd of 3yr $30,000 pledge)
5,000	Bakersfield Museum of Art, Bakersfield, CA
2,000	East Texas Oil Museum, Kilgore, TX

Civic & Public Affairs

10,000	Bakersfield Centennial Plaza, Bakersfield, CA
5,000	Private Sectors Initiative, Houston, TX
2,500	Forward Midland, Midland, TX

Education

25,000	American Geological Institute Foundation, Houston, TX
19,860	National Merit Scholarship, Evanston, IL
5,000	Bakersfield College Foundation - Library, Bakersfield, CA -- (Fourth payment of 4 yr. $20,000 commitment)
5,000	South Elementary School, Midland, Midland, TX
5,000	Stockdale High School, Bakersfield, CA
5,000	Tulsa University, Tulsa, OK -- Minority Engineers Partnership scholarship (1998 Commitment)
5,000	Tulsa University, Tulsa, OK -- Minority Engineers Partnership scholarship (1997 payment)
4,000	Junior Achievement of Longview, Longview, TX
2,500	Simon Estes Education Foundation, Tulsa, OK
1,250	Cal State University Bakersfield Foundation, Bakersfield, CA -- Scholastic
1,200	Taft College Foundation, Taft, CA

Environment

2,500	Project Clean Air, Bakersfield, CA
2,000	Texas Wildlife Rehabilitation Coalition, Houston, TX

Health

5,000	Susan B. Komen Breast Cancer Foundation, Houston, TX
2,000	St. Francis Hospital of Tulsa, Tulsa, OK
1,500	American Heart Association, Houston, TX
1,000	American Cancer Society, Houston, Houston, TX
1,000	Driscoll Foundation, Corpus Christi, TX
1,000	Leukemia Society of America, Houston, Houston, TX
1,000	Mercy Hospital Foundation, Bakersfield, CA
1,000	National Multiple Sclerosis Society, Wichita, Wichita, KS
1,000	San Joaquin Hospital Foundation, Bakersfield, CA

Religion

1,000	Area Missions Outreach Services, Midland, Midland, TX

Science

8,000	Offshore Energy Center, Houston, TX
2,500	California Living Museum (CALM), Bakersfield, CA
2,500	Kern County Science Foundation, Bakersfield, CA

Social Services

76,973	United Way, Kern County (Bakersfield & Elk Hills), Bakersfield, CA
40,137	United Way, Texas Gulf Coast, Houston, TX
25,000	United Way, Tulsa Area, Tulsa, OK
21,678	United Way, Midland, Midland, TX
10,000	American Red Cross (disaster relief), Houston, TX
10,000	Golden Empire Gleaners, Bakersfield, CA
10,000	Pyles Boys Camp, Valencia, CA
6,000	Girl Scouts, Tulsa (4th of 4yr pledge: $25,000), Tulsa, OK
3,000	Parent Child Center of Tulsa, Tulsa, OK
2,500	CASA - (Court Appointed Special Advocates), Bakersfield, CA
2,000	Big Brothers/ Big Sisters of Fort Bend County, Richmond, TX
2,000	Big Brothers & Sisters, Greater Houston, Houston, TX
1,500	Midland/Lee Youth Centers, Midland, TX
1,197	United Way of Seward County, Liberal, KS
1,000	Assistance League, Bakersfield, CA
1,000	Boy Scouts of America - Southern Sierra Council, Bakersfield, CA
1,000	Camp for All Foundation, Houston, TX
1,000	Langham Creek YMCA, Houston, TX

OCCIDENTAL PETROLEUM CORP.

Company Contact

Los Angeles, CA
Web: http://www.oxy.com

Company Description

Revenue: US$7,610,000,000 (1999)
Employees: 14,270
Fortune Rank: 235, per FORTUNE Magazine's list of 500 Largest U.S. Corporations (1999).
FF 235
SIC(s): 1311 Crude Petroleum & Natural Gas, 1382 Oil & Gas Exploration Services, 2819 Industrial Inorganic Chemicals Nec, 2869 Industrial Organic Chemicals Nec.

Operating Locations

Bolivia; Libyan Arab Jamahiriya; Peru; United Kingdom

Occidental Petroleum Charitable Foundation

Giving Contact

Ms. Elizabeth Bellamy, Secretary
Occidental Petroleum Charitable Foundation
10889 Wilshire Boulevard
Los Angeles, CA 90024
Phone: (310)208-8800
Fax: (310)443-6977

Description

Founded: 1959
EIN: 166052784
Organization Type: Corporate Foundation
Giving Locations: for corporate direct giving, operating locations; for foundation, nationally.
Grant Types: Employee Matching Gifts, General Support, Multiyear/Continuing Support, Scholarship.
Note: Matches gifts for education, primarily higher education.

Financial Summary

Total Giving: $600,000 (2000 approx); $600,000 (1999); $505,551 (1998). Note: Contributes through foundation only. 1998 Giving includes foundation ($232,035); matching gifts ($193,514); United Way ($80,000).
Giving Analysis: Giving for 1997 includes: foundation matching gifts ($203,755); foundation ($128,510); foundation grants to United Way ($80,000); 1998: foundation ($232,035); foundation matching gifts ($193,516); foundation grants to United Way ($80,000)
Assets: $195,923 (1998); $76,690 (1997); $19,147 (1996)
Gifts Received: $624,500 (1998); $507,000 (1997); $297,000 (1996). Note: Contributions are received from the Occidental Petroleum Corp.

Typical Recipients

Arts & Humanities: Museums/Galleries, Music, Performing Arts, Visual Arts
Civic & Public Affairs: African American Affairs, Business/Free Enterprise, Chambers of Commerce, Ethnic Organizations, Public Policy, Urban & Community Affairs, Women's Affairs
Education: Colleges & Universities, Community & Junior Colleges, Education Associations, Engineering/Technological Education, Legal Education, Medical Education, Minority Education, Private Education (Precollege), Religious Education, Science/ Mathematics Education, Student Aid
Environment: Environment-General, Resource Conservation
Health: AIDS/HIV, Cancer, Emergency/Ambulance Services, Health Organizations, Hospitals, Single-Disease Health Associations
International: Trade
Religion: Dioceses, Jewish Causes, Ministries
Social Services: United Funds/United Ways, Youth Organizations

Contributions Analysis

Giving Priorities: Education, mainly through matching gifts; united funds and youth organizations; civic organizations; and the environment.
Civic & Public Affairs: 2%. Supports legal programs and various community groups.
Education: 64%. Majority of funding is in the form of matching gifts. Primarily supports colleges and universities.
Environment: 8%. Supports environmental concerns.
Social Services: 26%. Grants primarily support united funds and youth organizations.

Application Procedures

Initial Contact: brief letter or proposal, not to exceed four pages
Application Requirements: amount requested; proposed use of funds; whether application is for one-time or multiyear support; basic nature, scope, and purpose of organization; primary objectives to be accomplished with funds; brief outline of methods used to accomplish objectives; evaluation of needs or problems organization addresses; proof of IRS tax-exempt status; most recent annual financial statements; and proposed budget for project
Deadlines: Between November 1 and December 1.

Restrictions

Organizations must be tax-exempt under Internal Revenue Code 501(c)(3).

Additional Information

Contributions to organizations whose activities are generally confined to the geographical area or the industry in which a division or subsidiary of Occidental Petroleum operates will not be considered by the foundation but may be considered by such divisions or subsidiaries.

The foundation reports that it will consider donation requests for the following: scholarships, capital funding, and restricted grants; capital drives for hospitals, community centers, etc., and organizations promoting national societal betterment.
Publications: Guidelines

Corporate Officials

Dr. Raymond Reza Irani: chairman, director, chief executive officer officer, director B Beirut, Lebanon 1935. ED American University Beirut BS (1953); University of Southern California PhD (1957). PRIM CORP EMPL chairman, director, chief executive officer: Occidental Petroleum Corp. CORP AFFIL director: Kaufman & Broad Home Corp.
Dr. Dale R. Laurance: president, senior operations officer, director B ON Canada 1946. ED Oregon State University BSChE (1967); University of Kansas MS (1971); University of Kansas PhD (1973). PRIM CORP EMPL president, senior operations officer, director: Occidental Petroleum Corp. CORP AFFIL director: Occidental Petrochemicals Inc.; officer: Occidental Petroleum Corp.; director: Occidental Chemical Holding Corp.; director: Jacobs Engineering Group Inc.; director: Leslie's Poolmart Inc.

Foundation Officials

Arthur Groman: president B Los Angeles, CA 1914. ED University of Southern California AB (1936); Yale University JD (1939). PRIM CORP EMPL senior partner: Mitchell, Silberberg & Knupp. CORP AFFIL director: Occidental Petroleum Corp. CLUB AFFIL Hillcrest Country Club.
Dr. Raymond Reza Irani: director (see above)
Dr. Dale R. Laurance: director (see above)
Rosemary Tomich: director CORP AFFIL director: Occidental Petroleum Corp.; Owner: A.S. Tomich Construction Co.; Owner: Hope Cattle Co.
Evelyn S. Wong: secretary-treasurer

Grants Analysis

Disclosure Period: calendar year ending 1997
Total Grants: $232,035*
Number of Grants: 13
Average Grant: $17,849
Highest Grant: $80,000
Typical Range: $10,000 to $50,000
***Note:** Giving excludes matching gifts; United Way.

Recent Grants

Note: Grants derived from 1997 Form 990.

Civic & Public Affairs

10,000 Resources for the Future, Washington, DC
2,000 NAACP
2,000 National Urban League, New York, NY
1,000 Catalyst, New York, NY

Education

60,000 Armand Hammer United World College, Montezuma, NM
33,510 National Merit Scholarship Corporation, Evanston, IL
10,000 Colorado School of Mines, Golden, CO
5,000 Southwestern University School of Law, Los Angeles, CA
2,000 United Negro College Fund, New York, NY
1,000 Inroads
1,000 National Action Council for Minorities in Engineering, New York, NY

Religion

1,000 Jewish National Fund Tree of Life

Social Services

80,000 United Way

OG&E Electric Services

Company Contact

Oklahoma City, OK
Web: http://www.oge.com

Company Description

Former Name: Oklahoma Gas & Electric Co.
Employees: 2,765
SIC(s): 1311 Crude Petroleum & Natural Gas, 4911 Electric Services, 4922 Natural Gas Transmission.

Nonmonetary Support

Type: Loaned Employees; Loaned Executives
Note: Nonmonetary support is provided by the company.

Corporate Sponsorship

Type: Arts & cultural events

Oklahoma Gas & Electric Co. Foundation

Giving Contact

Erma Elliot, Secretary & Treasurer
Oklahoma Gas & Electric Co. Foundation
Box 321
Oklahoma City, OK 73101
Phone: (405)553-3196
Fax: (405)553-3567

Description

Founded: 1957
EIN: 736093572
Organization Type: Corporate Foundation
Giving Locations: OK headquarters and operating communities.
Grant Types: Capital, Employee Matching Gifts, General Support, Scholarship.

Financial Summary

Total Giving: $895,814 (1998); $785,785 (1997); $813,665 (1996). Note: Contributes through foundation only.
Giving Analysis: Giving for 1994 includes: foundation ($582,255); foundation matching gifts ($33,294); 1996: foundation ($755,817); foundation grants to United Way ($57,848); 1997: foundation ($739,667); foundation matching gifts ($46,118);
Assets: $1,118,252 (1998); $1,123,768 (1997); $1,396,378 (1996)
Gifts Received: $800,000 (1998); $400,000 (1997); $400,000 (1996). Note: In 1998, contributions were received from Oklahoma Gas and Electric Co.

Typical Recipients

Arts & Humanities: Arts Associations & Councils, Arts Funds, Arts Institutes, Ballet, Ethnic & Folk Arts, Arts & Humanities-General, Historic Preservation, History & Archaeology, Libraries, Museums/Galleries, Music, Theater
Civic & Public Affairs: Botanical Gardens/Parks, Community Foundations, Economic Development, Civic & Public Affairs-General, Municipalities/Towns, Professional & Trade Associations, Urban & Community Affairs, Zoos/Aquariums
Education: Business Education, Colleges & Universities, Community & Junior Colleges, Economic Education, Education-General, Private Education (Precollege), Public Education (Precollege), Science/Mathematics Education, Secondary Education (Public), Special Education
Environment: Resource Conservation
Health: Children's Health/Hospitals, Clinics/Medical Centers, Emergency/Ambulance Services, Health Organizations, Heart, Hospitals, Medical Research, Public Health
International: International Affairs
Religion: Religious Welfare
Science: Science Museums
Social Services: Camps, Community Service Organizations, Emergency Relief, Family Planning, Family Services, People with Disabilities, Recreation & Athletics, Scouts, Senior Services, Special Olympics, YMCA/YWCA/YMHA/YWHA, Youth Organizations

Contributions Analysis

Giving Priorities: Colleges and universities in Oklahoma; museums and arts funds; youth organizations; hospitals, medical research, and pediatric health; and economic and community development.
Arts & Humanities: 28%. Supports historic preservation, museums, and arts funds.
Civic & Public Affairs: 13%. Economic and community development are typical areas of funding, with support also going to environmental, urban, and community affairs.
Education: 46%. Supports colleges and universities, public and private secondary schools. Large grants consistently are given to Oklahoma City University, the University of Oklahoma, and Oklahoma State University.
Health: 3%. Funds hospitals, medical research, and pediatric health.
Religion: 4%. Supports religious causes.
Science: 2%. Supports science museums.
Social Services: 4%. Primary concern is youth organizations. Other interests include community services, family planning, recreation and athletics, and organizations concerned with the elderly and children.

Application Procedures

Initial Contact: Send a brief letter.
Application Requirements: Include an outline of the proposed project, amount requested, and proof of 501(c)(3) status.
Deadlines: None.

Restrictions

Does not support fraternal organizations, individuals, political or lobbying groups, or religious organizations for sectarian purposes. Preference given to organizations in service areas.

Foundation Officials

Erma B. Elliott: secretary, treasurer PRIM CORP EMPL secretary: OG&E Electric Services ADD CORP EMPL vice president, corporate secretary: OG&E Energy Corp.
Steven Moore: president B Sayre, OK 1946. ED University of Oklahoma BBA (1968); University of Oklahoma JD (1971). PRIM CORP EMPL chairman, president, chief executive officer, director: OGE Energy Corp.
A. M. Strecker: vice president, director B Seiling, OK 1943. ED Oklahoma State University BSEE (1971). PRIM CORP EMPL senior vice president finance: OG&E Electric Services. CORP AFFIL senior vice president: Oklahoma Gas & Electric Co.

Grants Analysis

Disclosure Period: calendar year ending 1998
Total Grants: $840,167*
Number of Grants: 73
Average Grant: $11,509
Highest Grant: $80,000
Typical Range: $100 to $6,000
***Note:** Giving excludes matching gifts.

Recent Grants

Note: Grants derived from 1997 Form 990.

Arts & Humanities

52,000 Allied Arts Foundation, Oklahoma City, OK
50,000 Friends of the Mansion, Oklahoma City, OK
25,000 Oklahoma City Philharmonic Orchestra, Oklahoma City, OK

10,000 Oklahoma City Philharmonic Orchestra, Oklahoma City, OK
6,000 Metropolitan Library System Endowment Fund, Oklahoma City, OK
6,000 Oklahoma City Philharmonic Orchestra, Oklahoma City, OK
5,000 Oklahoma Heritage Association, Oklahoma City, OK
3,500 Lyric Theatre, Oklahoma City, OK
3,000 Preservation El Reno, El Reno, OK
2,500 Ballet Oklahoma, Oklahoma City, OK
2,500 McLoud Friends of the Library, McLoud, OK

Civic & Public Affairs
20,000 Integris Foundation, Oklahoma City, OK
15,000 Oklahoma Zoological Society, Oklahoma City, OK
5,000 Automobile Alley, Oklahoma City, OK
2,500 Norman Community Foundation, Norman, OK

Education
60,000 Oklahoma Christian University of Science and Arts, Oklahoma City, OK
50,000 Oklahoma City University, Oklahoma City, OK
50,000 Oklahoma State University Foundation, Stillwater, OK
50,000 University of Oklahoma Foundation, Norman, OK
20,000 Oklahoma School of Science and Mathematics, Oklahoma City, OK
10,000 Oklahoma City Public Schools Foundation, Oklahoma City, OK
8,000 Oklahoma Baptist University, Shawnee, OK
6,666 Northeastern State University, Muskogee, OK
5,000 Langston University, Langston, OK
5,000 Oklahoma State University Foundation, Stillwater, OK
5,000 St. Gregory's College, Shawnee, OK
5,000 University of Oklahoma Foundation, Norman, OK
3,500 Oklahoma State University Foundation, Stillwater, OK
3,000 Murray State College Foundation, Tishomingo, OK
3,000 Oklahoma State University Foundation, Stillwater, OK
3,000 University of Oklahoma Foundation, Norman, OK
2,500 Oklahoma Council on Economic Education, Edmond, OK
2,500 Seminole State College, Seminole, OK -- Lloyd Simmons Training Facility

Environment
5,000 Nature Conservancy, Tulsa, OK

Health
16,667 Shawnee Regional Hospital, Shawnee, OK
16,667 Shawnee Regional Hospital, Shawnee, OK
15,000 Pauls Valley General Hospital Foundation, Pauls Valley, OK
10,000 Oklahoma Medical Research Foundation, Oklahoma City, OK
5,000 Gregory Kistler Treatment Center for Children, Fort Smith, AR
5,000 Mercy Health Center, Oklahoma City, OK
5,000 Southwest Medical Center, Oklahoma City, OK

Religion
25,000 Salvation Army, Oklahoma City, OK
3,000 Salvation Army, Oklahoma City, OK

Science
10,000 Omniplex, Oklahoma City, OK
4,000 Omniplex, Oklahoma City, OK

Social Services
80,000 National Cowboy Hall of Fame, Oklahoma City, OK
10,000 Hatbox Sports Complex, Muskogee, OK
3,000 YMCA, Oklahoma City, OK
2,500 Redbud Classic, Oklahoma City, OK
2,500 YWCA, Oklahoma City, OK

OHIO NATIONAL LIFE INSURANCE CO.

Company Contact

Cincinnati, OH

Company Description

Income: US$1,400,000,000
Employees: 600
SIC(s): 6311 Life Insurance, 6321 Accident & Health Insurance.

Nonmonetary Support

Type: Donated Equipment; Workplace Solicitation

Ohio National Foundation

Giving Contact

Anthony G. Esposito, 2nd Vice President, Human Resources
PO Box 237
Cincinnati, OH 45201
Phone: (513)794-6594

Description

Founded: 1987
EIN: 311230164
Organization Type: Corporate Foundation
Giving Locations: OH: Cincinnati
Grant Types: Capital, Employee Matching Gifts, General Support, Multiyear/Continuing Support, Research, Scholarship.

Financial Summary

Total Giving: $500,000 (1997 approx); $260,740 (1996); $325,012 (1995)
Assets: $1,925,055 (1996); $1,563,712 (1995); $869,180 (1993)
Gifts Received: $143,374 (1996); $500,000 (1995)

Typical Recipients

Arts & Humanities: Arts Centers, Arts Festivals, Arts Funds, Arts Institutes, Film & Video, Arts & Humanities-General, Libraries, Museums/Galleries, Music, Performing Arts, Public Broadcasting, Theater
Civic & Public Affairs: African American Affairs, Botanical Gardens/Parks, Chambers of Commerce, Community Foundations, Civic & Public Affairs-General, Housing, Inner-City Development, Law & Justice, Urban & Community Affairs, Women's Affairs, Zoos/Aquariums
Education: Arts/Humanities Education, Business Education, Colleges & Universities, Continuing Education, Education Funds, Education-General, Legal Education, Literacy, Minority Education, Religious Education, Student Aid
Health: AIDS/HIV, Alzheimers Disease, Cancer, Children's Health/Hospitals, Clinics/Medical Centers, Diabetes, Eyes/Blindness, Health-General, Health Policy/Cost Containment, Heart, Hospices, Hospitals, Medical Rehabilitation, Medical Research, Multiple Sclerosis, Public Health
Religion: Religion-General, Jewish Causes, Ministries, Religious Welfare, Social/Policy Issues
Science: Scientific Research
Social Services: Community Centers, Food/Clothing Distribution, Recreation & Athletics, Shelters/Homelessness, Substance Abuse, United Funds/United Ways, YMCA/YWCA/YMHA/YWHA, Youth Organizations

Application Procedures

Initial Contact: Send a brief letter of inquiry.
Application Requirements: a description of organization and proof of tax-exempt status.
Deadlines: None.

Restrictions

Does not support individuals, religious organizations for sectarian purposes, or political or lobbying groups.

Corporate Officials

Ronald J. Dolan: senior vice president, chief financial officer, directorc B Cincinnati, OH 1947. ED University of Cincinnati (1969); University of Michigan (1970). PRIM CORP EMPL senior vice president, chief financial officer, director: Ohio National Life Insurance Co.
David B. O'Maley: chairman, president, chief executive officer, director PRIM CORP EMPL chairman, president, chief executive officer, director: Ohio National Life Insurance Co.

Foundation Officials

Howard C. Becker: trustee PRIM CORP EMPL vice president: Ohio National Life Insurance Co.
Joseph P. Brom: vice president, trustee
Ronald J. Dolan: trustee (see above)
Anthony G. Esposito: secretary, trustee PRIM CORP EMPL senior vice president human resources: Ohio National Life Insurance Co.
David B. O'Maley: president, trustee (see above)
Stuart G. Summers: assistant secretary, trustee

Grants Analysis

Disclosure Period: calendar year ending 1996
Total Grants: $260,740
Number of Grants: 121
Highest Grant: $33,103
Typical Range: $50 to $5,000

Recent Grants

Note: Grants derived from 1997 Form 990.

Arts & Humanities
20,000 Cincinnati Institute of Fine Arts, Cincinnati, OH -- operating support
19,000 Fine Arts Fund, Cincinnati, OH -- operating support
10,000 Cincinnati Symphony Orchestra, Cincinnati, OH -- operating support
5,000 Cincinnati Arts Festival, Cincinnati, OH -- operating support

Civic & Public Affairs
14,200 Urban League, Cincinnati, OH -- operating support
10,062 Living Arrangements for Developmentally Disabled, Cincinnati, OH -- operating support
10,000 Cincinnati Zoo and Botanical Gardens, Cincinnati, OH -- operating support
10,000 Greater Cincinnati Foundation, Cincinnati, OH -- operating support
5,000 Greater Cincinnati 2008 Amateur Sports Association, Cincinnati, OH -- operating support

Education
7,000 American College, Bryn Mawr, PA -- support program development
6,000 Junior Achievement, Cincinnati, OH -- operating support
5,000 Ohio Foundation of Independent Colleges, Columbus, OH -- operating support

Health
31,670 Life and Health Insurance Foundation

	for Education, Washington, DC -- operating support
7,000	Children's Hospital Medical Center, Cincinnati, OH -- capital fund
6,400	Hospice, Cincinnati, OH -- operating support

Religion

10,000	Good Samaritan Foundation, Cincinnati, OH -- capital fund
5,000	US Catholic Conference, St. Joseph Home, Cincinnati, OH -- operating support

Social Services

100,000	United Way, Cincinnati, OH -- operating support
10,700	United Way, Cincinnati, OH -- support Loaned Executive Program
4,740	YWCA, Cincinnati, OH -- operating support

OKLAHOMA PUBLISHING CO.

Company Contact

Oklahoma City, OK

Company Description

Employees: 2,500
SIC(s): 2711 Newspapers.

The Oklahoman Foundation

Giving Contact

Linda Brown, Executive Assistant
The Oklahoman Foundation
PO Box 25125
Oklahoma City, OK 73125
Phone: (405)475-3298
Fax: (405)475-3128

Description

Founded: 1990
EIN: 731363152
Organization Type: Corporate Foundation. Supports preselected organizations only.
Giving Locations: OK: Oklahoma City
Grant Types: General Support, Matching.

Financial Summary

Total Giving: $1,240,000 (1998); $1,170,000 (1997); $981,000 (1996). Note: Contributes through foundation only.
Giving Analysis: Giving for 1996 includes: foundation ($841,000); foundation grants to United Way ($140,000); 1997: foundation ($1,020,000); foundation grants to United Way ($150,000); 1998: foundation ($1,090,000); foundation grants to United Way ($150,000)
Assets: $16,685,746 (1998); $16,198,497 (1997); $13,714,560 (1996)
Gifts Received: $850,000 (1997); $700,000 (1996); $800,000 (1995). Note: Contributions were received from the Oklahoma Publishing Co.

Typical Recipients

Arts & Humanities: Arts Funds, Historic Preservation, History & Archaeology, Museums/Galleries
Civic & Public Affairs: Botanical Gardens/Parks, Economic Development, Professional & Trade Associations, Public Policy
Education: Colleges & Universities, Science/Mathematics Education
Health: Children's Health/Hospitals, Clinics/Medical Centers
Religion: Ministries, Religious Welfare
Science: Science Museums
Social Services: Animal Protection, Child Abuse, Child Welfare, Community Service Organizations, People with Disabilities, Recreation & Athletics, Scouts, United Funds/United Ways, YMCA/YWCA/YMHA/YWHA

Contributions Analysis

Arts & Humanities: 43%. Major support for the National Cowboy Hall of Fame. Also supports various arts organizations, including an arts fund.
Civic & Public Affairs: 2%.
Education: 15%. Funds a local university and a school of science and math.
Health: 5%.
Science: 4%. Supports Omiplex Science Museum.
Social Services: 31%. Supports the United Way, the YMCA, and community service organizations.
Note: Total contributions made in 1998.

Restrictions

Grants are not made to individuals.

Corporate Officials

Edward Lewis Gaylord: chairman, chief executive officer, director, publisher B Denver, CO 1919. ED Oklahoma City University LLD; Stanford University AB (1941). PRIM CORP EMPL chairman, chief executive officer, director, publisher: Oklahoma Publishing Co. CORP AFFIL president: Sun Resources Inc.; president: OPUBCO Properties Inc.; president: OPUBCO Resources Inc.; president: OPUBCO Development Co.; president: OPUBCO International Ltd.; chairman: Grand Ole Opry Tour Inc.; chairman: Opryland USA Inc.; chairman: Gaylord Entertainment Co.; chairman: Gayno Inc.; president: Gaillardia Residential Community; chairman: Gaylord Broadcasting Co.; chairman: C Tri Inc.; partner: Cimarron Coal Co.; chairman, chief executive officer: Broadmoor Hotel Inc. NONPR AFFIL member: Oklahoma Chamber of Commerce; member: Southern Newspaper Publishers Association. CLUB AFFIL chairman: Broadmoor Golf Club.

Foundation Officials

Christine Gaylord Everest: trustee PRIM CORP EMPL vice president, director: Oklahoma Publishing Co. CORP AFFIL director: Gaylord Entertainment Co.
Edward K. Gaylord, II: trustee B 1957. PRIM CORP EMPL president: Oklahoma Publishing Co. CORP AFFIL president: Connect Oklahoma Inc.; vice chairman: Gaylord Entertainment Co.
Edward Lewis Gaylord: trustee (see above)

Grants Analysis

Disclosure Period: calendar year ending 1998
Total Grants: $1,090,000*
Number of Grants: 13
Average Grant: $49,167*
Highest Grant: $500,000
Typical Range: $10,000 to $75,000
***Note:** Giving excludes United Way. Average grant figure excludes the highest grant.

Recent Grants

Note: Grants derived from 1997 Form 990.

Arts & Humanities

35,000	Allied Arts Foundation, Oklahoma City, OK
20,000	Crystal Cathedral Ministries, Orange, CA

Education

155,000	Oklahoma Christian University of Science and Arts, Oklahoma City, OK
50,000	Oklahoma School Science and Math, Oklahoma City, OK
15,000	Oklahoma State University Foundation, Stillwater, OK

Religion

50,000	City Rescue Mission, Oklahoma City, OK

Science

50,000	Omniplex Science Museum, Oklahoma City, OK

Social Services

150,000	United Way, Oklahoma City, OK
100,000	Oklahoma Goodwill Industries, Oklahoma City, OK
25,000	YMCA, Oklahoma City, OK
10,000	American Quarterhorse Foundation, Amarillo, TX
10,000	US Olympic Committee, Dallas, TX

OLD KENT BANK

Company Contact

Elmhurst, IL

Company Description

Assets: US$2,104,400,000
Employees: 590

Old Kent Foundation

Giving Contact

Steven D. Crandall, Secretary & Trustee
Old Kent Foundation
1 Vandenberg Center
Grand Rapids, MI 49503
Phone: (616)771-5363

Description

Founded: 1993
EIN: 383083066
Organization Type: Corporate Foundation
Giving Locations: MI: Western Michigan
Grant Types: General Support.

Financial Summary

Total Giving: $757,958 (1997); $655,446 (1996); $924,400 (1995). Note: 1997 Giving includes United Way.
Assets: $411,851 (1997); $1,130,179 (1996); $724,297 (1995)
Gifts Received: $1,000,000 (1996); $1,000,004 (1994); $100,000 (1993). Note: In 1996, contributions were received from Old Kent Bank.

Typical Recipients

Arts & Humanities: Arts Associations & Councils, Arts Institutes, History & Archaeology, Libraries, Museums/Galleries, Music, Opera
Civic & Public Affairs: Botanical Gardens/Parks, Chambers of Commerce, Community Foundations, Economic Development, Housing, Zoos/Aquariums
Education: Business Education, Colleges & Universities, Community & Junior Colleges, Education-General, Preschool Education, Private Education (Precollege), Student Aid
Health: Hospices
Religion: Ministries, Religious Welfare
Social Services: Animal Protection, Community Centers, Community Service Organizations, Family Services, Scouts, Senior Services, United Funds/United Ways, YMCA/YWCA/YMHA/YWHA

Application Procedures

Initial Contact: Send brief letter of inquiry, including a description of organization, amount requested, purpose of funds sought, recently audited financial statements, and proof of tax-exempt status. Committee meets every two weeks to consider proposals.

Restrictions

Contributions are restricted to western Michigan for charitable, scientific, literary, and educational purposes.

Corporate Officials

Kevin T. Kabat: vice chairman, president, chief executive officer PRIM CORP EMPL vice chairman, president: Old Kent Bank.

Janet S. Nisbett: senior vice president, controller PRIM CORP EMPL senior vice president, controller: Old Kent Bank.

Robert L. Sadler: president, vice chairman, director B Beloit, KS 1935. ED Baker University AB (1958); Indiana University MBA (1959); Rutgers University Stonier Graduate School of Banking (1970). PRIM CORP EMPL president, vice chairman, director: Old Kent Bank. NONPR AFFIL member: Delta Mu Delta; member: Sigma Iota Epsilon; chairman: Davenport College Business; member: American Bankers Association. CLUB AFFIL University Club; Cascade Country Club.

David J. Wagner: chairman, president, chief executive officer B Cincinnati, OH 1954. ED Indiana University BA (1975); Indiana University MBA (1976). PRIM CORP EMPL chairman, president, chief executive officer: Old Kent Finance Corp. CORP AFFIL chairman, director: Old Kent Bank.

Foundation Officials

Steven D. Crandall: senior vice president, secretary
Kevin T. Kabat: trustee (see above)
Janet S. Nisbett: treasurer, trustee (see above)
David J. Wagner: treasurer (see above)

Grants Analysis

Disclosure Period: calendar year ending 1997
Total Grants: $757,958
Typical Range: $1,000 to $20,000

Recent Grants

Note: Grants derived from 1997 Form 990.

Arts & Humanities

35,000	Grand Rapids Children's Museum, Grand Rapids, MI
32,500	Grand Rapids Symphony, Grand Rapids, MI
22,000	Opera Grand Rapids, Grand Rapids, MI
15,000	Urban Institute for Contemporary Arts, Grand Rapids, MI
7,500	Arts Council, Grand Rapids, MI
5,000	Gerald R. Ford Foundation, Grand Rapids, MI
5,000	Platt River Community Library, Greenville, MI

Civic & Public Affairs

55,000	Greater Grand Rapids Chamber Foundation, Grand Rapids, MI
25,000	Downtown Management Board, Grand Rapids, MI
25,000	Grand Rapids Foundation, Grand Rapids, MI
22,000	Local Initiatives Support Corporation, New York, NY
17,000	John Ball Zoo, Grand Rapids, MI
13,000	Frederick Meijer Gardens, Grand Rapids, MI
10,000	Jellema House, Grand Rapids, MI
7,500	Kalamazoo Neighborhood Housing Services, Kalamazoo, MI
7,500	Niles Community Development Corporation, Niles, MI

Education

33,000	Grand Valley State University, Allendale, MI
10,000	CEO Michigan Child Education Opportunity Fund, Grand Rapids, MI
10,000	Grand Rapids Foundation, Grand Rapids, MI -- support Youth Enrichment Scholarship Program
8,125	Junior Achievement, Grand Rapids, MI
7,500	Grand Rapids Community College Foundation, Grand Rapids, MI

Health

10,000	Hospice of Southeastern Michigan, Southfield, MI

Religion

15,000	Mel Trotter Ministries, Grand Rapids, MI
10,000	Salvation Army, Grand Rapids, MI

Social Services

110,000	Heart of West Michigan United Way, Grand Rapids, MI
47,250	United Way, Kalamazoo, MI
20,000	YMCA, Grand Rapids, MI -- capital campaign
12,000	Reach, Grand Rapids, MI
10,000	Humane Society, Grand Rapids, MI
7,000	United Way, Niles, MI

OLD NATIONAL BANK EVANSVILLE

Company Contact

Evansville, IN
Web: http://www.oldnational.com

Company Description

Assets: US$1,240,000,000
Employees: 500
SIC(s): 6021 National Commercial Banks.
Parent Company: Old National Bancorp.

Nonmonetary Support

Type: Cause-related Marketing & Promotion; Donated Equipment; In-kind Services; Loaned Employees; Loaned Executives
Volunteer Programs: The company encourages employee volunteerism through an informal volunteer program.
Contact: Melva Thomas, Marketing Coordinator

Old National Bank Charitable Trust

Giving Contact

Prudence Pekinpaugh, Public Relations Representative
Old National Bank in Evansville
PO Box 207
Evansville, IN 47702
Phone: (812)464-1441
Fax: (812)464-1505
Email: prudence_pekinpaugh@oldnational.com

Description

Founded: 1957
EIN: 356015583
Organization Type: Corporate Foundation. Supports preselected organizations only.
Giving Locations: IL: Gibson County, Perry County, Posey County, Spencer County, Vandeburg County, Wabash County, Warrick County, White County; KY: Henderson County
Grant Types: Capital, Challenge, Conference/Seminar, General Support, Operating Expenses, Project.

Financial Summary

Total Giving: $451,401 (1998); $233,102 (1996); $304,193 (1995). Note: Contributes through foundation only.
Giving Analysis: Giving for 1996 includes: foundation ($179,932); foundation grants to United Way ($53,170); 1997: foundation ($348,418); foundation grants to United Way ($4,000); 1998: foundation ($344,401); foundation grants to United Way ($107,000)
Assets: $3,038,928 (1998); $1,380,491 (1996); $1,360,133 (1995)
Gifts Received: $400,000 (1997); $180,000 (1996); $631,936 (1995)

Typical Recipients

Arts & Humanities: Arts Associations & Councils, Community Arts, Dance, Arts & Humanities-General, Historic Preservation, History & Archaeology, Libraries, Literary Arts, Museums/Galleries, Music, Performing Arts, Public Broadcasting, Theater
Civic & Public Affairs: African American Affairs, Business/Free Enterprise, Clubs, Community Foundations, Economic Development, Civic & Public Affairs-General, Hispanic Affairs, Housing, Inner-City Development, Minority Business, Municipalities/Towns, Parades/Festivals, Philanthropic Organizations, Professional & Trade Associations, Safety, Urban & Community Affairs, Zoos/Aquariums
Education: Afterschool/Enrichment Programs, Arts/Humanities Education, Business Education, Colleges & Universities, Education Funds, Elementary Education (Private), Engineering/Technological Education, Education-General, Medical Education, Preschool Education, Private Education (Precollege), Public Education (Precollege), Religious Education, Secondary Education (Private), Special Education, Student Aid
Environment: Environment-General, Resource Conservation
Health: Adolescent Health Issues, Children's Health/Hospitals, Clinics/Medical Centers, Emergency/Ambulance Services, Health-General, Health Organizations, Home-Care Services, Hospitals, Medical Rehabilitation, Respiratory, Single-Disease Health Associations
Religion: Churches, Religion-General, Ministries, Religious Organizations, Religious Welfare
Science: Science Museums
Social Services: Animal Protection, At-Risk Youth, Community Service Organizations, Day Care, Delinquency & Criminal Rehabilitation, Family Planning, Family Services, Food/Clothing Distribution, People with Disabilities, Recreation & Athletics, Scouts, Senior Services, Shelters/Homelessness, Social Services-General, Substance Abuse, United Funds/United Ways, YMCA/YWCA/YMHA/YWHA, Youth Organizations

Contributions Analysis

Arts & Humanities: 8%. Supports Evansville area arts organizations, including museums, theaters, music, and arts councils.
Civic & Public Affairs: 22%. Supports community affairs organizations, development, zoos, and housing.
Education: 24%. Major support goes to colleges and universities. Other interests include private and public education at the elementary and secondary school levels.
Health: 4%. Supports medical rehabilitation, health centers, and various health organizations.
Religion: 4%. Supports Christian religious welfare organizations.
Social Services: 38%. Primarily supports the United Way and youth organizations.
Note: Total contributions made in 1998.

Application Procedures

Initial Contact: Send a one-page letter.
Application Requirements: Include a description of organization, amount requested, who will benefit from the program or project, and proof of tax-exempt status.
Deadlines: None.

Review Process: Requests for support are evaluated on an ongoing basis; the foundation requests additional information as necessary.
Decision Notification: The foundation's board meets in March, June, September, and December; requests may take up to six months from time of receipt for complete review and determination.

Restrictions

Does not support individuals, political or lobbying groups, or organizations outside operating areas.

Additional Information

Separate banks administer independent programs.

Corporate Officials

Michael R. Hinton: president, chief operating officer, director B Evansville, IN 1954. ED University of Evansville (1975); University of Evansville (1982). PRIM CORP EMPL president, chief operating officer, director: Old National Bank of Evansville ADD CORP EMPL director: Old National Service Corp. Evansville; director: Old National Trust Corp. NONPR AFFIL director: Saint Marys Medical Center; trustee: University Evansville; secretary, treasurer, director: Mission Health Systems Inc.
James A. Risinger: chairman, chief executive officer B Logansport, IN 1948. ED North Carolina State University BA (1971); Rutgers University Stonier Graduate School of Banking (1989). PRIM CORP EMPL chairman, chief executive officer: Old National Bank of Evansville ADD CORP EMPL chairman, chief executive officer: Ad National Bancorp.

Grants Analysis

Disclosure Period: calendar year ending 1998
Total Grants: $344,401*
Number of Grants: 56
Average Grant: $6,150
Highest Grant: $40,000
Typical Range: $3,000 to $10,000
***Note:** Giving excludes United Way.

Recent Grants

Note: Grants derived from 1997 Form 990.

Arts & Humanities

6,300	Evansville Philharmonic Orchestra, Evansville, IN
2,500	Arts Council of Southwest Indiana, Evansville, IN
2,000	Evansville Civic Theater, Evansville, IN
2,000	Tales and Scales, Evansville, IN
1,500	Evansville Dance Theater, Evansville, IN
1,000	Reitz Home Preservation Society, Evansville, IN

Civic & Public Affairs

20,000	Habitat for Humanity, Evansville, IN
20,000	Rapp Grainary Owen Foundation
10,000	Evansville Downtown Development, Evansville, IN
5,000	Local Initiatives Support Corporation, Evansville, IN
3,500	Evansville Freedom Festival, Evansville, IN
3,000	Operation City Beautiful, Evansville, IN
2,000	Junior League, Evansville, IN
1,000	Town of Newburgh Summerfest, Newburgh, IN

Education

80,000	Schlottman Scholarships
20,000	University of Southern Indiana Presidential Scholarship, Evansville, IN
10,000	Signature Learning Center
8,333	Indiana University of Medicine, Bloomington, IN
8,333	University of Evansville Compete Experience Campaign, Evansville, IN
7,500	Children's Learning Center
6,000	Independent Colleges of Indiana Foundation, Indianapolis, IN
3,333	Evansville Catholic High School Board, Evansville, IN
3,000	Catholic Education Foundation, Evansville, IN
3,000	Evansville Day School, Evansville, IN
2,000	Ivy Tech Foundation, Indianapolis, IN
2,000	University of Evansville Art Department, Evansville, IN
1,500	Junior Achievement

Health

5,000	Welborn Hospital Foundation
3,000	Easter Seal Society, Honolulu, HI
2,000	Easter Seal Society, Evansville, IN
1,125	St. Mary's Medical Center Foundation
1,000	Southwest Indiana Easter Seal Telethon, Evansville, IN

Religion

10,000	Salvation Army
4,500	Center City Corp
3,000	First Baptist Church, Evansville, IN
2,500	Evansville Rescue Mission, Evansville, IN
2,000	United Methodist Youth Home
1,500	Lincoln Avenue Community Development Company

Science

1,500	Evansville Museum of Arts and Science, Evansville, IN

Social Services

31,000	YMCA, Evansville, IN
5,000	Southwest Indiana Council on Aging, Evansville, IN
4,000	United Way Southwestern Indiana, Evansville, IN
3,500	Raintree Girl Scout Council, Evansville, IN
3,500	YMCA, Evansville, IN
3,000	Youth Leadership
3,000	Youth Resources of Southwest Indiana, Evansville, IN
2,500	Sustainable Evansville Echo House
2,500	Youth Care Center
1,000	Evansville ARC Foundation, Evansville, IN
1,000	Hope, Evansville, IN

OLIN CORP.

Company Contact

Norwalk, CT
Web: http://www.olin.com

Company Description

Profit: US$139,900,000
Employees: 7,400 (1999)
SIC(s): 2812 Alkalies & Chlorine, 2819 Industrial Inorganic Chemicals Nec, 2821 Plastics Materials & Resins, 2865 Cyclic Crudes & Intermediates.

Operating Locations

Australia: Olin Australia Ltd., Geelong, Saint Leonards; Belgium: N.V. Olin Europe SA, Brussels; N.V. Olin Hunt Products, Saint-Niklaas; Bermuda: Nutmeg Insurance Ltd., Hamilton; Brazil: Nordesclor SA, Recife, Pernambuco; Olin Brazil Ltda., Sao Paulo; Canada: Olin Canada Inc., Mississauga; France: Hydrochim SA, Amboise; Olin SA, Charles de Gaulle; Olin Microelectronic Materials SA, Roissy Charles de Gaulle; Germany: Langengerg Kupfer und Messingwerke GmbH, Langenberg; OCG Microelectronic Materials GmbH, Ratingen; Olin GmbH, Ratingen; Schwermetall Halbzeugwerk GmbH and Co. KG, Stolberg; Hong Kong: Olin Industrial (Hong Kong) Ltd., Kowloon; Ireland: Olin Chemicals B.V., Swords; Italy: OCG Microelectronic Materials Srl, Milan; Japan: Yamaha-Olin Metal Corporate, Shizuoka-ken; Asahi-Olin Ltd., Tokyo; Fuji-Hunt Electronics Technology Co. Ltd., Tokyo; Kyodo TDI Ltd. Co., Tokyo; Olin Japan, Inc., Tokyo; Mexico: Olin Quimica SA de CV, Mexico; New Zealand: Olin Corporate N.Z. Ltd., Manukau, Aukland; Republic of South Africa: Olin (Proprietary) Ltd., Johannesburg; Aquachlor (Proprietary) Ltd., Kempton Park; Singapore: Olin Pte., Ltd. Singapore, Singapore; United Kingdom: Judd-Olin (U.K.) Ltd., Coventry, West Midlands; Olin UK Ltd., Droitwic, Worcester; OCG Microelectronic Materials Ltd., Worcester; Venezuela: Etoxyl C.A., Caracas; Olin Quimica, SA, Caracas; Productora de Alcoholes Hidratados, Caracas

Nonmonetary Support

Contact: Carmella Piacentini, Manager Corporate Contributions
Note: Annual competitive award program for long-term significant employee, retiree or family member volunteer affiliation.

Olin Corp. Charitable Trust

Giving Contact

Carmella V. Piacentini, Administrator
Olin Corp. Charitable Trust
501 Merritt 7
PO Box 4500
Norwalk, CT 06856-4500
Phone: (203)750-3301
Fax: (203)750-3065
Web: http://www.olin.com/about/charitable.asp

Description

EIN: 436022750
Organization Type: Corporate Foundation
Giving Locations: communities where employees work and live; some support for national organizations.
Grant Types: Award, Capital, Challenge, Conference/Seminar, Department, Emergency, Employee Matching Gifts, Endowment, Fellowship, Multiyear/Continuing Support, Project.
Note: Employee matching gift ratio: 1 to 1 for active employees; 0.5 to 1 for retirees.

Financial Summary

Total Giving: $1,500,000 (2000 approx); $2,000,000 (1999 approx); $2,000,000 (1998 approx). Note: Contributes through corporate direct giving program and foundation. Giving includes trust.
Assets: $2,500,000 (2000 approx); $6,975,079 (1997); $7,382,310 (1996)

Typical Recipients

Arts & Humanities: Arts Associations & Councils, Arts Centers, Arts Institutes, Community Arts, Dance, Historic Preservation, Libraries, Museums/Galleries, Music, Opera, Performing Arts, Public Broadcasting, Theater, Visual Arts
Civic & Public Affairs: African American Affairs, Business/Free Enterprise, Chambers of Commerce, Civil Rights, Minority Business, Professional & Trade Associations, Public Policy, Urban & Community Affairs, Zoos/Aquariums
Education: Business Education, Business-School Partnerships, Colleges & Universities, Community & Junior Colleges, Elementary Education (Public), Engineering/Technological Education, Education-General, Literacy, Medical Education, Minority Education, Private Education (Precollege), Public Education (Precollege), Science/Mathematics Education, Student Aid
Environment: Air/Water Quality, Environment-General, Protection, Resource Conservation

Health: Emergency/Ambulance Services, Health Organizations, Hospices, Hospitals, Medical Rehabilitation, Mental Health, Nursing Services, Single-Disease Health Associations
International: Foreign Educational Institutions, International Affairs, International Environmental Issues
Science: Science Museums, Scientific Centers & Institutes
Social Services: Community Centers, Community Service Organizations, Family Services, Food/Clothing Distribution, Shelters/Homelessness, Substance Abuse, United Funds/United Ways, Volunteer Services, Youth Organizations

Contributions Analysis

Giving Priorities: Education, with emphasis on science and technology; programs involving employee volunteers and impacting communities in which employees live; and conservation, environmental education, and environmental research.
Arts & Humanities: Less than 5%. Major support has gone to opera associations and music organizations. Also supports theaters, the performing arts, museums, libraries, ballet, and art centers. Predominant means of arts support is matching gifts program.
Civic & Public Affairs: 10% to 15%. Recipients have included local community affairs associations; minority and urban affairs groups; economics, business, free enterprise, and public policy organizations; public safety agencies; and environmental affairs organizations.
Education: 45% to 50%. Primary support to higher education institutions, with emphasis on engineering, science, and technology. Private secondary schools are supported through matching gifts. Minority and pre-college programs also supported. The remainder supports educational associations, including scholarship programs. Sponsors matching gifts program for higher and secondary educational institutions.
Environment: About 10%. Supports environmental education, conservation,environmental research.
Health: 25% to 30%. Primary interests are hospitals and united funds. Other areas of interest include organizations for the handicapped,drug and alcohol education, child welfare, and community service. Limited support to medical research and rehabilitation and pediatric health.
International: Less than 5%. Emphasis on international affairs organizations.

Application Procedures

Initial Contact: one- or two-page letter
Application Requirements: a description of organization, amount requested, purpose of funds sought, recently audited financial statement, and proof of tax-exempt status
Deadlines: None.
Review Process: initial review to determine relation to priorities, areas of interest, and geographic proximity
Decision Notification: ongoing

Restrictions

Foundation does not support loans, dinners or special events, fraternal organizations, goodwill advertising, individuals, political or lobbying groups, or religious organizations for sectarian purposes.
Does not provide general support to member agencies of united funds. May consider capital campaign support.

Corporate Officials

Donald Wayne Griffin: chairman, president, chief executive officer, director B Evansville, IN 1937. ED Syracuse University; Indiana University BA (1954-1957); University of Evansville BA (1961). PRIM CORP EMPL chairman, president, chief executive officer, director: Olin Corp. CORP AFFIL director: Rayonier Timberlands LP; director: Riverbend Bancshares Inc.; director: Rayonier Forest Resources Co.; director: Rayonier Inc.; director: AC Nielsen Corp.; director: Illinois State Bank E Alton. NONPR AFFIL director: Southwest Illinois Industry Association; director: Wildlife Management Institute; director: Small Arms Ammunition Manufacturer; director: National Shooting Sports Foundation; life member: Navy League U.S.; member: Illinois Chamber of Commerce; director: Leadership Council Southwest Illinois; director: Buffalo Bill Historical Center; director: Chemical Manufacturers Association; member: American Society Metals; member: Association U.S. Army.
Peter C. Kosche: senior vice president corporate affairs PRIM CORP EMPL senior vice president corporate affairs: Olin Corp.
Anthony W. Ruggiero: executive vice president, chief financial officer ED Fordham University BS (1963); Columbia University MBA (1964). PRIM CORP EMPL executive vice president, chief financial officer: Olin Corp.

Foundation Officials

Donald Wayne Griffin: trustee (see above)
Peter C. Kosche: trustee (see above)
Carmella V. Piacentini: administrator

Grants Analysis

Disclosure Period: calendar year ending 1997
Total Grants: $1,892,177
Number of Grants: 1,500 (approx)
Average Grant: $1,261 (approx)
Highest Grant: $200,000 (approx)
Typical Range: $50 to $5,000

Recent Grants

Note: Grants derived from 1996 Form 990.

Arts & Humanities

10,000	E.G. Fisher Public Library

Civic & Public Affairs

60,000	Maritime Aquarium, Norwalk, CT
50,000	Inroads Incorporated
30,000	Conference Board, New York, NY
25,000	American Chemical Society, Detroit, MI
20,000	Cleveland Bradley County Chamber Foundation
10,000	American Chemical Society, Detroit, MI

Education

200,000	Corporate Education Partnership, Godfrey, IL
33,814	Washington County Board of Education
30,000	Queen Creek United School District
25,000	National Consortium for Graduate Degrees for Minorities in Engineering, Notre Dame, IN
24,000	East Alton Elementary School District
23,246	Rochester City School District
22,470	Bradley County School System
22,000	University of California Berkeley, Berkeley, CA
20,000	Crawford County School District
20,000	University of Connecticut, Storrs, CT
20,000	University of Missouri Rolla Department of Metallurgical Engineering, Rolla, MO
18,723	Calcasieu Parish School System
18,000	Meade County Board of Education
17,800	Wakula County School Board, HI
16,150	Cheshire Education Foundation, Cheshire, CT
13,740	National Merit Scholarship Corporation, Evanston, IL
12,000	Fairfield University, Fairfield, CT
10,525	Norwalk Community Technical College Foundation, Norwalk, CT
10,000	Drexel University, Philadelphia, PA
9,000	Meade County Board of Education
8,500	Alton Community United School
7,083	Washington State University Foundation, Pullman, WA
6,644	Cornell University, Ithaca, NY
6,050	Harvard University, Cambridge, MA
6,000	Cheshire Education Foundation, Cheshire, CT
6,000	Connecticut Academy for Education in Math, Science, and Technology, Middletown, CT
6,000	Town of Cheshire School System
6,000	Washington County Board of Education

Environment

10,000	Clean Sites, Alexandria, VA
7,500	Student Conservation Association, Arlington, VA

Health

7,000	Family Service and Visiting Nurse Association

International

12,500	Global Environmental Management Initiative, Washington, DC
12,500	Global Environmental Management Initiative, Washington, DC
10,000	Co-operation Ireland, New York, NY

Science

12,500	Science Museum of Connecticut, West Hartford, CT

Social Services

70,000	United Way Partnership
30,000	United Way
22,750	Bradley County United Way
15,000	Jackson County United Way, Independence, MO
15,000	United Way King County, Seattle, WA
14,180	United Way Southwestern Alabama, AL
9,000	United Way Central Indiana, Indianapolis, IN
7,500	United Way York County, York, PA

ONEOK, INC.

Company Contact

Tulsa, OK
Web: http://www.oneok.com

Company Description

Revenue: US$949,890,000
Employees: 2,061
SIC(s): 1311 Crude Petroleum & Natural Gas, 4923 Gas Transmission & Distribution, 6719 Holding Companies Nec.

Giving Contact

Ginny Creveling, Administrator, Corporate Responsibility
PO Box 871
Tulsa, OK 74102-0871
Phone: (918)588-7000

Description

Organization Type: Corporate Giving Program
Grant Types: Capital, Employee Matching Gifts, General Support, Multiyear/Continuing Support, Project.

Financial Summary

Total Giving: $1,000,000 (2000 approx); $1,000,000 (1999 approx); $1,000,000 (1998)

Typical Recipients

Arts & Humanities: Arts & Humanities-General
Education: Colleges & Universities, Community & Junior Colleges, Education-General, Leadership Training, Secondary Education (Private), Secondary Education (Public)
Environment: Energy, Environment-General
Health: Health-General
Social Services: Social Services-General

Application Procedures

Initial Contact: Send a full proposal.
Application Requirements: Description of organization, amount requested, purpose of funds sought, recently audited financial statement, board list, and proof of tax-exempt status.

Restrictions

Does not support individuals, religious organizations for sectarian purposes, political or lobbying groups, or organizations outside operating areas.

Corporate Officials

Larry W. Brummett: chairman, chief executive officer, director PRIM CORP EMPL chairman, chief executive officer, director: ONEOK Inc.
James C. Kneale: chief financial officer PRIM CORP EMPL chief financial officer: ONEOK Inc.
David L. Kyle: president PRIM CORP EMPL president: ONEOK Inc.

Grants Analysis

Disclosure Period: calendar year ending
Total Grants: $1,000,000 (approx)*
Typical Range: $5,000 to $50,000
***Note:** Giving total provided by organization.

ORACLE CORP.

Company Contact

Redwood Shores, CA
Web: http://www.oracle.com

Company Description

Revenue: US$8,827,300,000 (1999)
Employees: 23,113
Fortune Rank: 195, per FORTUNE Magazine's list of 500 Largest U.S. Corporations (1999).
FF 195
SIC(s): 3571 Electronic Computers, 3572 Computer Storage Devices, 7371 Computer Programming Services, 7372 Prepackaged Software.
Parent Company: Oracle Systems Corp.

Giving Contact

Rosalie Gann, Director, Giving Programs
Oracle Corporate Giving Program
500 Oracle Parkway
MS-50P-11
Redwood City, CA 94065
Phone: (650)506-7000
Fax: (650)506-7200
Email: lames@us.oracle.com

Alternate Contact

Shannon Mollner
Phone: (650)375-8881
Email: smollner@appliedcom.com

Description

Organization Type: Corporate Giving Program
Giving Locations: primarily operating locations.

Giving Philosophy

'The Oracle Corporate Giving Program extends the Oracle employee tradition of supporting charitable causes to the corporate level. Through the Corporate Giving Program, Oracle responds directly to the financial needs of medical research, endangered animal protection, environmental protection, and K-12 education. By donating funds to qualified nonprofit organizations and institutions that support these causes, Oracle gives back to the communities in which it operates, and invests in the future of our global community. Through the Corporate Giving Program, Oracle Corporation contributes to the legacy of goodwill established by Oracle employees throughout the world. With their continued support and input, Oracle makes a difference.' *Oracle in the Community* 1997

Contributions Analysis

Giving Priorities: Environmental protection, endangered animal protection, medical research, and K-12 educational programs.
Education: About 60%. Supports K-12 education, with an emphasis on math, science and technology. Has a major commitment to improve technology in the classroom through the Oracle's Promise foundation.
Environment: About 15%. Funding goes to endangered animal protection. 5% to 10%. The remaining funds support enivronmental protection, with an emphasis on education and preservation of open space.
Health: About 15%. Supports medical research, with an emphasis on cancer, AIDS and neuroscience.

Application Procedures

Initial Contact: request application guidelines
Application Requirements: completed application; and proposal (no longer than five pages), including a description of support requested, description of agency and program, population and geographic areas served, proposed starting date and duration, organization and project budgets, a list of key staff members and their backgrounds, any past involvement with company either through donations or volunteer efforts, project objectives, plans for evaluation, and proof of tax-exempt status
Deadlines: June 1,December 1
Decision Notification: awards are sent in late May, late August, late November and late February
Notes: To apply for the Oracle Volunteer Program send a letter of inquiry or a proposal addressed to the Oracle Volunteer Program. Include verification of tax-exempt status; name and mission of agency; volunteer job description; whether current agency volunteers are employees; name, address, and telephone number of contact; and whether the agency has liability insurance.

Restrictions

The company does not support programs or projects directly, fund-raising activities, charitable dinners, sporting events, marketing, brochures or loans.

Additional Information

Oracle is in the process of establishing the Oracle Mentoring Program, which will mobilize its employees to develop mentoring relationships with economically disadvantaged youth grades 4-12.
In 1997 the company formed Oracle's Promise, a nonprofit foundation chartered with placing a network computer on every child's desk. The company has committed $100 million towards this project in conjunction with America's Promise - The Alliance for Youth program. The company also has a companion program called Oracle's Challenge: Help Us Help, designed to recruit individuals, corporation and governments to get involved by adopting students, classrooms to entire schools in their community.

Corporate Officials

Lawrence J. Ellison: chairman, chief executive officer, director, president B New York, NY 1944. ED University of Illinois; University of Chicago BS (1966). PRIM CORP EMPL chairman, chief executive officer, director, president: Oracle Corp. CORP AFFIL systems architect: Amdahl Inc.; director: Apple Computer Inc.
Jeffrey O. Henley: executive vice president, chief financial officer, director B Phoenix, AZ 1944. ED University of California, Santa Barbara BA (1966); University of California, Los Angeles MBA (1967). PRIM CORP EMPL executive vice president, chief financial officer, director: Oracle Corp. NONPR AFFIL member: Financial Executives Institute; member: Sigma Phi Epsilon.

ORANGE & ROCKLAND UTILITIES, INC.

Company Contact

Pearl River, NY
Web: http://www.oru.com

Company Description

Assets: US$1,313,600,000
Employees: 1,501
SIC(s): 4911 Electric Services, 4924 Natural Gas Distribution.

Nonmonetary Support

Type: Donated Equipment

Giving Contact

Neil Winter, Manager, Corporate Programs
1 Blue Hill Plaza
Pearl River, NY 10965
Phone: (914)352-6000

Description

Organization Type: Corporate Giving Program
Giving Locations: headquarters and operating communities.
Grant Types: Award, Challenge, Employee Matching Gifts, General Support, Multiyear/Continuing Support, Scholarship, Seed Money.

Financial Summary

Total Giving: $290,000 (1997 approx); $275,000 (1996); $350,000 (1993). Note: Contributes through corporate direct giving program only.

Typical Recipients

Civic & Public Affairs: Chambers of Commerce, Employment/Job Training, Civic & Public Affairs-General, Professional & Trade Associations
Education: Business Education, Community & Junior Colleges, Elementary Education (Public), Engineering/Technological Education, Education-General, Science/Mathematics Education
Health: Cancer, Health-General, Heart, Hospitals, Medical Research, Respiratory
Science: Science-General, Science Museums
Social Services: People with Disabilities, Social Services-General, United Funds/United Ways, Volunteer Services

Application Procedures

Initial Contact: a brief letter of inquiry
Application Requirements: a description of organization, amount requested, purpose of funds sought, recently audited financial statement, and proof of tax-exempt status

Restrictions

Does not support individuals, religious organizations for sectarian purposes, political or lobbying groups, or organizations outside operating areas.

Corporate Officials

R. Lee Haney: senior vice president, chief financial officer ED Brigham Young University BS (1970); Brigham Young University MBA (1972). PRIM CORP EMPL senior vice president, chief financial officer: Orange & Rockland Utilities, Inc.
D. Louis Peoples: vice chairman, chief executive officer, director B Kansas City, MO 1940. ED Stanford University (1963); Harvard University (1972). PRIM CORP EMPL vice chairman, chief executive officer, director: Orange & Rockland Utilities, Inc. NONPR AFFIL director: Electric Power Research Institute; member: Empire State Electric Energy Research Corp.; member: Edison Electric Institute.
H. Kent Vanderhoef: chairman, director PRIM CORP EMPL chairman, director: Orange & Rockland Utilities, Inc.

Grants Analysis
Disclosure Period: calendar year ending 1996
Typical Range: $1,000 to $2,500

Recent Grants
Note: Grants derived from 1996 grants list.

Arts & Humanities
Neversink Museum

Civic & Public Affairs
Leadership Orange
Orange County Citizens Foundation

Education
Educational Foundation of OCCC
Junior Achievement

Health
American Cancer Society
American Lung Association
Epilepsy Society of Southern New York

Social Services
Police Chief's Foundation of Rockland County
Rockland Council on Alcohol and Drugs

Orscheln Co.

Company Contact
Moberly, MO

Company Description
Employees: 600
SIC(s): 3451 Screw Machine Products, 3544 Special Dies, Tools, Jigs & Fixtures, 3714 Motor Vehicle Parts & Accessories, 7699 Repair Services Nec.

Orscheln Industries Foundation, Inc.

Giving Contact
Gerald A. Orscheln, Director
Orscheln Industries Foundation, Inc.
PO Box 698
Moberly, MO 65270
Phone: (816)263-4377
Fax: (816)269-3520

Description
Founded: 1968
EIN: 237115623
Organization Type: Corporate Foundation
Giving Locations: MO: especially Randolph County
Grant Types: General Support, Scholarship.

Financial Summary
Total Giving: $1,300,000 (fiscal year ending September 30, 1999 approx); $1,064,205 (fiscal 1998 approx); $1,288,052 (fiscal 1996). Note: Contributes through foundation only.
Giving Analysis: Giving for fiscal 1996 includes: foundation scholarships ($39,500); foundation grants to United Way ($19,597); fiscal 1998: foundation scholarships ($105,250); foundation grants to United Way ($30,657)
Assets: $16,359,718 (fiscal 1998); $13,447,588 (fiscal 1996); $12,792,318 (fiscal 1993)
Gifts Received: $3,282,680 (fiscal 1998); $410,141 (fiscal 1996); $373,513 (fiscal 1993). Note: Contributions are received from the Alkin Company, GAO, and David Orscheln.

Typical Recipients
Arts & Humanities: History & Archaeology, Theater
Civic & Public Affairs: Botanical Gardens/Parks, Business/Free Enterprise, Civic & Public Affairs-General, Urban & Community Affairs
Education: Agricultural Education, Colleges & Universities, Community & Junior Colleges, Medical Education, Private Education (Precollege), Public Education (Precollege), Religious Education, Secondary Education (Private), Secondary Education (Public), Student Aid
Environment: Sanitary Systems
Health: Alzheimers Disease, Arthritis, Health Funds, Health Organizations, Hospitals, Prenatal Health Issues, Public Health, Single-Disease Health Associations
Religion: Churches, Dioceses, Religious Organizations, Religious Welfare, Seminaries, Social/Policy Issues
Social Services: Child Welfare, Community Service Organizations, Day Care, Day Care, Food/Clothing Distribution, Scouts, United Funds/United Ways, YMCA/YWCA/YMHA/YWHA, Youth Organizations

Contributions Analysis
Giving Priorities: Primary emphasis on religious causes and education.
Arts & Humanities: 1%.
Education: 34%. Supports local schools and colleges, as well as religious colleges. Also sponsors scholarship awards program for Randolph County High School seniors, and provides scholarships to children of employees.
Health: 2%. Funds support hospitals, single-disease health organizations, and similar health groups.
Religion: 56%. Majority supports Catholic and other religious institutions in Missouri. Also contributes to a Catholic diocese, several parishes and church fund drives, and religious service organizations.
Social Services: 7%. Grants are made to the United Way, child welfare organizations, youth groups, community centers, and a variety of other programs.
Note: Total contributions in fiscal 1998.

Application Procedures
Initial Contact: Send a brief letter or proposal.
Application Requirements: Include a description of organization, amount requested, purpose of funds sought, and proof of tax-exempt status.
Deadlines: None, for general grants; April 1 for scholarships.

Corporate Officials
Donald W. Orscheln: director, chairman B 1925. PRIM CORP EMPL director, chairman: Orscheln Co. CORP AFFIL trustee: Computerized Business Systems; director: Orbseal LLC.

Foundation Officials
Donald W. Orscheln: secretary (see above)
Gerald A. Orscheln: president B 1927. PRIM CORP EMPL chairman, director: Orscheln Farm & Home Supply. CORP AFFIL president: Computerized Business Systems; director: Orbseal LLC.
Phillip A. Orscheln: director PRIM CORP EMPL director: Orscheln Management Co.
William L. Orscheln: treasurer B 1950. ED Central Methodist College BA (1972). PRIM CORP EMPL president, treasurer, director: Orscheln Farm & Home LLC. CORP AFFIL vice president, finance: Computerized Business Systems; president, director: Orscheln Co.

Grants Analysis
Disclosure Period: fiscal year ending September 30, 1998
Total Grants: $928,298*
Number of Grants: 118
Average Grant: $7,867
Highest Grant: $141,043
Typical Range: $1,000 to $10,000
***Note:** Giving excludes scholarship; United Way.

Recent Grants
Note: Grants derived from fiscal 1998 Form 990.

Arts & Humanities

10,000 General Omar N. Bradley Memorial, Inc., Moberly, MO -- General Purpose

Education

67,100 Moberly Area Community College Foundation, Moberly, MO -- General Purpose
39,262 Rockhurst High School, Kansas City, MO -- General Purpose
29,000 4-H Scholarships -- Scholarships
29,000 FFA Scholarships -- Scholarships
20,000 Creighton University, Omaha, NE -- General Purpose
12,500 University of Missouri, Columbia, MO -- Scholarship
12,000 St. Joseph School, Salisbury, MO -- General Purpose
8,000 St. Peter's Catholic School, Fulton, MO -- General Purpose
6,000 Central Christian Coll of the Bible, Moberly, MO -- Scholarship
6,000 Missouri Valley College, Marshall, MO -- General Purpose
5,000 Benedictine College, Atchison, KS -- General Purpose
5,000 Carroll College Foundation, Helena, MT -- General Purpose
5,000 Donnelly College, Kansas City, MO -- General Purpose
5,000 Fontbonne College, St. Louis, MO -- General Purpose
5,000 Kansas Newman College, Wichita, KS -- General Purpose
5,000 Maryville University of St. Louis, St. Louis, MO -- General Purpose
5,000 Rockhurst College, Kansas City, MO -- General Purpose
5,000 St. Mary College, Leavenworth, KS -- General Purpose
5,000 School Sisters of Notre Dame, St. Louis, MO -- General Purpose
5,000 University of Mossouri-Arthritis Center, Columbia, MO -- Scholarship
4,900 Maur Hill Prep School, Atchison, KS -- General Purpose
4,500 Stephens College, Columbia, MO -- General Purpose

Health

5,500 Moberly Regional Health Foundation, Moberly, MO -- General Purpose
5,000 Arthritis Found., Eastern Mosouri Chapter, St. Louis, MO -- General Purpose
4,250 Alzheimer's Association -- General Purpose

Religion

141,043 St. Pius X Building Fund, Moberly, MO -- General Purpose
80,500 St. Vincent De Paul Society -- General Purpose
50,000 Immaculate Conception Parish, Montgomerycity, MO -- General Purpose
50,000 St. Ann Catholic Church, Warsaw, MO -- General Purpose
37,000 Our Lady of Lourdes Parish, Columbia, MO -- General Purpose
25,000 Newman Center, Columbia, MO -- General Purpose
24,000 St. James Catholic Church, Liberty, MO -- General Purpose
18,000 Diocese of Jefferson City, Jefferson City, MO -- General Purpose
13,350 Our Lady of the Lake, Lake of Ozarks, MO -- General Purpose
12,975 Our Lady of Joy, Carefree, AZ -- General Purpose
10,000 St. Francis Xavier Church, Jefferson City, MO -- General Purpose

8,400	St. Anthony's Church, Camdenton, MO -- General Purpose
5,000	Church of the Little Flower, Browning, MT -- General Purpose
5,000	Kenrick-Glennon Seminary, St. Louis, MO -- General Purpose
4,500	Emmaus Catholic Church, Austin, TX -- General Purpose
Social Services	
30,000	Comm Day Care Learning Center Inc, Moberly, MO -- General Purpose
10,800	Great Rivers Council, Boy Scouts, Columbia, MO -- General Purpose
10,000	Assistance League of Kansas City, Kansas City, MO -- General Purpose
6,564	Boys & Girls Club -- General Purpose
6,000	Children's Foundation of Mid-America, Inc., St. Louis, MO -- General Purpose

OSBORNE ENTERPRISES

Company Contact
Chattanooga, TN

Company Description
Employees: 56

Weldon F. Osborne Foundation

Giving Contact
Harold S. Wilson, Executive Director
Weldon F. Osborne Foundation
209 Uptain Bldg.
571 Uptain Road
Chattanooga, TN 37411
Phone: (423)510-0390

Description
EIN: 626026442
Organization Type: Corporate Foundation
Giving Locations: TN: Chattanooga
Grant Types: General Support, Matching, Scholarship.

Financial Summary
Total Giving: $430,000 (fiscal year ending June 30, 1998 approx); $34,063 (fiscal 1997); $450,000 (fiscal 1996). Note: 1997 Giving includes United Way ($1,000).
Assets: $1,260,205 (fiscal 1997); $868,375 (fiscal 1994); $767,498 (fiscal 1992)
Gifts Received: $450,211 (fiscal 1997); $40,000 (fiscal 1994); $40,000 (fiscal 1992)

Typical Recipients
Civic & Public Affairs: Business/Free Enterprise, Clubs, Economic Development, Urban & Community Affairs
Education: Education Funds, Elementary Education (Private), Health & Physical Education, Leadership Training, Private Education (Precollege), Public Education (Precollege), Religious Education, Secondary Education (Private), Secondary Education (Public), Student Aid
Health: Hospitals
Religion: Ministries, Religious Welfare
Social Services: Big Brother/Big Sister, Community Service Organizations, Crime Prevention, Delinquency & Criminal Rehabilitation, Food/Clothing Distribution, Recreation & Athletics, Scouts, Special Olympics, United Funds/United Ways, Veterans

Application Procedures
Initial Contact: Send letter requesting application form. Requesting organizations must be tax-exempt under Section 501(c)(3).

Restrictions
Grants are not made to individuals.

Additional Information
Publications: Application Form

Corporate Officials
Gene Burnett: chief financial officer, president, chief executive officer PRIM CORP EMPL chief financial officer: Osborne Enterprises.
C. Duffy Franck: chairman, president, chief executive officer PRIM CORP EMPL chairman, president, chief executive officer: Osborne Enterprises.

Foundation Officials
C. Duffy Franck: assistant secretary (see above)
Robert E. Knight: treasurer
Ray C. Marlin: president
J. M. Skurlock: vice president
Harold S. Wilson: executive director

Grants Analysis
Disclosure Period: fiscal year ending June 30, 1997
Total Grants: $33,063*
Number of Grants: 17
Average Grant: $1,945
Highest Grant: $3,000
Typical Range: $600 to $4,000
***Note:** Giving excludes United Way.

Recent Grants
Note: Grants derived from fiscal 1997 Form 990.

Civic & Public Affairs	
730	Siskin 365 Club, Chattanooga, TN -- operating fund
300	East Ridge Revitalization Program, Chattanooga, TN -- planning workshop meeting
Education	
3,000	Public School Bible Study Committee, Chattanooga, TN -- operating fund
2,000	Our Lady of Perpetual Help Catholic School, Chattanooga, TN -- educational financial aid
2,000	Scenic Land School, Chattanooga, TN -- educational financial aid
1,000	Girls Preparatory School, Chattanooga, TN -- educational financial aid
900	Hixson High School AJROTC, Hixson, TN
Health	
2,500	Sisters of Charity, Memorial Hospital, Chattanooga, TN -- capital campaign
Religion	
3,000	Chattanooga Prison Ministries, Chattanooga, TN -- operating fund
3,000	Salvation Army, Chattanooga, TN -- operating fund
2,000	Contact Ministries, Chattanooga, TN -- operating fund
Social Services	
2,500	Hosanna Community House, Chattanooga, TN -- operating fund
2,133	Community Kitchen, Chattanooga, TN -- operating fund
2,000	Chattanooga Area Veterans, Chattanooga, TN -- national cemetery brochure
2,000	Chattanooga Big Brothers and Sisters Association, Chattanooga, TN -- operating fund
2,000	Special Olympics, Chattanooga, TN -- operating fund
2,000	Sports, Arts, and Recreation, Chattanooga, TN -- operating fund
1,000	United Way, Chattanooga, TN -- operating fund

OSHKOSH B'GOSH, INC.

Company Contact
Oshkosh, WI
Web: http://www.oshkoshbgosh.com

Company Description
Employees: 4,700
SIC(s): 2325 Men's/Boys' Trousers & Slacks, 2326 Men's/Boys' Work Clothing, 2369 Girls'/Children's Outerwear Nec.

Corporate Sponsorship
Type: Arts & cultural events; Festivals/fairs; Music & entertainment events; Pledge-a-thon; Sports events

Oshkosh B'Gosh Foundation Inc.

Giving Contact
Michael D. Wachtel, Executive Vice President
Oshkosh B'Gosh Inc.
112 Otter Ave.
Oshkosh, WI 54901
Phone: (920)231-8800
Fax: (920)231-8621

Description
EIN: 391525020
Organization Type: Corporate Foundation
Giving Locations: operating locations.
Grant Types: General Support, Scholarship.
Note: Scholarships are available for high school graduates in the communities in which Oshkosh B'Gosh, Inc. plants or facilities are located.

Financial Summary
Total Giving: $331,309 (1998); $328,054 (1997); $337,005 (1996). Note: Contributes through foundation only.
Giving Analysis: Giving for 1996 includes: foundation grants to United Way ($49,369); foundation scholarships ($38,750); 1997: foundation scholarships ($101,250); foundation grants to United Way ($33,329); 1998: foundation ($195,934); foundation scholarships ($98,875); foundation grants to United Way ($36,500)
Assets: $722,380 (1998); $948,173 (1997); $779,871 (1996)
Gifts Received: $400,000 (1997); $450,000 (1996); $295,000 (1995). Note: Contributions are received from Oshkosh B'Gosh, Inc.

Typical Recipients
Arts & Humanities: Arts Associations & Councils, Arts Centers, Arts Festivals, Community Arts, Dance, Libraries, Museums/Galleries, Music, Opera, Performing Arts, Public Broadcasting
Civic & Public Affairs: Botanical Gardens/Parks, Business/Free Enterprise, Chambers of Commerce, Community Foundations, Civic & Public Affairs-General, Housing, Parades/Festivals, Philanthropic Organizations, Professional & Trade Associations, Public Policy, Urban & Community Affairs, Zoos/Aquariums
Education: Agricultural Education, Business Education, Colleges & Universities, Education Funds, Elementary Education (Private), Education-General, Literacy, Medical Education, Minority Education, Private Education (Precollege), Public Education (Precollege), Public Education (Precollege), Science/Mathematics Education, Student Aid, Vocational & Technical Education
Environment: Environment-General, Watershed
Health: Cancer, Children's Health/Hospitals, Clinics/Medical Centers, Diabetes, Emergency/Ambulance Services, Eyes/Blindness, Health Organizations,

Heart, Medical Rehabilitation, Mental Health, Respiratory, Single-Disease Health Associations, Speech & Hearing
International: International-General, International Environmental Issues, International Organizations, International Relief Efforts
Religion: Jewish Causes
Science: Science Museums
Social Services: At-Risk Youth, Big Brother/Big Sister, Camps, Child Abuse, Child Welfare, Community Service Organizations, Day Care, Domestic Violence, Family Services, Family Services, People with Disabilities, Recreation & Athletics, Scouts, Senior Services, Sexual Abuse, Special Olympics, United Funds/United Ways, YMCA/YWCA/YMHA/YWHA, Youth Organizations

Contributions Analysis

Arts & Humanities: 20%. The Paine Art Center and Arboretum in Oshkosh, WI, receives major support. Music and dance are also funded.
Civic & Public Affairs: 1%. Supports community affairs and organizations.
Education: 41%. Supports colleges and universities and educational foundations and programs. A significant amount is devoted to scholarships, awarded to high school graduates from cities with company operating locations.
Health: 16%. Supports hospitals, health societies, and single-disease health associations.
International: 2%. Supports international organizations.
Social Services: 20%. Major support goes to the United Way. Additional funds support community service organizations and youth activities.
Note: Total contributions in 1998.

Application Procedures

Initial Contact: Send brief letter.
Application Requirements: Include a description of organization; amount requested and purpose of funds sought; audited financial statement; and proof of tax-exempt status.
Deadlines: None.
Notes: The foundation reports there are no standard application procedures for grants. Scholarship applicants should contact the foundation for a formal application form. Deadlines for scholarship applications are determined by each participating college.

Restrictions

The foundation only supports organizations where a corporate office or sewing facility is located.

Corporate Officials

Douglas W. Hyde: chairman, president, chief executive officer B 1950. PRIM CORP EMPL chairman, president, chief executive officer: Oshkosh B'Gosh, Inc.
David L. Omachinski: chief financial officer, treasurer, vice president B Appleton, WI 1952. ED University of Wisconsin BA (1974). PRIM CORP EMPL chief financial officer, treasurer, vice president: Oshkosh B'Gosh Inc. CORP AFFIL director: White Clover Dairy; director: Archorbank SSB; director: Fox Cities Bank. NONPR AFFIL member: Knights of Columbus; member: Rotary International; treasurer: Art Paine Center & Arboretum; member: Financial Executive Institute; member: American Institute CPAs.
Michael D. Wachtel: chief operating officer B 1954. ED University of Wisconsin Pharmacy (1977). PRIM CORP EMPL chief operating officer: Oshkosh B'Gosh, Inc.

Foundation Officials

David L. Omachinski: (see above)
Michael D. Wachtel: president (see above)
William Wyman: director

Grants Analysis

Disclosure Period: calendar year ending 1998
Total Grants: $195,934*
Number of Grants: 43
Average Grant: $4,557
Highest Grant: $47,000
Typical Range: $500 to $5,000
***Note:** Giving excludes scholarship; United Way.

Recent Grants

Note: Grants derived from 1998 Form 990.

Arts & Humanities

47,000	Paine Art Center Arboretum, Oshkosh, WI
10,000	GR Opera House Fund, Oshkosh, WI
5,000	Oshkosh Symphony, Oshkosh, WI
1,550	United Performing Arts Fund, Milwaukee, WI
1,000	Pick of the Crop Dance, Buffalo, NY
500	Green Lake Festival of Music, Green Lake, WI
384	Oshkosh Fine Arts, Oshkosh, WI
250	Oshkosh Area Community Band, Oshkosh, WI

Civic & Public Affairs

1,500	Habitat for Humanity of Oshkosh, Inc., Oshkosh, WI
1,000	Bay-Lakes Council, Menasha, WI
1,000	Project Soar, Oshkosh, WI

Education

22,000	UWO Foundation, Oshkosh, WI
5,750	Junior Achievement of Oshkosh, Oshkosh, WI
5,000	Emma Willard School, Troy, NY
1,000	American Apparel Education, Arlington, VA
1,000	Oshkosh Area School District, Oshkosh, WI
500	Odyssey of the Mind, Oshkosh, WI
450	WMC Foundation Inc, Madison, WI
250	CBAA Scholarship Fund, Oshkosh, WI

Environment

500	Fox-Wolf Basin 2000, Appleton, WI

Health

31,000	Mercy Medical Center Foundation, Oshkosh, WI
5,000	Children's Hospital Foundation, Neenah, WI
5,000	The Imus Ranch, Riborn, NM
4,000	Easter Seal Society of Wisconsin, Madison, WI
2,500	American Red Cross, Oshkosh, WI
2,000	American Cancer Society, Appleton, WI
1,800	Center for the Deaf & Hard of Hearing, Milwaukee, WI
1,000	Ronald McDonald House, Wauwatosa, WI
250	UFCW Leukemia Research Fund, Milwaukee, WI
150	American Diabetes Association, Oshkosh, WI

International

500,000	Comite Amigos De Guarderias Infantiles Y Salas Cunas, Sula, Honduras

Social Services

36,500	United Way, Oshkosh, WI
10,000	Kids in Distressed Situations, Moorestown, NJ
5,000	Boys Girls Club of Oshkosh, Oshkosh, WI
5,000	Child Welfare League of America, New York, NY
3,500	Regional Domestic Abuse Services, Inc., Neenah, WI
3,000	Child Care Resource & Referral of Winnebago County, Oshkosh, WI
2,000	Oshkosh YMCA, Oshkosh, WI
1,000	Fox River Area Girl Scouts, Appleton, WI
1,000	Rawhide Boys Ranch, New London, WI
1,000	Special Olympics of Wisconsin, Madison, WI
500	Oshkosh Family Inc., Oshkosh, WI
500	Sexual Abuse Services Inc., Oshkosh, WI
100	Oshkosh Big Brothers, Oshkosh, WI

OUTBOARD MARINE CORP.

Company Contact

Waukegan, IL
Web: http://www.omc-online.com

Company Description

Profit: US$84,300,000
Employees: 8,449
SIC(s): 3519 Internal Combustion Engines Nec, 3732 Boat Building & Repairing.

Operating Locations

Includes plant and division locations.

OMC Foundation

Giving Contact

Gary Beckett, Director, Public Affairs & Communications
100 Sea Horse Dr.
Waukegan, IL 60085
Phone: (847)689-6200
Fax: (847)689-5555

Description

Founded: 1945
EIN: 396037139
Organization Type: Corporate Foundation
Giving Locations: headquarters and operating communities.
Grant Types: Employee Matching Gifts, Project, Scholarship.

Financial Summary

Total Giving: $245,235 (fiscal year ending September 30, 1997); $274,666 (fiscal 1996); $250,247 (fiscal 1994). Note: 1997 Giving includes matching gifts ($72,429); scholarship ($43,500); United Way ($83,076).
Assets: $5,504,493 (fiscal 1997); $4,731,877 (fiscal 1996); $4,057,430 (fiscal 1994)
Gifts Received: $2,500,000 (fiscal 1990); $1,087,500 (fiscal 1989). Note: In 1990, contributions were received from Outboard Marine Corp.

Typical Recipients

Arts & Humanities: Arts Institutes, Libraries, Museums/Galleries, Performing Arts, Public Broadcasting
Civic & Public Affairs: Community Foundations, Economic Development, Civic & Public Affairs-General, Housing, Public Policy, Urban & Community Affairs, Zoos/Aquariums
Education: Colleges & Universities, Community & Junior Colleges, Engineering/Technological Education, Minority Education, Private Education (Precollege), Vocational & Technical Education
Environment: Air/Water Quality, Environment-General, Resource Conservation
Health: Cancer, Clinics/Medical Centers, Hospitals
Religion: Bible Study/Translation
Social Services: At-Risk Youth, Community Service Organizations, Delinquency & Criminal Rehabilitation, Recreation & Athletics, Scouts, Substance

Abuse, United Funds/United Ways, YMCA/YWCA/YMHA/YWHA

Application Procedures

Initial Contact: Send a brief letter of inquiry including a description of organization, amount requested, purpose of funds sought, and proof of tax-exempt status.
Deadlines: September.

Restrictions

Initial consideration is given to privately supported colleges and universities located in or serving the areas in which Outboard Marine Corp. facilities are located. Does not support individuals, religious organizations for sectarian purposes, political or lobbying groups, or organizations outside operating areas.

Corporate Officials

Harold W. Bowman: chairman, president, chief executive officer, director PRIM CORP EMPL chairman, president, chief executive officer, director: Outboard Marine Corp.
George Louis Schueppert: chief financial officer, executive vice president B Merrill, WI 1938. ED University of Wisconsin BBA (1961); University of Chicago MBA (1969). PRIM CORP EMPL chief financial officer, executive vice president: Outboard Marine Corp. NONPR AFFIL vice chairman, director: De Paul University Government Assistance Project; chairman, finance committee, director: Great Books Foundation; board advisors: CPAs Pub Interest. CLUB AFFIL dir, chmn membership comm: Economic Club Chicago.

Foundation Officials

Harold W. Bowman: president (see above)
Henry H. Hegel: director
Richard H. Medland: director

Grants Analysis

Disclosure Period: fiscal year ending September 30, 1997
Total Grants: $46,230*
Number of Grants: 14
Average Grant: $2,231*
Highest Grant: $15,000
Typical Range: $100 to $1,000
***Note:** Giving excludes matching gifts; scholarship; United Way. Average grant figure excludes highest grant.

Recent Grants

Note: Grants derived from fiscal 1997 Form 990.

Civic & Public Affairs

15,000	Waukegan Downtown Association, Waukegan, WI
5,000	Cooperative Housing Foundation, Silver Spring, MD
4,000	Greater Beloit Community Foundation, Beloit, WI

Education

7,000	Columbia University, New York, NY
6,965	Suomi College, Hancock, MI
5,000	University of Detroit Mercy, Detroit, MI
4,500	Hobart and William Smith Colleges
4,300	Northwestern University, Evanston, IL
4,000	Ball State University Foundation, Muncie, IN
3,600	Ezell-Harding Christian School
3,000	David Lipscomb University, Nashville, TN
2,600	Lake Forest College, Lake Forest, IL

Environment

5,000	Great Lakes Fishing Council

Health

4,087	Lake County American Cancer Society, Gurnee, IL

Religion

3,460	Moody Bible Institute

Social Services

23,258	United Way Gordon County, Calhoun, GA
20,848	United Way Lake County, Green Oaks, IL
16,849	United Way, Milwaukee, WI
4,748	United Way Yancey County, Burnsville, NC
4,463	United Way Kenosha County, Kenosha, WI

Overnite Transportation Co.

Company Contact

Richmond, VA

Company Description

Revenue: US$967,000,000
Employees: 14,300
SIC(s): 4213 Trucking Except Local.
Parent Company: Union Pacific Corp., Dallas, TX, United States

Operating Locations

Operates throughout the USA.

Nonmonetary Support

Type: Donated Equipment

Corporate Sponsorship

Value: $50,000
Type: Arts & cultural events; Pledge-a-thon; Festivals/fairs

Giving Contact

Mark Goodwin, Vice President, General Counsel
Overnite Transportation Co.
PO Box 1216
Richmond, VA 23218-1216
Phone: (804)231-8860
Fax: (804)231-8752

Description

Organization Type: Corporate Giving Program
Giving Locations: principally near operating locations and to national organizations.
Grant Types: General Support.
Note: Employee matching gift ratio: 2 to 1 for education institutions. Employee matching gift ratio: 1 to 1 for cultural institutions.

Financial Summary

Total Giving: Contributes through corporate direct giving program only.

Typical Recipients

Arts & Humanities: Museums/Galleries, Performing Arts, Theater
Civic & Public Affairs: Economic Development, Urban & Community Affairs
Education: Business Education, Economic Education
Environment: Environment-General
Social Services: United Funds/United Ways

Restrictions

The company does not support individuals, religious organizations for sectarian purposes, or political or lobbying groups.

Corporate Officials

Mark B. Goodwin: vice president, general counselo PRIM CORP EMPL vice president, general counsel: Overnite Transportation Co.
Leo H. Suggs: director, chairman, chief executive officer B 1934. ED Biltmore College. PRIM CORP EMPL director, chairman, chief executive officer: Overnite Transportation Co. CORP AFFIL president: Overnite Corp.; chairman: Overnite Holding Inc.

Overseas Shipholding Group Inc.

Company Contact

New York, NY

Company Description

Revenue: US$408,800,000
Employees: 2,200
SIC(s): 4412 Deep Sea Foreign Transportation of Freight.

OSG Foundation

Giving Contact

Luis Alicea, Secretary
OSG Foundation
1114 Avenue of the Americas
511 5th Ave.
New York, NY 10017
Phone: (212)578-1822
Fax: (212)578-1832

Alternate Contact

Phone: (212)953-4100

Description

EIN: 133099337
Organization Type: Corporate Foundation. Supports preselected organizations only.
Giving Locations: NY: New York metropolitan area
Grant Types: Endowment, General Support, Professorship.

Financial Summary

Total Giving: $956,051 (1998); $849,745 (1997); $1,055,783 (1996). Note: Contributes through foundation only.
Assets: $23,521 (1998); $4,663 (1997); $4,493 (1996)
Gifts Received: $975,000 (1998); $850,000 (1997); $212,500 (1996). Note: Contributions were received from Glander International, Inc. and OSG Bulk Ships, Inc.

Typical Recipients

Arts & Humanities: Arts Associations & Councils, Arts Centers, Arts Outreach, Dance, Ethnic & Folk Arts, Film & Video, Historic Preservation, Libraries, Museums/Galleries, Music, Performing Arts, Public Broadcasting, Theater, Visual Arts
Civic & Public Affairs: Botanical Gardens/Parks, Ethnic Organizations, Gay/Lesbian Issues, Civic & Public Affairs-General, Law & Justice, Philanthropic Organizations, Professional & Trade Associations, Safety, Urban & Community Affairs, Women's Affairs
Education: Business Education, Colleges & Universities, Continuing Education, Education Reform, Engineering/Technological Education, Environmental Education, Education-General, International Studies, Legal Education, Medical Education, Private Education (Precollege), Religious Education, Secondary Education (Private)
Environment: Energy, Environment-General
Health: AIDS/HIV, Cancer, Children's Health/Hospitals, Clinics/Medical Centers, Diabetes, Geriatric Health, Heart, Hospitals, Medical Research, Mental Health, Respiratory, Single-Disease Health Associations, Transplant Networks/Donor Banks
International: Foreign Arts Organizations, Foreign Educational Institutions, Health Care/Hospitals, Human Rights, International Organizations, International

Relations, International Relief Efforts, Missionary/Religious Activities
Religion: Churches, Jewish Causes, Religious Organizations, Religious Welfare
Science: Scientific Centers & Institutes
Social Services: Camps, Child Welfare, Community Service Organizations, People with Disabilities, Recreation & Athletics, Shelters/Homelessness, Substance Abuse, United Funds/United Ways, Youth Organizations

Contributions Analysis

Giving Priorities: Hospitals, colleges and universities, philanthropic organizations, and various arts groups. Has supported U.S.-based affiliates of organizations in Israel and international relations.
Arts & Humanities: 2%. Supports museums, symphonies, and arts centers.
Civic & Public Affairs: 1%. Funds are divided between philanthropic organizations, housing, and child welfare.
Education: 2%. Majority of grants benefit colleges and universities. Substantial interest in arts education and medical education.
Health: 71%. Highest grants were given to Mount Sinai Medical Center, and NuBeth Israel Medical Center. Remaining funds benefit medical research and single-disease health organizations.
International: 1%. Supports international relations and religious activities.
Religion: 22%. Majority of funding supports Jewish causes.
Social Services: 1%.
Note: Total contributions made in 1998.

Corporate Officials

Morton Peter Hyman: president, director B New York, NY 1936. ED Cornell University BA (1956); Cornell University LLD (1959). PRIM CORP EMPL president, director: Overseas Shipholding Group Inc. ADD CORP EMPL president, director: Overseas Discount Corp. NONPR AFFIL member: Order Coif; member: Phi Kappa Phi; member: New York State Bar Association; fellow: New York Academy Medicine. CLUB AFFIL Harmonie Club.

Foundation Officials

Morton Peter Hyman: vice president, director (see above)
Michael A. Recanati: executive vice president, director B New York, NY 1957. PRIM CORP EMPL executive vice president, director: Overseas Shipholding Group Inc. CORP AFFIL member: I Fushion Holdings LLC; executive vice president: Maritime Overseas Corp.
Raphael Recanati: president, director B Salonica, Greece 1924. PRIM CORP EMPL chairman: PEC Israel Economic Corp. CORP AFFIL chairman, managing director: IDB Bankholding Corp. Ltd.; chairman, managing director: IDB Development Corp. Ltd.

Grants Analysis

Disclosure Period: calendar year ending 1998
Total Grants: $956,051
Number of Grants: 60
Average Grant: $5,936*
Highest Grant: $250,000
Typical Range: $100 to $15,000
***Note:** Average grant excludes three highest grants.

Recent Grants

Note: Grants derived from 1997 Form 990.

Arts & Humanities

10,000	Carnegie Hall Society, New York, NY
5,000	Baltimore Symphony Orchestra, Baltimore, MD
5,000	Young Audiences, New York, NY
3,000	Carnegie Hall Society, New York, NY
3,000	Film Society of Lincoln Center, New York, NY
2,500	Lincoln Center for Performing Arts, New York, NY
2,500	Lincoln Center for Performing Arts, New York, NY
2,500	Lincoln Center for Performing Arts, New York, NY
2,500	Museum of Modern Art, New York, NY
1,500	Dance Theater Foundation, New York, NY
1,500	Museum of Modern Art, New York, NY
1,000	Channel 13

Civic & Public Affairs

1,000	Financial Accounting Foundation, Norwalk, CT

Education

5,000	City University Graduate School Energy Forum
3,500	New York Medical College, New York, NY
2,000	University of Chicago, Chicago, IL
2,000	University of Chicago, Chicago, IL

Health

250,000	Mount Sinai Medical Center, New York, NY
100,000	New England Deaconess Hospital, Boston, MA
50,000	Beth Israel Medical Center Foundation, New York, NY
46,145	Beth Israel Medical Center, New York, NY
25,000	Beth Israel Medical Center Foundation, New York, NY
25,000	Psychoanalytic Research and Development Fund, Bronx, NY
25,000	St. Luke's-Roosevelt Hospital Center, New York, NY
10,000	Beth Israel Medical Center Foundation, New York, NY
3,000	United Hospital Fund, New York, NY
3,000	United Hospital Fund, New York, NY
2,500	Diabetes Research Institute Foundation, Miami, FL
2,500	Muscular Dystrophy Association
1,500	New York Easter Seal Society, New York, NY
1,000	American Cancer Society
1,000	Mental Health Association of New York and Bronx Counties, NY

International

5,000	Appeal of Conscience Foundation, New York, NY
5,000	Appeal of Conscience Foundation, New York, NY
5,000	French Institute Alliance Francaise, New York, NY
5,000	French Institute Alliance Francaise, New York, NY
1,000	American Friends of Bezalel Academy of Arts and Design
1,000	American Friends of Bezalel Academy of Arts and Design

Religion

50,000	Ort, New York, NY
40,000	United Jewish Appeal, New York, NY
40,000	United Jewish Appeal, New York, NY
35,000	Jewish Publication Society of America, Philadelphia, PA
25,000	Jewish Publication Society of America, Philadelphia, PA
15,000	B'nai B'rith Foundation, Union, NY
5,000	Jewish Museum, New York, NY
2,500	Jewish Publication Society of America, Philadelphia, PA
2,000	Blessed Sacrament Church, Jamaica Plains, MA

Social Services

2,000	Happiness is Camping, Bronx, NY
1,000	Beginning with Children Foundation, New York, NY
1,000	Citizens Committee for Children, New York, NY
1,000	Citizens Committee for Children, New York, NY
1,000	Citizens Committee for Children, New York, NY
1,000	Henry Street Settlement, New York, NY

OWENS CORNING

Company Contact

Toledo, OH
Web: http://www.owenscorning.com

Company Description

Revenue: US$5,048,000,000 (1999)
Employees: 21,000
Fortune Rank: 323, per FORTUNE Magazine's list of 500 Largest U.S. Corporations (1999).
FF 323
SIC(s): 2821 Plastics Materials & Resins, 3052 Rubber & Plastics Hose & Belting, 3069 Fabricated Rubber Products Nec, 3229 Pressed & Blown Glass Nec.

Operating Locations

Belgium: European Owens-Corning Fiberglas SA, Brussels; N.V. Owens-Corning SA, Brussels; Brazil: Owens-Corning Fibergals AS Limitada, Sao Paulo; Canada: Owens-Corning Ontario Holdings Inc., Mississauga; Owens-Corning Canada, Scarborough; People's Republic of China: Owens-Corning Changchun Guan Dao Co. Ltd., Changchun, Jillin Province; Owens-Corning (Guangzhou) Fiberglas Co. Ltd., Guangdong; Nanjing Owens Corning XPS Foam Co. Ltd., Nanjing, Jiangsu; Owens-Corning (Shanghai) Fiberglas Co. Ltd., Pudong, Shanghai; Colombia: Owens Corning Andercol Tuberias, Medellin; Germany: Owens-Corning Eternit Rohre GmbH, Aachen; Deutsche Owens-Corning Galsswool GmbH, Taunusstein; India: Owens-Corning (India) Ltd., New Delhi; Italy: Owens Corning Polypan SPA, Turin; LMP Impianti Sri, Volpiano; Republic of Korea: LG Owens Corning, Seoul; Mexico: Vitro-Fibras SA, Mexico; Norway: Owens-Corning Fiberglas Norway AS, Birkeland; Republic of South Africa: Owens Corning South Africa Pty Ltd., Springs; Saudi Arabia: Amiantit Fibreglass Industries Ltd., Dammam; Arabian Fiberlass Insulation Co., Dammam; Spain: Owens Corning Building Materials Espana SA, Barcelona; Owens-Corning Tubs, SA, Tarragona; Turkey: Owens-Corning Yapi Merkezi Boru Sanayi Ve Ticaret AS, Istanbul; United Kingdom: Owens-Corning Fiberglas (U.K.) Ltd., Ascot, Berkshire; Kitsons Insulation Products (U.K.) Ltd., Leicester; Owens-Corning Veil U.K., Ltd., Liversedge, West Yorkshire; Scanglas Ltd., Runcorn; Owens-Corning Building Products UK Ltd., Saint Helens, Merseyside; Owens-Corning Fibergals (G.B.) Ltd., Wrexham, North Wales; Uruguay: Owens-Corning Fiberglas SA, Montevideo; Zimbabwe: Owens-Corning Pipe (Africa) Pvt. Ltd., Harare

Nonmonetary Support

Value: $300,000 (1995)
Type: Donated Products; In-kind Services
Volunteer Programs: The company sponsors volunteer programs for United Way and Junior Achievement.
Note: Foundation provides nonmonetary support.

Corporate Sponsorship

Value: $1,500,000
Type: Arts & cultural events
Note: Sponsorship includes United Way and fundraisers.

Owens Corning Foundation, Inc.

Giving Contact

Mr. Emerson J. Ross, President, Treasurer
Owens Corning Foundation, Inc.
One Owens Corning Parkway
Toledo, OH 43659
Phone: (419)248-7972
Fax: (419)248-6227

Description

EIN: 341270856
Organization Type: Corporate Foundation
Giving Locations: headquarters and operating communities.
Grant Types: Employee Matching Gifts.

Giving Philosophy

'The Owens-Corning Contribution Program is designed primarily to benefit the communities in which our major business facilities and larger employee groups reside. Programs benefiting these communities and company employees in the area of Health and Human Services, Education, Arts and Culture and Civic Organizations are considered for annual support or program grants.' *Owens Corning Fiberglas Corp., General Giving Guidelines*

Financial Summary

Total Giving: $2,400,000 (1999 approx); $1,400,000 (1998); $1,540,050 (1997). Note: Contributes through corporate direct giving program and foundation. 1997 Giving includes corporate direct giving; foundation; domestic subsidiaries; nonmonetary support.
Giving Analysis: Giving for 1998 includes: foundation ($1,400,000)
Assets: $5,000,000 (1998 approx); $7,164,124 (1996); $571,818 (1995)
Gifts Received: $7,513,063 (1996); $9,645 (1995); $31,790 (1994)

Typical Recipients

Arts & Humanities: Arts Associations & Councils, Arts Centers, Community Arts, Museums/Galleries, Music, Opera, Public Broadcasting
Civic & Public Affairs: African American Affairs, Asian American Affairs, Clubs, Housing, Parades/Festivals, Philanthropic Organizations, Urban & Community Affairs, Women's Affairs
Education: Afterschool/Enrichment Programs, Business Education, Colleges & Universities, Community & Junior Colleges, Education Funds, Education Reform, Gifted & Talented Programs, Minority Education, Public Education (Precollege), Student Aid
Health: Cancer, Medical Research, Mental Health, Preventive Medicine/Wellness Organizations, Respiratory
International: Foreign Educational Institutions, Health Care/Hospitals, International Organizations, International Relations, International Relations, International Relief Efforts
Science: Scientific Centers & Institutes
Social Services: Community Centers, Emergency Relief, Scouts, Substance Abuse, United Funds/United Ways, YMCA/YWCA/YMHA/YWHA, Youth Organizations

Contributions Analysis

Giving Priorities: Human service organizations; colleges and universities, with emphasis on business, science, and engineering; business and free enterprise and civil rights; and various arts organizations. Company reports foreign subsidiaries make contributions to local organizations. Program is unstructured and independent of domestic contributions, which do not support international activities.
Arts & Humanities: 6%. Museums and galleries, music, and the performing arts receive funding. Also supports arts associations and community arts groups.
Civic & Public Affairs: 15%. Primary interests are business and free enterprise organizations and civil rights groups. Also supports organizations concerned with safety, public policy, and environmental, urban, and women's affairs.
Education: About 40%. Emphases include colleges and universities; business, economic, and engineering education; public and private precollegeeducation programs; at-risk children's achievement programs; junior achievement; and minority education. Other interests include faculty development, literacy, community and junior colleges, and science and technology education.
Health: 39%. Priority is affordable housing. Supports human service organizations in communities with major employee populations. Also supports united funds, community centers, and organizations concerned with domestic violence and substance abuse. Other interests include youth organizations, family services, the aged, and deliquency and crime. Supports health organizations, hospitals, and health-care cost containment.
International: Company's foreign subsidiaries make contributions to international organizations.
Note: Total contributions made in 1998.

Application Procedures

Initial Contact: written request
Application Requirements: a description of organization; description of program, including population served, objectives, and proposed timeline; contact name, phone number, and address; amount requested; most recent and if statement; proof of tax-exempt status, and measurement criteria
Deadlines: August.
Review Process: foundation board committee reviews requests quarterly: applicant organizations are notified of committee's decision within one month

Restrictions

Generally does not support debt retirement or endowment campaigns; individuals; religious organizations for sectarian purposes; political organizations or those influencing legislation; or promoting ideological points of view; travel expenses; or organizations without IRS tax exempt status.

Additional Information

Publications: Annual Giving Report

Corporate Officials

Glen Harold Hiner, Jr.: chairman, chief executive officer, director B Morgantown, WV 1934. ED West Virginia University BS (1957); West Virginia University (1989). PRIM CORP EMPL chairman, chief executive officer, director: Owens Corning. CORP AFFIL director: Huntsman Corp.; director: Prudential Insurance Co. American; director: Delsan Industries Inc.; director: Dana Corp. NONPR AFFIL member: Business Roundtable; director: Toledo Symphony Orchestra; member: Business Council. CLUB AFFIL Toledo Country Club; Toledo Club; Inverness Club; The Links Club.

Giving Program Officials

Emerson J. Ross: treasurer PRIM CORP EMPL leader community relations: Owens Corning.

Foundation Officials

Charles H. Dana: president, chairman
William F. Dent: assistant secretary
Robert E. Donald: director
Dennis Jarvela: secretary
George E. Kiemle: director
Emerson J. Ross: treasurer (see above)
Jeremiah M. Sullivan: director

Grants Analysis

Disclosure Period: calendar year ending 1998
Total Grants: $1,400,000*
Number of Grants: 274 (approx)
Average Grant: $5,110
Highest Grant: $125,000
Typical Range: $5,000 to $10,000
***Note:** Grants analysis provided by foundation.

Recent Grants

Note: Grants derived from 1998 Form 990.

Arts & Humanities

25,000	Toledo Cultural Arts Center, Inc., Toledo, OH -- Educational
15,000	Toledo Museum of Art, Toledo, OH -- Charitable
10,000	Arts Commission of Greater Toledo, Toledo, OH -- Charitable
10,000	Toledo Symphony, Toledo, OH -- Charitable
7,000	Toledo Opera, Toledo, OH -- Charitable
5,000	WGTE Public Broadcasting Foundation of Northwest Ohio, Toledo, OH -- Charitable

Civic & Public Affairs

12,500	Local Initiatives Support Corp., Toledo, OH -- Charitable
10,834	Local Initiatives Support Corp., Toledo, OH -- Charitable
10,000	Citifest, Inc., Toledo, OH -- Charitable
10,000	Gifts in Kind International, Alexandria, VA -- Charitable
5,000	Peninsula Habitat for Humanity, Menlo Park, CA -- Charitable
1,000	Gifts in Kind International, Alexandria, VA -- Charitable

Education

18,000	Junior Achievement of Northwest Ohio, Toledo, OH -- Educational
13,420	National Merit Scholarship Corporation, Chicago, IL -- Educational
12,500	The Coalition for Quality Education, Toledo, OH -- Educational
12,000	University of Toledo EXCEL & PREP TECH, Toledo, OH -- Educational
10,000	Junior Achievement International, Colorado Springs, CO -- Educational
6,500	Foundation for Exceptional Children, Toledo, OH -- Charitable
5,000	Anderson College, Anderson, SC -- Educational
5,000	Executive Leadership Foundation, Washington, DC -- Charitable
5,000	Tri-County Technical College, Pendleton, SC -- Educational
4,500	Newark City Schools, Newark, OH -- Educational

Health

40,000	City of Hope, Los Angeles, CA -- Charitable
10,000	Memorial Sloan-Kettering-Cancer Center, New York, NY -- Charitable

International

25,000	International Foundation for Education and Self-Help, Phoenix, AZ -- Educational
12,270	The Foundation of Guelph General Hospital, Guelph, ON, Canada -- Charitable
9,401	Association of Universities & Colleges of Canada, Ottawa, ON, Canada -- Educational
8,175	Carmel College, St. Helens, England -- Educational
7,293	Guelph & Wellington United Way, Guelph, ON, Canada -- Charitable
5,000	Joint Center for Political and Economic Studies, Washington, DC -- Educational
5,000	Junior Achievement Botswana, Gaborone, Botswana -- Educational

Social Services

190,000	United Way of Greater Toledo, Toledo, OH -- Charitable
46,000	United Way of Licking County, Newark, OH -- Charitable
42,500	United Way of Amarillo, Amarillo, TX -- Charitable
42,000	United Way of Licking County, Newark, OH -- Charitable
37,000	Foothills United Way, Anderson, SC -- Charitable
28,000	United Way, Elkhart, IN -- Charitable
27,000	Boy Scouts of America, Irving, TX -- Charitable
20,000	United Way of Aiken County, Aiken, SC -- Charitable
20,000	United Way of Aiken Cty, Aiken, SC -- Charitable
20,000	YMCA of Greater Toledo, Toledo, OH -- Charitable
17,000	United Way of Huntingdon County, Huntingdon, PA -- Charitable
15,000	United Way of Wyandotte County, Inc., Kansas City, KS -- Charitable
11,000	United Way of Santa Clara County, Santa Clara, CA -- Charitable
10,000	Metro United Way, Louisville, KY -- Charitable
8,500	United Way, Atlanta, GA -- Charitable
7,000	United Way of West Ellis County, Waxahachie, TX -- Charitable
5,500	United Way of Northeastern NY, Delmar, NY -- Charitable
5,000	Catawba County United Way, Hickory, NC -- Charitable
5,000	United Way of Comal County, New Braunfels, TX -- Charitable

OWENS-ILLINOIS INC.

Company Contact

Toledo, OH

Company Description

Revenue: US$5,786,700,000 (1999)
Employees: 30,800
Fortune Rank: 293, per FORTUNE Magazine's list of 500 Largest U.S. Corporations (1999).
FF 293
SIC(s): 3089 Plastics Products Nec, 3221 Glass Containers, 3466 Crowns & Closures, 3821 Laboratory Apparatus & Furniture.

Nonmonetary Support

Type: Donated Equipment; In-kind Services

Giving Contact

LaDonna Smith, Contributions Administrator
Owens-Illinois, Inc.
1 Seagate
Toledo, OH 43666
Phone: (419)247-1188
Fax: (419)247-1322

Description

Organization Type: Corporate Giving Program
Giving Locations: headquarters and operating communities.
Grant Types: Employee Matching Gifts, General Support.

Financial Summary

Total Giving: Contributes through corporate direct giving program only.

Typical Recipients

Arts & Humanities: Arts & Humanities-General
Civic & Public Affairs: Civic & Public Affairs-General
Education: Education-General, Minority Education
Health: Health-General
Social Services: Social Services-General

Contributions Analysis

Note: Support for minority education is given only in areas of company operation.

Application Procedures

Initial Contact: a brief letter of inquiry
Application Requirements: a description of organization, amount requested, purpose of funds sought, audited financial statement, and proof of tax-exempt status
Deadlines: None.

Restrictions

The company does not support trips, tours, or special events.

Corporate Officials

Joseph Henry Lemieux: chairman, chief executive officer, director B Providence, RI 1931. ED Stonehill College (1949-1950); University of Rhode Island (1950-1951); Bryant College BBA (1957). PRIM CORP EMPL chairman, chief executive officer, director: Owens-Illinois Inc. ADD CORP EMPL chairman: ACL America Holdings Inc.; chairman: Owens-Illinois Closure Inc.; chairman: Owens-Illinois Labels Inc.; president, director: Owens-Brockway Glass Container; president, director: Owens-Brockway Packaging Inc.; chairman: Owens-Brockway Plastics Inc. CORP AFFIL director: National City Northwest; director: Ohio Citizens Bank; director: Health Care & Retirement Corp.; director: National City Corp.; director: HCR Manor Care Inc. NONPR AFFIL trustee: Bryant College; member: Glass Pkg Institute. CLUB AFFIL Inverness Club.

Giving Program Officials

LaDonna Smith: contributions administrator

PACCAR INC.

Company Contact

Bellevue, WA
Web: http://www.paccar.com

Company Description

Revenue: US$9,021,000,000 (1999)
Employees: 10,163
Fortune Rank: 189, per FORTUNE Magazine's list of 500 Largest U.S. Corporations (1999).
FF 189
SIC(s): 3533 Oil & Gas Field Machinery, 3711 Motor Vehicles & Car Bodies, 5012 Automobiles & Other Motor Vehicles, 5013 Motor Vehicle Supplies & New Parts.

Operating Locations

Australia; Canada; Mexico; United Kingdom

Nonmonetary Support

Type: Loaned Employees; Workplace Solicitation
Note: Workplace solicitation is for United Way only.

PACCAR Foundation

Giving Contact

Dennis Sather, Corporate Service Manager
PACCAR Foundation
PO Box 1518
Bellevue, WA 98009
Phone: (206)455-7400
Fax: (206)455-7421

Description

Founded: 1951
EIN: 916030638
Organization Type: Corporate Foundation. Supports preselected organizations only.
Giving Locations: headquarters and operating communities.
Grant Types: Capital, Department, Employee Matching Gifts, Endowment, General Support.
Note: Employee matching gift ratio: 1 to 1 to educational institutions and organizationanizations supporting educational purposes.

Financial Summary

Total Giving: $2,653,279 (1999 approx); $3,875,267 (1998); $2,944,834 (1996). Note: Contributes through foundation only.
Giving Analysis: Giving for 1995 includes: foundation ($3,077,544); foundation matching gifts ($59,572); 1996: foundation ($2,142,457); foundation grants to United Way ($802,377); 1998: foundation ($2,353,950); foundation grants to United Way ($937,424); foundation fellowships ($500,000); foundation matching gifts ($83,893)
Assets: $13,158,445 (1998); $10,337,822 (1996); $9,295,544 (1995)
Gifts Received: $3,000,000 (1998); $2,500,000 (1996); $2,500,000 (1995). Note: Contributions are received from PACCAR Inc.

Typical Recipients

Arts & Humanities: Arts Associations & Councils, Arts Funds, Historic Preservation, History & Archaeology, Libraries, Museums/Galleries, Music, Opera, Performing Arts, Public Broadcasting, Theater, Visual Arts
Civic & Public Affairs: Botanical Gardens/Parks, Business/Free Enterprise, Economic Policy, Employment/Job Training, Housing, Law & Justice, Municipalities/Towns, Public Policy, Safety, Urban & Community Affairs, Zoos/Aquariums
Education: Arts/Humanities Education, Business Education, Colleges & Universities, Community & Junior Colleges, Economic Education, Education Associations, Education Funds, Engineering/Technological Education, Education-General, Minority Education, Private Education (Precollege), Science/Mathematics Education, Secondary Education (Private), Secondary Education (Public), Vocational & Technical Education
Health: AIDS/HIV, Cancer, Children's Health/Hospitals, Clinics/Medical Centers, Emergency/Ambulance Services, Health Organizations, Hospitals, Medical Research, Mental Health, Research/Studies Institutes
International: International Relations
Religion: Dioceses, Religious Organizations, Religious Welfare
Science: Science Museums, Scientific Centers & Institutes, Scientific Organizations
Social Services: Child Welfare, Community Centers, Community Service Organizations, Day Care, Family Services, Food/Clothing Distribution, People with Disabilities, Scouts, Senior Services, Substance Abuse, United Funds/United Ways, YMCA/YWCA/YMHA/YWHA, Youth Organizations

Contributions Analysis

Giving Priorities: United funds, colleges and universities and independent college funds, the arts, civic organizations, and hospitals.
Arts & Humanities: 18%. Supports arts funds, theater, historical organizations, and cultural campaigns.
Civic & Public Affairs: 2%. Supports municipalities, business and free enterprises, and public policy groups.
Education: 35%. Primarily supports colleges and universities, including major support to independent college foundations. Also awards matching grants and supports economic education.
Health: 6%. Funds youth and children's hospitals.

Social Services: 39%. Funding is provided to United Way, YMCA's, and youth organizations.

Application Procedures

Initial Contact: Submit a proposal.
Application Requirements: Include evidence of 501(c)(3) status, description of goals and programs; background data on key personnel, exact amount requested, budget information, and list of other corporate contributions.
Deadlines: None.
Decision Notification: Quarterly.

Restrictions

Foundation does not support individual dinners or special events, fraternal organizations, goodwill advertising, political or lobbying groups, or religious organizations for sectarian purposes. Proposals for program funds, operating budgets, and fundraising events are seldom funded.

Corporate Officials

Gerald Grinstein: director emeritus, director B Seattle, WA 1932. ED Yale College BA (1954); Harvard University Law School LLB (1957). PRIM CORP EMPL non-executive chairman board, director: Delta Air Lines ADD CORP EMPL director: PACCAR Inc. CORP AFFIL director: Sundstrand Corp.; director: Imperial Sugar Co.; director: Pittston Co.; non-executive chairman board, director: Delta Air Lines; director: Imperial Holly Corp.; director: Browning-Ferris Industries Inc. NONPR AFFIL director: Henry M. Jackson Foundation.
David J. Hovind: president, director B 1940. ED University of Washington BA (1964); Stanford University Executive Program (1984). PRIM CORP EMPL president, director: PACCAR Inc.
Charles McGee Pigott: chairman emeritus, director B Seattle, WA 1929. ED Stanford University BS (1951). PRIM CORP EMPL chairman emeritus, director: PACCAR Inc. ADD CORP EMPL chairman: PACCAR Automotive Distribution Co. CORP AFFIL director: Seattle Times Co.; director: Boeing Co.; director: Chevron Corp. NONPR AFFIL member: Business Council.

Foundation Officials

G. Glen Morie: secretary, treasurer B Woodbury, NJ 1942. ED Bowdoin College BBA (1964); University of Pennsylvania LLB (1967). PRIM CORP EMPL vice president, general counsel, secretary: PACCAR Inc. ADD CORP EMPL secretary: PACCAR Automotive Distribution Co.; secretary: PACCAR Automotive Inc. NONPR AFFIL member: American Corporate Counsel Association; member: American Society of Corporate Secretaries; member: American Bar Association.
Charles McGee Pigott: president, director (see above)
John Wilson Pitts: director B Victoria, BC Canada 1926. ED McGill University (1949); Harvard University (1951). PRIM CORP EMPL president, chief executive officer: MacDonald Dettwiler. CORP AFFIL director: Canada Trust; director: PACCAR Inc.; director: BC Sugar Refinery Ltd.; director: BC Telephone Co. Ltd.
(H.) Dennis Sather: corporate service manager
James Hooker Wiborg: director B Seattle, WA 1924. ED University of Washington BA (1946). PRIM CORP EMPL chairman, chairman executive committee, director: Univar Corp. CORP AFFIL director: Prime Source Corp.; director: Tacoma Moving Storage Co.; director: Penwest Ltd.; director: Brandrud Furniture Inc.; director: PACCAR Inc.

Grants Analysis

Disclosure Period: calendar year ending 1998
Total Grants: $2,353,950*
Number of Grants: 86
Average Grant: $27,372
Highest Grant: $150,000
Typical Range: $2,000 to $25,000

*Note: Giving excludes United Way, matching gifts, and fellowships.

Recent Grants

Note: Grants derived from 1996 Form 990.

Arts & Humanities

150,000	Seattle Symphony, Seattle, WA
125,000	Blanchet High School Library Media Resource Center, Seattle, WA
120,000	Corporate Council for the Arts, Seattle, WA
58,333	A Contemporary Theater, Seattle, WA
50,000	Seattle Repertory Theater, Seattle, WA
33,333	Kirkland Performance Center, Kirkland, WA
25,000	On the Boards, Seattle, WA
16,668	KCTS Association, Seattle, WA -- Fund for Programming Excellence
16,668	Seattle Children's Theater, Seattle, WA

Civic & Public Affairs

35,000	American Enterprise Institute for Public Policy Research, Washington, DC
15,000	Council on Competitiveness, Washington, DC
10,000	Economics America, Washington Council on Economic Education, Seattle, WA

Education

125,000	Seattle Preparatory School, Seattle, WA
111,000	Lakeside School, Seattle, WA
100,000	Holy Names Academy, Seattle, WA
90,000	Independent Colleges of Washington, Seattle, WA
83,333	Bellevue Community College Foundation, Bellevue, WA
33,333	Washington State University, Pullman, WA -- Campaign WSU
25,000	Bellarmine Preparatory School, Tacoma, WA -- Heritage II Campaign
20,000	Partnership for Learning, Seattle, WA
20,000	University of Washington School of Business Administration, Seattle, WA
16,050	Texas Independent College Fund, Fort Worth, TX
15,000	Pilchuck Glass School, Seattle, WA
15,000	Renton Technical College Foundation, Renton, WA
12,550	Tennessee Foundation for Independent Colleges Fund, Brentwood, TN
12,000	National Action Council for Minorities in Engineering, New York, NY
10,440	Ohio Foundation of Independent Colleges, Columbus, OH

Health

100,000	Virginia Mason Foundation, Seattle, WA
50,000	Ryther Child Center, Seattle, WA -- capital campaign
33,333	Eastside Mental Health, Bellevue, WA
25,000	American Red Cross, Seattle, WA
24,300	Skagit Valley Hospital Foundation, Mount Vernon, WA
20,000	Fred Hutchinson Cancer Research Center, Seattle, WA
12,500	Providence Medical Center Foundation of Seattle, Seattle, WA

Religion

50,000	Archdiocese of Seattle, Immaculate Conception Painting Foundation, Seattle, WA

Science

12,750	Pacific Science Center, Seattle, WA

Social Services

474,977	United Way King County, Seattle, WA
89,940	United Way Denton County, Denton, TX
84,150	United Way Nashville and Middle Tennessee, Nashville, TN
70,000	United Way Ross County-Chillicothe, Chillicothe, OH
50,000	Children's Home Society, Seattle, WA
39,000	YWCA of Seattle-King County, Seattle, WA
33,333	Seattle Children's Home, Seattle, WA
25,000	Boys and Girls Clubs of Snohomish County, Everett, WA
25,000	Eastside Adult Day Center, Bellevue, WA
23,890	Boy Scouts of America, Oakland, CA
15,220	United Way, Tulsa, OK
15,050	United Way Hays County, San Marcos, TX
15,000	Children's Services of Snow Valley, Snoqualmie, WA
12,500	Southwest Youth and Family Services, Seattle, WA

PACIFIC CENTURY FINANCIAL CORP.

Company Contact

Honolulu, HI
Web: http://www.boh.com

Company Description

Former Name: Bancorp Hawaii, Inc.
Assets: US$14,400,000,000 (1999)
Employees: 5,134 (1999)
SIC(s): 6022 State Commercial Banks, 6712 Bank Holding Companies.

Corporate Sponsorship

Type: Arts & cultural events; Festivals/fairs; Music & entertainment events; Sports events
Contact: Debby Staton, Vice President

Pacific Century Financial Charitable Foundation

Giving Contact

Cheryl Ritchie
Pacific Century Financial Charitable Foundation
130 Merchant Street
Honolulu, HI 96813-4426
Phone: (808)538-4525
Fax: (808)538-4647

Description

Founded: 1981
EIN: 990210467
Organization Type: Corporate Foundation. Supports preselected organizations only.
Former Name: Bank of Hawaii Charitable Foundation (1997).
Giving Locations: HI: Honolulu
Grant Types: Capital, Employee Matching Gifts, Endowment, General Support.

Financial Summary

Total Giving: $1,500,000 (1999 approx); $1,500,000 (1998 approx); $1,000,000 (1996). Note: Contributes through corporate direct giving program and foundation. 1996 Giving includes foundation ($1,327,412); United Way ($211,250).
Assets: $11,053,558 (1996); $11,336,954 (1995); $9,295,774 (1994)
Gifts Received: $23,500 (1996); $1,215,000 (1995); $565,500 (1994). Note: Foundation receives contributions from Bancorp Hawaii.

Typical Recipients

Arts & Humanities: Arts Centers, Ethnic & Folk Arts, Arts & Humanities-General, Historic Preservation, History & Archaeology, Museums/Galleries, Music, Opera, Performing Arts, Public Broadcasting, Theater, Visual Arts

Civic & Public Affairs: Asian American Affairs, Botanical Gardens/Parks, Business/Free Enterprise, Community Foundations, Employment/Job Training, Civic & Public Affairs-General, Housing, Parades/Festivals, Philanthropic Organizations, Public Policy, Rural Affairs, Urban & Community Affairs
Education: Agricultural Education, Arts/Humanities Education, Business Education, Colleges & Universities, Faculty Development, Education-General, Literacy, Private Education (Precollege), Public Education (Precollege), Religious Education, Science/Mathematics Education, Secondary Education (Private), Student Aid
Environment: Environment-General, Resource Conservation
Health: Children's Health/Hospitals, Clinics/Medical Centers, Emergency/Ambulance Services, Health Organizations, Hospitals, Medical Rehabilitation, Mental Health, Multiple Sclerosis
International: Foreign Arts Organizations, Foreign Educational Institutions
Religion: Churches, Dioceses, Religious Welfare
Science: Science Museums
Social Services: At-Risk Youth, Child Welfare, Community Centers, Community Service Organizations, Day Care, Domestic Violence, Family Services, Food/Clothing Distribution, People with Disabilities, Recreation & Athletics, Scouts, Senior Services, Shelters/Homelessness, Social Services-General, United Funds/United Ways, YMCA/YWCA/YMHA/YWHA, Youth Organizations

Contributions Analysis

Giving Priorities: Education, cultural arts centers, and hospitals.
Arts & Humanities: About 20%. Supports community and cultural arts centers on two islands. The remainder goes to museums and theater.
Civic & Public Affairs: (United Funds & United Way) Support goes to food and clothing distribution, community centers, YMCA, and child welfare. About 40%. Major support goes to the Kaukini Foundation. Alsosupports neighborhood associations.
Education: About 20%. Equally supports colleges, private academies, and public education. Additional support goes to a literacy fund.
Health: About 20%. Recipients include hospitals and medical centers.

Additional Information

In April of 1997, Bancorp Hawaii, Inc. changed its name to Pacific Century Financial Corp.

Corporate Officials

Richard J. Dahl: president B 1951. ED University of Idaho (1973). PRIM CORP EMPL president: Bank Hawaii ADD CORP EMPL treasurer: BankHawaii International.
Lawrence M. Johnson: president B Honolulu, HI 1940. ED Bradley University (1961); University of Hawaii (1963). PRIM CORP EMPL president: Pacific Century Financial Corp. ADD CORP EMPL chairman, president, chief executive officer: BankHawaii International. CORP AFFIL director, chairman: Bank Hawaii; member: HI Community Reinvestment Corp. NONPR AFFIL director: East West Center; director: Hawaii Pacific University.

Grants Analysis

Disclosure Period: calendar year ending 1996
Total Grants: $1,327,412
Number of Grants: 81 (approx)
Average Grant: $16,803
Highest Grant: $107,500
Typical Range: $2,000 to $20,000

Recent Grants

Note: Grants derived from 1996 Form 990.

Arts & Humanities

45,000	Hawaii Labor Heritage Council, Honolulu, HI -- first of two payments for Ilwu mural restoration Project
25,000	Mission Houses Museum
16,000	Polynesian Cultural Center, Laie, HI -- for Sterling Scholar Program
10,000	Friends of Pearl Harbor, Honolulu, HI
10,000	Hawaii Theater Center, Honolulu, HI

Civic & Public Affairs

25,000	Marimed Foundation, Honolulu, HI -- for Kailana-Tole Mour Program
25,000	Palama Settlement, Honolulu, HI -- for Centennial contribution
20,000	Namakuli Neighborhood Housing Services, Namakuli, HI
10,000	First Night Honolulu, Honolulu, HI
10,000	Japanese Cultural Center of Hawaii, Honolulu, HI
5,000	Better Business Bureau, Honolulu, HI -- for technology upgrade project
5,000	Friends of Honolulu City Lights, Honolulu, HI
4,000	Hawaii Community Foundation, Honolulu, HI
3,030	Moanalua Gardens Foundation, Honolulu, HI -- for Na Makani O Moanalua newsletter
3,000	Agricultural Leadership Foundation of Hawaii, HI -- support for Ag Day

Education

25,000	Honolulu Waldorf School, Honolulu, HI
20,000	Maryknoll Schools, Honolulu, HI
15,000	University of Arizona Phoenix Alumni Club, Tucson, AZ
12,500	Trinity Christian School
10,000	University of Hawaii College of Education, Honolulu, HI
10,000	University of Hawaii Foundation, Honolulu, HI -- for Pacific Business Center Program
6,274	Hawaii State 4-H Livestock Committee, HI -- for three steers
5,000	Honolulu Academy of Arts, Honolulu, HI -- support Workers An Archaeology of the Industrial Age program
5,000	University of Hawaii Foundation, Honolulu, HI -- for History, Culture, and Power in the Pacific Conference
4,608	University of Hawaii Foundation, Honolulu, HI -- for Harry and Myra Scholarships
4,500	University of Hawaii Manoa College of Education, Manoa, HI -- scholarships
4,000	Iolani School, Honolulu, HI
3,000	University of Arizona Yuma Alumni Club, Tucson, AZ
2,500	Punahou School, Honolulu, HI
2,500	University of Hawaii Foundation, Honolulu, HI

Environment

10,000	Nature Conservancy, Honolulu, HI -- for Corporate Council for the Environment

Health

25,000	Wilcox Hospital Foundation, Lihue, HI
20,000	North Hawaii Community Hospital, Kamuela, HI
20,000	Rehabilitation Hospital of the Pacific, Honolulu, HI
15,000	Hamakua Health Center, Hamakua, HI -- program support
5,000	American Red Cross Hawaii Chapter, Honolulu, HI -- for Community Humanitarians of Hawaii Campaign
4,000	Multiple Sclerosis Society Hawaii Islands Chapter, HI -- first of two payments on pledge

Social Services

107,500	United Way Statewide Association Hawaii, Honolulu, HI -- second quarter corporate donation
106,250	United Way Statewide Association Hawaii, Honolulu, HI -- fourth quarter payment on pledge
105,000	United Way Statewide Association Hawaii, Honolulu, HI -- third quarter donation
20,000	Goodwill Industries, Honolulu, HI
20,000	Susannah Wesley Community Center, Honolulu, HI
12,500	YMCA, Maui, HI
10,000	Hawaii Canoe/Kayak Team, HI
10,000	Kauai Food Bank, Kauai, HI
5,000	Boys and Girls Club, Honolulu, HI
5,000	Domestic Violence Clearninghouse and Legal Hotline, Honolulu, HI -- for Plan for Your Life project
5,000	Friends of the Natatorium
3,000	Augustine Educational Foundation, Kaneohe, HI -- support A Walk In Time project, Walk-A-Thon, sponsor events for disadvantaged children
3,000	Lanikai Canoe Club, Lanikai, HI

PACIFIC ENTERPRISES

Company Contact

Los Angeles, CA

Company Description

Revenue: US$2,588,000,000
Profit: US$203,000,000
Employees: 7,643
SIC(s): 1521 Single-Family Housing Construction, 4923 Gas Transmission & Distribution, 6552 Subdividers & Developers Nec, 6719 Holding Companies Nec.

Operating Locations

Operates throughout southern California.

Giving Contact

Carolyn Williams, Manager, Public Affairs
555 W. 5th St., ML28H5
Los Angeles, CA 90013
Phone: (213)244-2555
Fax: (213)244-8254
Email: crwilliams@semtpra.com

Description

Organization Type: Corporate Giving Program
Giving Locations: headquarters and operating communities.
Grant Types: Employee Matching Gifts.

Financial Summary

Total Giving: $476,000 (1994); $421,625 (1993); $1,336,578 (1992). Note: 1992 figure does not include a $1,100,000 contribution to the United Way. Company reported in 1993 that contributions budget was being significantly cut back.

Application Procedures

Initial Contact: Send a brief letter of inquiry. Include a description of organization, amount requested, purpose of funds sought, recently audited financial statement, and proof of tax-exempt status.

Restrictions

Does not support individuals, religious organizations for sectarian purposes, or political or lobbying groups.

Additional Information

Publications: Guidelines

Corporate Officials

Larry J. Dagley: senior vice president, chief financial officerc B Waco, TX 1948. ED Baylor University (1970). PRIM CORP EMPL senior vice president, chief financial officer: Pacific Enterprises. CORP AFFIL partner,manager audit div: Arthur Anderson & Co.; senior vice president,contr: Transco Energy Co.

Richard Donald Farman: chairman, chief executive officer B San Francisco, CA 1935. ED Stanford University BA (1957); Stanford University LLB (1963). PRIM CORP EMPL chairman, chief executive officer: Sempra Energy. CORP AFFIL director: Union Bank; director: Sentinel Group Funds; director: Assoc Electric & Gas Insurance Services Ltd. NONPR AFFIL member: Pacific Coast Gas Association; chairman: Public Service Sta KCET-TV; member: National Petroleum Council; member: Los Angeles Area Chamber of Commerce; director: National Business Higher Education Forum; member: Interstate Natural Gas Association America; member executive committee, director: American Gas Association. CLUB AFFIL mem: Los Angeles Country Club; mem: California Club.

Willis B. Wood, Jr.: chairman, chief executive officer, director B Kansas City, MO 1934. ED University of Tulsa BS (1957); Harvard University (1983); Pepperdine University JD (1996). NONPR AFFIL director, member business council: Sustainable Energy Future; trustee: University Southern California; member: Society Petroleum Engineers; trustee: Southwest Museum; director: Pacific Council International Affairs; member: Pacific Energy Association; member: National Association Manufacturers; member: Pacific Coast Gas Association; trustee: Harvey Mudd College; director: Los Angeles World Affairs Council; chairman, trustee: California Medical Center Foundation; member: Chamber of Commerce California State; member: American Gas Association. CLUB AFFIL Hacienda Golf Club; California Club; Center Club.

PACIFIC GAS AND ELECTRIC CO.

Company Contact

San Francisco, CA
Web: http://www.pge.com/about_us/communities/giving.html

Company Description

Revenue: US$9,610,000,000
Profit: US$1,338,900,000
Employees: 21,000
SIC(s): 4911 Electric Services, 4925 Gas Production & Distribution Nec, 4941 Water Supply.

Nonmonetary Support

Value: $285,000 (1996); $100,000 (1993); $100,000 (1992)
Type: Donated Equipment; Donated Products; In-kind Services; Loaned Executives
Note: 1997 nonmonetary support $250,000. Company also donates real estate.

Corporate Sponsorship

Type: Arts & cultural events
Note: Sponsorship is limited to the San Francisco Symphony, Opera, and Ballet.

Giving Contact

Tricia L. Capri, Senior Program Manager, Corporate Contributions
Pacific Gas and Electric Co.
Mail Code B29C
PO Box 770000
San Francisco, CA 94177
Phone: (415)973-9172
Fax: (415)973-8239
Email: tlch@pge.com

Alternate Contact

77 Bea
San Francisco, CA 94105
Phone: 800-743-5000

Description

Organization Type: Corporate Giving Program
Giving Locations: CA: Northern and Central California (company's service area)
Grant Types: Capital, Employee Matching Gifts, General Support, Scholarship.
Note: Employee matching gifts support education. Company contributes to limited civic functions.

Giving Philosophy

'At PG&E we have an active Contributions Program that makes grants to non-profit organizations in our service area of Northern and Central California. Our goal is to strengthen the economic and social vitality of the communities where we operate and our employees live and work.' *Contributions Program, How To Apply*

Financial Summary

Total Giving: $8,947,000 (1997); $9,385,000 (1996 approx); $9,381,000 (1995 approx). Note: Contributes through corporate direct giving program only. 1997 Giving includes corporate direct giving. 1996 Giving includes corporate direct giving; nonmonetary support. 1995 Giving includes corporate direct giving.

Typical Recipients

Arts & Humanities: Arts Centers, Ethnic & Folk Arts, Museums/Galleries, Music, Performing Arts
Civic & Public Affairs: Economic Development, Employment/Job Training, Urban & Community Affairs, Women's Affairs
Education: Colleges & Universities, Engineering/Technological Education, Minority Education, Science/Mathematics Education
Environment: Environment-General
Social Services: Shelters/Homelessness, United Funds/United Ways, Youth Organizations

Contributions Analysis

Giving Priorities: Programs that promote employability and economic self-sufficiency; education in math, science, engineering, and technical fields; federated campaigns; and AIDS research.
Civic & Public Affairs: 50% to 55%. Includes organizations that promote job training and placement programs and community economic development activities that stimulate businesses and job development. Also supports an emergency preparedness and response program.
Education: 15% to 20%. Supports higher education and innovative K-12 programs, especially those that focus on math, science, environmental stewardship, and emergency preparedness. Also supports programs that encourage students to stay in school.
Environment: Less than 5%. Limited support to programs that promote environmental quality and the protection of natural resources.
Social Services: 25% to 30%. Limited support to partnerships with organizationslike the American Red Cross that mobilize communities and increase their ability to prepare for emergencies.

Application Procedures

Initial Contact: brief written proposal, preferably two to four pages plus attachments
Application Requirements: organization's name, address, phone number, and contact person; brief description and history, accomplishments, and goals; description of program; area and number of people served; how organization or proposed project fits into company's charitable priorities; how project's outcome will be measured; amount requested and purpose for which grant will be used; copy of 501(c)(3) document; current operating budget; current and anticipated funding sources; list of governing board members and chief management officers; and involvement of volunteers, including PG&E employees
Deadlines: October 31.
Review Process: initial review by the local business office; final decision by contributions committee
Evaluative Criteria: extent to which project meets priority areas and program objectives, benefit of organization to company service area and customers, project promotes cultural diversity, capacity to address cross-section of broad community interest, alleviation of under-funded needs, evidence of nondiscriminatory policy, involvement of company employees
Decision Notification: contributions committee meets quarterly; decisions may take three months

Restrictions

PG&E does not make contributions to individuals, except for through the college scholarship program; for contest tickets, raffles, or other prize-oriented activities; to churches, synagogues, or other religious groups for sectarian activities; to fraternal organizations; to political or lobbying groups; to reduce debts or past operating deficits; for underwriting of films, television or video productions; reducing or donating the cost of gas and electric services; endowment funds; organizations outside of service area; hospitals or medical organizations; sports tournaments; trips or tours; talent or beauty contests; academic chairships or fellowships; or conferences.
Company prefers not to fund multiyear grants.
Company does not respond to requests that are not in writing.

Additional Information

PG&E has a college scholarship program: call (415) 973-8555 for information.
In limited cases, PG&E may donate surplus real estate, temporary use of real estate, printing, vehicles, furniture, computer equipment, or other miscellaneous items not needed for our operations. The company also donates used computers to the Detwiler Foundation, which provides them to schools only: call (800) 939-6000 for information.
Local offices may make contributions; grants are usually less than $1,000.
Publications: Guidelines

Corporate Officials

Barbara Coull Williams: vice president human resources PRIM CORP EMPL vice president human resources: Pacific Gas & Electric Co.

Giving Program Officials

Lee Callaway: vice president public relations B Montgomery, AL 1936. ED Vanderbilt University (1958); Stanford University (1977). PRIM CORP EMPL vice president: Pacific Gas & Electric Co.
Tricia L. Capri: senior program manager
Gordon Smith: president, chief executive officer

Grants Analysis

Disclosure Period: calendar year ending
Typical Range: $1,000 to $15,000

PACIFIC MUTUAL LIFE INSURANCE CO.

Company Contact

Newport Beach, CA
Web: http://www.pacificlife.com

Company Description

Revenue: US$4,548,900,000 (1999)
Employees: 2,500
Fortune Rank: 353, per FORTUNE Magazine's list of 500 Largest U.S. Corporations (1999).
FF 353
SIC(s): 6311 Life Insurance, 6321 Accident & Health Insurance, 6371 Pension, Health & Welfare Funds, 6799 Investors Nec.

Nonmonetary Support

Value: $122,577 (1996); $217,742 (1995); $158,958 (1992)
Type: Donated Equipment; In-kind Services
Note: Nonmonetary support is provided by the company. 1997 nonmonetary support $198,143.

Corporate Sponsorship

Type: Music & entertainment events

Pacific Mutual Charitable Foundation

Giving Contact

Robert G. Haskell, President
Pacific Mutual Charitable Foundation
700 Newport Center Drive
Newport Beach, CA 92660
Phone: (949)640-3787
Fax: (949)640-7614
Web: http://www.pacificlife.com/corporate/community

Description

EIN: 953433806
Organization Type: Corporate Foundation
Giving Locations: CA primarily to organizations in areas with large concentrations of company employees; some funding nationally.
Grant Types: Award, Capital, Employee Matching Gifts, General Support, Multiyear/Continuing Support.
Note: Employee matching gift ratio: 1 to 1 for higher education.

Giving Philosophy

'Pacific Mutual's charitable giving program is driven by a belief in the ability of the community to define and solve its own problems--given the resources to do so. As social issues have become more complex, our grantmaking process has evolved in strategy and emphasis. We have chosen to focus some of our charitable dollars on issues of particular concern to us and have sought partnerships with organizations effectively addressing those concerns. Additionally, we have placed emphasis on the problems of children and youth.

'In addition to our growing interest in and support of children's issues, we continue to make annual grants that address a broad spectrum of social problems. Grants are made to organizations that address health needs and provide human services. Grants are also made to organizations that use the arts to stimulate creativity and innovation, as well as to groups that strengthen the community through education and civic programs. In all cases, the programs and organizations we support are committed to giving individuals and families the tools needed to improve their lives and achieve their goals.

'In all our efforts, we are constantly energized by the accomplishments of our grantees. The organizations we support work diligently to enhance the quality of our lives, and to ameliorate some of society's most pressing problems.' *Report on Community Involvement*

Financial Summary

Total Giving: $2,400,000 (1999 approx); $2,000,000 (1998 approx); $1,909,275 (1997). Note: Contributes through corporate direct giving program and foundation. 1997 Giving includes corporate direct giving ($175,826); foundation ($1,535,306); nonmonetary support.
Assets: $21,625,693 (1996); $20,462,640 (1995); $19,388,217 (1994)
Gifts Received: $6,372,707 (1997); $30,281 (1996); $21,336 (1995). Note: Contributions were received from Pacific Mutual Life Insurance Company.

Typical Recipients

Arts & Humanities: Arts Associations & Councils, Arts Centers, Arts Festivals, Arts Funds, Arts Institutes, Ballet, Dance, Ethnic & Folk Arts, Film & Video, Arts & Humanities-General, Historic Preservation, Libraries, Museums/Galleries, Music, Opera, Performing Arts, Public Broadcasting, Theater
Civic & Public Affairs: Asian American Affairs, Botanical Gardens/Parks, Civil Rights, Clubs, Community Foundations, Economic Development, Economic Policy, Employment/Job Training, Civic & Public Affairs-General, Hispanic Affairs, Housing, Law & Justice, Legal Aid, Municipalities/Towns, Nonprofit Management, Professional & Trade Associations, Public Policy, Safety, Urban & Community Affairs, Women's Affairs, Zoos/Aquariums
Education: Business Education, Business-School Partnerships, Colleges & Universities, Continuing Education, Economic Education, Education Funds, Education Reform, Education-General, Health & Physical Education, Leadership Training, Medical Education, Minority Education, Private Education (Precollege), Public Education (Precollege), School Volunteerism, Secondary Education (Public), Special Education, Student Aid
Environment: Environment-General, Wildlife Protection
Health: AIDS/HIV, Alzheimers Disease, Cancer, Children's Health/Hospitals, Emergency/Ambulance Services, Eyes/Blindness, Geriatric Health, Health Policy/Cost Containment, Health Organizations, Heart, Hospices, Hospitals, Medical Research, Medical Training, Mental Health, Multiple Sclerosis, Nutrition, Public Health, Single-Disease Health Associations, Speech & Hearing
International: Health Care/Hospitals, International Environmental Issues, Missionary/Religious Activities
Religion: Religious Welfare
Science: Science Museums, Scientific Centers & Institutes
Social Services: At-Risk Youth, Child Abuse, Child Welfare, Community Service Organizations, Counseling, Day Care, Delinquency & Criminal Rehabilitation, Domestic Violence, Emergency Relief, Family Planning, Family Services, Food/Clothing Distribution, Homes, People with Disabilities, Recreation & Athletics, Senior Services, Shelters/Homelessness, Social Services-General, Substance Abuse, United Funds/United Ways, Veterans, Volunteer Services, YMCA/YWCA/YMHA/YWHA, Youth Organizations

Contributions Analysis

Arts & Humanities: 15% to 20%. Supports museums, symphonies, ballets, gardens and musical endeavors.
Civic & Public Affairs: Less than 5%. Includes support for cultural diversity programs, urban affairs, community development organizations, and ecological and environmental concerns.
Education: 30% to 35%. Supports universities, graduate schools and drop-out programs. Also includes matching gifts to institutions of higher learning.
Health: 45% to 50%. Supports the United Way, shelters, hospitals and single disease organizations such as the American Cancer Society and the American Heart Association. Funding also goes to children's advocacy groups and AIDS education/home care.
Note: Foundation chooses five to seven specific areas of focus annually in December. Priorities may change according to these areas of focus.

Application Procedures

Initial Contact: letter or proposal
Application Requirements: documentation of 501(c)(3) status; one-page a description of organization and project, including needs and objectives; one-page budget for project, including personnel and operating costs, list of other contributors and levels of funding, and amount requested; one-page current budget for organization, including specific sources of revenue and any contingency funds; one-page description of volunteer support; and list of board of directors and advisory board members and staff
Deadlines: August 1 through September 16, for consideration for the following calendar year's budget
Evaluative Criteria: type of activity being promoted; population affected; how regional issues are confronted; how progress can be documented; supportiveness of public welfare; need served by proposed activity and duplication of function; benefit to or involvement of employees
Decision Notification: December; announcements made after January 1 with payment made before the end of February

Restrictions

Foundation does not support individuals; political parties, candidates, or partisan political organizations; professional associations; veterans and labor organizations, fraternal organizations, athletic clubs, or social clubs; religious organizations for sectarian or denominational purposes, except for programs that are available to anyone; or operating expenses for member agencies of United Way, except under special circumstances.

Additional Information

Generally prefers to make annual grants. Organizations may reapply annually, but grants typically are made to one organization for no more than three consecutive years.
The foundation reports that each year it selects five to seven areas of special focus (e.g. AIDS, homelessness, Hispanic needs) and makes major grants in that focus area. These grants are usually made later in the calendar year after the foundation has done considerable research. research.
Publications: Community Involvement Report

Corporate Officials

Marianne Beaz: vice president client service & pension investments PRIM CORP EMPL vice president client service & pension investments: Pacific Mutual Life Insurance Co.
Anthony J. Bonno: senior vice president human resources PRIM CORP EMPL senior vice president human resources: Pacific Mutual Life Insurance Co.
David R. Carmichael: senior vice president, general counsel, director PRIM CORP EMPL senior vice president, general counsel, director: Pacific Mutual Life Insurance Co. CORP AFFIL senior vice president: Pacific Life Insurance Co.; director: PM Group Life Insurance Co.
Richard Michael Ferry: chairman B Ravenna, OH 1937. ED Kent State University BS (1959). PRIM CORP EMPL chairman: Korn/Ferry International. CORP AFFIL director: Mellon First Business Bank; director: Pacific Life Insurance Co.; director: Avery Dennison Corp.; director: Dole Food Co. Inc. NONPR AFFIL director: Hugh O'Brian Youth Foundation; trustee: Saint Johns Health Center; director: Catholic Charities; director: California Community Foundation; trustee: California Institute Technology.
Marc Scott Franklin: senior vice president strategic planning B Norwalk, CT 1959. ED Claremont McKenna College (1982); University of Chicago (1982). PRIM CORP EMPL senior vice president strategic planning: Pacific Mutual Life Insurance Co.
Donald Eugene Guinn: chairman emeritus B Wellington, KS 1932. PRIM CORP EMPL chairman emeritus: Pacific Telesis Group. CORP AFFIL director: BankAmerica Corp.; director: Dial Corp.

Robert G. Haskell: senior vice president public affairs B Orange, CA 1952. ED University of Southern California (1974); University of Southern California (1979). PRIM CORP EMPL senior vice president public affairs: Pacific Mutual Life Insurance Co.

Ignacio Eugenio Lozano, Jr.: chairman B San Antonio, TX 1927. ED University of Notre Dame AB (1947). PRIM CORP EMPL chairman: La Opinion. CORP AFFIL director: Sempra Energy; director: Southern California Gas Co.; director: Pacific Enterprises; director: Pacific Life Insurance Co.; chairman: Lozano Communications; ltd. partner: Lozano Enterprises; director: Walt Disney Co.

Charles Allen Lynch: chairman, director B Denver, CO 1927. ED Yale University BS (1950). PRIM CORP EMPL chairman, director: Fresh Choice Inc.

Audrey L. Milfs: vice president, corporate secretary, director B 1945. PRIM CORP EMPL vice president, corporate secretary, director: Pacific Mutual Life Insurance Co. CORP AFFIL secretary: Pacific Mutual Distributors.

Charles Daly Miller: chairman, director B Hartford, CT 1928. ED Johns Hopkins University (1949). PRIM CORP EMPL chairman, director: Avery Dennison Corp. CORP AFFIL director: Pacific Mutual Life Insurance Co.; director: Nationwide Health Properties Inc.; director: Davidson & Associates Inc.; director: Great Western Finance Corp.; chairman, director: Avery Dennison Decorative Films. NONPR AFFIL director: Edison International.

Donn Biddle Miller: president, chief executive officer B Gallipolis, OH 1929. ED Ohio Wesleyan University BA (1951); University of Michigan JD (1954); Harvard University (1974). PRIM CORP EMPL president, chief executive officer: Pearson-Sibert Oil Co. of Texas. CORP AFFIL director: Pacific Life Insurance Co. NONPR AFFIL vice chairman, director: Automobile Club Southern California.

Jacqueline C. Morby: managing partner B Sacramento, CA 1937. ED Stanford University BA (1959); Simmons Colorado Graduate School of Management MBA (1978). PRIM CORP EMPL managing partner: TA Associates, Inc. CORP AFFIL director: Pacific Life Corp.; director: BLP Group Inc.; director: HVL Inc.; director: Ansys Inc.; director: Axx Trend Techs Inc. NONPR AFFIL member: Massachusetts Governments Council Growth & Technology; member: National Venture Capital Organization; trustee: Chatham College.

J. Fernando Niebla: chairman, chief executive officer B Nigales, Mexico 1940. ED University of Arizona BS; University of Southern California MS (1970). PRIM CORP EMPL chairman, chief executive officer: Infotec Commercial Systems Inc. CORP AFFIL director: Pacer Infotec Inc.; director: Union Bancal Corp.

Richard Morris Rosenberg: chairman, chief executive officer (retired) B Fall River, MA 1930. ED Suffolk University BS (1952); Golden Gate University MBA (1963); Golden Gate College LLB (1966). PRIM CORP EMPL chairman, chief executive officer (retired): BankAmerica Corp. CORP AFFIL director: Potlatch Corp.; director: SBC Corp.; director: Airborne Freight Corp.; director: Northrop Grumman Corp. NONPR AFFIL director: San Francisco Symphony; director: United Way America; trustee: California Institute Technology. CLUB AFFIL Hillcrest Country Club; Rainier Club.

Glenn Stanley Schafer: president, director B Saint Johns, MI 1949. ED Michigan State University (1971); University of Detroit (1975). PRIM CORP EMPL president, director: Pacific Mutual Life Insurance Co. ADD CORP EMPL chief financial officer: Pacific Financial Asset Management Corp.; director: Pacific Life & Annuity Co.; president: Pacific Mutual Holding Co. CORP AFFIL director: PIMCO Advisor LP. NONPR AFFIL member: Financial Executive Institute; fellow: Life Management Institute; director: Court Appointed Special Advocates; member: American Institute of Certified Public Accountant.

Thomas C. Sutton: chairman, chief executive officer, director B Atlanta, GA 1942. ED University of Toronto BS (1965); Harvard University (1982). PRIM CORP EMPL chairman, chief executive officer, director: Pacific Mutual Life Insurance Co. CORP AFFIL chairman: PM Group Life Insurance Co.; director: Pimco Advisor LP; chairman: Pacific Lifecorp; director: Pacific Mutual Distributors; director: Pacific Finance Asset Management Corp.; director: Edison International; director: Newhall Land & Farming Co. NONPR AFFIL fellow: Society Actuaries; member affiliates advisory board: University California Irvine School Management; member: Pacific Studies Actuarial Club; member: American Academy of Actuaries.

Khanh T. Tran: senior vice president, chief financial officer, director B Saigon, Vietnam 1956. ED Whittier College (1977); University of California (1980). PRIM CORP EMPL senior vice president, chief financial officer, director: Pacific Mutual Life Insurance Co. CORP AFFIL member: Life Office Management Association; member: Treasury Management Association; member: Finance Executive Institute; member: Finance Officer Group.

James R. Ukropina: partner B Fresno, CA 1937. ED Stanford University (1959); University of Southern California Law School (1965). PRIM CORP EMPL partner: O'Melveny & Myers. CORP AFFIL director: Pacific Mutual; director: Lockheed Martin Corp.; director: Pacific Life Insurance Co. NONPR AFFIL member: Los Angeles County Bar Association; trustee: Stanford University; member: Beta Theta Pi; member: American Bar Association. CLUB AFFIL Annandale Golf Club; California Club.

Raymond L. Watson: vice chairman PRIM CORP EMPL vice chairman: Irvine Co. CORP AFFIL director: Walt Disney Co.

Foundation Officials

Edward R. Byrd: chief financial officer PRIM CORP EMPL Chief Financial Officer: Pacific Mutual Distributor.
Cynthia Dillion: director
Robert G. Haskell: president, director (see above)
Michael T. McLaughlin: general counsel
Audrey L. Milfs: secretary (see above)
Michele Myszka: vice president
Thomas C. Sutton: chairman, director (see above)

Grants Analysis

Disclosure Period: calendar year ending 1997
Total Grants: $1,535,306*
Number of Grants: 138
Average Grant: $11,125
Highest Grant: $140,000
Typical Range: $2,500 to $10,000 and $10,000 to $50,000
***Note:** Giving excludes corporate direct giving.

Recent Grants

Note: Grants derived from 1998 Form 990.

Arts & Humanities

70,000	Smithsonian Institution, Washington, DC
35,000	Orange County Museum of Art, Newport Beach, CA -- capital campaign
20,000	Leland Stanford Mansion Foundation, Inc., Sacramento, CA -- capital campaign
15,000	Huntington Library, Society of Fellows, The, Huntington, CA
10,000	Multicultural Arts Council of Orange County, Irvine, CA
10,000	Orange County Museum of Art, Newport Beach, CA
10,000	Orange County Performing Arts Center, Costa Mesa, CA
10,000	Saint Joseph Ballet, Santa Ana, CA -- capital campaign
10,000	South Coast Repertory, Costa Mesa, CA

Civic & Public Affairs

15,000	Orange County Community Foundation, Costa Mesa, CA -- Teen 2000 Fund
12,500	Drowning Prevention Foundation, Danville, CA
10,000	Taller San Jose, San Jose, CA
10,000	Women's Transitional Living Center, Duluth, MN -- capital campaign
8,575	Public Law Center, Santa Ana, CA

Education

150,000	Health Education Activities, Limited, Jackson, MI
50,000	Parent Institute for Quality Education, San Diego, CA
25,000	Independent Colleges of Southern California, Los Angeles, CA
12,500	Educational Foundation, Inc., Georgia State University, Atlanta, GA
10,000	California State University, Fullerton, Fullerton, CA
10,000	Chapman University, Orange, CA -- capital campaign
10,000	EdSource, Menlo Park, CA
10,000	Orange Coast College Foundation, Los Angeles, CA
10,000	Orange Coast College Foundation, Los Angeles, CA -- reach program
10,000	Rolling Readers U.S.A., San Diego, CA
10,000	University of California, Irvine, Irvine, CA -- gsm mba fellowship
6,000	Huntington Beach Union High School District, Fountain Valley High School, Huntington Beach, CA

Environment

75,000	Whale Conservation Institute, Lincoln, MA
15,000	FISH-Harbor Area, Inc., Continuum of Care Coalition, Newport Beach, CA
10,000	Environmental Nature Center, Newport Beach, CA -- capital campaign

Health

80,000	Public Health Foundation Enterprises, Inc., Los Angeles, CA
10,000	AIDS Services Foundation, Orange County, Irvine, CA
10,000	Children's Hospital Foundation of Orange County, Orange, CA
10,000	Interval House, Long Beach, CA
7,500	American Red Cross, Orange County Chapter, Los Angeles, CA

Science

35,000	Discovery Science Center, Ocala, FL -- capital campaign
10,000	Discovery Science Center, Ocala, FL
10,000	Orange County Marine Institute, Dana Point, CA

Social Services

245,933	United Way of Orange County, Garden Grove, CA
173,500	Orange County Human Relations Council, Orange, CA
20,000	United Way of Orange County, Garden Grove, CA -- needs assessment
15,000	Court Appointed Special Advocates of Orange County, Inc., Orange, CA
10,000	Casa Teresa, Orange, CA
10,000	Center for the Improvement of Child Caring, Studio City, CA
10,000	Human Options, Capital Campaign, South Laguna, CA
10,000	STOP-GAP, Los Angeles, CA
10,000	YMCA of Orange County, Orange, CA
7,500	Girls and Boys Clubs of Garden Grove, Garden Grove, CA
7,500	Save Our Youth, Knoxville, TN
7,500	YWCA of Central Orange County, Orange, CA
7,000	Camp Fire Boys and Girls, Orange County Council, Tustin, CA

PACIFICARE HEALTH SYSTEMS

Company Contact

3120 Lake Center Dr.
Santa Ana, CA 92704
Phone: (714)825-5200
Fax: (714)825-5045
Web: http://www.pacificare.com

Company Description

Assets: US$4,884,000,000 (1999)
Profit: US$278,500,000 (1999)
Employees: 8,800 (1999)
Fortune Rank: 171, per FORTUNE Magazine's list of 500 Largest U.S. Corporations (1999).
FF 171

PacifiCare Health System Foundation

Giving Contact

Riva Gebel, Director
PacifiCare Foundation
3120 Lake Center Dr.
Mail Stop LC01-320
PO Box 25186
Santa Ana, CA 92799
Phone: (714)825-5233
Fax: (714)825-5028

Description

Founded: 1996
EIN: 330473608
Organization Type: Corporate Foundation
Giving Locations: CA: within company service area; FL: within company service area; OK: within company service area; OR: within company service area; TX: within company service areas; WA: within company service areas

Giving Philosophy

'The PacifiCare Foundation's mission is to improve the quality of lives of the disadvantaged or underserved in geographical areas where PacifiCare Health Systems does business, providing support in keeping with the company's vision, values, and commitment to nurturing healthy lifestyles.
'The Foundation focuses primarily on causes dedicated to improving mental and physical well-being, including programs which increase access to health-care; wellness programs for youth and seniors; education; and human and social services.
'The PacifiCare Foundation has been purposefully structured to manage and direct the philanthropic contributions of the corporation and its employees, so that collectively we can have the greatest positive impact on the communities in which we work and live.'
Guidelines for Charitable Giving

Financial Summary

Total Giving: $3,000,000 (fiscal year ending September 30, 1999 approx); $2,500,000 (fiscal 1998 approx); $1,826,322 (fiscal 1996). Note: Contributes through corporate direct giving program and foundation. 1996 Giving includes corporate direct giving ($571,456); foundation ($1,222,866) United Way ($32,000). 1995 Giving includes foundation.
Assets: $1,562,405 (fiscal 1996); $3,897,787 (fiscal 1995)
Gifts Received: $358,914 (fiscal 1996); $2,909,370 (fiscal 1995). Note: In fiscal 1996, contributions were received from C. William Wood ($6,200). In fiscal 1995, contributions were received from PacifiCare of California ($1,000,000), PacifiCare Health Systems ($750,000), Terry Hartshorn PacifiCare Health Systems ($750,000), Terry Hartshorn ($131,527), Hal C. Hylton ($20,000), and C. William Wood ($5,000); miscellaneous contributions under $5,000 each, totaling $1,002,843 also were received.

Typical Recipients

Arts & Humanities: Museums/Galleries, Public Broadcasting
Civic & Public Affairs: Community Foundations, Economic Development, Civic & Public Affairs-General, Hispanic Affairs, Women's Affairs
Education: Education-General, Public Education (Precollege), Special Education
Health: Adolescent Health Issues, AIDS/HIV, Alzheimers Disease, Cancer, Children's Health/Hospitals, Clinics/Medical Centers, Geriatric Health, Health Organizations, Heart, Hospitals, Long-Term Care, Preventive Medicine/Wellness Organizations, Public Health, Single-Disease Health Associations
International: Missionary/Religious Activities
Religion: Churches, Religious Welfare
Social Services: Animal Protection, At-Risk Youth, Big Brother/Big Sister, Child Abuse, Child Welfare, Community Service Organizations, Crime Prevention, Domestic Violence, Food/Clothing Distribution, People with Disabilities, Recreation & Athletics, Senior Services, United Funds/United Ways, Volunteer Services, Youth Organizations

Contributions Analysis

Education: Focuses on elementary, junior and senior high school programs that promote self-esteem, encourage academic achievement and the development of specific skill, literacy programs, training programs and programs that improve the effectiveness of the educational system.
Health: Supports programs with a focus on prevention, health educationprograms, programs that promote access to health care, and programs that improve the quality of health-care for targeted populations. Supports programs targeted to meet the needs of the homeless and hungry, shelters that address the needs of targeted populations, and other social service programs.
Social Services: Includes support to child care, youth activity programs, programs to support at-risk youth, and counseling programs. Supports senior social services, nutrition, education, volunteer, and adult day care programs.
Note: Above priorities are for the foundation.

Application Procedures

Initial Contact: call or write to request guidelines, application form, and checklist; then completed form with two copies of a two- five-page proposal
Application Requirements: background information and qualifications of organization; description of problem, need, or issue addressed; complete description of project, including goals, objectives, timeline, staffing, and evaluation procedures; geographic area served by project; line item budget showing project costs, and description of how future funding will be secured; cover letter signed by chief executive officer, summarizing project, problem addressed, and amount requested, with contact information; proof of tax-exempt status; most recent audited financial statement; current operating bud get and specific project budget; most recent Form 990; list of major sources of funding, with amounts; list of board members; other support materials
Deadlines: January 1 or July 1
Review Process: proposals reviewed by foundation staff, then forwarded to an Employee Allocation Committee for review; committees make recommendations to foundation board of directors
Decision Notification: board meets in March and September, decisions announced in Mid-March and Mid-September

Restrictions

Grants are only considered to nonprofit, tax-exempt organizations serving company market areas, and which have been in existence at least two years.
Grants are not considered for the following: arts/cultural programs, professional or technical associations, annual or capital campaigns, research, endowments, conferences, individuals, private foundations, programs which promote religious doctrine, sponsorship of special events, scholarship, challenge grants, capital campaigns or multiple year requests. special events, scholarship, challenge grants, capital campaigns or multiple year requests.

Additional Information

Organizations may re-apply annually; only one grant may be received per organization per year.
Publications: Annual Report; Application Form and Guidelines

Foundation Officials

Brad A. Bowlus: member PRIM CORP EMPL regional vice president western region: PacifiCare Health Systems Inc. CORP AFFIL president, chief executive officer: PacifiCare California; president: PacifiCare Operation Inc.
Jeffrey M. Folick: member ED University of California, Los Angeles BS. CORP AFFIL executive vice president, chief operating officer: Pacificare Health Systems Inc.; director: Pacificare Pharmacy Center; chairman: Pacificare Behavioral Health.
Nick Franklin: member PRIM CORP EMPL senior vice president, public affairs: PacifiCare Health Systems Inc.
Riva Gebel: director
Terry O'Dell Hartshorn: chairman B 1944. ED University of California, Los Angeles BS (1967); University of California, Los Angeles MS (1979). PRIM CORP EMPL chairman: PacifiCare Health Systems Inc. CORP AFFIL chairman: PacifiCare Operations; president, chief executive officer: UniHealth America; director: PacifiCare Life Health Insurance.
Alan R. Hoops: member B 1947. ED University of California, Los Angeles BA (1969); University of Washington MS (1973). PRIM CORP EMPL president, chief executive officer, director: PacifiCare Health System Inc. CORP AFFIL secretary: PacifiCare Oregon.
Wanda Lee: member PRIM CORP EMPL senior vice president corporate human resources: PacifiCare Health Systems Inc.
Robert Lloyd: member
Bill Wood: president

Grants Analysis

Disclosure Period: fiscal year ending September 30, 1996
Total Grants: $1,222,866*
Number of Grants: 149
Average Grant: $8,152
Highest Grant: $32,000
Typical Range: $2,000 to $10,000
***Note:** Giving excludes United Way.

Recent Grants

Note: Grants derived from fiscal 1996 Form 990.

Arts & Humanities

10,000 Los Angeles Children's Museum, Los Angeles, CA

Civic & Public Affairs

10,000 Area Chapter, Houston, TX
10,000 Casa Teresa, Orange, CA
10,000 Economic Development Corporation, Long Beach, CA
10,000 Unicorn Centers, San Antonio, TX

Education

32,000 Newport Mesa Unified School District, Newport Beach, CA
22,372 Pasadena Unified School District, Pasadena, CA
10,000 Cassata Learning Center, Dallas, TX
10,000 Happy Hands Education Center, Tulsa, OK

10,000	Mardan Foundation of Educational Therapy, Irvine, CA
8,450	Evergreen Middle School, Everett, WA
Health	
24,000	St. Joseph Hospital Foundation, Orange, CA
10,000	AIDS Arms, Dallas, TX
10,000	Alzheimer's Association, Dallas, TX
10,000	American Cancer Society, San Antonio, TX
10,000	American Heart Association, Irvine, CA
10,000	Autistic Treatment Center, Dallas, TX
10,000	Glendale Adventist Medical Center, Glendale, CA
10,000	In Need of Treatment, Oklahoma City, OK
10,000	Memorial Foundation, Riverside, CA
10,000	Neighborhood Health Clinics, Portland, OR
10,000	RAIN Regional AIDS Interfaith Network, Oklahoma City, OK
10,000	St. Clare's Home, Escondido, CA
10,000	Special Care, Oklahoma City, OK
Religion	
10,000	Catholic Charities of Orange County, Santa Ana, CA
Social Services	
32,000	United Way Orange County, Irvine, CA
11,000	Oklahoma City Food Bank, Oklahoma City, OK
10,400	Child Advocates, Houston, TX
10,245	Blind Children's Learning Center, Santa Ana, CA
10,150	Boys and Girls Club, Buena Park, CA
10,000	Big Brothers of Orange County, Tustin, CA
10,000	Boys Club of Fountain Valley, Huntington Beach, CA
10,000	Boys and Girls Clubs, San Antonio, TX
10,000	Boys Hope, Girls Hope, Laguna Niguel, CA
10,000	Canon Area Residential Center, Anaheim, CA
10,000	Child Abuse Council of Orange County, Laguna Hills, CA
10,000	Child Advocates, San Antonio, TX
10,000	Children Now, Oakland, CA
10,000	Compass Community Services, San Francisco, CA
10,000	Court-Appointed Special Advocates of Orange County, Orange, CA
10,000	Covenant House of California, Hollywood, CA
10,000	Cypress Police Department, Cypress, CA
10,000	Friends of Child Advocates, Monterey Park, CA
10,000	Girls Incorporated of Newport News, Casa Mesa, CA
10,000	Haven Hills, Canoga Park, CA
10,000	Loaves and Fishes, Portland, OR
10,000	Los Angeles Regional Food Bank, Los Angeles, CA
10,000	San Bernardino Child Advocacy Program, San Bernardino, CA
10,000	Texas Association for Retarded Citizens, San Antonio, TX
10,000	Volunteer Center, Los Angeles, CA

PACIFICORP

Company Contact

Portland, OR
Web: http://www.pacificorp.com

Company Description

Revenue: US$9,442,500,000
Employees: 15,216
SIC(s): 1041 Gold Ores, 1044 Silver Ores, 1094 Uranium, Radium & Vanadium Ores, 4911 Electric Services.

Nonmonetary Support

Type: Donated Equipment; Workplace Solicitation
Note: Nonmonetary support is provided by the company.

Corporate Sponsorship

Value: $75,000
Type: Arts & cultural events; Festivals/fairs
Note: Supports a program called SMART: Start Making a Reader Today.

PacifiCorp Foundation

Giving Contact

Alan Richardson, II, Executive Director
PacifiCorp Foundation
825 NE Multnomah, Suite 2000
Portland, OR 97232
Phone: (503)813-7257
Fax: (503)813-7249
Email: ernie.bloch@pacificorp.com
Web: http://www.pacificorp.com/paccomp/commsvc

Description

Founded: 1988
EIN: 943089826
Organization Type: Corporate Foundation
Giving Locations: CA: Northern California; ID; NV; OR; UT; WA; WY
Grant Types: Capital, Emergency, General Support, Matching, Multiyear/Continuing Support.

Giving Philosophy

In 1998, PacifiCorp created the Foundation to formalize its charitable contributions to ensure the health and vitality of our communities. The Foundation became the major philanthropic arm of PacifiCorp, Pacific Power and Utah Power -- a way to invest in the long term health of the communities where PacifiCorp serves and the company's employees and their families live.' Foundation brochure

Financial Summary

Total Giving: $2,800,000 (2000 approx); $3,434,739 (1998); $2,843,895 (1997). Note: Contributes through corporate direct giving program and foundation.
Giving Analysis: Giving for 1997 includes: foundation ($2,413,494); corporate direct giving ($347,394); international subsidiaries ($190,000); 1998: foundation ($2,508,446); foundation grants to United Way ($583,431); corporate direct giving ($342,862)
Assets: $40,595,543 (1998); $46,774,108 (1997); $32,748,120 (1996). Note: 1998 assets include January to June 30.
Gifts Received: $3,303,081 (1998); $3,784,220 (1996); $12,544,510 (1995). Note: Contributions are received from Pacific Power & Light Co., Pacific Telecom, Inc. and PacifiCorp Holdings, Inc.

Typical Recipients

Arts & Humanities: Arts Associations & Councils, Ballet, Historic Preservation, Libraries, Museums/Galleries, Music, Opera, Performing Arts, Public Broadcasting, Theater
Civic & Public Affairs: African American Affairs, Community Foundations, Economic Development, Employment/Job Training, Civic & Public Affairs-General, Housing, Rural Affairs, Urban & Community Affairs
Education: Afterschool/Enrichment Programs, Business Education, Colleges & Universities, Education Funds, Education-General, Public Education (Precollege), Science/Mathematics Education
Environment: Energy, Environment-General, Resource Conservation, Wildlife Protection
Health: Children's Health/Hospitals, Emergency/Ambulance Services, Health Organizations, Hospitals, Public Health
International: International Organizations
Science: Science Museums
Social Services: At-Risk Youth, Child Welfare, Community Centers, Community Service Organizations, Family Planning, People with Disabilities, Recreation & Athletics, Scouts, Shelters/Homelessness, United Funds/United Ways, Youth Organizations

Contributions Analysis

Giving Priorities: United funds; youth groups; colleges and universities; cultural enrichment; and health and human services.
Arts & Humanities: 10%. Supports the performing arts, the visual arts, historic preservation, and public broadcasting.
Civic & Public Affairs: 3%. Funds community chests, parks, recreation facilities, crime prevention, chemical dependency treatment and prevention programs, and senior citizens centers.
Education: 21%. Provides funds to educational and research institutions, both public and private, from elementary through university level.
Health: 4%. Supports medical centers and hospitals.
Social Services: 61%. Funds youth organizations, United Way runaway youth services, and domestic violence treatment and prevention.
Note: Total contributions made in 1998.

Application Procedures

Initial Contact: Send a one-page summary and a proposal of no more than 10 pages (including attachments) to foundation; contact appropriate subsidiary or local manager.
Application Requirements: Include a description of organization, amount requested, purpose of funds sought, recently audited financial statement, proof of tax-exempt status; connection to PacifiCorp and/or its business units; budget for activity or project; the percentage of the total operating budget that the project budget would represent; itemized amounts of financial support requested by other donors, or already pledged or contributed by other donors, and indication if it is a matched grant; and the way in which funds would be applied.
Deadlines: March 15 for education and research organizations; June 15 for civic and community grants; September 15 for arts and cultural organizations; December 15 for health, welfare, youth, community chests, and united appeals.
Review Process: Most contributions are made by the foundation on the recommendation of each subsidiary; recommendations are considered four times per year.

Restrictions

Foundation grants are not made to any non-charitable purpose; establishment or support of endowments; operating deficits; individuals; to religious organizations for religious purposes; political organizations, campaigns, or candidates for political office; organizations that discriminate against individuals on the basis of creed, color, sex, age, national origin or veteran status; veterans' or fraternal organizations for operating purposes; sponsorship or advertising that directly benefits marketing or sales programs of PacifiCorp or its operating companies; establishment or support of endowments; coverage of operating deficits; memberships in chambers of commerce; and taxpayer associations and other bodies whose activities directly benefit PacifiCorp or its operating companies.

Additional Information

Direct giving by the company will go only to organizations that are ineligible for grants under foundation guidelines. Subsidiaries and divisions of PacifiCorp that contribute to the PacifiCorp Foundation include

Pacific Power, Pacific Telecom, and PacifiCorp Holdings, Inc.
Subsidiaries: Pacific Power, 920 SW 6th Ave., Portland, OR 97204 (503) 464-5000; Pacific Telecom, 805 Broadway, Box 9901, Vancouver, WA 98669, (360) 905-5800; PacifiCorp Holdings, Inc., 825 NE Multnomah, Suite 775, Portland, OR 97232.
PacifiCorp merged with Scottish Power in November 1999. 825 NE Multnomah, Suite 775, Portland, OR 97232.
PacifiCorp merged with Scottish Power in November 1999.

Corporate Officials

John A. Bohling: senior vice president, chief financial officer B Salt Lake City, UT 1943. ED University of Utah BSEE (1968); University of Delaware MBA (1972). PRIM CORP EMPL senior vice president: PacifiCorp.
Keith Robert McKennon: chairman, president B Condon, OR 1933. ED Oregon State University BS (1955). PRIM CORP EMPL chairman, president: PacifiCorp. NONPR AFFIL trustee: National Legal Center Public Interest; member executive committee: Society Chemical Industry; trustee: Keystone Center.
Richard T. O'Brien: executive vice president, chief operating officer ED Chicago State University BA (1976); Portland State University JD (1985). PRIM CORP EMPL executive vice president, chief operating officer: PacifiCorp.
William E. Peressinni: senior vice president, chief financial officer B Great Falls, MT 1956. PRIM CORP EMPL vice president, treasurer: PacifiCorp; senior vice president, chief financial officer: Pacificorp Financial Services Inc. CLUB AFFIL Oswego Club; University Club; Alpha Delta Phi.

Foundation Officials

John A. Bohling: board member (see above)
Pamela Bradford: assistant secretary
Tom Imeson: chairman, director PRIM CORP EMPL vice president public affairs & communications: Public Affairs & Communications.
Lenore Martin: secretary
Keith Robert McKennon: member (see above)
Richard T. O'Brien: member (see above)
William E. Peressinni: treasurer (see above)
Alan Richardson: executive director
Dennis P. Steinberg: board member PRIM CORP EMPL senior vice president: PacifiCorp Inc.

Grants Analysis

Disclosure Period: calendar year ending 1998
Total Grants: $2,508,446*
Number of Grants: 373
Average Grant: $5,409
Highest Grant: $220,000
Typical Range: $500 to $5,000
***Note:** Giving excludes corporate direct giving; international subsidiaries; United Way.

Recent Grants

Note: Grants derived from 1997 Form 990.

Arts & Humanities

40,000	Oregon State University Foundation, Corvallis, OR -- OSU Library campaign
38,000	Utah Symphony Society, Salt Lake City, UT -- general program support
37,500	Oregon Ballet Theater, Portland, OR -- leadership challenge grant for new and increased giving towards annual operating support
33,334	Westminster College, Salt Lake City, UT -- additional capital campaign for construction of a new library
30,000	Southern Utah University, Cedar City, UT -- funding for SUU's centennial celebration
25,000	Oregon Symphony Association, Portland, OR -- annual operating support
25,000	Portland Art Museum, Portland, OR -- capital campaign for complete purchase of adjacent property
25,000	Utah Shakespeare Festival, Cedar City, UT -- general production support
24,000	University of Utah, Salt Lake City, UT -- support for public broadcasting stations KUER radio and KUED television
20,000	University of Alaska Museum, AK -- capital campaign for museum expansion
16,666	Utah Opera Company, Salt Lake City, UT -- consolidation and renovation of new facilities from five separate locations to one warehouse
16,350	Ballet West, Salt Lake City, UT -- annual general support
15,000	Portland Art Museum, Portland, OR -- sponsor Museum Family Sunday to honor Martin Luther King, Jr.
15,000	Portland Opera Association, Portland, OR -- annual operating support
14,730	Utah Opera Company, Salt Lake City, UT -- annual support
12,500	Alliance of Redding Museums, Redding, CA -- capital campaign for construction of a major museum complex
12,500	Library Foundation, Portland, OR -- capital and operating grants for library functions
12,500	Oregon Ballet Theater, Portland, OR -- leadership challenge grant for new and increased giving towards annual operating support
12,500	Oregon Ballet Theater, Portland, OR -- annual support
12,500	Portland Center Stage, Portland, OR -- tickets to neighborhood groups
12,500	Sevier Valley Applied Technology Center, Richfield, UT -- capital request for architectural drawings to design and build a performing arts center

Civic & Public Affairs

25,000	Neighborhood Partnership Fund of the Oregon Community, Portland, OR -- community development in low-income neighborhoods
12,500	Black United Fund, Portland, OR -- annual operating support
12,500	Identify Clark County Campaign, Vancouver, WA -- capital campaign for construction of a special events center in Clark County

Education

70,500	Oregon Independent College Foundation, Portland, OR -- annual support
40,000	University of Utah, Salt Lake City, UT -- construction of the C. Roland Christensen Center at the David Eccles School of Business
25,467	Self Enhancement, Portland, OR -- capital campaign for new building
20,000	Portland Public Schools Foundation, Portland, OR -- funding for development, major grants, and a major fundraiser
17,000	University of Wyoming Foundation, Laramie, WY -- general program support
15,000	Junior Achievement of Columbia Empire, Portland, OR -- annual support
12,500	Marylhurst College, Marylhurst, OR -- capital campaign for renovation of Flavia Hall

Environment

15,000	Nature Conservancy Great Basin Field Office, Salt Lake City, UT -- capital request for Utah Land Legacy Campaign
15,000	Sustainable Northwest, Portland, OR -- community partnership projects in rural Oregon
12,500	Ducks Unlimited, Rancho Cordova, CA -- Bear Lake National Wildlife Refuge restoration

International

25,000	World Masters Games, Portland, OR -- operating support

Social Services

112,111	United Way of the Great Salt Lake Area, Salt Lake City, UT -- general program support
60,072	United Way of the Columbia-Willamette, Portland, OR
55,000	United Way of the Columbia-Willamette, Portland, OR
55,000	United Way of the Columbia-Willamette, Portland, OR -- annual support
55,000	United Way of the Columbia-Willamette, Portland, OR -- annual support
28,667	Goodwill Industries of the Columbia-Willamette, Portland, OR -- capital campaign for a major facility renewal project
25,000	STARS Foundation, Salem, OR -- an abstinence-based pregnancy prevention program using peer mentors in rural Oregon
25,000	United Way of Yakima County, Yakima, WA -- operating support
20,000	Oregon Children's Foundation, Portland, OR -- three-year, $60,000 grant to fund the SMART program in 11 Oregon counties
20,000	Woodland Community Swimming Pool Committee, Woodland, WA -- capital project to fund construction of a recreational facility to include a swimming pool
18,576	United Way of Southeastern Utah, Price, UT -- general program support
16,000	Boy Scouts of America Cascade Pacific Council, Portland, OR -- annual operating support
15,557	United Way of Natrona County, Casper, WY
15,500	United Way of Lewis County, Centralia, WA -- general program support
12,500	Whitefish Community Center, Whitefish, MT -- capital campaign to construct a community center

Paine Webber

Company Contact

1285 Avenue of the Americas
New York, NY 10019
Phone: (212)713-2000
Email: comments@painewebber.com
Web: http://www.painewebber.com

Company Description

Employees: 16,105
SIC(s): 6211 Security Brokers & Dealers, 6719 Holding Companies Nec.
Parent Company: Paine Webber Group, Inc., 1285 Ave. of the Americas, New York, NY, United States

Paine Webber Foundation

Giving Contact

Susan Clark, Contact
PaineWebber Foundation
Phone: (212)713-2807
Fax: (212)713-1380

Description

Founded: 1879
EIN: 046032804
Organization Type: Corporate Foundation

Giving Locations: NY: New York
Grant Types: General Support, Research.

Financial Summary
Total Giving: $902,750 (1997); $800,208 (1994); $330,683 (1993). Note: Contributes through foundation only.
Assets: $30,110,551 (1997); $16,993,006 (1995); $13,549,280 (1994)
Gifts Received: $8,028,750 (1997); $1,941,091 (1993); $2,870,885 (1992)

Typical Recipients
Arts & Humanities: Arts Associations & Councils, Arts Centers, Libraries, Museums/Galleries, Music, Theater
Civic & Public Affairs: Botanical Gardens/Parks, Clubs, Community Foundations, Employment/Job Training, Civic & Public Affairs-General, Municipalities/Towns, Women's Affairs
Education: Business Education, Colleges & Universities, Education Associations, Education Reform, Legal Education, Minority Education, Private Education (Precollege), Religious Education, Student Aid
Environment: Environment-General
Health: AIDS/HIV, Arthritis, Cancer, Children's Health/Hospitals, Diabetes, Emergency/Ambulance Services, Hospices, Hospitals, Medical Research, Public Health, Single-Disease Health Associations, Transplant Networks/Donor Banks
International: Foreign Educational Institutions, International Development, International Relief Efforts
Religion: Churches, Dioceses, Jewish Causes, Ministries, Religious Organizations, Religious Welfare
Social Services: Animal Protection, At-Risk Youth, Child Welfare, Community Service Organizations, Counseling, Day Care, Family Services, Food/Clothing Distribution, People with Disabilities, Recreation & Athletics, Shelters/Homelessness, Social Services-General, Substance Abuse, YMCA/YWCA/YMHA/YWHA, Youth Organizations

Contributions Analysis
Giving Priorities: Grants are made to support education, health, civic improvement programs, arts & culture, housing, and the environment.
Arts & Humanities: 55%. Major support for the New York Public Library.
Civic & Public Affairs: 2%. Employment/job training, clubs, and botanical gardens.
Education: 3%. Primary support for colleges and universities.
Health: 35%. Major support for the Memorial Sloan-Kettering Cancer Center.
International: 1%. International education and international relief.
Religion: 1%. Jewish welfare organizations.
Social Services: 3% Emphasis on the homeless and people with disabilities.
Note: Total contributions in 1997.

Application Procedures
Initial Contact: Brief typewritten letter of inquiry on organization's letterhead.
Application Requirements: Include a description of organization, amount requested, and proof of tax-exempt status.
Deadlines: December 1

Corporate Officials
Regina A. Dolan: chief financial officer, vice president director B 1955. PRIM CORP EMPL chief financial officer, senior vice president: PaineWebber Group Inc. ADD CORP EMPL chief financial officer: Paine Webber Inc.
Joseph J. Grano, Jr.: president B Hartford, CT 1948. PRIM CORP EMPL president: PaineWebber Group Inc. CORP AFFIL president: PaineWebber Inc.
Donald Baird Marron: chairman, chief executive officer, director B Goshen, NY 1934. ED City University of New York Bernard M. Baruch College (1949-1951); City University of New York Bernard M. Baruch College (1955-1957). PRIM CORP EMPL chairman, chief executive officer, director: Paine Webber Group Inc. ADD CORP EMPL chairman, chief executive officer: Paine Webber Inc. CORP AFFIL co-founder: Data Resources. NONPR AFFIL director: New York City Partnership; member: President Committee Arts & Humanities; member board overseers: Memorial Sloan-Kettering Cancer Center; vice chairman board trustee: Museum Modern Art; member: Council Foreign Relations; member: Governor School & Business Alliance Task Force; director: Business Committee Arts.
Ronald M. Schwartz: executive vice president, director PRIM CORP EMPL executive vice president, director: PaineWebber Group Inc.

Foundation Officials
Regina A. Dolan: trustee (see above)
Donald Baird Marron: trustee (see above)
Ronald M. Schwartz: trustee (see above)

Grants Analysis
Disclosure Period: calendar year ending 1997
Total Grants: $902,750
Number of Grants: 27
Average Grant: $24,110*
Highest Grant: $500,000
Typical Range: $300,000 to $500,000
***Note:** Average grant excludes two highest grants totaling $800,000.

Recent Grants
Note: Grants derived from 1997 Form 990.

Arts & Humanities

500,000 New York Public Library, New York, NY

Civic & Public Affairs

5,000 Gildas Club, New York, NY
5,000 Hewlett House, Garden City, NY
5,000 Jobs for the Future, Boston, MA
5,000 New York Botanical Garden, Bronx, NY

Education

5,000 Bates College Parents Fund, Lewistown, ME
5,000 Bristow High School Class of '40 Scholarship Fund, Bristow, OK
5,000 Colgate University, Hamilton, NY
5,000 Queens College Foundation, Flushing, NY
2,500 Mount Tamalpais School, Mill Valley, CA
250 New York University, New York, NY

Health

300,000 Memorial Sloan-Kettering Cancer Center, New York, NY
5,000 Christ Hospital, Jersey City, NJ
5,000 Northwestern Memorial Foundation, Chicago, IL
5,000 Outer Cape Health Services, Truro, MA
2,500 Leukemia Society of America, New York, NY

International

5,000 US Committee for United World Colleges, New York, NY
1,000 UNICEF, New York, NY

Religion

4,000 Interfaith Council for the Homeless, Plainfield, NJ
3,000 Combined Jewish Philanthropies, Boston, MA
2,500 Combined Jewish Philanthropies, Boston, MA
2,000 Friends of Harvard-Radcliffe Hillel, Cambridge, MA

Social Services

5,000 Coalition for the Homeless, New York, NY
5,000 Federation of Organizations for the Mentally Disabled, West Islip, NY
5,000 Just One Break, New York, NY
5,000 National Elite Gymnastics Team Booster Club, Austin, TX
5,000 Partnership for the Homeless, New York, NY

Pan-American Life Insurance Co.

Company Contact
New Orleans, LA

Company Description
Premiums: US$448,210,000
Employees: 1,080
SIC(s): 6311 Life Insurance, 6321 Accident & Health Insurance, 6324 Hospital & Medical Service Plans.

Nonmonetary Support
Value: $5,000 (1994)
Type: Donated Equipment; In-kind Services; Loaned Employees

Corporate Sponsorship
Value: $50
Note: Sponsors health care and people-oriented nonprofit organizations and events.

Giving Contact
Eileen Lumar-Johnson, Second Vice President, Corporate Communications
Pan-American Life Insurance Co.
Pan-American Life Center
New Orleans, LA 70130
Phone: (504)566-3100
Fax: (504)566-3381

Description
Founded: 1911
Organization Type: Corporate Giving Program
Giving Locations: headquarters area only.
Grant Types: Capital, Conference/Seminar, Endowment, General Support, Multiyear/Continuing Support.

Financial Summary
Total Giving: Contributes through corporate direct giving program only.

Typical Recipients
Arts & Humanities: Museums/Galleries, Public Broadcasting
Civic & Public Affairs: Business/Free Enterprise
Education: Business Education, Colleges & Universities
Health: Medical Rehabilitation, Medical Research
Religion: Churches
Social Services: Community Service Organizations, Shelters/Homelessness, United Funds/United Ways, Youth Organizations

Contributions Analysis
Arts & Humanities: About 5%. Supports local museums and public broadcasting.
Civic & Public Affairs: About 10%. Funding supports business and the free enterprise system in the local community.
Health: About 25%. Contributes to medical research and health services.
Social Services: About 60%. Major support is given to the United Way, community and volunteer services, and youth organizations.

Application Procedures

Initial Contact: a brief letter of inquiry
Application Requirements: a description of organization, amount requested, purpose of funds sought, and proof of tax-exempt status
Deadlines: before October 1 of each year

Restrictions

Does not support individuals or organizations outside operating areas.

Additional Information

Primarily gives to organizations and events that are health-related or that will benefit people.

Corporate Officials

George Frank Purvis, Jr.: chairman, president, chief executive officer, director B Rayville, LA 1914. ED Kemper Military School and College AA (1932); Louisiana State University LLB (1935). PRIM CORP EMPL chairman, president, chief executive officer, director: Pan-American Life Insurance Co. ADD CORP EMPL director, president: Compania DeSeguros Panamerica South America; vice president, director: Pan-America International Insurance Corp.; president: Pan-America deColumbia Compania de-Sequros deVida South America. CORP AFFIL director: Republic Airlines Inc.; director: Southern-Republic Airlines; chairman, board governors: International Insurance Seminars Inc.; chairman: International Reinsurance Co.; director: First Commerce Corp.; director: First National Bank Commerce. NONPR AFFIL director: Summer Pop Concerts; president: YMCA; member advisory board: Salvation Army; chairman: S.S. Huebner Foundation Insurance Education; member: Phi Delta Phi; member board commissioners: Port New Orleans; director: New Orleans Philharmonic Symphony Society; member: Omicron Delta Kappa; member: Louisiana Law Institute; member: New Orleans Association Life Underwriters; member: Louisiana Association Legal Research Life Insurance Companies; member: Louisiana Bar Association; member: Insurance Economics Society America; member: International Trade Administration; director: Family Service Society New Orleans; member: Health Insurance Association America; director: Council Better Louisiana; member: Delta Kappa Epsilon; chairman: Business Task Force Education Inc.; member: Chamber of Commerce Greater New Orleans Area; member advisory board: Baptist Hospital; director: Bureau Government Research New Orleans; member: American Life Convention; member: Association Life Insurance Council; member: American Bar Association; member: American Judicature Society.
John Kenneth Roberts, Jr.: president, chief executive officer, director B Omaha, NE 1936. ED University of Iowa BA (1958). PRIM CORP EMPL president, chief executive officer, director: Pan-American Life Insurance Co. CORP AFFIL director: Whitney National Bank New Orleans; chairman: Panarem Inc.; director: Whitney Holding Corp. NONPR AFFIL member: American Academy of Actuaries; fellow: Society Actuaries.

Giving Program Officials

Eileen Lumar-Johnson: vice president PRIM CORP EMPL second vice president corporate communications: Pan-American Life Insurance Co.

PARK NATIONAL BANK

Company Contact

Newark, OH
Web: http://www.parknationalbank.com

Company Description

Assets: US$914,000,000
Employees: 400
SIC(s): 6021 National Commercial Banks.
Parent Company: Park National Corp.

Park National Corp. Foundation

Giving Contact

Stuart N. Parsons, Trust Officer
PO Box 3500
Newark, OH 43058-3500
Phone: (614)349-8451

Description

EIN: 316249406
Organization Type: Corporate Foundation. Supports preselected organizations only.
Giving Locations: OH
Grant Types: General Support.

Financial Summary

Total Giving: $257,753 (1996); $68,500 (1990)
Assets: $6,286,088 (1996); $1,181,484 (1989)
Gifts Received: $20 (1996)

Typical Recipients

Arts & Humanities: Ballet, Community Arts, Historic Preservation, History & Archaeology, Music, Performing Arts, Theater
Civic & Public Affairs: Botanical Gardens/Parks, Business/Free Enterprise, Chambers of Commerce, Community Foundations, Economic Development, Housing, Municipalities/Towns, Parades/Festivals
Education: Arts/Humanities Education, Business Education, Colleges & Universities, Education Associations, Education Funds, Education Reform, Education-General, Minority Education, Private Education (Precollege), Public Education (Precollege)
Health: Cancer, Emergency/Ambulance Services, Hospitals, Mental Health, Prenatal Health Issues, Public Health
International: International Organizations
Religion: Churches
Social Services: Camps, Community Service Organizations, Domestic Violence, Family Services, Recreation & Athletics, Scouts, Senior Services, United Funds/United Ways, YMCA/YWCA/YMHA/YWHA

Restrictions

Does not support individuals, political or lobbying groups, or organizations outside operating areas.

Corporate Officials

David C. Bowers: senior vice president, chief financial officer PRIM CORP EMPL senior vice president, chief financial officer: Park National Corp.
C. Daniel DeLawder: president, director PRIM CORP EMPL president, director: Park National Bank.
William Thompson McConnell: chairman, ceo B Zanesville, OH 1933. ED Denison University BA (1955); Northwestern University MBA (1959). PRIM CORP EMPL chairman, ceo: Park National Corp. CORP AFFIL chairman, director: Park National Bank; director: Consolidated Computer Center; director: Freight Services. NONPR AFFIL member: Newark Area Chamber of Commerce; member: Ohio Bankers Association.

Foundation Officials

C. Daniel DeLawder: president (see above)
William Thompson McConnell: chairman (see above)
Stuart N. Parsons: secretary, treasurer, director B Johnstown, OH 1942. ED Ohio State University (1964-1969). PRIM CORP EMPL senior vice president, trust officer: Park National Corp.

Grants Analysis

Disclosure Period: calendar year ending 1996
Number of Grants: 42
Highest Grant: $53,333
Typical Range: $1,000 to $10,000

Recent Grants

Note: Grants derived from 1997 Form 990.

Arts & Humanities

3,333	Utica County Historical Society, Utica, OH

Civic & Public Affairs

54,500	Licking County Foundation, Newark, OH
10,000	Ohio Chamber of Commerce Education, Columbus, OH
5,000	COSI, Columbus, OH
5,000	East Mound Community Development, Newark, OH

Education

50,000	Newark Campus Development Fund, Newark, OH
10,000	Par Excellence Learning Center, Newark, OH
6,000	St. Peter's Schools, Mansfield, OH
5,000	Lexington Local Schools, Lexington, OH
2,500	Ohio Foundation of Independent Colleges, Columbus, OH

Health

5,000	American Red Cross, Newark, OH
5,000	Licking Memorial Health Foundation, Newark, OH
2,700	Ohio Cancer Research, Columbus, OH

Social Services

60,000	United Way Licking County, Newark, OH
15,000	United Way Richland County, Mansfield, OH
10,000	Boy Scouts of America, Newark, OH
10,000	Family Counseling Services, Newark, OH
7,400	United Way Fairfield County, Lancaster, OH
5,000	Olivedale Senior Citizens, Lancaster, OH
2,500	Camp O'Bannon, Newark, OH

PARKER HANNIFIN CORP.

Company Contact

Cleveland, OH
Web: http://www.parker.com

Company Description

Revenue: US$4,958,800,000 (1999)
Employees: 38,928 (1999)
Fortune Rank: 328, per FORTUNE Magazine's list of 500 Largest U.S. Corporations (1999).
FF 328
SIC(s): 3494 Valves & Pipe Fittings Nec, 3593 Fluid Power Cylinders & Actuators, 3594 Fluid Power Pumps & Motors, 3599 Industrial Machinery Nec.

Operating Locations

Argentina: Parker Hannifin Argentina SAIYC, Villa Maipu, Buenos Aires; Australia: Parker Hannifin (Australia) Pty. Ltd., Castle Hill; Parker Hannifin Corporate Hose Division, Wodonga; Austria: Parker Ermeto GmbH, Marchtrenk; Parker Hannifin NMF GmbH, Vienna; Parker-Ermento GmbH, Wiener Neustadt; Belgium: Parker Hannifin NV, Brussels, Brabant; Brazil: Parker Hannifin Industria e Comercio Ltda., Jacarei; Canada: Parker Hannifin Canada, Beamsville; Seal Group, Mississauga; People's Republic of China: Parker Aerospace Beijing, Beijing; Parker Hannifin Hong Kong Ltd., Beijing, Shanghai; Parker Hannifin Motion and Control Co. Ltd., Shanghai; Czech Republic: Parker Hannifin Corporate, Prague; Denmark: Polar Seals ApS, Espergaerde; Parker Hannifin Danmark A/S, Ishoj, Copenhagen; England: Parker Hannifin plc, Watferd, Hertshire; Finland: Parker Hannifin Oy, Urjala AS; Parker hannifin Oy (Finland), Vantaa;

France: Parker Hannifin RAK, Contamine-Sur-Arve; Telemecanique, Evreux Cedex; VOAC Hydraulics S.A., LES MUREAUX Cedex; Parker Hannifin, Paris, Cedex; Parker Hannafin RAK, SA, Pontarlier, Cedex; Parker Hannifin RAK SA, Ville la Grand, Haute Savoie; Polyflex France S.A., Wissembourg; Germany: Parker Hannifin GmbH, Beilefeld, Nordrhein-Westfalen, Berlin, Bietigheim-Bissingen, Chemnitz, Dortmund, Frankfurt; Parker Hannifin GmbH (CIC), Grunberg-Queckborn; Parker Hannifin GmbH, Kaarst; Parker Hannifin GmbH (CLD), Koln; Parker Hannifin GmbH, Lampertheim, Leinfelden-Echterdingen, Limbach; Parker Bertea Aeiospace (Abex Division), Mainz-Kastel; Parker Hannifin GmbH (Schrader Bellows), Mettmann; Parker Hannifin GmbH (HPD), Muecke; Parker Hannifin GmbH, Muenchen, Offenburg; Parker Praedifa GmbH (O-Ring Division), Pleidelsheim; Hungary: Parker Hannifin Corporate, Budapest; India:, Mumbai; Italy: Parker Seals SpA, Ardo; Parker Hannifin SpA, Arsago Seprio, Corsico, Lombardia, Gessate; Republic of Korea: H.S. Parker Air Conditioning Componenets Co. Ltd., Chonan-Gun, Choong Nam; H.S. Parker Co. Ltd., Kyoungnam; Parker Hannifin Korea Ltd., Seoul; Mexico: Parker Automotive de Mexico SA de CV, Apodaca; Parker Seal de Matamoros, Matamoros; Brownsville Rubber Co. SA de CV, Matamoros; Brownsville Rubber Co. SA de CV, Matamoros; Climate Control Division, Monterrey; Parker Zenith, Monterrey; Parker Seal de Baja SA de CV, Tijuana; Schrader Bellows, Toluca; Parker Fluid Connectors De Mexico SA de CV, Toluca de Lerdo; Malaysia: Parker Hannifin Singapore Pte Ltd., Petaling Jaya, Selongor; Netherlands: Parker Sempress Pneimatic BV, Hndrik-Ido-Ambacht; Parker Hannifin BV, Hoogezand, Oldenzaal, Overijssel; Norway: Parker Hannifin A/S, Aalesund, Kokstad, Bergen, Langhus, Stavanger; New Zealand: Parker Hannifin Ltd., Auckland; Parker Enzed (New Zealand) Ltd., Mt. Wellington, Auckland; Philippines: Parker Hannifin Singapore Pte Ltd., Ayala Alabang, Muntinlupa City; Poland: Parker Hannifin Corporate, Warsaw; Parker Hannifin Sp. z.o.o., Wroclaw; Russia: Parker Hannifin Corporate, Moscow; Republic of South Africa: Paker Hannifin Africa pty Ltd., Kempton Park; Spain: VOAC Hydraulics SA, Madrid; Parker Hannifin Espana SA, Torrejon de Ardoz, Madrid; Sweden: Voac Hydraulics Norden AB, Boras; Parker Hannifin Sweden, Spanga, Sundsvall; Parker Hannifin AB, Ulricehamm, Alvsborg; Switzerland: Parker Hannifin Lucifer SA, Carouge Geneva; Thailand: Parker Hannifin Thailand Co. Ltd., Huaykwang, Bangkok; Taiwan: Parker Hannifin Taiwan Co. Ltd., Taipei; United Kingdom: Parker Hannifin plc, Barnstaple, Devon, Bridgtown Cannock, Staffs, Dewsbury, West Yorkshire, Hellaby, Rotherham, South Yorks; Parker Hannifin Corporate, Hemel Hempstead, Hertfordshire; Parker Hannifin plc, Marlow, Bucks; Parker Digiplan Plc, Poole, Dorset; VOAC Hydraulics Ltd., West Yorkshire; Parker Hannifin plc, Wetherby Road, Derby; Venezuela: Parker Hannifin de Venezuela SA, Caracas; Parker Hannafin de Venezuela, SA, Puerto Ordaz, Edo. Bolivar

Parker Hannifin Foundation

Giving Contact

Millie Hosler, Administrative Assistant
Parker-Hannifin Foundation
6035 Parkland Boulevard
Cleveland, OH 44124-1290
Phone: (216)896-3000
Fax: (216)896-4057

Description

EIN: 346555686
Organization Type: Corporate Foundation. Supports preselected organizations only.
Giving Locations: nationally.
Grant Types: Capital, Employee Matching Gifts, General Support, Scholarship.
Note: Employee matching gift ratio: 2 to 1 to higher education. Scholarships are awarded through the National Merit Scholarship Program.

Financial Summary

Total Giving: $1,900,000 (fiscal year ending June 30, 1999 approx); $1,959,925 (fiscal 1997); $1,716,949 (fiscal 1996). Note: Contributes through foundation only. Fiscal 1997 Giving includes foundation ($1,025,196); matching gifts ($509,504); United Way ($425,225).
Assets: $54,319 (fiscal 1997); $558,213 (fiscal 1996); $121,399 (fiscal 1995)
Gifts Received: $1,444,486 (fiscal 1997); $2,143,401 (fiscal 1996); $964,600 (fiscal 1995)

Typical Recipients

Arts & Humanities: Arts Centers, Arts Institutes, Ballet, Historic Preservation, Libraries, Museums/Galleries, Music, Opera, Performing Arts, Theater
Civic & Public Affairs: Community Foundations, Economic Development, Employment/Job Training, Civic & Public Affairs-General, Municipalities/Towns, Parades/Festivals, Public Policy, Safety, Urban & Community Affairs, Zoos/Aquariums
Education: Business Education, Business-School Partnerships, Colleges & Universities, Community & Junior Colleges, Continuing Education, Education Funds, Education Reform, Engineering/Technological Education, Education-General, Minority Education, Secondary Education (Public), Student Aid
Health: Children's Health/Hospitals, Emergency/Ambulance Services, Health Funds, Health Organizations, Hospitals, Medical Research, Mental Health, Nursing Services, Outpatient Health Care
Science: Science Museums, Scientific Centers & Institutes
Social Services: Community Centers, Scouts, Senior Services, Shelters/Homelessness, Substance Abuse, United Funds/United Ways, Volunteer Services, YMCA/YWCA/YMHA/YWHA, Youth Organizations

Contributions Analysis

Giving Priorities: Colleges, universities, and higher education funds; economic development; United Way drives and youth organizations; hospitals; and theater groups. Company has provided limited support to U.S.-based organizations with an international focus. Headquarters is not involved with contributions programs in Europe. The person to contact for foreign subsidiary contributions is Leszek Marcinowicz, Vice President of Human Resources (England), phone: 011-44-442-238, fax: 011-44-442-238-111.
Arts & Humanities: About 15%. Major support goes to theater groups. Other recipients include arts centers, museums, and music and dance groups.
Civic & Public Affairs: 35% to 40%. Emphasis is on economic development organizations. Other recipients include environmental affairs organizations and police and fire departments in plant communities.
Education: About 40%. Funds matching gifts to educational institutions. Major support is provided to colleges, universities, and funds for higher education. Focus on economic education.
Health: About 10%. Focus is on hospitals. Other interests include single-disease health organizations, clinics, and medical centers. Remaining funds support ambulance services, pediatrichealth, mental health, and medical research programs.
Social Services: 1% to 5%. Majority of funds go to United Way drives in plant communities. Also provides substantial support to youth organizations, particularly to local Boy Scouts/Girl Scouts, YMCA/YWCA, and Junior Achievement chapters. Other recipients include organizations concerned with child welfare, the handicapped, and recreation and athletics, as well as local chapters of the SalvationArmy and the Red Cross.

Corporate Officials

Duane E. Collins: president, chief executive officer, director B 1936. ED Harvard University; University of Wisconsin BSME (1961). PRIM CORP EMPL president, chief executive officer, director: Parker Hannifin Corp. ADD CORP EMPL president: Parker De Puerto Rico Inc. CORP AFFIL director: Sherwin-Williams Co.; director: National City Bank; officer: National City Corp. NONPR AFFIL trustee: Cleveland YMCA; director: Greater Cleveland Growth Association.
Patrick Streeter Parker: chairman, director B Cleveland, OH 1929. ED Williams College BA (1951); Harvard University MBA (1953). PRIM CORP EMPL chairman, director: Parker Hannifin Corp. NONPR AFFIL trustee: Case Western Reserve University. CLUB AFFIL Union Club; Country Club; Pepper Pike Club.

Foundation Officials

Duane E. Collins: vice president, trustee (see above)
Patrick Streeter Parker: president, trustee (see above)

Grants Analysis

Disclosure Period: fiscal year ending June 30, 1997
Total Grants: $1,025,196*
Number of Grants: 315 (approx)
Average Grant: $3,255
Highest Grant: $225,000
Typical Range: $250 to $5,000
***Note:** Giving excludes matching gifts; United Way.

Recent Grants

Note: Grants derived from fiscal 1997 Form 990.

Arts & Humanities

40,000	Cleveland Orchestra, Cleveland, OH
10,000	Playhouse Square Foundation, Cleveland, OH
9,000	Cleveland Museum of Art, Cleveland, OH
5,000	Cleveland Ballet, Cleveland, OH
5,000	Cleveland Playhouse Foundation, Cleveland, OH

Civic & Public Affairs

30,000	Cleveland Tomorrow, Cleveland, OH
20,000	Atlantic Foundation, Cleveland, OH
20,000	Cleveland Fund, Cleveland, OH
16,668	Cleveland Bicentennial Commission, Cleveland, OH
10,000	East Tennessee Foundation, Greeneville, TN
10,000	National Legal Center for Public Interest, Cleveland, OH
5,000	Greater Cleveland Roundtable, Cleveland, OH

Education

100,000	University of California Irvine Executive Roundtable, Irvine, CA
100,000	University of Illinois, Cleveland, OH
30,000	ADSME FPST Division, Cleveland, OH
28,572	John Carroll University, University Heights, OH
25,000	Florida A&M University, Tallahassee, FL
25,000	United Negro College Fund, Cleveland, OH
25,000	University of California Irvine Graduate Fellowship, Irvine, CA
24,000	Ursuline College, Cleveland, OH
15,000	United Negro College Fund, Cleveland, OH
15,000	University of Cincinnati College of Engineers, Cleveland, OH
14,250	National Merit Scholarship Corporation, Evanston, IL
14,000	California State Polytechnic University, Pomona, CA
10,000	Junior Achievement, Cleveland, OH
8,000	University of New Hampshire, Cleveland, OH

7,500 University of Wisconsin Foundation, Richnert Park, CA
5,000 Fluid Power Educational Foundation, Cleveland, OH
5,000 Jacksonville State University, Jacksonville, AL
5,000 Purdue University Office of Industry, Cleveland, OH
5,000 University of California Irvine Graduate School, Irvine, CA
5,000 University of Tennessee Martin School of Business, Greenfield, TN
4,500 Central Carolina Community College, Sanford, SC

Health
20,000 Visiting Nurse Association, Cleveland, OH
7,600 Newark Wayne Community Hospital Foundation, Lyons, NY
5,000 Grantsburg Hospital, Irvine, CA
5,000 Hoag Memorial Hospital, Irvine, CA
5,000 Ronald McDonald House, Cleveland, OH

Science
130,331 Great Lakes Museum of Science, Environment, and Technology, Cleveland, OH
10,000 Inventure Place, Cleveland, OH

Social Services
255,000 United Way, Cleveland, OH
17,000 United Way, Kalamazoo, MI
16,000 Boy Scouts of America, Irvine, CA
15,000 United Way Orange County, Irvine, CA
10,000 United Way Wayne County, Lyons, NY
8,000 United Way Green County, Greenville, IN
7,500 United Way Lorain County, Elyria, OH
5,000 United Way Crusade of Mercy, Des Plaines, IL
5,000 United Way Long Island, Smithtown, NY
5,000 United Way Lorain County, Elyria, OH

PATAGONIA INC.

Company Contact

Ventura, CA
Web: http://www.patagonia.com

Company Description

Employees: 603 (1999)
SIC(s): 5961 Catalog & Mail-Order Houses.
Parent Company: Lost Arrow Inc.

Nonmonetary Support

Value: $500,000 (1996); $150,000 (1994)
Type: Cause-related Marketing & Promotion; Donated Products; In-kind Services; Loaned Employees; Loaned Executives; Workplace Solicitation
Contact: Karel Malloy, Product Donations Coordinator
Note: Products are retail value.

Giving Contact

Jil Zilligen, Environmental Programs Director
Patagonia Environmental Grant Program
PO Box 150
Ventura, CA 93002-0150
Phone: (805)643-8616
Fax: (805)667-4835
Email: jil_zilligen@patagonia.com

Alternate Contact

John Sterling
Email: john_sterling@patagonia.com

Description

Organization Type: Corporate Giving Program
Giving Locations: nationally; Europe;.
Grant Types: Employee Matching Gifts, General Support, Project.

Giving Philosophy

'Patagonia designs and distributes clothing for active use in the outdoors. When we're not in the office, we take to the mountains, to climb or ski the backbowls, to paddle a wild stretch of river or cast a fly into its riffles, to surf in the ocean or raise a sail there. We see the wildlands we love so dearly being polluted, shorelines altered, streambeds eroded and silted over, the forest clear cut, and everywhere we see less wildlife and fewer wild fish. The world we love best is disappearing.'

'That is why those of us who work here share a strong commitment to protecting undomesticated lands and rivers. Each year we pledge 1% of our sales to the preservation and restoration of the natural environment. We call it our Earth Tax. The Environmental Grants Program falls within this 1% framework.' *Patagonia Environmental Grant Program: Guidelines*

Financial Summary

Total Giving: $1,253,749 (fiscal year ending April 30, 1999); $1,225,824 (fiscal 1998); $1,551,212 (fiscal 1997). Note: Contributes through corporate direct giving program only. Giving includes corporate direct giving; international subsidiaries; nonmonetary support.

Typical Recipients

Civic & Public Affairs: Public Policy
Education: Environmental Education
Environment: Air/Water Quality, Forestry, Environment-General, Protection, Research, Resource Conservation, Watershed, Wildlife Protection
International: International Environmental Issues, International Organizations
Social Services: Family Planning, Shelters/Homelessness

Contributions Analysis

Giving Priorities: The Tides Foundation, San Francisco, CA, researches and distributes Patagonia's international grants. Patagonia brings to them ideas on groups it would like to support in foreign lands where it does business. Tides Foundation then checks on tax status and organizational ability.
Environment: 100%. Contributions fund grassroots activist organizations with direct action agendas. Patagonia seeks locally based groups working with passion to protect biological diversity and habitat integrity. Giving categories are as follows: Biodiversity; Forests; Water; International; Social/Political/Environmental; Education; Extraction; and Media/Publication.
International: The company contributes to international organizations through international subsidiaries.

Application Procedures

Initial Contact: Submit a letter of inquiry requesting grant guidelines.
Application Requirements: Include a description of organization, proof of tax-exempt status, how money would be used, the organization's accomplishments, mission, goals and how organization will go about achieving them; detailed project and program budgets.
Deadlines: April 30 and August 31.
Review Process: After the company receives a proposal, it will mail an acknowledgement including a decision date.
Decision Notification: Company awards two rounds of grants, in September and January.
Notes: First-time recipients can expect grants of $2,000 to $5,000. The company responds best to straight-forward, brief, typewritten letters, and will not accept proposals sent by express mail. Company prefers that nonprofits not call requesting status of proposal.

Restrictions

Does not fund scientific research, general environmental education efforts, land acquisition, endowment funds, political campaigns, organizations without 501(c)3 status, dinners or special events, fraternal organizations, religious organizations for sectarian purposes, or member agencies of united funds.

Additional Information

Company donates 10% of pre-tax profits or 1% of sales, whichever is greater, to preserving and restoring the natural environment.
Publications: Grant Guidelines

Corporate Officials

Yvon Chouinard: owner, principal B Lewiston, ME 1938. PRIM CORP EMPL owner, principal: Lost Arrow. CORP AFFIL president: Patagonia Inc. NONPR AFFIL member national council: Environmental Defense Fund.
Neil Edwards: chief financial officer PRIM CORP EMPL chief financial officer: Patagonia Inc.
Eve Jursch: chief executive officer PRIM CORP EMPL chief executive officer: Patagonia Inc.

Giving Program Officials

John Sterling: PRIM CORP EMPL environmental program associate: Patagonia Inc.
Jil Zilligen: PRIM CORP EMPL environmental program director: Patagonia Inc.

Grants Analysis

Disclosure Period: fiscal year ending April 30, 1999
Total Grants: $1,253,749
Number of Grants: 240
Average Grant: $5,224
Highest Grant: $25,000
Typical Range: $3,000 to $10,000

Recent Grants

Note: Grants derived from fiscal 1997 Annual Report.

Environment
100,000 Environmental Defense Center, Santa Barbara, CA -- to establish branch office
47,068 Pesticide Action Network, San Francisco, CA -- to promote organic practices in cotton industry
30,000 Ecotrust, Portland, OR -- to restore Chinook River Watershed
20,000 Friends of the River, Sacramento, CA -- to stop construction of Auburn Dam, to advocate responsible flood control, floodplain management
20,000 Peregrine Fund, Boise, ID -- support Wetlands Conservation Project
18,000 Sustainable Cotton Project, Newman, CA -- public education on organic cotton
15,000 Mothers and Others for a Livable Planet, New York, NY -- operating support, program support
15,000 Wildlands Project, Tucson, AZ
14,000 Save America's Forests, Washington, DC -- to repeal timber salvage rider, to counter timber industry's attempt to establish destructive legislation
12,000 Palouse-Clearwater Environmental Institute, Moscow, ID -- support farm tours
12,000 RESTORE The North Woods, Concord, MA -- support Maine Woods National Park Campaign
11,000 Bay Area Nuclear Waste Coalition, San Francisco, CA -- support public awareness of Ward Valley issue
10,000 Fairview Gardners, Goleta, CA -- to place conservation easement on its land
10,000 Food and Water, Walden, VT -- to stop use of pesticides and biotechnology products

10,000	Green Mountain Forest Watch, Brattleboro, VT -- to protect Lamb Rook roadless area
10,000	Living on Earth, Cambridge, MA -- to support broadcast
10,000	Nature Conservancy, Lander, WY -- to develop managed grazing program at Red Canyon Ranch
10,000	Nature Conservancy, Salt Lake City, UT -- to purchase Dugout Ranch
10,000	Oregon Natural Resources Council, Portland, OR -- prevent building of Milltown Hill Dam
9,000	Alaska Clean Water Alliance, Haines, AK -- to ensure water quality standards
9,000	Public Lands Council, Spokane, WA -- support conservation initiatives
8,100	Alliance for the Wild Rockies, Missoula, MT -- to secure ecological integrity of the Northern Rockies bioregion
8,000	California Wilderness Coalition, Davis, CA -- preserve California's biodiversity by protecting its wildlands
8,000	Community Alliance with Family Farmers, Davis, CA -- support Lighthouse Farm Network
8,000	Georgia Center for Law in the Public Interest, Athens, GA -- to create model TMDL program
8,000	Nature Conservancy, Helena, MT
8,000	Ohio Valley Environmental Coalition, Huntington, WV -- to halt proposed pulp mill
8,000	Oregon Trout, Portland, OR -- support wild fish advocacy program
8,000	Willapa Alliance, South Bend, WA -- program support, public education, natural resource management, sustainable economic development
7,700	Environmental Protection Information Center, Garberville, CA -- to protect Headwaters Forest
7,000	Green Institute, North New Portland, ME -- public education
7,000	IDA Conservation League, Boise, ID -- to protect IDA's wilderness areas
7,000	Northwest Ecosystem Alliance, Bellingham, WA -- support endangered species protection campaign
7,000	Payette Forest Watch, McCall, ID -- to protect IDA's Payette National Forest
7,000	Southeast Alaska Conservation Council, Juneau, AK -- to defend Tongass National Forest from loggers
7,000	Wildlands Center for Preventing Roads, Missoula, MT -- to develop road restoration guide, national directory of road fighting activists
6,000	Southern Appalachian Biodiversity Project, Asheville, NC -- to revise the southern Appalachian region's National Forest management plans

International

30,000	Institute for Agriculture and Trade Policy, Minneapolis, MN -- for watershed organizing program, Organic Cotton Monitor
30,000	Steelhead Society of British Columbia, Coquitlam, BC, Canada -- support communications project
15,000	RARE Center for Tropical Conservation, Philadelphia, PA -- computer equipment, training
10,000	Ecotrust Canada, Nanaimo, BC, Canada -- general support
10,000	Nanakila Institute, Kitamaat Village, BC, Canada -- to protect Greater Kitlope Ecosystem
10,000	Pumalin Park Project, San Francisco, CA -- to acquire Chilean forest land
10,000	Rivers Canada, White Rock, BC, Canada -- to publish newsletter, develop national database for river activists
10,000	Sanoe Vivant/Doubs Vivant, Besancon, France -- to stop canal project on Rhone River
10,000	Sierra Legal Defense Fund, Coquitlam, BC, Canada -- for full enforcement of new Forest Practices Codes
10,000	SOS Loire Vivante, Le Puy en Velay, France -- to protect salmon populations in Lorie and Allier Rivers
8,000	International Society for Ecology and Culture, Berkeley, CA -- to counter conventional development in Ladakh
7,000	Canadian Parks and Wilderness Society, Toronto, ON, Canada -- to save remaining white pine forests of Algoma Highlands
7,000	Sea Turtle Restoration Project, Forest Knolls, CA -- consumer education component of Turtle-Safe Campaign

PECO ENERGY CO.

Company Contact
Philadelphia, PA
Web: http://www.peco.com

Company Description
Revenue: US$5,434,000,000 (1999)
Employees: 6,815
Fortune Rank: 306, per FORTUNE Magazine's list of 500 Largest U.S. Corporations (1999).
FF 306
SIC(s): 4931 Electric & Other Services Combined.

Nonmonetary Support
Type: Donated Equipment; In-kind Services; Loaned Employees; Loaned Executives

Corporate Sponsorship
Value: $5,000
Type: Arts & cultural events; Festivals/fairs; Music & entertainment events

Giving Contact
Anne Baker, Manager, Corp. Contributions
PECO Energy Co.
2301 Market Street, 7th Floor
Philadelphia, PA 19103
Phone: (215)841-4124
Fax: (215)841-4040

Description
Organization Type: Corporate Giving Program
Giving Locations: PA: Bucks County, Chester County, Delaware County, Montgomery County, York County
Grant Types: Capital, General Support, Operating Expenses.

Financial Summary
Total Giving: $3,000,000 (1999 approx); $3,000,000 (1998 approx). Note: Contributes through corporate direct giving program only.

Typical Recipients
Arts & Humanities: Arts Funds, Dance, Ethnic & Folk Arts, Libraries, Music, Opera
Civic & Public Affairs: Housing, Law & Justice, Urban & Community Affairs
Education: Business Education, Colleges & Universities, Community & Junior Colleges, Education Funds, Education-General, Public Education (Precollege)
Environment: Environment-General
Health: Hospitals
Social Services: Child Welfare, United Funds/ United Ways

Contributions Analysis
Arts & Humanities: Dance, music, opera, and general arts funding.
Civic & Public Affairs: Supports civic and public affairs.
Education: Supports education initiatives.
Environment: Supports environment programs and organizations.
Health: Supports various health and welfare programs.
Social Services: Focus on crime prevention, youth organizations.
Note: Supports traditional funding categories across the board.

Application Procedures
Initial Contact: brief letter
Application Requirements: a description of organization and its mission; detailed description of project and amount requested; list of organization's board of directors, trustees, officers, and other key people and their affiliations; copy of current year's organizational budget and/or project budget; and copy of 501(c)(3) letter of determination
Deadlines: None.

Corporate Officials
Corbin Asahel McNeill, Jr.: president, chief executive officer, director, chairman B Santa Fe, NM 1939. ED United States Naval Academy BS (1962); Naval Nuclear Power School (1962-1963); University of California at Berkeley (1975-1976); Syracuse University (1983-1984). PRIM CORP EMPL president, chief executive officer, director, chairman: PECO Energy Co. CORP AFFIL president, chief executive officer, chairman: Philadelphia Electric Co.; president: Adwin Equipment Co.; president, director: Adwin Realty Co. NONPR AFFIL director: Drexel University; director: Nuclear Utility Management Resources Council; director: American Nuclear Energy Council; member: American Nuclear Society; director: American Gas Association.

Foundation Officials
Anne Baker: manager corporate contributions

Grants Analysis
Disclosure Period: calendar year ending

PELLA CORP.

Company Contact
Pella, IA
Web: http://www.pella.com

Company Description
Employees: 5,065 (1999)
SIC(s): 2431 Millwork, 3231 Products of Purchased Glass.

Corporate Sponsorship
Type: Arts & cultural events; Festivals/fairs; Music & entertainment events
Contact: Beth Wilson, Director, Public Affairs

Pella Rolscreen Foundation

Giving Contact
Mary Van Zante, Director
Pella Rolscreen Foundation
102 Main Street
Pella, IA 50219
Phone: (515)628-1000

Fax: (515)628-6487

Description

EIN: 237043881
Organization Type: Corporate Foundation
Giving Locations: IA: Carroll County, Mahaska County, Marion County, Page County, Story County
Grant Types: Capital, Conference/Seminar, Employee Matching Gifts, Endowment, General Support.
Note: Employee matching gift ratio: 1 to 1.

Financial Summary

Total Giving: $1,800,000 (1999 approx); $2,053,159 (1998); $1,652,225 (1997). Note: Contributes through corporate direct giving program and foundation. Giving includes foundation.
Giving Analysis: Giving for 1997 includes: corporate matching gifts ($410,000); corporate scholarships ($388,184); 1998: corporate matching gifts ($422,000)
Assets: $15,000,000 (1999 approx); $15,000,000 (1998 approx); $15,538,356 (1997)
Gifts Received: $1,644,028 (1997); $1,260,475 (1995)

Typical Recipients

Arts & Humanities: Arts Associations & Councils, Arts Centers, Historic Preservation, History & Archaeology, Libraries, Literary Arts, Museums/Galleries, Music, Opera, Performing Arts, Public Broadcasting, Theater, Visual Arts
Civic & Public Affairs: Botanical Gardens/Parks, Business/Free Enterprise, Chambers of Commerce, Clubs, Economic Development, Housing, Municipalities/Towns, Parades/Festivals, Safety, Urban & Community Affairs, Zoos/Aquariums
Education: Business Education, Colleges & Universities, Community & Junior Colleges, Education Funds, Education Reform, Elementary Education (Private), Engineering/Technological Education, Faculty Development, Education-General, Preschool Education, Private Education (Precollege), Public Education (Precollege), Science/Mathematics Education, Secondary Education (Private), Secondary Education (Public), Special Education, Student Aid, Vocational & Technical Education
Environment: Forestry, Environment-General
Health: AIDS/HIV, Clinics/Medical Centers, Emergency/Ambulance Services, Hospitals, Outpatient Health Care, Transplant Networks/Donor Banks
Religion: Churches, Ministries, Religious Organizations, Religious Welfare
Science: Scientific Centers & Institutes
Social Services: Camps, Child Abuse, Child Welfare, Community Centers, Community Service Organizations, Crime Prevention, Day Care, Family Services, Food/Clothing Distribution, People with Disabilities, Recreation & Athletics, Scouts, Senior Services, Substance Abuse, United Funds/United Ways, Volunteer Services, YMCA/YWCA/YMHA/YWHA, Youth Organizations

Contributions Analysis

Giving Priorities: Capital grants and scholarships to Iowa colleges and universities, economic development, recreation and athletic organizations, and the arts.
Arts & Humanities: 9%. Primarily supports historical organizations, museums, and libraries.
Civic & Public Affairs: 10%. Interests include economic development, municipalities, and environmental affairs.
Education: About 41%. Majority of education funds support colleges and universities in Iowa as scholarships and capital grants. Other interests include education funds and private and public precollege education. Also sponsors a scholarship program for children of company employees.
Environment: 4%. Supports conservation projects.
Health: 15%. Funding supports hospitals, emergency services, and single-disease health associations.
Social Services: 21%. Most contributions are made to recreational and athletic programs and centers, and to religious welfare organizations. Also supports child welfare, community service organizations, and united funds.
Note: About 30% of grants are distributed through matching gifts. Total contributions made in 1997.

Application Procedures

Initial Contact: Submit a full proposal.
Application Requirements: Include a description of organization, statement of need, amount requested, purpose of funds sought, project budget, recently audited financial statement, and proof of tax-exempt status.
Deadlines: None; board meets quarterly.

Restrictions

Grants are not made to individuals, except to children of employees under scholarship program. Product donations are not made.

Corporate Officials

William J. Anderson: assistant secretarys B Fort Dodge, IA 1946. ED Northeast Missouri State University (1969). PRIM CORP EMPL assistant secretary: Pella Corp.
Gary M. Christensen: president B 1943. PRIM CORP EMPL president: Pella Corp. CORP AFFIL director: Butler Manufacturing Co.
Joan Kuyper Farver: chairman emeritus, director B 1919. ED Grinnell College BA (1941). PRIM CORP EMPL chairman emeritus, director: Pella Corp.
David Munn: assistant secretary
Mary Van Zante: corporate communications PRIM CORP EMPL corporate communications: Pella Corp.

Foundation Officials

William J. Anderson: secretary (see above)
Gary M. Christensen: president, director (see above)
Charles Farver: treasurer, director CORP AFFIL director: Pella Corp.
Joan Kuyper Farver: director (see above)
Mary Van Zante: director (see above)

Grants Analysis

Disclosure Period: calendar year ending 1998
Total Grants: $1,631,159*
Number of Grants: 204
Average Grant: $7,995
Typical Range: $500 to $10,000
***Note:** Giving excludes matching gifts. Analysis was provided by foundation.

Recent Grants

Note: Grants derived from 1997 Form 990.

Arts & Humanities

44,500 Living History Farms, Urbandale, IA -- new visitor's center
25,000 Pella Opera House Commission, Pella, IA -- programming support
20,000 National Sprint Car Hall of Fame and Museum, Knoxville, IA -- Complete the Dream project

Civic & Public Affairs

66,487 Iowa State Fair Blue Ribbon Foundation, Des Moines, IA -- Pella Plaza project
30,000 Sesquicentennial, Des Moines, IA -- education program
3,000 Pella Chamber Foundation, Pella, IA

Education

216,667 Central College, Pella, IA -- scholarship program
20,000 Iowa Architecture Foundation, Des Moines, IA -- Education in the Schools project
20,000 Shenandoah High School, Shenandoah, IA -- remodeling project
17,742 Catholic High School, Carroll, IA -- expansion project
15,000 Iowa College Foundation, Des Moines, IA -- general operating grant
12,675 Pella Christian High School, Pella, IA -- Excellence in School program
12,500 Iowa State University Department of Industry and Manufacturing, Ames, IA -- lab equipment
12,500 Iowa State University Industrial Technology Department, Ames, IA
12,275 Iowa Academy of Science, Cedar Falls, IA -- science medals
12,000 William Penn College, Oskaloosa, IA -- education development program
6,000 Iowa State University Foundation, Ames, IA -- scholarship funds
5,750 University of Iowa, Iowa City, IA -- scholarship fund
5,000 Camp Sunnyside, Pella, IA -- camping scholarship fund
5,000 Knoxville Education Foundation, Knoxville, IA -- new computers
3,506 Pella Community School District, Pella, IA -- National Honor Society Luncheon
3,201 Glidden-Ralston Community Schools, Glidden, IA -- Excellence in Teaching program
3,000 Sully Christian School, Sully, IA -- new computer project
2,750 Shenandoah Community High School, Shenandoah, IA -- window replacement project
2,484 Oskaloosa Community High School, Oskaloosa, IA -- special education project
2,400 Business Horizons, Des Moines, IA -- scholarship fund

Environment

20,500 City of Pella, Pella, IA -- land purchase
11,000 Greater Shenandoah Foundation, Shenandoah, IA -- tree planting project
6,000 Iowa Natural Heritage Foundation, Des Moines, IA -- Complete Iowa Trails program
2,500 Iowa Environmental Council, Des Moines, IA

Health

101,500 Pella Regional Health Center, Pella, IA -- expansion project
20,000 St. Anthony Regional Hospital, Carroll, IA -- expansion project
12,500 Manaska County Hospital, Oskaloosa, IA -- expansion project
5,000 City of Pleasantville Emergency Medical Services, Pleasantville, IA -- new equipment
2,600 Caring Foundation, Des Moines, IA

Religion

2,500 New Sharon Methodist Church, New Sharon, IA -- new elevator project

Social Services

139,198 City of Pella, Pella, IA -- new soccer complex
12,000 Iowa Games, Ames, IA -- annual sponsorship
7,000 Capital Area Child Care Center, Carroll, IA -- new building
5,000 City of Oskaloosa, Oskaloosa, IA -- police department equipment
5,000 Forest Lake Camp and Conference Center, Ottumwa, IA -- capital project
5,000 Homestead, Woodstock, VT -- building project
4,500 Turning Point, Knoxville, IA -- capital project
4,000 Knoxville Police Department, Knoxville, IA -- new equipment

3,500 United Way, Carroll, IA -- annual grant
3,500 United Way, Oskaloosa, IA -- annual grant
3,500 United Way, Shenandoah, IA -- annual grant
3,000 Pella Task Force Against Drug and Alcohol Abuse, Pella, IA
2,500 YMCA, Oskaloosa, IA -- new equipment
2,000 Boy Scouts of America Mid-Iowa Council, Des Moines, IA

PEMCO CORP.

Company Contact

Bluefield, VA

Company Description

Employees: 100
SIC(s): 6311 Life Insurance, 7359 Equipment Rental & Leasing Nec, 7374 Data Processing & Preparation.

PEMCO Foundation

Giving Contact

Kathy Dykstra, Foundation Administrator
PEMCO Foundation
325 Eastlake Ave. E.
Seattle, WA 98109
Phone: (206)628-4094

Description

EIN: 916072723
Organization Type: Corporate Foundation
Giving Locations: WA
Grant Types: General Support, Scholarship.

Financial Summary

Total Giving: $1,000,000 (fiscal year ending June 30, 1998 approx); $939,096 (fiscal 1997); $994,395 (fiscal 1996). Note: Contributes through foundation only. 1997 Giving includes foundation ($661,236); matching gifts ($1,885); scholarship ($207,683); United Way ($68,292).
Assets: $100,521 (fiscal 1997); $683,289 (fiscal 1996); $1,033,406 (fiscal 1995)
Gifts Received: $340,719 (fiscal 1997); $608,055 (fiscal 1996); $900,285 (fiscal 1995). Note: In fiscal 1997, contributions were received from the PEMCO Mutual Insurance Co. ($535,000), Washington School Employees Credit Union ($95,719), Evergreen Bank ($45,000), and Teachers Foundation ($200,000).

Typical Recipients

Arts & Humanities: Arts Associations & Councils, Ballet, History & Archaeology, Museums/Galleries, Music, Public Broadcasting, Theater
Civic & Public Affairs: Business/Free Enterprise, Clubs, Community Foundations, Economic Policy, Civic & Public Affairs-General, Hispanic Affairs, Housing, Professional & Trade Associations, Urban & Community Affairs
Education: Business Education, Colleges & Universities, Community & Junior Colleges, Education Associations, Education Funds, Education Reform, Faculty Development, Education-General, Literacy, Private Education (Precollege), Public Education (Precollege), Secondary Education (Public), Student Aid, Vocational & Technical Education
Health: Cancer, Children's Health/Hospitals, Clinics/Medical Centers, Emergency/Ambulance Services, Health-General, Geriatric Health, Health Funds, Heart, Home-Care Services, Hospices, Hospitals, Kidney, Medical Rehabilitation, Multiple Sclerosis, Research/Studies Institutes, Respiratory, Single-Disease Health Associations, Trauma Treatment
Religion: Churches, Religious Organizations, Religious Welfare
Science: Scientific Centers & Institutes
Social Services: Big Brother/Big Sister, Camps, Child Welfare, Community Service Organizations, Crime Prevention, Day Care, Domestic Violence, Food/Clothing Distribution, People with Disabilities, Scouts, Senior Services, Special Olympics, United Funds/United Ways, Volunteer Services, Youth Organizations

Contributions Analysis

Arts & Humanities: Less than 5%. Museums, and history and arts councils.
Civic & Public Affairs: 5% to 10%. Business, community affairs, and community funds.
Education: About 30%. Public and private secondary education, foundations, and individual scholarships.
Health: 20% to 25%. Health funds, hospices, medical centers, medical rehabilitation, and single-disease organizations.
Religion: Less than 5%. Religious welfare.
Science: About 5%. Science centers.
Social Services: 20% to 25%. United Way, youth organizations, people with disabilities, senior services, child welfare, and family services.

Application Procedures

Initial Contact: Send a brief letter of inquiry.
Deadlines: None.
Decision Notification: notice of approval, rejection, or request for more information usually within two months
Notes: Prior period transcripts are required before current funds can be released. Scholarship funds are distributed through educational associations.

Restrictions

Scholarships restricted to state of Washington residents at time of acceptance.

Foundation Officials

Sandra Kurack: vice president, trustee NONPR AFFIL president: Washington School Employes Credit Union.
Stanley W. McNaughton, Junior: assistant treasurer PRIM CORP EMPL president: Pemco Mutual Insurance Co.
Astrid I. Thompson: president, trustee

Grants Analysis

Disclosure Period: fiscal year ending June 30, 1997
Total Grants: $661,236*
Number of Grants: 172
Average Grant: $3,936*
Highest Grant: $65,258
Typical Range: $250 to $5,000
***Note:** Giving excludes scholarship, matching gifts, and United Way. Average grant figure excludes highest grant.

Recent Grants

Note: Grants derived from fiscal 1997 Form 990.

Arts & Humanities

10,000 Bellarmine Heritage Fund, Tacoma, WA
10,000 Nordic Heritage, Seattle, WA
5,000 Intiman Theater Company, Seattle, WA
5,000 Pacific Northwest Ballet, Seattle, WA

Civic & Public Affairs

22,350 Providence Foundation, Seattle, WA
10,400 Hispanic Academic Achievers, Pasco, WA
6,000 Washington State Chapter Neuof, Lynnwood, WA
5,500 Northwest District Exchange, Seattle, WA
5,000 Millionaire Club, Seattle, WA
5,000 Washington Business Week, Olympia, WA

Education

31,000 Alliance for Education, Seattle, WA
25,000 Independent Colleges of Washington, Seattle, WA
20,000 Blanchet High School, Seattle, WA
20,000 Seattle Preparatory School, Seattle, WA
12,000 Junior Achievement, Mercer Island, WA
10,000 Assumption-St. Bridget School, Seattle, WA
10,000 Bellevue Community College, Bellevue, WA
10,000 Heritage College, Toppenish, WA
10,000 Institute for Motivational Reading, Seattle, WA
10,000 RCH Technical Institute, Seattle, WA
5,000 Centrum, Seattle, WA
5,000 Washington State Retired Teachers, Olympia, WA
4,000 Causer's Children's College Fund

Health

30,000 Children's Hospital Foundation, Seattle, WA
25,000 American Parkinson's Disease Fund, Seattle, WA
11,000 Snohomish County Search and Rescue, Edmonds, WA
10,500 Elderhealth Northwest, Seattle, WA
10,000 Hope Heart Institute, Seattle, WA
10,000 Make-A-Wish Foundation, Seattle, WA
10,000 Pacific Northwest Cancer Foundation, Kirkland, WA
10,000 Snohomish County Search and Rescue, Edmonds, WA
5,500 Northwest Burn Foundation, Seattle, WA
5,000 American Red Cross, Seattle, WA
5,000 Evergreen Hospice, Kirkland, WA
5,000 Multiple Sclerosis Association, Seattle, WA

Religion

10,000 St. Joseph Capital Campaign, Seattle, WA
5,300 Catholic Charities, Seattle, WA
5,000 Salvation Army, Seattle, WA
5,000 Union Gospel Mission, Seattle, WA

Science

30,000 Pacific Science Center, Seattle, WA

Social Services

62,257 United Way King County, Seattle, WA
15,000 Senior Services of Seattle and King County, Seattle, WA
15,000 Washington State Law Enforcement, Pullman, WA
7,500 Executive Service Corp of Washington, Seattle, WA
5,000 Boy Scouts of America Chief Seattle Council, Seattle, WA
5,000 First Avenue Service Center, Seattle, WA
5,000 Guide Dogs for the Blind, San Rafael, CA
5,000 Youthcare, Seattle, WA
4,500 Seattle Milk Fund, Seattle, WA
4,000 Ryther Child Center, Seattle, WA

PENN MUTUAL LIFE INSURANCE CO.

Company Contact

Horsham, PA 19044
Web: http://www.pennmutual.com

Company Description

Assets: US$6,620,000,000
Employees: 739
SIC(s): 6311 Life Insurance.

Nonmonetary Support

Type: Donated Equipment; In-kind Services; Loaned Employees; Loaned Executives; Workplace Solicitation

Giving Contact

Donna Beath, Assistant to Chairman & Chief Executive Officer
C3A
600 Dresher Rd.
Horsham, PA 19044
Phone: (215)956-8060
Fax: (215)956-8347

Description

Organization Type: Corporate Giving Program
Giving Locations: headquarters area only.
Grant Types: Award, Capital, Conference/Seminar, Employee Matching Gifts, General Support, Matching, Multiyear/Continuing Support, Operating Expenses, Scholarship.

Financial Summary

Total Giving: $500,000 (2000 approx); $480,000 (1999 approx); $500,000 (1998 approx). Note: Contributes through corporate direct giving program and foundation. Giving includes corporate direct giving; foundation; nonmonetary support. 1997 & 1998 Giving includes corporate direct giving.

Typical Recipients

Arts & Humanities: Arts & Humanities-General
Civic & Public Affairs: Civic & Public Affairs-General
Education: Education-General
Health: Health-General
Science: Science-General
Social Services: Social Services-General

Application Procedures

Initial Contact: Brief letter of inquiry.
Application Requirements: Description of organization, amount requested, purpose of funds sought, and proof of tax-exempt status.

Restrictions

Does not support individuals, religious organizations for sectarian purposes, or organizations outside operating areas.

Corporate Officials

Nancy S. Brodie: executive vice president, chief financial officer B Cleveland, OH 1951. ED Cleveland State University (1975). PRIM CORP EMPL executive vice president, chief financial officer: Penn Mutual Life Insurance Co. CORP AFFIL president, director: Independence Square Properties; chief financial officer: Penn Insurance & Annuity Co.
Robert E. Chappell: chairman, chief executive officer PRIM CORP EMPL chairman, chief executive officer: Penn Mutual Life Insurance Co. CORP AFFIL director: PH Glatfelter Co.; director: Quaker Chemical Corp.; director: Janney Montgomery Scott.
Daniel Toran: president PRIM CORP EMPL president: Penn Mutual Life Insurance Co.

Giving Program Officials

Donna Beath: PRIM CORP EMPL director contributions: Penn Mutual Life Insurance Co.

Grants Analysis

Disclosure Period: calendar year ending 2000
Total Grants: $500,000 (approx)
Typical Range: $1,000 to $2,500

J.C. Penney Co., Inc.

 Number 36 of Top 100 Corporate Givers

Company Contact

Plano, TX
Web: http://www.jcpenney.net

Company Description

Revenue: US$32,510,000,000 (1999)
Profit: US$594,000,000
Employees: 205,000
Fortune Rank: 36, per FORTUNE Magazine's list of 500 Largest U.S. Corporations (1999).
FF 36
SIC(s): 5311 Department Stores, 5961 Catalog & Mail-Order Houses.

Operating Locations

Operates 1,752 stores in the USA and Puerto Rico.

Nonmonetary Support

Value: $4,500,000 (1996); $5,687,778 (1995); $5,000,000 (1994)
Type: Cause-related Marketing & Promotion; Donated Equipment; Donated Products; In-kind Services
Volunteer Programs: In order to enhance employees' volunteer activites, the company sponsors the James Cash Penney Award for Community Service, which rewards outstanding employees who volunteer; and the Associate Involvement Fund, which provides contributions for organizations where associates volunteer. Employees volunteer for Adopt-A-School, Junior Achievement, and March of Dimes programs. 'Just Caring People' clubs are also formed by company units to organize employee volunteerism.
Note: Company provides nonmonetary support through local store managers. In-kind gifts at fair market value.

Corporate Sponsorship

Type: Arts & cultural events; Festivals/fairs
Note: Sponsors educational events. Each store handles sponsorships independently.

J.C. Penney Co. Fund

Giving Contact

Jeannette Siegel, Community Relations and Contributions Manager
JCPenney Co., Inc.
PO Box 10001
Dallas, TX 75301-8101
Phone: (972)431-1349
Fax: (972)431-1355
Email: jsiegel@jcpenney.com
Web: http://www.jcpenney.net/company/commrel/index.htm

Description

EIN: 133274961
Organization Type: Corporate Foundation
Giving Locations: headquarters and operating communities.
Grant Types: Employee Matching Gifts, General Support, Matching.
Note: Employee matching gift ratio: 1 to 1 for gifts to higher education only.

Giving Philosophy

'JCPenney is committed to being a socially responsible business partner, both nationally and in the communities in which we do business. JCPenney recognizes a basic relationship between business and society. They are mutually dependent and need one another to exist. .. The first social responsibility of a business is accomplished by the fact that it exists -- and so creates jobs, products and services necessary to society. The second social responsibility of a business is to prosper and grow -and so contribute in an ongoing way to the health of society. The third social responsibility of business is accomplished through well-conceived, well implemented involvement in community improvement efforts, including financial support for effective and efficient charitable and civic activities.' Corporate Contributions Guidelines

Financial Summary

Total Giving: $28,000,000 (fiscal year ending March 31, 2000 approx); $28,000,000 (fiscal 1999 approx); $27,800,000 (fiscal 1998). Note: Contributes through corporate direct giving program and foundation. Fiscal 1998 Giving includes foundation ($24,000,000); nonmonetary support. Fiscal 1997 Giving includes corporate direct giving ($33,997,285); foundation ($1,715).
Giving Analysis: Giving for fiscal 1998 includes: corporate direct giving ($22,800,000); nonmonetary support ($3,400,000); domestic subsidiaries ($1,400,000); foundation ($200,000)
Assets: $6,879,460 (fiscal 1998); $7,161,261 (fiscal 1997); $7,047,124 (fiscal 1996)

Typical Recipients

Arts & Humanities: Arts Associations & Councils, Dance, Museums/Galleries, Music, Opera, Performing Arts, Public Broadcasting, Theater
Civic & Public Affairs: Business/Free Enterprise, Civil Rights, Economic Development, Employment/ Job Training, Civic & Public Affairs-General, Hispanic Affairs, Nonprofit Management, Philanthropic Organizations, Public Policy, Safety, Urban & Community Affairs, Women's Affairs, Zoos/Aquariums
Education: Business Education, Business-School Partnerships, Colleges & Universities, Community & Junior Colleges, Economic Education, Education Reform, Elementary Education (Private), Education-General, Literacy, Minority Education, Preschool Education, Public Education (Precollege), Special Education
Health: Emergency/Ambulance Services, Health Organizations, Hospitals
Social Services: Day Care, Food/Clothing Distribution, People with Disabilities, Recreation & Athletics, Shelters/Homelessness, Social Services-General, Substance Abuse, United Funds/United Ways, Volunteer Services, Youth Organizations

Contributions Analysis

Giving Priorities: Local United Way drives, precollege education and dropout prevention, civic activities, and various arts organizations.
Arts & Humanities: About 5%. Includes support for arts associations and councils, and performing arts.
Civic & Public Affairs: About 10%. Grants made to local philanthropic organizations, employment and job training, and business councils.
Education: About 20% to 25%. Primarily supports precollege education, focusing on curriculum-based afterschool programs. Colleges, universities, and business education also receive support. Supports scholarship and teacher development programs.
Social Services: 50% to 55%. Includes support for local United Way and youth organizations.

Application Procedures

Initial Contact: Submit a brief written proposal.
Application Requirements: Include a description of organization; specific request, including expected outcomes, program milestones with target dates, evaluation plan, and strategy to secure full funding; project budget; list of board members, with affiliations; list of other funding organizations; recently audited financial statement, IRS Form 990; proof of tax-exempt status; most recent annual report, describing goals and accomplishments.
Deadlines: None.
Evaluative Criteria: Prefers organizations that demonstrate efficient management, serve a broad sector of the community, have an identifiable impact on the community, are striving to broaden their base of support, have proven record of success, provide direct services to clients, and national projects that have a multiplier effect by benefiting local organizations across the country.

Decision Notification: Minor grants of $5,000 or less are made throughout the year; major grants follow quarterly meetings of public affairs committee or the management committee.
Notes: Local organizations should apply through the managers of local stores or facilities.

Restrictions

Does not support individuals, religious or membership organizations (unless activity of benefit to entire community), goodwill advertising, testimonial dinners or other fundraising events, international projects, conferences and seminars, pilot projects, or film and video projects.

Additional Information

Company has operating locations in nearly all 50 states.
Priorities established by company headquarters; budget goals based on resources available. Through 'Associate Involvement Fund,' JCPenney units make small grants to organizations where employees are actively involved. National grants are fewer and larger and focus on 'multiplier' organizations that increase effectiveness of local agencies.
Contributions to individual colleges and universities, hospitals, and community-based organizations are normally made by local units. and community-based organizations are normally made by local units.

Corporate Officials

Robin Caldwell: director community relationss & corporate image PRIM CORP EMPL director community relations: J.C. Penney Co., Inc.
Marilee J. Cumming: president PRIM CORP EMPL president: J.C. Penney Co. Inc.
Gale Duff-Bloom: president co. communications & corporate image PRIM CORP EMPL president co. communications & corporate image: J.C. Penney Co. Inc.
James E. Oesterreicher: chairman, chief executive officer, director B Saginaw, MI 1941. ED Michigan State University BS (1964). PRIM CORP EMPL chairman, chief executive officer, director: J.C. Penney Co. Inc. CORP AFFIL director: Texas Utilities Co.; director: TXU; director: Brinker International Inc. NONPR AFFIL director: Presbyterian Healthcare Systems; director: Presbyterian Hospital Plano; director: Childrens Presbyterian Healthcare Center; director: Presbyterian Healthcare Center North.

Giving Program Officials

Jeannette Siegel

Grants Analysis

Disclosure Period: fiscal year ending March 31, 1998
Total Grants: $200,000 (approx)*
Number of Grants: 12 (approx)
Highest Grant: $50,000
Typical Range: $2,000 to $20,000
***Note:** Giving excludes corporate direct giving; nonmonetary support.

Recent Grants

Note: Grants derived from 1996 Form 990.

Civic & Public Affairs

15,000	Gifts in Kind America, Alexandria, VA
15,000	Jobs for America's Graduates, Alexandria, VA
12,500	Committee for Economic Development, New York, NY
12,000	TTARA Research Foundation
4,000	Independent Sector, Washington, DC

Education

50,000	Center for Leadership in School Reform, Louisville, KY
30,000	Junior Achievement
25,000	WAVE
24,000	University of Texas, Austin, TX
10,000	National Center for Family Literacy, Louisville, KY
10,000	Texas Business and Education Coalition, TX

Social Services

8,000	National Executive Service Corps, New York, NY

PENNSYLVANIA POWER & LIGHT

Company Contact

Allentown, PA

Company Description

Assets: US$9,371,000,000
Employees: 6,428
SIC(s): 4911 Electric Services.

Giving Contact

Don Bernhard, Manager, Econ Development, Community Affairs
Pennsylvania Power & Light
2 N. Ninth St.
Allentown, PA 18101
Phone: (610)774-5458
Fax: (610)774-6503

Description

Organization Type: Corporate Giving Program
Giving Locations: locally in service areas.
Grant Types: Employee Matching Gifts, General Support.
Note: Matches gifts to educational institutions, $25 to $1,000 annually per employee.

Giving Philosophy

'At PP&L, community involvement means being a responsible and responsive corporate citizen. It means caring about cultural and civic values in our communities, and operating our business in harmony with those values.'
'Community involvement means corporate monetary contributions to organizations serving those who live where we serve. It means PP&L people provide leadership roles in United Way campaigns and other community fundraisers; it means making useful community service a part of the job description of those who work closely with community leaders and economic development partners; it means encouraging employees to be involved during their off-work hours; and it means setting a good example by making community service and involvement a corporate value.' *Pennsylvania Power & Light Annual Report 1991*

Financial Summary

Total Giving: $4,700,000 (1997 approx). Note: Contributes through corporate direct giving program only.

Typical Recipients

Arts & Humanities: Arts & Humanities-General
Civic & Public Affairs: Civic & Public Affairs-General
Education: Education-General
Health: Health-General
Social Services: Social Services-General

Application Procedures

Initial Contact: a brief letter of inquiry and full proposal
Application Requirements: a description of organization, amount requested, purpose of funds sought, audited financial statement, and proof of tax-exempt status
Deadlines: None.

Restrictions

Does not support individuals, religious organizations for sectarian purposes, or political or lobbying groups.

Additional Information

Company reports that their corporate giving program is fairly static giving, only to local and to traditional community programs with no targeted areas of interest.

Corporate Officials

William F. Hecht: chairman, president, chief executive officer director B New York, NY 1943. ED Lehigh University BSEE (1964); Lehigh University MSEE (1970). PRIM CORP EMPL chairman, president, chief executive officer: Pennsylvania Power & Light. CORP AFFIL chairman, chief executive officer: PP&L Spectrum; president: Realty Co. Pennsylvania Inc.; chairman, president, chief executive officer: PP&L Resources Inc.; chairman, chief executive officer: PP& L Global; chairman, president, chief executive officer: PP&L Inc. NONPR AFFIL director: National Association Manufacturer; director: Nuclear Energy Institute; trustee: Lehigh Valley Hospital; trustee: Lehigh University; director: Lehigh Valley Economic Development Corp.; director: Edison Electric Institute.
Francis A. Long: executive vice president, chief operating officer, director B 1941. ED Northeastern University BS (1963). PRIM CORP EMPL executive vice president, chief operating officer, director: Pennsylvania Power & Light ADD CORP EMPL executive vice president, chief operating officer, director: PP&L Resources, Inc.; vice president, secretary, director: PP& L Global.

Foundation Officials

Don Bernhard: manager economic development & community affairs PRIM CORP EMPL Pennsylvania Power & Light.

Grants Analysis

Disclosure Period: calendar year ending

PENNZOIL-QUAKER STATE CO.

Company Contact

Houston, TX
Web: http://www.pennzoil.com

Company Description

Former Name: Pennzoil Co.
Employees: 13,200 (1999)
SIC(s): 1311 Crude Petroleum & Natural Gas, 1479 Chemical & Fertilizer Mining Nec, 2911 Petroleum Refining, 6794 Patent Owners & Lessors.

Nonmonetary Support

Type: Cause-related Marketing & Promotion
Note: Company donated $10 million worth of land in 1989.

Giving Contact

Barbara Tambakakis, Coordinator, Contributions & Community Relations
Pennzoil-Quaker State Co.
PO Box 2967
Houston, TX 77252-2967
Phone: (713)546-8590

Description

Organization Type: Corporate Giving Program
Giving Locations: communities in which company has plants, warehouses, or refineries; rarely gives nationally, internationally.
Grant Types: General Support, Research.
Note: Employee matching gift ratio: 1 to 1 for gifts to education, up to $5,000 annually.

Giving Philosophy

'Pennzoil Company seeks to be a good corporate citizen and neighbor in the communities where we live and work. One of the ways we demonstrate our corporate citizenship is through the support of organizations which work to improve the quality of life and the general welfare of our employees and the citizens of our home communities. The well-being and vitality of the nation's communities clearly affect the company, its stockholders and employees. For this reason, and because we have an obligation to share our resources with others in the community, we contribute to education, health, cultural, civic and other charitable organizations whose programs promote this well-being and vitality. The policy is administered so as to provide the greatest benefit to the company, its stockholders and employees.' Corporate Contributions Policy, Pennzoil Co.

Financial Summary

Total Giving: $1,600,000 (1999 approx); $1,600,000 (1998 approx); $1,600,000 (1997 approx). Note: Contributes through corporate direct giving program only.

Typical Recipients

Arts & Humanities: Arts Associations & Councils, Arts Centers, Arts Festivals, Community Arts, Dance, Historic Preservation, Libraries, Museums/Galleries, Music, Opera, Performing Arts, Public Broadcasting, Theater
Civic & Public Affairs: Public Policy, Safety, Urban & Community Affairs, Zoos/Aquariums
Education: Business Education, Colleges & Universities, Engineering/Technological Education, Science/Mathematics Education, Student Aid
Health: Emergency/Ambulance Services, Health Organizations, Hospices, Hospitals, Medical Rehabilitation, Medical Research, Single-Disease Health Associations
Social Services: Child Welfare, Community Service Organizations, Delinquency & Criminal Rehabilitation, Emergency Relief, People with Disabilities, Shelters/Homelessness, Substance Abuse, United Funds/ United Ways, Youth Organizations

Contributions Analysis

Giving Priorities: Higher education, health, social welfare, and culture.
Arts & Humanities: About 15%. Supports performing and visual arts, museums, zoos, libraries, and other cultural activities that are broadly supported and that benefit a large segment of the population in local communities.
Civic & Public Affairs: 5% to 10%. Supports selected organizations that work to improve the quality of life in company communities.
Education: About 50%. Emphasis is on accredited colleges and universities in communities where company has significant operations, where it recruits employees, or where research relevant to company's business is conducted. Related disciplines including accounting, geology, and engineering are priorities. Also administers matching gifts program.
Health: About 10%. Supports local hospitals, clinics, rehabilitation centers, and other health-related organizations. Contributions are restricted to building programs, equipment additions, or unusual research programs. Contributions to single-disease health associations also may be considered.
Social Services: About 15%. Local united funds are principal vehicles of support. Well-established, widely supported service organizations (including those for the handicapped) that are not members of united funds are also eligible forconsideration.

Application Procedures

Initial Contact: written request; no telephone inquiries will be accepted
Application Requirements: a description of organization, amount requested, purpose of funds sought, recently audited financial statement, copy of 501(c)(3) statement
Deadlines: before fall, when budget is completed; proposals received after the budgeting process are not likely to be considered until the following year
Evaluative Criteria: causes supported should fulfill a corporate obligation to communities in which company has a presence and should benefit a wide segment of the population

Restrictions

Company generally does not support strictly sectarian or denominational religious activities, secondary schools, veterans' or fraternal organizations, individual testimonial dinners, donations that are not tax-deductible, charitable advertising, or donations of products.
Does not generally contribute to member agencies of united funds.

Additional Information

The company was formed by the 1998 merger of Pennzoil and Quaker State.
Publications: Guidelines

Corporate Officials

James Leonard Pate: chairman, chief executive officer, director B Mount Sterling, IL 1935. ED Monmouth College BA (1963); University of Indiana MBA (1967). PRIM CORP EMPL chairman, chief executive officer, director: Pennzoil-Quaker State Co. CORP AFFIL president, chief executive officer, director: Pennzoil Products Co.; president, director: Richland Development Corp.; president: Pennzoil Petro Pipeline Co.; director: Pennzoil Exploration Products Co.; president: Pennzoil International Co.; director: Bowater Inc. NONPR AFFIL member: Senate Monmouth College; member: Society Social Political Science; board governors: Rice University; fellow: Royal Economic Society; director: National Petroleum Council; member: Pi Gamma Mu; director: American Petroleum Institute.

Giving Program Officials

Barbara Tambakakis: contributions coordinator

Grants Analysis

Disclosure Period: calendar year ending 1996
Total Grants: $1,292,880

PENTAIR INC.

Company Contact

St. Paul, MN
Web: http://www.pentair.com

Company Description

Employees: 9,770
SIC(s): 2992 Lubricating Oils & Greases, 3482 Small Arms Ammunition, 3546 Power-Driven Handtools, 3553 Woodworking Machinery.

Nonmonetary Support

Value: $5,000 (1993)
Type: Donated Products
Note: 1997 nonmonetary support ($3,000 est.).

Pentair Foundation

Giving Contact

Jeanne Benson, Foundation Manager
Pentair Inc. Water Edge Plaza
Water Edge Plaza
1500 County Rd., B2 W
St. Paul, MN 55113-3105
Phone: (612)636-7920
Fax: (612)639-5203

Description

Organization Type: Corporate Foundation
Giving Locations: MN: Minneapolis metropolitan area, St. Paul metropolitan area headquarters and operating communities.
Grant Types: Capital, Employee Matching Gifts, General Support.
Note: Employee matching gift ratio: 2 to 1 up to $100; 1 to 1 up to $5,000.

Giving Philosophy

'The Pentair Foundation's mission is to provide philanthropic support in communities where Pentair operations are located by investing in programs which offer long-term solutions to community issues.' Pentair Establishes Foundation of Charitable Giving (company news release) March 1998.

Financial Summary

Total Giving: $2,500,000 (1997 approx); $2,368,527 (1996); $1,468,533 (1995). Note: Contributes through foundation only. 1997 Giving includes corporate direct giving. 1996 Giving includes corporate direct giving ($1,526,007); domestic subsidiaries ($842,520).

Typical Recipients

Arts & Humanities: Arts & Humanities-General
Civic & Public Affairs: Civic & Public Affairs-General
Education: Education-General
Health: Health-General
Social Services: Social Services-General

Contributions Analysis

Arts & Humanities: Funds programs that provide a solid cultural base and offer opportunities to experience art in many different forms. Supports development and preservation of artistic and cultural traditions; broadening and expanding the audience base for the arts so they are accessible for all; and development and expansion of programs that offer educational and developmental opportunities in literature, music, and theater.
Civic & Public Affairs: Supports mentoring and tutoring opportunities for youth, together with general guidance and recreation; programs which encourage economic self-reliance among individuals; job training for youth, the disadvantaged, and the disabled; and low-income housing.
Education: Supports elementary, secondary, and higher education programsthat provide innovative education opportunities for youth; target socially and economically disadvantaged youth; bring business concepts, practices, and principles into the classroom; provide a trade curriculum to add skilled workers to the work force; and address environmental values, including resource and wildlife conservation and preservation.
Health: Supports programs which ensure access to adequate health care and health care education, including rehabilitation services for thedisabled, particularly youth; effective, low-cost health care services for those who are unable to afford adequate health care; and educational information and promotion of sound physical and mental health and development.

Application Procedures

Initial Contact: call or write for guidelines and application form
Deadlines: March 1; June 1; October 1
Review Process: Proposals are reviewed by a board comprised of representatives from Pentair's corporate headquarters and its subsidiaries

Restrictions

Does not support individuals; religious, political, professional, or fraternal organizations; organizations or causes whose purpose or activities conflict with the Pentair Code of Business Conduct; organizations or projects under guidance or control of a fiscal agent; or organizations receiving more than 40% of operating budget from an umbrella organization.

Additional Information
The Pentair Foundation was established in 1998 to continue the company's charitable giving activities. The foundation reports that its focus will be on community and education.

Corporate Officials
Winslow Hurlbert Buxton: chairman, president, chief executive officer, director B Coral Gables, FL 1939. ED University of Washington BS (1961). PRIM CORP EMPL chairman, president, chief executive officer, director: Pentair Inc. CORP AFFIL director: Toro Co.; director: Willamette Industries Inc.; director: Bemis Co. Inc.

Giving Program Officials
Jeanne Benson: PRIM CORP EMPL foundation manager: Pentair Inc.

Grants Analysis
Disclosure Period: calendar year ending
Typical Range: $1,000 to $10,000

PEOPLES BANK

Company Contact
Eatonton, GA
Web: http://www.peoples.com

Company Description
Employees: 29
Parent Company: Peoples Mutual Holdings

Nonmonetary Support
Type: Donated Equipment; In-kind Services; Loaned Employees

Corporate Sponsorship
Note: Sponsors events and causes.

Giving Contact
Phyllis F. Cannata, Community Relations Manager
People's Bank
850 Main St.
Bridgeport, CT 06604
Phone: (203)338-2606
Fax: (203)338-2502

Description
Organization Type: Corporate Giving Program
Giving Locations: CT
Grant Types: Employee Matching Gifts, General Support.
Note: Employee matching gift ratio: 1 to 2.

Financial Summary
Total Giving: Contributes through corporate direct giving program only.

Typical Recipients
Arts & Humanities: Museums/Galleries, Performing Arts, Public Broadcasting, Theater
Civic & Public Affairs: Economic Development, Housing
Education: Colleges & Universities, Elementary Education (Private), Preschool Education, Public Education (Precollege)
Social Services: Day Care, Homes, Shelters/Homelessness, United Funds/United Ways, Volunteer Services

Contributions Analysis
Arts & Humanities: 15% to 20%. Support favors museums, performing arts, theater, and public broadcasting.
Civic & Public Affairs: (Housing & Neighborhood Revitalization) 15% to 20%. Supports homes and housing projects and localeconomic development.
Education: 15% to 20%. Supports colleges and universities, elementary schools, preschool education, and public education.
Social Services: About 40%. Major support goes to United Ways. Other recipients include day care services and homeless shelters.

Application Procedures
Initial Contact: a brief letter of inquiry and full proposal
Application Requirements: a description of organization, amount requested, purpose of funds sought, recently audited financial statement, and proof of tax-exempt status
Deadlines: None.

Restrictions
Does not support individuals, religious organizations for sectarian purposes, or political or lobbying groups.

Additional Information
Publications: Annual Report

Corporate Officials
James Biggs: president community relations B 1940. ED Dartmouth College (1962); Columbia University (1963). PRIM CORP EMPL president: People's Bank. CORP AFFIL director: Peoples Mutual Holdings.
Phyllis F. Cannata: manager community relations PRIM CORP EMPL manager community relations: People's Bank.
David Ellis Adams Carson: chairman, chief executive officer B Birkenhead, England 1934. ED University of Michigan BBA (1955). PRIM CORP EMPL chairman, chief executive officer: People's Bank. CORP AFFIL president, chief executive officer, director: Peoples Mutual Holdings; director: United Illuminating Co.

Grants Analysis
Disclosure Period: calendar year ending
Typical Range: $100 to $2,500

PEOPLES ENERGY CORP.

Company Contact
Chicago, IL
Web: http://www.pecorp.com

Company Description
Assets: US$1,783,800,000
Employees: 2,804
SIC(s): 4924 Natural Gas Distribution, 6719 Holding Companies Nec.

Nonmonetary Support
Type: Donated Equipment; In-kind Services; Loaned Employees; Loaned Executives

Corporate Sponsorship
Value: $200
Type: Arts & cultural events

Giving Contact
Andre F. Garner, Manager, Community Affairs
Peoples Energy Corp.
130 E. Randolph Dr.
Chicago, IL 60601
Phone: (312)240-4002
Fax: (312)240-4389

Alternate Contact
Marilyn Randell-Ellis, Corporate Contributions Representative

Description
Organization Type: Corporate Giving Program
Giving Locations: company service area.
Grant Types: Award, Capital, Employee Matching Gifts, General Support, Multiyear/Continuing Support.
Note: Employee matching gift ratio: 2 to 1 for gifts to primary and secondary schools and hospitals; 1 to 1 for gifts to other eligible institutions.

Financial Summary
Total Giving: $1,000,000 (1997 approx); $978,000 (1996 approx); $944,931 (1995). Note: Contributes through corporate direct giving program only.

Typical Recipients
Arts & Humanities: Arts Associations & Councils, Arts Institutes, Dance, Ethnic & Folk Arts, Historic Preservation, Libraries, Museums/Galleries, Opera, Performing Arts, Public Broadcasting, Theater
Civic & Public Affairs: Civil Rights, Economic Development, Economic Policy, Employment/Job Training, Housing, Law & Justice, Professional & Trade Associations, Urban & Community Affairs, Women's Affairs, Zoos/Aquariums
Education: Colleges & Universities, Community & Junior Colleges, Elementary Education (Private), Literacy, Private Education (Precollege), Public Education (Precollege)
Health: Health Organizations, Hospitals
Science: Observatories & Planetariums
Social Services: Child Welfare, Community Centers, Community Service Organizations, Family Services, Homes, Senior Services, Shelters/Homelessness, United Funds/United Ways, Volunteer Services, Youth Organizations

Contributions Analysis
Arts & Humanities: About 5% to 10%. Supports museums, historical societies, libraries, visual and performing arts.
Civic & Public Affairs: 20% to 25%. Support of civic and neighborhood causes includes study and research projects. Support of programs in the areas of social services, housing, employment, education, and economic development is designed to help economically distressed neighborhoods and communities.
Education: About 25%. Invests in higher education -- public and private colleges and universities -- by making annual contributions to selected institutions. In addition, support goes to outreach efforts, such as educational television and community outreach programs within the public school system.
Health: 30% to 35%. Generally, contributions go to programs through the Metropolitan Crusade of Mercy and various United Way funds. Other donations are earmarked for health and welfare agencies, hospitals, research projects, and medical programs.

Application Procedures
Initial Contact: letter requesting guidelines and application form, then written proposal
Application Requirements: letter of inquiry should include: name, full mailing address, and telephone number of organization; background and purpose of the organization; type of request (operating or capital); description of project or program for which funding is requested; amount requested; geographical area served; proof of tax-exempt status; names of officers and directors, with affiliations; and number of professional, clerical, and volunteer staff members
Deadlines: None.
Review Process: all requests are reviewed by the contributions staff; this review process sometimes includes a visit to the soliciting agency and an evaluation of audited financial statements; gathered information then is evaluated against the company's overall contribution policies and grants are disbursed to those who qualify
Evaluative Criteria: background of the organization, organization's legal status, how the program will benefit the community, whether the organization receives broad community support, quality of organization's leadership, and organization's financial status; whether organization has clearly stated objectives,

long-range planning, active participation of board members, and plans for expanding the support base
Decision Notification: applications are reviewed in December, April, and August

Restrictions

Contributions will not be made to individuals; organizations not eligible for tax-deductible support; organizations that discriminate by race, color, creed, or national origin; political organizations or campaigns; organizations whose prime purpose is to influence legislation; religious organizations for purely sectarian purposes; agencies or institutions owned and operated by local, state, or federal governments; trips or tours; or special occasion or goodwill advertising.

Additional Information

Requests for specific capital or endowment purposes are generally limited to 0.5% of total amount sought.
Publications: Contribution Guidelines; Application Form

Corporate Officials

J. Bruce Hasch: president, chief operating officer, director ED University of Nebraska BS (1960); University of Chicago MBA (1976). PRIM CORP EMPL president, chief operating officer, director: People's Energy Corp. CORP AFFIL vice chairman: Peoples Energy Services Corp.; president, chief operating officer: Peoples Gas, Light & Coke Co.; president, chief operating officer: North Shore Gas Co.
Marilyn Randell-Ellis: senior community affairs representative PRIM CORP EMPL senior community affairs representative: People's Energy Corp.
Desiree Glapion Rogers: vice president community affairs B New Orleans, LA 1959. ED Wellesley College BS (1981); Harvard University MBA (1985). PRIM CORP EMPL vice president community affairs: People's Energy Corp. CORP AFFIL vice president corporate communications: Peoples Gas, Light & Coke Co. NONPR AFFIL director: Smithsonian Institute; director: WTTW Channel 11; director: National Museum Natural History; trustee: Museum Contemporary Art; director: Museum Science & Industry; chairman: Chicago Children's Museum; trustee: Harvard Business School Club Chicago. CLUB AFFIL Economic Club; Wellesley Club.
Richard Edward Terry: chairman, chief executive officer, director B Green Bay, WI 1937. ED Saint Norbert College BA (1959); University of Wisconsin LLB (1964). PRIM CORP EMPL chairman, chief executive officer, director: People's Energy Corp. CORP AFFIL director: Peoples Gas, Light & Coke Co.; director: North Shore Gas Co.; chairman: Peoples Energy Service Corp.; director: Harris Bankmont Inc.; director: Harris Trust & Savings Bank; director: Harris Bankcorp Inc.; director: Amsted Industries Inc.; director: Harris Bank-Oakbrook Terrace. NONPR AFFIL trustee: Saint Norbert College; trustee: Saint Xavier University; member: National Petroleum Council; director: Peoples Gas & Light Co.; director: Institute Gas Technology; member: Midwest Gas Association; director: Illinois Council Economic Education; member business advisory council: Chicago Urban League; treasurer: DePaul University; director: Chicago Museum Science & Industry; member: Chicago United; member: Chicago Area Central Comm; director: Chicago Chamber of Commerce; director: Big Shoulders Fund; director: American Gas Association. CLUB AFFIL Mid-America Club; University Club; Commercial Club; Economic Club; Chicago Club.

Giving Program Officials

Andre F. Garner: PRIM CORP EMPL manager community affairs: People's Energy Corp.
Andre F. Garner: manager communication affairs

PEPSICO, INC.

 Number 86 of Top 100 Corporate Givers

Company Contact

Purchase, NY
Web: http://www.pepsico.com

Company Description

Revenue: US$20,367,000,000 (1999)
Profit: US$1,993,000,000
Employees: 150,000
Fortune Rank: 76, per FORTUNE Magazine's list of 500 Largest U.S. Corporations (1999).
FF 76
SIC(s): 2052 Cookies & Crackers, 2086 Bottled & Canned Soft Drinks, 2087 Flavoring Extracts & Syrups Nec, 2096 Potato Chips & Similar Snacks.

Operating Locations

Argentina: Pepsi-Cola Argentina, S.A.C.I., Buenos Aires; Australia: PepsiCo. Australia Pty Ltd., Melbourne; Bermuda: Anderson Hill Insurance Ltd., Hamilton; Pepsi-Cola (Bermuda) Ltd., Hamilton; Pepsi-Cola International Ltd., Hamilton; Brazil: Seven-Up Concessiones SA, Buenos Aires; Chile: Pepsi-Cola Chile Consultores Ltda., Santiago; France: Pepsi-Cola de France, S.A.R.L., Paris; Germany: Florida International; Pepsi-Cola GmbH, Munich; India: Pepsi Foods Private Ltd., Channo, Patiala; Ireland: Pepsi-Cola Manufacturing, Cork, County Cork; The Concentrate Co. of Ireland, Dublin; Seven-Up Ireland Ltd., Dublin; Mexico: Sabritas SA de CV, Ciudad de Mexico; Pepsico de Mexico, SA de CV, Mexico; Temati SA de CV, Tijuana; Netherlands: feven-Up Nederlands NV, Bussum; Frito-Lay Finance NV, Curacao; Paine Corporate NV, Curacao; PARCO NV, Curacao; PEI NV, Curacao; Pepsi-Cola NV, Curacao; PepsiCo Finance (Antilles A) NV, Curacao; PepsiCo Finance (Antilles B) NV, Curacao; PepsiCo. Capital Corporate, NV, Curacao; Philippines: Pepsi-Cola Far East Trade, Manilla; Seven-Up Philippines, Inc., Metro Manilla; Spain: Pepsi-Cola de Espana, SA, Madrid; Productos Pepsi Co., SA, Madrid; United Kingdom: Walker's Crisps, Ltd., Leicester; PepsiCo Holdings Ltd. (UK), London; PepsiCo World Trading Co., London; Seven-Up Europe Ltd., London; Smith's Crisps, Ltd., Reading, Berkshire; Smiths Crisps Ltd., Reading, Berkshire; Pepsi-Co Internatioanl, Surrey; Uruguay: Emboltelladora del Uruguay, SA, Montevideo

Nonmonetary Support

Type: Donated Products
Volunteer Programs: Contributions are matched dollar for dollar to institutions and organizations that are determined tax-exempt by the I.R.S. When an employee volunteers in addition to a financial contribution, the foundation will double the match. Employee Community Involvement Grants are made to non-profit organizations where employees volunteer.

PepsiCo Foundation, Inc.

Giving Contact

Ms. Jacqueline R. Millan, Manager, Corporate Contributions
PepsiCo Foundation
700 Anderson Hill Road
Purchase, NY 10577
Phone: (914)253-3153
Fax: (914)253-3553

Description

Founded: 1962
EIN: 136163174
Organization Type: Corporate Foundation
Giving Locations: headquarters and operating communities.
Grant Types: Employee Matching Gifts, General Support, Project, Scholarship.
Note: Employee matching gift ratio: 1 to 1; 2 to 1 if employee volunteers in the organization. Majority of grants are initiated by employees volunteering in non-profit organisation.

Financial Summary

Total Giving: $8,334,805 (1998); $8,331,527 (1997); $9,733,732 (1996). Note: Contributes through foundation only.
Giving Analysis: Giving for 1996 includes: foundation ($3,779,332); foundation matching gifts ($2,498,552); foundation grants to United Way ($2,115,058); foundation scholarships ($1,340,781); 1997: foundation matching gifts ($2,861,034); foundation grants to United Way ($2,172,054); foundation scholarships ($1,493,514); 1998: foundation ($2,781,420); foundation grants to United Way ($1,860,820); foundation matching gifts ($1,850,445); foundation scholarships ($1,842,120)
Assets: $33,561,134 (1998); $38,941,775 (1997); $31,627,893 (1996)
Gifts Received: $1,000,000 (1998); $14,000,000 (1997); $14,000,000 (1996). Note: Contributions received from PepsiCo, Inc.

Typical Recipients

Arts & Humanities: Arts Associations & Councils, Arts Centers, Film & Video, Historic Preservation, History & Archaeology, Libraries, Museums/Galleries, Music, Opera, Performing Arts, Public Broadcasting, Theater
Civic & Public Affairs: African American Affairs, Botanical Gardens/Parks, Business/Free Enterprise, Economic Development, Ethnic Organizations, Civic & Public Affairs-General, Hispanic Affairs, Housing, Minority Business, Professional & Trade Associations, Public Policy, Urban & Community Affairs
Education: Business Education, Business-School Partnerships, Colleges & Universities, Continuing Education, Economic Education, Education Associations, Education Reform, Engineering/Technological Education, Education-General, Medical Education, Minority Education, Private Education (Precollege), Secondary Education (Public), Student Aid
Environment: Forestry, Resource Conservation
Health: Cancer, Children's Health/Hospitals, Health Organizations, Hospitals, Multiple Sclerosis
International: Foreign Educational Institutions, International-General, Health Care/Hospitals, Human Rights, International Affairs, International Development, International Organizations, International Peace & Security Issues, International Relations, International Relief Efforts, Trade
Religion: Churches, Religious Welfare
Science: Science Museums, Scientific Organizations
Social Services: Child Welfare, Community Service Organizations, Family Planning, People with Disabilities, Scouts, Substance Abuse, United Funds/United Ways

Contributions Analysis

Giving Priorities: Education and social services. Company's overseas operations make contributions; however, in-country managers are autonomous in setting priorities and selecting recipients. Domestically, the foundation is restricted from making contributions outside the United States. Has supported select policy and international affairs organizations.
Arts & Humanities: 2%. Supports opera, dance, theater, museums, and historical societies.
Civic & Public Affairs: 7%. Funds the National Urban League, community and neighborhood affairs.
Education: 58%. Support is given to major colleges and universities; education programs for minorities, including scholarships and leadership development; and scholarships for children of employees.

Social Services: 29%. Provides major support to the United Way. Also supports youth organizations, senior services and other social service organizations.
Note: Contributions analysis reflects contributions made in 1998, excluding matching gifts.

Application Procedures

Initial Contact: Send a written request.
Application Requirements: Include a statement of organization's objectives, proposed use and primary objective of grant, history of organization's achievements, list of officers and directors, copy of IRS 501(c)(3) letter, and financial statements.
Deadlines: None.
Evaluative Criteria: The foundation focuses on projects where Pepsico employees are actively involved as volunteers.

Restrictions

The foundation does not provide grants to individuals.

Additional Information

PepsiCo is the parent company of a number of operating divisions, at the following addresses: Frito-Lay, Inc., 7701 Legacy Dr., Plano, TX 75024, phone: (214) 334-7000; Pizza Hut, Inc., 17841 Dallas Parkway, Dallas, TX 75240; Taco Bell Corp., 17901 Von Karman, Irvine, CA 92714, phone: (714) 863-4500; Pepsi-Cola Co., Somers, NY 10589, phone: (914) 767-6000; and KFC, 1441 Gardiner Ln., Louisville, KY 40213. phone: (502)456-8300. Contributions activity is handled at each division based on community needs.
Organizations recommended by PepsiCo employees are also eligible for grants and will be considered.
Publications: Foundation Guidelines

Corporate Officials

Roger A. Enrico: chairman, chief executive officer, directorars, general counsel B 1944. ED Babson College BSBA (1965). PRIM CORP EMPL chairman, chief executive officer, director: PepsiCo, Inc. CORP AFFIL president, chief executive officer: PepsiCo Worldwide Beverages; director: Prudential Insurance Co. America; director: Dayton Hudson Corp.; president: Pepsi Cola Bottling Co.; director: A.H. Belo Corp. NONPR AFFIL director: Babson College Corp.; director: Lincoln Center for the Performing Arts.
Matthew M. McKenna: senior vice president, treasurer B Washington, DC 1950. ED Hamilton College (1972); Georgetown University (1978). PRIM CORP EMPL senior vice president, treasurer: PepsiCo, Inc.
Jacqueline R. Millan: manager corporate contributions PRIM CORP EMPL manager corporate contributions: PepsiCo, Inc.
Robert Francis Sharpe, Jr.: senior vice president public affairs, general counsel B Long Branch, NJ 1952. ED DePauw University BA (1975); Purdue University BSE (1975); Wake Forest University JD (1978). PRIM CORP EMPL senior vice president public affairs, general counsel: PepsiCo Inc. CORP AFFIL director: Whitman Corp. NONPR AFFIL member: North Carolina Bar Association; member board visitors: Wake Forest University; member board visitors: DePauw University; member: Forsyth County Bar Association; member: American Corporate Counsel Association; member: Atlanta Bar Association; member: American Bar Association.

Foundation Officials

Roger A. Enrico: chairman (see above)
Kathleen Allen Luke: secretary PRIM CORP EMPL vice president: PepsiCo Inc.
Matthew M. McKenna: treasurer (see above)
Jacqueline R. Millan: vice president, manager corporate contributions (see above)

Grants Analysis

Disclosure Period: calendar year ending 1998
Total Grants: $2,781,420*
Number of Grants: 129
Average Grant: $13,917*
Highest Grant: $1,000,000
Typical Range: $1,000 to $50,000
***Note:** Giving excludes matching gifts; scholarship; United Way. Average grant figure excludes highest grant.

Recent Grants

Note: Grants derived from 1998 Form 990.

Arts & Humanities

60,000	Metropolitan Opera, New York, NY
32,500	Westchester Arts Council, White Plains, NY
25,000	American Film Institute, New York, NY

Civic & Public Affairs

70,000	National Urban League, New York, NY
50,000	Lead Program in Business, New York, NY
30,000	Western Association of Food Chains, Los Angeles, CA
25,000	Westchester County, Westchester, NY
20,000	NAACP, New York, NY
15,000	Aspira, Washington, DC
15,000	National Council of Negro Women, Washington, DC
15,000	National Urban League, New York, NY
14,000	Congressional Hispanic Caucus, Washington, DC

Education

1,349,240	National Merit Scholarship Corp, Evanston, NY
1,000,000	University of Maryland, Baltimore, MD
286,500	Citizens Scholarship Foundation, Oxford, NY
200,000	Augustana College, Rock Island, IL
200,000	Texas Christian University, Fort Worth, TX
170,900	Citizens Scholarship Foundation, Oxford, NY
126,595	Fairfield University, Fairfield, CT
100,000	Boule Foundation, Toledo, OH
70,000	Cornell University, Ithaca, NY
28,000	Culinary Institute of America, Hyde Park, NY
25,000	Purchase College Foundation, Purchase, NY
20,000	Wake Forest University, Salem, NC
15,000	NAFEO, Silver Spring, MD

Health

25,000	Multiple Sclerosis Society, New York, NY

International

25,000	International Foundation for Education and Self-Help, Phoenix, AZ
20,000	Trilateral Commission, New York, NY
5,000	International Executive Service Corps, Stamford, CT
1,000	Americares, New York, NY

Science

20,000	American Council on Science/Health, New York, NY

Social Services

165,407	United Way of Westchester-Putnam, White Plains, NY
125,470	United Way of Metropolitan Dallas, Dallas, TX
115,327	United Way of Metropolitan Dallas, Dallas, TX
95,494	United Way of Metropolitan Dallas, Dallas, TX
77,387	United Way of Metropolitan Dallas, Dallas, TX
65,205	United Way of Metropolitan Dallas, Dallas, TX
64,166	United Way of Westchester-Putnam, White Plains, NY
57,354	United Way of Westchester-Putnam, White Plains, NY
52,225	United Way of Westchester-Putnam, White Plains, NY
39,339	United Way of Westchester-Putnam, White Plains, NY
33,633	United Way of Westchester-Putnam, White Plains, NY
28,505	United Way of Westchester-Putnam, White Plains, NY
26,095	United Way of Orange County, Garden Grove, CA
25,970	United Way of Westchester-Putnam, White Plains, NY
19,405	United Way of Clinton County, Frankfort, IN
19,197	United Way of Clinton County, Frankfort, IN
17,983	United Way of Clinton County, Frankfort, IN
14,481	United Way of Clinton County, Frankfort, IN
13,663	United Way of Metropolitan Tarrant County, Fort Worth, TX
13,315	United Way of Kern County, Bakersfield, CA
12,580	United Way of King County, Seattle, WA

PerkinElmer, Inc.

Company Contact

Wellesley, MA 02481
Phone: (781)237-5100
Web: http://www.perkinelmer.com

Company Description

Former Name: EG&G, Inc. (1999).
Revenue: US$1,420,000,000
Employees: 15,000
SIC(s): 3675 Electronic Capacitors, 3676 Electronic Resistors, 3823 Process Control Instruments.

PerkinElmer Foundation

Giving Contact

Administrator
PerkinElmer Foundation
45 William Street
Wellesley, MA 02481
Phone: (781)237-5100
Fax: (781)431-4183

Description

EIN: 042683042
Organization Type: Corporate Foundation
Former Name: EG&G Foundation (1999).
Giving Locations: nationally.
Grant Types: General Support.

Financial Summary

Total Giving: $3,400,000 (fiscal year ending June 30, 1999 approx); $3,400,000 (fiscal 1998 approx); $347,250 (fiscal 1997). Note: Contributes through foundation only. 1997 Giving includes United Way ($21,500).
Assets: $5,938,764 (fiscal 1997); $5,875,913 (fiscal 1996); $5,890,611 (fiscal 1995)

Typical Recipients

Arts & Humanities: Arts Associations & Councils, Arts Institutes, Ballet, Historic Preservation, History & Archaeology, Museums/Galleries, Music, Performing Arts, Public Broadcasting, Theater
Civic & Public Affairs: African American Affairs, Business/Free Enterprise, Civil Rights, Economic Development, Employment/Job Training, Hispanic Affairs, Housing, Law & Justice, Legal Aid, Philanthropic Organizations, Public Policy, Urban & Community Affairs, Zoos/Aquariums

Education: Business Education, Colleges & Universities, Community & Junior Colleges, Education Associations, Education Reform, Engineering/Technological Education, Education-General, International Exchange, International Studies, Private Education (Precollege), Science/Mathematics Education, Vocational & Technical Education
Environment: Environment-General
Health: Cancer, Children's Health/Hospitals, Clinics/Medical Centers, Diabetes, Emergency/Ambulance Services, Health Organizations, Hospitals, Medical Rehabilitation, Medical Research, Preventive Medicine/Wellness Organizations, Single-Disease Health Associations
International: Foreign Arts Organizations, International Affairs
Religion: Religious Welfare
Science: Science Museums
Social Services: Community Centers, Community Service Organizations, Family Planning, Food/Clothing Distribution, People with Disabilities, Special Olympics, Substance Abuse, United Funds/United Ways, Volunteer Services, Youth Organizations

Contributions Analysis

Arts & Humanities: 7%. Funds performing arts, musems, and arts.
Civic & Public Affairs: 11%. Contributes to environmental affairs, law and justice, and international affairs.
Education: 61%. Supports nationally recognized colleges and universities, vocational schools, junior colleges, and engineering education.
Health: 5%. Funding supports cancer research and treatment, and hospitals.
International: 3%. Funds the International Museum of Photography.
Science: About 1%. Funds a science museum.
Social Services: 11%.

Application Procedures

Initial Contact: Write for application form.
Application Requirements: Tax-exempt form.
Deadlines: None.

Additional Information

In October 1999, EG&G, Inc. changed its name to PerkinElmer, Inc. PerkinElmer, Inc. encompasses EG&G's Instruments, Life Sciences, Optoelectronics, and Fluid Sciences businesses and the recently purchased PerkinElmer Analytical Instruments business.

Corporate Officials

John F. Alexander: senior vice president, chief financial officer B Pittsburgh, PA 1956. ED Indiana University of Pennsylvania BS (1978); Rider College MBA (1988). PRIM CORP EMPL senior vice president, chief financial officer: EG&G, Inc. NONPR AFFIL member: Financial Executives Institute.
Murray Gross: senior vice president, general counsel, clerk B New York, NY 1936. ED Florida Southern College BS (1958); Brooklyn Law School JD (1961). PRIM CORP EMPL senior vice president, general counsel, clerk: EG&G, Inc. ADD CORP EMPL secretary: EG&G Instruments Inc. CORP AFFIL director: East River Housing Corp. NONPR AFFIL member: American Bar Association; member: American Society of Corporate Secretaries.
John Michael Kucharski: chairman, chief executive officer, director B Milwaukee, WI 1936. ED Marquette University BSEE (1958); George Washington University JD (1965). PRIM CORP EMPL chairman, chief executive officer, director: EG&G, Inc. CORP AFFIL director: State Street Bank & Trust Co.; director: State Street Boston Corp.; director: New England Electric System; chairman: EG&G Holdings Inc.; director: Nashua Corp.
E. Lavonne Lewis: vice president human resources PRIM CORP EMPL vice president human resources: EG&G, Inc.

Foundation Officials

John F. Alexander: trustee (see above)
Murray Gross: trustee (see above)
John Michael Kucharski: trustee (see above)
E. Lavonne Lewis: trustee (see above)

Grants Analysis

Disclosure Period: fiscal year ending June 30, 1997
Total Grants: $325,750*
Number of Grants: 115
Average Grant: $2,833
Highest Grant: $30,000
Typical Range: $500 to $3,000
***Note:** Giving excludes United Way.

Recent Grants

Note: Grants derived from fiscal 1997 Form 990.

Arts & Humanities

10,000 Boston Ballet, Boston, MA
5,000 Boston Symphony Orchestra, Boston, MA
2,500 Museum of Fine Arts, Boston, MA
2,500 New England Conservatory of Museums, Boston, MA
2,500 Old Sturbridge Village, Sturbridge, MA

Civic & Public Affairs

10,000 New England Aquarium, Boston, MA
5,000 New England Legal Foundation, Boston, MA
5,000 Washington Center, Washington, DC
3,000 EG and G Foundation, Wellesley, MA
3,000 EG and G Foundation, Wellesley, MA
3,000 EG and G Foundation, Wellesley, MA
2,500 Massachusetts Coalition, Boston, MA
2,500 Urban League, Roxbury, MA
1,500 Washington Legal Foundation, Washington, DC

Education

30,000 Maldef, Los Angeles, CA
25,000 Marquette University, Milwaukee, WI
25,000 Marquette University, Milwaukee, WI
25,000 Wheeling Jesuit University, Wheeling, WV
25,000 Wheeling Jesuit University, Wheeling, WV
20,000 University of California Berkeley, Berkeley, CA
20,000 West Virginia University Foundation, Morgantown, WV
7,500 Belmont Hill School, Belmont, MA
3,250 University of Texas Foundation, Austin, TX
3,250 University of Texas Foundation, Austin, TX
2,000 Advancement Foundation, Saratoga, CA
2,000 Japan-American Student Conference, Washington, DC
1,500 Junior Achievement, Boston, MA
1,500 Ulster Community College, Stone Ridge, NY
1,000 Johns Hopkins University, Baltimore, MD
1,000 University of Maryland Foundation, College Park, MD

Health

10,000 Lahey Clinic Foundation, Burlington, MA
2,000 Dana Lesher Benefit Fund, Henderson, NV
1,000 Cape Canaveral Hospital, Cocoa Beach, FL
1,000 Children's Clinic, Long Beach, CA
1,000 Children's Hospital of Orange County, Orange, CA
1,000 Hope Rehabilitation Services, San Jose, CA
1,000 Kingston Hospital, Kingston, NY

International

10,000 International Museum of Photography, Rochester, NY

Science

2,500 Museum of Science, Boston, MA

Social Services

10,500 United Way Massachusetts Bay, Boston, MA
7,500 Planned Parenthood, Palm Beach, FL
5,000 United Way Brevard County, Cocoa Beach, FL
2,500 Executive Service Corps, Boston, MA
2,500 Partnership for a Drug-Free America, New York, NY
2,500 United Fund of Anderson County, Oak Ridge, TN
1,000 California Special Olympics, Santa Monica, CA
1,000 Joy Junction, Albuquerque, NM
1,000 Joy Junction, Albuquerque, NM
1,000 United Way Mononcalia, Morgantown, WV
1,000 United Way Virginia Peninsula, Hampton, VA

PFIZER INC.

 Number 3 of Top 100 Corporate Givers

Company Contact

New York, NY
Web: http://www.pfizer.com

Company Description

Revenue: US$16,204,000,000 (1999)
Employees: 17,652 (1999)
Fortune Rank: 107, per FORTUNE Magazine's list of 500 Largest U.S. Corporations (1999).
FF 107
SIC(s): 2833 Medicinals & Botanicals, 2834 Pharmaceutical Preparations, 3841 Surgical & Medical Instruments, 3842 Surgical Appliances & Supplies.

Operating Locations

Belgium: Cadsand Medica N.V., Herent; Brazil: Laboratorios Pfizer Ltd., Sao Paulo, Guuarulhos; France: Orsim, S.A., Orsay, Cedex; Netherlands: Van Cadsand Beheer B.V., Bussum; Taiwan: Pfizer Trading Corporate, Taipei

Nonmonetary Support

Value: $63,900,000 (1996); $25,900,000 (1994); $9,351,860 (1992)
Type: Donated Products
Contact: Kim Frawley, Manager Product Donations
Note: Nonmonetary contributions include donations of medicine and equipment to emergecy relief and disaster aid. Product donations at fair market value. 1997 nonmonetary support $82.2 million.

Corporate Sponsorship

Type: Arts & cultural events; Pledge-a-thon

Pfizer Foundation

Giving Contact

Christopher Perez, Grants Coordinator
Pfizer Inc.
235 E. 42nd St.
New York, NY 10017-5755
Phone: (212)573-1758
Fax: (212)573-2883
Web: http://www.pfizer.com/pfizerinc/philanthropy

Description

EIN: 136083839
Organization Type: Corporate Foundation
Giving Locations: NY: New York principally near operating locations and to national organizations.

Grant Types: Award, Employee Matching Gifts, General Support, Multiyear/Continuing Support.
Note: Employee matching gift ratio: 1 to 1.

Giving Philosophy

'As a major global health care company, Pfizer is committed to finding solutions to society's most pressing health care problems through the discovery, development and advancement of innovative products, services, and programs that help people live longer, healthier and more productive lives.
'This mission extends to our Contributions Program, which seeks to support strategic partnerships with organizations in the health field. The Company also gives priority to medicine and health in other areas of its contributions program, including especially education, scientific research, human services and international affairs.
'In addition, our contributions and other corporate support programs seek to improve the quality of life by providing financial and other forms of assistance to civic and cultural organizations that are national in scope or serve communities where Pfizer employees live and work. Because we recognize the critical importance of innovation, quality, cost-effectiveness, enterprise and partnerships to our own business, we place a special emphasis on supporting community programs that demonstrate the importance of these values in helping to solve society's problems.' *Pfizer Inc. Contributions Program Mission Statement*

Financial Summary

Total Giving: $120,000,000 (1999 approx); $123,910,000 (1998); $106,340,000 (1997). Note: Contributes through corporate direct giving program and foundation.
Giving Analysis: Giving for 1997 includes: corporate direct giving ($21,750,000); foundation ($2,390,000); 1998: corporate direct giving ($120,807,800); foundation ($3,102,200)
Assets: $299,363,201 (1998); $13,000,000 (1997 approx); $12,000,000 (1996 approx)
Gifts Received: $300,000,000 (1998)

Typical Recipients

Arts & Humanities: Arts Associations & Councils, Arts Centers, Arts Funds, Dance, Historic Preservation, History & Archaeology, Libraries, Museums/Galleries, Music, Opera, Performing Arts, Public Broadcasting, Theater
Civic & Public Affairs: Asian American Affairs, Botanical Gardens/Parks, Business/Free Enterprise, Civil Rights, Economic Development, Economic Policy, Employment/Job Training, Hispanic Affairs, Housing, Law & Justice, Legal Aid, Municipalities/Towns, Professional & Trade Associations, Public Policy, Safety, Urban & Community Affairs, Women's Affairs, Zoos/Aquariums
Education: Business Education, Business-School Partnerships, Colleges & Universities, Colleges & Universities, Community & Junior Colleges, Economic Education, Education Associations, Education Funds, Education Reform, Elementary Education (Private), Elementary Education (Public), Engineering/Technological Education, Faculty Development, Education-General, International Exchange, International Studies, Leadership Training, Legal Education, Literacy, Medical Education, Minority Education, Private Education (Precollege), Public Education (Precollege), Science/Mathematics Education, Secondary Education (Public), Student Aid
Environment: Environment-General, Resource Conservation
Health: Adolescent Health Issues, AIDS/HIV, Children's Health/Hospitals, Clinics/Medical Centers, Emergency/Ambulance Services, Geriatric Health, Health Funds, Health Organizations, Hospices, Hospitals, Medical Rehabilitation, Medical Research, Mental Health, Public Health, Single-Disease Health Associations, Transplant Networks/Donor Banks
International: Foreign Arts Organizations, Foreign Educational Institutions, Health Care/Hospitals, International Development, International Peace & Security Issues, International Relations
Science: Science Museums, Scientific Centers & Institutes, Scientific Labs, Scientific Research
Social Services: Child Welfare, Community Centers, Community Service Organizations, Counseling, Delinquency & Criminal Rehabilitation, Emergency Relief, Family Services, Food/Clothing Distribution, People with Disabilities, Recreation & Athletics, Senior Services, Shelters/Homelessness, Substance Abuse, United Funds/United Ways, Volunteer Services, Youth Organizations

Contributions Analysis

Arts & Humanities: 4%. Priority is given to arts and cultural organizations identified as making a positive contribution to the cultural life of a Pfizer operating community. Cultural organizations eligible for funding include, but are not limited to, art education programs; museums; aquariums; performing arts organizations; cultural and performing arts centers. Programs that strive to develop working relationships between business and the arts community also are funded.
Civic & Public Affairs: 10%. Grants support programs such as community organizations and development, botanical gardens, and nonprofit management assistance providers. Through this fund, the company invests in nonprofit organizations dedicated to breaking the cycle of poverty through innovative, entrepreneurial programs that create wealth in local communities. Focus is on New York City.
Education: 26%. Preference given to schools at which Pfizer recruits; to schools located in Pfizer facility communities; to educational programs that relate to the company's business operations in math and science-based disciplines; and programs that provide training and other resources to teachers in science and math.
Environment: 1%. Funds wildlife conservation and protection.
Health: 44%. Supports patient education programs; programs that help people live healthier, more productive lives; therapeutic programs including those targeting hypertension, diabetes and depression; community health centers; social service providers; technical assistance providers; health communications technology to provide access to up-to-date health information; projects for changing the health care system; maternal and child health; and women's health issues.
Science: 9%. Supports New York Academy of Sciences, New York Hall of Science, Chicago Academy of Sciences, and California Academy of Sciences.
Social Services: 4%. Funds youth and social services.
Note: Total contributions made in 1998.

Application Procedures

Initial Contact: Send a a brief letter of inquiry not more than three pages.
Application Requirements: Include a description of organization; amount requested; purpose of funds sought; annual report and financial statement.
Deadlines: None.
Notes: Grant requests should be directed to company's philanthropy programs at the above address.

Restrictions

Does not support individuals; veterans, political, fraternal, labor, or sectarian religious organizations; antibusiness organizations; private foundations; organizations which are not tax-exempt; or independent agencies that duplicate work of United Way member agencies.
Both the company and the foundation only consider applicants meeting requirements of Internal Revenue Code Section 501(c)(3); foundation requires that applicants also meet requirements of Section 509(a)(1), (2), or (3). foundation requires that applicants also meet requirements of Section 509(a)(1), (2), or (3).

Additional Information

Generally, the company sponsors local organizations in company operating communities.
Gives special consideration to programs at which employees volunteer.
Disaster aid generally dispensed through established international relief organizations. Contact operating divisions for information on nonmonetary support, and contact the corporate office for product donations.
In February 2000, Pfizer Inc. announced plans to merge with Warner-Lambert Co.

Corporate Officials

Constantine Louis Clemente: executive vice president corporate affairs, secretary, corporate counsel B New York, NY 1937. ED College of the Holy Cross AB (1958); Columbia University LLB (1961). PRIM CORP EMPL executive vice president corporate affairs, secretary, corporate counsel: Pfizer Inc. NONPR AFFIL director: Project Hope; member executive committee: U.S. Council International Business; director: American Women's Economic Development Corp.; director: Fisk University.
Henry A. McKinnell, PhD: president, chief operating officer B 1942. PRIM CORP EMPL president, chief operating officer: Pfizer Inc. ADD CORP EMPL president: Pfizer Pharmaceuticals Group. CORP AFFIL director: Dun & Bradstreet Corp.
John F. Niblack, PhD: vice chairman PRIM CORP EMPL vice chairman: Pfizer Inc.
William Campbell Steere, Jr.: chairman, chief executive officer, director B Ann Arbor, MI 1936. ED University of California, Santa Barbara (1956); Stanford University BS (1959). PRIM CORP EMPL chairman, chief executive officer, director: Pfizer Inc. CORP AFFIL director: WNET-TV; director: New York University Medical Center; director: Texaco Inc.; director: Federal Reserve Bank New York; director: Minerals Technologies Inc.; director: Dow Jones & Co. Inc. NONPR AFFIL chairman: Pharmaceutical Manufacturer Association; member, director: Pharmaceutical Research & Manufacturer America; board overseers: Memorial Sloan-Kettering Cancer Center; trustee: New York Botanical Garden; director: Business Council; member: Business Roundtable. CLUB AFFIL University Club; New York Yacht Club.

Giving Program Officials

Paula Luff: senior program officer PRIM CORP EMPL manager corporate philanthropy programs: Pfizer Inc.
Rick Luftglass: PRIM CORP EMPL assistant director: Pfizer Inc.
Sarah Williams: assistant director

Foundation Officials

Constantine Louis Clemente: chairman (see above)
Terence Joseph Gallagher: secretary, director B New York, NY 1934. ED Manhattan College BA (1955); Harvard University JD (1958); New York University LLM (1966). PRIM CORP EMPL vice president, assistant secretary, attorney: Pfizer Inc. CORP AFFIL secretary, director: Adforce Inc. NONPR AFFIL member: Independent Order Sons Malta; member: New York State Bar Association; trustee: Business Advisory Council Federal Reports; director: Calvary Hospital Fund; member: American Bar Association; director: American Society of Corporate Secretaries.
James Richard Gardner: vice president B Wellsville, NY 1944. ED United States Military Academy BS (1966); Princeton University MA (1968); Long Island University MBA (1977); Princeton University PhD (1977); United States Army War College (1989). NONPR AFFIL member: USMA Association Graduates; member: West Point Society New York; member advisory committee: Princeton University Department Astrophysical Science; member: Planning Forum;

member advisory council: Princeton University Center International Studies; member: North American Society Corporate Planning; member: Phi Kappa Phi; director: Boy Scouts America Greater New York Council; member: National Investor Relations Institute.
Charles Hardwick: chief operating officer
Kevin Keating: treasurer PRIM CORP EMPL treasurer: Pfizer Overseas Inc.
Jay Kosminsky: president PRIM CORP EMPL executive director communications philanthhropy: Pfizer Inc.
Paula Luff: senior program officer (see above)

Grants Analysis

Disclosure Period: calendar year ending 1998
Total Grants: $3,102,200
Number of Grants: 60
Average Grant: $51,703
Highest Grant: $250,000
Typical Range: $5,000 to $75,000

Recent Grants

Note: Grants derived from 1997 Form 990.

Arts & Humanities

50,000	Carnegie Hall, New York, NY
25,000	Channel Thirteen/WNET, New York, NY
20,000	Brooklyn Children's Museum, Brooklyn, NY

Civic & Public Affairs

300,000	New York Botanical Garden/Chair in Botanical Sciences, New York, NY
50,000	Organizations (COSSMHO), Washington, DC
36,000	Chinatown Health Center, New York, NY
35,000	La Clinica del Carino, Hood River, OR
30,000	Asian Health Services, Oakland, CA

Education

125,000	St. Lawrence University, New York, NY
100,000	National Academy of Sciences, Washington, DC
40,000	New Visions for Public Schools, New York, NY
40,000	New York Academy of Sciences, New York, NY
30,000	Fisk University, Nashville, TN
30,000	Rockefeller University, New York, NY
30,000	Tufts University, Boston, MA
25,000	Black Student Fund, Washington, DC
25,000	Center for Educational Innovation, New York, NY
25,000	Impact II - The Teachers' Network, New York, NY
25,000	NYC Outward Bound, New York, NY
21,000	Friends of the High School for Environmental Studies, New York, NY
20,000	Public Education Association, New York, NY
15,000	Columbia University, College of Physicians & Surgeons, New York, NY
15,000	Summerbridge National, San Francisco, CA
12,165	Project STIR/City University, New York, NY

Health

50,000	East Liberty Family Health Center, East Liberty, PA
50,000	Lamprey Health Care, New Market, NH
50,000	Philadelphia Health Services, Philadelphia, PA
50,000	Primary Care Development Corporation, New York, NY
50,000	South of Market Health Center, San Francisco, CA
47,000	Institute for Urban Family Health, New York, NY
47,000	Regional Medical Center at Lubec, Lubec, ME
47,000	Venice Family Clinic, Venice, CA
45,000	Southern Illinois Health Care Foundation, St. Louis, IL
41,000	Healthnet Community Health Centers, Indianapolis, IN
41,000	Nevada Rural Health Centers, Carson City, NV
38,000	Fairhaven Community Health Center, Fairhaven, CT
38,000	Sun Life Family Health Center, Casa Grande, AZ
35,000	Church Health Center, Memphis, TN
35,000	Ebenezer Medical Outreach, Cabell County, WV
35,000	Interfaith Family Health Center, Bellingham, WA
35,000	NonProfit Clinic Consortium, Washington, DC
32,000	Neighborhood Family Practice, Cleveland, OH
25,000	Arthur Ashe Institute, Brooklyn, NY
25,000	March of Dimes, National, Spartanburg, SC
10,000	Anson Regional Medical Services, Wadesboro, NC

Science

250,000	Massachusetts Institute of Technology, Boston, MA
23,700	Liberty Science Center, Jersey City, NJ
15,000	Columbus Center, Baltimore, MD

Social Services

35,000	Boston Health Care for the Homeless, Boston, MA
35,000	Health Care for the Homeless of Maryland, Baltimore, MD

PHARMACIA &UPJOHN, INC.

Company Contact

Bridgewater, NJ
Web: http://wwww.pnu.com

Company Description

Former Name: Upjohn Co.
Revenue: US$7,252,600,000 (1999)
Employees: 31,700
Fortune Rank: 244, per FORTUNE Magazine's list of 500 Largest U.S. Corporations (1999).
FF 244
SIC(s): 2833 Medicinals & Botanicals, 2834 Pharmaceutical Preparations, 2879 Agricultural Chemicals Nec, 2899 Chemical Preparations Nec.
Parent Company: Pharmacia & Upjohn, 67 Anma Rd., Windsor, BR, England

Operating Locations

CT: Pharmacia & Upjohn, Inc., North Haven; IA: O's Gold Seed Co., Aplington; MI: Pharmacia & Upjohn, Kalamazoo; Pharmacia & Upjohn Adria Laboratories, Kalamazoo; Pharmacia & Upjohn Central, Kalamazoo; Pharmacia & Upjohn, Inc., Kalamazoo; Pharmacia & Upjohn Inter-American Corp., Kalamazoo; Pharmacia & Upjohn Intl. Inc., Kalamazoo; Pharmacia & Upjohn Pharmaceutical Division, Kalamazoo; TUCO Animal Health, Kalamazoo; MN: Pharmacia & Upjohn Deltec, Inc., Arden Hills; NJ: Pharmacia & Upjohn Corporate Services, Piscataway; Pharmacia & Upjohn U.S. Inc., Piscataway; PR: Pharmacia & Upjohn, Inc.; Pharmacia & Upjohn Manufacturing Co., Arecibo; WI: Pharmacia & Upjohn, Hartland

Nonmonetary Support

Value: $14,849,000 (1995); $4,792,000 (1994); $7,404,000 (1993)
Type: Cause-related Marketing & Promotion; Donated Products; In-kind Services; Loaned Employees; Loaned Executives
Note: 1995 nonmonetary support consisted of about $14.7 million in product wholesale value,& approximately $149,000 in in-kind donations, equipment, and misc. furniture.

Corporate Sponsorship

Note: Sponsors fundraising events, cause-related marketing partnerships, and meetings. Contact co. regarding sponsorships.

Pharmacia & Upjohn Foundation

Giving Contact

Phillip C. Carra, Secretary
Pharmacia & Upjohn Foundation
7000 Portage Rd.
Kalamazoo, MI 49001
Phone: (616)833-7181
Fax: (616)833-6418

Description

EIN: 382784862
Organization Type: Corporate Foundation
Giving Locations: MI: Kalamazoo headquarters and operating communities; internationally; product donations go only to Third World countries.
Grant Types: Capital, Challenge, Employee Matching Gifts, General Support, Multiyear/Continuing Support.
Note: General support given in local communities only. Matching gifts made to educational institutions only.

Giving Philosophy

'Philanthropic programs work against the backdrop of complex societal needs and the inter-relationships of government, the private sector, nonprofit institutions and others who devote their time to bettering our world. While we strive to position limited resources as a powerful change agent, society's problems continue to grow. Therefore, we must work together by leveraging resources and investing in creative solutions..Pharmacia and Upjohn and the Foundation look forward to the future partnering with others to help people live longer and fuller lives by meeting medical needs through innovative research and development and investing to make our world better.' *Making a Difference: Contributions Programs 1995,* Pharmacia and Upjohn

Financial Summary

Total Giving: $5,500,000 (1999 approx); $5,000,000 (1998 approx); $4,822,560 (1997). Note: Contributes through corporate direct giving program and foundation.
Giving Analysis: Giving for 1995 includes: foundation ($5,832,913); corporate direct giving ($2,600,000); 1996: foundation ($5,144,831); foundation grants to United Way ($308,690); 1997: foundation ($4,073,652); foundation grants to United Way ($808,908)
Assets: $17,273,290 (1996); $22,424,412 (1995); $25,687,160 (1994)
Gifts Received: $1,000,000 (1995); $4,000,000 (1994). Note: In 1995, contributions were received from Pharmacia & UpJohn.

Typical Recipients

Arts & Humanities: Arts Associations & Councils, Arts Funds, Arts Institutes, Arts Outreach, Community Arts, Ethnic & Folk Arts, Historic Preservation, History & Archaeology, Museums/Galleries, Music, Performing Arts, Theater, Visual Arts
Civic & Public Affairs: African American Affairs, Business/Free Enterprise, Civil Rights, Community

Foundations, Economic Development, Employment/ Job Training, Housing, Municipalities/Towns, Parades/Festivals, Professional & Trade Associations, Public Policy, Safety, Urban & Community Affairs, Women's Affairs, Zoos/Aquariums
Education: Afterschool/Enrichment Programs, Business Education, Colleges & Universities, Community & Junior Colleges, Economic Education, Education Funds, Education Reform, Engineering/ Technological Education, Faculty Development, Education-General, Health & Physical Education, Medical Education, Minority Education, Public Education (Precollege), Science/Mathematics Education, Student Aid
Environment: Environment-General, Resource Conservation
Health: AIDS/HIV, Cancer, Emergency/Ambulance Services, Health Organizations, Hospices, Hospitals, Medical Research, Mental Health, Nursing Services, Nutrition, Prenatal Health Issues, Public Health, Research/Studies Institutes, Single-Disease Health Associations, Transplant Networks/Donor Banks
International: Foreign Arts Organizations, Foreign Educational Institutions, Health Care/Hospitals, International Development
Religion: Ministries, Religious Welfare
Science: Scientific Centers & Institutes, Scientific Organizations
Social Services: Animal Protection, At-Risk Youth, Camps, Emergency Relief, Family Planning, Family Services, Food/Clothing Distribution, People with Disabilities, Recreation & Athletics, Senior Services, Substance Abuse, United Funds/United Ways, Volunteer Services, YMCA/YWCA/YMHA/YWHA, Youth Organizations

Contributions Analysis

Giving Priorities: Education, health, united funds, civic organizations, culture, the environment, and opportunities for minorities and the disadvantaged. International donations are primarily in the form of pharmaceutical products and vegetable and agronomic seeds. Donations are made through charitable organizations assisting developing countries, including World Vision Relief & Development, MAP, Inc., Direct Relief International, and the Red Cross. The company also provides financial support to organizations dedicated to aiding other countries such as Project HOPE and Blessings International. Product contributions are made to relieve suffering in the aftermath of catastrophes and to relieve chronic inability to obtain pharmaceuticals through normal commercial channels. Vegetable and agronomic seeds are provided to established and reputable organizations which aid people in areas suffering from insufficient food supplies or catastrophic crop failures. In recognition of the threat of unbridled population growth, the company also supports agencies that are dealing effectively with this problem, both in the United States and in other countries. The selected agencies are those that carry out an educational function in the field of human fertility.
Arts & Humanities: About 2%. Supports symphonies, arts funds, performing arts, and arts institutes.
Civic & Public Affairs: About 15%. Zoos, housing, urban and community affairs, and women's causes.
Education: About 31%. Primarily to colleges and universities.
Health: About 14%. Formed the Arrow partnership with doctors, nurses, and Native American volunteers in order to provide health care services in remote areas of the American West. Health care, prevention of drug and alcohol abuse, educational programs.
Social Services: 28%. Focus on the United Way and family services.
Note: Total contributions in 1997.

Application Procedures

Initial Contact: Request guidelines, then submit a written proposal.
Application Requirements: Include 501(c)(3) tax status, audited financial statements, and budgets; a complete proposal description; a list of funders and a list of board members; and if appropriate, also include a plan to evaluate results.
Deadlines: None.
Review Process: The initial recommendation is made by the administrator of corporate contributions; final decisions are made by the corporate contributions committee.
Evaluative Criteria: The foundation has established priorities that reflect Pharmacia and Upjohn's commitment to the quality of life and concern for communities where employees and their families live and work; the foundation board emphasizes health care, education, and civic projects in its funding decisions.
Decision Notification: The contributions committee meets monthly. The foundation makes an effort to respond within 60 days of application receipt; the budget for the following year is drafted in August; nonbudgeted discretionary funds are extremely limited and rarely available
Notes: Requests for clinical research grants or product-related research should be directed to company's Research and Development offices. Funding requests for public policy research should be directed to the Public Affairs area. Do not make telephone calls during the evaluation process.

Restrictions

Arts and culture grants, community improvements, or local projects will be considered only where company facilities are located.
Does not give grants to individuals; social organizations; political action committees or candidates; religious institutions (except for non-sectarian, humanitarian services), churches, or veterans organizations; travel funds for tours, expeditions, or trips; tickets, tables, or any social events; or school-related sports or band events and activities. Grants are made for one year only, except in the case of capital grants. In no case will the company commit funds for more than five years.
No grants can be made that directly benefit the company.

Additional Information

In 1995, Upjohn merged with Pharmacia AB, a Swedish pharmaceutical and biotechnology company, to form Pharmacia & Upjohn. In 2000, Pharmacia and Upjohn merged with Monsanto to form Pharmacia Corp.
Publications: Annual Report; Application Guidelines; Application Form

Corporate Officials

Phillip C. Carra: vice president public relations business ED Kalamazoo College (1969); Western Michigan University (1972). PRIM CORP EMPL vice president public relations: Pharmacia & Upjohn, Inc.
Donald R. Parfet: senior vice president associated business B Kalamazoo, MI 1952. ED University of Arizona BA (1975); University of Michigan MBA (1977). PRIM CORP EMPL senior vice president associated business: Pharmacia & Upjohn, Inc. CORP AFFIL treasurer: Gull Lake Marine Center Inc.; treasurer: Oakleys Catering LLC.

Foundation Officials

Steven J. Aschelman: vice president, treasurer
Charles H. Bibart: director
Phillip C. Carra: director (see above)
Donald R. Parfet: president (see above)

Grants Analysis

Disclosure Period: calendar year ending 1997
Total Grants: $4,073,652*
Number of Grants: 101
Average Grant: $40,333
Highest Grant: $487,500
Typical Range: $1,000 to $50,000
***Note:** Giving excludes United Way.

Recent Grants

Note: Grants derived from 1997 Form 990.

Arts & Humanities

200,000 Kalamazoo Symphony Society, Kalamazoo, MI -- third payment on a three-year, $650,000 pledge
100,000 Kalamazoo Foundation, Kalamazoo, MI -- third payment on a five-year, $500,000 grant for the Civic Campaign Fund
50,000 Irving S. Gilmore International Keyboard Festival, Kalamazoo, MI
45,000 Kalamazoo Foundation, Kalamazoo, MI -- Sutherland Park/Annen Sports Complex
30,000 Kalamazoo Symphony Society, Kalamazoo, MI -- support for educational outreach programs
18,000 Kalamazoo Institute of Arts, Kalamazoo, MI -- general support
15,000 Kalamazoo Civic Players, Kalamazoo, MI
11,000 Kalamazoo Institute of Arts, Kalamazoo, MI -- artist outreach

Civic & Public Affairs

200,000 Binder Park Zoological Society, Battle Creek, MI -- final payment on a five-year, $1 million grant for capital expansion
125,000 Local Initiatives Support Corporation, Kalamazoo, MI -- first payment on a two-year, $250,000 grant for the Kalamazoo Program
87,500 Greater Kalamazoo Telecity USA, Kalamazoo, MI -- second payment on a two-year, $175,000 grant for expansion of programs
50,000 Women's Education Coalition, Kalamazoo, MI -- second payment on a $100,000 pledge
35,000 MRC Industries, Kalamazoo, MI -- Pathways capital campaign
22,500 Forum for Kalamazoo County, Kalamazoo, MI -- unrestricted program support
15,000 High on America Air Show, Kalamazoo, MI -- unrestricted program support

Education

333,333 Western Michigan University, Kalamazoo, MI -- second payment on a three-year, $1 million grant for science campaign
300,000 University of Michigan, Ann Arbor, MI -- second payment on a five-year, $1.5 million grant for Capital/Endowment Campaign
100,000 Spelman College, Atlanta, GA -- final payment on a five-year, $500,000 grant for the expansion of the science center
88,750 Kalamazoo College, Kalamazoo, MI -- Science Grasp program
55,000 Michigan Colleges Foundation, Southfield, MI -- support for Michigan liberal arts colleges
50,000 PhRMA Foundation, Washington, DC -- fellowships
40,000 University of Rochester College of Arts and Sciences, Rochester, NY -- third payment on a five-year, $200,000 pledge for Marshall Gates Faculty Scholar Award
39,380 National Merit Scholarship Corporation, Evanston, IL
20,500 American Foundation for Pharmaceutical Education, Rockville, MD -- fellowship in toxicology and graduate scholarship
20,000 Alma College, Alma, MI -- microscopes for student labs
20,000 Kalamazoo College, Kalamazoo, MI -- annual fund support

20,000 National Medical Fellowships, New York, NY -- minority scholarships
20,000 University of Kansas, Lawrence, KS -- third payment on a $100,000 grant for Biosciences Research Building
20,000 Western Michigan University, Kalamazoo, MI -- annual fund support
15,000 Junior Achievement, Kalamazoo, MI -- unrestricted program support
10,000 Campbell University School of Pharmacy, Buies Creek, NC -- building project
10,000 College Fund/UNCF, Detroit, MI -- unrestricted support

Health

200,000 Healthy Futures, Kalamazoo, MI -- first payment on a five-year, $1 million grant for program support
125,000 Hospice Care of Southwest Michigan, Kalamazoo, MI -- first payment on a three-year, $350,000 pledge
85,000 American Red Cross, Kalamazoo, MI -- first payment on a three-year, $250,000 grant for Building a Stronger Red Cross campaign
50,000 New York Academy of Medicine Center for Epidemiology Studies, New York, NY -- second payment on a three-year, $150,000 grant for urban epidemiologic studies
27,000 Foundation for Biomedical Research, Washington, DC -- unrestricted program support
20,000 National Alopecia Areata Foundation, San Rafael, CA -- support for research and educational programs
10,000 Michigan Society for Medical Research, Ann Arbor, MI -- educational programs

International

15,000 Project Hope, Millwood, VA -- unrestricted program support

Social Services

487,500 Greater Kalamazoo United Way, Kalamazoo, MI -- second and third quarterly payments on a $975,000 pledge
243,750 Greater Kalamazoo United Way, Kalamazoo, MI -- first quarterly payment on a $975,000 pledge for unrestricted program support
52,658 United Way, San Juan, PR -- unrestricted grant
50,000 Family Institute, Kalamazoo, MI -- unrestricted support
50,000 Family Institute, Kalamazoo, MI -- remainder of second payment on a three-year, $300,000 grant for program support
50,000 Family Institute, Kalamazoo, MI -- final payment on a $300,000 pledge
50,000 Family Institute, Kalamazoo, MI -- advance on future pledge
35,000 Kalamazoo Humane Society, Kalamazoo, MI -- support for A Century of Compassion campaign
25,000 Greater Kalamazoo United Way, Kalamazoo, MI -- one-time donation recognizing employee campaign commitment
20,000 Planned Parenthood, Kalamazoo, MI -- educational programs

PHELPS DODGE CORP.

Company Contact

Phoenix, AZ
Web: http://www.phelpsdodge.com

Company Description

Acquired: Cyprus Amax (1999).
Revenue: US$3,114,400,000 (1999)
Employees: 13,924
Fortune Rank: 493, per FORTUNE Magazine's list of 500 Largest U.S. Corporations (1999).
FF 493
SIC(s): 1021 Copper Ores, 2819 Industrial Inorganic Chemicals Nec, 2895 Carbon Black, 3331 Primary Copper.

Operating Locations

Austria: Phelps Dodge Eldra GmbH, Mureck, Steiermark; Phelps Dodge Industries GmbH, Vienna; Belgium: Hudson Wire Co., Puurs, Anvers; Canada: Columbian Chemicals Canada Ltd., Hamilton; Accuride Canada, London; Ashfork Mines Ltd., Toronto; Phelps Dodge Corp. of Canada Ltd., Toronto; Chile: Cobre Cerrillos SA, Santiago; Cocesa Ingenieria y Construccion SA, Santiago; Compania Contractual Minera Ojos Del Salado SA, Santiago; Compania Minera Ojos del Saldo SA, Santiago; Costa Rica: Conducen SA, Heredia; Ecuador: Cables Electricos Ecuatorianos SA, Quito, Pichincha; France: Columbian Carbone International France, Rungis, Val-de-Marne; Germany: Columbian Carbon Deutschland GmbH, Hannover, Niedersachsen; Columbian Chemicals Europa GmbH, Hannover, Niedersachsen; Hungary: Columbia Tiszai Koromgyarto KFT, Tiszaujvaros; Italy: Columbian Carbon Europa SRL, Trecate, Piemonte; Mexico: Accuride de Mexico SA de CV, San Nicholas de los Garza; Panama: Alambres y Cables de Panama SA, Panama City; Philippines: Columbian Carbon (Philippines), Makati, Rizal; Spain: Columbian Carbon Spain SA, Gajano, Cantabria; Thailand: Thai Copper Rod Ltd., Samrong Nua; Venezuela: Alambres y Cables Venezolanos CA, Valencia, Carabobo; Conductores y Aluminio CA, Valencia, Carabobo; Industria de Conductores Electricos CA, Valencia, Carabobo

Nonmonetary Support

Value: $1,317,000 (1993)
Type: Donated Products; In-kind Services

Phelps Dodge Foundation

Giving Contact

Ann Gibson, Community Affairs
Phelps Dodge Foundation
2600 N. Central Ave.
Phoenix, AZ 85004
Phone: (602)234-8100
Fax: (602)234-8082
Web: http://www.phelpsdodge.com/index-community.html

Description

EIN: 136077350
Organization Type: Corporate Foundation
Giving Locations: communities where company maintains major operating facilities.
Grant Types: Employee Matching Gifts, General Support, Multiyear/Continuing Support, Scholarship.
Note: Limited multiyear/continuing support is provided.

Giving Philosophy

'It is our responsibility, and our privilege, to support the communities where we have operations. We don't just talk about our Tradition of Giving. We experience it. We experience it each time one of the Phelps Dodge scholarship recipients graduates from college; when a premature baby is cared for in one of the community hospitals near our mining operations; when a visually impaired individual learns a meaningful work skill; and when an audience applauds their symphony orchestra. .. Through the Phelps Dodge Foundation, corporate contributions, and an employee matching gifts program, we share our support among four areas: education, health and welfare, civic activities and culture and art. In addition, many people benefit from Phelps Dodge employees who volunteer their time, money and other resources to assist the communities where they live and work. . . .' *A Tradition of Giving 1992-1993*

Financial Summary

Total Giving: $2,000,000 (1999 approx); $1,553,397 (1998); $1,605,625 (1997). Note: Contributes through corporate direct giving program and foundation.
Giving Analysis: Giving for 1997 includes: foundation ($848,710); foundation scholarships ($393,227); foundation matching gifts ($363,688); 1998: foundation ($824,247); foundation scholarships ($379,150); foundation matching gifts ($350,000)
Assets: $18,407,619 (1998); $16,624,800 (1997); $15,026,211 (1996)
Gifts Received: $500,000 (1995)

Typical Recipients

Arts & Humanities: Arts Associations & Councils, Arts Centers, Arts Funds, Ballet, Community Arts, History & Archaeology, Libraries, Museums/Galleries, Music, Opera, Performing Arts, Public Broadcasting, Theater
Civic & Public Affairs: Botanical Gardens/Parks, Business/Free Enterprise, Civil Rights, Economic Development, Economic Policy, Law & Justice, Public Policy, Safety, Urban & Community Affairs, Zoos/Aquariums
Education: Business Education, Colleges & Universities, Community & Junior Colleges, Economic Education, Education Associations, Education Funds, Engineering/Technological Education, Health & Physical Education, International Exchange, Medical Education, Minority Education, Private Education (Precollege), Science/Mathematics Education, Student Aid
Environment: Environment-General
Health: Cancer, Children's Health/Hospitals, Clinics/Medical Centers, Geriatric Health, Health Funds, Health Organizations, Hospitals, Kidney, Medical Research, Medical Training
International: Health Care/Hospitals, International Peace & Security Issues, International Relations, International Relief Efforts
Religion: Religious Organizations, Religious Welfare
Science: Science Museums, Scientific Centers & Institutes
Social Services: Community Service Organizations, Family Planning, Recreation & Athletics, Scouts, Senior Services, Shelters/Homelessness, United Funds/United Ways, Youth Organizations

Contributions Analysis

Giving Priorities: Education, health, social welfare, and culture and the arts. Company's international giving is decentralized and autonomous. Foreign operating companies are responsible for making contributions in locales directly from operating budgets. Contributions are considered a cost of doing business overseas and decisions are made at the local level and are based on local community needs.
Arts & Humanities: 25%. Funding supports symphonies, opera, museums, performing arts, and historical preservation. Limited support to art funds and centers.
Education: 34%. Majority of funding supports scholarships to colleges and universities. Funding also emphasizes scientific, technological, mining, and business education. Interests include minority and independent college funds, community colleges, and medical education.
Health: 11%. Support goes to youth hospitals and children's health.
Note: Matching gifts, equal to 25% to 30% of annual grants, are made to educational, non-profit voluntary hospitals, family issues, cultural organizations and institutions. Total contributions in 1998.

Application Procedures

Initial Contact: Send a brief letter on the organization's letterhead.

Application Requirements: Include a description of organization, amount requested, purpose of funds sought, recently audited financial statement, and proof of tax-exempt status.
Deadlines: June.
Decision Notification: The budget is determined at the annual meeting held in September.

Restrictions

Does not support individuals, political or lobbying groups, dinners or special events, or goodwill advertising.

Additional Information

Company matches employee contributions to accredited colleges and universities, including junior colleges; privately financed, nonprofit accredited secondary schools; voluntary hospitals; museums; performing arts organizations; botanical gardens; public broadcasting services; or zoological societies.
Publications: A Tradition of Giving

Corporate Officials

S. David Colton: senior vice president, general counsel ED Brigham Young University BA; Brigham Young University J. Reuben Clark College of Law JD. PRIM CORP EMPL senior vice president, general counsel: Phelps Dodge Corp. NONPR AFFIL member: American Bar Association; member: Utah State Bar Association.
Manuel J. Iraola: senior vice president, director B 1948. ED Sacred Heart University MBA; University of Puerto Rico BS. PRIM CORP EMPL senior vice president, director: Phelps Dodge Corp. ADD CORP EMPL president: Phelps Dodge Industries. NONPR AFFIL director: National Association Manufacturers; member: Thunderbird Graduate School International Management Global Council.
Ramiro G. Peru: senior vice president, chief financial officer B Morenci, AZ 1956. ED University of Arizona BS (1978). PRIM CORP EMPL senior vice president, chief financial officer: Phelps Dodge Corp.
David L. Pulatie: senior vice president human resources ED Arizona State College BS; Northern Arizona University MA.
Timothy R. Snider: senior vice president ED Northern Arizona University BS. PRIM CORP EMPL senior vice president: Phelps Dodge Corp. ADD CORP EMPL president: Phelps Dodge Mining Co.
Gregory W. Stevens: vice president, treasurer ED Yale University BA. PRIM CORP EMPL vice president, treasurer: Phelps Dodge Corp.
Robert C. Swan: vice president, secretary PRIM CORP EMPL vice president, secretary: Phelps Dodge Corp.
J. Steven Whisler: chairman, president, chief executive officer B 1954. ED Colorado School of Mines MS; University of Colorado BS; University of Denver College of Law JD. PRIM CORP EMPL chairman, president, chief executive officer: Phelps Dodge Corp. CORP AFFIL director: Burlington Northern Santa Fe Corp.; director: Southern Peru Copper Corp. NONPR AFFIL chairman: Copper Development Association; member: Mining Metallurgical Society America; member: American Institute Mining Engineers.

Foundation Officials

Tracy L. Bame: manager community affairs ED University of Arizona BA. PRIM CORP EMPL manager community affairs: Phelps Dodge Corp. NONPR AFFIL director: Phoenix Body Positive; director: Waste Not; director: Fresh Start Women's Foundation.
Paul W. Douglas: director B Springfield, MA 1926. ED Princeton University AB (1948). CORP AFFIL director: Phelps Dodge Corp.; trustee: US Trust Co. of New York; director: New York Life Insurance Co.
William Augustus Franke: director B Bryan, TX 1937. ED Stanford University BA (1959); Stanford University LLB (1961). PRIM CORP EMPL chairman, president, chief executive officer: America West Airlines Inc. ADD CORP EMPL chairman, chief executive officer: America West Holdings Corp.; president, owner: Franke & Inc. CORP AFFIL director: Phelps Dodge Corp.; chairman: Engineer and Fabricators Co.; managing partner: Newbridge Latin American LLP; director: Beringer Wine Estates; director: Central Newspapers Inc.; director: Airplanes Ltd.; chairman, trustee: Airplanes United States Trust. NONPR AFFIL member: Chief Executives Organization; member: Washington Bar Association; member: American Bar Association; member: Arizona State University School Business; director: Air Transport Association. CLUB AFFIL Paradise Valley Country Club; Phoenix Country Club; Arizona Club; Desert Mountain Country Club.
Rodney A. Prokop: assistant treasurer PRIM CORP EMPL director investor relations: Phelps Dodge Corp.
Mary K. Sterling: secretary PRIM CORP EMPL shareholder relations officer, assistant vice president secretary: Phelps Dodge Corp.
Robert C. Swan: president (see above)

Grants Analysis

Disclosure Period: calendar year ending 1998
Total Grants: $824,247*
Number of Grants: 109 (approx)
Average Grant: $7,562
Highest Grant: $80,000 (approx)
Typical Range: $1,000 to $20,000
***Note:** Giving excludes matching gifts; scholarships.

Recent Grants

Note: Grants derived from 1997 Form 990.

Arts & Humanities

175,000	Phoenix Symphony Orchestra, Phoenix, AZ
100,000	Opera Association, Albuquerque, NM
50,000	Ballet Arizona, Phoenix, AZ
25,000	Arizona Opera Company, Phoenix, AZ
25,000	Arizona Theater Company, Phoenix, AZ
25,000	Friends of the Phoenix Public Library, Phoenix, AZ
25,000	Heard Museum, Phoenix, AZ
25,000	Phoenix Art Museum, Phoenix, AZ
15,000	Actors Theater, Phoenix, AZ
6,000	New Mexico Symphony Orchestra, Albuquerque, NM
5,000	Embassy Theater Foundation, Fort Wayne, IN
5,000	Mimbres Regional Arts Council, Silver City, NM
5,000	Museum of Northern Arizona, Flagstaff, AZ
5,000	Tucson Museum of Art, Tucson, AZ
5,000	Tucson Symphony Orchestra, Tucson, AZ
3,500	Metropolitan Museum of Art, New York, NY
3,000	Silver City Museum, Silver City, NM

Civic & Public Affairs

10,000	Headwaters Park, Fort Wayne, IN

Education

67,000	University of Arizona, Tucson, AZ -- scholarships
50,000	American Graduate School of International Management, Glendale, AZ -- scholarships
38,000	Arizona State University, Tempe, AZ -- scholarships
37,127	National Merit Scholarship Corporation, Evanston, IL -- Phelps Dodge Scholarships
30,000	Colorado School of Mines, Golden, CO -- scholarships
25,000	Maricopa Community College Foundation, Tempe, AZ -- scholarships
22,400	Northern Arizona University, Flagstaff, AZ -- scholarships
20,000	United Negro College Fund, New York, NY
15,000	Western New Mexico University, Silver City, NM -- scholarships
10,000	Indiana Institute of Technology, Fort Wayne, IN -- scholarships
10,000	New Mexico State University, Las Cruces, NM -- scholarships
10,000	New Way School, Scottsdale, AZ -- scholarships
10,000	Science Central, Fort Wayne, IN
10,000	University of New Mexico, Albuquerque, NM -- scholarships
10,000	University of Texas El Paso, El Paso, TX -- scholarships
8,450	National Merit Scholarship Corporation, Evanston, IL -- Phelps Dodge Merit Scholarships
8,000	Georgia Institute of Technology, Atlanta, GA -- scholarships
7,500	Orme School, Meyer, AZ -- scholarships
6,000	Montana Tech Foundation, Butte, MT -- scholarships
5,000	American Industrial Hygiene Association Foundation, Fairfax, VA -- scholarships
5,000	Hopkinsville Community College, Hopkinsville, KY
5,000	National Merit Scholarship Corporation, Evanston, IL -- Phelps Dodge Achievement Scholarships
5,000	New Mexico Highlands University, Las Vegas, NM -- scholarships
5,000	New Mexico Institute of Mining and Technology, Socorro, NM -- scholarships
5,000	University of New Mexico Robert O. Anderson Graduate School of Management, Albuquerque, NM
3,000	Grand Canyon University, Phoenix, AZ -- scholarships
2,500	University of Arizona American Indian Graduate Scholarship Fund, Tucson, AZ

Health

25,000	St. Joseph's Hospital and Medical Center, Phoenix, AZ
5,000	Phoenix Children's Hospital, Phoenix, AZ

International

10,000	International Centers for Human Development, Tucson, AZ
10,000	International Centers for Human Development, Tucson, AZ

Social Services

55,000	Valley of the Sun United Way, Phoenix, AZ
5,000	Homeward Bound, Phoenix, AZ

PHEONIX FINANCIAL GROUP

Company Contact

Atlanta, GA

Company Description

Former Name: Abrams Industries.
Employees: 300
SIC(s): 6200 Security & Commodity Brokers.

Pheonix Foundation

Giving Contact

Maria Ornelas, Director
Pheonix Foundation
2090 Palm Beach Lakes Blvd., Suite 700
West Palm Beach, FL 33409
Phone: (561)640-5898

Description

Founded: 1957
EIN: 586036725
Organization Type: Corporate Foundation. Supports preselected organizations only.
Giving Locations: FL

Financial Summary

Total Giving: $500,000 (1999 approx); $500,000 (1998); $500,000 (1997)
Assets: $678,926 (1996); $619,836 (1994); $491,145 (1993)
Gifts Received: $115,000 (1994). Note: In 1994, contributions were received from Abrams Fixture Corp. ($71,875) and Abrams Construction ($43,125).

Typical Recipients

Education: Colleges & Universities, Economic Education, Engineering/Technological Education, Education-General, Leadership Training, Minority Education, Science/Mathematics Education, Student Aid
Social Services: Camps, Family Services, Scouts, Shelters/Homelessness, United Funds/United Ways, Volunteer Services, YMCA/YWCA/YMHA/YWHA, Youth Organizations

Corporate Officials

Thomas Abrams: chairman, president, chief executive officer, chief financial officer PRIM CORP EMPL chairman, president, chief executive officer, chief financial officer: Pheonix Financial.

Foundation Officials

A. R. Abrams: director
B. W. Abrams: president
E. M. Abrams: vice president, director
J. A. Abrams: director
Thomas Abrams: founder (see above)
Virlyn B. Moore, Jr.: director B 1911. ED Emory University BHP; University of Georgia LLB. NONPR AFFIL president emeritus: Woodrow Wilson College Law.
Maria Ornelas: director
Joseph H. Rubin: director

Grants Analysis

Disclosure Period: calendar year ending 1996
Total Grants: $127,815
Number of Grants: 82
Average Grant: $1,559
Highest Grant: $29,000
Typical Range: $25 to $25,000

Recent Grants

Note: Grants derived from 1996 Form 990.

Arts & Humanities

1,250 Woodruff Arts Center, Atlanta, GA

Education

29,000 Notre Dame Foundation, Notre Dame, IN
28,600 West Point Fund, West Point, NY -- Bernard W. Abrams 1947 Endowment Fund
1,500 Atlanta Outward Bound Center, Atlanta, GA
1,000 Boy and Girls Clubs, Atlanta, GA -- for West Point Math and Science Camp
1,000 Georiga Council on Economic Education, Atlanta, GA

Health

1,000 St. Jude's Recovery Center

Religion

25,000 Atlanta Jewish Federation, Atlanta, GA
2,000 Atlanta Jewish Federation, Atlanta, GA -- for the William Breman Jewish Heritage Museum
2,000 Temple Kehillat Chaim -- to honor Bill Marcus
1,950 National Conference of Christians and Jews, Atlanta, GA
1,850 American Jewish Committee, Atlanta, GA
1,000 American ORT, Atlanta, GA -- to honor Bill Marcus
1,000 Anti-Defamation League Torch of Liberty, Atlanta, GA
900 National Conference of Christians and Jews, Atlanta, GA -- for Anytown Camp
870 Anti-Defamation Appeal, Atlanta, GA

Social Services

12,100 United Way, Atlanta, GA
5,000 United Way, Atlanta, GA
1,000 Boy Scouts of America Atlanta Council, Atlanta, GA
600 YMCA Butler Street

Philip Morris Companies Inc.

Company Contact

New York, NY

Company Description

Revenue: US$61,751,000,000 (1999)
Profit: US$5,372,000,000
Employees: 144,000
Fortune Rank: 9, per FORTUNE Magazine's list of 500 Largest U.S. Corporations (1999).
FF 9
SIC(s): 2013 Sausages & Other Prepared Meats, 2082 Malt Beverages, 2111 Cigarettes, 6719 Holding Companies Nec.

Operating Locations

Australia: Sungold Dairies Propietary Ltd., Melbourne; Kraft Holdings Ltd., Melbourne; Philip Morris (Australia) Ltd., Melbourne; Kraft Foods Ltd., Milsons Point; Philip Morris Ltd., Moorabbin; Brazil: Embare Industries Alimenticias, Rio de Janeiro; Canada: Kraft Ltd.-Kraft Limitee, Montreal; Denmark: Kraft Foods A/S, Copenhagen; France: Kraft Jacobs Suchard, Velizy-Villacoublay; Germany: Philip Morris GmbH, Minich; Ireland: Dowdall, O'Mahoney and Co. Ltd., Dublin; Italy: Superpila S.p.A.; Japan: Philip Morris K.K., Tokyo; Philippines: Kraft Foods Inc., Manila; Switzerland: Philip Morris EEC, Lausanne; Philip Morris EFTA (Eastern Europe, Middle East and Africa), Lausanne; Fabriques de Tabac Reunis SA, Neuchatel; United Kingdom: Kraft Jacobs Suchard, Cheltenham Glos; Philip Morris/Cash and Carry Ltd., London
Note: Includes all of Kraft General Foods locations.

Nonmonetary Support

Value: $13,000,000 (1995); $16,500,000 (1992); $16,500,000 (1991)
Type: Donated Equipment; Donated Products; In-kind Services
Note: Nonmonetary donations are distributed through local plant committees. Companyestimates nonmonetary support 30% of cash contributions. Kraft Food products are donated.

Corporate Sponsorship

Type: Arts & cultural events; Festivals/fairs; Music & entertainment events; Sports events
Contact: Ina Broeman, Director, Event Marketing
Note: Sponsors the Arizona State Fair, Virginia Slims Tennis Tournament, and Marlboro Motor Racing.

Giving Contact

Karen Brosius, Director, Corporate Contributions
Philip Morris Companies Inc.
120 Park Avenue
New York, NY 10017
Phone: (917)663-3631
Fax: (917)663-5396

Description

Founded: 1919
Organization Type: Corporate Giving Program
Giving Locations: principally near operating locations and to national organizations.
Grant Types: Employee Matching Gifts, General Support, Project.
Note: Employee matching gift ratio: 2 to 1 and 1 to 1, depending on the amount of the gift.

Giving Philosophy

'We think of our support as a socially responsible investment. For as each project, small or large, improves the quality of life, it helps create a more vibrant marketplace.' Philip Morris Companies Inc.

Financial Summary

Total Giving: $68,000,000 (1995 approx); $45,000,000 (1994 approx); $55,500,000 (1993). Note: Contributes through corporate direct giving program only. 1995 Giving includes domestic and international subsidiaries; nonmonetary support.

Typical Recipients

Arts & Humanities: Arts Associations & Councils, Dance, Arts & Humanities-General, Museums/Galleries, Performing Arts, Theater, Visual Arts
Civic & Public Affairs: Civil Rights, Employment/Job Training, Legal Aid, Philanthropic Organizations, Public Policy, Women's Affairs
Education: Arts/Humanities Education, Colleges & Universities, Community & Junior Colleges, Education Associations, Education Funds, Education Reform, Engineering/Technological Education, Literacy, Minority Education
Environment: Environment-General
Social Services: Emergency Relief, Food/Clothing Distribution, Senior Services

Contributions Analysis

Giving Priorities: Education, the arts, health, social services, and civic interests. Company supports U.S.-based nonprofit organizations with an international focus, but the value of that support is not released by the company. Each foreign operating company has its own contributions budget, but may seek help from headquarters if the request can be channeled through a U.S.-based nonprofit. Primary focus areas include the arts, particularly the visual arts; hunger and nutrition; and education, with an emphasis on teacher development and education. Foreign operating companies often modify their priorities to fit the needs of the communities in which they operate. contributed more than $2 million to domestic and international initiatives in environmetaleducation, water conservation, improvement of farming and agrigcultural methods, and solid waste management. The Philip Morris Institute for Public Policy Research, a nonprofit organization that promotes debate of European issues such as employment, regional security and monetary union, sponsored its first conference, 'Trends in World Trade.' The company also funded the first 'Eco-Design Europe' competition in Brussels, supported human service organizations in Europe and Canada, and provide disaster relief aid to refugees in Rwanda, Colombia, and Japan, as well as the U.S.
Arts & Humanities: Arts organizations have traditionally been the most visible in the program. With innovation as a guide, company supports a wide variety of arts organizations with emphasis on visual arts and dance. Gives funding to organizations or programs that present breakthroughideas and explore new ground in artistic expression; tour one or more Philip Morris locations, especially visual or performing arts groups; use art to stimulate learning; expand access to arts among the under-served and disadvantaged populations; and alternative arts organizations that introduce and nurture emerging talent. To a lesser extent, supports museums, theaters, music groups, and key cultural institutions in operating communities.

Civic & Public Affairs: Company promotes community-building, sustenance, and empowerment. Supports programs designed to increase mutual acceptance between diverse groups; organizations that focus on the advancement of women,particularly in the workplace; and programs tailored to the needs of groups new to American society.
Education: Education grants are limited and reserved for special projects only. Company's interest in educating the future work force focuses on teacher education, training, and recruitment. Funds programs that support, enhance, andprepare educators for their new and varied roles in the future. Company prefers programs with new approaches to teacher training, creative teaching, professional and leadership development, or management training for superintendents and principals. Also seeks projects that give special opportunities for minorities in higher education. Further interests include adult literacy projects and the replication of the Gateway program. Considers K-12 education reform that connects families and schools.
Environment: Aware of its dependency on earth's well-being and productivity, company supports environmental concerns that address the sustainability of water, food, and soil resources and the effectivemanagement of solid waste. Interests include development of sustainable agricultural practices and environmentally sound farming techniques; environmental impacts of the food supply; protection of nation's water resources; improvement of quality and quantity of world's food supply; and integrated waste management. Also supports collaboration among corporate, public, conservation, and academic communities in development of public policies and programs.
Health: Company is committed to addressing the plight of the hungry andmalnourished, especially children and families. Grants are made under two initiatives--Food for Thought and Helping the Helpers. Under the Food for Thought initiative, company addresses the important connection between nutritional status of children and their ability to learn. Through the Helping the Helpers initiative, company supports innovative approaches to improving private voluntary programs that feed the hungry. Proposals under this banner include organizations with ancillary services to their food programs, such as job-training or housing assistance; innovative programs; organizations that address the food requirements of a particularpopulation, like the elderly or children; and primary distribution programs or food banks. Does not consider academic research projects in this area. Funds AIDS care, research, and education. Interests include direct care to People With AIDS, especially the nutritional needs of these people; educational outreach and prevention programs; and research through organizations that provide seed grants.
International: Company also contributes to U.S.-based nonprofits with an international focus and to international organizations through foreign subsidiaries. Contact R. Staley for more information.
Social Services: Company supportsprograms and organizations dealing with domestic violence issues.

Application Procedures

Initial Contact: letter or brief proposal; local or regional requests should be forwarded to the nearest Philip Morris operating company
Application Requirements: purpose of organization and activities or project, description of needs to be addressed, plans for implementation and evaluation, management techniques, sources of income, population served, proof of tax-exempt status, copy of recent annual report, current total budget figures, list of board of directors, list of other corporate support, and an audited financial statement; for gift renewals, include a progress report
Deadlines: None; suggests sending proposals far in advance of funding deadlines to be included in giving budget
Review Process: proposals are evaluated by corporate contributions department
Evaluative Criteria: program management and budget; sources of income; distinctive features of population served; community impact and relationship to Philip Morris' corporate goals and priorities, including assisting institutions that enrich the quality of life in communities in which Philip Morris has a special interest; ability to carry out project; applicant's continued commitment to program; and plan to measure progress and outcomes; for social, educational, and environmental proposals, also impact beyond immediate boundaries; new approaches to problem solving; model for other programs; contribute to existing knowledge about an issue
Decision Notification: as necessary throughout the year
Notes: Application procedures are for general grants only. Applications which fall under the company's Focus Giving priorities need additional information. Refer to Philip Morris's Corporate Contributions Policy and Guidelines for further information.

Restrictions

Philip Morris does not support religious organizations or churches; fraternal groups or veterans organizations; political parties, lobbying groups, or candidates for public office; youth-related organizations; or member agencies of united funds.
Company also does not give grants to individuals; to organizations for the underwriting of productions, fund-raising galas, benefits, or dinners; to organizations which discriminate on the basis of race, creed, gender, sexual preference, or national origin; one-time or annual events, such as conferences; or film, video, or television projects.
Philip Morris generally does not support capital campaigns, endowments, athletic or sports-related activities, travel funds, building fund drives, or research for specific diseases or disease-prevention (with the exception of AIDS).
In cases where funds go to nonprofit programs in foreign countries, funding must be through a U.S.-based 501(c)(3) organization.

Additional Information

Philip Morris acquired General Foods Corp. and General Foods Fund in 1985 and Kraft and the Kraft Foundation in 1988. The two companies and their giving programs were merged to form Kraft General Foods in 1989.
In 1992, Philip Morris consolidated and unified all subsidiaries, giving procedures and priorities to each, including Kraft General Foods, which formerly ran a separate giving program. The Philip Morris name has also been added to the Kraft General Foods Foundation, but the foundation is now used sparingly.
National organizations should contact Manager, Corporate Contributions, at headquarters. Operating companies will accept proposals in their headquarters' communities and key operating locations for regional or local organizations. The locations and contacts for Philip Morris operating companies are listed below.
Kraft General Foods, Director, Corporate Contributions, 3 Lakes Drive, Northfield, IL 60093-2758.
Miller Brewing Company, Community Relations Representative, 3939 West Highland Blvd., Milwaukee, WI 53201.
Mission Viejo Company, Manager, Corporate Affairs, 26137 La Paz Road, Mission Viejo, CA 92691.
Philip Morris International, Corporate Affairs, 800 Westchester Ave., Rye Brook, NY 10573-1301.
Philip Morris USA, Manager, Corporate Affairs, 120 Park Ave., New York, NY 10017.
Publications: Corporate Contributions Policy and Guidelines; Corporate Contributions AIDS Giving Guidelines; Hunger and Nutrition Guidelines

Corporate Officials

Geoffrey Cyril Bible: chairman, chief executive officer, director B Canberra, NW Australia 1937. ED Chartered Institute Management Accountants UK; Institute of Chartered Accountants Australia; Waverly College. PRIM CORP EMPL chairman, chief executive officer, director: Philip Morris Companies Inc. ADD CORP EMPL president: Kraft General Foods. NONPR AFFIL director: Lincoln Center Performing Arts; director: New York Stock Exchange Inc.; trustee: American Graduate School International Management.
Louis C. Camilleri: chief financial officer, senior vice president B 1956. PRIM CORP EMPL chief financial officer, senior vice president: Philip Morris Companies Inc.

Giving Program Officials

Richard A. Brown: manager corporate contributions
Tom Collamore: vice president
Stephanie French: vice president

Grants Analysis

Disclosure Period: calendar year ending
Typical Range: $2,500 to $10,000

Recent Grants

Note: Grants derived from 1994 grants list.

Education

70,000 National Board for Professional Teaching Standards, Detroit, MI

Philips Electronics North America Corp.

Company Contact

New York, NY

Company Description

Former Name: North American Philips Corp.
Employees: 30,000
SIC(s): 3315 Steel Wire & Related Products, 3579 Office Machines Nec, 3589 Service Industry Machinery Nec, 3651 Household Audio & Video Equipment.
Parent Company: Philips Electronics NV, Groenewoudseweg 1, Eindhoven, Netherlands

Operating Locations

CA: Philips Electronics North America Corp.; Application Specific Products Group, Sunnyvale; Linear Div., Sunnyvale; Microprocessor & Microcontroller Div., Sunnyvale; Military Products Div., Sunnyvale; Philips Semiconductors, Sunnyvale; Semi-Custom Products Div., Sunnyvale; Standard Products Group, Sunnyvale; Airvision, Valencia; CO: Philips Laser Magnetic Storage, Colorado Springs; CT: Philips Electronics North America Corp.; Philips Automotive Electronics, Cheshire; Philips Medical Systems North America Co., Shelton; Beauty Care Div., Stamford; Coffemaker Div., Stamford; Health Care Div., Stamford; Home Products Div., Stamford; Norelco Consumer Products Co., Stamford; Razor Div., Stamford; DE: Philips Electronics North America Corp.; Philips & Dupont Optical Co., Wilmington; FL: Philips Electronics North America Corp.; Philips Components, Jupiter; Philips Circuit Assemblies, Riviera Beach; GA: Philips Speech Processing,, Atlanta; IA: Optimage Interactive Services Co., Des Moines; IL: Advance Transformer Co., Chicago; Chicago Magnet Wire Corp., Elk Grove Village; Musser Div., La Grange; Edax International, Prairie View; Advance Transformer Co., Rosemont; IN: Philips Electronics North America Corp.; KS: TH Agriculture & Nutrition Co., Kansas City; MA: Philips Electronics North America Corp.; N.A.P. Commercial Electronics Corp., Waltham; ME: Philips Electronics North America Corp.; MI: Philip Display Components, Ann Arbor; MN: Philips Electronics North America Corp.; NJ: Philips Electronics North America Corp.; Philips Electronics Instruments Co., Mahwah; CSD, Inc., Piscataway; Philips Lighting, Somerset;

Radiant Lamp, Somerset; V-L Service Lighting, Somerset; NY: Philips Electronics North America Corp.; Philips Laboratories, Briarcliff Manor; Philips Broadband Networks, Manlius; American Color & Chemical Corp., New York; Philips Credit Corp., New York; Philips Electronics North America Corp., New York; PolyGram Holding, New York; OH: Philips Electronics North America Corp.; RI: Philips Electronics North America Corp.; Philips Components-Discrete Products Division, Slatersville; TN: Philips Consumer Electronics, Knoxville; TX: Philips Electronics North America Corp.; Philips Information Systems, Dallas

Nonmonetary Support

Type: Donated Products

Giving Contact

Philips Electronics North American Corporate Contributions Program
1251 Avenue of the Americas
New York, NY 10020
Phone: (212)536-0500

Description

Founded: 1979
Organization Type: Corporate Giving Program
Giving Locations: operating areas.
Grant Types: Employee Matching Gifts, Scholarship.

Financial Summary

Total Giving: $215,500 (1995); $210,785 (1994); $209,000 (1993). Note: Contributes through corporate direct giving program only.
Assets: $20,202 (1995); $12,652 (1994); $10,437 (1993)
Gifts Received: $223,050 (1995); $213,000 (1994); $212,000 (1993)

Typical Recipients

Arts & Humanities: Museums/Galleries
Civic & Public Affairs: Economic Development
Education: Colleges & Universities, Engineering/Technological Education, Medical Education, Student Aid
Health: Hospitals
Social Services: United Funds/United Ways, Youth Organizations

Application Procedures

Initial Contact: a brief letter of inquiry; application form required
Deadlines: None.
Notes: Company provides scholarships to individuals.

Additional Information

The Philips Electronics North American Foundation has ceased operations. The company now gives directly.

Corporate Officials

Bill Curran: executive vice president, chief financial officerc PRIM CORP EMPL executive vice president, chief financial officer: Philips Electronics North America Corp.
Stephen C. Tumminello: president, chief executive officer, director B Paterson, NJ 1936. ED Stanford University Executive Program; Fairleigh Dickinson University BS (1958). PRIM CORP EMPL president, chief executive officer, director: Philips Electronics North America Corp. CORP AFFIL director: J. M. Huber Corp. NONPR AFFIL trustee: John F. Kennedy Medical Center; director: National Association Manufacturer; trustee: Fairleigh Dickinson University; member: American Institute CPAs.

Giving Program Officials

Robert F. Matthews: president
Warren T. Oates, Jr.: secretary PRIM CORP EMPL secretary, director: Mobil International Petroleum Corp.
Robert N. Smith: vice president

PHILLIPS PETROLEUM CO.

 Number 81 of Top 100 Corporate Givers

Company Contact

Bartlesville, OK
Web: http://www.phillips66.com

Company Description

Revenue: US$13,852,000,000 (1999)
Employees: 17,300 (1999)
Fortune Rank: 126, per FORTUNE Magazine's list of 500 Largest U.S. Corporations (1999). FF 126
SIC(s): 1311 Crude Petroleum & Natural Gas, 1382 Oil & Gas Exploration Services, 2992 Lubricating Oils & Greases.

Operating Locations

Belgium: Phillips Petroleum Chemicals SA, Overijse; Tessenderlo Plant, Tessenderlo; England: Phillips Petroleum Co. Europe-Africa, Woking; Norway: Phillips Petroleum Co. Norway, Tananger; Singapore: Phillips Petroleum Singapore, Singapore

Nonmonetary Support

Value: $117,000 (1993); $300,000 (1986)

Corporate Sponsorship

Type: Sports events
Note: Sponsors educational events ,specifically, Math Counts.

Giving Contact

Clara Bradley, Administrator
Phillips Petroleum Co.
Phillips Building, 16th Floor
Bartlesville, OK 74004
Phone: (918)661-6171
Fax: (918)662-1347
Email: cgbradl@ppco.com

Description

Organization Type: Corporate Giving Program
Giving Locations: headquarters and operating communities.
Grant Types: Award, Employee Matching Gifts, Fellowship, General Support.

Giving Philosophy

'Phillips Petroleum Company's philanthropic activities are consistent with good corporate citizenship. We believe that as companies grow and prosper, they should invest in programs that help build human potential and quality of life.' *Phillips Petroleum Company, Contributions Annual Report*

Financial Summary

Total Giving: $9,200,000 (1999 approx); $9,275,000 (1998); $9,200,000 (1997 approx). Note: Contributes through corporate direct giving program only. 1998 Giving includes domestic subsidiaries ($8,854,000); international subsidiaries ($421,000). 1997 Giving includes corporate direct giving.
Assets: $353,599 (1995); $45,177 (1994); $496,876 (1993)
Gifts Received: $5,850,000 (1995); $5,050,000 (1994); $6,500,000 (1993)

Typical Recipients

Arts & Humanities: Arts Associations & Councils, Arts Centers, Arts Funds, Arts Institutes, Community Arts, Dance, Historic Preservation, Museums/Galleries, Music, Opera, Performing Arts, Public Broadcasting, Theater
Civic & Public Affairs: Business/Free Enterprise, Civil Rights, Economic Development, Economic Policy, Employment/Job Training, Law & Justice, Legal Aid, Municipalities/Towns, Professional & Trade Associations, Public Policy, Safety, Urban & Community Affairs
Education: Agricultural Education, Business Education, Business-School Partnerships, Colleges & Universities, Community & Junior Colleges, Economic Education, Education Associations, Education Funds, Education Reform, Elementary Education (Private), Engineering/Technological Education, Environmental Education, Faculty Development, Education-General, Health & Physical Education, International Exchange, International Studies, Literacy, Medical Education, Minority Education, Public Education (Precollege), Science/Mathematics Education, Secondary Education (Public), Special Education, Student Aid, Vocational & Technical Education
Environment: Environment-General, Research, Resource Conservation, Wildlife Protection
Health: Clinics/Medical Centers, Geriatric Health, Health Organizations, Hospitals, Medical Rehabilitation, Medical Research, Mental Health, Nutrition, Public Health
International: International Development, International Peace & Security Issues, International Relations
Religion: Religious Welfare
Science: Scientific Centers & Institutes, Scientific Organizations, Scientific Research
Social Services: Child Welfare, Community Centers, Community Service Organizations, Crime Prevention, Domestic Violence, Emergency Relief, Family Services, Food/Clothing Distribution, People with Disabilities, Recreation & Athletics, Scouts, Senior Services, Substance Abuse, United Funds/United Ways, YMCA/YWCA/YMHA/YWHA, Youth Organizations

Contributions Analysis

Giving Priorities: Higher education, health, social welfare, and civic interests. Limited support for international organizations. Interests include international economics, foreign relations, and international public policy commissions.
Arts & Humanities: 5% to 10%. Arts associations, including almost one-third to educational television. Other interests include art centers, theater, and historical societies. Programs which introduce K-12 students to the arts and humanities are favored.
Civic & Public Affairs: 5% to 10%. Organizations involoved with energy industry-related issues, tourism in operating communities, and international relations and trade. Special emphasis on theheadquarters community, Bartlesville, OK.
Education: 50% to 55%. Primarily reflects the interests of the company, such as engineering and geoscience. Fellowship and research grants account for about one-tenth of this support and encompass agronomy and graduate education and research in chemistry, engineering, geophysics, geology, combustion, and polymer science. Significant support also goes to colleges and universities for miscellaneous purposes including scholarships; programs in chemistry, science, and technology; and unrestricted operating support. Educational contributions are limited to schools or organizations whose location, facilities, or curricula are beneficial to the communities from whichthe company recruits. Company also sponsors a matching gifts program and a scholarship program for employees' children. Also funds educational film series to promote interest in mathematics and science careers. Phillips is the national sponsor of the U.S. Swimming and Mathcounts.

Environment: 10% to 15%. Wildlife and Audubon conservatories.
Health: About 10%. United funds, community services, substance abuse prevention, and health agencies. Emphasis on Oklahoma and Texas.
Social Services: 5% to 10%. Youth organizations, including child welfare programs, boys' and girls' clubs, Junior Achievement, and boy and girl scouts in locations where company operates.

Application Procedures

Initial Contact: brief summary of proposal, include proof of 501(c)(3) status; if proposal meets criteria and availability of funds, more complete information may be requested
Application Requirements: full proposal should include proof of charitable 501(c)(3) status; clear statement of goals, objectives, activities, performance measures and geographic scope, particularly as it relates to Phillips; names and affiliations of officers, trustees, or board of directors, including whether anyone is an employee, retiree, or board member of Phillips or its subsidiaries; number and total compensation of paid employees; number of volunteers; sources of current income; list of other corporations, foundations, or government agencies from which funding is currently requested; list of organizations and foundations contributing to organization during previous 12 months; brief description of project for which funding is requested and how long funds will be needed; description of what grant is expected to accomplish, how program is administered, and how it will be evaluated; and program budget, geographical scope, and special funding costs, if any
Deadlines: unsolicited requests: accepted from June 1 to August 31 for funding in the next fiscal year, requests received outside of this period may not be answered

Restrictions

Company generally does not support individuals; sectarian or denominational/religious organizations or institutions, other than universities and colleges already receiving aid through taxation; specific disease-oriented organizations; national organizations where support can be made locally; political candidates or organizations; veterans or service clubs, except for community-wide programs; trips, tours, tickets, or banquets; endowment or bricks and mortar.

Corporate Officials

W. Wayne Allen: chairman, chief executive officer, director B 1936. ED Oklahoma State University BS (1959); Oklahoma State University MME (1969). PRIM CORP EMPL chairman, chief executive officer, director: Phillips Petroleum Co.
Charles L. Bowerman: executive vice president, director B Crawfordsville, IN 1939. ED Wabash College AB (1961). PRIM CORP EMPL executive vice president, director: Phillips Petroleum Co. CLUB AFFIL Masons Club.
James J. Mulva: president, chief operating officer, director B Oshkosh, WI 1946. ED University of Texas BBA (1968); University of Texas MBA (1969). PRIM CORP EMPL president, chief operating officer, director: Phillips Petroleum Co. CORP AFFIL chairman: Phillips Gas Co. NONPR AFFIL member: American Petroleum Institute; member: National Association Manufacturer.

Grants Analysis

Disclosure Period: calendar year ending 1996
Total Grants: $8,300,000*
Number of Grants: 700
Typical Range: $1,000 to $10,000
***Note:** Giving excludes 900 matching gifts. Grants analysis provided by company.

Recent Grants

Note: Grants derived from 1996 Form 990.

Arts & Humanities

75,000	Oklahoma Educational Television Authority, Oklahoma City, OK
68,334	Philbrook Museum of Art, Tulsa, OK
25,000	OK Mozart, Bartlesville, OK
25,000	Tulsa Philharmonic, Tulsa, OK

Civic & Public Affairs

100,000	Ethics Resources Center, Washington, DC
79,000	Tamu Development Foundation, College Station, TX
25,000	American Institute of Chemical Engineers, New York, NY
15,000	Committee for Economic Development, New York, NY
15,000	National Center for State Courts, Williamsburg, VA

Education

201,000	Oklahoma State University, Stillwater, OK
158,750	Bartlesville Independent School District 30, Bartlesville, OK
100,000	Georgia Institute of Technology Foundation, Atlanta, GA
100,000	University of Oklahoma, Norman, OK
94,700	University of Texas Austin, Austin, TX
72,000	Texas Tech University Department of Family Medicine, Amarillo, TX
66,000	University of Tulsa Foundation, Tulsa, OK
43,800	Texas Tech University, Lubbock, TX
42,000	Colorado School of Mines Foundation, Golden, CO
40,000	Bartlesville Wesleyan College, Bartlesville, OK
40,000	National Environmental Education and Training Foundation, Washington, DC
40,000	Water Education for Teachers, Bozeman, MT
30,000	Center for Environmental Education, Stillwater, OK
25,000	Frank Phillips College, Borger, TX
25,000	Mathcounts Foundation, Alexandria, VA
24,000	Iowa State University, Ames, IA
23,000	University of Arkansas Foundation, Fayetteville, AR

Environment

50,000	Nature Conservancy, Tulsa, OK
45,000	National Fish and Wildlife Foundation, Washington, DC

Health

125,000	Laird Center, Marshfield Clinic, Marshfield, WI
25,000	Green Country Free Clinic, Bartlesville, OK
25,000	Washington County Eldercare, Bartlesville, OK
16,000	Family Care Services, Bartlesville, OK

Religion

100,000	Salvation Army, Oklahoma City, OK

Science

25,000	George Miksch Sutton Avian Research Center, Bartlesville, OK
19,330	George Sutton Avian Research Center, Bartlesville, OK

Social Services

300,000	National Forensic League, Ripon, WI
60,000	Boys and Girls Clubs of America, Atlanta, GA
47,000	Alcohol and Drug Center, Bartlesville, OK
37,500	Boys and Girls Club, Bartlesville, OK
34,452	Brazoria County United Way, Angleton, TX
30,000	Washington County Senior Citizens, Dewey, OK
28,435	United Way Texas Gulf Coast, Houston, TX
26,273	Bartlesville Community Center, Bartlesville, OK
25,000	Texas County Family YMCA, Guymon, OK
22,000	Hutchinson County United Way, Borger, TX
22,000	US Swimming, Colorado Springs, CO
21,000	Women and Children in Crisis, Bartlesville, OK
20,000	Girl Scouts of America Bluestem Council, Bartlesville, OK -- for Christmas Food Baskets
18,000	United Way Texas Gulf Coast, Houston, TX
17,500	Boy Scouts of America Cherokee Area Council, Bartlesville, OK

Phoenix Home Life Mutual Insurance Co.

Company Contact

Hartford, CT
Web: http://www.phl.com

Company Description

Revenue: US$3,193,700,000 (1999)
Employees: 3,800
Fortune Rank: 479, per FORTUNE Magazine's list of 500 Largest U.S. Corporations (1999).
FF 479
SIC(s): 6311 Life Insurance.

Nonmonetary Support

Type: Cause-related Marketing & Promotion

Corporate Sponsorship

Type: Sports events
Contact: Tina Muzzey, Assistant Vice President Public Affairs
Note: Sponsors Special Olympics.

Phoenix Foundation

Giving Contact

Kathleen Riordan, Giving Program Coordinator
Phoenix Foundation
1 American Row
Hartford, CT 06115
Phone: (860)403-5000
Fax: (860)403-5755

Description

Organization Type: Corporate Foundation
Giving Locations: CT: Enfield, Hartford; MA: Greenfield; NY: Albany
Grant Types: Employee Matching Gifts, General Support.
Note: Employee matching gift ratio: 1 to 1.

Giving Philosophy

'Phoenix Home Life is committed to the effort to improve society through the thoughtful application of financial and human resources.. Phoenix Home Life's contributions program focuses on two specific priority areas: youth and community economic development in our headquarters communities of Hartford and Enfield, CT; Greenfield, MA; and Albany, NY.'

Financial Summary

Total Giving: $1,100,000 (1999 approx); $1,100,000 (1998 approx); $850,000 (1995 approx). Note: Contributes through corporate direct giving program and foundation. Giving includes matching gifts. 1998 Giving includes corporate direct giving ($300,000); foundation ($800,000).

Typical Recipients
Civic & Public Affairs: Housing
Education: Education-General
Health: Health-General
Social Services: United Funds/United Ways

Application Procedures
Initial Contact: written request
Application Requirements: description of agency and its objectives; amount requested and how it will be used; organization budget for upcoming year; description of other support received, including support received from the United Way or any government entities; account of staff size, including qualifications; statement of organization's board's composition; copy of most recent annual report; demonstration that organization serves one of the giving areas; description of how organization measures progress towards its goals; and proof of tax-exempt status
Deadlines: before September 1
Decision Notification: requests are considered during the fourth quarter of each calendar year; company will notify agencies of outcome during the following year's first quarter

Additional Information
Publications: Guidelines

Corporate Officials
Robert William Fiondella: chairman, president, chief executive officer B Bristol, CT 1942. ED Providence College AB (1964); University of Connecticut School of Law JD (1968). PRIM CORP EMPL chairman, president, chief executive officer: Phoenix Home Life Mutual Insurance Co. ADD CORP EMPL director, president: OML International Insurance Ltd.; president: PM Holdings Inc.; president: Phl Variable Insurance Co.; president, director, chairman: Phoenix America Life Insurance Co.; director, president: Phoenix Investment Partners Ltd. CORP AFFIL director: Phoenix Investment Council Ltd.; director: PXRE Corp.; director: Phoenix Equity Planning Corp.; director: Phoenix Charter Oak Trust; director: Phoenix Duff & Phelps Corp.; director: WS Griffith & Co. Inc.; director: Life Insurance Council New York; director: Barnes Group Inc.; director: Advest Group; chairman, director: America Phoenix Corp. NONPR AFFIL director: Special Olympics World Summer Games; member advisor board: WKND Greater Hartford Initiative; director: Special Olympics International; member steering committee: Mayor Peter's Hartford Americorps; director: Saint Francis Hospital Medical Center; chairman east regional fundraising: Little League Center; member: Connecticut Children's Center Campaign Our Children; director, chairman: Greater Hartford Chamber of Commerce; member, director: Connecticut Business & Industry Association; cochairman: Community Cancer Center Building Fund, Johnson Memorial; member: Connecticut Bar Association.

Giving Program Officials
Jane Driscoll: vice president PRIM CORP EMPL director public affairs: Phoenix Home Life Mutual Insurance Co.

Foundation Officials
Jane Driscoll: vice president (see above)
Kathleen Riordan: giving coord

PHYSICIANS MUTUAL INSURANCE CO.

Company Contact
Omaha, NE
Web: http://www.pmic.com/

Company Description
Assets: US$897,000,000
Employees: 1,200
SIC(s): 6321 Accident & Health Insurance.

Nonmonetary Support
Type: Donated Equipment; In-kind Services; Loaned Executives; Workplace Solicitation

Corporate Sponsorship
Type: Arts & cultural events; Festivals/fairs; Music & entertainment events; Pledge-a-thon; Sports events
Contact: Jerome Coon, Treasurer

Physicians Mutual Insurance Co. Foundation

Giving Contact
Jerome Coon, Secretary/Treasurer
PMIC Foundation
2600 Dodge St.
Omaha, NE 68131
Phone: (402)633-1000
Fax: (402)633-1096

Description
EIN: 363424068
Organization Type: Corporate Foundation
Giving Locations: NE
Grant Types: Capital, Emergency, Endowment, General Support, Operating Expenses, Scholarship.

Financial Summary
Total Giving: $260,000 (fiscal year ending November 30, 2000 approx); $245,000 (fiscal 1999 approx); $230,120 (fiscal 1998). Note: Contributes through corporate direct giving program and foundation.
Giving Analysis: Giving for fiscal 1997 includes: foundation ($189,652); foundation grants to United Way ($51,000); fiscal 1998: foundation ($176,320); foundation grants to United Way ($53,800)
Assets: $1,000,000 (fiscal 2000 approx); $1,100,000 (fiscal 1999 approx); $1,129,972 (fiscal 1998)

Typical Recipients
Arts & Humanities: Arts Associations & Councils, Arts Funds, Ballet, History & Archaeology, Libraries, Museums/Galleries, Music, Opera, Public Broadcasting, Theater
Civic & Public Affairs: African American Affairs, Chambers of Commerce, Community Foundations, Ethnic Organizations, Hispanic Affairs, Housing, Native American Affairs, Parades/Festivals, Philanthropic Organizations, Public Policy, Safety, Urban & Community Affairs, Women's Affairs, Zoos/Aquariums
Education: Agricultural Education, Business Education, Business-School Partnerships, Colleges & Universities, Community & Junior Colleges, Continuing Education, Economic Education, Education Funds, Elementary Education (Private), Elementary Education (Public), Faculty Development, Education-General, Literacy, Minority Education, Private Education (Precollege), Religious Education, Secondary Education (Private), Special Education
Environment: Environment-General
Health: Alzheimers Disease, Arthritis, Cancer, Children's Health/Hospitals, Diabetes, Emergency/Ambulance Services, Health-General, Health Policy/Cost Containment, Health Organizations, Heart, Hospices, Hospitals, Long-Term Care, Medical Research, Multiple Sclerosis, Nursing Services, Public Health, Respiratory, Single-Disease Health Associations
International: International Relations, International Relief Efforts
Religion: Churches, Dioceses, Jewish Causes, Religious Organizations, Religious Welfare
Social Services: At-Risk Youth, Big Brother/Big Sister, Camps, Child Welfare, Community Service Organizations, Counseling, Delinquency & Criminal Rehabilitation, Emergency Relief, Family Services, Food/Clothing Distribution, People with Disabilities, Recreation & Athletics, Refugee Assistance, Scouts, Senior Services, Shelters/Homelessness, Social Services-General, Substance Abuse, United Funds/United Ways, Volunteer Services, YMCA/YWCA/YMHA/YWHA, Youth Organizations

Contributions Analysis
Giving Priorities: Supports public and private education; medical facilities and projects; welfare of the elderly and financially oppressed and united funds; civic organizations and community groups; and local fine arts organizations.
Arts & Humanities: 2%. Supports public broadcasting, fine arts and historical preservation.
Civic & Public Affairs: 26%. Supports community foundations and civic policy.
Education: 30%. Supports colleges, universities and higher education.
Health: 4%. Supports hospitals single-disease organizations, and healthcare associations.
Religion: 7%. Supports religious organizations.
Social Services: 31%. Supports alcohol and drug prevention, family services, boys and girls clubs, and United Way.
Note: Total contributions made in 1998.

Application Procedures
Initial Contact: a brief letter of inquiry
Application Requirements: a description of organization, amount requested, purpose of funds sought, and proof of tax-exempt status
Deadlines: None.

Restrictions
Does not support individuals or political or lobbying groups.

Corporate Officials
Bill R. Benson: executive vice president, chief financial officer PRIM CORP EMPL executive vice president, chief financial officer: Physicians Mutual Insurance Co.
Arnold W. Lempka, MD: chairman, director B Tecumseh, NE 1927. ED Creighton University MD (1941). PRIM CORP EMPL chairman, director: Physicians Mutual Insurance Co. CORP AFFIL chairman: Physicians Life Insurance Co. NONPR AFFIL fellowshiplow: American College Surgeons; member: American Medical Association.
Robert A. Reed: president, chief executive officer B 1939. ED Creighton University BA (1961). PRIM CORP EMPL president, chief executive officer: Physicians Mutual Insurance Co.

Foundation Officials
Bill R. Benson: vice president (see above)
Jerome J. Coon: treasurer PRIM CORP EMPL treasurer: Physicians Mutual Insurance Co.
Stewart Crosbie: secretary
John B. Davis, MD: director B Omaha, NE 1922. ED Yale University (1941-1943); Yale University (1946-1947); University of Nebraska MD (1951). PRIM NONPR EMPL associate professor surgery: University Northeast Medical College. CORP AFFIL co-owner, president: Miracle Hill Golf & Tennis Center; director: Physicians Mutual Insurance Co.
William R. Hamsa, MD: director, assistant secretary PRIM CORP EMPL partner: Hamsa, O'Neil & Ferlic. CORP AFFIL director: Physicians Mutual Insurance Co.
Arnold W. Lempka, MD: director (see above)
Harry W. McFadden, Jr. MD: assistant treasurer, director CORP AFFIL director: Physicians Mutual Insurance Co.
Robert A. Reed: president, director (see above)

John D. Woodbury, MD: director CORP AFFIL director: Physicians Mutual Insurance Canada.

Grants Analysis

Disclosure Period: fiscal year ending November 30, 1998
Total Grants: $176,320*
Number of Grants: 55
Average Grant: $3,206
Highest Grant: $53,100
Typical Range: $100 to $25,000
***Note:** Giving excludes United Way.

Recent Grants

Note: Grants derived from fiscal 1998 Form 990.

Arts & Humanities

25,000	Heritage - Joslyn Foundation, Omaha, NE -- 6
2,000	Omaha Symphony Association, Omaha, NE -- 6
1,500	Trans-Mississippi Exposition Historical Association, Omaha, NE -- 5
1,000	Omaha Chamber Foundation, Omaha, NE
300	Nebraska Public TV, Lincoln, NE

Civic & Public Affairs

5,000	Nebraska Community Foundation, Lincoln, NE
2,000	River City Roundup and Rodeo, Omaha, NE -- 5
300	Urban League of Nebraska, Lincoln, NE -- 5
225	Madd, Irving, TX -- 5
200	Fraternal Order of Police, Lincoln, NE -- 5

Education

53,100	Creighton University, Omaha, NE -- 2
20,000	AK-SAR-BEN Foundation, Omaha, NE -- 5
5,250	Duchesne Academy, Omaha, NE -- 2
4,500	Roncalli Catholic High School, Omaha, NE -- 2
3,000	Direct Marketing Education Foundation, New York, NY -- 1
2,500	University of Nebraska Great Plains Studies, Lincoln, NE -- 1
2,000	Nebraska Independent College Foundation, Omaha, NE -- 1
1,000	University of Nebraska Foundation, Lincoln, NE -- 1
800	Junior Achievement, Omaha, NE -- 5
500	Skutt Catholic High School, Omaha, NE -- 2
500	United Negro College Fund, Omaha, NE -- 2
500	UNO Lady Mav Club, Omaha, NE -- 1
300	Metropolitan Community College Foundation, Omaha, NE -- 1
300	Teacher Recognition Day, Omaha, NE -- 1
200	Omaha Literacy Council, Omaha, NE -- 4

Environment

500	Fontenelle Forest Association, Omaha, NE -- 5

Health

2,500	United Cerebral Palsy, New York, NY -- 3
1,550	American Cancer Society, Omaha, NE -- 3
1,000	Alzheimers Association, Omaha, NE -- 3
1,000	Juvenile Diabetes Foundation, Omaha, NE -- 3
500	Bergan Mercy Hospital, Omaha, NE -- 3
250	Easter Seals Nebraska, Omaha, NE -- 5
250	Make-A-Wish Foundation of Nebraska Inc., Omaha, NE -- 4
250	Muscular Dystrophy Assn, Omaha, NE -- 3

Religion

5,500	The Salvation Army, Omaha, NE -- 4
1,250	Lutheran Family Services of Nebraska, Omaha, NE -- 4

Social Services

53,800	United Way, Omaha, NE -- 4
5,500	YMCA Downtown, Omaha, NE -- 5
5,000	Boys Town, Boys Town, NE -- 2
5,000	Franciscan Adult Day Center, Omaha, NE -- 4
5,000	Mid-America Council, BSA, Omaha, NE -- 5
2,000	American Red Cross, Omaha, NE -- 3
2,000	Family Service, Omaha, NE -- 4
1,000	Camp Fire Boys and Girls, Omaha, NE -- 5
1,000	Nebraska Council to Prevent Alcohol & Drug Abuse, Lincoln, NE -- 3
1,000	Y W C A Capital Campaign, Omaha, NE -- 5
500	Big Brothers Big Sisters of the Midlands, Omaha, NE -- 5
500	Child Saving Institute, Omaha, NE -- 3
400	The Food Bank, Lincoln, NE -- 4
300	College World Series, Omaha, NE -- 5

PIEPER POWER ELECTRIC CO.

Company Contact

Milwaukee, WI

Company Description

Operating Revenue: US$65,000,000
Employees: 600
SIC(s): 1731 Electrical Work.

Pieper Power Electric Foundation

Giving Contact

Barbara Jones, Executive Secretary
Pieper Power Electric Foundation
5070 North 35th Street
Milwaukee, WI 53209-5302
Phone: (414)462-7700
Fax: (414)462-3589

Description

EIN: 396124770
Organization Type: Corporate Foundation
Giving Locations: WI: Milwaukee
Grant Types: Conference/Seminar, Employee Matching Gifts, General Support, Scholarship.
Note: Employee matching gift ratio: 2 to 1.

Giving Philosophy

'Pieper Power Electric Foundation will pass back to the community, as allowed by each Company policy, prosperity received through its Companies. It will support any operating needs of programs that are available to the entire population. It is our intention to positively respond to each request from a valid organization to encourage those providing the services their quest to make this a better neighborhood, community and world. In this learning process, what the giver experiences in the development of the community may ultimately be more valuable than the services rendered.' Foundation Guidelines, 1997

Financial Summary

Total Giving: $225,000 (1999 approx); $296,587 (1998); $299,878 (1997). Note: Contributes through foundation only.

Giving Analysis: Giving for 1998 includes: foundation ($277,758); foundation grants to United Way ($17,300); foundation matching gifts ($1,560)
Assets: $54,554 (1998); $27,018 (1997); $141,080 (1996)
Gifts Received: $378,190 (1998); $414,026 (1997); $238,729 (1996). Note: In 1995, contributions were received from Pieper Electric, Inc.

Typical Recipients

Arts & Humanities: Arts Associations & Councils, Arts Centers, Ballet, Historic Preservation, History & Archaeology, Museums/Galleries, Music, Opera, Performing Arts, Theater
Civic & Public Affairs: Economic Development, Civic & Public Affairs-General, Hispanic Affairs, Housing, Nonprofit Management, Parades/Festivals, Professional & Trade Associations, Urban & Community Affairs, Zoos/Aquariums
Education: Arts/Humanities Education, Business Education, Business-School Partnerships, Colleges & Universities, Engineering/Technological Education, Education-General, Private Education (Precollege), Public Education (Precollege), Vocational & Technical Education
Environment: Wildlife Protection
Health: Children's Health/Hospitals, Clinics/Medical Centers, Multiple Sclerosis, Research/Studies Institutes, Speech & Hearing
Religion: Religious Welfare
Social Services: Child Welfare, Community Centers, Community Service Organizations, Domestic Violence, Family Planning, Family Services, Food/Clothing Distribution, Recreation & Athletics, Scouts, United Funds/United Ways, Youth Organizations

Contributions Analysis

Arts & Humanities: About 15%. Arts museums, the ballet, orchestra, and theater.
Civic & Public Affairs: 20% to 25%. Foundations and community support programs.
Education: About 20%. Supports specific schools, school districts, and pre-collegiate programs.
Health: 5% to 10%. Major grant to the Ronald McDonald House.
Religion: Less than 5%.
Science: About 5%. Supports wildlife centers.
Social Services: About 30%. Primarily supports Boy Scouts of America, Boys and Girls Clubs, and the United Way

Application Procedures

Initial Contact: Send a written request.
Application Requirements: Include any of the following depending on size of grant: a list of the board of directors; a copy of an annual budget, expenses and a resonable definition of the mission of the organization; examination of the percentage of funds used for promotion, as opposed to the actual services from the mission of the organization; a copy of long-range plans and goals, and accomplished goals.
Deadlines: August 1 for the following year.
Review Process: Foundation reviews requests in the fall.
Decision Notification: By December 31.

Restrictions

Does not generally support capital programs or religious organizations.

Additional Information

As a policy, the foundation allocates 10% of pre-tax profits to charitable organizations.
Publications: Guidelines

Corporate Officials

Norman R. Doll: president, chief executive officer, director PRIM CORP EMPL president: Pieper Power Electric Co.

Ronnie T. Hinson: president PRIM CORP EMPL president: Pieper Power Electric Co. CORP AFFIL president: Metropower Inc.
Thomas Ohlgart: secretary PRIM CORP EMPL secretary: Pieper Electric Inc.
Richard R. Pieper: chairman, chief executive officer, director B 1936. ED University of Miami. PRIM CORP EMPL chairman, chief executive officer, director: Pieper Electric Inc.

Foundation Officials

Mary Ellen Doll: vice president
Thomas Ohlgart: treasurer (see above)
Richard R. Pieper: secretary (see above)
Suzanne Pieper: vice president

Grants Analysis

Disclosure Period: calendar year ending 1998
Total Grants: $277,758*
Number of Grants: 390 (approx)
Average Grant: $712 (approx)
Highest Grant: $11,500
Typical Range: $20 to $12,000
***Note:** Giving excludes United Way; matching gifts.

Recent Grants

Note: Grants derived from 1997 Form 990.

Arts & Humanities

10,000	Museum of Arts and Sciences, Macon, GA
5,000	Pabst Theater, Milwaukee, WI
3,500	Friends of East Troy Railroad, East Troy, WI
2,600	Milwaukee Art Museum, Milwaukee, WI
2,500	Waukesha Symphony Orchestra, Waukesha, WI
1,600	First Stage, Milwaukee, WI
1,500	Albany Museum of Art, Albany, NY
1,500	Woodruff Arts Center, Atlanta, GA
1,200	Milwaukee Ballet, Milwaukee, WI

Civic & Public Affairs

18,000	Lightspan Partnership
10,000	Electrical Contracting Foundation, Bethesda, MD
5,500	Next Door Foundation, Milwaukee, WI
5,000	Neighborhood House, Milwaukee, WI
2,000	Wisconsin NGA Host Committee, WI
1,500	Phoebe Foundation, Albany, GA

Education

10,000	South Georgia Technical Institute, Americus, GA
7,300	Junior Achievement
5,000	PAVE, San Diego, CA
5,000	Urban Day School, Milwaukee, WI
3,000	Milwaukee Trade and Technical High, Milwaukee, WI
2,770	Harambee Community School
2,000	Albany State Fund, Albany, NY
2,000	Glendale River Hills School District

Environment

10,000	Northwoods Wildlife Center

Health

10,000	Ronald McDonald House
2,500	St. Luke's Medical Center, Phoenix, AZ
1,500	Georgia Speech Center, GA
1,200	National Multiple Sclerosis Society, New York, NY

Religion

4,000	Milwaukee Catholic Home, Milwaukee, WI
1,500	Salvation Army

Social Services

11,000	Boy Scouts of America
8,300	United Way, Milwaukee, WI
5,000	Rosalie Manor
4,500	Boys and Girls Club
2,750	Boy Scouts of America
2,750	Boy Scouts of America
2,500	Boy Scouts of America
2,500	Drucker Foundation, New York, NY
2,000	Boys and Girls Club
2,000	Boys and Girls Clubs
2,000	Boys and Girls Clubs, Albany, NY
1,500	Boy Scouts of America
1,500	Boy Scouts of America, Atlanta, GA
1,500	United Way
1,500	United Way
1,500	United Way, Columbus, NE
1,500	United Way Southwest Georgia, Albany, GA
1,200	Hunger Task Force, Milwaukee, WI
1,200	Planned Parenthood of Wisconsin, Milwaukee, WI
1,100	Gathering

PILLSBURY CO.

Company Contact

200 S. Sixth St.
Minneapolis, MN 55402-1404
Phone: (612)330-4966
Fax: (612)330-5200
Web: http://www.pillsbury.com

Company Description

Employees: 13,400
SIC(s): 2024 Ice Cream & Frozen Desserts, 2033 Canned Fruits & Vegetables, 2037 Frozen Fruits & Vegetables, 2045 Prepared Flour Mixes & Doughs.
Parent Company: Diageo Plc, 8 Henrietta Place, London, United Kingdom

Operating Locations

AZ: Pillsbury Co., Tempe; CA: Pillsbury Co., Los Angeles, Tulare; FL: Pillsbury Co., Medley; Burger King Corp., Miami; IA: Roush Products Co., Cedar Rapids; ID: Idaho Potato Operations, Shelley; Pillsbury Co., Shelley; IL: Pillsbury Co., Belvidere, Geneva; IN: Pillsbury Co., New Albany; MD: Pillsbury Co., Federalsburg; ME: Pillsbury Co., Portland; MN: Pillsbury Co., Chanhassen, Eden Prairie; Grand Metropolitan Foodservice, Minneapolis; Green Giant International, Minneapolis; Haagen-Dazs Co., Minneapolis; Pillsbury Bakeries & Foodservice, Minneapolis; Pillsbury Co., Minneapolis; Pillsbury Co., Minneapolis; Pillsbury Grain Export, Minneapolis; MO: Pillsbury Co., Hannibal, Joplin; NJ: Haagen-Dazs, Teaneck; Pillsbury Co., Vineland; NY: Grand Metropolitan Community Services-USA, New York; OH: Pillsbury Co., Martel, Wellston; Totino's/Wellston, Wellston; PA: Pillsbury Co., Allentown; TN: Pillsbury Co., Murfreesboro; WI: Pillsbury Co., Poplar

Nonmonetary Support

Value: $10,000,000 (1991); $6,000,000 (1990); $4,700,000 (1989)
Type: Cause-related Marketing & Promotion; Donated Equipment; Donated Products; In-kind Services
Note: About $10,000,000 annually in nonmonetary support. Principally gives food products to the Second Harvest Network of food banks.

Corporate Sponsorship

Range: less than $50,000
Note: Sponsors events for disabled children.

Pillsbury Co. Foundation

Giving Contact

Rebecca L. Erdahl, Vice President, Community Relations
Pillsbury Co.
200 South, 6th Street
Minneapolis, MN 55402-1464
Phone: (612)330-7230
Fax: (612)330-4923
Web: http://www.pillsbury.com/about/foundation.asp

Description

Founded: 1957
EIN: 416021373
Organization Type: Corporate Foundation
Giving Locations: headquarters and operating communities.
Grant Types: General Support, Project, Scholarship.

Giving Philosophy

'The Pillsbury Company has a history of leadership in the communities where we operate, with an interest in strengthening and developing healthy communities, vibrant economies and a well-educated workforce. In support of this community commitment, Pillsbury philanthropic and volunteerism efforts are targeted toward the healthy development of youth, with an emphasis on helping today's young people--and tomorrow's workforce--achieve self-sufficiency.'
'Pillsbury's charitable giving and active employee and retiree volunteer programs have helped Pillsbury achieve the broad scope of its mission: To be known by its shareholders, trade customers, consumers, employees and communities as the Best Food Company in the world. Pillsbury's charitable contributions are more than 2% of pretax profits. Over half of all employees participate in the company's volunteer programs.'
New Initiatives: 'Kids and Caring Adults' is a new emphasis based on research and observations of well-regarded experts in the field of youth development. The goal is to establish benchmarks that will allow the company to accelerate the very best of these initiatives to the benefit of young people.

Financial Summary

Total Giving: $4,303,321 (fiscal year ending September 30, 1998); $4,527,238 (fiscal 1997); $4,503,748 (fiscal 1996). Note: Contributes through foundation only.
Giving Analysis: Giving for fiscal 1996 includes: foundation grants to United Way ($906,604); fiscal 1997: foundation grants to United Way ($1,090,873); fiscal 1998: foundation grants to United Way ($1,013,853)
Assets: $3,560,594 (fiscal 1998); $3,909,601 (fiscal 1997); $4,279,273 (fiscal 1996)
Gifts Received: $3,722,798 (fiscal 1998); $3,852,382 (fiscal 1997); $3,818,510 (fiscal 1996). Note: Foundation receives funds from Pillsbury Co.

Typical Recipients

Arts & Humanities: Arts Institutes, Community Arts, Museums/Galleries, Music, Public Broadcasting, Theater
Civic & Public Affairs: African American Affairs, Asian American Affairs, Botanical Gardens/Parks, Chambers of Commerce, Civil Rights, Community Foundations, Economic Development, Employment/Job Training, Hispanic Affairs, Housing, Municipalities/Towns, Native American Affairs, Public Policy, Safety, Urban & Community Affairs, Women's Affairs
Education: Afterschool/Enrichment Programs, Business Education, Colleges & Universities, Community & Junior Colleges, Economic Education, Education Reform, Elementary Education (Private), Environmental Education, Education-General, Literacy, Minority Education, Preschool Education, Private

Education (Precollege), Public Education (Precollege), Student Aid, Vocational & Technical Education
Environment: Environment-General
Health: Children's Health/Hospitals, Clinics/Medical Centers, Hospitals, Medical Rehabilitation, Nutrition, Prenatal Health Issues
International: International Development
Religion: Churches, Religion-General, Religious Welfare
Science: Science Museums
Social Services: At-Risk Youth, Big Brother/Big Sister, Child Welfare, Community Centers, Community Service Organizations, Crime Prevention, Day Care, Delinquency & Criminal Rehabilitation, Emergency Relief, Family Planning, Family Services, Food/Clothing Distribution, Recreation & Athletics, Scouts, United Funds/United Ways, Volunteer Services, YMCA/YWCA/YMHA/YWHA, Youth Organizations, Youth Organizations

Contributions Analysis

Giving Priorities: Disadvantaged youth.
Civic & Public Affairs: 11%. Organizations and programs that offer educational and employment skills young people need to achieve self-sufficiency. Typically funds school and community organization education programs, academic support, career awareness/work readiness, life skills, and employment programs.
Education: 10%. Funds public and private education.
Health: 1%. Supports health initiatives targeting young people.
Religion: 5%. Funds churches and religious welfare.
Social Services: 73%. Supports organizations that build and sustain ongoing relationships with caring adults and at-risk young people. Typically funds mentoring programs.
Note: Total contributions in fiscal 1998.

Application Procedures

Initial Contact: Send a brief letter requesting an application.
Application Requirements: Full proposal should include a completed application, including mission of organization; description of program; what foundation focus area it supports; specific goals and objectives of program; what measures determine the program's success; how many individuals are served; how many people are in organization; demographic information, and any specific cultural orientation of group; organizational and program budgets; list of other funders with dollar amounts; program cost per participant; percentage of budget used for administrative purposes; history of financial contributions from Pillsbury; percentage of program budget that makes up organization budget; qualifications of staff who will implement program; number of staff and active volunteers; any volunteer opportunities for company employees; copy of 501(c)(3) tax-exempt letter; list of board directors and their affiliations; and a recent audited financial statement.
Deadlines: For Skills for Education and Employment grants, January 15; and for Youth Development grants, March 15.
Review Process: An initial review is conducted by staff to determine whether proposal matches contributions guidelines; eligible requests are either forwarded to the contributions committee at the headquarters or to local committees for consideration and funding decisions.
Evaluative Criteria: Priority is given to programs that provide services that directly impact the focus areas and programs with Pillsbury employee or retiree volunteer involvement; programs that demonstrate performance outcomes related to self-sufficiency; and programs with volunteer opportunities for employees.

Restrictions

Does not support organizations without 501(c)(3) status; religious organizations for sectarian purposes; scholarships, except through company scholarship program; capital or endowment campaigns; sponsorship or fund-raising requests; propaganda or lobbying efforts; research of all kinds; or individuals.

Additional Information

Grand Metropolitan subsidiaries include Burger King, Haagen-Dazs, Pearle Inc., and Heublein, which separately provide giving to nonprofit organizations.
Company reports it is a member of the greater Minneapolis Chamber of Commerce Keystone Club, contributing more than 2% of its pretax profits.
Company reports that the foundation is being downsized and localized.
Publications: Guidelines; Application

Corporate Officials

Luis J. de Ocejo: senior vice president human resourceseo PRIM CORP EMPL senior vice president human resources: Pillsbury Co.
Paul S. Walsh: chairman, president, chief executive officer PRIM CORP EMPL chairman, president, chief executive officer: Pillsbury Co. CORP AFFIL director: Ceridian Corp.; director: FDX Corp.

Giving Program Officials

Rebecca Erdahl: executive director PRIM CORP EMPL vice president community relations: Pillsbury Co.

Foundation Officials

Luis J. de Ocejo: president, director (see above)
Rebecca Erdahl: executive director (see above)
Lionell Nowell: secretary-treasurer
Paul S. Walsh: director (see above)

Grants Analysis

Disclosure Period: fiscal year ending September 30, 1997
Total Grants: $3,289,468*
Number of Grants: 341
Average Grant: $9,647
Highest Grant: $246,263
Typical Range: $500 to $30,000
***Note:** Giving excludes United Way.

Recent Grants

Note: Grants derived from fiscal 1998 Form 990.

Civic & Public Affairs

90,000	Project for Pride in Living, Inc., Minneapolis, MN
60,000	Metropolitan Economic Development Association, Minneapolis, MN.
45,000	Minneapolis American Indian Center, Minneapolis, MN
30,000	Harriet Tubman Center, Minneapolis, MN
30,000	Neighborhood Involvement Program, Minneapolis, MN
30,000	Twin Cities One to One, Minneapolis, MN
25,000	Geneva Community Chest, Geneva, IL
20,000	NAACP/Minneapolis Branch, Minneapolis, MN

Education

50,000	The Institute for Education and Advocacy, Minneapolis, MN
50,000	Minneapolis Public Schools, Minneapolis, MN
45,000	Minneapolis Public Schools, Minneapolis, MN
45,000	Summit Academy, OIC, Minneapolis, MN
35,000	Dunwoody Institute, Minneapolis, MN
35,000	University of St. Thomas, St. Paul, MN
30,000	Athletes Committed to Educating Students, Minneapolis, MN
25,000	Junior Achievement of The Upper Midwest, Inc., Minneapolis, MN

Health

30,000	YouthCARE, Minneapolis, MN

Religion

40,000	Catholic Charities, Minneapolis, MN
35,000	Plymouth Christian Youth Center, Minneapolis, MN
26,000	Greater Minneapolis Council of Churches, Minneapolis, MN
25,000	Greater Minneapolis Council of Churches, Minneapolis, MN
20,000	Greater Minneapolis Council of Churches, Minneapolis, MN

Social Services

550,000	United Way of Minneapolis, Minneapolis, MN
246,263	Big Brothers/Big Sisters of America, Philadelphia, PA
239,980	Boys & Girls Clubs of America, Atlanta, GA
150,000	Big Brothers/Big Sisters of America, Philadelphia, PA
100,000	Boys & Girls Club of Minneapolis, Minneapolis, MN
79,799	United Way of Rutherford County, Murfreesboro, TN
70,000	The City, Inc., Minneapolis, MN
65,000	Big Brothers/Big Sisters of Greater Minneapolis, Minneapolis, MN
50,000	Kinship of Greater Minneapolis, Minneapolis, MN
50,000	Second Harvest National Food Bank Network, Chicago, IL
45,000	Girl Scout Council of Greater Minneapolis, Minneapolis, MN
42,919	United Way of the Mark Twain Area, Hannibal, MO
40,000	Boy Scouts of America, Viking Council, Minneapolis, MN
40,000	Sabathani Community Center, Minneapolis, MN
39,062	United Way of Boone County, Belvidere, IL
36,198	United Way of Jackson County, Jackson, OH
35,530	United Way of Joplin, Joplin, MO
35,000	Loring Nicollet-Bethlehem Community Centers, Inc., Minneapolis, MN
35,000	Minneapolis Youth Diversion Program, Minneapolis, MN
33,749	United Way of Minneapolis, Minneapolis, MN
30,000	Child Relief & You Inc., Mercerville, NJ
30,000	Pillsbury Neighborhood Services, Inc., Minneapolis, MN
25,000	Children's Home Society of Minnesota, St. Paul, MN
25,000	Elaine M. Stately Peacemaker Center, Minneapolis, MN
25,000	Phyllis Wheatley Community Center, Minneapolis, MN
25,000	YMCA of Metro Minneapolis, Minneapolis, MN
25,000	Youth Trust, Minneapolis, MN
21,269	United Way of Grayson County, Inc., Sherman, TX

PIONEER GROUP

Company Contact

Boston, MA

Company Description

Revenue: US$198,700,000
Employees: 2,120
SIC(s): 6289 Security & Commodity Services Nec, 6719 Holding Companies Nec.

Nonmonetary Support

Type: Donated Equipment

Giving Contact

Janine Hall, Administrative Corporate Services
60 State St., 5th Fl.
Boston, MA 02109
Phone: (617)742-7825
Fax: (617)422-4207

Description

Organization Type: Corporate Giving Program
Giving Locations: headquarters and operating communities.
Grant Types: Employee Matching Gifts, General Support.

Financial Summary

Total Giving: $250,000 (1999 approx); $240,000 (1998 approx); $224,578 (1997)

Typical Recipients

Arts & Humanities: Arts Institutes, Ballet, Community Arts, Arts & Humanities-General, Museums/Galleries, Music, Opera, Performing Arts
Civic & Public Affairs: Economic Policy, Civic & Public Affairs-General
Education: Education-General
Environment: Environment-General
Health: Clinics/Medical Centers, Health-General
Science: Science Museums
Social Services: Shelters/Homelessness, Social Services-General, United Funds/United Ways

Application Procedures

Initial Contact: Send a brief letter of inquiry.
Application Requirements: a description of organization, amount requested, and purpose of funds sought.

Restrictions

Does not support religious organizations for sectarian purposes or political or lobbying groups.

Additional Information

Company reports 60% of contributions support health and human services, 22% support the arts, 10% support civic affairs, and 8% support education.

Corporate Officials

John Francis Cogan, Jr.: president, chief executive officer, director B Boston, MA 1926. ED Harvard College AB (1949); Harvard University Law School JD (1952). PRIM CORP EMPL president, chief executive officer, director: Pioneer Group. CORP AFFIL chairman: Teberebie Goldfields Ltd.; president, director: Pioneer Mutual Funds; president, director: Pioneering Management Corp.; director: ICI Mutual Insurance Co.; director: Pioneer Capital Corp.; chairman: Hale & Dorr; trustee: Boston Medical Center; director: Fiduciary Counseling Inc. NONPR AFFIL director: Walker Home Children; director: Wendell P Clark Memorial Association; member: National Association Securities Dealers; member: Massachusetts Bar Association; chairman, trustee: Museum Fine Arts; member: International Bar Association; chairman board governors: Investment Co. Institute; trustee: Boston Symphony Orchestra; member: Boston Estate Planning & Business Counsel; member: Boston Probate & Estate Planning Forum; member: American Bar Association; member: Boston Bar Association.
William H. Keough: senior vice president, chief financial officer B Framingham, MA 1937. ED Boston College (1959); Northeastern University (1967). PRIM CORP EMPL senior vice president, chief financial officer: Pioneer Group. NONPR AFFIL national director: Financial Executives Institute; member tax & acct committee: Investment Co. Institute.

Grants Analysis

Disclosure Period: calendar year ending
Typical Range: $100 to $999

Recent Grants

Note: Grants derived from 1998 Form 990.

Arts & Humanities
Boston Ballet, Boston, MA
Boston Symphony, Boston, MA
Children's Museum, Boston, MA
Museum of Fine Arts, Boston, MA

Civic & Public Affairs
Committee for Fair Taxation, Boston, MA
Massachusetts Tax Foundation, Boston, MA

Health
Boston Medical Center, Boston, MA

Science
Museum of Science, Boston, MA

Social Services
Pine Street Inn, Boston, MA
United Way Massachusetts Bay, Boston, MA

Pioneer Hi-bred International, Inc.

Company Contact

800 Capital Sq.
400 Locust St.
Des Moines, IA 50306
Phone: (515)248-4800
Fax: (515)248-4999
Web: http://www.pioneer.com

Company Description

Employees: 5,025
SIC(s): 0111 Wheat, 0115 Corn, 0116 Soybeans, 0119 Cash Grains Nec.
Parent Company: E.I. du Pont de Nemours & Co., Wilmington, DE, United States

Operating Locations

Argentina: Pioneer Argentina SA, Buenos Aires; Semillas Meriel, Buenos Aires; Australia: Pioneer Hi-Bred Australia Pty. Ltd., Toowoomba; Austria: Pioneer Overseas GmbH, Parndorf; Pioneer Saaten AG, Parndorf; Brazil: Empreendimentos Agricola Pioneer Ltda., Santa Cruz do Sul; Pioneer Agricultura Ltda., Santa Cruz do Sul; Pioneer Sementes Ltda., Santa Cruz do Sul; Canada: Pioneer Hi-Bred Limited, Chatham; Chile: Semillas Pioneer Chile Ltda., Santiago; Egypt: MISR Pioneer Seed Co. SAE, Cairo; France: Service Genetiques SARL, Auxonne; GIE Pioneer France, Oucques; Pioneer France Mais SA, Toulouse; Germany: Pioneer Saaten GmbH, Buxtehude; Indonesia: PT Pioneer Hibrida Indonesia, Surabaya; India: Pioneer Biogene, Pvt. Ltd., Janakpur; Italy: Pioneer Hi-Bred Italia SpA, Parma; Japan: Pioneer Hi-Bred Japan Co. Ltd., Tokyo; Mexico: Hibridos Pioneer de Mexico SA de CV, Guadalajara; Investigaciones Pioneer S de RL de CV, Guadalajara; Spain: Semillas Pioneer SA, Seville; Thailand: Pioneer Hi-Bred (Thailand) Co. Ltd., Bangkok; Pioneer Overseas Corp., Sara Buri; Turkey: Pioneer Tohumculuk AS, Istanbul; Venezuela: Hibreven Hibridos Venezolanos SA, Valencia

Nonmonetary Support

Value: $2,870 (1995); $85,000 (1993); $85,000 (1990)
Type: Donated Products; In-kind Services
Note: Nonmonetary support is provided by the company.

Corporate Sponsorship

Type: Arts & cultural events; Music & entertainment events; Sports events

Giving Contact

Eric P. Fogg, Program Manager & Community Investment
Pioneer Hi-Bred International, Inc.
800 Capital Square, Suite 800
400 Locust St.
Des Moines, IA 50309-2340
Phone: (515)334-6813
Fax: (515)248-4842
Email: foggep@phibred.com

Description

Organization Type: Corporate Giving Program
Giving Locations: headquarters and operating communities.
Grant Types: Award, Capital, Employee Matching Gifts, Matching.
Note: Employee matching gift ratio: 2 to 1.

Giving Philosophy

'Pioneer Hi-Breed International, Inc., is committed to helping improve the quality of life in the communities where its customers and employees live and work through philanthropic investments. Community Investment is the philanthropic resource base of Pioneer. The specific objectives are to invest the Company's resources in programs that add economic or social value to its communities and Company stakeholders, to expand the Company's reputation as a good corporate citizen, and to initiate collaborative funding programs that address rural economic and social issues.' *Pioneer Hi-Bred International, Inc., Community Investment Program, 1997*

Financial Summary

Total Giving: $5,000,000 (1998 approx); $7,200,000 (1997 approx); $6,892,827 (1996). Note: Contributes through corporate direct giving program only. 1997 Giving includes domestic and international subsidiaries. 1995 Giving includes nonmonetary support.

Typical Recipients

Arts & Humanities: Community Arts, Dance, Opera, Performing Arts
Civic & Public Affairs: Economic Development, Employment/Job Training, Rural Affairs
Education: Agricultural Education, Colleges & Universities, Science/Mathematics Education
International: International Organizations
Social Services: United Funds/United Ways

Contributions Analysis

Giving Priorities: Rural initiatives, conservation, higher education, health, social welfare, the performing arts, historic preservation, and international agriculture. Company began an internationl giving program in 1991. Supports programs designed to increase international agricultural development and farmer health programs.
Civic & Public Affairs: Supports programs designed to facilitate and enhance rural community development and economics.
Education: Supports programs designed to strengthen leadership within agriculture, or research that will benefit agriculture. Supports agricultural resources management programs, particularly at colleges from which company recruits employees.
Environment: Funds projects and programs designed to preserve land and farm communities.
Health: Supports programs, such as job training, that provideopportunities for young people to develop values and skills needed to become self-reliant and productive. Supports rural health care programs and services that deal with preventive health care and farm safety. Interested in health-related programs designed to provide adequate care at reduced cost.
International: Provides support to programs designed to increase international agricultural development and health programs for farmers.
Note: Also has an employee volunteer grant program.

Application Procedures

Initial Contact: written proposal of 3 pages or less, including an executive summary of the program, sent to local Pioneer office
Application Requirements: history of organization; statement of current projects, including population served; purpose of grant and amount requested; funding sources, an audited financial statement, copy of budget; proof of tax-exempt status; list of board of directors, and trustees, including board financial and volunteer support; history of Pioneer employee involvement in organization; means of evaluating program's effectiveness; contact name, address and telephone number of representative to whom correspondence should be addressed
Deadlines: September 30, December 30, March 30, and June 30 for next quarterly meeting
Evaluative Criteria: program based on community need; cooperation with other community-based programs; ability to meet goals with positive results; effective leadership; broad-based support; programs that involve customers, growers, employees and community leaders; projects that are within the company's focus areas; and pertinence of request to Pioneer's core business
Decision Notification: requests reviewed at quarterly meetings in October, January, April, and July
Notes: Company does not respond to verbal requests or to requests that are not addressed to a specific person.

Restrictions

Company does not support non tax-exempt organizations; emergency funding; athletic activities; individuals; health associations that do not provide direct services; political organizations; elected officials; marketing or advertising; organizations that conflict with company's interest or values; or religious organizations that promote a particular doctrine.

Corporate Officials

John D. James: senior vice president, director research B 1945. PRIM CORP EMPL senior vice president: Pioneer Hi-Bred International, Inc.
Charles S. Johnson: president, chief executive officer, chairman B 1938. ED Iowa State University BS (1965). PRIM CORP EMPL president, chief executive officer, chairman: Pioneer Hi-Bred International, Inc. CORP AFFIL director: Gaylord Container Corp.
Doctor Richard Lynn McConnell: senior vice president, director research B Sterling, CO 1950. ED Colorado State University BS (1972); Colorado State University MS (1974); University of Nebraska PhD (1978). PRIM CORP EMPL senior vice president, director research: Pioneer Hi-Bred International, Inc.

Giving Program Officials

Steven Daugherty: PRIM CORP EMPL director government affairs: Pioneer Hi-Bred International, Inc.
Eric P. Fogg: manager community investments
W. Thomas Phillips: director community investments

Foundation Officials

Charles S. Johnson: president, chief executive officer (see above)

Grants Analysis

Disclosure Period: calendar year ending 1996
Total Grants: $6,892,827
Typical Range: $2,500 to $10,000

PIONEER NATURAL RESOURCES

Company Contact

Amarillo, TX

Company Description

Former Name: Mesa Inc.
Employees: 321
SIC(s): 1311 Crude Petroleum & Natural Gas.

Operating Locations

Principal operating facilities are located in southwest Kansas and the western panhandle of Texas.

Nonmonetary Support

Type: Donated Equipment; Loaned Employees; Loaned Executives

Corporate Sponsorship

Type: Arts & cultural events
Note: Supports Christmas projects.

Giving Contact

Corporate Contributions
Pioneer Natural Resource
1400 Williams Square West
5205 North O'Conner
Irving, TX 75039
Phone: (972)969-4024
Fax: (972)444-4328

Description

Organization Type: Corporate Giving Program
Giving Locations: headquarters area only.
Grant Types: General Support.

Financial Summary

Total Giving: $275,000 (1996 approx); $300,000 (1995 approx); $300,000 (1994 approx). Note: Contributes through corporate direct giving program only.

Typical Recipients

Arts & Humanities: Arts & Humanities-General
Civic & Public Affairs: Civic & Public Affairs-General
Education: Education-General
Health: Health-General
Social Services: Social Services-General

Application Procedures

Initial Contact: send letter of inquiry
Application Requirements: a description of organization, amount requested, purpose of funds sought, recently audited financial statement, and proof of tax-exempt status

Giving Program Officials

Mitch Contreras: PRIM CORP EMPL director corporate contributions: Mesa Inc.

PITNEY BOWES INC.

Company Contact

Stamford, CT

Company Description

Revenue: US$4,547,500,000 (1999)
Employees: 28,625
Fortune Rank: 354, per FORTUNE Magazine's list of 500 Largest U.S. Corporations (1999).
FF 354
SIC(s): 2677 Envelopes, 2679 Converted Paper Products Nec, 2761 Manifold Business Forms, 3579 Office Machines Nec.

Nonmonetary Support

Type: Cause-related Marketing & Promotion; In-kind Services; Loaned Employees; Workplace Solicitation
Note: Company also donates assets to the United Way.

Corporate Sponsorship

Value: $10,000
Type: Arts & cultural events; Festivals/fairs; Music & entertainment events

Giving Contact

Polly O'Brien, Director, Community Affairs
Pitney Bowes Inc., World Headquarters
1 Elmcroft Rd.
Stamford, CT 06926-0700
Phone: (203)351-6669
Fax: (203)351-6303
Email: obrienpo@pb.com

Description

Organization Type: Corporate Giving Program
Giving Locations: headquarters and operating communities.
Grant Types: Capital, Emergency, Employee Matching Gifts, General Support, Loan, Matching, Multiyear/Continuing Support, Project.

Financial Summary

Total Giving: $3,700,000 (1999 approx); $3,502,000 (1998 approx); $3,400,000 (1997 approx). Note: Contributes through corporate direct giving program only. 1998 Giving includes corporate direct giving. 1996 Giving includes corporate direct giving ($3,036,243); domestic subsidiaries ($181,827).
Assets: $6,000,000 (1990)

Typical Recipients

Arts & Humanities: Arts Centers, Community Arts
Civic & Public Affairs: Civil Rights, Employment/Job Training, Housing, Urban & Community Affairs, Women's Affairs
Education: Colleges & Universities, Education Funds, Elementary Education (Private), Literacy, Minority Education, Science/Mathematics Education
Health: Hospitals
Social Services: Community Service Organizations, Day Care, Shelters/Homelessness, United Funds/United Ways

Contributions Analysis

Giving Priorities: Hospitals, community service, united funds, and education.
Arts & Humanities: Less than 5%. Supports various arts activities near corporate operating locations.
Civic & Public Affairs: About 15%. Supports urban affairs, civil rights, and communitydevelopment.
Education: About 20%. Interests include Head Start and similar programs; school-wide and grade-wide tutorial programs; parenting skills and guidance programs; and before- and after-school programs that provide activities and enrichment. Other interests include high school mathematics and science programs.
Health: About 45%. Supports United Way and human service organizations involved in developing affordable housing via building or renovation, as well as those that provide temporary shelter.

Application Procedures

Initial Contact: proposal to headquarters
Application Requirements: brief history of organization, including its objectives; amount requested, amount requested from other corporations, and total amount required; purpose of funds sought, and whether the request is for capital or operating support; complete financial information, including organization's budget, balance sheet, and operating statement with sources of revenue, expenses, and fund balance; description of program and proposed outcome; proof of tax-exempt status; list of board of directors
Deadlines: None.
Notes: Corporate contributions are administered at headquarters. Each branch, operating unit, and subsidiary has smaller budget (primarily for United Way and local community projects).

Restrictions

Does not purchase tickets or advertising space or support conference attendance, dinners or other special events, auctions, sporting events, single-disease health associations, travel expenses, fraternal organizations, individuals, political or lobbying groups, or religious organizations for sectarian purposes.

Pitney Bowes Inc. does not make product donations.

Corporate Officials

Marc C. Breslawsky: president, chief operating officer, general counsel, chairman B New York, NY 1942. ED New York University BA (1963). PRIM CORP EMPL president, chief operating officer: Pitney Bowes Inc. ADD CORP EMPL director: Pitney Bowes Credit Corp. CORP AFFIL director: CR Bard Inc.; director: United Illuminating Co.

Michael J. Critelli: vice president, secretary, general counsel, chairman B Newark, NJ 1948. ED University of Wisconsin BA (1970); Harvard University JD (1974). PRIM CORP EMPL vice president, secretary, general counsel, chairman: Pitney Bowes Inc. ADD CORP EMPL president: Pitney Bowes Credit Corp. CORP AFFIL director: Eaton Corp.

Giving Program Officials

Polly O'Brien: director community affairs PRIM CORP EMPL director, corporate affairs: Pitney Bowes Inc.

Grants Analysis

Disclosure Period: calendar year ending
Typical Range: $2,500 to $5,000

PITTWAY CORP.

Company Contact

Chicago, IL
Web: http://www.pittway.com

Company Description

Employees: 6,800
SIC(s): 2721 Periodicals, 3669 Communications Equipment Nec, 5085 Industrial Supplies, 6531 Real Estate Agents & Managers.

Pittway Corp. Charitable Foundation

Giving Contact

Mr. King Harris, Vice President & Director
Pittway Corp. Charitable Foundation
200 S. Wacker Dr., Suite 700
Chicago, IL 60606
Phone: (312)831-1070
Fax: (312)831-0808

Description

EIN: 366149938
Organization Type: Corporate Foundation
Giving Locations: emphasis on communities near company's manufacturing sites.
Grant Types: Capital, Employee Matching Gifts, General Support, Multiyear/Continuing Support.

Financial Summary

Total Giving: $1,600,000 (fiscal year ending February 28, 1998 approx); $1,218,857 (fiscal 1997); $1,224,801 (fiscal 1996). Note: Contributes through corporate direct giving program and foundation. 1997 Giving includes foundation ($1,153,857); United Way ($65,000).
Assets: $10,509,005 (fiscal 1997); $6,530,994 (fiscal 1996); $5,983,791 (fiscal 1993)
Gifts Received: $4,562,932 (fiscal 1997); $1,200,000 (fiscal 1996); $1,000,000 (fiscal 1993)

Typical Recipients

Arts & Humanities: Arts Associations & Councils, Arts Centers, Arts Festivals, Arts Institutes, Historic Preservation, History & Archaeology, Museums/Galleries, Music, Opera, Performing Arts, Public Broadcasting, Theater, Visual Arts
Civic & Public Affairs: Civil Rights, Community Foundations, Economic Development, Civic & Public Affairs-General, Housing, Law & Justice, Philanthropic Organizations, Professional & Trade Associations, Public Policy, Safety, Urban & Community Affairs, Women's Affairs, Zoos/Aquariums
Education: Arts/Humanities Education, Business Education, Colleges & Universities, Economic Education, Education Associations, Education Funds, Elementary Education (Private), Engineering/Technological Education, International Studies, Literacy, Medical Education, Minority Education, Private Education (Precollege), Science/Mathematics Education, Secondary Education (Private), Social Sciences Education, Student Aid
Health: Alzheimers Disease, Cancer, Clinics/Medical Centers, Health Funds, Hospices, Hospitals, Medical Rehabilitation, Medical Research, Mental Health, Nursing Services, Prenatal Health Issues, Single-Disease Health Associations
International: International Affairs, International Relations
Religion: Jewish Causes, Religious Welfare
Science: Observatories & Planetariums, Scientific Labs, Scientific Organizations
Social Services: At-Risk Youth, Child Welfare, Community Service Organizations, Day Care, Delinquency & Criminal Rehabilitation, Family Planning, Family Services, Food/Clothing Distribution, People with Disabilities, Substance Abuse, United Funds/United Ways, YMCA/YWCA/YMHA/YWHA, Youth Organizations

Contributions Analysis

Giving Priorities: Health, social welfare, education, and civic interests.
Arts & Humanities: 5% to 10%. Emphasis on public broadcasting, museums, history,and arts institutes.
Civic & Public Affairs: 10% to 15%. Majority of funding supports economic development. Other interests include business and free enterprise and urban and community programs.
Education: 20% to 25%. Supports colleges and universities, early education, literacy programs, and education funds.
Health: 10% to 15%. Funds support hospitals, various single-disease health organizations, mental health, and other facilities.
Religion: 5% to 10%. Religious causes.
Social Services: 35%. Focuses on programs working to break the intergenerational transmission of poverty. Family planning and family services receive much of this funding, as well as united funds. Child welfare, food and clothing distribution, and youth organizations are also supported.

Application Procedures

Initial Contact: brief letter or proposal
Application Requirements: a description of organization, amount requested, purpose of funds sought, recently audited financial statement, and proof of tax-exempt status
Deadlines: December 31 for payment in following year

Restrictions

The foundation does not support individuals or organizations located outside the United States.

Corporate Officials

Leo A. Guthart: vice chairman, director B New York, NY 1937. ED Harvard University AB (1958); Harvard University MBA (1960); Harvard University (1966). PRIM CORP EMPL vice chairman, director: Pittway Corp. ADD CORP EMPL chairman, chief executive officer: Pittway Security Group. CORP AFFIL director: Aptagroup; chairman: Cylink Corp. NONPR AFFIL director: Long Island Research Institute; director: Long Island Venture Fund; honorary member: Beta Gamma Sigma; director: Acorn Fund; Alarm Industries Research Education Foundation. CLUB AFFIL Harvard Club; Racquet Club.

Irving Brooks Harris: chairman executive committee, director B Saint Paul, MN 1910. ED Yale University AB (1931). PRIM CORP EMPL chairman executive committee, director: Pittway Corp. CORP AFFIL president: William Harris & Co.; chairman: William Harris Investors; director: Teva Pharmaceuticals Industries Ltd.; chairman: Acorn Fund; chairman: Harris Realty. NONPR AFFIL president, co-founder, chairman emeritus: Ounce Prevention Fund; trustee: University Chicago; member: National Academy Sciences; trustee: National Center Clinical Infant Programs; chairman advisory board: Illinois Department Children & Family Services Training Institute; special counselor select committee children: Illinois General Assembly; chairman advisory board: Illinois Competitive Access Reimbursement Equity Program; chairman emeritus: Family Focus Inc.; vice chairman: Governments Task Force Future Mental Health Illinois; president emeritus: Erickson Institute; trustee: Chicago Education Television Association; honorary chairman: Chicago Pediatric Society; member: American Orthopsychiatric Association; honorary fellow: American Academy Pediatrics; trustee: American Jewish Committee; fellow: American Academy of Arts & Sciences. CLUB AFFIL Standard Club; Mid-Day Club; Saddle & Cycle Club; Commercial Club.

King William Harris: president, chief executive officer B Minneapolis, MN 1943. ED Harvard University BA (1965); Harvard University MBA (1969). PRIM CORP EMPL president, chief executive officer: Pittway Corp.

Richard Neison Harris: chairman, director B Saint Paul, MN 1915. ED Yale University AB (1936). PRIM CORP EMPL chairman, director: Pittway Corp. CORP AFFIL chairman, director: Standard Shares.

Foundation Officials

E. David Coolidge, III: vice president B 1943. ED Williams College (1965); Harvard University (1967). PRIM CORP EMPL chief executive officer: William Blair & Co. CORP AFFIL director: Pittway Corp.

Paul Richard Gauvreau: treasurer B Chicago, IL 1939. ED Loyola University BSc (1961); University of Chicago MBA (1976). PRIM CORP EMPL vice president finance, treasurer: Pittway Corp. ADD CORP EMPL treasurer, director: Industries Publishing Co.; treasurer, director: BRK Electronics; treasurer: Curtin & Pease Inc.; treasurer: Domestic International Sales Corp.; vice president,treasurer,director: Family Gard Inc.; vice president,treasurer, director: Penton Publishing Co.; vice president, treasurer: Pittway Corp. Canada Ltd.; president, chief executive officer, director: Pittway Real Estate Inc.; president, director: Pittway Leasing Co.; treasurer, director: Power Publishing &CPN.

Irving Brooks Harris: chairman, director (see above)

King William Harris: vice president, director (see above)

Richard Neison Harris: president, director (see above)

William W. Harris: director B 1940. ED Wesleyan University BA (1961); Massachusetts Institute of Technology Ph.D (1977). CORP AFFIL director: Cylinck Corp.; director: Pittway Corp. NONPR AFFIL director: Kids Fund; treasurer, founder: KIDSPAC; founder, president: Children's Research and Education Institute Inc.

William Zermuehlen: secretary PRIM CORP EMPL assistant secretary: Pittway Corp. CORP AFFIL assistant secretary: Fire Lite Alarms Inc.; secretary: Pittway International Ltd.

Grants Analysis

Disclosure Period: fiscal year ending February 28, 1996
Total Grants: $1,224,801
Number of Grants: 347
Average Grant: $3,530
Highest Grant: $275,000
Typical Range: $500 to $10,000

Recent Grants

Note: Grants derived from fiscal 1997 Form 990.

Arts & Humanities

38,000	Museum of Contemporary Art, Chicago, IL
10,000	National Public Radio, Washington, DC
8,444	WBEZ Chicagoland Public Radio, Chicago, IL
5,196	Art Institute, Chicago, IL
5,000	Chicago Children's Museum, Chicago, IL
5,000	Facing History and Ourselves National Foundation, Brookline, MA
5,000	Paramount Arts Center, Aurora, IL
4,608	Metropolitan Museum of Art, New York, NY
3,470	WTTW/Channel 11, Chicago, IL
3,170	WVIZ TV, Cleveland, OH

Civic & Public Affairs

84,000	Erikson Institute, Chicago, IL
15,000	City Year Chicago, Chicago, IL
10,000	Chicago '96 Democratic Convention, Chicago, IL
8,000	Marklund Charities, Saint Charles, IL
5,000	Brookings Institution, Washington, DC
5,000	People for the American Way, Washington, DC
5,000	Stony Brook Foundation, Stony Brook, NY

Education

117,100	University of Chicago, Chicago, IL
32,000	University of Illinois, Urbana, IL
17,000	Hofstra University, Hempstead, NY
11,000	University of Maryland, College Park, MD
11,000	Worcester Polytechnical Fire Engineering Program, Worcester, MA
8,500	University of New Haven, New Haven, CT
7,500	Business Press Education Foundation, Cleveland, OH
7,000	Illinois Math and Science Academy, Aurora, IL
5,000	Scholarship and Guidance Association, Chicago, IL
5,000	State University of New York Engineering 500, Geneseo, NY
4,000	Columbia College, Chicago, IL
3,000	Ohio Foundation of Independent Colleges, Columbus, OH

Health

75,000	Ounce School-Based Medical Clinic, Chicago, IL
25,000	National Center for Clinical Infant Programs, Washington, DC
13,400	Rehabilitation Institute Foundation, Chicago, IL
10,000	Chicago Health Center, Chicago, IL
6,220	Leukemia Society of America, Cleveland, OH
5,000	Hope Lodge American Cancer Society, Cleveland, OH
5,000	North Shore Hospital, Long Island, NY

Religion

55,900	Family Focus, Chicago, IL

Social Services

200,000	Ounce of Prevention Fund, Chicago, IL
52,500	United Way Services, Chicago, IL
25,000	Planned Parenthood, Chicago, IL
15,000	Alan Guttmacher Institute, New York, NY
12,400	Chicago United, Chicago, IL
8,000	Court Appointed Special Advocates, Kane County, IL
7,100	Chicago Lighthouse for the Blind, Chicago, IL
6,000	Glen School for Boys, Saint Charles, IL
6,000	Greater Chicago Food Depository, Chicago, IL
5,000	Juvenile Protection Association, Chicago, IL
5,000	United Way Long Island, Melville, NY
3,000	Tri-City Family Services, Saint Charles, IL
3,000	United Way Aurora, Cleveland, OH

PLAYBOY ENTERPRISES INC.

Company Contact

Chicago, IL

Company Description

Revenue: US$247,249,000
Employees: 643
SIC(s): 2721 Periodicals, 4841 Cable & Other Pay Television Services, 5961 Catalog & Mail-Order Houses, 6794 Patent Owners & Lessors.

Nonmonetary Support

Value: $450,000 (1998); $1,000,000 (1997); $783,000 (1996)
Type: Donated Products
Note: Nonmonetary support is in the form of printing and design services and public service ads in Playboy magazine.

Corporate Sponsorship

Value: $5,000
Type: Pledge-a-thon; Other
Note: Supports AIDS-related fund raisers, literacy organizations, and social change issues.

Playboy Foundation

Giving Contact

Cleo F. Wilson, Executive Director
Playboy Foundation
680 N. Lake Shore Dr.
Chicago, IL 60611
Phone: (312)751-8000
Fax: (312)266-8506
Email: giving@playboy.com
Web: http://www.playboy.com/corporate/foundation/index.html

Description

Organization Type: Corporate Foundation
Giving Locations: nationally.
Grant Types: Employee Matching Gifts, General Support, Matching, Multiyear/Continuing Support.
Note: Employee matching gift ratio: 1 to 1.

Giving Philosophy

'The Playboy Foundation seeks to foster social change by confining it grants and other support to project of national impact and scope involved in fostering open communication about, and research into, human sexuality, reproductive health and rights; protecting and fostering civil rights and civil liberties in the United States for all people, including women, people affected and impacted by HIV/AIDS, gays and lesbians, racial minorities, the poor and the disadvantaged; and eliminating censorship and protecting freed of expression.' www.playboy.com

Financial Summary

Total Giving: $900,000 (1999); $815,235 (1998); $1,422,571 (1997). Note: Contributes through corporate direct giving program and foundation.
Giving Analysis: Giving for 1998 includes: nonmonetary support ($450,000); foundation ($300,000); corporate direct giving ($65,235)

Typical Recipients

Arts & Humanities: Community Arts, Ethnic & Folk Arts, Public Broadcasting
Civic & Public Affairs: Civil Rights, First Amendment Issues, Law & Justice, Legal Aid, Philanthropic Organizations, Public Policy, Women's Affairs
Education: Journalism/Media Education
Health: Medical Research, Single-Disease Health Associations
Social Services: Community Service Organizations, Delinquency & Criminal Rehabilitation, Domestic Violence, Family Planning, People with Disabilities, Refugee Assistance, Senior Services, Shelters/Homelessness, Youth Organizations

Contributions Analysis

Giving Priorities: Reproductive rights, civil rights, and eliminating censorship.

Application Procedures

Initial Contact: written request for funding
Application Requirements: a description of organization, including a summary of its background, purpose, objectives, and experience in the area for which funds are sought; amount requested; purpose of funds sought; audited financial statements; proof of tax-exempt status; itemized project budget and proposed funding sources; names and qualifications of people involved with the project; organizational expenses and income for previous, current, and coming fiscal year; list of board members, their titles, outside affiliations, and phone numbers
Deadlines: None.
Review Process: board of directors generally meets in the fall to consider proposals

Restrictions

Does not support individuals; religious organizations for sectarian purposes; scholarships or fellowships; endowments; social services, including residential care, clinics, treatment or recreation programs; national health, welfare, educational or cultural organizations, or their state or local affiliates; government agencies or projects; or capital campaigns.

Additional Information

Publications: Foundation Annual Report; Newsletter

Corporate Officials

Dennis S. Bookshester: chairman, chief executive officerdirector, international publishing PRIM CORP EMPL chairman, chief executive officer: Cutanix Corp.s. CORP AFFIL director: Playboy Enterprises Inc.; director: Sundance Homes Inc.; director: Modagrafics Inc.; director: Evans Inc.; director: Fruit of Loom; director: Arthur Treacher's Inc.
David I. Chemerow: executive vice president, chief financial officer B Washington, DC 1951. ED Dartmouth College BS (1973); Dartmouth College Amos Tuck Graduate School of Business Administration MBA (1975). PRIM CORP EMPL executive vice president, chief financial officer: GT Interactive Software Corp. CORP AFFIL director: Dunhams Athleisure Corp.; director: Playboy Enterprises Inc.; director: American Specialty Retailing Group.
Christie Ann Hefner: chairman, chief executive officer B Chicago, IL 1952. ED Brandeis University BA (1974). PRIM CORP EMPL chairman, chief executive officer: Playboy Enterprises, Inc. ADD CORP EMPL

director: Playboy Clubs International Inc.; chairman: Playboy.com. CORP AFFIL director: Sealy Corp. NONPR AFFIL member: Voters Choice; member: Young President Organization; member: Phi Beta Kappa; director: Rush-Presbyterian-Saint Lukes Medical Center; director: Magazine Publishers Association; director: National Coalition Crime Delinquency; director: Goodman Theatre; member: Chicago Network; member: Comm 200; director: Brandeis University; director: American Civil Liberties Union Illinois Chapter; member: Brandeis National Womens Comm.

Hugh Marston Hefner: founder, chairman emeritus B Chicago, IL 1926. ED University of Illinois BS (1949). PRIM CORP EMPL founder, chairman emeritus: Playboy Enterprises, Inc. CORP AFFIL publ, editor-in-chief: Playboy Magazine.

Jeffrey M. Jenest: senior vice president new business development B Boston, MA 1952. ED Stanford University BA (1974); Harvard University MBA (1978). PRIM CORP EMPL executive Vice President new business: Playboy Enterprises, Inc.

James R. Petersen: senior staff writer, Playboy Magazine

Cindy Rakowitz: vice president public relations PRIM CORP EMPL vice president public relations: Playboy Enterprises, Inc.

Sol Rosenthal: counsel B Baltimore, MD 1934. ED Princeton University AB (1956); Harvard University JD (1959). PRIM CORP EMPL counsel: Blanc, Williams, Johnston & Kronstadt. CORP AFFIL arbitrator: Writers Guild America; negotiator: Writers Guild Association of Talent Agents; director: Playboy Enterprises Inc.; arbitrator: American Film Marketing Association; arbitrator: Directors Guild of America; member entertainment panel: American Arbitration Association. NONPR AFFIL member: Los Angeles County Bar Association; member: Phi Beta Kappa; member: California Bar Association; member: Los Angeles Copyright Society; member: American Bar Association; member: Beverly Hills Bar Association; member: Academy Television Arts & Sciences.

Richard Stuart Rosenzweig: executive vice president, director B Appleton, WI 1935. ED Northwestern University BS (1957); Harvard University Advanced Management Program (1975). PRIM CORP EMPL executive vice president, director: Playboy Enterprises, Inc. CORP AFFIL advisory board: West Hollywood Marketing Corp.; director: I Bahcall Industries; president: Playboy Jazz Festivals. NONPR AFFIL member: University California Los Angeles Chancellor's Associates; member, chairman: University California Los Angeles Legislation Network; director: Southern California ACLU; member: Town Hall California; member: President's Circle; member: Public Affairs Council; director: Periodical & Book Association America; director: Maple Center; director: Museum Contemporary Art; member president council, contemporary arts council: Los Angeles Museum Contemporary Art; member: Los Angeles Public Affairs Officers Association; member: Los Angeles County Music Center; trustee: Los Angeles Film Exposition; director: International Institute Kidney Diseases UCLA; member: Craft & Folk Art Museum; member: Founders Circle of Music Center; member, chairman: Beverly Hills Fine Art Commission; director: Children of the Night; member, director: Beverly Hills Chamber of Commerce; member: Beverly Hills Economic Development Council; member: American Marketing Association; member: American Cinematheque; member 2nd decade council: American Film Institute. CLUB AFFIL member, director: Variety Southern California Club.

Howard Shapiro: executive vice president, general counsel B Chicago, IL 1947. ED University of Illinois BA (1968); DePaul University JD (1973). PRIM CORP EMPL executive vice president, general counsel: Playboy Enterprises, Inc. ADD CORP EMPL vice president, assistant secretary: Critics Choice Video Inc.

David Walker: editorial director, international publishing OCCUPATION editorial director, international publishing.

Giving Program Officials

Jeffrey M. Jenest: director (see above)
James R. Petersen: director (see above)
James Peterson: (see above)
Cindy Rakowitz: director (see above)
Howard Shapiro: director (see above)
David Walker: director (see above)

Foundation Officials

Christie Ann Hefner: director (see above)
Jeffrey M. Jenest: director (see above)
Burton Joseph: chairman, director ED City University of New York.
Cindy Rakowitz: director (see above)
Howard Shapiro: director (see above)
Cleo Francine Wilson: executive director B Chicago, IL 1943. ED University of Illinois (1976). PRIM CORP EMPL executive director: Playboy Enterprises Inc. PRIM NONPR EMPL executive director: Playboy Foundation. CORP AFFIL director: American Civil Liberties Union Illinois Chapter. NONPR AFFIL director: Center of Intuitive & Outsider Art; director: National Coalition Against Censorship.

Grants Analysis

Disclosure Period: calendar year ending 1998
Total Grants: $300,000*
Typical Range: $5,000 to $10,000
*Note: Giving excludes Corporate, Nonmonetary. Grants analysis provided by foundation.

Recent Grants

Note: Grants derived from 1998 Annual Report.

Civic & Public Affairs

freedoms and reconnect citizens to democracy, New York, NY -- to establish the Hugh M. Hefner Fund for the Bill of Rights

National Coalition Against Censorship, New York, NY -- ongoing support for its efforts to end attacks on expression

People for the American Way, Washington, DC -- ongoing support to create a broad-based movement to bridge social divisions, counter political extremism, and advance fundamental freedoms

Education

Reuben Salizar Bilingual Academy, Chicago, IL -- support elementary school that serves poor children whose first language is not English

Social Services

Broadway Theatre Institute, New York, NY -- for ticket purchase and food for children living in a homeless shelter

God's Love we Deliver, New York, NY -- for meal delivery and support for homebound people with HIV/AIDs

PNC Bank

Company Contact

Philadelphia, PA
Web: http://www.pncbank.com

Company Description

Former Name: Provident National Bank.
Employees: 25,400
Parent Company: PNC Financial Services Group, Pittsburgh, PA, United States

Nonmonetary Support

Type: Donated Equipment; Donated Products; In-kind Services

Corporate Sponsorship

Type: Arts & cultural events; Festivals/fairs; Music & entertainment events; Pledge-a-thon

Giving Contact

David Washington, Manager, Public Affairs
PNC Bank
1600 Market St.
Philadelphia, PA 19103-1015
Phone: (215)585-7453
Fax: (215)585-8271

Description

Organization Type: Corporate Giving Program
Grant Types: Capital, Employee Matching Gifts, General Support, Operating Expenses.

Financial Summary

Total Giving: Contributes through corporate direct giving program only.

Typical Recipients

Arts & Humanities: Arts Outreach, Arts & Humanities-General
Civic & Public Affairs: Business/Free Enterprise, Economic Development, Employment/Job Training, Civic & Public Affairs-General, Housing
Education: Colleges & Universities, Education-General, Literacy
Health: Adolescent Health Issues, Health-General, Hospitals
Social Services: Community Service Organizations, Shelters/Homelessness, Social Services-General

Contributions Analysis

Arts & Humanities: About 25%. Funds programs which encourage collaboration between arts associations. Also considers programs that introduce Delaware Valley young people to the arts through arts outreach.
Civic & Public Affairs: 30% to 35%. Contributes to agencies which advance construction or rehabilitation of low- or moderate-income housing. Other interests include economic development, small business initiatives, and low- and moderate-income job retention. Funds programs which work to improve the quality of life in the region and government services.
Education: 20% to 25% of contributions. Supports programs which advance literacy, encourage self-reliance and self-sufficiency, and prepareyouths to enter workforce.
Health: 15% to 20%. Funds programs designed to elimite homelessness, and improve the health and psychological well-being of urban youth. Also supports hospitals.

Application Procedures

Initial Contact: call or write for application form
Application Requirements: organization name and address; contact person's name, title, and telephone; amount requested; geographic area served and population served; list of staff members and board members; purpose of grant; need and relevance served; community support; coordination of services; method of evaluation; future support, including use of PNC support; evidence of competence; and list of prior funding
Deadlines: None.
Decision Notification: decisions are made on a quarterly basis

Restrictions

Does not fund political candidates or religious organizations for sectarian purposes.
Generally does not support United Way member agencies.

Additional Information
Publications: Application Form

Corporate Officials
Richard Leonard Smoot: chairman B Dayton, KY 1940. ED University of Colorado BA (1963); University of Cincinnati MA (1964); Duke University (1974-1975). PRIM CORP EMPL chairman: PNC Bank Corp. CORP AFFIL director: P H Glatfelter Co. NONPR AFFIL vice chairman: Philadelphia Orchestra Association; president: PNC Bank National Association; secretary: Episcopal Community Services.

Giving Program Officials
Donald Lee Haskin: vice president B Wilmington, DE 1945. ED Temple University BS (1973). PRIM CORP EMPL vice president public affairs: PNC Bank Corp. NONPR AFFIL director: Settlement Music School; member: Society Professional Journalists; director: Center Literacy; vice president external affairs: Regional Performing Arts Center.

PNC BANK KENTUCKY INC.

Company Contact
Louisville, KY

Company Description
Former Name: Citizens Fidelity Bank & Trust Co.
Assets: US$5,045,400,000
Employees: 2,412
Parent Company: PNC Financial Services Group, Pittsburgh, PA, United States

Nonmonetary Support
Value: $50,000 (1989); $3,500 (1988)
Type: Loaned Employees

PNC Bank Foundation

Giving Contact
Ms. Traci Orman, Vice President, Community Relations
PNC Bank Kentucky, Inc.
Citizens Plz.
500 W. Jefferson St.
Louisville, KY 40202
Phone: (502)581-2016
Fax: (502)581-7461

Alternate Contact
Mia Hallett, Vice President, Manager
1 Oliver Plaza, 29th Floor
Pittsburgh, PA 15222-2602
Phone: (412)762-7076

Description
EIN: 310999030
Organization Type: Corporate Foundation
Former Name: Citizens Fidelity Foundation.
Giving Locations: headquarters and operating communities only.
Grant Types: Capital, Endowment, Matching, Project, Seed Money.

Giving Philosophy
'The PNC Bank Foundation is committed to the enrichment and growth of the communities it serves. Its philanthropic intent is to empower the people in those markets to maximize their human potential. Recognizing that communities thrive and flourish through creative problem-solving, the PNC Bank Foundation seeks to contribute the necessary funds to seed the ideas, support the initiatives and encourage the leadership of those organizations where imagination and determination are at work enhancing the lives of the people they serve.' *PNC Foundation Report*

Financial Summary
Total Giving: $1,500,000 (fiscal year ending October 31, 1997 approx); $1,500,000 (fiscal 1996 approx); $1,700,000 (fiscal 1995 approx). Note: Contributes through foundation only.

Typical Recipients
Arts & Humanities: Arts Centers, Arts Funds, Ballet, Museums/Galleries, Opera, Visual Arts
Civic & Public Affairs: Economic Development, Housing, Urban & Community Affairs
Education: Business-School Partnerships, Minority Education, Public Education (Precollege), Student Aid
Social Services: Food/Clothing Distribution, People with Disabilities, United Funds/United Ways

Contributions Analysis
Giving Priorities: Human service, education, the arts, civic development, health, and religion.
Arts & Humanities: 15% to 20%. Interests includes performing arts, ballet, opera, museums, arts centers, and arts funds.
Civic & Public Affairs: 20% to 25%. Interests include housing and community beautification programs, including Operation Brightside, Habitat for Humanity, and Sunny Side Pride.
Education: About 15%. Interests include minority education, public education, Junior Achievement, and summer employment programs. Alsosupports colleges and universities in PNC communities with funds for research, academics, and athletics.
Social Services: About 45%. Major support for the United Way. Other interests include food distribution for the hungry, and the Special Olympics.

Application Procedures
Initial Contact: brief letter requesting proposal guidelines
Application Requirements: description of the organization; amount requested; period covered; program for which funding is requested; when, where, and how services are to be delivered; target group served or to be served; plan for measuring results; whether funding from umbrella organizations is expected; budget information; personnel information; proof of tax-exempt status; audited financial statements; list of board of directors; list of officers and compensation; descriptive literature
Deadlines: prior to the first day of each month
Decision Notification: decisions are made quarterly

Restrictions
Company does not give to political candidates or causes, individuals, or goodwill advertising.
Generally, does not fund member agencies of the United Way or the Fund for the Arts.
Does not give to national organizations unless the program would benefit the local community.
Funds must benefit community where PNC Bank Corp. has a meaningful presence.

Additional Information
The Citizens Fidelity Foundation was dissolved in late 1991 as part of the changes that ensued after Citizens Fidelity Bank & Trust Co. was acquired by PNC Financial Corp.
Company reports that funds are predominantly awarded to organizations within the PNC Bank service area: Jefferson, Oldham, and Hardin Counties of Kentucky and Clark and Floyd Counties of Indiana.
Publications: Pnc Bank Community Involvement Report

Corporate Officials
Michael Neal Harreld: president, chief executive officer B Louisville, KY 1944. ED University of Louisville BA (1966); University of Louisville Law School JD (1969). PRIM CORP EMPL president, chief executive officer: PNC Bank of Kentucky Inc.

Giving Program Officials
Traci Orman: PRIM CORP EMPL vice president community relations: PNC Bank of Kentucky Inc.

Grants Analysis
Disclosure Period: fiscal year ending October 31,
Typical Range: $1,000 to $10,000

PNC FINANCIAL SERVICES GROUP

 Number 73 of Top 100 Corporate Givers

Company Contact
Pittsburgh, PA
Web: http://www.pnc.com

Company Description
Former Name: Pittsburgh National Bank; PNC Bank Corp. (2000).
Revenue: US$7,666,000,000 (1999)
Profit: US$1,264,000,000 (1999)
Employees: 12,413
Fortune Rank: 230, per FORTUNE Magazine's list of 500 Largest U.S. Corporations (1999).
FF 230
SIC(s): 6021 National Commercial Banks.

SUBSIDIARY COMPANIES
PA: PNC Bank, Philadelphia

PNC Bank Foundation

Giving Contact
Mia Hallett, Vice President and Manager
PNC Bank Foundation
Two PNC Plaza, 34th Fl.
Pittsburgh, PA 15222
Phone: (412)762-7076
Fax: (412)705-1062

Description
Founded: 1970
EIN: 251202255
Organization Type: Corporate Foundation
Giving Locations: areas served by PNC Bank Corp. and affiliates.
Grant Types: Capital, Employee Matching Gifts, General Support, Multiyear/Continuing Support.

Financial Summary
Total Giving: $10,793,250 (1998); $10,714,366 (1997); $10,556,162 (1996). Note: Contributes through foundation only. 1997 Giving includes matching gifts ($305,950); United Way ($1,779,583).
Giving Analysis: Giving for 1998 includes: foundation ($10,793,250)
Assets: $25,690,369 (1997); $30,914,047 (1996); $36,036,888 (1995)
Gifts Received: $8,559,680 (1995); $4,896,626 (1994); $25,000,000 (1993). Note: Foundation receives contributions from PNC Bank Corp.

Typical Recipients
Arts & Humanities: Arts Associations & Councils, Arts Centers, Arts Festivals, Arts Funds, Ballet, Community Arts, Arts & Humanities-General, Historic Preservation, History & Archaeology, Libraries, Literary Arts, Museums/Galleries, Music, Opera, Performing Arts, Public Broadcasting, Theater
Civic & Public Affairs: African American Affairs, Business/Free Enterprise, Clubs, Community Foundations, Economic Development, Economic Policy,

Employment/Job Training, Civic & Public Affairs-General, Housing, Legal Aid, Municipalities/Towns, Parades/Festivals, Philanthropic Organizations, Professional & Trade Associations, Public Policy, Safety, Urban & Community Affairs, Zoos/Aquariums
Education: Arts/Humanities Education, Business Education, Colleges & Universities, Community & Junior Colleges, Education Associations, Education Funds, Faculty Development, Education-General, Literacy, Preschool Education, Private Education (Precollege), Student Aid
Environment: Environment-General, Resource Conservation
Health: Cancer, Children's Health/Hospitals, Health Organizations, Hospices, Hospitals, Long-Term Care, Medical Rehabilitation, Single-Disease Health Associations
International: International Development
Religion: Jewish Causes, Ministries, Religious Welfare
Science: Science Museums, Scientific Centers & Institutes
Social Services: Child Welfare, Community Centers, Community Service Organizations, Delinquency & Criminal Rehabilitation, Domestic Violence, Family Services, Food/Clothing Distribution, People with Disabilities, Recreation & Athletics, Scouts, Senior Services, Shelters/Homelessness, United Funds/United Ways, Youth Organizations

Contributions Analysis

Giving Priorities: Social welfare, education, and civic interests.
Arts & Humanities: 20% to 25%. Supports local symphony organizations and music groups, public broadcasting, libraries, performing arts, museums, opera, and arts associations, festivals, and centers.
Civic & Public Affairs: 15% to 20%. Primary support to economic development and urban affairs. Other interests include international affairs, public policy, economics, civil rights, women's interests, and business and free enterprise.
Education: 5% to 10%. Major support goes to local colleges and universities. Also gives to public and private precollege education, minority education, and education funds. Also matches employee gifts to colleges and universities.
Health: Less than 5%. Primarily supports local hospitals. Other interests include single-disease health associations, health funds and organizations, medical rehabilitation, and pediatric health.
Religion: 5% to 10%. Funds community service related religious groups.
Social Services: 40% to 45%. Most of this supports united funds in southwestern Pennsylvania. Also contributes to organizations concerned with youth, the elderly, the disabled, food distribution, community and family services, religious welfare, and emergency relief.

Application Procedures

Initial Contact: Send a brief letter or proposal.
Application Requirements: Include a description of organization, amount requested, purpose of funds sought, description of group's qualifications, recently audited financial statement, proof of tax-exempt status, and list of officers and directors.
Deadlines: None.

Restrictions

Foundation does not award scholarships or make grants to individuals.

Additional Information

The company changed its name from Pittsburgh National Bank to PNC Bank Corp. and the foundation from Pittsburgh National Bank Foundation to PNC Bank Foundation.

Corporate Officials

Walter Emmor Gregg, Junior: senior executive vice president finance & administration B Utica, NY 1941. ED University of Pittsburgh BS (1968); University of Pittsburgh JD (1973). PRIM CORP EMPL senior executive vice president finance & administration: PNC Financial Corp. CORP AFFIL director: Watson Healthcare Inc.; director: PNC Bridge Capital Inc.; director: PNC Venture Corp.; executive vice president: PNC Bancorp Inc.; chairman: PNC Bank Corp.; director: Pittsburgh National Leasing Corp. NONPR AFFIL director: Pennsylvania Institute CPAs; director: Sewickley YMCA; member: National Association Accts; member: Pen Bar Association; member: American Bar Association; director: DT Watson Rehabilitation Hospital; director: America Institute CPA; member: America Society Corp. Secretary; member: Allegheny County Bar Association. CLUB AFFIL Duquesne Club.
Thomas H. O'Brien, Jr.: chairman, chief executive officer PRIM CORP EMPL chairman, chief executive officer: PNC Bank Corp. CORP AFFIL director: Bell Atlantic Corp.
James Edward Rohr: chief executive officer, president, director B Cleveland, OH 1948. ED University of Notre Dame BA (1970); Ohio State University MBA (1972). PRIM CORP EMPL chief executive officer, president, director: PNC Bank Corp. CORP AFFIL president: PNC Mortgage Bank National Association; director: Private Export Funding Corp.; chairman: PNC Bank Pittsburgh; director: Equitable Resources Inc.; president: PNC Bank National Association; director: Allegheny Teledyne Inc.; director: Allegheny Ludlum Corp. NONPR AFFIL director: United Way; member: Young President Organization; director: Student Loan Marketing Association; member advisory board: Salvation Army; director: Shadyside Hospital; vice chairman: Pennsylvania Business Roundtable; director: Greater Pittsburgh Council Boy Scouts America; chairman: National Flag Foundation; director: Cultural Trust; director: Carnegie Mellon University; chairman: Civic Light Opera; member: American Bankers Association; member: Bankers Roundtable; member: Allegheny Conference. CLUB AFFIL director: Duquesne Club.

Foundation Officials

Mia Hallett: manager
William Johns: treasurer, secretary distribution committee
Thomas R. Moore: secretary, counsel

Grants Analysis

Disclosure Period: calendar year ending 1998
Total Grants: $10,793,250
Number of Grants: 1496 (approx)
Average Grant: $10,334
Highest Grant: $374,933
Typical Range: $500 to $50,000

Recent Grants

Note: Grants derived from 1997 Form 990.

Arts & Humanities

250,000	Philadelphia Orchestra, Philadelphia, PA
225,000	Pittsburgh Symphony Society, Pittsburgh, PA
152,500	Greater Louisville Fund for Arts, Louisville, KY
100,000	Pittsburgh Cultural Trust, Pittsburgh, PA
75,000	Garden State Arts Center Foundation, Holmdel, NJ
65,000	Wilma Theater, Philadelphia, PA
51,000	J.B. Speed Art Museum, Louisville, KY
50,185	Ohio Center for Performing Arts, Cincinnati Association, Cincinnati, OH
50,000	Avenue of the Arts, Philadelphia, PA
50,000	Freedom Theater, Philadelphia, PA
45,000	Cincinnati Art Museum, Cincinnati, OH
43,200	Fine Arts Fund, Cincinnati, OH
35,000	Kentucky Center for Arts, Louisville, KY
32,500	Free Library, Philadelphia, PA
30,000	Civic Light Opera, Pittsburgh, PA

Civic & Public Affairs

325,000	Greater Philadelphia First Foundation, Philadelphia, PA
285,548	Pennsylvania Horticultural Society, Erie, PA
140,000	Pittsburgh Partnership for Neighborhood Development, Pittsburgh, PA
110,000	Acorn Housing Corporation, Philadelphia, PA
90,000	Citizen Policy and Education Fund, Hackensack, NY
78,000	Manchester Citizen's Corporation, Pittsburgh, PA
60,000	Louisville Zoo, Louisville, KY
60,000	Mon Valley Progress Council, Monessen, PA
50,000	Greater Louisville Economic Development Partnership, Louisville, KY
38,000	Allegheny Conference on Community Development, Pittsburgh, PA
35,000	Committee for Economic Growth, Wilkes-Barre, PA
32,500	Delaware Valley Community Reinvestment Fund, Philadelphia, PA
31,667	Urban League, Pittsburgh, PA
30,000	Cecil B. Moore Avenue Community Development Corporation, Philadelphia, PA

Education

100,000	Settlement Music School, Philadelphia, PA
80,000	Carnegie Mellon University, Pittsburgh, PA
50,000	Drexel University, Philadelphia, PA
50,000	Early Childhood Initiative, Pittsburgh, PA
49,998	Xavier University, Cincinnati, OH
49,800	University of Cincinnati, Cincinnati, OH
35,000	Indiana University of Pennsylvania, Indiana, PA
35,000	King's College, Wilkes-Barre, PA
35,000	University of Scranton, Scranton, PA
30,000	College of Mount St. Joseph, Cincinnati, OH

Environment

50,000	Save Our Waterfront, Camden, NJ

Health

50,000	Bayley Place, Cincinnati, OH
40,000	Center Community Hospital, State College, PA

International

40,000	Latin American Economic Development Association, Camden, NJ

Religion

70,000	Federation for Allied Jewish Appeal, Philadelphia, PA

Social Services

929,021	United Way of Southwestern Pennsylvania, Pittsburgh, PA
174,569	United Way, Cincinnati, OH
126,000	United Way, Wilmington, DE
90,000	United Way of Lackawanna County, Scranton, PA
83,975	United Way of Wyoming Valley, Wilkes-Barre, PA
81,073	United Way of Tri-State, New York, NY

POLAROID CORP.

Company Contact

Cambridge, MA
Web: http://www.polaroid.com

Company Description

Employees: 10,046
SIC(s): 3861 Photographic Equipment & Supplies.

Nonmonetary Support

Value: $50,000 (1992); $98,000 (1990)
Type: Donated Products
Contact: Jill Healy, Senior Administrator
Note: Foundation provides photographic equipment for projects which help the disadvantagedor where immediate access to images is vital, i.e. disaster relief;animal rescue

Corporate Sponsorship

Note: Sponsors business related events through community relations at various sites.

Polaroid Foundation

Giving Contact

Donna F. Eidson, Executive Director
Polaroid Foundation
784 Memorial Drive
Cambridge, MA 02139
Phone: (781)386-9400
Fax: (781)386-9818
Email: Polaroid.Foundation@polaroid.com

Description

EIN: 237152261
Organization Type: Corporate Foundation
Giving Locations: MA: Boston metropolitan area, Cambridge, New Bedford including surrounding area, Waltham internationally for product donations; nationally for product donations; nationally: considers funding outside of Massachusetts to historically black educational instituations.
Grant Types: Employee Matching Gifts, General Support, Operating Expenses, Project, Seed Money.

Giving Philosophy

'Within the community, the Polaroid Foundation invests resources where we determine that we can make the greatest difference in helping disadvantaged children and adults to develop skills that enable them to create full and self-sufficient lives. We fully understand that we cannot do what others must do for themselves. We want, however, to do what we can to make resources available to those who actively seek to realize their potential and to develop themselves and others.'
'Polaroid favors programs that help participants gain measurable skills through hands-on practice, training and experience. These skills enable participants to make significant and long-lasting improvements in their lives.' *Polaroid Foundation Guidelines*

Financial Summary

Total Giving: $1,400,000 (1997 approx); $1,850,000 (1996); $2,266,681 (1995). Note: Contributes through corporate direct giving program and foundation. Giving includes foundation. 1996 Giving includes foundation ($1,189,977); matching gifts ($324,642); scholarship ($25,500); United Way ($217,500).
Assets: $19,000,000 (1997 approx); $1,441,964 (1996); $1,255,909 (1995)
Gifts Received: $1,747,390 (1996); $2,240,468 (1995); $2,314,382 (1994). Note: Gifts are received from Polaroid Corporation.

Typical Recipients

Arts & Humanities: Arts Associations & Councils, Arts Centers, Arts Funds, Arts Institutes, Arts Outreach, Ballet, Community Arts, Dance, Ethnic & Folk Arts, Historic Preservation, History & Archaeology, Libraries, Museums/Galleries, Music, Opera, Performing Arts, Public Broadcasting, Theater, Visual Arts
Civic & Public Affairs: African American Affairs, Asian American Affairs, Civil Rights, Community Foundations, Economic Development, Employment/ Job Training, Ethnic Organizations, Housing, Law & Justice, Minority Business, Municipalities/Towns, Nonprofit Management, Philanthropic Organizations, Public Policy, Safety, Urban & Community Affairs, Women's Affairs
Education: Arts/Humanities Education, Business Education, Colleges & Universities, Community & Junior Colleges, Continuing Education, Education Reform, Elementary Education (Private), Engineering/Technological Education, Faculty Development, Education-General, Health & Physical Education, Leadership Training, Literacy, Medical Education, Minority Education, Preschool Education, Private Education (Precollege), Public Education (Precollege), Science/ Mathematics Education, Secondary Education (Public), Special Education, Student Aid, Vocational & Technical Education
Environment: Environment-General
Health: AIDS/HIV, Clinics/Medical Centers, Diabetes, Eyes/Blindness, Hospices, Hospitals, Medical Research, Mental Health, Nursing Services, Public Health, Speech & Hearing
International: Human Rights
Religion: Religious Welfare, Social/Policy Issues
Science: Scientific Labs, Scientific Organizations
Social Services: At-Risk Youth, Camps, Child Welfare, Community Service Organizations, Counseling, Crime Prevention, Day Care, Domestic Violence, Family Services, Food/Clothing Distribution, People with Disabilities, Recreation & Athletics, Shelters/ Homelessness, United Funds/United Ways, YMCA/ YWCA/YMHA/YWHA, Youth Organizations

Contributions Analysis

Giving Priorities: Social welfare and education.
Arts & Humanities: 5% to 10%. Funding to historical and arts museums and public television.
Civic & Public Affairs: 10% to 35%. Community support Massachusetts.
Education: 30% to 35%. Primarily technical colleges, universities, and program support for educational incentives.
Health: 10% to 15%. Health associations and healthcare centers.
Religion: Less than 5%.
Social Services: 35% to 40%. YMCA, women's shelters, United Way and programs for children.

Application Procedures

Initial Contact: call or write to request application form and guidelines, then full proposal
Application Requirements: cover letter summary in narrative form, on organization's letterhead; completed application form; brief history of program including mission and major accomplishments; background of key personnel and list of board members; with affiliations; outline of project including goals, constituents served, community need to be met, and desired outcomes; project's implementation, assessment and evaluation; skills participants will gain from program; long-term effects of program; annual budget for project and organization; proof of tax-exempt status; list of funding sources and amounts solicited and received; and most recently audited financial statement
Deadlines: None; grants are reviewed from November to July each year
Review Process: requests go through a preliminary screening by employee volunteers and then to a subcommittee for a full review; site visits are often included
Evaluative Criteria: programs help participants gain measurable skills through hands-on practice, training, and experience
Decision Notification: reviews take three to four months
Notes: Foundation accepts the AGM Common Proposal Format. Do not call regarding status of proposal; applicants will be notified in writing of the decision.

Restrictions

The foundation does not make more than one grant to a recipient in any calendar year or make contributions commitments beyond the current funding year. The foundation does not support advertisements; individuals; political or lobbying groups; religious organizations for sectarian purposes; dinners; special events; research; or sponsor events. Foundation rarely makes grants to national organizations.
No product donations can be made to fundraisers, short-term events, prizes, raffles, booths, fairs, or auctions. events, prizes, raffles, booths, fairs, or auctions.

Additional Information

Publications: Guidelines; Application Form

Corporate Officials

Gary Thomas DiCamillo: chairman, chief executive officer, director B Niagara Falls, NY 1950. ED Rensselaer Polytechnic Institute BS (1973); Harvard University MBA (1975). PRIM CORP EMPL chairman, chief executive officer, director: Polaroid Corp. NONPR AFFIL member: Rensselaer Alumni Association; member: Water Quality Association; member board governors: New England Aquarium; trustee: Medical Science Center; trustee: Museum Science Boston; member: Hardware Marketing Council; member: Maryland Academy Science; member: DIY Research Institute; trustee: Greater Baltimore Committee. CLUB AFFIL Wianno Club; Willowbend Club; Skokie Country Club; Maryland Club; Rensselaer Polytechnic Institute Club; Harvard Club; L'Hirondelle Club; Brae Burn Country Club; Elkridge Club.
Joseph G. Parham, Jr.: senior vice president, human resources PRIM CORP EMPL senior vice president, human resources: Polaroid Corp.

Foundation Officials

Donna Furlong Edison: executive director
Thomas Michael Lemberg: secretary B Detroit, MI 1946. ED Princeton University BA (1966); Yale University LLB (1969). PRIM CORP EMPL vice president, secretary, general counsel: Lotus Development Corp. CORP AFFIL senior vice president, general counsel: Polaroid Corp. NONPR AFFIL member: Phi Beta Kappa; chairman government affairs committee: Software Pubs Association; member, director: Bus Software Alliance.
Ralph M. Norwood: treasurer B Rochester, NH 1943. ED University of New Hampshire (1965); University of Virginia (1967). PRIM CORP EMPL vice president, treasurer: Polaroid Corp. NONPR AFFIL member: American Institute CPAs.
Joseph G. Parham, Jr.: president (see above)

Grants Analysis

Disclosure Period: calendar year ending 1996
Total Grants: $1,189,977
Number of Grants: 235
Average Grant: $5,064
Highest Grant: $203,500
Typical Range: $10,000 to $25,000

Recent Grants

Note: Grants derived from 1996 Form 990.

Arts & Humanities

25,000 Facing History and Ourselves National

Foundation, Brookline, MA -- program support

10,000	Art Institute, Boston, MA -- student aid
10,000	Museum of African American History, Detroit, MI -- for film and video productions
10,000	Somerville Community Access Television, Somerville, MA -- program support

Civic & Public Affairs

25,000	Associated Grantmakers of Massachusetts, Boston, MA -- program support
22,500	Community Works, Boston, MA -- support Workplace Federated Giving Campaign
10,000	One With One, Boston, MA
7,500	Community Foundation of Southeastern Massachusetts, New Bedford, MA -- program support
6,100	Town of Lexington, Lexington, MA -- purchase equipment
5,495	Town of Dartmouth, Dartmouth, MA -- program support
5,000	Associated Grantmakers of Massachusetts, Boston, MA
5,000	Boston Asian Youth Essential Service, Boston, MA
5,000	Massachusetts Youth Teenage Unemployment Reduction Network, Brockton, MA -- program support

Education

34,000	Rensselaer Polytechnic Institute Walker Laboratory, Troy, NY -- capital campaign
24,222	American College Testing, Iowa City, IA -- student aid
19,454	National Merit Scholarship Corporation, Evanston, IL -- student aid
16,000	Rensselaer Polytechnic Institute Walker Laboratory, Troy, NY -- capital renovations of Walker Laboratory
15,000	American College Testing, Iowa City, IA -- student aid
15,000	University of Massachusetts Foundation, Amherst, MA -- for internships
10,000	Boston Partners in Education, Boston, MA -- program support
10,000	Don Bosco Technical High School -- for student aid, science program expansion
10,000	North Carolina A&T University Department of Chemical Engineering, Greensboro, NC
10,000	Northeastern University, Boston, MA -- capital campaign
10,000	Northeastern University, Boston, MA -- capital campaign
10,000	Sargent College of Allied Health Professions -- program support
10,000	Tuskegee University Business and Industry Cluster, Tuskegee, AL -- student aid
10,000	Worcester Polytechnic Institute Electrical and Computer Engineering Department, Worcester, MA -- capital campaign
10,000	Worcester Polytechnic Institute Electrical and Computer Engineering Department, Worcester, MA -- capital campaign
10,000	Xavier University of Louisiana Department of Chemistry, New Orleans, LA -- for equipment
7,500	Concord Academy, Concord, MA -- program support
7,000	United Negro College Fund, New York, NY
5,000	Thompson Island Outward Bound Education Center, Boston, MA -- program support

Health

20,000	Combined Health Appeal of Massachusetts, Dedham, MA -- support Workplace Federated Giving Campaign
20,000	Massachusetts Eye and Ear Infirmary, Boston, MA -- capital campaign
10,000	Cambridge Mental Health Association, Cambridge, MA -- program support
10,000	Cambridge Mental Health Association, Cambridge, MA -- program support
9,950	Foundation for Children With AIDS, Roxbury, MA -- seed money to purchase books
6,860	St. Luke's Hospital, New Bedford, MA -- program support
5,000	Health Care of Southeastern Massachusetts, Abington, MA -- program support
5,000	Windsor House Adult Day Health Care Centers

Religion

5,000	Interseminarian, Boston, MA -- support Project Place
5,000	Urban Revival, City of Life/Vida Urbana, Jamaica Plain, MA

Social Services

203,500	United Way Eastern New England Chapter -- support Workplace Federated Giving Campaign
20,000	Parents United for Child Care, Boston, MA -- program support
12,800	Our Sisters Place -- program support
10,000	United Way, New Bedford, MA -- program support
10,000	YMCA, Cambridge, MA -- program support
7,500	Italian Home for Children, Jamaica Plain, MA -- program support
6,000	Dorchester House Multiservice Center, Dorchester, MA
5,500	Sojourner House, Roxbury, MA -- program support

Portland General Electric Co.

Company Contact

Portland, OR
Web: http://www.pge-online.com

Company Description

Assets: US$3,398,200,000
Employees: 2,587
SIC(s): 4911 Electric Services.
Parent Company: Enron Corp., Houston, TX, United States

Nonmonetary Support

Value: $20,000 (1992); $50,000 (1991); $100,000 (1990)
Type: Donated Equipment; Donated Products; Inkind Services; Loaned Executives
Note: Company also donates the use of its facilities.

Corporate Sponsorship

Type: Arts & cultural events; Festivals/fairs; Music & entertainment events; Pledge-a-thon; Sports events
Contact: Elene Donaldson, Corporate Communications Coordinator, Events

PGE-Enron Foundation

Giving Contact

Gwyneth Gamble Booth, Chairman
PGE Enron Foundation
121 Southwest Salmon Street
One World Trade Center, 9th Fl.
Portland, OR 97204
Phone: (503)464-8818
Fax: (503)464-2223

Description

Organization Type: Corporate Foundation
Giving Locations: OR: emphasis on service area
Grant Types: Capital, General Support, Multiyear/Continuing Support, Project, Scholarship.

Financial Summary

Total Giving: $1,233,534 (1998); $1,332,617 (1997); $275,000 (1996 approx). Note: Contributes through corporate direct giving program and foundation.
Giving Analysis: Giving for 1998 includes: foundation ($1,006,599); foundation grants to United Way ($226,935)

Typical Recipients

Arts & Humanities: Arts Festivals, Arts Institutes, Dance, Ethnic & Folk Arts, Music, Opera, Performing Arts, Public Broadcasting
Civic & Public Affairs: Economic Development, Housing, Professional & Trade Associations, Urban & Community Affairs
Education: Business Education, Colleges & Universities, Community & Junior Colleges, Continuing Education, Education Funds, Science/Mathematics Education, Student Aid
Environment: Environment-General
Health: Public Health
Science: Science Exhibits & Fairs, Scientific Organizations
Social Services: Child Welfare, Community Centers, Community Service Organizations, Delinquency & Criminal Rehabilitation, Emergency Relief, Food/Clothing Distribution, People with Disabilities, Senior Services, Shelters/Homelessness, Substance Abuse, United Funds/United Ways, Volunteer Services, Youth Organizations

Contributions Analysis

Giving Priorities: Health, social welfare, higher education, and civic interests.
Arts & Humanities: 35%. Arts and cultural organizations.
Civic & Public Affairs: 3%. Municipal affairs, wildlife preservation, and chambers of commerce.
Education: 15%. Primarily supports independent college funds. Recipients also include energy education programs, higher education and graduate centers, and health science education programs. Science scholarships and curricula support for science education in public schools.
Environment: 5%.
Health: 42%. Majority of funds support united funds and social welfare programs. Also supports youth organizations and food distribution programs. Limited support to hospitals and clinics. Also funds small, local clinics and public health organizations for minorities.

Application Procedures

Initial Contact: a brief letter of inquiry
Application Requirements: a description of organization (including mission statement, purpose, history of accomplishments, governance, area and population served and role of volunteers), a copy of your one-page project description signed by the executive directory and amount requested, project budget, purpose of funds sought, recently audited financial statement, proof of 501 (c)(3) tax-exempt status
Deadlines: None.
Review Process: requests for less than $2,500 reviewed by internal committee; requests for $2,500 or more reviewed by board of directors
Evaluative Criteria: community need, economic development potential, company goals
Decision Notification: response usually follows within 90 days of submittal; committee meets quarterly

Notes: PGE contributions packet includes an annual report, application form, community involvement information, and a community statement of philosophy.

Restrictions

Does not support individuals, fraternal or political groups, religious organizations for sectarian purposes, or goodwill advertising.

Additional Information

In 1997, Portland General Electric Co. was acquired by Enron Corp.
Contributions budget for the following year is set in the fall.
Publications: Guidelines; Annual Report

Giving Program Officials

Fred D. Miller: vice president public affairs PRIM CORP EMPL vice president public affairs: Portland General Electric Co. CORP AFFIL president: 121 Southwest Salmon Street Corp.

Foundation Officials

Gwyneth Gamble Booth: chairman
Carole Morse: manager

Grants Analysis

Disclosure Period: calendar year ending 1998
Total Grants: $1,006,599*
Number of Grants: 127
Average Grant: $7,926
Highest Grant: $300,000
Typical Range: $500 to $5,000
***Note:** Giving excludes United Way. Grants analysis derived from 1998 annual report.

Recent Grants

Note: Grants derived from 1993 grants list.

Arts & Humanities
Friends of the Children's Museum, Lattabra, CA
Interstate Firehouse Cultural Theater -- student matinee series
Morrison Center for Performing Arts, Boise, ID
Oregon Art Institute, Portland, OR
Oregon Ballet Theater, Portland, OR
Oregon Symphony, Portland, OR

Civic & Public Affairs
Black United Fund, Detroit, MI

Education
Environmental Education Association
I Have A Dream Foundation, Dallas, TX
Junior Achievement
Oregon Governor's School for Citizen Leadership, Portland, OR
Oregon Independent College Foundation, Portland, OR
Oregon Science Teachers Association, Portland, OR

Environment
American Fisheries Society, Bethesda, MD
Audubon Society, Audubon, NJ
Nature Conservancy, Arlington, VA

Health
ASAP Treatment Services, Portland, OR
Healthbridge Northwest, Portland, OR

Religion
Union Gospel Mission Shelter for Women and Children

Social Services
Business Youth Exchange
Citizens for a Drug-Free Oregon, Portland, OR
Community Energy Project
Imagination Celebration for Homeless Teens
Oregon Children's Foundation, Portland, OR
Salvation Army Greenhouse United Way, Portland, OR
Stop Oregon Litter and Vandalism, Portland, OR
Transition Projects Youth Shelter
YWCA Leadership Forum

POTLATCH CORP.

Company Contact

San Francisco, CA
Web: http://www.potlatchcorp.com

Company Description

Employees: 6,800 (1999)
SIC(s): 2421 Sawmills & Planing Mills--General, 2426 Hardwood Dimension & Flooring Mills, 2435 Hardwood Veneer & Plywood, 2493 Reconstituted Wood Products.

Potlatch Foundation II

Giving Contact

Hugh Travaille, Foundation President
Potlatch Corp.
601 West Riverside Avenue, Suite 1100
Spokane, WA 99201
Phone: (509)835-1519
Fax: (509)835-1559
Email: foundation@potlatchcorp.com
Web: http://www.potlatchcorp.com/company/foundations/html

Description

EIN: 942948030
Organization Type: Corporate Foundation
Giving Locations: AR; CA: San Francisco; ID; MN
Grant Types: Employee Matching Gifts, General Support, Scholarship.

Giving Philosophy

'Potlatch Foundation II makes grants in a number of fields ranging from education to community health to youth services and cultural activities.'

Financial Summary

Total Giving: $1,100,000 (1999 approx); $1,104,291 (1998); $375,846 (1997). Note: Contributes through foundation only. 1997
Giving Analysis: Giving for 1997 includes: foundation ($519,224); 1998: foundation ($369,133)
Assets: $594,244 (1998); $519,224 (1997); $381,279 (1996)
Gifts Received: $1,206,950 (1998); $402,000 (1997); $1,303,350 (1996). Note: Contributions are received from the Potlatch Corp.

Typical Recipients

Arts & Humanities: Dance, Museums/Galleries, Music, Opera, Performing Arts
Civic & Public Affairs: Economic Development
Education: Business Education, Colleges & Universities, Education Associations, Engineering/Technological Education, Environmental Education, Literacy, Science/Mathematics Education
Environment: Environment-General
Health: Hospitals
Science: Scientific Centers & Institutes
Social Services: Child Welfare, United Funds/United Ways, Youth Organizations

Contributions Analysis

Giving Priorities: Higher education, the performing arts, museums, hospitals, and youth organizations.
Arts & Humanities: Less than 5%. Performing arts centers and museums.
Civic & Public Affairs: 10% to 15%. Local economic development and environmental efforts.
Education: 50% and 55%. Supports the Potlatch Foundation for Higher Education, which provides for scholarships, colleges and universities, and pre-college education.
Health: 5% to 10%. Hospitals.
Social Services: 5% to 10%. Primarily interested in youth organizations.

Application Procedures

Initial Contact: For general grants, written request; for scholarships, write for application packet.
Deadlines: None, for general grants; February 15 for scholarships.

Restrictions

Grants are not made to organizations serving only a specific group of people.

Additional Information

The Potlatch Foundation II contributes funds to The Potlatch Foundation for Higher Education. Officially, the foundation is not considered a program under the Potlatch Foundation II, it is considered a separate foundation.
'The Potlatch Foundation for Higher Education (PFHE) awards undergraduate scholarships to qualified students whose permanent residence is within 30 miles of major Potlatch facilities. Applicants must be qualified to attend an accredited college, university, or higher education institution. Scholarships are not awarded for graduate study.
'Trustees of PFHE select scholarship recipients on the basis of character, leadership qualities, scholastic achievement and ability, and financial need. Recipients may pursue any studies leading to a bachelor's degree or a course of instruction that meets trustees' approval. Scholarships of $1,400 per year are renewable annually during a regular four-year undergraduate college course, subject to the trustees' discretion. Payments are made to the student's education institution in equal amounts in August and December of each academic year for which the scholarship is awarded.
'Application packets are available between October 1 and December 15 of each year. High schools near Potlatch facilities usually maintain a supply of applications, but an application packet can be obtained from the same contact as that of the Potlatch Foundation II.' Potlatch Corporate Overview
In 1998, PFHE awarded $369,133 in scholarships, the foundation assets were $36,042, and they received $382,200 in contributions from The Potlatch Foundation II. II.
Publications: Annual Report

Corporate Officials

Betty R. Fleshman: secretary B Sapulpa, OK 1949. ED Northeastern State University (1971). PRIM CORP EMPL secretary: Potlatch Corp. CORP AFFIL secretary: Duluth & Northeastern Rr Co.
Charles R. Pottenger: group vice president pulp & paperboard group B 1939. ED Institute of Paper Chemistry MS; Institute of Paper Chemistry PhD; University of Minnesota MS. PRIM CORP EMPL group vice president pulp & paperboard group: Potlatch Corp.
John M. Richards: chairman, chief executive officer, director B 1937. ED Stanford University BA (1959); Harvard University MBA (1961). PRIM CORP EMPL chairman, chief executive officer, director: Potlatch Corp.
Louis Pendelton Siegel: chairman, president, chief executive officer, chief operating officer B Richmond, VA 1942. ED Dartmouth College AB (1967). PRIM CORP EMPL chairman, president, chief executive officer, chief operating officer: Potlatch Corp.
Gerald L. Zuehlke: treasurer PRIM CORP EMPL treasurer: Potlatch Corp. CORP AFFIL treasurer: Duluth & Northeastern Railroad Co.

Foundation Officials

Ralph M. Davisson: trustee B Portland, OR 1941. ED Stanford University AB (1964); University of Oregon Law School JD (1967). PRIM CORP EMPL vice president, general counsel: Potlatch Corp.

Barbara M. Failing: trustee PRIM CORP EMPL vice president employee relations: Potlatch Corp.

Betty R. Fleshman: secretary (see above)

George Frederick Jewett, Jr.: trustee B Spokane, WA 1927. ED Dartmouth College BA (1950); Harvard University MBA (1952). PRIM CORP EMPL vice chairman, director: Potlatch Corp.

Charles R. Pottenger: trustee (see above)

Sandra Theresa Powell: trustee B Orofino, ID 1944. ED Idaho State University BS (1966). PRIM CORP EMPL senior vice president, finance, chief financial officer: Potlatch Corp. CORP AFFIL vice president: Duluth & Northeastern Railroad Co. NONPR AFFIL member: Idaho Society Certified Public Accountants; member: Idaho State Board Accounting; member: American Institute CPAs.

John M. Richards: trustee (see above)

Louis Pendelton Siegel: vice president, trustee (see above)

Thomas J. Smiekar: trustee

Hubert Duane Travaille: president, trustee B Bangkok, Thailand 1939. ED University of Michigan (1961); New York University (1970). PRIM CORP EMPL vice president public affairs: Potlatch Corp.

Gerald L. Zuehlke: treasurer (see above)

Grants Analysis

Disclosure Period: calendar year ending 1998
Total Grants: $369,133
Number of Grants: 524
Average Grant: $700

Recent Grants

Note: Grants derived from 1994 Form 990.

Education

10,000	University of Arkansas Fayetteville Business Administration, Fayetteville, AR
10,000	University of IDA Business Administration, Boise, ID
10,000	University of IDA Chemical Engineering, Boise, ID
10,000	University of IDA Wood Utilization, Boise, ID
10,000	University of Minnesota Twin Cities Forestry Research, Minneapolis, MN
8,000	University of Arkansas Monticello Forestry, Monticello, AR
4,000	University of Washington, Washington Pulp and Paper Foundation, Seattle, WA
3,000	North Carolina State University Pulp and Paper Foundation, Raleigh, NC
2,400	University of Minnesota Twin Cities Paper Science and Engineering, Minneapolis, MN
2,000	University of Minnesota Twin Cities Institute of Technology Department of Chemical Engineering, Minneapolis, MN
1,500	College of St. Scholastica Department of Accounting, Duluth, MN
1,500	University of Minnesota Duluth, College of Science and Engineering, Chemical Engineering, Duluth, MN
1,500	University of North Dakota Department of Engineering, Grand Forks, ND
1,500	University of Wisconsin Stevens Point, Pulp and Paper Technology, Stevens Point, WI

Science

2,500	Institute of Paper Science and Technology, Atlanta, GA

POTOMAC ELECTRIC POWER CO.

Company Contact

Washington, DC
Web: http://www.pepco.com/home.html

Company Description

Revenue: US$2,476,000,000 (1999)
Employees: 3,716 (1999)
SIC(s): 4911 Electric Services.

Giving Contact

William T. Torgerson, Chairman, Contributions Committee
Potomac ElectricPower Co.
1900 Pennsylvania Ave., NW, Rm 841
Washington, DC 20068
Phone: (202)872-2365
Fax: (202)261-7889

Description

Organization Type: Corporate Giving Program
Giving Locations: DC: Washington company service area of greater Washington DC
Grant Types: Capital, Project.

Financial Summary

Total Giving: Contributes through corporate direct giving program only.

Typical Recipients

Arts & Humanities: Arts Associations & Councils, Arts Centers, Dance, Historic Preservation, Libraries, Museums/Galleries, Music, Opera, Performing Arts, Public Broadcasting, Theater

Civic & Public Affairs: Business/Free Enterprise, Civil Rights, Employment/Job Training, Municipalities/Towns, Urban & Community Affairs, Women's Affairs

Education: Colleges & Universities, Education Associations, Education Funds, Literacy, Minority Education, Public Education (Precollege), Science/Mathematics Education, Student Aid

Environment: Environment-General

Health: Health Organizations, Hospices, Hospitals, Medical Research, Single-Disease Health Associations

International: International Peace & Security Issues

Religion: Churches, Religious Organizations

Social Services: Animal Protection, Child Welfare, Community Service Organizations, Family Services, Food/Clothing Distribution, People with Disabilities, Recreation & Athletics, Senior Services, Shelters/Homelessness, Substance Abuse, United Funds/United Ways, Youth Organizations

Contributions Analysis

Giving Priorities: Social welfare, united funds, the arts, and education.

Arts & Humanities: 30% to 35%. Nationally known performing arts centers in Washington, D.C. commonly receive large grants. Interests also include music and opera, theater, public broadcasting, libraries, and historic preservation.

Education: 15% to 20%. Extensive support is given to colleges anduniversities; also supports education funds, minority and scientific education, student aid, and literacy.

Health: 5% to 10%. Interests include hospitals, hospices, health organizations, and pediatric health.

Social Services: 35% to 40%. Main priority is united funds. The remainder supports organizations dealing with youth, the elderly, drug and alcohol abuse, the disabled, and employment.

Application Procedures

Initial Contact: written proposal

Application Requirements: a description of organization, including goals, structure, and sources of funding; amount requested, purpose of funds sought; proof of tax-exempt status

Deadlines: None, but proposal should be submitted well in advance of need.

Review Process: Contributions Committee reviews request on a case-by-case basis

Restrictions

Funds only organizations in company's service territory; does not provide operating funds.

Giving Program Officials

William T. Torgerson: managing B Annapolis, MD 1944. ED Princeton University BA (1966); University of Maryland JD (1973). PRIM CORP EMPL senior vice president external affairs, general counsel: Potomac Electric Power Co. CORP AFFIL senior vice president: Constellation Energy Corp.

PPG INDUSTRIES, INC.

Company Contact

One PPG Place
Pittsburgh, PA 15272
Phone: (412)434-3131
Web: http://www.ppg.com

Company Description

Revenue: US$7,757,000,000 (1999)
Employees: 32,500 (1999)
Fortune Rank: 227, per FORTUNE Magazine's list of 500 Largest U.S. Corporations (1999).
FF 227
SIC(s): 2812 Alkalies & Chlorine, 2851 Paints & Allied Products, 2869 Industrial Organic Chemicals Nec, 2891 Adhesives & Sealants.

Operating Locations

Argentina: PPG Industries Argentina, Pilar; Australia: PPG Industries Australia, Clayton; Transitions Optical, Lonsdale; Belgium: PPG Packaging Coatings Benelux, Brussels; Brazil: PPG Industrial do Brasil, Cajamar, Sumare; Transitions Optical do Brasil, Sumare; Canada: PPG Canada Inc., Alliston, Beauharnois, Hawkesbury, Kitchener; PPG Canada, Mississauga; PPG Canada Inc., Oshawa, Owen Sound; Chemfil Canada Ltd., Windsor; PPG Canada, Winnepeg; England: PPG Industries (UK), Birmingham; PPG Packaging (UK), London (Silvertown); PPG Industries (UK), Wigan; France: Sipsy Chimie Fine, Avrille; Gonfreville Coatings, Gonfreville; PPG Industries France, Saultain; Germany: PPG Industries Lacke, Saarwellingen; PPG Industries Lackfabrik, Weingarten, Rheinland-Pfalz; PPG Industries Lacke, Wuppertal; Ireland: Transitions Optical, Tuam; Italy: PPG Industries Italia, Baranzate di Bollate, Caivano; Ampaspace, Casaletto Vaprio, Lombardia; PPG Industries Italia, Genoa; PPG Industries Italia, Milan, Quattordio; Mexico: PPG Industries de Mexico, Altamira; PPG Industries de Mexico, San Juan del Rio; Netherlands: PPG Chemicals, Delfzijl; PPG Industries Fiber Glass, Hoogezand; PPG Coatings, Tiel; Philippines: Transitions Optical Phillipines, Laguna; Spain: PPG Iberica, Rubi, Cataluna; Turkey: PPG Industries Kimya Sanayi ve Ticaret, Bursa; Taiwan: Taiwan Chlorine Industries, Kaohsiumg; PPG Industries Taiwan, Sanyi

Nonmonetary Support

Type: In-kind Services

Volunteer Programs: Sponsors the GIVE Program to recognize employee involvement in volunteerism. Employees may apply for one grant of $250 annually to benefit an eligible non-profit organization for whom they volunteer.

Note: Nonmonetary support is contributed in the form of administrative services.

Corporate Sponsorship

Type: Arts & cultural events; Sports events
Contact: Carol Wilkins, Manager, Communications & Motorsports

PPG Industries Foundation

Giving Contact

Ms. Sue Sloan, Program Officer
PPG Industries Foundation
Phone: (412)434-2962

Description

EIN: 256037790
Organization Type: Corporate Foundation
Giving Locations: PA: Pittsburgh headquarters and operating communities; nationally.
Grant Types: Capital, Department, Emergency, Employee Matching Gifts, General Support, Multiyear/ Continuing Support, Operating Expenses, Project.
Note: Employee matching gift ratio: 1 to 1 up to $10,000 per eligible donor per organization.

Giving Philosophy

'The Foundation shares a unique role in American philanthropy with other corporate contributions programs. As a 'corporate' foundation, it must be sensitive to many publics: employees, shareholders, plant communities, customers, government, minorities, the needy and those who advocate for them, and civic institutions seeking to shape the future of our society.' PPG Industries Foundation Annual Report

Financial Summary

Total Giving: $4,817,329 (1998); $4,795,805 (1997); $4,551,185 (1996). Note: Contributes through corporate direct giving program and foundation.
Giving Analysis: Giving for 1996 includes: foundation ($2,637,364); foundation matching gifts ($1,076,096); foundation grants to United Way ($837,725); 1998: foundation ($2,690,329); foundation matching gifts ($1,227,000); foundation grants to United Way ($900,000)
Assets: $19,088,188 (1997); $16,426,243 (1996); $15,536,150 (1995)
Gifts Received: $5,240,153 (1996); $5,236,099 (1995); $213,499 (1993). Note: Foundation receives contributions from PPG Industries in the form of cash and administrative services.

Typical Recipients

Arts & Humanities: Arts Associations & Councils, Arts Festivals, Ballet, Community Arts, Dance, Historic Preservation, History & Archaeology, Libraries, Literary Arts, Museums/Galleries, Music, Opera, Performing Arts, Public Broadcasting
Civic & Public Affairs: Botanical Gardens/Parks, Business/Free Enterprise, Civil Rights, Economic Development, Economic Policy, Employment/Job Training, Housing, Law & Justice, Municipalities/Towns, Professional & Trade Associations, Public Policy, Safety, Urban & Community Affairs, Women's Affairs, Zoos/Aquariums
Education: Business Education, Business-School Partnerships, Colleges & Universities, Community & Junior Colleges, Economic Education, Education Associations, Education Funds, Engineering/Technological Education, Environmental Education, Faculty Development, Minority Education, Private Education (Precollege), Public Education (Precollege), Science/ Mathematics Education, Secondary Education (Public), Student Aid
Environment: Environment-General
Health: Clinics/Medical Centers, Emergency/Ambulance Services, Health Policy/Cost Containment, Health Organizations, Hospitals, Long-Term Care, Medical Rehabilitation, Mental Health, Nursing Services, Public Health, Single-Disease Health Associations
International: International Relations
Religion: Jewish Causes, Religious Welfare
Science: Observatories & Planetariums, Science Exhibits & Fairs, Scientific Centers & Institutes, Scientific Organizations
Social Services: Child Welfare, Community Centers, Community Service Organizations, Day Care, Family Services, Food/Clothing Distribution, Homes, People with Disabilities, Scouts, Senior Services, Shelters/ Homelessness, United Funds/United Ways, Volunteer Services, YMCA/YWCA/YMHA/YWHA, Youth Organizations

Contributions Analysis

Giving Priorities: Social welfare, higher education, and culture.
Arts & Humanities: 8%. Pittsburgh arts organizations, including symphonies, libraries, and museums. Also supports local performing arts organizations and public broadcasting.
Civic & Public Affairs: 8%. Research, education, and the dissemination of information related to the areas of economic education and development, and public policy issues. Large grants are awarded to support economic development and public policy groups. Other recipients include business and free enterprise, and civil rights groups.
Education: 36%. Most grants support higher education, with emphasis on private colleges and universities, especially those in plant communities and those with engineering and science programs. Of special interest are science-based efforts that attract students to chemistry, business, and engineering; education for minorities; and support of studentsachieving high academic standards. Other areas receiving major gifts include college funds, minority engineering and other education associations, and precollege education. Awards include capital and operating support.
Health: 6%. Improved patient care, effective deliveryof services, and educational programs.
Social Services: 45%. Primarily United Way campaigns, which receive about two-thirds of human service funds. An additional priority is funding programs through employee volunteer allocations. Other grants are allocated for capital projects and special programs to provide support for new facilities and changing services.

Application Procedures

Initial Contact: one- to two-page letter to foundation if organizations are located in Pittsburgh area or are national in scope; organizations serving communities where PPG facilities are located should direct inquiries to local PPG agent
Application Requirements: brief outline of purpose of organization; organization's mission statement; population it serves, including project benefit; grant's purpose; project summary; schedule of implementation; methods of evaluation; most recent audited financial statement; financial analysis for the project; list of board members and their affiliations; proof of tax-exempt status; amount requested and rationale; and person in charge of the project and their qualifications
Deadlines: None; requests are reviewed year-round.
Review Process: screening committee reviews appeals quarterly; committee decides on grants of less than $10,000; board reviews grants of more than $10,000
Evaluative Criteria: correspondence of applicant's goal to foundation's priorities; available resources; financial need of organization; foundation's past experience with organization; applicant's capability and reputation; funds available from other funders; duplication of work; population served; proposal's clarity and breadth; and practices of other corporate funders

Restrictions

No grant application for less than $100 will be considered. Foundation does not support operating funds of United Way agencies; political activities or organizations; individuals; endowments; organizations outside the United States or its territories; projects which would directly benefit PPG Industries, Inc.; advertising in benefit publications; sectarian groups for religious purposes; and telephone solicitations.
Company gives directly to charities under the Pennsylvania Neighborhood Assistance Act in the Pittsburgh area.
Company gives directly to charities under the Pennsylvania Neighborhood Assistance Act in the Pittsburgh area.

Additional Information

To ensure sensitivity to local needs in PPG plant communities, the foundation has developed a local agent system. Approximately 40 company managers, most of whom live in PPG plant communities, have been designated as local agents for the foundation. Once a year agents recommend a budget for contributions in their communities to a screening committee for presentation to the foundation board.
Publications: Foundation Annual Report

Corporate Officials

Frank A. Archinaco: executive vice president ED Seton Hall University MBA; Villanova University BA. PRIM CORP EMPL executive vice president: PPG Industries, Inc.
Russell L. Crane: senior vice president B Independence, KS. ED University of Kansas BS. PRIM CORP EMPL senior vice president: PPG Industries, Inc. CORP AFFIL director: Lobon Policy Association. NONPR AFFIL director: Employment Policy Foundation.
William H. Hernandez: senior vice president B Pittsburgh, PA 1948. ED University of Pennsylvania Wharton School BA (1970); Harvard University Graduate School of Business Administration MBA (1973). PRIM CORP EMPL senior vice president: PPG Industries, Inc. NONPR AFFIL member: Institute of Management Accountants; member: National Association Accts; member: Conference Board Council Financial Executive; member: Financial Executives Institute.
Raymond W. LeBoeuf: director, chairman, chief executive officer B Chicago, IL 1946. ED Northwestern University BA (1967); University of Illinois MBA (1970). PRIM CORP EMPL director, chairman, chief executive officer: PPG Industries, Inc. CORP AFFIL chairman: Keeler & Long Inc.; director: Praxair Inc. NONPR AFFIL director: Magee-Women's Hospital; trustee: Robert Morris College; member: Financial Executives Institute.
E. Kears Pollock: executive vice president B Marion Center, PA. ED Carnegie Mellon University BS (1962); Carnegie Mellon University MS (1964); Duquesne University JD (1970). PRIM CORP EMPL executive vice president: PPG Industries, Inc. NONPR AFFIL member: Society Automotive Engineers; member: Society Manufacturing Engineers; director: Pittsburgh Ballet Theatre; director: Chemical Manufacturers Association; director: National Paint & Coatings Association; member: American Intellectual Property Law Association; director: Carnegie Mellon University; member: American Bar Association; member: American Institute Chemical Engineers.

Foundation Officials

Frank A. Archinaco: director (see above)
Russell L. Crane: director (see above)
William H. Hernandez: director (see above)
Dan W. Kiener: member screening committee B Rocky River, OH 1951. ED Georgetown University BS (1974); Columbia University MBA (1976). PRIM CORP EMPL treasurer: PPG Industries Inc. CORP AFFIL director: Pittsburgh Corning Corp. NONPR AFFIL member: Financial Executives Institute.
Raymond W. LeBoeuf: director (see above)

Richard B. Leggett: member screening committee B Mobile, AL. ED Auburn University BS (1971). PRIM CORP EMPL vice president flatglass: PPG Industries Inc. NONPR AFFIL director: Pittsburgh Zoo.
Donna Magill: member screening committee
Maurice V. Peconi: member screening committee B New Kensington, PA. ED Duquesne University MBA; Duquesne University BS. PRIM CORP EMPL vice president: PPG Industries Inc. NONPR AFFIL director: Pittsburgh Childrens Museum.
E. Kears Pollock: director (see above)
Roslyn Rosenblatt: chairman, executive director
Sue Sloan: program officer
Kevin F. Sullivan: member screening committee B Baltimore, MD. ED Case Western Reserve University; Franklin and Marshall College. PRIM CORP EMPL vice president: PPG Industries Inc. NONPR AFFIL director: Society Plastics Industry.

Grants Analysis

Disclosure Period: calendar year ending 1998
Total Grants: $2,690,329*
Number of Grants: 609
Average Grant: $4,418
Highest Grant: $500,000
Typical Range: $1,000 to $20,000
***Note:** Grant analysis provided by foundation. Giving excludes matching gifts; United Way.

Recent Grants

Note: Grants derived from 1996 Form 990.

Arts & Humanities

75,000 Historical Society of Western Pennsylvania, Pittsburgh, PA
50,000 Historical Society of Western Pennsylvania, Pittsburgh, PA
50,000 Pittsburgh Symphony Society, Pittsburgh, PA
50,000 QED Communications, Pittsburgh, PA
35,000 Pittsburgh Cultural Trust, Pittsburgh, PA
31,000 Carnegie Library, Pittsburgh, PA
20,000 Pittsburgh Children's Museum, Pittsburgh, PA
20,000 Pittsburgh Opera, Pittsburgh, PA
17,500 River City Brass Band, Pittsburgh, PA
15,000 Pittsburgh Ballet Theater, Pittsburgh, PA

Civic & Public Affairs

50,000 City of Lake Charles, Lake Charles, LA
25,000 Allegheny Conference and Community Development, Pittsburgh, PA
25,000 Monmouth Valley Initiative, Homestead, PA
25,000 Pennsylvania Institute of Certified Public Accountants, Philadelphia, PA
20,000 Pennsylvania's Southwest Association, PA
20,000 Zoological Society, Pittsburgh, PA
18,000 Pennsylvania Economy League, Harrisburg, PA

Education

309,170 National Merit Scholarship Corporation, Evanston, IL
100,000 Carnegie Mellon University Chemistry Department, Pittsburgh, PA
50,000 Community College of Allegheny County, Pittsburgh, PA
50,000 Robert Morris College, Pittsburgh, PA
30,000 Rhode Island University Foundation, RI
25,000 Florida A&M University, Tallahassee, FL
25,000 Manufacturing Institute, Washington, DC
25,000 Pittsburgh Voyager, Pittsburgh, PA
25,000 University of Pittsburgh, Pittsburgh, PA
20,000 Langley High School, Pittsburgh, PA
18,450 Junior Achievement, Pittsburgh, PA
15,000 National Action Council for Minorities in Engineering, New York, NY

Health

30,000 Magee Women's Health Foundation, Pittsburgh, PA

Religion

30,000 Salvation Army, Pittsburgh, PA
30,000 United Jewish Federation, Pittsburgh, PA

Science

100,000 Carnegie Science Center, Pittsburgh, PA

Social Services

500,000 United Way Southwestern Pennsylvania, Pittsburgh, PA
64,500 United Way Southwest Louisiana, Lake Charles, LA
30,000 Girl Scouts of America Southwestern Pennsylvania, Pittsburgh, PA
28,500 United Way, Huntsville, AL
25,000 Goodwill Industries, Pittsburgh, PA
25,000 Miryam's, Pittsburgh, PA
25,000 United Way, Decatur, GA
25,000 YMCA, Pittsburgh, PA
24,000 United Way, Carlisle, PA
20,000 Family Communications, Pittsburgh, PA
20,000 United Fund, Lexington, NC
20,000 United Way, Oak Creek, WI
20,000 United Way West Crawford County, Meadville, PA
20,000 YMCA, Lexington, NC
17,250 United Way, Cleveland, OH
17,000 United Way, Altoona, PA
15,000 Arc of Allegheny, PA

PRAXAIR

Company Contact

Danbury, CT
Web: http://www.praxair.com

Company Description

Revenue: US$4,639,000,000 (1999)
Employees: 23,000
Fortune Rank: 347, per FORTUNE Magazine's list of 500 Largest U.S. Corporations (1999).
FF 347
SIC(s): 2813 Industrial Gases.

Praxair Foundation

Giving Contact

Nigel D. Muir, President & Director
Praxair Foundation
39 Old Ridgebury Rd.
Danbury, CT 06810-5113
Phone: (203)837-2000
Fax: (203)837-2550

Description

Founded: 1995
EIN: 061413665
Organization Type: Corporate Foundation

Financial Summary

Total Giving: $663,258 (fiscal year ending November 30, 1997); $369,245 (fiscal 1996); $194,283 (fiscal 1995)
Assets: $630,260 (fiscal 1997); $675,233 (fiscal 1996); $1,123,590 (fiscal 1995)
Gifts Received: $589,478 (fiscal 1997); $1,318,333 (fiscal 1995). Note: In fiscal 1995, contributions were received from Praxair, Inc. ($185,000) and Linde Gases of the Mid-Atlantic ($1,133,333).

Typical Recipients

Civic & Public Affairs: Botanical Gardens/Parks, Business/Free Enterprise, Economic Development, Civic & Public Affairs-General, Hispanic Affairs, Legal Aid, Minority Business, Professional & Trade Associations, Urban & Community Affairs, Women's Affairs
Education: Business Education, Colleges & Universities, Education Funds, Engineering/Technological Education, Education-General, Medical Education, Student Aid, Vocational & Technical Education
Environment: Environment-General, Resource Conservation
Health: AIDS/HIV, Cancer, Children's Health/Hospitals, Clinics/Medical Centers, Emergency/Ambulance Services, Hospices, Hospitals, Medical Rehabilitation, Single-Disease Health Associations, Transplant Networks/Donor Banks
International: Health Care/Hospitals
Religion: Jewish Causes, Religious Welfare
Science: Science Exhibits & Fairs, Science Museums
Social Services: At-Risk Youth, Community Centers, Community Service Organizations, Crime Prevention, Day Care, Family Services, Scouts, United Funds/United Ways, YMCA/YWCA/YMHA/YWHA, Youth Organizations

Application Procedures

Initial Contact: The foundation has no formal grant application procedure or application form.
Deadlines: None.
Review Process: Requests are reviewed every 3-4 weeks.

Corporate Officials

John A. Clerico: chief financial officer, chief executive officer PRIM CORP EMPL chief financial officer: Praxair.
Edgar G. Hotard: president PRIM CORP EMPL president: Praxair.
Horst William Lichtenberger: chairman, chief executive officer B Yugoslavia 1935. ED University of Iowa BA (1957); University of Iowa BS (1959); State University of New York MBA (1962). PRIM CORP EMPL chairman, chief executive officer: Praxair. NONPR AFFIL member: American Iron & Steel Institute; member: Chemical Manufacturers Association.

Foundation Officials

John A. Anello: treasurer
Robert Bassett: secretary
John A. Clerico: chief financial officer
Nigel D. Muir: president, director PRIM CORP EMPL vice president communications: Praxair.
S. Mark Seymour: director
J. Robert Vipond: director PRIM CORP EMPL vice president, controller: Praxair.

Grants Analysis

Disclosure Period: fiscal year ending November 30, 1997
Total Grants: $663,258
Number of Grants: 72
Average Grant: $9,212
Highest Grant: $40,000
Typical Range: $500 to $5,000

Recent Grants

Note: Grants derived from fiscal 1997 Form 990.

Civic & Public Affairs

60,000 Inroads, Saint Louis, MO
10,000 Botanical Gardens

Education

40,000 College Fund
40,000 University of Buffalo Foundation, Buffalo, NY
10,000 Occupational School Fund
10,000 University of Iowa Foundation, Iowa City, IA
8,000 Foundation of University of Medicine and Dentistry, NJ
7,500 Foundation of University of Medicine and Dentistry, NJ

Environment

8,800 Connecticut Audubon Center, CT

Health

30,000	Danbury Hospital Development Fund, Danbury, CT
16,000	Datahr Rehabilitation Institute, Danbury, CT
12,000	American Red Cross

International

20,000	Heart to Heart International
10,000	Operation Smile, Norfolk, VA

Religion

7,500	Anti-Defamation League, New York, NY

Science

8,000	Putnam Children's Discovery Center, Carmel, NY

Social Services

160,207	United Way
10,000	Horizons
10,000	Phoenix House
8,250	Boy Scouts of America

Premark International Inc.

Company Contact

1717 Deefield Rd.
Deerfield, IL 60015
Phone: (847)405-6000
Fax: (847)405-6013
Web: http://www.premarkintl.com

Company Description

Profit: US$237,600,000
Employees: 16,300
SIC(s): 2891 Adhesives & Sealants, 3089 Plastics Products Nec, 3565 Packaging Machinery, 3596 Scales & Balances Except Laboratory.
Parent Company: Illinois Tool Works, Inc., 3600 W. Lake Ave., Glenview, IL, United States

Nonmonetary Support

Value: $77,000 (1996)
Type: Donated Equipment
Note: Company also donates surplus and support services.

Giving Contact

Isabelle Goossen, Vice President & Treasurer
Premark International Inc.
1717 Deerfield Road
Deerfield, IL 60015
Phone: (847)405-6218
Fax: (847)405-6311

Description

Organization Type: Corporate Giving Program
Giving Locations: nationally.
Grant Types: Employee Matching Gifts, Fellowship, General Support, Scholarship.
Note: Employee matching gift ratio: 1 to 1, up to $3,500.

Giving Philosophy

'Premark International, Inc. supports good corporate citizenship throughout its diverse organization. While the company's high-quality products and services and equitable employment practices provide the most effective benefits for communities, our contributions program adds another dimension to corporate citizenship. By maintaining a close relationship between corporate and community well-being, we strengthen the social fabric as a whole.' Objectives and Guidelines for Charitable Giving

Financial Summary

Total Giving: $350,000 (1997 approx); $327,000 (1996 approx); $293,800 (1995). Note: Contributes through corporate direct giving program only. 1996 Giving includes corporate direct giving; nonmonetary support.

Typical Recipients

Education: Education-General

Contributions Analysis

Education: Supports education from preschool to accredited four-year colleges, universities, and professional institutions. Supports operating, research, and capital needs, and scholarships and fellowships.
Health: Supports nonprofit organizations dedicated to the physical and emotional well-being of people of all ages, with a focus on community and economic development, and the needs of minorities, women, and people with disabilities. Supports alcohol and substance abuse rehabilitation; United Way; health and human service agencies; nutrition, health, and wellness programs; senior citizens; and youth groups.

Application Procedures

Initial Contact: written proposal
Application Requirements: general program information, including a statement of the history, purpose, and achievements of the organization; proposal, including an indication of how program innovatively responds to an important need, is supported by the targeted constituency it intends to serve; and is cost effective; budgets for the organization and program, for current and previous fiscal years; audited financial statement; proof of tax-exempt status; list of officers and board members; list of other donors; list of accrediting agencies, as appropriate; statement of fundraising expenses
Deadlines: None.
Review Process: cooperate contributions committee reviews and awards contributions

Restrictions

Company will not fund individuals; organizations with a limited constituency, such as fraternal or veterans' groups; sectarian religious groups; political or lobbying groups; travel, tuition, and registration fees; membership dues; goodwill advertising; loan; or tickets for dinners, sporting events, or other fundraising benefits.

Additional Information

Company is committed to contributing a maximum of 2% of domestic pretax net income.
Publications: Objectives and Guidelines for Charitable Giving

Corporate Officials

James M. Ringler: chairman, president, chief executive officer, director B 1945. ED State University of New York Buffalo BS (1967); State University of New York Buffalo MBA (1968). PRIM CORP EMPL chairman, president, chief executive officer, director: Premark International Inc. ADD CORP EMPL president: Hobart International Holdings; president: Hobart Sales & Service Inc.; president, chief operating officer, director: Tappan Co. CORP AFFIL director: Reynolds Metals Co.; director: Union Carbide Corp.

Giving Program Officials

Isabelle C. Goossen: PRIM CORP EMPL vice president, treasurer: Premark International Inc.

Premier Dental Products Co.

Company Contact

Norristown, PA
Web: http://www.premusa.com

Company Description

Employees: 175
SIC(s): 5047 Medical & Hospital Equipment.

Julius and Ray Charlestein Foundation

Giving Contact

Morton Charlestein, President
Julius & Ray Charlestein Foundation
3600 Horizon Drive
King of Prussia, PA 19406
Phone: 888-773-6872
Fax: (610)239-6172

Description

Founded: 1963
EIN: 232310090
Organization Type: Corporate Foundation. Supports preselected organizations only.
Giving Locations: PA nationally.
Grant Types: General Support.

Financial Summary

Total Giving: $355,074 (fiscal year ending June 30, 1997); $275,937 (fiscal 1996); $452,979 (fiscal 1994). Note: Contributes through foundation only.
Assets: $3,592,357 (fiscal 1997); $3,365,021 (fiscal 1996); $3,359,236 (fiscal 1994)
Gifts Received: $34,750 (fiscal 1997); $100,000 (fiscal 1994); $100,000 (fiscal 1993). Note: In fiscal 1997, contributions were received from Premier Dental Products Company. In fiscal 1994, foundation received contributions from Premier Dental Products Co.

Typical Recipients

Arts & Humanities: Arts Associations & Councils, Historic Preservation, Museums/Galleries, Music, Performing Arts, Theater
Civic & Public Affairs: Chambers of Commerce, Clubs, Economic Development, Employment/Job Training, Ethnic Organizations, Civic & Public Affairs-General, Municipalities/Towns
Education: Colleges & Universities, Education-General, Medical Education, Minority Education, Private Education (Precollege), Religious Education, Science/Mathematics Education, Special Education, Student Aid
Health: Alzheimers Disease, Children's Health/Hospitals, Diabetes, Eyes/Blindness, Geriatric Health, Health Organizations, Hospitals (University Affiliated), Medical Rehabilitation, Medical Research, Nursing Services, Public Health, Single-Disease Health Associations
International: Foreign Educational Institutions, Health Care/Hospitals, International Organizations, International Relief Efforts, Missionary/Religious Activities
Religion: Jewish Causes, Religious Organizations, Religious Welfare, Seminaries, Social/Policy Issues, Synagogues/Temples
Science: Scientific Centers & Institutes
Social Services: Camps, Community Centers, Community Service Organizations, Family Planning, Food/Clothing Distribution, People with Disabilities, Recreation & Athletics, Social Services-General, Youth Organizations

Contributions Analysis

Education: 25% to 30%. Primarily Jewish universities, secondary education, and religious education.
Health: About 15%. Single-disease health associations, medical centers, and health foundations.
International: 5% to 10%. Foreign education institutions, missionary activities, and people with disabilities.
Religion: 45% to 50%. Variety of Jewish organizations.

Corporate Officials

Morton Charlestein: president PRIM CORP EMPL president: Premier Dental Products Co.

Foundation Officials

Morton Charlestein: president (see above)
Ellyn C. Phillips: executive director NONPR AFFIL director: Amyotrophic Lateral Sclerosis Association.

Grants Analysis

Disclosure Period: fiscal year ending June 30, 1997
Total Grants: $355,074
Number of Grants: 97
Average Grant: $3,661
Highest Grant: $120,000
Typical Range: $300 to $10,000

Recent Grants

Note: Grants derived from fiscal 1997 Form 990.

Arts & Humanities

5,000 Regional Performing Arts Center, Philadelphia, PA
577 Mann Music Center, Philadelphia, PA
500 Please Touch Museum, Philadelphia, PA

Civic & Public Affairs

500 Philadelphia Opportunities Industrialization Corp, Philadelphia, PA

Education

20,000 Akiba Hebrew Academy, Merion Station, PA
2,500 Solomon Schechter Day School, Bala Cynwyd, PA
1,500 CCFA, Feasterville, PA
1,000 Grantz College, Melrose Park, PA
1,000 Har Zion Religious School, Penn Valley, PA
500 Overbrook School for the Blind, Philadelphia, PA
500 Temple University, Philadelphia, PA

Health

25,000 ALS Association, Blue Bell, PA
2,000 Charcot Marie Tooth Association, Upland, PA
1,000 ALS Association, Blue Bell, PA
1,000 Children's Hospital Foundation, Philadelphia, PA
1,000 Philadelphia Geriatric Center, Philadelphia, PA
500 Tay Sachs and Allied Disease Research, Jenkintown, PA
500 Temple University Hospital, Philadelphia, PA

International

30,000 American Friends of Hebrew University, Philadelphia, PA
5,000 American Friends of Weizmann Institute of Science, Philadelphia, PA
5,000 Jaffa Institute, Gladwyne, PA
1,000 Israel Guide Dog Center for the Blind, Warrington, PA
500 USA Chabad Children of Chernobyl, New York, NY

Religion

120,000 Jewish Federation, Philadelphia, PA
25,000 Har Zion Temple, Penn Valley, PA
20,000 American Interfaith Institute, Philadelphia, PA
20,000 Camp Ramah in Poconos, Jenkintown, PA
9,166 Jewish Federation, Philadelphia, PA
5,000 Jewish National Fund, Philadelphia, PA
5,000 Jewish Theological Seminary, Philadelphia, PA
3,000 Har Zion Temple, Penn Valley, PA
3,000 Har Zion Temple, Penn Valley, PA
2,500 Jewish Theological Seminary, Philadelphia, PA
2,500 Operation Understanding, Philadelphia, PA
2,000 Adath Jeshurun, Elkins Park, PA
1,000 B'nai B'rith Foundation, Philadelphia, PA
1,000 Germantown Jewish Center, Philadelphia, PA
1,000 Salvation Army, Philadelphia, PA
1,000 Temple Beth Zion, Royal Palm Beach, FL
750 Jewish Community Center, Philadelphia, PA
750 National Museum of American Jewish History, Philadelphia, PA
550 Youth Symposium of the Holocaust, Philadelphia, PA
500 Manna, Philadelphia, PA
500 Mansorti, Philadelphia, PA
500 Mansorti, Philadelphia, PA
500 Mansorti, Philadelphia, PA

Social Services

5,000 Woodrock, Philadelphia, PA
1,000 Philabundance, Philadelphia, PA
500 Kosher Meals on Wheels, Philadelphia, PA
500 Police Athletic League, Philadelphia, PA

PREMIER INDUSTRIAL CORP.

Company Contact

Cleveland, OH

Company Description

Employees: 4,300
SIC(s): 2842 Polishes & Sanitation Goods, 2899 Chemical Preparations Nec, 2992 Lubricating Oils & Greases, 3429 Hardware Nec.

Premier Industrial Foundation

Giving Contact

Morton Mandell, Chief Executive Officer
Premier Industrial Foundation
2829 Euclid Avenue
Cleveland, OH 44115
Phone: (216)875-6500
Fax: (216)875-6580

Description

Founded: 1953
EIN: 346522448
Organization Type: Corporate Foundation
Giving Locations: OH: Northeast Ohio with emphasis on Cleveland
Grant Types: Capital, General Support, Project, Scholarship.

Financial Summary

Total Giving: $714,424 (1996); $736,021 (1995); $856,722 (1994). Note: Contributes through foundation only. 1996 Giving includes foundation ($553,919); scholarship ($14,850); United Way ($145,655).
Assets: $41,105 (1996); $362,767 (1995); $127,466 (1994)
Gifts Received: $420,000 (1996); $975,000 (1995); $450,000 (1994). Note: Contributions are received from Premier Industrial Corp.; In 1996, contributions were received from Premier Industrial Corp. ($100,000) and Premier Farnell ($320,000).

Typical Recipients

Arts & Humanities: Arts Associations & Councils, Arts Centers, Arts Institutes, Arts Outreach, Ballet, Dance, Historic Preservation, History & Archaeology, Libraries, Museums/Galleries, Music, Opera, Performing Arts, Public Broadcasting, Theater
Civic & Public Affairs: African American Affairs, Clubs, Community Foundations, Economic Development, Employment/Job Training, Civic & Public Affairs-General, Municipalities/Towns, Nonprofit Management, Parades/Festivals, Philanthropic Organizations, Professional & Trade Associations, Safety, Urban & Community Affairs, Women's Affairs, Zoos/Aquariums
Education: Afterschool/Enrichment Programs, Business Education, Colleges & Universities, Economic Education, Education Associations, Education Funds, Education Reform, Education-General, Medical Education, Minority Education, Science/Mathematics Education, Student Aid
Environment: Environment-General, Resource Conservation
Health: AIDS/HIV, Clinics/Medical Centers, Emergency/Ambulance Services, Eyes/Blindness, Health Organizations, Hospices, Hospitals, Nursing Services, Public Health
International: International Affairs
Religion: Jewish Causes, Religious Organizations, Religious Welfare, Social/Policy Issues
Science: Science Museums, Scientific Centers & Institutes
Social Services: Child Welfare, Community Centers, Community Service Organizations, Crime Prevention, Domestic Violence, Emergency Relief, Food/Clothing Distribution, Homes, Recreation & Athletics, Scouts, Substance Abuse, United Funds/United Ways, Volunteer Services, YMCA/YWCA/YMHA/YWHA, Youth Organizations

Contributions Analysis

Giving Priorities: Social welfare, civic interests, health, and education.
Arts & Humanities: 5% to 10%. Museums, libraries, historical societies, and other arts centers. Support also goes to performing arts groups including theatre and music.
Civic & Public Affairs: About 30%. Philanthropic organizations, community-oriented groups such as safety councils, and zoological and nature organizations.
Education: About 30%. Higher education, including universities, technical schools, education funds, and commissions. Other recipients includeindependent programs such as Junior Achievement.
Religion: 5% to 10%. Religious welfare and Jewish organizations, including Jewish Community Federation and National Conference of Christians and Jews.
Social Services: 20% to 25%. Organizations that build homes and supply clothing to the needy, volunteer organizations, children's recreation groups such as Boy Scouts, and United Way organizations. Neighborhood and regional revitalization is a priority.

Application Procedures

Initial Contact: brief letter or proposal; no formal application form is used
Application Requirements: description of project and justification for grant; amount and terms of request; pertinent financial information; IRS exemption status, including copy of exemption letter; if available, appraisal of the requesting organization by a standard-setting organization
Deadlines: None.
Review Process: foundation board meets bimonthly
Evaluative Criteria: quality of nonprofit management; neighborhood and regional revitalization are priorities
Decision Notification: within two months

Additional Information

Company reports that it is in the process of restructuring at the time of publication.

Corporate Officials

Jack N. Mandel: director, treasurer B Austria 1911. ED Cleveland College; Fenn College (1930-1933).

PRIM CORP EMPL director: Premier Farnell PLC. CORP AFFIL founder, chairman finance committee: Premier Industries Corp. NONPR AFFIL trustee: Tel Aviv University Museum Diaspora; trustee: Temple Woodruff Foundation; member executive committee: National Conference Christians & Jews; life trustee: S Broward Jewish Federation; honorary trustee: Hebrew University; president: Montefiore Home Aged; member executive committee: Florida Society Blind; life trustee: Cleveland Jewish Welfare Foundation; trustee: Cleveland Playhouse; president advisory board: Barry University. CLUB AFFIL Commede Club; Emerald Hills Country Club; Beachmont Country Club.

Morton Leon Mandel: deputy chairman B Cleveland, OH 1921. ED Case Western Reserve University (1939-1940); Pomona College (1943). PRIM CORP EMPL deputy chairman: Premier Farnell PLC. CORP AFFIL chairman: MCM Electronics Inc.; chairman: Parkwood Corp.

Philip Stuart Sims: vice chairman, treasurer B Cleveland, OH 1927. ED Case Western Reserve University (1956). PRIM CORP EMPL vice chairman, treasurer: Premier Industries Corp.

Foundation Officials

Morton Leon Mandel: trustee (see above)

Grants Analysis

Disclosure Period: calendar year ending 1996
Total Grants: $553,919*
Number of Grants: 36
Average Grant: $15,387
Highest Grant: $135,500
Typical Range: $500 to $20,000
***Note:** Giving excludes scholarship; United Way. Average grant excludes the highest grant.

Recent Grants

Note: Grants derived from 1996 Form 990.

Arts & Humanities

30,000 Musical Arts Association, Cleveland, OH
10,000 Cleveland Playhouse, Cleveland, OH
3,000 Playhouse Square Foundation, Cleveland, OH
1,000 Young Audiences, Cleveland, OH
100 Cleveland Restoration Society, Cleveland, OH

Civic & Public Affairs

135,500 Neighborhood Progress, Cleveland, OH
82,000 Midtown Corridor, Cleveland, OH
43,332 Cleveland Bicentennial, Cleveland, OH
15,000 Cleveland Tomorrow, Cleveland, OH
10,000 Cleveland Initiative, Cleveland, OH
5,000 Independent Sector, Cleveland, OH
2,000 Greater Cleveland Roundtable, Cleveland, OH
1,300 Orville Development Fund, Wooster, OH
1,000 Youth Opportunities, Cleveland, OH
500 Miles Ahead, Cleveland, OH

Education

50,000 Case Western Reserve University, Cleveland, OH
12,000 Neighborhood Center, Cleveland, OH
7,500 University Circle, Cleveland, OH
5,000 John Carroll University, University Heights, OH
4,500 Ohio Foundation of Independent Colleges, Columbus, OH
2,000 Cleveland Scholarship Programs, Cleveland, OH
1,000 Northeast Ohio Council on Higher Education, Cleveland, OH
800 Junior Achievement Wayne County, Orrville, OH
750 Junior Achievement, Cleveland, OH
500 Cleveland Initiative for Education, Cleveland, OH

Environment

7,000 Clean Land Ohio, Cleveland, OH

Health

2,500 Free Clinic, Cleveland, OH

Religion

30,000 Jewish Community Federation, Cleveland, OH
5,000 First Presbyterian Society, Cleveland, OH
2,500 Catholic Charities, Cleveland, OH
1,000 Salvation Army, Cleveland, OH

Science

33,333 Great Lakes Museum of Science, Cleveland, OH

Social Services

101,055 United Way, Cleveland, OH
50,000 YMCA, Cleveland, OH
18,350 United Way Crusade of Mercy, Chicago, IL
16,000 United Way, Wooster, OH
4,100 United Way, Dayton, OH
2,400 United Way Central Indiana, Indianapolis, IN
2,000 United Way Community Services, Detroit, MI
1,750 United Way Cherokee County, Gaffney, SC
500 Girl Scouts of America Lake Erie Council, Cleveland, OH
500 YWCA, Cleveland, OH

T. Rowe Price Associates

Company Contact

PO Box 17630
Baltimore, MD 21297-1302
Phone: 800-225-5132
Email: info@troweprice.com
Web: http://www.troweprice.com

Company Description

Revenue: US$586,100,000
Employees: 2,587
SIC(s): 6282 Investment Advice.

Corporate Sponsorship

Type: Arts & cultural events; Festivals/fairs; Music & entertainment events; Pledge-a-thon

T. Rowe Price Associates Foundation

Giving Contact

Brenda K. Ashworth, Program Director
T. Rowe Price Associates Foundation
100 E. Pratt St., 8th Fl.
Baltimore, MD 21202
Phone: (410)345-3603
Fax: (410)685-2806

Alternate Contact

Albert C. Hubbard, Jr., President

Description

EIN: 521231953
Organization Type: Corporate Foundation
Giving Locations: headquarters and operating communities.
Grant Types: Capital, Employee Matching Gifts, General Support, Multiyear/Continuing Support.
Note: Employee matching gift ratio: 1:1.

Giving Philosophy

The foundation concentrates grantmaking in the following categories: Civic and Community Interest; Health and Welfare; Education, Secondary and Higher; and Culture and the Arts.

Financial Summary

Total Giving: $1,400,000 (1998 approx); $1,750,637 (1997); $1,475,834 (1996). Note: Contributes through corporate direct giving program and foundation.
Giving Analysis: Giving for 1996 includes: foundation grants to United Way ($110,800); 1997: foundation grants to United Way ($123,000)
Assets: $15,700,000 (1998 approx); $16,033,998 (1997); $12,054,741 (1996)
Gifts Received: $2,269,142 (1997); $4,215,267 (1996); $1,700,050 (1995). Note: Contributions are received from T. Rowe Price Associates.

Typical Recipients

Arts & Humanities: Arts Festivals, Arts Funds, Arts Institutes, Community Arts, Historic Preservation, History & Archaeology, Libraries, Museums/Galleries, Music, Opera, Public Broadcasting, Theater
Civic & Public Affairs: Botanical Gardens/Parks, Community Foundations, Economic Development, Civic & Public Affairs-General, Housing, Professional & Trade Associations, Public Policy, Urban & Community Affairs, Zoos/Aquariums
Education: Arts/Humanities Education, Business Education, Colleges & Universities, Education Funds, Elementary Education (Private), Education-General, Literacy, Minority Education, Private Education (Precollege), Public Education (Precollege), Secondary Education (Private), Student Aid
Environment: Environment-General, Resource Conservation
Health: Emergency/Ambulance Services, Health Organizations, Heart, Hospitals, Single-Disease Health Associations
Religion: Jewish Causes, Religious Welfare
Science: Science Museums
Social Services: Child Abuse, Child Welfare, Community Service Organizations, Family Services, Food/Clothing Distribution, People with Disabilities, Recreation & Athletics, Scouts, Shelters/Homelessness, United Funds/United Ways, Youth Organizations

Contributions Analysis

Giving Priorities: Education, the arts, and social welfare.
Arts & Humanities: 33%. Theaters, museums, galleries, music, art associations, and historic preservation.
Civic & Public Affairs: 9%. Public policy, community foundations, and urban and community affairs.
Education: 34%. Colleges and universities, public and private schools for precollege education, art education, business education, religious education, literacy, education scholarship funds, minority education, and Junior Achievement.
Religion: 2%. Supports Dominican and Jewish organizations.
Science: 2%. Supports a children's museum.
Social Services: 22%. United Way chapters, community centers, community service organizations, child welfare, shelters for abused women and children, and food distribution.
Note: Total contributions in 1997.

Application Procedures

Initial Contact: Send a brief letter or proposal.
Application Requirements: Include a description of the organization, with a brief history; copy of IRS determination letter; latest audited financial report; current operating budget and sources of income; list of organization's board members; annual report; and number of paid and volunteer employees. Information regarding the particular program should include purpose and objectives; needs to be addressed; population served; plan of action and timeframe; qualifications of administrators; total funding required and projected sources; and amount requested.
Deadlines: None.

Notes: All requests should be in writing.

Restrictions

Company does not support individuals, religious organizations for sectarian purposes, or political or lobbying groups. No support is given to organizations which are not tax-exempt, or to United Way/Combined Health Agency organizations (although capital campaigns will be considered).

Corporate Officials

George A. Roche: chairman, president B Rochester, NY 1941. ED Georgetown University (1963); Harvard University Graduate School of Business Administration MBA (1966). PRIM CORP EMPL chairman, president: T. Rowe Price Associates Inc. CORP AFFIL director: Telecommunications Inc.; president: TRP Finance Inc.; president, director: T Rowe Price New Era Fund Inc.

Foundation Officials

Brenda K. Ashworth: program director
Stephen W. Boesel: vice president, secretary, treasurer B Niles, OH 1944. ED Baldwin-Wallace College (1968); University of Denver (1969). PRIM CORP EMPL managing director: T.Rowe Price Associates Inc. ADD CORP EMPL vice president: T.Rowe Price New Era Fund Inc.
Jacquelin Hrabowski: vice president, trustee
Albert C. Hubbard, Jr.: chairman, president
Mary J. Miller: vice president, trustee PRIM CORP EMPL vice president: T. Rowe Price. CORP AFFIL managing director: T. Rowe Price Associates Inc.
Brian C. Roger: vice president, trustee

Grants Analysis

Disclosure Period: calendar year ending 1997
Total Grants: $1,750,637
Number of Grants: 404
Average Grant: $4,333
Highest Grant: $151,470
Typical Range: $500 to $5,000

Recent Grants

Note: Grants derived from 1997 Form 990.

Arts & Humanities

151,470 Walters Art Gallery, Baltimore, MD
88,850 Baltimore Museum of Art, Baltimore, MD
71,615 Center Stage, Baltimore, MD
30,640 Baltimore Symphony Orchestra, Baltimore, MD
30,000 Maryland Institute College of Art, Baltimore, MD
26,400 Maryland Historical Society, Baltimore, MD
10,000 Preservation Society
9,000 Baltimore Opera Company, Baltimore, MD

Civic & Public Affairs

50,000 Baltimore Community Foundation, Baltimore, MD
20,000 Enterprise Foundation, Columbia, MD
12,630 Constellation Foundation, Baltimore, MD
12,000 Parks and People Foundation, Baltimore, MD
9,000 Maryland Zoological Society, Baltimore, MD
8,500 Jeremy School, Owings Mills, MD

Education

100,000 Notre Dame Loyalty and Endowment Fund, West Haven, CT
30,100 College Bound Foundation, Baltimore, MD
30,000 Baltimore Educational Scholarship Trust, Baltimore, MD
21,300 Harvard University Graduate School of Business Administration, Cambridge, MA
20,650 Boston College, Chestnut Hill, MA
20,094 St. Paul's School, Brooklandville, MD
19,900 Gilman School, Baltimore, MD
16,500 Independent College Fund, Baltimore, MD
15,000 University of Baltimore Educational Foundation, Baltimore, MD
14,500 South Baltimore Learning Center, Baltimore, MD
14,400 University of Richmond, Richmond, VA
12,250 Garrison Forest School, Owings Mills, MD
11,200 Coppin State College, Baltimore, MD
11,125 Wake Forest University, Winston-Salem, NC
11,030 Loyola College, Baltimore, MD
10,125 Goucher College, Towson, MD
10,000 Lycoming College, Williamsport, PA
9,750 Fund for Educational Excellence, Baltimore, MD
9,070 Baltimore Hebrew University, Baltimore, MD
9,000 Teach Baltimore, Baltimore, MD
8,650 Stanford University, Stanford, CA
8,500 Johns Hopkins University School of Arts and Sciences, Baltimore, MD
8,000 Virginia Military Institute Foundation, Lexington, VA
7,800 St. Ignatius Loyola Academy, Baltimore, MD

Religion

10,000 Adrian Dominican Sisters
10,000 Associated Jewish Community

Science

30,000 Port Discovery Children's Museum, Baltimore, MD

Social Services

100,000 United Way of Central Maryland, Baltimore, MD
75,000 Police Athletic League
15,000 Maryland Food Bank, Baltimore, MD
11,250 Paul's Place, Baltimore, MD
11,000 United Way of Hillsborough County, Tampa, FL
10,000 Girl Scouts of America of Central Maryland, Baltimore, MD
10,000 National Organization on Disability, Washington, DC
10,000 Woodbourne Foundation, Baltimore, MD
9,000 United Way, Los Angeles, CA

PRICEWATERHOUSECOOPERS

Company Contact

New York, NY
Web: http://www.pwcglobal.com

Company Description

Former Name: Price Waterhouse.
Employees: 48,723
SIC(s): 8721 Accounting, Auditing & Bookkeeping, 8742 Management Consulting Services.

Operating Locations

Corporate headquarters in New York City; local offices maintained throughout the USA.

PricewaterhouseCoopers Foundation

Giving Contact

Mr. Larry P. Scott, Executive Director
PricewaterhouseCoopers Foundation
400 Campus Drive
PO Box 988
Florham Park, NJ 07932
Phone: (973)236-5113
Fax: (973)236-5714

Description

EIN: 136119208
Organization Type: Corporate Foundation. Supports preselected organizations only.
Giving Locations: nationally.
Grant Types: Department, Fellowship, Multiyear/Continuing Support.

Giving Philosophy

'The PW Foundation was established in 1956 to formalize the firm's long-standing commitment to supporting the advancement of accounting and business education. The Foundation's mission embraces two essential principles: fulfillment of our professional responsibility to support that part of the academic community devoted to excellence in accounting and business education and related research; enhancement of the quality of graduates attracted to the profession.' Pricewaterhouse Foundation Initiatives Supporting Higher Education

Financial Summary

Total Giving: $2,250,000 (2000 approx); $2,250,000 (1999 approx); $1,000,000 (1998 approx). Note: Contributes through corporate direct giving program and foundation.
Assets: $33,164 (1996); $33,014 (1995); $33,099 (1994)
Gifts Received: $150 (1996); $200 (1993); $9,570 (1992). Note: Foundation received contributions from Howard Dudley Murphy.

Typical Recipients

Education: Business Education, Colleges & Universities, Education Associations

Contributions Analysis

Giving Priorities: Education..
Education: Sole priority, 100%. Supports accounting and business education at colleges and universities nationwide. Interests include projects for analysis and restructuring of accounting curriculum, development of business information technology, and the advancement of minorities in careers in public accounting. Also provides direct grants for teaching fellowships, lecture series, awards programs and professional seminars. Maintains an employee matching gifts program. Occasional support for education and business associations and funds (less than 5% of total grants). Educational support targeted to schools from which company recruits prospective employees.

Application Procedures

Initial Contact: Send a brief letter or proposal to nearest local practice office.
Application Requirements: A description of organization, amount requested, purpose of funds sought, proof of tax-exempt status.
Deadlines: None.
Review Process: If proposal has the support of the local practice office, it is submitted to foundation directors for review at next scheduled meeting at foundation's national office.
Evaluative Criteria: Primarily, the quality of the school for which support is sought; specifically, the quality of the school's accounting and business education program.
Decision Notification: Generally, in August; additional meetings scheduled throughout the year.
Notes: Foundation does give to some preselected organizations as well.

Restrictions

All giving is restricted to educational activities. Foundation does not support individuals directly and does not give outside the United States and its possessions.

Additional Information

In July of 1998, Price Waterhouse and Coopers & Lybrand merged to form PricewaterhouseCoopers.

Corporate Officials

Frances Engoran: director, senior partner PRIM CORP EMPL director: PricewaterhouseCoopers.
Marie Gerke: secretary PRIM CORP EMPL secretary: PricewaterhouseCoopers.
James J. Schiro: chairman, senior partner B 1946. ED Dartmouth College Amos Tuck School Executive Program; Saint John's University BS (1995). PRIM CORP EMPL chairman, senior partner: PricewaterhouseCoopers. NONPR AFFIL board governors: World Economic Forum; member united states firm management committee: World Firms General Council; treasurer, executive committee: U.S. Council International Business; member: New York State Society Public Accountants; member, board directors: Regional Plan Association; member leadership committee: Lincoln Center Consolidated Corporate Fund; chairman finance committee, board trustees: McCarter Theatre Princeton New Jersey; chairman: Business Improvement Distribution Task Force New York City Partnership/Chamber of Commerce; member New York steering committee: Accountants Coalition Liability Reform; member: American Institute CPAs.

Giving Program Officials

Larry P. Scott: PRIM CORP EMPL executive director: PricewaterhouseCoopers.

Foundation Officials

Robert Brown: director
Richard P. Kearns: vice president PRIM CORP EMPL partner, partner affairs: PricewaterhouseCoopers LLP.
Norman Walker: president

Grants Analysis

Disclosure Period: calendar year ending
Typical Range: $5,000 to $10,000

PRINCIPAL FINANCIAL GROUP

Company Contact

Des Moines, IA
Web: http://www.principal.com

Company Description

Revenue: US$7,659,200,000 (1999)
Employees: 16,275
Fortune Rank: 232, per FORTUNE Magazine's list of 500 Largest U.S. Corporations (1999).
FF 232
SIC(s): 6159 Miscellaneous Business Credit Institutions, 6282 Investment Advice, 6311 Life Insurance, 6321 Accident & Health Insurance.

Operating Locations

Principal Financial Group and subsidiaries operate throughout the USA.

Nonmonetary Support

Value: $710,145 (1997); $619,189 (1996); $200,000 (1993)
Type: Donated Equipment
Contact: Steve Thilges, Community Relations Associate
Note: Nonmonetary support is provided by the company to local organizations only. 1997 support valued at $710,145.

Corporate Sponsorship

Type: Arts & cultural events
Contact: Gabrielle Malettr
Community Relations Consultant

Principal Financial Group Foundation, Inc.

Giving Contact

Ms. Michele Walstrom, Contributions Consultant
Principal Financial Group
711 High St.
Des Moines, IA 50392-0150
Phone: (515)247-5111
Fax: (515)246-5475
Email: bassett.kendra@principal.com

Alternate Contact

Lori Hess
Phone: (515)247-5091
Email: hess.lori@principal.com

Description

Founded: 1987
EIN: 421312301
Organization Type: Corporate Foundation
Giving Locations: IA: Des Moines occasional nationally and internationally; operating locations.
Grant Types: Capital, Employee Matching Gifts, General Support, Project.
Note: Employee matching gift ratio: 1 to 1 to higher education and United Way.

Giving Philosophy

'The Principal Financial Group Foundation, Inc., was created in 1987 for the purpose of supporting various scientific, educational, health and welfare, and civic and cultural organizations. The Foundation continues the corporate contributions program established by the Principal Financial Group. Its primary objective is to support, through charitable contributions, selected nonprofit organizations, primarily within the greater Des Moines area. .. The objectives, priorities and programs of the Foundation seek to reflect the needs and concerns of the community and environment in which the Principal Financial Group operates.' Guidelines for Grant Making, The Principal Financial Group Foundation, Inc.

Financial Summary

Total Giving: $4,500,657 (1999 approx); $3,910,946 (1998); $6,485,021 (1997). Note: Contributes through corporate direct giving program and foundation.
Giving Analysis: Giving for 1998 includes: foundation ($3,910,946); foundation grants to United Way ($894,396); foundation matching gifts ($612,909)
Assets: $92,061,555 (1998); $21,427,008 (1997); $12,850,685 (1996)
Gifts Received: $70,000,030 (1998); $9,999,963 (1997)

Typical Recipients

Arts & Humanities: Arts Centers, Ballet, Community Arts, Dance, History & Archaeology, Libraries, Music, Opera, Performing Arts, Public Broadcasting, Theater
Civic & Public Affairs: Botanical Gardens/Parks, Business/Free Enterprise, Civil Rights, Community Foundations, Economic Development, Employment/Job Training, Housing, Parades/Festivals, Urban & Community Affairs, Women's Affairs, Zoos/Aquariums
Education: Agricultural Education, Business Education, Business-School Partnerships, Colleges & Universities, Community & Junior Colleges, Education Funds, Elementary Education (Public), Faculty Development, Literacy, Minority Education, Preschool Education, Private Education (Precollege), Public Education (Precollege), Science/Mathematics Education, Student Aid
Environment: Environment-General, Wildlife Protection
Health: AIDS/HIV, Cancer, Children's Health/Hospitals, Emergency/Ambulance Services, Health Policy/Cost Containment, Health Organizations, Hospices, Medical Research, Mental Health, Respiratory, Single-Disease Health Associations
International: International Affairs, International Peace & Security Issues, International Relations
Religion: Religious Welfare
Science: Scientific Centers & Institutes
Social Services: At-Risk Youth, Child Welfare, Community Service Organizations, Day Care, Family Planning, Family Services, Food/Clothing Distribution, People with Disabilities, Recreation & Athletics, Scouts, Senior Services, Shelters/Homelessness, Substance Abuse, United Funds/United Ways, Volunteer Services, YMCA/YWCA/YMHA/YWHA, Youth Organizations

Contributions Analysis

Giving Priorities: Science, education, health, welfare, civic and culture.
Arts & Humanities: 11%. Support of the greater Des Moines area and selected visual and performing arts organizations, museums, cultural centers, public television, arts-related organizations, and other cultural groups.
Civic & Public Affairs: 12%. Supports civic and public policy.
Education: 28%. Support of local universities and colleges, the Iowa College Foundation, various actuarial scholarships and programs at select universities, economic education programs, and education-related organizations. Matching Grant program for employees and qualified agents/brokers of The Principal Financial Group.
Environment: 2%. Environmental, Recreation, & Tourism: Support of local, statewide, and national organizations addressing environmental, social, economic, or business issues which enhance the quality of life in the community.
Health: 3%.
Religion: 6%. Supports religious causes and organizations.
Social Services: 38%. Support of health and human services agencies or organizations, national health organizations, and special projects.

Application Procedures

Initial Contact: contact the foundation to receive a form to return with the proposal, then submit proposal (include ten copies with the original)
Application Requirements: Letter outlining proposal, purpose, sponsoring organization, anticipated budget, amount specifically requested from foundation; itemized budget, including contributions received and anticipated expenses; other sources of funding; most recent IRS Form 990; audited financial statement; fundraising expenses; a description of organization, including goals, geographic scope, number of paid employees and volunteers, and total salary expense; names and affiliations of officers and directors associated with organization and project; frequency of board meetings; plan for evaluation; proof of tax-exempt status; evaluation of previous year's foundation funding, if applicable.
Deadlines: March 1 for health & human services, June 1 for education, September 1 for arts and culture, and December 1 for environment, recreation, and tourism.
Decision Notification: Review process generally takes six to ten weeks.
Notes: Original application must be sent along with nine copies for review. One copy of the audited financial statements and annual report need to be submitted with grant proposal.

Restrictions

Does not support athletic, fraternal, social or veterans' organizations; conference, seminar, or festival

participation; individuals; endowments; political parties or causes; trade, industry, or professional organizations; sectarian religious organizations; fellowships; individual K-12 schools; libraries; scholarships, fellowships, internships through school; goodwill advertising; capital fund drives for hospitals or health care facilities; grantmaking bodies (except for United Way and independent college funds); private foundations; organizations whose activities are mostly international; social organizations tax-supported organizations; or operating expenses of programs receiving United Way support. foundations; organizations whose activities are mostly international; social organizations tax-supported organizations; or operating expenses of programs receiving United Way support.

Additional Information

Grant renewals are not automatic, and the foundation expects an annual report from all grant recipients. The foundation was formerly known as the Principal Foundation.

Publications: Guidelines; Social Responsibility Report

Corporate Officials

David J. Drury: chief executive officer, chairman B Marshalltown, PA 1944. ED Iowa State University of Science & Technology (1966). PRIM CORP EMPL chief executive officer, chairman: Principal Mutual Life Insurance Co. CORP AFFIL chairman: Principal Life Insurance Co.; chairman: Principal Mutual Holding Co.; chairman: Principal Holding Co.; chairman: Principal Financial Group; chairman: Principal Financial Services; director: Coventry Health Care Inc. NONPR AFFIL director: Health Insurance Association America; president emeritus: Iowa Life Health Insurance Association; member: Drake University; director: American Council Capital Formation; member: American Council Life Insurance Tax Steering Committee; fellow: American Academy of Actuaries.

Mary Gesiriech: contributions coordinator PRIM CORP EMPL contributions coordinator: Principal Financial Group.

Thomas J. Graf: chief actuary PRIM CORP EMPL chief actuary: Principal Mutual Life Insurance Co. CORP AFFIL senior vice president: Principal Financial Groupp; senior vice president: Principal Life Insurance Co.; director: Coventry Health Care Inc.

Barry Griswell: president PRIM CORP EMPL president: Principal Financial Group. CORP AFFIL president: Principal Life Insurance Co.

Foundation Officials

Tom Gaard: chairman

Mary Gesiriech: contributions coordinator (see above)

Libby Jacobs: secretary

Grants Analysis

Disclosure Period: calendar year ending 1998
Total Grants: $2,403,641*
Number of Grants: 163
Average Grant: $14,746
Highest Grant: $220,138
Typical Range: $5,000 to $25,000
***Note:** Giving excludes matching gifts; United Way.

Recent Grants

Note: Grants derived from 1997 Form 990.

Arts & Humanities

75,000 Living History Farms, Urbandale, IA -- capital campaign
48,667 Des Moines Symphony, Des Moines, IA -- payment on three-year pledge for cultural support
35,000 Des Moines Art Center, Des Moines, IA
35,000 Des Moines Metropolitan Opera, Des Moines, IA -- to underwrite Merry Widow
25,000 Living History Farms, Urbandale, IA -- support educational programs
20,000 Des Moines Art Center, Des Moines, IA -- bridge funding for operating support

Civic & Public Affairs

120,000 Iowa State Fair Blue Ribbon Campaign, Des Moines, IA -- capital campaign for Blue Ribbon Campaign
66,666 Blank Park Zoo, Des Moines, IA -- capital campaign
66,666 Greater Des Moines Housing Trust Fund, Des Moines, IA
30,000 Greater Des Moines Foundation, Des Moines, IA -- operating support
25,000 Neighborhood Finance Corporation, Des Moines, IA -- support Hispanic and Vietnamese mortgage loan originator
16,000 Home, Des Moines, IA -- support for 975 26th Street

Education

200,000 Drake University, Des Moines, IA -- support New Campaign
75,000 Grand View College, Des Moines, IA -- to reduce interest rate
72,500 Grand View College, Des Moines, IA -- support for Drumm Center
70,000 Iowa College Foundation, Des Moines, IA
50,200 Drake University, Des Moines, IA -- support Actuarial Science, Distinguished Professorship, annual support, head start
50,000 Des Moines Business-Education Alliance, Des Moines, IA -- payment on three-year pledge
40,000 Central College, Pella, IA -- payment on five-year pledge for educational support
30,000 Grand View College, Des Moines, IA -- annual fund
25,000 Simpson College, Indianola, IA -- scholarships, annual fund
20,000 Science Center, Des Moines, IA -- support daily programs of informal science education
20,000 United Negro College Fund, New York, NY -- support Campaign 2000
16,000 Life and Health Insurance Medical Research Fund, Washington, DC -- scholarships, research
15,000 William Penn College, Oskaloosa, IA -- support Literacy Tutoring Project

Environment

50,000 Iowa Natural Heritage Foundation, Des Moines, IA
25,000 Iowa Natural Heritage Foundation, Des Moines, IA -- bridge funding for Protecting Iowa's Wild Places

Health

34,600 American Red Cross Central Iowa Chapter, Des Moines, IA -- capital campaign
15,000 American Lung Association, Des Moines, IA -- support Open Airways for Schools

International

20,000 Council for International Understanding, Des Moines, IA -- support Global Iowa IV

Religion

25,000 Lutheran Social Services, Des Moines, IA -- support Link Iowa Project
20,000 Catholic Charities, Des Moines, IA -- support St. Joseph Emergency Family Shelter
15,000 Churches United, Des Moines, IA -- support Overnight Emergency Shelter Program
15,000 Salvation Army, Des Moines, IA -- support Homeless Breakfast Program

Social Services

220,946 United Way of Central Iowa, Des Moines, IA -- support 1996-97 campaign
204,438 United Way of Central Iowa, Des Moines, IA -- support 1996-97 campaign
204,438 United Way of Central Iowa, Des Moines, IA -- support 1996-97 campaign
166,461 United Way of Central Iowa, Des Moines, IA -- support 1996-97 campaign
40,000 Civic Center, Des Moines, IA
37,500 Convalescent Home for Children, Johnston, IA
25,000 Youth Emergency Services and Shelter, Des Moines, IA -- capital campaign
25,000 YWCA, Des Moines, IA
20,000 Des Moines Coalition for the Homeless, Des Moines, IA -- support Transitional Housing Program
20,000 Goodwill Industries of Central Iowa, Des Moines, IA -- payment on three-year pledge for Supported Employment Program, transportation for disabled individuals to employment
20,000 North Iowa Girl Scout Council, Mason City, IA -- capital fund drive for Camp Tanglefoot
20,000 Planned Parenthood, Des Moines, IA -- operating support
20,000 YMCA, Des Moines, IA -- operating support
20,000 YMCA, Des Moines, IA -- support YMCA Camp
15,000 Youth Law Center, Des Moines, IA -- support legal resources
15,000 YWCA, Des Moines, IA -- support Child Care Scholarships

PROCTER &GAMBLE CO.

 Number 10 of Top 100 Corporate Givers

Company Contact

Cincinnati, OH
Web: http://www.pg.com

Company Description

Revenue: US$38,125,000,000 (1999)
Profit: US$3,780,000,000
Employees: 110,000
Fortune Rank: 23, per FORTUNE Magazine's list of 500 Largest U.S. Corporations (1999).
FF 23
SIC(s): 2033 Canned Fruits & Vegetables, 2045 Prepared Flour Mixes & Doughs, 2076 Vegetable Oil Mills Nec, 2841 Soap & Other Detergents.

Operating Locations

Australia: Procter & Gamble Australia, Villawood; Austria: Procter & Gamble Austria GmbH, Vienna; TEMPO-Vertiebsges fur hygienische, Vienna; Belgium: Procter & Gamble Health and Beauty Care Belgium, Brussels; Socofidex, Brussels; Procter & Gamble Benelux SA, Strombeek-Bever; Brazil: Richardson-Vicks do Brasil Quimica e Farmaceutica Ltda., Rio de Janiero; Canada: Procter & Gamble Inc., Grand Prarie, Hamilton, Mississauga, North York; People's Republic of China: Procter & Gamble Personal Cleansing (Tianjin) Ltd., Tianjin, Chiba; Czech Republic: Rakona, Prague; England: Noxell Corp. (U.K.) Ltd.; Procter & Gamble (Health & Beauty Care) Ltd., Borrklands; Vick International Ltd., Egham; Procter & Gamble (H & B Care) Ltd. - Manufacturing Division, Saffron Waldon, Skelmersdale; Finland: Oy Richardson-Vicks AB, Helsinki; France: Laboratoire LaChartre SA, Neuilly; Procter & Gamble France SNC, Neully-sur-Seine; TEMPO SANYS SA, Saint Ouen; Germany: Pantene GmbH; Westdeutsche Welpappenfabrik GmbH, Dusseldorf; Wick Pharma, Gross-Gerau; Dressin Kosmetik-u Pharma GmbH, Kulmbach; Procter & Gamble Health & Beauty Care Germany, Mainz; Mechanische Weberei und Zwirnerei Rosenhammer GmbH, Nuremberg; Temca

Chemische Union GmbH, Nuremberg; VP-Schickedanz AG, Nuremberg; Richardson GmbH, Schwalbach; Procter & Gamble GmbH, Schwalbach, Taunas; Greece: Procter & Gamble Greece, Athens; Indonesia: P.T. Richardson-Vicks Indonesia, Jakarta; India: Procter & Gamble India, Mumbai; Ireland: R-V Chemicals Ltd., Nenagh; Italy: Nelsen SpA, Gattatico; Procter & Gamble Health and Beauty Care South Europe, Rome; Procter & Gamble Italia SpA, Rome; Procter & Gamble Pescara Technical Center SpA, San Giovanni Teatino, Abruzzi; Japan: Nippon Vicks K.K., Osaka; Max Factor K.K., Tokyo; Mexico: Richardson-Vicks SA de CV, Mexico; Malaysia: Procter & Gamble (Malaysia), Petaling Jaya, Selangor; Netherlands Antilles: Richardson-Vicks (Overseas) France NV, Curacao; Netherlands: Procter & Gamble Health & Beauty Care Scnadinavia, Amersfoot; TEMPO ROPARKO BV, Zwijndrecht; New Zealand: Richardson-Vicks Ltd., Auckland; Peru: Procter & Gamble of Peru, Lima; Philippines: Procter & Gamble Phillipines Inc., Metro Manila; Portugal: Procter & Gamble Portugal; Singapore: Procter & Gamble (Singapore) Pte. Ltd., Singapore; Spain: Procter & Gamble Espana SA, Madrid; Richardson-Vicks SA, Madrid; Tempo Espana SA y Cia SeC, Madrid; Sweden: Richardson-Vicks AB, Stockholm; Switzerland: Blendax-Richardson AG, Basel; Bess Hygiene AG, Bern; Procter & Gamble AG, Geneva; Thailand: Richardson-Vicks Ltd., Bangkok; United Kingdom: Procter & Gamble Laundry Cleaning & Paper Products Benelux, Egham, Surrey; Procter & Gamble Ltd., Newcastle upon Tyne; Venezuela: Procter & Gamble Venezuela, CA, Caracas; Procter & Gamble de Venezuela CA, Caracas

Nonmonetary Support

Value: $8,517,909 (1996); $11,048,012 (1995); $10,656,000 (1993)
Type: Donated Equipment; Donated Products; Loaned Executives
Note: 1998 nonmonetary support $4,700,000. 1997 nonmonetary support $6,960,076. Company has also donated land.

Corporate Sponsorship

Value: $3,675,000 (1997); $3,272,000 (1995)
Type: Arts & cultural events; Sports events

Procter & Gamble Fund

Giving Contact

Brenda Ratliss, Contributions & Community Relations
The Procter & Gamble Fund
PO Box 599
Cincinnati, OH 45201-0599
Phone: (513)945-8454
Web: http://www.pg.com/docCommunity/

Description

EIN: 316019594
Organization Type: Corporate Foundation
Giving Locations: headquarters and operating communities, nationally and internationally.
Grant Types: Capital, Employee Matching Gifts, General Support.
Note: Employee matching gift ratio: 2 to 1.

Giving Philosophy

'Proctor & Gamble has always considered its interests to be inseparable from those of its employees. We feel the same way about the needs of our communities--whether we're helping to nurture the arts, to improve our schools and universities, or to meet the needs of our less-fortunate neighbors, we at P&G are committed to doing what's right and good for the communities in which we live and work.' Procter & Gamble Summary of Contributions 1993

Financial Summary

Total Giving: $73,245,604 (fiscal year ending June 30, 1999); $66,859,204 (fiscal 1998); $87,024,065 (fiscal 1997). Note: Contributes through corporate direct giving program and foundation.
Giving Analysis: Giving for fiscal 1999 includes: international subsidiaries ($27,049,150); foundation ($26,752,493); nonmonetary support ($6,165,236); corporate direct giving ($5,132,560); domestic subsidiaries ($4,782,800); foundation program-related investments ($3,363,365)
Assets: $13,409,571 (fiscal 1996); $12,249,704 (fiscal 1995); $19,061,123 (fiscal 1994)
Gifts Received: $19,000,000 (fiscal 1996); $17,825,551 (fiscal 1995); $15,468,750 (fiscal 1994). Note: Fund receives contributions from the Proctor & Gamble Co.

Typical Recipients

Arts & Humanities: Arts Associations & Councils, Arts Centers, Arts Funds, Arts Institutes, Ballet, Historic Preservation, Museums/Galleries, Music, Opera, Performing Arts, Theater
Civic & Public Affairs: African American Affairs, Business/Free Enterprise, Chambers of Commerce, Community Foundations, Economic Development, Economic Policy, Employment/Job Training, Housing, Municipalities/Towns, Parades/Festivals, Professional & Trade Associations, Public Policy, Safety, Urban & Community Affairs, Women's Affairs, Zoos/Aquariums
Education: Business Education, Business-School Partnerships, Colleges & Universities, Economic Education, Education Funds, Education Reform, Engineering/Technological Education, Faculty Development, Education-General, International Studies, Legal Education, Minority Education, Public Education (Precollege), Religious Education, Science/Mathematics Education, Secondary Education (Public), Special Education, Student Aid
Environment: Environment-General, Resource Conservation
Health: Cancer, Emergency/Ambulance Services, Health Organizations, Hospitals, Nutrition
International: International Affairs
Science: Science Museums
Social Services: Child Welfare, Community Centers, Community Service Organizations, Food/Clothing Distribution, People with Disabilities, Recreation & Athletics, Scouts, Shelters/Homelessness, Special Olympics, Substance Abuse, United Funds/United Ways, Volunteer Services, YMCA/YWCA/YMHA/YWHA, Youth Organizations

Contributions Analysis

Giving Priorities: Education, hospitals, human services, civic groups, the arts, the environment, religious groups, and science. Domestic interests include international policy, management, environmental affairs, and exchange programs. However, overseas subsidiaries administer independent programs that include cash and product donations. Interests include civic organizations; the environment; health and social services, particularly child health; and international affairs. In 1997, cash contributions in Latin America totaled $1,117,640 and donations of products, equipment, or personnel was valued at $765,718. In Mexico and Brazil, the company focuses on education programs. In Columbia, the company assisted in the purchase of medical equipment for a local hospital and renovation of a school for low-income families. In Peru, the company and its employees support a local center for abandoned children. In Asia, cash contributions ($5,438,973) and donations of products, equipment, or personnel ($310,616) totaled $5,749,589. Contributions were made in China, Australia, India, Japan, Indonesia, Singapore, and Thailand. In Europe, the Middle East, and Africa, cash contributions ($5,703,334) and donations of products, equipment, or personnel ($579,689) totaled $6,293,023. Contributions were made in the Czech Republic, Germany, Pakistan, Russia, Sweden, Spain, and the U.K.
Arts & Humanities: 5% to 10%. Promotes cultural enrichment, educational programs, and entertainment. Supports theater, dance, music, and the visual arts.
Civic & Public Affairs: About 10%. Goals are to promote economic stimulation and enrichment for all parts of the community. Supports youth programs, chambers of commerce, the Urban League, libraries, zoos, and museums.
Education: 55% to 60%. Major support to scholarship programs and grants to public and private colleges and universities. Also supports employee matching gifts; public policy, research, and economic education organizations; scholarships for employees' children, and K-12 initiatives.
Environment: Less than 5%. Gives to the Nature Conservancy, Audubon Society, Center for Marine Conservation, and Keep America Beautiful.
Health: About 25%. Supports United Way, the Salvation Army, Red Cross, hospitals, food banks, and social service agencies.
International: Company's foreign subsidiaries provide cash and nonmonetary contributions to the communities in which they operate. Priorities vary according to community needs.

Application Procedures

Initial Contact: Brief letter or proposal.
Application Requirements: Include a description of organization, amount requested, purpose of funds sought, recently audited financial statement, and proof of tax-exempt status.
Deadlines: None.
Review Process: Requests are reviewed by trustees upon receipt.
Evaluative Criteria: Programs that promote continued growth and prosperity of business and society as a whole, and help enhance the quality of life in communities with a concentration of employees.

Restrictions

Fund does not support individuals, goodwill advertising, dinners or special events, fraternal or political organizations, religious organizations for sectarian purposes, or endowments.

Additional Information

Company also specializes in disposable diapers, cellulose pulp, chemicals, shortenings, oils, cake mixes, peanut butter, potato chips, coffee, tea, animal feed, and personal care products.
Publications: Global Contributions Report

Corporate Officials

Durk I. Jager: chairman, president, chief executive PRIM CORP EMPL chairman, president, chief executive: Procter & Gamble Co.
John E. Pepper, Jr.: chairman executive committee B Pottsville, PA 1938. ED Yale University BA (1960). PRIM CORP EMPL chairman executive committee: Procter & Gamble Co. CORP AFFIL director: Xerox Corp.; director: Motorola Inc. NONPR AFFIL trustee: Yale Corp.; member advisory council: Yale School Management; member: Soap & Detergent Association; member: Grocery Manufacturer America; director: National Alliance Business; co-chairman: Cincinnati Youth Collaborative; co-chairman: Governments Education Council Ohio; trustee: Cincinnati Medicine Institute; member scholarship committee: Cincinnati Business Committee; trustee: Cincinnati Council World Affairs; trustee: Christ Church Endowment Fund; trustee: Cincinnati Art Museum; trustee: Center Strategic & International Studies; member: American Society Corporate Executives. CLUB AFFIL Yale Club; Queen City Club; Commercial Club; Commonwealth Club.
Robert Louis Wehling: global marketing, government relations officer B Chicago, IL 1938. ED Denison

University BA (1960). PRIM CORP EMPL global marketing, government relations officer: Procter & Gamble Co. CORP AFFIL co-founder: USA Today. NONPR AFFIL member: Phi Beta Kappa; trustee: United Way Cincinnati; trustee: Ohio School Development Corp.; trustee executive committee: Greater Cincinnati Chamber of Commerce; member: Mayor's Commission Children; member allocations committee: Fine Arts Fund; participant: Governments Education Management Council; vice chairman: Downtown Cincinnati Inc.; director: Education Excellence Partnership; executive committee: Cincinnati Youth Collaborative; co-founder: Coalition of Education Initiatives; member: Association National Advertisers; member education task force: Business Roundtable; campaign director: Advertising Council. CLUB AFFIL Commonwealth Club; Queen City Club.

Giving Program Officials

Carol G. Talbot: vice president, secretary PRIM CORP EMPL associate director, contributions communication relations educational services: Procter & Gamble Co.

Foundation Officials

Richard A. Bachhuber, Jr.: vice president, trustee
Clayton Dale: trustee
Charlotte R. Otto: vice president, trustee PRIM CORP EMPL senior vice president public affairs: Procter & Gamble Co.
Carol G. Talbot: vice president, secretary (see above)
Robert Louis Wehling: president, trustee (see above)

Grants Analysis

Disclosure Period: fiscal year ending June 30, 1999
Total Grants: $26,752,493*
Number of Grants: 550 (approx)
Typical Range: $5,000 to $50,000
***Note:** Giving excludes matching gifts. Giving includes foundation only.

Recent Grants

Note: Grants derived from fiscal 1997 Form 990.

Arts & Humanities

250,000 Cincinnati Symphony Orchestra, Cincinnati, OH
245,000 Museum Center Foundation, Cincinnati, OH
125,000 Cincinnati Institute of Fine Arts, Cincinnati, OH
125,000 Cincinnati Institute of Fine Arts, Cincinnati, OH
125,000 Cincinnati Institute of Fine Arts, Cincinnati, OH
125,000 Cincinnati Institute of Fine Arts, Cincinnati, OH
115,000 Cincinnati Ballet Company, Cincinnati, OH
100,000 Cincinnati Playhouse in the Park, Cincinnati, OH
100,000 Cincinnati Symphony Orchestra, Cincinnati, OH
100,000 Museum Center Foundation, Cincinnati, OH
75,000 Museum of Television and Radio, New York, NY

Civic & Public Affairs

244,000 City of Cincinnati, Cincinnati, OH
215,000 Greater Cincinnati Foundation, Cincinnati, OH
200,000 Zoological Society, Cincinnati, OH
185,000 Spire Foundation, Cincinnati, OH
166,667 National Council of Negro Women, Washington, DC
100,000 Greater Cincinnati Housing Alliance, Cincinnati, OH
100,000 National Underground Railroad Center, Cincinnati, OH
100,000 National Urban League, New York, NY
100,000 Sawyer Point Endowment

Education

724,291 Educational Testing Service, Princeton, NJ
250,000 New American Schools Development Corp, Arlington, VA
200,000 United Negro College Fund, Fairfax, VA
157,000 Junior Achievement, Colorado Springs, CO
157,000 Junior Achievement, Colorado Springs, CO
150,000 National Board for Professional Development, Southfield, MI
143,211 Junior Achievement, Colorado Springs, CO
140,000 Cornell University, Ithaca, NY
127,000 Northwestern University, Evanston, IL
122,000 University of Pennsylvania, Philadelphia, PA
117,000 Harvard University, Cambridge, MA
110,000 Purdue Foundation, West Lafayette, IN
100,000 National Board for Professional Development, Southfield, MI
97,000 Ohio State University, Columbus, OH
97,000 University of Michigan Ann Arbor, Ann Arbor, MI
93,000 University of Illinois Foundation, Urbana, IL
91,000 University of Cincinnati, Cincinnati, OH
90,000 Indiana University Foundation, Bloomington, IN

Environment

200,000 Nature Conservancy, Washington, DC

Health

200,000 American Red Cross, Washington, DC

Social Services

641,250 United Way and Community Chest, Cincinnati, OH
641,250 United Way and Community Chest, Cincinnati, OH
630,000 United Way and Community Chest, Cincinnati, OH
173,000 United Way Central Maryland, Baltimore, MD
150,000 YWCA, Cincinnati, OH
120,000 Cincinnati Youth Collaborative, Cincinnati, OH
108,060 United Way Brown County, Green Bay, WI
105,000 United Way Southwest Georgia, Albany, GA
100,000 Greater Cincinnati 2008 Amateur Sports, Cincinnati, OH
100,000 Neediest Kids of All, Cincinnati, OH

PROCTER &GAMBLE CO., COSMETICS DIVISION

Company Contact

Hunt Valley, MD
Web: http://www.pg.com

Company Description

Former Name: Noxell Corp.
SIC(s): 2844 Toilet Preparations.
Parent Company: Procter & Gamble Co., Cincinnati, OH, United States

Nonmonetary Support

Note: Employee matching gift ratio: 2 to 1.

Procter & Gamble Cosmetics Foundation

Giving Contact

Cheryl G. Hudgins, Public Affairs Manager
Procter & Gamble Cosmetic Foundation
11050 York Rd.
Hunt Valley, MD 21030
Phone: (410)785-7300
Fax: (410)316-8025

Description

Founded: 1951
EIN: 526041435
Organization Type: Corporate Foundation
Giving Locations: MD: Baltimore metropolitan area some support to nationally organizations with local chapters.
Grant Types: Capital, Challenge, Employee Matching Gifts, Endowment, General Support, Research, Scholarship.

Financial Summary

Total Giving: $433,369 (fiscal year ending June 30, 1996); $173,605 (fiscal 1994); $907,670 (fiscal 1992). Note: All contributions are made through the foundation.
Assets: $965,540 (fiscal 1996); $928,993 (fiscal 1994); $1,307,583 (fiscal 1992)
Gifts Received: $275,000 (fiscal 1996). Note: In 1996, contributions were received from Noxell Corp.

Typical Recipients

Arts & Humanities: Arts Centers, Arts Festivals, Arts Institutes, Dance, Historic Preservation, Libraries, Museums/Galleries, Music, Opera, Performing Arts, Public Broadcasting, Theater, Visual Arts
Civic & Public Affairs: African American Affairs, Business/Free Enterprise, Chambers of Commerce, Civil Rights, Clubs, Community Foundations, Economic Development, Employment/Job Training, Civic & Public Affairs-General, Housing, Law & Justice, Municipalities/Towns, Nonprofit Management, Philanthropic Organizations, Professional & Trade Associations, Safety, Urban & Community Affairs, Women's Affairs, Zoos/Aquariums
Education: Arts/Humanities Education, Business Education, Business-School Partnerships, Colleges & Universities, Economic Education, Education Associations, Education Funds, Elementary Education (Public), Engineering/Technological Education, Education-General, Health & Physical Education, Literacy, Medical Education, Minority Education, Private Education (Precollege), Religious Education, Science/Mathematics Education, Secondary Education (Private), Secondary Education (Public), Student Aid
Health: AIDS/HIV, Cancer, Children's Health/Hospitals, Clinics/Medical Centers, Diabetes, Emergency/Ambulance Services, Health Organizations, Hospitals, Medical Rehabilitation, Mental Health, Nursing Services, Public Health, Respiratory, Single-Disease Health Associations
International: International Affairs, International Relations
Science: Science Museums, Scientific Centers & Institutes, Scientific Research
Social Services: At-Risk Youth, Child Welfare, Community Service Organizations, Domestic Violence, Family Services, Food/Clothing Distribution, People with Disabilities, Recreation & Athletics, Senior Services, Shelters/Homelessness, Substance Abuse, United Funds/United Ways, Volunteer Services, YMCA/YWCA/YMHA/YWHA, Youth Organizations

Application Procedures

Initial Contact: Send a brief letter of inquiry and a proposal.
Application Requirements: a description of organization, amount requested, purpose of funds sought,

other contributors, recently audited financial statement, current budget, list of officers and directors, and proof of tax-exempt status.
Deadlines: None.
Review Process: The board meets semiannually.

Restrictions

Does not support individuals or political or lobbying groups.

Foundation Officials

Marc S. Pritchard: president PRIM CORP EMPL general manager: Proctor & Gamble Co. Cosmetics & Fragrance Division. CORP AFFIL vice president: Proctor & Gamble.

Grants Analysis

Disclosure Period: fiscal year ending June 30, 1996
Number of Grants: 63
Highest Grant: $50,000
Typical Range: $1,000 to $5,000

Recent Grants

Note: Grants derived from fiscal 1997 Form 990.

Arts & Humanities

17,975	Baltimore Symphony Orchestra, Baltimore, MD
15,000	American Visionary Art Museum, Baltimore, MD
15,000	Center Stage, Baltimore, MD
5,000	Maryland Art Place, Baltimore, MD

Civic & Public Affairs

9,300	Cosmetic Executive Women, Women In Need

Education

25,000	College Bound Foundation, Baltimore, MD
22,000	Maryland Business Roundtable for Education, MD
20,000	Independent College Fund of Maryland, Baltimore, MD
13,641	St. Paul's School for Girls, Brooklandville, MD
13,100	Junior Achievement of Central Maryland, Baltimore, MD
10,000	Institute for Christian and Jewish Studies, Baltimore, MD
5,000	Goucher College, Towson, MD

Health

20,000	American Cancer Society, Baltimore, MD
7,680	Susan G. Komen Breast Cancer Foundation, Dallas, TX

Science

27,500	Maryland Science Center, Baltimore, MD
25,000	Port Discovery Children's Museum
7,500	Columbus Center, Baltimore, MD

Social Services

22,500	Kennedy Krieger Institute, Baltimore, MD
20,000	United Way Central Maryland, Baltimore, MD
7,500	House of Ruth, Baltimore, MD

PROGRESSIVE CORP.

Company Contact

Mayfield Village, OH
Web: http://www.progressive.com

Company Description

Revenue: US$6,124,200,000 (1999)
Employees: 8,679
Fortune Rank: 286, per FORTUNE Magazine's list of 500 Largest U.S. Corporations (1999).
FF 286
SIC(s): 6331 Fire, Marine & Casualty Insurance, 6719 Holding Companies Nec.

Nonmonetary Support

Value: $129,270 (1994)

Giving Contact

Betty J. Powers, Executive Assistant
Progressive Corp.
6300 Wilson Mills Road
Mayfield Village, OH 44143
Phone: (440)461-5000
Fax: (440)446-7088

Description

Organization Type: Corporate Giving Program. Supports preselected organizations only.
Giving Locations: headquarters and operating communities.
Grant Types: General Support.

Giving Philosophy

'Progressive is a company that succeeds by taking risks. We go after market segments other companies avoid or refuse to enter. We have been very successful in creating new products and identifying new markets. We are organized to give maximum entrepreneurial responsibility and freedom to our people. We reward risk-taking, honesty, innovation and creativity. We recognize performance evaluated against objectives. In 1993, we are confining our contributions to the United Way.' Progressive Contributions Program Information

Financial Summary

Total Giving: $3,000,000 (1996 approx); $1,314,750 (1994); $189,919 (1993). Note: Contributes through corporate direct giving program only. 1996 Giving includes corporate direct giving; domestic and international subsidiaries.

Typical Recipients

Social Services: United Funds/United Ways

Contributions Analysis

Giving Priorities: Education, united funds, the arts, and economic development.

Corporate Officials

Peter Benjamin Lewis: chairman, president, chief executive officer, director B Cleveland, OH 1933. ED Princeton University AB (1955). PRIM CORP EMPL chairman, president, chief executive officer, director: Progressive Corp. CORP AFFIL president: United Financial Adjusting Co.; president: Progressive SPLty Insurance Co.; chairman, chief executive officer: Progressive SPLty Life Insurance Co.; chairman: Progressive Northwestern; chairman: Progressive Southeastern Insurance Co.; chairman: Progressive Northern Insurance Co.; vice president: Progressive County Mutual Insurance Co.; president: Progressive Max Insurance Co.; chairman: Progressive Casualty Insurance Co.; chairman, chief executive officer: Progressive Casualty Life Insurance Co.; chairman, chief executive officer: Progressive America Life Insurance Co.; chairman: Progressive American Insurance Co. NONPR AFFIL member: Society Chartered Property & Casualty Underwriters. CLUB AFFIL Cleveland Racquet Club.

Giving Program Officials

Betty Jean Powers: PRIM CORP EMPL executive assistant: Progressive Southeastern Insurance.

Grants Analysis

Disclosure Period: calendar year ending

PROMUS HOTEL CORP.

Company Contact

Memphis, TN
Web: http://www.promus.com

Company Description

Revenue: US$266,630,000
Employees: 7,800
SIC(s): 7011 Hotels & Motels.

Nonmonetary Support

Type: Cause-related Marketing & Promotion; Donated Equipment; Donated Products; In-kind Services; Loaned Employees; Loaned Executives; Workplace Solicitation

Giving Contact

Joyce McKinney
Promus Hotel Corp.
755 Crossover Lane
Memphis, TN 38117
Phone: (901)374-5000
Fax: (901)374-5543
Email: info@promus.com

Description

Organization Type: Corporate Giving Program
Giving Locations: headquarters and operating communities.
Grant Types: Award, Employee Matching Gifts, General Support.
Note: Employee matching gift ratio: 1 to 1.

Giving Philosophy

'Corporations have a responsibility to the community. They should contribute more than just jobs and income. As community leaders, they have an obligation to use their human and financial resources to improve the quality of education, provide help and hope for the less fortunate, create a stronger economic environment, encourage artistic development, and make an investment in the community's future through personal involvement and financial contribution.' *Community Relations Annual Report Fulfilling our Commitment to Memphis*

Financial Summary

Total Giving: Contributes through corporate direct giving program only.

Typical Recipients

Arts & Humanities: Arts Funds, Museums/Galleries, Music, Opera, Public Broadcasting, Theater
Civic & Public Affairs: Economic Development, Economic Policy, Urban & Community Affairs
Education: Colleges & Universities, Minority Education
Environment: Environment-General
Social Services: United Funds/United Ways

Contributions Analysis

Giving Priorities: Education, business improvement, health, and human service.
Arts & Humanities: 15% to 20%. Most funding is channeled through the Memphis Arts Council. Also underwrites major cultural events, including Russian Religious Art. Also supports public broadcasting station. Sponsorsemployee matching gifts to public broadcasting.
Civic & Public Affairs: 20% to 25%. Funding is concentrated on improving the quality of life and the business climate in Memphis. Featured programs have included a lecture seriesby national leaders, and

Adopt-A-Neighbor (including beautification of common areas, Easter-egg hunts, and sports for teenagers). Other interests include the Memphis Area Chamber of Commerce and Leadership Memphis.
Education: 30% to 35%. Primary concern is education in the Memphis community. Through the Adopt-A-School program, the corporation has provided leadership, assistance, and guidance to elementary schools such as the Springdale Magnet School. Also supports Junior Achievement. Company has established a new program for minority education in the Memphis, TN, area and will expand program into other areas where company has a significant presence. Matches employee gifts to colleges and universities.
Health: 15% to 20%. Concentration is on the United Way. Other interests include the aged, family services, child welfare, mental health, the handicapped, and traditional youth organizations.

Application Procedures

Initial Contact: brief letter
Application Requirements: a description of organization, amount requested, purpose of funds sought, recently audited financial statement, proof of tax-exempt status
Deadlines: None.
Review Process: requests reviewed as received by staff of community relations department; evaluation process is informal

Restrictions

Does not support dinners or special events, religious or veterans organizations, individuals, health agencies, or member agencies of United Way.

Additional Information

Company sold its Holiday Inns, Inc. subsidiary in 1990 and changed its name from Holiday Corp. to The Promus Companies.
Promus Companies includes Hampton Inn, Embassy Suites, and Homewood Suites.
In 1995 Harrah's split from the Promus Companies to form Harrah's Entertainment, Inc.
In 1997, Promus Hotels and Doubletree Hotels Corp. merged.
Subsidiaries of Promus Companies handle grant requests for the areas in which they are located.
Employees and executives are active volunteers in community groups including Junior Achievement, Chamber of Commerce, Visitors Bureau, Memphis Arts Council, Leadership Memphis, Christian Brothers College, WKNO, and the Private IndustryCouncil.

Corporate Officials

Philip Glen Satre: chairman, president, chief executive officer, director B Palo Alto, CA 1949. ED Stanford University BA (1971); University of California, Davis JD (1975); Massachusetts Institute of Technology (1982). PRIM CORP EMPL chairman, president, chief executive officer, director: Harrahs Entertainment Inc. ADD CORP EMPL chief executive officer: Harrah's Atlantic City Inc.; president, chief executive officer: Harrahs Operating Co. Inc.; president, chief executive officer, director: Harrahs Las Vegas Inc.; president director: Harrahs Laughlin Inc.; chairman: Ocean Showboat Inc.; chairman: Showboat Operating Co. CORP AFFIL director: Star City Pty Ltd. NONPR AFFIL member: Stanford University Alumni Association; member: Young President Organization; member: Stanford Athletic Board; member: Order Coif; member: Phi Kappa Phi; member: Nevada Bar Association; member: California Bar Association; director, trustee: National Judicial College; member: Business Roundtable; member: American Bar Association.

Giving Program Officials

Mary Jane Fuller: PRIM CORP EMPL director public affairs: The Promus Companies Inc.
Ben C. Peternell: B Fort Wayne, IN 1945. ED Hanover College BA (1968); Indiana University MBA (1970). PRIM CORP EMPL senior vice president human resources: Harrahs Entertainment Inc. CORP AFFIL senior vice president: Harrahs Operating Co. Inc.; director: Promus Hotel Corp.
Colin V. Reed: PRIM CORP EMPL director: The Promus Companies Inc.

Grants Analysis

Disclosure Period: calendar year ending
Typical Range: $10,000 to $125,000

Providence Journal-Bulletin Co.

Company Contact

Providence, RI

Company Description

Employees: 3,700
SIC(s): 2711 Newspapers, 4833 Television Broadcasting Stations, 4841 Cable & Other Pay Television Services.

Nonmonetary Support

Type: Donated Equipment; In-kind Services
Note: Annual nonmonetary support is approximately $10,000.

Corporate Sponsorship

Type: Arts & cultural events; Festivals/fairs; Music & entertainment events

Providence Journal Charitable Foundation

Giving Contact

Mary Ellen Ahern, Community Services and Gift Committee Director
Providence Journal Charitable Foundation
75 Fountain Street
Providence, RI 02902-9985
Phone: (401)277-7597
Fax: (401)277-7529
Email: mary_ellen_ahern@projo.com

Alternate Contact

M. Isabel Rego, Community Services Administrator,
Phone: (401)277-7514

Description

EIN: 056015372
Organization Type: Corporate Foundation
Giving Locations: MA; RI
Grant Types: Capital, General Support, Multiyear/Continuing Support, Scholarship, Seed Money.

Financial Summary

Total Giving: $1,000,000 (1999 approx); $1,000,000 (1998 approx); $1,071,184 (1996). Note: Contributes through foundation only. 1996 Giving includes foundation ($841,184); United Way ($230,000). 1995 Giving includes foundation ($604,449); United Way ($250,000)
Assets: $5,279,826 (1996); $5,478,089 (1995); $5,214,400 (1994)
Gifts Received: $350,123 (1994); $3,515,353 (1992). Note: Gifts are received from Colony Communications.

Typical Recipients

Arts & Humanities: Arts Appreciation, Arts Associations & Councils, Arts Centers, Ballet, Historic Preservation, History & Archaeology, Libraries, Museums/Galleries, Music, Performing Arts, Public Broadcasting, Theater
Civic & Public Affairs: African American Affairs, Business/Free Enterprise, Community Foundations, Economic Development, Civic & Public Affairs-General, Housing, Legal Aid, Municipalities/Towns, Parades/Festivals, Professional & Trade Associations, Urban & Community Affairs, Women's Affairs, Zoos/Aquariums
Education: Arts/Humanities Education, Business Education, Colleges & Universities, Education Funds, Education-General, Literacy, Private Education (Precollege), Public Education (Precollege), Secondary Education (Private), Special Education, Student Aid
Environment: Environment-General, Resource Conservation, Watershed
Health: Adolescent Health Issues, AIDS/HIV, Cancer, Emergency/Ambulance Services, Health Organizations, Hospices, Hospitals, Nursing Services, Single-Disease Health Associations
International: International Affairs
Religion: Churches, Religious Welfare
Social Services: Child Welfare, Community Centers, Community Service Organizations, Family Planning, Food/Clothing Distribution, People with Disabilities, Scouts, Senior Services, Sexual Abuse, Substance Abuse, United Funds/United Ways, Youth Organizations

Contributions Analysis

Giving Priorities: Social welfare, education, the arts, economic development, the environment, hospitals, and single disease health organizations.
Arts & Humanities: 10% to 15%. Grants support performing arts groups, libraries, public broadcasting, philharmonic orchestras, and historic preservation.
Civic & Public Affairs: 5% to 10%. Environment is a major area of concern; trade associations, housing, public parks, and economic developmentgroups also receive funding.
Education: About 15%. Local colleges and universities, preparatory schools, and Junior Achievement receive support.
Health: 15% to 20%. Supports hospitals, single-disease health organizations, and adolescent health associations.
Social Services: 40% to 45%. Majority of funding supports the United Way. Other interests include religious welfare, youth organizations, food banks and shelters, and women's and family services.

Application Procedures

Initial Contact: written proposal
Application Requirements: mission statement and objectives; project description; total project, and amount requested; other sources of funding, and other companies approached; a copy of IRS 501 (c)(3); recent financial statements; list of board of directors
Deadlines: January 31; April 30; July 31; October 31
Review Process: three-member committee reviews requests
Decision Notification: quarterly

Corporate Officials

Stephen Hamblett: chairman, chief executive officer, publisher B Nashua, NH 1934. ED Harvard University BA (1957). PRIM CORP EMPL chairman, chief executive officer, publisher: Providence Journal-Bulletin Co. CORP AFFIL director: A.H. Belo Corp.
Mary Ellen Haren: director public relations PRIM CORP EMPL director public relations: Providence Journal-Bulletin Co.

Foundation Officials

Stephen Hamblett: trustee (see above)
Howard Sutton: president B Irvington, NJ 1950. ED University of Notre Dame (1972); Providence College (1978). PRIM CORP EMPL president, general manager, assistant publisher: The Providence Journal. CORP AFFIL president: Rhode Island Monthly Communication.

Grants Analysis

Disclosure Period: calendar year ending 1996
Total Grants: $841,184*
Number of Grants: 64
Average Grant: $13,143
Highest Grant: $80,000
Typical Range: $5,000 to $25,000
***Note:** Giving excludes United Way.

Recent Grants

Note: Grants derived from 1996 Form 990.

Arts & Humanities

50,000	Rhode Island Historical Society, Providence, RI
20,000	Providence Performing Arts Center, Providence, RI
18,750	Children's Museum, Providence, RI
16,000	Trinity Repertory Company, Providence, RI
10,000	Channel 36 Foundation, Providence, RI
10,000	Providence Preservation Society, Providence, RI
10,000	Providence Public Library, Providence, RI
10,000	Rhode Island Philharmonic Orchestra, Providence, RI
5,000	Langston Hughes Center for the Arts and Education, Providence, RI
4,000	Rhode Island Museum of Art, Providence, RI

Civic & Public Affairs

30,000	City Year Rhode Island, Providence, RI
25,000	American Press Institute Endowment Campaign, Reston, VA
25,000	Center for Design and Business
25,000	Rhode Island Zoological Society, Providence, RI
12,500	Local Initiatives Support Corporation, Providence, RI
10,000	First Night, Providence, RI
10,000	Keep Providence Beautiful, Providence, RI
10,000	Providence Foundation, Providence, RI
5,000	Providence Waterfront Festival, Providence, RI
4,000	Times2, Providence, RI
4,000	United Black and Brown Fund of Rhode Island, RI
3,500	American Press Institute, Reston, VA
2,500	American Society of Newspaper Editors Foundation, Washington, DC
2,500	Justice Assistance, Providence, RI
2,500	Leadership Rhode Island Educational Foundation, Providence, RI

Education

75,000	Public Education Fund, Providence, RI
40,000	Providence College, Providence, RI
6,600	Community Preparatory School, Providence, RI
5,700	South Providence Tutorial, Providence, RI
5,000	University of Rhode Island, Kingston, RI
4,500	Junior Achievement Rhode Island, Providence, RI
3,334	St. Andrew's School, Barrington, RI
3,000	Latino Dollars for Scholars of Rhode Island Foundation, RI

Environment

12,500	Save the Bay, Providence, RI
2,500	American Audubon Society of Rhode Island, RI

Health

80,000	Rhode Island Hospital, Providence, RI
15,000	Memorial Hospital of Rhode Island, Pawtucket, RI
10,000	Rhode Island Project AIDS, Providence, RI
10,000	St. Joseph's Hospital, Providence, RI
8,333	Roger Williams Hospital, Providence, RI
5,000	Daily Care Nurses, Providence, RI

Religion

6,666	St. Mary's Home for Children, Providence, RI
5,000	Episcopal Conference Center
2,500	Salvation Army, Providence, RI

Social Services

230,000	United Way Southeastern New England, Providence, RI
14,000	Planned Parenthood, Providence, RI
10,000	Rhode Island Anti-Drug Coalition, Providence, RI
5,000	Boy Scouts of America National Council, Irving, TX
5,000	Rhode Island Rape Crisis Center, Providence, RI
5,000	Share Our Strength

Provident Companies, Inc.

Company Contact

Chattanooga, TN
Web: http://www.providentcompanies.com/

Company Description

Former Name: Provident Life & Accident Insurance Co. of America.
Revenue: US$3,904,000,000
Employees: 1,964

Operating Locations

Operates throughout the USA and 4 Canadian provinces.

Nonmonetary Support

Value: $20,000 (1995); $20,000 (1994)
Type: Donated Equipment; Loaned Executives
Note: Donated equipment goes to schools and charities; executives are loaned to United Way.

Corporate Sponsorship

Type: Arts & cultural events; Sports events

Giving Contact

Thomas A.H. White, Vice President, Corporate Investor Relations
Provident Companies, Inc.
1 Fountain Square
Chattanooga, TN 37402
Phone: (423)755-8996
Fax: (423)755-3194

Description

Organization Type: Corporate Giving Program
Giving Locations: headquarters and operating communities.
Grant Types: Employee Matching Gifts.
Note: Employee matching gift ratio: 1 to 1 for gifts to 501(c)(3) organizations; 2 to 1 for gifts to education only.

Financial Summary

Total Giving: $1,350,000 (1999 approx); $1,350,000 (1998 approx); $1,300,000 (1997 approx). Note: Contributes through corporate direct giving program only. 1996 Giving includes corporate direct giving ($493,835); matching gifts ($50,000); United Way ($254,500).

Typical Recipients

Arts & Humanities: Arts Associations & Councils, Arts Festivals, Arts Funds, Libraries, Museums/Galleries, Music, Opera, Performing Arts, Visual Arts
Civic & Public Affairs: Civil Rights, Clubs, Economic Development, Economic Policy, Housing, Parades/Festivals, Urban & Community Affairs, Zoos/Aquariums
Education: Business Education, Colleges & Universities, Community & Junior Colleges, Economic Education, Education Reform, Education-General, Health & Physical Education, Literacy, Private Education (Precollege), Public Education (Precollege), Science/Mathematics Education, Student Aid
Environment: Environment-General, Resource Conservation
Health: Health Organizations, Heart
Science: Science Exhibits & Fairs, Science Museums
Social Services: Big Brother/Big Sister, Community Service Organizations, Food/Clothing Distribution, Recreation & Athletics, Scouts, Shelters/Homelessness, Substance Abuse, United Funds/United Ways, Youth Organizations

Contributions Analysis

Arts & Humanities: About 15% Major support to the Allied Arts Fund.
Civic & Public Affairs: 10 to 15%. Supports community programs in Chattanooga, TN
Education: 20% to 25%. Major support to the University of Tennessee Chattanooga, junior achievement, and the Community Foundation of Chatanooga, TN.
Environment: Less than 5%. Supports environmental learning programs.
Health: Less than 5%. Supports single-disease foundations and associations.
Science: About 5%. Supports science fairs and museums.
Social Services: 35% to 40%. Majority of support to United Way and programs for disadvantaged youth.

Application Procedures

Initial Contact: a brief letter of inquiry
Application Requirements: a description of organization, amount requested, purpose of funds sought, audited financial statement, and proof of tax-exempt status
Deadlines: apply by early fall for funding the next year

Restrictions

Does not support individuals. Gives limited multiyear grants.

Corporate Officials

J. Harold Chandler: chairman, president, chief executive officer B Belton, SC 1949. ED Wofford College (1971); University of South Carolina MBA (1972). PRIM CORP EMPL chairman, president, chief executive officer: Provident Companies, Inc. ADD CORP EMPL president: Provident National Assurance Co.; president, chief executive officer, director: Provident Life & Accident Insurance Co.; president: Provident Life & Casualty Insurance Co. CORP AFFIL director: Herman Miller Inc.; director: Storage Technology Corp.; director: AmSouth Bancorp; director: Healthsource Inc.
Thomas R. Watjen: vice chairman, chief financial officer B Lansing, MI 1954. ED Virginia Military Institute (1976); University of Virginia Darden School of Business Administration MBA (1981). PRIM CORP EMPL vice chairman, chief financial officer, director: Provident Companies, Inc. ADD CORP EMPL executive vice president: Unum Provident Corp.
Thomas A. H. White: vice president corporate relations B Knoxville, TN 1958. ED University of the South (1980); Vanderbilt University (1982). PRIM CORP EMPL vice president corporate relations: Provident Companies, Inc.

Giving Program Officials

Jeffrey G. McCall: vice president (see above)
Thomas A. H. White: (see above)

Grants Analysis

Disclosure Period: calendar year ending 1996
Total Grants: $493,835*
Number of Grants: 98
Average Grant: $5,039
Highest Grant: $75,000
Typical Range: $500 to $1,500 and $10,000 to $20,000
***Note:** Giving excludes matching gifts; United Way.

Recent Grants

Note: Grants derived from 1996 grants list.

Arts & Humanities

60,000	Allied Arts Fund, Chattanooga, TN
15,000	Friends of the Festival Riverbend, Chattanooga, TN
15,000	Friends of the Festival Riverbend, Chattanooga, TN
7,500	Chattanooga Symphony and Opera Association, Chattanooga, TN
2,500	Chattanooga Regional History Museum, Chattanooga, TN
2,500	Chattanooga Symphony and Opera Association, Chattanooga, TN -- for gala
2,500	Chattanooga Symphony and Opera Association, Chattanooga, TN
2,500	Chattanooga Symphony and Opera Association, Chattanooga, TN -- for gala

Civic & Public Affairs

17,500	Habitat for Humanity, Chattanooga, TN -- support for disadvantaged
15,000	Tennessee 200 Bicentennial Celebration Folk Festival, TN
10,000	Chattanooga Summit, Chattanooga, TN
10,000	Junior League, Chattanooga, TN
10,000	Tennessee Aquarium, Chattanooga, TN
5,000	Air Show 1996, Chattanooga, TN
5,000	Chattanooga Downtown Partner, Chattanooga, TN -- for 1996 Nooner
5,000	Chattanoogans for Tax Fairness, Chattanooga, TN
2,000	Tennessee 200 Bicentennial Celebration Folk Festival, TN
1,500	A Night To Remember IX, Chattanooga, TN

Education

75,000	University of Tennessee Chattanooga, Chattanooga, TN
20,000	Junior Achievement, Chattanooga, TN
17,500	Community Foundation, Chattanooga, TN -- Provident Scholarships
15,000	Community Foundation, Chattanooga, TN -- Provident Scholarships
14,000	University of Tennessee, Knoxville, TN -- for UTC Rowing Team
10,000	READ, Chattanooga, TN
5,000	Better Schools Committee, Chattanooga, TN -- for school system merger
5,000	Georgia State University, Atlanta, GA
3,000	STARS -- educational
3,000	University of Tennessee, Knoxville, TN -- for Athletics River City Classic
2,500	Community Foundation, Chattanooga, TN -- educational
2,500	Community Foundation, Chattanooga, TN -- educational

Environment

10,000	Ecology Channel, Chattanooga, TN -- for Chatanooga Earth Day 1996
5,000	Nature Conservancy, Chattanooga, TN
5,000	Southern Environmental Law Center, Charlottesville, VA
2,000	Tennessee River Gorge Trust, Chattanooga, TN

Health

2,500	American Heart Association, Chattanooga, TN
2,500	Siskin Memorial Foundation, Chattanooga, TN -- for StarNight '96
2,000	American Heart Association, Chattanooga, TN
2,000	Siskin Memorial Foundation, Chattanooga, TN -- for Phonathon

Science

35,000	Creative Discovery Museum, Chattanooga, TN
1,500	Chattanooga Regional Science Fair, Chattanooga, TN

Social Services

63,500	United Way, Chattanooga, TN
63,500	United Way, Chattanooga, TN
63,500	United Way, Chattanooga, TN
63,500	United Way, Chattanooga, TN
7,500	Girls, Incorporated, Chattanooga, TN -- for disadvantaged
5,000	Big Brothers and Big Sisters, Chattanooga, TN -- for disadvantaged
5,000	Boys Club, Chattanooga, TN -- for Steak 'N Burger Dinner
2,500	Girl Scouts of America, Chattanooga, TN -- civic
2,000	Chattanooga Community Kitchen, Chattanooga, TN -- for 'Fast Day Week '96
2,000	Chattanooga Sports and Events Committee, Chattanooga, TN -- for Ukrainian Gym

PROVIDENT MUTUAL LIFE INSURANCE CO.

Company Contact

Berwin, PA

Company Description

Assets: US$3,240,000,000
Employees: 1,200
SIC(s): 6311 Life Insurance, 6321 Accident & Health Insurance.

Nonmonetary Support

Range: $15,000 - $20,000
Type: In-kind Services
Note: In-kind services are in the form of printing services performed for nonprofit groups.

Giving Contact

Kathy Hopson, Administrative Assistant to Chief Executive Officer
Provident Mutual Life Insurance Co.
1000 Chesterbrook Boulevard
Berwyn, PA 19312
Phone: (610)407-1501
Fax: (610)407-1718

Description

Organization Type: Corporate Giving Program
Giving Locations: PA: Philadelphia metropolitan area
Grant Types: Employee Matching Gifts.

Financial Summary

Total Giving: $500,000 (2000 approx); $500,000 (1999 approx); $500,000 (1998 approx). Note: Contributes through corporate direct giving program only.

Typical Recipients

Arts & Humanities: Arts & Humanities-General
Civic & Public Affairs: Civic & Public Affairs-General
Education: Education-General
Health: Health-General
Social Services: Social Services-General

Application Procedures

Initial Contact: a brief letter of inquiry
Application Requirements: a description of organization, amount requested, purpose of funds sought, recently audited financial statement, and proof of tax-exempt status
Deadlines: must be submitted by early fall

Corporate Officials

Robert Kloff: president, chief executive officer PRIM CORP EMPL president, chief executive officer: Provident Mutual Life Insurance Co.

Giving Program Officials

Kathy Hopson: administrative assistant

PRUDENTIAL INSURANCE CO. OF AMERICA

★ Number 43 of Top 100 Corporate Givers

Company Contact

Newark, NJ
Web: http://www.prudential.com

Company Description

Revenue: US$26,618,000,000 (1999)
Profit: US$813,000,000 (1999)
Employees: 92,966
Fortune Rank: 48, per FORTUNE Magazine's list of 500 Largest U.S. Corporations (1999).
FF 48
SIC(s): 6311 Life Insurance, 6321 Accident & Health Insurance, 6331 Fire, Marine & Casualty Insurance.

Nonmonetary Support

Value: $250,000 (1996); $186,000 (1995); $2,500,000 (1993)
Type: Donated Equipment; In-kind Services; Loaned Employees; Loaned Executives
Contact: Emma Perry, Community Relations Consultant
Note: 1997 employee volunteer hours totaled 76,011. 1997 nonmonetary support: $250,000.

Corporate Sponsorship

Range: less than $8,200,000 (1998)
Type: Arts & cultural events; Festivals/fairs; Music & entertainment events; Sports events
Contact: Emma Perry-White, Community Relations Consultant
Note: Company also sponsors fundraising dinners and golf outings.

Prudential Foundation

Giving Contact

Lata Reddy, Secretary
Prudential Foundation
Prudential Plaza
751 Broad Street, 15th Floor
Newark, NJ 07102-3777
Phone: (973)802-7354
Fax: (973)802-3345

Description

EIN: 222175290
Organization Type: Corporate Foundation
Giving Locations: NJ: particularly Newark headquarters and operating communities; nationally.
Grant Types: Employee Matching Gifts, General Support, Multiyear/Continuing Support.
Note: Employee matching gift ratio: 2 to 1 for the first $100 donated; 1 to 1 for donations of $101 to $5,000. Contact for matching gift information: (800) 554-5846.

Giving Philosophy

'The Community Resources area created in 1996 is a powerful combination of three units: the Prudential Foundation, an independent nonprofit grantmaking

organization funded by contributions from the Prudential Insurance Company of America; the Social Investment Program, which originates and manages socially beneficial investments for Prudential and the Prudential Foundation; and Local Initiatives, which coordinates employee volunteerism and helps communities identify and solve problems.

'Through Community Resources, Prudential is achieving greater impact with its community outreach efforts. Community Resources is focusing sharply on three important categories of need--Ready to Learn, Ready to Work, Ready to Live--to help individuals and communities build the skills they need to be more productive and self-sufficient.' *Prudential Community Resources 1996*'Prudential's Social Investment Program makes socially responsible investments in the areas of affordable housing, economic development, minority entrepreneurship, community health and safety, and education.

'The Social Investment Program originates investments for the Prudential Insurance Company of America and the Prudential Foundation. The program is authorized to originate annually an average of $25 million of new social investments for Prudential. By year-end 1997, more than $685 million in equity and debt investments had been provided to nonprofit and for-profit ventures. Currently outstanding investments benefit individuals in 288 cities in 29 states.' *Overview of Prudential's Social Investment Program*

Financial Summary

Total Giving: $25,045,110 (1999 approx); $21,770,100 (1998 approx); $18,984,386 (1997). Note: Contributes through corporate direct giving program and foundation. 1997 Giving includes corporate direct giving ($6,512,646); foundation ($13,000,446); matching gifts ($2,089,072); United Way ($3,372,368). 1996 Giving includes corporate direct giving ($3,400,000); foundation ($11,995,945,945); matching gifts ($2,239,234); United Way ($3,165,863); volunteer grants ($553,250); nonmonetary support.

Assets: $129,631,000 (1996); $145,764,000 (1995); $140,675,773 (1994)

Typical Recipients

Arts & Humanities: Arts Associations & Councils, Arts Centers, Arts Funds, Arts Institutes, Community Arts, Historic Preservation, History & Archaeology, Libraries, Museums/Galleries, Music, Opera, Performing Arts, Public Broadcasting

Civic & Public Affairs: African American Affairs, Botanical Gardens/Parks, Business/Free Enterprise, Civil Rights, Economic Development, Economic Policy, Employment/Job Training, Hispanic Affairs, Housing, Law & Justice, Legal Aid, Municipalities/Towns, Nonprofit Management, Professional & Trade Associations, Public Policy, Safety, Urban & Community Affairs, Women's Affairs

Education: Afterschool/Enrichment Programs, Arts/Humanities Education, Business Education, Colleges & Universities, Community & Junior Colleges, Continuing Education, Economic Education, Education Associations, Education Funds, Education Reform, Elementary Education (Private), Elementary Education (Public), Engineering/Technological Education, Faculty Development, Education-General, Health & Physical Education, Journalism/Media Education, Leadership Training, Legal Education, Literacy, Medical Education, Minority Education, Preschool Education, Private Education (Precollege), Public Education (Precollege), Religious Education, School Volunteerism, Science/Mathematics Education, Secondary Education (Private), Social Sciences Education, Special Education, Student Aid, Vocational & Technical Education

Environment: Environment-General

Health: AIDS/HIV, Children's Health/Hospitals, Clinics/Medical Centers, Emergency/Ambulance Services, Geriatric Health, Health Policy/Cost Containment, Health Organizations, Hospitals, Medical Rehabilitation, Medical Training, Mental Health, Public Health, Research/Studies Institutes

International: Human Rights, International Relations

Religion: Religious Welfare

Social Services: At-Risk Youth, Child Abuse, Child Welfare, Community Centers, Community Service Organizations, Counseling, Crime Prevention, Day Care, Delinquency & Criminal Rehabilitation, Emergency Relief, Family Planning, Family Services, Food/Clothing Distribution, Homes, People with Disabilities, Recreation & Athletics, Scouts, Senior Services, Shelters/Homelessness, Substance Abuse, United Funds/United Ways, Veterans, Volunteer Services, Youth Organizations

Contributions Analysis

Giving Priorities: Education, United Way, community development, health care, human services, government, and civic affairs.

Civic & Public Affairs: (Ready to Work) 15% to 20%. Promotes job entry skills that are acquired through initiatives that focus on school-to-worktransition, workforce development and welfare-to-work; job creation strategies that include access to capital, nonprofit/for-profit ventures, adult and youth entrepreneurship, financial training, business attraction/development/retention; decent, affordable housing that is created through programs that focus on either housing strategies or neighborhood-based activities.

Education: (Ready to Learn) 15% to 20%. Supports education efforts that strengthen early childhood education initiatives; support professional development for preK-3 teachers; build strong school leadership, with a particular emphasis on parental involvement; provide school-based health and human services that reduce the barriers to learning; or create safe school environments through conflict resolution programs. Within this framework, the foundation emphasizes the creation of model schools, arts education, and literacy.

Social Services: Company also gives directly through its Social Investment Program. Areas of emphasis are affordable housing, economic revitalization, and minority entrepreneurship, community health and safety, and education. Support is in the form of loans.

Application Procedures

Initial Contact: contact foundation for application form

Application Requirements: 3-page concept paper (optional); completed application form; proof of tax-exempt status; latest audited financial statement; itemized budget of project; breakdown of current funding sources, including the amount received from each source; and names and qualifications of those conducting the project

Deadlines: None.

Review Process: proposals reviewed continuously; grants that exceed $200,000 are reviewed by the Board of Trustees, which meets in April, August and December

Evaluative Criteria: evaluate organization's ability to direct project; identify specific and measurable short- and long-term objectives; demonstrate that approach is the most effective; develop a complete and realistic budget; ability to continue program after funding ceases; and evaluate outcome of project

Decision Notification: grants up to $200,000: decisions made within 30 days of receipt of application; for grants over $200,000: decisions made by Board of Trustees in April, August, and December

Notes: Foundation requests that no faxed applications or videotapes be sent. Do not phone for application status.

Restrictions

Grants are not made to veterans, labor, religious, political, fraternal, or athletic groups, except when program benefits or provides services to the community at large; individuals; organizations that do not have 501(c)(3) status; general operating support for single-disease health organizations, except local AIDS groups; goodwill advertising; or fundraising events.

Does not fund capital campaigns, annual fund drives, or endowments.

Additional Information

Every three years foundation staff examines public and nonprofit environments, in order to direct foundation grant-making procedures, and reviews and revises foundation's strategic plan accordingly.

Publications: Prudential Community Resources; Application Form; Guidelines

Corporate Officials

Arthur Frederick Ryan: chairman, chief executive officer B Brooklyn, NY 1942. ED Providence College BA (1963). PRIM CORP EMPL chairman, chief executive officer: The Prudential Insurance Co. of America. CORP AFFIL director, member policy & planning committee, chairman: Depository Trust Co. NONPR AFFIL vice chairman operations division, vice chairman government relations council: American Bankers Association; program manager: CHIPS Same Day Settlement New York Clearing House.

Giving Program Officials

Pindaros Roy Vagelos: trustee B Westfield, NJ 1929. ED University of Pennsylvania AB (1950); Columbia University MD (1954). CORP AFFIL director: Prudential Insurance Co. North America; chairman, director: Regeneron Pharmaceuticals Inc.; director: PepsiCo; director: Prudential Insurance Co. America; director: Boeing Corp.; director: Estee Lauder Companies Inc. NONPR AFFIL director: New Jersey Center Performing Arts; trustee, chairman board: University Pennsylvania; member: Institute Medicine; member: National Academy Sciences; member: Business Roundtable; trustee: Danforth Foundation; member: American Philosophical Society; member: American Society Biological Chemists; member: American Academy of Arts & Sciences; member: American Chemical Society.

Foundation Officials

Martin A. Berkowitz: comptroller

Peter Bushyeager: vice president

Michele S. Darling: chairman

Carolyne Kahle Davis, PhD: trustee B Penn Yan, NY 1932. ED Johns Hopkins University BS (1954); Syracuse University MS (1965); Syracuse University PhD (1972). CORP AFFIL director: Pharmaceutical Marketing Services Inc.; director: Prudential Insurance Co. America; director: Minimed Sylmar; director: Beverly Enterprises; director: Merck & Co. Inc.; director: Beckman Instruments. NONPR AFFIL vis com: University Michigan Medical Center; trustee: University Pennsylvania Medical Center; member: Phi Delta Kappa; member: Sigma Theta Tau; member: National Academy Sciences Institute Medicine; member: National League Nursing; vis com: Medical University South Carolina.

Jon F. Hanson: trustee PRIM CORP EMPL chairman: Hampshire Management Co. CORP AFFIL director: United Water Resources Inc.; director: Prudential Insurance Co. North America; director: United Water New Jersey; director: Neuman Health Services; director: Orange & Rockland Utilities Inc.; director: Consolidated Delivery Logistics. NONPR AFFIL chairman: National Football Foundation.

Gabriella Morris: president

Mary Puryear: program officer culture & arts

Lata Reddy: secretary

Arthur Frederick Ryan: trustee (see above)

Grants Analysis

Disclosure Period: calendar year ending 1997

Total Grants: $18,984,386*

Number of Grants: 422

Average Grant: $10,000

Highest Grant: $500,000
Typical Range: $10,000 to $20,000
***Note:** Giving excludes corporate direct giving. Analysis provided by foundation.

Recent Grants

Note: Grants derived from 1996 Form 990.

Arts & Humanities

342,000 Children's Television Network, New York, NY
200,000 Children's Television Workshop, New York, NY

Civic & Public Affairs

250,000 Manhattan Institute for Policy Research Center for Educational Innovation, New York, NY
125,000 Advertising Council, New York, NY
100,000 Hispanic Designers, Washington, DC
100,000 Local Initiatives Support Corporation, Newark, NJ
100,000 National Puerto Rican Coalition, Washington, DC
85,000 City of Philadelphia Commission on Human Relations, Philadelphia, PA
75,000 Center for Community Change, Washington, DC
50,000 Committee for Economic Development, New York, NY
50,000 Committee for Economic Development, New York, NY
50,000 Community Loan Fund of New Jersey, Trenton, NJ
50,000 Delaware Valley Community Fund, Philadelphia, PA
50,000 Enterprise Foundation, Columbia, MD

Education

320,210 Columbia University Graduate School of Journalism, New York, NY
200,000 New American Schools Development Corporation, Arlington, VA
150,000 Educators for Social Responsibility, New York, NY
150,000 Reading is Fundamental, Washington, DC
125,000 Community Training and Assistance Center, Boston, MA
125,000 Independent College Fund of New Jersey, Summit, NJ
125,000 New Jersey Institute of Technology, Newark, NJ
125,000 Recruiting New Teachers, Belmont, MA
113,198 Citizens Scholarship Foundation of America, Saint Peter, MN
100,000 Los Angeles Educational Partnership, Los Angeles, CA
100,000 United Negro College Fund, Minneapolis, MN
75,000 Institute for Educational Leadership, Washington, DC
75,000 Institute for Educational Leadership, Washington, DC
70,000 Rutgers University Center for Strategic Urban Community Leadership, Camden, NJ
60,000 Work, Achievement, Values, and Education, Washington, DC
50,000 Chad School, Newark, NJ

Health

85,000 Black Leadership Commission AIDS, New York, NY
71,000 Hastings Center, Princeton, NJ
62,701 Yale University Child Study Center, New Haven, CT

International

75,000 Joint Center for Political and Economic Studies, Washington, DC

Religion

75,000 Protestant Community Centers, Newark, NJ

Social Services

1,850,000 United Way Tri-State, New York, NY
276,100 United Way Southeastern Pennsylvania, Philadelphia, PA
208,000 United Way, Minneapolis, MN
195,000 Children's Express Foundation, Washington, DC
164,125 Police Executive Research Forum, Washington, DC
138,100 United Way Northeast Florida, Jacksonville, FL
130,000 Trust for Public Land Playground Initiative, Newark, NJ
125,000 Food Research and Action Center, Washington, DC
100,000 Kids Corporation, Morristown, NJ
90,000 Child Welfare League of America, Washington, DC
80,000 Adoption Center of Delaware Valley, Philadelphia, PA
75,000 Children's Defense Fund, Washington, DC
75,000 Children's Home Society of New Jersey, Trenton, NJ
60,000 Boys and Girls Clubs of America, Atlanta, GA
58,500 Association for Children of New Jersey, Newark, NJ

PRUDENTIAL SECURITIES INC.

Company Contact

New York, NY
Web: http://www.prusec.com

Company Description

Former Name: Prudential-Bache Securities.
Revenue: US$3,400,000,000
Employees: 17,000
SIC(s): 6211 Security Brokers & Dealers.
Parent Company: Prudential Insurance Co. of America, Newark, NJ, United States

Operating Locations

Australia: Bache Nominees Pty. Ltd., Melbourne; Corcarr Funds Management Ltd. Dormant, Melbourne; Corcarr Management Pty. Ltd., Melbourne; Corcarr Nominees Pty. Ltd., Melbourne; Corcarr Superannuation Pty. Ltd., Melbourne; Divisplit Nominees Pty. Ltd., Melbourne; PBML Custodian Ltd., Melbourne; Prudential-Bache Capital Funding (Australia) Ltd., Melbourne; Prudential-Bache Nominees P/L, Melbourne; Prudential-Bache Securities (Australia) Ltd., Melbourne; Prudential Securities Group Inc., Melbourne; British Virgin Islands: Prudential Asia Fund Management Ltd., Road Town, Tortola; Canada: Otip/Raeo Insurance Co., Scarborough; P I C Realty Canada Ltd., Scarborough; Prudential of America General Insurance Co. (Canada), Scarborough; Prudential Fund Management Canada Ltd., Toronto; Prudential Insurance of America, Toronto; France: Prudential Bache Internationale SA, Paris, Ville-de-Paris; Germany: Pruential-Bache Securities (Germany) Inc. Niederlassung Hamburg, Hamburg; Hong Kong: Prudential Asia Fund Management Ltd., Central District; Prudential Asia Fund Managers Hong Kong Ltd., Central District; Prudential Asia Investments Ltd., Central District; Prudential Asset Management Asia Hong Kong Ltd., Central District; Prudential-Bache Capital Funding Asia (Hong Kong) Ltd., Central District; Prudential-Bache Forex (Hong Kong) Ltd., Central District; Prudential-Bache Futures (Hong Kong) Ltd., Central District; Prudential-Bache Nominees (Hong Kong) Ltd., Central District; Prudential-Bache Securities Asia Pacific Ltd., Central District; Prudential-Bache Securities (Hong Kong) Ltd., Central District; Italy: Pricoa Vita SPA, Milano, Lombardia; Japan: Prudential Investment Advisory Co. Ltd., Tokyo; Prudential Life Insurance Co. Ltd., Tokyo; Republic of Korea: Prudential Life Insurance Co. of Korea, Chung-Gu, Seoul; Luxembourg: Gateway Holdings SA, Luxembourg; Global Income Fund Management Co. SA, Luxembourg; Global Series Fund II Managment Co. SA, Luxembourg; Jennison Long Bond Management Co. SA, Luxembourg; Pricoa International SA, Luxembourg; Prudential-Bache Intl Bank SA, Luxembourg; Prudential-Bache Securities (Luxembourg), Luxembourg; Monaco: Prudential Bache Securities Inc., Monaco; Netherlands: Prudential-Bache Securities (Holland), Amsterdam, Noord-Holland; Prudential-Bache Capital Funding BV, Haarlem, Noord-Holland; Singapore: Pama (Singapore) Pte. Ltd., Singapore; Prudential-Bache Securities Asia Pacific Ltd., Singapore; Simmons (Southeast Asia) Private Ltd., Singapore; Spain: Prudential-Bache Securities Agencia de Valores SA, Madrid; United Kingdom: Prudential-Bache Forex (United Kingdom) Ltd., London; Prudential-Bache International (United Kingdom) Ltd., London; Prudential-Bache Intl Ltd., London

Nonmonetary Support

Type: In-kind Services

Corporate Sponsorship

Type: Sports events

Prudential Securities Foundation

Giving Contact

Elizabeth A. Longley, Vice President
Prudential Securities Foundation
1 Seaport Plaza
New York, NY 10292
Phone: (212)214-4884
Fax: (212)214-5541

Description

EIN: 136193023
Organization Type: Corporate Foundation
Giving Locations: NY
Grant Types: Emergency, General Support.

Financial Summary

Total Giving: $724,384 (fiscal year ending January 31, 1996); $1,023,906 (fiscal 1995); $890,430 (fiscal 1994). Note: Contributes through foundation only.
Assets: $57,191 (fiscal 1996); $51,368 (fiscal 1995); $371,174 (fiscal 1993)
Gifts Received: $730,307 (fiscal 1996); $704,245 (fiscal 1995); $1,242,499 (fiscal 1993)

Typical Recipients

Arts & Humanities: Ethnic & Folk Arts, History & Archaeology, Libraries, Museums/Galleries, Music, Performing Arts, Public Broadcasting, Theater
Civic & Public Affairs: African American Affairs, Botanical Gardens/Parks, Business/Free Enterprise, Civil Rights, Economic Development, Civic & Public Affairs-General, Housing, Law & Justice, Municipalities/Towns, Public Policy, Urban & Community Affairs, Women's Affairs, Zoos/Aquariums
Education: Business Education, Colleges & Universities, Economic Education, Education Associations, Education Funds, Education-General, Literacy, Minority Education, School Volunteerism, Student Aid
Environment: Environment-General
Health: Arthritis, Children's Health/Hospitals, Health Organizations, Heart, Hospitals, Medical Research, Mental Health, Single-Disease Health Associations, Transplant Networks/Donor Banks
International: International Peace & Security Issues, Missionary/Religious Activities
Religion: Churches, Jewish Causes, Religious Organizations, Religious Welfare, Synagogues/Temples

Social Services: Big Brother/Big Sister, Community Service Organizations, Crime Prevention, Food/Clothing Distribution, People with Disabilities, Scouts, Senior Services, Shelters/Homelessness, Substance Abuse, United Funds/United Ways, YMCA/YWCA/YMHA/YWHA, Youth Organizations

Contributions Analysis

Giving Priorities: Limited funding goes to international houses, organizations that promote good will between nations, and policy study organizations.
Arts & Humanities: 15% to 20%. Libraries and museums receive major support. Also contributes to orchestras, opera, arts associations, and art education.
Civic & Public Affairs: 5% to 10%. Legal aid, business organizations, chambers ofcommerce, parks, and civil rights.
Education: 10% to 15%. Colleges and universities, literacy programs, scholarship funds, and education associations.
Health: 5% to 10%. Most contributions go to hospitals and single-disease health associations. Foundations involved with mental health, children, cancer, general health, emergency relief, and fitness also receive funding.
Religion: Less than 5%. Churches, synagogues, and religious organizations.
Social Services: 45% to 50%. Over half of funding supports United Way chapters, and other youth organizations receive substantial contributions. Other interests include athletic organizations, substance abuse education, and food distribution.

Application Procedures

Initial Contact: brief letter describing program
Deadlines: None.

Corporate Officials

Elizabeth A. Longley: 1st vice presidenteo, director PRIM CORP EMPL 1st vice president: Prudential Securities Inc.
Leland B. Paton: president capital marketings, director, member executive committee B Worcester, MA 1943. PRIM CORP EMPL president capital marketings, director, member executive committee: Prudential Securities Inc. CORP AFFIL member: New York Stock Exchange Inc.; director: Prudential Securities Group Inc.; director: Chicago Board Options Exchange; exchange officer: America Stock Exchange Inc. NONPR AFFIL member: Securities Industry Association; member: Securities Industry Institute; member: American Marketing Association; director: Riverdale Country School. CLUB AFFIL Mid-Ocean Club; Long Cove Club; Bond Club; Harvard Club; Apawanis Club.
Hardwick Simmons: president, chief executive officer, director B Baltimore, MD 1940. ED Harvard University BA (1962); Harvard University MBA (1966). PRIM CORP EMPL president, chief executive officer, director: Prudential Securities Inc. CORP AFFIL president, chief executive officer, director: Prudential Securities Group Inc.; chief executive officer, director: Prudential Capital & Investment Services; president: First Financial Fund Inc. NONPR AFFIL director: Chicago Board Options Exchange. CLUB AFFIL Bond Club.

Foundation Officials

Elizabeth A. Longley: vice president corporate affairs (see above)
Nathalie P. Maio: vice president, secretary

Grants Analysis

Disclosure Period: fiscal year ending January 31, 1996
Total Grants: $724,384
Number of Grants: 52
Average Grant: $13,930
Highest Grant: $300,000
Typical Range: $1,000 to $15,000

Recent Grants

Note: Grants derived from 1996 Form 990.

Arts & Humanities

50,000	South Street Seaport Museum, New York, NY
25,000	Carnegie Hall, New York, NY
20,000	South Street Seaport Museum, New York, NY
10,000	Lincoln Center Consolidated Corp, New York, NY
10,000	Metropolitan Museum of Art, New York, NY
7,500	Historic Hudson Valley, New York, NY
5,000	National Museum of the American Indian, Washington, DC
2,500	WNET/Channel 13, New York, NY

Civic & Public Affairs

35,000	New York City Partnership Foundation, New York, NY
25,000	Central Park Conservancy, New York, NY
5,000	Parks Council, New York, NY
1,000	Public Policy Institute, Albany, NY
1,000	SLE Foundation
500	Uniform Law Foundation, Chicago, IL
250	Better Business Bureau Foundation

Education

21,460	National Merit Scholarship Corp, Evanston, IL
11,424	SIA Foundation for Economic Education
10,000	Prep for Prep, New York, NY
10,000	United Negro College Fund, New York, NY
5,000	A Better Chance, Boston, MA
5,000	Fund for New York City Public Education, New York, NY
5,000	Securities Industry Foundation for Economic Education, New York, NY
5,000	Stern School of Business, New York, NY
5,000	University of Miami Arthur J. Hall Memorial Scholarship, Miami, FL
4,000	Financial Women's Association of New York Educational Fund, New York, NY
3,500	SIA New York District Economic Education Foundation, NY
1,000	Marymount College, Tarrytown, NY
1,000	New York City School Volunteer Program, New York, NY

Health

30,000	New York Downtown Hospital, New York, NY
23,225	Children's Hospital Fund, New York, NY
6,000	Buoniconti Fund to Cure Paralysis, Miami, FL
1,775	Children's Hospital Fund, New York, NY
1,500	New York Blood Center, New York, NY
1,200	Children's Hospital Fund, New York, NY
1,000	American Heart Association Wall Street Run, New York, NY
500	American Paralysis Association, Short Hills, NJ

International

2,000	Business Executives for National Security, Washington, DC
1,500	Boys Town Jerusalem, Washington, DC

Religion

15,000	Cardinals Committee of the Laity, New York, NY
3,600	Wall Street Division of United Jewish Appeal Federation, New York, NY

Social Services

300,000	United Way Tri-State, New York, NY
10,000	Big Brothers and Big Sisters, New York, NY
10,000	Boy Scouts of America, New York, NY
7,500	Hale House for the Promotion of Human Potential, New York, NY
6,000	Boys Club, New York, NY
5,500	Phoenix House Development Fund, New York, NY
5,000	New York Police and Fire Widows and Children's Benefit Fund, New York, NY
4,000	Citymeals-on-Wheels, New York, NY
2,500	Girls Club, New York, NY
1,000	Shake-A-Leg, Newport, RI

Public Service Co. Of Oklahoma

Company Contact

Tulsa, OK

Company Description

Employees: 1,477
SIC(s): 4911 Electric Services.
Parent Company: Central & South West Corp.

Corporate Sponsorship

Type: Arts & cultural events; Music & entertainment events; Sports events
Note: Sponsors the Special Olympics in Oklahoma.

Giving Contact

Fran Gutierrez, Corporate Contributions Coordinator
Public Service Co. of Oklahoma
PO Box 201
Tulsa, OK 74102
Phone: (918)599-2000
Fax: (918)599-3479

Description

Organization Type: Corporate Giving Program
Giving Locations: OK: Southeastern and Southwestern Oklahoma
Grant Types: General Support.

Financial Summary

Total Giving: $900,000 (2000 approx); $900,000 (1999 approx); $900,000 (1998 approx). Note: Contributes through corporate direct giving program only.

Typical Recipients

Arts & Humanities: Arts & Humanities-General
Civic & Public Affairs: Civic & Public Affairs-General
Education: Education-General
Health: Health-General
Social Services: Social Services-General

Application Procedures

Initial Contact: a brief letter of inquiry
Application Requirements: a description of organization, amount requested, purpose of funds sought, recently audited financial statements, proof of tax-exempt status, and percent that United Way funds make up of total budget, if applicable
Deadlines: proposals should be received at least 90 days in advance of need

Restrictions

Does not support individuals; religious organizations for sectarian purposes; political or lobbying groups; controversial organizations, membership-only or discriminatory groups; athletic group funds or disease-related organizations.

Additional Information

The company announced plans to merge with American Electric Power in 2000.
Publications: Annual Report

Corporate Officials

Pete Churchwell: president manager, director PRIM CORP EMPL president: Public Service Co. of Oklahoma.

William McKamey: general manager, director B Worland, VA 1946. ED Clark College (1970); University of Virginia (1991). PRIM CORP EMPL general manager, director: Public Service Co. of Oklahoma.

Giving Program Officials

Vaughn Conrad: PRIM CORP EMPL director, manager Tulsa: Public Service Co. of Oklahoma.
Carole Hicks: manager PRIM CORP EMPL manager business development: Public Service Co. of Oklahoma.

PUBLIC SERVICE ELECTRIC &GAS CO.

Company Contact

Newark, NJ

Company Description

SIC(s): 4931 Electric & Other Services Combined.
Parent Company: Public Service Enterprise Group Inc., 80 Park Plaza, Newark, NJ, United States

Nonmonetary Support

Type: Donated Equipment; Donated Products; In-kind Services; Loaned Executives

Corporate Sponsorship

Type: Arts & cultural events; Other
Note: Sponsors an economic development program.

Public Service Electric & Gas Foundation

Giving Contact

Eileen Leahy, Manager, Corporate Contributions
Public Service Electric& Gas Foundation
80 Park Plz., Mail Code TI0C
Newark, NJ 07101
Phone: (973)430-7000
Fax: (973)430-5867

Description

Organization Type: Corporate Foundation
Giving Locations: nationally for education grants; primarily in service area.
Grant Types: Capital, Challenge, Employee Matching Gifts, General Support, Project, Scholarship, Seed Money.

Giving Philosophy

'PSE&G's philosophy of strategic philanthropy focuses on three critical areas: **Children's Issues** (initiatives that address the well being of children and focus on the improvement of our educational system), **Economic Development** (urban revitalization and affordable housing) and the **Environment** (proper use of energy, pollution prevention and natural resource conservation). These areas of focus have been selected since they are of high priority for New Jersey citizens and are also of strategic business importance to the company.'

Financial Summary

Total Giving: $3,400,000 (1999 approx); $3,000,000 (1998 approx); $2,400,000 (1995 approx). Note: Contributes through corporate direct giving program and foundation. Giving includes foundation. 1998 Giving includes corporate direct giving ($1,500,000); foundation ($1,500,000).

Typical Recipients

Arts & Humanities: Arts Centers, Arts Funds, Historic Preservation, Libraries, Museums/Galleries, Performing Arts, Public Broadcasting, Theater
Civic & Public Affairs: Economic Development, Employment/Job Training, Housing, Law & Justice, Professional & Trade Associations, Public Policy, Safety, Urban & Community Affairs, Women's Affairs
Education: Business Education, Colleges & Universities, Community & Junior Colleges, Elementary Education (Private), Engineering/Technological Education, Minority Education, Private Education (Precollege), Public Education (Precollege), Science/Mathematics Education
Environment: Environment-General
Health: Emergency/Ambulance Services, Hospitals
Science: Science Exhibits & Fairs, Scientific Centers & Institutes
Social Services: Child Welfare, Community Service Organizations, Counseling, Delinquency & Criminal Rehabilitation, Food/Clothing Distribution, People with Disabilities, Recreation & Athletics, Senior Services, Substance Abuse, United Funds/United Ways, Youth Organizations

Contributions Analysis

Giving Priorities: Social service, education, civic concerns, the arts, and health care.
Arts & Humanities: 5% to 10%. Funds cultural programs in urban communities.
Civic & Public Affairs: About 30%. Focuses on economic development, urban improvement projects, and the environment.
Education: 25% to 30%. Primarily supports higher education, including minority education, educational funds, capital campaigns.
Health: About 35%. Major support goes to United Way agencies. Also supports hospitals and youth organizations.

Application Procedures

Initial Contact: letter accompanied by full proposal
Application Requirements: a description of organization and project, budget, and proof of tax-exempt status
Deadlines: None.
Decision Notification: continuously

Restrictions

Does not support individuals, member agencies of united funds, political or lobbying groups, or religious organizations for sectarian purposes.

Additional Information

Publications: Corporate Responsiblity Report

Corporate Officials

Lawrence R. Codey: president, chief operating officercorporate responsibility B Montclair, NJ 1944. ED Saint Peter's College BS (1966); Seton Hall University JD (1969); Rutgers University Graduate School of Business MBA (1975). PRIM CORP EMPL president, chief operating officer: Public Service Electric & Gas Co. CORP AFFIL director: United Water Mid-Atlantic Utilities; director: United Water Resources Inc.; director: Trust Co. New Jersey; director: Public Service Enterprise Group Inc.; director: Sealed Air Corp.
E. James Ferland: chairman, president, chief executive officer B Boston, MA 1942. ED Harvard University; University of Maine BSME (1964); University of New Haven MBA (1979). PRIM CORP EMPL chairman, president, chief executive officer, director: Public Service Enterprise Group Inc. CORP AFFIL director: Public Service Resources Corp.; chairman, chief executive officer, director: Public Service Electric & Gas Co.; chairman, chief executive officer, director: PSEG Energy Technologies Inc.; director: PSEG Global Inc.; director: Hartford Steam Boiler Inspection & Insurance Co.; director: HSB Group Inc.; director: First Fidelity Bancorp; director: Foster Wheeler Corp.; chairman, chief executive officer: Enterprise Diversified Holdings Inc. NONPR AFFIL member: Edison Electric Institute; director: Nuclear Energy Institute; director: Association of Edison Illuminating Companies; director: Committee for Economic Development; member: American Gas Association.
Maria B. Pinho: general manager corporate responsibility PRIM CORP EMPL general manager corporate responsibility: Public Service Enterprise Group Inc.

Foundation Officials

Alfred C. Koeppe: senior vice president corporate services & external affairs ED Rutgers University BA; Seton Hall University JD. PRIM CORP EMPL president, chief executive officer: Bell Atlantic New Jersey. CORP AFFIL director: Digital Solutions Inc.
Eileen Leahy: manager corporate contributions

Grants Analysis

Disclosure Period: calendar year ending
Typical Range: $1,000 to $5,000

Recent Grants

Note: Grants derived from 1993 grants list.

Civic & Public Affairs

125,000	Community Agencies Corp of New Jersey, Newark, NJ
125,000	Princeton Center Leadership Training, Lawrenceville, NJ

PUBLIX SUPERMARKETS

★ Number 61 of Top 100 Corporate Givers

Company Contact

1936 George Jenkins Blvd.
Lakeland, FL 33815
Web: http://www.publix.com

Company Description

Revenue: US$13,068,900,000 (1999)
Profit: US$462,400,000 (1999)
Employees: 112,325 (1999)
Fortune Rank: 137, per FORTUNE Magazine's list of 500 Largest U.S. Corporations (1999).
FF 137
SIC(s): 5411 Grocery Stores.

Publix Supermarkets Charities

Giving Contact

Carol Jenkins Barnett, Chairperson
PO Box 407
Lakeland, FL 33802
Phone: (941)688-1188
Web: http://www.publix.com/comm_involvement.htm

Description

Founded: 1967
EIN: 596194119
Organization Type: Family Foundation
Giving Locations: AL; FL; GA; SC
Grant Types: Capital, Challenge, Employee Matching Gifts, General Support, Multiyear/Continuing Support, Operating Expenses, Project, Scholarship.

Giving Philosophy

The George W. Jenkins Foundation primarily supports social services organizations with youth priorities. Youth alternative organizations, boys and girls clubs, children's homes, and child development councils, and education are major priorities.

Financial Summary

Total Giving: $16,000,000 (1999 approx); $14,000,000 (1998 approx); $12,385,890 (1997)
Assets: $261,928,143 (1997); $237,868,081 (1996)

Gifts Received: $2,850,350 (1997); $50,257,597 (1996); $89,820,733 (1990). Note: In 1996, contributions were received from Florida Combined Life Insurance Co., the estate of Mr. George Jenkins, and various donors.

Typical Recipients

Arts & Humanities: Arts Associations & Councils, Arts Centers, Arts Festivals, Community Arts, Museums/Galleries, Performing Arts, Public Broadcasting, Theater
Civic & Public Affairs: African American Affairs, Chambers of Commerce, Economic Policy, Municipalities/Towns, Public Policy, Rural Affairs, Zoos/Aquariums
Education: Colleges & Universities, Community & Junior Colleges, Economic Education, Minority Education, Private Education (Precollege), Public Education (Precollege), Secondary Education (Private), Student Aid
Environment: Environment-General
Health: Cancer, Emergency/Ambulance Services, Geriatric Health, Hospices, Hospitals, Single-Disease Health Associations, Transplant Networks/Donor Banks
International: Foreign Arts Organizations, International Affairs
Religion: Churches, Ministries, Religious Organizations, Religious Welfare
Science: Observatories & Planetariums, Science Museums, Scientific Centers & Institutes
Social Services: At-Risk Youth, Child Welfare, Community Service Organizations, Emergency Relief, Family Planning, Family Services, Food/Clothing Distribution, Homes, People with Disabilities, Scouts, Shelters/Homelessness, Substance Abuse, United Funds/United Ways, YMCA/YWCA/YMHA/YWHA, Youth Organizations

Contributions Analysis

Giving Priorities: Youth and education.
Arts & Humanities: 5%. Funds art festivals, and children, youth and art museums.
Civic & Public Affairs: 8%. Supports future farmers of Florida, county zoo in Atlanta, public affairs, and the Florida aquarium.
Education: 26%. Colleges and universities in Florida.
Health: 1%. American Cancer Society, and the Marrow Foundation.
International: 2%. International museum of art.
Religion: About 1%.
Science: 4%. Science center and Museum of Science and Industry.
Social Services: 53%. Funds United Way, childrens services, YMCA, the homeless, family services, and the handicapped.
Note: Contributions were made in 1996.

Application Procedures

Initial Contact: The foundation requests applications be made in writing.
Application Requirements: Applicants should include the purpose of the request, a copy of 501(c)(3) determination letter from IRS, and the latest financial statement of the organization.
Deadlines: None.

Restrictions

Grants are not made to individuals.

Corporate Officials

Carol Jenkins Barnett: treasurer, director CORP AFFIL director: Publix Supermarkets Inc.
Hoyt R. Barnett: executive vice president, director B Raleigh, NC 1943. ED Florida Southern College BS (1965). PRIM CORP EMPL executive vice president, director: Publix Supermarkets Inc. CLUB AFFIL president: Lone Pine Golf Club.
Carolyn C. Day: assistant secretary B 1945. PRIM CORP EMPL assistant secretary: Publix Super Markets Inc.
Tina Johnson: treasurer, director B 1959. PRIM CORP EMPL treasurer, director: Publix Super Markets Inc.

Grants Analysis

Disclosure Period: calendar year ending 1997
Total Grants: $12,385,890
Number of Grants: 2011 (approx)
Average Grant: $6,159
Highest Grant: $750,000
Typical Range: $1,000 to $10,000

Recent Grants

Note: Grants derived from 1996 Form 990.

Arts & Humanities

225,000	Miami Youth Museum, Miami, FL
50,000	John and Mable Ringling Museum of Art Foundation, Sarasota, FL
42,000	Children's Museum, Atlanta, GA
30,000	Arts Festival Association, Atlanta, GA

Civic & Public Affairs

300,000	Florida Aquarium, Tampa, FL
100,000	National Right to Work Legal Defense Foundation, Springfield, VA
50,000	Atlanta Fulton County Zoo, Atlanta, GA
50,000	Future Farmers of Florida Foundation, Haines City, FL

Education

1,000,000	Florida Southern College, Lakeland, FL
400,000	Florida Southern College, Lakeland, FL
100,000	All Saints Academy
92,000	University of South Florida Foundation, Tampa, FL
71,000	Inroads, Tampa Bay, FL
50,000	Stetson University, De Land, FL
39,200	University of South Florida Foundation, Tampa, FL

Health

50,000	Marrow Foundation, Minneapolis, MN
45,000	American Cancer Society, Tampa, FL

International

100,000	Carter Center, Atlanta, GA
49,000	International Museum of Cartoon Art, Boca Raton, FL

Religion

50,000	First United Methodist Church, Atlanta, GA

Science

200,000	Orlando Science Center, Orlando, FL
50,000	Museum of Science and Industry, Chicago, IL

Social Services

500,000	Take Stock in Children
468,800	United Way Central Florida, Highland City, FL
400,000	Boy Scouts of America Gulf Stream Council, FL
243,900	United Way, Atlanta, GA
222,400	United Way Broward County, Fort Lauderdale, FL
192,500	United Way Dade County, Miami, FL
175,000	YMCA, Lakeland, FL
155,500	United Way Heart of Florida, Orlando, FL
121,600	United Way Palm Beach County, Palm Beach, FL
115,700	United Way Hillsborough County, Tampa, FL
110,800	United Way Pinellas County, Saint Petersburg, FL
100,000	Community Partnership for the Homeless, Atlanta, GA
74,100	United Way Northeast Florida, Jacksonville, FL
63,600	United Way Lee County
60,000	United Way Tallahassee, Tallahassee, FL
58,400	United Way Volusia County, Daytona Beach, FL
56,800	United Way Sarasota County, Sarasota, FL
52,900	United Way Brevard County, Cocoa, FL
50,000	Florida Family Council, Tampa, FL
40,000	Boy Scouts of America Gulf Ridge Council
38,800	United Way Collier County, Naples, FL
33,800	United Way Alachua County, Gainesville, FL
33,000	United Way Manatee County, Bradenton, FL
30,900	United Way Charlotte County, Port Charlotte, FL
30,000	Paul Anderson Youth Home, Vidalia, GA
29,800	United Way Lake-Sumter County, Leesburg, FL
25,500	United Way Columbus-Muscogee
25,000	Polk County Association for Handicapped Citizens, Lakeland, FL

Puget Sound Energy (PSE) Inc.

Company Contact

Bellevue, WA

Company Description

Former Name: Puget Sound Power & Light and Washington Natural Gas.
Assets: US$3,269,000,000
Profit: US$123,100,000
Employees: 3,050

Corporate Sponsorship

Type: Arts & cultural events; Festivals/fairs; Music & entertainment events

Giving Contact

Heather Wangaard
Puget Sound Energy Inc.
Corporate Relations OBC-11E
PO Box 97034
Bellevue, WA 98009-9734
Phone: (425)462-3799
Fax: (425)462-3355
Email: hwanga@puget.com

Alternate Contact

Phone: 888-225-5773

Description

Organization Type: Corporate Giving Program
Giving Locations: PSE service areas.
Grant Types: General Support, Matching.

Financial Summary

Total Giving: $900,000 (1999); $1,100,000 (1998 approx); $650,000 (1997). Note: Contributes through corporate direct giving program only.

Contributions Analysis

Arts & Humanities: Organizations that enrich the communities we serve with music, theater, literature, and visual arts
Civic & Public Affairs: Programs that focus on the protection, improvement, and economichealth of our communities
Education: Private and public higher education institutions, with an emphasis on those programs that focus on educating tomorrow's workforce
Environment: Programs that work to balance environmental and economic needs
Health: Programs that serve the basic health and welfare needs in communities the co. serves

Application Procedures

Initial Contact: Send a written request.

Application Requirements: Proof of 501(c)(3) status; specific amount with explanation of how funds will be spent; description of the organization and specific program for which funding is sought; organization's complete name, address, telephone number, and contact name; explanation of how program benefits the community; description of geographical area and people served by the organization or program; list of key board members or directors and their biographical data; and a list of any other corporate contributors.

Deadlines: None.

Review Process: Proposals reviewed by the Corporate Relations Manager (CRM) of the territory in which an organization is located.

Evaluative Criteria: Any request above $1,500 must be approved by the PSE Corporate Contributions Committee.

Decision Notification: The Corporate Contributions Committee meets quarterly.

Restrictions

The foundation does not fund organizations without 501(c)(3) tax-exempt status; individual or team projects and tickets for prize-oriented activities; group travel expenses; churches or other religious organizations whose programs support a specific religious doctrine; fraternal or labor organizations; political organizations; tax-supported educational institutions; K-12 schools; national or international organizations; advertising or mass-mailings; organizations that are themselves grant-making bodies, endowment funds, or foundations; hospitals and medical research programs. funds, or foundations; hospitals and medical research programs.

Additional Information

In 1995, Puget Sound Energy Co. was formed by the merger of Puget Power and Light Co. and Washington Natural Gas Co.

Company is less likely to fund organizations that are heavily supported by United Way, or Corporate Council for the Arts, due to the company's major contributions to their campaigns.

The company is currently restructuring their guidelines and giving priorities. giving priorities.

Grants Analysis

Disclosure Period: calendar year ending

Typical Range: $500 to $1,000

Pulitzer Publishing Co.

Company Contact

St. Louis, MO

Company Description

Revenue: US$472,339,000

Employees: 2,400

SIC(s): 2711 Newspapers, 4832 Radio Broadcasting Stations, 4833 Television Broadcasting Stations.

Corporate Sponsorship

Type: Arts & cultural events

Note: Sponsors writing contest.

Pulitzer Publishing Co. Foundation

Giving Contact

Mr. Ronald H. Ridgway, Secretary & Treasurer
Pulitzer Publishing Co. Foundation
900 North Tucker Boulevard
St. Louis, MO 63101
Phone: (314)340-8000
Fax: (314)340-3133

Description

EIN: 436052854

Organization Type: Corporate Foundation

Giving Locations: MO: St. Louis metropolitan area

Grant Types: Capital, Endowment, General Support, Project, Scholarship.

Financial Summary

Total Giving: $530,000 (1998 approx); $601,083 (1997); $540,761 (1996). Note: Contributes through foundation only. 1996 Giving includes United Way ($100,000). 1995 Giving includes United Way ($95,000).

Assets: $761,102 (1997); $708,962 (1996); $680,578 (1995)

Gifts Received: $598,833 (1997); $535,011 (1996); $472,144 (1995). Note: In 1997, contributions were received from Pulitzer Broadcasting Co.($556,833); WESH Television, Inc. ($17,000); and Star Publishing ($12,000). In 1996, the foundation received gifts from KCCI Television, Inc., Pulitzer Broadcasting Co., Star Publishing Co., WDSU Television, Inc., and WESH Television, Inc. In 1995, the foundation received gifts from Pulitzer Publishing Co.

Typical Recipients

Arts & Humanities: Arts Appreciation, Arts Associations & Councils, Arts Centers, Arts Funds, Arts Institutes, Dance, Ethnic & Folk Arts, Arts & Humanities-General, Historic Preservation, History & Archaeology, Libraries, Museums/Galleries, Music, Opera, Performing Arts, Public Broadcasting, Theater, Visual Arts

Civic & Public Affairs: African American Affairs, Asian American Affairs, Botanical Gardens/Parks, Business/Free Enterprise, Civil Rights, Clubs, Economic Development, Employment/Job Training, First Amendment Issues, Civic & Public Affairs-General, Professional & Trade Associations, Public Policy, Urban & Community Affairs, Women's Affairs, Zoos/Aquariums

Education: Arts/Humanities Education, Business Education, Colleges & Universities, Education Funds, Education-General, International Exchange, Journalism/Media Education, Legal Education, Medical Education, Minority Education, Private Education (Precollege), Public Education (Precollege), Science/Mathematics Education, Special Education, Student Aid, Vocational & Technical Education

Environment: Environment-General

Health: AIDS/HIV, Cancer, Children's Health/Hospitals, Emergency/Ambulance Services, Home-Care Services, Hospices, Hospitals, Long-Term Care, Mental Health, Respiratory, Single-Disease Health Associations

International: Human Rights, International Organizations, International Relations

Religion: Churches, Dioceses, Jewish Causes, Religious Organizations, Religious Welfare

Science: Scientific Centers & Institutes

Social Services: Child Welfare, Community Service Organizations, Emergency Relief, Family Planning, Family Services, Food/Clothing Distribution, Homes, Recreation & Athletics, Scouts, Senior Services, United Funds/United Ways, YMCA/YWCA/YMHA/YWHA, Youth Organizations

Contributions Analysis

Giving Priorities: The arts, higher education, social service, civic affairs, hospitals, single disease health associations, and churches.

Arts & Humanities: About 35%. Primarily St. Louis area cultural institutions. Major support goes to the St. Louis Symphony. Remaining funds, in grants generally ranging from $1,000 to $5,000, support historic preservation, music, opera, theater, arts funds and associations, and dance.

Civic & Public Affairs: About 5%. Press associations, First Amendment issues, business/free enterprise organizations, and botanical gardens.

Education: About 35%. Colleges and universities, principally in St. Louisand elsewhere in Missouri. Remaining funds support journalism studies, education funds, minority education, technical education, and student aid. Grants typically range from $1,000 to $10,000. Scholarships are limited to St. Louis area minority students who are either high school graduates or in junior college. Scholarships are for attending the University of Missouri Journalism School.

Social Services: 20% to 25%. Majority of funding supports the United Way of Greater St. Louis. Also supports traditional youth organizations, community services, employment, emergency relief, and the aged.

Application Procedures

Initial Contact: brief letter or proposal

Application Requirements: a description of organization, amount requested, purpose of funds sought, recently audited financial statement, proof of tax-exempt status

Deadlines: None.

Restrictions

Applications from individuals are not accepted.

Corporate Officials

Cole C. Campbell: editorewspaper operations B Roanoke, VA. ED University of North Carolina BA. PRIM CORP EMPL editor: Saint Louis Post Dispatch. NONPR AFFIL journalism advisory board: Norfolk State University.

Michael Edgar Pulitzer: chairman, president, chief executive officer, director B Saint Louis, MO 1930. ED Harvard University AB (1951); Harvard University LLB (1954). PRIM CORP EMPL chairman, president, chief executive officer, director: Pulitzer Publishing Co. CORP AFFIL chairman: WESH Television Inc.; chairman, president, chief executive officer, publisher: Star Publishing Co.; chairman: WDSU Television Inc.; president: Pulitzer Ventures Inc.; chairman: Southwest Oregon Publishing Co.; chairman: Pulitzer Broadcasting Co.; chairman: Pulitzer Community Newspapers; vice chairman, director: KKLT-FM; vice chairman, director: KTAR-AM; chairman: KCCI Television Inc.; chairman, director: KETV Television Inc.; publisher: Arizona Daily Star. NONPR AFFIL trustee: Saint Louis University. CLUB AFFIL Saint Louis Country Club; Mountain Oyster Club.

Ronald H. Ridgway: senior vice president B 1938. ED Ohio State University. PRIM CORP EMPL senior vice president: Pulitzer Publishing Co. CORP AFFIL vice president: Star Publishing Co.; treasurer: WESH Television Inc.; vice president finance: KETV Television Inc.; senior vice president fin, director: Saint Louis Post Dispatch.

Nicholas G. Tenniman, IV: vice president newspaper operations PRIM CORP EMPL vice president newspaper operations: Pulitzer Publishing Co.

Foundation Officials

Cole C. Campbell: director (see above)

Terrance C.Z. Egger: director ED Augustana College. PRIM CORP EMPL vice president: Pulitzer Publishing Co.

Michael Edgar Pulitzer: chairman, president, chief executive officer (see above)

Ronald H. Ridgway: secretary, treasurer, director (see above)

Nicholas G. Tenniman, IV: director (see above)

Grants Analysis

Disclosure Period: calendar year ending 1997

Total Grants: $601,083

Number of Grants: 91

Average Grant: $6,605

Highest Grant: $100,000

Typical Range: $250 to $10,000

Recent Grants

Note: Grants derived from 1997 Form 990.

Arts & Humanities

100,000	Grand Center, St. Louis, MO -- support J. Pulitzer Memorial
50,000	St. Louis Symphony Society, St. Louis, MO
12,000	Arts and Education Fund, St. Louis, MO
7,500	Forum for Contemporary Arts, St. Louis, MO -- operating support
7,500	Opera Theater, St. Louis, MO -- operating support
5,000	KETC/Channel 9, St. Louis, MO -- capital campaign
5,000	Mercantile Library, St. Louis, MO -- capital campaign
3,000	Missouri Historical Society, St. Louis, MO
2,500	Circus Arts Foundation, St. Louis, MO -- operating support
2,000	Sheldon Arts Foundation, St. Louis, MO -- capital campaign
1,500	Dance St. Louis, St. Louis, MO -- operating support
1,500	Magic House, St. Louis, MO -- capital campaign
1,000	Center of Contemporary Arts, St. Louis, MO
1,000	Historical League, Tempe, AZ -- Gala Fundraiser support

Civic & Public Affairs

15,000	St. Louis Zoo Foundation, St. Louis, MO -- support six-year pledge
3,500	Focus, St. Louis, MO
2,000	Women's Self-Help Center, St. Louis, MO
1,500	Grace Hill Neighborhood, St. Louis, MO -- operating support
1,000	Greater St. Louis Association of Black Journalists, St. Louis, MO
1,000	Reporters Committee for Freedom of Press, Washington, DC -- support Jack Nelson Fellowship Fund

Education

100,000	Columbia University School of Journalism, New York, NY -- support Pulitzer New World Room
50,000	St. Louis University, St. Louis, MO
12,000	University of Missouri Columbia, Columbia, MO -- support scholarships
5,000	Mary Institute and St. Louis Country Day School, St. Louis, MO
5,000	Neiman Foundation at Harvard University, Cambridge, MA -- support five-year pledge
5,000	University of Missouri St. Louis, St. Louis, MO -- operating support
5,000	University of San Diego, San Diego, CA -- operating support
3,500	Ranken Technical College, St. Louis, MO -- support five-year pledge
3,333	St. Louis Priory School, St. Louis, MO -- capital campaign
3,000	Network for Educational Development, St. Louis, MO
2,500	University of Missouri Columbia, Columbia, MO -- support New Directions for News
1,000	Central Institute for Deaf, St. Louis, MO -- operating support
1,000	Journalism Foundation, St. Louis, MO
1,000	Today and Tomorrow Education Foundation, St. Louis, MO
1,000	United Negro College Fund, Fairfax, VA

Environment

5,000	Missouri Coalition for Environment, St. Louis, MO -- support underwriting speaker visit
2,500	Gateway Trailnet, St. Louis, MO

Health

2,500	AIDS Foundation, St. Louis, MO

International

1,000	World Press Freedom Committee, Reston, VA

Religion

2,500	Anti-Defamation League A World of Difference Institute, St. Louis, MO
2,500	Jewish Federation, St. Louis, MO
2,000	Salvation Army, St. Louis, MO -- operating support

Science

7,500	St. Louis Science Center, St. Louis, MO -- capital campaign

Social Services

100,000	United Way, St. Louis, MO
10,000	Dwight Davis Tennis Center, St. Louis, MO -- support renovation of Forest Park Courts
7,500	Butterfly House and Education Center, St. Louis, MO -- pledge support
7,500	Jackie Joyner-Kersee Youth Center Foundation, St. Louis, MO -- support three-year pledge
5,000	St. Louis Cardinals Community Fund, St. Louis, MO
5,000	YMCA, St. Louis, MO -- support five-year pledge
1,000	Paraquad, St. Louis, MO

Putnam Investments

Company Contact

Boston, MA
Web: http://www.putnaminv.com

Company Description

Revenue: US$750,000,000
Employees: 3,600
SIC(s): 6726 Investment Offices Nec.
Parent Company: Marsh & McLennan Companies, 1166 Avenue of the Americas, New York, NY, United States

Putnam Investors Fund

Giving Contact

Margaret Leipsitz, Manager, Community Relations
Assistant Vice President
Putnam Investments
c/o Public Relations
1 Post Office Square, Mail Stop A-4-E
Boston, MA 02109
Phone: (617)292-1000 ext 14611
Fax: (617)760-8048

Alternate Contact

Phone: (617)760-1586

Description

EIN: 043175266
Organization Type: Corporate Foundation. Supports preselected organizations only.
Giving Locations: MA: Boston, Quincy
Grant Types: General Support, Operating Expenses, Project.

Financial Summary

Total Giving: $552,608 (1997); $800,000 (1996); $514,125 (1995). Note: Contributes through corporate direct giving program and foundation. 1997 Giving includes foundation ($492,608); United Way ($60,000). 1996 Giving includes foundation; matching gifts ($100); United Way ($60,000).
Assets: $1,325,204 (1997); $334,892 (1996); $296,179 (1995)
Gifts Received: $1,400,000 (1997); $580,000 (1996); $450,000 (1995). Note: Foundation receives gifts from Putnam Investment Management.

Typical Recipients

Arts & Humanities: Arts Centers, Arts Outreach, Ballet, Historic Preservation, History & Archaeology, Libraries, Museums/Galleries, Music, Performing Arts, Public Broadcasting, Theater
Civic & Public Affairs: Botanical Gardens/Parks, Clubs, Community Foundations, Economic Policy, Employment/Job Training, Civic & Public Affairs-General, Housing, Minority Business, Philanthropic Organizations, Professional & Trade Associations, Urban & Community Affairs, Women's Affairs, Zoos/Aquariums
Education: Arts/Humanities Education, Business Education, Colleges & Universities, Engineering/Technological Education, Education-General, Literacy, Minority Education, Preschool Education, Private Education (Precollege), Public Education (Precollege), Secondary Education (Public), Student Aid, Vocational & Technical Education
Environment: Environment-General, Resource Conservation
Health: AIDS/HIV, Arthritis, Cancer, Children's Health/Hospitals, Clinics/Medical Centers, Diabetes, Heart, Hospices, Hospitals, Medical Research, Multiple Sclerosis, Prenatal Health Issues, Single-Disease Health Associations
International: Health Care/Hospitals, International Affairs, International Development, International Organizations, International Relief Efforts, Missionary/Religious Activities
Religion: Jewish Causes, Religious Welfare
Science: Science Museums
Social Services: At-Risk Youth, Big Brother/Big Sister, Camps, Child Abuse, Child Welfare, Community Service Organizations, Counseling, Family Services, Food/Clothing Distribution, People with Disabilities, Recreation & Athletics, Scouts, Shelters/Homelessness, Social Services-General, United Funds/United Ways, YMCA/YWCA/YMHA/YWHA, Youth Organizations

Contributions Analysis

Arts & Humanities: 5% to 10%. Boston area arts and cultural organizations receive funding. Interests include the fine arts, museums, public broadcasting, music, and dance.
Civic & Public Affairs: About 25%. Supports neighborhood associations, especially those that help youth gain employment skills.
Education: 15% to 20%. Primarily supports secondary education and programs that help minorities achieve academically.
Health: 10% to 15%. Major support for community health centers. Also funds hospitals, pediatric health, and local chapters of single-disease health associations.
International: Less than 5%. Funds groups affiliated with Ireland.
Religion: Less than 5%. Supports religious welfare organizations.
Social Services: About 35%. Supports youth organizations, the United Way, and organizations assisting the disabled and at-risk.

Additional Information

The company reported that it gives the majority of its annual contributions to a pass-through nonprofit organization which distributes the funds.

Corporate Officials

Richard M. Cutler: vice chairman, director, chief executive officer B Dover, MA 1920. ED Harvard University (1943). PRIM CORP EMPL vice chairman, director: Putnam Investments.
Nancy Fisher: director public relations PRIM CORP EMPL director public relations: Putnam Investments.

Lawrence Jay Lasser: president, chief executive officer, director B 1942. ED Antioch College (1965); Harvard University MBA (1967). PRIM CORP EMPL president, chief executive officer, director: Putnam Investments. CORP AFFIL vice president: Putnam New York Tax Exempt Fund; trustee: Putnam Investors Fund; trustee: Putnam Mutual Funds; director: Putnam Income Fund; president: Putnam Investment Management Inc.; vice president: Putnam Convertible Income Growth Trust; director: Putnam High Income Convertible; director: Putnam Advisory Co., Inc.; director: Putnam American Government; director: Marsh & McLennan Companies Inc. NONPR AFFIL director: United Way Massachusetts Bay; trustee: Vineyard Open Land Foundation; board governor executive committee: Investment Co. Institute; member, board overseers: Museum Fine Arts; trustee: Beth Israel/Deaconess Medical Center.

George Putnam, Jr.: chairman, president, chief executive officer B Manchester, MA 1926. ED Harvard University AB (1949); Harvard University MBA (1951). PRIM CORP EMPL chairman, president, chief executive officer: Putnam Management Co. CORP AFFIL chairman: Putnam Investment Management Inc.; chairman: Putnam Investments; chairman, president: Putnam Group of Mutual Funds; director: Putnam Advisory Co., Inc.; director: Putnam Finance Services Co. Inc.; director: Marsh & McLennan Companies Inc.; director: McMoran Oil & Gas Inc.; director: Houghton Mifflin Co.; director: Freeport-McMoRan Copper & Gold Inc.; director: Freeport-McMoRan Inc.

Foundation Officials

Robert W. Burke: president, chief executive officer PRIM CORP EMPL vice president human resources: Putnam Investments. CORP AFFIL director: Putnam Advisory Co. Inc.

Lawrence Jay Lasser: president, chief executive officer (see above)

Grants Analysis

Disclosure Period: calendar year ending 1997
Total Grants: $492,608*
Number of Grants: 133
Average Grant: $3,704
Highest Grant: $70,000
Typical Range: $500 to $10,000
***Note:** Giving excludes United Way.

Recent Grants

Note: Grants derived from 1997 Form 990.

Arts & Humanities

15,000	Museum of Fine Arts, Boston, MA
12,500	Museum of Fine Arts, Boston, MA
5,000	Boston Crusader Drum and Bugle Corps, Boston, MA
5,000	National Trust for Historical Preservation, Washington, DC
5,000	Wang Center for Performing Arts, Boston, MA
5,000	WGBH, Boston, MA
5,000	WGBH, Boston, MA
2,500	Boston Crusader Drum and Bugle Corps, Boston, MA
2,500	Boston Symphony Orchestra, Boston, MA
2,500	Lyric Stage, Boston, MA

Civic & Public Affairs

15,000	PSCA
7,500	Massachusetts Taxpayers Foundation, Boston, MA
5,000	Youthbuild, Boston, MA
2,500	Andonna Society, Andover, MA
2,500	Shed, Andover, MA
2,000	Boston Foundation Blackwell Fund, Boston, MA

Education

65,000	Citizens Schools
27,000	Greater Lawrence School to Careers Partnership, Lawrence, MA
10,000	Columbia Business School, New York, NY
10,000	Harvard Business School, Cambridge, MA
10,000	Massachusetts Institute of Technology, Cambridge, MA
10,000	University of Chicago, Chicago, IL
10,000	University of Pennsylvania, Philadelphia, PA
5,000	National Head Start Association, Alexandria, VA
2,500	Junior Achievement, Boston, MA
2,000	Rashi School
2,000	Town of Franklin School Department, Franklin, MA

Environment

5,000	Massachusetts Audubon Society, Lincoln, MA

Health

25,000	Boston Marathon Jimmy Fund, Boston, MA
10,000	Juvenile Diabetes Association, Boston, MA
5,000	Boston Children's Hospital, Boston, MA
5,000	Children's Hospital Medical Center, Boston, MA
2,500	AIDS Action Committee
2,500	Trinity Hospice

International

2,500	Americares Foundation, New Canaan, CT

Religion

2,500	Salvation Army, Boston, MA

Social Services

70,000	Bridge Over Troubled Waters, Boston, MA
60,000	United Way Massachusetts Bay, Boston, MA
50,000	YWCA, Boston, MA
13,000	Family Service Association, Lawrence, MA
10,000	Lawrence Boys and Girls Club, Lawrence, MA
5,000	Big Brother Association, Boston, MA
5,000	Big Brothers and Big Sisters, Boston, MA
5,000	Jimmy Fund
2,500	Big Brother Association, Boston, MA
2,500	FUQUA MBA Games
2,500	Professional Center for Handicapped Children, Andover, MA
2,500	Project Bread Walk for Hunger, Boston, MA
2,000	Community Servings, Boston, MA
2,000	Strive

QUAKER CHEMICAL CORP.

Company Contact

Conshohocken, PA

Company Description

Employees: 835
SIC(s): 2821 Plastics Materials & Resins, 2841 Soap & Other Detergents, 2842 Polishes & Sanitation Goods, 2899 Chemical Preparations Nec.

Nonmonetary Support

Type: Loaned Employees; Loaned Executives

Quaker Chemical Foundation

Giving Contact

Kathleen Lasota, Secretary
Quaker Chemical Foundation
Elm and Lee Sts.
Conshohocken, PA 19428
Phone: (610)832-4127
Fax: (610)832-4282

Description

EIN: 236245803
Organization Type: Corporate Foundation
Giving Locations: headquarters and operating communities.
Grant Types: Employee Matching Gifts, General Support.
Note: Employee matching gift ratio: 1 to 1 for education, health and welfare, cultural organisation, and civic and community affairs, up to $1,000 annually.

Financial Summary

Total Giving: $278,635 (fiscal year ending June 30, 1998); $264,922 (fiscal 1997); $255,327 (fiscal 1996). Note: Contributes through foundation only.
Giving Analysis: Giving for fiscal 1996 includes: foundation matching gifts ($62,500); fiscal 1997: foundation matching gifts ($54,540); foundation scholarships ($41,628)
Assets: $535,895 (fiscal 1998); $648,527 (fiscal 1997); $293,448 (fiscal 1996)
Gifts Received: $147,000 (fiscal 1998); $527,800 (fiscal 1997); $259,000 (fiscal 1996). Note: Contributions were received from the Quaker Chemical Corporation.

Typical Recipients

Arts & Humanities: Arts Associations & Councils, Arts Centers, Arts Funds, Arts Outreach, Ballet, Community Arts, Historic Preservation, History & Archaeology, Libraries, Museums/Galleries, Music, Opera, Performing Arts
Civic & Public Affairs: Economic Development, Employment/Job Training, Urban & Community Affairs, Women's Affairs, Zoos/Aquariums
Education: Arts/Humanities Education, Colleges & Universities, Community & Junior Colleges, Engineering/Technological Education, Environmental Education, Literacy, Private Education (Precollege), Special Education, Student Aid, Vocational & Technical Education
Environment: Environment-General
Health: Health Organizations, Hospices, Hospitals, Medical Research, Nursing Services, Nutrition, Single-Disease Health Associations
International: Health Care/Hospitals, International Organizations, International Relations
Religion: Religious Welfare
Science: Science Museums, Scientific Centers & Institutes
Social Services: At-Risk Youth, Child Welfare, Community Service Organizations, Counseling, Food/Clothing Distribution, Homes, People with Disabilities, Recreation & Athletics, Scouts, Sexual Abuse, United Funds/United Ways, Volunteer Services, Youth Organizations

Contributions Analysis

Arts & Humanities: 10% to 15%. Supports arts outreach, opera, arts funds, library funds, and art centers.
Civic & Public Affairs: About 5%. Emphasis is on women's affairs, job training, and community affairs.
Education: About 65%. Majority of education contributions are in the form of scholarships to employees and individuals in the community. Focus is on chemistry and the physical sciences. Other funding supports colleges and universities.

Health: 10% to 15%. Funding supports hospital foundations, nursing services, and health organizations. Also funds family services, counseling, food distribution, and victims of sexual abuse.

Application Procedures

Initial Contact: Request guidelines, then send written grant application.
Application Requirements: Grant applications must include: project description with a pro-forma budget; annual operating budget and audited financial statements; list of funding sources, including past major contributors with amounts, recent applications with results, and anticipated future funding sources; list of board members and officers.
Deadlines: April 30.

Restrictions

Distributions limited to tax-exempt organizations in geographic locations where the corporation has operations in the United States.
Generally does not support brick and mortar projects.

Additional Information

Publications: Guidelines

Corporate Officials

Ronald James Naples: president, chief executive officer, director B Passaic, NJ 1945. ED United States Military Academy BS (1967); Tufts University Fletcher School of Law & Diplomacy MA (1972); Harvard University MBA (1974). PRIM CORP EMPL president, chief executive officer, director: Quaker Chemical Corp. CORP AFFIL director: Advanta Corp. NONPR AFFIL member: President Commission White House Fellows; director: University Arts; member: Harvard Business School Alumni Association; director: Philadelphia Museum Art; vice chairman, director: Free Library Philadelphia Federation; vice chairman: Greater Philadelphia First Corp.; director: Foreign Policy Research Institute; director: Childrens Hospital Philadelphia; member advisory board: Fletcher School Law & Diplomacy; member: Association Grads U.S. Military Academy. CLUB AFFIL Pyramid Club; Racquet Club; Harvard Business School Philadelphia Club.

Foundation Officials

Katherine N. Coughenour: trustee
Edwin J. Delattre: trustee CORP AFFIL director: Quaker Chemical Corp.
Alan J. Keyser: trustee
Kathleen Lasota: secretary
Karl Henry Spaeth: chairman, trustee B Philadelphia, PA 1929. ED Haverford College AB (1951); Oxford University (1955); Harvard University JD (1958). PRIM CORP EMPL vice president, secretary: Quaker Chemical Corp. CORP AFFIL secretary: SB Decking Inc. CLUB AFFIL Philadelphia Cricket Club; Philadelphia Club.
Jane Williams: trustee

Grants Analysis

Disclosure Period: fiscal year ending June 30, 1997
Total Grants: $168,699*
Number of Grants: 122
Average Grant: $1,383
Highest Grant: $4,000
Typical Range: $400 to $3,000
***Note:** Giving excludes scholarship; matching gifts.

Recent Grants

Note: Grants derived from fiscal 1997 Form 990.

Arts & Humanities

25,000 Philadelphia Orchestra, Philadelphia, PA
12,000 Free Library, Philadelphia, PA
4,000 Philadelphia Orchestra, Philadelphia, PA
2,500 Opera Company, Philadelphia, PA
2,500 Philadelphia Museum of Art, Philadelphia, PA
2,500 University of Pennsylvania Museum, Philadelphia, PA
2,000 Bach Festival, Philadelphia, PA
2,000 William Jeanes Memorial Library of Whitemarsh, Layfayette Hill, PA
1,500 Academy of Music, Philadelphia, PA
1,500 Creative Artists Network, Philadelphia, PA
1,500 Detroit Symphony Orchestra Hall, Detroit, MI
1,500 Young Audiences of Eastern Pennsylvania, Philadelphia, PA
1,000 Atwater Kent Museum, Philadelphia, PA
1,000 Historical Society of Pennsylvania, Philadelphia, PA
1,000 Library Company, Philadelphia, PA
1,000 Mann Music Center, Philadelphia, PA
1,000 Pennsylvania Ballet, Philadelphia, PA

Civic & Public Affairs

3,000 Metropolitan Career Center, Philadelphia, PA
2,000 Colonial Neighborhood Council, Conshohocken, PA
1,500 Philadelphia Futures, Philadelphia, PA
1,500 Women's Association for Women's Alternatives, Wawa, PA
1,500 Zoological Society, Philadelphia, PA
1,000 Central Philadelphia Development Corp, Philadelphia, PA

Education

8,000 Yale University, New Haven, CT
4,000 Drexel University, Philadelphia, PA
4,000 Georgia Institute of Technology, Atlanta, GA
4,000 Stanford University, Stanford, CA
4,000 University of California Berkeley, Oakland, CA
4,000 University of Michigan, Detroit, MI
3,967 Michigan State University, Detroit, MI
3,215 Auburn University, Auburn, PA
2,500 Bryn Mawr College, Bryn Mawr, PA
2,000 Academy of Notre Dame DeNamur, Villanova, PA
2,000 Virginia Tech University, Roanoke, VA
1,750 Pennsylvania School for the Deaf, Philadelphia, PA
1,500 Academy of Vocal Arts, Philadelphia, PA
1,500 Dartmouth College, Hanover, NH
1,500 Emory University, Atlanta, GA
1,500 Jason Costello for University of La Verne, Fremont, CA
1,000 Schuylkill Center for Environmental Education, Philadelphia, PA

Health

1,500 Wissahickon Hospice, Philadelphia, PA

International

2,000 International House, Philadelphia, PA
1,500 International Visitors Council, Philadelphia, PA
1,500 SEE International, Santa Barbara, CA

Religion

1,500 Methodist Children's Home Society, Detroit, MI

Science

1,500 Academy of Natural Sciences, Philadelphia, PA
1,500 Franklin Institute Science Museum, Philadelphia, PA

Social Services

2,000 Colonial Meals on Wheels, Conshohocken, PA
1,500 RSVP, Plymouth Meeting, PA
1,500 Voyage House, Philadelphia, PA

QUANEX CORP.

Company Contact

Houston, TX

Company Description

Profit: US$12,400,000
Employees: 3,345 (1999)
SIC(s): 3312 Blast Furnaces & Steel Mills, 3317 Steel Pipe & Tubes, 3341 Secondary Nonferrous Metals, 3365 Aluminum Foundries.

Nonmonetary Support

Type: Donated Equipment; Donated Products

Quanex Foundation

Giving Contact

Paul Kraft, Manager, Corporate Administration
1900 West Loop S., Suite 1500
Houston, TX 77027
Phone: (713)961-4600

Description

Founded: 1951
EIN: 366065490
Organization Type: Corporate Foundation
Giving Locations: TX
Grant Types: General Support.

Financial Summary

Total Giving: $200,000 (1998); $216,000 (1997); $194,359 (1996)
Assets: $3,292,080 (1996); $2,730,300 (1995); $2,131,451 (1994)
Gifts Received: $500,000 (1996); $200,000 (1995); $52,205 (1994)

Typical Recipients

Arts & Humanities: Arts Funds, Museums/Galleries, Music, Performing Arts, Public Broadcasting, Theater
Civic & Public Affairs: Chambers of Commerce, Clubs, Community Foundations, Economic Development, Civic & Public Affairs-General, Law & Justice, Municipalities/Towns, Parades/Festivals, Professional & Trade Associations, Rural Affairs, Safety, Urban & Community Affairs
Education: Agricultural Education, Business Education, Colleges & Universities, Community & Junior Colleges, Education Funds, Elementary Education (Private), Engineering/Technological Education, Literacy, Minority Education, Preschool Education, Private Education (Precollege), Public Education (Precollege), Secondary Education (Private), Secondary Education (Public), Student Aid
Health: AIDS/HIV, Cancer, Children's Health/Hospitals, Clinics/Medical Centers, Diabetes, Emergency/Ambulance Services, Health Organizations, Heart, Hospices, Hospitals, Kidney, Medical Research, Nutrition, Public Health, Single-Disease Health Associations
Religion: Ministries, Religious Welfare, Social/Policy Issues
Science: Science Museums
Social Services: Big Brother/Big Sister, Community Service Organizations, Crime Prevention, People with Disabilities, Recreation & Athletics, Scouts, Senior Services, Shelters/Homelessness, Special Olympics, United Funds/United Ways, YMCA/YWCA/YMHA/YWHA, Youth Organizations

Application Procedures

Initial Contact: The foundation has no formal grant application procedure or application form. Submit a full proposal.
Deadlines: October 31.

Restrictions

Does not support individuals, religious organizations for sectarian purposes, political or lobbying groups, or organizations outside operating areas.

Corporate Officials

Vernon E. Oechsle: president, chief executive officer PRIM CORP EMPL president, chief executive officer: Quanex Corp.

Foundation Officials

Vernon E. Oechsle: vice president, director (see above)
J. K. Peery: president, director
Wayne Myron Rose: treasurer, director B Washington, DC 1946. ED University of Illinois (1968); University of Illinois (1972). PRIM CORP EMPL vice president, chief financial officer: Quanex Corp.

Grants Analysis

Disclosure Period: calendar year ending 1996
Number of Grants: 164
Highest Grant: $21,660
Typical Range: $300 to $6,000

Recent Grants

Note: Grants derived from 1997 Form 990.

Arts & Humanities

3,500 Quad City Symphony Orchestra, Davenport, IA
2,500 Society for Performing Arts, Houston, TX

Civic & Public Affairs

10,000 Houston Livestock Show and Rodeo, Houston, TX
9,200 Fort Bend County Fair, Rosenberg, TX
3,000 ABET, Boca Raton, FL
2,500 Houston Forum, Houston, TX

Education

20,075 National Merit Scholarship Corporation, Evanston, IL
5,000 I Have A Dream, Houston, TX
3,000 Junior Achievement, Davenport, IA
3,000 St. Katherine's-St. Mark's College Prep School, Bettendorf, IA

Health

5,000 Juvenile Diabetes Foundation, Houston, TX
2,500 Juvenile Diabetes Foundation, Houston, TX
2,500 Juvenile Diabetes Foundation, Houston, TX

Religion

5,000 Active Faith, South Lyon, MI
2,500 Interfaith Ministries, Houston, TX

Social Services

25,775 United Way Texas Gulf Coast, Houston, TX
5,800 United Way, Jackson, MI
4,500 United Way, Fort Smith, AR
3,262 United Way Rice Lake, Rice Lake, WI
3,262 United Way Rice Lake, Rice Lake, WI

QUESTAR CORP.

Company Contact

Salt Lake City, UT
Web: http://www.questarcorp.com

Company Description

Assets: US$1,816,200,000
Employees: 2,452
SIC(s): 1311 Crude Petroleum & Natural Gas, 4923 Gas Transmission & Distribution.

Nonmonetary Support

Value: $87,500 (1996); $100,000 (1993)
Type: Donated Equipment; In-kind Services; Loaned Employees; Loaned Executives
Note: 1997 nonmonetary support $100,000.

Corporate Sponsorship

Type: Arts & cultural events; Sports events; Music & entertainment events; Pledge-a-thon
Note: Sponsored events include AIDS walks, the March of Dimes, and Special Olympics.

Giving Contact

Janice W. Bates, Director, Community Affairs
Questar Corp.
180 East 1st South Street
PO Box 45433
Salt Lake City, UT 84145-0433
Phone: (801)324-5435
Fax: (801)324-5483
Email: janb@questar.com

Description

Organization Type: Corporate Giving Program
Giving Locations: CO: limited funding; OK: limited funding; TX: limited funding; UT; WY
Grant Types: Capital, Emergency, General Support, Scholarship.

Financial Summary

Total Giving: $800,000 (2000 approx); $800,000 (1999 approx); $850,000 (1998 approx). Note: Contributes through corporate direct giving program only. 1998, 1997, and 1996 Giving includes corporate direct giving; nonmonetary support.

Typical Recipients

Arts & Humanities: Museums/Galleries, Music, Opera, Theater
Civic & Public Affairs: Legal Aid, Zoos/Aquariums
Education: Business Education, Colleges & Universities
Environment: Environment-General
Health: Health Organizations, Hospitals
Science: Science Exhibits & Fairs
Social Services: Child Welfare, Food/Clothing Distribution, People with Disabilities, Shelters/Homelessness, United Funds/United Ways, Volunteer Services, Youth Organizations

Contributions Analysis

Giving Priorities: Primary support for education, health care, and the arts. Also supports civic causes.
Arts & Humanities: 20% to 25%. Funding goes to arts festivals, dance and music, historic preservation, museums and galleries, and performing arts.
Civic & Public Affairs: 10% to 15%. Funds programs for better government and economic development.
Education: About 30%. Business education, career and vocational education, colleges and universities, and economic education are all supported.
Health: 25% to 30%. Support goes to hospitals, medical rehabilitation, single-disease health associations, child welfare, community service organizations, traditional youth groups, the United Way, and food and clothing distribution.

Application Procedures

Initial Contact: Submit a brief letter of inquiry.
Application Requirements: Include a description of organization, amount requested, purpose of funds sought, recently audited financial statements, board of directors list (including salaries), and proof of tax-exempt status.
Deadlines: None.
Decision Notification: The board meets every five to six weeks.

Restrictions

Does not support individuals, religious organizations for sectarian purposes, or fraternal organizations. Will not support national health organizations unless it can be determined that funds will remain in the company's service area.

Corporate Officials

R. D. Cash: chairman, president, chief executive officer, director B Shamrock, TX 1942. ED Texas Technology University BS (1966). PRIM CORP EMPL chairman, president, chief executive officer, director: Questar Corp. CORP AFFIL chief executive officer, director: Universal Resources Corp.; chief executive officer, director: Wexpro Co.; chairman, director: Questar Pipeline Co.; chairman, director: Questar Gas Management Co.; chairman, director: Questar InfoComm Inc.; chairman, director: Questar Energy Trading Co.; chairman, director: Questar Gas Co.; chairman, director: Celsius Energy Co.; chairman, director: Questar Energy Services Inc.
Clyde Mont Heiner: executive vice president B Wendell, ID 1938. ED Columbia University BA (1960); Columbia University BS (1961); Stanford University MBA (1966). PRIM CORP EMPL executive vice president: Questar Corp. CORP AFFIL president, chief executive officer, director: Questar InfoComm Inc.; president, chief executive officer, director: Questar Synfuels Corp.; vice president, director: Entrada Industries Inc.; president, chief executive officer, director: Interstate Land Corp.
Stephen E. Parks: vice president, treasurer, chief financial officer ED University of Utah MBA; University of Utah BS. PRIM CORP EMPL vice president, treasurer, chief financial officer: Questar Corp. CORP AFFIL vice president, treasurer, chief financial officer: Universal Resources Corp.; vice president, treasurer, chief financial officer: Wexpro Co.; chief financial officer: Questor Gas Co.; vice president, treasurer, chief financial officer: Questar InfoComm Inc.; vice president, chief financial officer, treasurer: Questar Pipeline Co.; chief financial officer: Entrada Industries Inc.

Giving Program Officials

Janice W. Bates: director PRIM CORP EMPL director community affairs & employee services: Questar Corp.

Foundation Officials

Janice W. Bates: director (see above)

Grants Analysis

Disclosure Period: calendar year ending
Typical Range: $1,000 to $5,000

RALPH'S GROCERY CO.

Company Contact

Compton, CA
Web: http://www.ralphs.com

Company Description

Employees: 15,000
SIC(s): 5411 Grocery Stores.

Nonmonetary Support

Value: $17,510 (1996)
Type: Donated Equipment; In-kind Services

Ralph's-Food 4 Less Foundation

Giving Contact

Jan Golleher, Program Director
Ralph's-Food 4 Less Foundation
1100 West Artesia Boulevard
Compton, CA 90220
Phone: (310)884-6250
Fax: (310)884-2590

Description

Founded: 1992
EIN: 330492352
Organization Type: Corporate Foundation
Giving Locations: CA: southern California
Grant Types: General Support.

Financial Summary

Total Giving: $6,720,000 (1999 approx); $2,896,800 (1998); $1,856,621 (1996)
Giving Analysis: Giving for 1998 includes: foundation ($2,896,800)
Assets: $339,086 (1998); $463,953 (1996); $659,926 (1995)
Gifts Received: $3,613,729 (1998); $2,035,415 (1996); $2,607,002 (1995). Note: In 1998, contributions were received from Western Union Financial Services ($200,000); Anheuser-Busch, Inc. ($124,293); Ralphs Grocery Co. ($40,000); and numerous other donors who contributed less than $40,000 each. In 1995, contributions were received from Anheuser-Busch ($154,000), Ralph's Grocery Co. ($855,000), Western Union ($400,000), Miller Brewing Co. ($63,335), and Coors Brewing ($95,500); numerous other donors contributed less than $50,000 each.

Typical Recipients

Arts & Humanities: Arts Festivals, Arts Institutes, Ethnic & Folk Arts, Film & Video, Historic Preservation, History & Archaeology, Libraries, Museums/Galleries, Music, Performing Arts, Theater
Civic & Public Affairs: African American Affairs, Economic Development, Civic & Public Affairs-General, Hispanic Affairs, Housing, Legal Aid, Public Policy, Urban & Community Affairs
Education: Afterschool/Enrichment Programs, Business Education, Colleges & Universities, Education Reform, Education-General, International Studies, Medical Education, Private Education (Precollege), Religious Education, Science/Mathematics Education, Special Education, Student Aid
Environment: Environment-General, Protection
Health: AIDS/HIV, AIDS/HIV, Cancer, Children's Health/Hospitals, Clinics/Medical Centers, Diabetes, Eyes/Blindness, Health Organizations, Multiple Sclerosis, Prenatal Health Issues, Single-Disease Health Associations
Religion: Churches, Jewish Causes, Missionary Activities (Domestic), Religious Organizations, Religious Welfare
Social Services: Child Abuse, Child Welfare, Community Service Organizations, Crime Prevention, Domestic Violence, Emergency Relief, Family Planning, Food/Clothing Distribution, People with Disabilities, Recreation & Athletics, Scouts, Substance Abuse, United Funds/United Ways, YMCA/YWCA/YMHA/YWHA, Youth Organizations

Contributions Analysis

Giving Priorities: Arts, social services, and health.
Arts & Humanities: Supports music, the performing arts, libraries, and arts funds/foundations.
Civic & Public Affairs: 8%. Funds urban leagues, public safety and legal aid.
Education: 3%. Supports colleges and universities.
Environment: 4%. Funds environmental protection initiatives.
Health: 18%. Supports children's health organizations, medical centers, and single-disease health organizations.
Religion: 3%. Supports religious welfare organizations.
Social Services: 26%. Supports day care, food distribution, family services, scouting, community sports, and violence and substance abuse prevention.
Note: Total contributions made in 1998.

Application Procedures

Initial Contact: Request application form and guidelines.
Deadlines: None.

Restrictions

Grangs are not made to memorial campaigns, political activities, endowment campaigns, or to fund programs that are discriminatory.

Corporate Officials

Wayne Bell: senior counsel, assistant secretary B Los Angeles, CA 1954. ED University of California, Los Angeles BA (1976); Loyola University JD (1979); Rutgers University (1992). PRIM CORP EMPL senior counsel, assistant secretary: Ralph's Grocery Co. NONPR AFFIL member: Legal Assistance Association; member: Los Angeles County Bar Association; member: California Bar Association; member: DC Bar Association.
Ron Burkle: chairman PRIM CORP EMPL chairman: Ralph's Grocery Co.
Sam Duncan: president PRIM CORP EMPL president: Ralph's Grocery Co.
George C Golleher: chief executive officer B Bethesda, MD 1948. ED California State University, Fullerton BA (1970). PRIM CORP EMPL chief executive officer: Ralph's Grocery Co. ADD CORP EMPL president: Food 4 Less Holdings Inc.; president: Food 4 Less of Southern California. CORP AFFIL director: Cala Co.; director: Cala Foods Inc.
John Stanley: senior vice president, chief financial officer PRIM CORP EMPL senior vice president, chief financial officer: Ralph's Grocery Co.

Foundation Officials

Darius Anderson: executive director
Wayne Bell: secretary (see above)
George C Golleher: president (see above)
Dennis Kyte: treasurer, chief financial officer
Mary Lou Wakefield: trustee

Grants Analysis

Disclosure Period: calendar year ending 1998
Total Grants: $2,896,800
Number of Grants: 209
Average Grant: $8,583*
Highest Grant: $1,000,000
Typical Range: $100 to $75,000
***Note:** Average grant figure excludes highest grant, which went to the Music Center of Los Angeles County.

Recent Grants

Note: Grants derived from 1998 Form 990.

Arts & Humanities

1,000,000	Music Center of Los Angeles County, Los Angeles, CA -- for the constrution of the walt disney concert hall
25,000	Music Center of Los Angeles County, Los Angeles, CA -- to support the caroline leonetti ahmanson endowment for arts education
20,000	Orange County Performing Arts, Costa Mesa, CA -- for the performing arts and the center's endowment fund
15,000	library foundation of los angeles, Los Angeles, CA -- a grant to support the los angeles public library's card campaign with a goal to increase community awareness of the many resources available at the l
10,000	East L.A. Classic Theatre, Los Angeles, CA -- to support the beyond borders literacy intervention pilot program to service 6-8th grade students learning English or experiencing academic difficulty
10,000	Getty House Foundation, Los Angeles, CA -- for getty house foundation's educational and enrichment programs for los angeles area school children

Civic & Public Affairs

100,000	National Urban League, Washington, DC -- to support ongoing training, educational programs and services for children, youth and their families
35,000	Los Angeles Urban League, Los Angeles, CA -- to support job training and placement programs
35,000	San Bernardino County Peace Officers' Memorial, Rancho Cucamonga, CA -- for the "officer down" memorial statues, first installment
25,000	Bet Tzedek-The House of Justice, Los Angeles, CA -- to support free legal services for the elderly, indigent and disabled in southern california
10,000	Coro Southern California, Los Angeles, CA -- for the public affairs awards dinner, with proceeds to benefit the coro fellows program.

Education

50,000	Learn, Los Angeles, CA -- to support operating expenses of school reform efforts
25,000	California State University Dominguez Hills, Carson, CA -- to support the southern california international business academy at gardena high school
10,000	American Academy of Allergy, Asthma & Immunology, Milwaukee, WI -- to sponsor the 'for richer or poorer' event with proceeds going to a children's asthma camp and the education and research trust
10,000	Rabbi Jacob Pressman Academy of Temple Beth American, Los Angeles, CA -- scholarship

Environment

100,000	Walden Woods Project, Lincoln, MA -- support the educational and research programs of the Thoreau Center
10,000	Global Green USA, Venice, CA -- to support the los angeles greening affordable housing initiative

Health

200,000	CaP Cure, Santa Monica, CA -- to support comprehensive research awards to seek a cure for prostate cancer
127,000	CaP Cure, Santa Monica, CA -- to support the scientific competitive awards program for prostate cancer research
50,000	Children's Diabetes Foundation, Los Angeles, CA -- to support the carousel of hope with proceeds to benefit special clinical programs and research at the barbara davis center for childhood diabetes
25,000	Cedars-Sinai Medical Center, Los Angeles, CA -- support the guess chair for community child health
25,000	Cedars-Sinai Medical Center, Los Angeles, CA -- to support the medical genetics birth-defects center
25,000	Nancy Davis Foundation for Multiple Sclerosis, Los Angeles, CA -- to sponsor the race to erase MS, with proceeds to benefit multiple sclerosis research and the center without walls, a symposium on multiple sclerosis
25,000	Pediatric AIDS Foundation, Los Angeles, CA -- to support research which will impact the diagnosis, treatment and prevention of HIV infection and its complications in infants and children
15,000	National Multiple Sclerosis Society/So Cal Chapter, Los Angeles, CA -- to support the MS dinner of champions with proceeds to benefit the chapter's mental/emotional health care program
10,000	Camp Ronald McDonald for Good Times, Los Angeles, CA -- to support

cost-free, medically-supervised camping and outdoor experiences for children with cancer and their families

10,000 Center for the Partially Sighted, Los Angeles, CA -- to support the vision rehabilitation program for older partially sighted adults

Religion

25,000 Industrial Areas Foundation, Newark, NJ -- for the active citizenship campaign in Southern California

10,000 Brotherhood Crusade, Los Angeles, CA -- to support community outreach programs to improved the quality of life in inner city commuinities

10,000 Catholic Charities of Los Angeles, Los Angeles, CA -- foundation hunger program grant for St. Margaret's Center to underwrite the expense of hiring a volunteer cordinator and purchasing additional food

10,000 Jewish Community Centers of Greater Los Angeles, Los Angeles, CA -- foundation hunger program grant for the SOVA kosher food pantry

10,000 Jewish Federation Council of Greater Los Angeles, Los Angeles, CA -- for the annual campaign of the unifed jewish fund

10,000 Salvation Army Southern California Headquarters, Los Angeles, CA -- foundation hunger program grant to help cover costs associated with the rental truck to facilitate the delivery of donated food to distribution sites

Social Services

200,000 D.A.R.E. America, Los Angeles, CA -- to support D.A.R.E. officer training and the publication and distribution costs of educational materials on substance abuse and violence

173,000 Do Something, Los Angeles, CA -- to recruit and train Community Coaches who will help motivate young people to become actively engaged in building better communities

100,000 Project Angel Food, Los Angeles, CA -- foundation hunger program grant to underwrite the lease of the facility and to support the frozen meal program

60,000 Project Angel Food, Los Angeles, CA -- foundation hHunger pProgram grant to help fund the frozen food program for people living with AIDS

30,000 Food Industry Crusade Against Hunger, Washington, DC -- foundation hunger program grant to support anti-hunger programs in southern california.

25,000 D.A.R.E. America, Los Angeles, CA -- for the publishing and distribution of educational material for programs that promotes alternatives to drugs, gangs and violence

25,000 Do Something, Los Angeles, CA -- A grant to support the National Do Something League.

25,000 Hugh O'Brian Youth Foundation, Los Angeles, CA -- to support youth leadership programs designed to enhance the knowledge of the democratic process, free enterprise system and volunteerism

25,000 Los Angeles Regional Foodbank, Los Angeles, CA -- foundation hunger program grant for the Children and Youth Fund

20,000 Project Angel Food, Los Angeles, CA -- foundation hunger program grant to underwrite the lease of the facility and to support the frozen meal program

15,000 Children's Institute International, Los Angeles, CA -- to support the champions of children gala with proceeds to benefit the programs and services to meet both the immediate and on-going needs of families

15,000 Watts Friendship Sports League, Los Angeles, CA -- to support the baseball program for inner-city youth ages 5 to 12 years old

10,000 Assistance League of Southern California Hilltopers Auxiliary, Los Angeles, CA -- to establish an infant & toddler day care program for low-income children, ages 0 to 3, at the learning cCenter for young children

10,000 Boy Scouts of America Los Angeles Area Council, Los Angeles, CA -- to support the after-class and learning for life programs

10,000 FASE, Los Angeles, CA -- to support the violence prevention program

10,000 Labor Community Services Food & Emergency Program, Los Angeles, CA -- foundation hunger program grant to expand food delivery program for unemployed, seniors, disabled and/or homeless families or individuals

Ralston Purina Co.

Company Contact

St. Louis, MO
Web: http://www.ralston.com

Company Description

Revenue: US$4,720,500,000 (1999)
Profit: US$505,100,000 (1999)
Employees: 22,435
Fortune Rank: 342, per FORTUNE Magazine's list of 500 Largest U.S. Corporations (1999).
FF 342
SIC(s): 2047 Dog & Cat Food, 3692 Primary Batteries--Dry & Wet.

Operating Locations

Belgium: Purina Protein Europe SA, Zaventem; Brazil: Purina Alimentos Ltda., Sau Paulo; Canada: Ralston Purina Canada Eveready Division, Mississauga; Ralston Purina Canada Inc., Mississauga; Ralston Purina Canada Agri-Division, Woodstock; France: Duquesne-Purina SA; Hungary: Purina-Hage Ltd., Budapest; Italy: Purina Italia SPA, Milan; Republic of Korea: Purina Korea Inc., Seoul; Mexico: Eveready de Mexico SA de CV, Mexico City; Industrias Purina, SA de CV, Mexico City; Netherlands: Ralston Purina Overseas Finance NV, Willemstad, Curacao; Singapore: Eveready Singapore Pte. Ltd., Singapore; Spain: Gallina Blanca Purina, Barcelona; United Kingdom: Energizer Eveready Ltd., London

Nonmonetary Support

Type: Cause-related Marketing & Promotion; Donated Equipment; Donated Products; In-kind Services; Loaned Employees; Loaned Executives; Workplace Solicitation

Ralston Purina Trust Fund

Giving Contact

Fred H. Perabo, Secretary
Ralston Purina Trust Fund
Checkerboard Square
St. Louis, MO 63164
Phone: (314)982-3234
Fax: (314)982-2752

Description

EIN: 431209652
Organization Type: Corporate Foundation
Giving Locations: MO: St. Louis headquarters and operating communities.
Grant Types: Capital, Employee Matching Gifts, Endowment, General Support, Project.

Giving Philosophy

'The Ralston Purina Trust Fund exists in recognition of the fact that conditions exist in St. Louis and in other communities where our company operates which affect the company as well as the population in general. We will consider support to not-for-profit, tax-exempt organizations which deal with genuine community needs, especially when the interests of the community and those of our shareholders intersect. We will focus our support on programs which address the needs of the disadvantaged.' Ralston Purina Trust Fund Contribution Guidelines

Financial Summary

Total Giving: $2,054,917 (fiscal year ending August 31, 1998); $1,794,400 (fiscal 1996); $1,787,150 (fiscal 1994). Note: Contributes through corporate direct giving program and foundation.
Giving Analysis: Giving for fiscal 1998 includes: foundation ($1,301,917); foundation grants to United Way ($753,000)
Assets: $28,342,439 (fiscal 1998); $24,065,899 (fiscal 1996); $17,517,445 (fiscal 1994)
Gifts Received: $3,750,000 (fiscal 1996); $1,000,000 (fiscal 1994); $1,000,000 (fiscal 1993). Note: Contributions are received from the Ralston Purina Company.

Typical Recipients

Arts & Humanities: Arts Associations & Councils, Arts Centers, Historic Preservation, History & Archaeology, Libraries, Museums/Galleries, Music, Performing Arts, Public Broadcasting, Theater
Civic & Public Affairs: African American Affairs, Botanical Gardens/Parks, Business/Free Enterprise, Chambers of Commerce, Civil Rights, Clubs, Community Foundations, Economic Development, Employment/Job Training, Housing, Municipalities/Towns, Nonprofit Management, Parades/Festivals, Professional & Trade Associations, Public Policy, Urban & Community Affairs, Zoos/Aquariums
Education: Arts/Humanities Education, Business Education, Colleges & Universities, Education Funds, Education-General, Literacy, Medical Education, Minority Education, Private Education (Precollege), Public Education (Precollege), Science/Mathematics Education, Secondary Education (Public), Special Education, Student Aid, Vocational & Technical Education
Environment: Environment-General
Health: Alzheimers Disease, Children's Health/Hospitals, Health Policy/Cost Containment, Health Organizations, Hospices, Hospitals, Medical Research, Nursing Services, Single-Disease Health Associations
International: International Relations
Religion: Jewish Causes, Religious Organizations, Religious Welfare, Social/Policy Issues
Science: Scientific Centers & Institutes
Social Services: Animal Protection, At-Risk Youth, Child Welfare, Community Service Organizations, Crime Prevention, Delinquency & Criminal Rehabilitation, Domestic Violence, Family Planning, Family Services, Food/Clothing Distribution, Homes, People with Disabilities, Recreation & Athletics, Scouts, Senior Services, Shelters/Homelessness, Substance Abuse, United Funds/United Ways, Volunteer Services, YMCA/YWCA/YMHA/YWHA, Youth Organizations

Contributions Analysis

Giving Priorities: Social service, education, the arts, health care, civil rights, public policy, and environmental affairs. Company does not release information on

charitable contributions. A review of the foundation's most recent Form 990 for 1994 does not provide evidence of contributions for international purposes.
Arts & Humanities: 9%. Supports museums.
Civic & Public Affairs: 12%. Supports urban affairs, parks, and chambers of commerce.
Education: 15%. Supports colleges and universities, scholarship programs, and Junior Achievement.
Health: 3%. Funds the Alzheimer's Association.
Religion: 7%. Supports Jewish concerns.
Social Services: 53%. Supports the United Way, humane societies, youth concerns, and service groups.
Note: Total contributions made in 1998.

Application Procedures

Initial Contact: Written proposal
Application Requirements: clear statement of need, timetable of accomplishment, background on organization and staff who would administer grant, plan for post-grant evaluation, proof of 501(c)(3) status, amount requested, detailed program budget, and copy of most recent financial statement
Deadlines: None.
Evaluative Criteria: project can be duplicated and has a prevention component
Decision Notification: proposals are reviewed quarterly

Restrictions

The fund does not support individuals; religious or politically partisan causes; projects that require funding outside the United States or its possessions; loans or investment funds; veterans or fraternal organizations, unless they furnish services to the general public; tickets for dinners, benefits, exhibits, conferences, sports events, or other short-term activities; advertisements; or underwriting of deficits or post-event funding.

Additional Information

Publications: Contribution Guidelines

Corporate Officials

W. Patrick McGinnis: co-chief executive officer B 1947. PRIM CORP EMPL co-chief executive officer: Ralston Purina Co.
J. Patrick Mulcahy: co-chief executive officer ED Cornell University MS (1966); Cornell University MBA (1967). PRIM CORP EMPL co-chief executive officer: Ralston Purina Co.

Foundation Officials

James Morton Neville: member board control B Minneapolis, MN 1939. ED University of Minnesota BA (1961); University of Minnesota JD (1964). PRIM CORP EMPL vice president, general counsel: Ralston Purina Co. NONPR AFFIL member: U.S. Supreme Court Bar Association; member: University Minnesota Law School Alumni Association; member: Psi Upsilon; member: Saint Louis Bar Association; member: Order Coif; member: Phi Delta Phi; member: Minnesota Bar Association; member: American Society of Corporate Secretaries; member: Hennepin County Bar Association; member: American Bar Association; member: American Corporate Counsel Association. CLUB AFFIL Noonday Club; Old Warson Country Club; Ladue Racquet Club.
Fred H. Perabo: secretary board control PRIM CORP EMPL director community affairs: Ralston Purina Co.
E. D. Richards: member board control
Charles S. Sommer: member board control ED Amherst College (1965); University of Virginia (1967).

Grants Analysis

Disclosure Period: fiscal year ending August 31, 1998
Total Grants: $1,301,917*
Number of Grants: 48
Average Grant: $27,123
Highest Grant: $750,000
Typical Range: $5,000 to $30,000

***Note:** Giving excludes United Way.

Recent Grants

Note: Grants derived from 1998 Form 990.

Arts & Humanities

70,000 KETC/Channel 9, St. Louis, MO
50,000 Missouri Historical society, St. Louis, MO
25,000 Arts & Education Council of Greater St. Louis, St. Louis, MO
20,000 Municipal Theatre Association of St. Louis, St. Louis, MO
20,000 St. Louis Symphony Orchestra, St. Louis, MO
6,000 The Magic House, St. Louis, MO
1,000 Clinton Art Association, Clinton, IA

Civic & Public Affairs

100,000 St. Louis 2004, St. Louis, MO
20,000 Forest Park Forever, Chicago, IL
20,000 St. Louis Zoo Foundation, St. Louis, MO
20,000 The Urban League of Metropolitan St. Louis, St. Louis, MO
15,000 V.P. Foundation, St. Louis, MO
5,000 Cross Community Coalition, Denver, CO

Education

230,000 Washington University, St. Louis, MO
20,000 Harris-Stowe State College, St. Louis, MO
20,000 St. Louis University High School, St. Louis, MO
18,600 Logos School, St. Louis, MO
15,000 Junior Achievement of Mississippi Valley, Inc., St. Louis, MO
10,000 Ranken Technical College, St. Louis, MO
9,317 National Merit Scholarship Corporation, Chicago, IL
5,000 United Negro College Fund, St. Louis, MO
2,000 Lindenwood University, St. Louis, MO
1,000 Clinton High School, Clinton, IA

Health

20,000 Brooks Memorial Hospital, Dunkirk, NY
15,000 Unity Health Hospice, St. Louis, MO
10,000 Alzheimer's Association, St. Louis, MO
10,000 Center of Living Home Health and Hospice, Asheboro, NC

Religion

52,000 Jewish Community Centers Association, St. Louis, MO
30,000 The Salvation Army, St. Louis, MO
10,000 The National Conference of Christians & Jews, St. Louis, MO
10,000 St. Patrick Center, St. Louis, MO
10,000 Today and Tomorrow Foundation, St. Louis, MO

Social Services

750,000 United Way of Great St. Louis, St. Louis, MO
200,000 Human Society of Missouri, St. Louis, MO
50,000 Girl Scout Council of Greater St. Louis, St. Louis, MO
45,000 American Youth Foundation, St. Louis, MO
40,000 YMCA of Greater St. Louis, St. Louis, MO
20,000 YMCA Southwest Illinois, Belleville, IL
10,000 Epworth Children's Home, St. Louis, MO
10,000 Jackie Joyner-Kersee Youth Center Foundation, East St. Louis, MO
10,000 Paraquad, St. Louis, MO
10,000 St. Louis Area Foodbank, St. Louis, MO
10,000 Support Dogs, Inc., St. Louis, MO
7,500 The Women's Safe House, St. Louis, MO
5,000 Court Appointed Special Advocates of St. Louis County, St. Louis, MO
5,000 Foster Care Coalition of Greater St. Louis, St. Louis, MO
5,000 Sunshine Mission, St. Louis, MO
3,000 Tri-Cities Area United Way, Granite City, IL
2,500 Boy Scouts of America, St. Louis, MO
2,000 Skyline Center, Inc., Clinton, IA

RAYONIER INC.

Company Contact

Stamford, CT
Web: http://www.rayonier.com

Company Description

Former Name: ITT Rayonier.
Employees: 2,300 (1999)
SIC(s): 2411 Logging, 2421 Sawmills & Planing Mills--General, 2611 Pulp Mills, 3087 Custom Compound of Purchased Resins.

Nonmonetary Support

Type: In-kind Services

Rayonier Foundation

Giving Contact

Jay A. Fredericksen, Vice President
Rayonier Foundation
1177 Summer Street
Stamford, CT 06905-5529
Phone: (203)348-7000
Fax: (203)964-4528

Description

Founded: 1952
EIN: 136064462
Organization Type: Corporate Foundation
Giving Locations: FL; GA; WA
Grant Types: Employee Matching Gifts, General Support, Scholarship.

Financial Summary

Total Giving: $575,585 (1996 approx); $420,000 (1995); $739,826 (1994). Note: Contributes through foundation only. 1996 Giving includes foundation ($390,795); scholarship ($121,080); United Way ($63,710). 1995 Giving includes foundation ($493,590); scholarship ($83,395); United Way ($109,435). 1994 Giving includes foundation ($662,753); scholarship ($77,073); United Way.
Assets: $4,455,452 (1996); $4,106,876 (1995); $3,175,313 (1994)
Gifts Received: $400,000 (1996); $873,000 (1995); $610,000 (1994). Note: Contributions received from Rayonier, Inc.

Typical Recipients

Arts & Humanities: Arts Associations & Councils, Arts Centers, Historic Preservation, History & Archaeology, Museums/Galleries, Music, Public Broadcasting
Civic & Public Affairs: Business/Free Enterprise, Economic Development, Economic Policy, Employment/Job Training, Municipalities/Towns, Philanthropic Organizations, Safety, Urban & Community Affairs
Education: Business Education, Colleges & Universities, Economic Education, Education Associations, Education Funds, Elementary Education (Public), Engineering/Technological Education, Environmental Education, Education-General, Legal Education, Minority Education, Preschool Education, Private Education (Precollege), Public Education (Precollege),

Science/Mathematics Education, Secondary Education (Public), Special Education, Student Aid, Vocational & Technical Education
Environment: Forestry, Environment-General
Health: Hospices, Hospitals, Mental Health
Religion: Religious Welfare
Social Services: Camps, Child Abuse, Child Welfare, Community Centers, Community Service Organizations, Counseling, Day Care, Delinquency & Criminal Rehabilitation, Domestic Violence, Emergency Relief, Food/Clothing Distribution, People with Disabilities, Recreation & Athletics, Scouts, Senior Services, Shelters/Homelessness, Substance Abuse, United Funds/ United Ways, Volunteer Services, YMCA/YWCA/ YMHA/YWHA, Youth Organizations

Contributions Analysis

Civic & Public Affairs: (United Funds & United Way) 10% to 15%. Support goes to united funds in giving areas. Less than 5%. Supports a variety of community service organizations, including youth groups, environmental groups, chambers of commerce, libraries, fine arts centers, music, and recreational organizations.
Education: 60% to 65%. Supports individual scholarship programs including the Black Scholar Awards, the Four Year Scholarship Program, the Timber County Scholarship Program, and the Rayonier College Scholarship. Other areas of interests include colleges and universities, elementary and secondary schools, and Head Start programs.
Health: Less than 5%. Contributes to hospitals andhealth-care organizations.
Social Services: 20% to 25%. Supports youth organizations and volunteer programs.

Application Procedures

Initial Contact: letter
Application Requirements: a description of organization and program, amount requested, and proof of tax-exempt status
Deadlines: November 30
Decision Notification: board meets in February; notification one month after meeting
Notes: Application forms are available for scholarship programs from the foundation.

Restrictions

In March 2000, Foundation reported that all funding will be targeted to Jacksonville, Florida when it relocates to Florida at an undisclosed time.

Additional Information

Foundation awards scholarships to outstanding black students residing within and graduating from a high school within Wayne County, GA, or Nassau County, FL. Also awards scholarships to outstanding students (without regard to race) residing within and graduating from a high school within Wayne, GA, Nassau, FL, and Mason, Clallam, and Grays Harbor, WA. Scholarship decisions are made locally. Contact foundation for more information and applications.
Company reports that it is no longer affiliated with ITT Corp.
Company reports that it is no longer affiliated with ITT Corp.

Corporate Officials

Ronald Martin Gross: chairman, president, chief executive officer, director B Cleveland, OH 1933. ED Ohio State University BA (1955); Harvard University Graduate School of Business Administration MBA (1960). PRIM CORP EMPL chairman, president, chief executive officer, director: Rayonier Inc. CORP AFFIL director: Pittston Co.; director: Rayonier Forest Resources Co.; director: Corn Products International Inc.; director: Lukens Inc.

Foundation Officials

MacDonald Auguste: treasurer B 1948. ED City University of New York BA (1976); Pace University MBA (1979). PRIM CORP EMPL treasurer: Rayonier Inc. CORP AFFIL treasurer: Rayonier Timberlands LP.
William S. Berry: director B Placerville, CA 1941. ED University of California at Berkeley BS (1964); University of Michigan MS (1965). PRIM CORP EMPL executive vice president forest resources & wood products: Rayonier Inc. CORP AFFIL president, director: Rayonier New Zealand.
John Beckman Canning: secretary B Chicago, IL 1943. ED Princeton University AB (1965); Columbia University LLB (1968). PRIM CORP EMPL corporate secretary, associate general counsel: Rayonier Inc. CORP AFFIL vice president, director: Beckman Bros. NONPR AFFIL member: Columbia University Law School Alumni Association; director: Stamford Symphony Orchestra; member: American Society of Corporate Secretaries; member: American Bar Association.
Jay A. Fredericksen: vice president CORP AFFIL vice president corp. relations: Rayonier Inc.
Ronald Martin Gross: chairman, president, director (see above)
Wallace L. Nutter: director B Astoria, OR 1944. ED University of Washington BA (1967); Harvard University Graduate School of Business Administration (1987). PRIM CORP EMPL president, chief operating officer, director: Rayonier Inc. CORP AFFIL director: Rayonier Forest Resources. NONPR AFFIL member board governments: National Council Paper Industry Air & Stream Improvement.
Wendy Pugnetti: assistant secretary

Grants Analysis

Disclosure Period: calendar year ending 1996
Total Grants: $390,795*
Number of Grants: 313 (approx)
Average Grant: $932*
Highest Grant: $100,000
Typical Range: $100 to $2,500
***Note:** Giving excludes scholarship; United Way. Average grant figure excludes highest grant.

Recent Grants

Note: Grants derived from 1996 Form 990.

Arts & Humanities

4,000	Stamford Symphony Society, Stamford, CT
2,000	Forks Timber Museum, Forks, WA

Civic & Public Affairs

2,700	City of Plummer, Plummer, ID
2,500	Cordova Volunteer Fire Department, Cordova, AL
2,000	Foundation for Private Enterprise Education, Olympia, WA
2,000	Lumber City Fire Department, Lumber City, GA
2,000	Nunez Fire Department, Nunez, GA
2,000	Wayne County Improvement, Jessup, GA

Education

121,080	Individual Scholarship Grants
100,000	University of Oklahoma, Norman, OK
10,000	Brunswick College, Brunswick, GA
10,000	University of Washington, Seattle, WA
6,000	Georgia Tech University, Atlanta, GA
5,000	Washington Agriculture and Forestry Foundation, Spokane, WA
5,000	Washington Science Teachers Association, Port Angeles, WA
5,000	Wayne County Education Foundation, Jessup, GA
4,000	University of Washington Pulp and Paper Foundation, Seattle, WA
3,650	Washington State University Foundation, Pullman, WA
2,750	Grays Harbor College Harbor, Aberdeen, WA
2,570	Ohio State University, Columbus, OH
2,500	ATI Foundation, Jessup, GA
2,500	Baruch College Fund, New York, NY
2,500	Kenyon College, Gambier, OH
2,500	New Mexico Military Institute Foundation, Roswell, NM
2,500	Northwest Nazarene College, Nampa, ID
2,500	Princeton University, Princeton, NJ
2,500	University of Washington, Seattle, WA
2,500	Wayne County Alternative School Program, Jessup, GA
2,375	Fernandina Beach High School Foundation, Fernandina Beach, FL
2,000	Duke University, Durham, NC
2,000	Port Angeles Education Foundation, Port Angeles, WA
2,000	Wishkah Valley School District, Aberdeen, WA

Environment

5,000	Florida Forestry Foundation, Tallahassee, FL
5,000	Foundation for Research on Economics and Environment, Bozeman, MT

Health

2,000	Nassau County Alliance for the Mentally Ill, Fernandina Beach, FL

Religion

2,500	Good Samaritan Center, Jesup, GA

Social Services

25,000	South Mason Youth Soccer Club, Shelton, WA
22,924	United Way, Stamford, CT
20,000	United Way Clallam County, Port Angeles, WA
9,000	United Way Northeast Florida, Jacksonville, FL
6,000	YMCA Florida's First Coast, Fernandina Beach, FL
5,000	Grays Harbor and Pacific County Food Bank, Aberdeen, WA
5,000	United Way Grays Harbour, Aberdeen, WA
3,000	Nassau County Volunteer Center, Fernandina Beach, FL
2,500	United Way Appling County, Baxley, GA
2,500	Wayne County Concerted Services, Jessup, GA
2,500	Wayne County Service Center, Jessup, GA
2,000	DARE, Jesup, GA
2,000	Port Angeles Food Bank, Port Angeles, WA
2,000	United Way Mason County, Mossyrock, WA

The Reader's Digest Association, Inc.

Company Contact

Pleasantville, NY
Web: http://www.readersdigest.com

Company Description

Profit: US$264,000,000
Employees: 6,000
SIC(s): 2721 Periodicals.

Nonmonetary Support

Volunteer Programs: Reader's Digest employees, employee spouses, and retirees can receive grants for nonprofit groups where they actively volunteer. The company operates a Double-Match Gift Program where employees and retirees may give up to $10,000 per year to charities of their choice.

Reader's Digest Foundation

Giving Contact

Jan Braun, Program Manager
Reader's Digest Foundation
1 Reader's Digest Rd.
Pleasantville, NY 10570
Phone: (914)244-5370
Fax: (914)244-7642

Description

EIN: 136120380
Organization Type: Corporate Foundation
Giving Locations: nationally.
Grant Types: Employee Matching Gifts, Multiyear/ Continuing Support, Scholarship.

Giving Philosophy

The Reader's Digest Foundation reports that their focus is currently on basic skills, literacy and library services targeting grades K-12.

Financial Summary

Total Giving: $3,500,000 (fiscal year ending June 30, 2000 approx); $3,500,000 (fiscal 1999 approx); $3,860,182 (fiscal 1998). Note: Contributes through corporate direct giving program and foundation.
Giving Analysis: Giving for fiscal 1998 includes: foundation matching gifts ($1,962,646); foundation ($1,651,236); foundation scholarships ($144,800); foundation program-related investments ($101,500)
Assets: $30,255,653 (fiscal 1998); $29,363,304 (fiscal 1997); $28,318,598 (fiscal 1996)
Gifts Received: $17,254 (fiscal 1997); $13,334 (fiscal 1996); $5,000 (fiscal 1995). Note: 1997 contribution received from DeWitt Wallace-Lila Acheson Wallace.

Typical Recipients

Arts & Humanities: Libraries, Museums/Galleries, Performing Arts, Theater
Civic & Public Affairs: Municipalities/Towns
Education: Afterschool/Enrichment Programs, Colleges & Universities, Education Associations, Education-General, Journalism/Media Education, Literacy, Minority Education, Public Education (Precollege), Student Aid
Health: Clinics/Medical Centers
Religion: Jewish Causes
Social Services: Senior Services

Contributions Analysis

Giving Priorities: Higher education and literacy programs.
Arts & Humanities: 31%. Primarily supports libraries.
Civic & Public Affairs: 21%. Supports community services.
Education: 23%. The company supports such initiatives as the Putnam Valley School's early intervention reading program, the Links to Literacy program, the Westchester Education Coalition, and the Horizons Student Summer Enrichment program. The company also maintains a national scholarship program and the Tall Tree Initiative for Libraries.
Health: 24%. Supports children's health organizations and a clinic.
Religion: 1%. Jewish causes.
Note: Contributions made in 1998. Percentages exclude matching gifts, scholarship, and volunteer program investments.

Application Procedures

Initial Contact: Send a brief letter.
Application Requirements: Include a description of project and the sponsoring organization; description of need, target group, and timetable; explanation of why funding would solve a problem and meet a need; the degree to which the program can generate long-term funding; a demonstration of how funding would have a direct impact on a social need; a description of community, public and private sector involvement (if applicable); a description of measurable outcomes and timetables; audited financial statements for the current year; current itemized budget for project and organization; total project cost, other funding sources, and total requested from foundation; and evidence of tax-exempt status and latest IRS Form 990.
Deadlines: April 1, August 1, and December 1, to be considered in the following month.
Review Process: If initial letter meets foundation guidelines, full proposals (due by the dates listed above) will be requested.

Restrictions

The foundation does not support individuals or religious, veterans', fraternal, political, environmental, or cultural organizations. Grants are not made for dinners, audiovisual productions, legislative or lobbying purposes, or to organizations that are not tax-exempt. The foundation generally does not support capital or endowment campaigns, medical research, health-related activities, international charities, local chapters of national organizations, conferences, publications, or annual operating costs. Funding is generally for the company's immediate geographical area. Some programs give nationally.

Additional Information

The foundation prefers to support direct service projects rather than grants for general support or to intermediary funding agencies.
Funding is usually made on a one-time basis, and exceptions are generally limited to a maximum of three consecutive years.
The foundation seeks to support those organizations that demonstrate responsible management and that provide timely reports to the directors of the foundation on the disposition of funds and program results. results.
Publications: Reader's Digest Foundation Annual Report

Corporate Officials

Milan Kofol: vice president, treasurer chief financial officer B 1950. ED Presbyterian College BA (1973); University of Pennsylvania Wharton School MBA (1975). PRIM CORP EMPL vice president, treasurer: The Reader's Digest Association, Inc.
James Phillip Schadt: chairman, president, chief executive officer, director B Saginaw, MI 1938. ED Northwestern University BA (1960). PRIM CORP EMPL chairman: Dailey Capital Management LP. CORP AFFIL chief executive officer, director: Readers Digest Publishing Inc. NONPR AFFIL trustee: Northwestern University; trustee: Norwalk Connecticut Hospital; member: Magazine Publishers Association; member: American Association Publishers; trustee: American Enterprise Institute. CLUB AFFIL Fairfield County Hunt Club; Johns Island Club; Fairfield Country Club; Blind Brook Country Club; Chicago Club.
Jack A. Smith: senior vice president PRIM CORP EMPL senior vice president: The Reader's Digest Association, Inc.
Paul A. Soden: senior vice president, secretary, general counsel B New York, NY 1944. ED Fordham University AB (1965); Fordham University JD (1968). PRIM CORP EMPL senior vice president, secretary, general counsel: The Reader's Digest Association, Inc. CORP AFFIL vice president: Readers Digest Latinoamerica SA. NONPR AFFIL member: New York State Bar Association; member advisor board: Whitehead Institution; trustee: Fordham University; member: American Bar Association. CLUB AFFIL Scarsdale Golf Club.
Stephen R. Wilson: executive vice president, chief financial officer B 1947. ED United States Naval Academy BA (1968); Harvard University MBA (1974). PRIM CORP EMPL executive vice president, chief financial officer: The Reader's Digest Association, Inc.

Foundation Officials

Jan Braun: program manager
Claudia L. Edwards: executive director
Milan Kofol: treasurer (see above)
Barbara J. Morgan: director PRIM CORP EMPL senior vice president: The Reader's Digest Association, Inc. ADD CORP EMPL vice president: Pegasus Sales Inc.
James Phillip Schadt: chairman, director (see above)
Mary Terry: assistant secretary

Grants Analysis

Disclosure Period: fiscal year ending June 30, 1998
Total Grants: $1,651,236*
Number of Grants: 68
Average Grant: $8,500*
Highest Grant: $432,069
Typical Range: $10,000 to $75,000
***Note:** Giving excludes matching gifts; scholarship; volunteer program-related investments. Average grant figure excludes three highest grants (totaling $1,098,736).

Recent Grants

Note: Grants derived from fiscal 1997 Form 990.

Arts & Humanities

400,000	Westchester Library System, Elmsford, NY
6,000	Street Theater, White Plains, NY
5,000	Norwalk Public Library, Norwalk, CT

Civic & Public Affairs

333,333	New York City Partnership Foundation, New York, NY

Education

61,041	Westchester Education Coalition, White Plains, NY
55,000	United Negro College Fund, New York, NY
50,000	Reading is Fundamental, Blank, NY
23,000	Learning Foundation, Blank, NY
18,000	College Careers, Yonkers, NY
15,000	Fairfield University, Fairfield, CT
15,000	Poughkeepsie City School District, Poughkeepsie, NY
15,000	White Plains City School District, White Plains, NY
10,000	Horizon Student Summer Enrichment, New Canaan, CT
10,000	Howard University, Washington, DC -- journalism scholarships
10,000	Stanford University, Stanford, CA -- journalism scholarships
10,000	Syracuse University, Syracuse, NY -- journalism scholarships
10,000	University of California, CA -- journalism scholarships
10,000	University of Illinois, Urbana, IL -- journalism scholarships
10,000	University of Indiana, Bloomington, IN -- journalism scholarships
10,000	University of Kansas, Lawrence, KS -- journalism scholarships
10,000	University of Minnesota, Minneapolis, MN -- journalism scholarships
10,000	University of Mississippi, University, MS -- journalism scholarships
10,000	University of Missouri, Columbia, MO -- journalism scholarships
10,000	University of North Carolina, NC -- journalism scholarships
10,000	University of Texas, Austin, TX -- journalism scholarships
10,000	University of Wisconsin, WI -- journalism scholarships
10,000	University of Wisconsin, WI -- journalism scholarships

8,500 Putnam Valley Central School District, Putnam Valley, NY
6,000 New Rochelle Public Schools, New Rochelle, NY

Religion
25,000 Westchester Jewish Community Services, Hartsdale, NY

Social Services
15,000 Westchester Office for the Aging, White Plains, NY

RED WING SHOE CO. INC.

Company Contact
Red Wing, MN

Company Description
Employees: 1,300
SIC(s): 3143 Men's Footwear Except Athletic.

Red Wing Shoe Co. Foundation

Giving Contact
Shirley L. Perkins, Secretary
Red Wing Shoe Co. Foundation
314 Main Street
Red Wing, MN 55066
Phone: (612)388-8211
Fax: (612)385-0897

Description
EIN: 416020177
Organization Type: Corporate Foundation
Giving Locations: MN: Minneapolis, Red Wing, St. Paul
Grant Types: Capital, General Support.

Financial Summary
Total Giving: $581,295 (1998); $354,877 (1997); $525,357 (1996). Note: Contributes through foundation only.
Giving Analysis: Giving for 1996 includes: foundation ($502,357); foundation grants to United Way ($23,000); 1997: foundation ($324,877); foundation grants to United Way ($30,000); 1998: foundation ($548,795); foundation grants to United Way ($32,500)
Assets: $1,039,276 (1998); $861,514 (1997); $804,768 (1996)
Gifts Received: $548,000 (1998); $242,000 (1997); $535,000 (1996). Note: Contributions are received from the Red Wing Shoe Co.

Typical Recipients
Arts & Humanities: Arts Associations & Councils, Arts Centers, Arts Institutes, Arts & Humanities-General, Historic Preservation, History & Archaeology, Libraries, Museums/Galleries, Music, Performing Arts, Public Broadcasting, Theater
Civic & Public Affairs: Botanical Gardens/Parks, Business/Free Enterprise, Chambers of Commerce, Clubs, Economic Development, Civic & Public Affairs-General, Housing, Law & Justice, Municipalities/Towns, Nonprofit Management, Public Policy, Safety, Urban & Community Affairs, Women's Affairs, Zoos/Aquariums
Education: Arts/Humanities Education, Business Education, Colleges & Universities, Economic Education, Education Associations, Education Funds, Education Reform, Environmental Education, Education-General, Public Education (Precollege), Science/Mathematics Education, Social Sciences Education, Special Education
Environment: Air/Water Quality, Environment-General, Resource Conservation, Wildlife Protection
Health: Cancer, Children's Health/Hospitals, Clinics/Medical Centers, Emergency/Ambulance Services, Health Organizations, Hospices, Medical Rehabilitation, Preventive Medicine/Wellness Organizations, Single-Disease Health Associations
International: International Development, International Environmental Issues, International Organizations
Religion: Religious Welfare
Science: Science Museums, Scientific Centers & Institutes
Social Services: Child Welfare, Community Centers, Community Service Organizations, Crime Prevention, Emergency Relief, People with Disabilities, Recreation & Athletics, Scouts, Substance Abuse, United Funds/United Ways, YMCA/YWCA/YMHA/YWHA, Youth Organizations

Contributions Analysis
Giving Priorities: Emphasis is placed on education and the arts. Social services and civic causes also are supported.
Arts & Humanities: 21%. Arts associations, historic preservation, orchestral music, and public broadcasting.
Civic & Public Affairs: 10%. City of Red Wing, national parks, Chambers of Commerce, and Native American affairs.
Education: 47%. Red Wing School District 256, colleges, economic education, and education reform.
Environment: 5%. Nature and trails organizations.
Health: 3%. Health organizations, single disease associations, and medical centers.
Religion: 1%. Retreat Center.
Social Services: 13%. Primarily supports the United Way. Youth organizations, family services, and Special Olympics also receive support.
Note: Total contributions in 1998.

Application Procedures
Initial Contact: Send a brief letter.
Application Requirements: Include a description of organization's activities or projects, and a copy of tax exemption certificate.
Deadlines: None.

Restrictions
Grants are not made to individuals.

Foundation Officials
Joseph P. Goggin: treasurer B 1935. PRIM CORP EMPL president, treasurer, secretary, director: Red Wing Hotel Co. ADD CORP EMPL president: Red Wing Hotel Corp. CORP AFFIL director: SB Foot Tanning Co.
Shirley L. Perkins: secretary
William J. Sweasy: president B 1953. PRIM CORP EMPL chairman: Red Wing Hotel Co.

Grants Analysis
Disclosure Period: calendar year ending 1998
Total Grants: $548,795*
Number of Grants: 59
Average Grant: $5,152*
Highest Grant: $250,000
Typical Range: $1,000 to $15,000
***Note:** Giving excludes United Way. Average grant figure excludes highest grant.

Recent Grants
Note: Grants derived from 1998 Form 990.

Arts & Humanities
40,000 T. B. Sheldon Auditorium, Red Wing, MN
5,000 KTCA, St. Paul, MN
4,000 National Trust for Historic Preservation, Washington, DC
3,000 Minnesota Historical Society, St. Paul, MN
2,500 The Ordway, St. Paul, MN
2,000 Red Wing Arts Association, Red Wing, MN -- Summer Concert
1,500 Anderson Center, Red Wing, MN -- Residency Progrm
1,500 Lake Pepin Players, Inc., Pepin, WI
1,500 Minnesota Orchestral Association, Minneapolis, MN
1,500 Minnesota Public Radio, St. Paul, MN
1,000 The Children's Theatre, Minneapolis, MN
1,000 Guthrie Theatre Foundation, Minneapolis, MN
1,000 The Minneapolis Institute of Arts, Minneapolis, MN
1,000 Minnesota Children's Museum, St. Paul, MN

Civic & Public Affairs
25,000 Minnesota Zoo, Apple Valley, MN -- General Fund
25,000 Southeastern Minnesota Initiative Fund, Owatonna, MN -- Youth Trust Fund
3,000 Red Wing Noontime Kiwanis, Red Wing, MN -- Iodine Deficiency Project
2,400 City of Red Wing, Red Wing, MN -- Youth Fund
2,000 Center of the American Experiment, Minneapolis, MN -- General Fund
1,350 Republican Eagle, Red Wing, MN -- Newspaper In Education Partnership
1,260 Minnesota Council on Foundations, Minneapolis, MN -- Membership

Education
250,000 Red Wing School District 256 Environmental Learning Center, Red Wing, MN -- Environmental Education
5,000 Gustavas Adolphus College, St. Peter, MN -- General Fund
5,000 Lake City Environmental Learning Center, Lake City, MN -- Environmental Education
3,000 Minnesota Academic Excellence Foundation, Minneapolis, MN
2,700 Business Economic Education Foundation, Minneapolis, MN
2,500 Red Wing School District 256, Red Wing, MN -- Arts Education
1,760 Red Wing Public Schools, Red Wing, MN -- Summer Enrichment Program
1,000 Red Wing School District 256, Red Wing, MN -- Music Education

Environment
25,000 Project Earth Sense Fund of Minnesota Foundation, Minneapolis, MN
1,500 Continental Divide Trail Alliance, Pine, CO
1,000 The Nature Conservancy, Minneapolis, MN

Health
5,000 Red Wing Hospice, Red Wing, MN
5,000 Wings of Wellness, Red Wing, MN
3,200 Courage Center, Golden Valley, MN
1,200 American Cancer Society, Red Wing, MN
1,000 Children's Hospitals & Clinic Foundation, Roseville, MN

International
5,000 Opportunity International, Oak Brook, IL -- Central America Disaster Recovery

Science
50,000 Science Museum of Minnesota, St. Paul, MN -- Capital Fund
7,000 Science Museum of Minnesota, St. Paul, MN

Social Services
19,000 United Way, Red Wing, MN -- General Fund

13,500 United Way, Danville, KY -- General Fund
12,000 Red Wing Baseball Association, Red Wing, MN -- State Tournament
10,000 Red Wing YMCA, Red Wing, MN
10,000 Villa Maria, Old Frontenac, MN -- Capital Fund
3,000 Red Wing Young Life, Red Wing, MN -- General Fund
2,500 Enhancements, Inc., Potosi, MO -- General Fund
1,100 Gamehaven Council Boy Scouts, Rochester, MN -- General Fund
1,100 YMCA of the Ozarks, Potosi, MO -- General Fund
1,000 Cannon Valley Girl Scouts, Red Wing, MN -- General Fund

Reebok International Ltd.

Company Contact

Stoughton, MA
Web: http://www.reebok.com

Company Description

Revenue: US$2,899,900,000 (1999)
Employees: 6,600 (1999)
SIC(s): 5136 Men's/Boys' Clothing, 5137 Women's/Children's Clothing, 5139 Footwear.

Operating Locations

Austria: Reebok Austria GmbH, Obertrum Am See; Rockport GmbH, Obertrum Am See; Belgium: Reebok Belgium SA, Brussels, Brabant; Canada: Reebok Canada, Aurora; France: Reebok France, Buc; Rockport SA, Buc; Germany: Reebok Deutschland GmbH, Oberhaching, Bayern; American Sports Sportartikel Vertriebs GmbH, Schenefeld, Schleswig-Holstein; Hong Kong: Reebok International-Asia/Pacific, Central District; Reebok Trading (Far East) Ltd., Tsim Sha Tsui, Kowloon; Italy: Reebok Italia SRL, Agrate Brianza, Lombardia; Rockport International Trading Co. Italy SRL, Scandicci, Toscana; Republic of Korea: Reebok Korea Technical Service Ltd., Pusan; Netherlands: Reebok International Finance BV, Amsterdam, Noord-Holland; Reebok Nederland BV, Leusden, Utrecht; Rockport (Nederland) BV, Leusden, Utrecht; Reebok Europe BV, Rotterdam, Zuid-Holland; Spain: Reebok Leisure SA, Elche, Alicante; United Kingdom: Reebok United Kingdom Ltd., Lancaster, Lancashire; Rockport Co. Ltd., Lancaster, Lancashire; Foster J W & Sons (Athletic Shoes) Ltd., Uxbridge, Middlesex; Reebok Eastern Trading Ltd., Uxbridge, Middlesex; Reebok International Ltd., Uxbridge, Middlesex; Reebok Sports Ltd., Uxbridge, Middlesex

Nonmonetary Support

Value: $321,326 (1998); $305,000 (1996)
Type: Donated Equipment; Donated Products
Note: Company provides nonmonetary support. Donates autographed sports equipment for fundraising.

Corporate Sponsorship

Type: Arts & cultural events; Festivals/fairs; Music & entertainment events; Pledge-a-thon; Sports events
Contact: Brenda Goodell, Vice President Marketing
Note: Sponsors events promoting human and civil rights.

The Reebok Human Rights Foundation

Giving Contact

Geri Noonan, Associate Manager
The Reebok Human Rights Foundation
100 Technology Center Drive
Stoughton, MA 02072
Phone: (781)401-7946
Fax: (781)401-48060
Email: geri.noonan@reebok.com

Description

EIN: 043073548
Organization Type: Corporate Foundation
Former Name: The Reebok Foundation (1999).
Giving Locations: MA: Boston internationally through Human Rights Awards; principally near operating locations and to national organizations.
Grant Types: Emergency, Employee Matching Gifts, General Support.
Note: Employee matching gift ratio: 1 to 1.

Giving Philosophy

'The Reebok Foundation was formed in 1986 to focus Reebok International Ltd.'s social concerns and to help organize and expand the company's commitment to socially responsible action.' Reebok Foundation Coordinator

Financial Summary

Total Giving: $1,595,000 (1999 approx); $1,499,636 (1998); $1,080,077 (1997). Note: Contributes through corporate direct giving program and foundation.
Giving Analysis: Giving for 1998 includes: foundation ($1,178,310); nonmonetary support ($321,326)
Assets: $8,041,953 (1998); $7,034,518 (1997); $7,252,914 (1996)
Gifts Received: $3,001,059 (1996); $21,420 (1995); $3,002,450 (1993). Note: Contributions were received from Reebok International, Inc.

Typical Recipients

Arts & Humanities: Arts Associations & Councils, Museums/Galleries, Public Broadcasting
Civic & Public Affairs: African American Affairs, Asian American Affairs, Business/Free Enterprise, Civil Rights, Civic & Public Affairs-General, Hispanic Affairs, Legal Aid, Municipalities/Towns, Philanthropic Organizations, Professional & Trade Associations, Urban & Community Affairs, Women's Affairs
Education: Community & Junior Colleges, Education Funds, Education-General, Minority Education, Public Education (Precollege)
Health: Children's Health/Hospitals, Clinics/Medical Centers, Public Health
International: Health Care/Hospitals, Human Rights, International Affairs, International Development, International Organizations, International Peace & Security Issues, International Relief Efforts, Missionary/Religious Activities
Religion: Jewish Causes, Religious Welfare
Science: Science Museums
Social Services: At-Risk Youth, Child Welfare, Community Centers, Domestic Violence, Family Services, Food/Clothing Distribution, Recreation & Athletics, Refugee Assistance, Social Services-General, United Funds/United Ways, YMCA/YWCA/YMHA/YWHA, Youth Organizations

Contributions Analysis

Giving Priorities: Underserved youth and human rights. Internationally, the Reebok Foundation supports organizations defending and extending human rights. Each year the company seeks nominations for its annual Reebok Human Rights Award, which honors activists under the age of 30 who have made an outstanding contribution toward the struggle for human rights.
Civic & Public Affairs: Company supports human rights organizations. The majority of company's international giving is through its Human Rights Award. Foundation supports a short list of major national organizations devoted to furthering the achievement of social and economic equality of communities of color. Grants are made by invitation only.
Social Services: Contributions go to organizations in Boston serving the needs of underserved youth population, especially programs that educate, improve self-esteem, and protect the rights of African-American, Hispanic and Asian people. New proposals are not currently being accepted for this program.

Application Procedures

Initial Contact: Send a written proposal.
Deadlines: None.
Evaluative Criteria: Contributions are awarded to organizations that provide equal access to the funding and equal opportunity, and do not discriminate based on race, religion or sex.
Notes: Most grants are made by invitation only.

Restrictions

Does not support individuals, political organizations, advertising/program books, event sponsorship, fraternal organizations, or medical research. Foundation only supports nonprofit, tax-exempt organizations.

Corporate Officials

James Jones: vice president, director
Robert Meers: director
Barry Nagler: director
Leo Vannoni: director

Foundation Officials

Sharon Cohen: executive director, trustee PRIM CORP EMPL vice president public affairs: Reebok International Ltd.
J. Kevin Duffy: director
James Jones: vice president, director (see above)
Robert Meers: director (see above)
Barry Nagler: director (see above)
Geri Noonan: associate manager
Leo Vannoni: director (see above)

Grants Analysis

Disclosure Period: calendar year ending 1998
Total Grants: $1,178,310*
Number of Grants: 214
Average Grant: $5,506
Highest Grant: $25,000
Typical Range: $1,000 to $25,000
***Note:** Giving excludes nonmonetary support. Analysis was provided by company.

Recent Grants

Note: Grants derived from 1996 Form 990.

Arts & Humanities

40,000 Artists for Humanity, Boston, MA

Civic & Public Affairs

70,000 City Year, Boston, MA
65,000 Action for Boston Committee, Boston, MA
50,000 Business for Social Responsibility, Boston, MA
33,600 Shelburne Community Council, Roxbury, MA
30,000 National Council of La Raza, Washington, DC
25,000 National Urban League, New York, NY
18,000 Association of Grantmakers of Massachusetts, Boston, MA
15,000 National Hispanic Leadership Agenda, Washington, DC
15,000 Puerto Rico Legal Defense, PR
10,000 Ms. Foundation for Women, New York, NY
10,000 NAACP
10,000 Ten Point Coalition
10,000 Urban League, Jacksonville, FL

Education

50,000 Citizens School
25,000 Society Education Fund
19,000 Thurgood Marshall School, New York, NY
12,000 Broad Meadows Middle School
12,000 Jackie Robinson Scholarships, New York, NY

Health
10,000 Ronald McDonald House

International
300,000 Lawyers Committee for Human Rights, New York, NY
45,000 Two-Ten International Footwear Foundation, Watertown, MA
30,000 Carter Center, Atlanta, GA
30,000 Physicians for Human Rights, Boston, MA
25,000 Association for Defense of Human Rights in Rwanda
25,000 Chitlak
25,000 Human Rights Watch, New York, NY
25,000 International Crisis Group, Washington, DC
25,000 Society of African Missions
25,000 Tibet Fund, New York, NY
25,000 Yay Asan Pendidikan
20,000 League of Latin American Cities
19,000 Latin American Human Rights
15,000 Fund for Peace, New York, NY
15,000 Lawyers Committee for Human Rights, New York, NY
10,000 Association San Martin de Porres

Religion
25,000 Anti-Defamation League, Boston, MA
10,000 Brockton Interfaith, Brockton, MA

Science
65,000 Computer Museum, Boston, MA

Social Services
65,000 Center for Development of Teenagers
65,000 YMCA, Boston, MA
50,000 United Way North East
45,000 All Dorchester Sports League, Dorchester, MA
45,000 United Way New England, Providence, RI
40,000 YMCA, Boston, MA
25,000 Boston Youth Fund, Boston, MA
20,000 Women's Committee for Refugees
10,000 Boys and Girls Club, Brockport, MA
10,000 Stoughton Youth Resources, Stoughton, MA
9,220 Youth on Board

REGIONS BANK

Company Contact

PO Box 10247
Birmingham, AL 35202-0247
Phone: (205)326-7090

Company Description

Parent Company: Regions Financial Corp., Birmingham, AL, United States

Regions Financial Corporation Foundation

Giving Contact

Rosemary Bruten
PO Box 1471
Little Rock, AR 72203-1471
Phone: (501)371-7000
Fax: (501)371-7413

Description

Founded: 1992
EIN: 710713678
Organization Type: Corporate Foundation

Financial Summary

Total Giving: $369,901 (1996)
Assets: $558,500 (1996); $544,310 (1992)
Gifts Received: $369,901 (1996)

Typical Recipients

Arts & Humanities: Arts Centers, Arts Funds, Arts & Humanities-General, Museums/Galleries, Music, Public Broadcasting, Theater
Civic & Public Affairs: African American Affairs, Botanical Gardens/Parks, Business/Free Enterprise, Chambers of Commerce, Clubs, Community Foundations, Economic Development, Employment/Job Training, Ethnic Organizations, Civic & Public Affairs-General, Housing, Inner-City Development, Law & Justice, Parades/Festivals, Professional & Trade Associations, Rural Affairs, Urban & Community Affairs, Women's Affairs
Education: Colleges & Universities, Economic Education, Education Associations, Education Funds, Education Reform, Elementary Education (Public), Faculty Development, Education-General, Journalism/Media Education, Leadership Training, Minority Education, Secondary Education (Public), Special Education, Student Aid
Environment: Forestry
Health: AIDS/HIV, Arthritis, Cancer, Children's Health/Hospitals, Clinics/Medical Centers, Health Organizations, Heart, Kidney, Medical Research, Mental Health, Respiratory
International: International-General, International Organizations
Religion: Churches, Religious Organizations
Science: Science-General, Scientific Research
Social Services: Animal Protection, Big Brother/Big Sister, Camps, Community Centers, Community Service Organizations, Counseling, Domestic Violence, Emergency Relief, Family Planning, Family Services, Food/Clothing Distribution, Homes, Recreation & Athletics, Scouts, Social Services-General, United Funds/United Ways, Volunteer Services, YMCA/YWCA/YMHA/YWHA, Youth Organizations

Contributions Analysis

Giving Priorities: Focus on civic concerns, the United Way, education, the arts, and health organizations.
Arts & Humanities: 7%. Supports symphonies, arts centers, and theater.
Civic & Public Affairs: 43%. Primarily for a chamber of commerce, economic development, urban affairs, and law and justice.
Education: 11%. Emphasis on colleges and universities, scholarship funds, and private secondary schools.
Health: 6%. Supports children's health, hospitals, and medical centers.
International: 2%.
Social Services: 31%. Primarily to the United Way.
Note: Total contributions made in 1996.

Grants Analysis

Disclosure Period: calendar year ending 1996
Total Grants: $369,901
Number of Grants: 249
Average Grant: $975*
Highest Grant: $50,000
***Note:** Average grant figure excludes five highest grants ($132,000).

Recent Grants

Note: Grants derived from 1997 Form 990.

Arts & Humanities
7,000 Arkansas Arts Center, Little Rock, AR -- Donation - Exhibit Sponsorship
5,000 Arkansas Museum of Science and History, Little Rock, AR -- General donation
5,000 Arkansas Repertory Theatre, Little Rock, AR -- General donation
5,000 Central High Museum, Little Rock, AR -- General donation
5,000 Central High School Museum, Little Rock, AR -- General donation
5,000 Children's Museum of Arkansas, Little Rock, AR -- General donation
2,000 Arkansas Celebration of the Arts, Little Rock, AR -- General donation
500 Old State House Museum, Little Rock, AR -- General donation
400 Old State House, Little Rock, AR -- General donation
250 Chancelors Benefit for the Arts UAPB, Pine Bluff, AR -- General donation
200 KABF Radio, Little Rock, AR -- General donation
100 Arkansas Humanities Council, Little Rock, AR -- General donation
100 Little Rock Oral Program, Little Rock, AR -- General donation

Civic & Public Affairs
25,000 Little Rock NOW, Little Rock, AR -- General donation
12,500 Downtown Partnership, Little Rock, AR -- General donation
7,000 Dunbar Magnet, Little Rock, AR -- Donation - Teacher grants
5,000 Arkansas Institute for Social Justice, Little Rock, AR -- Donation - Home Counseling
5,000 Institute for Social Justice, Little Rock, AR -- General donation
4,000 Hot Springs Development Foundation -- General donation
3,000 Arkansas Easter Seal Society, Little Rock, AR -- General donation
2,500 Farm and Ranch Club, Little Rock, AR -- General donation
2,500 Urban League of Arkansas, Little Rock, AR -- General donation
2,000 Watershed, Little Rock, AR -- General donation
1,666 Wylewood (Searcy), Searcy, AR -- General donation
1,500 UCP, Little Rock, AR -- General donation
1,000 Arkansas Rice Depot, Little Rock, AR -- General donation
1,000 Comerstone Project, Little Rock, AR -- General donation
1,000 Department of Parks and Tourism, Little Rock, AR -- General donation
1,000 EMOBA, Little Rock, AR -- General donation
1,000 Governors Conference on the Family, Little Rock, AR -- General donation
1,000 Greater LR Chamber of Commerce, Little Rock, AR -- General donation
1,000 NCCJ, Little Rock, AR -- General donation
1,000 NLR Woman's Club, North Little Rock, AR -- General donation
1,000 Paint Your Heart Out, Little Rock, AR -- General donation
1,000 Summerset, North Little Rock, AR -- General donation
750 Heart of Arkansas Travel Association, Little Rock, AR -- General donation
750 RSVP, Little Rock, AR -- General donation
570 Cooperative Extension Service/UALR, Little Rock, AR -- General donation
500 Annual Author Symposium, Little Rock, AR -- General donation
500 Arkansas Bar Association, Little Rock, AR -- General donation
500 Arkansas Good Roads and Transportation Council -- General donation
500 Arkansas State Highway and Transportation Department, Little Rock, AR -- General donation
500 The Arkopolis Foundation -- General donation
500 Association of Arkansas Counties, Little Rock, AR -- General donation

500	Clinton Birthplace, Hope, AR -- General donation
500	Dining For Life, Little Rock, AR -- General donation
500	Ducks Unlimited, Sherwood, AR -- General donation
500	HOBY, Little Rock, AR -- General donation
500	Hoopfest, Little Rock, AR -- General donation
500	Housing Authority of NLR, North Little Rock, AR -- General donation
500	Kiwanis Activities, Little Rock, AR -- General donation
500	Lakeside Booster Club -- General donation
500	Martin Luther King Commission, Little Rock, AR -- General donation
500	Oasis Renewal, Little Rock, AR -- General donation
500	Parents Club, Little Rock, AR -- General donation
400	Arkansas Poultry Federation, Little Rock, AR -- General donation
300	Watershed, Little Rock, AR -- General donation
298	Lonoke County Fair and Livestock Association, Lonoke, AR -- General donation
250	Arkansas Rural Development Commission, Little Rock, AR -- General donation
250	Arkansas Tennis Association, Little Rock, AR -- General donation
250	Arkansas Trial Lawyers Association, Little Rock, AR -- General donation
250	City of Wrighsville, Wrightsville, AR -- General donation
250	Downtown Partnership, Little Rock, AR -- General donation
250	Little Rock Black Nurses, Little Rock, AR -- General donation
250	Little Rock Sister Cities, Little Rock, AR -- General donation
250	Mayors Christmas Tree Fund, Little Rock, AR -- General donation
250	NAACP, Little Rock, AR -- General donation
250	NLR Woman's Club, North Little Rock, AR -- General donation
250	Pulaski County 4-H Foundation, Little Rock, AR -- General donation
250	SCAN, Little Rock, AR -- General donation
250	Southwest Little Rock Christmas Parade Committee, Little Rock, AR -- General donation
250	Wolfe Street Foundation, Little Rock, AR -- General donation
200	Little Rock Ducks Unlimited, Little Rock, AR -- General donation
200	Little Rock Police Department, Little Rock, AR -- General donation
200	Little Rock Town Meeting on Africa, Little Rock, AR -- General donation
200	National Wild Turkey Federation, Jacksonville, AR -- General donation
100	American Society of Association Executives, Washington, AR -- General donation
100	Arkansas Department of Human Services, Little Rock, AR -- General donation
100	Committee on Women's Concern, Little Rock, AR -- General donation
100	England Housing Authority, England, AR -- General donation
100	League of Women Voters, Little Rock, AR -- General donation
100	League of Women Voters Pulaski County, Little Rock, AR -- General donation
100	LRSD- Hippy Program, Little Rock, AR -- General donation
100	NAACP Win, Little Rock, AR -- General donation
100	SALSA, Sherwood, AR -- General donation
100	UAPB/AMN Alumni Association, Little Rock, AR -- General donation
100	W. Harold Law Society, Little Rock, AR -- General donation
60	EMOBA, Little Rock, AR -- General donation
50	Cumberland Towers, Little Rock, AR -- General donation
50	EMOBA, Little Rock, AR -- General donation
50	Greater LR Chamber of Commerce, Little Rock, AR -- General donation

Education

10,000	University of Arkansas Medical Systems, Little Rock, AR -- General donation
5,000	Hendrix College, Conway, AR -- General donation
5,000	Philander Smith College, Little Rock, AR -- General donation
5,000	University of Arkansas Little Rock Foundation, Little Rock, AR -- General donation
5,000	University of Arkansas at Pine Bluff, Pine Bluff, AR -- Donation - New Stadium
3,000	Independent College Fund of Arkansas, North Little Rock, AR -- General donation
2,000	Arkansas Council on Economics Education, Little Rock, AR -- General donation
2,000	Lyon College, Batesville, AR -- General donation
1,500	Baker Elementary, Little Rock, AR -- General donation
1,500	Junior League of NLR, North Little Rock, AR -- General donation
1,125	University of Arkansas Little Rock School of Law, Little Rock, AR -- General donation
1,000	Arkansas Leadership Builders, Fayetteville, AR -- General donation
1,000	Jessville Public School -- General donation
1,000	NLR Community Scholarship Fund, North Little Rock, AR -- General donation
1,000	Shorter College, Little Rock, AR -- General donation
1,000	Single Parent Scholarship, Springdale, AR -- General donation
500	Arkansas Educational Television Network, Conway, AR -- General donation
500	Arkansas Tech University, Little Rock, AR -- General donation
500	Cutter Morning Star School -- General donation
500	Economic Summit-Bridging the Gap for Education Committee -- General donation
500	National Dunbar Alumni Association, Hot Springs, AR -- General donation
300	Arkansas School Boards Association, Little Rock, AR -- General donation
300	NLR Public School District, North Little Rock, AR -- General donation
250	Talladega College, Talladega, AL -- General donation
250	University of Arkansas Little Rock, Little Rock, AR -- General donation
200	Zeta Phi Beta Sorority, Little Rock, AR -- General donation
150	Leadership of Greater LR, Little Rock, AR -- General donation
150	McClellan Community Education, Little Rock, AR -- General donation
100	Alpha Kappa Alpha Sorority, Little Rock, AR -- General donation
100	J.A. Fair High School, Little Rock, AR -- General donation
100	Jacksonville and North Pulaski Schools, Jacksonville, AR -- General donation
100	Little Rock School District, Little Rock, AR -- General donation
100	NLR High School West Campus, North Little Rock, AR -- General donation
100	UAMS College of Nursing, Little Rock, AR -- General donation
50	Daisy Bates Elementary School, Little Rock, AR -- General donation

Environment

200	Hensley Community Park, Hensley, AR -- General donation

Health

1,000	American Cancer Society, Little Rock, AR -- General donation
1,000	Central Arkansas Community AIDS Partnership, Little Rock, AR -- General donation
1,000	Cystic Fibrosis Foundation, Little Rock, AR -- General donation
1,000	Muscular Dystrophy Association, Little Rock, AR -- General donation
750	American Diabetes Association, Little Rock, AR -- General donation
500	American Heart Association, Little Rock, AR -- General donation
210	Arthritis Foundation, Little Rock, AR -- General donation
200	American Lung Association, Little Rock, AR -- General donation
200	National Kidney Foundation, Little Rock, AR -- General donation
100	American Lung Association, Little Rock, AR -- General donation
100	Arkansas Youth Suicide Prevention Committee, Little Rock, AR -- General donation
100	Helping People with AIDS, Little Rock, AR -- General donation

International

5,000	Winrock International, Morrilton, AR -- General donation

Religion

6,000	Ouachita Baptist, Arkadelphia, AR -- General donation
3,750	Fellowship of Christian Athletes, Little Rock, AR -- General donation
3,350	First Christian Church, El Dorado, AR -- General donation
1,000	St. Vincent Foundation, Little Rock, AR -- General donation
250	Mount St.Mary's, Little Rock, AR -- General donation
50	Bethel AME Church, North Little Rock, AR -- General donation
25	Longley Baptist Church, Little Rock, AR -- General donation

Science

1,250	Aerospace Education Center, Little Rock, AR -- General donation
100	Parkview Arts and Science, Little Rock, AR -- General donation

Social Services

85,000	United Way, Little Rock, AR -- Donation - Pledge
5,000	Home Ownership Partners of Arkansas, Little Rock, AR -- Donation - Home Counseling
5,000	Humane Society of Pulaski County, Little Rock, AR -- General donation
5,000	In Affordable Housing, Little Rock, AR -- General donation

5,000 YMCA, North Little Rock, AR -- General donation
3,750 Centers for Youth and Families, Little Rock, AR -- General donation
2,500 Carelink, North Little Rock, AR -- General donation
1,000 Arkansas Community Organization for Reform Now, Little Rock, AR -- Donation - Bank Fair
1,000 North Garland County Boys and Girls Club -- General donation
1,000 Ouachita Area Council-Boy Scouts of America -- General donation
1,000 Professional Counseling Associates, Little Rock, AR -- General donation
1,000 Professional Counselling Associates, Little Rock, AR -- General donation
1,000 Salvation Army, Oklahoma City, OK -- General donation
1,000 We Care of Pulaski County, Wrightsville, AR -- General donation
750 Treatment Homes, Inc., Little Rock, AR -- General donation
500 American Red Cross, Little Rock, AR -- General donation
500 Arkansas Advocates for Children and Families, Little Rock, AR -- General donation
500 Environmental Youth Team, Little Rock, AR -- General donation
500 Salvation Army -- General donation
500 Ymca-Future 500, Little Rock, AR -- General donation
500 YWCA, Little Rock, AR -- General donation
375 Med Camps, Little Rock, AR -- General donation
300 Big Brother Big Sister, North Little Rock, AR -- General donation
250 Arkansas Advocates for Children and Families, Little Rock, AR -- General donation
250 Boy Scouts of America, Little Rock, AR -- General donation
250 Family Service Agency, Little Rock, AR -- General donation
250 Planned Parenthood of Greater Arkansas, Little Rock, AR -- General donation
250 Volunters in Public Schools, Little Rock, AR -- General donation
200 Arkansas Sheriffs Boys and Girls Ranch, Batesville, AR -- General donation
200 Habitat for Humanity, Little Rock, AR -- General donation
200 The Step Up Center, Little Rock, AR -- General donation
200 Treatment Homes, Inc., Little Rock, AR -- General donation
100 Advocates for Battered Women, Little Rock, AR -- General donation
100 Advocates and Relatives for Kids, North Little Rock, AR -- General donation
100 Little Rock Racquet Club, Little Rock, AR -- General donation
100 NLR Girls Softball Association -- General donation
100 NLR Independent Social Services Center, North Little Rock, AR -- General donation
100 Young Life, Little Rock, AR -- General donation

REGIONS FINANCIAL CORP.

Company Contact

Birmingham, AL

Company Description

Former Name: Regent Financial Co.;
Acquired:.
Revenue: US$3,391,800,000 (1999)
Profit: US$525,400,000 (1999)
Fortune Rank: 453, per FORTUNE Magazine's list of 500 Largest U.S. Corporations (1999).
FF 453
SIC(s): 6022 State Commercial Banks, 6035 Federal Savings Institutions, 6712 Bank Holding Companies.

SUBSIDIARY COMPANIES

AL: Regions Bank, Birmingham

Nonmonetary Support

Type: Cause-related Marketing & Promotion; Donated Equipment; In-kind Services; Loaned Employees; Loaned Executives; Workplace Solicitation

Giving Contact

Ms. Artist McMicken, Assistant Corporate Chairperson
Regions Financial Co.
PO Box 10247
Birmingham, AL 35202
Phone: (205)326-7168
Fax: (205)326-7099

Description

Organization Type: Corporate Giving Program
Giving Locations: AL: especially small communities headquarters and operating communities.
Grant Types: General Support.

Financial Summary

Total Giving: Contributes through corporate direct giving program only.

Typical Recipients

Arts & Humanities: Arts & Humanities-General
Civic & Public Affairs: Civic & Public Affairs-General
Education: Education-General
Health: Health-General
Social Services: Social Services-General

Application Procedures

Initial Contact: Send a letter outlining the proposal.
Application Requirements: Include a description of organization, amount requested, purpose of funds sought, recently audited financial statement, and proof of tax-exempt status.
Deadlines: None.

Additional Information

The company divides its operating area into five regions. Each makes requests for expenditures.
In 1997, the company's name was changed from Regent Financial Company to Regions Financial Corporation. In 1994, the company's name was changed from First Alabama Bancshares to Regent Financial Company.

Corporate Officials

Richard David Horsley: vice chairman, executive financial officer, director B Birmingham, AL 1942. ED University of Alabama (1964). PRIM CORP EMPL vice chairman, executive financial officer, director: Regions Financial Co. CORP AFFIL vice chairman, executive financial officer, director: First Alabama Bancshares Inc.
Carl E. Jones, Jr.: president, chief executive officer PRIM CORP EMPL president, chief executive officer: Regions Financial Co.
James Stanley Mackin: chairman, chief executive officer B Birmingham, AL 1932. ED Auburn University (1954). PRIM CORP EMPL chairman, chief executive officer: Regions Financial Co.

Giving Program Officials

James Stanley Mackin: B Birmingham, AL 1932. ED Auburn University (1954). PRIM CORP EMPL chairman, chief executive officer: Regions Financial Co.
Artist McMicken: PRIM CORP EMPL executive assistant: Regions Financial Co.

REGIS CORP.

Company Contact

Minneapolis, MN

Company Description

Revenue: US$927,100,000 (1999)
Employees: 31,000 (1999)
SIC(s): 7231 Beauty Shops.

Regis Foundation

Giving Contact

Mr. Myron Kunin, President
Regis Foundation
7201 Metro Boulevard
Minneapolis, MN 55439
Phone: (612)947-7777
Fax: (612)947-7900

Description

Founded: 1981
EIN: 411410790
Organization Type: Corporate Foundation
Giving Locations: MN: Minneapolis
Grant Types: General Support, Scholarship.
Note: Scholarship program is administered by the Minneapolis Board of Education.

Financial Summary

Total Giving: $852,201 (fiscal year ending June 30, 1998); $597,002 (fiscal 1996); $497,000 (fiscal 1994). Note: Contributes through foundation only.
Giving Analysis: Giving for fiscal 1997 includes: foundation ($582,002); foundation grants to United Way ($15,000); fiscal 1998: foundation ($842,201); foundation grants to United Way ($10,000)
Assets: $316 (fiscal 1998)
Gifts Received: $852,517 (fiscal 1998); $597,002 (fiscal 1996); $497,000 (fiscal 1994). Note: Foundation receives contributions from Regis Corp.

Typical Recipients

Arts & Humanities: Arts Associations & Councils, Arts Centers, Arts Institutes, Arts & Humanities-General, Museums/Galleries, Music, Opera, Theater
Civic & Public Affairs: Community Foundations, Civic & Public Affairs-General, Housing, Urban & Community Affairs
Education: Business Education, Colleges & Universities, Education Associations, Student Aid
Health: Cancer
Religion: Jewish Causes, Religious Organizations, Synagogues/Temples
Social Services: Child Welfare, Community Service Organizations, United Funds/United Ways, YMCA/YWCA/YMHA/YWHA, Youth Organizations

Contributions Analysis

Giving Priorities: Supports social services organizations, education, and the arts.
Arts & Humanities: 14%. Supports art museums and a theater.
Civic & Public Affairs: 1%. Supports housing initiatives and other civic causes.
Education: 32%. Funds universities and scholarship funds.
Religion: 7%. Contributes to Jewish organizations.
Social Services: 1%. Supports United Way.
Note: Total contributions in 1998.

Application Procedures

Initial Contact: Submit a brief letter of inquiry.
Application Requirements: Include a description of organization, amount requested, and purpose of funds sought.
Deadlines: None.
Notes: Applications for scholarships are available at Minneapolis public high schools.

Corporate Officials

Myron Kunin: chairman, director B Minneapolis, MN 1928. ED University of Minnesota BA (1949). PRIM CORP EMPL chairman, director: Regis Corp. CORP AFFIL ltd. partner: Rosepointe Housing; director: Supercuts Inc.; president: Regis Collection Inc.; chairman, principal stockholder: Curtis Squire Inc.; president: Red River Broadcasting Corp.

Foundation Officials

Frank E. Evangelist: secretary B 1936. PRIM CORP EMPL senior vice president finance, secretary, director: Regis Corp.
Bert M. Gross: assistant secretary B 1929. PRIM CORP EMPL secretary: Kurt Manufacturing Co. CORP AFFIL legal counsel: Phillips Gross & Aaron Pennsylvania.
Jack Holewa: vice president
Myron Kunin: president (see above)

Grants Analysis

Disclosure Period: fiscal year ending June 30, 1996
Total Grants: $842,201*
Number of Grants: 16
Average Grant: $36,013*
Highest Grant: $302,000
Typical Range: $10,000 to $25,000
***Note:** Giving excludes United Way. Average grant figure excludes highest grant.

Recent Grants

Note: Grants derived from fiscal 1998 Form 990.

Arts & Humanities

50,000 Minneapolis Institute of Arts, Minneapolis, MN
34,000 Walker Art Center, Minneapolis, MN
32,500 Minneapolis Institute of Arts, Minneapolis, MN
2,000 Minnesota Childrens Museum, Minneapolis, MN
1,750 Guthrie Theater, Minneapolis, MN

Civic & Public Affairs

8,200 Northern Clay Center, St. Paul, MN
4,000 Community Housing, Minneapolis, MN

Education

112,000 Saint Cloud University, St. Cloud, MN
80,000 Minneapolis Board of Education, Minneapolis, MN -- Scholarship Fund
75,000 Univ of Minnesota, Minneapolis, MN
5,000 Curtis Carlson School of Management, Minneapolis, MN -- Scholarship Fund

Religion

21,961 Fritz Hirschberger, Elizabeth town, PA
20,000 Sholom Foundation, Minneapolis, MN
15,000 Knoxville Holocaust, Knoxville, TN

Social Services

10,000 United Way, Minneapolis, MN

REI-RECREATIONAL EQUIPMENT, INC.

Company Contact

Kent, WA
Web: http://www.rei.com

Company Description

Employees: 5,524 (1999)
SIC(s): 2399 Fabricated Textile Products Nec, 5699 Miscellaneous Apparel & Accessory Stores, 5941 Sporting Goods & Bicycle Shops, 5961 Catalog & Mail-Order Houses.

Nonmonetary Support

Type: Donated Equipment; Donated Products
Note: Annual nonmonetary support is approximately $150,000.

Corporate Sponsorship

Type: Sports events

Giving Contact

David Jayo, Grants Administrator
Recreational Equipment, Inc.
PO Box 1938
Sumner, WA 98390-0800
Phone: (253)395-3780
Fax: (253)395-8135

Description

Organization Type: Corporate Giving Program
Giving Locations: operating locations, United States & Canada.
Grant Types: Award, General Support.

Financial Summary

Total Giving: $785,567 (1997); $716,170 (1995); $660,000 (1994 approx). Note: Contributes through corporate direct giving program only.

Typical Recipients

Environment: Environment-General
Social Services: Community Service Organizations, Recreation & Athletics

Contributions Analysis

Giving Priorities: Environmental causes and civic concerns.
Civic & Public Affairs: About 35%. Grants awarded to nonprofit organizations that promote safe participation in outdoor muscle-powered sports and outdoor education programs. Supports programs that increase access and encourage involvement, in outdoor activities, including climbing, camping, backpacking, winter sports, bicycling, paddling, and hiking. Supports education-based programs for all ages that address specific safety issues and proper care for outdoor resources; outdoor recreational activities for children ages 5-18 who would otherwise not have such an opportunity; programs that increase access to outdoor activities and encourage involvement for all people; and organizations working on outdoor recreation public policy initatives.
Environment: About 65%. Supports advocacy issues which moblize citizen support to influence public policy to protect and enhance opportunities for outdoor recreation; building a constituency base to advocate for the outdoors and its recreational uses, including strategies to build new alliances with outdoor users, youth, senior citizens, minorities, local goverment and other non-traditional conservation constituencies; lobbying of Congress representatives for protection of outdoor recreationl areas; mediation of conflict between muscle-powered recreationists, particularly hikers/campers,climbers, bicyclists, skiers and paddlers; and technology to increase advocacy effectiveness and organize grass-roots volunteers through communications technology, including hardware and technical training.

Application Procedures

Initial Contact: Call and request an application form.
Application Requirements: An application must be complete and include a detailed line item budget, a copy of IRS tax-exempt letter. For a community recreation grant, also include a copy of insurance certificate and a one-page cover letter in organizations letterhead; and for a conservation grant, also include project goals, strategies and how they will be measured, and up to three pieces of supportive material.
Deadlines: Proposals are due by the 10th of each month for consideration the following month; no grants are considered in November or December.
Review Process: Acknowledgement of application and decision will be sent via mail.
Evaluative Criteria: A project must show measurable progress over one or two years. The effort should be quantifiable, with specific goals, objectives, action plans, and methods of evaluation; and include a legislative element.
Decision Notification: Monthly, from February to November.
Notes: Faxed copies will not be considered. Company requests that applicants not make inquiries during the evaluation of a proposal.

Restrictions

Grants are not made for film, video, or book production; for-profit organizations; start-up costs; annual fund drives; operational administrative costs; team or individual sponsorships; projects not directly related to muscle-powered outdoor recreation; trail construction or maintenance; projects outside the United States; discriminatory organizations; operational administrative costs; start up costs for new organizations; research and education unless it is for specific advocacy on an issue; third-party fund raising; or campaigns for elected or appointed officials. for elected or appointed officals.

Additional Information

Programs that do not qualify for grants may still be eligible for discounts on quality outdoor gear and clothing. Groups in need may contact REI's Commercial Sales Department at 1-800-258-4567.
REI stores organize and fund an annual service project, relying on volunteer commitment to perform local conservation-oriented work. Efforts are wide-reaching, from cleaning up Seattle's Lake Union by kayak, to building trail sections along San Francisco's Bay Area Ridge Trail.
Other community involvement activities include free education clinics and demo days to inform and assist members and customers with outdoor pursuits, providing informational publications and brochures, and dedicating retail space for environmental centers for information and learning centers for conservation and environmental issues.
Publications: Corporate Contributions Program Guidelines; Application Forms

Corporate Officials

Dennis Madsen: chief executive officer PRIM CORP EMPL chief executive officer: REI-Recreational Equipment, Inc.

Giving Program Officials

David Jayo: grants administrator

Grants Analysis

Disclosure Period: calendar year ending 1997
Total Grants: $785,567
Typical Range: $1,000 to $3,000

REILLY INDUSTRIES, INC.

Company Contact

Indianapolis, IN

Company Description

Employees: 850
SIC(s): 2812 Alkalies & Chlorine, 2821 Plastics Materials & Resins, 2822 Synthetic Rubber, 2865 Cyclic Crudes & Intermediates.

Corporate Sponsorship

Type: Arts & cultural events; Festivals/fairs; Music & entertainment events; Pledge-a-thon

Reilly Foundation

Giving Contact

Rand Brooks, Trustee
Reilly Foundation
300 North Meridian Street, Suite 1500
Indianapolis, IN 46204-1763
Phone: (317)248-6464
Fax: (317)248-6472

Description

Founded: 1962
EIN: 352061750
Organization Type: Corporate Foundation
Giving Locations: company operating locations.
Grant Types: Employee Matching Gifts, General Support, Scholarship.

Financial Summary

Total Giving: $400,000 (2000 approx); $400,000 (1999 approx); $424,878 (1998). Note: Contributes through foundation only.
Giving Analysis: Giving for 1998 includes: foundation ($335,923); foundation grants to United Way ($76,500); foundation matching gifts ($12,455)
Assets: $1,509,351 (1998); $1,779,687 (1997); $704,728 (1995)
Gifts Received: $600,000 (1998); $600,000 (1997); $700,000 (1995). Note: Contributions were received from Reilly Industries.

Typical Recipients

Arts & Humanities: Arts Associations & Councils, Arts Outreach, Ballet, Museums/Galleries, Music, Opera, Performing Arts, Theater
Civic & Public Affairs: Civic & Public Affairs-General, Housing, Public Policy, Zoos/Aquariums
Education: Business Education, Colleges & Universities, Community & Junior Colleges, Economic Education, Education Associations, Education Funds, Elementary Education (Public), Engineering/Technological Education, Private Education (Precollege), Public Education (Precollege), Student Aid, Vocational & Technical Education
Environment: Resource Conservation
Health: Cancer, Children's Health/Hospitals, Clinics/Medical Centers, Health Organizations, Hospitals, Long-Term Care, Medical Rehabilitation, Medical Research, Transplant Networks/Donor Banks
International: Foreign Arts Organizations
Religion: Ministries, Religious Organizations, Religious Welfare, Seminaries
Science: Scientific Centers & Institutes
Social Services: At-Risk Youth, Camps, Child Welfare, Community Centers, Community Service Organizations, Day Care, Family Planning, Family Services, Food/Clothing Distribution, Homes, People with Disabilities, Scouts, Senior Services, Shelters/Homelessness, Special Olympics, United Funds/United Ways, YMCA/YWCA/YMHA/YWHA, Youth Organizations

Contributions Analysis

Arts & Humanities: 13%. Supports museums, galleries, and performing arts.
Civic & Public Affairs: 23%. Supports zoos and leadership development.
Education: 27%. Supports colleges, universities, and secondary education. Education funds and associations also receive support. Foundation offers scholarships and an employee matching gifts program.
Environment: 1%. Supports conservation efforts.
Health: 8%. Funds health centers, community hospitals, and long-term healthcare.
Religion: 2%. Supports religious welfare and seminaries.
Social Services: 26%. Funding primarily supports the United Way. Other interests include youth activities, child welfare, homelessness, and food distribution.
Note: Total contributions made in 1998.

Application Procedures

Initial Contact: Write a letter of intent.
Application Requirements: For grant requests: a description of organization and project, amount requested, and purpose of funds sought. For scholarship requests: tuition receipts and grade reports.
Deadlines: None.
Review Process: Trustees review requests at quarterly meetings.

Restrictions

Scholarship awards are limited to children of qualified employees.

Corporate Officials

Robert D. McNeeley: president, director, director B 1944. ED Purdue University BS (1967). PRIM CORP EMPL president, director: Reilly Industries, Inc. CORP AFFIL polytechnical: Solar Aluminum Technology Services.
Thomas E. Reilly, Jr.: chairman, chief executive officer, director B 1939. ED Stanford University BA (1961); Harvard University Graduate School of Business Administration MBA (1963). PRIM CORP EMPL chairman, chief executive officer, director: Reilly Industries, Inc. CORP AFFIL director: Lilly Industries Inc.; director: Bank One Corp. NONPR AFFIL director: Methodist Hospital of Indiana.

Foundation Officials

Rand Brooks: trustee
Elizabeth C. Reilly: trustee
Thomas E. Reilly, Jr.: trustee (see above)
Clarke L. Wilhelm: chairman

Grants Analysis

Disclosure Period: calendar year ending 1998
Total Grants: $335,923*
Number of Grants: 66
Average Grant: $5,090
Highest Grant: $40,000
Typical Range: $100 to $7,500
***Note:** Giving excludes matching gifts; United Way.

Recent Grants

Note: Grants derived from 1997 Form 990.

Arts & Humanities

17,500	Indianapolis Symphony Orchestra, Indianapolis, IN
16,000	Bifeborg Museum
3,000	Greensboro Symphony Orchestra, Greensboro, NC
2,750	Indianapolis Museum of Art, Indianapolis, IN
2,000	Indiana Repertory Theater, Indianapolis, IN
1,000	Arts Council, Indianapolis, IN

Civic & Public Affairs

40,000	Reed Memorial Association
32,000	Indianapolis Zoological Society, Indianapolis, IN
15,000	Life Leadership Development, Indianapolis, IN
1,000	Habitat for Humanity

Education

52,019	Wayne Township School District
24,000	Associated Colleges of Indiana, Indianapolis, IN
18,500	Butler University, Indianapolis, IN
17,500	Junior Achievement Central Indiana, IN
10,500	Earlham College, Richmond, IN
6,500	Guilford Technical Community College, Jamestown, NC
4,000	Ohio Foundation of Independent Colleges, Columbus, OH
2,500	Junior Achievement
1,000	LaSalle Academy
1,000	Texas Independent Colleges Fund, Fort Worth, TX
1,000	Wake Forest University, Winston-Salem, NC

Environment

2,500	Nature Conservancy, Arlington, VA

Health

10,000	St. Francis Health Care Foundation, Honolulu, HI
7,500	St. Augustine's Home for Aged
3,000	Pleasant Run Children's Hospital, Indianapolis, IN
3,000	Pleasant Run Children's Hospital, Indianapolis, IN
3,000	St. Francis Health Care Foundation, Honolulu, HI
2,500	Crossroads Rehabilitation Center, Indianapolis, IN
1,500	Healthnet Community Health Center
1,000	Riley Cancer Research

International

1,000	Ballet Internationale
1,000	International Violin Competition

Religion

11,500	Christian Care Aid Society
2,000	Society of St. Vincent de Paul

Social Services

76,000	United Way Central Indiana, Indianapolis, IN
5,000	Hoosier Capital Girl Scout Council, Indianapolis, IN
3,000	Meals on Wheels, New York, NY
2,500	Boy Scouts of America, Indianapolis, IN
2,000	Girls, Incorporated, Greenwich, CT
2,000	Indianapolis Retirement Home, Indianapolis, IN
2,000	Noble Centers, Indianapolis, IN
2,000	Our House
1,500	Boys and Girls Clubs, Indianapolis, IN
1,250	Day Nursery
1,000	Center for Leadership
1,000	Child Advocates, Houston, TX
1,000	Guardian Home Foundation
1,000	Indianapolis Civic Center, Indianapolis, IN
1,000	YMCA, Indianapolis, IN
1,000	YWCA, Indianapolis, IN

William B. Reily &Co., Inc.

Company Contact

New Orleans, LA

Company Description

Employees: 1,200
SIC(s): 2035 Pickles, Sauces & Salad Dressings, 2079 Edible Fats & Oils Nec, 2095 Roasted Coffee, 5141 Groceries--General Line.

Reily Foundation

Giving Contact

Robert D. Reily, President
Reily Foundation
640 Magazine St.
New Orleans, LA 70130
Phone: (504)524-6131
Fax: (504)539-5417

Description

EIN: 726029179
Organization Type: Corporate Foundation
Giving Locations: LA
Grant Types: Capital, General Support.

Financial Summary

Total Giving: $1,000,000 (1998 approx); $1,213,165 (1997); $1,243,860 (1996). Note: Contributes through foundation only. 1996 Giving includes United Way ($121,000).
Giving Analysis: Giving for 1996 includes: foundation ($1,122,860); foundation grants to United Way ($121,000); 1997: foundation ($1,072,165); foundation grants to United Way ($141,000)
Assets: $9,678,674 (1997); $7,482,935 (1996); $7,495,231 (1993)
Gifts Received: $2,700,000 (1997); $1,175,400 (1996); $1,200,000 (1993). Note: Contributions were received from the Reily Foods Company and The Standard Companies, Inc.

Typical Recipients

Arts & Humanities: Arts Associations & Councils, Arts Centers, Arts Funds, Historic Preservation, Museums/Galleries, Music, Opera, Public Broadcasting
Civic & Public Affairs: Botanical Gardens/Parks, Business/Free Enterprise, Community Foundations, Economic Development, Employment/Job Training, Civic & Public Affairs-General, Housing, Municipalities/Towns, Nonprofit Management, Parades/Festivals, Professional & Trade Associations, Public Policy, Safety, Urban & Community Affairs
Education: Business Education, Colleges & Universities, Community & Junior Colleges, Education Associations, Education Funds, Education Reform, Elementary Education (Private), Elementary Education (Public), Faculty Development, Education-General, Literacy, Minority Education, Private Education (Precollege), Public Education (Precollege), Religious Education, Science/Mathematics Education
Environment: Environment-General, Wildlife Protection
Health: AIDS/HIV, Clinics/Medical Centers, Health Organizations, Hospitals, Single-Disease Health Associations
Religion: Churches, Religious Welfare
Science: Scientific Organizations
Social Services: At-Risk Youth, Child Welfare, Community Service Organizations, Crime Prevention, Day Care, Delinquency & Criminal Rehabilitation, Family Planning, Family Services, Food/Clothing Distribution, Homes, People with Disabilities, Scouts, United Funds/United Ways, YMCA/YWCA/YMHA/YWHA, Youth Organizations

Contributions Analysis

Arts & Humanities: 17%. Emphasis on arts funds, museums, orchestras, historic preservation, and public broadcasting.
Civic & Public Affairs: 27%. Majority of funding supports community foundations, public policy, botanical gardens, and professional trade associations in New Orleans.
Education: 18%. Supports universities; public and private, secondary and elementary education; education reform; minority education; and Junior Achievement.
Health: 2%. Single-disease health organizations, hospitals and clinics receive support.
Religion: 11%. Focus on religious welfare organizations and churches.
Social Services: 25%. Provides funding for United Way, youth groups, family services, crime prevention, and food distribution. Also supports criminal rehabilitation and at-risk youth.

Application Procedures

Initial Contact: send a full proposal
Application Requirements: a description of organization, amount requested, purpose of funds sought, recently audited financial statement, and proof of tax-exempt status
Deadlines: None.

Restrictions

Does not support individuals, religious organizations for sectarian purposes, political or lobbying groups, or organizations outside operating areas.

Corporate Officials

Harold M. Herrmann: chief financial officer, director B 1935. PRIM CORP EMPL chief financial officer: William B. Reily & Co., Inc. CORP AFFIL director: Reily Foods Co.; director: Standard Co. Inc.
H. Eustis Reily: secretary, director PRIM CORP EMPL secretary, director: William B. Reily & Co., Inc.
Robert D. Reily: vice president, director B 1927. ED Tulane University (1946-1949). PRIM CORP EMPL vice president, director: William B. Reily & Co., Inc.
William Boatner Reily, III: president, chief executive officer, director B 1928. ED Tulane University (1947-1950). PRIM CORP EMPL president, chief executive officer, director: William B. Reily & Co., Inc.

Foundation Officials

Joan Coulter: secretary, treasurer
H. Eustis Reily: director (see above)
Robert D. Reily: president, director (see above)
William Boatner Reily, III: director (see above)

Grants Analysis

Disclosure Period: calendar year ending 1997
Total Grants: $1,072,165*
Number of Grants: 77
Average Grant: $13,924
Highest Grant: $90,000
Typical Range: $5,000 to $25,000
***Note:** Giving excludes United Way.

Recent Grants

Note: Grants derived from 1996 Form 990.

Arts & Humanities

85,000	Louisiana Philharmonic Orchestra, New Orleans, LA
33,000	Louisiana Children's Museum, New Orleans, LA
30,000	New Orleans Museum of Art, New Orleans, LA
25,000	Preservation Resource Center
20,000	New Orleans Opera Foundation, New Orleans, LA

Civic & Public Affairs

59,500	Greater New Orleans Foundation, New Orleans, LA
50,000	Bicentennial Endowment Campaign, New Orleans, LA
50,000	Metrovision Partnership Foundation, New Orleans, LA
30,000	National Right to Work, Springfield, VA
20,000	NOCCA
13,500	Bureau of Governmental Research, New Orleans, LA
10,000	Southeastern Development Foundation, Hammond, LA
5,000	Center for Effective Nonprofit Management
5,000	Parkway Partners, New Orleans, LA

Education

75,000	Tulane University, New Orleans, LA
50,000	Metairie Park Country Day School, Metairie, LA
37,500	Advocates for Science and Mathematics Education, New Orleans, LA
35,000	Metropolitan Area Committee, New Orleans, LA
30,000	Delgado Community College, New Orleans, LA
13,000	St. George's Episcopal School, New Orleans, LA
10,000	Louise McGehee School
10,000	Louisiana Center for Development and Learning, LA
8,000	Helen Edwards Elementary School
7,110	Start the Adventures in Reading, New Orleans, LA
5,000	James Lewis Extension School
5,000	Teach for America, New Orleans, LA

Environment

35,000	Southern Animal Foundation, New Orleans, LA

Health

25,000	Touro Infirmary, New Orleans, LA
15,000	Grace House, New Orleans, LA

Religion

15,000	Sister Servants of Mary
12,500	Crescent City Youth for Christ, New Orleans, LA
10,000	Archbishop's Community Appeal, New Orleans, LA
10,000	Interfaith Sponsoring Committee, New Orleans, LA
10,000	Jeremiah Group
7,000	Pleasant Valley Baptist Church
5,000	New Orleans Mission, New Orleans, LA
5,000	Salvation Army, New Orleans, LA

Social Services

121,000	United Way, New Orleans, LA
50,000	Kingsley House, New Orleans, LA
25,000	Planned Parenthood Louisiana, New Orleans, LA
25,000	YMCA, New Orleans, LA
23,000	Kalorama Foundation
20,000	New Orleans Police Foundation, New Orleans, LA
12,500	Poydras Home, New Orleans, LA
10,000	Boy Scouts of America, New Orleans, LA
10,000	Goodwill Industries
8,000	Second Harvesters, New Orleans, LA
7,500	Covenant House, New Orleans, LA
5,000	Metropolitan Crime Commission, New Orleans, LA
5,000	New Orleans Outreach, New Orleans, LA

REINHART INSTITUTIONAL FOODS

Company Contact

La Crosse, WI

Company Description

Employees: 650
SIC(s): 5046 Commercial Equipment Nec, 5141 Groceries--General Line.

Corporate Sponsorship

Value: $1,000

D. B. and Marjorie Reinhart Family Foundation

Giving Contact

Nancy Hengel, Director
D. B. and Marjorie Reinhart Family Foundation
PO Box 2228
La Crosse, WI 54602-2228
Phone: (608)782-4999
Fax: (608)782-5084

Alternate Contact

Marjorie A. Reinhart

Description

EIN: 391564353
Organization Type: Corporate Foundation. Supports preselected organizations only.
Giving Locations: WI
Grant Types: General Support.

Financial Summary

Total Giving: $484,555 (fiscal year ending August 31, 1998); $185,438 (fiscal 1997); $345,929 (fiscal 1996). Note: Contributes through foundation only.
Giving Analysis: Giving for fiscal 1997 includes: foundation grants to United Way ($30,000)
Assets: $14,015,860 (fiscal 1998); $6,023,279 (fiscal 1997); $5,717,774 (fiscal 1996)
Gifts Received: $7,829,534 (fiscal 1998); $50,000 (fiscal 1997); $50,000 (fiscal 1996). Note: Contributions are received from Reinhart Institutional Foods and Marjorie A. Reinhart.

Typical Recipients

Arts & Humanities: Arts Associations & Councils, Arts Centers, Arts Funds, Historic Preservation, History & Archaeology, Libraries, Music, Public Broadcasting
Civic & Public Affairs: Clubs, Civic & Public Affairs-General, Parades/Festivals, Public Policy, Safety, Urban & Community Affairs
Education: Colleges & Universities, Elementary Education (Public), Education-General, Medical Education, Preschool Education, Private Education (Precollege), School Volunteerism, Student Aid, Vocational & Technical Education
Environment: Air/Water Quality
Health: Cancer, Children's Health/Hospitals, Clinics/Medical Centers, Diabetes, Emergency/Ambulance Services, Eyes/Blindness, Heart, Hospitals, Medical Research, Prenatal Health Issues, Public Health, Single-Disease Health Associations
International: International Relations, International Relief Efforts
Religion: Churches, Dioceses, Religious Organizations, Religious Welfare, Social/Policy Issues
Social Services: Big Brother/Big Sister, Community Centers, Community Service Organizations, Crime Prevention, People with Disabilities, Recreation & Athletics, Scouts, Special Olympics, Substance Abuse, United Funds/United Ways, YMCA/YWCA/YMHA/YWHA, Youth Organizations

Contributions Analysis

Giving Priorities: Primary support for education, social services, the arts, health organizations, and religious welfare.
Arts & Humanities: 16%. Arts funds, music, historical societies, and public broadcasting.
Civic & Public Affairs: Primarily for urban and community affairs.
Education: About 28%. Emphasis on colleges and universities and education associations.
Health: 15%. Primarily supports the Children's Hospital of Milwaukee, WI.
Religion: About 13%. Funding supports the Diocese of La Crosse, churches, and religious welfare organizations.
Social Services: 24%. Supports community services, traditional youth organizations, and children's services.
Note: Total contributions made in 1997.

Additional Information

Please note that the family foundation is legally a separate entity from Reinhart Institutional Foods.

Foundation Officials

Gerald Edward Connolly: trustee (see above)
Nancy Hengel: director
Marjorie A. Reinhart: trustee

Grants Analysis

Disclosure Period: fiscal year ending August 31, 1997
Total Grants: $155,438*
Number of Grants: 41
Average Grant: $3,791
Highest Grant: $25,000
Typical Range: $1,000 to $12,500
***Note:** Giving excludes United Way.

Recent Grants

Note: Grants derived from 1997 Form 990.

Arts & Humanities

10,000	United Fund for Arts and Humanities, La Crosse, WI
10,000	United Fund for Arts and Humanities, La Crosse, WI
5,000	Friends of Shell Lake Library, Shell Lake, WI
1,000	La Crosse Boy Choir, La Crosse, WI
1,000	Philharmonic Center for Arts, Naples, FL
1,000	Washburn County Historical Society, Shell Lake, WI
1,000	Wisconsin Public Television, Madison, WI

Civic & Public Affairs

5,000	Dr. Thomas Haggai Foundation, High Point, NC
2,000	Rotary Lights, La Crosse, WI
568	La Crosse Regional Quality Council, La Crosse, WI
500	Skyrockers, La Crosse, WI

Education

25,000	Horatio Alger Association, Washington, DC
7,000	Viterbo College, La Crosse, WI -- educational support
5,700	Viterbo College, La Crosse, WI -- educational support
5,000	CESA Foundation, Onalaska, WI -- educational support
5,000	Ladysmith Elementary School Playground, Ladysmith, WI
2,000	Mount Senario College, Ladysmith, WI -- educational support
1,000	Western Wisconsin Technical College, La Crosse, WI -- educational support
500	CVTC Foundation, Eau Claire, WI -- educational support

Health

20,000	Milwaukee Children's Hospital, Milwaukee, WI -- medical support
5,000	Children's Hospital Foundation, Milwaukee, WI -- medical support
1,500	March of Dimes Birth Defects Foundation, Madison, WI
200	Gundersen Foundation for Heart, La Crosse, WI -- medical support

International

200	German International Relations Committee, La Crosse, WI

Religion

10,000	Diocese of La Crosse, La Crosse, WI
10,000	St. Joseph's Parish, Rice Lake, WI
1,112	St. Patrick's Parish, Onalaska, WI
1,089	St. Patrick's Parish, Onalaska, WI
1,000	Birthright, La Crosse, WI
570	Birthright, La Crosse, WI
100	Birthright, La Crosse, WI
100	Good News, La Crosse, WI

Social Services

15,000	CHILEDA, La Crosse, WI
10,000	United Way, La Crosse, WI
5,000	Rotary Foundation, La Crosse, WI
5,000	Special Olympics, La Crosse, WI
5,000	YMCA, La Crosse, WI
1,000	Boys and Girls Clubs, La Crosse, WI
1,000	Coulee Council on Alcohol, La Crosse, WI
1,000	Ragar Association for Blind, Milwaukee, WI
450	Onalaska Youth Hockey, Onalaska, WI
450	Onalaska Youth Hockey, Onalaska, WI
50	Big Brothers and Big Sisters, La Crosse, WI

RELIANT ENERGY INC.

Company Contact

PO Box 1700
Houston, TX 77251
Web: http://www.reliantenergy.com

Company Description

Former Name: Houston Industries, Inc. (1999).
Revenue: US$15,302,800,000 (1999)
Profit: US$1,482,500,000 (1999)
Employees: 8,891
Fortune Rank: 114, per FORTUNE Magazine's list of 500 Largest U.S. Corporations (1999).
FF 114
SIC(s): 4841 Cable & Other Pay Television Services, 4911 Electric Services, 5063 Electrical Apparatus & Equipment, 6719 Holding Companies Nec.

Nonmonetary Support

Type: Donated Equipment; In-kind Services; Loaned Employees; Loaned Executives

Reliant Energy Foundation

Giving Contact

Robert Gibbs, Director, Corporate Community Relations
Reliant Energy Foundation
PO Box 4567
Houston, TX 77210
Phone: (713)207-8058
Fax: (713)207-0207
Email: cathy.guy@reliantenergy.com
Web: http://www.reliantenergy.com/community/default.asp

Description

Founded: 1997
EIN: 760537222
Organization Type: Corporate Foundation
Former Name: Houston Industries, Inc. (1999).
Giving Locations: headquarters and operating communities.
Grant Types: Capital, General Support, Research, Seed Money.

Financial Summary

Total Giving: Contributes through corporate direct giving program and foundation. Company does not disclose contributions figures.
Assets: $21,724,004 (1997)

Typical Recipients

Arts & Humanities: Arts Associations & Councils, Arts Funds, Community Arts, Dance, Ethnic & Folk Arts, Historic Preservation, Libraries, Museums/Galleries, Music, Performing Arts, Public Broadcasting, Theater
Civic & Public Affairs: Business/Free Enterprise, Economic Development, Law & Justice, Municipalities/Towns, Professional & Trade Associations, Public Policy, Safety, Urban & Community Affairs, Women's Affairs, Zoos/Aquariums
Education: Colleges & Universities, Community & Junior Colleges, Economic Education, Literacy, Minority Education

Environment: Environment-General
Health: Health Organizations, Hospitals, Medical Research, Mental Health, Single-Disease Health Associations
Science: Scientific Organizations
Social Services: Child Welfare, Community Centers, Community Service Organizations, Delinquency & Criminal Rehabilitation, Family Services, People with Disabilities, Refugee Assistance, Senior Services, Substance Abuse, United Funds/United Ways, Volunteer Services, Youth Organizations

Contributions Analysis

Giving Priorities: Civic affairs, higher education, health, science, social service, elderly, and united funds.
Note: Former giving priorities are listed above. The company reports that it is currently undergoing an evaluation to determine future funding priorities.

Application Procedures

Initial Contact: Submit a letter and proposal.
Application Requirements: Include a description of organization; amount requested; purpose; recently audited financial statement; proof of tax-exempt status; list of officers and directors; and list of past contributors.
Deadlines: By July for following year's budget.

Restrictions

Does not support dinners or special events, fraternal organizations, individuals, political or lobbying groups, or religious organizations for sectarian purposes.

Corporate Officials

Robert W. Harvey: vice chairman, executive vice president, chief financial officer PRIM CORP EMPL vice chairman: Reliant Energy Inc.
Lee W. Hogan: vice chairman, executive vice president PRIM CORP EMPL vice chairman, executive vice president: Reliant Energy Inc.
R. Steve Letbetter: chairman, president, chief executive officer PRIM CORP EMPL chairman, president, chief executive officer: Reliant Energy Inc.
Stephen W. Naeve: vice chairman, executive vice president, chief financial officer PRIM CORP EMPL vice chairman, executive vice president, chief financial officer: Reliant Energy Inc.
Donald D. Sykora: director B Stamford, TX 1930. ED University of Houston BBA (1957); South Texas College of Law JD (1969). PRIM CORP EMPL director: TransTexas Corp. CORP AFFIL director: Pool Energy Services Co.; director: Powell Industries Inc.

Giving Program Officials

Robert Gibbs: PRIM CORP EMPL director corporate & community relations: Reliant Energy Inc.

RELIANT ENERGY MINNEGASCO

Company Contact

Minneapolis, MN

Company Description

Employees: 470
SIC(s): 4911 Electric Services.
Parent Company: Diversified Energies, Inc., United States

Nonmonetary Support

Value: $10,000 (1996); $185,000 (1992); $3,500 (1990)
Type: Donated Equipment; In-kind Services; Loaned Employees; Loaned Executives; Workplace Solicitation

Corporate Sponsorship

Value: $12,000
Type: Arts & cultural events; Festivals/fairs
Note: Supports business-related community events.

Giving Contact

Angela Dawson, Communications Administrator
Reliant Energy Minnegasco
800 LaSalle Ave.
PO Box 59038
Minneapolis, MN 55459-0038
Phone: (612)321-4702
Fax: (612)321-5137
Email: Angela_R_Dawson@reliantenergy.com

Alternate Contact

Phone: (612)321-4550
Note: Contact number for guidelines.

Description

Organization Type: Corporate Giving Program
Giving Locations: MN: only within company service areas
Grant Types: Employee Matching Gifts, Fellowship, General Support, Project.
Note: Employee matching gift ratio: 1 to 1 for gifts to public broadcasting and post secondary educational institutions.

Giving Philosophy

'An energy company like Minnegasco can't operate in a vacuum. The health and well-being of our company depends on the health and well-being of our customers - and the community in which they live and work. Each year, we reinvest a fixed percentage of our pretax profits and employee volunteerism efforts in a variety of community building programs.' *Minnegasco, Energy To Build Better Communities*

Financial Summary

Total Giving: $522,000 (2000 approx); $522,000 (1999 approx); $522,000 (1998). Note: Contributes through corporate direct giving program only.

Typical Recipients

Civic & Public Affairs: Environmental Affairs (General), Housing, Urban & Community Affairs
Education: Engineering/Technological Education, Environmental Education
Environment: Environment-General
Social Services: Community Service Organizations, United Funds/United Ways

Contributions Analysis

Giving Priorities: United funds and youth groups, higher education in Minnesota and neighboring states, the arts, and community development.
Civic & Public Affairs: 50% to 55%. Majority of funds are committed to the United Way and the Salvation Army's HeatShare program. The remainder is targeted to major arts programs in the Twin Cities metro area and nonprofit organizations whose boards are served by Minnegasco executives. (Housing & Neighborhood Revitalization) About 25%. Funds organizations that build, develop, and revitalize affordable, energy-efficient housing, and programs that educate homeowners on energy conservation.
Education: 10% to 15%. Goal is to expand opportunities for technical and environmental education. Supports scholarship programs in math, science, and environmental programs at numerous colleges, universities, and technical schools in service area.
Environment: 10% to 15%. Goal is to promote a cleaner, safer environment. Supports environmental programs and initiatives that address public policy and advocacy, as well as education and awareness.

Application Procedures

Initial Contact: call or write for guidelines and Minnesota Common Grant Application Form, then full proposal
Application Requirements: completed application form, including the following attachments: financial statements from most recent fiscal year; organization and project budgets; list of solicited funding sources, including dollar amounts and whether funds are committed, pending, or anticipated; list of board members and affiliations; one-paragraph description of key staff, including qualifications relevant to specific request; copy of current IRS determination letter indicating tax-exempt status
Deadlines: August 5; for discretionary funds: March 15, July 15, and November 15
Review Process: preliminary review made by the Communications Department to determine which proposals meet guidelines; board meets in October
Evaluative Criteria: the extent to which the program furthers the objectives of Minnegasco's charitable contributions program; the capacity of the applicant to enact the proposed program and achieve the desired results, sustain program, and evaluate results; track record of achieving results; community support; fiscal stability; volunteer opportunities for employees, and current employee involvement; need for company's technical and professional support
Decision Notification: applicants are notified November 30
Notes: Organizations that are not sure if they meet requirements are encouraged to send a preliminary letter of inquiry.

Restrictions

No grants are made for programs or organizations outside the Minnegasco geographic service territory, religious or political purposes, individuals, travel, conferences, fundraising activities, multiyear requests (except in special circumstances), national fund drives, or athletic programs.

Additional Information

Contributions solely intended for capital campaigns, endowments, contingencies, reserve purposes or deficit financing are not normally favored.
Pledges are made for one year at a time.
Contributions to organizations supported by the United Way or similar groups will only be considered for a specific program not funded by the umbrella organization.
Discretionary Funds are awarded on a first-come, first-served basis until funds are depleted. An employee committee reviews proposals three times a year.
Publications: Application Form; Guidelines; Annual Report

Corporate Officials

Angela Dawson: communications administration PRIM CORP EMPL communications administration: Minnegasco.

Giving Program Officials

Patty Peterson: PRIM CORP EMPL communications assistant: Minnegasco.

Grants Analysis

Disclosure Period: calendar year ending 1997
Total Grants: $522,000
Number of Grants: 46
Average Grant: $8,711*
Highest Grant: $130,000
Typical Range: $1,000 to $10,000
***Note:** Average grant figure excludes highest grant.

RELIASTAR FINANCIAL CORP.

Company Contact

Minneapolis, MN
Web: http://www.reliastar.com

Company Description

Former Name: Northwestern National Life Insurance Co.
Assets: US$24,926,900,000 (1999)
Profit: US$253,600,000 (1999)
Employees: 3,467
Fortune Rank: 500, per FORTUNE Magazine's list of 500 Largest U.S. Corporations (1999).
FF 500
SIC(s): 6311 Life Insurance.

SUBSIDIARY COMPANIES

VA: ReliaStar/United Services Life Co., Arlington

Nonmonetary Support

Value: $205,000 (1994); $150,000 (1993); $60,000 (1992)
Type: Donated Equipment; In-kind Services; Loaned Employees; Loaned Executives
Volunteer Programs: ReliaStar offers employees a variety of opportunities to volunteer their time and talents to help others in the community. These programs include tutoring, food and clothing distribution, and community cleanup.
Note: Nonmonetary support is provided by company. A limited amount of cause-related marketing & promotion is available. Workplace solicitation is for United Way only.

Corporate Sponsorship

Type: Sports events
Note: Sponsors men's and women's collegiate sports.

ReliaStar Foundation

Giving Contact

Teresa K. Egge, Community Relations & Reliastar Foundation Director
ReliaStar Financial Corp.
20 Washington Avenue South
Minneapolis, MN 55401
Phone: (612)342-7443
Fax: (612)342-3578
Email: terry.egge@reliastar.com

Description

Organization Type: Corporate Foundation
Giving Locations: near headquarters and subsidiaries, and to a limited number of national organizations in health fields.
Grant Types: Capital, Conference/Seminar, Employee Matching Gifts, Endowment, General Support, Matching, Multiyear/Continuing Support, Scholarship.
Note: Employee matching gift ratio: 2 to 1 for the first $200. Research grants are limited.

Giving Philosophy

'The Priorities of the ReliaStar Foundation reflect the current needs of our communities as they coincide with the interests of the company.' The primary focus of the foundation is support of the school-to-work transition programs for high school students. 'Under the affiliate programs, contributions are made to nonprofit organizations in the broad categories of Education, Urban and Civic Affairs, Health, and Culture, with priority given to Youth and Education issues.' Reliastar Grant Application Guidelines

Financial Summary

Total Giving: $3,500,000 (2000 approx); $3,500,000 (1999 approx); $2,500,000 (1997 approx). Note: Contributes through corporate direct giving program and foundation.

Typical Recipients

Arts & Humanities: Museums/Galleries, Music, Performing Arts, Public Broadcasting
Civic & Public Affairs: Economic Development, Employment/Job Training, Urban & Community Affairs, Women's Affairs
Education: Business Education, Colleges & Universities, Community & Junior Colleges, Economic Education, Elementary Education (Private), Literacy, Minority Education, Public Education (Precollege)
Health: Health Funds
Social Services: United Funds/United Ways

Contributions Analysis

Giving Priorities: Focus on economic independence and affordable housing in communities where the company operates. Also supports preschool through higher education, United Way, urban and civic organizations, wellness programs, and the arts.
Arts & Humanities: 5% to 10%. Priority given to organizations providing free or subsidized access to low-income people, the elderly, or school children. Primary recipients include museums, the performing arts,and public broadcasting.
Civic & Public Affairs: (United Funds & United Way) 20% to 25%. Supports the United Way in communities with significant numbers of employees. 5% to 10%. Funds a wide range of activities including youth, self-sufficiency, strengthening families, housing, job development, youth, community service,economic development, and minority affairs.
Education: 55% to 60%. Supports preschool through higher education in the areas of business, economics, and minority education. Priority is given to programs supporting youth, women, people of color, disabled people, and people of low income. Focuses on preparing young people for the workforce. Also offers a matching gift program for post-secondary education and a scholarship program for dependents of employees.
Health: 5% to 10%. Supports basic health care for low-income people, drug and alcohol rehabilitation; services for the physically, mentally, and emotionally challenged; and wellness, health, and nutrition for the elderly, children, and teen mothers.

Application Procedures

Initial Contact: Call or write for guidelines; then submit a written proposal.
Application Requirements: Include a cover letter of no more than 3 pages, outlining history and description of the organization; its mission, goals and objectives; amount requested; purpose for which funds are sought; method for evaluating the outcome of the project; information, attached as appendices, should include: recently audited financial statement; copy of tax-exempt status letter; list of board members; other sources of secured and pending funding and amounts; resume of executive director; current budget, including sources of revenue and expenses; and a recent annual report.
Deadlines: None.
Evaluative Criteria: Considerations include: the management and fiscal capability to carry out the program for which funds were requested; the objectives of the program; and the extent to which the request is consistent with the foundation's priorities.
Notes: Requests for nonmonetary support and volunteers have special requirements. Contact foundation for more information. See Additional Information on where to submit requests for Washington, Virginia and New York areas.

Restrictions

Does not support dinners or special events; fraternal, social, or labor organizations; goodwill advertising; individuals; political or lobbying groups, trips, benefits, performances, or fundraising activities; conferences (unless meeting directly addresses company's giving priorities); or religious organizations for sectarian purposes. In health, does not support hospitals, capital drives, research, or single-disease health associations.

The company funds causes only in its immediate operating areas. funds causes only in its immediate operating areas.

Additional Information

The Northwestern National Life Foundation was established in 1991. Its focus is on education and youth, particularly in the areas of school reform, workforce readiness, and learning readiness.
The ReliaStar Financial Corporation was formerly known as the Northwestern National Life Insurance Company.
Submit requests in Arlington, Virginia to: United Services Life, David Roe, Chief Executive Officer, 4601 Fairfax Drive, Arlington, Virginia 22203.
For Seattle Washington: Northern Life, Barb Rochon, Corporate Contribution Coordinator, 1110 Third Avenue, Seattle, Washington 98101.
For Woodbury, New York: Bankers Security Life, David Sloan, Executive Vice President and Chief Operating Officer, 1000 Woodbury Road, Suite 102, Woodbury, New York 11797.
Publications: Guidelines

Corporate Officials

Teresa K. Egge: director community relationsrc PRIM CORP EMPL director community relations: ReliaStar Financial Corp.
Susan W. A. Mead: vice president B White Plains, NY 1950. ED University of Minnesota (1976); College of Saint Thomas (1977). PRIM CORP EMPL vice president: ReliaStar Financial Corp. NONPR AFFIL member: Life Community Association.
Robert C. Solipante: senior vice president PRIM CORP EMPL senior vice president: ReliaStar Financial Corp.
John Gosney Turner: chairman, chief executive officer, director B Springfield, MA 1939. ED Amherst College BA (1961). PRIM CORP EMPL chairman, chief executive officer, director: ReliaStar Financial Corp. CORP AFFIL director: Washington Square Capital Inc.; chairman, chief executive officer, director: ReliaStar Life Insurance Co.; chairman: ReliaStar United Services Life Insurance Co.; chairman: ReliaStar Bankers Security Life Insurance Co.; director: Northern Life Insurance Co.; director: Northstar Investment Management Corp. NONPR AFFIL director: Health Insurance Association America; director: Life & Health Insurance Medical Research Fund; director: Carlson School of Management; chairman: American Council Life Insurance.

Foundation Officials

Michael Dubes: membership B Dubuque, IA 1942. ED Iowa State University BS (1966); American College MS (1981); Harvard University (1987). CORP AFFIL chairman: NWNL Management Corp. NONPR AFFIL member: National Association Life Underwriters; member enterprise council management committee: Northern Life; member: Gen Agents & Managers Association; member: Life Insurance Marketing & Research Association; director: Boys & Girls Clubs Minneapolis; member: Certified Fin Planner; member: American Society Chartered Life Underwriters; member: Agency Offs Round Table. CLUB AFFIL Rotary Club; Variety Iowa Club; Interlochen Country Club; Metro Breakfast Club; Harvard Business School Minnesota Club.
Teresa K. Egge: director (see above)
Dewey Ingham: membership
Susan W. A. Mead: director (see above)
John Gosney Turner: director (see above)
Ruth Weber-Kelley: membership

Grants Analysis

Disclosure Period: calendar year ending
Typical Range: $1,000 to $5,000

Revlon Inc.

Company Contact

New York, NY

Company Description

Employees: 14,300
SIC(s): 2844 Toilet Preparations, 5122 Drugs, Proprietaries & Sundries.
Parent Company: MacAndrews & Forbes Holdings Inc., New York, NY, United States

Nonmonetary Support

Type: Donated Products

Corporate Sponsorship

Note: Sponsors women's cancer clinics and research programs via events such as the Fire & Ice Ball and the Revlon Run/Walk for Women.

Revlon Foundation Inc.

Giving Contact

Joan Horton, Corporate Events
Revlon, Inc.
625 Madison Avenue
New York, NY 10022
Phone: (212)527-5000
Fax: (212)527-6977

Alternate Contact

Revlon Foundation, Inc.,
35 East 62nd Street
New York, NY 10021

Description

Founded: 1955
EIN: 136126130
Organization Type: Corporate Foundation. Supports preselected organizations only.
Giving Locations: headquarters and operating communities; nationally.
Grant Types: Employee Matching Gifts, General Support, Project.

Giving Philosophy

'Revlon is the world's best known brand of cosmetics and personal care products. Beyond external beauty, Revlon is concerned about women's lives and well-being and has dedicated both support and financial resources to critical health issues, including breast and ovarian cancer, skin cancer, fertility and AIDs.'

Financial Summary

Total Giving: $5,066,897 (1998); $3,414,613 (1997); $4,033,732 (1996). Note: Contributes through corporate direct giving program and foundation.
Giving Analysis: Giving for 1995 includes: foundation matching gifts ($44,626); 1996: foundation matching gifts ($57,162); 1997: foundation matching gifts ($62,613);
Assets: $0 (1998); $5,985 (1997); $80,886 (1996)
Gifts Received: $4,793,425 (1998); $3,421,758 (1997); $4,033,757 (1996). Note: Gifts are received from Revlon Group Inc.

Typical Recipients

Arts & Humanities: Arts Centers, History & Archaeology, Libraries, Museums/Galleries, Music, Performing Arts, Public Broadcasting, Theater
Civic & Public Affairs: African American Affairs, Civic & Public Affairs-General, Philanthropic Organizations, Public Policy, Urban & Community Affairs, Women's Affairs
Education: Business Education, Colleges & Universities, Education Funds, Medical Education, Minority Education, Private Education (Precollege), Religious Education, Science/Mathematics Education, Social Sciences Education, Student Aid
Health: AIDS/HIV, Cancer, Clinics/Medical Centers, Hospitals, Single-Disease Health Associations
International: Foreign Educational Institutions, International Development, International Organizations
Religion: Jewish Causes, Religious Organizations, Religious Welfare, Synagogues/Temples
Social Services: Community Service Organizations, People with Disabilities, Shelters/Homelessness, United Funds/United Ways, Volunteer Services, YMCA/YWCA/YMHA/YWHA

Contributions Analysis

Giving Priorities: Primarily higher education; also health organizations, performing arts, and minority causes.
Arts & Humanities: 2%. Supports a performing arts center.
Civic & Public Affairs: 3%. Gives to African-American affairs groups and to urban affairs.
Education: 83%. Supports colleges and universities. Matching grants also are made in the area of education.
Health: 12%. Support goes to medical centers.
Note: Total contributions made in 1997.

Corporate Officials

Ronald H. Dunbar: senior vice president human resources, director B 1938. PRIM CORP EMPL senior vice president human resources, director: Revlon Inc. ADD CORP EMPL vice president human resources: Revlon Consumer Products Corp.; senior vice president: Revlon Holdings Inc.
William J. Fox: executive vice president, chief financial officer B 1957. PRIM CORP EMPL executive vice president, chief financial officer: Revlon Inc. ADD CORP EMPL chief financial officer: Revlon International Corp.; executive vice president, chief financial officer: Revlon Consumer Products Corp.; executive vice president, chief financial officer: Revlon Holdings Inc.
Joan Horton: corporate events PRIM CORP EMPL corporate events: Revlon Inc.
Wade Hampton Nichols, III: executive vice president, general counsel B Bronxville, NY 1942. ED Yale University BA (1964); Columbia University LLB (1967). PRIM CORP EMPL executive vice president, general counsel: Revlon Inc. ADD CORP EMPL executive vice president, general counsel: MacAndrews & Forbes Holdings Inc.; executive vice president, general counsel: Revlon Consumer Products Corp.; senior vice president, general counsel: Revlon Holdings Inc.
Bruce Slovin: president, director B New York, NY 1935. ED Cornell University BA (1957); Harvard University Law School JD (1960). PRIM CORP EMPL president, director: MacAndrews & Forbes Holdings ADD CORP EMPL president, director: MacAndrews & Forbes Group Inc.; president, chief operating officer, director: Revlon Group Inc. CORP AFFIL director: Oak Hill Sportswear Corp.; chairman executive committee: Revlon Inc.; officer: Meridian Sports Inc.; director: Moore Medical Corp.; director: Four Star International Inc.; director: Gulf Resources & Chemical Corp.; vice chairman: Andrews Group Inc.; director: Cantel Industries Inc.

Foundation Officials

James T. Conroy: senior vice president
Carl J. Deddens: vice president, treasurer
Anna Marie Dellafave: assistant secretary
Ronald H. Dunbar: vice president (see above)
William J. Fox: senior vice president (see above)
Howard Gittis: director B Philadelphia, PA 1934. ED University of Pennsylvania BS (1955); University of Pennsylvania School of Law LLB (1958). PRIM CORP EMPL vice chairman, chief administrative officer: MacAndrews & Forbes Holdings Inc. ADD CORP EMPL vice chairman: Andrews Group Inc.; vice chairman: Consolidated Cigar Holdings; director: MacAndrews & Forbes Group Inc.; vice chairman: Mafco Consolidated Group Inc. CORP AFFIL director: RGI Group Inc.; director: Sunbeam Corp.; director: Revlon Holdings Inc.; director: Revlon Inc.; director: New World Television; director: Revlon Consumer Products Corp.; director: Jones Apparel Group Inc.; director: Loral Space & Communications Ltd.
Richard E. Halperin: president B New York, NY 1954. ED Boston University BS (1976); New England School of Law JD (1979). PRIM CORP EMPL executive vice president, special counsel to chairman: MacAndrews & Forbes Group Inc. ADD CORP EMPL executive vice president, special counsel to chairman: Revlon Group Inc. CORP AFFIL president: ROP Aviation.
Gerry Roth Kessel: assistant treasurer
Robert K. Kretzman: vice president, secretary PRIM CORP EMPL vice president, secretary, deputy general counseling: Revlon Inc.
Wade Hampton Nichols, III: vice president (see above)
Ronald Owen Perelman: director B Greensboro, NC 1943. ED University of Pennsylvania BA (1964); University of Pennsylvania Wharton School MBA (1966). PRIM CORP EMPL chairman, president, chief executive officer, director: Revlon Group Inc. ADD CORP EMPL chairman board: Andrews Group Inc.; president: First Nationwide Holdings Inc.; chairman: MacAndrews & Forbes Group Inc.; chairman, chief executive officer, director: McAndrews & Forbes Holdings Inc.; chairman: RGI Group Inc.; chairman: Revlon Inc.; chairman: Revlon International Corp.; director: Revlon Consumer Products Corp.; chairman: Revlon Holdings Inc. CORP AFFIL chief executive officer: Meridian Sport Holdings DE Corp.; chairman: National Health Laboratories Inc.; chairman: Mafco Consolidated Group Inc.; chairman, chief executive officer, director: Mafco Holdings Inc.
Hope Grittis Sheft: vice president

Grants Analysis

Disclosure Period: calendar year ending 1997
Total Grants: $3,352,000*
Number of Grants: 15
Average Grant: $223,467
Highest Grant: $1,250,000
Typical Range: $1,000 to $400,000
***Note:** Giving excludes matching gifts.

Recent Grants

Note: Grants derived from 1997 Form 990.

Arts & Humanities

50,000	Kennedy Center for the Performing Arts, Washington, DC

Civic & Public Affairs

30,000	NAACP, New York, NY
20,000	National Urban League, New York, NY

Education

1,250,000	University of California Los Angeles, Los Angeles, CA
1,125,000	Princeton University, Princeton, NJ -- support for Judaic Studies
200,000	Columbia University Business School, New York, NY
75,000	Spence School, New York, NY
60,000	Princeton University, Princeton, NJ -- support Judaic Studies
50,000	Park East Day School, New York, NY
50,000	United Negro College Fund, New York, NY
25,000	Spence School, New York, NY
5,000	National Hispanic Scholarship Fund, Novato, CA

Health

400,000	New York Hospital Cornell Medical Center, New York, NY
10,000	John F. Kennedy Medical Center, Edison, NJ

Religion
2,000 Hillel, New York, NY

Reynolds Metals Co.

Company Contact
Richmond, VA
Web: http://www.rmc.com

Company Description
Revenue: US$4,796,000,000 (1999)
Profit: US$124,000,000 (1999)
Employees: 7,544
Fortune Rank: 335, per FORTUNE Magazine's list of 500 Largest U.S. Corporations (1999).
FF 335
SIC(s): 2819 Industrial Inorganic Chemicals Nec, 2869 Industrial Organic Chemicals Nec, 2899 Chemical Preparations Nec, 3334 Primary Aluminum.

Operating Locations
Operates internationally in Australia, Europe, Central and South America, Bermuda, Canada, Jamaica, and the Philippines.

Nonmonetary Support
Type: Donated Equipment
Note: The company donates equipment and scrap metal.

Reynolds Metals Co. Foundation

Giving Contact
Linda E. Fowler, Administrator
Reynolds Metals Co. Foundation
6601 West Broad Street
Richmond, VA 23230
Phone: (804)281-2222
Fax: (804)281-4160

Description
EIN: 541084698
Organization Type: Corporate Foundation
Giving Locations: headquarters and operating communities.
Grant Types: Award, General Support, Multiyear/Continuing Support, Project.

Giving Philosophy
'Purpose and Objectives: to support the maintenance or improvement of the quality of life in the geographic areas served by the Foundation; to support the initiation of or sustain organizations whose principles and purposes coincide with goals of the Foundation; and to gain proper recognition for the Foundation's contributions from the organizations being supported.' Reynolds Metals Company Foundation Policies and Guidelines

Financial Summary
Total Giving: $770,025 (1998); $1,031,478 (1997); $969,040 (1996). Note: Contributes through corporate direct giving program and foundation.
Giving Analysis: Giving for 1996 includes: foundation ($518,760); foundation matching gifts ($271,073); foundation grants to United Way ($179,207); 1997: foundation ($855,971); foundation matching gifts ($279,003); foundation grants to United Way ($175,507); 1998: foundation matching gifts ($387,093); foundation ($243,700); foundation grants to United Way ($139,232)
Assets: $13,902,432 (1999); $14,067,807 (1998); $13,436,011 (1997)
Gifts Received: $638,000 (1996)

Typical Recipients
Arts & Humanities: Arts Associations & Councils, Arts Centers, Arts Festivals, History & Archaeology, Libraries, Museums/Galleries, Music, Opera, Performing Arts, Public Broadcasting, Theater
Civic & Public Affairs: African American Affairs, Botanical Gardens/Parks, Business/Free Enterprise, Economic Development, Economic Policy, Civic & Public Affairs-General, Housing, Municipalities/Towns, Philanthropic Organizations, Professional & Trade Associations, Public Policy, Safety, Urban & Community Affairs, Zoos/Aquariums
Education: Business Education, Colleges & Universities, Community & Junior Colleges, Economic Education, Education Associations, Education Funds, Education Reform, Elementary Education (Private), Engineering/Technological Education, Minority Education, Private Education (Precollege), Public Education (Precollege), Science/Mathematics Education, Secondary Education (Public), Student Aid
Environment: Environment-General, Wildlife Protection
Health: Children's Health/Hospitals, Emergency/Ambulance Services, Hospitals, Medical Rehabilitation, Medical Research, Public Health, Single-Disease Health Associations, Transplant Networks/Donor Banks
International: Health Care/Hospitals
Religion: Religious Organizations, Religious Welfare
Science: Science Museums, Scientific Centers & Institutes
Social Services: Child Welfare, Community Service Organizations, Day Care, Domestic Violence, Food/Clothing Distribution, People with Disabilities, Recreation & Athletics, Scouts, Shelters/Homelessness, Substance Abuse, United Funds/United Ways, YMCA/YWCA/YMHA/YWHA, Youth Organizations

Contributions Analysis
Giving Priorities: Education, social welfare, civic concerns, hospitals, health foundations, single disease health associations, and the arts.
Arts & Humanities: 14%. Supports museums, symphonies, opera, historical societies, and public broadcasting.
Civic & Public Affairs: 6%. Supports economic development, safety, and urban affairs.
Education: 50%. Major support goes to colleges and universities with strong business, science, and engineering programs, and to middle and secondary schools and organizations which demonstrate initiative in preparing and recruiting quality students for those career tracks. The foundation sponsors a matching gifts program for graduate or professional schools, four-year colleges, two-year junior or community colleges, and independent and public secondary schools.
Health: 2%. Primary interest is the American Red Cross and hospitals.
Social Services: 27%. Major support for the United Way; also YMCAs.
Note: Total contributions in 1998.

Application Procedures
Initial Contact: Request guidelines, then written proposal.
Application Requirements: Organization's purpose, history of achievement, description of program activities and goals for current year, IRS determination letter, current budget information showing income and expenditures, list of board of directors, use for requested funds.
Deadlines: October 1.
Evaluative Criteria: Organization is tax-exempt; request is within scope of contributions policy; addresses priority area; provides needed service to wide segment of population; sound, well-developed program answering need in designated area; current activities of organization further stated objectives and aims; good reputation in community; efficient and honest management, active board, and competent leadership; strong financial status; reasonable fund-raising and administrative expenses; nonduplication of services already funded; degree of corporate and community support; interest of civic and business leaders.

Restrictions
Foundation generally does not support causes and organizations outside communities in which Reynolds operates; religious organizations for sectarian purposes; veterans, fraternal, or similar organizations, unless contribution will benefit entire community; conferences, trips, or tours; operating expenses of member agencies of united funds; advertising, tickets, or tables for benefits; public or private preschool and primary educational institutions; duplicated funds during the same year; athletics, athletic clubs, or athletic scholarships; or organizations acting as fundraising agents for others (excluding United Way). Foundation will make no contributions to political or lobbying groups, or to individuals. athletic clubs, or athletic scholarships; or organizations acting as fundraising agents for others (excluding United Way). Foundation will make no contributions to political or lobbying groups, or to individuals.

Additional Information
Publications: Policies and Guidelines; Application Form

Corporate Officials
D. Michael Jones: senior vice president, general counselc B Smithfield, NC 1953. ED University of North Carolina BA (1975); University of North Carolina JD (1978). PRIM CORP EMPL senior vice president, general counsel: Reynolds Metals Co. ADD CORP EMPL vice president, general couns, director: Bakers Choice Products Inc.; vice president: Reynolds Aluminum Deutschland. NONPR AFFIL member: Association General Counsel; member: Washington Society CPA's; member: American Corp. Counsel Association.
Randolph Nicklas Reynolds: vice chairman, executive officer, director B Louisville, KY 1941. ED Bellarmine College BA (1966); University of Louisville (1967-1968). PRIM CORP EMPL vice chairman, executive officer, director: Reynolds Metals Co. ADD CORP EMPL president, director: Malakoff Industries Inc.; president: Reynolds International Inc.; president: Reynolds Wheels International. CORP AFFIL president, director: Reynolds International Service Co.; director: First Union Corp.; chairman: Ramco Manufacturing Co.; director: Dominion National Bank; director: Eskimo Pie Corp.; director: Dominion Bankshares Corp. NONPR AFFIL member: Virginia Commonwealth Foundation.
William Gray Reynolds, Jr.: vice president government relations & public affairs B New York, NY 1939. ED University of Pennsylvania BA (1962); University of Virginia JD (1965). PRIM CORP EMPL vice president government relations & public affairs: Reynolds Metals Co. CORP AFFIL director: Wachovia Corp.
Henry S. Savedge, Jr.: executive vice president, chief financial officer, director B Dendron, VA 1933. ED University of Richmond BS (1955); Stanford University (1984). PRIM CORP EMPL executive vice president, chief financial officer, director: Reynolds Metals Co. ADD CORP EMPL chief financial officer, executive vice president, director: Bakers Choice Products Inc.; chief financial officer: RMC Properties Ltd.

Foundation Officials
Janice M. Bailey: vice president
Donna C. Dabney: secretary B Watseka, IL 1947. ED Southern Illinois University (1969); University of Virginia (1980). PRIM CORP EMPL secretary, assistant general counsel: Reynolds Metals Co. ADD CORP EMPL secretary: Reynolds International Inc.;

secretary: Reynolds Aluminum Deutschland. NONPR AFFIL member: American Corporate Counsel Association; member: American Society of Corporate Secretaries; member: American Bar Association.
Carol L. Dillon: assistant secretary PRIM CORP EMPL assistant general counsel, chief litigation counsel: Reynolds Metals Co.
Douglas M. Jerrold: vice president B Brooklyn, NY 1950. ED Hamilton College (1972); Rutgers University (1973). PRIM CORP EMPL vice president tax affairs: Reynolds Metals Co.
D. Michael Jones: vice president, director (see above)
Randolph Nicklas Reynolds: director (see above)
William Gray Reynolds, Jr.: director (see above)
D. Brickford Rider: president
Henry S. Savedge, Jr.: executive vice president, director (see above)
Jeremiah J. Sheehan: chairman, director B New York, NY 1938. ED Hunter College BA; University of Chicago. PRIM CORP EMPL chairman, chief executive officer, director: Reynolds Metals Co. ADD CORP EMPL president: Latas De Aluminio Reynolds; chairman: Reynolds International Inc. CORP AFFIL director: Universal Corp.; director: International Paper Co.; director: Union Camp Corp.; director: Federation Reserve Bank Richmond. NONPR AFFIL director, trustee: Virginia Commonwealth University School Engineering Foundation; member board trustees: Virginia Foundation Independent Colleges; member advisory council: University Richmond Claiborne Robins School Business; member: Virginia Business Council; member: Richmond Management Roundtable; director: Richmond Met Coalition Against Drugs; trustee: Conference Board; member: Advisory Council Rev Estimates State Virginia; member: Business Roundtable.
Julian Howard Taylor: vice president, treasurer, director B Emporia, KS 1943. ED Earlham College (1961-1962); Emporia State University BA (1965); Iowa State University PhD (1969). PRIM CORP EMPL vice president, treasurer: Reynolds Metals Co. ADD CORP EMPL treasurer: RMC Properties Ltd.; treasurer: Reynolds International; treasurer: Reynolds Aluminum Deutschland Inc. CORP AFFIL treasurer, director: Southern Graphics System Inc.
J. Wilt Wagner: director B 1942. ED University of Florida BS (1963); Richmond College MA Comm (1970).

Grants Analysis

Disclosure Period: calendar year ending 1998
Total Grants: $243,700*
Number of Grants: 69
Average Grant: $3,532
Highest Grant: $60,000
Typical Range: $1,000 to $25,000
***Note:** Giving excludes matching gifts; United Way.

Recent Grants

Note: Grants derived from 1998 Form 990.

Arts & Humanities

10,000	Virginia Historical Society, Richmond, VA
5,000	Richmond Symphony, Richmond, VA
5,000	Theatre Virginia, Richmond, VA
5,000	Virginia Museum of Fine Arts, Richmond, VA
5,000	Virginia Opera, Richmond, VA
1,500	South Texas Public Broadcasting System, Inc., Corpus Christi, TX

Civic & Public Affairs

25,000	Richmond Riverfront Development Corporation, Richmond, VA
10,000	Lewis Ginter Botanical Garden, Richmond, VA
10,000	Maymont Foundation, Richmond, VA
5,000	Metropolitan Business Foundation, Richmond, VA -- (MAPS Program)
5,000	The Richmond Forum, Richmond, VA
2,000	Financial Accounting Foundation, Hartford, CT
2,000	Foundation for Public Affairs, Washington, DC

Education

25,000	Virginia Foundation for Independent Colleges, Richmond, VA
16,000	Reynolds School District, Troutdale, OR -- (Scholarship, Excellence in Education)
12,000	Students in Free Enterprise, Springfield, MO
10,000	Longview Independent School District, Longview, WA -- (Longview Reduction)
5,000	Clarkson University - American Indian Program, Potsdam, NY -- (St. Lawrence Reduction)
5,000	The College Fund/UNCF, Fairfax, VA
5,000	Junior Achievement of Central Virginia, Inc., Richmond, VA
5,000	Virginia Council on Economic Education, Richmond, VA
3,500	Richmond Area Program for Minorities in Engineering Virginia State University, Petersburg, VA
2,500	The Virginia College Fund, Richmond, VA
2,170	Goza Junior High & Arkadelphia High Schools, Arkadelphia, AR -- (Excellence in Education - Gum Springs)
1,800	Peake Elementary School, Arkadelphia, AR -- (Excellence in Education - Gum Springs)
1,405	Massena Central School, Massena, NY -- (Excellence in Education - Massena)
1,200	Junior Achievement of South Texas, San Antonio, TX

Environment

11,000	Keep America Beautiful, Stamford, CT

Health

5,000	American Red Cross, Washington, DC
5,000	American Red Cross, Greater Richmond Chapter, Richmond, VA
5,000	Hospital Hospitality House, Inc., Richmond, VA

Science

50,000	Science Museum of Virginia Foundation, Richmond, VA

Social Services

60,000	United Way Services, Richmond, VA
50,000	YMCA of Greater Richmond, Richmond, VA
18,000	United Way of Shoals, Florence, AL
14,000	United Way of Cowlitz County, Longview, WA -- (Longview Reduction)
10,250	Metro United Way, Louisville, KY -- (Louisville 1, 15 and Louisville Laminating)
8,000	United Way of Coastal Bend, Corpus Christi, TX
6,000	United Way of Southwest Louisiana, Lake Charles, IL
5,850	United Way of St. Lawrence County, Ogdensburg, NY -- (St. Lawrence Reduction)
5,000	Metro Richmond Coalition Against Drugs, Richmond, VA
3,600	Stateline United Way, Beloit, MI -- (Beloit Plant)
3,100	United Way of Columbia-Willamette, Portland, OR -- (Troutdale)
2,750	United Way of DeKalb County, Auburn, IN
2,500	Alabama Child Caring Foundation, Birmingham, AL
2,500	YMCA of the Colombia-Willamette, Portland, OR
2,000	Metro United Way, Louisville, KY -- (Southern Graphics)
2,000	United Way of Clark County, Arkadelphia, AR -- (Gum Springs)
1,800	United Way of Franklin County, Malone, NY -- (St. Lawrence)
1,632	United Way of Garland County, Hot Springs, AR -- (Hot Springs)

REYNOLDS &REYNOLDS CO.

Company Contact

Dayton, OH
Web: http://www.reyrey.com

Company Description

Revenue: US$1,563,000,000 (1999)
Employees: 9,083 (1999)
SIC(s): 2752 Commercial Printing--Lithographic, 3571 Electronic Computers, 8299 Schools & Educational Services Nec.

Nonmonetary Support

Type: Donated Equipment; In-kind Services; Loaned Executives; Workplace Solicitation
Note: Nonmonetary support is provided by the company.

Corporate Sponsorship

Value: $5,000
Type: Arts & cultural events
Note: Sponsors health and human services fundraising events, banquets, and dinners.

Reynolds & Reynolds Co. Foundation

Giving Contact

Alice Davisson, Administrator
Reynolds & Reynolds Co. Foundation
PO Box 2608
Dayton, OH 45401
Phone: (937)485-4409
Fax: (937)485-3831

Description

EIN: 311168299
Organization Type: Corporate Foundation
Giving Locations: OH
Grant Types: General Support, Project.
Note: Also supports programs.

Giving Philosophy

'The Reynolds and Reynolds Company has a strong tradition of giving as we carry out our social and economic responsibility to the communities in which we operate. By combining the corporation's resources with the talent and energy of our employees, Reynolds impacts a great number of organizations and programs that meet the communities' growing needs. Our attention is concentrated on promoting a healthy environment and ensuring the quality of life for the people of our communities.' The Reynolds & Reynolds Company Foundation

Financial Summary

Total Giving: $640,000 (fiscal year ending September 30, 2000 approx); $640,000 (fiscal 1999 approx); $638,900 (fiscal 1998). Note: Contributes through corporate direct giving program and foundation. Giving includes foundation.
Assets: $624,535 (fiscal 1998); $1,013,000 (fiscal 1997); $834,546 (fiscal 1996)

Gifts Received: $600,000 (fiscal 1996); $796,431 (fiscal 1995); $800,000 (fiscal 1994). Note: Foundation receives contributions from Reynolds & Reynolds Company.

Typical Recipients

Arts & Humanities: Arts Associations & Councils, Arts Centers, Arts Funds, Arts Institutes, Ballet, Community Arts, Dance, Ethnic & Folk Arts, History & Archaeology, Museums/Galleries, Music, Opera, Performing Arts, Public Broadcasting, Theater, Visual Arts

Civic & Public Affairs: African American Affairs, Botanical Gardens/Parks, Business/Free Enterprise, Clubs, Community Foundations, Economic Development, Employment/Job Training, Civic & Public Affairs-General, Municipalities/Towns, Parades/Festivals, Philanthropic Organizations, Urban & Community Affairs, Women's Affairs

Education: Business Education, Colleges & Universities, Education Funds, Education Reform, Education-General, Literacy, Public Education (Precollege), Secondary Education (Private), Student Aid

Environment: Protection

Health: Arthritis, Cancer, Children's Health/Hospitals, Emergency/Ambulance Services, Health Organizations, Hospices, Trauma Treatment

Science: Science Museums

Social Services: Community Service Organizations, Scouts, Senior Services, United Funds/United Ways, YMCA/YWCA/YMHA/YWHA, Youth Organizations

Contributions Analysis

Giving Priorities: Major emphasis on the arts and social services. Also supports education and civic concerns.

Arts & Humanities: 40% to 45%. Foundation supports a variety of arts and cultural organizations that enrich the quality of life for area residents. Major recipients include the Culture Works, the Dayton Museum of Natural History, and other arts organizations in Dayton, OH.

Civic & Public Affairs: 5% to 10%. Grants encourage strategic community economic development in company's operating areas, including community foundations and the Dayton Urban League.

Education: 10% to 15%. Funding emphasizes support for programs geared toward at-risk children in grades K-12. Foundation allocates funds to educational institutions and nonprofit organizations that help keepchildren in school and prepare them for employment, college, technical training, or the military.

Health: Less than 5%. Supports Hospice of Dayton.

Social Services: 35% to 40%. Majority of support reaches the United Way.

Application Procedures

Initial Contact: Send a brief letter requesting an application form and guidelines.

Application Requirements: Submit a completed grant application, including mission or purpose of the organization; statement of need and a description of how the proposed program will meet that need; goals of program; population served; amount requested and how it will be used; any other sources of funding and amounts; plans for permanent financial support, plans for evaluating and reporting results; if organization has received funds from the foundation previously; and the name of the contact person, along with his or her address and phone number. Include the following attachments: a copy of the organization's 501(c)(3) tax-exemption letter from the IRS and a 509(a)(1) letter, if established prior to 1975; the organization's most recent year-end financial statement; a copy of the organization's current operating budget and current sources of income; the names and occupations of the board of trustees and officers; and the organization's annual report or other relevant publications.

Deadlines: None.

Review Process: Written requests are reviewed by the foundation staff for merit and completeness; acceptable proposals are presented to the foundation's board of trustees for further review; applications are reviewed quarterly.

Evaluative Criteria: Priority is given to socially responsible programs that have an impact upon the local community, and that fit into the total contributions program of the company.

Decision Notification: The foundation's fiscal year begins in October and applications are reviewed quarterly thereafter. The foundation attempts to respond to all grant applications within three months of receipt.

Restrictions

Foundation does not contribute to organizations without tax-exempt status; sectarian organizations having a predominantly religious purpose; individuals; political parties, offices, or candidates; fraternal or veterans' organizations; individual primary or secondary schools; organizations which cannot provide adequate accounting records or procedures; courtesy advertising; tax-supported colleges and universities for operating purposes; funding for deficits or debt retirement; or endowments.

Organizations receiving funds through the United Way generally are not considered for additional gifts towards operations, programs, or capital campaigns. In general, organizations repeating a request in the same fiscal year will not be considered for additional funding. An approved grant does not necessarily indicate that continued support will automatically be available the following year. Grant requests must be resubmitted annually unless otherwise stipulated.

Additional Information

Publications: Foundation Guidelines; Application Form

Corporate Officials

David Richard Holmes: chief executive officer, chief operating officer, directororms B Salt Lake City, UT 1940. ED Stanford University BA (1963); Northwestern University MBA (1965). PRIM CORP EMPL chief executive officer, chief operating officer, director: Reynolds & Reynolds Co. ADD CORP EMPL chairman, chief executive officer, director: Reyna Financial Corp. CORP AFFIL chairman: Station WDPR-FM; director: DPL Inc.; director: NCR Corp.; director: Bank One. NONPR AFFIL co-chairman: Downtown Dayton Partnership; chairman: YMCA; chairman: Dayton Performing Arts Fund; member: Dayton Philharmonic Orchestra Association; member: Dayton Business Committee Area Progress Council; member: Dayton Chamber of Commerce; member: Area Progress Council; member: American Management Association. CLUB AFFIL Dayton Country Club; American Yacht Club.

Dale L. Medford: vice president corporate finance, chief financial officer B Dayton, OH 1950. ED Miami University BS (1972). PRIM CORP EMPL vice president corporate finance, chief financial officer: Reynolds & Reynolds Co. ADD CORP EMPL vice president finance, chief financial officer: Formcraft Inc.; treasurer: Reyna Capital Corp. NONPR AFFIL member: Financial Executives Institute; member: National Investor Relations Institute; member: American Institute CPAs.

Tom Suttmiller: senior vice president auto forms PRIM CORP EMPL senior vice president auto forms: Reynolds & Reynolds Co.

Foundation Officials

Tony Orme: trustee
Cathy Ponitz: trustee
Doug Strasser: trustee
Gillis West: trustee
Mona Yezbak: trustee

Grants Analysis

Disclosure Period: fiscal year ending September 30, 1996
Total Grants: $486,145
Number of Grants: 37
Average Grant: $8,297*
Highest Grant: $187,440
Typical Range: $500 to $20,000
***Note:** Average grant figure excludes highest grant.

Recent Grants

Note: Grants derived from fiscal 1997 Form 990.

Arts & Humanities

15,000	Cultural Works, Dayton, OH
15,000	Dayton Visual Arts, Dayton, OH
12,750	Victoria Theater, Dayton, OH
10,000	Dayton Philharmonic, Dayton, OH
6,500	WPTD/Channel 12/16
2,500	WPTD/Channel 12/16
1,000	Black Cultural Festival

Civic & Public Affairs

20,000	Urban League, Jacksonville, FL
10,000	Celebrate Dayton, Dayton, OH
2,500	LEAD
2,250	Intercart Marketing
1,139	Mercer County Civic Foundation, Celina, OH

Education

31,995	Citizen's Scholarship Fund, Dayton, OH

Environment

2,500	Lead Poisoning

Health

5,000	Hospice, Dayton, OH
2,500	Children's Medical Center, Dayton, OH

Social Services

200,000	United Way, Dayton, OH
10,000	Other Place, Dayton, OH
9,000	United Way, Celina, OH
821	United Way, Hagerstown, MD

R.J. Reynolds Tobacco

Company Contact

401 N. Main St.
Winston-Salem, NC 27101
Phone: (336)741-5000
Fax: (336)741-4238
Web: http://www.rjrt.com

Company Description

Revenue: US$11,394,000,000 (1999)
Profit: US$2,343,000,000 (1999)
Employees: 7,900 (1999)
Fortune Rank: 155, per FORTUNE Magazine's list of 500 Largest U.S. Corporations (1999).
FF 155
SIC(s): 2024 Ice Cream & Frozen Desserts, 2035 Pickles, Sauces & Salad Dressings, 2038 Frozen Specialties Nec, 2043 Cereal Breakfast Foods.
Parent Company: Nabisco Group Holdings, Parsippany, NJ, United States

Operating Locations

Argentina: Nabisco Argentina SA, Buenos Aires; Brazil: Industria e Comercio de Productos Alimenticios Cerqueirense Ltda., Cerqueira Cesar; Iracema Industrias de Caju Ltda., Fortaleza; Gumz Alimentos S/A Industria e Comercio, Jaragua do Sul; Companhia Productos Pilar, Recife; Industrias Alimenticias Maguary SA, Rio de Janeiro; Leite Gloria do Nordeste Ltda., Rio de Janeiro; Produtos Alimenticios Fleischmann & Royal Ltda., Rio de Janeiro; Canada: Nabisco Ltd., Etobicoke; Chile: Nabisco Royal Chile Limitada, Santiago; Colombia: Landers y Cia SA, Medellin, Antioquia; Nabisco Royal Colombiana Inc., Palmira; Costa Rica: Golden SA, San Jose; England: Gem: Global

Event Management Ltd., London; International Nabisco Brands Ltd., London; Guatemala: Dely SA, Guatemala City; Productos Confitados Salvavidas de Guatemala SA, Guatemala City; Hong Kong: Nabisco Hong Kong Ltd., Causeway Bay; R J Reynolds Tobacco International (Hong Kong) Ltd., Wan Chai; RJR Nabisco China Ltd., Wan Chai; Jamaica: West Indies Yeast Co. Ltd., Spanish Town; Japan: R J Reynolds/ MC Tobacco Co. Ltd., Tokyo; Malaysia: RJ Reynolds Bhd., Kuala Lumpur, Selangor; Peru: Nabisco Peru SA, Lima; Poland: RJ Reynolds Tobacco-Poland Ltd., Piaseczno; Portugal: Nabisco Iberia Lda., Carnaxide, Oeiras; Spain: Galletas Fontaneda SA, Aguilar De Campoo, Palencia; Nabisco Europe Middle East & Africa Trading SA, Barcelona, Cataluna; R J Reynolds Tobacco Co. SAE, El Paso; Carnes y Conservas Espanolas SA, Madrid; Marbu SA, Montornes del Valles, Cataluna; Nabisco Iberia SL, Montornes del Valles, Cataluna; Galletas Artiach SA, Orozco, Vizcaya; Sweden: R J Reynolds Scandinavia AB, Danderyd, Stockholm; Switzerland: R J Reynolds Tobacco AG, Dagmersellen, Lucerne; R J Reynolds Finance SA, Geneva; Nabisco Trading AG, Zug; Tunisia: Royal Food Products SA, Hammam Lif; Turkey: RJ Reynolds Tutun Sanayi AS, Istanbul; United Kingdom: Nabisco Brands (United Kingdom) Ltd., Maidenhead, Berkshire; Nabisco Pension Trust Ltd., Manchester, Greater Manchester; Nabisco Brands Trading Ltd., Reading, Berkshire; Venezuela: Royal Productos Alimenticios CA, La Victoria, Aragua; Galletera Tejerias SA, Tejerias, Aragua

Note: Operates throughout the USA.

Nonmonetary Support

Value: $4,000,000 (1989); $6,600,000 (1988); $6,400,000 (1987)

Type: Donated Equipment; Donated Products; In-kind Services; Workplace Solicitation

Note: Nonmonetary support consists primarily of product donations to Second Harvest food bank.

Corporate Sponsorship

Type: Arts & cultural events; Sports events

Contact: Heidi Gurian, Director, Corporate Projects

RJR Nabisco Foundation

Giving Contact

Linda I. Elkes, Executive Director
Nabisco Foundation
1301 Avenue of the Americas
New York, NY 10019
Phone: (212)258-5600
Fax: (212)969-9001

Description

EIN: 581681920

Organization Type: Corporate Foundation

Giving Locations: headquarters and operating communities; nationally.

Grant Types: Capital, Challenge, Department, Employee Matching Gifts, Fellowship, General Support, Operating Expenses, Project, Research, Scholarship.

Note: Matching gifts are for arts and education only.

Financial Summary

Total Giving: $5,000,000 (1998 approx); $5,703,314 (1997); $5,515,923 (1996). Note: Contributes through corporate direct giving program and foundation.

Giving Analysis: Giving for 1996 includes: foundation ($6,559,738); foundation matching gifts ($1,055,615); foundation grants to United Way ($11,000); 1997: foundation ($5,038,571); foundation matching gifts ($1,030,355); foundation scholarships ($410,521); foundation grants to United Way ($11,000); 1998: foundation (approx $5,000,000)

Assets: $50,256,136 (1997); $51,124,159 (1996); $51,221,072 (1995)

Typical Recipients

Arts & Humanities: Arts Associations & Councils, Arts Centers, Community Arts, Dance, Ethnic & Folk Arts, Historic Preservation, History & Archaeology, Libraries, Literary Arts, Museums/Galleries, Music, Opera, Performing Arts, Public Broadcasting, Theater, Visual Arts

Civic & Public Affairs: African American Affairs, Asian American Affairs, Botanical Gardens/Parks, Business/Free Enterprise, Chambers of Commerce, Clubs, Economic Development, Economic Policy, Employment/Job Training, Civic & Public Affairs-General, Hispanic Affairs, Housing, Law & Justice, Legal Aid, Municipalities/Towns, Parades/Festivals, Philanthropic Organizations, Professional & Trade Associations, Public Policy, Rural Affairs, Safety, Urban & Community Affairs, Women's Affairs

Education: Agricultural Education, Arts/Humanities Education, Business Education, Business-School Partnerships, Colleges & Universities, Education Funds, Education Reform, Elementary Education (Private), Elementary Education (Public), Engineering/Technological Education, Faculty Development, Education-General, International Exchange, Leadership Training, Medical Education, Minority Education, Preschool Education, Private Education (Precollege), Public Education (Precollege), School Volunteerism, Science/Mathematics Education, Secondary Education (Private), Secondary Education (Public), Special Education, Student Aid, Vocational & Technical Education

Health: AIDS/HIV, Cancer, Children's Health/Hospitals, Clinics/Medical Centers, Emergency/Ambulance Services, Geriatric Health, Hospices, Hospitals, Medical Research

International: Foreign Educational Institutions, Health Care/Hospitals, International Affairs, International Peace & Security Issues, International Relations, International Relief Efforts

Religion: Jewish Causes, Religious Welfare

Social Services: Camps, Child Welfare, Community Centers, Community Service Organizations, Counseling, Crime Prevention, People with Disabilities, Recreation & Athletics, Scouts, Senior Services, Shelters/Homelessness, Substance Abuse, United Funds/ United Ways, Volunteer Services, YMCA/YWCA/ YMHA/YWHA, Youth Organizations

Contributions Analysis

Giving Priorities: Public education, private colleges, university research, minority issues, museums, symphonies, and art centers. Limited support for international relief agencies. Contributions abroad are handled by R.J. Reynolds Tobacco International.

Arts & Humanities: 16%. Supports museums, opera, theater, and historical societies.

Civic & Public Affairs: 50%. Supports minority and women's groups, legal aid, chambers of commerce, and city partnerships and foundations.

Education: 21%. Supports colleges, universities and research.

Health: 5%. Supports the American Red Cross, single disease health organizations, and medical centers.

Social Services: 6%.

Note: Total contributions in 1997. Majority of general grants are provided directly by the company.

Application Procedures

Initial Contact: preliminary letter

Application Requirements: proposed project, including analysis of purpose, need, goals, timetable for completion, and evaluative criteria; background information on organization, including governing board and qualifications of proposed leaders; financial information, including evidence of tax-exempt status, latest audited financial statement, and budget; list of other sources of funding and plan for future support

Deadlines: None.

Review Process: review of preliminary request by internal advisory group; if of interest, proposal submitted to contributions committee and additional information solicited

Decision Notification: committee meets once each quarter

Restrictions

Does not support athletic groups, social clubs, fraternal or veterans organizations; labor or political organizations; educational institutions already supported through fundraising organizations such as the United Negro College Fund or the Independent College Fund; sectarian or denominational religious groups; marathons or similar sports events; endowments or revolving funds; courtesy advertising or raffle tickets; conferences, workshops, seminars or trips; and production or distribution of audio-visual materials.

Corporate Officials

Steven F. Goldstone: chairman, chief executive officer, directoride communications ED New York University JD (1967); Pennsylvania University BA (1967). PRIM CORP EMPL chairman, chief executive officer, director: RJR Nabisco Holdings Corp. CORP AFFIL chairman: Nabisco Inc.; chairman: RJR Nabisco Inc.

Suzanne Jenney: assistant secretary PRIM CORP EMPL assistant secretary: RJR Nabisco Inc.

David Rickard: chief financial officer B 1946. PRIM CORP EMPL chief financial officer: RJR Nabisco Inc. CORP AFFIL chief financial officer: RJR Nabisco Holdings Corp.

Jason H. Wright: senior vice president worldwide communications PRIM CORP EMPL senior vice president worldwide communications: RJR Nabisco Inc.

Giving Program Officials

Linda I. Elkes: executive director PRIM CORP EMPL vice president human resources & administration: RJR Nabisco Holding Corp.

Joellen M. Shiffman: PRIM CORP EMPL director philanthropy: RJR Nabisco Inc.

Foundation Officials

William Apostolides: assistant treasurer
Linda I. Elkes: executive director (see above)
Steven F. Goldstone: chairman (see above)
Thomas M. Sansone: assistant treasurer
W. Read Smith: assistant secretary
David Ternlieb: secretary
Jason H. Wright: president (see above)

Grants Analysis

Disclosure Period: calendar year ending 1997
Total Grants: $4,251,438*
Number of Grants: 116
Average Grant: $19,578*
Highest Grant: $2,000,000
Typical Range: $20,000 to $100,000
***Note:** Giving excludes matching gifts; United Way; scholarships. Average grant figure excludes highest grant.

Recent Grants

Note: Grants derived from 1997 Form 990.

Arts & Humanities

333,333	Strategic Air Command Memorial Society, Omaha, NE
150,000	Faberge Arts Foundation, Washington, DC
75,000	Aldrich Museum of Contemporary Art, Ridgefield, CT
20,000	Museum for African Art, New York, NY
15,000	Roundabout Theatre Company, New York, NY
8,000	Poet's & Writers, Inc., New York, NY
7,500	Manhattan Theatre Club, New York, NY
5,000	New York City Opera, The, New York, NY

Civic & Public Affairs

875,428 Matching Gifts Program - Education
333,333 New York City Partnership Foundation Inc., New York, NY
333,333 New York City Partnership Foundation Inc., New York, NY
154,927 Matching Gifts Program - Arts, New York, NY
65,000 Congressional Hispanic Caucus, Washington, DC
32,000 Women's Research & Education Institute, Washington, DC
25,000 Congressional Black Caucus Foundation, Washington, DC
25,000 Washington Legal Foundation, Washington, DC
15,000 Cato Institute, Washington, DC
15,000 Heritage Foundation, Washington, DC
10,000 Catalyst, New York, NY
5,000 Financial Accounting Foundation, Norwalk, CT
5,000 Huntington Township Chamber of Commerce, Huntington, NY
5,000 Legal Aid Society, New York, NY
5,000 Peace Parks Club
5,000 Robert A. Toigo Foundation, Sacramento, CA
5,000 Women Executives in State Government, Washington, DC

Education

396,521 National Merit Scholarships, Evanston, IL
250,000 National Board for Professional Teaching Standards, Southfield, MI
56,000 University of Notre Dame, Notre Dame, IN
25,000 Consortium for Graduate Study in Management, St. Louis, MO
14,000 University of Notre Dame; Lou Holtz Scholarship, Notre Dame, IN
13,722 College Scholarship Service
12,500 Milton Academy, Milton, MA
10,000 Ohio State University, Columbus, OH
10,000 Prep for Prep, New York, NY
10,000 Seton Hall University, South Orange, NJ
5,000 Bloomfield College, Bloomfield, NJ
5,000 Institute for Educational Leadership Inc., Washington, DC
5,000 Norwalk Community-Technical College Fdn., Norwalk, CT
5,000 Studio in a School Association Inc., New York, NY
NC Central University Foundation, Durham, NC

Health

100,000 American Red Cross - National, Washington, DC
32,500 Gay Men's Health Crisis, New York, NY
10,000 American Red Cross - Greater New York, New York, NY
10,000 AmeriCares, New Canaan, CT
5,000 AIDS Walk Washington Whitman Walker Clinic, Washington, DC
5,000 Columbia Hospital, Washington, DC
5,000 Columbus Hospital Foundation, Newark, NJ
5,000 Gerwin Jewish Geriatric Foundation, Inc., Commack, NY
5,000 Hipple Cancer Research Center, Dayton, OH
5,000 National AIDS Fund, Washington, DC
5,000 New York University Medical Center, New York, NY
5,000 Presbyterian Hospital (Babies & Children's), New York, NY
5,000 Ronald McDonald House, New York, NY

International

5,000 Seeds of Peace, New York, NY

Religion

50,000 Jewish Committee, Brooklyn, NY
5,000 Episcopal Charities, New York, NY

Social Services

110,000 Institute for Youth Development, Washington, DC
21,500 Boy Scouts of America - Greater NY Council, New York, NY
15,500 Young Adult Institute, Inc., New York, NY
13,500 Sheltering Arms Childrens Service, New York, NY
12,500 YMCA of Greater New York, New York, NY
11,500 Just One Break, Inc., New York, NY
11,000 United Way
7,500 Happiness is Camping, Bronx, NY
5,000 Girl Scout Council of Greater New York, New York, NY
5,000 Institute of Youth Development, CT
5,000 Junior Achievement - National, Colorado Springs, CO
5,000 Volunteer Consulting Group, New York, NY
5,000 Youth Renewal Fund, New York, NY

RICH PRODUCTS CORP.

Company Contact

Buffalo, NY

Company Description

Employees: 7,000
SIC(s): 2037 Frozen Fruits & Vegetables, 2038 Frozen Specialties Nec, 2053 Frozen Bakery Products Except Bread.

Rich Family Foundation

Giving Contact

David A. Rich, Executive Director
Rich Family Foundation
1150 Niagara Street
Buffalo, NY 14213
Phone: (716)878-8363
Fax: (716)878-8775

Description

Founded: 1961
EIN: 166026199
Organization Type: Corporate Foundation
Giving Locations: NY: Buffalo
Grant Types: General Support.

Financial Summary

Total Giving: $499,610 (1997); $582,524 (1996); $326,183 (1995). Note: Contributes through foundation only.
Giving Analysis: Giving for 1995 includes: foundation ($302,268); foundation grants to United Way ($23,915); 1996: foundation ($553,574); foundation grants to United Way ($28,950); 1997: foundation ($452,895); foundation grants to United Way ($46,715)
Assets: $2,695,630 (1997); $1,791,557 (1996); $1,644,265 (1995)
Gifts Received: $970,000 (1997); $420,000 (1996); $420,000 (1995). Note: In 1995, contributions were received from Rich Products Corporation. In 1997, contributions were received from Rich Products Corporation and Robert E. Rich.

Typical Recipients

Arts & Humanities: Arts Associations & Councils, Arts Centers, Arts Institutes, Historic Preservation, History & Archaeology, Libraries, Museums/Galleries, Music, Performing Arts, Public Broadcasting, Theater
Civic & Public Affairs: Botanical Gardens/Parks, Business/Free Enterprise, Clubs, Economic Development, Civic & Public Affairs-General, Professional & Trade Associations, Urban & Community Affairs, Zoos/Aquariums
Education: Arts/Humanities Education, Business Education, Colleges & Universities, Continuing Education, Leadership Training, Legal Education, Literacy, Private Education (Precollege), Religious Education, Special Education, Student Aid
Environment: Wildlife Protection
Health: Alzheimers Disease, Cancer, Children's Health/Hospitals, Clinics/Medical Centers, Diabetes, Emergency/Ambulance Services, Health Organizations, Heart, Hospitals, Medical Rehabilitation, Multiple Sclerosis, Prenatal Health Issues, Public Health, Single-Disease Health Associations
International: Missionary/Religious Activities
Religion: Churches, Dioceses, Jewish Causes, Religious Organizations, Religious Welfare, Social/Policy Issues
Social Services: Animal Protection, Child Welfare, Community Centers, Community Service Organizations, Family Services, Food/Clothing Distribution, Recreation & Athletics, Substance Abuse, United Funds/United Ways, Youth Organizations

Contributions Analysis

Arts & Humanities: 7%. Contributes to music, performing arts, libraries and historical societies.
Civic & Public Affairs: 12%. Supports the Greater Buffalo Development Foundation, community affairs organizations, and professional associations.
Education: 35%. Supports the University of Buffalo Foundation in New York, NY, the Frozen Food Scholarship Fund and other regional colleges and universities.
Environment: 1%.
Health: 6%. Funds hopitals and single-disease health associations.
Religion: 14%. Primarily supports the Dioceses of Western New York, Buffalo, NY. Also funds St. Paul's Cathedral and the Anti-Defamation League of B'nai B'rith.
Social Services: 25%. The United Way receives the majority of grants. Also supports child welfare organizations.

Application Procedures

Initial Contact: formal letter of request
Deadlines: None.

Corporate Officials

David A. Rich: vice president, secretary, director B Buffalo, NY 1944. ED Bradley University (1970). PRIM CORP EMPL vice president, secretary, director: Rich Products Corp. ADD CORP EMPL vice president: BR Guest Ltd.; vice president: Bison Baseball Inc.; secretary: Palm Beach National Golf Country Club; treasurer: Wichita Baseball Inc. CORP AFFIL director: Rich Communications Corp. NONPR AFFIL executive director, director: Rich Foundation; member: Rotary International.
Janet W. Rich: vice president, director B 1914. PRIM CORP EMPL vice president, director: Rich Products Corp.
Robert E. Rich, Sr.: founder, chairman, director B Buffalo, NY 1913. ED University of Buffalo (1935). PRIM CORP EMPL founder, chairman, director: Rich Products Corp. CORP AFFIL chairman, director: Palm Beach National Golf & Country Club; chairman: Wichita Baseball Inc.; director: Marine Midland Trust Co.; chairman, director: B.R. Guest Ltd.; chairman, director: Casa Di Bertacchi Corp.; chairman: Bison Baseball Inc.
Robert E. Rich, Jr.: president, director B Buffalo, NY 1941. ED University of Rochester MBA; Williams College (1963). PRIM CORP EMPL president, director: Rich Products Corp. ADD CORP EMPL president:

BR Guest Ltd.; president: Bison Baseball Inc.; president: Palm Beach National Golf Country Club; president: Wichita Baseball Inc. CORP AFFIL vice chairman: Casa Di Bertacchi Corp. NONPR AFFIL vice chairman, director: Buffalo Sabres Hockey Club.

Foundation Officials

David A. Rich: executive director (see above)
Janet W. Rich: assistant secretary (see above)
Robert E. Rich, Sr.: president, treasurer (see above)
Robert E. Rich, Jr.: secretary (see above)

Grants Analysis

Disclosure Period: calendar year ending 1997
Total Grants: $452,895*
Number of Grants: 149
Average Grant: $2,384*
Highest Grant: $100,000
Typical Range: $100 to $5,000
*Note: Giving excludes United Way. Average grant figure excludes highest grant.

Recent Grants

Note: Grants derived from 1997 Form 990.

Arts & Humanities

25,000 Buffalo Fine Arts Academy, Buffalo, NY
8,000 Library Foundation of Buffalo and Erie County, Buffalo, NY

Civic & Public Affairs

50,000 SFSF Invest in Us Campaign
2,500 Buffalo Foundation, Buffalo, NY
2,000 Roswell Park Alliance Foundation, Buffalo, NY

Education

100,000 University of Buffalo Foundation, Buffalo, NY
25,000 Johnson and Wales University, Providence, RI
10,000 Minnesota Life College, Eden Prairie, MN
5,000 Campaign for the Sisters of Mercy and Trocaire College
5,000 Canisius College Presidents Council, Buffalo, NY
5,000 D'Youville College, Buffalo, NY
5,000 Frozen Food Scholarship Fund
2,500 Joe Lee Scholarship Foundation
2,000 Williams College Alumni Fund, Williamstown, MA

Environment

5,000 George Bush/Cheeca Lodge Bonefish Tournament

Health

10,000 Sisters Hospital Foundation
6,000 Independent Health Foundation, Buffalo, NY
5,000 Juvenile Diabetes Foundation, New York, NY
2,500 Children's Hospital, Buffalo, NY
2,000 March of Dimes

Religion

50,000 Christ Our Healer, Buffalo, NY
5,000 Elijah House
5,000 Salvation Army School for Officer Training, Atlanta, GA
3,300 Prayer and Praise Fellowship, Buffalo, NY
2,000 Genesee Orleans Ministry of Concern, Albion, NY

Social Services

17,750 United Way of Buffalo and Erie County, NY
15,000 Boys and Girls Clubs of America -- All Books for Children campaign
6,000 United Way of Buffalo and Erie County, NY
6,000 United Way of Buffalo and Erie County, NY
5,000 Western New York United Against Drug and Alcohol Abuse, Buffalo, NY
5,000 Western New York United Against Drug and Alcohol Abuse, Buffalo, NY
5,000 Western New York United Against Drug and Alcohol Abuse, Buffalo, NY
5,000 Western New York United Against Drug and Alcohol Abuse, Buffalo, NY
5,000 Western New York United Against Drug and Alcohol Abuse, Buffalo, NY
5,000 Western New York United Against Drug and Alcohol Abuse, Buffalo, NY
5,000 Western New York United Against Drug and Alcohol Abuse, Buffalo, NY
5,000 Western New York United Against Drug and Alcohol Abuse Foundation, Buffalo, NY
5,000 Western New York United Against Drug and Alcohol Abuse Foundation, Buffalo, NY
2,500 Boys and Girls Clubs, Buffalo, NY
2,500 Kelly for Kids
2,500 Operation Kindness
2,500 United Way of Erie County
2,500 United Way of Erie County
2,200 United Way of Rutherford County, Spindale, NC
2,000 United Way Palm Beach Community Chest, West Palm Beach, FL
2,000 United Way Palm Beach Community Chest, West Palm Beach, FL
1,939 United Way of Fox Cities
1,939 United Way of Fox Cities
1,939 United Way of Fox Cities
1,939 United Way of Fox Cities

RIGGS BANK NA

Company Contact

Washington, DC
Web: http://www.riggsbank.com

Company Description

Assets: US$351,303,000
Employees: 1,428
SIC(s): 6021 National Commercial Banks, 6082 Foreign Trade & International Banks, 6282 Investment Advice, 6712 Bank Holding Companies.
Parent Company: Riggs National Corp.

Corporate Sponsorship

Type: Arts & cultural events; Festivals/fairs; Music & entertainment events; Pledge-a-thon; Sports events
Contact: Timothy Coughlin, President

Giving Contact

Amy Hurley, Corporate Events Manager
Riggs National Bank of Washington, D.C.
800 17th Street, NW, 2nd Floor
Washington, DC 20074
Phone: (202)835-4495
Fax: (202)835-5184

Description

Organization Type: Corporate Giving Program
Giving Locations: DC: Washington metropolitan area
Grant Types: General Support.

Financial Summary

Total Giving: $500,000 (2000 approx); $500,000 (1999 approx); $500,000 (1998 approx). Note: Contributes through corporate direct giving program only.
Assets: $6,000,000 (2000 approx); $6,000,000 (1999 approx); $5,846,426 (1997)

Typical Recipients

Arts & Humanities: Arts & Humanities-General, Music, Performing Arts
Civic & Public Affairs: Civic & Public Affairs-General
Education: Education-General
Health: Clinics/Medical Centers, Kidney, Single-Disease Health Associations
Social Services: Social Services-General

Contributions Analysis

Arts & Humanities: Supports organizations that provide artistic enrichment to the community or reach underserved audiences, including museums and visual and performing arts groups.
Civic & Public Affairs: Supports organizations committed to the safety, welfare, and well-being of the community. Physical revitalization of the community; economic development; groups with monitor legal, consumer, and governmental issues; boys and girls clubs; and community associations are supported. Supports organizations dedicated to affordable housing initiatives, neighborhood development, small-business development and enhancement, and job training and development programs.
Education: Supports formal education and community-based organizations for educational purposes.
Health: Supports mental and physical medical care and basic human services. Supports hospitals, clinics, food banks, shelters for the homeless, and federated campaigns.

Application Procedures

Initial Contact: Write to request guidelines, then submit a formal request.
Application Requirements: Include a brief statement of history, purpose, and goals of organization and program; proof of tax-exempt status; organization's most recent operating budget; most recent audited financial statements, or annual report; list of officers and board members; and list of other donors and levels of support.
Deadlines: None.
Evaluative Criteria: The project must be financially and administratively stable and efficient, with non-duplication of services. Priority is given to programs that benefit a large number of individuals and have relevance to the bank's corporate mission.
Decision Notification: Within four to six weeks of receipt of the proposal.
Notes: Telephone and fax inquiries are not encouraged.

Restrictions

Company prefers to donate to individual organizations, rather than umbrella groups or foundations. Rarely gives to United Way-supported organizations. Multi-year commitments should not be expected.
No grants are made to fraternal organizations, political parties or candidates, political action committees, propaganda organizations, or individuals.
Serves the immediate metropolitan D.C. area only. or individuals.
Serves the immediate metropolitan D.C. area only.

Additional Information

Most grants are awarded to charitable organizations which do business with Riggs Bank.
Publications: Guidelines

Corporate Officials

Joe Lewis Allbritton: chairman, chief executive officer B D'Lo, MS 1924. ED Baylor University LLB (1949); Baylor University JD (1969). PRIM CORP EMPL chairman, chief executive officer: Perpetual Corp. CORP AFFIL chairman: WSET Inc.; chairman: Westfield Thoroughbreds Inc.; chairman: Westfield Management Corp.; chairman: Westfield News Advertiser Inc.; chairman: University Bancshares Inc.; chairman: Westfield Investments Inc.; chairman board, chairman executive committee: TV AlabamaInc.; chairman: Riggs National Bank Washington DC; chairman, chief executive officer: Riggs National Corp.; chairman: Riggs Bank Europe Ltd.; chairman: Riggs Bank NA; chairman: Riggs Asia Ltd.;

chairman: Perfin Corp.; director: Pierce National Life Insurance Co.; chairman: KTUL Television Inc.; chairman: Lazy Lane Farms Inc.; chairman: KATV Television Inc.; chairman: JLA Partners Inc.; chairman: Jobaro Corp.; chairman: Harrisburg Television Inc.; chairman: Houston Financial Services Ltd.; chairman: Great Cumberland Investments Ltd.; chairman: Allwin Inc.; chairman: First Charleston Corp.; chairman: Allfino Inc.; chairman: Allnewsco Inc.; chairman: Allbritton News Bureau; chairman: Allbritton Group Inc.; chairman: Allbritton Jacksonville Inc.; chairman: Allbritton Birmingham Corp.; chairman: Allbritton Communications Co.; chairman: 78 Inc.; chairman: Allbritton 2600 Carlyle Inc. NONPR AFFIL trustee: National Geographic Society; member: Texas Bar Association; member: Greater Washington Board Trade; trustee: George Bush Presidential Foundation; trustee: Fed City Council; member: Association Reserve City Bankers.

Timothy C. Coughlin: president B Fort Dodge, IA 1951. ED Iowa Central Community College (1970); University of South Dakota (1973). PRIM CORP EMPL president: Riggs Bank NA.

R. M. Williams: president, director PRIM CORP EMPL president, director: Riggs National Bank.

RITE AID CORP.

Company Contact

Camp Hill, PA
Web: http://www.riteaid.com

Company Description

Former Name: HarCo Drug.
Revenue: US$12,731,900,000 (1999)
Profit: US$143,700,000 (1999)
Fortune Rank: 142, per FORTUNE Magazine's list of 500 Largest U.S. Corporations (1999).
FF 142
SIC(s): 5531 Automobile & Home Supply Stores, 5912 Drug Stores & Proprietary Stores, 5942 Book Stores, 8099 Health & Allied Services Nec.

Giving Contact

Gayle Rife, Corporate Contributions Coordinator
Rite Aid Corp.
PO Box 3165
Harrisburg, PA 17105
Phone: (717)761-2633
Fax: (717)731-4737

Description

Organization Type: Corporate Giving Program
Giving Locations: operating locations.
Grant Types: General Support.

Giving Philosophy

'Rite Aid Corporation's roots are in the neighborhood drugstore. We understand that being a good neighbor is about more than offering customers quality products and service; it's about taking an active role in the communities we call home. Rite Aid supports programs and projects in the communities we serve. Rite Aid currently operates drug stores in 27 eastern and western states and the District of Columbia. While we strive to support charitable organizations and programs throughout all of these communities, we place greatest emphasis on those in which Rite Aid has a significant presence.'

Financial Summary

Total Giving: Contributes through corporate direct giving program only. Company does not disclose contributions figures.

Contributions Analysis

Giving Priorities: Health and medical, social services, education, the arts, and civic services.

Application Procedures

Initial Contact: Submit a written request on organization letterhead.
Application Requirements: Include the name and address of the requesting organization on letterhead; background information on the history, purpose and leadership of the organization; contact person's name; amount requested; purpose of the contributions; list of other corporate contributors; and any marketing and promotional plans.
Decision Notification: Allow at least four to six weeks for processing; all funding decisions are communicated in writing.

Restrictions

Religious organizations or programs; individuals; sporting events; agencies that receive United Way funding in areas where Rite Aid has contributed to the United Way campaign during the past 12 months; agencies that belong to other umbrella organizations that are supported by Rite Aid; organizations or programs that have received funding from Rite Aid during the past 12 months (with the acception of approved capital campaign contributions); travel for individuals or groups

Additional Information

The company reports that it is not making grants for the foreseeable future as it undergoes a financial restructuring.

Corporate Officials

Martin Lehrman Grass: chairman, chief executive officer, director B Harrisburg, PA 1954. ED University of Pennsylvania BA (1976); Cornell University MBA (1978). PRIM CORP EMPL chairman, chief executive officer, director: Rite Aid Corp. CORP AFFIL vice chairman, treasurer: Super Rite Foods; director: Tesco Technology Inc.; chairman: Rite Aid West Virginia Inc.; chairman: Rite Aid South Carolina Inc.; chairman: Rite Aid Virginia Inc.; president: Rite Aid Rome Distribution Center; chairman: Rite Aid Ohio Inc.; chairman: Rite Aid Pennsylvania Inc.; chairman: Rite Aid North Carolina Inc.; chairman: Rite Aid New Jersey Inc.; chairman: Rite Aid New York Inc.; chairman: Rite Aid New Hampshire Inc.; chairman: Rite Aid Massachusetts Inc.; chairman: Rite Aid Michigan Inc.; chairman: Rite Aid Maryland Inc.; chairman: Rite Aid Indiana Inc.; chairman: Rite Aid Maine Inc.; chairman: Rite Aid Idaho Inc.; chairman: Rite Aid Florida Inc.; chairman: Rite Aid Georgia Inc.; chairman: Rite Aid Corp. Kentucky; chairman: Perry Drug Stores Inc.; chairman: Rite Aid Connecticut Inc.; director: Mercantile Bankshares Corp.

Timothy J. Noonan: president, chief operating officer, director B 1941. ED Niagara University BS (1963); Albany Medical College (1966). PRIM CORP EMPL president, chief operating officer, director: Rite Aid Corp. CORP AFFIL president: Rite Aid New Hampshire Inc.; president: Rite Aid Pennsylvania Inc.; president: Rite Aid Corp. Kentucky; president: Rite Aid Idaho Inc.

Giving Program Officials

Amy Johnson: corporate communications manager PRIM CORP EMPL director public relations: Rite Aid Corp.

ROCHESTER GAS & ELECTRIC CORP.

Company Contact

Rochester, NY
Web: http://www.rge.com

Company Description

Assets: US$1,207,500,000 (1999)
Employees: 2,333 (1999)
SIC(s): 4911 Electric Services, 4931 Electric & Other Services Combined.

Nonmonetary Support

Type: Loaned Executives
Note: The company loans executives to the United Way only.

Giving Contact

Lydia Boddie-Neal, Manager Corporate Contributions
Rochester Gas & ElectricCorp.
89 East Avenue
Rochester, NY 14649-0001
Phone: (716)724-8790
Fax: (716)724-8799

Description

Organization Type: Corporate Giving Program
Giving Locations: Finger Lakes region.
Grant Types: Award, General Support.

Financial Summary

Total Giving: Contributes through corporate direct giving program only.

Typical Recipients

Arts & Humanities: Arts Centers, Arts & Humanities-General, Museums/Galleries, Music, Public Broadcasting, Theater
Civic & Public Affairs: Economic Development, Urban & Community Affairs
Education: Colleges & Universities
Health: Hospitals
Social Services: United Funds/United Ways

Application Procedures

Initial Contact: Send a brief letter of inquiry.
Application Requirements: Include a description of organization, amount requested, purpose of funds sought, recently audited financial statement, and proof of tax-exempt status.
Deadlines: None.

Restrictions

Contributions are strictly limited to the Rochester and Finger Lakes areas in New York.
Does not support individuals, religious organizations for sectarian purposes, political or lobbying groups, or organizations outside operating areas. Also does not support organizations funded by the United Way.

Corporate Officials

Roger W. Kober: chairman, chief executive officer, director B Webster, NY 1933. ED Clarkson University (1955); Rochester Institute Technology (1983). PRIM CORP EMPL chairman, chief executive officer, director: Rochester Gas & Electric Corp. CORP AFFIL director: Home Properties New York. NONPR AFFIL vice president: Empire State Electric Energy Resources.

Thomas S. Richards: chairman, president, chief executive officer PRIM CORP EMPL chairman, president, chief executive officer: Rochester Gas & Electric Corporate.

Giving Program Officials

Lydia Boddie-Neal: manager corporate contributions

Thomas Swartz: chairman contributions committee PRIM CORP EMPL department manager public communications: Rochester Gas & Electric Corp.

ROCKWELL INTERNATIONAL CORP.

★ Number 100 of Top 100 Corporate Givers

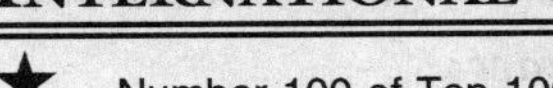

Company Contact

Costa Mesa, CA
Web: http://www.rockwell.com

Company Description

Revenue: US$7,043,000,000 (1999)
Profit: US$562,000,000 (1999)
Employees: 41,200 (1999)
Fortune Rank: 247, per FORTUNE Magazine's list of 500 Largest U.S. Corporations (1999).
FF 247
SIC(s): 3465 Automotive Stampings, 3493 Steel Springs Except Wire, 3555 Printing Trades Machinery, 3679 Electronic Components Nec.

Operating Locations

Argentina: Rockwell Automation Argentina -- Allen-Bradley/Rockwell Software, Buenos Aires; Australia: Rockwell Electric Commerce Australia, North Sydney; Belgium: Rockwell Automation -- Allen-Bradley/Rockwell Software, Brussels; Brazil: Rockwell Collins do Brasil Ltda., Sao Jose dos Campos; Rockwell Automation do Brasil -- Allen-Bradley/Rockwell Software, Sau Paulo; Canada: Rockwell Automation Canada -- Dodge/Reliance, Bramalea; Rockwell Automation Canada -- Allen-Bradley/Rockwell Software, Cambridge; Rockwell Electronic Commerce Canada, North York; Rockwell Collins of Canada, Ottawa; Chile: Rockwell Automation Chile, Las Condes, Santiago; People's Republic of China: Rockwell, Beijing; Colombia: Rockwell Colombia -- Allen-Bradley/Rockwell Software, Bogota; England: Rockwell Electronic Commerce, Caldecotte, Milton Keyes; Rockwell Collins (U.K.), Earley, Reading; France: Rockwell Automation -- Dodge/Reliance, Annecy; Rockwell Collins France, Blagnac; Rockwell Automation, Velizy-Villacoublay; Germany: Rockwell Automation/Dodge Europe, Elztal-Dallau; Rockwell Automation -- Allen-Bradley/Rockwell Software, Haan-Gruiten; Rockwell Collins Deutschland, Heusemstamm; Hong Kong: Rockwell Automation Asia Pacific -- Allen-Bradley/Rockwell Software, Causeway Bay; India: Rockwell Automation -- Allen-Bradley/Rockwell Software, Delhi; Japan:, Tokyo; Rockwell Electronic Commerce, Tokyo; Republic of Korea: Rockwell Automation Korea, Seoul; Mexico: Rockwell Automation de Mexico -- Allen-Bradley/Rockwell Software, Bosques de las Lomas; Rockwell Automation - Dodge/Reliance Electric Dodge de Mexico, El Salto; Republic of South Africa: Rockwell Automation -- Allen-Bradley/Rockwell Software, Midrand; Rockwell Electronic Commerce, Midrand; Singapore: Rockwell Automation Southeast Asia, Singapore; Rockwell Collins, Singapore; Spain: Rockwell Automation, Barcelona; United Arab Emirates: Rockwell Automation -- Allen-Bradley/Rockwell Software, Dubai; Venezuela: Rockwell Automation de Venezuela -- Allen-Bradley/Rockwell Software, Caracas

Nonmonetary Support

Value: $1,000,000 (1995); $3,500,000 (1993)
Type: Cause-related Marketing & Promotion; Donated Equipment; Donated Products; In-kind Services; Loaned Employees
Note: Company provides nonmonetary support.

Corporate Sponsorship

Type: Festivals/fairs; Arts & cultural events; Pledge-a-thon; Sports events
Note: Contact area contributions/community relations coordinator. Sponsors cultural events, PBS fundraisers, Habitat for Humanity, and Christmas in April.

Rockwell International Corp. Trust

Giving Contact

Tracy Sigman, Administrator
Rockwell International Corp. Trust
600 Anton Boulevard, Ste. 700
PO Box 5090
Costa Mesa, CA 92628-5090
Phone: (714)424-4640
Fax: (714)424-4217

Alternate Contact

Phone: (714)424-4361
Fax: (714)424-4314

Description

EIN: 251072431
Organization Type: Corporate Foundation
Giving Locations: headquarters and operating communities; nationally to education.
Grant Types: Capital, Employee Matching Gifts, General Support, Multiyear/Continuing Support.
Note: Employee matching gift ratio: 1 to 1 to accredited colleges and accredited public and private elementary and high schools. Company will match gifts of more than $25 to a maximum of $10,000 per employee annually.

Financial Summary

Total Giving: $6,911,225 (1998); $9,000,000 (1997 approx); $9,600,000 (1996 approx). Note: Contributes through corporate direct giving program and foundation.
Giving Analysis: Giving for 1998 includes: foundation ($5,029,776); foundation grants to United Way ($1,215,800); foundation matching gifts ($665,649)
Assets: $8,550,587 (1998); $12,800,000 (1996 approx); $3,900,000 (1995 approx)
Gifts Received: $8,500,000 (1994); $8,000,000 (1993). Note: Contributions received from Rockwell International Corporation.

Typical Recipients

Arts & Humanities: Arts Associations & Councils, Arts Centers, Arts Festivals, Arts Funds, Arts Institutes, Community Arts, Dance, Historic Preservation, History & Archaeology, Libraries, Museums/Galleries, Music, Opera, Performing Arts, Public Broadcasting, Theater
Civic & Public Affairs: African American Affairs, Asian American Affairs, Business/Free Enterprise, Chambers of Commerce, Civil Rights, Economic Development, Economic Policy, Employment/Job Training, Hispanic Affairs, Housing, Law & Justice, Legal Aid, Municipalities/Towns, Nonprofit Management, Professional & Trade Associations, Public Policy, Safety, Urban & Community Affairs, Urban & Community Affairs, Women's Affairs, Zoos/Aquariums
Education: Business Education, Colleges & Universities, Community & Junior Colleges, Continuing Education, Economic Education, Education Associations, Education Funds, Education Reform, Engineering/Technological Education, Faculty Development, Education-General, Gifted & Talented Programs, International Studies, Literacy, Minority Education, Private Education (Precollege), Public Education (Precollege), Science/Mathematics Education, Special Education, Student Aid, Vocational & Technical Education
Environment: Environment-General
Health: Cancer, Children's Health/Hospitals, Emergency/Ambulance Services, Health Policy/Cost Containment, Health Organizations, Hospices, Hospitals, Medical Rehabilitation, Mental Health, Public Health, Single-Disease Health Associations
International: International Affairs, International Peace & Security Issues, International Relations
Religion: Bible Study/Translation, Churches, Religious Welfare
Science: Science Exhibits & Fairs, Science Museums, Scientific Centers & Institutes, Scientific Organizations
Social Services: Child Welfare, Community Service Organizations, Counseling, Delinquency & Criminal Rehabilitation, Domestic Violence, Emergency Relief, Family Services, People with Disabilities, Recreation & Athletics, Scouts, Shelters/Homelessness, Substance Abuse, United Funds/United Ways, Volunteer Services, YMCA/YWCA/YMHA/YWHA, Youth Organizations

Contributions Analysis

Giving Priorities: Colleges and universities, engineering education, minority education, youth organizations, religious welfare, the arts, economic development, international affairs, medical research, and hospitals. Rockwell supports organizations in operating communities worldwide, disbursed directly by the company, through the Rockwell International Corp. Trust, and the Rockwell International Canadian Trust. The company has formal contributions programs in Australia, Brazil, Canada, China, France, Germany, Japan, Mexico, and the United Kingdom. Priorities domestically and internationally are the same. Education receives about half of all contributions, supporting colleges and universitites from which company recruits, to schools whose research programs are of interest to Rockwell, and to schools located in communities where Rockwell maintains major facilities.Also supports community funds, health organizations and hospitals, human service contributions, civic affairs, and culture and the arts. In 1995, overseas contributions were more than $1 million.
Arts & Humanities: About 5% to 10%. Primarily funds museums and arts institutes (particularly in corporate communities). Arts centers, public broadcasting, symphony orchestras, cultural and performing arts organizations, theaters, and libraries also supported.
Civic & Public Affairs: (United Funds & United Way) 15% to 20%. Supports United Ways in areas where the company operates. About 5% to 10%. Supports community development, public policy research, as well as urban coalitions. Other interests include job training and placement services and conservation, environmental, andecological organizations.
Education: About 50%. Primarily supports colleges, universities and community schools, with emphasis on schools from which the company recruits. Also supports independent college funds, minority programs, schools with excellent research programs, merit scholarships for children of employees, and education associations. Other interests include math and science education, and improving K-12 education. Also administers a substantial matching gifts program.
Health: About 10%. Support for organizations in company operating locations. Health grants include health organizations and medical research. Human service funding includes youth groups, community service organizations, YMCAs/YWCAs, disability assistance programs, senior and disadvantaged services, and disaster relief.
International: About 10% to 15% of overall corporate contributions. Company has established formal contributions programs in Australia, Brazil, Canada, China, France, Germany, Japan, Mexico, and the UnitedKingdom. Contact person and giving program priorities vary for each country.

Application Procedures

Initial Contact: Send a brief letter or proposal.
Application Requirements: Information should include a description of organization, amount requested, purpose of funds sought, recently audited financial statement, proof of tax-exempt status, list of other funding sources.
Deadlines: None.
Decision Notification: Within 90 days of receipt of proposal.
Notes: National and Los Angeles organizations should submit applications to the above address; organizations outside of Los Angeles should contact manager of nearest facility.

Restrictions

Does not support individuals, fraternal organizations, political or lobbying groups, goodwill advertising, or religious organizations for sectarian purposes.

Corporate Officials

W. Michael Barnes: senior vice president finance & planning, chief financial officer B 1938. ED Texas A&M University BA; Texas A&M University MA; Texas A&M University PhD (1968). PRIM CORP EMPL senior vice president finance & planning, chief financial officer: Rockwell International Corp. NONPR AFFIL member: Council Financial Executives.

Donald Ray Beall: director B Beaumont, CA 1938. ED University of California, Los Angeles; San Jose State University BS (1960); University of Pittsburgh MBA (1961). PRIM CORP EMPL director: Rockwell International Corp. ADD CORP EMPL president: Collins International Service Corp. CORP AFFIL chairman: Procter & Gamble Co.; chairman: Times Mirror Co.; director: Conexant Systems Inc.; director: Meritor Automotive Inc.; director: BP Amoco Corp. NONPR AFFIL fellow: American Institute Aeronautics & Astronautics; fellow: Society Manufacturing Engineers.

William Joseph Calise, Junior: senior vice president, secretary, general counsel B New York, NY 1938. ED Bucknell University BA (1960); Columbia University JD (1963); Columbia University MBA (1963). PRIM CORP EMPL senior vice president, secretary, general counsel: Rockwell International Corp. NONPR AFFIL member: Association Bar New York City. CLUB AFFIL Rockefeller Center Club; Duquesne Club.

Donald H. Davis, Jr.: president, chief executive officer, chairman B 1939. ED Texas A&M University BSME (1962); Texas A&M University MBA (1963). PRIM CORP EMPL president, chief executive officer, chairman: Rockwell International Corp. CORP AFFIL director: Ingram Micro Inc.

Joseph H. Garrett, Junior: vice president government & international operations PRIM CORP EMPL vice president government & international operations: Rockwell International Corp.

Earl S. Washington: senior vice president communications B Los Angeles, CA. ED California State University BS. PRIM CORP EMPL senior vice president communications: Rockwell International Corp.

Foundation Officials

W. Michael Barnes: member trust committee (see above)

William Joseph Calise, Junior: (see above)

John A. Coleman: assistant secretary

Donald H. Davis, Jr.: chairman trust committee (see above)

Earl S. Washington: secretary (see above)

Grants Analysis

Disclosure Period: calendar year ending 1998

Total Grants: $5,029,776 (approx)

Number of Grants: 1344 (approx)

Average Grant: $3,742 (approx)

Highest Grant: $250,000

Typical Range: $2,000 to $25,000

Note: Number of grants and Average grants are estimates.

Recent Grants

Note: Grants derived from 1999 Form 990.

International

50,000 Hoover Institution on War, Peace, and Revolution, Stanford, CA

ROHM &HAAS CO.

Company Contact

100 Independence Mall West
Philadelphia, PA 19106-2399
Phone: (215)592-3000
Fax: (215)592-3377
Web: http://www.rohmhaas.com

Company Description

Acquired: Morton International (1999).

Revenue: US$5,339,000,000 (1999)

Profit: US$249,000,000 (1999)

Employees: 21,500 (1999)

Fortune Rank: 310, per FORTUNE Magazine's list of 500 Largest U.S. Corporations (1999).

FF 310

SIC(s): 2821 Plastics Materials & Resins, 2869 Industrial Organic Chemicals Nec, 2879 Agricultural Chemicals Nec, 3089 Plastics Products Nec.

SUBSIDIARY COMPANIES

IL: Morton International Inc., Chicago

Nonmonetary Support

Value: $260,000 (1991); $140,000 (1990); $300,000 (1988)

Type: Donated Equipment; Donated Products; In-kind Services; Loaned Employees; Loaned Executives

Note: Company sponsored employee volunteer programs include Dollars for Doers and volunteer recognition programs.

Giving Contact

Alexandra Samuels, Manager, Civic & Philanthropic Affairs
Rohm & Haas Co.
Corp. Social Investment
100 Independence Mall West
Philadelphia, PA 19106-2399
Phone: (215)592-3644
Fax: (215)592-6808

Description

Organization Type: Corporate Giving Program

Giving Locations: principally near operating locations and to national organizations; where employees live.

Grant Types: Capital, Challenge, Department, Employee Matching Gifts, Fellowship, General Support, Operating Expenses, Project, Scholarship, Seed Money.

Giving Philosophy

'A key component of the Rohm and Haas vision is that the public views the company as a valued corporate citizen and good neighbor. In this regard, Rohm and Haas has a long history of making meaningful investments in programs and activities designed to improve the communities where our employees live and we do business. These investments include not only our funds but also our time, energy and talents of our many employee volunteers. Our employee volunteers significantly extend the reach of our involvement and support that we can provide in our communities.'

'In addition to responding to requests for assistance that we receive, we have been proactive in our outreach and support of our nonprofit partners' programs which address high priority community needs. All requests are given careful consideration. Most of our investments are focused around Education and Health and Human Services.' 1999 *Rohm and Haas and the Community*

Financial Summary

Total Giving: $4,000,000 (2000 approx); $4,000,000 (1999 approx); $2,900,000 (1998 approx). Note: Contributes through corporate direct giving program only.

Typical Recipients

Arts & Humanities: Arts & Humanities-General

Civic & Public Affairs: Civic & Public Affairs-General

Education: Education-General

Environment: Environment-General

Health: Health-General

Social Services: Social Services-General

Contributions Analysis

Giving Priorities: Health and human services, education, civic and community improvement, and culture and the arts.

Arts & Humanities: 5% to 10%. Funding primarily supports Philadelphia arts organizations, including public broadcasting stations, music groups, and museums.

Civic & Public Affairs: 10% to 15%. Typically funds organizations concerned with civil rights, urban affairs, business and free enterprise,

Education: About 55%. Support for higher education includes programs that encourage minority youths to enter the fields of chemistry and engineering. Also supports career and vocational training programs, economic education, and matching gifts to precollege and higher education.

Health: About 25% of total annual contributions. Primaily supports united funds in company operating locations, the handicapped and youth.

Application Procedures

Initial Contact: Submit a written request.

Application Requirements: Include the organization's name and purpose; length of service; funding sources; current objectives and priorities; a statement of need for support, including background, objectives, time period, budget, key staff, results expected, and general plan for funding; proof of tax-exempt status; and annual report and descriptive literature as available (project outlines, programs, brochures, etc.).

Deadlines: None.

Review Process: After reviewing proposal, additional information may be requested or a site visit may be arranged.

Evaluative Criteria: Company considers various community needs; relevance of those needs to the company and employees; likelihood of a favorable impact through contributions of money, time, or leadership; and the likelihood of involvement reflecting favorably on company.

Decision Notification: Company is able to provide a decision in a four- to six-week period.

Restrictions

Company does not support fraternal, labor, social, religious or veteran organizations, political or lobbying groups, religious organizations for sectarian purposes, or individuals.

Company severely limits its contributions to fundraising dinners, testimonials to prominent individuals, and complimentary advertising in program booklets.

Company minimizes its support of national appeals and capital programs.

Company minimizes its support of national appeals and capital programs.

Additional Information

Community activity guidelines set by corporate management; individual plants determine scope of program and specific activities.

Rohm and Haas tries to channel employees into community activities supported by company.

Contributions are not awarded on the basis of indefinitely continuing or unquestioned support. Even when multiyear pledges are made, Rohm and Haas retains right to terminate support if appropriate.

Rohm and Haas occasionally provides seed money grants, usually as an outright gift or in the form of a matching or challenge grant.

Corporate Officials

Brian McPeak: manager corporate community affairs PRIM CORP EMPL manager corporate community affairs: Rohm & Haas Co.

James Lawrence Wilson: chairman, chief executive officer, director B Rosedale, MS 1936. ED Vanderbilt University BSME (1958); Harvard University MBA (1963). PRIM CORP EMPL chairman, chief executive

officer, director: Rohm & Haas Co. CORP AFFIL director: Mead Corp.; director: Vanguard Group Investment Companies; director: Cummins Engine Co. Inc. NONPR AFFIL chairman: Phil High School Academy; trustee: Vanderbilt University; member: Chemical Manufacturers Association.

Giving Program Officials

Brian McPeak: (see above)

Grants Analysis

Disclosure Period: calendar year ending
Typical Range: $1,000 to $5,000

Roseburg Forest Products Co.

Company Contact

Roseburg, OR
Web: http://www.rfpco.com

Company Description

Employees: 3,950
SIC(s): 2421 Sawmills & Planing Mills--General, 2436 Softwood Veneer & Plywood, 2493 Reconstituted Wood Products.
Parent Company: RLC Industries Co.

Nonmonetary Support

Type: Donated Products

Corporate Sponsorship

Type: Arts & cultural events; Festivals/fairs; Music & entertainment events; Pledge-a-thon

Giving Contact

Ron Burgess, Chief Financial Officer
Roseburg Forest Products Co.
PO Box 1088
Roseburg, OR 97470
Phone: (541)679-3311
Fax: (541)679-6540

Alternate Contact

Lori Cockreham, Secretary to Chief Financial Officer

Description

Organization Type: Corporate Giving Program
Giving Locations: headquarters and operating communities.
Grant Types: General Support.

Financial Summary

Total Giving: $4,000,000 (fiscal year ending March 31, 1996 approx); $3,000,000 (fiscal 1995 approx). Note: Contributes through corporate direct giving program only. Giving includes corporate direct giving; nonmonetary support.

Application Procedures

Initial Contact: Request an application form.
Application Requirements: Submit completed application including purpose of organization and project, amount requested, date funds are needed, and any other relevant material.
Deadlines: None.

Corporate Officials

Ron Burgess: chief financial officer PRIM CORP EMPL chief financial officer: Roseburg Forest Products Co.
Kenneth W. Ford: chairman B 1908. PRIM CORP EMPL chairman: Roseburg Forest Products Co. CORP AFFIL chairman, director: RLC Industries; chairman: Roseburg Lumber Co.

Grants Analysis

Disclosure Period: fiscal year ending March 31,

Rouse Co.

Company Contact

Columbia, MD

Company Description

Revenue: US$831,900,000
Employees: 4,287
SIC(s): 1531 Operative Builders, 6512 Nonresidential Building Operators.

Nonmonetary Support

Value: $50,000 (1998)
Type: Donated Equipment; In-kind Services; Loaned Employees

Corporate Sponsorship

Value: $1,000
Type: Arts & cultural events; Festivals/fairs; Music & entertainment events; Pledge-a-thon

Rouse Co. Foundation

Giving Contact

Margaret P. Mauro, Executive Director, Secretary & Trustee
Rouse Co. Foundation
10275 Little Patuxent Pkwy.
Columbia, MD 21044
Phone: (410)992-6375
Fax: (410)992-6363
Email: mpm@therousecompany.com

Description

Founded: 1967
EIN: 526056273
Organization Type: Corporate Foundation
Giving Locations: MD: Central Maryland area
Grant Types: Capital, Challenge, Department, Employee Matching Gifts, Endowment, General Support, Matching, Multiyear/Continuing Support, Operating Expenses, Project, Scholarship, Seed Money.

Financial Summary

Total Giving: $1,400,000 (1999 approx); $1,200,000 (1998); $997,832 (1996). Note: Contributes through foundation only.
Giving Analysis: Giving for 1996 includes: foundation ($882,832); foundation grants to United Way ($115,000); 1999: foundation ($1,400,000); nonmonetary support ($50,000)
Assets: $5,400,000 (1999 approx); $5,736,477 (1996); $4,651,161 (1995)
Gifts Received: $1,424,000 (1996); $815,984 (1995); $174,176 (1993). Note: Contributions are received from the Rouse Co.

Typical Recipients

Arts & Humanities: Arts Associations & Councils, Arts Centers, Arts Funds, Arts Institutes, Community Arts, Dance, Ethnic & Folk Arts, Historic Preservation, Libraries, Literary Arts, Museums/Galleries, Music, Opera, Performing Arts, Public Broadcasting, Theater, Visual Arts
Civic & Public Affairs: Botanical Gardens/Parks, Economic Development, Employment/Job Training, Civic & Public Affairs-General, Housing, Public Policy, Zoos/Aquariums
Education: Arts/Humanities Education, Business Education, Colleges & Universities, Community & Junior Colleges, Education Funds, Education Reform, Education-General, Legal Education, Minority Education, Social Sciences Education, Student Aid
Environment: Resource Conservation
Health: Clinics/Medical Centers, Hospices, Hospitals, Prenatal Health Issues, Preventive Medicine/ Wellness Organizations
International: International Relations
Religion: Ministries, Religious Welfare
Science: Scientific Centers & Institutes
Social Services: Child Welfare, Community Service Organizations, Domestic Violence, Family Services, Food/Clothing Distribution, Homes, People with Disabilities, Senior Services, Sexual Abuse, Shelters/ Homelessness, Substance Abuse, United Funds/ United Ways, Volunteer Services, YMCA/YWCA/ YMHA/YWHA, Youth Organizations

Contributions Analysis

Arts & Humanities: 15% to 20%. Supports the performing arts, orchestra, and museum.
Civic & Public Affairs: 10% to 15%. Funds community services, housing, and foundations.
Environment: Less than 1%. Supports nature conservation.
Religion: Less than 5%. Supports religious philanthropic activities.
Science: About 10%. Funds science centers.
Social Services: 15% to 20%. Supports United Way, foundations, and youth services.

Application Procedures

Initial Contact: Written or telephone request.
Application Requirements: Include amount requested and intended use; a brief a description of organization, its history and activities; the name(s) and qualifications of the person(s) who will administer the grant; a copy of the most recent tax-exemption ruling statement from the IRS; goals and objectives for project or program; population to be served; schedule for implementation; and method of evaluating its effectiveness.
Deadlines: None.

Restrictions

Does not support religious programs, endowments, individuals, or political advocacy. Organizations must be tax-exempt under 501(c)(3) or 509(a).

Additional Information

Publications: Informational Brochure (including Application Guidelines)

Corporate Officials

Anthony W. Deering: chairman, chief executive officer chief financial officer B 1945. ED Drexel University BS (1969); University of Pennsylvania MBA (1971). PRIM CORP EMPL chairman, chief executive officer: Rouse Co. CORP AFFIL president: Village Cross Keys Inc.; president: White Marsh Mall Inc.; president: Rouse-Tampa Inc.; treasurer: Salem Mall Inc.; president: Rouse-Oakwood Shopping Center; chief financial officer: Rouse Philadelphia Inc.; president: Rouse-Milwaukee Inc.; president: Rouse Missouri Holding Co.; chief financial officer: Rouse Management Service Corp.; chairman: Rouse Marshalltown Center; senior vice president: Rouse Co. Saint Louis Inc.; senior vice president: Rouse Co. Texas Inc.; president: Rouse Co. Oregon Inc.; officer: Rouse Co. Owings Mills Inc.; chief financial officer: Rouse Co. Ohio Inc.; treasurer: Rouse Co. Massachusetts Inc.; president: Rouse Co. Michigan Inc.; president: Rouse Co. Florida Inc.; president: Rouse Co. Illinois Inc.; director: Plymouth Meeting Mall Inc.; president: Rouse Co. Colorado Inc.; senior vice president: North Star Mall Inc.; president: Paramus Park Inc.; senior vice president: Hanendale Mall Inc.; president: Louisville Shopping Center; chairman: Exton Square Inc.; treasurer: Governor's Square Inc.; president: Columbia Mall Inc.; chief financial officer: Columbia Management Inc.; chief financial officer: Charlottetown Inc.
Jeffrey H. Donahue: senior vice president, chief financial officer ED University of Pennsylvania MBA; Cornell University (1966). PRIM CORP EMPL senior vice president, chief financial officer: Rouse Co.

CORP AFFIL vice president: Village Cross Keys Inc.; chief financial officer: Woodbridge Center Inc.; chief financial officer: Rouse-Tampa Inc.; treasurer: Salem Mall Inc.; chairman: Rouse Marshalltown Center; treasurer: Rouse Philadelphia Inc.; chief financial officer: Rouse Hotel Management Inc.; chief financial officer: Rouse Management Service Corp.; chief financial officer: Rouse Co. New Jersey Inc.; trustee: Rouse Co. Owings Mills Inc.; trustee: North Star Mall Inc.; vice president: Rouse Co. Massachusetts Inc.; chief financial officer: Exton Square Inc.; vice president: Governor's Square Inc.; vice president: Charlottetown Inc.

Foundation Officials

Anthony W. Deering: chairman, president, trustee (see above)

Margaret Mauro: executive director, secretary, trustee

Douglas A. McGregor: trustee B 1942. ED Rutgers University BA (1963); Case Western Reserve University JD (1967). PRIM CORP EMPL executive vice president development & Cope: The Rouse Co. CORP AFFIL president: Rouse-Teachers Properties Inc.; executive vice president: Woodbridge Center Inc.; executive vice president: North Star Mall Inc.; executive vice president: Rouse Co. Owings Mills Inc.

Grants Analysis

Disclosure Period: calendar year ending 1996
Total Grants: $882,832*
Number of Grants: 52
Average Grant: $16,978
Highest Grant: $100,000
Typical Range: $5,000 to $50,000
***Note:** Giving excludes United Way.

Recent Grants

Note: Grants derived from 1996 Form 990.

Arts & Humanities

50,000	Baltimore Center for the Performing Arts, Baltimore, MD -- operating support
25,000	Baltimore Symphony Orchestra, Baltimore, MD -- for endowment
25,000	Baltimore Symphony Orchestra, Baltimore, MD -- annual support
16,667	Baltimore City Life Museums, Baltimore, MD -- capital campaign pledge payment
15,000	Baltimore Museum of Art, Baltimore, MD -- project support
15,000	B&O Railroad Museum, Baltimore, MD -- capital campaign
10,000	Baltimore Chamber Orchestra, Baltimore, MD -- annual support
10,000	Baltimore Museum of Industry, Baltimore, MD -- capital campaign
10,000	Baltimore Opera Company, Baltimore, MD -- for annual giving
5,000	National Trust for Historic Preservation, Washington, DC -- annual support

Civic & Public Affairs

50,000	Jubilee Housing, Washington, DC -- operating support
20,000	BUILD, Baltimore, MD -- annual support
10,000	Ladew Topiary Gardens, Monkton, MD -- capital campaign
10,000	National Aquarium in Baltimore, Baltimore, MD -- capital campaign
10,000	Neighborhood Housing Services, Baltimore, MD -- operating support
7,000	Parks and People Foundation, Baltimore, MD -- capital campaign
5,000	Aspen Institute, Washington, DC -- operating support
5,000	Jamestown Foundation, Washington, DC -- operating support
5,000	Sandtown Habitat for Humanity, Baltimore, MD -- operating support

Education

100,000	Maryland Institute, Baltimore, MD -- for MJD Scholarship Fund
30,000	College Bound Foundation, Baltimore, MD -- endowment, scholarships
20,000	BEST, Baltimore, MD -- for Rouse scholarships
20,000	Goucher College, Baltimore, MD -- capital campaign
20,000	Maryland Institute, Baltimore, MD -- capital campaign
20,000	University of Maryland, College Park, MD -- to endow William Donald Shaefer Chair
16,666	University of Maryland College of Business, College Park, MD -- endowment
16,666	University of Maryland School of Law, Baltimore, MD -- endowment
15,000	Fund for Educational Excellence, Baltimore, MD -- operating support
10,000	BEST, Baltimore, MD -- annual support
10,000	Independent College Fund of Maryland, Baltimore, MD -- scholarships
4,500	Fund for Johns Hopkins, Baltimore, MD -- project support
4,500	Living Classrooms, Baltimore, MD -- operating support
4,000	Maryland Institute College of Art, Baltimore, MD -- annual support

Environment

5,000	Chesapeake Bay Foundation, Annapolis, MD -- annual support
5,000	Nature Conservancy, Chevy Chase, MD -- project support

Health

46,000	Howard County Hospital, Columbia, MD -- capital campaign
20,000	GBMC, Baltimore, MD -- capital campaign
20,000	University of Maryland Medical Center, Baltimore, MD -- capital campaign
12,000	Wellness Center, Baltimore, MD -- operating support

Religion

25,000	St. Ambrose Housing Aid Center, Baltimore, MD -- operating support
5,000	Episcopal Social Ministries, Baltimore, MD -- annual support
5,000	Franciscan Center, Baltimore, MD -- operating support

Science

83,333	Constellation Foundation, Baltimore, MD -- capital campaign
14,000	Maryland Science Center, Baltimore, MD -- capital campaign

Social Services

115,000	United Way Central Maryland, Baltimore, MD -- for human services, health grants
20,000	Kennedy Krieger Institute, Baltimore, MD -- research
10,000	Chimes, Baltimore, MD -- operating support
7,500	Columbia Foundation, Columbia, MD -- annual support
5,000	Family Life Center, Columbia, MD -- annual support
5,000	YMCA Central Maryland, Ellicott City, MD -- capital campaign

ROYAL &SUNALLIANCE USA, INC.

Company Contact

Charlotte, NC
Web: http://www.royalsunalliance-usa.com

Company Description

Former Name: Royal Insurance Co. of America.
Premiums: US$1,671,157,000
Employees: 3,982
SIC(s): 6719 Holding Companies Nec.
Parent Company: Royal & SunAlliance Insurance Group Plc, 30 Berkeley Sq., London, United Kingdom

Operating Locations

CO: Royal & SunAlliance USA, Inc.; CT: Royal & SunAlliance USA, Inc.; FL: Royal & SunAlliance USA, Inc.; GA: Royal & SunAlliance USA, Inc.; KS: Royal & SunAlliance USA, Inc.; MA: Royal & SunAlliance USA, Inc.; MD: Royal & SunAlliance USA, Inc.; ME: Royal & SunAlliance USA, Inc.; NC: American and Foreign Insurance Co., Charlotte; Commericial Marketing Systems, Charlotte; Globe Indemnity Co., Charlotte; Newark Insurance Co., Charlotte; Royal Indemnity Co., Charlotte; Royal Insurance, Charlotte; Royal Insurance Co. of America, Charlotte; Royal Life Insurance Co. of America, Charlotte; Royal & SunAlliance USA, Inc., Charlotte; Safeguard Insurance Co., Charlotte; NH: Royal & SunAlliance USA, Inc.; NJ: Royal & SunAlliance USA, Inc.; NY: Royal & SunAlliance USA, Inc.; Phoenix Assurance of New York, New York; Royal Life Insurance Co. of America, New York; Sun Alliance USA, New York; Sun Insurance Co. of New York, New York; PA: Royal & SunAlliance USA, Inc.; SD: Milbank Insurance Co., Milbank; TX: Royal & SunAlliance USA, Inc.; UT: Royal & SunAlliance USA, Inc.; VA: Royal & SunAlliance USA, Inc.

Nonmonetary Support

Value: $25,000 (1994)
Type: Cause-related Marketing & Promotion; Donated Equipment; In-kind Services
Volunteer Programs: Company actively encourages employee volunteerism, including an Education Week. Special consideration is given to requests for funding if an employee is involved in the organization in a meaningful voluntary capacity.

Corporate Sponsorship

Type: Other

Royal & SunAlliance Insurance Foundation, Inc.

Giving Contact

Fred Dabney, Executive Director
Royal & SunAlliance Insurance Foundation, Inc.
9300 Arrowpoint Blvd.
PO Box 1000
Charlotte, NC 28201-1000
Phone: (704)522-2056
Fax: (704)522-2055

Description

Founded: 1989
EIN: 561658178
Organization Type: Corporate Foundation
Giving Locations: areas where producers, employees, and customers reside.
Grant Types: Employee Matching Gifts, General Support, Multiyear/Continuing Support.
Note: Employee matching gift ratio: 1 to 1 up to $1,000 for gifts to higher education only.

Giving Philosophy

'We believe that Royal Insurance should be a vital, contributing part of the community. We recognize and accept our responsibility of corporate citizenship. .. Our objective is to help build the environment in which health, welfare, educational, and cultural institutions will continue to thrive and prosper to the good of the community, the corporation, and its employees. It is our policy, therefore, to contribute to recognized, tax-exempt organizations whose services benefit the

communities in which our principal producers, customers, and facilities are situated, and where our largest groups of employees reside. Our contributions may take the form of direct financial contributions, gifts-in-kind, and encouraging our employees to contribute time and talent.' Royal Insurance Foundation Annual Report

Financial Summary

Total Giving: $800,000 (2000 approx); $845,000 (1999 approx); $505,000 (1998 approx). Note: Contributes through corporate direct giving program and foundation.
Giving Analysis: Giving for 1997 includes: foundation ($293,878); foundation grants to United Way ($136,312); foundation matching gifts ($34,369); 1998: foundation ($505,000); 1999: foundation ($845,000);
Assets: $327,451 (1997); $245,535 (1995); $89,381 (1993)
Gifts Received: $490,000 (1997); $475,000 (1995); $475,000 (1993)

Typical Recipients

Arts & Humanities: Arts Appreciation, Arts Associations & Councils, Arts Centers, Community Arts, Dance, Ethnic & Folk Arts, Arts & Humanities-General, Historic Preservation, Libraries, Museums/Galleries, Music, Opera, Performing Arts, Public Broadcasting, Theater, Visual Arts
Civic & Public Affairs: African American Affairs, Business/Free Enterprise, Civil Rights, Economic Development, Civic & Public Affairs-General, Housing, Public Policy, Safety
Education: Business Education, Colleges & Universities, Community & Junior Colleges, Continuing Education, Education Funds, Education Reform, Elementary Education (Private), Education-General, Literacy, Minority Education, Preschool Education, Private Education (Precollege), Public Education (Precollege), Science/Mathematics Education
Environment: Environment-General
Health: Adolescent Health Issues, Cancer, Children's Health/Hospitals, Emergency/Ambulance Services, Health-General, Geriatric Health, Health Funds, Health Organizations, Heart, Home-Care Services, Hospices, Hospitals, Mental Health, Public Health, Single-Disease Health Associations
Religion: Ministries, Religious Welfare
Science: Science Museums
Social Services: Child Abuse, Child Welfare, Community Centers, Community Service Organizations, Counseling, Crime Prevention, Family Services, Homes, People with Disabilities, Recreation & Athletics, Refugee Assistance, Senior Services, Shelters/Homelessness, Social Services-General, Special Olympics, Substance Abuse, United Funds/United Ways, Volunteer Services, YMCA/YWCA/YMHA/YWHA, Youth Organizations

Contributions Analysis

Giving Priorities: Social services, arts and humanities, health orgs, and education.
Arts & Humanities: 31%. Significant grants made to an annual arts and sciences fund drive to support multiple arts groups.
Civic & Public Affairs: 3%. Supports public broadcasting, crime prevention, minority organizations, low-income housing.
Education: 10%. Supports universities, colleges, and education funds. Focus on business and insurance courses. Also supports early childhood intervention, drop-out prevention, and Junior Achievement.
Health: 11%. Interests include the homeless, the developmentally and mentally disabled, the elderly, and health organizations.
Religion: 2%.
Science: 1%.
Social Services: 42%. Supports United Way, Special Olympics and children's organizations.
Note: Total contributions in 1997.

Application Procedures

Initial Contact: Write for application form, then written proposal.
Application Requirements: Include completed application; what makes Royal & SunAlliance an appropriate donor; list of current board of directors; schedule of board meetings; budgetary information; sources of income, with amounts; proof of IRS tax-exemption; and current financial statement.
Deadlines: None.
Evaluative Criteria: Priority is given to education, health, and human service organizations, and to geographic areas where the largest numbers of the company's producers, customers, and employees reside; also favors requests from organizations when an employee is involved in a meaningful voluntary capacity.

Restrictions

Does not support individuals, religious organizations for sectarian purposes, political or lobbying groups, organizations outside operating areas, fraternal organizations, medical research, veterans' organizations, broadcast fundraising, or endowments. With few exceptions, does not support operating funds of United Way member agencies nor other Foundations which support various organizations.
No funding may be secured through telephone solicitation or direct mail marketing. Contributions also will not be made to an organization solely because a company officer or employee is involved in fundraising efforts. fundraising efforts.

Additional Information

Royal & Sun Alliance was created in 1996 with the merger of two of Britain's biggest insurance companies, Royal Insurance and Sun Alliance.
The majority of contributions stay within the state of North Carolina and are decided upon at corporate headquarters. Field offices across the United States have autonomy to make smaller discretionary donations. At the headquarters, the board of directors meets quarterly to vote on all expenditures of over $2,500.
Capital funding requests are presented for consideration once per year at the annual meeting of the board of directors. Priority is given to industry-related projects.
Publications: Application Guidelines; Brochure

Corporate Officials

Terry Broderick: president technology executive
Fred E. Dabney, II: vice president corporate communications B Harrisburg, IL 1937. ED Southern Illinois University BA (1958). PRIM CORP EMPL vice president corporate communications: Royal & SunAlliance USA, Inc. NONPR AFFIL member: Public Relations Society America; chairman: University Radio Foundation; member: International Association of Business Communications; president emeritus: Insurance Marketing Communication Association; president emeritus: Insurance Public Relations Council; member: Insurance Institute Property Loss Reduction.
Wendy Harrigan: information technology executive
Elizabeth McLaughlin: chairman PRIM CORP EMPL chairman: Royal & SunAlliance USA, Inc.
Joyce W. Wheeler: vice president, corporate secretary B Durham, NC 1951. ED Albright College (1973); University of Houston (1980). PRIM CORP EMPL vice president, corporate secretary: Royal & SunAlliance USA, Inc. CORP AFFIL corporate secretary: Royal Surplus Lines Insurance Co.; corporate secretary: Safeguard Insurance Co.; section: Royal Group Inc.

Foundation Officials

Terry Broderick: director (see above)
Fred E. Dabney, II: executive director (see above)
Allan Dixon: director
Wendy Harrigan: director (see above)
Philip E. Kline: treasurer, director B Vandalia, OH. PRIM CORP EMPL treasurer: Royal & SunAlliance USA, Inc. CORP AFFIL treasurer: American & Foreign Insurance Co.
Elizabeth McLaughlin: chairman (see above)
Joyce W. Wheeler: secretary (see above)

Grants Analysis

Disclosure Period: calendar year ending 1998
Total Grants: $501,158*
Number of Grants: 119
Average Grant: $4,211
Typical Range: $1,000 to $5,000
***Note:** Giving excludes matching gifts. Grants analysis provided by foundation.

Recent Grants

Note: Grants derived from 1997 Form 990.

Arts & Humanities

50,000	Arts and Science Council, Charlotte, NC
35,000	Arts and Science Council, Charlotte, NC
5,000	Charlotte Symphony, Charlotte, NC
5,000	Mint Museum, Charlotte, NC
5,000	South Street Seaport Museum, New York, NY
3,000	North Carolina Dance Theater, Charlotte, NC
3,000	Theater Charlotte, Charlotte, NC
3,000	WCAV Radio
2,500	Charlotte Choral Society, Charlotte, NC
2,000	Afro-American Cultural Center, Charlotte, NC
2,000	Children's Theater, Charlotte, NC
1,500	Opera Carolina, Charlotte, NC

Civic & Public Affairs

3,000	Programs for Accessible Living
2,500	100 Black Men, Charlotte, NC
2,500	Charlotte Emergency Housing, Charlotte, NC
1,500	Mecklenburg City Council, Charlotte, NC

Education

15,000	Charlotte-Mecklenberg Education Foundation, Charlotte, NC -- capital campaign
7,500	Onondaga Community College, Syracuse, NY
5,000	Communities in Schools, Houston, TX
5,000	Junior Achievement, Charlotte, NC
2,500	Carolina Computer Access Center, Charlotte, NC
2,500	Independent College Fund, Syracuse, NY

Health

25,000	Presbyterian Hospital, New York, NY -- capital campaign
5,000	Teen Health Connection, Charlotte, NC
3,000	Mental Health Association
3,000	Ronald McDonald House, Manhattan, NY
2,000	American Heart Association, Nashville, TN
1,500	Huntingtons Disease Society of America, New York, NY

Religion

5,000	St. Mark's -- capital campaign
1,500	Crisis Assistance Ministry, Charlotte, NC

Science

3,000	Discovery Place, Charlotte, NC

Social Services

27,500	United Way of Central Carolinas, Charlotte, NC -- first quarter pledge
27,500	United Way of Central Carolinas, Charlotte, NC -- fourth quarter pledge
27,500	United Way of Central Carolinas, Charlotte, NC -- third quarter pledge
27,500	United Way of Central Carolinas, Charlotte, NC -- second quarter pledge

10,000	YWCA, Charlotte, NC -- capital campaign
5,000	Council for Children
5,000	Special Olympics, NC
3,000	Alexander Children's Center, Charlotte, NC
3,000	The Relatives
3,000	YMCA, Charlotte, NC
3,000	YWCA
2,500	Special Olympics, NC
2,500	United Way, New York, NY
2,500	United Way, New York, NY
2,500	United Way of Long Island, Deer Park, NY
2,000	United Way, Atlanta, GA
1,800	United Way of Central New York, Syracuse, NY
1,500	Marty Celic Running Festival
1,425	United Way of King County, Seattle, WA

RUBBERMAID INC.

Company Description

Parent Company: Newell Rubbermaid Inc., Freeport, IL, United States

Nonmonetary Support

Type: Donated Products
Note: Contact President and General Manager, Home Products Division for information.

Rubbermaid Foundation

Giving Contact

Kay Butler, Administrator
Rubbermaid Foundation
1147 Akron Rd.
Wooster, OH 44691-0800
Phone: (330)264-6464
Fax: (330)287-2864

Alternate Contact

Richard G. Gates, President of Foundation

Description

EIN: 341533729
Organization Type: Corporate Foundation
Giving Locations: headquarters and operating communities.
Grant Types: Capital, Employee Matching Gifts, Scholarship.
Note: Employee matching gift ratio: 1 to 1 for education institutions. Scholarships are available.

Financial Summary

Total Giving: $700,000 (1999 approx); $700,000 (1998 approx); $625,965 (1997). Note: Contributes through corporate direct giving program and foundation.
Giving Analysis: Giving for 1997 includes: foundation ($374,169); foundation grants to United Way ($165,000); foundation matching gifts ($86,796)
Assets: $1,132,084 (1997); $1,958,513 (1996); $2,624,133 (1995)
Gifts Received: $125,100 (1997); $1,000,000 (1993). Note: Contributions were received from Rubbermaid Incorporated.

Typical Recipients

Arts & Humanities: Arts Associations & Councils, Arts Centers, Historic Preservation, History & Archaeology, Literary Arts, Museums/Galleries
Civic & Public Affairs: African American Affairs, Business/Free Enterprise, Community Foundations, Economic Development, Economic Policy, Employment/Job Training, Civic & Public Affairs-General, Housing, Law & Justice, Philanthropic Organizations, Professional & Trade Associations, Women's Affairs
Education: Agricultural Education, Business Education, Colleges & Universities, Community & Junior Colleges, Economic Education, Education Associations, Education Funds, Education Reform, Elementary Education (Public), Engineering/Technological Education, Education-General, Minority Education, Private Education (Precollege), Public Education (Precollege), Science/Mathematics Education, Secondary Education (Public)
Health: Cancer, Children's Health/Hospitals, Clinics/ Medical Centers, Emergency/Ambulance Services, Health Organizations, Hospices, Hospitals
Religion: Bible Study/Translation, Ministries, Religious Organizations, Religious Welfare, Seminaries
Science: Scientific Centers & Institutes
Social Services: At-Risk Youth, Child Welfare, Community Centers, Community Service Organizations, Day Care, Homes, People with Disabilities, Substance Abuse, United Funds/United Ways, YMCA/ YWCA/YMHA/YWHA, Youth Organizations

Contributions Analysis

Giving Priorities: Education, business and advertising councils, minority organizations, the arts, and social services.
Arts & Humanities: 2%. Major interests include historic preservation, art appreciation, and the literary arts.
Civic & Public Affairs: 7%. Interests include professional and trade associations, business and free enterprise. A majority of this type of giving is in the form of general operating support.
Education: 48%. Most educational giving is provided in the form of matching gifts to universities and colleges.
Environment: 1%. Supports a wilderness center.
Health: 2%. Primarily supports hospitals, clinics, and children's health.
Social Services: 35%. Majority of support goes to local United Ways, Boy Scouts, and other social services agencies located in areas where Rubbermaid operates.
Note: Priorities reflect foundation giving only, and include matching gifts. Total contributions in 1997.

Application Procedures

Initial Contact: Letter of request to foundation's president.
Application Requirements: Details about project, amount requested, background of organization, proof of IRS status.
Deadlines: None.
Review Process: Proposals are reviewed by the foundation committee, which meets approximately once per month.
Decision Notification: Foundation will announce its decision at least 30 days after receipt of proposal.

Restrictions

Foundation does not support individuals or organizations not tax exempt under IRS guidelines. Grants go only to those organizations near Rubbermaid operating locations.
Only requests from organizations located in Wayne County and Wooster, OH, will be considered. Subsidiary locations can submit requests to the foundation.

Additional Information

Organizations that do not meet IRS guidelines for tax-exemption may be able to obtain some funds directly from Rubbermaid Inc., as long as they fulfill geographic and focus criteria.
In 1999, Newell and Rubbermaid Inc. merged to form Newell Rubbermaid Inc. Rubbermaid Inc. is now a subsidiary of Newell Rubbermaid Inc.

Corporate Officials

Charles A. Carroll: president, chief operating officer, director B 1949. PRIM CORP EMPL president, chief operating officer, director: Rubbermaid Inc. CORP AFFIL chief operating officer: Rubbermaid Cortland Inc.; president: Rubbermaid Specialty Products Inc.
John W. Dean, III: vice president, treasurer B Johnstown, PA 1956. ED Clarion University of Pennsylvania BS (1978); Kent State University MBA (1982). PRIM CORP EMPL vice president, treasurer: Rubbermaid Inc. CORP AFFIL treasurer: Rubbermaid Commercial Products; treasurer: Rubbermaid Cortland Inc.; vice president, treasurer, director: Little Tikes Co.
Michael E. Naylor: senior vice president operations B Melton Mowbray, England 1939. ED University of Durham Kings (1961). PRIM CORP EMPL senior vice president operations: Rubbermaid Inc. NONPR AFFIL member: Society Automotive Engineers; member: Society Plastics Engineers.
David L. Robertson: senior vice president human resources B 1945. PRIM CORP EMPL senior vice president human resources: Rubbermaid Inc. ADD CORP EMPL executive vice president human resources & corporate law: Weirton Steel Corp.
Wolfgang Rudolph Schmitt: chairman, chief executive officer, director B Koblenz, Germany 1944. ED Otterbein College BA (1966); Harvard University Graduate School of Business Administration AMP (1986). PRIM CORP EMPL chairman, chief executive officer, director: Rubbermaid Inc. CORP AFFIL president: Rubbermaid Cortland Inc.; director: Kimberly-Clark Corp.; director: Parker-Hannifin Corp. NONPR AFFIL director: Otterbein College.
George C. Weigand: chief financial officer, senior vice president B 1951. ED University of Akron BS (1973). PRIM CORP EMPL chief financial officer, senior vice president: Rubbermaid Inc. CORP AFFIL senior vice president: Rubbermaid Cleaning Products; senior vice president: Rubbermaid Commercial Products.

Foundation Officials

William H. Pfund: trustee B Monroe, WI 1953. ED Princeton University (1975). PRIM CORP EMPL vice president investor relations and corporate communication: Rubbermaid Inc.
Martha Roblee: trustee
George C. Weigand: vice president, trustee (see above)

Grants Analysis

Disclosure Period: calendar year ending 1997
Total Grants: $374,169*
Number of Grants: 49
Average Grant: $7,636
Highest Grant: $140,000
Typical Range: $1,000 to $10,000
***Note:** Giving excludes matching gifts; United Way.

Recent Grants

Note: Grants derived from 1997 Form 990.

Arts & Humanities

3,000	Power of the Pen, Richfield, OH
3,000	Wayne Center for the Arts, Wooster, OH
3,000	Wayne Center for the Arts, Wooster, OH
1,800	University of Pennsylvania Press Inc., Philadelphia, PA

Civic & Public Affairs

35,000	Greater Wayne County Foundation Inc., Wooster, OH
5,000	Jobs for America's Graduates, Alexandria, VA
5,000	Ohio Business Week Foundation, Columbus, OH

Education

140,000	The College of Wooster, Wooster, OH
20,000	Ohio Foundation of Independent Colleges Inc., Columbus, OH
15,000	Students in Free Enterprise, Springfield, MO

11,000	Junior Achievement Inc., Orrville, OH
8,670	College of Wooster, Wooster, OH
5,000	Amherst College Trustees, Amherst, MA
5,000	Carnegie Mellon University, Pittsburgh, PA
5,000	College Foundation, NY
5,000	Cowley County Community Junior College, KS
5,000	Eaton Elementary, Eaton, OH
5,000	Michigan State University Foundation, E Lansing, MI
5,000	University of Toledo, Toledo, OH
4,538	Trustees of William Jewell College, Liberty, MO
3,084	Baldwin-Wallace College, Berea, OH
3,000	Tri-County Education Service Center, Wooster, OH
2,635	University of Cincinnati Foundation, Cincinnati, OH
2,503	Apple Creek Elementary, Apple Creek, OH
2,500	CMA Educational & Industrial Dev. Institute, Columbus, OH
2,500	The College of Wooster, Wooster, OH
2,000	Franklin Elementary, Wooster, OH
2,000	University of North Carolina, Chapel Hill, NC
2,000	University of Tennessee Research Corporation, TN
1,750	Harvard University, Cambridge, MA
1,625	North Carolina State University Foundation Inc., Raleigh, NC
1,600	Otterbein College, Westerville, OH
1,500	Apple Creek Elementary, Apple Greek, OH
1,500	Northwestern Local Schools, West Salem, OH
1,500	Regents of the University of Michigan, Ann Arbor, MI
1,500	United Negro College Fund, Cleveland, OH
1,500	United States Military Academy Alumni Assoc., Annapolis, MD
1,500	Waynedale High School, Apple Greek, OH

Health

10,000	Children's Hospital Medical Center, OH
5,000	American Red Cross Blood Services, Cleveland, OH

Religion

20,000	Wooster Interfaith Housing Corporation, Wooster, OH
10,000	The Salvation Army, Wooster, OH
1,500	Calvin Theological Seminary, Grand Rapids, MI

Social Services

37,500	United Way of Wooster, Wooster, OH
37,500	United Way of Wooster, Wooster, OH
37,500	United Way of Wooster, Wooster, OH
37,500	United Way of Wooster, Wooster, OH
15,000	Boys' Village Inc., Smithville, OH
15,000	Children's Grand Prix of Minnesota, Minneapolis, MN
15,000	United Way of Wooster, Inc., Wooster, OH
15,000	Youth Development Center, Inc., Winchester, VA
2,610	YMCA-Canton Area, Tippecanoe, OH
1,500	Orrville Area Boys & Girls Club., Inc., Orrville, OH

RUDDICK CORP.

Company Contact

Charlotte, NC
Web: http://www.ruddick.com

Company Description

Employees: 20,200
SIC(s): 2284 Thread Mills, 5411 Grocery Stores, 6719 Holding Companies Nec.

SUBSIDIARY COMPANIES

NC: Harris-Teeter, Matthews

Dickson Foundation

Giving Contact

Colleen Colbert, Secretary & Treasurer
Dickson Foundation
Number 1800, Two First Union Ctr.
Charlotte, NC 28282
Phone: (704)372-5404
Fax: (704)372-6409

Description

EIN: 566022339
Organization Type: Corporate Foundation
Giving Locations: FL; GA; NC; SC; TN
Grant Types: General Support.

Financial Summary

Total Giving: $2,400,000 (2000 approx); $2,400,000 (1999 approx); $4,201,805 (1998). Note: Contributes through foundation only.
Giving Analysis: Giving for 1998 includes: foundation ($4,129,805); foundation grants to United Way ($45,000); foundation scholarships ($27,000)
Assets: $58,301,472 (1998); $53,617,481 (1997); $46,315,395 (1996)

Typical Recipients

Arts & Humanities: Arts Funds, Community Arts, Arts & Humanities-General, History & Archaeology, Museums/Galleries, Performing Arts, Theater
Civic & Public Affairs: Botanical Gardens/Parks, Community Foundations, Civic & Public Affairs-General, Housing, Parades/Festivals, Philanthropic Organizations, Urban & Community Affairs
Education: Afterschool/Enrichment Programs, Business Education, Colleges & Universities, Community & Junior Colleges, Environmental Education, Faculty Development, Leadership Training, Medical Education, Private Education (Precollege), Science/Mathematics Education, Secondary Education (Private), Student Aid
Environment: Environment-General, Resource Conservation
Health: Clinics/Medical Centers, Health Organizations, Heart, Hospices, Hospitals, Medical Research, Single-Disease Health Associations
Religion: Churches, Religious Organizations, Religious Welfare
Science: Science Museums
Social Services: Child Welfare, Community Service Organizations, Food/Clothing Distribution, Scouts, Senior Services, Substance Abuse, United Funds/United Ways, YMCA/YWCA/YMHA/YWHA, Youth Organizations

Contributions Analysis

Giving Priorities: Education, arts, and health.
Arts & Humanities: 17%. More than half of the funding in this category supports the North Carolina Performing Arts Center in Charlotte. Other interests include the North Carolina Dance Theater, the Arts and Science Council in Charlotte, NC, and community arts centers.
Civic & Public Affairs: 2%. Funds the North Carolina Zoological Society, business and free enterprise, minority affairs, municipalities, and community affairs.
Education: 60%. Primarily in the form of support for colleges and universities in North Carolina, specifically the University of North Carolina, Wake Forest University, and North Carolina University. Also supports education funds, faculty development, medical education, and secondary schools.
Health: 13%. Primarily supports the Arthritis Research Center in Chapel Hill, NC. Cancer research, hospitals and hospices also receive support.
Social Services: 7%. Family and youth services.
Note: Contributions made in 1998.

Application Procedures

Initial Contact: Send a brief letter of inquiry.
Application Requirements: A description of organization, amount requested, and purpose of funds.
Deadlines: None.

Restrictions

Does not support individuals. Provides primarily local giving.

Corporate Officials

Alan Thomas Dickson: chairman B Charlotte, NC 1931. ED North Carolina State College BS (1953); Harvard University MBA (1955). PRIM CORP EMPL chairman: Ruddick Corp. CORP AFFIL director: Sonoco Products Co.; director: Teal Aviation Inc.; chairman: Ruddick Corp.; chairman, director: Linville Resorts Inc.; director: NationsBank Corp.; director: Lance Inc.; director: Bassett Furniture Industries North Carolina; director: Harris Teeter Inc.; director: Bassett Furniture Industries Inc.; chairman: America & Efird Mills Inc.; director: BankAmerica Corp.

Foundation Officials

Alan Thomas Dickson: president (see above)
Rush S. Dickson, III: vice president B 1954. ED Washington & Lee University (1976); Vanderbilt University (1978). PRIM CORP EMPL senior vice president: Harris-Teeter.
Rush Stuart Dickson: chairman B Charlotte, NC 1929. ED Davidson College (1951). PRIM CORP EMPL chairman: Harris-Teeter PRIM NONPR EMPL chairman executive committee: Ruddick Co. CORP AFFIL director: Textron Inc.; director: United Dominion Industries Ltd.; director: Ruddick Investment Co.; director: PCA International Inc.; chairman executive committee: Ruddick Corp.; director: First Union Corp.; director: Harris Teeter Inc.; director: America & Efird Mills Inc.; director: Dimon Inc.
Thomas W. Dickson: vice president B 1955. ED University of Virginia BA (1977); Colgate University Darden School of Business Administration MBA (1980). PRIM CORP EMPL president: Ruddick Corp.
Alison Scott: director

Grants Analysis

Disclosure Period: calendar year ending 1998
Total Grants: $4,129,805*
Number of Grants: 358
Average Grant: $11,536
Highest Grant: $200,000
Typical Range: $1,000 to $10,000
***Note:** Giving excludes scholarships, United Way.

Recent Grants

Note: Grants derived from 1997 Form 990.

Arts & Humanities

50,000	Endowment of the Arts
50,000	Endowment of the Arts
50,000	North Carolina Performing Arts Center, Charlotte, NC
30,000	Museum of the New South, Charlotte, NC
20,000	North Carolina Museum of Art, Raleigh, NC

Civic & Public Affairs

40,000	Central Piedmont Community Council
20,000	Blue Ridge Leadership Conference, NC
20,000	Brookgreen Gardens, Murrells Inlet, SC
10,000	Habitat for Humanity, Charlotte, NC

Education

100,000	Davidson College, Davidson, NC -- support chair RSD
50,000	Charlotte Country Day School, Charlotte, NC
50,000	Charlotte Latin School, Charlotte, NC
50,000	Davidson College, Davidson, NC -- support Dr. Kuykendall Scholarship
50,000	McCallie School, Chattanooga, TN
30,000	Hollins College, Roanoke, VA
25,000	Davidson College, Davidson, NC
25,000	Providence Day School, Charlotte, NC
25,000	Queens College, Charlotte, NC
25,000	Queens College, Charlotte, NC
20,000	Darden Graduate School of Business
20,000	Darden Graduate School of Business
20,000	Furman University, Greenville, SC
20,000	Johnson C. Smith University, Charlotte, NC
20,000	Outward Bound School
20,000	Queens College, Charlotte, NC -- support McColl Business School
20,000	St. Catherine's School, Richmond, VA
20,000	Salem College, Winston-Salem, NC
20,000	South Carolina Governor's School for Science and Math, Hartsville, SC
20,000	University of North Carolina Chapel Hill Business School, Chapel Hill, NC
20,000	University of North Carolina Greensboro, Greensboro, NC
20,000	Washington and Lee University, Lexington, VA
15,000	Wingate College, Wingate, NC
10,000	Belmont Abbey -- capital campaign
10,000	Charlotte Latin School, Charlotte, NC
10,000	Gethsemane Enrichment Program
10,000	Junior Achievement, Charlotte, NC

Environment

20,000	Nature Conservancy of Wild North Carolina, NC

Health

50,000	Carolinas Heart Institute
25,000	Presbyterian Hospital Foundation, Charlotte, NC
10,000	Bowman Gray Medical Center -- support Equation for Progress

Religion

20,000	St. Mary's, Burlington, WI

Science

20,000	Exploris, Raleigh, NC
10,000	Discovery Place, Charlotte, NC

Social Services

50,000	Gaston County Family YMCA
50,000	YMCA
25,000	Boy Scouts of America Mecklenburg County Council, Charlotte, NC
20,000	Summit House, Greensboro, NC
10,000	Alexander Children's Center, Charlotte, NC
10,000	Dalton Village Outreach Center, Charlotte, NC
10,000	Metrolina Food Bank, Charlotte, NC

RUSSER FOODS

Company Contact

Buffalo, NY

Company Description

Employees: 180
SIC(s): 2013 Sausages & Other Prepared Meats, 5147 Meats & Meat Products.
Parent Company: Zemco Industries

Russer Foods/Zemsky Family Trust

Giving Contact

Howard Zemsky, President
Russer Foods
665 Perry St.
Buffalo, NY 14210
Phone: (716)826-6400
Fax: (716)826-9183

Alternate Contact

6420 Southeast Harbor Cir.
Stuart, FL 34996-1958
Fax: (786)826-5138
Note: Zemsky Family Trust address.

Description

Founded: 1987
EIN: 112867625
Organization Type: Corporate Foundation
Giving Locations: NY: Buffalo
Grant Types: General Support.

Financial Summary

Total Giving: $180,125 (1998); $144,160 (1997); $195,350 (1996). Note: Contributes through foundation only.
Giving Analysis: Giving for 1997 includes: foundation ($143,160); foundation grants to United Way ($1,000); 1998: foundation ($179,125); foundation grants to United Way ($1,000)
Assets: $560,170 (1998); $531,104 (1997); $405,133 (1996)
Gifts Received: $150,000 (1998); $223,312 (1997); $237,778 (1996). Note: Contributions are received from Russer Foods.

Typical Recipients

Arts & Humanities: Arts Centers, Arts Festivals, Ballet, Dance, History & Archaeology, Libraries, Museums/Galleries, Music, Performing Arts, Public Broadcasting, Theater
Civic & Public Affairs: Botanical Gardens/Parks, Civil Rights, Community Foundations, Employment/Job Training, Civic & Public Affairs-General, Municipalities/Towns, Parades/Festivals, Urban & Community Affairs, Zoos/Aquariums
Education: Arts/Humanities Education, Colleges & Universities, Private Education (Precollege), Religious Education, Student Aid
Environment: Wildlife Protection
Health: Arthritis, Cancer, Children's Health/Hospitals, Diabetes, Geriatric Health, Health Organizations, Heart, Hospices, Hospitals, Medical Research, Multiple Sclerosis, Prenatal Health Issues, Research/Studies Institutes, Respiratory, Single-Disease Health Associations
International: Missionary/Religious Activities
Religion: Jewish Causes, Religious Welfare, Synagogues/Temples
Science: Science Museums
Social Services: Camps, Child Welfare, Community Service Organizations, Domestic Violence, Family Services, Food/Clothing Distribution, People with Disabilities, Recreation & Athletics, Scouts, Senior Services, Special Olympics, Substance Abuse, United Funds/United Ways, YMCA/YWCA/YMHA/YWHA

Contributions Analysis

Giving Priorities: Religious organizations, education, health, art, social studies and civic.
Arts & Humanities: 46%. Supports theater, orchestra, and festivals.
Civic & Public Affairs: 4%. Supports community activities.
Education: 4%. Supports education programs.
Health: 14%. Funds hospitals, single-disease associations.
Religion: 24%. Supports religious community centers and associations.
Social Services: 8%. Supports United Way, and youth programs, and preventative education.
Note: Total contributions made in 1998.

Application Procedures

Initial Contact: Send a brief letter of inquiry.
Application Requirements: Include purpose of funds sought and proof of tax-exempt status.
Deadlines: None.
Notes: Foundation does not accept applications.

Restrictions

Grants are not made to individuals.

Corporate Officials

Howard Zemsky: president B 1959. ED Michigan State University (1981). PRIM CORP EMPL president: Zemco Industries Inc. Delaware.
Sam Zemsky: chairman, director B 1926. PRIM CORP EMPL chairman, director: Zemco Industries Inc. Delaware.

Foundation Officials

Howard Zemsky: trustee (see above)
Sam Zemsky: trustee (see above)
Shirley Zemsky: trustee

Grants Analysis

Disclosure Period: calendar year ending 1998
Total Grants: $179,125*
Number of Grants: 58
Average Grant: $3,088
Highest Grant: $37,000
Typical Range: $500 to $7,500
***Note:** Giving excludes United Way.

Recent Grants

Note: Grants derived from 1998 Form 990.

Arts & Humanities

37,000	Buffalo Philharmonic Orchestra, Buffalo, NY
12,250	Studio Arena Theater, Buffalo, NY
10,000	Studio Arena Endowment, Buffalo, NY
5,000	Buffalo/Erie County Historical Society, Buffalo, NY
4,400	Buffalo Philharmonic Womens Committee, Buffalo, NY
3,000	Atlantic Classical Orchestra, Stuart, FL
2,750	Albright Knox Art Gallery, Buffalo, NY
2,000	Irish Classical Theater
2,000	Jacobs Pillow, Becket, MA -- (Scholarship)
1,000	Chautauqua Institute, Chautauqua, NY
1,000	Library Foundation of Martin City, Stuart, FL
1,000	Naples Players, The, Naples, FL
500	Miami City Ballet, Miami, FL
500	Sheas Performing Art Center, Buffalo, NY
500	Williamstown Art Conservation Center, Williamstown, MA
500	Williamstown Theater Festival, Williamstown, MA
500	WPBT 2, Miami, FL

Civic & Public Affairs

3,000	Tanglewood Annual Fund, Boston, MA
1,750	National Conference, The, Los Angeles, CA
1,600	Leadership Buffalo, Buffalo, NY
1,200	Roswell Park Alliance, Buffalo, NY
1,000	Buffalo Niagara Partnership Found., Buffalo, NY

Education

2,500	South Area Illegible Text Schecter Day School, Stoughton, MA

1,500	Buffalo Prep, Buffalo, NY
500	D'Youville Pres. Scholarship Endowment, Buffalo, NY
500	Elmwood Franklin School, Buffalo, NY
400	St. Joseph's Collegiate Institute, Buffalo, NY
250	Daeman College, Amherst, NY

Health

12,500	Children's Hospital, Buffalo, NY
4,000	Arthritis Foundation of WNY, New York, NY
3,000	Muscular Dystrophy Association, New York, NY
2,000	Daniel Heumann Fund for Spinal Research, Miami, FL
1,275	Leukemia Society of America, Buffalo, NY
1,000	Council on Aging - Martin County, Stuart, FL
1,000	March of Dimes, Buffalo, NY
500	American Heart Association, Buffalo, NY
500	Gwen Knapp Center for Lupus, Chicago, IL
500	Independent Health Found., Buffalo, NY
500	Memorial Sloan Kettering Cancer Center, New York, NY
500	Walk to Cure Diabetes, New York, NY

Religion

25,000	Reform Congregation of Stuart, Stuart, FL
10,000	National Yiddish Book Center, Amherst, MA
5,000	Jewish Federation of Greater Buffalo, Buffalo, NY
1,000	Simon Wiesenthal Center, New York, NY
1,000	Temple Beth Zion, Palm Beach, FL

Social Services

7,500	Boy Scouts, New York, NY
1,000	King Urban Life Center, Buffalo, NY
1,000	United Way, Buffalo, NY
500	Camp Endeavor, Dundee, FL
500	Sisters Hospital Found., Buffalo, NY
500	YWCA of Western N.Y., Buffalo, NY

RUTLEDGE HILL PRESS

Company Contact

211 Seventh Avenue
Nashville, TN 37219-1823
Phone: (615)244-2700

Company Description

Employees: 45
SIC(s): 2731 Book Publishing.

Rutledge Hill Press Foundation

Giving Contact

James R. Powell, President
Rutledge Hill Press Foundation
1920 Oak Hills Drive
Colorado Springs, CO 80919
Phone: (719)594-9836

Description

Founded: 1993
EIN: 621486303
Organization Type: Corporate Foundation

Financial Summary

Total Giving: $136,394 (1998); $139,435 (1997); $214,820 (1996)
Giving Analysis: Giving for 1996 includes: foundation ($214,820); 1997: foundation ($113,600); foundation matching gifts ($25,835); 1998: foundation ($122,632); foundation matching gifts ($13,762)
Assets: $337,729 (1998); $477,990 (1997); $583,783 (1996)

Typical Recipients

Arts & Humanities: Libraries
Civic & Public Affairs: Native American Affairs, Urban & Community Affairs
Education: Colleges & Universities, Minority Education, Religious Education, Secondary Education (Public)
Health: Prenatal Health Issues, Preventive Medicine/Wellness Organizations
International: Foreign Educational Institutions, International-General, International Development, International Organizations, International Relations, International Relief Efforts, Missionary/Religious Activities
Religion: Bible Study/Translation, Churches, Religion-General, Ministries, Religious Welfare
Social Services: Community Service Organizations

Contributions Analysis

Giving Priorities: Religious ministries and organizations, inner city and international literacy programs, and international organizations.
Education: 14%. Funds inner city college readiness programs and Christian colleges.
International: 32%. Supports international ministries and outreach programs.
Religion: 54%. Supports Christian Ministries, youth organizations and biblical translation.
Note: Total contributions made in 1998.

Application Procedures

Initial Contact: Send a brief letter of inquiry.
Deadlines: None.

Corporate Officials

John P. Finnegan: chief financial officer, publisher PRIM CORP EMPL chief financial officer: Rutledge Hill Press.
Bill Jayne: president PRIM CORP EMPL president: Rutledge Hill Press.
Lawrence Mynatt Stone: chairman, publisher B Baltimore, MD 1945. ED University of Iowa BA (1968). PRIM CORP EMPL chairman, publisher: Rutledge Hill Press.

Foundation Officials

Don Finto: director
William Lane: director
Ronald Pitkin: director
James R. Powell: president
Lawrence Mynatt Stone: secretary, treasurer (see above)

Grants Analysis

Disclosure Period: calendar year ending 1998
Total Grants: $122,632*
Number of Grants: 18
Average Grant: $6,813
Highest Grant: $20,000
Typical Range: $2,500 to $25,000
*Note: Giving excludes matching gifts.

Recent Grants

Note: Grants derived from 1998 Form 990.

Civic & Public Affairs

16,500	Interdev, Seattle, WA -- Fund Consultancy for Strategic Evangelism Pla
6,500	Urban Promise, Camden, NJ -- Support College Readiness Program of Inner City

Education

10,000	Gordon College, Wenham, MA -- General

International

15,000	Operation Mobilization, Tyrone, GA -- Fundraising Program for Publishing Indian
10,000	African Enterprises, Republic of South Africa -- General
10,000	Audio Scriptures International, Holland, MI -- Matching Funds for Study Guide in 18 Language
6,142	International Christian Ministries, Bakersfield, CA -- Fund 3 Educational Projects of Icm in Kenya
5,000	International Reconciliation Coalition, Ventura, CA -- General
5,000	Sem. Library, Costa Rica -- General
1,000	Cuba Project, Washington, DC -- General
1,000	Magazine Training Institute, Oradea, Romania -- General

Religion

20,000	Franklin House, Franklin, TN -- General
10,000	Reconciling Raleigh, Raleigh, NC -- General
7,500	Bay Road Church, New York -- General
3,762	Raleigh International Church, Raleigh, NC -- Matching Grant for "Reconciling Raleigh"
2,330	Wycliffe Translators, Waxhaw, NC -- General
310	Youth for Christ, Memphis, TN -- General

RYDER SYSTEM, INC.

Company Contact

Miami, FL

Company Description

Revenue: US$5,363,900,000 (1999)
Profit: US$419,600,000 (1999)
Fortune Rank: 309, per FORTUNE Magazine's list of 500 Largest U.S. Corporations (1999).
FF 309
SIC(s): 4212 Local Trucking Without Storage, 4213 Trucking Except Local, 4731 Freight Transportation Arrangement, 7513 Truck Rental & Leasing Without Drivers.

Nonmonetary Support

Value: $65,000 (1991); $70,000 (1990); $65,000 (1989)
Type: Donated Equipment; In-kind Services; Loaned Employees; Workplace Solicitation
Volunteer Programs: Company actively supports employee volunteerism, and encourages management to volunteer in organizations it supports.
Note: Company also donates the use of facilities.

Ryder System Charitable Foundation

Giving Contact

Ross Roadman, Executive Director
Ryder System Charitable Foundation
3600 NW 82nd Ave.
Miami, FL 33166
Phone: (305)593-3726
Fax: (305)593-4579

Description

EIN: 592462315
Organization Type: Corporate Foundation
Giving Locations: CA: Los Angeles through community initiative program; FL: Dade County, Miami metropolitan area Miami; GA: Atlanta through community initiative program; MO: St. Louis through community initiative program; OH: Cincinnati through community

initiative program; TX: Dallas through community initiative program
Grant Types: Employee Matching Gifts, General Support.
Note: Employee matching gift ratio: 1 to 1.

Giving Philosophy

'Ryder System supports a broad cross-section of organizations and activities in the Greater Miami area, where its headquarters is located. This support grows out of a strong interest in the enhancement of the community, to the end that the quality of life in the Greater Miami area is perceived and acknowledged to be a superior environment in which to live and work.' *A Statement of Policy on Charitable Contributions, Ryder System*

Financial Summary

Total Giving: $955,908 (1997); $2,300,000 (1996); $2,500,000 (1995 approx). Note: Contributes through corporate direct giving program and foundation.
Giving Analysis: Giving for 1997 includes: foundation ($580,608); foundation grants to United Way ($376,148); foundation gifts to individuals ($22,000)
Assets: $19,218 (1997); $67,209 (1996); $313,834 (1993)
Gifts Received: $905,175 (1997); $1,525,201 (1996); $2,260,168 (1993). Note: The foundation receives gifts from Ryder System, Inc.

Typical Recipients

Arts & Humanities: Arts Associations & Councils, Arts Centers, Arts Funds, Ballet, Dance, History & Archaeology, Literary Arts, Museums/Galleries, Music, Opera, Performing Arts, Theater
Civic & Public Affairs: African American Affairs, Botanical Gardens/Parks, Community Foundations, Economic Development, Civic & Public Affairs-General, Housing, Professional & Trade Associations, Public Policy, Safety, Urban & Community Affairs
Education: Arts/Humanities Education, Business Education, Business-School Partnerships, Colleges & Universities, Community & Junior Colleges, Education Funds, Education Reform, Engineering/Technological Education, Faculty Development, Education-General, Legal Education, Minority Education, Public Education (Precollege), Science/Mathematics Education, Student Aid
Health: Children's Health/Hospitals, Hospitals, Research/Studies Institutes, Single-Disease Health Associations
International: International Peace & Security Issues
Religion: Ministries, Religious Welfare
Social Services: Child Welfare, Family Services, Recreation & Athletics, Scouts, Social Services-General, Substance Abuse, United Funds/United Ways, Volunteer Services, YMCA/YWCA/YMHA/YWHA, Youth Organizations

Contributions Analysis

Giving Priorities: Health, social welfare, colleges and universities, cultural organizations, and civic organizations.
Arts & Humanities: 31%. Provides basic support to numerous established organizations. Priority is broadening access to cultural events to school children, the economically disadvantaged, and others.
Civic & Public Affairs: 5%. Supports community centers, urban leagues and junior achievement.
Education: 22%. Supports public and private educational programs from kindergarten through graduate school. Contributes to educational programs and employment opportunities for minorities in America.
Health: 1%. Supports children's health organizations.
Social Services: 41%. Provides funding for private social service agency programs; revitalizing communities through economic development programs and improved housing facilities; and providing counseling services and other coping mechanisms to those in crisis situations.
Note: Total contributions in 1997.

Application Procedures

Initial Contact: Send a concise letter of request.
Application Requirements: General a description of organization, including goals, purposes, and significant past projects; description and budget of the project for which funding is sought; specific amount requested, and sources and amount of other funding obtained for requested purpose; most recent financial statements; current organizational budget; statement of fundraising expenses; list of officers and board members, with affiliations; and proof of tax-exempt status.
Deadlines: None, but it is recommended that requests be submitted during the first half of the calendar year.
Decision Notification: Allow 90 to 120 days for processing; grant decisions are finalized in third quarter of year.

Restrictions

Does not support religious organizations for religious purposes; political or legislative groups; veterans' or fraternal organizations; individuals; fundraising events including sponsorship, ticket purchases, or goodwill advertising; single-disease health organizations; capital programs, endowment funds, or loan programs; or health-care facilities.

Corporate Officials

Mitchell Anthony Burns: chairman, president, chief executive officer B Las Vegas, NV 1942. ED Brigham Young University BS (1964); University of California at Berkeley MBA (1965). PRIM CORP EMPL chairman, president, chief executive officer: Ryder System, Inc. CORP AFFIL chairman, president, chief executive officer: Ryder Truck Rental Inc.; chairman, secretary, director: Transit Management Tucson; director: Pfizer Inc.; Ryder Energy Distr Corp.; director: Chase Manhattan Corp.; director: JC Penney Co. Inc.; director: Chase Manhattan Bank. NONPR AFFIL trustee: University Miami; member, board visitors graduate schoolbusiness administration: University North Carolina Chapel Hill; member: Business Roundtable; trustee, vice chairman: National Urban League; member: Bus Higher Education Forum; member: Business Council; member national advisory council sch management: Brigham Young University.
John R. Haddock: senior vice president marketing ED Harvard University Graduate School of Business Administration MBA; University of Birmingham BS. PRIM CORP EMPL senior vice president marketing: Ryder System, Inc. ADD CORP EMPL senior vice president: Ryder Truck Rental Inc.
Edwin Allen Huston: vice chairman, director B Dayton, OH 1938. ED Amherst College AB (1960); Harvard University MBA (1962). PRIM CORP EMPL vice chairman, director: Ryder System, Inc. CORP AFFIL trustee: WPBT Channel 2; director: Unisys Corp. NONPR AFFIL president, trustee: Ft Lauderdale Art Museum; vice president: Transit Management Tucson. CLUB AFFIL Lauderdale Yacht Club; Coral Ridge Country Club.
Thomas E. McKinnon: executive vice president human resources ED Wayne State University; Western Michigan University. PRIM CORP EMPL executive vice president human resources: Ryder System, Inc. ADD CORP EMPL vice president human resources: Unisys Corp.

Foundation Officials

Mitchell Anthony Burns: president, director (see above)
Dwight D. Denny: director B Winston-Salem, NC 1943. ED University of North Carolina BBA (1966). PRIM CORP EMPL executive vice president development: Ryder System, Inc. CORP AFFIL president: Ryder Puerto Rico Inc.
R. Ray Goode: director ED Pennsylvania State University; University of Charleston. PRIM CORP EMPL vice president public affairs: Ryder System, Inc. CORP AFFIL director: A. Duda & Sons. NONPR AFFIL director: South Miami Hospital; trustee: University Miami; vice president: Dade County Youth Fair & Expo; director: AvMed; trustee: Baptist Health System.
James B. Griffin: director ED Pennsylvania State University BA. PRIM CORP EMPL president: Ryder Transportation Services ADD CORP EMPL president: Ryder Truck Rental Inc.
John R. Haddock: board member (see above)
James Michael Herron: secretary, director B Chicago, IL 1934. ED University of Missouri AB (1955); Northwestern University (1958-1959); Washington University JD (1961); Harvard University (1982). PRIM CORP EMPL senior executive vice president, general counsel: Ryder System, Inc. ADD CORP EMPL president: Ryder Services Corp. NONPR AFFIL chairman: New World School Arts; member national council: Washington University School Law; first vice president, director executive commission: Florida Grand Opera; member: Missouri Bar Association; director: Fiduciary Trust International South; member: Florida Bar Association; member: Dade County Bar Association; member: Association Bar New York City; director: Bar Association Metropolitan Saint Louis; member: American Trucking Association; director: American Trucking Association Litigation Center; member: American Bar Association; member: American Society of Corporate Secretaries. CLUB AFFIL Royal Palm Tennis Club.
Edwin Allen Huston: vice president, director (see above)
Thomas E. McKinnon: director (see above)
Larry S. Mulkey: director PRIM CORP EMPL president: Ryder Integrated Logistics Inc. CORP AFFIL president: Ryder Student Transportation Services.
Gerald R. Riordan: director B 1949. ED Niagara University BS (1971); University of Miami MBA (1973). PRIM CORP EMPL president: Ryder Transportation Inc.
Ross Roadman: executive director
Gina S. Russ: assistant secretary B 1954. PRIM CORP EMPL attorney: Ryder System, Inc. CORP AFFIL secretary: Piercing Pagoda Florida.
Randall E. West: director PRIM CORP EMPL president: Ryder Automotive Operations. CORP AFFIL president: Commercial Carriers Inc.

Grants Analysis

Disclosure Period: calendar year ending 1997
Total Grants: $557,760*
Number of Grants: 162
Average Grant: $3,443
Highest Grant: $50,000
Typical Range: $25 to $10,000
***Note:** Giving excludes gifts to individuals for disaster relief; United Way.

Recent Grants

Note: Grants derived from 1997 Form 990.

Arts & Humanities

50,000	Florida Grand Opera, Miami, FL
40,000	Concert Association, Miami Beach, FL
40,000	New World Symphony, Miami Beach, FL
40,000	New World Symphony, Miami Beach, FL
30,000	National Foundation for Advancement in the Arts, Miami, FL
25,000	Florida Philharmonic Orchestra, Fort Lauderdale, FL
25,000	Miami Art Museum, Miami, FL
9,650	Mesquite Arts Council, Mesquite, NV
5,000	Coconut Grove Playhouse, Coconut Grove, FL
5,000	Historical Association, Miami, FL

Civic & Public Affairs

25,000	Fairchild Tropical Gardens, Miami, FL
10,000	Alpharetta Community
10,000	Urban League, Jacksonville, FL
5,000	National Child Labor Commission, New York, NY
500	Riverside House

Education

50,000	New American Schools, Arlington, VA
15,000	Institute for Education, Washington, DC
15,000	University of Utah, Salt Lake City, UT
10,000	National Guild of Community Schools
7,500	Florida Memorial College, Miami, FL
7,500	Junior Achievement
7,500	University of Charleston, Charleston, WV
5,000	Broward Education Foundation, Fort Lauderdale, FL
5,000	Consortium for Graduate Study in Management, St. Louis, MO
5,000	Johns Hopkins University, Baltimore, MD
2,500	College Assistance Program, Coral Gables, FL
2,500	Haas School of Business
2,500	Junior Achievement
1,500	Chet Jordan Scholarship Fund
1,000	FIU Foundation

Health

1,000	Make-A-Wish Foundation
500	Center for Childhood Development

Social Services

125,000	United Way of Dade County, Miami, FL
125,000	United Way of Dade County, Miami, FL
125,000	United Way of Dade County, Miami, FL
10,000	Family Christian Association, Miami Shores, FL
5,000	Boys and Girls Clubs
5,000	YMCA, Miami, FL
848	Cedar Valley United Way, Waterloo, IA
300	United Way

S.G. COWEN

Company Contact

1221 Avenue of the Americas
New York, NY 10020
Phone: (212)278-6000
Fax: (212)278-5452
Web: http://www.cowen.com

Company Description

Formed by Merger of: SG USA (1998);
Former Name:.
Revenue: US$400,000,000
Employees: 1,600
SIC(s): 6211 Security Brokers & Dealers.
Parent Company: Societe Generale Group, 29 Boulevard Haussmann, Paris, France

Corporate Sponsorship

Type: Arts & cultural events; Sports events

Cowen Foundation

Giving Contact

Robert M. Greenberger, Director, Taxes
S.G. Cowen & Co.
New York, NY

Description

Founded: 1990
EIN: 133550779
Organization Type: Corporate Giving Program. Supports preselected organizations only.
Giving Locations: NY; PA
Grant Types: General Support.

Financial Summary

Total Giving: $617,226 (1995); $742,845 (1994); $423,127 (1993). Note: Contributes through corporate direct giving program only.
Assets: $377,483 (1995); $33,766 (1994); $22,319 (1993)
Gifts Received: $960,250 (1995); $760,403 (1994); $440,765 (1993). Note: In 1995, contributions were received from Cowen & Co. ($945,136), Gerald P. Kaminsky ($4,076), and Judy Cowen ($11,038).

Typical Recipients

Arts & Humanities: Arts Associations & Councils, Ballet, Museums/Galleries, Music, Opera, Performing Arts, Theater, Visual Arts
Civic & Public Affairs: Business/Free Enterprise, Civic & Public Affairs-General, Public Policy, Women's Affairs
Education: Arts/Humanities Education, Business Education, Colleges & Universities, Economic Education, Minority Education, Private Education (Precollege), Religious Education, Secondary Education (Private), Student Aid
Health: Cancer, Children's Health/Hospitals, Diabetes, Eyes/Blindness, Health Organizations, Heart, Hospitals, Hospitals (University Affiliated), Single-Disease Health Associations, Transplant Networks/Donor Banks
International: Missionary/Religious Activities
Religion: Churches, Jewish Causes, Religious Organizations, Religious Welfare
Science: Science Museums, Scientific Labs
Social Services: Child Welfare, Community Service Organizations, Crime Prevention, Family Services, Food/Clothing Distribution, People with Disabilities, Recreation & Athletics, United Funds/United Ways, Youth Organizations

Corporate Officials

Joseph M. Cohen: chairman, chief executive officer director B New York, NY 1937. ED University of Pennsylvania (1964); Columbia University (1965). PRIM CORP EMPL chairman, chief executive officer: Cowen & Co.
Raymond K. Moran: chief operating officer, managing director PRIM CORP EMPL chief operating officer, managing director: Cowen & Co.
Charles T. Peterson: chief financial officer, managing director B Bronxville, NY 1932. ED Manhattan College (1958). PRIM CORP EMPL chief financial officer, managing director: Cowen & Co.

Foundation Officials

Joseph M. Cohen: president, director (see above)
Robert M. Greenberger: secretary, treasurer PRIM CORP EMPL director tax: Cowen & Co.
Raymond W. Merritt: assistant treasurer PRIM CORP EMPL executive partner: Willkie, Farr & Gallagher.
Creighton Houck Peet: vice president, director B New York, NY 1938. ED Tufts University (1961); University of Pennsylvania (1963). PRIM CORP EMPL managing director: Cowen & Co.
Peter W. Schmidt: assistant treasurer
Stephen Robert Weber: director B Kansas City, MO 1938. ED University of Pennsylvania (1960); Harvard University (1962). PRIM CORP EMPL managing director investment research: Cowen & Co.

Grants Analysis

Disclosure Period: calendar year ending 1995
Total Grants: $607,726*
Number of Grants: 307
Average Grant: $1,973
Highest Grant: $45,500
Typical Range: $25 to $10,000
*Note: Giving excludes United Way.

Recent Grants

Note: Grants derived from 1995 Form 990.

Arts & Humanities

12,500	Second Stage Theater, New York, NY
10,755	Metropolitan Museum of Art, New York, NY
5,800	Boston Symphony Orchestra, Boston, MA
4,350	Soho Partnership, New York, NY

Civic & Public Affairs

5,000	One-to-One, New York, NY
4,900	Wall Street Council, New York, NY
4,500	Buhl Foundation, New York, NY

Education

10,000	Rye Country Day School, Rye, NY
7,500	Milton Academy Annual Fund, Milton, MA
5,550	Harvard Business School Fund, Cambridge, MA
5,250	Harvard College Fund, Cambridge, MA
5,000	A Better Chance, New York, NY
5,000	Marymount Manhattan College, New York, NY
5,000	University of Pennsylvania, Philadelphia, PA
3,500	Baruch College Fund, New York, NY
2,500	Economic Education Foundation, New York, NY

Health

45,500	Glaucoma Foundation, New York, NY
20,500	American Italian Foundation for Cancer Research, New York, NY
12,000	National Pediculosis Association, Newton, MA
8,200	St. Jude's Children's Research Hospital, Memphis, TN
3,950	American Heart Association, New York, NY
3,750	Interstitial Cystitus Association, New York, NY
3,160	United Cerebral Palsy Association, Cleveland, OH
3,050	American Cancer Society, Albany, NY
3,050	American Cancer Society, New York, NY
3,000	Beth Israel Hospital, Boston, MA
2,600	North Shore University Hospital, Manhasset, NY

International

2,500	Jerusalem Torah Institute, Brooklyn, NY

Religion

20,825	United Jewish Appeal Federation, New York, NY
9,250	Anti-Defamation League, New York, NY
8,000	Our Lady of Grace, Brooklyn, NY
7,000	St. Patrick's Church, Staten Island, NY
5,500	American Jewish Committee, New York, NY
5,000	St. Bernadette, Brooklyn, NY
5,000	St. Francis Cabrini Catholic Church, Brooklyn, NY
5,000	Yeshiva Chasdei Torah, Brooklyn, NY
3,000	Church of the Cure of ARS, Merrick, NY
3,000	St. Luke's Mothers Club
3,000	Seton Foundation, Staten Island, IL

Science

25,000	Jackson Laboratory, Bar Harbor, ME
5,000	Museum of Natural History, New York, NY

Social Services

13,915	Judge Baker Children's Center, Boston, MA
6,000	United Way, New York, NY
4,860	Hillsborough Auxiliary of the Family Service Agency, Hillsborough, CA
4,500	Youth Enternet of America, Washington, DC

4,150	New York Police and Fire Widows and Children's Benefit Fund, New York, NY
3,600	Boys Club, New York, NY
3,600	Staten Island Center for Independent Living, Staten Island, NY
3,000	United Way Massachusetts Bay, Boston, MA
2,500	Gary Klinsky Children's Center, Brooklyn, NY

S&T BANCORP

Company Contact

Indiana, PA

Company Description

Income: US$115,330,000
Employees: 560
SIC(s): 6022 State Commercial Banks, 6712 Bank Holding Companies.

S&T Bancorp Charitable Foundation

Giving Contact

James C. Miller, President
Main Office
PO Box 190
Indiana, PA 15701-0190
Phone: (724)465-1443

Description

Founded: 1993
EIN: 251716950
Organization Type: Corporate Foundation
Giving Locations: headquarters and operating communities.
Grant Types: Capital, General Support, Scholarship.

Financial Summary

Total Giving: $281,275 (1998); $207,205 (1997); $214,550 (1996)
Giving Analysis: Giving for 1998 includes: foundation ($218,525); foundation grants to United Way ($62,750)
Assets: $933,537 (1998); $1,137,605 (1997); $457,040 (1996)
Gifts Received: $34,500 (1998); $814,475 (1997); $100,000 (1996). Note: In 1996, contributions were received from S&T Bank.

Typical Recipients

Arts & Humanities: Arts Associations & Councils, Arts Festivals, Ballet, History & Archaeology, Libraries, Museums/Galleries, Music
Civic & Public Affairs: Business/Free Enterprise, Clubs, Economic Development, Civic & Public Affairs-General, Municipalities/Towns, Parades/Festivals, Professional & Trade Associations, Safety, Urban & Community Affairs
Education: Agricultural Education, Business Education, Colleges & Universities, Community & Junior Colleges, Education Reform, Education-General, Preschool Education, Public Education (Precollege), Student Aid
Health: Cancer, Children's Health/Hospitals, Clinics/Medical Centers, Diabetes, Heart, Hospitals, Nursing Services, Public Health
Religion: Religious Welfare
Social Services: Big Brother/Big Sister, Child Welfare, Community Centers, Community Service Organizations, People with Disabilities, Recreation & Athletics, Scouts, Senior Services, United Funds/United Ways, Veterans, YMCA/YWCA/YMHA/YWHA

Contributions Analysis

Giving Priorities: Social services, art, education, health, and civic organizations.
Arts & Humanities: 16%. Supports historical societies, arts councils, museums, dance, symphonies, and libraries.
Civic & Public Affairs: 9%. Supports community and economic development, fire departments, and community fairs.
Education: 11%. Supports colleges, Head Start, and economic education.
Health: 10%. Supports single-disease health organizations, hospitals and medical centers, and children's health issues.
Religion: 2%. Funds religious welfare organizations and churches.
Social Services: 52%. Funds senior services, youth organizations, community centers, and United Way.
Note: Total contributions made in 1998.

Application Procedures

Initial Contact: Submit a written application.
Application Requirements: Include the amount requested and purpose of funds sought.
Deadlines: None.
Review Process: The contributions committee meets monthly.

Restrictions

Does not support organizations outside bank's marketing area.

Additional Information

Trust(s): S&T Bank

Corporate Officials

Robert D. Duggan: chairman, chief executive officer chief financial officer PRIM CORP EMPL chairman, chief executive officer: S&T Bancorp.
James C. Miller: president, director PRIM CORP EMPL president, director: S&T Bancorp.
Robert E. Rout: senior vice president, chief financial officer PRIM CORP EMPL senior vice president, chief financial officer: S&T Bancorp.

Foundation Officials

Robert D. Duggan: chairman (see above)
James C. Miller: president (see above)
Bruce W. Salome: vice president PRIM CORP EMPL executive vice president trust service: S&T Bancorp.

Grants Analysis

Disclosure Period: calendar year ending 1998
Total Grants: $218,125*
Number of Grants: 87
Average Grant: $2,512
Highest Grant: $47,000
Typical Range: $1,000 to $5,000
***Note:** Giving excludes United Way, scholarship.

Recent Grants

Note: Grants derived from 1997 Form 990.

Arts & Humanities

6,600	James M. Steward Museum Foundation, Indiana, PA
5,000	Indiana Symphony Society, Indiana, PA -- concert support
3,000	Indiana Arts Council, Indiana, PA -- support arts festival
1,000	Indiana County Sports Hall of Fame, Indiana, PA
1,000	Reynoldsville War Memorial, Reynoldsville, PA
800	Indiana Symphony Series, Indiana, PA -- concert support

Civic & Public Affairs

10,000	Punxsy Regional Development Corporation, Punxsutawney, PA
5,000	Celebration '97, Indiana, PA
3,000	DuBois Volunteer Fire Department, DuBois, PA
2,000	Indiana County Fair Association, Indiana, PA
2,000	Westmoreland Economic Development Corporation, Greensburg, PA
1,000	Habitat for Humanity of Indiana County, Indiana, PA
700	Saltsburg Borough, River's Edge Development, Saltsburg, PA

Education

36,000	Foundation for Indiana University of Pennsylvania, Indiana, PA
6,400	Excellence Foundation, PA
5,000	Indiana University of Pennsylvania Foundation, Indiana, PA -- support Nell Jack Classic
1,000	DuBois Educational Foundation, DuBois, PA -- scholarships
750	Junior Achievement of Southwest Pennsylvania, Johnstown, PA

Health

5,000	Keystone Rehabilitation Systems, Indiana, PA
2,000	American Cancer Society, Indiana, PA
1,700	Make-A-Wish Foundation of Western Pennsylvania, Pittsburgh, PA -- support for Indiana County area
1,000	American Heart Association, Pittsburgh, PA
1,000	Children's Hospital, Pittsburgh, PA -- capital campaign
1,000	United Cerebral Palsy, Spring Church, PA
1,000	Visiting Nurse Association Hospice Foundation, Indiana, PA
750	American Diabetes Association, Mechanicsburg, PA
700	Indiana County Cancer Coalition, Indiana, PA

Religion

5,000	Salvation Army, DuBois, PA
2,000	Unity Presbyterian Church, Pittsburgh, PA
1,000	Open Door, Indiana, PA

Social Services

21,000	United Way Indiana County, Indiana, PA
12,500	White Township Recreation Complex, Indiana, PA
11,500	DuBois Area United Way, DuBois, PA
6,180	East Suburban YMCA, Indiana, PA -- general support, building campaign
5,250	Brookville Area United Fund, Brookville, PA -- capital campaign
5,000	DuBois Soccer Association, DuBois, PA
5,000	Millcraft Charity Golf Classic, Canonsburg, PA
2,500	Westmoreland County Special Olympics, Greensburg, PA
2,500	Westmoreland Human Services, Greensburg, PA
2,000	YMCA of Kiski Valley, Vandergrift, PA
1,500	Aging Services, Indiana, PA
1,500	Big Brothers and Big Sisters, Greensburg, PA
1,250	Goodwill Industries of North Central Pennsylvania, DuBois, PA
1,200	Boy Scouts of America Penn's Woods Council, Seward, PA
1,000	Alice Paul House, Indiana, PA
1,000	Boy Scouts of America Bucktail Council, DuBois, PA
1,000	Handicapped Children's Christmas Party, Indiana, PA -- support for Christmas party
1,000	Kiwanis Gold Tournament, Indiana, PA
1,000	Lincoln Park Athletic and Enrichment, Pittsburgh, PA

1,000 United Way Westmoreland County, Greensburg, PA

SAFECO CORP.

 Number 84 of Top 100 Corporate Givers

Company Contact

Seattle, WA
Web: http://www.safeco.com

Company Description

Revenue: US$6,717,100,000 (1999)
Profit: US$252,200,000 (1999)
Employees: 11,000 (1999)
Fortune Rank: 259, per FORTUNE Magazine's list of 500 Largest U.S. Corporations (1999).
FF 259
SIC(s): 6159 Miscellaneous Business Credit Institutions, 6211 Security Brokers & Dealers, 6311 Life Insurance, 6719 Holding Companies Nec.

Nonmonetary Support

Type: Donated Equipment
Contact: Tom Murphy

Corporate Sponsorship

Value: $100,000
Type: Arts & cultural events; Festivals/fairs

Giving Contact

Rose Lincoln, Manager Community Relations
SAFECO Corp.
SAFECO Plaza
Seattle, WA 98185
Phone: (206)545-5015
Fax: (206)545-5730
Email: roslin@afeco.com

Description

Organization Type: Corporate Giving Program
Giving Locations: headquarters and operating communities in the United States.
Grant Types: Award, Capital, Challenge, Employee Matching Gifts, General Support, Operating Expenses.
Note: Company matches employee gifts to local organisation and the United Way.

Giving Philosophy

'SAFECO believes in America's neighborhoods. That's why we've positioned our community involvement to maximize our impact in the communities where we do business. We develop and fund programs that target and support the social concerns of America's neighborhoods. These social investments support business goals, enhance SAFECO's reputation as an active community partner, contribute to healthy economic development, and demonstrate our commitment to social responsibility by placing resources back into our communities.
'SAFECO actively partners with innovative, dynamic organizations in communities where we live and work. We use our employee expertise and philanthropic resources to make social investments with the same care and concern that SAFECO brings to its businesses. Our partnerships reflect employee values, business interests and community needs.
'Our investments are targeted to the following funding areas: creating safe and vigorous neighborhoods; maintaining engaged and proud neighborhoods; supporting economically secure neighborhoods; promoting stable and friendly neighborhoods.' SAFECO Community Relations Guidelines.

Financial Summary

Total Giving: $8,200,000 (1999 approx); $8,600,000 (1998 approx); $8,100,000 (1997 approx). Note: Contributes through corporate direct giving program only.

Typical Recipients

Arts & Humanities: Arts Funds, Community Arts, Dance, Historic Preservation, Libraries, Museums/Galleries, Opera, Performing Arts, Public Broadcasting, Visual Arts
Civic & Public Affairs: Economic Development, Employment/Job Training, Housing, Nonprofit Management, Public Policy, Safety, Urban & Community Affairs, Zoos/Aquariums
Education: Arts/Humanities Education, Business Education, Colleges & Universities, Continuing Education, Economic Education, Education Associations, Elementary Education (Private), Literacy, Minority Education, Private Education (Precollege), Public Education (Precollege)
Environment: Environment-General
Health: Health Policy/Cost Containment, Health Organizations, Mental Health, Nutrition, Public Health, Single-Disease Health Associations
Social Services: Community Service Organizations, Day Care, Delinquency & Criminal Rehabilitation, Emergency Relief, People with Disabilities, Senior Services, Shelters/Homelessness, Substance Abuse, United Funds/United Ways, Volunteer Services, Youth Organizations

Contributions Analysis

Giving Priorities: Health, social welfare, the arts, education, and civic organizations.
Arts & Humanities: 10% to 15%. Interests include theater, music, dance, museums, arts federations, visual arts, and community festivals.
Civic & Public Affairs: About 30%. Supports economic development, public safety, civic improvement; neighborhood development.
Education: About 20%. Interests include adult education, job readiness, and consumer education in financial areas.
Social Services: 30% to 35%. Major support goes to United Way in operating communities. Supports traditional social services, youth development, family relationships, and natural disaster preparedness.

Application Procedures

Initial Contact: Call or write for application and guidelines, then full proposal of four pages or less, plus attachments.
Application Requirements: Include cover letter; completed application form; how project meets guidelines and criteria; organization's mission statement and purpose, history of accomplishments, governance, area and population served, and role of volunteers (if a collaboration, describe lead agency and relation to others); needs statement, acknowledging existing similar projects, and how proposed project differs, and any efforts to work cooperatively; proposal, including how needs will be addressed, projected goals, objectives, timeline, anticipated impact, population to benefit, how work will be monitored and success evaluated, potential and actual sources of current support, and plan for future support; the following attachments: proof of tax-exempt status, list of board members with affiliations, key organizational staff with titles and functions, IRS Form 990, most recent audited financial statement, one-page summary of actual income and expenses for the past two years, listing of funding sources and amounts for those years, organization's operating budget, detailed project budget, letters from collaborating agencies (if appropriate).
Deadlines: None.
Review Process: All requests are evaluated, either at home office or branch office.
Evaluative Criteria: Program's capability and soundness of financial management and fiscal policies; competency and policy-making authority of board of directors; demonstration that program does not represent unnecessary duplication of services; program is designed to promote self-sufficiency, focuses on prevention rather treatment of problems; can sustain itself beyond company funding; and the organization promotes collaboration between other organizations and individuals.
Decision Notification: Candidates are notified within six weeks of review of proposal.
Notes: Application should be sent to nearest company office.

Restrictions

As a general rule, SAFECO does not make contributions to individuals; projects or programs operating outside the United States; national programs; endowment funds; religious, fraternal, or political groups or projects; general fundraising events; goodwill advertising; loans or investments; film or video production; operating deficits or debt retirement; health education, research, or prevention; amateur arts; individual K-12 public schools; amateur sports teams or athletic scholarships; conferences; research; or fraternal, professional, or membership organizations.

Additional Information

Company was founded in 1923 as a property and casualty insurance company. Today, they've added life and health insurance; real estate management and investments and commercial credit and asset management to their list of operations.
Company sets aside approximately two percent of pre-tax income annually for contributions programs.
Company will consider requests from communities where significant numbers of SAFECO employees live and work.
Contributions are given for one year with no implied renewals.
Company may require recipients to provide an audited financial statement at year's end and periodic reports on the project.
Publications: Boomerang Giving: Flight Instruction Manual (guidelines)

Corporate Officials

Boh A. Dickey: president, chief operating officerrelations B Helena, MT 1944. ED University of Montana (1966). PRIM CORP EMPL president, chief operating officer: SAFECO Corp. ADD CORP EMPL executive vice president: Safeco Insurance Co. America; executive vice president, director: Safeco Insurance Co. Illinois. CORP AFFIL chairman: SAFECO Mutual Funds.
Roger Harry Eigsti: chairman, chief executive officer B Vancouver, WA 1942. ED Linfield College BS (1964). PRIM CORP EMPL chairman, chief executive officer: SAFECO Corp. CORP AFFIL director: Washington Mutual Inc.; director: SAFECO Properties Inc.; director: SAFECO Surplus Lines Insurance Co.; director: SAFECO National Life Insurance; director: SAFECO Life Insurance Co.; director: SAFECO National Insurance Co.; chairman: SAFECO Credit Co. Inc.; chairman: SAFECO Insurance Co. America; director: GSL Corp.; director: General America Corp. Texas; chairman: General Insurance Co. America; director: First National Insurance Co. America; director, chairman: General America Corp.; director: FB Beattie & Co. Inc. NONPR AFFIL business director: Seattle Repertory Theatre; president: Westminster Chapel of Bellevue; chairman budget revision committee: Seattle Chamber of Commerce; member: American Institute CPAs; director: Life Office Management Association. CLUB AFFIL Central Park Tennis Club; Mercer Island Country Club.
Gordon C. Hamilton: vice president public relations PRIM CORP EMPL vice president public relations: SAFECO Insurance Companies.

Giving Program Officials

Boh A. Dickey: member contributions committee B Helena, MT 1944. ED University of Montana (1966).

PRIM CORP EMPL president, chief operating officer: SAFECO Corp. ADD CORP EMPL executive vice president: Safeco Insurance Co. America; executive vice president, director: Safeco Insurance Co. Illinois. CORP AFFIL chairman: SAFECO Mutual Funds.

Roger Harry Eigsti: member contributions committee B Vancouver, WA 1942. ED Linfield College BS (1964). PRIM CORP EMPL chairman, chief executive officer: SAFECO Corp. CORP AFFIL director: Washington Mutual Inc.; director: SAFECO Properties Inc.; director: SAFECO Surplus Lines Insurance Co.; director: SAFECO National Life Insurance; director: SAFECO Life Insurance Co.; director: SAFECO National Insurance Co.; chairman: SAFECO Credit Co. Inc.; chairman: SAFECO Insurance Co. America; director: GSL Corp.; director: General America Corp. Texas; chairman: General Insurance Co. America; director: First National Insurance Co. America; director, chairman: General America Corp.; director: FB Beattie & Co. Inc. NONPR AFFIL business director: Seattle Repertory Theatre; president: Westminster Chapel of Bellevue; chairman budget revision committee: Seattle Chamber of Commerce; member: American Institute CPAs; director: Life Office Management Association. CLUB AFFIL Central Park Tennis Club; Mercer Island Country Club.

Gordon C. Hamilton: member contributions committee PRIM CORP EMPL vice president public relations: SAFECO Insurance Companies.

Rose Hurley: vice president human resources

Michele Kemper: member

Dan Wolfe: member

Grants Analysis

Disclosure Period: calendar year ending

Recent Grants

Note: Grants derived from 1994 partial grants list.

Civic & Public Affairs

100,000	Intercollegiate Center for Nursing Education

SAFEGUARD SCIENTIFICS

Company Contact

Wayne, PA

Company Description

Revenue: US$2,953,300,000 (1999)
Employees: 5,400 (1999)
SIC(s): 6799 Investors Nec.

Safeguard Scientifics Foundation

Giving Contact

Gerald Hogan, Director, Corporate Administration
435 Devon Pk. Dr., No. 800
Wayne, PA 19087
Phone: (610)293-0600

Description

EIN: 232571278
Organization Type: Corporate Foundation. Supports preselected organizations only.
Grant Types: General Support.

Financial Summary

Total Giving: $1,000,000 (1999 approx); $1,099,505 (1998); $509,386 (1997)
Assets: $319,436 (1995); $772,688 (1991)
Gifts Received: $374,590 (1995). Note: In 1995, contributions were received from the Safeguard Scientifics, Inc.

Typical Recipients

Arts & Humanities: Arts Associations & Councils, Ballet, Arts & Humanities-General, Museums/Galleries, Music, Performing Arts, Theater
Civic & Public Affairs: Botanical Gardens/Parks, Business/Free Enterprise, Community Foundations, Economic Development, Civic & Public Affairs-General, Housing, Municipalities/Towns, Philanthropic Organizations, Urban & Community Affairs, Women's Affairs
Education: Arts/Humanities Education, Colleges & Universities, Economic Education, Secondary Education (Public), Special Education
Environment: Environment-General
Health: AIDS/HIV, Children's Health/Hospitals, Diabetes, Emergency/Ambulance Services, Health Organizations, Heart, Medical Rehabilitation, Single-Disease Health Associations
International: Health Care/Hospitals
Religion: Religious Welfare
Science: Science Museums, Scientific Centers & Institutes
Social Services: Community Service Organizations, Crime Prevention, Recreation & Athletics, Scouts, United Funds/United Ways, Youth Organizations

Contributions Analysis

Giving Priorities: Education, the arts, health organizations, and civic and public affairs.
Arts & Humanities: 19%. Supports performing arts, humanities councils, and museums.
Civic & Public Affairs: 11%. Supports community and economic development, women's affairs, housing issues, and gardens/parks.
Education: 54%. Supports colleges and universities, secondary and special education, and economic and arts education.
Health: 16%. Supports children's health, and single-disease health associations.
Note: Total contributions made in 1998.

Restrictions

Does not support political or lobbying groups.

Corporate Officials

Donald R. Caldwell: president, chief operating officer, director PRIM CORP EMPL president, chief operating officer, director: Safeguard Scientifics.

Warren Van Dyke Musser: chairman, chief executive officer, director B Harrisburg, PA 1926. ED Lehigh University BS (1949). PRIM CORP EMPL chairman, chief executive officer, director: Safeguard Scientifics. CORP AFFIL chairman: Tech Leaders Management; director: Sanchez Computer Associates; director: Rabbit Software Corp.; founder, general partner: Radnor Venture Ptnr; director: Gandalf Techs; director: QVC Network; director: CenterCore; chairman, director: CompuCom System. NONPR AFFIL member: World Business Council.

Foundation Officials

Deirdre Blackburn: secretary
Donald R. Caldwell: vice president (see above)
Warren Van Dyke Musser: president, director (see above)
Charles A. Root: vice president, director

Grants Analysis

Disclosure Period: calendar year ending 1998
Total Grants: $1,099,505
Typical Range: $500 to $250,000

Recent Grants

Note: Grants derived from 1997 Form 990.

Arts & Humanities

62,500	Regional Performing Arts Center
25,000	Academy of Music, Philadelphia, PA
12,500	American Music Theater Festival, Philadelphia, PA
10,000	American Music Theater Festival, Philadelphia, PA
10,000	Philadelphia Museum of Art, Philadelphia, PA
5,000	Arden Theater Company
5,000	Pennsylvania Ballet, Philadelphia, PA

Civic & Public Affairs

40,000	City Year, Boston, MA
8,000	Friends of Philadelphia Parks, Philadelphia, PA
7,500	Committee for Economic Development, New York, NY
7,500	Committee for Economic Development, New York, NY
5,000	Fund for Philadelphia, Philadelphia, PA
5,000	Habitat for Humanity
5,000	Jack and Jill of America Foundation, Houston, TX

Education

25,000	Temple University, Philadelphia, PA
25,000	Temple University, Philadelphia, PA
25,000	Temple University, Philadelphia, PA
20,000	Pennsylvania Partnership for Economic Education, PA
10,000	Los Angeles Academy of Fine Arts, Los Angeles, CA -- US artists support
9,500	Pennsylvania Academy of Fine Arts, Philadelphia, PA
5,000	Institute for Arts Education
5,000	Pennsylvania School for Deaf, Philadelphia, PA

Health

15,000	Juvenile Diabetes Foundation, New York, NY
10,000	American Red Cross
5,000	AIDS Fund, Norfolk, VA
5,000	American Red Cross
5,000	Juvenile Diabetes Foundation, New York, NY
5,000	Moss Rehabilitation Hospital, Philadelphia, PA -- support Wheelchair Tennis Tournament

Social Services

10,000	Philadelphia Tennis Patrons Association, Wayne, PA
5,000	Crime Prevention Association

SAFEWAY INC.

Company Contact

Pleasanton, CA
Web: http://www.safeway.com

Company Description

Acquired: Randall's Food Markets (1999).
Revenue: US$28,860,000,000 (1999)
Profit: US$970,900,000 (1999)
Employees: 170,000 (1999)
Fortune Rank: 40, per FORTUNE Magazine's list of 500 Largest U.S. Corporations (1999).
FF 40
SIC(s): 5411 Grocery Stores.

Operating Locations

Canada: Canada Safeway Ltd., Calgary

Nonmonetary Support

Type: Donated Products; Loaned Employees
Note: Annual nonmonetary support is approximately $11,000,000. Support consists of food and beverage donations.

Corporate Sponsorship

Type: Festivals/fairs; Arts & cultural events
Contact: Renee Mitchell, Public Affairs Coordinator

Giving Contact

Craig Muckle, Manager, Public Affairs
Safeway Inc.
4551 Forbes Boulevard
Lanham, MD 20706
Phone: (301)918-6803

Alternate Contact

Mary Kirby
Phone: (301)918-6807

Description

Organization Type: Corporate Giving Program
Giving Locations: headquarters and operating communities.
Grant Types: General Support.

Financial Summary

Total Giving: Contributes through corporate direct giving program only. Company does not disclose contributions figures.

Typical Recipients

Civic & Public Affairs: Employment/Job Training
Religion: Churches
Social Services: Food/Clothing Distribution, Shelters/Homelessness

Contributions Analysis

Giving Priorities: Company giving program is highly decentralized, with individual stores donating products to community-based human service programs in the United States and Canada. Cash donations are made to enhance job skills for youth and other similar causes.
Civic & Public Affairs: Cash donations are made to enhance job skills for youth, and other similar causes.
Education: Company's Tapes for Education program donated equipment to schools in exchange for collected Safeway register tapes.
Health: Donates to the National Easter Seal Society.
Social Services: Company donates food to charities such as Second Harvest, homeless shelters, and church groups.

Application Procedures

Initial Contact: Submit a brief letter.

Additional Information

Contact division public affairs managers for specific information.
--Denver Division: (303) 843-7671
--Eastern Division: (301) 918-6807
--Northern California Division: (510) 498-2201
--Phoenix Division: (602) 894-4129
--Portland Division: (503) 657-6287
--Seattle Division: (206) 455-6374
--Canada Division: (204) 946-4230

Corporate Officials

Steven A. Burd: president, chief executive officer, chairman, director B Valley City, ND 1949. ED Carroll College (1971); University of Wisconsin (1973). PRIM CORP EMPL president, chief executive officer, chairman, director: Safeway Inc.
Peter Alden Magowan: president, managing general partner B New York, NY 1942. ED Stanford University BA (1964); Oxford University MA (1966); Johns Hopkins University (1967-1968). PRIM CORP EMPL president, managing general partner: San Francisco Giants. CORP AFFIL director: Safeway Inc.; director: Vons Companies Inc.; director: Caterpillar Inc.; director: Chrysler Corp.

SAINT PAUL COMPANIES INC.

Company Contact

385 Washington St.
St. Paul, MN 55102
Phone: (651)310-7911
Fax: (651)310-8294
Web: http://www.stpaul.com

Company Description

Revenue: US$8,641,400,000 (1999)
Profit: US$834,000,000 (1999)
Fortune Rank: 204, per FORTUNE Magazine's list of 500 Largest U.S. Corporations (1999).
FF 204
SIC(s): 6331 Fire, Marine & Casualty Insurance.

SUBSIDIARY COMPANIES

IL: The John Nuveen Co., Chicago

Nonmonetary Support

Type: Donated Equipment; Loaned Employees; Workplace Solicitation
Contact: Ron McKinley, Vice President
Phone: (612)310-2623
Note: The company also provides printing services to nonprofits.

Giving Contact

Deb Anderson, Community Affairs Administrator
St. Paul Companies, Inc.
385 Washington Street, MC514D
St. Paul, MN 55102
Phone: (612)310-7757
Fax: (612)310-2327

Description

Organization Type: Corporate Giving Program
Giving Locations: MN: some statewide giving, Minneapolis, St. Paul headquarters and operating communities national and international organizations; low priority.
Grant Types: Capital, Employee Matching Gifts, Endowment, Fellowship, General Support, Matching, Multiyear/Continuing Support, Project.
Note: Employee matching gift ratio: 1:1; 2:1 to organisation with 50 hours of employee volunteer time.

Giving Philosophy

'To accomplish its business mission, The St. Paul is dependent on a healthy and vital social, economic and political environment. It, therefore, has a responsibility to all its stockholders to actively participate in creating that environment. One way it does this is through its community affairs programs. The St. Paul's effort is directed towards building the capacity of individuals and institutions in the communities in which we operate to improve the quality of life for all citizens, with a major focus on aiding disadvantaged people to participate fully in the mainstream of American life.' *Contributions Program Guidelines*

Financial Summary

Total Giving: $10,963,612 (1997); $11,029,965 (1996); $8,829,084 (1995). Note: Contributes through corporate direct giving program only.
Giving Analysis: Giving for 1996 includes: corporate direct giving ($10,311,881); corporate matching gifts ($718,084); 1997: corporate direct giving ($9,375,625); corporate matching gifts ($920,221); corporate grants to United Way ($610,351); domestic and international subsidiaries ($57,415)

Typical Recipients

Arts & Humanities: Arts Associations & Councils, Arts Centers, Arts Funds, Arts Institutes, Arts Outreach, Community Arts, Dance, Ethnic & Folk Arts, History & Archaeology, Libraries, Literary Arts, Museums/Galleries, Music, Performing Arts, Public Broadcasting, Theater
Civic & Public Affairs: African American Affairs, Asian American Affairs, Business/Free Enterprise, Chambers of Commerce, Clubs, Economic Development, Employment/Job Training, Civic & Public Affairs-General, Hispanic Affairs, Housing, Native American Affairs, Nonprofit Management, Urban & Community Affairs, Women's Affairs
Education: Arts/Humanities Education, Business Education, Colleges & Universities, Community & Junior Colleges, Education Reform, Faculty Development, International Studies, Leadership Training, Literacy, Minority Education, Private Education (Precollege), Public Education (Precollege), Social Sciences Education, Student Aid
Health: Adolescent Health Issues, AIDS/HIV, Cancer, Clinics/Medical Centers
International: International Affairs
Religion: Religious Welfare
Science: Science Museums
Social Services: At-Risk Youth, Child Welfare, Community Centers, Community Service Organizations, Day Care, Emergency Relief, Family Services, Recreation & Athletics, Senior Services, United Funds/ United Ways, Volunteer Services, YMCA/YWCA/ YMHA/YWHA, Youth Organizations

Contributions Analysis

Giving Priorities: Minority education, housing, and international organizations.
Arts & Humanities: 23%. Supports a variety of art groups to ensure expression of diverse cultures and to enhance efforts in education and neighborhood development. Funding includes annual operating support on a three-year basis, capital support (excluding endowment) and special project funds for activities that advance the company's other community affairs goals. Interests include museums, music and art funds, which combine resources to support small- and medium-sized organizations.
Civic & Public Affairs: 31%. Focus on low-income housing opportunities, leadership skills, and economic viability of city neighborhoods. Interests include philanthropic organizations, neighborhood development, neighborhood-based health clinics, and housing. Company sponsors the Leadership Initiatives in Neighborhoods (LIN) Program, which provides grants to individuals who do community action work. Goals are to encourage citizen participation in, and improve the effectiveness of, the nonprofit voluntary. sector. Foucs includes improving financial development capabilities, enhancing informaiton management systems, consolidation administrative functions and project activities with other nonprofits, and improving lleadership opportunities. Interests include nonprofit management, volunteer services, ethnic/minority organizations ans youth organizations.
Education: About 24%. General operating support to private colleges and secondary schools in Minnesota through federated fund drives; support of private college capital and endowment fund drives in Minnesota; support of community-based education, including early childhood development, K-12 initiatives, and employment programs, and support of opportunities for minorities.
Science: 10%. Funds science museums.
Social Services: 12%. Major support for the United Way.
Note: Total contributions in 1997.

Application Procedures

Initial Contact: Call or write to request application packet; one-page letter describing the request for funding.
Application Requirements: Submit a completed application, with the following attachments: list of board members and affiliations; proof of tax-exemption and Minnesota Charities Registration; most recent audited financial statement; organizational chart; current year

organizational budget; current project budget; summary of financial or volunteer involvement with company; sources and amounts of organization revenue; letter of intent to act as fiscal agent; any other relevant information.
Deadlines: The first of December, March, June and September.
Review Process: Staff committee conducts initial review and prepares research report for executive management.
Evaluative Criteria: Clear program description, quality delivery of needed service, willingness to cooperate with others in community, broad base of support, probability that objectives will be met, effective program evaluation, sound fiscal policies, complete financial disclosure, reasonable administrative overhead, competence and involvement of directors, qualifications of staff and volunteers, participation of groups being served, potential for broader application of program; participation of company employees in meaningful voluntary capacities.
Decision Notification: Committee meets quarterly to review proposals; it takes two to four months to fully consider each request.
Notes: All the information listed in the application requirements must be included for request to be considered. Organizations seeking funds for programs that have not previously received funding from The St. Paul Cos. should begin the process by submitting a one-page project summary describing the new request. Organizations outside of the Saint Paul-Minneapolis area should send inquiries to the nearest regional office. Send a copy to the Community Affairs Department at the above address. Saint Paul will respond to initial request within two weeks to determine whether a full application should be submitted.

Restrictions

Contribution funds, will not be used for religious organizations unless seeking funds in the direct interest of the entire community; veterans, fraternal, political, or lobbying organizations; hospitals or other health services funded by third-party reimbursements; benefits or fundraisers; advertising; individuals; and scholarships to individuals unless part of ongoing scholarship program of an educational institution or other nonprofit organization, which selects the scholarship recipients. Generally no grants are made to organizations which are part of a United Way or other federated giving drive to which company is contributing, except to provide funding for management, technical assistance, housing, or education for communities of color. The company will not replace public funding or fund programs that appear to be responsibility of the government.
Low priority is given to national and international organization, disease-specific organizations, and events.

Additional Information

Corporate contributions currently average about 2% of pretax operating earnings averaged over a three-year period.
Regional offices have separate giving programs.
St. Paul Companies completed its merger with USF&G Corp. in April 1998. USF&G and St. Paul had combined revenues of $9.6 billion in 1997.
Publications: Community Affairs Distribution Report; Grant Application; Partners in Giving - St. Paul's Matching Gift Program Brochure; Guidelines; Application Information

Corporate Officials

James E. Gustafson: president, chief operating officerofficer B 1946. ED University of South Dakota BA (1965-1969). PRIM CORP EMPL president, chief operating officer: Saint Paul Companies Inc. CORP AFFIL president: General Reinsurance Service Corp.; chairman: National Reinsurance Corp.
Karen Himle: vice president corporate committee PRIM CORP EMPL vice president corporate committee: St. Paul Companies Inc.
Douglas West Leatherdale: chairman, chief executive officer, president B Morden, MB Canada 1936. ED United College (Canada) BA (1957). PRIM CORP EMPL chairman, chief executive officer, president: Saint Paul Companies Inc. ADD CORP EMPL president, director: St Paul Mercury Insurance Co.; chairman: St Paul Surplus Lines Insurance Co. CORP AFFIL director: Saint Paul Risk Services Inc.; director: United HealthCare Corp.; director: Saint Paul Real Estate Illinois Inc.; director: Saint Paul Plymouth Center Inc.; director: Saint Paul Properties Inc.; principal: Saint Paul Medicine Lblty Insurance Co.; director: Saint Paul Oil & Gas Corp.; chairman: Saint Paul Insurance Connecticut Inc.; director: Saint Paul Land Resources Inc.; president, director: Saint Paul Guardian Insurance Co.; chairman: Saint Paul Fire & Marine Insurance Co.; director: Saint Paul Fire & Marine Insurance Co. (UK) Ltd.; director: Ramsey Insurance Co.; director: Saint Paul Finance Group Inc.; director: Northern Studies Power Co.; director: John Nuveen & Co. Inc.; director: National Insurance Wholesalers; director: Carlyle Capital LP; director: Graham Resources Inc.; director: Atwater McMillian; director: 77 Water Street Inc.; director: Athena Assurance Co. NONPR AFFIL member: Financial Executives Institute; member: Twin Cities Society Security Analysts; member: American Insurance Association; trustee: Carleton College. CLUB AFFIL Minnesota Club.
Paul J. Liska: executive vice president, chief financial officer B 1956. ED University of Notre Dame BBA (1977); Northwestern University MM (1983). PRIM CORP EMPL executive vice president, chief financial officer: Saint Paul Companies Inc. ADD CORP EMPL executive vice president: Saint Paul Insurance Co. Inc.; executive vice president: Saint Paul Fire & Mar Insurance Co.; chief financial officer: Saint Paul Mercury Insurance Co.; chief financial officer: Fidelty & Guaranty Insurance; director: John Nuveen Corp.; chief financial officer: Seaboard Surety Co. CORP AFFIL director: Renaissance Reinsurance. NONPR AFFIL director: Walker Art Center.
Mary Pickard: community affairs officer PRIM CORP EMPL community affairs officer: St. Paul Companies Inc.

Giving Program Officials

Deb Anderson: manager PRIM CORP EMPL communication affairs administrator: Saint Paul Companies Inc.
Ron McKinley: PRIM CORP EMPL program manager community affairs: St. Paul Companies Inc.

Grants Analysis

Disclosure Period: calendar year ending 1997
Total Grants: $9,375,625*
Number of Grants: 349
Average Grant: $26,864
Highest Grant: $500,000
Typical Range: $5,000 to $55,000
***Note:** Giving excludes United Way, matching gifts, and domestic and international subsidiary giving.

Recent Grants

Note: Grants derived from 1995 Annual Report.

Arts & Humanities

250,000	Minnesota Orchestral Association, Minneapolis, MN -- third payment of $1.25 million to support endowment campaign
200,000	Artspace Projects, Minneapolis, MN -- support creation of National Project Development Fund
150,000	KTCA Twin Cities Public Television, Saint Paul, MN -- funding for history series
69,000	United Arts Council, Saint Paul, MN -- support for COMPAS, Graywolf Press, Greater Twin Cities Youth Symphony, Minnesota Museum of American Art, Schubert Club, Theater de la Jeune Lune programs
50,000	Minnesota Historical Society, Saint Paul, MN -- support to develop video and computer tutorials in Ronald Hubbs Center
50,000	St. Paul Chamber Orchestra Society, Saint Paul, MN -- support for Connect curriculum
40,000	American Composers Forum, Saint Paul, MN -- research
40,000	Ordway Music Theater, Saint Paul, MN -- first payment of $80,000 to support performing arts
40,000	St. Paul Chamber Orchestra Society, Saint Paul, MN -- annual support
40,000	Teatro Del Pueblo, Saint Paul, MN -- general support
40,000	United Arts Services, Saint Paul, MN -- support for federated fund drive

Civic & Public Affairs

200,000	Family Housing Fund of Minneapolis and St. Paul, Minneapolis, MN -- support for research to address problems of low-income housing
100,000	Local Initiatives Support Corp, New York, NY -- second payment of $300,000 grant to provide up-front financing and technical assistance to housing nonprofits in St. Paul
100,000	United Cambodian Association of Minnesota, Saint Paul, MN -- capital support
90,000	Commonbond Communities, Saint Paul, MN -- support for Torre de San Miguel Advantage Center
75,000	Habitat for Humanity, Minneapolis, MN -- support for St. Paul Homeownership Development Collaboration
75,000	Management Assistance Program of Nonprofits, Saint Paul, MN -- support for Technology Partnership Fund
68,411	Top Brass Partners in Giving, Saint Paul, MN -- for St. Paul companies match
50,000	Commonbond Communities, Saint Paul, MN -- capital support
50,000	Communities of Color Institute for Organizational Development, Minneapolis, MN -- support for Community Fellows Program
50,000	Stairstep Foundation, Minneapolis, MN -- support programs
50,000	University of St. Thomas Center for Nonprofits, Saint Paul, MN -- support to increase management capabilities of nonprofit practitioners
45,000	Chicanos Latinos Unidos En Servicios, Minneapolis, MN -- support for vocational and educational programs
45,000	Ramsey County Opportunities Industrialization Center, Saint Paul, MN -- operating support
35,000	North End Area Revitalization, Saint Paul, MN -- final payment of $105,000 to promote commercial revitalization
35,000	St. Paul Coalition for Community Development, Saint Paul, MN -- to collaborate and enhance neighborhood-based economic and housing development
35,000	Selby Area Community Development Corp, Saint Paul, MN -- three-year support
35,000	Thomas-Dale District 7 Community Council, Saint Paul, MN -- support affordable housing efforts
35,000	Womenventure, Saint Paul, MN -- support career development program for women

Education

75,000	Minnesota Private College Fund, Saint Paul, MN -- scholarships
65,400	Minnesota Inclusiveness Program, Plymouth, MN -- support Minnesota SEED Project

65,000 Minnesota Minority Education Partnership, Minneapolis, MN -- two year support for creation of Institute for Multicultural Connections
60,000 Minnesota Independent School Fund, Saint Paul, MN -- support for Students of Color Scholarships
50,000 College of St. Benedict, Saint Joseph, MN -- final payment of $150,000 grant for scholarships
50,000 Concordia College, Saint Paul, MN -- final payment of $150,000 grant for capital campaign
50,000 Minnesota Minority Education Partnership, Minneapolis, MN -- to increase success of students of color in Minnesota schools
50,000 Summit University Education Consortium, Saint Paul, MN -- support tutoring and academic support services for African American students in East Metro area
50,000 University of Minnesota Carlson School of Management, Minneapolis, MN -- second of $250,000 to support new business school facility
42,375 University of Minnesota Leadership for Black Women, Minneapolis, MN -- second payment of $84,750 to support programs
40,000 Concordia College ARTS-US, Saint Paul, MN -- support for four multicultural education programs

Religion

75,000 Catholic Charities, Minneapolis, MN -- capital support

Science

45,000 Science Museum of Minnesota, Saint Paul, MN -- two year support for science and technology museum

Social Services

622,402 Partners in Giving, Saint Paul, MN -- St. Paul companies match for employees program
410,000 United Way St. Paul Area, Saint Paul, MN -- support of over 220 programs
138,074 United Way Field Offices, Minneapolis, MN -- St. Paul companies commitment to match employee pledges
50,000 Earthstar Project, Saint Paul, MN -- support for development of Elders Lodge apartments
50,000 Sabathani Community Center, Minneapolis, MN -- capital support
50,000 United Way Minneapolis, Minneapolis, MN -- operating support
50,000 YMCA Metropolitan Minneapolis, Minneapolis, MN -- support of Commitment to Values capital campaign
45,000 Project for Pride in Living, Minneapolis, MN -- capital support

SALOMON SMITH BARNEY

Company Contact

New York, NY
Web: http://www.smithbarney.com

Company Description

Profit: US$457,000,000
Employees: 36,293
SIC(s): 2911 Petroleum Refining, 6211 Security Brokers & Dealers, 6221 Commodity Contracts Brokers & Dealers, 6719 Holding Companies Nec.
Parent Company: Citigroup, New York, NY, United States

Operating Locations

Australia: Saloman Brothers Australia Ltd., Sydney; Canada: Saloman Brothers Canada, Toronto; France: Saloman Brothers SA, Paris, Ville-de-Paris; Germany: Saloman Brothers AG, Frankfurt, Hessen; Saloman Brothers Finance Corp., Frankfurt, Hessen; Saloman Brothers Kapitalanlage-GmbH, Frankfurt, Hessen; Saloman Brothers Services GmbH, Frankfurt, Hessen; Hong Kong: Derby Metals Ltd., Central District; Phibro Energy Hong Kong Ltd., Central District; Ireland: Saloman Brothers Asset Management (Ireland) Ltd., Dublin; Japan: Saloman Brothers Asia Ltd. Tokyo Branch, Tokyo; Republic of Korea: Salomon Brothers, Chung-Gu, Seoul; Singapore: Phibro Trading Pte. Ltd., Singapore; Saloman Brothers Singapore Pte. Ltd., Singapore; Spain: Saloman Brothers Internacional Ltd., Madrid; Switzerland: Phibro Energy AG (Auflosung), Zug; Philipp Brothers AG, Zug; Saloman (International) Finance AG, Zug; Scanports Shipping Ltd., Zug; Shipalks Shipping AG, Zug; Saloman Brothers Finanz AG, Zurich; United Kingdom: T MC Mortgage Securities Plc, Epsom, Surrey; Saloman Brothers International Operations Jersey Ltd., Jersey, Channel Islands; Anglo Chemical Metals Ltd., London; Carisgreen Ltd., London; Hilsrest Ltd., London; PE Ltd., London; Phibro Bullion Ltd., London; Phibro Energy Marketing Ltd., London; Phibro GmbH, London; Phibro Holdings Ltd., London; Phibro-Salomon Nominees Ltd., London; Philipp Brothers Bullion Ltd., London; Philipp Brothers Futures Ltd., London; Saloman Brothers Asset Management Ltd., London; Saloman Brothers Europe Ltd., London; Saloman Brothers International Ltd., London; Saloman Brothers UK Equity Ltd., London; Saloman Brothers (United Kingdom) Ltd., London; SB Funding Ltd., London; SB Residential Plc, London; SBI Ltd., London; T M C Portfolio Services Ltd., London; T M C Private Placements Ltd., London; T MC Mortgage Securities Plc, London; Wadecharles & Co. Ltd., London; SB Placement Ltd., Woking, Surrey; T MC Mortgage Securities Plc, Woking, Surrey

Giving Contact

Ms. Jane E. Heffner, Vice President, Corporate Contributions
Salomon Smith Barney Community Investment Program
153 E. 53rd Street
New York, NY 10043
Phone: (212)816-8682
Web: http://www.smithbarney.com/abt_sb/community/index.html

Alternate Contact

Patricia Byrne
Phone: (212)793-8885

Description

Organization Type: Corporate Foundation
Former Name: Salomon Foundation.
Former Name: Traveler's Group Foundation.
Former Name: Traveler's Foundation.
Giving Locations: headquarters and operating communities; nationally.
Grant Types: Employee Matching Gifts, General Support, Scholarship.
Note: Employee matching gift ratio: 1 to 1.

Giving Philosophy

'The Salomon Smith Barney Community Investment Program (CIP) is a national initiative that fosters ongoing partnerships between Salomon Smith Barney and community organization through a powerful combination of financial contributions and employee involvement. Since its inception in 1994, CIP has supported a variety of projects ranging from education and financial literacy to community development and art enhancement.. CIP has grown to include over 440 outreach programs.' Solomon Smith Barney web site

Financial Summary

Total Giving: $11,336,073 (1997); $4,300,000 (1996 approx); $4,200,000 (1995 approx). Note: Contributes through corporate direct giving program only.
Giving Analysis: Giving for 1998 includes: foundation ($11,336,073)
Assets: $7,835,584 (1997); $23,639,516 (1995); $17,539,615 (1994)
Gifts Received: $4,500,000 (1997); $638,445 (1995); $17,332,588 (1994). Note: Contributions are received from Salomon Brothers, Inc., and Salomon Brothers Holding Corp.

Typical Recipients

Arts & Humanities: Ballet, Historic Preservation, Libraries, Museums/Galleries, Music, Opera, Performing Arts, Public Broadcasting, Theater, Visual Arts
Civic & Public Affairs: Economic Development, Employment/Job Training, Law & Justice, Legal Aid, Women's Affairs, Zoos/Aquariums
Education: Arts/Humanities Education, Business Education, Economic Education, Elementary Education (Private), Literacy, Minority Education, Public Education (Precollege)
Health: Hospitals, Medical Research, Single-Disease Health Associations
Science: Scientific Centers & Institutes
Social Services: Delinquency & Criminal Rehabilitation, Emergency Relief, Family Planning, Food/Clothing Distribution, Recreation & Athletics, Substance Abuse, Youth Organizations

Contributions Analysis

Giving Priorities: Education, child welfare, community development, museums, the arts, and health. Domestically and worldwide, company primarily supports higher education. While headquarters approves budgets for overseas affiliates, in-country managers are autonomous in choosing recipients for support. Some support domestically for public policy organizations. The budget for overseas contributions is about $250,000 annually.
Arts & Humanities: 27%. Supports the Old Station House Association.
Civic & Public Affairs: 1%. Grants were given to The Fulbright Foundation and the Japan Society.
Education: 6%. Awards given to the Capital Partners for Education and The Inner City Scholarship Foundation.
Health: 6% Grant given to The Hartford Hospital.
Religion: 27%. Grant given to The Asylum Hill Congregational Church.
Social Services: 12%. Funds given to the YMCA of Greater New York, and the National Committee to Prevent Child Abuse.
Note: Total contributions made in 1997. Contributions were made by the Traveler's Foundation. The company now gives directly through the Salomon Smith Barney Community Investment Program.

Application Procedures

Initial Contact: Contact the company for specific guidelines.
Deadlines: None.

Restrictions

Fraternal organizations, political or lobbying groups, or religious groups for sectarian purposes are not considered for contributions.

Additional Information

Travelers Foundation and Citicorp Foundation merged to form Citigroup Foundation in 1999. Salomon Smith Barney now gives directly through its Community Investment Program.

Corporate Officials

James R. Dimon: president, chief operating officer, chief financial officer B New York, NY 1956. ED Tufts University BA (1978); Harvard University Graduate

School of Business Administration MBA (1982). PRIM CORP EMPL president, chief operating officer, chief financial officer: The Travelers Inc. ADD CORP EMPL president: Primerica Corp.; president: Travelers Group Inc. CORP AFFIL director: Tricon Global Restaurants Inc.

Deryck C. Maughan: co-chairman, co-chief executive officer B Consett, England 1947. ED University of London Kings College BA (1969); Stanford University MBA (1978). PRIM CORP EMPL co-chairman, co-chief executive officer: Salomon Smith Barney ADD CORP EMPL president: Salomon Brothers Realty Corp. CORP AFFIL director: Salomon Brothers Inc.; chairman: Salomon Forex Inc.; vice chairman: Citigroup Inc.; officer: New York Stock Exchange Inc.

Giving Program Officials

Jane E. Heffner: vice president PRIM CORP EMPL vice president corporate contributions: Salomon Brothers Inc.

Grants Analysis

Disclosure Period: calendar year ending 1997
Total Grants: $942,917
Number of Grants: 9
Average Grant: $32,153*
Highest Grant: $250,000
Typical Range: $10,000 to $50,000
***Note:** Average grant excludes three highest grants totaling $750,000.

Typical Recipients

Arts & Humanities: Arts & Humanities-General
Civic & Public Affairs: Civic & Public Affairs-General
Education: Education-General
Health: Health-General
Social Services: Social Services-General

Application Procedures

Initial Contact: letter
Application Requirements: Include a description of organization, amount requested, purpose of funds sought, recently audited financial statement, and proof of tax-exempt status.
Deadlines: None.

Corporate Officials

Gordon M. Anderson: chairman, chief executive officer B Los Angeles, CA 1932. ED Glendale College AA (1951); University of Southern California BSME (1954). PRIM CORP EMPL chairman: Santa Fe International Corp.

Sted Garber: president, chief executive officer PRIM CORP EMPL president, chief executive officer: Santa Fe International Corp.

Giving Program Officials

Gordon M. Anderson: B Los Angeles, CA 1932. ED Glendale College AA (1951); University of Southern California BSME (1954). PRIM CORP EMPL chairman: Santa Fe International Corp.

Sted Garber: PRIM CORP EMPL president, chief executive officer: Santa Fe International Corp.

John J. Mika: B Bethlehem, PA 1938. ED University of Pennsylvania (1960). PRIM CORP EMPL vice president administration & corporate affairs: Santa Fe International Corp. CORP AFFIL president: SFIC Properties Inc.

SANTA FE INTERNATIONAL CORP.

Company Contact

Dallas, TX

Company Description

Employees: 4,400
SIC(s): 1381 Drilling Oil & Gas Wells, 1382 Oil & Gas Exploration Services, 6519 Real Property Lessors Nec.
Parent Company: Kuwait Petroleum Corp., PO Box 26565, Safat, Kuwait

Operating Locations

CA: Santa Fe Drilling Co., Alhambra; Santa Fe for Engineering & Petroleum Projects Co. K.S.C., Alhambra; Santa Fe International Corp., Alhambra; Santa Fe Shaft Drilling Co., Alhambra; SFIC Properties, Alhambra; Santa Fe International Corp., Live Oak; LA: Santa Fe International Corp., Houma, Lafayette; OK: Santa Fe International Corp., Oklahoma City, Tulsa; TX: Santa Fe International Corp., Dallas; Santa Fe International Corp., Dallas; Santa Fe Minerals, Dallas; Santa Fe International Corp., Giddings; Santa Fe Offshore Construction Co., Houston; Sphere Supply, Houston

Giving Contact

John J. Mika, Vice President, Corporate Affairs
Santa Fe International Corp.
Two Lincoln Centre
5420 LBJ Freeway, Suite 1100
Dallas, TX 75240-2648
Phone: (972)701-7820
Fax: (972)701-7600

Description

Organization Type: Corporate Giving Program
Grant Types: General Support.

Financial Summary

Total Giving: Contributes through corporate direct giving program only.

SARA LEE CORP.

 Number 27 of Top 100 Corporate Givers

Company Contact

Chicago, IL
Web: http://www.saralee.com

Company Description

Revenue: US$20,012,000,000 (1999)
Profit: US$1,191,000,000 (1999)
Employees: 138,000 (1999)
Fortune Rank: 79, per FORTUNE Magazine's list of 500 Largest U.S. Corporations (1999).
FF 79
SIC(s): 2011 Meat Packing Plants, 2013 Sausages & Other Prepared Meats, 2032 Canned Specialties, 2038 Frozen Specialties Nec.

Operating Locations

Australia: Kiwi Brands Pty. Ltd., Clayton; Sara Lee Personal Products Australia, North Sydney; Sara Lee Holdings, Sydney; Canada: Sara Lee Hosiery, Montreal; Canadelle, Inc., Saint Leonard; Denmark: Merrild Kaffe, Kolding; England: Kitchens of Sara Lee--United Kingdom, Bridlington, East Yorkshire; Pretty Polly Limited, Sutton in Ashfield; France: Brossard, Bievres; Dim SA, Levallois-Perret; Biscuiterie Vinchon-Jeanette SA, Paris; Desobry SA, Paris; Driehoek, Paris; Germany: Vatter, Schongau; Hong Kong: Sara Lee Corp.-Asia, Wan Chai; Hungary: Compack Douwe Egberts RT, Budapest; Italy: Maglificio Bellia SpA, Biella; Filodoro, Casalmorana; Playtex Europe, Rome; Japan: Nihon Sara Lee, Tokyo; Upxon, Inc., Tokyo; Mexico: Manufacturas Mallorca SA; House of Fuller, SA de CV, Mexico; Rinbros, SA, Mexico; Sara Lee Knit Products-Mexico, Mexico; Estelar SA de CV, Mexico City; Kir Alimentos, SA de CV, Monterrey; Netherlands: Sara Lee Personal Products Europe, Bunnik; Sara Lee Processed Meats-Europe, Bunnik; Sara Lee/DE, Utrecht; Kortman Intradel, Veenendaal; Philippines: Intercon Garments Inc., Metro Manila, Makati; Republic of South Africa: South African Hosiery Co. Ltd., Johannesburg; Avroy Shlain Cosmetics (Pty.), Kramerville; Kiwiw Brands South Africa, Natal; Playtex South Africa, Natal; Singapore: Sara Lee/DE Asia, Singapore; Spain: Cruz Verde-Legrain, Barcelona; Sans, SA, Barcelona; United Kingdom: Sara Lee Household & Personal Care--U.K., Slough

SUBSIDIARY COMPANIES

NC: Sara Lee Hosiery, Inc., Winston-Salem

Nonmonetary Support

Value: $23,420,000 (1999); $20,834,000 (1997); $8,000,000 (1996)
Type: Donated Products
Note: The estimated value for fiscal 1999 is at cost.
Volunteer Programs: Company maintains a 15 to 20 person 'Employee Volunteerism Committee,' which is responsible for organizing approximately eight programs per year. Also sponsors a 'Board Placement Program,' through which company executives in the Chicago area are recruited to serve on nonprofit boards. These organizations also may be eligible for a $1,000 grant.
Note: Various division-level personnel are responsible for nonmonetary distributions.

Corporate Sponsorship

Type: Arts & cultural events; Sports events
Contact: Patrick Sheahan, Deputy Directory
Sara Lee Foundation
Note: Sponsors the Olympics.

Sara Lee Foundation

Giving Contact

Robin Tryloff, Executive Director
Sara Lee Foundation
3 First National Plaza
Chicago, IL 60602-4260
Phone: (312)558-8448
Fax: (312)419-3192
Web: http://www.saraleefoundation.org

Description

EIN: 363150460
Organization Type: Corporate Foundation
Giving Locations: IL: Chicago metropolitan area principally near operating locations and to national organizations.
Grant Types: Award, Employee Matching Gifts, General Support.
Note: Employee matching gift ratio: 2 to 1 up to $1,000 per employee annually. Employee matching gift ratio: 1 to 1 up to $10,000.

Giving Philosophy

'In this era of expanding social needs, corporations have an obligation not merely to act, but also to act wisely. In order to make the most of opportunities to help meet community needs, companies must respond with the same dedication to performance that characterizes their business operations. At Sara Lee Corporation, this commitment begins with a directive that says our managers must use high standards of responsibility in relating to our employees and the public. One of the ways in which Sara Lee Corporation demonstrates this sense of responsibility is through corporate-wide contributions programs. The Sara Lee Foundation administers a major portion of these programs. In addition to the Foundation's programs, our operating companies and divisions administer giving programs based on their assessment of needs in the communities where they operate. Both at the corporate and the division level, we seek to enhance the impact of our actions in two ways: by forming active partnerships with particularly effective local organizations, and by providing not merely financial support,

but also the personal involvement of our employees.'
Sara Lee Foundation

Financial Summary

Total Giving: $19,000,000 (fiscal year ending July 03, 2000 approx); $42,698,000 (fiscal 1999); $31,900,000 (fiscal 1998 approx)
Giving Analysis: Giving for fiscal 1996 includes: foundation ($5,400,322); domestic subsidiaries ($4,445,000); corporate direct giving ($2,760,000); nonmonetary support ($2,644,678); international subsidiaries ($834,000); fiscal 1997: nonmonetary support ($20,834,000); foundation ($5,980,735); domestic subsidiaries ($2,986,000); corporate direct giving ($2,704,000); international subsidiaries ($1,136,000); fiscal 1999: nonmonetary support ($23,420,000); foundation ($8,739,000); corporate direct giving ($5,176,000); domestic subsidiaries ($3,700,000) international subsidiaries ($1,663,000)
Assets: $21,076,698 (fiscal 1998); $30,483,583 (fiscal 1996); $11,400,000 (fiscal 1995 approx)
Gifts Received: $2,619,883 (fiscal 1998); $16,510,721 (fiscal 1996). Note: Contributions are received from Sara Lee Corp.

Typical Recipients

Arts & Humanities: Arts Associations & Councils, Arts Centers, Arts Festivals, Arts Funds, Arts Institutes, Community Arts, Dance, Ethnic & Folk Arts, Film & Video, Historic Preservation, History & Archaeology, Libraries, Museums/Galleries, Music, Opera, Performing Arts, Public Broadcasting, Theater, Visual Arts
Civic & Public Affairs: African American Affairs, Asian American Affairs, Civil Rights, Economic Development, Employment/Job Training, Civic & Public Affairs-General, Hispanic Affairs, Housing, Law & Justice, Legal Aid, Philanthropic Organizations, Professional & Trade Associations, Public Policy, Urban & Community Affairs, Women's Affairs, Women's Affairs, Zoos/Aquariums
Education: Arts/Humanities Education, Business Education, Colleges & Universities, Education Associations, International Exchange, Literacy, Minority Education, Student Aid
Health: Cancer, Health Organizations, Hospitals, Nutrition, Prenatal Health Issues
International: Human Rights, International Peace & Security Issues, International Relations
Religion: Religious Welfare
Science: Observatories & Planetariums, Science Museums
Social Services: Child Welfare, Community Centers, Community Service Organizations, Counseling, Day Care, Domestic Violence, Family Planning, Family Services, Food/Clothing Distribution, Homes, People with Disabilities, Refugee Assistance, Senior Services, Shelters/Homelessness, Substance Abuse, United Funds/United Ways, Volunteer Services, YMCA/YWCA/YMHA/YWHA, Youth Organizations

Contributions Analysis

Giving Priorities: The disadvantaged, arts organizations, and international organizations. Contributions by foreign subsidiaries are handled independently, designed to address local community needs. Contact individual international subsidiaries for funding information. Canadian budget is largest. Total contributions by overseas companies in fiscal 1999 was $1,663,000. Domestically, the foundation has supported U.S.-based organizations with an international focus.
Arts & Humanities: About 30%. Provides cash support for new, emerging arts groups as well as for major, established institutions in Chicago. 35% to 40%. Funds performing arts, libriaries, art institutes and the arts.
Civic & Public Affairs: 10% to 15%. Supports housing, women causes, jobs, and community services.
Education: 10% to 15%. Supports educational programs, colleges and universities.
International: Sara Lee Corporation contributes to international organizations through its foreign subsidiaries. Contact individual international subsidiaries for details. This support is included in above totals.
Science: Less than 5%. Funds the Museum of National History and the Museum of Science and Industry.
Social Services: 35% to 40%. Seeks to fund organizations addressing issues of the disadvantaged with vision, dignity, and effectiveness, with emphasis on assisting the hungry and the homeless and women.
Note: Above priorities are for the foundation. In addition to foundation's programs, operating companies and divisions administer giving programs based on assessment of needs in the communities where they operate. They contribute cash and product donations to local and national organizations. Divisions and employees also participate in community-based projects.

Application Procedures

Initial Contact: Send a brief letter, or call requesting annual contributions report and application; to apply to divisions, call local division for information.
Application Requirements: Along with your application, submit most recently audited financial statement, current operating budget, annual report (or other materials summarizing programs), list of directors and their affiliations, proof of tax-exempt status, and list of public and private support of $500 or more received during the most recently completed fiscal year.
Deadlines: No later than first working day of March or September for consideration at quarterly meetings held after those months.
Review Process: Acknowledgment of receipt is sent to applicant. If proposal meets guidelines, it is placed on foundation agenda. If proposal does not meet guidelines, it is declined. Foundation staff reviews approved proposals and schedules meetings and site visits, if needed. Foundation discusses applicants at quarterly board meetings and approves or rejects requests.
Evaluative Criteria: Proposals are evaluated based on relevance to the foundation's priorities; unique contribution of the applicant; the ability of the project to reach underserved communities, populations, or audiences; innovation; leadership; effectiveness; feasibility and perceived need for services or the project; community support and involvement; sound management; and employee involvement.
Decision Notification: Applications are acknowledged upon receipt and organizations are notified by letter of the foundation's decision after quarterly meetings.
Notes: Proposals must be submitted on the foundation's application form.

Restrictions

The following are not eligible for grants: capital and endowment campaigns; individuals; organizations with a limited constituency, such as fraternal or veterans groups; organizations that limit services to members of one religious group or seek to propagate a particular belief or creed; political organizations or groups promoting one ideological view; elementary or secondary schools, either public or private; single-disease health organizations; tickets to dinners and other events; goodwill advertising in yearbooks or dinner programs; or national or international organizations with limited relationship to local Sara Lee operations. national or international organizations with limited relationship to local Sara Lee operations.

Additional Information

Company has operating locations in nearly all 50 states. Sara Lee's contributions program is decentralized. About two-fifths of total contributions are made by the foundation, which is the main philanthropic vehicle for the Chicago corporate office. The remainder is distributed by divisions, which administer their own programs, including nonmonetary giving and volunteer services.
Organizations should not submit a contribution application more than once in any 12-month period. Grants are not automatically renewed, and recipients desiring renewed support should submit a request approximately two months prior to the anniversary of their grant(s). A renewal request should include the organization's most recent audited financial statement, current year's operating budget, updated board of directors list, and summary of how the previous year's grant was used. An application form is not necessary for grant renewal requests.
Sara Lee maintains a policy that annual cash and product contributions shall represent at least 2% of domestic pretax income.
At the corporate and division levels, company forms active partnerships with particularly effective local organizations and encourages employee involvement.

Corporate Officials

John Henry Bryan: chairman vice president, chief financial officer, chief administrative officer B West Point, MS 1936. ED Rhodes College BA (1958); State University of New York Graduate School of Business Administration MS (1960). PRIM CORP EMPL chairman: Sara Lee Corp. CORP AFFIL director: General Motors Corp.; director: Bank One Corp.; director: BP Amoco Corp. NONPR AFFIL trustee: Rush-Presbyterian-Saint Lukes Medical Center; trustee, vice chairman executive committee: University Chicago; member: President Committee Arts & Humanities; member trustee council: National Gallery Art; board governors: National Womens Economic Alliance; trustee: Committee for Economic Development; member: Grocery Manufacturer America; chairman: Chicago Council Foreign Relations; chairman business advisory council: Chicago Urban League; member: Business Roundtable; chairman: Catalyst; director: Business Committee Arts; member: Business Council; treasurer, trustee: Art Institute of Chicago.
C. Steven McMillan: president, chief executive officer PRIM CORP EMPL president, chief executive officer: Sara Lee Corp.
Cary D. McMillan: executive vice president, chief financial officer, chief administrative officer PRIM CORP EMPL executive vice president, chief financial officer, chief administrative officer: Sara Lee Corp.
Robin Tryloff: director community relations PRIM CORP EMPL director community relations: Sara Lee Corp.

Foundation Officials

John Henry Bryan: director (see above)
David B. Ellis: assistant treasurer
Patrick M. Sheahan: deputy director
Judith A. Sprieser: vice president, treasurer
Robin Tryloff: executive director (see above)

Grants Analysis

Disclosure Period: fiscal year ending July 03, 1999
Total Grants: $3,929,000*
Number of Grants: 350
Average Grant: $10,000
Highest Grant: $250,000
Typical Range: $2,500 to $25,000
***Note:** Giving excludes corporate direct giving; domestic and international subsidiaries; matching gifts; United Way; nonmonetary support. Grants analysis provided by the foundation.

Recent Grants

Note: Grants derived from fiscal 1998 Form 990.

Arts & Humanities

250,000	Hubbard Street Dance Chicago, Chicago, IL
250,000	Museum of Contemporary Art, Chicago, IL
125,000	Art Institute of Chicago*The, Chicago, IL
100,000	Mexican Fine Arts Center Museum, Chicago, IL

100,000 Shakespeare Repertory, Chicago, IL
85,298 Arts Council-Winston-Salem, Winston Salem, NC
75,000 Arts & Business Council of Chicago, Chicago, IL
35,000 Art Institute of Chicago*The, Chicago, IL
26,000 Orchestral Association*, Chicago, IL
25,000 John F. Kennedy Center for the Performing Arts, Washington, DC
25,000 Lyric Opera of Chicago, Chicago, IL
25,000 Pegasus Players, Chicago, IL
25,000 Steppenwolf Theatre Company, Chicago, IL
23,431 Arts Council-Winston-Salem, Winston Salem, NC
20,000 Grantmakers in the Arts, Philadelphia, PA
15,000 Chicago Historical Society, Chicago, IL
15,000 Chicago Humanities Festival, Chicago, IL
15,000 Chicago Public Library Foundation, Chicago, IL
15,000 Chicago Theatre Group, Inc., Chicago, IL

Civic & Public Affairs

25,000 Catalyst, Chicago, IL
25,000 Donors Forum of Chicago, Chicago, IL
25,000 Taylor Institute, Chicago, IL
20,000 Chicago Urban League, Chicago, IL
20,000 Women's Self-Employment Project, Chicago, IL
15,000 El Valor Corporation, Chicago, IL

Education

75,000 University of Chicago*, Chicago, IL
50,000 United Negro College Fund, Inc., Chicago, IL
48,730 National Merit Scholarship Corporation, Evanston, IL
42,417 Wake Forest University, Winston Salem, NC
22,000 Columbia College-Chicago, Chicago, IL
15,000 Chicago Academy for the Arts*The, Chicago, IL
15,000 Chicago Arts Partnerships in Education, Chicago, IL

Health

50,000 Northwestern Memorial Hospital, Chicago, IL
34,312 March of Dimes Birth Defects-Western, Statesville, NC
31,726 March of Dimes Birth Defects, Winston-Salem, NC
25,000 Food Research and Action Center, Washington, DC
25,000 Gilda's Club Chicago, Chicago, IL

International

15,000 Chicago Council on Foreign Relations, Chicago, IL

Science

20,000 Museum of Science and Industry, Chicago, IL

Social Services

460,000 United Way/Crusade of Mercy, Inc., Chicago, IL
100,000 Children's Defense Fund, New York, NY
52,180 Youth for Understanding, Washington, DC
50,745 Youth for Understanding, Washington, DC
50,000 Erie Neighborhood House, Chicago, IL
44,000 Youth Guidance, Chicago, IL
40,000 Second Harvest, Chicago, IL
25,000 Alternatives For Girls, Detroit, MI
25,000 Family Violence Prevention Fund, San Francisco, CA
25,000 Spectrum Youth and Family Services, Hoffman Estates, IL
20,000 YMCA - Metropolitan Chicago, Chicago, IL

SARA LEE HOSIERY, INC.

Company Contact

Winston-Salem, NC

Company Description

Former Name: Hanes Hosiery.
SIC(s): 2251 Women's Hosiery Except Socks.
Parent Company: Sara Lee Corp., Chicago, IL, United States

Corporate Sponsorship

Type: Sports events

Giving Contact

Sandy Foreman, Accounting Manager
Sara Lee Hosiery, Inc.
5650 University Parkway
Winston-Salem, NC 27105
Phone: (336)519-7355
Fax: (336)519-3241
Email: contributions@slkp.com

Description

Organization Type: Corporate Giving Program
Giving Locations: headquarters and operating communities.
Grant Types: Award, Capital, Emergency, Employee Matching Gifts, General Support.
Note: Employee matching gift ratio: 2 to 1 up to $1,000; 1 to 1 from $1,000 to a maximum of $10,000.

Financial Summary

Total Giving: $2,500,000 (2000 approx); $2,500,000 (1999 approx); $200,000 (1997 approx). Note: Contributes through corporate direct giving program only.

Typical Recipients

Arts & Humanities: Arts Appreciation, Arts Associations & Councils, Arts Funds, Community Arts, Film & Video, Historic Preservation, Libraries, Literary Arts, Museums/Galleries, Music, Performing Arts, Public Broadcasting, Visual Arts
Civic & Public Affairs: Business/Free Enterprise, Civil Rights, Economic Development, Civic & Public Affairs-General, Philanthropic Organizations, Urban & Community Affairs
Education: Business Education, Community & Junior Colleges, Education Funds, Elementary Education (Private), Education-General, Literacy, Minority Education, Preschool Education, Private Education (Precollege)
Environment: Environment-General
Health: Emergency/Ambulance Services, Health-General, Health Organizations, Hospices, Hospitals, Public Health
Religion: Churches
Social Services: Animal Protection, Child Welfare, Community Service Organizations, Counseling, Day Care, Domestic Violence, Emergency Relief, Family Services, Food/Clothing Distribution, People with Disabilities, Refugee Assistance, Senior Services, Shelters/Homelessness, Social Services-General, Substance Abuse, United Funds/United Ways, Volunteer Services, Youth Organizations

Contributions Analysis

Civic & Public Affairs: 67%. Supports minority and women's programs.
Social Services: 33%. Supports children's programs.
Note: Total contributions made in 1999.

Application Procedures

Initial Contact: letter of inquiry
Application Requirements: a description of organization, amount requested, purpose of funds sought, recently audited financial statement, and proof of tax-exempt status
Deadlines: June 30

Restrictions

The company does not support national or statewide United Way recipients, churches, political organizations, individuals, or clubs.

Corporate Officials

Ken Dobbins: chief financial officer L'Eggs PRIM CORP EMPL chief financial officer L'Eggs: Sara Lee Hosiery, Inc.

Grants Analysis

Disclosure Period: calendar year ending
Typical Range: $50 to $5,000

SBC COMMUNICATIONS INC.

 Number 16 of Top 100 Corporate Givers

Company Contact

San Antonio, TX
Web: http://www.sbc.com

Company Description

Former Name: Southwestern Bell Corp.;
Acquired:.
Revenue: US$49,489,000,000 (1999)
Profit: US$8,159,000,000 (1999)
Employees: 61,540
Fortune Rank: 12, per FORTUNE Magazine's list of 500 Largest U.S. Corporations (1999).
FF 12
SIC(s): 4813 Telephone Communications Except Radiotelephone, 6719 Holding Companies Nec.

SUBSIDIARY COMPANIES

IL: Ameritech Corp., Chicago

Corporate Sponsorship

Type: Arts & cultural events; Festivals/fairs; Music & entertainment events; Pledge-a-thon; Sports events
Contact: Cappy Ritter, Corporate Manager

SBC Foundation

Giving Contact

Gloria Delgado, President
SBC Foundation
175 East Houston, Suite 200
San Antonio, TX 78205
Phone: 800-591-9663
Fax: (210)351-2259
Web: http://www.sbc.com/Commuity/SBC_Foundation/Home.html

Alternate Contact

Sue Sonke, Corporate Manager
Phone: 800-591-9663

Description

EIN: 431353948
Organization Type: Corporate Foundation
Former Name: Southwestern Bell Foundation.
Formed by Merger of: PacTel Foundation (1998).
Giving Locations: AR; CA; CT; DC; IL: central Illinois, Chicago; KS; MD: Baltimore; MA: western Massachusetts, Boston; MO; NV; NY: Upstate; OK; RI; TX nationally.
Grant Types: Award, Capital, Conference/Seminar, Emergency, Employee Matching Gifts, Endowment, General Support, Multiyear/Continuing Support, Project, Scholarship.
Note: Employee matching gift ratio: 1 to 1 to higher education and cultural institutions.

Giving Philosophy

'The foundation reflects a commitment to being involved for the long-term in advancing the welfare of society. It embodies a desire to be a leader in exploring new approaches to major public agenda issues. Also, it indicates the willingness of one of the most successful companies in the telecommunications industry to address tough community concerns proactively and with an innovative spirit.

'We see our efforts as investments in progress, particularly in towns and cities served by SBC Communications and its subsidiaries. We like to think of ourselves as facilitators who help communities search for lasting solutions to critical and complex problems. And thanks to a unique combination of extensive local presence, leadership expertise, employee volunteers, and financial resources, we are well-positioned to understand local needs and make a difference where it counts.

'The Foundation contributes to many types of nonprofit organizations. We believe the best way to magnify the effect of our giving is to concentrate on specific areas of interest, on problems where we can hope to make a significant impact, within the general categories of education, civic affairs, health and welfare, and culture and the arts.' Contribution Guidelines

Financial Summary

Total Giving: $102,000,000 (2000 approx); $93,500,000 (1999 approx); $55,000,000 (1998 approx). Note: Contributes through foundation and corporate direct giving.

Giving Analysis: Giving for 1997 includes: foundation ($20,600,000); corporate direct giving ($9,300,000); 1998: foundation ($31,400,000); corporate direct giving ($23,600,000); foundation grants to United Way ($6,200,000); foundation scholarships ($2,700,000); foundation matching gifts ($1,500,000)

Assets: $398,400,000 (1999 approx); $204,700,000 (1998 approx); $100,900,000 (1997 approx)

Gifts Received: $33,100,000 (1999); $129,000,000 (1994); $14,000,000 (1992). Note: Contributions are received from SBC Communications Inc. and its subsidiaries.

Typical Recipients

Arts & Humanities: Arts Appreciation, Arts Associations & Councils, Arts Centers, Arts Festivals, Arts Funds, Arts Institutes, Community Arts, Dance, Ethnic & Folk Arts, Historic Preservation, History & Archaeology, Libraries, Museums/Galleries, Music, Opera, Performing Arts, Public Broadcasting, Theater

Civic & Public Affairs: African American Affairs, Botanical Gardens/Parks, Clubs, Community Foundations, Economic Development, Employment/Job Training, Ethnic Organizations, Civic & Public Affairs-General, Hispanic Affairs, Municipalities/Towns, Parades/Festivals, Public Policy, Urban & Community Affairs, Zoos/Aquariums

Education: Arts/Humanities Education, Business Education, Colleges & Universities, Community & Junior Colleges, Education Associations, Education Funds, Education Reform, Engineering/Technological Education, Faculty Development, Education-General, Literacy, Medical Education, Minority Education, Public Education (Precollege), School Volunteerism, Science/Mathematics Education, Student Aid, Vocational & Technical Education

Health: Cancer, Children's Health/Hospitals, Emergency/Ambulance Services, Health Organizations, Hospitals, Medical Research, Mental Health

International: Foreign Educational Institutions

Religion: Religious Welfare

Science: Scientific Centers & Institutes

Social Services: Child Welfare, Community Centers, Community Service Organizations, Family Services, People with Disabilities, Scouts, Senior Services, Shelters/Homelessness, Special Olympics, United Funds/United Ways, Volunteer Services, YMCA/YWCA/YMHA/YWHA, Youth Organizations

Contributions Analysis

Giving Priorities: Education and community economic development; also arts and cultural outreach, and health and human services.

Arts & Humanities: About 10%. Supports initiatives that promote cultural and arts education, broaden access to arts and cultural activities and help promote community pride. Areas of focus include broad-based performing arts and cultural programs that promote cultural diversity and community outreach, and partnerships between arts and cultural institutions and schools that provide educational programs for K-12 students and underserved communities.

Civic & Public Affairs: About 20%. Supports initiatives designed to promote the sustained economic growth of our communities and build the capacity of community-based organizations to serve their clients. Areas of focus are programs that broaden economic growth opportunities for the whole community; technology-based programs that enhance a community's infrastructure or improve the efficiency and productivity of community-based organizations; community coalitions that stimulate business retention and expansion, especially in economically disadvantaged areas; programs that address adult literacy, job training and leadership skill development.

Education: 37%. Supports K-12 and higher education initiatives that can improve and strengthen the education process, produce sustained improvement in student learning, broaden educational opportunity and increase the potential for each student to succeed. Areas of focus include programs that support strategic and systemic change in K-12 education and can be linked to improved student achievement; programs that integrate innovative approaches to instruction with a focus on creative technology applications for enhanced learning and improved school effectiveness; programs that support at-risk students and encourage parental involvement in student achievement; public or private colleges and universities with an emphasis on collaborations to improve teacher preparedness, expand the use of technology in the classroom, promote excellence in math, science, and engineering, and support student success and achievement.

Social Services: 21%. Funds the United Way.

Note: Total contributions in 1998.

Application Procedures

Initial Contact: Obtain a grant application from the foundation. Completed applications should be prefaced with a brief cover letter; grant requests of a local or statewide nature should be sent to local subsidiary or division; requests of a regional or national nature should be addressed directly to the Foundation.

Application Requirements: Include proof of tax-exempt status; description of how project fits with foundation's priorities; total project budget and amount requested; brief statement of history and accomplishments; statement of current objectives, including problem being addressed, program budget and amount sought; linkage of project's goals to the foundation's priorities; timetable for implementation and description of expected results; details of fund-raising plans, including sources, amounts, and commitments; plans for sustaining activities after conclusion of foundation support; annual report or budget for organization, showing all income sources and expenditures; list of board members; list of accrediting agencies; one-page evaluation component detailing how project success will be measured; line-item budget for project.

Deadlines: June 1 for higher education grants. None for other grant requests.

Review Process: All requests will be evaluated within four to six weeks after receipt; requesting organization may be contacted for additional information.

Evaluative Criteria: The foundation prefers to fund organizations in operating areas, project-specific proposals within areas of interest, projects that directly impact human needs and have the potential to be self-sustaining and adaptable to other settings, projects that stimulate partnerships among community organizations, and projects with well-defined goals, a clear picture of the need addressed, and specific tracking and evaluation procedures. Organizations seeking support should demonstrate clearly stated objectives, long-range planning, active participation of the governing board, strategies and plans to move from dependency on any one source of support, sound financial principles and practices, and close monitoring of programs.

Notes: Organizations are asked not to submit a proposal more than once in a 12-month period.

Restrictions

Foundation does not support private foundations or organizations without tax-exempt status; organizations that practice discrimination by race, color, creed, sex, age, or national origin; hospital operating funds or capital funds; operating expenses for organizations supported by the United Way; individuals; political activities or organizations; religious organizations for sectarian purposes; fraternal, veteran, or labor groups when serving only their memberships; disease specific organizations; individual K-12 schools or districts, local school systems or school-system foundations; sports programs or events; cause-related marketing; donation of products or services; or special occasion goodwill advertising and ticket or dinner purchases.

Additional Information

Foundation states a preference for organizations that operate in corporate operating locations and in communities where a significant number of employees live; project-oriented proposals rather than requests for grants to underwrite operating or capital budgets; projects that promote citizen participation and volunteerism; projects that generate public awareness and offer opportunities to leverage contributions; projects that address human needs and whose services are provided directly rather than through intermediary organizations; and projects that develop leadership skills.

SBC Communications is in the process of purchasing Ameritech Corp.

In 1998, the company acquired Pacific Telesis (PacTel) and that company's foundation. The PacTel Foundation was merged into the SBC Foundation.

Publications: Contributions Guidelines

Corporate Officials

Janet Kendall: associate vice presidentc, chief executive officer PRIM CORP EMPL associate vice president: SBC Communications Inc.

Donald E. Kiernan, Sr.: senior vice president, chief financial officer, treasurer B Trumbull, CT 1940. ED Boston College BS (1962); Florida State University MBA (1970). PRIM CORP EMPL senior vice president, chief financial officer, treasurer: SBC Communications Inc. CORP AFFIL director: Southwest Bell Mobile Systems; director: Southwest Bell Telephone Co.

Edward E. Whitacre, Jr.: chairman, director, chief executive officer B Ennis, TX 1941. ED Texas Technology University BS (1964). PRIM CORP EMPL chairman, director, chief executive officer: SBC Communications Inc. CORP AFFIL president: Southwest Bell Telephone Co.; director: Emerson Electric Co.; director: May Department Stores Co.; director: Anheuser-Busch Companies Inc.; director: Burlington Northern Santa Fe Corp. NONPR AFFIL trustee: Southwest Research Institute; board regents: Texas Technology University & Health Science; member: Learning National Advisory Board; member executive board national council & southern reg: Boy Scouts America.

Foundation Officials

Royce S. Caldwell: director B 1939. ED Abilene Christian University BBA (1961). PRIM CORP EMPL president, chief executive officer, director: Southwest

Bell Operations. CORP AFFIL president: SBC Communications Inc.; president, ceo: Southwest Bell Telephone Co.

Cassandra Colvin Carr: director B Champaign, IL 1944. ED Vanderbilt University BA (1966); University of Texas MA (1973). PRIM CORP EMPL senior vice president human resources, director: SBC Communications Inc. ADD CORP EMPL officer: Southwestern Bell Telephone Co. CORP AFFIL director: Yellow Corp.; director: Destec Energy Inc. NONPR AFFIL member: National Association Corp. Treas; commissioner: Saint Louis Regional Conv Sports Complex Authority; trustee: Foundation Womens Resources; director: Conference Board; member: Financial Executives Institute; director: Arch Funds Inc. CLUB AFFIL Forest Hills Country Club; Saint Louis Club.

Gloria Delgado: president

James D. Ellis: director B 1943. ED University of Iowa BBA (1965); University of Missouri JD (1968). PRIM CORP EMPL senior executive vice president, general counsel: SBC Communications Inc. ADD CORP EMPL secretary: Southwestern Bell Telephone Co. CORP AFFIL director: Southwest Bell Mobile Systems.

Charles E. Foster: director B 1936. ED University of Oklahoma BSME (1961); Washington University (1967). PRIM CORP EMPL group president: SBC Communications Inc. CORP AFFIL director: Southwest Bell Mobile Systems; director: Southwest Bell Telephone Co.

Karen E. Jennings: director

Janet Kendall: chairman (see above)

Donald E. Kiernan, Sr.: director (see above)

Linda S. Mills: director

Harold E. Rainbolt: vice president, secretary B Norman, OK 1929. ED University of Oklahoma (1951); University of Oklahoma (1957). PRIM CORP EMPL chairman: BancFirst Corp. CORP AFFIL director: Sonic Corp.; director: Trend Venture Corp.

Larry Walther: chairman

Roger W. Wohlert: vice president, treasurer PRIM CORP EMPL treasurer: SBC Asset Management Inc.

Grants Analysis

Disclosure Period: calendar year ending 1996
Total Grants: $17,302,143*
Number of Grants: 902 (approx)
Average Grant: $19,182
Highest Grant: $1,051,958
Typical Range: $1,000 to $50,000
***Note:** Giving excludes matching gifts; United Way.

Recent Grants

Note: Grants derived from 1996 Form 990.

Arts & Humanities

200,000	Symphony Society, San Antonio, TX
150,000	Brooks Heritage Foundation, Brooks, TX
150,000	San Antonio Public Library Foundation, San Antonio, TX
125,000	Museum of Fine Arts, Houston, TX
100,000	San Antonio Museum of Art, San Antonio, TX
75,000	Dallas Museum of Art, Dallas, TX
75,000	National Cowboy Hall of Fame and Western Heritage Center, Oklahoma City, OK

Civic & Public Affairs

120,000	Oklahoma City Economic Development Foundation, Oklahoma City, OK
100,000	Variety Club, Saint Louis, MO

Education

1,051,958	Citizens Scholarship Foundation of America, Saint Peter, MN
1,051,958	Citizens Scholarship Foundation of America, Saint Peter, MN
996,084	Citizens Scholarship Foundation of America, Saint Peter, MN
400,000	Dallas Education Center, Dallas, TX
300,000	University of Texas San Antonio, San Antonio, TX
250,000	Washington University, Saint Louis, MO
225,000	Texas A&M Foundation, College Station, TX
150,000	Trinity University, San Antonio, TX
120,000	Texas Independent College Fund, Fort Worth, TX
100,000	Dallas Education Center, Dallas, TX
100,000	Florida A&M University Foundation, Tallahassee, FL
100,000	St. Mary's University, San Antonio, TX
100,000	Texas A&M Foundation, College Station, TX
100,000	Texas A&M University Foundation, College Station, TX
100,000	Texas A&M University Foundation, College Station, TX
100,000	Texas Technical University Foundation, Lubbock, TX
100,000	University of Missouri, Saint Louis, MO
100,000	University of Texas Austin, Austin, TX
100,000	University of Texas Pan American Foundation, Edinburg, TX
80,000	Westark Community College Foundation, Fort Smith, AR
78,563	Harvard University, Cambridge, MA
75,000	Junior Achievement South Texas, San Antonio, TX
75,000	Texas Technical University Foundation, Lubbock, TX

Health

90,000	Capper Foundation for Crippled Children, Topeka, KS

Religion

75,000	Valley Interfaith Alliance, McAllen, TX

Science

80,000	Mind Science Foundation, San Antonio, TX

Social Services

392,500	United Way, Saint Louis, MO
392,500	United Way, Saint Louis, MO
267,500	United Way Texas Gulf Coast, Houston, TX
267,500	United Way Texas Gulf Coast, Houston, TX
236,250	United Way, Dallas, TX
236,250	United Way, Dallas, TX
200,000	United Way San Antonio and Bexar County, San Antonio, TX
200,000	United Way San Antonio and Bexar County, San Antonio, TX
100,000	YMCA San Antonio and the Hill Country, San Antonio, TX
90,500	Heart of America United Way, Kansas City, MO
90,500	Heart of America United Way, Kansas City, MO
87,500	United Way Plains, Wichita, KS
80,000	United Way, Tulsa, OK
80,000	United Way Metropolitan Tarrant County, Fort Worth, TX
80,000	United Way Metropolitan Tarrant County, Fort Worth, TX

SCANA Corp.

Company Contact

Columbia, SC
Web: http://www.scana.com

Company Description

Assets: US$5,685,000,000 (1999)
Employees: 4,697 (1999)
SIC(s): 4939 Combination Utility Nec, 6719 Holding Companies Nec.

SUBSIDIARY COMPANIES

SC: South Carolina Electric & Gas Co., Columbia

Nonmonetary Support

Type: Donated Equipment; Loaned Employees; Loaned Executives

Corporate Sponsorship

Type: Arts & cultural events; Festivals/fairs; Music & entertainment events; Pledge-a-thon; Sports events
Note: Only sponsors events in central South Carolina.

Giving Contact

Joann Butler, Manager, Corp. Affairs
SCANA Corp.
1426 Main Street
Columbia, SC 29201
Phone: (803)217-9394
Fax: (803)217-9469

Description

Organization Type: Corporate Giving Program
Giving Locations: SC: only in company operating locations in central SC
Grant Types: Capital.

Financial Summary

Total Giving: Contributes through corporate direct giving program only.

Typical Recipients

Arts & Humanities: Arts & Humanities-General
Civic & Public Affairs: Civic & Public Affairs-General
Education: Education-General
Health: Health-General
Social Services: Social Services-General

Contributions Analysis

Education: Supports this state program that consolidates school and social service resources to rescue at-risk youth. Supports medical students to become primary care physicians and practice in the smaller communities of the state; provides stipends to student doctors.

Application Procedures

Initial Contact: Send a brief letter of inquiry.
Application Requirements: Include a description of organization, amount requested, purpose of funds sought, recently audited financial statement, and proof of tax-exempt status.
Deadlines: The budget is fixed by the first of the year. Requests for funding are best received during the last half of the year.

Restrictions

Does not support organizations without 501(c)(3) status or organizations outside company's operating area.
Only gives to capital projects located in the central South Carolina area.

Giving Program Officials

Joann Butler: PRIM CORP EMPL coordinator community service: SCANA Corp.

Schering-Plough Corp.

Company Contact

Madison, NJ
Web: http://www.sch-plough.com

Company Description

Revenue: US$9,176,000,000 (1999)
Profit: US$2,110,000,000 (1999)
Fortune Rank: 185, per FORTUNE Magazine's list of 500 Largest U.S. Corporations (1999).
FF 185

SIC(s): 2833 Medicinals & Botanicals, 2834 Pharmaceutical Preparations, 2836 Biological Products Except Diagnostic, 2844 Toilet Preparations, 3842 Surgical Appliances & Supplies, 3851 Ophthalmic Goods, 6719 Holding Companies Nec.

Operating Locations

Brazil: Schering Plough Brasil, Sau Paulo, Caixa; England: Plough (UK) Ltd., London; Schering-Plough Holdings Ltd., London; Scholl (UK) Ltd., London; Norway: Norsk Schering A/S, Stabekk

Nonmonetary Support

Type: Donated Equipment; Donated Products; In-kind Services
Volunteer Programs: Provides small grants through its Dollar for Volunteer program most used by employees and their families, American Red Cross, health-care services to low-income working people, and university schools of pharmacy.

Corporate Sponsorship

Type: Arts & cultural events; Festivals/fairs
Contact: Joseph Starkey, Manager Community Affairs
Note: Co. sponsors health fairs, art exhibitions, and charity drives.

Schering-Plough Foundation

Giving Contact

Christine Fahey, Assistant Secretary
Schering-Plough Foundation
One Giralda Farms
Madison, NJ 07940-1010
Phone: (973)822-7414
Fax: (973)822-7349

Alternate Contact

Andrew Hageman
Phone: (973)822-7000
Note: For direct contributions.

Description

EIN: 221711047
Organization Type: Corporate Foundation
Giving Locations: principally near operating locations and to national organizations.
Grant Types: Capital, Employee Matching Gifts, Endowment, Fellowship, General Support, Multiyear/Continuing Support, Professorship, Research, Scholarship, Seed Money.
Note: Employee matching gift ratio: 1 to 1 for secondary and higher education, hospitals and hospices.

Giving Philosophy

'Schering-Plough Corporation believes it is in the best interest of the company to be active corporate citizens in the communities in which we have facilities and in which our employees live.'
'This responsibility has many facets. It includes participation in the public policy process; support for a myriad of national, state and local organizations through our philanthropic activities; and leadership in community partnerships both domestically and internationally.' Foundation & Community Affairs.

Financial Summary

Total Giving: $2,300,000 (1999 approx); $2,300,000 (1998 approx); $2,660,088 (1997). Note: Contributes through corporate direct giving program and foundation.
Giving Analysis: Giving for 1997 includes: foundation ($2,266,746); foundation matching gifts ($393,342); 1998: foundation (approx $2,300,000); 1999: foundation (approx $2,300,000)
Assets: $18,200,000 (1999 approx); $18,200,000 (1998 approx); $20,082,461 (1997)
Gifts Received: $1,500,000 (1997); $1,500,000 (1996); $1,500,000 (1995). Note: The foundation receives gifts from the Schering-Plough Corp.

Typical Recipients

Arts & Humanities: Arts Associations & Councils, Arts Centers, Arts Festivals, Arts Funds, Community Arts, Dance, Ethnic & Folk Arts, Arts & Humanities-General, Historic Preservation, Libraries, Museums/Galleries, Music, Performing Arts, Theater
Civic & Public Affairs: Civil Rights, Community Foundations, Economic Development, Hispanic Affairs, Housing, Nonprofit Management, Philanthropic Organizations, Professional & Trade Associations, Public Policy, Zoos/Aquariums
Education: Arts/Humanities Education, Business Education, Colleges & Universities, Education Associations, Education Funds, Engineering/Technological Education, Faculty Development, Education-General, Health & Physical Education, Literacy, Medical Education, Minority Education, Preschool Education, Private Education (Precollege), Science/Mathematics Education, Student Aid
Health: Cancer, Children's Health/Hospitals, Clinics/Medical Centers, Emergency/Ambulance Services, Health Policy/Cost Containment, Hospices, Hospitals, Long-Term Care, Medical Rehabilitation, Medical Research, Medical Training, Mental Health, Public Health, Research/Studies Institutes, Single-Disease Health Associations, Transplant Networks/Donor Banks
International: Health Care/Hospitals, International Peace & Security Issues, International Relations
Religion: Churches, Religious Welfare
Science: Scientific Centers & Institutes, Scientific Labs, Scientific Research
Social Services: Child Welfare, Family Services, Substance Abuse, United Funds/United Ways, YMCA/YWCA/YMHA/YWHA, Youth Organizations

Contributions Analysis

Giving Priorities: Education, health-related education, civic welfare, public policy, culture, the arts, and health care. Company has supported U.S.-based nonprofits with international operations in the areas of health and development. Foreign operating companies have limited contributions budget. Headquarters reports that the international contributions are very decentralized. Headquarters requires each foreign operating facility to administer a contributions program, but no guidelines or priorities have been established.
Arts & Humanities: 6%. Support is awarded to galleries, museums, arts centers, exhibitions and performing arts organizations.
Civic & Public Affairs: 5%. Supports civic affairs, including affordable housing, women's shelters, public policy, and the environment.
Education: 48%. Supports higher and secondary education. Interests include medical and pharmaceutical schools, medical research, and public health education. Also awards funding to establish scholarships in the natural sciences and biomedical studies and to support traditional scholarship programs and education funds. Also supports management education, education associations, and student aid programs.
Health: 34%. Supports hospitals and health-care programs most used by employees and their families, American Red Cross, health-care services to low-income working people, and university schools of pharmacy.
Science: 5%. Supports science research and laboratories.
Social Services: 2%. Supports YMCAs, anti-drug campaigns, and other social service organizations.
Note: Total contributions in 1997.

Application Procedures

Initial Contact: Letter or proposal on organization letterhead.
Application Requirements: Specific purpose of funds sought, background information on requesting organization, major programs and services rendered, proof of tax-exempt status, latest audited financial statement, program budget (if application relates to specific activity); supporting material (including annual report) is desirable.
Deadlines: July 1 for foundation only.
Evaluative Criteria: Primary focus is support of institutional activities and programs devoted to improving health-care delivery.
Decision Notification: Requests are reviewed continually; board meets annually in the fall.
Notes: Requests that do not include the information above will be returned to applicants.

Restrictions

Grants are not made to individuals.

Additional Information

Occasionally makes product donations, primarily to assist efforts of U.S. organizations working in developing countries. Surplus equipment is made available to organizations in operating communities.
Foundation historically pays grants for annual support in the fourth quarter of the year.

Corporate Officials

Paul Cesan: president, chief operating officer PRIM CORP EMPL president, chief operating officer: Schering-Plough Corp.
Richard Jay Kogan: chairman, chief executive officer B New York, NY 1941. ED City University of New York BA (1963); New York University MBA (1968). PRIM CORP EMPL chairman, chief executive officer: Schering-Plough Corp. ADD CORP EMPL president: Canji Inc.; president: Schering Plough Veterinary; president: Schering-Plough Products Inc.; president: Syntro Corp. CORP AFFIL director: Colgate-Palmolive Co.; director: DNAX Research Institute Molecular Cell Biology; director: Atlantic Mutual Companies; director: Bank New York Co. Inc. NONPR AFFIL member: Pharmaceutical Research & Manufacturer Association America; trustee: Saint Barnabas Medical Center; member: Council Foreign Relations; member, board overseers: New York University Stern School Business.

Foundation Officials

Hugh Alfred D'Andrade: trustee, member B Metuchen, NJ 1938. ED Rutgers University BA (1961); Columbia University LLB (1964). PRIM CORP EMPL vice chairman, chief administrative officer: Schering-Plough Corp. CORP AFFIL director: Autoimmune Inc. NONPR AFFIL member: American Bar Association.
Christine Fahey: assistant secretary
Andrew F. Hageman: secretary PRIM CORP EMPL manager corporate philanthropy: Schering-Plough Corp.
Richard J. Kinney: president PRIM CORP EMPL staff vice president public affairs: Schering-Plough Corp.
Richard Jay Kogan: trustee, member (see above)
E. Kevin Moore: treasurer PRIM CORP EMPL vice president, treasurer: Schering-Plough Corp.
Jack L. Wyszomierski: trustee, member B 1955. ED Carnegie Mellon University BS (1977); Carnegie Mellon University MS (1978). PRIM CORP EMPL executive vice president, chief financial officer: Schering-Plough Corp. CORP AFFIL chief financial officer: Canji Inc.

Grants Analysis

Disclosure Period: calendar year ending 1997
Total Grants: $2,266,746
Number of Grants: 56
Average Grant: $40,478
Highest Grant: $300,000
Typical Range: $10,000 to $30,000
Note: Grants analysis derived from 1997 form 990.

Recent Grants

Note: Grants derived from 1997 Form 990.

Arts & Humanities

50,000 Cleveland Bradley Regional Museum, Cleveland, TN
25,000 Newark Museum, Newark, NJ
20,000 Crossroads Theater Company, New Brunswick, NJ
15,000 Paper Mill Playhouse, Milburn, NJ
12,500 Montclair Art Museum, Montclair, NJ

Civic & Public Affairs

60,000 Pharmaceutical Manufacturers Association
25,000 Elizabeth Development Company, Elizabeth, NJ
25,000 Enterprise Foundation, Columbia, MD

Education

100,000 Foundation of University of Medicine and Dentistry, Newark, NJ
100,000 University of Michigan College of Pharmacy, Ann Arbor, MI
90,000 University College Cork
75,000 Baruch College, New York, NY
71,824 National Merit Scholarship Corporation, Evanston, IL
50,000 Education and Research Trust
50,000 Fairleigh Dickinson University, Teaneck, NJ
50,000 Independent College Fund, Little Rock, AR
50,000 New Jersey Institute of Technology, Newark, NJ
50,000 New York University Stern School of Business, New York, NY
50,000 Occupational Physicians Scholarship Fund, New York, NY
50,000 St. Mary's University, San Antonio, TX
30,000 College Fund/UNCF
30,000 Douglass College
30,000 Early Childhood Learning Centers, NJ
30,000 Marymount Manhattan College, New York, NY
25,000 University of Wisconsin Foundation, Madison, WI
20,000 Drew University, Madison, NJ
16,000 Stanford University, Stanford, CA
15,000 Quality Education for Minorities, Washington, DC
15,000 Tufts University, Medford, MA
12,500 University of Minnesota, Minneapolis, MN
10,750 Blair Academy, Blairstown, NJ
10,000 American Foundation for Pharmaceutical Education, North Plainsfield, NJ
10,000 Bloomfield College, Bloomfield, NJ
10,000 Florida A&M University, Sarasota, FL
10,000 Physician Assistant Foundation
10,000 Rutgers Preparatory School, Somerset, NJ

Health

300,000 Children's Health Fund, New York, NY
250,000 American Red Cross
50,000 Morristown Memorial Hospital Health Foundation, Morristown, NJ
50,000 People-to-People Health Foundation, Millwood, VA
25,000 Children's Specialized Hospital, Mountainside, NJ
25,000 Church Health Center, Memphis, TN
25,000 University of Texas M.D. Anderson Cancer Center, Houston, TX
20,000 Mental Health Association, NJ
10,000 High Hopes Therapeutic Riding
10,000 Plainfield Health Center, Plainfield, NJ

Science

90,172 Life Sciences Research Foundation, Baltimore, MD
30,000 Cold Spring Harbor Laboratory, Cold Spring Harbor, NY

Social Services

35,000 Partnership for a Drug-Free America
10,000 Sussex County YMCA

MARCUS SCHLOSS &CO.

Company Contact

New York, NY

Company Description

Employees: 38
SIC(s): 6200 Security & Commodity Brokers.

Rexford Fund

Giving Contact

Douglas Schloss, Chairman & Chief Executive Officer
1 Whitehall Street, 17th Floor
New York, NY 10004
Phone: (212)483-1500
Fax: (212)363-7265

Description

Founded: 1967
EIN: 136222049
Organization Type: Corporate Foundation. Supports preselected organizations only.
Giving Locations: NY

Financial Summary

Total Giving: $280,000 (2000 approx); $280,000 (1999); $247,646 (1998)
Assets: $3,786,983 (1998); $3,751,758 (1997); $2,645,570 (1996)
Gifts Received: $1,258,094 (1997); $405,600 (1996); $488,990 (1995)

Typical Recipients

Arts & Humanities: Arts Associations & Councils, Arts Funds, Dance, Libraries, Literary Arts, Museums/Galleries, Music, Performing Arts, Theater
Civic & Public Affairs: Botanical Gardens/Parks, Business/Free Enterprise, Community Foundations, Civic & Public Affairs-General, Urban & Community Affairs
Education: Arts/Humanities Education, Business Education, Colleges & Universities, Literacy, Minority Education, Private Education (Precollege), Public Education (Precollege), Secondary Education (Private), Special Education
Environment: Environment-General, Resource Conservation, Wildlife Protection
Health: Cancer, Clinics/Medical Centers, Emergency/Ambulance Services, Health Organizations, Hospices, Hospitals, Mental Health, Multiple Sclerosis, Public Health, Single-Disease Health Associations
International: Foreign Arts Organizations, Foreign Educational Institutions, International Peace & Security Issues
Religion: Churches, Jewish Causes, Religious Organizations, Religious Welfare, Synagogues/Temples
Social Services: Child Welfare, Community Service Organizations, Day Care, Family Planning, Family Services, Food/Clothing Distribution, People with Disabilities, Scouts, Shelters/Homelessness, Substance Abuse, United Funds/United Ways, YMCA/YWCA/YMHA/YWHA, Youth Organizations

Contributions Analysis

Giving Priorities: Arts organizations, social services, civic affairs, and education.
Arts & Humanities: 31%. Funds art and history museums, theater and other performing arts, and libraries.
Civic & Public Affairs: 9%. Supports parks and conservatories, community clubs, and community loan funds.
Education: 22%. Funds colleges and universities, nursery and primary education, and scholarship funds.
Environment: 3%. Funds land trusts and planting fields.
Health: 2%. Supports a food allergy organization, emergency/ambulatory services, medical centers, and single-disease health organizations.
Religion: 10%. Provides support for religious welfare organizations and Jewish and Christian places of worship.
Social Services: 23%. Supports family and youth centers.
Note: Total contributions made in 1998.

Restrictions

Does not support individuals.

Corporate Officials

James C. Cusumano: chief financial officer PRIM CORP EMPL chief financial officer: Marcus Schloss & Co.
Douglas Schloss: chairman, chief executive officer PRIM CORP EMPL chairman, chief executive officer: Marcus Schloss & Co.
Richard Schloss: president PRIM CORP EMPL president: Marcus Schloss & Co.

Foundation Officials

Douglas Schloss: secretary (see above)
Richard Schloss: treasurer (see above)
Alan S. Sexter: president

Grants Analysis

Disclosure Period: calendar year ending 1998
Total Grants: $247,646
Number of Grants: 193
Average Grant: $1,283
Highest Grant: $25,000
Typical Range: $50 to $20,000

Recent Grants

Note: Grants derived from 1997 Form 990.

Arts & Humanities

10,000 White Columns, New York, NY
4,375 Lincoln Center for Performing Arts, New York, NY
3,700 American Craft Museum, New York, NY

Civic & Public Affairs

25,000 Genesis Community Loan Fund, Bristol, ME
15,000 ICI, New York, NY
5,000 ICI, New York, NY

Education

15,000 St. Bernard's School, New York, NY
12,000 St. John's University, Jamaica, NY
10,000 Brearley School, New York, NY
10,000 Salisbury School Annual Fund, Salisbury, CT
5,000 Union Settlement Association, New York, NY

Health

10,000 Columbia University Health Sciences Division, New York, NY

International

10,000 Business Executives for National Security, Washington, DC

Religion

19,000 Grace Lutheran Church, Forest Hills, NY
10,000 Ramaz KJ 2000 Fund, New York, NY
4,000 St. John's Bread of Life, Brooklyn, NY
4,000 St. Mary's Children and Family Services, Syosset, NY

Social Services

25,500 Family Dynamics, New York, NY
20,000 Family Dynamics, New York, NY
5,000 Family Dynamics, New York, NY

SCHLUMBERGER LTD. (USA)

Company Contact

New York, NY
Web: http://www.slb.com

Company Description

Profit: US$886,600,000
Employees: 57,000
SIC(s): 1389 Oil & Gas Field Services Nec, 3824 Fluid Meters & Counting Devices, 3825 Instruments to Measure Electricity, 7374 Data Processing & Preparation.
Parent Company: Schlumberger Ltd., 42 rue Saint-Dominique, Paris, France

Operating Locations

CA: Schlumberger Ltd., Mountain View, Oxnard, San Jose; CT: Schlumberger Ltd., Bridgeport; GA: Schlumberger Industries-Electricity Management, Norcross; Schlumberger Ltd., Norcross; MI: Schlumberger CAD/CAM Division, Ann Arbor; Schlumberger Ltd., Ann Arbor; NY: Schlumberger Ltd., Elmsford, New York; Schlumberger Ltd., New York; OR: Schlumberger Ltd., Medford; PA: Schlumberger Ltd., Archbold; TX: Schlumberger Ltd., Dallas; Dowell Schlumberger Inc., Houston; Geco Geophysical Co., Inc., Houston; Schlumberger Ltd., Houston; Schlumberger Well Services, Houston; Anadrill, Sugar Land
Note: Operates internationally.

Schlumberger Foundation

Giving Contact

Arthur W. Alexander, Secretary & Treasurer
Schlumberger Foundation
277 Park Avenue
New York, NY 10172-0266
Phone: (212)350-9400
Fax: (212)350-9440

Description

EIN: 237033142
Organization Type: Corporate Foundation
Giving Locations: NY: New York nationally to education.
Grant Types: Capital, Fellowship, General Support, Professorship, Project, Research, Scholarship.

Financial Summary

Total Giving: $1,000,000 (1999 approx); $1,367,710 (1998); $1,000,000 (1996 approx). Note: Contributes through foundation only.
Giving Analysis: Giving for 1998 includes: foundation gifts to individuals ($411,932); foundation fellowships ($206,783); foundation scholarships ($172,995)
Assets: $24,076,945 (1998)

Typical Recipients

Arts & Humanities: Arts Centers, Ballet, Dance, Ethnic & Folk Arts, Historic Preservation, Libraries, Literary Arts, Museums/Galleries, Music, Opera, Performing Arts, Public Broadcasting, Theater
Civic & Public Affairs: Botanical Gardens/Parks, Economic Development, Economic Policy, Legal Aid, Minority Business, Nonprofit Management, Professional & Trade Associations, Women's Affairs
Education: Arts/Humanities Education, Colleges & Universities, Economic Education, Education Associations, Engineering/Technological Education, Faculty Development, International Studies, Medical Education, Minority Education, Private Education (Precollege), Public Education (Precollege), Science/Mathematics Education, Special Education, Student Aid
Environment: Environment-General, Resource Conservation, Wildlife Protection
Health: Alzheimers Disease, Cancer, Eyes/Blindness, Hospices, Hospitals, Medical Research, Single-Disease Health Associations
International: Foreign Educational Institutions
Science: Science Museums, Scientific Centers & Institutes
Social Services: Community Service Organizations, Day Care, Family Planning, Family Services, Food/Clothing Distribution, People with Disabilities, Shelters/Homelessness, Substance Abuse, Youth Organizations

Contributions Analysis

Giving Priorities: Colleges and universities, cancer research, music, museums, and social service organizations.
Arts & Humanities: About 7%. Majority of support funds music and museums. Dance organizations, arts centers, and performing arts organizations also receive support.
Civic & Public Affairs: 3%. Environmental efforts, women's issues, and law and justice are supported.
Education: 73%. Funding primarily supports colleges and universities for professorships, research programs, and facilities grants. Interest is also shown in minority education, and scholarships and fellowships.
Environment: Less than 5%. Supports conservation efforts.
Health: 5% to 10%. Interests include geriatric health, single-disease health associations, and hospitals.
Science: 5% to 10%. Funding supports the Houston Museum of Natural Science.
Social Services: 5% to 10%. Supports community service organizations with emphasis on neighborhoods and homelessness. Youth clubs and people with disabilities also receive funding.

Application Procedures

Initial Contact: brief letter or proposal
Application Requirements: a description of organization, amount requested, purpose of funds sought, recently audited financial statement, and proof of tax-exempt status
Deadlines: None.

Restrictions

Grants are generally limited to colleges and universities emphasizing engineering and natural sciences, and cultural institutions.

Additional Information

According to Schlumberger Ltd., it has three headquarters: Paris, France; The Hague, Netherlands; and New York, NY.

Corporate Officials

Dugald Euan Baird: chairman, president, chief executive officer B Aberdeen, Scotland 1937. ED Aberdeen University (1955); Cambridge University BA (1960); Trinity College (1957-1960); Aberdeen University LLD (1995). PRIM CORP EMPL chairman, president, chief executive officer: Schlumberger Ltd. CORP AFFIL director: BOC Group.
Arthur Lindenauer: executive vice president, chief financial officer B New York, NY 1937. ED Dartmouth College BA (1958); Dartmouth College Amos Tuck Graduate School of Business Administration MBA (1959). PRIM CORP EMPL executive vice president, chief financial officer: Schlumberger Ltd. ADD CORP EMPL president: Schlumberger Technology Corp.; president: Schlumberger Electricities. NONPR AFFIL member: American Institute CPAs.

Foundation Officials

Arthur W. Alexander: secretary-treasurer PRIM CORP EMPL vice president, director personnel: Schlumberger Ltd.
George Hiram Jewell: director B Fort Worth, TX 1922. ED University of Texas BA (1942); University of Texas LLB (1950). PRIM CORP EMPL counsel: Baker & Botts, LLP. NONPR AFFIL member: Phi Delta Phi; trustee: Texas Childrens Hospital; member: Phi Beta Kappa; fellow: American College Tax Counsel; member: Order Coif; fellow: American Bar Foundation; member: American Bar Association. CLUB AFFIL Old Baldy Club; Houston Country Club; Coronado Country Club; Eldorado Country Club.
Pierre Marcel Schlumberger: director B 1943. ED Yale University BA (1963); Southern Methodist University LLD (1966). CLUB AFFIL Argyle Club.
Roy Ray Shourd: president B East Saint Louis, IL 1927. ED University of Missouri (1950). PRIM CORP EMPL executive vice president drilling & products: Schlumberger Ltd. NONPR AFFIL member: American Petroleum Institute.

Grants Analysis

Disclosure Period: calendar year ending 1998
Total Grants: $576,000*
Number of Grants: 49
Average Grant: $9,714
Highest Grant: $50,000
Typical Range: $1,000 to $15,000
***Note:** Giving excludes scholarships; fellowships; and targeted technical grants to individuals.

Recent Grants

Note: Grants derived from 1996 Form 990.

Arts & Humanities

14,000	Museum of American Folk Art, New York, NY
10,000	Carnegie Hall Society, New York, NY
8,000	Whitney Museum of American Art, New York, NY
5,000	Houston University Blaffer Gallery, Houston, TX
5,000	John F. Kennedy Center Corporate Fund, Washington, DC
5,000	Metropolitan Museum of Art, New York, NY
2,500	Pierpont Morgan Library, New York, NY
2,000	WNET/Channel 13, New York, NY

Civic & Public Affairs

8,000	National Women's Political Caucus, Washington, DC
7,000	Legal Aid Society, New York, NY
3,000	Economics America, New York, NY
1,000	Committee for Economic Development, New York, NY

Education

50,000	Harvard University, Cambridge, MA
40,000	Columbia University Earth Sciences, New York, NY
40,000	Massachusetts Institute of Technology, Cambridge, MA
40,000	University of California Berkeley, Berkeley, CA
30,000	Colorado School of Mines, Golden, CO
30,000	Georgia Institute of Technology, Atlanta, GA
30,000	Georgia Institute of Technology Foundation, Atlanta, GA
30,000	Rice University, Houston, TX
25,000	Spelman College, Atlanta, GA
16,000	New York University Center for French Civilization and Culture, New York, NY
12,000	Landmark College, Putney, VT
10,000	Awty International School, Houston, TX
10,000	Briarwood School, Houston, TX
10,000	National Action Council for Minorities in Engineering, New York, NY
8,000	Bank Street College of Education, New York, NY
7,500	University of Texas Medical School Houston, Houston, TX
7,000	Texas A&M University, College Station, TX
5,000	California Institute of Technology, Pasadena, CA

5,000 Occupational Physician's Scholarship Fund, Schiller Park, IL
4,000 University of Texas Dallas, Richardson, TX
3,000 Institute of International Education, Houston, TX

Environment
10,000 National Fish and Wildlife Foundation, Washington, DC

Health
25,000 Memorial Sloan-Kettering Cancer Center, New York, NY
10,000 Manhattan Eye, Ear, and Throat Hospital, New York, NY
8,100 Duke University Eye Center, Durham, NC
6,000 Tourette Syndrome Association, Bayside, NY
5,000 Don and Sybil Harrington Cancer Center, Amarillo, TX

Science
50,000 Houston Museum of Natural Science, Houston, TX

Social Services
15,000 Jacob A. Riis Neighborhood Settlement House, Long Island City, NY
15,000 League for the Hard of Hearing, New York, NY
15,000 Partnership for the Homeless, New York, NY
10,000 The Door A Center of Alternatives, New York, NY
8,000 National Children's Eye Care Foundation, Dallas, TX
7,000 Odyssey House Texas, Houston, TX
5,000 Boys and Girls Club of America, New York, NY
5,000 Family Service Center, Houston, TX
5,000 Planned Parenthood, New York, NY
1,000 We Can, New York, NY

CHARLES SCHWAB &CO., INC.

Company Contact

San Francisco, CA
Web: http://www.schwab.com

Company Description

SIC(s): 6211 Security Brokers & Dealers.
Parent Company: The Charles Schwab Corp., United States

Nonmonetary Support

Value: $63,000 (1996); $50,000 (1993)
Type: Donated Equipment; In-kind Services
Note: Foundation provides nonmonetary support. Application procedure is the same as for printing. In-kind services are for printing only.

Corporate Sponsorship

Type: Arts & cultural events; Pledge-a-thon; Sports events
Note: Sponsors AIDS walks, races to fight breast cancer, and similar events. Marketing department sponsors the PGA.

Charles Schwab Corp. Foundation

Giving Contact

Karen Ens, Manager, Community Relations
Charles Schwab & Co., Inc.
101 Montgomery St., 26th Floor
San Francisco, CA 94104
Phone: (415)636-5860
Fax: (415)627-7112
Email: karen.ens@schwab.com

Description

EIN: 943192615
Organization Type: Corporate Foundation
Giving Locations: CA: San Francisco communities where there are Schwab branch offices.
Grant Types: Capital, Conference/Seminar, Emergency, Employee Matching Gifts, General Support, Multiyear/Continuing Support, Project.
Note: Employee matching gift ratio: 2 to 1.

Giving Philosophy

'The Charles Schwab Corp. Foundation was established to honor the Company's commitment to improve the quality of life in the communities in which we live and work by supporting a broad range of charitable services and programs. The Foundation also endeavors to support Schwab employees' community involvement and to foster long-term corporate social responsibility through the visibility of our philanthropic programs.' Foundation Application Guidelines

Financial Summary

Total Giving: $1,975,980 (fiscal year ending June 30, 1997); $1,466,101 (fiscal 1996); $1,700,000 (fiscal 1995 approx). Note: Contributes through corporate direct giving program and foundation. Fiscal 1997 Giving includes foundation ($1,052,816); matching gifts ($923,164). 1996 Giving includes corporate direct giving ($330,000); foundation ($1,466,101).
Assets: $6,417,423 (fiscal 1997); $3,129,538 (fiscal 1996)
Gifts Received: $5,267,483 (fiscal 1997); $4,100,000 (fiscal 1996)

Typical Recipients

Arts & Humanities: Arts Associations & Councils, Arts Centers, Arts Festivals, Arts Outreach, Ballet, Community Arts, Ethnic & Folk Arts, Libraries, Museums/Galleries, Music, Opera, Performing Arts, Public Broadcasting
Civic & Public Affairs: African American Affairs, Asian American Affairs, Botanical Gardens/Parks, Business/Free Enterprise, Civil Rights, Clubs, Community Foundations, Economic Development, Employment/Job Training, Civic & Public Affairs-General, Hispanic Affairs, Housing, Nonprofit Management, Philanthropic Organizations, Professional & Trade Associations, Urban & Community Affairs, Women's Affairs, Zoos/Aquariums
Education: Afterschool/Enrichment Programs, Business Education, Colleges & Universities, Economic Education, Elementary Education (Public), Faculty Development, Leadership Training, Minority Education, Private Education (Precollege), Public Education (Precollege), School Volunteerism, Science/Mathematics Education, Secondary Education (Private), Secondary Education (Public), Special Education, Student Aid, Vocational & Technical Education
Environment: Environment-General, Resource Conservation, Wildlife Protection
Health: AIDS/HIV, Cancer, Children's Health/Hospitals, Clinics/Medical Centers, Diabetes, Emergency/Ambulance Services, Home-Care Services, Hospices, Kidney, Medical Research, Multiple Sclerosis, Nursing Services, Prenatal Health Issues, Single-Disease Health Associations, Transplant Networks/Donor Banks
International: Health Care/Hospitals, International Environmental Issues, International Organizations
Religion: Jewish Causes, Ministries, Religious Welfare
Science: Science Museums, Scientific Centers & Institutes
Social Services: Animal Protection, Big Brother/Big Sister, Child Welfare, Community Service Organizations, Day Care, Domestic Violence, Emergency Relief, Family Planning, Family Services, Food/Clothing Distribution, People with Disabilities, Recreation & Athletics, Senior Services, Shelters/Homelessness, United Funds/United Ways, Volunteer Services, YMCA/YWCA/YMHA/YWHA, Youth Organizations

Contributions Analysis

Arts & Humanities: 21%. Emphasis on educational and community-based programs.
Civic & Public Affairs: 23%. Supports environmental affairs, nonprofit organizations, and public concerns.
Education: 12%. Contributions support K-12 education.
Health: 10%. Supports health-care and human service organizations, with the exception of hospitals. Major interests are youth groups, AIDS education and information, women's issues, and organizations which respond to community needs and underserved populations.
Religion: 1%. Supports religious causes.
Science: 2%. Funds science education programs, and the Arizona Science Center.
Social Services: 32%.Supports Meals on Wheels, Big Brothers and Big Sisters, retarded children association, and food banks.

Application Procedures

Initial Contact: call or write for guidelines, then formal proposal
Application Requirements: mission statement, program objectives, how funds will be used, population served, plan for evaluation; amount requested; current operating budget; list of staff members; list of board of directors; list of foundation and corporate funders; most recent annual report or Form 990; written materials or publicity; proof of tax-exempt status
Deadlines: None.
Decision Notification: applicants will receive a written response within 60 days of receipt

Restrictions

Foundation does not fund: organizations which are not tax-exempt; fundraising events; goodwill advertising; individuals; religious or sectarian organizations; political or lobbying organizations; non-charitable athletic and sports programs; fraternal organizations; private foundations; cause-related marketing; video production; sponsorship or promotional events; conferences; or discriminatory organizations.
Foundation does not provide capital, challenge and seed funding, or grants to higher education and hospitals, except in very limited circumstances. Grants are generally not made to single-disease organizations or for medical research.

Additional Information

The Charles Schwab Corporation Foundation was created in December 1993.
Publications: Program Guidelines

Corporate Officials

David Steven Pottruck: president, chief executive officer, director B 1948. ED University of Pennsylvania BA (1970); University of Pennsylvania MBA (1972). PRIM CORP EMPL president, chief executive officer, director: Charles Schwab & Co., Inc. CORP AFFIL president, chief operating officer: Charles Schwab Corp.; director: Preview Travel Inc.; director: Intel Corp.; director: McKesson Corp.; director: Decibel Instruments Inc. NONPR AFFIL trustee: University Pennsylvania.
Steven L. Scheid: executive vice president, chief financial officer B 1953. ED Michigan State University. PRIM CORP EMPL executive vice president, chief financial officer: Charles Schwab Corp.
Charles R. Schwab: chairman, co-chief executive officer, director B Sacramento, CA 1937. ED Stanford University MBA (1959); Stanford University MBA (1961). PRIM CORP EMPL chairman, co-chief executive officer, director: Charles Schwab & Co., Inc. CORP AFFIL director: Siebel Systems, Inc.; director: TransAmerica Corp.; chairman: Schwab Holding Inc.;

director: AirTouch Communications Inc.; director: The Gap Inc.
Lawrence J. Stupski: president, vice chairman, chief operating officer, director ED Yale University JD (1971). PRIM CORP EMPL president, vice chairman, chief operating officer, director: Charles Schwab & Co., Inc. CORP AFFIL vice chairman: Schwab Holding Inc.

Giving Program Officials

Karen Ens: PRIM CORP EMPL manager community relations: Charles Schwab & Co., Inc.

Foundation Officials

Charles R. Schwab: chairman (see above)
Lawrence J. Stupski: chief financial officer, secretary (see above)

Grants Analysis

Disclosure Period: fiscal year ending June 30, 1997
Total Grants: $1,052,816*
Number of Grants: 451
Average Grant: $2,334
Highest Grant: $150,000
Typical Range: $1,000 to $10,000
***Note:** Giving excludes matching gifts.

Recent Grants

Note: Grants derived from fiscal 1997 Form 990.

Arts & Humanities

40,000	San Francisco Museum of Modern Art, San Francisco, CA
25,000	Committee to Restore the Opera House, San Francisco, CA -- capital campaign
19,800	San Francisco Symphony, San Francisco, CA -- to sponsor newsletter
15,000	University of California Regents, Berkeley, CA -- support Asian American Studies Library
10,000	Library Foundation, San Francisco, CA
5,000	Center for the Arts, Escondido, CA -- support Education and Community Program request
5,000	Friends of the Chinatown Library, Los Angeles, CA
5,000	Metropolitan Opera Association, New York, NY
5,000	Minnesota Museum of American Art, St. Paul, MN
5,000	San Francisco Ballet Association, San Francisco, CA
5,000	Scottsdale Cultural Council, Scottsdale, AZ

Civic & Public Affairs

25,000	Golden Gate National Parks Association, San Francisco, CA -- support Presidio restoration
25,000	Jobs for California Graduates, Merced, CA
25,000	National Park Foundation, New York, NY
25,000	National Park Foundation, New York, NY -- support Yosemite Restoration
20,000	East Bay Zoological Society, Center for Science and Environmental Education, Oakland, CA
10,000	National Foundation for Teaching Entrepreneurship -- support Youth Entrepreneurship
5,607	New Way Workers -- support CBO Mapping Project
5,000	Chinatown Manpower Project, New York, NY
5,000	Christmas in April -- support annual JOBS Project
5,000	Habitat for Humanity of the East Bay

Education

10,000	Junior Achievement of the Bay Area, South San Francisco, CA
10,000	Outward Bound -- support Pinnacle Scholarship Program
10,000	United Negro College Fund, New York, NY
8,070	William R. DeAvila Elementary School
7,500	City College of San Francisco, San Francisco, CA -- support for Transition Center
7,500	San Francisco State University Foundation, San Francisco, CA -- support minority scholarships
5,000	Detwiler Foundation, San Francisco, CA -- support Computers for Schools Program
5,000	RCH, Detroit, MI
5,000	San Francisco School Volunteers, San Francisco, CA -- support School to Business Program
5,000	Stanford University, Stanford, CA
5,000	Teach for America of the Bay Area

Health

15,000	American National Red Cross, Alexandria, VA -- support for Northern California flood relief
15,000	American National Red Cross, Alexandria, VA -- support relief for Midwest floods
15,000	American National Red Cross, Alexandria, VA -- support Northern Plains Flooding
10,000	American National Red Cross, Alexandria, VA -- support for Northern California flood relief
5,000	American Cancer Society Chinese Chapter
5,000	American National Red Cross, Alexandria, VA -- support relief efforts in Puerto Rico from Hurricane Hortense

Religion

7,000	Union Rescue Mission, Los Angeles, CA

Science

7,000	Exploratorium, San Francisco, CA -- support educational outreach
5,000	Arizona Science Center, Phoenix, AZ

Social Services

150,000	US Ski Team Foundation, Park City, UT -- to sponsor Disabled Ski Team
25,000	San Francisco Food Bank, San Francisco, CA -- capital campaign
12,000	Aim High, San Francisco, CA -- support summer program
5,000	Asian Youth Center
5,000	Association of Retarded Citizens, San Francisco, CA
5,000	Big Brothers and Big Sisters, San Francisco, CA
5,000	Meals on Wheels, San Francisco, CA
5,000	Russell Home for Atypical Children, Orlando, FL
5,000	YMCA of Central Florida, FL

SCHWEBEL BAKING CO.

Company Contact

Youngstown, OH

Company Description

Employees: 1,180
SIC(s): 2000 Food & Kindred Products.

Schwebel Family Foundation

Giving Contact

Joseph Schwebel, President
PO Box 6018
Youngstown, OH 44501
Phone: (330)783-2860

Description

Founded: 1989
EIN: 341600311
Organization Type: Corporate Foundation
Giving Locations: OH
Grant Types: General Support, Scholarship.

Giving Philosophy

The foundation provides 'charitable contributions to worthy organizations as needed.' Schwebel Family Foundation IRS Form 990-PF 1998

Financial Summary

Total Giving: $240,000 (1999 approx); $190,333 (1998); $232,500 (1997)
Giving Analysis: Giving for 1997 includes: foundation ($232,500); 1998: foundation ($180,033); foundation grants to United Way ($10,300)
Assets: $6,425,843 (1998); $5,631,946 (1997); $4,253,924 (1996)
Gifts Received: $510,135 (1997); $1,157,744 (1996); $611,526 (1994). Note: In 1996, contributions were received from Schwebel Baking Co.

Typical Recipients

Arts & Humanities: Arts Associations & Councils, Ballet, Music, Performing Arts, Public Broadcasting
Civic & Public Affairs: Botanical Gardens/Parks, Civic & Public Affairs-General, Hispanic Affairs, Urban & Community Affairs
Education: Business Education, Colleges & Universities, Education Funds, Education-General, Public Education (Precollege), Social Sciences Education, Special Education, Student Aid
Health: Cancer, Children's Health/Hospitals, Diabetes, Health Organizations, Heart, Hospices, Hospitals, Multiple Sclerosis, Single-Disease Health Associations
Religion: Jewish Causes, Religious Welfare
Social Services: Child Welfare, Community Centers, Community Service Organizations, Counseling, Family Services, Food/Clothing Distribution, People with Disabilities, Recreation & Athletics, Shelters/Homelessness, United Funds/United Ways, YMCA/YWCA/YMHA/YWHA, Youth Organizations

Contributions Analysis

Giving Priorities: Education, social services, health, and religion.
Arts & Humanities: 5%. Funds arts councils and a theater.
Civic & Public Affairs: 4%. Supports a junior league and other civic organizations.
Education: 25%. Supports colleges and universities, public schools, and arts education.
Health: 22%. Supports single-disease health organizations, hospitals, hospice, and health funds.
Religion: 22% Funds Jewish organizations.
Social Services: 22%. Supports the United Way, youth organizations, YMCAs, substance abuse organizations, planned parenthood, and food distribution services.
Note: Total contributions made in 1998.

Application Procedures

Initial Contact: Submit an application form.
Deadlines: November 30; by the end of November each year, the determination has been made for giving for the following year.

Restrictions

Applications are restricted to within a 250 mile radius from the foundation.

Corporate Officials

Joseph M. Schwebel: president, director B Youngstown, OH 1939. ED University of Pennsylvania (1960). PRIM CORP EMPL president, director: Schwebel Baking Co. CORP AFFIL 1st vice president,

director: Quality Bakers America Corp. NONPR AFFIL director: American Bakers Association; chairman: American Institute Baking.
Frances Solomon: chairman, director PRIM CORP EMPL chairman, director: Schwebel Baking Co.

Foundation Officials

Joseph M. Schwebel: trustee (see above)
Frances Solomon: trustee (see above)
Alyson Winick: trustee

Grants Analysis

Disclosure Period: calendar year ending 1998
Total Grants: $180,033*
Number of Grants: 69
Average Grant: $2,148*
Highest Grant: $34,000
Typical Range: $100 to $15,000
***Note:** Giving excludes United Way. Average grant figure excludes highest grant.

Recent Grants

Note: Grants derived from 1997 Form 990.

Arts & Humanities

5,000	Youngstown Symphony Society, Youngstown, OH
3,000	Educational Television Association, Cleveland, OH
2,500	North East Education Television of Ohio, Kent, OH
2,000	Youngstown Playhouse, Youngstown, OH
1,500	Ballet Western Reserve, Youngstown, OH

Education

50,000	Ohio State University Foundation, Columbus, OH
31,250	Youngstown State University, Youngstown, OH

Health

10,000	Easter Seal Society, Youngstown, OH
7,500	Pittsburgh Children's Hospital, Pittsburgh, PA
2,650	American Cancer Society, Youngstown, OH
2,500	Diabetes Association, Cleveland, OH
2,500	Tods Children's Fund, Western Reserve Health Fund, Youngstown, OH

Religion

35,000	Youngstown Area Jewish Federation, Youngstown, OH
2,500	Bellefaire Jewish Children, Youngstown, OH

Social Services

23,500	Giant Eagle LPGA Classic, Youngstown, OH
8,000	Mahoning Valley United Way, Youngstown, OH
5,500	Boys and Girls Club, Youngstown, OH
3,000	Chili Open Golf Classic, Youngstown, OH
3,000	Mahoning Valley Safe Kids Coalition, Youngstown, OH
3,000	Mill Creek Children's Center, Youngstown, OH

SCIENTIFIC-ATLANTA, INC.

Company Contact

Norcross, GA
Web: http://www.sciatl.com

Company Description

Employees: 5,343
SIC(s): 3663 Radio & T.V. Communications Equipment.

Nonmonetary Support

Value: $10,000 (1994)
Type: Cause-related Marketing & Promotion; Donated Equipment; Donated Products; In-kind Services; Loaned Employees; Loaned Executives; Workplace Solicitation

Giving Contact

Bill McCargo, Community Directory of Relations
Scientific-Atlanta Inc.
One Technology Pkwy.
Norcross, GA 30092
Phone: (770)903-4607
Fax: (770)903-4881
Email: bill.mccargo@sciatl.com

Description

Organization Type: Corporate Giving Program
Giving Locations: headquarters and operating communities.
Grant Types: Award, Capital, Challenge, Employee Matching Gifts, General Support, Matching, Multiyear/Continuing Support.
Note: Employee matching gift ratio: 1 to 1; program for officers matches gifts 2 to 1.

Financial Summary

Total Giving: $1,200,000 (2000 approx); $1,000,000 (1999); $800,000 (1998). Note: Contributes through corporate direct giving program only.

Typical Recipients

Arts & Humanities: Arts & Humanities-General
Civic & Public Affairs: Civic & Public Affairs-General
Education: Education-General
Health: Health-General

Contributions Analysis

Arts & Humanities: 10% to 15%.
Civic & Public Affairs: About 15%.
Education: 25%.
Health: 35%.

Application Procedures

Initial Contact: a brief letter of inquiry
Application Requirements: a description of organization and purpose of funds sought
Deadlines: None.

Restrictions

Restricts giving to 501(c)(3) organizations.

Corporate Officials

William Everette Eason, Jr.: senior vice president, corporate secretary, general counsel B Elizabeth City, NC 1943. ED Duke University BA (1965); Duke University JD (1968). PRIM CORP EMPL senior vice president, corporate secretary, general counsel: Scientific-Atlanta, Inc. CORP AFFIL partner: Paul Hastings Janofsky & Walker. NONPR AFFIL counselor: Metropolitan Atlanta Olympic Games Authority; trustee: Woodward Academy; member: Georgia Bar Association; member: Leadership Atlanta. CLUB AFFIL Georgian Club; Capital City Club.
H. Allen Ecker: president subscriber systems B Athens, GA 1935. ED Georgia Institute of Technology BEE (1957); Georgia Institute of Technology MSEE (1959); Ohio State University PhD (1965). PRIM CORP EMPL president subscriber systems: Scientific-Atlanta, Inc.
Julian W. Eidson: vice president, controller B 1939. ED North Georgia College BS (1961); North Georgia College MBA (1971). PRIM CORP EMPL vice president, controller: Scientific-Atlanta, Inc.
Wallace G. Haislip: senior vice president finance, chief financial officer, treasurer ED Old Dominion University BS (1971). PRIM CORP EMPL senior vice president finance, chief financial officer, treasurer: Scientific-Atlanta, Inc.
Brian C. Koenig: senior vice president human resources B Portland, ME 1947. ED University of Charleston (1969); West Virginia University (1973). PRIM CORP EMPL senior vice president human resources: Scientific-Atlanta, Inc. NONPR AFFIL member: Human Resources Management Association; member: Senior Personnel Association.
James F. McDonald: president, chief executive officer B Louisville, KY 1941. ED University of Kentucky BSEE (1963); University of Kentucky MEE (1964). PRIM CORP EMPL president, chief executive officer: Scientific-Atlanta, Inc. CORP AFFIL director: American Business Products Inc.; director: Burlington Resources Inc.
Steven K. Necessary: senior vice president marketing B Kansas City, MO 1956. ED Georgia Institute of Technology (1978); Harvard University (1982). PRIM CORP EMPL senior vice president marketing: Scientific-Atlanta, Inc. NONPR AFFIL member: Society Cable Telecommunications Engineers; member: Women Cable TV; member: Christian Cable; director: Gwinnett Ballet Theatre.
Conrad J. Wredberg, Junior: senior vice president, chairman, corp. operating committee PRIM CORP EMPL senior vice president, chairman, corp. operating committee: Scientific-Atlanta, Inc.

Giving Program Officials

Bill McCargo: director community relations

E.W. SCRIPPS CO.

Company Contact

Cincinnati, OH
Web: http://www.scripps.com

Company Description

Employees: 6,700
SIC(s): 2711 Newspapers.

Corporate Sponsorship

Type: Arts & cultural events
Contact: Judy Clabes, President & Chief Executive Officer

Scripps Howard Foundation

Giving Contact

Patty Cottingham, Executive Director
Scripps Howard Foundation
312 Walnut Street
PO Box 5380
Cincinnati, OH 45201
Phone: (513)977-3035
Fax: (513)977-3800
Email: cottingham@scripps.com
Web: http://www.scripps.com/foundation

Description

EIN: 316025114
Organization Type: Corporate Foundation
Giving Locations: OH: operating locations, Cincinnati metropolitan area nationally, with emphasis on operating locations; particularly Greater Cincinnati, OH.
Grant Types: Award, Capital, Conference/Seminar, Employee Matching Gifts, Endowment, Fellowship, General Support, Multiyear/Continuing Support.
Note: Scholarships are awarded to students preparing for careers in print and electronic journalism. Matches gifts to educational institutions.

Giving Philosophy

'Here at the Scripps Howard Foundation we are 'Always Learning..Always Changing.'

'We watch with satisfaction the impact of our literacy program on thousands of new readers across the country. We come to realize that goals in learning to read are deeply personal matters. We learn that the wonder of understanding a simple traffic sign becomes a conquest that inspires the new reader to persevere to higher levels.

'We learn what our college scholarship students come to know, that getting the scholarship is just the first step. Making maximum use of it takes dedication and hard work by the scholar, and continued encouragement and support from us.

'We constantly seek new ways to help career journalists and communicators to realize what continuing education can mean to them. One of the environmental reporters taking time out for a year to go back to campus as a Ted Scripps Fellow brought the point into sharp focus: 'I found myself learning things I have never thought about, never knew I didn't know.'

'We assist those who wish to learn by providing financial support to cost-effective projects. Programs that offer opportunities, raise awareness and instill in the recipient pride of accomplishment are the essence of our mission..' *Always Learning, Always Changing, Progress Report of Scripps Howard Foundation*

Financial Summary

Total Giving: $2,900,000 (1999 approx); $2,975,069 (1998); $2,700,000 (1997 approx). Note: Contributes through corporate direct giving program and foundation.

Giving Analysis: Giving for 1998 includes: foundation scholarships ($375,500); foundation matching gifts ($146,500)

Assets: $50,476,823 (1996); $34,979,279 (1995); $27,104,184 (1994)

Gifts Received: $15,500,677 (1996); $538,449 (1995); $11,842,815 (1994). Note: In 1994, donations were received from Scripps Howard, Inc ($11,291,925), Naoma Lowensohn Estate ($25,000), Robert P. Scripps ($273,400), Jack R. Howard ($20,000) Scripps Howard Broadcasting Company ($10,000), Edward W. Scripps, Jr. ($65,000), Cindy S. & Nathan Leising ($125,000) and miscellaneous contributors ($32,490)

Typical Recipients

Arts & Humanities: Arts Centers, Arts Festivals, Arts Funds, History & Archaeology, Libraries, Literary Arts, Museums/Galleries, Music, Performing Arts, Public Broadcasting, Theater

Civic & Public Affairs: African American Affairs, Botanical Gardens/Parks, Business/Free Enterprise, Chambers of Commerce, Economic Development, Employment/Job Training, First Amendment Issues, Civic & Public Affairs-General, Housing, Minority Business, Professional & Trade Associations, Public Policy, Urban & Community Affairs, Women's Affairs

Education: Arts/Humanities Education, Business Education, Colleges & Universities, Economic Education, Education Funds, Elementary Education (Public), Engineering/Technological Education, Environmental Education, Journalism/Media Education, Legal Education, Literacy, Minority Education, Preschool Education, Private Education (Precollege), Religious Education, Science/Mathematics Education, Secondary Education (Public), Special Education, Student Aid, Vocational & Technical Education

Environment: Environment-General

Health: Emergency/Ambulance Services, Preventive Medicine/Wellness Organizations

International: Foreign Arts Organizations, Human Rights, International Affairs, International Relations

Religion: Dioceses, Religious Welfare

Science: Science Museums

Social Services: Big Brother/Big Sister, Child Welfare, Community Service Organizations, Food/Clothing Distribution, People with Disabilities, Scouts, Substance Abuse, United Funds/United Ways, YMCA/YWCA/YMHA/YWHA

Contributions Analysis

Giving Priorities: Journalism education, journalism awards, and literacy.

Civic & Public Affairs: 48%. The Fund supports various charitable organizations that improve the quality of life in operating areas particularly through the Greater Cincinnati Fund. Supports educational institutions that produce potential employees, readers or viewers; or that promote strong community conscience and encourage alternatives in education. Social welfare organizations which make significant contributions to the disadvantaged are supported, including the United Way, the Salvation Army, food banks, and scouting and Big Brothers. Supports civic organizations that promote leadership, community involvement, good government, sound public policy, free speech or journalism.

Education: 21%. Awards scholarships and internships to full-time undergraduate students preparing for careers in journalism. Preference is given to students with continuing interest and work in the field of journalism, prior recipients, and students residing in or attending schools located in communities served by company operations. The Robert P. Scripps Graphic Arts Grant is awarded to graphic arts majors who, in the opinion of college authorities, have the potential for becoming newspaper production administrators. Also matches employee gifts to educational institutions.

Application Procedures

Initial Contact: Send a full proposal.

Application Requirements: Include a description of organization, recently audited financial statement, a description of the program for which support is requested, including rationale, a detailed projected budget, schedule of implementation, methods of evaluating and reporting results, and qualification of program manager, describe other sources of funding, include a copy of the IRC Section 501(c)(3) determination letter issued by the IRS to the organization, and give names and affiliations of members of the organization's Board of Directors or other governing body.

Deadlines: None.

Review Process: Decisions are based on written proposals; personal interviews are discouraged.

Evaluative Criteria: For scholarships: good scholastic standing, interest in journalism and evidence of work in this field, letters of recommendation from faculty or employer, financial need, willingness of student to pay part of educational expenses, U.S. citizenship; for grants: programs which impact communities where company operates, are measurable with stated goals and objectives, demonstrate effectiveness and innovation, can serve as models, and can be eventually self-supporting.

Decision Notification: Proposals will be reviewed and applicants notified within 90 days after receipt of all required information.

Restrictions

Contributions for capital needs, including renovation, equipment and construction, are not encouraged except in special circumstances; specific projects and programs are preferred over general operating funds. In general, only one contribution a year will be made to any single organization, including support for fundraising events. Multi-year contributions are discouraged. The foundation normally does not provide support to organizations that receive United Way or Fine Arts funding because of on-going support of both United Way and the Fine Arts Fund.

The foundation does not make contributions to individuals, religious organizations unless they are engaged in a significant program benefiting the entire community, political causes or candidates, or anti-business organizations; foundation does not purchase courtesy advertising, support organizations that discriminate on the basis of race, creed, religion, gender or national origin; fund private foundations, organizations not qualifying as IRC Section 501(c)(3) organizations, or veterans', fraternal, or labor groups.

Additional Information

Capital requests are not encouraged; specific programs or projects are favored over operating support. The Scripps Howard Foundation was incorporated in 1962, as a charitable nonprofit organization.

Publications: Scripps Howard Foundation Progress Report; Guidelines for Scholarships; Special Journalism Grants and Awards

Corporate Officials

William Robert Burleigh: president, chief executive officer, director B Evansville, IN 1935. ED Marquette University BA (1957). PRIM CORP EMPL president, chief executive officer, director: E.W. Scripps Co. CORP AFFIL director: Xtek Inc.; president, chief executive officer: Scripps Howard Newspapers; director: Evansville Courier Co. Inc.; director: Ohio National Financial Services. NONPR AFFIL member: American Society Newspaper Editors. CLUB AFFIL Cincinnati Literacy Club; Queen City Club; Cincinnati Commercial Club; Cincinnati Country Club.

John Hunter Burlingame: executive partner B Milwaukee, WI 1933. ED University of Wisconsin BS (1960); University of Wisconsin LLB (1963). PRIM CORP EMPL partner: Baker & Hostetler. CORP AFFIL director: E.W. Scripps Co. NONPR AFFIL trustee: Cleveland Playhouse; trustee: Edward W. Scripps Trust; member: Cleveland Bar Association; trustee: Cleveland Orchestra; member: American Bar Association. CLUB AFFIL Shoreby Club; Union Club.

Daniel J. Castellini: senior vice president finance & administration, chief financial officer B 1940. ED University of Notre Dame BS (1962); Xavier University MBA (1973). PRIM CORP EMPL senior vice president finance & administration, chief financial officer: E.W. Scripps Co. ADD CORP EMPL vice president: Evansville Courier Co. Inc.; treasurer: Sripps Howard Broadcasting Co.

Judy G. Clabes: president, chief executive officer B Henderson, KY 1945. ED University of Kentucky BA (1967); Indiana State University MPA (1984).

Colleen Christner Conant: branch manager B Oklahoma City, OK 1947. ED Oklahoma City University MusB (1970). PRIM CORP EMPL branch manager: EW Scripps Co. CORP AFFIL chief executive officer: Boulder Publishing Inc.

Frank Gardner: senior vice president PRIM CORP EMPL senior vice president: E.W. Scripps Co. CORP AFFIL senior vice president: Scripps Howard Broadcasting Co.

Alan M. Horton: senior vice president newspapers ED Yale University (1965). PRIM CORP EMPL senior vice president newspapers: E.W. Scripps Co.

Lawrence Arthur Leser: chairman, director B Cincinnati, OH 1935. ED Xavier University BS (1957). PRIM CORP EMPL chairman, director: E.W. Scripps Co. ADD CORP EMPL director: Evansville Courier Co. Inc.; chairman, president, chief executive officer, director: Scripps Howard Inc.; president, chief executive officer, director: Scripps Howard Broadcasting Co. CORP AFFIL director: Union Central Life Insurance Co.; member national advisory board: Chemical Bank; director: Heekin Can Co. Inc.; director: AK Steel Holding Corp. NONPR AFFIL director: Newspaper Advertising Bureau; director: Xavier University.

Daniel Joseph Meyer: chairman, president, chief executive officer, director B Flint, MI 1936. ED Purdue University BSEE (1958); Indiana University MBA (1963). PRIM CORP EMPL chairman, president, chief executive officer, director: Cincinnati Milacron, Inc. CORP AFFIL director: Valenite Inc.; director: Star Banc Corp.; director: Milacron Marketing Co.; director: E.W. Scripps Co.; director: Milacron International Marketing Co.; director: Hubbell Inc.; director: Milacron Inc.; chairman, director: Cincinnati Milacron Marketing Co.; director: Cincinnati Bell Inc. NONPR AFFIL member: American Institute CPAs. CLUB AFFIL Kenwood Country Club.

Nicholas Biddle Paumgarten: managing director B Philadelphia, PA 1945. ED University of Pennsylvania BA (1967); Columbia University MBA (1971). PRIM CORP EMPL managing director: J.P. Morgan & Co. Inc. CORP AFFIL director: E.W. Scripps Co.

J. Robert Routt: vice president, controller B 1954. ED University of Kentucky BS. PRIM CORP EMPL vice president, controller: E.W. Scripps Co.

Charles Edward Scripps: chairman executive committee, director, vice president B San Diego, CA 1920. ED College of William & Mary (1938-1940); Pomona College (1940-1941). PRIM CORP EMPL chairman executive committee, director, vice president: E.W. Scripps Co. CORP AFFIL director: Scripps Howard Broadcasting Co.; trustee: Edward W. Scripps Trust; director: Evansville Courier Co. Inc. NONPR AFFIL member national board advisors: Salvation Army; member: Theta Delta Chi; member: CAP; trustee: Freedoms Foundation.

Paul K. Scripps: vice president, director PRIM CORP EMPL vice president, director: E W Scripps Co.

Robert P. Scripps, Jr.: B 1918. NONPR AFFIL trustee: Edward W. Scripps Trust.

Craig Clayton Standen: senior vice president corporate development B Camden, NJ 1942. ED Denison University BA (1964); Northwestern University MBA (1966). PRIM CORP EMPL senior vice president corporate development: E.W. Scripps Co. NONPR AFFIL member, director: President Association Advertising Council New York; senior vice president: Scripps Howard Broadcasting Co.; director: ARC Cincinnati Chapter; director: Junior Achievement. CLUB AFFIL Ivy Hills Country Club; Kenwood Country Club; Darien Country Club.

Ronald W. Tysoe: vice chairman, director B 1953. ED University of British Columbia (1978). PRIM CORP EMPL vice chairman, director: Federated Department Stores, Inc. CORP AFFIL director: E.W. Scripps Co.

Julie Ann Wrigley: director PRIM CORP EMPL director: E.W. Scripps Co.

Foundation Officials

William Robert Burleigh: member (see above)
Daniel J. Castellini: treasurer (see above)
Judy G. Clabes: president, chief executive officer, trustee, member (see above)
Colleen Christner Conant: trustee (see above)
Deborah Cooper: administrator
Patty Cottingham: executive director
Pamela (Howard) Gumprecht: trustee ED Sarah Lawrence College (1963). CLUB AFFIL Cosmopolitan Club.
Julia Scripps Heidt: trustee
Paul Frederick Knue: trustee B Lawrenceburg, IN 1947. ED Murray State University BS (1969). PRIM CORP EMPL editor: E.W. Scripps Co. ADD CORP EMPL editor: Cincinnati Post. NONPR AFFIL member: Associated Press Managing Editors Association; trustee: Associated Press Society Ohio; member: American Society Newspaper Editors.
Cindy Scripps Leising: member
Lawrence Arthur Leser: member (see above)
Nicholas Biddle Paumgarten: member (see above)
Sue Porter: trustee
J. Robert Routt: trustee (see above)
Charles Edward Scripps: member (see above)
Edward Wyllis Scripps, II: member (see above)
Maggie Scripps: member
Paul K. Scripps: trustee (see above)
Dan King Thomasson: vice president, trustee B Shelbyville, IN 1933. ED Indiana University BS (1956); Colorado State University (1959). PRIM CORP EMPL editor: Scripps Howard News Service ADD CORP EMPL vice president: E.W. Scripps Co.; vice president: Scripps Howard Newspapers Cincinnati. NONPR AFFIL trustee: Franklin College; member: White House Correspondents Association; president: Raymond Clapper Foundation; member: American Society Newspaper Editors. CLUB AFFIL Washington Golf & Country Club; Sigma Delta Chi; University Club Washington; Overseas Press Club; Gridiron Society Club; National Press Club.
Ronald W. Tysoe: member (see above)

Grants Analysis

Disclosure Period: calendar year ending 1998
Total Grants: $2,453,069*
Typical Range: $1,000 to $10,000
***Note:** Giving excludes matching gifts; scholarships.

JOSEPH E. SEAGRAM & SONS, INC.

Company Contact

New York, NY

Company Description

Employees: 18,000
SIC(s): 2084 Wines, Brandy & Brandy Spirits, 2085 Distilled & Blended Liquors.
Parent Company: Seagram Co. Ltd., 1430 Peel St., Montreal, PQ, Canada

Operating Locations

CA: Seagram Classics Wine Co., San Mateo; Universal Studios, Universal City; DC: Joseph E. Seagram & Sons, Inc., Washington; FL: Tropicana North America, Bradenton; Seagram Latin America, Coral Gables; IL: Joseph E. Seagram & Sons, Inc., Des Plaines, Rolling Meadows; IN: Joseph E. Seagram & Sons, Inc., Lawrenceburg; KY: Joseph E. Seagram & Sons, Inc., Louisville; MD: Joseph E. Seagram & Sons, Inc., Baltimore; NY: Joseph E. Seagram & Sons, Inc., New Hyde Park; House of Seagram, New York; Joseph E. Seagram & Sons, Inc., New York; Seagram Asia Pacific/Global Duty Free, New York; Seagram Beverage Co., New York; Seagram Beverage Group, New York; Seagram Chateau & Estate Wines Co., New York; Joseph E. Seagram & Sons, Inc., New York; Seagrams Spirits and Wine Group, New York; Seagrams Corp. Research & Development, White Plains; OH: Joseph E. Seagram & Sons, Inc., Hamilton

Nonmonetary Support

Type: Donated Products

Samuel Bronfman Foundation/Joseph E. Seagram & Sons, Inc. Fund

Giving Contact

Richard Marker, Vice President
Joseph E. Seagram & Sons, Inc.
375 Park Avenue, 5th Floor
New York, NY 10152-0192
Phone: (212)572-7240

Alternate Contact

Dawn Daly Walsh
Phone: (212)572-7701
Fax: (212)572-7591
Note: Alternate contact is for the Joseph E. Seagram & Sons, Inc. Fund, which the company also runs.

Description

Founded: 1951
EIN: 136084708
Organization Type: Corporate Foundation
Giving Locations: NY: New York
Grant Types: Challenge, Employee Matching Gifts, Fellowship, General Support, Professorship, Research.

Financial Summary

Total Giving: $8,000,000 (1998 approx); $7,500,000 (1996); $9,188,582 (1995). Note: Contributes through foundation only. 1995 Giving includes the Samuel Bronfman Foundation ($6,688,582); the Joseph E. Seagram & Sons, Inc. Fund ($2,500,000).
Assets: $26,472,677 (1996); $27,871,812 (1995); $9,682,245 (1994)
Gifts Received: $1,284,420 (1996); $23,327,500 (1995); $5,060,561 (1994). Note: Receives contributions from Seagram Distillers Charitable Trust, Joseph E. Seagram & Sons, Inc., Kirin Brewery Co. Ltd., and miscellaneous donations.

Typical Recipients

Arts & Humanities: Arts Associations & Councils, Arts Centers, Arts Funds, Dance, Ethnic & Folk Arts, Libraries, Museums/Galleries, Music, Performing Arts, Public Broadcasting, Theater
Civic & Public Affairs: African American Affairs, Business/Free Enterprise, Civil Rights, Ethnic Organizations, Civic & Public Affairs-General, Legal Aid, Municipalities/Towns, Public Policy, Urban & Community Affairs, Women's Affairs
Education: Arts/Humanities Education, Business Education, Colleges & Universities, Education Funds, Education Reform, Faculty Development, Education-General, International Exchange, International Studies, Medical Education, Minority Education, Private Education (Precollege), Public Education (Precollege), Religious Education, Science/Mathematics Education, Social Sciences Education, Student Aid
Health: AIDS/HIV, Cancer, Clinics/Medical Centers, Medical Research, Mental Health
International: Foreign Arts Organizations, Foreign Educational Institutions, Health Care/Hospitals, Human Rights, International Affairs, International Organizations, International Peace & Security Issues, International Relations, Missionary/Religious Activities
Religion: Jewish Causes, Religious Organizations, Religious Welfare
Social Services: At-Risk Youth, Camps, Child Welfare, Community Service Organizations, Day Care, Emergency Relief, Family Services, Food/Clothing Distribution, Substance Abuse, Youth Organizations

Contributions Analysis

Giving Priorities: Medical research, international organizations, education, historical societies, and public affairs organizations. Supports Jewish-related organizations and provides fellowships for East-West studies.

Application Procedures

Initial Contact: letter
Application Requirements: reason for requesting support, amount needed, and proof of tax-exempt status
Deadlines: None.
Notes: Further information will be requested if foundation is interested.

Restrictions

Does not support individuals.

Corporate Officials

Edgar Miles Bronfman: chairman vice president, general counsel, secretary B Montreal, PQ Canada 1929. ED Williams College (1946-1949); McGill University BA (1951). PRIM CORP EMPL chairman: Joseph E. Seagram & Sons, Inc. CORP AFFIL chairman: Seagram Co. Ltd. NONPR AFFIL director: Weizmann Institute Science; president: World Jewish Congress; chairman: US-USSR Trade Economic Council; president: North American Consortium Free Market Study; member: United Jewish Appeal Federation; member: Foreign Policy Association; member: Hundred Years Association New York; member: Council Communication Economic Development; member: Council Foreign Relations; member: Center

International-American Relations; member international advisory board: Columbia University School International & Public Affairs; member: Business Committee Arts; chairman, trustee: B'nai B'rith Anti-Defamation League New York; member, board overseers: B'nai B'rith International Trust; member executive committee: American Jewish Congress; director: American Technician Society; chairman: American Jewish Committee.

Edgar Miles Bronfman, Jr.: president, chief executive officer B 1955. PRIM CORP EMPL president, chief executive officer: Joseph E. Seagram & Sons, Inc. ADD CORP EMPL president: Seagram Enterprises Inc. CORP AFFIL director: United States of America Networks Inc.

Robert W. Matschullat: vice chairman, chief financial officer B 1948. PRIM CORP EMPL vice chairman, chief financial officer: Joseph E. Seagram & Sons, Inc. CORP AFFIL director: Clorox Co.; director: Trans-America Corp.

Daniel R. Paladino: executive vice president, general counsel, secretary B New York, NY 1943. ED Fordham University BS (1965); New York University JD (1968). PRIM CORP EMPL executive vice president, general counsel, secretary: Joseph Seagram & Sons Inc. ADD CORP EMPL president: Distillers Products Sls Ma Corp.; secretary: J.E. Seagram Corp.; vice president: Seagram Co. Ltd.; secretary: Seagram Enterprises Inc.

Foundation Officials

Charles Rosner Bronfman: trustee B Montreal, PQ Canada 1931. ED Trinity College (1951). PRIM CORP EMPL co-chairman, chairman executive committee, director: The Seagram Co. CORP AFFIL chairman: Claridge Israel Inc.; director: Power Corp. Canada.

Edgar Miles Bronfman, Jr.: trustee (see above)

Edgar Miles Bronfman: chairman, trustee (see above)

Samuel Bronfman, II: president, trustee B 1954. PRIM CORP EMPL chairman: Sterling Vineyards Inc. CORP AFFIL president: Domaine Mumm Inc.

Claire Cullen: secretary PRIM CORP EMPL director corporate philanthropy: Joseph E. Seagram & Sons, Inc.

Patricia Glazer: trustee PRIM CORP EMPL director public affairs: Joseph E. Seagram & Sons, Inc.

Robert W. Matschullat: trustee (see above)

Daniel R. Paladino: trustee (see above)

David G. Sacks: trustee B New York, NY 1924. ED Columbia University AB (1944); Columbia University LLB (1948). CORP AFFIL director: Seagram Co. Ltd.

Grants Analysis

Disclosure Period: calendar year ending 1996
Total Grants: $3,022,020
Number of Grants: 78
Average Grant: $37,948*
Highest Grant: $1,000,000
Typical Range: $5,000 to $20,000 and $25,000 to $100,000
***Note:** Average grant excludes highest grant. Grants analysis covers first half of 1996.

Recent Grants

Note: Grants derived from 1996 Form 990.

Arts & Humanities

50,000	Education Broadcasting Corporation, New York, NY
30,000	Lincoln Center for Performing Arts, New York, NY
25,000	Carnegie Hall Society, New York, NY
15,000	Alvin Alley Dance Theater Foundation, New York, NY
15,000	Theater for a New Audience, New York, NY
10,000	Arts Connection, New York, NY
10,000	California Afro-American Museum, Los Angeles, CA
10,000	Museum of African American History, Detroit, MI
10,000	St. Helena Library

Civic & Public Affairs

30,000	Catalyst, New York, NY
10,000	Citizens Advice Bureau, Bronx, NY
10,000	Foundation for Ethnic Understanding, New York, NY
10,000	Marion G. Obemauer Memorial Fund

Education

172,000	Columbia University Graduate School of Business, New York, NY
50,000	Teach for America, New York, NY
50,000	United Negro College Fund, New York, NY
40,000	Columbia University Teachers College, New York, NY
22,500	Clark University, Worcester, MA
20,000	Prep for Prep, New York, NY
15,000	Algebra Project, Boston, MA
15,000	Bronfman Fellowships Prep School Initiative, New York, NY
15,000	Classroom, New York, NY
15,000	Studio in a School Association, New York, NY
10,000	Johns Hopkins University Paul H. Nitze School of Advanced International Studies, Baltimore, MD -- for Middle East Studies Program
10,000	New School for Social Research Robert J. Milano Graduate School of Management and Urban Policy, New York, NY
10,000	Providence College, Providence, RI
10,000	Third Street Music School Settlement
10,000	University of Pennsylvania Joseph H. Lauder Institute, Philadelphia, PA

Health

25,000	Gay Men's Health Crisis, New York, NY
25,000	New York University Medical Center, New York, NY -- support Stephen E. Banner Fund for Lung Cancer Research
10,000	Hudson Guild, New York, NY
10,000	St. Aloysius Education Clinic

International

1,000,000	World Jewish Congress American Section, New York, NY
409,270	Bronfman Youth Fellowship in Israel, New York, NY
30,000	Foreign Policy Association, New York, NY
10,000	Emanuel Foundation for Hungarian Culture, New York, NY

Religion

200,000	Foundation for Jewish Campus Life, Washington, DC
135,000	Anti-Defamation League of B'nai B'rith, New York, NY
25,000	Jewish Heritage Programs, New York, NY
13,900	Bronfman Library of Jewish Classics, New York, NY
10,000	Cathedral of St. John of the Divine
10,000	Jewish Museum, San Francisco, CA

Social Services

150,000	Boggy Creek Gang Camp, Winter Park, FL
55,000	United Neighborhood Houses, New York, NY
20,000	Child Care, New York, NY
20,000	Project Reach Youth, New York, NY
10,000	Citizens Committee for Children, New York, NY
10,000	Food for All
10,000	Hammonds House, Atlanta, GA
10,000	Project Reach Youth, New York, NY

G.D. SEARLE &CO.

Company Contact

Skokie, IL

Company Description

Employees: 9,400 (1999)
SIC(s): 2834 Pharmaceutical Preparations.
Parent Company: Monsanto Co., St. Louis, MO, United States

Nonmonetary Support

Type: Donated Products

Corporate Sponsorship

Value: $30,000
Type: Arts & cultural events; Music & entertainment events
Note: Sponsors the Chicago Symphony.

Searle Charitable Trust

Giving Contact

Judith Vandervort, Trust Administrator
Searle Charitable Trust
5200 Old Orchard Road
Skokie, IL 60077
Phone: (847)581-6769
Fax: (847)581-4032

Description

EIN: 366785886
Organization Type: Corporate Foundation
Giving Locations: nationally, with emphasis on operating communities.
Grant Types: Employee Matching Gifts, General Support.

Financial Summary

Total Giving: $424,040 (1998); $541,860 (1997); $482,607 (1996). Note: Contributes through foundation only.
Giving Analysis: Giving for 1996 includes: foundation ($410,650); foundation matching gifts ($71,957); 1997: foundation ($541,860)
Assets: $80,872 (1998); $4,374 (1997); $43,932 (1996)
Gifts Received: $500,000 (1998); $500,000 (1997); $475,000 (1996). Note: The foundation receives contributions from G. D. Searle & Co.

Typical Recipients

Arts & Humanities: Arts Associations & Councils, Arts Festivals, Arts Institutes, Museums/Galleries, Music, Opera, Performing Arts, Theater
Civic & Public Affairs: Business/Free Enterprise, Economic Development, Economic Policy, Employment/Job Training, Civic & Public Affairs-General, Law & Justice, Legal Aid, Professional & Trade Associations, Public Policy, Urban & Community Affairs, Women's Affairs, Zoos/Aquariums
Education: Agricultural Education, Business Education, Colleges & Universities, Community & Junior Colleges, Economic Education, Medical Education, Preschool Education, Public Education (Precollege), Science/Mathematics Education
Environment: Environment-General
Health: AIDS/HIV, Cancer, Clinics/Medical Centers, Health Organizations, Heart, Medical Research, Nursing Services, Public Health, Single-Disease Health Associations
International: Health Care/Hospitals
Science: Science Museums, Scientific Centers & Institutes, Scientific Organizations
Social Services: At-Risk Youth, Child Welfare, Delinquency & Criminal Rehabilitation, Senior Services, Special Olympics, United Funds/United Ways, Volunteer Services, Youth Organizations

Contributions Analysis

Arts & Humanities: 29%. Supports museums, historical societies, and the performing arts and fine arts.

Civic & Public Affairs: 7%. Supports a zoo, a legal foundation, 4-H programs, and workforce development.
Education: 27%. Provides funding for medical education, primary and secondary education, and junior achievement.
Health: 27%. Funds single-disease health organizations, patient rights, and medical research.
Religion: 1%. Funds religious welfare.
Social Services: 8%. Supports family services, homeless shelters, and youth foundations.
Note: Total contributions made in 1998.

Application Procedures

Initial Contact: Send a brief letter or proposal.
Application Requirements: Include a description of organization, amount requested, purpose of funds sought, recently audited financial statement, proof of tax-exempt status. There is no formal application policy.
Deadlines: None.
Decision Notification: The board meets on as-needed basis.

Restrictions

No grants awarded to individuals, sectarian religious groups, political organizations, or organizations supported by United Way Crusade of Mercy.
Company does not award scholarships or 'brick and mortar' grants.

Corporate Officials

Robert Lee Bogomolny: senior vice president, general counsel, secretary B Cleveland, OH 1938. ED Harvard University AB (1960); Harvard University LLB (1963). PRIM CORP EMPL senior vice president, general counsel, secretary: G.D. Searle & Co. CORP AFFIL member: Biotechnology Development Corp. NONPR AFFIL member: Food & Drug Law Institute; member: Pharmaceutical Research & Manufacturer America; member: American Corporate Counsel Association; member: American Bar Association.
Richard U. De Schutter: chairman, chief executive officer B Detroit, MI 1940. ED University of Arizona BS (1963-1964); University of Arizona MS (1965). PRIM CORP EMPL chairman, chief executive officer: G.D. Searle & Co. CORP AFFIL vice chairman: Monsanto Co.

Foundation Officials

Robert Lee Bogomolny: director (see above)
Richard U. De Schutter: director (see above)

Grants Analysis

Disclosure Period: calendar year ending 1998
Total Grants: $424,040
Number of Grants: 110
Average Grant: $3,855
Highest Grant: $35,000
Typical Range: $1,000 to $5,000

Recent Grants

Note: Grants derived from 1996 Form 990.

Arts & Humanities

25,000	Chicago Symphony Orchestra, Chicago, IL
25,000	Chicago Symphony Orchestra, Chicago, IL
25,000	Ravinia Festival Association, Highland Park, IL
15,000	North Shore Center for Performing Arts, NY
10,000	Chicago Children's Theater, Chicago, IL
7,500	Goodman Theater, Chicago, IL
5,000	Chicago Children's Museum, Chicago, IL
5,000	Lake Forest Symphony, Lake Forest, IL
5,000	Lake Forest Symphony, Lake Forest, IL
1,000	Art Institute, Chicago, IL

Civic & Public Affairs

25,000	Orchard Village
25,000	Watts Foundation Community Trust, Hawthorne, CA
10,000	Media Institute, New York, NY
7,500	Infinity Plus, Oak Park, IL
5,000	American Enterprise Institute for Public Policy Research, Washington, DC
4,000	IIFAR
2,500	American Chemical Society, Detroit, MI
2,500	John G. Shedd Aquarium, Chicago, IL
1,500	Women's Board of Heartland Alliance
1,000	Brookfield Zoo, Brookfield, IL
1,000	Lincoln Park Zoological Society, Chicago, IL
1,000	National Consumers League, Washington, DC

Education

15,000	Chicago and Cook County 4-H Foundation, Chicago, IL
10,000	Columbia University, New York, NY
10,000	Columbia University, New York, NY
10,000	Junior Achievement, Chicago, IL
10,000	Lake Forest College, Lake Forest, IL
10,000	Morehouse School of Medicine, Atlanta, GA
10,000	Morehouse School of Medicine, Atlanta, GA
10,000	Philadelphia College of Pharmacy and Science, Philadelphia, PA
10,000	University of Illinois, Environmental, Health, and Safety Fellowship, Urbana, IL
5,000	Chicago Public Schools Student Science Fair, Chicago, IL
2,000	National Lekotek Center, Evanston, IL

Environment

3,000	Hastings Center, Briarcliff Manor, NY

Health

15,000	Tufts Center for the Study of Drug Development, Medford, MA
5,000	AIDS Foundation, Chicago, IL
5,000	Crohn's and Colitis Foundation of America, New York, NY
5,000	National Council on Patient Information and Education, Washington, DC
5,000	National Kidney Cancer Association, Evanston, IL
5,000	Rush North Shore Medical Center, Chicago, IL
4,000	Combined Health Appeal, Saint Louis, MO
2,000	American Heart Association
1,000	Health for Humanity, Glencoe, IL

International

10,000	Jones Foundation for Reproductive Medicine

Science

5,000	American Council on Science and Health, New York, NY
2,750	Museum of Science and Industry, Chicago, IL

Social Services

3,100	Reach Volunteer Action Program
3,000	Boys Hope and Girls Hope
2,500	A Safe Place Lake County Crisis Center
2,500	Special Olympics, IL

SEARS, ROEBUCK AND CO.

Company Contact

Hoffman Estates, IL
Web: http://www.sears.com

Company Description

Revenue: US$41,071,000,000 (1999)
Profit: US$1,453,000,000 (1999)
Employees: 324,000 (1999)
Fortune Rank: 16, per FORTUNE Magazine's list of 500 Largest U.S. Corporations (1999).
FF 16
SIC(s): 5311 Department Stores.

Operating Locations

Canada: Sears Canada, Inc., Toronto; Mexico: Sears de Mexico, Col Santa Fe de Quajimalpa

Corporate Sponsorship

Type: Music & entertainment events; Festivals/fairs; Sports events
Note: The company sponsors a variety of events, including music concerts, circuses, and state fairs.

Sears, Roebuck and Co. Foundation

Giving Contact

Sonya Jackson, Vice President
Sears, Roebuck and Co. Foundation
3333 Beverly Road, BC-110A
Hoffman Estates, IL 60179
Phone: (847)286-1314
Fax: (847)286-5918

Description

EIN: 366032266
Organization Type: Corporate Foundation
Giving Locations: IL: Chicago operating locations.
Grant Types: General Support, Project.

Giving Philosophy

'Throughout its history, Sears has had a long-standing commitment to corporate responsibility, including providing contributions to non-profit organizations. Participating in the communities where it does business is a fundamental policy and practice for the company.' 1996 Contributions Guidelines

Financial Summary

Total Giving: $22,000,000 (1999 approx); $16,400,000 (1997 approx); $15,000,000 (1996 approx). Note: Contributes through corporate direct giving program and foundation. 1997 Giving includes corporate direct giving; foundation ($211,896). 1996 Giving includes foundation ($1,100,000). 1995 Giving includes corporate direct giving; foundation.
Assets: $2,880,239 (1997); $2,897,279 (1996); $2,430,869 (1993)
Gifts Received: $2,300 (1996); $1,350,000 (1993); $575 (1991)

Typical Recipients

Civic & Public Affairs: Employment/Job Training, Professional & Trade Associations
Education: Arts/Humanities Education, Business Education, Colleges & Universities, Education-General, Minority Education
Social Services: Community Service Organizations, United Funds/United Ways

Contributions Analysis

Giving Priorities: Woman, family and racial inclusiveness.
Note: Corporate contributions respond to major grant requests from national organizations or activities in the Chicago area. Priority is given to projects that have a direct measurable impact on multiple communities where company operates.
Local community contributions are provided by local store managers. United Way is the primaryorganization supported at the local level.

Application Procedures

Initial Contact: submit request in writing
Application Requirements: a description of organization's purpose, history, and programs; brief explanation of the issue the organization is attempting to address; how the proposed program relates to company funding priorities; a line-item program budget; most recent audited financial statement; list of all sources of income; list of governing board members and their affiliations; copy of 501(c)(3) tax-exempt status from IRS; copy of most recent Form 990
Deadlines: None.
Review Process: requests are reviewed throughout the year to determine eligibility and relationship to funding priorities
Evaluative Criteria: supports programs which are which are responsive to diverse social needs; additional considerations are annual budget, program priorities and geographic scope; and special interest in programs that offer volunteer opportunities
Decision Notification: Sears, Roebuck and Co. Foundation board meets quarterly; corporate contributions committees meet periodically each year; ineligible organizations will be notified immediately
Notes: Funding renewals are not automatic and cannot be guaranteed from year to year.

Restrictions

Grants generally do not support individuals; political, labor, social, veterans', or fraternal organizations; religious organizations or endeavors, unless the program benefits a large segment of the community; goodwill advertising in journal or dinner programs; disease-specific organizations; research projects; or programs outside the United States.

Additional Information

During the 1990s, Sears will continue to emphasize and fully integrate education in each of its funding priorities. The goal is to serve as a catalyst to create a holistic approach to education. Funding will be used as a strategic tool to leverage opportunities for greater impact within and between the organizations supported.

Corporate Officials

John Connolly: manager community relationsrs PRIM CORP EMPL manager community relations: Sears, Roebuck and Co.
E. Ronald Culp: vice president public affairs B 1947. ED Indiana State University BS (1970). PRIM CORP EMPL vice president public affairs: Sears, Roebuck and Co.
Alan J. Lacy: president credit B 1953. ED Emory University MBA (1972); Georgia Institute of Technology BSIM (1975). PRIM CORP EMPL president credit: Sears, Roebuck and Co. CORP AFFIL president: National Tire Battery.
Arthur C. Martinez: chairman, chief executive officer, president B New York, NY 1939. ED Polytechnic University BS (1960); Harvard University MBA (1965). PRIM CORP EMPL chairman, chief executive officer, president: Sears, Roebuck and Co. CORP AFFIL director: Sprout Venture Capital Group; director: Western Auto Supply Co.; chairman: National Tire Battery; director: Northwestern Memorial Hospital; director: BP Amoco Corp.; department chairman: Federal Reserve Bank Chicago; director: Ameritech Corp. NONPR AFFIL trustee: Orchestra Association Chicago Symphony Orhcestra; trustee: Polytech University; director: National Urban League; advisory board: Northwestern University Kellogg Graduate School Business Management; chairman: National Minority Supplier Development Council Inc.; member, chairman: National Retail Federation; trustee: Art Institute; director: Defenders Wildlife.

Giving Program Officials

Amelia Kohm: administrator PRIM CORP EMPL administrator corporate community relations: Sears, Roebuck and Co.
Shawnelle Richie: PRIM CORP EMPL corporate community relations manager: Sears, Roebuck and Co.
Joanie Valdez: PRIM CORP EMPL manager community relations: Sears, Roebuck and Co.

Foundation Officials

John Connolly: vice president (see above)
E. Ronald Culp: president (see above)
Susan Duchak: vice president PRIM CORP EMPL community relations manager: Sears, Roebuck and Co.
Sonya Jackson: president
Rita P. Wilson: director B Philadelphia, PA 1946. ED Saint Paul's College (1968). PRIM CORP EMPL senior vice president corporate communications, director: Ameritech Corp.

Grants Analysis

Disclosure Period: calendar year ending
Typical Range: $10,000 to $100,000

Recent Grants

Note: Grants derived from 1996 Form 990.

Education

250,000 United Negro College Fund, New York, NY

Social Services

100,000 Gloria Estefan Foundation, Miami Beach, FL -- provide aid to underprivileged

SEAWAY FOOD TOWN, INC.

Company Contact

Maumee, OH
Web: http://www.foodtownonline.com

Company Description

Employees: 5,024 (1999)
SIC(s): 5411 Grocery Stores, 5912 Drug Stores & Proprietary Stores.

Operating Locations

Company operates 24 Food Town Supermarkets, 20 Food Town Plus Supermarkets, and 22 discount drug stores under the name of 'Pharm.'

Nonmonetary Support

Type: Cause-related Marketing & Promotion; Donated Equipment; Donated Products; In-kind Services
Note: Nonmonetary support provided by company.

Corporate Sponsorship

Type: Arts & cultural events; Festivals/fairs; Music & entertainment events; Sports events

Giving Contact

Ms. Pat Nowak, Director, Public Relations & Community Affairs
Seaway Food Town, Inc.
1020 Ford Street
Maumee, OH 43537
Phone: (419)893-9401
Fax: (419)891-4907

Description

Organization Type: Corporate Giving Program
Giving Locations: MI: Southeastern Michigan; OH: Northwest Ohio headquarters area only.
Grant Types: General Support, Multiyear/Continuing Support.

Financial Summary

Total Giving: Contributes through corporate direct giving program only.

Typical Recipients

Arts & Humanities: Arts Appreciation, Arts Associations & Councils, Arts Centers, Arts Festivals, Community Arts, Ethnic & Folk Arts, Libraries, Museums/Galleries, Opera, Performing Arts, Public Broadcasting, Theater, Visual Arts
Civic & Public Affairs: Philanthropic Organizations, Zoos/Aquariums
Education: Colleges & Universities, Elementary Education (Private), Literacy
Health: Geriatric Health, Health Organizations, Hospitals, Nutrition
Religion: Churches, Synagogues/Temples
Science: Science Exhibits & Fairs
Social Services: Child Welfare, Community Centers, Community Service Organizations, Domestic Violence, Food/Clothing Distribution, Recreation & Athletics, Shelters/Homelessness, Substance Abuse, Youth Organizations

Contributions Analysis

Arts & Humanities: About 20%. Contributes to art associations, museums, community and folk arts, libraries, performing arts, and public broadcasting.
Civic & Public Affairs: About 15%. Primary support for philanthropic organizations.
Education: About 10%. Colleges and universities, elementary education, and literacy programs are the primary recipients.
Health: About 10%. Support for hospitals and health organizations with emphasis on geriatric health.
Religion: About 20%. Recipients include churches and synagogues.
Social Services: About 25%. Supports child services and youth organizations, community centers, drug rehabilitation programs, homeless shelters and recreation programs.

Application Procedures

Initial Contact: Submit a brief letter of inquiry and full proposal.
Application Requirements: Include a description of organization, amount requested, purpose of funds sought, and proof of tax-exempt status.
Deadlines: One month in advance of date that funds are needed.

Restrictions

Does not support individuals, political or lobbying groups, or organizations outside operating areas.

Corporate Officials

Richard B. Iott: president, chief executive officer, director B Columbus, OH 1951. ED Hillsdale College. PRIM CORP EMPL president, chief executive officer, director: Seaway Food Town, Inc. CORP AFFIL president: Gruber's Food Town Inc.; president: VF Inc.; president: Buckeye Discount Inc.; president: Food Town Inc.
Wallace D. Iott: chairman, director B 1915. PRIM CORP EMPL chairman, director: Seaway Food Town, Inc. CORP AFFIL chairman: Gruber's Food Town Inc.; chairman: VP Inc.; chairman: Buckeye Discount Inc.; chairman: Custer Pharmacy Inc.

Giving Program Officials

Pat Nowak: PRIM CORP EMPL director public relations & community affairs: Seaway Food Town, Inc.

Grants Analysis

Disclosure Period: calendar year ending
Typical Range: $2,500 to $5,000

SECURITY BENEFIT LIFE INSURANCE CO.

Company Contact

Topeka, KS

Web: http://www.securitybenefit.com

Company Description

Employees: 600
SIC(s): 6153 Short-Term Business Credit, 6311 Life Insurance, 6321 Accident & Health Insurance.

Nonmonetary Support

Type: Donated Equipment; In-kind Services

Corporate Sponsorship

Type: Arts & cultural events; Music & entertainment events
Contact: Vanette Davis, Marketing Communications

Security Benefit Life Insurance Co. Charitable Trust

Giving Contact

Krysta Congrove, Contact
Security Benefit Life Insurance Co. Charitable Trust
700 Southwest Harrison Street
Topeka, KS 66636-0001
Phone: (785)431-3215

Description

Founded: 1976
EIN: 486211612
Organization Type: Corporate Foundation
Giving Locations: KS: Topeka some giving in other areas of Kansas
Grant Types: General Support, Matching.

Financial Summary

Total Giving: $300,435 (1998); $250,000 (1997 approx); $249,735 (1996). Note: Contributes through foundation only.
Giving Analysis: Giving for 1996 includes: foundation ($200,635); foundation grants to United Way ($49,100); 1998: foundation ($270,191); foundation grants to United Way ($30,244)
Assets: $1,794,880 (1998); $770,756 (1996)
Gifts Received: $333,840 (1998); $367,500 (1996); $275,185 (1993). Note: Contributions were received from Security Benefit Life Industry Co.

Typical Recipients

Arts & Humanities: Arts Associations & Councils, Arts Centers, Ballet, Dance, History & Archaeology, Museums/Galleries, Music, Performing Arts, Public Broadcasting, Theater
Civic & Public Affairs: African American Affairs, Clubs, Employment/Job Training, Civic & Public Affairs-General, Hispanic Affairs, Housing, Parades/ Festivals, Professional & Trade Associations, Public Policy, Urban & Community Affairs, Women's Affairs, Zoos/Aquariums
Education: Business Education, Colleges & Universities, Economic Education, Education Associations, Education Funds, Environmental Education, Faculty Development, Education-General, Minority Education, Public Education (Precollege), Secondary Education (Private), Secondary Education (Public)
Environment: Resource Conservation
Health: Cancer, Children's Health/Hospitals, Diabetes, Emergency/Ambulance Services, Health Organizations, Hospices, Single-Disease Health Associations
Science: Scientific Research
Social Services: Animal Protection, Big Brother/Big Sister, Child Welfare, Community Service Organizations, Family Planning, Family Services, People with Disabilities, Scouts, United Funds/United Ways, Volunteer Services, YMCA/YWCA/YMHA/YWHA, Youth Organizations

Contributions Analysis

Arts & Humanities: 24%. Supports arts organizations in Topeka.
Civic & Public Affairs: 12%. Gives to the United Way, the Boy Scouts of America, and Big Brothers and Big Sisters. Also supports women's resources, community affairs, and Friends of the Topeka Zoo.
Education: 17%. Major support given to colleges and secondary schools, primarily in Topeka, KS.
Health: 6%. Major support to the Menninger Foundation of Topeka, KS.
Science: 4%. Supports the Life Sciences Research and Education Center.
Social Services: 37%. Supports scout troops, youth and senior organizations, and animal welfare.
Note: Total contributions made in 1998.

Application Procedures

Initial Contact: Send a brief letter.
Deadlines: None.

Additional Information

The trust lists Security Benefit Trust Company as a corporate trustee.

Corporate Officials

Howard R. Fricke: president, director B 1936. PRIM CORP EMPL president, director: Security Benefit Life Insurance Co. CORP AFFIL president: Security Distributor Inc. Co. LLC; president: Security Management; president, director: Security Benefit Group Inc.; director: Oneok Inc.; director: Payless Shoe Source Inc.

Foundation Officials

Howard R. Fricke: trustee (see above)

Grants Analysis

Disclosure Period: calendar year ending 1998
Total Grants: $270,191*
Number of Grants: 81
Average Grant: $3,336
Highest Grant: $30,000
Typical Range: $300 to $4,500
***Note:** Giving excludes United Way.

Recent Grants

Note: Grants derived from 1998 Form 990.

Arts & Humanities

30,000	Topeka Civic Theatre, Topeka, KS
10,000	Topeka Performing Arts Center, Topeka, KS
5,000	Topeka Civic Theatre, Topeka, KS
5,000	Topeka Civic Theatre, Topeka, KS
5,000	Topeka Symphony Society, Topeka, KS
3,000	Topeka Festival Singers, Topeka, KS
1,000	Kanu, Lawrence, KS

Civic & Public Affairs

7,500	Spirit of Topeka, Topeka, KS
4,000	Shelfered Living, Topeka, KS
3,000	Every Woman's Resource Center, Topeka, KS
2,500	Every Woman's Resource Center, Topeka, KS
2,500	Junior League of Topeka, Topeka, KS
2,500	Project Topeka, Topeka, KS
1,500	Living the Dream Committee, Topeka, KS
1,500	Sales & Marketing Executives Seminar, Topeka, KS
1,000	Capper Foundation, Topeka, KS
1,000	Capper Foundation, Topeka, KS
1,000	Friends of the Zoo, Topeka, KS

Education

13,000	Washburn University, Topeka, KS
5,000	United Negro College Fund, St. Louis, MO
4,000	Kansas State Department of Education, Manhattan, KS
3,000	Kansas Teacher of the Year, Uniontown, KS
2,500	Illinois Wesleyan University, Bloomington, IL
2,500	Topeka Public Schools Foundation, Topeka, KS
2,500	University of Kansas Endowment Association, Lawrence, KS
2,000	Kansas Independent College Fund, Topeka, KS
2,000	Kansas State University Foundation, Manhattan, KS
1,500	Ascension Education Corporation, Overland, KS
1,250	Kansas State University Foundation, Manhattan, KS
1,000	Junior Achievement of Northeast Kansas, Topeka, KS

Health

5,000	American Cancer Society, Topeka, KS
4,500	American Red Cross, Topeka, KS
2,500	March of Dimes, Topeka, KS
1,000	Florence Crittenton, Topeka, KS
1,000	Juvenile Diabetes Association, Shawnee, KS

Science

10,000	Life Sciences Research and Education Center, Topeka, KS

Social Services

30,000	United Way of Greater Topeka, Topeka, KS
20,000	Kaw Valley Girl Scouts, Topeka, KS
10,000	YMCA, Topeka, KS
10,000	YMCA, Topeka, KS
4,000	Boy Scout Council Jayhawk Area, Topeka, KS
3,200	Big Brothers/Big Sisters of Topeka, Topeka, KS
3,000	CASA, Topeka, KS
2,500	Boy Scout Council Jayhawk Area, Topeka, KS
2,500	Kansas Families for Kids, Topeka, KS
2,000	Topeka North Outreach, Topeka, KS
1,500	Topeka Association for Retarded Citizens (TARC), Topeka, KS
1,500	Topeka Youth Project, Topeka, KS
1,000	CASA, Topeka, KS
1,000	Helping Hands Humane Society, Topeka, KS

Security Life Of Denver Insurance Co.

Company Contact

Denver, CO

Company Description

Revenue: US$2,880,400,000
Employees: 650
SIC(s): 6311 Life Insurance.
Parent Company: Internationale Nederlanden U.S. Insurance Holdings, Inc.
Parent Income: US$4,110,000,000

Operating Locations

CA: Security Life of Denver Insurance Co.; CO: Security Life of Denver Insurance Co., Denver; Security Life of Denver Insurance Co., Denver; FL: Security Life of Denver Insurance Co.; GA: Security Life of Denver Insurance Co.; KS: Security Life of Denver Insurance Co.; MA: Security Life of Denver Insurance Co.; TX: Security Life of Denver Insurance Co.

Nonmonetary Support

Type: Donated Equipment; Workplace Solicitation

Giving Contact

Kristin Jewett, Marketing Promotions Consultant
Security Life of Denver
Security Life Center
1290 Broadway
Denver, CO 80203
Phone: (303)894-4949
Email: kjewett@sld-ins.com

Description

Organization Type: Corporate Giving Program
Giving Locations: CO: emphasis on Denver states where there is an agent.
Grant Types: Capital, Employee Matching Gifts, General Support, Multiyear/Continuing Support, Operating Expenses, Project.

Financial Summary

Total Giving: $255,000 (1999 approx); $225,000 (1998 approx); $300,000 (1997 approx). Note: Contributes through corporate direct giving program only.

Typical Recipients

Arts & Humanities: Arts Associations & Councils, Arts Outreach, Ballet, Arts & Humanities-General, Historic Preservation, History & Archaeology, Libraries, Museums/Galleries, Music, Opera, Public Broadcasting
Civic & Public Affairs: Botanical Gardens/Parks, Chambers of Commerce, Environmental Affairs (Conservation), Urban & Community Affairs, Zoos/Aquariums
Education: Afterschool/Enrichment Programs, Arts/Humanities Education, Business Education, Elementary Education (Private), Elementary Education (Public), Education-General, Literacy
Health: AIDS/HIV, Cancer, Eyes/Blindness, Health-General, Single-Disease Health Associations
Religion: Jewish Causes
Social Services: At-Risk Youth, Domestic Violence, Emergency Relief, Food/Clothing Distribution, People with Disabilities, Recreation & Athletics, Senior Services, Social Services-General, United Funds/United Ways, Youth Organizations

Application Procedures

Initial Contact: Send a brief letter of inquiry.
Application Requirements: Include a description of organization, amount requested, purpose of funds sought, and time frame within which contribution is needed.

Restrictions

Does not support political or lobbying groups or religious organizations for sectarian purposes.

Corporate Officials

Stephen Christopher: president, chief operating officer PRIM CORP EMPL president, chief operating officer: Security Life Denver Insurance Co. CORP AFFIL director: First Ing Life Insurance of New York. NONPR AFFIL director: Professional Examination Service.

Grants Analysis

Disclosure Period: calendar year ending
Typical Range: $1,000 to $5,000

Recent Grants

Note: Grants derived from 1996 grants list.

Arts & Humanities

Colorado Symphony Orchestra, Denver, CO
Denver Public Library, Denver, CO

Civic & Public Affairs

Bayaud Industries, Denver, CO
Oneday Foundation, Denver, CO

Education

Denver Public Schools, Denver, CO
Metro State College, Denver, CO

Environment

Volunteers for Outdoor Colorado, Denver, CO

Social Services

Community Resources, Denver, CO
Food Bank of the Rockies, Denver, CO
Safe House of Denver, Denver, CO

SEGA OF AMERICA INC.

Company Contact

Redwood City, CA
Web: http://www.sega.com

Company Description

Employees: 900
SIC(s): 5045 Computers, Peripherals & Software.
Parent Company: Sega Enterprises Ltd., 2-12, Haneda, Ohta-ku, Tokyo, Japan

Operating Locations

CA: Sega of America, Redwood City; Sega of America Inc., Redwood City

Nonmonetary Support

Value: $78,000 (1995)
Type: Donated Equipment; Donated Products
Note: 1995 corporate nonmonetary support ($40,000 est.) and foundation nonmonetary support ($38,000). 1997 nonmonetary support ($50,000 est.).

Corporate Sponsorship

Note: Company sponsors events pertaining to youth education and health.

Sega Foundation

Giving Contact

Trizia Hill, Director
Sega Foundation
255 Shoreline Drive, State 200
Redwood City, CA 94065
Phone: (650)701-6000

Description

Founded: 1992
EIN: 946648255
Organization Type: Corporate Foundation
Giving Locations: CA: San Francisco Bay Area of Alameda County, San Francisco Bay Area of Santa Clara County, San Francisco Bay area of San Francisco, San Francisco Bay area of San Mateo County nationally--some foundation-initiated programs may be national in scope; San Francisco Bay area of Contra Costa County.
Grant Types: Employee Matching Gifts, Project.
Note: Employee matching gift ratio: 1 to 1 with $100 minimum and $1,000 maximum annually.

Giving Philosophy

'The Sega Foundation was founded out of concern for the life long well being of American children, and a commitment to empower youth for the challenges of their generation. The Foundation believes education and health are critical elements to preparing children and youth to be leaders and visionaries in the twenty-first century. The Sega Foundation pursues innovative programs with potential for adaptation, and those efforts being made on behalf of under served populations.' Sega Foundation Mission Statement

Financial Summary

Total Giving: $413,968 (fiscal year ending March 31, 1998); $400,000 (fiscal 1997); $622,991 (fiscal 1996). Note: Contributes through foundation only. Giving includes nonmonetary support.
Assets: $268,185 (fiscal 1998); $779,080 (fiscal 1997); $1,390,873 (fiscal 1996)
Gifts Received: $139,936 (fiscal 1998); $68,429 (fiscal 1997); $580,728 (fiscal 1996). Note: Foundation receives contributions from Sega of America Inc.

Typical Recipients

Arts & Humanities: Arts Outreach, Film & Video, Libraries, Visual Arts
Civic & Public Affairs: Asian American Affairs, Community Foundations, Nonprofit Management, Philanthropic Organizations, Professional & Trade Associations, Public Policy
Education: Afterschool/Enrichment Programs, Arts/Humanities Education, Colleges & Universities, Education Associations, Education Reform, Elementary Education (Public), Faculty Development, Education-General, Literacy, Minority Education, Private Education (Precollege), Public Education (Precollege), School Volunteerism, Science/Mathematics Education, Secondary Education (Public), Special Education, Student Aid, Vocational & Technical Education
Health: AIDS/HIV, Cancer, Children's Health/Hospitals, Clinics/Medical Centers, Diabetes, Health Organizations, Heart, Hospitals, Prenatal Health Issues, Respiratory, Single-Disease Health Associations
International: Foreign Educational Institutions, International Relief Efforts
Religion: Religious Welfare
Science: Scientific Centers & Institutes, Scientific Organizations
Social Services: Camps, Child Abuse, Child Welfare, Community Service Organizations, Emergency Relief, Family Planning, Family Services, Food/Clothing Distribution, Recreation & Athletics, Scouts, Shelters/Homelessness, Substance Abuse, United Funds/United Ways, Volunteer Services, YMCA/YWCA/YMHA/YWHA, Youth Organizations

Contributions Analysis

Giving Priorities: Social services, education, and health receive approximately equal support.
Arts & Humanities: 1%.
Education: 32%. The foundation contributes to educational programs that seek to integrate technology into the curriculum and school culture, programs that supplement school curriculum and improve learning, and teacher development programs. Applicants should be prepared to demonstrate project's impact on systemic change efforts. While classroom use of technology is a high priority, the foundation prefers to fund comprehensive technology programs, not necessarily the purchase of hardware. The foundation also supports youth HIV/AIDS programs, primarily focusing on education and prevention.
Health: 32%. Supports health programs that provide medical services to children, preferably in the context of enduring and meaningful access to care, and programs that improve pediatric care through resources and training for pediatricians, nurses, and others who care for children. Another area of focus is the pediatric AIDS crisis.
International: 1%.
Social Services: 34%. Funds programs to prevent child abuse, Boys and Girls Clubs, and other youth-related social services.
Note: Total contributions in 1998.

Application Procedures

Initial Contact: Telephone, written, or e-mail inquiry for guidelines.
Application Requirements: Application should include a cover sheet, with date of application, organization name, purpose of grant, organization mission statement, address, phone and fax numbers, e-mail address, executive director, contact person and title, amount requested, total project budget, and project name; brief proposal summary; background information, including a description of organization's history

and mission, need to be addressed, current programs and accomplishments, population served, and relationships with other organizations; a funding request, including the length of the project; methods of evaluation; and a copy of the IRS tax-exempt letter, project budget, current annual operating budget, and a copy of the most recent Form 990.
Deadlines: September 30.
Review Process: Based on information provided in response to guidelines, foundation may request more information, a meeting with staff members, and/or site visit; foundation staff may then recommend programs for consideration and approval by the trustees.
Evaluative Criteria: Foundation pursues innovative approaches to problems with measurable outcomes and ongoing programs with potential for dissemination and adaptation, rather than programs seeking to test new ideas; requests should be project-oriented with specific, measurable activity goals for the organization and outcome goals for the population served; grants are awarded only to charitable or educational organizations addressing youth education and health issues.
Decision Notification: Board of trustees meets quarterly; small grants or grants made to local charitable organizations may be approved by the board at any time; grant review process may take several months.
Notes: Approximately 90% of grants are initiated by the foundation. The remaining 10% of the budget is set aside for small grants, ranging from $500 to $2,500, distributed to applying organizations that work in the San Francisco Bay area. Grantees are required to provide periodic financial and program reports.

Restrictions

Prefers not to fund general operations of specific schools, endowments, fund-raising events, research projects, single-disease or single-medical issue programs (except in certain cases under the foundation's matching gift program), or multiple-year grant commitments.
Does not make grants to individuals or private shareholders. Also does not fund organizations where a substantial part of activities is carrying on propaganda or otherwise attempting to influence legislation, sectarian or denominational religious activities; or organizations that discriminate on the basis of race, sex, or color.
Grants are awarded only to charitable organizations as defined by Section 501(c)(3) of the IRS code.
No equipment or games are donated to raffles, auctions, or similar sales.

Additional Information

The foundation was established in March 1992 with monies from Sega of America, Redwood City, CA, and Sega Enterprises, Tokyo, Japan. Sega prefers to fund innovative and effective programs that impact relatively large numbers of children, particularly those efforts being made in major urban areas. When possible, Sega will collaborate with other funding sources. Programs should demonstrate a specific need for Sega support, and be well-managed, well-organized, and effectively implemented. Programs also should demonstrate flexibility and adaptability, as well as include indicators of effectiveness to allow thoughtful evaluation that will guide the program's evolution over time.
Publications: Guidelines

Corporate Officials

Ted Hoff: executive vice president sales & marketing, director PRIM CORP EMPL executive vice president sales & marketing, director: Sega of America Inc.

Foundation Officials

Trizia L. Hill: director
Ted Hoff: trustee (see above)
Shoichiro Irimajri: trustee
David Rosen: trustee CORP AFFIL director: Sega Enterprises.
Bernie Stolar: trustee B Munich, Germany 1946. PRIM CORP EMPL president: Sega of America Inc. CORP AFFIL director: Interactive Light.
Shinobu Toyoda: trustee CORP AFFIL director: Sega America Inc.

Grants Analysis

Disclosure Period: fiscal year ending March 31, 1998
Total Grants: $413,968
Number of Grants: 114
Average Grant: $3,631
Highest Grant: $52,000
Typical Range: $200 to $2,500 and $10,000 to $25,000

Recent Grants

Note: Grants derived from 1998 Form 990.

Arts & Humanities

2,500 San Jose Public Library Foundation, San Jose, CA -- Youth reading resources

Education

50,000 JASON Foundation, Waltham, MA -- Interactive Telecommunications/Education program
25,260 Bay Area School Reform Collaborative, San Francisco, CA -- Multimedia technologies in schools
25,000 National Foundation for the Improvement of Education, Washington, DC -- Instructional technology & curriculum development
10,000 Plugged In, East Palo Alto, CA -- instructional technologies for youth
8,500 World Link Foundation, San Francisco, CA -- School-based Virtual expeditions
3,000 Bay Area School Reform Collaborative, San Francisco, CA -- School tech. program support
1,956 Future Scientists and Engineers of America, Anaheim, CA -- Science/engineering competition
1,500 Santa Fe Elementary School, Oakland, CA -- Literacy project

Health

35,000 Children's Health Fund, New York, NY -- medical services for homeless children
24,280 Elizabeth Glaser Pediatric AIDS Foundation, Santa Monica, CA -- emergency
18,525 Sabriya's Castle of Fun Foundation, Los Angeles, CA -- hospitalized children
10,083 The Children's Health Fund, New York, NY -- homeless children's services
7,500 Children's Benefit Fund, Inc., Rochelle Park, NJ -- health services for needy children
5,849 Elizabeth Glaser Pediatric AIDS Foundation, Santa Monica, CA -- children affected by aids
3,718 National Children's Cancer Society, St. Louis, MO -- computers for hospitalized cancer patients
3,199 Children's Health Council, New York, NY -- youth services
2,500 May View Community Health Center, Pa.lo Alto, CA -- medical services for children
2,500 San Mateo County Health Services, San Mateo, CA -- nutrition counseling services
2,500 Sunburst Projects, Petaluma, CA -- camp program for hiv affected children
2,500 Watts Foundation Community Trust, Hawthorne, CA -- mobile medical services for homeless children
1,833 Ronald McDonald House at Stanford, Palo Alto, CA
1,000 Adult & Child Guidance Center, San Jose, CA -- hiv/aids education
1,000 American Heart Assoc. of San Mateo Cnty., Burlingame, CA -- youth heart power program
1,000 Easter Seal Society of The Bay Area, San Francisco, CA -- services for children with disabilities
1,000 Juvenile Diabetes, San Francisco, CA

International

2,500 Global Education Partnership, Oakland, CA -- entrepreneurial business skill building using technology

Social Services

52,000 National Committee To Prevent Child Abuse, Chicago, IL -- healthy families child abuse prevention program
19,241 Boys & Girls Clubs of of N. San Mateo County, South San Francisco, CA -- youth services
7,000 Foundation of America, San Diego, CA -- youth community service program
6,317 Friends for Youth, Redwood City, CA -- youth mentoring
5,000 Omega Boys Club, San Francisco, CA -- life skills program
3,717 Boys & Girls Club of Metro Atlanta, Atlanta, GA -- youth services
3,213 Boys & Girls Club of Chicago, Chicago, IL -- youth services
3,199 Child Abuse Prevention Center, Palo Alto, CA -- child abuse prevention services
3,081 Boys & Girls Club of Snohomish County, Everett, WA -- youth services
2,897 Metro Phoenix Boys & Girls Club, Glendale, AZ -- youth services
2,655 Boys & Girls Club of N.E. Florida, Jacksonville, FL -- youth services
2,500 Child Advocates of Santa Clara & San Mateo County, San Jose, CA -- foster children advocate services
2,500 Emergency Housing Consortium, San Jose, CA -- healthy families safe families program
2,500 Friends for Youth, Redwood City, CA -- youth mentoring
2,283 Madison Square Boys & Girls Club, New York, NY -- youth services
2,045 Boys & Girls Club of King County, Seattle, WA -- youth services
1,488 Children's Aid Society, New York, NY -- youth services
1,290 East Bay Outreach Project/UC Berkeley, Berkeley, CA -- youth entrepreneur program
1,238 Street Level Youth Media, Chicago, IL -- computer access program
1,000 Assistance League Of Santa Clara County, Los Altos, CA -- to purchase shoes & socks for school kids
1,000 Mid-Peninsula YWCA, Palo Alto, CA -- parenting education
1,000 Project Open Hand, San Francisco, CA -- children's meals program
1,000 Raphael House, San Francisco, CA -- homeless children's services
500 Child Abuse Prevention Council, Walnut Creek, CA -- child abuse prevention services

SEMPRA ENERGY

Company Contact

San Diego, CA
Web: http://www.sempra.com

Company Description

Former Name: San Diego Gas & Electric.
Assets: US$11,270,000,000 (1999)
Profit: US$394,000,000 (1999)
Fortune Rank: 307, per FORTUNE Magazine's list of 500 Largest U.S. Corporations (1999).
FF 307
SIC(s): 4931 Electric & Other Services Combined.

Nonmonetary Support

Value: $100,000 (1996); $820,000 (1994); $35,000 (1992)
Type: Cause-related Marketing & Promotion; Donated Equipment; In-kind Services; Workplace Solicitation
Volunteer Programs: The company promotes employee volunteerism through Team San Diego Gas & Electric, a group of nearly 1,200 employees and family members who volunteer in hands-on community service projects.

Corporate Sponsorship

Type: Arts & cultural events; Festivals/fairs; Music & entertainment events; Sports events

Giving Contact

Corporate Community Relations Department
Sempra Energy
101 Ash St.
San Diego, CA 92101-3017
Phone: (619)696-4297
Fax: (619)696-1868
Email: community@sempra.com

Alternate Contact

Phone: 877-SEMPRA-9
Note: Toll free number.

Description

Organization Type: Corporate Giving Program
Giving Locations: CA: Southern California
Grant Types: Conference/Seminar, Emergency, Employee Matching Gifts, Project.

Giving Philosophy

'We are dedicated to taking a leadership role in promoting health, furthering education and environmental protection, and stimulating economic vitality, while enhancing the quality of life in communities where we do business. Throughout all of our companies, we give preference to requests that embrace diversity which allows us to work in partnership with businesses, governmental and community leaders to meet community needs and attain measurable outcomes and results.' *Sempra Community Service*

Financial Summary

Total Giving: $4,000,000 (1997 approx); $3,594,278 (1996); $3,417,275 (1995). Note: Contributes through corporate direct giving program only. Giving includes corporate direct giving; memberships; local economic development. 1996 Giving includes nonmonetary support.
Giving Analysis: Giving for 1997 includes: corporate direct giving ($2,250,000)

Typical Recipients

Arts & Humanities: Arts Centers, Arts Festivals, Arts Funds, Arts Institutes, Community Arts, Dance, Ethnic & Folk Arts, Historic Preservation, Libraries, Museums/Galleries, Music, Opera, Performing Arts, Theater, Visual Arts
Civic & Public Affairs: Economic Development, Employment/Job Training, Legal Aid, Professional & Trade Associations, Safety, Zoos/Aquariums
Education: Arts/Humanities Education, Business Education, Colleges & Universities, Economic Education, Education Funds, Elementary Education (Private), Engineering/Technological Education, Health & Physical Education, Literacy, Medical Education, Minority Education, Preschool Education, Science/Mathematics Education
Environment: Environment-General
Health: Geriatric Health, Health Organizations, Hospices, Hospitals, Medical Research, Mental Health, Single-Disease Health Associations
Science: Observatories & Planetariums, Science Exhibits & Fairs, Scientific Organizations
Social Services: Child Welfare, Community Centers, Community Service Organizations, Counseling, Day Care, Delinquency & Criminal Rehabilitation, Emergency Relief, Family Services, Food/Clothing Distribution, People with Disabilities, Recreation & Athletics, Senior Services, Shelters/Homelessness, Substance Abuse, United Funds/United Ways, Volunteer Services, Youth Organizations

Contributions Analysis

Arts & Humanities: About 15%. Supports arts appreciation, artassociations, art centers, visual arts, opera and music, and historic preservation. Emphasis is on making the arts accessible to underserved or disadvantaged groups.
Civic & Public Affairs: About 20%. Supports consumer affairs, economic development, environmental affairs, urban and community affairs, and ethnic and minority affairs. Emphais on crime prevention.
Education: 25% to 30%. Primary support goes to business education, colleges and universities, elementary education, literacy programs, and minority education.
Health: 35% to 40%. Supports the aged and geriatric health, hospices and hospitals, medical research, single-disease health associations, child welfare, community centers and community service organizations, family services, and traditional youth organizations. Major emphasis is on drug abuse prevention.

Application Procedures

Initial Contact: Call or write for guidelines, then submit a written request.
Application Requirements: Include name of organization, contact person and title, address, phone and fax number; a description of organization, including purpose, size and audience served; description of program or project, with target audience: ethnicity, number of people, age, etc.; amount requested; geographic area served; description of need, including relevant research; budget for the project, including personnel, operating and direct costs; list of other contributors and funding levels; method of evaluation; current budget for organization, including revenue sources and reserve or contingency funds; description of volunteer support; list of board members, advisory board, and staff; proof of tax-exempt status; description of how SDG&E's participation will be highlighted; and tax I.D. number.
Deadlines: None.
Evaluative Criteria: Project is in one of company's focus areas; builds alliances between businesses, nonprofits, schools and media; delivers specific benefits or services to community; provides company with leadership opportunity; demonstrates commitment to measuring results. The company prefers to make direct contributions, rather than to other grant-making organizations; to fund programs that reach consumers or businesses with direct benefits; and to fund single-year efforts as opposed to multi-year commitments.
Decision Notification: Applicants are notified on a monthly basis.

Restrictions

The company generally does not provide funds for general operating expenses; travel expenses; loans or loan guarantees; debt reduction or past operating deficits; liquidating an organization; reducing or donating the cost of any gas or electric service that other customers must pay for (except for customers who are helped through our winter assistance program); building funds or capital campaigns.
No grants are made to individuals; private foundations or endowment funds; grantmaking organizations; discriminatory organizations; sectarian religious activities or political activities.
No grants are made to individuals; private foundations or endowment funds; grantmaking organizations; discriminatory organizations; sectarian religious activities or political activities.

Additional Information

The company provides for corporate and regional contributions. Corporate contributions dollars exist to support community-wide organizations and activities that benefit citizens throughout the markets where they do business. Regional contributions dollars exist to support organizations and activities that benefit citizens living within certain geographic areas of the community.
The company supports the Employee Contributions Club, which funds local community projects, and a holiday food drive.
Publications: Guidelines; Annual Review

Corporate Officials

Donald E. Felsinger: president, chief executive officer B Safford, AZ 1947. ED University of Arizona (1972). PRIM CORP EMPL president, chief executive officer: San Diego Gas & Electric Co. CORP AFFIL member: Pacific Coast Gas Association; director: Institute Medical Quality; director: Calstart; director: Institute America. NONPR AFFIL director: Edison Electric Institute.

Giving Program Officials

Molly Cartmill: director corporate contributions PRIM CORP EMPL community affairs manager: Sempra Energy.

Grants Analysis

Disclosure Period: calendar year ending
Typical Range: $1,000 to $50,000

SENTINEL COMMUNICATIONS CO.

Company Contact

Orlando, FL

Company Description

Employees: 1,400
SIC(s): 2711 Newspapers, 2752 Commercial Printing--Lithographic.
Parent Company: Tribune Co.

Nonmonetary Support

Value: $385,000 (1995)
Type: Cause-related Marketing & Promotion; Donated Equipment; Donated Products; In-kind Services; Loaned Employees

Corporate Sponsorship

Type: Arts & cultural events; Festivals/fairs

Orlando Sentinel Charities Fund

Giving Contact

Cindy Spraker, Community Relations Manager
Sentinel Communications Co.
633 North Orange Avenue, MP68
Orlando, FL 32801-1349
Phone: (407)420-5591
Fax: (407)420-5758

Description

Organization Type: Corporate Foundation
Giving Locations: FL: Central Florida
Grant Types: Capital, Employee Matching Gifts, General Support, Project.
Note: Employee matching gift ratio: 2 to 1.

Financial Summary

Total Giving: Contributes through corporate direct giving program and foundation.
Assets: $1,600,000 (1995 approx); $1,200,000 (1994 approx); $1,100,000 (1993 approx)

Typical Recipients

Arts & Humanities: History & Archaeology
Civic & Public Affairs: African American Affairs, Housing, Safety, Urban & Community Affairs, Women's Affairs
Education: Colleges & Universities, Community & Junior Colleges, Journalism/Media Education, Literacy, Public Education (Precollege)
Environment: Environment-General
Health: Health Organizations, Hospices, Public Health
International: International Organizations
Religion: Jewish Causes, Religious Welfare
Social Services: Child Welfare, Community Service Organizations, Family Services, Food/Clothing Distribution, Homes, People with Disabilities, Senior Services, Shelters/Homelessness, Social Services-General, United Funds/United Ways, Youth Organizations

Contributions Analysis

Education: Supports adult literacy programs; and programs for school-age students that are independent of publicschools.
Health: Funding goes to programs designed to help and encourage people living with a physical or mental disability.
Social Services: Supports programs and protective services designed to improve the well-being and living conditions for senior citizens; and that enable the elderly to remain independent, productive citizens. Funding goes to programs that strengthen or support the family stucture; abuse prevention and intervention programs; and parenting education programs. Supports food banks and programs that support community hunger relief; and shelter programs that help individuals and families break the cycle of homelessness to become productive members of society.
Note: Grants are also made from The Orlando Sentinel Santa Children's Fund to organizations providing basic necessities and program services for children in the following areas: toys and holiday gifts for needy children ages 12 and under; food shelter and clothing for needy children; physical or sexual abuse pevention; recreation for children with special needs; drug and alcohol abuse prevention; prgrams for children considered to be at-risk as a result of physical, emotional, economic or environmental disadvatage; child care for economicallydisadvantaged; and programs that provide medical assistance to impoverished children.

Application Procedures

Initial Contact: a brief letter of inquiry
Application Requirements: a description of organization, amount requested, purpose of funds sought, and proof of tax-exempt status
Deadlines: for Orlando Sentinel Charities Fund: March 1; for Sentinel Santa Fund: August 15
Evaluative Criteria: long-term, positive impact on community; reflect racial and cultural diversity of citizens; meet the needs of targeted and under-served populations
Decision Notification: for Orlando Sentinel Charities Fund, in August or October; for Sentinel Santa Fund, in December or February

Restrictions

Typically does not make grants for administrative salaries and personnel costs; legal aid societies; political, advocacy or lobbying groups; groups that have received more than three annual consecutive grants; sponsorships or promotional activities; religious organizations for sectarian purposes; individuals; medical treatment programs; medical or health-related organizations; or capital requests for building or major improvements.

Additional Information

No less than 95% of the Sentinel Santa funding will be directed to programs for children ages 12 and younger. Up to 5% may be directed to programs for children ages 15 and under.
In 1990, the Robert R. McCormick Tribune Foundation began supplementing both the Orlando Sentinel Charities Fund and the Sentinel Santa Fund.
Publications: Guidelines; Annual Report

Corporate Officials

John Puerner: president, chief executive officer B 1952. PRIM CORP EMPL president, chief executive officer: Sentinel Communications Co. ADD CORP EMPL vice president, director marketing & development: Chicago Tribune Co.; president, publisher: Orlando Sentinel; president, chief executive officer: Orlando Sentinel Communications Co.

Giving Program Officials

Cindy Spraker: community relations manager

Grants Analysis

Disclosure Period: calendar year ending
Typical Range: $2,500 to $25,000

Recent Grants

Note: Grants derived from 1993 grants list.

Arts & Humanities

12,000 Orange County Historical Society, Orlando, FL

Civic & Public Affairs

22,500 Junior League of Orlando, Winter Park, Orlando, FL
10,000 Association to Preserve Eatonville Community, Eatonville, FL
10,000 Habitat for Humanity, Seminole
10,000 Homes In Partnership, Apopka, FL
8,500 Women's Residential and Counseling Center, Orlando, FL
5,000 Central Florida Crime Line Program, Orlando, FL
5,000 Seminole County Better Living, Longwood, FL
3,500 Foundation for Osceola Foundation
2,200 East Orange Community Action, Orlando, FL

Education

6,000 Valencia Community College Displaced Homemakers, Valencia, FL
4,000 Adult Literacy League, Orlando, FL

Health

10,000 Guardian Care, Orlando, FL

International

2,500 Rotary International

Religion

15,000 Christian Service Center
10,000 Catholic Social Services
10,000 Jewish Community Center

Social Services

35,000 Coalition for the Homeless, Orlando, FL
14,700 B.E.T.A.
11,500 House Next Door, De Land, FL
10,000 Friends of CITE, Orlando, FL
10,000 Lake County Association for Retarded Citizens, Leesburg, FL
10,000 Parent Resource Center
8,215 Boys and Girls Clubs of Central Florida, Orlando, FL
5,000 Osceola County Council on Aging, Kissimmee, FL
5,000 Rainbow Charitable Services, Orlando, FL
2,130 Citrus Council of Girl Scouts, Winter Park, FL

SENTRY INSURANCE, AMUTUAL CO.

Company Contact

Stevens Point, WI
Web: http://www.sentry-insurance.com

Company Description

Assets: US$3,032,000,000
Profit: US$188,000,000
Employees: 4,314
SIC(s): 6311 Life Insurance.

Nonmonetary Support

Note: Undisclosed amounts of nonmonetary support are given by the company.

Sentry Insurance Foundation Inc.

Giving Contact

Marg Coker-Nelson, Executive Director, Vice President
Sentry Insurance A Mutual Co.
1800 N Point Dr.
Stevens Point, WI 54481
Phone: (715)346-6000
Fax: (715)346-6405

Description

EIN: 391037370
Organization Type: Corporate Foundation
Giving Locations: nationally; areas with large employee populations.
Grant Types: Employee Matching Gifts, General Support, Scholarship.

Financial Summary

Total Giving: $639,549 (1998); $639,686 (1997); $655,815 (1996). Note: Contributes through foundation only.
Giving Analysis: Giving for 1997 includes: foundation grants to United Way ($112,800)
Assets: $2,016,989 (1998); $1,846,335 (1997); $5,331 (1996)
Gifts Received: $670,750 (1998); $2,510,155 (1997); $652,928 (1996). Note: Contributions are received from Sentry Insurance, A Mutual Co.

Typical Recipients

Arts & Humanities: Arts Associations & Councils, Community Arts, History & Archaeology, Libraries, Music, Public Broadcasting, Theater
Civic & Public Affairs: Business/Free Enterprise, Chambers of Commerce, Clubs, Community Foundations, Employment/Job Training, Civic & Public Affairs-General, Housing, Public Policy, Urban & Community Affairs
Education: Business Education, Colleges & Universities, Community & Junior Colleges, Economic Education, Education Funds, Engineering/Technological Education, Education-General, Gifted & Talented Programs, Minority Education, Private Education (Precollege), Public Education (Precollege), Religious Education, Science/Mathematics Education,

Secondary Education (Private), Secondary Education (Public), Student Aid
Environment: Environment-General, Wildlife Protection
Health: Cancer, Health Organizations, Heart, Hospitals, Medical Research, Public Health
International: Health Care/Hospitals
Religion: Religious Organizations, Religious Welfare, Seminaries
Social Services: Animal Protection, At-Risk Youth, Camps, Community Service Organizations, Delinquency & Criminal Rehabilitation, People with Disabilities, Recreation & Athletics, Scouts, Special Olympics, Substance Abuse, United Funds/United Ways, Veterans, YMCA/YWCA/YMHA/YWHA, Youth Organizations

Contributions Analysis

Arts & Humanities: 33%. Matches employee gifts.
Civic & Public Affairs: About 13%.
Education: 30%.
Health: 2%.
Social Services: 18%. Supports the United Way.
Note: Analysis provided by foundation. Total contributions in 1998.

Application Procedures

Initial Contact: Send letter of request.
Application Requirements: Include description of program and amount of contribution sought.
Deadlines: None.

Corporate Officials

William J. (Bill) Lohr: vice president financen resources PRIM CORP EMPL vice president finance: Sentry Insurance A Mutual Co. CORP AFFIL treasurer: Sentry Fund Inc.; treasurer: Sentry Life Insurance Co.
Greg Mox: vice president human resources PRIM CORP EMPL vice president human resources: Sentry Insurance, A Mutual Co.
Dale R. Schuh: president, chief executive officer ED Lawrence University. PRIM CORP EMPL president, chief executive officer: Sentry Insurance, A Mutual Co. CORP AFFIL chairman: Sentry Life Insurance Co.

Foundation Officials

William R. Beversdorf: vice president PRIM CORP EMPL vice president human resources: Sentry Insurance A Mutual Co.
Marg Coker-Nelson: executive director, vice president
William J. (Bill) Lohr: treasurer (see above)
Greg Mox: president, director (see above)
Bill O'Reilly: secretary, treasurer

Grants Analysis

Disclosure Period: calendar year ending 1998
Total Grants: $178,855*
Number of Grants: 41
Average Grant: $4,362
Highest Grant: $60,000
Typical Range: $100 to $10,000
***Note:** Giving excludes matching gifts, scholarship, and United Way.

Recent Grants

Note: Grants derived from 1998 Form 990.

Arts & Humanities

3,100	Central Wisconsin Symphony Orchestra, Stevens Point, WI
500	American Players Theatre, Spring Green, WI
500	Portage County Historical Society, Stevens Point, WI

Civic & Public Affairs

10,000	Stevens Point/Plover Area Chamber Foundation, Inc, Stevens Point, WI
5,000	Wisconsin Manufacturers & Commerce, Madison, WI
2,500	Community Foundation of Portage County, Stevens Point, WI
1,080	Wisconsin Taxpayers Alliance, Milwaukee, WI
750	Project Equality of Wisconsin, Milwaukee, WI
500	Central Wisconsin Habitat for Humanity, Stevens Point, WI
500	Wisconsin Lions Foundation, Inc, Rosholt, WI

Education

56,000	University of Wisconsin Stevens Point Foundation, Stevens Point, WI
25,000	Wisconsin Foundation of Independent Colleges, Milwaukee, WI
16,000	University of Wisconsin Eau Claire Foundation, Eau Claire, WI
16,000	University of Wisconsin Oshkosh Foundation, Osh Kosh, WI
16,000	University of Wisconsin Whitewater Foundation, Whitewater, WI
14,000	University of Wisconsin Green Bay Foundation, Green Bay, WI
14,000	University of Wisconsin Stevens Point Foundation, Stevens Point, WI
12,000	Lawrence University, Appleton, WI
11,000	Drake University, Des Moines, IA
10,000	University of Wisconsin Platteville Foundation, Platteville, WI
3,000	Insurance Education Foundation, Indianapolis, IN
3,000	Portage County Junior Achievement, Stevens Point, WI
2,000	University of Wisconsin Madison Foundation, Madison, WI
1,750	Wisconsin Center for Academically Talented Youth, Madison, WI
1,000	Mid-State Technical College, Wisconsin Rapids, WI
1,000	Wisconsin Council on Economic Education, Milwaukee, WI
700	University of Wisconsin Actuarial Science, Madison, WI
500	Junior Achievement of Arizona, Phoenix, AZ
500	Pacelli High School, Stevens Point, WI
500	United Negro College Fund, Milwaukee, WI
500	Wisconsin Academic Decathlon, Green Bay, WI
400	Evans Scholarship Foundation, Golf, IL

Health

5,000	Marshfield Medical Research, Marshfield, WI
2,500	St Michaels Foundation, Stevens Point, WI
1,675	Vince Lombardi Cancer Fund, Clark, NJ
500	American Heart Association, Milwaukee, WI

Religion

1,000	Fellowship of Christian Athletes, Marshfield, WI

Social Services

109,500	United Way of Portage County, Stevens Point, WI
60,000	Portage County YMCA, Stevens Point, WI
7,500	Rawhide, New London, WI
2,500	United Way of Richmond, Virginia, Richmond, VA
2,500	Wisconsin Special Olympics, Milwaukee, WI
1,000	Portage County Humane Society, Stevens Point, WI
700	Sentry Cares, Stevens Point, WI
500	Boys & Girls Club, Milwaukee, WI
500	Camp Hope, Stevens Point, WI
500	Home-Free, Stevens Point, WI
250	United Way of Central New York, Syracuse, NY
250	United Way of Greater Milwaukee, Milwaukee, WI
250	United Way of Minneapolis Area, Minneapolis, MN

SERVCO PACIFIC

Company Contact

Honolulu, HI

Company Description

Employees: 930
SIC(s): 5013 Motor Vehicle Supplies & New Parts, 5044 Office Equipment, 5064 Electrical Appliances--Television & Radio, 5112 Stationery & Office Supplies, 5511 New & Used Car Dealers.

Servco Foundation

Giving Contact

Sandra C. H. Wong, Corporate Secretary
PO Box 2788
Honolulu, HI 96803
Phone: (808)521-6511

Description

Founded: 1986
EIN: 990248256
Organization Type: Corporate Foundation
Giving Locations: HI nationally;.

Financial Summary

Total Giving: $210,000 (fiscal year ending June 30, 2000 approx); $260,000 (fiscal 1999 approx); $210,574 (fiscal 1998)
Giving Analysis: Giving for fiscal 1998 includes: foundation ($210,574)
Assets: $5,477,027 (fiscal 1998); $4,229,730 (fiscal 1996); $3,578,676 (fiscal 1995)
Gifts Received: $4,807 (fiscal 1992). Note: In fiscal 1992, contributions were received from Servco Pacific, Inc.

Typical Recipients

Arts & Humanities: Ballet, Ethnic & Folk Arts, Arts & Humanities-General, Museums/Galleries, Theater
Civic & Public Affairs: African American Affairs, Asian American Affairs, Civic & Public Affairs-General, Parades/Festivals
Education: Agricultural Education, Arts/Humanities Education, Business Education, Colleges & Universities, Community & Junior Colleges, Education-General, Gifted & Talented Programs, International Studies, Private Education (Precollege), Public Education (Precollege)
Health: Cancer, Clinics/Medical Centers, Diabetes, Emergency/Ambulance Services, Health-General, Heart, Hospitals, Medical Rehabilitation, Single-Disease Health Associations
International: Foreign Educational Institutions, International-General, International Relations
Religion: Churches, Religion-General, Religious Welfare, Synagogues/Temples
Social Services: Big Brother/Big Sister, Child Abuse, Community Centers, Community Service Organizations, Family Services, Food/Clothing Distribution, Scouts, Social Services-General, Substance Abuse, United Funds/United Ways, Veterans, YMCA/YWCA/YMHA/YWHA, Youth Organizations

Application Procedures

Initial Contact: Send a brief letter of inquiry. For scholarship requests, write for formal application.
Application Requirements: Include information on the purpose of funds sought, and proof of tax-exempt 501(c)(3) status.
Deadlines: None.

Restrictions
The foundation does not provide funds to political or lobbying groups.

Additional Information
Awards scholarships for higher education to spouses and children of Servco Pacific employees.

Corporate Officials
Mark H. Fukunaga: chief executive officer, chairman B Honolulu, HI. ED Pomona College (1978); University of Chicago JD (1982). PRIM CORP EMPL chief executive officer, chairman: Servco Pacific Inc. CORP AFFIL chairman, chief executive officer: Pola Cosmetics; chairman, chief executive officer: Service Motors; chairman, chief executive officer: Film Services Hawaii; chairman, chief executive officer: Motor Imports.

Foundation Officials
Patrick D. Ching: treasurer
Eric S. Fukunaga: president, director PRIM CORP EMPL president, chief operating officer: Servco Pacific Inc.
Mark H. Fukunaga: chairman, director (see above)
Jean H. Nakagawa: vice president, director B Honolulu, HI 1943. ED University of Hawaii (1965); University of Hawaii (1968). PRIM CORP EMPL executive vice president research & planning, director: Servco Pacific Inc. CORP AFFIL director: Servco Fin Corp. NONPR AFFIL member: Pacific Asian Affairs Council; member: Planning Executives Institute; member: Organization Women Leaders; member: Hawaii Economic Association; member: Hawaii Society Corp. Planners; director: American Red Cross; member devel committeem: Hawaii Baptist Academy; member: American Marketing Association.
George S. Sakurai: vice president, director
Sandra C. H. Wong: secretary

Grants Analysis
Disclosure Period: fiscal year ending June 30, 1998
Total Grants: $210,574
Typical Range: $100 to $6,000

Recent Grants
Note: Grants derived from fiscal 1996 Form 990.

Arts & Humanities

6,000	Contemporary Arts Museum, Honolulu, HI
5,000	Japanese American National Museum, Honolulu, HI
2,000	Hawaii Children's Museum, Honolulu, HI
2,000	Hawaii Theater Center, Honolulu, HI

Civic & Public Affairs

8,500	Japanese Cultural Center of Hawaii, Honolulu, HI
2,000	First Night Honolulu, Honolulu, HI

Education

11,000	University of Hawaii Foundation, Honolulu, HI
4,000	Honolulu Academy of Arts, Honolulu, HI
2,500	Hawaii Baptist Academy, Honolulu, HI

Health

2,500	American Red Cross Hawaii Chapter, Honolulu, HI
2,000	Kuakini Medical Center, Honolulu, HI

Religion

5,000	Harris United Methodist Church, Honolulu, HI

Social Services

10,000	Aloha United Way, Honolulu, HI
3,000	Boy Scouts of America Aloha Council, Honolulu, HI
2,500	Palama Settlement, Honolulu, HI
2,000	Big Brothers and Big Sisters, Honolulu, HI
2,000	Child and Family Services, Honolulu, HI
2,000	Prevent Child Abuse Hawaii, Honolulu, HI
2,000	Susannah Wesley Community Center, Honolulu, HI
2,000	YWCA, Honolulu, HI

ServiceMaster Co.

Company Contact
Downers Grove, IL
Web: http://www.servicemaster.com

Company Description
Revenue: US$5,703,500,000 (1999)
Profit: US$173,000,000 (1999)
Employees: 51,740 (1999)
Fortune Rank: 295, per FORTUNE Magazine's list of 500 Largest U.S. Corporations (1999).
FF 295
SIC(s): 0782 Lawn & Garden Services, 7217 Carpet & Upholstery Cleaning, 7299 Miscellaneous Personal Services Nec, 8741 Management Services.

Nonmonetary Support
Type: Donated Products

ServiceMaster Foundation

Giving Contact
Claire Buchan, Vice President, Corporate Communications
1 ServiceMaster Way
Downers Grove, IL 60515
Phone: (708)271-1300

Alternate Contact
Jean McGuffey, Secretary to the Chairman.

Description
Founded: 1987
EIN: 363529559
Organization Type: Corporate Foundation. Supports preselected organizations only.
Giving Locations: headquarters area only.
Grant Types: General Support.

Financial Summary
Total Giving: $277,000 (1996); $223,000 (1993); $125,450 (1992)
Assets: $4,467,042 (1996); $942,313 (1993); $509,527 (1992)
Gifts Received: $377,827 (1993); $246,440 (1992); $132,820 (1991)

Typical Recipients
Arts & Humanities: Arts & Humanities-General
Civic & Public Affairs: Business/Free Enterprise, Clubs, Employment/Job Training, Civic & Public Affairs-General, Inner-City Development, Public Policy, Urban & Community Affairs, Women's Affairs
Education: Colleges & Universities, Education-General, Private Education (Precollege), Religious Education, Secondary Education (Public)
Environment: Environment-General
Health: Health-General
International: Foreign Educational Institutions, Health Care/Hospitals, International Organizations, International Relief Efforts, Missionary/Religious Activities
Religion: Churches, Ministries, Religious Welfare
Social Services: Community Service Organizations, Family Services, Social Services-General, Youth Organizations

Contributions Analysis
Giving Priorities: The foundation supports international missionary activities, international development and relief, and other international organizations. Overseas operating locations make contributions from their own budgets. These contributions are generally small and are not coordinated through corporate headquarters except for reporting purposes.

Corporate Officials
Carlos H. Cantu: president, chief executive officer, director PRIM CORP EMPL president, chief executive officer, director: ServiceMaster Co.
Ernest J. Mrozek: executive vice president, chief financial officer B Chicago, IL 1953. ED University of Illinois BS (1976). PRIM CORP EMPL executive vice president, chief financial officer: ServiceMaster Co. NONPR AFFIL member: American Institute CPAs; member: Financial Executives Institute.
Charles William Pollard, Jr.: chairman, director B Chicago, IL 1938. ED Wheaton College BA (1960); Northwestern University JD (1963). PRIM CORP EMPL chairman, director: ServiceMaster Co. CORP AFFIL director: Provident Life & Accident Insurance Co.; director: Herman Miller. NONPR AFFIL director: Wheaton College.
Charles W. Stair: vice chairman international, director PRIM CORP EMPL vice chairman international, director: ServiceMaster Co.

Foundation Officials
Kenneth N. Hansen: director
Robert F. Keith: treasurer B 1956. PRIM CORP EMPL president: ServiceMaster Consumer Services Co.
Charles William Pollard, Jr.: president, director (see above)
Vernon T. Squires: vice president, secretary PRIM CORP EMPL senior vice president, general counsel: ServiceMaster Co.

Grants Analysis
Disclosure Period: calendar year ending 1996
Total Grants: $277,000
Number of Grants: 15
Average Grant: $10,143*
Highest Grant: $135,000
Typical Range: $3,000 to $25,000
***Note:** Average grant figure excludes highest grant.

Recent Grants
Note: Grants derived from 1996 Form 990.

Civic & Public Affairs

10,000	Americans United for Life, Chicago, IL
10,000	Pioneer Clubs, Wheaton, IL
7,000	Koinonia House, HI

Education

135,000	Northwestern University, Evanston, IL
20,000	Russian-American Christian University, Silver Spring, MD
10,000	Calvin College, Grand Rapids, MI
5,000	Circle Rock Academy, Chicago, IL
5,000	Eastern College, Saint Davids, PA

International

25,000	MAP International, Wheaton, IL
25,000	MAP International, Wheaton, IL
10,000	English Language Institute of China, San Dimas, CA
10,000	English Language Institute of China, San Dimas, CA
10,000	Operation Mobilization Ships, Peachtree, GA
10,000	Operation Mobilization Ships, Peachtree, GA
5,000	International Aid, Spring Lake, MI
5,000	International Aid, Spring Lake, MI

Religion

10,000	Outreach Community Ministries
5,000	Lawndale Christian Development, Chicago, IL

Social Services

10,000	Drucker Foundation, New York, NY

7-ELEVEN, INC.

Company Contact

Dallas, TX

Company Description

Former Name: Southland Corp. (1999).
Employees: 32,368 (1999)
SIC(s): 5411 Grocery Stores, 5999 Miscellaneous Retail Stores Nec.
Parent Company: Ito-Yokado Co. Ltd., 1-4, Shibakoen 4-chome Minato-ku, Tokyo, Japan

Operating Locations

CA: Southland Corp.; Southland Corp., San Diego; CO: Southland Corp., Denver; CT: Southland Corp.; DC: Southland Corp.; DE: Southland Corp.; FL: Southland Corp., Orlando; IL: Southland Corp.; IN: Southland Corp.; KS: Southland Corp.; MA: Southland Corp.; MI: Southland Corp., Novi; MO: Southland Corp.; NC: Southland Corp.; NH: Southland Corp.; NJ: Southland Corp., Great Meadows; NV: Southland Corp., Las Vegas; NY: Southland Corp., Smithtown; OH: Southland Corp.; PA: Southland Corp., Willow Grove; RI: Southland Corp.; TX: 7-Eleven Stores, Dallas; Central Division, Dallas; Southland Corp., Dallas; Southland Corp., Dallas; UT: Southland Corp., Salt Lake City; VA: Atlantic Division, Alexandria; Southland Corp., Virginia Beach; WI: Southland Corp.; WV: Southland Corp.

Nonmonetary Support

Value: $3,000,000 (1996)
Type: Cause-related Marketing & Promotion; Donated Products; Loaned Executives; Workplace Solicitation

Corporate Sponsorship

Note: Sponsors reading-related events.

Giving Contact

Sharon Neal, Manager, Community Affairs
The Southland Corp.
2711 North Haskell Avenue
Dallas, TX 75204
Phone: (214)828-7480
Fax: (214)828-7090
Web: http://www.7-eleven.com

Description

Organization Type: Corporate Giving Program
Former Name: Southland Corp. (1999).
Giving Locations: TX: Dallas operating locations.
Grant Types: General Support, Project.

Giving Philosophy

'Since its founding, the company has provided assistance to a variety of health and social welfare, educational, community and cultural programs both nationally and through 7-Eleven stores in neighborhoods throughout the country.

'Southland's attitude toward community involvement parallels its merchandising strategy of anticipating and responding promptly to customers' needs. As a part of their neighborhood, 7-Eleven stores have an active, people-to-people interest in the communities where they are located.

'We believe 'doing business' means more than selling merchandise 24 hours a day. It means being involved and doing our part as a good neighbor to help better the community in whatever way we can.

'It means caring about people and demonstrating that concern through the quality of all our actions. It means doing what we can to assure that our neighbors, our customers and our employees and franchisees will be able to increase the opportunities available to their children.

'We believe that every one of us was helped by and learned from those who came before us. It is our privilege rather than our obligation to extend a hand to our neighbors through our contributions and volunteer activities in order to build a better future together.'
The Southland Corporation Community Contributions Guidelines

Financial Summary

Total Giving: $6,393,243 (1998 approx); $750,000 (1997 approx); $3,750,000 (1996 approx). Note: Contributes through corporate direct giving program only.
Giving Analysis: Giving for 1996 includes: nonmonetary support ($3,000,000); corporate direct giving ($750,000); 1997: corporate direct giving ($750,000); 1998: nonmonetary support ($4,814,877); domestic subsidiaries ($1,008,205); corporate direct giving ($570,161)

Typical Recipients

Arts & Humanities: Arts & Humanities-General
Civic & Public Affairs: Civic & Public Affairs-General
Education: Education-General, Literacy
Social Services: Social Services-General

Contributions Analysis

Civic & Public Affairs: Supports education, arts, and other programs that recognize the rich cultural diversity of company communities and promote better understanding among cultures throughout America. A specific interest is in projects and programs that serve ethnic and inner-city constituents. Supports community-based organizations. In addition to other activities, several geographic divisions of the 7-Eleven stores sponsor the 'People Who Read Achieve' campaign, a campaign that addresses literacy issues. Goals of the program are to raise awareness of the literacy problem and to support nonprofit groups that promote literacy. Crime prevention is also supported through Operation Chill: law enforcement officers award coupons for free slurpee drinks to young people exhibiting positive behavior.
Education: Supports programs that promote literacy as a key to economic empowerment, personal betterment, and self-sufficiency. Also supports programs that encourage English skills for those for whom English is a second language.

Application Procedures

Initial Contact: Call (800) 711-1FAX, to request guidelines (document 906), then written proposal.
Application Requirements: Send brief description of project or event for which you are requesting funds; anticipated outcomes; project budget and amount requested; population served; project timetable; organization's officers, key staff, and directors, including affiliations; proof of tax-exempt status; and a description of how organization will acknowledge Southland/7-Eleven support.
Deadlines: None; decisions are generally made within forty-five days of receipt of application
Notes: Video and audio tapes are not accepted.

Restrictions

Does not make political contributions.
Giving generally is restricted to a specific project, program, or event rather than to general operating support, capital, or endowment campaigns.
Also does not support individuals, scholarship funds, conventions, advertising, journals, social and fundraising events, or organizations that discriminate on the basis of race, religion, sex, or national origin.
Company typically does not make multiyear commitments and giving is subject to annual review and evaluation.

Additional Information

Ito-Yokado Co. Ltd. has a 64% investment in the Southland Corp. The Southland Corp. conducts business principally under the name 7-Eleven.
Publications: Contributions Guidelines

Corporate Officials

James W. Keyes: executive vice president, chief operating officerc B Passaic, NJ 1941. PRIM CORP EMPL executive vice president, chief operating officer: Southland Corp.
Clark J. Matthews, II: president, chief executive officer, director B Arkansas City, KS 1936. ED Southern Methodist University BA (1959); Southern Methodist University JD (1961). PRIM CORP EMPL president, chief executive officer, director: Southland Corp. ADD CORP EMPL president: 7 Eleven Inc.; president: 7 Eleven Sales Corp. NONPR AFFIL member: Pi Alpha Delta; member: Texas Bar Association; member: American Judicature Society; member: Dallas Bar Association; member: Alpha Tau Omega; member: American Bar Association. CLUB AFFIL DeMolay Club.

Giving Program Officials

Sharon Neal: PRIM CORP EMPL manager community affairs: Southland Corp.

Grants Analysis

Disclosure Period: calendar year ending
Typical Range: $500 to $2,000

SHAKLEE CORP.

Company Contact

San Francisco, CA
Web: http://www.shaklee.com

Company Description

Employees: 1,850
SIC(s): 2023 Dry, Condensed & Evaporated Dairy Products, 2834 Pharmaceutical Preparations, 2841 Soap & Other Detergents, 2842 Polishes & Sanitation Goods.
Parent Company: Yamanouchi Pharmaceutical Co. Ltd., 3-11 Nihonbashi-Honcho, 2-chome, Chuo-ku, Tokyo, Japan

Operating Locations

CA: Shaklee U.S., La Palma; Shaklee Corp., San Francisco; Shaklee U.S., San Francisco; Shaklee U.S., San Francisco; IL: Shaklee U.S., Bedford Park; NJ: Shaklee U.S., Dayton; NY: Yamanouchi U.S.A., White Plains; OR: Bear Creek Corp., Medford; Bear Creek Gardens, Medford; Bear Creek Stores, Medford; Harry and David, Medford; Jackson & Perkins, Medford; Shaklee U.S., Medford; Orchids Etc., Milwaukie

Nonmonetary Support

Value: $99,390 (1996); $59,192 (1995); $63,869 (1994)
Type: Donated Equipment; Donated Products; In-kind Services; Loaned Employees
Note: 1997 nonmonetary support $135,495. Nonmonetary support is provided through the foundation.

Corporate Sponsorship

Range: less than $300,000
Type: Sports events
Note: Sponsors educational events.

Shaklee Cares

Giving Contact

Karin Topping, Director, Public Relations
Shaklee U.S.
4747 Willow Road
Pleasanton, CA 94588
Phone: (925)924-2000
Fax: (925)924-2862
Email: ktopping@aol.com
Note: Ms. topping may be reached at extension 2007.

Description

Organization Type: Corporate Foundation
Giving Locations: principally near operating locations and to national organizations.
Grant Types: Award, Employee Matching Gifts, General Support, Matching, Multiyear/Continuing Support, Project, Scholarship.

Giving Philosophy

'Shaklee Corporation is committed to improving society in the communities in which company employees live and work. The Company believes that business should share the responsibility for bettering the community and demonstrates and encourages this commitment through philanthropic activities in the areas of health, art and culture, welfare, civic activities and higher education.' Community Involvement, Shaklee Corporation

Financial Summary

Total Giving: $500,000 (fiscal year ending March 31, 1999 approx); $490,000 (fiscal 1996). Note: Contributes through corporate direct giving program and foundation.
Assets: $89,052 (fiscal 1997); $56,604 (fiscal 1996); $32,071 (fiscal 1995)
Gifts Received: $213,759 (fiscal 1997); $164,447 (fiscal 1996); $98,372 (fiscal 1995). Note: Contributions received from Shaklee Corp. and individuals.

Typical Recipients

Arts & Humanities: Museums/Galleries, Music, Opera, Performing Arts
Civic & Public Affairs: Business/Free Enterprise, Zoos/Aquariums
Education: Colleges & Universities, Education Funds, Health & Physical Education, Student Aid
Environment: Environment-General
Health: Nutrition
International: International Relief Efforts
Social Services: Emergency Relief, Food/Clothing Distribution, Recreation & Athletics, United Funds/United Ways, Youth Organizations

Contributions Analysis

Giving Priorities: Health and fitness, art and culture, and education.
Arts & Humanities: 10% to 15%. Funding emphasizes the performing arts.
Civic & Public Affairs: About 5%.
Education: About 10%. Supports colleges, universities, and independent college funds; also offers scholarships to children of company employees and sales leaders, and matches employee contributions to educational institutions and charitable organizations.
Health: About 65%. This is the highest priority, with contributions allocated for health promotion, nutrition, and physical fitness, as well as environmental wellness. Also funds annual federated drives supporting human service agencies, such as united funds, youth organizations, and food banks.
International: 15% to 20%. Contributions go to U.S.-based nonprofit organizations with an international focus.

Application Procedures

Initial Contact: Submit a typewritten letter no longer than two pages.
Application Requirements: Include a description of the organization with history, function, goals, and objectives; description and specific objectives of current program or project for which funds are being requested; amount requested, specific uses for grant, and benefits expected; geographic area and persons served by organization, program, or project.
Deadlines: None.
Review Process: If initial staff review is promising; a full proposal and formal application will be requested.
Evaluative Criteria: Organizations requesting grants must have proof of IRS 501(c)(3) status, serve a broad group of people in a geographic area where employees and their families can derive direct benefits; have adequate staff of professional personnel; show evidence of volunteer support; report regularly to a board of directors; and provide evidence of financial responsibility and operating integrity, including the use of proper fundraising and control of administrative costs.
Decision Notification: The contributions committee meets quarterly.
Notes: Applications for disaster relief from Shaklee Cares are accepted anytime; contact foundation by letter.

Restrictions

Contributions generally not considered for individuals (except through Shaklee Cares); research; capital or building funds; sectarian or religious institutions that do not serve the general public on a nondenominational basis; political groups; conferences or seminars; fraternal orders, veterans, or labor groups; contests, raffles, or prize-oriented events; goodwill advertising; or organizations primarily funded through united funds or federated campaigns.

Additional Information

Publications: Guidelines Sheet; Annual Report

Corporate Officials

Edward W. Beck: senior vice president, general counsel, secretary, director B Atchison, KS 1944. ED Yale University BA (1967); Harvard University JD (1972). PRIM CORP EMPL senior vice president, general counsel, secretary, director: Shaklee Corp. CORP AFFIL secretary: Harry David Co.; director: Bear Creek Corp. NONPR AFFIL member: San Francisco Yale Alumni Association; member law committee: United Way Bay Area Campaign; trustee, member executive committee: San Francisco Conservatory Music; member: San Francisco Bar Association; member: San Francisco Chamber of Commerce; member: California Bar Association; member: American Society of Corporate Secretaries; member: Bay Area General Counsel Group; member: American Corporate Counsel Association; member: American Bar Association.
Kay Childs: vice president human resources
Masa Inone: executive vice president
Charles Lee Orr: president, chief executive officer B Philadelphia, PA 1943. ED Wesleyan University BA (1965); University of Connecticut MBA (1969). PRIM CORP EMPL president, chief executive officer: Shaklee Corp.
James H. Whittam: executive vice president, Shaklee Companies PRIM CORP EMPL executive vice president: Shaklee Companies.

Giving Program Officials

Kay Childs: director (see above)
Masa Inone: director (see above)
Karin Topping: (see above)
James H. Whittam: director (see above)

Grants Analysis

Disclosure Period: fiscal year ending March 31, 1997
Typical Range: $1,000 to $10,000

Sharp Electronics Corp.

Company Contact

Mahwah, NJ
Web: http://sharp-usa.com

Company Description

Employees: 2,300
SIC(s): 3631 Household Cooking Equipment, 3651 Household Audio & Video Equipment, 5044 Office Equipment, 5064 Electrical Appliances--Television & Radio.
Parent Company: Sharp Corp. (Japan), 22-22, Nagaike-cho, Abeno-ku, Osaka, Japan

Operating Locations

CA: Sharp Electronics Corp., Carson; Sharp Digital Information Products Inc., Irvine; Perkins Corp., San Jose; Sharp Electronics Corp., San Jose; FL: Sharp Electronics Corp., Miami; GA: Sharp Electronics Corp., Southeast Regional Office, Lawrenceville; IL: Sharp Electronics Corp., Midwest Regional Office, Romeoville; MA: Sharp Electronics Corp., Burlington; NJ: Sharp Electronics Corp., Mahwah; Sharp Electronics Corp., Mahwah; NY: Icon Office Solutions, New York; TN: Sharp Manufacturing Co. of America, Memphis; TX: Sharp Electronics Corp., Dallas; VA: Sharp Electronics Corp., Alexandria; WA: Sharp Flat Display Manufacturing Co., Camas; Sharp Laboratories of America, Camas; Sharp Microelectronics Technology Inc., Camas

Giving Contact

Robert Garbutt, Vice President, Human Resources
1 Sharp Plz.
PO Box 650
Mahwah, NJ 07430
Phone: (201)529-8200
Fax: (201)529-8413

Description

Organization Type: Corporate Giving Program
Giving Locations: headquarters and operating communities.

Financial Summary

Total Giving: $385,000 (1994)

Typical Recipients

Education: Colleges & Universities
Social Services: Community Service Organizations, United Funds/United Ways, Youth Organizations

Application Procedures

Initial Contact: Initial contact may be a brief letter of inquiry; however, unsolicited requests are not encouraged.

Restrictions

Does not support individuals, religious organizations for sectarian purposes, or political or lobbying groups.

Corporate Officials

Barry Kay: chief financial officer, president, chief executive officer PRIM CORP EMPL chief financial officer: Sharp Electronics Corp.
Toshiahi Urushisako: chairman, president, chief executive officer PRIM CORP EMPL chairman, president, chief executive officer: Sharp Electronics Corp.

Grants Analysis

Disclosure Period: calendar year ending
Typical Range: $1,000 to $2,500

SHAW INDUSTRIES INC.

Company Contact

Dalton, GA

Company Description

Revenue: US$4,107,700,000 (1999)
Profit: US$228,000,000 (1999)
Fortune Rank: 387, per FORTUNE Magazine's list of 500 Largest U.S. Corporations (1999).
FF 387
SIC(s): 2273 Carpets & Rugs.

Nonmonetary Support

Type: Donated Equipment

Giving Contact

Carl Rollins, Vice President, Administration
Shaw Industries, Inc.
PO Box 2138
Dalton, GA 30722
Phone: (706)278-3812
Fax: (706)275-1129
Email: crollins@shawinc.com
Web: http://www.shawinc.com

Description

Organization Type: Corporate Giving Program
Giving Locations: headquarters and operating communities.
Grant Types: General Support.

Financial Summary

Total Giving: Contributes through corporate direct giving program only.

Typical Recipients

Arts & Humanities: Arts & Humanities-General
Civic & Public Affairs: Civic & Public Affairs-General
Education: Education-General
Health: Health-General
Social Services: Social Services-General

Application Procedures

Initial Contact: Send a brief letter of inquiry.
Application Requirements: Include a description of organization, amount requested, purpose of funds sought, and proof of tax-exempt status.
Deadlines: None.

Corporate Officials

Vance D. Bell: executive vice president operations PRIM CORP EMPL executive vice president operations: Shaw Industries Inc.
Kenneth G. Jackson: executive vice president, chief financial officer PRIM CORP EMPL executive vice president, chief financial officer: Shaw Industries Inc.
William Norris Little: vice chairman, director B Marshville, NC 1931. ED University of North Carolina (1955). PRIM CORP EMPL vice chairman, director: Shaw Industries Inc.
Julian D. Saul: president ED Georgia Institute of Technology BS (1962). PRIM CORP EMPL president: Shaw Industries Inc.
Julian D. Saul: president PRIM CORP EMPL president: Shaw Industries Inc.
Julius C. Shaw, Jr.: executive vice president corporate communications PRIM CORP EMPL executive vice president corporate communications: Shaw Industries Inc.
Robert E. Shaw: chairman, chief executive officer B Cartersville, GA 1931. ED University of the South. PRIM CORP EMPL chairman, chief executive officer: Shaw Industries Inc. CORP AFFIL director: Oxford Industries Inc.; president: Shaw Investments Inc.; chairman: Agricola Inc.

Giving Program Officials

Carl P. Rollins: vice president administration

SHAW'S SUPERMARKETS, INC.

Company Contact

East Bridgewater, MA
Web: http://www.shaws.com

Company Description

Employees: 17,800
SIC(s): 5411 Grocery Stores.
Parent Company: J. Sainsbury Plc, Stamford House, Stamford Street, London, England

Operating Locations

CT: Shaw's Supermarkets, Inc.; MA: Shaw's Supermarkets, Inc.; ME: Shaw's Supermarkets, Inc., Portland; NH: Shaw's Supermarkets, Inc.; NJ: Shaw's Supermarkets, East Bridgewater

Nonmonetary Support

Type: Donated Products

Shaw's Supermarkets Charitable Foundation

Giving Contact

Bernard J. Rogan, Corporate Communications Director
Shaw's Supermarkets, Inc.
140 Laurel Street
PO Box 600
East Bridgewater, MA 02333
Phone: (508)350-3316
Fax: (508)350-3112

Description

Founded: 1959
EIN: 016008389
Organization Type: Corporate Foundation
Giving Locations: CT; ME; MA; NH; RI headquarters and operating communities.
Grant Types: Capital, Challenge, General Support.

Giving Philosophy

'Since its founding in 1860, Shaw's Supermarkets, Inc. has understood that with the privilege of community membership and support comes responsibility; responsibility to act in the best interest of the community and to be active and helpful where it is most needed.
'Of particular importance to us are youth and social services, the arts, and education.
'Contributions are made on three levels: neighborhood, regional, and corporate.
'Neighborhood projects are those that have a direct effect on the quality of life in an individual store area, and are determined by the local store.
'Regional donations are for those projects that impact more than one store location area, and are determined by the management of Shaw's region offices (limited to $500 each).
'Contributions of over $500 are considered corporate donations and are coordinated through Shaw's corporate offices in East Bridgewater, Masschusetts.'

Financial Summary

Total Giving: $447,000 (fiscal year ending July 31, 1998); $501,583 (fiscal 1997); $211,150 (fiscal 1996). Note: Contributes through corporate direct giving program and foundation.
Giving Analysis: Giving for fiscal 1997 includes: foundation grants to United Way ($382,250); fiscal 1998: foundation grants to United Way ($288,000)
Assets: $1,531,686 (fiscal 1998); $1,588,550 (fiscal 1997); $1,755,234 (fiscal 1996)
Gifts Received: $300,000 (fiscal 1998); $250,000 (fiscal 1997); $250,000 (fiscal 1996). Note: Contributions are received from Shaw's Supermarkets.

Typical Recipients

Arts & Humanities: Arts Appreciation, Arts Associations & Councils, Arts Funds, Arts Outreach, Historic Preservation, History & Archaeology, Libraries, Museums/Galleries, Music, Public Broadcasting, Theater
Civic & Public Affairs: Business/Free Enterprise, Community Foundations, Economic Development, Civic & Public Affairs-General, Safety, Urban & Community Affairs, Zoos/Aquariums
Education: Colleges & Universities, Education Funds, Environmental Education, Secondary Education (Public)
Environment: Environment-General
Health: Children's Health/Hospitals, Clinics/Medical Centers, Emergency/Ambulance Services, Geriatric Health, Health Organizations, Hospitals, Nursing Services, Public Health, Single-Disease Health Associations
Science: Science Museums
Social Services: Child Welfare, Community Service Organizations, Food/Clothing Distribution, Recreation & Athletics, Senior Services, United Funds/ United Ways, YMCA/YWCA/YMHA/YWHA, Youth Organizations

Contributions Analysis

Giving Priorities: Contributions are directed toward the United Way, Second Hearvest Food Banks in New England, and capital development and scholarship programs. Store-based funding goes to non-profit youth service organizations, local activities, and neighborhood projects.
Arts & Humanities: 9%. Supports museums, libraries, and performing arts an arts fund, primarily in New England.
Civic & Public Affairs: 4%. Supports community development and civic organizations.
Health: 2%. Interests include hospitals, and other health organizations.
Science: 5%. Funds a science museum.
Social Services: 80%. Supports the United Way of New England, traditional youth organizations, community services, and Second Harvest Food Bank.
Note: Total contributions in fiscal 1998.

Application Procedures

Initial Contact: For regional requests in Maine, New Hampshire, Vermont and the Greater Boston area of Massachusetts, contact: Regional Vice President, Northern Region Office, Shaw's Supermarkets, Inc., P.O. Box 3566 Portland, ME 04104 For requests in Connecticut, Rhode Island and all other parts of Massachusetts, contact: Regional Vice President, Southern Region Office, Shaw's Supermarkets, Inc., P.O. Box 300 South Easton, MA 02375. For corporate funding, contact: Senior Vice President, Operations Shaw's Supermarkets, Inc., 140 Laurel St., East Bridgewater, MA 02333.
Application Requirements: Include proof of 501(c)(3) status and full description of event or cause with request.

Additional Information

Fleet Bank of Maine is the trust's corporate trustee.

Corporate Officials

David Brimner: chairman vice president administration, treasurer, director PRIM CORP EMPL chairman: Shaw's Supermarkets, Inc.
Ross McLaren: chief executive officer PRIM CORP EMPL chief executive officer: Shaw's Supermarkets, Inc.
Scott W. Ramsay: executive vice president administration, treasurer, director PRIM CORP EMPL executive vice president administration, treasurer, director:

Shaw's Supermarkets, Inc. ADD CORP EMPL treasurer: Shaw Equipment Corp.

Foundation Officials

Scott W. Ramsay: trustee (see above)

Grants Analysis

Disclosure Period: fiscal year ending July 31, 1998
Total Grants: $159,000*
Number of Grants: 31
Average Grant: $5,129
Highest Grant: $20,000
Typical Range: $1,000 to $10,000
***Note:** Giving excludes United Way.

Recent Grants

Note: Grants derived from 1998 Form 990.

Arts & Humanities

5,000 Center for Maine History Campaign, Portland, ME
5,000 Friends of Pembroke Libraries, Pembroke, MA
5,000 Friends of Pembroke Libraries, Pembroke, MA
5,000 Portland Museum of Art, Portland, MA
5,000 Young Audiences of Massachusetts, Cambridge, MA
3,000 Bangor Public Library, Bangor, ME
3,000 Plymouth Plantation, Plymouth, MA
3,000 Shaw's Supermarkets, Inc., East Bridgewater, MA
2,500 Children's Museum of Plymouth, Plymouth, MA
2,500 Mayor's Office of Cultural Affairs
2,000 Greater Hartford Arts Council, Hartford, CT

Civic & Public Affairs

10,000 Buttonwood Park Zoological Society, Inc.
5,000 East Bridgewater Fire Department
2,500 Brockton 21st Century Corporation, Brockton, MA

Health

5,000 Concord Hospital, Concord, NH
3,000 Community Nurse Association of Fairhaven, Fairhaven, MA

Science

20,000 Museum of Science, Boston, MA

Social Services

185,500 United Ways of New England, Boston, MA
40,000 United Way of Greater Portland, Portland, ME
10,000 Middleboro YMCA, Middleboro, MA
10,000 Old Colony YMCA, Middleboro, MA
10,000 YMCA of Greater New Bedford, New Bedford, MA
9,000 United Way of York County, Kennebunk, MA
7,500 UWCA/CHA, Hartford, CT
6,850 United Way of Merrimack County, Concord, NH
5,800 United Way of Mid-Coast Maine, Bath, MA
5,000 Casco Bay Regional YMCA, Portland, ME
5,000 New England Food Foundation, West Roxbury, MA
5,000 Northern York County Family YMCA, Biddeford, MA
5,000 South Norfolk County Association of Retarded Citizens, Inc., Westwood, MA
4,700 United Way of Androscoggin County, Lewrston, ME
4,000 Hockomock Area YMCA, North Attleboro, MA
3,500 United Way of Eastern Fairfield County, Bridgeport, CT
3,400 United Way of the Upper Valley, Lebanon, NH
3,000 Cheshire County YMCA, Keene, NH
3,000 Lakes Region United Way, Inc., Laconia, NH
2,800 United Way of the Upper Valley, Lebanon, NH
2,500 United Way of Mid-Maine, Inc., Waterville, MA
2,300 United Way of Kennebec Valley, Augusta, MA
2,100 Monadnock United Way, Keene, NH
2,100 United Way Northern New Hampshire, Berlin, NE
2,100 United Way of Southbridge, Southbridge, MA
2,000 Down East Family YMCA, Ellsworth, ME
2,000 Milestone House, Inc., Bridgewater, MA
1,800 Monadnock United Way, Keene, NH
1,800 United Way of Northern New Hampshire, Berlin, NH
1,750 United Way Central Naugatuck Valley, Watterbury, CT
1,750 United Way of Greater New Haven, New Haven, CT
1,750 United Way of Southeastern Conneticut, Gales Ferry, CT
1,750 United Way of Southington, Inc., Southington, CT
1,750 United Way West Central Connecticut, Bristol, CT

JOHN F. SHEA CO.

Company Contact

Walnut, CA

Company Description

SIC(s): 1622 Bridge, Tunnel & Elevated Highway, 1623 Water, Sewer & Utility Lines.

J. F. Shea Co. Foundation

Giving Contact

Ronald L. Lakey, Chief Financial Officer
J.F. Shea Co. Foundation
655 Brea Canyon Road
Walnut, CA 91789
Phone: (909)594-0941
Fax: (909)869-0849

Alternate Contact

Michelle Pennington

Description

Founded: 1967
EIN: 952554052
Organization Type: Corporate Foundation. Supports preselected organizations only.
Giving Locations: AZ; CA
Grant Types: General Support.

Financial Summary

Total Giving: $192,749 (1998); $184,040 (1997); $2,000,000 (1995 approx). Note: Contributes through corporate direct giving program and foundation.
Giving Analysis: Giving for 1995 includes: foundation ($1,130,147); corporate direct giving ($869,853); 1997: foundation ($181,540); foundation grants to United Way ($2,500); 1998: foundation ($189,249); foundation grants to United Way ($3,000)
Assets: $157,619 (1998); $286,537 (1997); $11,374 (1995)
Gifts Received: $2,776 (1998); $13,748 (1997); $745,634 (1995). Note: Contributions were received from John F. Shea Co.

Typical Recipients

Arts & Humanities: Ballet, Libraries, Museums/Galleries, Music, Public Broadcasting
Civic & Public Affairs: Business/Free Enterprise, Clubs, Economic Development, Employment/Job Training, Civic & Public Affairs-General, Hispanic Affairs, Housing, Law & Justice, Legal Aid, Professional & Trade Associations, Urban & Community Affairs, Women's Affairs
Education: Business Education, Colleges & Universities, Elementary Education (Public), Education-General, Private Education (Precollege), Public Education (Precollege), Science/Mathematics Education, Secondary Education (Private), Secondary Education (Public)
Environment: Environment-General
Health: Arthritis, Cancer, Children's Health/Hospitals, Emergency/Ambulance Services, Eyes/Blindness, Hospitals, Hospitals (University Affiliated), Kidney, Multiple Sclerosis, Nutrition, Single-Disease Health Associations, Speech & Hearing, Transplant Networks/Donor Banks
Religion: Churches, Dioceses, Missionary Activities (Domestic), Religious Organizations, Religious Welfare, Synagogues/Temples
Social Services: Animal Protection, Big Brother/Big Sister, Child Welfare, Community Service Organizations, Domestic Violence, People with Disabilities, Recreation & Athletics, Scouts, Senior Services, Shelters/Homelessness, Special Olympics, United Funds/United Ways, YMCA/YWCA/YMHA/YWHA, Youth Organizations

Contributions Analysis

Giving Priorities: Primary support for education and social services.
Arts & Humanities: 1%. Focus on museums, libraries, public broadcasting, and arts outreach.
Civic & Public Affairs: 3%. Women's affairs, community affairs, and job training receive support.
Education: 52%. Majority of funding supports school districts in California and Arizona.
Health: 8%. Supports single-disease health organizations, hospitals, and children's health.
Religion: 4%. Supports religious welfare and other religious organizations.
Social Services: 32%. Emphasis on United Way, youth organizations, domestic violence, and family services.
Note: Total contributions in 1998.

Restrictions

Does not support individuals.

Corporate Officials

Edmund H. Shea, Jr.: executive vice president PRIM CORP EMPL executive vice president: JF Shea Co. Inc. ADD CORP EMPL vice president: Shasta Electric Inc. CORP AFFIL director: Adac Laboratories.
John F. Shea: chief executive officer, director B 1927. PRIM CORP EMPL chief executive officer, director: Shasta Electric Inc. ADD CORP EMPL president, chief executive officer: John F Shea Co.

Foundation Officials

Ronald L. Lakey: secretary
Edmund H. Shea, Jr.: secretary (see above)
John F. Shea: president (see above)
Peter O. Shea: treasurer

Grants Analysis

Disclosure Period: calendar year ending 1998
Total Grants: $189,249*
Number of Grants: 49
Average Grant: $3,862
Highest Grant: $25,000
Typical Range: $250 to $10,000
***Note:** Giving excludes United Way.

Recent Grants

Note: Grants derived from 1998 Form 990.

Arts & Humanities

1,000 Kixe-Pbs, Los Angeles, CA
250 Friends of Banning Museum, Wilmington, CA

Civic & Public Affairs

2,500 Aasco, Inc., Sacramento, CA
2,500 Shasta County Women's Refuge, Shasta, CA
1,000 Siskiyou Opportunity Center, Mount Shasta, CA
500 San Diego Knights of Columbus, San Diego, CA

Education

25,000 Franklin McKinley School District, San Jose, CA
25,000 Franklin Mckinley School District, San Jose, CA
21,985 Bourgade High School, Phoenix, AZ
9,089 Bourgade High School, Phoenix, AZ
7,500 Lutheran Burbank School District, Santa Rosa, CA
5,000 O'Farrell Community School, San Diego, CA
3,000 Capistrano Unified School District, San Clemente, CA
2,000 Monte Vista School, Pasadena, CA
1,000 Chandler Unified School District, Chandler, AZ
250 St. Francis of Assisi School, Bend, OR

Environment

250 Urban Land Foundation, Washington, DC
250 Urban Land Foundation, Washington, DC

Health

5,000 Children's Hospital, Los Angeles, CA
3,400 St. Elizabeth Emergency Room, Lafayette, IN
2,500 Leukemia Society of America, Los Angeles, CA
2,500 Mercy Hospital, Los Angeles, CA
1,000 National Kidney Foundation, Los Angeles, CA
750 The National MS Society, Los Angeles, CA
250 Arizona Organ Donor Bank, Phoenix, AZ

Religion

2,000 Salvation Army, Los Angeles, CA
1,500 Jesuit Charities Gold Tournament
1,500 Rescue Mission, Los Angeles, CA
1,000 Yreka Salvation Army Committee, Yreka, CA
500 Trinity Temple, Anderson, SC
300 St. Pauls ECDC, St. Paul, MN
250 The Helper's Club of St. John of God, Los Angeles, CA

Social Services

25,000 Young Life, Los Angeles, CA
5,475 Orange County Council Boy Scouts, Irvine, CA
5,000 Kids Included Together, Del Mar, CA
5,000 Ymca of Orange County, Orange, CA
5,000 Ymca of Santa Clarita Valley, Santa Clarita, CA
2,500 Big Brother Big Sisters, San Diego, CA
2,500 United Way of Shasta County, Redding, CA
2,500 Ymca of San Diego County, San Diego, CA
2,000 Senior Nutrition Program, Los Angeles, CA
1,500 Siskiyou Domestic Violence Association, Yreka, CA
1,000 Bia Cares, Los Angeles, CA
1,000 Haven Humane Society, Redding, CA
1,000 Shasta Senior Nutrition Program, Shasta, CA
1,000 Summit League, Saratoga, CA
1,000 United Way, Los Angeles, CA
250 Arizona Baseball Charities, Paradise Valley, AZ
200 McDowell Mountain Ranch Soccer Club, Scottsdale, AZ
200 Sisters' Fund for Youth, Santa Ana, CA

SHELL OIL CO.

★ Number 40 of Top 100 Corporate Givers

Company Contact

Houston, TX
Web: http://www.shellus.com

Company Description

Employees: 31,637
SIC(s): 1311 Crude Petroleum & Natural Gas, 2819 Industrial Inorganic Chemicals Nec, 2822 Synthetic Rubber, 2879 Agricultural Chemicals Nec.
Parent Company: Royal Dutch/Shell Group of Companies, Carel Van Bylandtlaan 16, The Hague, Netherlands

Operating Locations

CA: Shell Oil Co., Bishop, Concord, Elk Grove, Livermore, Los Angeles, Madera, Martinez, Moreno Valley, Riverside, San Bruno, San Jose, Van Nuys, Willows; CT: Shell Oil Co., Bridgeport; DC: Shell Oil Co., Washington; FL: Shell Oil Co., Fort Lauderdale, Bradenton, Holly Hill, Melbourne, Miami, New Port Richey, North Port, Ocala, Tampa; GA: Shell Oil Co., Atlanta, Nashville; HI: Shell Oil Co., Honolulu, Kahului; IL: Shell Oil Co., Mount Auburn, Arlington Heights, Berwyn, Chatham, Effingham, Harristown, Sibley, Skokie; IN: Shell Oil Co., Hammond; KY: Shell Oil Co., Louisville; LA: Shell Oil Co., Gibson, Golden Meadow, Kenner, Metairie; LL&E Petroleum Marketing, New Orleans; Shell Oil Co., Norco, Plaquemine; MA: Shell Oil Co., Fall River, West Boylston, Westwood, Worcester; MD: Shell Oil Co., Rockville; MI: Shell Oil Co., Farmington Hills, Grand Haven, Jackson, South Boardman, Spring Lake; MN: Shell Oil Co., Minneapolis; MO: Shell Oil Co., Saint Louis; MS: Shell Oil Co., Collins, Columbus, Jackson, Pelahatchie; NJ: Shell Oil Co., Swearen; NV: Shell Oil Co., Reno; NY: Shell Oil Co., Jamaica; Billiton Metals, Inc., New York; Shell Oil Co., New York; OH: Shell Oil Co., Cincinnati, Columbus, Dayton, Lima, Sunbury, Tipp City, Westerville, Willoughby; PA: Shell Oil Co., Pittsburgh; SC: Shell Oil Co., Spartanburg; TN: Shell Oil Co., Knoxville; TX: Shell Oil Co., Mount Pleasant, Baytown, Deer Park, Douglassville; Criterion Catalyst Co. L.P., Houston; Shell Chemical Co., Houston; Shell Development Co., Houston; Shell Oil Co., Houston; Shell Oil Co., Houston; Shell Pipe Line Corp., Houston; Tejas Gas Corp., Houston; Shell Oil Co., Pharr, Seminole, Sugar Land; VA: Shell Oil Co., Reston
Note: Operates internationally.

Nonmonetary Support

Type: Loaned Employees; Loaned Executives
Note: Contact the Manager of Corporate Relations for nonmonetary support information.

Corporate Sponsorship

Type: Sports events
Contact: Mr. E. Schmitz, Manager, Advertising & Sales Promotion
Note: Sponsors national football and racing events.

Shell Oil Co. Foundation

Giving Contact

Terry Garland, Administrative Assistant
Shell Oil Co. Foundation
One Shell Plaza
Box 2099
Houston, TX 77252
Phone: (713)241-1595
Fax: (713)241-3329
Note: Terry Garland's direct line is: (713)241-7514.

Alternate Contact

Betty Lynn McHam, Corporate Secretary

Description

Founded: 1953
EIN: 136066583
Organization Type: Corporate Foundation
Giving Locations: nationally, with emphasis on communities where Shell employees are located.
Grant Types: Capital, Department, Employee Matching Gifts, General Support, Operating Expenses, Project, Research.
Note: Employee matching gift ratio: 2 to 1 up to $500; 1 to 1 up to $5,000 per employee annually, for higher education only.

Giving Philosophy

'Since its beginning in the United States in 1912, Shell Oil Company has followed a policy of contributing to philanthropies that promise to benefit large and diverse groups of Americans and of supporting programs designed to improve education. As our organization grew, so did our commitment to this policy. It was to support this growing commitment that the Shell Oil Company Foundation was founded in 1953.' Pattern for Giving, 1992

Financial Summary

Total Giving: $24,799,427 (1998); $20,732,949 (1997); $22,310,573 (1996). Note: Contributes through corporate direct giving program and foundation.
Giving Analysis: Giving for 1995 includes: foundation ($12,733,426); foundation matching gifts ($1,712,491); 1996: foundation ($19,277,403); foundation matching gifts ($2,366,800); foundation scholarships ($666,370); 1997: foundation ($15,306,671); foundation scholarships ($3,052,445); foundation matching gifts ($2,373,833)
Assets: $67,153,995 (1998); $62,921,689 (1997); $45,996,625 (1996)
Gifts Received: $22,092,398 (1998); $13,079,260 (1997); $35,549,740 (1996). Note: Foundation receives gifts from the Shell Oil Company and its subsidiaries.

Typical Recipients

Arts & Humanities: Arts Centers, Arts Festivals, Arts Outreach, Ballet, Dance, Historic Preservation, History & Archaeology, Libraries, Museums/Galleries, Music, Opera, Performing Arts, Theater
Civic & Public Affairs: African American Affairs, Botanical Gardens/Parks, Business/Free Enterprise, Civil Rights, Clubs, Community Foundations, Economic Development, Economic Policy, Employment/Job Training, Hispanic Affairs, Housing, Law & Justice, Parades/Festivals, Public Policy, Rural Affairs, Safety, Urban & Community Affairs, Women's Affairs, Zoos/Aquariums
Education: Business Education, Colleges & Universities, Economic Education, Education Associations, Education Funds, Education Reform, Elementary Education (Private), Engineering/Technological Education, Faculty Development, Education-General, Health & Physical Education, International Studies,

Journalism/Media Education, Legal Education, Medical Education, Minority Education, Private Education (Precollege), Public Education (Precollege), Science/ Mathematics Education, Secondary Education (Public), Student Aid
Environment: Environment-General, Resource Conservation
Health: Children's Health/Hospitals, Clinics/Medical Centers, Eyes/Blindness, Health Funds, Health Organizations, Heart, Hospices, Hospitals, Hospitals (University Affiliated), Medical Rehabilitation, Medical Research, Mental Health, Single-Disease Health Associations
International: International Organizations, International Peace & Security Issues, International Relations
Religion: Ministries, Religious Welfare
Science: Science Exhibits & Fairs, Science Museums, Scientific Centers & Institutes, Scientific Organizations
Social Services: Child Welfare, Community Centers, Community Service Organizations, Delinquency & Criminal Rehabilitation, Emergency Relief, Family Services, Food/Clothing Distribution, People with Disabilities, Recreation & Athletics, Scouts, Senior Services, Shelters/Homelessness, Substance Abuse, United Funds/United Ways, Volunteer Services, Youth Organizations

Contributions Analysis

Giving Priorities: Higher education, health and welfare, culture and the arts, and civic and public affairs. Supports public policy organizations, overseas development, and organizations that aid other countries. Requests from Shell affiliates overseas are minimal. Shell's parent company, headquartered in London, England, handles contributions by foreign subsidiaries.
Arts & Humanities: About 10%. Primarily gives in communities where company employees live. Supports a variety of disciplines, with emphasis on cultural centers, music, museums, public TV/radio, dance, art councils, performing arts, theaters, and libraries.
Civic & Public Affairs: 5% to 10%. Interest in national and local development, community improvement, research organizations, environmental efforts, public policy, justice and law, and minority needs.
Education: 45% to 50%. Emphasis on support of higher education through established programs (by invitation only). Shell Doctoral Fellowships encourage outstanding students to seek teaching careers in engineering and the sciences. Shell Faculty Career Initiation Funds support untenured faculty in science and engineering research. Shell Departmental Grants are designed to strengthen activities in specified areas related to teaching and/or research. Shell Career Counseling Grants are used to enhance career counseling and placement activities in colleges and universities with well-established programs. Focus on precollege math and science programs. Shell Incentive Funds are targeted to undergraduate minority students, with emphasis on technical and business education. National education funds, education organizations, and economic education receive substantial support. Also sponsors matching gifts program, and scholarships for children of employees.
Health: About 35%. Primary support goes to united funds. Support also goes to national health agencies, national welfare agencies, youth organizations and local health and welfare agencies. A priority is hospitals which serve employees, particularly through capital support.

Application Procedures

Initial Contact: Send a brief letter.
Application Requirements: Include a description of structure, purpose, history, and programs of organization; summary of need and proposed use for support; detailed financial data on organization (independent audit, budget, sources of income, breakdown of expenditures by program, administration, and fund raising); copies of forms 501(c)(3), 509(a), and 990; list of donors, and level of support.
Deadlines: None; contributions are planned in advance for each calendar year.

Restrictions

Foundation prefers not to contribute to capital campaigns of national organizations; endowment or development funds; special requests from colleges and universities or state or area college fundraising associations; or hospital operating expenses.
Does not support individuals, dinners or special events, fraternal organizations, goodwill advertising, political or lobbying groups, or religious organizations for sectarian purposes.
Does not support education capital or project requests.

Additional Information

Companies participating in the Shell Oil Co. Foundation include Shell Oil Co.; Shell Offshore, Inc.; Shell Pipe Line Corp.; Shell Western E&P, Inc.; Pecten Chemicals, Inc.; Pecten International Co.; and Pecten Middle East Services Co.
Publications: Foundation Annual Report

Corporate Officials

Michael Howard Grasley: senior vice president B Barberton, OH 1937. ED University of Kentucky MS; Ohio University (1958); University of Florida PhD (1963). PRIM CORP EMPL senior vice president: Shell Oil Co. NONPR AFFIL director: Chemical Manufacturers Association; member: Society Chemical Industry.

Foundation Officials

Bruce E. Bernard: director B 1945. ED Louisiana State University BS. PRIM CORP EMPL vice president: Shell Oil Co. CORP AFFIL partner: Smackover-Shell Ltd. Partnership.
Jack N. Doherty: senior vice president, member executive committee, director
Michael Howard Grasley: member executive committee, director (see above)
H. R. Hutchins: secretary
S. Allen Lackey: director B Jackson, MS 1942. ED University of Mississippi BBA (1963); University of Mississippi JD (1968). PRIM CORP EMPL vice president, general counsel: Shell Oil Co.
B. W. Levan: vice president, director B Saint Louis, IL 1941. ED Southern Illinois University (1964); University of Illinois MS (1966). PRIM CORP EMPL vice president human resources: Shell Oil Co.
James McClay Morgan: member executive committee, director B Burgettstown, PA 1947. ED Pennsylvania State University BS (1969); Case Western Reserve University MBA (1974). PRIM CORP EMPL senior vice president: Shell Oil Co. Products Division.
Jere Paul Parrish: president, chairman executive committee, director B Lovington, NM 1941. ED University of Texas BS (1965). PRIM CORP EMPL president: Shell Oil Co.
Fred M. Rabbe: senior admin representative B 1928. PRIM CORP EMPL owner: Rabbe Oil Co.
Steven Charles Stryker: director B Omaha, NE 1944. ED University of Iowa BS (1967); University of Iowa JD (1969); Northwestern University Kellogg Graduate School of Business Administration (1969-1970); DePaul University (1971). PRIM CORP EMPL vice president, general tax counsel: Shell Oil Co.
P. G. Turberville: vice president, director B 1951. ED Aberdeen University MA (1972). PRIM CORP EMPL vice president finance: Shell Oil Co.

Grants Analysis

Disclosure Period: calendar year ending 1997
Total Grants: $15,306,671*
Number of Grants: 1,100 (approx)
Average Grant: $13,915 (approx)
Highest Grant: $2,840,000
Typical Range: $1,000 to $35,000
***Note:** Giving excludes matching gifts; scholarships.

Recent Grants

Note: Grants derived from 1997 Form 990.

Arts & Humanities

290,000 Children's Museum, Houston, TX
250,000 Houston Symphony Society, Houston, TX
200,000 Houston Museum of Fine Arts, Houston, TX
100,000 Houston Symphony Society, Houston, TX
100,000 National Gallery of Art, Washington, DC
80,000 Houston Museum of Fine Arts, Houston, TX
50,000 Alley Theater, Houston, TX
50,000 Houston Grand Opera, Houston, TX

Civic & Public Affairs

170,000 Friends of the Zoo, New Orleans, LA
100,000 National Fund for US Botanic Garden, Washington, DC
85,000 American Enterprise Institute for Public Policy Research, Washington, DC

Education

1,000,000 Baylor College of Medicine, Houston, TX
427,233 National Merit Scholarship Corporation, Evanston, IL
400,000 Tulane University Educational Fund, New Orleans, LA
250,000 Texas A&M University Development Foundation, College Station, TX
200,000 University of Houston, Houston, TX
160,000 Tulane University Educational Fund, New Orleans, LA
150,000 Society of Organizational Learning, Cambridge, MA
120,000 National Action Council for Minorities in Engineering, New York, NY
120,000 University of St. Thomas, Houston, TX
100,000 Loyola University, New Orleans, LA
100,000 University of Houston, Houston, TX
100,000 William Marsh Rice University, Houston, TX
75,000 Rice University, Houston, TX
74,000 Junior Achievement, Colorado Springs, CO
60,000 Education Foundation of Harris County, Houston, TX
56,250 Los Angeles Scholars Program, Los Angeles, CA
50,000 Occupational Physicians Scholarship Fund, Schiller Park, IL
50,000 Spring Branch Education Foundation, Houston, TX
50,000 Texas Health Science Center, Houston, TX
50,000 United Negro College Fund, New York, NY
50,000 University of Alabama, University, AL

Environment

100,000 Nature Conservancy, Arlington, VA

Health

200,000 M.D. Anderson Hospital Tumor Institute, Houston, TX
100,000 Carter Center/River Blindness Center, Atlanta, GA

International

150,000 Visions of a Better World USA, Oak Brook, IL

Religion

50,000 Salvation Army, Houston, TX

Science

160,000 Museum of Medical Science Foundation, Health Adventure, Houston, TX

75,000 American Geological Institute, Houston, TX
50,000 Houston Museum of Natural Science and B.B. Planetarium, Houston, TX

Social Services
2,840,000 United Way of Texas Gulf Coast, Houston, TX
425,000 United Way, New Orleans, LA
250,000 Points of Light Foundation Connect America Program, Washington, DC
150,000 United Way Partnership, Alton, IL
100,000 Houston Parks Board Junior Golf Program, Houston, TX
87,500 Capital Area United Way, Baton Rouge, LA
75,000 United Way, New Orleans, LA
60,000 United Way of the Bay Area, San Francisco, CA
57,225 United Way of Kern County, Bakersfield, CA
50,000 Sam Houston Area Council Boy Scouts of America, Houston, TX

SHELTER MUTUAL INSURANCE CO.

Company Contact
Columbia, MO

Company Description
Employees: 1,600
SIC(s): 6311 Life Insurance, 6321 Accident & Health Insurance.

Shelter Insurance Foundation

Giving Contact
Raymond E. Jones, Secretary & Director
Shelter Insurance Foundation
1817 West Broadway
Columbia, MO 65218
Phone: (573)214-4290
Fax: (573)446-5727

Description
Founded: 1981
EIN: 431224155
Organization Type: Corporate Foundation
Giving Locations: AK; CO; IL; IN; IA; KS; KY; LA; MS; MO: Columbia; OK; TN
Grant Types: General Support, Research, Scholarship.

Financial Summary
Total Giving: $400,000 (fiscal year ending June 30, 2000 approx); $400,000 (fiscal 1999 approx); $400,000 (fiscal 1998 approx). Note: Contributes through corporate direct giving program and foundation.
Giving Analysis: Giving for fiscal 1997 includes: foundation scholarships ($295,250)
Assets: $4,373,607 (fiscal 1997); $3,223,118 (fiscal 1994); $1,708,554 (fiscal 1993)
Gifts Received: $485,725 (fiscal 1997); $1,771,870 (fiscal 1994); $210,140 (fiscal 1993). Note: Contributions are received from Shelter Life Insurance Co. and Shelter Mutual Insurance Co.

Typical Recipients
Arts & Humanities: History & Archaeology, Music
Civic & Public Affairs: Clubs, Civic & Public Affairs-General, Housing, Parades/Festivals, Public Policy, Safety, Urban & Community Affairs
Education: Arts/Humanities Education, Business Education, Colleges & Universities, Education Associations, Education-General, Legal Education, Public Education (Precollege), Secondary Education (Public), Special Education, Student Aid
Health: Alzheimers Disease, Children's Health/Hospitals, Medical Research, Single-Disease Health Associations
Religion: Religious Welfare
Social Services: Child Welfare, Community Service Organizations, Crime Prevention, People with Disabilities, Scouts, Senior Services, Youth Organizations

Contributions Analysis
Giving Priorities: Major scholarship funding and support for colleges and universities. Some support for social services and civic causes.
Civic & Public Affairs: 2%. Focus on housing and urban affairs.
Education: 93%. Almost all funding went towards scholarships.
Social Services: 5%. Supports scouting, crime prevention, and programs for the elderly.
Note: Total contributions in 1997.

Application Procedures
Initial Contact: Send a preliminary letter to the foundation.
Application Requirements: Include a brief description of the request.
Deadlines: None.
Notes: Corporate grants are made only through scholarships by a local Shelter Insurance agent for local high schools in that area.

Corporate Officials
Max J. Dills: director PRIM CORP EMPL director: Shelter Mutual Insurance Co.
Robert J. Feller: vice president B Cairo, IL 1941. ED Western Illinois University (1964). PRIM CORP EMPL vice president: Shelter Mutual Insurance Co.
Raymond E. Jones: executive vice president, secretary B Chillocothe, MO 1941. ED Missouri State University (1962). PRIM CORP EMPL executive vice president, secretary: Shelter Mutual Insurance Co. CORP AFFIL secretary: Daniel Boone Underwriters LLC.
Gustav J. Lehr: chairman, director B 1930. PRIM CORP EMPL chairman, director: Shelter Mutual Insurance Co. CORP AFFIL chairman: Daniel Boone Underwriters LLC; chairman, director: Shelter General Insurance Co.
John W. Lenox: president, chief executive officer, director PRIM CORP EMPL president, chief executive officer, director: Shelter Mutual Insurance Co. CORP AFFIL president: Shelter Financial Services; president: Shelter General Insurance Co.
David C. Mattson: director PRIM CORP EMPL director: Shelter Mutual Insurance Co.

Foundation Officials
Robert T. Cox: director PRIM CORP EMPL executive: Ace Manufacturing & Parts Co. CORP AFFIL director: Shelter Financial Services.
J. Donald Duello: president, treasurer, director B 1943. ED University of Missouri, Columbia (1961-1965). PRIM CORP EMPL vice president finance: Shelter Financial Services. CORP AFFIL vice president: Shelter General Insurance Co.
Jerry French: director
Raymond E. Jones: secretary, director (see above)
Gustav J. Lehr: vice president, director (see above)
John W. Lenox: director (see above)
Joe Moseley: director
James A. Offutt: director B Mexico, MO 1934. ED University of Missouri. PRIM CORP EMPL executive vice president, director: Shelter Mutual Insurance Co. CORP AFFIL director: Shelter Financial Services; vice president: Shelter General Insurance Co.

Grants Analysis
Disclosure Period: fiscal year ending June 30, 1997
Total Grants: $56,563*
Number of Grants: 20
Average Grant: $2,828
Highest Grant: $8,333
Typical Range: $250 to $6,000
***Note:** Giving excludes scholarship.

Recent Grants
Note: Grants derived from fiscal 1997 Form 990.

Arts & Humanities
1,000 Spiro Historical Society, Spiro, OK

Civic & Public Affairs
2,500 Advent Enterprises, Columbia, MO
2,500 Missouri Heads Up, Columbia, MO
200 Fair Missouri Foundation, Columbia, MO -- educational
200 Hodgen Fire Department, Hodgen, OK

Education
5,250 University of Missouri Columbia, Columbia, MO
5,000 Southwest Missouri State University, Springfield, MO
4,000 Columbia College, Columbia, MO
4,000 Stephens College, Columbia, MO
4,000 University of Southwestern Louisiana, Lafayette, LA
3,030 University of Missouri Columbia Law School Foundation, Columbia, MO
2,000 Columbia Public School Foundation, Columbia, MO
1,200 University of Missouri Columbia Department of Music Friends of Music, Columbia, MO
1,000 Assistance League Mid-Missouri, Columbia, MO -- educational
1,000 Wheatland R-II Schools, Hermitage, MO

Health
2,500 Children's Miracle Network Telethon, Columbia, MO

Religion
350 Christian Record Services, Lincoln, NE

Social Services
8,333 Boy Scouts of America Great Rivers Council, Columbia, MO -- educational
6,500 Albia Police Department, Albia, IA
2,000 Lenoir Retirement Community, Columbia, MO

SHERWIN-WILLIAMS CO.

Company Contact
Cleveland, OH

Company Description
Revenue: US$5,003,800,000 (1999)
Profit: US$303,900,000 (1999)
Employees: 24,822 (1999)
Fortune Rank: 326, per FORTUNE Magazine's list of 500 Largest U.S. Corporations (1999).
FF 326
SIC(s): 2816 Inorganic Pigments, 2819 Industrial Inorganic Chemicals Nec, 2851 Paints & Allied Products, 2869 Industrial Organic Chemicals Nec.

Sherwin-Williams Foundation

Giving Contact
Barbara Gadosik, Director, Corporate Contributions
Sherwin-Williams Foundation
101 Prospect Avenue Northwest
Cleveland, OH 44115

Phone: (216)566-2511
Fax: (216)566-3266

Description

EIN: 346555476
Organization Type: Corporate Foundation
Giving Locations: headquarters and operating communities, primarily Cleveland.
Grant Types: Capital, Employee Matching Gifts, General Support.

Financial Summary

Total Giving: $980,028 (1998); $947,993 (1997); $815,000 (1996). Note: Contributes through foundation only.
Giving Analysis: Giving for 1996 includes: foundation grants to United Way ($211,450); foundation matching gifts ($147,853); 1997: foundation grants to United Way ($213,845); foundation matching gifts ($170,588); 1998: foundation grants to United Way ($207,125); foundation matching gifts ($173,668); foundation gifts to individuals ($6,200)
Assets: $14,786,239 (1998); $14,594,742 (1997); $14,426,366 (1996)
Gifts Received: $660,000 (1996); $1,000,000 (1995); $4,000,000 (1994). Note: Foundation receives contributions from Sherwin-Williams Co.

Typical Recipients

Arts & Humanities: Ballet, Arts & Humanities-General, Historic Preservation, History & Archaeology, Libraries, Museums/Galleries, Music, Opera, Performing Arts, Theater
Civic & Public Affairs: Community Foundations, Economic Development, Economic Policy, Employment/Job Training, Civic & Public Affairs-General, Municipalities/Towns, Parades/Festivals, Professional & Trade Associations, Public Policy, Safety, Urban & Community Affairs
Education: Business Education, Business-School Partnerships, Colleges & Universities, Economic Education, Education Funds, Education-General, Medical Education, Minority Education, Preschool Education, Private Education (Precollege), Science/Mathematics Education, Student Aid, Vocational & Technical Education
Health: Cancer, Emergency/Ambulance Services, Hospices, Hospitals, Hospitals (University Affiliated), Long-Term Care, Medical Rehabilitation, Public Health, Single-Disease Health Associations
Religion: Churches, Dioceses, Jewish Causes, Religious Welfare
Science: Science Museums, Scientific Centers & Institutes
Social Services: Big Brother/Big Sister, Community Centers, Crime Prevention, Family Services, People with Disabilities, Recreation & Athletics, Shelters/Homelessness, United Funds/United Ways, Volunteer Services, YMCA/YWCA/YMHA/YWHA, Youth Organizations

Contributions Analysis

Giving Priorities: Health, social welfare, education, and civic and cultural organizations.
Arts & Humanities: 10%. Museums, art associations, and performing arts associations in Cleveland, OH, area.
Civic & Public Affairs: 17%. Development programs for Cleveland, OH, professional associations, sports and recreation, and matching gifts for volunteer leaders.
Education: 40%. More than half of education support is given in the form of matching gifts. Also supports universities, independent college funds, and official scholarship programs.
Health: 33%. Funds the United Way in operating locations. Youth, the disabled, and other human services organizations also receive support.
Note: Total contributions in 1998.

Application Procedures

Initial Contact: Send a written proposal.
Application Requirements: Include a description of organization, including its structure, purpose, and history; amount requested; purpose of funds sought; operating budget; detailed description of current programs and activities; description of project, including community needs to be addressed, program objectives, activities to be undertaken, timetable, fully defined project budget, and sources of committed and pending support; current operating budget with income and expenditures; current list of donors and amounts received; list of officers and directors; recent annual report; most recently audited financial statement; annual report; and proof of tax-exempt status.
Deadlines: None.

Restrictions

Foundation does not support endowments, individuals, research, religious or political organizations, dinners or special events, fraternal organizations, goodwill advertising, member agencies of united funds, sports programs, or elementary and secondary education. Only organizations serving company operating areas receive support.

Corporate Officials

John Gerald Breen: chairman, chief executive officer, directortreasurer, chief financial officer B Cleveland, OH 1934. ED John Carroll University BS (1956); Case Western Reserve University MBA (1961). PRIM CORP EMPL chairman, chief executive officer, director: Sherwin-Williams Co. ADD CORP EMPL director: Contract Trnsp Systems Co. CORP AFFIL director: National City Bank; director: Parker-Hannifin Corp.; director: Goodyear Tire & Rubber Co.; director: Mead Corp. CLUB AFFIL Pepper Pike Club; Union Club; Cleveland Skating Club.
Thomas Allen Commes: president, chief operating officer, director B Aurora, IL 1942. ED Saint Thomas College BA (1964). PRIM CORP EMPL president, chief operating officer, director: Sherwin-Williams Co. CORP AFFIL director: Centerior Energy Corp.; officer: KeyCorp.
Thomas E. Hopkins: vice president human resources ED Malone College (1978); Cleveland State University (1982). PRIM CORP EMPL vice president human resources: Sherwin-Williams Co. NONPR AFFIL member: Students Free Enterprise.
Larry John Pitorak: senior vice president finance, treasurer, chief financial officer B Chardon, OH 1946. ED Thiel College BA (1969); Cleveland-Marshall College of Law JD (1974). PRIM CORP EMPL senior vice president finance, treasurer, chief financial officer: Sherwin-Williams Co. CORP AFFIL director: Fifth Third Bank; treasurer: Contract Transportation System Co. NONPR AFFIL trustee: Thiel College.

Foundation Officials

John Gerald Breen: president, trustee (see above)
Thomas Allen Commes: assistant secretary, trustee (see above)
Barbara Gadosik: director corporate contributions PRIM CORP EMPL director corporate contributions: Sherwin-Williams Co.
Thomas E. Hopkins: assistant secretary, trustee (see above)
Larry John Pitorak: secretary, treasurer, trustee (see above)

Grants Analysis

Disclosure Period: calendar year ending 1998
Total Grants: $593,035*
Number of Grants: 136
Average Grant: $4,361
Highest Grant: $47,500
Typical Range: $1,000 to $15,000
***Note:** Giving excludes matching gifts, grants to volunteers, and United Way.

Recent Grants

Note: Grants derived from 1998 Form 990.

Arts & Humanities

20,000	Great Lakes Museum, Cleveland, OH
18,000	Musical Arts Association, Cleveland, OH
10,000	Cleveland Playhouse, Cleveland, OH
10,000	Rock and Roll Hall of Fame and Museum, Inc., Cleveland, OH
7,000	New Cleveland Opera Company, Cleveland, OH
5,000	Cleveland Museum of Art, Cleveland, OH
5,000	Cleveland Restoration Society, Cleveland, OH
5,000	Ohio Historical Foundation, Columbus, OH
4,500	Old Stone Historical Preservation Society, Inc., Cleveland, OH
3,000	Cleveland Public Library, Cleveland, OH
3,000	Great Lakes Theater Festival, Cleveland, OH
2,500	Cleveland Ballet, Cleveland, OH

Civic & Public Affairs

47,500	Cleveland Tomorrow, Inc., Cleveland, OH
3,000	P M Foundation, Cleveland, OH

Education

50,000	Construction Education Foundation, Rosslyn, VA
30,000	Case Western Reserve University, School of Medicine, Cleveland, OH
30,000	John Carroll University, University Heights, OH -- Capital Campaign
25,000	Students in Free Enterprise, Springfield, MO
22,500	Ohio Foundation of Independent Colleges, Inc., Columbus, OH
20,000	Cleveland Scholarship Programs, Inc. - S-W Scholarship, Cleveland, OH
20,000	Ursuline College, Pepper Pike, OH
5,800	Eastern Michigan University, Ypsilanti, MI
5,000	David N. Myers College, Cleveland, OH
5,000	Langston University Development Fund, Langston, OK
4,000	United Negro College Fund, Cleveland, OH
3,000	Texas Independent College Fund, Ft. Worth, TX
2,500	Berea College, Berea, KY
2,500	Cleveland Center for Economic Education, Cleveland, OH

Health

20,000	University Hospitals of Cleveland, Cleveland, OH
10,000	American Red Cross, Cleveland, OH
5,300	American Red Cross, Cleveland, OH
4,000	Hospice of the Western Reserve, Inc., Cleveland, OH
3,000	Edward W. Mccready Memorial Hospital, Crisfield, MD
3,000	Health Hill Hospital, Cleveland, OH
3,000	United Cerebal Palsy of Cleveland, Cleveland, OH

Religion

25,000	Diocese of Cleveland, Cleveland, OH
25,000	Diocese of Cleveland, Cleveland, OH
3,000	Catholic Charities Corp./Jennings Hall, Inc., Garfield Hts., OH

Science

3,000	National Invention Center, Inc., Akron, OH

Social Services

172,000	United Way Services, Inc., Cleveland, OH
20,000	Young Men's Christian Association, Cleveland, OH

11,615	United Way/Crusade of Mercy, Chicago, IL
5,000	Center for Familes and Children, Cleveland, OH
5,000	Greater Cleveland Neighborhood Centers Association, Cleveland, OH
4,850	United Way of Metropolitan Atlanta, Atlanta, GA
4,800	United Way of Metropolitan Dallas, Dallas, TX
3,720	United Way of the Lower Eastern Shore, Inc., Salisbury, MD
2,790	United Way of the Bluegrass, Lexington, KY
2,500	Big Brother/Big Sisters of America, Philadelphia, PA
2,500	Volunteers of America, Cleveland, OH

Shoney's Inc.

Company Contact

Nashville, TN
Web: http://www.shoneys.com

Company Description

Employees: 29,000
SIC(s): 5812 Eating Places, 6794 Patent Owners & Lessors.

Operating Locations

Shoney's has restaraunts in 1,865 locations in 35 states. Divisions include Captain D's, Lee's Famous Recipe Chicken, Pargo's, BarbWire's Steakhouses.

Nonmonetary Support

Type: Cause-related Marketing & Promotion; Donated Products; In-kind Services
Note: Schools and community organizations receive support through in-kind donations.

Corporate Sponsorship

Type: Arts & cultural events; Music & entertainment events; Sports events
Contact: Betty Marshall, Senior Vice President

Giving Contact

Sue Downs, Director, Corporate & Community Affairs
Shoney's Inc.
1727 Elm Hill Pike
Nashville, TN 37210
Phone: (615)231-2891
Fax: (615)231-2621
Email: sue_downs@shoneys.com

Description

Organization Type: Corporate Giving Program
Giving Locations: headquarters and operating communities.
Grant Types: General Support, Scholarship.

Financial Summary

Total Giving: $250,000 (1999 approx); $250,000 (1998 approx); $250,000 (1997 approx). Note: Contributes through corporate direct giving program only.

Typical Recipients

Arts & Humanities: Arts Festivals, Arts Institutes, Community Arts, Ethnic & Folk Arts, Music, Opera, Performing Arts, Public Broadcasting, Theater
Civic & Public Affairs: Employment/Job Training, Civic & Public Affairs-General
Education: Business Education, Colleges & Universities, Community & Junior Colleges, Education Funds, Elementary Education (Private), Preschool Education, Private Education (Precollege), Public Education (Precollege), Student Aid
Health: Health Funds, Health Organizations, Hospitals, Public Health
Religion: Churches
Science: Science Exhibits & Fairs
Social Services: Child Welfare, Community Centers, Community Service Organizations, Counseling, Day Care, Delinquency & Criminal Rehabilitation, Domestic Violence, Emergency Relief, Family Services, Food/Clothing Distribution, Homes, Substance Abuse, United Funds/United Ways, Volunteer Services, Youth Organizations

Contributions Analysis

Arts & Humanities: About 10%. Interests include festivals, art institutes, community arts, ethnic arts, performing arts, music, opera, theater, and public broadcasting.
Civic & Public Affairs: About 35%. Supports civic and public affairs groups near headquarters and operating locations.
Education: 40% to 45%. Recipients include public and private education, business education, colleges and universities, community colleges, education funds, and scholarship programs. The company is also an active supporter of United Negro College Fund and is a sponsor of the annual Bootstrap Awards Scholarship Program.
Health: About 10%. Supports health funds, hospitals, health organizations, mental health, and public health.

Application Procedures

Initial Contact: Letter of inquiry.
Application Requirements: Include a description of organization, amount requested, purpose of funds sought, recently audited financial statement, and proof of tax-exempt status.
Deadlines: None; apply four weeks prior to any event.
Review Process: Contributions committee reviews requests weekly.
Evaluative Criteria: Grantees are educationally focused, family oriented, research focused, or distributed on a broad-scale to social organizations.

Restrictions

The company does not support telemarketing or telephone solicitations; semi-professional athletic sponsorships; political parties, candidates; or issues; beauty pageants; independent film or video productions; individuals; picnics or celebrations for other for-profit companies; or scholarships other than the Bootstrap Awards.

Additional Information

The company also operates Bootstraps Awards, Inc., a nonprofit scholarship program. Annual college tuition scholarships are presented to five high school seniors from Middle Tennessee. Scholarships are also available for children of Shoney's Inc. employees. For scholarship information, contact Linda Bloodworth.

Corporate Officials

J. Michael Bodnar: president, chief executive officer PRIM CORP EMPL president, chief executive officer: Shoney's Inc.
Betty J. Marshall: senior vice president B Youngstown, OH 1950. ED Youngstown State University. PRIM CORP EMPL senior vice president: Shoney's Inc.

Giving Program Officials

Sue Downs: (see above)
Betty J. Marshall: (see above)

Sierra Pacific Industries

Company Contact

Redding, CA
Web: http://www.sierrapacificind.com

Company Description

Employees: 2,500
SIC(s): 2421 Sawmills & Planing Mills--General, 2431 Millwork.

Corporate Sponsorship

Type: Arts & cultural events; Festivals/fairs; Music & entertainment events; Pledge-a-thon; Sports events

Sierra Pacific Foundation

Giving Contact

Becky Riley
Sierra Pacific Foundation
PO Box 496028
Redding, CA 96049-6028
Phone: (530)378-8000
Fax: (916)378-8109

Description

Founded: 1978
EIN: 942574178
Organization Type: Corporate Foundation. Supports preselected organizations only.
Giving Locations: headquarters and operating communities.
Grant Types: General Support, Scholarship.

Giving Philosophy

'The Foundation was organized to provide scholarships to dependent children of Sierra Pacific crew members and to provide financial assistance to local communities, specifically those communities where Sierra Pacific Industries operates facilities.' Sierra Pacific Foundation statement

Financial Summary

Total Giving: $301,166 (fiscal year ending June 30, 1998); $4,875 (fiscal 1997); $706,919 (fiscal 1996). Note: Contributes through foundation only.
Giving Analysis: Giving for fiscal 1996 includes: foundation ($640,959); foundation scholarships ($65,960); fiscal 1998: foundation ($214,041); foundation scholarships ($87,125)
Assets: $1,001,522 (fiscal 1998); $129,352 (fiscal 1997); $1,319,326 (fiscal 1996)
Gifts Received: $200 (fiscal 1998); $528,240 (fiscal 1996); $500,705 (fiscal 1995). Note: In fiscal 1996, contributions were received from Sierra Pacific Industries ($500,000) and the Memorial for Ida. C. Emmerson ($22,812).

Typical Recipients

Arts & Humanities: Arts Associations & Councils, Arts Centers, Libraries, Museums/Galleries, Music, Opera, Public Broadcasting
Civic & Public Affairs: Botanical Gardens/Parks, Business/Free Enterprise, Chambers of Commerce, Clubs, Civic & Public Affairs-General, Parades/Festivals, Rural Affairs, Safety, Urban & Community Affairs, Women's Affairs
Education: Agricultural Education, Colleges & Universities, Elementary Education (Public), Education-General, Private Education (Precollege), Public Education (Precollege), Secondary Education (Public), Student Aid
Environment: Environment-General, Resource Conservation, Wildlife Protection
Health: Cancer, Health Organizations, Heart, Hospices, Medical Research, Nutrition, Single-Disease Health Associations, Transplant Networks/Donor Banks
International: International Relief Efforts
Religion: Churches, Religious Welfare
Science: Science Museums

Social Services: Child Welfare, Community Service Organizations, Crime Prevention, Food/Clothing Distribution, Recreation & Athletics, Scouts, Senior Services, Shelters/Homelessness, Youth Organizations

Contributions Analysis

Giving Priorities: Education and civic organizations are priorities.
Arts & Humanities: 7%. Supports community arts groups.
Civic & Public Affairs: 23%. Support goes to community groups such as hospitals, fire districts, schools, and educational television stations.
Education: 55%. Scholarships are awarded to children of employees for higher education.
Environment: 3%.
Health: 2%.
International: 1%.
Social Services: 9%. Supports scouts and community youth organizations.
Note: Total contributions made in 1998.

Application Procedures

Initial Contact: Obtain a contribution request form from nearest Sierra Pacific office or by calling (530) 378-8000.
Deadlines: March 31.

Restrictions

Scholarships are restricted to dependent children of Sierra Pacific employees.

Corporate Officials

A. A. Emmerson: president B 1929. PRIM CORP EMPL president: Sierra Pacific Industries.
George Emmerson: vice president B 1956. ED Oregon State University (1978). PRIM CORP EMPL vice president: Sierra Pacific Industries.
Mark D. Emmerson: chief financial officer PRIM CORP EMPL chief financial officer: Sierra Pacific Industries.

Foundation Officials

Carolyn Emmerson Dietz: chairman, president B 1959.
George Emmerson: director (see above)
Mark D. Emmerson: treasurer (see above)

Grants Analysis

Disclosure Period: fiscal year ending June 30, 1998
Total Grants: $214,041*
Number of Grants: 202
Average Grant: $1,060
Highest Grant: $15,000
Typical Range: $25 to $5,000
***Note:** Giving excludes scholarships.

Recent Grants

Note: Grants derived from fiscal 1997 Form 990.

Arts & Humanities

1,000 San Francisco Opera Association, San Francisco, CA -- community assistance

Health

200 Leukemia Society of America, San Francisco, CA -- for welfare assistance
100 American Heart Association -- for welfare assistance

International

2,600 World Images for Children, Blackhawk, CA -- community support

Religion

500 Community Presbyterian Church, Danville, CA -- support community church
125 East Bay Youth for Christ, Concord, CA -- community support

Social Services

150 Lynne Leach for Assembly, Walnut Creek, CA -- community support
100 Assistance League, Walnut Creek, CA -- for welfare assistance
100 Shelter, Concord, CA -- community support

SIERRA PACIFIC RESOURCES

Company Contact

Reno, NV
Web: http://www.sierrapacific.com

Company Description

Revenue: US$606,120,000
Employees: 1,840
SIC(s): 4924 Natural Gas Distribution, 4931 Electric & Other Services Combined, 6719 Holding Companies Nec.

Nonmonetary Support

Value: $9,498 (1996)
Type: In-kind Services

Corporate Sponsorship

Type: Pledge-a-thon
Contact: Greg Lambert, Director
Note: Sponsors Walk America and Adopt-a-Park.

Sierra Pacific Resources Charitable Foundation

Giving Contact

Karen Foster, Foundation Administrator
Sierra Pacific Power Co.
PO Box 10100
Reno, NV 89520-0040
Phone: (775)834-3070
Fax: (775)834-4339
Email: kfoster@sppc.com

Description

Founded: 1988
EIN: 880244735
Organization Type: Corporate Foundation
Giving Locations: CA: Northeastern California; NV: Northern Nevada headquarters and operating communities.
Grant Types: Employee Matching Gifts, General Support.
Note: Employee matching gift ratio: 1 to 1 for donations to Special Assistance Fund for Energy (SAFE).

Financial Summary

Total Giving: $300,000 (2000 approx); $300,000 (1999 approx); $270,000 (1998 approx). Note: Contributes through corporate direct giving program and foundation.
Giving Analysis: Giving for 1995 includes: foundation ($255,662); foundation grants to United Way ($31,250); 1997: foundation ($278,504); foundation grants to United Way ($33,750)
Assets: $252,128 (1997); $156,408 (1995); $169,064 (1994)
Gifts Received: $333,565 (1997); $262,000 (1995); $225,000 (1994). Note: Contributions received from Sierra Pacific Resources.

Typical Recipients

Arts & Humanities: Arts Associations & Councils, Arts Centers, Arts Funds, Community Arts, Ethnic & Folk Arts, Arts & Humanities-General, Libraries, Museums/Galleries, Music, Opera, Public Broadcasting, Theater
Civic & Public Affairs: African American Affairs, Business/Free Enterprise, Clubs, Economic Development, Civic & Public Affairs-General, Hispanic Affairs, Municipalities/Towns, Native American Affairs, Parades/Festivals, Professional & Trade Associations, Safety, Urban & Community Affairs, Women's Affairs
Education: Agricultural Education, Business Education, Colleges & Universities, Community & Junior Colleges, Education Reform, Elementary Education (Public), Engineering/Technological Education, Education-General, Legal Education, Public Education (Precollege), Religious Education, Science/Mathematics Education
Environment: Forestry, Environment-General, Resource Conservation, Wildlife Protection
Health: Children's Health/Hospitals, Diabetes, Emergency/Ambulance Services, Heart, Hospitals, Mental Health, Respiratory, Single-Disease Health Associations
Science: Scientific Research
Social Services: Camps, Community Service Organizations, Crime Prevention, Delinquency & Criminal Rehabilitation, Family Planning, Food/Clothing Distribution, People with Disabilities, Recreation & Athletics, Scouts, Senior Services, Social Services-General, United Funds/United Ways, YMCA/YWCA/YMHA/YWHA, Youth Organizations

Contributions Analysis

Giving Priorities: Emphasis on social services, education, and civic concerns.
Arts & Humanities: About 2%. Supports classical music and local arts councils.
Civic & Public Affairs: 9%. Supports chambers of commerce, fire departments, minority affairs, and parks and recreation.
Education: 25%. Primarily supports colleges and universities, with an emphasis on technology, mining and geology, and environmental science; supports scholarship funds and women's education. Also supports preK-12 education, with emphasis on math and science.
Environment: 7%. Supports mostly environmental education and resource conservation and development.
Health: 5%. Supports the United Way and the Red Cross, single-disease organizations, food banks, and social service agencies focusing on the elderly, the disabled, and the abused.
Social Services: 52%. Supports scouting, 4-H, and YMCAs. Also supports athleticand recreational activities.

Application Procedures

Initial Contact: Submit a brief letter of inquiry.
Deadlines: None.

Restrictions

The foundation does not make grants to individuals and does not fund scholarships, athletic or sporting events/teams, and does not fund religious organizations. Grants are limited to areas of service.

Additional Information

Publications: Annual Report

Corporate Officials

Malyn K. Malquist: chairman vice president, chief financial officer B Artesia, CA 1952. ED Brigham Young University (1976); Brigham Young University (1978). PRIM CORP EMPL chairman: Sierra Pacific Resources. CORP AFFIL senior vice president: Sierra Pacific Power Co.; president: Sierra Water Development; president: Siera Energy Co.
William E. Peterson: general counsel B 1943. ED College of the Holy Cross; North Carolina State University BA; University of South Carolina. PRIM CORP EMPL secretary: Sierra Energy Co. ADD CORP EMPL general counsel: Sierra Pacific Power Co. CORP AFFIL senior vice president, general counsel, corp. secretary: Sierra Pacific Resources.
Mark A. Ruelle: senior vice president, chief financial officer ED University of North Dakota BA; University of North Dakota MBA. PRIM CORP EMPL senior vice

president, chief financial officer: Sierra Pacific Resources. CORP AFFIL chief financial officer: Sierra Pacific Power Co. NONPR AFFIL member: National Association Business Economists; member: Planning Forum; member strategic planning committee: Edison Electric Institute; member: American Gas Association.

Foundation Officials

Karen Foster: secretary, administrator

Grants Analysis

Disclosure Period: calendar year ending 1997
Total Grants: $278,504*
Number of Grants: 119
Average Grant: $2,340
Highest Grant: $11,250
Typical Range: $20 to $10,000
***Note:** Giving excludes United Way.

Recent Grants

Note: Grants derived from 1997 Form 990.

Arts & Humanities

1,000 Sierra Arts Foundation, Reno, NV
1,000 Western Folklife Center, Elko, NV
550 Nevada Opera Association, Reno, NV

Civic & Public Affairs

3,500 Nevada Hispanic Services, Reno, NV
2,500 National Alliance
2,500 Northern Nevada Black Cultural Awareness Society, Reno, NV
1,850 Northern Nevada Black Cultural Awareness Society, Reno, NV
1,000 Nevada Women's Fund, Reno, NV
500 Pyramid Lake Pow-Wow
500 Renaissance Project Foundation, New York, NY
500 Salt Lake Tahoe Women's Center
400 Harmony Manor
300 Project Mana, Incline Village, NV
300 Tahoe Tallac Association, South Lake Tahoe, CA

Education

10,000 TMCC Applied Technology Center
7,500 University of Nevada Reno Foundation, MacKay School of Mines, Reno, NV
7,500 University of Nevada Reno Foundation, MacKay School of Mines, Reno, NV
5,000 Partners in Education, Chicago, IL
4,150 Junior Achievement of Northern Nevada, NV
2,000 Lake Tahoe Community College, CA
500 Kings Beach Elementary

Environment

7,500 Environmental Learning 2000
1,000 Environmental Leadership, Reno, NV
1,000 Great Basin Bird Observatory
500 National Forest Foundation, Arlington, VA

Health

2,500 Juvenile Diabetes Foundation, New York, NY
1,750 American Lung Association
1,200 American Heart Association
1,000 American Red Cross
500 Barton Memorial Hospital, South Lake Tahoe, CA
500 Tahoe Nordic Search and Rescue Team, Tahoe City, CA

Social Services

11,250 United Way of Northern Nevada, Reno, NV
11,250 United Way of Northern Nevada, Reno, NV
11,250 United Way of Northern Nevada, Reno, NV
10,000 Truckee Meadows Food Partnership, Reno, NV
9,457 Boy Scouts of America
9,428 Sierra Nevada Girl Scout Council, Reno, NV
5,000 Elko Snowbowl
2,500 Step 2, Reno, NV
2,000 YMCA
500 Boys and Girls Club of Western Nevada, NV
500 Carson City Sheriff's Department, Carson City, NV
500 El Dorado County Sheriff
500 High Sierra Seniors
500 Incline Ice Foundation, Incline Village, NV
500 Police Activities League, San Francisco, CA
500 YMCA of the Sierra, Reno, NV
400 Washoe Association for Retarded Citizens, Reno, NV
350 Food Bank of Northern Nevada, Reno, NV
300 Ray Schuckman's Sports Complex

J.R. Simplot Co.

Company Contact

Boise, ID

Company Description

Employees: 10,000
SIC(s): 0219 General Livestock Nec, 2034 Dehydrated Fruits, Vegetables & Soups, 2037 Frozen Fruits & Vegetables, 2873 Nitrogenous Fertilizers.

J.R. Simplot Foundation

Giving Contact

Connie Shields, Executive Secretary, Public Relations Department
PO Box 27
Boise, ID 83707
Phone: (208)336-2110

Description

EIN: 826003437
Organization Type: Corporate Foundation. Supports preselected organizations only.
Giving Locations: headquarters and operating communities.
Grant Types: General Support, Scholarship.

Financial Summary

Total Giving: $399,532 (fiscal year ending September 30, 1996); $60,087 (fiscal 1993). Note: Company does not disclose contributions figures. Company primarily gives directly.
Assets: $422 (fiscal 1996); $2,766 (fiscal 1993); $73 (fiscal 1992)
Gifts Received: $397,000 (fiscal 1996); $63,000 (fiscal 1993). Note: In fiscal 1996, contributions were received from the J.R. Simplot Co.

Typical Recipients

Arts & Humanities: Arts & Humanities-General, Libraries, Museums/Galleries, Music, Opera, Public Broadcasting
Civic & Public Affairs: Economic Development, Civic & Public Affairs-General, Hispanic Affairs, Legal Aid, Professional & Trade Associations, Rural Affairs, Urban & Community Affairs
Education: Agricultural Education, Arts/Humanities Education, Business Education, Colleges & Universities, Economic Education, Environmental Education, Education-General, Science/Mathematics Education, Student Aid, Vocational & Technical Education
Environment: Air/Water Quality, Environment-General, Resource Conservation
Health: Cancer, Clinics/Medical Centers, Diabetes, Health Organizations, Prenatal Health Issues
Religion: Religious Welfare
Science: Science Exhibits & Fairs
Social Services: Community Centers, Community Service Organizations, Recreation & Athletics, United Funds/United Ways, YMCA/YWCA/YMHA/YWHA, Youth Organizations

Restrictions

Does not support individuals, religious organizations for sectarian purposes, or political or lobbying groups.

Corporate Officials

Stephen A. Beebe: president, chief executive officer, director B 1945. ED University of Idaho JD. PRIM CORP EMPL president, chief executive officer, director: JR Simplot Co.
Dennis Mogensen: chief financial officer PRIM CORP EMPL chief financial officer: JR Simplot Co.
John Richard Simplot: chairman, founder B Dubuque, IA 1909. PRIM CORP EMPL chairman, founder: JR Simplot Co. CORP AFFIL director: Micron Tech; director: Morrison Knudsen Corp.; director: Continental Life & Accident Co.; director: First Security Corp.

Foundation Officials

James D. Crawford: treasurer B Boise, ID 1950. PRIM CORP EMPL controller: JR Simplot Co.
Ronald Norman Graves: secretary B Caldwell, ID 1942. ED College of Idaho BA (1965); University of Idaho JD (1968); Stanford University (1992). PRIM CORP EMPL secretary, general counsel: JR Simplot Co. CORP AFFIL vice president, secretary: Simplot Canada; vice president, secretary: Simplot Livestock Co. NONPR AFFIL director: United Way Ada County; member advisory board: University Idaho Business School; director: Ronald McDonald House Idaho; member: Idaho Bar Association; director, member: Mountain Sts Legal Foundation; director: Funhdsy; member: American Bar Association; member: American Corporate Counsel Association; director: Albertson College Idaho.
Donald J. Simplot: vice president B 1935. PRIM CORP EMPL vice president, director: JR Simplot Co. CORP AFFIL director: Micron Tech; president: Simplot Fin Corp.
John Richard Simplot: president (see above)

Grants Analysis

Disclosure Period: fiscal year ending September 30, 1996
Number of Grants: 59
Highest Grant: $100,000
Typical Range: $1,000 to $10,000

Recent Grants

Note: Grants derived from fiscal 1997 Form 990.

Arts & Humanities

18,000 Ballet Idaho Dance Company, Boise, ID -- program sponsorship
11,963 Boise State University Foundation, Boise, ID -- for the McCain Library Endowment Fund
7,500 Boise Opera, Boise, ID -- sponsorship of Children's Chorus
6,500 Boise Philharmonic Association, Boise, ID -- sponsorship of Youth Symphony
6,000 Western Folklife Center, Elko, NV
2,000 Idaho Public Television, Boise, ID -- matching grant

Civic & Public Affairs

12,500 Boise River Festival, Boise, ID
4,000 Junior League, Boise, ID
2,750 Idaho Business Week, Boise, ID
2,500 Caldwell Economic Development Council, Caldwell, ID -- for economic development

2,000 Blue Ribbon Coalition, Pocatello, ID
2,000 Idaho Agriculture Summit, Boise, ID
2,000 Leadership Idaho Agriculture Foundation, Meridian, ID
1,092 Canyon County Fair, Nampa, ID -- livestock sale

Education
33,333 Ester Simplot Performing Arts Academy, Boise, ID -- expansion campaign
29,215 University of Idaho, Moscow, ID -- scholarships and Veterinary Medicine Teaching Center
12,000 College of Southern Idaho, Twin Falls, ID -- technology scholarships
9,500 Idaho State University, Boise, ID -- golf tournament and health learning program scholarship
3,500 Pesky Center for Learning Enrichment, Boise, ID -- scholarship
2,500 Idaho Council on Economic Education, Boise, ID
2,500 University of North Dakota, Grand Forks, ND -- scholarship
2,000 Pacific Lutheran University, Tacoma, WA -- scholarship
2,000 Ricks College, Rexburg, ID -- scholarship
1,200 Boise State University Radio Network, Boise, ID
1,000 Albertson College, Boise, ID -- scholarship
1,000 Massachusetts Institute of Technology, Cambridge, MA -- scholarship
1,000 National Future Farmers of America Foundation, Madison, WI
1,000 Oregon State University, Corvallis, OR -- scholarship
1,000 Pensacola Christian College, Pensacola, FL -- scholarship
1,000 University of California Irvine, Irvine, CA -- scholarship
1,000 University of Florida College of Law, Gainesville, FL -- scholarship
1,000 University of Northern Colorado, Greeley, CO -- scholarship
1,000 University of Washington, Bothell, WA -- scholarship
1,000 Utah State University, Logan, UT -- scholarship
1,000 Washington State University, Pullman, WA -- scholarship

Environment
2,000 National Wilderness Institute, Washington, DC -- endangered species research
1,000 National 4-H Wildlife, Pocatello, ID -- Habitat Evaluation Contest program

Health
1,600 Tri-Cities Hospice House, Kennewick, WA

Religion
7,000 St. Luke's Foundation, Boise, ID -- Challenge Team and Light of Philanthropy fundraiser
5,100 St. Alphonsus Foundation, Boise, ID -- Festival of Trees fundraiser
5,000 Salvation Army, Nampa, ID -- building fund

Social Services
10,000 City of Hermiston, Hermiston, ID -- for community center
10,000 Girl Scouts of America Silver Sage Council, Boise, ID -- Friendship Square renovation
10,000 Treasure Valley United Way, Boise, ID -- Ada County agencies support
3,000 Children's Home Society, Boise, ID
2,500 Mini-Cassia Community Chest, Mini-Cassia, ID
2,000 Twin Falls WCA, Twin Falls, ID -- Twin Award support
2,000 Vera House, Syracuse, WY
1,500 Idaho Hall of Fame Humanitarian, Boise, ID -- World Sports Athletic Fund
1,000 McCall Ski Racing Team, McCall, ID

SIMPSON INVESTMENT CO.

Company Contact
Seattle, WA

Company Description
Employees: 83
SIC(s): 6719 Holding Companies Nec.
Parent Company: Kamilche Co.

Operating Locations
Operates in various cities and towns in the above states.

Nonmonetary Support
Value: $20,707 (1998); $519,520 (1997); $664,556 (1996)
Type: Donated Products
Volunteer Programs: The company sponsors a United Way 'Day of Caring' program where employees volunteer their time to help a designated United Way organization.
Note: Donated products include paper.

Matlock Foundation

Giving Contact
Colleen Musgrave, Administrator
Simpson Fund
1301 5th Ave., No. 2800
Seattle, WA 98101
Phone: (206)224-5198
Fax: (206)224-5060
Email: cmusgra@smpsn.com

Description
EIN: 916029303
Organization Type: Corporate Foundation
Giving Locations: CA: Del Norte County, Humboldt County; OR: Lincoln County, Tillamook County, North Portland; WA: Grays Harbor, King County, Mason County, Pierce County, Thurston County
Grant Types: Capital, Emergency, Employee Matching Gifts, General Support, Seed Money.
Note: Employee matching gift ratio: 1 to 1.

Financial Summary
Total Giving: $1,000,000 (2000 approx); $1,000,000 (1999 approx); $870,483 (1998). Note: Contributes through corporate direct giving program and foundation.
Giving Analysis: Giving for 1998 includes: foundation ($595,056); domestic subsidiaries ($196,615); corporate direct giving ($58,105); nonmonetary support ($20,707)
Assets: $1,320 (1993); $13,642 (1992); $188,860 (1989)
Gifts Received: $574,975 (1997); $658,336 (1996); $946,576 (1995). Note: Contributions were received from Simpson Investment Company, Simpson Paper Company, Simpson Timber Company, and Pacific Western Extruded Plastics Company.

Typical Recipients
Arts & Humanities: Arts Associations & Councils, Arts Institutes, Arts & Humanities-General, Historic Preservation, History & Archaeology, Libraries, Museums/Galleries, Music, Opera, Performing Arts, Theater
Civic & Public Affairs: African American Affairs, Botanical Gardens/Parks, Community Foundations, Economic Development, Civic & Public Affairs-General, Municipalities/Towns, Professional & Trade Associations, Safety, Urban & Community Affairs, Zoos/Aquariums
Education: Agricultural Education, Business Education, Colleges & Universities, Community & Junior Colleges, Continuing Education, Economic Education, Education Funds, Education Reform, Elementary Education (Private), Engineering/Technological Education, Environmental Education, Education-General, Private Education (Precollege), Public Education (Precollege), School Volunteerism, Science/Mathematics Education, Student Aid
Environment: Forestry, Environment-General, Resource Conservation, Wildlife Protection
Health: Children's Health/Hospitals, Clinics/Medical Centers, Emergency/Ambulance Services, Geriatric Health, Health Organizations, Hospices, Hospitals, Nursing Services, Trauma Treatment
International: International Relief Efforts
Religion: Churches, Dioceses, Ministries, Religious Welfare
Science: Science Exhibits & Fairs, Scientific Centers & Institutes
Social Services: At-Risk Youth, Child Abuse, Child Welfare, Community Centers, Community Service Organizations, Family Services, Food/Clothing Distribution, Recreation & Athletics, Scouts, Senior Services, Sexual Abuse, Shelters/Homelessness, Substance Abuse, United Funds/United Ways, Youth Organizations

Contributions Analysis
Giving Priorities: United funds, youth groups, and other social service organizations; colleges and universities; the arts, with emphasis on museums and galleries; civic organizations; and health agencies including hospitals and hospices.
Civic & Public Affairs: About 20%. Foundation support focuses on zoological societies and the community.
Education: 10% to 15%. Colleges and universities are primary recipients.
Environment: 5% to 10%. Emphasis is placed on forestry and conservation.
Health: 5% to 10%. Interests include hospitals.
Social Services: About 45%. Most support goes to united funds, shelters, and food banks.

Application Procedures
Initial Contact: Letter or telephone call requesting grant application.
Application Requirements: Completed application form; copy of IRS 501(c)(3) tax exempt letter; list of other donors, including names and amounts; list of board of directors; operating budget of organization for previous year and current year-to-date; and project/program budget.
Deadlines: Annual grant-making cycle begins in April.
Evaluative Criteria: The degree of support from Simpson employees; amount of enthusiasm in the community for the organization or drive; relative size and importance of company operations in the community and balance among Simpson communities; total amount being raised in the overall campaign, compared with the request being made of Simpson; needs of organization or program for which funding is requested; amount of previous Simpson contributions to the organization; amount committed by other companies, foundations, and/or governments (projects should demonstrate broad-based community support); and proximity of the requesting organization to the company operations or headquarters. When possible, contributions will support organizations of interest to or recommended by Simpson employees. The Fund prefers to make capital contributions or provide one-time 'seed money' for programs.
Decision Notification: Meetings are held in June and November to review grant applications.

Restrictions

Does not support individuals or provide funds for endowments or loans.

Additional Information

Foundation is sponsored by Simpson Investment Company and its subsidiaries, which include Simpson Paper Company, Simpson Timber Company, and Pacific Western Extruded Plastics Company. Matlock Foundation does not make grants, but allocates money to the Simpson Fund for giving.
Publications: Application Form

Corporate Officials

Maureen Frisch: vice president public affairs PRIM CORP EMPL vice president public affairs: Simpson Investment Co.
Colin Moseley: chairman, chief executive officer B 1960. ED Northwestern University MBA (1988). PRIM CORP EMPL chairman, chief executive officer: Simpson Investment Co.
Charles F. Pollnow, Jr.: chief financial officer B 1962. ED Princeton University BA; Stanford University MBA. PRIM CORP EMPL chief financial officer: Simpson Investment Co. ADD CORP EMPL chief financial officer: Simpson Paper Co.
William Garrard Reed, Jr.: director B 1939. ED Duke University; Harvard University Graduate School of Business Administration MBA (1969). PRIM CORP EMPL director: Simpson Investment Co. CORP AFFIL director: PACCAR Inc.; director: SAFECO Corp.; director: Microsoft Corp.

Foundation Officials

Kim Bishop: director
Maureen Frisch: president, director (see above)
Colin Moseley: director (see above)
Susan R. Moseley: director
Colleen Musgrave: administrator
Charles F. Pollnow, Jr.: treasurer, director (see above)
William Garrard Reed, Jr.: director (see above)
Raymond P. Tennison: director PRIM CORP EMPL president, chief executive officer: Simpson Paper Co.

Grants Analysis

Disclosure Period: calendar year ending 1998
Total Grants: $595,056*
Number of Grants: 225
Average Grant: $1,250
Highest Grant: $36,829
Typical Range: $500 to $5,000
***Note:** Giving excludes corporate direct giving; domestic subsidiaries; non. Grants analysis provided by foundation.

Recent Grants

Note: Grants derived from 1997 Form 990.

Arts & Humanities

7,500	North Coast Repertory Theater, Eureka, CA
6,000	Alliance of Redding Museums, Redding, CA
6,000	Corporate Council for the Arts, Seattle, WA

Civic & Public Affairs

10,000	Gilman Volunteer Fire Department, Gilman, VT
6,100	Kenton Action Plan, Portland, OR
5,000	Fort Dick Fire Protection District, Fort Dick, CA
5,000	Point Defiance Zoo and Aquarium, Tacoma, WA
5,000	Safe Streets Campaign, Tacoma, WA
5,000	Tacoma Urban League, Tacoma, WA
4,400	Washington Pulp and Paper Foundation, Seattle, WA
4,000	Humboldt County Fire/Arson Investigation Unit, Fortuna, CA
3,300	Providence St. Peter Foundation, Olympia, WA

Education

50,000	Grays Harbor College, Aberdeen, WA
10,000	Agriculture and Forestry Education Foundation, Spokane, WA
10,000	University of Washington Tacoma, Tacoma, WA -- Next Step Scholars Endowment Fund
10,000	Washington Pulp and Paper Foundation, Seattle, WA -- Robert J. Seidl Scholarship Fund
8,000	Communities in Schools, Pasadena, CA
5,000	Independent Colleges, Seattle, WA
5,000	Lunenburg School District, Lunenburg, VT
4,500	Miami University Pulp and Paper Foundation, Oxford, OH
3,600	St. Joseph Elementary School, Pomona, CA
3,500	University of Maine Pulp and Paper Foundation, Orono, ME

Environment

8,500	Rowdy Creek Fish Hatchery, Smith River, CA
3,300	Olympic Wildlife Rescue Project, McCleary, WA

Health

16,952	Grays Harbor Public Hospital, McCleary, WA
5,548	Mason County Department of Emergency Services, Shelton, WA

International

15,000	Habitat for Humanity International, Shelton, WA

Religion

3,250	Pomona Valley Council of Churches, Pomona, CA

Science

6,000	Pacific Science Center, Seattle, WA

Social Services

57,539	United Way of King County, Seattle, WA
21,000	United Way of Mason County, Shelton, WA
16,000	United Funds of Humboldt County, Eureka, CA
14,500	United Way of the Texas Gulf Coast, Houston, TX
12,454	Orick Community Services, Orick, CA
11,300	United Way of Pierce County, Tacoma, WA
10,600	United Way of Northern California, Redding, CA
10,000	Boys and Girls Club of Humboldt County, Eureka, CA
10,000	South Mason Youth Soccer Club, Shelton, WA
9,000	United Way of Grays Harbor, Aberdeen, WA
5,000	Boy Scouts of America Pacific Harbors Council, Tacoma, WA
5,000	Boys and Girls Club of North Mason, Belfair, WA
5,000	Del Norte Senior Center, Crescent City, CA
5,000	McKinleyville Senior Center, McKinleyville, CA
5,000	North Coast Substance Abuse Council, Eureka, CA
5,000	United Way of Del Norte County, Crescent City, CA
4,750	Humboldt Women for Shelter, Arcata, CA
4,000	Pomona Boys Club, Pomona, CA
3,960	North Country United Way, Lisbon, NH
3,692	North Coast Garden for Children, Arcata, CA
3,375	United Way of Pierce County, Tacoma, WA

SIT INVESTMENT ASSOCIATES, INC.

Company Contact

Minneapolis, MN

Company Description

Operating Revenue: US$15,000,000
Employees: 50
SIC(s): 6282 Investment Advice.

SIT Investment Associates Foundation

Giving Contact

Paul Rasmussen, Chief Financial Officer
4600 Norwest Center
90 S. 7th St.
Minneapolis, MN 55402
Phone: (612)332-3223
Fax: (612)342-2018

Description

EIN: 411468021
Organization Type: Corporate Foundation. Supports preselected organizations only.
Giving Locations: MN
Grant Types: General Support.

Financial Summary

Total Giving: $354,863 (1996); $196,930 (1994); $188,640 (1993)
Assets: $8,429,077 (1996); $4,811,864 (1993); $2,746,541 (1990)
Gifts Received: $300,000 (1996); $600,105 (1993); $501,500 (1990). Note: In 1993, contributions were received from SIT Investment Associates.

Typical Recipients

Arts & Humanities: Arts Institutes, Community Arts, History & Archaeology, Museums/Galleries, Music, Opera, Performing Arts
Civic & Public Affairs: African American Affairs, Business/Free Enterprise, Civic & Public Affairs-General, Housing, Native American Affairs, Nonprofit Management, Philanthropic Organizations, Public Policy, Urban & Community Affairs, Women's Affairs
Education: Arts/Humanities Education, Business Education, Colleges & Universities, Economic Education
Health: Children's Health/Hospitals, Emergency/Ambulance Services, Health Organizations, Heart, Hospices, Medical Rehabilitation, Single-Disease Health Associations
International: Foreign Educational Institutions, Health Care/Hospitals, International Development, International Organizations
Religion: Ministries, Religious Welfare
Social Services: At-Risk Youth, Child Welfare, Community Centers, Community Service Organizations, Counseling, Day Care, Delinquency & Criminal Rehabilitation, Family Services, Food/Clothing Distribution, Homes, People with Disabilities, Recreation & Athletics, Shelters/Homelessness, Substance Abuse, United Funds/United Ways, YMCA/YWCA/YMHA/YWHA, Youth Organizations

Restrictions

Does not support individuals, religious organizations for sectarian purposes, or political or lobbying groups.

Corporate Officials

Peter L. Mitchelson: president, director, director PRIM CORP EMPL president, director: SIT Investment Assoc.

Paul E. Rasmussen: chief financial officer PRIM CORP EMPL chief financial officer: SIT Investment Assoc.
Eugene C. Sit: chairman, chief executive officer, director PRIM CORP EMPL chairman, chief executive officer, director: SIT Investment Assoc.

Foundation Officials
Debra K. Beaudet: officer
Gloria A. Heyer: director
Peter L. Mitchelson: director (see above)
Paul E. Rasmussen: officer (see above)
Debra A. Sit: director
Eugene C. Sit: director (see above)

Grants Analysis
Disclosure Period: calendar year ending 1996
Number of Grants: 151
Highest Grant: $25,000
Typical Range: $100 to $5,000

Recent Grants
Note: Grants derived from 1997 Form 990.

Arts & Humanities
25,000 Minneapolis Institute of Arts, Minneapolis, MN
20,000 Minneapolis Institute of Arts, Minneapolis, MN
14,000 Minnesota Historical Society, St. Paul, MN
12,500 Minnesota Orchestral Association, Minneapolis, MN

Civic & Public Affairs
10,000 American Experiment -- support annual dinner
7,500 Elim Transitional Housing, Minneapolis, MN
5,000 American Experience
5,000 American Indian Housing, Minneapolis, MN
4,000 Loring-Nicollet-Bethlehem, Minneapolis, MN
4,000 Marie Sandvik Center, Minneapolis, MN

Education
10,000 Minneapolis College of Art and Design, Minneapolis, MN
10,000 Walter A. Haas School of Business -- support Dean's Fund
3,500 DePaul University, Chicago, IL
3,000 Minneapolis College of Art and Design, Minneapolis, MN

Health
10,000 Community Emergency Services
6,500 Minneapolis Heart Institute Foundation, Minneapolis, MN
3,000 Courage Center, Golden Valley, MN -- support Guardians of Courage

International
250,000 University of Toronto, Toronto, ON, Canada
5,000 Minnesota International Center, Minneapolis, MN
5,000 Salzburg Seminar, Middlebury, VT

Religion
15,000 Lutheran Social Services, Fort Wayne, IN
15,000 Salvation Army
7,000 Housing Resource Program, Lutheran Social Services
4,000 Our Saviour's Housing

Social Services
25,000 Second Harvest Food Bank, Chicago, IL
20,000 Emergency Foodshelf Network, Minneapolis, MN
12,000 United Way
10,000 Sharing and Caring Hands, Minneapolis, MN
5,000 Loaves and Fishes, Greenville, SC
5,000 Minneapolis Crisis Nursery, Minneapolis, MN

SLANT/FIN CORP.

Company Contact
Greenvale, NY
Web: http://www.slantfin.com

Company Description
Employees: 500
SIC(s): 3433 Heating Equipment Except Electric, 3585 Refrigeration & Heating Equipment, 3634 Electric Housewares & Fans.

Slant/Fin Foundation

Giving Contact
Ray Blaquiere, Controller
Slant/Fin Corp.
100 Forest Dr.
Greenvale, NY 11548
Phone: (516)484-2600 ext 384
Fax: (516)484-8906

Description
Founded: 1985
EIN: 112752009
Organization Type: Corporate Foundation. Supports preselected organizations only.
Giving Locations: NY nationally.
Grant Types: General Support.

Financial Summary
Total Giving: $271,363 (fiscal year ending June 30, 1998 approx); $235,295 (fiscal 1997); $218,448 (fiscal 1996). Note: Contributes through foundation only.
Assets: $114,641 (fiscal 1998); $200,250 (fiscal 1996); $316,151 (fiscal 1995)
Gifts Received: $260,000 (fiscal 1998); $90,000 (fiscal 1996); $374,384 (fiscal 1995). Note: Contributions received from Slant/Fin Corp.

Typical Recipients
Arts & Humanities: Arts Appreciation, Arts Associations & Councils, Arts Centers, Arts Funds, Historic Preservation, Libraries, Literary Arts, Museums/Galleries, Music, Opera, Performing Arts, Theater, Visual Arts
Civic & Public Affairs: African American Affairs, Civil Rights, Community Foundations, Economic Development, Ethnic Organizations, Civic & Public Affairs-General, Housing, Law & Justice, Philanthropic Organizations, Professional & Trade Associations, Public Policy, Safety, Urban & Community Affairs, Zoos/Aquariums
Education: Colleges & Universities, Community & Junior Colleges, Education Funds, Engineering/Technological Education, Education-General, Gifted & Talented Programs, Medical Education, Minority Education, Preschool Education, Religious Education, Science/Mathematics Education, Secondary Education (Public)
Environment: Environment-General
Health: Cancer, Children's Health/Hospitals, Clinics/Medical Centers, Geriatric Health, Hospices, Hospitals, Medical Rehabilitation, Medical Research, Single-Disease Health Associations
International: Foreign Educational Institutions, Health Care/Hospitals, International Affairs, International Environmental Issues, International Organizations, International Peace & Security Issues, International Relations, Missionary/Religious Activities
Religion: Jewish Causes, Religious Organizations, Religious Welfare, Seminaries, Synagogues/Temples
Social Services: Animal Protection, Child Welfare, Community Centers, Community Service Organizations, Food/Clothing Distribution, Homes, People with Disabilities, Recreation & Athletics, Refugee Assistance, Senior Services, Shelters/Homelessness, United Funds/United Ways, YMCA/YWCA/YMHA/YWHA, Youth Organizations

Contributions Analysis
Giving Priorities: Jewish organizations receive majority of support. About 10% of contributions go to U.S.-based organizations affiliated with organizations in Israel.
Arts & Humanities: 2%. Interests include art associations, museums, music, and performing arts.
Civic & Public Affairs: 2%. Emphasis on community development and civic affairs.
Education: 6%. Supports colleges, universities, and foundations.
Health: 3%. Supports hospitals, medical centers, and single-disease health associations.
International: 2%. Funds educational institutions, foreign policy, medical centers, and youth programs in Israel.
Religion: 84%. Funds a variety of Jewish organizations and causes, including the United Jewish Appeal Federation, the American Technion Society, and the Anti-defamation League.
Social Services: 1%.
Note: Total contributions made in 1998.

Corporate Officials
Ray Blaquiere: controller finance PRIM CORP EMPL controller: Slant/Fin Corp.
Donald P. Brown: executive vice president, treasurer, director B 1937. ED New York University. PRIM CORP EMPL executive vice president, treasurer, director: Slant/Fin Corp.
Melvin Dubin: chairman B Brooklyn, NY 1923. ED New York University BSEE (1946). PRIM CORP EMPL chairman: Slant/Fin Corp. CORP AFFIL chairman: Greenvale Marketing Corp.; president: Slant/Fin-Hidron Ltd.
John Svitek: vice president finance B 1937. PRIM CORP EMPL vice president finance: Slant/Fin Corp.

Foundation Officials
Delcy Brooks: secretary, director B 1927. PRIM CORP EMPL secretary: Slant/Fin Corp.
Donald P. Brown: treasurer, director (see above)
Melvin Dubin: president, director (see above)
John Svitek: vice president, director (see above)

Grants Analysis
Disclosure Period: fiscal year ending June 30, 1998
Total Grants: $271,363
Number of Grants: 80
Average Grant: $2,165*
Highest Grant: $100,300
Typical Range: $50 to $5,000
***Note:** Average grant figure excludes highest grant.

Recent Grants
Note: Grants derived from fiscal 1997 Form 990.

International
15,000 PEF Israel Endowment Funds, New York, NY
6,000 Thanks to Scandinavia, New York, NY
5,250 Jewish Institute for National Security Affairs, Washington, DC
5,000 American Friends of Nishmat, New York, NY
5,000 American Friends of Sanz Medical Center, New York, NY
5,000 One Israel Fund Yesha Heartland, New York, NY
3,000 American Friends of Israel Arts and Science Academy, New York, NY
2,500 Jerusalem Fellowships, Monsey, NY
2,000 American Friends of Shalom Center, New York, NY

1,300	American Friends of Open University of Israel, New York, NY
1,000	American Associates of Ben Gurion University, New York, NY
1,000	Americans for Safe Israel, New York, NY
1,000	Friends of the Israel Defense Forces, New York, NY
1,000	Thanks to Scandinavia, New York, NY

A.O. Smith Corp.

Company Contact

Milwaukee, WI
Web: http://www.aosmith.com

Company Description

Employees: 13,000
SIC(s): 3089 Plastics Products Nec, 3443 Fabricated Plate Work--Boiler Shops, 3523 Farm Machinery & Equipment, 3714 Motor Vehicle Parts & Accessories.

Operating Locations

Bermuda; Canada; Ireland; Mexico; Netherlands

A.O. Smith Foundation, Inc.

Giving Contact

Edward J. O'Connor, Secretary
A.O. Smith Foundation
11270 West Park Place
Milwaukee, WI 53223-0971
Phone: (414)359-4042
Fax: (414)359-4064

Description

Founded: 1955
EIN: 396076724
Organization Type: Corporate Foundation
Giving Locations: communities where company has manufacturing facilities.
Grant Types: Capital, Employee Matching Gifts, General Support, Operating Expenses, Project, Scholarship.

Financial Summary

Total Giving: $1,000,000 (fiscal year ending June 30, 2000 approx); $1,000,000 (fiscal 1999 approx); $1,000,000 (fiscal 1998 approx). Note: Contributes through corporate direct giving program and foundation. Giving includes foundation; matching gifts; United Way.
Assets: $116,659 (fiscal 1991); $788,300 (fiscal 1990); $14,766 (fiscal 1989)

Typical Recipients

Arts & Humanities: Arts Funds, Dance, Historic Preservation, Libraries, Museums/Galleries, Music, Performing Arts
Civic & Public Affairs: Business/Free Enterprise, Civil Rights, Economic Development, Nonprofit Management, Safety, Urban & Community Affairs
Education: Business Education, Colleges & Universities, Community & Junior Colleges, Economic Education, Education Funds, Engineering/Technological Education, Literacy, Medical Education, Minority Education, Student Aid
Environment: Environment-General
Health: Emergency/Ambulance Services, Hospitals, Medical Rehabilitation, Mental Health, Public Health
Social Services: Child Welfare, Community Centers, Community Service Organizations, Family Services, Homes, People with Disabilities, Recreation & Athletics, Senior Services, Shelters/Homelessness, Substance Abuse, United Funds/United Ways, Youth Organizations

Contributions Analysis

Giving Priorities: Social welfare, colleges and universities, civic causes, and health organizations.
Civic & Public Affairs: About 28%.
Education: 29%. Emphasis on colleges and universities and independent college funds.
Health: 5%.
Social Services: 38%. Major emphasis on the United Way.
Note: Total contributions in 1999.

Application Procedures

Initial Contact: Send a letter or proposal on the organization's letterhead.
Application Requirements: Include name, location, and a description of organization; proof of tax-exempt status; geographic area served; explanation of activity for which support is sought; amount requested; description of benefits to be achieved and who will receive them; budget, including other sources of income; and plans for reporting results.
Deadlines: By October 30 to be considered for following year's budget; requests are reviewed in the order that they are received.
Review Process: The foundation is governed by a four-member board, including the company's vice president of human resources & public affairs.
Decision Notification: The board meets annually in June, with special meetings held periodically when necessary.
Notes: Also forward any printed materials describing your organization that may lend support to the application.

Restrictions

The foundation does not make contributions to politically active organizations seeking to influence legislation, nor does it fund individuals.

Additional Information

A.O. Smith Corp. employees are encouraged to take an active part in civic affairs.

Corporate Officials

John J. Kita: vice president, treasurer, controller, director PRIM CORP EMPL vice president, treasurer, controller: A.O. Smith Corp.
Robert Joseph O'Toole: chairman, president, chief executive officer, director B Chicago, IL 1941. ED Loyola University BS (1961). PRIM CORP EMPL chairman, president, chief executive officer, director: A.O. Smith Corp. CORP AFFIL director: Protection Mutual Insurance Co.; director: Smith Fiberglass Products Inc.; director: FM Global Insurance; director: Firstar Bank NA; director: Firstar Corp.; director: Briggs & Stratton Corp.

Foundation Officials

John J. Kita: treasurer (see above)
Edward J. O'Connor: secretary, director B Saint Louis, MO. ED Saint Louis University (1962). PRIM CORP EMPL vice president human resources & public affairs: A.O. Smith Corp.
Robert Joseph O'Toole: director (see above)
Arthur O. Smith: president B 1930. CORP AFFIL director: AO Smith Corp.; chairman, chief executive officer: Smith Investment Co.; director: Central Studies Distributing Service Inc.

Grants Analysis

Disclosure Period: fiscal year ending June 30, 1994
Total Grants: $718,240
Number of Grants: 211
Average Grant: $3,404

SmithKline Beecham Corp.

 Number 32 of Top 100 Corporate Givers

Company Contact

Philadelphia, PA
Web: http://www.sb.com

Company Description

Employees: 54,000
SIC(s): 2834 Pharmaceutical Preparations, 8071 Medical Laboratories, 8741 Management Services.
Parent Company: SmithKline Beecham Plc, SB House, Great West Rd., Brentford, Middlesex, England

Operating Locations

AZ: SmithKline Beecham Corp., Scottsdale; CA: SmithKline Beecham Corp., Fresno, Irvine, Roseville; FL: SmithKline Beecham Corp., Orlando, Sarasota; SmithKline Beecham Labs, Tallahassee; GA: SmithKline Beecham Labs, Norcross; SmithKline Beecham Corp., Smyrna; ID: SmithKline Beecham Corp., Pocatello; IL: SmithKline Beecham Corp., Crystal Lake, Lisle, Oak Brook, Rolling Meadows; MA: SmithKline Beecham Corp., Newton Center; MD: SmithKline Beecham Corp., Rockville; MN: Diversified Pharmaceutical Services, Edina; NC: SmithKline Beecham Corp., Greensboro, Mooresville; NE: SmithKline Beecham Labs, Lincoln; NJ: SmithKline Beecham Corp., Kirkwood Vrhes, Marlton, Parsippany, Piscataway; NY: SmithKline Beecham Corp., Highland Mills, New York, Wappingers Falls; PA: SmithKline Beecham Corp., Conshohocken; SmithKline Beecham Clinical Laboratories, King of Prussia; SmithKline Beecham Corp., Philadelphia; SmithKline Beecham Corp., Philadelphia; SmithKline Beecham Pharmaceuticals, Philadelphia; SmithKline Beecham Consumer Healthcare, U.S., Pittsburgh; SmithKline Beecham Corp., Pittsburgh; SC: SmithKline Beecham Corp., Myrtle Beach; TN: Affiliated Laboratories, Bristol; SmithKline Beecham Corp., Bristol; SmithKline Beecham Laboratories, Bristol; SmithKline Beecham Pharmaceuticals, Cordova; SmithKline Beecham Corp., Johnson City, Knoxville; TX: SmithKline Beecham Corp., Arlington; SmithKline Beecham Labs, Houston; SmithKline Beecham Corp., San Antonio; WA: SmithKline Beecham Corp., Vancouver, Wenatchee; WI: SmithKline Beecham Corp., Milwaukee

Nonmonetary Support

Value: $15,000,000 (1998); $1,100,000 (1996)
Type: Donated Equipment; Donated Products
Contact: Jean Glenn, Manager, Community Partnership
Email: jean.glenn@sb.com
Note: 1997 nonmonetary support: $15,060,000 (product).

SmithKline Beecham Foundation

Giving Contact

Doug Bauer, Director, Community Partnership
SmithKline Beecham
One Franklin Plz.
PO Box 7929
Philadelphia, PA 19101-7929
Phone: (215)751-4668
Fax: (215)751-7655
Email: doug.bauer@sb.com
Web: http://www.sb.com/company/community

Description

Founded: 1967
EIN: 232120418
Organization Type: Corporate Foundation
Giving Locations: internationally; nationally.
Grant Types: Award, Employee Matching Gifts, General Support, Project.
Note: Employee matching gift ratio: 1 to 1 to education, health care organizations, and the arts.

Financial Summary

Total Giving: $27,597,050 (1999); $28,443,732 (1998 approx); $27,400,917 (1997). Note: Contributes through corporate direct giving program and foundation.
Giving Analysis: Giving for 1997 includes: nonmonetary support ($15,060,000); international subsidiaries ($7,113,500); corporate direct giving ($4,144,598); foundation ($1,082,819); 1998: nonmonetary support ($15,000,000); international subsidiaries ($7,713,545); corporate direct giving ($4,430,187); foundation ($1,300,000)
Assets: $1,627,051 (1996); $1,833,440 (1995); $1,574,636 (1994)
Gifts Received: $1,172,722 (1995); $3,963,836 (1994); $5,151,500 (1993). Note: Foundation receives contributions from SmithKline Beecham Corporation.

Typical Recipients

Arts & Humanities: Arts Associations & Councils, Arts Outreach, Ballet, Ethnic & Folk Arts, History & Archaeology, Libraries, Museums/Galleries, Music, Opera, Theater
Civic & Public Affairs: Economic Policy, Employment/Job Training, Municipalities/Towns, Nonprofit Management, Philanthropic Organizations, Professional & Trade Associations, Public Policy, Urban & Community Affairs, Women's Affairs, Zoos/Aquariums
Education: Arts/Humanities Education, Business Education, Colleges & Universities, Education Funds, Education-General, International Exchange, Literacy, Medical Education, Private Education (Precollege), Science/Mathematics Education, Student Aid
Environment: Environment-General
Health: AIDS/HIV, Cancer, Emergency/Ambulance Services, Health Funds, Health Organizations, Long-Term Care, Medical Research, Single-Disease Health Associations
International: Foreign Educational Institutions, Health Care/Hospitals, International Organizations, International Relations
Science: Scientific Centers & Institutes, Scientific Labs, Scientific Organizations
Social Services: Camps, Crime Prevention, People with Disabilities, Substance Abuse, United Funds/United Ways, Volunteer Services, Youth Organizations

Contributions Analysis

Giving Priorities: North American operations focus giving on better access to better healthcare; European operations fund children's health issues; other international subsidiaries focus on health education and mobilization. Company supports U.S.-based nonprofit organizations with international focus. Interest include international development, public policy, and international exchange.
Arts & Humanities: Supports arts institutions primarily in London and the greater Philadelphia area. Emphasis is on health-related programming in a cultural context.
Civic & Public Affairs: Supports a discourse about health care issues, and communitywide efforts that create further awareness about various health issues.
Health: About 90%. Four Community Partnership Management Teams govern grant making in this area. Priorities are: for North America: better access to better health care; Europe: children's health issues; International: health-care education and mobilization; Corporate: excellence in community based health-care. The majority of grants are initiated by the company and do not result from unsolicited applications. Company donates products to medical nonprofits, and offers the Community Health Impact Awards, which acknowledge and reward excellence in the nonprofit health-care community.
Science: Science education is a priority, including hands-on, inquiry-based science education for youth.
Note: Impact Awards are given to groups in Philadelphia, the United Kingdom, and Canada.

Application Procedures

Initial Contact: Send a two- to three-page letter of inquiry.
Application Requirements: Include a summary a description of organization; a summary of the proposed project or program with description of the problem to be addressed, the proposed solution, how it relates to SB's focus, and how SB products and volunteers (if appropriate) can be incorporated; the amount requested and the proposed project budget (with all other anticipated sources of income); a plan to measure and evaluate program results; and a contact name, address, phone number, fax number and e-mail address if available.
Deadlines: None.
Review Process: Letter of inquiry is reviewed by a staff person, who will contact organization for full proposal.
Notes: Company rarely supports unsolicited grant proposals, but prefers to initiate partnerships.

Restrictions

No grants are made to the following: deficit financing or debt retirement; capital campaigns, chairs, or endowments; individuals; political, labor, religious, fraternal, athletic or veterans' organizations; fund-raising events and associated advertising; conferences and symposia; lobbying groups; or universities or free-standing scientific research centers.

Additional Information

A merger between SmithKline Beecham and Glaxo Wellcome is expected to be finalized in summer 2000.
Publications: Guidelines Sheet; Annual Report

Corporate Officials

Douglas Bauer: director community partnership PRIM CORP EMPL director community partnership: SmithKline Beecham Corp.
James Hill: senior vice president corporate affairs PRIM CORP EMPL senior vice president corporate affairs: SmithKline Beecham Corp.
Jan Leschly: chief executive officer PRIM CORP EMPL chief executive officer: SmithKline Beecham PLC. CORP AFFIL director: CBS Corp.; chief executive officer: SmithKline Beecham International Co.; chairman: Brit Pharma Group. NONPR AFFIL director: Pharmaceutical Research & Manufacturer America; trustee: Pharmaceutical Research & Manufacturer Financial for Infectious Diseases; member dean's advisory council: Emory Business School.
Peter Walters: chairman B Birmingham, England 1931. PRIM CORP EMPL chairman: SmithKline Beecham PLC. CORP AFFIL director: National Westminster Bank USA; chairman: Blue Circle Industries PLC; chairman: Midland Bank. NONPR AFFIL member: Indiana Society Council.

Foundation Officials

Carol Ashe: secretary, general counsel
Douglas Bauer: executive director (see above)
Robert Carr, MD: president
Eileen A. Laksh: treasurer, director

Grants Analysis

Disclosure Period: calendar year ending 1996
Total Grants: $3,764,180*
Number of Grants: 49
Average Grant: $76,820
***Note:** Giving excludes international subsidiaries; matching gifts; nonmonetary support.

Recent Grants

Note: Grants derived from 1995 Form 990.

Arts & Humanities

30,000	Montgomery County-Norristown Public Library, Norristown, PA -- expansion funds

Education

60,000	American Association of Colleges of Pharmacy, Alexandria, VA
35,406	Cornell University College of Veterinary Medicine, Ithaca, NY -- third and final payment of three-year $105,406 grant, to initiate a conceptually novel graduate program in cellular and molecular medicine
30,000	Montgomery County-Norristown Public Library, Norristown, PA -- Science in the Summer programs
23,698	Montgomery County-Norristown Public Library, Norristown, PA -- Science in the Summer programs
21,903	Bucks County Free Library and District Center, Doylestown, PA -- Science in the Summer programs
19,719	Chester County Library, Exton, PA -- Science in the Summer programs
17,077	Delaware County Library System, Brookhaven, PA -- Science in the Summer programs
14,242	Free Library of Philadelphia, Philadelphia, PA -- Science in the Summer programs
8,000	Montgomery County-Norristown Public Library, Norristown, PA -- Science in the Summer programs

JM SMUCKER CO.

Company Contact

Orrville, OH
Web: http://www.smucker.com

Company Description

Employees: 1,900 (1999)
SIC(s): 2033 Canned Fruits & Vegetables, 2038 Frozen Specialties Nec, 2087 Flavoring Extracts & Syrups Nec, 2099 Food Preparations Nec.

Nonmonetary Support

Value: $394,000 (1991); $250,000 (1990); $200,000 (1989)
Type: Cause-related Marketing & Promotion; Donated Products

Giving Contact

Maribeth Badertscher, Manager, Employee Training & Development
J.M. Smucker Co.
Strawberry Lane
Orrville, OH 44667
Phone: (330)682-0015
Fax: (330)684-3475
Email: info@smucker.com

Description

Organization Type: Corporate Giving Program
Giving Locations: emphasis on five-county area surrounding headquarters; operating locations.
Grant Types: General Support.

Financial Summary

Total Giving: Contributes through corporate direct giving program only.

Typical Recipients

Arts & Humanities: Performing Arts, Public Broadcasting
Civic & Public Affairs: Urban & Community Affairs
Education: Colleges & Universities, Elementary Education (Private)
Health: Health Organizations
Social Services: Community Service Organizations

Contributions Analysis

Giving Priorities: Higher education, public policy, and cultural organizations.
Arts & Humanities: 5% to 10%. Supports business-sponsored arts funds, performing arts centers, libraries, public broadcasting, and the visual and performing arts.
Civic & Public Affairs: About 35%. Supports national public policy research organizations and community improvement efforts.
Education: About 50%. Supports accredited institutions of higher education, state and local education fund-raising associations, minority education funds, and economic education.
Health: Less than 5%. Support includes national health and human service organizations such as the American Cancer Society, the American Red Cross, and the National Committee to Prevent Child Abuse.

Application Procedures

Initial Contact: Submit a brief letter or proposal.
Application Requirements: Include a description of organization, amount requested, purpose of funds sought, recently audited financial statement, and proof of tax-exempt status.
Deadlines: None.

Additional Information

Company's goal is to donate 2% of pretax profits to charitable activities.

Corporate Officials

Cathy Hogan: director change management PRIM CORP EMPL director change management: JM Smucker Co.
Timothy Paul Smucker: chairman, director B Wooster, OH 1944. ED College of Wooster BA (1967); University of Pennsylvania Wharton School MBA (1969). PRIM CORP EMPL chairman, director: JM Smucker Co. CORP AFFIL chairman: AF Murch Co.; director: Smucker Quality Beverages; director: Kellogg Co.; president: HB DeViney Co. Inc.; director: Huntington Bancshares Inc.

Grants Analysis

Disclosure Period: calendar year ending
Typical Range: $500 to $2,000

Smurfit-Stone Container Corp.

Company Contact

150 N. Michigan Avenue
Chicago, IL 60601
Phone: (312)346-6600
Fax: (312)580-2272
Web: http://www.smurfit-stone.net

Company Description

Former Name: Jefferson Smurfit Corp.
Revenue: US$7,386,000,000 (1999)
Profit: US$157,000,000 (1999)
Employees: 36,300 (1999)
Fortune Rank: 240, per FORTUNE Magazine's list of 500 Largest U.S. Corporations (1999).
FF 240
SIC(s): 2411 Logging, 2493 Reconstituted Wood Products, 2631 Paperboard Mills, 2657 Folding Paperboard Boxes.
Parent Company: Jefferson Smurfit Group Plc, Beech Hill, Clonskeagh, Dublin 4, DU, Ireland

Operating Locations

AR: Smurfit-Stone Container Corp.; CA: Smurfit-Stone Container Corp.; DE: Smurfit Plastic Packaging Div., Wilmington; FL: Smurfit-Stone Container Corp.; GA: Smurfit-Stone Container Corp.; IN: Smurfit-Stone Container Corp.; KS: Smurfit-Stone Container Corp.; KY: Smurfit-Stone Container Corp.; MI: Smurfit-Stone Container Corp.; MO: Carton Division, Saint Louis; Jefferson Smurfit Consumer Packaging Div., Saint Louis; Jefferson Smurfit Corp., Saint Louis; Jefferson Smurfit Folding Carton & Boxboard Mills Div., Saint Louis; Mill Division, Saint Louis; Smurfit Packaging Corp., Saint Louis; NC: Smurfit-Stone Container Corp.; NY: Smurfit-Stone Container Corp.; Orlandi, Farmingdale; OH: Smurfit-Stone Container Corp.; OR: Smurfit-Stone Container Corp.; Newberg Division, Newberg; Oregon City Division, Oregon City; Smurfit Newsprint Corp., Oregon City; TX: Smurfit-Stone Container Corp.; UT: Smurfit-Stone Container Corp.; WI: Smurfit-Stone Container Corp.

Corporate Sponsorship

Type: Arts & cultural events; Festivals/fairs; Music & entertainment events; Pledge-a-thon; Sports events

Jefferson Smurfit Corp. Charitable Trust

Giving Contact

Pam Bazzell, Corporate Secretary
Smurfit-Stone Container Corp.
8182 Maryland Avenue
St. Louis, MO 63105
Phone: (314)746-1151
Fax: (314)746-1259

Alternate Contact

Phone: (314)746-1204

Description

Founded: 1951
EIN: 436023508
Organization Type: Corporate Foundation
Giving Locations: MO: St. Louis
Grant Types: General Support.

Financial Summary

Total Giving: $702,900 (1998); $901,433 (1997); $1,039,067 (1996). Note: Contributes through foundation only.
Giving Analysis: Giving for 1996 includes: foundation ($1,006,067); foundation grants to United Way ($33,000); 1998: foundation ($644,900); foundation grants to United Way (approx $58,000)
Assets: $5,011,786 (1998); $3,481,393 (1997); $2,680,114 (1996)
Gifts Received: $1,650,000 (1998); $1,350,000 (1997); $2,950,000 (1996). Note: In 1996 and 1998, foundation received contributions from the Jefferson Smurfit Corp.

Typical Recipients

Arts & Humanities: Arts Associations & Councils, Ballet, Dance, Arts & Humanities-General, Museums/Galleries, Music, Theater
Civic & Public Affairs: Economic Development, Civic & Public Affairs-General, Municipalities/Towns, Parades/Festivals, Professional & Trade Associations, Public Policy, Urban & Community Affairs, Zoos/Aquariums
Education: Agricultural Education, Business Education, Colleges & Universities, Education Funds, Education-General, Minority Education, Private Education (Precollege), Special Education, Student Aid, Vocational & Technical Education
Environment: Environment-General, Wildlife Protection
Health: Alzheimers Disease, Cancer, Children's Health/Hospitals, Mental Health, Multiple Sclerosis, Single-Disease Health Associations
Religion: Jewish Causes, Religious Organizations, Religious Welfare, Social/Policy Issues
Science: Scientific Centers & Institutes
Social Services: At-Risk Youth, Child Welfare, Community Service Organizations, Scouts, United Funds/United Ways, YMCA/YWCA/YMHA/YWHA, Youth Organizations

Contributions Analysis

Giving Priorities: Education, social servies, the arts, civic organizations, and health causes.
Arts & Humanities: 18%. Supports various arts organizations located in the St. Louis area.
Civic & Public Affairs: 9%. Supports economic development.
Education: 29%. Supports colleges and universities, agriculture education, and business education.
Health: 8%. Interests include single-disease health associations.
Religion: 5%. Supports religious welfare organizations.
Social Services: 28%. Awards major support to Boys Hope; also supports the United Way and youth organizations.
Note: Total contributions made in 1998.

Application Procedures

Initial Contact: Send letter and a brief proposal.
Application Requirements: Include a description of organization, amount requested, who benefits from programs or projects, and time frame.
Deadlines: None.
Review Process: Contributions committee meets monthly to review requests.

Restrictions

The foundation will only award grants for religious, charitable, scientific, literary or other education purposes as defined by federal legislation.

Additional Information

The company was formed in 1998 by the merger of Jefferson Smurfit and Stone Container.
The company reports that Boatmen's Trust Company serves as a corporate trustee for the trust.

Corporate Officials

Richard William Graham: president, chief executive officer, chief operating officer, director B Philadelphia, PA 1934. ED Lafayette College BS (1956); University of Pennsylvania MBA (1957-1959). PRIM CORP EMPL president, chief executive officer, chief operating officer, director: Smurfit-Stone Container Corp. CORP AFFIL director: JM Smucker Co.; director: Mercantile Bank Saint Louis NA.
Patrick J. Moore: vice president ED DePaul University BBA (1981). PRIM CORP EMPL vice president: Smurfit-Stone Container Corp.
Michael William J. Smurfit: chairman B 1936. PRIM CORP EMPL chairman: Smurfit-Stone Container Corp. CORP AFFIL chairman: JSCE Inc.; chairman: Michigan Canada & Tube Inc.; chairman: Jefferson Smurfit Corp. United States; chairman, chief executive officer: Jefferson Smurfit Group PLC.

Foundation Officials

Jack Straw: member administration committee PRIM CORP EMPL vice president: Smurfit-Stone Container Corp.

Grants Analysis

Disclosure Period: calendar year ending 1998
Total Grants: $644,900*
Typical Range: $5,000 to $30,000
***Note:** Giving excludes United Way.

Recent Grants

Note: Grants derived from 1996 Form 990.

Arts & Humanities

15,000	St. Louis Symphony Orchestra, Saint Louis, MO
12,500	Sheldon Arts Foundation, Saint Louis, MO
5,000	Arts and Education Council, Saint Louis, MO
5,000	Repertory Theater, Saint Louis, MO
3,000	Dance St. Louis Ballet Ball, Saint Louis, MO
1,500	St. Louis Art Museum Foundation, Saint Louis, MO

Civic & Public Affairs

20,000	Campaign for Greater St. Louis, Saint Louis, MO
12,000	Greater St. Louis Area, Saint Louis, MO
10,000	National Conference, Saint Louis, MO
3,000	Confluence St. Louis, Saint Louis, MO

Education

100,000	St. Louis University, Saint Louis, MO
100,000	St. Louis University, Saint Louis, MO
25,000	Washington University, Saint Louis, MO
25,000	Washington University, Saint Louis, MO
25,000	Washington University, Saint Louis, MO
19,000	University of Missouri Rolla, Rolla, MO
10,000	Glenwood School for Boys, Glenwood, IL
5,000	Evans Scholars Foundation, Golf, IL
3,400	Good Shepherd School, Pacifica, CA
2,500	Junior Achievement, Saint Louis, MO
2,500	United Negro College Fund, Saint Louis, MO

Health

8,000	American Cancer Society, Saint Louis, MO
5,000	St. Louis Children's Hospital, Saint Louis, MO

Religion

15,000	Jewish Community Centers Association, Saint Louis, MO
1,000	Salvation Army Tree of Lights, Saint Louis, MO

Science

20,000	St. Louis Science Center, Saint Louis, MO
20,000	St. Louis Science Center, Saint Louis, MO

Social Services

150,000	YMCA, Saint Louis, MO
135,334	Boys Hope/Girls Hope, Saint Louis, MO
135,333	Boys Hope/Girls Hope, Saint Louis, MO
60,000	YMCA, Saint Louis, MO
33,000	United Way, Saint Louis, MO
31,000	Boys Hope/Girls Hope, Saint Louis, MO
5,000	Assistance League, Saint Louis, MO
5,000	Girl Scout Council, Saint Louis, MO
5,000	Mathews Dickey Boys Club, Saint Louis, MO
4,500	YMCA, Saint Louis, MO
1,500	Hugh O'Brian Youth Foundation, Los Angeles, CA

Solo Cup Co.

Company Contact

Highland Park, IL

Company Description

Employees: 3,000
SIC(s): 2656 Sanitary Food Containers, 3089 Plastics Products Nec.
Parent Company: SCC Holding Co.

Solo Cup Foundation

Giving Contact

Ronald L. Whaley, Foundation Administrator
Solo Cup Foundation
1700 Old Deerfield Road
Highland Park, IL 60035
Phone: (847)831-4800
Fax: (847)831-5849

Description

Founded: 1959
EIN: 366062327
Organization Type: Corporate Foundation
Giving Locations: IL
Grant Types: Capital, General Support, Operating Expenses, Project, Research, Scholarship.

Financial Summary

Total Giving: $2,239,400 (fiscal year ending March 31, 1997); $2,950,863 (fiscal 1996). Note: Contributes through foundation only.
Giving Analysis: Giving for fiscal 1996 includes: foundation scholarships ($88,000)
Assets: $11,068 (fiscal 1997); $1,313,828 (fiscal 1996)
Gifts Received: $1,163,291 (fiscal 1997); $2,272,570 (fiscal 1996); $7,732,473 (fiscal 1989). Note: Contributions received from Solo Cup Co. and Joseph L. Hulseman.

Typical Recipients

Arts & Humanities: Arts & Humanities-General, Performing Arts, Theater
Civic & Public Affairs: Employment/Job Training, Civic & Public Affairs-General, Philanthropic Organizations, Urban & Community Affairs
Education: Business Education, Gifted & Talented Programs, Preschool Education, Private Education (Precollege), Religious Education, Science/Mathematics Education, Secondary Education (Private), Student Aid
Health: Cancer, Children's Health/Hospitals, Hospitals, Prenatal Health Issues, Public Health, Single-Disease Health Associations
International: Missionary/Religious Activities
Religion: Churches, Dioceses, Jewish Causes, Ministries, Missionary Activities (Domestic), Religious Organizations, Religious Welfare
Social Services: At-Risk Youth, Community Centers, Community Service Organizations, Delinquency & Criminal Rehabilitation, Family Services, Food/Clothing Distribution, People with Disabilities, Scouts, Senior Services, Social Services-General, Substance Abuse, United Funds/United Ways, Volunteer Services, YMCA/YWCA/YMHA/YWHA, Youth Organizations

Contributions Analysis

Civic & Public Affairs: Less than 5%. Supports civic funding initiatives, such as Old St. Patrick's Renaissance Campaign, Chicago, IL.
Education: 40% to 45%. Funds private precollege education.
Health: Less than 5%. Supports hospitals and medical research.
Religion: 10% to 15%. Supports Roman Catholic churches and missionary activities.
Social Services: 40% to 45%. Majority of funding supports the Salvation Army in Washington, DC; Baltimore, MD; and Chicago, IL. Also funds homes for the disabled, substance abuse recovery programs, religious welfare, and youth groups.
Note: Total contributions in fiscal 1997.

Application Procedures

Initial Contact: Send a full proposal.
Application Requirements: Include a description of organization, amount requested, purpose of funds sought, audited financial statement, and proof of tax-exempt status.
Deadlines: None.

Restrictions

Does not support individuals or political or lobbying groups.

Corporate Officials

John F. Hulseman: vice president manufacturing, secretary, director B 1930. PRIM CORP EMPL vice president manufacturing, secretary, director: Solo Cup Co.
Robert L. Hulseman: president, chief executive officer, director B 1932. PRIM CORP EMPL president, chief executive officer, director: Solo Cup Co.

Foundation Officials

John F. Hulseman: vice president (see above)
Robert L. Hulseman: president (see above)
Ronald L. Whaley: foundation administrator ED Illinois State University. PRIM CORP EMPL vice president, treasurer, director: SCC Holding Co. CORP AFFIL vice president: Quality Inks Inc.; vice president, treasurer, director: Solo Cup Co.; vice president: Business Leases Inc.

Grants Analysis

Disclosure Period: fiscal year ending March 31, 1997
Total Grants: $2,239,400
Number of Grants: 48
Average Grant: $46,654
Highest Grant: $250,000
Typical Range: $5,000 to $50,000

Recent Grants

Note: Grants derived from 1997 Form 990.

Arts & Humanities

25,000	Jesuit High School, Portland, OR -- for Performing Arts Center
13,000	Wisemnear West Theater, Cleveland, OH -- capital improvements
5,000	Urban Gateways, Chicago, IL -- for cultural enrichment program

Civic & Public Affairs

20,000	Victory 2000, Winnetka, IL
15,000	Iowa CCI, Des Moines, IA

Education

250,000	St. Scholastica Academy, Chicago, IL
233,714	Congregation of the Passion, Chicago, IL -- for school expansion project
200,000	Johns Hopkins School of Medicine, Baltimore, MD -- for scientist fund
150,000	Benedictine School, Ridgely, MO
50,000	John Carroll University, University Heights, OH -- for Management and Marketing Center
40,000	Notre Dame De La Baie Academy, Green Bay, WI
30,000	Immaculate Conception School, Bronx, NY -- computer project
29,800	Christ the King School, Bronx, NY -- for computer project, Aquinas Program
25,000	Mother Seton School, Emmitsburg, MD -- for school bus
19,491	Sacred Heart School, Bronx, NY -- for Aspire Project
18,000	Cleveland Central Catholic High School, Cleveland, OH -- scholarships, computer project
15,000	St. John School Development Fund, Westminster, MD -- computer project

Health

250,000 Larabida Children's Hospital, Chicago, IL -- for case management program
50,000 Memorial Sloan-Kettering Cancer Center, New York, NY
25,000 Highland Park Hospital Foundation, Highland Park, IL -- for birthing center
25,000 Little Sisters of the Poor, Palatine, IL -- for health care program
5,000 American Cancer Society, Gurnee, IL -- support Relay for Life Event

International

10,000 Jesuit International Mission, Chicago, IL -- for Christo Rey Project

Religion

110,000 Saints Faith, Hope and Charity, Winnetka, IL -- for Charity Fund, Sharing Fund
75,000 Old St. Patrick's Church, Chicago, IL -- for renovations
50,000 St. Michael the Archangel Parish, Chicago, IL
50,000 St. Procudus Church, Chicago, IL -- for park project
30,000 Franciscan Center, Baltimore, MD -- for building campaign
25,000 Benet Hill Monastery, Colorado Springs, CO
25,000 Our Lady of Joy, Carefree, AZ
25,000 St. Bede Priory, Eau Claire, WI
25,000 St. Columbanus Church, Chicago, IL
10,000 Daughters of Charity, Emmitsburg, MD -- for outreach project
10,000 Redemptoristine Nuns, Liguori, MO -- for repairs, expansion
10,000 St. Peter and Paul Catholic Church, Easton, MD -- annual fund
5,000 Jesuite Volunteer Corps of the Midwest, Detroit, MI -- for volunteer program
5,000 St. Ann Catholic Church, Warsaw, MO -- for new church project

Social Services

50,000 Boys Hope, Saint Louis, MO
50,000 Hazelden, Center City, MN
50,000 Hazelden, Chicago, IL -- for the Chicago Project
25,000 Beans and Bread, Baltimore, MD -- for meal program
15,000 Shore Community Services, Skokie, IL -- for van
12,000 A Safe Place, Waukegan, IL
10,000 Executive Service Corps, Chicago, IL
10,000 United Fund of Talbot County, Easton, MD
5,000 Boy Scouts of America, Wilmington, DE -- for renovation project
5,000 Jeanne Jugan Residence, Newark, DE
2,500 YMCA, Chicago, IL -- annual campaign

SONOCO PRODUCTS CO.

Company Contact

Hartsville, SC
Web: http://www.sonoco.com

Company Description

Revenue: US$2,788,100,000
Profit: US$164,500,000
Employees: 19,000
SIC(s): 2421 Sawmills & Planing Mills--General, 2499 Wood Products Nec, 2631 Paperboard Mills, 2679 Converted Paper Products Nec.

Operating Locations

Operates 165 branch or manufacturing facilities in the U.S., 25 in Canada, and 78 in other foreign countries.

Nonmonetary Support

Type: Donated Equipment; Donated Products

Sonoco Foundation

Giving Contact

Joyce Beasley, Manager, Community Affairs
Sonoco Foundation
One North 2nd Street, Mail Stop A09
Hartsville, SC 29550
Phone: (843)383-7851
Fax: (843)383-7008
Email: joyce.beasley@sonoco.com
Web: http://www.sonoco.com/sonoco_foundation.htm

Description

EIN: 570752950
Organization Type: Corporate Foundation
Giving Locations: SC counties in which employees reside.
Grant Types: Award, Emergency, Employee Matching Gifts, Endowment, General Support, Matching, Multiyear/Continuing Support, Project, Research, Scholarship.
Note: Employee matching gift ratio: 1 to 1 for higher education.

Giving Philosophy

'Sonoco Products Company continues, through its philanthropic and business endeavors, to demonstrate its commitment to social responsibility. The corporation views its contribution program as an investment to improve the quality of life, especially in communities where Sonoco has operations. The Sonoco Foundation, the principal conduit for corporate contributions of Sonoco Products Company, is responsive to human needs through its support of quality projects and programs within its priority areas of funding. The Foundation's grant program currently focuses on education, health and welfare, arts and culture and the environment. The Foundation supports higher education institutions that supply Sonoco Products Company's future leaders and technologists. The vast majority of these funds support United States institutions with a local, rather than a national, perspective.' *Guidelines for Grant Consideration*

Financial Summary

Total Giving: $1,750,198 (1998); $2,018,809 (1997); $2,171,628 (1996). Note: Contributes through corporate direct giving program and foundation. Giving includes foundation.
Giving Analysis: Giving for 1998 includes: foundation ($1,666,648); foundation grants to United Way ($83,550)
Assets: $2,842 (1998); $458,143 (1997); $31,719 (1996)
Gifts Received: $1,295,000 (1998); $2,445,300 (1997); $1,956,200 (1996). Note: Contributions received from Sonoco Products Co.

Typical Recipients

Arts & Humanities: Arts Associations & Councils, Arts Centers, Arts Festivals, Arts Funds, Arts Institutes, Community Arts, Dance, Arts & Humanities-General, Historic Preservation, History & Archaeology, Libraries, Museums/Galleries, Music, Opera, Performing Arts, Public Broadcasting, Theater
Civic & Public Affairs: African American Affairs, Botanical Gardens/Parks, Business/Free Enterprise, Clubs, Economic Development, Civic & Public Affairs-General, Housing, Municipalities/Towns, Parades/Festivals, Professional & Trade Associations, Public Policy, Safety, Urban & Community Affairs, Women's Affairs
Education: Arts/Humanities Education, Business Education, Business-School Partnerships, Colleges & Universities, Community & Junior Colleges, Economic Education, Education Funds, Education Reform, Elementary Education (Private), Elementary Education (Public), Engineering/Technological Education, Faculty Development, Education-General, Health & Physical Education, Minority Education, Private Education (Precollege), Public Education (Precollege), Science/Mathematics Education, Secondary Education (Public), Student Aid
Environment: Forestry, Environment-General
Health: Cancer, Children's Health/Hospitals, Emergency/Ambulance Services, Eyes/Blindness, Health-General, Health Organizations, Hospitals, Medical Rehabilitation, Medical Research, Mental Health, Multiple Sclerosis, Research/Studies Institutes, Single-Disease Health Associations
Science: Science Exhibits & Fairs
Social Services: Camps, Child Welfare, Community Centers, Community Service Organizations, Domestic Violence, Emergency Relief, Family Services, Homes, Recreation & Athletics, Scouts, Shelters/Homelessness, Social Services-General, Special Olympics, Substance Abuse, United Funds/United Ways, Volunteer Services, YMCA/YWCA/YMHA/YWHA, Youth Organizations

Contributions Analysis

Giving Priorities: Focuses on education and health and welfare; also supports arts and culture and civic concerns.
Arts & Humanities: 3%. Supports historic preservation, museums, arts councils, and arts festivals.
Civic & Public Affairs: 8%. Majority of giving supports urban and community development projects designed to improve and revitalize communities, and promote the general well-being of all citizens.
Education: 60%. Primarily supports colleges and universities, college funds, private and public secondary education, business education, and humanities education. Focus is on institutions from which the company recruits.
Environment: Less than 1%. Supports local environmental and conservation efforts.
Health: 1%. Single-disease health associations and emergency services.
Social Services: 28%. Emphasis on YMCAs and the United Way.
Note: Total contributions in 1998.

Application Procedures

Initial Contact: Request application guidelines, then send an application letter (no more than 3 pages).
Application Requirements: Include name, address, telephone number and IRS tax-exempt classification of organization; summary of the purpose of funds, and evidence of need; amount of money requested and its proposed use.
Deadlines: None.
Review Process: Foundation reviews applications quarterly.

Restrictions

Foundation supports selected activities in the form of one-time or, on occasion, multi-year grants. One time grants receive the strongest consideration.
Requests for grants for the following are ineligible: projects in areas where the company has no operations; individuals; private foundations; courtesy advertising, testimonial dinners; loans or investments, pledges longer than five years, automatic renewal of grants; lobbying for political purposes; projects which are sensitive, controversial or harmful, or which pose a potential conflict of interest to the company; organizations that discriminate in any way and are inconsistent with national equal opportunity policies.
The foundation generally does not contribute to the following: intermediary funding agencies that channel monies to donee organizations, except the United Way; projects that consist simply of fund-raising events; grants to cover operating deficits; memorials;

national organizations where local or regional chapters are supported; endowments; fraternal, social, labor or veterans' organizations; memberships; conferences, workshops, or seminars; 'brick and mortar' building grants.
Foundation prefers not to be the only funding source for a project.

Corporate Officials

Peter C. Browning: chief executive officer, president, director ED Colgate University BA (1963); University of Chicago MBA (1976). PRIM CORP EMPL chief executive officer, president, director: Sonoco Products Co. CORP AFFIL director: Wachovia Bank & Trust; director: Pelican Co.; director: Phoenix Home Life Mutual Insurance Co.; director: Lowe's Co. Inc. NONPR AFFIL member executive: Pee Dee Area County Boy Scouts America; trustee: Presbyterian Hospital Foundation; member board visitors: McCall School business/Queens College; member: National Association Manufacturer; member: Conference Board; director: Darlington County Community in School; trustee: Coker College; member council: Chicago Graduate School. CLUB AFFIL member: Quail Hollow Country Club; member: DeBordieu Country Club.

Charles Westfield Coker: vice president B Florence, SC 1933. ED Princeton University BA (1955); Harvard University MBA (1957). PRIM CORP EMPL vice president: Sonoco Products Co. ADD CORP EMPL president: Sonoco Puerto Rico Inc. CORP AFFIL director: Sara Lee Corp.; director: Springs Industries Inc.; director: Carolina Power & Light Co.; director: NCNB Corp.; director: BankAmerica Corp. NONPR AFFIL director: Hollings Cancer Center; member: Palmetto Business Forum. CLUB AFFIL Rotary Club.

Harris E. DeLoach, Junior: executive vice president, director B Columbia, SC 1944. ED University of South Carolina BBA (1966); University of South Carolina JD (1969). PRIM CORP EMPL executive vice president, director: Sonoco Products Co. CORP AFFIL director: Sebro Plastics Inc. NONPR AFFIL member: Rotary International; member: South Carolina Bar Association; member: Darlington County Bar Association; member: Hartsville Chamber of Commerce; member: 4th Jud. Cir. Association South Carolina; member: American Bar Association.

Frank Trent Hill, Jr.: vice president, chief financial officer B Greensboro, NC 1952. ED University of North Carolina BS (1974). PRIM CORP EMPL vice president, chief financial officer: Sonoco Products Co. CORP AFFIL director: Trion Inc.

Harry J. Moran: executive vice president B Pasadena, CA 1932. ED Loyola University (1954). PRIM CORP EMPL executive vice president: Sonoco Products Co. CORP AFFIL president, director: Sonoco Containers Canada; director: Sonoco France; director: Sonoca Latin America; director: Engraph Corp.; director: Keating Corp.; chairman: CMB-Sonoco Europe.

Foundation Officials

Charles Westfield Coker: trustee (see above)
Frank Trent Hill, Jr.: trustee (see above)
Charles J. Hupfer: trustee B 1946. ED University of North Carolina, Charlotte MS; University of North Carolina BS (1968). PRIM CORP EMPL vice president, secretary, treasurer: Sonoco Products Co. ADD CORP EMPL treasurer: Speciality Packaging Group Inc.

James Herbert Shelley: chairman B Columbia, SC 1943. ED University of South Carolina BA (1965); University of South Carolina JD (1969). PRIM CORP EMPL staff vice president personnel & industrial relations: Sonoco Products Co. CORP AFFIL chairman: Sonopal. NONPR AFFIL trustee: South Carolina Business & Industry Policy Education Committee. CLUB AFFIL Hartsville Country Club; Prestwood Club.

Grants Analysis

Disclosure Period: calendar year ending 1998
Total Grants: $1,666,648*
Number of Grants: 272
Average Grant: $6,127
Highest Grant: $500,000
Typical Range: $500 to $10,000
***Note:** Giving excludes United Way.

Recent Grants

Note: Grants derived from 1997 Form 990.

Arts & Humanities

16,666	Governors Mansion Foundation
5,000	Arts and Science Council, Charlotte, NC
2,500	Hartsville High School Bands, Hartsville, SC

Civic & Public Affairs

20,000	Town of Society Hill
10,000	American Legion Post 53
5,000	State Development Board -- special events
4,000	Columbia Urban League, Columbia, SC

Education

500,000	Trinity Collegiate School, Florence, SC
380,000	Governors School for Science and Mathematics
125,000	Thomas E. Hart Academy
100,000	Independent Colleges and Universities, Taylors, SC
50,000	Coker College, Darlington, SC
50,000	Packaging Education Forum, Herndon, VA
25,000	Management Education Alliance, Fort Mill, SC
21,000	Independent Colleges and Universities, Taylors, SC
20,000	North Carolina State University, Raleigh, NC
20,000	Queens College Hugh McColl School of Business
16,887	Coker College, Darlington, SC
15,747	Coker College, Darlington, SC
10,000	Communities in Schools for Darlington County
10,000	Wofford College, Spartanburg, SC
8,333	South Carolina Business Center for Excellence in Education, SC
6,885	Coker College, Darlington, SC
6,000	Junior Achievement of Central South Carolina, SC
5,000	Coker College, Darlington, SC
5,000	College Fund/UNCF
5,000	Pee Dee Education Foundation, Florence, SC
3,325	Clemson University, Clemson, SC
2,930	Wofford College, Spartanburg, SC
2,700	University of North Carolina Chapel Hill, Chapel Hill, NC
2,500	Campaign for Clemson
2,500	Sonovista Elementary School
2,200	Carolina Elementary School
2,100	Hartsville Junior High School, Hartsville, SC

Environment

5,000	Palmetto Project of Darlington County, Sumter, SC

Health

250,000	Shriners Hospital for Children
10,000	National Multiple Sclerosis Society, New York, NY
5,000	Hollings Cancer Center

Social Services

72,000	Hebron Colony and Grace Home, Boone, NC
20,000	McBee Scouting and Community Center
10,000	Irish Children's Summer Program
10,000	Lydia Red Sox Baseball Team
10,000	Putting Families First Foundation
10,000	Snoopy Super Summer Day Camp
10,000	Southeastern Baseball Classic
10,000	Special Olympics, SC
5,000	American Legion Post 53 Baseball
5,000	Hartsville Country Club Junior Golf Foundation, Hartsville, SC
3,000	Hartsville Alert Center, Hartsville, SC
3,000	Hartsville Dixie Boys Baseball, Hartsville, SC

SONY ELECTRONICS

Company Contact

Park Ridge, NJ
Web: http://www.sony.com

Company Description

SIC(s): 3571 Electronic Computers, 3572 Computer Storage Devices, 3577 Computer Peripheral Equipment Nec, 3651 Household Audio & Video Equipment.
Parent Company: Sony Corp. of America

Operating Locations

AL: Sony Electronics, Dothan; AZ: Materials Research Corp., Gilbert, Phoenix; CA: Merv Griffin Enterprises, Beverly Hills; Columbia Tri-Star Home Video, Burbank; Sony Trans Com Systems, Costa Mesa; Columbia Pictures, Culver City; Columbia Tri-Star Film Distributors International, Culver City; Columbia Tri-Star International Releasing Corp., Culver City; Columbia Tri-Star International Television, Culver City; Culver Studios, Culver City; Sony Pictures Entertainment, Culver City; Sony Pictures Entertainment Television Group, Culver City; Sony Pictures Studios, Culver City; TriStar Pictures, Culver City; Sony Electronics, Cypress; Sony Logistics Service Co., Long Beach; Guber Peters Entertainment Co., Los Angeles; Sony Electronics, San Diego; Sony Engineering & Manufacturing of America, San Diego; Sony Electronics, San Jose; Sony Microelectronics, San Jose; Materials Research Corp., Santa Clara; Sony Music Entertainment, Santa Monica; FL: Sony Electronics, Boca Raton; Sony Professional Products Co., Boca Raton; Sony Electronics, Miami; GA: Sony Electronics, Atlanta; IL: Sony Electronics, Chicago; IN: Digital Audio Disc Corp., Terre Haute; MO: Materials Research Corp., Bridgeton; NJ: Business & Professional Products Group, Montville; Sony Consumer Sales Products Co., Paramus; Sony Communications Products, Park Ridge; Sony Consumer Audio Products Co., Park Ridge; Sony Consumer Display Products Co., Park Ridge; Sony Consumer Video Products Co., Park Ridge; Sony Electronics, Park Ridge; Sony Electronics, Park Ridge; Sony Information Systems Co., Park Ridge; Sony Magnetic Products Co., Park Ridge; Sony Service Co., Park Ridge; Sony Electronics, Teaneck; NY: Materials Research Corp., Congers; Process Equipment, Congers; Columbia House Music Club, New York; Columbia Pictures Merchandising, New York; Loews Theatre Management Corp., New York; Sony Component Products Co., New York; Sony Electronics, New York; Sony Music Entertainment, New York; Sony U.S.A., New York; Quality Metals, Orangeburg; Hybrid Products, Pearl River; PA: Sony Display Systems, Mount Pleasant; TN: Sony Music Nashville, Nashville; TX: Materials Research Corp., Dallas; Sony Electronics, San Antonio; Sony Microelectronics, San Antonio
Note: Operates 122 sites in 25 states.

Nonmonetary Support

Range: $100,000 - $350,000
Type: Donated Products

Sony U.S.A. Foundation Inc.

Giving Contact

Ken Nees, President
Sony Electronics Inc.
1 Sony Drive
Park Ridge, NJ 07656-8002

Phone: (201)930-6097
Fax: (201)930-4762
Note: Mr. Nees direct line is: (201)833-6870.

Description

EIN: 237181637
Organization Type: Corporate Foundation
Giving Locations: headquarters and operating communities; nationally.
Grant Types: Employee Matching Gifts, General Support, Scholarship.
Note: Employee matching gift ratio: 1 to 1 to education, hospitals, and cultural institutions.

Giving Philosophy

'As Sony's American philanthropic efforts enter their third decade, the company is dedicated to being even more responsive to community needs, primarily in locations where Sony has facilities, by fostering partnerships with worthy causes and institutions, funding special programs, and encouraging further employee involvement.' *A History of Giving, A Future of Partnership*, Sony Charitable Contributions Program Guidelines

Financial Summary

Total Giving: $1,280,298 (1998); $1,232,202 (1997); $1,500,000 (1996). Note: Contributes through corporate direct giving program and foundation.
Giving Analysis: Giving for 1996 includes: foundation ($1,500,000); 1997: foundation ($1,232,202); 1998: foundation ($830,822); foundation grants to United Way ($296,833); foundation matching gifts ($114,343); foundation scholarships ($38,300)
Assets: $2,399,658 (1998); $2,317,455 (1997); $2,297,777 (1996)
Gifts Received: $976,184 (1998); $1,050,000 (1997); $1,350,000 (1996). Note: Foundation received contributions from Sony Electronics Inc.

Typical Recipients

Arts & Humanities: Arts Associations & Councils, Arts Outreach, Historic Preservation, Museums/Galleries, Music, Opera, Performing Arts, Public Broadcasting, Theater, Visual Arts
Civic & Public Affairs: African American Affairs, Asian American Affairs, Business/Free Enterprise, Chambers of Commerce, Community Foundations, Economic Development, Employment/Job Training, Ethnic Organizations, Civic & Public Affairs-General, Nonprofit Management, Philanthropic Organizations, Professional & Trade Associations, Public Policy, Urban & Community Affairs
Education: Arts/Humanities Education, Business Education, Colleges & Universities, Community & Junior Colleges, Education Funds, Education Reform, Engineering/Technological Education, Environmental Education, Education-General, International Exchange, International Studies, Literacy, Minority Education, Private Education (Precollege), Public Education (Precollege), Science/Mathematics Education, Secondary Education (Public), Special Education, Student Aid
Environment: Environment-General, Resource Conservation, Wildlife Protection
Health: Children's Health/Hospitals, Emergency/Ambulance Services, Eyes/Blindness, Health Organizations, Hospitals, Medical Rehabilitation, Mental Health, Multiple Sclerosis, Prenatal Health Issues, Preventive Medicine/Wellness Organizations, Public Health
International: Foreign Arts Organizations, International Affairs, International Development, International Relations
Religion: Churches, Jewish Causes, Religious Welfare
Science: Science Museums, Scientific Centers & Institutes
Social Services: Child Abuse, Child Welfare, Community Service Organizations, Family Services, People with Disabilities, Recreation & Athletics, Scouts, United Funds/United Ways, Volunteer Services, Youth Organizations

Contributions Analysis

Giving Priorities: Social welfare, colleges and universities, ethnic and minority organizations, and arts and culture.
Arts & Humanities: 3%. Supports music, opera, museums, and public broadcasting in New York City.
Civic & Public Affairs: 18%. Supports urban and community affairs including civic organizations, foundations, and employment training. Includes efforts to promote the advancement and recognition of minorities.
Education: 31%. Funding supports institutions and programs that bring commitment and innovation to the task of strengthening education at the primary and secondary school levels, with consideration also given to selected higher education initiatives. Also supports efforts that promote literacy and basic educational competency, and encouragement of the technical and scientific skills required of tomorrow's work force. Also funds arts education. Scholarships are awarded to the children of employees.
Social Services: 48%. Majority of funds support the United Way. Additional funding supports health associations and social service organizations.
Note: Above priorities are for Sony USA Foundation in 1998. Sony Corp. of America subsidiaries run independent giving programs.

Application Procedures

Initial Contact: Send a written request.
Application Requirements: Include a brief written a description of organization, including its legal name, history, activities, purpose, and proof of 501(c)(3) status; a history of previous support from Sony Electronics, the Sony USA Foundation, Inc., or a Sony business unit; amount requested; and the purpose for which grant is requested.
Deadlines: None.
Review Process: Requests and supporting materials are reviewed; if the request is within the foundation's guidelines and program priorities, and available funds permit consideration of the request, the organization may be asked to provide more complete information before a decision is made.
Decision Notification: Notification of grant request approval or rejection is made within three months of receipt of all proposal material.
Notes: Company does not respond to telephone follow-ups.

Restrictions

Does not support organizations that discriminate on the basis of race, color, creed, gender, religion, age, or national origin; partisan political organizations, committees, or candidates and public office holders; religious organizations; labor unions; endowment or capital campaigns of national organizations; organizations whose prime purpose is to influence legislation or whose mission is outside of the United States; testimonial dinners; for-profit publications seeking advertisements; individuals seeking self-advancement; or foreign or non-U.S. organizations.
Foundation will not consider funding for more than one proposal per organization per year.

Additional Information

Sony Pictures Entertainment administers an independent program geared toward education and the arts. Requests for information must be in writing and can be sent to Janice Pober, Vice President, Corporate Affairs, Sony Pictures Entertainment, 10202 W Washington Blvd., Culver City, CA, 90232-3195. Sony Music Entertainment Press also administers an independent program. Requests for information must be in writing and can be sent to Public Relations, 500 Madison Ave., 20th Fl., New York, NY, 10022-3211, (212) 833-7141.
Publications: Program Guidelines

Corporate Officials

John Briesch: president consumer products group PRIM CORP EMPL president consumer products group: Sony Electronics Inc.
Masaaki Morita: CORP AFFIL chairman, chief executive officer: Sony Electronics; chairman: Sony Trans Communication; deputy president, rep director, director: Sony Corp. Japan.
Kenneth L. Nees: senior vice president, secretary B 1940. ED University of Maryland BA (1962). PRIM CORP EMPL senior vice president: Sony Corp. ADD CORP EMPL secretary: Sony Corp. of America; secretary, director: Sony Magnetic Products Inc.

Giving Program Officials

Leslie Gaffney: community affairs representative

Foundation Officials

Howard Paul Burak: secretary, director B New York, NY 1934. ED Cornell University BS (1954); Columbia University LLB (1957). PRIM CORP EMPL partner: Rosenman & Colin. CORP AFFIL director: Sony Music Entertainment Inc.; director: Sony Pictures Entertainment Inc.; director: Sony Corp. America. NONPR AFFIL member: International Bar Association; member: New York State Bar Association; member: Fed Bar Council; member: American Bar Association; member: Association Bar New York City. CLUB AFFIL University Club.
Tadasu Kawai: director B 1944. PRIM CORP EMPL deputy president, director: Sony Electronics. CORP AFFIL president, director: Sony Software Corp.
Masaaki Morita: chairman, director (see above)
Kenneth L. Nees: president, assistant secretary, director (see above)

Grants Analysis

Disclosure Period: calendar year ending 1998
Total Grants: $830,822*
Number of Grants: 389
Average Grant: $1,884*
Highest Grant: $100,000
Typical Range: $100 to $3,000
***Note:** .Giving excludes matching gifts; scholarship; United Way. Average grant figure excludes highe t grant.

Recent Grants

Note: Grants derived from 1998 Form 990.

Arts & Humanities

10,000	New Jersey Center for Visual Arts, New York, NY
10,000	Salon De Virtuosi Inc., New York, NY
5,000	San Diego Opera, San Diego, CA

Civic & Public Affairs

100,000	Greater San Diego Chamber of Commerce, San Diego, CA
25,000	National Action Council for Minorities, New York, NY
10,000	Kessler Foundation, Inc., West Orange, NJ
10,000	National Urban League, Inc., New York, NY
10,000	San Diego Nihongo Kyoiku Shinkoka, San Diego, CA
5,000	100 Black Men of New Jersey, Inc., East Orange, NJ
5,000	Council of Better Business Bureaus, Arlington, VA
5,000	Gifts in Kind International, Alexandria, VA
5,000	Lead San Diego, Inc., San Diego, CA
5,000	Partnership in Philanthropy, New York, NY
5,000	Reading Alabama, Inc., Rye Brook, NY

Education

50,000	Minorities in Engineering, Inc., New York, NY

38,300	National Merit Scholarship Corp., Chicago, IL
25,000	Troy State University, Troy, AL
20,000	Council of the Great City Schools, New York, NY
15,000	Consortium for Graduate Study in Management, St. Louis, MO
10,000	Brearley School, New York, NY
10,000	College Fund/UNCF, New York, NY
10,000	Santa Clara Unified School District, Santa Clara, CA
10,000	Troy State University, Troy, AL
10,000	University of Alabama, Birmingham, AL
8,000	College Fund/UNCF, New York, NY
7,000	San Antonio Education Partnership, San Antonio, TX
5,000	Citizenship Education Fund, Washington, DC
5,000	Electronic Industries Foundation, Arlington, VA
5,000	Hispanic Scholarship Fund, San Francisco, CA
5,000	Morgan State University Foundation, Baltimore, MD
5,000	Northview High School, Covina, CA
5,000	University of California, San Diego, CA
5,000	University of California at San Diego, San Diego, CA
5,000	Washington Center, Washington, DC
Health	
50,000	American Red Cross, New York, NY
10,000	Pascack Valley Hospital Foundation, Westwood, NJ
5,000	American Red Cross, New York, NY
5,000	Children's PKU Network, San Diego, CA
5,000	March of Dimes, New York, NY
5,000	Wellness Community, San Diego, San Diego, CA
5,000	West Bergen Mental Healthcare, West Bergen, NJ
International	
7,425	AFS Intercultural Programs, Inc., New York, NY
Social Services	
141,000	United Way of Bergen County, Fairlawn, NJ
50,000	United Way of San Diego County, San Diego, CA
50,000	Wiregrass United Way, Inc., Dothan, AL
20,833	United Way of Santa Clara County, Santa Clara, CA
15,000	United Way of San Antonio & Bexar, San Antonio, TX
9,200	Casa De Amparo, San Luis Rey, CA
5,000	Access Living, Chicago, IL
5,000	Aloha United Way, Honolulu, HI
5,000	Aloha United Way, Honolulu, HI
5,000	Boy Scouts of America, New York, NY

SOTHEBY'S INC.

Company Contact

New York, NY
Web: http://www.sothebys.com

Company Description

Former Name: Sotheby's Holdings, Inc.
Employees: 450
SIC(s): 7389 Business Services Nec.
Parent Company: Sotheby's Service Corp.

Nonmonetary Support

Type: In-kind Services

Corporate Sponsorship

Type: Arts & cultural events

Giving Contact

Katherine Ross, Senior Vice President & Director Museum Services
Sotheby's
1334 York Avenue
New York, NY 10021
Phone: (212)894-1137
Fax: (212)606-1116

Description

Organization Type: Corporate Giving Program
Giving Locations: headquarters only.
Grant Types: Department, General Support, Project.

Financial Summary

Total Giving: $250,000 (2000 approx); $250,000 (1999 approx). Note: Contributes through corporate direct giving program only.

Typical Recipients

Arts & Humanities: Arts Institutes
Civic & Public Affairs: Civic & Public Affairs-General
Education: Arts/Humanities Education

Contributions Analysis

Arts & Humanities: 90%. Primary emphasis is on arts organizations, arts education, and museums.
Civic & Public Affairs: 10%. Supports various civic organizations.

Application Procedures

Initial Contact: Send a brief letter of inquiry.
Application Requirements: Include a description of organization, amount requested, purpose of funds sought, audited financial statement, and proof of tax-exempt status.
Deadlines: None.

Restrictions

Does not support individuals, religious organizations for sectarian purposes, or political or lobbying groups.

Corporate Officials

Richard Erik Oldenburg: chairman, president B Stockholm, Sweden 1933. ED Harvard University AB (1954). PRIM CORP EMPL chairman: Sotheby's North & South America. NONPR AFFIL director emeritus, honorary trustee: Museum Modern Art.
William Ruprecht: chief executive officer, president PRIM CORP EMPL chief executive officer, president: Sotheby's Inc.

Giving Program Officials

Katherine Ross: PRIM CORP EMPL vice president, director museum services: Sotheby's Inc.

Grants Analysis

Disclosure Period: calendar year ending
Typical Range: $2,500 to $10,000

SOUTH BEND TRIBUNE CORP.

Company Contact

South Bend, IN

Company Description

Employees: 270
SIC(s): 2711 Newspapers.
Parent Company: Schurz Communications

Schurz Communications Foundation

Giving Contact

Todd F. Schurz, President
225 West Colfax Avenue
South Bend, IN 46626
Phone: (219)236-1773
Fax: (219)236-1765

Description

Founded: 1940
EIN: 356024357
Organization Type: Corporate Foundation
Giving Locations: IN: South Bend
Grant Types: General Support.

Financial Summary

Total Giving: $201,950 (1998); $205,650 (1996); $174,600 (1995)
Giving Analysis: Giving for 1998 includes: foundation grants to United Way ($46,400)
Assets: $795,418 (1998); $715,363 (1996); $833,911 (1995)
Gifts Received: $57,588 (1998); $56,213 (1996); $77,923 (1995). Note: The company receives contributions from the South Bend Tribune ($32,400) and WSBT ($23,813).

Typical Recipients

Arts & Humanities: Arts Centers, Arts Festivals, Historic Preservation, History & Archaeology, Libraries, Museums/Galleries, Music, Performing Arts, Public Broadcasting
Civic & Public Affairs: Botanical Gardens/Parks, Community Foundations, Economic Development, Civic & Public Affairs-General, Municipalities/Towns, Parades/Festivals, Urban & Community Affairs
Education: Business Education, Colleges & Universities, Education Funds, Private Education (Precollege)
Health: Hospices
Social Services: Child Welfare, United Funds/United Ways, YMCA/YWCA/YMHA/YWHA, Youth Organizations

Contributions Analysis

Giving Priorities: Support for the United Way and social services, the arts, civic causes, and education.
Arts & Humanities: 28%. Historical societies, museums, arts centers, music, and arts festivals.
Civic & Public Affairs: 16%. Primarily for community foundations and economic development.
Education: 13%. Colleges and universities and business education.
Social Services: Emphasis on the United Way; also supports child welfare and youth organizations.

Application Procedures

Initial Contact: The foundation has no formal grant application procedure or application form.
Deadlines: None.

Corporate Officials

Mark Hocker: chief financial officer, controller, editor, director PRIM CORP EMPL chief financial officer, controller: South Bend Tribune Corp.
Todd F. Schurz: president, publisher, editor, director PRIM CORP EMPL president, publisher, editor, director: South Bend Tribune Corp.

Foundation Officials

James D. Freeman: vp
James Montgomery Schurz: president B South Bend, IN 1933. ED Stanford University (1956). PRIM CORP EMPL senator vice president newspapers, director: Schurz Communs.
Todd F. Schurz: vice president (see above)
E. Berry Smith: secretary, treasurer

Grants Analysis

Disclosure Period: calendar year ending 1996
Total Grants: $159,250*
Number of Grants: 18
Average Grant: $8,847
Highest Grant: $40,000
Typical Range: $500 to $10,000
***Note:** Giving excludes United Way.

Recent Grants

Note: Grants derived from 1996 Form 990.

Arts & Humanities

40,000	Northern Indiana Historical Society, South Bend, IN
10,000	College Football Hall of Fame
5,000	South Bend Regional Museum of Art, South Bend, IN
1,000	Colfax Cultural Center
1,000	South Bend Symphony Orchestra, South Bend, IN
500	Carnival of the Arts

Civic & Public Affairs

20,000	Community Foundation of St. Joseph County, South Bend, IN
10,000	Logan
3,000	Local Initiatives Support Group, South Bend, IN

Education

15,000	University of Notre Dame, South Bend, IN -- outreach program
6,000	Junior Achievement
5,000	Holy Cross College

Health

750	Hospice, South Bend, IN

Social Services

30,750	United Way, South Bend, IN
30,000	Madison Center for Children
13,650	United Way, South Bend, IN
10,000	Building for Youth Campaign, South Bend, IN
1,000	United Way, Niles, MI
1,000	United Way, Niles, MI
1,000	United Way Southwest Michigan, MI

SOUTHEASTERN MUTUAL INSURANCE CO.

Company Contact

Louisville, KY

Company Description

Assets: US$140,000,000
Employees: 650
SIC(s): 6324 Hospital & Medical Service Plans.

Anthem Foundation, Inc.

Giving Contact

Nancy Purcell, Secretary
Anthem Foundation, Inc.
9901 Linn Station Road
Louisville, KY 40223
Phone: (317)488-6169
Fax: (317)339-5483

Description

Founded: 1990
EIN: 611191499
Organization Type: Corporate Foundation
Giving Locations: KY
Grant Types: Employee Matching Gifts, Project.

Financial Summary

Total Giving: $292,700 (1998); $378,955 (1997); $274,000 (1996). Note: Contributes through foundation only.
Giving Analysis: Giving for 1997 includes: foundation grants to United Way ($27,000); foundation matching gifts ($1,955); 1998: foundation grants to United Way ($31,000); foundation matching gifts ($6,200)
Assets: $6,268,038 (1998); $6,159,917 (1997); $6,170,254 (1996)
Gifts Received: $12,000 (1998); $12,000 (1997); $12,000 (1996). Note: Contributions are received from SpectraCare.

Typical Recipients

Arts & Humanities: Arts Festivals, Arts Funds, Ballet, History & Archaeology, Libraries, Museums/Galleries, Music, Opera, Public Broadcasting, Theater
Civic & Public Affairs: African American Affairs, Botanical Gardens/Parks, Business/Free Enterprise, Economic Development, Civic & Public Affairs-General, Municipalities/Towns, Professional & Trade Associations, Public Policy, Urban & Community Affairs, Women's Affairs
Education: Arts/Humanities Education, Business Education, Colleges & Universities, Community & Junior Colleges, Economic Education, Education Funds, Education Reform, Education-General, Leadership Training, Medical Education, Minority Education, Private Education (Precollege), Public Education (Precollege), Religious Education, Secondary Education (Public), Special Education, Student Aid
Environment: Environment-General, Resource Conservation
Health: AIDS/HIV, Cancer, Children's Health/Hospitals, Clinics/Medical Centers, Emergency/Ambulance Services, Health Organizations, Heart, Hospitals, Medical Rehabilitation, Multiple Sclerosis, Nursing Services, Prenatal Health Issues, Preventive Medicine/Wellness Organizations, Public Health, Respiratory, Single-Disease Health Associations, Trauma Treatment
Religion: Dioceses, Religious Organizations, Religious Welfare
Science: Scientific Centers & Institutes
Social Services: At-Risk Youth, Camps, Child Abuse, Child Welfare, Community Service Organizations, Food/Clothing Distribution, Scouts, Senior Services, Special Olympics, Substance Abuse, United Funds/United Ways, YMCA/YWCA/YMHA/YWHA

Contributions Analysis

Giving Priorities: Education is the foundation's major priority. Also supports human services, child development, and community improvement programs.
Arts & Humanities: 9%. Supports arts funds.
Civic & Public Affairs: 13%. Funds community groups and economic education.
Education: 17%. Supports higher education and matching gifts.
Health: 37%. Health education and single-disease associations receive funding.
Social Services: 25%. Funds the United Way and youth and human services.
Note: Total contributions in 1998.

Application Procedures

Initial Contact: Request application form.
Deadlines: None.

Foundation Officials

Travis L. Cochran: member
David R. Frick: chairman PRIM CORP EMPL executive vice president: Anthem Insurance Companies. CORP AFFIL officer: Anthem Companies Inc.; officer: Anthem Life Insurance Co.
Frank Beard Hower, Jr.: vice chairman B Louisville, KY 1928. ED Centre College of Kentucky AB (1950). CORP AFFIL director: Falls City Industries Inc.; director: Loma Linda Corp.; director: Bank One Kentucky Corp.; director: Churchill Downs Inc.; director: Anthem Insurance Companies; director: Alliant Health System Inc.; director: American Life Insurance Co. NONPR AFFIL member: Robert Morris Associates; director, chairman: University Louisville; chairman: Regional Airport Authority Louisville & Jefferson County; treasurer: Louisville Orchestra Inc.; chairman: Norton Kosair Childrens Hospital Inc.; chairman: Louisville Development Committee; vice chairman: Kentucky & Tennessee District Export Council; member: Louisville Chamber of Commerce; chairman, trustee: Kentucky Independent College Fund; member: Association Reserve City Bankers; trustee: Center College; member: American Bankers Association; member: American Kentucky Bankers Association; member: Actors Theatre Board.
James Lemaster: president B 1938. PRIM CORP EMPL president: Giovanni's Pizza Inc. ADD CORP EMPL president: Truck Maintenance Corp.
George Martin: treasurer
Ellen Monroe: assistant secretary PRIM CORP EMPL secretary: Outsourced Administration System Inc.
Nancy L. Purcell: secretary PRIM CORP EMPL secretary: Anthem Companies Inc. CORP AFFIL secretary: Anthem Health Indiana; secretary: Anthem Insurance Companies.
Tracy Whitman: secretary

Grants Analysis

Disclosure Period: calendar year ending 1998
Total Grants: $255,500*
Number of Grants: 21
Average Grant: $12,167
Highest Grant: $42,500
Typical Range: $5,000 to $15,000
***Note:** Giving excludes matching gifts, United Way.

Recent Grants

Note: Grants derived from 1998 Form 990.

Arts & Humanities

25,000	Fund for the Arts, Louisville, KY -- Human Services
10,000	UK Basketball Museum, Lexington, KY -- Health Education

Civic & Public Affairs

30,000	Greater Louisville Economic Foundation, Louisville, KY -- Economic Education
10,000	Women 4 Women, Louisville, KY -- Health Education
3,000	Leadership Kentucky Foundation, Frankfort, KY -- Education
1,500	Leadership Louisville Foundation, Louisville, KY -- Education

Education

10,000	The Pritchard Commettee for Academic Excellence, Lexington, KY -- Education
9,000	Bellarmine College, Louisville, KY -- Education
1,500	Christian Academy of Louisville, Louisville, KY -- Education - Matching Gifts Program
1,200	Bellarmine College, Louisville, KY -- Education - Matching Gifts Program
600	University of Louisville Foundation, Louisville, KY -- Education - Matching Gifts Program
500	Highview Baptist School, Louisville, KY -- Education - Matching Gifts Program
500	Pitt Academy, Louisville, KY -- Education - Matching Gifts Program
500	Transylvania University, Lexington, KY -- Education - Matching Gifts Program
300	Spalding University, Louisville, KY -- Education - Matching Gifts Program
250	Berea College, Berea, KY -- Education - Matching Gifts Program

250 Midway College, Midway, KY -- Education - Matching Gifts Program
150 Ursuline Campus Schools, Louisville, KY -- Education - Matching Gifts Program
100 Campbellsville University, Campbellsville, KY -- Education - Matching Gifts Program
100 Murray State University, Marray, KY -- Education - Matching Gifts Program
100 St. Xavier High School, Louisville, KY -- Education - Matching Gifts Program
50 University of Kentucky, Louisville, KY -- Education - Matching Gifts Program
25 Centre College of Kentucky, Danville, KY -- Education - Matching Gifts Program
25 Owensboro Catholic High School, Owensboro, KY -- Education - Matching Gifts Program
25 Pikeville College, Pikeville, KY -- Education - Matching Gifts Program
25 Western Kentucky University Foundation Bowling, Green, KY -- Education - Matching Gifts Program

Health
42,500 Kentucky Academy of Family Physicians Foundation, Louisville, KY -- Health Education
25,000 American Heart Association, Louisville, KY -- Education
25,000 Community Health Alliance, Louisville, KY -- Health Education
10,000 The American Lung Association, Louisville, KY -- Health Education
10,000 Health Kentucky, Inc., Louisville, KY -- Health Education
5,000 Brain Injury Association of Kentucky, Louisville, KY -- Health Education
3,000 Children's Hospital Foundation, Louisville, KY -- Health Education
3,000 National Multiple Sclerosis Society, Louisville, KY -- Health Education

Social Services
20,000 Metro United Way, Louisville, KY -- Human Services
11,000 United Way of the Bluegrass, Lexington, KY -- Human Services
10,000 Kentucky Council on Child Abuse, Inc, Lexington, KY -- Human Services
9,000 Paris/Bourbon County YMCA, Lexington, KY -- Education
6,000 YMCA, Louisville, KY -- Human Services
6,000 Young Men's Christian Association of Central Kentucky -- Human Services
2,500 Lincoln Heritage Council, Louisville, KY -- Human Services

SOUTHERN CALIFORNIA GAS CO.

Company Contact
Los Angeles, CA

Company Description
Employees: 8,484
SIC(s): 1311 Crude Petroleum & Natural Gas, 1382 Oil & Gas Exploration Services.
Parent Company: Pacific Enterprises, Los Angeles, CA, United States

Nonmonetary Support
Volunteer Programs: Company supports the Volunteer Incentive Program.

Corporate Sponsorship
Value: $500,000
Type: Festivals/fairs

Giving Contact
Carolyn R. Williams, Manager, Public Affairs
Southern California Gas Co.
555 West 5th Street, ML 28H5
PO Box 3249
Los Angeles, CA 90013-1011
Phone: (213)244-2555
Fax: (213)689-2092
Note: Contact's extension is 2555.

Alternate Contact
Kathy Lavin, Contributions Analyst
Phone: (619)696-2069

Description
Organization Type: Corporate Giving Program
Giving Locations: CA: awards grants only to organizations and activities within company's service area in Central and Southern California
Grant Types: General Support, Project.

Giving Philosophy
'The strategic goal of Southern California Gas' Charitable Contributions Program is: To contribute dollars and services to organizations which principally adress the company's stated outreach targets and, at the same time, maintain the company's good business relationships in communities where it operates.' Southern California Gas Co.

Financial Summary
Total Giving: $2,700,000 (1996 approx); $1,500,000 (1995 approx); $1,300,000 (1994 approx). Note: Contributes through corporate direct giving program only.

Typical Recipients
Civic & Public Affairs: Urban & Community Affairs, Women's Affairs
Education: Engineering/Technological Education, Literacy, Minority Education, Public Education (Precollege), Science/Mathematics Education
Environment: Environment-General
Health: Health Funds
Science: Science Exhibits & Fairs

Contributions Analysis
Giving Priorities: Economic self-sufficiency, leadership development, ethnic groups, urban affairs, and public education.
Civic & Public Affairs: Supports economic vitality and competitiveness, business retention, growth management, and community economic revitalization. Supports programs which address social and political trends resulting from shifting demographics, including leadership development, consumer-oriented community-based programs, small business development for women and minorities, education reform, and education outreach in computer science, math, and engineering.
Environment: Supports environmental education, environmental quality, and air quality.

Application Procedures
Initial Contact: Submit a written request (not to exceed four pages, plus attachments).
Application Requirements: Include background of organization, with objectives, target groups, programs, and accomplishments to date; nature and purpose of project; amount requested; organizational and project financial statements for the last two years; proof of tax-exempt status; how project will be evaluated; list of board members and affiliations; funding sources and amounts for the project; how project fits funding criteria; and a description of how the program benefits the community.
Deadlines: None.
Evaluative Criteria: The program must significantly enhance a community's social, economic, or cultural well-being; be service-oriented or educational in nature; be located within service territory (southern and central California); have effective management and a successful track record; and have tax-exempt status. It also must meet giving criteria.
Decision Notification: Decisions are announced in February, May, and September.

Restrictions
Does not fund endowments or third-party scholarship programs.
Does not support individuals, commercial profit-making groups, fraternal groups, capital campaigns, sectarian religious institutions, political organizations, fundraising activities, team sponsorships, academic research projects, or most health and human services and arts groups.

Additional Information
Company rarely makes multiyear grants.
Contributions usually are unrestricted.

Corporate Officials
Warren I. Mitchell: president, director B Los Angeles, CA 1937. ED Pepperdine University BSAS (1963); Pepperdine University MBA (1965). PRIM CORP EMPL president, director: Southern California Gas Co. CORP AFFIL director: Calstart; chairman: San Diego Gas Electric Co. NONPR AFFIL chairman: Natural Gas Vehicle Coalition; 1st vice chairman, director: Pacific Coast Gas Association; director: Gas Research Institute; director: Institute Gas Technology; member: American Gas Association; director: Employers Group.

Giving Program Officials
Carolyn R. Williams: public affairs manager

Grants Analysis
Disclosure Period: calendar year ending
Typical Range: $250 to $5,000

SOUTHERN CO. SERVICES INC.

Company Contact
Birmingham, AL
Web: http://www.southernco.com

Company Description
Employees: 3,207
SIC(s): 8711 Engineering Services, 8721 Accounting, Auditing & Bookkeeping, 8742 Management Consulting Services.
Parent Company: South Corp.

Nonmonetary Support
Type: Donated Equipment; In-kind Services; Loaned Employees

Giving Contact
Susan Harrell, Supervisor Community Affairs
Southern Co. Services, Inc.
270 Peachtree Street
Atlanta, GA 30303
Phone: (404)506-0563
Fax: (404)506-0584

Description
Organization Type: Corporate Giving Program
Giving Locations: headquarters and operating communities.
Grant Types: Employee Matching Gifts, General Support.

Giving Philosophy

'Recognizing its own responsibilities to be a good corporate citizen, Southern Company Services has a modest charitable contributions program for itself and the Southern Company. The program is administered by the community affairs department which reviews applications and recommends to the public relations department the disposition of funds . .. Some other programs in the area of social responsibility in which the company participates are educational matching gift program for higher education, the adopt-a-school program, and encouragement of a great deal of employee personal commitment of time and funds to community activities. The company's aim is to enhance the quality of life and provide benefits to the citizens and communities served by the Southern Electric System.' *Charitable Contributions Programs and Guidelines*

Financial Summary

Total Giving: Contributes through corporate direct giving program only.

Typical Recipients

Civic & Public Affairs: Civic & Public Affairs-General
Education: Education-General
Health: Health-General
Social Services: Social Services-General

Application Procedures

Initial Contact: Send a one page letter.
Application Requirements: Included contact name, address, and phone number; IRS classification; a description of organization and its objectives; amount sought; and the intended purpose of the project.
Deadlines: None.
Review Process: After the initial review, the organization will be notified if a full proposal is required.
Evaluative Criteria: The organization must have IRS 501(c)(3) tax-exempt status, an independent functioning board of directors, competent executive staff, and be financially stable. Applications must be submitted in writing.

Restrictions

Does not contribute to individuals; political organizations, candidates or activities; lobbying organizations; labor organizations; veteran, or fraternal, organizations; religious organizations, unless project benefits the entire community; and organizations without 501 (c)(3) status.
Also does not make grants in the form of advertising, deficit reduction, or to colleges and universities other than matching gifts.
Gives only 'one time' contributions, rather than multi-year contributions. The company prefers not to be a single, or part of a limited number of sources of support for a program. The project must fall within the scope of company's program. The proposed program must have community support, achievable goals, and avoid duplication of services.

Additional Information

Each of the five electric utilities--Alabama Power Co., Georgia Power Co., Gulf Power Co., Mississippi Power Co., and Savannah Electric and Power--has its own charitable contributions program, which is carried on independently with separate applications and guidelines.
Publications: Charitable Contributions Policy Statement; Application Guidelines

Corporate Officials

David R. Altman: vice president corporate communicationso B Vanesville, OH 1952. ED Georgia State University (1974). PRIM CORP EMPL vice president corporate communications: Southern Co.
Alfred William Dahlberg, III: chairman, president, chief executive officer B Atlanta, GA 1940. ED Georgia State University BBA (1970). PRIM CORP EMPL chairman, president, chief executive officer: Southern Co. CORP AFFIL director: Trust Co. Georgia; director: Trust Co. Bank; director: Southern Electronic Generating Co.; director: SunTrust Banks Inc.; director: Southern Co. Services Inc.; director: Protective Life Corp.; member: Southeastern Electric Exchange; president, director: Piedmont-Forrest Corp.; director: Electric Power Research Institute; director: Equifax Inc. NONPR AFFIL member: Edison Electric Institute.
Paul J. De Nicola: president, chief executive officer B 1949. ED Mississippi State University BSEE. PRIM CORP EMPL president, chief executive officer: Southern Co. Services Inc. CORP AFFIL director: Gulf Power Co.; executive vice president, director: Southern Co. Inc.

Giving Program Officials

Dora Brandt: PRIM CORP EMPL public relations assistant: Southern Co. Services Inc.
Lynn M. Williams: PRIM CORP EMPL senior communications specialist: Southern Co. Services Inc. CORP AFFIL secretary: SCANA Resources Inc.; secretary: ServiceCare Inc.; secretary: SCANA Propane Services Inc.; secretary: SCANA Petroleum Resources; secretary: SCANA Propane Gas Inc.; corporate secretary: SCANA Corp.; secretary: SCANA Energy Marketing Inc.; secretary: SCANA Communications Inc.; secretary: Primesouth Inc.; secretary: SC Pipeline Corp.

Foundation Officials

David R. Altman: (see above)

SOUTHERN NEW ENGLAND TELEPHONE CO.

Company Contact

New Haven, CT
Web: http://www.snet.com

Company Description

Also Known As: SNET.
Employees: 9,500
SIC(s): 4813 Telephone Communications Except Radiotelephone, 4899 Communications Services Nec.
Parent Company: Southern New England Telecommunications Corp.

Nonmonetary Support

Value: $200,000 (1993); $200,000 (1992); $200,000 (1990)
Type: Donated Equipment; In-kind Services; Loaned Executives

Corporate Sponsorship

Type: Arts & cultural events; Festivals/fairs; Music & entertainment events; Sports events

Giving Contact

Kathleen Buccy, Manager, Contributions
SNET
310 Orange Street
New Haven, CT 06510
Phone: (203)771-3114
Fax: (203)865-5198

Description

Organization Type: Corporate Giving Program
Giving Locations: CT: New Haven
Grant Types: Capital, Conference/Seminar, Employee Matching Gifts.
Note: Employee matching gift ratio: 1 to 1.

Giving Philosophy

'As part of our commitment to Connecticut's educational systems, SNET believes that active participation and leadership in statewide efforts is essential. SNET is represented on several of the statewide educational committees and, as the employer of a large employee base, has representation on many local educational and non-profit committees. SNET has established a proud tradition of supporting education and has developed a close relationship with the State Department of Education as well as local educational communities, being a strong business partner and a leader in telecommunications.' SNET Web site

Financial Summary

Total Giving: $10,000,000 (1999 approx); $10,000,000 (1998 approx)

Typical Recipients

Arts & Humanities: Arts Associations & Councils, Dance, Libraries, Music, Performing Arts, Theater
Civic & Public Affairs: Economic Development, Public Policy
Education: Colleges & Universities, Community & Junior Colleges, Education Associations, Engineering/Technological Education, Literacy, Minority Education, Private Education (Precollege), Science/ Mathematics Education
Health: Hospitals
Social Services: Child Welfare, Community Service Organizations, People with Disabilities, Senior Services, Substance Abuse, United Funds/United Ways, Youth Organizations

Contributions Analysis

Giving Priorities: Health and social services, technical education, and the arts.
Education: Focus is on technical edcuation. Company grant programs include 'Narrowing the Digital Divide,' to improve computer literacy in adults through grants to colleges, universities, and technical schools; a grant to the University of Connecticut for research in information technology; small grants supporting high school band and music programs; and free Internet access and websites for Connecticut schools and libraries. The companies also funds Amistad America, SeniorNet Learning Centers, the Sporting Geography education program, the Celebration of Excellence Program (recognizing outstanding teachers), and educational conferences. SNET is a business partner with Katherine Brennan School.

Application Procedures

Initial Contact: Send a letter or proposal.
Application Requirements: Include a description of organization, amount requested, purpose of funds sought, recently audited financial statement, proof of tax-exempt status, and other corporate funding sources.
Deadlines: None.
Review Process: Field offices submit recommendations on local applicants and forward them to their director or contributions manager; proposals for pledges or large grants are forwarded to corporate contributions manager.
Evaluative Criteria: Management efficiency, community support, relation to communications industry, lack of duplication of services, need of service, justification of expenses, potential to provide public recognition of company.
Decision Notification: Applicants are notified within two months of submission of application.

Restrictions

Company does not support endowments; fraternal, political, or religious organizations; member agencies of united funds; goodwill advertising; or individuals.

Additional Information

SNET merged with Southwestern Bell Communications in fourth quarter of 1998.

Corporate Officials
Kathleen Buccy: director external relationsrc, chief executive officer PRIM CORP EMPL director external relations: Southern New England Telephone Co.
Daniel Joseph Miglio: chairman, president, director, chief executive officer B Philadelphia, PA 1940. ED University of Pennsylvania Wharton School BS (1962). PRIM CORP EMPL chairman, president, director, chief executive officer: Southern New England Telecommunications Corp. CORP AFFIL director: Aristotle Corp. NONPR AFFIL chairman: Southern New England Telephone Co. Political Action Comm; member executive committee, director: U.S. Telephone Association; member: Kappa Alpha; director: New Haven Symphony Orch; finance chairman: Connecticut Joint Council Economic Education. CLUB AFFIL University Club Hartford; University of Pennsylvania of Greater Hartford Club.

Giving Program Officials
Toni Boulay: PRIM CORP EMPL staff associate matching gifts: Southern New England Telephone Co.
Kathleen Buccy: director PRIM CORP EMPL director external relations: Southern New England Telephone Co.
Linda D. Hershman: vice president B Pittsburgh, PA 1947. ED University of Pittsburgh (1967); University of Connecticut School of Law (1970). PRIM CORP EMPL vice president external affairs: Southern New England Telephone Co. CORP AFFIL member board director: Colony Savings Bank; vice president: Southern New England Telecom Corp.

Grants Analysis
Disclosure Period: calendar year ending
Typical Range: $500 to $1,000

SOUTHWEST GAS CORP.

Company Contact
Las Vegas, NV

Company Description
Assets: US$1,560,300,000
Employees: 2,424
SIC(s): 4924 Natural Gas Distribution.

Nonmonetary Support
Value: $13,141 (1998)
Type: Donated Products; In-kind Services; Loaned Executives
Volunteer Programs: The company sponsors an employee volunteer team that works on various projects.
Contact:
Contact operating division through the Consumer and Community Affairs Department.
Note: The company and foundation give nonmonetary support. 1997 nonmonetary support totaled $24,000. Volunteer teams are involved in walk-a-thons and house refurbishing for the disadvantaged.

Southwest Gas Corp. Foundation

Giving Contact
Suzanne Farinas, Assistant to the Chief Executive Officer
Southwest Gas Corp.
PO Box 98510
Las Vegas, NV 89193-8510
Phone: (702)876-7247

Description
EIN: 942988564
Organization Type: Corporate Foundation
Giving Locations: AZ: Southern and Central Arizona; CA: Barstow, Big Bear, Victorville; NV: Northern and Southern Nevada (except Reno)
Grant Types: Capital, Employee Matching Gifts, General Support, Multiyear/Continuing Support.
Note: Employee matching gift ratio: 1 to 1 up to $2,500, for gifts to two- or four-year colleges and universities.

Financial Summary
Total Giving: $410,000 (1999 approx); $511,575 (1998); $423,776 (1997). Note: Contributes through corporate direct giving program and foundation.
Giving Analysis: Giving for 1997 includes: foundation ($386,208); corporate direct giving ($37,568); 1998: foundation ($414,432); foundation grants to United Way ($57,568); nonmonetary support ($13,141); corporate direct giving ($9,002)
Assets: $1,381,783 (1998); $1,243,801 (1997); $1,197,116 (1996)
Gifts Received: $550,000 (1998); $383,478 (1997); $380,000 (1996). Note: Contributions were received from the Southwest Gas Corporation.

Typical Recipients
Arts & Humanities: Arts Associations & Councils, Arts Funds, Ballet, Community Arts, Dance, Film & Video, Historic Preservation, Museums/Galleries, Music, Opera, Performing Arts, Public Broadcasting, Theater
Civic & Public Affairs: African American Affairs, Botanical Gardens/Parks, Chambers of Commerce, Clubs, Economic Policy, Employment/Job Training, Civic & Public Affairs-General, Hispanic Affairs, Housing, Law & Justice, Legal Aid, Native American Affairs, Parades/Festivals, Philanthropic Organizations, Public Policy, Urban & Community Affairs
Education: Arts/Humanities Education, Business Education, Colleges & Universities, Community & Junior Colleges, Legal Education, Literacy, Private Education (Precollege), Public Education (Precollege)
Environment: Environment-General, Research, Resource Conservation, Wildlife Protection
Health: Arthritis, Cancer, Children's Health/Hospitals, Clinics/Medical Centers, Diabetes, Emergency/Ambulance Services, Eyes/Blindness, Heart, Hospices, Hospitals, Medical Research, Prenatal Health Issues, Respiratory, Single-Disease Health Associations
Religion: Jewish Causes, Religious Organizations, Religious Welfare
Science: Science Museums, Scientific Centers & Institutes, Scientific Labs
Social Services: At-Risk Youth, Big Brother/Big Sister, Child Welfare, Community Service Organizations, Domestic Violence, Family Services, Food/Clothing Distribution, Food/Clothing Distribution, People with Disabilities, Recreation & Athletics, Scouts, Special Olympics, United Funds/United Ways, Volunteer Services, YMCA/YWCA/YMHA/YWHA, Youth Organizations

Contributions Analysis
Arts & Humanities: 10% to 15%. Support includes local orchestras, symphonies, museums, public broadcasting, and performing arts.
Civic & Public Affairs: 5% to 10%. Funding supports a variety of legal and business associations, youth programs, safety programs.
Education: 35% to 40%. Yout and education program emphasizes universities, colleges, and literacy. Supports youth agencies, scholarships, and scouting.
Environment: Less than 5%. Funds environmental and scientific research organizations, land and wildlife preservation, forestry, and air and water quality.
Health: About 10%. Funds single-disease health associations and university medical centers.
Social Services: 30% to 35%. Majority of funding supports the United Way. Also supports community service organizations, a volunteer center, seniors, low-income services, shelters and food banks, and emergency relief.

Application Procedures
Initial Contact: Send a written request.
Application Requirements: Include a description of organization; amount requested; overview of program or project, including purpose, targeted population, evaluation strategies, anticipated results, budget, other sources of funding, and timeline; recently audited financial statement; list of board members and key staff; current or past company involvement, including employee volunteers; and proof of tax-exempt status.
Deadlines: None.
Review Process: Requests are reviewed at the corporate level or by the Division Contributions Committee.
Evaluative Criteria: Evidence of sound fiscal policies and management, collaborative efforts with similar programs, non-duplication of services, relevance to company's business interests, long-term benefits for community, involvement of employees.
Notes: Request should be sent to local Consumer & Community Affairs Department.

Restrictions
Grants are not made to individuals, team or extracurricular school events, tournament fundraisers, trips or tours, churches or religious organizations, discriminatory organizations, endowments or foundations, hospital operating funds, non-tax-exempt organizations, or groups located outside company service area.

Additional Information
Publications: Guidelines

Corporate Officials
George C. Biehl: senior vice president, chief financial officer, corporate secretary, director B 1947. ED Ohio State University BS (1969); Columbia University MBA (1972). PRIM CORP EMPL senior vice president, chief financial officer, corporate secretary, director: Southwest Gas Corp.
Suzanne Farinas: assistant to chief executive officer, assistant corporate secretary PRIM CORP EMPL assistant to chief executive officer: Southwest Gas Corp.
Michael O. Maffie: president, chief executive officer, director B Los Angeles, CA 1948. ED University of Southern California BS (1969); University of Southern California MBA (1971). PRIM CORP EMPL president, chief executive officer, director: Southwest Gas Corp. CORP AFFIL director: Del Webb Corp.; director: Norwest Bank Nevada; director: Boyd Gaming Corp.
Thomas R. Sheets: vice president, general counsel ED Ashland College BS (1973); Toledo JD (1975). PRIM CORP EMPL vice president, general counsel: Southwest Gas Corp.

Foundation Officials
George C. Biehl: trustee (see above)
Michael O. Maffie: trustee (see above)
Thomas R. Sheets: trustee (see above)

Grants Analysis
Disclosure Period: calendar year ending 1998
Total Grants: $454,007*
Number of Grants: 264
Average Grant: $1,436*
Highest Grant: $75,000
Typical Range: $100 to $2,500
***Note:** Giving excludes United Way. Average grant figure excludes highest grant.

Recent Grants
Note: Grants derived from 1998 Form 990.

Arts & Humanities

7,500	Nevada Dance Theater, Las Vegas, NV
5,000	Phoenix Symphony, Phoenix, AZ
3,700	West Valley Fine Arts Council, Litchfield Park, AZ

3,000	Heard Museum, Phoenix, AZ
3,000	Phoenix Art Museum, Phoenix, AZ
2,500	Sierra Arts Foundation, Reno, NV
2,000	Yuma Ballet Theatre, Yuma, AZ

Civic & Public Affairs

25,000	Campaign for Prospect Park, New York, NY
14,000	Laub Foundation, Las Vegas, NV
4,750	National Conference, Los Angeles, CA
3,000	Gaming Entertainment Research, Kansas City, MO
2,500	Mountain States Legal Foundation, Denver, CO

Education

75,000	ASU Foundation/CASB, Tempe, AZ
10,630	University of Nevada, Las Vegas, Las Vegas, NV
10,000	Northern Arizona University, Flagstaff, AZ
5,000	Great Basin College, Elko, NV
5,000	National Judicial College, Reno, NV
5,000	Nevada School of the Arts, Las Vegas, NV
3,443	Junior Achievement, Phoenix, AZ
2,250	Victor Valley College, Victorville, CA
2,000	Community College of Southern Nevada, Las Vegas, NV

Environment

2,500	Nature Conservancy, San Francisco, CA

Health

10,000	Barrow Neurological Foundation, Phoenix, AZ
5,400	American Heart Association, Phoenix, AZ
5,000	St. Luke's Board of Visitors, Phoenix, AZ
4,800	American Diabetes Association, Phoenix, AZ
4,500	American Red Cross, Phoenix, AZ
3,000	Juvenile Diabetes Foundation, Phoenix, AZ
2,850	Arthritis Foundation, Phoenix, AZ
2,750	American Cancer Society, Phoenix, AZ
2,500	American Lung Association, Phoenix, AZ
2,250	March of Dimes, Las Vegas, NV
2,000	St. Mary Hospital Foundation, Langhorne, PA

Religion

11,347	Salvation Army, Phoenix, AZ
2,500	Anti-Defamation League, Reno, NV

Science

5,000	Desert Research Institute, Reno, NV
2,500	Lied Discovery Children's Museum, Las Vegas, NV

Social Services

57,568	United Way, Phoenix, AZ
19,725	Boys and Girls Club, Denver, CO
8,452	Boy Scouts of America, Phoenix, AZ
6,080	YMCA, Chicago, IL
5,025	Tumbleweed Center for Youth Development, Phoenix, AZ
5,000	Assistance League of Las Vegas, Las Vegas, NV
3,000	Happy Trails Foundation, Apple Valley, CA
2,800	Community Food Bank, Phoenix, AZ
2,650	Big Brothers/Big Sisters, Phoenix, AZ
2,500	Community Information Referral, Phoenix, AZ
2,500	Frontier Girl Scouts Council, Las Vegas, NV
2,500	M.A.S.H. Village, Las Vegas, NV
2,000	Greater Las Vegas Inner-City Games, Las Vegas, NV

SOVEREIGN BANK

Company Contact

Wyomissing, PA
Web: http://www.sovereignbank.com

Company Description

Assets: US$22,000,000,000
Employees: 4,100
SIC(s): 6035 Federal Savings Institutions.
Parent Company: Sovereign Bancorp

Nonmonetary Support

Type: Cause-related Marketing & Promotion; Donated Equipment; Donated Products; In-kind Services; Workplace Solicitation

Sovereign Bank Foundation

Giving Contact

John Killen, Manager
Sovereign Bank Foundation
PO Box 12646
Reading, PA 19612
Phone: (610)320-8504

Alternate Contact

1130 Berkshire Boulevard
Wyomissing, PA 19610
Phone: (610)320-8400

Description

EIN: 232548113
Organization Type: Corporate Foundation
Giving Locations: NJ: Mercer County bank or service areas.
Grant Types: Capital, General Support, Multiyear/Continuing Support.

Financial Summary

Total Giving: $400,000 (1999 approx); $375,917 (1998); $275,175 (1997)
Giving Analysis: Giving for 1997 includes: foundation ($247,076); foundation grants to United Way ($27,410); foundation matching gifts ($825); 1998: foundation ($334,950); foundation grants to United Way ($35,600); foundation matching gifts ($5,367)
Assets: $100 (1991); $1,773 (1990)
Gifts Received: $376,031 (1998); $275,311 (1997); $170,983 (1996). Note: The foundation receives contributions from Sovereign Bank.

Typical Recipients

Arts & Humanities: Arts Festivals, Arts Outreach, Community Arts, Historic Preservation, Libraries, Museums/Galleries, Music, Opera, Public Broadcasting
Civic & Public Affairs: African American Affairs, Asian American Affairs, Business/Free Enterprise, Civil Rights, Economic Development, Ethnic Organizations, Gay/Lesbian Issues, Hispanic Affairs, Housing, Inner-City Development, Municipalities/Towns, Native American Affairs, Nonprofit Management, Parades/Festivals, Philanthropic Organizations, Urban & Community Affairs, Women's Affairs
Education: Afterschool/Enrichment Programs, Colleges & Universities, Community & Junior Colleges, Literacy, Minority Education, Student Aid
Environment: Environment-General
Health: AIDS/HIV, Clinics/Medical Centers, Hospitals, Public Health
Religion: Religious Welfare, Social/Policy Issues
Social Services: Child Welfare, Community Centers, Community Service Organizations, Crime Prevention, Domestic Violence, Emergency Relief, Family Planning, Family Services, Food/Clothing Distribution, Homes, People with Disabilities, Sexual Abuse, Shelters/Homelessness, United Funds/United Ways, Volunteer Services, YMCA/YWCA/YMHA/YWHA

Contributions Analysis

Giving Priorities: Civic, social services, education, and arts organizations.
Arts & Humanities: 13%. Supports libraries, museums, and performing arts.
Civic & Public Affairs: 60%. Supports housing and community and economic development.
Education: 8%. Supports colleges and universities.
Religion: 2%. Supports interfaith organizations.
Social Services: 17%. Supports the United Way, homeless shelters, and youth organizations.
Note: Total contributions were made in 1997.

Application Procedures

Initial Contact: Send a full proposal.
Application Requirements: Include a description of organization, needs of the project, population served, and a listing of the directors of the organization.
Deadlines: None.

Restrictions

Does not support individuals, religious organizations for sectarian purposes, political or lobbying groups, organizations outside operating areas, organizations that are not tax-exempt/nonprofit, or beauty scholarship pageants.

Additional Information

Publications: Guidelines Brochure

Corporate Officials

Richard E. Mohn: chairman, director PRIM CORP EMPL chairman, director: Sovereign Bank. CORP AFFIL chairman: Cloister Spring Water Co.
Jay S. Sidhu: president, chief executive officer PRIM CORP EMPL president, chief executive officer: Sovereign Bank.

Foundation Officials

Gail Dawson-White: mgr
Stewart B. Kean: director
Howard D. Mackey: director
Richard E. Mohn: director (see above)
Elizabeth B. Rothermel: director
Jay S. Sidhu: director (see above)
Lawrence M. Thompson, Jr.: president

Grants Analysis

Disclosure Period: calendar year ending 1998
Total Grants: $334,950*
Number of Grants: 110
Average Grant: $3,045
Highest Grant: $30,000
Typical Range: $500 to $10,000
***Note:** Giving excludes matching gifts, United Way.

Recent Grants

Note: Grants derived from 1997 Form 990.

Arts & Humanities

5,000	Bethlehem Musikfest Association, Bethlehem, PA -- support Banana Factory Capital Campaign
5,000	Bethlehem Musikfest Association, Bethlehem, PA -- sponsorship
5,000	Reading Public Museum, Reading, PA -- second payment on three-part pledge

Civic & Public Affairs

15,000	New Jersey Citizen Action, Hackensack, NJ -- operating support
10,000	Perth Amboy Redevelopment Agency, Perth Amboy, NJ -- first payment on three-part pledge for operating support
9,000	Lancaster Housing Opportunity Partnership, Lancaster, PA -- annual drive

6,000	Neighborhood Housing Service, Reading, PA -- operating support
5,000	Community Action Committee of the Lehigh Valley, Bethlehem, PA -- support home ownership
5,000	Elizabeth Development Company, Elizabeth, NJ -- operating support
5,000	Partnership for Small Business Development, Philadelphia, PA -- support Bucks County Micro Loan Program
5,000	SACA Development Corporation, Lancaster, PA -- support construction, rehabilitation costs
5,000	Trenton Business Assistance Corporation, Trenton, NJ -- support technical assistance, lending services
4,000	Isles, Trenton, NJ -- support Affordable Housing Program

Education

6,000	Alvernia College, Reading, PA -- capital campaign

Environment

15,000	Isles, Trenton, NJ -- support Capital Housing Resource Center

Religion

6,000	Salvation Army, Allentown, PA -- capital campaign

Social Services

8,000	United Way Berks County, Reading, PA -- annual support
5,500	United Way Lancaster County, Lancaster, PA -- annual support
5,000	Pennsylvania Crime Prevention Officers' Association, Reading, PA -- sponsor Crime Prevention Video Tape
5,000	YMCA Reading and Berks County, Reading, PA -- support Glenside Day Camp Program

SPRINGS INDUSTRIES, INC.

Company Contact

Fort Mill, SC
Web: http://www.springs.com

Company Description

Employees: 17,500 (1999)
SIC(s): 2211 Broadwoven Fabric Mills--Cotton, 2221 Broadwoven Fabric Mills--Manmade, 2231 Broadwoven Fabric Mills--Wool, 2262 Finishing Plants--Manmade.

Nonmonetary Support

Value: $6,000 (1996); $6,682 (1993)
Type: Donated Equipment; Donated Products; In-kind Services; Loaned Employees
Note: Nonmonetary support 1997 ($4,000).

Corporate Sponsorship

Value: $1,000
Type: Arts & cultural events
Note: Sponsors benefit dinners for health-related causes, scholarship programs, and Junior Achievement.

Giving Contact

Mr. Robert L. Thompson, Vice President, Public Affairs
Springs Industries, Inc.
PO Box 70
Ft. Mill, SC 29716
Phone: (803)547-3736
Fax: (803)547-3740

Description

Organization Type: Corporate Giving Program
Giving Locations: principally near operating locations and to national organizations.
Grant Types: Capital, Emergency, Employee Matching Gifts, Endowment, General Support, Matching, Multiyear/Continuing Support.
Note: Employee matching gift ratio: 2 to 1 up to $50; 1 to 1 thereafter.

Financial Summary

Total Giving: $1,025,000 (1999 approx); $1,050,000 (1998); $939,049 (1997). Note: Contributes through corporate direct giving program only.
Giving Analysis: Giving for 1997 includes: corporate direct giving ($935,049); nonmonetary support ($4,000)

Typical Recipients

Arts & Humanities: Arts Associations & Councils, Arts Festivals, Community Arts, Museums/Galleries, Visual Arts
Civic & Public Affairs: Business/Free Enterprise, Economic Development, Employment/Job Training, Professional & Trade Associations, Public Policy
Education: Business Education, Colleges & Universities, Economic Education, Education Associations, Faculty Development, Minority Education, Preschool Education, Public Education (Precollege)
Environment: Environment-General
Health: Hospices, Hospitals, Single-Disease Health Associations
Science: Science Exhibits & Fairs
Social Services: Community Centers, Emergency Relief, Family Services, Substance Abuse, United Funds/United Ways, Volunteer Services, Youth Organizations

Contributions Analysis

Giving Priorities: Education and business.
Arts & Humanities: About 10%. Priorities include arts associations and historic preservation. Other interests include a museum, galleries, and community arts.
Civic & Public Affairs: 20% to 25%. Primary interest is organizations concerned with business or free enterprise. Interests also include economic development, professional and trade associations, and public policy organizations.
Education: 50% to 55%. Major priorities include improvement in higher education and adult education. Other interests include business education, elementary and secondary education, economic education, and public and private education organizations.
Health: 5% to 10%. Major welfare interests include community service, family service, and youth organizations. Major health interests include hospitals and single disease health associations. Smaller contributions go to organizations promoting health care cost containment, child welfare, drug and alcohol abuse prevention, and united funds.

Application Procedures

Initial Contact: Send a brief letter.
Application Requirements: Include a description of organization, amount requested, purpose of funds sought, recently audited financial statement, proof of tax-exempt status, relationship to company interests.
Deadlines: None.

Restrictions

Does not give to special events, fraternal organizations, goodwill advertising, individuals, member agencies of united funds, political or lobbying groups, or religious organizations.

Corporate Officials

Crandall Close Bowles: president, chief executive officer, chairman, director B 1947. ED Wellesley College BA (1969); Columbia University MBA (1973). PRIM CORP EMPL president, chief executive officer, chairman, director: Springs Industries, Inc. NONPR AFFIL director: Juvenile Diabetes Foundation International.
William K. Easley: senior vice president
Stephen Paul Kelbley: executive vice president B Tiffin, OH 1942. ED Heidelberg College (1964). PRIM CORP EMPL executive vice president: Springs Industries, Inc. NONPR AFFIL director: Connectivity Technologies Inc.; director: Glenayre Technologies Inc.
Robert W. Moser: executive vice president B Rock Hill, SC 1938. ED Clemson University BS (1961); Winthrop College MBA (1975). PRIM CORP EMPL executive vice president: Springs Industries, Inc. CORP AFFIL president: Bath Manufacturing.
Thomas P. O'Connor: executive vice president PRIM CORP EMPL executive vice president: Springs Industries, Inc.
Robert L. Thompson: vice president public affairs B Adel, GA 1937. ED Furman University BA (1960). PRIM CORP EMPL vice president public affairs: Springs Industries, Inc. CORP AFFIL comptroller, director corporate planning: Oryx Energy Co.

Giving Program Officials

Crandall Close Bowles: president B 1947. ED Wellesley College BA (1969); Columbia University MBA (1973). PRIM CORP EMPL president, chief executive officer, chairman, director: Springs Industries, Inc. NONPR AFFIL director: Juvenile Diabetes Foundation International.
Robert W. Moser: B Rock Hill, SC 1938. ED Clemson University BS (1961); Winthrop College MBA (1975). PRIM CORP EMPL executive vice president: Springs Industries, Inc. CORP AFFIL president: Bath Manufacturing.
Robert L. Thompson: secretary B Adel, GA 1937. ED Furman University BA (1960). PRIM CORP EMPL vice president public affairs: Springs Industries, Inc. CORP AFFIL comptroller, director corporate planning: Oryx Energy Co.
Elizabeth 'Betty' M. Turner: public relations director

Grants Analysis

Disclosure Period: calendar year ending 1997
Total Grants: $935,049*
Number of Grants: 838
Average Grant: $1,116
Typical Range: $500 to $1,500
***Note:** Giving excludes nonmonetary support. Grants analysis provided by company.

Recent Grants

Note: Grants derived from 1997 Form 990.

Arts & Humanities

20,450	Lancaster County Council of the Arts, Lancaster, SC -- payment on grant
15,000	Children's Theater, Charlotte, NC

Civic & Public Affairs

1,000	Chester Shrine Club
1,000	Flat Creek Volunteer Fire Department, Thompsons Station, TN
1,000	Jackson Shrine Club
1,000	Lewis Fire Protection Association
1,000	York County Crescent Shrine Club

Education

40,000	Fort Mill School District, Fort Mill, SC -- LEAP program
30,554	Lancaster County School District, Lancaster, SC -- payment on grant, for school assistance programs
29,000	Lancaster County School District, Lancaster, SC -- Project Success at Barr Street Middle School
20,451	Chester County Department of Education, Chester, SC -- payment on grant, for school assistance programs
17,250	Communities in Schools of Lancaster County
11,955	Fort Mill School District 4, Fort Mill, SC -- payment on grant, for school assistance programs
6,800	University of Lancaster -- summer camp program

6,500 Lancaster County School District, Lancaster, SC -- homework center at Clinton Elementary School
5,000 Clemson University, Clemson, SC -- College Week for Senior Citizens
2,000 Fort Mill Elementary School, Fort Mill, SC

Health
15,000 Healthy Mothers Healthy Babies
2,185 Fort Mill Care Center, Fort Mill, SC

Religion
2,000 First Presbyterian Church, Kershaw, SC
1,500 Van Wyck Presbyterian Church
1,000 Macedonia Missionary Church, Kershaw, SC
1,000 Pineview Baptist Church, Kershaw, SC
1,000 Trinity Pentecostal Holiness Church, Lancaster, SC
500 Pleasant Plain Baptist Church, Kershaw, SC
500 Zoar United Methodist Church, Charlotte, NC

Social Services
300,000 Leroy Springs and Company, Fort Mill, SC -- payment on grant, for Springmaid Beach 4 Million Project
20,000 United Way Fund, Lancaster, SC -- payment on grant
18,040 YMCA Camp Thunderbird
15,000 Harvest Hope Food Bank, Columbia, SC
10,000 United Way Fund of Chester -- payment on grant
7,000 Lancaster County Council on Aging, Lancaster, SC
7,000 United Way Fund of East Mill -- payment on grant
5,392 York County Board of Disabilities and Special Needs, Rock Hill, SC
2,500 Boy Scouts of America Troop 1 of Buford
1,500 Rock Hill District 3 -- Parent to Parent program
1,000 Columbus Parker Track Club
450 Lancaster Disabilities and Special Needs Board, Lancaster, SC

SPRINT CORP.

Company Contact

Westwood, KS
Web: http://www.sprint.com

Company Description

Former Name: United Telecommunication Inc.
Revenue: US$19,930,300,000 (1999)
Employees: 48,024
Fortune Rank: 81, per FORTUNE Magazine's list of 500 Largest U.S. Corporations (1999).
FF 81
SIC(s): 2741 Miscellaneous Publishing, 4812 Radiotelephone Communications, 4813 Telephone Communications Except Radiotelephone, 5065 Electronic Parts & Equipment Nec.

Nonmonetary Support

Type: Donated Equipment; In-kind Services; Loaned Executives
Note: Nonmonetary Support Range: $10,000 to $300,000. Nonmonetary support is provided through the company.

Corporate Sponsorship

Type: Arts & cultural events
Contact: Julie Hershey, Manager, Corporate Relations

Sprint Foundation

Giving Contact

David P. Thomas, Executive Director
Sprint Foundation
2330 Shawnee Mission Parkway
Westwood, KS 66205
Phone: (913)624-3343
Fax: (913)624-3490
Web: http://www.sprint.com/sprint/overview/commun

Description

EIN: 481062018
Organization Type: Corporate Foundation
Giving Locations: principally near operating locations and to national organizations; also to areas where the company's subsidiaries have major concentrations of employees.
Grant Types: Capital, Employee Matching Gifts, General Support.
Note: Employee matching gift ratio: 2 to 1 for first $500 matched; 1 to 1 for $500 to $10,000 annually.

Giving Philosophy

'The foundation's charitable giving program emphasizes support of local and regional organizations in those communities in which the corporation has a major presence. Support of national organizations with a broad sphere of interest will be considered on a case by case basis.' Sprint Foundation Contribution Guidelines.

'Funding Priorities:

'Education: The Foundation's emphasis on education centers on support of activities that will prepare people for the challenges of the workplace and enable them to be productive participants in the economy. It addresses educational needs an initiatives covering the childhood through early adult years. Support of higher education is focused principally in the Sprint Employee Matching Gift Program and in a targeted scholarship program addressing career development for the telecommunications industry. Grantmaking priorities include programs that encourage innovation and the use of technology in the classroom, enhance the quality of education for minorities and/or the disadvantaged, and encourage employee and public support of education.

'Arts and Culture: The Foundation supports visual and performing arts organizations, museums and other cultural organizations and activities which have effective outreach programs that broaden cultural experiences for the general public, particularly youth and non-traditional audiences.

'Community Improvement: The Foundation's principal support of community service organizations which provide social or human services will be directed through the United Way. Special project grants targeted to encourage resource-sharing efforts among non-profit agencies also will be considered.

'Youth Development: The Foundation's support of youth organizations will be targeted to drug and alcohol education, minority youth endeavors, broad scale community youth activities focused on building leadership and social skills, and to programs which promote business an economic education for youth.'

Financial Summary

Total Giving: $6,578,395 (1998); $6,183,376 (1997); $5,000,000 (1996). Note: Contributes through corporate direct giving program and foundation.
Giving Analysis: Giving for 1997 includes: foundation grants to United Way ($805,000); 1998: foundation matching gifts ($1,041,003); foundation grants to United Way ($1,039,500)
Assets: $9,700,750 (1998); $15,250,385 (1997); $17,439,925 (1996)
Gifts Received: $268,000 (1997); $153,000 (1996); $22,058 (1995). Note: Foundation receives contributions from Sprint Corporation.

Typical Recipients

Arts & Humanities: Arts Associations & Councils, Arts Centers, Arts Festivals, Arts Institutes, Ballet, Arts & Humanities-General, Historic Preservation, Museums/Galleries, Music, Opera, Performing Arts, Public Broadcasting, Theater
Civic & Public Affairs: Business/Free Enterprise, Chambers of Commerce, Community Foundations, Economic Development, Employment/Job Training, Civic & Public Affairs-General, Hispanic Affairs, Law & Justice, Legal Aid, Parades/Festivals, Urban & Community Affairs, Zoos/Aquariums
Education: Business Education, Colleges & Universities, Community & Junior Colleges, Education Associations, Education Reform, Engineering/Technological Education, Education-General, Literacy, Minority Education, Private Education (Precollege), Public Education (Precollege), Science/Mathematics Education, Secondary Education (Private), Special Education, Vocational & Technical Education
Health: Cancer, Children's Health/Hospitals, Public Health
International: Foreign Arts Organizations, Health Care/Hospitals, International Affairs
Religion: Social/Policy Issues
Science: Scientific Centers & Institutes
Social Services: Camps, Child Welfare, Community Service Organizations, Food/Clothing Distribution, Scouts, United Funds/United Ways, Volunteer Services, Youth Organizations

Contributions Analysis

Giving Priorities: Education, the performing arts, united funds, youth, and minority programs.
Arts & Humanities: 17%. Supports major visual and performig arts organizations, museums and other cultural organizations, and activities which have effective outreach programs that broaden the cultural experience of the general public and bring cultural opportunity to the economically disadvantaged.
Civic & Public Affairs: 23%. Supports economic development, legal and women's issues, and civic organizations. Special project grants targeted to encourage resource-sharing efforts among not-for-profit agencies are also considered.
Education: 30%. Supports activities that will prepare people for the challenges of the workplace and enable them to be productive participants in the economy by addressing educational needs and initiatives covering the childhood through early adult years. Targets public school renewal and reform, programs that enhance educational opportunities for minorities and/or the disadvantaged, excellence in teaching and retention of quality educators, encourages employee and public support of education, and the use of new communications technology in education. Also sponsors matching gifts program.
Health: 2%. Supports medical centers.
Social Services: 29%. Supports youth organizations with drug and alcohol education, minority youth endeavors, community youth activities, and United Way.
Note: Total contributions in 1998.

Application Procedures

Initial Contact: Call or write to request guidelines, then full proposal.
Application Requirements: Include background information on the organization, description of project which the funding will support, proposed project budget, information on other sources of support, current financial statements, proof of tax-exempt status.
Deadlines: None.
Review Process: Major contributions considered by foundation directors.
Decision Notification: Board meets quarterly; applicants typically receive an initial response within three or four weeks.
Notes: Guidelines are also found on company's web site.

Restrictions

Company does not support fraternal, labor, or veterans' organizations; individuals; hospitals; neighborhood associations; political or lobbying groups; or religious organizations.

Additional Information

Subsidiaries and regional offices administer their own charitable giving programs. Contact the public relations department of the nearest office for more information.

Corporate Officials

William Todd Esrey: chairman, chief executive officerrelations B Philadelphia, PA 1940. ED Denison University BA (1961); Harvard University MBA (1964). PRIM CORP EMPL chairman, chief executive officer: Sprint Corp. CORP AFFIL chairman, chief executive officer: United Telecommunications Inc.; director: Panhandle Eastern Corp.; chairman: Sprint United Management Co.; director: General Mills Inc.; director: PanEnergy Corp.; director: ExxonMobil Corp.; director: Equitable Life Assurance Society US; director: Everen Capital Corp.; director: Equitable Companies Inc.; director: Equitable Life Assurance; director: Duke Energy Corp.; president: Centel Corp.; chairman: Central Telephone Co. Illinois. NONPR AFFIL director: Midwest Research Committee for Economic Development; member: Phi Beta Kappa. CLUB AFFIL Mission Hills Country Club; River Club; Kansas City Country Club; The Links Club.

Donald George Forsythe: vice president corporate relations B Emmetsburg, IA 1938. ED University of Iowa BA (1960); Rockhurst College MBA (1978). PRIM CORP EMPL vice president corporate relations: Sprint Corp. CORP AFFIL vice president: United Telecommunications Inc. NONPR AFFIL member: National Investor Relations Institute; member: Sigma Delta Chi.

Foundation Officials

James Richard Devlin: director B Camden, NJ 1950. ED New Jersey Institute of Technology BS (1972); Fordham University JD (1976). PRIM CORP EMPL executive vice president external affairs, general counsel: Sprint Corp. CORP AFFIL director: Transfinancial Holdings Inc. NONPR AFFIL member: Fed Communications Bar Association; member board overseers: New Jersey Institute Technology; member: American Bar Association; director: American Arbitration Association.

Donald George Forsythe: executive director (see above)

Len J. Lauer: president PRIM CORP EMPL senior vice president brand management & public relations: Sprint Corp.

Mary Jeannine Strandjord: director B Kansas City, MO 1945. ED University of Kansas BSBA (1968); University of Missouri (1976). PRIM CORP EMPL senior vice president, treasurer: Sprint Corp. CORP AFFIL vice president: Utelcom Inc.; vice president: United States Telecom Inc.; vice president, treasurer: United Telecommunications Inc.; treasurer: Sprint United Management Co.; treasurer: UCOM Inc.; director: DST Corp.; treasurer: Sprint International Caribbean Inc.; treasurer: Centel Corp.; treasurer: Central Telephone Co. NONPR AFFIL member executive committee, acct advisory council: Kansas University Lawrence; treasurer: State Health Center Foundation; member: American Institute CPAs; member: Financial Executives Institute; director: American Century Mutual Funds. CLUB AFFIL Blue Hills Country Club.

Grants Analysis

Disclosure Period: calendar year ending 1998
Total Grants: $5,538,895*
Number of Grants: 286
Average Grant: $15,926
Highest Grant: $1,000,000
Typical Range: $500 to $20,000

***Note:** Giving excludes United Way. Giving includes matching gifts. Average grant figure excludes highest grant. Number of grants is approximate.

Recent Grants

Note: Grants derived from 1998 grants list.

Arts & Humanities

1,000,000	Kansas City Royals Succession Plan, Kansas City, MO -- Royals Succession Plan
150,000	Kansas City Art Institute, Kansas City, MO -- technology project challenge grant
100,000	Kansas City Symphony, Kansas City, MO -- concert underwriting
78,000	Kansas City Public Television, Kansas City, MO -- local programming support

Civic & Public Affairs

200,000	Friends of the Zoo, Kansas City, MO -- KC signature film for IMAX
75,000	Zoo Atlanta, Atlanta, GA -- Conservation Action Resource Center

Education

150,000	The Jason Foundation for Education, Waltham, MA -- operating support
125,000	The Learning Exchange, Kansas City, MO -- interdisciplinary entrepreneurship program
75,000	The Learning Exchange, Kansas City, MO -- BE2 school to career initiative
50,000	Florida Gulf Coast University (Fort Myers), Ft. Myers, FL -- distance learning grant
50,000	National Technical Institute for the Deaf, Rochester, MN -- capital grant for videoconferencing technology

Social Services

675,000	Heart of America United Way, Kansas City, MO
100,000	The Welfare to Work Partnership (D.C.), Washington, DC -- operating support
75,000	Heart of America United Way, Kansas City, MO -- enhanced information system
70,000	Heart of America United Way, Kansas City, MO
50,000	Boys & Girls Clubs of America, Richardson, TX -- corporate campaign and underwriting
50,000	Greater Los Angeles Council on Deafness, Inc., Los Angeles, CA -- telecommunications project
50,000	Youthnet, Kansas City, MO -- operating support
45,000	United Way of Metropolitan Dallas, Dallas, TX
12,000	Crusade of Mercy-United Way, Chicago, IL

Sprint/United Telephone

Company Contact

Mansfield, OH

Company Description

Former Name: United Telephone Co. of Indiana and Ohio.
SIC(s): 4813 Telephone Communications Except Radiotelephone.
Parent Company: Sprint Corp., Westwood, KS, United States

Corporate Sponsorship

Type: Arts & cultural events; Sports events
Contact: John Eitelgeorge, General Manager, Community Relations

Giving Contact

Dave Brown, Budget Administrator & Public Affairs Manager
Sprint/United Telephone
PO Box 3555
Mansfield, OH 44907
Phone: (419)755-8370
Fax: (419)755-8118

Description

Organization Type: Corporate Giving Program
Giving Locations: limited to areas of service.
Grant Types: Employee Matching Gifts, General Support.

Financial Summary

Total Giving: $300,000 (1996 approx); $300,000 (1995 approx); $3,275,738 (1994). Note: Contributes through corporate direct giving program only. 1996 and 1995 Giving includes corporate direct giving; nonmonetary support.

Typical Recipients

Arts & Humanities: Arts Centers, Ballet, Arts & Humanities-General, Museums/Galleries, Music, Opera, Public Broadcasting, Theater
Civic & Public Affairs: Business/Free Enterprise, Community Foundations, Civic & Public Affairs-General, Legal Aid, Professional & Trade Associations, Urban & Community Affairs, Zoos/Aquariums
Education: Business Education, Colleges & Universities, Education Reform, Education-General, Minority Education, Public Education (Precollege)
Health: Children's Health/Hospitals, Emergency/Ambulance Services, Health-General
International: Foreign Educational Institutions, International Affairs
Science: Scientific Centers & Institutes, Scientific Organizations
Social Services: Child Welfare, Crime Prevention, Homes, Social Services-General, United Funds/United Ways

Application Procedures

Initial Contact: Call the company for an application form.
Application Requirements: Include a description of organization, amount requested, purpose of funds sought, recently audited financial statements, and proof of tax-exempt status.
Deadlines: None.

Restrictions

Does not support individuals or religious organizations for sectarian purposes.
Only donates in geographical service area.

Additional Information

Sprint/United Telephone's giving program is separate from the Sprint Foundation in Westwood, KS.

Corporate Officials

Randy W. Osler: president B 1947. ED Webster University MBA (1968). PRIM CORP EMPL president: Sprint Corp. ADD CORP EMPL president: United Telephone Co. Indiana; president: United Telephone Co. Ohio.

Giving Program Officials

John Eitelgeorge: PRIM CORP EMPL general manager community relations: Sprint/United Telephone.

Foundation Officials

Randy W. Osler: president (see above)

SPX Corp.

Company Contact

Muskegon, MI

Company Description

Former Name: Sealed Power Corp.
Employees: 7,125
SIC(s): 3423 Hand & Edge Tools Nec, 3429 Hardware Nec,- 3491 Industrial Valves, 3544 Special Dies, Tools, Jigs & Fixtures.

Corporate Sponsorship

Type: Arts & cultural events; Festivals/fairs; Music & entertainment events; Pledge-a-thon

SPX Foundation

Giving Contact

Tina Betlejewski, President
SPX Foundation
700 Terrace Point Drive
Muskegon, MI 49443-3301
Phone: (231)724-5000
Fax: (231)724-5720

Description

Founded: 1984
EIN: 386058308
Organization Type: Corporate Foundation
Giving Locations: primarily in plant communities.
Grant Types: Capital, Employee Matching Gifts, General Support.

Financial Summary

Total Giving: $417,957 (1998); $400,000 (1996 approx); $337,920 (1995)
Giving Analysis: Giving for 1998 includes: foundation matching gifts ($226,383); foundation grants to United Way ($77,425)
Assets: $376,311 (1998); $194,097 (1995); $526,308 (1994)
Gifts Received: $781,632 (1994); $392,641 (1993); $205,948 (1991). Note: In 1994, contributions of $780,332 were received from SPX Corp., and $1,300 received from First Chicago.

Typical Recipients

Arts & Humanities: Arts Centers, Arts Festivals, Arts & Humanities-General, Libraries, Museums/Galleries, Music, Performing Arts, Public Broadcasting, Theater
Civic & Public Affairs: Business/Free Enterprise, Clubs, Economic Development, Economic Policy, Civic & Public Affairs-General, Housing, Municipalities/Towns, Nonprofit Management, Parades/Festivals, Professional & Trade Associations, Urban & Community Affairs, Women's Affairs
Education: Business Education, Colleges & Universities, Community & Junior Colleges, Education Funds, Engineering/Technological Education, Education-General, Minority Education, Public Education (Precollege), Science/Mathematics Education
Health: Diabetes, Emergency/Ambulance Services, Health-General, Health Organizations, Hospitals
Religion: Churches, Religious Organizations, Religious Welfare
Science: Scientific Centers & Institutes, Scientific Organizations
Social Services: Child Abuse, Community Service Organizations, Crime Prevention, Family Planning, Family Services, Food/Clothing Distribution, People with Disabilities, Scouts, Social Services-General, Special Olympics, Substance Abuse, United Funds/ United Ways, YMCA/YWCA/YMHA/YWHA, Youth Organizations

Contributions Analysis

Giving Priorities: Focus on social services, health organizations, and education.
Arts & Humanities: About 5%. Major support to art museums, theaters, music, public radio, and the performing arts.
Civic & Public Affairs: Less than 1%. Supports local iniatives and chambers of commerce.
Education: About 17%. Primarily supports community colleges and public and private higher education. Interests also include business, science, and minority education. Company also matches employee gifts to higher education.
Health: 31%. Supports community hospitals and cancer research.
Social Services: 47%. Supports the United Way and youth organizations.
Note: Total contributions made in 1998.

Application Procedures

Initial Contact: Send a letter of inquiry.
Application Requirements: Include a description of organization, amount requested, purpose of funds sought, and proof of tax-exempt status.
Deadlines: None.

Corporate Officials

Tina L. Betlejewski: manager corporate communications, chief financial officer PRIM CORP EMPL manager corporate communications: SPX Corp.
John B. Blystone: chairman, president, chief executive officer, director B Erie, PA 1953. ED University of Pittsburgh BS (1975). PRIM CORP EMPL chairman, president, chief executive officer, director: SPX Corp. CORP AFFIL director: Worthington Indiana Inc.
Patrick J. O'Leary: vice president finance, treasurer, chief financial officer PRIM CORP EMPL vice president finance, treasurer, chief financial officer: SPX Corp.

Foundation Officials

Tina L. Betlejewski: secretary, trustee (see above)
John B. Blystone: (see above)
Christopher J. Kearney: trustee ED DePaul University; Notre Dame College. PRIM CORP EMPL vice president, secretary, general counsel: SPX Corp.
Stephen A. Lison: vice president, trustee B Pittsburgh, PA 1940. ED Miami University (1962); University of Pittsburgh (1973). PRIM CORP EMPL vice president human resources: SPX Corp.
Patrick J. O'Leary: secretary, treasurer (see above)

Grants Analysis

Disclosure Period: calendar year ending 1998
Total Grants: $191,575*
Number of Grants: 17
Average Grant: $8,848*
Highest Grant: $50,000
Typical Range: $250 to $10,000
***Note:** Giving excludes matching gifts; United Way. Average grant figure excludes highest grant.

Recent Grants

Note: Grants derived from 1995 Form 990.

Arts & Humanities

18,800	West Shore Symphony, Muskegon, MI
15,000	Cherry County Playhouse
12,650	Muskegon Museum of Art, Muskegon, MI
3,500	Music in Owatonna, Owatonna, MN
2,500	Jackson Symphony Orchestra, Jackson, MI
2,000	Friends of Hackley Library, Muskegon, MI

Civic & Public Affairs

10,000	Michigan First, Lansing, MI
5,000	Every Woman's Place, Muskegon, MI
2,500	Jackson Alliance, Jackson, MI
1,500	Southeastern Minnesota Initiative, Owatonna, MN
500	Council of Michigan Foundations, Grand Haven, MI

Education

30,000	Muskegon Community College, Muskegon, MI
25,000	Grand Valley State University, Allendale, MI
20,000	University of Michigan, Ann Arbor, MI
18,000	AWDA University, Kansas City, MO
1,000	United Negro College Fund, New York, NY

Religion

3,333	City Rescue Mission, Muskegon, MI

Social Services

67,500	United Way Muskegon County, Muskegon, MI
20,675	United Way Steele County, Owatonna, MN
9,143	Greater Kalamazoo United Way, Kalamazoo, MI
6,608	United Way Jackson County, Jackson, MI
6,337	Cass County United Way, Dowagiac, MI
5,079	Montpelier Area United Fund, Montpelier, OH
5,000	Boy Scouts of America
3,855	United Way Southeastern Michigan, Detroit, MI
1,949	Steuben County United Way, Angola, IN
1,000	Lakeshore Center for Independent Living, Holland, MI
1,000	YFCA Partner with Youth
208	Gratiot County United Way, MI
182	DeKalb County United Way

Square Dco.

Company Contact

Palatine, IL
Web: http://www.squared.com

Company Description

Employees: 15,000
SIC(s): 3497 Metal Foil & Leaf, 3499 Fabricated Metal Products Nec, 3612 Transformers Except Electronic, 3613 Switchgear & Switchboard Apparatus.
Parent Company: Schneider SA, 64-70 Ave. Jean-Baptiste Clement, Boulogne-Billancourt, Cedex, France

Operating Locations

AL: Square D Co., Clanton, Leeds; CA: Square D Co., Bakersfield; Square D Co., Costa Mesa; Square D Co.-Pacifico, San Ysidro; FL: Square D Co., Clearwater; Square D Co., Clearwater; Square D Co.-Assembly Operations, Clearwater; GA: Square D Co., Atlanta, Norcross; IA: Square D Co., Cedar Rapids; Square D Co., Cedar Rapids; IL: Square D Co., Niles, Palatine; Square D Co., Palatine; Square D Co., Schiller Park; Square D Co., Schiller Park; IN: Square D Co., Huntington, Peru; Square D Co., Peru; KY: Square D Co., Florence, Lexington; Square D Co., Lexington; MA: Schneider Automation, North Andover; MO: Square D Co., Columbia; Square D Co., Columbia; NC: Square D Co., Asheville; Square D Co., Knightdale; Square D Co.-Control Products, Knightdale; Square D Co., Monroe; Square D Co., Monroe; Square D Co., Raleigh; NE: Square D Co., Lincoln; Square D Co., Lincoln; NJ: Square D Co., Secaucus; OH: Square D Co., Middletown; Square D Middletown Plant, Middletown; Square D Co., Oxford; Square D Oxford Plant, Oxford; PA: Square D Co., Harrisburg; SC: Square D Co., Columbia; Square D Co., Columbia; Square D Co., Seneca; Square D Seneca Plant, Seneca; TN: Square D Co., Memphis; Square D Co.-Central Distribution Center, Memphis; Square D Co., Nashville; Electrical Distribution Business, Smyrna; Square D Co., Smyrna; Square D Co., Smyrna; TX: Square D Co., Fort Worth; Square D Co., Bedford, Dallas; Square D Co., Mesquite; WA: Square D Co., Mercer Island; WI: Square D Automation Products, Milwaukee; Square D Co., Milwaukee; Square D Co., Milwaukee; Square D Co.-Transformer

Business Division, Milwaukee; Square D Co., Oshkosh; Square D Co., Oshkosh

Nonmonetary Support

Value: $40,000 (1995)
Type: Donated Equipment
Contact: Tammy Sittinger, Foundation Coordinator

Corporate Sponsorship

Type: Arts & cultural events; Sports events
Contact: Larry Brand
Human Resources

Square D Foundation

Giving Contact

James R. White, Secretary
Square D Foundation
1415 South Roselle Road
Palatine, IL 60067
Phone: (847)397-2610
Fax: (847)397-2804

Description

EIN: 366054195
Organization Type: Corporate Foundation
Giving Locations: manufacturing facility communities.
Grant Types: Capital, Employee Matching Gifts, General Support.

Financial Summary

Total Giving: $2,000,000 (1999 approx); $2,882,072 (1998); $1,685,781 (1997). Note: Contributes through foundation only.
Giving Analysis: Giving for 1997 includes: foundation matching gifts ($234,972); foundation grants to United Way ($219,972); 1998: foundation grants to United Way ($272,998); foundation matching gifts ($218,626)
Assets: $21,483 (1998); $143,265 (1996); $334,277 (1995)
Gifts Received: $2,804,105 (1998); $1,874,550 (1997); $961,000 (1996). Note: Foundation receives contributions from the Square D Company.

Typical Recipients

Arts & Humanities: Arts Associations & Councils, Arts Centers, Arts Festivals, Arts Funds, Arts Institutes, Dance, Libraries, Museums/Galleries, Music, Opera, Public Broadcasting, Theater
Civic & Public Affairs: Botanical Gardens/Parks, Business/Free Enterprise, Legal Aid, Minority Business, Parades/Festivals, Rural Affairs, Safety, Urban & Community Affairs
Education: Arts/Humanities Education, Business Education, Colleges & Universities, Community & Junior Colleges, Economic Education, Education Funds, Elementary Education (Public), Engineering/Technological Education, Education-General, Minority Education, Public Education (Precollege), Student Aid
Health: Cancer, Children's Health/Hospitals, Clinics/Medical Centers, Emergency/Ambulance Services, Health Funds, Hospitals, Long-Term Care, Medical Research, Mental Health, Single-Disease Health Associations
Social Services: At-Risk Youth, Child Welfare, Community Centers, Community Service Organizations, Emergency Relief, Food/Clothing Distribution, Homes, People with Disabilities, Recreation & Athletics, Senior Services, United Funds/United Ways, YMCA/YWCA/YMHA/YWHA, Youth Organizations

Contributions Analysis

Giving Priorities: Colleges and universities, social welfare, and hospitals.
Arts & Humanities: 1%. Museums, arts councils, arts festivals, and arts funds.
Education: 63%. Primarily supports colleges and universities. Also supports education funds, scholarships, endowments for faculty, acquisition of equipment, and operating support. Interests include engineering, business, economics, and minority education. Matching gifts account for limited funding. Supports the National Merit Scholarship Corporation for children of employees.
Health: About 6%. Interests include hospitals, single-disease health associations, medical research, and geriatric health.
Social Services: 30% to 35%. Supports united funds and child welfare, as well as youth organizations, rural affairs, and community service organizations. About 10% of giving is in the form of matching gifts.
Note: Total contributions made in 1998.

Application Procedures

Initial Contact: Submit a brief letter or proposal.
Application Requirements: Include a description of organization, amount requested, evaluative plans, purpose of funds sought, recently audited financial statement, proof of tax-exempt status, operating budget for the current year showing breakdown of expenses and sources of income, members of the agency's governing board, and corporate and foundation contributors and amount each has contributed in the last calendar year.
Deadlines: Submit proposals to local Square D facilities/plants between June and August for funding during the next calendar year.
Evaluative Criteria: The organization must provide a general public service and be supported by the public. Grant should be for non-controversial purposes. Effective management, adequate budgetary controls, and proof of an annual audit are required.
Decision Notification: Contributions budget is established in the fourth quarter for the following year.

Restrictions

Does not make contributions to religious organizations (except where support is used for nondenominational social service); political groups and organizations; labor unions and organizations; organizations making requests by telephone; organizations listed by the U.S. Attorney General as subversive or front organizations; or individuals.
Since foundation supports United Way in corporate communities, donations normally are not made to organizations receiving support through United Way.

Corporate Officials

Charles W. Denny: president, chief executive officer, directort B 1935. ED Wesleyan University BA (1958); Northwestern University MBA (1960). CORP AFFIL director: Southwire Co.; director: Woodhead Industries Inc.; director: Cherry Corp.; president, chief executive officer: Groupe Schneider NA.
Walter W. Kurczewski: vice president, secretary, general counsel B 1943. ED University of Illinois AB (1965); University of Michigan JD (1968). PRIM CORP EMPL vice president, secretary, general counsel: Square D Co.
Frank P. Sullivan: vice president sales & marketing B 1953. ED Harvard University BA (1974); University of Chicago MBA (1980). PRIM CORP EMPL vice president sales & marketing: Square D Co.

Foundation Officials

R. P. Fiorani: vice president, director
Walter W. Kurczewski: president, director (see above)
Dick O'Shanna: vice president, director
Tammy Sittinger: coord
Frank P. Sullivan: vice president, director (see above)
James R. White: secretary, director
Jo Ellyn Willis: vice president, director

Grants Analysis

Disclosure Period: calendar year ending 1998
Total Grants: $2,391,374*
Number of Grants: 243 (approx)
Average Grant: $5,749*
Highest Grant: $1,000,000
Typical Range: $1,000 to $6,000
***Note:** Giving excludes matching gifts; United Way. Average grant excludes highest grant.

Recent Grants

Note: Grants derived from 1997 Form 990.

Civic & Public Affairs

25,000	National Minority Supplier Development Council Conference, New York, NY
15,000	Chicago Bar Foundation, Chicago, IL
15,000	National Electrical Safety Foundation, Rosslyn, VA
15,000	National Park Foundation, New York, NY

Education

125,000	Targeted Universities
70,000	Lawndale Community School, Chicago, IL
50,000	Iowa State University, Ames, IA
20,000	Targeted Universities
20,000	Targeted Universities
20,000	Targeted Universities
20,000	Targeted Universities
20,000	Targeted Universities
20,000	Targeted Universities
20,000	Targeted Universities
20,000	Touch the Future, Long Beach, CA
18,250	National Merit Scholarship Corporation, Evanston, IL
15,000	Northern Illinois University, DeKalb, IL
15,000	Wake County Communities in School, Raleigh, NC
10,000	District 15 Educational Foundation, Palatine, IL
10,000	Lakewood Elementary School, Tomball, TX
10,000	Marquette University, Milwaukee, WI
8,500	Junior Achievement of Eastern North Carolina
8,000	Harper College Two Plus One Scholarships

Health

25,000	Good Shepherd Hospital, Barrington, IL
20,000	Mental Health Association, Chicago, IL
15,000	Alexian Brothers Medical Center
15,000	La Rabida Children's Hospital and Research Center, La Rabida, IL
10,000	American Cancer Society of Palatine
10,000	City of Hope, Duarte, CA
10,000	St. Joseph's Home for Elderly

Social Services

50,700	United Way of Asheville and Buncombe County, Asheville, NC
50,000	Triangle United Way, Morrisville, NC
25,000	Buehler YMCA
24,400	United Way of the Bluegrass, Lexington, KY
23,100	United Way of Lincoln and Lancaster County
21,300	United Way of East Central Iowa, Cedar Rapids, IA
20,000	United Way of the Midlands
16,567	Home of the Sparrow, Barrington, IL
14,900	United Way of Miami County, Peru, IN
14,400	Columbia Area United Way, Columbia, MO
11,000	United Way of Rutherford County, Spindale, NC
10,500	United Way of Oconee County
10,000	Palatine Celtic Soccer Club
10,000	Palatine Township Senior Citizen Center, Palatine, IL

10,000 United Way of Asheville and Buncombe County, Asheville, NC
9,000 United Way of Oxford Ohio and Vicinity, Oxford, OH
8,500 United Way of Central Carolinas, Charlotte, NC
7,200 Middletown Area United Way, Middletown, OH
7,000 Northwest Special Recreation Association
6,000 Alliance Award Community Service

STANDARD PRODUCTS CO.

Company Contact

Dearborn, MI

Company Description

Employees: 10,350
SIC(s): 3011 Tires & Inner Tubes, 3053 Gaskets, Packing & Sealing Devices, 3069 Fabricated Rubber Products Nec, 3089 Plastics Products Nec.

Standard Products Co. Charitable Foundation

Giving Contact

S. Carol Dwyer, Secretary
Standard Products Co. Charitable Foundation
2401 South Gulley Road
Dearborn, MI 48124
Phone: (313)791-2172

Description

Founded: 1984
EIN: 341440117
Organization Type: Corporate Foundation
Giving Locations: headquarters and operating communities.
Grant Types: Capital, Employee Matching Gifts, General Support.

Giving Philosophy

'The Standard Products Co. Charitable Foundation exists for the purpose of fulfilling the charitable and community obligations of The Standard Products Co. (and its subsidiaries) to the communities in which they have plants or other operations and to advance the interests of the Company and its subsidiaries in such communities. Such obligations include, but are not limited to, support of local United Way programs, local hospitals and other institutions, facilities, or programs used by company employees.' *Guidelines*

Financial Summary

Total Giving: $594,366 (fiscal year ending June 30, 1998); $242,148 (fiscal 1997); $233,385 (fiscal 1996). Note: Contributes through foundation only. Fiscal 1998 giving includes a contribution of Standard Products Co. publicly traded stock, valued at $326,536, to Harvard University.
Giving Analysis: Giving for fiscal 1997 includes: foundation grants to United Way ($132,000); foundation ($101,435); foundation matching gifts ($8,713); fiscal 1998: foundation ($146,253); foundation grants to United Way ($121,550)
Assets: $1,840,668 (fiscal 1998); $2,135,495 (fiscal 1997); $2,092,447 (fiscal 1996)
Gifts Received: $109,000 (fiscal 1996); $300,000 (fiscal 1995); $300,000 (fiscal 1994). Note: Contributions received from Standard Products Co.

Typical Recipients

Arts & Humanities: Music, Public Broadcasting, Theater
Civic & Public Affairs: Community Foundations, Economic Development, Employment/Job Training, Civic & Public Affairs-General, Housing, Municipalities/Towns, Parades/Festivals, Urban & Community Affairs, Women's Affairs
Education: Agricultural Education, Business Education, Colleges & Universities, Community & Junior Colleges, Economic Education, Education Funds, Faculty Development, Minority Education, Private Education (Precollege), Public Education (Precollege), Student Aid, Vocational & Technical Education
Environment: Energy, Environment-General
Health: Children's Health/Hospitals, Clinics/Medical Centers, Emergency/Ambulance Services, Health Organizations, Hospitals, Medical Research, Prenatal Health Issues, Single-Disease Health Associations, Transplant Networks/Donor Banks
Religion: Religious Welfare
Social Services: Community Centers, Community Service Organizations, Food/Clothing Distribution, People with Disabilities, Scouts, Special Olympics, Substance Abuse, United Funds/United Ways, YMCA/YWCA/YMHA/YWHA, Youth Organizations

Contributions Analysis

Giving Priorities: Focus on social services, the arts, health, education, and civic affairs.
Arts & Humanities: 14%.
Civic & Public Affairs: 8%. Supports economic development and urban and community affairs organizations.
Education: 12%. Supports higher education and literacy programs.
Health: 13%. Primarily supports hospitals.
Social Services: 53%. Most grants are given to the United Way. Also supports community and family service organizations.
Note: Percentages reflect all contributions made in 1998 except stock contribution of $326,536.

Application Procedures

Initial Contact: Submit a typed proposal of no more than five pages.
Application Requirements: Requests for general operations or a capital campaign should include: the specific sum requested, why the funds are needed, how they will be raised from other sources, how they will be used, and how publicity for support will be developed. Requests for specific programs should include: the community need to be addressed, specific goals and objectives, how the objectives will be met (including a schedule), a plan for evaluation and reporting results, and suggestions for publicizing grant support. All requests should also include a brief description of the organization (including legal name, history, mission, and activities) and the name and qualifications of those administering the organization or program. Supporting materials that should also be included with all requests include: a list of organization's officers/directors or trustees; a copy of the groups most recent financial statement; an annual budget (showing expenses and income by sources); a list of corporations/foundations contributing to the group in the past year; a copy of the tax-exempt ruling from the IRS; and a copy of the group's most recent IRS Form 990.
Deadlines: None.

Restrictions

Does not make grants to individuals, fraternal organizations, other private foundations, or for religious or political purposes.

Additional Information

Publications: Guidelines

Corporate Officials

Charles F. Nagy: treasurer, chief operating officer, director B Cleveland, OH 1951. ED University of Toledo BS (1973); University of Toledo MBA (1974). PRIM CORP EMPL treasurer: Standard Products Co.
James Sims Reid, Jr.: chairman, director B Cleveland, OH 1926. ED Harvard University AB (1948); Harvard University JD (1951). PRIM CORP EMPL chairman, director: Standard Products Co. NONPR AFFIL trustee: John Carroll University; trustee: Musical Arts Association Cleveland.
Donald R. Sheley, Junior: vice president finance, chief financial officer B Vincennes, IN 1942. ED Vincennes University AB (1962); Indiana University BS (1964); University of Chicago MBA (1971). PRIM CORP EMPL vice president finance, chief financial officer: Standard Products Co. CORP AFFIL director: National Standard Co.
Theodore K. Zampetis: president, chief operating officer, director B Samos, Greece 1945. ED University of Toledo BBA (1978); University of Toledo MBA (1980). PRIM CORP EMPL president, chief operating officer, director: Standard Products Co. CORP AFFIL executive chairman: Standard Products Ltd.; president: Westborn Service Center Inc.; chairman: Standard Products International; director: Shiloh Industries Inc.; vice chairman, director: Standard Products (Canada) Ltd.; director: Oliver Rubber Co.; director: Shiloh Corp.; director: Holm Industries Inc.; director: National City Bank.

Foundation Officials

John C. Brandmahl: trustee PRIM CORP EMPL vice president human resources: Standard Products Co.
Carol Dwyer: secretary PRIM CORP EMPL executive secretary: Standard Products Co.
Charles F. Nagy: trustee (see above)
James Sims Reid, Jr.: chairman, president (see above)
Donald R. Sheley, Junior: treasurer, trustee (see above)

Grants Analysis

Disclosure Period: fiscal year ending June 30, 1998
Total Grants: $146,253*
Number of Grants: 76
Average Grant: $1,924
Highest Grant: $20,000
Typical Range: $100 to $5,000
***Note:** Giving excludes United Way.

Recent Grants

Note: Grants derived from fiscal 1997 Form 990.

Arts & Humanities

2,000 Detroit Symphony Orchestra, Detroit, MI
1,200 WMHT Education Telecommunications, Schenectady, NY
1,000 Kentucky Educational Television, Lexington, KY

Civic & Public Affairs

1,700 Cleveland Tomorrow Project, Cleveland, OH

Education

5,000 Case Western Reserve University, Cleveland, OH
5,000 David N. Myers College, Cleveland, OH
4,000 Gaylord Community Schools, Gaylord, MI
3,000 North Carolina Wesleyan College, Rocky Mount, NC
2,500 Nash Community College, Rocky Mount, NC
2,500 Ohio Foundation of Independent Colleges, Columbus, OH
2,000 Cleveland Scholarship Program, Cleveland, OH
2,000 Spartanburg Technical College, Spartanburg, SC
2,000 Wayne Community College, River Rouge, MI
1,500 Midlands Technical College, Columbia, SC
1,000 Junior Achievement Winnsboro
1,000 Otsego County 4-H Program, MI

Environment

1,000 Energy Outlet

Health

3,000	Otsego County Memorial Hospital, Gaylord, MI
2,500	Athens Regional Medical Center, Athens, GA
2,500	St. Mary's Health Care Center
2,000	Randolph Hospital, Asheboro, NC
1,500	Fairfield Memorial Hospital, Fairfield, IL
1,000	American Red Cross Disaster Relief

Religion

1,000	Providence House, New York, NY

Social Services

20,000	United Way Southeastern Michigan, Detroit, MI
19,000	United Way, Cleveland, OH
14,000	United Way Otsego County
10,000	United Way Scott County, Scottsburg, IN
8,000	United Way Northeast Georgia, Athens, GA
7,500	United Way, Rocky Mount, NC
7,000	United Way, Dallas, TX
7,000	United Way Wayne County, Richmond, IN
6,700	United Way, Schenectady, NY
6,000	United Way, Asheboro, NC
6,000	United Way Bluegrass, Lexington, KY
5,000	Boys and Girls Club, Rocky Mount, NC
5,000	United Way Griffin-Spalding County, Griffin, GA
5,000	YMCA Scott County
4,500	United Way Winnsboro
3,000	United Way Piedmont, Woodruff, SC
2,500	Athens Boys and Girls Club, Athens, GA
2,500	Boy Scouts of America, Detroit, MI
2,500	Center on Addiction and Substance Abuse, Cleveland, OH
2,500	United Way Bay Area, San Francisco, CA
2,000	Bethlehem Community Center, Columbia, SC
2,000	Boy Scouts of America Indian Waters Council, Milwaukee, WI
2,000	WINOC
1,500	United Way, Salisbury, MD
1,385	South Carolina Special Olympics, Columbia, SC
1,000	Rocky Bottom Camp of the Blind, Columbia, SC

Standard Register Co.

Company Contact

Dayton, OH
Web: http://www.stdreg.com

Company Description

Revenue: US$903,200,000
Employees: 6,201
SIC(s): 2672 Coated & Laminated Paper Nec, 2761 Manifold Business Forms, 3579 Office Machines Nec.

Operating Locations

Includes plant locations

Sherman-Standard Register Foundation

Giving Contact

Kathryn A. Lamme, Corp. vice president, secretary and deputy general counsel
600 Albany Street
Dayton, OH 45408
Phone: (937)443-1540
Fax: (937)221-3431

Description

Founded: 1955
EIN: 316026027
Organization Type: Corporate Foundation. Supports preselected organizations only.
Giving Locations: OH
Grant Types: General Support.

Giving Philosophy

The foundation focuses on programs benefiting children and youth in the local geographic area around Dayton, OH.

Financial Summary

Total Giving: $241,478 (fiscal year ending November 30, 1998); $213,663 (fiscal 1996); $190,473 (fiscal 1995)
Giving Analysis: Giving for fiscal 1998 includes: foundation ($144,428); foundation grants to United Way ($97,050)
Assets: $1,501,928 (fiscal 1998); $1,310,280 (fiscal 1996); $1,204,449 (fiscal 1995)
Gifts Received: $250,000 (fiscal 1998); $250,000 (fiscal 1996); $250,000 (fiscal 1995). Note: In fiscal 1996 and 1998, contributions were received from the Standard Register Co.

Typical Recipients

Arts & Humanities: Arts Associations & Councils, Arts Centers, Arts Funds, Arts Institutes, Community Arts, Libraries, Music
Civic & Public Affairs: Botanical Gardens/Parks, Clubs, Economic Development, Employment/Job Training, Civic & Public Affairs-General, Native American Affairs, Safety, Women's Affairs
Education: Business Education, Colleges & Universities, Community & Junior Colleges, Education Associations, Education Funds, Education-General, Health & Physical Education, Minority Education
Health: Cancer, Children's Health/Hospitals, Clinics/Medical Centers, Emergency/Ambulance Services, Health Funds, Hospices, Hospitals, Public Health
Religion: Religious Organizations, Religious Welfare
Science: Science Museums
Social Services: Big Brother/Big Sister, Community Service Organizations, Counseling, Recreation & Athletics, Scouts, Senior Services, United Funds/United Ways, YMCA/YWCA/YMHA/YWHA, Youth Organizations

Contributions Analysis

Giving Priorities: Social services, religious organizations, and educational organizations.
Arts & Humanities: 8%. Supports arts organizations and institutes.
Civic & Public Affairs: 2%. Supports women's causes.
Education: 10%. Provides funds for high schools and Junior Achievement.
Health: 3%. Funds home health care, treatment centers, and the American Red Cross.
Religion: 22%. Major support for the Catholic Campaign.
Science: 4%. Funds a science museum.
Social Services: 51%. Supports the United Way, scouting, and suicide prevention.
Note: Total contributions made in fiscal 1998.

Corporate Officials

Craig J. Brown: senior vice president administration, treasurer, chief financial officer B Findlay, OH 1949. ED Bowling Green State University (1971). PRIM CORP EMPL senior vice president administration, treasurer, chief financial officer: Standard Register Co.
Paul H. Granzow: chairman, director B 1927. ED University of Cincinnati LLB (1950). PRIM CORP EMPL chairman, director: Standard Register Co. CORP AFFIL partner: Turner Granzow & Hollenkamp; senior vice president, director: Western Paper & Manufacturing Co.
Kathryn A. Lamme: PRIM CORP EMPL corporate vice president/secretary, general counsel: Standard Register Co.
Peter Stoddard Redding: president, chief executive officer, director B Brooklyn, NY 1938. ED University of Maryland BA (1960); Georgia State University MS (1974). PRIM CORP EMPL president, chief executive officer, director: Standard Register Co. NONPR AFFIL trustee: Human Race Theatre; trustee: Vitoria Theater Association; trustee: Childrens Medical Center. CLUB AFFIL Dayton Country Club; Orinda Country Club; Country Club North.

Foundation Officials

Roy W. Begley, Jr.: trustee
Craig J. Brown: treasurer (see above)
Peter Stoddard Redding: trustee (see above)
Charles F. Sherman: president
James L. Sherman: vice president PRIM CORP EMPL member compensation committee, director: Standard Register Co.
John Q. Sherman, II: trustee
Ronald Zlotnik: trustee

Grants Analysis

Disclosure Period: fiscal year ending November 30, 1998
Total Grants: $144,428*
Number of Grants: 25
Average Grant: $3,935*
Highest Grant: $50,000
Typical Range: $200 to $15,000
***Note:** Giving excludes United Way. Average grant figure excludes highest grant.

Recent Grants

Note: Grants derived from fiscal 1997 Form 990.

Arts & Humanities

15,000	Dayton Art Institute, Dayton, OH
8,000	Anthenaeum of Ohio, OH
4,000	Culture Works

Civic & Public Affairs

10,000	Nike Miami Valley Open, Springboro, OH
5,000	Womanline

Education

7,500	Junior Achievement, Dayton, OH
6,000	Chaminade-Julienne
5,000	Ohio Foundation of Independent Colleges, Columbus, OH

Health

10,500	Samaritan Health Foundation, Dayton, OH
8,000	American Cancer Society
7,500	American Red Cross Dayton and Montgomery Counties, OH

Social Services

57,500	United Way, Dayton, OH
10,000	United Way -- for building renovations
8,250	United Way York County, York, PA
5,000	Boys and Girls Clubs of Shelby
5,000	Frankly County Family YMCA
5,000	United Way Licking County, Newark, OH
4,200	United Way FAY
4,000	United Fund of Addison County
3,400	United Way KIR

The Stanley Works

Company Contact

New Britain, CT
Web: http://www.stanleyworks.com

Company Description

Profit: US$59,100,000
Employees: 18,000

SIC(s): 2542 Partitions & Fixtures Except Wood, 3315 Steel Wire & Related Products, 3429 Hardware Nec, 3442 Metal Doors, Sash & Trim.

Operating Locations

Australia: Stanley-Bostitch Pty. Ltd., Ingleburn, Kent Town; Stanley Bostitch Pty. Ltd., Mulgrave; Stanley Works Pty. Ltd., West Heidelberg; Belgium: Stanley Works Belgium NV, Aalter, Flandre-Orientale; Canada: Stanley Home Decor Canada Ltd., Brampton; Stanley Tools, Burlington; Colombia: Herramientas Stanley SA, Palmira; Denmark: Stanley Vearktyj APS, Skovlunde, Ribe; France: Sicfo Stanley, Besancon, Doubs; Stanley Works Ltd., Les Essarts Le Roi, Yvelines; Stanley Nirva, Marquette Lez Lille, Nord; Stanley Bostitch, Morangis; Bostitch SA (Societe de Fabrication), Rupt Sur Moselle, Vosges; Germany: Stanley Germany Inc. Zweigniederlassung Essen, Essen; Bostitch GmbH, Norderstedt, Hamburg; Friess GmbH, Wieseth, Bayern; Hong Kong: Stanley Works (Hong Kong) Ltd., Central District; Italy: Acrimo Italia SRL, Figino Serenza, Lombardia; Stanley Tools SpA, Figino Serenza, Lombardia; Stanley Works Italia SpA, Figino Serenza, Lombardia; Mexico: Herramientas Stanley SA de CV, Puebla; New Zealand: Stanley Tools (New Zealand) Ltd., Te Rapa; Spain: Stanley Iberia SA, Barcelona, Cataluna; Switzerland: Bostitch AG, Zurich; Bostitch (Europe) AG, Zurich; Taiwan: Stanley Works Asia/Pacific Ltd., Linkou; Chiro Tool Manufacturing Corp., Taya Hsiang, Taichung; United Kingdom: Stanley Works Ltd., Bracknell, Berkshire; R J Lendrum Ltd., Bridgnorth, Shropshire; Acmetrack Ltd., East Grinstead, West Sussex; Alpha Handles Ltd., Leeds, West Yorkshire; KJ Tool Co. Ltd., Leeds, West Yorkshire; Mosley-Stone Ltd., Leeds, West Yorkshire; Sentinal Forge Ltd., Leeds, West Yorkshire; Stone Brothers (Brushes) Ltd., Leeds, West Yorkshire; Pear Tree Tools Ltd., Sowerby Bridge, West Yorkshire; Mosleye (Brushes) Ltd., Stockport, Cheshire; Dudley Shearing Sales Ltd., Sunderland, Tyne & Wear

Nonmonetary Support

Value: $150,000 (1992); $150,000 (1991); $150,000 (1990)
Type: Donated Products; Workplace Solicitation
Note: Nonmonetary support is approximately $150,000 annually.

Giving Contact

Cheryl B. Farmer, Contributions Administrator
The Stanley Works
1000 Stanley Drive
New Britain, CT 06053
Phone: (860)225-5111

Description

Organization Type: Corporate Giving Program
Giving Locations: operating location communities.
Grant Types: Capital, Challenge, Employee Matching Gifts, General Support, Operating Expenses, Seed Money.
Note: Employee matching gift ratio: 1 to 1.

Giving Philosophy

'Stanley provides support for worthy projects and programs operating in communities where the company has operating facilities, the majority if which are targeted to enhance the volunteer efforts of Stanley employees.'
'Areas of support include: sweat equity and co-operative housing and neighborhood revitalization; education; health and human services; and the arts.' Stanley Works Contribution Program

Financial Summary

Total Giving: $2,000,000 (1999 approx); $1,535,000 (1998 approx); $1,553,653 (1997). Note: Contributes through corporate direct giving program only.
Giving Analysis: Giving for 1998 includes: foundation matching gifts ($439,158)
Assets: $4,523 (1993); $1,246,241 (1992); $1,468,588 (1991)

Typical Recipients

Arts & Humanities: Arts Associations & Councils, Community Arts, Dance, Arts & Humanities-General, Libraries, Museums/Galleries, Music, Opera, Performing Arts, Public Broadcasting, Theater
Civic & Public Affairs: African American Affairs, Business/Free Enterprise, Community Foundations, Economic Policy, Employment/Job Training, Civic & Public Affairs-General, Housing, Urban & Community Affairs
Education: Business Education, Colleges & Universities, Economic Education, Elementary Education (Private), Elementary Education (Public), Engineering/Technological Education, Literacy, Minority Education, Public Education (Precollege), Science/ Mathematics Education
Environment: Environment-General, Resource Conservation
Health: Cancer, Children's Health/Hospitals, Emergency/Ambulance Services, Hospitals, Medical Research
International: International Development
Religion: Churches, Religious Welfare
Science: Science Exhibits & Fairs
Social Services: Community Service Organizations, Family Services, Homes, People with Disabilities, Shelters/Homelessness, Substance Abuse, United Funds/United Ways, Youth Organizations

Contributions Analysis

Giving Priorities: Higher education, health, social welfare, and arts and humanities. Foreign subsidiaries make contributions directly, but data is not tracked.

Application Procedures

Initial Contact: Send a brief letter or proposal.
Application Requirements: Include a description of organization and how it will affect Stanley employees, amount requested, purpose of funds sought, recently audited financial statement, proof of 501(c)(3) tax-exempt status, identification of company employees involved with organization.
Deadlines: Contact foundation for current deadlines.
Review Process: Reviews grant request three times a year.
Evaluative Criteria: Involvement of company personnel with organization; organization's qualifications to provide services; company's feeling of responsibility to organization or community; operate in a Stanley community; endorsement of local company management; organization's service population.

Restrictions

No funds will be given outside communities where Stanley has operations.
Company does not fund national organizations, operating funds, research projects, athletic programs, health research organizations, endowment funds, organizations which are not tax-exempt, private foundations, or individuals.

Additional Information

In 1999, the company announced that new giving program guidelines were being prepared for the 2000 grant cycle.
Publications: Guidelines Sheet; Annual Report; grants List

Corporate Officials

Scott Bannell: advertising and brand manager

Giving Program Officials

Scott Bannell: director (see above)
Cheryl B. Farmer: (see above)

Grants Analysis

Disclosure Period: calendar year ending
Typical Range: $1,000 to $5,000

Recent Grants

Note: Grants derived from 1993 Form 990.

Arts & Humanities

40,000	New Britain Institute, New Britain, CT -- library
23,000	Greater Hartford Arts Council, Hartford, CT
10,000	Connecticut Public Broadcasting, Hartford, CT
10,000	Horace Bushnell Memorial Hall, Hartford, CT
10,000	Horace Bushnell Memorial Hall, Hartford, CT
10,000	New Britain Institute, New Britain, CT -- library
10,000	New Britain Museum of American Art, New Britain, CT
10,000	New Britain Museum of American Art, New Britain, CT
5,000	New Britain Museum of American Art, New Britain, CT

Civic & Public Affairs

20,000	Local Initiatives Support Corp
10,000	Habitat for Humanity of Providence, Providence, RI
10,000	Neighborhood Housing Services of New Britain, New Britain, CT
8,000	Clinton Foundation, Clinton, CT
7,500	Hartford Area Habitat for Humanity, Hartford, CT
5,000	Neighborhood Housing Services of New Britain, New Britain, CT

Education

50,000	Constructive Workshops, New Britain, CT
25,000	Central Connecticut State University Foundation, New Britain, CT
20,000	Connecticut Pre-Engineering Program, Storrs, CT
10,000	University of Connecticut, Storrs, CT
8,000	Central Connecticut State University Foundation, New Britain, CT
8,000	Junior Achievement of North Central Connecticut, Hartford, CT
6,202	Chatfield College
5,214	Harvard University, Cambridge, MA

Environment

8,000	Save the Bay, Boston, MA

Health

100,000	City of Hope, Duarte, CA
40,000	New Britain Memorial Hospital, New Britain, CT
20,000	Clinton Memorial Hospital Fund, Clinton, CT
10,000	Greater Hartford Easter Seal Society, Hartford, CT
8,971	American Red Cross Central Connecticut Chapter, New Britain, CT
6,000	Community Mental Health Affiliates, Bristol, VA

Religion

5,000	Our Lady of Mercy Church, Daly City, CA

Social Services

50,000	Boys and Girls Club of New Britain, New Britain, CT
20,599	United Way/Combined Health Appeal, Hartford, CT
20,599	United Way/Combined Health Appeal, Hartford, CT
20,598	United Way/Combined Health Appeal, Hartford, CT
20,598	United Way/Combined Health Appeal, Hartford, CT
15,413	United Way Southeastern New England, Providence, RI

12,500	YMCA Newton County
11,267	United Way Services, Cleveland, OH
10,226	United Way Greater Lee County, NC
10,000	Foodshare, Hartford, CT
10,000	Rhode Island Anti-Drug Coalition, Providence, RI
10,000	United Way Capital Region
8,092	United Way Sayette County
7,940	New Horizons, La Crosse, WI
6,666	Family Services, Fort Worth, TX
6,585	United Way Bennington County, Bennington, VT
6,298	United Way Greater Wichita Falls, Wichita Falls, TX
5,507	United Way Wyandotte County, Kansas City, KS
5,000	Big Brothers of Rhode Island, Providence, RI

STAR BANK NA

Company Contact

Cincinnati, OH

Company Description

Employees: 3,850
SIC(s): 6021 National Commercial Banks.
Parent Company: Firstar Corp., 777 East Wisconsin Avenue, Milwaukee, WI, United States

Nonmonetary Support

Value: $250,000 (1995)
Type: Cause-related Marketing & Promotion; Donated Equipment; In-kind Services
Contact: Jane Ludwig

Corporate Sponsorship

Range: less than $2,100,000
Type: Arts & cultural events; Festivals/fairs; Music & entertainment events; Sports events
Note: Sponsors community development events.

Star Bank NA, Cincinnati Foundation

Giving Contact

Cynthia Booth, Senior Vice President & Director of Community Outreach
Star Bank, NA
425 Walnut St., ML CN-WN-09 AD
PO Box 1038
Cincinnati, OH 45202-1038
Phone: (513)632-4404
Fax: (513)632-4279

Description

EIN: 316079013
Organization Type: Corporate Foundation
Giving Locations: IN; KY; OH
Grant Types: Capital, Department, Endowment, General Support, Matching, Project.

Giving Philosophy

'Star Bank seeks to be a good corporate citizen in the Greater Cincinnati area by being responsive to the broader needs of the community. Accordingly, a planned program of contributions to nonprofit organizations is carried out by the Bank in the interests of the Bank, its employees, shareholders, customers, and the community at large.' Star Bank, N.A. Foundation Guidelines

Financial Summary

Total Giving: $1,978,434 (1998); $1,697,453 (1997); $1,576,173 (1996). Note: Contributes through corporate direct giving program and foundation.
Giving Analysis: Giving for 1996 includes: foundation ($1,576,173); 1997: foundation ($1,256,663); foundation grants to United Way ($440,790); 1998: foundation ($1,567,484); foundation grants to United Way ($410,950)
Assets: $7,155,419 (1998); $2,218,711 (1997); $2,295,280 (1996)
Gifts Received: $6,523,410 (1998); $1,400,000 (1997); $2,196,000 (1996). Note: Contributions are received from Star Bank.

Typical Recipients

Arts & Humanities: Arts Centers, Arts Festivals, Arts Funds, Arts Institutes, Historic Preservation, History & Archaeology, Libraries, Museums/Galleries, Music, Opera, Public Broadcasting, Theater
Civic & Public Affairs: African American Affairs, Botanical Gardens/Parks, Business/Free Enterprise, Chambers of Commerce, Community Foundations, Economic Development, Employment/Job Training, Housing, Municipalities/Towns, Parades/Festivals, Philanthropic Organizations, Professional & Trade Associations, Urban & Community Affairs, Zoos/Aquariums
Education: Arts/Humanities Education, Business Education, Colleges & Universities, Economic Education, Education Associations, Education Funds, Education-General, Medical Education, Private Education (Precollege), Public Education (Precollege), Religious Education, Secondary Education (Public), Special Education, Student Aid
Health: Cancer, Children's Health/Hospitals, Clinics/Medical Centers, Eyes/Blindness, Health Organizations, Heart, Hospitals, Medical Research, Single-Disease Health Associations
International: International Affairs
Religion: Jewish Causes, Religious Organizations, Religious Welfare, Social/Policy Issues, Synagogues/Temples
Social Services: Camps, Child Welfare, Community Centers, Community Service Organizations, Counseling, Food/Clothing Distribution, People with Disabilities, Recreation & Athletics, Scouts, Senior Services, United Funds/United Ways, YMCA/YWCA/YMHA/YWHA, Youth Organizations

Contributions Analysis

Giving Priorities: Social services, art, civic organizations, and education.
Arts & Humanities: 22%. Supports fine and performing arts and museums.
Civic & Public Affairs: 20%. Supports chambers of commerce, community foundations, and housing.
Education: 14%. Funds higher education and junior achievement.
Health: 6%. Funds hospitals and homecare services.
Religion: 9%. Supports Jewish and Christian organizations.
Social Services: 29%. Supports youth groups and organizations, including scouts, sports groups, and Boys and Girls Clubs. Also funds organizations dealing with chemical dependency and the United Way.
Note: Contributions made in 1998.

Application Procedures

Initial Contact: Send a written proposal.
Application Requirements: Include a description and contact information of the organization, services provided and population served, amount requested, description of project/activity for which funds are sought, names of administrative officers and governing board, balance sheet and annual operating statement, proof of tax-exempt status, copy of most recent IRS Form 990, project budget, percentage of budget received from United Way, government funding, other sources, and recipients.
Deadlines: None.
Decision Notification: Committee meets bimonthly, makes recommendations to board of directors.

Restrictions

Contributions will not be made to partisan political organizations, religious organizations for services limited to their membership, controversial social causes, agencies that are beneficiaries of united appeal and fine arts funds (with the exception of capital grants), individuals, or institutions supported principally by taxes (except specific programs at publicly funded educational institutions), or organizations which discriminate on the basis of race, creed, color, sex, age, or national origin.
Grants will generally not be made to organizations outside the greater Cincinnati, Cleveland, and Hamilton areas. No grants are made to organizations which are not tax-exempt.

Corporate Officials

Daniel B. Benhase: executive vice presidentchairman PRIM CORP EMPL executive vice president: Star Bank NA. CORP AFFIL executive vice president: Star Banc Corp.
Samuel M. Cassidy: director B Lexington, KY 1932. ED Duke University (1958); University of Cincinnati (1962). PRIM CORP EMPL director: Star Bank NA. CORP AFFIL director: Star Banc Corp.
Jerry A. Gundhofer: chairman, director B 1945. ED Loyola Marymount University (1967). PRIM CORP EMPL chairman, director: Star Bank NA. CORP AFFIL president, chief executive officer: Star Banc Corp.
Thomas J. Lakin: regional chairman B Cincinnati, OH 1942. ED University of Cincinnati BA (1965); Salmon P. Chase College of Law JD (1969). PRIM CORP EMPL regional chairman: Star Bank NA. CLUB AFFIL Rotary Club.

Giving Program Officials

Cynthia Booth: senior vice president, director community outreach

Foundation Officials

Daniel B. Benhase: treasurer (see above)
Michael J. Bohman: trustee
James Ralph Bridgeland, Jr.: trustee B Cleveland, OH 1929. ED University of Akron BA (1951); Harvard University MA (1955); Harvard University JD (1957). PRIM CORP EMPL partner: Taft, Stettinius & Hollister. CORP AFFIL director, member executive committee: Star Banc Cincinnati; director, member executive committee: Star Banc Corp.; director: SHV North America Inc.; director: David J. Joseph Co.; director: Seinau-Fisher Studios Inc.; director: Robert A. Cline Co.; director: Art Stamping Inc. NONPR AFFIL member: Ohio Bar Association; instructor: University Cincinnati; trustee: Hillside Trust; member: Harvard University Alumni Association; member: Harvard University Law School Association; president, trustee: Cincinnati Symphony Orchestra; trustee: Cincinnati Institute Fine Arts; trustee: Cincinnati Opera; member: Cincinnati Bar Association; member: American Arbitration Association; member: American Bar Association. CLUB AFFIL mem: Queen City Club; mem: Harvard Club; mem: Cincinnati Literacy Club; mem: Commonwealth Club.
Jerry A. Gundhofer: vice president (see above)
Joseph Page Hayden, Jr.: trustee B Cincinnati, OH 1929. ED Miami University BSBA (1951); University of Cincinnati Law School (1952). PRIM CORP EMPL chairman, chief executive officer, director: Midland Co. CORP AFFIL director, chairman audit committee, member executive committee: Star Bank NA; director, member executive committee: Star Banc Corp. NONPR AFFIL member: Sigma Chi; member president council: Xavier University; trustee: Miami University Ohio Foundation; Chairman: MG Transport Service Inc.; member business advisory committee: Miami University Ohio; chief executive officer: American Family Home Insurance Co. CLUB AFFIL Useppa Island Club; Queen City Club; University Club; Metropolitan Club; Hyde Golf Club; Lemon Bay Golf Club; Boca Grande Club; Commonwealth Club; Bankers Club; Boca Bay Pass Club.

Thomas John Klinedinst, Jr.: trustee B Cincinnati, OH 1942. ED Georgetown University BA (1965). CORP AFFIL president, chairman, chief executive officer, director: Thomas E Wood Inc.; executive committee: USI Insurance Service Corp.; director: Star Banc Corp.; director: Star Bank NA Association; president: Ohio CAP Insurance Co. Ltd. NONPR AFFIL member: Independent Insurance Agents Association Ohio; director: Project Encor; director: Employers Resource Association; director: Franciscan U.S. Department of Health and Human Services Systems Ohio Valley; trustee: Cincinnati Better Business Bureau. CLUB AFFIL Rotary Club; Friars Club; Queen City Club; Cincinnati Country Club.

Thomas J. Lakin: president (see above)

Grants Analysis

Disclosure Period: calendar year ending 1998
Total Grants: $1,567,484*
Number of Grants: 119
Average Grant: $13,172
Highest Grant: $100,000
Typical Range: $2,500 to $15,000
***Note:** Giving excludes United Way.

Recent Grants

Note: Grants derived from 1997 Form 990.

Arts & Humanities

58,000 Fine Arts Fund, Cincinnati, OH
50,000 Cincinnati Symphony Orchestra, Cincinnati, OH -- support Second Century Fund Campaign
30,000 Cincinnati Art Museum, Cincinnati, OH
30,000 Greater Cincinnati Arts and Education Center, Cincinnati, OH -- support Campus OTR

Civic & Public Affairs

60,000 Cincinnati Zoo and Botanical Garden, Cincinnati, OH
50,000 Urban League, Jacksonville, FL -- support capital fund campaign
30,000 Greater Cincinnati Chamber of Commerce, Cincinnati, OH -- support Blue Chip Campaign
16,666 Greater Cincinnati Tall Stacks Commission, Cincinnati, OH
15,000 Columbia Tusculum Economic Development Corporation, Cincinnati, OH -- support community center
10,121 Famicos Foundation, Cleveland, OH
10,000 Athenaeum of Ohio, Our Faith Our Future, OH -- support Preserving Affordable Housing
10,000 Dayton Urban League, Dayton, OH
10,000 Greater Cincinnati Housing Association, Cincinnati, OH
10,000 National Underground Railroad Freedom Center, Cincinnati, OH
7,864 Neighborhood Progress, Cleveland, OH

Education

75,000 Xavier College of Business Arts -- capital campaign
51,900 University of Cincinnati Foundation, Cincinnati, OH
50,000 Greater Cincinnati Foundation for the Greater Cincinnati Scholarship Association, Cincinnati, OH
50,000 Hebrew Union College, Cincinnati, OH
17,333 College of Mount St. Joseph, Cincinnati, OH -- support Vision 2000 Campaign
16,456 Northern Kentucky University, Highland Heights, KY
15,000 Joy Experimental Learning
12,180 Thomas More College, Crestview Hills, KY
10,000 Catholic Inner-City Schools Education Fund
10,000 Lehman High School, Sidney, OH -- support 21st Century Fund Campaign
9,000 Junior Achievement, Cincinnati, OH

Health

60,000 Children's Hospital -- capital campaign
20,000 Ohio Cancer Research Associates, Columbus, OH
15,000 Good Samaritan Hospital
8,334 St. Elizabeth Hospital, Appleton, WI -- support Cancer Care Center

Religion

40,000 St. John's Social Service Center
16,666 Isaac M. Wise Temple -- support restoration project
10,000 Franciscan Sisters of the Poor, Warwick, NY
10,000 St. Joseph Home, Cincinnati, OH
8,000 Jewish Federation, Philadelphia, PA

Social Services

275,000 United Way
50,000 United Way -- supplemental support
30,000 United Way, Cleveland, OH
26,500 United Way
20,000 Sisters of Charity Capital Campaign -- support Bayley Place
20,000 United Way -- supplemental support
15,000 Greater Cincinnati 2008 Amateur Sports Association, Cincinnati, OH -- support Olympics
15,000 YMCA, Cincinnati, OH
12,005 YMCA, Cleveland, OH
10,000 Boy Scouts of America Dan Beard Council -- support 1997 Challenge Camping Program
10,000 Cincinnati Youth Collaborative, Cincinnati, OH
10,000 Greater Cincinnati 2008 Amateur Sports Association, Cincinnati, OH -- support Olympic Committee
10,000 Tender Mercies, Norwood, OH
9,135 YWCA -- capital campaign
8,700 United Way of Butler County, Butler, PA

Starwood Hotels & Resorts Worldwide, Inc.

Company Contact

777 Westchester Ave.
White Plains, NY 10604
Phone: (914)640-8100
Fax: (914)640-8310
Web: http://www.starwoodhotels.com

Company Description

Former Name: ITT Corp.
Revenue: US$4,700,000,000 (1999)
Employees: 130,000 (1999)
Fortune Rank: 311, per FORTUNE Magazine's list of 500 Largest U.S. Corporations (1999).
FF 311
SIC(s): 7011 Hotels & Motels, 7375 Information Retrieval Services, 7929 Entertainers & Entertainment Groups, 7997 Membership Sports & Recreation Clubs.

Operating Locations

Austria: Sheraton International GmbH, Salzburg, Salzburg; Canada: Caesars World International Marketing Corp. of Canada, Toronto; Hong Kong: ITT Sheraton International (Hong Kong) Ltd., Tsim Sha Tsui, Kowloon; Ireland: ITT Sheraton Reservations Corp., Cork; Italy: CIGA Hotels Italia SpA, Milano, Lombardia; CIGA Resort SRL, Milano, Lombardia; CIGA Service SpA, Milano, Lombardia; CIGA SpA, Milano, Lombardia; CIGA Sport SpA, Milano, Lombardia; Sheraton Hotels Italia SRL, Milano, Lombardia; Japan: CIGA Hotels International Ltd., Tokyo; Mexico: Hoteles Sheraton SA de CV, Ciudad de Mexico; Netherlands: Hotel Maatschappij Oudamsterdam BV, Amsterdam, Noord-Holland; ITT Publitec Research & Development BV, Amsterdam, Noord-Holland; Pulitzer Monumenten BV, Amsterdam, Noord-Holland; CIGA Hotels Netherlands BV, Noordwijk, Zuid-Holland; Peru: Hoteles Sheraton Del Peru SA, Lima; United Kingdom: Sheraton Management Corp., Basingstoke, Hampshire; Caesars Palace Ltd., London; M H (General Partner) Ltd., London; Venezuela: Sheraton De Venezuela CA, La Guaira, Distrito Federal

Giving Contact

Dan Gibson, Senior Vice President Corporate Affairs
Starwood Hotels & Resorts Worldwide, Inc.
777 Westchester Avenue
White Plains, NY 10604
Phone: (914)640-8100
Fax: (914)640-8134

Alternate Contact

Kathy Contis

Description

Organization Type: Corporate Giving Program
Giving Locations: headquarters and operating communities.
Grant Types: Employee Matching Gifts, General Support.

Financial Summary

Total Giving: $1,500,000 (1997 approx); $1,500,000 (1996 approx); $1,500,000 (1995 approx). Note: Contributes through corporate direct giving program only.

Typical Recipients

Arts & Humanities: Arts Associations & Councils, Arts Centers, Arts Funds, Dance, Museums/Galleries, Music, Opera, Public Broadcasting
Civic & Public Affairs: Business/Free Enterprise, Civil Rights, Economic Development, Economic Policy, Employment/Job Training, Civic & Public Affairs-General, Housing, Urban & Community Affairs, Women's Affairs, Zoos/Aquariums
Education: Arts/Humanities Education, Business Education, Colleges & Universities, Economic Education, Engineering/Technological Education, Education-General, Literacy, Minority Education, Preschool Education, Private Education (Precollege), Science/Mathematics Education, Secondary Education (Public), Student Aid, Vocational & Technical Education
Environment: Environment-General
Health: Emergency/Ambulance Services, Geriatric Health, Hospices, Hospitals, Medical Research, Nutrition, Single-Disease Health Associations
International: International Peace & Security Issues
Science: Scientific Organizations
Social Services: Child Welfare, Community Service Organizations, Day Care, Delinquency & Criminal Rehabilitation, Domestic Violence, Emergency Relief, Food/Clothing Distribution, People with Disabilities, Recreation & Athletics, Senior Services, Shelters/Homelessness, Substance Abuse, United Funds/United Ways, Volunteer Services, Youth Organizations

Contributions Analysis

Giving Priorities: Education, social welfare, health, civic interests, and the arts. Limited support to U.S.-based nonprofit organizations with an international focus. Company supports disaster relief efforts and international development. Foreign subsidiary managers make contributions at their own discretion. Headquarters does not track giving overseas, but substantial contributions must be approved by management at headquarters. Otherwise, international operating facilities report contributions generally.
Arts & Humanities: Supports a variety of local arts groups, centers, and funds. Also supports museums and public broadcasting.
Civic & Public Affairs: Sponsors awards and assistance program to recognize and support ideas for local

civic improvement. Also supports civil rights and minority affairs groups and urban affairs organizations.
Education: Highest priority. Areas of interest include independent and minority college funds, business education, and education associations. Also supports programs in creative management and computer technology. Administers matching gifts program.
Health: Supports a variety of medical research programs, as well as hospitals and other health organizations.
Social Services: Emphasis on youth programs. Also supports organizations concerned with the disabled, emergency relief, alcohol and drug abuse, the aged, community service, and delinquency and crime.

Application Procedures

Initial Contact: Submit a brief letter or proposal.
Application Requirements: Include a description of organization, amount requested, purpose of funds sought, recently audited financial statement, proof of tax-exempt status, and list of major activities and services rendered by organization.
Deadlines: None.

Corporate Officials

Robert A. Bowman: president, chief operating officer ED Harvard University BS (1977); University of Pennsylvania MBA (1979). PRIM CORP EMPL president, chief operating officer, director: ITT Corp. CORP AFFIL director: People's Bank & Trust; president, chief operating officer: ITT Destinations Inc. NONPR AFFIL member executive board: University Pennsylvania.
Ronald C. Brown: executive vice president, chief financial officer ED London School of Economics LLM; Osgoode Hall Law School LLB. PRIM CORP EMPL executive vice president, chief financial officer: Starwood Hotels & Resorts Worldwide, Inc. ADD CORP EMPL president: Sonoran Hotel Advisors.
Robert F. Cotter: chief operating officer PRIM CORP EMPL chief operating officer: Starwood Hotels & Resorts Worldwide Inc.
Barry S. Sternlicht: chairman, chief executive officer PRIM CORP EMPL chairman, chief executive officer: Starwood Hotels & Resorts Worldwide, Inc.

Giving Program Officials

Cathy Cornish: manager corporate giving
Dan Gibson: senior vice president corporate affairs

Grants Analysis

Disclosure Period: calendar year ending

STATE FARM MUTUAL AUTOMOBILE INSURANCE CO.

 Number 99 of Top 100 Corporate Givers

Company Contact

Bloomington, IL
Web: http://www.statefarm.com

Company Description

Profit: US$1,034,100,000 (1999)
Fortune Rank: 15, per FORTUNE Magazine's list of 500 Largest U.S. Corporations (1999).
FF 15
SIC(s): 6331 Fire, Marine & Casualty Insurance.
Parent Company: State Farm Insurance Companies

Nonmonetary Support

Type: Donated Equipment; Donated Products; In-kind Services
Volunteer Programs: Company-sponsored volunteer programs include loaned executives for United Way campaigns, Junior Achievement advisors, and Red Cross Blood drives. Interested employees complete a questionnaire, then receive a newsletter of volunteer activities. Employees participate in activities on their own initiative.
Note: The company provides nonmonetary support.

State Farm Companies Foundation

Giving Contact

Jill A. Jones, Assistant Secretary
State Farm Companies Foundation
One State Farm Plz., SC3
Bloomington, IL 61710-0001
Phone: (309)766-2161
Fax: (309)766-2314
Email: jill.jones.A3RI@statefarm.com

Description

Founded: 1963
EIN: 366110423
Organization Type: Corporate Foundation
Giving Locations: near major offices.
Grant Types: Capital, Employee Matching Gifts, Endowment, Fellowship, Matching, Multiyear/Continuing Support, Scholarship.
Note: Employee matching gift ratio: 1 to 1 up to $1,000 per contribution. Matching and employee ma tching gifts are for four-year colleges and universities only.

Giving Philosophy

'The State Farm Companies Foundation was founded in 1963 to respond to the many requests State Farm receives for financial support from nonprofit organizations.
'The Foundation's financial resources are primarily directed toward supporting higher education through our scholarship programs and grants to colleges and universities.
'We award limited grants to community, human service and health agencies in locations with large State Farm employee populations . . .' --State Farm Companies Foundation Grants and Scholarships Statement

Financial Summary

Total Giving: $9,000,000 (1999 approx); $10,050,899 (1998); $7,167,543 (1997). Note: Contributes through corporate direct giving program and foundation.
Giving Analysis: Giving for 1997 includes: foundation ($2,747,871); foundation matching gifts ($1,898,850); foundation scholarships ($1,534,570); foundation grants to United Way ($986,253); 1998: foundation ($6,202,875); foundation matching gifts ($2,480,576); foundation grants to United Way ($1,108,198); foundation fellowships ($179,250); foundation gifts to individuals ($80,000)
Assets: $83,174,321 (1998); $37,838,299 (1997); $42,550,057 (1996)
Gifts Received: $56,000,026 (1998); $4,750,000 (1993); $3,000,000 (1992). Note: Foundation received contributions from State Farm Life Insurance Co. and State Farm Mutual Automobile Insurance Co.

Typical Recipients

Arts & Humanities: Arts Associations & Councils, History & Archaeology, Public Broadcasting, Theater
Civic & Public Affairs: African American Affairs, Economic Policy, Employment/Job Training, Law & Justice, Native American Affairs, Professional & Trade Associations, Public Policy, Safety, Zoos/Aquariums
Education: Arts/Humanities Education, Business Education, Colleges & Universities, Community & Junior Colleges, Economic Education, Education Associations, Education Funds, Medical Education, Minority Education, Private Education (Precollege), Science/Mathematics Education, Student Aid
Health: Cancer, Children's Health/Hospitals, Clinics/Medical Centers, Hospitals, Medical Rehabilitation, Public Health
Religion: Religious Welfare
Social Services: Child Welfare, Community Service Organizations, Family Services, Substance Abuse, United Funds/United Ways, YMCA/YWCA/YMHA/YWHA

Contributions Analysis

Giving Priorities: Education and social services.
Arts & Humanities: 3%. Supports arts and culture organizations with an emphasis on history museums and societies.
Civic & Public Affairs: 1%. Funds leadership foundations, law organizations and women's organizations.
Education: 66%. Supports colleges and universities, insurance education, fellowships, and doctoral awards.
Health: 3%. Funds medical programs.
Social Services: 27%. Supports the United Way, youth activities, and a wide variety of health and human service organizations.
Note: Total contributions made in 1998.

Application Procedures

Initial Contact: Send a written proposal.
Application Requirements: Include description and purpose of the project; amount requested; project action plan and time frame; expected results; total cost and budget; sources and levels of expected funding; annual report; recently audited financial statement; copies of IRS 501(c)(3) and 509(a)1, 2, or 3 rulings; and fund-raising campaign time frame.
Deadlines: None.

Restrictions

Does not support seminars or conferences, or individuals (other than for scholarships).

Additional Information

Scholarship, fellowship, and doctoral program grants have specific deadlines for submission. These dates may be obtained from the foundation.
Publications: Foundation Contributions Report

Corporate Officials

John Coffey: senior vice president, vice chairman, chief operating officer, director B Pekin, IL. PRIM CORP EMPL senior vice president: State Farm Mutual Automobile Insurance Co. ADD CORP EMPL vice president: State Farm General Insurance Co.; vice president: State Farm Fire & Casualty Co.
Edward Barry Rust, Jr.: chairman, president, chief executive officer, director B Chicago, IL 1950. ED Lawrence University (1968-1969); Illinois Wesleyan University BS (1972); Southern Methodist University JD (1975); Southern Methodist University MBA (1975). PRIM CORP EMPL chairman, president, chief executive officer, director: State Farm Mutual Automobile Insurance Co. CORP AFFIL director, member executive committee, member investment committee: State Farm Life Insurance Co.; president, director: State Farm Investment Management Corp.; director, member executive committee, member investment committee: State Farm Life & Annuity Co.; chairman, president, chief executive officer: State Farm Insurance Companies; president, director: State Farm International Services Inc.; director, member executive committee, member investment committee: State Farm Fire & Casualty Co.; director, member executive committee, member investment committee: State Farm General Insurance Co. NONPR AFFIL member: Texas State Bar Association; member business advisory council: University Illinois College Commerce & Business Administration; trustee: Illinois Wesleyan University; member, trustee: Insurance Institute America; member: Business Roundtable; member: Illinois Bar Association; member: American Enterprise Institute; member: American Institute Property &

Liability Underwriters; member: American Bar Association.

Laura P. Sullivan: vice president, secretary, counsel B Des Moines, IA 1947. ED Cornell University BA (1971); Drake University JD (1972). PRIM CORP EMPL vice president, secretary, counsel: State Farm Mutual Automobile Insurance Co. CORP AFFIL secretary: State Farm Lloyds Inc.; vice president, secretary, counsel: State Farm Life Insurance Co.; assistant treasurer, director: State Farm Indemnity Co.; vice president, secretary, counsel, director: State Farm Life & Accident Assurance Co.; secretary, vice president, counsel, director: State Farm General Insurance Co.; vice president, secretary, counsel: State Farm Annuity & Life Insurance Co.; secretary, vice president, counsel: State Farm Fire & Casualty Co. NONPR AFFIL director: Insurance Institute Highway Safety; member: Iowa Bar Association; member: American Corporate Counsel Association; member: American Bar Association.

Vincent Joseph Trosino: executive vice president, vice chairman, chief operating officer, director B Upland, PA 1940. ED Villanova University (1962); Illinois State University (1973). PRIM CORP EMPL executive vice president, vice chairman, chief operating officer, director: State Farm Mutual Automobile Insurance Co. CORP AFFIL vice chairman, member executive committee, director: State Farm Life Insurance Co.; vice chairman, member, executive committee: State Farm Mutual Insurance Co.; director member executive committee: State Farm Life Co.; director: State Farm Life & Accident Assurance Co.; director: State Farm Life & Annuity Co.; director: State Farm International Services; director: State Farm Investment Management Corp.; member executive committee director: State Farm Fire Casualty Co.; director: State Farm General Insurance Co.

Foundation Officials

John Coffey: vice president programs (see above)

Jill Jones: assistant secretary

Roger Scott Joslin: treasurer B Bloomington, IL 1936. ED Miami University BS (1958); University of Illinois JD (1961). PRIM CORP EMPL senior vice president, treasurer: State Farm Mutual Automobile Insurance Co. ADD CORP EMPL treasurer: State Farm General Insurance Co.; vice president, treasurer, director: State Farm International Services Inc.; vice president, treasurer, director: State Farm Investment Management Corp.; treasurer: State Farm County Mutual Insurance Co. Texas; vice president, treasurer, director: State Farm Lloyds Inc.; vice president, treasurer, director: State Farm Municipal Bond Fund Inc. CORP AFFIL director: State Farm Life Insurance Co.; vice president, treasurer, director: State Farm Interim Fund Inc.; director: State Farm Life & Accident Assurance Co.; chairman: State Farm Fire & Casualty Co.; vice president, treasurer, director: State Farm Growth Fund Inc.; director: State Farm Annuity & Life Insurance Co.; vice president, treasurer, director: State Farm Balanced Fund Inc. NONPR AFFIL chairman board trustees: Natural Disaster Coalition.

John Killian: assistant treasurer PRIM CORP EMPL vice president: State Farm General Insurance Co.

Larry Phillips: assistant vice president programs

Edward Barry Rust, Jr.: chairman, president, director (see above)

Laura P. Sullivan: vice president, secretary, director (see above)

Vincent Joseph Trosino: assistant secretary (see above)

Grants Analysis

Disclosure Period: calendar year ending 1998
Total Grants: $6,202,875*
Number of Grants: 205
Average Grant: $19,420*
Highest Grant: $1,241,128
Typical Range: $2,000 to $50,000
***Note:** Giving excludes matching gifts; fellowships; gifts to individuals; and United Way. Average grant figure excludes two highest grants, totaling $2,241,128.

Recent Grants

Note: Grants derived from 1997 Form 990.

Arts & Humanities

105,000 McLean County Historical Society, Bloomington, IL
20,000 Illinois Shakespeare Festival Theater Project, Normal, IL

Civic & Public Affairs

25,000 Miller Park Zoological Society, Bloomington, IL
25,000 Students Against Drunk Driving, Marlborough, MA
20,000 American Indian College Fund, New York, NY

Education

1,278,236 National Merit Scholarship Corporation, Evanston, IL
229,585 Illinois Wesleyan University Minority Enrichment Program, Bloomington, IL
100,000 Howard University, Washington, DC
100,000 Illinois State University, Normal, IL
100,000 Illinois State University College of Business, Normal, IL
50,000 University of Wisconsin, Whitewater, WI
35,000 University of Virginia, Charlottesville, VA
33,333 Auburn University, Auburn, AL
33,333 University of Georgia Foundation, Athens, GA
25,000 Bradley University Centennial Campaign, Peoria, IL
25,000 Frederick Community College, Frederick, MD
25,000 Frederick Community College Fund, Frederick, MD
25,000 Insurance Education Foundation, Normal, IL
25,000 Mennonite College of Nursing, Bloomington, IL
25,000 Middle Tennessee State University, Murfreesboro, TN
25,000 Millikin University, Decatur, IL
25,000 National Council on Economic Education, New York, NY
25,000 Skidmore College, Saratoga Springs, NY
25,000 University of Georgia Foundation, Atlanta, GA
23,000 National Hispanic Scholarship Fund, Novato, CA
20,000 Hood College, Frederick, MD
20,000 Illinois State University Actuarial Science Program, Normal, IL
20,000 Mississippi State University, Jackson, MS
20,000 S.S. Huebner Foundation of Insurance Education, Philadelphia, PA
20,000 University of Illinois, Urbana, IL
20,000 University of Missouri College of Business and Public Administration, Columbia, MO
20,000 University of Southwest Louisiana, Lafayette, IN

Health

200,000 Community Cancer Center, Bloomington, IL
35,000 Chilton Memorial Hospital, Pompton Plains, NJ
25,000 Oaklawn Hospital, Marshall, MI
25,000 Southern Methodist University School of Law, Dallas, TX
25,000 Tippecanoe Community Health Clinic, Lafayette, IN
25,000 Valley Children's Hospital Foundation, Fresno, CA

Social Services

50,000 Children's Foundation, Bloomington, IL
48,276 United Way Central Florida, Highland City, FL
45,084 United Way, Passaic, NJ
44,455 United Way Passaic County, Paterson, NJ
41,994 Kern County United Way, Bakersfield, CA
29,826 United Way, Dallas, TX
28,750 United Way, Dallas, TX
28,656 United Way Crusade of Mercy, Chicago, IL
26,928 United Way McLean County, Bloomington, IL
25,000 Partnership for a Drug-Free America, New York, NY
23,976 United Way Valley of the Sun, Phoenix, AZ
21,708 United Way Licking County, Newark, OH

STATE STREET BANK & TRUST CO.

Company Contact

Boston, MA
Web: http://www.statestreet.com

Company Description

SIC(s): 6022 State Commercial Banks, 6282 Investment Advice.
Parent Company: State Street Boston Corp.

Operating Locations

Australia: State Street Australia, Limited; State Street Bank and Trust Co. -- Sydney, Sydney; State Street Global Advisors, Australia, Limited, Sydney; Belgium: State Street Bank and Trust Co. -- Brussels, Brussels; State Street Global Advisors Brussels, Brussels; Canada: Fiducie State Street, Montreal; State Street Global Advisors, Ltd., Montreal; State Street Global Advisors, Limited, Montreal; State Street Fund Services Toronto, Inc., Toronto; State Street Global Advisors, Limited, Toronto; State Street Trust Co., Canada, Toronto, Vancouver; Chile: State Street Global Advisors Chile, Las Condes, Santiago; Cayman Islands: State Street Cayman Trust Co., NV, Grand Cayman; England: State Street Bank Europe, Limited, London; State Street Bank and Trust Co. -- London, London; State Street Global Advisors, United Kingdom, Limited, London; State Street Unit Trust Management Limited, London; France: State Street Banque, SA, Montpellier; State Street Banque SA, Paris; Germany: State Street Bank GmbH, Munich; State Street Investment GmbH, Munich; Hong Kong: State Street Bank and Trust Co.; State Street Global Advisors (HK), Ltd.; Ireland: Bank of Ireland Securities, Dublin; Japan: State STR Trust and Banking Co., Limited, Tokyo; State Street Bank and Trust Co. -- Tokyo, Tokyo; State Street Global Advisors, (Japan) Co., Ltd., Tokyo; Republic of Korea: State Street Bank and Trust Co. -- Seoul, Seoul; Luxembourg: State Street Luxembourg, SA; Netherlands Antilles: State Street Curacao Trust Co., NV; Netherlands: State Street Amsterdam, Amsterdam; New Zealand: State Street New Zealand, Limited, Wellington; Scotland: State Street Bank Trustees Limited, Edinburgh; Singapore: State Street Bank PTE Ltd., Singapore; Switzerland: State Street Bank and Trust Co., Zurich; Taiwan: State Street Bank and Trust Co. -- Taipei, Taipei; United Arab Emirates: State Street Bank and Trust Co., Dubai

Nonmonetary Support

Type: Cause-related Marketing & Promotion; Donated Equipment; In-kind Services; Loaned Employees; Loaned Executives

Corporate Sponsorship

Value: $370,064 (1998)
Type: Arts & cultural events; Music & entertainment events
Contact: Diane Smith, Events Coordinator
Note: Company sponsors selected non-profit organization benefits.

State Street Foundation

Giving Contact

George A. Bowman, Jr., Vice President, Community Affairs
State Street Foundation
225 Franklin Street
Boston, MA 02110-2804
Phone: (617)664-3381
Fax: (617)451-6315
Email: gabowman@statestreet.com

Alternate Contact

Ms. Lilo Navales de Garne, Program Office
Phone: (617)664-3156
Email: lmnavales@statestreet.com

Description

EIN: 046401847
Organization Type: Corporate Foundation
Giving Locations: MA: Boston including surrounding communities
Grant Types: Capital, Challenge, Employee Matching Gifts, General Support, Project.

Financial Summary

Total Giving: $8,000,000 (1999 approx); $5,938,171 (1998); $4,400,000 (1996 approx). Note: Contributes through foundation only.
Giving Analysis: Giving for 1998 includes: foundation grants to United Way ($1,000,000); foundation matching gifts ($179,000)
Assets: $3,520,416 (1995); $3,306,611 (1994); $3,865,917 (1992)
Gifts Received: $4,254,000 (1995); $2,000,000 (1994); $3,266,900 (1992). Note: Contributions are received from State Street Bank & Trust.

Typical Recipients

Arts & Humanities: Arts Associations & Councils, Arts Centers, Arts Institutes, Arts Outreach, Ballet, Community Arts, Dance, Ethnic & Folk Arts, Historic Preservation, History & Archaeology, Libraries, Museums/Galleries, Music, Opera, Performing Arts, Theater
Civic & Public Affairs: African American Affairs, Asian American Affairs, Business/Free Enterprise, Civil Rights, Clubs, Economic Development, Economic Policy, Employment/Job Training, Hispanic Affairs, Housing, Law & Justice, Municipalities/Towns, Nonprofit Management, Public Policy, Safety, Urban & Community Affairs, Women's Affairs, Zoos/Aquariums
Education: Afterschool/Enrichment Programs, Arts/Humanities Education, Business Education, Business-School Partnerships, Colleges & Universities, Continuing Education, Economic Education, Education Funds, Education Reform, Elementary Education (Private), Engineering/Technological Education, Faculty Development, Education-General, Leadership Training, Literacy, Medical Education, Minority Education, Preschool Education, Private Education (Precollege), Public Education (Precollege), School Volunteerism, Science/Mathematics Education, Secondary Education (Public), Student Aid, Vocational & Technical Education
Health: Adolescent Health Issues, Cancer, Children's Health/Hospitals, Clinics/Medical Centers, Diabetes, Geriatric Health, Health Policy/Cost Containment, Health Organizations, Hospitals, Medical Rehabilitation, Mental Health
International: Health Care/Hospitals, International Affairs, International Relief Efforts
Religion: Jewish Causes
Science: Science Museums
Social Services: Animal Protection, Child Abuse, Child Welfare, Community Centers, Community Service Organizations, Counseling, Delinquency & Criminal Rehabilitation, Domestic Violence, Family Services, Homes, People with Disabilities, Recreation & Athletics, Refugee Assistance, Scouts, Shelters/Homelessness, Social Services-General, United Funds/United Ways, YMCA/YWCA/YMHA/YWHA, Youth Organizations

Contributions Analysis

Giving Priorities: Neighborhood revitalization, education, job traning and development, and youth programs. Supports international relief agencies.
Civic & Public Affairs: 10%. Supports initiatives to increase housing availability for low and moderate income persons and make their neighborhoods safer, more prosperous places to live and work.
Education: 37%. Supports initiatives to improve educational quality and opportunities for students in areas where State Street has operations. Funds programs that help students succeed and prepare for advancement to higher education, and that increase jobs and job opportunities. Funds adult/family literacy and job skills training and development initiatives that help prepare under-employed and displaced workers to participate successfully in the changing workforce.
Health: 14%.
Social Services: 28%. Supports initiatives addressing high school dropout prevention and teen pregnancy and parenting issues; major support for the United Way.
Note: Total contributions in 1998.

Application Procedures

Initial Contact: Call or write for guidelines, then send full proposal.
Application Requirements: Include executive summary (two-page maximum) on organization's letterhead, including: statement of project's principal objective; expected measurable outcome; total project budget, including dollar amount requested and any other anticipated sources of funding; description of population to be affected; project's timetable; name and telephone number of director, and primary contact person; proposal (six-page maximum), including: profile of organization and mission statement; description of the project to be funded; project's purpose; project's history and measures of success; services to be provided; cost to users of the services; profile of the population to be served; primary short-and long-term objectives; description of how the stated objectives will be achieved and the results quantified; plan for sustaining project after funding has ended; the following attachments: brief paragraph indicating size of budget for project, amount raised to date, prior and current funders, and list of proposals currently outstanding; proof of tax-exempt status; detailed projected budget for project and organization; list of board members and key officers with business affiliations; audited financial statements or Form 990 for the most recent two years, and sources of corporate and foundation support for those years; and other supporting material.
Deadlines: None.
Review Process: Funding decisions are made quarterly, in March, June, September, and December.
Decision Notification: About 90 days after receipt.
Notes: Also accepts the Associated Grantmakers of Massachusetts grant application form. Organizations may submit a funding request during a calendar year in which they are not receiving payments from a prior grant awarded.

Restrictions

Foundation does not support scholarships, fellowships, research projects; emergency cash flow; deficit spending; or debt liquidation; seed money or start-up programs; trips, tours, or transportation expenses; or films or videos.
Foundation seldom makes multiyear grants, or for general operating support.

Additional Information

Publications: Guidelines

Corporate Officials

George A. Bowman, Jr.: vice president community affairs PRIM CORP EMPL vice president community affairs: State Street Bank & Trust Co.
Marshall Nichols Carter: chairman, chief executive officer B Newport News, VA 1940. ED United States Military Academy BScE (1962); United States Navy Post Graduate School MS (1970); George Washington University MA (1976). PRIM CORP EMPL chairman, chief executive officer: State Street Bank & Trust Co. CORP AFFIL executive: State Street Corp.; director: Euroclear; chairman, president, chief executive officer, director: State Street Boston Corp.; director: AlliedSignal Inc.; director: Cedel (Luxembourg). NONPR AFFIL member executive committee: Livraison Valeurs Mobilieres; director: Project Orbis International; member: International Society Securities Administration; member working group: Group 30.
David Anthony Spina: president, chief operating officer B New York, NY 1942. ED College of the Holy Cross BS (1964); Harvard University MBA (1972). PRIM CORP EMPL president, chief operating officer: State Street Bank & Trust Co. CORP AFFIL chief financial officer, treasurer, vice chairman: State Street Boston Corp.; president, chief operating officer: State Street Corp.

Foundation Officials

George A. Bowman, Jr.: foundation manager, vice president (see above)
Lilo Navales de Garne: foundation officer

Grants Analysis

Disclosure Period: calendar year ending 1995
Total Grants: $3,143,579*
Number of Grants: 236
Average Grant: $13,320
Highest Grant: $100,000
Typical Range: $3,000 to $25,000
***Note:** Giving excludes matching gifts; United Way.

Recent Grants

Note: Grants derived from 1996 Form 990.

Arts & Humanities

25,000	Huntington Theater Company, Huntington, NY -- education programs directed to Boston's schools
20,000	American Academy of Arts and Sciences, Cambridge, MA -- operating support
20,000	Boston Public Library Foundation, Boston, MA -- support of the student reading and creating writing program
20,000	Boston Public Library Foundation, Boston, MA -- support of the student reading promotion program
15,000	Artists for Humanity, Boston, MA -- operating support
15,000	Community Music Center, Boston, MA -- support of the Intensive Study project
15,000	Community Music Center, Boston, MA -- support of the Intensive Study project

Civic & Public Affairs

100,000	Metropolitan Boston Housing Partnership, Boston, MA -- operating support
50,000	Action for Boston Community Development, Boston, MA -- support of assistance program
35,000	City Year, Boston, MA -- team sponsorship

25,000 Working Capital, Miami, FL -- support of the Metro Boston Initiative
22,000 Organization for a New Equality, Boston, MA -- for the luncheon and awards dinner
20,000 Habitat for Humanity, Boston, MA -- for low-income affordable housing development in Dorchester-Roxbury
20,000 Habitat for Humanity, Kansas City, MO -- support of the sponsorship of construction of a sponsor house
20,000 Inquilinos Boricuas in Action -- support of child care project and day center project
20,000 Nuestra Comunidad Development Corporation, Roxbury, MA -- operating support
20,000 One With One, Boston, MA -- support of Entrances Office Work Program
15,000 Codman Square Neighborhood Development Corporation, Dorchester, MA -- operating support
15,000 Commonwealth Zoological Corporation, Boston, MA -- support of the Wildlife on Wheels program
15,000 Massachusetts Alliance for Small Contractors, Boston, MA -- operating support

Education

45,000 Suffolk University, Boston, MA -- support of the Financial Industry in the 21st Century project
40,000 Boston University Academy, Boston, MA -- challenge grant
29,400 Inner-City Scholarship Fund, Boston, MA -- support of Inner-City Business Advisors Program
25,000 A Better Chance, Boston, MA -- college preparatory program for minority students
25,000 Boston Partners in Education School Volunteers for Boston, Boston, MA -- support of the AquaSmarts program
25,000 Boston Partners in Education School Volunteers for Boston, Boston, MA -- support of the AquaSmarts program
25,000 Boston Renaissance Charter School, Boston, MA -- support of the Junior Academy science laboratory
25,000 A Different September Foundation, Boston, MA -- to further expand funding resources
25,000 Harvard University John Shornstein Center, Cambridge, MA -- for support of the project on economics and journalism
25,000 Thompson Island Outward Bound Education Center, Boston, MA -- support of summer Institute and Island School
20,000 Lesson One Foundation, Boston, MA -- support of ECSS program
20,000 Massachusetts Pre-Engineering Program, Boston, MA -- support of Camp Tech
20,000 Organization for a New Equality, Boston, MA -- for the Economic Literacy Campaign of Kansas City
17,500 Citywide Educational Coalition, Boston, MA -- operating support
15,000 Boston Music Education Collaborative, Boston, MA -- to support pilot program

Health

150,000 Harbor Health Services -- support of the Healthy Start to Head Start Program

International

25,000 Orbis International, Houston, TX -- operating support
25,000 Orbis International, Houston, TX -- operating support
20,000 International Institute, Boston, MA -- support of counseling and cultural programs
20,000 International Institute, Boston, MA -- support of counseling and cultural programs

Science

25,000 Computer Museum, Boston, MA -- support of the Clubhouse Program

Social Services

25,000 Girl Scouts of America Patriots Trail Council, MA -- to support the Girls Bank program
25,000 Operation Outreach -- support of programs
25,000 Pine Street Inn, Boston, MA -- support of the Paul Sullivan Housing Program
25,000 South Shore YMCA, MA -- Germantown neighborhood program
25,000 Training -- Support Against Domestic Violence Project
20,000 Girl Scouts of America Patriots Trail Council, MA -- to support Haitian-Hispanic-Asian outreach and the Girls Bank
15,000 Colonel Daniel More Boys and Girls Club, Dorchester, MA -- support of inner-city riding program
15,000 Haitian Multiservice Center -- support of study center and adult education program
15,000 Lawyers Clearinghouse on Affordable Housing and Homelessness -- support of nonprofit assistance project
15,000 Massachusetts Caring for Children, Boston, MA -- support of children in the program during one year
15,000 Massachusetts Coalition of Battered Women Service Groups, Boston, MA -- support of income self-sufficiency program

STEELCASE INC.

Company Contact

Grand Rapids, MI
Web: http://www.steelcase.com

Company Description

Employees: 19,000
SIC(s): 2521 Wood Office Furniture, 2522 Office Furniture Except Wood, 2531 Public Building & Related Furniture, 3577 Computer Peripheral Equipment Nec.

Nonmonetary Support

Value: $700,000 (1990); $700,000 (1989); $700,000 (1988)
Type: Donated Products; In-kind Services
Contact: Howard Sutton, Vice President of Corporate Relations
Note: The company provides nonmonetary support.

Corporate Sponsorship

Value: $600,000 (1997)
Type: Arts & cultural events; Festivals/fairs; Pledge-a-thon
Contact: Howard Sutton, Vice President, Corporate Relations

Steelcase Foundation

Giving Contact

Ms. Susan Broman, Executive Director
Steelcase Foundation
PO Box 1967, CH-4E
Grand Rapids, MI 49501-1967
Phone: (616)246-4695
Fax: (616)475-2200

Alternate Contact

Phone: (616)246-9860

Description

EIN: 386050470
Organization Type: Corporate Foundation
Giving Locations: communities in which company has manufacturing operations.
Grant Types: Award, Capital, Employee Matching Gifts, General Support, Matching, Multiyear/Continuing Support, Project.
Note: Employee matching gift ratio: 1 to 1 for gifts to educational institutions.

Giving Philosophy

'In general, foundation contributions and grants are limited to local projects or programs in the areas of Steelcase Inc. manufacturing plants. In this way, the foundation seeks to improve the health, educational, recreational, and environmental opportunities for residents of these Steelcase communities.' *Annual Report, Steelcase Foundation*

Financial Summary

Total Giving: $6,624,615 (1998); $5,932,785 (1997); $5,115,512 (1996). Note: Contributes through corporate direct giving program and foundation.
Giving Analysis: Giving for 1996 includes: foundation matching gifts ($240,348); 1997: foundation grants to United Way ($10,000); 1998: foundation grants to United Way ($1,500,000); foundation matching gifts ($316,209); foundation scholarships ($64,500)
Assets: $113,851,313 (1998); $100,221,502 (1997); $87,685,747 (1996)
Gifts Received: $6,000,000 (1998); $5,000,000 (1997); $5,000,000 (1996). Note: Contributions are received from Steelcase, Inc.

Typical Recipients

Arts & Humanities: Arts Associations & Councils, Arts Centers, Arts Institutes, Ballet, Dance, Ethnic & Folk Arts, Historic Preservation, History & Archaeology, Libraries, Literary Arts, Museums/Galleries, Music, Opera, Performing Arts, Public Broadcasting, Theater
Civic & Public Affairs: African American Affairs, Botanical Gardens/Parks, Business/Free Enterprise, Community Foundations, Economic Development, Civic & Public Affairs-General, Hispanic Affairs, Housing, Native American Affairs, Urban & Community Affairs, Women's Affairs, Zoos/Aquariums
Education: Arts/Humanities Education, Business Education, Colleges & Universities, Community & Junior Colleges, Education Funds, Environmental Education, Leadership Training, Preschool Education, Private Education (Precollege), Public Education (Precollege), Student Aid
Health: Children's Health/Hospitals, Clinics/Medical Centers, Emergency/Ambulance Services, Geriatric Health, Health Policy/Cost Containment, Health Organizations, Hospices, Medical Rehabilitation, Mental Health, Nutrition, Prenatal Health Issues, Public Health, Single-Disease Health Associations
Religion: Churches, Ministries, Religious Organizations, Religious Welfare
Social Services: Animal Protection, Camps, Child Abuse, Child Welfare, Community Centers, Community Service Organizations, Counseling, Delinquency & Criminal Rehabilitation, Domestic Violence, Emergency Relief, Family Planning, Family Services, Food/Clothing Distribution, Homes, People with Disabilities, Recreation & Athletics, Scouts, Senior Services, Shelters/Homelessness, Substance Abuse, United Funds/United Ways, Volunteer Services, YMCA/YWCA/YMHA/YWHA, Youth Organizations

Contributions Analysis

Giving Priorities: Social welfare, museums, the arts, and elementary and secondary education.

Arts & Humanities: 9%. Supports theaters, ballet, museums, and arts centers. The Grand Rapids symphony is a major recipient.
Civic & Public Affairs: 2%. Supports community and economic development programs, and zoological and horticultural societies.
Education: 12%. Funds colleges, universities, and higher education foundations. Company also matches employee gifts to education.
Health: 9%. Supports the Easter Seal Society and the Red Cross. Also funds local health organizations.
Social Services: 52%. Supports United Way, child welfare, and family services.
Note: Total contributions in 1998. Special consideration is given to requests involving the disadvantaged, the disabled, youth, or the elderly.

Application Procedures

Initial Contact: Send letter requesting application.
Application Requirements: Letter should be on organizational letterhead, signed by the chief executive, and include: description of organization and project, expected results, amount requested, copy of IRS 501(c)(3) nonprofit certification.
Deadlines: Contact foundation for the next deadline.

Restrictions

The foundation does not make grants to individuals, organizations that have received a foundation grant in the last 12 months, fraternal organizations, political or lobbying groups, for conferences or seminars, or for dinners or special events.
Donations to religiously-affiliated programs are made only when the objectives benefit the entire community. Programs with substantial religious overtones of a sectarian nature are not considered.
Foundation does not support groups that discriminate against people because of race, sex, disability, or national origin.
Foundation does not support groups that discriminate against people because of race, sex, disability, or national origin.

Additional Information

The foundation and company endeavor to support organizations in which company employees are board members, volunteers, or clients, or where employees are part of the benefiting community.
The foundation prefers to participate with others in providing financial support for a project and occasionally will structure its grants to encourage broad support by others.
Old Kent Bank and Trust Company serves as a corporate trustee for the foundation.
Foundation requires reports from recipients detailing financial accounting of grant expenditures and accomplishments.
Publications: Annual Report

Corporate Officials

James P. Hackett: president, chief executive officer B 1955. ED University of Michigan BA (1977). PRIM CORP EMPL president, chief executive officer: Steelcase Inc. CORP AFFIL president, chief executive officer: Steelcase North American.
David Dyer Hunting, Jr.: director B Grand Rapids, MI 1926. ED University of Michigan (1948). PRIM CORP EMPL director: Steelcase Inc.
Frank Henry Merlotti: director B Herrin, IL 1926. PRIM CORP EMPL director: Steelcase Inc.
Peter M. Wege: vice chairman, director B Grand Rapids, MI 1921. ED University of Michigan. PRIM CORP EMPL vice chairman, director: Steelcase Inc.

Foundation Officials

Susan Broman: executive director
James P. Hackett: trustee (see above)
David Dyer Hunting, Jr.: trustee (see above)
Frank Henry Merlotti: trustee (see above)
Robert Cunningham Pew, II: trustee B Syracuse, NY 1923. ED Wesleyan University BA. PRIM CORP EMPL chairman emeritus: Steelcase Inc. CORP AFFIL director: Old Kent Financial Corp.; director: Foremost Corp. America. NONPR AFFIL director: Michigan Strategic Fund; director: National Organization Disability; director: Grand Rapids Employers Association; board control: Grand Valley State College; member: Governments Commission Jobs & Economic Development; director: Grand Rapids Chamber of Commerce; director: Economic Development Corp. Grand Rapids; member: Chi Psi. CLUB AFFIL University Club; Lost Tree Club; Peninsular Club; Kent Country Club.
Howard Sutton: trustee B Chicago, IL 1936. ED Michigan State University BA (1958). NONPR AFFIL member: Association National Advertisers; member: Business & Professional Advertisers Association; member: American Advertising Federation; member: American Marketing Association.
Peter M. Wege: trustee (see above)
Kate Pew Wolters: trustee

Grants Analysis

Disclosure Period: calendar year ending 1998
Total Grants: $4,743,906*
Number of Grants: 113
Average Grant: $33,428*
Highest Grant: $1,000,000
Typical Range: $5,000 to $100,000
***Note:** Giving excludes United Way, matching gifts, scholarship. Average grant figure excludes highest grant.

Recent Grants

Note: Grants derived from 1997 Form 990.

Arts & Humanities

1,000,000 Ryerson Library Foundation, Grand Rapids, MI
135,000 St. Cecilia Music Society, Grand Rapids, MI
125,000 Urban Institute of Contemporary Art, Grand Rapids, MI
113,300 Grand Rapids Symphony, Grand Rapids, MI
75,000 Grand Rapids Art Museum, Grand Rapids, MI
60,000 Arts Council, Grand Rapids, MI
60,000 Arts Council, Grand Rapids, MI
25,000 Opera Grand Rapids, Grand Rapids, MI
21,715 West Michigan Public Broadcasting, Grand Rapids, MI

Civic & Public Affairs

50,000 Neighborhood Housing Services, Asheville, NC
32,500 Limestone Area Community Foundation, Athens, AL
25,000 Grand Rapids Urban League, Grand Rapids, MI
25,000 Oakdale Neighbors, Grand Rapids, MI
22,118 Direction Center, Grand Rapids, MI
20,000 West Grand Neighborhood Organization, Grand Rapids, MI

Education

300,000 Aquinas College, Grand Rapids, MI
150,000 Calvin College, Grand Rapids, MI
100,000 St. Andrew's School, Grand Rapids, MI
52,500 National Merit Scholarship Corporation, Evanston, IL
39,345 Adams Christian School, Wyoming, MI
25,000 Grand Rapids Community College Fund, Grand Rapids, MI
25,000 Intervention Center for Early Childhood, Santa Ana, CA
23,000 Junior Achievement of Michigan Great Lakes, Grand Rapids, MI
18,440 Cutlerville Christian School, Grand Rapids, MI

Health

50,000 Health Intervention Services, Grand Rapids, MI
44,000 Gerontology Network Resources, Grand Rapids, MI
25,000 American Red Cross, Grand Rapids, MI
25,000 American Red Cross, Grand Rapids, MI

Religion

400,000 Salvation Army, Grand Rapids, MI
250,000 Mel Trotter Ministries, Grand Rapids, MI
50,000 Grace Christian Reformed Church, Grand Rapids, MI
50,000 Salvation Army of Asheville-Buncombe County, Asheville, NC
40,000 Inner-City Christian Federation, Grand Rapids, MI
40,000 St. John's Home, Grand Rapids, MI
25,000 Degage Ministries, Grand Rapids, MI
17,000 United Methodist Community House, Grand Rapids, MI

Social Services

490,300 Heart of Western Michigan United Way, Grand Rapids, MI
382,688 Child and Family Resource Council, Grand Rapids, MI
175,000 Camp Blodgett, Grand Rapids, MI
166,667 YMCA, Grand Rapids, MI
125,000 Grand Rapids REACH, Grand Rapids, MI
125,000 Humane Society, Grand Rapids, MI
75,000 Goodwill Industries of Greater Grand Rapids, Grandville, MI
54,304 Planned Parenthood Center of West Michigan, Grand Rapids, MI
30,000 Association for the Blind and Visually Impaired, Grand Rapids, MI
20,000 Grand Rapids Youth Commonwealth, Grand Rapids, MI
20,000 Life Guidance Services, Grand Rapids, MI
20,000 One Way House, Grand Rapids, MI
20,000 Orange County Human Relations Council, Santa Ana, CA
19,000 YMCA, Grand Rapids, MI

Stone Container Corp.

Company Contact

Chicago, IL

Company Description

Profit: US$255,500,000
Employees: 24,000
SIC(s): 1311 Crude Petroleum & Natural Gas, 2493 Reconstituted Wood Products, 2499 Wood Products Nec, 2653 Corrugated & Solid Fiber Boxes.

Stone Foundation

Giving Contact

Jerome N. Stone, Contact
Stone Foundation
150 North Michigan Avenue
Chicago, IL 60601
Phone: (312)346-6600

Alternate Contact

Joyce Bopp, Travel Manager/Foundation Secretary

Description

Founded: 1948
EIN: 366063761
Organization Type: Corporate Foundation
Giving Locations: IL: Chicago nationally.
Grant Types: Capital, General Support, Matching, Project, Scholarship.

Financial Summary

Total Giving: $954,333 (1998); $842,118 (1997); $959,885 (1996). Note: Contributes through foundation only.

Giving Analysis: Giving for 1996 includes: foundation ($730,485); foundation scholarships ($96,000); foundation grants to United Way ($82,150); foundation matching gifts ($51,250); 1997: foundation ($794,118); foundation matching gifts ($48,000); 1998: foundation ($772,333); foundation matching gifts ($650,000); foundation scholarships ($100,000); foundation grants to United Way ($82,000)

Assets: $1,402,397 (1998); $2,210,375 (1997); $1,729,953 (1996)

Gifts Received: $42,500 (1998); $1,046,900 (1997); $1,072,400 (1996). Note: In 1998 contributions were received from Norman Stone Family Foundation ($10,500); James H. Stone ($7,500); Roger & Susan Stone Family Foundation ($15,400); Laimbeer Packaging Corp.; Jerome H. Stone Family Foundation; Avery Stone; Matt Kaplan; Laimbeer Packaging Corporate; and miscellaneous contributors.

Typical Recipients

Arts & Humanities: Arts Centers, Arts Institutes, Historic Preservation, History & Archaeology, Libraries, Museums/Galleries, Music, Opera, Performing Arts, Public Broadcasting, Theater

Civic & Public Affairs: Botanical Gardens/Parks, Business/Free Enterprise, Chambers of Commerce, Clubs, Economic Development, Employment/Job Training, Civic & Public Affairs-General, Hispanic Affairs, Law & Justice, Legal Aid, Philanthropic Organizations, Urban & Community Affairs, Women's Affairs, Zoos/Aquariums

Education: Arts/Humanities Education, Business Education, Colleges & Universities, Economic Education, Education Associations, Education Funds, Education-General, International Studies, Journalism/Media Education, Legal Education, Minority Education, Private Education (Precollege), Science/Mathematics Education, Secondary Education (Private), Special Education, Student Aid

Environment: Air/Water Quality, Forestry, Environment-General, Resource Conservation

Health: Alzheimers Disease, Cancer, Children's Health/Hospitals, Clinics/Medical Centers, Diabetes, Emergency/Ambulance Services, Eyes/Blindness, Hospitals, Long-Term Care, Medical Rehabilitation, Medical Research, Mental Health, Multiple Sclerosis, Single-Disease Health Associations

International: Foreign Educational Institutions, International Affairs, International Environmental Issues, International Relations, Missionary/Religious Activities

Religion: Jewish Causes, Religious Organizations, Religious Welfare

Science: Science Museums

Social Services: Child Welfare, Community Centers, Community Service Organizations, Emergency Relief, Family Planning, Food/Clothing Distribution, People with Disabilities, Scouts, Shelters/Homelessness, Substance Abuse, United Funds/United Ways, Volunteer Services, YMCA/YWCA/YMHA/YWHA, Youth Organizations

Contributions Analysis

Giving Priorities: Jewish philanthropy, the arts, colleges and universities, and social welfare.

Arts & Humanities: 25%. Priorities include music, museums, theaters, and arts institutes and centers.

Civic & Public Affairs: 4%. Supports economic development, environmental issues, community affairs, and foundations.

Education: 21%. Contributions support colleges and universities in the Chicago area, with interest shown in business, law, and scientific education. Grants also benefit scholarship funds and education associations. Scholarships are available for children of active, full-time employees with two or more years of service.

Health: 2%. Interests include hospitals and single-disease health associations.

Religion: 37%. Supports Jewish causes and religious welfare organizations.

Social Services: 11%. Support is primarily provided to the United Way. Remaining funds focus on homelessness, child welfare, and youth organizations.

Application Procedures

Initial Contact: Send a brief letter or proposal.

Application Requirements: Include a description of organization, amount requested, purpose of funds sought, recently audited financial statement, and proof of tax-exempt status; for scholarships, include an application form., high school transcripts, and records of nationally administered test.

Deadlines: None, for grants; April 1 for scholarships.

Restrictions

Scholarships are available only to children of active, full-time employees with more than two years service to the company.

Corporate Officials

Roger Warren Stone: chairman, president, chief executive officer, director B Chicago, IL 1935. ED University of Pennsylvania BS (1957). PRIM CORP EMPL chairman, president, chief executive officer, director: Stone Container Corp. CORP AFFIL director: Morton International Inc.; director: Option Care Inc.; director: McDonald's Corp. NONPR AFFIL member: Mid-American Comm; board overseers: University Pennsylvania Wharton School Business; member advisor counselor: Economic Development; fellow: Lake Forest Academy; member: Chicago Council Foreign Relations; trustee: Chicago Symphony Orchestra; director: American Forest & Paper Association; member: Chicago Comm. CLUB AFFIL Tavern Club; Lake Shore Country Club; Standard Club; Commercial Club; Economic Club.

Foundation Officials

Jerome H. Stone: vice president, secretary, treasurer B Chicago, IL 1913. ED DePaul University; Northwestern University (1934). CORP AFFIL director: Solar Press; chairman emeritus: Stone Container Corp.

Marvin N. Stone: director B Chicago, IL 1909. ED Northwestern University. PRIM CORP EMPL ltd. partner: General Hardware.

Roger Warren Stone: president (see above)

Grants Analysis

Disclosure Period: calendar year ending 1998
Total Grants: $772,333*
Number of Grants: 50
Average Grant: $5,124*
Highest Grant: $331,500
Typical Range: $1,000 to $10,000
***Note:** Giving excludes matching gifts; scholarship; United Way. Average grant excludes three highest grants.

Recent Grants

Note: Grants derived from 1996 Form 990.

Arts & Humanities

100,000	Chicago Symphony Lyric Opera, Chicago, IL
55,200	Museum of Contemporary Art, Los Angeles, CA
22,000	Chicago Public Library Foundation, Chicago, IL
10,000	Caramoor Center for Music and Arts, Katonah, NY
10,000	Norton Museum of Art
5,000	Missouri Theater Project, Missouri Symphony Society, MO
2,500	Chicago Cultural Center Foundation, Chicago, IL

Civic & Public Affairs

25,000	El Valor
5,000	Community of Economic Development, Chicago, IL
3,000	Chicago Horticultural Society, Chicago, IL
1,000	Career Resource Center, Chicago, IL
1,000	Chicago Commons, Chicago, IL
500	Allendale Association, Lake Villa, IL

Education

13,750	Junior Achievement, Chicago, IL
13,750	Junior Achievement, Chicago, IL
10,000	Dartmouth College, Hanover, NH
8,335	Kellogg School of Management, Chicago, IL
3,000	Roosevelt University, Chicago, IL
2,500	Chicago State University, Chicago, IL
1,000	DePaul University, Chicago, IL
1,000	Hadley School for Blind, Winnetka, IL
1,000	Junior Achievement of Southeast Texas, TX
1,000	Yeshiva University, New York, NY
350	Josephenium High School, Chicago, IL

Environment

5,000	GIRF
1,000	Lake Forest Open Lands, Lake Forest, IL
1,000	Nature Conservancy, Arlington, VA

Health

50,000	Cap Care
5,000	Rush-Presbyterian Medical Center, Chicago, IL
5,000	St. Joseph's Hospital and Care
5,000	United Cerebral Palsy, New York, NY
2,050	Lake Forest Hospital, Lake Forest, IL
1,000	National Osteoporosis Foundation, Washington, DC
100	American Red Cross, Chicago, IL
100	Children's Memorial Hospital, Chicago, IL

International

25,000	Conservation International, Washington, DC
5,000	American Ireland Fund, Boston, MA
2,600	Chicago Council on Foreign Relations, Chicago, IL
500	American Committee for Weizmann Institute of Science, New York, NY

Religion

301,408	Jewish United Fund, Chicago, IL
2,550	National Conference of Christians and Jews
2,500	American Jewish Committee, New York, NY

Social Services

65,000	United Way, Chicago, IL
17,000	United Way Crusade of Mercy, Chicago, IL
5,000	Boys and Girls Clubs of America, New York, NY
5,000	Hugh O'Brien Youth Foundation, Wichita, KS
3,050	Voices for Illinois Children, Chicago, IL
2,000	Boys and Girls Club, Chicago, IL
1,000	Center for New Horizons, Chicago, IL
400	Love Louise, Chicago, IL

STONE &WEBSTER INC.

Company Contact

New York, NY
Web: http://www.stoneweb.com

Company Description

Income: US$1,000,000,000
Employees: 6,000

SIC(s): 1629 Heavy Construction Nec, 6792 Oil Royalty Traders, 8711 Engineering Services, 8742 Management Consulting Services.

Nonmonetary Support

Type: Loaned Employees; Workplace Solicitation

Giving Contact

John Smith, Secretary, Contributions Committee
Stone & Webster, Inc.
245 Summer Street
Boston, MA 02210
Phone: (617)589-5111
Fax: (617)589-2156

Description

Organization Type: Corporate Giving Program
Giving Locations: MA; NY: New York
Grant Types: Conference/Seminar, Emergency, Employee Matching Gifts, General Support, Multiyear/Continuing Support.
Note: The company matches employee gifts from $50 to $5,000.

Financial Summary

Total Giving: Contributes through corporate direct giving program only.

Typical Recipients

Arts & Humanities: Arts Centers
Civic & Public Affairs: Business/Free Enterprise
Education: Business Education
Health: Health Organizations
Social Services: Community Centers

Contributions Analysis

Note: Minimally supports civic and public affairs, health and human services, and arts organizations.

Application Procedures

Initial Contact: Send a brief letter of inquiry.
Application Requirements: Include a description of organization, amount requested, purpose of funds sought, audited financial statement, and proof of tax-exempt status.
Deadlines: None.

Restrictions

Does not support political or lobbying groups.

Grants Analysis

Disclosure Period: calendar year ending
Typical Range: $1,000 to $2,500

STONECUTTER MILLS CORP.

Company Contact

Spindale, NC

Company Description

Employees: 1,150
SIC(s): 2221 Broadwoven Fabric Mills--Manmade, 2261 Finishing Plants--Cotton, 2262 Finishing Plants--Manmade, 2269 Finishing Plants Nec.

Stonecutter Foundation

Giving Contact

Van H. Lonon, Staff Assistant
Stonecutter Foundation
Dallas Street
Spindale, NC 28160
Phone: (828)286-2341
Note: Van Lonon may be reached at extension 21.

Description

EIN: 566044820
Organization Type: Corporate Foundation
Giving Locations: NC
Grant Types: General Support, Scholarship.

Financial Summary

Total Giving: $450,000 (fiscal year ending March 31, 2000 approx); $450,000 (fiscal 1999 approx). Note: Contributes through foundation only.
Assets: Annual Asset Range: $5,500,000 to $6,750,000.
Gifts Received: $72,420 (fiscal 1993); $39,700 (fiscal 1992); $26,155 (fiscal 1991)

Typical Recipients

Arts & Humanities: Libraries, Museums/Galleries
Civic & Public Affairs: Business/Free Enterprise, Civil Rights, Employment/Job Training, Civic & Public Affairs-General, Housing, Municipalities/Towns, Public Policy, Safety
Education: Agricultural Education, Arts/Humanities Education, Colleges & Universities, Community & Junior Colleges, Education Associations, Education Funds, Elementary Education (Private), Elementary Education (Public), Engineering/Technological Education, Education-General, Private Education (Precollege), Public Education (Precollege), Religious Education, Science/Mathematics Education, Secondary Education (Public)
Environment: Environment-General, Resource Conservation
Health: Hospices, Hospitals, Medical Research
Religion: Churches, Dioceses, Religious Organizations
Science: Science Museums
Social Services: Child Welfare, Community Service Organizations, Crime Prevention, Domestic Violence, Homes, Recreation & Athletics, Scouts, United Funds/United Ways, Youth Organizations

Contributions Analysis

Giving Priorities: Focus on higher education. Also supports civic causes, religious welfare, social services, and health organizations.
Arts & Humanities: 2%. Libraries and museums.
Civic & Public Affairs: 8%. Employee legal affairs, economic development, and housing.
Education: 67%. Emphasis on colleges and universities and private secondary education.
Health: 5%. Hospices and medical research.
Religion: 10%. Supports churches and religious welfare.
Science: About 1%. Science museums.
Social Services: 7%. Focus on scouting, the United Way, and crime prevention.
Note: Total contributions in fiscal 1997.

Application Procedures

Initial Contact: Request an application form.
Deadlines: None.

Restrictions

Loans are restricted to residents of local area.

Additional Information

Publications: Application Form

Corporate Officials

James R. Cowan: chairman, president, chief executive officer, director B 1945. ED University of North Carolina BS (1967); Indiana University MS (1973). PRIM CORP EMPL chairman, president, chief executive officer, director: Stonecutter Mills Corp. CORP AFFIL chairman: Mitchell Co.
James M. Perry: vice chairman B 1927. ED Clemson University BS (1947). PRIM CORP EMPL vice chairman: Stonecutter Mills Corp.

Foundation Officials

James R. Cowan: vice president, director (see above)
Z. E. Dobbins: president, director
Van H. Lonon: treasurer PRIM CORP EMPL staff assistant: Stonecutter Mills Corp.
Mark L. Summey: director
K. S. Tanner, Jr.: director CORP AFFIL director: Stonecutter Mills Corp.
Thomas P. Walker: secretary B 1929. ED Berea College BA; University of North Carolina JD. PRIM CORP EMPL vice chairman, secretary, director: Stonecutter Mills Corp. CORP AFFIL president: Mitchell Co.

Grants Analysis

Disclosure Period: fiscal year ending March 31, 1997
Typical Range: $500 to $25,000

Recent Grants

Note: Grants derived from 1997 Form 990.

Arts & Humanities

5,000 Spindale Public Library, Spindale, NC
1,500 Rutherford County Farm Museum, Forest City, NC

Civic & Public Affairs

10,000 National Right to Work Legal, Springfield, VA -- employee rights protection
7,500 Jesse Helms Center, Wingate, NC -- to promote free enterprise education
5,000 Rutherford County Habitat for Humanity, Rutherfordton, NC -- low-income housing
2,275 Town of Spindale, Spindale, NC
1,500 Business Foundation of North Carolina, Chapel Hill, NC
1,000 Blue Ridge Assembly, Black Mountain, NC
1,000 Thermal Belt Habitat for Humanity, Tryon, NC -- low-income housing

Education

150,000 Isothermal Community College Foundation, Spindale, NC
25,000 Isothermal Community College Foundation, Spindale, NC
7,500 Isothermal Community College Foundation, Spindale, NC
5,000 Asheville School, Asheville, NC
5,000 Independent College Fund of North Carolina, Raleigh, NC
5,000 Montreat College, Montreat, NC
4,800 Chase High School, Forest City, NC
4,000 Brevard College, Brevard, NC
4,000 Gardner-Webb University, Boiling Springs, NC
3,000 Rutherfordton-Spindale Central High School, Rutherfordton, NC
3,000 Spindale Elementary School, Spindale, NC
2,500 Education Foundation for the Fashion Industry, New York, NY
2,500 Institute of Textile Technology, Charlottesville, VA
1,500 North Carolina Textile Foundation, Raleigh, NC
1,500 Rutherfordton-Spindale Central High School, Rutherfordton, NC
1,300 Harris School, Forest City, NC
1,000 Greensboro College, Greensboro, NC
1,000 Hillsdale College, Hillsdale, MI
1,000 Philadelphia School of Textiles, Philadelphia, PA
1,000 Warren Wilson College, Swannanoa, NC

Environment

1,000 Mountain Retreat Association, Montreat, NC

Health
10,000 Hospice of Rutherford County, Forest City, NC
5,000 Heinerman Medical Research Foundation, Charlotte, NC
1,500 Hospice of Rutherford County, Forest City, NC

Religion
10,000 Spindale First Baptist Church, Spindale, NC
5,000 Crestview Baptist Church, Shelby, NC
5,000 Pleasant Grove United Methodist Church, Forest City, NC
5,000 Spencer Baptist Church, Spindale, NC
5,000 Spindale First United Methodist Church, Spindale, NC
3,000 Forest City Church of the Nazarene, Forest City, NC
1,000 Spindale Church of the Brethren, Spindale, NC

Science
1,000 Discovery Place, Charlotte, NC
1,000 Sohiele Museum of Natural History, Gastonia, NC

Social Services
10,000 Girl Scouts of America Pioneer Council, Gastonia, NC -- youth training
5,000 Girl Scouts of America Pioneer Council, Gastonia, NC
4,000 Boy Scouts of America Piedmont Council, Gastonia, NC
2,700 United Way Rutherford County, Spindale, NC
1,500 Rutherford County Sheriff Department, Rutherfordton, NC
1,500 Town of Spindale Police Department, Spindale, NC
1,000 Crime Stoppers of Rutherford County, Rutherfordton, NC

STORAGE TECHNOLOGY CORP.

Company Contact
Louisville, CO
Web: http://www.stortek.com

Company Description
Employees: 8,300
SIC(s): 3577 Computer Peripheral Equipment Nec.

Nonmonetary Support
Type: Donated Equipment; In-kind Services
Volunteer Programs: Employees actively volunteer for a variety of corporate-sponsored activities, including Meals on Wheels, Boy Scouts, community hospitals, food banks, high schools and elementary schools, 4-H clubs, and wildlife and rescue groups. The company initiated the Volunteers in Partnership with the Community (VIP.COM) program in 1998. The program not only encourages employees to volunteer commitments, but also generates additional funds from the company for nonprofit organizations to which employees dedicate time.

Corporate Sponsorship
Type: Festivals/fairs

StorageTek Foundation

Giving Contact
Arlyce K. Lewis, Manager, Community Relations
Storage Technology Corp.
2270 S 88th St., MS-4341
Louisville, CO 80028-4310
Phone: (303)673-6833
Fax: (303)673-8876

Description
EIN: 841168359
Organization Type: Corporate Foundation
Giving Locations: headquarters area only.
Grant Types: Employee Matching Gifts, General Support, Scholarship.
Note: Employee matching gift ratio: .5 to 1 for gifts to higher education and the United Way.

Financial Summary
Total Giving: $1,109,038 (1998); $768,728 (1997); $1,892,328 (1996). Note: Contributes through corporate direct giving program and foundation.
Giving Analysis: Giving for 1997 includes: foundation ($740,648); foundation matching gifts ($22,852); foundation grants to United Way ($5,228); 1998: foundation ($955,221); foundation grants to United Way ($116,827); foundation matching gifts ($36,990)
Assets: $275,933 (1998); $814,172 (1996); $1,938,337 (1995)
Gifts Received: $682,000 (1998); $750,000 (1996); $2,436,134 (1995). Note: Contributions received from Storage Technology Corp.

Typical Recipients
Arts & Humanities: Arts Appreciation, Arts Centers, Dance, Arts & Humanities-General, Libraries, Museums/Galleries, Music, Performing Arts, Public Broadcasting, Theater
Civic & Public Affairs: Business/Free Enterprise, Community Foundations, Economic Policy, Civic & Public Affairs-General, Housing, Native American Affairs, Professional & Trade Associations, Urban & Community Affairs, Women's Affairs
Education: Arts/Humanities Education, Business Education, Colleges & Universities, Continuing Education, Education Associations, Education Funds, Education Reform, Engineering/Technological Education, Education-General, Leadership Training, Literacy, Minority Education, Preschool Education, Private Education (Precollege), Public Education (Precollege), Science/Mathematics Education, Special Education, Student Aid
Health: Arthritis, Cancer, Children's Health/Hospitals, Clinics/Medical Centers, Emergency/Ambulance Services, Health-General, Health Funds, Health Organizations, Heart, Hospices, Hospitals, Medical Rehabilitation, Mental Health, Multiple Sclerosis, Nutrition, Public Health, Single-Disease Health Associations, Transplant Networks/Donor Banks
Religion: Jewish Causes
Science: Science Museums
Social Services: At-Risk Youth, Big Brother/Big Sister, Child Welfare, Community Service Organizations, Domestic Violence, Emergency Relief, Family Services, Food/Clothing Distribution, Homes, People with Disabilities, Recreation & Athletics, Recreation & Athletics, Scouts, Shelters/Homelessness, Social Services-General, Special Olympics, Substance Abuse, United Funds/United Ways, Volunteer Services, YMCA/YWCA/YMHA/YWHA, Youth Organizations

Contributions Analysis
Giving Priorities: Health and human services, education, and arts.
Arts & Humanities: 8%. Supports orchestras, outreach programs, arts education, and children's programs. Supports projects that extend cultural opportunities that benefit a broad population base and enhance the quality of life.
Education: 29%. Supports Junior Achievement, scholarships, leadership and outreach programs, women and minority engineering programs, computer labs and networking, educational media, matching gifts, and Boulder Valley public schools. Focus is on innovative programs that strengthen the educational process in the areas of science, math, engineering, management, and technology. Supports literacy, including computer literacy and reading skills.
Social Services: 61%. Support includes health and human services. Major support to the YMCA in Boulder, CO.
Note: Total contributions made in 1998.

Application Procedures
Initial Contact: Send a written proposal.
Application Requirements: Include a description and background of organization, project description and purpose, objectives of organization and project, amount requested and purpose of funds sought, unique aspects of project, project budget, funding sources and amounts, list of board members and officers with affiliations, current and/or proposed income and expense budget, recently audited financial statement, and proof of tax-exempt status.
Deadlines: None.
Evaluative Criteria: The foundation may request additional information and a site visit.
Decision Notification: Evaluation generally takes 2 to 3 months.

Restrictions
The company does not support individuals, religious organizations for sectarian purposes, political or lobbying groups, fraternal organizations, general operating budgets receiving more than 40% of budget from United Way, or trips or tours.

Corporate Officials
David C. Lacey: executive vice president, chief financial officero, director B Alameda, CA 1946. ED University of California at Berkeley AB (1969); University of California (1974). PRIM CORP EMPL executive vice president, chief financial officer: Storagetek International Corp.
Mark McGregor: vice president, treasurer ED Texas A&M University BA (1964). PRIM CORP EMPL vice president, treasurer: Storage Technology Corp.
David E. Weiss: chairman, president, chief executive officer, director B 1944. ED University of Colorado BA (1967); University of Colorado MBA (1989); University of Colorado MA (1989). PRIM CORP EMPL chairman, president, chief executive officer, director: Storage Technology Corp.

Foundation Officials
Michael Klatman: president PRIM CORP EMPL vice president corporate communications: Storage Technology Corp.
David C. Lacey: chief financial officer, director (see above)
Arlyce K. Lewis: vice president PRIM CORP EMPL manager community relations: Storage Technology Corp.
Mark McGregor: vice president, treasurer (see above)
Lizbeth Stenmark: assistant secretary

Grants Analysis
Disclosure Period: calendar year ending 1998
Total Grants: $955,221*
Number of Grants: 143
Average Grant: $6,680
Highest Grant: $100,000
Typical Range: $1,000 to $20,000
***Note:** Giving excludes matching gifts; United Way.

Recent Grants
Note: Grants derived from 1998 Form 990.

Arts & Humanities
16,100 Rocky Mountain PBS, Denver, CO
14,452 Louisville Public Library Foundation, Louisville, CO
10,000 The Dairy Center for the Arts, Boulder, CO
10,000 Denver Art Museum, Denver, CO
9,200 World of Wonder Children's Museum, Louisville, CO
6,000 Collage Children's Museum, Boulder, CO

5,000 Colorado Dance Festival, Inc., Boulder, CO
5,000 Colorado Shakespeare Festival, Boulder, CO

Civic & Public Affairs

15,000 Colorado Minority Engineering Association, Denver, CO
6,525 Denver Organizing Committee, Denver, CO
5,000 Attention Homes, Boulder, CO
5,000 Colorado Minority Engineering Association, Denver, CO
5,000 Longmont Coalition for Women in Crisis, Longmont, CO
5,000 Ponce Neighborhood Housing Service, Ponce, PR

Education

25,000 Junior Achievement-Rocky Mountain, Denver, CO
15,000 Rocky Mountain News In Education Foundation, Denver, CO
10,000 Foundation for Boulder Valley Schools, Boulder, CO
10,000 University of Colorado at Boulder, Boulder, CO
10,000 University of Colorado at Boulder, Boulder, CO
9,505 Boulder Country Day Preschool/Kindergarten, Boulder, CO
9,260 National Merit Scholarship Corporation, Evanston, IL
5,000 Regis University, Denver, CO

Health

100,000 Colorado Therapeutic Riding Center, Boulder, CO
25,000 American Red Cross, San Juan, PR
15,000 St. Anthony Health Foundation, Denver, CO
9,390 National Multiple Sclerosis Society, Greeley, CO
7,500 Colorado Therapeutic Riding Center, Boulder, CO
5,000 American Heart Association, Denver, CO
5,000 United Cerebral Palsy of Colorado, Inc., Denver, CO

Religion

18,000 Jewish Community Center Of Denver, Denver, CO

Social Services

82,500 YMCA of Boulder Valley, Boulder, CO
50,000 Boy Scouts-Longs Peak Council, Inc., Greeley, CO
50,000 Community Food Share, Boulder, CO
30,839 Boulder County United Way, Boulder, CO
25,705 Boulder County United Way, Boulder, CO
22,535 Boulder County United Way, Boulder, CO
19,561 Boulder County United Way, Boulder, CO
10,000 Big Brothers Big Sisters, Denver, CO
10,000 Club 1360, Boulder, CO
8,250 Boy Scouts-Longs Peak Council, Inc., Greeley, CO
7,506 Boulder County United Way, Boulder, CO
7,000 National Sports Center for the Disabled, Denver, CO
5,000 Boys Hope/Girls Hope, Aurora, CO
5,000 Cenikor Foundation, Inc., Lakewood, CO
5,000 Colorado Foundation For Families And Children, Denver, CO
5,000 Eldora Special Recreation Program, Boulder, CO
5,000 Emergency Family Assistance Association, Boulder, CO
5,000 Instituto Ponceno del Hogar, Ponce, PR
5,000 Longmont YMCA, Longmont, CO

STREAR FARMS CO.

Company Contact

Denver, CO

Strear Family Foundation

Giving Contact

Leonard Strear, Chairman, President & Chief Executive Officer
6825 E. Tennessee Ave., Suite 235
Denver, CO 80224
Phone: (303)399-4631
Fax: (303)388-9125

Description

Founded: 1987
EIN: 841078190
Organization Type: Corporate Foundation. Supports preselected organizations only.
Giving Locations: CO
Grant Types: General Support.

Financial Summary

Total Giving: $244,196 (fiscal year ending September 30, 1998); $170,281 (fiscal 1997); $136,737 (fiscal 1995)
Assets: $9,177,123 (fiscal 1998); $9,241,675 (fiscal 1997); $4,631,330 (fiscal 1995)
Gifts Received: $302,963 (fiscal 1998); $440,000 (fiscal 1997); $123,092 (fiscal 1995). Note: In fiscal 1998, contributions were received from Strear Farms Co.

Typical Recipients

Arts & Humanities: Arts Associations & Councils, Museums/Galleries, Public Broadcasting, Theater
Civic & Public Affairs: Botanical Gardens/Parks, Civil Rights, Civic & Public Affairs-General, Zoos/Aquariums
Education: Arts/Humanities Education, Colleges & Universities, Education Reform, Elementary Education (Private), Private Education (Precollege), Religious Education, Secondary Education (Private)
Environment: Environment-General
Health: Cancer, Children's Health/Hospitals, Diabetes, Hospitals, Medical Research, Speech & Hearing
International: Health Care/Hospitals, International Relations, Missionary/Religious Activities
Religion: Jewish Causes, Religious Organizations, Religious Welfare, Social/Policy Issues, Synagogues/Temples
Science: Science Museums
Social Services: Child Welfare, Food/Clothing Distribution, Substance Abuse, United Funds/United Ways, YMCA/YWCA/YMHA/YWHA

Corporate Officials

Leonard Strear: chairman, president, chief executive officer PRIM CORP EMPL chairman, president, chief executive officer: Strear Farms Co.

Foundation Officials

Leonard Strear: president (see above)
Michael Strear: vice president, secretary

Grants Analysis

Disclosure Period: fiscal year ending September 30, 1998
Total Grants: $244,196

Recent Grants

Note: Grants derived from fiscal 1997 Form 990.

Arts & Humanities

2,400 Loveland High Plains Art Council, Loveland, CO

Civic & Public Affairs

6,993 Shalom Park, Denver, CO
3,500 Ascent, Denver, CO

Education

12,000 Rocky Mountain Hebrew Academy, Denver, CO
10,410 Art Student League, Denver, CO
2,000 Beth Jacob High School, Denver, CO

Health

7,000 Longmont United Hospital Care Center, Longmont, CO
3,000 AMC Cancer Research Center, Lakewood, CO
1,500 Hear Now, Denver, CO

International

2,000 Western Center for Russian Jewry, Denver, CO

Religion

41,000 Allied Jewish Federation, Denver, CO
25,200 Jewish Community Center, Denver, CO
12,141 Congregation Emanu-El, Denver, CO
3,600 Talmudic Research Institute, Denver, CO
3,600 Yeshiva Toras Chaim, Denver, CO
2,915 Congregation Har Ha Shem, Boulder, CO
2,500 Anti-Defamation League of B'nai B'rith, Denver, CO
2,000 Jewish National Fund, Pittsburgh, PA
1,100 American Jewish Committee, Denver, CO

Social Services

2,000 Kempe Children's Foundation, Denver, CO

STRIDE RITE CORP.

Company Contact

191 Spring Street
Lexington, MA 02173

Company Description

Employees: 2,400 (1999)
SIC(s): 3143 Men's Footwear Except Athletic, 3144 Women's Footwear Except Athletic, 3149 Footwear Except Rubber Nec, 5661 Shoe Stores.

Nonmonetary Support

Range: $900,000 - $1,000,000
Type: Donated Equipment; Donated Products
Contact: John Zelliher
Note: Nonmonetary support is handled through the corporation (see alternate address).

Stride Rite Foundation

Giving Contact

Ellen Sahl, Contact
Stride Rite Foundation
Review Committee
400 Atlantic Avenue
Boston, MA 02110
Phone: (617)574-4169
Fax: (617)574-6595

Description

Founded: 1953
EIN: 046059887
Organization Type: Corporate Foundation

Giving Locations: MA: Boston, Cambridge operating locations.
Grant Types: Capital, Employee Matching Gifts, Multiyear/Continuing Support, Operating Expenses, Scholarship.

Giving Philosophy

'The Stride Rite Foundation Review Committee provides funding for the operational activities of nonprofit organizations aimed at benefiting underprivileged inner-city children and families in the City of Boston and the City of Cambridge. Other giving is addressed through an employee matching gift program and corporate contributions to the United Way of Massachusetts Bay and other United Way chapters where company facilities are located. We therefore do not respond positively to special fundraising requests for operating support of United Way affiliates. Much of the Foundation's funding is dedicated to supporting Stride Rite sponsored charitable projects, which include funding of The Stride Rite Children's Center, The Stride Rite Intergenerational Center, The Stride Rite Public Service Programs at Harvard University and Northeastern University and other company sponsored charitable programs.' *The Stride Rite Foundation Guidelines for the Review Committee*

Financial Summary

Total Giving: $1,100,000 (fiscal year ending September 30, 1999 approx); $1,138,946 (fiscal 1998); $1,133,452 (fiscal 1997). Note: Contributes through corporate direct giving program and foundation.
Giving Analysis: Giving for fiscal 1997 includes: foundation ($1,075,057); foundation grants to United Way ($33,000); foundation matching gifts ($25,395); fiscal 1998: foundation ($1,072,278); foundation grants to United Way ($43,000); foundation matching gifts ($23,668)
Assets: $7,309,346 (fiscal 1998); $8,911,334 (fiscal 1997); $7,835,806 (fiscal 1996)
Gifts Received: $234,889 (fiscal 1998); $255,964 (fiscal 1997); $267,863 (fiscal 1996). Note: Contributions are received from the Stride Rite Philanthropic Foundation.

Typical Recipients

Arts & Humanities: Arts Associations & Councils, Arts Centers, Arts Festivals, Arts Institutes, Arts Outreach, Ballet, Community Arts, Dance, Arts & Humanities-General, Museums/Galleries, Music, Opera, Performing Arts, Public Broadcasting, Theater
Civic & Public Affairs: Botanical Gardens/Parks, Clubs, Community Foundations, Economic Development, Employment/Job Training, Civic & Public Affairs-General, Hispanic Affairs, Law & Justice, Philanthropic Organizations, Public Policy, Urban & Community Affairs, Women's Affairs, Zoos/Aquariums
Education: Afterschool/Enrichment Programs, Arts/Humanities Education, Colleges & Universities, Community & Junior Colleges, Education Funds, Education Reform, Education Reform, Education-General, Leadership Training, Literacy, Private Education (Precollege), Public Education (Precollege), Religious Education, School Volunteerism, Science/Mathematics Education, Student Aid
Environment: Resource Conservation
Health: Children's Health/Hospitals, Hospitals, Nursing Services
International: International Organizations, International Relief Efforts
Religion: Churches, Ministries, Religious Welfare
Science: Science Museums, Scientific Centers & Institutes
Social Services: Animal Protection, At-Risk Youth, Big Brother/Big Sister, Camps, Child Abuse, Child Welfare, Community Centers, Community Service Organizations, Counseling, Day Care, Delinquency & Criminal Rehabilitation, Family Services, Homes, People with Disabilities, Recreation & Athletics, Scouts, Senior Services, Shelters/Homelessness, Substance Abuse, United Funds/United Ways, Volunteer Services, YMCA/YWCA/YMHA/YWHA, Youth Organizations

Contributions Analysis

Giving Priorities: Child welfare and higher education.
Arts & Humanities: 2%. Grants often support museums, art centers, theater, dance, operas, and symphonies.
Civic & Public Affairs: 17%. Recipients include civic and public affairs groups and community organizations.
Education: 27%. Majority of funding supports precollege education. Other interests include higher education funded through Stride Rite's employee matching gift program.
Health: 3%. Primarily supports child welfare organizations. Recipients also include child recreational groups, including volunteer groups and community centers.
International: 1%.
Religion: 1%.
Social Services: 49%. Supports United Way, Big Brothers/Big Sisters, and children and family social service organizations.
Note: Total contributions made in 1998.

Application Procedures

Initial Contact: request for Grant Request Summary Form and the Stride Rite Foundation Application Procedure Checklist
Application Requirements: completed Grant Request Summary Form; statement of request (not to exceed five pages), include a brief description of program, program evaluation for the past year, relationship between program, agency's other activities and any parent organization; a copy of IRS determination letter Section 501(c)(3), including determination of non-private foundation status; brief description of agency background, accomplishments, mission and goals; detailed program budget; detailed agency budget; most recent audited financial statement; annual report; fundraising strategy, including list of last full year funders/amounts; names and positions of board members; calendar of events relating to the project for which the funding is sought; and if reapplying for funding, a two-page report on the use of prior funding
Deadlines: None.
Review Process: committee reviews proposals once per month
Evaluative Criteria: heavy emphasis on child welfare organizations in the Boston/Cambridge area; review committee takes notice of organizations which reach large numbers of children, have low costs per unit of service, and utilize volunteers
Decision Notification: responds within 90 days of each meeting
Notes: Foundation only reviews one proposal per organization during a calendar year.

Restrictions

Requests will not be considered for conferences, film production, scholarships, travel loans, research projects, curriculum development, publications, national organizations, construction projects, day care programs, or advertising.
The foundation generally does not support medical institutions, or long-term residential treatment facilities.
Grants are not made directly to individuals; individual public, private, or charter schools; or religious or political organizations.
Proposals that benefit children indirectly are not favorably reviewed.
Foundation giving is generally restricted to programs involving children, favoring the greater Boston area.

Additional Information

The foundation was endowed by the Stride Rite Philanthropic Foundation in 1995. The Philanthropic Foundation's assets were $4,256,239, and it's giving was $464,557 in 1995.

Foundation Officials

Arnold Selig Hiatt: chairman, director B Worcester, MA 1927. ED Harvard University BA (1948). CORP AFFIL director: Cabot Corp.; director: Dreyfus Fund. NONPR AFFIL chairman: Business Social Responsibility; trustee: Isabella Stewart Gardner Museum; member: American Footwear Industry Association.
Ellen Sahl: assistant to chairman

Grants Analysis

Disclosure Period: fiscal year ending September 30, 1998
Total Grants: $1,072,278*
Number of Grants: 92
Average Grant: $3,742*
Highest Grant: $386,000
Typical Range: $1,000 to $5,000
***Note:** Giving excludes United Way; matching gifts. Average grant excludes three highest grants ($739,228).

Recent Grants

Note: Grants derived from fiscal 1998 Form 990.

Arts & Humanities

3,000 The Computer Museum, Boston, MA
2,500 Artists for Humanity, Boston, MA
2,500 Cooperative Artists, Cambridge, MA
2,500 DAnce Collective, Mass Movement, Boston, MA
2,500 MJT Dance Company, Boston, MA
2,500 Museum of Fine Arts, Boston, MA
2,500 Very Special Arts, Boston, MA

Civic & Public Affairs

153,226 Stride Rite Phillanthropic Foundation, Lexington, MA
5,000 Strive/Boston Employment Service, Boston, MA
3,000 The B.E.L.L. Found, Cambridge, MA
3,000 Boston Urban Gardeners, Boston, MA
2,500 Anthony Spinazzola Foundation, Stoughton, MA
2,500 Casa Myma Vazquez, Boston, MA
2,500 New England Aquarium, Boston, MA
2,500 Project STEP, Inc., Boston, MA

Education

200,000 Harvard University, Cambridge, MA -- Phillips Brooks House Associates
50,000 BSR Education Fund, San Francisco, CA
3,000 Boston Algebra in Middle Schools, Boston, MA
3,000 Boston Partners in Education, Boston, MA
3,000 Project 10 East, Inc., Cambridge, MA
3,000 Summerbridge Cambridge, Cambridge, MA
2,500 Northeastern University, Boston, MA
2,500 Reach Out and Read, Boston, MA
2,500 Thompson Island Outward Bound, Boston, MA
2,500 WEATOC, Inc., Boston, MA

Health

30,000 Magic Me/Boston I, Boston, MA

International

15,000 Two Ten International Footwear Foundation, Boston, MA

Social Services

386,000 Stride Rite Foundation Children's Center, Lexingfon, MA
40,000 United Way of Massachusetts, Boston, MA
10,000 Cambridge School Volunteers, Cambridge, MA
9,300 Initiatives for Children, Houston, TX
5,000 Adolescant Consultation Services, Boston, MA

5,000	Cambridge Family and Children's Services, Boston, MA
4,000	Bridge Over Troubled Water, Boston, MA
3,500	YMCA Training Inc., Boston, MA
3,000	Boston Aging Concerns, Boston, MA
3,000	Families First Parenting Programs, Cambridge, MA
3,000	Handl-Kids, Boston, MA
3,000	United Way of Merrimack, Merrimack, NH
2,785	Pan Massachusetts Challenge, Boston, MA
2,500	Big Brother Association of Boston, Boston, MA
2,500	Big Sister Association of Boston, Boston, MA
2,500	Executive Service Corps, Boston, MA
2,500	Youth Advocacy Program, Detroit, MI

Student Loan Marketing Association

Company Contact
Washington, DC
Web: http://www.salliemae.com

Company Description
Also Known As: Sallie Mae.
Assets: US$47,629,900,000
Profit: US$496,400,000
Employees: 4,792
SIC(s): 6111 Federal & Federally-Sponsored Credit, 6159 Miscellaneous Business Credit Institutions.

Nonmonetary Support
Type: Cause-related Marketing & Promotion; Donated Equipment; In-kind Services; Loaned Employees; Loaned Executives

Corporate Sponsorship
Value: $5,000
Type: Arts & cultural events; Pledge-a-thon; Sports events

Sallie Mae Trust for Education

Giving Contact
Christopher Greene, Director of Corporate Philanthropy
Sallie Mae
11600 Sallie Mae Drive
Reston, VA 20193
Phone: (703)810-5175
Fax: (703)810-3106
Email: christopher.b.greene@slma.com

Alternate Contact
Marcia Rose Fuoss, Program Coordinator
Phone: (703)810-5373
Email: marciarose.fuoss@slma.com

Description
Organization Type: Corporate Giving Program
Giving Locations: FL: Panama City; KS: Lawrence; PA: Wilkes-Barr; TX: Killeen; VA: Reston primarily at headquarters and operating communities.
Grant Types: Award, Conference/Seminar, Emergency, Employee Matching Gifts, General Support, Matching, Multiyear/Continuing Support.
Note: Employee matching gift ratio: 3 to 1 for higher education; 2 to 1 for primary education, health and human services, and civic and community organizations; 1 to 1 for arts and culture organizations and United Way and federated campaigns.

Giving Philosophy
'The mission of the Sallie Mae Trust for Education is to: educate the general public about the value of education in individual lives and to society; strengthen the nation's college access and preparatory programs for at-risk youth; recognize outstanding teachers and encourage their retention in the field; and elevate the understanding of the role of the private sector in the national educational agenda.
'This mission is accomplished through: grants to individuals and institutions whose work in education is making a difference; development consumer education initiatives on the college financing process; support for research and training programs focused on educational issues through the Trust's non-profit affiliate, the Sallie Mae Education Institute; and employee volunteer activities.' *Sallie Mae Trust for Education Fact Sheet*

Financial Summary
Total Giving: $6,975,000 (1998 approx); $5,000,000 (1997 approx). Note: Contributes through Sallie Mae Trust for Education only.
Giving Analysis: Giving for 1998 includes: nonmonetary support ($1,975,000); corporate grants to United Way (approx $250,000)

Typical Recipients
Arts & Humanities: Arts & Humanities-General
Civic & Public Affairs: Civic & Public Affairs-General
Education: Education-General
Social Services: Social Services-General

Contributions Analysis
Giving Priorities: The trust focuses on education, including college access and preparatory programs for at-risk youth, consumer education on the college financing process, education finance research, and recognition and retention of outstanding teachers.

Application Procedures
Initial Contact: Call or write for guidelines.
Application Requirements: Send a brief (less than three pages) synopsis of the organization and the specific program to be funded; program success criteria; plans for evaluation; proof of tax-exempt status; and name, address, phone number, and e-mail address of contact person.
Deadlines: None.

Restrictions
Does not support religious organizations for sectarian purposes, political or lobbying groups, or individuals. Organizations must have 501(c)(3) status.

Additional Information
The Sallie Mae Trust for Education was established in 1999.

Corporate Officials
Lawrence Alan Hough: president, chief executive officer B Janesville, WI 1944. ED Stanford University (1966); Massachusetts Institute of Technology Sloan School of Management (1973). PRIM CORP EMPL president, chief executive officer: Student Loan Marketing Association. NONPR AFFIL chairman: Shakespeare Theatre Co.
Tracy McMahon: vice president

Stupp Brothers Bridge &Iron Co.

Company Contact
St. Louis, MO

Company Description
Employees: 700
SIC(s): 3441 Fabricated Structural Metal.

Stupp Brothers Bridge & Iron Co. Foundation

Giving Contact
Robert P. Stupp, Trustee
Stupp Brothers Bridge & Iron Co. Foundation
120 S. Central Ave., Suite 1650
St. Louis, MO 63105
Phone: (314)638-5000
Fax: (314)721-6334

Description
EIN: 237412437
Organization Type: Corporate Foundation. Supports preselected organizations only.
Giving Locations: MO
Grant Types: General Support.

Financial Summary
Total Giving: $637,055 (fiscal year ending October 31, 1998); $573,680 (fiscal 1997); $394,130 (fiscal 1996). Note: Contributes through foundation only.
Giving Analysis: Giving for fiscal 1997 includes: foundation ($503,680); foundation grants to United Way ($70,000); fiscal 1998: foundation ($567,055); foundation grants to United Way ($70,000)
Assets: $12,736,515 (fiscal 1998); $11,864,384 (fiscal 1997); $10,498,424 (fiscal 1996)

Typical Recipients
Arts & Humanities: Arts Associations & Councils, Arts Outreach, Arts & Humanities-General, History & Archaeology, Libraries, Museums/Galleries, Performing Arts
Civic & Public Affairs: Botanical Gardens/Parks, Clubs, Economic Development, Municipalities/Towns, Parades/Festivals, Philanthropic Organizations, Professional & Trade Associations, Urban & Community Affairs, Zoos/Aquariums
Education: Arts/Humanities Education, Business Education, Colleges & Universities, Education Funds, Education-General, Minority Education, Private Education (Precollege), Science/Mathematics Education, Secondary Education (Private)
Health: Cancer, Children's Health/Hospitals, Health Organizations, Hospices, Hospitals, Medical Research, Public Health, Single-Disease Health Associations
International: International Environmental Issues
Religion: Churches, Jewish Causes, Religious Organizations, Religious Welfare
Science: Science Museums, Scientific Centers & Institutes
Social Services: Animal Protection, At-Risk Youth, Camps, Child Welfare, Community Service Organizations, Family Planning, Family Services, Homes, People with Disabilities, Recreation & Athletics, Scouts, Senior Services, Special Olympics, Substance Abuse, United Funds/United Ways, YMCA/YWCA/YMHA/YWHA, Youth Organizations

Contributions Analysis
Arts & Humanities: 3%. Funds the historical society, performing arts, and the artists guild.
Civic & Public Affairs: 16%. Primarily supports the Capital Area United Givers Campaign and Tower Grove Park. Zoos, botanical gardens, and specialized foundations also received support.
Education: 46%. Colleges, universities, and secondary schools received support, as well as education funds and foundations.
Health: 4%. Funds children's hospitals, Hospice House, and health care concerns.
Religion: 13%. Mainly supports churches.
Science: 1%. Supports the Academy of Science and the St. Louis Science Center.
Social Services: 18%. Major support is given to the United Way. Other interests include traditional youth

organizations, community service groups, and child welfare.

Note: Total contributions made in fiscal 1998.

Corporate Officials

Erwin P. Stupp, Jr.: chairman, director B 1926. PRIM CORP EMPL chairman: Stupp Brothers Inc.

John P. Stupp, Jr.: executive vice president, chief operating officer, director B 1950. PRIM CORP EMPL executive vice president, chief operating officer, director: Stupp Brothers Inc. CORP AFFIL director: Atrion Corp.

Robert P. Stupp: president, director B Saint Louis, MO 1930. ED Washington University (1952). PRIM CORP EMPL president, director: Stupp Brothers Bridge & Iron Co. CORP AFFIL president: Stupp Metals; director: Laclede Gas Co.; senior vice president: Stupp Corp.; president: Builders Engr Co.; president: Fulton Iron Works International. NONPR AFFIL member: American Society Testing & Materials; member: Ancient Free Accepted Masons; fellow: American Society Civil Engineers; director: American Institute Steel Construction.

Foundation Officials

Erwin P. Stupp, Jr.: trustee (see above)
John P. Stupp, Jr.: trustee (see above)
Robert P. Stupp: trustee (see above)

Grants Analysis

Disclosure Period: fiscal year ending October 31, 1998
Total Grants: $567,055*
Number of Grants: 174
Average Grant: $3,259
Highest Grant: $140,750
Typical Range: $200 to $10,000
***Note:** Giving excludes United Way.

Recent Grants

Note: Grants derived from 1999 Form 990.

Arts & Humanities

3,250	Missouri Historical Society, St. Louis, MO
3,196	Arts & Education Council of St. Louis, St. Louis, MO
2,500	Magic House, St. Louis, MO
1,600	St. Louis Artists Guild, St. Louis, MO

Civic & Public Affairs

41,500	Tower Grove Park, St. Louis, MO
17,000	John Burroughs Foundation, St. Louis, MO
10,345	Safari Club International, Fenton, MO
7,700	St. Louis Zoo Friends Association, St. Louis, MO
3,500	VP Fair Foundation, St. Louis, MO
3,000	Missouri Botanical Garden, St. Louis, MO
2,180	Baton Rouge Green Association, Baton Rouge, LA
2,004	St. Louis 2004 Corporation, St. Louis, MO

Education

140,750	Mary Institute and St. Louis Country Day School, St. Louis, MO
27,845	College School Association, St. Louis, MO
21,345	Washington University, St. Louis, MO
15,750	AISC Education Foundation, Chicago, IL
15,750	Community School Association, St. Louis, MO
12,500	Episcopal High School, Baton Rouge, LA
10,345	Washington University School of Medicine, St. Louis, MO -- Cardiovascular
10,345	Washington University School of Medicine, St. Louis, MO -- Herpetic Keratitus
10,345	Washington University School of Medicine, St. Louis, MO -- Diabetic Research
10,345	Washington University School of Medicine, St. Louis, MO -- Gastroenterology
6,000	Lehigh University, Lehigh, PA
5,000	Missouri Colleges Fund, St. Louis, MO
4,800	William Jewel College, Liberty, MO
2,200	Academy of Science of St. Louis, St. Louis, MO
2,000	Junior Achievement of Mississippi Valley, Inc., St. Louis, MO
2,000	Louisiana Independent College Fund, Baton Rouge, LA
2,000	St. Louis University, St. Louis, MO
2,000	United Negro College Fund, St. Louis, MO

Health

10,345	Barnes - Jewish, Inc., St. Louis, MO
10,345	Missouri Baptist Health Care, St. Louis, MO
5,500	St. Louis Children's Hospital, St. Louis, MO
5,100	Shriners Hospital for Crippled Children, St. Louis, MO
2,500	Unity Health Hospice House, St. Louis, MO

Religion

24,350	Church of St. Michael & St. George, St. Louis, MO
7,500	St. Paul's Episcopal Church, St. Louis, MO
3,000	First Unitarian Church of St. Louis, St. Louis, MO
2,000	Salvation Army, St. Louis, MO

Science

3,000	St. Louis Science Center, St. Louis, MO

Social Services

50,000	United Way of Greater St. Louis, St. Louis, MO
20,000	Capital Area United Way, Baton Rouge, LA
10,345	Camp Leelanau & Kohahna Foundation, Maple City, MI
5,600	Boy Scouts of America, St. Louis, MO
5,400	Boys and Girls Town of Missouri, St. Louis, MO
3,200	Young Men's Christian Association of the Ozarks, Springfield, MO
2,000	Anti-Drug Abuse Education Fund, St. Louis, MO
2,000	Young Men's Christian Association, South County Branch, Wakefield, RI
1,600	Boys Club of St. Louis, St. Louis, MO
1,500	Family Care Center of Carondelet, Carondelet, MO

Subway Sandwich Shops, Inc.

Company Contact

Milford, CT
Web: http://www.subway.com

Company Description

SIC(s): 7311 Advertising Agencies.
Parent Company: Subway Franchise World Headquarters

Nonmonetary Support

Type: Donated Products

Giving Contact

Michele Klotzer, Public & Community Relations Director
Subway Franchise World Headquarters
325 Bic Drive
Milford, CT 06460
Phone: (203)877-4281
Fax: (203)876-6674

Description

Organization Type: Corporate Giving Program
Giving Locations: headquarters; nationally.
Grant Types: General Support.

Financial Summary

Total Giving: Company does not disclose contributions figures.

Typical Recipients

Education: Business-School Partnerships, Colleges & Universities, Education-General
Health: Multiple Sclerosis
Social Services: Food/Clothing Distribution, People with Disabilities, Senior Services

Application Procedures

Initial Contact: There are no formal application guidelines. Send a brief letter to the company.
Deadlines: None.

Additional Information

Company reports that approximately 99% of Subway restaurants are franchised.

Corporate Officials

Fred DeLuca: vice president B 1947. ED University of Bridgeport (1969). PRIM CORP EMPL vice president: Doctor's Associates Inc. CORP AFFIL president: Subway Equipment Leasing Corp.

Giving Program Officials

Michele Klotzer: manager PRIM CORP EMPL public & community relations director: Subway Franchise World Headquarters.

Sumitomo Bank

Company Contact

New York, NY

Company Description

SIC(s): 6081 Foreign Banks--Branches & Agencies.
Parent Company: Sumitomo Bank, Ltd., 6-5 Kitahama 4-chome, Chuo-ku, Osaka, Japan

Operating Locations

NY: Sumitomo Bank, New York Branch, New York

Sumitomo Bank Global Foundation

Giving Contact

Yasuhiko Imai, Assistant Treasurer
277 Park Ave.
New York, NY 10172
Phone: (212)224-4031

Description

Founded: 1995
EIN: 133766226
Organization Type: Corporate Foundation
Giving Locations: internationally, with emphasis on Asian countries;;;.

Financial Summary

Total Giving: $900,000 (1999 approx); $718,926 (1998); $213,932 (1997). Note: 1996 Giving includes scholarship ($131,700).
Assets: $11,314,677 (1996); $11,282,031 (1995); $10,138,210 (1994)
Gifts Received: $10,139,057 (1994). Note: In 1994, contributions were received from Sumitomo Bank.

Typical Recipients

Education: Student Aid
International: Foreign Educational Institutions

Application Procedures

Initial Contact: For direct contributions, the company has no formal application procedures and generally preselects recipients. For scholarship program, request application guidelines. Foundation may ask applicants to submit complete biographical records and supporting materials, including a report on academic and professional careers; a detailed statement of academic plans; a statement of plans and commitments after completion of academic program; letters of reference; lists of extracurricular activities; and any other information as may be requ ested by the selections committee. Applicant may also be required to demonstrate financial need for grant funds.

Restrictions

Recipients must be enrolled at an educational institution approved by the foundation or at which the foundation has established a scholarship grant program. The Foundation does not make grants to individuals.

Additional Information

In 1995, scholarships were provided for attendance at Thammasat University, Bangkok, Thailand; Chulalongkorn University, Bangkok, Thailand; Indonesia University, Jakarta, Indonesia; Airlangga University, Surabaya, Indonesia; Gadjah Mada University, Yogakarta, Indonesia; Padjadjaran University, Bandung, Indonesia; Peking University, Beijing, China; Zhongshan University, Quangdong, China; Peoples University of China, Beijing, China; University of International Business and Economics, Beijing, China; Beijing Foreign Studies University, Beijing, China; and Tsinghua University, Beijing, China.

Corporate Officials

Jane Hutta: general counsel, assistant treasurer, staff attorney PRIM CORP EMPL general counsel, assistant treasurer, staff attorney: Sumitomo Bank.
Ryuzo Kodama: director, head Americas Division PRIM CORP EMPL director, head Americas Division: Sumitomo Bank.
Natsuo Okada: president PRIM CORP EMPL president: Sumitomo Bank Securities. CORP AFFIL president: Sumitomo Bank Capital Markets.
Robert A. Rabbino, Jr.: joint general manager PRIM CORP EMPL joint general manager: Sumitomo Bank.
D. Scarborough Smith, III: joint general manager PRIM CORP EMPL joint general manager: Sumitomo Bank.
Nancy Z. Smith: vice president PRIM CORP EMPL vice president: Sumitomo Bank.

Foundation Officials

Jane Hutta: secretary (see above)
Ryuzo Kodama: director (see above)
Natsuo Okada: president, director (see above)
Robert A. Rabbino, Jr.: director (see above)
D. Scarborough Smith, III: director (see above)
Nancy Z. Smith: treasurer (see above)

Grants Analysis

Disclosure Period: calendar year ending 1996
Total Grants: $258,485*
Number of Grants: 1
Typical Range: $100,000 to $250,000
***Note:** Giving excludes scholarship.

Recent Grants

Note: Grants derived from 1996 Form 990.

Education

9,000 Airlangga University -- scholarship grant program

International

258,485 China Institute of Finance and Banking, People's Republic of China -- scholarship grant program
24,000 Chulalongkorn University, Bangkok, People's Republic of China -- scholarship grant program
24,000 Thammasat University -- scholarship grant program
11,000 Indonesia University -- scholarship grant program
9,000 Gajahmada University -- scholarship grant program
9,000 Padjajaran University -- scholarship grant program
8,000 Khon Kaen University -- scholarship grant program
4,000 Beijing Foreign Studies University, Beijing, People's Republic of China -- scholarship grant program
4,000 Dalian University of Foreign Languages -- scholarship grant program
4,000 Guangdong Foreign Studies University -- scholarship grant program
4,000 Guangdong Foreign Studies University -- scholarship grant program
4,000 Liaoning University -- scholarship grant program
4,000 People's University of China, People's Republic of China -- scholarship grant program
4,000 University of International Business and Economics -- scholarship grant program
4,000 Zhongshan University, Zhongshan, People's Republic of China -- scholarship grant program
3,700 China Institute of Finance and Banking, People's Republic of China -- scholarship grant program
2,000 Tsinghua University -- scholarship grant program

SUN MICROSYSTEMS INC.

Company Contact

Palo Alto, CA
Web: http://www.sun.com

Company Description

Revenue: US$11,726,300,000 (1999)
Employees: 18,785 (1999)
Fortune Rank: 150, per FORTUNE Magazine's list of 500 Largest U.S. Corporations (1999).
FF 150
SIC(s): 3577 Computer Peripheral Equipment Nec, 7371 Computer Programming Services, 7372 Prepackaged Software.

Operating Locations

Australia: Sun Microsystems Australia Pty.-Sydney, Artarmon, NSW; Sun Microsystems Australia Pty-Brisbane, Chapel Hill, QLD; Sun Microsystems of Australia Pty., Chatswood, NSW; Sun Microsystems Australia Pty.-Melbourne, Melbourne, VIC; Sun Microsystems Australia Pty.-Adelaide, Norwood, SA; Sun Microsystems Australia Pty.-Perth, Subiaco, WA; Sun Microsystems Australia Pty.-Canberra, Turner, ACT; Belgium: BIM SA, Everberg; Canada: Sun Microsystems of Canada, Calgary; Sun Microsystems of Canada-Edmonton, Edmonton; Sun Microsystems of Canada, Markham; Sun Microsystems of Canada-Ottawa, Ottawa; Sun Microsystems of Canada-Eastern Canada, Saint-Laurent; Sun Microsystems of Canada-Vancouver, Vancouver; Sun Microsystems of Canada-Winnipeg, Winnipeg; People's Republic of China: Sun Microsystems of California (Services), Beijing; Finland: Sun Microsystems AB, Espoo; France: Sun Microsystems France, Velizy-Villacoublay; Germany: Sun Microsystems GmbH, Grasbunn, Bayern; Hong Kong: Sun Microsystems of California, Hong Kong; Italy: Sun Microsystems Italia SpA, Milan; Japan: Nihon Sun Microsystems KK, Ibaraki, Tokyo; Republic of Korea: Sun Microsystems of California, Seoul; Netherlands: Sun Microsystems Nederland BV, Amersfoort, Utrecht; Philippines: Philippine Sunsystems Products Inc., Manila; Singapore: Sun Microsystems of California, Singapore; Spain: Sun Microsystems Iberica SA, Madrid; Sweden: Sun Microsystems AB, Solna; Switzerland: Sun Microsystems (Suisse) SA, Gland; Sun Microsystems (Schweiz) AG, Schwerzenbach, Zurich; Thailand: Sun Microsystems of California, Bangkok; Taiwan:, Taipei; United Kingdom: Sun Microsystems Europe Inc., Bagshot, Surrey; Sun Microsystems Ltd., Camberley, Surrey
Note: Operates offices in 63 foreign countries, including Brazil, China, Japan, Norway, Peru, Singapore, and the United Kingdom.

Nonmonetary Support

Type: Donated Products; In-kind Services; Workplace Solicitation
Volunteer Programs: Sun Microsystem's Community Action Volunteer Program provides employees with a wide range of volunteer opportunities. Through the Open Gateways program, employees volunteer to provide technical support and training for schools and teachers to make meaningful use of technology in the classroom. Employee volunteers also participate in the Sun Foundation's grant review process. Worldwide Volunteer Week allows for more concentrated efforts by company volunteers.
Note: Workplace solicitation is offered to the United Way Progressive Way, Earth Share/Environmental Federation, International service agencies, combined health appeal, and community works.

Corporate Sponsorship

Type: Sports events
Note: Sponsors the World Cup and America's Cup tournaments.

Sun Microsystems Foundation, Inc.

Giving Contact

Gary F. Serda, Manager, Corporate Affairs
Sun Microsystems Foundation, Inc.
Mail Stop UPAL01-462
901 San Antonio Road
Palo Alto, CA 94303
Phone: (650)336-0487
Fax: (650)856-2114
Email: corpaffr@corp.sun.com

Description

Founded: 1990
EIN: 770244198
Organization Type: Corporate Foundation
Giving Locations: CA: South San Francisco Bay Area; CO: Denver the Front Page Communities (up to and including Longmont); MA: Merrimack Valley West Lothian District.
Grant Types: Emergency, Employee Matching Gifts, Multiyear/Continuing Support.
Note: Employee matching gift ratio: 1 to 1, up to $1,000 per employee per year.

Giving Philosophy

'Effective community development calls for long-term commitment. It requires focused, meaningful programs that enable a community to develop from within. It's an investment in potential -- a process of building people's capacity to participate fully in society. .. Sun's community involvement programs are based on the premise that Sun is part of the community, not apart from it. With this in mind, the company's efforts focus on people in surrounding communities in need. Sun's programs are designed to enable those who historically have been least positioned to help themselves get on the economic ladder.'

'Through direct grants, coordinated volunteer efforts, and more, Sun's programs provide support for economic improvement of surrounding communities through job training, education, leadership development, and business enterprise development. Sun is working with community-based organizations, intermediary groups, community-based development corporations, and other nonprofits to achieve these ends.' *Sun Corporate Affairs Community Involvement Programs* pamphlet

Financial Summary

Total Giving: $1,228,623 (fiscal year ending June 30, 1998); $1,643,241 (fiscal 1997); $1,079,346 (fiscal 1996). Note: Contributes through foundation only.
Giving Analysis: Giving for fiscal 1996 includes: foundation ($1,075,975); foundation grants to United Way ($3,371); fiscal 1997: foundation ($1,049,655); foundation matching gifts ($593,586); fiscal 1998: foundation matching gifts ($775,322); foundation ($453,301)
Assets: $4,187,000 (fiscal 1998); $3,792,794 (fiscal 1997); $2,899,150 (fiscal 1996)
Gifts Received: $1,394,506 (fiscal 1998); $2,247,166 (fiscal 1997); $739,650 (fiscal 1996). Note: In 1998, contributions were received from Sun Microsystems Inc. and Robert F. Sproull.

Typical Recipients

Arts & Humanities: Museums/Galleries, Opera
Civic & Public Affairs: Asian American Affairs, Business/Free Enterprise, Chambers of Commerce, Community Foundations, Economic Development, Employment/Job Training, Civic & Public Affairs-General, Housing, Law & Justice, Municipalities/Towns, Public Policy, Urban & Community Affairs, Women's Affairs, Zoos/Aquariums
Education: Business Education, Colleges & Universities, Community & Junior Colleges, Education Associations, Elementary Education (Public), Engineering/Technological Education, Education-General, Minority Education, Private Education (Precollege), Public Education (Precollege), Science/Mathematics Education, Secondary Education (Private), Secondary Education (Public), Student Aid, Vocational & Technical Education
Environment: Environment-General, Resource Conservation
Health: AIDS/HIV, Cancer, Children's Health/Hospitals, Emergency/Ambulance Services, Heart, Hospitals
International: Foreign Educational Institutions, International Affairs, International Environmental Issues
Religion: Ministries, Religious Welfare
Science: Science Museums
Social Services: Big Brother/Big Sister, Community Centers, Community Service Organizations, Counseling, Day Care, Delinquency & Criminal Rehabilitation, Family Services, Food/Clothing Distribution, People with Disabilities, Recreation & Athletics, United Funds/United Ways, YMCA/YWCA/YMHA/YWHA, Youth Organizations

Contributions Analysis

Giving Priorities: Pre-college education, civic organizations, and religious causes.
Civic & Public Affairs: 10% to 15%. Supports projects that close the gap in the current employment development system; projects which help reverse conditions of high unemployment and low income; provide job placement and counseling; work closely with the industry; and provide training for occupations that are in high demand.
Education: 55% to 60%. Supports 7-12 education which prepares young people for the workforce and for lifelong learning. Supported programs incorporate target population's needs and interests; programs designed to increase education; projects that reverse unsatisfactory academic school performance; engage students in activities that enable them to make experiential connections between learning and real life; foster motivation and improve academic skills; and improve college readiness. Also supports higher education through equipment donations, collaborative and sponsored research; and university affiliate programs.
Health: Less than 5%. Funds children's hospitals.
International: Less than 5%. Funds international programs and world wildlife.
Religion: 5% to 10%. Funds religious causes.
Science: Less than 5%. Funds go to the San Jose Discovery Museum.

Application Procedures

Initial Contact: Request guidelines, then submit a three-page concept paper.
Application Requirements: Included the organization's mission and goals; description of the target population, project, and rationale; amount requested; plan for evaluation; roles and responsibilities of key project participants; qualifications of key staff; and proof of tax-exempt status.
Deadlines: For concept papers: May 15 or November 15; for full proposal: July 15 or Janурay 15.
Review Process: If the organization's concept paper is accepted, the organization will be invited within one month of concept paper deadline to submit full proposal; nonprofit organizations will then have one month to prepare a full proposal; a committee of Sun employee volunteers will evaluate proposals and make recommendations to the Corporate Affairs department.
Evaluative Criteria: The foundation considers whether the project falls within giving priorities; whether the organization services the populations and communities where company has majority of work force; and whether the program serves an emerging population.
Decision Notification: For invitations for full proposals: 2lJune 15 or 2lDecember 15; grants are awarded in mid-to-late September or mid-to-late March.
Notes: Company reports funding cycle will take approximately three months.

Restrictions

Foundation does not fund fundraising activities, such as benefits, charitable dinners, or sporting events; goodwill advertising; religious, fraternal, or sports organizations; political causes, candidates, organizations, or campaigns; books, magazines, or articles in professional journals; endowments or capital campaigns; hospitals, health, and disease-specific organizations; purchase of capital equipment; requests for general operating support; or individuals.
An institution may receive no more than three grants for a single project. Previous grant recipients may not apply for additional funding until terms or prior grant have been met and final report submitted.
No grants are made over $50,000.

Additional Information

The company provides hardware resources to eligible organizations that help define and create future of computer and information technology through the Academic Equipment Grants Program.
Publications: Program Guidelines

Corporate Officials

Scott G. McNealy: chairman, chief executive officer, director B Columbus, IN 1954. ED Harvard University BA (1976); Stanford University Graduate School of Business Administration MBA (1980). PRIM CORP EMPL chairman, chief executive officer, director: Sun Microsystems Inc.

Foundation Officials

Kenneth M. Alveres: president
Michael E. Lehman: director B 1950. ED University of Wisconsin BA (1974). PRIM CORP EMPL vice president, chief financial officer: Sun Microsystems Inc.
Michael H. Morris: secretary, director B 1948. ED Northwestern University BA (1970); University of Michigan JD (1974). PRIM CORP EMPL vice president, general counsel, secretary: Sun Microsystems Inc.
Gary F. Serda: manager corporate affairs
Mark Vermilion: executive director

Grants Analysis

Disclosure Period: fiscal year ending June 30, 1997
Total Grants: $1,049,655*
Number of Grants: 146
Average Grant: $7,189
Highest Grant: $82,050
Typical Range: $1,000 to $25,000
*Note: Giving excludes matching gifts.

Recent Grants

Note: Grants derived from fiscal 1997 Form 990.

Civic & Public Affairs

50,000	Center for Employment Training, San Jose, CA -- economic development, employment
35,000	Emergency Housing, San Jose, CA -- human services
30,000	Women's Center, Vienna, VA -- human services
12,500	City Year, San Jose, CA -- school support
10,000	WATCH, Milpitas, CA -- economic development, employment

Education

50,000	Massachusetts Networks, Cambridge, MA -- school support
50,000	Peninsula Community Foundation, San Mateo, CA -- school support
50,000	Society of Women Engineers, Sunnyvale, CA -- school support
49,700	Plugged In, East Palo Alto, CA -- school support
40,000	CIS, 49ers Academy, East Palo Alto, CA -- school support
38,000	San Jose State University Foundation, San Jose, CA -- support school
35,000	Milpitas High School, Milpitas, CA -- school support
29,340	Merrimack College, North Andover, CA -- school support
25,000	East Side High School District, San Jose, CA -- support school
25,000	Merrimack Education Center, Chelmsford, MA -- school support
25,000	Peninsula Community Foundation, San Mateo, CA -- school support
25,000	Santa Clara County Office, San Jose, CA -- school support
23,000	Peninsula Omega YC, Menlo Park, CA -- school support
20,000	Peninsula Bridge Program, Menlo Park, CA -- school support
17,500	Sacred Heart Community Service, San Jose, CA -- school support
15,000	Coalition for A Better Acre, Lowell, MA -- school support
15,000	MESA, Oakland, CA -- school support
15,000	NAFT, San Mateo, CA -- school support
13,894	Fremont Union High School, Sunnyvale, CA -- school support
10,000	American Leadership Forum, Los Altos, CA -- scholarships, fellowships
1,050	Hayward High School, Hayward, CA -- school support
1,000	Agassiz Elementary School, Jamaica Plain, MA -- school support
1,000	Bromfield School, Harvard, MA -- school support
1,000	Eisenhower Elementary, Santa Clara, CA -- school support

1,000 Gate School, Acton, MA -- school support
1,000 Grandin Miller Elementary, San Jose, CA -- school support
1,000 Longfellow Elementary, Albuquerque, NM -- school support
1,000 Thomas Russell Middle School, Milpitas, CA -- school support
1,000 Toyon Elementary School, San Jose, CA -- school support
1,000 Turn of the River School, Stamford, CT -- school support
1,000 Venice High School, Los Angeles, CA -- school support
1,000 Vernonia High School, Vernonia, CA -- school support

Environment
2,229 Nature Conservancy, Arlington, VA -- environmental

Health
9,000 Children's Hospital Foundation, Columbus, OH -- hospital support

International
12,250 St. Kentigen's Academy, West Lothian, England -- school support
9,030 Armadale Academy, Armadale, Scotland
6,925 Mappa Mondo, Hollano, Honduras -- educational
1,100 World Wildlife Fund, Washington, DC -- environmental

Religion
82,050 Catholic Charities, San Jose, CA -- economic development, employment

Science
20,000 San Jose Discovery Museum, San Jose, CA -- economical development, employment

Social Services
40,000 Acre Day Care, Lowell, MA -- economic development, employment
30,000 YWCA, Lawrence, MA -- school support
25,000 Bay Area Community Resources, Larkspur, CA -- school support
25,000 United Way of Merrimack, Lawrence, MA -- human services
1,500 Family Giving Tree, Palo Alto, CA -- human services

SUNMARK CAPITAL CORP.

Company Contact

St. Louis, MO

Company Description

SIC(s): 2064 Candy & Other Confectionery Products, 2068 Salted & Roasted Nuts & Seeds.

Sunmark Foundation

Giving Contact

Kathryn Ruzicka, Executive Secretary
Sunmark Foundation
16100 Chesterfield Parkway West, Suite 395
Chesterfield, MO 63017
Phone: (636)537-4800

Description

Founded: 1964
EIN: 436061564
Organization Type: Corporate Foundation. Supports preselected organizations only.
Giving Locations: nationally.
Grant Types: General Support.

Financial Summary

Total Giving: $400,000 (fiscal year ending January 31, 2000 approx); $2,000 (fiscal 1999); $395,000 (fiscal 1998 approx). Note: Contributes through foundation only.
Assets: $2,389,123 (fiscal 1999); $1,990,081 (fiscal 1997); $2,351,853 (fiscal 1996)
Gifts Received: $700,000 (fiscal 1996); $350,000 (fiscal 1994); $304,706 (fiscal 1991). Note: Contributions are received from Menlo F. Smith.

Typical Recipients

Arts & Humanities: Film & Video, Public Broadcasting
Civic & Public Affairs: Business/Free Enterprise, Civil Rights, Clubs, Economic Development, Economic Policy, Law & Justice, Legal Aid, Nonprofit Management, Philanthropic Organizations, Professional & Trade Associations, Public Policy, Rural Affairs, Women's Affairs
Education: Business Education, Colleges & Universities, Economic Education, Education Associations, Education Funds, Education Reform, Education-General, Journalism/Media Education, Legal Education, Social Sciences Education
International: International Development, International Peace & Security Issues, International Relations
Religion: Religious Organizations, Religious Welfare, Social/Policy Issues
Social Services: Animal Protection, Community Service Organizations, Youth Organizations

Contributions Analysis

Giving Priorities: Emphasis on free market enterprise, public policy, and education.
Arts & Humanities: 1%. Focus on public broadcasting.
Civic & Public Affairs: 48%. Funding supports free market enterprise, public policy, economic policy, and professional trade associations.
Education: 10%. Focus on colleges and universities, business education, education foundations, journalism, and economic education.
International: 36%. Supports international enterprise development and security policy.
Religion: 3%. Social policy and religious organizations receive support.
Social Services: 2%. Funds social services.
Note: In fiscal 1999, the foundation awarded one grant, to the Junior Achievement of the Mississippi Valley in Hazelwood, MO.

Restrictions

The foundation supports tax-exempt organizations for research purposes only. The foundation does not make grants to individuals.

Additional Information

The foundation supports organizations that work to preserve and develop the free enterprise system and its basic underlying principles of individual freedom and responsibility, private property, and limited constitutional government. It does not support activities outside this field of interest and does not support general charity appeals.

Foundation Officials

Stephanie Lee: trustee
John Prentis: trustee
John Reed: trustee
Menlo F. Smith: trustee

Grants Analysis

Disclosure Period: fiscal year ending January 31, 1997
Total Grants: $610,515
Number of Grants: 41
Average Grant: $14,891
Highest Grant: $212,815
Typical Range: $1,000 to $10,000

Recent Grants

Note: Grants derived from 1997 Form 990.

Arts & Humanities
5,000 Radio America, Richmond Heights, MO

Civic & Public Affairs
60,000 National Right to Work Legal Fund, Springfield, VA
35,000 Heritage Foundation, Washington, DC
25,000 Center on National Labor Policy, North Springfield, VA
25,000 National Institute for Labor Relations, Springfield, VA
25,000 Young America's Foundation, Herndon, VA
15,000 Cato Institute, Washington, DC
15,000 National Center for Neighborhood Enterprise, Washington, DC
13,000 Atlas Economic Research Foundation, Fairfax, VA
12,000 Capitol Research Center, Washington, DC
10,000 Sutherland Institute
7,000 Leadership Institute, Springfield, VA
6,000 Hudson Institute, Indianapolis, IN
5,000 American Legislative Exchange Council, Washington, DC
5,000 Institute for Political Economy, Washington, DC
5,000 National Coalition for Protection
4,000 Independent Women's Forum, Arlington, VA
4,000 Locke Institute
4,000 National Foundation for Teaching Entrepreneurs
4,000 Students for Free Enterprise, Springfield, MO
3,000 Philanthropy Roundtable, Indianapolis, IN
3,000 Reason Foundation, Santa Monica, CA
2,000 American Enterprise Institute, Washington, DC
2,000 American Spectator Educational Foundation, Arlington, VA
2,000 Discussion Club, Saint Louis, MO

Education
8,000 George Mason University Foundation Law and Economics Center, Fairfax, VA
8,000 Hillsdale College, Hillsdale, MI
8,000 Intercollegiate Studies Institute, Bryn Mawr, PA
8,000 National Journalism School, Education, and Research Institute
7,000 Center for Study of American Business
7,000 Foundation for Economic Education, Irvington, NY
7,000 Fund for American Studies, Washington, DC
4,000 Center for Education Reform, Washington, DC
3,000 George Mason University Foundation, Fairfax, VA -- for Bennett Research
1,200 Junior Achievement Mississippi Valley, Hazelwood, MO

International
212,815 International Enterprise Development Foundation -- for Enterprise Mentors
8,000 Center for Security Policy, Washington, DC

Religion
10,000 Acton Institute for the Study of Religion and LIberty, Grand Rapids, MI
10,000 Christian Anti-Communism Crusade, Long Beach, CA
500 Cardinal Mindszenty Foundation, Saint Louis, MO

Social Services
12,000 Institute for Humane Studies, Fairfax, VA

Sunoco Inc.

Company Contact
Philadelphia, PA

Company Description
Former Name: Sun Co. Inc.
Revenue: US$8,485,000,000 (1999)
Profit: US$97,000,000 (1999)
Employees: 12,150
Fortune Rank: 211, per FORTUNE Magazine's list of 500 Largest U.S. Corporations (1999).
FF 211
SIC(s): 1311 Crude Petroleum & Natural Gas, 1321 Natural Gas Liquids, 2911 Petroleum Refining, 4612 Crude Petroleum Pipelines.

Nonmonetary Support
Value: $100,000 (1991)
Type: Cause-related Marketing & Promotion; Workplace Solicitation
Note: The company provides workplace solicitation for the United Way only.

Corporate Sponsorship
Type: Arts & cultural events; Music & entertainment events; Pledge-a-thon

Giving Contact
Barbara Nearon, Contributions Administrator
Sunoco Inc.
1801 Market Street
Philadelphia, PA 19103
Phone: (215)977-3401
Fax: (215)246-8562

Description
Organization Type: Corporate Giving Program
Giving Locations: PA: Philadelphia operating locations.
Grant Types: Employee Matching Gifts, General Support.

Giving Philosophy
'Sun Company believes that its Corporate Contributions Program is a key part of the Company's response to the public's economic and social needs. The purpose of this program, then, is to help improve the intellectual, economic, social, and cultural environments in those communities within the continental United States where the corporation has a major presence.' Sun Contributions Programs

Financial Summary
Total Giving: $2,000,000 (2000 approx); $2,000,000 (1999 approx); $2,000,000 (1998 approx). Note: Contributes through corporate direct giving program only.

Typical Recipients
Arts & Humanities: Arts Associations & Councils, Arts Centers, Dance, Museums/Galleries, Music, Performing Arts
Civic & Public Affairs: Business/Free Enterprise, Economic Development, Employment/Job Training, Public Policy, Urban & Community Affairs
Education: Business Education, Colleges & Universities, Education Associations, Engineering/Technological Education, Literacy, Minority Education, Public Education (Precollege), Science/Mathematics Education, Student Aid
Health: Hospitals, Public Health
Social Services: Community Service Organizations, Emergency Relief, People with Disabilities, Senior Services, Substance Abuse, United Funds/United Ways, Youth Organizations

Contributions Analysis
Giving Priorities: Higher education, economic development, employment opportunities, health, and social welfare. Company does not make contributions for international purposes either domestically or through foreign operating companies.
Arts & Humanities: 10% to 15%. Museums, theaters, dance companies, and visual and performing arts programs.
Civic & Public Affairs: 15% to 20%. Organizations that promote economic development and employment opportunities. (Public Policy) About 15%. Nonpartisan organizations engaged in public policy issues and economic research important to company interests; groups promoting government efficiency; and organizations concerned with the allocation of public funds.
Education: About 25%. Major support to higher education. Other recipients include minority education and education associations.
Health: 30% to 35%. Primarily supports the United Way. Also supports hospitals, community service organizations, and youth organizations.

Application Procedures
Initial Contact: Send a letter to the company's headquarters or a local Sun facility.
Application Requirements: Include a brief history of the organization, list of key management and board members, number of paid employees and volunteers, annual report or update of activities, latest audited financial report, current operating budget and sources of income, and copy of current tax-exempt status. Requests for program support also should include purpose and objective; need addressed; population served; plan of action and time frame; qualifications of administrators; total funding required; and projected sources, evaluative criteria, and utilization of results.
Deadlines: None.
Evaluative Criteria: Proposals are judged according to the incidence and severity of the problem; level of funding available from other sources; likelihood that a Sun grant will bring about a desired solution; and the ability to effect a long-term solution.

Restrictions
Company does not support political parties or candidates, individuals, or organizations that are not tax-exempt; generally does not support veterans, labor, religious, fraternal, or athletic groups; goodwill advertising or benefit fund raisers; or funding to cover continuing operating deficits.

Additional Information
Contributions program focuses on needs of company's operating locations, primarily in the Philadelphia area. In view of the company's restructuring and budget reductions, new grant applications are not encouraged at this time.

Corporate Officials
Robert Henderson Campbell: chairman, chief executive officer B Pittsburgh, PA 1937. ED Princeton University BS (1959); Carnegie Mellon University MS (1961); Massachusetts Institute of Technology MA (1978). PRIM CORP EMPL chairman, chief executive officer: Sunoco Inc. CORP AFFIL director: Philadelphia National Bank; director: Hershey Foods Corp.; director: CIGNA Corp.; director: Elwyn Institute. NONPR AFFIL member: American Petroleum Institute.
Don Drosdick: president PRIM CORP EMPL president: Sunoco Inc.
Kenneth D. Hill: vice president B Bryn Mawr, PA 1938. ED Temple University (1958); University of Pennsylvania (1972); Harvard University PMD (1980). PRIM CORP EMPL vice president: Sunoco Inc.
Sheldon Lee Thompson: senior vice president, chief administrative officer B Minneapolis, MN 1938. ED University of Minnesota BS (1960); University of Minnesota MS (1962); Harvard University Advanced Management Program (1983). PRIM CORP EMPL senior vice president, chief administrative officer: Sunoco Inc. ADD CORP EMPL senior vice president, chief administrative officer: Sun Co. Inc. NONPR AFFIL trustee: Temple University School Podiatric Medicine Foundation; member executive education advisory board: University Pennsylvania Wharton School Business; trustee: Philadelphia Orchestra Association; trustee: Philadelphia Theatre Co.; trustee: Arts Business Council; member executive committee: Greater Philadelphia Chamber of Commerce; trustee: Academy Natural Science; member: Alche.

Giving Program Officials
Barbara Nearon: contributions administration

Grants Analysis
Disclosure Period: calendar year ending

Suntrust Bank Atlanta

Company Contact
Atlanta, GA
Web: http://www.suntrust.com

Company Description
Former Name: Trust Co. Bank.
Employees: 2,850
SIC(s): 6022 State Commercial Banks.
Parent Company: SunTrust Banks, Inc., Atlanta, GA, United States

Operating Locations
Operates numerous branches in Fulton and Dekalb counties.

Nonmonetary Support
Type: Donated Equipment; Loaned Employees; Loaned Executives; Workplace Solicitation
Contact: Ed Bishop, Vice President
Note: Company provides nonmonetary support.

Corporate Sponsorship
Type: Arts & cultural events; Festivals/fairs; Pledge-a-thon; Sports events
Note: Sponsors fundraising events (charity balls, etc.). Individual department heads make sponsorship decisions.

SunTrust Bank Atlanta Foundation

Giving Contact
Mr. William R. Bowdoin, Jr., First Vice President/Secretary
SunTrust Bank Atlanta Foundation
Mail Code 041
PO Box 4418
Atlanta, GA 30302
Phone: (404)588-8246
Fax: (404)230-5550

Description
EIN: 586026063
Organization Type: Corporate Foundation
Giving Locations: GA: Atlanta metropolitan area
Grant Types: Capital, Employee Matching Gifts, General Support, Operating Expenses, Project, Research, Seed Money.

Giving Philosophy
'Trust Company of Georgia Foundation was established in 1959 to provide a continuing means of supporting worthwhile educational, cultural, and human services programs in our community. Trust Company

supports the healthy development of metropolitan Atlanta through Foundation donations based on a positive philosophy of good corporate citizenship and an awareness of economic interdependence between the bank and its home community.' Trust Company of Georgia Foundation Summary of Policies

Financial Summary

Total Giving: $1,800,000 (1999 approx); $1,742,718 (1998); $2,285,171 (1997). Note: Contributes through corporate direct giving program and foundation.
Giving Analysis: Giving for 1997 includes: foundation ($1,272,495); foundation grants to United Way ($1,012,676); 1998: foundation ($1,167,268); foundation grants to United Way ($575,450)
Assets: $19,696,229 (1998); $18,232,561 (1997); $15,927,323 (1996)
Gifts Received: $2,225,000 (1997); $795,238 (1996). Note: Gifts received from SunTrust Bank; cash for matching charitable donations.

Typical Recipients

Arts & Humanities: Arts Appreciation, Arts Associations & Councils, Arts Centers, Arts Festivals, Arts Funds, Ballet, Community Arts, Dance, Ethnic & Folk Arts, Historic Preservation, History & Archaeology, Libraries, Museums/Galleries, Music, Opera, Performing Arts, Public Broadcasting, Theater
Civic & Public Affairs: Botanical Gardens/Parks, Business/Free Enterprise, Chambers of Commerce, Civil Rights, Community Foundations, Economic Development, Economic Policy, Employment/Job Training, Civic & Public Affairs-General, Housing, Law & Justice, Legal Aid, Municipalities/Towns, Nonprofit Management, Public Policy, Safety, Urban & Community Affairs, Women's Affairs, Zoos/Aquariums
Education: Arts/Humanities Education, Business Education, Colleges & Universities, Economic Education, Education Funds, Engineering/Technological Education, International Exchange, International Studies, Legal Education, Medical Education, Minority Education, Private Education (Precollege), Public Education (Precollege), Religious Education, Science/Mathematics Education, Special Education, Vocational & Technical Education
Environment: Environment-General, Resource Conservation
Health: Alzheimers Disease, Children's Health/Hospitals, Clinics/Medical Centers, Emergency/Ambulance Services, Geriatric Health, Health Organizations, Hospitals, Medical Rehabilitation, Medical Training, Mental Health, Nursing Services, Public Health, Single-Disease Health Associations
Religion: Jewish Causes
Science: Scientific Centers & Institutes
Social Services: Child Welfare, Community Centers, Community Service Organizations, Counseling, Delinquency & Criminal Rehabilitation, Domestic Violence, Emergency Relief, Family Services, Food/Clothing Distribution, Homes, People with Disabilities, Recreation & Athletics, Senior Services, Shelters/Homelessness, Substance Abuse, United Funds/United Ways, Youth Organizations

Contributions Analysis

Giving Priorities: Social welfare, education, the arts, and civic affairs.
Arts & Humanities: 17%. Supports major Atlanta arts organizations and centers through direct grants and arts funds. Interests include dance, history, and public broadcasting.
Civic & Public Affairs: 8%. Interests include urban and community affairs, economic development, municipalities, philanthropic organizations, botanical gardens, and zoos.
Education: 23%. Primarily supports colleges and universities. Private schools are also major recipients, including religious institutions. The remainder supports business and economic education, minority education, international studies, and secondary education. Also sponsors matching gifts program.
Health: 2%. Supports medical clinics and the American Red Cross.
Religion: 2%. Funds the Atlanta Jewish Federation.
Social Services: 48%. Supports human service organizations primarily through the United Way of Metropolitan Atlanta. Other interests include youth organizations, child welfare, community service organizations, family services, and recreation and athletics.
Note: Total contributions made in 1998.

Application Procedures

Initial Contact: Request guidelines and Fact Sheet from the foundation.
Application Requirements: Submit the completed Fact Sheet for grant consideration. Include the following supporting materials: IRS determination letter, list of board of directors and their affiliations, relevant financial material, and case statement or other concise supporting material.
Deadlines: November 30, March 31, or August 31.
Review Process: Applications are summarized and presented quarterly to the distribution committee.
Evaluative Criteria: Emphasis on metropolitan Atlanta, community benefit, project/community coordination and support, timeliness and precedence, organization management and governance, grant multiplier effect, human value and self-help emphasis, and financial management.
Decision Notification: Notification made by letter following meetings held in January, May, and October.

Restrictions

Foundation does not make loans or grants for maintenance or debt service. Does not support political organizations, churches, or individuals.

Additional Information

Nonmatching grants may be made to national organizations, but must benefit the metropolitan Atlanta area.
The committee expects periodic program reports from recipients.
Publications: Application Guidelines

Corporate Officials

William R. Bowdoin, Jr.: first vice president B Birmingham, AL 1944. ED University of Georgia (1966). PRIM CORP EMPL first vice president: SunTrust Bank Atlanta. CORP AFFIL director: Suntrust Bank Northwest Georgia N.A.
Robert R. Long: chairman B 1937. ED Auburn University (1959); Harvard University (1967). PRIM CORP EMPL chairman: SunTrust Bank Atlanta ADD CORP EMPL director: SunTrust Service Corp.; chairman: SunTrust Bank Georgia Inc.

Foundation Officials

William R. Bowdoin, Jr.: secretary (see above)
L. Phillip Humann: member PRIM CORP EMPL director: SunTrust Bank Atlanta. CORP AFFIL director: SunTrust Banks Georgia Inc.; chairman, chief executive officer: SunTrust Banks Inc.; director: Haverty Furniture Companies Inc.; director: Coca-Cola Enterprises Inc.; director: Equifax Inc.
Robert R. Long: chairman (see above)
John William Spiegel: member B Indianapolis, IN 1941. ED Wabash College (1963); Emory University (1965). PRIM CORP EMPL executive vice president, chief financial officer: SunTrust Bank Atlanta. CORP AFFIL director: Rock Tennessee Texas Co.; executive vice president: SunTrust Banks Georgia Inc.; director: Rock Tenn Co. CLUB AFFIL Cherokee Town & Country Club.
Edward Jenner Wood: member B Danville, VA 1951. ED University of North Carolina (1974); Georgia State University (1984). PRIM CORP EMPL executive vice president, trust & Investment Services: SunTrust Banks Inc. CORP AFFIL director: Crawford & Co.; director: Oxford Industries Inc.; director: Cotton Studies Life Insurance Co.

Grants Analysis

Disclosure Period: calendar year ending 1998
Total Grants: $1,167,268*
Number of Grants: 608
Average Grant: $1,920
Highest Grant: $125,000
Typical Range: $3,000 to $5,000
*Note: Giving excludes United Way.

Recent Grants

Note: Grants derived from 1998 Form 990.

Arts & Humanities

125,000	Woodruff Arts Center, Atlanta, GA
20,000	Telfair Museum Of Art, Savannah, GA
18,450	Woodruff Arts Center, Atlanta, GA
13,839	Woodruff Arts Center, Atlanta, GA
10,000	Classic Center, Athens, GA
7,560	High Museum Of Art, Atlanta, GA
7,500	Atlanta Historical Society, Inc., Atlanta, GA
7,190	High Museum Of Art, Atlanta, GA

Civic & Public Affairs

25,000	The Atlanta Project, Atlanta, GA
12,500	Atlanta Neighborhood Development Partnership, Atlanta, GA
10,000	Macon 2000, Macon, GA
10,000	Newtown Macon, Inc., Macon, GA
10,000	Research Atlanta, Atlanta, GA
7,500	Atlanta Botanical Garden, Atlanta, GA
7,500	Zoo Atlanta, Atlanta, GA
7,500	Zoo Atlanta, Atlanta, GA
6,762	Zoo Atlanta, Atlanta, GA
6,250	Wesley Wood, Atlanta, GA

Education

50,000	Emory University Business School, Atlanta, GA
20,000	Junior Achievement Of Greater Atlanta, Atlanta, GA
20,000	United Negro College Fund, New York, NY
17,500	Inroads Atlanta, Atlanta, GA
15,848	Emory University, Atlanta, GA
12,500	Georgia State University Foundation, Atlanta, GA
11,500	Girls Preparatory School, Chattanooga, TN
10,363	Georgia Institute Of Technology, Atlanta, GA
10,046	The Lovett School, Atlanta, GA
10,000	Benedictine Military School, Savannah, GA
10,000	The Georgia Foundation For Independent Colleges, Inc., Atlanta, GA
10,000	Mercer University, Macon, GA
10,000	Savannah Country Day School, Savannah, GA
10,000	Wesleyan College, Macon, GA
9,982	University Of Georgia, Athens, GA
9,455	Emory University, Atlanta, GA
9,000	UNCF For Spelman College, Atlanta, GA
8,775	Westminster Schools, Atlanta, GA
7,500	Morehouse School Of Medicine, Atlanta, GA
7,500	Southern Wesleyan University, Central, SC
7,500	Westminster Schools, Atlanta, GA
6,244	University Of Virginia, Charlottesville, VA

Environment

7,500	The Nature Conservancy Of Georgia, Atlanta, GA -- Operating Grant

Health

10,000	American Red Cross, Atlanta, GA
10,000	American Red Cross, Metropolitan Atlanta Chapter, Atlanta, GA
7,500	John Tracy Clinic, Los Angeles, CA

Religion

20,000	The Atlanta Jewish Federation, Atlanta, GA

Social Services

270,725	United Way of Metropolitan Atlanta, Atlanta, GA
270,725	United Way Of Metropolitan Atlanta, Atlanta, GA
25,000	United Way Of Metro Atlanta Alexis D. Tocqueville Society, Atlanta, GA
22,500	The Bobby Dodd Coach Of the Year Foundation, Inc., Atlanta, GA
8,500	Northeast Georgia United Way, Athens, GA

SUNTRUST BANKS OF FLORIDA

Company Contact

Orlando, FL

Company Description

Former Name: SunBank N.A.
Assets: US$22,567,000,000
Profit: US$565,500,000
Employees: 7,900
SIC(s): 6022 State Commercial Banks, 6712 Bank Holding Companies.
Parent Company: SunTrust Banks, Inc., Atlanta, GA, United States

SunTrust Banks Foundation

Giving Contact

Ms. Pat Seita, Vice President & Trust Officer
SunTrust Banks of Florida
400 Park Avenue South, No. 200
Winter Park, FL 32789
Phone: (407)621-6266
Fax: (407)621-6272

Description

EIN: 596877429
Organization Type: Corporate Foundation
Giving Locations: FL
Grant Types: Capital, Endowment, General Support, Multiyear/Continuing Support.

Financial Summary

Total Giving: $250,000 (1999 approx); $1,163,333 (1998); $281,987 (1997). Note: Contributes through foundation only.
Assets: $9,000,000 (1999 approx); $11,341,268 (1998); $9,426,671 (1997)
Gifts Received: $1,163,080 (1998); $275,000 (1997); $122,288 (1996). Note: The foundation receives contributions from Suntrust Banks, Inc.

Typical Recipients

Arts & Humanities: Historic Preservation, Libraries, Museums/Galleries
Civic & Public Affairs: Zoos/Aquariums
Education: Colleges & Universities, Literacy, Student Aid
Health: Cancer, Clinics/Medical Centers
International: Foreign Arts Organizations
Science: Scientific Centers & Institutes
Social Services: Child Welfare, Family Services, Substance Abuse

Contributions Analysis

Giving Priorities: Focus on education and science.
Arts & Humanities: 1%. Supports historical society.
Civic & Public Affairs: 1%. Funds a zoo.
Education: 87%. Funding supports colleges and universities, student aid, and literacy near operating locations in Florida.
Health: 1%. Funds the TMH Regional Medical Center Foundation.
Science: 10%. Funds the Orlando Science Center.
Note: Total contributions made in 1998.

Application Procedures

Initial Contact: Send a brief letter.
Application Requirements: Include proof of tax-exempt status of organization.
Deadlines: None.

Restrictions

Foundation gives specifically to scientific, literary, and educational institutions.

Additional Information

SunBank N.A. is corporate trustee for the foundation.

Corporate Officials

Pat Seita: vice president, trust officer PRIM CORP EMPL vice president, trust officer: SunTrust Banks of Florida.

Foundation Officials

Hunt Deutfa: secretary
Pat Seita: contact (see above)

Grants Analysis

Disclosure Period: calendar year ending 1998
Total Grants: $1,163,333
Number of Grants: 6
Average Grant: $11,667*
Highest Grant: $1,000,000
Typical Range: $3,000 to $25,000
***Note:** Average grant excludes the two highest grantss totaling ($1,116,666).

Recent Grants

Note: Grants derived from 1998 Form 990.

Arts & Humanities

7,500	historical association of southern florida, Miami, FL -- operational

Civic & Public Affairs

12,500	Zoological Society of Florida, Miami, FL -- operational

Education

1,000,000	Rollins College Multi-Year Grant, Winter Park, FL
16,667	Bethune-Cookman College, Daytona Beach, FL

Health

10,000	TMH Regional Medical Center, Tallahassee, FL

Science

116,666	Orlando Science Center, Orlando, FL

SUPERVALU, INC.

Company Contact

Eden Prairie, MN
Web: http://www.supervalu.com

Company Description

Former Name: SuperValu Stores;
Acquired:.
Revenue: US$17,420,500,000 (1999)
Profit: US$191,300,000 (1999)
Employees: 44,800
Fortune Rank: 99, per FORTUNE Magazine's list of 500 Largest U.S. Corporations (1999).
FF 99
SIC(s): 5141 Groceries--General Line.

SUBSIDIARY COMPANIES

VA: Richfood Holdings, Glen Allen

Nonmonetary Support

Type: Donated Products; In-kind Services

Giving Contact

Anika Haganson, Contributions Coordinator & Administrator
SuperValu, Inc.
PO Box 990
Minneapolis, MN 55440
Phone: (612)828-4430
Fax: (612)828-4838

Description

Organization Type: Corporate Giving Program
Giving Locations: MN: Minneapolis-St. Paul some the Twin Cities organizations in the company's general service area.
Grant Types: Employee Matching Gifts, General Support, Operating Expenses, Project.

Giving Philosophy

'The employees, customers, and shareholders of SUPERVALUE INC. are an integral part of the communities where SUPERVALU does business. As members of the community, the company is continually looking for ways to strengthen these communities as places to work and live.
'SUPERVALU provides essential products for consumers' daily needs and generates employment for tens of thousands of people through its business activities. To further strengthen the environment in which it operates, the company supports a wide variety of charitable initiatives with special emphasis on hunger and educational efforts.
'As a significant force in the food chain, SUPERVALU has selected hunger and nutrition related issues as a focus of its charitable giving program. In addition, because SUPERVALU also knows the value of a well-educated work force, education is both key to an individual's ability to generate income and avoid hunger, and as a major employer, SUPERVALU also focuses its efforts on education.' Contributions Guidelines

Financial Summary

Total Giving: $2,000,000 (2000 approx); $2,000,000 (1999 approx); $1,642,000 (1997). Note: Contributes through corporate direct giving program only.

Typical Recipients

Arts & Humanities: Community Arts
Civic & Public Affairs: Employment/Job Training, Law & Justice
Education: Colleges & Universities
Environment: Environment-General
Social Services: People with Disabilities, Substance Abuse, Youth Organizations

Contributions Analysis

Education: Supports business, political, and cooperative education programs; programs designed to build knowledge and leadership skills of youth; and urban projects relating to the employability of youth.
Social Services: Supports the United Way in the headquarters area, and organizations providing assistance to minority, physically challenged, disabled, and disadvantaged persons. Also supports organizations programs aimed at promotion of nutrition and organizations established to educate and train people to enter the workforce.

Application Procedures

Initial Contact: Write to receive guidelines, then submit a full written application.
Application Requirements: The completed application form should include a cover letter on organization letterhead with brief history, objectives, and current

activities of the organization; description of the program or activity for which funds are being requested, and verification of its need; proposed method of evaluating the program or activity; amount of request, including other funding sources and funds received; copy of the organization's most recent financial report, audited if possible; current operating budget and a proposed budget, if the project will occur during the following fiscal year; list of the organization's board of directors and their affiliations; brief resume of the individual who serves as administrator for the program; and proof of tax-exempt status.
Deadlines: Requests for support should be made one month prior to meeting dates February 15, May 15, August 15, and November 15 for disbursement in the following year.
Evaluative Criteria: Criteria include: clear description of the program; quality delivery of a needed service; potential benefit to a substantial segment of the community; results which are predictable and can be evaluated; broad-based community support; competent, qualified staff and board; and fiscal and management capability to carry out program.
Decision Notification: The budget for donations is prepared in October for the fiscal year beginning the following March.
Notes: First-time applicants are encouraged to submit a brief letter of inquiry prior to a full proposal. Quarterly meetings are held in March, June, September, and December.

Restrictions

The company does not support political, lobbying, or religious groups; veteran, fraternal, or labor organizations; advertising; individuals; capital campaigns; or travel.
Serves the Minneapolis-St. Paul metropolitan area only.

Additional Information

SuperValu was formerly known as Super Valu Stores.
Publications: Program Guidelines; Application Form

Corporate Officials

T. Andrew Herring: vice president
Michael William Wright: chairman, president, chief executive officer, director B Minneapolis, MN 1938. ED University of Minnesota BA (1961); University of Minnesota JD (1963). PRIM CORP EMPL chairman, president, chief executive officer, director: SuperValu, Inc. CORP AFFIL director: Norwest Corp.; chairman: SuperValu Transportation Inc.; director: Musicland Stores Corp.; director: SC Johnson & Co. Inc.; director: The Musicland Group; director: Honeywell Inc.; chairman: CUB Foods Green Bay Inc.; director: Food Distributors International; director: Cargill Inc. NONPR AFFIL director, member: International Center for Companies of the Food Trade and Industry; director: National American Wholesale Growers Association Inc.; chairman: Food Marketing Institute.

Susquehanna-Pfaltzgraff Co.

Company Contact

York, PA

Company Description

Revenue: US$1,230,000,000
Employees: 7,000
SIC(s): 3262 Vitreous China Table & Kitchenware, 3269 Pottery Products Nec, 4832 Radio Broadcasting Stations.

Nonmonetary Support

Type: Donated Equipment; Donated Products; In-kind Services; Loaned Employees; Loaned Executives; Workplace Solicitation

Susquehanna-Pfaltzgraff Foundation

Giving Contact

John L. Finlayson, Vice President, Finance & Administration
140 East Market Street
York, PA 17401
Phone: (717)848-5500
Fax: (717)771-1440

Description

Founded: 1966
EIN: 236420008
Organization Type: Corporate Foundation
Giving Locations: headquarters and operating communities.
Grant Types: Capital, Challenge, Emergency, Endowment, General Support, Multiyear/Continuing Support, Operating Expenses, Project.

Financial Summary

Total Giving: $350,000 (2000 approx); $350,000 (1999 approx); $351,797 (1998). Note: Contributes through foundation only.
Giving Analysis: Giving for 1998 includes: foundation ($286,747); foundation grants to United Way ($65,050)
Assets: $1,325,712 (1998); $1,230,749 (1997); $1,037,466 (1996)
Gifts Received: $350,000 (1998); $275,000 (1997); $340,000 (1996). Note: Contributions were received from Pfaltzgraff Co., Cable TV of York, Radio San Francisco, KNBR, KLIF Co., Radio Metroplex, KRBE Co., Susquehanna Radio Corp., Radio Indianapolis, and Indianapolis Radio License Co., Radio Cincinnati.

Typical Recipients

Arts & Humanities: Arts Associations & Councils, Community Arts, Arts & Humanities-General, Historic Preservation, History & Archaeology, Music, Opera, Public Broadcasting, Theater
Civic & Public Affairs: Chambers of Commerce, Community Foundations, Civic & Public Affairs-General, Nonprofit Management, Urban & Community Affairs
Education: Agricultural Education, Colleges & Universities, Education Funds, Education-General, Health & Physical Education, Minority Education, Private Education (Precollege), Public Education (Precollege), Secondary Education (Private), Student Aid, Vocational & Technical Education
Environment: Resource Conservation, Wildlife Protection
Health: Children's Health/Hospitals, Eyes/Blindness, Health-General, Hospitals, Public Health, Single-Disease Health Associations
International: International Organizations
Religion: Churches, Religious Welfare, Seminaries
Science: Science-General, Science Museums
Social Services: Animal Protection, Community Service Organizations, Recreation & Athletics, Scouts, Social Services-General, United Funds/United Ways, YMCA/YWCA/YMHA/YWHA

Contributions Analysis

Giving Priorities: Social services, civic and public affairs, art, and education.
Arts & Humanities: 17%. Supports museums, theaters, and historical societies.
Civic & Public Affairs: 22%. Funds community foundations.
Education: 16%. Funds colleges, minority education, and private primary and secondary schools.
Environment: 5%. Supports conservation districts, rails to trails projects, and environmental protection.
Health: 2%. Supports a hospital.
Religion: 4%. Supports a seminary and the Brethren Home Foundation.
Social Services: 34%. Supports the United Way, youth organizations, Make a Difference conferences, and YMCAs.
Note: Total contributions made in 1998.

Application Procedures

Initial Contact: Send a brief letter of inquiry.
Application Requirements: Outline need for funds sought.
Deadlines: None.

Restrictions

Does not support individuals, religious organizations for sectarian purposes, political or lobbying groups, or organizations outside operating areas.

Corporate Officials

George N. Appell: treasurer B 1926. PRIM CORP EMPL treasurer: Susquehanna Pfaltzgraff Co.
Louis J. Appell, Jr.: president B 1924. ED Harvard University (1947). PRIM CORP EMPL president: Susquehanna-Pfaltzgraff Co. CORP AFFIL chairman: Susquehanna Media Co.; chairman: Susquehanna Radio Corp.; chairman: Radio Metroplex Inc.; chairman: SBC Cable Co.; chairman: Pfaltzgraff Co.; chairman: Pfaltzgraff Outlet Co.; chairman: Casco Cable Televising Inc.
John L. Finlayson: vice president finance & administration PRIM CORP EMPL vice president finance & administration: Susquehanna-Pfaltzgraff Co. CORP AFFIL vice president: Susquehanna Media Co.; vice president: Susquehanna Radio Corp.; vice president: Susquehanna Cable Co.; vice president: Pfaltzgraff Outlet Co.; vice president: SBC Cable Co.; vice president: Pfaltzgraff Co.
Mike Sibol: director PRIM CORP EMPL director: Susquehanna-Pfaltzgraff Co.
William H. Simpson: president B Ithaca, NY 1941. ED United States Air Force Academy (1963); Harvard University (1966). PRIM CORP EMPL president: Pfaltzgraff Co. CORP AFFIL president: Pfaltzgraff Outlet Co.; vice president manufacturing: Susquehanna Pfalzgraff Co.

Foundation Officials

George N. Appell: vice president (see above)
Louis J. Appell, Jr.: president (see above)
Helen A. Norton: vice president B 1931. PRIM CORP EMPL vice president: Susquehanna Pfaltzgraff Co.
William H. Simpson: secretary (see above)

Grants Analysis

Disclosure Period: calendar year ending 1998
Total Grants: $286,747*
Number of Grants: 37
Average Grant: $7,750
Highest Grant: $32,500
Typical Range: $1,000 to $30,000
***Note:** Giving excludes United Way.

Recent Grants

Note: Grants derived from 1997 Form 990.

Arts & Humanities

18,000	York Little Theater, York, PA
16,000	York County Heritage Rail Trail, York, PA
15,000	Maryland and Pennsylvania Railroad Preservation Society, York, PA
5,000	Preservation Pennsylvania, York, PA
5,000	Yorkarts Capital Campaign, York, PA
1,000	St. Rose of Lima Church York Ecumenical Choir, York, PA
250	Heritage of Hope, Hope, IN

Civic & Public Affairs

32,500	York Foundation, York, PA
7,000	Golden Vision Foundation, York, PA
3,333	Penn Mar Organization, York, PA
1,667	York Foundation York Nonprofit Management Development Center, York, PA

Education

30,000	Campaign for York College, York, PA
5,000	Christian School, York, PA
5,000	Health Education Center, York, PA
5,000	York Foundation York City Schools, York, PA
2,000	York Country Day School, York, PA
1,500	Foundation for Independent Colleges, Mechanicsburg, PA
1,500	York County 4-H Center, York, PA
1,000	Lycoming College, Williamsport, PA
1,000	York Catholic High School, York, PA
500	United Negro College Fund, Harrisburg, PA

Environment

1,000	Brunswick Topsam Land Trust, Brunswick, ME
500	York Wildcare, York, PA

Health

20,000	Byrnes Health Education Center, York, PA

Religion

7,500	Brethren Home Foundation, York, PA
7,000	Make a Difference Pennsylvania Central Conference United Church of Christ, York, PA
5,000	Lancaster Theological Seminary, Lancaster, PA

Social Services

57,000	United Way York County, York, PA
6,000	Penn Laurel Girl Scout Council, York, PA
5,000	Boy Scouts of America York Adams Area Council, York, PA
2,700	United Way Lycoming, Williamsport, PA
1,500	York County Society for Prevention of Cruelty to Animals, York, PA
1,000	Dream Fund, Dallas, TX
800	United Way Mid-Coast Maine, Bath, ME
750	United Way, Atlanta, GA
500	Little League Baseball International Headquarters, Williamsport, PA
500	United Way Adams County, York, PA
335	YMCA, Williamsport, PA

SVERDRUP CORP.

Company Contact

Maryland Heights, MO

Company Description

Employees: 5,000
SIC(s): 8711 Engineering Services, 8712 Architectural Services, 8741 Management Services.

Sverdrup Corp. Charitable Trust

Giving Contact

Thomas E. Wehrle, Treasurer
13723 Riverport Drive
Maryland Heights, MO 63043
Phone: (314)466-3439

Description

Founded: 1951
EIN: 436023499
Organization Type: Corporate Foundation
Giving Locations: MO: Saint Louis nationally.
Grant Types: General Support, Scholarship.

Financial Summary

Total Giving: $321,909 (1998); $318,753 (1996); $220,650 (1994)
Giving Analysis: Giving for 1998 includes: foundation ($230,709); foundation grants to United Way ($91,200)
Assets: $743,679 (1998); $1,069,431 (1996); $1,007,911 (1994)
Gifts Received: $250,000 (1996); $200,000 (1994). Note: In 1996, contributions were received from Sverdrup Corp.

Typical Recipients

Arts & Humanities: Arts Associations & Councils, Arts Centers, Dance, History & Archaeology, Museums/Galleries, Music, Opera, Theater
Civic & Public Affairs: Botanical Gardens/Parks, Clubs, Civic & Public Affairs-General, Parades/Festivals, Professional & Trade Associations
Education: Colleges & Universities, Community & Junior Colleges, Engineering/Technological Education, Private Education (Precollege), Secondary Education (Private), Vocational & Technical Education
Health: Cancer, Children's Health/Hospitals, Single-Disease Health Associations
Religion: Religious Welfare
Science: Scientific Centers & Institutes
Social Services: At-Risk Youth, Child Welfare, Family Services, Scouts, United Funds/United Ways, YMCA/YWCA/YMHA/YWHA, Youth Organizations

Contributions Analysis

Giving Priorities: Social services, education, and arts organizations.
Arts & Humanities: 22%. Supports performing arts, museums, and historical societies.
Civic & Public Affairs: 9%. Funds professional trade organizations, county fairs, and a zoo.
Education: 23%. Funds scholarship funds, colleges and universities, high schools, and Junior Achievement.
Health: 3%. Supports single-disease health organizations and the American Red Cross.
Religion: 2%. Supports religious welfare organizations aimed at children and families.
Science: 1%. Funds a science center.
Social Services: 40%. Supports the United Way, youth clubs, and YMCAs.
Note: Total contributions made in 1998.

Application Procedures

Initial Contact: Send a written proposal.
Application Requirements: State activity of organization, purpose of funds sought, budget, current financial statements, and proof of tax-exempt status.
Deadlines: None.

Restrictions

Grants are not made to individuals or to organizations not having 501(c)(3) exemption.

Additional Information

Trust(s): Boatmen's Trust Co

Corporate Officials

Richard Eugene Beumer: president PRIM CORP EMPL president: Sverdrup Corp.
R. J. Messey: senior vice president, chief financial officer PRIM CORP EMPL senior vice president, chief financial officer: Sverdrup Corp.
A. F. Morrison: senior vice president, secretary PRIM CORP EMPL senior vice president, secretary: Sverdrup Corp.
Thomas E. Wehrle: treasurer PRIM CORP EMPL treasurer: Sverdrup Corp.
J. D. Whitfield: vice chairman PRIM CORP EMPL vice chairman: Sverdrup Corp.

Foundation Officials

A. F. Morrison: mem (see above)
H. G. Schwartz, Jr.: mem
Thomas E. Wehrle: mem (see above)

Grants Analysis

Disclosure Period: calendar year ending 1998
Total Grants: $230,709*
Number of Grants: 63
Average Grant: $3,662
Highest Grant: $20,000
Typical Range: $100 to $15,000
***Note:** Giving excludes United Way.

Recent Grants

Note: Grants derived from 1997 Form 990.

Arts & Humanities

20,000	St. Louis Symphony Society, St. Louis, MO
15,000	Arts and Education Council, St. Louis, MO
5,000	AEDC Heritage Foundation
5,000	American Society
5,000	St. Louis Art Museum Foundation, St. Louis, MO
4,000	Repertory Theater
3,000	Dance St. Louis, St. Louis, MO
2,500	Missouri Historical Society, St. Louis, MO
1,500	Air Force Armament Museum

Civic & Public Affairs

5,000	ASCE Building
5,000	Fair St. Louis
5,000	St. Louis Zoo Foundation, St. Louis, MO
4,000	Missouri Botanical Garden, St. Louis, MO
4,000	Missouri Botanical Garden, St. Louis, MO
2,500	Behlmann's TFK
2,500	St. Louis County
2,000	Civil Engineering
2,000	Focus St. Louis

Education

15,000	University of Tennessee, Knoxville, TN
10,000	Washington University, St. Louis, MO
10,000	Washington University Medical School, St. Louis, MO
9,000	Webster University, Webster Groves, MO
7,143	Motlow State Community College
5,000	Missouri Society of Professionals Educational Foundation, Jefferson City, MO
5,000	Prep for Prep, New York, NY
3,000	McNarmara Scholarship Fund, Grosse Pointe Farms, MI
3,000	University of Kansas, Lawrence, KS
2,500	Junior Achievement
2,200	Missouri Colleges Fund, Jefferson City, MO
2,000	Alpha Scholastic Foundation
2,000	University of West Florida, Pensacola, FL
1,800	Junior Achievement
1,300	United Negro College Fund, New York, NY

Health

10,000	Leukemia Society of America
10,000	St. Louis Children's Hospital, St. Louis, MO
3,750	American Heart Association
2,500	American Red Cross
2,500	Cystic Fibrosis Foundation, Philadelphia, PA

Religion

5,000	Episcopal Church, St. Louis, MO
5,000	Jewish Community Center
5,000	Lutheran Children's Home

Science

5,000	St. Louis Science Center, St. Louis, MO

Social Services

87,000	United Way
11,655	Boy Scouts of America
5,000	Boys Hope-Girls Hope
5,000	Girl Scouts of America, St. Louis, MO
5,000	LFCS Salute to Baseball
4,200	Boy Scouts of America Greater St. Louis Council
3,000	YMCA, St. Louis, MO
1,500	United Way King County, Seattle, WA

Synovus Financial Corp.

Company Contact

Columbus, GA

Company Description

Assets: US$8,612,300,000
Employees: 9,489 (1999)
SIC(s): 6029 Commercial Banks Nec, 6211 Security Brokers & Dealers, 7374 Data Processing & Preparation.

Corporate Sponsorship

Type: Arts & cultural events; Festivals/fairs; Music & entertainment events; Sports events
Contact: Sandy Coolick, Vice President, Marketing

Synovus Charitable Trust

Giving Contact

Sam Wellborn, Chairman and Chief Executive Officer
Synovus Foundation
PO Box 120
Columbus, GA 31902
Phone: (706)649-2679
Fax: (706)649-5986

Description

EIN: 237024198
Organization Type: Corporate Foundation
Giving Locations: GA: Columbus
Grant Types: Capital, General Support.

Financial Summary

Total Giving: $1,300,000 (1999 approx); $992,020 (1998); $761,480 (1997). Note: Contributes through foundation only.
Giving Analysis: Giving for 1997 includes: foundation ($561,480); foundation grants to United Way ($200,000); 1998: foundation ($772,020); foundation grants to United Way ($220,000)
Assets: $800 (1998); $25 (1997); $1,506 (1996)
Gifts Received: $993,036 (1998); $758,500 (1997); $483,000 (1996). Note: The foundation receives contributions from Total System SVC, Synovus Financial, CB&T Bancshares and Synovus Trust.

Typical Recipients

Arts & Humanities: Arts Associations & Councils, Arts Centers, Arts Festivals, Historic Preservation, History & Archaeology, Museums/Galleries, Music, Opera, Theater
Civic & Public Affairs: African American Affairs, Community Foundations, Economic Development, Employment/Job Training, Civic & Public Affairs-General, Housing, Municipalities/Towns, Parades/Festivals, Philanthropic Organizations, Public Policy, Urban & Community Affairs, Women's Affairs, Zoos/Aquariums
Education: Colleges & Universities, Economic Education, Education Associations, Education Funds, Education Reform, Engineering/Technological Education, Education-General, Legal Education, Literacy, Medical Education, Minority Education, Private Education (Precollege), Private Education (Precollege), Public Education (Precollege), Special Education, Student Aid
Environment: Air/Water Quality, Protection
Health: Alzheimers Disease, Cancer, Children's Health/Hospitals, Clinics/Medical Centers, Emergency/Ambulance Services, Eyes/Blindness, Geriatric Health, Health Organizations, Heart, Hospices, Hospitals, Long-Term Care, Medical Rehabilitation, Mental Health, Multiple Sclerosis, Outpatient Health Care, Single-Disease Health Associations
International: International Affairs
Religion: Churches, Religious Organizations, Religious Welfare
Science: Science Museums
Social Services: Animal Protection, Child Abuse, Child Welfare, Community Centers, Community Service Organizations, Counseling, Domestic Violence, Family Services, Homes, Recreation & Athletics, Scouts, Senior Services, Shelters/Homelessness, Special Olympics, Substance Abuse, United Funds/United Ways, YMCA/YWCA/YMHA/YWHA, Youth Organizations

Contributions Analysis

Giving Priorities: Social service organizations, civic and community affairs, and education.
Arts & Humanities: 4%. Funds the Shakespeare Georgia Festival, music, and historic handcrafts.
Civic & Public Affairs: 29%. Emphasis is on community affairs and development.
Education: 16%. Supports various education institutions, including colleges and scholarship funds.
Environment: 2%.
Health: 5%. Contributions favor medical centers and community-focused health organizations.
Religion: 4%. Funds religious causes.
Social Services: 40%. Funding supports United Way, youth organizations, recreation, and family services.
Note: Total contributions made in 1998.

Application Procedures

Initial Contact: Send a letter of application.
Application Requirements: Include a description of organization, amount requested, purpose of funds sought, audited financial statement, and proof of tax-exempt status.
Deadlines: None.

Restrictions

Does not support organizations that are not tax-exempt or groups which do not directly benefit the Columbus, GA, area.

Corporate Officials

James Hubert Blanchard: chairman, chief executive officer, president, chief operating officer B Augusta, GA 1941. ED University of Georgia BBA (1963); University of Georgia LLB (1965). PRIM CORP EMPL chairman, chief executive officer: Synovus Financial Corp. CORP AFFIL director: Synovus Data Corp.; chairman executive committee: Total System Service Inc.; director: Hardaway Co.; chairman executive committee, director: Hotel Columbus; director: WC Bradley Co.; director: Columbus Bank & Trust Co.; director: BellSouth Corp.
Stephen L. Burts, Jr.: president, treasurer, chief financial officer B Atlanta, GA 1953. ED Columbus College (1976). PRIM CORP EMPL president, treasurer, chief financial officer: Synovus Financial Corp.
James D. Yancey: vice chairman, director, president, chief operating officer B 1941. ED Rutgers University Stonier Graduate School of Banking (1973). PRIM CORP EMPL vice chairman, director, president, chief operating officer: Synovus Financial Corp. CORP AFFIL director: Shoneys Inc.; director: Total System Services Inc.; director: First Community Bank of Tifton; director: National Bank of South Carolina.

Foundation Officials

Nancy Buntin: vice president finance
William L. Slaughter, Jr.: vice president
Sam M. Wellborn: president PRIM CORP EMPL manager: Columbus Bank & Trust Co. CORP AFFIL director: Flint Electric Membership Corp.

Grants Analysis

Disclosure Period: calendar year ending 1998
Total Grants: $772,020*
Number of Grants: 54
Average Grant: $14,297
Highest Grant: $260,000
Typical Range: $5,000 to $25,000
***Note:** Giving excludes United Way.

Recent Grants

Note: Grants derived from 1998 Form 990.

Arts & Humanities

25,000	Springer Opera House, Columbus, GA
5,000	Historic Columbus Foundation, Columbus, GA
5,000	Infantry Museum, Fort Benning, GA
5,000	Westville, Inc, Lumpkin, GA
500	Columbus Boy Choir, Columbus, GA
500	Georgia Shakespeare Festival, Atlanta, GA

Civic & Public Affairs

260,000	Community Projects Foundation, Inc., Columbus, GA
22,500	Uptown Columbus Foundation, Columbus, GA
6,500	Urban League, Atlanta, GA
250	Chattahoochee Flint Heritage Highway, Warm Springs, GA

Education

50,000	Brookstone School Fund Raising Campaign, Columbus, GA
42,875	Columbus College Foundation, Columbus, GA -- General Development Fund
20,000	Achievement Academy, Columbus, GA
12,000	University of Georgia, Athens, GA
10,000	Muscogee Educational Excellence, Columbus, GA
10,000	Troy State University, Troy, AL
7,595	Andrew College, Cuthbert, GA
5,000	United Negro College Fund, Columbus, GA
2,000	Georgia Council on Economic Education, Atlanta, GA
1,500	Georgia Foundation for Independent Colleges, Atlanta, GA
1,000	Morehouse School of Medicine, Atlanta, GA
500	Fort Valley State College, Fort Valley, GA
500	St. Mary's Road UMC - RIF Program, Columbus, GA

Environment

2,500	Chattahoochee Riverkeeper, Columbus, GA

Health

35,000	Roosevelt Warm Springs Development Fund, Inc., Warm Springs, GA
5,000	Juvenile Diabetes Foundation, Atlanta, GA
5,000	Ronald Mcdonald House, Columbus, GA
2,400	American Heart Association, Atlanta, GA
600	National Multiple Sclerosis Society, Atlanta, GA

Religion

20,000	Carpenter's Way Ranch, Columbus, GA
20,000	Valley Rescue Mission, Columbus, GA
500	Good Shepherd Therapeutic Center, Warm Springs, GA

200 First Presbyterian Church, Atlanta, GA
100 Britt David Baptist Church, Atlanta, GA
100 Wesley United Methodist Church, Minneapolis, MN

Social Services
220,000 United Way, Inc., Columbus, GA
40,000 Boys Club of Columbus and Phenix City, Columbus, GA
40,000 Open Door Community Center, Columbus, GA
30,000 Y.M.C.A., Atlanta, GA
10,000 The Greater Columbus Sports & Events Council, Columbus, GA
10,000 Stewart Community Home, Columbus, GA
7,200 House of T.I.M.E., Inc., Columbus, GA
7,000 B.R.I.D.G.E., Atlanta, GA
2,500 Georgia Caring Program for Children, Inc., Atlanta, GA
1,000 Columbus Regional Chartered Council on Child Abuse, Columbus, GA
1,000 Muscogee County Special Olympics, Columbus, GA
500 Columbus Community Resource Center, Columbus, GA
250 Georgia High School Rodeo, Meansville, GA
250 Muscogee County Humane Society, Columbus, GA

TACO BELL CORP.

Company Contact
17901 Von Karman
Irvine, CA 92614
Phone: (949)863-4500
Fax: (949)863-2246
Web: http://www.tacobell.com

Company Description
SIC(s): 5812 Eating Places, 6794 Patent Owners & Lessors.
Parent Company: Tricon Global Restaurants Inc., 1441 Gardiner Lane, Louisville, KY, United States

Operating Locations
Operates more than 4,000 Taco Bell restaurants throughout the United States.

Nonmonetary Support
Note: Contact local restaurant.

Corporate Sponsorship
Type: Arts & cultural events; Festivals/fairs; Music & entertainment events; Sports events
Note: Sponsors minority affairs.

Taco Bell Foundation

Giving Contact
Laurie Gannon, Manager, Public Affairs
Taco Bell Foundation
17901 Von Karman Avenue
Irvine, CA 92614-6221
Phone: (949)863-4944
Fax: (949)863-2246

Description
Founded: 1993
Organization Type: Corporate Foundation
Giving Locations: CA: Southern California
Grant Types: Project.

Financial Summary
Total Giving: Contributes through corporate direct giving program and foundation.

Typical Recipients
Education: Education-General
Health: Emergency/Ambulance Services, Health Organizations
Religion: Religious Welfare
Social Services: At-Risk Youth, Child Welfare, Community Service Organizations, Emergency Relief, Youth Organizations

Contributions Analysis
Social Services: 100%.

Application Procedures
Initial Contact: contact co. for guidelines
Review Process: formal committee reviews applications

Restrictions
Applications for general grants are no longer available.

Additional Information
Funds are committed entirely to the Boys & Girls Club through the year 2001. The foundation is not accepting other proposals at this time.
The foundation bases giving on an annual evaluation of previously funded projects and new grant requests; grants should not be assumed as a precedent for future support.
The foundation prefers to make one-time grants rather than multi-year commitments.
In 1997, Tricon Global Restaurants Inc. became the parent company of Taco Bell. PepsiCo. was the previous parent company of KFC.

Corporate Officials
John E. Martin: chairman, chief executive officer B 1945. ED Middlebury College BS (1967). PRIM CORP EMPL chairman, chief executive officer: Taco Bell Worldwide. CORP AFFIL chairman, chief executive officer: Taco Bell Corp.; president, director: Taco Caliente Inc.; director: The Good Guys Inc.

Foundation Officials
Laurie Gannon: manager public affairs
John E. Martin: chairman (see above)

Grants Analysis
Disclosure Period: calendar year ending

Recent Grants
Note: Grants derived from 1993 grants list.

Health
160,000 American Red Cross-Greater Miami Chapter, FL

Religion
150,000 Catholic Community Services, Miami, FL -- to establish a permanent health care clinic for the public in Miami

J.T. TAI AND CO.

Company Contact
New York, NY

J.T. Tai and Co. Foundation, Inc.

Giving Contact
Ping Y. Tai, Co-President & Co-Treasurer
Tai andCo.Foundation, Inc. (J. T.)
18 E. 67th St.
New York, NY 10021
Phone: (212)288-5242
Fax: (212)737-4105

Description
EIN: 133157279
Organization Type: Corporate Foundation
Giving Locations: NY Northeastern United States.
Grant Types: General Support.

Financial Summary
Total Giving: $1,094,498 (1997); $780,645 (1996); $600,000 (1995)
Assets: $30,304,049 (1997); $24,358,995 (1996); $19,221,709 (1995)
Gifts Received: $8,500 (1992); $788 (1991); $4,286 (1990)

Typical Recipients
Civic & Public Affairs: Civic & Public Affairs-General, Urban & Community Affairs
Education: Colleges & Universities, Community & Junior Colleges, Engineering/Technological Education, Education-General, Health & Physical Education, International Exchange, Medical Education, Vocational & Technical Education
Health: Cancer, Children's Health/Hospitals, Clinics/Medical Centers, Emergency/Ambulance Services, Health Organizations, Heart, Hospitals, Medical Research, Public Health
International: Foreign Educational Institutions, International Relations, International Relief Efforts
Religion: Churches, Religious Organizations
Social Services: At-Risk Youth, Community Service Organizations, People with Disabilities

Contributions Analysis
Civic & Public Affairs: 2%. Supports community programs.
Education: 69%. Primarily supports colleges, universities, and medical schools throughout the country.
Health: 17%. Majority of funding supports cancer research. Also, supports other single-disease health organizations and hospitals.
International: 5%. Emphasis on international relief efforts and hospitals.
Religion: 4%. Supports Chinese Christian organizations and Chinese churches.
Social Services: 3%. Focuses on at-risk youth and community service organizations.

Application Procedures
Initial Contact: Send brief letter of inquiry.
Application Requirements: Description of program and proposed purpose for funds.
Deadlines: None.

Corporate Officials
Ping Y. Tai: co-president PRIM CORP EMPL co-president: J.T. Tai and Co.

Foundation Officials
Y. C. Chen: assistant secretary
F. Richard Hsu: secretary
Ping Y. Tai: co-president, co-treasurer (see above)
Yuan Tai: co-president, co-treasurer

Grants Analysis
Disclosure Period: calendar year ending 1997
Total Grants: $1,094,498
Number of Grants: 45
Average Grant: $15,869*
Highest Grant: $180,000
Typical Range: $1,000 to $15,000
***Note:** Average grant figure excludes three highest grants ($428,000).

Recent Grants
Note: Grants derived from 1997 Form 990.

Civic & Public Affairs
15,000 BROADWAY COMMUNITY INC, New York, NY
10,000 ODYSSEY FOUNDATION, New York, NY

Education

128,000 COLUMBIA UNIVERSITY, Columbia, SC
120,000 NEW YORK UNIVERSITY, New York, NY
83,000 JOHN HOPKIN UNIVERSITY, Baltimore, MD
66,000 HARVARD MEDICAL SCHOOL, Boston, MA
50,000 CORNELL UNIVERSITY MEDICAL COLLEGE, Ithaca, NY
50,000 NY COLLEGE OF PODIATRIC MEDICINE, New York, NY
47,000 BROWN UNIVERSITY, Manhattan, NY
46,000 BOSTON UNIVERSITY, Boston, MA
40,000 PENN STATE UNIVERSITY, McKeesport, PA
30,000 DARTMOUTH MEDICAL SCHOOL, Hanover, NH
30,000 HARVARD SCHOOL OF PUBLIC HEALTH, Boston, MA
10,000 MANHATTAN COLLEGE, New York, NY
6,000 TULANE UNIVERSITY, New Orleans, LA
5,000 GEORGETOWN UNIVERSITY, Georgetown, TX
5,000 HAVERFORD COLLEGE, Haverford, PA
4,000 PACE UNIVERSITY, New York, NY
4,000 RUTGERS UNIVERSITY, Camden, NJ
3,928 UNIVERSITY OF SOUTH FLORIDA, Tampa, FL
3,000 BROOKLYN COLLEGE, Brooklyn, NY
3,000 CORNELL UNIVERSITY, Ithaca, NY
3,000 GEORGIA SOUTHERN UNIVERSITY, Statesboro, GA
3,000 HAHNEMANN UNIVERSITY, Philadelphia, PA
3,000 LOUISIANA STATE UNIVERSITY, Alexandria, LA
3,000 UNIVERSITY OF MEDICINE & DENTISTRY OF NJ, Brunswick, NJ
2,000 ALBERT EINSTEIN COLLEGE OF MEDICINE, New York, NY
2,000 GEORGE WASHINGTON UNIVERSITY, Washington, DC
1,433 DUTCHESS COMMUNITY COLLEGE, NY
512 HIGHLINE COMMUNITY COLLEGE, Des Moines, WA

Health

40,000 CHINATOWN CLINIC, New York, NY
30,000 AMERICAN CANCER SOCIETY
30,000 AMERICAN HEART ASSOCIATION
20,000 AMERICAN RED CROSS IN GREATER NY, New York, NY
20,000 CHEMOTHERAPY FOUNDATION
20,000 MEMORIAL SLOAN-KETTERING CANCER SOCIET, New York, NY
10,000 MT. SINAI HOSPITAL, Chicago, IL
10,000 VILLAGE CENTER FOR CARE, New York, NY

International

30,000 US COMMITTE FOR UNICEF, New York, NY
20,000 CHINA INSTITUTE, New York, NY

Religion

30,000 CHINESE BIBLE CHURCH, Los Angeles, CA
10,000 ST. ANN CHURCH, Boulder Junction, WI
5,000 CHURCH IN NY CITY, New York, NY

Social Services

20,000 COVENANT HOUSE
20,000 LIGHTHOUSE, New York, NY

TAMKO ROOFING PRODUCTS

Company Contact

Joplin, MO

Company Description

Employees: 1,300
SIC(s): 2952 Asphalt Felts & Coatings.

E.L. Craig Foundation

Giving Contact

Ethel Mae Humphreys, President
E. L. Craig Foundation
PO Box 1404
Joplin, MO 64802
Phone: (417)624-6644

Description

Founded: 1960
EIN: 446015127
Organization Type: Corporate Foundation. Supports preselected organizations only.
Giving Locations: MO: Joplin nationally.
Grant Types: Research.

Financial Summary

Total Giving: $348,940 (fiscal year ending July 31, 1998). Note: Contributes through foundation only.
Assets: $5,855,173 (fiscal 1998); $5,700,957 (fiscal 1993); $4,945,980 (fiscal 1991)
Gifts Received: $77,000 (fiscal 1993); $200,000 (fiscal 1991); $100,000 (fiscal 1990). Note: Contributions were received from the Ethel Mae C. Humphreys Revocable Trust and the J.P. Humphreys Revocable Trust.

Typical Recipients

Arts & Humanities: Music, Theater
Civic & Public Affairs: Business/Free Enterprise, Civil Rights, Economic Policy, Civic & Public Affairs-General, Housing, Law & Justice, Nonprofit Management, Public Policy, Urban & Community Affairs
Education: Colleges & Universities, Economic Education, Education-General, Legal Education, Private Education (Precollege), Science/Mathematics Education, Secondary Education (Public), Social Sciences Education
Health: Cancer, Hospitals, Public Health, Single-Disease Health Associations
International: Human Rights, International Relations
Religion: Churches, Ministries, Religious Welfare
Social Services: Community Service Organizations, Crime Prevention, People with Disabilities, Scouts, Senior Services, Special Olympics, Youth Organizations

Contributions Analysis

Giving Priorities: Youth services, education foundations, and civic organizations.
Civic & Public Affairs: 11%. Supports business institutions, as well as policy groups and think-tanks.
Education: 86%. Recipients include colleges and universities, educational foundations, and MathCounts.
Social Services: 3%. Supports Boy Scouts and Girl Scouts.
Note: Total contributions made in 1998.

Restrictions

Company does not support individuals.

Additional Information

The foundation reports that it gives preference to non-tax supported organizations.
The company changed its name from Tamko Asphalt Products to Tamko Roofing Products.

Corporate Officials

David Craig Humphreys: president, chief operating officer, director B 1956. ED New York University MBA; University of Miami JD; University of the South BS. PRIM CORP EMPL president, chief operating officer, director: Tamko Roofing Products Inc. CORP AFFIL president: Tamko Ennis Inc.
Ethel Mae Craig Humphreys: chairman, chief executive officer B 1927. ED Monticello College (1946); University of Kansas AB (1948). PRIM CORP EMPL chairman, chief executive officer: Tamko Roofing Products.

Foundation Officials

Sarah Humphreys Atkins: vice president B 1958. ED Southern Methodist University MA; University of the South. CORP AFFIL director: Tamko Roofing Products Inc.
David Craig Humphreys: secretary-treasurer (see above)
Ethel Mae Craig Humphreys: president (see above)

Grants Analysis

Disclosure Period: fiscal year ending July 31, 1998
Total Grants: $348,940
Number of Grants: 14
Average Grant: $24,924
Highest Grant: $250,000
Typical Range: $100 to $10,000

Recent Grants

Note: Grants derived from 1997 Form 990.

Civic & Public Affairs

80,000 National Right to Work Legal Defense Foundation, Springfield, VA
50,000 Institute for Civil Society, Washington, DC
25,000 US Term Limits Foundation, Washington, DC
20,000 Landmark Legal Foundation, Herndon, VA
10,000 Center for Independent Thought, New York, NY
5,000 Consumer Alert, Washington, DC
5,000 Local Philosophy and Policy Foundation, Bowling Green, OH
5,000 Mackinac Center for Public Policy, Midland, MI
4,420 Institute for Policy Renovation
2,500 Philanthropic Roundtable, Washington, DC
500 Defenders of Property Rights, Arlington, VA

Education

25,000 Kansas University Endowment Association, Lawrence, KS
25,000 New York University, New York, NY
200 MSFF Education Foundation, Joplin, MO

Health

1,600 Mercy Health Resource Library, Joplin, MO
100 Hisharo Hospital, Indianapolis, IN

International

25,000 Future of Freedom Federation, Fairfax, VA

Religion

500 First Community Church, Joplin, MO
200 Bella Vista Baptist Church, Bella Vista, AR
100 Calvary Presbyterian Church, Wichita, KS

Social Services

1,200 Boy Scouts of America Black Warrior Council, Tuscaloosa, AL
100 Law Enforcement Torch Fund, Tuscaloosa, AL

100 National Sports Center for the Disabled, Kinter Park, CO
40 Kansas Special Olympics, Wichita, KS

Tampa Electric Co.

Company Contact
Tampa, FL

Company Description
Revenue: US$1,094,865,000
Employees: 2,836
SIC(s): 4911 Electric Services.
Parent Company: TECO Energy, Inc.

TECO Energy Foundation

Giving Contact
Julius Hobbes, Director, Corporate Relations
Teco Energy Foundation
PO Box 111
Tampa, FL 33601
Phone: (813)228-4273
Fax: (813)228-1691

Description
Organization Type: Corporate Foundation
Giving Locations: headquarters and operating communities.
Grant Types: General Support.

Financial Summary
Total Giving: Contributes through corporate direct giving program only.

Typical Recipients
Arts & Humanities: Arts & Humanities-General
Civic & Public Affairs: Civic & Public Affairs-General
Education: Education-General
Health: Health-General

Contributions Analysis
Arts & Humanities: 20% to 25%.
Civic & Public Affairs: 15% to 20%.
Education: 30% to 35%.
Health: 25% to 30%.

Application Procedures
Initial Contact: request application form
Application Requirements: completed application, recently audited financial statement or Form 990, list of current board of directors, itemized annual budget, and proof of tax-exempt status
Deadlines: the fifteenth of January, April, June, and September
Review Process: foundation reviews applications quarterly, in April, June, August, and November

Restrictions
Does not support individuals, religious organizations for sectarian purposes, political or lobbying groups, or organizations outside operating areas.

Additional Information
Publications: Contributions Guidelines; Community Improvement Partnership Brochure; Fact Sheet

Corporate Officials
Michelle Adler: director community services PRIM CORP EMPL director community service: Tampa Electric Co.
Girard F. Anderson: chairman, chief executive officer, president B Grand Rapids, MI 1932. ED University of Florida BSChE (1959). PRIM CORP EMPL chairman, chief executive officer, president: TECO Energy Inc. CORP AFFIL director: Sun Bank Tampa Bay; chairman: Tampa Electric Co.; chief operating officer: Peoples Gas Co.
Wayne W. Hopkins: vice president corporate communications B Atlanta, GA 1947. ED Georgia State University (1973). PRIM CORP EMPL vice president corporate communications: TECO Energy Inc. CORP AFFIL vice president corporate communication: Tampa Electric Co.

Giving Program Officials
Julius Hobbes: director PRIM CORP EMPL director corporate relations: Tampa Electric Co.

Grants Analysis
Disclosure Period: calendar year ending
Typical Range: $50 to $1,000

Tandy Corp.

Company Contact
Fort Worth, TX

Company Description
Revenue: US$4,126,200,000 (1999)
Profit: US$297,900,000 (1999)
Employees: 49,300
Fortune Rank: 382, per FORTUNE Magazine's list of 500 Largest U.S. Corporations (1999).
FF 382
SIC(s): 5065 Electronic Parts & Equipment Nec, 5731 Radio, Television & Electronics Stores.

Operating Locations
Operates throughout the USA.

Giving Contact
Lynn M. Platania, Director, Community Relations
Tandy Corp.
1800 One Tandy Center
Ft. Worth, TX 76102
Phone: (817)390-3700
Fax: (817)415-3500

Description
Organization Type: Corporate Giving Program
Grant Types: Employee Matching Gifts, General Support.
Note: Employee matching gift ratio: 2 to 1 up to $500 per employee annually. Company does not offer multiyear/continuing support.

Financial Summary
Total Giving: Contributes through corporate direct giving program only. Company does not disclose contributions figures.

Typical Recipients
Arts & Humanities: Performing Arts
Education: Education-General, Private Education (Precollege), Public Education (Precollege)
Social Services: Child Welfare

Application Procedures
Initial Contact: brief letter
Deadlines: before October 31

Restrictions
Company funds only 501(c)(3) organizations.

Corporate Officials
John Vinson Roach, II: chairman, director B Stamford, TX 1938. ED Texas Christian University BA (1961); Texas Christian University MBA (1965). PRIM CORP EMPL chairman, director: Tandy Corp. CORP AFFIL director: Justin Industries Inc. NONPR AFFIL chairman: Texas Christian University; director: Van Cliburn Foundation. CLUB AFFIL Colonial Country Club; Fort Worth Country Club; City Club.

Giving Program Officials
Lynn M. Platania: director community relations

Target Corp.

 Number 29 of Top 100 Corporate Givers

Company Contact
777 Nicollet Mall
Minneapolis, MN 55402-2055
Phone: (612)370-6948
Fax: (612)370-5502
Web: http://www.targetcorp.com

Company Description
Revenue: US$33,702,000,000 (1999)
Profit: US$1,144,000,000 (1999)
Employees: 214,000 (2000)
Fortune Rank: 32, per FORTUNE Magazine's list of 500 Largest U.S. Corporations (1999).
FF 32
SIC(s): 5331 Variety Stores.
Parent Company: Dayton Hudson, Minneapolis, MN, United States
Parent Revenue: US$33,702,000,000 (1999)

SUBSIDIARY COMPANIES
CA: Mervyn's California, Hayward; MN: Dayton Hudson, Minneapolis; IL: Marshall Field's, Chicago

Nonmonetary Support
Type: Cause-related Marketing & Promotion; Donated Equipment; Donated Products
Note: Contact local store for details.

Corporate Sponsorship
Type: Arts & cultural events; Festivals/fairs
Contact: Debbie Estes, director, events marketing
Note: Sponsors events for social causes.

Giving Contact
Ann Aronson, Director, Community Relations
Target Stores
PO Box 1392
Minneapolis, MN 55440-1392
Phone: (612)304-8721
Fax: (612)304-5660

Description
Organization Type: Corporate Giving Program
Giving Locations: headquarters and operating communities.
Grant Types: Project.

Giving Philosophy
'As a major national retailer, service is central to our business. But that's only the beginning. We also serve our communities, and strive to improve the quality of life for our employees and customers. As a result, we are an active participant in the communities where we operate stores. It's the way we do business. .. Our financial resources focus on programs that will have direct, positive effects on families. Through partnerships with local nonprofit organizations, our Good Neighbor Volunteer Program, and Target funding, we can work together to improve the quality of life that all of us enjoy.' *Building Community Partnerships Application Brochure*

Financial Summary
Total Giving: $30,000,000 (1998 approx); $19,600,000 (1997); $11,000,000 (1996 approx). Note: Contributes through corporate direct giving program only.

Typical Recipients

Arts & Humanities: Arts Festivals, Community Arts, Dance, Ethnic & Folk Arts, Museums/Galleries, Music, Opera, Performing Arts, Theater, Visual Arts
Social Services: Domestic Violence, Family Services

Contributions Analysis

Arts & Humanities: Supports programs which provide quality arts experiences for family audiences through art exhibits, classes, performances, and arts-in-education programs. Specific interests are in programs that are appealing and accessible to family audiences,are affordable for families (low price, ticket subsidy or free), and which bring arts to schools or school children to the arts.
Education: Provides scholarships to high school seniors who have shown a commitment to education, community volunteer service, and close family involvement.
Social Services: Supports organizations offering programs that provide long-term impact in strengthening families. Specifically, emphasizes programs that teach skills promoting effective family relationships, including parenting education, family counseling and support groups, and effective communication; or that prevent violence and neglect in family relationships, including the prevention of child abuse and domestic violence.

Application Procedures

Initial Contact: application guidelines available through local Target Stores or from headquarters (for nearest store, call 800-800-8800); if your organization and project meet criteria, submit a grant proposal to the local Target store team leader
Application Requirements: two- to three-page project description, including a description of the activity, event, or project; the need for the program; how the program will enrich and strengthen families in Target communities; a description of organization's main audience; an explanation of the expected outcome or result of the program; program impact; how results will be measured and evaluated; the proposed time frame; project budget information that details the various expenses and anticipated income sources; and plans if Target is unable to fund the full amount requested; a current, annual operating budget for the organization that lists income and expenses; a list of major business donors that includes their contributions level; a list of the organization's board of directors; the most recent audited financial statement for the organization; and a copy of the IRS ruling on the organization's nonprofit 501(c)(3) status
Deadlines: while grants are made throughout the year, applicants are encouraged to submit proposals between March 1 and November 1
Review Process: art funding is decided at the district level; store team leaders review social action requests and make recommendations to Target headquarters
Decision Notification: decisions usually are made within two or three months

Restrictions

Company does not make grants to programs outside Target communities; community foundations; endowment funds or capital fund drives; religious organizations; healthcare rehabilitation organizations; housing programs; treatment programs, i.e., medical, substance abuse, or alcohol abuse; individuals; athletic teams or events; fundraisers or tickets for benefit dinners; or advertising purposes.
Social service agencies with religious affiliations are eligible for grants if the proposed project does not advocate religious beliefs or practices, or restrict participation on the basis of religion.
Merchandise contributions, discounts, or gift certificates are not provided in lieu of grants.

Additional Information

Company donates 5% of federally taxable income to programs that meet social and cultural needs. Target is the largest operating company of the Dayton Hudson Corp. (see separate entry).
Company hosts an annual holiday party for senior citizens and persons with disabilities.
Most grants support specific programs, but general operating support will be considered when an organization's overall mission matches company's funding guidelines.
Grants are renewable, based upon an evaluation of achieved results, continuing need, and available funds.
Organizations that are funded by United Way are not excluded from applying for a grant.
Publications: Contributions Guidelines

Corporate Officials

Larry Gilpin: executive vice presidento, director B Benton, IL 1943. ED Louisiana State University; Western Kentucky University BS (1965); University of Kentucky MBA (1971). PRIM CORP EMPL executive vice president: Dayton Hudson Corp.
Robert J. Ulrich: chairman, chief executive officer, director B Minneapolis, MN 1944. ED University of Minnesota (1967); Stanford University Executive Program (1978). PRIM CORP EMPL chairman, chief executive officer, director: Dayton Hudson Corp. PRIM NONPR EMPL chairman, chief executive officer, director: Target Stores. CORP AFFIL director: Tricon Global Restaurants Inc.

Giving Program Officials

Linnea Rynders: grant administrator
Elia E. Tello: community relations representative

Grants Analysis

Disclosure Period: calendar year ending 1997
Total Grants: $19,600,000*
Number of Grants: 4,000
Average Grant: $4,900
Typical Range: $1,000 to $5,000
***Note:** Figures are approximate and were provided by the co.

TCF National Bank Minnesota

Company Contact

Minneapolis, MN
Web: http://www.tcfbank.com

Company Description

Former Name: TCF Banking & Savings FSB.
Assets: US$3,632,600,000
SIC(s): 6035 Federal Savings Institutions.
Parent Company: TCF Financial Corp.

Corporate Sponsorship

Type: Festivals/fairs; Pledge-a-thon

TCF Foundation

Giving Contact

Rebecca Escalante
TCF Foundation
801 Marquette Ave.
Minneapolis, MN 55402
Phone: (612)745-2750

Alternate Contact

TCF Bank Wisconsin
500 W. Brown Deer Road
Milwaukee, WI 53217-1698

Description

EIN: 411659826
Organization Type: Corporate Foundation
Giving Locations: headquarters and operating communities.
Grant Types: Department, Employee Matching Gifts, General Support, Operating Expenses.
Note: Employee matching gift ratio: 1 to 1 for most charitable 501(c)(3) organizations.

Giving Philosophy

'TCF Financial Corporation believes that contributions should be an investment in the future of the people in the communities it serves. The financial health of a company is dependent upon the social environment of the communities in which it operates as well as upon the economic environment. Business has an obligation to support private philanthropy, particularly when failing to do so might well result in a government assuming responsibility for a service or function that could be more efficiently and humanely provided by the private sector. The societal needs that can be met in part through the philanthropic activities of companies are widespread and varied. TCF Financial believes that prudence dictates that it concentrate its philanthropy in those specific geographical areas in which it has an immediate and long-range interest and some expertise. By doing so, the Corporation has reasonable assurance that there will be both short-term and long-range benefit from its philanthropy.' *TCF Foundation Contribution Guidelines*

Financial Summary

Total Giving: $2,000,000 (1999 approx); $2,000,000 (1998 approx); $1,300,000 (1997 approx)
Giving Analysis: Giving for 1996 includes: foundation ($902,328); corporate direct giving ($350,000); foundation grants to United Way ($96,466); foundation matching gifts ($24,802)
Assets: $791,907 (1996); $360,291 (1995); $249,240 (1994)
Gifts Received: $1,623,483 (1996); $1,100,100 (1995); $1,084,828 (1994). Note: Contributions are received from TCF Bank Minnesota.

Typical Recipients

Arts & Humanities: Arts Associations & Councils, Arts Centers, Arts Funds, Arts Institutes, Arts & Humanities-General, Libraries, Museums/Galleries, Music, Opera, Performing Arts, Public Broadcasting, Theater
Civic & Public Affairs: African American Affairs, Business/Free Enterprise, Chambers of Commerce, Economic Development, Employment/Job Training, Civic & Public Affairs-General, Housing, Law & Justice, Municipalities/Towns, Nonprofit Management, Professional & Trade Associations, Safety, Urban & Community Affairs, Women's Affairs
Education: Business Education, Business-School Partnerships, Colleges & Universities, Community & Junior Colleges, Education Associations, Education Funds, Faculty Development, Education-General, Private Education (Precollege), Science/Mathematics Education, Secondary Education (Public), Student Aid
Health: Clinics/Medical Centers, Health-General, Health Funds, Health Organizations, Heart, Hospitals, Medical Rehabilitation, Public Health
International: International Organizations
Religion: Ministries, Religious Organizations, Religious Welfare
Science: Observatories & Planetariums, Science Museums
Social Services: Child Welfare, Community Centers, Community Service Organizations, Recreation & Athletics, Scouts, Senior Services, Shelters/Homelessness, Social Services-General, Substance Abuse, United Funds/United Ways, Volunteer Services, YMCA/YWCA/YMHA/YWHA, Youth Organizations

Contributions Analysis

Arts & Humanities: 5%. Supports museums, arts associations, and the performing arts in communities where company operates.

Civic & Public Affairs: 35%. Supports housing, welfare reform, and economic development.

Education: 20%. Supports business education at secondary and college levels.

Social Services: 35%. Supports the United Way, youth groups, community centers, and senior services.

Application Procedures

Initial Contact: Include a a brief letter of inquiry written grant request.

Application Requirements: Include a description of organization; list of board members, including information on people who will manage project; audited financial statements, current budget, and next year's budget; mission statement and summary of long-range plans; purpose of contribution requested and relationship to plans; list of major contributors and amounts given; how project relates to foundation's interests and guidelines; methods of evaluating program's effectiveness; company employee involvement; sources of income, current and planned; copy of IRS 501(c)(3) tax-exemption determination letter.

Deadlines: None.

Evaluative Criteria: Charitable grants are made (with few exceptions) only to tax-exempt 501(c)(3) organizations; special consideration is given to those institutions supported by the employees of TCF Financial Corporation or its subsidiaries through their personal contributions of time and/or money.

Decision Notification: Most funding decisions will require at least sixty days for review.

Notes: In Minnesota, all requesters are required to use the Minnesota Common Grant application form. Grant requests may be directed to offices in Michigan, Illinois, Wisconsin, or Minnesota.

Restrictions

The foundation does not make grants to individuals, political parties or candidates, lobbying groups, individual churches or sectarian activities, advertising or subsidizing publications, or social events of otherwise qualified organizations.

Support will be given only to organizations that are able to provide evidence of 501(C)(3) tax-exempt status.

Foundation does not award multi-year grants.

Grants are only made to organizations located in areas where TCF has a bank office. Grants are made to United Way campaigns in communities where TCF has well-established offices.

Additional Information

TCF Bank Minnesota, FSB, was formerly named TCF Bank Savings, FSB.

Publications: Community Affairs Report; Grant Request Guidelines

Corporate Officials

William Allen Cooper: chairman, director chief financial officer, treasurer B Detroit, MI 1943. ED Wayne State University BS (1967). PRIM CORP EMPL chairman, director: TCF Bank Minnesota FSB. CORP AFFIL principal: TCF finance Insurance Agency; chairman, director: TCF Fin Corp. NONPR AFFIL member: American Institute CPAs.

Thomas A. Cusick: chairman B Detroit, MI 1944. ED University of Detroit (1971); Rutgers University Stonier Graduate School of Banking (1977). PRIM CORP EMPL chairman: TCF Bank Minnesota FSB. CORP AFFIL vice chairman, chief operating officer: TCF Fin Corp.; chairman: TCF National Bank Minnesota; director: Damark International.

Lynn A. Nagorske: executive vice president, chief financial officer, treasurer B Windom, MN 1956. ED Mankato State University BS (1977). PRIM CORP EMPL executive vice president, chief financial officer, treasurer: TCF Bank Minnesota FSB. CORP AFFIL chairman: TCF Mortgage Corp.; director: Winthrop Resources Corp.; treasurer: Great Lakes National Bank; president: TCF Fin Corp.

Foundation Officials

Peter Bell: president PRIM CORP EMPL executive vice president: TCF Financial Corp. ADD CORP EMPL executive vice president: TCF National Bank Minnesota.

Morgan Brown: senior community affairs officer

Rebecca Escalante: community affairs officer

Grants Analysis

Disclosure Period: calendar year ending 1996

Total Grants: $902,328*

Number of Grants: 269

Average Grant: $3,354

Highest Grant: $60,000

Typical Range: $100 to $5,000

***Note:** Giving excludes corporate direct giving; matching gifts; United Way.

Recent Grants

Note: Grants derived from 1996 Form 990.

Arts & Humanities

8,000	Artspace -- operating support
5,000	Minneapolis Institute of Arts, Minneapolis, MN
4,000	United Arts Fund, Minneapolis, MN -- for expenses

Civic & Public Affairs

60,000	Community Reinvest -- for community development
60,000	Urban Ventures Leadership Foundation, Minneapolis, MN -- for Kitchen Incubator
60,000	Women's Venture, New York, NY -- for community development
24,000	Twin Cities Neighborhood, Saint Paul, MN -- for community development
20,000	Jeremiah Program, Minneapolis, MN -- for community development
15,000	Family Housing Fund, Minneapolis, MN -- for community development
10,000	City of Minneapolis, Minneapolis, MN -- for employment
10,000	Frogtown Action Alliance, Saint Paul, MN -- capital campaign
10,000	Greater Minneapolis Metro, Minneapolis, MN -- for community development
10,000	Overcoming Poverty, Mankato, MN -- for community development
7,500	Minneapolis Foundation, Minneapolis, MN -- Minnesota Future Fund
5,000	CommonBond Community Fund
5,000	Harriet Tubman Women -- capital campaign
5,000	St. Paul Chamber of Commerce, Saint Paul, MN -- support Prepare St. Paul
5,000	Twin Cities Opportunities Industrialization Corp, Saint Paul, MN -- for education
5,000	Whittier Housing Fund
4,000	Simpson Housing Services
3,500	Lyndale Development
3,500	Lyndale Neighborhood
3,000	Community Action and Home Buyer Education
3,000	Powderhorn Community Fund

Education

26,216	Patrick Henry High School, Minneapolis, MN -- for 1995-96
25,000	Minnesota Private, Saint Paul, MN -- for education
24,743	Patrick Henry High School, Minneapolis, MN -- for computers
10,000	University of Minnesota, Minneapolis, MN -- for Carlson School of Management
8,500	Citizens Scholarships, Minneapolis, MN -- for education
8,098	Patrick Henry High School, Minneapolis, MN -- for Liberty Parent
6,000	Junior Achievement, Minneapolis, MN -- for education
5,000	Project 120 -- for scholarships
3,695	Patrick Henry High School, Minneapolis, MN
3,000	Patrick Henry High School, Minneapolis, MN

Health

30,000	Courage Center, Golden Valley, MN -- for human service
6,000	HealthFund of Minneapolis, Minneapolis, MN -- for human services
5,000	Minneapolis Heart, Minneapolis, MN -- for human services

Religion

10,000	Union Gospel Mission, Minneapolis, MN -- for WorkNet Program
8,000	Presbyterian Homes -- for human services
5,000	Our Saviours Lutheran -- for shelter

Science

5,500	Science Museum -- for education

Social Services

25,000	Project for Pride in Living, Minneapolis, MN -- for HOMS program
18,501	United Way, Minneapolis, MN -- for human services
18,501	United Way, Minneapolis, MN -- for human services
10,000	W. Harry Davis Foundation, Minneapolis, MN -- for human services
7,500	Minnesota Children, MN -- capital campaign
5,000	Boy Scouts of America Viking Council, MN -- for education
5,000	Chrysalis, Minneapolis, MN -- capital campaign
5,000	Hallie Q. Brown Community Center, Saint Paul, MN -- for human services
5,000	Hammer Residences, Wayzata, MN -- for human services

TEKTRONIX, INC.

Company Contact

Wilsonville, OR

Web: http://www.tek.com

Company Description

Employees: 8,392

SIC(s): 2759 Commercial Printing Nec, 3575 Computer Terminals, 3825 Instruments to Measure Electricity, 3829 Measuring & Controlling Devices Nec.

Operating Locations

Operates offices in 25 states, the District of Columbia, and internationally.

Nonmonetary Support

Value: $400,000 (1996)

Type: Donated Equipment; Donated Products

Contact: Patty Larkins, Program Manager

Tektronix Foundation

Giving Contact

Jill Powers Kirk, Executive Director
Tektronix Foundation
2660 Southwest Parkway
PO Box 1000, M.S. 63-813
Wilsonville, OR 97070-1000
Phone: (503)685-2862

Fax: (503)685-4017

Description

EIN: 936021540
Organization Type: Corporate Foundation
Giving Locations: CA: Southwestern Washington; OR: Northwestern Oregon
Grant Types: Employee Matching Gifts, General Support, Project, Research, Scholarship.
Note: Employee matching gift ratio: 1 to 1 for gifts to education, the arts, and conservation. Scholarships are provided for dependents of employees only.

Financial Summary

Total Giving: $1,100,000 (1999 approx); $1,122,018 (1998); $1,229,329 (1997). Note: Contributes through corporate direct giving program and foundation. Giving includes foundation.
Giving Analysis: Giving for 1996 includes: foundation matching gifts ($212,491); 1998: foundation grants to United Way ($285,000); foundation matching gifts ($188,358); foundation scholarships ($37,600)
Assets: $2,257,096 (1998); $1,997,391 (1997); $2,282,878 (1996)
Gifts Received: $1,100,000 (1998); $1,100,000 (1997); $1,100,000 (1996). Note: Contributions are received from Tektronix, Inc.

Typical Recipients

Arts & Humanities: Arts Associations & Councils, Arts Institutes, Ballet, History & Archaeology, Libraries, Museums/Galleries, Music, Opera, Performing Arts, Public Broadcasting, Theater
Civic & Public Affairs: Business/Free Enterprise, Economic Development, Economic Policy, Civic & Public Affairs-General, Hispanic Affairs, Native American Affairs, Urban & Community Affairs, Zoos/Aquariums
Education: Arts/Humanities Education, Business Education, Colleges & Universities, Community & Junior Colleges, Economic Education, Education Funds, Engineering/Technological Education, Environmental Education, Education-General, Minority Education, Private Education (Precollege), Public Education (Precollege), Science/Mathematics Education, Student Aid
Environment: Environment-General, Resource Conservation
Health: Emergency/Ambulance Services, Hospitals
Science: Science Exhibits & Fairs, Science Museums
Social Services: Child Welfare, Community Service Organizations, United Funds/United Ways, Youth Organizations

Contributions Analysis

Giving Priorities: Higher education and social welfare, with lesser interests in the arts and civic causes.
Arts & Humanities: 21%. Majority supports arts outreach programs, which combine arts and education. Also supports Oregon arts groups, with an emphasis on Portland. Matches gifts to art and culture.
Civic & Public Affairs: 15%. Supports the Portland Metro Zoo and minority and employment programs.
Education: 26%. Major support is awarded to colleges and universitites emphasizing technical, business, and computer science education. Also supports K-12 education, focusing on math, physical sciences, and supplementary programs. Matches gifts to education, and provides scholarships for employees' children.
Social Services: 38%. Majority supports the United Way; also funds youth organizations.
Note: Total contributions in 1998.

Application Procedures

Initial Contact: Send a letter of inquiry or full proposal.
Application Requirements: Include a description of organization, amount requested, description of project and purpose of funds sought, recently audited financial statement, and proof of tax-exempt status.
Deadlines: None.

Corporate Officials

James F. Dalton: vice president, general counsel, secretary ED Boston College JD (1985). PRIM CORP EMPL vice president, general counsel, secretary: Tektronix Inc.
Michele Potter Marchesi: vice president corporate communications & human resources PRIM CORP EMPL vice president corporate communications & human resources: Tektronix, Inc.
Jerome J. Meyer: chairman, chief executive officer B Caledonia, MN 1938. ED Hamline University (1956-1958); University of Minnesota BA (1960). PRIM CORP EMPL chairman, chief executive officer: Tektronix, Inc. CORP AFFIL director: Standard Insurance Co.; director: Esterline Technologies Corp.; director: Portland General Electric Co.; director: Enron Corp.; director: AMP Inc. NONPR AFFIL trustee: Willamette University; director: YMCA; trustee: Oregon Graduate Institute; director: Oregon Business Council; trustee: Oregon Childrens Foundation. CLUB AFFIL Oregon Golf Club.
Douglas C. Shafer: president, America operations B Portland, OR 1959. ED Portland State University (1981); University of Oregon (1987). PRIM CORP EMPL president, America operations: Tektronix, Inc.

Foundation Officials

James F. Dalton: chairman, trustee (see above)
Jill Powers Kirk: executive director PRIM CORP EMPL director community affairs: Tektronix Inc.
Michele Potter Marchesi: trustee (see above)
Douglas C. Shafer: trustee (see above)
Robert L. Vance: trustee B 1943. ED Wichita State University; Wichita State University MBA. PRIM CORP EMPL vice president information system: Tektronix Inc.

Grants Analysis

Disclosure Period: calendar year ending 1998
Total Grants: $611,033*
Number of Grants: 46
Average Grant: $13,283
Highest Grant: $60,000
Typical Range: $300 to $25,000
***Note:** Giving excludes matching gifts, scholarship, United Way.

Recent Grants

Note: Grants derived from 1997 Form 990.

Arts & Humanities

75,000	Portland Art Museum, Portland, OR
30,000	Portland Art Museum, Portland, OR
25,000	Oregon Ballet Theater, Portland, OR
25,000	Oregon Symphony Association, Portland, OR
25,000	Portland Art Museum, Portland, OR
10,000	Artists Repertory Theater, Portland, OR
10,000	Portland Center Stage, Portland, OR
10,000	Portland Opera Association, Portland, OR
10,000	Portland Repertory Theater, Portland, OR
10,000	Portland Youth Philharmonic, Portland, OR
10,000	Tygres Heart Shakespeare Company
5,000	Chamber Music Northwest, Portland, OR
5,000	Northwest Business Community for the Arts, Portland, OR
5,000	Oregon Children's Theater, Portland, OR
5,000	Oregon Historical Society, Portland, OR
5,000	Portland Baroque Orchestra, Portland, OR

Civic & Public Affairs

45,000	Portland Metro Zoo, Portland, OR
10,000	Oregon Council for Hispanic Achievement, Portland, OR
10,000	SOLV

Education

50,000	Oregon Independent College Foundation, Portland, OR
50,000	Oregon State University, Corvallis, OR
34,000	96 Tek Kids Scholarship
30,000	Saturday Academy, Portland, OR
15,000	Maryhurst College
4,000	Oregon State University, Corvallis, OR
3,400	Central Oregon Service to Community Scholarships
3,200	Saturday Academy Women in Science, Portland, OR
2,500	Junior Achievement, Omaha, NE
2,000	MathCounts, Alexandria, VA
1,400	Tek Kids Scholarships
1,100	Tek Kids Scholarships
1,000	Mount Hood Community College
800	96 Tek Kids Scholarship
300	Lyman Gilmore Middle School
100	Lyman Gilmore Middle School

Science

50,000	Oregon Museum of Science and Industry, Portland, OR

Social Services

71,250	United Way, Portland, OR
71,250	United Way, Portland, OR
71,250	United Way, Portland, OR
5,000	Boys and Girls Club, Bakersfield, CA
4,000	93 Child of Tek

TELCORDIA TECHNOLOGIES

Company Contact

Morristown, NJ
Web: http://www.bellcore.com

Company Description

Former Name: Bell Communs. Res.
Employees: 5,270
SIC(s): 8742 Management Consulting Services.
Parent Company: Science Applications International Corp., San Diego, CA, United States

Nonmonetary Support

Type: Donated Equipment; In-kind Services

Corporate Sponsorship

Type: Music & entertainment events

Giving Contact

Ron Reichmann, Manager, Corporate Contributions
Telcordia Technologies
445 South Street, Room 1C3526
Morristown, NJ 07960
Phone: (973)829-2177
Fax: (973)829-2159

Description

Founded: 1984
Organization Type: Corporate Giving Program
Giving Locations: headquarters area only.
Grant Types: Capital, General Support, Matching, Multiyear/Continuing Support, Research, Scholarship, Seed Money.

Financial Summary

Total Giving: $350,000 (2000 approx); $350,000 (1999 approx). Note: Contributes through corporate direct giving program only.

Typical Recipients

Arts & Humanities: Arts Associations & Councils
Civic & Public Affairs: Professional & Trade Associations
Education: Colleges & Universities
Health: Emergency/Ambulance Services, Hospitals
Social Services: United Funds/United Ways

Contributions Analysis

Arts & Humanities: About 10%. Supports arts associations.
Civic & Public Affairs: 10% to 15%. Includes grants to professional and trade associations.
Education: Approximately 50%. Focus is on colleges and universities.
Health: About 25%. Primarily supports the United Way, hospitals, and emergency services.

Application Procedures

Initial Contact: written proposal
Application Requirements: description and mission of organization, amount requested, purpose of funds sought, budget and audited financial statements, support from other sources, and proof of tax-exempt status
Deadlines: None.

Restrictions

The company does not support individuals, religious organizations for sectarian purposes, political or lobbying groups, organizations not eligible for tax-deductible support, organizations that discriminate for any reason, or national health organizations other than United Way. The company also does not consider requests for donations or prizes for fundraising events.

Corporate Officials

Sanjiv Ahuja: president, chief operating officer, director PRIM CORP EMPL president, chief operating officer, director: Bell Communications Research.
Stephen Chappell: corporate vice president PRIM CORP EMPL corporate vice president: Bell Communications Research (Bellcore).
John E. Glancy: corporate executive vice president, chairman B 1946. ED University of Pittsburgh BS (1968); Cornell University MS (1970); Cornell University MS (1970); Cornell University PhD (1972). PRIM CORP EMPL corporate executive vice president, chairman: Science Applications International Corp. ADD CORP EMPL vice chairman: Telcordia.
N. Michael Groves: vice president, general counsel
Robert Wendell Lucky: corporate vice president B Pittsburgh, PA 1936. ED Purdue University BSEE (1957); Purdue University MS (1959); Purdue University PhD (1961). PRIM CORP EMPL corporate vice president: Bell Communications Research (Bellcore). NONPR AFFIL member science advisory board: United States Air Force; member: University California, Santa Barbara; fellow: IEEE; member: NAE; director: Computer Museum; member: European Academy Arts Science; member: American Academy of Arts & Sciences; member: Community Society.
Ward Reed: corporate vice president, chief financial officer PRIM CORP EMPL corporate vice president, chief financial officer: Bell Communications Research.
Ron Riehmann: manager corporate contributions PRIM CORP EMPL manager corporate contributions: Bell Communications Research.
Jerry Roberto: president PRIM CORP EMPL president: Bell Communications Research (Bellcore).
Robert J. Singsank: corporate vice president PRIM CORP EMPL corporate vice president: Bell Communications Research (Bellcore).
Richard C. Smith: chief executive officer, director ED Vanderbilt University BE; Yale University MA; Yale University PhD; Yale University MS. PRIM CORP EMPL chief executive officer: Telcordia Technologies ADD CORP EMPL senior vice president: Sprint Corp.
John Andrew Warner, III: director B New Haven, CT 1946. ED Princeton University BA (1968); Northwestern University MS (1971). ADD CORP EMPL senior vice president, chief financial officer: NCCI.

TELEFLEX INC.

Company Contact

Limerick, PA

Company Description

Employees: 9,800
SIC(s): 3625 Relays & Industrial Controls, 3812 Search & Navigation Equipment, 3841 Surgical & Medical Instruments.

Operating Locations

Sermatech International Inc. operates 4 plants in locations.

Teleflex Foundation

Giving Contact

Thelma A. Fretz, Vice President & Secretary
Teleflex Foundation
155 S. Limerick Rd.
Limerick, PA 19468
Phone: (610)948-5100

Description

EIN: 232104782
Organization Type: Corporate Foundation. Supports preselected organizations only.
Giving Locations: headquarters and operating communities.
Grant Types: Employee Matching Gifts, General Support.

Financial Summary

Total Giving: $250,000 (1997 approx); $271,984 (1996); $259,267 (1995)
Assets: $1,452,731 (1996); $993,413 (1995); $931,597 (1994)
Gifts Received: $525,000 (1996); $200,000 (1995); $580,125 (1994)

Typical Recipients

Arts & Humanities: Ballet, Arts & Humanities-General, History & Archaeology, Libraries, Museums/Galleries, Music
Civic & Public Affairs: Business/Free Enterprise, Civic & Public Affairs-General, Housing, Zoos/Aquariums
Education: Arts/Humanities Education, Business Education, Colleges & Universities, Economic Education, Education-General, Private Education (Precollege), Public Education (Precollege)
Health: Health-General, Hospices, Nursing Services, Public Health
International: International Affairs, International Organizations
Science: Scientific Centers & Institutes
Social Services: Child Welfare, Community Service Organizations, Scouts, Senior Services, Social Services-General, Special Olympics, YMCA/YWCA/YMHA/YWHA, Youth Organizations

Restrictions

Does not support individuals, religious organizations for sectarian purposes, political or lobbying groups, or organizations outside operating areas.

Corporate Officials

Lennox K. Black: chairman, director B Montreal, PQ Canada 1930. ED Royal Naval College (1949); McGill University (1952). PRIM CORP EMPL chairman, director: Teleflex. CORP AFFIL director: TFX Engineering; director: Westmoreland Coal Co.; director: Quaker Chemical Corp.; director: Penn Virginia Corp.; director: Pep Boys; director: Envirite Corp.
David Scott Boyer: president, chief executive officer, director B Detroit, MI 1942. ED Saint Joseph's College BS (1964); University of Detroit (1965); Harvard University Graduate School of Business Administration (1976). PRIM CORP EMPL president, chief executive officer, director: Teleflex.
Harold L. Zuber, Jr.: vice president, chief financial officer PRIM CORP EMPL vice president, chief financial officer: Teleflex.

Foundation Officials

Lennox K. Black: president (see above)

Grants Analysis

Disclosure Period: calendar year ending 1996
Total Grants: $271,984
Number of Grants: 183
Average Grant: $1,486
Highest Grant: $25,500
Typical Range: $500 to $5,000

Recent Grants

Note: Grants derived from 1995 Form 990.

Arts & Humanities

30,250	Philadelphia Orchestra Association, Philadelphia, PA
7,750	Philadelphia Museum of Art, Philadelphia, PA
5,000	Bucks County Historical Society, Doylestown, PA
5,000	Philadelphia Singers, Philadelphia, PA
3,000	Pennsylvania Ballet, Philadelphia, PA
2,500	Wissahickon Valley Public Library, North Wales, PA
2,200	Mann Music Center, Philadelphia, PA
2,000	Philomel Concerts, Philadelphia, PA
2,000	Please Touch Museum, Philadelphia, PA

Civic & Public Affairs

5,000	Habitat for Humanity, New Ipswich, NH
5,000	Philadelphia Zoological Gardens, Philadelphia, PA
3,000	Handisoft Foundation, Philadelphia, PA
2,500	California Business Week Foundation, Oxnard, CA

Education

10,000	Gwynedd Mercy College, Gwynedd Valley, PA
5,000	Eufaula Education Foundation, Eufaula, PA
4,025	Thomas Jefferson University, Philadelphia, PA
4,000	Sacred Heart School, Conroe, TX
4,000	Willis Independent School District, Willis, TX
3,500	Maryland Institute College of Art, Baltimore, MD
3,250	Economics and Entrepreneurship Education, Philadelphia, PA
2,400	Foundation for Free Enterprise Education, Erie, PA

Health

3,000	Creative Health Services, Pottstown, PA
2,500	Community Visiting Nurse Services, Phoenixville, PA
2,500	Hospice, Charlotte, NC

International

2,500	World Affairs Council, Philadelphia, PA
2,000	International House of Philadelphia, Philadelphia, PA

Science

2,000	Academy of Natural Sciences, Philadelphia, PA

Social Services

6,085	YMCA, Phoenixville, PA
5,000	Child Welfare League of America, Washington, DC
5,000	North Penn Valley Boys and Girls Club, Lansdale, PA
3,000	Need In Deed, Philadelphia, PA
2,250	Boy Scouts of America Valley Forge Council, Valley Forge, PA
2,100	Pennsylvania Special Olympics, Exton, PA
2,000	Fellowship Farms, Pottstown, PA
2,000	Senior Adult Activity Center of Montgomery County, Norristown, PA

TEMPLE-INLAND INC.

Company Contact

Diboll, TX

Company Description

Revenue: US$4,063,000,000 (1999)
Profit: US$99,200,000 (1999)
Fortune Rank: 393, per FORTUNE Magazine's list of 500 Largest U.S. Corporations (1999).
FF 393
SIC(s): 2421 Sawmills & Planing Mills--General, 2611 Pulp Mills, 2621 Paper Mills, 6719 Holding Companies Nec.

Temple-Inland Foundation

Giving Contact

Mr. Evonne Nerren, Secretary & Treasurer
Temple-Inland Foundation
303 S Temple Dr.
PO Box N
Diboll, TX 75941
Phone: (409)829-1721
Fax: (409)829-7406

Description

EIN: 751977109
Organization Type: Corporate Foundation
Giving Locations: headquarters.
Grant Types: Employee Matching Gifts, General Support, Scholarship.

Financial Summary

Total Giving: $3,200,000 (fiscal year ending June 30, 1999 approx); $3,200,000 (fiscal 1998 approx); $2,928,203 (fiscal 1997). Note: Contributes through foundation only. Giving includes matching gifts; scholarship.
Assets: $3,018,345 (fiscal 1997); $2,493,445 (fiscal 1996); $5,578,702 (fiscal 1995)
Gifts Received: $2,975,000 (fiscal 1997); $3,775,000 (fiscal 1996); $1,950,000 (fiscal 1995)

Typical Recipients

Arts & Humanities: Arts Associations & Councils, Ethnic & Folk Arts, Libraries, Museums/Galleries, Theater
Civic & Public Affairs: African American Affairs, Clubs, Community Foundations, Employment/Job Training, Housing, Law & Justice, Municipalities/Towns, Public Policy, Safety, Urban & Community Affairs, Zoos/Aquariums
Education: Business Education, Colleges & Universities, Elementary Education (Private), Engineering/Technological Education, Education-General, Preschool Education, Private Education (Precollege), Public Education (Precollege), Religious Education, Secondary Education (Private), Secondary Education (Public), Vocational & Technical Education
Environment: Forestry, Environment-General, Resource Conservation, Wildlife Protection
Health: Children's Health/Hospitals, Clinics/Medical Centers, Health Organizations, Hospices, Hospitals, Medical Research
Religion: Seminaries
Science: Science Museums
Social Services: Camps, Child Welfare, Community Service Organizations, Crime Prevention, Family Services, Food/Clothing Distribution, People with Disabilities, Shelters/Homelessness, Substance Abuse, United Funds/United Ways, Volunteer Services, YMCA/YWCA/YMHA/YWHA, Youth Organizations

Contributions Analysis

Giving Priorities: Scholarships, museums, libraries, health, and youth organizations.
Note: Grant awards comprise 55% to 60% of total foundation giving; employee scholarships and other scholastic awards, 20% to 25%; and matching gifts, 15% to 20%.

Application Procedures

Initial Contact: request application form, then written request
Application Requirements: completed application form, a description of organization; amount requested; purpose of funds sought; recently audited financial statements; proof of tax-exempt status
Deadlines: None.

Restrictions

Does not provide support to individuals; fraternal or veterans organizations; political or lobbying groups; or religious organizations.

Additional Information

Inland Container, a subsidiary, also maintains a foundation.
Publications: Application Form

Corporate Officials

Clifford J. Grum: director, chairman, chief executive officerlt B Davenport, IA 1934. ED Austin College BA (1956); University of Pennsylvania Wharton School MBA (1958). PRIM CORP EMPL director, chairman, chief executive officer: Temple-Inland Inc. ADD CORP EMPL president: Guaranty Holdings Inc.; director: Inland Paperboard and Packg; director: Temple-Inland Financial Service; chairman: Temple-Inland Forest Products Corp.; chairman: Temple-Inland Paperboard Specialty. CORP AFFIL director: Tupperware Corp. Inc.; director: Trinity Industries Inc.; director: Cooper Industries Inc.; chairman,director: Guaranty Federal Bank FSB. NONPR AFFIL trustee: Austin College.
Doyle Simons: director investor relations PRIM CORP EMPL director investor relations: Temple Inland Inc.

Foundation Officials

Clifford J. Grum: director (see above)
Kenneth M. Jastrow, II: director B 1947. ED University of Texas BA (1970); University of Texas MBA (1971). PRIM CORP EMPL president, chief operating officer: Temple-Inland Inc. ADD CORP EMPL chairman, president: Lumbermans Investment Corp. CORP AFFIL chairman, chief executive officer: Temple-Inland Financial Services Inc.; chairman, chief executive officergroup vice president financial services: Temple-Inland Mortgage Corp.; chairman: Knutson Mortgage Corp.; chairman: Guaranty Federal Bank FSB; director: Inland Paperboard Packaging; chairman: Capitol Mortgage Bankers Inc.
Harold C. Maxwell: director B 1940. ED Texas A&M University (1963). PRIM CORP EMPL group vice president: Temple-Inland Inc. ADD CORP EMPL group vice president, director: Temple-Inland Forest Products Corp. CORP AFFIL director: Inland Paperboard Packaging.
Evonne Nerren: secretary, treasurer
Doyle Simons: president (see above)
Roger B. Smart: vice president
Jack C. Sweeny: director PRIM CORP EMPL vice president forest division: Temple-Inland Inc.
Arthur Temple, III: director B Texarkana, AR 1920. ED University of Texas, Austin (1937-1938). PRIM CORP EMPL chairman, chief executive officer: Exeter Investment Co. ADD CORP EMPL treasurer: Demcp Manufacturing Co. CORP AFFIL director: Temple-Inland Financial Services Inc.; chairman: Temple-Inland Inc.; director: Guaranty Federal Bank FSB; director: Contractors Supplies Inc.; chairman, director: First Bank & Trust East Texas.
M. Richard Warner: director B Lufkin, TX 1951. ED Baylor University BBA (1974); Baylor University JD (1975). PRIM CORP EMPL vice president, secretary, general counsel: Temple-Inland Inc. ADD CORP EMPL vice president, corporate secretary: Guaranty Holdings Inc.; vice president, corporate secretary, director: Inland Paperboard Packaging Inc.; vice president, director: Temple-Inland Financial Services Inc.; vice president, corporate secretary, director: Temple-Inland Food Services Inc.; vice president, corporate secretary, director: Temple-Inland Forest Products Corp.; vice president, corporate secretary, director: Temple-Inland Realty Inc.

Grants Analysis

Disclosure Period: fiscal year ending June 30, 1997
Total Grants: $1,532,252*
Number of Grants: 777
Average Grant: $1,972
Highest Grant: $78,244
Typical Range: $500 to $4,500
***Note:** Giving excludes gifts to individuals; United Way.

Recent Grants

Note: Grants derived from fiscal 1997 Form 990.

Arts & Humanities

50,000	Austin Children's Museum, Austin, TX
25,100	T.L.L. Temple Memorial Library, Diboll, TX
9,058	Museum of East Texas, Lufkin, TX
8,000	Ensemble Theater, Houston, TX

Civic & Public Affairs

71,000	Diboll Booster Club, Diboll, TX
21,000	City of Pineland, Pineland, TX
13,040	Friends of the Ellen Trout Zoo, Lufkin, TX
13,000	City of Zavalla, Zavalla, TX
10,300	Lake Rayburn Volunteer Fire Department, Sam Rayburn, TX

Education

78,244	University of Texas Austin, Austin, TX
68,643	Texas A&M University, College Station, TX
50,000	Angelina College, Lufkin, TX
46,632	Stephen F. Austin State University, Nacogdoches, TX
25,000	Pineland Early Learning Center, Pineland, TX
22,775	Indiana University Foundation, Bloomington, IN
22,293	University of Houston, Houston, TX
20,150	Little Cypress Mauriceville, Orange, TX
19,903	St. Patrick Catholic School, West Memphis, AR
19,813	Lamar University, Beaumont, TX
16,450	Clemson University, Clemson, SC
14,800	Baylor University, Waco, TX
14,000	Model High School, Rome, GA
12,050	Olivet Nazarene University, Kankakee, IL
11,615	Junior Achievement, Indianapolis, IN
10,000	Augusta Technical Institute, Augusta, GA
9,700	Hudson Independent School District, Lufkin, TX

8,500	McNeese State University, Lake Charles, LA
8,288	University of Alabama, Tuscaloosa, AL
7,915	Purdue University, West Lafayette, IN
7,650	St. Stephen's Episcopal School, Austin, TX
6,600	University of Southern Wisconsin, Madison, WI
6,456	University of Evansville, Evansville, IN
6,300	Auburn University, Auburn, AL
6,300	Austin College, Austin, TX
6,150	University of Southern Mississippi, Hattiesburg, MS
6,075	Millsep College, Jackson, MS
Environment	
10,000	Texas Forestry Association, Lufkin, TX
Health	
41,495	Ronald McDonald House, Austin, TX
17,355	Hospice in the Pines, Lufkin, TX
7,650	Scott and White Memorial Hospital, Temple, TX
Religion	
8,450	Dallas Theological Seminary, Dallas, TX
Science	
7,000	Natural History Museum, Athens, GA
Social Services	
68,410	Boys and Girls Clubs, Galveston, TX
50,707	United Way Angeline County, Lufkin, TX
33,740	United Way Capital Area, Austin, TX
25,000	Alcohol and Drug Abuse Council, Lufkin, TX
25,000	Partners Resource Network, Beaumont, TX
10,000	Hardin County Sheriff's Department, Kountze, TX
9,500	Goodwill Industries, Evansville, IN
9,417	United Way, Beaumont, TX

TENET HEALTHCARE CORP.

Company Contact

Santa Barbara, CA
Web: http://www.tenethealth.com

Company Description

Revenue: US$10,880,000,000 (1999)
Profit: US$249,000,000 (1999)
Fortune Rank: 158, per FORTUNE Magazine's list of 500 Largest U.S. Corporations (1999).
FF 158
SIC(s): 8062 General Medical & Surgical Hospitals, 8063 Psychiatric Hospitals, 8069 Specialty Hospitals Except Psychiatric.

Operating Locations

Operates health care facilities in various overseas locations.

Corporate Sponsorship

Type: Arts & cultural events; Festivals/fairs; Music & entertainment events; Sports events

Tenet Healthcare Foundation

Giving Contact

Barbara Luton, Executive Director
Tenet Healthcare Foundation
PO Box 31907
Santa Barbara, CA 93105-1907
Phone: (805)563-6865
Fax: (805)898-9104
Email: foundation@tenethealth.com

Description

Organization Type: Corporate Foundation
Giving Locations: principally near operating locations and to national organizations.
Grant Types: Award, Capital, Employee Matching Gifts, Endowment, General Support, Matching.
Note: Matches gifts to qualified local, regional, and national organizations that hold 501 (c)(3) tax exempt status.

Giving Philosophy

'Tenet directs its corporate charitable contributions primarily to nonprofit organizations engaged in beneficial healthcare activities to improve the quality of life where employees live and work. The major share of resources is devoted to programs in support of healthcare projects. Some support is given to higher and secondary education, with emphasis on research and healthcare. The company sponsors an employee educational matching gift program.'

Financial Summary

Total Giving: $6,500,000 (2000 approx); $5,451,355 (1999); $1,738,745 (1998). Note: Giving includes corporate direct giving; foundation giving.
Giving Analysis: Giving for 1998 includes: foundation ($4,767,232); corporate direct giving ($684,123)

Typical Recipients

Civic & Public Affairs: Nonprofit Management
Education: Colleges & Universities, Medical Education, Minority Education
Health: Health Organizations, Medical Research, Medical Training, Mental Health, Nursing Services, Single-Disease Health Associations
Social Services: Child Welfare, Community Centers, People with Disabilities, Senior Services, Youth Organizations

Contributions Analysis

Giving Priorities: National and local health organizations, health-related education, and united funds and youth organizations.
Education: Funding goes to programs leading to careers in medicine, nursing, or health care administration; institutions that train future health care professionals, and provide continuing education of health care professionals; and programs to support advancement and improvement of health care education.
Health: Majority of support goes to health care projects and programs, including organizations that improve the efficiency of the healthcare delivery system; organizations that promote individual and community education in health; organizations and institutions the develop medical research programs, publications, conferences and seminars; organizations that seek to develop cures for debilitating diseases and conditions; and human service programs that benefit the aging, the handicapped, and persons unable to obtain adequate medical care.

Application Procedures

Initial Contact: Call or write for application, then send full proposal.
Application Requirements: Include a general letter with organization's history, project description, and project budget; completed application; list of board of directors, current budget and financial statement, annual report, most recent audited financial report, last year's IRS Form 990, and IRS Form 501(c)(3).
Deadlines: None.
Evaluative Criteria: Priority is given to single-year funding, projects which eliminate duplication and encourage collaboration, model projects that can be replicated, and projects with a clear specific purpose that can be evaluated; emphasis placed on organizations recommended by Tenet facilities and regional offices.
Decision Notification: Approximately 90 days after receipt of request.

Restrictions

Contributions are not generally made to individuals; fraternal, labor, political, or veterans groups; religious or sectarian institutions; travel expenses, or cultural exchange programs for individuals; direct funding for hospital operations; discharge of operating deficits or to retire debts; or contributions to one organization for support of the programs of another.

Corporate Officials

Jeffrey C. Barbakow: chairman, chief executive officer, director B Los Angeles, CA 1944. ED San Jose State University BS (1966); University of Southern California MBA (1968). PRIM CORP EMPL chairman, chief executive officer, director: Tenet Healthcare Corp. ADD CORP EMPL principal: Tenet Health System Medical.

Foundation Officials

Barbara B. Luton: executive director NONPR AFFIL director: Santa Barbara Museum Art.

Grants Analysis

Disclosure Period: calendar year ending
Typical Range: $2,000 to $10,000

TENNANT CO.

Company Contact

Minneapolis, MN

Company Description

Employees: 2,127 (1999)
SIC(s): 2842 Polishes & Sanitation Goods, 2843 Surface Active Agents, 2851 Paints & Allied Products, 3589 Service Industry Machinery Nec.

Nonmonetary Support

Type: Donated Equipment
Volunteer Programs: The Volunteer Gift-Matching Program was established to recognize the volunteer work of company employees. The program matches 40 hours or more per year of volunteer hours to a single agency with a $200 gift, if that agency would otherwise be eligible for foundation grants. In 1997, the program supported over 850 hours of volunteer work by TENNANT employees.
Contact: Roger Hale, Foundation President

Corporate Sponsorship

Type: Arts & cultural events

TENNANT Co. Foundation

Giving Contact

Carol A. Van Lith, Secretary/Administrator
TENNANT Co. Foundation
PO Box 1452
Minneapolis, MN 55440
Phone: (612)540-1209
Fax: (612)540-1616
Email: carol.vanlith@tennantco.com

Description

Founded: 1973
EIN: 237297045
Organization Type: Corporate Foundation
Giving Locations: headquarters and operating communities.
Grant Types: Capital, Emergency, Employee Matching Gifts, General Support, Operating Expenses, Scholarship.
Note: Employee matching gift ratio: 2 to 1 for the first $200 to higher education and public broadcasting; 1 to 1 up to $1,500 for all other gifts to nonprofits.

Giving Philosophy

'The Management of TENNANT firmly believes that corporate responsibility involves the corporation's involvement in the total life of the communities in which it operates. To this end, the TENNANT Foundation has focused its contributions efforts in three major areas: Community/Conservation and Health Needs, Cultural Activities and Educational Programs.' *TENNANT Foundation Annual Report*

Financial Summary

Total Giving: $429,937 (1998); $339,187 (1997); $338,439 (1996). Note: Contributes through foundation only.
Giving Analysis: Giving for 1997 includes: foundation ($150,108); foundation grants to United Way ($131,485); foundation matching gifts ($57,594); 1998: foundation ($209,034); foundation grants to United Way ($134,996); foundation matching gifts ($51,907)
Assets: $1,669,814 (1998); $1,426,359 (1997); $1,230,056 (1996)
Gifts Received: $601,460 (1998); $478,658 (1997); $1,267,000 (1996). Note: Contributions are received from TENNANT Co.

Typical Recipients

Arts & Humanities: Arts Centers, Arts Institutes, Dance, History & Archaeology, Literary Arts, Museums/Galleries, Music, Opera, Performing Arts, Public Broadcasting, Theater
Civic & Public Affairs: Economic Development, Employment/Job Training, Civic & Public Affairs-General, Housing, Philanthropic Organizations, Urban & Community Affairs, Women's Affairs, Zoos/Aquariums
Education: Business Education, Colleges & Universities, Education Funds, Education Reform, Education-General, International Studies, Minority Education, Public Education (Precollege), Special Education, Student Aid, Vocational & Technical Education
Environment: Air/Water Quality, Environment-General
Health: Clinics/Medical Centers, Health Policy/Cost Containment, Health Organizations, Medical Rehabilitation, Mental Health, Single-Disease Health Associations
International: Human Rights, International Organizations, International Relief Efforts
Religion: Religious Welfare
Science: Science Museums
Social Services: At-Risk Youth, Child Welfare, Community Centers, Community Service Organizations, Domestic Violence, Family Planning, Family Services, People with Disabilities, Refugee Assistance, Shelters/Homelessness, Substance Abuse, United Funds/United Ways, YMCA/YWCA/YMHA/YWHA, Youth Organizations

Contributions Analysis

Giving Priorities: Supports social services, the arts, education, and civic organizations.
Arts & Humanities: 20% to 25%. Supports Minneapolis/St. Paul area arts organizations. Interests include the performing arts, opera, music, and public broadcasting. Company matches employee gifts to cultural organizations.
Civic & Public Affairs: 5% to 10%. Supports youth organizations, housing, shelters, neighborhood improvement projects, citizens groups and women's issues.
Education: 5% to 10%. Supports public and private higher education and education organizations. Company matches employee gifts to education. Company also sponsors a scholarship program for eligible children of employees.
Health: Less than 5%.
International: Less than 5%.
Religion: Less than 5%.
Science: Less than 5%.
Social Services: 55% to 60%. Supports learning disabilities, children services, YMCA, food for the hungry, and the United Way. Company matches employee gifts to the United Way.

Application Procedures

Initial Contact: Call or write requesting application guidelines; then written proposal.
Application Requirements: Include name, address, contact person, and telephone number of the organization, and date of application; history and general purpose of the organization, including a description of current programs and program statistics; purpose of request, including evidence of need, proposed achievements, method of evaluation, and expected long-range results; amount of request, including where other funds are being sought and pledges received to date; description of how project will be funded on an ongoing basis, if necessary; budget history and program budget, including cur rent operating budget and audited financial statement; evidence of IRS tax-exempt status and Minnesota Charities Registration (if applicable); and list of board of directors.
Deadlines: Four weeks prior to board meeting dates in March, June, September, and December; contact foundation for exact dates.
Review Process: Board of directors meets quarterly to consider requests; proposals are first researched by a consultant through a process that may include on-site evaluations and written reviews.
Evaluative Criteria: Ability to serve the special needs of a given community and have proven to have a significant impact upon that community; reasonable project and organizational objectives including long-range plans and a method of program evaluation; prior receipt of broad-based community support; sound fiscal policies; competent management staff, and an involved board of directors. Priority is given to organizations with company employee volunteers, organizations serving company communities, and organizations which have already received grants from the foundation.

Restrictions

Does not support organizations located outside the Minneapolis or western suburb area, except in areas where company has a concentration of employees; agencies also funded through umbrella organizations; organizations and programs designed to influence legislation or elect candidates to public office; national organizations without active local chapters; religious organizations for religious purposes; individuals; elementary and secondary schools; trips or tours; or tickets, tables, or advertising for benefit purposes.

Additional Information

It is expected that the foundation will continue to limit new funding in order to ensure that adequate monies are available to fund ongoing commitments.
Publications: Annual Report (including Application Guidelines)

Corporate Officials

Roger Loucks Hale: chairman B Plainfield, NJ 1934. ED Brown University BA (1956); Harvard University Graduate School of Business Administration MBA (1961). PRIM CORP EMPL chairman: TENNANT Co. CORP AFFIL vice chairman, director: Dayton Hudson Corp.; director: United States Bancorp. NONPR AFFIL member: Machinery & Allied Products Institute; director: Minnesota Business Partnership.

Foundation Officials

Richard M. Adams: director B 1948. PRIM CORP EMPL vice president, chief acctg officer: Tennant Co.
Barbara A. Clarity: director
Roger Loucks Hale: president (see above)
Joseph A. Shaw: treasurer, director
William Strang: vice president

Grants Analysis

Disclosure Period: calendar year ending 1998
Total Grants: $209,034*
Number of Grants: 83
Average Grant: $2,518
Highest Grant: $34,000
Typical Range: $1,000 to $5,000
***Note:** Giving excludes matching gifts; United Way.

Recent Grants

Note: Grants derived from 1998 Form 990.

Arts & Humanities

8,334	Minnesota Opera, Minneapolis, MN
6,000	Minnesota Orchestral Association, Minneapolis, MN
5,500	Walker Art Center, Minneapolis, MN
5,000	KTCA-TV, Minneapolis, MN
4,500	Guthrie Theater, Minneapolis, MN
4,200	Minnesota Public Radio, Minneapolis, MN
4,000	Minneapolis Institute of Arts, Minneapolis, MN
3,000	KTCA-TV, Minneapolis, MN
2,500	KTCA-TV, Minneapolis, MN
2,500	Minnesota Opera, Minneapolis, MN
2,000	Children's Theater Company, Minneapolis, MN
2,000	Minnesota Childrens Museum, Minneapolis, MN
2,000	St. Paul Chamber Orchestra, St. Paul, MN
1,500	Child's Play Theater, Edina, MN
1,500	Jungle Theater, Minneapolis, MN
1,500	Minnesota Chorale, Minneapolis, MN
1,500	Plymouth Music Series, Minneapolis, MN

Civic & Public Affairs

2,000	Citizen's League, Minneapolis, MN
2,000	Loring Nicollet Bethlehem, Minneapolis, MN
1,500	Employment Action Center, Minneapolis, MN
1,500	Neighborhood Involvement Project, Minneapolis, MN
1,500	Project for Pride in Living, Minneapolis, MN
1,500	Simpson Housing Development, Minneapolis, MN

Education

10,000	Minnesota Private College Fund, Minneapolis, MN
7,500	U of M - Carlson School of Management, Minneapolis, MN
3,500	Institute for Education and Advocacy, Minneapolis, MN
3,000	Page Educational Foundation, Minneapolis, MN
3,000	U of M - Carlson School of Management, Minneapolis, MN
2,500	U of M - Carlson School of Management, Minneapolis, MN
2,000	Dunwoody Institute, Minneapolis, MN
1,500	English Learning Center, Minneapolis, MN
1,500	Learning Disabilities Association, Minneapolis, MN

Environment

2,000	Nature Conservancy, Minneapolis, MN

Health

2,500	Courage Center, Golden Valley, MN

International

1,609	United Way of Montreal, Montreal, PQ, Canada

Religion

2,000	Catholic Charities, Minneapolis, MN

Science

2,000	Science Museum of Minnesota, St. Paul, MN

Social Services

34,000	YMCA, Minneapolis, MN
30,250	United Way of Minneapolis, Minneapolis, MN
30,250	United Way of Minneapolis, Minneapolis, MN
30,250	United Way of Minneapolis, Minneapolis, MN
30,250	United Way of Minneapolis, Minneapolis, MN
5,000	Boys and Girls Club, Minneapolis, MN
3,800	Children's Home Society, Minneapolis, MN
3,000	C.E.A.P., Minneapolis, MN
3,000	United Way of Orange County, Irvine, CA
2,000	C.E.A.P., Minneapolis, MN
2,000	Reuben Lindh Family Services, Minneapolis, MN
1,964	United Way of Metro Atlanta, Atlanta, GA
1,710	United Way of Camden County, Kingsland, GA

TENNECO AUTOMOTIVE

Company Contact

Greenwich, CT
Web: http://www.tenneco.com

Company Description

Former Name: Tenneco Inc. (1999).
Revenue: US$3,279,000,000 (1999)
Employees: 23,600
Fortune Rank: 469, per FORTUNE Magazine's list of 500 Largest U.S. Corporations (1999).
FF 469
SIC(s): 6719 Holding Companies Nec.

Operating Locations

Argentina: Tenneco Automotive, Buenos Aires, Rosario; Australia:, Adelaide, Sydney; Belgium:, St. Truide; Brazil:, Mogi Mirim, Sao Paolo; Canada:, Cambridge, Owen Sound; People's Republic of China:, Beijing, Dalian; Czech Republic:, Lazne Bel Hodkovice; Denmark:, Middelfart; France:, Etain, Laval, Wissembo; Germany: Tenneco Packaging, Bopfingen; Tenneco Automotive, Buerstadt, Edenkobe; Tenneco Packaging, Elsfeth, Halle, Hamburg, Linlar, Rohrdorf, Warburg; Tenneco Automotive, Zwickau; Hungary: Tenneco Packaging, Akko, Budapest, Hibbutz Ga'; India: Tenneco Automotive, Hosur, Madras, Pondicherry; Italy: Tenneco Packaging, Ossago, Pisticci; Japan:, Kyoto; Tenneco Automotive, Yokohama; Tenneco Packaging, Yokohama; Mexico: Tenneco Automotive, Celaya, Puebla, Queretaro, Reynosa, San Pedrito; Netherlands: Tenneco Packaging, Eerbeck, Naarden; New Zealand: Tenneco Automotive, Lower Hutt; Poland: Tenneco Packaging, Gliwice; Portugal: Tenneco Automotive, Palmela; Romania: Tenneco Packaging, Bucharest, Buchin; Republic of South Africa: Tenneco Automotive, Pretoria; Singapore:; Spain: Tenneco Packaging, Aoiz; Tenneco Automotive, Ermua, Gijon, Valencia; Sweden:, Vittaryd; Switzerland: Tenneco Packaging, Belp; Turkey: Tenneco Automotive, Corlu; United Kingdom:, Birmingham; Tenneco Packaging, Bristol; Tenneco Automotive, Burnley; Tenneco Packaging, Caerphilly, Winsford; Tenneco Automotive, Cardiff; Tenneco Packaging, Great Yarm, Livingston, Stanley; Tenneco Automotive, Tredegar

Nonmonetary Support

Value: $400,000 (1995); $200,000 (1994); $400,000 (1993)
Type: Cause-related Marketing & Promotion; Donated Equipment; In-kind Services; Loaned Employees; Loaned Executives
Contact: Gloria Moritz, Committee Affairs Representative

Corporate Sponsorship

Value: $600,000
Type: Festivals/fairs; Sports events
Note: Sponsors the Houston-Tenneco Marathon and arts events.

Giving Contact

Chris Gable, Community Affairs
Tenneco Inc.
1275 King St.
Greenwich, CT 06831
Phone: (203)863-1000
Fax: (203)863-1146

Description

Organization Type: Corporate Giving Program
Giving Locations: headquarters and operating communities.
Grant Types: Capital, Conference/Seminar, Department, Employee Matching Gifts, Endowment.
Note: Employee matching gift ratio: 1 to 1 for gifts to educational institutions and arts and cultural organizations.

Financial Summary

Total Giving: $6,200,000 (1997 approx); $6,525,311 (1996); $6,316,987 (1995). Note: Contributes through corporate direct giving program only. Giving includes corporate direct giving; international subsidiaries.
Assets: $450,000 (1995 approx); $415,000 (1994 approx); $400,000 (1992)

Typical Recipients

Arts & Humanities: Arts Associations & Councils, Arts Centers, Arts Festivals, Arts Funds, Community Arts, Dance, Historic Preservation, Libraries, Museums/Galleries, Music, Opera, Performing Arts, Public Broadcasting, Theater, Visual Arts
Civic & Public Affairs: Business/Free Enterprise, Employment/Job Training, Housing, Law & Justice, Professional & Trade Associations, Public Policy, Safety, Urban & Community Affairs, Women's Affairs, Zoos/Aquariums
Education: Business Education, Colleges & Universities, Community & Junior Colleges, Economic Education, Education Associations, Education Funds, Engineering/Technological Education, Faculty Development, Literacy, Minority Education, Public Education (Precollege), Science/Mathematics Education, Student Aid
Environment: Environment-General
Health: Emergency/Ambulance Services, Health Organizations, Hospices, Hospitals, Medical Research, Mental Health, Nutrition, Single-Disease Health Associations
Science: Science Exhibits & Fairs
Social Services: Animal Protection, Community Centers, Community Service Organizations, Delinquency & Criminal Rehabilitation, Emergency Relief, Food/Clothing Distribution, People with Disabilities, Senior Services, Shelters/Homelessness, Substance Abuse, United Funds/United Ways, Volunteer Services, Youth Organizations

Contributions Analysis

Giving Priorities: Higher education, social welfare, health, civic and public affairs, and arts and humanities. Like the domestic giving program, contributions by foreign operating companies are decentralized. Local managers submit budgets for approval to corporate headquarters; however, priorities are based on community needs. Some emphasis is on health and human service organizations.
Arts & Humanities: About 10%. Includes visual and performing arts organizations, libraries, museums, cultural centers, arts funds, or councils and the like. Includes support for public radio and television if funded from the contributions budget.
Civic & Public Affairs: About 10%. Includes support for national organizations in public-policy research (Forum for International Policy); national community improvements (Committee for Economic Development, Enterprise Foundation, Points of Light Foundation); national environment (Nature Conservacy, Keep America Beautiful); national justice and law organizations (Independent Sector, Council for Excellence in Government); municipal or statewide improvements (Forward Wisconsin, Western Pennsylvania Conservancy); local community improvements (neighborhood or community-based groups); housing programs; economic development and employment (private industry councils, job training programs); local legal systems and services research (Legal Aid Society); local environment and ecology (zoos, parks, conservation activities); and other local civic and community organizations. Includes local projects such as transportation, housing law and order, fire prevention, grants tolocal or state governments, and support of study groups to resolve social problems. Supports United Way.
Education: About 55%. Includes support for institutions of higher education, precollege educational institutions, state and local educational fund-raising groups, economic education groups and education-related organizations. Program support for research projects funded from the contributions budget is included; however, support of contractual university research is generally excluded. Educational programs such as employee tuition-refund plans are excluded when funded out of the personnel, public relations, or other expense budgets.
Health: About 25%. Includes support for national health organizations (American Cancer Society, Leukemia Society of America, Multiple Sclerosis); national human service orgainzations (American Red Cross, National Committee for Prevention of Child Abuse); national youth organizations (Boys Clubs of America); support for hospitals; local youth organizations (Boys Clubs, Boy or Girl Scouts, YMCA); and other local health and human services agencies. Other interests are agencies concerned with safety, recreation, family planning, drug abuse and disaster relief.

Application Procedures

Initial Contact: Send a brief letter or proposal on organization's letterhead to contributions coordinator at divisional company operating most prominently in the geographic area; for Houston area and national activities, send brief letter or proposal to John Castellani, executive vice president.
Application Requirements: Include a description of the organization, amount requested, purpose of funds sought, expected outcomes, proof of tax-exempt status, financial report, board of directors, and budget for project.
Deadlines: August 15.
Review Process: Proposals are recorded and reviewed by the Contributions Committee, and recommendations made to senior management.
Decision Notification: January.

Restrictions

Company does not give to political or lobbying groups; religious organizations; or individuals.

Additional Information

Each operating location administers its own contributions program. Together these local programs account for around 50% of overall Tenneco giving.

Corporate Officials

John Castellani: executive vice presidento, director B Syracuse, NY 1951. ED Union College (1972).

PRIM CORP EMPL executive vice president: Tenneco Inc. NONPR AFFIL trustee: Business-Industry Politcal Action Committee.
Arthur H. House: senior vice president corporate affairs PRIM CORP EMPL senior vice president corporate affairs: Tenneco Inc.
Dana George Mead: chairman, chief executive officer, director B Cresco, IA 1936. ED United States Military Academy BS (1957); Massachusetts Institute of Technology PhD (1967). PRIM CORP EMPL chairman, chief executive officer, director: Tenneco Inc. CORP AFFIL director: Zurich Life Insurance; director: Zurich Group; director: Zurich Insurance; director: Unisource Worldwide Inc.; director: Tennessee Gas Pipeline Co.; director: Textron Inc.; director: Pfizer Inc.; director: Newport News Shipbuilding & Drydock; director: Newport News Shipbuilding Inc.; director: Logistics Management Institute; director: Case Corp. NONPR AFFIL member: President Commission White House Fellowships West Point Society; member: West Point Society New York; director: National Association Manufacturer; trustee: George C Marshall Foundation; member: Massachusetts Institute Technology Visiting Committee on Political Science; member: Council Foreign Relations; member: American Society Corporate Executives; trustee: Association Grads W Point. CLUB AFFIL University Club; Metro Club; Greenwich City Club; Greenwich Country Club; Blind Brook Club.

Giving Program Officials

Ethel Samuels: PRIM CORP EMPL contributions coordinator: Tenneco Inc.
Jo Ann Swinney: PRIM CORP EMPL director community affairs: Tenneco Inc.

Grants Analysis

Disclosure Period: calendar year ending 1996
Total Grants: $6,525,311
Typical Range: $1,000 to $10,000

TENNECO PACKAGING

Company Contact

Evanston, IL

Company Description

Former Name: Packaging Corp. of America.
Employees: 20,000
SIC(s): 2421 Sawmills & Planing Mills--General, 2611 Pulp Mills, 2631 Paperboard Mills, 2653 Corrugated & Solid Fiber Boxes.
Parent Company: Tenneco Automotive, Greenwich, CT, United States

Operating Locations

Operates in 100 field locations.

Nonmonetary Support

Type: Cause-related Marketing & Promotion; Donated Products

Giving Contact

Warren Hazelton, Director, Corporate Relations
Packaging Corp. of America
1900 West Field Ct.
Lake Forest, IL 60045
Phone: (847)492-6968
Fax: (847)570-3034

Description

Organization Type: Corporate Giving Program
Giving Locations: headquarters and operating communities.
Grant Types: Award, Emergency, Employee Matching Gifts, General Support, Scholarship.

Financial Summary

Total Giving: Contributes through corporate direct giving program only.

Typical Recipients

Arts & Humanities: Community Arts, Arts & Humanities-General, Libraries, Museums/Galleries, Public Broadcasting
Civic & Public Affairs: Civic & Public Affairs-General, Municipalities/Towns
Education: Arts/Humanities Education, Business Education, Colleges & Universities, Economic Education, Elementary Education (Private), Engineering/Technological Education, Education-General, Minority Education, Public Education (Precollege), Science/Mathematics Education, Special Education
Health: Emergency/Ambulance Services, Health-General, Hospices, Hospitals, Nursing Services, Single-Disease Health Associations
Social Services: Community Service Organizations, Emergency Relief, Food/Clothing Distribution, Recreation & Athletics, Shelters/Homelessness, Social Services-General, United Funds/United Ways, Youth Organizations

Contributions Analysis

Arts & Humanities: Less than 5%. Supports community arts, libraries, museums, andpublic broadcasting.
Civic & Public Affairs: 10% to 15%. Favors municipalities and community affairs.
Education: About 40%. Primary interests include business, minority, public, and science and technology education. Also contributes to colleges and universities and special education.
Health: About 35%. Focus is on youth centers, nursing services, and community service organizations.
Note: About 10% of funding is set aside for contingency within the four categories above. The company's program is highly decentralized across more than 100 locations. Local charitable organizations may make requests to community representatives at the nearest plant. Small contributions are at the discretion of the plant; larger requests are forwarded to corporate headquarters with recommendations for support.

Application Procedures

Initial Contact: a brief letter of inquiry
Application Requirements: a description of organization, amount requested, purpose of funds sought, recently audited financial statement, and proof of tax-exempt status
Deadlines: None; annual budget developed in July
Notes: No phone calls will be accepted, and local requests must be made through local operating facilities.

Restrictions

The company does not support individuals, religious organizations for sectarian purposes, or political or lobbying groups.

Corporate Officials

Robert A. Page: chief financial officer, director B 1951. ED Lamar University BS (1974). PRIM CORP EMPL chief financial officer: Tenneco Inc. CORP AFFIL chief financial officer: Tenneco Packaging Inc.
Paul T. Stecko: president, director B 1944. ED University of Pittsburgh MBA; University of Pittsburgh MS; Pennsylvania State University BS (1966). PRIM CORP EMPL president, director: Tenneco Inc. CORP AFFIL president: Tenneco Packaging Inc.; president: Tenneco Packaging Supply Services.

Giving Program Officials

Warren Hazelton: director PRIM CORP EMPL director corporate relations: Tenneco Packaging Inc.

Grants Analysis

Disclosure Period: calendar year ending
Typical Range: $500 to $2,500

TENSION ENVELOPE CORP.

Company Contact

Kansas City, MO

Company Description

Employees: 1,650
SIC(s): 2677 Envelopes.

Operating Locations

Includes plant locations.

Tension Envelope Foundation

Giving Contact

Eliot S. Berkley, Secretary
Tension Envelope Foundation
819 East 19th Street, 3rd Floor
Kansas City, MO 64108
Phone: (816)471-3800
Fax: (816)283-1498

Description

Founded: 1954
EIN: 446012554
Organization Type: Corporate Foundation
Giving Locations: MO
Grant Types: General Support.

Financial Summary

Total Giving: $246,650 (fiscal year ending November 30, 1998); $271,150 (fiscal 1997); $252,850 (fiscal 1996). Note: Contributes through foundation only.
Giving Analysis: Giving for fiscal 1997 includes: foundation ($200,700); foundation grants to United Way ($70,450); fiscal 1998: foundation ($164,200); foundation grants to United Way ($70,450); foundation scholarships ($12,000)
Assets: $3,751,568 (fiscal 1998); $3,000,000 (fiscal 1997 approx); $2,900,838 (fiscal 1996)
Gifts Received: $120,000 (fiscal 1998); $295,500 (fiscal 1997); $267,000 (fiscal 1996). Note: In 1997, contributions were received from Tension Envelope Corp.

Typical Recipients

Arts & Humanities: Arts Centers, Arts Institutes, Community Arts, Dance, Museums/Galleries, Public Broadcasting, Theater
Civic & Public Affairs: Botanical Gardens/Parks, Business/Free Enterprise, Community Foundations, Civic & Public Affairs-General, Housing, Professional & Trade Associations, Urban & Community Affairs, Women's Affairs, Zoos/Aquariums
Education: Business Education, Business-School Partnerships, Colleges & Universities, Community & Junior Colleges, Continuing Education, Economic Education, Education Funds, Education Reform, Education-General, Minority Education, Private Education (Precollege), Public Education (Precollege), Vocational & Technical Education
Environment: Environment-General
Health: Clinics/Medical Centers, Health Organizations, Hospices, Hospitals, Mental Health, Public Health
International: International Affairs, International Relations, International Relief Efforts, Missionary/Religious Activities
Religion: Jewish Causes, Religious Organizations, Religious Welfare, Social/Policy Issues, Synagogues/Temples
Social Services: Child Welfare, Community Service Organizations, Crime Prevention, Domestic Violence, Family Planning, Family Services, People with Disabilities, Shelters/Homelessness, Substance Abuse,

United Funds/United Ways, Volunteer Services, YMCA/YWCA/YMHA/YWHA, Youth Organizations

Contributions Analysis

Arts & Humanities: 4%. Museums, public broadcasting, and a symphony are supported.
Education: 13%. Primarily supports colleges and universities with several donations to scholarship funds. Also supports continuing education.
Health: 1%. Medical centers, clinics, and hospices.
Religion: 37%. Majority of funding supports the Jewish Federation of Kansas City. Other recipients include Jewish women's groups, family services, and some non-Jewish religious welfare groups.
Social Services: 46%. Funds the United Way, family planning, and family and youth services.
Note: Total contributions in 1998.

Application Procedures

Initial Contact: Send a brief letter of request.
Application Requirements: Include a description of organization activities, amount of support requested, purpose of funds sought, a copy of tax-exempt certificate, and a copy of the budget.
Deadlines: None.
Decision Notification: Foundation reviews requests as received and will notify applicants.

Restrictions

Grants are not made to individuals.

Corporate Officials

Eugene Bertram Berkley: chairman, director B Kansas City, MO 1923. ED Duke University BA (1948); Harvard University Graduate School of Business Administration MBA (1950). PRIM CORP EMPL chairman, director: Tension Envelope Corp. CORP AFFIL director: Tension Envelope Corp. New York; director: Reference Press. NONPR AFFIL director: National Youth Information Network; director: Travelfest; director: National Minority Supplier Development Council; advisory board: National Parks & Conservation Association; director: Institute Entrepreneurial Leadership Inc.; advisory board: National History Museum; member: Flexographic Technology Association; Business Roundtable Apartment Social Service; member: Envelope Manufacturer Association America. CLUB AFFIL Oakwood Country Club; Homestead Country Club.
Richard L. Berkley: treasurer, secretary, director B 1931. PRIM CORP EMPL treasurer, secretary, director: Tension Envelope Corp.
William S. Berkley: president, chief executive officer, director B Kansas City, MO 1956. ED Colorado College BA (1974-1978); Dartmouth College Amos Tuck Graduate School of Business Administration (1979-1981). PRIM CORP EMPL president, chief executive officer, director: Tension Envelope Corp. CORP AFFIL director: Reference Press.
Walter L. Hiersteiner: vice chairman B Des Moines, IA 1918. ED University of Iowa BA (1939); Harvard University LLB (1942). PRIM CORP EMPL vice chairman: Tension Envelope Corp.

Foundation Officials

Eliot S. Berkley: secretary
Eugene Bertram Berkley: treasurer (see above)
Richard L. Berkley: president (see above)
William S. Berkley: director (see above)
Walter L. Hiersteiner: vice president (see above)
Abraham E. Margolin: director B Saint Joseph, MO 1907. ED Washington University LLD; Washington University JD. PRIM CORP EMPL attorney: Gage & Tucker. CORP AFFIL director: UMB Mortgage Co.; director: Tension Envelope Corp. NONPR AFFIL member: United States Supreme Court Historical Society; member: World Jewish Congress; member board governors: Research Mental Health Foundation; life member: Truman Medicine Center; member: Metropolitan Kansas City Bar ASN; member: Missouri Bar Association; life member: Menorah Medicine Center; member: Heritage Foundation; director, vice president: Jewish Federation Greater Kansas City; member board governors: Hebrew Academy Kansas City; member board governors: City Trust Kansas City; member: Federation Bar Association; member: Cato Institute; member: ATLA; president council, fellow: Brandeis University; governor: American Royal Association; member advisory board: Anti-Defamation League B'nai B'rith; member national executive council: American Joint Distribution Committee; member: American Judicature Society; member: American Jewish Congress; member: American Bar Association; member national executive council: American Jewish Committee. CLUB AFFIL Oakwood Golf & Country Club; Kansas City Club.

Grants Analysis

Disclosure Period: fiscal year ending November 30, 1998
Total Grants: $164,200*
Number of Grants: 93
Average Grant: $1,766
Highest Grant: $65,000
Typical Range: $250 to $3,000
*Note: Giving excludes United Way, scholarships.

Recent Grants

Note: Grants derived from fiscal 1998 Form 990.

Arts & Humanities

3,250 KCPT-19, Kansas City, MO
2,500 Center for Contemporary Arts in St. Louistom Hillman, St. Louis, MO
1,000 Johnson County Museum, Shawnee, KS
1,000 KCUR-FM 89.3 (UMKC), Kansas City, MO
1,000 Starlight Theatre, Kansas City, MO

Civic & Public Affairs

2,500 Friends of the Zoo, Kansas City, MO
1,000 Local Investment Group (LINC), Kansas City, MO
1,000 Mocsa, Kansas City, MO
1,000 VICA - Kansas City, Kansas City, MO

Education

5,000 Bank St. College of Education, New York, NY
2,500 Be2:School-to-Career, Kansas City, MO
2,500 Partnership for Outstanding Schools, Jefferson City, MO
2,500 Wildwood Outdoor Ed Center, Lacygne, KS
2,000 Central MO State University, Warrensburg, MO
2,000 Kansas State University, Manhattan, KS
2,000 Learning Exchange, Kansas City, MO
2,000 University of Kansas, Lawrence, KS
1,400 Iowa College Foundation, Des Moines, IA
1,000 Baker University, Baldwin, KS
1,000 Central City School Fund, Kansas City, MO
1,000 Fort Hays State University, Hayes, KS
1,000 Junior Achievement of Middle America, Kansas City, MO
1,000 Long Island University, Brooklyn, NY
1,000 MO College Fund, Jeffcty, MO
1,000 National Council Economic Educ., New York, NY
1,000 No. Carolina State University, Raleigh, NC
1,000 Pembroke Hill School, Kansas City, MO
1,000 Rockhurst College, Kansas City, MO
1,000 Rutgers College, New Brunswick, NJ
1,000 United Negro College, New York, NY
1,000 University of Iowa, Iowa City, IA

Health

1,000 Mental Health Association/Heartland, Kansas City, KS

International

500 International Relations Council, Kansas City, MO

Religion

65,000 Jewish Federation of KC, Overland Park, KS
10,000 Jewish Federation KC - Ladies, Overland Park, KS
5,000 Midwest Center for Holocaust Education, Inc., Overland Park, KS
4,500 Jewish Federation of Greater Des Moines, Ames, IA
2,500 The Temple Congregation B'Nai Jehudah, Kansas City, MO
2,000 National Council of Jewish Women, Shawnee Mission, KS
1,000 Jewish Family & Children Services, Overland Park, KS
1,000 Sacred Heart Southern Missions Housing, Walls, MS
1,000 Salvation Army, Kansas City, MO

Social Services

55,000 Heart of America United Way, Kansas City, MO
6,000 United Way of Central Iowa, Des Moines, IA
6,000 United Way of MPLS, Minneapolis, MN
3,000 Kansas Children's SVC. League, Wichita, KS
2,500 Planned Parenthood - KC, Kansas City, MO
2,500 Safehome, Inc., Overland Park, KS
2,500 YMCA, Kansas City, MO
1,650 United Way of Tarrant County, Ft Worth, TX
1,500 United Way Shelby Company, Memphis, TN
1,000 Heart of America Family Services, Kansas City, KS

TESORO HAWAII

Nonmonetary Support

Type: Cause-related Marketing & Promotion; Donated Equipment; Donated Products
Volunteer Programs: Tesoro Petroleum encourages employees to volunteer in community organizations and company-sponsored events through its Team Tesoro volunteer program.

Giving Contact

Andrea L. Simpson, Tesoro Corporate Contribution Committee
Tesoro Petroleum Corp.
300 Concord Plaza Dr.
San Antonio, TX 78216-6999
Phone: (210)283-2801
Web: http://www.energypeople.com/community/index.html

Description

Founded: 1986
Organization Type: Corporate Foundation
Former Name: BHP Hawaii Foundation.
Giving Locations: headquarters and operating communities.
Grant Types: Capital, Employee Matching Gifts, General Support, Operating Expenses, Project, Seed Money.

Giving Philosophy

'Corporate philanthropy and volunteerism are deep-rooted traditions at Tesoro as we enter our 35th anniversary year. It has been our belief that success is measured not only by our bottom line but also by our reputation as a responsible corporate citizen. We will earn the respect and patronage of the communities we serve by being responsible not only in the way we

conduct our business, but in the ways we give back to our communities. This means both in monetary contributions and in our community service activities with our Team Tesoro employee volunteers.

'As just one example, we are a meaningful contributor in the United Way programs in each of our communities and support a wide range of other programs and charities. The majority of our support focuses on education and improving the quality of life for the children in the communities we live in and serve. Yet, the charitable contributions programs we have in each of our communities span a fairly wide range of charities.'*A Letter from Tesoro's CEO: Treasuring our Community*

Financial Summary

Total Giving: Makes contributions through a corporate direct giving program.

Giving Analysis: Giving for 1996 includes: foundation ($290,325); foundation matching gifts ($9,675); 1997: foundation grants to United Way ($128,500); foundation matching gifts ($4,355); 1998: foundation grants to United Way ($96,500); foundation matching gifts ($12,898)

Typical Recipients

Arts & Humanities: Arts Associations & Councils, Arts Outreach, Film & Video, Arts & Humanities-General, Museums/Galleries, Music, Opera, Performing Arts, Public Broadcasting, Theater, Visual Arts

Civic & Public Affairs: Asian American Affairs, Botanical Gardens/Parks, Clubs, Employment/Job Training, Civic & Public Affairs-General, Housing, Nonprofit Management, Safety, Urban & Community Affairs, Women's Affairs, Zoos/Aquariums

Education: Agricultural Education, Arts/Humanities Education, Business Education, Colleges & Universities, Economic Education, Elementary Education (Public), Engineering/Technological Education, Education-General, Gifted & Talented Programs, Preschool Education, Private Education (Precollege), Public Education (Precollege), Science/Mathematics Education, Secondary Education (Private), Secondary Education (Public)

Environment: Environment-General, Resource Conservation, Wildlife Protection

Health: Cancer, Children's Health/Hospitals, Clinics/Medical Centers, Emergency/Ambulance Services, Eyes/Blindness, Health Policy/Cost Containment, Hospices, Hospitals, Mental Health, Nutrition

International: Foreign Arts Organizations, International Affairs, International Environmental Issues, International Relations

Religion: Religious Welfare, Seminaries

Science: Science Museums

Social Services: Animal Protection, Child Welfare, Community Centers, Community Service Organizations, Counseling, Day Care, Emergency Relief, Food/Clothing Distribution, People with Disabilities, Recreation & Athletics, Scouts, Scouts, Shelters/Homelessness, Special Olympics, Substance Abuse, United Funds/United Ways, YMCA/YWCA/YMHA/YWHA, Youth Organizations

Contributions Analysis

Giving Priorities: Emphasis is on environment and education. Health, social welfare, and culture and the arts are also funded. Company makes contributions to nonprofit organizations in international marketplace. Foundation supports international studies, cultural centers, and an international film festival.

Arts & Humanities: 10%. Emphasis is on music, public broadcasting, and museums and art galleries. Interests also include arts associations and centers, historic preservation and restoration, and the performing arts.

Civic & Public Affairs: 4%.

Education: 14%. Primarily funds colleges and universities through matching, capital, and general support grants. Other interests include international studies and business, economic, and engineering education. Company also administers a scholarship program for children of employees.

Environment: 9%. Funds are directed toward nature centers and recycling.

Health: 1%.

International: 7%.

Religion: 1%.

Social Services: 54%. Interests include United Way, community service organizations, shelters, and family services. Health support is directed primarily toward hospitals and single-disease associations. Other interests include public health, nutrition, and health maintenance. Supports youth organizations and groups concerned with child welfare.

Note: Total contributions made in 1998.

Application Procedures

Initial Contact: Send a full proposal to appropriate regional Corporate Contribution Committee member.

Application Requirements: Include a business plan with a brief description of organization and its purpose; summary of project's need, plan of action, benefit to community, population served, and evaluation methods; budget for organization and proposed projects, including percentages used for fundraising; list of directors; proof of tax-exempt status, and any data supporting the program's success.

Deadlines: None.

Review Process: The Board of Trustees for the Tesoro Corporate Contribution Committee will meet periodically to review grant applications for the current year.

Restrictions

Grants are not made for scholarships or tuition aid; travel expenses; programs directed to an individual; or activites of churches or religious organizations. In teneral, grants are not awarded to sporting activities or conferences/seminars. Multi-year commitments are generally not made.

Additional Information

Proposals should be mailed to the appropriate regional Tesoro Corporate Contribution Committee contact:

San Antonio: Andrea L. Simpson, Tesoro Corporate Contribution Committee, 300 Concord Plaza Dr., San Antonio, TX 78216; 210-283-2801

Anchorage: William F. Miller, Tesoro Corporate Contribution Committee, 3230 'C' St., Anchorage, AK 99519; 907-561-5521

Kenai: Heidi Peterson, Tesoro Corporate Contribution Committee, Mile 22, Kenai Spur Hwy., Kenai, AK 99611; 907-776-8191

Anacortes: Rene Guckenburg, Tesoro Corporate Contribution Committee, PO Box 700, Anacortes, WA 98221; 360-293-9126

Hawaii: Shere Saneishi-Kim, Tesoro Corporate Contribution Committee, PO Box 3379, Honolulu, HI 96842

Seattle: Rob Donovan, Tesoro Contribution Committee, 3450 S. 344th Way, Ste. 100, Auburn, WA 98001; 800-473-1123

In May 1998, Tesoro Petroleum Corp. acquired BHP Hawaii.

Publications: Guidelines Sheet; Report on Community Investments

Corporate Officials

Faye Watanabe Kurren: president PRIM CORP EMPL president: Tesoro Hawaii Corp. CORP AFFIL secretary: Hawaii Energy Resources Inc.; secretary: Tesoro South Pacific Petro Co.; secretary: BHP Petroleum Trading & Marketing; secretary: BHP Hawaii Inc.; vice president: BHP Petroleum Pacific Islands.

Foundation Officials

George E. Bates: treasurer B 1943. ED University of Hawaii BS (1967); University of Hawaii MBA (1981). PRIM CORP EMPL vice president: BHP Hawaii Inc. CORP AFFIL vice president: Tesoro Hawaii Corp.; vice president: Tesoro South Pacific Petro Co.; vice president: BHP Petroleum Pacific Islands.

Thomas A. Clark: trustee B 1940. PRIM CORP EMPL vice president: Gasco Inc. CORP AFFIL vice president: BHP Hawaii Inc.

Sherelee Saneishi-Kim: secretary

Andrea Lynn Simpson: president B Altadena, CA 1948. ED University of Southern California BA (1969); University Colorado Boulder School Marketing (1977); University of Southern California MS (1983). PRIM CORP EMPL vice president corporate communications: Tesoro Hawaii Corp. NONPR AFFIL member: University Southern California Alumni Association; member: Utilities Communicators International; member: Public Relations Society America; member: International Public Relations Association; trustee: Kapiolani Medical Center; director: Hawaii Strategic Development Corp.; member: Honolulu Advertising Federation; director: Hawaii Public Television; member: Hawaii Jaycees; advisory director: Hawaii Kids Work; member advisory board: Girl Scouts U.S. Council Hawaii; director: Hanahavoli School; director: Childrens Discovery Center; member: Alpha Phi; member: American Marketing Association; director: Aloha Council Boy Scouts America. CLUB AFFIL Rotary Club; Outrigger Canoe Club; Pacific Club.

Heidi Karin Wild: trustee B Detroit, MI 1948. ED Western Michigan University BA (1971); University of Michigan MBA (1985). PRIM CORP EMPL director marketing: BHP Petroleum Americas. CORP AFFIL director: Makiki Park Place Condominium Association; president, director: BHP Hawaii Federal Credit Union. NONPR AFFIL member: University Hawaii MBA Alumni Group; member: Western Michigan Alumni Association; member advisory board: University Hawaii College Business; member: U.S. Air Force Civilian Advisory; member: University Hawaii Alumni Association; member: Navy League; member: Beta Gamma Sigma; member: Hawaii Chamber of Commerce. CLUB AFFIL PRI Golf Club.

Jim R. Yates: trustee PRIM CORP EMPL vice president: BHP Hawaii. CORP AFFIL vice president: Gasco Inc.

Recent Grants

Arts & Humanities

10,000	Asian/Pacific Foundation of Hawaii, Honolulu, HI
7,500	Honolulu Theatre for Youth, Honolulu, HI -- Kai Wai Ola Production
5,000	Hawaii Opera Theatre, Honolulu, HI -- HOT TEXT - 1997/98 Season

Civic & Public Affairs

5,000	Moanalua Gardens Foundation, Honolulu, HI -- Hawaii Environmental Education Curriculum
2,500	Coast Guard Foundation, Stonington, CT -- Operating support in Hawaii
1,000	Hawaii Lions Foundation, Honolulu, HI -- For the Lions Eye help program
100	Honolulu Theatre for Youth, Honolulu, HI -- BHP Hawaii Foundation's Matching Gifts to Non-Profit Organizations Plan

Education

10,000	University of Hawaii Foundation, Honolulu, HI -- Environmental Engineering Laboratory equipment
5,000	Junior Achievement of Maui, Honolulu, HI -- Business education program
4,000	Close Up Foundation, Alexandria, VA -- 1998 programs
3,000	Le Jardin Academy, Kailua, HI -- For capital costs
2,500	Chaminade University, Honolulu, HI -- For the integrated computer data base system
1,250	Iolani School, Honolulu, HI -- BHP Hawaii Foundation's Matching Gifts to Education Plan

1,100 Iolani School, Honolulu, HI -- BHP Hawaii Foundation's Matching Gifts to Education Plan
1,000 Academy of The Pacific, Honolulu, HI -- Athletic equipment
500 Kainalu Elementary School, Kailua, HI -- BHP Hawaii Foundation's Matching Gifts to Education Plan
500 Kalanianaole School Foundation, Papaikou, HI -- BHP Hawaii Foundation's Matching Gifts to Education Plan
500 University of Hawaii Foundation, Honolulu, HI -- Business Night-Outstanding Masters of Business Administration Student in International Business
500 University of Redlands Hawaii Scholarship Fund/HCF, Honolulu, HI -- BHP Hawaii Foundation's Matching Gifts to Education Plan
400 Hawaii Pacific University, Honolulu, HI -- BHP Hawaii Foundation's Matching Gifts to Education Plan
375 Hawaii Baptist Academy, Honolulu, HI
280 United States Merchant Marine Academy Foundation Inc/Development Fund, Kings Point, NY -- BHP Hawaii Foundation's Matchig Gifts to Education Plan
250 Aikahi Elementary School, Kailua, HI -- BHP Hawaii Foundation's Matching Gifts to Education Plan
200 Sacred Hearts Academy, Honolulu, HI -- BHP Hawaii Foundation's Matching Gifts to Education Plan
200 United States Merchant Marine Academy Foundation Inc., Kings Point, NY -- BHP Hawaii Foundation's Matching Gifts to Education Plan
175 Hawaii Baptist Academy, Honolulu, HI -- BHP Hawaii Foundation's Matching Gifts to Education Plan
100 Hawaii Pacific University, Honolulu, HI -- BHP Hawaii Foundation's Matching Gifts to Education Plan

Environment

20,000 Hawaii Nature Center, Honolulu, HI -- BHP/HNC volunteer partnership program

Health

1,000 Kalihi-Palama Health Center, Honolulu, HI -- Operating support

International

15,000 Earthtrust, Kailua, HI -- Project Delphis web site
2,000 Pacific and Asian Affairs Council, Honolulu, HI -- Model APEC 2020

Religion

900 Graduate Theological Union/American Baptist Seminary of The West, Berkeley, CA -- BHP Hawaii Foundation's Matching Gifts to Education Plan
100 Salvation Army, Hawaiian and Pacific Islands Division, Honolulu, HI -- BHP Hawaii Foundation's Matching Gifts to Non-Profit Organizations Plan
40 Salvation Army, Hawaiian and Pacific Islans Division, Honolulu, HI -- BHP Hawaii Foundation's Matching Gifts to Non-Profit Organizations Plan

Social Services

86,000 Aloha United Way, Honolulu, HI
10,000 Girl Scout Council of Hawaii, Honolulu, HI -- "Be your Best..the Earth Matters" project
6,500 Hawaii Island United Way, Hilo, HI -- 1997/99 fund drive
5,000 Boy Scouts of America, Maui County Council, Wailuku, HI -- Capital campaign
5,000 Hawaii Special Olympics, Honolulu, HI -- 1998 Summer Games Opening Ceremony
4,000 Maui United Way, Wailuku, HI -- 1997/98 corporate campaign
1,000 Friends of the Children's Advocacy Center of West Hawaii, Kailua-Kona, HI -- For child abuse emergency and treatment needs
1,000 Samaritan Counseling Center of Hawaii, Honolulu, HI -- Operating support
100 American Red Cross, Hawaii State Chapter, Honolulu, HI -- BHP Hawaii Foundation's Matching Gifts to Non-Profit Organizations
100 Samaritan Counseling Center of Hawaii, Honolulu, HI -- BHP Hawaii Foundation's Matching Gifts to Non-Profit Organizations Plan

TEXACO INC.

★ Number 24 of Top 100 Corporate Givers

Company Contact

White Plains, NY
Web: http://www.texaco.com

Company Description

Revenue: US$35,690,000,000 (1999)
Profit: US$1,177,000,000 (1999)
Employees: 28,957
Fortune Rank: 28, per FORTUNE Magazine's list of 500 Largest U.S. Corporations (1999).
FF 28
SIC(s): 1311 Crude Petroleum & Natural Gas, 1381 Drilling Oil & Gas Wells, 1382 Oil & Gas Exploration Services, 2992 Lubricating Oils & Greases.

Operating Locations

Australia: Texaco Australia, Perth; Belgium: SA Texaco Belgium, NV, Brussels; Barbados: Texaco Eastern Caribbean Limited, Warrens, St. Michael; Brazil: Texaco Brasil SA, Rio De Janeiro; People's Republic of China: Texaco China BV, Beijing; Colombia: Texaco Petroleum Co. Colombian Division, Bogota; Ireland: Texaco (Ireland) Ltd., Ballsbridge; Kuwait: Saudi Arabian Texaco Inc., Al-Zour (Mina Saud); Nigeria: Texaco Nigeria Plc, Lagos; Scotland: Texaco North Sea UK Co., Aberdeen; Singapore: Texaco International Trader Inc., Singapore; United Kingdom: Texaco Limited, Canary Wharf, London

Nonmonetary Support

Value: $6,200,000 (1998); $7,500 (1987)
Type: Donated Equipment; In-kind Services; Loaned Executives

Corporate Sponsorship

Type: Arts & cultural events; Music & entertainment events; Sports events
Contact: Diane Herzman, Manager of Sponsorships

Texaco Foundation

Giving Contact

Mr. Kieran Murray, Secretary
Texaco Foundation
2000 Westchester Ave.
White Plains, NY 10650
Phone: (914)253-4000 ext 7398
Fax: (914)253-4655
Email: contributions@texaco.com

Description

EIN: 133007516
Organization Type: Corporate Foundation
Giving Locations: headquarters and operating communities, and national organizations.
Grant Types: Department, Employee Matching Gifts, Fellowship, Project, Research, Scholarship.
Note: Employee matching gift ratio: 1 to 1 up to $10,000.

Giving Philosophy

'Since our founding in 1902, Texaco has been providing energy and energy products to the world. As a successful global company, we also contribute to a vibrant, energetic society through Texaco's focused giving to people and institutions in communities where we work and live.

'When we speak of Texaco's philanthropic giving, focus has become a key word since we embarked on a strategic review of our grant making in 1997. Until then, we had given broadly, with special emphasis on the arts, education and the environment. As a result of our strategic review, we recast Texaco's priorities for giving beginning in 1998.

'The first of these focal areas is Early Childhood Education. Our response in this critical area is guided by two simple beliefs: Early childhood learning is critical to sustained educational achievement; (and) the workforce of the next century must include a diverse pool of qualified scientists and engineers.'

'The second focal area for Texaco's philanthropic giving is Leadership Development. This program focuses on supporting skill development and management training programs for the leaders of nonprofit organizations and, to a lesser extent, local businesses.'

'The third focal area is Texaco in the Community. This program, like our Leadership Development initiative, reflects Texaco's commitment to support the communities in which we operate and where our employees live and work.' *Contributing to an Energized Society--Texaco*

Financial Summary

Total Giving: $23,000,000 (2000 approx); $33,880,428 (1998); $11,728,810 (1997). Note: Contributes through corporate direct giving program and foundation.
Giving Analysis: Giving for 1997 includes: corporate grants to United Way ($1,807,535); corporate matching gifts ($1,555,136); foundation scholarships ($867,084); 1998: corporate direct giving ($16,531,917); foundation ($6,939,500); nonmonetary support ($6,200,000); corporate grants to United Way ($1,800,000); corporate matching gifts ($1,491,393); foundation scholarships ($917,618)
Assets: $11,400,045 (1998); $13,558,027 (1997); $13,958,241 (1996)
Gifts Received: $5,500,000 (1998); $11,100,000 (1997); $13,850,000 (1996). Note: Contributions were received from Texaco Incorporated.

Typical Recipients

Arts & Humanities: Arts Associations & Councils, Arts Festivals, Arts Funds, Ballet, Community Arts, Dance, History & Archaeology, Libraries, Literary Arts, Museums/Galleries, Music, Opera, Performing Arts
Civic & Public Affairs: African American Affairs, Botanical Gardens/Parks, Business/Free Enterprise, Civil Rights, Economic Development, Economic Policy, Employment/Job Training, Housing, Law & Justice, Legal Aid, Municipalities/Towns, Philanthropic Organizations, Public Policy, Safety, Urban & Community Affairs, Women's Affairs, Zoos/Aquariums
Education: Arts/Humanities Education, Business Education, Colleges & Universities, Community & Junior Colleges, Education Associations, Education Funds, Education Reform, Engineering/Technological Education, Environmental Education, Education-General, Health & Physical Education, International Studies, Legal Education, Literacy, Medical Education, Minority Education, Private Education (Precollege), Public

Education (Precollege), Religious Education, Science/Mathematics Education, Secondary Education (Public), Special Education, Student Aid
Environment: Air/Water Quality, Energy, Forestry, Environment-General, Resource Conservation, Wildlife Protection
Health: Cancer, Children's Health/Hospitals, Clinics/Medical Centers, Diabetes, Emergency/Ambulance Services, Health Organizations, Hospices, Hospitals, Hospitals (University Affiliated), Medical Rehabilitation, Medical Research, Medical Training, Public Health, Research/Studies Institutes, Respiratory, Transplant Networks/Donor Banks
International: Foreign Educational Institutions, Health Care/Hospitals, International Affairs, International Development, International Environmental Issues, International Relations, International Relief Efforts, Missionary/Religious Activities
Science: Observatories & Planetariums, Science Museums, Scientific Centers & Institutes, Scientific Labs, Scientific Organizations, Scientific Research
Social Services: Child Welfare, Community Service Organizations, Delinquency & Criminal Rehabilitation, Emergency Relief, People with Disabilities, Recreation & Athletics, Senior Services, Shelters/Homelessness, Substance Abuse, United Funds/United Ways, Volunteer Services, Youth Organizations

Contributions Analysis

Giving Priorities: Early childhood education; leadership development; and community support for the communities in which Texaco operates and Texaco employees live and work.
Civic & Public Affairs: Supports leadership development and community support to address critical needs and support organizations that are working to improve the quality of life in communities where Texaco operates and where its employees live and work.
Education: Supports early childhood education through two programs. Early Notes: The Sound of Children Learning is a comprehensive music education program which begins in the earliest grades to help improve student learning and expore the possible connection of music to skills vital to later success in math and science. Tough Science: Hands-on Learning for Kids and Communities is an elementary school program that is aimed at retaining children's natural inquisitiveness through the use of interactive instruction and involvement.

Application Procedures

Initial Contact: Call, write or see corporate Web site for application information, then send a full proposal.
Application Requirements: Proposal should include a two-page summary of the organization's project or program objective, amount of money requested, and the funding period; a brief statement of history and accomplishments to date; a list of members of board of directors; the most recent annual report; proof of tax-exempt status; total operating budget for the current year; and a list of other corporate, foundation, and government support.
Deadlines: None.
Review Process: If the foundation is interested in a proposal, more detailed information will be requested.

Restrictions

The foundation does not make grants to: individuals; religious, veteran or fraternal organizations; fundraising events, telethons, races, or benefits; capital campaigns, endowments, or building fund drives; political or lobbying organizations; organizations that discriminate on the basis of race, creed, gender, sexual preference or national origin; organizations already supported through United Way contributions; publications or courtesy advertising; film, video, or television projects; specific productions or concerts; or purchasing of instruments or other equipment.

Additional Information

Texaco Foundation offers a four-year college scholarship program to children of employees. The fund generally solicits proposals from organizations working within elementary childhood education, particularly those located in key Texaco locations. Unsolicited proposals will be accepted, but a favorable decision is less likely.

Corporate Officials

John Doss Ambler: vice president investor relations & shareholder service B Buena Vista, VA 1934. ED Virginia Polytechnic Institute & State University BS (1956). PRIM CORP EMPL vice president: Texaco Inc.
Michael N. Ambler: general tax counsel PRIM CORP EMPL general tax counsel: Texaco Inc.
Peter I. Bijur: chairman, chief executive officer B New York, NY 1942. ED University of Pittsburgh BA (1964); Columbia University MBA (1966). PRIM CORP EMPL chairman, chief executive officer: Texaco Inc. CORP AFFIL director: International Paper Co. NONPR AFFIL director: New York University Medical Center; fellow: Royal Society Arts; member: National Petroleum Council; managing director: New York Botanical Garden; managing director: Metropolitan Opera; trustee: Middlebury College; fellow: Institute Petroleum; member: Conference Board; member: Council Foreign Relations; member: Business Council; member: Business Roundtable; director, member management committee: American Petroleum Institute. CLUB AFFIL Country Club New Canaan.
Elizabeth Patience Smith: vice president investor relations & shareholder service B New York, NY 1949. ED Bucknell University BA (1971); Georgetown University JD (1976). PRIM CORP EMPL vice president investor relations & shareholder service: Texaco Inc. CORP AFFIL trustee: Inroads Fairfield Westchester Counties Inc. NONPR AFFIL member: Petroleum Investors Relations Association; director: Westchester Education Coalition; member: National Investor Relations Institute; member: Investor Relations Institute; member, board trustee: Marymount College.

Giving Program Officials

Anne T. Dowling: executive director

Foundation Officials

Kjestine M. Anderson: director PRIM CORP EMPL vice president, corporate communication, secretary: Texaco Inc.
George Batauick: comptroller
John Brademas: chairman B Mishawaka, IN 1927. ED Harvard University BA (1949); Oxford University DPhil (1954). PRIM NONPR EMPL president emeritus: New York University. CORP AFFIL director: Texaco Inc.; director: RCA/NBC; director: Scholastic Corp.; director: NYNEX Corp.; director: Oxford University Press; director: Loews Corp. NONPR AFFIL member, board advisors: Woodrow Wilson Center International Scholars; member central committee: World Council Churches; trustee: University Notre Dame; member: Study National Needs Biomed & Behavioral Research; board advisors: Trilateral Commission; trustee: Spelman College; senator: Phi Beta Kappa; member: Smithsonian Institute National Board; director: Alexander S. Onassis Public Benefit Foundation; director: New York Stock Exchange Inc.; president emeritus: New York University; member: National Advisory Council Public Service; member: National Committee Student Financial Assistance; chairman advisory committee: National Advisory Committee Fighting Back; member board visitors department : Massachusetts Institute Technology; member: National Academy Sciences; chairman board director: Federal Reserve Bank New York; member board overseers: Harvard University; board advisors: Emory University Carter Center; director: Council Aid Education; board advisors: Dumbarton Oaks Research Library; director: Center National Policy; trustee: Committee for Economic Development; director: Carnegie Endowment National Commission American & New World; director: Berlitz International Inc.; director: Carnegie Commission Science Technology & Government; director: Aspen Institute; director: Athens College (Greece); member: American Legion; director: American Council Arts; member, board directors: American Council Education; director: Academy Educational Development; fellow: American Academy of Arts & Sciences. CLUB AFFIL Ahepa Club; Masons Club.
John J. Coppinger, Jr.: assistant comptroller
Anne T. Dowling: executive director (see above)
Dr. Franklyn Green Jenifer: trustee ED Howard University (1965); University of Maryland PhD (1970). PRIM NONPR EMPL president: University of Texas at Dallas. CORP AFFIL director: Texaco Inc.
Robert E. Koch: vice president
James F. Link: treasurer PRIM CORP EMPL treasurer: Texaco Inc. NONPR AFFIL vice president: Iona College.
Kieran Murray: president
Robert C. Oelkers: director PRIM CORP EMPL comptroller, vice president: Texaco Inc. CORP AFFIL senior vice president: Texaco Refining & Mktg; controller: Texaco Trading Trnsp; chief financial officer: Texaco Overseas Holdings Inc.
Elizabeth Patience Smith: director (see above)
John E. Tuohy: general counsel
Howard Stanley Vogel: tax counsel B 1934. PRIM CORP EMPL general attorney: Texaco Inc. CORP AFFIL president, director: 169 East 69th Corp. NONPR AFFIL member: American Bar Association. CLUB AFFIL Princeton Club.

Grants Analysis

Disclosure Period: calendar year ending 1998
Total Grants: $6,939,500*
Number of Grants: 75
Average Grant: $40,267*
Highest Grant: $2,000,000
Typical Range: $1,000 to $50,000
***Note:** Giving excludes corporate direct giving, matching gifts, scholarship, United Way, nonmonetary support. Average grant excludes two highest grants totaling $4,000,000.

Recent Grants

Note: Grants derived from 1998 Form 990.

Arts & Humanities

2,000,000 Metropolitan Opera Association, New York, NY
150,000 American Museum of Natural History, New York, NY
150,000 The Library of Congress, Washington, DC
80,000 The Children's Museum of Houston, Houston, TX
50,000 Houston Grand Opera Association Inc., Houston, TX
50,000 The Museum of Fine Arts, Houston, Houston, TX
40,000 Museum of the Southwest, Midland, TX
35,000 Louisiana Philharmonic Orchestra, New Orleans, LA
25,000 Stepping Stones Museum for Children, Norwalk, CT

Civic & Public Affairs

150,000 The New York Botanical Garden, Bronx, NY
75,000 42nd Street Development Corporation, New York, NY
75,000 Denver Zoological Foundation, Denver, CO
35,000 Denver Zoological Foundation, Denver, CO
30,000 Business Council for International Understanding, New York, NY
25,000 KPMG Peat Marwick Foundation, Montvale, NJ

Education

2,000,000 University of Notre Dame, Notre Dame, IN
236,961 Texaco Foundation Scholarship - 1995 Program, White Plains, NY
222,500 Texaco Foundation Scholarship Program, White Plains, NY
210,000 Texaco Foundation Scholarship Program, White Plains, NY
207,500 Texaco Foundation Scholarship Program, White Plains, NY
100,000 United Negro College Fund, Fairfax, VA
75,000 Institute for Educational Inquiry, Seattle, WA
75,000 University of Florida Foundation, Gainsville, FL
58,000 Bank Street College of Education, New York, NY
50,000 American Geological Institute Foundation, Houston, TX
40,000 University of Notre Dame - Center for Catalysis, Notre Dame, IN
40,000 University of Rochester, Eastman School of Music, Rochester, NY
37,500 Levine School of Music, Washington, DC
35,000 University of South Carolina, Columbia, SC
30,000 Boston College, Chestnut Hill, MA
30,000 Education Through Music, Incorporated, New York, NY
30,000 Marymount College, Tarrytown, NY
25,000 College of New Rochelle, New Rochelle, NY
25,000 Education Foundation of Harris County, Houston, TX

Environment

85,000 The Audubon Institute, New Orleans, LA
50,000 Central Park Conservancy, New York, NY
50,000 Wildlife Conservation Society, Bronx, NY

Health

125,000 Music Intelligence Neural Development Institute, Irvine, CA
100,000 Memorial Sloan-Kettering Cancer Society, New York, NY
100,000 Music Intelligence Neural Development Institute, Irvine, CA
50,000 Norwalk Hospital Foundation, Norwalk, CT
25,000 New York University Medical Center, New York, NY

International

25,000 American Foundation for the University of the West Indies, Jamaica, WI
25,000 Operation Smile International, Norfolk, VA

Science

115,000 Houston Museum of Natural Science, Houston, TX
75,000 Kern County Science Foundation, Bakersfield, CA
50,000 New York Hall of Science, Corona Park, NY
25,000 Houston Museum of Natural Science, Houston, TX
25,000 Offshore Energy Center, Houston, TX

Social Services

25,000 Save the Children Federation, Westport, CT

TEXAS GAS TRANSMISSION CORP.

Company Contact

Owensboro, KY

Company Description

Employees: 1,155
SIC(s): 4922 Natural Gas Transmission, 5171 Petroleum Bulk Stations & Terminals.
Parent Company: Williams, Tulsa, OK, United States

Nonmonetary Support

Value: $25,000 (1996)
Type: Donated Equipment; In-kind Services; Loaned Employees

Corporate Sponsorship

Type: Arts & cultural events; Festivals/fairs; Music & entertainment events; Pledge-a-thon; Sports events

Giving Contact

Robert Carlton, Director, Human Resources & Administration
Texas Gas Transmission Corp.
3800 Frederica Street
Owensboro, KY 42301
Phone: (502)926-8686
Fax: (502)683-5373

Alternate Contact

Cindy Huston

Description

Organization Type: Corporate Giving Program
Giving Locations: headquarters and operating communities.
Grant Types: Employee Matching Gifts, General Support, Multiyear/Continuing Support, Operating Expenses.

Financial Summary

Total Giving: $750,000 (1997 approx); $950,000 (1996 approx); $950,000 (1995 approx). Note: Contributes through corporate direct giving program only.

Typical Recipients

Arts & Humanities: Arts Associations & Councils, Arts Centers, Arts Festivals, Arts Funds, Community Arts, Dance, Museums/Galleries, Music, Theater
Civic & Public Affairs: Economic Development, Economic Policy, Housing, Urban & Community Affairs
Education: Business Education, Colleges & Universities, Community & Junior Colleges
Health: Health-General
Social Services: Child Welfare, Community Service Organizations, Counseling, Day Care, Delinquency & Criminal Rehabilitation, Domestic Violence, Food/Clothing Distribution, People with Disabilities, Recreation & Athletics, Senior Services, Shelters/Homelessness, Substance Abuse, United Funds/United Ways, Volunteer Services, Youth Organizations

Application Procedures

Initial Contact: a brief letter of inquiry
Application Requirements: purpose of funds sought and proof of tax-exempt status
Deadlines: None.

Restrictions

Company does not support religious organizations for sectarian purposes.

Corporate Officials

Keith E. Bailey: chairman, president, director, chief executive officer B Kansas City, MO 1942. ED Missouri School of Mines & Metallurgy BS (1964); University of Missouri (1981). PRIM CORP EMPL chairman, president, director, chief executive officer: The Williams Companies Inc. CORP AFFIL chief executive officer: Williams Information Services Corp.; chairman: Williams Colorado Solutions; chairman: Williams Holdings Delaware; president: Touchstar Technologies LLC; director: Transco Energy Co.; executive: Northwest Pipeline Corp.; president: Rainbow Resources; chairman: Mapco Inc.; president, chief operating officer: Northwest Central Pipeline Co.; director: Apco Argentina Inc.; director: Bank Oklahoma Tulsa. NONPR AFFIL member: National Society Professional Engineers; member: Southern Gas Association; member: National Association Corrosion Engineers; member: Association Oil Pipelines; member: Interstate Natural Gas Association America; member: American Petroleum Institute.
Kim Roland Cocklin: senior vice president B Massillon, OH 1951. ED Wichita State University BS (1973); Wichita State University MA (1975); Washburn University JD (1981). PRIM CORP EMPL senior vice president: Texas Gas Transmission Corp. NONPR AFFIL member: American Bar Association.
Beverly H. Griffith: general counsel B Louisville, KY 1954. ED University of Mississippi BA (1976); University of Kentucky JD (1979). PRIM CORP EMPL general counsel: Texas Gas Transmission Corp. CLUB AFFIL Junior League Owensboro Club.
Gary D. Lauderdale: senior vice president, general manager B Holland, IN 1945. ED University of Evansville BS (1967); University of Evansville MBA (1974). PRIM CORP EMPL senior vice president, general manager: Texas Gas Transmission Corp. CORP AFFIL senior vice president, general manager: Williams Gas Pipeline-Central; senior vice president, general manager: Williams Gas Pipeline-Texas Gas; senior vice president, general manager: Texas Gas.
Norris E. McDivitt: vice president operations & engineering B 1932. ED Louisiana College BS (1961). PRIM CORP EMPL vice president operations & engineering: Texas Gas Transmission Corp.
E. Jack Ralph: vice president finance, controller B Hammond, IN 1940. ED Western Kentucky University BS (1970); University of Evansville MBA (1973). PRIM CORP EMPL vice president finance, controller: Texas Gas Transmission Corp. ADD CORP EMPL vice president: Williams Gas Pipeline Texas Gas.

Foundation Officials

Brian Edward O'Neill: B San Diego, CA 1935. ED United States Naval Academy BS (1957); University of Texas LLB (1965). PRIM CORP EMPL president, chief executive officer: Williams Gas Pipelines.

TEXAS INSTRUMENTS INC.

Company Contact

Dallas, TX
Web: http://www.ti.com

Company Description

Revenue: US$9,486,000,000 (1999)
Profit: US$1,406,000,000 (1999)
Employees: 35,948
Fortune Rank: 180, per FORTUNE Magazine's list of 500 Largest U.S. Corporations (1999).
FF 180
SIC(s): 3399 Primary Metal Products Nec, 3571 Electronic Computers, 3575 Computer Terminals, 3674 Semiconductors & Related Devices.

Operating Locations

Belgium: NV Texas Instruments Belgium SA, Brussels; Canada: Texas Instruments Canada, Ottawa; England: Texas Instruments Limited, Bedford; France: Texas Instruments France SA, Villeneuve-Loubet; Germany: Texas Instruments Deutschland GmbH, Freising; Hong Kong: Texas Instruments Asia Ltd., Hong Kong; Italy: Texas Instruments Italia SpA, Cittaducale; Japan: Texas Instruments Japan Ltd., Tokyo; Netherlands: Texas Instruments Holland BV, Almelo; Singapore: Texas Instruments Singapore (Pte.), Singapore; Sweden: Texas Instruments International Trade Corp., Stockholm; Switzerland: Texas Instruments (Switzerland) AG

Nonmonetary Support

Type: Donated Equipment; Loaned Employees; Loaned Executives

Note: Nonmonetary support is provided under company's direct giving program. The company sponsors a $1.2 million equipment cost-sharing with TX colleges.

Texas Instruments Foundation

Giving Contact

Mrs. Ann Minnis, Grants Administrator
Texas Instruments Foundation
PO Box 650311, M/S 3906
Dallas, TX 75265
Phone: (972)917-4505
Fax: (972)917-4583

Alternate Contact

Manager Corporate University Relations
PO Box 655474
M/S 8219
Phone: (972)480-6873

Description

EIN: 756038519
Organization Type: Corporate Foundation
Giving Locations: TX: emphasis on Texas-based organizations, Dallas nationally.
Grant Types: Capital, Challenge, Conference/Seminar, Employee Matching Gifts, General Support, Operating Expenses, Research.
Note: Employee matching gift ratio: 1 to 1.

Financial Summary

Total Giving: $4,000,000 (1999 approx); $3,225,903 (1998); $3,389,994 (1997). Note: Contributes through corporate direct giving program and foundation.
Giving Analysis: Giving for 1997 includes: corporate direct giving ($2,215,581); foundation grants to United Way ($733,000); foundation ($441,413); 1998: foundation ($2,036,923); foundation grants to United Way ($1,188,980)
Assets: $28,170,566 (1998); $25,121,387 (1997); $21,926,637 (1996)
Gifts Received: $4,200,000 (1998); $3,500,000 (1997); $5,000,000 (1995). Note: The foundation receives gifts from Texas Instruments Incorporated.

Typical Recipients

Arts & Humanities: Arts Centers, Arts Funds, Arts & Humanities-General, Libraries, Museums/Galleries, Music, Opera, Performing Arts, Public Broadcasting, Theater
Civic & Public Affairs: African American Affairs, Community Foundations, Economic Policy, Employment/Job Training, Hispanic Affairs, Nonprofit Management, Zoos/Aquariums
Education: Business Education, Colleges & Universities, Community & Junior Colleges, Economic Education, Education Associations, Education Funds, Education Reform, Elementary Education (Public), Engineering/Technological Education, Faculty Development, Education-General, Medical Education, Minority Education, Preschool Education, Private Education (Precollege), Public Education (Precollege), Science/Mathematics Education, Social Sciences Education, Special Education, Student Aid
Environment: Environment-General
Health: Clinics/Medical Centers, Hospitals, Hospitals (University Affiliated), Medical Research, Nursing Services, Research/Studies Institutes
International: Foreign Educational Institutions
Religion: Ministries, Religious Welfare
Science: Science Museums
Social Services: Community Centers, Community Service Organizations, Counseling, Day Care, People with Disabilities, Scouts, Shelters/Homelessness, Substance Abuse, United Funds/United Ways, Volunteer Services, YMCA/YWCA/YMHA/YWHA, Youth Organizations

Contributions Analysis

Giving Priorities: Education, social welfare, arts and humanities, and health. The Texas Instrument Foundation's mission statement states that the foundation supports organizations within and without the United States. However, contributions abroad are rare. The company is exploring expanding contributions overseas.
Arts & Humanities: 2%. Funds performing arts, music and cultural centers.
Civic & Public Affairs: 11%. Funds minority affairs.
Education: 25%. Supports educational programs, colleges and universities.
Health: 3%. Funds child development centers, medical centers, and aerobic research institute.
Science: Supports science museums.
Social Services: 40%. Major support given to United Way, also supports youth services.
Note: Foundation giving analysis for 1998; excludes employee matching gifts.

Application Procedures

Initial Contact: Send a brief letter (no longer than two pages).
Application Requirements: Include a description of the organization, population served, amount requested, purpose of funds sought, recently audited financial statement, cop of tax-exempt status letter.
Deadlines: None.
Decision Notification: Foundation board meets four times a year: March, June, September, December; applicants notified of grant decision within three weeks; company contributions board reviews and makes decisions as requests are received.

Restrictions

Foundation does not support individuals, political organizations, causes, candidates or campaigns, religious groups, or Athletic initiatives.

Corporate Officials

Richard John Agnich: senior vice president, secretary, general counsel B Eveleth, MN 1943. ED Stanford University AB (1965); University of Texas JD (1969). PRIM CORP EMPL senior vice president, secretary, general counsel: Texas Instruments Inc. NONPR AFFIL member: Southwest Legal Foundation; member: Texas Bar Association; trustee: Childcare Group; member: Dallas Bar Association; member: American Society of Corporate Secretaries; trustee: Austin College; member: American Bar Association.
William Andrew Aylesworth: chief financial officer, treasurer B Gary, IN 1942. ED Cornell University BEE (1965); Carnegie Mellon University MS (1967). PRIM CORP EMPL chief financial officer, treasurer: Texas Instruments Inc. CORP AFFIL director: Arkwright Mutual Insurance Co. NONPR AFFIL member: Financial Executives Institute.
Thomas James Engibous: president, chief executive officer, chairman, director B Saint Louis, MO 1953. ED Purdue University BSEE (1975); Purdue University MSEE (1976). PRIM CORP EMPL president, chief executive officer, chairman, director: Texas Instruments Inc. CORP AFFIL president: Texas Instruments Phillipines. NONPR AFFIL member visitors committee: Purdue University Engineering; trustee: Southern Methodist University; member: Dallas Citizens Council; member: Institute Electrical & Electronics Engineers; member: Business Roundtable; director: Catalyst; member: Business Council.
Win Skiles: senior vice president B Louisville, KY 1941. ED Baylor University (1963); University of Texas (1968). PRIM CORP EMPL senior vice president: Texas Instruments Inc.

Foundation Officials

Richard John Agnich: director (see above)
William Andrew Aylesworth: treasurer (see above)
Thomas James Engibous: director (see above)
Ann Minnis: grants administrator, director
James Mitchell: director
Liston Michael Rice, Jr.: president, director public affairs B Dallas, TX 1927. ED University of Texas (1948-1949).
Win Skiles: vice president (see above)
Cynthia Stewart: secretary

Grants Analysis

Disclosure Period: calendar year ending 1998
Total Grants: $2,036,923*
Number of Grants: 45
Average Grant: $32,657*
Highest Grant: $600,000
Typical Range: $2,000 to $50,000
***Note:** Giving excludes United Way. Average grant figure excludes highest grant.

Recent Grants

Note: Grants derived from 1998 Form 990.

Arts & Humanities

50,000	Dallas Symphony Association, TX, Dallas, TX -- Public
15,000	The Dallas Opera, Dallas, TX -- Public
10,000	Dallas Children's Theater, Inc., Dallas, TX -- Public

Civic & Public Affairs

300,000	Dallas Urban League, Dallas, TX -- Public
50,000	The Dallas Foundation, Dallas Reading Plan(DISD), Dallas, TX -- Public
20,000	Dallas Zoological Society, Dallas, TX -- Public
10,000	Latino Cultural Center, Dallas, TX -- Public
5,000	The Center for Nonprofit Management, Dallas, TX -- Public

Education

400,000	Dallas Public Schools, 3rd Grade Reading Initiative, Dallas, TX -- Public
70,500	SMU Learning Therapy Center, Dallas, TX -- Public
55,650	Texas A&M University Foundation, College Station, TX -- Public
53,650	University of Texas at Arlington - Community Srvs Dev Center, Arlington, TX -- Public
27,500	Jr. Achievement of Dallas, Dallas, TX -- Public
25,000	Mckinney Education Foundation, Mckinney, TX -- Public
24,476	University of Texas School of Public Affairs, Austin, TX -- Public
20,000	University of Dallas, Dallas, TX -- Public
13,000	Austin College, Sherman, TX -- Public
10,000	University of Texas at Dallas, Richardson, TX -- Public
5,000	Dallas Can Academy, Dallas, TX -- Public
5,000	National Action Council for Minorities in Engineering, Inc., New York, NY -- Public
5,000	National Hispanic Scholarship Fund, The, California -- Public
4,000	Lubbock Christian University, Lubbock, TX -- Public
2,500	University of Kentucky - Chandler Medical/Markey Cancer, Lexington, KY -- Public
2,000	Jr. Achievement of Grayson County, Inc., Sherman, TX-- Public
1,500	Council for Advancement and Support of Education, Washington, DC -- Public

Health
10,000 The Cooper Institute for Aerobics Research, Dallas, TX -- Public
5,000 Baylor Medical Center at Garland, Garland, TX -- Public

International
3,000 Friends of the American Schools in Japan, Inc., Tokyo, Japan -- Public

Religion
20,000 The Salvation Army, Dallas, TX -- Public
5,000 Shelter Ministries of Dallas - Genesis Women's Shelter, Dallas, TX -- Public

Science
600,000 Southwest Museum of Science and Technology, Dallas, TX -- Public

Social Services
879,800 United Way of Metropolitan Dallas, Dallas, TX -- Public
149,600 United Way of Eastern New England, Attleboro, MA -- Public
97,647 Headstart of Greater Dallas, Dallas, TX -- Public
58,800 United Way of Texas Gulf Coast, Houston, TX -- Public
42,500 United Way of Grayson County, Sherman, TX -- Public
35,000 Circle Ten Council, Boy Scouts of America, Dallas, TX -- Public
26,800 United Way of Lubbock, Lubbock, TX -- Public
20,000 YMCA of Metropolitan Dallas, Dallas, TX -- Public
19,100 United Way of Woodford County, Versailles, KY -- Public
12,500 Dare to Dream Foundation, Dallas, TX -- Public
10,000 Daytop Village Foundation, Inc., Dallas, TX -- Public
10,000 Tejas Girl Scount Council, Dallas, TX -- Public
10,000 YWCA, Dallas, TX -- Public
7,400 United Way of Midland, Midland, TX -- Public
5,000 Boys & Girls Clubs of Sherman, Sherman, TX -- Public
4,000 Boys & Girls Clubs of Collin County, McKinney, TX -- Public
2,600 United Way of Odessa, Odessa, TX -- Public
1,380 United Way of Santa Clara County, Santa Clara, CA -- Public
1,000 United Way of Grand Traverse Area, Central Lake, MI -- Public

TEXTRON INC.

Company Contact
Providence, RI
Web: http://www.textron.com

Company Description
Revenue: US$11,579,000,000 (1999)
Profit: US$2,226,000,000 (1999)
Employees: 64,000 (1999)
Fortune Rank: 154, per FORTUNE Magazine's list of 500 Largest U.S. Corporations (1999).
FF 154
SIC(s): 2771 Greeting Cards, 2782 Blankbooks & Looseleaf Binders, 2844 Toilet Preparations, 3728 Aircraft Parts & Equipment Nec.

Corporate Sponsorship
Type: Arts & cultural events; Music & entertainment events; Sports events

Textron Charitable Trust

Giving Contact
Ellie Weston, Contributions Coordinator
Textron Charitable Trust
40 Westmintster Street
Providence, RI 02903
Phone: (401)457-2430
Fax: (401)457-3598

Description
EIN: 256115832
Organization Type: Corporate Foundation
Giving Locations: headquarters and operating communities.
Grant Types: Capital, Employee Matching Gifts, General Support, Scholarship.

Giving Philosophy
'The mission of the Textron Charitable Contributions Program is to fulfill Textron Inc.'s commitment to responsible corporate citizenship by helping to improve the quality of life in communities where Textron employees live and work. Textron views its public responsibility as an integral part of its business and is concerned with public issues and community needs. In order to leverage its philanthropic investments, Textron encourages and supports the work of its employee volunteers.' Textron Charitable Trust guidelines

Financial Summary
Total Giving: $2,872,935 (1997); $2,847,669 (1996); $2,900,000 (1995). Note: Company gives through charitable trust only.
Giving Analysis: Giving for 1997 includes: foundation ($1,451,238); foundation matching gifts ($1,321,697); foundation grants to United Way ($100,000)
Assets: $7,607,445 (1997); $7,946,594 (1996); $10,545,380 (1995)
Gifts Received: $2,000,000 (1997); $3,000,000 (1995); $3,000,000 (1994). Note: Contributions received from Textron Corporation.

Typical Recipients
Arts & Humanities: Arts Appreciation, Arts Associations & Councils, Arts Centers, Arts Funds, Arts Institutes, Community Arts, Dance, Historic Preservation, Libraries, Museums/Galleries, Music, Opera, Performing Arts, Public Broadcasting, Theater
Civic & Public Affairs: Business/Free Enterprise, Chambers of Commerce, Civil Rights, Economic Development, Economic Policy, Employment/Job Training, Civic & Public Affairs-General, Housing, Law & Justice, Legal Aid, Municipalities/Towns, Professional & Trade Associations, Public Policy, Safety, Urban & Community Affairs, Women's Affairs, Zoos/Aquariums
Education: Arts/Humanities Education, Business Education, Colleges & Universities, Community & Junior Colleges, Economic Education, Education Associations, Education Funds, Education Reform, Engineering/Technological Education, Education-General, International Studies, Legal Education, Literacy, Medical Education, Minority Education, Private Education (Precollege), Public Education (Precollege), Science/Mathematics Education, Student Aid, Vocational & Technical Education
Environment: Air/Water Quality, Environment-General
Health: Cancer, Children's Health/Hospitals, Health Policy/Cost Containment, Health Organizations, Hospices, Hospitals, Medical Rehabilitation, Prenatal Health Issues, Single-Disease Health Associations
International: Foreign Educational Institutions, Human Rights, International Affairs, International Organizations, International Peace & Security Issues, International Relations
Religion: Missionary Activities (Domestic), Religious Welfare
Science: Science Exhibits & Fairs, Scientific Centers & Institutes
Social Services: Child Welfare, Community Centers, Community Service Organizations, Counseling, Emergency Relief, Family Planning, Food/Clothing Distribution, People with Disabilities, Recreation & Athletics, Refugee Assistance, Scouts, Senior Services, Shelters/Homelessness, Special Olympics, Substance Abuse, United Funds/United Ways, Volunteer Services, Youth Organizations

Contributions Analysis
Giving Priorities: Student financial aid, united funds, arts centers, music, and hospitals.
Arts & Humanities: 4%. Funds the arts centers and music receive primarysupport. Other interests include arts associations, dance, historical preservation and restoration, and museums and galleries. Also includes matching gifts to arts institutions and organizations.
Civic & Public Affairs: 11%. Organizations involved in civil rights, women's issues and urban development.
Education: 53%. Majority of funding consists of matching grants. Substantial amounts also support student aid organizations, such as the National Merit Scholarship program and College Scholarship Service. Limited support goes to colleges, universities, and minority education.
Health: 18%. Hospitals receive the largest amount of health care funds, through both general support and matching grants. Health organizations, single-disease health associations, hospices, and pediatric health also are supported.
International: 2%. Supports political organizations.
Religion: 1%. Funds religious philanthropy.
Science: 1%. Funds a scientific institute.
Social Services: 9%. Support typically includes scouting organizations, youth employment services, and YMCA/YWCAs and united funds.

Application Procedures
Initial Contact: brief letter or proposal
Application Requirements: statement of purposes and objectives of the organization; history of the programs of the organization; list of the organization's officers, board of directors, and staff; annual operating budget for the organization for the year in which the project will occur; audited financial statements for the most recently completed year; description of the program or project that is the subject of the proposal and how it relates to the needs of the community; budget for the program or project that is the subject of the proposal; dollar level of support requested; copy of tax-exempt determination letter from the Internal Revenue Service; list of other sources approached for financial assistance and amounts received
Deadlines: None.
Evaluative Criteria: proposals will be evaluated on consistency with focus and mission of Textron's contributions program; purpose and impact of proposed request; and involvement of Textron employees
Decision Notification: contributions committee meets quarterly

Restrictions
Does not support individuals, including political candidates; endowment funds; educational or hospital capital or operating expenses; requests intended to reduce operating deficits; fund-raising appeals from churches, seminaries, or other religious organizations; operating funds of United Way member agencies; or organizations that are not 501(c)(3) tax-exempt.

Additional Information
Grant recipients are required to complete a post-grant application form and adhere to terms of the grant. A

fiscal and program summary must be submitted upon completion of the project.
Rhode Island Hospital Trust National Bank serves as a corporate trustee of the trust.

Corporate Officials

John D. Butler: executive vice president, chief human resources officer ED Michigan State University. PRIM CORP EMPL executive vice president, chief human resources officer: Textron Inc.
Lewis B. Cambell: chairman, chief executive officer, director B 1946. ED Duke University BS (1968). PRIM CORP EMPL chairman, chief executive officer, director: Textron Inc. CORP AFFIL president, chief operating officer: Davidson Textron Inc.; director: Textron Financial Corp.; director: Bristol-Myers Squibb Co.; director: Citizens Financial Group Inc.; director: Avco Financial Service Inc.; director: Bell Helicopter Textron Inc.; executive vice president, chief operating officer: Avco Corp.
John A. Janitz: president, chief executive officer, chairman ED Eastern Michigan University; Villanova University. PRIM CORP EMPL president, chief executive officer, chairman: Textron Automotive Co. NONPR AFFIL member: Society Automotive Engineers.
Donald McGrath: director community affairs PRIM CORP EMPL director community affairs: Textron Inc.

Grants Analysis

Disclosure Period: calendar year ending 1997
Total Grants: $2,872,935
Number of Grants: 1,500 (approx)
Average Grant: $1,915 (approx)
Highest Grant: $150,000
Typical Range: $100 to $500 and $1,000 to $5,000
Note: Grants analysis is approximate.

Recent Grants

Note: Grants derived from 1997 Form 990.

Arts & Humanities

15,000	Springfield Library & Museums, Springfield, MA
12,000	Museum of Art, RISD, Providence, RI
10,000	Kennedy Center for the Performing Arts, Washington, DC
10,000	Museum of Art, RISD, Providence, RI
10,000	Phillips Collection, Washington, DC
10,000	Trinity Repertory Company, Providence, RI

Civic & Public Affairs

75,000	Greater Providence, Providence, RI
40,000	Local Initiatives Support Corporation, Providence, RI
25,000	Employment Policy Foundation, Washington, DC
20,000	City Year Rhode Island, Providence, RI
18,750	Marine Corps Command Staff, Quantico, VA
12,500	Urban Collaborative, Providence, RI

Education

150,000	Davidson College, Davidson, NC
109,533	Providence College, Providence, RI
100,000	Duke University, Durham, NC
75,000	Public Education Fund, Providence, RI
56,375	Educational Testing Service, Princeton, NJ
51,910	National Merit Scholarship, Evanston, IL
25,000	Council for Excellence, Washington, DC
25,000	University of Rhode Island Foundation, Providence, RI
20,000	Heridian International Center, Washington, DC
19,523	Educational Testing Service, Princeton, NJ
18,750	NAACP Legal Defense Fund, New York, NY
17,400	Texas Christian University, Fort Worth, TX
16,466	College of the Holy Cross, Worcester, MA
15,010	College Fund/UNCF, Dallas, TX
15,000	Florida State University, Tallahassee, FL
15,000	Pennsylvania State University, University Park, PA
15,000	Providence College, Providence, RI
15,000	Providence College, Providence, RI
15,000	Rhode Island School of Design, Providence, RI
15,000	University of Virginia FunD, Charlottesville, VA
12,000	Atlanta Christian College, East Point, GA
12,000	Johns Hopkins University, Baltimore, MD
12,000	University of Virginia Law School Foundation, Charlottesville, VA
11,000	Providence College, Providence, RI
11,000	Villanova University, Villanova, PA
10,601	University of Kentucky, Lexington, KY
10,000	College of William & Mary, Williamsburg, VA
10,000	Flint Hill School, Oakton, VA
10,000	Muskegon County Catholic Education Foundation, Muskegon, MI
10,000	Pennsylvania College of Technology, Williamsport, PA
10,000	Rhode Island Children's Crusade for Higher Education, Providence, RI
10,000	Rhode Island Legal-Educational Partnership, Providence, RI
10,000	St. Sebastian's School, Needham, MA
10,000	Spring Arbor College, Spring Arbor, MI
10,000	Union Springs Academy, Union Springs, NY

Environment

10,000	Save the Bay, Providence, RI

Health

123,493	Scottish Rite Hospital, Dallas, TX
75,157	Cook Children's Medical Center, Fort Worth, TX
50,000	Rhode Island Hospital, Providence, RI
25,000	Sargent Rehabilitation Center, Warwick, RI
13,882	Shriners Hospital, Houston, TX
13,333	Shriners Hospital - Burns Institute, Galveston, TX
11,406	Dana-Farber, Inc., Boston, MA

International

12,600	Irish American Partnership, Boston, MA
10,000	Center for Security Policy, Washington, DC
10,000	Center for Strategic and International Studies, Inc., Washington, DC

Religion

10,000	Salvation Army, Washington, DC
10,000	Vision of Hope, Cranston, RI

Science

10,000	Manufacturing Institute, Washington, DC

Social Services

100,000	United Way of Southeastern New England, Providence, RI
25,000	Narragansett Council Boy Scouts, Providence, RI
25,000	Rhode Island Decathalon, Warwich, RI
10,000	Elmwood Community Center, Providence, RI
10,000	Special Olympics Rhode Island, Warwick, RI

THERMO ELECTRON CORP.

Company Contact

Waltham, MA
Web: http://www.thermo.com

Company Description

Revenue: US$4,303,800,000 (1999)
Employees: 23,600
Fortune Rank: 369, per FORTUNE Magazine's list of 500 Largest U.S. Corporations (1999).
FF 369
SIC(s): 3443 Fabricated Plate Work--Boiler Shops, 3471 Plating & Polishing, 3479 Metal Coating & Allied Services, 3629 Electrical Industrial Apparatus Nec.

Operating Locations

Germany: Thermo Instrument Systems GmbH, Dortmund; Termoquest Analytische Systeme GmbH, Egelsbach, Hessen; Lindner GmbH Fabrik Elektrischer Lampen Und Apparate, Eggolsheim, Bayern; Gould Electronics GmbH, Eichstetten; Gould International GmbH, Eichstetten; ESM Eberline Instruments Strahlen-Und Unweltmesstechnik GmbH, Erlangen, Bayern; Gebr Haake GmbH, Karlsruhe, Baden-Wuerttemberg; Unterstuetzungskasse GmbH der Firma Gebrueder Haake GmbH, Karlsruhe, Baden-Wuerttemberg; Nicolet-Eme GmbH, Klein Ostheim, Bayern; Spectra-Physics GmbH, Kranichstein; Pharos Holdings GmbH, Weiterstadt; Spectra Precision GmbH, Weiterstadt; VG Instruments GmbH, Wiesbaden; Greece: Electrotechnic Hellas SA, Manika, Euboea; Hong Kong: Thermo Instrument Systems (F.E.) Limited, Aberdeen; Dynex Technology (Asia), Cheung Sha Wan, Kowloon; Spectra-Physics Scanning Systems, Hong Kong; VG Instruments Asia Ltd., Hong Kong; Italy: Spectra-Physics S.R.L., Cascina; VG Instruments Group Ltd., Milan; Comtest Italy, Turin; Geotronics Italia SPA, Vimercate; Japan: K.K. Geotronics, Omiya, Saitama; Thermo Electron Nippon Co., Ltd., Osaka; Spectra-Physics KK, Tokyo; Republic of Korea: VG Instruments Korea Ltd., Seoul; Netherlands: Thermo Instrument Systems BV, Breda; This Analytical BV, Breda, Noord-Brabant; This Automation BV, Breda, Noord-Brabant; Nicolet Technologies BV, Dongen, Noord-Brabant; Saroph Holdings BV, Eindhoven; Spectra-Physics BV, Eindhoven; Rutter & Co. BV, Enschede, Overijssel; Grond en Watersaneringstechniek Nederland BV, Farmsum, Groningen; Thermospectra BV, Naarden, Noord-Holland; This Scientific BV, Sliedrecht, Zuid-Holland; Finnigan MAT Benelux, Veenendaal; VG Instruments BV, Weesp; This Gas Analysis Systems BV, Weesp, Noord-Holland; This Lab Systems BV, Weesp, Noord-Holland; Thermo Voltek Europe BV, Zoeterwoude, Zuid-Holland; Thermo Votek Corp., Zoeterwoude-Rijndijk; Norway: Nobel Elektroikk A/S, Oslo; Thermomedics Detection Scandinavia AS, Oslo, Akershus; Philippines: Geotronics AB, Pasay; Singapore: AB Pharos Marine Pte. Ltd.; Spain: Agrolaser SA, Madrid; Geotronics SAn Zonen BV, Madrid; Spectra Physics SA, Madrid; Sweden: Chemtronics AB, Bohus; Geotronics Scandinavia AB, Danderyd; Finnigan MANT AB, Hagersten; Nobel Elektronik AB, Karlskoga; Spectra-Physics Laserplane AB, Malmo; Permanova Lasersystem AB, Ostersund; AB Pharos Marine, Stockholm; Spectra-Physics AB, Stockholm; VG Instruments AB, Stockholm; AB Pharos Marine, Vastra Frolunda; Switzerland: Spectra-Physics AG, Basel; United Kingdom: VG Data Systems Ltd., Altrincham, Cheshire; VG Laboratory Systems Ltd., Altrinham, Cheshire; Nobel Systems Ltd., Bedford; Spectra-Physics Holding Plc, Brentford, Middlesex; Thermo Black Clawson Ltd., Bury, Lancashire; Vickerys Ltd., Bury, Lancashire; VG Instruments Plc, Crawley, W. Sussex; VG Precision Ltd., Crawley, W. Sussex; PH Russell Ltd., Cupar, Fife; Winterburn Ltd., Dartford, Kent; VG Microscopes Ltd., East Grinstead, W. Sussex; VG Scientific Ltd., East Grinstead, W. Sussex; VG Semicon Ltd., East Grinstead, W. Sussex; Vacuum Generators Ltd., Hastings, E. Sussex; VG Electronics Ltd., Hastings, E. Sussex; VG Electrovac Ltd., Hastings, E. Sussex; VG Engineering (Hastings) Ltd.,

Hastings, E. Sussex; VG Special Systems Ltd., Hastings, E. Sussex; Spectra-Physics Ltd., Hemel Hempstead, Herts; Turboflex Ltd., High Wycombe, Buckinghamshire; Geotronics Ltd., Huntingdon, Cambridgeshire; Thermospectra Ltd., Ilford Essex; Vickery Holdings Ltd., London; VG GAs Analysis Systems Ltd., Middlewich, Cheshire; S Gregson & Sons Ltd., Peterborough, Cambridgeshire; Tru-Lon Printed Circuits (Royston) Ltd., Royston, Hertfordshire; VG Engineering (Telford) Ltd., Telford; Comtest Ltd., Thame, Oxfordshire; VG Microtech Ltd., Uckfield, E. Sussex

Corporate Sponsorship

Value: $200,000
Type: Arts & cultural events; Other

Thermo Electron Foundation

Giving Contact

Patricia Gibbs, Administrator
Thermo Electron Foundation
81 Wyman Street
Waltham, MA 02451
Phone: (617)622-1000
Fax: (617)622-1183

Description

Founded: 1986
EIN: 222778152
Organization Type: Corporate Foundation
Giving Locations: headquarters area only.
Grant Types: Capital, General Support.

Financial Summary

Total Giving: $400,000 (2000 approx); $398,000 (1999 approx); $327,500 (1998). Note: Contributes through corporate direct giving program and foundation.
Giving Analysis: Giving for 1999 includes: foundation (approx $398,000)
Assets: $450,000 (1999 approx)
Gifts Received: Contributions are received from Thermo Electron Corp.

Typical Recipients

Arts & Humanities: Arts Centers, Ballet, Dance, Historic Preservation, Libraries, Museums/Galleries, Music, Performing Arts, Public Broadcasting, Theater
Civic & Public Affairs: Business/Free Enterprise, Civil Rights, Economic Development, Economic Policy, Employment/Job Training, Civic & Public Affairs-General, Legal Aid, Municipalities/Towns, Native American Affairs, Philanthropic Organizations, Professional & Trade Associations, Public Policy, Urban & Community Affairs
Education: Business Education, Colleges & Universities, Community & Junior Colleges, Economic Education, Engineering/Technological Education, Education-General, Health & Physical Education, Literacy, Private Education (Precollege), Religious Education, Science/Mathematics Education
Environment: Environment-General, Resource Conservation
Health: AIDS/HIV, Clinics/Medical Centers, Emergency/Ambulance Services, Hospices, Hospitals
International: International Development, International Environmental Issues, International Organizations, International Relations, International Relief Efforts
Religion: Jewish Causes, Religious Welfare
Science: Observatories & Planetariums, Science Exhibits & Fairs, Science Museums, Scientific Research
Social Services: Child Welfare, Community Service Organizations, Counseling, Emergency Relief, Food/Clothing Distribution, People with Disabilities, Scouts, Senior Services, Shelters/Homelessness, Substance Abuse, United Funds/United Ways, Volunteer Services

Contributions Analysis

Giving Priorities: Civic organizations, economic and public policy, the arts, higher education, health organizations, and international causes.
Arts & Humanities: 15% to 20%. Supports museums, public broadcasting, theater, and music.
Civic & Public Affairs: 40% to 45%. Supports urban and community affairs, municipalities and towns, and economic and public policy.
Education: 15% to 20%. Recipients include Harvard Business School, National Academy of Engineering, and Wentworth Institute of Technology.
Health: 10% to 15%. Supports hospitals, medical centers, and AIDS research.
International: 10% to 15%. Recipients include International Institute for Energy Conservation, International Center in New York, and Institute for International Economics.

Application Procedures

Initial Contact: Send a letter to the foundation.
Application Requirements: Include a description of organization, amount requested, purpose of funds sought, and proof of tax exempt status.
Deadlines: None.

Restrictions

Does not support individuals, religious organizations for sectarian purposes political or lobbying groups, or organizations outside operating areas.

Corporate Officials

Dr. George Nicholas Hatsopoulos: founder, chairman, chief executive officer, director B Athens, Greece 1927. ED Massachusetts Institute of Technology BS (1949); Massachusetts Institute of Technology MS (1950); Massachusetts Institute of Technology (1956). PRIM CORP EMPL founder, chairman, chief executive officer, director: Thermo Electron Corp. CORP AFFIL director: Thermoquest Inc.; director: ThermoTrex Corp.; director: Thermo Power Corp.; director: Thermo Process System; director: Thermo Instrument System Inc.; director: Thermo Optek Corp.; director: Thermo Ecotek Corp.; director: Thermo Fibertek Inc.; director: Thermedics Inc.; director: Thermo Cardiosys; chairman: FI Instruments Inc.; advisory council: International Center New York Inc.; director: Bolt Beranek & Newman. NONPR AFFIL member: Pi Tau Sigma; member: Sigma Xi; director: NRC Board Science Technology Economic Policy; council: National Academy Engineering; director, executive committee: National Bureau Economic Research; trustee: Maliotis Foundation; member vis committee department mech engineering: Massachusetts Institute Technology; member advisory board program technology economic policy: Harvard University John F Kennedy School Government; fellow: Institute Electrical & Electronics Engineers; chairman: College Yr in Athens; director: Concord Coalition; overseer: Boston Museum Science; trustee: Center Policy Research; fellow: American Service Metals; fellow: American Society Mechanical Engineers; director executive committee, member: American Business Conference; director: American Council Capital Formation; fellow: AIAA; fellow: American Academy of Arts & Sciences. CLUB AFFIL Commonwealth Club Boston.
John Nicholas Hatsopoulos: retired president B Athens, Greece 1934. ED Athens College BS; Northwestern University (1959). PRIM CORP EMPL retired president: TMD Securities Corp. CORP AFFIL chief financial officer: Thermo Instrument System Inc.; chief financial officer: Thermo Power Corp.; chief financial officer: Thermo Fibertek Inc.; chief financial officer: Thermedics Inc.; vice president, chief financial officer, director: Thermo Cardiosys; director: Lois/USA.

Foundation Officials

Robert V. Aghababian: committee member PRIM CORP EMPL assistant secretary, director: Nicolet Instrument Corp. CORP AFFIL assistant secretary: Noran Instrument Inc.
Fred Florio: committee member
Patricia E. Gibbs: committee administrator
Dr. George Nicholas Hatsopoulos: committee member (see above)
John Nicholas Hatsopoulos: committee member (see above)
Paul F. Kelleher: committee member B Boston, MA 1942. ED Bentley College BS (1970); Boston College MBA (1975). PRIM CORP EMPL senior vice president: Thermo Electron Corp. CORP AFFIL officer: Thermoquest Corp.; officer: ThermoTrex Corp.; officer: Thermo Sentron Inc.; officer: Thermo Terratech Inc.; officer: Thermo Optek Corp.; officer: Thermo Remediation Inc.; officer: Thermo Instrument System Inc.; officer: Thermo Bioanalysis Corp.; controller: Thermo Fibertek Inc.; officer: Thermedics Inc.; assistant secretary: Noran Instrument Inc.; officer: Onix Systems Inc.; assistant secretary: Nicolet Instrument Corp.
Linda C. Nordberg: committee member

Grants Analysis

Disclosure Period: calendar year ending 1998
Total Grants: $327,500
Typical Range: $250 to $5,000

Recent Grants

Note: Grants derived from 1994 Form 990.

Arts & Humanities

10,000	Boston Symphony Orchestra, Boston, MA
5,000	DeCordova Museum, Boston, MA
5,000	Museum of Fine Arts, Boston, MA
3,000	WGBH, Boston, MA
2,500	Boston Ballet, Boston, MA
1,000	Boston Children's Theater, Boston, MA
1,000	Pine Street Inn, Boston, MA

Civic & Public Affairs

25,000	ILSI
15,000	Concord Coalition, Washington, DC
10,000	Concord Coalition, Washington, DC
10,000	Thera Foundation
3,000	Boston Private Industry Council, Boston, MA
3,000	City Year, Boston, MA
2,500	Committee for a Responsible Federal Budget, Washington, DC
2,000	ASFA Fund
2,000	Committee for Citizens Awareness, Washington, DC
2,000	Massachusetts Taxpayers Foundation, Boston, MA
2,000	National Conference, Tulsa, OK
2,000	Pioneer Institute for Public Policy Research, Boston, MA

Education

20,000	Harvard Business School, Cambridge, MA
5,000	National Academy of Engineering, Washington, DC
5,000	Wentworth Institute of Technology, Boston, MA

Health

5,000	AIDS Action Committee, Boston, MA
5,000	Lahey Clinic Foundation, Burlington, MA
5,000	Waltham/Weston Hospital, Waltham, MA
2,000	American Red Cross Massachusetts Bay, Boston, MA
1,000	Newton Wellesley Hospital, Newton, MA

International

7,500	International Institute for Energy Conservation, Washington, DC

7,500	International Institute for Energy Conservation, Washington, DC
3,000	International Center in New York, New York, NY
3,000	International Center in New York, New York, NY
2,500	Institute for International Economics, Washington, DC
2,500	Institute for International Economics, Washington, DC
2,500	Japan Society of Boston, Boston, MA
2,500	Japan Society of Boston, Boston, MA
2,000	AmeriCares Foundation, New Canaan, CT
2,000	AmeriCares Foundation, New Canaan, CT

Religion

2,000	Salvation Army, Boston, MA

Science

3,000	Massachusetts State Science Fair, Boston, MA
3,000	Scientific Research Society
1,000	Museum of Science, Boston, MA

Social Services

1,500	Boy Scouts of America Minuteman Council
1,500	Northeast Home for Little Wanderers, Boston, MA
1,000	Narconon Drug Prevention
1,000	Santas Kitchen, Boston, MA -- Project Bread

THOMASVILLE FURNITURE INDUSTRIES INC.

Company Contact

Thomasville, NC
Web: http://www.thomasville.com

Company Description

Employees: 7,000
SIC(s): 2511 Wood Household Furniture, 2512 Upholstered Household Furniture, 2514 Metal Household Furniture.
Parent Company: Armstrong World Industries, Inc., Lancaster, PA, United States

Nonmonetary Support

Value: $125,000 (1996)
Type: Donated Equipment; Donated Products; Loaned Employees; Loaned Executives
Volunteer Programs: Thomasville employees volunteer in Communities in Schools and Chamber programs and in local shool systems and YMCA's.

Thomasville Furniture Industries Foundation

Giving Contact

Vickie Holder, General Manager
Thomasville Furniture Industries Foundation
PO Box 339
Thomasville, NC 27361-0339
Phone: (336)472-4000
Fax: (336)472-4085
Email: vholder@thomasville.com

Description

Founded: 1960
EIN: 566047870
Organization Type: Corporate Foundation
Giving Locations: NC
Grant Types: Award, Endowment, General Support.

Financial Summary

Total Giving: $250,000 (1999 approx); $267,944 (1998); $67,775 (1997). Note: Contributes through corporate direct giving program and foundation. 1997 Giving includes scholarship.
Assets: $5,079,176 (1998); $4,722,453 (1997); $4,140,904 (1996)
Gifts Received: $2,257 (1997). Note: Gifts received in 1997 include those from a Thomasville employee.

Typical Recipients

Arts & Humanities: Arts Associations & Councils, Arts Festivals, Community Arts, Libraries, Museums/Galleries, Music, Performing Arts, Theater
Civic & Public Affairs: Economic Development, Civic & Public Affairs-General, Housing
Education: Arts/Humanities Education, Colleges & Universities, Community & Junior Colleges, Education Funds, Elementary Education (Public), Environmental Education, Education-General, International Studies, Literacy, Minority Education, Private Education (Precollege), Public Education (Precollege), Science/Mathematics Education, Secondary Education (Public), Student Aid
Health: Emergency/Ambulance Services, Hospitals, Medical Research
Religion: Religious Welfare
Science: Scientific Centers & Institutes
Social Services: Animal Protection, Child Welfare, Community Centers, Community Service Organizations, Crime Prevention, Family Services, Recreation & Athletics, United Funds/United Ways, YMCA/YWCA/YMHA/YWHA, Youth Organizations

Contributions Analysis

Arts & Humanities: About 15 to 20%. Performing arts, libraries, and museums and galleries.
Education: 55% to 60%. Scholarships to colleges and universities.
Social Services: 20 to 25%. Primarily to Children's Center in Lexington, NC.

Application Procedures

Initial Contact: Send a a brief letter of inquiry and a full proposal.
Deadlines: None.

Restrictions

Does not support individuals, religious organizations for sectarian purposes, political or lobbying groups, or organizations outside operating areas.

Additional Information

Company provides scholarships to children of employees.

Corporate Officials

Ronald G. Berrier: vice president, treasurer, assistant secretaryc B Winston-Salem, NC 1943. ED High Point College (1965). PRIM CORP EMPL vice president, treasurer, assistant secretary: Thomasville Furniture Industries Inc.
D. Paul Dascoli: chief financial officer, vice president B Providence, RI 1960. ED Providence College (1982). PRIM CORP EMPL chief financial officer, vice president: Thomasville Furniture Industries Inc.
Christian J. Pfaff: chairman, president, chief executive officer, director PRIM CORP EMPL chairman, president, chief executive officer, director: Thomasville Furniture Industries Inc.

Foundation Officials

Vickie Holder: general manager, administrator operations

Grants Analysis

Disclosure Period: calendar year ending 1998
Total Grants: $267,944
Number of Grants: 140
Average Grant: $1,914
Highest Grant: $20,636
Typical Range: $50 to $500 and $1,000 to $5,000

Recent Grants

Note: Grants derived from 1997 Form 990.

Arts & Humanities

2,000	Davidson County-Thomasville City Theater Cooperative, Thomasville, NC
1,000	Chair City Players, Thomasville, NC

Education

3,200	Eastern Music Festival Scholarships, Greensboro, NC
475	South Davidson High School, Denton, NC -- support Destination North Carolina program
473	Wallburg Elementary School Foundation
431	Ledford Middle School, Thomasville, NC -- support Herbally Yours Program
397	Silver Valley Elementary, Lexington, NC -- support Look at Me I'm TV Free program
371	Thomasville High School, Thomasville, NC -- support Tailor Made Tiles program
294	Liberty Drive School, Thomasville, NC -- support African Shekere program
250	Thomasville Primary School, Thomasville, NC -- support Reading All Night Program
228	Extended Day School, Lexington, NC -- support Angel/Bear/Tooth Fairy/Sun Fun Project
212	Ledford Middle School, Thomasville, NC -- support As We See It program
200	Denton Elementary School, Denton, NC -- support Magic Mural Maker program
200	Thomasville Middle School, Thomasville, NC -- support Language is All Around Us Program
186	Thomasville Primary School, Thomasville, NC -- support Postcard Geography program
176	Fair Grove Elementary School, Thomasville, NC -- support Back Door Natural Habitat program
167	Thomasville Primary School, Thomasville, NC -- support Book Bag Buddies program
165	Thomasville Educational Program, Thomasville, NC -- support Bag-O-Math program
161	Thomasville Senior High, Thomasville, NC -- support Foreign Language Week International
160	East Davidson High School, Thomasville, NC -- support Hands on US History program
160	Thomasville Primary School, Thomasville, NC -- support TFI Mini-Grants go International
150	Thomasville Primary School, Thomasville, NC -- support Celebrating Good Character program
135	Fair Grove Elementary School, Thomasville, NC -- support Beaded Learner Program
102	East Davidson High School, Thomasville, NC -- support Stock Market Game
99	Liberty Drive School, Thomasville, NC -- support Wish You Were Here program
92	Wallburg Elementary, Winston-Salem, NC -- support Dabbing into Spring program
75	Thomasville Primary School, Thomasville, NC -- support Have Writing Will Travel Program
60	Denton Elementary School, Denton, NC -- support Integalactic Art Program

60 Fair Grove Elementary School, Thomasville, NC -- support Hands on History program
57 Fair Grove Elementary School, Thomasville, NC -- support Motor Articulation Program
50 Liberty Drive School, Thomasville, NC -- support Read Along with Me program
46 Denton Elementary School, Denton, NC -- support Oobleck What in the World is That program

Social Services

1,490 YMCA West Forsyth Branch, Clemmons, NC -- to underwrite employee memberships
670 YMCA, Winston-Salem, NC -- to underwrite employee memberships
500 Children's Center, Lexington, NC -- support Remember This Program
160 Children's Center, Lexington, NC -- support Seeing is Believing program
146 Flowers by Neil, Thomasville, NC -- program support
145 Children's Center, Lexington, NC -- support Hooded with no Chill program
78 Children's Center, Lexington, NC -- support Fit Is It Program
77 Children's Center, Lexington, NC -- support Painting But No Brushes program
65 Children's Center, Lexington, NC -- support Fore Program
65 Children's Center, Lexington, NC -- support What's My Name Program
64 Davidson County Children's Center, Lexington, NC -- support Cooking for Learning Chapter 4
56 Children's Center, Lexington, NC -- support special needs program
55 Children's Center, Lexington, NC -- support Animals Everywhere
55 Davidson County Children's Center, Lexington, NC -- support Grab and Snap program
55 Davidson County Children's Center, Lexington, NC -- support Band Aides Session II
45 Children's Center, Lexington, NC -- support Spinning program
43 Children's Center, Lexington, NC -- support Smelling Good Gourds program
43 Children's Center, Lexington, NC -- support Art on Wheels program

J. Walter Thompson Co.

Company Contact

New York, NY
Web: http://www.jwtworld.com

Company Description

Revenue: US$7,000,000,000
Employees: 7,300
SIC(s): 7311 Advertising Agencies.
Parent Company: WPP Group Plc, 27 Farm Street, London, GL, England

Operating Locations

AZ: Winona Research, Phoenix; J. Walter Thompson Co., Scottsdale; CA: J. Walter Thompson Co., Los Angeles; Mendoza, Dillon & Associates, Newport Beach; J. Walter Thompson Co., San Diego; SBG Enterprises, San Francisco; J. Walter Thompson Co., San Francisco; DC: RTCdirect, Washington; J. Walter Thompson & Co., Washington; Timmons & Co., Washington; FL: J. Walter Thompson Co., Coral Gables; GA: J. Walter Thompson Co., Atlanta; IL: J. Walter Thompson Co., Chicago; MI: J. Walter Thompson Co., Detroit; MO: J. Walter Thompson Co., Saint Ann; NJ: J. Walter Thompson Co., Cherry Hill; HLS Corp., Little Falls; Einson Freeman, Paramus; CommonHealth USA, Parsippany; Thomas G. Ferguson Associates, Parsippany; NY: J. Walter Thompson Co., Fairport; Anspach Grossman Enterprise, New York; Carl Byoir & Associates, New York; Hill & Knowlton, New York; J. Walter Thompson Co., New York; MRB Group, New York; Ogilvy & Mather Worldwide, New York; Pace Advertising, New York; Simmons, New York; Walker Group/CNI Inc., New York; WPP Group USA, New York; OH: J. Walter Thompson Co., Cincinnati, Columbus; TX: J. Walter Thompson Co., Dallas; UT: J. Walter Thompson Co., Salt Lake City

Nonmonetary Support

Value: $730,249 (1996); $880,000 (1994)
Type: In-kind Services; Loaned Employees; Loaned Executives; Workplace Solicitation
Note: The company also provides nonmonetary support in the form of creative work/services.

J. Walter Thompson Co. Fund

Giving Contact

Donald Gammon, Partner
466 Lexington Ave.
New York, NY 10017
Phone: (212)210-7000
Fax: (212)210-6852

Description

EIN: 136020644
Organization Type: Corporate Foundation
Giving Locations: nationally.
Grant Types: Employee Matching Gifts, General Support.
Note: Employee matching gift ratio: 1 to 1 to higher education, up to $2,500 annually.

Financial Summary

Total Giving: $1,700,000 (fiscal year ending November 30, 1999 approx); $289,154 (fiscal 1998); $1,579,082 (fiscal 1996). Note: Contributes through corporate direct giving program and foundation.
Giving Analysis: Giving for fiscal 1996 includes: corporate direct giving ($630,249); foundation ($189,644); foundation matching gifts ($28,940); fiscal 1998: foundation ($207,057); foundation grants to United Way ($50,000); foundation matching gifts ($32,098)
Assets: $998,707 (fiscal 1998); $1,322,240 (fiscal 1996); $897,166 (fiscal 1994)
Gifts Received: $200,000 (fiscal 1996); $200,000 (fiscal 1994). Note: Contributions received from J. Walter Thompson.

Typical Recipients

Arts & Humanities: Arts Centers, Arts Festivals, Arts Funds, Ballet, Dance, Arts & Humanities-General, Historic Preservation, Libraries, Museums/Galleries, Music, Performing Arts, Theater
Civic & Public Affairs: African American Affairs, Botanical Gardens/Parks, Business/Free Enterprise, Economic Development, Civic & Public Affairs-General, Municipalities/Towns, Professional & Trade Associations, Public Policy, Safety, Women's Affairs
Education: Business Education, Colleges & Universities, Education Funds, Education Reform, Engineering/Technological Education, Education-General, International Exchange, Medical Education, Minority Education, Private Education (Precollege), Social Sciences Education, Student Aid
Environment: Environment-General, Resource Conservation
Health: Cancer, Clinics/Medical Centers, Diabetes, Heart, Hospitals, Medical Research, Speech & Hearing
International: International Organizations, International Relations, Trade
Religion: Jewish Causes, Religious Organizations
Science: Science Museums, Scientific Research
Social Services: At-Risk Youth, Community Centers, Crime Prevention, Recreation & Athletics, Scouts, Social Services-General, Substance Abuse, United Funds/United Ways, Youth Organizations

Contributions Analysis

Giving Priorities: Higher education, museums, hospitals, and civic.
Arts & Humanities: 27%. Supports museums, music, and theater. Funds established performing and visual arts institutions with national/international reputations.
Civic & Public Affairs: 15%. Supports civic affairs and public policy.
Education: 19%. Supports higher education. Support of education is almost entirely through a matching gift program for employees. Certain scholarship programs receive support, but must be associated with the co.
Health: 7%. Supports hospitals, American Red Cross and juvenile diabetes.
International: 5%.
Social Services: 25%. Major support given to United Way.
Note: Requests in areas other than the arts and education are considered by the relevant offices of the co. Such contributions in most cases are made to organizations that in some way are connected with the co.'s business or because the request is client-related. Total contributions made in 1998.

Application Procedures

Initial Contact: Submit a a brief letter of inquiry.
Application Requirements: Include proof of tax-exempt status.
Deadlines: None.

Restrictions

Does not support individuals, religious organizations for sectarian purposes, or political or lobbying groups.

Corporate Officials

Christopher Jones: chief executive officer, director PRIM CORP EMPL chief executive officer: J. Walter Thompson Co.
Peter A. Schweitzer: president B Chicago, IL 1939. ED University of Michigan BA (1961); Western Michigan University MBA (1967). PRIM CORP EMPL president: J. Walter Thompson Co. NONPR AFFIL member: American Association Advertising Agencies.
Lewis J. Trencher: chief operating officer, director B 1952. ED New York Law School JD; New York University BS; New York University MBA. PRIM CORP EMPL chief operating officer, director: J. Walter Thompson Co.

Foundation Officials

Donna Matteo: secretary, treasurer
Susan Mirsky: vice president, director B New York, NY 1939. ED Smith College BA (1961); New York University (1961-1962). PRIM CORP EMPL senior vice president, worldwide personnel director: J. Walter Thompson Co. NONPR AFFIL member: New York Human Research Planners; member: New York Personnel Management Association; advisory member: Boys Harbor; member directors committee: Mount Sinai Medical Center.
Lewis J. Trencher: chairman, director (see above)

Grants Analysis

Disclosure Period: fiscal year ending November 30, 1998
Total Grants: $207,057*
Number of Grants: 37
Average Grant: $5,596
Highest Grant: $15,000
Typical Range: $1,000 to $10,000

***Note:** Giving excludes matching gifts and United Way.

Recent Grants

Note: Grants derived from fiscal 1996 Annual Report.

Arts & Humanities

10,000	Library of Congress James Madison Council, Washington, DC
10,000	National Actors Theater, New York, NY
9,015	Lincoln Center Consolidated Corporate Fund, New York, NY
5,000	Business Committee for the Arts, New York, NY
5,000	Museum of Radio and Television
5,000	Museum of Radio and Television
2,290	Metropolitan Museum of Art, New York, NY
2,224	Museum of Modern Art, New York, NY
1,250	Carnegie Hall, New York, NY
1,250	Carnegie Hall Corporate Fund, New York, NY
1,000	American Advertising Museum
1,000	New York Philharmonic, New York, NY
1,000	Whitney Museum of American Art, New York, NY
740	New York Landmarks Conservancy, New York, NY

Civic & Public Affairs

9,000	Advertising Council, New York, NY
9,000	New Jersey Network of Business and Professional Women, River Edge, NJ
5,000	Central Park Conservancy, New York, NY
4,000	James Webb Young Fund, Saratoga Springs, NY
3,750	Catalyst, New York, NY

Education

5,000	Jason Foundation for Education, Waltham, MA
4,725	National Merit Scholarship Corp, Evanston, IL
4,300	University Settlement, New York, NY
2,575	University of Michigan School of Business, Ann Arbor, MI
2,500	Lawrence University, Appleton, WI
2,500	Mount Holyoke College, South Hadley, MA
2,500	St. Paul's School
2,500	Skidmore College, Saratoga Springs, NY
1,500	Branson School, Ross, CA
1,500	Syracuse University, Syracuse, NY
1,000	Albert Einstein College of Medicine of Yeshiva University, Bronx, NY
950	Humboldt State University, Arcata, CA
675	Yale University, New Haven, CT
650	Columbia College and University, New York, NY
615	Brown University, Providence, RI
550	Bryn Mawr College, Bryn Mawr, PA

Health

10,000	Society of the New York Hospital Fund, New York, NY
5,000	Cancer Care
3,900	American Heart Association, New York, NY
1,000	American Heart Association, New York, NY
1,000	Catholic Medical Center, Jamaica, NY
1,000	Juvenile Diabetes Foundation New York Chapter, New York, NY
700	Children's Hearing Institute

International

1,000	Netherland-America Foundation, New York, NY
1,000	Operation Smile, Norfolk, VA

Religion

4,000	United Jewish Appeal Federation, New York, NY
1,500	Anti-Defamation League, New York, NY

Science

1,000	American Museum of Natural History, New York, NY

Social Services

50,000	United Way, New York, NY
4,500	Phoenix House Development Fund, New York, NY
1,000	Silver Shield Foundation, New York, NY

TICKETMASTER CORP.

Company Contact

Los Angeles, CA

Company Description

Operating Revenue: US$161,300,000
Employees: 4,905
SIC(s): 7922 Theatrical Producers & Services, 7999 Amusement & Recreation Nec.
Parent Company: Ticketmaster Group, Inc.

Ticketmaster Foundation

Giving Contact

Claire Rothman, Executive Vice President & General Manager, Western Region
3701 Wilshire Blvd., 7th Floor
Los Angeles, CA 90010
Phone: (310)360-6000
Fax: (310)383-8714

Description

Founded: 1994
EIN: 954390694
Organization Type: Corporate Foundation. Supports preselected organizations only.

Financial Summary

Total Giving: $591,790 (1996); $507,048 (1995)
Assets: $22,393 (1996); $13,474 (1995); $183,871 (1994)
Gifts Received: $589,352 (1996); $483,692 (1995). Note: In 1995 and 1997, contributions were received from various Ticketmaster locations.

Typical Recipients

Arts & Humanities: Arts & Humanities-General, Libraries, Music, Performing Arts
Civic & Public Affairs: Business/Free Enterprise, Civic & Public Affairs-General, Urban & Community Affairs
Education: Colleges & Universities, Preschool Education
Environment: Forestry
Health: AIDS/HIV, Children's Health/Hospitals, Clinics/Medical Centers, Diabetes, Medical Research, Multiple Sclerosis, Respiratory
International: International Development, International Environmental Issues
Religion: Jewish Causes, Religious Welfare
Social Services: Community Service Organizations, Recreation & Athletics

Corporate Officials

Peter B. Knepper: senior vice president, chief financial officer PRIM CORP EMPL senior vice president, chief financial officer: Ticketmaster Corp.
Fredric D. Rosen: president, chief executive officer PRIM CORP EMPL president, chief executive officer: Ticketmaster Corp.

Foundation Officials

Ned S. Goldstein: secretary
Peter B. Knepper: chief financial officer (see above)
Fredric D. Rosen: president (see above)

Grants Analysis

Disclosure Period: calendar year ending 1996
Total Grants: $591,790
Number of Grants: 152
Average Grant: $3,893
Highest Grant: $25,000
Typical Range: $1,000 to $5,000

Recent Grants

Note: Grants derived from 1996 Form 990.

Arts & Humanities

10,000	Musicares Foundation, Santa Monica, CA
5,000	Library Foundation, San Francisco, CA

Civic & Public Affairs

25,000	APLA
15,000	Crossroads Foundation
12,500	APLA
10,000	LA Committee, Los Angeles, CA

Education

25,000	University of California Los Angeles Foundation, Los Angeles, CA
10,000	University of California Los Angeles Foundation, Los Angeles, CA
6,250	Center for Early Education, West Hollywood, CA

Health

25,000	Children's Diabetes Foundation
25,000	Nancy Davis Foundation for Multiple Sclerosis, Aspen, CO
15,000	Pediatric AIDS Foundation, Chicago, IL
10,000	Asthma and Allergy Foundation
10,000	Elton John AIDS Foundation, Atlanta, GA
10,000	Starbright Foundation, Los Angeles, CA
8,000	Race to Erase Multiple Sclerosis

International

10,000	California-Israel Chamber of Commerce, CA

Religion

15,000	Jewish Defense Fund
15,000	National Conference of Christians and Jews, New York, NY

Social Services

10,000	Crossroads, Fort Wayne, IN

TIMES MIRROR CO.

Company Contact

Los Angeles, CA
Web: http://www.tm.com

Company Description

Revenue: US$3,215,800,000 (1999)
Profit: US$259,100,000 (1999)
Employees: 27,700
Fortune Rank: 477, per FORTUNE Magazine's list of 500 Largest U.S. Corporations (1999).
FF 477
SIC(s): 2711 Newspapers, 2721 Periodicals, 2731 Book Publishing, 4841 Cable & Other Pay Television Services.

Nonmonetary Support

Value: $27,352 (1988); $5,710 (1987)
Type: Donated Equipment; Donated Products; In-kind Services

Times Mirror Foundation

Giving Contact

Bonnie Hill, President
Times Mirror Foundation
Times Mirror Square
Los Angeles, CA 90053
Phone: (213)237-2922
Fax: (213)237-2116

Description

EIN: 956079651
Organization Type: Corporate Foundation
Giving Locations: CA: nonprofits located in Southern CA headquarters and operating communities.
Grant Types: Capital, Employee Matching Gifts, General Support, Multiyear/Continuing Support, Project, Scholarship.
Note: Employee matching gift ratio: 1 to 1. Company will match gifts made by employees and retirees with a minimum contribution of $25 and a maximum of $10,000 annually. The company grants scholarships to children of Times Mirror employees.

Giving Philosophy

'The mission of The Times Mirror Foundation is to support nonprofit organizations that measurably improve the quality of life in communities where Times Mirror does business. The Foundation gives priority to programs that improve the quality of journalism, education and literacy, strengthen the fabric of the community, or enhance cultural appreciation and understanding.' Application Guidelines and Procedures

Financial Summary

Total Giving: $3,700,000 (1997 approx); $1,879,000 (1995); $6,723,000 (1994 approx). Note: Contributes through corporate direct giving program and foundation. 1995 Giving includes foundation.
Assets: $7,358,434 (1995); $9,523,694 (1990); $18,183,490 (1989)

Typical Recipients

Arts & Humanities: Arts Associations & Councils, Arts Centers, Arts Institutes, Dance, Ethnic & Folk Arts, Arts & Humanities-General, Historic Preservation, Libraries, Museums/Galleries, Music, Performing Arts, Public Broadcasting, Theater
Civic & Public Affairs: African American Affairs, Asian American Affairs, Botanical Gardens/Parks, Chambers of Commerce, Civil Rights, Economic Development, Economic Policy, Employment/Job Training, First Amendment Issues, Civic & Public Affairs-General, Hispanic Affairs, Housing, Legal Aid, Minority Business, Municipalities/Towns, Native American Affairs, Nonprofit Management, Parades/Festivals, Professional & Trade Associations, Public Policy, Urban & Community Affairs, Women's Affairs, Zoos/Aquariums
Education: Arts/Humanities Education, Business Education, Business-School Partnerships, Colleges & Universities, Education Funds, Education Reform, Engineering/Technological Education, Faculty Development, Education-General, International Studies, Journalism/Media Education, Literacy, Minority Education, Public Education (Precollege), Student Aid, Vocational & Technical Education
Environment: Environment-General
Health: Cancer, Diabetes, Emergency/Ambulance Services, Eyes/Blindness, Health-General, Respiratory
International: Foreign Arts Organizations, International Affairs, International Organizations, International Relations
Science: Science Museums
Social Services: Camps, Child Welfare, Community Centers, Community Service Organizations, Domestic Violence, Family Services, Food/Clothing Distribution, Homes, People with Disabilities, Recreation & Athletics, Scouts, Senior Services, United Funds/United Ways, Volunteer Services, YMCA/YWCA/YMHA/YWHA, Youth Organizations

Contributions Analysis

Giving Priorities: Higher education, television and radio, the arts, social welfare, and media related organizations.
Arts & Humanities: 20%. Primary beneficiaries include community television and public radio stations, museums, music centers, and major performing arts centers. Other interests include symphonies and orchestras, theater, arts festivals, American folk arts, community arts groups, and libraries.
Civic & Public Affairs: 30% to 35%. Special interests include journalism, the press, First Amendment, and other media-related concerns. Other recipients in this category include conservation groups, civil rights and women's affairs organizations, public policy research organizations, zoos, and business and free enterprise groups.
Education: 25% to 30%. Communications, the arts, teaching, computers, independent and minority college funds, educational youth organizations, precollege schools, arts institutes, and minority scholarship assistance.
Health: 10% to 15%. Primarily supports united funds. Other community service concerns include youth agencies, shelters for homeless women and youth, child welfare, community centers, religious welfare, services for the disabled, and family planning. Health interests include hospitals, mental health, medical schools, and health organizations.
Note: Above priorities reflect combined foundation and direct giving priorities. Subsidiaries give both directly and through the foundation in their operating areas; other direct and foundation grants concentrate on Southern California organizations. Foundation grants typically range from $2,500 to $25,000, while company grants are usually $2,500 or less. Also provides matching gifts in the areas of education,cultural, conservation, and hospitals.

Application Procedures

Initial Contact: Call for guidelines and a grant summary form, which must accompany a full proposal.
Application Requirements: Include a description of organization, its purpose, programs, and project to be considered; statement of the problem the project will address; qualifications of personnel; program goals; methodology; evaluation procedures; proof of tax-exempt status; list of current supporting organizations and amount of support; and organizational budget for current and upcoming fiscal years.
Deadlines: by April 15 or October 15; board meets in June and December.
Notes: Organizations in areas served by Times Mirror subsidiaries with significant employee presence should submit requests to subsidiary directly.

Restrictions

Company and foundation do not provide grants for religious, political or fraternal purposes, to veteran or labor groups, for events, or to individuals.
Repeat grant requests will not be considered within a one-year time period.

Additional Information

Grant requests to the Times Mirror Co. are considered as they are received. Company's grants are generally smaller than the foundation's and may include support for fund-raising events. Application criteria and eligibility are similar to those for the foundation.
The foundation makes grants to nonprofit organizations in regions where Times Mirror operating companies are located, a listing of which is located on their website.
Times Mirror also gives through 26 operating units, including the Los Angeles Times, CA; Newsday, Long Island, NY; and The Baltimore Sun Newspaper, MD.
Publications: Contributions Annual Report

Corporate Officials

Kathryn M. Downing: executive vice presidents, chief executive officer ED Lewis & Clark College; Stanford University. PRIM CORP EMPL executive vice president: The Times Mirror Co. PRIM NONPR EMPL president, chief executive officer: Los Angeles Times ADD CORP EMPL president: Mosby Inc.; president, chief executive officer: Mosby Matthew Bender. NONPR AFFIL member: American Association Publishers; director: Friends Law Library Congress.
Bonnie Guiton Hill: vice president B Springfield, IL 1941. ED Mills College BA (1974); California State University, Hayward MS (1975); University of California at Berkeley EdD (1985). PRIM CORP EMPL vice president: The Times Mirror Co. PRIM NONPR EMPL senior vice president, communications & public affairs: Los Angeles Times. CORP AFFIL director: NA-South Dakota Regulation Inc.; director: Niagara Mohawk Power Corp.; director: Hershey Foods Corp.; director: Louisiana-Pacific Corp.; director: AK Steel Corp.; director: Crestar Financial Corp. NONPR AFFIL director: Joint Center Political Economic Studies; director: National Urban League.
Steven J. Schoch: vice president, treasurer B St. Louis, MO 1958. ED Tufts University (1981); Dartmouth College (1986). PRIM CORP EMPL vice president, treasurer: The Times Mirror Co. ADD CORP EMPL president, chief executive officer: Times Mirror Resource Management Co.
Mark Hinckley Willes: chairman, president, chief executive officer B Salt Lake City, UT 1941. ED Columbia University AB (1963); Columbia University PhD (1967). PRIM CORP EMPL chairman, president, chief executive officer: The Times Mirror Co. CORP AFFIL director: Ryder System Inc.; director: Talbots Inc.; director: Black & Decker Corp.; publisher: Los Angeles Times.

Giving Program Officials

Stephen Charles Meier: vice chairman B Los Angeles, CA 1950. ED Occidental College (1972); Harvard University MBA (1977). PRIM CORP EMPL vice president public & government affairs, corporate secretary: The Times Mirror Co.

Foundation Officials

Kathryn M. Downing: vice chairman (see above)
Bonnie Guiton Hill: president, chief executive officer (see above)
Stephen Charles Meier: vice chairman (see above)
Steven J. Schoch: treasurer, chief financial officer (see above)
Mark Hinckley Willes: chairman (see above)
Donald Franklin Wright: director B Saint Paul, MN 1934. ED University of Minnesota BME (1957); University of Minnesota MBA (1958). PRIM CORP EMPL executive vice president: The Times Mirror Co. CORP AFFIL chairman: Times Mirror Magazines Inc.; president, chief executive officer: Los Angeles Times. NONPR AFFIL vice chairman: Los Angeles Area Council Boy Scouts America; University Minnesota Alumni Association; director: Associates California Institute Technology; honorary member: Claremont University Graduate School; member: American Newspaper Publishers Association. CLUB AFFIL City Bunker Hill Club.

Grants Analysis

Disclosure Period: calendar year ending 1995
Total Grants: $1,879,000
Number of Grants: 53
Average Grant: $27,000*
Highest Grant: $475,000
Typical Range: $1,000 to $12,000 and $25,000 to $50,000
***Note:** Average grant figure excludes highest grant.

Recent Grants

Note: Grants derived from 1995 Form 990.

Arts & Humanities

250,000	Huntington Library, Huntington, CA -- three-year pledge
100,000	Museum of Contemporary Art, Los Angeles, CA -- three-year pledge
75,000	Los Angeles County Museum of Art, Los Angeles, CA
25,000	Horace Bushnell Memorial Hall, Hartford, CT
25,000	KCET, Los Angeles, CA
25,000	Museum of Television and Radio, New York, NY -- three-year pledge
20,000	Lincoln Center for Performing Arts, New York, NY
20,000	Orange County Performing Arts Center, Costa Mesa, CA
10,000	Museum of Contemporary Art, Los Angeles, CA
10,000	Wadsworth Athenaeum, Hartford, CT -- five-year pledge
10,000	Woodbury Library -- library automation
5,000	Brooklyn Museum, Brooklyn, NY
5,000	California Institute of the Arts, Valencia, CA
5,000	Metropolitan Museum of Art, New York, NY
4,000	Aman Folk Ensemble, Los Angeles, CA
2,500	KCRW Foundation, Los Angeles, CA
2,500	Los Angeles Chamber Orchestra, Los Angeles, CA
2,500	New York Public Library, New York, NY
2,500	South Coast Repertory Theater, Costa Mesa, CA

Civic & Public Affairs

20,000	American Press Institute, Reston, VA
20,000	Asme Foundation, New York, NY
20,000	Los Angeles Urban League, Los Angeles, CA
10,000	Foundation for American Communications, Los Angeles, CA
10,000	Missouri Botanical Gardens, Saint Louis, MO -- five-year pledge
5,000	Reporters Committee for Freedom of the Press, Washington, DC
2,500	Plaza De La Raza, Los Angeles, CA

Education

150,000	Independent Colleges of Southern California, Los Angeles, CA
100,000	United Negro College Fund, New York, NY -- three-year pledge
75,000	Loyola Marymount University, Los Angeles, CA
50,000	LEARN, York, PA -- two-year pledge, for 2000 Partnership
30,000	Maynard Institute of Journalism
25,000	California State University Northridge Trust Fund, School of Education, Northridge, CA -- four-year pledge
20,000	United Negro College Fund, New York, NY
15,000	Tomas Rivera Center, Claremont, CA
15,000	Tri-School Consortium
15,000	University of California Los Angeles, Los Angeles, CA -- LEAD Program in Business
10,000	Don Bosco Technical Institute
10,000	Princeton University, Princeton, NJ -- three-year pledge
5,000	Allentown College of St. Francis de Sales, Allentown, PA -- two-year pledge
5,000	National Hispanic Scholarship Fund, Baltimore, MD
5,000	Reading Is Fundamental
5,000	University of California Los Angeles Graduate School of Management, Los Angeles, CA
2,500	University of Missouri St. Louis, Saint Louis, MO -- three-year pledge

International

7,500	International Press Institute, Melville, NY

Social Services

475,000	United Way, Los Angeles, CA
75,000	Music Center United Fund, Los Angeles, CA
60,000	United Way Orange County, Irvine, CA
25,000	Camp Courant, Hartford, CT -- four-year pledge
5,000	Youth News Service, Los Angeles Bureau, Los Angeles, CA
2,500	Los Angeles Girl Scout Council, Los Angeles, CA

THE TIMKEN CO.

Company Contact

Canton, OH

Company Description

Employees: 19,130
SIC(s): 3312 Blast Furnaces & Steel Mills, 3562 Ball & Roller Bearings.

The Timken Co. Charitable Trust

Giving Contact

Mr. Ward J. Timken, Office of Vice President
Timken Co. Charitable Trust
1835 Dueber Avenue Southwest
Canton, OH 44706
Phone: (330)471-4062
Fax: (330)471-4041

Description

EIN: 346534265
Organization Type: Corporate Foundation
Giving Locations: communities where company operates plants, with an emphasis on Ohio.
Grant Types: Capital, Emergency, General Support, Multiyear/Continuing Support, Project, Research.
Note: Maximum multiyear support: 5 years.

Giving Philosophy

'The Timken Company Charitable Trust contributes funds to organizations created or organized in the United States and operated exclusively for charitable, scientific, veteran rehabilitation service, literary or educational purposes.' Timken Company Charitable Trust

Financial Summary

Total Giving: $7,500,000 (1999 approx); $910,345 (1998); $784,780 (1997). Note: Contributes through corporate direct giving program and foundation.
Giving Analysis: Giving for 1997 includes: foundation grants to United Way ($399,355); foundation ($385,425); 1998: foundation ($479,639); foundation grants to United Way ($430,706)
Assets: $3,819,585 (1998); $2,981,283 (1996); $1,809,445 (1995)
Gifts Received: $1,800,000 (1996); $1,500,000 (1995); $600,000 (1994). Note: The trust receives contributions from The Timken Co.

Typical Recipients

Arts & Humanities: Arts Associations & Councils, Arts Funds, Arts & Humanities-General, Historic Preservation, Museums/Galleries, Theater
Civic & Public Affairs: African American Affairs, Business/Free Enterprise, Chambers of Commerce, Clubs, Economic Development, Economic Policy, Civic & Public Affairs-General, Housing, Law & Justice, Municipalities/Towns, Philanthropic Organizations, Urban & Community Affairs, Zoos/Aquariums
Education: Business Education, Colleges & Universities, Continuing Education, Education Associations, Education Funds, Education Reform, Engineering/Technological Education, Education-General, Minority Education, Public Education (Precollege), Science/Mathematics Education, Secondary Education (Public)
Environment: Environment-General, Resource Conservation
Health: Arthritis, Emergency/Ambulance Services, Health Organizations
Science: Science Museums
Social Services: Animal Protection, Community Service Organizations, Crime Prevention, Food/Clothing Distribution, Scouts, Substance Abuse, United Funds/United Ways, Youth Organizations

Contributions Analysis

Giving Priorities: United funds, food distribution, and education.
Arts & Humanities: 7%. Arts funds.
Civic & Public Affairs: 6%. Supports foundations and community programs.
Education: 34%. Education reform, Junior Achievement, business education, and several colleges and universities. An educational fund gives scholarships only to children of employees.
Health: 1%. Healthcare organizations.
Science: 3%. Funds Inventure Place.
Social Services: 49%. United Way agencies in various Ohio communities.
Note: Total contributions made in 1998.

Application Procedures

Initial Contact: By letter, including proposal.
Application Requirements: Include a description of organization; amount and purpose of request; proof of tax exemption.
Deadlines: None.
Review Process: Applications are received throughout the year and reviewed by trustee advisors.
Evaluative Criteria: All proposals will be considered, though most grants awarded to civil and charitable organizations where company plants are located.
Decision Notification: Generally within one to two months after receipt of proposal.

Restrictions

Timken Co. Trust generally does not fund religious organizations.

Corporate Officials

Robert J. Lapp: vice president public affairsfr PRIM CORP EMPL vice president governmentaland public affairs: Timken Co.
John J. Schubach: senior vice president strategic management B 1935. ED Case Western Reserve University (1962); Harvard University (1969). PRIM CORP EMPL senior vice president strategic management: Timken Co.
Ward Jackson Timken: vice president, director, officer B Canton, OH 1942. ED University of Arizona (1966); Stanford University (1985). PRIM CORP EMPL vice president, director, officer: Timken Co. NONPR AFFIL member: Educational Enhancement Partnership.
William Robert Timken, Jr.: chairman, president, chief executive officer, director B Canton, OH 1938. ED Stanford University BA (1960); Harvard University MBA (1962). PRIM CORP EMPL chairman, president, chief executive officer, director: Timken Co. CORP AFFIL director: Tejas Holdings LLC; chairman: Timken Latrobe Steel; director: Aeroquip-Vickers Inc.; director: Diebold Inc.

Foundation Officials

Gene E. Little: trustee, advisor B 1943. ED Dartmouth College MBA; Kenyon College BS (1965); University of Akron (1973). PRIM CORP EMPL senior vice president finance: Timken Co. CORP AFFIL director: Easco Aluminum; director: Easco Inc.

John J. Schubach: trustee, advisor (see above)
Ward Jackson Timken: vice president (see above)

Grants Analysis

Disclosure Period: calendar year ending 1998
Total Grants: $479,639*
Number of Grants: 33
Average Grant: $14,553
Highest Grant: $75,000
Typical Range: $500 to $15,000
***Note:** Giving excludes United Way.

Recent Grants

Note: Grants derived from 1997 Form 990.

Arts & Humanities

40,000 Fund for the Arts, Canton, OH -- operating support
25,000 Automotive Hall of Fame, Midland, MI -- operating support
2,500 Canton Palace Theater, Canton, OH -- operating support
500 Canton Preservation Society, Canton, OH -- operating support

Civic & Public Affairs

2,500 Canton Pestonal Chamber of Commerce, Canton, OH -- operating support
2,120 Canton Regional Chamber Foundation, Canton, OH -- operating support
2,000 Frontiers of Canton, Canton, OH -- operating support
2,000 Tryon Rotary of Polk County, Tryon, NC -- operating support
1,500 NAACP of Cherokee County, Caffney, SC -- operating support
1,000 AHTS Council, Caffney, SC -- operating support
500 Junior League, Canton, OH -- operating support

Education

75,000 Stark County College of Technology, North Canton, OH -- operating support
50,000 Education Enhancement Partnership, Canton, OH -- operating support
50,000 Ohio Foundation of Independent Colleges, Columbus, OH -- operating support
25,115 Stark State College Foundation, North Canton, OH -- operating support
25,000 Junior Achievement of Stark County, Canton, OH -- operating support
18,000 Walsh University, North Canton, OH -- operating support
2,000 Junior Achievement of Buckhus County, Buckhus, OH -- operating support
1,800 Independent Colleges and Universities, Columbia, SC -- operating support
900 Mineral High School District Operating Fund, Mineral, OH
750 Independent Colleges, Raleigh, NC -- operating support
500 Junior Achievement of North Central Ohio, Mansfield, OH -- operating support

Environment

18,000 Natural Concerns -- operating support
3,500 Wilderness Central, Filmont, OH -- operating support

Health

2,000 American Red Cross of Central Stark County, Canton, OH -- operating support
500 Arthritis Foundation, Canton, OH -- operating support

Social Services

255,000 United Way of Central Stark County, Canton, OH -- operating support
24,000 United Way of the Buckhus Area, Buckhus, OH -- operating support
21,000 United Way of Westmoreland County, Greensburg, PA -- operating support
20,000 United Way of Cherokee County, Caffney, SC -- operating support
15,000 Boy Scouts of America Buckeye Council, Canton, OH -- operating support
15,000 United Way of Lincoln County, Lincolnton, NC -- operating support
14,800 United Way of Franklin County, Columbus, OH -- operating support
10,000 United Way, Detroit, MI -- operating support
6,750 United Way of Central Virginia, Lynchburg, VA -- operating support
6,500 United Way, Wooster, OH -- operating support
5,500 United Way of Tuscarawas County, New Philadelphia, OH -- operating support
5,000 United Way, Ashboro, NC -- operating support
4,700 United Way of Ashland County, Midland, OH -- operating support
1,300 United Way, Atlanta, GA -- operating support
1,200 United Way, Chicago, IL -- operating support
1,200 United Way, Eaton, OH -- operating support
1,000 United Way of Rutherford County, Spindale, NC -- operating support
900 United Way, Philadelphia, PA -- operating support
875 United Way, Dallas, TX -- operating support
800 United Way, Columbus, OH -- operating support
600 United Way, Reno, NV -- operating support
500 United Way, Hartford, CT -- operating support
500 United Way, Houston, TX -- operating support
500 United Way, Los Angeles, CA -- operating support

THE TIMKEN CO.

Company Contact

Canton, OH

Company Description

Employees: 19,130
SIC(s): 3312 Blast Furnaces & Steel Mills, 3562 Ball & Roller Bearings.

Timken Co. Educational Fund

Giving Contact

Debra K. Rankine, Manager, Staffing Services
1835 Dueber Avenue SW
Canton, OH 44706
Phone: (330)471-3933

Description

Founded: 1957
EIN: 346520257
Organization Type: Corporate Foundation
Grant Types: Scholarship.

Financial Summary

Total Giving: $370,558 (1998); $422,811 (1997); $409,874 (1996)
Giving Analysis: Giving for 1998 includes: foundation scholarships ($370,558)
Assets: $2,128,212 (1998); $1,493,027 (1996); $415,160 (1989)
Gifts Received: $1,200,000 (1996). Note: In 1996, contributions were received from the Timken Co.

Application Procedures

Initial Contact: Information and applications are available from company.

Additional Information

Provides scholarships to children and dependent stepchildren of associates or retirees of the Timken Co. and its subsidiaries.

Foundation Officials

Robert L. Leibensperger: trustee
Gene E. Little: secretary, treasurer, trustee B 1943. ED Dartmouth College MBA; Kenyon College BS (1965); University of Akron (1973). PRIM CORP EMPL senior vice president finance: Timken Co. CORP AFFIL director: Easco Aluminum; director: Easco Inc.
Ward Jackson Timken: president B Canton, OH 1942. ED University of Arizona (1966); Stanford University (1985). PRIM CORP EMPL vice president, director, officer: Timken Co. NONPR AFFIL member: Educational Enhancement Partnership.

TITAN INDUSTRIAL CORP.

Company Contact

New York, NY

Company Description

Employees: 55
SIC(s): 5051 Metals Service Centers & Offices.

Titan Industrial Foundation

Giving Contact

Marian Cassese, Assistant to the Chairman
555 Madison Ave., 10th Fl.
New York, NY 10022
Phone: (212)421-6700

Description

Founded: 1951
EIN: 136066216
Organization Type: Corporate Foundation. Supports preselected organizations only.
Giving Locations: NY
Grant Types: Endowment, General Support.

Financial Summary

Total Giving: $333,081 (fiscal year ending November 30, 1997); $164,913 (fiscal 1996); $192,377 (fiscal 1995)
Assets: $2,641,234 (fiscal 1997); $1,167,457 (fiscal 1996); $1,148,974 (fiscal 1995)
Gifts Received: $230,781 (fiscal 1995); $117,312 (fiscal 1994); $17,500 (fiscal 1993). Note: In fiscal 1995, contributions were received from the Titan Industrial Corp. ($100,000) and Jerome Siegel ($130,781).

Typical Recipients

Arts & Humanities: Arts Associations & Councils, Arts Centers, Arts Institutes, Dance, Ethnic & Folk Arts, Film & Video, Arts & Humanities-General, Historic Preservation, Libraries, Museums/Galleries, Music, Opera, Performing Arts, Theater
Civic & Public Affairs: Civic & Public Affairs-General, Legal Aid, Public Policy, Urban & Community Affairs, Women's Affairs

Education: Business Education, Colleges & Universities, Community & Junior Colleges, Education-General, International Exchange, Literacy, School Volunteerism
Environment: Wildlife Protection
Health: AIDS/HIV, Cancer, Clinics/Medical Centers, Eyes/Blindness, Health Organizations, Hospitals, Research/Studies Institutes, Single-Disease Health Associations
International: Foreign Arts Organizations, Human Rights, International Organizations, International Peace & Security Issues, International Relations, Missionary/Religious Activities
Religion: Jewish Causes, Religious Organizations, Religious Welfare, Synagogues/Temples
Social Services: Big Brother/Big Sister, Camps, Child Welfare, Community Service Organizations, Day Care, Family Services, Food/Clothing Distribution, People with Disabilities, Social Services-General, United Funds/United Ways, YMCA/YWCA/YMHA/YWHA, Youth Organizations

Restrictions

Does not support individuals.

Corporate Officials

Michael Stuart Levin: president, chief executive officer, director B New York, NY 1950. ED University of Wisconsin BA (1972); Harvard University MBA (1974). PRIM CORP EMPL president, chief executive officer: Titan IndustriesCorp. CORP AFFIL member counc foreign rels, director: Aiesec USA. NONPR AFFIL member: Council Foreign Relations; chairman: Erick Hawkins Dance Foundation. CLUB AFFIL New York Yacht Club; Mashomack Fish & Game Preserve Club; Milbrook Golf and Tennis Club; Gulfstream PC Club.
Jerome A. Siegel: chairman, treasurer, director PRIM CORP EMPL chairman, treasurer, director: Titan IndustriesCorp.

Foundation Officials

Jerome A. Siegel: president, treasurer (see above)

Grants Analysis

Disclosure Period: fiscal year ending November 30, 1997
Total Grants: $333,081
Number of Grants: 90
Average Grant: $1,495*
Highest Grant: $200,000
Typical Range: $20 to $10,000
***Note:** Average grant figure excludes highest grant.

Recent Grants

Note: Grants derived from fiscal 1997 Form 990.

Arts & Humanities

20,000	American Craft Museum, New York, NY
2,000	Film Society of Lincoln Center, New York, NY
2,000	Jazz at Lincoln Center, New York, NY
1,500	Friends of Arts and Preservation in Embassies, Washington, DC
1,500	Lincoln Center Theater, New York, NY

Education

200,000	Sarah Lawrence College, Bronxville, NY
10,000	Sarah Lawrence College, Bronxville, NY
5,000	Alpha Bata Gamma, Westchester Community College, Valhalla, NY
5,000	Westchester Community College Foundation, Valhalla, NY
1,000	Harvard Business School Fund, Cambridge, MA

Health

5,000	White Plains Hospital Center, White Plains, NY
2,000	Robert J. Liest Scleroderma Fund, New York, NY
1,500	Cystic Fibrosis Foundation, New York, NY

Religion

7,000	United Jewish Appeal Federation Women's Division, New York, NY
5,000	Westchester Reform Temple, Scarsdale, NY
2,000	Metropolitan New York Coordination Council on Jewish Poverty, New York, NY
1,765	Westchester Reform Temple, Scarsdale, NY

Social Services

15,000	Big Brothers and Big Sisters, New York, NY
10,000	92nd Street YM-YWHA, New York, NY
2,000	92nd Street YM-YWHA, New York, NY

TJX Companies, Inc.

Company Contact

Framingham, MA
Web: http://www.tjx.com

Company Description

Revenue: US$7,949,100,000 (1999)
Profit: US$521,700,000 (1999)
Employees: 62,000 (1999)
Fortune Rank: 196, per FORTUNE Magazine's list of 500 Largest U.S. Corporations (1999).
FF 196
SIC(s): 5699 Miscellaneous Apparel & Accessory Stores.

Nonmonetary Support

Range: $150,000 - $500,000
Type: Cause-related Marketing & Promotion; Donated Equipment; Donated Products; In-kind Services; Workplace Solicitation

TJX Foundation, Inc.

Giving Contact

Christine Strickland, Foundation Administrator
TJX Foundation, Inc.
770 Cochituate Road
Route 1E
Framingham, MA 01701
Phone: (508)390-3199
Fax: (508)390-2091

Description

EIN: 042399760
Organization Type: Corporate Foundation
Giving Locations: MA: Boston principally near operating locations and to national organizations.
Grant Types: Capital, Challenge, Endowment, General Support, Project, Scholarship.

Giving Philosophy

'The primary mission of our contribution program is to help needy families and children. We also support services in the community where we do business that help promote sound mental and physical health, provide shelter, enhance education and job readiness and build community ties.' TJX Contribution Program Mission Statement

Financial Summary

Total Giving: $2,500,000 (fiscal year ending January 31, 1998 approx); $992,392 (fiscal 1997); $723,482 (fiscal 1996). Note: Contributes through corporate direct giving program and foundation. 1997 Giving includes foundation ($971,392); United Way ($21,000). 1996 Giving includes foundation ($673,482); United Way ($50,000).
Assets: $1,155,987 (fiscal 1997); $1,127,716 (fiscal 1996); $202,248 (fiscal 1995)
Gifts Received: $1,000,000 (fiscal 1997); $1,675,000 (fiscal 1996); $900,000 (fiscal 1995). Note: Contributions received from TJX Companies, Inc.

Typical Recipients

Arts & Humanities: Arts Associations & Councils, Arts Centers, Arts Funds, Arts Institutes, Community Arts, Dance, Historic Preservation, History & Archaeology, Museums/Galleries, Performing Arts, Public Broadcasting, Theater
Civic & Public Affairs: African American Affairs, Business/Free Enterprise, Civil Rights, Community Foundations, Employment/Job Training, Civic & Public Affairs-General, Hispanic Affairs, Housing, Law & Justice, Municipalities/Towns, Philanthropic Organizations, Public Policy, Urban & Community Affairs, Women's Affairs
Education: Business Education, Colleges & Universities, Education Associations, Education Funds, Elementary Education (Private), Education-General, Legal Education, Medical Education, Minority Education, Private Education (Precollege), Public Education (Precollege), Religious Education, Special Education, Student Aid
Health: AIDS/HIV, Cancer, Children's Health/Hospitals, Clinics/Medical Centers, Diabetes, Emergency/Ambulance Services, Health Organizations, Heart, Hospices, Hospitals, Medical Rehabilitation, Mental Health, Nursing Services, Prenatal Health Issues, Public Health, Single-Disease Health Associations
International: Human Rights, International Relief Efforts
Religion: Jewish Causes, Ministries, Religious Welfare
Science: Scientific Centers & Institutes
Social Services: Camps, Child Welfare, Community Centers, Community Service Organizations, Counseling, Crime Prevention, Domestic Violence, Family Services, Food/Clothing Distribution, Homes, People with Disabilities, Scouts, Shelters/Homelessness, Substance Abuse, United Funds/United Ways, Volunteer Services, Youth Organizations

Contributions Analysis

Giving Priorities: United funds, youth and child welfare, colleges and universities, and health.
Arts & Humanities: 4%. Proposals that bring art or artists to new audiences; also supports initiatives that encourage people, especially the handicapped, elderly, young, or disadvantaged, to express themselves through art.
Civic & Public Affairs: 10%. Programs which promote improved race relations, communitydevelopment and housing.
Education: 14%. Programs that benefit children of preschool age through college, which provide scholarship or vocational education for the disadvantaged; strengthen leadership in public schools; teach people to speak, read, and write English; and encourage collaboration between community agencies and schools.
Health: 35%. Health-care to underserved populations; seeks programs that provide early and comprehensive prenatal services, immunizations and health screening for children who lack them, and preventative care and alternatives to hospitalization.
International: 15%. Support international children's services.
Religion: 4%. Majority of support goes to Jewish causes.
Social Services: 18%. Families and children are main beneficiaries. Priority to programs that strengthen the family unit, help single-parent families, encourage families to adopt or accept foster children, and help the physically impaired; also Programs that provide shelter for victims of domestics violence.

Application Procedures

Initial Contact: submit requests in writing, maximum four pages

Application Requirements: description of the organization and its purpose, objective of grant and its target group, evidence of need for such program, organization's experience with similar problems, method of evaluation, program budget and amount sought, federal IRS tax-exempt letter, most recent audited financial statement, current operating budget, list of board of directors, a list of contributors and amounts received in last fiscal year, age of organization, ethnic background.
Deadlines: None.
Evaluative Criteria: program within targeted areas of interest, as outlined above
Decision Notification: committee meets periodically to consider proposals; decisions are made within 60 to 90 days of receiving proposal

Restrictions

TJX generally will not support individuals, political groups, religious organizations for sectarian purposes, public policy research projects or advocacy, conferences/seminars, publications, international organizations, travel, cash reserves, environmental issues, unrestricted grants, seed money, education loans, fellowships, endowments, or capital/renovation campaigns.

Additional Information

TJX Foundation had been known as the Zayre Foundation until fiscal year 1989.
The TJX Companies, Inc. consists of four operating divisions: The Marmaxx Group (T.J. Maxx and Marshalls), Winners, HomeGoods and T.K. Maxx (in Europe).

Corporate Officials

Bernard Cammarata: president, chief executive officer, director B Brooklyn, NY 1940. PRIM CORP EMPL president, chief executive officer, director: TJX Companies, Inc.
Donald G. Campbell: executive vice president, chief financial officer B 1951. PRIM CORP EMPL executive vice president, chief financial officer: TJX Companies, Inc.
Sherry Lang: vice president & director investor relations PRIM CORP EMPL vice president & director investor relations: TJX Companies, Inc.
Richard G. Lesser: executive vice president, chief operating officer, director B Boston, MA 1935. ED Northeastern University BS. PRIM CORP EMPL executive vice president, chief operating officer, director: TJX Companies, Inc. CORP AFFIL president, chief executive officer: Marshall's Inc.; director: Reebok International Ltd.; president, director: Marmaxx Group.
John Martin Nelson: chairman, director B New York, NY 1931. ED Wesleyan University AB (1953); Harvard University MBA (1959). PRIM CORP EMPL chairman, director: TJX Companies. CORP AFFIL treasurer: Robert L. Cristofaro MD; director: Stockery & Yale Inc.; director: Eaton Vance Corp.; director: Brown & Sharpe Manufacturing Co.; director: Commerce Holdings Inc.; director: Aquila Biopharmaceuticals Inc. NONPR AFFIL director: Worcester Municipal Research Bureau; chairman: Worcester Polytech Institute; chairman: Worcester Art Music; trustee: Worcester Foundation Biomedical Research; chairman: Memorial Health Care; director: University Massachusetts Medical Center Foundation Inc.; director: Alliance for Education.
Virginia Nelson: corporate communications manager PRIM CORP EMPL corporate communications manager: TJX Companies, Inc.

Foundation Officials

Bernard Cammarata: president (see above)
Donald G. Campbell: treasurer, director (see above)
Sherry Lang: director (see above)
Richard G. Lesser: chief operating officer, director (see above)

Grants Analysis

Disclosure Period: fiscal year ending January 31, 1997
Total Grants: $971,392*
Number of Grants: 157
Average Grant: $6,187
Highest Grant: $118,272
Typical Range: $1,000 to $10,000
*Note: Giving excludes United Way.

Recent Grants

Note: Grants derived from 1997 Form 990.

Arts & Humanities

20,000 Wang Center for Performing Arts, Boston, MA
10,000 Worcester Art Museum, Worcester, MA
5,000 Artists for Humanity, Boston, MA

Civic & Public Affairs

17,500 City Year, Boston, MA
17,500 City Year, Boston, MA
10,000 Planning Office of Urban Affairs, Boston, MA
10,000 Project Renewal, New York, NY
5,000 Association for the Advancement of Mexican Americans, Houston, TX
5,000 Boston Can, Boston, MA
5,000 Hope New England, Woburn, MA
5,000 Jobs for Youth, Boston, MA
5,000 Women's Educational and Industrial Union, Boston, MA

Education

25,000 Brandeis University, Waltham, MA
15,000 Bentley College, Waltham, MA
15,000 Boston College, Chestnut Hill, MA
10,500 Northeastern University, Boston, MA
10,000 Catholic Schools Foundation, Boston, MA
10,000 National Merit Scholarship Corporation, Evanston, IL
8,000 United Negro College Fund, New York, NY
5,000 Francis Ouimet Caddie Scholarship, Weston, MA
5,000 Mother Caroline Academy
5,000 Public Education Foundation, Evansville, IN
5,000 University of Massachusetts Urban Scholar Program, Amherst, MA

Health

50,000 Roxbury Community Health Center, Roxbury, MA
40,000 St. Jude's Children's Research Hospital, Memphis, TN
25,000 American Red Cross, Boston, MA
25,000 Beth Israel Hospital, Boston, MA
25,000 Lahey Hitchcock Clinic, Lebanon, NH
24,500 Massachusetts Easter Seals Society, Boston, MA
20,000 American Red Cross, Boston, MA
15,000 Deaconess Hospital, Boston, MA
15,000 Massachusetts Easter Seals Society, Boston, MA
10,000 AIDS Action Committee, Boston, MA
10,000 Dana Farber Cancer Institute, Boston, MA
7,000 March of Dimes Birth Defects Foundation, New York, NY
5,000 AIDS Action Committee, Boston, MA
5,000 Brigham and Women's Hospital, Boston, MA

International

118,272 Save the Children Federation, Dallas, TX

Religion

25,000 Combined Jewish Philanthropies, Boston, MA
5,000 Catholic Charities, Boston, MA
5,000 New England Holocaust Memorial Committee, Boston, MA

Social Services

65,000 Family Violence Prevention Fund, San Francisco, CA
20,000 United Way Metrowest, Framingham, MA
16,000 Parent's Choice, Newton, MA
10,000 Greater Boston Food Bank, Boston, MA
10,000 Massachusetts Coalition of Battered Women's Service, Boston, MA
5,000 Massachusetts Coalition for the Homeless, Boston, MA
5,000 New England Home for Little Wanderers, Chestnut Hill, MA
5,000 San Diego Youth and Community Services, San Diego, CA
5,000 Why Me, Worcester, MA

TMC Investment Co.

Company Contact

Pittsburgh, PA
Web: http://www.tippins.com

Company Description

Parent Company: Tippins Inc.

Tippins Foundation

Giving Contact

George W. Tippins, Trustee
Tippins Foundation
435 Butler St.
Pittsburgh, PA 15223
Phone: (412)781-7600
Fax: (412)782-7210

Description

EIN: 256282382
Organization Type: Corporate Foundation
Giving Locations: PA
Grant Types: General Support.

Financial Summary

Total Giving: $250,640 (1998); $310,450 (1997); $236,800 (1996). Note: Contributes through foundation only.
Giving Analysis: Giving for 1996 includes: foundation ($206,800); foundation grants to United Way ($30,000); 1997: foundation ($295,450); foundation grants to United Way ($15,000); 1998: foundation ($250,640)
Assets: $37,722 (1998); $19,161 (1997); $78,580 (1996)
Gifts Received: $250,000 (1998); $250,000 (1997); $250,022 (1996). Note: Contributions are received from TMC Investment Co.

Typical Recipients

Arts & Humanities: Arts Associations & Councils, Ballet, History & Archaeology, Libraries, Museums/Galleries, Music, Public Broadcasting, Theater
Civic & Public Affairs: Civic & Public Affairs-General, Municipalities/Towns, Public Policy, Safety, Urban & Community Affairs, Women's Affairs
Education: Business Education, Colleges & Universities, Economic Education, Education Funds, Engineering/Technological Education, Education-General, Minority Education, Private Education (Precollege), Special Education
Environment: Air/Water Quality, Watershed
Health: Alzheimers Disease, Arthritis, Cancer, Children's Health/Hospitals, Clinics/Medical Centers, Diabetes, Emergency/Ambulance Services, Health Organizations, Heart, Hospitals, Kidney, Medical

Rehabilitation, Public Health, Single-Disease Health Associations
Religion: Churches, Religious Welfare
Social Services: Animal Protection, Community Service Organizations, Counseling, Delinquency & Criminal Rehabilitation, Family Services, People with Disabilities, Recreation & Athletics, Scouts, Shelters/Homelessness, Social Services-General, United Funds/United Ways, YMCA/YWCA/YMHA/YWHA

Application Procedures

Initial Contact: Send a written request.
Application Requirements: Include a description of organization, purpose of funds sought, amount requested, proof of tax-exempt status.
Deadlines: None.

Foundation Officials

Charles J. Queenan, Jr.: trustee PRIM CORP EMPL senior counsel: Kirkpatrick & Lockhart. CORP AFFIL director: Crane Co.; director: Allegheny Teledyne Inc.; director: Babcock Lumber Co. NONPR AFFIL director: Allegheny-Singer Research Institute.
Carolyn H. Tippins: trustee
George W. Tippins: trustee

Grants Analysis

Disclosure Period: calendar year ending 1998
Total Grants: $250,640
Number of Grants: 51
Average Grant: $4,915
Highest Grant: $25,000
Typical Range: $500 to $20,000

Recent Grants

Note: Grants derived from 1997 Form 990.

Arts & Humanities

5,000	Carnegie Museums, Pittsburgh, PA
5,000	Pittsburgh Cultural Trust, Pittsburgh, PA
1,000	Pittsburgh Ballet Theater, Pittsburgh, PA
1,000	Pittsburgh Public Theater, Pittsburgh, PA
1,000	Pittsburgh Symphony Orchestra, Pittsburgh, PA
1,000	Westmoreland Museum of Art, Greensburg, PA
1,000	WQED, Pittsburgh, PA
500	Fort Ligonier Association, Ligonier, PA
500	Historical Society of West Pennsylvania, Pittsburgh, PA
500	Ligonier Valley Library, Ligonier, PA

Civic & Public Affairs

10,000	Heritage Foundation, Washington, DC
5,000	Women's Center and Shelter, Pittsburgh, PA
1,000	Founder's Trust, Pittsburgh, PA
1,000	United Fire Companies, Ligonier, PA

Education

100,000	Carnegie Mellon University, Pittsburgh, PA
25,000	Extra Mile Educational Foundation, Pittsburgh, PA
5,000	Fox Chapel Country Day School, Pittsburgh, PA
5,000	Pennsylvania Council on Economic Education, Harrisburg, PA
5,000	Shady Side Academy, Pittsburgh, PA
5,000	University of Pittsburgh Joseph Katz School of Business, Pittsburgh, PA
1,000	Allegheny College, Meadville, PA
1,000	Negro Educational Emergency Drive, Pittsburgh, PA
1,000	Valley School, Ligonier, PA
500	Academy at Ocean Reef, Key Largo, FL

Environment

1,000	Loyalhanna Watershed Association, Ligonier, PA

Health

20,000	American Red Cross, Pittsburgh, PA
20,000	Children's Hospital, Pittsburgh, PA
15,000	Juvenile Diabetes Foundation, Pittsburgh, PA
2,000	Alzheimer's Association, Pittsburgh, PA
2,000	American Cancer Society, Pittsburgh, PA
2,000	American Heart Association, Pittsburgh, PA
2,000	National Parkinson's Foundation, Pittsburgh, PA
1,000	Bradley Center, Pittsburgh, PA
1,000	Ocean Reef Medical Center, Key Largo, FL
500	Arthritis Foundation, Pittsburgh, PA
500	National Kidney Foundation, Pittsburgh, PA
300	Fox Chapel Ambulance, Pittsburgh, PA
250	Ligonier Valley Ambulance, Latrobe, PA

Religion

25,000	Salvation Army, Pittsburgh, PA
5,000	Fox Chapel Presbyterian Church, Pittsburgh, PA
2,000	St. Margaret Memorial Fund, Pittsburgh, PA

Social Services

15,000	United Way Southwest Pennsylvania, Pittsburgh, PA
5,000	Ligonier Valley YMCA, Ligonier, PA
4,000	Western Pennsylvania School for the Blind, Pittsburgh, PA
1,000	Girl Scouts of America Southwest Pennsylvania, Pittsburgh, PA
1,000	Goodwill Industries, Pittsburgh, PA
1,000	Whale's Tale, Pittsburgh, PA
500	Animal Friends, Pittsburgh, PA
500	Animal Rescue League, Pittsburgh, PA
500	Western Pennsylvania Humane Society, Pittsburgh, PA

TOLEDO BLADE CO.

Company Contact

Toledo, OH

Company Description

Employees: 600
SIC(s): 2711 Newspapers.
Parent Company: Blade Communications

Blade Foundation

Giving Contact

William Block, Jr., President & Trustee
Blade Foundation
541 N. Superior St.
Toledo, OH 43660
Phone: (419)724-6000

Description

EIN: 346559843
Organization Type: Corporate Foundation
Giving Locations: OH: Toledo
Grant Types: General Support, Scholarship.

Financial Summary

Total Giving: $248,929 (1996); $195,789 (1995); $202,214 (1994). Note: 1996 Giving includes scholarship ($6,000); United Way ($55,000).
Assets: $250,000 (1996); $176,154 (1995); $160,832 (1994)
Gifts Received: $200,000 (1995); $150,000 (1994); $126,510 (1993). Note: In 1995, contributions were received from Blade Communications.

Typical Recipients

Arts & Humanities: Arts Associations & Councils, Arts Centers, Ballet, Community Arts, History & Archaeology, Libraries, Literary Arts, Museums/Galleries, Music, Opera, Public Broadcasting, Theater
Civic & Public Affairs: African American Affairs, Botanical Gardens/Parks, Business/Free Enterprise, Clubs, Economic Development, Employment/Job Training, First Amendment Issues, Civic & Public Affairs-General, Housing, Municipalities/Towns, Parades/Festivals, Professional & Trade Associations, Public Policy, Urban & Community Affairs, Women's Affairs, Zoos/Aquariums
Education: Business Education, Colleges & Universities, Education Funds, Literacy, Medical Education, Minority Education, Private Education (Precollege), Public Education (Precollege), Student Aid
Environment: Resource Conservation
Health: Arthritis, Children's Health/Hospitals, Clinics/Medical Centers, Multiple Sclerosis, Preventive Medicine/Wellness Organizations, Respiratory, Single-Disease Health Associations
International: International Affairs, International Relief Efforts
Religion: Jewish Causes, Ministries, Religious Organizations, Religious Welfare
Social Services: Child Welfare, Community Centers, Community Service Organizations, Family Planning, Food/Clothing Distribution, Recreation & Athletics, Scouts, United Funds/United Ways, Volunteer Services, YMCA/YWCA/YMHA/YWHA, Youth Organizations

Application Procedures

Initial Contact: send proposal
Application Requirements: a description of organization, amount requested, purpose of funds sought, and proof of tax-exempt status

Restrictions

Does not support: individuals, religious organizations for sectarian purposes, political or lobbying groups, or organizations outside operating areas.

Additional Information

Provides scholarships to children or legal dependents of full-time employees with at least three years employment with the Toledo Blade.

Corporate Officials

Allan James Block: director B Toledo, OH 1954. ED University of Pennsylvania (1977). PRIM CORP EMPL director: Toledo Blade Co. CORP AFFIL director: PG Publishing Co.; president: Blade Broadcasting Co.; director: C-SPAN. NONPR AFFIL trustee: Medical College Ohio. CLUB AFFIL Pennsylvania Club; Toledo Club; Metropolitan Club.
William Block, Jr.: president, director B New Haven, CT 1944. ED Trinity College BA (1967); Washington & Lee University JD (1972). PRIM CORP EMPL president, director: Toledo Blade Co. CORP AFFIL president: Pittsburgh Post-Gazette-Sun-Telegraph. NONPR AFFIL director: Toledo Symphony; director: United Way Toledo; director: Toledo Museum Art; member: Old Newsboys Goodfellow Association; president: Read for Literacy; member, director: Ohio Newspaper Association. CLUB AFFIL Toledo Club; Toledo Press Club.
William Block: chairman, director B New York, NY 1915. ED Yale University AB (1936). PRIM CORP EMPL chairman, director: Toledo Blade Co. CORP AFFIL chairman: Pittsburgh Post-Gazette-Sun-Telegraph; chairman board: PG Publishing Co.; co-publ: Pittsburgh Post Gazette; member board advisor: H John Heinz III Sch Pub Policy & Management. NONPR AFFIL director: Maumee Valley Historical Society; member: Society Professional Journalists; director: Inland Press Associates; member: International Press Institute; director: Gateway Music; director: Historical Society Western Pennsylvania; member: American Society Newspaper Editors;

trustee emeritus: American Assembly; member: American Newspaper Publishers Association; sponsor: Allegheny Conference Community Development.

Foundation Officials

Gary J. Blair: treasurer, trustee
Allan James Block: vice president, trustee (see above)
John Robinson Block: vice president, trustee B Toledo, OH 1954. ED Yale University BA (1977). PRIM CORP EMPL co-publisher, editor-in-chief, european corresp: Toledo Blade Co. CORP AFFIL vice president, director: PG Pub Co.; co-publ: Pittsburgh Post-Gazette; executive vice president, director: Blade Communication; co-publ, director: Monterey Peninsula Herald. NONPR AFFIL member: American Society Newspaper Editors; member: Society Professional Journalists. CLUB AFFIL mem: Belmont Country Club; mem: Yale Club.
William Block, Jr.: president, trustee (see above)
William Block: vice president, trustee (see above)
Sandra Chavez: secretary, trustee
Laneta Goings: vice president, trustee

Grants Analysis

Disclosure Period: calendar year ending 1996
Total Grants: $187,929*
Number of Grants: 85
Average Grant: $1,761*
Highest Grant: $40,000
Typical Range: $300 to $2,000
***Note:** Giving excludes scholarship; United Way. Average grant excludes highest grant.

Recent Grants

Note: Grants derived from 1996 Form 990.

Arts & Humanities

9,950	Toledo Symphony, Toledo, OH
5,000	Rutherford B. Hayes Presidential Center, Fremont, OH
3,800	Public Broadcasting Foundation of Northwest Ohio, Toledo, OH
2,500	Inland Press Foundation, Park Ridge, IL
2,500	Toledo Opera Association, Toledo, OH

Civic & Public Affairs

10,000	Local Initiatives Support Corporation, New York, NY
4,500	Toledo Classic, Toledo, OH
4,000	Junior League, Toledo, OH

Education

20,000	Maumee Valley Country Day School, Toledo, OH
11,000	Read for Literacy, Toledo, OH
3,000	Ohio Foundation of Independent Colleges, Columbus, OH
2,500	Medical College of Ohio Foundation, Toledo, OH
2,000	Press Club Scholarship Foundation, Toledo, OH

Health

8,125	Ronald McDonald Children's Charities, Toledo, OH

Religion

7,000	Jewish Federation, Toledo, OH

Social Services

55,000	United Way, Toledo, OH
40,000	Volunteers of America, Toledo, OH
6,000	YMCA, Toledo, OH
2,000	Boy Scouts of America, Toledo, OH
2,000	Planned Parenthood, Toledo, OH

TOMKINS INDUSTRIES, INC.

Company Contact

Dayton, OH
Web: http://www.tomkinsindustries.com

Company Description

Former Name: Philips Industries.
Employees: 10,348
SIC(s): 2431 Millwork, 3052 Rubber & Plastics Hose & Belting, 3084 Plastics Pipe, 3442 Metal Doors, Sash & Trim.
Parent Company: Tomkins Plc

Operating Locations

AZ: Kreuger Division, Tucson; Tomkins Industries, Inc., Tucson; CA: Lasco Bathware, Anaheim; Tomkins Industries, Inc., Anaheim, Irwindale; Red Wing Co., San Jose; CO: Gates Corp., Denver; Gates Rubber Co., Denver; Stant Corp., Denver; IN: Tomkins Industries, Inc., Albion; Dexter Axle Division, Elkhart; Shelter Products Group, Elkhart; Tomkins Industries, Inc., Elkhart, Indianapolis, Lebanon; KS: Mid-West Conveyor Co., Kansas City; Tomkins Industries, Inc., Kansas City; MA: Smith & Wesson Corp., Springfield; MI: Dearborn Fabricating & Engineering Co., Detroit; Defabco Installation, Detroit; Tomkins Industries, Inc., Three Rivers; MO: Gates Rubber Co., Charleston; Ruskin Division, Grandview; Swartwout Industries, Grandview; Gates Rubber Co., Poplar Bluff; NY: Red Wings, Fredonia; OH: Tomkins Industries, Inc., Mount Sterling, Amelia; Mayfran International, Cleveland; Tomkins Industries, Inc., Cleveland; Lau Div., Dayton; Tomkins Corp., Dayton; Tomkins Industries, Dayton; Residential Products Group, Malta; Tomkins Industries, Inc., Malta; Integrated Material Handling Co., Mount Sterling; PA: Tomkins Industries, Inc., Selinsgrove; TN: Murray Ohio Manufacturing Co., Brentwood; TX: Tomkins Industries, Inc., Clarksville; J & J Register Division, El Paso; Tomkins Industries, Inc., El Paso; Titus Products Div., Richardson; WI: Integrated Material Handling Co., Oshkosh

Tomkins Corp. Foundation

Giving Contact

Greg Kirchhoff, Vice President
Tomkins Industries Foundation
4801 Springfield Street
Dayton, OH 45431
Phone: (937)476-0359
Fax: (937)476-0439

Alternate Contact

Greg Kirchhoff, Corporate Controller

Description

Founded: 1989
EIN: 311207183
Organization Type: Corporate Foundation
Former Name: Philips Industries Foundation.
Giving Locations: OH: Dayton
Grant Types: Employee Matching Gifts, General Support.

Financial Summary

Total Giving: $390,888 (fiscal year ending April 30, 1996); $401,469 (fiscal 1995); $349,254 (fiscal 1994). Note: Contributes through foundation only. 1996 Giving includes foundation ($356,507); matching gifts ($34,381). 1995 Giving includes foundation ($355,531); matching gifts ($45,938).
Assets: $3,978,454 (fiscal 1996); $3,957,082 (fiscal 1995); $4,145,798 (fiscal 1994)
Gifts Received: $1,750,000 (fiscal 1996). Note: Contributions are received from Jesse Philips Foundation.

Typical Recipients

Arts & Humanities: Arts Associations & Councils, Community Arts, Dance, History & Archaeology, Libraries, Literary Arts, Music, Performing Arts, Public Broadcasting, Theater
Civic & Public Affairs: African American Affairs, Business/Free Enterprise, Employment/Job Training, Civic & Public Affairs-General, Housing, Municipalities/Towns, Philanthropic Organizations, Professional & Trade Associations, Safety, Urban & Community Affairs, Women's Affairs
Education: Agricultural Education, Arts/Humanities Education, Business Education, Colleges & Universities, Education Associations, Education Funds, Engineering/Technological Education, Education-General, Literacy, Minority Education, Private Education (Precollege), Public Education (Precollege), Religious Education, School Volunteerism, Science/Mathematics Education, Student Aid, Vocational & Technical Education
Health: Alzheimers Disease, Cancer, Children's Health/Hospitals, Clinics/Medical Centers, Diabetes, Emergency/Ambulance Services, Health Organizations, Hospices, Hospitals, Medical Research, Prenatal Health Issues, Public Health, Single-Disease Health Associations
Religion: Religious Organizations, Religious Welfare
Science: Science Museums, Scientific Centers & Institutes
Social Services: Animal Protection, Child Abuse, Child Welfare, Community Centers, Community Service Organizations, Family Services, Food/Clothing Distribution, People with Disabilities, Recreation & Athletics, Scouts, Special Olympics, Substance Abuse, United Funds/United Ways, YMCA/YWCA/YMHA/YWHA, Youth Organizations

Contributions Analysis

Arts & Humanities: 5% to 10%. Supports the performing arts, including symphonies, theater, and dance. Also supports museums and libraries.
Education: 30% to 35%. Aids public and private education (precollege), student aid, colleges and universities, literacy, technical and engineering education, business education, religious education, and agricultural education.
Health: 5% to 10%. Funds emergency services, prenatal health issues, hospitals and hospices,and a variety of health care groups, including the American Cancer Society and the March of Dimes.
Social Services: 50% to 55%. Supports the United Way, YMCAs, community service organizations, child abuse prevention services, child welfare, animal protection, people with disabilities, food and clothing distribution, and recreational and athletic associations.

Corporate Officials

Dan Disser: chief financial officer, chief executive officer B 1960. PRIM CORP EMPL chief financial officer: Tomkins Industries, Inc. ADD CORP EMPL chief financial officer: RHM Holdings Inc.; chief financial officer: Tomkins Corp.
Ian Duncan: deputy chairman, managing director finance B 1946. PRIM CORP EMPL deputy chairman, managing director finance: Tomkins PLC. CORP AFFIL director: Murray Inc.; director: Tomkins Industries Inc.; treasurer: Colorado Board Room; director: Gates Corp.
Anthony John Reading: president, chief executive officer B London, England 1943. PRIM CORP EMPL president, chief executive officer: Tomkins Industries, Inc. CORP AFFIL chief executive officer: Tomkins Corp.; director: Tomkins Plc.; president: RHM Holdings United States of America Inc.; president: Conergics Corp.; director: Murray Inc.; chief executive officer: Carriage House Fruit Co.

Foundation Officials

Dan Disser: vice president (see above)
Ian Duncan: trustee (see above)
Gregory Hutchings: trustee
Greg Kirchhoff: vice president PRIM CORP EMPL consultant: Tomkins Corp. ADD CORP EMPL consultant: Tomkins Industries Inc.
Anthony John Reading: president, trustee (see above)

Grants Analysis

Disclosure Period: fiscal year ending April 30, 1996
Total Grants: $356,507*
Number of Grants: 60
Average Grant: $4,356*
Highest Grant: $99,485
Typical Range: $500 to $6,000
***Note:** Giving excludes matching gifts. Average grant figure excludes the highest grant.

Recent Grants

Note: Grants derived from fiscal 1996 Form 990.

Arts & Humanities

2,000	Springfield Symphony Orchestra, Springfield, MA
2,000	Tennessee Foundation for Performing Arts, TN
1,000	Culture Works, Dayton, OH
1,000	Detroit Historical Society, Detroit, MI
500	Dayton Bach Society, Dayton, OH
500	Victoria Theater Association, Dayton, OH

Civic & Public Affairs

7,700	Habitat for Humanity
1,000	Dayton Fund for Home Rehabilitation, Dayton, OH
1,000	Dayton Urban League, Dayton, OH
1,000	National Alliance of Business, Washington, DC
500	Fredonia Fire Department, Lanett, AL

Education

30,397	National Merit Scholarship Corporation, Evanston, IL
25,000	Lawrence County Education Foundation, Lawrence, TN
21,000	Dayton-Montgomery County Scholarship Fund, Dayton, OH
7,600	Junior Achievement, Dayton, OH
5,000	Fredonia College Foundation, Fredonia, NY
5,000	University of Cincinnati Scholarship Fund, Cincinnati, OH
3,000	Ohio Foundation of Independent Colleges, Columbus, OH
3,000	Springfield Technical College Foundation, Springfield, MA
3,000	Western New England College, Springfield, MA
2,000	College of Our Lady of the Elms
1,500	Springfield School Volunteers, Springfield, MA
600	Missouri Colleges Fund, Jefferson City, MO

Health

8,000	American Red Cross, Dayton, OH
7,500	Hospice of Ponca City, Ponca City, OK
6,700	ASHRAE Research Fund, Atlanta, GA
3,000	Geisinger Foundation, Danville, PA
2,500	Houlton Regional Health Services, Houlton, ME
2,500	March of Dimes Birth Defects
2,500	Ronald McDonald House, Dayton, OH
1,500	Children's Medical Center, Dallas, TX
500	Alzheimer's Association, Philadelphia, PA
500	Muscular Dystrophy Association, Dayton, OH

Religion

1,000	House of Bread

Science

1,000	American Association for the Advancement of Science, Washington, DC
500	Dayton Museum of Natural History, Dayton, OH

Social Services

99,485	United Way, Dayton, OH
63,350	United Response, Dayton, OH
9,500	Boy Scouts of America, Dayton, OH
4,000	YMCA, Chicago, IL
2,500	Jimmy Fund, Boston, MA
2,000	Massachusetts Special Olympics, Hathorne, MA
1,500	Children's Study Home, Dayton, OH
1,500	Girl Scouts of America
1,500	Narconon, Los Angeles, CA
1,000	Food Industry Crusade Against Hunger, Washington, DC
1,000	Martha O'Bryan Center, Nashville, TN
1,000	Second Harvest Food Bank, Chicago, IL
1,000	YWCA
500	Goodwill Industries, Dayton, OH

TORCHMARK CORP.

Company Contact

Birmingham, AL

Company Description

Assets: US$9,800,000,000
Employees: 6,270
SIC(s): 6282 Investment Advice, 6311 Life Insurance, 6321 Accident & Health Insurance, 6331 Fire, Marine & Casualty Insurance.

Nonmonetary Support

Type: Cause-related Marketing & Promotion; Donated Equipment; In-kind Services
Note: All nonmonetary support provided by individual branches.

Corporate Sponsorship

Type: Arts & cultural events; Festivals/fairs; Sports events

Giving Contact

Carol McCoy, Associate Counsel & Secretary
Torchmark Corp.
2001 3rd Avenue South
Birmingham, AL 35233
Phone: (205)325-4243
Fax: (205)325-4198

Description

Organization Type: Corporate Giving Program
Giving Locations: AL: Birmingham
Grant Types: Capital, Employee Matching Gifts, General Support, Professorship, Project.
Note: The company has a matching gifts program for United Way only.

Financial Summary

Total Giving: $949,627 (1997); $763,639 (1996); $750,513 (1995). Note: Contributes through corporate direct giving program only.

Typical Recipients

Arts & Humanities: Arts Funds, Community Arts, Dance, Historic Preservation, Museums/Galleries, Music, Opera, Performing Arts
Civic & Public Affairs: Business/Free Enterprise, Civil Rights, Safety
Education: Colleges & Universities
Health: Health Organizations, Hospitals, Medical Rehabilitation, Single-Disease Health Associations
Science: Science Exhibits & Fairs
Social Services: Community Service Organizations, Emergency Relief, People with Disabilities, United Funds/United Ways, Youth Organizations

Contributions Analysis

Giving Priorities: Social welfare, colleges and universities, and health.
Education: About 30%. Colleges and universities.
Health: About 20%. Health organizations in the Birmingham area.
Social Services: About 35%. United appeals in communities where home office and district offices are located.

Application Procedures

Initial Contact: brief letter or proposal
Application Requirements: budget, area served by project or organization, amount requested, purpose of organization, list of officers and directors, copy of letter with 501(c)(3) number, and most recent annual report and financial statement
Deadlines: None.

Restrictions

Very few contributions are made outside the state of Alabama.

Corporate Officials

C. B. Hudson: chairman, chief executive officer

Giving Program Officials

Carol McCoy: B Florence, AL 1954. ED University of Alabama (1976); University of Alabama (1979). PRIM CORP EMPL associate counsel, corporate secretary: Torchmark Corp. NONPR AFFIL member: American Society of Corporate Secretaries; member: National Association Stock Plan Professionals; member: American Bar Association; member: American Corporate Counsel Association.

Grants Analysis

Disclosure Period: calendar year ending
Typical Range: $100 to $2,000

TORO CO.

Company Contact

Bloomington, MN

Company Description

Revenue: US$1,051,200,000
Employees: 3,911
SIC(s): 3523 Farm Machinery & Equipment, 3524 Lawn & Garden Equipment.

Nonmonetary Support

Type: Donated Equipment; Donated Products; In-kind Services; Loaned Employees

Toro Foundation

Giving Contact

Ellen Watson, Community Relations
8111 Lyndale Ave. S.
Bloomington, MN 55420-1196
Phone: (612)888-8801

Description

Founded: 1989
EIN: 363593618
Organization Type: Corporate Foundation
Giving Locations: headquarters and operating communities.
Grant Types: Employee Matching Gifts, General Support.

Financial Summary

Total Giving: $310,000 (1999 approx); $370,750 (1998); $295,000 (1997)
Giving Analysis: Giving for 1997 includes: foundation ($178,648); foundation grants to United Way ($116,352); 1998: foundation ($213,111); foundation grants to United Way ($135,634); foundation matching gifts ($22,005)

Assets: $801,831 (1998); $915,419 (1997); $972,412 (1996)
Gifts Received: $228,500 (1998); $200,000 (1997); $200,000 (1996). Note: Foundation receives contributions from the Toro Co.

Typical Recipients

Arts & Humanities: Arts Associations & Councils, History & Archaeology, Museums/Galleries, Music, Public Broadcasting, Theater
Civic & Public Affairs: Clubs, Civic & Public Affairs-General, Legal Aid, Parades/Festivals, Urban & Community Affairs
Education: Business Education, Colleges & Universities, Community & Junior Colleges, Education Reform, Environmental Education, Education-General, Private Education (Precollege), Public Education (Precollege), Secondary Education (Public), Student Aid
Environment: Environment-General
Health: Cancer, Emergency/Ambulance Services, Public Health
International: Foreign Educational Institutions, International Environmental Issues, International Organizations
Social Services: Community Service Organizations, Food/Clothing Distribution, People with Disabilities, Recreation & Athletics, Substance Abuse, United Funds/United Ways, YMCA/YWCA/YMHA/YWHA, Youth Organizations

Application Procedures

Initial Contact: Send a brief letter of inquiry.
Application Requirements: Include a description of organization, amount requested, proof of tax-exempt status, purpose of funds sought, how the purpose will be achieved by the grant, evidence that the people proposing a project are able to carry it to completion, a specific budget for the project, operating budget, major donor list.
Deadlines: None.

Restrictions

Does not support individuals, religious organizations for sectarian purposes, political or lobbying groups, or organizations outside operating areas.

Additional Information

Company promotes employees volunteerism through participation in local projects, schools, and neighborhood improvement.

Corporate Officials

David H. McIntosh: co-president PRIM CORP EMPL co-president: Toro Co.
Kendrick B. Melrose: chairman, co-president, chief executive officer, director B Orlando, FL 1940. ED Princeton University BS (1962); University of Chicago MBA (1967). PRIM CORP EMPL chairman, co-president, chief executive officer, director: Toro Co.

Foundation Officials

David H. McIntosh: director (see above)
Larry McIntyre: director
Kendrick B. Melrose: director (see above)
Karen Meyer: director
Katherine Nelson: secretary
Donald St. Dennis: president

Grants Analysis

Disclosure Period: calendar year ending 1998
Total Grants: $213,111*
Number of Grants: 126
Average Grant: $1,691
Highest Grant: $32,500
Typical Range: $100 to $50,000
***Note:** Giving excludes matching gifts, United Way.

Recent Grants

Note: Grants derived from 1997 Form 990.

Arts & Humanities

10,000	Guthrie Theater, Minneapolis, MN
5,000	Cottonwood Historical Society
5,000	Northwest Delta Arts Council
3,500	Shakopee Arts Council, Shakopee, MN
3,056	KTCA Television
3,000	Pioneer Public Television

Civic & Public Affairs

5,000	Nadacia Nase Deti
2,500	National Legal Center for the Public Interest, Washington, DC

Education

5,000	Citizens Scholarship Foundation, Lancaster, PA
5,000	English Learning Center
4,500	Oxford Middle School
3,500	Crown Jewel Foundation, Golden Valley, MN
3,500	Lafayette County School
2,400	Trinity School

Health

21,000	American Red Cross
8,000	St. Francis Health Care Foundation, Poughkeepsie, NY
5,000	Cancer Kids Fund

Social Services

115,000	United Way, Minneapolis, MN
3,500	Loaves and Fishes, Greenville, SC
2,500	Youth Frontiers, Minneapolis, MN

TOSHIBA AMERICA INC.

Company Contact

New York, NY
Web: http://www.toshiba.com

Company Description

Employees: 8,000
SIC(s): 3578 Calculating & Accounting Equipment, 3594 Fluid Power Pumps & Motors, 3631 Household Cooking Equipment, 5064 Electrical Appliances--Television & Radio.
Parent Company: Toshiba Corp., 1-1 Shibaura 1-chome Minato-ku, Tokyo, Japan

Operating Locations

CA: Toshiba America, Irvine; Toshiba America Electronic Components, Inc., Irvine; Toshiba America Inc., Irvine; Toshiba America Information Systems, Inc., Irvine; Toshiba International Corp. Utility Div., San Francisco; Toshiba America Inc., South San Francisco, Tustin; Toshiba America Medical Systems, Inc., Tustin; HI: Toshiba America Inc., Honolulu; IN: Enceratec, Inc., Columbus; NJ: Toshiba America Consumer Products, Inc., Wayne; Toshiba America Inc., Wayne; NY: Toshiba America Inc., Horseheads; Toshiba Display Devices, Horseheads; Toshiba America Capital Corp., New York; Toshiba America Inc., New York; Toshiba America Inc., New York; SD: Toshiba America Inc., Mitchell; TX: Toshiba America Inc., Houston; VA: Dominion Semiconductor L.L.C., Manassas
Note: Above lists locations where company has major manufacturing facilities; Toshiba America, Inc., and its subsidiaries operate in 30 states nationwide.

Corporate Sponsorship

Type: Sports events
Contact: Kenjiro Ishihara, Vice President

Toshiba America Foundation

Giving Contact

Program Officer
Toshiba America Foundation
126 E. 56th St., 28th Fl.
New York, NY 10022
Phone: (212)588-0820
Fax: (212)588-0824
Email: foundation@tai.toshiba.com

Description

Founded: 1990
EIN: 133596612
Organization Type: Corporate Foundation
Giving Locations: nationally; may give preference to schools and organizations in operating locations.
Grant Types: Award, Project.

Giving Philosophy

'The Toshiba America Foundation is a U.S., private, corporate-sponsored, not-for-profit grant making organization dedicated to supporting education programs and activities in the United States.'
'The mission of the Toshiba America Foundation is to contribute to the quality of life and productivity of U.S. communities by investing in projects designed by and with classroom teachers to improve science and science-related education for students in grades seven through twelve.' *Helping Classroom Teachers Improve Science Education*

Financial Summary

Total Giving: $520,000 (fiscal year ending March 31, 1999 approx); $514,835 (fiscal 1998); $519,910 (fiscal 1997). Note: Contributes through corporate direct giving program and foundation. Giving includes foundation.
Assets: $10,667,137 (fiscal 1998); $10,655,874 (fiscal 1997); $10,617,146 (fiscal 1996)
Gifts Received: $144,732 (fiscal 1997); $1,167,254 (fiscal 1996); $1,182,403 (fiscal 1995). Note: Contributions are received from Toshiba America, Inc.

Typical Recipients

Civic & Public Affairs: Botanical Gardens/Parks
Education: Agricultural Education, Elementary Education (Public), Engineering/Technological Education, Environmental Education, Faculty Development, Private Education (Precollege), Public Education (Precollege), Science/Mathematics Education, Secondary Education (Public)
Environment: Environment-General
International: Foreign Arts Organizations, Foreign Educational Institutions, International Environmental Issues
Science: Science Museums, Scientific Centers & Institutes, Scientific Research
Social Services: YMCA/YWCA/YMHA/YWHA, Youth Organizations

Application Procedures

Initial Contact: request application guidelines before preparing a proposal
Application Requirements: proposal cover form required; foundation guidelines require the following information for proposals (in as few pages as possible): names, addresses, and phone numbers of the organization and its project officer(s); self-assessment of alternative ways of reaching the same objectives; student-oriented objectives of the project and how they are to be measured; time period for reaching objectives; management plan showing how people, money, facilities, and time will be managed to reach objectives; line item budget reflective of management plan; proposed evaluation of the success of the project;

narrative establishing the credibility of the organization including proof of not-for-profit status not-for-profit status

Deadlines: throughout the year for proposals of $5,000 or less (decisions on smaller grants are postponed in March and September); prior to February 1 for March meeting and prior to August 1 for September meeting for larger grants

Review Process: proposals are reviewed by staff; president makes decisions on grants less than $5,000; for grants over $5,000, president makes recommendations to board of directors for action

Decision Notification: board meets in March and September to make decisions about proposals of more than $5,000

Notes: While certain information described above is required for proposal review, applicants may include additional information if it is essential to making the case for support.

Restrictions

The foundation does not support dinners or special events; fraternal organizations; goodwill advertising; individuals; member agencies of united funds; political or lobbying groups; religious organizations for sectarian purposes; or organizations that discriminate against women, minorities, older Americans, or the handicapped.

The foundation is interested in supporting time-limited projects/programs only, and therefore will not contribute to capital projects, endowments, or general operations. Also, requests for contributions for conferences, independent study, fund-raising events, or similar activities will not be considered.

The foundation does not generally provide grants for computer hardware, curriculum inventions, teacher training, salaries, facility maintenance, textbooks, creation of video or computer materials, or education research.

Summer projects will not be considered unless they are proven to be an integral part of the academic year curriculum as an extension of or prerequisite to a classroom project.

Additional Information

The Toshiba America Foundation was established in April 1990, marking the 25th anniversary of Toshiba America, Inc. Financial support for the foundation has been provided by the company's five independent companies. The Toshiba America Foundation board of trustees includes the chairman of Toshiba America, Inc., and the presidents of the five independent companies.

Toshiba America partners with the National Science Teachers Association in the ExploraVision Awards competition for teachers and students in grades K-12.

The foundation requires grantees to file a final report at the end of the funded project.

Toshiba America also makes direct corporate contributions through company departments.

Guidelines include specific information on how to write a proposal.

In April 1999, Toshiba Corporation and Carrier Corporation announced the formation of a global strategic alliance in the heating, ventilation, air conditioning, and refrigeration industry.

Publications: Foundation Guidelines; Annual Report

Corporate Officials

Katsufumi Nomura: treasurer, chief executive officer PRIM CORP EMPL treasurer: Toshiba America Inc.

Shunichi Yamashita: president, chief executive officer PRIM CORP EMPL president, chief executive officer: Toshiba America Inc.

Foundation Officials

John Anderson: secretary B 1945. ED College of the Holy Cross (1967). PRIM CORP EMPL secretary: Toshiba America Inc.

Hideo Ito: director PRIM CORP EMPL manager, chairman: Toshiba America Electronic Components.

Masamichi Katsurada: director PRIM CORP EMPL president: Toshiba America Medical Systems Inc.

Atsutoshi Nishida: director PRIM CORP EMPL vice chairman: Toshiba America Inc. CORP AFFIL president: Toshiba America Information Systems Inc.

Katsufumi Nomura: treasurer (see above)

Teruyuki Sugizaki: director B 1941. ED Waseda University (1964). PRIM CORP EMPL director: Toshiba Corp. CORP AFFIL president: Toshiba International Corp.

John Sumansky: president

Toshihide Yasui: director B 1953. PRIM CORP EMPL president: Toshiba Hawaii Inc. CORP AFFIL director: Toshiba America Information Systems Inc.

Grants Analysis

Disclosure Period: fiscal year ending March 31, 1997

Total Grants: $519,910

Number of Grants: 71

Average Grant: $7,323

Highest Grant: $50,000

Typical Range: $2,000 to $10,000

Recent Grants

Note: Grants derived from 1997 Form 990.

Civic & Public Affairs

5,000 New York Botanical Garden, Bronx, NY

Education

50,000 National Service Teachers Association, Washington, DC -- for Toshiba/NSTA Exploravision Awards

20,000 National Science Teachers Association, Washington, DC -- for Exploravision Awards Manual

18,180 Fund for New York City Public Education, New York, NY -- for Toshiba Math and Science Grants

15,000 San Francisco Unified School District, San Francisco, CA -- for Biotechnology-Science and Health Academy

13,400 California State University at Chico, Chico, CA -- for hand-on science lab

12,000 Elk Hill Farm, Goochland, VA -- for computerized learning system

11,100 Notre Dame High School, Belmont, CA -- for biotechnology

10,590 Ulster County Board of Cooperative Educational Services, NY -- for Interdisciplinary Hybrid Electric Vehicle Project

10,100 Papillion-LaVista High School, Papillion, NE -- for use of computer in Physics classroom

10,000 Broadway Middle School, Elmira, NY -- for math/science greenhouse

10,000 Communities in Schools, Dallas, TX -- support Year of Discovery

10,000 High School for Leadership and Public Service, New York, NY -- for chemistry project

10,000 Pahokee Middle Senior High School, Pahokee, FL -- for Lake Quality Monitoring Project

9,750 Horscheads High School, Horsenheads, NY -- for Fostering Independent Science Inquiry

9,410 Mitchell High School, Mitchell, SD -- for Environmental Impact Analysis of James River/Mitchell Lake Watershed

9,000 Friendship Christian School, Lebanon, TN -- support for Project TAMS

8,800 Holy Name of Jesus School, New Orleans, LA -- microscopes for middle school

8,490 Coral Gables Senior High School, Coral Gables, FL -- for Expanding Our Horizon program

8,350 Gooding Public Schools, Gooding, ID -- for Mechanical Universe and Beyond

8,100 West Philadelphia Catholic High School, Philadelphia, PA -- for science, technology, urban chemistry students

8,000 Grigsby Middle School, Granite City, IL -- for Physics, Science, Math, and Technology programs

7,960 Tallwood High School, Virginia Beach, VA -- for Tallwood Bridging Science and Math

7,500 Cypress Falls High School, Cypress-Fairbanks Independent School District, Houston, TX -- for Science Performance Task Project Phase II

7,370 Ganesha High School, Pomona, CA -- support Classroom to the Field

7,200 Cheltanham High School, Wyncote, PA -- support Using Interactive Technology to Enhance Learning of Human Physiology

7,200 Lakota Freshman School, West Chester, OH -- for Operation RESTORE

7,000 Garden City High School, Garden City, NJ -- for Living Science Project

6,000 Maria High School, Chicago, IL -- for Science Software Access

5,880 Minneapolis South High School, Minneapolis, MN -- for Cornerstone Science Program

5,000 Benjamin Mays High School, Atlanta, GA -- for Integration of Physics and the Computer

5,000 Cypress Falls High School, Cypress-Fairbanks Independent School District, Houston, TX -- for Sciences Performances

5,000 Lanier Middle School, Houston, TX -- support Solar Quest

5,000 Muskegon Area Intermediate School District, Muskegon, MI -- for Amusement Park Physics

4,820 Pickens County Middle School, Jasper, GA -- for Life Science Live

4,680 John V. Lindsay Wildcat Academy, New York, NY -- support for TCAT

4,650 Rachel Carson Intermediate School, Flushing, NY -- for Toshiba Green

4,600 Landmark Middle School, Jacksonville, FL -- for Keys to Success program

4,500 Central Senior High School, Cape Girardeau, MO -- for bio-chemical productions

4,480 Pioneer Middle School, Walla Walla, WA -- support for Maximizing the Science Curriculum

4,350 Fulton Junior High School, Fulton, MS -- support Teaching an Integrated Science Curriculum Through Interactive Technology

4,335 David Lipscomb High School, Nashville, TN -- for video microscopy

4,270 Arlington High School, Riverside, CA -- for James River Reserve Project

4,160 New Vistas Academy, Brooklyn, NY -- for Science in Action program

International

15,000 Royal Ontario Museum, Toronto, ON, Canada -- for Science Happens Here

10,000 Academia Mexicana de Professores de Ciencia Naturales, Mexico -- support Strategies for Supporting Innovative Teaching

10,000 Human Dolphin Institute, Panama City Beach, FL -- for Community Environmental Awareness and Education Program

Science

13,500 Discovery Science Center, Santa Ana, CA -- for resource enhancement modules

Social Services

12,000 Girls, Incorporated, New York, NY -- support Urban Girls

9,000 YMCA, Dallas, TX -- for CASA shelters, Science Partners

Toyota Motor Sales U.S.A., Inc.

Company Contact

Torrance, CA
Web: http://www.toyota.co.jp

Company Description

Employees: 70,000
SIC(s): 6141 Personal Credit Institutions.
Parent Company: Toyota Motor Corp., 1, Toyota-cho, Toyota, Aichi Pref., Japan

Operating Locations

CA: New United Motor Manufacturing Inc., Fremont; Denso Sales California, Long Beach; TABC, Inc., Long Beach; Calty Design Research, Inc., Newport Beach; Toyota Lift, Inc., Santee; Toyota Motor Credit Corp., Torrance; Toyota Motor Sales, U.S.A., Inc., Torrance; Toyota Motor Sales U.S.A., Inc., Torrance; IL: Nippondenso of Los Angeles (Chicago), Des Plaines; IN: Toyota Industrial Equipment Mfg., Columbus; KY: Toyota Motor Manufacturing, U.S.A., Georgetown; Toyota Motor Corp., Supplier Support Center, Lexington; MI: Toyota Technical Center, USA, Inc., Ann Arbor; Toyota Motor Corp., Southfield; NY: Toyota Motor Corporate Services of North America, New York

Nonmonetary Support

Type: Cause-related Marketing & Promotion; Donated Equipment; Donated Products
Contact: Steve Silbiger, Corporate Contributions Specialist
Note: Fiscal 1997 nonmonetary support $200,000.

Toyota U.S.A. Foundation

Giving Contact

Gloria Jahn, Corporate Manager, Corporate Philanthropy
Toyota Motor Sales, USA, Inc.
19001 South Western Avenue
Torrance, CA 90509
Phone: (310)618-4000
Fax: (310)618-7809
Note: The foundation's Web address is http://www.toyota.com/foundation

Alternate Contact

Tracy Underwood, Corporate Contributions

Description

Founded: 1987
EIN: 953255038
Organization Type: Corporate Foundation
Giving Locations: nationally for foundation contributions; major operating facility areas for corporate contributions.
Grant Types: Emergency, Employee Matching Gifts, Fellowship, General Support, Matching, Project.
Note: Employee matching gift ratio: 1 to 1 for education only.

Giving Philosophy

'For 40 years, Toyota Motor Sales, USA, Inc. has been a leader in the effort to improve the quality of life in the United States. By providing financial resources and encouraging employee volunteerism, Toyota has become a partner in enhancing communities nationwide.'
'The company strives to provide the highest quality products, the highest quality service and the highest degree of professionalism in administering its contributions program.'
'Under the umbrella of 'Highways to Learning,' education is the underlying focus of Toyota's corporate giving. In addition, Toyota supports various nonprofit organizations whose fundamental goals are to provide services that better the lives of all members of society.'
'Toyota seeks to support projects where its contributions will make a significant impact. In addition, Toyota has a proud tradition of supporting its employees who are active volunteers in their communities.' *Corporate Contributions Guidelines*

Financial Summary

Total Giving: $1,560,000 (fiscal year ending June 30, 1998 approx); $14,444,625 (fiscal 1997 approx); $16,645,000 (fiscal 1996 approx). Note: Contributes through corporate direct giving program and foundation. Fiscal 1997 Giving includes corporate direct giving (12,927,000); foundation ($1,517,625). 1996 Giving includes corporate direct giving; foundation ($1,260,877); domestic subsidiaries.
Assets: $27,320,675 (fiscal 1997); $25,088,352 (fiscal 1996 approx); $22,505,806 (fiscal 1995)
Gifts Received: $2,200,000 (fiscal 1997); $2,529,000 (fiscal 1996); $1,500,000 (fiscal 1995). Note: Contributions received from Toyota Motor Sales USA, Inc.

Typical Recipients

Arts & Humanities: Arts Appreciation, Arts Associations & Councils, Arts Centers, Arts Institutes, Arts Outreach, Film & Video, Arts & Humanities-General, Museums/Galleries, Music, Opera, Performing Arts, Public Broadcasting, Theater
Civic & Public Affairs: Botanical Gardens/Parks, Hispanic Affairs, Native American Affairs, Public Policy, Zoos/Aquariums
Education: Afterschool/Enrichment Programs, Arts/Humanities Education, Colleges & Universities, Community & Junior Colleges, Continuing Education, Economic Education, Education Funds, Education Reform, Elementary Education (Private), Engineering/Technological Education, Environmental Education, Faculty Development, Education-General, Leadership Training, Literacy, Minority Education, Private Education (Precollege), Public Education (Precollege), Science/Mathematics Education
Environment: Energy, Environment-General, Wildlife Protection
Health: Health Organizations, Nutrition
Science: Observatories & Planetariums, Science Museums, Scientific Centers & Institutes
Social Services: Child Welfare, People with Disabilities, Substance Abuse

Contributions Analysis

Giving Priorities: Elementary and secondary education, social welfare, arts and humanities, and civic organizations.
Civic & Public Affairs: 35% to 40%. Grants are made to supportthe social well-being of communities in which Toyota has a major presence. These contributions are made to organizations which have a wide reach and a significant impact on society. Examples of areas eligible for support are: health and human services, civic and community development, and culture and arts.
Education: 45% to 50%. Priority is given to programs which enhance the opportunity to pursue a quality education, with emphasis on pre-collegiate studies. Major Toyota-branded programs include Toyota Tapestry, Toyota Time, Toyota Fmily Learning Centers and Toyota Community Scholars Programs.
Environment: 10% to 15%. Funds the National Wildlife Federation.

Application Procedures

Initial Contact: contact the foundation or the company for application form
Application Requirements: for the foundation, include completed application form, most recent audited financial statement, line item project budget; line item organization budget, a copy of the most recent 990 Form, copy of IRS tax exempt letter; list of board of directors roster with addresses and business affiliations, annual report and/or news clippings (if available); for corporate giving, include a completed application form, a 1-2 page letter program summary, amount requested, project budget, organization's budget for the current year, list of board of directors with affiliations, copy of the IRS tax-exemption letter, and the most recent 990 Form
Deadlines: None.
Decision Notification: 90 days for corporate contributions; up to six months for foundation requests

Restrictions

Toyota does not fund organizations that are not recognized as 501(c)(3) by the IRS; discriminate by race, creed, color, sex, age or national origin; fraternal organizations, labor organizations or religious groups; political parties, candidates, publications or lobbying activities; advertising; or individuals.
The foundation also does not fund routine expenses, operating costs, annual fund drives, or deficit reductions; does not consider grants to endowments, capital campaigns, construction, fundraising events, conferences, meals, or travel; does not provide direct funds to K-12, public, or private schools.

Additional Information

Requests for corporate contributions of up to $5,000 should be sent to Toyota's Corporate Employee Contribution Committee, Toyota Motor Sales, U.S.A., Inc., at the above address. All other requests should be submitted to the Community Relations Department. Toyota will consider only one request per year from an organization.
Elaborate and lengthy requests are not encouraged. Telephone inquiries are accepted only to clarify Toyota contributions guidelines and verify mailing address information. Evaluations of proposals are not made over the phone.
Meetings with organizations requesting contributions are not encouraged.
Toyota formalized a corporate giving and community relations program in 1973, contributing to various U.S. organizations and activities in support of the goals of the company and its employees.
The three main centers for contributions are: Toyota Motor Sales U.S.A., Inc., Community Relations, 19001 S. Western Ave., Torrance, CA 90509; Toyota Motor Corporate Services of North America, Inc., Public Affairs, 9 W 57th St., New York, NY 10019; Toyota Manufacturing U.S.A., Inc., 1001 Cherry Blossom Way, Georgetown, KY 40324; Toyota Technical Center, U.S.A., Inc., Public Affairs, 1588 Woodbridge Ave., Ann Arbor, MI 48105.
The company sponsors organizations that significantly enhance a community's social and economic well-being; contributions are generally unrestricted grants for everyday operations. Company prefers to make direct grants, rather than fund events.
Publications: Application Forms for Foundation and Corporate Contributions; Guidelines for Foundation and Corporate Contributions

Corporate Officials

Yale Gieszl: executive vice president, treasurer B 1941. PRIM CORP EMPL executive vice president: Toyota Motor Sales USA, Inc. CORP AFFIL director: Toyota Motor Credit Corp.; director: Toyota Motor Insurance Services.
Yoshio Ishizaka: president, chief executive officer PRIM CORP EMPL president, chief executive officer: Toyota Motor Sales USA, Inc. CORP AFFIL president: Toyota Motor Credit Corp.
Tom Nishiyama: senior vice president, treasurer PRIM CORP EMPL senior vice president, treasurer: Toyota Motor Sales USA, Inc.

Jim Olson: senior vice president external affairs PRIM CORP EMPL senior vice president external affairs: Toyota Motor Sales USA, Inc.
C. Yamaguchi: senior vice president, treasurer PRIM CORP EMPL senior vice president, treasurer: Toyota Motor Sales U.S.A., Inc.

Giving Program Officials

Gloria Jahn: corporate manager philanthropy
William Pauli: PRIM CORP EMPL national manager corporate philanthropy: Toyota Motor Sales USA, Inc.

Foundation Officials

Yale Gieszl: executive vice president (see above)
Yoshio Ishizaka: president (see above)
William Plourde: senior vice president
Doug West: senior vice president, coordinating officer CORP AFFIL director: Toyota Motor Credit Corp.
C. Yamaguchi: senior vice president, treasurer (see above)

Grants Analysis

Disclosure Period: fiscal year ending June 30, 1997
Total Grants: $1,517,625*
Number of Grants: 16
Average Grant: $94,852
Highest Grant: $400,000
Typical Range: $20,000 to $100,000
*Note: Giving excludes Company gives directly.

Recent Grants

Note: Grants derived from fiscal 1997 Form 990.

Civic & Public Affairs

400,000 National Park Foundation, Washington, DC -- to underwrite Park Labs
150,000 Wildlife Conservation Society New York Zoological Society, Bronx, NY -- for teacher training in Habitat Ecology Learning Program
50,000 Brooklyn Botanic Garden, Brooklyn, NY -- for Discovery Carts Program

Education

150,000 Claremont Graduate School, Claremont, CA -- to assess student learning, for changes in teaching
100,000 Los Angeles Educational Partnership, Los Angeles, CA -- to expand and enhance Toyota Math and Science grants
100,000 National Public Radio, Washington, DC -- for Science Friday Kids Connection
75,000 KCET Center for Professional Development, Los Angeles, CA -- to expand MATHLINE program
60,000 Ohio University, Athens, OH -- for Science and Mathematics Robotics Training Program
50,000 Council for Basic Education, Washington, DC -- for Principals Leadership Academy
50,000 Pacific Science Center, Seattle, WA -- support Toyota Teacher's Program
50,000 Utah Museum of Natural History, Salt Lake City, UT -- for two-year support of Youth Teaching Youth program
40,000 Economics America, Louisville, KY -- to train Kentucky high school teachers in comprehensive curriculum
22,625 Illinois Institute of Technology Armour College of Engineering and Science, Chicago, IL -- for Year-Long Technology Learning Enhancement Program
20,000 Clemson University Division of Agriculture and Natural Resources, Clemson, SC -- three-year grant to underwrite Teaching Kids about the Environment program
20,000 Summerbridge National, San Francisco, CA -- to expand national educational program

Environment

180,000 National Wildlife Federation, Vienna, VA -- support for Wolf Tracks program

TRACE INTERNATIONAL HOLDINGS, INC.

Company Contact

New York, NY

Company Description

Former Name: 21 International Holdings, Inc.
Employees: 19,600
SIC(s): 3661 Telephone & Telegraph Apparatus, 5812 Eating Places, 7389 Business Services Nec.

Trace International Holdings, Inc. Foundation

Giving Contact

Judith G. Hershon, Vice President
Trace International Holdings, Inc. Foundation
375 Park Ave.
New York, NY 10152
Phone: (212)715-8619
Fax: (212)593-1363

Description

EIN: 222518739
Organization Type: Corporate Foundation. Supports preselected organizations only.
Giving Locations: NY: New York
Grant Types: General Support.

Financial Summary

Total Giving: $408,888 (1997); $347,061 (1996); $335,693 (1995). Note: Contributes through foundation only.
Assets: $16,100 (1997); $62,032 (1996); $9,080 (1995)
Gifts Received: $360,000 (1997); $395,000 (1996); $320,000 (1995). Note: 1997 contributions were received from Trace International Holdings, Inc. and The Ralph J. and Shirley Shapiro Fund.

Typical Recipients

Arts & Humanities: Arts Associations & Councils, Arts Centers, Arts Institutes, Ballet, Dance, Ethnic & Folk Arts, Film & Video, Historic Preservation, History & Archaeology, Libraries, Literary Arts, Museums/Galleries, Music, Opera, Performing Arts, Public Broadcasting, Theater
Civic & Public Affairs: Botanical Gardens/Parks, Business/Free Enterprise, Civil Rights, Economic Development, Civic & Public Affairs-General, Legal Aid, Municipalities/Towns, Professional & Trade Associations, Public Policy, Urban & Community Affairs, Women's Affairs
Education: Arts/Humanities Education, Business Education, Colleges & Universities, Continuing Education, Education-General, Medical Education, Minority Education, Private Education (Precollege), Religious Education, Social Sciences Education
Health: Alzheimers Disease, Cancer, Children's Health/Hospitals, Clinics/Medical Centers, Emergency/Ambulance Services, Eyes/Blindness, Geriatric Health, Health Organizations, Hospitals, Hospitals (University Affiliated), Medical Research, Single-Disease Health Associations
International: Foreign Arts Organizations, Foreign Educational Institutions, Human Rights, International Affairs, International Organizations, International Peace & Security Issues, International Relations, Missionary/Religious Activities
Religion: Jewish Causes, Religious Welfare, Synagogues/Temples
Science: Science Museums
Social Services: Animal Protection, At-Risk Youth, Camps, Child Welfare, Community Centers, Community Service Organizations, Emergency Relief, Family Services, Food/Clothing Distribution, People with Disabilities, Recreation & Athletics, Refugee Assistance, Scouts, Shelters/Homelessness, United Funds/United Ways, YMCA/YWCA/YMHA/YWHA, Youth Organizations

Contributions Analysis

Giving Priorities: Museums, colleges and universities, medical research, child welfare and youth organizations, and some civic organizations.
Arts & Humanities: 15% to 20%. Major recipients include museums, libraries, dance, and art centers.
Civic & Public Affairs: Less than 5%. Funding supports organizations for the improvement of New York City.
Education: 5% to 10%. Primarily supports colleges and universities in theNortheast. Educational foundations also receive grants.
Health: 10% to 15%. Grants concentrate on medical research with some support to single-disease health organizations.
International: About 35% Funding supports several international organizations in New York.
Religion: 15% to 20%. Funding primarily supports Jewish organizations in New York City.
Social Services: 5% to 10%. Majority of grants made to child welfareorganizations. Organizations that give aid to the homeless also receive support.

Corporate Officials

Marshall Stuart Cogan: chairman, president, chief executive officer, director B Boston, MA 1937. ED Harvard University AB (1959); Harvard University MBA (1962). PRIM CORP EMPL chairman, president, chief executive officer, director: Trace International Holdings, Inc. CORP AFFIL chairman: United Jeep Eagle Chrysler Plymouth; chief executive officer: United Nissan Inc.; director, chairman, chief executive officer: United Auto Group Inc.; vice chairman, chairman executive committee: Foamex; chairman: Foamex Capital Corp.; chief executive officer: Atlanta Toyota Inc.
Saul S. Sherman: vice chairman, director B 1917. ED University of Chicago BA (1939). PRIM CORP EMPL vice chairman, director: Trace International Holdings, Inc. CORP AFFIL director: Allied Products Corp.

Foundation Officials

Marshall Stuart Cogan: director (see above)
Joan Moore Flood: assistant treasurer B Hampton, VA 1941. ED North Texas State University BMus (1963); Southern Methodist University (1967-1968); North Texas State University (1977); Texas Woman's University (1978-1979); University of Dallas (1985-1986). PRIM CORP EMPL corporate transactions paralegal: Jones, Day, Reavis & Pogue. NONPR AFFIL member: American Bar Association; member: Texas Bar Association.
Judith G. Hershon: vice president
Frank Murtagh: assistant treasurer
Robert N. Nelson: treasurer B 1945. ED Manhattan College BBA (1968). PRIM CORP EMPL vice president finance, chief financial officer: Trace International Holdings, Inc.
Philip N. Smith, Jr.: secretary B 1942. ED University of Maryland BS (1964); George Washington University Law School (1967). PRIM CORP EMPL vice president, general secretary: Trace International Holdings, Inc. CORP AFFIL vice president, general counsel, secretary: Foamex International Inc.; senior vice president, general counsel, assistant secretary: United Auto Group Inc.

Grants Analysis

Disclosure Period: calendar year ending 1997
Total Grants: $408,088
Number of Grants: 72
Average Grant: $4,134*
Highest Grant: $115,176
Typical Range: $1,000 to $10,000
***Note:** Average grant excludes highest grant.

Recent Grants

Note: Grants derived from 1997 Form 990.

Arts & Humanities

50,000	Museum of Modern Art, New York, NY
5,000	New York Chamber Symphony, New York, NY
2,400	Parrish Art Museum, New York, NY
2,000	Brooklyn Academy of Music, Brooklyn, NY
2,000	New York City Opera, New York State Theater, New York, NY
1,000	Whitney Museum of Art, New York, NY

Civic & Public Affairs

4,970	National Abortion Rights Action League, Washington, DC
3,500	Central Park Conservancy, New York, NY
2,500	New York City 100, New York, NY
1,500	Project Renewal, New York, NY

Education

10,000	Prep for Prep, New York, NY
9,450	Trinity School, New York, NY
5,050	Brown University, Providence, RI
4,000	Columbia University, New York, NY
2,500	Studio in a School, New York, NY
1,500	Junior Achievement, New York, NY
1,000	Wellesley College, Wellesley, MA

Health

17,260	Breast Cancer Research Foundation, New York, NY
5,500	New York University Medical Center, New York, NY
5,000	Barrow Neurological Foundation, Phoenix, AZ
5,000	New York Hospital Cornell Medical Center, New York, NY
5,000	Samuel Waxman Cancer Research Foundation, New York, NY
3,000	Mount Sinai Medical Center, New York, NY
2,500	Cystic Fibrosis Foundation, New York, NY
2,500	SLE Foundation, New York, NY
2,200	Alzheimer's Association, Chicago, IL

International

115,176	American Friends of the Israel Museum, New York, NY
10,000	Lawyers Committee for Human Rights, New York, NY
4,550	American Committee for the Weizmann Institute of Science, New York, NY
3,750	Worldesign Foundation, New York, NY
1,200	American-Israel Cultural Foundation, New York, NY

Religion

15,000	B'nai B'rith Foundation, New York, NY
14,500	United Jewish Appeal Federation, New York, NY
5,000	Aleph Society, New York, NY
5,000	Partners for Jewish Life Network, New York, NY
5,000	United Jewish Appeal Federation, New York, NY
4,950	Central Synagogue, New York, NY
4,850	International Sephardic Education Foundation, New York, NY
2,650	Jewish Board of Family and Children's Services, New York, NY
2,500	Yeshiva University Museum, New York, NY
1,680	Jewish Museum, New York, NY

Science

1,450	American Museum of Natural History, New York, NY

Social Services

10,850	92nd Street YMCA, New York, NY
5,000	Horizons Initiative, Dorchester, MA
3,882	Children's Defense Fund, Washington, DC
3,500	Summer Camp, New York, NY
2,500	Ackerman Institute for Family Therapy, New York, NY
2,000	Friends in Deed, New York, NY
2,000	Group for the South Fork, Bridgehampton, NY
2,000	Scan New York Foundation, New York, NY

TRANSAMERICA CORP.

Company Contact

600 Montgomery St.
San Francisco, CA 94111
Phone: (415)983-4000
Web: http://www.transamerica.com

Company Description

Revenue: US$6,428,600,000 (1998)
Employees: 9,200 (1998)
SIC(s): 6282 Investment Advice.
Parent Company: AEGON NV, Mariahoeveplein 50, The Hague, Netherlands

Nonmonetary Support

Value: $154,000 (1989); $160,000 (1988)
Type: Donated Equipment; In-kind Services
Note: Nonmonetary support is provided by the company. 1997 Nonmonetary Amount: $10,000.

Corporate Sponsorship

Value: $2,500
Type: Arts & cultural events; Festivals/fairs; Sports events
Note: Sponsors golf tournaments and health fairs.

Transamerica Foundation

Giving Contact

Ms. Mary M. Sawai, Program Director
Transamerica Foundation
600 Montgomery Street
San Francisco, CA 94111
Phone: (415)983-4333
Fax: (415)983-4234

Description

EIN: 943034825
Organization Type: Corporate Foundation
Giving Locations: primarily in operating areas.
Grant Types: Employee Matching Gifts, General Support.

Financial Summary

Total Giving: $3,174,000 (1998 approx); $3,095,330 (1997); $2,204,084 (1996). Note: Contributes through corporate direct giving program and foundation. 1997 Giving includes foundation ($1,802,699); matching gifts (998,949); scholarships ($94,033); United Way ($198,650). 1996 Giving includes corporate direct giving ($469,912); foundation ($874,533); matching gifts ($768,872); scholarships ($90,767). 1995 Giving includes foundation ($880,840); matching gifts ($761,608); scholarships ($87,117).
Assets: $51,700,000 (1999 approx); $50,636,007 (1998); $46,879,640 (1997)

Typical Recipients

Arts & Humanities: Arts Associations & Councils, Arts Festivals, Arts Institutes, Ballet, Dance, Ethnic & Folk Arts, Historic Preservation, Libraries, Literary Arts, Museums/Galleries, Music, Opera, Performing Arts, Public Broadcasting, Theater
Civic & Public Affairs: African American Affairs, Asian American Affairs, Botanical Gardens/Parks, Business/Free Enterprise, Community Foundations, Economic Development, Employment/Job Training, Civic & Public Affairs-General, Housing, Legal Aid, Nonprofit Management, Philanthropic Organizations, Public Policy, Urban & Community Affairs, Zoos/Aquariums
Education: Business Education, Colleges & Universities, Economic Education, Education Associations, Education Funds, Elementary Education (Private), Legal Education, Minority Education, Preschool Education, Private Education (Precollege), Science/Mathematics Education, Secondary Education (Private), Secondary Education (Public), Special Education, Vocational & Technical Education
Environment: Environment-General, Resource Conservation, Wildlife Protection
Health: AIDS/HIV, Cancer, Clinics/Medical Centers, Emergency/Ambulance Services, Health Funds, Health Organizations, Heart, Hospices, Hospitals, Medical Research, Mental Health, Single-Disease Health Associations
International: International Peace & Security Issues
Religion: Churches, Jewish Causes, Religious Welfare
Science: Observatories & Planetariums, Science Museums, Scientific Centers & Institutes
Social Services: At-Risk Youth, Camps, Child Welfare, Community Centers, Community Service Organizations, Counseling, Family Services, Food/Clothing Distribution, People with Disabilities, Recreation & Athletics, Scouts, Senior Services, Shelters/Homelessness, United Funds/United Ways, YMCA/YWCA/YMHA/YWHA, Youth Organizations

Contributions Analysis

Giving Priorities: Health, social welfare, education, and culture and the arts.
Arts & Humanities: 25% to 30%. Museums, orchestras, public broadcasting, and libraries.
Civic & Public Affairs: 10%. Nonprofit management, ethnic organizations, and community affairs organizations.
Education: 10% to 15%. Majority disbursed as employee matching gifts to precollege and college education. Interests also include economic education and education funds.
Environment: 5% to 10%. Environmental organizations in operating area.
Health: 5% to 10%. Homelessness relief and housing, food distribution programs, and shelters; community service organizations and groups concerned with child welfare and drug abuse prevention; and religious welfare.
Science: Less than 5%. Funds given to the California Academy ofSciences, and science education.
Social Services: 30%. Supports Boy Scouts of America, children services, food banks, adult services, elder care, and the United Way.
Note: Percentages reflect combined foundation and direct giving priorities.

Application Procedures

Initial Contact: brief letter or proposal
Application Requirements: a description of organization, amount requested, purpose of funds sought, recently audited financial statement, proof of tax-exempt status, and a list of board of directors
Deadlines: None.
Decision Notification: within three to six months

Restrictions

Does not support individuals; political, religious, or fraternal organizations; advertisements in charitable publications; or loans. Foundation primarily supports organizations in the San Francisco Bay area.

Additional Information

Company reports that certain aspects of the giving program are undergoing changes and that giving may be somewhat curtailed in the future.

Corporate Officials

Burton Edward Broome: vice president, controller B New York, NY 1935. ED Fordham University BS (1963); University of California MBA (1964). PRIM CORP EMPL vice president, controller: TransAmerica Corp. CORP AFFIL director: TransAmerica Home First Corp.; member executive committee: ARC Reins Corp. NONPR AFFIL chairman advisory council: Second Financial Reporting Institute; member professional acctg program: University California Berkeley; member: California Society CPA's; member: Financial Executives Institute; member: American Institute CPAs. CLUB AFFIL Commonwealth Club.

Shirley H. Buccieri: senior vice president

Patricia T. Clarey: vice president

Edgar Harold Grubb: executive vice president, chief financial officer B Harrisburg, PA 1939. ED Pennsylvania State University BA (1961); California State University, Fullerton MBA (1967). PRIM CORP EMPL executive vice president, chief financial officer: TransAmerica Corp. CORP AFFIL director: TransAmerica Occidental Life Insurance Co.; director: TransAmerica Finance Corp.; director: TransAmerica Insurance Corp. California; director: TransAmerica Business Technical Corp. NONPR AFFIL member: Financial Executives Institute; director: Mills College; member: American Institute CPAs.

Frank Casper Herringer: president, chief executive officer, director, chairman B Brooklyn, NY 1942. ED Dartmouth College AB (1964); Dartmouth College MBA (1965). PRIM CORP EMPL president, chief executive officer, director, chairman: TransAmerica Corp. CORP AFFIL director: Union Oil Co. California; director: Unocal Corp.; director: TransAmerica Leasing Inc.; director: TransAmerica Occidental Life Insurance Co.; director: TransAmerica Fin Corp.; director: Charles Schwab Corp.; director: Trans America Insurance Corp. California. NONPR AFFIL trustee: California Pacific Medical Center; member: Phi Beta Kappa. CLUB AFFIL San Francisco Golf Club; Olympic Club; Pacific-Union Club; Cypress Point Club.

Foundation Officials

Burton Edward Broome: vice president, treasurer (see above)

Shirley H. Buccieri: vice president, secretary (see above)

Patricia T. Clarey: president (see above)

Edgar Harold Grubb: director (see above)

Frank Casper Herringer: vice chairman, director (see above)

Richard Neal Latzer: vice president, director B New York, NY 1937. ED University of Pennsylvania BA (1959); University of Pennsylvania MA (1961). PRIM CORP EMPL senior vice president, chief investment officer: TransAmerica Corp. CORP AFFIL president, chief executive officer, director: TransAmerica Realty Services Inc.; chairman investment committee, chief investment officer, director: TransAmerica Occidental Life Insurance Co.; director: TransAmerica Realty Investment Corp.; director, member investment committee: TransAmerica Life Insurance Co. Canada; chief executive officer, president, director: TransAmerica Investment Services Inc.; chairman investment committee, chief investment officer, director: TransAmerica Life & Annuity Co.; member investment committee, director: TransAmerica Insurance Group; director: TransAmerica Cash Reserve Inc.; director: TransAmerica Income Shares; chief investment officer, member investment committee: TransAmerica Assurance Co. NONPR AFFIL member: Chartered Financial Analysts; member: Security Analysts San Francisco.

Mary Sawai: assistant secretary

Grants Analysis

Disclosure Period: calendar year ending 1997
Total Grants: $1,802,699*
Number of Grants: 178
Average Grant: $10,127
Highest Grant: $110,000
Typical Range: $1,000 to $15,000
***Note:** Giving excludes matching gifts; scholarships; United Way.

Recent Grants

Note: Grants derived from 1997 Form 990.

Arts & Humanities

94,000	North Carolina Dance Theater, Charlotte, NC
60,000	Museum of the New South, Charlotte, NC
50,000	Arts and Science Council, Charlotte, NC
34,100	Charlotte Symphony Orchestra Society, Charlotte, NC
33,334	KQED, San Francisco, CA
30,500	Arts and Science Council, Charlotte, NC
25,000	Library Foundation, San Francisco, CA
20,000	Fine Arts Museums, San Francisco, CA
15,000	San Francisco Ballet, San Francisco, CA
15,000	San Francisco Opera, San Francisco, CA
15,000	San Francisco Symphony, San Francisco, CA
10,000	Arts and Science Council, Charlotte, NC
10,000	Japanese American National Museum, Los Angeles, CA
10,000	KQED, San Francisco, CA
10,000	Public Library of Charlotte and Mecklenburg, NC
10,000	San Francisco Art Institute, San Francisco, CA

Civic & Public Affairs

75,000	Golden Gate National Parks Association, San Francisco, CA
50,000	Foundation for the Carolinas, Charlotte, NC
10,000	100 Black Men, Charlotte, NC
10,000	Discovery Pride
10,000	San Francisco Zoological Society, San Francisco, CA

Education

50,000	Johnson Smith University
43,750	University of North Carolina Charlotte, Charlotte, NC
25,000	Fordham University School of Law, Bronx, NY
25,000	Seattle Avenue Preschool
20,000	Central Piedmont and South College Fund
10,000	Opera Carolina, Charlotte, NC

Environment

110,000	Yosemite Fund
16,100	Marine Mammal Center, San Francisco, CA

Health

31,700	United Way Heart America, Overland Park, KS
30,000	Glide Memorial Foundation, San Francisco, CA
25,000	California Hospital Medical Center Foundation, Los Angeles, CA
10,000	University of South Carolina Comprehensive Cancer Center, Columbia, SC

Science

40,000	California Academy of Sciences, San Francisco, CA
10,000	Charlotte Mecklenburg Education Foundation, Charlotte, NC

Social Services

66,800	United Way, Los Angeles, CA
60,000	United Way Bay Area, San Francisco, CA
50,000	Boy Scouts of America
40,000	Aviva Center, Los Angeles, CA
37,500	Charlotte Regional Sports Commission, Charlotte, NC
35,000	Jubilee West, San Francisco, CA
30,000	Hillsides Home for Children
25,000	San Francisco Food Bank, San Francisco, CA
25,000	YMCA
20,000	Fred Finch Youth Center
15,000	Mothers of Murdered Offspring
15,000	United Way, Dallas, TX
14,050	United Way Central Carolinas, Charlotte, NC
10,000	Age Center Alliance, Palo Alto, CA
10,000	Charlotte Regional Sports Commission, Charlotte, NC

TRUE NORTH COMMUNICATIONS, INC.

Company Contact

Chicago, IL
Web: http://www.bozell.com

Company Description

Former Name: Foote, Cone & Belding Communications.
Gross Operating Earnings: US$7,500,000,000
Employees: 4,369
SIC(s): 7311 Advertising Agencies.
Parent Company: Associated Communications

True North Foundation

Giving Contact

Mitch Engle, President of Associated Communication Companies & Foundations
True North Foundation
101 East Erie Street
Chicago, IL 60611-2897
Phone: (312)751-7000
Web: http://www.truenorth.com

Description

Founded: 1947
EIN: 366116701
Organization Type: Corporate Foundation
Former Name: Foote, Cone & Belding Foundation.
Giving Locations: IL: Chicago; NY: New York
Grant Types: General Support, Multiyear/Continuing Support, Operating Expenses.

Financial Summary

Total Giving: $690,310 (1998); $170,650 (1997); $299,900 (1996). Note: Contributes through foundation only.
Giving Analysis: Giving for 1996 includes: foundation ($292,400); foundation grants to United Way ($7,500); 1997: foundation ($143,150); foundation scholarships ($20,000); foundation grants to United Way ($7,500); 1998: foundation ($639,310); foundation ($567,210); foundation grants to United Way ($123,100); foundation grants to United Way ($123,000)
Assets: $91,722 (1998); $50,540 (1997); $11,245 (1996)
Gifts Received: $731,750 (1998); $210,000 (1997); $280,000 (1996). Note: Contributions are received from True North Communications.

Typical Recipients

Arts & Humanities: Arts Associations & Councils, Arts Festivals, Arts Funds, Arts Institutes, Community Arts, Dance, Arts & Humanities-General, History & Archaeology, Museums/Galleries, Music, Opera, Performing Arts, Theater
Civic & Public Affairs: African American Affairs, Chambers of Commerce, Civic & Public Affairs-General, Parades/Festivals, Professional & Trade Associations, Public Policy, Urban & Community Affairs, Women's Affairs, Zoos/Aquariums
Education: Arts/Humanities Education, Business Education, Business-School Partnerships, Colleges & Universities, Education-General, International Studies, Leadership Training, Medical Education, Minority Education, Preschool Education, Religious Education, Science/Mathematics Education, Special Education, Student Aid
Environment: Forestry, Environment-General
Health: Cancer, Diabetes, Hospices, Hospitals, Multiple Sclerosis, Public Health, Single-Disease Health Associations
International: International Affairs, International Relations, International Relief Efforts
Religion: Churches, Dioceses, Jewish Causes, Religious Organizations, Religious Welfare
Science: Science Museums, Scientific Centers & Institutes
Social Services: At-Risk Youth, Child Welfare, Community Service Organizations, Crime Prevention, Day Care, Family Services, Food/Clothing Distribution, People with Disabilities, Recreation & Athletics, Scouts, Senior Services, Shelters/Homelessness, Social Services-General, Special Olympics, United Funds/United Ways, Volunteer Services, YMCA/YWCA/YMHA/YWHA, Youth Organizations

Application Procedures

Initial Contact: Send a written request on organization's letterhead.
Deadlines: None.

Corporate Officials

John B. Balousek: president, director, director PRIM CORP EMPL president, director: True North Communications, Inc. CORP AFFIL president, chief operating officer: Foote Cone Belding Communications Inc.; chief operating officer: True North Technologies.
Gregory W. Blaine: chief operating officer B 1948. ED Ohio State University (1971). PRIM CORP EMPL chief operating officer: True North Communications, Inc. CORP AFFIL chief executive officer: T N Technology INC.
W. Bruce Mason: chairman, chief executive officer, director B Chicago, IL 1939. ED Saint John's University BA (1961); University of Chicago MBA (1963). PRIM CORP EMPL chairman, chief executive officer, director: True North Communications, Inc. CORP AFFIL chairman, chief executive officer, director: Foote Cone Belding. NONPR AFFIL member: American Association Advertising Agencies.

Foundation Officials

Terry M. Ashwill: vice president, director B 1945. ED Oregon State University MBA. PRIM CORP EMPL executive vice president, director: Foote Cone Belding Advg Development. CORP AFFIL executive vice president, chief financial officer: True North Communications Inc.
John B. Balousek: vice president, director (see above)
Gregory W. Blaine: president, director (see above)
Jack Boland: vice president, director B 1956. PRIM CORP EMPL executive vice president: Foote Cone & Belding Inc. CORP AFFIL executive vice president: Foote Cone Belding Advertising; executive, president: True North Communications Inc.
Dale F. Perona: secretary, treasurer B 1945. ED Illinois State University BS; Illinois State University MS. CORP AFFIL vice president, treasurer, secretary, officer: True North Communications Inc.

Grants Analysis

Disclosure Period: calendar year ending 1998
Total Grants: $567,210*
Number of Grants: 113
Average Grant: $5,020
Highest Grant: $30,000
Typical Range: $50 to $10,000
***Note:** Giving excludes United Way.

Recent Grants

Note: Grants derived from 1998 Form 990.

Arts & Humanities

25,000	American Museum of Natural History, New York, NY -- underwriter table at dinner
20,000	The American Craft Museum, New York, NY
14,000	Philadelphia Festivals of the Arts, Philadelphia, PA -- tables at the marian anderson award
10,000	Lincoln Center for the Performing Arts, Inc., New York, NY -- patron table
10,000	Metropolitan Museum of Art, New York, NY -- table at the art gala benefit
10,000	National Actors Theatre, New York, NY -- patron table at 1998 broadway frolic
10,000	New Jersey Performing Arts Center, Newark, NJ -- table at first anniversary gala
8,000	Chicago Symphony Orchestra, Chicago, IL
7,000	State of Historical Society of Wisconsin, Madison, WI -- final payment toward $35,000 grant
6,000	Lyric Opera of Chicago, Chicago, IL -- 2nd payment toward $30,000 pledge
6,000	Steppenwolf Theatre Company, Chicago, IL -- sponsor table at the benefit
5,000	American Craft Museum, New York, NY -- patron table at 1998 visionaries
5,000	Business Committee for the Arts, Inc., New York, NY -- annual corporate membership

Civic & Public Affairs

30,000	The Leadership Fund, Washington, DC
25,000	NYC Partnership and Chamber of Commerce, New York, NY -- table in annual benefit
20,000	Advertising Council Inc., New York, NY -- three year pledge
15,000	Advertising Council Incorporated, New York, NY -- benefactor table at award dinner
15,000	New York City Partnership & Chamber of Commerce, New York, NY
15,000	One-to-One/The National Mentoring Partnership, Washington, DC -- table at the benefit
10,000	Catalyst, New York, NY -- awards dinner
7,500	Advertising Council, New York, NY -- patron table at award dinner
7,500	Target Omaha, Omaha, NE -- 1st payment of $22,500 pledge
5,000	Big, New York, NY
5,000	Center for Communications, New York, NY -- table in annual benefit lucheon
5,000	Chicago Foundation for Women, Chicago, IL -- table sponsorship in annual luncheon

Education

20,000	Morehouse School of Medicine, Atlanta, GA -- 2nd payment of a $100,000 pledge
10,000	Business Leaders Organized for Catholic Schools, Phildelphia, PA
10,000	New School University, New York, NY
10,000	New York City Outward Bound Center, New York, NY -- patron table at fourth annual benefit
5,000	Educational Foundation for the Fashion Industries, New York, NY -- patron table at annual award dinner

Environment

10,000	National Forest Foundation, Arlington, VA

Health

25,000	Juvenile Diabetes Foundation, New York, NY -- sponsor at the 1998 walk
10,000	Cancer Research Institute, New York, NY -- annual awards dinner
10,000	The Jimmie Heuga Center, Edwards, CO
10,000	New York Hospital/Cornell Medical Center, New York, NY -- 2nd payment of a $50,000 pledge
10,000	Southampton Hospital, New York, NY
5,000	National Multiple Sclerosis Society, New York, NY

International

10,000	Business Council for the United Nations, New York, NY -- annual corporate membership
6,000	International Rescue Committee, New York, NY -- sponsor table at freedom award dinner

Religion

5,000	Christian Action Guild, Golden, CO -- annual donation

Social Services

25,000	Tomorrow's Children Fund & CJ Foundation, New York, NY
20,000	United Way of New York City, New York, NY -- annual pledge
20,000	United Way of NYC, New York, NY -- pledge
10,000	Boys & Girls Clubs of America, New York, NY -- chairman's dinner
10,000	YAI/National Institute for People with Disabilities, New York, NY -- sponsorship table
10,000	YMCA of Greater New York, New York, NY -- sponsor table at the benefit
8,000	United Way of SEPA, Chicago, IL -- t&p 1997 corporate gift
5,000	Child Care Action Campaign, New York, NY -- patron table at 15th anniversary celebration
5,000	Child Welfare League of America, Chicago, IL
5,000	Citizen's Crime Commission, New York, NY -- annual donation

TRUE OIL CO.

Company Contact

Casper, WY

Company Description

Employees: 87

True Foundation

Giving Contact

Cherie Miller, Secretary
True Foundation
PO Box 2360
Casper, WY 82602
Phone: (307)237-9301

Description

EIN: 836004596
Organization Type: Corporate Foundation. Supports preselected organizations only.

Giving Locations: WY
Grant Types: General Support, Scholarship.

Financial Summary

Total Giving: $225,547 (fiscal year ending November 30, 1997); $259,092 (fiscal 1996); $226,697 (fiscal 1994). Note: Contributes through foundation only.
Assets: $2,333,751 (fiscal 1997); $2,364,575 (fiscal 1996); $2,633,147 (fiscal 1994)
Gifts Received: $2,512,000 (fiscal 1991); $9,600 (fiscal 1990); $9,600 (fiscal 1989)

Typical Recipients

Arts & Humanities: Historic Preservation, History & Archaeology, Museums/Galleries, Music, Opera, Performing Arts, Public Broadcasting, Theater
Civic & Public Affairs: Botanical Gardens/Parks, Business/Free Enterprise, Clubs, Economic Development, Economic Policy, Civic & Public Affairs-General, Housing, Law & Justice, Legal Aid, Professional & Trade Associations, Public Policy
Education: Agricultural Education, Colleges & Universities, Community & Junior Colleges, Economic Education, Education Funds, Education-General, Private Education (Precollege), Public Education (Precollege)
Environment: Energy, Environment-General, Resource Conservation, Wildlife Protection
Health: Alzheimers Disease, Cancer, Children's Health/Hospitals, Clinics/Medical Centers, Diabetes, Emergency/Ambulance Services, Health Funds, Hospitals, Medical Rehabilitation, Medical Research, Public Health, Respiratory, Single-Disease Health Associations
Religion: Churches, Religious Organizations, Religious Welfare
Social Services: Child Welfare, Community Service Organizations, Crime Prevention, Food/Clothing Distribution, Recreation & Athletics, United Funds/United Ways, YMCA/YWCA/YMHA/YWHA, Youth Organizations

Contributions Analysis

Civic & Public Affairs: 50% to 55%. Supports united funds, community service organizations, religious welfare, and youth organizations. Less than 5%. Funds legal aid and research, economic policy, and public policy.
Education: 15% to 20%. Supports colleges, universities, and funds for scholarships.
Health: 20% to 25%. Medical rehabilitation centers, cancer treatment centers, and children's hospitals receive funding.

Additional Information

All funds are committed for the foreseeable future, due to the lengthy depression in the oil and gas industry.

Corporate Officials

David True: partner B 1950. PRIM CORP EMPL partner: True Oil Co. CORP AFFIL partner: True Geothermal Energy Co.; partner: True Ranches; vice president, director: Toolpushers Supply Co.; partner: True Drilling Co.; partner: Eighty-Eight Oil Co.; officer: Hilltop National Bank Mountain Plaza; vice president, director: Austin Powder Co.; vice president, director: Black Hills Trucking Inc.
Diemer True: partner B 1946. PRIM CORP EMPL partner: True Oil Co. CORP AFFIL partner: True Geothermal Energy Co.; partner: True Ranches; partner: True Drilling Co.; director: Hilltop National Bank Mountain Plaza; president, director: Toolpushers Supply Co.; secretary: Fire Creek Oil Co.; officer: Hilltop National Bank; president, director: Black Hills Trucking Inc.; partner: Eighty-Eight Oil Co.
Jean Durland True: partner B Olney, IL 1915. PRIM CORP EMPL partner: True Oil Co. CORP AFFIL secretary, director: Belle Fouche Pipeline Co. NONPR AFFIL member: Casper Area Chamber of Commerce; member: Rocky Mountain Oil & Gas Association; member: Alpha Gamma Delta. CLUB AFFIL member: Petroleum Club; member: Casper Country Club.

Foundation Officials

Jean Durland True: trustee (see above)

Grants Analysis

Disclosure Period: fiscal year ending November 30, 1996
Total Grants: $259,092
Number of Grants: 126
Average Grant: $2,056
Highest Grant: $28,600
Typical Range: $25 to $11,200

Recent Grants

Note: Grants derived from fiscal 1996 Form 990.

Arts & Humanities

6,100	Nicolaysen Art Museum, Casper, WY
5,600	Council for Public Television Channel Six, Denver, CO
5,000	Museum of the Rockies, Bozeman, MT
2,000	Central City Opera House Association, Denver, CO

Civic & Public Affairs

10,000	Mountain States Legal Foundation, Denver, CO
10,000	US Business and Industrial Council Education Foundation, Washington, DC
5,000	National Cattleman's Foundation, Englewood, CO
2,500	Capital Research Center, Washington, DC
1,500	Casper Rotary Club Foundation, Casper, WY
1,000	Heritage Foundation, Washington, DC
1,000	National Legal Center for Public Interest, Washington, DC

Education

28,600	University of Wyoming Foundation, Laramie, WY
3,750	University of Wyoming, Laramie, WY
3,500	Casper College Foundation, Casper, WY
2,500	Montana State University Alumni Association, Bozeman, MT
2,500	Rocky Mountain College, Billings, MT
1,500	Casper College, Casper, WY
1,500	Chadron State College, Chadron, NE
1,500	Eastern Wyoming College, Torrington, WY
1,250	Wyoming State 4-H Foundation, Laramie, WY
1,000	Hillsdale College, Hillsdale, MI

Environment

5,000	Jefferson Energy Foundation, Washington, DC

Health

20,500	Central Wyoming Cancer Treatment and Hospice Center, Casper, WY
15,100	Gottsche Foundation, Thermopolis, WY
10,000	Wyoming Medical Center Foundation, Casper, WY
5,600	Children's Hospital Foundation, Casper, WY
3,000	Caring Center, Casper, WY
2,000	Blue Envelope Health Fund, Casper, WY
1,000	American Diabetes Association, Casper, WY
1,000	American Diabetes Association, Casper, WY
1,000	Converse County Hospital Foundation, Douglas, WY
1,000	Luthercare, Casper, WY

Religion

7,150	St. Mark's Episcopal Church, Casper, WY
2,000	Cathedral Home for Children, Laramie, WY
2,000	Mother Seton Housing, Casper, WY
2,000	Wyoming Fellowship of Christian Athletes, Casper, WY
1,100	Salvation Army, Casper, WY
1,000	Casper Youth for Christ, Casper, WY
1,000	St. Joseph's Children's Home, Torrington, WY

Social Services

24,317	United Way Natrona County, Casper, WY
10,000	Stacy Marie True Memorial Trust, Casper, WY
5,000	Trooper Foundation, Casper, WY
3,500	YMCA, Casper, WY
2,000	Boys and Girls Clubs of America, Casper, WY
2,000	Meals on Wheels Foundation, Casper, WY
2,000	National Cowboy Hall of Fame, Oklahoma City, OK
1,000	Hugh O'Brian Youth Foundation, Los Angeles, CA
1,000	Theodore Roosevelt Medora Foundation, Medora, ND
1,000	Trooper Promotions, Casper, WY
1,000	Wyoming Children's Society, Cheyenne, WY

Trustmark Insurance Co.

Company Contact

Lake Forest, IL
Web: http://www.trustmark.com

Company Description

Former Name: Benefit Trust Life Insurance Co.
Assets: US$639,000,000
Employees: 1,425
SIC(s): 6321 Accident & Health Insurance.

Nonmonetary Support

Value: $149,231 (1998); $574,353 (1996); $180,158 (1995)
Type: Cause-related Marketing & Promotion; Donated Equipment; In-kind Services; Loaned Employees; Loaned Executives

Trustmark Foundation

Giving Contact

Ray Haase, Chairman
400 Field Dr.
Lake Forest, IL 60045
Phone: (847)615-1500
Fax: (847)615-5860

Description

EIN: 363330631
Organization Type: Corporate Foundation. Supports preselected organizations only.
Giving Locations: headquarters and operating communities.
Grant Types: Award, Employee Matching Gifts, General Support, Multiyear/Continuing Support, Research.

Financial Summary

Total Giving: $568,687 (1998); $582,605 (1997); $573,760 (1996). Note: Contributes through foundation only.
Giving Analysis: Giving for 1996 includes: foundation ($278,920); foundation grants to United Way ($103,185); 1997: foundation ($477,053); foundation grants to United Way ($105,552); 1998: foundation

($235,695); nonmonetary support ($149,231); foundation grants to United Way ($109,900); foundation matching gifts ($73,861)
Assets: $2,667,520 (1998); $2,902,590 (1997); $1,693,236 (1996)
Gifts Received: $149,231 (1998); $1,658,432 (1997); $715,945 (1996). Note: In 1993, contributions were received from Benefit Trust Life Insurance Co. In 1998, Foundation received gifts in kind.

Typical Recipients

Arts & Humanities: Arts Festivals, Community Arts, Arts & Humanities-General, Museums/Galleries, Music, Performing Arts, Theater
Civic & Public Affairs: Clubs, Community Foundations, Economic Development, Civic & Public Affairs-General, Parades/Festivals, Urban & Community Affairs, Zoos/Aquariums
Education: Business Education, Colleges & Universities, Community & Junior Colleges, Continuing Education, Education-General, Minority Education, Private Education (Precollege), Special Education, Student Aid
Health: Adolescent Health Issues, AIDS/HIV, Clinics/Medical Centers, Diabetes, Health-General, Hospices, Hospitals, Medical Research, Prenatal Health Issues, Preventive Medicine/Wellness Organizations, Single-Disease Health Associations
Religion: Jewish Causes, Religious Welfare
Social Services: Child Welfare, Community Centers, Community Service Organizations, Delinquency & Criminal Rehabilitation, Domestic Violence, Family Services, Homes, People with Disabilities, Recreation & Athletics, Sexual Abuse, Shelters/Homelessness, Social Services-General, Substance Abuse, United Funds/United Ways, Volunteer Services, Youth Organizations

Contributions Analysis

Arts & Humanities: 5%.
Civic & Public Affairs: 1%. Supports community services.
Education: 20%. Supports various colleges and universities-- mostly within Illinois, Wisconsin, and Indiana-- and often to programs associated with technology, finance or actuarial studies, and minority scholarships and endowments.
Health: 4%. Company supports medical research, health education and research organizations.
Social Services: 46%. Supports family and youth services, United Way and social services.
Note: Total contributions in 1998.

Additional Information

The Trustmark Companies commit 2% of earnings to charity each year.
Publications: Foundation Annual Report

Corporate Officials

Donald Matthew Peterson: president, chief executive officer, director B Mount Vernon, NY 1936. ED LaSalle College BA (1958). PRIM CORP EMPL president, chief executive officer, director: Trustmark Insurance Co. CORP AFFIL chairman: Trustmark Insurance Co. Mutual; director: Trustmark Life Insurance Co.; chairman: Trustco Inc.; director: Coresource Inc.; director: Star Marketing & Admin. NONPR AFFIL member: National Association Life Underwriters; director: United Way Lake County Illinois; member: National Association Health Underwriters; director: Lake Forest Graduate School Management; director: Lake Forest Hospital; member, director: Health Insurance Association America; director: Illinois Life Insurance Council; director: Barat College; member: American Academy of Actuaries; member, director: American Council Life Insurance. CLUB AFFIL North Shore Country Club; Pelican Nest Golf Club; Executive Club; Conway Farms Golf Club; Economic Club Chicago.

Foundation Officials

Richard D. Batten: trustee PRIM CORP EMPL treasurer: Trustmark Insurance Co. Mutual. CORP AFFIL vice president: Trustmark Life Insurance Co.
Ralph John Eckert: trustee B Milwaukee, WI 1929. ED University of Wisconsin BS (1951). PRIM CORP EMPL chairman emeritus: Trustmark Life Insurance Co. CORP AFFIL chairman: Trustmark Insurance Co. Mutual; director: Prin Preservation Mutual Funds. NONPR AFFIL member: Illinois Life Insurance Council; fellow: Society Actuaries; member: Illinois Life & Health Insurance Guaranty Association; member: American Council Life Insurance; member: Health Insurance Association America; member: American Academy of Actuaries. CLUB AFFIL Masons Club.
Frank G. Gramm, III: trustee PRIM CORP EMPL senior vice president: Trustmark Insurance Co. CORP AFFIL director: Coresource Inc.; vice president: Trustmark Life Insurance Co.
Maurice R. Haase: chairman, trustee
Donald Matthew Peterson: trustee (see above)

Grants Analysis

Disclosure Period: calendar year ending 1998
Total Grants: $235,695*
Number of Grants: 63 (approx)
Average Grant: $3,741
Highest Grant: $43,000
Typical Range: $1,000 to $10,000
***Note:** Giving excludes United Way; nonmonetary support; matching gifts.

Recent Grants

Note: Grants derived from 1998 Form 990.

Arts & Humanities

5,000	Friends of the Milwaukee Public Museum, WI
2,000	National Museum of Women in the Arts, Washington, DC

Civic & Public Affairs

5,000	Ravinia Festival Association, Highland Park, IL
3,000	Lincoln Park Zoological Gardens, Chicago, IL
1,000	Greater Kenosha Area Foundation, Kenosha, WI

Education

18,690	Trustmark Foundation Scholarships, Lake Forest, IL
13,000	College of Lake County Foundation, Grayslake, IL
7,000	Barat College, Lake Forest, IL
5,000	Illinois State University Foundation, Carbondale, IL
5,000	Lake Forest Graduate School of Management, Lake Forest, IL
3,500	J.L. Kellogg Graduate School of Management, Evanston, IL
3,000	North Park University, Chicago, IL
3,000	Youngstown State University Foundation, Youngstown, OH
2,500	University of Wisconsin Foundation, Madison, WI
2,000	Ball State University Foundation, Muncie, IL
2,000	Purdue University, West Lafayette, IN
2,000	United Negro College Fund, Chicago, IL
2,000	University of Michigan Foundation, Ann Arbor, MI

Health

3,000	Howard Brown Memorial Clinic, Chicago, IL
2,500	AIDSCARE, Inc., Chicago, IL
2,500	Lake Forest Hospital, Lake Forest, IL
2,500	Provena St. Therese medical Center, Waukegan, IL
1,643	Lake Forest Hospital, Lake Forest, IL -- (Printed material)

Religion

7,000	Lutheran Social Services of Illinois, Chicago, IL
3,000	Catholic Charities of Lake County, Waukegan, IL

Social Services

115,665	Community IMPACT, Palo Alto, CA -- (Volunteer time, printed material)
65,000	Lake County United Way, Green Oaks, IL
43,000	Community IMPACT, Palo Alto, CA
31,369	United Way, Lake Forest, IL -- (Loaned Executives, printed material)
25,000	Crusade of Mercy, Chicago, IL
16,125	Lake County Races, Highland Park, IL
7,500	Greensleeves Youth Project, Chicago, IL
6,400	Freeport United Way, Freeport, IL
6,000	Santa Monica Track Foundation, Santa Monica, CA
4,500	United Way of Kenosha County, Kenosha, WI
4,000	Howard Area Community Center, Chicago, IL
4,000	Interfaith House, Chicago, IL
4,000	Lake County Council Against Sexual Assault (LaCASA), Gurnee, IL
3,500	Omni Youth Services, Cook & Lake Counties, Buffalo Grove, IL
3,500	A Safe Place, Waukegan, IL
3,000	Family Services of North Lake County, Waukegan, IL
3,000	Family Services of South Lake County, Barrington, IL
3,000	United Way of Greater St. Joseph County, South Bend, IN
3,000	Youngstown/Mahoning Valley United Way, Youngstown, OH
2,500	Northern Illinois Council on Alcohol & Sexual Abuse, Lake County, Gurnee, IL
2,500	Youth & Family Counselling, Lake County, Waukegan, IL
2,500	Youth Service Project, Chicago, IL
2,000	Executive Service Corp of Chicago, Chicago, IL
2,000	Kenosha Youth Foundation, Kenosha, WI
2,000	United Way of Lake Forest, Lake Forest, IL

TRUSTMARK NATIONAL BANK

Company Contact

Jackson, MS
Web: http://www.trustmark.com

Company Description

Assets: US$5,193,700,000
Employees: 2,334
SIC(s): 6021 National Commercial Banks.
Parent Company: Trustmark Corp.

Nonmonetary Support

Type: Cause-related Marketing & Promotion; Donated Equipment; In-kind Services; Loaned Employees; Loaned Executives

Corporate Sponsorship

Type: Arts & cultural events

Giving Contact

Gray Wiggers, First Vice President
Trustmark National Bank
248 East Capitol Street
Jackson, MS 39201
Phone: (601)354-5942
Fax: (601)949-2313

Description

Organization Type: Corporate Giving Program
Giving Locations: headquarters and operating communities.
Grant Types: General Support.

Financial Summary

Total Giving: Contributes through corporate direct giving program only.

Typical Recipients

Arts & Humanities: Arts & Humanities-General
Civic & Public Affairs: Civic & Public Affairs-General
Education: Education-General
Health: Health-General
Social Services: Social Services-General

Application Procedures

Initial Contact: a brief letter of inquiry
Application Requirements: a description of organization, amount requested, purpose of funds sought, recently audited financial statement, and proof of tax-exempt status
Deadlines: None.
Notes: Only provides funding to organizations in the company's local area.

Corporate Officials

Frank R. Day: chairman B 1931. PRIM CORP EMPL chairman: Trustmark National Bank. CORP AFFIL principal: Smith County Bank; chairman: Trustmark Corp.
Richard G. Hickson: chief executive officer PRIM CORP EMPL chief executive officer: Trustmark National Bank ADD CORP EMPL president: Trustmark Corp.

TRW INC.

 Number 91 of Top 100 Corporate Givers

Company Contact

Cleveland, OH
Web: http://www.trw.com

Company Description

Revenue: US$16,969,000,000 (1999)
Profit: US$468,800,000 (1999)
Employees: 78,000 (1999)
Fortune Rank: 103, per FORTUNE Magazine's list of 500 Largest U.S. Corporations (1999).
FF 103
SIC(s): 3562 Ball & Roller Bearings, 3679 Electronic Components Nec, 3714 Motor Vehicle Parts & Accessories, 3761 Guided Missiles & Space Vehicles.

Operating Locations

Australia: TRW Carr Pty. Ltd., Hendon; Duly & Hansford Ltd., Marrickville; TRW Australia Holdings Ltd., Marrickville; TRW Sipea SpA, Marrickville; Austria: TRW Beteiligungs GmbH, Bergheim, Brabant; TRW Occupant Restraint Systems GmbH, Bergheim, Brabant; Belgium: TRW, Brussels, Brabant; Canada: TRW Vehicle Safety Systems Ltd., Midland; TRW Canada Ltd., St. Catherines; Quality Safety Systems Co., Windsor; Czech Republic: TRW Autoelektronika Spol S R O, Benesov u Prahy; France: Occupant Restraint Systems France SA, Ecouflant, Maine-et-Loire; TRW Carr France, Ingwiller, Bas-Rhin; TRW France SA, Longvic, Cote D'Or; TRW Electrotechnique Automobile SA, Osny, Val d'Oise; TRW Module Systems SA, Osny, Val d'Oise; TRW Composants Moteurs, Schirmeck, Bas-Rhin; Germany: TRW Occupant Restraint Systems GmbH, Aldorf, Baden-Wuerttemberg; TRW Deutschland GmbH, Barsinghausen, Niedersachsen; TRW Fahrwerksysteme GmbH & Co. KG, Duesseldorf; TRW Nelson Bolzenschweisstechnik GmbH & Co. KG, Gevelsberg; TRW Nelson Bolzenschweisstechnik Verwaltungs GmbH, Gevelsberg; TRW Automotive Electronics & Components GmbH & Co. KG, Radolfzell, Baden-Wuerttemberg; Italy: TRW Italia SpA, Gardone Val Trompia, Lombardia; TRW Sabelt SpA, Moncalieri, Piemonte; Japan: TRW Steering Systems Japan Co. Ltd., Kasugai, Aichi; TRW Overseas Tokyo, Tokyo; Mexico: TRW Occupant Restraints de Chihuahua SA de CV, Chihuahua; TRW Vehicle Safety System de Mexico SA de CV, Reynosa; Netherlands: TRW Financial Systems Nederland BV, Nieuwegein, Utrecht; TRW Overseas Finance NV, S'Gravenhage, Zuid-Holland; Face Holding BV, Veldhoven, Noord-Brabant; Face Industrial Automation BV, Veldhoven, Noord-Brabant; Face Industrial Electronics BV, Veldhoven, Noord-Brabant; Logisticon BV, Veldhoven, Noord-Brabant; Spain: TRW Direcciones de Vehiculos SA, Pamplona, Navarra; TRW Occupant Restraint Systems SA, Quintanaortuna; Thailand: Fuji Serina Valve Co. Ltd., Bangkok; Taiwan: TRW Electronic Components Co., Shulin; United Kingdom: TRW United Carr Ltd., Aylesbury, Buckinghamshire; TRW Steering Systems Ltd., Clevedon, Avon; TRW Ceramics Ltd., Derby, Derbyshire; TRW Occupant Restraint Systems Ltd., Derby, Derbyshire; TRW Transportation Electronics Ltd., Houghton-Le-Spring; TRW Remanufactured Steering Systems Ltd., Luton, Bedfordshire; TRW Automotive Systems Ltd., Wednesbury, West Midlands; TRW United Kingdom Ltd., Wednesday, West Midlands

Nonmonetary Support

Type: In-kind Services; Loaned Employees; Loaned Executives

Corporate Sponsorship

Type: Arts & cultural events; Sports events; Other
Note: Company sponsors the Harvest for Hunger and Hunger Network.

TRW Foundation

Giving Contact

Alan F. Senger, Vice President
TRW Foundation
1900 Richmond Road
Cleveland, OH 44124
Phone: (216)291-7160
Fax: (216)291-7632

Alternate Contact

Laura L. Johnson, Manager
Phone: (216)291-7166

Description

EIN: 346556217
Organization Type: Corporate Foundation
Giving Locations: principally near operating locations and to national organizations and internationally organizations.
Grant Types: Award, Capital, Employee Matching Gifts, Fellowship, General Support, Operating Expenses, Professorship, Project, Research, Scholarship.
Note: Employee matching gift ratio: 1 to 1 for individual gifts of $25 to $5,000 to U.S. educational institutions arts and cultural organizations annually.

Giving Philosophy

'Giving is focused on: Organizations meeting human service, cultural, and educational needs of those communities in which TRW employees live and work; selected organizations whose programs serve the broad interests of society and are consistent with the business goals and objectives of TRW Inc.; and selected educational institutions with engineering, technical/ science and/or business administration programs.'
1996 Grants List

Financial Summary

Total Giving: $8,000,000 (1999 approx); $7,994,582 (1998); $15,244,709 (1997). Note: Contributes through corporate direct giving program and foundation.
Giving Analysis: Giving for 1997 includes: foundation ($15,244,709); 1998: foundation ($7,394,582); corporate direct giving ($600,000)
Assets: $21,845,513 (1997); $25,904,297 (1995); $25,957,827 (1994)
Gifts Received: $11,156,394 (1995); $15,814,908 (1994). Note: Contributions received from TRW Inc.

Typical Recipients

Arts & Humanities: Arts Associations & Councils, Ballet, Community Arts, Ethnic & Folk Arts, Arts & Humanities-General, History & Archaeology, Museums/Galleries, Music, Opera, Performing Arts, Public Broadcasting, Theater
Civic & Public Affairs: African American Affairs, Business/Free Enterprise, Community Foundations, Economic Development, Economic Policy, Employment/Job Training, Civic & Public Affairs-General, Municipalities/Towns, Parades/Festivals, Professional & Trade Associations, Public Policy, Safety, Urban & Community Affairs, Women's Affairs
Education: Arts/Humanities Education, Business Education, Colleges & Universities, Community & Junior Colleges, Education Funds, Education Reform, Engineering/Technological Education, Faculty Development, Education-General, Minority Education, Preschool Education, Public Education (Precollege), Science/Mathematics Education, Student Aid
Environment: Environment-General
Health: Alzheimers Disease, Children's Health/Hospitals, Clinics/Medical Centers, Emergency/Ambulance Services, Health Policy/Cost Containment, Health Organizations, Hospices, Hospitals, Hospitals (University Affiliated), Medical Rehabilitation, Mental Health, Research/Studies Institutes
International: International Affairs
Religion: Churches, Religious Welfare
Science: Science Museums, Scientific Centers & Institutes, Scientific Organizations
Social Services: Child Welfare, Community Service Organizations, Day Care, Family Services, Food/ Clothing Distribution, People with Disabilities, Recreation & Athletics, Scouts, Senior Services, Shelters/ Homelessness, United Funds/United Ways, Volunteer Services, YMCA/YWCA/YMHA/YWHA, Youth Organizations

Contributions Analysis

Giving Priorities: Education, united funds, health, social welfare, and civic and cultural organizations. Contributions to domestic organizations support public policy. For example, has supported the Atlantic Council, the Council on Competitiveness, and the Institute for International Economics. Overseas. In 1997, the company's foreign grants allocation totaled more than $200,000.
Arts & Humanities: 14%. Supports professional trade associations, economic development, and urban and community affairs. Cultural support includes the performing arts, museums, theaters, arts centers, and dance and music groups.
Civic & Public Affairs: (United Funds & United Way) 21%. Supports United Ways in company operating locations and in areas with a significant number of TRW employees.
Education: 40%. Supports colleges and universities. Special interests include mathematics, engineering, computer science, and business education. Also funds minority education and scholarship programs.
Health: 10%. Supports research institutes, emergency services, hospitals, youth organizations, and volunteer services.

Note: In addition to foundation giving, the company also makes direct grants. Foundation generally represents about 90% of the total TRW contributions program. Direct giving priorities are the same as those of the foundation.

Application Procedures

Initial Contact: Send proposal letter.
Application Requirements: Include brief outline of project, how it relates to the business of TRW Inc. and the objectives of the TRW Foundation. If the foundation is interested, it will request: brief a description of organizations, evidence of IRS tax-exempt status, purpose of funds sought, itemized project or program budget, list of committed financial supporters of project, how publicity will be developed, list of board of directors and officers and their affiliates, and copy of most recent Form 990.
Deadlines: The foundation accepts and reviews grant requests throughout the year, although calendar year budget cycle begins in September.

Restrictions

Grants are not made to groups with unusually high fund-raising expenses; fraternal, political, or labor organizations; religious organizations for sectarian purposes; individuals; endowments; or medical research organizations.
Grants are limited to organizations defined as tax-exempt under section 501(c) of the IRS code.

Additional Information

Publications: Annual Report

Corporate Officials

Joseph T. Gorman: chairman, chief executive officer B Rising Sun, IN 1937. ED Kent State University BA (1959); Yale University LLB (1962). PRIM CORP EMPL chairman, chief executive officer: TRW Inc. CORP AFFIL director: Reminger & Reminger Co.; member advisory board: BP America Inc.; director: Procter & Gamble Co.; director: Aluminum Co. North America. NONPR AFFIL director: United States-China Business Council; trustee: United Way Services; member: Prince Wales Business Leaders Forum; member: Trilateral Commission; member: Ohio Governments Education Management Council; member: President's Export Council; director: New American Schools Development Corp.; chairman: International Trade & Investment Task Force; trustee: Museum Arts Association; member: Council Foreign Relations; member: Defense Institute Initiative Steering Committee; member: Conference Board; member: Council Competitiveness; member: Competitiveness Policy Council; trustee: Cleveland Tomorrow; trustee: Committee for Economic Development; trustee: Cleveland Institute Art; trustee: Cleveland Playhouse; member: Center Strategic & International Studies; trustee: Cleveland Clinic Foundation; member: Business Roundtable; member: Business Council; director: Business Higher Education Forum.

Foundation Officials

Laura L. Johnson: manager PRIM CORP EMPL manager: TRW Inc.
Howard V. Knicely: president B Parkersburg, WV 1936. ED Marietta College BS (1958); West Virginia University MS (1960). PRIM CORP EMPL executive vice president human resources: TRW Inc. CORP AFFIL director: Morrison Products Inc. NONPR AFFIL chairman: U.S. Council International Business; member: West Virginia University College Business Economics; member: National Academy Human Resources; member: Society Human Resources Management; director: Kettering University; director: Labor Policy Association; member: BRT Employee Relations Committee.
Alan F. Senger: vice president PRIM CORP EMPL vice president: TRW Inc.

Grants Analysis

Disclosure Period: calendar year ending 1998
Total Grants: $7,394,582*
Number of Grants: 305 (approx)
Average Grant: $23,931 (approx)
Highest Grant: $500,000
Typical Range: $5,000 to $50,000
*Note: Giving excludes matching gifts. Grants analysis provided by foundation.

Recent Grants

Note: Grants derived from 1997 Form 990.

Arts & Humanities

260,000	Allen Theatre, Cleveland, OH
250,000	Musical Arts Association, Cambridge, MA
225,000	Wolf Trap for Performing Arts, Vienna, VA
185,000	Rainbow Children's Museum, Cleveland, OH
101,000	Cleveland Play House, Cleveland, OH
93,000	Cleveland Museum of Natural History, Cleveland, OH
93,000	Michigan Opera Theatre, Detroit, MI
61,500	Automotive Hall of Fame, Dearborn, MI
45,500	Cleveland Ballet, Cleveland, OH
35,000	WVIZ-TV Cleveland, Cleveland, OH

Civic & Public Affairs

5,750,000	Cleveland Foundation, Cleveland, OH
458,480	Matching Gifts to Education
175,053	Matching Gifts to Arts & Culture
149,100	Cleveland Tomorrow, Cleveland, OH
50,000	National Safe Kids Campaign, Washington, DC
40,000	Society of Automotive Engineers, Bloomfield, MI

City Year Cleveland, Cleveland, OH

Education

462,000	Case Western Reserve University, Cleveland, OH
433,000	California State University, Carson, CA
274,000	GMI Engineering & Management Institute, Flint, MI
186,000	Caltech, Pasadena, CA
186,000	New American Schools Development Corporation, Arlington, VA
177,300	University of Michigan, Ann Arbor, MI
175,000	West Virginia University, Morgantown, WV
100,000	University of Southern California, Los Angeles, CA
75,000	Cleveland Initiative for Education, Cleveland, OH
75,000	Cleveland Scholarship Programs, Cleveland, OH
68,000	Redondo Beach School District, Redondo Beach, CA
60,000	Cleveland Scholarship Programs, Cleveland, OH
60,000	United Negro College Fund, Fairfax, VA
40,000	Cornerstone Schools, Detroit, MI
38,000	Kent State University, Kent, OH
35,200	USA Today, Arlington, VA
35,000	Urban Community School, Cleveland, OH

Health

180,000	Hanna Perkins Center, Cleveland, OH
136,700	University Hospitals, Cleveland, OH
50,000	American Red Cross, Cleveland, OH

Science

350,000	Great Lakes Science Center, Cleveland, OH
93,000	Arizona Science Center, Phoenix, AZ
65,000	Alabama Space & Rocket Center, Huntsville, AL

Social Services

615,000	United Fund - Cleveland, Cleveland, OH
219,000	Detroit United Fund, Detroit, MI
132,000	Mesa United Fund, Mesa, AZ
125,000	Los Angeles United Fund, Los Angeles, CA
95,000	YMCA, Cleveland, OH
76,713	Manager of Volunteers
60,000	Center for Families & Childrens, Cleveland, OH
46,000	Santa Clara United Fund, Santa Clara, CA
37,700	Lafayette United Fund, Lafayette, IN
35,500	Boy Scouts of America, Sequoyah Council, Johnson City, TN

TU ELECTRIC CO.

Company Contact

Dallas, TX

Company Description

Assets: US$18,794,900,000
Employees: 6,474
SIC(s): 4911 Electric Services.
Parent Company: Texas Utilities Co., Dallas, TX, United States

Giving Contact

Ms. Jerry Larmay, Community Affairs Manager
TU Electric Co.
Care of TU Services
1506 Commerce, Suite 14 W
Dallas, TX 75201
Phone: (214)812-7110
Fax: (214)812-7320

Description

Organization Type: Corporate Giving Program
Giving Locations: headquarters and operating communities.
Grant Types: General Support.

Financial Summary

Total Giving: Contributes through corporate direct giving program only.

Typical Recipients

Arts & Humanities: Community Arts, Museums/Galleries, Performing Arts, Public Broadcasting, Theater
Civic & Public Affairs: Business/Free Enterprise, Economic Development, Professional & Trade Associations, Safety, Urban & Community Affairs, Zoos/Aquariums
Education: Colleges & Universities, Community & Junior Colleges
Environment: Environment-General
Health: Hospitals
Science: Scientific Organizations
Social Services: United Funds/United Ways

Contributions Analysis

Giving Priorities: Higher education, economic development, the environment, and the arts.

Application Procedures

Initial Contact: letter
Application Requirements: a description of organization, amount requested, purpose of funds sought, recently audited financial statement, proof of tax-exempt status
Deadlines: None.

Corporate Officials

Terry Griffin: senior vice presidento, director PRIM CORP EMPL senior vice president: Texas Utilities Service Inc.

Erle Allen Nye: chairman, chief executive officer, director B Fort Worth, TX 1937. ED Texas A&M University BEE (1959); Southern Methodist University JD (1965). PRIM CORP EMPL chairman, chief executive officer, director: Texas Utilities Co. CORP AFFIL chairman, chief executive officer: TU Electric; president: TU Services; chairman, chief executive officer: Texas Utilities Properties Inc.; chairman, chief executive officer: Texas Utilities Fuel Co.; chairman, chief executive officer: Texas Utilities Mining Co.; chairman: Texas Utilities Australia Pty Ltd.; chairman, chief executive officer: Texas Utilities Communications Inc.; chief executive officer: Basic Resources Inc.; chairman, chief executive officer: Chaco Energy Co. NONPR AFFIL member: Science Place; member: Texas State Bar Association; member advisory board: Salvation Army Dallas County; member: Dallas Foundation; member: Dallas Together Forum; member: Dallas Chamber of Commerce; member: Dallas Committee Foreign Relations; member: Dallas Bar Association; member: American Bar Association; member board: Boys & Girls Clubs America.

Giving Program Officials

Jerry Larmay: manager

TUCSON ELECTRIC POWER CO.

Company Contact

Tucson, AZ
Web: http://www.tucsonelectric.com

Company Description

Assets: US$2,568,500,000
Employees: 1,175
SIC(s): 4911 Electric Services.

Nonmonetary Support

Value: $500,000 (1995)
Type: Cause-related Marketing & Promotion; Donated Equipment; In-kind Services; Loaned Employees
Note: Donated equipment is in the form of used power poles and used office equipment.

Corporate Sponsorship

Type: Arts & cultural events; Festivals/fairs; Sports events
Note: Sponsors local Earth Day Festival.

Giving Contact

Sharon B. Foltz, Director, Community Relations
Tucson ElectricPower Co.
PO Box 711-DA 102
Tucson, AZ 85702
Phone: (520)884-3740
Fax: (520)770-2005
Email: foltz@primenet.com

Description

Organization Type: Corporate Giving Program
Giving Locations: company service area.
Grant Types: Capital, General Support.

Financial Summary

Total Giving: Contributes through corporate direct giving program only.

Typical Recipients

Arts & Humanities: Performing Arts, Theater
Civic & Public Affairs: Civic & Public Affairs-General
Education: Education-General
Social Services: Social Services-General, Youth Organizations

Application Procedures

Initial Contact: a brief letter of inquiry
Application Requirements: a description of organization, including specific objectives and expected outcomes, and timetable of the project; amount requested; size and composition of the population to be served by the program; recently audited financial statements; proof of tax-exempt status; description of how company's support will be acknowledged
Deadlines: July 1 of year prior to the year for which funds are being requested
Evaluative Criteria: impact on the community and on TEP; employee volunteer involvement; broad-based community impact; programmatic strength and financial viability of applicant

Restrictions

Does not support individuals; fraternal, social or veterans' organizations; religious organizations for sectarian purposes, political or lobbying groups; individual schools K-12 (all schools in TEP service area are offered safety, environmental, and science related curricula and supplemental resources at no charge); organizations serving people suffering from a single disease or medical condition, or for medical research; endowments; travel funds of any kind; adult sports; programs outside TEP service territory/employee community, or agencies that contribute more than 10% of budget to outside service territory.
Giving is restricted to service territory and predetermined focus, and TEP cannot donate electricity or electric service.

Corporate Officials

Ira R. Adler: executive vice president, chief financial officero, director B Mineola, NY 1950. ED Northwestern University BA (1972); University of Denver MSBA (1973). PRIM CORP EMPL executive vice president, chief financial officer: Tucson Electric Power Co. CORP AFFIL chairman, president, chief executive officer: Tucson Resources Inc.; executive vice president, director: UniSource Energy Corp.; executive vice president, chief financial officer: MEH Corp.; director: Nations Energy Corp.
Jim Tignatelli: chairman, president, chief executive officer, director PRIM CORP EMPL chairman, president, chief executive officer, director: Tucson Electric Power Co.

Giving Program Officials

Sharon B. Foltz: PRIM CORP EMPL director community relations: Tucson Electric Power Co.

Grants Analysis

Disclosure Period: calendar year ending

Recent Grants

Note: Grants derived from 1994 partial grants list.

Social Services

20,000 Tucson Metropolitan Ministries, Tucson, AZ

TYSON FOODS INC.

Company Contact

Springdale, AR
Web: http://www.tyson.com

Company Description

Revenue: US$7,362,900,000 (1999)
Profit: US$230,100,000 (1999)
Employees: 69,000 (1999)
Fortune Rank: 241, per FORTUNE Magazine's list of 500 Largest U.S. Corporations (1999).
FF 241
SIC(s): 0251 Broiler, Fryer & Roaster Chickens, 2048 Prepared Feeds Nec, 5144 Poultry & Poultry Products.

Tyson Foundation, Inc.

Giving Contact

Cheryl J. Tyson, President
Tyson Foundation, Inc.
2210 Oaklawn Dr.
Springdale, AR 72762-6999
Phone: (501)290-4955
Fax: (501)290-7984
Web: http://www.tysonfoundation.org

Description

EIN: 237087948
Organization Type: Corporate Foundation
Giving Locations: AR
Grant Types: General Support.

Giving Philosophy

'The Tyson Foundation exists to help Americans improve their quality of life through education. The Foundation is a private foundation, established in 1967. Through a grant process, numerous educational projects are funded annually in the communities in which we operate. The Foundation seeks to give back to these communities in an effort to ensure both their success and the success of their citizens for generations to come.' Foundation Brochure

Financial Summary

Total Giving: $1,336,856 (1998); $1,084,492 (1997); $816,081 (1996). Note: Contributes through foundation only.
Giving Analysis: Giving for 1996 includes: foundation ($615,700); foundation scholarships ($200,381); 1997: foundation ($860,300); foundation scholarships ($224,192); 1998: foundation ($1,140,450); foundation scholarships ($196,406)
Assets: $23,491,722 (1998); $22,963,991 (1997); $24,750,426 (1996)
Gifts Received: $12,000 (1998); $18,000 (1997); $30,000 (1996). Note: Contributions are received from Tyson Foods, Inc.

Typical Recipients

Arts & Humanities: Arts Associations & Councils, Arts Centers, Community Arts, Arts & Humanities-General, Museums/Galleries, Music
Civic & Public Affairs: Business/Free Enterprise, Economic Development, Economic Policy, Municipalities/Towns, Professional & Trade Associations, Safety, Urban & Community Affairs
Education: Agricultural Education, Arts/Humanities Education, Business Education, Colleges & Universities, Economic Education, Education Funds, Faculty Development, Education-General, Literacy, Medical Education, Minority Education, Private Education (Precollege), Public Education (Precollege), Science/Mathematics Education, Secondary Education (Public), Special Education, Student Aid
Environment: Environment-General, Wildlife Protection
Health: Children's Health/Hospitals, Emergency/Ambulance Services, Health Organizations, Heart, Single-Disease Health Associations
International: International Environmental Issues
Social Services: Community Centers, Community Service Organizations, Family Services, Food/Clothing Distribution, Homes, Recreation & Athletics, Scouts, Sexual Abuse, Substance Abuse, United Funds/United Ways, Youth Organizations

Contributions Analysis

Arts & Humanities: 1%.
Education: 44%. Support goes to educational projects including a large scholarship program, colleges and universities.
Environment: 35%. Funds environmental causes.
Social Services: 20%. Supports youth services.

Application Procedures

Initial Contact: For individual scholarships, send written request for preprinted application form and instructions; for other grants, send brief written request for information, outlining nature of project. If project meets initial criteria, foundation will send complete proposal guidelines.
Deadlines: April 20 for fall semester.

Additional Information

Publications: Application Form

Corporate Officials

Donald John Tyson: senior chairmano, director B Olathe, KS 1930. ED University of Arkansas. PRIM CORP EMPL senior chairman: Tyson Foods Inc. CLUB AFFIL Elks Club.
John H. Tyson: chairman, chief executive officer, president, director B 1953. ED Southern Methodist University BS (1975). PRIM CORP EMPL chairman, chief executive officer, president, director: Tyson Foods Inc. ADD CORP EMPL vice president: Tyson Breeders Inc.; vice chairman, president: Tyson Farms Texas Inc.; senior vice president: Tyson Seafood Group. CORP AFFIL senior vice president: Arctic AK Fisheries Corp.; chairman: Hudson Foods Inc.
Donald E. Wray: president, chief operating officer, director B 1937. ED University of Arkansas BS (1959). PRIM CORP EMPL president, chief operating officer, director: Tyson Foods Inc. CORP AFFIL senior vice president: Tyson Seafood Group.

Foundation Officials

James Burton Blair: trustee B Elkins, AR 1935. ED University of Arkansas BA (1955); University of Arkansas LLB (1957); University of Arkansas JD (1957). PRIM CORP EMPL general counsel: Tyson Foods Inc. CORP AFFIL director: Tyson Export Sales Inc.; director: Holly Farms Corp. NONPR AFFIL fellow: Arkansas Bar Association Foundation; trustee: University Arkansas; fellow: American College Trial Lawyers; member: Arkansas Bar Association; member: American Bar Association.
Joe F. Starr: trustee PRIM CORP EMPL director: Tyson Foods Inc.
Cheryl F. Tyson: trustee
John H. Tyson: trustee (see above)

Grants Analysis

Disclosure Period: calendar year ending 1998
Total Grants: $1,140,450*
Number of Grants: 27
Average Grant: $28,479*
Highest Grant: $400,000
Typical Range: $1,000 to $50,000
***Note:** Giving excludes scholarship. Average grant figure excludes highest grant.

Recent Grants

Note: Grants derived from 1998 Form 990.

Arts & Humanities

1,500	Rogers Historical Museum, Rogers, AR

Education

250,000	University of Arkansas Press Fund, Little Rock, AR
100,000	University of Arkansas at Pine Bluff, Pine Bluff, AR
50,000	Southern Arkansas University, Magnolia, AR
25,000	Johnson and Wales University, Providence, RI
11,200	Bethany Lutheran College, Mankato, MN
10,000	Arkansas School for the Deaf, Little Rock, AR
10,000	Independent College Fund of Arkansas, Little Rock, AR
10,000	The New School, Fayetteville, AR
5,000	The Bridge School, Los Angeles, CA
5,000	Broken Bow Public Schools, Broken Bow, NE
5,000	Springdale High School Band, Springdale, AR
5,000	University of Arkansas Foundation - Lady Razorbacks, Fayetteville, AR
3,500	Missouri Colleges Fund, St. Louis, MO
3,000	Haworth Public Schools, Haworth, OK
2,500	Arkansas Council on Economic Education, Lit, AR
2,500	Charleston Outdoor Classroom Project, Charleston, WV
2,500	Students in Free Enterprise, Springfield, MO
2,000	Westville School System, Westville, OK
500	London Elementary School, Walnut Cove, NC
250	Gentry Public Schools, Gentry, AR

Environment

400,000	International Game Fish Association, Palm Beach, FL

Social Services

200,000	Harvey and Bernice Jones Center for Families, Little Rock, AR
25,000	Arkansas Single Parent Scholarship Fund, Springdale, AR
5,000	Mount Magazine Girl Scout Council, Inc., Fort Smith, AR
5,000	National Council on Alcoholism and Drug Abuse, St. Louis, MO
1,000	Single Parent Scholarship Fund, Springdale, AR

UKROP'S SUPER MARKETS

Company Contact

Richmond, VA

Company Description

Employees: 5,185 (1999)
SIC(s): 5411 Grocery Stores.

Corporate Sponsorship

Type: Arts & cultural events; Festivals/fairs; Music & entertainment events; Pledge-a-thon; Sports events
Note: 10% of pretaxed dollars goes towards sponsorships.

Ukrop Foundation

Giving Contact

Gail Long, Assistant to the President
Ukrop's Super Markets
600 Southlake Boulevard
Richmond, VA 23236
Phone: (804)794-2401
Fax: (804)379-7368

Description

Founded: 1983
EIN: 541206389
Organization Type: Corporate Foundation
Giving Locations: VA: Richmond
Grant Types: General Support, Scholarship.

Financial Summary

Total Giving: $809,539 (fiscal year ending June 30, 1998); $599,427 (fiscal 1996); $802,883 (fiscal 1995). Note: Contributes through foundation only.
Assets: $12,572,579 (fiscal 1998); $8,281,564 (fiscal 1996); $6,306,692 (fiscal 1995)
Gifts Received: $8,896 (fiscal 1998); $333,291 (fiscal 1996); $194,344 (fiscal 1995). Note: Contributions are received from Ukrop's Super Markets.

Typical Recipients

Arts & Humanities: Arts Associations & Councils, Arts Funds, Community Arts, Ethnic & Folk Arts, Historic Preservation, History & Archaeology, Museums/Galleries, Opera, Theater
Civic & Public Affairs: African American Affairs, Business/Free Enterprise, Chambers of Commerce, Clubs, Economic Development, Civic & Public Affairs-General, Housing, Municipalities/Towns, Public Policy, Urban & Community Affairs, Zoos/Aquariums
Education: Afterschool/Enrichment Programs, Business Education, Colleges & Universities, Community & Junior Colleges, Education Funds, Education Reform, Education-General, Literacy, Medical Education, Minority Education, Private Education (Precollege), Public Education (Precollege), Religious Education, School Volunteerism, Science/Mathematics Education, Student Aid
Environment: Environment-General
Health: Cancer, Emergency/Ambulance Services, Hospitals, Medical Research, Public Health, Single-Disease Health Associations
International: International Organizations
Religion: Churches, Ministries, Religious Organizations, Religious Welfare
Science: Science Museums, Scientific Centers & Institutes, Scientific Organizations, Scientific Research
Social Services: Child Welfare, Community Service Organizations, Delinquency & Criminal Rehabilitation, Family Services, Food/Clothing Distribution, Homes, Recreation & Athletics, Shelters/Homelessness, Special Olympics, United Funds/United Ways, YMCA/YWCA/YMHA/YWHA, Youth Organizations

Contributions Analysis

Arts & Humanities: 5% to 10%. Primarily supports historic preservation.
Civic & Public Affairs: About 25%. Major support to business and economic development organizations. Also supports community affairs organizations, clubs, and housing.
Education: About 35%. Funds colleges and universities, with emphasis on business education; community-school partnerships; and literacy.
Religion: Less than 5%. Supports churches and religious organizations.
Science: Less than 5%. Mainly supports the Virginia Biotechnology Research Park and miscellaneous science organizations.
Social Services: 10% to 15%. Major support goes to the United Way. Also supports recreation, athletics programs, community service organizations, and the disabled.

Application Procedures

Initial Contact: Send a letter of inquiry.
Application Requirements: Include a description of organization, amount requested, proof of tax-exempt status, time frame for project, description of benefits of project or program, and list of board of directors.
Deadlines: November 15.

Corporate Officials

Gail Long: assistant to vice chairman PRIM CORP EMPL assistant to vice chairman: Ukrop's Super Markets.
James E. Ukrop: vice chairman, chief executive officer B 1937. PRIM CORP EMPL vice chairman, chief executive officer: Ukrop's Super Markets Inc. CORP AFFIL director: Owens & Minor Inc.; director: Richfood Holdings Inc.
Joseph Edward Ukrop: chairman B 1914. PRIM CORP EMPL chairman: Ukrop's Super Markets.
Robert S. Ukrop: president, chief operating officer B 1947. PRIM CORP EMPL president, chief operating officer: Ukrop's Super Markets. CORP AFFIL director: Hilb Rogal Hamilton.

Foundation Officials

Joseph N. Melton, Jr.: treasurer, director PRIM CORP EMPL treasurer: Ukrop's Super Markets.
Jacqueline L. Ukrop: director, secretary PRIM CORP EMPL secretary: Ukrop's Super Markets.
James E. Ukrop: vice chairman, chief executive officer, director (see above)
Joseph Edward Ukrop: director (see above)
Robert S. Ukrop: president, chief operating officer, director (see above)

Grants Analysis

Disclosure Period: fiscal year ending June 30, 1996
Total Grants: $599,427
Number of Grants: 151
Average Grant: $3,970
Highest Grant: $104,250
Typical Range: $1,000 to $8,000

Recent Grants

Note: Grants derived from fiscal 1997 Form 990.

Arts & Humanities

30,000	Valentine Museum, Richmond, VA
25,000	Arts Council, Richmond, VA
6,000	Black History Museum and Cultural Center, Richmond, VA
2,500	Hanover Tavern Foundation, Hanover, VA
2,000	Virginia Museum of Fine Arts Foundation, Richmond, VA
1,500	Historic Richmond Foundation, Richmond, VA

Civic & Public Affairs

40,519	Metropolitan Business Foundation, Richmond, VA
10,000	Richmond Renaissance, Richmond, VA
3,000	Bainbridge and Blackwell Community Development, Richmond, VA
2,500	Short Pump Center Building Fund, Glen Allen, VA
2,000	Single-Room Occupancy Housing, Richmond, VA
1,400	Ashland Hanover Chamber of Commerce, Ashland, VA

Education

51,000	Virginia State University, Richmond, VA
36,085	College of William and Mary, Williamsburg, VA
22,351	University of Richmond, Richmond, VA
20,351	College of William and Mary Athletic Education Foundation Scholarship Fund, Williamsburg, VA
15,000	Communities in Schools, Richmond, VA
13,000	Communities in Schools, Chesterfield, VA
10,000	Stargate, Richmond, VA
10,000	Virginia Foundation for Independent Colleges, Richmond, VA
5,500	University of Virginia Darden School of Business, Charlottesville, VA
5,240	Davidson College, Davidson, NC
5,000	Furman University, Greenville, SC
5,000	Medical College of Virginia Virginia Commonwealth University Hospital, Richmond, VA
5,000	Virginia Business Higher Education, Richmond, VA
3,500	Medical College of Virginia Foundation, Richmond, VA
3,500	New Community School, Richmond, VA
2,500	Montreat College, Montreat, NC
2,500	Read Center, Richmond, VA
2,500	Virginia College Fund, Richmond, VA
1,500	Mathematics and Science Center Foundation, Richmond, VA

Environment

2,500	Maymont Foundation, Richmond, VA

Health

8,500	Manchester Volunteer Rescue Squad, Chesterfield, VA
1,750	Bensley Bermuda Rescue Squad, Chester, VA

Religion

10,000	Popular Springs Baptist Church, Richmond, VA
5,000	Good Samaritan Inn, Richmond, VA
5,000	Sacred Heart Center, Richmond, VA
5,000	Virginia Baptist Homes, Culpeper, VA
4,000	Athletes for Jesus, Richmond, VA
3,500	Cross Over Ministry, Richmond, VA

Social Services

41,750	United Way Services, Richmond, VA
25,000	Central Virginia Food Bank, Richmond, VA
25,000	NOVA of Virginia Aquatics, Richmond, VA
25,000	Richmond Sports Backers, Richmond, VA
25,000	Richmond Sports Backers, Richmond, VA
25,000	YMCA, Richmond, VA
10,000	Police Athletic League, Richmond, VA
2,500	Ashland Youth Recreation Association, Ashland, VA
2,500	YMCA Northern Virginia, Richmond, VA
2,000	William Byrd Community House, Richmond, VA

ULTRAMAR DIAMOND SHAMROCK CORP.

Company Contact

San Antonio, TX
Web: http://www.diasham.com

Company Description

Former Name: Diamond Shamrock Corp.
Revenue: US$11,079,200,000 (1999)
Profit: US$173,200,000 (1999)
Employees: 17,200
Fortune Rank: 157, per FORTUNE Magazine's list of 500 Largest U.S. Corporations (1999).
FF 157
SIC(s): 2911 Petroleum Refining, 5411 Grocery Stores, 5541 Gasoline Service Stations.

Corporate Sponsorship

Value: $250,000
Type: Arts & cultural events; Music & entertainment events
Note: Sponsors tournaments and galas.

Giving Contact

Caroline Green, Director, Government & Public Affairs
Ultramar Diamond Shamrock Corp.
PO Box 696000
San Antonio, TX 78269-6000
Phone: (210)592-2000
Fax: (210)370-4320

Alternate Contact

Phone: (210)641-8780
Note: Alternate phone number is a recorded message on application procedures.

Description

Organization Type: Corporate Giving Program
Giving Locations: CO; LA; NM; TX
Grant Types: General Support, Matching, Multiyear/Continuing Support.

Giving Philosophy

'As an integral part of its public relations, Diamond Shamrock is committed to providing reasonable financial support to certain organizations that endeavor to improve our economic and social environment.'
Corporate Contributions Policy Guidelines

Financial Summary

Total Giving: $600,000 (1997 approx); $600,000 (1996 approx); $550,000 (1995 approx). Note: Contributes through corporate direct giving program only. Giving includes domestic subsidiaries.

Typical Recipients

Arts & Humanities: Arts & Humanities-General, Libraries
Civic & Public Affairs: Economic Development, Civic & Public Affairs-General
Education: Business Education, Education-General
Health: Emergency/Ambulance Services, Health-General
Social Services: Community Centers, Social Services-General

Application Procedures

Initial Contact: written request
Application Requirements: name and purpose of organization, amount requested, description of project funded, and financial background
Deadlines: None.
Evaluative Criteria: effectively addresses an important community need that is not adequately funded; structured to achieve anticipated results and fiscal responsibility; does not duplicate services already in place; uses ethical methods of publicity, promotion, solicitation, and management of funds; appropriate recognition given to company's identification, reputation, and public relations; must have 501 (c)(3) status
Decision Notification: corporate contributions committee meets every six weeks. A written response will be sent to each non-profit organization requesting funds.
Notes: Organizations applying for the employee recommendation grant should send a written proposal with the employee's recommendation. Recommendation grants are made on the last working day of March, June, September, and December. Proposals should be sent at least eight weeks prior to event deadline. All requests will be responded to after committee determination.

Restrictions

The company does not support individuals, religious organizations for sectarian purposes, political or lobbying groups, ticket mailings, or telephone solicitation fund-raising activities.
Only organizations exempt under 501(c)(3) of the IRS code are eligible for funding.

Additional Information

Company does not accept phone calls for initial contact.
In December 1996, Diamond Shamrock merged with Ultramar to become the Ultramar Diamond Shamrock Corp.
Publications: Corporate Contributions Policy Guidelines

Corporate Officials

Robert Sheldon Beadle: senior vice president corporate development B Orange, NJ 1949. ED Cornell University (1971); Cornell University (1976). PRIM CORP EMPL senior vice president corporate development: Ultramar Diamond Shamrock Corp.
Paul Eisman: senior vice president refining Southwest B Bad Krevznach, Germany 1955. ED Texas Technology University BS (1978). PRIM CORP EMPL senior vice president refining Southwest: Ultramar Diamond Shamrock Corp. ADD CORP EMPL vice president: Diamond Shamrodk Refining Marketing Co. CORP AFFIL director: Ultramar Inc.

Timothy Jon Fretthold: executive vice president, general counsel, director B Berea, OH 1949. ED Yale University BA (1971); Case Western Reserve University JD (1975). PRIM CORP EMPL executive vice president, general counsel, director: Ultramar Diamond Shamrock Corp. CORP AFFIL vice president, director: Petroleum/Chemical Environmental Services; senior vice president, general counsel: Ultramar Diamond Shamrock Refining & Marketing Co.; executive vice president, secretary, general counsel: National Convenience Stores Inc.
Christopher Havens: senior vice president PRIM CORP EMPL senior vice president: Ultramar Diamond Shamrock Corp. CORP AFFIL president: Ultramar Energy Inc.
Mary Heartman: vice president PRIM CORP EMPL vice president: Ultramar Diamond Shamrock Corp.
Roger Roy Hemminghaus: chairman, director B Saint Louis, MO 1936. ED Purdue University (1954-1956); Auburn University BS (1958); Louisiana State University (1963-1966). PRIM CORP EMPL chairman, director: Ultramar Diamond Shamrock Corp. CORP AFFIL director: Southwest Public Service Co.; chairman: National Convenience Stores Inc.; director: New Century Energies Inc.; director: Lubys Cafeterias Inc.; director: Federal Reserve Bank San Antonio; director: InterFirst Bank NA; chairman: DS Splitter Inc.; president, director: Diamond Shamrock Refining & Marketing Co.; chairman: Diamond Shamrock Stations. NONPR AFFIL member: San Antonio Chamber of Commerce; member: Tau Beta Pi; member: Phi Lambda Upsilon; member: Naval Architects & Marine Engineers; member: Phi Kappa Phi; director: National Petroleum Council; member: American Petroleum Institute; member: Kappa Alpha; member: American Institute Chemical Engineers; member: American Chemical Society. CLUB AFFIL Plaza Club; Fair Oaks Country Club; Petroleum Club.
William R. Klesse: executive vice president operations B Morristown, NJ 1946. ED University of Dayton (1968); West Texas State University (1973). PRIM CORP EMPL executive vice president operations: Ultramar Diamond Shamrock Corp. CORP AFFIL executive vice president: National Convenience Stores Inc.; president: Ultramar Inc.; senior vice president: Diamond Shamrock Refining & Marketing Co.
Diane Skillrud: assistant to chairman PRIM CORP EMPL assistant to chairman: Ultramar Diamond Shamrock Corp.

Grants Analysis
Disclosure Period: calendar year ending
Typical Range: $1,000 to $10,000

UNILEVER HOME & PERSONAL CARE U.S.A.

Company Contact
Greenwich, CT
Web: http://www.unilever.com

Company Description
Former Name: Chesebrough-Ponds.
Employees: 2,500
SIC(s): 2834 Pharmaceutical Preparations, 2844 Toilet Preparations, 3842 Surgical Appliances & Supplies.
Parent Company: Unilever Plc, PO Box 68, Blackfriars, London, England

Operating Locations
CA: Unilever Home & Personal Care U.S.A.; CT: Unilever Home & Personal Care U.S.A., Clinton; Unilever Home & Personal Care USA, Trumbull; IL: Unilever Home & Personal Care U.S.A., Chicago; MO: Unilever Home & Personal Care U.S.A., Jefferson City; PR: Unilever Home & Personal Care U.S.A., Las Piedras

Nonmonetary Support
Value: $398,000 (1995); $500,000 (1994)
Type: Donated Products
Contact: Elizabeth Cummiskey, Manager, Corporate Contributions
Note: Co. provides nonmonetary support.

Corporate Sponsorship
Type: Arts & cultural events; Music & entertainment events
Contact: Walter Luckett, Manager, Corporate Contributions

Chesebrough Foundation

Giving Contact
Walter Luckett, Manager, Corporate Contributions
Unilever Home & Personal Care U.S.A.
75 Merritt Boulevard
Trumbull, CT 06611
Phone: (203)381-2445

Description
EIN: 223043105
Organization Type: Corporate Foundation
Giving Locations: neighborhoods and communities near corporate headquarters and operating locations.
Grant Types: Award, Capital, Employee Matching Gifts, General Support.
Note: Employee matching gift ratio: 1 to 1.

Giving Philosophy
'Our commitment to help improve society begins with our company's ability to operate successfully as a vibrant, profitable business serving employees and consumers. At the same time, we recognize that public service is necessary for business to function effectively. Examples must be set which perpetuate a healthy community in which to live and work. At Chesebrough-Pond's, we are actively engaged in programs designed to achieve social improvement. We are especially supportive of activities which provide educational opportunities, particularly for the underprivileged--and we support and maintain a keen interest in vital health, welfare, civic and cultural programs..' *Programs for People: A Social Responsibility*

Financial Summary
Total Giving: $746,000 (1996 approx); $764,523 (1995); $569,773 (1994). Note: Contributes through foundation only. Giving includes foundation; matching gifts. 1995 Giving includes foundation ($667,884); matching gifts ($46,833); United Way ($49,806).
Assets: $8,739 (1994); $352,466 (1993)
Gifts Received: $761,031 (1995); $226,188 (1994); $501,738 (1993). Note: In 1993 and 1994, the foundation received shares of Colgate-Palmolive stock from Calvin-Klein Cosmetic Corp.

Typical Recipients
Arts & Humanities: Arts Centers, Arts Institutes, History & Archaeology, Libraries, Museums/Galleries, Music, Opera, Performing Arts, Public Broadcasting, Theater
Civic & Public Affairs: African American Affairs, Business/Free Enterprise, Civil Rights, Economic Development, Employment/Job Training, Civic & Public Affairs-General, Hispanic Affairs, Housing, Minority Business, Municipalities/Towns, Native American Affairs, Urban & Community Affairs
Education: Arts/Humanities Education, Business Education, Business-School Partnerships, Colleges & Universities, Economic Education, Education Associations, Education Funds, Engineering/Technological Education, Education-General, Medical Education, Minority Education, Private Education (Precollege), Science/Mathematics Education, Student Aid, Vocational & Technical Education
Environment: Air/Water Quality, Environment-General
Health: Adolescent Health Issues, Cancer, Clinics/ Medical Centers, Emergency/Ambulance Services, Health Organizations, Hospitals
International: International Relief Efforts
Religion: Religious Organizations, Religious Welfare
Science: Science Museums
Social Services: Big Brother/Big Sister, Child Welfare, Community Service Organizations, Counseling, Emergency Relief, Food/Clothing Distribution, Recreation & Athletics, Scouts, Senior Services, Shelters/ Homelessness, Special Olympics, Substance Abuse, United Funds/United Ways, Volunteer Services, YMCA/YWCA/YMHA/YWHA, Youth Organizations

Contributions Analysis
Giving Priorities: Education, community service, arts and culture, and minority programs.
Arts & Humanities: About 10%. Provides selective sponsorship and financial assistance to local performing and fine arts groups, including matching gifts.
Civic & Public Affairs: Less than 5%. Emphasis is on supporting community-based social service programs which benefit the underpriviledged, the homeless, theelderly and children. Preference is given to programs and activites not funded by the government or through the United Way. Support also goes to the Jackie Robinson Scholarship program which is awarded to college-bound minority students; the National Urban League particulalry in the area of education, includes support for the Black Executive Exchange Program (BEEP); Opportunities Industralization Center (OIC) which has been a positive force in helping unerprivlidged and under-educated Americans enter a system of gainful employment; provides scholarships for Native American youths through the American Indian Science and Engineering Society (AISES); andthrough a program of identifying and developing long term relationships with qualified minority suppliers of materials and services, including in-kind support.
Education: 90% to 95%. Support is focused on basic literacy programs, scholarships and fellowship grants to accredited institutions of higher learning; job skills training for the underemployed; and innovative programs designed to encourage youths in primary, middle and high schools to achieve excellence. Preference is given to programs and institutions which serve a broad population.

Application Procedures
Initial Contact: call to request guidelines and application
Application Requirements: completed application, organization's statement of purpose, description of goals, current activities, description of special activities, audience served and number of people participating, anticipated long term benefits, and other pertinent information
Deadlines: August 31 for funding in the proceeding year
Review Process: questionnaires are reviewed by the corporate contributions committee which meets annually in the Fall
Decision Notification: organizations will be notified by mail of funding decision
Notes: Requests must be submitted by the executive director or other key official.

Restrictions
Company does not provide grants for endowments. Company only considers requests from not-for-profit, nonpolitical, nonsectarian organizations that possess IRS 501(c)(3) status.

Additional Information
In October 1997, Unilever NV merged three of its consumer products businesses in the US to form a single company known as Unilever Home & Personal

Care USA (HPC-USA). Joining forces were Chesebrough-Pond's, Greenwich, CT; Helene Curtis, Chicago, IL; and Lever Brothers, New York, NY. HPC-USA is part of Unilever's Home & Personal Care North America Business Group, which also includes Elizabeth Arden, Calvin Klein Cosmetics, and Lever Pond's Canada.
As of July 1998, the foundation's name was still the Chesebrough Foundation.

Corporate Officials

Robert M. Phillips: president PRIM CORP EMPL president: Unilever Home & Personal Care U.S.A. CORP AFFIL president: Elizabeth Arden Interamerica; president: Unilever Home & Personal Care North America; president: Chesebrough-Ponds Manufacturing.

Foundation Officials

Anthony Chiafari: director
Elizabeth Cummiskey: foundation contact
Melvin H. Kurtz: secretary, director B New York, NY 1936. ED City University of New York BSChE (1959); Fordham University JD (1963). CORP AFFIL vice president, general counsel, secretary, director: Chesebrough-Ponds U.S.A. Co. NONPR AFFIL committee member: Patent & Trademark Off; director: Stamford Symphony Orchestra; member: New York Bar Association; member: New York Patent Law Association; member: American Bar Association; member: International Patent & Trademark Association.
Walter Lockett: manager corporate contributions
James W. McCall: president, director PRIM CORP EMPL vice president personnel & public relations: Chesebrough-Pond's U.S.A. CORP AFFIL vice president: Conopco Inc.
Robert Orlando: assistant treasurer
Barbara Tarasovich: treasurer

Grants Analysis

Disclosure Period: calendar year ending 1995
Total Grants: $667,884*
Number of Grants: 147
Average Grant: $4,543
Highest Grant: $83,500
Typical Range: $1,000 to $5,000
***Note:** Giving excludes matching gifts; United Way.

Recent Grants

Note: Grants derived from 1995 Form 990.

Arts & Humanities

12,000	Bruce Museum, Greenwich, CT
8,000	Stamford Symphony Orchestra, Stamford, CT
6,000	Metropolitan Opera Association, New York, NY
5,500	Westport Arts Center, Westport, CT
5,000	WNET/Channel 13, New York, NY
2,500	Greenwich Library, Greenwich, CT

Civic & Public Affairs

28,000	Opportunities Industrialization Center, Philadelphia, PA
17,500	National Urban League, New York, NY
10,000	Habitat for Humanity, Trumbull, CT
6,000	American Indian Science and Engineering Society, Boulder, CO
5,500	Urban League of Southwestern Fairfield County, Stamford, CT
5,000	Aspira of Connecticut, Bridgeport, CT
5,000	Opportunities Industrialization Corp, New London, CT
5,000	Opportunities Industrialization Corp, Waterbury, CT

Education

83,500	Jackie Robinson Foundation, New York, NY
25,000	Fashion Institute of Technology, New York, NY
12,000	National Medical Fellowships, New York, NY
10,000	Charles Smith Jr. Educational Center, Bridgeport, CT
10,000	Norwalk Community Technical College, Norwalk, CT
7,500	University of New Haven Engineering Scholarships, West Haven, CT
7,000	Fairfield University, Fairfield, CT
5,000	Lincoln University, Jefferson City, MO
5,000	Tufts College School for Dental Medicine, Medford, MA
5,000	University of Connecticut Chemistry Scholarships, Storrs, CT
3,000	Lincoln University Scholarships, Jefferson City, MO
3,000	Missouri Colleges Fund, Jefferson City, MO

Environment

5,000	Sound Waters, Stamford, CT

Health

75,000	Princess Grace Hospital Foundation, New York, NY
15,000	Middlesex Hospital, Portland, CT
10,000	American Cancer Society Dreamball, New York, NY
5,000	Greenwich Hospital Cancer Center, Greenwich, CT
3,500	American Red Cross, Greenwich, CT
2,500	Vitam Youth Treatment Center, Norwalk, CT

International

2,500	AmeriCares, New Canaan, CT

Religion

5,400	Cardinal Shehan Center, Bridgeport, CT
5,000	St. Luke's Community Center, Stamford, CT
2,500	Thomas Merton House, Bridgeport, CT

Science

2,500	Discovery Museum, Bridgeport, CT

Social Services

75,000	Kids in Crisis, Cos Cob, CT
32,000	Big Brothers and Big Sisters of America, Philadelphia, PA
20,000	United Way, Greenwich, CT
10,500	United Way Middlesex County, Middletown, CT
10,000	United Way, Jefferson City, MO
5,000	Pacific House, Stamford, CT
5,000	United Way, Raeford, CT
4,500	Hotline, Greenwich, CT
4,000	United Way Eastern Fairfield County, Bridgeport, CT
3,000	Big Brothers and Big Sisters of Southwestern Connecticut, New Haven, CT
3,000	YMCA, Greenwich, CT
2,500	Special Olympics, Plainville, CT

UNILEVER UNITED STATES, INC.

Company Contact

New York, NY
Web: http://www.unilever.com

Company Description

Revenue: US$8,969,733,000
Employees: 30,000
SIC(s): 7389 Business Services Nec.
Parent Company: Unilever NV, Rotterdam, Netherlands
Parent Revenue: US$45,180,000,000

Operating Locations

CA: Unilever United States, Inc.; Lawry's Foods, Monrovia; Adolph's Ltd., North Hollywood; Ablestik Laboratories, Rancho Dominguez; CT: Unilever United States, Inc., Clinton; Chesebrough-Pond's USA, Greenwich; UMEX Co., Greenwich; Unilever United States, Inc., Greenwich; Ragu Foods, Inc., Trumbull; FL: Unilever United States, Inc., Jacksonville; IL: Helene Curtis Industries, Chicago; Unichema U.S.A., Chicago; Quest, Itasca; Crossfield Chemical, Joliet; Van den Bergh Foods Co., Lisle; Custom Farm Seed, Momence; IN: Unilever United States, Inc.; MA: Gorton Group, Gloucester; Emerson & Cuming Specialty Polymers, Lexington; MD: Unilever United States, Inc.; Lever, Baltimore; Quest International Flavors & Foods, Owings Mills; MI: Diversey Lever, Plymouth; MO: Unilever United States, Inc.; Lever, Saint Louis; NJ: National Starch and Chemical Co., Bridgewater; Quest International Fragrances, Budd Lake; Unilever Research & Development Co., Edgewater; Permabond International, Englewood; Lipton Co., Englewood Cliffs; Unilever United States, Inc., Englewood Cliffs; NY: Calvin Klein Cosmetics Co., New York; Elizabeth Arden Co., New York; Lever Brothers Co., New York; Lever Brothers Household Products Div., New York; Lever Brothers Industrial Div., New York; Parfums International Ltd., New York; Unilever United States, New York; OH: DuBois Chemicals, Cincinnati; PR: Unilever United States, Inc.; TN: Alco Chemical, Chattanooga; WA: Quest, Kent; WI: Good Humor/Breyers Ice Cream, Green Bay

Nonmonetary Support

Type: Cause-related Marketing & Promotion; Donated Equipment; Donated Products

Unilever Foundation

Giving Contact

John T. Gould, Jr., Director, Corporate Affairs
Unilever United States, Inc.
390 Park Avenue
New York, NY 10022
Phone: (212)906-4694
Fax: (212)906-4666

Description

Founded: 1952
EIN: 136122117
Organization Type: Corporate Foundation
Giving Locations: headquarters and operating communities.
Grant Types: Emergency, Employee Matching Gifts, General Support.

Financial Summary

Total Giving: $4,000,000 (2000 approx); $3,000,000 (1999 approx); $1,477,000 (1996 approx). Note: Contributes through foundation only. 1995 Giving includes United Way ($325,400).
Assets: $499,968 (1995); $122,103 (1994); $331,539 (1993)
Gifts Received: $1,273,563 (1995); $1,321,875 (1994); $1,206,425 (1993). Note: In 1995, the foundation received contributions from the sale of 20,500 shares of Colgate Palmolive Co. stock.

Typical Recipients

Arts & Humanities: Arts Centers, Arts Institutes, Historic Preservation, Libraries, Museums/Galleries, Music, Performing Arts, Public Broadcasting, Theater
Civic & Public Affairs: African American Affairs, Botanical Gardens/Parks, Business/Free Enterprise, Civil Rights, Economic Development, Economic Policy, Employment/Job Training, Civic & Public Affairs-General, Municipalities/Towns, Nonprofit Management, Professional & Trade Associations, Public Policy, Safety, Urban & Community Affairs, Zoos/Aquariums
Education: Agricultural Education, Business Education, Business-School Partnerships, Colleges & Universities, Economic Education, Education Associations, Elementary Education (Private), Engineering/Technological Education, International Studies, Literacy, Medical Education, Minority Education, Private

Education (Precollege), Public Education (Precollege), Science/Mathematics Education, Student Aid
Environment: Environment-General
Health: Children's Health/Hospitals, Health Organizations, Hospitals, Single-Disease Health Associations, Trauma Treatment
International: Health Care/Hospitals, Human Rights, International Affairs, International Relations, International Relief Efforts
Religion: Religious Welfare
Science: Science Museums, Scientific Organizations
Social Services: Community Centers, Community Service Organizations, Day Care, Food/Clothing Distribution, People with Disabilities, Recreation & Athletics, Senior Services, Shelters/Homelessness, Substance Abuse, United Funds/United Ways, YMCA/YWCA/YMHA/YWHA, Youth Organizations

Contributions Analysis

Giving Priorities: Civic and community affairs, education, environmental concerns, and health.
Civic & Public Affairs: 46%. Interests include community improvement, the environment, legal organization, economic development and public policy.
Education: 26%. Supports school programs for K-12 children; scholarships for children of employees and minorities; colleges, universities and graduate schools that have research, recruiting, scholarship programs or special minority-help programs; programs that combat illiteracy; job training or retraining program; scientific research groups whose activities are directly related to the participating companies interest; consumer and economic research and education programs; and programs that promote free enterprise.
Environment: 23%. Supports sustainable development of agriculture, clean water, and fisheries. Interest in recycling programs.
Health: 5%. Supports United Way campaigns; hospitals and health care facilities; homeless and feeding programs; programs that address needs of minorities, the disadvantaged and victims of domestic violence; programs for the prevention and treatment of substance abuse; youth and senior citizens groups; and organizations that are directly related to participating companies' interest.

Application Procedures

Initial Contact: letter or proposal on organization's letterhead and signed by its chief executive officer
Application Requirements: the grant's purpose, background information on the organization, the most recent annual report, a copy of the current operating budget, proof of tax-exempt status
Deadlines: None; budget is determined annually in February.
Evaluative Criteria: makes contributions to organizations with clearly defined, achievable goals that have demonstrated their effectiveness and fiscal responsibility.

Restrictions

The foundation does not support labor organizations; veterans groups for fraternal/social purposes; political activities; capital campaigns (other than hospitals in facilities locations); operating funds of member agencies of United Way; individuals; goodwill advertising; fundraising events and testimonial dinners; or sectarian religious organizations.

Corporate Officials

Richard A. Goldstein: president, chief executive officer, director B Boston, MA 1942. ED Boston University LLB; University of Massachusetts BBA (1963); Harvard University LLM (1968). PRIM CORP EMPL president, chief executive officer, director: Unilever US, Inc. ADD CORP EMPL chairman: Lipton Co.
John T. Gould, Jr.: director corporate affairs B Brunswick, ME 1938. ED Bowdoin College (1960). PRIM CORP EMPL director corporate affairs: Unilever US, Inc. NONPR AFFIL director: Public Affairs Council; member: Public Relations Society America; director: National Council Economic Education; director: National Press Foundation; director: International Food Information Council. CLUB AFFIL Overseas Press Club; National Press Club.

Foundation Officials

Carollyn Albstein: treasurer
John T. Gould, Jr.: vice president (see above)
Thomas J. Hoolihan: secretary
T. Keith Rowland: director
Paul W. Wood: president

Grants Analysis

Disclosure Period: calendar year ending 1995
Total Grants: $948,922*
Number of Grants: 287
Average Grant: $3,306
Highest Grant: $93,405
Typical Range: $1,000 to $5,000
*Note: Giving excludes United Way.

Recent Grants

Note: Grants derived from 1995 Form 990.

Arts & Humanities

15,000	Mount Rushmore Preservation Fund, Rapid City, SD
10,000	Lincoln Center for Performing Arts, New York, NY
10,000	New York Public Library, New York, NY
8,000	Metropolitan Museum of Art, New York, NY

Civic & Public Affairs

20,000	National Park Foundation, New York, NY
17,500	State Legislative Leaders Foundation, Centerville, MA
15,000	Citizens Research Education Network, Hartford, CT
12,000	National Governors Association Center for Policy Research, Washington, DC
10,000	American Enterprise Institute for Public Policy Research, Washington, DC
10,000	Citizens for a Sound Economy, Washington, DC
10,000	National Press Foundation, Washington, DC
10,000	NJBISEC

Education

93,405	National Merit Scholarship Corp, Evanston, IL
20,000	Massachusetts Institute of Technology Sloan School of Management, Cambridge, MA
10,000	Columbia Business School, New York, NY
10,000	Columbia Business School, New York, NY -- scholarship
10,000	Cornell University College of Agriculture and Life Science, Ithaca, NY
10,000	Duke University, Durham, NC -- scholarship
10,000	Duke University, Durham, NC
10,000	Lehigh University Chemistry Department, Bethlehem, PA
10,000	New York University, New York, NY
10,000	New York University, New York, NY -- scholarship
10,000	Northwestern University, Evanston, IL
10,000	Northwestern University, Evanston, IL -- scholarship
10,000	United Negro College Fund, New York, NY
10,000	University of Michigan, Ann Arbor, MI
10,000	University of Michigan, Ann Arbor, MI -- scholarship
10,000	University of Pennsylvania Trustees, Philadelphia, PA
10,000	University of Pennsylvania Trustees, Philadelphia, PA
10,000	Yale University Department of Dermatology, New Haven, CT

Health

18,000	New York Hospital, New York, NY -- Patient Database Fund
7,500	Johns Hopkins Children's Center, Baltimore, MD

International

20,000	Freedom House, New York, NY
15,000	African Medical and Research Foundation, New York, NY
12,000	International Food Information Council, Washington, DC

Science

10,000	American Museum of Natural History, New York, NY

Social Services

35,000	United Way, Tri-State, NY
26,000	Lake Area United Way, Griffith, IN
20,000	Jackie Robinson Foundation, New York, NY
15,000	Doe Fund, New York, NY
15,000	Jericho Project, New York, NY
13,000	United Way Bergen County, Oradell, NJ
10,000	Binding Together, New York, NY
10,000	Citymeals on Wheels, New York, NY
10,000	Food for Survival, New York, NY
10,000	Hope Community, New York, NY
10,000	United Way Central Maryland, Baltimore, MD
8,000	United Way Bartow County, Cartersville, GA
7,500	United Way Ohio Valley, Owensboro, KY
7,500	United Way Will County, Joliet, IL

UNION CAMP CORP.

Company Contact

Wayne, NJ
Web: http://www.unioncamp.com

Company Description

Revenue: US$4,502,900,000
Employees: 19,268

Nonmonetary Support

Value: $20,000 (1990); $20,000 (1989); $20,000 (1988)
Type: Donated Products; Loaned Employees

Union Camp Charitable Trust

Giving Contact

Phyllis M. Epp, Manager, Community & State Relations
Union Camp Corp.
1600 Valley Road
Wayne, NJ 07470
Phone: (201)628-2482
Fax: (201)628-2349

Description

EIN: 136034666
Organization Type: Corporate Foundation
Giving Locations: principally near operating locations and to national organizations.
Grant Types: Award, Capital, Employee Matching Gifts, Endowment, Fellowship, General Support, Matching, Scholarship.

Financial Summary

Total Giving: $2,370,854 (1997); $2,460,171 (1996); $2,052,725 (1995). Note: Contributes through corporate direct giving program and foundation. Giving includes foundation. 1996 Giving includes United Way ($433,253).
Assets: $1,803,090 (1996); $1,200,870 (1995); $214,934 (1994)
Gifts Received: $3,000,000 (1996); $3,000,000 (1995); $1,700,000 (1994). Note: Trust receives contributions from the Union Camp Corp.

Typical Recipients

Arts & Humanities: Arts Associations & Councils, Arts Festivals, Arts Funds, Community Arts, Ethnic & Folk Arts, Historic Preservation, Libraries, Literary Arts, Museums/Galleries, Music, Public Broadcasting, Theater, Visual Arts
Civic & Public Affairs: Business/Free Enterprise, Economic Development, Economic Policy, Employment/Job Training, Civic & Public Affairs-General, Law & Justice, Legal Aid, Municipalities/Towns, Professional & Trade Associations, Public Policy, Safety, Urban & Community Affairs, Women's Affairs, Zoos/Aquariums
Education: Agricultural Education, Business Education, Business-School Partnerships, Colleges & Universities, Community & Junior Colleges, Continuing Education, Economic Education, Education Associations, Education Funds, Elementary Education (Private), Elementary Education (Public), Engineering/Technological Education, Environmental Education, Faculty Development, Legal Education, Literacy, Medical Education, Minority Education, Preschool Education, Private Education (Precollege), Public Education (Precollege), Religious Education, Science/Mathematics Education, Secondary Education (Private), Secondary Education (Public), Social Sciences Education, Special Education, Student Aid, Vocational & Technical Education
Environment: Air/Water Quality, Environment-General, Resource Conservation
Health: Children's Health/Hospitals, Clinics/Medical Centers, Emergency/Ambulance Services, Geriatric Health, Health Funds, Health Organizations, Hospices, Hospitals, Medical Rehabilitation, Medical Research, Medical Training, Mental Health, Nursing Services, Single-Disease Health Associations
Religion: Churches, Religious Organizations, Religious Welfare, Synagogues/Temples
Science: Science Exhibits & Fairs, Scientific Organizations
Social Services: Child Welfare, Community Centers, Community Service Organizations, Counseling, Day Care, Delinquency & Criminal Rehabilitation, Domestic Violence, Emergency Relief, Family Planning, Family Services, Homes, People with Disabilities, Recreation & Athletics, Scouts, Senior Services, Shelters/Homelessness, Substance Abuse, United Funds/United Ways, Volunteer Services, YMCA/YWCA/YMHA/YWHA, Youth Organizations

Contributions Analysis

Giving Priorities: Education, health, social welfare, and civic organizations.
Arts & Humanities: 5% to 15%. Public broadcasting, theater festivals, and libraries.
Civic & Public Affairs: 15% to 20%. Environmental affairs groups, fire and safety organizations, economics and economic development, law and justice, public policy, civil rights, and free enterprise.
Education: 40% to 50%. Higher education institutions, with emphasis on scientific and technological institutes; paper industry-related education; and elementary and secondary education, independent and minority college funds, scholarships, and education associations. Also administers a matching gifts program in education.
Health: 30% to 40%. United funds, youth organizations, children's and community hospitals, and single-disease health associations. The remainder is disbursed among employment and job training, children's homes, medical rehabilitation, emergency and ambulance services,delinquency and crime councils, the disabled, and religious welfare.

Application Procedures

Initial Contact: brief letter or proposal
Application Requirements: a description of organization, amount requested, purpose of funds sought, recently audited financial statement, proof of tax-exempt status
Deadlines: None.
Decision Notification: monthly

Corporate Officials

Jerry Hunter Ballengee: president, chief operating officer, director B Martinsville, VA 1937. ED Virginia Polytechnic Institute & State University BSME (1962); Xavier University MBA (1974). PRIM CORP EMPL president, chief operating officer, director: Union Camp Corp. CORP AFFIL director: Goulds Pumps Inc.; director: United Cities Gas Co.; director: Chicago Bridge Iron Co. NONPR AFFIL member: Paper Industry Management Association; member, director: Tech Association Pulp & Paper Industry; trustee: Institute Paper Science Technology.
Thomas G. Lambrix: senior vice president communications & public affairs PRIM CORP EMPL senior vice president communications & public affairs: Union Camp Corp.
William Craig McClelland: chairman, chief executive officer, director B Orange, NJ 1934. ED Princeton University AB (1952); Harvard University MBA (1965). PRIM CORP EMPL chairman, chief executive officer, director: Union Camp Corp. CORP AFFIL director: Quaker State Oil Refining Corp.; director: Quaker State Corp.; director: PNC Bank Corp.; director: PNC Fin Corp.; director: Hammermill Paper Co.; director: International Paper Co.; director: Allegheny Ludlum Corp.; director: Allegheny Teledyne Inc. NONPR AFFIL director: Pittsburgh Theological Seminary.
Sydney N. Phin: director human resources PRIM CORP EMPL director human resources: Union Camp Corp.
James M. Reed: vice chairman, chief financial officer, director B New Sharon, IA 1933. ED Simpson College BSBA (1954). PRIM CORP EMPL vice chairman, chief financial officer, director: Union Camp Corp. CORP AFFIL director: Martin Marietta Materials Inc.; director: Savannah Foods & IDS Inc.; director: Bush Boake Allen Inc.

Foundation Officials

Jerry N. Carter: trustee PRIM CORP EMPL senior vice president human resources: Union Camp Corp.
William Craig McClelland: trustee (see above)
James M. Reed: trustee (see above)

Grants Analysis

Disclosure Period: calendar year ending 1996
Total Grants: $2,026,918*
Number of Grants: 1,492
Average Grant: $1,359
Highest Grant: $161,500
Typical Range: $50 to $50,000
***Note:** Giving excludes United Way.

Recent Grants

Note: Grants derived from 1996 Form 990.

Arts & Humanities

50,000 University of Virginia Darden School of Business, Charlottesville, VA -- Camp Library
25,000 Alabama Shakespeare Festival, Montgomery, AL
10,000 New Jersey Symphony, Newark, NJ

Civic & Public Affairs

25,000 Riordan Foundation, Los Angeles, CA
15,000 American Enterprise Institute for Public Policy Research, Washington, DC
12,000 Atlantic Legal Foundation, New York, NY
10,000 Adhesive and Sealant Council Education Foundation, Washington, DC

Education

161,500 Educational Testing Service, Princeton, NJ -- Sponsored Scholarship Programs
30,000 Georgia Tech Pulp and Paper Foundation, School of Chemical Engineering, Atlanta, GA
26,000 Savannah Christian Prep School, Savannah, GA
25,000 Autauga County Vocational Education, Prattville, AL
25,000 Royce Learning Center, Savannah, GA
24,000 Georgia 4-H Foundation, Eatonton, GA
20,871 College Scholarship Service, Princeton, NJ
20,549 Georgia Southern University, Statesboro, GA
20,000 Clemson University Power Electronics Lab, Clemson, SC
20,000 Educational Testing Service, Princeton, NJ -- Sponsored Scholarship Programs
19,792 Georgia Southern University, Statesboro, GA
18,778 Armstrong Atlantic State College, Savannah, GA
17,000 Virginia Foundation for Independent Colleges, Lynchburg, VA
13,000 Franklin City Schools New Horizons Club, Franklin, VA
11,500 P.D. Camp Community College Education Environment Institute, Franklin, VA
10,000 Auburn University Pulp and Paper Foundation, Auburn, AL
10,000 Miami University Pulp and Paper Foundation Fellowship, Oxford, OH
10,000 National Future Farmers of America Foundation, Madison, WI
10,000 North Carolina State University Pulp and Paper Foundation, Raleigh, NC
10,000 University of Massachusetts, Amherst, MA -- Chemical Engineering Fellowship Fund
10,000 University of South Carolina Chemical Engineering, Columbia, SC
9,000 Inroads, Charlotte, NC

Environment

10,000 Champions of the Environment, Columbia, SC
10,000 Conservation Fund, Arlington, VA
10,000 Conservation Fund, Arlington, VA
10,000 Nature Conservancy, Arlington, VA

Health

12,500 TYMC, Prattville, AL
10,000 Memorial Sloan-Kettering Hospital, New York, NY
10,000 Valley Hospital, Ridgewood, NJ

Social Services

242,807 United Way Coastal Empire, Savannah, GA
43,077 United Way, Franklin, VA
43,000 United Way Autauga County, Prattville, AL
42,000 United Way Midlands, Columbia, SC
22,924 United Way Passaic County, Paterson, NJ
17,650 United Way Piedmont, Spartanburg, SC
15,000 SPARK/United Way Passaic County, Wayne, NJ -- WPW Communication Campaign
15,000 YMCA, Montgomery, AL -- first of five payments

13,200	Boy Scouts of America, Columbia, SC
13,000	James L. Camp, Jr. YMCA, Franklin, VA -- sustaining membership
13,000	United Way Passaic County, Paterson, NJ
11,533	United Way, Savannah, GA
10,000	Hudson Hill Community Center, Savannah, GA
10,000	United Fund Tuscarawas County, Dover, OH

Union Carbide Corp.

Company Contact

Danbury, CT
Web: http://www.unioncarbide.com

Company Description

Revenue: US$5,870,000,000 (1999)
Profit: US$291,000,000 (1999)
Employees: 11,627
Fortune Rank: 292, per FORTUNE Magazine's list of 500 Largest U.S. Corporations (1999).
FF 292
SIC(s): 2819 Industrial Inorganic Chemicals Nec, 2821 Plastics Materials & Resins, 2833 Medicinals & Botanicals, 2869 Industrial Organic Chemicals Nec.

Operating Locations

Argentina: Union Carbide Argentina, Buenos Aires; Austria: Union Carbide Austria GmbH, Vienna; Belgium: Union Carbide Benelux NV, Antwerp; Brazil: Union Carbide do Brasil SA, Sao Paulo; Ecuador: UCAR Polimeros y Quimicos CA, Guayaquil; India: Union Carbide Indonesia PT, Jakarta; Japan: Union Carbide Japan KK, Tokyo; Republic of Korea: Union Carbide Chemicals Korea Ltd., Seoul; Philippines: Union Carbide Phillipines (Far East) Inc., Metroa Manila, Makati; Republic of South Africa: Union Carbide South Africa, Johannesburg; Singapore: Union Carbide Asia Pacific Inc., Singapore; Switzerland: Union Carbide (Europe) SA, Geneva; Venezuela: Union Carbide Comercial CA, Caracas

Nonmonetary Support

Range: $50,000 - $130,000
Type: Donated Equipment; In-kind Services; Workplace Solicitation
Volunteer Programs: Company sponsors an employee volunteer mentoring program for children.

Union Carbide Foundation

Giving Contact

Deborah Surat, Manager, Corporate Contributions
Union Carbide Corp.
39 Old Ridgebury Road
L4-507
Danbury, CT 06817
Phone: (203)794-6945

Alternate Contact

George H. Buchanan
Phone: (203)794-7044

Description

EIN: 223064103
Organization Type: Corporate Foundation
Giving Locations: CT: Danbury; LA: Taft; NJ: Bound Brook, Edison, Weston Canal; SC: South Charleston; TX: Seadrift, Texas City; WV: Kanawa Valley nationally.
Grant Types: General Support.

Financial Summary

Total Giving: $2,843,810 (1998); $2,525,235 (1997); $4,255,955 (1996). Note: Contributes through corporate direct giving program and foundation.
Giving Analysis: Giving for 1996 includes: corporate direct giving ($2,670,000); foundation ($1,589,955); 1997: foundation ($1,655,235); corporate direct giving ($870,000); 1998: foundation ($1,690,810); corporate direct giving ($743,841); domestic and international subsidiaries ($225,000); corporate grants to United Way ($184,159)
Assets: $21,047,312 (1998); $19,078,494 (1997); $13,115,708 (1996)
Gifts Received: $3,760,000 (1997); $3,895,000 (1996); $1,675,000 (1995). Note: Contributions are received from Union Carbide Corp.

Typical Recipients

Arts & Humanities: Arts Centers, Libraries, Museums/Galleries, Performing Arts, Public Broadcasting
Civic & Public Affairs: African American Affairs, Business/Free Enterprise, Employment/Job Training, Hispanic Affairs, Law & Justice, Legal Aid, Minority Business, Nonprofit Management, Parades/Festivals, Professional & Trade Associations, Public Policy, Safety, Urban & Community Affairs, Women's Affairs
Education: Business Education, Business-School Partnerships, Colleges & Universities, Continuing Education, Economic Education, Education Associations, Education Funds, Education Reform, Engineering/Technological Education, Environmental Education, Faculty Development, Education-General, International Exchange, International Studies, Literacy, Medical Education, Minority Education, Private Education (Precollege), Public Education (Precollege), School Volunteerism, Science/Mathematics Education, Special Education, Student Aid, Vocational & Technical Education
Environment: Environment-General, Resource Conservation, Watershed, Wildlife Protection
Health: Clinics/Medical Centers, Home-Care Services, Hospices, Hospitals, Medical Rehabilitation
International: International Environmental Issues
Science: Science Exhibits & Fairs, Science Museums, Scientific Centers & Institutes, Scientific Organizations, Scientific Research
Social Services: At-Risk Youth, Child Welfare, Community Centers, Community Service Organizations, Emergency Relief, Family Services, People with Disabilities, United Funds/United Ways, Volunteer Services, YMCA/YWCA/YMHA/YWHA, Youth Organizations

Contributions Analysis

Giving Priorities: Education, United Way, hospitals, environment, public policy research, and arts. International giving is not a priority. Has supported the World Environment Center and the World Wildlife Fund. Union Carbide also supports the Global Environmental Management Initiative, a group of 23 leading corporations fostering environmental excellence by business worldwide.
Arts & Humanities: 2%. Promotes museums and libraries.
Civic & Public Affairs: 14%. Supports public policy research and safety organizations; diversity is a priority.
Education: 60%. Highest priority, with support going to public education reform and secondary and elementary programs that promote math, science, and engineering. Particular interest in encouraging minority students, women, and at-risk youth in engineering education and careers.
Environment: 7%. Supports environmental preservation.
Health: 16%. Supports united funds, youth programs, hospices, and health related issues.
Note: Total contributions in 1998.

Application Procedures

Initial Contact: Send a brief letter of inquiry.
Application Requirements: Include goals of organization; purpose of project; amount of money requested; budget (include sources of revenue and expenses); expected results of project and how success will be measured; proof of tax-exempt status; explanation of why project is important to Union Carbide (Board of Directors looks for proposals that are sponsored by company operating sites).
Deadlines: January 1 and July 1.
Review Process: Contributions office evaluates and makes recommendations to foundation board.
Evaluative Criteria: Project applicability to foundation's giving priorities, management sponsorship, employee volunteer participation.
Decision Notification: Foundation's board of directors meets in the spring and fall.

Restrictions

Company does not support fraternal organizations; goodwill advertising; individuals; lobbying, advertising, or capital campaigns; public-supported health organizations; religious organizations for sectarian purposes; athletic, labor or veterans groups; dinners; or organizations outside the U.S. Company does not offer sponsorships.

Additional Information

Organizations that receive grants are expected to provide progress reports, as well as a final report.
Grants are not automatically renewed and are not guaranteed from year to year.
Nonmonetary support is decentralized at various locations, handled by plant managers, employee relations administrators, and community affairs representatives.
Company prefers to initiate contact with organizations working in areas of interest, rather than being contacted by organizations.
Contacts for grants at local company facilities: Marion Jones, Bound Brook, NJ, (908)563-5872. Linda Sprick, Danbury, CT, (203)794-6983. Fred McKenzie, Edison, NJ, (908)248-6055. Kathleen Hunt, Seadrift, TX, (512)553-3058. Thad Epps, S. Charleston, WV, (304)747-5487. Stanley Roy Dufrene, Taft, LA, (504)468-4472. Jim Hockersmith, Texas City, TX, (409)948-5269. Ellie Hall, Weston Canal, NJ, (908)271-2021.
In August 1999, Union Carbide Corp. and Dow Chemcial Co. announced the approval of a definitive merger agreement. The anticipated closing date of the merger is the second quarter of 2000.
Publications: Charitable Contributions Brochure

Corporate Officials

William H. Joyce: chairman, president, chief executive officer, chief operating officer B Greensburg, PA 1935. ED Pennsylvania State University BS (1957); New York University MBA (1971); New York University PhD (1984). PRIM CORP EMPL chairman, president, chief executive officer, chief operating officer: Union Carbide Corp. ADD CORP EMPL president: Union Carbide Inter America. CORP AFFIL director: Reynolds Metals Co.; director: CVS Corp. NONPR AFFIL member: Society Plastics Engineers; trustee: Universitys Research Association; member: Institute Electrical & Electronics Engineers; member: National Academy Engineering; director: American Plastics Council.

Foundation Officials

Joseph S. Byck: vice president B Stamford, CT 1941. ED Princeton University (1962); Columbia University (1967). PRIM CORP EMPL vice president: Union Carbide Corp. NONPR AFFIL member: American Chemical Society.
Sue DeCarlo: treasurer
John MacDonald: president PRIM CORP EMPL assistant corporate secretary: Union Carbide Corp.
Elen Malloy: secretary

Elen Molloy: secretary
Deborah Surat: assistant secretary PRIM CORP EMPL manager corporate contributions: Union Carbide Corp.

Grants Analysis

Disclosure Period: calendar year ending 1998
Total Grants: $1,690,810*
Number of Grants: 225
Average Grant: $7,515
Highest Grant: $150,000
Typical Range: $1,000 to $10,000
***Note:** Giving includes foundation giving only.

Recent Grants

Note: Grants derived from 1998 Form 990.

Arts & Humanities

20,000 Center for the Arts and Sciences of West Virginia, Charleston, WV -- Planetarium & Sunrise Museum

Civic & Public Affairs

15,000 Industrial Relations Council on GOALS, East Lansing, MI
10,000 Center on Work and Family, Boston, MA -- Issue Papers
10,000 Harvard Center for Risk Analysis, Boston, MA

Education

75,000 St. Charles Parish School Board, Luling, LA
75,000 St. Charles Parish School Board, Luling, LA
60,000 American Institute of Chemical Engineers, New York, NY
45,000 National Consortium - GEM PhD Eng. Program, Notre Dame, IN -- PhD Engineering Program
35,000 Education Alliance, Charleston, WV
30,000 National Action Council for Minorities in Engineering, New York, NY
30,000 National Consortium - GEM MS Program, Notre Dame, IN -- Masters Engineering Program
30,000 National Society of Black Engineers, Alexandria, VA
30,000 Thurgood Marshall Scholarship Fund, New York, NY
21,500 Pennsylvania State University, University Park, PA
21,500 West Virginia University, Morgantown, WV
20,000 Kanawha County Schools - BEAMS Program, Charleston, WV
20,000 National Institute for Chemical Studies, Charleston, WV
16,500 Ohio State University, Columbus, OH
16,000 Keystone Science School, Keystone, CO
15,000 Bell School Reform Network, McLean, VA -- School Reform
15,000 United Negro College Fund, Inc., CT
15,000 University of Minnesota, Minneapolis, MN
11,500 Georgia Tech Foundation, Atlanta, GA
11,500 Howard University, Washington, DC
11,500 Louisiana State University, Baton Rouge, LA
11,500 Mississippi State University, Mississippi State, MS
11,500 North Carolina State University, Raleigh, NC
11,500 Purdue University, West Lafayette, IN
11,500 Texas A&M University, College Station, TX
11,500 University of Houston, Houston, TX
11,500 University of Kentucky, Lexington, KY
11,500 University of Texas in Austin, Austin, TX
11,500 Virginia Polytechnic Institute, VA
10,300 Bloomington Ind. School District, Bloomington, TX -- School Reform
10,000 Danbury Public School - Mentoring Program, Danbury, CT
10,000 Massachusetts Institute of Technology, Cambridge, MA
10,000 Peat, Marwick, Mitchell Foundation - PhD Project, Montvale, NJ -- The PhD Project
10,000 Plainfield Board of Education, Plainfield, NJ -- Simulated Mission

Environment

12,500 Galveston Bay Foundation, Webster, TX

Health

25,000 Danbury Hospital Development Fund, Danbury, CT
25,000 Datahr Rehabilitation Institute, Brookfield, CT -- Employment Services Program

Science

20,000 American Council on Science & Health, New York, NY
15,000 Talcott Mountain Science Center, Avon, CT -- GLOBE Program
14,250 Environmental and Occupational Health Science Institute, Newark, NJ -- Tox-RAP Program
10,000 Science Horizons, Inc., Ridgefield, CT -- Science Fair and Community Forum
10,000 Sunrise Science Museum, Charleston, WV
9,950 The Mountain Institute, Franklin, WV -- Appalachian Program

Social Services

20,000 Mainland Youth at Risk, Texas City, TX
8,000 Family Alliance Non-Profit Corporation, Delran, NJ

UNION PACIFIC CORP.

 Number 85 of Top 100 Corporate Givers

Company Contact

Dallas, TX
Web: http://www.up.com

Company Description

Revenue: US$11,273,000,000 (1999)
Profit: US$810,000,000 (1999)
Employees: 54,800
Fortune Rank: 156, per FORTUNE Magazine's list of 500 Largest U.S. Corporations (1999).
FF 156
SIC(s): 1081 Metal Mining Services, 1311 Crude Petroleum & Natural Gas, 1382 Oil & Gas Exploration Services, 6719 Holding Companies Nec.

Corporate Sponsorship

Type: Arts & cultural events; Festivals/fairs
Note: Co. sponsors events located in communities that have a large employee base.

Union Pacific Foundation

Giving Contact

Darlynn Herweg, Director
Union Pacific Foundation
1416 Dodge Street, Room 802
Omaha, NE 68179
Phone: (402)271-5600
Fax: (402)271-5477
Web: http://www.up.com/found/index.htm

Description

EIN: 136406825
Organization Type: Corporate Foundation
Giving Locations: AR; CA; CO; DE; DC: Washington; FL; GA; ID; IL; IN; IA; KS; LA; MD; MI; MN; MS; MT; NE; NV; NJ; NM; NY; NC; OH; OK; OR; PA; TN; TX; UT; VA; WA; WI
Grant Types: Award, Capital, Challenge, Employee Matching Gifts, General Support, Multiyear/Continuing Support, Project.
Note: Employee matching gift ratio: 2 to 1 for educational institutions; 1 to 1 for cultural institutions.

Giving Philosophy

'Union Pacific Foundation administers the wide-ranging philanthropic activities of Union Pacific Corporation and its operating Companies -Union Pacific Railroad and Union Pacific Resources Company. Union Pacific Corporation believes that the well-being of the communities in which its employees work and live is an integral part of its own success. To this end, the Foundation's activities are concentrated in geographic areas where there is a significant Union Pacific presence, which is principally in the West. Of particular interest to the Foundation are projects or programs that will either permanently reduce operating costs or produce increased income for the recipient.' Union Pacific Foundation

Financial Summary

Total Giving: $8,500,000 (1999 approx); $8,500,000 (1998 approx); $8,500,000 (1997 approx). Note: Contributes through corporate direct giving program and foundation. 1996 Giving includes foundation United Way.
Assets: $10,271,548 (1996); $1,625,740 (1994); $2,004,802 (1993)
Gifts Received: $858,095 (1996); $7,200,000 (1993). Note: Contributions received from Union Pacific Corporation and affiliated Companies.

Typical Recipients

Arts & Humanities: Arts Associations & Councils, Arts Funds, Arts Outreach, Ballet, Dance, Historic Preservation, History & Archaeology, Libraries, Museums/Galleries, Music, Opera, Performing Arts, Public Broadcasting, Theater
Civic & Public Affairs: Botanical Gardens/Parks, Business/Free Enterprise, Economic Development, Professional & Trade Associations, Public Policy, Urban & Community Affairs, Zoos/Aquariums
Education: Afterschool/Enrichment Programs, Agricultural Education, Arts/Humanities Education, Business Education, Colleges & Universities, Community & Junior Colleges, Economic Education, Education Funds, Engineering/Technological Education, Faculty Development, Legal Education, Literacy, Minority Education, Religious Education, Science/Mathematics Education, Secondary Education (Public), Social Sciences Education, Special Education, Student Aid
Environment: Air/Water Quality, Environment-General, Research, Resource Conservation, Wildlife Protection
Health: Alzheimers Disease, Cancer, Children's Health/Hospitals, Clinics/Medical Centers, Emergency/Ambulance Services, Health Organizations, Hospices, Hospitals, Long-Term Care, Medical Rehabilitation, Medical Research, Mental Health, Prenatal Health Issues
Religion: Religious Organizations, Religious Welfare
Science: Scientific Centers & Institutes
Social Services: Child Welfare, Community Centers, Community Service Organizations, Domestic Violence, Family Services, Food/Clothing Distribution, Homes, People with Disabilities, Recreation & Athletics, Scouts, Senior Services, Shelters/Homelessness, Substance Abuse, United Funds/United Ways, YMCA/YWCA/YMHA/YWHA, Youth Organizations

Contributions Analysis

Giving Priorities: Social welfare, higher education, and the arts.

Arts & Humanities: 10% to 15%. Supports a broad range of activities andorganizations with emphasis on museums and performing arts groups. Grants most often awarded for specific project support.
Education: About 30%. Support is given largely to private colleges and universities and independent college funds. Also supports a variety of programs through capital projects, annual giving funds, scholarships, and special research projects related to company business.
Environment: About 5%. Supports resource conservation and wildlife protection.
Health: 5% to 10%. Grants awarded largely to hospitals for building, equipment, or project support. Also supports hospices and rehabilitation facilities.
Social Services: About 40%. United funds receive the majority of support. Remaining grants emphasize youth organizations and child welfare groups, as well as services for the handicapped and the disadvantaged, and a variety of other community service agencies.

Application Procedures

Initial Contact: letter; application form sent by the foundation
Application Requirements: description of the organization, purpose of funds sought
Deadlines: August 7 for application form for consideration in the following year
Review Process: if initial letter indicates organization's request complies with foundation guidelines, a formal grant request form is sent to the organization to be completed and returned with supplementary data, including recently audited financial statements, 501(c)(3) determination letter, and description of financial support from other businesses
Evaluative Criteria: leadership such that financial support will be used to optimum effect, significant public support of activities, non-duplication of activities of other organizations supported by foundation, corporate presence in community served by organization, evidence of other corporate support
Decision Notification: board meets annually in January

Restrictions

Does not support organizations not eligible for tax-exempt status under Section 501(c)(3) of the IRS Code; specialized national health or welfare organizations other than through United Way; political organizations; organizations engaged in influencing legislation; religious organizations that are sectarian or denominational in purpose; veterans organizations, labor groups, social clubs, or fraternal organizations; individuals; dinners or special events; goodwill advertising; or grant-making organizations, except allied arts funds and independent college associations.
Only reviews requests for support of capital projects from organizations funded by United Way.

Corporate Officials

Darlynn Herweg: director PRIM CORP EMPL director: Union Pacific Corp.

Foundation Officials

Robert F. Starzel: president PRIM CORP EMPL senior vice president corp. relations: Union Pacific Corp. CORP AFFIL officer: Saint Louis Southwest Railway Co.

Grants Analysis

Disclosure Period: calendar year ending 1996
Total Grants: $8,522,400
Number of Grants: 1,032 (approx)
Average Grant: $7,614*
Highest Grant: $250,000
Typical Range: $1,000 to $20,000
***Note:** Average grant excludes four highest grants, all of which were given to the United Way ($250,000), ($165,000), ($150,000), ($130,000).

Recent Grants

Note: Grants derived from 1996 Form 990.

Arts & Humanities

200,000 Western Heritage Museum, Omaha, NE
120,000 United Arts, Omaha, NE
100,000 Performing Arts, Fort Worth, TX -- to assist with design and construction of new arts center
100,000 Wyoming Transportation Museum Corporation, Cheyenne, WY -- restoration of depot
50,000 Chicago Historical Society, Chicago, IL -- for exhibition on life and career of Abraham Lincoln
30,000 National Western Historical Trails Center, Council Bluffs, IA -- to help underwrite exhibits and displays
25,000 Stanford Mansion Project, Sacramento, CA -- restoration project
25,000 Utah Symphony, Salt Lake City, UT -- for educational outreach programs

Civic & Public Affairs

33,000 Elmwood Park Zoo, Norristown, PA
30,500 City of Rawlings Downtown Development Authority, Rawlings, WY -- support for downtown renovations
25,000 City of Boise Depot Campaign, Boise, ID
25,000 Friends of the Zoo, Kansas City, MO -- support for the African Plains Exhibit

Education

125,000 Creighton University, Omaha, NE -- Capital Campaign 2000
80,000 Texas Christian University, Fort Worth, TX -- to help create a campus-wide computer network system
75,000 American Institute for Managing Diversity, Atlanta, GA -- to establish a research division
75,000 United Negro College Fund, Fairfax, VA -- support for capital campaign and endowment fund
67,000 United Negro College Fund, Fairfax, VA
50,000 IDA State University Foundation, Pocatello, ID -- support for the Union Pacific Non-Traditional Student Scholarship Endowment
50,000 Whitworth College, Spokane, WA -- to assist with construction of book store
40,000 Southern Methodist University Edwin L. Cox School of Business, Dallas, TX -- scholarships for MBA candidates
35,000 Nebraska Independent College Foundation, Omaha, NE
30,000 Ak-Sar-Ben Agricultural Youth Foundation, Omaha, NE -- youth scholarships and youth agricultural activities
25,000 Florida A&M University, Tallahassee, FL -- to establish scholarship endowment fund
25,000 St. Louis University, Saint Louis, MO -- to establish an endowed scholarship fund for students in the Colleges of Art and Sciences and the School of Business Administration
25,000 Stanford University, Stanford, CA -- restoration of facilities
25,000 Summerbridge Diversity Program, Fort Worth, TX -- tutoring program for minorities
25,000 University of Arkansas Pine Bluff, Pine Bluff, AR -- to help establish scholarship endowment fund
25,000 University of Michigan, Ann Arbor, MI -- support for the MBA Domestic Corps Program

Environment

30,000 BEAR Project, Evanston, WY -- to help construct pedestrian bridge along river corridor
25,000 Missouri Botanical Garden, Saint Louis, MO -- for research projects

Health

37,500 Uinta Medical Foundation, Evanston, WY -- to establish an endowment fund
25,000 Baptist Medical Center, Kansas City, MO -- to assist with construction of ambulatory service center

Religion

50,000 Salvation Army Eastern Pennsylvania, Philadelphia, PA -- for the Building to Build Lives capital campaign

Science

30,000 Academy of Natural Sciences, Philadelphia, PA

Social Services

250,000 United Way Midlands, Omaha, NE
165,000 United Way Crusade Mercy, Chicago, IL
150,000 United Way Metropolitan Tarrant County, Fort Worth, TX
130,000 United Way, Saint Louis, MO
65,000 United Way Mid-Plains, North Platte, NE
65,000 United Way Pulaski County, Little Rock, AR
60,000 United Way Heart of America, Kansas City, MO
55,000 United Way Southeastern IDA, Pocatello, ID
50,000 Food Bank of Greater Tarrant County, Fort Worth, TX -- to assist with expansion of facilities
48,000 United Way, Salt Lake City, UT
40,000 Boy Scouts of America, Irving, TX -- to assist with construction of new administration building at High Adventure Sea Base
40,000 Boy Scouts of America, Irving, TX -- to assist with dormitory at High Adventure Sea Base
30,000 United Way Columbia-Willamette, Portland, OR
30,000 United Way Laramie County, Cheyenne, WY
30,000 United Way Lehigh, Northampton, and Warren Counties, Lehigh Valley, PA
25,000 Boys and Girls Club, El Dorado, AR -- construction of soccer fields

UNION PLANTERS CORP.

Company Contact

Memphis, TN
Web: http://www.upbank.com

Company Description

Revenue: US$993,000,000
Employees: 2,990
SIC(s): 6021 National Commercial Banks, 6712 Bank Holding Companies.

Nonmonetary Support

Type: Cause-related Marketing & Promotion; Donated Equipment; In-kind Services; Workplace Solicitation

Giving Contact

Deborah Hester, Director of Employee & Community Relations
6200 Poplar Ave.
Memphis, TN 38119
Phone: (901)580-6000

Description

Organization Type: Corporate Giving Program
Giving Locations: headquarters and operating communities.
Grant Types: General Support.

Financial Summary

Total Giving: $746,276 (1994)

Typical Recipients

Arts & Humanities: Arts Festivals, Arts & Humanities-General, History & Archaeology, Museums/Galleries, Public Broadcasting, Theater
Civic & Public Affairs: Civic & Public Affairs-General
Education: Education-General
Environment: Wildlife Protection
Science: Science Museums
Social Services: Scouts, United Funds/United Ways

Application Procedures

Initial Contact: Send a brief letter of inquiry.
Application Requirements: a description of organization, amount requested, and purpose of funds sought.

Restrictions

Does not support individuals, religious organizations for sectarian purposes, political or lobbying groups, organizations outside operating areas, or any organizations previously supported for three consecutive years.

Additional Information

Value of nonmonetary support is approximately $200,000.

Corporate Officials

Jackson W. Moore: president, director, director B Birmingham, AL 1948. ED University of Alabama BS (1970); Vanderbilt University JD (1973). PRIM CORP EMPL president, director: Union Planters Corp. CORP AFFIL director: PSB Bancshares; director: Union Planters National Bank. NONPR AFFIL trustee, president cabinet: University Alabama; chairman: Vanderbilt Law School; director: Memphis Emmaus Comm; director: Boy Scouts America; director: Memphis Development Network Foundation. CLUB AFFIL Memphis Country Club; Memphis Hunt & Polo Club.
John W. Parker: executive vice president, chief financial officer PRIM CORP EMPL executive vice president, chief financial officer: Union Planters Corp.
Benjamin W. Rawlins, Jr.: chairman, chief executive officer, director B 1938. ED Vanderbilt University BA (1961); Georgia State University MBA (1969). PRIM CORP EMPL chairman, chief executive officer, director: Union Planters Corp. CORP AFFIL chairman, president: Union Planters National Bank.

Grants Analysis

Disclosure Period: calendar year ending
Total Grants: $746,276
Typical Range: $2,500 to $5,000

Recent Grants

Note: Grants derived from 1995 grants list.

Arts & Humanities
Dixon Art Gallery, Memphis, TN
Memphis Arts Festival, Memphis, TN
Orpheum Theater, Memphis, TN
Southern Heritage Classic, Memphis, TN
WKND-TV, Memphis, TN

Civic & Public Affairs
MIFA, Memphis, TN

Environment
Ducks Unlimited, Memphis, TN

Science
IMAX Theater, Memphis, TN

Social Services
Boy Scouts of America, Memphis, TN
United Way, Memphis, TN

UNISYS CORP.

Company Contact

Blue Bell, PA
Web: http://www.unisys.com

Company Description

Revenue: US$7,544,600,000 (1999)
Profit: US$510,700,000 (1999)
Employees: 33,200
Fortune Rank: 236, per FORTUNE Magazine's list of 500 Largest U.S. Corporations (1999).
FF 236
SIC(s): 3571 Electronic Computers, 3572 Computer Storage Devices, 3575 Computer Terminals, 3577 Computer Peripheral Equipment Nec.

Operating Locations

Argentina: Unisys, Buenos Aires, Mendoza, Montevedio-Uruguay, Rosario; Australia:, Adelaide, Brisbane, Burwood, Canberra; BankWest, Leederville; Unisys, Melbourne, Murarrie, North Ryde; Unisys Australia Head Office, North Sydney; Unisys, Perth, Silverwater, South Bank; Austria:, Dornbirn, Graz, Innsbruck, Klagenfurt, Linz, Salzburg, Wien (Vienna)ord-Holland; Belgium:, Brussels, Luxemburg; Brazil:, Belem, Belo Horizonte, Brasilia, Curitiba, Emrj, Fortaleza, Goiania, Londrina, Manaus, Matriz Vitoria, Natal, Porto Alegre, Recife, Rio de Janeiro, Salvador, Sao Luis; Unisys Informatica, Vitoria; Bulgaria: Bulgaria Head Office, Sofia; Canada: Unisys, Calgary, Edmonton, Fredericton, Halifax, London, Montreal, Ottawa, Pickering, Quebec City, Toronto; Unisys Canada CSG Office, Winnepeg; Chile: Unisys, Santiago; People's Republic of China:, Beijing, Guangzhou, Shanghai; Colombia:, Baranquilla, Bogota, Cali, Medellin; Cote d'Ivoire:, Abidjan; Czech Republic: Unisys Customer Service (Czech Republic), Prague; Unisys Headquarters (Czech Republic), Prague; Finland: Unisys, Espoo, Turku; France:, Bordeaux, La Defense, Lilly, Marseille, Nancy, Nantes, Saint Paul de Vence, Valbonne, Villers Ecalles; Germany:, Berlin, Hamburg, Hannover, Muenchen, Nuernberg, Ratingen, Stuttgart, Sulzbach; Hungary:, Budapest; Indonesia: UWT Inc, Jakarta; India: Pharma Search, Mumbai; Unisys, New Delhi; Italy:, Genova, Milano, Napoli, Padova, Roma; Japan: Unisys Japan, Ltd., Ebisu; Nihon Unisys, Ltd., Toyosu; Republic of Korea: Unisys, Yoido-Dong; Malaysia:, Kual Lumpur; Netherlands:, Amsterdam, Coengebuow, Deventer, Eindhoven, Rotterdam, Sassenheim; Norway:, Oslo; New Zealand:, Auckland, Wellington; Pakistan:, Karachi; Peru:, Lima; Philippines:, Makati City, Manila; Poland: Unisys Poland, Warsaw; Portugal: Unisys, Lisboa, Oporto; Russia:, Moscow; Republic of South Africa:, Cape Town, Durban, Pietermaritzburg, Port Elizabeth, Pretoria, Windhoek; Senegal:, Dakar; Singapore: Unisys -- Asia Division Headquarters; Slovakia: Unisys, Bratislava; Spain:, Barcelona, Bilbao, Madrid, Sevilla, Zaragoza; Sweden:, Alingsas, Goteborg, Kalmar, Linkoping, Lund, Orebro; Unisys Head Office (Sweden), Solna; Switzerland: Unisys, Basel, Bern, Geneve, Lausanne, Luzern, Manno, St. Gallen, Zug, Zurich; Thailand:, Bangkok; Taiwan:, Kaohsiung, Taichung, Taipei; United Kingdom:, Altrincham; UPSL Girobank Centre, Bootle; Unisys, Bristol, Glasgow, Heron House, London, Leeds; UPSL Prescott Street, London; Unisys Data Centre, Miton Keynes; Unisys, Slough, Stockport, Uxbridge; UPSL Girobank Quayside Centre, Wigan; Venezuela: Unisys, Caracas, Maracaibo, Valencia; Vietnam: Unisys Vietnam, Hanoi

Nonmonetary Support

Value: $500,000 (1993); $250,000 (1990)
Type: In-kind Services

Giving Contact

David Curry, Vice President, Corporate Public Affairs
Unisys Corp.
PO Box 500, M.S. A2-13
Blue Bell, PA 19424
Phone: (215)986-2867
Fax: (215)986-2312

Description

Organization Type: Corporate Giving Program
Giving Locations: headquarters and operating communities.
Grant Types: General Support.

Financial Summary

Total Giving: Contributes through corporate direct giving program only.

Typical Recipients

Arts & Humanities: Museums/Galleries
Civic & Public Affairs: Public Policy
Education: Science/Mathematics Education
Science: Science Exhibits & Fairs
Social Services: United Funds/United Ways

Contributions Analysis

Giving Priorities: Higher education, health and human services, civic and community services, and culture and the arts. Limited support to U.S. nonprofit organizations with an international focus. At the corporate level, the contributions program has been restructured and focuses on science and technology education and literacy. International contributions are expanding. Foreign operating facilities make contributions in their regions, with contributions by overseas subsidiaries in 1993 totaling $300,000.
Arts & Humanities: 10% to 15%. Supports community cultural institutions that promote greater appreciation of culture and the arts. Contributions concentrated in operating locations.
Civic & Public Affairs: 10% to 15%. Supports organizations whose purpose is to ensure the availability of adequate community services as well as a safe and stable environment for employees, customers, and shareholders. Areas of interest include civic organizations that support youth, neighborhood revitalization, and community development. Also supportsorganizations that work to improve the business climate in areas where the corporation conducts business.
Education: About 70%. Highest priority is science/technology literacy, through educational programming in science museums.
Health: 5% to 10%. Giving is focused on united funds.
International: Unisys foreign subsidiaries contribute to international organizations.

Application Procedures

Initial Contact: brief letter
Application Requirements: background of organization (history, record of accomplishments, evidence of fulfilling existing need); structure and board of directors of organization; campaign goal; other corporate support; timetable; method of solicitation; fundraising costs as percentage of total budget; total annual budget; annual report, preferably independently audited, including sources and use of funds (new organizations should provide certified public accountant's statement attesting to installation of proper financial system); and proof of tax-exempt status
Deadlines: before June 30
Review Process: staff receives requests and forwards applicable proposals to contributions committee
Evaluative Criteria: fit with overall contributions program goals
Decision Notification: proposals declined or accepted for further consideration in writing within 30 days

Restrictions

Company does not support individuals, dinners or special events, member agencies of united funds, political or lobbying groups, fraternal groups, or religious organizations for sectarian purposes.

Additional Information

The company reports that it rarely supports unsolicited requests.

The corporation will support the following types of grants: operating (undesignated funds given in general support); program (funds designated for implementation of a specific program); and major non-recurring requests that will have significant impact on the community.

Giving Program Officials

David R. Curry: vice president corporate contributions PRIM CORP EMPL vice president public affairs: Unisys Corp.

Grants Analysis

Disclosure Period: calendar year ending
Typical Range: $10,000 to $200,000

UNITED AIRLINES INC.

Company Contact

Elk Grove Village, IL
Web: http://www.ual.com

Company Description

SIC(s): 4512 Air Transportation--Scheduled.
Parent Company: UAL Corp., Elk Grove Township, IL, United States

Operating Locations

Argentina: United Airlines Argentina; Australia: United Airlines Australia; Belgium: United Airlines Belgium, Brussels, Brabant; Bermuda: Four Star Insurance Co. Ltd., Hamilton; Brazil: United Airlines Brazil; Chile: United Airlines Chile; People's Republic of China: United Airlines People's Republic of China; Costa Rica: United Airlines Costa Rica; El Salvador: United Airlines El Salvador; France: United Airlines France; Germany: United Airlines Germany; Guam: United Worldwide Corp., Upper Tumon; Hong Kong: United Airlines Hong Kong, Central District; India: United Airlines India; Ireland: United Airlines, Dublin; Italy:, Milano, Lombardia; Republic of Korea: United Airlines Korea; Mexico: United Airlines Mexico; New Zealand: United Airlines New Zealand; Peru: United Airlines Peru; Thailand: United Airlines Thailand; Taiwan: United Airlines Taiwan; United Kingdom: United Airlines United Kingdom, Hounslow, Greater London; Uruguay: United Airlines Uruguay

Nonmonetary Support

Value: $400,000 (1996); $2,000,000 (1991); $1,000,000 (1989)
Volunteer Programs: Co. sponsors employee volunteer programs such as: Believers Program-an educational mentoring and tutoring program; Habitat for Humanity; Take Your Community to Work Day; and AIDS walks.
Through its United We Care Program, co. also awards grants to organizations where employees volunteer.
Note: 1997 nonmonetary support valued at $2,200,000. Co. provides nonmonetary support through air transportation.

Corporate Sponsorship

Type: Arts & cultural events
Contact: Eileen Sweeney, Manager, corporate affairs
Note: Sponsors educational programs.

United Airlines Foundation

Giving Contact

Eileen M. Younglove, Manager-Contributions
United Airlines Foundation
PO Box 66100
Chicago, IL 60666
Phone: (847)700-5714
Fax: (847)700-7345
Email: uafoundation@UAL.com

Description

EIN: 366109873
Organization Type: Corporate Foundation
Giving Locations: internationally; focusing on major cities served by the company.
Grant Types: Department, Employee Matching Gifts, General Support, Multiyear/Continuing Support, Project.

Giving Philosophy

'The United Airlines Foundation has as its mission to define, develop, and communicate United Airlines corporate value of a commitment to community service. We will sponsor and support projects and programs that improve the quality of life in the communities we serve and where our employees live and work. United employees will recognize and take pride in United's civic leadership. United Airlines will be known in each of our cities, and by our customers and shareholders, for our community service.' United Airlines Foundation Contributions Guidelines.

Financial Summary

Total Giving: $2,964,809 (1998); $6,000,000 (1997 approx); $4,635,730 (1996). Note: Contributes through corporate direct giving program and foundation.
Giving Analysis: Giving for 1997 includes: foundation ($1,783,000); foundation grants to United Way ($1,026,800); corporate direct giving ($918,355); foundation scholarships ($71,845); 1998: foundation ($1,957,809); foundation grants to United Way ($1,007,000)
Assets: $3,497,777 (1998); $3,176,321 (1997); $3,871,970 (1996)
Gifts Received: $3,216,557 (1998); $2,632,332 (1997); $2,500,000 (1996)

Typical Recipients

Arts & Humanities: Arts Associations & Councils, Arts Funds, Arts Institutes, Ballet, Dance, Ethnic & Folk Arts, Libraries, Museums/Galleries, Music, Opera, Theater
Civic & Public Affairs: African American Affairs, Botanical Gardens/Parks, Business/Free Enterprise, Civil Rights, Clubs, Community Foundations, Economic Development, Employment/Job Training, Housing, Safety, Urban & Community Affairs, Women's Affairs, Zoos/Aquariums
Education: Afterschool/Enrichment Programs, Arts/Humanities Education, Business Education, Business-School Partnerships, Colleges & Universities, Education Funds, Education Reform, Education-General, Literacy, Minority Education, Minority Education, Private Education (Precollege), Public Education (Precollege), School Volunteerism, Science/Mathematics Education, Student Aid
Environment: Environment-General, Resource Conservation
Health: Alzheimers Disease, Cancer, Children's Health/Hospitals, Heart, Hospitals, Medical Research, Single-Disease Health Associations
International: International Development, International Environmental Issues, International Relief Efforts
Religion: Dioceses, Religious Welfare
Science: Observatories & Planetariums, Science Exhibits & Fairs, Science Museums, Scientific Centers & Institutes
Social Services: Child Welfare, Community Centers, Community Service Organizations, Crime Prevention, Delinquency & Criminal Rehabilitation, Emergency Relief, Recreation & Athletics, Senior Services, United Funds/United Ways, Volunteer Services, Volunteer Services, YMCA/YWCA/YMHA/YWHA, Youth Organizations

Contributions Analysis

Giving Priorities: Social welfare, education, museums, the arts, healthcare and science.
Arts & Humanities: 16%. Keen interest in projects designed to introduce young people to museums, music, dance, and other creative areas. Also supports museums and libraries.
Civic & Public Affairs: 10%. Programs that directly improve life in the community. Funds Habitat for Humanity projects around the world and supports their mission of decent, affordable housing for all.
Education: 13%. Tutoring and mentoring systems, Adopt-a-School projects, and School To Work initiatives.
Health: 4%. Programs that help individuals with disabilities and disease through grants, airline tickets for medical transport, and employee volunteerism.
International: 5%. Supports international foundations and organizations.
Science: 13%. Funds science centers and museums.
Social Services: 39%. Majority of funds go to United Way chapters across the United States and Canada.
Note: United customers can donate their Mileage Plus Miles to help global organizations such as Special Olympics, The Red Cross, Habitat for Humanity, Makes A Wish, and Shriners Children's Hospitals to transport staff and patients. Total contributions made in 1998.

Application Procedures

Initial Contact: Submit the proposal--typewritten--on organization letterhead.
Application Requirements: Include a one-page executive summary; project summary; date and duration of project; location of activity; target beneficiaries; number of people served; financial, human, and transportation resources requested; intended use of funds, tickets or volunteers; benefits to the community; how program fits company's philanthropic strategy; ability to attract other donors due to company's participation; background and programs; copy of IRS tax-exempt letter; list of board of directors; contributors; annual report; previous and current year budget; and other supporting documents.
Deadlines: None.
Review Process: Foundation and corporate contributions committee review proposals and conduct thorough evaluations of selected programs to be reviewed by the board of directors at meetings in the Spring and Fall.
Evaluative Criteria: Innovative or unusual approach to meeting stated objectives; ability of program to attract or stimulate the support of others; capacity to deal with fundamental issues of critical importance; potential for improvement of society through replication or institutional change.
Decision Notification: Allow at least 90 days prior to any publication and/or event deadlines for review and response; foundation will send a written response stating that the proposal has been accepted, declined, or is pending further consideration.
Notes: Do not send video tapes to the foundation. Supporting documentation will not be returned.

Restrictions

The United Airlines Foundation does not provide in-kind gifts or funding in the following areas: capital or building grants, development campaigns, individuals, political or fraternal organizations, United Way funded

agencies, individual public or private schools, or churches.

Additional Information

United Airlines supports Habitat for Humanity and Ronald McDonald House Charities through soliciting foreign coins from international customers on their return flights.

Publications: Foundation and Corporate Giving Guidelines

Corporate Officials

David A. Coltman: senior vice president marketing B London, England 1942. ED Eton College (1960); Edinburgh University (1965). PRIM CORP EMPL senior vice president marketing: United Airlines Inc. ADD CORP EMPL president, chairman: United Vacation Inc. NONPR AFFIL chairman: Edinburgh W Wide Investment Trust.

James E. Goodwin: president, chief operating officer, director B 1944. ED Salem College BA. PRIM CORP EMPL president, chief operating officer, director: UAL Corp. CORP AFFIL president: United Airlines Inc.

Gerald Greenwald: chairman, chief executive officer, director B St. Louis, MO 1935. ED Princeton University BA (1957); Wayne State University MBA (1962). PRIM CORP EMPL chairman, chief executive officer, director: UAL Corp. CORP AFFIL director: Aetna Inc.; director: Time Warner Inc. NONPR AFFIL member: Economic College Chicago; director: Princeton.

Douglas A. Hacker: senior vice president finance, chief financial officer B 1955. ED Princeton University BA; Harvard University School of Business MBA (1981). PRIM CORP EMPL senior vice president finance, chief financial officer: United Airlines Inc. CORP AFFIL senior vice president, chief financial officer: UAL Corp.

William P. Hobgood: senior vice president, human resources ED Florida State University BA; George Washington University MBA; Harvard University Senior Managers in Government; University of Louisville JD. PRIM CORP EMPL senior vice president, human resources: UAL Corp. CORP AFFIL senior vice president human resources: United Airlines Inc.

John D. Kiker: vice president corporate communications PRIM CORP EMPL vice president corporate communications: United Airlines Inc.

Francesca M. Maher: senior vice president, general counsel, secretary B Chicago, IL 1957. ED Loyola University JD; Loyola University BA. PRIM CORP EMPL senior vice president, general counsel, secretary: UAL Corp. CORP AFFIL secretary: United Vacations Inc.; senior vice president, general counsel, secretary: United Airlines Inc.; secretary: United Aviation Fuels Corp. Del; secretary: Mileage Plus Inc. NONPR AFFIL director: United Center Community Economic Development Fund; director: YMCA Metropolitan Chicago; member: American Bar Association.

Stuart I. Oran: senior vice president international B 1950. ED Cornell University BS; University of Chicago Law School JD. PRIM CORP EMPL senior vice president international: UAL Corp. CORP AFFIL senior vice president international: United Airlines Inc.

Eileen M. Younglove: contributions manager PRIM CORP EMPL contributions manager: United Airlines Inc.

Giving Program Officials

Eileen A. Sweeney: manager PRIM CORP EMPL manager civic affairs: United Airlines Inc.

Foundation Officials

Stuart I. Oran: director (see above)

Eileen M. Younglove: secretary (see above)

Grants Analysis

Disclosure Period: calendar year ending 1998

Total Grants: $1,957,809*

Number of Grants: 106

Average Grant: $18,470

Highest Grant: $250,000

Typical Range: $2,500 to $25,000

***Note:** Giving excludes corporate direct giving, scholarship, United Way, nonmonetary support.

Recent Grants

Note: Grants derived from 1998 Form 990.

Arts & Humanities

250,000	Chicago Symphony/Lyric Opera Facilities Fund, Chicago, IL
125,000	The Orchestral Association Chicago Symphony Orchestra, Chicago, IL -- 1998-1999 Season Support Program
25,000	Los Angeles Philharmonic Association, Los Angeles, CA
21,500	Library Foundation of Los Angeles, Los Angeles, CA
20,000	Art Institute of Chicago, Chicago, IL -- Second Century Campaign
15,000	Beem Foundation, Los Angeles, CA
10,000	Hubbard Street Dance, Chicago, IL -- ChicagoCommunity Outreach Program
10,000	Steppenwolf Theatre Company, Chicago, IL

Civic & Public Affairs

60,000	Lincoln Park Zoological Society, Chicago, IL -- Heart of the Zoo Capital Campaign (Final pmt. On 5-yr. Pledge of $300,000)
50,000	NAACP Special Contribution Fund, Baltimore, MD -- 1998 Program
46,212	Habitat for Humanity Newark, Newark, NJ
30,000	John G. Shedd Aquarium, Chicago, IL
20,000	East Bay Habitat for Humanity, Oakland, CA
10,000	Chicago Horticultural Society, Glencoe, IL -- Chicago Botanic GardensGateway to the Future Campaign(Final pmt. On 5-yr. Pledge of $50,000)

Education

72,597	National Merit Scholarship Corporation, Evanston, IL -- 1998-1999 Scholarships
70,000	I Have A Dream Foundation, Chicago, IL -- United Airlines Believers Program
20,000	Corporate/Community Schools of America, Chicago, IL
20,000	Wonder of Reading, Los Angeles, CA
15,000	The Transportation CenterNorthwestern University, Evanston, IL
10,000	Chicago Communities in Schools, Chicago, IL
10,000	The College Fund/United Negro College Fund, Chicago, IL
10,000	LA's Best (Better Educated Students for Tomorrow), Los Angeles, CA
7,500	Colorado UpLIFT, Denver, CO

Health

75,000	Muscular Dystrophy Association, Tucson, AZ -- 1998 Support Program
25,000	Alzheimer's Association, Chicago, IL -- Research Grant

International

85,000	Habitat for Humanity International, Americus, GA -- Habitat for Humanity Great Britain
50,000	Conservation International Foundation, Washington, DC

Science

250,000	Denver's Ocean Journey, Inc., Denver, CO
100,000	Museum of Science and Industry, Chicago, IL
20,000	California Museum Foundation New California Science Center, Los Angeles, CA

Social Services

1,007,000	United Way, National
270,000	United Way/Crusade of Mercy, Chicago, IL
255,000	The United Way, San Francisco, CA
105,000	Mile High United Way, Inc., Denver, CO
100,000	United Way, Inc., Los Angeles, CA
70,000	United Way of the National Capital Area, Washington, DC
56,000	United Way of Tri-State, New York, NY
50,000	Chicago Inner-City Games Foundation, Chicago, IL
50,000	Children's Memorial Foundation, Chicago, IL
30,000	United Way of King County, Seattle, WA
20,000	Aloha United Way, Honolulu, HI
20,000	United Way of Dade County, Inc., Miami, FL
15,000	Need Foundation, LaGrange, IL
15,000	United Way of Central Indiana, Indianapolis, IN
10,000	The Big Shoulders Fund, Chicago, IL
10,000	Center for Conflict Resolution Juvenile Mediation Project, Chicago, IL
10,000	Points of Light Foundation, Washington, DC
10,000	YMCA of Metropolitan Chicago, Chicago, IL
5,000	United Way of Massachusetts Bay, Inc., Boston, MA

UNITED CO.

Company Contact

Bristol, VA

Company Description

Former Name: United Coal Co.

Employees: 1,100

SIC(s): 1221 Bituminous Coal & Lignite--Surface, 1222 Bituminous Coal--Underground, 2522 Office Furniture Except Wood, 3446 Architectural Metal Work.

United Coal Co. Charitable Foundation

Giving Contact

William Miller, Vice President, Marketing & Communications
PO Box 1280
Bristol, VA 24203
Phone: (540)466-3322
Fax: (540)645-1427

Description

Founded: 1986

EIN: 541390453

Organization Type: Corporate Foundation. Supports preselected organizations only.

Giving Locations: VA

Grant Types: General Support.

Financial Summary

Total Giving: $1,783,546 (1998); $1,919,534 (1997); $1,225,542 (1996). Note: Contributes through foundation only.

Giving Analysis: Giving for 1998 includes: foundation ($1,783,546)

Assets: $2,858,907 (1998); $2,714,776 (1997); $1,923,253 (1996)

Gifts Received: $1,766,338 (1998); $2,090,259 (1997); $968,008 (1996). Note: Contributions are received from the United Co.

Typical Recipients

Arts & Humanities: Arts Centers, Museums/Galleries, Theater

Education: Arts/Humanities Education, Colleges & Universities, Health & Physical Education, Legal Education, Private Education (Precollege), Student Aid

Health: Cancer, Clinics/Medical Centers
Social Services: Child Welfare, Community Service Organizations, Scouts, YMCA/YWCA/YMHA/YWHA, Youth Organizations

Contributions Analysis

Arts & Humanities: 2%. Supports arts centers and museums.
Civic & Public Affairs: 2%.
Education: 69%. Supports colleges and universities.
Health: 10%. Supports Wellmont Health Systems facilities.
Social Services: 12%. Supports YMCAs and youth organizations.
Note: Total contributions made in 1998.

Corporate Officials

Lois A. Clarke: executive vice president finance, chief financial officer PRIM CORP EMPL executive vice president finance, chief financial officer: United Co. CORP AFFIL treasurer: Virginia Metal Industries.
J. Thomas Fowlkes: president B 1943. PRIM CORP EMPL president: United Co. CORP AFFIL president: United Energy Corp.; chief executive officer: United Oil Minerals Inc.
James W. McGlothlin: chairman, chief executive officer B 1940. ED College of William & Mary BA (1962); College of William & Mary JD (1964). PRIM CORP EMPL chairman, chief executive officer: United Co. CORP AFFIL chairman: United Oil Minerals Inc.; director: Virginia Metal Industries; director: Dominion Bankshares Corp.; chairman: United Central Industrial Sup Co.; director: Blue Ridge Industrial Sup Co.; director: CSX Corp.; director: Bassett Furniture Industries Inc.; director: Birmingham Steel Corp.

Foundation Officials

Wayne L. Bell: secretary CORP AFFIL secretary: United Energy Corp.; secretary: Virginia Metal Industries; secretary: Blue Ridge Industrial Supply Co.
Lois A. Clarke: treasurer (see above)
J. Thomas Fowlkes: president (see above)
James W. McGlothlin: chief executive officer (see above)

Grants Analysis

Disclosure Period: calendar year ending 1998
Total Grants: $1,696,897*
Number of Grants: 13
Average Grant: $130,530
Highest Grant: $500,000
Typical Range: $15,000 to $250,000
***Note:** Giving excludes misc. grants of $10,000 or less, totaling $86,649.

Recent Grants

Note: Grants derived from 1997 Form 990.

Arts & Humanities

25,000 Barter Foundation, Abingdon, VA -- support theater renovations, endowments, operating support
20,000 William King Regional Arts Center, Abingdon, VA -- support exhibits, classes and workshops, outreach programs for third graders, support visiting artists
15,000 Museum of Fine Arts, Boston, MA -- support museum projects

Education

558,000 College of William and Mary, Williamsburg, VA -- program support, building restoration, library expansion
500,000 Emory and Henry College, Emory, VA -- support liberal arts program
250,500 Mountain Mission School, Grundy, VA -- support school, scholarship program
100,000 Clinch Valley College, Wise, VA -- support liberal arts program
100,000 Milligan College, Milligan College, TN -- support occupational therapy program
19,600 Sullins Academy, Bristol, VA -- support curriculum enhancements, operating support, scholarship program, gym renovation project
15,000 King College, Bristol, TN -- scholarships

Social Services

110,094 Buchanan County YMCA, Grundy, VA -- activities support
25,000 Boy Scouts of America Sequoyah Council, Johnson City, TN -- program support
19,370 Project Santa Fund, Grundy, VA -- Christmas party and gifts for underprivileged children
15,000 YWCA, Bristol, TN -- support child care program

UNITED DISTILLERS & VINTNERS NORTH AMERICA

Company Contact

Hartford, CT
Web: http://www.diageo.com/operatingcomps/UDV.htm

Company Description

Employees: 2,200
SIC(s): 2084 Wines, Brandy & Brandy Spirits, 2085 Distilled & Blended Liquors, 5182 Wines & Distilled Beverages.
Parent Company: Diageo Plc, 8 Henrietta Place, London, United Kingdom

Operating Locations

CA: United Distillers & Vintners North America, Alameda, Menlo Park; Guinness Southern Div., Newport Beach; Beaulieu Vineyard, Rutherford; United Distillers & Vintners North America, San Mateo; CT: United Distillers & Vintners North America, Farmington; Guinness Import Co., Stamford; UDV North America, Stamford; DC: United Distillers & Vintners North America, Washington; FL: Central/Southern Div., Coral Gables; IL: United Distillers & Vintners North America, Rosemont; MA: United Distillers & Vintners North America, Canton; MI: United Distillers & Vintners North America, Allen Park; NJ: Carillon Importers, Teaneck; NY: Eastern Div., New York; Schiefflin Somerset Co., New York; TN: Tennessee Dickel Distilling Co., Tullahoma

Nonmonetary Support

Value: $50,000 (1989); $50,000 (1988)
Type: Donated Products
Note: Nonmonetary support is provided by the company.

Corporate Sponsorship

Type: Arts & cultural events; Festivals/fairs
Contact: Jack Shea, Vice President, External Affairs

Giving Contact

UDV North America
PO Box 778
Hartford, CT 06142-0778
Phone: (860)702-4000
Fax: (860)702-4029

Alternate Contact

John Shea, Vice President External Affairs
Note: Alternate contact is for direct gifts only.

Description

Founded: 1960
Organization Type: Corporate Giving Program
Former Name: Heublein Foundation Inc.
Giving Locations: principally near operating locations and to national organizations.
Grant Types: Employee Matching Gifts, General Support, Scholarship.
Note: Employee matching gift ratio: 1 to 1. Scholarships are available to Heublein employees only.

Financial Summary

Total Giving: $640,412 (1997); $974,956 (1996); $1,000,000 (1995). Note: Contributes through corporate direct giving program only. 1997 Giving includes foundation. 1996 Giving includes foundation
Assets: $556,543 (1997); $257,231 (1996); $179,504 (1995)
Gifts Received: $840,312 (1997); $987,399 (1996); $1,061,366 (1995). Note: Contributions are received from Heublein, Inc.

Typical Recipients

Arts & Humanities: Arts Associations & Councils, Ballet, Arts & Humanities-General, Historic Preservation, History & Archaeology, Libraries, Museums/Galleries, Music, Performing Arts, Public Broadcasting, Theater, Visual Arts
Civic & Public Affairs: Botanical Gardens/Parks, Business/Free Enterprise, Economic Development, Employment/Job Training, Civic & Public Affairs-General, Housing, Philanthropic Organizations, Public Policy, Urban & Community Affairs
Education: Afterschool/Enrichment Programs, Arts/Humanities Education, Business Education, Colleges & Universities, Continuing Education, Economic Education, Engineering/Technological Education, Education-General, Literacy, Minority Education, Public Education (Precollege), Science/Mathematics Education, Social Sciences Education, Student Aid
Environment: Environment-General, Resource Conservation
Health: AIDS/HIV, Children's Health/Hospitals, Health Funds, Health Organizations, Hospitals, Prenatal Health Issues
International: Foreign Educational Institutions
Religion: Churches, Religious Welfare, Seminaries
Science: Scientific Centers & Institutes
Social Services: Big Brother/Big Sister, Camps, Child Abuse, Child Welfare, Community Centers, Community Service Organizations, Counseling, Emergency Relief, Family Services, Food/Clothing Distribution, People with Disabilities, Recreation & Athletics, Scouts, Shelters/Homelessness, Special Olympics, Substance Abuse, United Funds/United Ways, Youth Organizations

Contributions Analysis

Giving Priorities: Education, social service, the arts, health care centers, and civic concerns.
Arts & Humanities: About 20%. A local arts council, museums, music, and historical preservation associations.
Civic & Public Affairs: 5% to 10%. Environmental, urban, andwomen's affairs organizations.
Education: 35% to 40%. Scholarship program for company employees' children, colleges and universities, economic and minority education, and education funds.
Health: 5% to 10%. Community health care centers, hospitals, and health organizations.
Religion: Less than 5%. Religious welfare programs.
Social Services: 25% to 30%. Major support goes to the United Way and other federated campaigns. Also funds youth organizations, shelters, food distribution programs, and other community service organizations.

Application Procedures

Initial Contact: brief letter and one copy of full proposal
Application Requirements: description of the organization, amount requested, purpose of funds sought, recently audited financial statement, and proof of tax-exempt status
Deadlines: None; board meets as required.

Restrictions

Does not support dinners or special events, fraternal organizations, goodwill advertising, individuals, member agencies of united funds, political or lobbying groups, or religious organizations for sectarian purposes.
Company stresses that they do not give outside of the local areas where the company has operations.

Additional Information

Publications: Scholarship Program Guidelines; Application Form

Corporate Officials

Jack Keenan: chief executive officer PRIM CORP EMPL chief executive officer: United Distillers & Vintners North America.

Giving Program Officials

Mark Larson: director
Rie Poirier: treasurer
David J. Scott: secretary B 1952. ED Saint Lawrence University JD (1975); Cornell University Law School (1978). PRIM CORP EMPL seniorvice president, general counsel, section: Medtronic Inc.
Peter M. Seremet: president PRIM CORP EMPL senior vice president external affairs: United Distillers & Vinters North America. CORP AFFIL vice president: International Distillers Vintners.

Grants Analysis

Disclosure Period: calendar year ending 1995
Total Grants: $1,162,592
Number of Grants: 442
Average Grant: $2,630
Highest Grant: $75,000
Typical Range: $100 to $5,000

Recent Grants

Note: Grants derived from 1996 Form 990.

Arts & Humanities

70,000	Greater Hartford Arts Council, Hartford, CT
35,000	Arts Mats for Parkville Kids Theater
13,000	Napa Valley Museum, Napa, CA
10,000	New England Villages, Pembroke, MA

Civic & Public Affairs

45,000	Walks Declare
10,000	Hartford Areas Ralley Together, Hartford, CT
10,000	Set Ranch Foundation
7,000	Connecticut Forum, Hartford, CT
3,000	Bushnell Park Foundation, Hartford, CT
3,000	Leadership Greater Hartford, Hartford, CT
3,000	Opportunities Industrialization Center, Menlo Park, CA
2,500	Revitalization Corps, Hartford, CT

Education

50,000	Bushnells Arts in Education
45,000	CPEP Connecticut Pre-Engineering Program, CT
30,000	Trinity College Outreach Program
15,000	Institute of Living Horticulture Therapy
13,500	St. Joseph College for Access Program
12,000	St. Joseph College Capital Campaign
11,000	Educational Testing Service, Princeton, NJ
10,000	Seneca State University, Seneca, NY
7,500	Literacy Volunteers of America, Syracuse, NY
6,000	California Pacific Scholarship Fund Northern California, CA
5,000	Central Connecticut State University, New Britain, CT -- for minority scholarships
5,000	East Farms School
5,000	School of Hartford Ballet, Hartford, CT
5,000	United Negro College Fund, New York, NY
5,000	West Middle School Committee, Hartford, CT
4,000	California Pacific Scholarship Fund Northern California, CA
4,000	Inroads
3,000	Trinity College of Connecticut Scholarship Program, CT

Environment

50,000	Riverfront Recapture, Hartford, CT

Health

35,000	St. Francis Hospital Violence Prevention Center
35,000	St. Francis Mount Sinai Hospitals
25,000	Connecticut Children's Medical Center, Hartford, CT
14,000	Hospital for Special Care, New Britain, CT
13,000	Hartford Action Plan on Infant Health, Hartford, CT

Religion

10,000	Salvation Army Homeless Prevention Program, Hartford, CT
5,000	Samaritan House, Hartford, CT
5,000	Samaritans of Capital Region, Hartford, CT
2,500	Immaculate Conception Church, Chicago, IL
2,500	Morey Housing for St. Elizabeth
2,000	Asylum Hill Christian Community, Hartford, CT

Science

30,000	Science Center of Connecticut, West Hartford, CT

Social Services

145,000	United Way New England, Providence, RI
22,000	United Way Southeastern Michigan, Detroit, MI
14,000	Camp Courant, Hartford, CT
14,000	United Way Bay Area, San Francisco, CA
10,000	Governor's Partnership Drugs Don't Work
5,000	Fidelco Guide Dog Foundation, Bloomfield, CT
2,500	Open Hearth Association, Hartford, CT

UNITED DOMINION INDUSTRIES, LTD.

Company Contact

Charlotte, NC
Web: http://www.uniteddominion.com

Company Description

Former Name: AMCA International Corp.
Employees: 11,000
SIC(s): 3441 Fabricated Structural Metal, 3442 Metal Doors, Sash & Trim, 3443 Fabricated Plate Work--Boiler Shops.

United Dominion Foundation

Giving Contact

Nancy Spurlock, Director, Corporate Communications
301 South College Street
Charlotte, NC 28202-6039
Phone: (704)347-6800
Fax: (704)347-6900

Description

EIN: 396044275
Organization Type: Corporate Foundation
Giving Locations: headquarters and operating communities.
Grant Types: Capital, Emergency, General Support, Project, Research.

Financial Summary

Total Giving: $298,939 (1996); $318,788 (1995); $335,800 (1994). Note: Contributes through corporate direct giving program and foundation. Giving includes foundation.
Assets: $377,927 (1996); $461,952 (1995); $379,992 (1994)
Gifts Received: $150,075 (1996); $324,377 (1995); $385,830 (1994). Note: Contributions received from United Dominion Industries.

Typical Recipients

Arts & Humanities: Arts Associations & Councils, Arts Centers, Libraries, Museums/Galleries, Music, Performing Arts, Public Broadcasting, Theater
Civic & Public Affairs: Chambers of Commerce, Economic Development, Civic & Public Affairs-General, Housing, Law & Justice, Nonprofit Management, Public Policy, Urban & Community Affairs, Zoos/Aquariums
Education: Business Education, Colleges & Universities, Education Funds, Education Reform, Preschool Education, Private Education (Precollege), Public Education (Precollege)
Environment: Resource Conservation
Health: Cancer, Children's Health/Hospitals, Hospices, Hospitals, Medical Research, Single-Disease Health Associations
International: International Affairs, International Relations
Social Services: Camps, Child Welfare, Community Service Organizations, Day Care, Domestic Violence, Family Planning, Family Services, People with Disabilities, Recreation & Athletics, Scouts, Senior Services, Substance Abuse, United Funds/United Ways, YMCA/YWCA/YMHA/YWHA, Youth Organizations

Contributions Analysis

Arts & Humanities: Major contributions of $30,000 or more have gone to the Arts and Science Council; **Civic & Public Affairs:** (United Funds & United Way) United Way, all in Charlotte, NC; **Education:** Charlotte Latin School, Queens College; **Health:** Presbyterian Hospital Foundation; **Social Services:** Habitat for Humanity.

Application Procedures

Initial Contact: a brief letter of inquiry
Application Requirements: statement of need and purpose of funds sought
Deadlines: None.

Additional Information

Company does not make contributions beyond its immediate operating communities.

Corporate Officials

William Ray Holland: chairman, chief executive officer, director B Ada, OK 1938. ED University of Denver BS (1960); University of Denver JD (1962). PRIM CORP EMPL chairman, chief executive officer, director: United Dominion Industries, Ltd. CORP AFFIL director: Morgan Products; chief executive officer: United Dominion Holdings Inc.; director: Lance Inc.; director: Coltec Industries Inc.; director: J.A. Jones Inc.
Robert L. Shaffer: vice president PRIM CORP EMPL vice president: United Dominion Industries Ltd.
Jan Karol Ver Hagen: president B Eau Claire, WI 1937. ED University of Wisconsin BSME (1961).

PRIM CORP EMPL president: United Dominion Industries, Ltd. CORP AFFIL director: Wolverine Tube Corp.; director: Wolverine Tube Inc.; vice chairman, president, chief operating officer, director: United Dominion Industries Ltd.

Foundation Officials

M. L. Bullard: secretary, director
B. B. Burns, Jr.: vice president, director PRIM CORP EMPL president: United Dominion Industries.
William Dries: vice president, director PRIM CORP EMPL executive vice president: United Dominion Industries.
Robert E. Drury: president, director B 1944. PRIM CORP EMPL executive vice president, chief administrative officer: United Dominion Industries, Ltd. CORP AFFIL director: Marley Co.; executive vice president: United Dominion Holdings Inc.; vice president: Core Industries; treasurer: Lee Engineering Co.
William Ray Holland: vice president, director (see above)
R. L. Magee: assistant secretary PRIM CORP EMPL assistant secretary: United Dominion Industries.
R. P. McKinney: assistant secretary PRIM CORP EMPL assistant secretary: United Dominion Industries.
Robert L. Shaffer: vice president, director (see above)

Grants Analysis

Disclosure Period: calendar year ending 1996
Total Grants: $298,939
Number of Grants: 28
Average Grant: $10,676
Highest Grant: $60,000
Typical Range: $1,000 to $60,000

Recent Grants

Note: Grants derived from 1996 Form 990.

Arts & Humanities

49,000	Arts and Science Council, Charlotte, NC
5,000	Mint Museum, Charlotte, NC
2,500	Children's Theater, Charlotte, NC
1,000	Blumenthal Performing Arts Center

Civic & Public Affairs

2,500	Center for Nonprofits
2,000	Christmas in April, Charlotte, NC
2,000	Leadership Charlotte, Charlotte, NC
1,000	Mecklenberg County Bar Summer Internship, NC
1,000	North Carolina Center for Public Policy Research, Raleigh, NC

Education

60,000	Queens College, Charlotte, NC
50,000	John A. Walker College of Business
20,000	Johnson C. Smith College Fund, Charlotte, NC
12,000	Arizona State University Foundation, Tempe, AZ
1,000	Lakewood Preschool Corporation, Charlotte, NC
500	Cities in Schools, Ardmore, OK

Environment

10,000	Nature Conservancy, Charlotte, NC

Health

40,000	Presbyterian Hospital Foundation, Charlotte, NC
1,000	Children's Miracle Network, Charlotte, NC

International

1,000	International House

Social Services

12,500	Charlotte Athletic Foundation, Charlotte, NC
10,000	YMCA Capital Campaign, Charlotte, NC
6,556	Boy Scouts of America Mecklenberg County Council, NC
2,500	Kids Voting, Tempe, AZ
2,383	Charlotte Mecklenburg Senior Centers, Charlotte, NC
1,000	Alexander Children's Home
1,000	Family Center, West Somerville, MA
1,000	YMCA Outreach, Charlotte, NC
500	Florence Crittenton Services

United Parcel Service Of America Inc.

 Number 19 of Top 100 Corporate Givers

Company Contact

Atlanta, GA
Phone: (404)828-6130
Web: http://www.ups.com

Company Description

Revenue: US$27,052,000,000 (1999)
Profit: US$883,000,000 (1999)
Employees: 339,000
Fortune Rank: 46, per FORTUNE Magazine's list of 500 Largest U.S. Corporations (1999).
FF 46
SIC(s): 4212 Local Trucking Without Storage, 6719 Holding Companies Nec.

Operating Locations

Headquarters is in Atlanta, Georgia. Operates both nationally and internationally.

Nonmonetary Support

Type: Loaned Executives; Workplace Solicitation
Note: Workplace solicitation is for United Way only.

UPS Foundation

Giving Contact

Ms. Evern Cooper, Executive Director
The UPS Foundation
55 Glenlake Pkwy., NE
Atlanta, GA 30328
Phone: (404)828-6374
Fax: (404)828-7435
Web: http://www.community.ups.com

Description

EIN: 136099176
Organization Type: Corporate Foundation
Giving Locations: nationally.
Grant Types: Employee Matching Gifts, Fellowship, Multiyear/Continuing Support, Professorship, Project, Research, Scholarship.
Note: Employee matching gift ratio: 1 to 1 for gifts to educational and cultural organisation. Scholarships are provided only for children of employees.

Giving Philosophy

'At United Parcel Service, our belief is that strong corporate commitment, backed by caring people, can help our community become a better place to live and work. .. We feel that The Foundation's success is measured by the number of lives it touches. By reaching out to those in need--in support of education, human services and health care--we can make a difference by enhancing the lives of others. Our goal is to serve the public by sharing our good fortune with those who are less fortunate.' *The UPS Foundation, Reaching Out*

Financial Summary

Total Giving: $42,723,327 (1998); $12,266,125 (1997); $26,452,886 (1996). Note: Contributes through corporate direct giving program and foundation. 1997 Giving includes foundation ($9,771,161); matching gifts ($983,138); scholarships ($1,511,826). 1996 Giving includes corporate direct giving ($1,200,000); foundation ($16,442,582); matching gifts ($810,617); scholarships ($1,526,368); United Way ($187,922).
Giving Analysis: Giving for 1998 includes: foundation ($30,493,791); foundation grants to United Way ($9,531,041); foundation scholarships ($1,568,248); foundation matching gifts ($1,130,247)
Assets: $53,519,816 (1998); $71,492,477 (1997); $73,822,349 (1996)
Gifts Received: $16,407,589 (1998); $6,738,215 (1996); $14,130,137 (1994). Note: In 1998, foundation received contributions from UPS of America, Inc.

Typical Recipients

Arts & Humanities: Arts Associations & Councils, Arts Centers, Arts Festivals, Arts Funds, Ballet, Historic Preservation, Literary Arts, Museums/Galleries, Music, Public Broadcasting
Civic & Public Affairs: African American Affairs, Botanical Gardens/Parks, Business/Free Enterprise, Chambers of Commerce, Clubs, Community Foundations, Economic Development, Employment/Job Training, Civic & Public Affairs-General, Hispanic Affairs, Housing, Nonprofit Management, Philanthropic Organizations, Public Policy, Safety, Urban & Community Affairs, Women's Affairs, Zoos/Aquariums
Education: Afterschool/Enrichment Programs, Business Education, Colleges & Universities, Community & Junior Colleges, Continuing Education, Economic Education, Economic Education, Education Associations, Education Funds, Education Reform, Elementary Education (Public), Engineering/Technological Education, Faculty Development, Education-General, International Studies, Leadership Training, Literacy, Medical Education, Minority Education, Private Education (Precollege), Public Education (Precollege), Science/Mathematics Education, Special Education, Student Aid, Vocational & Technical Education
Health: AIDS/HIV, Medical Rehabilitation, Nursing Services, Single-Disease Health Associations
International: Health Care/Hospitals, Human Rights, International Affairs, International Peace & Security Issues
Religion: Churches, Ministries, Religious Welfare, Social/Policy Issues
Science: Science Museums, Scientific Centers & Institutes, Scientific Organizations
Social Services: At-Risk Youth, Big Brother/Big Sister, Child Abuse, Child Welfare, Community Centers, Community Service Organizations, Day Care, Domestic Violence, Emergency Relief, Family Services, Food/Clothing Distribution, People with Disabilities, Senior Services, Shelters/Homelessness, Special Olympics, United Funds/United Ways, Volunteer Services, YMCA/YWCA/YMHA/YWHA, Youth Organizations

Contributions Analysis

Giving Priorities: Social welfare, education, and civic organizations.
Arts & Humanities: 5%. Historical societies, arts funds, and libraries.
Civic & Public Affairs: 28%. Funds women's group, ethnic organizations, urgan leagues, support for the disabled and blind, African American affairs, and foundations.
Education: 44%. Supports academic research, programs that raise the level of educational effectiveness, enhance the quality of instruction, family learning opportunities, and school involvement projects. Scholarship Programs include The Citizen's Scholarship Foundation of America, Inc. and The National Merit Scholarship Corporate.
Religion: 1%. Churches and religious community assistance efforts.
Social Services: 21%. Supports programs for families and children in crisis, food shelters, the economically or culturally disadvantaged, the physically or mentally challenged, and community development

programs, YMCA's, United Way, and domestic violence.

Application Procedures

Initial Contact: Send a proposal in concise letter form, no more than two pages in length.

Application Requirements: Include the description and mission of organization and project; needs addressed by program; goals and objectives; how objectives will be achieved and evaluated; total cost; amount requested; sources of future support; alternate funding sources and dollar amounts; current budget; audited financial statement; annual report; and proof of tax-exempt status.

Deadlines: September 1.

Review Process: Preliminary review by executive director and appropriate grant committees; final review by board of trustees.

Evaluative Criteria: Impact on number of people served and quality of service.

Restrictions

Does not support individuals; religious organizations or theological functions for sectarian purposes.

Rarely supports capital campaigns, endowments or operating expenses. UPS partnered with 15 other corporations to help the Orphan Foundation of America Project which is a national leadership and scholarship program for foster youth.

Additional Information

Publications: Annual Report; Guidelines

Corporate Officials

Robert J. Clanin: senior vice president, chief financial officer, treasurer, director B Toluca, IL 1944. ED Bradley University BS (1966). PRIM CORP EMPL senior vice president, chief financial officer, treasurer, director: United Parcel Service of America Inc. ADD CORP EMPL vice president: United Parcel Service New York Corp.; treasurer: United Parcel Service Ohio. CORP AFFIL director: Oversees Partner Ltd. NONPR AFFIL co-chair: Georgia Council Economic Education.

Thomas H. Weidemeyer: senior vice president, director B Brooklyn, NY 1947. ED California State University BA; Western State University JD. PRIM CORP EMPL senior vice president, director: United Parcel Service of America Inc. CORP AFFIL president: United Parcel Service Inc. Ohio; president, chief operating officer, director: UPS Airlines.

Foundation Officials

Don R. Fischer: trustee PRIM CORP EMPL vice president, director: United Parcel Service Truck Leasing Inc.

John J. Kelley: vice chairman PRIM CORP EMPL senior vice president, director: United Parcel Service of America Inc.

Thomas H. Weidemeyer: trustee (see above)

Grants Analysis

Disclosure Period: calendar year ending 1998
Total Grants: $30,493,761*
Number of Grants: 3,306 (approx)
Average Grant: $13,224
Highest Grant: $698,333
Typical Range: $10,000 to $75,000
***Note:** Giving excludes matching gifts, scholarship, United Way.

Recent Grants

Note: Grants derived from 1998 Form 990.

Arts & Humanities

300,000	Woodruff Arts Center, Atlanta, GA
200,000	Greater Atlanta Chamber Foundation, Inc., Atlanta, GA
125,000	American Battle Monuments Commission, Arlington, VA

Civic & Public Affairs

698,333	The Carter Center, Inc., Atlanta, GA
518,000	National Urban League, Inc., Washington, DC
350,000	Hands on Atlanta, Inc., Atlanta, GA
300,000	100 Black Men of America, Inc., Atlanta, GA
290,000	National Black Child Development Institute, Inc., Washington, DC
265,000	National Association for the Advancement of Colored People, Salem, OR
200,005	100 Black Men of America, Inc., Atlanta, GA
200,000	National Council of La Raza, Washington, DC
194,085	Work, Achievement, Values and Education, Washington, DC
175,000	Gifts in Kind Inc., Alexandria, VA
165,000	American Enterprise Institute, Washington, DC
140,000	Women's Employment Network, Inc., Kansas City, MO
125,000	Atlanta - Fulton County Zoo, Inc., Atlanta, GA
125,000	Greater Louisville Foundation, Inc., Louisville, KY
120,000	Catalyst for Women, Inc., Dallas, TX

Education

1,449,748	National Merit Scholarship Corporation, Evanston, IL
555,555	Kentucky School Reform Corporation, Lexington, KY
430,000	Georgia State University Foundation, Inc., Atlanta, GA
350,000	The Chief Executive Leadership Institute, Washington, DC
350,000	University of Louisville Foundation, Inc., Louisville, KY
300,000	Georgia Partnership for Excellence in Education, Inc., Atlanta, GA
300,000	The Georgia Partnership for Excellence in Education, Inc., Atlanta, GA
250,000	Main Line Academy, Haverford, PA
222,648	Georgia Council on Economic Education, Atlanta, GA
200,000	Georgia School Boards Association, Inc., Lawrenceville, GA
200,000	Junior Achievement, Inc., Atlanta, GA
200,000	National Board for Professional Teaching Standards, Inc., Washington, DC
200,000	New American Schools Development Corporation, Arlington, VA
200,000	University of Notre Dame, Notre Dame, IN
190,000	Inroads, Inc., Milwaukee, WI
180,000	Junior Achievement, Inc., Atlanta, GA
169,325	Laubach Literacy Action, Syracuse, NY
160,931	National Center for Family Literacy, Louisville, KY
125,000	Clarke School for the Deaf, North Hampton, MA

Religion

175,000	United States Catholic Conference, Roanoke, VA

Social Services

604,000	United Way of Metropolitan Atlanta, Inc., Atlanta, GA
439,425	United Way of America, Alexandria, VA
300,000	YMCA of Metropolitan Atlanta, Inc., Atlanta, GA
293,000	Big Brothers/Big Sisters of America, Philadelphia, PA
200,000	Georgia Special Olympics, Inc., Atlanta, GA
200,000	United Way of America, Alexandria, VA
162,386	Points of Light Foundation, Washington, DC
150,000	1999 Special Olympics World Summer Games, Raleigh, NC
150,000	Boys & Girls Clubs of Metro Atlanta, Inc., Atlanta, GA
150,000	The Bridge Family Center of Atlanta, Inc., Atlanta, GA
150,000	Heritage Foundation, Thomasville, GA
125,000	Big Brothers/Big Sisters of Metro Atlanta, Inc., Atlanta, GA

UNITED SERVICES AUTOMOBILE ASSOCIATION

Company Contact

USAA Bldg.
9800 Fredericksburg Rd.
San Antonio, TX 78288
Phone: (210)498-2211
Fax: (210)498-9940
Web: http://www.usaa.com

Company Description

Foreign Name: USAA
Revenue: US$8,319,100,000 (1999)
Profit: US$765,000,000 (1999)
Employees: 21,754 (1999)
Fortune Rank: 217, per FORTUNE Magazine's list of 500 Largest U.S. Corporations (1999).
FF 217
SIC(s): 6099 Functions Related to Deposit Banking, 6211 Security Brokers & Dealers, 6282 Investment Advice, 6331 Fire, Marine & Casualty Insurance.

USAA Foundation, A Charitable Trust

Giving Contact

Amy D. Cannefax, Trust Representative
9800 Fredericksburg Rd., Tax Dept. F3E
San Antonio, TX 78288-0115
Phone: (210)498-0702

Description

Founded: 1994
EIN: 746423382
Organization Type: Corporate Foundation. Supports preselected organizations only.
Giving Locations: headquarters and operating communities.

Financial Summary

Total Giving: $7,637,088 (fiscal year ending June 30, 1997); $4,797,150 (fiscal 1996); $953,065 (fiscal 1995). Note: Contributes through foundation only. 1997 Giving includes United Way ($1,870,431).

Assets: $155,503,465 (fiscal 1997); $133,412,541 (fiscal 1996); $79,178,741 (fiscal 1995)

Gifts Received: $349 (fiscal 1997); $40,539,661 (fiscal 1996); $75,466,991 (fiscal 1995). Note: In fiscal 1996, contributions were received from United Services Autombile Association. 17 other donors each contributed $700 or less.

Typical Recipients

Arts & Humanities: Community Arts, Libraries, Museums/Galleries, Music, Performing Arts, Theater
Education: Colleges & Universities, Community & Junior Colleges, Health & Physical Education
Health: Cancer, Children's Health/Hospitals, Emergency/Ambulance Services, Hospitals
Religion: Jewish Causes, Religious Welfare
Social Services: At-Risk Youth, Scouts, United Funds/United Ways, YMCA/YWCA/YMHA/YWHA

Additional Information
Trust(s): USAA Federal Savings Bank

Corporate Officials
Robert T. Herres: chairman, chief executive officer B Denver, CO 1932. ED United States Naval Academy BS (1954); Air Force Institute Technology MS (1960); George Washington University MPA (1965). PRIM CORP EMPL chairman, chief executive officer: United Services Automobile Association. CORP AFFIL chairman: USAA Real Estate Co.; chairman, chief executive officer: USAA General Indemnity Co.; chief executive officer: USAA Investment Trust; chairman, chief executive officer: USAA. NONPR AFFIL director: Trinity University; director: U.S. Naval Academy Foundation; director: National Association Independent Insurers; director: Insurance Institute Highway Safety; national chairman: Junior Achievement; director: Insurance Information Institute; director: Atlantic Council U.S.; member executive board: Boy Scouts America.

Josue Robles: chief financial officer PRIM CORP EMPL chief financial officer: USAA Life Insurance Co. CORP AFFIL chief financial officer, senior vice president, treasurer: USAA Capital Corp.

Foundation Officials
Barbara B. Gentry: trustee rep

Grants Analysis
Disclosure Period: fiscal year ending June 30, 1997
Total Grants: $5,766,637*
Number of Grants: 386
Average Grant: $8,480*
Highest Grant: $2,502,000
Typical Range: $500 to $100,000
***Note:** Giving excludes United Way. Average grant figure excludes highest grant.

Recent Grants
Note: Grants derived from fiscal 1997 Form 990.

Arts & Humanities
241,700 San Antonio Museum of Art, San Antonio, TX
125,000 San Antonio Symphony, San Antonio, TX
107,500 Las Casas Foundation, San Antonio, TX
51,500 McNay Art Museum, San Antonio, TX
50,500 United Services Organization, Washington, DC
50,000 Arts San Antonio!, San Antonio, TX

Education
2,502,000 University of Texas Health Science Center, San Antonio, TX
161,000 Alamo Community College District Foundation, San Antonio, TX
50,000 Abilene Christian University, Abilene, TX

Health
335,000 Cancer Therapy and Research Center, San Antonio, TX
200,000 Santa Rosa Children's Hospital, San Antonio, TX
85,000 American Red Cross, San Antonio, TX

Religion
116,000 Salvation Army, San Antonio, TX
50,000 Campus of the San Antonio Jewish Community, San Antonio, TX

Social Services
1,483,422 United Way San Antonio and Bexar County, San Antonio, TX
136,653 United Way Hillsborough County, Tampa, FL
133,500 YMCA San Antonio and Hill County, San Antonio, TX
83,486 United Way, Sacramento, CA
68,220 United Way South Hampton Roads, Virginia Beach, VA
60,479 Pike's Peak United Way, El Paso and Teller County, Colorado Springs, CO

U.S. BANCORP

 Number 18 of Top 100 Corporate Givers

Company Contact
601 Second Avenue South
Minneapolis, MN 55402
Phone: (612)973-1111
Fax: (612)973-2446
Web: http://www.usbank.com

Company Description
Former Name: First Bank System.
Revenue: US$8,435,400,000 (1999)
Profit: US$1,506,500,000 (1999)
Employees: 11,997
Fortune Rank: 212, per FORTUNE Magazine's list of 500 Largest U.S. Corporations (1999).
FF 212
SIC(s): 6022 State Commercial Banks, 6712 Bank Holding Companies.

SUBSIDIARY COMPANIES
MN: U.S. Bancorp Piper Jaffray, Minneapolis

Nonmonetary Support
Value: $239,055 (1996); $55,000 (1995); $269,507 (1993)
Type: Donated Equipment
Note: For nonmonetary support contact nearest company office.

Corporate Sponsorship
Type: Arts & cultural events; Sports events
Note: Employee volunteerism includes Junior Achievement, Habitat for Humanity, American Red Cross, and public television and radio.

Giving Contact
U.S. Bancorp
601 Second Avenue South
Minneapolis, MN 55402-4302
Phone: (612)973-4996
Fax: (612)973-2446
Web: http://www.usbank.com/comm_relations

Description
EIN: 411359579
Organization Type: Corporate Giving Program
Giving Locations: MN: Minneapolis operating locations.
Grant Types: Capital, Employee Matching Gifts, General Support.
Note: Employee matching gift ratio: 1 to 1 up to $500 per employee per year. Higher education gifts are matched up to $2,500 per employee per year.

Giving Philosophy
'Communities benefit from our contributions to economic expansion and improved quality of life. U.S. Bank, through its corporate giving, connects to its communities by providing support to organizations that (1) improve the educational and economic opportunities of targeted individuals and families, and (2) enhance the cultural and artistic life of the communities in which we live and work.
'Funding Priorities:
'Economic Opportunity: Affordable Housing: We support organizations that support the preservation, rehabilitation and construction of quality affordable housing that assists low and moderate income populations; programs that provide home buyer counseling and related economic education to individuals and families with low to moderate incomes. Support for Programs Working with Individuals: We support work entry and specific skills training programs that focus on low to moderate income adults; broad child care and transportation initiatives that offer solutions related to the needs of people transitioning from welfare-to-work (no direct service), i.e., child care and transportation (no funding provided for individual, stand-alone providers); programs that assist low and moderate income individuals in development of life skills that are essential to successful self-sufficiency, especially skills related to managing personal finances; programs that assist particular disadvantaged populations in seeking and retaining employment. Support for Programs Working with Businesses: We support organizations that develop and deliver innovative programs in these areas (with emphasis on low and moderate income communities): small business development and expansion, commercial revitalization, and job creation.
'Cultural and Artistic Enrichment: We fund programs that: build audiences of arts organizations; bring the arts to underserved populations; bring select and limited civic amenities to underserved, rural communities; promote the arts in education.
'Education: We fund organizations that work in collaboration with K-12 schools (public or private) that develop and/or deliver innovative programs addressing dropout prevention economic education, mentoring, and curriculum innovation. Priority is given to programs that reach a broad number of students, bring together community resources, and can, if successful, be replicated. No funding is provided for individual K-12 schools.
'United Way: U.S. Bank supports the United Way as an effective means of meeting human service needs in our communities where the United Way operates.'
1998 Corporate Giving Grant Guideline

Financial Summary
Total Giving: $44,000,000 (1998 approx); $38,000,000 (1997 approx); $9,226,508 (1996). Note: Contributes through corporate direct giving program only.
Giving Analysis: Giving for 1998 includes: corporate direct giving (approx $39,640,000); corporate grants to United Way (approx $2,200,000); foundation ($1,151,368); corporate matching gifts (approx $1,000,000)
Assets: $242,372 (1998); $837,596 (1997); $129,129 (1996 approx)
Gifts Received: $1,048,009 (1998)

Typical Recipients
Arts & Humanities: Arts Centers, Arts Institutes, Museums/Galleries, Music, Opera, Performing Arts, Public Broadcasting, Theater
Civic & Public Affairs: Community Foundations, Economic Development, Employment/Job Training, Civic & Public Affairs-General, Housing
Education: Business Education, Colleges & Universities, Economic Education, Elementary Education (Private), Minority Education, Private Education (Precollege), Public Education (Precollege)
Health: AIDS/HIV, Children's Health/Hospitals, Clinics/Medical Centers, Diabetes, Emergency/Ambulance Services, Multiple Sclerosis, Prenatal Health Issues, Research/Studies Institutes
Religion: Religious Welfare, Seminaries
Social Services: Animal Protection, Child Welfare, Community Service Organizations, Day Care, Food/Clothing Distribution, People with Disabilities, Scouts, United Funds/United Ways, YMCA/YWCA/YMHA/YWHA, Youth Organizations

Contributions Analysis
Giving Priorities: Affordable housing, economic opportunity, K-12 public education, and artistic and cultural enrichment.
Arts & Humanities: 20% to 25%. Major arts and cultural institutions, with operating budgets over 2 million.

Civic & Public Affairs: Less than 5%.
Education: 35% to 40%. Public education, adult education, especially in distressed areas.
Health: 30% to 35%. Majority of funds support the American Red Cross. Other funds support children's health, and AIDS awareness.
Religion: Less than 5%. Religious causes.
Social Services: About 5%. Funds youth services, animal services, and social services.

Application Procedures

Initial Contact: Contact company for funding guidelines and deadlines, to request a grant application, and for appropriate state contact person.
Evaluative Criteria: Service to local area; sponsorship and participation of bank employees; innovation in meeting unfulfilled community needs.

Restrictions

Funding restrictions include (but are not limited to) organizations that are not tax exempt under paragraph 501(c)(3) of the U.S. Internal Revenue Code; organizations outside of U.S. Bancorp communities; individuals; travel and related expenses; endowment campaigns; deficit reduction; religious organizations for religious purposes; organizations designed primarily to lobby; fundraising events or sponsorships; medically oriented charities; organizations receiving United Way funding; individual K-12 schools; 'pass through' organizations or other foundations, merchant associations, chamber memberships, or chamber programs; academic, medical, or scientific research; and political campaigns. organizations or other foundations, merchant associations, chamber memberships, or chamber programs; academic, medical, or scientific research; and political campaigns.

Additional Information

In 1997, First Bank System acquired US Bancorp of Portland, OR. The merged company is called US Bancorp.
Publications: Community Responsibility Report; Guidelines

Corporate Officials

Gerry B. Cameron: chairman, directorrcial banking & institutional finance B Grandview, WA 1938. PRIM CORP EMPL chairman, director: U.S. Bancorp. CORP AFFIL director: Tektronix Inc.; director: Blue Cross & Blue Shield Oregon; director: Regence Group. NONPR AFFIL director: Oregon Industrial College Foundation Inc.; chairman advisory board: Pacific Rim Bankers Program; director: Oregon Business Council; member: Bankers Roundtable; director: Benchmark Group; director: American Bankers Association.
John R. Danielson: senior vice president investor & corporate relations B 1944. PRIM CORP EMPL senior vice president investor & corporate relations: U.S. Bancorp.
Gary T. Duim: vice chairman commercial banking & private financial ****B 1943. PRIM CORP EMPL vice chairman commercial banking & private financial service: U.S. Bancorp.
David P. Grandstrand: senior vice president, treasurer B 1955. PRIM CORP EMPL senior vice president, treasurer: U.S. Bancorp.
John Francis Grundhofer: president, chief executive officer, director B Los Angeles, CA 1939. ED Loyola University (1960); University of Southern California (1964). PRIM CORP EMPL president, chief executive officer, director: U.S. Bancorp ADD CORP EMPL chairman: U.S. Bank N.A. CORP AFFIL director: Minnesota Mutual Life Insurance Co.; director: Irvine Apartment Community Inc.; director: Minnesota Marketing; director: Donaldson Co. Inc. NONPR AFFIL director: Horatio Alger Association; chairman: Minnesota Business Partnership.
Philip G. Heasley: president, chief operating officer B 1949. ED Baruch College MBA; Marist College BA. PRIM CORP EMPL president, chief operating officer: U.S. Bancorp ADD CORP EMPL president: Retail Product Group.
J. Robert Hoffmann: executive vice president, chief credit officer B 1945. PRIM CORP EMPL executive vice president, chief credit officer: U.S. Bancorp ADD CORP EMPL vice president: US Bank N.A.
Susan E. Lester: executive vice president, chief financial officer B Evergreen Park, IL 1956. ED University of Dayton (1977); University of Chicago (1984). PRIM CORP EMPL executive vice president, chief financial officer: U.S. Bancorp ADD CORP EMPL chief financial officer: U.S. Bank NA.
Lee R. Mitau: executive vice president, general counsel, secretary B Saint Paul, MN 1948. ED Dartmouth College AB (1969); University of Minnesota JD (1972). PRIM CORP EMPL executive vice president, general counsel, secretary: U.S. Bancorp. CORP AFFIL director: HB Fuller Co.
John M. Murphy, Jr.: chairman, chief investment officer B 1948. PRIM CORP EMPL chairman, chief investment officer: U.S. Bank Trust National Association.
David J. Parrin: senior vice president, controller B 1955. PRIM CORP EMPL senior vice president, controller: U.S. Bancorp.
Daniel C. Rohr: executive vice president commercial & business banking B 1946. PRIM CORP EMPL executive vice president commercial & business banking: U.S. Bancorp.
Robert H. Sayre: executive vice president human resources B 1939. PRIM CORP EMPL executive vice president human resources: U.S. Bancorp ADD CORP EMPL executive vice president: United States Bank Trust Gnat Association.
Robert D. Sznewajs: vice chairman retail banking B 1946. PRIM CORP EMPL vice chairman retail banking: U.S. Bancorp.
Richard A. Zona: vice chairman commercial banking & institutional finance B Chicago Heights, IL 1944. ED Roosevelt University (1969). PRIM CORP EMPL vice chairman commercial banking & institutional finance: U.S. Bancorp. CORP AFFIL director: Jostens Inc.; vice chairman: US Bank NA; vice president: First Bank Montana National Association; vice president: First Trust National Association.

Grants Analysis

Disclosure Period: calendar year ending 1998
Total Grants: $1,151,368*
Number of Grants: 1,500 (approx)
Average Grant: $768
Highest Grant: $21,800
Typical Range: $500 to $20,000
***Note:** Giving excludes corporate direct giving, matching gifts, United Way.

Recent Grants

Note: Grants derived from 1998 Form 990.

Arts & Humanities

50,000	Minnesota Orchestra, Minneapolis, MN
13,548	Idaho Public Television, Boise, ID
10,986	Minnesota Public Radio, St Paul, MN
10,740	Twin Cities Public Tv, Minneapolis, MN
7,050	Seattle Symphony, Seattle, WA
4,063	Oregon Public Broadcasting, Portland, OR
3,975	Minneapolis Institute of Arts, Minneapolis, MN
3,668	St Paul Chamber Orchestra, St Paul, MN

Civic & Public Affairs

3,000	Central Minnesota Community Foundation, St Cloud, MN

Education

50,000	Carlson School of Management, Minneapolis, MN
20,000	Montana State University Foundation, Bozeman, MT
8,529	University of Oregon Foundatio, Eugene, OR
8,208	College of Saint Benedict, St Joseph, MN
7,725	Dartmouth College, Hanover, NH
7,449	Boise State University Foundation, Boise, ID
6,561	Breck School, Minneapolis, MN
6,100	Portland State University Foundation, Portland, OR
6,049	Concordia College, Moorhead, MN
5,735	University of Minnesota, Minneapolis, MN
5,679	St Olaf College, Northfield, MN
5,225	Hamline University, St Paul, MN
5,050	Cretin-Derham Hall High School, St Paul, MN
4,892	Mankato State University, Mankato, MN
4,769	Totino-Grace High School, Fridley, MN
4,437	University of Minnesota, Minneapolis, MN
4,364	Calvin Christian School, Sioux Falls, SD
4,200	College of St Catherine, St Paul, MN
4,043	Marquette University, Milwaukee, WI
3,875	Carleton College, Northfield, MN
3,750	Creighton University University Relations, Omaha, NE
3,639	Gustavus Adolphus College, St Peter, MN
3,600	Harvard University, Cambridge, MA
3,600	Seattle Pacific University, Seattle, WA
3,575	Kansas University Endowment Association, Lawrence, KS
3,500	Columbia University, New York, NY
3,250	Mount Holyoke College, South Hadley, MA
3,250	Smith College, Northampton, MA
3,150	Gonzaga University, Spokane, WA
3,146	Minneapolis College of Art & Design, Minneapolis, MN
3,050	Academy of the Holy Angels, Richfield, MN
3,050	Augsburg College Ave, Minneapolis, MN
3,000	Cole Christian School, Boise, ID

Health

4,320	Providence Medical Center Foundation of Seattle, Seattle, WA
4,011	American Diabetes Association, Portland, OR
3,895	National Multiple Sclerosis, Minneapolis, MN

Religion

3,350	Salvation Army Brooklyn Center, Brooklyn Center, MN

Social Services

5,200	Animal Humane Society, Golden Valley, MN
3,895	Second Harvest St Paul Food Bank, St Paul, MN
3,475	Oregon Food Bank, Portland, OR
3,300	Vanessa Behan Crisis Nursery, Spokane, WA
3,200	Sharing & Caring Hands, Minneapolis, MN

U.S. Bancorp Piper Jaffray

Company Contact

222 South Ninth Street
Minneapolis, MN 55402
Web: http://www.piperjaffray.com

Company Description

Former Name: Piper Jaffray & Hopwood; Piper Jaffray Companies, Inc. (1999).
Revenue: US$601,900,000
Employees: 3,182

SIC(s): 6211 Security Brokers & Dealers, 6719 Holding Companies Nec.
Parent Company: U.S. Bancorp, 601 Second Avenue South, Minneapolis, MN, United States

Nonmonetary Support

Value: $10,744 (1996); $40,000 (1995)
Type: Donated Equipment; In-kind Services
Contact: Brenda Cich, Administrative Assistant
Email: bcich@pjc.com
Note: 1997 nonmonetary support $15,000. Company provides nonmonetary support. In-kind services are in the form of printing or meeting services; support should be requested by an employee.

Corporate Sponsorship

Range: less than $125,000
Type: Arts & cultural events; Festivals/fairs; Music & entertainment events; Pledge-a-thon; Sports events
Note: Sponsors golf tournaments, music and film festivals, and dinner fundraisers.

Piper Jaffray Companies Foundation

Giving Contact

Marina Lyon, Director, Public Affairs
U.S. Bancorp Piper Jaffray
Phone: (612)342-5501
Fax: (612)342-6085
Web: http://www.piperjaffray.com/pj/pj_ci.asp

Alternate Contact

Chris Kewitch, Community Affairs

Description

Founded: 1993
EIN: 411734808
Organization Type: Corporate Foundation
Former Name: Piper Jaffray Companies Inc. (2000).
Giving Locations: MN: Twin Cities area headquarters.
Grant Types: Capital, Employee Matching Gifts, Endowment, General Support, Operating Expenses.
Note: Employee matching gift ratio: 1 to 1 to accredited educational institutions and nonprofit organisation, with a minimum of $25 and maximum of $1,000 annually.

Giving Philosophy

'The Foundation supports organizations with programs that enhance the lives of people living and working in communities where we have offices.
'Within this broad framework, our primary interest is supporting organizations that assist people in helping themselves. Our highest priority is family stability programs (including such areas as housing, family violence, responsible parenting), early childhood development, job training/career development, and youth development.
'Healthy communities are composed of many elements. While support for human service organizations is our main interest, we recognize that civic involvement and arts and cultural experiences enhance the quality of life. For this reason, the Foundation will also consider requests from organizations that increase citizen understanding or involvement in civic affairs, or that enhance the artistic and cultural life of the community.' *Community Support Guidelines*

Financial Summary

Total Giving: $2,750,000 (1998 approx); $2,500,000 (1997 approx); $2,284,876 (1996). Note: 1998 giving reflects four additional grants made from October 1 to December 31, 1998. Contributes through corporate direct giving program and foundation.
Giving Analysis: Giving for 1996 includes: corporate direct giving ($1,231,010); foundation ($656,370); domestic subsidiaries ($397,496); 1997: foundation ($592,805); foundation grants to United Way ($143,500); 1998: foundation ($421,946); foundation grants to United Way ($115,000)
Assets: $4,107,798 (1998); $3,766,845 (1997); $2,388,532 (1996). Note: 1998 asset figure reflects change of accounting period from September 30 to December 31.
Gifts Received: $181,018 (1998); $1,561,243 (1997); $273,750 (1996). Note: Contributions are received from Piper Jaffray Cos.

Typical Recipients

Arts & Humanities: Arts Centers, Arts Festivals, Arts Institutes, Film & Video, Arts & Humanities-General, Libraries, Museums/Galleries, Music, Opera, Performing Arts, Public Broadcasting, Theater
Civic & Public Affairs: Business/Free Enterprise, Chambers of Commerce, Community Foundations, Economic Development, Employment/Job Training, Civic & Public Affairs-General, Housing, Native American Affairs, Nonprofit Management, Urban & Community Affairs, Women's Affairs, Zoos/Aquariums
Education: Arts/Humanities Education, Business Education, Colleges & Universities, Economic Education, Education Funds, Education Reform, Elementary Education (Private), Education-General, Gifted & Talented Programs, Leadership Training, Minority Education, Private Education (Precollege), Public Education (Precollege), Student Aid, Vocational & Technical Education
Environment: Environment-General, Resource Conservation
Health: Cancer, Children's Health/Hospitals, Emergency/Ambulance Services, Hospitals, Long-Term Care, Medical Rehabilitation, Multiple Sclerosis, Public Health
International: Health Care/Hospitals
Religion: Churches, Dioceses, Jewish Causes, Ministries, Religious Welfare, Social/Policy Issues
Science: Science Museums
Social Services: At-Risk Youth, Big Brother/Big Sister, Child Welfare, Community Centers, Community Service Organizations, Domestic Violence, Emergency Relief, Family Planning, Family Services, Food/Clothing Distribution, People with Disabilities, Recreation & Athletics, Scouts, Shelters/Homelessness, Social Services-General, United Funds/United Ways, Volunteer Services, YMCA/YWCA/YMHA/YWHA, Youth Organizations

Contributions Analysis

Giving Priorities: Highest priority is to support long-term improvement in the lives of socio-economically disadvantaged families with children.
Arts & Humanities: 15%. Funds art museums, opera, public radio, film institute, and performing art.
Civic & Public Affairs: 20%. Funds community services, zoological society, and neighborhood services.
Education: 9%. Funds educational programs, preparatory schools, and colleges.
Health: 6%. Funds children's hospitals, health services, and the American Red Cross.
International: 2%. International services.
Science: 3%. Minnesota Science Museum.
Social Services: 45%. Funds youth and children services, YMCA, YWCA, and human services.

Application Procedures

Initial Contact: organizations in the Minneapolis/St. Paul metropolitan area may request general operating support by completing an application form from the Foundation; organizations in the Twin Cities area requesting capital support should submit a proposal and supporting material to the foundation; organizations outside the Twin Cities area requesting capital support should submit a proposal to the nearest branch office.
Application Requirements: Both operating and capital support requests should include a cover letter with a summary and amount requested; recent annual report; current operating budget; list of major supporters; recent audited financial statement; copy of IRS 501(c)(3) determination letter; current list of officers, board members and key staff; and a list of contributions received (for capital requests only).
Deadlines: October 31 or May 31, for general operating support; April 30 for capital requests.
Review Process: Organizations are notified within three weeks of application receipt whether or not their applications will be reviewed.
Applications scheduled for review by the Foundation board are assigned a reviewer to discuss the application with a representative from the applying organization. After information is gathered and analyzed, the Foundation board meets and makes a decision.
Evaluative Criteria: In evaluating requests, the committee considers the petitioning organization's: organizational effectiveness, including helping individuals or improving the civic or cultural life of the community; evaluating and maintaining a set value of outcomes; qualified staff members; financial stability and operating efficiency, including fund-raising ability; ongoing support; responsible governing body, including evidence of long-range plans, a good reputation, active and sensitive board members; and Piper Jaffray employee involvement; capital requests are also considered based on how important project is to community.
Decision Notification: Requests are considered during meetings held in February, May, and September.

Restrictions

Foundation will not support the following: programs expansion; specific program costs; event sponsorships; ticket purchases at fundraising events; travel; expenses associated with team competition; basic and applied research.
Also not funded are: health or disease-specific organizations; individuals; newly formed nonprofit organizations; religious organizations for religious purposes; political, veteran, service or fraternal organizations; public or private K-12 schools; public or private higher education institutions; emergency memberships, or 501(c)(4) or (6) organizations.
The Minnesota Common Grant Application Form is not accepted.
Support for higher education is provided through the U.S. Bancorp Community and Higher Education Matching Gift Program.

Additional Information

In 1999, the foundation began the Youth Employment Strategies (YES) initiative. This two-year initiative will provide for effective employment training programs for disadvantaged youth and young adults.
The foundation reports that in 2000 more than 50% of charitable giving will be distributed by the U.S. Bancorp Piper Jaffray Foundation. Remainder of funds are distributed through branch offices and through corporate giving programs.
Publications: Community Involvement Report; Community Affairs Annual Report; Application Form and; Community Support Guidelines

Corporate Officials

Karen M. Bohn: chief executive officera relations manager B Grand Forks, ND 1953. ED University of North Dakota (1975); University of North Dakota (1976). PRIM CORP EMPL chief executive officer: Piper Jaffray Companies. CORP AFFIL officer: United States Piper Jaffray Inc.; director: Universal Hospital Service; director: Bcbsm Inc.; director: Blue Cross & Blue Shield Minnesota.
Andrew S. Duff: president B Minneapolis, MN 1957. ED Tufts University (1980). PRIM CORP EMPL president: Piper Jaffray Companies Inc.
Marina Lyon: director public affairs PRIM CORP EMPL director public affairs: Piper Jaffray Companies Inc.

Addison Lewis Piper: chairman, chief executive officer, director B Minneapolis, MN 1946. ED Williams College BA (1968); Stanford University MBA (1972). PRIM CORP EMPL chairman, chief executive officer, director: Piper Jaffray Companies Inc. CORP AFFIL director: Piper Trust Co.; chairman: United States Piper Jaffray Inc.; chairman, chief executive officer, chairman management committee: Piper Jaffray & Hopwood Inc.; ltd. partner: BGD5 Ltd. Partnership; director: Greenspring Co.; director: Allina Health System Inc. NONPR AFFIL director: Minnesota Business Partnership; member: Securities Industry Association; director: Abbott-Northwestern Hospital; treasurer: CARE Foundation Minneapolis. CLUB AFFIL Woodhill Country Club; Minneapolis Club; Ventana Canyon; Country Club Rockies.
Deborah K. Roesler: chief financial officer B 1954. PRIM CORP EMPL chief financial officer: Piper Jaffray Inc. CORP AFFIL chief financial officer: United States Piper Jaffray Inc.
Maria Verven: media relations manager

Foundation Officials

Karen M. Bohn: president (see above)
Teresa Bonner: vice president
Ann Brookman: director
Brenda M. Cich: secretary CORP AFFIL personnel: Piper Jaffray Inc.
William H. Ellis: director B 1942. ED DePauw University BA (1964); University of Oregon MBA (1966). PRIM CORP EMPL president, chief operating officer: Piper Jaffray Companies Inc. CORP AFFIL chairman: American Government Income Fund.
Paula Fadden: director
Dee Gore: director
Kathy Henderson: treasurer
Steve Hird: director
Warren Kelly: director
Marina Lyon: vice president PRIM CORP EMPL director public affairs: Piper Jaffray Companies Inc.
Annette Minor: director
Addison Lewis Piper: director (see above)
Dave Shehan: director

Grants Analysis

Disclosure Period: calendar year ending 1998
Total Grants: $428,342*
Number of Grants: 149
Average Grant: $2,894
Highest Grant: $250,000*
Typical Range: $1,000 to $15,000
***Note:** Giving excludes United Way, corporate direct giving, and highest grant.

Recent Grants

Note: Grants derived from 1998 Form 990.

Arts & Humanities

8,000	Saint Paul Chamber Orchestra, St. Paul, MN
7,500	Minneapolis Institute of Arts, Minneapolis, MN
7,500	Minnesota Public Radio, St. Paul, MN
6,000	Guthrie Theater, Minneapolis, MN
5,000	Independent Feature Project, Minneapolis, MN
5,000	The Lawrence Arts Center, Lawrence, KS -- building
5,000	Minnesota Museum of American Art, St. Paul, MN
4,200	The Minnesota Opera, Minneapolis, MN
4,000	Children's Theatre Company, Minneapolis, MN
4,000	Minnesota Museum of American Art, St. Paul, MN
3,500	Minnesota Children's Museum, St. Paul, MN
3,000	Minnesota Children's Museum, St. Paul, MN
2,500	Plymouth Music Series, Minneapolis, MN

Civic & Public Affairs

50,000	Minnesota Zoo, Apple Valley, MN
15,500	Zoological Society of Milwaukee, Milwaukee, WI
6,500	Minnesota Accounting Aid Society, Minneapolis, MN
5,000	Mercy Housing, Inc., Denver, CO
3,000	Women Venture, St. Paul, MN
2,750	Twin Cities Habitat for Humanity, Minneapolis, MN
2,500	Metropolitan Economic Development, Minneapolis, MN -- Ec

Education

14,000	Business Economics Education, Minneapolis, MN
10,000	Junior Achievement of the U, Minneapolis, MN
8,500	Minnesota Private College Foundation, St. Paul, MN
2,750	United Negro College Fund, Minneapolis, MN
2,500	Iowa College Foundation, Des Moines, IA

Environment

2,500	The Nature Conservancy of, Minneapolis, MN

Health

25,000	Abbott Northwestern Hospital, Minneapolis, MN
2,500	Neighborhood Health Care Network, St. Paul, MN

International

10,000	CARE Foundation, Plymouth, MN

Religion

2,500	St. Stephen's Church, Minneapolis, MN

Science

5,500	Science Museum of Minnesota, St. Paul, MN

Social Services

85,000	United Way of Minneapolis, Minneapolis, MN
27,500	United Way of the St. Paul Area, St. Paul, MN
15,000	Bridging, Inc., Bloomington, MN
12,000	Greater Minneapolis Council, Minneapolis, MN
10,000	West Coast Children's Center, El Cerrito, CA
5,000	Emergency Shelters of Apple, Appleton, WI
5,000	Girl Scout Council of Greate, Minneapolis, MN
4,000	Family & Children's Service, Minneapolis, MN
3,500	CommonBond Communities, St. Paul, MN
3,500	Minneapolis Youth Trust, Minneapolis, MN
3,000	Crisis Connection, Minnepolis, MN
3,000	Minneapolis Urban League, Minneapolis, MN
3,000	Planned Parenthood of Minnestoa, St. Paul, MN
2,500	Big Brothers and Sisters of G, Minneapolis, MN
2,500	People Serving People, Inc., Minneapolis, MN
2,500	St. Croix Area United Way, Stillwater, MN
2,500	Southeastern Minnesota Initiative, Owatonna, MN
2,500	YWCA of Minneapolis, Minneapolis, MN
1,500	People Serving People, Inc., Minneapolis, MN

United States Sugar Corp.

Company Contact

Clewiston, FL

Company Description

Employees: 2,700
SIC(s): 0133 Sugarcane & Sugar Beets, 0161 Vegetables & Melons.

United States Sugar Corp. Charitable Trust

Giving Contact

Robert Coker, Contact
United States Sugar Corp. Charitable Trust
PO Box 1207
Clewiston, FL 33440
Phone: (941)983-8121
Fax: (941)983-9827

Description

Founded: 1952
EIN: 596142825
Organization Type: Corporate Foundation
Giving Locations: headquarters and operating communities.
Grant Types: Capital, Emergency, Fellowship, General Support, Professorship, Project.

Financial Summary

Total Giving: $500,000 (fiscal year ending October 31, 1999 approx); $319,314 (fiscal 1998); $406,377 (fiscal 1997). Note: Contributes through corporate direct giving program and foundation.
Giving Analysis: Giving for fiscal 1997 includes: foundation ($396,377); foundation grants to United Way ($10,000); fiscal 1998: foundation ($309,314); foundation grants to United Way ($10,000)
Assets: $190,301 (fiscal 1998); $6,623 (fiscal 1997); $156,788 (fiscal 1996)
Gifts Received: $500,000 (fiscal 1998); $250,000 (fiscal 1997)

Typical Recipients

Arts & Humanities: Arts Associations & Councils, Arts Outreach, Libraries, Museums/Galleries
Civic & Public Affairs: African American Affairs, Business/Free Enterprise, Chambers of Commerce, Clubs, Community Foundations, Economic Development, Economic Policy, Civic & Public Affairs-General, Housing, Law & Justice, Legal Aid, Municipalities/Towns, Nonprofit Management, Philanthropic Organizations, Professional & Trade Associations, Public Policy, Rural Affairs, Safety, Urban & Community Affairs
Education: Afterschool/Enrichment Programs, Agricultural Education, Arts/Humanities Education, Business Education, Colleges & Universities, Community & Junior Colleges, Economic Education, Education Associations, Education Funds, Education Reform, Elementary Education (Private), Elementary Education (Public), Environmental Education, Literacy, Preschool Education, Private Education (Precollege), Public Education (Precollege), Science/Mathematics Education, Secondary Education (Public), Special Education, Student Aid
Environment: Environment-General, Resource Conservation
Health: Alzheimers Disease, Cancer, Children's Health/Hospitals, Clinics/Medical Centers, Diabetes, Emergency/Ambulance Services, Eyes/Blindness, Health Organizations, Heart, Hospices, Hospitals, Medical Rehabilitation, Mental Health, Public Health, Single-Disease Health Associations
International: International Relations

Religion: Churches, Religious Welfare
Science: Science Exhibits & Fairs, Scientific Centers & Institutes, Scientific Organizations
Social Services: Big Brother/Big Sister, Child Welfare, Community Centers, Community Service Organizations, Day Care, Family Services, People with Disabilities, Recreation & Athletics, Scouts, Shelters/Homelessness, Substance Abuse, United Funds/United Ways, YMCA/YWCA/YMHA/YWHA, Youth Organizations

Contributions Analysis

Civic & Public Affairs: 11%. Majority of funds support municipalities. Also supports business/free enterprise programs, environmental affairs, philanthropic organizations, and public policy.
Education: 74%. More than one-half of giving supports colleges and universities. Other areas of interest include agricultural education, business education, education administration and funds, health and physical education, and public education (elementary and precollege).
Health: 4%. Supports hospitals and single-disease health associations.
Social Services: 10%. Child welfare and youth organizations, community centers, the disabled, family services, legal aid, and united funds receive contributions.
Note: Total contributions in 1998.

Application Procedures

Initial Contact: Send a full proposal.
Application Requirements: Include a description of organization; amount requested and purpose of funds sought; recently audited financial statement; and proof of tax-exempt status.
Deadlines: None; trustees meet four times a year.

Additional Information

United States Sugar Corp. reports that its direct giving applies only to organizations located near company's headquarters.

Corporate Officials

J. Nelson Fairbanks: president, chief executive officer, director B 1936. PRIM CORP EMPL president, chief executive officer, director: United States Sugar Corp. CORP AFFIL director: Florida East Coast Industries Inc.; president, director: US Corrulite Corp.
James E. Terrill: executive vice president B Houston, TX 1944. ED Louisiana State University BS. PRIM CORP EMPL executive vice president: United States Sugar Corp. CORP AFFIL executive vice president, director: US Corrulite Corp.
Charles B. Webb, Jr.: vice chairman B 1928. PRIM CORP EMPL vice chairman: United States Sugar Corp. CORP AFFIL director: National Enterprises Inc.

Grants Analysis

Disclosure Period: fiscal year ending October 31, 1998
Total Grants: $309,314*
Number of Grants: 48
Average Grant: $4,985
Highest Grant: $75,000
Typical Range: $1,000 to $20,000
***Note:** Giving excludes United Way. Average grant figure excludes highest grant.

Recent Grants

Note: Grants derived from 1999 Form 990.

Arts & Humanities

500 Labelle Free Library, Inc., Labelle, FL -- Library Expansion Program

Civic & Public Affairs

8,000 City of Clewiston, Clewiston, FL -- Purchase of Equipment for Volunteer Fire Dept.
5,000 City of Moore Haven, Moore Haven, FL -- Playground Equipment
5,000 Montura - Flaghole Volunteer Fire Department, Clewiston, FL -- Purchase Equipment for Volunteer Fire Department
2,500 Central County Water Control District, Clewiston, FL -- Playground Equipment
2,500 Charity Challenge, Inc., Altamonte Springs, FL -- Unrestricted Grant
1,500 Montgomery County Economic Council, Winona, MS -- Unrestricted Grant
1,000 Alexander W. Dreyfoos, Jr. Charitable Foundation, Inc., West Palm Beach, FL -- Unrestricted Grant
1,000 Drive Smart Florida, Orlando, FL -- Unrestricted Grant
1,000 Florida Sheriff's Association, Tallahassee, FL -- Annual Conference
1,000 Horticulture Society of South Florida, West Palm Beach, FL -- Unrestricted Grant
500 David L. Singer Memorial Foundation, Inc., N. Miami Beach, FL -- Special Olympics

Education

75,000 Florida Independent College Fund, Inc., St. Augustine, FL -- Scholarship Program
37,314 Hendry County Board of Public Instruction, Labelle, FL -- Alternative School Funding
25,000 Glades Day School, Inc., Belle Glade, FL -- Unrestricted Grant
25,000 Liberty City Charter School Project, Inc., Coral Gables, FL -- Private Sector Matching for Florida's 1st Charter School
20,000 Florida 4-H Club Foundation, Inc., Gainsville, FL -- Environmental Education Program
12,500 Hendry Public Schools Foundation, Inc., Labelle, FL -- Clewiston Athletic Program
6,000 Junior Achievement of the Palm Beaches, Inc., Riviera Beach, FL -- Applied Business and Economics Courses
5,000 Florida Future Farmers of America Foundation, Inc., Haines City, FL -- Unrestricted Grant
5,000 Hendry County Board of Public Instruction, Labelle, FL -- Labelle High School Expansion of Football Facilities
2,500 Education Partnership of Palm Beach County, Inc., West Palm Beach, FL -- World Class Schools Academy Program
2,500 Florida Council on Economic Education, Inc., Tampa, FL -- Unrestricted Grant
2,500 Hendry Public Schools Foundation, Inc., Labelle, FL -- Golden Apple Awards Dinner
2,500 Hendry Public Schools Foundation, Inc., Labelle, FL -- Drug Awareness Retreat
2,500 Hendry Public Schools Foundation, Inc., Labelle, FL -- Clewiston High School Business Lab
2,500 Hendry Public Schools Foundation, Inc., Labelle, FL -- Labelle Athetic Program
2,500 Ransom Everglades School, Inc., Coconut Grove, FL -- "Summerbridge" Miami
1,500 Glades County School District, Moore Haven, FL -- Athletic Program
1,500 Winona Public Schools, Winona, MS -- "Excellence in Education" Foundation
1,000 Edison Community College Foundation, Inc., Ft. Myers, FL -- Unrestricted Grant
1,000 Labelle High School, Labelle, FL -- Purchase of Athletic Equipment
1,000 Lake City Community College Foundation Inc., Lake City, FL -- Landscape and Cancer Research Programs
1,000 The Progressive School, West Palm Beach, FL -- Unrestricted Grant
500 Hendry County School Board, Labelle, FL -- Clewiston Youth Wrestling Club

Health

5,000 Hendry Regional Medical Center, Clewiston, FL -- Hendry Healthy Kids
2,500 United Cerebral Palsy of Southwest Florida, Inc., Cape Coral, FL -- Unrestricted Grant
1,500 Tyler Holmes Memorial Hospital, Winona, MS -- Unrestricted Grant

International

1,000 The Nations Association Inc., Fort Myers, FL -- Unrestricted Grant

Science

3,000 American Council on Science and Health, New York, NY -- Unrestricted Grant

Social Services

10,000 Boys and Girls Clubs of Palm Beach County Inc., West Palm Beach, FL -- Unrestricted Grant
10,000 United Way of Palm Beach County, Inc., West Palm Beach, FL -- Unrestricted Grant
5,000 Boy Scouts of America, Inc., Palm Beach Gardens, FL -- Unrestricted Grant
2,500 The Arc, Riviera Beach, FL -- Unrestricted Grant
2,500 Clewiston Little League, Inc., Clewiston, FL -- Equipment, Insurance, Uniforms
2,500 Clewiston Youth Football Association, Inc., Clewiston, FL -- Youth Football Program
2,000 Children's Inn at National Institute of Health, Bethesda, MD -- Unrestricted Grant
1,500 Dole Foundation, Washington, DC -- Unrestricted Grant

United States Trust Co. Of New York

Company Contact

New York, NY
Web: http://www.ustrust.com

Company Description

Revenue: US$445,560,000
Employees: 2,250
SIC(s): 6022 State Commercial Banks, 6036 Savings Institutions Except Federal, 6282 Investment Advice, 6289 Security & Commodity Services Nec.
Parent Company: U.S. Trust Corp.

Nonmonetary Support

Type: Donated Equipment; In-kind Services
Contact: Maureen Nuget, Vice President

Corporate Sponsorship

Value: $175,000
Type: Arts & cultural events

U.S. Trust Corp. Foundation

Giving Contact

Carol A. Strickland, Chairman, Corporate Contributions Committee
U.S. Trust Corp. Foundation
114 West 47th Street
New York, NY 10036-1532
Phone: (212)852-1400
Fax: (212)852-1341
Email: foundation@ustrust.com

Description

EIN: 136072081
Organization Type: Corporate Foundation
Giving Locations: NY: New York metropolitan area
Grant Types: Employee Matching Gifts, General Support, Project.
Note: Employee matching gift ratio: 1 to 1 up to $2,000 annually to eligible educational institutions.

Giving Philosophy

'U.S. Trust's corporate contributions should enhance the well-being of the Corporation, supporting worthy organizations in the Corporation's primary market areas. These organizations include cultural and educational institutions, and health, human services, civic, housing-related and urban affairs organizations which assist in building or maintaining an improved quality of life for all citizens of such areas.' *Corporate Contribution Policy, United States Trust Company of New York*

Financial Summary

Total Giving: $500,000 (2000 approx); $486,423 (1998); $437,762 (1997). Note: Contributes through foundation only.
Giving Analysis: Giving for 1996 includes: foundation matching gifts ($173,840); 1997: foundation matching gifts ($140,798); foundation grants to United Way ($50,000); 1998: foundation matching gifts ($161,423); foundation grants to United Way ($50,000)
Assets: $17,768 (1998); $15,317 (1997); $4,734 (1996)
Gifts Received: $485,796 (1998); $447,000 (1997); $395,000 (1996)

Typical Recipients

Arts & Humanities: Arts Associations & Councils, Arts Centers, Arts Funds, Ballet, Community Arts, Dance, Historic Preservation, Museums/Galleries, Music, Opera, Performing Arts, Public Broadcasting, Theater, Visual Arts
Civic & Public Affairs: Business/Free Enterprise, Economic Development, Employment/Job Training, Housing, Legal Aid, Minority Business, Nonprofit Management, Public Policy, Rural Affairs, Urban & Community Affairs, Zoos/Aquariums
Education: Arts/Humanities Education, Business Education, Colleges & Universities, Education-General, International Studies, Literacy, Minority Education, Preschool Education, Private Education (Precollege), Public Education (Precollege), Secondary Education (Private), Special Education, Student Aid, Vocational & Technical Education
Environment: Environment-General
Health: AIDS/HIV, Cancer, Children's Health/Hospitals, Geriatric Health, Health Policy/Cost Containment, Health Funds, Health Organizations, Hospitals, Long-Term Care, Medical Rehabilitation, Nursing Services, Nutrition
Religion: Jewish Causes, Religious Welfare, Seminaries
Social Services: Child Welfare, Community Centers, Community Service Organizations, Delinquency & Criminal Rehabilitation, Family Services, Food/Clothing Distribution, Homes, People with Disabilities, Senior Services, Shelters/Homelessness, Substance Abuse, United Funds/United Ways, Volunteer Services, Youth Organizations

Contributions Analysis

Arts & Humanities: 31%. Contributions are equally distributed between cultural jewels of New York City and institutions supporting the work of emerging artists. U.S. Trust is interested in institutions which make their art accessible to all New Yorkers. Recent grants have been directed toward the New Victory Theater, The New York Public Library, the Theatre Development Fund, and Lincoln Center for the Performing Arts.
Civic & Public Affairs: 15%. Supports economic development and community and neighborhood organizations.
Education: 33%. U.S. Trust's funding to education is provided exclusively through employee participation in the matching gift program.
Health: 2%. Supports children's health.
Social Services: 18%. A substantial portion of the trust's support for human services is allocated through the United Way system.
Note: Total contributions in 1998.

Application Procedures

Initial Contact: Request guidelines, then send a written proposal.
Application Requirements: Include a concise description of organization including legal name, history, purpose, activities; purpose for which the grant is requested; amount requested and list of other sources of financial support, including foundations, corporations, and government grants; copy of IRS determination letter indicating 501(c)(3) tax-exempt status; copy of organization's most recently audited financial statement and form 990; primary goals including a statement of service area and population to which the program is primarily directed; list of officers and board members and their affiliations; budget for current year including sources of projected income and breakdown of actual income versus expense year to date; and description of how the program will be evaluated, including procedures and criteria.
Deadlines: Grant requests are grouped by program area and scheduled for review by the Corporate Contributions Committee during either the first half or second half of the year; all culture and arts grant proposals received by April 1 in any calendar year will be assured consideration for Foundation funding in the first half of the year; civic and community proposals received by September 1 will be assured funding consideration in the second half of the year.
Review Process: Grant proposals are reviewed by the Corporate Contributions Committee.
Evaluative Criteria: Preference is given to organizations which demonstrate: ability to solve problems and provide direct services; innovativeness of programs; broad-based community support; involvement of U.S. Trust employees; reliance on private support, as opposed to tax-supported organizations; self-sufficiency of participants; large number of constituents served; efficiency and effective administration of funds and programs; ability to become self-sufficient rather than dependent on yearly renewals of support; long-term solutions versus short-term remedies; stimulate broader participation and multiply the impact of the funds provided by attracting other contributors; nondiscriminatory practices; volunteer support; support being sought by an organization throughout the community and to the prospects for obtaining this support.
Decision Notification: Organizations applying for a grant receive an acknowledgement of their proposal within two weeks of receipt; grants are disbursed before June 30 or December 31 each year.
Notes: Program will accept the New York Area Common application form. Proposals will not be considered by the Committee until all requested information is received. Proposals that remain incomplete two months after receipt has been acknowledged will be discarded.

Restrictions

The company does not make grants to individuals for educational or any other purpose; religious, veterans', fraternal or labor organizations unless engaged in a significant project benefitting the entire community; organizations, projects or programs outside the United States; political organizations, political candidates, or in support of political activity; organizations requesting support for courtesy advertising, festival participation, telethons, marathons, races, benefits or events, fund-raising dinners, sponsorship of publications or athletic teams; or national associations and member agenices of the United Way and other organizations supported by an umbrella organization.

Additional Information

The foundation selects primarily Manhattan community grants in the area of housing. For job training initiatives, candidates are chosen from the five boroughs of New York City and Nassau County, Long Island.

Corporate Officials

Martha L. Dinerstein: managing director, head marketing & corporate communications PRIM CORP EMPL managing director, head marketing & corporate communications: United States Trust Co. of New York. NONPR AFFIL member: New York Junior League; director: Womens Economic Roundtable; member: Advertising Women New York; member: Financial Womens Association.
John L. Kirby: chief financial officer PRIM CORP EMPL chief financial officer: U.S. Trust Corp.
Jeffrey Stuart Maurer: president, chief operating officer, director B New York, NY 1947. ED Alfred University BA (1969); New York University MBA (1975); Saint John's University JD (1976). PRIM CORP EMPL president, chief operating officer, director: United States Trust Corp. New York.
H. Marshall Schwarz: chairman, chief executive officer B New York, NY 1936. ED Harvard University BA (1958); Harvard University MBA (1961). PRIM CORP EMPL chairman, chief executive officer: United States Trust Co. of New York. CORP AFFIL director: Bowne & Co. Inc.; director: Atlantic Mutual Companies. NONPR AFFIL trustee: Milton Academy; director: United Way New York City; trustee: Columbia University Teachers College; chairman: American Red Cross Greater New York City.
Frederick B. Taylor: vice chairman, chief investment officer B Albany, NY 1941. ED Wesleyan University BA (1963); University of Pennsylvania Wharton School MBA (1965). PRIM CORP EMPL vice chairman, chief investment officer: United States Trust Co. of New York. CORP AFFIL vice chairman, chief investment officer: US Trust Corp.

Foundation Officials

Carol A. Strickland: chairman corporate contributions committee B Cold Spring, NY 1949. ED Skidmore College BA (1972); New York University (1978). PRIM CORP EMPL corp. secretary, senior vice president: United States Trust Co. of New York. CORP AFFIL corporate secretary, senior vice president: US Trust Corp. NONPR AFFIL member: American Society of Corporate Secretaries.

Grants Analysis

Disclosure Period: calendar year ending 1998
Total Grants: $275,000*
Number of Grants: 25
Average Grant: $11,000
Highest Grant: $40,000
Typical Range: $5,000 to $12,500
***Note:** Giving excludes matching gifts; United Way.

Recent Grants

Note: Grants derived from 1997 Form 990.

Arts & Humanities

40,000	Metropolitan Museum of Art, New York, NY
15,000	Concert Artists Guild, New York, NY
15,000	Lincoln Center for Performing Arts, New York, NY
10,000	Bronx Council on the Arts, Bronx, NY
10,000	Lar Lubovitch Dance Company
10,000	New York Landmarks Conservancy, New York, NY
7,500	Theater Development Fund, New York, NY

5,000	Big Apple Circus, New York, NY
5,000	Manhattan Theater Club, New York, NY
5,000	New Victory Theater, Burbank, CA
5,000	New York Foundation for the Arts, New York, NY
5,000	Riverside Symphony

Civic & Public Affairs

12,500	Neighborhood 2000 Fund, New York, NY
5,000	Advertising Council, New York, NY
5,000	National Center for Disability Services, Albertson, NY
5,000	Nonprofit Facilities Fund, New York, NY
5,000	Times Square, New York, NY

Education

10,000	Cooper Union for the Advancement of Science and the Arts, New York, NY
2,000	Boston College, Chestnut Hill, MA
2,000	Chadwick School, Peninsula, CA
2,000	French American School, Larchmont, NY
2,000	Miss Porter's School, Farmington, CT
2,000	Perlman Jewish Day School, Wynnewood, PA
2,000	Pomona College, Claremont, CA
2,000	University of Southern California, Los Angeles, CA
2,000	Vassar College, Poughkeepsie, NY
1,750	St. Francis Preparatory School, Fresh Meadows, NY
1,500	Bates College, Lewiston, ME
1,500	Clairbourn School, San Gabriel, CA
1,400	Skidmore College, Saratoga Springs, NY
1,312	Wheaton College, Wheaton, IL
1,250	Union College, Barbourville, KY
1,050	Polytechnic School, Pasadena, CA
1,000	Albertus Magnus College, New Haven, CT
1,000	Alfred University, Alfred, NY
1,000	Highland Park Independent School District Education Foundation, Dallas, TX
1,000	New York University, New York, NY
1,000	St. Paul's School, Concord, NH
950	Delores Mission School, Los Angeles, CA
600	Middlesex School, Concord, MA
544	Princeton University, Princeton, NJ
500	Northwest Indian College Foundation, Bellingham, WA
500	St. Ann School, West Palm Beach, FL
500	St. Luke's Education Foundation, Bronx, NY

Health

10,000	Children's Health Fund, New York, NY
10,000	Hebrew Home for the Aged at Riverdale, New York, NY
7,500	God's Love We Deliver, New York, NY

Religion

2,000	Cathedral Preparatory Seminary, Elmhurst, NY

Social Services

50,000	United Way, New York, NY
12,500	Bridge Fund, New York, NY

UNITED TECHNOLOGIES CORP.

Company Contact

One Financial Plaza
Hartford, CT 06103
Phone: (860)728-7000
Fax: (860)728-7979
Web: http://www.utc.com

Company Description

Revenue: US$25,242,000,000 (1999)
Profit: US$1,531,000,000 (1999)
Employees: 178,800 (1999)
Fortune Rank: 57, per FORTUNE Magazine's list of 500 Largest U.S. Corporations (1999).
FF 57
SIC(s): 3511 Turbines & Turbine Generator Sets, 3519 Internal Combustion Engines Nec, 3534 Elevators & Moving Stairways, 3721 Aircraft.

Operating Locations

Argentina: Ascensores Otis Saici Y F, Buenos Aires; Australia: Sanscord Pty. Ltd., Bayswater; Pratt & Whitney Canada (A 'Asia) Pty. Ltd., Eagle Farm; United Technologies Pty. Ltd., Minto; Carrier Air Conditioning (Holdings) Ltd., Rozelle; Carrier Services Management System Pty. Ltd., Rozelle; Otis Elevator Co. Pty. Ltd., Sydney; Desair Holdings Pty. Ltd., Wembley; Direct Engineering Services Pty. Ltd., Wembley; Frigopol (Australia) Pty. Ltd., Wembley; Portslade Pty. Ltd., Wembley; Austria: Carrier Transicold Austria GmbH, Linz, Oberosterreich; Carrier GmbH, Vienna; Otis GmbH, Vienna; Belgium: Climatech NV, Aartselaar, Anvers; Evapo NV, Antwerpen, Anvers; Carrier SA, Brussels, Brabant; Otis NV, Dilbeek, Brabant; Brunei Darussalam: Q-Carrier (B) Sdn. Bhd., Seria; Brazil: Springer Carrier SA, Canoas; Climazon Industrial Ltda., Manaus; Springer Carrier SA, Sao Paulo; Canada: Pratt & Whitney Canada, Longueuil; Otis Canada, Oakville; United Technologies Pratt & Whitney Canada International, Ottawa; Colombia: International Elevator, Bogota, Cundinamarco; Czech Republic: Avia-Hamilton Standard Aviation Ltd.; Tranza Otis A S, Breclav; Denmark: Otis A/S, Herlev, Copenhagen; France: Ratier-Figeac; Monitor SA, Argenteuil, Val d'Oise; Profroid Industries SA, Aubagne, Bouches-du-Rhone; Profroid SA, Aubagne, Bouches-du-Rhone; Generale Frigorifique France, Bagnolet, Seine-St.-Denis; Cryokit France SA, Bedee, Ille-et-Vilaine; Carrier Transicold France SA, Boos; Carrier Transicold Europe SA, Cergy, Val d'Oise; CFA Ile De France, Cergy, Val d'Oise; Otis, Courbevoie, Hauts-de-Seine; United Technologies Holdings, Courbevoie, Hauts-de-Seine; United Technologies SAS, Courbevoie, Hauts-de-Seine; Carrier Transicold Industries SA, Franqueville St. Pierre; Frigiking France, Franqueville St. Pierre; United Technologies Automotive (France), Garches, Hauts-de-Seine; Distribution Composants D'Ascenseurs (Ste De), Gennevilliers, Hauts-de-Seine; Sangalli (Ascenseurs Walter), Grenoble, Isere; HVH BLB, L'Hay Les Roses, Val-de-Marne; Automatismes et de Services (Cie d'), Meudon, Hauts-de-Seine; Carrier SA, Montluel, Ain; EMA, Nice, Alpes-Maritimes; Technologie (Ste. Offranvillaise de), Offranville, Seine-Maritime; Ascenseurs France Logique, Paris, Ville-de-Paris; Froid Industriel (Ste De), Paris, Ville-de-Paris; Carrier European et Transcontinental Operations, Puteaux, Hauts-de-Seine; Otis Europe SA, Puteaux, Hauts-de-Seine; Pratt & Whitney, Puteaux, Hauts-de-Seine; Ascenseurs (Cie Francaise D'), St. Benoit; Portis SA, Voisins le Bretonneux; Poma Otis Systemes de Transport, Voreppe, Isere; Germany: United Technologies Research Center GmbH, Aachen, Nordrhein-Westfalen; Otis GmbH, Berlin; Liftec Aufzugservice GmbH, Braunschweig, Niedersachsen; United Technologies Automotive (Deutschland) GmbH, Cologne, Nordrhein-Westfalen; Mahler Aufzuege GmbH, Essen; Nordmicroelektronik Feinmechanik AG, Frankfurt, Hessen; United Technologies Holding GmbH, Frankfurt, Hessen; Nord-Micro, Frankfut; Carrier Transicold Deutschland GmbH & Co. KG, Georgsmarienhuette; UT Loewe Automotive Electronics GmbH, Kronach, Bayern; Holland Heating Deutschland GmbH, Linden, Hessen; Hans Winkler Aufzuege GmbH, Maintal, Hessen; Oth Aufzuege GmbH, Munich, Bavaria; Suetrak Transportkaelte GmbH Nord, Oststeinbek; Suetrak Transportkaelte GmbH, Renningen, Baden-Wuerttemberg; Otis Escalator GmbH, Stadthagen, Niedersachsen; Carrier GmbH, Unterschleissheim, Bayern; Guam: Carrier Guam, Harmon; Hong Kong: Carrier Transicold Hong Kong Ltd., Central District; Otis Elevator Co. (Hong Kong) Ltd., Quarry Bay; Carrier Comfort Co. Ltd., Sha Tin; Carrier Hong Kong Ltd., Sha Tin; Otis Far East Holdings Ltd., Wan Chai; Hungary: Otis Felvono KFT, Budapest; United Technologies Automotive (Hungary) KFT, Godollo, Pest; India: Otis Elevator Co. (India) Ltd., Mumbai; Ireland: ILS Irish Lift Services Ltd., Dublin; Pratt & Whitney Ireland Holdings, Rathcoole; PWA International Ltd., Rathcoole; Italy: Carrier Frimar SRL, Alessandria; Eisner Carlo SpA, Cusago, Lombardia; Microtecnica SpA, Torino, Piemonte; Microtecnica, Turin; Carrier SpA, Villasanta, Lombardia; Japan: General Aircon Tecnica, Tokyo; Nippon Building Systems Service Co. Ltd., Tokyo; Toyo Carrier Engineering Co. Ltd., Tokyo; United Technologies International Operations, Tokyo; Carrier Transicold Japan Ltd., Yokohama, Kanagawa; Luxembourg: General Technic - Otis SARL, Howald; Mexico: United Technologies Automotive Electrical Systems de Mexico SA de CV, Chihuahua; Carrier Transicold de Mexico SA de CV, Ciudad de Mexico; Elevadores Otis SA de CV, Ciudad de Mexico; Carrier Mexico SA de CV, Monterrey, Santa Catarina; Malaysia: Carrier International Sdn. Bhd., Bandar Baru Bangi, Selangor; Carrier Malaysia Sdn. Bhd., Petaling Jaya, Selangor; ICI Paints (Malaysia) Sdn. Bhd., Petaling Jaya, Selangor; Netherlands: Ascon Krebber & Buitenhuis VH Liftservice BV, Amersfoort, Utrecht; Otis BV, Amsterdam, Noord-Holland; Carrier BV, Hazerswoude Rijndijk; United Technologies Holdings BV, Hazerswoude Rijndijk; Otis Pacific Holdings BV, Heerhugowaard, Noord-Holland; Pratt & Whitney Overhaul & Repair Center (Europe) BV, Limburg; Noord-Brabant/Evapo Groep BV, Nuenen, Noord-Brabant; Noord-Brabant Komponenten BV, Nuenen, Noord-Brabant; Noord-Brabant Unitbouw BV, Nuenen, Noord-Brabant; Carrier Transicold Netherlands BV, Rotterdam, Zuid-Holland; Euromicro Microtecnica BV, S'Gravenhage, Zuid-Holland; United Technology BV, Vlaardingen, Zuid-Holland; HH-Redec BV, Waalwijk, Noord-Brabant; Holland Conditioning BV, Waalwijk, Noord-Brabant; Holland Heating Carrier BV, Waalwijk, Noord-Brabant; Norway: Otis AS, Oslo, Akershus; New Zealand: Carrier Air Conditioning (New Zealand) Ltd. Carrier Zonepak Ltd., East Tamaki, Auckland; Otis Elevator Co. Ltd., Parnell, Auckland; Papua New Guinea: Carrier Air Conditioning Papua New Guinea Pty. Ltd., Boroko; Portugal: Carrier Portugal Ar Condicionado Lda., Carnaxide, Oeiras; Otis Elevadores SA, Mem Martins, Sintra; A Reparadora de Ascensores Imperio Lda., Mem Martins, Sintra; Inelda Industria Nacional de Elevadores Lda., Rio de Mouro, Sintra; United Technologies Automotive (Portugal) Automovel Lda., Valongo; Russia: Hamilton Standard-Nauka; Sikorsky; Singapore: Carrier Singapore (Pte) Ltd., Singapore; Carrier Transicold Singapore Pte. Ltd., Singapore; Otis Elevator Co. (Singapore) Pte. Ltd., Singapore; Otis Elevator Construction & Installation Co. (Singapore) Pte. Ltd., Singapore; Pratt & Whitney Canada (SEA) Pte. Ltd., Singapore; Turbine Overhaul Services Pte. Ltd., Singapore; Spain: Iberfrio Carrier SA, Alcobendas, Madrid; Mantenimiento de Ascensores SL, Barcelona, Cataluna; Sutrak Iberica SL, La Ampolla, Tarragona; Ascensores Angulo SA, Madrid; Carrier Espana SA, Madrid; Conventi SA, Madrid; Inmobiliaria Zie SA, Madrid; Zardoya Otis SA, Madrid; Ascensores Ingar SA, Maracena, Granada; Ascensores Eguren SA, Munguia, Vizcaya; Ascensores Serra SA, Olot, Gerona; Mecanismos Auxiliares Industriales SA, Valls, Cataluna; Switzerland: Otis Switzerland, Fribourg; Carrier-Winner SA, Geneva; UT Holding SA, Geneva; Vallift Otis SA, Sion, Valais; Thailand: Link Carlyle Co. Ltd., Bangkok; Taiwan: Carricon Enterprises Co. Ltd., Taipei; Carrier Taiwan Co. Ltd., Taipei; United Kingdom: United Steering Systems Clifford Ltd., Birmingham, West Midlands; United Steering Systems Elmgrove Ltd., Birmingham, West Midlands; ERS (Lifts & Escalators) Ltd., Bromley, Kent; P & W C

Aircraft Services (United Kingdom) Ltd., Farnborough, Hampshire; Combined Lift Services (Merseyside) Ltd., Leicester, Leicestershire; Evans Lifts Ltd., Leicester, Leicestershire; Manor Lifts Ltd., Leicester, Leicestershire; Wadsworth Lifts Ltd., Leicester, Leicestershire; British Elevators Ltd., London; British Lifts Ltd., London; Carrier Pension Trustee Ltd., London; English Lifts Ltd., London; Gnitrow Ltd., London; Hall Lifts & Escalators Ltd., London; Otis Elevator Pension Trustee Ltd., London; Otis Plc, London; Porn & Dunwoody (Lifts) Ltd., London; SKG (United Kingdom) Ltd., London; Strategic Planning Associates Starplan SA, London; Waygood Lifts Ltd., London; United Technologies Automotive (United Kingdom) Ltd., Peterborough, Cambridgeshire; Britannia Lift & Automation Ltd., Sheerness, Kent; Carrier Transicold United Kingdom Ltd., Warrington, Cheshire; Carrier Holdings Ltd., Westerham, Kent; Takepine Ltd., Westerham, Kent; Carrier European & Transcontinental Operations Ltd., Woking, Surrey; Carrier Transcontinental Co. Ltd., Woking, Surrey; Pita Ltd., Woking, Surrey; United Technologies Finance (UK) Ltd., Woking, Surrey; United Technologies Holdings Plc, Woking, Surrey

SUBSIDIARY COMPANIES

CT: Hamilton Sundstrand Corp., Windsor Locks

Nonmonetary Support

Value: $5,800 (1990); $1,000,000 (1989); $1,334,159 (1987)
Type: In-kind Services

Giving Contact

Jacqueline F. Strayer, Director, Contribution & Communication Services
United Technologies Corp.
One Financial Plaza
Hartford, CT 06101
Phone: (860)728-7943
Fax: (860)728-7022

Alternate Contact

Leah Bailey, Contributions and Matching Gifts Administrator
Phone: (860)728-7848

Description

Organization Type: Corporate Giving Program
Giving Locations: CT: East Hartford, Hartford, Middletown, Stratford, Windsor Lock; DC: Washington; FL: Palm Beach; IN: Bloomington; MI: Dearborn; NY: Syracuse communities with major facilities and substantial employee residence population.
Grant Types: Capital, Employee Matching Gifts.
Note: Employee matching gift ratio: 1 to 1 to colleges, universities, private secondary schools, and environmental organisation. Public broadcasting, libraries, and cultural organisation are also eligible for matching gifts.

Giving Philosophy

'The increasing needs of our communities, shifts in governmental support, as well as slowing business charitable contributions, require a change in traditional American corporate philanthropy. . . . We believe that our contributions can only make a meaningful impact by targeting specific issues and focusing community-wide support on solutions. . . . We intend to increase the number of collaborative grants among non-profit agencies. By making more than one organization accountable for the development and administration of a project, we increase the number of people working toward a single solution..' United Technologies Contributions Focus

Financial Summary

Total Giving: $14,088,381 (1997); $12,800,000 (1996 approx); $11,500,000 (1994). Note: Contributes through corporate direct giving program only. 1997 Giving includes corporate direct giving ($14,085,309); international subsidiaries ($3,072).

Typical Recipients

Arts & Humanities: Arts Appreciation, Arts Centers, Community Arts, Historic Preservation, Museums/Galleries, Music, Opera, Performing Arts
Civic & Public Affairs: Business/Free Enterprise, Law & Justice, Public Policy, Urban & Community Affairs, Women's Affairs
Education: Business Education, Colleges & Universities, Community & Junior Colleges, Engineering/Technological Education, Literacy, Minority Education, Public Education (Precollege), Science/Mathematics Education
Environment: Environment-General
Health: Health Policy/Cost Containment, Health Organizations, Hospitals
Science: Science Exhibits & Fairs
Social Services: Child Welfare, Community Service Organizations, Family Services, Food/Clothing Distribution, People with Disabilities, Senior Services, Substance Abuse, Volunteer Services, Youth Organizations

Contributions Analysis

Giving Priorities: Education, health, social welfare, culture and the arts, and civic organizations. Company's overseas subsidiaries make grants directly to local organizations to improve community services and education totaling more than $1.5 million annually. Overseas programs are handled independently. Domestically, any contributions for international purposes would have to fall under the company's general focus in the areas of math and science within operating communities. Consequently, such contributions are rare. Company has sponsored a program with Junior Achievement that promotes an understanding of international trade and business issues.
Arts & Humanities: 10% to 15%. National touring museum exhibitions, art education, dance companies, opera, historical societies, art centers, libraries, museums, public radio and television, and historic architectural restoration projects.
Civic & Public Affairs: 10% to 15%. Primarily organizations involved in community development activities in operating locations.Supports civic projects, minority and women's programs, and public policy organizations. Particular interest in agencies willing to form alliances with other groups to improve the community.
Education: 45%. Colleges and universities, including company's 22 'focus' schools. Emphasis is on institutions from which company recruits employees and quality engineering programs, including those directed at women and minorities. Other interests include basic research related to company's fields of business and continuing education for company employees. Additional support provided through precollegiate math and science programs and teacher enrichment programs. Education is the company's major priority.
Health: 20% to 25%. Major support to United Ways and hospitals. Also supports preventive medical treatment groups and activities for the mentally and physically handicapped,senior citizens, youth groups, and health care cost containment. Some funding seeks to establish links between traditional funding areas; for example, funding for a human service organization might be contingent on help they provide an educational or civic group. Grants favored in states where company has operations.

Application Procedures

Initial Contact: brief letter
Application Requirements: a description of organization; amount and purpose of grant requested; most recent financial statement; list of directors; how program objectives will be achieved, including evidence of need for project; proof that organization can achieve project's purpose; project budget; current major donor listing with dollar amounts and anticipated funding sources for future project support; proof of tax-exempt status
Deadlines: August 1, for following year
Review Process: initial review conducted by contributions office; final decision made by corporate contributions committee
Decision Notification: all funding decisions made during fourth quarter; notification generally not made before February 5 of following year
Notes: All funding applications must be received by mail.

Restrictions

Does not support partisan political organizations; individuals; religious organizations for sectarian purposes; controversial social causes; organizations which are the recipients of federated drives to which company already contributes; or endowment campaigns.

Corporate Officials

George A. L. David: chairman, president, chief executive officer, chief operating officer B Bryn Mawr, PA 1942. ED Harvard University BA (1965); University of Virginia MBA (1967). PRIM CORP EMPL chairman, president, chief executive officer, chief operating officer: United Technologies Corp. NONPR AFFIL chairman: United States-ASEAN Council Business Technology; trustee: Wadsworth Atheneum; director: Institute International Economics; chairman: National Minority Supplier Development Council Inc.

Giving Program Officials

Jacqueline Strayer: director corporate contributions

Grants Analysis

Disclosure Period: calendar year ending
Typical Range: $2,000 to $30,000

UNITED WISCONSIN SERVICES

Company Contact

Milwaukee, WI
Web: http://www.uwz.com

Company Description

Assets: US$836,100,000
Employees: 1,202
SIC(s): 6321 Accident & Health Insurance, 8099 Health & Allied Services Nec.

Corporate Sponsorship

Type: Arts & cultural events; Festivals/fairs; Music & entertainment events; Sports events

United Wisconsin Services Foundation

Giving Contact

Tom Luljak, Executive Director
United Wisconsin Services Foundation
401 West Michigan Street
Milwaukee, WI 53203
Phone: (414)226-5756
Fax: (414)226-2637

Description

Founded: 1984
EIN: 391514703
Organization Type: Corporate Foundation
Giving Locations: WI
Grant Types: General Support, Multiyear/Continuing Support, Operating Expenses, Scholarship.

Financial Summary

Total Giving: $539,804 (1997); $574,791 (1996); $625,289 (1995). Note: Contributes through foundation only. 1996 Giving includes foundation ($503,181); United Way ($71,610). 1995 Giving includes matching gifts; United Way ($65,820).

Assets: $5,768,735 (1997); $5,521,400 (1996); $5,617,514 (1995)

Gifts Received: $100 (1995); $2,800,000 (1994); $275,000 (1992). Note: In 1995, contributions were received from Blue Cross & Blue Shield United of Wisconsin.

Typical Recipients

Arts & Humanities: Arts Associations & Councils, Arts Festivals, Community Arts, Dance, History & Archaeology, Libraries, Museums/Galleries, Music, Opera, Performing Arts, Public Broadcasting, Theater

Civic & Public Affairs: African American Affairs, Business/Free Enterprise, Chambers of Commerce, Community Foundations, Economic Development, Economic Policy, Employment/Job Training, Parades/Festivals, Professional & Trade Associations, Public Policy, Safety, Urban & Community Affairs, Women's Affairs

Education: Business Education, Colleges & Universities, Continuing Education, Education Funds, Education Reform, Faculty Development, Education-General, Gifted & Talented Programs, Literacy, Medical Education, Minority Education, Social Sciences Education, Student Aid, Vocational & Technical Education

Environment: Environment-General

Health: Alzheimers Disease, Arthritis, Cancer, Children's Health/Hospitals, Clinics/Medical Centers, Eyes/Blindness, Geriatric Health, Health Policy/Cost Containment, Health Organizations, Heart, Medical Research, Mental Health, Prenatal Health Issues, Public Health, Respiratory, Single-Disease Health Associations

International: Foreign Arts Organizations, International Environmental Issues

Religion: Religious Welfare

Social Services: Community Centers, Community Service Organizations, Family Services, Food/Clothing Distribution, Recreation & Athletics, Scouts, Senior Services, Substance Abuse, United Funds/ United Ways, Volunteer Services, YMCA/YWCA/ YMHA/YWHA, Youth Organizations

Contributions Analysis

Arts & Humanities: About 20%. Supports cultural education, museums, and theaters.

Civic & Public Affairs: About 40%. Funds go to organizations to assist the aging, Junior Achievement, veterans programs, food for the needy programs, and the prevention of family violence.

Education: 10% to 15%. Supports scholarship funds and other educational programs.

Health: About 10%. Supports children's health education programs, mental health associations, and research studies.

Social Services: 15% to 20%. Majority of support given to the United Way. Also funds, Big Brother and Big Sisters, and the Boys and Girls Club.

Application Procedures

Initial Contact: a letter requesting guidelines and application form

Deadlines: None.

Restrictions

Does not support individuals.

Foundation considers requests from religious organizations and institutions only when the resulting impact of the project is not primarily denominational.

Foundation considers requests from provider organizations and institutions (hospitals, clinics) only when the resulting impact of the project can be proven to benefit an entire community/region, or supports an employee's involvement with that organization.

Foundation considers requests for building projects or capital campaigns only when having a special interest to the purposes of the foundation.

Foundation does not support grant requests from member agencies of the United Way or the United Performing Arts Fund.

Additional Information

Contributions support nonprofit, charitable organizations with proof of 501(c)(3) status. Emphasis is on health and wellness activities, as well as other activities that add to the quality of life.

Contributions are awarded on a one-time basis without commitment to future giving.

Affiliates of United Wisconsin Services include Blue Cross & Blue Shield United of Wisconsin, Compcare Health Services Insurance Corp., Dentacare, Take Control Inc., Meridian Resource Corp., United Government Services, United Heartland, American Medical Security, Proservices, United Wisconsin Group, United Wisconsin Insurance Co., and United Wisconsin Life Insurance Co.

Publications: Guidelines; Application Form

Corporate Officials

Thomas R. Hefty: chairman, president, chief executive officer B 1947. ED University of Wisconsin BA (1968); Johns Hopkins University MA (1969); University of Wisconsin Law School JD (1973). PRIM CORP EMPL chairman, president, chief executive officer: United Wisconsin Services Inc. CORP AFFIL chairman, president: United Wisconsin Proservices; chief executive officer: Valley Health Plan; chairman: United Wisconsin Life Insurance; president: United Heartland Inc.; chairman: United Wisconsin Insurance Co.; chief executive officer: Meridian Resources Corp.; chairman, president: Take Control; chairman: Meridian Managed Care Inc.; chairman: Blue Cross & Blue Shield United Wisconsin; chairman: Compcare Health Services Insurance Corp.

Penny Siewert: vice president regional services PRIM CORP EMPL vice president regional services: United Wisconsin Services ADD CORP EMPL vice president: Meridian Resource Corp.; vice president: Meridian Managed Care Inc.; secretary: Unity Health Plans Insurance. CORP AFFIL officer: Blue Cross & Blue Shield United.

Essie M. Whitelaw: president, chief operating officer B 1948. ED Utica College. PRIM CORP EMPL president, chief operating officer: Blue Cross & Blue Shield United of Wisconsin. CORP AFFIL director: WICOR; director: Universal Foods Corp.; president: American Medical Security Group; vice president: Compcare Health Services. NONPR AFFIL vice chairman: Metropolitan Milwaukee Association.

Foundation Officials

Roger Formisano: vice president PRIM CORP EMPL president, chief operating officer: Compcare Health Services Insurance Corp. CORP AFFIL executive vice president, chief operating officer: United Wisconsin Services; vice president: Valley Health Plan; vice president: United Wisconsin Insurance Co.; vice president: United Wisconsin Life Insurance; president: Meridian Resources Corp.; director: United Heartland Inc.; president, chief operating officer: Meridian Managed Care Inc.

Mark Howard Granoff: vice president B Brooklyn, NY 1946. ED City University of New York BA (1968); City University of New York MA (1972). PRIM CORP EMPL president, chief operating officer: United Wisconsin Group. CORP AFFIL executive president: United Wisconsin Life Insurance; vice president: United Wisconsin Service; vice president: Blue Cross & Blue Shield United Wisconsin; president: United Wisconsin Insurance Co.

Thomas R. Hefty: chairman, president, chief executive officer (see above)

Tom Luljak: executive director PRIM CORP EMPL director corporate communications: United Wisconsin Services.

Penny Siewert: vice president, secretary, treasurer (see above)

Essie M. Whitelaw: vice president (see above)

Grants Analysis

Disclosure Period: calendar year ending 1997

Total Grants: $539,804

Number of Grants: 137

Average Grant: $3,940

Highest Grant: $71,000

Typical Range: $500 to $10,000

Recent Grants

Note: Grants derived from 1996 Form 990.

Arts & Humanities

66,243	United Performing Arts Center, Milwaukee, WI
25,000	Channel 10/36 Friends, Milwaukee, WI -- underwrite programming
10,000	Betty Brinn Children's Museum, Milwaukee, WI
5,000	Friends of Eager Free Public Library, Evansville, VA -- funding of new addition
5,000	Ko-Thi Dancer Company, Milwaukee, WI
4,500	United Performing Arts Fund, Milwaukee, WI -- sponsorship of performance card
4,000	Skylight Opera Theater, Milwaukee, WI
3,900	WUWM Public Radio, Milwaukee, WI -- underwrite programming
3,500	State Historical Society of Wisconsin, Madison, WI
2,200	Milwaukee Art Museum, Milwaukee, WI -- art acquisition fund

Civic & Public Affairs

25,000	Charitable, Educational, and Scientific Education Foundation, Madison, VA -- gun safety program
25,000	Charitable, Educational, and Scientific Education Foundation, Madison, VA -- child safe trigger lock program
15,000	New Hope Project, Milwaukee, WI
10,000	Greater Milwaukee Committee, Milwaukee, WI
5,000	Milwaukee Redevelopment Corporation, Milwaukee, WI
5,000	Stevens Point-Piovet Area Chamber Foundation, Stevens Point, WI
3,000	Madison Community Foundation, Madison, VA -- leadership awards
3,000	Milwaukee Foundation, Milwaukee, WI -- job initiative
3,000	MMAC Community Support Foundation, Milwaukee, WI
3,000	WTA, Madison, WI -- study of taxpayer equities
2,250	WMC Foundation Business World, Madison, WI
2,230	Milwaukee Urban League, Milwaukee, WI -- Black and White Ball
2,000	Institute of Human Relations, Milwaukee, WI

Education

25,000	Wisconsin Foundation for Independent Colleges, Milwaukee, WI -- economic impact study
20,000	University of Wisconsin Extension, Madison, WI -- scholarships
15,000	Greater Milwaukee Education Trust, Milwaukee, WI
15,000	University of Wisconsin Extension, Madison, WI -- We the People sponsorship
10,000	Junior Achievement Southeast Wisconsin, Milwaukee, WI
10,000	Medical College of Wisconsin, Milwaukee, WI -- Healthcare '98
5,000	Wisconsin Foundation for Independent Colleges, Milwaukee, WI -- social and economic impact study

3,000	Blackhawk Technical College Foundation, Janesville, WI
2,500	Journey House, Milwaukee, WI -- education opportunities
2,500	Wisconsin League for Nursing, Milwaukee, WI -- scholarships

Health

16,650	Health Education Center of Wisconsin, Milwaukee, WI
15,000	Health Education Center of Wisconsin, Milwaukee, WI
5,000	March of Dimes Birth Defects Foundation, New York, NY -- Walk America
2,500	Alzheimer's Association of Southwest Wisconsin, Madison, WI
2,000	American Heart Association of Wisconsin, Appleton, WI -- Heart Walk

International

10,000	African World Festival, Milwaukee, WI
5,000	Milwaukee World Festival, Milwaukee, WI

Social Services

58,000	United Way, Milwaukee, WI
5,000	Southeastern Wisconsin Area Agency on Aging, Brookfield, WI
5,000	United Way Portage County, Stevens Point, WI
3,500	United Way Northern Rock County, Janesville, WI
3,000	Volunteer Center, Milwaukee, WI -- employee volunteer program
2,500	Boy Scouts of America Milwaukee County Council, Milwaukee, WI -- breakfast benefit
2,500	Boys and Girls Club, Milwaukee, WI
2,500	L E Phillips Senior Center, Eau Claire, WI
2,500	Meridula Gridiron Club, Madison, WI -- membership campaign
2,500	Walker's Point Youth and Family Center, Milwaukee, WI -- transitional living program

UNIVERSAL FOODS CORP.

Company Contact

Milwaukee, WI

Company Description

Employees: 4,035

SIC(s): 2034 Dehydrated Fruits, Vegetables & Soups, 2087 Flavoring Extracts & Syrups Nec, 2099 Food Preparations Nec.

Operating Locations

Includes division locations.

Nonmonetary Support

Value: $273,000 (1995); $1,400,000 (1994); $1,600,000 (1993)

Type: Donated Equipment; Donated Products; In-kind Services

Note: 1997 nonmonetary support $70,000. The company donates yeast and frozen potatoes.

Corporate Sponsorship

Value: $500

Type: Arts & cultural events; Festivals/fairs

Universal Foods Foundation

Giving Contact

Carl L. Zaar, Secretary & Treasurer
Universal Foods Foundation
433 E Michigan St.
Milwaukee, WI 53202-5106

Phone: (414)347-3895
Fax: (414)347-4783

Alternate Contact

Phone: 800-558-9892

Description

EIN: 396044488

Organization Type: Corporate Foundation. Supports preselected organizations only.

Giving Locations: headquarters and operating communities.

Grant Types: Award, Capital, Conference/Seminar, Department, Emergency, Employee Matching Gifts, Endowment, General Support, Matching, Multiyear/Continuing Support.

Note: Employee matching gift ratio: 1 to 1 for gifts to postsecondary educational institutions, up to $3,000 per school annually for gifts made by employees and directors.

Financial Summary

Total Giving: $990,304 (fiscal year ending September 30, 1998); $850,000 (fiscal 1997 approx); $676,641 (fiscal 1996). Note: Contributes through corporate direct giving program and foundation.

Giving Analysis: Giving for fiscal 1997 includes: foundation (approx $700,000); corporate direct giving (approx $50,000); domestic subsidiaries (approx $30,000); fiscal 1998: foundation ($779,754); foundation grants to United Way ($210,550)

Assets: $10,525,727 (fiscal 1998); $10,200,000 (fiscal 1997 approx); $9,802,184 (fiscal 1996)

Gifts Received: $350,000 (fiscal 1990); $730,000 (fiscal 1989). Note: Gifts were received from Universal Foods Corp.

Typical Recipients

Arts & Humanities: Arts Institutes, Historic Preservation, Museums/Galleries, Music, Opera, Performing Arts, Public Broadcasting, Theater

Civic & Public Affairs: Economic Development, Employment/Job Training, Civic & Public Affairs-General, Urban & Community Affairs, Zoos/Aquariums

Education: Arts/Humanities Education, Business Education, Colleges & Universities, Education Funds, Education Reform, Engineering/Technological Education, Education-General, Literacy, Medical Education, Private Education (Precollege), Public Education (Precollege), Science/Mathematics Education, Secondary Education (Public), Student Aid, Vocational & Technical Education

Environment: Wildlife Protection

Health: Cancer, Children's Health/Hospitals, Clinics/Medical Centers, Heart, Hospitals, Medical Research, Transplant Networks/Donor Banks

Religion: Religious Welfare

Science: Science Museums

Social Services: Community Service Organizations, People with Disabilities, Scouts, United Funds/United Ways, YMCA/YWCA/YMHA/YWHA, Youth Organizations

Contributions Analysis

Arts & Humanities: 25%. Supports historic preservation, museums, and performing arts.

Civic & Public Affairs: 2%. Recipients include zoos, economic development programs, and philanthropic organizations.

Education: 20%. Major support goes to colleges and universities, with some emphasis on medical and education. Other recipients include literacy groups and education funds.

Health: 4%. Primarily supports hospitals, but funding also goes to medical research and United Way agencies.

Religion: 2%. Funds religious welfare agencies.

Social Services: 48%. Supports the United Way and youth organizations.

Note: Total contributions in fiscal 1998.

Corporate Officials

Richard F. Hobbs: vice president administration B Racine, WI 1947. ED University of Wisconsin BBA (1970); Marquette University MBA (1978). PRIM CORP EMPL vice president administration: Universal Foods Corp. NONPR AFFIL member: American Institute CPAs.

Kenneth Paul Manning: president B New York, NY 1942. ED Rensselaer Polytechnic Institute BSME (1963); George Washington University (1965-1966); American University MBA (1968). PRIM CORP EMPL president: Universal Foods Corp. CORP AFFIL director: Firstar Corp.; director: Firstar Trust Co.; director: Badger Meter Inc.

Foundation Officials

Richard Carney: vice president PRIM CORP EMPL vice president human resources: Universal Foods Corp.

Richard F. Hobbs: vice president, director (see above)

Kenneth Paul Manning: president, director (see above)

Carl L. Zaar: secretary, treasurer, director CORP AFFIL director internal audit: Universal Foods Corp.

Grants Analysis

Disclosure Period: fiscal year ending September 30, 1998

Total Grants: $779,754*

Number of Grants: 325 (approx)

Average Grant: $399

Highest Grant: $50,000

Typical Range: $25 to $5,000

***Note:** Giving excludes United Way.

Recent Grants

Note: Grants derived from fiscal 1998 Form 990.

Arts & Humanities

50,000	Milwaukee Art Museum, Milwaukee, WI
20,000	Marcus Center for the Performing Arts, Milwaukee, WI
10,000	Betty Brinn Childrens Museum, Milwaukee, WI
10,000	Betty Brinn Children's Museum, Milwaukee, WI
10,000	Cathedral Preservation Foundation
9,350	Milwaukee Art Museum, Milwaukee, WI
8,500	Milwaukee Art Museum, Milwaukee, WI
5,000	St. Louis Symphony Orchestra, St. Louis, MO

Civic & Public Affairs

35,000	UPAF, Milwaukee, WI
10,000	New Hope Project, Milwaukee, WI
5,000	Forward Wisconsin, Milwaukee, WI
5,000	Milwaukee Redevelopment Corp, Milwaukee, WI

Education

20,000	Alverno College, Milwaukee, WI
20,000	Alverno College, Milwaukee, WI
17,000	University of Wisconsin Foundation, Milwaukee, WI
15,980	National Merit Scholarship Corporation, Chicago, IL
10,000	Cardinal Stritch College, Milwaukee, WI
10,000	Cardinal Stritch College, Milwaukee, WI
10,000	PAVE, Milwaukee, WI
10,000	The UWM Foundation, Milwaukee, WI
7,000	Alverno College, Milwaukee, WI
5,000	Dominican High School, Milwaukee, WI
5,000	Marquette University, Milwaukee, WI
5,000	Medical College of Wisconsin, Milwaukee, WI
5,000	Medical College of Wisconsin, Milwaukee, WI
5,000	Purdue University/Industrial Associates, Indianapolis, IN
5,000	St. Louis Symphony Community Music School, St. Louis, MO

5,000	University of Wisconsin - Milwaukee, Milwaukee, WI
5,000	Urban Day School, Milwaukee, WI
5,000	UW-Whitewater Foundation, Inc., Whitewater, WI
Health	
10,000	Children's Hospital of Wisconsin, Milwaukee, WI
10,000	Emanuel Medical Center, Portland, OR
5,000	JHU Broccoli Aortic Center, Baltimore, MD
Science	
10,000	Discovery World Museum/ IMAX Theatre, Milwaukee, WI
Social Services	
109,700	United Way of Greater Milwaukee, Milwaukee, WI
29,600	United Way of Greater St. Louis, St. Louis, MO
20,000	Boys & Girls Clubs of Greater Milwaukee, Milwaukee, WI
20,000	Boys & Girls Clubs of Milwaukee, Milwaukee, WI
20,000	YMCA, Milwaukee, WI
20,000	YMCA of Metro Milwaukee, Milwaukee, WI
16,200	United Way of Central Indiana, Indianapolis, IN
12,500	United Way of Merced Area, Merced, CA
7,550	United Way of Central Maryland, Baltimore, MD
6,750	Dixon Area United Way, Dixon, IL
6,000	Goodwill Industries of Southeast Wisconsin, Milwaukee, WI
6,000	United Way of Greater Milwaukee, Milwaukee, WI
5,900	United Way of Dixon, Dixon, IL
5,800	United Way of Stanislaus County, Modesto, CA
5,000	YMCA of Greater Milwaukee, Milwaukee, WI

UNIVERSAL LEAF TOBACCO CO., INC.

Company Contact

Richmond, VA
Web: http://www.universalcorp.com

Company Description

Employees: 14,100
SIC(s): 5159 Farm-Product Raw Materials Nec.
Parent Company: Universal Corp.

Universal Leaf Foundation

Giving Contact

Nancy G. Powell, Manager, Corporate Relations
Universal Leaf Foundation
PO Box 25099
Richmond, VA 23260
Phone: (804)359-9311
Fax: (804)254-3594

Description

EIN: 510162337
Organization Type: Corporate Foundation
Giving Locations: NC; VA headquarters and operating communities.
Grant Types: General Support, Matching.

Financial Summary

Total Giving: $473,746 (fiscal year ending June 30, 1997); $647,574 (fiscal 1996); $399,173 (fiscal 1995). Note: Contributes through corporate direct giving program and foundation. Fiscal 1997 Giving includes foundation ($303,745); matching gifts ($124,001); United Way ($46,000). 1996 Giving includes corporate direct giving ($215,520); foundation ($312,836); domestic and international subsidiaries ($34,514); matching gifts ($84,704).
Assets: $14,491,875 (fiscal 1997); $11,473,457 (fiscal 1996); $8,681,690 (fiscal 1995)
Gifts Received: $1,500,000 (fiscal 1992); $4,949,278 (fiscal 1991); $372,500 (fiscal 1990). Note: Contributions are traditionally received from Universal Leaf Tobacco Co.

Typical Recipients

Arts & Humanities: Arts Associations & Councils, Arts Centers, Arts Festivals, Ballet, Community Arts, Dance, Historic Preservation, History & Archaeology, Museums/Galleries, Music, Performing Arts, Public Broadcasting, Theater
Civic & Public Affairs: Botanical Gardens/Parks, Business/Free Enterprise, Chambers of Commerce, Economic Development, Economic Policy, Employment/Job Training, Civic & Public Affairs-General, Housing, Municipalities/Towns, Philanthropic Organizations, Professional & Trade Associations, Public Policy, Urban & Community Affairs, Zoos/Aquariums
Education: Business Education, Business-School Partnerships, Colleges & Universities, Community & Junior Colleges, Economic Education, Education Funds, Elementary Education (Private), Education-General, Minority Education, Private Education (Precollege), Public Education (Precollege), Religious Education, Science/Mathematics Education, Secondary Education (Private), Student Aid
Environment: Environment-General
Health: Children's Health/Hospitals, Emergency/Ambulance Services, Eyes/Blindness, Health Funds, Health Organizations, Kidney, Multiple Sclerosis, Single-Disease Health Associations, Transplant Networks/Donor Banks
International: Human Rights
Religion: Religious Organizations, Religious Welfare, Social/Policy Issues
Science: Science Museums, Scientific Research
Social Services: Animal Protection, Child Welfare, Community Centers, Community Service Organizations, Family Planning, Family Services, Food/Clothing Distribution, Homes, People with Disabilities, Recreation & Athletics, Scouts, United Funds/United Ways, YMCA/YWCA/YMHA/YWHA, Youth Organizations

Contributions Analysis

Arts & Humanities: 10% to 15%. Area arts councils, ballet and symphony, local historic preservation leagues, and regional museums dealing with local culture and tradition.
Civic & Public Affairs: 20% to 25%. Economic development, a tobacco foundation, housing, and community affairs.
Education: 25% to 30%. Education funds, universities, middle schools, high schools, and economic education.
Health: About 25%. Primarily professional sporting tournaments and United Way agencies. Also contributes to Red Cross, National Multiple Sclerosis Society, health organizations, SPCA, boys homes, and other community service organizations.
Science: 5% to 10%. Scientific research and science museums.

Application Procedures

Initial Contact: written proposal
Application Requirements: amount, purpose, copy of tax exemption letter, a description of organization detailing its history and charitable purposes, list of officers/directors, names of other corporations contributing and the average gift amount, and most recent audited financial statements
Deadlines: None.
Review Process: requests reviewed by committee
Evaluative Criteria: considerations based on individual merits; preference given to agencies located in areas where company has a physical presence

Restrictions

Foundation does not support individuals, political or lobbying efforts, or make loans.

Corporate Officials

Gordon Lee Crenshaw, II: chairman emeritus, general counsel, assistant secretary B Richmond, VA 1922. ED Harvard University; University of Virginia BA (1943). PRIM CORP EMPL chairman emeritus: Universal Corp. CORP AFFIL director: Southwest Tobacco Co. Inc.
Henry Howze Harrell: chairman, chief executive officer, director B Richmond, VA 1939. ED Commonwealth College; Washington & Lee University AB (1961). PRIM CORP EMPL chairman, chief executive officer, director: Universal Corp. ADD CORP EMPL president: Processors Inc.; president, director: Southern Processor Inc. CORP AFFIL director: Jefferson Bankshares Inc. NONPR AFFIL member: Omicron Delta Kappa; member: Phi Beta Kappa; chairman: Lewis Ginter Botanical Garden; member, board visitors: James Madison University. CLUB AFFIL Deep Run Hunt Club; Forum Club; Commonwealth Club; Country Club Virginia.
James M. White, III: senior vice president, general counsel, assistant secretary B 1938. ED Washington & Lee University BA (1960); College of William & Mary Marshall-Wythe School & Law College BCL (1966). PRIM CORP EMPL secretary, general counsel, vice president: Universal Corp. ADD CORP EMPL assistant secretary: Deli Universal Inc.; senior vice president, general counsel, assistant secretary: Universal Leaf Tobacco Co. Inc. NONPR AFFIL member: Richmond Bar Association; member: Virginia State Bar Association.

Foundation Officials

Wallace Lee Chandler: vice president, director B Mecklenburg County, VA 1927. ED Elon College AB (1949); Smithdeal College of Law LLB (1953). PRIM CORP EMPL director: Universal Corp. CORP AFFIL director: Lawyers Title Insurance Co.; director: Life Virginia Series Funds.
Gordon Lee Crenshaw, II: member (see above)
Ollin Kemp Dozier: treasurer B Rocky Mount, NC 1929. ED Duke University (1947-1949); United States Military Academy BE (1953); Harvard University MBA (1958). PRIM NONPR EMPL adj professor: Virginia Commonwealth University. CORP AFFIL member investment advisor council: Virginia Retirement System. NONPR AFFIL member: Financial Executives Institute; adj professor: Virginia Commonwealth University. CLUB AFFIL Country Club Virginia; University Club New York City.
Henry Howze Harrell: director (see above)
Francis V. Lowden, III: secretary B Richmond, VA 1942. ED University of Virginia (1965); University of Virginia JD (1968). PRIM CORP EMPL assistant secretary: Universal Corp. ADD CORP EMPL secretary, treasurer, director: Lancaster Leaf Tobacco Co. Pennsylvania; secretary, director: Maclin-Zimmer-McGill Tobacco Co. Inc.; secretary, associate general counsel, vice president: Universal Leaf Tobacco Co. Inc.
Nancy G. Powell: vice president, director
Thomas R. Towers: president, director B 1925. CORP AFFIL director: Universal Corp.
James M. White, III: general counsel (see above)

Grants Analysis

Disclosure Period: fiscal year ending June 30, 1997
Total Grants: $303,745*

Number of Grants: 113
Average Grant: $2,688
Highest Grant: $25,000
Typical Range: $100 to $5,000
***Note:** Giving excludes matching gifts; United Way.

Recent Grants

Note: Grants derived from fiscal 1997 Form 990.

Arts & Humanities

3,500 Richmond Symphony, Richmond, VA
3,015 Theater Virginia, Richmond, VA
3,000 Virginia Museum of Fine Arts Foundation, Richmond, VA
3,000 WCVE/Channel 23
2,250 Valentine Museum, Richmond, VA

Civic & Public Affairs

10,000 Local Initiatives Support Corporation, Richmond, VA
10,000 Richmond Renaissance, Richmond, VA
6,500 Richmond Forum, Richmond, VA
5,250 Metropolitan Business Foundation, Richmond, VA
3,000 North Carolina Tobacco Foundation, Raleigh, NC
3,000 Virginia Institute of Political Leadership, VA
2,500 Balanced Federal System Foundation

Education

25,000 Virginia Foundation for Independent Colleges, Richmond, VA
15,000 James Madison University, Harrisonburg, VA
14,000 Independent College Fund of North Carolina, Winston-Salem, NC
10,000 Jamestown Yorktown Educational Foundation, Jamestown, VA
6,000 Hampden Sydney College, VA
5,000 St. Catherine's School
5,000 St. Christopher's School Foundation, Richmond, VA
5,000 Trinity Episcopal High School
5,000 Virginia Business Higher Education Council, VA
5,000 Virginia College Fund, Richmond, VA
5,000 Virginia Commonwealth University, Richmond, VA
4,803 Thompson Middle School, Richmond, VA
3,000 Randolph Macon College, Ashland, VA
2,500 Longwood College Foundation, Farmville, VA
2,500 St. Michael's Episcopal School
2,500 William and Mary Endowment Association
2,000 Barton College, Wilson, NC
2,000 Belmont Abbey College, Belmont, NC
2,000 Junior Achievement Central Virginia, Richmond, VA

Environment

5,500 Maymont Foundation, Richmond, VA

Health

11,000 American Red Cross, Richmond, VA
5,000 Children's Hospital, Richmond, VA
3,500 National Multiple Sclerosis Society Virginia Chapter, Richmond, VA
2,500 Manakin Volunteer Fire and Rescue, VA
2,500 Virginia Blood Services, Richmond, VA

Religion

2,500 Sacred Heart Center

Social Services

46,000 United Way, Richmond, VA
10,000 YMCA Capital Campaign, Richmond, VA
7,000 YMCA, Richmond, VA
4,000 Central Virginia Food Bank, Richmond, VA
3,000 Richmond Society for Prevention of Cruelty to Animals, Richmond, VA
3,000 Virginia Home for Boys, Richmond, VA
2,800 Boy Scouts of America Robert E. Lee Council, Richmond, VA
2,500 YMCA Johnson County
2,200 Virginia League for Planned Parenthood, Richmond, VA
2,000 Boys and Girls Clubs, Richmond, VA
2,000 Goodwill Industries, Richmond, VA
2,000 Tennis Opportunity Program, Richmond, VA

UNIVERSAL STUDIOS

Company Contact

Universal City, CA
Web: http://www.universalstudios.com

Company Description

Employees: 15,000
SIC(s): 2396 Automotive & Apparel Trimmings, 2731 Book Publishing, 2741 Miscellaneous Publishing, 7812 Motion Picture & Video Production.
Parent Company: Seagram Co. Ltd., 1430 Peel St., Montreal, PQ, Canada

Operating Locations

CA: Universal Studios, Anaheim, Glendale; Geffen Records, Los Angeles; Winterland Productions, San Francisco; MCA Records, Universal City; MCA/Universal Merchandising, Universal City; Merchandising Corp. of America, Universal City; UNI Distribution Corp., Universal City; Universal Amphitheatre, Universal City; Universal Studios, Universal City; Universal Studios Development Co., Universal City; Universal Studios Enterprises, Universal City; Universal Studios Hollywood, Universal City; Universal Studios Home Entertainment Group, Universal City; Universal Studios Music Entertainment Group, Universal City; Universal Studios New Ventures, Universal City; Universal Studios Publishing Group, Universal City; Universal Studios Recreation Services Group, Universal City; Universal Studios Television Ltd., Universal City; Universal Studios TV, Universal City; Universal Studios Videodisc, Universal City; Womp's Restaurant Bar & Grill, Universal City; Yosemite Concession Services Co., Yosemite National Park; FL: Universal Studios, Orlando; IL: Universal Studios Mfg., Pinckneyville; MI: Universal Studios, Grand Rapids; NJ: Spencer Gifts, Egg Harbor Township; NY: Universal Studios Mfg., Gloversville; Berkeley Publishing Group, New York; G.P. Putnam Sons, New York; GRP Records, New York; October Films, New York; Universal Film Exchanges, Inc., New York; Universal Studios Distributing Co., New York; PA: Universal Studios, Pittsburgh

Nonmonetary Support

Type: Donated Equipment; Donated Products; In-kind Services; Loaned Employees

Corporate Sponsorship

Type: Arts & cultural events; Music & entertainment events; Pledge-a-thon

Universal Studios Foundation

Giving Contact

Nancy Nemecek, Manager
Universal Studios Foundation
100 Universal City Plaza, Suite LRW/3
Universal City, CA 91608
Phone: (818)866-3099
Fax: (818)866-1506
Email: unistudios@isearch.com

Description

Founded: 1956
EIN: 136096061
Organization Type: Corporate Foundation
Giving Locations: CA: Los Angeles; NY: New York major operating locations.
Grant Types: Award, Capital, Emergency, Employee Matching Gifts, General Support, Multiyear/Continuing Support, Project.

Financial Summary

Total Giving: $800,000 (1999 approx); $982,500 (1998); $347,000 (1997). Note: Contributes through foundation only.
Giving Analysis: Giving for 1997 includes: foundation grants to United Way ($15,000); 1998: foundation grants to United Way ($18,000)
Assets: $1,000,000 (1999 approx); $14,234,999 (1998); $13,450,684 (1997)
Gifts Received: $23,109 (1998); $663 (1997); $6,000 (1995). Note: Foundation receives gifts from Universal Studios and its subsidiaries.

Typical Recipients

Arts & Humanities: Arts Associations & Councils, Arts Centers, Arts Funds, Arts Institutes, Ballet, Dance, Film & Video, Historic Preservation, Libraries, Literary Arts, Museums/Galleries, Music, Performing Arts, Public Broadcasting, Theater
Civic & Public Affairs: African American Affairs, Botanical Gardens/Parks, Business/Free Enterprise, Civil Rights, Community Foundations, Economic Development, Employment/Job Training, Civic & Public Affairs-General, Housing, Law & Justice, Philanthropic Organizations, Professional & Trade Associations, Public Policy, Urban & Community Affairs, Women's Affairs
Education: Arts/Humanities Education, Business Education, Colleges & Universities, Community & Junior Colleges, Community & Junior Colleges, Education Associations, Education Funds, Education Reform, Education-General, International Studies, Legal Education, Literacy, Medical Education, Minority Education, Student Aid
Environment: Environment-General, Resource Conservation
Health: Cancer, Children's Health/Hospitals, Clinics/Medical Centers, Diabetes, Emergency/Ambulance Services, Eyes/Blindness, Health Organizations, Hospitals, Medical Research, Mental Health, Multiple Sclerosis, Single-Disease Health Associations
Religion: Jewish Causes
Science: Scientific Centers & Institutes
Social Services: Big Brother/Big Sister, Child Welfare, Community Centers, Community Service Organizations, Counseling, Delinquency & Criminal Rehabilitation, Emergency Relief, Family Planning, Family Services, Food/Clothing Distribution, People with Disabilities, Recreation & Athletics, Scouts, Senior Services, Substance Abuse, United Funds/United Ways, Veterans, Volunteer Services, YMCA/YWCA/YMHA/YWHA, Youth Organizations

Contributions Analysis

Giving Priorities: The arts, entertainment-industry charities, civic organizations, education, and health.
Arts & Humanities: 26%. Arts centers, libraries, museums, theaters, arts institutes, and dance.
Civic & Public Affairs: 24%. Provides funding for ethnic affairs, civil rights, urban and consumer affairs, housing, jobs, economics, public policy, and industry-affiliated organizations.
Education: 25%. Art, medical, minority, and business and management education.
Health: 8%. Single-disease health associations, with major interests in cancer and cystic fibrosis; health relief organizations; medical centers; and hospitals.
Religion: 2%.
Social Services: 15%. Supports the United Way and youth activities.
Note: Total contributions in fiscal 1998.

Application Procedures

Initial Contact: Send a letter or preliminary proposal of not more than three pages.
Application Requirements: Include a description of organization and purpose for which support is sought; attach copy of 501(c)(3) not-for-profit IRS determination letter.
Deadlines: None.
Notes: If the foundation is interested in pursuing the possibility of working with the organization, it may request the following information: a statement of objectives, activities, accomplishments, and geographic scope; a list of the names and business or professional affiliations of the organization's officers and board of directors or trustees, the number of board meetings held in the previous year, and whether or not board members are compensated; number and total compensation of paid employees and the number of volunteer workers; a current itemized budget based on total anticipated funds (fund-raising costs should be shown); a list of sources of current income, including the amount received from each source, listing the corporations, foundations, and government agencies that are current sources of major funding; current audited financial statements; a detailed description of the specific program for which support is requested, including an explanation of what the grant is expected to accomplish, how the program will be carried out, and the method or procedure that will be used to evaluate the effec tiveness of the program; and a signed statement that the organization will furnish periodic reports indicating the use of any funds provided by the foundation.

Restrictions

Does not support individuals; film, television, or video projects; group trips; private foundations; political campaigns; ad journals; or fund-raising dinners or events.

Additional Information

Seagram's has an 80% investment in Universal Studios and Matsushita has a 20% investment in the company.
Publications: Application Guidelines

Corporate Officials

Ronald Meyer: president, director B 1945. PRIM CORP EMPL president, director: Universal Studios.

Foundation Officials

Nancy Nemecek: manager corporate communications, public affairs

Grants Analysis

Disclosure Period: calendar year ending 1998
Total Grants: $964,500*
Number of Grants: 53
Average Grant: $18,189
Highest Grant: $100,000
Typical Range: $10,000 to $50,000
***Note:** Giving excludes United Way.

Recent Grants

Note: Grants derived from 1998 Form 990.

Arts & Humanities

100,000	Geffen Playhouse, Los Angeles, CA
100,000	Motion Picture & TV Fund Found, Woodand Hills, CA
25,000	The Acting Company, New York, NY
25,000	American Museum of the Moving Image, New York, NY
15,000	Ford Theatre Foundation, Los Angeles, CA
10,000	Boston Film Video Foundation, Boston, MA -- for benefit of Montage Entertainment
10,000	Venture West Theatre Company, Los Angeles, CA
5,000	Barnstormers Theatre, Tamworth, NH
5,000	KCET Business Partners, Los Angeles, CA
5,000	Los Angeles Chamber Ballet, Los Angeles, CA
5,000	Los Angeles Children's Museum, Los Angeles, CA
5,000	Music Center Unified Fund, Los Angeles, CA

Civic & Public Affairs

60,000	Permanent Charities of the Entertainment Industries, Studio City, CA
50,000	The Kyle Foundation Inc., Oroville, CA
25,000	Economic Alliance of the SFV, Van Nuys, CA
24,000	L. A. Works, Los Angeles, CA
15,000	WATTS Foundation Community Trust, Los Angeles, CA
12,500	Habitat for Humanity, Los Angeles, CA
5,000	Ryman Carroll Foundation, Los Angeles, CA
3,500	Catalyst, New York, NY

Education

62,000	The Lew Wasserman Scholarship Foundation, Universal City, CA
26,500	Regents of the University of California, Los Angeles, CA
25,000	LA Educational Alliance for Restructuring Now, Los Angeles, CA
25,000	New York University, New York, NY
25,000	Southwest Community College Foundation, Los Angeles, CA
20,000	Princeton University, Princeton, NJ
10,000	WAVE, New York, NY
7,500	Academy of Television Arts and Sciences, Burbank, CA
7,500	LA Educational Alliance for Restructuring Now, Los Angeles, CA
5,000	Operation Unity, Los Angeles, CA

Environment

10,000	Central Park Conservancy, New York, NY
10,000	Central Park Conservancy, New York, NY

Health

50,000	The Fulfillment Fund, Los Angeles, CA
25,000	Mayo Foundation for Medical Education and Research, Rochester, MN
20,000	Cystic Fibrosis Foundation, Los Angeles, CA
10,000	National Multiple Scherosis Society/ Southern California Chapter, Los Angeles, CA
10,000	Research to Prevent Blindness, New York, NY
5,000	Project 9865, Los Angeles, CA

Religion

20,000	Simon Wiesenthal Center, Los Angeles, CA

Social Services

20,000	Big Brothers of Greater Los Angeles, Los Angeles, CA
18,000	United Way of Atlantic County, Egg Harbor, NJ
10,000	The Human Family Educational, Pacific Palisades, CA
10,000	LA Shares, Los Angeles, CA
5,000	Children of the Night, Los Angeles, CA
5,000	Los Angeles Regional Food Bank, Los Angeles, CA
5,000	Meeting Each Need with Dignity, Pacoima, CA
5,000	Mid Valley Family YMCA, Palo Alto, CA
5,000	National Veterans Foundation, Los Angeles, CA
5,000	North Valley Family YMCA, Mission Hills, CA
5,000	SFV Girl Scouts, Chatsworth, CA

UNOCAL CORP.

Company Contact

El Segundo, CA
Web: http://www.unocal.com

Company Description

Revenue: US$5,003,000,000 (1999)
Profit: US$137,000,000 (1999)
Employees: 7,880 (1999)
Fortune Rank: 282, per FORTUNE Magazine's list of 500 Largest U.S. Corporations (1999).
FF 282
SIC(s): 1311 Crude Petroleum & Natural Gas, 1321 Natural Gas Liquids, 2911 Petroleum Refining, 2992 Lubricating Oils & Greases.

Operating Locations

Canada: Unocal Canada Limited, Calgary; India: Unocal Geothermal of Indonesia Ltd., Jakarta; Unocal Indonesia, Ltd., Jakarta; Netherlands: Unocal Netherlands, Hague; Philippines: Phillippine Geothermal Inc., Manila; Thailand: Unocal Thailand, Bangkok

Unocal Foundation

Giving Contact

Tina Cardoza, Director, Administration
Unocal Foundation
2141 Rosecrans Ave., Suite 4000
El Segundo, CA 90245
Phone: (310)726-7726
Fax: (310)726-7873

Description

EIN: 956071812
Organization Type: Corporate Foundation
Giving Locations: nationally, with preference given to locations with Unocal corporate facilities.
Grant Types: Challenge, Department, Employee Matching Gifts, Fellowship, General Support, Professorship, Project, Research, Scholarship.
Note: Employee matching gift ratio: 1 to 1 for education, up to $5,000 per employee annually.

Giving Philosophy

'The Foundation's program is largely one of support of charitable, educational, scientific and cultural programs that work to enhance the quality of life -- especially at the local level. The program gives preference to well managed charitable organizations in areas where Unocal employees live and work.' Unocal Foundation Annual Report

Financial Summary

Total Giving: $2,000,000 (fiscal year ending January 31, 1999 approx); $2,000,000 (fiscal 1998 approx); $1,762,290 (fiscal 1997). Note: Contributes through corporate direct giving program and foundation. 1997 Giving includes foundation ($1,060,700); matching gifts ($196,919); United Way ($504,671).1996 Giving includes foundation. 1995 Giving includes foundation ($1,123,366); United Way ($540,191); matching gifts ($196,276).
Assets: $3,379,909 (fiscal 1997); $3,522,829 (fiscal 1995); $3,859,519 (fiscal 1994)
Gifts Received: $800,000 (fiscal 1997); $2,000,000 (fiscal 1995); $6,336,000 (fiscal 1994). Note: In fiscal year 1997, the foundation received contributions from Union Oil Company of California.

Typical Recipients

Arts & Humanities: Arts Centers, Arts Funds, Arts Institutes, Community Arts, Dance, Historic Preservation, Libraries, Museums/Galleries, Music, Opera, Performing Arts, Theater
Civic & Public Affairs: African American Affairs, Botanical Gardens/Parks, Business/Free Enterprise,

Civil Rights, Clubs, Economic Development, Economic Policy, Employment/Job Training, Hispanic Affairs, Housing, Law & Justice, Legal Aid, Minority Business, Nonprofit Management, Parades/Festivals, Philanthropic Organizations, Professional & Trade Associations, Public Policy, Safety, Urban & Community Affairs, Women's Affairs
Education: Agricultural Education, Arts/Humanities Education, Business Education, Colleges & Universities, Continuing Education, Economic Education, Education Associations, Education Funds, Education Reform, Engineering/Technological Education, Faculty Development, Education-General, International Exchange, International Studies, Leadership Training, Legal Education, Medical Education, Minority Education, Private Education (Precollege), Public Education (Precollege), Science/Mathematics Education, Secondary Education (Public), Social Sciences Education, Student Aid
Environment: Energy, Environment-General, Resource Conservation
Health: Arthritis, Children's Health/Hospitals, Clinics/Medical Centers, Emergency/Ambulance Services, Health Organizations, Hospitals, Medical Rehabilitation, Medical Research, Medical Training, Mental Health, Single-Disease Health Associations
International: International Affairs, International Organizations, International Relations
Religion: Religious Welfare
Science: Science Exhibits & Fairs, Science Museums, Scientific Centers & Institutes, Scientific Organizations
Social Services: At-Risk Youth, Big Brother/Big Sister, Camps, Child Welfare, Community Service Organizations, Crime Prevention, Family Services, Food/Clothing Distribution, Homes, People with Disabilities, Recreation & Athletics, Scouts, Social Services-General, Special Olympics, Substance Abuse, United Funds/United Ways, Volunteer Services, YMCA/YWCA/YMHA/YWHA, Youth Organizations

Contributions Analysis

Giving Priorities: Health, social welfare, higher education, civic affairs, and the arts. Has supported U.S.-based nonprofit organizations such as the Asia Society and the Carter Center. Overseas subsidiaries administer independent, unstructured contributions programs totaling less than $1 million annually.
Civic & Public Affairs: 10% to 15%. Supports minority business, minority affairs, and economic and community development. Other civic interests include public policy, civil rights, and environmental affairs. Arts supportemphasizes museums related to science. Other interests include music, theater, and performing arts.
Education: About 35% to 40%. Company-defined category of Educational Research includes grants to help sustain and initiate activities in higher education, including faculty programs at university engineering departments nationwide, and geological and petrochemicalstudies. Education grants are also disbursed through the company's matching gifts program for employees, retirees, and company directors. Also gives graduate and undergraduate scholarships and fellowships that aim to strengthen student interest in disciplines vital to the petroleum industry. Supports regional associations of independent colleges. Awards scholarships to children of employees.
Health: 45% to 50% of total annual contributions. Funding supports United Way, youth organizations, people with disabilities hospital programs and health institutions. Supports programs to keep inner city youth out of gangs and other programs for at-risk youth. Also supports medical centers.
International: Less than 5%. Funds international affairs, educational research and quality improvement, and scholarships to non-U.S. employees. Also offers International Fellowship in Petroleum Studies.
Note: In 1997, the foundation was revising its grantmaking focus. Guidelines were not available at the time of publication.

Application Procedures

Initial Contact: request guidelines, then brief letter
Application Requirements: background of organization, including its goals and objectives; necessity/purpose of grant; amount budgeted for project; most recent audited financial statement and annual report; current year's budget; evaluative criteria; other organizations solicited and amounts received, pledged, or anticipated; copy of IRS determination letter; copy of most recent IRS Form 990
Deadlines: contact Foundation for deadlines

Restrictions

Foundation does not support grants to individuals; elementary or secondary education; political or lobbying groups; veterans, fraternal, sectarian, social, religious, athletic, choral, band, or similar groups; courtesy advertising; conferences, films, or contests; supplemental operating support for organizations eligible for united funds; governmental agencies or departments; or trade, business, or professional associations; most capital campaigns or endowments.
Grants are not renewed automatically; a request for support must be submitted each year. submitted each year.

Corporate Officials

Roger C. Beach: chairman, chief executive officer, directorrlt & communications B Lincoln, NE 1936. ED Colorado School of Mines BS (1961). PRIM CORP EMPL chairman, chief executive officer, director: Unocal Corp. ADD CORP EMPL chairman: Union Oil Co. of California. NONPR AFFIL chairman board trustees: National 4-H Council; member: Presidents Interchange Executive Alumni Association.
Michael Thacher: general manager public relations & communications PRIM CORP EMPL general manager public relations & communications: Unocal Corp.

Foundation Officials

Barry S. Andrews: secretary
MacDonald G. Becket: trustee
Claude Stout Brinegar: trustee B Rockport, CA 1926. ED Stanford University BA (1950); Stanford University MS (1951); Stanford University PhD (1954). CORP AFFIL board directors: Maxicare Health Plans Inc.; director: CSX Corp.; founding director: Conrail Inc.; founding director: Consolidated Rail Corp. NONPR AFFIL member: Phi Beta Kappa; member: Sigma Xi; chairman: California Citizens Compensation Commission; member: American Petroleum Institute. CLUB AFFIL Southport Yacht Club; Boothbay Harbor Yacht Club; Georgetown Club.
Christina Cardoza: administrator
Darrell D. Chessum: treasurer PRIM CORP EMPL treasurer, director: Unocal International Corp. CORP AFFIL treasurer: Poco Graphite Inc.
Karen Ann Sikkema: president, trustee B Kalamazoo, MI 1946. ED Kalamazoo College (1968); University of Michigan (1970). PRIM CORP EMPL external affairs: Unocal Corp. CORP AFFIL vice president: Union Oil Co. California.

Grants Analysis

Disclosure Period: fiscal year ending January 31, 1997
Total Grants: $1,060,700*
Number of Grants: 197
Average Grant: $5,384
Highest Grant: $176,000
Typical Range: $1,000 to $8,000
***Note:** Giving excludes matching gifts; United Way.

Recent Grants

Note: Grants derived from 1997 Form 990.

Arts & Humanities

25,000	Orange County Center for Performing Arts, Costa Mesa, CA
20,000	Los Angeles Music Center Unified Fund, Los Angeles, CA
10,000	Library Foundation, Los Angeles, CA
10,000	South Coast Repertory, Costa Mesa, CA
5,000	Anchorage Museum Association, Anchorage, AK
5,000	Business Arts Fund, Houston, TX
5,000	Friends of the Santa Maria Public Library, Santa Maria, CA
5,000	San Luis Obispo Friends of the Library, San Luis Obispo, CA

Civic & Public Affairs

10,000	Kids Care Fair, Los Angeles, CA
5,000	Cato Institute, Washington, DC
5,000	Competitive Enterprise Institute, Washington, DC
5,000	El Nido Services, Los Angeles, CA
5,000	Heartland Institute, Palatine, IL
5,000	Heritage Foundation, Washington, DC
5,000	Pacific Legal Foundation, Sacramento, CA
4,000	Gulfway Hobby Airport Rotary Club Charitable Foundation, Houston, TX

Education

176,000	National 4-H Council, Chevy Chase, MD
86,500	Citizens Scholarship Foundation of America, Saint Peter, MN
50,000	California State Polytechnic University, Pomona, CA
50,000	Colorado School of Mines, Golden, CO
25,000	Harvey Mudd College, Claremont, CA
25,000	Texas A&M University, College Station, TX
25,000	Texas A&M University, College Station, TX
12,000	University of Southwestern Louisiana, Lafayette, LA
10,000	Los Angeles Educational Partnership, Los Angeles, CA
10,000	National Academy of Engineering Fund, Washington, DC
7,500	Fort Bond Independent School District, Sugar Land, TX
7,500	Learn, Los Angeles, CA
5,500	Fort Bond Independent School District, Sugar Land, TX
5,000	Cook Inlet Academy, Soldotna, AK
5,000	University of Illinois, Urbana, IL

Environment

25,000	Sea and Sage Audubon Society, Santa Ana, CA
10,000	National Energy Education Development Project, Reston, VA

Health

5,000	American Red Cross, Anchorage, AK

Science

5,000	Natural History Museum, Los Angeles, CA

Social Services

494,671	United Way Campaign, Los Angeles, CA
25,000	Questa Youth and Family Center, Questa, NM
20,000	Boys and Girls Clubs of Arcadiana, Lafayette, LA
20,000	Hollenbeck Police Business Council, Los Angeles, CA
15,000	Boy Scouts of America, Los Angeles, CA
15,000	Girl Scouts of America, Los Angeles, CA
10,000	Five Acres Boys and Girls Aid Society, Altadena, CA
10,000	United Way Orange County, Irvine, CA
10,000	YMCA, Los Angeles, CA
10,000	YMCA, Stafford, TX
7,500	Big Sisters, Los Angeles, CA
7,500	Volunteer Center of Greater Orange County, Huntington Beach, CA

5,000	Children's Bureau of Southern California, Los Angeles, CA
5,000	Friends of Child Advocates, Monterey Park, CA
5,000	RM Pyles Boys Camp, Valencia, CA

UNUMPROVIDENT

Company Contact

Portland, ME
Web: http://www.unum.com

Company Description

Formed by Merger of: UNUM AND Provident Companies Inc. (1999).
Revenue: US$9,242,500,000 (1999)
Employees: 6,700
Fortune Rank: 184, per FORTUNE Magazine's list of 500 Largest U.S. Corporations (1999).
FF 184
SIC(s): 6311 Life Insurance, 6321 Accident & Health Insurance, 6324 Hospital & Medical Service Plans, 6719 Holding Companies Nec.

Nonmonetary Support

Value: $75,000 (1988)
Type: Donated Equipment; Donated Products; In-kind Services; Loaned Employees; Workplace Solicitation
Note: The company provides nonmonetary support. Workplace solicitation is for the United Way and Red Cross Blood Drives. Loaned employees to the United Way only. Donates equipment.

Corporate Sponsorship

Type: Arts & cultural events; Festivals/fairs; Music & entertainment events
Contact: Carol Ebeazer, Vice President, Corp. Communications, UNUM Corp.

UNUM Foundation

Giving Contact

Laurie H. Taylor, Grant Administrator
UNUM Foundation
2211 Congress St., P 349
Portland, ME 04122
Phone: (207)770-4378
Fax: (207)770-4510

Description

EIN: 237026979
Organization Type: Corporate Foundation
Giving Locations: ME: Portland
Grant Types: Award, Capital, Challenge, Employee Matching Gifts, Multiyear/Continuing Support, Project, Scholarship, Seed Money.
Note: Employee matching gift ratio: 1 to 1 for gifts to higher education and public broadcasting.

Giving Philosophy

'At UNUM we have long recognized that our success is linked to the health of our various environments. That is why we believe so strongly in Corporate Public Involvement. Corporate Public Involvement will promote UNUM's Visions and Values.. through effective participation and investment in the issues influencing the social and economic health of our corporate communities. This means much more than simply responding to community needs. It also means getting involved in helping to shape important public policy issues and committing the financial, material, and human resources necessary to have an impact. In order to maximize these efforts, we strive to allocate resources to the issues and environments where we can truly make a difference.' UNUM Charitable Foundation

Financial Summary

Total Giving: $2,200,000 (1999 approx); $1,831,586 (1998); $1,846,178 (1997). Note: Contributes through corporate direct giving program and foundation.
Giving Analysis: Giving for 1997 includes: foundation ($1,212,885); foundation grants to United Way ($474,962); foundation matching gifts ($102,481); foundation scholarships ($55,850); 1998: foundation ($1,191,410); foundation grants to United Way ($470,362); foundation matching gifts ($123,514); foundation scholarships ($46,300)
Assets: $3,500,000 (1999 approx); $2,123,570 (1998); $1,807,530 (1997)
Gifts Received: $2,249,000 (1998); $548,000 (1997); $1,384,000 (1996). Note: In 1998, contributions were received from Unum Life Insurance of America contributed $1,988,000, First Unum Life Insurance Co. contributed $221,000 and Colonial Life and Accident Insurance Co. $40,000.

Typical Recipients

Arts & Humanities: Arts Associations & Councils, Dance, Historic Preservation, History & Archaeology, Museums/Galleries, Music, Performing Arts, Public Broadcasting
Civic & Public Affairs: Business/Free Enterprise, Civil Rights, Economic Development, Employment/Job Training, Civic & Public Affairs-General, Law & Justice, Legal Aid, Municipalities/Towns, Public Policy, Urban & Community Affairs, Zoos/Aquariums
Education: Agricultural Education, Business Education, Colleges & Universities, Economic Education, Education Associations, Education Reform, Education-General, Leadership Training, Private Education (Precollege), Public Education (Precollege), Science/Mathematics Education, Student Aid, Vocational & Technical Education
Environment: Forestry, Environment-General
Health: AIDS/HIV, Alzheimers Disease, Clinics/Medical Centers, Emergency/Ambulance Services, Health Policy/Cost Containment, Medical Rehabilitation, Medical Research
International: International Peace & Security Issues
Social Services: Child Welfare, Community Service Organizations, Domestic Violence, Family Services, Food/Clothing Distribution, People with Disabilities, Recreation & Athletics, Scouts, Senior Services, United Funds/United Ways, YMCA/YWCA/YMHA/YWHA, Youth Organizations

Contributions Analysis

Civic & Public Affairs: 21%. Support is for initiatives that promote economic development and leadership within the state of Maine and enhance the role of art organizations as economic enterprises.
Education: 38%. Support is directed to programs focused on long-term, systemic restructuring K-12 public schools that are committed to outcome-based education, accountability, and community involvement. Also provides scholarships.
Social Services: 41%. Funds are primarily given to United Way organizations in company headquarters, and in affiliate and field office communities. Funding for programs that help the elderly maintain their independence and quality of life. Initiatives with an emphasis on intergenerational collaborations will be given a high priority.
Note: Total contributions made in 1998.

Application Procedures

Initial Contact: Submit a brief concept paper (not more than two pages).
Application Requirements: Include a statement of purpose of the project; any UNUM employee knowledgeable of the project; statement of project's importance and relevance to foundation priorities; total project budget, sources of funding, and amount requested; list of organization's officers and board of directors; proof of tax-exempt status.
Deadlines: None, for concept papers.
Review Process: Foundation staff reviews concept paper, and responds within 30 days; organizations may be asked to submit a full proposal.
Evaluative Criteria: Ability to stimulate others in the private or public sector to participate in problem solving; advance innovative approaches for addressing defined, recognized needs; nonduplication of other efforts; will produce measurable, cost-effective results; demonstrated ability to obtain future project funding; includes a strategy for leveraging other resources and support; good leadership, sound management, and a commitment to lasting change; people affected by problem have a role in its solution.
Decision Notification: Ongoing.

Restrictions

The foundation does not support individuals, political organizations or candidates, religious organizations or activities, athletics, fundraising events such as testimonial dinners and walk-a-thons, annual operating expenses, conferences, seminars, endowments, goodwill advertising, or United Way member agencies except in emergency situations.
The foundation supports capital campaigns in Portland, South Portland, and Westbrook, ME only. Portland, and Westbrook, ME only.

Additional Information

Requests for non-cash contributions program are reviewed by the foundation and the internal contributor whose services or skills are being requested.
Publications: Annual Report; Guidelines

Corporate Officials

Anne Dinsmore: senior vice president PRIM CORP EMPL senior vice president: UNUM Corp.
Carol A. Eleazer: vice president corporate communications PRIM CORP EMPL vice president corporate communications: UNUM Corp.
Matthew Gilligan: vice president PRIM CORP EMPL vice president: UNUM Corp.
Robert Hecker: second vice president human resources PRIM CORP EMPL second vice president human resources: UNUM Corp.
Barry W. Larman: vice president tax PRIM CORP EMPL vice president tax: UNUM Corp.
Timothy Wayne Ludden: vice president, treasurer, cash manager B Lincoln, ME 1940. ED Bentley College (1964). PRIM CORP EMPL vice president, treasurer, cash manager: UNUM Provident Corp. ADD CORP EMPL internal audit: Bendix Corp.; treasurer: Claims Service International; internal audit, systems, analysts supervisor: Northern Paper Co.
Donna T. Mundy: senior vice president B Bangor, ME 1949. ED University of Maine (1971). PRIM CORP EMPL senior vice president: Unum Provident Corp.
James F. Orr, III: chairman B Minneapolis, MN 1943. ED Villanova University BA (1962); Boston University MA (1969). PRIM CORP EMPL chairman: UnumProvident Corp. ADD CORP EMPL chief operating officer, chairman, director: Cincinnati Bell Inc.; director: Claims Services International; chairman: Colonial Companies Inc.; director: Colonial Life & Accident Insurance Co.; chairman, director: First UNUM Life Insurance Co.; chief executive officer, president, director: UNUM Corp.; president, director: UNUM Holding Corp.; chairman, chief executive officer: UNUM Life Insurance Co. America. CORP AFFIL director: Nashua Corp.
Daniel Redmond: vice president PRIM CORP EMPL vice president: UNUM Corp.

Foundation Officials

Wendolyn C. Clarke: assistant secretary
Carol A. Eleazer: vice president, trustee (see above)
Robert B. Fast: trustee PRIM CORP EMPL Duncanson & Holt Services Inc.
Matthew Gilligan: trustee (see above)
Robert Hecker: trustee (see above)
Barry W. Larman: tax director (see above)
Janine M. Manning: secretary, clerk

Donna T. Mundy: vice president, trustee (see above)
James F. Orr, III: president, trustee (see above)
Daniel Redmond: trustee (see above)

Grants Analysis

Disclosure Period: calendar year ending 1998
Total Grants: $1,191,410*
Number of Grants: 259
Average Grant: $4,600
Highest Grant: $100,000
Typical Range: $2,000 to $50,000
***Note:** Giving excludes matching gifts; scholarship; United Way.

Recent Grants

Note: Grants derived from 1997 Form 990.

Arts & Humanities

50,000	Victoria Museum
35,000	Portland Observatory Restoration, Portland, ME
25,000	Portland Museum of Art, Portland, ME
15,000	Portland Stage Company, Portland, ME
10,000	Community Television Network
10,000	Maine Arts, Portland, ME

Civic & Public Affairs

50,000	National Alliance of Business, Washington, DC
26,150	Key Leadership Decisions Institute
25,000	Portland Partnership, Portland, ME
20,000	Portland West Neighborhood Planning Council, Portland, ME
15,000	Gulf of Maine Aquarium Development Corporation, Portland, ME
15,000	Maine Center for Enterprise Development, ME
15,000	Maine Development Foundation, Augusta, ME
10,000	City of Portland, Portland, ME
10,000	Committee for Economic Development, New York, NY
10,000	Media Works, Boston, MA
10,000	Portland Partnership, Portland, ME
10,000	Susan Curtis Foundation, Portland, ME

Education

83,000	University of Maine Orono, Orono, ME
69,940	University of Southern Maine, Gorham, ME
55,350	Citizens Scholarship Foundation of America
50,000	Maine School Administration, ME
37,275	Scarborough School of Development
33,500	University of Southern Maine, Gorham, ME
30,000	Maine School Administration, ME
22,300	University of Southern Maine, Gorham, ME
20,000	Institute for Civic Leadership, Portland, ME
17,750	Falmouth Public Schools
17,155	Portland Public Schools, Portland, OR
15,000	Maine Coalition for Excellence in Education, Augusta, ME
10,000	Junior Achievement, Portland, ME
10,000	Maine Coalition for Excellence in Education, Augusta, ME

Health

100,000	Maine Medical Center, Portland, ME
18,500	Life and Health Insurance Medical Research Fund, Washington, DC
15,000	Alzheimer's Disease and Related Disorders
9,000	Alzheimer's Disease and Related Disorders

Social Services

375,000	United Way, Portland, ME
23,000	YMCA
20,000	Sweetser Children's Services, Saco, ME
20,000	United Way, Portland, ME
20,000	Wayne Evening Soup Kitchen
17,000	YWCA, Portland, ME
15,000	Maine Center for the Blind and Visually Impaired, Portland, ME
14,335	United Way of Westchester, White Plains, NY
13,908	United Way Crusade of Mercy
13,541	Pine Tree Society for Handicapped Children and Adults, Bath, ME
12,810	United Way of Central New Jersey, Milltown, NJ
10,500	Gifford School, Weston, MA
10,000	Youth Education Through Sports, Portland, ME
8,000	Case Management for Youth, Portland, ME

UPN CHANNEL 50

Company Contact

2152 North Elston
Chicago, IL 60614

Company Description

SIC(s): 2759 Commercial Printing Nec.

WPWR-TV Channel 50 Foundation

Giving Contact

Marcia Lipetz, Executive Director
WPWR-TV Channel 50 Foundation
Phone: (773)292-5016

Description

Founded: 1992
EIN: 363805338
Organization Type: Corporate Foundation
Giving Locations: IL: Chicago including metropolitan area; IN: Northwest part of the state

Financial Summary

Total Giving: $1,259,750 (fiscal year ending February 28, 1997)
Assets: $54,233,444 (fiscal 1997)
Gifts Received: $22,029,420 (fiscal 1997). Note: In fiscal 1997, contributions were received from Newsweb Corp. ($8,503,228) and Fred Eychaner ($13,526,192).

Typical Recipients

Arts & Humanities: Ballet, Dance, Museums/Galleries, Music, Public Broadcasting, Theater
Civic & Public Affairs: Botanical Gardens/Parks, Employment/Job Training, Civic & Public Affairs-General, Public Policy, Urban & Community Affairs
Education: Arts/Humanities Education

Application Procedures

Initial Contact: Submit two-page letter of intent. Include audited financial statements, current year budget, list of directors, any relevant publications, annual report, and a copy of IRS determination letter of 501(c)(3) status.
Deadlines: May 1 and November 1. Grants are made in June and December.

Restrictions

Limited to arts, arts education, advocacy, and domestic violence organizations.

Foundation Officials

Marcia Lipetz: secretary-treasurer

Grants Analysis

Disclosure Period: fiscal year ending February 28, 1997
Total Grants: $1,259,750
Typical Range: $1,000 to $5,000

Recent Grants

Note: Grants derived from fiscal 1997 Form 990.

Arts & Humanities

70,000	Joffrey Ballet, Chicago, IL
65,000	Joffrey Ballet, Chicago, IL
50,000	WYIN/Channel 56, Merrilville, IN
33,000	Child's Play Touring Theater, Chicago, IL
25,000	Music and Dance Theater, Chicago, IL
15,000	SCT Productions, Chicago, IL -- for Dance Chicago '96
10,000	DuPage Children's Museum, Wheaton, IL
10,000	Northwest Indiana Symphony Society, Munster, IN

Civic & Public Affairs

15,000	Friends of the Parks, Chicago, IL
12,500	Center for Intuitive and Outsider, Chicago, IL
10,000	Erikson Institute, Chicago, IL -- for Project Match
10,000	Grand Cal Task Force, Whiting, IN
10,000	Illinois Coalition for Immigrants, Chicago, IL
10,000	Women Employed Institute, Chicago, IL

Education

30,000	Chicago Arts Partnership in Education, Chicago, IL

Health

50,000	Mount Sinai Hospital Medical Center, Chicago, IL

Social Services

40,000	United Way Lake Area, Griffith, IN
20,000	Taylor Institute, Chicago, IL
15,000	Horizons Community Services, Chicago, IL
15,000	Youth Communications, Chicago, IL

US BANK, WASHINGTON

Company Contact

Seattle, WA
Web: http://www.usbank.com

Company Description

Assets: US$5,956,500,000
Employees: 2,300
SIC(s): 6035 Federal Savings Institutions.
Parent Company: First Bank System (Minneapolis, MN), Minneapolis, MN, United States

Nonmonetary Support

Value: $53,550 (1996)
Type: Donated Equipment; Donated Products; Workplace Solicitation
Note: Workplace solicitation is for United Way only.

Corporate Sponsorship

Type: Arts & cultural events; Festivals/fairs; Sports events
Note: No organized program; sponsorships are held separately from corporate giving.

Giving Contact

Juliet Joy Ziegler, Vice President & Manager, Community Relations
1420 5th Avenue, Suite 800
PO Box 720 WWH658
Seattle, WA 98111-0720
Phone: (206)344-2360
Fax: (206)340-8554
Email: juliet.ziegler@usbank.com

Description

Organization Type: Corporate Giving Program
Giving Locations: WA
Grant Types: Capital, Employee Matching Gifts, General Support.

Financial Summary

Total Giving: $2,300,000 (1997 approx); $1,750,000 (1996 approx); $1,400,000 (1995 approx). Note: Contributes through corporate direct giving program only.

Typical Recipients

Arts & Humanities: Arts Associations & Councils, Arts Centers, Arts Festivals, Arts Funds, Arts Outreach, Ballet, Community Arts, Dance, Ethnic & Folk Arts, Arts & Humanities-General, Historic Preservation, Libraries, Museums/Galleries, Music, Opera, Performing Arts, Theater, Visual Arts
Civic & Public Affairs: African American Affairs, Asian American Affairs, Business/Free Enterprise, Chambers of Commerce, Civil Rights, Economic Development, Employment/Job Training, Ethnic Organizations, Gay/Lesbian Issues, Civic & Public Affairs-General, Hispanic Affairs, Housing, Inner-City Development, Native American Affairs, Professional & Trade Associations, Public Policy, Urban & Community Affairs, Women's Affairs, Zoos/Aquariums
Education: Afterschool/Enrichment Programs, Business Education, Business-School Partnerships, Colleges & Universities, Economic Education, Education Reform, Education-General, Literacy, Minority Education, Preschool Education, Special Education
Health: Adolescent Health Issues, AIDS/HIV, Cancer, Children's Health/Hospitals, Health-General, Hospices, Mental Health, Prenatal Health Issues
Science: Science Museums
Social Services: At-Risk Youth, Camps, Child Welfare, Community Centers, Community Service Organizations, Counseling, Day Care, Domestic Violence, Emergency Relief, Family Services, Food/Clothing Distribution, Homes, People with Disabilities, Refugee Assistance, Senior Services, Sexual Abuse, Shelters/Homelessness, Social Services-General, Substance Abuse, United Funds/United Ways, Volunteer Services, YMCA/YWCA/YMHA/YWHA, Youth Organizations

Application Procedures

Initial Contact: Call local branch or corporate headquarters for information.

Restrictions

Foundation does not make grants to individuals, religious organizations for sectarian purposes, political or lobbying groups, travel expenses, or organizations outside operating areas.

Additional Information

In 1997, First Bank System acquired U.S. Bancorp of Portland, OR. The merged company is called U.S. Bancorp. Until the two companies are fully integrated in 1998, the companies will be identified by their former names.

Corporate Officials

Phyllis J. Campbell: president private financial services B Spokane, WA 1951. ED Washington State University (1973); University of Washington (1987). PRIM CORP EMPL president private financial services: United States Bank, Washington. CORP AFFIL director: SAFECO Corp.; executive vice president: US Bancorp; director: Puget Sound Energy Co.; director: Puget Sound Power Light Co.
Juliet Joy Ziegler: community relations manager PRIM CORP EMPL community relations manager: U.S. Bank, Washington.

Grants Analysis

Disclosure Period: calendar year ending 1997
Total Grants: $2,300,000 (approx)
Typical Range: $1,000 to $5,000

Recent Grants

Note: Grants derived from 1995 grants list.

Arts & Humanities
Tears of Joy Theater, Vancouver, WA
Tri-Cities Corporate Council for Arts, Pasco, WA

Civic & Public Affairs
Center for Ethical Leadership, Seattle, WA
Local Initiatives Support Corp, Seattle, WA
Sean Humphrey House, Bellingham, WA
Women Helping Women, Spokane, WA
Woodland Park Zoo, WA

Education
Powerful Schools, Seattle, WA

Social Services
Spokane Food Bank, Spokane, WA
YMCA, Olympia, WA

US West, Inc.

 Number 37 of Top 100 Corporate Givers

Company Contact

Englewood, CO
Web: http://www.uswf.com

Company Description

Revenue: US$13,182,000,000 (1999)
Profit: US$1,342,000,000 (1999)
Employees: 61,047
Fortune Rank: 134, per FORTUNE Magazine's list of 500 Largest U.S. Corporations (1999).
FF 134
SIC(s): 4812 Radiotelephone Communications, 4813 Telephone Communications Except Radiotelephone.

Corporate Sponsorship

Type: Arts & cultural events; Festivals/fairs; Music & entertainment events

US West Foundation

Giving Contact

Larry Nash, Director, Administration
U.S. WEST Foundation
1801 California St., Suite 1360
Denver, CO 80202-2658
Phone: (303)896-1266
Fax: (303)896-4982
Email: Lnash@uswest.com

Description

EIN: 840978668
Organization Type: Corporate Foundation
Giving Locations: 14 western states served by company.
Grant Types: Conference/Seminar, Department, Employee Matching Gifts, General Support, Multiyear/Continuing Support, Project.
Note: Employee matching gift ratio: 1 to 1.

Giving Philosophy

'The US West Foundation was formed in July 1988, inheriting a tradition of giving that dates back more than a century. Today, we continue to build upon the traditions of community support and corporate social responsibility. Our mission is to provide new approaches and directions in supporting programs that improve quality of life. Since money alone does not always answer need, we continually seek fresh and innovative ways to solve problems.' Foundation Annual Report

Financial Summary

Total Giving: $22,000,000 (1999 approx); $27,349,520 (1998); $28,648,771 (1997). Note: Contributes through foundation only.
Assets: $40,000,000 (1999 approx); $44,582,443 (1998); $41,590,436 (1997)
Gifts Received: $24,716,390 (1998); $24,949,244 (1997); $26,467,933 (1995). Note: Contributions are received from US West and its subsidiaries.

Typical Recipients

Arts & Humanities: Arts Associations & Councils, Arts Funds, Ballet, Ethnic & Folk Arts, Film & Video, Historic Preservation, History & Archaeology, Museums/Galleries, Music, Opera, Public Broadcasting, Theater, Visual Arts
Civic & Public Affairs: Business/Free Enterprise, Chambers of Commerce, Community Foundations, Economic Development, Employment/Job Training, Civic & Public Affairs-General, Hispanic Affairs, Law & Justice, Native American Affairs, Nonprofit Management, Public Policy, Rural Affairs, Urban & Community Affairs, Women's Affairs
Education: Afterschool/Enrichment Programs, Business Education, Business-School Partnerships, Colleges & Universities, Community & Junior Colleges, Economic Education, Education Associations, Education Funds, Engineering/Technological Education, Faculty Development, Education-General, International Studies, Leadership Training, Minority Education, Preschool Education, Science/Mathematics Education, Social Sciences Education, Student Aid, Vocational & Technical Education
Environment: Environment-General, Wildlife Protection
Health: Alzheimers Disease, Emergency/Ambulance Services
Religion: Ministries, Religious Welfare
Science: Observatories & Planetariums, Science Museums, Scientific Centers & Institutes
Social Services: Child Welfare, Community Centers, Community Service Organizations, Family Services, United Funds/United Ways, Youth Organizations

Contributions Analysis

Giving Priorities: Human services, united funds, education, economic develompment, and the arts.
Arts & Humanities: 2%. Supports a wide range of cultural and artistic expression. Major interests include culturally diverse works that extend access to other audiences through electronic communications. Extends cultural opportunities by sponsoring performances, exhibits, outreach, or other access through communications technologies, especially in rural areas.
Civic & Public Affairs: About 19%. Interested in programs and organizations that advance economic development and small business support. Provides information access and technical assistance to enhance and grow small business. Encourages strategic planningsurrounding economic development connections between communities. Attempts to educate citizens of diverse cultural backgrounds to value the strength and to build leadership within the cultural fabric of their communities.
Education: 49%. Primary focus of the foundation. Looks for opportunities to improve education and to provide equity in education for all students. Interested in developing partnerships such as those including universities and K-12 educators and those involving business, social service agencies, and school systems. Specifically, major interests include early childhood education, diversity and greater sensitivity to

difference, and expansion of interdisciplinary technology in the classroom.
Health: 2%. Special emphasis is given to promoting collaborative efforts that encourage connections and cooperation between agencieswithin city, state, or region.
Science: 3%. Science centers.
Social Services: 25%. Primary support for the United Way.

Application Procedures

Initial Contact: Submit a proposal, not to exceed ten pages, to one of four operating offices (Colorado office only accepts proposals on a referral basis--unsolicited proposals sent to Colorado office will not be considered).
Application Requirements: Include name of organization, mailing address, telephone number, contact person, list of organization's board of directors, and copy of IRS form 501(c)(3).
Deadlines: Deadlines vary according to giving category: arts and culture, February; education, May; human services, August; civic and community improvement, October.
Evaluative Criteria: The foundation considers projects that promote economic self-reliance; advance equal opportunity; expand opportunities in rural areas; encourage cooperative efforts among charitable organizations, government and business; improve the viability and management of nonprofits; leverage grant dollars with funds from other sources; offer solutions to chronic social problems; address emerging social issues; can be replicated in other communities; and encourage the use of volunteers, including US West employees.
Decision Notification: Quarterly; notification is usually sent no later than 60 days after the respective category deadline.
Notes: Foundation only accepts proposals for the General Grants category of giving.

Restrictions

Foundation does not fund political campaigns; telephone service or communications equipment; computer hardware or software; individuals; fraternal organizations, clubs, school organizations, and school athletic funds; general operating budgets of organizations that receive more than 40% of their budget from the United Way; religious organizations for sectarian purposes; international organizations; national health agencies or their local affiliates; general operating budgets of tax-supported educational institutions; debt retirement or operational deficits; foundations that are themselves grantmaking bodies; or trips and tours. operational deficits; foundations that are themselves grantmaking bodies; or trips and tours.

Additional Information

The US WEST Foundation was formed in July 1988 and began making grants in 1989. The foundation serves to combine US WEST's giving program with those of its subsidiaries, Mountain Bell, Pacific Northwest Bell, and Northwestern Bell, which have now been combined into one company, US WEST Communications. The foundation also gives on behalf of the holding company's other subsidiaries, which include companies involved in cellular communications, and advanced technologies.
Publications: Us West Foundation Review

Corporate Officials

Betsy J. Bernard: executive vice president retail mkts secretary PRIM CORP EMPL executive vice president retail mkts: US West Inc.
Cliff Dodd: executive vice president systems integration PRIM CORP EMPL executive vice president systems integration: US West Inc.
Mark D. Roellig: executive vice president, general counsel, secretary PRIM CORP EMPL executive vice president, general counsel, secretary: US West Inc.
Allan R. Spies: executive vice president, chief financial officer PRIM CORP EMPL executive vice president, chief financial officer: US West Inc.
Solomon D. Trujillo: president, chief executive officer ED University of Wyoming BS; University of Wyoming MBA. PRIM CORP EMPL chairman, president, chief executive officer: United States West Inc. director: National Security Telecom Council CORP AFFIL director: Bank America; director: Dayton Hudson Corp. NONPR AFFIL director: Thomas Rivera Policy Institute; director: World Economic Forum; advisory: Services Policy Advisory Committee; chairman council seminars: Hispanic Americans Business Community; advisor: Office Press; member corp. advisors: Council LaRaza; chairman board trustees: Center New West; fellow: Claremont Graduate University; trustee: Aspen Institute.

Foundation Officials

Laurence J. Nash: director
Jane Prancan: vice president PRIM CORP EMPL director corporate community affairs: U.S. West Inc.
Janet Rash: grants manager
Solomon D. Trujillo: president (see above)

Grants Analysis

Disclosure Period: calendar year ending 1998
Total Grants: $20,203,429*
Number of Grants: 2,342 (approx)
Average Grant: $8,627
Highest Grant: $592,250
Typical Range: $1,000 to $25,000
***Note:** Giving includes United Way.

Recent Grants

Note: Grants derived from 1997 Form 990.

Arts & Humanities

150,000	Denver Art Museum, Denver, CO
85,450	Corporate Council for the Arts, Seattle, WA

Civic & Public Affairs

923,005	NFIE, Washington, DC
320,100	NFIE, Washington, DC
316,000	Nebraska Community Foundation, Lincoln, NE
297,756	Nebraska Community Foundation, Lincoln, NE
115,510	Southeast Idaho Council of Governments, Pocatello, ID
64,000	Greater Omaha Chamber Foundation, Omaha, NE

Education

520,180	University of Northern Iowa, Cedar Falls, IA
473,800	Mankato State University, Mankato, MN
409,500	University of Northern Iowa, Cedar Falls, IA
400,000	University of Colorado Denver Foundation, Denver, CO
370,260	University of Northern Colorado Foundation, Greeley, CO
357,000	Arizona State University, Tempe, AZ
333,338	Arizona State University, Tempe, AZ
294,000	Mankato State University, Mankato, MN
225,000	Colorado State University Foundation, Fort Collins, CO
216,300	Valley City State University, Valley City, ND
200,000	Arizona State University, Tempe, AZ
200,000	Children's Television Resource and Education Center, San Francisco, CA
192,166	Montana State University, Bozeman, MT
151,200	Cooperative Education Services, Albuquerque, NM
150,000	Applied Information Management Institute, Omaha, NE
140,450	Cooperative Education Services, Albuquerque, NM
138,600	Montana State University, Bozeman, MT
114,968	Small Business High Technology Institute, Phoenix, AZ
85,000	University of Colorado Denver Foundation, Denver, CO
76,597	Valley City State University, Valley City, ND
75,012	Creighton University, Omaha, NE
75,000	Independent Colleges, Seattle, WA
70,000	Oregon Independent Colleges Foundation, Portland, OR
60,000	College Fund/UNCF, Fairfax, VA

Health

115,000	American Red Cross, Washington, DC
100,000	American Red Cross, St. Paul, MN

Religion

150,000	Denver Urban Ministries, Denver, CO
100,000	Mount St. Vincent Home, Denver, CO
100,000	Salvation Army Divisional Headquarters, Brooklyn Center, MN

Science

160,000	Arizona Science Center, Phoenix, AZ
150,000	Oregon Innovation Center, Portland, OR

Social Services

463,445	United Way of King County, Seattle, WA
310,000	United Way, Minneapolis, MN
242,000	United Way of the Midlands, Omaha, NE
230,000	United Way Valley of the Sun, Phoenix, AZ
228,473	United Way of King County, Seattle, WA
228,472	United Way of King County, Seattle, WA
185,000	United Way of Columbia-Willamette, Portland, OR
125,200	Mile High United Way, Denver, CO
125,200	Mile High United Way, Denver, CO
120,000	United Way of Central Iowa, Des Moines, IA
109,000	United Way, St. Paul, MN

USAA Life Insurance Co.

Company Contact

San Antonio, TX
Web: http://www.usaa.com

Company Description

Employees: 875
SIC(s): 6311 Life Insurance.

USAA Foundation, A Charitable Trust

Giving Contact

Barbara Gentry, Vice President, Community Affairs
The USAA Foundation
c/o Community Relations (D-3-E)
Office of the Chairman
9800 Fredericksburg Rd.
San Antonio, TX 78288-0115
Phone: (210)498-1225
Fax: (210)498-8216

Description

EIN: 746363461
Organization Type: Corporate Foundation
Giving Locations: TX operating locations.
Grant Types: General Support, Scholarship.

Giving Philosophy

'As a service-oriented company, USAA takes pride in over seven decades of supporting efforts to improve the educational level, the economic well-being, and

the quality of life in the communities in which our employees live and work.' USAA Foundation Contributions Guidelines

Financial Summary

Total Giving: $6,233,186 (1995); $872,987 (1993); $1,910,908 (1992). Note: Contributes through foundation only.
Assets: $2,952,293 (1993); $3,022,927 (1992)
Gifts Received: $2,351 (1995); $1,413,613 (1993); $2,019,632 (1992). Note: In fiscal 1993, contributions were received from United Services Automobile Association.

Typical Recipients

Arts & Humanities: Libraries, Museums/Galleries, Music, Opera, Public Broadcasting, Theater
Education: Business Education, Colleges & Universities, Education-General, Private Education (Precollege)
Health: Cancer, Children's Health/Hospitals, Medical Research
Religion: Religious Welfare
Science: Scientific Research
Social Services: United Funds/United Ways, YMCA/YWCA/YMHA/YWHA

Contributions Analysis

Arts & Humanities: Museums and cultural centers, public radio and television stations, and visual and performing arts organizations.
Civic & Public Affairs: New businesses and new community services.
Education: Organizations committed to improving education and supporting the literacy effort, as well scholarship assistance in school programs.
Health: Research and treatment institutions primarily in the San Antonio area. Areas include research in cancer, heart disease, diabetes, genetics, Alzheimer's disease, and AIDS.
Social Services: United Way, health care facilities, youth organizations, services for the elderly and disadvantaged, and family support agencies.

Application Procedures

Initial Contact: written request
Application Requirements: a description of organization, including purpose, history, and current activities; proof of IRS tax-exempt status; current budget, including sources of income (an audited report is preferred); list of key management personnel and members of the board of directors; purpose and objectives of the program; segment of the community served by the program; how objectives will be achieved and in what time frame; total funding needed and projected sources; amount requested from foundation; method of evaluating the program's success; and plans for the future
Deadlines: None.
Review Process: proposals reviewed by contributions committee
Evaluative Criteria: organizations must provide bona fide credentials relative to assistance provided in priority areas; applications considered on an individual basis to determine if they fit within approved criteria

Restrictions

Requests for monetary assistance are not generally approved for individuals, religious organizations, beauty pageants, or transportation to parades, festivals, and similar activities.

Corporate Officials

Robert T. Herres: chairman, chief executive officer B Denver, CO 1932. ED United States Naval Academy BS (1954); Air Force Institute Technology MS (1960); George Washington University MPA (1965). PRIM CORP EMPL chairman, chief executive officer: United Services Automobile Association. CORP AFFIL chairman: USAA Real Estate Co.; chairman, chief executive officer: USAA General Indemnity Co.; chief executive officer: USAA Investment Trust; chairman, chief executive officer: USAA. NONPR AFFIL director: Trinity University; director: U.S. Naval Academy Foundation; director: National Association Independent Insurers; director: Insurance Institute Highway Safety; national chairman: Junior Achievement; director: Insurance Information Institute; director: Atlantic Council U.S.; member executive board: Boy Scouts America.
Josue Robles: chief financial officer PRIM CORP EMPL chief financial officer: USAA Life Insurance Co. CORP AFFIL chief financial officer, senior vice president, treasurer: USAA Capital Corp.
Edwin L. Rosane: president B 1936. ED United States Air Force Academy BS (1959); Southern Methodist University MS (1972). PRIM CORP EMPL president: USAA Life Insurance Co.

Foundation Officials

Amy D. Cannefax: trust representative
Hansford Tillman Johnson: trustee B Aiken, SC 1936. ED United States Air Force Academy BS (1959); Stanford University MS (1967); University of Colorado MBA (1970); National War College (1975-1976). PRIM CORP EMPL vice president: EG&G. CORP AFFIL president: EG&G Technical Services. NONPR AFFIL member: Order Daedalians; member: Society American Military Engineers; trustee: March Dimes; director: Cancer Therapy Research Center.

Grants Analysis

Disclosure Period: calendar year ending 1995
Total Grants: $6,233,186
Number of Grants: 95
Average Grant: $45,034*
Highest Grant: $2,000,000
Typical Range: $1,000 to $1,000,000
***Note:** Average grant figure excludes highest grant.

Recent Grants

Note: Grants derived from 1995 Form 990.

Arts & Humanities

270,000 San Antonio Symphony Society, San Antonio, TX -- for arts and education
210,000 San Antonio Museum of Art, San Antonio, TX -- for arts and education
75,000 Texas Public Radio, Riverwald, San Antonio, TX -- for the arts
50,000 Arts San Antonio, San Antonio, TX -- for the arts
50,000 Las Casas Foundation, San Antonio, TX -- for the arts

Education

400,000 US Military Academy Association of Graduates, West Point, NY
105,400 Junior Achievement National Headquarters, Colorado Springs, CO -- for education
80,000 Our Lady of the Lake University, San Antonio, TX
50,000 Insurance Education Foundation, Indianapolis, IN -- for education
50,000 Trinity University, San Antonio, TX
35,000 San Antonio Academy, San Antonio, TX

Health

2,000,000 Southwest Foundation for Biomedical Research, San Antonio, TX -- for medical research
250,000 Cancer Therapy and Research Center, San Antonio, TX -- for medical research
65,000 Children's Hospital Foundation, San Antonio, TX -- for human services

Religion

100,000 Salvation Army, San Antonio, TX -- for human services

Social Services

1,361,406 United Way San Antonio and Bexar County, San Antonio, TX -- for human services
100,517 United Way Sacramento Area, Sacramento, CA -- for human services
100,000 YMCA, San Antonio, TX -- for human services
55,773 Pikes Peak United Way, Colorado Springs, CO -- for human services
52,923 United Way South Hampton Roads, Virginia Beach, VA -- for human services

USG CORP.

Company Contact

Chicago, IL
Web: http://www.usg.com

Company Description

Revenue: US$3,600,000,000 (1999)
Profit: US$421,000,000 (1999)
Employees: 13,700
Fortune Rank: 437, per FORTUNE Magazine's list of 500 Largest U.S. Corporations (1999).
FF 437
SIC(s): 2621 Paper Mills, 2891 Adhesives & Sealants, 3275 Gypsum Products, 3296 Mineral Wool.

Operating Locations

Australia: USG Interiors Australia Pty. Ltd., Smithfield; Belgium: USG Interiors Coordination Centre SA, Aubange, Luxembourg; USG Interiors (Donn) SA, Aubange, Luxembourg; USG Interiors (Europe) SA, Aubange, Luxembourg; Bermuda: Gypsum Transportation Ltd., Hamilton; Canada: CGC, Inc., Mississauga; CNG Distribution Ltd., Mississauga; USG Canadian Mining Ltd., Mississauga; Donn Canada Ltd., Oakville; France: USG France SA, Dreux, Eure-et-Loir; Germany: USG Interiors Eastern Manufacturing Bauelemente GmbH, Telgte, Nordrhein-Westfalen; Donn Products GmbH, Viersen, Nordrhein-Westfalen; Italy: USG Italia SRL, Rodano, Lombardia; Mexico: Yeso Panamericano SA de CV, Ciudad de Mexico; Malaysia: USG Interiors (Far East) Sdn. Bhd., Petaling Jaya, Selangor, Subang, Selangor; Netherlands: Alabaster Engineering (Nederland) BV, Amsterdam, Noord-Holland; USG Netherlands BV, Amsterdam, Noord-Holland; Dinero Reinvertido BV, Rotterdam, Zuid-Holland; Red Top Technology (Nederland) BV, Rotterdam, Zuid-Holland; New Zealand: USG Interiors Pacific Ltd., Mt. Wellington, Auckland, Wellington; Spain: USG Interiors Espana SL, Madrid; United Kingdom: USG Europe Ltd., London; USG (UK) Ltd., Peterlee, Durham

USG Foundation

Giving Contact

Harold E. Pendexter, Jr., President
USG Foundation, Inc.
PO Box 6721
Chicago, IL 60680-6721
Phone: (312)606-4297
Fax: (312)606-5316

Alternate Contact

Margaret Clark

Description

EIN: 362984045
Organization Type: Corporate Foundation
Giving Locations: IL: nationally, with emphasis on corporate operating locations
Grant Types: Capital, Employee Matching Gifts, General Support, Scholarship.

Giving Philosophy

'USG Corporation recognizes a special responsibility to the complex society in which it exists. Just as a business operation affects the communities in which it operates, the vitality of these communities affects

the ability of a business enterprise to function. .. The social, educational, and cultural vitality of local communities promotes a healthy environment for neighbors, employees and their families, and the business community. Viewed from this perspective, contributions become an investment in learning how to cooperate and participate actively in improving the quality of life.' *The USG Foundation, Inc.* '..assistance promotes a positive, pro-active community environment for our employees, their families and friends and for the business community at large. In other words, contributions from the USG Foundation became an investment in a higher quality of life for us all.'

Financial Summary

Total Giving: $667,356 (1998); $492,626 (1997); $371,489 (1996). Note: 1996 Giving includes matching gifts ($56,822); United Way ($58,592).
Giving Analysis: Giving for 1998 includes: foundation ($521,605); foundation matching gifts ($89,380); foundation grants to United Way ($59,016)
Assets: $932,485 (1998); $932,485 (1997); $637,990 (1996)
Gifts Received: $1,000,000 (1998); $750,000 (1997); $500,000 (1996). Note: Contributions received from USG Corp.

Typical Recipients

Arts & Humanities: Arts Associations & Councils, Arts Institutes, Historic Preservation, History & Archaeology, Libraries, Museums/Galleries, Music, Opera, Public Broadcasting, Theater
Civic & Public Affairs: African American Affairs, Chambers of Commerce, Civil Rights, Economic Development, Employment/Job Training, Civic & Public Affairs-General, Hispanic Affairs, Housing, Law & Justice, Legal Aid, Public Policy, Safety, Urban & Community Affairs, Women's Affairs, Zoos/Aquariums
Education: Business Education, Colleges & Universities, Economic Education, Education Associations, Education-General, International Studies, Minority Education, Public Education (Precollege), Student Aid
Health: AIDS/HIV, Cancer, Clinics/Medical Centers, Diabetes, Eyes/Blindness, Health Organizations, Heart, Hospices, Hospitals, Long-Term Care, Medical Research, Mental Health, Public Health, Single-Disease Health Associations
International: International Organizations, International Relations, Missionary/Religious Activities
Religion: Jewish Causes, Ministries, Religious Welfare, Social/Policy Issues
Science: Science Museums
Social Services: Camps, Community Service Organizations, Crime Prevention, Delinquency & Criminal Rehabilitation, Emergency Relief, Family Services, Food/Clothing Distribution, People with Disabilities, Scouts, Substance Abuse, United Funds/United Ways, Volunteer Services, YMCA/YWCA/YMHA/YWHA, Youth Organizations

Contributions Analysis

Giving Priorities: Company makes limited contributions in Canada, geographically near its subsidiaries.
Arts & Humanities: 24%. Performing arts, museums, and historical and zoological societies
Civic & Public Affairs: 21%. Crime prevention, youth organizations, family services, and housing services.
Education: 26%. Organizations committed to educational improvement, colleges and universities, and scholarship programs.
Health: 26%. United Way, single-disease associations, hospitals, youth services, and disability services.

Application Procedures

Initial Contact: Full proposal.
Application Requirements: Include statement of need or problem and summary of background; amount requested and how it will be used; copy of IRS determination letter and most recent financial statements; list of board members; detailed description of proposed project, its purpose, and qualifications of organization to obtain objectives; goals and plan to achieve goals; supporting literature.
Deadlines: None.
Review Process: Foundation staff reviews all written proposals.
Evaluative Criteria: Evaluation of how the proposed program can effectively respond to societal needs, relevance in daily life, impact upon business and the future, and how grant will fit into the total contributions program.
Decision Notification: Board meets quarterly; responds within two months.
Notes: The foundation gives preference to relevant programs in which employees actively participate.

Restrictions

The foundation does not contribute to sectarian organizations having an exclusively religious nature; individuals; political parties, offices, or candidates; fraternal or veterans organizations; primary or secondary schools; organizations that cannot provide adequate accounting records or procedures; or courtesy advertising. In general, organizations already receiving funds through united campaigns will not be considered for additional support.

Corporate Officials

Eugene Bernard Connolly, Jr.: chairman emeritus B New York, NY 1932. ED Hofstra University BS (1954); Hofstra University MBA (1964). PRIM CORP EMPL chairman emeritus: USG Corp. CORP AFFIL director: Zenith Electronics Corp.; director: LaSalle National Bank; director: The Pepper Companies. NONPR AFFIL vice chairman: Lake Forest Graduate School Management.
Richard Harrison Fleming: chief financial officer, senior vice president B Milwaukee, WI 1947. ED University of the Pacific BA (1969); Dartmouth College MBA (1971). PRIM CORP EMPL chief financial officer, senior vice president: USG Corp. ADD CORP EMPL president, treasurer, director: USG Foreign Investments Ltd.; vice president, treasurer, director: USG Interiors Inc. CORP AFFIL director: Child Welfare League America; director: Family Care Services Metropolitan Chicago.
Harold E. Pendexter, Jr.: senior vice president, chief administrative officer B Portland, ME 1934. ED Bowdoin College AB (1957). PRIM CORP EMPL senior vice president, chief administrative officer: USG Corp. ADD CORP EMPL director: USG Interiors Inc.
Donald E. Roller: executive vice president PRIM CORP EMPL executive vice president: USG Corp. CORP AFFIL director: L & W Supply Corp.; president: La Mirada Product Co. Inc.

Foundation Officials

Richard Harrison Fleming: treasurer, trustee (see above)
Matthew P. Gonring: vice president, trustee B West Bend, WI 1955. ED University of Wisconsin (1977); American University (1978). PRIM CORP EMPL vice president corporate communications: USG Corp. NONPR AFFIL member: National Association Manufacturer; professor: Northwestern University.
Peter K. Maitland: director B 1941. PRIM CORP EMPL vice president: USG Corp.
Harold E. Pendexter, Jr.: president, director (see above)
Donald E. Roller: vice president (see above)
Susan K. Torrey: secretary PRIM CORP EMPL vice president, assistant secretary, director: USG Interiors Inc.

Grants Analysis

Disclosure Period: calendar year ending 1998
Total Grants: $521,605*
Number of Grants: 93
Average Grant: $5,609
Highest Grant: $30,000
Typical Range: $1,000 to $7,000
***Note:** Giving excludes matching gifts; United Way.

Recent Grants

Note: Grants derived from 1997 Form 990.

Arts & Humanities

20,000 Victory Garden Theater, Chicago, IL
15,000 Naperville Heritage Society, Naperville, IL
12,500 Lyric Opera, Chicago, IL
10,000 Chicago Children's Museum, Chicago, IL
8,000 Chicago Symphony Orchestra, Chicago, IL
7,500 Chicago Opera Theater, Chicago, IL
2,500 Chicago Historical Society, Chicago, IL

Civic & Public Affairs

7,500 Neighborhood Housing Services, New York, NY
5,950 Chicago Urban League, Chicago, IL
5,000 Lake Front Single-Room Occupancy Corporation, Chicago, IL
3,500 Chicago Zoological Society, Brookfield, IL
3,000 Chicago Councils Urban Affairs, Chicago, IL
2,500 Better Government Association, Chicago, IL
2,500 Employment Policy Foundation, Washington, DC
2,000 Latino Institute, Chicago, IL

Education

15,935 National Merit Scholarship Corporation, Evanston, IL
15,000 Bowdoin College, Brunswick, ME
7,500 University of Illinois Foundation, Urbana, IL
5,000 Institute of International Education, New York, NY
5,000 Lake Forest Graduate School of Management, Lake Forest, IL
5,000 Loyola University, New Orleans, LA
3,000 Illinois Council on Economic Education, Dekalb, IL
3,000 Junior Achievement, Chicago, IL
2,500 Inroads, Chicago, IL
2,500 Midtown Educational Foundation, Chicago, IL

Health

10,000 Rush-Presbyterian St. Luke's Medical Center, Chicago, IL
7,000 American Liver Foundation, Cedar Grove, NJ
5,000 Northwestern Memorial Hospital, Chicago, IL
4,000 American Heart Association, Wichita Falls, TX
2,500 Auxiliary of Condell
2,500 National Conference
2,000 Options for People, Chicago, IL

International

5,000 Kiwanis International Foundation, Indianapolis, IN
5,000 Kiwanis International Foundation, Indianapolis, IN

Religion

5,000 Coventry Children's Home

Science

8,600 Museum of Science and Industry, Chicago, IL
5,000 Discovery 2000, Birmingham, AL

Social Services

61,248 United Way Crusade of Mercy, Chicago, IL
10,000 Chicago Crime Commission, Chicago, IL

10,000	Chicago United, Chicago, IL
5,000	Camp Fire Illinois Prairie Council, IL
5,000	Youth Guidance, Chicago, IL
3,500	Executive Service Corps, Chicago, IL
3,000	Abraham Lincoln Center, Chicago, IL
3,000	Boys and Girls Club, Chicago, IL
3,000	Donka, Wheaton, IL
3,000	Equip for Equality, Chicago, IL
3,000	Juvenile Protection Association
2,500	Chicago Cares, Chicago, IL
2,500	YMCA, Chicago, IL
2,000	Heartland Alliance for Human Needs and Rights, Chicago, IL

UST INC.

Company Contact

Greenwich, CT

Company Description

Former Name: U.S. Tobacco Co.
Employees: 3,500
SIC(s): 2084 Wines, Brandy & Brandy Spirits, 2111 Cigarettes, 2121 Cigars, 6719 Holding Companies Nec.

Nonmonetary Support

Value: $153,000 (1996); $1,000 (1994)
Type: Donated Products

Corporate Sponsorship

Type: Arts & cultural events; Festivals/fairs; Music & entertainment events; Sports events
Contact: Nancy Mitchell, Administrative Assistant
Note: Sponsors auto races, golf tournaments, fishing tournaments, and rodeos in small and rural communities.

Giving Contact

Geraldine K. Morgan, Manager, Corporate Contributions & Community Relations
UST Inc.
100 W Putnam Ave.
Greenwich, CT 06830
Phone: (203)622-3696
Fax: (203)863-7284

Description

Organization Type: Corporate Giving Program
Giving Locations: headquarters and operating communities; on rare occasions will consider awards to national organizations.
Grant Types: Capital, Challenge, Conference/Seminar, Emergency, Employee Matching Gifts, Endowment, General Support, Loan, Project, Scholarship.
Note: Employee matching gift ratio: 2 to 1.

Financial Summary

Total Giving: $6,000,000 (1996 approx); $6,000,000 (1995 approx); $5,505,000 (1994 approx). Note: Contributes through corporate direct giving program only. 1996 and 1994 Giving includes corporate direct giving; nonmonetary support.

Typical Recipients

Arts & Humanities: Public Broadcasting, Theater
Civic & Public Affairs: Law & Justice, Urban & Community Affairs
Education: Colleges & Universities, Minority Education
Health: Health Organizations, Medical Research
Social Services: Community Service Organizations, Domestic Violence, Family Services, Senior Services, Substance Abuse

Contributions Analysis

Giving Priorities: Health and sciences, education, arts and humanities, and civic and public affairs.

Application Procedures

Initial Contact: letter and proposal
Application Requirements: a description of organization, amount requested, purpose of funds sought, recently audited financial statement, and proof of tax-exempt status
Deadlines: None.

Restrictions

Company does not fund individuals, political or lobbying groups, or religious organizations for sectarian purposes.

Additional Information

Company changed its name to UST Inc. from U.S. Tobacco Co. in January 1988.

Corporate Officials

Robert E. Barrett: executive vice president, general counsel B Brooklyn, NY 1938. ED C. W. Post University BA; Syracuse University MA. PRIM CORP EMPL executive vice president: UST Inc. CORP AFFIL president: UST Enterprise Inc.
Vincent A. Gierer, Jr.: chairman, president, chief executive officer, director B Bronx, NY 1947. ED Iona College BBA (1969). PRIM CORP EMPL chairman, president, chief executive officer, director: UST Inc. ADD CORP EMPL chairman: International Wine Spirits Ltd. NONPR AFFIL member: American Management Association; member: Financial Executives Institute; member: American Institute CPAs.
Richard H. Verheij: executive vice president, general counsel B 1958. ED Case Western Reserve University BA (1980); Case Western Reserve University JD (1983). PRIM CORP EMPL executive vice president, general counsel: UST Inc.

Giving Program Officials

Robert E. Barrett: chairman B Brooklyn, NY 1938. ED C. W. Post University BA; Syracuse University MA. PRIM CORP EMPL executive vice president: UST Inc. CORP AFFIL president: UST Enterprise Inc.
Valerie T. Held: vice president
Geraldine K. Morgan: PRIM CORP EMPL manager corporate contributions & community relations: UST Inc.
Albert J. Tortorella: PRIM CORP EMPL senior vice president corporate communications & public affairs: UST Inc.

Foundation Officials

Garnis W. Hagen: vice president PRIM CORP EMPL vice president: U.S. Tobacco Co.
Mark A. Rozelle: vice president PRIM CORP EMPL vice president: UST Inc.

Grants Analysis

Disclosure Period: calendar year ending 1996
Total Grants: $6,000,000 (approx)
Typical Range: $1,000 to $2,500

USX CORP.

 Number 97 of Top 100 Corporate Givers

Company Contact

Pittsburgh, PA
Web: http://www.usx.com

Company Description

Revenue: US$25,610,000,000 (1999)
Profit: US$698,000,000 (1999)
Employees: 32,862
Fortune Rank: 51, per FORTUNE Magazine's list of 500 Largest U.S. Corporations (1999).
FF 51
SIC(s): 1311 Crude Petroleum & Natural Gas, 2911 Petroleum Refining, 3312 Blast Furnaces & Steel Mills, 5051 Metals Service Centers & Offices.

Operating Locations

Canada: Met-Chem Canada, Montreal; Ireland: Marathon Petroleum Hibernia Ltd., Cork; Netherlands: CLAM Petroleum Co., Hague; Norway: Marathon Petroleum Norge AS, Oslo, Akershus; United Kingdom: Brae Gas Marketing Co. Ltd., London; Marathon International Petroleum (Great Britain) Ltd., London; Marathon Oil North Sea (Great Britain) Ltd., London; Marathon Petroleum (UK) Ltd., London; Marathon Service (Great Britain) Ltd., London; Marathon Oil (UK) Ltd., Montrose, Tayside

USX Foundation, Inc.

Giving Contact

Mr. James L. Hamilton, III, General Manager
USX Foundation, Inc.
600 Grant St., Rm. 685
Pittsburgh, PA 15219-4776
Phone: (412)433-5237
Fax: (412)433-6847

Description

EIN: 136093185
Organization Type: Corporate Foundation
Giving Locations: nationally, with emphasis on communities where USX Corp. and its subsidiaries operate.
Grant Types: Capital, Employee Matching Gifts, General Support, Matching.
Note: Matching grants awarded for education only.

Giving Philosophy

'USX Foundation, Inc. (the Foundation) is a nonprofit membership corporation founded in Delaware in 1953. The purpose of the Foundation is to provide support in a planned and balanced manner for educational, scientific, charitable, civic, cultural and health needs and to assist in meeting those and other major needs through support of selected organizations and projects. Priority is given to organizations and projects which serve the major operating areas of USX Corporation.' *USX Foundation Annual Report*

Financial Summary

Total Giving: $7,208,342 (fiscal year ending November 30, 1998); $5,801,935 (fiscal 1997); $5,323,315 (fiscal 1996). Note: Contributes through foundation only.
Giving Analysis: Giving for fiscal 1996 includes: foundation scholarships ($821,566); foundation matching gifts ($800,849); fiscal 1997: foundation grants to United Way ($1,363,500); foundation matching gifts ($859,337); fiscal 1998: foundation grants to United Way ($1,538,500); foundation matching gifts ($938,192); foundation scholarships ($649,850); foundation fellowships ($31,000)
Assets: $9,985,138 (fiscal 1998); $6,393,773 (fiscal 1997); $5,959,550 (fiscal 1996)
Gifts Received: $8,460,094 (fiscal 1998); $6,000,000 (fiscal 1997); $5,000,000 (fiscal 1996). Note: Contributions received from USX Corp.

Typical Recipients

Arts & Humanities: Arts Associations & Councils, Arts Centers, Arts Festivals, Ballet, Dance, Historic Preservation, History & Archaeology, Libraries, Museums/Galleries, Music, Opera, Performing Arts, Public Broadcasting, Theater
Civic & Public Affairs: Asian American Affairs, Business/Free Enterprise, Community Foundations, Economic Policy, Employment/Job Training, Civic & Public Affairs-General, Law & Justice, Professional & Trade Associations, Public Policy, Urban & Community Affairs

Education: Arts/Humanities Education, Business Education, Colleges & Universities, Community & Junior Colleges, Economic Education, Education Associations, Education Reform, Elementary Education (Public), Engineering/Technological Education, Environmental Education, Legal Education, Minority Education, Public Education (Precollege), Science/Mathematics Education, Special Education, Student Aid, Vocational & Technical Education
Environment: Environment-General
Health: Health Organizations, Medical Rehabilitation, Mental Health, Single-Disease Health Associations, Trauma Treatment
Religion: Religious Organizations, Religious Welfare
Science: Science Museums, Scientific Centers & Institutes, Scientific Organizations
Social Services: At-Risk Youth, Community Centers, Community Service Organizations, Delinquency & Criminal Rehabilitation, Family Services, Homes, People with Disabilities, Scouts, Senior Services, Substance Abuse, United Funds/United Ways, YMCA/YWCA/YMHA/YWHA, Youth Organizations

Contributions Analysis

Giving Priorities: Education and social welfare. Limited support to international affairs organizations through public policy and environmental contributions. For example, has supported the International Bird Rescue Research Center, the World Wildlife Fund, the World Affairs Council, and International Executive Service Corps.
Arts & Humanities: 5%. Support is allocated to the performing arts, particularly symphonies and operas. Other interests include museums and historic restoration.
Civic & Public Affairs: (Public Policy) 1%. Limited support is awarded to public affairs concerns, which target national and regional organizations, including support to public policy research organizations and organizations concerned with legal matters and the judiciary system. Limited support is also offered to organizations concerned with international affairs.
Education: 69%. Supports a broad spectrum of higher educational programs. Interests include stimulating voluntary educational support, supporting private institutions, and assisting higher education associations. About one-third of education funds is awarded in the form of matching gifts. The foundation supports scholarship programs for employees' children and college and university scholarship funds.
Environment: 1%.
Health: 2%. Health funding supported rehabilitation centers and single-disease associations.
Social Services: 23%. Primarily supports the United Way; also funds community centers and youth groups.
Note: Total contributions in 1998.

Application Procedures

Initial Contact: Send a concise letter or executive summary.
Application Requirements: Include a description of project and its goals; organization's mission and need, and projected outcomes; a copy of the organization's Internal Revenue Service certification of tax-exempt status under Section 501(c)(3) of Internal Revenue Code; a copy of the organization's current budget and its most recent audited financial report; the estimated cost of the project and the amount requested, with explanation of the need for funds in relation to the total requirements of the project and available resources; a statement of sources of aid in hand (if any) and the amount of committed support; a statement of sources of anticipated aid, i.e., prospective contributors that have been solicited and the amounts requested and/or prospective contributors still to be solicited; a list of the organization's chief executives and members of the Board of Directors/Trustees, with affiliations; the signature of an authorized executive of the tax-exempt organization; and a signed statement of approval by the chief executive of the parent organization if the application originates in a subdivision of such entity.
Deadlines: January 15 for public, cultural, and scientific requests; April 15 for aid to education; July 15 for health and human services requests.
Notes: Organizations in the Pittsburgh area may use the Common Grant Application format of the Grantmakers of Western Pennsylvania. Requests for personal interviews and site visits are accommodated as Foundation staff schedules permit.

Restrictions

The foundation does not award grants to individuals or to religious organizations for religious purposes. Additionally, grants are not awarded for economic development projects; conferences, seminars or symposia; travel; exhibits; special events; fund-raising events; publication of papers, books or magazines; or production of films, videotapes or other audiovisual materials.
Grants are generally not awarded for K-12 education, individual research projects, or organizations receiving United Way support.
Organizations seeking ongoing support must reapply each year in accordance with the above application deadlines.

Additional Information

Publications: Foundation Annual Report

Corporate Officials

James H. Fix: assistant comptrollero PRIM CORP EMPL assistant comptroller: USX Corp.
Gary Allen Glynn: president B Springfield, VT 1946. ED University of Vermont BS (1968); University of Pennsylvania MBA (1970). PRIM CORP EMPL president: USX and Carnegie Pension Fund. NONPR AFFIL chairman finance committee: General Services Board Alcoholic Anonymous; member: New York Society Security Analysts; member: Financial Executives Institute; member: Association Investment Management & Research. CLUB AFFIL Tuxedo Club; Metro Club; Metro Opera Association; Drones Club; Economic Club New York.
Gretchen R. Haggerty: vice president, treasurer B 1955. ED Case Western Reserve University BS; Duquesne University JD. PRIM CORP EMPL vice president, treasurer: USX Corp. ADD CORP EMPL vice president accounting and finance: United States Steel Group.
James L. Hamilton, III: general manager PRIM CORP EMPL general manager: USX Corp.
Robert M. Hernandez: vice chairman, chief financial officer, director B Pittsburgh, PA 1944. ED University of Pittsburgh AB (1966); University of Pennsylvania Wharton School MBA (1968). PRIM CORP EMPL vice chairman, chief financial officer, director: USX Corp. ADD CORP EMPL chairman: RTI International Metals Inc. CORP AFFIL director: America Casualty Excess Ltd.
Lewis B. Jones: vice president, partner B 1943. ED Oklahoma State University BBA (1966). PRIM CORP EMPL vice president, partner: USX Corp.
John T. Mills: vice president, tax counsel PRIM CORP EMPL senior vice president finance administration: Marathon Oil Co.
John L. Richmond: assistant treasurer PRIM CORP EMPL assistant treasurer: USX Corp.
Dan D. Sandman: senior vice president human resources, secretary, general counsel B 1949. ED Ohio State University BA (1970); Ohio State University JD (1973). PRIM CORP EMPL senior vice president human resources, secretary, general counsel: USX Corp.
Thomas J. Usher: chairman, chief executive officer B Reading, PA 1942. ED University of Pittsburgh BS (1964); University of Pittsburgh MS (1965); University of Pittsburgh PhD (1971). PRIM CORP EMPL chairman, chief executive officer: USX Corp. CORP AFFIL director: PP&G Industries Inc.; director: Transtar Inc.; director: PNC Bank Corp. NONPR AFFIL chairman: United States-Korea Business Council; trustee: University Pittsburgh; member: Dinamo Ovia; chairman: U.S.-Japan Business Council; member: America Iron Steel Engineers; member, chairman: America Iron Steel Institute. CLUB AFFIL Rolling Rock Club; Laurel Valley Country Club; Oakmont Country Club; Double Eagle Club; Duquesne Club; Burning Tree Club.

Foundation Officials

Victor Gene Beghini: trustee B Greensboro, PA 1934. ED Pennsylvania State University BS (1956); Harvard University Graduate School of Business Administration (1974). CORP AFFIL president: Marathon Petroleum Sakhalin; vice chairman, director: USX Corp.; director: Baker Hughes Inc.
M. Sharon Cassidy: assistant secretary B Latrobe, PA 1946. ED Wheeling Jesuit University BS (1968); university of Pittsburg JD (1974). PRIM CORP EMPL general counsel: United States Steel & Carnegie Pension Fund. NONPR AFFIL member: American Bar Association; advisory: Pension Benefit Guaranty Capital.
Patricia P. Funaro: program administrator
Gary Allen Glynn: vice president (see above)
James L. Hamilton, III: general manager (see above)
Marilyn A. Harris: trustee
Robert M. Hernandez: trustee (see above)
David A. Lynch: assistant secretary
Craig D. Mallick: assistant secretary
Dan D. Sandman: trustee (see above)
Thomas J. Usher: chairman board trustees (see above)
Paul J. Wilhelm: trustee B 1941. ED Carnegie Mellon University BS (1964). PRIM CORP EMPL president: United States Steel Group. CORP AFFIL director: USX Corp.

Grants Analysis

Disclosure Period: fiscal year ending November 30, 1998
Total Grants: $4,051,800*
Number of Grants: 200
Average Grant: $7,798
Highest Grant: $2,500,000
Typical Range: $1,000 to $25,000
***Note:** Giving excludes matching gifts; scholarship; fellowships; United Way. Average grant figure excludes highest grant.

Recent Grants

Note: Grants derived from fiscal 1997 Form 990.

Arts & Humanities

150,000	The Carnegie, Pittsburgh, PA -- capital campaign
55,000	Pittsburgh Symphony, Pittsburgh, PA
50,000	Alabama Symphony, Birmingham, AL -- capital campaign
50,000	Pittsburgh Symphony, Pittsburgh, PA -- capital campaign
40,000	Historical Society of Western Pennsylvania, Pittsburgh Regional History Center, Pittsburgh, PA -- capital campaign

Civic & Public Affairs

50,000	UPMC Braddock, Braddock, PA -- capital campaign

Education

200,000	Pennsylvania State University College of Earth and Mineral Science, University Park, PA -- operating support
200,000	University of Cincinnati College of Law, Cincinnati, OH -- capital campaign
50,000	Ohio University, Athens, OH -- scholarships
35,000	Inroads, Saint Louis, MO -- operating support

35,000	University of Minnesota Minerals Research Chair, Minneapolis, MN -- capital campaign
30,000	Duquesne University, Pittsburgh, PA -- support Celebration of Excellence Campaign
25,000	Birmingham-Southern College Birmingham Environmental Center, Birmingham, AL -- capital campaign
25,000	Carnegie Mellon University, Pittsburgh, PA -- capital campaign
25,000	Cornell University, Ithaca, NY -- capital campaign
25,000	Montana Tech University, Butte, MT -- capital campaign
25,000	Rose-Hulman Institute of Technology Chemical Engineering Department, Terre Haute, IN -- capital campaign
25,000	University of Pittsburgh, Pittsburgh, PA -- capital campaign
20,400	Inroads, Saint Louis, MO -- operating support
20,000	Communities in Schools, Pittsburgh, PA -- operating support
20,000	Houston Independent School District, Houston, TX -- operating support for Browning Elementary School
20,000	Ivy Tech State College, Gary, IN -- capital campaign
20,000	Robert Morris College, Pittsburgh, PA -- capital campaign
15,000	Allegheny Valley School, Pittsburgh, PA -- capital campaign
15,000	Alvernia College, Pittsburgh, PA -- support Faith in the Future
15,000	Junior Achievement Southeast Texas Chapter, Houston, TX -- operating support

Religion

20,000	Coalition for Christian Outreach, Pittsburgh, PA -- capital campaign
20,000	Coaliton for Christian Outreach, Pittsburgh, PA -- operating support
20,000	Holy Family Institute, Pittsburgh, PA -- capital campaign

Science

15,000	American Geological Institute, Houston, TX -- operating support

Social Services

350,000	United Way Southwestern Pennsylvania, Pittsburgh, PA -- operating support
350,000	United Way Southwestern Pennsylvania, Pittsburgh, PA -- operating support
187,500	Lake Area United Way, Griffith, IN -- operating support
187,500	Lake Area United Way, Griffith, IN -- operating support
70,000	United Way Hancock County, Findlay, OH -- operating support
70,000	United Way Hancock County, Findlay, OH -- operating support
62,500	United Way Texas Gulf Coast, Houston, TX -- operating support
62,500	United Way Texas Gulf Coast, Houston, TX -- operating support
55,000	United Way Central Alabama, Birmingham, AL -- operating support
55,000	United Way Central Alabama, Birmingham, AL -- operating support
50,000	Boy Scouts of America Sam Houston Area Council, Houston, TX -- capital campaign
40,000	Girl Scouts of America, Pittsburgh, PA -- capital campaign
30,000	YWCA, Pittsburgh, PA -- capital campaign
22,500	United Way Clark and Champaign Counties Ohio, Springfield, OH -- operating support
22,500	United Way Clark and Champaign Counties Ohio, Springfield, OH -- operating support
22,000	United Way Bucks County, Fairless Hills, PA -- operating support
22,000	United Way Bucks County, Fairless Hills, PA -- operating support
13,500	United Way Northeastern Minnesota, Chisholm, MN -- operating support
13,500	United Way Northeastern Minnesota, Chisholm, MN -- operating support
12,500	United Way, Dallas, TX -- operating support

VALERO ENERGY CORP.

Company Contact

San Antonio, TX

Company Description

Revenue: US$7,691,200,000 (1999)
Employees: 2,519 (1999)
Fortune Rank: 229, per FORTUNE Magazine's list of 500 Largest U.S. Corporations (1999).
FF 229
SIC(s): 2911 Petroleum Refining, 4923 Gas Transmission & Distribution.

Nonmonetary Support

Value: $52,469 (1990)
Type: Donated Equipment; In-kind Services; Loaned Executives
Note: In-kind services consist of printing services for a number of nonprofit organizations in San Antonio.

Corporate Sponsorship

Type: Arts & cultural events; Festivals/fairs; Pledge-a-thon

Giving Contact

Mary Rose Brown, Vice President Corporate Communications
Valero Energy Corp.
1 Valero Pl.
San Antonio, TX 78212
Phone: (210)370-2000
Fax: (210)370-2327

Description

Organization Type: Corporate Giving Program
Giving Locations: headquarters and operating communities.
Grant Types: Capital, Challenge, Emergency, Employee Matching Gifts, Endowment, Fellowship, General Support, Multiyear/Continuing Support, Project, Research, Seed Money.

Financial Summary

Total Giving: Contributes through corporate direct giving program only.

Typical Recipients

Arts & Humanities: Arts Appreciation, Arts & Humanities-General
Education: Agricultural Education
Environment: Environment-General
Health: Emergency/Ambulance Services
Social Services: Food/Clothing Distribution, Senior Services

Application Procedures

Initial Contact: Send a brief letter of inquiry.
Application Requirements: Include a description of organization, amount requested, purpose of funds sought, audited financial statement, and proof of tax-exempt status.
Deadlines: None.
Decision Notification: Contributions meetings are held monthly.

Corporate Officials

Edward Charles Benninger, Jr.: president, chief financial officercommunications B Chicago, IL 1942. ED Texas Technology University BBA (1965). PRIM CORP EMPL president, chief financial officer: Valero Energy Corp. ADD CORP EMPL president: Valero Corp. Service Co.; executive vice presidents: Valero Marketing & SUP Co.; president: Valero Refining & Marketing Co.; president: Valero Refining Co. Texas. CORP AFFIL chairman, president, chief executive officer: Valero Natural Gas Co.
Mary Rose Brown: vice president corporate communications PRIM CORP EMPL vice president corporate communications: Valero Energy Corp.
William Eugene Greehey: chairman, chief executive officer, director B Fort Dodge, IA 1936. ED Saint Mary's University BA (1960). PRIM CORP EMPL chairman, chief executive officer, director: Valero Energy Corp. ADD CORP EMPL chairman, chief executive officer: Valero Refining Co.; chairman: Valero Refining Co. - Texas; chairman, chief executive officer: Valero Refining Marketing Co. CORP AFFIL director: Santa Fe Energy Resources Inc.; director: Weatherford International Inc.

Giving Program Officials

Mary Rose Brown: vice president corporate communications (see above)
Luis Adolpho de la Garza: (see above)

VALMONT INDUSTRIES, INC.

Company Contact

Valley, NE
Web: http://www.valmont.com

Company Description

Employees: 4,868
SIC(s): 3523 Farm Machinery & Equipment, 3612 Transformers Except Electronic, 3648 Lighting Equipment Nec.

Corporate Sponsorship

Type: Arts & cultural events

Valmont Foundation

Giving Contact

Ed Burchfield, Executive Secretary
Valmont Foundation
One Valmont Plaza
Omaha, NE 68154-5215
Phone: (402)963-1050
Fax: (402)963-1095
Email: elb2@valmont.com

Description

Founded: 1976
EIN: 362895245
Organization Type: Corporate Foundation
Giving Locations: NE limited giving nationally.
Grant Types: Capital, General Support.

Giving Philosophy

'The mission of the Valmont Contributions Program is to help improve the quality of life in communities in which Valmont employees live and work. Our goal is to make contributions where they will be most effectively used to help accomplish this mission.' Valmont Contributions Program Guidelines

Financial Summary

Total Giving: $420,337 (fiscal year ending February 28, 1998); $374,733 (fiscal 1997); $408,737 (fiscal 1996). Note: Contributes through foundation only.

Giving Analysis: Giving for fiscal 1996 includes: foundation ($318,517); foundation grants to United Way ($90,200); fiscal 1997: foundation ($288,933); foundation grants to United Way ($85,800); fiscal 1998: foundation ($320,182); foundation grants to United Way ($100,155)
Assets: $17,996 (fiscal 1998); $63,416 (fiscal 1997); $69,477 (fiscal 1996)
Gifts Received: $372,413 (fiscal 1998); $420,170 (fiscal 1997); $450,042 (fiscal 1996). Note: Contributions are received from Valmont Industries.

Typical Recipients

Arts & Humanities: Arts Associations & Councils, Arts Funds, Ballet, Ethnic & Folk Arts, Arts & Humanities-General, History & Archaeology, Libraries, Museums/Galleries, Music, Performing Arts, Public Broadcasting, Theater
Civic & Public Affairs: Botanical Gardens/Parks, Business/Free Enterprise, Chambers of Commerce, Clubs, Community Foundations, Economic Development, Ethnic Organizations, Civic & Public Affairs-General, Parades/Festivals, Professional & Trade Associations, Rural Affairs, Urban & Community Affairs, Women's Affairs, Zoos/Aquariums
Education: Agricultural Education, Business Education, Colleges & Universities, Community & Junior Colleges, Economic Education, Education Funds, Engineering/Technological Education, Education-General, Literacy, Minority Education, Private Education (Precollege), Religious Education, Student Aid
Environment: Resource Conservation, Wildlife Protection
Health: AIDS/HIV, Arthritis, Children's Health/Hospitals, Emergency/Ambulance Services, Heart, Hospitals, Kidney, Medical Rehabilitation, Nutrition, Single-Disease Health Associations
Religion: Religious Organizations, Religious Welfare, Social/Policy Issues
Science: Science Exhibits & Fairs
Social Services: At-Risk Youth, Child Welfare, Crime Prevention, Family Services, People with Disabilities, Recreation & Athletics, Scouts, Senior Services, Substance Abuse, United Funds/United Ways, YMCA/YWCA/YMHA/YWHA, Youth Organizations

Contributions Analysis

Arts & Humanities: 14%. Funds museums, zoos, the arts, activities associated with supported institutions, and organizations and events directly supporting the arts.
Civic & Public Affairs: 11%. Supports service and youth organizations, community activities, community service organizations, and activities associated with community service organizations and events.
Education: 24%. Educational institutions, activities associated with educational institutions, and organizations participating directly with educational institutions receive support.
Health: 3%. Health care institutions, activities associated with health care institutions, and organizations assisting those in need.
Religion: 6%. Funds Christian organizations.
Social Services: 42%. Supports the United Way and youth groups.
Note: Total contributions made in 1998.

Application Procedures

Initial Contact: Send a written request, maximum of three pages.
Application Requirements: Include statement of organization's objectives; description of proposed use of contribution; Valmont employee involvement, if any; evidence of tax-exempt status defined under section 501(c)(3) of the Internal Revenue Code; list of officers and directors; and other significant donors.
Deadlines: None.
Notes: Please do not phone or fax requests.

Restrictions

The foundation does not make contributions to individuals; organizations with a limited constituency, such as clubs or fraternal and social organizations; support for any type of travel or tours for individuals or groups; or for-profit organizations.
Valmont will generally not consider contributions for organizations in communities where Valmont does not have an operational presence; multi-year funding for a program or project beyond three years; underwriting or sponsorship of specific radio or television programming; emergency operating support for an organization; or athletic events. underwriting or sponsorship of specific radio or television programming; emergency operating support for an organization; or athletic events.

Additional Information

Publications: Guidelines

Corporate Officials

Mogens C. Bay: chairman, chief executive officer chief financial officer B 1953. PRIM CORP EMPL chairman, chief executive officer: Valmont Industries, Inc. CORP AFFIL director: Inacom Corp.; director: ConAgra Inc. NONPR AFFIL director: Nebraska Health Systems.
Edward Burchfield
Robert B. Daugherty: director B 1922. PRIM CORP EMPL director: Valmont Industries, Inc. NONPR AFFIL trustee: Hastings College Foundation.
Terry James McClain: senior vice president, chief financial officer B Osmond, NE 1948. ED Wayne State University BS (1970); University of South Dakota MBA (1971). PRIM CORP EMPL senior vice president, chief financial officer: Valmont Industries, Inc. NONPR AFFIL member: Financial Executives Institute.

Foundation Officials

Robert B. Daugherty: president (see above)
Thomas P. Egan, Jr.: officer B 1948. ED Creighton University BSBA (1971); Creighton University JD (1973). PRIM CORP EMPL vice president, corporate counsel, secretary: Valmont Industries, Inc. CORP AFFIL secretary: Microflect Co. Inc.
Terry James McClain: director (see above)
Brian C. Stanley: officer B 1942. PRIM CORP EMPL vice president, controller: Valmont Industries, Inc.

Grants Analysis

Disclosure Period: fiscal year ending February 28, 1998
Total Grants: $320,182*
Number of Grants: 66
Average Grant: $4,851
Highest Grant: $25,000
Typical Range: $500 to $10,000
***Note:** Giving excludes United Way.

Recent Grants

Note: Grants derived from fiscal 1998 Form 990.

Arts & Humanities

25,000 United Arts Omaha, Omaha, NE
6,250 Rose D. Lumkin Performing Arts Center
6,000 Omaha Children's Museum, Omaha, NE
5,000 Joslyn Art Museum, Omaha, NE
5,000 Omaha Public Library Foundation, Omaha, NE
4,000 National Western Historical Trails Center, Council Bluffs, IA
4,000 Shakespeare on the Green
2,500 Constitutional Heritage Institute
1,000 El Museo Latino, Omaha, NE -- building fund drive

Civic & Public Affairs

18,000 Omaha Zoo Foundation, Omaha, NE
10,000 Knights of Ak-Sar-Ben River City Roundup
10,000 Omaha Chamber Foundation, Omaha, NE -- Target Omaha
2,000 League of Women Voters, Louisville, KY
1,500 Omaha 100, Omaha, NE
1,500 Omaha Minority Purchasing Council, Omaha, NE
1,200 Greater Omaha Chamber Foundation, Omaha, NE
1,000 Nebraska Young Farmers and Ranchers Educational Association, Lincoln, NE

Education

25,000 Creighton University, Omaha, NE
15,000 Dana College, Blair, NE
12,000 College of St. Mary, Omaha, NE -- scholarship program
10,000 Hastings College Foundation, Hastings, NE
8,400 Nebraska Independent Colleges Foundation, Omaha, NE
5,000 Jesuit Middle School
5,000 Wayne State Foundation, Wayne, NE
3,600 Junior Achievement of the Midlands, Fremont, NE
3,500 Creighton Preparatory School
3,500 Omaha Literacy Council, Omaha, NE
2,000 Nebraska Mesa College of Engineering and Technology, NE
1,500 Madonna School
1,460 Christian Urban Education Service
1,000 Metropolitan Community College Foundation, Kansas City, MO

Health

10,000 American Red Cross Heartland Chapter
5,000 Nebraska AIDS Project, Pamaha, NE

Religion

15,000 Salvation Army
5,000 Omaha Campus for Hope-United Catholic Social Services, Omaha, NE
2,000 Lutheran Family Services, Denver, CO
1,000 Fellowship of Christian Athletes

Social Services

99,935 United Way of the Midlands
20,000 Boy Scouts of America Mid-America Council, Kansas City, MO
16,500 Fremont Area United Way
10,000 Quality Living, Omaha, NE
5,000 Family Service
5,000 Fremont Family YMCA
5,000 Waterloo-Valley Recreation Association
2,500 Youth Emergency Services
2,000 Girls, Incorporated
1,500 Cornhusker State Games, Lincoln, NE
1,500 Edmonson Youth Outreach Program
1,000 Girl Scouts of America
1,000 Nebraska Council to Prevent Alcohol and Drug Abuse, Lincoln, NE

VALSPAR CORP.

Company Contact

Minneapolis, MN

Company Description

Employees: 2,800
SIC(s): 2851 Paints & Allied Products.

Operating Locations

Includes plant and division locations.

Nonmonetary Support

Value: $402,000 (1996)
Type: Donated Products
Note: Foundation donated $850,000 of nonmonetary support in fiscal 1998.

Valspar Foundation

Giving Contact

Gwen Leifeld, Administrator
Valspar Foundation
1700 Foshay Tower
821 Marquette Ave.
Minneapolis, MN 55402
Phone: (612)337-5903
Fax: (612)337-5904
Email: gleifeld@valspar.com

Description

EIN: 411363847
Organization Type: Corporate Foundation
Giving Locations: communities with manufacturing facilities only.
Grant Types: General Support, Scholarship.

Financial Summary

Total Giving: $660,969 (fiscal year ending September 30, 1998); $1,400,000 (fiscal 1997); $1,083,858 (fiscal 1996). Note: 1996 Giving includes foundation ($547,307); scholarship ($45,000); United Way ($89,551).
Giving Analysis: Giving for fiscal 1998 includes: foundation ($485,726); foundation grants to United Way ($115,243); foundation gifts to individuals ($60,000)
Assets: $1,775,725 (fiscal 1998); $1,599,352 (fiscal 1997); $703,402 (fiscal 1996)
Gifts Received: $606,825 (fiscal 1998); $1,408,050 (fiscal 1997); $300,000 (fiscal 1992). Note: In 1998, contributions were received from Valspar Corporation ($605,000) and Employees of The Valspar Corporation on behalf of The Lonnie Jones Family ($1,825).

Typical Recipients

Arts & Humanities: Arts Centers, Arts Funds, Arts Institutes, Community Arts, Historic Preservation, Music, Opera, Performing Arts, Public Broadcasting, Theater
Civic & Public Affairs: Economic Development, Employment/Job Training, Housing, Rural Affairs, Safety, Urban & Community Affairs
Education: Business Education, Colleges & Universities, Economic Education, Education Funds, Education-General, Private Education (Precollege), Science/Mathematics Education
Health: Cancer, Hospitals, Medical Research, Single-Disease Health Associations
Science: Science Museums
Social Services: Big Brother/Big Sister, Child Welfare, Community Service Organizations, People with Disabilities, Shelters/Homelessness, United Funds/United Ways, YMCA/YWCA/YMHA/YWHA, Youth Organizations

Contributions Analysis

Arts & Humanities: About 10%.
Civic & Public Affairs: About 45%. Funding supports areas near operating facilities.
Education: 10% to 15%. Supports scholarships for employees' children.
Social Services: 20% to 25%. The majority of support goes to various United Ways.
Note: Total contributions made in 1997.

Application Procedures

Initial Contact: Written request for application form.
Application Requirements: Include a description of organization, specific use of requested gift, budget information, list of officers and board members, and proof of tax-exempt status.
Deadlines: October 1.

Restrictions

No contributions are made to political campaigns, or religious, ethnic, fraternal, labor, or veterans' causes. For children of Valspar Corporate, those who apply for scholarships must be entering or attending a secondary institution as a full-time student.

Additional Information

Publications: Guidelines

Corporate Officials

Rolf Engh: senior vice president, general counsel, secretary ED University of Minnesota BA (1976); William Mitchell College of Law JD (1982). PRIM CORP EMPL senior vice president, general counsel, secretary: Valspar Corp.
Gary E. Gardner: vice president human resources & public affairs B 1950. ED State University of New York BA (1968). PRIM CORP EMPL vice president human resources & public affairs: Valspar Corp.
Paul C. Reyelts: vice president finance, chief financial officer B Davenport, IA 1946. ED Harvard University BA (1968); Harvard University MBA (1975). PRIM CORP EMPL vice president finance, chief financial officer: Valspar Corp. ADD CORP EMPL president: Color Corp. of America. CORP AFFIL director: Winthrop Resources Corp.
Richard M. Rompala: president, chief executive officer, director, chairman B Pittsburgh, PA 1946. ED Columbia University BA (1968); Columbia University BS (1969); Harvard University MBA (1975). PRIM CORP EMPL president, chief executive officer, director, chairman: Valspar Corp. CORP AFFIL officer: Olin Asahi Interconnect Tech; director: Olin Corp.; director: Kerr-McGee Corp.
Deborah D. Weiss: vice president, treasurer PRIM CORP EMPL vice president, treasurer: Valspar Corp.

Foundation Officials

Rolf Engh: secretary (see above)
Gary E. Gardner: vice president, assistant treasurer (see above)
Paul C. Reyelts: vice president, assistant secretary (see above)
Richard M. Rompala: vice president (see above)
Deborah D. Weiss: treasurer (see above)
C. Angus Wurtele: president B Minneapolis, MN 1934. ED Yale University BA (1956); Stanford University MBA (1961). CORP AFFIL director: IDS Mutual Fund Group; director: Spectro Alloys Corp.; secretary, director: FFS Inc.; director: General Mills Inc.; director: Bemis Co. Inc. NONPR AFFIL member, director: National Paint & Coatings Association; member advisory council: Stanford University Graduate School Business; member: American Business Conference. CLUB AFFIL Minneapolis Club.

Grants Analysis

Disclosure Period: fiscal year ending September 30, 1998
Total Grants: $485,726*
Number of Grants: 107
Average Grant: $4,540
Highest Grant: $50,000
Typical Range: $100 to $4,000
***Note:** Giving excludes gifts to individuals; United Way.

Recent Grants

Note: Grants derived from fiscal 1997 Form 990.

Arts & Humanities

10,000 Minnesota Orchestral Association, Minneapolis, MN
8,333 Minnesota Opera, Minneapolis, MN
7,500 Guthrie Theater, Minneapolis, MN
7,500 Minneapolis Institute of Arts, Minneapolis, MN
7,500 Minnesota Orchestral Association, Minneapolis, MN
7,500 St. Paul Chamber Orchestra, Saint Paul, MN
7,500 Walker Art Center, Minneapolis, MN
4,000 Children's Theater Company, Minneapolis, MN
4,000 Minnesota Opera, Minneapolis, MN
4,000 Twin Cities Public Television, Saint Paul, MN -- social services
3,500 Minnesota Public Radio, Saint Paul, MN

Civic & Public Affairs

15,000 CLEARCorps Project, Baltimore, MD
10,000 NEXT Innovations, Minneapolis, MN
10,000 Project for Pride in Living, Minneapolis, MN
7,000 Greater Minneapolis Metropolitan Housing Corporation, Minneapolis, MN
6,000 Twin Cities Neighborhood Housing Services, Minneapolis, MN -- social services
5,500 Community Design Center, Minneapolis, MN
4,500 Powderhorn Community Council, Minneapolis, MN

Education

15,000 Calvin Academy of Learning, Roseville, MN -- educational
6,667 Curtis L. Carlson School of Management and Business, Minneapolis, MN
6,250 Duquesne University Computer Academy, Pittsburgh, PA
5,000 University of Minnesota, Minneapolis, MN
4,500 Minnesota Private College Fund, Saint Paul, MN
3,500 Business Economics Education Foundation, Minneapolis, MN

Health

20,000 City of Hope, Los Angeles, CA
10,000 Lutheran General Hospital, Cancer Care Center, Park Ridge, IL -- social services

Religion

3,500 Northside Common Ministries, Pittsburgh, PA

Science

10,000 Science Museum of Minnesota, Saint Paul, MN
7,500 Science Museum of Minnesota, Saint Paul, MN

Social Services

22,838 United Way, Minneapolis, MN
22,834 United Way, Minneapolis, MN
22,834 United Way, Minneapolis, MN
19,887 United Way, Minneapolis, MN
10,000 YMCA, Minneapolis, MN
10,000 Youth Trust, Minneapolis, MN
6,200 United Way, Minneapolis, MN
5,000 Lifeworks Services, Eagan, MN -- social services
5,000 Variety Children's Association, Minneapolis, MN -- social services
4,500 Mom's House, Pittsburgh, PA
4,311 United Way Crusade of Mercy, Chicago, IL
4,000 Big Brothers and Big Sisters of Beaver County, Monaca, PA
4,000 Contact Pittsburgh, Pittsburgh, PA
3,500 YMCA Metro Internship Program, Minneapolis, MN
3,416 United Way Rock River Valley, Rockford, IL
3,416 United Way Rock River Valley, Rockford, IL
3,359 United Way Rock River Valley, Rockford, IL
3,308 United Way Southwestern Pennsylvania, Pittsburgh, PA
3,308 United Way Southwestern Pennsylvania, Pittsburgh, PA
3,100 United Way Southwestern Pennsylvania, Pittsburgh, PA
3,000 Lazarus Tomb, Arnold, PA -- social services

VAN LEER HOLDING

Company Contact
Norwalk, CT

Company Description
Employees: 2,070
SIC(s): 2655 Fiber Cans, Drums & Similar Products, 3000 Rubber & Miscellaneous Plastics Products, 3085 Plastics Bottles, 3411 Metal Cans, 3412 Metal Barrels, Drums & Pails.

Van Leer U.S. Foundation

Giving Contact
Marvin Witham, Treasurer
Van Leer U.S. Foundation
101 Merritt 7
Norwalk, CT 06856
Phone: (203)849-4128
Fax: (203)849-4133

Description
EIN: 222517923
Organization Type: Corporate Foundation. Supports preselected organizations only.

Financial Summary
Total Giving: $178,500 (1998); $346,400 (1996); $648,000 (1995). Note: Contributes through corporate direct giving program and foundation.
Giving Analysis: Giving for 1998 includes: foundation ($178,500)
Assets: $454 (1998); $386 (1996); $284 (1995)
Gifts Received: $178,500 (1998); $346,785 (1996); $648,288 (1995). Note: Contributions received from the Bernard Van Leer (UK) Trust ($178,500) and the Chinet Co.

Typical Recipients
Civic & Public Affairs: Community Foundations, Housing, Native American Affairs
Education: Colleges & Universities
Health: Medical Research, Public Health
International: Health Care/Hospitals, International Relief Efforts
Religion: Jewish Causes
Social Services: Crime Prevention, Day Care, Family Planning, Family Services

Contributions Analysis
Education: 26%. Funds colleges and universitites.
Social Services: 74%. Supports community organizations and programs for children and families.
Note: Total contributions made in 1998.

Restrictions
Grants are not made to individuals.

Corporate Officials
William de Vlugt: chairman, chief executive officer, chief financial officer PRIM CORP EMPL chairman: Van Leer Holding.
Alexander J. Schuit: president, chief executive officer, chief financial officer PRIM CORP EMPL president, chief executive officer, chief financial officer: Van Leer Holding Inc. CORP AFFIL chief executive officer: Chinet Co.

Foundation Officials
Marvin Witham: treasurer

Grants Analysis
Disclosure Period: calendar year ending 1998
Total Grants: $178,500
Number of Grants: 5
Average Grant: $35,700
Highest Grant: $67,300
Typical Range: $30,000 to $70,000

Recent Grants
Note: Grants derived from 1998 Form 990.

Education

40,100	Pacific Oaks College, Pasadena, CA -- anti-bias education
5,900	University of Illinois, Champaign, IL -- meta web site

Social Services

67,300	Southwest Community Organization, Baltimore, MD -- securing child futures
35,200	Village for Family & Children, Hartford, CT -- securing child futures
30,000	Moore Community House, Biloxi, MS -- mississippi child care

VANGUARD GROUP

Company Contact
Valley Forge, PA

Company Description
Assets: US$470,000,000,000
Employees: 8,000
SIC(s): 6726 Investment Offices Nec.

Vanguard Group Foundation

Giving Contact
Ralph K. Packard, Principal & Chief Financial Officer
PO Box 2600
Valley Forge, PA 19482-2600
Phone: (610)669-1000

Description
Founded: 1994
EIN: 232699769
Organization Type: Corporate Foundation

Financial Summary
Total Giving: $872,646 (1996). Note: 1996 Giving includes United Way ($28,460).
Assets: $3,072,310 (1996); $368,675 (1994)
Gifts Received: $2,055,781 (1996). Note: In 1996, contributions were received from Vanguard Money Market Reserves, Inc., Vanguard Index Trust, and Vanguard/Wellington Fund, Inc.

Typical Recipients
Arts & Humanities: Ballet, Arts & Humanities-General, History & Archaeology, Libraries, Theater
Civic & Public Affairs: Urban & Community Affairs, Zoos/Aquariums
Education: Colleges & Universities, Economic Education, Private Education (Precollege)
Environment: Resource Conservation
Social Services: United Funds/United Ways

Application Procedures
Initial Contact: Send letter requesting guidelines and 'Summary of Request' form.

Corporate Officials
John C. Bogle: senior chairmano PRIM CORP EMPL senior chairman: Vanguard Group.
John J. Brennan: chairman, chief executive officer B Boston, MA 1954. ED Dartmouth College AB (1976); Harvard University MBA (1980). PRIM CORP EMPL chairman, chief executive officer: Vanguard Group. CORP AFFIL director: ICI Mutual Insurance Co. NONPR AFFIL member: Financial Executives Institute; government, executive vice president, member: Mutual Fund Education Alliance.
Ralph K. Packard: chairman, chief financial officer PRIM CORP EMPL chairman, chief financial officer: Vanguard Group.

Foundation Officials
John C. Bogle: chairman (see above)
John J. Brennan: president (see above)
Raymond J. Kaplinsky: secretary PRIM CORP EMPL senior vice president, secretary: Vanguard Group.
Ralph K. Packard: treasurer (see above)

Grants Analysis
Disclosure Period: calendar year ending 1996
Total Grants: $844,186*
Number of Grants: 493 (approx)
Average Grant: $1,513*
Highest Grant: $100,000
Typical Range: $50 to $1,500
***Note:** Giving excludes United Way. Average grant figure excludes highest grant.

Recent Grants
Note: Grants derived from 1996 Form 990.

Arts & Humanities

100,000	National Constitution Center, Philadelphia, PA
25,050	Free Library, Philadelphia, PA
17,500	Arden Theater Company, Philadelphia, PA
10,000	Village of the Arts and Humanities, Philadelphia, PA
7,525	Philadelphia Ballet, Philadelphia, PA

Civic & Public Affairs

60,730	Zoological Society, Philadelphia, PA
50,000	Greater Philadelphia First CAC, Philadelphia, PA
7,500	West Philadelphia Partnership, Philadelphia, PA

Education

59,500	Blair Academy, Browns Mills, NJ
10,000	Committee for Economic Education, New York, NY
8,500	Harvard University, Cambridge, MA
8,190	Vanderbilt University, Nashville, TN

Environment

13,125	Nature Conservancy, Philadelphia, PA

Health

27,600	American Cancer Society, Philadelphia, PA
25,000	American Red Cross, Philadelphia, PA

International

7,500	World Affairs Council, Philadelphia, PA

Science

13,911	Academy of Natural Sciences, Philadelphia, PA

Social Services

25,000	YMCA, Philadelphia, PA
10,000	Project HOME, Philadelphia, PA
10,000	United Way SEPA, Philadelphia, PA -- for Day of Caring

VARIAN MEDICAL SYSTEMS, INC.

Company Contact
Palo Alto, CA
Web: http://www.varian.com/vms

Company Description
Former Name: Varian Associates Inc.
Employees: 6,900

SIC(s): 3821 Laboratory Apparatus & Furniture, 3826 Analytical Instruments, 3844 X-Ray Apparatus & Tubes.

Nonmonetary Support

Value: $650,000 (1990); $650,000 (1989); $650,000 (1988)
Type: Donated Equipment; In-kind Services; Loaned Employees; Loaned Executives
Note: Nonmonetary Support Range: $350,000 to $1,000,000. Equipment donations are handled directly by divisions & subsidiaries. Figures do not include value of equipment donations.

Giving Contact

Corporate Contributions
Varian Medical Systems, Inc.
3100 Hansen Way
Palo Alto, CA 94304
Phone: (650)493-4000
Fax: (650)424-5358

Description

Organization Type: Corporate Giving Program
Giving Locations: headquarters and operating communities.
Grant Types: Challenge, Employee Matching Gifts, Endowment, Fellowship, General Support, Multiyear/Continuing Support, Professorship, Research, Scholarship, Seed Money.

Financial Summary

Total Giving: $335,000 (1996 approx); $388,000 (1995 approx); $350,000 (1994). Note: Contributes through corporate direct giving program only.

Typical Recipients

Arts & Humanities: Arts Appreciation, Arts Festivals, Historic Preservation, Museums/Galleries
Civic & Public Affairs: Nonprofit Management, Public Policy, Women's Affairs
Education: Business Education, Colleges & Universities, Elementary Education (Private), Engineering/Technological Education, Faculty Development, Minority Education, Public Education (Precollege), Science/Mathematics Education, Student Aid
Environment: Environment-General
Health: Health Organizations, Mental Health, Public Health
Science: Science Exhibits & Fairs, Scientific Organizations
Social Services: Child Welfare, Community Service Organizations, Counseling, Delinquency & Criminal Rehabilitation, Family Services, People with Disabilities, Recreation & Athletics, Senior Services, Shelters/Homelessness, United Funds/United Ways, Youth Organizations

Contributions Analysis

Education: About 50%. Colleges and universities with strong programs in engineering, science, business, and medicine, as well as to those institutions that participate in scientific research important to company.
Health: About 40%. United Way fund drives in operating locations, as well as special projects. Company also matches employee donations to the United Way. Limited support to non-United Way organizations, provided services do not duplicate United Way efforts.

Application Procedures

Initial Contact: write co. for guidelines

Additional Information

Varian Associates Inc. split up into three independent public companies in 1999: Varian Medical Systems, Varian Inc., and Varian Semiconductor Equipment Associates, Inc. Each company is likely to establish some form of giving program.

For Varian Inc. inquiries, contact: Arthur W. Homan, secretary, Varian Inc., 3120 Hansen Way, Palo Alto, CA 94304-1030, (650) 213-8000.
For Varian Semiconductor Equipment Associates, Inc., contact: G. Dennis Key, vice president, sales and marketing, 35 Dory Rd., Gloucester, MA 01930, (978) 282-2000. Dennis Key, vice president, sales and marketing, 35 Dory Rd., Gloucester, MA 01930, (978) 282-2000.

Corporate Officials

Elisha M. Finney: vice president finance, chief financial officersl, vice president PRIM CORP EMPL vice president finance, chief financial officer: Varian Medical Systems, Inc.
Timothy E. Guertin: vice president B 1949. ED University of California BS. PRIM CORP EMPL vice president: Varian Medical Systems, Inc.
Robert H. Kluge: president B 1946. PRIM CORP EMPL president: Varian Medical Systems, Inc. ADD CORP EMPL branch manager: Varian Associates Inc.
Richard M. Levy: president, chief executive officer B Cincinnati, OH 1938. ED Dartmouth College (1960); University of California (1964). PRIM CORP EMPL president, chief executive officer: Varian Medical Systems, Inc. NONPR AFFIL member: American Electronics Association.
Joseph Baschon Phair: corporate secretary, general counsel, vice president B New York, NY 1947. ED university of San Francisco BA (1970); University of San Francisco JD (1973). PRIM CORP EMPL corporate secretary, general counsel, vice president: Varian Medical Systems, Inc. NONPR AFFIL member: Saint Vincent de Paul Development Council; member: Silicon Valley Association General Counsel; member: Bay Area General Counsel Group. CLUB AFFIL member: Olympic Club.

Grants Analysis

Disclosure Period: calendar year ending
Typical Range: $250 to $1,000

VESPER CORP.

Company Contact

Bala-Cynwyd, PA

Company Description

Employees: 1,271
SIC(s): 3400 Fabricated Metal Products.
Parent Company: Arrowhead Holdings Corp.

Vesper Foundation

Giving Contact

John V. Curci, Vice President & Treasurer
Vesper Corp.
8223 Brecksville Rd., Suite 100
Brecksville, OH 44141
Phone: (440)838-4700
Fax: (440)838-4702

Description

EIN: 236251198
Organization Type: Corporate Foundation. Supports preselected organizations only.
Giving Locations: nationally, focusing on the Northeast USA.
Grant Types: General Support.

Financial Summary

Total Giving: $1,000,000 (1999 approx); $1,152,312 (1998); $517,200 (1997). Note: Contributes through foundation only.
Giving Analysis: Giving for 1997 includes: foundation ($509,200); foundation grants to United Way ($8,000); 1998: foundation ($1,145,812); foundation grants to United Way ($6,500)
Assets: $5,475,740 (1998); $5,300,945 (1997); $4,186,230 (1996)
Gifts Received: $1,100,000 (1998); $1,400,000 (1997); $1,000,000 (1996)

Typical Recipients

Arts & Humanities: Arts & Humanities-General, Historic Preservation, History & Archaeology, Libraries, Literary Arts, Museums/Galleries, Performing Arts
Civic & Public Affairs: Botanical Gardens/Parks, Clubs, Civic & Public Affairs-General, Municipalities/Towns, Philanthropic Organizations, Urban & Community Affairs
Education: Arts/Humanities Education, Colleges & Universities, Continuing Education, Elementary Education (Public), Engineering/Technological Education, Private Education (Precollege), School Volunteerism, Secondary Education (Private), Secondary Education (Public), Vocational & Technical Education
Environment: Environment-General, Resource Conservation
Health: Cancer, Hospitals, Hospitals (University Affiliated), Single-Disease Health Associations
International: Missionary/Religious Activities
Religion: Churches, Religious Organizations, Religious Welfare, Seminaries
Social Services: Animal Protection, At-Risk Youth, Recreation & Athletics, Special Olympics, United Funds/United Ways, Youth Organizations

Contributions Analysis

Arts & Humanities: 6%. Supports libraries, museums, and historic preservation.
Civic & Public Affairs: 22%. Supports zoos and parks.
Education: 44%. Supports colleges and universities and art education.
Environment: 21%. Supports wetlands conservation.
Health: 3%.
Religion: 1%.
Science: 1%.
Social Services: 2%. Primarily supports United Way, youth organizations, and animal shelters.
Note: Total contributions made in 1998.

Corporate Officials

James Benenson, Jr.: chairman, president, director B Moultrie, GA 1936. ED Massachusetts Institute of Technology BS (1958); Yale University (1960). PRIM CORP EMPL chairman, president, director: Vesper Corp. CORP AFFIL James Benenson & Co. Inc.; chairman: Arrowhead Holdings Corp. NONPR AFFIL member: Horticultural Society New York; member: New York Botanical Garden Society Cincinnati; member: Century Association. CLUB AFFIL Racquet Club; Bucks Harbor Yacht Club; New York Yacht Club.
John V. Curci: chief financial officer B 1944. ED Dyke College (1963). PRIM CORP EMPL chief financial officer: Vesper Corp. CORP AFFIL treasurer: Columbia Gear Co.; treasurer: Farval Lubrication Systems; vice president, treasurer, chief financial officer: Arrowhead Holdings Corp.; treasurer: Cleveland Gear Co.

Foundation Officials

James Benenson, Jr.: trustee (see above)
John V. Curci: trustee (see above)

Grants Analysis

Disclosure Period: calendar year ending 1998
Total Grants: $1,145,812*
Number of Grants: 34
Average Grant: $33,700
Highest Grant: $400,000
Typical Range: $150 to $50,000
***Note:** Giving excludes United Way.

Recent Grants

Note: Grants derived from 1997 Form 990.

Arts & Humanities

40,000	American Independence Museum
20,000	Smith Cove Preservation Trust, Ellsworth, ME
12,500	Mercantile Library, New York, NY
11,000	Mount Vernon, Alexandria, VA
2,000	Essex Winter Series, Essex, CT
500	Athenaeum, Philadelphia, PA

Civic & Public Affairs

82,500	New York Botanical Garden, Bronx, NY
25,000	Pact 2000, South Portland, ME
20,000	Horticultural Society, New York, NY
3,500	Society of the Cincinnati NH, Boston, MA
500	Avon Fire and Rescue, Avon, MN

Education

120,000	Tabor Academy Annual Fund, Marion, MA
50,000	Hotchkiss School, New York, NY
50,000	Massachusetts Institute of Technology, Cambridge, MA
12,000	Yale University Graduate School, New Haven, CT
10,000	Grace Church School, New York, NY
5,000	Avon Parent-Teacher's Association, Avon, MN
1,000	Wellesley College, Boston, MA
500	Pennsylvania Academy of Fine Arts, Philadelphia, PA

Environment

15,000	Wetlands Foundation, Ellsworth, ME
500	Friends of Holbrook Sanctuary, Brooksville, ME

Health

1,500	Muscular Dystrophy Association, Peoria, IL
500	American Cancer Society, New York, NY

Religion

10,000	Simpsonwood United Methodist Church, Norcross, GA
5,000	Holy Apostles Soup Kitchen, New York, NY

Social Services

5,000	Funds for the Animals, New York, NY
5,000	Northeast Sailing Association, South Portland, ME
5,000	United Way, Saint Cloud, MN
3,000	United Way Services, Cleveland, OH
400	Friends of Craig Brook, Brooksville, ME
300	Pennsylvania Special Olympics, Norristown, PA

VIACOM INC.

Company Contact

1515 Broadway
New York, NY 10036
Phone: (212)258-6000
Fax: (212)258-6464
Web: http://www.viacom.com

Company Description

Former Name: Viacom International Inc.;
Acquired:.
Revenue: US$12,858,800,000 (1999)
Profit: US$334,000,000 (1999)
Employees: 126,820 (1999)
Fortune Rank: 141, per FORTUNE Magazine's list of 500 Largest U.S. Corporations (1999).
FF 141
SIC(s): 4800 Communications, 7800 Motion Pictures.

SUBSIDIARY COMPANIES

NY: CBS Corp., New York; Simon & Schuster

Viacom Foundation

Giving Contact

George J. Smith, Jr., Trustee
1515 Broadway, 32nd Fl.
New York, NY 10036
Phone: (212)258-6000
Fax: (212)258-6354

Description

Organization Type: Corporate Foundation

Financial Summary

Total Giving: $392,530 (fiscal year ending October 31, 1995). Note: Contributes through corporate direct giving program and foundation. 1995 Giving includes foundation.
Gifts Received: $15,647 (fiscal 1995). Note: Receives contributions from Viacom, Inc.

Corporate Officials

Sumner Murray Redstone: chairman B Boston, MA 1923. ED Harvard University BA (1944); Harvard University LLB (1947). PRIM CORP EMPL chairman: Viacom Inc. ADD CORP EMPL chairman, president, chief executive officer: National Amusements Inc. NONPR AFFIL member: Theatre Owners America; director: TV Academy Arts & Sciences Foundation; member: New England Medical Center; member executive committee: Will Rogers Memorial Fund; director: Motion Picture Pioneers; member executive committee: National Association Theatre Owners; member: Massachusetts General Hospital Corp.; judge: John F. Kennedy Profile Courage Award Committee; member: Massachusetts Bar Association; member: Harvard University Law School Association; member presidential advisory committee arts: John F. Kennedy Library Foundation; overseer: Dana Farber Cancer Institute; lecturer: Harvard Law School; chairman: Corp. Commn Edn Technology; trustee: Childrens Cancer Research Foundation; member executive board: Combined Jewish Philanthropies Greater Boston; sponsor: Boston Museum Science; visiting professor: Brandeis University; member: Boston Bar Association; overseer: Boston Museum Fine Arts; director; Boston Arts Festival; member: American Judicature Society; chairman: Art Lending Library; member: American Bar Association. CLUB AFFIL Masons Club; University Club; Harvard Club.

Grants Analysis

Disclosure Period: fiscal year ending October 31, 1995
Total Grants: $392,530*
Number of Grants: 18
Average Grant: $21,807
***Note:** Grants analysis is approximate.

VODAFONE AIRTOUCH PLC

Company Contact

The Courtyard
2-4 London Rd.
Newbury RG14 1JX, United Kingdom
Phone: ENG 1635 33-251

Fax: ENG 1635 45-713
Web: http://www.vodafone-airtouch-plc.com

Company Description

Acquired: AirTouch Communications (1999);
Former Name:.
Revenue: US$5,415,000,000 (1999)
Employees: 12,642 (1999)
SIC(s): 3661 Telephone & Telegraph Apparatus, 6719 Holding Companies Nec.

AirTouch Communications Foundation

Giving Contact

Mark Hickey, Executive Director
Airtouch Communications Foundation
1 California St., 17th Fl.
San Francisco, CA 94111-5401
Phone: (415)658-2300
Fax: (415)658-2332

Description

Founded: 1993
EIN: 680315367
Organization Type: Corporate Foundation
Formed by Merger of: Vodafone Group (1999).
Giving Locations: AZ; CA: San Francisco, Walnut Creek; CO; DC: Washington; GA: Atlanta; ID; IA; MI; MN; NE; NM; ND; OH; OR; TX: Dallas; UT; WA; WY areas where company provides cellular and paging operations under the AirTouch name.

Giving Philosophy

'Wireless communications create a world in which people have the power and ability to connect anytime, anywhere. It's a world where people are never out of range of loved ones, vital information or emergency help.'

At AirTouch Communications Foundation, our goal is to reflect that world through our grant-making, which is aimed at helping people work together to improve the security of their lives and the lives of those around them. We fund programs that strengthen connections and communications between people and organizations in communities in which AirTouch has a presence. *AirTouch Communications Foundation Guidelines and Application Procedures*

Financial Summary

Total Giving: $886,200 (1998); $649,445 (1996); $498,350 (1995). Note: Fiscal 1996 Giving includes scholarship ($16,000); United Way ($255,000).
Giving Analysis: Giving for 1998 includes: foundation grants to United Way ($330,000)
Assets: $19,865,148 (1996); $16,913,415 (1995); $13,629,236 (1994)
Gifts Received: $1,181,240 (1996); $357,812 (1995); $1,281,683 (1994). Note: In 1996, contributions were received from Airtouch Communications, Inc. and Airtouch Cellular.

Typical Recipients

Arts & Humanities: Arts Associations & Councils, Arts Funds, Ballet, Ethnic & Folk Arts, History & Archaeology, Libraries, Museums/Galleries, Music, Opera, Performing Arts
Civic & Public Affairs: Employment/Job Training, Housing, Nonprofit Management, Professional & Trade Associations, Public Policy
Education: Arts/Humanities Education, Business Education, Education Funds, Elementary Education (Public), Education-General, International Studies, Literacy, Science/Mathematics Education, Student Aid
Environment: Environment-General
Health: AIDS/HIV, Eyes/Blindness, Public Health
International: International Relations, International Relief Efforts
Religion: Religious Welfare
Social Services: Emergency Relief, Family Planning, Family Services, Recreation & Athletics, Scouts, United Funds/United Ways, Volunteer Services

Contributions Analysis

Giving Priorities: Safe communities, transitional assistance, the arts, health services, educational institutions, and environmental programs.
Arts & Humanities: 21%. Funds art museums and associations, ballet, opera, and other performing arts.
Civic & Public Affairs: 16%. Funds public safety, community foundations, and public policy.
Education: 5%. Supports minority education and programs for the disadvantaged.
Social Services: 58%. Major support for the United Way. Other interests include youth organizations and welfare transition groups.
Note: Total contributions made in 1998.

Application Procedures

Initial Contact: Send a letter requesting detailed guidelines.
Application Requirements: To apply for support, send a letter that includes background information about organization and its mission, the population served, and its unique role in the community; a description of the program or project for which funds are requested, including evidence of need, project budget, and how success will be measured; and a description of how you will report program/project results to the foundation. Also attach a copy of 501(c)(3) determination letter; a current operating budget, including a list of committed and pending sources of income; a copy of the most recent Form 990 and most recent audited financial statements, if available; and a list of organization's board of directors and their affiliations.
Deadlines: None.
Evaluative Criteria: Preference is given to organizations that: seek and achieve excellence in their leadership, client service, operations and results; have an open and cooperative relationship with other community groups in order to most effectively solve problems and avoid duplication of effort and resources; seek funding for projects that are central to their missions; can show how their programs and projects achieve their intended results; are committed to sustaining the positive results of their work.
Decision Notification: The foundation will review and respond to proposals within 4 to 6 weeks.

Restrictions

The foundation generally does not make grants to support capital or endowment campaigns, fundraising events or goodwill advertising (including benefits), sports activities, cause-related marketing, memberships, emergency appeal or regranting organizations. The foundation does not provide any AirTouch Communications products or services, nor does it support individuals; political organizations; religious organizations seeking grants for sectarian purposes; fraternal, veteran or labor groups; individual K-12 schools or school districts; or medical clinics or hospitals. In addition, the foundation will not support organizations that practice unlawful discrimination in the provision of services.

Additional Information

Priority areas are: 'Safe Communities,' which includes support of efforts that promote neighborhood security through citizen involvement and that enhance the personal safety of the most vulnerable members of society, and 'Transitional Assistance,' which includes support of programs and projects that forge connections between people and give them the tools to become contributing and productive members of society.
In 1999, Vodaphone Group acquired AirTouch Communications. The company is now known as Vodaphone AirTouch Plc.
In 1999, Vodaphone Group acquired AirTouch Communications. The company is now known as Vodaphone AirTouch Plc.
Publications: Guidelines; Foundation Application Procedures; Foundation Grants Report

Corporate Officials

Margaret G. Gill: senior vice president legal and external affairs PRIM CORP EMPL senior vice president legal and external affairs: Airtouch Communications.
Samuel L. Ginn: chairman, chief executive officer, director B Saint Clair, AL 1937. ED Auburn University BS (1959); Stanford University MS (1968). PRIM CORP EMPL chairman, chief executive officer, director: Airtouch Communications. NONPR AFFIL member international advisory council: Institute International Studies; trustee: Mills College. CLUB AFFIL Rams Hill Country Club; World Trade Club; Blackhawk Country Club; Pacific-Union Club; Bankers Club.
Arun Sarin: president, chief operating officer, vice chairman, vice president PRIM CORP EMPL chief executive USA/Asia Pacific: Vodafone Airtouch PLC. CORP AFFIL director: Cisco Systems Inc.

Foundation Officials

Susan Diekman: executive director ED Stanford University BA (1966); Stanford University ME (1967).
Samuel L. Ginn: chairman, director (see above)
M. Hickey: president, director
J. Neels: director
Arun Sarin: director (see above)

Grants Analysis

Disclosure Period: calendar year ending 1998
Total Grants: $556,200*
Number of Grants: 74
Average Grant: $7,516
Highest Grant: $25,000
Typical Range: $5,000 to $25,000
***Note:** Giving excludes United Way.

Recent Grants

Note: Grants derived from 1996 Form 990.

Arts & Humanities

25,000 San Francisco Ballet, San Francisco, CA -- first payment on $50,000 grant, for support of production at Pasadena Civic Auditorium
25,000 Smuin Ballet, San Francisco, CA -- support of Christmas Ballet
15,000 John F. Kennedy Center for Performing Arts, Washington, DC -- sponsorship of presentation of San Francisco Ballet
15,000 San Francisco Ballet, San Francisco, CA -- to partially underwrite premiere of new work
12,500 Library Foundation, San Francisco, CA -- second payment on $25,000 grant, for support of Children's Center of New Main Library
10,000 San Francisco Museum of Modern Art, San Francisco, CA -- support of exhibition

Civic & Public Affairs

15,000 League of Women Voters of California Education Fund, San Francisco, CA -- to sponsor the National Student-Parent Mock Election activities

Education

25,000 Detwiler Foundation, La Jolla, CA -- first payment on $50,000 grant, for support of Computers for Schools program
10,000 Bay Area Women's and Children's Center, San Francisco, CA -- support of Community Services Center of Tenderloin Elementary School
10,000 Disney GOALS, Anaheim, CA -- support of Growth Opportunities through Athletics, Learning, and Science program

Religion

10,000 Congregational Management Foundation, Washington, DC -- support of educational programs
7,000 Congregational Hispanic Caucus Institute, Washington, DC -- support of Summer Internship Program

Social Services

105,000 United Way Bay Area, San Francisco, CA
40,500 United Way Orange County, Irvine, CA
29,500 United Way, Los Angeles, CA
15,000 Boy Scouts of America San Francisco Bay Area Council, Oakland, CA -- final payment on $30,000 grant, to support inner-city neighborhood Scouting and Learning for Life programs
15,000 United Way, Lilburn, GA
15,000 United Way, Sacramento, CA
15,000 United Way San Diego County, San Diego, CA
9,000 United Way, Dallas, TX

VULCAN MATERIALS CO.

Company Contact

Birmingham, AL

Company Description

Employees: 6,971 (1999)
SIC(s): 1422 Crushed & Broken Limestone, 1423 Crushed & Broken Granite, 2812 Alkalies & Chlorine, 2865 Cyclic Crudes & Intermediates.

Nonmonetary Support

Type: Donated Equipment; Donated Products; In-kind Services; Loaned Employees; Loaned Executives; Workplace Solicitation
Note: Nonmonetary support is provided by the company.

Corporate Sponsorship

Type: Arts & cultural events; Festivals/fairs; Music & entertainment events; Pledge-a-thon

Vulcan Materials Co. Foundation

Giving Contact

Mary S. Russom, Administrator, Community Affairs
Vulcan Materials Co.
PO Box 530187
Birmingham, AL 35253-0187
Phone: (205)298-3229

Description

EIN: 630971859
Organization Type: Corporate Foundation
Giving Locations: states in which company has operations.
Grant Types: Capital, Department, Emergency, Employee Matching Gifts, Endowment, Fellowship, General Support, Multiyear/Continuing Support, Project, Research, Scholarship, Seed Money.
Note: Employee matching gift ratio: 1 to 1 for hospitals and cultural organizations; 2 to 1 to educational institutions. Annual limit of $10,000 per employee.

Financial Summary

Total Giving: $2,182,001 (fiscal year ending November 30, 1998); $2,202,981 (fiscal 1997); $1,941,981 (fiscal 1996). Note: Contributes through corporate direct giving program and foundation.
Giving Analysis: Giving for fiscal 1997 includes: foundation ($1,677,083); foundation grants to United Way ($525,898); fiscal 1998: foundation ($1,497,195); foundation grants to United Way ($529,956); foundation scholarships ($154,850)
Assets: $7,429,487 (fiscal 1998); $5,918,541 (fiscal 1997); $3,062,027 (fiscal 1996)

Gifts Received: $3,144,500 (fiscal 1998); $2,748,964 (fiscal 1997); $2,250,000 (fiscal 1996). Note: Contributions are received from Vulcan Materials Company.

Typical Recipients

Arts & Humanities: Arts Associations & Councils, Arts Centers, Arts Festivals, Arts Funds, Arts Institutes, Ballet, Community Arts, Dance, Ethnic & Folk Arts, Historic Preservation, History & Archaeology, Libraries, Literary Arts, Museums/Galleries, Music, Opera, Performing Arts, Public Broadcasting, Theater, Visual Arts
Civic & Public Affairs: African American Affairs, Botanical Gardens/Parks, Business/Free Enterprise, Civil Rights, Clubs, Economic Development, Economic Policy, Civic & Public Affairs-General, Municipalities/Towns, Public Policy, Urban & Community Affairs, Zoos/Aquariums
Education: Arts/Humanities Education, Business Education, Business Education, Colleges & Universities, Economic Education, Education Funds, Education Reform, Elementary Education (Private), Engineering/Technological Education, Education-General, Literacy, Minority Education, Public Education (Precollege), Science/Mathematics Education, Special Education, Student Aid
Environment: Environment-General, Resource Conservation, Sanitary Systems
Health: Cancer, Children's Health/Hospitals, Clinics/ Medical Centers, Health Organizations, Mental Health
International: International Organizations
Religion: Jewish Causes, Religious Welfare
Science: Science Exhibits & Fairs, Science Museums
Social Services: Animal Protection, Child Welfare, Community Centers, Community Service Organizations, Counseling, Delinquency & Criminal Rehabilitation, Emergency Relief, Emergency Relief, Family Services, Food/Clothing Distribution, People with Disabilities, Recreation & Athletics, Scouts, Senior Services, Shelters/Homelessness, Substance Abuse, United Funds/United Ways, YMCA/YWCA/YMHA/ YWHA, Youth Organizations

Contributions Analysis

Giving Priorities: Education, health, social welfare, the arts, and civic interests.
Arts & Humanities: 26%. Large grants support theater and neighborhood growth/economic development projects. Also supports museums, arts festivals, and public broadcasting. Civic interests include business, safety, and urban affairs organizations.
Civic & Public Affairs: 6%. Interests include economic development, public policy, and urban and community affairs.
Education: 34%. Supports educational interests in operating areas, including education funds, scholarships, public and private precollege education, and minority education.
Environment: 2%. Funds conservation organizations.
Health: About 1%. Supports hospitals.
Religion: 3%. Funds religious philanthropic groups and ministries.
Social Services: 27%. Primarily gives to united funds. Also interested in programs for unemployed youth, employment, and youth organizations.
Note: Total contributions made in fiscal 1998.

Application Procedures

Initial Contact: Send a one or two-page letter.
Application Requirements: Include a description of organization, amount requested, purpose of funds sought, recently audited financial state proof of tax-exempt status.
Deadlines: None; applications acted upon throughout the year.
Review Process: Proposals are reviewed by secretary/treasurer of foundation; if proposal meets guidelines, it is usually referred to appropriate division office for recommendation by local contributions committee; if proposal is appropriate for decision in headquarters office in Birmingham, AL, it is approved or rejected by secretary/treasurer, president, or full board of trustees, depending on amount of request.
Evaluative Criteria: Relative benefit to community; type of project; financial soundness; organizational efficiency.
Decision Notification: Varies, depending on disposition of the proposal.
Notes: Company does not respond to telephone solicitations.

Restrictions

No grants are awarded to groups with discriminatory practices.
Does not give grants to individuals, fraternal organizations, member agencies of united funds, political or lobbying groups, or religious organizations for sectarian purposes; does not support goodwill advertising, dinners, or special events.

Giving Program Officials

Mary S. Russom: secretary, treasurer PRIM CORP EMPL administrator committee affairs: Vulcan Materials Co.

Foundation Officials

Reter J. Clemins, III: trustee
William Frank Denson, III: president B Birmingham, AL 1943. ED University of Montevallo BA (1965); Emory University JD (1968). PRIM CORP EMPL senior vice president law, secretary: Vulcan Material Co. NONPR AFFIL member: American Bar Association; trustee: University Montevallo; member: Alabama State Bar. CLUB AFFIL Kiwanis Club Birmingham; Willow Point Golf & Country Club; Birmingham Country Club.
John A. Heilala: trustee B Detroit, MI 1940. ED Pennsylvania State University (1962); Washington University (1965). PRIM CORP EMPL president: Vulcan Materials Co., Chloralkali Unit.
Donald M. James: chairman B 1949. ED University of Alabama BS (1971); University of Alabama MBA (1973); University of Virginia JD (1977). PRIM CORP EMPL chairman, chief executive officer, director: Vulcan Materials Co.
Terry W. Reese: assistant treasurer B Huntsville, AL 1942. ED University of Tennessee (1970). PRIM CORP EMPL assistant treasurer, director taxes: Vulcan Materials Co. NONPR AFFIL member: National Association Accts; member: Tax Executives Institute; member: Institute of Management Accountants.
Mary S. Russom: secretary, treasurer (see above)

Grants Analysis

Disclosure Period: fiscal year ending November 30, 1998
Total Grants: $1,497,195*
Number of Grants: 557
Average Grant: $2,688
Highest Grant: $104,800
Typical Range: $1,000 to $10,000
***Note:** Giving excludes scholarships, United Way.

Recent Grants

Note: Grants derived from fiscal 1998 Form 990.

Arts & Humanities

104,800	Metropolitan Arts Council, Birmingham, AL
100,000	Birmingham Museum of Art, Birmingham, AL
45,000	Metropolitan Arts Council, Birmingham, AL
38,000	McWane Center, Birmingham, AL
20,000	Ascension Parish Library Board, Baton Rouge, LA
10,000	Columbus Museum, Inc., Columbus, GA
10,000	Exploration Place, Wichita, KS
10,000	National Guard Historical Society, Birmingham, AL

Civic & Public Affairs

30,000	Birmingham Botanical Society, Birmingham, AL
25,000	Village of Sussex
11,500	Urban League of Wichita, Inc., Wichita, KS
10,000	Region 2020, Inc., Birmingham, AL

Education

83,333	Birmingham-Southern College, Birmingham, AL
50,000	University of Montevallo Foundation, Montevallo, AL
31,250	Wichita State University, Wichita, KS
20,800	National Merit Scholarship Corporation, Chicago, IL
20,000	Brenau University, Gainesville, GA
20,000	Rocks Build America Foundation, Washington, DC
20,000	University of Chicago, Chicago, IL
20,000	Wichita State University, Wichita, KS
16,750	University of Alabama at Birmingham, Birmingham, AL
16,000	University of Tennessee, Knoxville, TN
15,000	A Research Foundation, Montgomery, AL
15,000	Columbus State University Foundation, Columbus, GA
15,000	Mississippi State University, Jackson, MS
13,500	Sepup, Berkeley, CA
13,000	Sepup, Berkeley, CA
12,800	Inroads, Birmingham, AL
12,000	Georgia Foundation for Independent Colleges, Inc., Atlanta, GA
12,000	United Negro College Fund, Inc., Atlanta, GA
11,500	Newman University, Wichita, KS
11,000	Tennessee Foundation for Independent Colleges, Nashville, TN
10,000	Junior Achievement of Greater Birmingham, Inc., Birmingham, AL

Health

10,000	American Cancer Society, Birmingham, AL

Religion

20,000	Jewish Community Center, Chicago, IL
10,000	Jewish Community Center, Chicago, IL
10,000	The Salvation Army, Birmingham, AL

Social Services

58,650	United Way of Central Alabama, Inc., Birmingham, AL
57,000	United Way of the Plains, Wichita, KS
37,500	United Way of Metropolitan Atlanta, Atlanta, GA
32,200	United Way of Central Alabama, Inc., Birmingham, AL
30,000	Young Women's Christian Association of Birmingham, Birmingham, AL
26,500	Capital Area United Way, Lansing, MI
24,150	United Way of Central Alabama, Inc., Birmingham, AL
22,356	United Way/Crusade of Mercy, Chicago, IL
21,450	United Way of Greater Chattanooga, Chattanooga, TN
18,000	United Way of Forsyth County, Winston Salem, NC
14,000	United Way of Columbus, Columbus, GA
12,620	United Way of Greater Knoxville, Knoxville, TN
12,000	Cahaba Girl Scout Council, Birmingham, AL
10,000	American Red Cross - Birmingham Area Chapter, Birmingham, AL

Wachovia Bank Of North Carolina Na

 Number 82 of Top 100 Corporate Givers

Company Contact

Winston-Salem, NC

Company Description

Employees: 8,200
SIC(s): 6021 National Commercial Banks, 6712 Bank Holding Companies.
Parent Company: Wachovia Corp.

Nonmonetary Support

Type: Loaned Executives
Note: Nonmonetary Support Range: $100,000. Nonmonetary Support Contact: local bank office.

The Wachovia Foundation, Inc.

Giving Contact

Will C. Mann, Contact
The Wachovia Foundation
100 North Main Street
Mail Code NC-37203
Winston-Salem, NC 27150-7131
Phone: (336)732-5426
Fax: (336)732-2509
Email: will.mann@wachovia.com

Description

EIN: 581485946
Organization Type: Corporate Foundation
Giving Locations: GA; NC; SC
Grant Types: Capital, Challenge, Conference/Seminar, Emergency, Endowment, Fellowship, General Support, Matching.

Financial Summary

Total Giving: $9,247,123 (1998); $7,612,197 (1997); $8,525,258 (1996). Note: Contributes through corporate direct giving program and foundation. Giving includes foundation.
Giving Analysis: Giving for 1998 includes: foundation ($8,091,478); foundation grants to United Way ($1,152,265); foundation matching gifts ($3,380)
Assets: $25,898,581 (1998); $14,777,132 (1997); $15,319,236 (1996)
Gifts Received: $1,950,000 (1998); $4,911,342 (1997); $5,090,003 (1993). Note: 1998 Contributions received from Wachovia Corporation.

Typical Recipients

Arts & Humanities: Arts Associations & Councils, Arts Centers, Arts Festivals, Arts Funds, Community Arts, Dance, Historic Preservation, History & Archaeology, Libraries, Museums/Galleries, Music, Opera, Performing Arts, Public Broadcasting
Civic & Public Affairs: African American Affairs, Botanical Gardens/Parks, Business/Free Enterprise, Chambers of Commerce, Civil Rights, Clubs, Community Foundations, Economic Development, Civic & Public Affairs-General, Housing, Municipalities/Towns, Philanthropic Organizations, Professional & Trade Associations, Public Policy, Urban & Community Affairs, Women's Affairs, Zoos/Aquariums
Education: Agricultural Education, Arts/Humanities Education, Business Education, Business-School Partnerships, Colleges & Universities, Economic Education, Education Funds, Elementary Education (Private), Engineering/Technological Education, Minority Education, Private Education (Precollege), Public Education (Precollege), Science/Mathematics Education, Secondary Education (Private), Student Aid
Environment: Environment-General, Resource Conservation, Wildlife Protection
Health: Emergency/Ambulance Services, Health Funds, Health Organizations, Hospices, Hospitals, Respiratory
International: Foreign Arts Organizations, International Environmental Issues, International Peace & Security Issues
Religion: Jewish Causes, Religious Organizations, Religious Welfare
Science: Scientific Centers & Institutes
Social Services: Child Welfare, Community Centers, Community Service Organizations, Day Care, Delinquency & Criminal Rehabilitation, Family Planning, Family Services, Food/Clothing Distribution, People with Disabilities, Recreation & Athletics, Scouts, Senior Services, Substance Abuse, United Funds/United Ways, YMCA/YWCA/YMHA/YWHA, Youth Organizations

Contributions Analysis

Giving Priorities: Economic development, community reinvestment, affordable housing, educational development and welfare of youth, economic and job skill education, united funds, and the arts. Limited support for U.S.-based nonprofit organizations with international focus.
Arts & Humanities: About 10%. Recipients include art programs and public television.
Civic & Public Affairs: 15% to 20%. Supports community organizations in North Carolina. (United Funds & United Way) 10% to 15%.
Education: About 20%. Primarily supports educational institutions in North Carolina.
Religion: Less than 5%.
Social Services: About 40%. Supports traditional youth organizations. Majorsupport goes to united funds in North Carolina.

Application Procedures

Initial Contact: Requests should be sent to officer in charge of nearest branch bank.
Application Requirements: Include a description of organization, its mission; the scope; budget, and leadership of fundraising project; amount requested, purpose of funds sought; leadership of organization; recently audited financial statement, proof of tax-exempt status, list of contributors.
Deadlines: Requests must be received by February 1, May 1, August 1, and November 1.
Review Process: Branch office requests forwarded to general offices with recommendation of officer in charge of branch. Foundation distributor committee meets quarterly.

Restrictions

Does not support individuals, political or lobbying groups, good will advertising, or religious organizations for sectarian purposes.

Corporate Officials

Leslie Mayo Baker, Jr.: president, chief executive officer, chairman B Brunswick, MD 1942. ED University of Richmond BA (1964); University of Virginia MBA (1969). PRIM CORP EMPL president, chief executive officer, chairman: Wachovia Corp. CORP AFFIL chairman: Wachovia Bank NC NA; director: Carolina Power & Light Co.; senior associates: Robert Morris Associates; trustee: Carolina Medicorp Inc. NONPR AFFIL trustee: Colgate Darden Graduate School; chairman: Elon College; member: American Bankers Council.
Clyatt E. Loflin, Jr.: trustee officer PRIM CORP EMPL trustee officer: Wachovia Corp.
Ed Loflin: assistant treasurer PRIM CORP EMPL assistant treasurer: Wachovia Bank of North Carolina NA.
J. Walter McDowell: president, chief executive officer, director B 1951. ED University of North Carolina BS (1973). PRIM CORP EMPL president, chief executive officer, director: Wachovia Bank of North Carolina NA. CORP AFFIL executive vice president: Wachovia Corp.

Foundation Officials

Leslie Mayo Baker, Jr.: chairman (see above)
J. Walter McDowell: director (see above)
G. Joseph Prendergast: director B 1945. ED Pace University MBA; Wesleyan University BA. PRIM CORP EMPL chairman: Wachovia Bank Georgia NA ADD CORP EMPL president: Wachovia Corp.; senior executive vice president: Wachovia Bank North Carolina NA; president: Wachovia Bank NA. CORP AFFIL director: Georgia Power Co.; director: Willamette Industries Inc.
Will B. Spence: director

Grants Analysis

Disclosure Period: calendar year ending 1998
Total Grants: $8,097,778*
Number of Grants: 675 (approx)
Average Grant: $11,997
Highest Grant: $250,000
Typical Range: $1,000 to $20,000
***Note:** Giving excludes United Way; matching gifts.

Recent Grants

Note: Grants derived from 1998 Form 990.

Arts & Humanities

140,000	Robert W. Woodruff Arts Center, Inc., Atlanta, GA -- 1997-1998 Campaign
100,000	The Lynnwood Foundation, Charlotte, NC -- Duke Mansion/William States Lee Leadership Institute
75,000	Arts & Science Council Charlotte and Mecklenburg, Charlotte, NC -- 1998 Annual Fund Drive
70,000	Arts Council Incorporated Winston-Salem Arts Council, Winston-Salem, NC -- 1998 Operational Budget for Member Agencies and Artists Grants
50,000	Mariners' Museum, Newport News, VA -- Support Access to Collections and Programs
50,000	South Carolina Archives and History Foundation, Columbia, SC -- Capital Campaign
40,000	Cultural Council of Richland and Lexington Counties, Columbia, SC -- Contribution
37,000	Arts & Science Council, Charlotte, NC -- 1997 Fund Drive/Affiliate Operating Support

Civic & Public Affairs

100,000	Forward Atlanta Campaign, Atlanta, GA -- 2nd of 6 payments
100,000	North Carolina Community Development Initiative, Inc., Raleigh, NC -- 2nd of 3 payments
50,000	The Atlanta Project, Atlanta, GA -- 2nd of 3 payements
50,000	East Lake Community Foundation, Inc., Atlanta, GA -- Final PMT/East Lake Golf Club & Community
50,000	North Carolina Business Committee for Education, Raleigh, NC -- 2nd of 3 PMTS/North Carolina Partnership for Excel
42,000	Georgia Corporation for Economic Development, Atlanta, GA -- General Operating Support
33,333	Atlanta Botanical Garden, Inc., Atlanta, GA -- 2nd of 3 PMTS/Grow the Great Urban Garden
30,000	Lake Lanier Canoe Kayak Club Legacy Campaign, Gainesville, GA
30,000	Richmond Renaissance Incorporated, Richmond, VA -- 1998 Annual Operating Budget

Education

100,000	Clemson University Foundation, Clemson, SC -- 1st of 5 PMTS/Wachovia Student Scholarship Prg.
100,000	Emory University, Atlanta, GA -- Capital Campaign-Goizueta Business School
100,000	Savannah College of Art and Design, Savannah, GA -- Establish Wachovia Scholars Program
100,000	Savannah College of Art & Design, Savannah, GA -- Establish Wachovia Scholars Scholarship
100,000	Savannah College of Art and Design, Savannah, GA -- Establish Wachovia Scholars Program
100,000	University of South Carolina, Columbia, SC -- 2nd of 5 PMTS/Bicentennial Campaign
75,000	Durham Technical Community College, Durham, NC -- Support Technology Capital Campaign
75,000	Georgia Institute of Technology, Atlanta, GA -- 1st of 2 PMTS/Management of Technology Program
50,000	Christopher Newport University, Newport News, VA -- Help Build World Class Center for the Arts
50,000	Duke University, Durham, NC -- 1st of 3 PMTS/Support Budgetary Efforts to Initiate the Duke Global Capital Markets Center
50,000	University of North Carolina, Chapel Hill, NC -- 3rd of 5 PMTS/The Second Century Campaign
50,000	Virginia Tech Foundation, Inc., Blacksburg, VA -- Va Tech Leadership Dev-Pamplin College of Bus
40,000	Duke University, Durham, NC -- 3rd of 5 PMTS/Fuqua School of Business-Thomas F. Keller Initiative
40,000	National Humanities Center Research, Triangle Park, NC -- 1st of 5 PMTS/ John Hope Franklin
33,000	Savannah College of Art and Design, Savannah, GA -- Establish Wachovia Scholars Program
33,000	Virginia Foundation for Independent Colleges, Richmond, VA -- Support 15 Private Colleges in Virginia
30,000	Governor's School for the Arts Foundation, Inc., Greenville, SC -- 2nd of 5 PMTS/Capital Campaign

Environment

100,000	Path Foundation, Inc., Atlanta, GA -- Phase II - Atlanta's Greenway Trail System
50,000	Campaign for Giant Pandas, Atlanta, GA

Health

116,667	Roper Foundation, Inc., Charleston, SC -- Family Care Project

International

50,000	ZZZ, Postfach, Switzerland -- PMT/Endow-Cap Constr-Strengthen Educ Infras

Religion

100,000	Atlanta Jewish Federation, Inc., Atlanta, GA -- 2nd of 3 PMTS/SPEC Community Capital Campaign

Social Services

300,000	United Way of Greater Richmond, Richmond, VA -- Support Adversely Impacted Agencies
200,000	North Carolina Partnership for Children, Inc., Raleigh, NC -- Smart Start, Third Installment
200,000	United Way of Forsyth County, Inc., Winston-Salem, NC -- 1997-1998 Campaign Contribution
162,500	United Way of Metropolitan Atlanta, Atlanta, GA -- 1st of 4 PMTS/1997-98 Campaign Contribution
162,500	United Way of Metropolitan Atlanta, Atlanta, GA -- 2nd of 4 PMTS/1997-98 Campaign Contribution
100,000	United Way of Forsyth County, Inc., Winston-Salem, NC -- "Challenge Grant"/ 1997 Additional Corp Support
98,000	United Way of the Midlands, Columbia, SC -- 1998 Contribution
50,000	Senior Services Inc., Winston-Salem, NC -- 1st of 5 PMTS/Campaign for Dignity
50,000	Senior Servicesinc., Winston-Salem, NC -- 1st of 5 PMTS/Campaign for Dignity
50,000	Senior Servicesinc., Winston-Salem, NC -- 1st of 5 PMTS/Campaign for Dignity
35,000	Trident United Way, Inc., Charleston, SC -- 1998 Contribution
31,500	United Way of Greenville County Incorporated, Greenville, SC -- 1998 Contribution
30,000	Oak Ranch, Inc., Sanford, NC -- Land Purchase-Establish Oak Ranch

WACHTELL, LIPTON, ROSEN &KATZ

Company Contact

New York, NY
Web: http://www.wlrk.com

Company Description

Revenue: US$220,000,000
Employees: 300
SIC(s): 8111 Legal Services.

Wachtell, Lipton, Rosen & Katz Foundation

Giving Contact

Hillary Rappaport, Coordinator, Charitable Contributions
Wachtell, Lipton, Rosen & Katz Foundation
51 West 52nd Street
New York, NY 10019
Phone: (212)403-1000
Fax: (212)403-2000

Description

Founded: 1981
EIN: 133099901
Organization Type: Corporate Foundation. Supports preselected organizations only.
Giving Locations: NY: New York metropolitan area
Grant Types: General Support.

Financial Summary

Total Giving: $2,913,166 (fiscal year ending September 30, 1997); $1,175,000 (fiscal 1996); $1,109,250 (fiscal 1994). Note: Contributes through foundation only.
Assets: $9,272,909 (fiscal 1997); $5,984,925 (fiscal 1996); $4,252,800 (fiscal 1994)
Gifts Received: $5,000 (fiscal 1997); $1,500,500 (fiscal 1996); $902,705 (fiscal 1993)

Typical Recipients

Arts & Humanities: Libraries, Museums/Galleries, Public Broadcasting
Civic & Public Affairs: Botanical Gardens/Parks, Law & Justice, Municipalities/Towns, Philanthropic Organizations
Education: Business Education, Colleges & Universities, Legal Education, Medical Education, Minority Education, Private Education (Precollege), Secondary Education (Private)
Environment: Wildlife Protection
Health: Geriatric Health, Hospitals (University Affiliated), Long-Term Care, Speech & Hearing
International: Foreign Educational Institutions, Missionary/Religious Activities
Religion: Jewish Causes, Religious Welfare, Seminaries
Social Services: Community Service Organizations, Shelters/Homelessness, United Funds/United Ways

Contributions Analysis

Giving Priorities: Education and social welfare. Supports organizations and funds affiliated with Jewish causes and Israel.
Civic & Public Affairs: 25%. Legal services, citizen committees, and local public affairs.
Education: 40% to 45%. Law schools, legal education programs and conferences, and private preparatory schools.
Health: Less than 5%. Supports medical centers.
International: Less than 5%. Funds international concerns.
Religion: 20% to 25%. Jewish causes and religious organizations in New York City.
Social Services: Less than 5%. Supports the homeless and social services.

Corporate Officials

Martin Lipton: partner partner B NJ 1931. ED University of Pennsylvania BS (1952); New York University LLB (1955). PRIM CORP EMPL partner: Wachtell, Lipton, Rosen & Katz. NONPR AFFIL president, board trustees: New York University Law School; director, chairman: Prep for Prep; vice chairman, board trustees: New York University; member council: American Law Institute; director: Institute Judicial Administration.
Leonard M. Rosen: senior partner PRIM CORP EMPL senior partner: Wachtell, Lipton, Rosen & Katz.
Herbert M. Wachtell: senior partner B 1932. ED New York University (1954); Harvard University LLM (1957). PRIM CORP EMPL senior partner: Wachtell, Lipton, Rosen & Katz.

Foundation Officials

Peter C. Cannellos: assistant vice president
David M. Einhorn: assistant vice president
Martin Lipton: president (see above)
Constance Monte: manager
Leonard M. Rosen: vice president, secretary (see above)
Herbert M. Wachtell: vice president, treasurer (see above)

Grants Analysis

Disclosure Period: fiscal year ending September 30, 1997
Total Grants: $2,913,166
Number of Grants: 34
Average Grant: $85,681
Highest Grant: $500,000
Typical Range: $5,000 to $100,000

Recent Grants

Note: Grants derived from fiscal 1999 Form 990.

International

47,000	Ohr Somayach International, New York, NY
25,000	American Friends of the Hebrew University, New York, NY

Waffle House Inc.

Company Contact

5986 Financial Drive
Norcross, GA 30071
Phone: 877-992-3353
Web: http://www.wafflehouse.com

Company Description

Employees: 10,000
SIC(s): 5812 Eating Places, 6719 Holding Companies Nec.

Waffle House Foundation, Inc.

Giving Contact

Alice Johnson, President
Waffle House Foundation, Inc.
5986 Financial Drive
PO Box 6450
Norcross, GA 30071
Phone: (770)729-5700
Fax: (770)729-5900

Description

EIN: 581477023
Organization Type: Corporate Foundation
Giving Locations: GA: Atlanta including metropolitan area
Grant Types: Project, Scholarship.

Financial Summary

Total Giving: $375,000 (fiscal year ending May 31, 2000 approx); $375,000 (fiscal 1999 approx); $296,569 (fiscal 1998). Note: Contributes through foundation only.
Giving Analysis: Giving for fiscal 1997 includes: foundation ($282,370); foundation scholarships ($19,251); fiscal 1998: foundation ($284,322); foundation scholarships ($12,247)
Assets: $268,938 (fiscal 1998); $258,284 (fiscal 1997); $256,870 (fiscal 1996)
Gifts Received: $303,696 (fiscal 1998); $301,227 (fiscal 1997); $283,115 (fiscal 1996). Note: The foundation receives contributions from Waffle House, Inc.

Typical Recipients

Arts & Humanities: Arts Centers, Ballet, Arts & Humanities-General, History & Archaeology, Performing Arts
Civic & Public Affairs: African American Affairs, Botanical Gardens/Parks, Business/Free Enterprise, Chambers of Commerce, Clubs, Community Foundations, Economic Development, Employment/Job Training, Civic & Public Affairs-General, Hispanic Affairs, Housing, Philanthropic Organizations, Safety, Urban & Community Affairs, Women's Affairs
Education: Business Education, Business-School Partnerships, Colleges & Universities, Economic Education, Education Reform, Elementary Education (Public), Engineering/Technological Education, Education-General, Literacy, Private Education (Precollege), Public Education (Precollege), School Volunteerism, Secondary Education (Private), Special Education
Environment: Forestry, Resource Conservation
Health: Alzheimers Disease, Cancer, Children's Health/Hospitals, Emergency/Ambulance Services, Eyes/Blindness, Health Organizations, Heart, Hospices, Hospitals, Medical Rehabilitation, Multiple Sclerosis, Nursing Services, Prenatal Health Issues, Preventive Medicine/Wellness Organizations, Single-Disease Health Associations, Trauma Treatment
Religion: Jewish Causes, Ministries, Missionary Activities (Domestic), Religious Organizations, Religious Welfare, Social/Policy Issues
Science: Science Museums, Scientific Centers & Institutes
Social Services: Animal Protection, At-Risk Youth, Big Brother/Big Sister, Camps, Child Abuse, Child Welfare, Community Service Organizations, Counseling, Delinquency & Criminal Rehabilitation, Domestic Violence, Family Services, Food/Clothing Distribution, People with Disabilities, Recreation & Athletics, Scouts, Senior Services, Sexual Abuse, Shelters/Homelessness, Special Olympics, YMCA/YWCA/YMHA/YWHA, Youth Organizations

Contributions Analysis

Civic & Public Affairs: 9%. Women's affairs, African American affairs, foundations, and housing.
Education: 8%. Funds K-12 education and literacy efforts.
Environment: 4%.
Health: 10%. Single-disease centers and foundations receive support.
Religion: 5%. Recipients include ministries, conferences, and religious charity.
Social Services: 64%. Funds family services and youth organizations, community service organizations, the homeless and domestic violence.
Note: Total contributions made in 1998.

Application Procedures

Initial Contact: Send a brief letter and any program material; contact foundation for scholarship guidelines and application.
Application Requirements: Include a description of organization, amount requested, purpose of funds sought, audited financial statement, and proof of tax-exempt status.
Deadlines: None, for general grants; April 1 for scholarships.
Evaluative Criteria: Scholarships are considered on a financial need; charitable contributions are considered based on need and program objective. Preference is given to Metro Atlanta charities.

Corporate Officials

Thomas F. Forkner: vice chairman, director B 1918. PRIM CORP EMPL vice chairman, director: Waffle House Inc.
Joe W. Rogers, Sr.: founder, chairman, director B 1919. PRIM CORP EMPL founder, chairman, director: Waffle House Inc.
Joe W. Rogers, Jr.: president, director B 1946. PRIM CORP EMPL president, director: Waffle House Inc.

Foundation Officials

Alice Johnson: president
John Michael McCarthy: vice president B Jackson, TN 1946. ED Georgia Institute of Technology (1968); University of Virginia (1973). PRIM CORP EMPL executive vice president, director: Waffle House Inc. CLUB AFFIL Rotary Club.

Grants Analysis

Disclosure Period: fiscal year ending May 31, 1998
Total Grants: $284,322*
Number of Grants: 51
Average Grant: $5,575
Highest Grant: $75,000
Typical Range: $100 to $15,000
***Note:** Giving excludes scholarship.

Recent Grants

Note: Grants derived from 1998 Form 990.

Civic & Public Affairs

16,667	East Lake Community Foundation, Atlanta, GA
5,000	Metropolitan Atlanta Community Foundation, Inc., Atlanta, GA
1,500	Habitat for Humanity, Atlanta, GA
500	Gwinnett Community Foundation, Norcross, GA
500	The Pat Cocciolone Fund, Atlanta, GA
100	Morehouse Chapter of NAACP, Atlanta, GA

Education

6,000	Wadsworth Elementary School, Decatur, GA
5,000	Communities in Schools of Atlanta, Inc., Atlanta, GA
5,000	Lawrenceville Elementary School, Lawrenceville, GA
2,500	Junior Achievement of Georgia, Inc., Atlanta, GA
1,500	Georgia Council on Economic Education, Atlanta, GA
1,000	Literacy Action, Inc., Atlanta, GA
850	The Atlanta Journal News for Kids, Atlanta, GA
500	The Winder-Barrow Certified Literate Community Coalition, Winder, GA
400	Glenwood Elementary School, Decatur, GA
100	Atlanta Area School for the Deaf, Clarkston, GA

Environment

10,000	Foundation of Wesley Woods, Atlanta, GA
500	Piedmont Park Conservancy, Atlanta, GA

Health

20,000	American Red Cross, Atlanta, GA
5,000	Gwinnett Hospital System Foundation, Lawrenceville, GA
1,500	American Sudden Infant Death Syndrome Institute, Atlanta, GA
1,000	Cystic Fibrosis Foundation, Atlanta, GA
500	American Lung Association, St. Petersburg, FL
500	Cystic Fibrosis Foundation, Atlanta, GA
500	March of Dimes - Georgia Chapter, Atlanta, GA
200	Georgia Firefighters Burn Foundation, Lawrenceville, GA
100	Alzheimer's Association, Atlanta, GA
100	March of Dimes - Georgia Chapter, Atlanta, GA

Religion

8,000	Missionaries of Charity, Atlanta, GA
5,674	Crossroads Community Ministries, Atlanta, GA
500	The National Conference Brotherhood/Sisterhood, Atlanta, GA

Social Services

75,000	Gwinnett County Boys & Girls Club, Lawrenceville, GA
46,881	Big Brothers - Big Sisters, Norcross, GA
10,685	Hope for Children, Inc., Marietta, GA
10,000	Georgians for Children, Atlanta, GA
10,000	North Atlanta Parents' Council, Atlanta, GA
7,500	Eagle Ranch, Chestnut Mountain, GA
6,000	Boy Scouts of America, Atlanta, GA
6,000	The Partnership Against Domestic Violence, Atlanta, GA
2,700	The Giving Tree, Decatur, GA
2,500	Gwinnett Children's Shelter, Inc., Lawrenceville, GA
1,000	The Atlanta Area Council, Boy Scouts of America, Atlanta, GA
1,000	DeKalb Rape Crisis Center, DeKalb, GA
1,000	Families of Children Under Stress, Atlanta, GA
1,000	YMCA of Georgia, Atlanta, GA
800	USO Golf 'Committee, Atlanta, GA
500	Marcus Institute, Atlanta, GA
200	Carver Homes Seniors Association, Atlanta, GA
140	Children's Restoration Network, Chamblee, GA

125	Nike Coach of the Year Clinic, Commerce, GA
100	Casa / Kappa Alpha Theta, Athens, GA

WAL-MART STORES, INC.

 Number 22 of Top 100 Corporate Givers

Company Contact

Bentonville, AR
Web: http://www.wal-mart.com

Company Description

Revenue: US$166,809,000,000 (1999)
Profit: US$5,377,000,000 (1999)
Fortune Rank: 2, per FORTUNE Magazine's list of 500 Largest U.S. Corporations (1999).
FF 2
SIC(s): 5311 Department Stores.

Operating Locations

Mexico: Wal-Mart Holding Co., Mexico City

Nonmonetary Support

Type: Donated Equipment; Donated Products; In-kind Services; Workplace Solicitation
Note: Co. provides checks to organizations in which employees volunteer a minimum of 15 hours per quarter.

Corporate Sponsorship

Note: Sponsors programs for Children's Miracle Network, United Way, Prevent Blindness, USA-Weekends, and Make a Difference Day.

Wal-Mart Foundation

Giving Contact

Emerson Goodwin, Foundation Director
Wal-Mart Foundation
702 Southwest Eighth Street
Bentonville, AR 72716-8071
Phone: (501)277-1905
Fax: (501)273-6850

Description

EIN: 716107283
Organization Type: Corporate Foundation
Giving Locations: headquarters and operating communities.
Grant Types: Employee Matching Gifts, Matching, Scholarship.

Giving Philosophy

'Through fund-raising for local charitable causes, sponsorship of youth scholarships and numerous other community projects, Wal-Mart associates demonstrate their commitment to positively influence the quality of life in their local communities. Although this philosophy is not always typical of chain stores, Wal-Mart associates believe that local stores should be just that -- local stores.' Wal-Mart Stores, Inc.: *Contributing to the Quality of Community Life*

Financial Summary

Total Giving: $50,000,000 (1999 approx); $37,047,484 (1998); $32,571,556 (1996). Note: Contributes through foundation only. Giving includes matching gifts; scholarship; United Way.
Assets: $8,850,203 (1996); $15,681,286 (1991); $9,332,875 (1990)
Gifts Received: $10,301,862 (1996). Note: In 1996, the foundation received contributions from United Way ($57,836); and Children'sMiracle Network ($10,244,026).

Typical Recipients

Arts & Humanities: Arts Centers, Arts Festivals, Community Arts, Dance, Historic Preservation, Libraries, Museums/Galleries, Music, Public Broadcasting, Theater
Civic & Public Affairs: African American Affairs, Business/Free Enterprise, Economic Development, Economic Policy, Housing, Law & Justice, Minority Business, Municipalities/Towns, Philanthropic Organizations, Professional & Trade Associations, Public Policy, Safety, Urban & Community Affairs, Women's Affairs, Zoos/Aquariums
Education: Agricultural Education, Business Education, Colleges & Universities, Community & Junior Colleges, Continuing Education, Economic Education, Education Associations, Education Funds, Elementary Education (Private), Engineering/Technological Education, Education-General, Literacy, Medical Education, Minority Education, Preschool Education, Public Education (Precollege), Religious Education, School Volunteerism, Science/Mathematics Education, Secondary Education (Public), Special Education, Student Aid
Environment: Environment-General, Resource Conservation
Health: Cancer, Children's Health/Hospitals, Emergency/Ambulance Services, Geriatric Health, Health Funds, Health Organizations, Hospices, Hospitals, Medical Rehabilitation, Medical Research, Mental Health, Nutrition, Public Health, Single-Disease Health Associations
Religion: Churches, Religious Welfare
Social Services: Animal Protection, Child Welfare, Community Centers, Community Service Organizations, Counseling, Day Care, Domestic Violence, Emergency Relief, Family Services, Food/Clothing Distribution, Homes, People with Disabilities, Recreation & Athletics, Senior Services, Shelters/Homelessness, Substance Abuse, United Funds/United Ways, Volunteer Services, Youth Organizations

Contributions Analysis

Giving Priorities: Social welfare and higher education.
Civic & Public Affairs: 9%. (United Funds & United Way) 25%.
Education: 17%.
Environment: 3%.
Social Services: 30%.

Application Procedures

Initial Contact: brief letter or proposal to foundation; or contact local store for application
Application Requirements: a description of organization, amount requested, purpose of funds sought, recently audited financial statement, and proof of tax-exempt status
Deadlines: None.
Notes: Company does not accept requests for direct grants. Address grant requests to the foundation only.

Restrictions

Wal-Mart Foundation only supports organizations that in some way benefit the communities in which their stores are located.
The foundation does not give grants to individuals, except student scholarships.

Additional Information

Wal-Mart Foundation awards one scholarship per year to a graduating high school senior in each of its store communities.
The Wal-Mart Community Involvement Program (CIP) allows each store to hold local fund-raisers on store premises for qualifying charities and organizations. Qualifying projects are matched up to $2,000.

Corporate Officials

Jay Allen: vice president corporate affairs PRIM CORP EMPL vice president corporate affairs: Wal-Mart Stores, Inc.
Paul R. Carter: executive vice president B Monticello, AR 1940. ED University of Arkansas BA (1964). PRIM CORP EMPL executive vice president: Wal-Mart Stores, Inc. ADD CORP EMPL president: Wal-Mart Realty Co.
Thomas Martin Coughlin: executive vice president B Cleveland, OH 1949. ED California State University BS (1972). PRIM CORP EMPL executive vice president: Wal-Mart Stores Inc. ADD CORP EMPL president, chief executive officer: Wal-Mart Stores Division.
David Dayne Glass: director B Liberty, MO 1935. ED Southwest Missouri State University BS (1959). CORP AFFIL director: Bank Bentonville; chairman, chief executive officer: Kansas City Royals Baseball Club.
John Menzer: executive vice president B Chicago, IL 1951. ED Loyola University BBA (1972); Loyola University MBA (1980). PRIM CORP EMPL executive vice president: Wal-Mart Stores Inc. ADD CORP EMPL executive vice president, chief operating officer, director: Ben Franklin Retail Stores. CORP AFFIL director: Merit Distribution Services; director: Professional Data Solutions; director: McLane/Western Inc.; director: McLane/Suneast Inc.; director: McLane/Sunwest Inc.; director: McLane/Southern California; director: McLane/Southern Inc.; director: McLane/Pacific Inc.; director: McLane/Mid Atlantic Inc.; director: McLane/Midwest Inc.; director: McLane Foods Inc.; director: McLane/High Plains Inc.; director: McLane Co. Inc.; director: McLane/Eastern Inc. NONPR AFFIL member: International Franchise Association; member: National Retail Merchants Association; member: Illinois State Society CPAs; member: American Institute CPAs; member: Financial Executives Institute.
Donald G. Soderquist: senior vice chairman, director B Chicago, IL 1934. ED Wheaton College BA (1955). PRIM CORP EMPL senior vice chairman, director: Wal-Mart Stores Inc. CORP AFFIL director: Servicemaster-Consumer Services; chief operating officer: Bud's Warehouse Outlets; director: First National Bank Rogers AR. NONPR AFFIL director: International Mass Retail Association.
S. Robson Walton: chairman, director B 1945. ED University of Arkansas (1966); Columbia University JD (1969). PRIM CORP EMPL chairman, director: Wal-Mart Stores, Inc. NONPR AFFIL trustee: Wooster College.

Foundation Officials

Thomas Martin Coughlin: member (see above)
David Dayne Glass: trustee (see above)
Bobby L. Martin: member B Giddeon, MO 1948. ED South Texas University (1969). PRIM CORP EMPL executive vice president: Wal-Mart Stores, Inc. CORP AFFIL president, chief executive officer: Wal-Mart International Division. NONPR AFFIL member: DPQA University AR; executive director: Gen Merchandise Advisory Council.
Donald G. Soderquist: trustee (see above)
S. Robson Walton: member (see above)

Grants Analysis

Disclosure Period: calendar year ending 1998
Total Grants: $37,047,484*
Number of Grants: 25,000 (approx)
Average Grant: $1,400
Highest Grant: $285,000
Typical Range: $100 to $2,000 and $10,000 to $20,000
***Note:** Grants analysis provided by co.

Recent Grants

Note: Grants derived from 1997 Form 990.

Civic & Public Affairs

943,884	Charities Funds Transfers, Alexandria, VA
864,878	Charities Funds Transfers, Alexandria, VA

859,533 Charities Funds Transfers, Alexandria, VA
536,690 Charities Funds Transfers, Alexandria, VA
536,690 Charities Funds Transfers, Alexandria, VA
535,011 Charities Funds Transfers, Alexandria, VA
535,011 Charities Funds Transfers, Alexandria, VA
30,000 Habitat for Humanity
27,740 National Minority Supplier Development Council, New York, NY
27,000 SADD Students Against Drunk Drivers
25,000 National Urban League, New York, NY
22,500 NAACP
20,000 Cruz Roja Americana Capitulo de Puerto Rico, PR

Education

200,000 United Negro College Fund, New York, NY
150,000 Students in Free Enterprise, Springfield, MO
87,500 Northwest Arkansas Community College Foundation, Bentonville, AR
75,000 West Point High School
75,000 West Point School System
58,500 University of the Ozarks, Clarksville, AR
51,000 National Future Farmers of America Foundation, Madison, WI
50,000 University of Texas Pan American, Edinburgh, TX
43,000 Head Start
39,000 Florida A&M University, Tallahassee, FL
30,000 Independent College Fund of Arkansas, Little Rock, AR
29,000 Satsuma High School Quarterback Club, Satsuma, AL
25,000 Thurgood Marshall Scholarship Fund, New York, NY
23,000 Danz Parent-Teacher Organization
17,000 Head Start

Health

12,670,447 Children's Miracle Network
357,143 Arkansas Children's Hospital, Little Rock, AR
65,000 Children's Miracle Network
25,000 Cancer Challenge, Bentonville, AR

Religion

19,000 Martins Creek Baptist Church

Social Services

150,000 National Center for Missing and Exploited Children, Arlington, VA
72,630 United Way, Bentonville, AR
65,414 Benton County United Way
60,582 Benton County United Way
57,734 United Way, Bentonville, AR
54,116 Benton County United Way
32,509 United Way, Lowell, MA
29,451 United Way, Lowell, MA
27,522 United Way, Lowell, MA
27,316 United Way, Rogers, AR
25,000 Boys and Girls Club Benton County
24,489 United Way Northern California, Redding, CA
24,371 United Way, Rogers, AR
22,332 Benton County United Way
20,000 Drug Abuse Resistance Education, Midland, TX
19,000 Hit and Run Sluggers
17,000 Family Service Centers

WALDBAUM'S SUPERMARKETS, INC.

Company Contact

Central Islip, NY

Company Description

Employees: 10,000
SIC(s): 5411 Grocery Stores.
Parent Company: Great Atlantic & Pacific Tea Co. Inc., Montvale, NJ, United States

Operating Locations

NY: Waldbaum's Supermarkets, Central Islip; Waldbaum's Supermarkets, Inc., Central Islip

Nonmonetary Support

Type: Donated Products

Giving Contact

Dee Perfido, Executive Secretary to the President
Waldbaum, Inc.
1 Hemlock St.
Central Islip, NY 11722
Phone: (516)233-8410
Fax: (516)233-8272

Description

Organization Type: Corporate Giving Program
Giving Locations: principally near operating locations and to national organizations.
Grant Types: General Support, Matching, Project, Scholarship.

Financial Summary

Total Giving: Contributes through corporate direct giving program only.

Typical Recipients

Arts & Humanities: Arts Associations & Councils, Community Arts, Museums/Galleries, Music
Education: Colleges & Universities, Private Education (Precollege), Student Aid
Religion: Religious Organizations
Social Services: Child Welfare, Community Service Organizations, Domestic Violence, Family Services, People with Disabilities, Senior Services, United Funds/United Ways, Youth Organizations

Application Procedures

Initial Contact: a brief letter of inquiry on organization's letterhead
Application Requirements: a description of organization, amount requested, and purpose for which the funds are sought
Deadlines: None.

Restrictions

Political and lobbying groups are not considered for charitable contributions.

Corporate Officials

Dave Smithies: president, director PRIM CORP EMPL president, director: Waldbaum's Supermarkets, Inc.

Giving Program Officials

Dave Smithies: president (see above)

WALGREEN CO.

Company Contact

Deerfield, IL
Web: http://www.walgreens.com

Company Description

Revenue: US$17,838,800,000 (1999)
Profit: US$624,100,000 (1999)
Employees: 85,000
Fortune Rank: 95, per FORTUNE Magazine's list of 500 Largest U.S. Corporations (1999). FF 95
SIC(s): 5912 Drug Stores & Proprietary Stores.

Operating Locations

Operates more than 1,700 stores in 30 states and Puerto Rico.

Nonmonetary Support

Type: In-kind Services

Walgreen Benefit Fund

Giving Contact

Edward King, Director of Trade & Corporate Relations
Walgreen Co.
200 Wilmot Road
Mail Stop 2255
Deerfield, IL 60015-4681
Phone: (847)940-2500
Fax: (847)940-2825

Description

EIN: 366051130
Organization Type: Corporate Foundation
Giving Locations: IL: Chicago including metropolitan area company operating locations.
Grant Types: General Support.

Financial Summary

Total Giving: $672,890 (fiscal year ending April 30, 1997); $426,198 (fiscal 1996); $3,500,000 (fiscal 1993 approx). Note: Contributes through corporate direct giving program and foundation. Annual Giving Range: $3,500,000 to $4,250,000 for corporate direct giving. 1996 Giving includes foundation ($426,198).
Assets: $16,876,748 (fiscal 1997); $16,275,092 (fiscal 1996); $12,656,887 (fiscal 1993)
Gifts Received: $14,731 (fiscal 1997); $11,032 (fiscal 1996)

Typical Recipients

Arts & Humanities: Arts Institutes, Museums/Galleries, Opera
Civic & Public Affairs: Business/Free Enterprise, Municipalities/Towns, Public Policy, Urban & Community Affairs, Women's Affairs, Zoos/Aquariums
Education: Colleges & Universities, Economic Education
Health: Hospitals, Mental Health, Single-Disease Health Associations
Social Services: Child Welfare, People with Disabilities, Substance Abuse, United Funds/United Ways, Youth Organizations

Contributions Analysis

Giving Priorities: Higher education, social welfare, health, civic interests, and the arts.

Application Procedures

Initial Contact: brief proposal
Application Requirements: organization name and address; name and phone for contact person; statement of history and purpose; budget for organization and specific project; copy of the most recent audited financial statement; list of board members; list of other contributors; demographic group(s) served; plans for media coverage; names of Walgreen employees involved in project; list of accrediting agencies, if applicable; and copy of IRS determination letter
Deadlines: None.
Evaluative Criteria: priority given to requests which most closely reflect the demographics of company's patients and employees
Decision Notification: 90 days after receipt of proposal; resubmit proposal if response is not received
Notes: Telephone inquiries and faxes are not accepted. Contact company for information regarding benefit funds distributed through the foundation.

Restrictions

The company does not make grants to individuals; fraternal, veteran, labor, or religious organizations

serving a limited constituency; sports teams or any sports-related activity; political, lobbying, or voter registration programs, or those supporting the candidacy of a particular individual; hospitals; capital campaigns or projects; national headquarters of single-disease agencies, except those identified through the company's annual special program; additional requests from organizations who have already received support within the previous 12 months; travel expenses; fund-raising benefits or program advertising; and organizations which might pose a conflict with corporate goals, products, customers, or employees.
In 1996, all grants made by the foundation were in the form of relief payments to individuals.

Corporate Officials

David W. Bernauer: president, chief operating officerfacilities development B Wadena, MN 1944. ED North Dakota State University BS (1967). PRIM CORP EMPL president, chief operating officer: Walgreen Co.
Vernon A. Brunner: executive vice president marketing B Chicago, IL 1940. ED University of Wisconsin (1963). PRIM CORP EMPL executive vice president marketing: Walgreen Co.
Louis Daniel Jorndt: president, chief executive officer, director B Chicago, IL 1941. ED Drake University BS (1963); University of New Mexico MBA (1974). PRIM CORP EMPL president, chief executive officer, director: Walgreen Co.
Glenn S. Kraiss: executive vice president store operations B Chicago, IL 1933. ED University of Illinois (1956). PRIM CORP EMPL executive vice president store operations: Walgreen Drug Co.
Roger L. Polark: senior vice president, chief financial officer B 1948. ED University of Northern Iowa BS (1970). PRIM CORP EMPL senior vice president, chief financial officer: Walgreen Co.
John A. Rubino: senior vice president human resources PRIM CORP EMPL senior vice president human resources: Walgreen Co.
William A. Shiel: senior vice president facilities development B Chicago, IL 1950. ED Marquette University (1972); DePaul University MBA (1976). PRIM CORP EMPL senior vice president facilities development: Walgreen Co. NONPR AFFIL member, trustee: International Council Shopping Centers.

Giving Program Officials

Kimary Lee: PRIM CORP EMPL manager public affairs: Walgreen Co.

Grants Analysis

Disclosure Period: fiscal year ending April 30, 1997
Total Grants: $672,890
Number of Grants: 609
Average Grant: $1,105
Typical Range: $200 to $5,000

Recent Grants

Note: Grants derived from fiscal 1994 Form 990.

Social Services

12,459 United Way St. Louis, Saint Louis, MO
12,409 Valley of the Sun United Way, Phoenix, AZ
11,719 United Way Massachusetts Bay, Boston, MA
11,553 United Way Dade County, Miami, FL
11,384 Valley of the Sun United Way, Phoenix, AZ
10,442 Metro United Way, Louisville, KY
10,278 Mile High United Way, Denver, CO
10,003 Broward County United Way, Fort Lauderdale, FL
9,429 Mile High United Way, Denver, CO
9,427 United Way
9,177 United Way Brower County
8,649 United Way
8,168 United Way New Orleans, New Orleans, LA
7,480 Hillsboughs City United Way
6,862 United Way Tampa, Tampa, FL
6,193 United Way Danville Area, Danville, IL
5,848 United Way Minneapolis, Minneapolis, MN
5,602 United Way Palm Beach County, Delray, FL
5,600 Greater Tucson United Way, Tucson, AZ
5,597 United Way Lake County, Mentor, OH
5,554 United Way Community Chest
5,203 Heart of Florida United Way, Orlando, FL
5,160 United Way Midlands
5,138 United Way Tucson, Tucson, AZ
5,002 United Way Pinellas County, Saint Petersburg, FL
4,773 Heart of Florida United Way, Orlando, FL
4,589 Fondos Unidos De Puerto Rico, PR
4,405 Lake Area United Way, Griffith, IN
4,199 United Way Central New Mexico, Albuquerque, NM
4,131 United Way Quad Cities, Rock Island, IL
3,554 Santa Clara United Way, Santa Clara, CA
3,051 Middle United Way
3,005 Volusia County United Way, Daytona Beach, FL
2,866 Central Iowa United Way, Des Moines, IA
2,735 Westport Weston United Way, Westport, CT
2,616 Lee County United Way
2,547 Pikes Peak United Way, Colorado Springs, CO
2,509 Metrowest United Way, Framingham, MA
2,385 Brevard United Way, Cocoa, FL
2,346 Bergen County United Way, Oradell, NJ
2,293 Allen County United Way, Fort Wayne, IN
2,293 Sarasota United Way, Sarasota, FL
1,902 St. Paul United Way, Saint Paul, MN
1,902 Siouxland United Way, Sioux City, IA
1,813 Manatee County United Way, Bradenton, FL
1,813 Yavapai County United Way, Prescott, AZ
1,626 Central Indiana United Way, Indianapolis, IN
1,537 Decatur and Macon United Way, Decatur, IL
1,537 Southwestern Indiana United Way, Evansville, IN
1,537 Will County United Way, Joliet, IL

WALTER INDUSTRIES INC.

Company Contact

Tampa, FL
Web: http://www.walterind.com

Company Description

Former Name: Hillsborough Holding Corp.
Employees: 7,584
SIC(s): 1521 Single-Family Housing Construction, 3321 Gray & Ductile Iron Foundries.

Operating Locations

Includes locations of operating companies.

Walter Foundation

Giving Contact

W. Kendall Baker, Trustee
Walter Foundation
1500 N Dale Mabry
PO Box 31601
Tampa, FL 33631-3601
Phone: (813)871-4168
Fax: (813)871-4094

Description

Founded: 1966
EIN: 596205802
Organization Type: Corporate Foundation
Giving Locations: FL: Tampa headquarters and operating communities.
Grant Types: General Support.

Financial Summary

Total Giving: $643,735 (fiscal year ending August 31, 1998); $415,400 (fiscal 1997); $370,905 (fiscal 1996). Note: Contributes through foundation only.
Giving Analysis: Giving for fiscal 1997 includes: foundation ($359,050); foundation grants to United Way ($56,350); fiscal 1998: foundation ($596,735); foundation grants to United Way ($47,000)
Assets: $13,411,021 (fiscal 1998); $13,237,037 (fiscal 1997); $10,934,458 (fiscal 1996)
Gifts Received: $367,385 (fiscal 1998); $667,020 (fiscal 1997); $56,120 (fiscal 1996). Note: Contributions are received from Walter Industries, Jim Walters Resources and U.S. Pipe and Foundry Co.

Typical Recipients

Arts & Humanities: Arts Centers, Ballet, Museums/Galleries, Music, Opera, Performing Arts, Visual Arts
Civic & Public Affairs: African American Affairs, Asian American Affairs, Botanical Gardens/Parks, Business/Free Enterprise, Clubs, Community Foundations, Economic Development, Employment/Job Training, Civic & Public Affairs-General, Philanthropic Organizations, Public Policy, Urban & Community Affairs, Women's Affairs, Zoos/Aquariums
Education: Arts/Humanities Education, Business Education, Colleges & Universities, Economic Education, Legal Education, Private Education (Precollege), Secondary Education (Private)
Environment: Environment-General
Health: Children's Health/Hospitals, Clinics/Medical Centers, Health Organizations, Heart, Hospices, Hospitals, Medical Research, Respiratory, Single-Disease Health Associations
Religion: Churches, Ministries, Religious Welfare
Social Services: Big Brother/Big Sister, Child Welfare, Community Service Organizations, Counseling, Recreation & Athletics, Scouts, Shelters/Homelessness, Substance Abuse, United Funds/United Ways, YMCA/YWCA/YMHA/YWHA, Youth Organizations

Contributions Analysis

Arts & Humanities: About 2%. Music and visual arts.
Civic & Public Affairs: 16%. Support goes to community foundations and neighborhood improvement.
Education: 55%. Major interests include Catholic education, colleges and universities, and private secondary education.
Health: 3%. Interests include cancer research, hospitals, clinics, and medical centers.
Religion: 5%. Ministries and churches.
Social Services: 30% to 35%. Majority of support goes to youth groups, including Boys and Girls Clubs, and the United Way.
Note: Total contributions in fiscal 1998.

Application Procedures

Initial Contact: Send a brief letter or proposal.
Application Requirements: Include a brief description of the organization, purpose for which funding is needed, and amount requested.
Deadlines: None.

Restrictions

Grant must be received as a qualified charitable gift.

Additional Information

The foundation administers funds for the U.S. Pipe and Foundry Co. and Jim Walters Resources. Both are subsidiaries of Walter Industries, Inc.

Corporate Officials

Richard E. Almy: executive vice president, chief operating officer, director B Seattle, WA 1942. ED University of Washington BS (1964); University of Washington BS (1965). PRIM CORP EMPL executive vice president, chief operating officer, director: Walter Industries Inc. CORP AFFIL president: JW Window Components Inc.; chief operating officer: JWI Holdings Corp.

Howard Longstreth Clark, Jr.: vice chairman B New York, NY 1944. ED Boston University BS (1967); Columbia University MBA (1968). PRIM CORP EMPL vice chairman: Lehman Brothers, Inc. CORP AFFIL director: Plasti-Line; director: Walter Industries Inc.; advisor: Fund America Companies Inc.; director: Maytag Corp.; director: American Enterprises Holdings Inc.; director: Compass International Service Corp. CLUB AFFIL Seminole Club; River Club; Round Hill Country Club; Nantucket Golf Club; Racquet & Tennis Club; Jupiter Island; The Links Club; Blind Brook Country Club.

James Bernard Farley: chairman emeritus, trustee B Pittsburgh, PA 1930. ED Duquesne University BBA (1953); Case Western Reserve University MBA (1961). PRIM CORP EMPL chairman emeritus, trustee: Mutual of New York. CORP AFFIL trustee: Mutual New York; director: Ashland Inc.; director: Harrahs Entertainment Co. NONPR AFFIL director: Conference Board New York.

Dean M. Fjelstul: senior vice president, chief financial officer B Decorah, IA 1942. ED Dartmouth College BA (1964); Columbia University MBA (1966). PRIM CORP EMPL senior vice president, chief financial officer: Walter Industries Inc. CORP AFFIL vice president: Southern Precision Corp.; vice president: Vestal Manufacturing Co.; treasurer: Mid-State Homes Inc.; chief financial officer: JWL Holdings Corp.; vice president: Mid-State Holdings Corp.; president: Jim Walter Computer Service; treasurer: JW Window Components Inc.; treasurer: Dixie Building Supplies Inc.; treasurer: Coast To Coast Advertising; vice president: Computer Holdings Corp.

Eliot M. Fried: managing director PRIM CORP EMPL managing director: Lehman Brothers, Inc. CORP AFFIL director: Bridgeport Machines Inc.

Perry Golkin: member PRIM CORP EMPL member: Kohlberg, Kravis, Roberts & Co., LLC. CORP AFFIL director: Primedia Inc.; director: Walter Industries Inc.; director: Films for the Humanities Science; director: K-III Prime Corp.

Frank A. Hult: vice president, controller, chief accounting officer B Chicago, IL 1951. ED University of South Florida (1973). PRIM CORP EMPL vice president, controller, chief accounting officer: Walter Industries Inc.

Kenneth Ernest Hyatt: chairman, president, chief executive officer, director B Canton, GA 1940. ED Georgia Institute of Technology BS (1962); Georgia Institute of Technology MS (1965). PRIM CORP EMPL chairman, president, chief executive officer, director: Walter Industries Inc. CORP AFFIL president: Mid-State Holdings Corp.; president: Mid-State Homes Inc.; director: Jim Walter Homes Inc.; chairman: JWI Holdings Corp.; director: Barnett Bank Tampa; president: Computer Holdings Corp. CLUB AFFIL Rotary Club.

James Lawrence Johnson: chairman emeritus B Vernon, TX 1927. ED Texas Technology University BBA (1949). PRIM CORP EMPL chairman emeritus: GTE Corp. CORP AFFIL director: Walter Industries Inc.; director: First Federal Savings & Loan Association; director: Mutual Life Insurance Co.; director: CellStar Corp.; director: BC Telecommunications Co.; director: Bloomington Unlimited. NONPR AFFIL member: Wesleyan Associates; member: Wesleyan University; member: National Association Accts; director: McLean County Association Commerce Industries; trustee, member advisory council: Mennonite Hospital; member advisory council: Illinois State University College Business; director: Illinois Telephone Association; member: Financial Executives Institute. CLUB AFFIL Rotary Club; Woodway Country Club; Bloomington Country Club; Crestwicke Country Club.

Robert W. Michael: senior vice president, group executive PRIM CORP EMPL senior vice president, group executive: Walter Industries Inc. CORP AFFIL president: Jim Walter Homes Inc.

Edward A. Porter: vice president, general counsel, secretary B Lansing, MI 1946. ED Michigan State University BA (1968); University of Michigan JD (1971). PRIM CORP EMPL vice president, general counsel, secretary: Walter Industries Inc. CORP AFFIL secretary: Jim Walter Resources Inc.; secretary: J W Windo Components Inc.; secretary: United States Pipe Foundry Co. Inc.; Vestal Manufacturing Co.; secretary: MidState Holdings Corp.; secretary: Southern Precision Corp.; secretary: Coast Coast Advertising; secretary: Dixie Building Supplies Inc.

Michael T. Tokarz: founding partner PRIM CORP EMPL founding partner: Kohlberg, Kravis, Roberts & Co., LLC. CORP AFFIL director: Primedia Inc.; director: Walter Industries Inc.; director: Evenflo & Spalding Holdings; director: IDEX Corp.

David L. Townsend: vice president administration B Wilmington, DE 1954. ED University of Delaware (1976). PRIM CORP EMPL vice president administration: Walter Industries Inc. NONPR AFFIL member: National Investor Relations Institute; member: Public Relations Society America; member: Leadership Tampa Alumni; member: Committee 100; member: Greater Tampa Chamber of Commerce.

Joseph J. Troy: vice president, treasurer PRIM CORP EMPL vice president, treasurer: Walter Industries Inc.

James W. Walter: chairman emeritus, founder, director B Lewes, DE 1922. PRIM CORP EMPL chairman emeritus, founder, director: Walter Industries Inc. CORP AFFIL director: Contel Cellular Inc.; director: General Tel & Electric Corp.; director: Anchor Glass Container Corp.

Foundation Officials

W. Kendall Baker: trustee B 1922.
James W. Walter: trustee (see above)
Robert A. Walter: trustee PRIM CORP EMPL secretary, treasurer, director: Booker & Co. Inc.

Grants Analysis

Disclosure Period: fiscal year ending August 31, 1998
Total Grants: $596,735*
Number of Grants: 138
Average Grant: $4,324
Highest Grant: $200,000
Typical Range: $500 to $5,000
***Note:** Giving excludes United Way.

Recent Grants

Note: Grants derived from 1997 Form 990.

Arts & Humanities

10,000	Tampa Museum of Art, Tampa, FL
5,000	Children's Museum, Tampa, FL
5,000	Tampa Ballet, Tampa, FL
2,350	Henry B. Plant Museum, Tampa, FL

Civic & Public Affairs

25,000	Life Skills Foundation, Gig Harbor, WA
20,000	Mosi Mosi Foundation, Union City, CA
5,000	Lowry Park Zoo, Tampa, FL
3,000	Cato Institute, Washington, DC
2,000	Tampa Hillsborough Urban League, Tampa, FL
1,000	Chiselers, Tampa, FL

Education

50,000	University of South Florida, Tampa, FL
20,000	Catholic Education Foundation
10,000	Tampa Preparatory School, Tampa, FL
10,000	University of Tampa, Tampa, FL
5,000	Florida Council on Economic Education, Tampa, FL
5,000	School of Tampa Ballet, Tampa, FL
4,500	Junior Achievement, Tampa, FL
4,500	St. John's Episcopal Day School
4,100	Junior Achievement, Birmingham, AL
2,100	Junior Achievement, Birmingham, AL

Health

23,900	University of San Francisco Center for Swallowing Disorders, San Francisco, CA
10,000	Pediatric Pulmonary Research and Education Fund
5,000	Hospice of Hillsborough County, Tampa, FL
5,000	Tampa General Hospital Foundation, Tampa, FL

Religion

10,000	Metropolitan Ministries, Tampa, FL
10,000	Salvation Army, Tampa, FL
1,500	National Conference of Christians and Jews

Social Services

40,000	Boys and Girls Clubs, Tampa, FL
6,250	United Way Community Chest of West Central Alabama, AL
6,250	United Way Community Chest of West Central Alabama, AL
5,000	Boy Scouts of America Gulf Ridge Council
5,000	Boys and Girls Clubs, Tampa, FL
5,000	United Way West Alabama, AL
4,500	United Way Hillsborough County, Tampa, FL
4,500	United Way Hillsborough County, Tampa, FL
4,500	United Way Hillsborough County, Tampa, FL
3,800	Boy Scouts of America Gulf Ridge Council
3,750	United Way Central Alabama, Birmingham, AL
3,750	United Way Central Alabama, Birmingham, AL
3,750	United Way Hillsborough County, Tampa, FL
3,500	Hope, Basin, WY
2,500	Big Brothers and Big Sisters, Tampa, FL
2,500	Boy Scouts of America, Tampa, FL
2,500	Spring of Tampa Bay, Tampa, FL
2,500	United Way Community Chest of West Central Alabama, AL
2,000	Boys Club, New York, NY
1,250	United Way, Chattanooga, TN
1,250	United Way, Chattanooga, TN
1,200	United Way Calhoun County, Anniston, AL
1,100	United Way Bay Area, San Francisco, CA

WARNER-LAMBERT CO.

 Number 55 of Top 100 Corporate Givers

Company Contact

Morris Plains, NJ
Web: http://www.warner-lambert.com

Company Description

Profit: US$1,733,200,000 (1999)
Employees: 41,000
Fortune Rank: 139, per FORTUNE Magazine's list of 500 Largest U.S. Corporations (1999).
FF 139
SIC(s): 2064 Candy & Other Confectionery Products, 2067 Chewing Gum, 2834 Pharmaceutical Preparations, 2844 Toilet Preparations.

Operating Locations

Australia: Parke-Davis Pty. Ltd., Caringbah; Austria: Substantia Gesellschaft mbH, Vienna; Belgium: SA Capsugel NV, Bornem; Warner-Lambert Belgium NV, Zaventum; Brazil: Warner-Lambert Industria E Comercio Ltda, Guarulhos; Canada: Warner-Lambert Canada, Inc., Scarborough; England: Warner-Lambert, Eastleigh; France: Societe Financiere et Commerciale de Cadillac, Colmar; Parke-Davis, Courbevoie; Germany: Goedecje AG, Berlin; Tetra Heimtierbedarf GmbH, Melle; Italy: Parke-Davis SpA, Milan; Mexico: Chicle Adams SA de CV, Mexico; Compania Medicinal La Campana, SA de CV, Mexico; Compania de Chicle Adams Inc., Pueblo; Netherlands: Schick Nederland BV, Amsterdam; Pakistan: Parke-Davis & Co., Limited, Sindh; Spain: Adams, SA, Barcelona; Parke-Davis SA, Barcelona; United Kingdom: Parke-Davis & Co., Ltd., Gwent; Hall Brothers (Whitefield) Limited, Radcliffe, Manchester; Venezuela: Laboratorios Substantia, CA, Caracas

Nonmonetary Support

Value: $2,000,000 (1995); $2,000,000 (1993)
Type: Donated Equipment; Donated Products; In-kind Services
Note: Nonmonetary support is handled at the local level. Nonmonetary Support Contact: local facility.

Corporate Sponsorship

Type: Arts & cultural events

Warner-Lambert Charitable Foundation

Giving Contact

Evelyn Self, Secretary
Warner-Lambert Charitable Foundation
201 Tabor Rd.
Morris Plains, NJ 07950
Phone: (973)540-2243
Fax: (973)540-3320

Description

Founded: 1969
EIN: 237038078
Organization Type: Corporate Foundation
Giving Locations: NJ: Morris Plains headquarters and operating communities.
Grant Types: Employee Matching Gifts, General Support, Multiyear/Continuing Support, Project.
Note: Employee matching gift ratio: 1 to 1, with the exception of sports programs and scholarships.

Financial Summary

Total Giving: $15,635,576 (1998); $7,600,000 (1996); $7,800,000 (1995 approx). Note: Contributes through corporate direct giving program and foundation.
Giving Analysis: Giving for 1995 includes: foundation ($4,025,600); corporate direct giving (approx $3,774,400); 1996: foundation ($3,604,455); foundation grants to United Way ($359,084); 1998: corporate direct giving (approx $13,300,000); foundation ($2,335,576)
Assets: $1,675,880 (1998); $1,711,331 (1996); $1,028,710 (1992)
Gifts Received: $1,374,750 (1998); $3,963,539 (1996); $4,115,000 (1995). Note: In 1998, contributions were received from Warner-Lamber Company.

Typical Recipients

Arts & Humanities: Arts Associations & Councils, Arts Centers, Arts Festivals, Ballet, Museums/Galleries, Music, Opera, Performing Arts
Civic & Public Affairs: African American Affairs, Business/Free Enterprise, Chambers of Commerce, Community Foundations, Economic Development, Economic Policy, Employment/Job Training, Civic & Public Affairs-General, Hispanic Affairs, Parades/Festivals, Philanthropic Organizations, Professional & Trade Associations, Public Policy, Urban & Community Affairs, Women's Affairs
Education: Arts/Humanities Education, Business Education, Colleges & Universities, Continuing Education, Economic Education, Education Associations, Education Funds, Engineering/Technological Education, Education-General, Gifted & Talented Programs, International Exchange, Legal Education, Medical Education, Minority Education, Private Education (Precollege), Science/Mathematics Education, Student Aid, Vocational & Technical Education
Health: Alzheimers Disease, Cancer, Children's Health/Hospitals, Clinics/Medical Centers, Geriatric Health, Health Funds, Health Organizations, Heart, Hospices, Hospitals, Medical Rehabilitation, Medical Research, Prenatal Health Issues, Public Health, Single-Disease Health Associations
International: Health Care/Hospitals, International Affairs
Religion: Religious Welfare
Science: Science Museums, Scientific Centers & Institutes, Scientific Research
Social Services: Child Welfare, Community Centers, Domestic Violence, People with Disabilities, Senior Services, Shelters/Homelessness, Special Olympics, Substance Abuse, United Funds/United Ways, YMCA/YWCA/YMHA/YWHA, Youth Organizations

Contributions Analysis

Giving Priorities: Education, social welfare, health, and civic interests. Domestically, the foundation generally does not support organizations with an international focus. International contributions come out of the corporate budget and overseas companies. The company's contributions guidelines state, 'As a global health care company, our community extends beyond United States boundaries. Recognizing the needs of terminally ill patients and their families, we will work with hospice organizations domestically and internationally to provide support and to enhance the understanding of the needs of terminal patients and their families. Corporate funding will be limited to special projects at the national/international level.'
However, overseas plant locations also make contributions out of their own operating budgets, with priorities established at the operating level. Employee volunteerism also is encourged overseas. In the early 1980s, Warner-Lambert established Tropicare, a program created to offer training to local health care providers and community leaders. In various ways, it provides instruction in basic therapeutic and preventive techniques for a wide range of tropical illnesses. Warner-Lambert initially invested $1 million to start Tropicare in Senegal, West Africa. Its success grew quickly, and the program was introduced by Warner-Lambert into Cameroon, Ivory Coast, Kenya, Nigera, and Zaire. Since 1991, the company also has donated pharmaceutical and personal care products valued at more the $6 million through Project Hope. Cash contributions by overseas manufacturing or research operations is more than $1.8 million annually. In accordance with local custom, however, assistance is more often given in voluntary service and product doantions.
Arts & Humanities: 13%. Areas of interest include performing arts, libraries, and museums.
Civic & Public Affairs: 10%. Funds economic development and employment programs.
Education: 58%. Supports literacy, at-risk youth, and scientific, medical, pharmaceutical, dental, and health-related education programs. Also contributes to higher education funds and associations. Some support for elementary and secondary education.
Health: 13%. Priority is research in cardiovascular disease, central nervous system disease, and women's health care. Supports health organizations, university medical centers, hospitals, pediatric health, health funds, medical education, rehabilitation, hospices, terminal illness, and mental health.
Social Services: 2%. Supports domestic abuse, drug rehabilitation and awareness, the homeless, youth organizations, the aged, and aid to the handicapped.
Note: Total contributions in 1998.

Application Procedures

Initial Contact: Call to request guidelines, then send written request.
Application Requirements: Include name and objective of the organization, amount requested, purpose of funds sought, recently audited financial statement, copy of current budget with operating costs, list of other supporters, list of board members, three specific goals to be accomplished within the next 18 months, statement of how funds will be used, date fiscal year closes, and proof of tax-exempt status.
Deadlines: None.
Review Process: Requests are reviewed by internal committee, which meets quarterly.
Decision Notification: Notification is sent out usually within 90 days.

Restrictions

Gives exclusively to charitable, scientific, literary, or educational organizations that qualify as tax exempt organizations.
Funds and products are not available for: trips, tours, airships, auctions; government-supported organizations; religious organizations for sectarian purposes; veteran organizations; political groups; or individuals. No grants are made for loans, business start-up funds, or individual scholarships.

Additional Information

In 1994, Warner-Lambert Company absorbed Parke-Davis Group.
Publications: Contributions Program Guidelines; Giving Something Back

Corporate Officials

Lodewijk J. R. de Vink: president, chief operating officer, director B 1945. ED Netherlands School of Business; Washburn University BBA (1968); American University MBA (1969). PRIM CORP EMPL president, chief operating officer, director: Warner-Lambert Co. CORP AFFIL director: Bell Atlantic Corp.
Raymond M. Fino: vice president human resources B Plainfield, NJ 1942. ED College of the Holy Cross (1964); Fordham University (1965). PRIM CORP EMPL vice president human resources: Warner-Lambert Co. CORP AFFIL manager: Continental Can Co.; regional personnel director: Sealtest Foods.
Melvin Russell Goodes: chairman, chief executive officer, director B Hamilton, ON Canada 1935. ED Queens University BComm (1957); University of Chicago MBA (1960). PRIM CORP EMPL chairman, chief executive officer, director: Warner-Lambert Co. ADD CORP EMPL president: Warner-Lambert Ltd. CORP AFFIL director: Unisys Corp.; officer: Chase Manhattan Bank; director: Chase Manhattan Corp.; director: Ameritech Corp. NONPR AFFIL member: Proprietary Association; trustee: Queens University; member: National Wholesale Druggists Association; member: Pharmaceutical Manufacturer Association; member: National Association Retail Druggists; member finance committee: National Council Economic Education; director: National Alliance Business; member: International Executive Service Corps. CLUB AFFIL Plainfield Country Club; Pine Valley Golf Club.
Ernest J. Larini: vice president, chief financial officer B 1943. ED Saint John's University MBA; University of Notre Dame BS. PRIM CORP EMPL vice president, chief financial officer: Warner-Lambert Co. ADD CORP EMPL chief financial officer, director: Warner-Lambert Ltd.

Foundation Officials

Lodewijk J. R. de Vink: director (see above)
Raymond M. Fino: second vice president (see above)
Stanley D. Grubman: secretary

Richard W. Keelty: chairman PRIM CORP EMPL senior vice president public affairs: Warner-Lambert Co.
Ernest J. Larini: chief financial officer (see above)
Steve Mock: director
Evelyn Self: director community affairs

Grants Analysis

Disclosure Period: calendar year ending 1998
Total Grants: $2,335,576
Number of Grants: 150
Average Grant: $10,695*
Highest Grant: $742,000
Typical Range: $2,000 to $50,000
***Note:** Average grant figure excludes highest grant.

Recent Grants

Note: Grants derived from 1998 Form 990.

Arts & Humanities

143,000 New Jersey Performing Arts Center, Newark, NJ
30,000 Metropolitan Opera Association, Inc., New York, NY
30,000 Metropolitan Opera Association, Inc., New York, NY
25,000 Morris Museum, Morristown, NJ
12,500 Ann Arbor Summer Festival, Ann Arbor, MI
12,500 Lincoln Center for the Performing Arts, New York, NY
10,000 New Jersey Ballet, West Orange, NJ

Civic & Public Affairs

75,000 PhRMA Foundation, Washington, DC
50,000 Jersey Battered Women Service, Inc., Morris Plains, NJ
12,500 Alice Paul Centennial Foundation, Inc., Mt. Laurel, NJ
12,500 Committee for Economic Development, New York, NY
12,500 Mrs. Wilson's House, Morristown, NJ
12,500 Prosperity New Jersey, Princeton, NJ -- Dome Project
10,000 Brookings Institution, The, Washington, DC
10,000 Families and Work Institute, New York City, NY
10,000 National Alliance of Business, Washington, DC

Education

742,000 University of Michigan, Ann Arbor, MI
50,000 University of Maryland School of Pharmacy, Baltimore, MD
50,000 University of Medicine & Dentistry of New Jersey, Newark, NJ
40,000 Independent College Fund of New Jersey, Summit, NJ
40,000 Lead Program in Business, New York City, NY
25,000 Consortium for Graduate Study in Management, St. Louis, MO
25,000 Medical Education for South African Blacks, New Brunswick, NJ
20,000 Tri-County Scholarship Fund, Maplewood, NJ
15,000 American Academy of Neurology Fellowships, Minneapolis, MN
15,000 Colonial Symphony-Bayley Ellard School, Madison, NJ
15,000 Howard University, Washington, DC
14,500 American Foundation for Pharmaceutical Education, North Plainfield, NJ
14,000 National Council on Economic Education, New York, NY
13,000 Oakland University, Rochester, MI
12,500 Occupational Physicians Scholarship Fund, Schiller Park, IL
10,000 County College of Morris Foundation, Randolph, NJ
10,000 Howard University, Washington, DC
10,000 Long Trail School, Dorset, VT
10,000 New Jersey Seeds, Hightstown, NJ
10,000 Pennsylvania State University, The, University Park, PA

Health

100,000 Morristown Memorial Health Foundation, Morristown, NJ
50,000 St. Joseph Mercy Hospital, Ann Arbor, MI
20,000 Alzheimer's Association, Chicago, IL
20,000 Association of Reproductive Health Professionals, Washington, DC
20,000 Foundation for Biomedical Research, Washington, DC
15,000 Overlook Hospital Foundation, Summit, NJ
15,000 Overlook Hospital Foundation, Summit, NJ
12,000 St. Joseph Mercy Hospital, Ann Arbor, MI
10,000 National Council on Patient Information & Education, Washington, DC

Religion

35,000 St. Clare's Riverside Foundation, Denville, NJ

Science

20,000 Ann Arbor Hands-On Museum, Ann Arbor, MI

Social Services

19,076 Youth For Understanding, Washington, DC
15,000 New Jersey Special Olympics, Piscataway, NJ

WASHINGTON MUTUAL, INC.

Company Contact

Irwindale, CA

Company Description

Former Name: Home Savings of America FSB.
Assets: US$49,902,000,000
Employees: 9,502
SIC(s): 6036 Savings Institutions Except Federal.

Nonmonetary Support

Value: $30,000 (1994); $52,000 (1990)
Type: Donated Equipment
Note: Company provides nonmonetary support.

Corporate Sponsorship

Value: $250,000 (1994)

Washington Mutual Bank Foundation

Giving Contact

Tim Otani, Vice President, Community Relations
Washington Mutual Bank Foundation
1201 Third Ave., WMT 1213
Seattle, WA 98101
Phone: (206)461-4663
Fax: (206)554-2778

Description

EIN: 911070920
Organization Type: Corporate Foundation
Giving Locations: OR: Western Oregon; WA company operating areas.
Grant Types: Employee Matching Gifts, General Support.
Note: Employee matching gift ratio: 1 to 1.

Giving Philosophy

'The Washington Mutual Foundation was created by the bank in 1979 to assist local communities served by Washington Mutual. The Foundation places primary focus on the areas of education, affordable housing, and health and human services. In addition, secondary issues of cultural enhancement and civic betterment are also considered.' 1993 Foundation Annual Report

Financial Summary

Total Giving: $10,000,000 (1999 approx); $8,000,000 (1998 approx); $2,377,439 (1997). Note: Contributes through corporate direct giving program and foundation.
Giving Analysis: Giving for 1995 includes: foundation ($980,215); foundation grants to United Way ($386,575); foundation matching gifts ($148,382); 1996: foundation ($1,186,861); foundation grants to United Way ($400,093); foundation matching gifts ($183,078); 1997: foundation ($1,538,222); foundation matching gifts ($423,517); foundation grants to United Way ($415,700)
Assets: $3,553,776 (1997); $2,750,611 (1996); $2,550,906 (1995)
Gifts Received: $3,000,000 (1997); $1,750,000 (1996); $1,500,000 (1995). Note: Contributions are received from Washington Mutual Bank.

Typical Recipients

Arts & Humanities: Arts Associations & Councils, Arts Centers, Ballet, Community Arts, Ethnic & Folk Arts, Libraries, Museums/Galleries, Music, Performing Arts, Public Broadcasting, Theater
Civic & Public Affairs: Asian American Affairs, Business/Free Enterprise, Economic Development, Employment/Job Training, Civic & Public Affairs-General, Hispanic Affairs, Housing, Native American Affairs, Public Policy, Urban & Community Affairs, Women's Affairs
Education: Agricultural Education, Arts/Humanities Education, Business Education, Colleges & Universities, Community & Junior Colleges, Economic Education, Education Funds, Education Reform, Elementary Education (Public), Faculty Development, Education-General, Leadership Training, Literacy, Minority Education, Preschool Education, Private Education (Precollege), Public Education (Precollege), Science/Mathematics Education, Special Education
Environment: Resource Conservation
Health: AIDS/HIV, Cancer, Children's Health/Hospitals, Clinics/Medical Centers, Emergency/Ambulance Services, Long-Term Care, Mental Health, Public Health
Religion: Religious Welfare
Science: Scientific Centers & Institutes
Social Services: Camps, Child Welfare, Community Centers, Community Service Organizations, Day Care, Domestic Violence, Family Services, Food/Clothing Distribution, Scouts, Senior Services, United Funds/United Ways, Volunteer Services, YMCA/YWCA/YMHA/YWHA, Youth Organizations

Contributions Analysis

Giving Priorities: Education, affordable housing, and health and human services.
Arts & Humanities: 5%. Museums, art associations, theater and the performingarts, art education.
Civic & Public Affairs: 37%. Supports rural and urban housing in areas where the company operates. Focus is on increasing the amount of long-term affordable housing in the community. Parks and recreation, legal issues, and minority concerns.
Education: 43%. Supports systemic change to improve the delivery of educational services to students, and encourages model K-12 programs that improve academic success in core subjects; supports programs which increase parental involvement, or train or diversify teaching corps.
Health: 7%. Health care delivery, children's health, and AIDS.

Social Services: 8%. Food banks, child welfare, and YM/YWCAs.
Note: Total contributions in 1997.

Application Procedures

Initial Contact: Contact the foundation by letter or phone to request application form.
Application Requirements: Submit completed grant application form along with any other fundraising efforts, most recent financial statement, and a copy of IRS letter of nonprofit status, a copy of audited financial statements.
Deadlines: Submit by January 1, to be notified by March 15; by April 1, to be notified by June 15; by July 1, to be notified by September 15; or by October 1, to be notified by December 15. Applications are reviewed at quarterly meetings.
Review Process: Requests are initially reviewed by the foundation's managing officer. Foundation board, which meets quarterly, decides grants totaling $10,000 and more; the contributions committee, which meets quarterly, decides grants that are less than $10,000.
Evaluative Criteria: Preference is given to organizations seeking partial rather than exclusive funding from the foundation. The foundation favors organizations with a past record, with emphasis on affordable housing, prevention-oriented strategies, family support programs, high-risk groups, and innovative models. The foundation favors organizations that have company employees involved in leadership roles in the organization.
Decision Notification: Quarterly; applicants are generally notified eight to ten weeks after receipt of application.

Restrictions

Does not support individuals; organizations without tax-exempt status; organizations which discriminate based on race, color, religion, creed, age, sex, national origin, or any reason; political organizations or groups that influence legislation; veterans organizations; labor organizations; or religious-oriented projects.
Does not provide funds, other than for capital campaigns, to organizations that already receive support from the United Way.
Organizations receiving funds from the Corporate Council for the Arts may not apply for operating expenses.
Accepts one application per organization per calendar year. Generally does not fund an organization for more than three successive years.
Foundation does not accept requests that are not made on application form.

Additional Information

The foundation receives its funds from the financial services companies of the Washington Mutual Financial Group (WMFG), including: Washington Mutual Savings Bank; Benefit Service Corp.; Composite Research & Management Co.; Murphey Favre, Inc.; Mutual Travel, Inc.; Washington Mutual, a Federal Savings Bank; Washington Mutual Insurance Services; and WM Life Insurance Co.
Publications: Foundation Annual Report

Corporate Officials

Kerry Kent Killinger: chairman, president, chief executive officer, director B Des Moines, IA 1949. ED University of Iowa BBA (1970); University of Iowa MBA (1971). PRIM CORP EMPL chairman, president, chief executive officer, director: Washington Mutual Inc. CORP AFFIL president: WM Financial Inc.; president, director, chief executive officer, chairman: Washington Mutual Savings Bank; director: Federal Home Loan Bank Seattle. NONPR AFFIL director: Washington Roundtable; director: Washington Savings League; member: Society Financial Analysts; member: Seattle Chamber of Commerce; director: Seattle Repertory Theatre; fellow: Life Management Institute; member: Alliance for Education. CLUB AFFIL Rotary Club.

Foundation Officials

Tim Otani: vice president community relations department

Grants Analysis

Disclosure Period: calendar year ending 1997
Total Grants: $1,538,222*
Number of Grants: 206
Average Grant: $7,467
Typical Range: $1,000 to $10,000
***Note:** Giving excludes matching gifts; United Way.

Recent Grants

Note: Grants derived from 1997 Form 990.

Civic & Public Affairs
25,000 Local Initiatives Support Corporation -- assist in building units of affordable housing
25,000 Washington Community Development Loan Fund, Seattle, WA -- to provide predevelopment loans to nonprofit housing organizations throughout the state of Washington

Education
40,000 Washington State University, Seattle, WA -- leadership for Washington Schools Program Initiatives to improve the quality of existing and future educational administrators

Health
5,000 Northwest AIDS Foundation, Seattle, WA -- to support educational efforts in the prevention of HIV and AIDS

WASHINGTON MUTUAL, INC.

Company Contact

Irwindale, CA

Company Description

Former Name: Home Savings of America FSB.
Assets: US$49,902,000,000
Employees: 9,502
SIC(s): 6036 Savings Institutions Except Federal.

Nonmonetary Support

Type: Cause-related Marketing & Promotion; Donated Equipment; In-kind Services; Loaned Employees; Loaned Executives

Corporate Sponsorship

Note: Company will consider sponsorships if they conform to giving guidelines.

Washington Mutual Fund

Giving Contact

Randy Robinson, Vice President, Corporate Giving & Committee Relations
Home Savings of America FSB
1000 Wilshire, 22nd Fl., 695
Los Angeles, CA 90017
Phone: (626)814-7924
Fax: (626)814-5659

Description

Organization Type: Corporate Foundation
Giving Locations: CA headquarters and operating communities.
Grant Types: Employee Matching Gifts, General Support.

Financial Summary

Total Giving: $4,700,000 (1999 approx); $4,700,000 (1998 approx); $2,000,000 (1997 approx). Note: Contributes through corporate direct giving program only. Giving includes nonmonetary support.

Typical Recipients

Arts & Humanities: Arts & Humanities-General
Civic & Public Affairs: Civic & Public Affairs-General, Housing
Education: Education-General
Health: Health-General, Medical Research, Single-Disease Health Associations
Social Services: Social Services-General, United Funds/United Ways, Youth Organizations

Contributions Analysis

Arts & Humanities: About 5%. General support for arts organizations in California.
Civic & Public Affairs: About 50%. The company's specific focus is on housing. Supports neighborhood improvement, community reinvestment, and diversity. (United Funds & United Way) About 5%. General support to various United Way chapters.
Education: About 20%. The company's main priority is its 'Career Awareness Program,' which focuses on the problem of high unemployment among teenagers.
Health: About 20%. Majority of funding supports Alzheimer's research and treatment. Also supports scouting. Includes support to youth programs, homeless centers, soup kitchens, health care, battered women's centers, daycare, and alcohol and drug recovery programs.

Application Procedures

Initial Contact: written proposal on organization's letterhead
Application Requirements: description of the organization; amount requested; purpose of funds sought; audited financial statement; and nonprofit tax identification number
Deadlines: None.

Restrictions

Does not support individuals, religious organizations, or political or lobbying groups.

Additional Information

Each branch office has its own contributions budget. Nominal requests should be submitted to nearest branch location, with larger requests approved by the contributions committee at headquarters.

Corporate Officials

Samantha Davies: vice president corporate communications PRIM CORP EMPL vice president corporate communications: Home Savings of America, FSB.
Wilbur Mekesson: senior vice president, director communication development PRIM CORP EMPL senior vice president, director communication development: Home Savings of America, FSB.
Charles Robert Rinehart: chairman, chief executive officer, director B South San Francisco, CA 1947. ED University of San Francisco BS (1968). PRIM CORP EMPL chairman, chief executive officer, director: H.F. Ahmanson & Co. CORP AFFIL director: LA Business Advisors; director: Home Savings of America FSB; director: Kaufman & Broad Home Corp. NONPR AFFIL member: Thrift Institute Advisory Council; member: Tustin Public School Foundation; director: Federation Home Loan Bank San Francisco; member advisory committee: Drug Use is Life Abuse; member: Fannie Mae National Advisory Council; fellow: Casualty Actuarial Society; member: American Academy of Actuaries; member: American Management Association.
Randy Robinson: first vice president PRIM CORP EMPL first vice president: Washington Mutual, Inc.

Giving Program Officials
Randy Robinson: vice president community relations (see above)

Grants Analysis
Disclosure Period: calendar year ending
Typical Range: $1,000 to $2,500

THE WASHINGTON POST

Company Contact
Washington, DC
Web: http://www.washpostco.com

Company Description
Employees: 7,300
SIC(s): 2711 Newspapers, 2721 Periodicals, 4833 Television Broadcasting Stations, 4841 Cable & Other Pay Television Services.

Nonmonetary Support
Note: The company provides occasional printing services.

Corporate Sponsorship
Type: Arts & cultural events; Festivals/fairs; Music & entertainment events
Contact: Virginia Rodriquez, Public Relations Director

Giving Contact
Lillie Lee, Assistant to Vice President, Communications
The Washington Post
1150 15th Street, NW
Washington, DC 20071-7300
Phone: (202)334-6834
Fax: (202)334-5609
Email: leel@washpost.com

Description
Organization Type: Corporate Giving Program
Giving Locations: DC: Washington metropolitan area
Grant Types: Employee Matching Gifts, General Support.
Note: Employee matching gift ratio: 2 to 1, for gifts to education; 1 to 1 for all other gifts.

Financial Summary
Total Giving: $1,000,000 (1998 approx); $3,300,000 (1996 approx). Note: Contributes through corporate direct giving program only.

Typical Recipients
Arts & Humanities: Museums/Galleries, Music, Opera, Performing Arts, Public Broadcasting
Civic & Public Affairs: Public Policy
Education: Colleges & Universities, Elementary Education (Public), Engineering/Technological Education, Faculty Development, Literacy, Preschool Education, Private Education (Precollege), Public Education (Precollege), Science/Mathematics Education, Secondary Education (Public), Student Aid
Social Services: Child Welfare, Community Service Organizations, United Funds/United Ways, Youth Organizations

Contributions Analysis
Giving Priorities: Health, social welfare, the arts, education, and civic interests.

Application Procedures
Initial Contact: call or write for guidelines, then written proposal
Application Requirements: cover sheet, including: organization name, mailing address, phone and fax numbers, name and title of proposal contact person, brief a description of organization and its purpose, summary of proposal, total cost of project, amount requested, previous funding from company, other specific sources and amounts of support for proposed project (committed and pending); application letter of no more than 5 pages, including: a description of organization and scope of its current activities, statement concerning need for project, statement of objectives of the project-specifically what it is intended to accomplish, description of the activities included in project and time table of accomplishment, overall cost of project, amount requested, and amounts, sources, and status of additional support; supporting documents, including: proof of tax-exempt status, project budget with sources of projected revenues and purpose of expenses, current annual operating budget with revenues and expenses, list of board members and officers with affiliations, most recent annual report, and relevant supporting documentation
Deadlines: applications must be received by the first Tuesday in March, June, September, or December
Review Process: contributions committee meets quarterly
Evaluative Criteria: projects serve the most needy and least able citizens of the community; to fill unmet societal needs or solve long-standing community problems; address key community issues and concerns in collaborative and imaginative ways
Decision Notification: written notification of decisions is made within 60 to 90 days of receipt
Notes: Company accepts the Washington Regional Association of Grantmakers Common Grant Application format. Faxed applications are not accepted. Applicants are discouraged from telephoning during the application review process.

Restrictions
Funding is rarely available for capital grants.
Generally, support is not awarded to individuals; religious organizations for religious purposes; meeting or conference expenses; national or other programs not directly serving Washington area needs; fraternal, membership, or veterans' organizations, athletic teams; volunteer fire/emergency services, or similar groups; political action or advocacy groups; multiyear grants; challenge grants; third-party fundraising efforts; research; or start-up projects.
Does not respond to form letters or mass-mailing appeals.

Additional Information
The Washington Post is a part of The Washington Post Company. The Company has a Contributions program which is run by Rima Calderon. Contact Ms. Calderon for charitable contributions guidelines for the Company.
Company donates approximately 1.5% of pretax earnings to charitable activities.
The Washington Post Company also contributes to The Washington Post Education Foundation, which makes scholarships and provides awards to teachers and principals for use in their schools. Contact the company for more information about this giving program.
Publications: Guidelines

Corporate Officials
Donald Edward Graham: chairman, chief executive officer, director, publisher B Baltimore, MD 1945. ED Harvard University BA (1966). PRIM CORP EMPL chairman, chief executive officer, director, publisher: Washington Post Co. NONPR AFFIL member: American Antiquarian Society.
Katharine Meyer Graham: chairman executive committee, director B New York, NY 1917. ED Vassar College (1934-1936); University of Chicago AB (1938). PRIM CORP EMPL chairman executive committee, director: Washington Post Co. CORP AFFIL trustee: Reuters Founders Share Co. Ltd.; co-chairman: International Herald Tribune. NONPR AFFIL life trustee: University Chicago; director, vice chairman: Urban Institute; member collectors committee: National Gallery Art; member: Overseas Development Council; member: Council Foreign Relations; honorary trustee: George Washington University; member: American Society Newspaper Editors; fellow: American Academy of Arts & Sciences. CLUB AFFIL National Press Club; Cosmopolitan Club; Metro Club; 1925 F Street Club.
Lillie Lee
Alan Gary Spoon: president, chief operating officer, director B Detroit, MI 1951. ED Massachusetts Institute of Technology BS (1973); Massachusetts Institute of Technology MS (1973); Harvard University JD (1976). PRIM CORP EMPL president, chief operating officer, director: Washington Post Co. CORP AFFIL director: International Herald Tribune; director: America Management System Inc. NONPR AFFIL member: New England Intercollegiate Sailing Association; director: Smithsonian Institute National Museum Natural History; member: International Newspaper Fin Executives; member: Financial Executives Institute.

Grants Analysis
Disclosure Period: calendar year ending 1996
Typical Range: $500 to $3,000
Note: Recents grants listed are from the Washington Post Company Educational Foundation.

Recent Grants
Note: Grants derived from 1998 Form 990.

Education

9,000	Drexel University, Philadelphia, PA -- Eastern High Sch.Scholarship
9,000	Spelman College, Atlanta, GA -- Eastern High Sch.Scholarship
8,000	N.Carolina Wesleyan College, Rocky Mount, NC -- Eastern High Sch.Scholarship
7,450	George Washington University, Washington, DC -- Eastern High Sch.Scholarship
7,000	Mt. Saint Mary's College, Emmitsburg, MD -- Eastern High Sch.Scholarship
7,000	University Pittsburgh, Pittsburgh, PA -- Eastern High Sch.Scholarship
6,500	Loyola College, Baltimore, MD -- Eastern High Sch.Scholarship
6,400	Hampton University, Hampton, VA -- Eastern High Sch.Scholarship
4,500	Ohio Wesleyan University, Delawarw, OH -- Eastern High Sch.Scholarship
3,600	Fairfax County Public Schools, Fairfax, VA -- Public Grant in Education Awd
3,000	Anne Arundel County Public Schools, Annapolis, MD -- Public Grant in Education Awd
3,000	DePauw University, Greencastle, IN -- Eastern High Sch.Scholarship
3,000	Georgetown University, Washington, DC -- Eastern High Sch.Scholarship
3,000	University District Columbia, Washington, DC -- Eastern High Sch.Scholarship
2,500	Carnegie Mellon University, Pittsburgh, PA -- Eastern High Sch.Scholarship
2,500	Drexel University, Philadelphia, PA -- Eastern High Sch.Scholarship
2,500	Frostburg State University, Frostburg, MD -- Eastern High Sch.Scholarship
2,500	Hampton University, Hampton, VA -- Eastern High Sch.Scholarship
2,500	N.Carolina Wesleyan College, Rocky Mount, NC -- Eastern High Sch.Scholarship
2,500	Spelman College, Atlanta, GA -- Eastern High Sch.Scholarship
2,500	Wesleyan University, Middletown, CT -- Eastern High Sch.Scholarship
2,100	Arlington Public Schools, Arlington, VA -- Public Grant in Education Awd

2,100 Frederick County Public Schools, Frederick, MD -- Public Grant in Education Awd
2,100 Prince William County Public Schools, Manassas, VA -- Public Grant in Education Awd
2,000 American University, Washington, DC -- Eastern High Sch.Scholarship
2,000 Clark Atlanta University, Atlanta, GA -- Eastern High Sch.Scholarship
2,000 Montgomery College, Takoma Park, MD -- Eastern High Sch.Scholarship
2,000 N.Carolina Wesleyan College, Rocky Mount, NC -- Eastern High Sch.Scholarship
2,000 University Central Flordia, Orlando, FL -- Eastern High Sch.Scholarship
1,800 Charles County Public Schools, La Plata, MD -- Public Grant in Education Awd
1,500 American University, Washington, DC -- Eastern High Sch.Scholarship
1,500 Calvert County Public Schools, Prince Frederick, MD -- Public Grant in Education Awd
1,500 Columbia Union College, Takoma Park, MD -- Eastern High Sch.Scholarship
1,500 Fisk University, Nashville, TN -- Eastern High Sch.Scholarship
1,500 Flordia A&M University, Tallahassee, FL -- Eastern High Sch.Scholarship
1,500 Flordia A&M University, Tallahassee, FL -- Eastern High Sch.Scholarship
1,500 Lincoln University, Lincoln University, PA -- Eastern High Sch.Scholarship
1,500 N.Carolina Wesleyan College, Rocky Mount, NC -- Eastern High Sch.Scholarship
1,500 St.Mary's County Public Schools, Leonardtown, MD -- Public Grant in Education Awd
1,500 University District Columbia, Washington, DC -- Eastern High Sch.Scholarship
1,500 University District Columbia, Washington, DC -- Eastern High Sch.Scholarship
1,500 Virginia Commonwealth University, Richmond, VA -- Eastern High Sch.Scholarship
1,000 Dudley Beauty College, Washington, DC -- Eastern High Sch.Scholarship
1,000 George Washington University, Washington, DC -- Eastern High Sch.Scholarship
1,000 High Point University, High Point, NC -- Eastern High Sch.Scholarship
1,000 Johnson C. Smith University, Charlotte, NC -- Eastern High Sch.Scholarship
1,000 Ohio State University, Columbus, OH -- Eastern High Sch.Scholarship
1,000 Ohio Wesleyan University, Delware, OH -- Eastern High Sch.Scholarship
1,000 University District Columbia, Washington, DC -- Eastern High Sch.Scholarship
1,000 University District Columbia, Washington, DC -- Eastern High Sch.Scholarship

WASHINGTON TRUST BANK

Company Contact

Spokane, WA

Company Description

Assets: US$1,240,100,000
Employees: 710
SIC(s): 6022 State Commercial Banks.
Parent Company: W.T.B. Financial Corp.

Nonmonetary Support

Type: Donated Products; In-kind Services

Corporate Sponsorship

Type: Arts & cultural events

Washington Trust Bank Foundation

Giving Contact

Susan Rowe-Adler, Director Community Affairs
Washington Trust Bank
PO Box 2127
Spokane, WA 99210
Phone: (509)353-3820

Description

EIN: 911145506
Organization Type: Corporate Foundation
Giving Locations: ID; WA: Spokane metropolitan area
Grant Types: General Support.

Financial Summary

Total Giving: $274,620 (1998); $333,001 (1997); $316,950 (1996). Note: Contributes through corporate direct giving program and foundation. Giving includes foundation.
Giving Analysis: Giving for 1998 includes: foundation ($205,620); foundation grants to United Way ($69,000)
Assets: $0 (1998); $24,456 (1997); $11,457 (1996)
Gifts Received: $250,164 (1998); $346,000 (1997); $325,000 (1996). Note: Contributions received from Washington Trust Bank.

Typical Recipients

Arts & Humanities: Arts Associations & Councils, Arts Centers, Ballet, Community Arts, History & Archaeology, Museums/Galleries, Music, Opera, Performing Arts, Theater
Civic & Public Affairs: Business/Free Enterprise, Chambers of Commerce, Civil Rights, Community Foundations, Employment/Job Training, Civic & Public Affairs-General, Housing, Legal Aid, Minority Business, Municipalities/Towns, Native American Affairs, Parades/Festivals, Safety, Urban & Community Affairs, Women's Affairs, Zoos/Aquariums
Education: Arts/Humanities Education, Business Education, Colleges & Universities, Community & Junior Colleges, Education Funds, Education Reform, Engineering/Technological Education, Education-General, Leadership Training, Private Education (Precollege), Secondary Education (Private), Special Education, Vocational & Technical Education
Environment: Environment-General, Protection, Resource Conservation
Health: AIDS/HIV, Cancer, Children's Health/Hospitals, Clinics/Medical Centers, Heart, Hospitals, Multiple Sclerosis, Nursing Services, Research/Studies Institutes
Religion: Churches, Religious Organizations, Religious Welfare
Science: Scientific Centers & Institutes
Social Services: At-Risk Youth, Child Welfare, Community Centers, Community Service Organizations, Counseling, Emergency Relief, Food/Clothing Distribution, People with Disabilities, Recreation & Athletics, Scouts, Senior Services, Shelters/Homelessness, Special Olympics, United Funds/United Ways, YMCA/YWCA/YMHA/YWHA, Youth Organizations

Contributions Analysis

Arts & Humanities: 17%. Primary support is for the Spokane Symphony in Spokane, WA. Other interests include a ballet company, civic theater, and concert and arts associations.
Civic & Public Affairs: 15%. Funds community foundations and civic and women's affairs.
Education: 23%. Major support to St. George's School in Spokane, WA. The remainder of funds support other universities, specialty schools, and education funds in Washington state.
Religion: 1%. Supports religious services.
Science: 1%. Funds the Pacific Science Center.
Social Services: 38%. Primary support goes to the United Way. Other support goes to traditional youth groups and community services.
Note: Total contribution in 1998.

Application Procedures

Initial Contact: Send a brief letter requesting a formal application, then send written proposal.
Application Requirements: Include the name and general purpose of the organization; proof of tax exemption; amount and purpose of funds requested; copy of current budget and the most recent financial statements showing sources of grants, contributions, and earned income, if any; and a list of officers and members of any advisory council or board.
Deadlines: None.

Restrictions

Generally limits giving to those areas where the company operates; its primary focus is on the immediate needs of local communities.

Corporate Officials

Peter F. Stanton: chairman, president, chief executive officer B 1956. PRIM CORP EMPL chairman, president, chief executive officer: Washington Trust Bank.
Philip H. Stanton: chief executive officer, director B 1931. ED Stanford University (1952); Gonzaga University Law School JD (1956). PRIM CORP EMPL chief executive officer, director: Washington Trust Bank Financial Corp. CORP AFFIL chairman: Washington Trust Bank. NONPR AFFIL member: Spokane County Bar Association; member: Washington Bar Association.
Lea Werner: senior vice president PRIM CORP EMPL senior vice president: Washington Trust Bank.

Giving Program Officials

Susan Rowe-Adler: director community affairs

Grants Analysis

Disclosure Period: calendar year ending 1998
Total Grants: $205,620*
Number of Grants: 35
Average Grant: $5,875
Highest Grant: $37,500
Typical Range: $1,000 to $10,000
***Note:** Giving excludes United Way.

Recent Grants

Note: Grants derived from 1998 Form 990.

Arts & Humanities

28,200 Spokane Symphony, Spokane, WA -- General Fund
13,520 Children's Museum of Spokane, Spokane, WA -- General Fund
2,500 Uptown Opera, Spokane, WA -- General Fund
1,000 North Central Washington Museum, Wenatchee, WA -- General Fund
1,000 Theatre Ballet of Spokane, Spokane, WA -- General Fund

Civic & Public Affairs

25,000 Mt. Spokane 2000, Spokane, WA -- General Fund
8,000 Snap, Spokane, WA -- General Fund
2,500 Wampum, Spokane, WA -- General Fund
2,000 Idaho Community Foundation, Coeur D'Alene, ID -- General Fund

1,000 Mid-City Concerns, Spokane, WA -- General Fund
1,000 SBASE, Spokane, WA -- General Fund
1,000 Women Helping Women Fund, Spokane, WA -- General Fund

Education
37,500 Saint George's School, Spokane, WA -- General Fund
11,000 Washington State University, Pullman, WA -- General Fund
8,000 North Idaho College Foundation, Coeur D'Alene, ID -- General Fund
2,750 Junior Achievement, Spokane, WA -- General Fund
2,000 Excel, Coeur D'Alene, ID -- General Fund
1,000 Spokane Scholars Foundation, Spokane, WA -- General Fund
1,000 Wenatchee Valley College Foundation, Wenatchee, WA -- General Fund

Environment
14,500 Supporters of the Center, Inc., Spokane, WA -- General Fund

Health
1,000 Ronald McDonald House, Spokane, WA -- General Fund

Religion
2,000 The Children's Ark, Spokane, WA -- General Fund

Science
2,750 Pacific Science Center, Seattle, WA -- General Fund

Social Services
65,000 United Way of Spokane, Spokane, WA -- General Fund
10,200 YWCA, Spokane, WA -- General Fund
7,500 Spokane Valley Junior Soccer, Spokane, WA -- General Fund
4,000 Spokane Food Bank, Spokane, WA -- General Fund
4,000 United Way of Chelan and Douglas Counties, Wenatchee, WA -- General Fund
2,500 Chase Youth Commission, Spokane, WA -- General Fund
2,500 Wenatchee Valley YMCA, Wenatchee, WA -- General Fund
2,100 Boy Scouts of America, Spokane, WA -- General Fund
2,000 Columbia Basin Foundation, Wenatchee, WA -- General Fund
1,500 Retired Senior Volunteer Program, Wenatchee, WA -- General Fund
1,100 Morning Star Boys Ranch, Spokane, WA -- General Fund

WASTE MANAGEMENT INC.

Company Contact
Oak Brook, IL

Company Description
Former Name: WMX Technologies Inc.
Revenue: US$13,257,400,000 (1999)
Employees: 65,000
Fortune Rank: 133, per FORTUNE Magazine's list of 500 Largest U.S. Corporations (1999).
FF 133
SIC(s): 4952 Sewerage Systems, 4953 Refuse Systems.

Operating Locations
Operates in 48 states and in more than 20 countries overseas.

Nonmonetary Support
Value: $826,000 (1994); $790,000 (1993); $768,000 (1992)
Type: In-kind Services; Workplace Solicitation
Note: Above figures include services donated by the company and its subsidiaries.

Corporate Sponsorship
Type: Arts & cultural events; Festivals/fairs; Music & entertainment events; Pledge-a-thon

Giving Contact
Jewel Sikes, Vice President, Communications
Waste Management, Inc.
1001 Fannin, Suite 4000
Houston, TX 77002
Phone: (713)512-77002

Description
Organization Type: Corporate Giving Program
Giving Locations: principally near operating locations and to national organizations.
Grant Types: Capital, Conference/Seminar, Employee Matching Gifts, Endowment, General Support, Multiyear/Continuing Support.
Note: Employee matching gift ratio: 2 to 1 for employee and retiree gifts of $50 or more to higher education institutions and environmental programs; 1 to 1 to other nonprofit organisation.

Giving Philosophy
'The philosophy behind Waste Management, Inc.'s contributions program is relatively simple: the Company believes that good corporate citizenship must go beyond that which is required by law or by custom. This belief is best expressed in Waste Management's Mission Statement. .. In pledging to 'promote a spirit of partnership with the communities and enterprises we serve as we strive to be a responsible neighbor,' the Company also commits itself and its resources to an ongoing relationship with the communities in which the Company operates and its people's lives. That basic partnership demands an active and aggressive program of shared responsibility for all elements that affect the quality of life in those communities.' Waste Management, Inc. (WMX Technologies, Inc.), Annual Report of Corporate Contributions

Financial Summary
Total Giving: $12,000,000 (1996 approx); $11,100,000 (1995 approx); $11,800,000 (1994 approx). Note: Contributes through corporate direct giving program only. 1996 Giving includes corporate direct giving ($6,850,000); matching gifts ($2,080,000); scholarship ($400,000); employee campaigns; domestic subsidiaries; nonmonetary support. 1995 and 1994 Giving includes corporate direct giving; domestic subsidiaries; matching gifts; scholarship; nonmonetary support.

Typical Recipients
Arts & Humanities: Arts Associations & Councils, Arts Festivals, Arts Funds, Arts Institutes, Historic Preservation, Museums/Galleries, Music, Opera, Performing Arts, Public Broadcasting, Theater
Civic & Public Affairs: Municipalities/Towns, Professional & Trade Associations, Safety, Urban & Community Affairs, Zoos/Aquariums
Education: Colleges & Universities, Education Funds, Elementary Education (Private), Engineering/Technological Education, Minority Education, Public Education (Precollege), Science/Mathematics Education
Environment: Environment-General
Health: Health Funds, Hospitals, Medical Research, Mental Health, Single-Disease Health Associations

Contributions Analysis
Giving Priorities: Social welfare, education, and the environment.
Civic & Public Affairs: About 50%. Focus is on improving quality of life for people in operating communities. Employee involvement and corporate contributions promote cultural enrichment, neighborhood development, and improved human services care. Grants have been made to performing arts, museums, child care, public safety, youth organizations, civic groups, and social service organizations.
Education: About 35%. Emphasis at local school level is on volunteerism, environmental education development, and involvement in school partnerships. Supports colleges, universities, elementary and secondary schools, public educational broadcasting, and other education-related organizationsand programs. Interests include scholarship programs, educational outreach tools, higher education programs for minorities, engineering and science programs, and environmental management and law studies.
Environment: About 15%. Promotes responsible use of natural resources and enhancement of the environment. Recipients include wildlife preservation organizations, pollution prevention and clean-up projects, environmental study groups, recycling programs, and conservation funds.

Application Procedures
Initial Contact: brief proposal summary to either the company headquarters or regional offices or local operating facilities; no telephone or E-mail solicitations
Application Requirements: one- or two-page proposal summary, including concise statement of need to be addressed; a description of organization, including history, mission statement, purpose, and goals; amount requested; purpose of funds sought, including need and explanation of how it fits within company's giving guidelines; recently audited financial statements or annual report; approved operating budget; project plan, including budget and method of evaluation; list of public and private contributors in most recent fiscal year; list of current trustees and board members and their affiliations; proof of tax-exempt status
Deadlines: None.
Evaluative Criteria: organization must have certification of 501(c)(3) status and be eligible to receive tax deductible gifts under Section 170(c) of the Internal Revenue Code; operate for the benefit of communities where company operates and/or in which employees live; provide services or benefits to a broad segment of the population without regard to race, creed, or sex; improve quality of life in community, including artistic and cultural activities

Restrictions
Does not support individuals; religious groups for sectarian purposes; veterans, fraternal, and labor organizations; or organizations that discriminate on the basis of race, sex, or religion. Does not support courtesy advertising.

Additional Information
Publications: Report on Community Investment

Corporate Officials
Herbert A. Getz: senior vice president, secretary, general counsel B Clinton, IA 1955. ED Illinois Wesleyan University BA (1977); Harvard University JD (1980). PRIM CORP EMPL senior vice president, secretary, general counsel: Waste Management Inc. ADD CORP EMPL chairman: NSC Corp.; secretary: Salem Waste Disposal Centre; secretary: WMX Technology Center Inc.; secretary: Waste Management Missouri; secretary: Waste Management Holdings.
Steve Miller: chief executive officer PRIM CORP EMPL chief executive officer: Waste Management Inc.

Giving Program Officials
Paul Pyrcik: PRIM CORP EMPL director community investment: Waste Management Inc.

Grants Analysis

Disclosure Period: calendar year ending 1996
Total Grants: $12,000,000 (approx)
Typical Range: $1,000 to $50,000

Recent Grants

Note: Grants derived from 1993 Annual Report.

Arts & Humanities

Art Institute of Chicago, Chicago, IL
Auditorium Theater Council, Chicago, IL
Chicago Educational Television Association/WTTW Cannel 11, Chicago, IL -- New Explorers series
Chicago Symphony Orchestra, Chicago, IL
Chicago Theater Group, Chicago, IL -- Goodman Theater
City of Chicago Department of Cultural Affairs, Chicago, IL -- Gallery 37
Lyric Opera of Chicago, Chicago, IL
Lyric Opera of Chicago, Chicago, IL
Maryland Institute College of Art, Baltimore, MD
Museum of Contemporary Art, Chicago, IL
National Public Radio, Washington, DC

Civic & Public Affairs

American Public Works Association, Kansas City, MO
Institute for Illinois, Washington, DC
John G. Shedd Aquarium Society, Chicago, IL

Education

Bradley University, Peoria, IL
Brenau College, Gainesville, GA
Calvin College, Grand Rapids, MI
Clemson University College of Engineering, Clemson, SC
Clemson University Foundation, Clemson, SC
DePaul University, Chicago, IL
Florida Southern College, Lakeland, FL
Hope College, Holland, MI
Illinois Institute of Technology, Chicago, IL
Illinois Wesleyan University, Bloomington, IL
Illinois Wesleyan University, Bloomington, IL
Indiana University Foundation, Bloomington, IN
John Carroll University, University Heights, OH
League of Women Voters Education Fund, Washington, DC
Leo High School, Chicago, IL
Marquette University, Milwaukee, WI
Massachusetts Institute of Technology, Cambridge, MA
Midtown Educational Foundation, Chicago, IL
Mississippi State University at Meridian, Meridian, MS
Mount Union College, Alliance, OH
NAACP Special Contribution Fund, New York, NY
Newberry College, Newberry, SC
North Central College, Naperville, IL
Northwestern University, Evanston, IL
Oklahoma Baptist University, Shawnee, OK
Phillips Academy, Andover, MA
Princeton University, Princeton, NJ
Roane State Community College Foundation, Harriman, TN
St. Ignatius College Prep, Chicago, IL
St. Thomas Aquinas High School Foundation, Fort Lauderdale, FL
Stonehill College, North Easton, MA
Timothy Christian Schools, Elmhurst, IL
Trinity Christian College, Palos Heights, IL
United Negro College Fund, New York, NY
University of Georgia Foundation, Athens, GA
University of Illinois Foundation, Urbana, IL
University of Notre Dame, Notre Dame, IN
University of South Carolina Academic and Athletic Scholarship Fund, Columbia, SC
Yale University, New Haven, CT

Environment

Center for Marine Conservation, Washington, DC
Ducks Unlimited, Memphis, TN
Ducks Unlimited South Carolina Chapter, Barnwell, SC
Environmental Careers Organization, Boston, MA
Keep America Beautiful, Stamford, CT
Keep Florida Beautiful, Tallahassee, FL
Keystone Center, Keystone, CO
National Audubon Society, New York, NY
National Audubon Society, New York, NY
National Wildlife Federation, Washington, DC
National Wildlife Federation, Washington, DC
Nature Conservancy, Arlington, VA
Project Together We Stand, Bowling Green, OH
US Conference of Mayors, Washington, DC -- waste management composting and office paper recycling projects
US Environmental Training Institute, Washington, DC
Wetland Habitat Alliance of Texas, Nacogdoches, TX
World Wildlife Fund, Washington, DC
World Wildlife Fund/The Conservation Foundation, Washington, DC

Health

Children's Memorial Foundation, Chicago, IL
EHS Good Samaritan Hospital, Downers Grove, IL
EHS Trinity Hospital, Chicago, IL
Hinsdale Hospital Foundation, Hinsdale, IL
Juvenile Diabetes Foundation, Chicago, IL
Lauderdale Lakes Alzheimer's Foundation, Fort Lauderdale, FL
McLaughlin Research Institute, Great Falls, MT
Nick and Marc Buoniconti Fund to Cure Paralysis, New York, NY
Oklahoma Easter Seal Society, Oklahoma City, OK
Rehabilitation Institute of Chicago, Chicago, IL
Robert Crown Center for Health Education, Hinsdale, IL

Science

Field Museum of Natural History, Chicago, IL
Franklin Institute Science Museum, Philadelphia, PA
Museum of Science and Industry, Chicago, IL

Social Services

Bethshan Association, Palos Heights, IL
Big Shoulders Fund, Chicago, IL
Boy Scouts of America, Chicago, IL -- Hoover Outdoor Education Center
Chicago United, Chicago, IL
Community House, Hinsdale, IL
Life Directions, Detroit, MI
United Way, Van Nuys, CA
United Way Crusade of Mercy, Hinsdale, IL
United Way Massachusetts Bay, Boston, MA
United Way Mesa County, Grand Junction, CO
United Way Midlands, Columbia, SC
United Way Niagara, Niagara Falls, NY
United Way Sonoma-Mendocina Lake, Santa Rosa, CA
United Way Southwest Louisiana, Lake Charles, LA

WAUSAU INSURANCE COMPANIES

Company Contact

Wausau, WI
Web: http://www.wausau.com

Company Description

Employees: 5,592
SIC(s): 6331 Fire, Marine & Casualty Insurance.
Parent Company: Employers Insurance of Wausau, A Mutual Co., Wausau, WI, United States
Parent Revenue: US$15,499,000,000 (1999)

Nonmonetary Support

Type: Donated Equipment; In-kind Services; Loaned Employees

Giving Contact

Lynn Kordus, Senior Public Relations Coordinator
Wausau Insurance Companies
2000 Westwood Drive
Wausau, WI 54401
Phone: 800-826-9781
Fax: (715)843-3690

Description

Organization Type: Corporate Giving Program
Giving Locations: WI: Marathon County, Wausau County some giving nationally.
Grant Types: Employee Matching Gifts, General Support.

Financial Summary

Total Giving: Contributes through corporate direct giving program only.

Typical Recipients

Arts & Humanities: Arts & Humanities-General
Civic & Public Affairs: Civic & Public Affairs-General
Education: Education-General
Health: Health-General
Social Services: Social Services-General

Contributions Analysis

Arts & Humanities: 10% to 15%. Local art centers and activities involving youths.
Civic & Public Affairs: 60% to 65%. Includes United Way.
Education: 15% to 20%. Local education.
Note: Health care, although not represented in a separate category, has gained importance in recent years.

Application Procedures

Initial Contact: a brief letter of inquiry
Application Requirements: a description of organization, amount requested, purpose of funds sought, audited financial statement, and proof of tax-exempt status
Deadlines: None.

Restrictions

Does not support individuals, religious organizations for purely sectarian purposes, political or lobbying groups, agencies which receive funding from the United Way, labor groups, or 'token requests.'

Additional Information

The company is restructuring and is in the process of going from operating in sixteen divisions in the United States to seven. The company awards grants in its operating communities. Final grant award decisions are made at local operating units after solicitation is initially approved at the company's headquarters office.
Employers Insurance of Wausau, Wausau Life Insurance Company's parent, is affiliated with Nationwide Mutual Insurance Co.; see the entry for Employers Insurance of Wausau, A Mutual Company, for more information. entry for Employers Insurance of Wausau, A Mutual Company, for more information.

Corporate Officials

Dimon Richard McFerson: chairman, chief executive officer B Los Angeles, CA 1937. ED University of California, Los Angeles (1959); University of Southern California (1972). PRIM CORP EMPL chairman, chief executive officer: Nationwide Mutual Insurance Co. ADD CORP EMPL president: Nationwide General Insurance Co. NONPR AFFIL member: American Institute CPAs.
David O. Miller: chairman PRIM CORP EMPL chairman: Wausau Insurance Companies. CORP AFFIL director: Scottsdale Insurance Co.; chairman: Wausau Preferred Health Insurance Co.; director: Nationwide Mutual Insurance Co.; director: Nationwide Life

Insurance Co.; director: Nationwide Mutual Fire Insurance Co.; director: Nationwide Financial Services; director: Nationwide General Insurance Co.; director: Nationwide Advisory Services; director: Allied Life Financial Corp.; director: Colonial Insurance Co. California.

Giving Program Officials

Lynn Kordus: coordinator PRIM CORP EMPL senior public relations coordinator: Wausau Insurance Companies.

WEBSTER BANK

Company Contact

Waterbury, CT

Company Description

SIC(s): 6035 Federal Savings Institutions.
Parent Company: Webster Financial Corp.

Harold Webster Smith Foundation Inc.

Giving Contact

Mike G. Bazinet
Webster Bank
PO Box 191
Waterbury, CT 06720
Phone: (203)755-1422

Description

EIN: 222947047
Organization Type: Corporate Foundation. Supports preselected organizations only.
Former Name: Webster Bank Foundation.
Giving Locations: CT
Grant Types: Employee Matching Gifts, General Support.

Financial Summary

Total Giving: $25,500 (fiscal year ending June 30, 1998); $548,486 (fiscal 1996); $26,500 (fiscal 1995)
Assets: $252,249 (fiscal 1998); $110,850 (fiscal 1996); $637,943 (fiscal 1995)
Gifts Received: $250,000 (fiscal 1998); $500,000 (fiscal 1994); $68,000 (fiscal 1991). Note: In 1998, contributions were received from Webster Financial Corp. In 1991 and 1994 contributions were received from Bristol Savings Bank.

Typical Recipients

Arts & Humanities: Community Arts, Museums/Galleries, Music, Performing Arts
Civic & Public Affairs: Chambers of Commerce, Community Foundations, Housing, Urban & Community Affairs
Education: Colleges & Universities, Community & Junior Colleges, Legal Education, Private Education (Precollege), Public Education (Precollege), Secondary Education (Private), Special Education
Environment: Energy, Resource Conservation
Health: Children's Health/Hospitals, Clinics/Medical Centers, Emergency/Ambulance Services, Health Organizations, Hospitals, Nursing Services, Public Health
Religion: Religious Welfare
Social Services: Community Service Organizations, Recreation & Athletics, United Funds/United Ways, YMCA/YWCA/YMHA/YWHA, Youth Organizations

Contributions Analysis

Giving Priorities: Civic organizations.
Civic & Public Affairs: 88%. Supports a chamber of commerce and community partnerships.
Health: 12%. Supports a hospital.
Note: Total contributions made in 1998.

Corporate Officials

John V. Brennan: executive vice president, chief financial officer PRIM CORP EMPL executive vice president, chief financial officer: Webster Bank.
Lee A. Gagnon: executive vice president, chief operating officer, secretary PRIM CORP EMPL executive vice president, chief operating officer, secretary: Webster Bank.
James C. Smith: chairman, chief executive officer PRIM CORP EMPL chairman, chief executive officer: Webster Bank.

Foundation Officials

Sherwood L. Anderson: director
John D. Benjamin: secretary
John V. Brennan: treasurer (see above)
Lee A. Gagnon: vice president (see above)
J. Gregory Hickey: director
Richard A. O'Brien: director
David J. Preleski: director
James C. Smith: president (see above)

Grants Analysis

Disclosure Period: fiscal year ending June 30, 1998
Total Grants: $25,500
Number of Grants: 4
Average Grant: $6,375
Highest Grant: $12,500
Typical Range: $25 to $5,000

Recent Grants

Note: Grants derived from fiscal 1997 Form 990.

Arts & Humanities

25,000 Shubert, New Haven, CT

Civic & Public Affairs

10,000 Greater Bristol Chamber of Commerce, Bristol, CT
10,000 Greater Bristol Chamber of Commerce, Bristol, CT
10,000 New Hampshire Neighborhood Housing Services, NH
5,000 Greater Bristol Chamber of Commerce, Bristol, CT

Health

10,000 Bristol Hospital Capital Campaign, Bristol, CT
10,000 Bristol Hospital Intensive Care Unit, Bristol, CT
2,000 Hospital for Special Care, New Britain, CT
1,000 Hospital for Special Care, New Britain, CT

Religion

5,000 United Methodist Homes of Connecticut, Shelton, CT

WEIL, GOTSHAL & MANGES CORP.

Company Contact

New York, NY
Web: http://www.weil.com

Company Description

Revenue: US$260,000,000
Employees: 1,600
SIC(s): 8111 Legal Services.

Corporate Sponsorship

Range: less than $1,000
Contact: Ira Millstein, President
Note: Sponsors Police/Fireman Child - Widow Fund, Boys Harbor.

Weil, Gotshal & Manges Foundation

Giving Contact

Jesse D. Wolff, Treasurer & Director
Weil, Gotshal & Manges Foundation
767 5th Ave.
New York, NY 10153
Phone: (212)310-8000

Description

Founded: 1983
EIN: 133158325
Organization Type: Corporate Foundation
Giving Locations: NY
Grant Types: General Support.

Financial Summary

Total Giving: $2,000,000 (1999 approx); $2,000,000 (1998 approx); $1,781,103 (1997). Note: Contributes through foundation only.
Giving Analysis: Giving for 1995 includes: foundation ($1,716,535); foundation grants to United Way ($162,750); 1997: foundation ($1,623,603); foundation grants to United Way ($157,500)
Assets: $8,344,099 (1997); $3,842,574 (1996); $3,880,037 (1995)
Gifts Received: $1,516,800 (1997); $1,500,000 (1996); $1,500,000 (1995). Note: In 1995, contributions were received from Weil, Gotshal & Manges LLP.

Typical Recipients

Arts & Humanities: Arts Centers, Dance, History & Archaeology, Libraries, Museums/Galleries, Music, Opera, Performing Arts, Public Broadcasting
Civic & Public Affairs: African American Affairs, Botanical Gardens/Parks, Business/Free Enterprise, Civil Rights, Economic Development, Economic Policy, Employment/Job Training, Ethnic Organizations, Civic & Public Affairs-General, Law & Justice, Legal Aid, Municipalities/Towns, Parades/Festivals, Public Policy, Urban & Community Affairs, Women's Affairs
Education: Arts/Humanities Education, Colleges & Universities, Education Reform, International Studies, Legal Education, Private Education (Precollege), Secondary Education (Private)
Environment: Environment-General
Health: AIDS/HIV, Cancer, Emergency/Ambulance Services, Heart, Medical Research, Prenatal Health Issues, Single-Disease Health Associations, Transplant Networks/Donor Banks
International: Foreign Educational Institutions, Human Rights, International Affairs, International Peace & Security Issues, International Relations, Missionary/Religious Activities
Religion: Dioceses, Jewish Causes, Religious Organizations, Religious Welfare
Social Services: At-Risk Youth, Big Brother/Big Sister, Camps, Child Welfare, Community Service Organizations, Crime Prevention, Emergency Relief, Family Planning, Family Services, Recreation & Athletics, Scouts, Shelters/Homelessness, United Funds/United Ways, Volunteer Services, YMCA/YWCA/YMHA/YWHA, Youth Organizations

Contributions Analysis

Giving Priorities: Primary support for Jewish causes and civic concerns.
Arts & Humanities: 2%. Performing arts, museums, symphonies, and libraries.
Civic & Public Affairs: 27%. Primarily for legal aid, parks, and urban affairs.
Education: 11%. Focus on Columbia Law School an private primary and secondary education.
Health: 19%.
International: 3%. Human rights and foreign relations organizations.

Religion: 41%. Major support for the United Jewish Appeal.
Social Services: 15%. The United Way, family services, and youth organizations.
Note: Total contributions in 1997.

Application Procedures

Initial Contact: a brief letter of inquiry
Application Requirements: a description of organization project; statement of purpose; budget; and schedule of activities
Deadlines: November 1

Corporate Officials

Ira M. Millstein: partner B New York, NY 1926. ED Columbia University BS (1947); Columbia University LLB (1949). PRIM CORP EMPL partner: Weil, Gotshal & Manges Corp. NONPR AFFIL chairman: New York City Partnership Policy Center; member: New York State Bar Association; member: National Association Corp. Directors; professor, chairman board advisors: Columbia University Center Law Economic Studies; member: Government Cuomo's Task Force on Pension Fund Investment; chairman board trustee: Center Park Conservancy; fellow: American Academy of Arts & Sciences; member: American Bar Association; vice chairman board overseers: Albert Einstein College of Medicine. CLUB AFFIL Metro Club; Quaker Ridge Golf Club.

Foundation Officials

Robert Todd Lang: chairman, director B New York, NY 1924. ED Yale University BA (1945); Yale University LLB (1947). PRIM CORP EMPL senior partner: Weil, Gotshal & Manges Corp. NONPR AFFIL chairman: Task Force Listing Standards Self Regulatory Organizations; member: Task Force Review Federal Securities Law; chairman: Task Force Hedge Funds; member: American Bar Association; member: Committee Federal Regulation Securities.
Harvey R. Miller: secretary, director B Brooklyn, NY 1933. ED Columbia University School of Law (1959). PRIM CORP EMPL partner: Weil, Gotshal & Manges Corp.
Ira M. Millstein: president, director (see above)
Jesse David Wolff: treasurer, director B Minneapolis, MN 1913. ED Dartmouth College BA (1935); Harvard University JD (1938). PRIM CORP EMPL counsel: Weil, Gotshal & Manges Corp. NONPR AFFIL trustee greater NY chapter: American Red Cross; member: Judge Advisory General Association; member: American Bar Association.

Grants Analysis

Disclosure Period: calendar year ending 1997
Total Grants: $1,623,603*
Number of Grants: 162
Average Grant: $10,022
Highest Grant: $550,000
Typical Range: $250 to $25,000
***Note:** Giving excludes United Way.

Recent Grants

Note: Grants derived from 1997 Form 990.

Arts & Humanities

15,000 Lincoln Center Consolidated Corporation
5,000 Children's Museum, New York, NY
5,000 Dallas Symphony Association, Dallas, TX
5,000 New York Public Library, New York, NY

Civic & Public Affairs

200,000 Legal Aid Society, New York, NY
50,000 Central Park Conservancy, New York, NY
25,000 Association of the Bar of the City of New York Fund, New York, NY
25,000 Community Studies, New York, NY
15,000 Central Park Conservancy, New York, NY
15,000 Lawyers Alliance, New York, NY
15,000 New York Lawyers for the Public Interest, New York, NY
15,000 Uniform Law Foundation, Chicago, IL
12,000 First Department Assigned Counsel Corporation, New York, NY
10,000 City Bar Fund
7,500 Washington Lawyers Committee for Civil Rights, Washington, DC
7,000 New York City Partnership Summer Jobs Program, New York, NY
5,000 Corporate Bar Fund, Stamford, CT
5,000 French Institute
5,000 Fund for Modern Courts, New York, NY
5,000 Justice Resource Center, New York, NY
5,000 Stern Grove Festival Association, San Francisco, CA

Education

150,000 Columbia Law School, New York, NY
10,000 Dominican Commercial High School
7,500 Our Lady of Fatima Parochial School
5,000 Columbia University Teachers College, New York, NY
5,000 Whitfield School, St. Louis, MO

Health

7,500 New York Blood Center, New York, NY

International

25,000 Lawyers Committee for Human Rights, New York, NY
10,000 Council on Foreign Relations, New York, NY
10,000 Seeds of Peace, Washington, DC
5,000 Business Council for the United Nations, New York, NY
5,000 Jerusalem Fund, Washington, DC

Religion

550,000 United Jewish Appeal Federation, New York, NY
25,000 Dallas Jewish Coalition, Dallas, TX
20,000 United Jewish Appeal Federation, New York, NY
17,000 Greater Miami Jewish Federation, Miami, FL
15,000 Jewish Federation, Houston, TX
10,000 Catholic Charities Diocese, Brooklyn, NY
10,000 Jewish Foundation for the Righteous, New York, NY
5,000 Jewish Federation, Dallas, TX
5,000 St. Luke's Community Services, Stamford, CT

Social Services

155,000 United Way, New York, NY
25,000 New York Police and Fire Widows and Children's Benefit, Uniondale, NY
10,000 Big Brothers and Big Sisters
10,000 Flames Neighborhood Youth Association, Brooklyn, NY
10,000 Girl Scouts of America
10,000 Randalls Island Sports Foundation, Albany, NY
6,000 CPR Institute for Dispute Resolution, New York, NY
5,000 Lawyers for Children, New York, NY
5,000 VOLS

WELLS FARGO &CO.

Company Contact

San Francisco, CA
Web: http://wellsfargo.com

Company Description

Revenue: US$21,795,000,000 (1999)
Profit: US$3,747,000,000 (1999)
Employees: 36,902
Fortune Rank: 68, per FORTUNE Magazine's list of 500 Largest U.S. Corporations (1999).
FF 68
SIC(s): 6021 National Commercial Banks, 6712 Bank Holding Companies.

Nonmonetary Support

Type: Donated Equipment; In-kind Services

Corporate Sponsorship

Contact: Lyna Faucett, Contact
Phone: (415)396-6409

Wells Fargo Foundation

Giving Contact

Mario Diaz, Vice President
Wells Fargo Foundation
455 Market Street, 0104-034
San Francisco, CA 94163
Phone: (415)222-5235
Fax: (415)975-6260

Description

EIN: 942549743
Organization Type: Corporate Foundation
Giving Locations: AZ; CA: headquarters and operating communities; CO; ID; NV; NM; OR; TX; UT; WA
Grant Types: Challenge, Employee Matching Gifts, General Support, Project.
Note: Employee matching gift ratio: 1 to 1.

Giving Philosophy

'As a corporate citizen in the communities in which it operates, Wells Fargo has a responsibility to the needs of those communities. The quality of life and education, and the economic health of our society are of vital interest to our organization and its staff. The Wells Fargo Foundation was created to support community activities, primarily in areas where the Company operates, that contribute to the economic and educational needs of these localities.' Wells Fargo & Co.

Financial Summary

Total Giving: $1,093,692 (1995); $1,249,564 (1994); $3,876,323 (1993). Note: Contributes through corporate direct giving program and foundation. 1995 and 1994 Giving includes foundation.
Assets: $574,253 (1995); $599,174 (1994); $495,585 (1993)
Gifts Received: $1,096,896 (1995); $1,427,254 (1994); $1,141,250 (1993). Note: Contributions are received from Wells Fargo & Company. In 1995 contributions were in the form of shares of Intuit, Inc.

Typical Recipients

Arts & Humanities: History & Archaeology, Music, Performing Arts
Civic & Public Affairs: Economic Development, Employment/Job Training, Housing, Urban & Community Affairs, Zoos/Aquariums
Education: Business Education, Colleges & Universities, Continuing Education, Economic Education, Education Funds, Elementary Education (Private), Minority Education, Public Education (Precollege)
Health: Single-Disease Health Associations
Social Services: Child Welfare, Community Service Organizations, Family Services, Food/Clothing Distribution, People with Disabilities, Senior Services, United Funds/United Ways, Volunteer Services, YMCA/YWCA/YMHA/YWHA, Youth Organizations

Contributions Analysis

Giving Priorities: Education and housing.
Civic & Public Affairs: Programs that help provide affordable housing for low and moderate income individuals; promote economic development by financing

small businesses or small farms that meet size eligibility standards for the SBA's Development Company Program or have gross annual revenues of $1,000,000 or less; provide job training programs that assist low and moderate income individuals to find and retain employment; or help revitalize or stabilize low and moderate income communities.

Education: Pre-kindergarten through twelfth grade institutions, as well as for nonprofits whose primary focus is to assist them, when the primary purpose of the grant is to promoteacademic achievement to low and moderate income students in the areas of math and science, literacy, and history of the American West. Also considers support of programs that work to encourage school partnerships with parents/guardians, the community in which the school is located, and the business community, as well as to programs that provide staff training for teachers and administrators working with low and moderate income students.

Social Services: Organizations whose work primarily benefits low and moderate income individuals. Issues of interest include child care, health services and education, and basic needs assistance.

Application Procedures

Initial Contact: written proposal, not exceeding five pages, that addresses funding criteria

Application Requirements: in addition, include a description of organization, including mission and major accomplishments; current operating budget and sources of funds; copy of tax-exempt letter from the IRS or non-profit designation as a governmental or tribal entity, as well as Taxpayer ID number; description of population to be served, including data used to identify income levels; project goals, project budget, objectives, timelines, expected outcomes, and evaluation criteria; and specific dollar amount requested

Deadlines: None.

Review Process: proposals given careful and serious consideration upon receipt

Evaluative Criteria: nonprofit tax-exempt organizations with 501(c)(3) and 170(b) designations; program capability, sound fiscal policies, responsible financial management, evidence of long-range planning, and effective use of volunteers; benefit to low and moderate income individuals; active board of directors; budget, financial statements, and a plan for funding beyond the period covered by the proposed contributions, particularly in the case of start-up requests; method of evaluating results of the proposed project

Decision Notification: within four to six weeks

Notes: incomplete proposals will not be considered and will be returned; binders, videos, and other unrequested materials should not be included and will not be returned if presented.

Restrictions

Applications will not be considered for individuals; including scholarship or fellowship assistance; for-profit entities, including start-up small businesses; endowments; equipment, including computer hardware and software; marketing activities such as sports or athletic groups; hospitals; vehicles; film or video projects, including documentaries; travel expenses, including student trips or tours; or promotional merchandise. The foundation also discourages requests for capital campaigns.

Additional Information

Proposals from organizations in Northern California, Nevada, Colorado, and New Mexico should be directed to Mario Diaz, Vice President, at the above address.

Proposals from organizations in Washington, Oregon, Idaho, Utah, and Texas should be directed to Pamela Irwin, Vice President, at the above address.

Proposals from organizations in Southern California and Arizona should be mailed to Jonathan Weedman, Vice President, Wells Fargo Foundation, 333 South Grand Avenue, 2064-014, Los Angeles, CA 90071; phone: (213)253-7118 or (602)378-7350; fax: (213)680-8856.

Foundation may require recipient to provide year-end audited financial statements and periodic reports on the project.

United Ways eligible for funding must have at least one full-time Wells Fargo & Company employee in their geographical service territory for funding to occur.

In 1996, Wells Fargo and Company purchased First Interstate Banks of Arizona, California, Oregon, Texas, and Washington.

Publications: Contributions Guidelines

Corporate Officials

Michael J. Gillfillan: vice chairman, chief executive officer B 1948. PRIM CORP EMPL vice chairman: Wells Fargo & Co.

Paul Mandeville Hazen: chairman, chief executive officer, director B Lansing, MI 1941. ED University of Arizona BA (1963); University of California at Berkeley MBA (1964). PRIM CORP EMPL chairman, chief executive officer, director: Wells Fargo & Co. ADD CORP EMPL chairman, chief executive officer: Wells Fargo Bank NA; trustee: Wells Fargo Mortgage & Equity Trust; officer: Wells Fargo Realty Advisors. CORP AFFIL president, chief operating officer, director: Real Estate Industries Group; director: Safeway Inc.; director: Phelps Dodge Corp.; director: AirTouch Communications Inc.; director: Pacific Telesis Group.

Charles M. Johnson: vice chairman B 1942. ED Ohio State University BS (1963); Stanford University MA (1978). PRIM CORP EMPL vice chairman: Wells Fargo & Co.

Clyde W. Ostler: vice chairman B 1947. ED University of California, San Diego BA (1968); University of Chicago MBA (1976). PRIM CORP EMPL vice chairman: Wells Fargo & Co.

William F. Zuendt: president, chief executive officer B 1946. ED Rensselaer Polytechnic Institute BA (1968); Stanford University MBA (1973). PRIM CORP EMPL president, chief executive officer: Wells Fargo & Co. CORP AFFIL director: 3Com Corp.; president: Wells Fargo Bank NA.

Foundation Officials

Iris S Chan: director PRIM CORP EMPL executive vice president: Wells Fargo Bank National Association.

Virginia Arana Greene: director

Tim Hanlon: president

Patricia Howze: director

Rodney L. Jacobs: chief financial officer B 1940. PRIM CORP EMPL president: Wells Fargo & Co. ADD CORP EMPL vice chairman, chief financial officer: Wells Fargo Bank NA.

Yung Lew: director PRIM CORP EMPL division manager: Wells Fargo Bank NA.

Diane Disney Miller: director B 1933. PRIM CORP EMPL owner, president, director: Retlaw Enterprises ADD CORP EMPL president: Silverado Vineyards.

Karen Wegmann: president, director B 1944. PRIM CORP EMPL executive vice president: Wells Fargo Bank NA.

Grants Analysis

Disclosure Period: calendar year ending 1995

Total Grants: $1,093,692*

Number of Grants: 53

Average Grant: $11,866*

Highest Grant: $476,662

Typical Range: $1,000 to $19,000

***Note:** Giving excludes Company gives directly. Average grant figure excludes highest grant.

Recent Grants

Note: Grants derived from 1995 Form 990.

Education

93,750	University of California, Berkeley, CA

Social Services

476,662	United Way Bay Area, San Francisco, CA
155,115	United Way Campaign, Los Angeles, CA
66,138	United Way San Diego County, San Diego, CA
61,815	United Way Santa Clara County, Santa Clara, CA
56,635	United Way Orange County, Irvine, CA
49,473	United Way, Sacramento, CA
16,110	United Way Sonoma/Mendocino/Lake, Santa Rosa, CA
15,268	United Way Napa/Solano, Vallejo, CA
10,245	United Way Fresno County, Fresno, CA
8,924	United Way Desert, Palm Springs, CA
8,378	United Way Stanislaus County, Modesto, CA
8,039	United Way San Joaquin County, Stockton, CA
7,564	United Way Ventura County, Ventura, CA
7,379	United Way Kern County, Bakersfield, CA
4,372	United Way Santa Cruz County, Capitola, CA
4,113	United Way Salinas Valley, Salinas, CA
3,757	United Way Monterey Peninsula, Monterey, CA
3,459	United Way Tulare County, Tulane, CA
3,136	United Way Butte/Glenn Counties, Chico, CA
2,749	United Way San Luis Obispo County, San Luis Obispo, CA
2,485	United Way Arrowhead, San Bernardino, CA
2,473	United Way Santa Barbara County, Santa Barbara, CA
2,161	United Way Desert, Palm Springs, CA
1,777	United Way Northern California, Redding, CA
1,584	United Way Merced Area, Merced, CA
1,517	United Way Yuba/Sutter, Marysville, CA
1,491	United Way Corona/Norco, Corona, CA
1,467	United Way Humboldt, Eureka, CA
1,464	United Way Madera County, Madera, CA
1,362	United Way Kings AID, Seattle, WA
1,308	United Way Mount Baldy Region, Los Angeles, CA
1,301	United Way Central Coast, Santa Maria, CA
1,267	United Way, Dallas, TX
948	United Way Mojave Desert, Barstow, CA
940	United Way East Valley, Redlands, CA
934	United Way Nevada County, Grass Valley, CA
851	United Way Woodland, Woodland, CA
806	United Way Crusade of Mercy, Chicago, IL
806	United Way Mile High, Denver, CO
792	United Way Tuolumne County, Sonora, CA
748	United Way Imperial County, El Centro, CA
724	United Way, Atlanta, GA
403	United Way National Capital Area, Washington, DC
309	United Way Lompoc Valley, Lompoc, CA
230	United Way Valley of the Sun, Phoenix, AZ
115	United Way Massachusetts Bay, Boston, MA
58	United Way, Minneapolis, MN
58	United Way, New York, NY
58	United Way Hemet San Jacinto Valley, San Jacinto, CA

WEST CO. INC.

Company Contact

Lionville, PA

Company Description

Former Name: West Co. Plastics Group.
Employees: 5,210
SIC(s): 3069 Fabricated Rubber Products Nec, 3089 Plastics Products Nec, 3469 Metal Stampings Nec, 3565 Packaging Machinery.

Corporate Sponsorship

Type: Arts & cultural events

Herman O. West Foundation

Giving Contact

Maureen Richards, Administrator
Herman O. West Foundation
101 Gordon Dr.
Exton, PA 19341-0645
Phone: (610)594-2900
Fax: (610)594-3011

Description

EIN: 237173901
Organization Type: Corporate Foundation
Giving Locations: FL; NJ; NC; PA headquarters and operating communities.
Grant Types: Capital, Emergency, Employee Matching Gifts, General Support, Multiyear/Continuing Support, Scholarship.
Note: Employee matching gift ratio: 1 to 1 up to $500 per employee annually, for secondary and higher education.

Giving Philosophy

Mission Statement: 'To provide financial assistance to nonprofit organizations serving the cultural, health, and public service needs of the areas and communities where the company maintains operations; to fund the company's employee scholarship program; and to encourage financial support to education through its matching gifts to education program.'

Financial Summary

Total Giving: $261,018 (1997); $311,988 (1996); $334,879 (1995). Note: Contributes through foundation only. 1997 Giving includes foundation ($121,300); matching gifts ($13,760); scholarship ($44,797); United Way ($81,161). 1996 Giving includes foundation ($152,150); matching gifts ($12,895): scholarship ($49,888); United Way ($97,055).
Assets: $242,760 (1996); $275,983 (1995); $246,920 (1994)
Gifts Received: $121,500 (1997); $272,940 (1996); $278,310 (1995). Note: In 1997, contributions were received from from the West Co. ($115,500) and others ($6,000).

Typical Recipients

Arts & Humanities: Arts Centers, Community Arts, Arts & Humanities-General, Historic Preservation, History & Archaeology, Libraries, Museums/Galleries, Music, Performing Arts, Theater
Civic & Public Affairs: Public Policy, Safety, Urban & Community Affairs, Zoos/Aquariums
Education: Arts/Humanities Education, Business-School Partnerships, Colleges & Universities, Community & Junior Colleges, Education Funds, Engineering/Technological Education, Medical Education, Minority Education, Private Education (Precollege), Public Education (Precollege), Secondary Education (Private), Student Aid
Health: Cancer, Children's Health/Hospitals, Emergency/Ambulance Services, Health Organizations, Hospitals, Medical Rehabilitation, Medical Research, Nursing Services, Prenatal Health Issues, Public Health, Trauma Treatment
International: Health Care/Hospitals, International Organizations
Science: Observatories & Planetariums, Science Museums, Scientific Centers & Institutes, Scientific Organizations
Social Services: Big Brother/Big Sister, Community Centers, Community Service Organizations, Family Planning, People with Disabilities, Scouts, Senior Services, Social Services-General, Substance Abuse, United Funds/United Ways, YMCA/YWCA/YMHA/YWHA

Contributions Analysis

Arts & Humanities: 5% to 10%. Recipients include theater, museums, orchestras, and arts councils.
Civic & Public Affairs: (United Funds & United Way) 25% to 30%. Supports United Way in operating areas. 20% to 25%. Supports community service agencies, YMCAs, nature centers, and a zoo.
Education: About 15%. Support goes to colleges and universities, minority education, and community education programs. Also supports an educational matching gifts program and provides scholarships.
Health: 20% to 25%. Focus on hospitals and health organizations.

Application Procedures

Initial Contact: written proposal
Application Requirements: a description of organization, and extent of services provided; recently audited financial statement, indicating sources of funds and how they are disbursed; future needs and services of program; and proof of tax-exempt status
Deadlines: None.

Restrictions

Foundation does not support individuals, political or lobbying groups, or organizations outside operating areas.

Corporate Officials

George R. Bennyhoff: senior vice president human resources B 1943. ED East Stroudsburg State University BS (1965). PRIM CORP EMPL senior vice president human resources: West Co., Inc.
Jerry E. Dorsey: executive vice president, chief operating officer B 1944. ED Assumption College; Fairleigh Dickinson University MBA. PRIM CORP EMPL executive vice president, chief operating officer: West Co., Inc.
Steven A. Ellers: chief financial officer PRIM CORP EMPL chief financial officer: West Co., Inc.
John Robert Gailey, III: vice president, general counsel, secretary B York, PA 1954. ED Haverford College (1976); Temple University (1986). PRIM CORP EMPL vice president, general counsel, secretary: West Co., Inc. CORP AFFIL director: American Society of Corporate Secretaries; secretary: Paco Pharmaceutical Services.
Stephen Michael Heumann: vice president, treasurer B Darby, PA 1941. ED Saint Joseph's University BA (1963); University of Pennsylvania Wharton School MBA (1969). PRIM CORP EMPL vice president, treasurer: West Co., Inc. NONPR AFFIL member: Financial Executives Institute.
William G. Little: chairman, president, chief executive officer, director B 1942. ED Dunedin Teachers College. PRIM CORP EMPL chairman, president, chief executive officer, director: West Co., Inc. CORP AFFIL president: West Co. of Puerto Rico.
Donald E. Morel: president PRIM CORP EMPL president: West Co., Inc.
Anna Mae Papso: vice president, controller B 1943. ED Drexel University BS (1966); Drexel University MBA (1972). PRIM CORP EMPL vice president, controller: West Co., Inc.

Foundation Officials

George R. Bennyhoff: chairman, trustee (see above)
Maureen Richards: administrator
Roffe Wake: trustee
Franklin West: trustee

Grants Analysis

Disclosure Period: calendar year ending 1997
Total Grants: $121,300*
Number of Grants: 40
Average Grant: $3,033
Highest Grant: $26,500
Typical Range: $500 to $5,000
***Note:** Giving excludes matching gifts, scholarship, United Way.

Recent Grants

Note: Grants derived from 1997 Form 990.

Arts & Humanities

5,000	Peoples Light and Theater Company, Malvern, PA
4,000	Philadelphia Museum of Art, Philadelphia, PA
2,000	Philadelphia Orchestra, Philadelphia, PA

Civic & Public Affairs

5,000	Cradle of Liberty Council, Philadelphia, PA
3,000	Zoological Society, Philadelphia, PA

Education

5,000	Foundation for Independent Colleges, Mechanicsburg, PA
3,000	East Carolina University, Greenville, NC
3,000	Philadelphia College of Pharmacy and Science, Philadelphia, PA
2,000	Bates College, Lewiston, ME
1,000	Albright College, Reading, PA
1,000	Boston University, Boston, MA
1,000	College of New Jersey, Ewing, NJ
1,000	Concordia College, Seward, NE
1,000	Concordia College, Seward, NE
1,000	Creighton University, Omaha, NE
1,000	Creighton University, Omaha, NE
1,000	Drew University, Madison, NJ
1,000	Drew University, Madison, NJ
1,000	Drew University, Madison, NJ
1,000	Drew University, Madison, NJ
1,000	George Washington University, Washington, DC
1,000	Gettysburg College, Gettysburg, PA
1,000	Harding University, Searcy, AR
1,000	Harding University, Searcy, AR
1,000	Harding University, Searcy, AR
1,000	Indiana University of Pennsylvania, Indiana, PA
1,000	Kenyon College, Gambier, OH
1,000	Lebanon Valley College, Annville, PA
1,000	Massachusetts Institute of Technology, Cambridge, MA
1,000	North Carolina State University, Raleigh, NC
1,000	Pennsylvania State University, University Park, PA
1,000	Southwest Texas State University, San Marcos, TX
1,000	University of Nebraska Kearney, Kearney, NE
1,000	University of Nebraska Lincoln, Lincoln, NE
1,000	University of Pennsylvania, Philadelphia, PA
1,000	University of Virginia, Richmond, VA
1,000	Villanova University, Villanova, PA

Health

26,500	Fox Chase Cancer Center, Philadelphia, PA
10,000	American Red Cross, Philadelphia, PA -- capital campaign

10,000	Brandywine Hospital and Trauma Center, Coatesville, PA
5,800	Community Visiting Nurse Services, Phoenixville, PA
Science	
3,000	Academy of Natural Sciences, Philadelphia, PA
3,000	Franklin Institute Science Museum, Philadelphia, PA
Social Services	
24,309	United Way, West Chester, PA
21,862	United Way, Pinellas, FL
16,923	United Way, Lenoir, NC
10,913	United Way, Lycoming, PA
10,000	Western Main Line YMCA, Exton, PA
5,035	United Way, Kearney, NE
2,000	Planned Parenthood of Chester County, West Chester, PA

WESTERN RESOURCES INC.

Company Contact

Topeka, KS
Web: http://www.wstnres.com

Company Description

Former Name: Kansas Gas & Electric Co.
Assets: US$6,647,800,000
Employees: 5,960
SIC(s): 4911 Electric Services, 4931 Electric & Other Services Combined, 4932 Gas & Other Services Combined.

Nonmonetary Support

Value: $1,000 (1998)
Type: Donated Equipment
Volunteer Programs: Community Partners is a voluntary program for active and retired Western Resources employees.
Contact: Michel Philipp, Foundation President
Note: Provides support through both the company and the foundation.

Corporate Sponsorship

Type: Arts & cultural events; Sports events
Note: Supports cultural events, children and elderly program, and environmental causes.

Western Resources Foundation

Giving Contact

Foundation President
Western Resources Foundation
PO Box 889
Topeka, KS 66601-0889
Phone: (913)575-1927
Fax: (913)575-6399
Web: http://www.wr.com

Description

Founded: 1991
Organization Type: Corporate Foundation
Giving Locations: headquarters and operating communities.
Grant Types: Capital, Emergency, Employee Matching Gifts, General Support, Multiyear/Continuing Support.
Note: The company sponsors Community Partners, a voluntary program for active and retired Western Resources employees.

Giving Philosophy

'Western Resources is highly visible as a provider of electric and natural gas service in most of Kansas and northeastern Oklahoma. We recognize a corporate responsibility to support worthy projects and organizations that contribute to the social and economic welfare of the communities and people within our service territory.' *Western Resources Foundation Policy Guide on Contributions*

Financial Summary

Total Giving: $1,159,824 (1999); $1,287,000 (1998); $1,127,755 (1997). Note: Contributes through foundation only.

Typical Recipients

Civic & Public Affairs: Employment/Job Training
Education: Colleges & Universities
Environment: Environment-General
Health: Public Health
Social Services: Community Service Organizations, Senior Services, United Funds/United Ways, Youth Organizations

Contributions Analysis

Civic & Public Affairs: 10% to 15%. Local public affairs and employment programs.
Education: 15% to 20%. Colleges and universities.
Environment: 15% to 20%. Environmental programs, especially those that are part of a nonpartisan effort in conjunction with federal, state, or local government.
Social Services: 50% to 55%. United Way and youth programs, especially those dealing with employment opportunity enhancement. Also contributes to groups dealing with the problems of aging.

Application Procedures

Initial Contact: Submit a full proposal.
Application Requirements: Include a description of organization, description of project, indication of number of people who will be affected by the project, other funding sources, IRS tax status, and contact person.
Deadlines: None.
Review Process: Requests are initially reviewed by the foundation president for appropriateness and compliance with foundation guidelines and procedures before being reviewed by the Western Resources Foundation board.
Evaluative Criteria: Preference will be given to programs which serve children and youth, especially programs which enhance employment opportunities for youth; health programs which relate to the general well-being of the community; programs which serve the elderly, particularly energy assistance programs; and programs that protect and enhance the environment. Preference will be given to one-time projects, or projects that will be self-sustaining after the initial contribution; organizations supported by Western Resources employees and their families; organizations willing to acknowledge foundation contributions; and projects for which the foundation is the principal sponsor. sponsor.

Restrictions

Does not support individuals, religious organizations for sectarian purposes, political or lobbying groups, or organizations outside operating areas. Contributions to such organizations as Boy Scouts and 4-H will only be made on a regional or national level. Does not support sport programs or trips.

Additional Information

Foundation was established in 1991.

Corporate Officials

Thomas L. Grennan: executive vice president electric operationsrp secretary PRIM CORP EMPL executive vice president electric operations: Western Resources Inc.
Carl M. Koupal, Jr.: executive vice president, chief administrative officer B Bonne Terre, MO 1953. ED Mineral Area College; University of Missouri, Columbia BS (1975); University of Missouri Law School JD (1978). PRIM CORP EMPL executive vice president, chief administrative officer: Western Resources Inc.
Douglas T. Lake: executive vice president, chief strategic officer PRIM CORP EMPL executive vice president, chief strategic officer: Western Resources Inc.
William B. Moore: executive vice president, chief financial officer, treasurer B Kansas City, MO 1952. ED Wichita State University (1974); Wichita State University BBA (1977). PRIM CORP EMPL executive vice president, chief financial officer, treasurer: Western Resources Inc. CORP AFFIL director: Intrust Bank NA.
Richard D. Terrill: executive vice president, general counsel, corp. secretary PRIM CORP EMPL executive vice president, general counsel, corp. secretary: Western Resources Inc.
David C. Wittig: chairman, president, chief executive officer PRIM CORP EMPL chairman, president, chief executive officer: Western Resources Inc.

Foundation Officials

Greg Greenwood: vice president, treasurer
Ron Holt: trustee
Carl M. Koupal, Jr.: trustee (see above)
William B. Moore: director (see above)
Betty Ott: secretary
Michel Philipp: president

WESTERN &SOUTHERN LIFE INSURANCE CO.

Company Contact

Cincinnati, OH

Company Description

Employees: 5,495
SIC(s): 6311 Life Insurance.

Western-Southern Foundation, Inc.

Giving Contact

Richard Taulbee, Assistant Treasurer
Western-Southern Foundation
400 Broadway
Cincinnati, OH 45202-3341
Phone: (513)629-2121

Description

Founded: 1990
EIN: 311259670
Organization Type: Corporate Foundation
Giving Locations: OH
Grant Types: General Support, Matching, Scholarship.

Financial Summary

Total Giving: $943,000 (fiscal year ending March 31, 1997); $898,503 (fiscal 1996); $649,084 (fiscal 1995). Note: Contributes through foundation only.
Giving Analysis: Giving for fiscal 1996 includes: foundation ($751,957); foundation grants to United Way ($146,546); fiscal 1997: foundation ($786,760); foundation grants to United Way ($156,240)
Assets: $40,084,116 (fiscal 1997); $26,242,912 (fiscal 1996); $12,529,047 (fiscal 1995)
Gifts Received: $107,063 (fiscal 1997); $68,695 (fiscal 1996); $10,094,446 (fiscal 1995). Note: Foundation receives contributions from Western-Southern, Columbus Life Charitable Trust, and Continental General.

Typical Recipients

Arts & Humanities: Arts Associations & Councils, Arts Funds, Arts Institutes, Film & Video, Historic Preservation, Libraries, Museums/Galleries, Music, Performing Arts, Public Broadcasting

Civic & Public Affairs: African American Affairs, Botanical Gardens/Parks, Business/Free Enterprise, Chambers of Commerce, Civil Rights, Community Foundations, Economic Development, Economic Policy, Employment/Job Training, Civic & Public Affairs-General, Housing, Professional & Trade Associations, Urban & Community Affairs, Women's Affairs, Zoos/Aquariums

Education: Business Education, Colleges & Universities, Economic Education, Education Funds, Education-General, Minority Education, Private Education (Precollege), Science/Mathematics Education, Special Education, Student Aid, Vocational & Technical Education

Health: Cancer, Diabetes, Emergency/Ambulance Services, Health Organizations, Hospices, Hospitals, Long-Term Care, Mental Health, Multiple Sclerosis, Single-Disease Health Associations

International: International Peace & Security Issues

Religion: Churches, Dioceses, Religious Organizations, Religious Welfare

Social Services: Child Welfare, Community Service Organizations, Homes, People with Disabilities, Scouts, Senior Services, Shelters/Homelessness, United Funds/United Ways, Youth Organizations

Contributions Analysis

Arts & Humanities: 24%. Majority of funding supports museums, arts funds, arts festivals, and historic preservation in Cincinnati, OH.

Civic & Public Affairs: 18%. Contributes to the Greater Cincinnati Foundation. Other recipients include a zoo and botanical garden, and professional and trade associations promoting the insurance business.

Education: 26%. Primarily supports higher education, with an emphasis on institutions located in Ohio. Other interests include minority and economic education.

Health: 10%. Emphasis is on single-disease health associations, long-term care, and preventative medicine.

Religion: 2%. Supports ministries, religious welfare, churches, and other religious organizations.

Social Services: 20%. Majority of funding supports various United Way agencies in Ohio. Other recipients include youth organizations and food and clothing distributors, and people with disabilities.

Note: Total contributions in 1997.

Application Procedures

Initial Contact: Send a brief letter.

Application Requirements: Include a description of organization and project, amount requested, and purpose of funds sought.

Deadlines: None.

Corporate Officials

John F. Barrett: president, chief executive officer, director B 1949. ED University of Cincinnati (1971). PRIM CORP EMPL president, chief executive officer, director: Western & Southern Life Insurance Co. ADD CORP EMPL president: Western Southern Life Assurance Co. CORP AFFIL director: Fifth Third Bank; director: Fifth Third Bancorp; director: Cincinnati Bell Inc.; director: Convergys Corp.; director: Andersons Inc. NONPR AFFIL vice chairmanr: Greater Cincinnati Chamber of Commerce.

J. Thomas Lancaster: vice president, treasurer PRIM CORP EMPL vice president, treasurer: Western & Southern Life Insurance Co.

Richard Taulbee: vice president B Cincinnati, OH 1951. ED University of Cincinnati (1974). PRIM CORP EMPL vice president: Western & Southern Life Insurance Co.

William Joseph Williams: chairman, director B Cincinnati, OH 1915. ED Georgetown University AB (1937); Harvard University (1938). PRIM CORP EMPL chairman, director: Western & Southern Life Insurance Co. CORP AFFIL director: Columbus Life Insurance Co. Ohio.

Foundation Officials

John F. Barrett: trustee (see above)

J. Thomas Lancaster: assistant treasurer (see above)

Richard Taulbee: assistant treasurer (see above)

William Joseph Williams: trustee (see above)

Grants Analysis

Disclosure Period: fiscal year ending March 31, 1997

Total Grants: $786,760*

Number of Grants: 151

Average Grant: $5,210

Highest Grant: $160,583

Typical Range: $50 to $5,000 and $10,000 to $100,000

*Note: Giving excludes United Way.

Recent Grants

Note: Grants derived from 1997 Form 990.

Arts & Humanities

100,000	Cincinnati Art Museum, Cincinnati, OH
50,600	Fine Arts Fund, Cincinnati, OH
33,333	Cincinnati Symphony Orchestra, Cincinnati, OH
20,000	Taft Museum, Cincinnati, OH
10,050	Old St. Mary's Preservation Fund, Kansas City, MO
2,000	WCET/Channel 48, Cincinnati, OH
1,600	United Arts, Omaha, NE
1,000	Syrian Shrine Circus

Civic & Public Affairs

50,000	Greater Cincinnati Foundation, Cincinnati, OH
40,000	Cincinnati Zoo and Botanical Gardens, Cincinnati, OH
20,000	Urban League, Cincinnati, OH
15,000	Downtown Cincinnati, Cincinnati, OH
10,000	Over the Rhine Foundation, Cincinnati, OH
8,000	Cincinnati Parks Board Foundation, Cincinnati, OH
5,000	Cincinnati Chamber of Commerce Foundation, Cincinnati, OH
5,000	Habitat for Humanity
5,000	Jack Rabe
5,000	Work Rehabilitation Center, Cincinnati, OH
2,500	Youth Employment Services
1,263	Million Dollar Round Table, Park Ridge, IL

Education

160,583	Xavier University, Cincinnati, OH
30,000	Life Education Fund, Washington, DC
10,150	Northern Kentucky University, Highland Heights, KY
10,100	Thomas More College, Crestview Hills, KY
7,805	Catholic Inner-City Schools Education Fund
6,200	CISE
3,075	Junior Achievement
3,000	Nebraska Independent College Foundation, Omaha, NE
2,500	Greater Cincinnati Center for Economic Education, Cincinnati, OH
2,375	College of Mount St. Joseph, Cincinnati, OH
2,000	College Fund/UNCF
2,000	Hoffman School
1,500	University of Cincinnati Foundation, Cincinnati, OH
1,285	University of Cincinnati, Cincinnati, OH

Health

67,500	Multiple Sclerosis Society
10,100	Hospice, Cincinnati, OH
5,000	Sisters of Notre Dame de Namur, Washington, DC
4,996	Louisiana Oncology Associates, Lafayette, LA
3,500	University Emergency Physicians

Religion

12,278	Salvation Army
5,000	Milford Spiritual Center
2,000	Franciscan Foundation
1,000	St. Joseph Orphanage

Social Services

152,489	United Way
10,000	Tender Mercies, Norwood, OH
3,751	United Way of the Midlands, Omaha, NE
3,705	Neediest Kids of All, Cincinnati, OH
3,000	Children's Home of Northern Kentucky, KY
2,500	Children's Fund of Beech Acres
2,000	Northern Kentucky Association for the Retarded, KY

WESTVACO CORP.

Company Contact

New York, NY

Company Description

Revenue: US$2,831,200,000 (1999)

Employees: 12,750 (1999)

SIC(s): 2611 Pulp Mills, 2621 Paper Mills, 2631 Paperboard Mills, 2653 Corrugated & Solid Fiber Boxes.

Operating Locations

Australia: Westvaco Pacific Pty. Ltd., North Sydney; Belgium: Westvaco Europe, SA, Brussels; Brazil: Rigesa, Ltda., Sau Paulo; Canada: Westvaco Canada, Ltd., Mississauga; Czech Republic: Westvaco Svitavy, SPOL, SRO, Svitany; Hong Kong: Westvaco Hong Kong, Ltd., Hong Kong; Japan: Westvaco Asia, KK, Tokyo

Nonmonetary Support

Note: Company gives nonmonetary support.

Westvaco Foundation Trust

Giving Contact

Roger Holmes, Secretary, Contributions Committee
Westvaco Corp.
299 Park Ave.
New York, NY 10171
Phone: (212)318-5288
Fax: (212)318-5070

Description

EIN: 136021319

Organization Type: Corporate Foundation

Giving Locations: headquarters and operating communities.

Grant Types: Capital, Emergency, Employee Matching Gifts, Endowment, Fellowship, General Support, Multiyear/Continuing Support.

Note: Employee matching gift ratio: 1 to 1.5 from $25 to $2,000 annually.

Financial Summary

Total Giving: $1,552,929 (fiscal year ending September 30, 1998); $2,500,000 (fiscal 1997 approx); $1,465,397 (fiscal 1996). Note: Contributes through corporate direct giving program and foundation.

Giving Analysis: Giving for fiscal 1996 includes: foundation grants to United Way ($1,182,810); foundation matching gifts ($282,587); fiscal 1998: foundation ($781,598); foundation grants to United Way ($564,037)
Assets: $7,263,558 (fiscal 1998); $10,373,762 (fiscal 1997); $8,494,884 (fiscal 1996)
Gifts Received: $1,500,000 (fiscal 1998); $1,500,000 (fiscal 1996); $1,100,000 (fiscal 1995). Note: The foundation receives contributions from Westvaco Corp.

Typical Recipients

Arts & Humanities: Arts Centers, Historic Preservation, History & Archaeology, Libraries, Museums/Galleries, Music, Opera, Performing Arts, Public Broadcasting, Theater
Civic & Public Affairs: African American Affairs, Botanical Gardens/Parks, Business/Free Enterprise, Civil Rights, Economic Development, Economic Policy, Employment/Job Training, Housing, Nonprofit Management, Professional & Trade Associations, Public Policy, Safety, Urban & Community Affairs, Women's Affairs, Zoos/Aquariums
Education: Business Education, Colleges & Universities, Community & Junior Colleges, Continuing Education, Education Associations, Education Funds, Elementary Education (Private), Engineering/Technological Education, International Studies, International Studies, Literacy, Medical Education, Minority Education, Private Education (Precollege), Religious Education, Science/Mathematics Education
Environment: Forestry, Environment-General, Resource Conservation, Wildlife Protection
Health: Cancer, Health Funds, Health Organizations, Hospitals, Medical Rehabilitation, Medical Research, Single-Disease Health Associations
International: Foreign Arts Organizations, International Development, International Relations
Religion: Religious Welfare
Science: Scientific Labs
Social Services: Animal Protection, Community Service Organizations, Counseling, People with Disabilities, Recreation & Athletics, Substance Abuse, United Funds/United Ways, YMCA/YWCA/YMHA/YWHA, Youth Organizations

Contributions Analysis

Giving Priorities: Social welfare, education, and health. Foundation supports U.S. organizations with an interest in international affairs and relations.
Arts & Humanities: 3%. Supports public broadcasting, opera, and arts funds.
Civic & Public Affairs: 14%. Supports public policy organizations, business and free enterprise, and urban and community affairs groups.
Education: 22%. Supports universities and colleges, education funds, technology and minority education, and education associations. Some interest in pulp and paper sciences and forestry. Also includes matching grants to educational institutions.
Environment: 9%. Primarily for conservation.
Health: About 4%. Primarily supports hospitals and medical centers. Other interests include single-disease health associations, health organizations, and medical research.
International: 1%. International development.
Social Services: About 47%. Primarily supports united funds. Recipients of smaller amounts include youth organizations, drug and alcohol programs, community service organizations, and recreation and athletics.
Note: Total contributions in fiscal 1998.

Application Procedures

Initial Contact: Send a brief letter or proposal.
Application Requirements: Include a description of organization, amount requested, purpose of funds sought, and proof of tax-exempt status.
Deadlines: None; July is the recommended time to apply.
Decision Notification: Usually within one month.
Notes: Program is decentralized; recommended procedure is to apply through company operating units rather than directly to the foundation.

Corporate Officials

William S. Beaver: treasurer, vice president B Lancaster, PA 1951. ED Dickinson College BA (1973); Harvard University MBA (1978). PRIM CORP EMPL treasurer, vice president: Westvaco Corp. CORP AFFIL treasurer: Westvaco Development Corp.
John A. Luke, Jr.: chairman, president, chief executive officer, director B New York, NY 1948. ED Lawrence University BA (1971); University of Pennsylvania Wharton School MBA (1979). PRIM CORP EMPL chairman, president, chief executive officer, director: Westvaco Corp. CORP AFFIL director: FM Global Insurance; director: Timken Co.; director: Arkwright Mutual Insurance Co.; director: Bank New York Co. Inc.; director: Arkwright Insurance Co. NONPR AFFIL board governors: NCASI; director: United Negro College Fund; trustee: Lawrence University; member: Council Foreign Relations; trustee: Institute Paper Science Technology; member executive committee, director: American Forest & Paper Association; director: Council Americas; director: America Society; chairman: American Forest Foundation. CLUB AFFIL University Club; Commonwealth Club; The Links Club.
James E. Stoveken, Jr.: senior vice president B 1939. ED University of Delaware BS (1968); University of Delaware MBA (1969). PRIM CORP EMPL senior vice president: Westvaco Corp.

Foundation Officials

William S. Beaver: trustee (see above)
James E. Stoveken, Jr.: trustee (see above)

Grants Analysis

Disclosure Period: fiscal year ending September 30, 1998
Total Grants: $781,598*
Number of Grants: 63
Average Grant: $12,406
Typical Range: $1,000 to $5,000
*Note: Giving excludes United Way; matching gifts.

Recent Grants

Note: Grants derived from fiscal 1998 Form 990.

Arts & Humanities

14,500 WPSD-TV Lions Club Telethon, New York, NY
10,000 Opera Orchestra of New York, New York, NY
8,500 LSP Governor's Mansion Foundation, Annapolis, MD

Civic & Public Affairs

50,000 South Carolina Aquarium, Charleston, SC
40,000 The New York Botanical Garden, New York, NY
25,000 Local Initiatives Support Corporation, New York
20,000 The English Speaking Union for the Luard Scholarship, New York, NY
15,000 American Enterprise Institute, Washington, DC
15,000 LSP the Heritage Foundation, Washington, DC
10,000 LSP W.E.B. Dubois Institute, Cambridge, MA
10,000 W.E.B. Dubois Institute, Cambridge, MA

Education

100,000 Clark Atlanta University, Atlanta, GA
50,000 United Negro College Fund, New York, NY
50,000 West Virginia University Foundation, Morgantown, WV
30,000 Eisenhower Exchange Fellowship, Philadelphia, PA
16,500 Rensselaer Polytechnic Institute, Rensselaer, NY
10,000 North Carolina State University-Pulp & Paper Foundation, Inc., Raleigh, NC
10,000 Prep for Prep, New York, NY
10,000 Wharton Partnership of the Wharton School, University of Pennsylvania, Philadelphia, PA
7,000 Miami University Pulp & Paper Foundation, Miami, OH

Environment

60,000 The Nature Conservancy, New York
20,000 The Annapolis Center for Environmental Quality, Annapolis, MD
20,000 Ducks Unlimited Habitat 2000 Campaign, Memphis, TN
15,000 The Nature Conservancy, Washington, DC

Health

50,000 Memorial Sloan-Kettering Cancer Center, New York, NY

International

12,000 The International Tennis Hall of Fame, Inc., New York, NY
7,500 Accion International, New York, NY

Social Services

100,000 Trident United Way, Charleston, SC
65,000 County United Way, New York, NY
49,930 United Way of Greater Richmond, Richmond, VA
45,000 Great Alleghany United Fund, Covington, VA
40,000 United Way of Pioneer Valley, Springfield, MA
37,709 United Way of Tri-State, New York, NY
36,496 United Way Services, New York, NY
25,000 Police Athletic League, New York, NY
24,400 United Way of Central Maryland, Baltimore, MD
21,010 United Way of Greater Los Angeles, Los Angeles, CA
18,870 United Way of Bradley County, Cleveland, TN
18,870 United Way of Delaware, Wilmington, DE
16,200 Trident United Way, Charleston, SC
15,500 LSP Ballard County United Appeal, New York, NY
13,000 United Way of Blair County, Altoona, PA
12,500 Paducah-Mccracken County United Way, Paducah, KY
10,850 United Way of Metropolitan Dallas Inc., Dallas, TX
9,420 United Way Capital Area, Austin, TX
9,360 United Way of Central Blair County Inc., Altoona, PA
8,520 United Way of Central Indiana, Indianapolis, IN
7,500 United Way, New York, NY
7,185 United Way of Metropolitan Atlanta Inc., Atlanta, GA
6,230 United Way of Lake County Inc, Waukegan, IL

WEYERHAEUSER CO.

Company Contact

Federal Way, WA
Web: http://www.weyerhaeuser.com

Company Description

Revenue: US$12,262,000,000 (1999)
Profit: US$527,000,000 (1999)
Employees: 35,000
Fortune Rank: 145, per FORTUNE Magazine's list of 500 Largest U.S. Corporations (1999).
FF 145

SIC(s): 2411 Logging, 2421 Sawmills & Planing Mills--General, 2431 Millwork, 2435 Hardwood Veneer & Plywood.

Operating Locations

Belgium: Weyerhauser SA, Brussels; Canada: Weyehauser Canada Ltd., Vancouver; Hong Kong: Weyehauser (Far East) Ltd., Wan Chai; Japan: Weyerhauser Japan Ltd., Tokyo

Nonmonetary Support

Value: $4,700,000 (1993)
Type: Cause-related Marketing & Promotion; Donated Equipment; Donated Products; Loaned Employees; Loaned Executives; Workplace Solicitation
Contact: Penny Paul, Executive Assistant
Note: Nonmonetary support is contributed directly through the company. Workplace solicitation is for the United Way only.

Corporate Sponsorship

Type: Arts & cultural events; Festivals/fairs; Sports events

Weyerhaeuser Co. Foundation

Giving Contact

Elizabeth A. Crossman, Vice President
Weyerhaeuser Co. Foundation
CH1L 32
PO Box 2999
Tacoma, WA 98477-2999
Phone: (253)924-3159
Fax: (253)924-3658

Description

EIN: 916024225
Organization Type: Corporate Foundation
Giving Locations: AL; AR; MS; NC; OK; OR; WA nationally, with emphasis on communities, particularly remote communities, in which company has significant numbers of employees.
Grant Types: Award, Capital, Department, Employee Matching Gifts, General Support, Project.
Note: Employee matching gift ratio: 1 to 1 for higher education only.

Giving Philosophy

'The Foundation's mission is: (1) to improve the quality of life in communities where Wyerhaeuser has a major presence, and (2) to provide leadership that increases public understanding of issues where society's needs intersect with the interest of the forest products industry.'
'The majority of the Foundation's giving is in the many, often rural, communities where Weyerhaeuser has a major presence and a significant number of employees. Priority is given to educational programs that improve the quality of public schools and promote public awareness of natural-resource management.'
'Our other priority is in those unique opportunities where society's needs and the interests of the forest products industry converge. Our priorities are: forestry practices; manufacturing's effects on air, land, and water; energy; international trade; resource utilization and conservation; and diversity.' *Weyerhaeuser Company Foundation 1994-96 Biennial Report*

Financial Summary

Total Giving: $6,732,356 (1997); $6,774,871 (1996); $5,403,442 (1995). Note: Contributes through corporate direct giving program and foundation. 1997 Giving includes foundation ($5,550,506); matching gifts ($134,317); United Way ($1,047,533).
Assets: $2,238,078 (1995); $7,496,235 (1994); $14,356,780 (1993)
Gifts Received: $12,500,000 (1995); $19,268 (1994); $13,150,932 (1993). Note: Foundation receives contributions from Weyerhaeuser Company.

Typical Recipients

Arts & Humanities: Arts Associations & Councils, Arts Funds, Community Arts, Dance, Historic Preservation, History & Archaeology, Libraries, Museums/Galleries, Music, Opera, Public Broadcasting, Theater
Civic & Public Affairs: African American Affairs, Business/Free Enterprise, Economic Development, Employment/Job Training, Housing, Legal Aid, Municipalities/Towns, Native American Affairs, Public Policy, Rural Affairs, Safety, Urban & Community Affairs, Zoos/Aquariums
Education: Business Education, Colleges & Universities, Community & Junior Colleges, Economic Education, Education Associations, Education Funds, Elementary Education (Private), Elementary Education (Public), Engineering/Technological Education, Environmental Education, Education-General, Minority Education, Private Education (Precollege), Public Education (Precollege), Science/Mathematics Education, Student Aid, Vocational & Technical Education
Environment: Forestry, Environment-General, Resource Conservation, Wildlife Protection
Health: Children's Health/Hospitals, Clinics/Medical Centers, Emergency/Ambulance Services, Hospices, Hospitals, Public Health
International: Foreign Educational Institutions, International Affairs, International Development, International Environmental Issues, International Relief Efforts
Religion: Churches
Science: Science Museums, Scientific Centers & Institutes
Social Services: Child Welfare, Community Centers, Community Service Organizations, Family Services, People with Disabilities, Recreation & Athletics, Scouts, Shelters/Homelessness, Substance Abuse, United Funds/United Ways, Volunteer Services, YMCA/YWCA/YMHA/YWHA, Youth Organizations

Contributions Analysis

Giving Priorities: Community services, education, public policy, and land management. Foundation and corporate contributions place high emphasis on community improvement services in rural and remote operating communities.
Arts & Humanities: Less than 5%. Special emphasis is placed on projects promotingrural access to the arts.
Civic & Public Affairs: 15% to 20%. Environmental segment includes support for public policy development that address ways to maintain a reasonable balancebetween environmental protection and a viable economy. Housing component promotes low-income and affordable housing, primarily to further public/private partnerships. Some awards are also made for projects that will have a significant impact on housing policies. The civic and community initiatives and facilities segment is limited to Weyerhaeuser's major communities, with emphasis on Seattle-Tacoma, WA area. In most cases, the foundation will not consider requests that are in excess of 10% of the project's cost. (United Funds & United Way) 15% to 20%.
Education: 25% to 30%. One-time grants to colleges and universities in Weyerhaeuser operating locations for research, curriculum, and for issues related to the forest products industry. Also supports curriculum improvement and scholarships to community colleges, usually in disciplines related to careers in the forest products industry. Elementary and secondary schools receive support for efforts leading to district-wide improvements in public schools. Two scholarship programs are offered for children of employees. Mississippi, Oklahoma, North Carolina, and Arkansas are current priorities.
Environment: 5%. Funds public land, forest foundation, and the environmental concerns.
Health: Less than 5%. Supports preventive health care services that show a reasonable promise of reducing costs. Grants for facilities are normally considered only in key Weyerhaeuser locales where no other services are available. No awards are made to national-level organizations. The foundation supports the United Way as the primary means for helping with critical human services.
International: 10% to 15%. Supports international Habitat for Humanity,international education, and international corrugated packaging.
Social Services: 10% to 15%. Housing, family services, and youth organizations.

Application Procedures

Initial Contact: call for application
Application Requirements: completed application, including: description of project and sponsoring organization; statement of why project is consistent with foundation guidelines; project cost, sources of funding, and amount requested; evidence of tax-exempt status
Deadlines: requests received after September may not be considered until budgets are established for the following year
Review Process: appropriate review committee is consulted and request is considered within budget constraints/local priorities
Evaluative Criteria: direct relevance to foundation's mission and geographic interests; evidence that project will address important need; innovative and cost-effective approaches; impact consistent with proposed expenditure; evidence that project does not duplicate other efforts; indication that other financial support likely will be available; demonstrated competence of administration and staff
Decision Notification: inquiries acknowledged as soon as possible (normally within 30 days); applicants should allow 90 to 120 days for a decision
Notes: If further consideration is warranted, foundation may ask for additional information or formal proposal; personal meetings or site visits are normally arranged only for projects that have passed initial application.

Restrictions

Does not support religious, sacramental, or theological purposes; political campaigns; to influence legislation; for tickets or tables at fundraising events; individuals; or direct grants to organizations already receiving foundation funds through an umbrella organization.
Discourages applications seeking to cover operating deficits; for services that the public sector should reasonably be expected to provide; to establish endowments or memorials; for research or conferences outside the forest products industry; for hospital building or equipment campaigns that will result in higher costs to health-care users; for services outside Weyerhaeuser operating area; for general administrative expenses; or for amounts that are clearly unrealistic given the foundation's total annual budget.
The foundation will not consider requests that do not meet its program and geographic criterion. If organizations are unsure about the presence of a Weyerhaeuser facility in their community, write or call the foundation for confirmation before submitting a grant request.

Additional Information

In 1998, the foundation launched a program that supports employee-initiated volunteer projects. Foundation makes cash grants only, with a $1,000 minimum. Normally, support is committed for one year at a time. Grants may be made to umbrella organizations or combined campaigns.
Publications: Biennial Report (includes Current Guidelines); Grant Application; Volunteer Employee Pamphlet

Corporate Officials

William R. Corbin: executive vice president timberlands & distribution PRIM CORP EMPL executive vice president timberlands & distribution: Weyerhaeuser Co. ADD CORP EMPL corporate executive: Weyerhaeuser International.

Richard C. Gozon: executive vice president pulp paper & packaging PRIM CORP EMPL executive vice president pulp paper & packaging: Weyerhaeuser Co. CORP AFFIL director: UGI Corp.; director: UGI Utilities Inc.; director: Amerisource Health Corp.

Steven Richard Hill: senior vice president human resources B Oakland, CA 1947. ED University of California at Berkeley BS (1969); University of California, Los Angeles MBA (1971). PRIM CORP EMPL senior vice president human resources: Weyerhaeuser Co. ADD CORP EMPL director: Weyerhaeuser - Canada.

Norman E. Johnson: senior vice president technology B 1933. ED Harvard University Advanced Management Program (1955); Oregon State University MS (1957); University of California at Berkeley PhD (1961). PRIM CORP EMPL senior vice president technology: Weyerhaeuser Co.

Thomas M. Luthy: senior vice president wood products PRIM CORP EMPL senior vice president wood products: Weyerhaeuser Co.

Sandy D. McDade: secretary B Seattle, WA 1952. ED Whitman College (1974); University of Puget Sound (1979). PRIM CORP EMPL secretary: Weyerhaeuser Co. NONPR AFFIL member: American Society of Corporate Secretaries.

Kenneth J. Stancato: vice president, controller B 1938. ED Colorado State University BS (1960). PRIM CORP EMPL vice president, controller: Weyerhaeuser Co..

William Charles Stivers: senior vice president, chief financial officer, treasurer B Modesto, CA 1938. ED Stanford University BA (1960); University of Southern California MBA (1963); Harvard University Graduate School of Business Administration (1977). PRIM CORP EMPL senior vice president, chief financial officer, treasurer: Weyerhaeuser Co. CORP AFFIL vice president fin, director: Weyerhaeuser Real Estate Co.; director: Protection Mutual Insurance Co.; president, director: S&S Land & Cattle Co.; director: First Interstate Bancorp; member national advisory board: Chase Manhattan Corp.; member: Chemical Banking Corp. NONPR AFFIL director: Pacific Rim Finance Center Graduate School Business, University Washington; trustee, chairman: Saint Francis Community Hospital; trustee: Franciscan Health Systems West; member management & steering committee: American Forest & Paper Association.

George Hunt Weyerhaeuser: director B Seattle, WA 1926. ED Yale University BSIE (1949). CORP AFFIL director: SAFECO Corp.; director: Chevron Corp.; director: Dietzgen Corp.; director: Boeing Co. NONPR AFFIL member: Business Roundtable; member: Washington State Business Roundtable; member: Business Council.

Foundation Officials

Mary L. Cabral: assistant controller

William R. Corbin: trustee (see above)

Elizabeth A. Crossman: vice president PRIM CORP EMPL director corporate contributions: Weyerhaeuser Co.

Richard C. Gozon: trustee (see above)

Steven Richard Hill: trustee (see above)

Mack L. Hogans: chairman, president, trustee B Abbeville, AL 1949. ED University of Michigan (1971); University of Washington (1976). PRIM CORP EMPL senior vice president corporate affairs: Weyerhaeuser Co.

Norman E. Johnson: trustee (see above)

C. Stephen Lewis: trustee B 1944. PRIM CORP EMPL president, chief executive officer: Weyerhaeuser Real Estate Co.

Sandy D. McDade: assistant secretary legal affairs (see above)

Susan M. Mersereau: trustee B Portland, OR 1946. ED Scripps College BA (1968); University of Chicago MA (1971); Antioch College MA (1990). PRIM CORP EMPL vice president: Weyerhaeuser Co. NONPR AFFIL director: King County United Way.

Kenneth J. Stancato: controller (see above)

William Charles Stivers: treasurer, trustee (see above)

Linda L. Terrien: assistant treasurer

Karen L. Veitenhans: secretary

George Hunt Weyerhaeuser: trustee (see above)

Robert B. Wilson: trustee

Grants Analysis

Disclosure Period: calendar year ending 1997
Total Grants: $5,550,506*
Number of Grants: 740
Average Grant: $7,501
Highest Grant: $281,980
Typical Range: $1,000 to $10,000
*Note: Giving excludes matching gifts; United Way.

Recent Grants

Note: Grants derived from 1997 Form 990.

Arts & Humanities

110,000 Corporate Council for Arts, Seattle, WA
50,000 Fayette County Memorial Library, Fayette, AL

Civic & Public Affairs

212,500 Local Initiatives Support Corporation
50,000 City of Idabel
50,000 Long Live the Kings, Redmond, WA
50,000 Resources for the Future, Washington, DC
50,000 Stop Oregon Litter and Vandalism, Portland, OR
35,000 American Council for Capital Formation Center for Policy Research, Washington, DC
33,000 Tacoma Urban League, Tacoma, WA
30,000 Pacific Legal Foundation, Sacramento, CA
25,000 City of Barnsville
25,000 Craven County, New Bern, NC
25,000 Willapa Alliance, South Bend, WA

Education

281,980 National Merit Scholarship Corporation, Evanston, IL
250,000 Oregon State University Foundation, Corvallis, OR
111,690 Citizens Scholarship Foundation of America, St. Peter, MN
50,000 Northwest Regional Educational Laboratory, Portland, OR
50,000 South Georgia Technical Institute Foundation, Americus, GA
50,000 University of Washington College of Forestry
32,000 Washington County Schools
30,000 University of Washington, Seattle, WA -- support College of Forest Resources
27,000 University of Arizona, Tucson, AZ
25,000 Seattle University, Seattle, WA
25,000 University of Wisconsin Stevens Point Paper Science Foundation, Stevens Point, WI

Environment

59,430 American Forest Foundation, Washington, DC
50,000 Trust for Public Land, New York, NY
30,000 Mountains to Sound Greenway Trust, Seattle, WA
29,870 American Forest Foundation, Washington, DC

Health

75,000 American Red Cross Seattle-King County Chapter
30,000 Arkansas Children's Hospital Foundation, Little Rock, AR

International

185,000 University of British Columbia, Vancouver, BC, Canada
185,000 University of British Columbia, Vancouver, BC, Canada
100,000 Habitat for Humanity International, Denver, CO
100,000 Habitat for Humanity International, Denver, CO
73,220 University of British Columbia, Vancouver, BC, Canada
73,220 University of British Columbia, Vancouver, BC, Canada
30,000 International Corrugated Packaging Foundation, Alexandria, VA
30,000 International Corrugated Packaging Foundation, Alexandria, VA
25,000 Habitat for Humanity International, Denver, CO
25,000 Habitat for Humanity International, Denver, CO

Science

75,000 Arkansas Museum of Science and History, Little Rock, AR
25,000 Discovery Institute

Social Services

180,510 United Way of Pierce County, Tacoma, WA
118,490 United Way of King County, Seattle, WA
100,000 United Way of Lane County, Eugene, OR
68,000 United Way of Cowlitz County, Longview, WA
60,000 United Way of Lane County, Eugene, OR
50,000 City of Federal Way Parks and Recreation Commission
30,000 Marshfield Area United Way, Marshfield, WI
30,000 United Way
28,305 United Way of Washington County
25,000 South King County Multi-Service Center, Federal Way, WA
25,000 United Way of Grays Harbor, Aberdeen, WA
25,000 United Way of Southwestern Oregon, Coos Bay, OR
24,300 Girl Scouts of America of Coastal Carolina, Goldsboro, NC

Whirlpool Corp.

Company Contact

Benton Harbor, MI
Web: http://www.whirlpoolcorp.com

Company Description

Revenue: US$10,511,000,000 (1999)
Profit: US$347,000,000 (1999)
Employees: 59,000
Fortune Rank: 164, per FORTUNE Magazine's list of 500 Largest U.S. Corporations (1999).
FF 164
SIC(s): 3582 Commercial Laundry Equipment, 3585 Refrigeration & Heating Equipment, 3631 Household Cooking Equipment, 3633 Household Laundry Equipment.

Operating Locations

Brazil: Embraco SA, Joinville; Multibras SA, Joinville, Sao Bernardo do Campo; Whirlpool do Brazil SA, Sau Paulo; Canada: Inglis Limited, Mississauga; Hong Kong: Whirlpool-Asia, Causeway Bay; Italy: Aspera Srl, Turin; Whirlpool Europe, Varese; Mexico: Vitromatic, SA de CV, Mexico

Whirlpool Foundation

Giving Contact

Colleen D. Keast, Executive Director
Whirlpool Foundation
2000 North M-63
Benton Harbor, MI 49022
Phone: (616)923-5000
Fax: (616)923-3214

Alternate Contact

Barbara A. Hall
Phone: (616)923-5580

Description

EIN: 386077342
Organization Type: Corporate Foundation
Giving Locations: operating locations.
Grant Types: Employee Matching Gifts, Project, Scholarship.
Note: Employee matching gift ratio: 1 to 1. Scholarships are for employees' children only.

Financial Summary

Total Giving: $4,953,489 (1997); $3,952,964 (1996); $6,086,651 (1995). Note: Contributes through corporate direct giving program and foundation. 1997 Giving includes foundation ($2,882,034); matching gifts ($779,235); scholarship ($353,000); United Way ($939,220).
Assets: $15,983,268 (1997); $17,680,202 (1996); $17,973,642 (1995)
Gifts Received: $2,000,000 (1996); $2,000,000 (1995). Note: Foundation receives gifts from Whirlpool Corp.

Typical Recipients

Arts & Humanities: Arts Associations & Councils, Arts Centers, Arts Funds, Arts Institutes, Ballet, Community Arts, Dance, Ethnic & Folk Arts, Arts & Humanities-General, Historic Preservation, History & Archaeology, Libraries, Literary Arts, Museums/ Galleries, Music, Opera, Performing Arts, Public Broadcasting, Theater, Visual Arts
Civic & Public Affairs: Botanical Gardens/Parks, Business/Free Enterprise, Civil Rights, Clubs, Community Foundations, Economic Development, Economic Policy, Employment/Job Training, First Amendment Issues, Civic & Public Affairs-General, Hispanic Affairs, Housing, Law & Justice, Municipalities/ Towns, Nonprofit Management, Professional & Trade Associations, Public Policy, Safety, Urban & Community Affairs, Women's Affairs
Education: Afterschool/Enrichment Programs, Arts/ Humanities Education, Business Education, Colleges & Universities, Community & Junior Colleges, Economic Education, Education Associations, Education Funds, Education Reform, Elementary Education (Private), Engineering/Technological Education, Education-General, International Studies, Journalism/Media Education, Literacy, Medical Education, Minority Education, Private Education (Precollege), Public Education (Precollege), Science/Mathematics Education, Secondary Education (Private), Social Sciences Education, Student Aid, Vocational & Technical Education
Environment: Environment-General
Health: Clinics/Medical Centers, Emergency/Ambulance Services, Health Organizations, Hospitals
International: Foreign Educational Institutions, Health Care/Hospitals, International Development, International Organizations, International Relations
Religion: Religious Welfare
Science: Science Exhibits & Fairs, Scientific Centers & Institutes, Scientific Organizations
Social Services: Animal Protection, Big Brother/Big Sister, Child Welfare, Community Centers, Community Service Organizations, Counseling, Day Care, Delinquency & Criminal Rehabilitation, Domestic Violence, Family Planning, Family Services, Food/Clothing Distribution, Homes, People with Disabilities, Recreation & Athletics, Senior Services, Shelters/ Homelessness, Social Services-General, Substance Abuse, United Funds/United Ways, Volunteer Services, YMCA/YWCA/YMHA/YWHA, Youth Organizations

Contributions Analysis

Giving Priorities: Community affairs, education, health, and social welfare. Currently, contributions to international organizations are limited. However, Whirlpool has begun to expand into a world market, and a global contributions program has been undertaken, including the expansion of its scholarship program into Canada. Program strategies focus on 'Helping Our Communities Build A Better World.' Contributions fall into three categories: lifelong learning, cultural diversity, and contemporary family life.
Arts & Humanities: 20% to 25% of citizenship grants. Primarily supports museums, arts centers, symphony orchestras, and arts institutes.
Civic & Public Affairs: About 10% of strategic grants. Support includes the anti-bias programs of the Raintree Girl Scout Council, Inc. of Evansville, Indiana and a training program for teachers and students that equips them with the skills necessary to teach others about diversity and mediate related conflicts. 10% to 15% of citizenship grants. Supportscommunity affairs organizations concerned with businesses, municipalities, housing, law and justice, environmental affairs, and economic development. (United Funds & United Way) About 30% of total grants. Foundation offers a one-to-one match for every dollar US-based employees contribute.
Education: 65% to 70% of strategic grants. Includes support to the Forum for Intercultural Communications to train Slovakian business women and entrepreneurs in management and free-market economy skills. Also, supports the 9 to 5 Working Women Education Fund, a career advancement training program for non-management and administrative support to women workers. 30% to 35% of citizenship grants. Supports colleges and universities, with interests in science, technological, business, minority education, arts and humanities education and higher education associations. Scholarships are given to children of employees whodemonstrate academic and personal excellence.
Health: 30% to 35% of citizenship grants. Supports traditional youth groups, community services, family planning, and programs for the handicapped, the elderly, and children.
Social Services: 25% to 30% of strategic grants. Support goes to the prevention of domestic violence, including an advertising campaign to raise awareness of domestic violence issues, and YMCAs to provide scholarship assistance to low-income families needing day care for their children.

Application Procedures

Initial Contact: brief letter or telephone call for guidelines and application form
Deadlines: January 31, April 1, July 1, and October 1

Restrictions

Does not support dinners or special events, fraternal organizations, goodwill advertising, individuals, political or lobbying groups, or religious organizations for sectarian purposes.

Corporate Officials

J. C. Anderson: vice president, president, chief executive officer, director PRIM CORP EMPL vice president: Whirlpool Corp.
Bradley John Bell: vice president, treasurer B Chicago, IL 1952. ED University of Illinois BS (1974); Harvard University Graduate School of Business Administration MBA (1978). PRIM CORP EMPL vice president, treasurer: Whirlpool Corp. CORP AFFIL director: Morgan Group Inc.; treasurer: Whirlpool Financial Corp. DE; director: Lynch Corp.
Bruce K. Berger: vice president corporate affairs PRIM CORP EMPL vice president corporate affairs: Whirlpool Corp.
William D. Marohn: vice chairman, director B Toledo, OH 1940. ED University of Toledo BSME (1964). PRIM CORP EMPL vice chairman, director: Whirlpool Corp. CORP AFFIL director: Michigan First.
David Ray Whitwam: chairman, president, chief executive officer, director B Madison, WI 1942. ED University of Wisconsin BS (1967). PRIM CORP EMPL chairman, president, chief executive officer, director: Whirlpool Corp. CORP AFFIL director: Combustion Engineering Inc.; director: PP&G Industries Inc. NONPR AFFIL member: National Council Housing Industries; president, director: Soup Kitchen; fellow: Aspen Institute; director: Conference Board. CLUB AFFIL Point O Woods Club.

Foundation Officials

J. C. Anderson: trustee (see above)
Bradley John Bell: treasurer (see above)
Bruce K. Berger: president, trustee (see above)
Frank Luongo: treasurer
Charles Daly Miller: trustee B Hartford, CT 1928. ED Johns Hopkins University (1949). PRIM CORP EMPL chairman, director: Avery Dennison Corp. CORP AFFIL director: Pacific Mutual Life Insurance Co.; director: Nationwide Health Properties Inc.; director: Davidson & Associates Inc.; director: Great Western Finance Corp.; chairman, director: Avery Dennison Decorative Films. NONPR AFFIL director: Edison International.
David E. Mitchell: trustee
Nancy T. Snyder: trustee
Jay Van Den Berg: trustee
J. Christopher Wyse: manager communications
Gloria Zamora: trustee

Grants Analysis

Disclosure Period: calendar year ending 1997
Total Grants: $2,882,034*
Number of Grants: 215 (approx)
Average Grant: $13,405*
Highest Grant: $1,598,045
Typical Range: $5,000 to $25,000
***Note:** Giving excludes matching gifts; scholarship; United Way. Grants analysis is approximate. Average grant figure excludes highest grant.

Recent Grants

Note: Grants derived from 1997 Form 990.

Arts & Humanities

50,000	Persephone Productions, Arlington, VA
31,492	Craftsmanship 2000, Tulsa, OK
15,100	LOFT, Benton Harbor, MI
15,000	Orchestral Association, Chicago Symphony Orchestra, Chicago, IL
10,000	Curious Kids Museum, Saint Joseph, MI

Civic & Public Affairs

1,598,045	Community Economic Development Center
164,000	9 to 5 Working Women Education Fund, Cleveland, OH
25,000	Ms. Foundation for Women, New York, NY
20,000	Foundation for the National Capital Region, Washington, DC
15,000	Knoxville Area Urban League, Knoxville, TN
15,000	Sandusky County Economic Development Corporation, Fremont, OH
10,000	National Hispanic Leadership Institute, Washington, DC

Education

75,100	Andrews University, Berrien Springs, MI
71,200	University of Michigan School of Business Administration, Ann Arbor, MI

68,400	Inroads Southwestern Michigan, MI
50,000	Twin City Area Catholic School Fund, Saint Joseph, MI
50,000	University of Evansville, Evansville, IN
50,000	University of Findlay, Findlay, OH
50,000	University of Notre Dame, South Bend, IN
40,000	Indiana University Foundation, Bloomington, IN
34,437	Michigan Technological University, Houghton, MI
25,000	Marion Area Partners in Education, Marion, OH
24,000	Berrien County Intermediate School District, Berrien Springs, MI
21,815	Laporte Community School Corporation, La Porte, IN
20,000	City University, Bellevue, WA
15,000	Consortium for Graduate Study in Management, Saint Louis, MO
15,000	Junior Achievement Berrien County, MI
10,000	Lake Michigan College Education Fund, Benton Harbor, MI
10,000	Purdue University, West Lafayette, IN

Health

56,000	American National Red Cross, Alexandria, VA
12,892	American Red Cross, Fort Smith, AR

International

20,000	Forum for Intercultural Communication, Washington, DC
10,000	Scuola Europea Varese

Religion

50,000	Christian Outreach Rehabilitation and Development Nonprofit Housing Corporation, Benton Harbor, MI
10,000	Rainbows, Schaumburg, IL

Social Services

423,327	United Way Southwestern Michigan, MI
119,438	United Way, Fort Smith, AR
83,292	United Way Southwestern Indiana, Evansville, IN
72,398	United Way Marion County, Marion, OH
56,304	United Way Hancock County, Findlay, OH
50,000	Family Violence Prevention Fund, San Francisco, CA
46,136	YMCA Benton Harbor/St. Joseph
44,400	United Way Sandusky County, Fremont, OH
42,216	United Way Oxford Lafayette County, Oxford, MS
20,000	YWCA Southeastern Michigan, MI
17,670	United Way Middle Tennessee, Nashville, TN
16,094	United Way Darke County, Greenville, OH
14,190	United Way, Tulsa, OK
14,000	YMCA, Findlay, OH
13,283	United Way, Knoxville, TN

WHITMAN CORP.

Company Contact

Rolling Meadows, IL
Web: http://www.whitmancorp.com

Company Description

Profit: US$133,500,000
Employees: 17,594
SIC(s): 6719 Holding Companies Nec.

Whitman Corp. Foundation

Giving Contact

Charles H. Connolly, President
Whitman Corp. Foundation
3501 Algonquin Road
Rolling Meadows, IL 60008
Phone: (847)818-5000
Fax: (847)818-5046

Description

EIN: 363610784
Organization Type: Corporate Foundation. Supports preselected organizations only.
Giving Locations: IL: Chicago nationally.
Grant Types: Challenge, Employee Matching Gifts, General Support.
Note: Challenge gifts are administered through the foundation's matching gifts program. Directors, directors emeriti, and full time employees of Whitman Corporation, excluding subsidiaries, are eligible.

Financial Summary

Total Giving: $588,813 (1998); $299,700 (1997); $362,565 (1996). Note: Contributes through foundation only.
Giving Analysis: Giving for 1998 includes: foundation matching gifts ($448,413); foundation ($100,400)
Assets: $5,244,251 (1998); $5,263,525 (1997); $4,198,934 (1996)
Gifts Received: $400,000 (1995); $300,000 (1994); $500,000 (1993). Note: Contributions received from the Whitman Corporation.

Typical Recipients

Arts & Humanities: Arts Festivals, Museums/Galleries, Music, Opera, Performing Arts, Theater
Civic & Public Affairs: Asian American Affairs, Clubs, Economic Development, Economic Policy, Ethnic Organizations, Civic & Public Affairs-General, Hispanic Affairs, Urban & Community Affairs, Women's Affairs, Zoos/Aquariums
Education: Arts/Humanities Education, Business Education, Colleges & Universities, Community & Junior Colleges, Continuing Education, Education Funds, Faculty Development, Education-General, Legal Education, Minority Education, Private Education (Precollege), Science/Mathematics Education, Secondary Education (Private), Secondary Education (Public), Student Aid
Health: Diabetes, Emergency/Ambulance Services, Eyes/Blindness, Health Policy/Cost Containment, Hospitals, Hospitals (University Affiliated), Medical Rehabilitation, Prenatal Health Issues, Single-Disease Health Associations
International: International Affairs, International Relations
Religion: Religious Organizations, Religious Welfare
Science: Science Museums
Social Services: At-Risk Youth, Child Abuse, Child Welfare, Community Service Organizations, Homes, People with Disabilities, Recreation & Athletics, Scouts, Shelters/Homelessness, United Funds/United Ways, YMCA/YWCA/YMHA/YWHA, Youth Organizations

Contributions Analysis

Giving Priorities: Education, and social welfare.
Arts & Humanities: 1%. Supports the symphony.
Civic & Public Affairs: 9%. Urban and community affairs.
Education: 57%. Includes matching gifts to educational institutions. Majority of funding supports colleges and universities nationwide.
Health: 4%. Emergency relief, health policy, hospitals, and single-disease health associations.
Social Services: 29%. United funds, YMCA's youth organizations, and child welfare.

Note: Total contributions in 1997.

Restrictions

Recipients must be 501 (c)(3) nonprofit organizations under IRS standards.

Corporate Officials

Thomas L. Bindley: executive vice president finance & administration B Terre Haute, IN 1943. ED Georgetown University BS (1965); Harvard University MBA (1969). PRIM CORP EMPL executive vice president finance & administration: Whitman Corp.
Bruce Stanley Chelberg: chairman, chief executive officer, director B Chicago, IL 1934. ED University of Illinois BS (1956); University of Illinois LLB (1958). PRIM CORP EMPL chairman, chief executive officer, director: Whitman Corp. CORP AFFIL chief executive officer: Whitman Leasing Inc.; director: Snap-On Tools Inc.; director: Northfield Laboratories Inc.; director: Snap-On Inc.; president: Equities Inc.; director: First Midwest Bank Corp. Inc. NONPR AFFIL member: Illinois Bar Association. CLUB AFFIL World Trade Club; Chicago Club; Metro Club.
Charles H. Connolly: senior vice president corporate affairs & investor relations B New York, NY 1934. ED Columbia University; Fordham University AB (1957). PRIM CORP EMPL senior vice president corporate affairs & investor relations: Whitman Corp. NONPR AFFIL member: Public Relations Society America; trustee: Saint Xavier College; member: Chicago Athletic Association; deacon: Chicago United Church.
William B. Moore: senior vice president, secretary, general counsel B 1941. ED Stanford University BA (1963); University of Illinois JD (1966). PRIM CORP EMPL senior vice president, secretary, general counsel: Whitman Corp. CORP AFFIL secretary: Whitman Leasing Inc.; secretary: IC Equities Inc. NONPR AFFIL member: American Society of Corporate Secretaries.
Lawrence James Pilon: senior vice president human resources B Detroit, MI 1948. ED Michigan State University (1970); University Michigan (1976). PRIM CORP EMPL senior vice president human resources: Whitman Corp.
Frank Thomas Westover: senior vice president B Bay City, MI 1938. ED University of Michigan BBA (1961); University of Michigan MBA (1962). PRIM CORP EMPL senior vice president: Whitman Corp. CORP AFFIL vice president: Whitman Leasing Inc.

Foundation Officials

Thomas L. Bindley: vice president, treasurer (see above)
Bruce Stanley Chelberg: director (see above)
Charles H. Connolly: president (see above)
William B. Moore: secretary (see above)
Frank Thomas Westover: director (see above)

Grants Analysis

Disclosure Period: calendar year ending 1998
Total Grants: $100,400*
Number of Grants: 29
Average Grant: $3,462
Highest Grant: $25,000
Typical Range: $1,000 to $5,000 and $10,000 to $35,000
***Note:** Giving excludes educational and matching gifts.

Recent Grants

Note: Grants derived from 1998 Form 990.

Arts & Humanities

2,500	The Goodman Theatre, Chicago, IL
2,000	The Sylvia and Danny Kay Playhouser at Hunter College, New York, NY
1,000	The Philbrook Museum of Art, Tulsa, OK

Civic & Public Affairs

25,000	Chicago Council on Urban Affairs, Chicago, IL

25,000	Chicago Council on Urban Affairs, Chicago, IL
10,000	Mexican American Legal Defense & Educational Fund, Chicago, IL
7,500	The Happiness Club, Schaumburg, IL
5,000	Organization of New City, Chicago, IL
5,000	Polish American Association, Chicago, IL
3,000	Chicago Council on Urban Affairs, Chicago, IL

Education

333,000	Roosevelt University, Chicago, IL
15,000	Community Youth Creative Learning Experience, Chicago, IL
15,000	University of Michigan, Ann Arbor, MI
11,000	University of Michigan, Ann Arbor, MI
10,000	J.L. Kellogg Graduate School of Management/Northwestern, Evanston, IL
10,000	Roosevelt University, Chicago, IL
6,188	Washington College, Chestertown, MD
6,000	Junior Achievement of Chicago, Chicago, IL
6,000	Wayland Academy, Beaver Dam, WI
5,000	The Chi Psi Educational Trust, Olympia Fields, IL
5,000	Georgetown University, Washington, DC
5,000	St. Xavier University, Chicago, IL
5,000	Wayland Academy, Beaver Dam, WI
4,000	Wayland Academy, Beaver Dam, WI
3,200	University of Michigan, Ann Arbor, MI
3,075	Oklahoma State University Foundation, Stillwater, OK
3,000	Yale University, New Haven, CT
2,000	St. Francis Grade School, Chicago, IL
2,000	University of Michigan, Ann Arbor, MI
2,000	Westchester Community College Foundation, Valhalia, NY
1,200	Wellesley College, Wellesley, MA
1,000	Cottey Junior College, Nevada, MO
1,000	The Kansas University Endowment Association, Lawrence, KS
1,000	The Kansas University Endowment Association, Lawrence, KS
1,000	Safer Foundation, Chicago, IL
1,000	St. Jude Grade School, Wauwatosa, WI
1,000	University of Chicago Section of Urology Rescue Fund, Chicago, IL

Health

3,000	Health & Medicine Policy Research Group, Chicago, IL
2,000	Chicago Health Policy Research Council, Chicago, IL
1,000	American Liver Foundation, Chicago, IL
1,000	Kilo Diabetes & Vascular Research Foundation, St. Louis, MO
1,000	Lake Forest Hospital, Lake Forest, IL

Social Services

5,000	CYCLE, Chicago, IL
5,000	Infant Welfare Society of Chicago, Chicago, IL
5,000	Infant Welfare Society of Chicago, Chicago, IL
3,000	YMCA of Metropolitan Chicago, Chicago, IL
2,000	Howe Association for Retarded Citizens, Oak Forest, IL
2,000	YWCA of Metropolitan Chicago/Leader Luncheon, Chicago, IL
1,000	Lawrence Hall Youth Services, Chicago, IL
1,000	Rainbow House, Inc., San Antonio, TX

WICOR, INC.

Company Contact

Milwaukee, WI

Company Description

Assets: US$1,010,100,000 (1999)
Employees: 3,524 (1999)
SIC(s): 1311 Crude Petroleum & Natural Gas, 3823 Process Control Instruments, 4924 Natural Gas Distribution, 6719 Holding Companies Nec.

Nonmonetary Support

Value: $32,770 (1998); $106,000 (1993)
Type: Donated Equipment; Donated Products; Inkind Services; Loaned Executives
Volunteer Programs: The foundation supports V.O.I.C.E., which is a volunteer program that identifies volunteer opportunities and coordinates companywide events.
Note: The company reports that furniture and retired equipment is donated to nonprofit organizations. The foundation supports weatherization of low-income residences.

Corporate Sponsorship

Type: Arts & cultural events; Festivals/fairs; Music & entertainment events
Contact: Loraine O'Brien, Marketing Communications

WICOR Foundation

Giving Contact

Carolyn Simpson, Foundation Coordinator
WICOR Foundation
626 E Wisconsin Ave.
Milwaukee, WI 53202-4609
Phone: (414)291-6565
Fax: (414)291-6361
Email: carolyn.simpson@wicor.com
Web: http://www.wicor.com

Description

EIN: 391522073
Organization Type: Corporate Foundation
Giving Locations: WI: Milwaukee headquarters and operating communities and service territories.
Grant Types: Capital, Conference/Seminar, Employee Matching Gifts, Endowment, General Support, Multiyear/Continuing Support.

Giving Philosophy

The foundation has four focus areas: Employment, Neighborhood Stabilization, Education, and Quality of Life. Employment giving focuses on 'programs that help bring the economically disadvantaged to full participation in the economy,' mainly by providing training and opportunities for women and minorities. Neighborhood Stabilization giving focuses on improving communities served by WICOR, increasing home ownership, improving housing, and the Share the Warmth Fund. Education giving is directed to public elementary schools, colleges, and educational outreach programs. Quality of Life grants are focused on youth, health, civic affairs, and the arts.

Financial Summary

Total Giving: $650,000 (1999 approx); $600,014 (1998); $619,815 (1997). Note: Contributes through foundation only.
Giving Analysis: Giving for 1997 includes: foundation grants to United Way ($162,620); 1998: foundation grants to United Way ($84,750)
Assets: $795,470 (1999); $424,059 (1998); $340,676 (1997)
Gifts Received: $650,000 (1998); $800,000 (1997); $643,219 (1996). Note: Contributions received from Wisconsin Gas Company ($550,000), WICOR, Inc. ($100,000).

Typical Recipients

Arts & Humanities: Arts Institutes, History & Archaeology, Libraries, Museums/Galleries, Music, Opera, Performing Arts, Theater
Civic & Public Affairs: Asian American Affairs, Botanical Gardens/Parks, Business/Free Enterprise, Community Foundations, Economic Development, Employment/Job Training, Civic & Public Affairs-General, Hispanic Affairs, Housing, Legal Aid, Nonprofit Management, Public Policy, Urban & Community Affairs, Women's Affairs, Zoos/Aquariums
Education: Business Education, Colleges & Universities, Economic Education, Education Reform, Elementary Education (Private), Elementary Education (Public), Engineering/Technological Education, Education-General, Leadership Training, Literacy, Medical Education, Minority Education, Private Education (Precollege), Public Education (Precollege), Student Aid
Environment: Environment-General
Health: Children's Health/Hospitals, Clinics/Medical Centers, Emergency/Ambulance Services, Health-General, Health Policy/Cost Containment, Hospitals, Transplant Networks/Donor Banks
Religion: Jewish Causes, Religious Organizations, Religious Welfare
Science: Science Museums
Social Services: Child Abuse, Child Welfare, Community Centers, Community Service Organizations, Domestic Violence, Family Services, Food/Clothing Distribution, Homes, People with Disabilities, Recreation & Athletics, Scouts, Social Services-General, Substance Abuse, United Funds/United Ways, Volunteer Services, YMCA/YWCA/YMHA/YWHA, Youth Organizations

Contributions Analysis

Arts & Humanities: 13%. Emphasis is on the United Performing Arts Fund in Milwaukee. Also supports museums, libraries, a symphony, and a theater.
Civic & Public Affairs: 28%. Supports the Zoological Society of Milwaukee County, a women's fund, nature centers, and community building. Employment is also an interest.
Education: 17%. Primarily supports higher education and medical education in Milwaukee. Also contributes to education funds, literacy programs, and public education.
Social Services: 42%. Major contributions are made to various United Ways. Other interests include traditional youth organizations, child welfare, community services, and Milwaukee inner-city agencies.

Application Procedures

Initial Contact: Call or write for application; then send a written proposal.
Application Requirements: Include legal name; completed application; address, and telephone number of organization; name of representative who can be contacted by telephone; statement of purpose and a brief history of organization, including past projects; description of overall program, including any collaboration with other nonprofit organizations; an explanation regarding specific request for support; most recent audited financial statement; itemized annual and project budget with projected revenues and expenses; list of funding sources contacted and funds received; copy of tax-exempt letter; list of current board of directors; description of unique facets of request and what differentiates it from other projects of the same nature; and a description of how results will be measured.
Deadlines: January 31, April 30, July 31, and October 31.
Decision Notification: Board meets quarterly, and decisions are made within four weeks following the meeting of the board.

Restrictions

Does not support individuals, religious organizations for sectarian purposes, political or lobbying groups, or organizations outside operating areas.

Additional Information

Publications: Fact Sheet; Annual Report; Application Form

Corporate Officials

James Charles Donnelly: vice president, chief executive officer, director B Boston, MA 1945. ED Northeastern University BS (1969); Northeastern University MBA (1974); Suffolk University JD (1978). PRIM CORP EMPL vice president: WICOR Inc.

George E. Wardeberg: president, chief executive officer, director B Barnsville, MN 1935. ED Bowling Green State University; Michigan State University BA (1957). PRIM CORP EMPL president, chief executive officer, director: WICOR, Inc. CORP AFFIL chairman: WICOR Energy; chairman, director: Wisconsin Gas Co.; director: Twin Disc Inc.; chairman, director: SHURflo Pump Manufacturing Co.; chairman, director: Sta-Rite Industries Inc.; chairman: Hypro Corp.; director: Marshall & Ilsley Bank; chairman: Fibredyne Inc.; chairman: Field Tech Inc.

Joseph P. Wenzler: senior vice president, chief financial officer B Fond du Lac, WI 1942. ED Marquette University BS (1964); University of Wisconsin MBA (1983). PRIM CORP EMPL senior vice president, chief financial officer: WICOR Inc. ADD CORP EMPL vice president, chief financial officer: Wisconsin Gas Co.; vice president: Fibredyne Inc.; vice president, treasurer: FieldTech Relations; treasurer, secretary: Hypro Corp.; treasurer, secretary: SHURflo Pump Manufacturing Co.; secretary: WICOR Energy.

Foundation Officials

James Charles Donnelly: vice president, director (see above)

Thomas F. Schrader: vice president, director B Indianapolis, IN 1950. ED Princeton University BS (1972); Princeton University MS (1978). PRIM CORP EMPL vice chairman, director: Wisconsin Gas Co. CORP AFFIL president, chief operating officer, director: WICOR Inc.; director: Firstar Trust Co.; director: Sta-Rite Industries Inc.; president: Field Tech Inc. NONPR AFFIL president: New Hope Project Inc.; director: Wisconsin Utilities Association; director: Goodwill Industries.

Carolyn Simpson: coordinator

George E. Wardeberg: president (see above)

Joseph P. Wenzler: secretary, treasurer (see above)

Grants Analysis

Disclosure Period: calendar year ending 1998
Total Grants: $600,014*
Number of Grants: 157
Average Grant: $3,822
Highest Grant: $156,000
Typical Range: $500 to $5,000
***Note:** Giving includes United Way. Grants analysis provided by foundation.

Recent Grants

Note: Grants derived from 1998 Form 990.

Arts & Humanities

42,500	United Performing Arts Fund, Milwaukee, WI
10,000	Marcus Center for the Performing Arts, Milwaukee, WI
10,000	Milwaukee Art Museum, Milwaukee, WI
5,000	Friends of the Pabst Theater, Milwaukee, WI
5,000	Milwaukee Symphony Orchestra, Milwaukee, WI

Civic & Public Affairs

15,000	Martin Luther King Economic Development Corp., Milwaukee, WI
10,000	Esperanza Unida, Milwaukee, WI
10,000	Milwaukee Foundation-Safe and Sound, Milwaukee, WI
10,000	Neighborhood Improvement Development Corp, Milwaukee, WI
10,000	The New Hope Project, Inc., Milwaukee, WI
7,500	Public Allies Milwaukee, Milwaukee, WI
5,000	Community Advocates, Milwaukee, WI
5,000	Habitat for Humanity-Milwaukee, Milwaukee, WI
5,000	Hmong American Friendship Association, Menomonie, WI
5,000	Lisbon Avenue Neighborhood Development, Milwaukee, WI
5,000	Neighborhood House of Milwaukee, Milwaukee, WI
5,000	Public Allies, Milwaukee, WI
5,000	Public Policy Forum, Milwaukee, WI
5,000	Spirit of Milwaukee, Milwaukee, WI
4,000	YW Housing, Inc., Milwaukee, WI
3,000	Project Equality of Wisconsin, Milwaukee, WI

Education

8,000	Alverno College, Milwaukee, WI
7,500	1290 Scholarship Fund,Inc., Milwaukee, WI
7,500	Medical College of Wisconsin, Milwaukee, WI
6,250	UWM Foundation, Milwaukee, WI
6,000	Junior Achievement of Wisconsin, Milwaukee, WI
5,000	Alverno College, Milwaukee, WI
5,000	Cardinal Stritch College, Milwaukee, WI
5,000	Marquette University, Milwaukee, WI
5,000	Milwaukee School of Engineering, Milwaukee, WI
5,000	Partners Advancing Values in Education, Milwaukee, WI
4,000	Urban Day School, Milwaukee, WI
2,500	UWM Foundation, Milwaukee, WI

Science

5,000	Discovery World, Milwaukee, WI

Social Services

39,000	United Way of Greater Milwaukee, Milwaukee, WI
39,000	United Way of Greater Milwaukee, Milwaukee, WI
39,000	United Way of Greater Milwaukee, Milwaukee, WI
39,000	United Way of Greater Milwaukee, Milwaukee, WI
20,000	YMCA of Metropolitan Milwaukee, Milwaukee, WI
12,000	YMCA of Metropolitan Milwaukee, Milwaukee, WI
10,000	La Causa, Inc., Milwaukee, WI
8,500	Milwaukee Community Service Corps, Milwaukee, WI
8,000	Boys and Girls Clubs, Milwaukee, WI
7,500	Northcott Neighborhood House, Milwaukee, WI
5,000	Boys and Girls Clubs of Greater Milwaukee, Milwaukee, WI
5,000	Second Harvest Food Bank of Wisconsin, Milwaukee, WI
5,000	Social Development Commission, Milwaukee, WI
3,000	St. Paul Home, Kaukauna, WI
3,000	YWCA of Greater Milwaukee, Milwaukee, WI
2,750	Milwaukee County Council-Boy Scouts of America, Milwaukee, WI

Wilbur-Ellis Co. & Connell Brothers Co.

Company Contact

San Francisco, CA
Web: http://www.wilbur-ellis.com

Company Description

Employees: 2,100
SIC(s): 5191 Farm Supplies.

Brayton Wilbur Foundation

Giving Contact

Brayton Wilbur, Jr., President
Brayton Wilbur Foundation
345 California St., 27th Floor
San Francisco, CA 94104
Phone: (415)772-4006
Fax: (415)772-4005

Description

Founded: 1947
EIN: 946088667
Organization Type: Corporate Foundation. Supports preselected organizations only.
Giving Locations: headquarters and operating communities.
Grant Types: Endowment, General Support.

Financial Summary

Total Giving: $200,000 (1999 approx); $238,000 (1998 approx); $665,750 (1997). Note: Contributes through foundation only.
Giving Analysis: Giving for 1996 includes: foundation ($316,600); foundation ($10,000); 1997: foundation ($655,750); foundation grants to United Way ($10,000)
Assets: $150,000 (1997); $7,538,329 (1996); $6,549,470 (1995)
Gifts Received: $150,000 (1996); $150,000 (1995); $100,000 (1994). Note: Contributions are received from Wilbur Ellis Co.

Typical Recipients

Arts & Humanities: Arts Associations & Councils, Arts Institutes, Ethnic & Folk Arts, Arts & Humanities-General, Historic Preservation, Libraries, Museums/Galleries, Music, Opera, Performing Arts, Theater, Visual Arts
Civic & Public Affairs: African American Affairs, Botanical Gardens/Parks, Clubs, Economic Development, Civic & Public Affairs-General, Municipalities/Towns, Urban & Community Affairs, Women's Affairs, Zoos/Aquariums
Education: Arts/Humanities Education, Colleges & Universities, Community & Junior Colleges, Education Funds, Education-General, International Studies, Legal Education, Private Education (Precollege), Public Education (Precollege), Religious Education, Science/Mathematics Education, Secondary Education (Private), Special Education
Environment: Air/Water Quality, Environment-General, Resource Conservation, Wildlife Protection
Health: Clinics/Medical Centers, Emergency/Ambulance Services, Health-General, Health Organizations, Hospices, Hospitals, Single-Disease Health Associations
International: Foreign Arts Organizations, Health Care/Hospitals, International Affairs, International Environmental Issues, International Organizations, International Peace & Security Issues, International Relations, Missionary/Religious Activities
Religion: Churches, Religious Organizations, Religious Welfare
Science: Scientific Centers & Institutes
Social Services: Animal Protection, Community Service Organizations, Family Planning, People with Disabilities, Recreation & Athletics, Shelters/Homelessness, Social Services-General, United Funds/United Ways

Contributions Analysis

Giving Priorities: Major support for the arts.
Arts & Humanities: 74%. Primary support for museums, opera, symphonies, arts associations, and art institutes.
Civic & Public Affairs: 3%. Aquariums, aboretums, and zoos.

Education: 8%. Private secondary schools and colleges and universitites.
Environment: 1%. Wildlife preservation and conservation.
Health: 4%. Medical centers and hospitals.
International: 2%. International security and foreign relief.
Religion: 4%. Religious welfare organizations.
Social Services: 4%. A sports foundation, the United Way, and community services.

Restrictions

Grants are not made to individuals.

Corporate Officials

Carter Pomeroy Thacher: chairman, director B 1926. PRIM CORP EMPL chairman, director: Wilbur-Ellis Co.
Herbert B. Tulley: vice president, chief financial officer, treasurer B 1943. PRIM CORP EMPL vice president, chief financial officer, treasurer: Wilbur-Ellis Co. & Connell Brothers Co. CORP AFFIL treasurer, director: KCAC Inc.
Brayton Wilbur, Jr.: president, chief executive officer B San Francisco, CA 1935. ED Yale University BA (1957); Stanford University MBA (1961). PRIM CORP EMPL president, chief executive officer: Wilbur-Ellis Co. CORP AFFIL executive vice president: Connell Bros Co. Ltd. NONPR AFFIL member: Council Foreign Relations; vice president: Sponsors Performing Arts Center; chairman, trustee: Asia Foundation. CLUB AFFIL Cypress Point Club; Pacific-Union Club; Bohemian Club; Burlingame Country Club.

Foundation Officials

Carter Pomeroy Thacher: vice president (see above)
Herbert B. Tulley: secretary, treasurer (see above)
Brayton Wilbur, Jr.: president (see above)

Grants Analysis

Disclosure Period: calendar year ending 1997
Total Grants: $655,750*
Number of Grants: 45
Average Grant: $7,722*
Highest Grant: $316,000
Typical Range: $500 to $13,500
***Note:** Giving excludes United Way. Average grant figure excludes highest grant.

Recent Grants

Note: Grants derived from 1997 Form 990.

Arts & Humanities

316,000	Asian Art Museum Foundation, San Francisco, CA
100,000	Committee to Restore the Opera House, San Francisco, CA
45,000	University of San Francisco, San Francisco, CA -- Gleeson Library expansion
13,250	San Francisco Museum of Modern Art, San Francisco, CA
6,000	San Francisco Symphony, San Francisco, CA
5,000	Library Foundation, San Francisco, CA
4,000	San Francisco Opera Association, San Francisco, CA
1,000	Oakland Museum Association, Oakland, CA
500	San Francisco Art Institute, San Francisco, CA
500	University of California Art Museum, Berkeley, CA

Civic & Public Affairs

7,500	Monterey Bay Aquarium, Monterey, CA
7,500	Strybing Arboretum Society, San Francisco, CA
1,000	San Francisco Zoological Society, San Francisco, CA
500	di Rosa Preserve, Napa, CA
500	San Francisco Planning and Urban Research Association, San Francisco, CA
250	League of Women Voters, San Francisco, CA

Education

10,000	Sacred Heart Schools, Atherton, CA
10,000	Vassar College, Poughkeepsie, NY
10,000	Yale Law School, New Haven, CT
5,000	Grinnell College, Grinnell, IA
5,000	Schools of the Sacred Heart, San Francisco, CA
5,000	University of San Francisco, San Francisco, CA -- St. Ignatius Church renovation
2,500	Marin Academy, San Rafael, CA
1,500	Urban School, San Francisco, CA
1,000	Graduate Theological Union, Berkeley, CA
500	University of San Francisco Center for the Pacific Rim, San Francisco, CA

Environment

5,000	Point Reyes Bird Observatory, Stinson Beach, CA
2,000	Napa County Land Trust, Napa, CA
2,000	Sonoma Land Trust, Santa Rosa, CA

Health

20,000	California Pacific Medical Center Foundation, San Francisco, CA
5,000	Shriners Hospital, San Francisco, CA
500	ALS Association, San Francisco, CA

International

10,000	Hoover Institution, Stanford, CA
10,000	Hoover Institution, Stanford, CA
2,250	Medical Mission Sisters, Hillsborough, CA
2,250	Medical Mission Sisters, Hillsborough, CA
2,000	Asia Foundation, San Francisco, CA
2,000	Asia Foundation, San Francisco, CA
1,000	American Himalayan Foundation, San Francisco, CA
1,000	American Himalayan Foundation, San Francisco, CA

Religion

12,000	Grace Cathedral, San Francisco, CA
6,000	Catholic Charities, San Francisco, CA
5,000	United Religions Initiative, San Francisco, CA
3,000	St. Anthony Foundation, San Francisco, CA
3,000	St. Luke's Church, San Francisco, CA

Social Services

13,500	Monterey Peninsula Golf Foundation, Monterey, CA
10,000	United Way, San Francisco, CA
2,500	Life Plan Center, San Francisco, CA
1,000	Assistance League, Indianapolis, IN
1,000	Raphael House, San Francisco, CA

JOHN WILEY &SONS

Company Contact

New York, NY
Web: http://www.wiley.com

Company Description

Revenue: US$432,000,000
Employees: 1,800
SIC(s): 2721 Periodicals, 2731 Book Publishing.

Nonmonetary Support

Type: Donated Products; Workplace Solicitation

Giving Contact

Deborah Wiley, Senior Vice President
605 3rd Ave.
New York, NY 10158
Phone: (212)850-6000

Description

Organization Type: Corporate Giving Program
Giving Locations: headquarters area only.

Financial Summary

Total Giving: $210,000 (fiscal year ending April 30, 1999 approx); $198,300 (fiscal 1998); $180,000 (fiscal 1997). Note: Figures do not include matching gift amounts.

Typical Recipients

Arts & Humanities: Ballet, Dance, Libraries, Museums/Galleries, Opera, Performing Arts, Public Broadcasting, Theater
Civic & Public Affairs: Botanical Gardens/Parks, Civil Rights, First Amendment Issues, Professional & Trade Associations, Zoos/Aquariums
Education: Arts/Humanities Education, Business Education, Colleges & Universities, Community & Junior Colleges, Continuing Education, Education Associations, Education Funds, Elementary Education (Private), Elementary Education (Public), Education-General, Legal Education, Literacy, Medical Education, Minority Education, Preschool Education, Private Education (Precollege), Public Education (Precollege), Science/Mathematics Education, Secondary Education (Private), Secondary Education (Public)
Environment: Resource Conservation, Wildlife Protection
Health: AIDS/HIV, Diabetes, Mental Health
International: Human Rights
Religion: Bible Study/Translation
Science: Science Museums, Scientific Centers & Institutes, Scientific Organizations
Social Services: Emergency Relief, Shelters/Homelessness

Application Procedures

Initial Contact: Send brief letter of inquiry, including a description of organization, amount requested, purpose of funds sought, and proof of tax-exempt status.
Deadlines: None.

Restrictions

Does not support individuals, film projects, religious organizations for sectarian purposes, or political or lobbying groups.

Additional Information

Contributions to education are made primarily through matching gift program.
Publications: Contributions Policy Statement

Corporate Officials

William J. Pesce: president, chief executive officer chief financial officer PRIM CORP EMPL president, chief executive officer: John Wiley & Sons.
Robert D. Wilder: executive vice president, chief financial officer PRIM CORP EMPL executive vice president, chief financial officer: John Wiley & Sons.
Bradford Wiley, II: chairman, director B Orange, NJ 1941. ED Columbia University (1965); Johns Hopkins University (1968). PRIM CORP EMPL chairman, director: John Wiley & Sons.
Deborah Wiley: vice chairman B 1946. ED Pine Manor College AA (1966); Boston University BA (1968); Harvard University (1983). PRIM CORP EMPL vice chairman: John Wiley & Sons.

Grants Analysis

Disclosure Period: fiscal year ending April 30, 1997
Total Grants: $180,000
Typical Range: $500 to $2,500

Recent Grants

Note: Grants derived from fiscal 1998 Form 990.

Arts & Humanities
Metropolitan Opera, New York, NY
Museum of Modern Art, New York, NY
New York Public Library, New York, NY

Civic & Public Affairs
Association of College and Research Libraries, Newton, MA
Central Park Conservancy, New York, NY

Education
Council for Aid to Education, New York, NY
National Association of Biology Teachers, Reston, VA

Health
Juvenile Diabetes Foundation, New York, NY

Religion
Library of Congress Center for the Book, Washington, DC

Science
American Institute of Physics, College Park, MD

WILLIAMS

Company Contact

Houston, TX
Web: http://www.williams.com

Company Description

Former Name: Transco Energy Co.
Employees: 4542
SIC(s): 1221 Bituminous Coal & Lignite--Surface, 1222 Bituminous Coal--Underground, 1311 Crude Petroleum & Natural Gas, 5172 Petroleum Products Nec.

Nonmonetary Support

Type: Loaned Employees; Workplace Solicitation
Note: Company reports that workplace solicitation is for the United Way only.

Corporate Sponsorship

Type: Music & entertainment events; Sports events

Giving Contact

Sylvia Schmidt, Manager, Community Affairs
Williams
2800 Post Oak Boulevard
Houston, TX 77056
Phone: (713)215-2348
Fax: (713)215-2340

Description

Organization Type: Corporate Giving Program
Giving Locations: headquarters and operating communities.
Grant Types: Capital, Employee Matching Gifts, General Support, Project, Scholarship.

Giving Philosophy

'Transco Energy Company's corporate philanthropy program reflects our strong commitment and sense of responsibility to the communities in which we do business and our employees live.
The primary focus of Transco's giving program is education with a secondary focus on United Way and the arts. Education is vital to the present workforce and to creating the workforce of the future. Similarly, the arts are an integral part of a balanced, well-rounded education. Based in Houston, Transco contributes a large portion of its budget to Houston-area organizations, but also makes grants throughout Transco's market area and field office locations and, in special cases, provides some national-level funding.' *Transco Energy Company: Building a Foundation for the Future*

Financial Summary

Total Giving: $1,500,000 (1998 approx); $1,300,000 (1997 approx); $1,050,000 (1995 approx). Note: Contributes through corporate direct giving program and foundation.

Typical Recipients

Arts & Humanities: Arts Centers, Community Arts, Dance, Ethnic & Folk Arts, Libraries, Museums/Galleries, Music, Opera, Performing Arts, Public Broadcasting, Theater, Visual Arts
Civic & Public Affairs: Business/Free Enterprise, Economic Development, Economic Policy, Employment/Job Training, Housing, Law & Justice, Public Policy, Urban & Community Affairs, Women's Affairs, Zoos/Aquariums
Education: Arts/Humanities Education, Business Education, Colleges & Universities, Community & Junior Colleges, Economic Education, Elementary Education (Private), Engineering/Technological Education, Literacy, Minority Education, Preschool Education, Public Education (Precollege), Science/Mathematics Education
Environment: Environment-General
Health: Hospices, Medical Research, Mental Health
Science: Science Exhibits & Fairs
Social Services: Child Welfare, Community Service Organizations, Delinquency & Criminal Rehabilitation, Domestic Violence, People with Disabilities, Recreation & Athletics, Substance Abuse, United Funds/United Ways, Youth Organizations

Contributions Analysis

Giving Priorities: Education, economic education, health, social welfare, culture and the arts, civic organizations, and youth activities.
Arts & Humanities: About 15%. Programs that benefit the greatest number of people in the community.
Civic & Public Affairs: 10% to 15%. Organizations that address diverse contemporary issues and challenges facing society, including conservation and preservation, crime prevention, community revitalizations, and thedevelopment of public policy.
Education: About 35%. Direct grants to colleges and universities where the company actively recruits and to those institutions that provide education to their employees; K-12 education with focus on adopt-a-school programs, character education, math, science, and technology education, and literacy; and economic education programs that promote the understanding of economics and the free enterprise systems. Additionally, the company matches employee gifts to eligible educational institutions and sponsors a scholarship program for employee children.
Health: Less than 5%. Organizations where employees are directly involved and hospitals near operating locations.
Social Services: About 35%. Majority to United Way. Also supports disaster relief efforts, programs for the disabled, prevention of child abuse, and youth organizations.

Application Procedures

Initial Contact: telephone call, brief letter, or proposal
Application Requirements: general purpose of organization and the population it serves; name of contact person and executive director; purpose for which organization is seeking funds; need for program; amount requested; number of Transco employees involved; names of directors and trustees, including affiliations; notation if organization is a United Way member; most recent financial statement; proposed annual budget; sources of funds, including government funding; identity and amounts of major donors; and copy of IRS 501(c)(3) determination letter
Deadlines: before December for following year's funding
Review Process: grants are distributed throughout the year
Evaluative Criteria: community needs; organization's adherence to sound management principles; and its function as an employer
Decision Notification: a two month review time is requested for each proposal

Restrictions

Company does not purchase benefit tickets; contribute to advertising space in souvenir books, programs, or benefit performances; offer loans or financial aid to individuals; or make grants to fraternal, political, veterans, or religious organizations, or to member agencies of united funds.
Also does not fund school sports activities or organizations in foreign countries.

Additional Information

No contribution is automatically renewable; company tries to rotate support in many categories among as many recipients as possible. Company suggests brief progress reports outlining use of contributions at 6-month intervals.
Company reports that it funds approximately 10 percent of all requests received.
Publications: Guidelines

Corporate Officials

Cuba Wadlington, Jr.: vice president B Saint Louis, MO 1943. ED Washington University BA (1972); Saint Louis University MBA (1975). PRIM CORP EMPL executive vice president, chief operating officer: Gas Pipeline ADD CORP EMPL chief operating officer: Northwest Pipeline Corp.; executive vice president: Pine Needle Operating Co.; vice president: Transc Gas Pipe Line Corp.; senior vice president, general manager: Transcontinental Gas Pipeline Corp. NONPR AFFIL director: Southern Gas Association.

Grants Analysis

Disclosure Period: calendar year ending
Typical Range: $1,000 to $5,000

WILLIAMS

Company Contact

Tulsa, OK
Web: http://www.williams.com

Company Description

Former Name: The Williams Companies (1997).
Revenue: US$8,364,100,000 (1999)
Profit: US$221,400,000 (1999)
Employees: 11,000
Fortune Rank: 215, per FORTUNE Magazine's list of 500 Largest U.S. Corporations (1999).
FF 215
SIC(s): 4613 Refined Petroleum Pipelines, 4922 Natural Gas Transmission, 6159 Miscellaneous Business Credit Institutions.

Nonmonetary Support

Value: $61,081 (1989); $75,890 (1988)
Type: In-kind Services; Loaned Executives; Workplace Solicitation

Corporate Sponsorship

Type: Arts & cultural events; Pledge-a-thon

The Williams Companies Foundation

Giving Contact

Sylvia Schmidt, Director, Community Relations
The Williams Companies Foundation
PO Box 2400
Tulsa, OK 74102
Phone: (918)573-2248

Description

EIN: 237413843
Organization Type: Corporate Foundation
Giving Locations: areas near company headquarters and operating communities.
Grant Types: Capital, Employee Matching Gifts, Endowment, General Support.

Financial Summary

Total Giving: $6,000,000 (1998 approx); $338,583 (1997); $6,423,000 (1996 approx). Note: Contributes through corporate direct giving program and foundation.
Giving Analysis: Giving for 1996 includes: corporate direct giving (approx $6,423,000); 1998: corporate grants to United Way (approx $6,000,000)
Assets: $20,951,556 (1998); $18,636,656 (1997); $8,276,553 (1991)
Gifts Received: $5,000,000 (1995). Note: The foundation receives contributions from The Williams Companies.

Typical Recipients

Arts & Humanities: Arts Associations & Councils, Arts Centers, Arts Institutes, Dance, Historic Preservation, History & Archaeology, Libraries, Museums/Galleries, Music, Opera, Performing Arts, Theater
Civic & Public Affairs: African American Affairs, Botanical Gardens/Parks, Business/Free Enterprise, Clubs, Economic Development, Housing, Law & Justice, Legal Aid, Philanthropic Organizations, Professional & Trade Associations, Public Policy, Rural Affairs, Safety, Urban & Community Affairs, Women's Affairs, Zoos/Aquariums
Education: Afterschool/Enrichment Programs, Agricultural Education, Arts/Humanities Education, Business Education, Colleges & Universities, Community & Junior Colleges, Economic Education, Education Associations, Education Funds, Elementary Education (Private), Education-General, Private Education (Precollege), Public Education (Precollege), Science/Mathematics Education, Secondary Education (Private), Student Aid
Environment: Environment-General, Resource Conservation, Wildlife Protection
Health: AIDS/HIV, Children's Health/Hospitals, Clinics/Medical Centers, Health Funds, Health Organizations, Hospitals, Prenatal Health Issues, Single-Disease Health Associations
International: International Relations
Religion: Social/Policy Issues
Science: Science Exhibits & Fairs, Scientific Organizations
Social Services: At-Risk Youth, Child Welfare, Community Service Organizations, Crime Prevention, Domestic Violence, Emergency Relief, Family Planning, Family Services, Food/Clothing Distribution, Homes, People with Disabilities, Recreation & Athletics, Shelters/Homelessness, Substance Abuse, United Funds/United Ways, YMCA/YWCA/YMHA/YWHA, Youth Organizations

Contributions Analysis

Giving Priorities: Health, social welfare, education, the arts, and civic interests.
Arts & Humanities: 10% to 15%. Performing arts organizations, museums, ethnic arts, and historical preservation.
Civic & Public Affairs: 15% to 20%. Primarily supports environmental affairs and urban and community affairs. Also supports business, philanthropy, minority affairs, public policy, and women's organizations.
Education: 20% to 25%. Majority of funds support colleges and universities. Remaining support goes to engineering and economic education, education funds, and business education.
Environment: 10% to 15%. Funds nature conservancy, prevention of cruelty to animals, tree planting, and the National Wildlife Art Museum.
Health: 10%. More than three-fourths supports united funds, American Red Cross, and family service organizations. Other interests include youth organizaions, drug and alcohol abuse, the disabled, and child welfare organizations. Health interests include medical centers, medical research, and single-disease health associations.
Religion: Less than 5%. Religious causes.
Social Services: 20% to 25%. Funds Meals on Wheels, children and youth services, YMCA, and social services.

Application Procedures

Initial Contact: Send a brief letter and one copy of a full proposal.
Application Requirements: Include a description of organization, amount requested, purpose of funds sought, recently audited financial statement, and proof of tax-exempt status.
Deadlines: None; board meets in June and December.
Decision Notification: Usually within two weeks of receipt of request.

Restrictions

Does not support fraternal organizations, goodwill advertising, individuals, political or lobbying groups, or religious organizations for sectarian purposes.

Additional Information

Williams Companies acquired Mapco Inc. in 1998/1999.

Corporate Officials

Keith E. Bailey: chairman, president, director, chief executive officer B Kansas City, MO 1942. ED Missouri School of Mines & Metallurgy BS (1964); University of Missouri (1981). PRIM CORP EMPL chairman, president, director, chief executive officer: The Williams Companies Inc. CORP AFFIL chief executive officer: Williams Information Services Corp.; chairman: Williams Colorado Solutions; chairman: Williams Holdings Delaware; president: Touchstar Technologies LLC; director: Transco Energy Co.; executive: Northwest Pipeline Corp.; president: Rainbow Resources; chairman: Mapco Inc.; president, chief operating officer: Northwest Central Pipeline Co.; director: Apco Argentina Inc.; director: Bank Oklahoma Tulsa. NONPR AFFIL member: National Society Professional Engineers; member: Southern Gas Association; member: National Association Corrosion Engineers; member: Association Oil Pipelines; member: Interstate Natural Gas Association America; member: American Petroleum Institute.
John C. Baumgarner, Jr.: senior vice president corporate development PRIM CORP EMPL senior vice president corporate development: The Williams Companies Inc.
David M. Higbee: secretary B Cedar City, UT 1944. ED Brigham Young University (1968); University of Chicago (1971). PRIM CORP EMPL secretary: The Williams Companies Inc. CORP AFFIL secretary: Williams Communications Stations LLC; secretary: Williams Energy Ventures Inc.; secretary: Transco Energy Co.
Sylvia Schmidt: director community relations PRIM CORP EMPL director community relations: Williams Companies.
William G. von Glahn: senior vice president, general counsel B Bronxville, NY 1943. ED University of North Carolina (1965); Washington University JD (1973). PRIM CORP EMPL senior vice president, general counsel: The Williams Companies Inc. ADD CORP EMPL senior vice president: Williams Communications Group.

Foundation Officials

Keith E. Bailey: president, director (see above)
John C. Baumgarner, Jr.: director (see above)
David M. Higbee: secretary, treasurer (see above)
Sylvia Smith: managing director
William G. von Glahn: director (see above)

Grants Analysis

Disclosure Period: calendar year ending 1998
Total Grants: $18,000,000 (approx)
Typical Range: $1,000 to $10,000
Note: Giving includes United Way.

Recent Grants

Note: Grants derived from 1997 Form 990.

Arts & Humanities

10,000	Tulsa Library Trust, Tulsa, OK -- support African American Resource Center
5,000	Black Gold Jr. Drum and Bugle Corporation, Tulsa, OK -- operating support
5,000	Oklahoma Heritage Association, OK -- operating support
1,000	Broken Arrow Community Playhouse, Broken Arrow, OK -- operating support
1,000	Local Motion Foundation, Tulsa, OK -- for collaboration with Gilcrease Museum
1,000	Sapulpa Community Theater, Sapulpa, OK -- operating support
562	Black Gold Drum and Bugle Corps, Tulsa, OK -- for printing

Civic & Public Affairs

25,000	Tulsa Zoo Friends, Tulsa, OK -- first payment on $100,000 pledge for Discovery Center
3,000	Metropolitan Tulsa Urban League, Tulsa, OK -- support Corporate Partnership Pledge
2,500	National Legal Career for the Public Interest, Washington, DC -- operating support
2,300	Committee for Citizen Awareness, Washington, DC -- to sponsor race
1,000	Habitat for Humanity, OK -- to relocate thrift shop
805	Park Friends, Tulsa, OK -- for light installation
500	Junior League, Tulsa, OK -- support Blooming Delas
500	Women in Communication, OK -- for paper stock

Education

11,700	Junior Achievement, Tulsa, OK -- operating support
5,000	Bishop Kedley High School, OK -- support Home Field Prescription Program
5,000	North Carolina School of the Arts, Winston-Salem, NC -- first payment on $15,000 pledge for scholarships
5,000	Thunderbird Challenge, OK -- support Thunderbird Youth Academy
5,000	Tulsa County 4-H Foundation, Tulsa, OK -- operating support
3,300	Junior Achievement, Tulsa, OK -- support Applies Business and Project Business Consultants
2,500	Riverfield Country Day School, Tulsa, OK -- support holiday dinner and auction
2,000	Oklahoma State University, Stillwater, OK -- scholarships
2,000	St. Louis University, Saint Louis, MO -- scholarships
1,000	Sapulpa Christian School, Sapulpa, OK -- for classroom enrichment

1,000	Tulsa Education Fund, Tulsa, OK -- operating support
949	Tulsa Public Schools, Tulsa, OK -- for printing costs
857	Tulsa Education Fund, Tulsa, OK -- for printing
500	Rogers University, OK -- operating support

Environment

7,200	Up With Trees, OK -- for tree planting
5,000	National Wildlife Art Museum, Jackson, WY -- support Wildlife Education Fund
5,000	Nature Conservancy, OK -- purchase land
5,000	Society for Prevention of Cruelty to Animals of Maryland, Annapolis, MD -- support Wildlife Rescue Facility
2,000	Nature Conservancy, OK -- support Corporate Council for the Environment luncheon

Health

10,000	Hillcrest Medical Center Foundation, Tulsa, OK -- replacement of check
5,000	Oklahoma Caring Foundation, Tulsa, OK -- health care for uninsured children
2,500	March of Dimes Birth Defects Foundation, New York, NY -- sponsor Gourmet Gala fundraiser
1,000	HIV Resource Consortium, Tulsa, OK -- operating support
1,000	Myasthenia Gravis Foundation, OK -- support indigent patient prescription program
500	Muscular Dystrophy Association, OK -- operating support

Religion

5,000	National Conference of Christians and Jews, New York, NY -- for Oklahoma Youth Project

Social Services

14,388	Companion Resources, OK -- support accessibility project
13,000	Twelve and Twelve Transition House, OK -- to replace air-conditioner units
5,000	Parent-Child Center, Tulsa, OK -- purchase new phone system
5,000	Project Get Together, Tulsa, OK -- school supplies
2,650	YMCA, Tulsa, OK -- support Kids to Camp
2,500	Tulsa Sports Commission, Tulsa, OK -- support TSC Winner Classic
2,000	Metropolitan Tulsa Citizens Crime Commission, Tulsa, OK -- operating support
2,000	Tulsa Meals on Wheels, Tulsa, OK -- operating support
1,250	Tulsa Court-Appointed Special Advocates, Tulsa, OK -- operating support

WINN-DIXIE STORES INC.

Company Contact

Jacksonville, FL

Company Description

Revenue: US$14,136,000,000 (1999)
Profit: US$182,300,000 (1999)
Employees: 132,000 (1999)
Fortune Rank: 123, per FORTUNE Magazine's list of 500 Largest U.S. Corporations (1999).
FF 123
SIC(s): 5411 Grocery Stores.

Corporate Sponsorship

Type: Arts & cultural events; Music & entertainment events; Sports events
Note: Sponsors HeartWalk.

Winn-Dixie Stores Foundation

Giving Contact

Lawrence H. May, President
Winn-Dixie Stores Foundation
5050 Edgewood Ct.
Jacksonville, FL 32254-3699
Phone: (904)783-5000
Fax: (904)783-5235

Alternate Contact

PO Box B
Jacksonville, FL 32203-0297

Description

EIN: 590995428
Organization Type: Corporate Foundation
Giving Locations: primarily in the company's 14-state trade area; generally within the Southern United States.
Grant Types: Employee Matching Gifts, General Support, Matching, Project, Research, Scholarship.
Note: Employee matching gift ratio: 1 to 1 for educational purposes, health-related causes, the United Way, and the arts.

Financial Summary

Total Giving: $3,842,066 (1998); $3,884,292 (1997); $3,358,530 (1996). Note: Contributes through corporate direct giving program and foundation.
Giving Analysis: Giving for 1997 includes: foundation matching gifts ($1,971,575); foundation ($1,529,567); foundation grants to United Way ($27,000); 1998: foundation ($1,967,028); foundation matching gifts ($1,868,738); foundation grants to United Way ($6,300)
Assets: $482,576 (1998); $290,918 (1997); $156,575 (1996)
Gifts Received: $4,000,000 (1998); $4,000,000 (1997); $3,000,000 (1996). Note: In 1998, contributions were received from Winn-Dixie Stores, Inc.

Typical Recipients

Arts & Humanities: Arts Festivals, History & Archaeology, Libraries, Music, Public Broadcasting
Civic & Public Affairs: African American Affairs, Business/Free Enterprise, Clubs, Economic Policy, Civic & Public Affairs-General, Law & Justice, Legal Aid, Public Policy, Urban & Community Affairs, Women's Affairs, Zoos/Aquariums
Education: Business Education, Colleges & Universities, Medical Education, Minority Education, Secondary Education (Public), Student Aid
Health: Alzheimers Disease, Cancer, Children's Health/Hospitals, Clinics/Medical Centers, Diabetes, Emergency/Ambulance Services, Heart, Hospices, Hospitals, Mental Health, Prenatal Health Issues, Public Health, Single-Disease Health Associations
Religion: Religious Organizations, Religious Welfare
Social Services: At-Risk Youth, Big Brother/Big Sister, Child Welfare, Community Service Organizations, Family Services, Food/Clothing Distribution, People with Disabilities, Recreation & Athletics, Scouts, Shelters/Homelessness, Special Olympics, Substance Abuse, United Funds/United Ways, YMCA/YWCA/YMHA/YWHA, Youth Organizations

Contributions Analysis

Giving Priorities: United Way, education, health, youth services, and arts.
Arts & Humanities: 5%.
Civic & Public Affairs: (United Funds & United Way) 2%.
Education: 2%. Support for colleges, associated college funds, and elementary and secondary schools. Support for minorities and the disabled, and some support for public broadcasting and substance abuse prevention.
Health: 49%. Supports hospitals, hospices, national disease associations, and mental health.
Social Services: 41%. Supports YMCA/YWCA, recreation, early childhood, Junior Achievement, scouting, and 4-H.
Note: About half of foundation giving is in the form of employee matching gifts. Total contributions madein 1998.

Application Procedures

Initial Contact: Submit a letter.
Application Requirements: Provide a description of organization, amount requested, purpose of funds sought, recently audited financial statement, and proof of tax-exempt status.
Deadlines: None, Board meets quarterly.
Notes: Applications should be sent to the nearest division office.

Restrictions

Funds only 501(c)(3) organizations near Winn-Dixie operating locations.
No grants are made to individuals, religious or political organizations; nor are contributions matched to fraternal, professional, social, or recreational groups. No grants (except for matching contributions) are made outside trade territories served by Winn-Dixie.

Additional Information

Publications: Guidelines; Annual Report

Corporate Officials

Andrew Dano Davis: vice president finance, chief financial officer B Henderson, AR 1945. ED Stetson University. PRIM CORP EMPL vice president: Winn-Dixie Stores Inc.
James Kufeldt: president, director B 1938. ED Anderson College BA (1960). PRIM CORP EMPL president, director: Winn-Dixie Stores Inc. ADD CORP EMPL president, director: Astor Products Inc.; president, director: Deep South Products Inc.; president, director: Dixie Packers Inc.
Larry H. May: vice president, director associate relations & human resources PRIM CORP EMPL vice president, director associate relations & human resources: Winn-Dixie Stores Inc.
Richard P. McCook: vice president finance, chief financial officer B Miami, FL 1953. ED Florida State University BS (1975); Florida State University M (1976). PRIM CORP EMPL vice president finance, chief financial officer: Winn-Dixie Stores Inc. NONPR AFFIL member: Financial Executives Institute; member: Florida Institute CPAs; member: American Institute CPAs. CLUB AFFIL River Club.
Charles H. McKellar: executive vice president, director B 1937. PRIM CORP EMPL executive vice president, director: Winn-Dixie Stores Inc.

Foundation Officials

David H. Bragin: treasurer, assistant secretary, director B 1944. ED University of Southern Florida BS (1972); University of Northern Florida MBA (1978). PRIM CORP EMPL treasurer: Winn-Dixie Stores Inc. CORP AFFIL treasurer: Winn-Dixie Raleigh Inc.; treasurer: Winn-Dixie Texas Inc.; treasurer: Winn-Dixie Montgomery Inc.; treasurer: Winn-Dixie LAInc.; treasurer: Winn-Dixie Midwest Inc.; treasurer: Winn-Dixie Charlotte Inc.; treasurer: Monterey Canning Co.; treasurer: Winn-Dixie Atlanta Inc.; treasurer: Dixie Packers Inc.; treasurer: Astor Products Inc.; director: Deep South Products Inc.
Andrew Dano Davis: vice president, director (see above)
Judith Dixon: secretary
James Kufeldt: vice president, director (see above)
Larry H. May: president, director (see above)
Richard P. McCook: vice president (see above)
Charles H. McKellar: vice president, director (see above)

T. L. Qualls: assistant secretary PRIM CORP EMPL director corporate acctg: Winn-Dixie Stores Inc.
Ellis Zahara: vice president

Grants Analysis

Disclosure Period: calendar year ending 1998
Total Grants: $1,967,028*
Number of Grants: 750 (approx)
Average Grant: $2,623
Highest Grant: $130,000
Typical Range: $100 to $5,000
***Note:** Giving excludes matching gifts; gifts to individuals; United Way.

Recent Grants

Note: Grants derived from 1998 Form 990.

Arts & Humanities

50,000 Jacksonville Chamber Foundation Inc, Jacksonville, FL
50,000 Jacksonville Chamber Foundation Inc, Jacksonville, FL
25,000 Jacksonville Symphony Association, Jacksonville, FL
11,000 Kentucky Shakespeare Festival, Louisville, KY

Civic & Public Affairs

35,000 National Urban League, New York, NY
25,000 Urban League, Jacksonville, FL

Education

50,000 University of North Florida Foundation, Jacksonville, FL

Health

157,362 American Cancer Society/American Heart Association, Louisville, KY
130,000 American Cancer Society, Miami, FL
95,480 American Cancer Society/American Heart Association, Montgomery, AL
69,264 American Cancer Society/American Heart Association, Charlotte, NC
67,313 American Cancer Society, Orlando, FL
63,326 American Cancer Society/American Heart Association, Miami, FL
56,634 American Cancer Society/American Heart Association
55,056 American Cancer Society/American Heart Association, New Orleans, LA
53,849 American Cancer Society/American Heart Association, Orlando, FL
52,000 American Red Cross, New Orleans, LA
50,000 American Red Cross-Disaster Relief, Orlando, FL
44,595 American Cancer Society/American Heart Association, Fort Worth, TX
42,977 American Cancer/Winn-Dixie Hope Lodge, Atlanta, GA
37,390 American Cancer Society/American Heart Association, Jacksonville, FL
35,000 American Cancer Society, Louisville, KY
34,340 American Cancer Society/American Heart Association, Atlanta, GA
30,000 American Red Cross-Disaster Relief Fund, Birmingham, AL
30,000 Ronald McDonald House, Jacksonville, FL
25,600 American Cancer Society, Orlando, FL
25,000 American Red Cross, Elizabethton, TN
21,132 American Cancer Society/American Heart Association, Raleigh, NC
17,900 Duke Childrens Hospital, Durham, NC
17,900 Duke Childrens Hospital, Durham, NC
10,530 United Cerebral Palsy of Central Florida, Orlando, FL
10,400 American Cancer Society/American Heart Association, Tampa, FL

Social Services

354,116 United Way, Louisville, KY
113,831 United Way, Charlotte, NC
76,416 United Way, Alexandria, VA
73,798 United Way, Montgomery, AL
53,809 United Way, Orlando, FL
51,790 United Way, Jacksonville, FL
50,951 United Way, Miami, FL
43,800 United Way, Fort Worth, TX
39,105 United Way, New Orleans, LA
30,000 YMCA of Florida's First Coast, Jacksonville, FL
25,706 United Way, Tampa, FL
25,000 Big Brothers/Big Sisters of South East Louisiana, New Orleans, LA
20,000 Police Athletic League, Jacksonville, FL
19,141 Boy Scouts of America-Central Florida, Orlando, FL
17,887 United Way, Raleigh, NC
17,807 United Way, Atlanta, GA
15,000 Girl Scouts-Citrus County Council, Winter Park, FL
12,000 Boy Scouts of America Ban Beard Council, Cincinnati, OH

WIREMOLD CO.

Company Contact

West Hartford, CT
Web: http://www.wiremold.com

Company Description

Employees: 681
SIC(s): 3643 Current-Carrying Wiring Devices, 3644 Noncurrent-Carrying Wiring Devices, 3646 Commercial Lighting Fixtures, 3648 Lighting Equipment Nec.

Wiremold Foundation

Giving Contact

JoAnn Mazzo, Secretary
Wiremold Foundation
60 Woodlawn St.
West Hartford, CT 06110
Phone: (860)233-6251
Fax: (860)523-3699

Description

Founded: 1967
EIN: 066089445
Organization Type: Corporate Foundation
Giving Locations: headquarters area only.
Grant Types: Employee Matching Gifts, General Support.

Financial Summary

Total Giving: $204,627 (1997); $197,832 (1996); $203,610 (1995). Note: 1997 Giving includes matching gifts.
Assets: $321,056 (1997); $269,220 (1996); $257,166 (1995)
Gifts Received: $252,000 (1997); $204,000 (1996); $204,000 (1995)

Typical Recipients

Arts & Humanities: Arts Associations & Councils, Ballet, Arts & Humanities-General, Historic Preservation, Libraries, Literary Arts, Museums/Galleries, Music, Performing Arts, Public Broadcasting
Civic & Public Affairs: African American Affairs, Employment/Job Training, Civic & Public Affairs-General, Housing, Public Policy, Urban & Community Affairs, Women's Affairs
Education: Business Education, Colleges & Universities, Education Funds, Education-General, International Exchange, Literacy, Minority Education, Student Aid
Environment: Environment-General, Watershed
Health: AIDS/HIV, Children's Health/Hospitals, Emergency/Ambulance Services, Health-General, Health Organizations, Hospitals, Public Health
Religion: Religious Welfare
Science: Science Museums, Scientific Centers & Institutes
Social Services: Camps, Child Welfare, Community Service Organizations, Family Services, Food/Clothing Distribution, People with Disabilities, Recreation & Athletics, Senior Services, Social Services-General, Special Olympics, United Funds/United Ways, Youth Organizations

Application Procedures

Initial Contact: The foundation has no formal grant application procedure or application form.
Deadlines: None.

Restrictions

Preference is given to written requests for capital and/or start-up campaigns over operating funds.

Corporate Officials

Arthur P. Byrne: chairman, president, chief executive officer, director PRIM CORP EMPL chairman, president, chief executive officer, director: Wiremold Co.
Orest J. Fiume: vice president finance, chief financial officer PRIM CORP EMPL vice president finance, chief financial officer: Wiremold Co.

Foundation Officials

Arthur P. Byrne: treasurer (see above)
Joan L. Johnson: secretary
John Davis Murphy: president
Robert H. Murphy: vice president

Grants Analysis

Disclosure Period: calendar year ending 1997
Total Grants: $195,626*
***Note:** Giving excludes matching gifts.

Recent Grants

Note: Grants derived from 1997 Form 990.

Arts & Humanities

16,000 Greater Hartford Arts Council, Hartford, CT
5,000 Mark Twain House, Hartford, CT
3,500 West Hartford Community Television, Hartford, CT
1,700 Hartford Symphony Orchestra, Hartford, CT
1,500 Connecticut Public Television and Radio, CT

Civic & Public Affairs

70,000 UWCA/CHA
3,000 Walks Foundation, Simsbury, CT
2,500 Connecticut Housing Investment Fund, Hartford, CT
1,500 Hartford Area Habitat for Humanity, Hartford, CT

Education

4,800 Junior Achievement of North Central Connecticut, Hartford, CT
3,000 New England Colleges Fund, Woburn, MA
2,500 Greater Hartford Interracial Scholarship Fund, Hartford, CT

Environment

1,500 Connecticut River Watershed Council, Easthampton, MA

Health

5,000 Campaign for St. Francis/Mount Sinai
3,000 American Red Cross, Hartford, CT

Religion

25,000 Salvation Army

Social Services

2,000 Camp Courant, Hartford, CT -- support 1996-98 capital campaign
2,000 Children in Placement
1,500 Camp Courant, Hartford, CT
1,500 Fidelco Guide Dog Foundation, Bloomfield, CT

WISCONSIN ENERGY CORP.

Company Contact

Milwaukee, WI
Web: http://www.wisenergy.com

Company Description

Assets: US$4,810,800,000
Employees: 4,514
SIC(s): 4911 Electric Services, 4923 Gas Transmission & Distribution, 6719 Holding Companies Nec.

Operating Locations

Operates throughout southeastern Wisconsin and the Upper Penninsula of Michigan.

Nonmonetary Support

Value: $100,000 (1989); $100,000 (1988); $100,000 (1987)

Corporate Sponsorship

Type: Arts & cultural events; Music & entertainment events

Wisconsin Energy Corp. Foundation, Inc.

Giving Contact

Barbara Karow, Foundation Coordinator
Wisconsin Energy Corp. Foundation, Inc.
231 West Michigan Street
PO Box 2046
Milwaukee, WI 53290
Phone: (414)221-2106
Fax: (414)221-2412
Email: WEC.Foundation@WEmail.wisenergy.com

Description

EIN: 391433726
Organization Type: Corporate Foundation
Giving Locations: headquarters and operating communities; grants may be made in other states.
Grant Types: Capital, Employee Matching Gifts, Endowment, General Support, Matching, Multiyear/Continuing Support.
Note: Employee matching gift ratio: 1 to 1.

Financial Summary

Total Giving: $3,500,000 (2000 approx); $3,900,000 (1999 approx); $4,023,295 (1998). Note: Contributes through foundation only.
Giving Analysis: Giving for 1998 includes: foundation ($2,819,732); foundation grants to United Way ($895,510); foundation matching gifts ($308,053)
Assets: $20,010,502 (1998); $17,224,919 (1997); $20,657,298 (1996)
Gifts Received: $5,161,930 (1998); $2,000,000 (1996). Note: In 1998, contributions were received from Wisconsin Electric Power Co. ($5,000,000) and Technical League (EMBA) ($161,930).

Typical Recipients

Arts & Humanities: Arts Associations & Councils, Arts Funds, Community Arts, Historic Preservation, Museums/Galleries, Music, Opera, Performing Arts, Public Broadcasting, Theater
Civic & Public Affairs: Botanical Gardens/Parks, Business/Free Enterprise, Civil Rights, Community Foundations, Economic Development, Employment/Job Training, Hispanic Affairs, Housing, Urban & Community Affairs, Zoos/Aquariums
Education: Arts/Humanities Education, Business Education, Colleges & Universities, Economic Education, Education Associations, Education Funds, Education Reform, Engineering/Technological Education, Leadership Training, Medical Education, Minority Education, Private Education (Precollege), Public Education (Precollege), Science/Mathematics Education, Secondary Education (Private), Secondary Education (Public), Social Sciences Education
Environment: Environment-General, Resource Conservation
Health: Children's Health/Hospitals, Clinics/Medical Centers, Health Organizations, Hospitals, Medical Rehabilitation, Medical Research, Mental Health, Public Health, Respiratory, Single-Disease Health Associations, Trauma Treatment
Religion: Religious Organizations, Religious Welfare
Science: Science Museums, Scientific Organizations
Social Services: Child Welfare, Community Centers, Community Service Organizations, Counseling, Family Services, Homes, People with Disabilities, Recreation & Athletics, Scouts, Senior Services, Shelters/Homelessness, United Funds/United Ways, YMCA/YWCA/YMHA/YWHA, Youth Organizations

Contributions Analysis

Giving Priorities: Social welfare, education, the arts, health, and civic interests.
Arts & Humanities: 21%. Performing arts, community arts, and arts centers. Museums also receive significant support.
Civic & Public Affairs: 27%. Environmental affairs, community development, civil rights, and business and free enterprise groups.
Education: 32%. Majority supports general programs at colleges and universities in Wisconsin. Other recipients include education reform programs, education funds, engineering programs, minority education, and business education projects. Also sponsors an employee matching gifts program for contributions to higher education institutions.
Health: 5%. Children's health, hospitals, and medical centers receive support.
Social Services: 12%. United Ways in Wisconsin communities, youth organizations, and community centers. Other interests include the aged and community service organizations.

Application Procedures

Initial Contact: Send a brief letter or proposal.
Application Requirements: Include a description of organization, including the purpose and activities of the requestor, amount requested, purpose of funds sought, recently audited financial statement, proof of tax-exempt status.
Deadlines: None.
Evaluative Criteria: Supports organizations that aid large numbers of Wisconsin residents.
Decision Notification: Most large grants awarded in November for following year.

Additional Information

The company's subsidiaries, Wisconsin Natural Gas Co. and Wisconsin Electric Power Co., also contribute to the foundation.

Corporate Officials

Richard A. Abdoo: chairman, president, chief executive officer B Port Huron, MI 1944. ED University of Dayton BSEE (1965); University of Detroit MA (1969). PRIM CORP EMPL chairman, president, chief executive officer: Wisconsin Energy Corp. CORP AFFIL chairman, chief executive officer: Witech Corp.; chairman, chief executive officer: Wispark Corp.; chairman, chief executive officer: Wisconsin Electric Power Co.; president, chief executive officer, director: Wisconsin Michigan Investment Corp.; director: Sunstrand Corp.; director: United Wisconsin Services; chairman, chief executive officer: Minergy Corp.; chief executive officer, director: Badger Service Co.; director: Marshall & Ilsley Corp. NONPR AFFIL member: American Economic Association.
Calvin H. Baker: vice president finance, chief financial officer B 1944. ED Franklin and Marshall College (1965); University of Chicago (1969). PRIM CORP EMPL vice president finance, chief financial officer: Wisconsin Electric Power Co. CORP AFFIL treasurer, chief financial officer: Wisconsin Energy Corp.; chief financial officer: Wispark Corp.
Richard R. Grigg: vice president B Waukegan, IL 1948. ED University of Wisconsin BSME (1970); University of Wisconsin MSME (1975). PRIM CORP EMPL vice president: Wisconsin Energy Corp. ADD CORP EMPL vice president, director: Wisconsin Electric Power Co.; vice president, director: Badger Service Co. CORP AFFIL vice president: Primergy Corp.; vice president: Wisconsin Energy Corp.
Jerry G. Remmel: chief financial officer, vice president, treasurer B 1931. ED Marquette University BS (1955); Marquette University MBA (1959). PRIM CORP EMPL chief financial officer, vice president, treasurer: Wisconsin Energy Corp. CORP AFFIL treasurer: Future Value Ventures Inc.; vice president finance, treasurer: Wisconsin Natural Gas Co.; vice president: Employees Mutual Savings Building Loan.

Foundation Officials

Richard A. Abdoo: president, director (see above)
Calvin H. Baker: treasurer, director (see above)
Susan Edwards: director
Joyce Feaster: assistant treasurer, assistant secretary ED University of Wisconsin BBA (1983); University of Wisconsin MS (1990). PRIM CORP EMPL assistant corporate section: Wisconsin Energy Corp. CORP AFFIL assistant treasurer: Wisconsin Electric Power Co.; assistant treasurer: Wisconsin Natural Gas Co.
Thomas Fering: secretary
Richard R. Grigg: director (see above)
Barbara Karow: foundation coordinator
Gordon A. Willis: assistant treasurer, assistant secretary B Milwaukee, WI 1938. ED University of Wisconsin, Milwaukee BA; University of Wisconsin, Milwaukee MBA (1961). PRIM CORP EMPL treasurer: Wisconsin Electric Power Co. CORP AFFIL assistant treasurer: WI Energy Corp.; treasurer: WI Natural Gas Co.; treasurer: Employees Mutual Savings Building Loan.

Grants Analysis

Disclosure Period: calendar year ending 1998
Total Grants: $2,819,732*
Number of Grants: 368
Average Grant: $7,662
Highest Grant: $374,510
Typical Range: $2,500 to $10,000
***Note:** Giving excludes matching gifts; United Way.

Recent Grants

Note: Grants derived from 1997 Form 990.

Arts & Humanities

300,000 United Performing Arts Fund, Milwaukee, WI
100,000 Milwaukee Symphony Orchestra, Milwaukee, WI
75,000 Discovery World Museum of Science, Economics, and Technology, Milwaukee, WI
75,000 Marcus Center for Performing Arts, Milwaukee, WI
50,000 Milwaukee Repertory Theater, Milwaukee, WI
40,000 Discovery World Museum of Science, Economics, and Technology, Milwaukee, WI

40,000 Friends of East Troy Railroad Museum, East Troy, WI
30,000 Milwaukee Art Museum, Milwaukee, WI
20,000 Friends of the Milwaukee Public Museum, Milwaukee, WI

Civic & Public Affairs
66,000 New Hope Project, Milwaukee, WI
45,000 Habitat for Humanity, Milwaukee, WI
25,000 Local Initiatives Support Corporation, Milwaukee, WI
20,000 Esperanza Unida, Milwaukee, WI
15,000 Greater Milwaukee Committee, Milwaukee, WI

Education
100,000 Partners Advancing Values in Education, Milwaukee, WI
50,000 Medical College of Wisconsin, Milwaukee, WI
50,000 Messmer High School, Milwaukee, WI
50,000 University of Wisconsin Milwaukee, Milwaukee, WI
50,000 Youth Leadership Academy, Milwaukee, WI
38,000 Wisconsin Foundation of Independent Colleges, Milwaukee, WI
35,000 Junior Achievement, Racine, WI
33,000 School Sisters of Notre Dame, Elm Grove, WI
30,000 Dominican High School, Milwaukee, WI
25,000 Cardinal Stritch College, Milwaukee, WI
25,000 Marquette University, Milwaukee, WI
25,000 Messmer High School, Milwaukee, WI
25,000 Michigan Technological University, Houghton, MI
25,000 Milwaukee School of Engineering, Milwaukee, WI
25,000 Mount Mary College, Milwaukee, WI
17,000 Inroads, St. Louis, MO

Environment
30,000 Nature Conservancy, Madison, WI
20,000 Trees for Tomorrow, Eagle River, WI

Health
35,000 Children's Hospital, Milwaukee, WI
25,000 Sinai Samaritan Medical Center, Milwaukee, WI
16,700 American Lung Association, Milwaukee, WI

Religion
31,616 St. Josephat Basilica, Milwaukee, WI
30,000 St. Francis Foundation, Milwaukee, WI

Social Services
700,000 United Way, Milwaukee, WI
62,500 YMCA, Milwaukee, WI
54,750 Racine Area United Way, Racine, WI
37,000 United Way of Waukesha County, Waukesha, WI
35,000 Boys and Girls Club, Milwaukee, WI
34,000 United Way of Fox Cities, Menasha, WI
28,000 Boy Scouts of America Milwaukee County Council, Milwaukee, WI
26,000 United Way, Kenosha, WI
25,000 Family Foundation of North America, Milwaukee, WI
25,000 Southside Milwaukee Emergency Shelter, Milwaukee, WI
25,000 YWCA, Milwaukee, WI
25,000 YWCA, Milwaukee, WI
20,000 Goodwill Industries of Southeastern Wisconsin, Milwaukee, WI

Wisconsin Power & Light Co.

Company Contact

Madison, WI
Web: http://www.alliantenergy.com

Company Description

Assets: US$1,299,000,000
Employees: 2,332
SIC(s): 4911 Electric Services, 4924 Natural Gas Distribution, 4941 Water Supply.
Parent Company: WPL Holdings, Inc.

Wisconsin Power & Light Foundation, Inc.

Giving Contact

Joann Healy, Foundation Administrator
Wisconsin Power & Light Foundation, Inc.
222 West Washington Avenue
PO Box 219
Madison, WI 53701-0192
Phone: (608)252-5545
Fax: (608)283-6991

Description

EIN: 391444065
Organization Type: Corporate Foundation
Giving Locations: WI: near headquarters and service areas (central and south central Wisconsin)
Grant Types: Capital, Employee Matching Gifts, General Support.
Note: Employee matching gift ratio: 1 to 1.

Giving Philosophy

'The foundation was established to provide contributions for charitable, scientific, literary or educational purposes in a manner that would help improve the quality of community life.' *Wisconsin Power & Light Foundation Annual Report*

Financial Summary

Total Giving: $719,078 (1997); $819,971 (1996); $915,162 (1995). Note: Contributes through corporate direct giving program and foundation. 1996 Giving includes foundation ($687,239); matching gifts ($19,609); scholarship ($2,800); United Way($110,323).
Assets: $11,189,331 (1997); $9,190,424 (1996); $8,181,248 (1995)
Gifts Received: $1,200,000 (1997); $1,300,000 (1996); $1,000,800 (1995). Note: Contributions received from Wisconsin Power & Light Company.

Typical Recipients

Arts & Humanities: Arts Centers, Arts Festivals, Community Arts, Historic Preservation, History & Archaeology, Libraries, Museums/Galleries, Music, Performing Arts, Public Broadcasting, Theater
Civic & Public Affairs: African American Affairs, Botanical Gardens/Parks, Business/Free Enterprise, Community Foundations, Economic Development, Economic Policy, Employment/Job Training, Civic & Public Affairs-General, Municipalities/Towns, Parades/Festivals, Professional & Trade Associations, Safety, Urban & Community Affairs
Education: Business Education, Colleges & Universities, Education Funds, Engineering/Technological Education, Education-General, Preschool Education, Private Education (Precollege), Student Aid, Vocational & Technical Education
Environment: Environment-General
Health: Cancer, Children's Health/Hospitals, Clinics/Medical Centers, Emergency/Ambulance Services, Health Organizations, Hospitals, Nursing Services, Public Health, Single-Disease Health Associations
Religion: Religious Welfare
Social Services: Child Welfare, Community Centers, Community Service Organizations, Emergency Relief, Family Services, Food/Clothing Distribution, People with Disabilities, Shelters/Homelessness, Social Services-General, United Funds/United Ways, YMCA/YWCA/YMHA/YWHA, Youth Organizations

Contributions Analysis

Giving Priorities: Education, health, social welfare, civic interests, and culture and art.
Arts & Humanities: 11%. Cultural interests include history, museums, and libraries. Art interests include performing arts events, music, dance, community-ensembles, small theaters, arts and crafts centers, and visual arts.
Civic & Public Affairs: 29%. Supports neighborhood improvement, community business funds, parks and environmental projects, community affairs, fire safety.
Education: 30%. Supports colleges and universities in areas where the company operates. Other interests include agricultural and technical programs, matching gifts, and scholarship funds.
Health: 29%. Most support goes to social services, with about one-third awarded to united fund drives in local communities. Also supports youth organizations, family services, nursing services, and hospitals.

Application Procedures

Initial Contact: brief letter or proposal
Application Requirements: name and history of organization, overview of proposed project, purpose of funds sought, proof of tax-exempt status, audited financial statement, and copy of current budget
Deadlines: by September for next year funding

Corporate Officials

Anthony J. Amato: senior vice presidento, director B Madison, WI 1951. ED University of Wisconsin, Madison (1973); University of Wisconsin, Madison (1976). PRIM CORP EMPL senior vice president: Wisconsin Power & Light Co.
Erroll Brown Davis, Jr.: president, chief executive officer, director B Pittsburgh, PA 1944. ED Carnegie Mellon University BSEE (1965); University of Chicago MBA (1967). PRIM CORP EMPL president, chief executive officer, director: Interstate Energy Corp. CORP AFFIL chief executive officer: Wisconsin Power & Light Co.; director: Sentry Insurance Co.; chief executive officer: Interstate Power Co.; director: PP&G Industries Inc.; chairman: Heartland Development Corp.; chief executive officer: IES Utilities; chief executive officer: Alliant Industries Inc.; director: BP Amoco Corp. NONPR AFFIL director: WI Manufacturing & Commerce; director: WI Utilities Association; member: Selective Service Board; director: Edison Electric Institute; director: Electric Power Research Institute; trustee: Carnegie Mellon University; director: Competitive Wisconsin Inc.; member: Association of Edison Illuminating Companies; member: American Gas Association; member: American Society Corporate Executives; member: American Association Blacks Energy.

Foundation Officials

Joanne Acomb: director
Anthony J. Amato: president, director (see above)
Linda Brei: vice president
Jo Ann Healy: administrator
Bill Howliski: director
Jules Nicolet: director
Jan Scott: director
Linda Taplin: director

Grants Analysis

Disclosure Period: calendar year ending 1997
Total Grants: $719,708*
Number of Grants: 800 (approx)
Average Grant: $898
Highest Grant: $94,897
Typical Range: $250 to $5,000
***Note:** Giving includes United Way; matching gifts; scholarship.

Recent Grants

Note: Grants derived from 1996 Form 990.

Arts & Humanities
5,000 Al Ringling Theater Friends, Baraboo, WI -- to upgrade stage rigging

5,000	American Players Theater, Spring Green, WI -- general support, educational programs
5,000	Children's Theater of Madison, Madison, WI -- 1996 program support, tickets
5,000	Circus World Museum, Baraboo, WI -- support C.P. Fox Wagon Restoration
5,000	Madison Children's Museum, Madison, WI -- second of two year pledge for Dance Program
5,000	Madison Civil Center, Madison, WI -- cultural programs
5,000	Monroe Street Fine Arts Center
5,000	Net Southwest Foundation, Fennimore, WI -- support project to network libraries in five counties
5,000	Very Special Arts, Muncie, IN -- second payment on two year pledge for Dance Program
2,000	Clown Hall of Fame
2,000	Wisconsin Public Radio, Madison, WI

Civic & Public Affairs

10,000	Urban League, Madison, WI -- 1996 program support
10,000	Wisconsin Sesquicentennial Commission, Madison, WI -- celebration support
5,000	Community Adolescent Program, Madison, WI -- for Parents in Youth Employment
5,000	Experimental Aircraft Association Aviation Foundation, Oshkosh, WI -- support for Young Eagles Program
3,600	Okee Community Park
3,500	Neighbor for Neighbor -- building funds
2,000	Opportunity Development Centers
2,000	Vocational Industries

Education

30,500	Citizens Scholarship Foundation, Lancaster, PA -- for 1996 scholarship program
25,000	Marquette University, Milwaukee, WI -- for corporate sponsorship
15,500	Board of Regents -- fellowship grant
10,000	Business World, Madison, WI -- for Business World, teachers scholarships
10,000	Village Partnership -- third of three year pledge
9,500	Ripon College, Ripon, WI -- annual support
8,000	Beloit College, Beloit, WI -- for Logan Museum
7,000	Marian College -- support campus computer network
5,000	Beloit College, Beloit, WI -- for Help Yourself Program
5,000	John Muir Academy, Madison, WI -- program support
5,000	Lakeland College, Sheboygan, WI -- to raise funds for college
4,500	University of Wisconsin Platteville, Platteville, WI -- support for engineering education
3,000	University of Wisconsin Platteville, Platteville, WI
1,000	Business and Education Council, Madison, WI

Health

10,000	Ripon Medical Center, Ripon, WI -- for 21 Century Building Campaign
5,000	Southern Madison Health Care Center -- second payment on three year pledge
5,000	Tomah Memorial Hospital, Tomah, WI -- annual support
2,000	American Red Cross, Madison, WI

Religion

5,000	Salvation Army -- second payment of three year pledge

Social Services

86,270	United Way Dane County, Madison, WI -- general support, educational programs
16,000	Stateline United Way, Beloit, WI
15,020	United Way North Rock County, Janesville, WI -- annual support
15,000	Village of Oakfield -- for disaster relief of July tornado
11,700	Forward Foundation, Janesville, WI -- for New Beginnings pledge
8,640	United Way -- for YES Payment
6,480	United Way, Sheboygan, WI -- annual support
5,076	Dodge County United Way -- for Beaver Dame, Mayville, Horicon
5,000	Madison Civic Center, Madison, WI -- for 1996 Cultural Heritage Series
5,000	Second Harvest Food Bank, Milwaukee, WI -- third payment on three year grant
5,000	YMCA, Madison, WI -- third payment on three year pledge for building fund
3,000	City of Madison Youth Program, Madison, WI -- management fees

WISCONSIN PUBLIC SERVICE CORP.

Company Contact

Green Bay, WI
Web: http://www.wpsr.com

Company Description

Assets: US$1,258,900,000
Employees: 2,578
SIC(s): 4911 Electric Services, 4924 Natural Gas Distribution.

Nonmonetary Support

Type: Cause-related Marketing & Promotion; Donated Equipment; Donated Products; Loaned Employees
Volunteer Programs: The company sponsors employee volunteer programs in association with the United Way at Work Committee, Adopt-a-Classroom, and the Lyle Kingston Environmental Group.

Wisconsin Public Service Foundation, Inc.

Giving Contact

Larry Weyers, President & Chief Executive Officer
Wisconsin Public Service Foundation, Inc.
PO Box 19001
Green Bay, WI 54307-9001
Phone: (920)448-7260
Fax: (414)433-1693
Web: http://www.wpsr.com/foundat/index.html

Description

EIN: 396075016
Organization Type: Corporate Foundation
Giving Locations: MI: Northern Michigan; WI: Northeast Wisconsin
Grant Types: Capital, Emergency, General Support, Scholarship.
Note: Employee matching gift ratio: 1 to 2.

Financial Summary

Total Giving: $925,000 (1999 approx); $828,522 (1998); $879,234 (1997). Note: Contributes through corporate direct giving program and foundation. Giving includes foundation.
Giving Analysis: Giving for 1997 includes: foundation scholarships ($176,800); foundation grants to United Way ($111,545); foundation matching gifts ($19,241); 1998: foundation scholarships ($184,100); foundation grants to United Way ($101,610); foundation matching gifts ($22,461)
Assets: $18,692,832 (1998); $16,682,052 (1997); $14,361,928 (1996)
Gifts Received: $230,000 (1998); $95,000 (1997); $300,000 (1995). Note: Contributions are received from Wisconsin Public Service Corp.

Typical Recipients

Arts & Humanities: Arts Festivals, Dance, Arts & Humanities-General, History & Archaeology, Libraries, Museums/Galleries, Music, Opera, Performing Arts, Theater
Civic & Public Affairs: Botanical Gardens/Parks, Business/Free Enterprise, Chambers of Commerce, Clubs, Community Foundations, Civic & Public Affairs-General, Housing, Municipalities/Towns, Philanthropic Organizations, Rural Affairs, Urban & Community Affairs, Women's Affairs, Zoos/Aquariums
Education: Agricultural Education, Business Education, Colleges & Universities, Education Funds, Engineering/Technological Education, Education-General, Medical Education, Minority Education, Public Education (Precollege), Science/Mathematics Education, Student Aid
Environment: Environment-General, Wildlife Protection
Health: Children's Health/Hospitals, Emergency/Ambulance Services, Health Organizations, Hospitals, Medical Rehabilitation, Prenatal Health Issues, Single-Disease Health Associations
Religion: Religious Welfare
Science: Science Museums
Social Services: Animal Protection, At-Risk Youth, Big Brother/Big Sister, Community Centers, Community Service Organizations, Day Care, Domestic Violence, Family Services, Homes, People with Disabilities, Recreation & Athletics, Scouts, Senior Services, Special Olympics, Substance Abuse, United Funds/United Ways, Volunteer Services, YMCA/YWCA/YMHA/YWHA, Youth Organizations

Contributions Analysis

Arts & Humanities: About 5%. Supports historical societies and historical preservation, music, dance, and museums.
Civic & Public Affairs: 16%. Funds cities, parks, and public affairs organizations.
Education: About 30%. Major support is for colleges and universities. Also funds health, technical, and religious education, and educational associations. Foundation makes scholarships, as well.
Environment: 8%. Interests include tree and wildlife preservation.
Health: 7%. Supports hospitals and health organizations.
Social Services: 34%. Supports united funds, Salvation Army, youth organizations including clubs, camps, sports, and Christian youth organizations, and family services.
Note: Total contributions in 1998.

Application Procedures

Initial Contact: Write for application form.
Application Requirements: Include organization name, explanation of organization, funds desired, and reason for request.
Deadlines: None.

Restrictions

Foundation only supports 501(c)(3) organizations.

Corporate Officials

Larry Lee Weyers: chief executive officer, chairman, director B Tecumseh, NE 1945. ED Doane College BA (1967); Columbia University ME (1971); Harvard University MBA (1975). PRIM CORP EMPL chief executive officer, chairman, director: Wisconsin Public Service Resources Corp. ADD CORP EMPL president, director, chief executive officer, chairman: WPS

Resources Corp.; vice president, director: WPS Energy Services Inc.; president, chief executive officer, director: WPS Power Development Inc.

Foundation Officials

D. P. Bittner: treasurer, assistant secretary ED Saint Norbert College BBA (1965); University of Wisconsin, Oshkosh MBA (1975). PRIM CORP EMPL senior vice president finance: Wisconsin Public Service Corp.
Francs Kicfer: secretary, assistant treasurer
Patrick D. Schrickel: vice president B Green Bay, WI 1944. ED Illinois Institute of Technology (1966); University of Wisconsin (1974). PRIM CORP EMPL executive vice president: Wisconsin Public Service Corp. CORP AFFIL executive vice president: Wisconsin Public Service Resources Corp.
Larry Lee Weyers: president, chief executive officer (see above)

Grants Analysis

Disclosure Period: calendar year ending 1998
Total Grants: $520,351*
Number of Grants: 119
Average Grant: $4,373
Highest Grant: $33,000
Typical Range: $1,000 to $10,000
***Note:** Giving excludes United Way, matching gifts, scholarship.

Recent Grants

Note: Grants derived from 1998 Form 990.

Arts & Humanities

10,000 Wisconsin History Foundation Inc., Madison, WI -- Operating
8,350 Green Bay Symphony Orch Inc., Green Bay, WI -- Operating
5,000 National Railroad Museum Inc., Green Bay, WI -- Capital
5,000 New Howard-Suamico Library Fund Inc., Green Bay, WI -- Operating

Civic & Public Affairs

15,000 Green Bay Botanical Garden Inc., Green Bay, WI -- Capital
10,000 Greater Green Bay Community Foundation Inc., Green Bay, WI -- Capital
10,000 Wausau Area Community Foundation Inc., Wausau, WI -- Capital
5,000 City of Rhinelander, Rhinelander, WI -- Capital
5,000 Greater Green Bay Community Foundation Inc., Green Bay, WI -- Operating
5,000 Green Bay Area Chamber of Commerce Foundation I, Green Bay, WI -- Operating
5,000 Green Bay Area Chamber of Commerce Foundation I, Green Bay, WI -- Capital
5,000 Neighborhood Housing Services of Green Bay Inc., Green Bay, WI -- Operating
5,000 Newcap Inc., Oconto, WI -- Capital
5,000 Wisconsin Lions Foundation Inc., Roshold, WI -- Capital

Education

40,500 University of Wisconsin - Madison, Madison, WI -- Scholarship-6000Ziemer
28,000 St. Norbert College, DePere, WI -- Scholarship-College
20,000 St. Norbert College, DePere, WI -- Capital
19,000 NWTC Educational Foundation, Green Bay, WI -- Scholarship-Tech/Stoll
16,700 WMC Foundation Inc. (The), Madison, WI -- Contribution-Scholarship
15,000 Bellin College of Nursing Inc., Green Bay, WI -- Operating
14,500 Marquette University, Milwaukee, WI -- Scholarship-College
12,500 Lawrence University, Appleton, WI -- Scholarship-College
10,000 Einstein Project Inc. (The), Green Bay, WI -- Operating
10,000 University of Wisconsin - Green Bay, Green Bay, WI -- Operating
9,295 University of Wisconsin Marinette County Foundation, Marinette, WI -- Capital
6,000 Carroll College, Waukesha, WI -- Scholarship-College
5,600 NWTC Educational Foundation, Green Bay, WI -- Scholarship-AgriBusiness
5,500 Michigan Technological University, Houghton, MI -- Scholarship-500Minority
5,000 Utility Business Education Coalition, Baltimore, MD -- Operating
5,000 Wisconsin Foundation of Independent Colleges Inc., Milwaukee, WI -- Operating

Environment

33,000 Trees for Tomorrow Inc., Eagle River, WI -- Capital
15,300 Trees for Tomorrow Inc., Eagle River, WI -- Operating

Health

20,000 American National Red Cross, Green Bay, WI -- Capital
15,000 NEW Curative Rehabilitation Inc., Green Bay, WI -- Capital
10,000 St. Vincent Hospital, Green Bay, WI -- Capital
5,000 Childrens Hospital Foundation Inc., Milwaukee, WI -- Operating

Social Services

87,000 United Way of Brown County, Green Bay, WI -- Operating
30,000 Young Mens Christian Association of Green Bay, Green Bay, WI -- Capital
25,000 Brown County Association for Retarded Citizens Inc., Green Bay, WI -- Capital
20,000 Family Service Association of Brown County Inc., Green Bay, WI -- Capital
10,000 Options for Independent Living Inc., Green Bay, WI -- Capital
10,000 Wisconsin Amateur Sports Corporation, Madison, WI -- Operating
9,000 United Way of Marathon County Inc., Wausau, WI -- Operating
6,000 Wausau YMCA Foundation Inc., Wausau, WI -- Capital
5,000 Boy Scouts of America Bay Lakes Council, Menasha, WI -- Capital
5,000 Door County YMCA Inc., Sturg Bay, WI -- Capital
5,000 Menominee Animal Shelter, Menominee, MI -- Capital
5,000 Stevens Point Area YMCA, St. Pt., WI -- Capital
5,000 Violence Intervention Project Inc., Kewaunee, WI -- Capital
5,000 Volunteer Center Inc., Green Bay, WI -- Capital

WITCO CORP.

Company Contact

Greenwich, CT

Company Description

Former Name: Witco Chemical Corp.
Employees: 7,200
SIC(s): 2869 Industrial Organic Chemicals Nec, 2899 Chemical Preparations Nec, 2951 Asphalt Paving Mixtures & Blocks, 2992 Lubricating Oils & Greases.

Robert I. Wishnick Foundation

Giving Contact

William Wishnick, President & Director
Robert I. Wishnick Foundation
1 American Lane
Greenwich, CT 06831
Phone: (212)371-1844

Description

EIN: 136068668
Organization Type: Corporate Foundation
Giving Locations: operating communities.
Grant Types: Conference/Seminar, Endowment, Fellowship, General Support, Research, Scholarship.

Financial Summary

Total Giving: $696,291 (1998); $750,000 (1997 approx); $699,488 (1996). Note: Contributes through foundation only.
Giving Analysis: Giving for 1998 includes: foundation ($696,291)
Assets: $8,387,248 (1998); $8,558,992 (1996); $8,855,258 (1995)
Gifts Received: $100,000 (1998); $200,000 (1994); $31,569 (1992). Note: Contributions are received from William Wishnick.

Typical Recipients

Arts & Humanities: Arts Associations & Councils, Arts Centers, Arts Festivals, Arts Institutes, Ballet, Dance, Arts & Humanities-General, Libraries, Museums/Galleries, Music, Opera, Performing Arts, Theater, Visual Arts
Civic & Public Affairs: Civil Rights, Clubs, Civic & Public Affairs-General, Law & Justice, Native American Affairs, Safety, Urban & Community Affairs, Women's Affairs
Education: Arts/Humanities Education, Business Education, Colleges & Universities, Engineering/Technological Education, Education-General, Legal Education, Medical Education, Minority Education, Preschool Education, Private Education (Precollege), Public Education (Precollege), School Volunteerism, Student Aid
Environment: Air/Water Quality, Environment-General
Health: AIDS/HIV, Cancer, Children's Health/Hospitals, Clinics/Medical Centers, Emergency/Ambulance Services, Geriatric Health, Home-Care Services, Hospitals, Medical Research, Multiple Sclerosis, Single-Disease Health Associations
International: Foreign Educational Institutions, Health Care/Hospitals, International Peace & Security Issues, International Relations, Missionary/Religious Activities
Religion: Churches, Jewish Causes, Religious Organizations, Religious Welfare, Synagogues/Temples
Science: Scientific Centers & Institutes, Scientific Organizations
Social Services: Animal Protection, Camps, Child Welfare, Community Service Organizations, Crime Prevention, Family Planning, Family Services, Homes, People with Disabilities, Recreation & Athletics, Scouts, Shelters/Homelessness, Social Services-General, United Funds/United Ways, Veterans, Youth Organizations

Contributions Analysis

Arts & Humanities: 25%. Interests include theaters, museums, ballet, and opera.
Civic & Public Affairs: 5%. Funds Native American issues and peace initiatives.
Education: 12%. Primarily supports colleges and universities, private secondary education, and art, science and math education programs.
Environment: 2%.

Health: 4%. Primary interests include hospitals, clinics and medical centers, and medical research.
Religion: 44%. Principal support goes to Jewish organizations and temples.
Social Services: 9%. Supports people with disabilities, family planning, programs protecting the homeless, and shelters.
Note: Total contributions in 1998.

Application Procedures

Initial Contact: Send a brief letter.
Application Requirements: Include a description of program, amount of funds requested.
Deadlines: None.
Decision Notification: Board meets quarterly; decisions take six to eight weeks.

Restrictions

Foundation does not support individuals or matching gifts. Loans are not made.

Additional Information

The foundation and corporation operate as separate entities.

Foundation Officials

Robert L. Bachner: director B 1934. ED Harvard University AB (1955); Harvard University JD (1958). PRIM CORP EMPL partner: Bachner, Tally, Polevoy & Misher.
Simeon Brinberg: director PRIM CORP EMPL senior vice president: BRT Realty Trust. CORP AFFIL director: Witco Corp.
Lisa Wishnick: director
William Wishnick: president, director B Brooklyn, NY 1924. ED Carnegie Institute of Technology; University of Texas BBA (1949). CORP AFFIL chairman emeritus, director: Witco Corp.

Grants Analysis

Disclosure Period: calendar year ending 1998
Total Grants: $696,291
Number of Grants: 122
Average Grant: $5,707
Highest Grant: $100,000
Typical Range: $250 to $10,000

Recent Grants

Note: Grants derived from 1998 Form 990.

Arts & Humanities

66,200	New York City Ballet, New York, NY -- General
18,000	National Dance Institute, New York, NY -- General
15,000	Eye on Dance/ Arts Resources in Collaboration, New York, NY -- General
11,450	Ballet West-Salt Lake City, Salt Lake City, UT -- General
9,525	Ballet Theater Foundation, New York, NY -- General
6,000	Institute at Deer Valley, Park City, UT -- General
6,000	Lincoln Center Theater, New York, NY -- General
6,000	Metropolitan Opera Association, New York, NY -- General
5,000	Foundation for Dance Promotion, New York, NY -- General
3,000	National Museum of American Indian/ Smithsonian, Washington, DC -- General

Civic & Public Affairs

17,000	Adopt a Native American Elder, Park City, UT -- General

Education

60,000	American Friends of The Hebrew University, New York, NY -- General
25,000	Crossroads School, New York, NY -- General
15,000	Monte Vista Intermediate School, Danville, CA -- General
10,000	Appleseed Foundation, Houston, TX -- General
10,000	Gregorian University Foundation, New York, NY -- General
8,200	ACA Camper Scholarship Program, Louisville, KY -- General
5,000	Blessed Sacrament Regional School, Tonawanda, NY -- General
5,000	Delbarton School, Morristown, NJ -- General
5,000	Los Angeles High School for the Arts, Los Angeles, CA -- General
5,000	University of Michigan, Ann Arbor, MI -- General
2,500	Polytechnic University, Brooklyn, NY -- General
2,500	The Thatcher School, Ojai, CA -- General

Environment

10,000	Environmental Defense Fund, New York, NY -- General
5,000	Farm Sanctuary, Inc., Watkins Glen, NY -- General

Health

13,000	Mt. Sinai Annual Trustee Campaign, New York, NY -- General
10,000	Mt. Sinai Medical Center Crystal Ball, New York, NY -- General
6,000	Darrell Gwynn Research Fund, Miami, FL -- General
6,000	International Center for the Disabled, New York, NY -- General
4,000	Self-help, New York, NY -- General
2,500	United People For Better Nursing Home Care, Arlington, NY -- General

International

35,000	Jerusalem Foundation, New York, NY -- General
10,000	Seeds of Peace, Washington, DC -- General

Religion

100,000	United Jewish Appeal, New York, NY -- General
15,000	Museum of Jewish Heritage, New York, NY -- General
13,000	Anti Defamation League, New York, NY -- General
7,500	Brotherhood Synagogue, New York, NY -- General
5,000	AJC-ADL Holocaust Foundation, San Francisco, CA -- General
5,000	AMCHA, New York, NY -- General
5,000	Descendants of the Shoah, Los Angeles, CA -- General
5,000	Leo Baeck Institute, New York, NY -- General
4,000	American Jewish Committee, New York, NY -- General
3,500	Church of the Woods, Lake Arrowhead, CA -- General
2,816	Temple Israel of New Rochelle, New Rochelle, NY -- General
2,500	Abundant Grace Fellowship Church, Toms River, NJ -- General

Social Services

15,000	Planned Parenthood of New York City, New York, NY -- General
5,000	National Ability Center of Park City, Park City, UT -- General
4,500	US Ski Team Foundation, Park City, UT -- General
3,000	Planned Parenthood of Park City, Park City, UT -- General
2,750	Alyn-American Society for Handicapped Children, New York, NY -- General

Wolverine World Wide

Company Contact

Rockford, MI

Company Description

Employees: 6,775
SIC(s): 3111 Leather Tanning & Finishing, 3143 Men's Footwear Except Athletic, 3144 Women's Footwear Except Athletic, 3149 Footwear Except Rubber Nec, 3151 Leather Gloves & Mittens.

Operating Locations

Includes division locations.

Nonmonetary Support

Type: Donated Products

Wolverine World Wide Foundation

Giving Contact

Robert Sedrowski, Vice President Human Resources
9341 Courtland Drive
Rockford, MI 49351
Phone: (616)866-5500

Description

EIN: 386056939
Organization Type: Corporate Foundation. Supports preselected organizations only.
Giving Locations: MI
Grant Types: Award, Capital, Challenge, Employee Matching Gifts, Endowment, General Support, Matching, Project, Research, Scholarship.

Financial Summary

Total Giving: $276,984 (1998); $190,931 (1997); $168,834 (1996)
Assets: $435,426 (1996); $309,904 (1995); $173,792 (1993)
Gifts Received: $259,435 (1996); $180,000 (1995); $62,650 (1993). Note: In 1996, contributions were received from Wolverine World Wide.

Typical Recipients

Arts & Humanities: Arts Associations & Councils, Arts & Humanities-General, Libraries, Music, Opera
Civic & Public Affairs: Botanical Gardens/Parks, Civic & Public Affairs-General, Parades/Festivals, Urban & Community Affairs
Education: Arts/Humanities Education, Business Education, Colleges & Universities, Economic Education, Education-General, Minority Education, Public Education (Precollege), Student Aid
Health: Clinics/Medical Centers, Emergency/Ambulance Services, Eyes/Blindness, Health-General
International: International Affairs, International Relief Efforts
Science: Science-General
Social Services: Child Welfare, Community Service Organizations, Family Services, Recreation & Athletics, Scouts, Social Services-General, United Funds/ United Ways

Additional Information

Trust(s): NBD Bank NA

Corporate Officials

Geoffrey B. Bloom: chairman, chief executive officer, director B Newton, MA 1941. ED Ursinus College (1963). PRIM CORP EMPL chairman, chief executive officer, director: Wolverine World Wide. NONPR AFFIL trustee: Kendall School Art & Design.

Stephen L. Gulis, Jr.: executive vice president, treasurer, chief financial officer PRIM CORP EMPL executive vice president, treasurer, chief financial officer: Wolverine World Wide.
Timothy O'Donovan: president PRIM CORP EMPL president: Wolverine World Wide.

Grants Analysis

Disclosure Period: calendar year ending 1996
Total Grants: $168,834
Number of Grants: 118
Highest Grant: $10,000
Typical Range: $25 to $10,000

Recent Grants

Note: Grants derived from 1996 Form 990.

Arts & Humanities

10,000	Opera Grand Rapids, Grand Rapids, MI
7,500	Grand Rapids Symphony, Grand Rapids, MI

Civic & Public Affairs

6,250	Michigan Botanic Garden, Grand Rapids, MI

Education

15,000	Kendall College of Art and Design, Evanston, IL
7,500	Chicago State University, Chicago, IL
7,500	University of Chicago, Chicago, IL
5,000	Rockford Education Foundation, Rockford, MI
4,500	Junior Achievement Campaign
2,500	Frolic Footwear Scholarship Program

International

10,000	Two/Ten International Footwear Foundation, Watertown, MA
7,000	Habitat for Humanity International, Denver, CO

Social Services

5,500	United Way Mecosta County, Big Rapids, MI
5,250	United Way Kent County, Grand Rapids, MI
5,250	United Way Kent County, Grand Rapids, MI
5,000	Grand Rapids Metro Soccer Complex, Grand Rapids, MI
5,000	North Kent Service Center
5,000	United Way Kent County, Grand Rapids, MI
5,000	United Way Kent County, Grand Rapids, MI
3,000	United Way Franklin County, Columbus, OH
2,500	Michigan Stand for Children, MI

WOODWARD GOVERNOR CO.

Company Contact

Rockford, IL
Web: http://www.woodward.com

Company Description

Employees: 3,765 (1999)
SIC(s): 3511 Turbines & Turbine Generator Sets, 3519 Internal Combustion Engines Nec, 3621 Motors & Generators, 3724 Aircraft Engines & Engine Parts.

Woodward Governor Co. Charitable Trust

Giving Contact

Thomas Winking, Contributions Committee Chairman
Woodward Governor Co. Charitable Trust
61111 North Second Street
Rockford, IL 61125
Phone: (815)877-7441
Fax: (815)639-6033

Description

EIN: 846025403
Organization Type: Corporate Foundation
Giving Locations: headquarters and operating communities.
Grant Types: Capital, Emergency, Multiyear/Continuing Support, Operating Expenses, Seed Money.

Financial Summary

Total Giving: $411,156 (1998); $430,190 (1997); $461,562 (1996). Note: Contributes through foundation only.
Giving Analysis: Giving for 1996 includes: foundation grants to United Way ($248,000); foundation ($215,562); 1997: foundation ($258,220); foundation grants to United Way ($171,970); 1998: foundation ($255,956); foundation grants to United Way ($155,200)
Assets: $8,045,253 (1998); $9,686,568 (1997); $9,627,784 (1996)
Gifts Received: $100,000 (1998); $100,000 (1997); $100,000 (1996). Note: In 1998, contributions were received from Woodward Governor Co.

Typical Recipients

Arts & Humanities: Arts Festivals, Arts & Humanities-General, Historic Preservation, Museums/Galleries, Performing Arts, Public Broadcasting, Theater
Civic & Public Affairs: African American Affairs, Botanical Gardens/Parks, Business/Free Enterprise, Economic Development, Employment/Job Training, Housing, Law & Justice, Legal Aid, Philanthropic Organizations, Public Policy, Safety, Urban & Community Affairs, Women's Affairs
Education: Business Education, Colleges & Universities, Elementary Education (Private), Engineering/Technological Education, Education-General, Literacy, Preschool Education, Private Education (Precollege), Secondary Education (Private), Secondary Education (Public), Vocational & Technical Education
Environment: Environment-General
Health: Alzheimers Disease, Cancer, Children's Health/Hospitals, Clinics/Medical Centers, Emergency/Ambulance Services, Geriatric Health, Health Organizations, Hospices, Hospitals, Medical Rehabilitation, Medical Research, Mental Health, Public Health, Research/Studies Institutes, Single-Disease Health Associations, Speech & Hearing
Religion: Religious Welfare
Science: Science Museums
Social Services: At-Risk Youth, Child Welfare, Community Centers, Community Service Organizations, Counseling, Crime Prevention, Emergency Relief, Family Services, Food/Clothing Distribution, Homes, People with Disabilities, Recreation & Athletics, Scouts, Senior Services, Shelters/Homelessness, Special Olympics, Substance Abuse, United Funds/United Ways, Volunteer Services, YMCA/YWCA/YMHA/YWHA, Youth Organizations

Contributions Analysis

Giving Priorities: The arts, united funds, and health.
Arts & Humanities: 5%. The arts, including symphonies and various museums.
Civic & Public Affairs: 6%. Children's recreational programs, including youth centers, volunteer programs such as Big Brother/Big Sister, and educational programs such as Junior Achievement. Housing, crime prevention, legal aid, and safety are also priorities.
Education: 12%. Educational programs including schools and literacy councils.
Health: 13%. Most recipients are single-disease health organizations. Funds also support the handicapped, mental health groups, and some clinics and hospitals.
Religion: 1%. Supports religious causes.
Science: 2%. Funds science museums, natural history museums and the discovery center.
Social Services: 61%. Food distribution centers, community services, minority groups, youth organizations, and various programs for child welfare.
Note: Total contributions made in 1998.

Application Procedures

Initial Contact: Send a brief letter.
Application Requirements: Include a description of organization and how it meets community needs and copy of unexpired IRS letter proving that contributions to organization are tax deductible.
Deadlines: None.
Review Process: No standard letter of application is required; after receipt of initial letter, foundation will send a request evaluation form to be completed and returned.
Evaluative Criteria: Seeks organizations that benefit company operating communities.
Decision Notification: Within eight weeks.

Restrictions

The foundation does not give to individuals, endowment funds, research, scholarships, fellowships, special projects, publications, or conferences.
The foundation does not give matching gifts or loans.
Almost all grants go to organizations in company operating areas.

Corporate Officials

John A. Halbrook: chief executive officer, chairman B 1945. PRIM CORP EMPL chief executive officer, chairman: Woodward Governor Co.

Foundation Officials

Roger Frey: trustee
George Mittendorf: trustee
Robert Reuterfors: trustee
Thomas Winking: chairman contributions committee

Grants Analysis

Disclosure Period: calendar year ending 1998
Total Grants: $255,956*
Number of Grants: 46
Average Grant: $5,564
Highest Grant: $25,000
Typical Range: $2,500 to $10,000
***Note:** Giving excludes United Way.

Recent Grants

Note: Grants derived from 1997 Form 990.

Arts & Humanities

5,000	New American Theater, Rockford, IL
5,000	Rockford Museum Association, Rockford, IL -- cultural, educational

Civic & Public Affairs

10,000	Rockford Park District, Rockford, IL -- research

Education

15,000	Rockford College, Rockford, IL -- educational
11,000	University of Wisconsin Foundation, Madison, WI -- educational
5,000	Rock Valley College Foundation, Rockford, IL -- educational
2,650	Barbara Olson School of Hope, Rockford, IL -- social welfare
2,500	Community Education Foundation of Rockford -- educational

2,500	Junior Achievement of Rockford -- social welfare
1,500	Junior Achievement of Rock Mountain-Northern Colorado, CO -- social welfare
1,000	St. Francis Primary School -- educational
1,000	Thompson R2-J Education Foundation, Loveland, CO -- educational
1,000	Thompson Valley Preschool, Loveland, CO -- educational
Health	
25,000	McKee Medical Center, Loveland, CO -- medical
20,000	Crusader Clinic -- medical, health
8,000	Northern Illinois Hospice Association, Rockford, IL -- medical research
5,000	Swedish American Hospital, Rockford, IL -- medical, health
3,500	American Red Cross of Larimer County -- social welfare
3,500	Larimer County Partners, Fort Collins, CO -- medical
1,800	Al-Care, Rockford, IL -- medical
1,800	Children's Development Center -- social welfare
1,500	Alzheimer's Association Rocky Mountain Chapter, CO -- medical
1,500	Children's Speech Therapy Center -- social welfare
Religion	
27,160	Rockford Rescue Mission, Rockford, IL -- social welfare
2,160	Salvation Army Food Pantry -- social welfare
Science	
15,000	Burpee Museum of Natural History, Rockford, IL -- cultural, educational
3,200	Discovery Center, Rockford, IL -- cultural, educational
3,000	Discovery Center Science Museum, Fort Collins, CO -- cultural, educational
Social Services	
80,000	United Way of Rockford -- social welfare
53,565	United Way, Fort Collins, CO -- social welfare
25,670	United Way of Loveland/Berthoud/Estes Park, Loveland, CO -- social welfare
17,000	YMCA, Rockford, IL -- recreational
7,060	Park Pantry -- social welfare
7,060	Rock River Valley Food Pantry, Rockford, IL -- social welfare
5,000	House of Neighborly Service -- social welfare
5,000	YMCA Partners with Youth, IL -- recreational
4,000	United Way of Boone County -- social welfare
4,000	United Way of Stateline -- social welfare
3,500	Project Self-Sufficiency, Columbus, IN -- social welfare
3,000	Boy Scouts of America Peak Council -- social welfare
2,690	RocVale Children's Home, Rockford, IL -- social welfare
2,500	Children's Justice Center, Tulsa, OK -- social welfare
2,500	Mill, Millville, NJ -- social welfare
2,500	Mold of Rockford -- social welfare
2,000	Larimer County Blind and Physical Handicapped -- social welfare
2,000	United Way of Rockford -- for needs assessment
2,000	United Way of Stephenson County -- social welfare
1,800	Family Advocate Project -- social welfare
1,510	United Way of Weld County, Greeley, CO -- social welfare
1,500	Girl Scouts of America Mountain Prairie Council -- social welfare

WM. JR. WRIGLEY CO.

Company Contact
Chicago, IL

Company Description
Employees: 7,300
SIC(s): 2067 Chewing Gum.

Wm. Jr. Wrigley Co. Foundation

Giving Contact
William M. Piet, Vice President
Wm. Wrigley Jr. Co. Foundation
410 North Michigan Avenue
Chicago, IL 60611
Phone: (312)645-3950
Fax: (312)661-1267

Alternate Contact
Phone: (312)645-3910

Description
EIN: 363486958
Organization Type: Corporate Foundation
Giving Locations: IL: Chicago nationally.
Grant Types: General Support.

Financial Summary
Total Giving: $1,617,196 (1998); $1,769,600 (1997); $1,650,000 (1996). Note: Contributes through foundation only.
Giving Analysis: Giving for 1996 includes: foundation ($1,154,500); foundation grants to United Way ($418,100); foundation matching gifts ($61,296); 1997: foundation ($1,270,800); foundation ($421,100); foundation matching gifts ($77,700); 1998: foundation ($1,136,750); foundation grants to United Way ($411,000); foundation matching gifts ($69,446)
Assets: $44,655,582 (1998); $41,746,128 (1997); $37,552,216 (1996)

Typical Recipients
Arts & Humanities: Museums/Galleries, Music, Performing Arts, Public Broadcasting
Civic & Public Affairs: African American Affairs, Chambers of Commerce, Civil Rights, Employment/Job Training, Civic & Public Affairs-General, Hispanic Affairs, Housing, Nonprofit Management, Philanthropic Organizations, Public Policy, Urban & Community Affairs
Education: Business Education, Colleges & Universities, Community & Junior Colleges, Education Associations, Education Funds, Engineering/Technological Education, International Exchange, Medical Education, Minority Education, Student Aid
Environment: Environment-General, Resource Conservation
Health: Alzheimers Disease, Clinics/Medical Centers, Diabetes, Health Funds, Health Organizations, Hospitals, Nursing Services, Prenatal Health Issues, Public Health, Single-Disease Health Associations
International: Foreign Educational Institutions, Human Rights
Religion: Religious Welfare
Social Services: Child Abuse, Child Welfare, Community Service Organizations, Delinquency & Criminal Rehabilitation, Domestic Violence, Food/Clothing Distribution, People with Disabilities, Senior Services, Substance Abuse, United Funds/United Ways, Youth Organizations

Contributions Analysis
Giving Priorities: Health, social welfare, civic and public affairs, and education.
Civic & Public Affairs: 19%. Supports NAACP, conservation associations, and neighborhood and community development.
Education: 11%. Funds groups concerned with minority education, education funds and nursing scholarships. Company provides scholarships for children of employees. Makes no direct grants to colleges or universities.
Environment: 3%. Supports Keep American Beautiful and Keep Chicago Beautiful.
Health: 25%. Supports medical centers, health care, single-disease associations, elder care, and American cancer Society.
International: 2%. Funds the Foundation for Educational Exchange Between Canada & USA.
Science: 2%. Supports Chicago Academy of Science, and Museum of Science & Industry.
Social Services: 38%. Supports United Way, youth and family services, child abuse prevention, and social services.
Note: Total contributions made in 1998.

Application Procedures
Initial Contact: Send a brief letter and proposal.
Application Requirements: Include a summary of program, audited financial statement, annual report, list of current contributors, IRS letter of tax-exempt certification, list of board of directors and their affiliations.
Deadlines: October 1 for consideration for the following year; considers emergency requests throughout the year.
Evaluative Criteria: Grants primarily directed to national basic health and welfare organizations.
Decision Notification: End of the year for the following year.

Restrictions
Does not support individuals, fraternal organizations, political or lobbying groups, religious organizations for sectarian purposes, member agencies of united funds, or goodwill advertising.

Additional Information
Organizations must be certified by the state in which they operate, and must qualify under IRS 501(c)(3) tax-exempt status.

Corporate Officials
Dushan Petrovich: vice president, chief executive officer, director B 1954. PRIM CORP EMPL vice president: Wm. Jr. Wrigley Co.
William M. Piet: vice president corporate affairs, secretary, assistant to president B Chicago, IL 1943. ED DePaul University BSc (1971); Northwestern University MBA (1974). PRIM CORP EMPL vice president corporate affairs, secretary, assistant to president: Wm. Jr. Wrigley Co. CORP AFFIL chairman: Four-Ten Corp.; director, member executive committee: Santa Catalina Island Co.
William Wrigley, Jr.: vice president, director B 1963. PRIM CORP EMPL vice president, director: Wm. Jr. Wrigley Co. CORP AFFIL officer: Amurol Confections Co.; director: JM Smucker Co. Inc.
William Wrigley: president, chief executive officer, director B Chicago, IL 1933. ED Yale University BA (1954). PRIM CORP EMPL president, chief executive officer, director: Wm. Jr. Wrigley Co. CORP AFFIL director: Zeno Air Inc.; director: Wrigley T.O.O. Russia; director: Wrigley Romania SRL; director: Wrigley doo Slovenia; director: Wrigley Poland SPZOO; director: Wrigley de Mexico SA; director: Wrigley Phillipines Inc.; general manager: Wrigley Gmb H; chairman: Wrigley Co. SA Spain; director: Wrigley Co. (Thailand) Ltd.; director: Wrigley Co. Ltd. UK; director: Wrigley Co. Propriety Ltd. Australia; director: Wrigley Co. Ltd. NZ; director: Wrigley Co. Ltd. HK; director: Wrigley Co. Ltd. Japan; director: Wrigley Chewing

Gum Co. Ltd. China; chairman: Weigert Co. SA; chairman, director: Wrigley (Cayman) Ltd.; director: Texaco Inc.; director, member corporate issues & nominating committee: America Home Products Corp.; chairman: Santa Catalina Island Co. NONPR AFFIL director: Grocery Manufacturer America.

Foundation Officials

Steve Huston: secretary B Morris, IL 1954. ED Illinois College BA (1977); John Marshall Law School JD (1980); Northwestern University MBA (1989). PRIM CORP EMPL counsel: William Wrigley Junior Co. NONPR AFFIL member: American Bar Association; member: Chicago Bar Association.

Dushan Petrovich: treasurer (see above)

William M. Piet: vice president, director (see above)

William Wrigley, Jr.: vice president, director (see above)

William Wrigley: chairman, director (see above)

Grants Analysis

Disclosure Period: calendar year ending 1998
Total Grants: $1,136,750*
Number of Grants: 88
Average Grant: $12,918
Highest Grant: $40,000
Typical Range: $1,000 to $15,000
***Note:** Giving excludes matching gifts; United Way.

Recent Grants

Note: Grants derived from 1997 Form 990.

Arts & Humanities

90,000 Wrigley Gospel Choir Awards
50,000 Wrigley Gospel Choir Awards
40,000 WGBH Educational Foundation, Springfield, MA
30,000 Wrigley Gospel Choir Awards

Civic & Public Affairs

35,000 Advertising Council, New York, NY
15,000 Chicago Urban League, Chicago, IL
15,000 NAACP Special Contribution Fund, Baltimore, MD
15,000 NAACP Special Contributions Fund, New York, NY
15,000 National Urban League, New York, NY
10,000 Better Government Association, Chicago, IL
10,000 Chicagoland Chamber of Commerce Foundation Youth Motivation Programs, Chicago, IL
10,000 Jobs for Youth, Chicago, IL
10,000 Latino Institute, Chicago, IL

Education

25,000 Associated Colleges of Illinois, Chicago, IL
25,000 National Hispanic Scholarship Fund, Novato, CA
20,000 Brenau College, Gainesville, GA
20,000 United Negro College Fund, New York, NY
16,000 Junior Achievement, Chicago, IL
15,000 Consortium for Graduate Study in Management, Saint Louis, MO
15,000 Loyola University Chicago, Chicago, IL
15,000 Schools of Nursing and Allied Health of Muhlenberg Regional Medical Center

Environment

20,000 Keep America Beautiful, Stamford, CT

Health

70,000 Oral Health America America's Fund for Dental Health, Chicago, IL
35,000 Northwestern Memorial Foundation, Chicago, IL
30,000 Health Watch
30,000 Health Watch
20,000 Erie Family Health Center, Chicago, IL
20,000 Oral Health America America's Fund for Dental Health, Chicago, IL
15,000 Alivio Medical Center, Chicago, IL
15,000 Alzheimer's Disease and Related Disorders Association, Chicago, IL
15,000 Juvenile Diabetes Foundation, New York, NY
15,000 March of Dimes Birth Defect Foundation
15,000 Muhlenberg Regional Medical Health, Plainfield, NJ
15,000 Northeast George Medical Center

International

30,000 Foundation for Educational Exchange Between Canada and the USA, ON, Canada
10,000 International Committee on Journalism, New York, NY

Religion

10,000 Salvation Army

Social Services

120,450 United Way Crusade of Mercy, Chicago, IL
120,450 United Way Crusade of Mercy, Chicago, IL
90,600 United Way Hall County, Gainesville, GA
25,000 National Committee for Prevention of Child Abuse, Chicago, IL
25,000 United Way Santa Cruz County, Capilos, CA
20,000 Food Industry Crusade Against Hunger, Washington, DC
19,200 United Way Bergen County, Fairlawn, NJ
19,200 United Way Schaumberg-Hoffman Estates
15,000 Little Friends, Naperville, IL
15,000 Second Harvest National Food Bank Network, Chicago, IL
14,500 United Way, Dallas, TX
11,700 United Way Bay Area, San Francisco, CA
10,000 National Committee for the Prevention of Child Abuse, Chicago, IL

WYMAN-GORDON CO.

Company Contact

Grafton, MA

Company Description

Employees: 3,650
SIC(s): 3462 Iron & Steel Forgings, 3463 Nonferrous Forgings.

Nonmonetary Support

Type: Loaned Executives
Note: Company participates in the United Way Loaned Executive Program.

Corporate Sponsorship

Type: Arts & cultural events; Festivals/fairs; Music & entertainment events; Sports events

Wyman-Gordon Foundation

Giving Contact

Wallace F. Whitney, Jr., Secretary & Treasurer
Wyman-Gordon Foundation
244 Worcester St.
North Grafton, MA 01536-8001
Phone: (508)839-4441
Fax: (508)839-7500

Description

EIN: 046142600
Organization Type: Corporate Foundation
Giving Locations: principally near operating locations and to national organizations.
Grant Types: Employee Matching Gifts, Fellowship, General Support, Scholarship, Seed Money.

Financial Summary

Total Giving: $323,844 (1997); $300,185 (1996); $316,878 (1995). Note: Contributes through foundation only.
Giving Analysis: Giving for 1995 includes: foundation ($310,080); foundation matching gifts ($6,798); 1997: foundation ($170,844); foundation grants to United Way ($153,000)
Assets: $7,192,210 (1997); $6,150,790 (1996); $5,817,798 (1995)

Typical Recipients

Arts & Humanities: Arts Appreciation, Ethnic & Folk Arts, Arts & Humanities-General, Historic Preservation, History & Archaeology, Libraries, Museums/Galleries, Music, Public Broadcasting, Theater
Civic & Public Affairs: Business/Free Enterprise, Chambers of Commerce, Clubs, Economic Development, Civic & Public Affairs-General, Housing, Legal Aid, Parades/Festivals, Professional & Trade Associations, Public Policy, Urban & Community Affairs
Education: Arts/Humanities Education, Business Education, Business-School Partnerships, Colleges & Universities, Community & Junior Colleges, Economic Education, Education Associations, Education Reform, Engineering/Technological Education, Education-General, Private Education (Precollege), Science/Mathematics Education, Student Aid
Environment: Environment-General
Health: AIDS/HIV, Cancer, Children's Health/Hospitals, Emergency/Ambulance Services, Health-General, Health Organizations, Hospitals, Medical Research, Multiple Sclerosis, Nursing Services, Public Health
Religion: Churches, Religious Welfare
Science: Science Exhibits & Fairs, Scientific Centers & Institutes, Scientific Research
Social Services: Child Welfare, Community Service Organizations, Family Services, People with Disabilities, Recreation & Athletics, Scouts, Senior Services, United Funds/United Ways, YMCA/YWCA/YMHA/YWHA, Youth Organizations

Contributions Analysis

Arts & Humanities: 5%. Contributes to museums and historic preservation, as well as general art activites.
Civic & Public Affairs: 10%. Supports community and civic needs in operating locations, including community groups, housing, and legal aid.
Education: 23%. Supports colleges, universities, and education associations, primarily in Massachusetts.
Health: 7%. Funds are awarded to public health associations, and for disease research and prevention.
Social Services: 52%. The majority of funding supports the United Way. Additional funds support traditional youth organizations and people with disabilities.

Application Procedures

Initial Contact: Submit a formal proposal.
Application Requirements: Include a description of the program and purpose of funds requested.
Deadlines: None.

Restrictions

Does not support individuals, religious organizations for sectarian purposes, or political or lobbying groups.

Corporate Officials

Edward J. Davis: chief financial officer, vice president, treasurer B Framingham, MA 1946. ED Harvard College (1968); University of Virginia (1973). PRIM CORP EMPL chief financial officer, vice president, treasurer: Wyman-Gordon Co. ADD CORP EMPL vice president: Wyman Gordon Forgings Inc.

David P. Gruber: president, chief executive officer, director B 1941. ED Ohio State University (1965). PRIM CORP EMPL president, chief executive officer, director: Wyman-Gordon Co. CORP AFFIL chief executive officer: Wyman-Gordon Inv Castings; director: State Street Corp.; director: Wyman-Gordon Forgings Inc. NONPR AFFIL trustee: Manufacturer Alliance Productivity & Innovation.

Foundation Officials

David P. Gruber: chairman, vice president, director (see above)
Jay Whelan: president
Wallace F. Whitney, Jr.: secretary, treasurer B 1943. PRIM CORP EMPL vice president, general counsel, secretary: Wyman-Gordon Co. CORP AFFIL secretary: Wyman-Gordon Inv Castings; secretary: Wyman-Gordon Forgings Inc. NONPR AFFIL chief executive officer: Worcester Performing Arts School.

Grants Analysis

Disclosure Period: calendar year ending 1997
Total Grants: $170,844*
Number of Grants: 74
Average Grant: $2,309*
Highest Grant: $150,000
Typical Range: $200 to $5,000
***Note:** Average grant figure excludes highest grant. Giving excludes United Way.

Recent Grants

Note: Grants derived from 1997 Form 990.

Arts & Humanities

5,000	Old Sturbridge Village, Sturbridge, MA
4,000	Worcester Historic Museum, Worcester, MA
2,000	WICN/90.5 Public Radio, Worcester, MA
1,000	Higgins Armory Museum, Worcester, MA
1,000	Worcester Art Museum, Worcester, MA
800	Worcester Forum Theater, Worcester, MA
500	American Antiquarian Society, Worcester, MA
500	Preservation Worcester, Worcester, MA
500	Preservation Worcester, Worcester, MA
500	WICN/90.5 Public Radio
500	Worcester Historic Museum, Worcester, MA

Civic & Public Affairs

20,000	Worcester Chamber of Commerce, Worcester, MA
5,000	Manufacturing Our Future
3,000	Worcester Community Housing Resources, Worcester, MA
2,000	New England Legal Foundation, Boston, MA
1,000	X-Prize Foundation, Rockville, MD
500	Junior League, Worcester, MA

Education

45,144	Worcester Polytechnic Institute Scholarship Program, Worcester, MA
5,000	FIERF
5,000	Worcester Polytechnic Institute, Worcester, MA
4,000	Nichols College, Dudley, MA
3,000	Northeastern University, Boston, MA
2,500	James E. Coyne Memorial Fund
2,000	Alliance for Education, Worcester, MA
1,000	Al Hamra Academy
1,000	Becker College, Leicester, MA
1,000	MSPCC
1,000	Worcester State College, Worcester, MA
500	Clark University, Worcester, MA
500	Junior Achievement of Central Massachusetts, MA
500	Performing Arts School, Worcester, MA

Environment

5,000	Massachusetts Audubon Society, Lincoln, MA
1,000	Massachusetts Audubon Society, Lincoln, MA

Health

10,000	Medical Society of Central Massachusetts
3,000	Research Bureau
2,000	Community Healthlink, Worcester, MA
2,000	Visiting Nurses Association, Worcester, MA
1,650	Worcester Society of Biomedical Research, Worcester, MA
1,000	Community Healthlink, Worcester, MA

Religion

1,000	First Congregational Church, Geneva, NE
1,000	First Congregational Church, Geneva, NE

Science

1,000	New England Science Center, Worcester, MA

Social Services

150,000	United Way of Central Massachusetts, Worcester, MA
3,000	United Way of Central Massachusetts, Worcester, MA
2,500	YOU
1,500	WAARC, Worcester, MA -- Lori Lajoie Golf Tournament
1,000	Dynamy, Worcester, MA -- annual campaign
500	Boy Scouts of America Camp Wanocksett
500	Family Services of Central Massachusetts
500	YMCA, Worcester, MA

XEROX CORP.

Company Contact

Stamford, CT
Web: http://www.xerox.com

Company Description

Revenue: US$19,228,000,000 (1999)
Profit: US$1,424,000,000 (1999)
Employees: 92,700
Fortune Rank: 87, per FORTUNE Magazine's list of 500 Largest U.S. Corporations (1999).
FF 87
SIC(s): 3577 Computer Peripheral Equipment Nec, 3578 Calculating & Accounting Equipment, 3579 Office Machines Nec, 5045 Computers, Peripherals & Software.

Operating Locations

Argentina: Xerox Argentina ICSA, Buenos Aires; Brazil: Xerox do Brasil SA, Rio de Janiero; Canada: Xerox Canada Holdings Inc., North York; Xerox Canada Ltd., North York; Chile: Xerox de Chile SA, Santiago; Ecuador: Xerox del Ecuador SA, Quito; England: Lyell Holdings Limited, Marlow; Xerox Limited, Marlow; Japan: Fuji Xerox Co. Ltd., Tokyo; Mexico: Xerox Mexicana SA, Mexico; Netherlands Antilles: Xerox Antillana NV, Curacao; Peru: Xerox del Peru, Lima; Republic of South Africa: Xerox South Africa, Islando; Switzerland: Xerox Limited AG, Zurich; Venezuela: Xerox de Colombia, Caracas

Nonmonetary Support

Value: $1,000,000 (1996); $1,000,000 (1994); $500,000 (1990)
Type: Donated Equipment; Loaned Employees; Workplace Solicitation
Contact: G. L. Watson, Vice President
Note: Nonmonetary support is provided by the company.

Corporate Sponsorship

Value: $500,000 (1994)
Type: Arts & cultural events; Sports events
Contact: Nancy Wiese, Director, Advertising

Xerox Foundation

Giving Contact

Joseph M. Cahalan, Vice President
Xerox Foundation
PO Box 1600
Stamford, CT 06904
Phone: (203)968-3445
Fax: (203)968-4312

Description

EIN: 060996443
Organization Type: Corporate Foundation
Giving Locations: nationally, with emphasis on operating locations.
Grant Types: Award, Department, Employee Matching Gifts, Fellowship, General Support, Matching, Multiyear/Continuing Support.
Note: Employee matching gift ratio: 1 to 1 for gifts from employees and/or their spouses to institutions of higher learning, up to $1,000 per institution annually.

Giving Philosophy

'The management of Xerox has in the past and continues to be committed to a policy of charitable contributions. This policy seeks to position the corporation as an active participant in society. We believe that a corporation today has institutional responsibilities that go beyond its primary economic role. These responsibilities include a concern for the communities around the country in which Xerox conducts business.' *The Xerox Foundation: Policy and Guidelines*

Financial Summary

Total Giving: $283,894 (1998); $238,598 (1997); $15,000,000 (1996). Note: Contributes through corporate direct giving program and foundation.
Assets: $10 (1998); $534 (1997); $419 (1996)
Gifts Received: $283,710 (1998); $238,500 (1997); $219,023 (1996). Note: In 1998, contributions were received from Xerox Corp.

Typical Recipients

Arts & Humanities: Arts Associations & Councils, Arts Centers, Arts Funds, Arts Institutes, Dance, Historic Preservation, Libraries, Museums/Galleries, Music, Opera
Civic & Public Affairs: Civil Rights, Economic Development, Economic Policy, Employment/Job Training, Housing, Professional & Trade Associations, Public Policy, Urban & Community Affairs, Women's Affairs
Education: Business Education, Colleges & Universities, Economic Education, Education Associations, Education Funds, Engineering/Technological Education, Literacy, Minority Education, Science/Mathematics Education, Student Aid, Vocational & Technical Education
Environment: Environment-General
Health: Health Policy/Cost Containment
International: Foreign Educational Institutions, Health Care/Hospitals, International Organizations, International Relations
Science: Scientific Organizations
Social Services: Child Welfare, Community Service Organizations, Domestic Violence, People with Disabilities, Senior Services, Shelters/Homelessness, Substance Abuse, United Funds/United Ways, Youth Organizations

Contributions Analysis

Giving Priorities: Education, civic interests, and the arts. According to foundation materials, Xerox 'makes

substantial contributions to multinational and international organizations that work to meet basic human needs, develop resources and capabilities, and preserve cultural integrity.' Worldwide, Xerox philanthropy tries to engage national leadership in addressing major social problems and to support programs in education, employability, and cultural affairs. Other areas of particular focus include programs responsive to the national concern for increased productivity, the application of information management technology and general education. Interests include public policy,foreign relations, health care, and development.

Education: 44%. Emphasis is on higher education. Makes large grants to colleges and universities located in communities where company has facilities. Interests include science, technology, and minority education. Also sponsors employee matching gifts.

International: 56%. Emphasis on higher education internationally.

Note: Total contributions made in 1998.

Application Procedures

Initial Contact: Submit a two- to three-page letter.

Application Requirements: Provide the legal name of organization, official contact person, proof of tax-exempt status, description of activities and programs, purpose of grant, benefits expected, plans for evaluation, projected budget, expected sources, amount of funds needed, and a copy of the latest annual financial statement.

Deadlines: None.

Review Process: The contributions committee reviews submissions collectively on a monthly basis; and makes recommendations to the board of trustees who meet quarterly.

Evaluative Criteria: Application to Xerox focus areas of Employee/Community Affairs, Science/Technology Education, Work Force Preparation, National Affairs, or Culture.

Decision Notification: Within 60 days of receipt.

Restrictions

Foundation does not support individuals; organizations supported by the United Way, unless permission has been granted by the United Way to conduct a capital fund drive or special benefit; political organizations or candidates; religious or sectarian groups; or municipal, county, state, federal, or quasi-governmental agencies.

Foundation does not provide capital grants (except in preselected locations with major company facilities) or endowments.

Additional Information

All requests from organizations that have previously received support will be evaluated based on their accomplishment of the objectives included in the initial request.

Corporate Officials

Paul Arthur Allaire: chairman, chief executive officer, chairman executive committee B Worcester, MA 1938. ED Worcester Polytechnic Institute BS (1960); Carnegie Mellon University MS (1966). PRIM CORP EMPL chairman, chief executive officer, chairman executive committee: Xerox Corp. CORP AFFIL director: Xerox Printing Co.; director: SmithKline Beecham PLC; director: Xerox Financial Services Inc.; director: Rank Xerox Ltd.; director: Sara Lee Corp.; director: JP Morgan & Co. Inc.; director: Morgan Guaranty Trust Co. New York; director: Fuji Xerox Co. Ltd.; director: Lucent Technologies Inc. NONPR AFFIL director: New York City Ballet; member: Tau Beta Pi; member: Eta Kappa Nu; member: National Academy Engineering; member: Council Competitiveness; member: Council Foreign Relations; director: Catalyst for Women Inc.

Allan E. Dugan: senior vice president corporate strategic service B Rochester, NY. ED Pennsylvania State University; University Toronto. PRIM CORP EMPL senior vice president corporate strategic service: Xerox Corp. CORP AFFIL director: Katun Corp.; director: Rochester Gas & Electric Corp.; director: Greater Rochester Health System Inc. NONPR AFFIL director: National Association Manufacturers; trustee: University Rochester; director: American European Chamber of Commerce.

John A. Lopiano: senior vice president ED New York University; United States Military Academy. PRIM CORP EMPL senior vice president: Xerox Corp. CORP AFFIL director: Inter Leaf Inc.

Mark B. Myers: senior vice president corporate research & technology B Winchester, IN 1938. ED Earlham College (1960); Pennsylvania State University (1964). PRIM CORP EMPL senior vice president corporate research & technology: Xerox Corp. CORP AFFIL director: SDL Inc.

Addison Barry Rand: executive vice president operations B Washington, DC 1944. ED American University BS; Stanford University MS. PRIM CORP EMPL executive vice president operations: Xerox Corp. ADD CORP EMPL chairman, chief executive officer: Avis Rent A Car Inc. CORP AFFIL director: Honeywell Inc.; director: Abbott Laboratories; director: Ameritech Corp. NONPR AFFIL member board overseers: Garth Fagan Dance Theatre; member board overseers: Rochester New York Philharmonic Orchestra.

Barry D. Romeril: executive vice president, chief financial officer B England 1943. ED Oxford University (1966). PRIM CORP EMPL executive vice president, chief financial officer: Xerox Corp. CORP AFFIL director: Xerox Credit Corp.; director: Xerox Financial Services Inc.; director: United States Surgical Corp.; director: Concert PLC; director: Fuji Xerox Co. Ltd.; director: Comcast United Kingdom Cable Partners Ltd.

G. Richard Thoman: president, chief operating officer B Tuscaloosa, AL 1944. ED McGill University BA (1966); Tufts University MA (1968); Tufts University PhD (1971). PRIM CORP EMPL president, chief operating officer: Xerox Corp. CORP AFFIL director: Fuji Xerox Co. Ltd.; director: Bankers Trust Co.; director: DaimlerChrysler; Union Bancaire Privee:. NONPR AFFIL member: Council Foreign Relations; member: School Management Yale University; member: America Society.

Foundation Officials

Paul Arthur Allaire: president (see above)
Joseph M. Cahalan: vice president
Allan E. Dugan: trustee (see above)
David E. Garnett: trustee
John A. Lopiano: trustee (see above)
Mark B. Myers: trustee (see above)
Addison Barry Rand: trustee (see above)
Martin S. Wagner: secretary, general counsel PRIM CORP EMPL assistant secretary: Xerox Corp.

Grants Analysis

Disclosure Period: calendar year ending 1998
Total Grants: $283,894
Number of Grants: 86
Average Grant: $3,301
Highest Grant: $32,394
Typical Range: $1,500 to $10,000

Recent Grants

Note: Grants derived from 1998 Form 990.

Education

3,000	Case Western Reserve University, Cleveland, OH
3,000	Cornell University, Ithaca, NY
3,000	George Washington University, Washington, DC
3,000	MIT, Cambridge, MA
3,000	MIT, Cambridge, MA
3,000	MIT, Cambridge, MA
3,000	MIT, Cambridge, MA
3,000	MIT, Cambridge, MA
3,000	MIT, Cambridge, MA
3,000	MIT, Cambridge, MA
2,500	Cornell University, Ithaca, NY
2,500	Devry Institute of Technology, Long Beach, CA
2,500	Georgia Institute of Technology, Atlanta, GA
2,500	Harvard University, Cambridge, MA
2,500	Illinois Institute of Technology, Chicago, IL
2,000	California Institute of Technology, Pasadena, CA
2,000	Cornell University, Ithaca, NY
2,000	Devry Institute of Technology, Decatur, GA
2,000	Devry Institute of Technology, Irving, TX
2,000	Loyola University, New Orleans, LA
2,000	MIT, Cambridge, MA
2,000	Northwestern University, Evanstown, IL
2,000	Stanford University, Stanford, CA
2,000	University of California, Los Angeles, CA
2,000	University of Texas, Austin, Austin, TX
2,000	University of Washington at Seattle, Seattle, WA
2,000	USC, Los Angeles, CA
1,500	Florida A&M University, Tallahassee, FL
1,500	Morehouse College, Atlanta, GA
1,500	Prairie View A& M University, Prairie View, TX
1,500	University of Alabama in Huntsville, Huntsville, AL
1,500	University of California, Los Angeles, CA
1,500	University of California - Berkeley, Berkeley, CA
1,500	University of Colorado at Boulder, Boulder, CO
1,500	University of Colorado at Boulder, Boulder, CO
1,500	University of Illinois at Urbana, Champaign, IL
1,500	University of Maryland, College Park, MD
1,500	University of Michigan, Ann Arbor, MI
1,500	University of North Carolina, Greensboro, NC
1,500	University of Tampa, Tampa, FL
1,500	Virginia State University, Petersburg, VA

International

32,394	International University of Japan, Yamato-machi, Japan
20,000	University of Barcelona, Barcelona, Spain
15,000	The Barretstown Gang Camp, Kildare, Ireland
15,000	Queen's University, Kingston, ON, Canada
15,000	Queen's University, Kingston, ON, Canada
15,000	University of Guelph, Guelph, ON, Canada
15,000	University of Seville, Seville, Spain
15,000	University of Toronto, Toronto, ON, Canada
15,000	University of Toronto, Toronto, ON, Canada

Yellow Corp.

Company Contact

Overland Park, KS

Company Description

Revenue: US$3,226,800,000 (1999)
Employees: 29,700
SIC(s): 4213 Trucking Except Local, 6719 Holding Companies Nec.

Nonmonetary Support

Type: In-kind Services; Workplace Solicitation
Note: Nonmonetary Support Range: $35,000 to $40,000. Workplace solicitation is only for the United Way.

Yellow Corp. Foundation

Giving Contact

Steve Richards, Managing Director
Yellow Corp. Foundation
10990 Roe Avenue
Overland Park, KS 66211-1213
Phone: (913)696-6123
Fax: (913)696-6116

Description

EIN: 237004674
Organization Type: Corporate Foundation
Giving Locations: MO: Kansas City headquarters and operating communities.
Grant Types: Capital, Employee Matching Gifts, General Support, Multiyear/Continuing Support, Operating Expenses, Project.

Giving Philosophy

'We feel it is our responsibility to improve the quality of life in the communities we serve, and in particular, in the city where we are headquartered. Yellow Freight and its employees support the various community programs through direct monetary contributions, volunteer efforts of employees, and the Yellow Corporate Foundation. By accepting responsibility for the quality of life in our communities, we not only ensure that our business will thrive in a healthy atmosphere, but that our families and neighbors will enjoy life to the fullest.' *Yellow Corporation, Inc., Community Relations Report*

Financial Summary

Total Giving: $184,910 (1998); $6,460 (1997); $477,658 (1996). Note: Contributes through corporate direct giving program and foundation. Giving includes foundation.
Assets: $402,433 (1998); $536,432 (1997); $527,247 (1996)

Typical Recipients

Arts & Humanities: Arts Associations & Councils, Arts Centers, Arts Institutes, Ballet, Community Arts, Dance, Arts & Humanities-General, Historic Preservation, Libraries, Museums/Galleries, Music, Opera, Performing Arts, Public Broadcasting, Theater, Visual Arts
Civic & Public Affairs: Economic Development, Urban & Community Affairs
Education: Agricultural Education, Arts/Humanities Education, Business Education, Colleges & Universities, Community & Junior Colleges, Economic Education, Environmental Education
Health: Cancer, Children's Health/Hospitals, Health Organizations, Public Health
Religion: Religious Welfare
Social Services: Camps, Crime Prevention, Scouts, United Funds/United Ways, Youth Organizations

Contributions Analysis

Giving Priorities: Focus is on youth education. Culture, the arts, health and social services also receive funding.
Arts & Humanities: 6%. Major interests include music, opera, and museums. Substantial support is also given to dance, arts associations, and public broadcasting. The foundation awards large grants to the Nelson Atkins Museum, the Kansas City Symphony, and the State Ballet of Missouri.
Civic & Public Affairs: 4%.
Education: 21%. Administers matching gifts program to accredited colleges and universities. Major interests include education concerned with traffic and logistics, business education, and arts education. Substantial funding is also awarded to education associations, economic education, literacy programs, and faculty development.
Health: 28%.
Social Services: 41%. Major interests include united funds, community centers, and youth organizations. Yellow Corporation matches United Way contributions.
Note: Total contributions made in 1998.

Application Procedures

Initial Contact: Send a letter.
Application Requirements: Include a description of organization, amount requested, purpose of funds sought, recently audited financial statement, proof of tax-exempt status.
Deadlines: None.
Review Process: Monthly review, follow-up questions, and/or site visits.
Decision Notification: Typically 30 to 60 days from receipt of proposal.

Restrictions

Foundation does not support fraternal organizations, goodwill advertising, individuals, political or lobbying groups, or religious organizations for sectarian purposes.

Additional Information

The foundation reports that they are in the process of reducing their contributions program. In the future, nearly all of the gifts will be issued to the United Way, groups in the Kansas City Area, and organizations that are current recipients of their contributions.
The Yellow Corporate Foundation was formerly known as the Yellow Freight System Foundation.

Corporate Officials

George Everett Powell, III: president, chief executive officer, director B Kansas City, MO 1948. ED Indiana University BSBA (1970). PRIM CORP EMPL president, chief executive officer, director: Yellow Corp. NONPR AFFIL trustee: Midwest Research Institute; member: Young President Organization; member: Kansas City Public Television.
Phillip A. Spangler: vice president, treasurer ED University of Kansas (1964). PRIM CORP EMPL vice president, treasurer: Yellow Corp. CORP AFFIL vice president, treasurer, director: Mission Supply Co.

Foundation Officials

Daniel L. Hornbeck: assistant secretary PRIM CORP EMPL secretary: Yellow Freight System Inc.
George Everett Powell, III: trustee (see above)
George Everett Powell, Jr.: trustee B Kansas City, MO 1926. ED Northwestern University (1946). PRIM CORP EMPL director: Butler Manufacturing Co. CORP AFFIL director: Colt Energy Inc. NONPR AFFIL member: Kansas City Chamber of Commerce; trustee, member executive committee: Midwest Research Institute; board governors: Kansas City Art Institute.
Phillip A. Spangler: treasurer, secretary (see above)

Grants Analysis

Disclosure Period: calendar year ending 1998
Total Grants: $184,910
Number of Grants: 16
Average Grant: $11,557
Highest Grant: $75,000
Typical Range: $1,000 to $20,000

Recent Grants

Note: Grants derived from 1997 Form 990.

Arts & Humanities

2,860	Lyric Opera, Kansas City, MO -- cultural, entertainment
500	KCPT/Channel 9, Kansas City, MO -- support educational auction

Civic & Public Affairs

500	Trucker Buddies, Arizona City, AZ -- support community development

Education

2,000	University of Missouri Kansas City, Kansas City, MO -- community development

Health

100	Leukemia Society of America, New York, NY -- Volunteer 100 Program

Social Services

100	Boy Scouts of America Jayhawk Area Council Troop 172 -- Volunteer 100 program
100	Boy Scouts of America Okaw Valley Council -- Volunteer 100 Program
100	Boy Scouts of America Troop 6 -- Volunteer 100 Program
100	Boy Scouts Heart of America Council, Kansas City, MO -- Volunteer 100 Program
100	Mathews-Dickey Boys Club, St. Louis, MO -- Volunteer 100 Program

York Federal Savings &Loan Association

Company Contact

York, PA
Web: http://www.yorkfed.com

Company Description

Employees: 465
SIC(s): 6035 Federal Savings Institutions.
Parent Company: York Financial Corp.

York Federal Savings & Loan Foundation

Giving Contact

Robert W. Pullo, Chairman & Chief Executive Officer
York Federal Savings & Loan Association
101 South George Street
PO Box 15068
York, PA 17405
Phone: (717)846-8777
Fax: (717)846-5590

Description

EIN: 232111139
Organization Type: Corporate Foundation
Giving Locations: PA: York
Grant Types: Employee Matching Gifts, General Support, Scholarship.

Financial Summary

Total Giving: $232,633 (fiscal year ending June 30, 2000 approx); $232,633 (fiscal 1999); $282,267 (fiscal 1998). Note: Contributes through foundation only.
Giving Analysis: Giving for fiscal 1996 includes: foundation grants to United Way ($33,500); fiscal 1997: foundation grants to United Way ($37,400); fiscal 1998: foundation grants to United Way ($68,450)
Assets: $215,391 (fiscal 2000 approx); $215,391 (fiscal 1999); $304,697 (fiscal 1998)
Gifts Received: $284,650 (fiscal 1998); $252,850 (fiscal 1997); $245,527 (fiscal 1996). Note: Contributions are received from York Federal Savings & Loan Assocation.

Typical Recipients

Arts & Humanities: Arts Associations & Councils, Arts Centers, Arts Festivals, Arts Funds, Community Arts, Ethnic & Folk Arts, Historic Preservation, History & Archaeology, Libraries, Museums/Galleries, Music, Performing Arts, Theater
Civic & Public Affairs: Business/Free Enterprise, Community Foundations, Employment/Job Training, Civic & Public Affairs-General, Hispanic Affairs, Housing, Minority Business, Parades/Festivals, Urban & Community Affairs
Education: Business Education, Colleges & Universities, Economic Education, Education Reform, Education-General, Literacy, Preschool Education, Private Education (Precollege), Public Education (Precollege), Student Aid, Vocational & Technical Education
Environment: Environment-General, Resource Conservation
Health: Children's Health/Hospitals, Clinics/Medical Centers, Emergency/Ambulance Services, Health Organizations, Heart, Hospices, Hospitals, Multiple Sclerosis, Prenatal Health Issues, Public Health, Single-Disease Health Associations
Religion: Churches, Jewish Causes, Religious Welfare
Science: Science Museums
Social Services: Camps, Child Welfare, Community Centers, Community Service Organizations, Crime Prevention, Family Services, People with Disabilities, Recreation & Athletics, Scouts, Sexual Abuse, Substance Abuse, United Funds/United Ways, YMCA/YWCA/YMHA/YWHA, Youth Organizations

Contributions Analysis

Arts & Humanities: 19%. Supports arts funds, music, and historical preservation.
Civic & Public Affairs: 12%. Interests include housing and urban affairs.
Education: 23%. Funds York College, public and private preK-12 schools, and health education.
Health: 4%. Supports the American Red Cross and single-disease health associations.
Social Services: 41%. Major funding for the United Way; also supports youth organizations.
Note: Total contributions in fiscal 1998.

Application Procedures

Initial Contact: Send a brief letter of inquiry.
Deadlines: None.

Restrictions

Company does not make grants to religious organizations for sectarian purposes.

Additional Information

Special initiatives are underway to address housing and the needs of low-income communities.

Corporate Officials

Robert A. Angelo: president, chief operating officer, director B 1947. ED LaSalle University PA; University of Baltimore JD. PRIM CORP EMPL president, chief operating officer: York Federal Savings & Loan Association. CORP AFFIL president: Y-F Service Corp. NONPR AFFIL director: York City School District Authority; member: York County Bar Association; member: Pennsylvania Bar Association.
Robert W. Pullo: chairman, chief executive officer, director B Cambridge, MA 1939. ED Williams College (1961-1962); Northeastern University (1960-1970). PRIM CORP EMPL chairman, chief executive officer, director: York Federal Savings & Loan Association. CORP AFFIL chairman: Y-F Service Corp.; president, chief executive officer, director: York Financial Corp. NONPR AFFIL director: York County Industrial Development Corp.; director: York Township Water Sewer Authority; member: Pennsylvania Association Savings Institute; director: York Area Enterprise Development Committee; president: Central Pennsylvania Savings Loan League; member: Mayor's Economic Advisory Council.

Foundation Officials

Robert A. Angelo: secretary (see above)
Cynthia A. Dotzel, CPA: trustee B 1955. CORP AFFIL director: York Federal Savings & Loan Association.
Robert W. Erdos: trustee CORP AFFIL director: York Federal Savings & Loan Association.
Randall A. Gross: trustee B 1944. ED University of Cincinnati MBA; University of Cincinnati BS. PRIM CORP EMPL president: RG Industries Inc. CORP AFFIL director: York Federal Savings & Loan Association. NONPR AFFIL chairman: York Area Chamber of Commerce.
Paul D. Mills: trustee B 1930. PRIM CORP EMPL owner: Willow Tree Farm. CORP AFFIL director: York Federal Savings & Loan Association. NONPR AFFIL member: Pennsylvania Horse Breeders Association.
James H. Moss: treasurer B Lancaster, PA 1953. ED Elizabethtown College (1977). PRIM CORP EMPL executive vice president, treasurer: York Federal Savings & Loan Association. CORP AFFIL treasurer: Y-F Service Corp.; vice president: York Financial Corp. NONPR AFFIL member: Fin Managers Society; member: Financial Executives Institute; member: American Institute CPAs.
Paul W. Moyer: trustee B 1929. PRIM CORP EMPL president: Moyer & Sons Inc.
Robert W. Pullo: president, trustee (see above)
Byron A. Ream: trustee
Robert L. Simpson: trustee B 1946. PRIM NONPR EMPL executive director: Crispus Attucks Association.
Carolyn E. Steinhauser: trustee B 1940. ED Middlebury College BA. CORP AFFIL director: York Federal Savings & Loan Association.
Hiram L. Wiest: trustee
Thomas W. Wolf: trustee B 1948. ED Dartmouth College BA; Massachusetts Institute of Technology PhD; University of London. CORP AFFIL director: York Federal Savings & Loan Association; chairman: York Financial Corp.; partner: Wolf Organization Inc.; treasurer: Wolf Supply Co.; president: Wolf Distributing Co. Baltimore; president: Wolf Distributing Co. Dover; treasurer: Wolf Distributing Co. Allentown.
William T. Wolf: trustee

Grants Analysis

Disclosure Period: fiscal year ending June 30, 1999
Total Grants: $232,633
Number of Grants: 70
Average Grant: $3,323
Highest Grant: $15,000
Typical Range: $150 to $10,000
Note: Grants analysis provided by foundation.

Recent Grants

Note: Grants derived from fiscal 1997 Form 990.

Arts & Humanities

10,000	York Little Theater, York, PA -- first of five payments on pledge
7,000	Maryland and Pennsylvania Railroad Preservation Society, York, PA -- second of three payments on pledge
5,500	Strand Capitol Performing Arts Center, York, PA -- corporate membership
5,000	York Little Theater, York, PA -- first of five payments on pledge
5,000	YorkArts, York, PA -- first of three payments on pledge
3,000	Allied Arts Fund, Harrisburg, PA -- corporate pledge
3,000	Strand Capitol Performing Arts Center, York, PA -- for Arts Alliance
2,500	Allied Arts Fund, Harrisburg, PA -- corporate campaign
2,500	Historical Society, York, PA -- for business membership
2,000	Hershey Public Library, Hershey, PA -- capital campaign
2,000	Junior Symphony Orchestra, York, PA
2,000	York Arts Festival, York, PA -- for Youth Arts Festival
1,750	Strand Capitol Performing Arts Center, York, PA -- for Day at the Strand

Civic & Public Affairs

15,000	York Foundation, York, PA -- final of five payments on pledge
6,666	Penn-Mar Organization, Maryland Line, MD -- second of three payments on pledge
5,000	Better York, York, PA
4,000	William C. Goodridge Business Resource Center, York, PA -- first of five payments on pledge
3,000	Harford Habitat for Humanity, Forest Hill, MD
2,500	Revolving Loan Fund, Bel Air, MD
2,500	R.G. Charitable Foundation, York, PA -- for Rock & Ride
2,000	York Hispanic Spanish American Center, York, PA -- for Hispanic Heritage Celebration
1,500	FIRST, York, PA -- for Aquo Primero Program
1,400	City of York, York, PA -- for First Annual 4th of July Celebration
1,000	Keep York Beautiful, York, PA -- campaign support
1,000	Lancaster Housing Opportunity Partnership, Lancaster, PA -- financial support
1,000	PACH Foundation, Harrisburg, PA

Education

10,000	Junior Achievement, York, PA -- for 1996-97 campaign
5,000	York City Dollars for Scholars Endowment Fund, York, PA -- first of five payments on pledge
5,000	York Country Day School, York, PA -- third of five payments on pledge
4,000	Dallastown School District, Dallastown, PA -- support Dollars for Scholars
4,000	Northeastern School District Scholarship Foundation, Manchester, PA -- second of five payments on pledge
1,000	Spring Grove Area Scholarship Foundation, Spring Grove, PA -- second of five payments on pledge

Environment

8,334	York County Heritage Rail/Trail, York, PA -- final of three payments on pledge

Health

3,000	York House Hospice, York, PA
2,500	Byrnes Health Education Center, York, PA -- Heart of Gold Sponsor
2,000	American Red Cross, York, PA -- for Technology Project

Religion

1,000	Christ Hope Community Church, York, PA -- for playground

Social Services

15,000	United Way York County, York, PA -- third of four payments on pledge
15,000	United Way York County, York, PA -- second of four payments on pledge
15,000	United Way York County, York, PA -- first of four payments on pledge
12,500	YMCA, York, PA -- for second half of first pledge
10,400	Crispus Attucks, York, PA -- for Youth Build
7,400	United Way York County, York, PA -- final of four payments on pledge
5,000	Boy Scouts of America, York, PA -- first of three payments on pledge
5,000	City of York, York, PA -- for Motorcycle Brigade

2,500 City of York, York, PA -- for Motorcycle Brigade
2,000 Crispus Attucks, York, PA -- fourth of five payments on pledge
1,350 City of York, York, PA -- for Motorcycle Brigade
1,000 Pennsylvania Coalition Against Rape, Harrisburg, PA -- first of three payments on pledge
1,000 White Rose Foundation, York, PA -- support Tennis for Kids

YOUNG &RUBICAM

Company Contact

New York, NY
Web: http://www.yr.com

Company Description

Gross Operating Earnings: US$13,564,000,000
Employees: 11,749
SIC(s): 7311 Advertising Agencies.

Young & Rubicam Foundation

Giving Contact

Young & Rubicam Foundation
285 Madison Avenue, 18th Floor
New York, NY 10017
Phone: (212)210-3000
Fax: (212)490-9073

Description

Founded: 1955
EIN: 136156199
Organization Type: Corporate Foundation. Supports preselected organizations only.
Giving Locations: NY
Grant Types: General Support, Matching.

Financial Summary

Total Giving: $750,000 (1999 approx); $750,000 (1998 approx); $583,283 (1996). Note: Contributes through foundation only. 1996 Giving includes foundation ($475,908); matching gifts ($107,375). 1995 Giving includes foundation ($683,581); matching gifts ($79,755).
Assets: $36,798 (1996); $59,785 (1995); $52,489 (1994)
Gifts Received: $563,301 (1996); $763,336 (1995); $541,285 (1994). Note: The foundation receives contributions from Young and Rubicam, Inc.

Typical Recipients

Arts & Humanities: Arts Associations & Councils, Arts Centers, Arts Funds, Dance, Arts & Humanities-General, History & Archaeology, Libraries, Museums/Galleries, Music, Opera, Performing Arts, Public Broadcasting, Theater, Visual Arts
Civic & Public Affairs: African American Affairs, Botanical Gardens/Parks, Business/Free Enterprise, Chambers of Commerce, Clubs, Economic Development, Economic Policy, Employment/Job Training, Ethnic Organizations, Civic & Public Affairs-General, Hispanic Affairs, Municipalities/Towns, Professional & Trade Associations, Public Policy, Rural Affairs, Urban & Community Affairs, Women's Affairs, Zoos/Aquariums
Education: Arts/Humanities Education, Business Education, Colleges & Universities, Economic Education, Education Funds, Engineering/Technological Education, Education-General, International Studies, Journalism/Media Education, Leadership Training, Literacy, Minority Education, Private Education (Precollege), Public Education (Precollege), Religious Education, Secondary Education (Private), Special Education, Student Aid
Health: AIDS/HIV, Cancer, Children's Health/Hospitals, Clinics/Medical Centers, Diabetes, Emergency/Ambulance Services, Geriatric Health, Heart, Hospitals, Medical Research, Multiple Sclerosis, Nursing Services, Prenatal Health Issues, Public Health, Respiratory, Single-Disease Health Associations, Transplant Networks/Donor Banks
International: Foreign Arts Organizations, Health Care/Hospitals, Human Rights, International Affairs, International Development, International Peace & Security Issues, International Relations, International Relief Efforts
Religion: Churches, Jewish Causes, Religious Organizations, Religious Welfare, Seminaries, Social/Policy Issues
Science: Science Museums
Social Services: Child Welfare, Community Service Organizations, Day Care, Family Planning, Family Services, Food/Clothing Distribution, People with Disabilities, Recreation & Athletics, Scouts, Social Services-General, Substance Abuse, United Funds/United Ways, YMCA/YWCA/YMHA/YWHA, Youth Organizations

Contributions Analysis

Arts & Humanities: 10% to 15%. Museums, theaters, and libraries.
Civic & Public Affairs: 10% to 15%. The Advertising Council, with other funding directed to community and economic development.
Education: 25% to 30%. Primarily in the form of employee matching gifts. Remaining support goes to education funds in New York, NY.
Health: About 10%. Hospitals, community service programs, and disease-specific foundations.
Social Services: 30% to 35%. United Way of New York City, youth organizations, and community services.

Restrictions

Does not support individuals, capital or endowment funds, scholarships, fellowships, operating budgets, continuing support, annual campaigns, seed money, emergency funds, deficit financing, special projects, research, publications, or conferences. Does not make loans.

Grants Analysis

Disclosure Period: calendar year ending 1996
Total Grants: $475,908*
Number of Grants: 119
Average Grant: $3,999
Highest Grant: $26,402
Typical Range: $500 to $10,000
***Note:** Giving excludes matching gifts.

Recent Grants

Note: Grants derived from 1997 Form 990.

Arts & Humanities

25,000 Boys Club of Harlem, New York, NY
17,500 Museum of Modern Art, New York, NY
10,000 New York Philharmonic, New York, NY
6,000 Museum of Television and Radio, New York, NY
5,000 Arts & Business Council, New York, NY
5,000 Carnegie Hall Society Inc., New York, NY
5,000 Kentucky Arts & Crafts Foundation, Louisville, KY

Civic & Public Affairs

20,000 National Ethnic Coalition, New York, NY
17,500 Advertising Council, New York, NY
13,000 New York City Partnership, New York, NY
10,000 New York Botanical Garden, New York, NY
10,000 N.O.W. Legal Defense, New York, NY
10,000 ORBIS, New York, NY
5,000 Chamber of Commerce, New York, NY
5,000 Chicago Zoological Society, Chicago, IL
5,000 Jobs for Youth, New York, NY

Education

25,000 American Academy of Achievement, CA
25,000 New York University, New York, NY
6,000 Marine Corps Scholarship Foundation, Skokie, IL
5,000 Inner City Foundation for Charity and Education, Old Greenwick, CT
5,000 National Council on Economic Education, Washington, DC
5,000 Thurgood Marshall Scholarship Fund, New York, NY

Health

30,441 United Cerebral Palsy Association, New London, CT
10,000 American Paralysis Foundation, Springfield, NJ
5,000 Arthur Ashe Institute, New York, NY
5,000 New York Academy of Medicine, New York, NY
5,000 New York Medical Center, New York, NY

International

10,000 United Nations Association, New York, NY

Religion

30,000 Jewish Theological Seminary, New York, NY
10,000 National Medical Fellowships, New York, NY
St. Vincents Society, New York, NY

Social Services

32,000 United Way, New York, NY
12,000 YMCA of Greater New York, New York, NY
10,000 Boy Scouts of America, New York, NY
10,000 Boys and Girls Club of America, New York, NY
10,000 YMCA, New York, NY
6,000 National Child Labor Committee, New York, NY
5,000 Graham Windam, New York, NY
3,000 United Way, Detroit, MI

H.B. ZACHRY CO.

Company Contact

San Antonio, TX

Company Description

Revenue: US$500,000,000
Employees: 7,000
SIC(s): 1622 Bridge, Tunnel & Elevated Highway.

The Zachry Foundation

Giving Contact

Pamela W. O'Connor, Executive Director
Zachry Foundation
310 South St. Mary's Street, Suite 2500
San Antonio, TX 78205
Phone: (210)554-4663
Fax: (210)554-4605

Description

Founded: 1960
EIN: 741485544
Organization Type: Corporate Foundation
Giving Locations: TX: higher education grants are given throughout the state, San Antonio
Grant Types: Capital, Challenge, Emergency, Multiyear/Continuing Support, Research.

Financial Summary

Total Giving: $557,225 (1996); $1,055,220 (1995); $513,645 (1994). Note: Contributes through foundation only. 1996 Giving includes United Way ($100,000).
Assets: $8,677,759 (1996); $8,465,502 (1995); $8,500,325 (1994)
Gifts Received: $205,000 (1996); $100,000 (1995); $1,000,000 (1994). Note: The foundation receives contributions from the H. B. Zachry Co.

Typical Recipients

Arts & Humanities: Arts Outreach, Ethnic & Folk Arts, Arts & Humanities-General, Historic Preservation, Libraries, Museums/Galleries, Music, Performing Arts, Public Broadcasting, Theater
Civic & Public Affairs: Botanical Gardens/Parks, Economic Development, Civic & Public Affairs-General, Housing, Municipalities/Towns, Nonprofit Management, Philanthropic Organizations, Urban & Community Affairs
Education: Afterschool/Enrichment Programs, Arts/Humanities Education, Business Education, Business-School Partnerships, Colleges & Universities, Community & Junior Colleges, Continuing Education, Economic Education, Elementary Education (Public), Engineering/Technological Education, Faculty Development, Education-General, Leadership Training, Literacy, Medical Education, Private Education (Precollege), Public Education (Precollege), Secondary Education (Public), Student Aid, Vocational & Technical Education
Health: Cancer, Children's Health/Hospitals, Clinics/Medical Centers, Diabetes, Health-General, Health Organizations, Hospitals, Hospitals (University Affiliated), Medical Rehabilitation, Medical Research
International: Foreign Arts Organizations, International Affairs, Missionary/Religious Activities
Religion: Jewish Causes, Religious Welfare
Science: Science-General, Observatories & Planetariums, Science Museums, Scientific Centers & Institutes, Scientific Research
Social Services: At-Risk Youth, Big Brother/Big Sister, Camps, Child Welfare, Community Centers, Community Service Organizations, Delinquency & Criminal Rehabilitation, Domestic Violence, Family Services, People with Disabilities, Scouts, Senior Services, Social Services-General, Substance Abuse, United Funds/United Ways, YMCA/YWCA/YMHA/YWHA, Youth Organizations

Contributions Analysis

Arts & Humanities: 10% to 15%. Performing arts, libraries, and museums and galleries.
Education: 30% to 40%. Public education, colleges and universities, and private education.
Social Services: 35% to 40%. United funds, child welfare, and family services.

Application Procedures

Initial Contact: a brief letter of inquiry or phone call to request application form, which is required for all proposals
Application Requirements: a description of organization, amount requested, and purpose of funds sought
Deadlines: February 15
Decision Notification: a preliminary review of agency proposals is conducted at the first board meeting held in late spring; organizations denied will be informed at this time and requests receiving interest and meriting further discussion are retained. Respective agencies are considered for funding at the second board meeting in mid-summer; majority of grants are determined and awarded at that time, and all agencies are notified in writing.
Notes: Proposals are accepted only during the first six weeks of the year.

Restrictions

Foundation does not support individuals, endowments, or organizations outside San Antonio for general grants or outside Texas for educational grants.

Corporate Officials

Bruce Benjamin Cloud, Sr.: vice chairman, director B Thomas, OK 1920. ED Texas A&M University BCE (1940). PRIM CORP EMPL vice chairman, director: H.B. Zachry Co. CORP AFFIL chairman: Bruce Cloud Equipment Co. Inc.; director: Dudley R. Cloud & Son Construction. NONPR AFFIL honorary life board member: Texas State Technology College Foundation; member: Texas Transportation Institute; member: Texas Society Professional Engineers; member: Texas Good Roads-Transportation Association; member: Texas Hotmix Paving Association; member: Texas Association General Contractors; member: Texas Congress Extension Service; member: San Antonio Chamber of Commerce; member: San Antonio Livestock Association; member: National Asphalt Paving Association; member: Nocturnal Adoration Society; member: Consult Contractors Council America; member: American Institute Management; member: American Management Association; member: Alpha Epsilon Chi; member: American Concrete Paving Association.
Charles E. Ebrom: director, vice president B 1931. PRIM CORP EMPL director, vice president: H.B. Zachry Co. International. CORP AFFIL treasurer: Zachry Inc.; director: Tower Life Insurance; vice president: Capitol Aggregates Inc. Delaware; president: Metropolitan Resources Inc. NONPR AFFIL director: Goodwill Industries San Antonio.
Peter S. Van Nort: president B 1937. PRIM CORP EMPL president: H.B. Zachry Co.
Henry Bartell Zachry, Jr.: chairman B Laredo, TX 1933. ED Texas A&M University BScE (1954). PRIM CORP EMPL chairman: Zachry Inc. CORP AFFIL chairman: H B Zachry Co. NONPR AFFIL director: Southwest Research Institute.

Foundation Officials

Charles E. Ebrom: treasurer, trustee (see above)
Murray Lloyd Johnson, Jr.: secretary, trustee B Lake Charles, LA 1940. ED Austin College (1962); University of Texas (1965). PRIM CORP EMPL vice president, general counsel, director: H.B. Zachry Co. NONPR AFFIL member: American Judicature Society; member: International Association Defense Counsel; member: American Bar Association.
Pamela O'Connor: executive director
Henry Bartell Zachry, Jr.: trustee (see above)
J. P. Zachry: president, trustee B 1937. PRIM CORP EMPL president: Tower Life Insurance Co.
Mollie Steves Zachry: trustee

Grants Analysis

Disclosure Period: calendar year ending 1996
Total Grants: $457,225*
Number of Grants: 41
Average Grant: $11,152
Typical Range: $2,000 to $25,000
***Note:** Giving excludes United Way.

Recent Grants

Note: Grants derived from 1996 Form 990.

Arts & Humanities

30,000	San Antonio Symphony, San Antonio, TX
30,000	Witte Museum, San Antonio, TX
25,000	San Antonio Museum of Art, San Antonio, TX
25,000	State Preservation Board
5,290	Youth Philharmonic Orchestras, San Antonio, TX
5,000	San Antonio Children's Museum, San Antonio, TX
4,800	McNay Art Museum, San Antonio, TX
3,000	Texas Public Radio, San Antonio, TX

Civic & Public Affairs

30,000	TSTI Development Foundation, Waco, TX
25,000	San Antonio Botanical Society, San Antonio, TX
5,000	City Year, San Antonio, TX
2,500	Say Sil, San Antonio, TX

Education

50,000	University of Texas Health Science Center, Houston, TX
25,000	Our Lady of the Lake University, San Antonio, TX
25,000	University of Texas San Antonio, San Antonio, TX
12,000	Trinity University, San Antonio, TX
10,000	San Antonio Pre-Freshman Engineering Program, San Antonio, TX
10,000	University of Texas San Antonio, San Antonio, TX
5,000	Character Education Institute, San Antonio, TX
5,000	St. Louis Catholic School, Austin, TX
4,000	Texas Council on Economic Education, Houston, TX
3,500	Communities in Schools, San Antonio, TX
3,000	Our Lady of the Lake University, San Antonio, TX
2,500	Our Lady of the Lake University, San Antonio, TX

Health

25,000	Cancer Therapy and Research Foundation of South Texas, San Antonio, TX
17,000	Texas Diabetes Institute, San Antonio, TX
6,000	Respite Care, San Antonio, TX
5,000	Santa Rosa Children's Hospital Foundation, San Antonio, TX

Religion

10,000	Good Samaritan Center, San Antonio, TX
2,500	Jewish Community Center, San Antonio, TX
2,000	Los Compadres de San Antonio Missions, San Antonio, TX

Science

5,000	9th International Congress on Genes, Gene Families, and Isozymes

Social Services

100,000	United Way San Antonio and Bexar County, San Antonio, TX
8,010	Advance, San Antonio, TX
5,000	Alamo Children's Advocacy Center, San Antonio, TX
5,000	Big Brothers and Big Sisters, Alamo, TX
5,000	Family Service Association, San Antonio, TX
5,000	San Antonio Council on Alcohol and Drug Abuse, San Antonio, TX
3,600	Youth Alternatives, San Antonio, TX
2,525	Boy Scouts of America Alamo Area Council, San Antonio, TX
2,500	Children's Habilitation Center, San Antonio, TX
2,500	San Antonio Lighthouse, San Antonio, TX

ZENITH ELECTRONICS CORP.

Company Contact

Glenview, IL
Web: http://www.Zenith.com

Company Description
Employees: 15,900

Nonmonetary Support
Value: $500,000 (1987)
Type: Donated Equipment; Donated Products; In-kind Services
Note: 1987 nonmonetary support $500,000.

Giving Contact
John I. Taylor, Director, Corporate Public Relations & Communications
Zenith Electronics Corp.
1000 Milwaukee Avenue
Glenview, IL 60025
Phone: (847)391-7000

Description
Organization Type: Corporate Giving Program
Giving Locations: nationally; preference is given to organizations located near corporate operating locations.
Grant Types: Capital, Fellowship, General Support, Research, Scholarship.

Giving Philosophy
'Zenith Electronics Corporation, as a responsible corporate citizen, makes contributions in the form of monetary donations, products, and employee participation to worthwhile and selected civic, community, cultural, educational, health, and welfare institutions and organizations.' Policy and Guidelines, Corporate Contributions Program, Zenith Electronics Corp.

Financial Summary
Total Giving: Contributes through corporate direct giving program only.

Typical Recipients
Arts & Humanities: Public Broadcasting
Civic & Public Affairs: Civil Rights
Education: Colleges & Universities
Health: Hospitals
Social Services: People with Disabilities, United Funds/United Ways, Youth Organizations

Contributions Analysis
Arts & Humanities: Less than 5%. Preference to public radio and television stations.
Civic & Public Affairs: (United Funds & United Way) Around 40% of budget. Supports United Ways and other federated campaigns in Chicago and other plant communities. Between 10% and 15%. Preference given to organizations that serve and involve minorities, the handicapped, and youth.
Education: Between 20% and 25%. Contributes to institutions where company recruits employees or with which there are significant corporate relationships, such as joint research projects, board leadership by Zenith executives, and employee involvement or benefits. Generally does not support precollegiate educational institutions.
Health: Between 15% and 20%. Priority given to hospitals serving Zenith plant communities or significant numbers of employees and their families.

Application Procedures
Initial Contact: Send a brief letter or proposal.
Application Requirements: Include a brief a description of organization, including purposes and objectives; amount requested and explanation of how funds will be used; most recently audited financial statement; current itemized budget; cop y of IRS determination letter; list of officers and directors; and other past funding sources.
Evaluative Criteria: Priorities are based on the size of the population served, improvement to the quality of life in company operating locations, and the participation of company employees.

Restrictions
Generally does not contribute to individuals, except in Zenith-sponsored scholarship or fellowship programs; organizations with excessive fund-raising costs; religious organizations; veterans groups, fraternal orders, or labor groups; preschool, primary, or secondary schools; loan or investment funds of any kind; or special occasion fund drives through advertising.

Giving Program Officials
John I. Taylor: director B Greencastle, IN 1958. ED DePauw University BA (1980); Northwestern University MS (1981). PRIM CORP EMPL director corporate public relations & communications: Zenith Electronics Corp. NONPR AFFIL member: Consumer Electronics Manufacturers Association.

Grants Analysis
Total Grants: $500,000
Typical Range: $500 to $1,000

ZILKHA &SONS

Company Contact
New York, NY

Zilkha Foundation, Inc.

Giving Contact
Ezra K. Zilkha, President
Zilkha Foundation
767 5th Avenue, Suite 4605
New York, NY 10153
Phone: (212)758-7750
Fax: (212)758-7803

Description
Founded: 1948
EIN: 136090739
Organization Type: Corporate Foundation. Supports preselected organizations only.
Giving Locations: NY: New York
Grant Types: General Support.

Financial Summary
Total Giving: $371,059 (fiscal year ending August 31, 1996); $471,906 (fiscal 1995); $682,485 (fiscal 1994). Note: Contributes through foundation only.
Assets: $2,611,708 (fiscal 1996); $1,251,747 (fiscal 1995); $1,616,467 (fiscal 1994)
Gifts Received: $1,698,759 (fiscal 1996); $3,090,375 (fiscal 1991); $320,000 (fiscal 1989)

Typical Recipients
Arts & Humanities: Arts Outreach, Ballet, Dance, Historic Preservation, History & Archaeology, Libraries, Museums/Galleries, Music, Opera, Performing Arts, Public Broadcasting, Theater
Civic & Public Affairs: Botanical Gardens/Parks, Ethnic Organizations, Civic & Public Affairs-General, Parades/Festivals, Philanthropic Organizations, Public Policy, Urban & Community Affairs, Women's Affairs
Education: Arts/Humanities Education, Colleges & Universities, Elementary Education (Private), Education-General, International Studies, Medical Education, Private Education (Precollege), Public Education (Precollege), Social Sciences Education, Student Aid
Health: AIDS/HIV, Alzheimers Disease, Cancer, Clinics/Medical Centers, Emergency/Ambulance Services, Geriatric Health, Hospitals, Hospitals (University Affiliated), Medical Research, Research/Studies Institutes, Transplant Networks/Donor Banks
International: Foreign Arts Organizations, Foreign Educational Institutions, Health Care/Hospitals, Human Rights, International Affairs, International Organizations, International Relations, International Relief Efforts, Missionary/Religious Activities
Religion: Jewish Causes, Religious Organizations, Religious Welfare, Seminaries, Synagogues/Temples
Science: Scientific Centers & Institutes
Social Services: Child Welfare, People with Disabilities, Recreation & Athletics, Scouts, Substance Abuse, United Funds/United Ways, YMCA/YWCA/YMHA/YWHA, Youth Organizations

Contributions Analysis
Arts & Humanities: About 35%. Support includes operas, libraries, museums, ballet, and historical preservation.
Education: 40% to 45%. Major support includes the Waterford Institute and universities.
Health: 5% to 10%. Supports hospitals, medical centers, and research.
International: Less than 5%. Minor funding is awarded to foreign educational institutions with American ties.
Religion: About 10%. Supports synagogues, Jewish philanthropies, and Jewish religious organizations.
Social Services: Less than 5%. Support goes to the disabled, youth groups, and housing.

Restrictions
Foundation does not support individuals.

Corporate Officials
Ezra Khedouri Zilkha: president B Baghdad, Iraq 1925. ED Wesleyan University AB (1947). PRIM CORP EMPL president: Zilkha & Sons. CORP AFFIL director: Milwaukee Land Co.; director: Newhall Land & Farming Co.; director: CIGNA Corp.; general partner: Heartland Partners; director: Cambridge Associates; director: Chicago Milwaukee Corp.; president: 3555 Intermediate Corp. NONPR AFFIL trustee: Lycee Francaise; trustee emeritus: Wesleyan University; chairman: International Center Disabled; trustee: Brookings Institution; member: Council Foreign Relations. CLUB AFFIL Travelers Club; Polo Club; Racquet & Tennis Club; Knickerbocker Club; Meadow Club.

Foundation Officials
Kathleen Quinlan: assistant secretary
Cecile E. Zilkha: vice president, secretary
Ezra Khedouri Zilkha: president, treasurer (see above)

Grants Analysis
Disclosure Period: fiscal year ending August 31, 1996
Total Grants: $371,059
Number of Grants: 69
Average Grant: $3,042*
Highest Grant: $164,235
Typical Range: $500 to $5,000
***Note:** Average grant figure excludes highest grant.

Recent Grants
Note: Grants derived from 1997 Form 990.

Arts & Humanities

134,890	Metropolitan Opera Guild, New York, NY
5,000	Ballet Theater Foundation, New York, NY
4,850	Pierpont Morgan Library, New York, NY
4,700	Frick Collection to Benefit Art Gallery, New York, NY
2,000	Young Audiences, New York, NY
1,500	Foundation for French Museum, New York, NY
1,050	New York Public Library, New York, NY
1,000	Folger Shakespeare Library, Washington, DC

1,000 Historic House, New York, NY
1,000 Metropolitan Museum of Art, New York, NY
1,000 Whitney Museum of American Art, New York, NY
500 Museum of Modern Art, New York, NY
425 Metropolitan Opera Club, New York, NY

Civic & Public Affairs

125,000 Brookings Institution, Washington, DC
10,000 Ronald Reagan Presidential Foundation, Los Angeles, CA
1,700 Versailles Foundation, New York, NY
1,000 Princess Grace Foundation US of America, New York, NY
500 Citizens Committee, New York, NY

Education

110,500 Wesleyan University, Middletown, CT
2,500 Middle East Studies Society
2,000 Spence School, New York, NY
500 School Choice Scholarships Foundation

Health

70,480 Hospital for Special Surgery, New York, NY
4,700 Alzheimer's Association, Philadelphia, PA
3,000 Southampton Hospital, Southampton, NY
500 Hospital for Joint Diseases, New York, NY
500 Judith Peabody Fund AIDS
250 Mayo Foundation, Rochester, MN
250 Southampton Village Volunteer Ambulance, Southampton, NY

International

41,183 French Institute Alliance Francaise, New York, NY
5,340 American Society of the French Legion of Honor, New York, NY
5,000 Lycee Francais de New York, New York, NY
3,000 Association of Canadian Studies in the US
3,000 Council on Foreign Relations, New York, NY
2,500 International Sephardic Educational Foundation, New York, NY
2,000 American Friends of Alliance Israelite
1,000 American Friends of Covent Garden and the Royal Ballet, New York, NY
1,000 American Friends of Israel Philharmonic Orchestra, Israel
1,000 American Friends of Paris Opera and Ballet, Paris, France
1,000 Sisterhood of the Spanish and Portuguese Synagogue
500 Refugees International, Washington, DC
500 UNICEF, New York, NY
230 Sisterhood of the Spanish and Portuguese Synagogue

Religion

10,000 Federation of Jewish Philanthropies, New York, NY
3,898 Congregation Shearith Israel, New York, NY
250 Congregation Bene Naharayim, New York, NY

Social Services

25,000 International Center for the Disabled, New York, NY
5,000 Center for Addiction and Substance Abuse, New York, NY
5,000 YWCA/YMHA Camp, New York, NY
500 Citizens Committee for Children, New York, NY

Zurn Industries, Inc.

Company Contact

Erie, PA

Company Description

Revenue: US$353,000,000
Employees: 5,100
SIC(s): 1629 Heavy Construction Nec, 1711 Plumbing, Heating & Air-Conditioning, 3084 Plastics Pipe, 6719 Holding Companies Nec.

Giving Contact

James A. Zurn, Senior Vice President
Zurn Industries, Inc.
One Zurn Place
Erie, PA 16514
Phone: (814)452-2111
Fax: (814)454-0524
Email: zrnind@zurn.com

Description

Organization Type: Corporate Giving Program
Giving Locations: PA
Grant Types: Capital, Emergency, Employee Matching Gifts, Endowment, General Support, Matching.
Note: Employee matching gift ratio: 1 to 1.

Financial Summary

Total Giving: $220,000 (1997 approx); $175,000 (1996 approx); $165,000 (1995 approx). Note: Contributes through corporate direct giving program only.

Typical Recipients

Arts & Humanities: Arts & Humanities-General
Civic & Public Affairs: Civic & Public Affairs-General
Education: Colleges & Universities, Elementary Education (Private), Education-General
Health: Health-General
Social Services: Social Services-General

Application Procedures

Initial Contact: contact company for application procedures

Restrictions

Does not support individuals, religious organizations for sectarian purposes, or political or lobbying groups.

Corporate Officials

Robert R. Womack: chairman, chief executive officer, director B Franklin, NC 1937. ED North Carolina State University BS (1959); University of California, Los Angeles MS (1969). PRIM CORP EMPL chairman, chief executive officer, director: Zurn Industries, Inc.

Giving Program Officials

James A. Zurn: B 1942. ED Dartmouth College BA (1964); Harvard University Graduate School of Business Administration MBA (1966). PRIM CORP EMPL senior vice president, director: Zurn Industries, Inc.

Grants Analysis

Disclosure Period: calendar year ending
Typical Range: $1,000 to $2,500

FUNDERS BY HEADQUARTERS STATE

The following index includes funders listed by the state in which their main office is located. Within each state, foundation/giving program names are listed in alphabetical order. Defunct or inactive organizations are not included in this list.

Alabama

Alabama Power Co.
Blount International, Inc.
Blue Cross & Blue Shield of Alabama
Compass Bank
Ebsco Industries, Inc.
MacMillan Bloedel Inc.
McWane Inc.
Regions Bank
Regions Financial Corp.
Southern Co. Services Inc.
Torchmark Corp.
Vulcan Materials Co.

Alaska

Alyeska Pipeline Service Co.
Cook Inlet Region

Arizona

America West Airlines, Inc.
Arizona Public Service Co.
Central Newspapers, Inc.
Dial Corp.
Globe Corp.
Phelps Dodge Corp.
Tucson Electric Power Co.

Arkansas

ALLTEL Corp.
Murphy Oil Corp.
Tyson Foods Inc.
Wal-Mart Stores, Inc.

California

Advanced Micro Devices, Inc.
American Honda Motor Co., Inc.
APL Ltd.
Apple Computer, Inc.
Atlantic Richfield Co.
Autodesk Inc.
Avery Dennison Corp.
Bechtel Group, Inc.
Beckman Coulter, Inc.
Bourns, Inc.
Broderbund Software, Inc.
Cadence Designs Systems, Inc.
Caesar's World, Inc.
California Bank & Trust
California Federal Bank, FSB
Callaway Golf Co.
Chevron Corp.
Clorox Co.
CNF Transportation, Inc.
Consolidated Electrical Distributors
Copley Press, Inc.
Deutsch Co.
Disney Co. (Walt)
Dreyer's Grand Ice Cream
Edison International
EMI Music Publishing
Farmers Group, Inc.
Fireman's Fund Insurance Co.
Fluor Corp.
Gallo Winery, Inc. (E&J)
Gap, Inc.
Genentech Inc.
Goodrich Aerospace - Aerostructures Group (B.F.)
Guess?
Hewlett-Packard Co.
Hofmann Co.
Hughes Electronics Corp.
Informix Software, Inc.
Intel Corp.
Jacobs Engineering Group
Knight Ridder
Levi Strauss & Co.
Litton Industries, Inc.
Mattel Inc.
Mazda North American Operations
McClatchy Co.
McKesson-HBOC Corp.
Mervyn's California
Mitsubishi Electric America
Nestle U.S.A. Inc.
New United Motor Manufacturing Inc.
Nissan North America, Inc.
Northrop Grumman Corp.
Occidental Oil and Gas
Occidental Petroleum Corp.
Oracle Corp.
Pacific Enterprises
Pacific Gas and Electric Co.
Pacific Mutual Life Insurance Co.
PacifiCare Health Systems
Patagonia Inc.
Potlatch Corp.
Ralph's Grocery Co.
Rockwell International Corp.
Safeway Inc.
Schwab & Co., Inc. (Charles)
Sega of America Inc.
Sempra Energy
Shaklee Corp.
Shea Co. (John F.)
Sierra Pacific Industries
Southern California Gas Co.
Sun Microsystems Inc.
Taco Bell Corp.
Tenet Healthcare Corp.
Ticketmaster Corp.
Times Mirror Co.
Toyota Motor Sales U.S.A., Inc.
Transamerica Corp.
Universal Studios
Unocal Corp.
Varian Medical Systems, Inc.
Washington Mutual, Inc.
Washington Mutual, Inc.
Wells Fargo & Co.
Wilbur-Ellis Co. & Connell Brothers Co.

Colorado

Ball Corp.
Coors Brewing Co.
Cyprus Amax Minerals Co.
Edwards Enterprise Software (J.D.)
Gates Rubber Corp.
Hensel Phelps Construction Co.
New Century Energies
Security Life of Denver Insurance Co.
Storage Technology Corp.
Strear Farms Co.
US West, Inc.

Connecticut

ABB Inc.
Aetna, Inc.
BankBoston-Connecticut Region
Barden Corp.
Barnes Group Inc.
Carrier Corp.
Champion International Corp.
Crane Co.
Deloitte & Touche
Dexter Corp.
Duracell International
Ensign-Bickford Industries
Fortune Brands, Inc.
General Electric Co.
General Reinsurance Corp.
Hamilton Sundstrand Corp.
Hartford (The)
Hartford Steam Boiler Inspection & Insurance Co.
Hubbell Inc.
Kaman Corp.
Loctite Corp.
NEBCO Evans
Newman's Own Inc.
Northeast Utilities
Olin Corp.
Phoenix Home Life Mutual Insurance Co.
Pitney Bowes Inc.
Praxair
Rayonier Inc.
Southern New England Telephone Co.
Stanley Works (The)
Subway Sandwich Shops, Inc.
Tenneco Automotive
Unilever Home & Personal Care U.S.A.
Union Carbide Corp.
United Distillers & Vintners North America
United Technologies Corp.
UST Inc.
Van Leer Holding
Webster Bank
Wiremold Co.
Witco Corp.
Xerox Corp.

Delaware

Bell Atlantic-Delaware, Inc.
Conectiv
du Pont de Nemours & Co. (E.I.)
Hercules Inc.

District of Columbia

Fannie Mae
GEICO Corp.
NASDAQ Stock Market
Potomac Electric Power Co.
Riggs Bank NA
Student Loan Marketing Association
The Washington Post

Florida

BankAtlantic Bancorp
Burger King Corp.
Carnival Corp.
CSR Rinker Materials Corp.
Eckerd Corp.
Florida Power Corp.
Florida Power & Light Co.
Florida Rock Industries
Grace & Co. (W.R.)
Gulf Power Co.
Harris Corp.
Publix Supermarkets
Ryder System, Inc.
Sentinel Communications Co.
SunTrust Banks of Florida
Tampa Electric Co.
United States Sugar Corp.
Walter Industries Inc.
Winn-Dixie Stores Inc.

Georgia

AFLAC Inc.
AGL Resources Inc.
Atlantic Investment Co.
BellSouth Corp.
BellSouth Telecommunications
Coca-Cola Co.
Colonial Oil Industries, Inc.
Cox Enterprises Inc.
Delta Air Lines, Inc.
Equifax Inc.
Georgia-Pacific Corp.
Georgia Power Co.
Gulfstream Aerospace Corp.
Harland Co. (John H.)
Home Depot, Inc.
Morris Communications Corp.
National Service Industries, Inc.
Peoples Bank
Pheonix Financial Group
Scientific-Atlanta, Inc.
Shaw Industries Inc.
SunTrust Bank Atlanta
Synovus Financial Corp.
United Parcel Service of America Inc.
Waffle House Inc.

Hawaii

Alexander & Baldwin, Inc.
Castle & Cooke Properties Inc.
First Hawaiian, Inc.
Hawaiian Electric Co., Inc.
Pacific Century Financial Corp.
Servco Pacific

Idaho

Albertson's Inc.
Boise Cascade Corp.
First Security Bank of Idaho NA
Idaho Power Co.
Morrison Knudsen Corp.
Simplot Co. (J.R.)

Illinois

Abbott Laboratories
Ace Hardware Corp.
Allstate Insurance Co.
AMCORE Bank Rockford
Ameritech Corp.
Ameritech Illinois
Amsted Industries Inc.
Aon Corp.
Archer-Daniels-Midland Co.
Bank One Corp.
Baxter International Inc.
Blair & Co. (William)
Boler Co.
BP Amoco Corp.
Brunswick Corp.
Burnett Co. (Leo)
Caterpillar Inc.
Chicago Board of Trade
Chicago Sun-Times, Inc.
Chicago Title Corp.
Chicago Tribune Co.
CLARCOR Inc.
CNA
Comdisco, Inc.
Commonwealth Edison Co.
Curtis Industries, Inc. (Helene)
Deere & Co.
DeKalb Genetics Corp.
Donnelley & Sons Co. (R.R.)
Duchossois Industries Inc.
First National Bank of Evergreen Park
FMC Corp.
Fort James Corp.
Galter Corp.
GATX Corp.
Grainger, Inc. (W.W.)
Grand Victoria Casino
Griffith Laboratories U.S.A.
Harris Trust & Savings Bank
Hartmarx Corp.
Heller Financial, Inc.
Hoffer Plastics Corp.
Household International Inc.
Illinois Power Co.
Illinois Tool Works, Inc.
Katten, Muchin & Zavis
Kemper National Insurance Companies
Kirkland & Ellis
Kraft Foods, Inc.
Marshall Field's
McDonald's Corp.
Montgomery Ward & Co., Inc.

Morton International Inc.
Motorola Inc.
Nalco Chemical Co.
NICOR Gas Co.
Northern Trust Co.
Old Kent Bank
Outboard Marine Corp.
Peoples Energy Corp.
Pittway Corp.
Playboy Enterprises Inc.
Premark International Inc.
Sara Lee Corp.
Searle & Co. (G.D.)
Sears, Roebuck and Co.
ServiceMaster Co.
Smurfit-Stone Container Corp.
Solo Cup Co.
Square D Co.
State Farm Mutual Automobile Insurance Co.
Stone Container Corp.
Tenneco Packaging
True North Communications, Inc.
Trustmark Insurance Co.
United Airlines Inc.
UPN Channel 50
USG Corp.
Walgreen Co.
Waste Management Inc.
Whitman Corp.
Woodward Governor Co.
Wrigley Co. (Wm. Jr.)
Zenith Electronics Corp.

Indiana

American General Finance
American United Life Insurance Co.
Ameritech Indiana
Arvin Industries, Inc.
Auburn Foundry
Central Soya Co.
Coachmen Industries, Inc.
Cummins Engine Co., Inc.
First Source Corp.
Ford Meter Box Co.
Franklin Electric Co.
Indiana Mills & Manufacturing
Inland Container Corp.
Journal-Gazette Co.
Kimball International, Inc.
Koch Enterprises, Inc.
Lilly & Co. (Eli)
Lincoln Financial Group
National City Bank of Cleveland
Northern Indiana Public Service Co.
Old National Bank Evansville
Reilly Industries, Inc.
South Bend Tribune Corp.

Iowa

AmerUS Group
Bandag, Inc.
Blue Cross & Blue Shield of Iowa
Employers Mutual Casualty Co.
GuideOne Insurance
HON Industries Inc.
Lee Enterprises
Maytag Corp.
Meredith Corp.
MidAmerican Energy Holdings Co.
Pella Corp.
Pioneer Hi-Bred International, Inc.

Principal Financial Group

Kansas

Cessna Aircraft Co.
Excel Corp.
INTRUST Financial Corp.
Koch Industries, Inc.
Lee Apparel Co.
Security Benefit Life Insurance Co.
Sprint Corp.
Western Resources Inc.
Yellow Corp.

Kentucky

Ashland, Inc.
Brown & Williamson Tobacco Corp.
Humana, Inc.
LG&E Energy Corp.
Mid-America Bank of Louisville
PNC Bank Kentucky Inc.
Southeastern Mutual Insurance Co.
Texas Gas Transmission Corp.

Louisiana

DSM Copolymer
Entergy Corp.
Freeport-McMoRan Inc.
Louisiana Land & Exploration Co.
McDermott Inc.
Pan-American Life Insurance Co.
Reily & Co., Inc. (William B.)

Maine

Bean, Inc. (L.L.)
Central Maine Power Co.
Hannaford Brothers Co.
UnumProvident

Maryland

AEGON U.S.A. Inc.
Constellation Energy Group, Inc.
Croft-Leominster
Crown Books
First Maryland Bancorp
Giant Food Inc.
ISE America
Lockheed Martin Corp.
Manor Care Health SVS, Inc.
Marriott International Inc.
McCormick & Co. Inc.
Price Associates (T. Rowe)
Procter & Gamble Co., Cosmetics Division
Rouse Co.

Massachusetts

Allmerica Financial Corp.
Analog Devices, Inc.
BankBoston Corp.
Boston Edison Co.
Boston Gas Co.
Boston Globe (The)
Cabot Corp.
Country Curtains, Inc.
Crane & Co., Inc.
Cummings Properties Management
Demoulas Supermarkets Inc.
Eastern Bank
Eastern Enterprises
Erving Industries
Fidelity Investments

FleetBoston Financial Corp.
Gillette Co.
Hancock Financial Services (John)
Harcourt General, Inc.
Houghton Mifflin Co.
Housatonic Curtain Co.
Kendall International, Inc.
Liberty Mutual Insurance Group
Little, Inc. (Arthur D.)
Lotus Development Corp.
Massachusetts Mutual Life Insurance Co.
Millipore Corp.
New England Bio Labs
New England Financial
Norton Co.
PerkinElmer, Inc.
Pioneer Group
Polaroid Corp.
Putnam Investments
Reebok International Ltd.
Shaw's Supermarkets, Inc.
State Street Bank & Trust Co.
Stride Rite Corp.
Thermo Electron Corp.
TJX Companies, Inc.
Wyman-Gordon Co.

Michigan

Alma Piston Co.
Ameritech Michigan
Blue Cross & Blue Shield of Michigan
Borman's Inc.
Citizens Bank-Flint
Comerica Inc.
Consumers Energy Co.
DaimlerChrysler Corp.
Detroit Edison Co.
Domino's Pizza Inc.
Dow Chemical Co.
Dow Corning Corp.
Erb Lumber Co.
Fabri-Kal Corp.
Federal-Mogul Corp.
Ford Motor Co.
General Motors Corp.
Gerber Products Co.
JSJ Corp.
Kellogg Co.
Kelly Services
Kmart Corp.
La-Z-Boy Inc.
Masco Corp.
Meijer, Inc.
Michigan Consolidated Gas Co.
SPX Corp.
Standard Products Co.
Steelcase Inc.
Whirlpool Corp.
Wolverine World Wide

Minnesota

Alliant Techsystems
Allianz Life Insurance Co. of North America
Andersen Corp.
Bemis Co., Inc.
Blue Cross & Blue Shield of Minnesota
Business Improvement
Cargill Inc.
Carlson Companies, Inc.
Cenex Harvest States
Dain Bosworth Inc.
Dayton Hudson
Deluxe Corp.

Donaldson Co., Inc.
Ecolab Inc.
Federated Mutual Insurance Co.
Fuller Co. (H.B.)
General Mills, Inc.
Graco, Inc.
Hickory Tech Corp.
Hubbard Broadcasting, Inc.
International Multifoods Corp.
Jostens, Inc.
Land O'Lakes, Inc.
Liberty Diversified Industries
Medtronic, Inc.
Minnesota Mining & Manufacturing Co.
Minnesota Mutual Life Insurance Co.
MTS Systems Corp.
National City Bank of Minneapolis
National Computer Systems, Inc.
Northern States Power Co.
Northwest Airlines, Inc.
Norwest Corp.
Pentair Inc.
Pillsbury Co.
Red Wing Shoe Co. Inc.
Regis Corp.
Reliant Energy Minnegasco
ReliaStar Financial Corp.
Saint Paul Companies Inc.
SIT Investment Associates, Inc.
SuperValu, Inc.
Target Corp.
TCF National Bank Minnesota
TENNANT Co.
Toro Co.
U.S. Bancorp
U.S. Bancorp Piper Jaffray
Valspar Corp.

Mississippi

Deposit Guaranty National Bank
MCI WorldCom, Inc.
Trustmark National Bank

Missouri

Ameren Corp.
Anheuser-Busch Companies, Inc.
Block, Inc. (H&R)
Brown Shoe Co., Inc.
Business Men's Assurance Co. of America
Butler Manufacturing Co.
Clark Refining & Marketing
Commerce Bancshares, Inc.
CPI Corp.
Edison Brothers Stores, Inc.
Emerson Electric Co.
Enterprise Rent-A-Car Co.
Furniture Brands International, Inc.
GenAmerica Corp.
Group Health Plan
Hallmark Cards Inc.
Hoechst Marion Roussel, Inc.
Independent Stave Co.
Jones & Co. (Edward D.)
Kellwood Co.
Laclede Gas Co.
Mallinckrodt Chemical, Inc.
Maritz Inc.
May Department Stores Co.
Mercantile Bank NA
MFA Inc.

Monsanto Co.
Orscheln Co.
Pulitzer Publishing Co.
Ralston Purina Co.
Shelter Mutual Insurance Co.
Stupp Brothers Bridge & Iron Co.
Sunmark Capital Corp.
Sverdrup Corp.
Tamko Roofing Products
Tension Envelope Corp.

Montana

Montana Power Co.

Nebraska

Ameritas Life Insurance Corp.
Commercial Federal Corp.
ConAgra, Inc.
IBP
Kiewit Sons' Inc. (Peter)
Mutual of Omaha Insurance Co.
National Bank of Commerce Trust & Savings
Northwest Bank Nebraska, NA
Physicians Mutual Insurance Co.
Valmont Industries, Inc.

Nevada

Sierra Pacific Resources
Southwest Gas Corp.

New Hampshire

Fisher Scientific
Kingsbury Corp.

New Jersey

AlliedSignal Inc.
American Standard Inc.
AT&T Corp.
Bard, Inc. (C.R.)
Becton Dickinson & Co.
Bestfoods
Campbell Soup Co.
Carillon Importers, Ltd.
Chubb Corp.
Church & Dwight Co., Inc.
Dun & Bradstreet Corp.
GPU Energy
GPU Inc.
Gucci America Inc.
Hoffmann-La Roche Inc.
Honeywell International Inc.
Johnson & Johnson
Lipton Co.
Mamiye Brothers
Matsushita Electric Corp. of America
Merck & Co.
Nabisco Group Holdings
National Starch & Chemical Co.
New Jersey Natural Gas Co.
Novartis Corporation
Pharmacia & Upjohn, Inc.
Prudential Insurance Co. of America
Public Service Electric & Gas Co.
Schering-Plough Corp.
Sharp Electronics Corp.
Sony Electronics
Telcordia Technologies
Union Camp Corp.
Warner-Lambert Co.

New York

ABC
Agrilink Foods, Inc.
Albany International Corp.
American Express Co.
American Retail Group
American Stock Exchange, Inc.
ASARCO Inc.
Associated Food Stores
Avon Products, Inc.
Banfi Vintners
Bank of New York Co., Inc.
Bausch & Lomb Inc.
Bell Atlantic Corp.
Bernstein & Co., Inc. (Sanford C.)
Bristol-Myers Squibb Co.
Brooklyn Union
Butler Capital Corp.
Calvin Klein
Cantor, Fitzgerald Securities Corp.
Carter-Wallace, Inc.
CBS Corp.
Central National-Gottesman
Century 21
Chase Manhattan Bank, NA
CIBC Oppenheimer
CIT Group, Inc. (The)
Citibank Corp.
Citigroup
Colgate-Palmolive Co.
Computer Associates International, Inc.
Continental Grain Co.
Corning Inc.
Credit Suisse First Boston
Daily News
Dow Jones & Co., Inc.
Eastman Kodak Co.
Ernst & Young, LLP
European American Bank
Fisher Brothers Cleaning Services
Forbes Inc.
Fortis, Inc.
Fox Entertainment Group
Frontier Corp.
Fuji Bank & Trust Co.
General Atlantic Partners II LP
Glickenhaus & Co.
Goldman Sachs Group
Golub Corp.
Guardian Life Insurance Co. of America
Hitachi America Ltd.
HSBC Bank USA
Industrial Bank of Japan Trust Co. (New York)
International Business Machines Corp.
International Flavors & Fragrances Inc.
International Paper Co.
Interpublic Group of Companies, Inc.
Jacobson & Sons (Benjamin)
KPMG Peat Marwick LLP
Leviton Manufacturing Co. Inc.
Liz Claiborne, Inc.
Loews Corp.
Macy's East Inc.
Manufacturers & Traders Trust Co.
Mark IV Industries
MBIA Inc.
McGraw-Hill Companies, Inc.
Merrill Lynch & Co., Inc.
Metropolitan Life Insurance Co.
MONY Group (The)
Morgan & Co. Inc. (J.P.)
Morgan Stanley Dean Witter & Co.
National Fuel Gas Distribution Corp.
NEC America, Inc.
New York Life Insurance Co.
New York Mercantile Exchange
New York State Electric & Gas Corp.
New York Stock Exchange, Inc.
New York Times Co.
Niagara Mohawk Holdings Inc.
Nomura Holding America
Orange & Rockland Utilities, Inc.
Overseas Shipholding Group Inc.
Paine Webber
PepsiCo, Inc.
Pfizer Inc.
Philip Morris Companies Inc.
Philips Electronics North America Corp.
PricewaterhouseCoopers
Prudential Securities Inc.
Reader's Digest Association, Inc. (The)
Revlon Inc.
Rich Products Corp.
Rochester Gas & Electric Corp.
Russer Foods
Salomon Smith Barney
Schloss & Co. (Marcus)
Schlumberger Ltd. (USA)
Seagram & Sons, Inc. (Joseph E.)
S.G. Cowen
Slant/Fin Corp.
Sotheby's Inc.
Starwood Hotels & Resorts Worldwide, Inc.
Stone & Webster Inc.
Sumitomo Bank
Tai and Co. (J.T.)
Texaco Inc.
Thompson Co. (J. Walter)
Titan Industrial Corp.
Toshiba America Inc.
Trace International Holdings, Inc.
Unilever United States, Inc.
United States Trust Co. of New York
Viacom Inc.
Wachtell, Lipton, Rosen & Katz
Waldbaum's Supermarkets, Inc.
Weil, Gotshal & Manges Corp.
Westvaco Corp.
Wiley & Sons (John)
Young & Rubicam
Zilkha & Sons

North Carolina

Bank of America
Barclays Capital
Belk Stores Services Inc.
BFGoodrich Co.
Blue Bell, Inc.
Branch Banking & Trust Co.
Burlington Industries, Inc.
Carolina Power & Light Co.
CCB Financial Corp.
Collins & Aikman Corp.
Cone Mills Corp.
Duke Energy
First Union Corp.
First Union National Bank, NA
Glaxo Wellcome Inc.
Lance, Inc.
Lowe's Companies
Nucor Corp.
Reynolds Tobacco (R.J.)
Royal & SunAlliance USA, Inc.
Ruddick Corp.
Sara Lee Hosiery, Inc.
Stonecutter Mills Corp.
Thomasville Furniture Industries Inc.
United Dominion Industries, Ltd.
Wachovia Bank of North Carolina NA

Ohio

AK Steel Corp.
American Electric Power
Ameritech Ohio
Andersons Inc.
Bardes Corp.
Barry Corp. (R.G.)
Battelle Memorial Institute
Borden, Inc.
Chemed Corp.
Cincinnati Bell Inc.
Cinergy Corp.
Cleveland-Cliffs, Inc.
Commercial Intertech Corp.
Cooper Tire & Rubber Co.
Dana Corp.
Danis Companies
Dayton Power and Light Co.
Diebold, Inc.
Duriron Co., Inc.
Eaton Corp.
Federated Department Stores, Inc.
Ferro Corp.
Fifth Third Bancorp
FirstEnergy Corp.
Forest City Enterprises, Inc.
GenCorp
Gosiger, Inc.
Hanna Co. (M.A.)
Huffy Corp.
Huntington Bancshares Inc.
Invacare Corp.
Key Bank of Cleveland
Kroger Co.
Lancaster Lens, Inc.
Lincoln Electric Co.
LTV Corp.
Lubrizol Corp. (The)
McDonald & Co. Securities, Inc.
Mead Corp.
Milacron, Inc.
Monarch Machine Tool Co.
MTD Products Inc.
National City Bank of Columbus
National City Corp.
National Machinery Co.
Nationwide Insurance Co.
NCR Corp.
Nordson Corp.
Ohio National Life Insurance Co.
Owens Corning
Owens-Illinois Inc.
Park National Bank
Parker Hannifin Corp.
Premier Industrial Corp.
Procter & Gamble Co.
Progressive Corp.
Reynolds & Reynolds Co.
Schwebel Baking Co.
Scripps Co. (E.W.)
Seaway Food Town, Inc.
Sherwin-Williams Co.
Smucker Co. (JM)
Sprint/United Telephone
Standard Register Co.
Star Bank NA
Timken Co. (The)
Timken Co. (The)
Toledo Blade Co.
Tomkins Industries, Inc.
TRW Inc.
Western & Southern Life Insurance Co.

Oklahoma

American Fidelity Corp.
Kerr-McGee Corp.
OG&E Electric Services
Oklahoma Publishing Co.
ONEOK, Inc.
Phillips Petroleum Co.
Public Service Co. of Oklahoma
Williams

Oregon

Freightliner Corp.
Jeld-wen, Inc.
Louisiana-Pacific Corp.
Nike, Inc.
Northwest Natural Gas Co.
PacifiCorp
Portland General Electric Co.
Roseburg Forest Products Co.
Tektronix, Inc.

Pennsylvania

Air Products and Chemicals, Inc.
Alcoa Inc.
Allegheny Technologies Inc.
AMETEK, Inc.
AMP Inc.
Aristech Chemical Corp.
Armstrong World Industries, Inc.
Bayer Corp.
Berwind Group
Bethlehem Steel Corp.
Binney & Smith Inc.
Binswanger Companies
Carpenter Technology Corp.
CertainTeed Corp.
CGU Insurance
CIGNA Corp.
Consolidated Natural Gas Co.
CSS Industries, Inc.
Duquesne Light Co.
Dynamet, Inc.
Elf Atochem North America, Inc.
Equitable Resources, Inc.
First Union Bank
Franklin Mint (The)
Giant Eagle Inc.
Harsco Corp.
Heinz Co. (H.J.)
Hershey Foods Corp.
Hunt Manufacturing Co.
IKON Office Solutions, Inc.
Kennametal, Inc.
Lehigh Portland Cement Co.
Mellon Financial Corp.
Merit Oil Corp.
Mine Safety Appliances Co.
National City Bank of Pennsylvania
PECO Energy Co.
Penn Mutual Life Insurance Co.
Pennsylvania Power & Light
PNC Bank
PNC Financial Services Group
PPG Industries, Inc.
Premier Dental Products Co.
Provident Mutual Life Insurance Co.
Quaker Chemical Corp.
Rite Aid Corp.
Rohm & Haas Co.
Safeguard Scientifics
S&T Bancorp
SmithKline Beecham Corp.
Sovereign Bank
Sunoco Inc.
Susquehanna-Pfaltzgraff Co.
Teleflex Inc.
TMC Investment Co.
Unisys Corp.
USX Corp.
Vanguard Group
Vesper Corp.
West Co. Inc.
York Federal Savings & Loan Association
Zurn Industries, Inc.

Rhode Island

Citizens Financial Group, Inc.
Cranston Print Works Co.
FM Global
Hasbro, Inc.
Hasbro, Inc.
Providence Journal-Bulletin Co.
Textron Inc.

South Carolina

Belk-Simpson Department Stores
Bowater Inc.
Colonial Life & Accident Insurance Co.
Evening Post Publishing Co.
Inman Mills
Leigh Fibers, Inc.
Liberty Corp.
Milliken & Co.
SCANA Corp.
Sonoco Products Co.
Springs Industries, Inc.

Tennessee

Bradford & Co. (J.C.)
Bridgestone/Firestone, Inc.
Conwood Co. LP
Dixie Group, Inc. (The)
Dollar General Corp.
Eastman Chemical Co.
FedEx Corp.
First American Corp.
First Tennessee National Corp.
Harrah's Entertainment Inc.
Ingram Industries Inc.
Maybelline, Inc.
Memphis Light Gas & Water Division
Nortel
North American Royalties
Osborne Enterprises

Promus Hotel Corp.
Provident Companies, Inc.
Rutledge Hill Press
Shoney's Inc.
Union Planters Corp.

Texas

7-Eleven, Inc.
Alcon Laboratories, Inc.
American General Corp.
Amgen, Inc.
AMR Corp.
Baker Hughes Inc.
Bank One, Texas-Houston Office
Bank One, Texas, NA
Belo Corp. (A.H.)
Browning-Ferris Industries Inc.
Burlington Northern Santa Fe Corp.
Burlington Resources, Inc.
Centex Corp.
Central & South West Services
Chase Bank of Texas
Compaq Computer Corp.
Conoco, Inc.
Contran Corp.
Cooper Industries, Inc.
EDS Corp.
El Paso Energy Co.
Exxon Mobil Corp.
FINA
Fort Worth Star-Telegram Inc.
Frito-Lay, Inc.
Frost National Bank
GTE Corp.
Halliburton Co.
Hunt Oil Co.
Kimberly-Clark Corp.
Kinder Morgn
Lennox International, Inc.
Lyondell Chemical Co.
Penney Co., Inc. (J.C.)
Pennzoil-Quaker State Co.
Pioneer Natural Resources
Quanex Corp.
Reliant Energy Inc.
Santa Fe International Corp.
SBC Communications Inc.
Shell Oil Co.
Tandy Corp.
Temple-Inland Inc.
Tesoro Hawaii
Texas Instruments Inc.
TU Electric Co.
Ultramar Diamond Shamrock Corp.
Union Pacific Corp.
United Services Automobile Association
USAA Life Insurance Co.
Valero Energy Corp.
Williams
Zachry Co. (H.B.)

Utah

Questar Corp.

Vermont

Ben & Jerry's Homemade Inc.
Carris Reels
Central Vermont Public Service Corp.
National Life of Vermont

Virginia

Bassett Furniture Industries
Burress (J.W.)
Chesapeake Corp.
Circuit City Stores, Inc.
Crestar Finance Corp.
CSX Corp.
Dominion Resources, Inc.
Ethyl Corp.
First Union Securities, Inc.
Freddie Mac
Gannett Co., Inc.
General Dynamics Corp.
Heilig-Meyers Co.
LandAmerica Financial Services
Landmark Communications Inc.
Navcom Systems
Newport News Shipbuilding
Norfolk Southern Corp.
Overnite Transportation Co.
PEMCO Corp.
Reynolds Metals Co.
Ukrop's Super Markets
United Co.
Universal Leaf Tobacco Co., Inc.

Washington

Airborne Freight Corp.
Alaska Airlines, Inc.
Avista Corporation
Boeing Co.
Microsoft Corp.
PACCAR Inc.
Puget Sound Energy (PSE) Inc.
REI-Recreational Equipment, Inc.
SAFECO Corp.
Simpson Investment Co.
US Bank, Washington
Washington Trust Bank
Weyerhaeuser Co.

West Virginia

Bell Atlantic Corp.-West Virginia

Wisconsin

Ameritech Wisconsin
Appleton Papers Inc.
Badger Meter, Inc.
Baird & Co. (Robert W.)
Banta Corp.
Bemis Manufacturing Co.
Briggs & Stratton Corp.
Bucyrus-Erie Co.
Charter Manufacturing Co.
Consolidated Papers, Inc.
CUNA Mutual Group
Employers Insurance of Wausau, A Mutual Co.
Extendicare Health Services
First Financial Bank
Firstar Bank Milwaukee NA
Fortis Insurance Co.
Giddings & Lewis
Grede Foundries
Green Bay Packaging
Harley-Davidson Co.
Harnischfeger Industries
Johnson Controls Inc.
Johnson & Son (S.C.)
Journal Communications, Inc.
Kohler Co.
Ladish Co., Inc.
Madison Gas & Electric Co.
Marcus Corp.
Marshall & Ilsley Corp.
Menasha Corp.
MGIC Investment Corp.
National Presto Industries, Inc.
Oshkosh B'Gosh, Inc.
Pieper Power Electric Co.
Reinhart Institutional Foods
Sentry Insurance, A Mutual Co.
Smith Corp. (A.O.)
United Wisconsin Services
Universal Foods Corp.
Wausau Insurance Companies
WICOR, Inc.
Wisconsin Energy Corp.
Wisconsin Power & Light Co.
Wisconsin Public Service Corp.

Wyoming

True Oil Co.

Funders By Operating Locations

The following index lists corporations by the states of their major operating locations. Within each state, company names are listed in alphabetical order.

Alabama

AFLAC Inc.
AGL Resources Inc.
Air Products and Chemicals, Inc.
Alabama Power Co.
Albany International Corp.
Alcoa Inc.
Alliant Techsystems
Apple Computer, Inc.
Armstrong World Industries, Inc.
Arvin Industries, Inc.
Battelle Memorial Institute
Baxter International Inc.
Belk Stores Services Inc.
BellSouth Telecommunications
Blount International, Inc.
Blue Bell, Inc.
Blue Cross & Blue Shield of Alabama
Boeing Co.
Boise Cascade Corp.
Bowater Inc.
BP Amoco Corp.
Briggs & Stratton Corp.
Browning-Ferris Industries Inc.
Butler Manufacturing Co.
Caterpillar Inc.
Champion International Corp.
Chevron Corp.
Circuit City Stores, Inc.
CLARCOR Inc.
Clorox Co.
Compass Bank
Computer Associates International, Inc.
ConAgra, Inc.
Cooper Industries, Inc.
CSX Corp.
Cummins Engine Co., Inc.
DaimlerChrysler Corp.
Dana Corp.
Deloitte & Touche
Delta Air Lines, Inc.
Dexter Corp.
Diebold, Inc.
du Pont de Nemours & Co. (E.I.)
Eastman Kodak Co.
Eaton Corp.
Eckerd Corp.
Ecolab Inc.
EDS Corp.
Elf Atochem North America, Inc.
Employers Mutual Casualty Co.
Equifax Inc.
Ernst & Young, LLP
Exxon Mobil Corp.
Fannie Mae
FMC Corp.
Forest City Enterprises, Inc.
Fort James Corp.
Fortune Brands, Inc.
Frontier Corp.
Gannett Co., Inc.
GEICO Corp.
GenCorp
General Motors Corp.
Georgia-Pacific Corp.
Georgia Power Co.
Gerber Products Co.
Goodrich Aerospace - Aerostructures Group (B.F.)
Halliburton Co.
Hamilton Sundstrand Corp.
Harley-Davidson Co.
Harsco Corp.
Hartmarx Corp.
Hercules Inc.
Hewlett-Packard Co.
Home Depot, Inc.
Humana, Inc.
Hunt Manufacturing Co.
IKON Office Solutions, Inc.
Inland Container Corp.
International Business Machines Corp.
International Paper Co.
Johnson Controls Inc.
Kendall International, Inc.
Kimball International, Inc.
Kimberly-Clark Corp.
KPMG Peat Marwick LLP
Lehigh Portland Cement Co.
Levi Strauss & Co.
Liberty Corp.
Lilly & Co. (Eli)
Lincoln Electric Co.
Litton Industries, Inc.
Lockheed Martin Corp.
Louisiana Land & Exploration Co.
Louisiana-Pacific Corp.
MacMillan Bloedel Inc.
Marcus Corp.
Matsushita Electric Corp. of America
McDonald & Co. Securities, Inc.
McWane Inc.
Mead Corp.
Minnesota Mining & Manufacturing Co.
Monsanto Co.
Montana Power Co.
Montgomery Ward & Co., Inc.
Morton International Inc.
Motorola Inc.
Nalco Chemical Co.
New York Times Co.
Norfolk Southern Corp.
Northrop Grumman Corp.
Novartis Corporation
Nucor Corp.
Occidental Petroleum Corp.
Olin Corp.
Oracle Corp.
Parker Hannifin Corp.
Regions Financial Corp.
Reynolds Metals Co.
Sara Lee Corp.
Scripps Co. (E.W.)
Sears, Roebuck and Co.
Shaw Industries Inc.
Sony Electronics
Southern Co. Services Inc.
Springs Industries, Inc.
Square D Co.
Standard Products Co.
Starwood Hotels & Resorts Worldwide, Inc.
State Farm Mutual Automobile Insurance Co.
Steelcase Inc.
Stone Container Corp.
Sun Microsystems Inc.
SuperValu, Inc.
Synovus Financial Corp.
Temple-Inland Inc.
Tenet Healthcare Corp.
Texas Instruments Inc.
Textron Inc.
Torchmark Corp.
Trustmark Insurance Co.
TRW Inc.
Tyson Foods Inc.
Union Camp Corp.
United Airlines Inc.
United Parcel Service of America Inc.
United Technologies Corp.
Unocal Corp.
USG Corp.
USX Corp.
Vulcan Materials Co.
Wal-Mart Stores, Inc.
Walter Industries Inc.
Weyerhaeuser Co.
Williams
Winn-Dixie Stores Inc.
Witco Corp.
Zurn Industries, Inc.

Alaska

Alyeska Pipeline Service Co.
Chevron Corp.
Commercial Intertech Corp.
Cook Inlet Region
Deloitte & Touche
Delta Air Lines, Inc.
Diebold, Inc.
Eastman Kodak Co.
Extendicare Health Services
Exxon Mobil Corp.
FedEx Corp.
Fisher Scientific
Fluor Corp.
FMC Corp.
General Mills, Inc.
International Business Machines Corp.
KPMG Peat Marwick LLP
Lincoln Financial Group
Minnesota Mining & Manufacturing Co.
Nalco Chemical Co.
PacifiCorp
Phillips Petroleum Co.
REI-Recreational Equipment, Inc.
Sara Lee Hosiery, Inc.
Tyson Foods Inc.
United Parcel Service of America Inc.
Unocal Corp.

Arizona

Air Products and Chemicals, Inc.
Albertson's Inc.
Alliant Techsystems
America West Airlines, Inc.
American Express Co.
American General Finance
American United Life Insurance Co.
Apple Computer, Inc.
Appleton Papers Inc.
Arizona Public Service Co.
ASARCO Inc.
Atlantic Richfield Co.
Badger Meter, Inc.
Bard, Inc. (C.R.)
Baxter International Inc.
Becton Dickinson & Co.
Ben & Jerry's Homemade Inc.
BFGoodrich Co.
Boeing Co.
Boise Cascade Corp.
Cadence Designs Systems, Inc.
Caterpillar Inc.
Central Newspapers, Inc.
Chase Manhattan Bank, NA
Circuit City Stores, Inc.
Citibank Corp.
CNF Transportation, Inc.
Computer Associates International, Inc.
ConAgra, Inc.
Cox Enterprises Inc.
Crane Co.
Cyprus Amax Minerals Co.
DaimlerChrysler Corp.
Dana Corp.
Deloitte & Touche
Delta Air Lines, Inc.
Deluxe Corp.
Dial Corp.
Diebold, Inc.
Dow Jones & Co., Inc.
Eastman Kodak Co.
Edison International
EDS Corp.
Emerson Electric Co.
Equifax Inc.
Ernst & Young, LLP
Evening Post Publishing Co.
Fannie Mae
Federated Mutual Insurance Co.
FedEx Corp.
Fifth Third Bancorp
Firstar Bank Milwaukee NA
FMC Corp.
Freightliner Corp.
Gannett Co., Inc.
GEICO Corp.
GenCorp
Georgia-Pacific Corp.
Gerber Products Co.
Globe Corp.
Grace & Co. (W.R.)
Hamilton Sundstrand Corp.
Harrah's Entertainment Inc.
Harris Trust & Savings Bank
Hartford (The)
Hewlett-Packard Co.
Home Depot, Inc.
Honeywell International Inc.
HSBC Bank USA
Hubbell Inc.
Humana, Inc.
IKON Office Solutions, Inc.
Intel Corp.
International Business Machines Corp.
Jeld-wen, Inc.
Kaman Corp.
Kimberly-Clark Corp.
Kroger Co.
Lee Enterprises
Lilly & Co. (Eli)
Lincoln Electric Co.
Litton Industries, Inc.
Lockheed Martin Corp.
Loews Corp.
Lotus Development Corp.
Marshall & Ilsley Corp.
Masco Corp.
Mattel Inc.
McClatchy Co.
McCormick & Co. Inc.
McKesson-HBOC Corp.
Mead Corp.
Medtronic, Inc.
Mellon Financial Corp.
Meredith Corp.
Mervyn's California
Metropolitan Life Insurance Co.
Microsoft Corp.
Minnesota Mining & Manufacturing Co.
Montgomery Ward & Co., Inc.
Morgan Stanley Dean Witter & Co.
Morrison Knudsen Corp.
Morton International Inc.
Motorola Inc.
Nestle U.S.A. Inc.
Northern Trust Co.
Northrop Grumman Corp.
Norton Co.
Norwest Corp.
Nucor Corp.
Olin Corp.
Parker Hannifin Corp.
PerkinElmer, Inc.
Phelps Dodge Corp.
Phillips Petroleum Co.
Pillsbury Co.
Pioneer Hi-Bred International, Inc.
Procter & Gamble Co.
Prudential Insurance Co. of America
Pulitzer Publishing Co.
REI-Recreational Equipment, Inc.
Reynolds Metals Co.
Sara Lee Corp.
Schwab & Co., Inc. (Charles)
Scripps Co. (E.W.)
Sears, Roebuck and Co.
S.G. Cowen
SmithKline Beecham Corp.
Sony Electronics
Stanley Works (The)
Starwood Hotels & Resorts Worldwide, Inc.

State Farm Mutual Automobile Insurance Co.
Stone Container Corp.
Target Corp.
Tenet Healthcare Corp.
Texas Instruments Inc.
Thompson Co. (J. Walter)
Times Mirror Co.
Tomkins Industries, Inc.
Trustmark Insurance Co.
TRW Inc.
Tucson Electric Power Co.
U.S. Bancorp Piper Jaffray
US West, Inc.
Varian Medical Systems, Inc.
Wal-Mart Stores, Inc.
Walgreen Co.
The Washington Post
Westvaco Corp.
Zenith Electronics Corp.

Arkansas

Aetna, Inc.
Air Products and Chemicals, Inc.
Alcoa Inc.
ALLTEL Corp.
Anheuser-Busch Companies, Inc.
Archer-Daniels-Midland Co.
AT&T Corp.
Badger Meter, Inc.
Ball Corp.
Baxter International Inc.
Belk Stores Services Inc.
Bemis Co., Inc.
Bestfoods
Bridgestone/Firestone, Inc.
Browning-Ferris Industries Inc.
Burlington Industries, Inc.
Campbell Soup Co.
Carrier Corp.
Computer Associates International, Inc.
ConAgra, Inc.
Cooper Industries, Inc.
Cooper Tire & Rubber Co.
DaimlerChrysler Corp.
Dana Corp.
Dayton Hudson
Deloitte & Touche
Diebold, Inc.
Donnelley & Sons Co. (R.R.)
Dow Chemical Co.
Dow Jones & Co., Inc.
du Pont de Nemours & Co. (E.I.)
Eastman Kodak Co.
EDS Corp.
Emerson Electric Co.
Entergy Corp.
Equifax Inc.
Ernst & Young, LLP
FedEx Corp.
Fort James Corp.
Gannett Co., Inc.
GenCorp
Georgia-Pacific Corp.
Gerber Products Co.
Goodrich Aerospace - Aerostructures Group (B.F.)
Hartmarx Corp.
Heinz Co. (H.J.)
Hercules Inc.
Illinois Tool Works, Inc.
Inland Container Corp.
International Business Machines Corp.
International Paper Co.
Johnson Controls Inc.
Johnson & Son (S.C.)
Kimberly-Clark Corp.
KPMG Peat Marwick LLP
La-Z-Boy Inc.
Levi Strauss & Co.
Liberty Corp.
Lincoln Electric Co.
Marcus Corp.
Mark IV Industries
Maybelline, Inc.
McDermott Inc.
McKesson-HBOC Corp.
Mead Corp.
Medtronic, Inc.
Monsanto Co.
Montgomery Ward & Co., Inc.
Murphy Oil Corp.
National Starch & Chemical Co.
Norton Co.
OG&E Electric Services
Oracle Corp.
Owens Corning
Parker Hannifin Corp.
Phelps Dodge Corp.
Pioneer Hi-Bred International, Inc.
Potlatch Corp.
PPG Industries, Inc.
Prudential Insurance Co. of America
Quanex Corp.
Reliant Energy Inc.
Reynolds Metals Co.
Rouse Co.
Sara Lee Corp.
SBC Communications Inc.
Schering-Plough Corp.
Smith Corp. (A.O.)
Smurfit-Stone Container Corp.
Starwood Hotels & Resorts Worldwide, Inc.
Stone Container Corp.
Sun Microsystems Inc.
Target Corp.
Temple-Inland Inc.
Tenet Healthcare Corp.
Tenneco Automotive
Timken Co. (The)
Torchmark Corp.
Tyson Foods Inc.
Union Camp Corp.
Union Pacific Corp.
United Parcel Service of America Inc.
Wal-Mart Stores, Inc.
Weyerhaeuser Co.
Whirlpool Corp.
Wolverine World Wide

California

7-Eleven, Inc.
ABB Inc.
Abbott Laboratories
ABC
Aetna, Inc.
Air Products and Chemicals, Inc.
Albertson's Inc.
Alcoa Inc.
Alexander & Baldwin, Inc.
Allegheny Technologies Inc.
Alliant Techsystems
Allianz Life Insurance Co. of North America
AlliedSignal Inc.
America West Airlines, Inc.
American Express Co.
American General Finance
American Honda Motor Co., Inc.
American United Life Insurance Co.
Ameritech Corp.
AMETEK, Inc.
Amgen, Inc.
AMP Inc.
AMR Corp.
Analog Devices, Inc.
Anheuser-Busch Companies, Inc.
APL Ltd.
Apple Computer, Inc.
Appleton Papers Inc.
Armstrong World Industries, Inc.
AT&T Corp.
Atlantic Richfield Co.
Autodesk Inc.
Avery Dennison Corp.
Avon Products, Inc.
Baker Hughes Inc.
Ball Corp.
Bandag, Inc.
Bank of America
Bank of New York Co., Inc.
Banta Corp.
Bard, Inc. (C.R.)
Barnes Group Inc.
Battelle Memorial Institute
Bausch & Lomb Inc.
Baxter International Inc.
Bayer Corp.
Bechtel Group, Inc.
Beckman Coulter, Inc.
Becton Dickinson & Co.
Belo Corp. (A.H.)
Bemis Co., Inc.
Ben & Jerry's Homemade Inc.
Bestfoods
BFGoodrich Co.
Blount International, Inc.
Boeing Co.
Boise Cascade Corp.
Bourns, Inc.
Bridgestone/Firestone, Inc.
Broderbund Software, Inc.
Browning-Ferris Industries Inc.
Brunswick Corp.
Bucyrus-Erie Co.
Burlington Industries, Inc.
Burnett Co. (Leo)
Butler Manufacturing Co.
Cadence Designs Systems, Inc.
Caesar's World, Inc.
California Bank & Trust
California Federal Bank, FSB
Callaway Golf Co.
Campbell Soup Co.
Cargill Inc.
Carnival Corp.
Carrier Corp.
Carris Reels
Carter-Wallace, Inc.
Castle & Cooke Properties Inc.
CertainTeed Corp.
Chase Manhattan Bank, NA
Chevron Corp.
Chicago Tribune Co.
Church & Dwight Co., Inc.
CIBC Oppenheimer
Circuit City Stores, Inc.
CIT Group, Inc. (The)
Citibank Corp.
Citizens Financial Group, Inc.
CLARCOR Inc.
Clorox Co.
CNF Transportation, Inc.
Collins & Aikman Corp.
Comdisco, Inc.
Comerica Inc.
Commercial Intertech Corp.
Compaq Computer Corp.
Computer Associates International, Inc.
ConAgra, Inc.
Cone Mills Corp.
Consolidated Electrical Distributors
Cooper Industries, Inc.
Cooper Tire & Rubber Co.
Copley Press, Inc.
Cox Enterprises Inc.
Crane Co.
CUNA Mutual Group
Curtis Industries, Inc. (Helene)
Daily News
DaimlerChrysler Corp.
Dana Corp.
Dayton Hudson
Deloitte & Touche
Delta Air Lines, Inc.
Deluxe Corp.
Deutsch Co.
Dexter Corp.
Diebold, Inc.
Disney Co. (Walt)
Dixie Group, Inc. (The)
Donaldson Co., Inc.
Donnelley & Sons Co. (R.R.)
Dow Chemical Co.
Dow Corning Corp.
Dow Jones & Co., Inc.
Dreyer's Grand Ice Cream
du Pont de Nemours & Co. (E.I.)
Dun & Bradstreet Corp.
Eastman Chemical Co.
Eastman Kodak Co.
Eaton Corp.
Ecolab Inc.
Edison Brothers Stores, Inc.
Edison International
EDS Corp.
Elf Atochem North America, Inc.
Emerson Electric Co.
EMI Music Publishing
Equifax Inc.
Ernst & Young, LLP
European American Bank
Exxon Mobil Corp.
Fannie Mae
Farmers Group, Inc.
Federated Department Stores, Inc.
FedEx Corp.
Ferro Corp.
Fireman's Fund Insurance Co.
Fisher Scientific
Fluor Corp.
FMC Corp.
Forest City Enterprises, Inc.
Fort James Corp.
Fortis, Inc.
Fox Entertainment Group
Franklin Mint (The)
Freddie Mac
Freightliner Corp.
Fuller Co. (H.B.)
Gallo Winery, Inc. (E&J)
Gannett Co., Inc.
Gap, Inc.
GATX Corp.
GEICO Corp.
GenCorp
Genentech Inc.
General Dynamics Corp.
General Electric Co.
General Mills, Inc.
General Motors Corp.
General Reinsurance Corp.
Georgia-Pacific Corp.
Gerber Products Co.
Giant Food Inc.
Gillette Co.
Goldman Sachs Group
Goodrich Aerospace - Aerostructures Group (B.F.)
Grace & Co. (W.R.)
Graco, Inc.
Grainger, Inc. (W.W.)
GTE Corp.
Guess?
Halliburton Co.
Hamilton Sundstrand Corp.
Harcourt General, Inc.
Harris Corp.
Harris Trust & Savings Bank
Harsco Corp.
Hartford (The)
Hasbro, Inc.
Heinz Co. (H.J.)
Heller Financial, Inc.
Hershey Foods Corp.
Hewlett-Packard Co.
Hickory Tech Corp.
Hitachi America Ltd.
Hoffmann-La Roche Inc.
Hofmann Co.
Home Depot, Inc.
HON Industries Inc.
Houghton Mifflin Co.
Household International Inc.
Hubbard Broadcasting, Inc.
Hubbell Inc.
Huffy Corp.
Hughes Electronics Corp.
Hunt Manufacturing Co.
IKON Office Solutions, Inc.
Illinois Tool Works, Inc.
Industrial Bank of Japan Trust Co. (New York)
Inland Container Corp.
Intel Corp.
International Business Machines Corp.
International Multifoods Corp.
International Paper Co.
Interpublic Group of Companies, Inc.
Jacobs Engineering Group
Johnson Controls Inc.
Johnson & Johnson
Johnson & Son (S.C.)
Jostens, Inc.
Kaman Corp.
Kemper National Insurance Companies
Kendall International, Inc.
Kimball International, Inc.
Kimberly-Clark Corp.
Kirkland & Ellis
Knight Ridder
KPMG Peat Marwick LLP
Kraft Foods, Inc.
La-Z-Boy Inc.
Land O'Lakes, Inc.
Lee Enterprises
Lehigh Portland Cement Co.
Lennox International, Inc.
Levi Strauss & Co.
Liberty Mutual Insurance Group
Lilly & Co. (Eli)
Lincoln Electric Co.
Lipton Co.
Little, Inc. (Arthur D.)
Litton Industries, Inc.

Liz Claiborne, Inc.
Lockheed Martin Corp.
Loews Corp.
Lotus Development Corp.
Louisiana-Pacific Corp.
Macy's East Inc.
Maritz Inc.
Mark IV Industries
Masco Corp.
Matsushita Electric Corp. of America
Mattel Inc.
May Department Stores Co.
Maybelline, Inc.
Maytag Corp.
Mazda North American Operations
McCormick & Co. Inc.
McGraw-Hill Companies, Inc.
MCI WorldCom, Inc.
McKesson-HBOC Corp.
Mead Corp.
Medtronic, Inc.
Mellon Financial Corp.
Merck & Co.
Meredith Corp.
Mervyn's California
Metropolitan Life Insurance Co.
Microsoft Corp.
Milacron, Inc.
Milliken & Co.
Minnesota Mining & Manufacturing Co.
Mitsubishi Electric America
Monsanto Co.
Montgomery Ward & Co., Inc.
Morgan & Co. Inc. (J.P.)
Morgan Stanley Dean Witter & Co.
Morrison Knudsen Corp.
Morton International Inc.
Motorola Inc.
Nalco Chemical Co.
National Starch & Chemical Co.
NCR Corp.
NEC America, Inc.
Nestle U.S.A. Inc.
New United Motor Manufacturing Inc.
New York Times Co.
Nissan North America, Inc.
Nomura Holding America
Nordson Corp.
Norfolk Southern Corp.
Nortel
Northern Trust Co.
Northrop Grumman Corp.
Norton Co.
Norwest Corp.
Novartis Corporation
Occidental Oil and Gas
Occidental Petroleum Corp.
Olin Corp.
Oracle Corp.
Oshkosh B'Gosh, Inc.
Owens Corning
Owens-Illinois Inc.
PACCAR Inc.
Pacific Enterprises
Pacific Gas and Electric Co.
Pacific Mutual Life Insurance Co.
Parker Hannifin Corp.
Patagonia Inc.
PepsiCo, Inc.
PerkinElmer, Inc.
Pfizer Inc.
Phelps Dodge Corp.
Philip Morris Companies Inc.
Philips Electronics North America Corp.
Pillsbury Co.
Pioneer Hi-Bred International, Inc.
Pittway Corp.
Playboy Enterprises Inc.
Polaroid Corp.
Potlatch Corp.
Premark International Inc.
Procter & Gamble Co.
Progressive Corp.
Prudential Insurance Co. of America
Quaker Chemical Corp.
Ralph's Grocery Co.
Ralston Purina Co.
REI-Recreational Equipment, Inc.
Revlon Inc.
Reynolds Metals Co.
Reynolds & Reynolds Co.
Reynolds Tobacco (R.J.)
Rich Products Corp.
Rockwell International Corp.
Rohm & Haas Co.
Roseburg Forest Products Co.
Rouse Co.
Ryder System, Inc.
SAFECO Corp.
Safeway Inc.
Salomon Smith Barney
Santa Fe International Corp.
Sara Lee Corp.
Sara Lee Hosiery, Inc.
Schering-Plough Corp.
Schlumberger Ltd. (USA)
Schwab & Co., Inc. (Charles)
Scientific-Atlanta, Inc.
Scripps Co. (E.W.)
Seagram & Sons, Inc. (Joseph E.)
Sears, Roebuck and Co.
Security Life of Denver Insurance Co.
Sega of America Inc.
Sempra Energy
S.G. Cowen
Shaklee Corp.
Sharp Electronics Corp.
Shaw Industries Inc.
Shea Co. (John F.)
Shell Oil Co.
Sherwin-Williams Co.
Simpson Investment Co.
Smith Corp. (A.O.)
SmithKline Beecham Corp.
Smucker Co. (JM)
Smurfit-Stone Container Corp.
Sony Electronics
Sotheby's Inc.
Southern California Gas Co.
Springs Industries, Inc.
Sprint Corp.
Square D Co.
Standard Products Co.
Stanley Works (The)
Starwood Hotels & Resorts Worldwide, Inc.
State Farm Mutual Automobile Insurance Co.
State Street Bank & Trust Co.
Steelcase Inc.
Stone Container Corp.
Sun Microsystems Inc.
SuperValu, Inc.
Taco Bell Corp.
Tandy Corp.
Target Corp.
Tektronix, Inc.
Teleflex Inc.
Temple-Inland Inc.
Tenet Healthcare Corp.
Tension Envelope Corp.
Texaco Inc.
Texas Instruments Inc.
Textron Inc.
Thompson Co. (J. Walter)
Times Mirror Co.
Timken Co. (The)
Tomkins Industries, Inc.
Torchmark Corp.
Toshiba America Inc.
Toyota Motor Sales U.S.A., Inc.
Transamerica Corp.
True North Communications, Inc.
TRW Inc.
Tyson Foods Inc.
Unilever Home & Personal Care U.S.A.
Unilever United States, Inc.
Union Camp Corp.
Union Carbide Corp.
Union Pacific Corp.
Unisys Corp.
United Airlines Inc.
United Distillers & Vintners North America
United Dominion Industries, Ltd.
United Parcel Service of America Inc.
U.S. Bancorp Piper Jaffray
United States Trust Co. of New York
United Technologies Corp.
Universal Foods Corp.
Universal Studios
Unocal Corp.
USG Corp.
Valspar Corp.
Varian Medical Systems, Inc.
Vodafone AirTouch Plc
Wal-Mart Stores, Inc.
Walgreen Co.
Washington Mutual, Inc.
Wells Fargo & Co.
Westvaco Corp.
Weyerhaeuser Co.
WICOR, Inc.
Wilbur-Ellis Co. & Connell Brothers Co.
Witco Corp.
Wrigley Co. (Wm. Jr.)
Wyman-Gordon Co.
Xerox Corp.
Young & Rubicam
Zenith Electronics Corp.
Zurn Industries, Inc.

Colorado

7-Eleven, Inc.
ABC
Aetna, Inc.
Air Products and Chemicals, Inc.
Albertson's Inc.
Alcoa Inc.
AlliedSignal Inc.
America West Airlines, Inc.
American United Life Insurance Co.
Amgen, Inc.
Anheuser-Busch Companies, Inc.
Appleton Papers Inc.
ASARCO Inc.
AT&T Corp.
Atlantic Richfield Co.
Autodesk Inc.
Badger Meter, Inc.
Ball Corp.
Battelle Memorial Institute
Baxter International Inc.
Bayer Corp.
Bemis Co., Inc.
Ben & Jerry's Homemade Inc.
Boise Cascade Corp.
BP Amoco Corp.
Bristol-Myers Squibb Co.
Browning-Ferris Industries Inc.
Burlington Resources, Inc.
Caterpillar Inc.
Chevron Corp.
Church & Dwight Co., Inc.
Compaq Computer Corp.
ConAgra, Inc.
Conoco, Inc.
Coors Brewing Co.
Cyprus Amax Minerals Co.
DaimlerChrysler Corp.
Dain Bosworth Inc.
Dayton Hudson
Deloitte & Touche
Deluxe Corp.
Diebold, Inc.
Donnelley & Sons Co. (R.R.)
Dow Jones & Co., Inc.
du Pont de Nemours & Co. (E.I.)
Dun & Bradstreet Corp.
Eastman Kodak Co.
Ecolab Inc.
EDS Corp.
Ernst & Young, LLP
Evening Post Publishing Co.
Fluor Corp.
FMC Corp.
Gates Rubber Corp.
GEICO Corp.
General Electric Co.
General Mills, Inc.
Georgia-Pacific Corp.
Gerber Products Co.
Graco, Inc.
Hamilton Sundstrand Corp.
Hartford (The)
Hensel Phelps Construction Co.
Hewlett-Packard Co.
Hitachi America Ltd.
Hoffmann-La Roche Inc.
Huffy Corp.
IKON Office Solutions, Inc.
Illinois Tool Works, Inc.
International Business Machines Corp.
International Multifoods Corp.
Kaman Corp.
Kemper National Insurance Companies
Kimberly-Clark Corp.
Kinder Morgn
Kirkland & Ellis
Knight Ridder
KPMG Peat Marwick LLP
Kroger Co.
Lilly & Co. (Eli)
Lincoln Electric Co.
Lincoln Financial Group
Litton Industries, Inc.
Lockheed Martin Corp.
Loews Corp.
Lotus Development Corp.
Louisiana Land & Exploration Co.
Louisiana-Pacific Corp.
May Department Stores Co.
Maytag Corp.
McGraw-Hill Companies, Inc.
MCI WorldCom, Inc.
Mead Corp.
Medtronic, Inc.
Mellon Financial Corp.
Mervyn's California
Microsoft Corp.
Minnesota Mining & Manufacturing Co.
Montana Power Co.
National Bank of Commerce Trust & Savings
NCR Corp.
NEC America, Inc.
Nestle U.S.A. Inc.
New Century Energies
Norfolk Southern Corp.
Norwest Corp.
Novartis Corporation
Occidental Oil and Gas
Occidental Petroleum Corp.
Oracle Corp.
PerkinElmer, Inc.
Pfizer Inc.
Philip Morris Companies Inc.
Philips Electronics North America Corp.
Phillips Petroleum Co.
Procter & Gamble Co.
Progressive Corp.
Ralston Purina Co.
REI-Recreational Equipment, Inc.
Reynolds Metals Co.
Rockwell International Corp.
Rouse Co.
Royal & SunAlliance USA, Inc.
SAFECO Corp.
Safeway Inc.
Saint Paul Companies Inc.
Schwab & Co., Inc. (Charles)
Scripps Co. (E.W.)
Security Life of Denver Insurance Co.
Shaw Industries Inc.
Sotheby's Inc.
Starwood Hotels & Resorts Worldwide, Inc.
State Farm Mutual Automobile Insurance Co.
Storage Technology Corp.
Sun Microsystems Inc.
SuperValu, Inc.
Target Corp.
Temple-Inland Inc.
Tenet Healthcare Corp.
Texaco Inc.
Texas Instruments Inc.
Times Mirror Co.
Timken Co. (The)
Tomkins Industries, Inc.
TRW Inc.
Ultramar Diamond Shamrock Corp.
Union Camp Corp.
Union Carbide Corp.
Union Pacific Corp.
Unisys Corp.
United Airlines Inc.
U.S. Bancorp
U.S. Bancorp Piper Jaffray
United Technologies Corp.
US West, Inc.
Valmont Industries, Inc.
Wal-Mart Stores, Inc.
Wells Fargo & Co.
Woodward Governor Co.
Zenith Electronics Corp.

Connecticut

7-Eleven, Inc.
ABB Inc.
ABC
Aetna, Inc.
Air Products and Chemicals, Inc.
Allegheny Technologies Inc.
Allianz Life Insurance Co. of North America
American Express Co.
American Standard Inc.
AMETEK, Inc.
Bank of New York Co., Inc.
BankBoston-Connecticut Region
BankBoston Corp.
Barden Corp.
Barnes Group Inc.
Bausch & Lomb Inc.
Baxter International Inc.
Bayer Corp.
Becton Dickinson & Co.
Ben & Jerry's Homemade Inc.
Browning-Ferris Industries Inc.
Campbell Soup Co.
Carnival Corp.
Carpenter Technology Corp.
CIGNA Corp.
Citibank Corp.
Citizens Financial Group, Inc.
CNF Transportation, Inc.
Commercial Intertech Corp.
Compaq Computer Corp.
Computer Associates International, Inc.
Cooper Industries, Inc.
Country Curtains, Inc.
Cox Enterprises Inc.
DaimlerChrysler Corp.
Dana Corp.
Deloitte & Touche
Delta Air Lines, Inc.
Dexter Corp.
Diebold, Inc.
Donnelley & Sons Co. (R.R.)
du Pont de Nemours & Co. (E.I.)
Duracell International
Eaton Corp.
Ecolab Inc.
EDS Corp.
Ernst & Young, LLP
Fannie Mae
FedEx Corp.
Fisher Brothers Cleaning Services
Fisher Scientific
FleetBoston Financial Corp.
Forbes Inc.
Fort James Corp.
Fortune Brands, Inc.
Freightliner Corp.
Gannett Co., Inc.
General Dynamics Corp.
General Electric Co.
General Motors Corp.
General Reinsurance Corp.
Georgia-Pacific Corp.
GTE Corp.
Harsco Corp.
Hartford (The)
Hartford Steam Boiler Inspection & Insurance Co.
Hershey Foods Corp.
Hewlett-Packard Co.
Home Depot, Inc.
HSBC Bank USA
Hubbell Inc.
Hunt Manufacturing Co.
IKON Office Solutions, Inc.
Illinois Tool Works, Inc.
Inland Container Corp.
International Business Machines Corp.
International Multifoods Corp.
Johnson & Johnson
Journal Communications, Inc.
Kaman Corp.
KPMG Peat Marwick LLP
Kraft Foods, Inc.
Lilly & Co. (Eli)
Litton Industries, Inc.
Loctite Corp.
Lotus Development Corp.
Marcus Corp.
Mark IV Industries
Massachusetts Mutual Life Insurance Co.
May Department Stores Co.
McClatchy Co.
McCormick & Co. Inc.
Medtronic, Inc.
Mellon Financial Corp.
Metropolitan Life Insurance Co.
Microsoft Corp.
Minnesota Mining & Manufacturing Co.
Morton International Inc.
Nationwide Insurance Co.
Nestle U.S.A. Inc.
New York Life Insurance Co.
New York Times Co.
Newman's Own Inc.
Northeast Utilities
Norton Co.
Olin Corp.
Owens-Illinois Inc.
Pacific Mutual Life Insurance Co.
Parker Hannifin Corp.
Pfizer Inc.
Pharmacia & Upjohn, Inc.
Philip Morris Companies Inc.
Philips Electronics North America Corp.
Phoenix Home Life Mutual Insurance Co.
Pitney Bowes Inc.
Pittway Corp.
Ralston Purina Co.
Rayonier Inc.
Reader's Digest Association, Inc. (The)
Rohm & Haas Co.
Royal & SunAlliance USA, Inc.
Saint Paul Companies Inc.
Salomon Smith Barney
Sara Lee Corp.
Schlumberger Ltd. (USA)
S.G. Cowen
Shaw's Supermarkets, Inc.
Shell Oil Co.
Southern New England Telephone Co.
Stanley Works (The)
Starwood Hotels & Resorts Worldwide, Inc.
State Street Bank & Trust Co.
Stone Container Corp.
Subway Sandwich Shops, Inc.
Sun Microsystems Inc.
Teleflex Inc.
Tenet Healthcare Corp.
Tenneco Automotive
Textron Inc.
Times Mirror Co.
Timken Co. (The)
True North Communications, Inc.
Unilever Home & Personal Care U.S.A.
Unilever United States, Inc.
Union Camp Corp.
Union Carbide Corp.
United Distillers & Vintners North America
United Dominion Industries, Ltd.
United Technologies Corp.
UST Inc.
Wal-Mart Stores, Inc.
Warner-Lambert Co.
The Washington Post
Webster Bank
Westvaco Corp.
Wiremold Co.
Witco Corp.
Woodward Governor Co.
Wyman-Gordon Co.
Xerox Corp.

Delaware

7-Eleven, Inc.
AlliedSignal Inc.
American Express Co.
AMETEK, Inc.
Armstrong World Industries, Inc.
Avon Products, Inc.
Bank of New York Co., Inc.
Bell Atlantic Corp.
Bell Atlantic-Delaware, Inc.
Blount International, Inc.
Campbell Soup Co.
CertainTeed Corp.
Chase Manhattan Bank, NA
CIBC Oppenheimer
Circuit City Stores, Inc.
Citibank Corp.
Citigroup
Conectiv
Country Curtains, Inc.
DaimlerChrysler Corp.
Dexter Corp.
du Pont de Nemours & Co. (E.I.)
Duke Energy
Eckerd Corp.
EMI Music Publishing
Equifax Inc.
Farmers Group, Inc.
FedEx Corp.
First Maryland Bancorp
First Union Bank
Fisher Scientific
Freightliner Corp.
Gannett Co., Inc.
General Motors Corp.
Georgia-Pacific Corp.
GPU Inc.
Heller Financial, Inc.
Hercules Inc.
Hewlett-Packard Co.
International Business Machines Corp.
Johnson Controls Inc.
Kimberly-Clark Corp.
KPMG Peat Marwick LLP
Morgan & Co. Inc. (J.P.)
National Presto Industries, Inc.
New York Life Insurance Co.
Philips Electronics North America Corp.
PNC Bank
Procter & Gamble Co.
Provident Mutual Life Insurance Co.
Saint Paul Companies Inc.
Sara Lee Corp.
Schering-Plough Corp.
Sears, Roebuck and Co.
Smurfit-Stone Container Corp.
Sovereign Bank
Westvaco Corp.

District of Columbia

7-Eleven, Inc.
Abbott Laboratories
ABC
Air Products and Chemicals, Inc.
Alcoa Inc.
American Electric Power
American Stock Exchange, Inc.
Ameritech Corp.
ASARCO Inc.
Ashland, Inc.
Banfi Vintners
Bayer Corp.
Bechtel Group, Inc.
Bell Atlantic Corp.
Ben & Jerry's Homemade Inc.
Bristol-Myers Squibb Co.
Burlington Industries, Inc.
Carolina Power & Light Co.
Caterpillar Inc.
Chicago Tribune Co.
Citibank Corp.
Crestar Finance Corp.
CSX Corp.
Dayton Hudson
Deloitte & Touche
Dow Chemical Co.
Dow Corning Corp.
Dow Jones & Co., Inc.
Dun & Bradstreet Corp.
Eastman Kodak Co.
Ecolab Inc.
EDS Corp.
Ernst & Young, LLP
Ethyl Corp.
FedEx Corp.
First Union Corp.
Fluor Corp.
FMC Corp.
Fox Entertainment Group
Freddie Mac
Gannett Co., Inc.
GenCorp
General Mills, Inc.
Gerber Products Co.
Giant Food Inc.
Goldman Sachs Group
Halliburton Co.
Harcourt General, Inc.
Hartford (The)
Heller Financial, Inc.
Hercules Inc.
Hewlett-Packard Co.
Humana, Inc.
Industrial Bank of Japan Trust Co. (New York)
International Business Machines Corp.
Interpublic Group of Companies, Inc.
Kimberly-Clark Corp.
Kirkland & Ellis
KPMG Peat Marwick LLP
Little, Inc. (Arthur D.)
Marriott International Inc.
MCI WorldCom, Inc.
Mead Corp.
Medtronic, Inc.
Merck & Co.
Microsoft Corp.
Minnesota Mining & Manufacturing Co.
Niagara Mohawk Holdings Inc.
Nike, Inc.
Norfolk Southern Corp.
Northern States Power Co.
Novartis Corporation
PerkinElmer, Inc.
Pfizer Inc.
Potomac Electric Power Co.
Prudential Insurance Co. of America
Reynolds Metals Co.
Reynolds Tobacco (R.J.)
Riggs Bank NA
Rite Aid Corp.
Rouse Co.
Scripps Co. (E.W.)
Seagram & Sons, Inc. (Joseph E.)
Sears, Roebuck and Co.
Shell Oil Co.
Sprint Corp.
Student Loan Marketing Association
Thompson Co. (J. Walter)
Times Mirror Co.
TJX Companies, Inc.
TRW Inc.
Union Carbide Corp.
Unisys Corp.
United Airlines Inc.
United Distillers & Vintners North America
United Technologies Corp.
Vodafone AirTouch Plc
The Washington Post
Xerox Corp.
Young & Rubicam

Florida

7-Eleven, Inc.
ABB Inc.
Advanced Micro Devices, Inc.
AEGON U.S.A. Inc.
Air Products and Chemicals, Inc.
Alcoa Inc.
America West Airlines, Inc.
American Express Co.
American United Life Insurance Co.
AMETEK, Inc.
Anheuser-Busch Companies, Inc.
Archer-Daniels-Midland Co.
AT&T Corp.
Avery Dennison Corp.
Bank of America
Bank of New York Co., Inc.
BankBoston-Connecticut Region
Battelle Memorial Institute
Bausch & Lomb Inc.
Baxter International Inc.
Bayer Corp.
Belk Stores Services Inc.
BellSouth Telecommunications
Bemis Co., Inc.
Ben & Jerry's Homemade Inc.
BFGoodrich Co.
Blue Bell, Inc.
Boeing Co.

Bridgestone/Firestone, Inc.
Bristol-Myers Squibb Co.
Browning-Ferris Industries Inc.
Burger King Corp.
Burnett Co. (Leo)
Cadence Designs Systems, Inc.
Cargill Inc.
Carnival Corp.
Caterpillar Inc.
CertainTeed Corp.
Champion International Corp.
Chase Manhattan Bank, NA
Chevron Corp.
Chicago Tribune Co.
Church & Dwight Co., Inc.
Circuit City Stores, Inc.
Citibank Corp.
CNA
CNF Transportation, Inc.
Coca-Cola Co.
Comerica Inc.
Compaq Computer Corp.
Computer Associates International, Inc.
ConAgra, Inc.
Cox Enterprises Inc.
Crane Co.
CSR Rinker Materials Corp.
CSX Corp.
DaimlerChrysler Corp.
Dana Corp.
Dayton Hudson
Deloitte & Touche
Delta Air Lines, Inc.
Deluxe Corp.
Diebold, Inc.
Disney Co. (Walt)
Donaldson Co., Inc.
Donnelley & Sons Co. (R.R.)
Dow Jones & Co., Inc.
du Pont de Nemours & Co. (E.I.)
Dun & Bradstreet Corp.
Duracell International
Eastman Chemical Co.
Eastman Kodak Co.
Eaton Corp.
Eckerd Corp.
Ecolab Inc.
EDS Corp.
Equifax Inc.
Ernst & Young, LLP
European American Bank
Extendicare Health Services
Fannie Mae
Federated Department Stores, Inc.
FedEx Corp.
Fifth Third Bancorp
First Union Corp.
Firstar Bank Milwaukee NA
Fisher Scientific
FleetBoston Financial Corp.
Florida Power Corp.
Florida Power & Light Co.
Florida Rock Industries
FMC Corp.
Forest City Enterprises, Inc.
Fortis, Inc.
Freightliner Corp.
Fuller Co. (H.B.)
Gannett Co., Inc.
GATX Corp.
GEICO Corp.
General Mills, Inc.
General Motors Corp.
Georgia-Pacific Corp.
Gerber Products Co.
Goldman Sachs Group
Grace & Co. (W.R.)
GTE Corp.
Halliburton Co.
Harcourt General, Inc.
Harris Corp.
Harris Trust & Savings Bank
Harsco Corp.
Hartford (The)
Hartford Steam Boiler Inspection & Insurance Co.
Heinz Co. (H.J.)
Heller Financial, Inc.
Hercules Inc.
Hewlett-Packard Co.
Hitachi America Ltd.
Honeywell International Inc.
Hubbard Broadcasting, Inc.
Humana, Inc.
Huntington Bancshares Inc.
IKON Office Solutions, Inc.
Inland Container Corp.
International Business Machines Corp.
International Multifoods Corp.
International Paper Co.
Interpublic Group of Companies, Inc.
Johnson Controls Inc.
Johnson & Johnson
Kaman Corp.
Kimberly-Clark Corp.
Knight Ridder
KPMG Peat Marwick LLP
Kraft Foods, Inc.
Land O'Lakes, Inc.
Levi Strauss & Co.
Lilly & Co. (Eli)
Lincoln Electric Co.
Lincoln Financial Group
Lipton Co.
Litton Industries, Inc.
Lockheed Martin Corp.
Lotus Development Corp.
Louisiana-Pacific Corp.
Macy's East Inc.
Marcus Corp.
Marshall & Ilsley Corp.
Maybelline, Inc.
Maytag Corp.
McCormick & Co. Inc.
Mead Corp.
Medtronic, Inc.
Menasha Corp.
Meredith Corp.
Mervyn's California
Metropolitan Life Insurance Co.
Microsoft Corp.
Minnesota Mining & Manufacturing Co.
Mitsubishi Electric America
Monsanto Co.
Morgan & Co. Inc. (J.P.)
Morris Communications Corp.
Morrison Knudsen Corp.
Morton International Inc.
Motorola Inc.
Nalco Chemical Co.
National City Corp.
Nationwide Insurance Co.
NEC America, Inc.
Nestle U.S.A. Inc.
New York Times Co.
Norfolk Southern Corp.
Northern Trust Co.
Northrop Grumman Corp.
Norwest Corp.
Novartis Corporation
Occidental Petroleum Corp.
Olin Corp.
Oracle Corp.
Outboard Marine Corp.
Owens Corning
Owens-Illinois Inc.
Pacific Mutual Life Insurance Co.
Parker Hannifin Corp.
PerkinElmer, Inc.
Phelps Dodge Corp.
Pheonix Financial Group
Philip Morris Companies Inc.
Philips Electronics North America Corp.
Pillsbury Co.
Pioneer Hi-Bred International, Inc.
Pitney Bowes Inc.
Pittway Corp.
Premark International Inc.
Progressive Corp.
Prudential Insurance Co. of America
Publix Supermarkets
Regions Financial Corp.
Revlon Inc.
Riggs Bank NA
Rockwell International Corp.
Rouse Co.
Royal & SunAlliance USA, Inc.
Ryder System, Inc.
Saint Paul Companies Inc.
Sara Lee Corp.
Schering-Plough Corp.
Schwab & Co., Inc. (Charles)
Scientific-Atlanta, Inc.
Scripps Co. (E.W.)
Seagram & Sons, Inc. (Joseph E.)
Security Life of Denver Insurance Co.
Sentinel Communications Co.
Sharp Electronics Corp.
Shell Oil Co.
Sherwin-Williams Co.
Smith Corp. (A.O.)
SmithKline Beecham Corp.
Smurfit-Stone Container Corp.
Sony Electronics
Sotheby's Inc.
Sprint Corp.
Square D Co.
Stanley Works (The)
Stone Container Corp.
Stone & Webster Inc.
Storage Technology Corp.
Sun Microsystems Inc.
SunTrust Banks of Florida
SuperValu, Inc.
Synovus Financial Corp.
Tampa Electric Co.
Teleflex Inc.
Tenet Healthcare Corp.
Texaco Inc.
Texas Instruments Inc.
Textron Inc.
Thompson Co. (J. Walter)
TJX Companies, Inc.
Transamerica Corp.
Trustmark Insurance Co.
Tyson Foods Inc.
Unilever United States, Inc.
Union Camp Corp.
Union Carbide Corp.
Union Planters Corp.
United Distillers & Vintners North America
United Parcel Service of America Inc.
United States Sugar Corp.
United States Trust Co. of New York
United Technologies Corp.
Universal Studios
USG Corp.
Valspar Corp.
Wal-Mart Stores, Inc.
Walgreen Co.
Walter Industries Inc.
The Washington Post
West Co. Inc.
Westvaco Corp.
Weyerhaeuser Co.
Whitman Corp.
Winn-Dixie Stores Inc.
Zurn Industries, Inc.

Georgia

Abbott Laboratories
Advanced Micro Devices, Inc.
AEGON U.S.A. Inc.
AFLAC Inc.
AGL Resources Inc.
Agrilink Foods, Inc.
Air Products and Chemicals, Inc.
Albany International Corp.
Alcoa Inc.
America West Airlines, Inc.
American Express Co.
American United Life Insurance Co.
Anheuser-Busch Companies, Inc.
Apple Computer, Inc.
Appleton Papers Inc.
Archer-Daniels-Midland Co.
Armstrong World Industries, Inc.
AT&T Corp.
Atlantic Investment Co.
Avery Dennison Corp.
Bandag, Inc.
Bard, Inc. (C.R.)
Barnes Group Inc.
Battelle Memorial Institute
Bausch & Lomb Inc.
Beckman Coulter, Inc.
Belk Stores Services Inc.
BellSouth Telecommunications
Boeing Co.
BP Amoco Corp.
Bridgestone/Firestone, Inc.
Briggs & Stratton Corp.
Brown & Williamson Tobacco Corp.
Browning-Ferris Industries Inc.
Brunswick Corp.
Burlington Industries, Inc.
Butler Manufacturing Co.
California Bank & Trust
Campbell Soup Co.
Carpenter Technology Corp.
Caterpillar Inc.
Central Soya Co.
CertainTeed Corp.
Champion International Corp.
Chevron Corp.
Chicago Tribune Co.
Church & Dwight Co., Inc.
CIBC Oppenheimer
CIT Group, Inc. (The)
Citigroup
Citizens Financial Group, Inc.
CLARCOR Inc.
Clorox Co.
CNF Transportation, Inc.
Coachmen Industries, Inc.
Collins & Aikman Corp.
Colonial Oil Industries, Inc.
Compaq Computer Corp.
Computer Associates International, Inc.
ConAgra, Inc.
Cooper Industries, Inc.
Cooper Tire & Rubber Co.
Coors Brewing Co.
Cox Enterprises, Inc.
CSR Rinker Materials Corp.
CSX Corp.
CUNA Mutual Group
Dayton Hudson
Deere & Co.
Deloitte & Touche
Delta Air Lines, Inc.
Deluxe Corp.
Diebold, Inc.
Donnelley & Sons Co. (R.R.)
Dow Corning Corp.
Dow Jones & Co., Inc.
DSM Copolymer
du Pont de Nemours & Co. (E.I.)
Duracell International
Eastman Kodak Co.
Eckerd Corp.
Ecolab Inc.
Edison Brothers Stores, Inc.
EDS Corp.
Elf Atochem North America, Inc.
Equifax Inc.
Ernst & Young, LLP
European American Bank
Exxon Mobil Corp.
Fannie Mae
Federated Department Stores, Inc.
Federated Mutual Insurance Co.
Ferro Corp.
Fireman's Fund Insurance Co.
First Union Corp.
Fisher Scientific
FMC Corp.
Fort James Corp.
Fortis, Inc.
Freddie Mac
Freightliner Corp.
Frontier Corp.
Fuller Co. (H.B.)
GEICO Corp.
GenAmerica Corp.
GenCorp
General Electric Co.
General Motors Corp.
General Reinsurance Corp.
Georgia-Pacific Corp.
Georgia Power Co.
Gerber Products Co.
Gillette Co.
Grace & Co. (W.R.)
Graco, Inc.
GTE Corp.
Gucci America Inc.
Gulfstream Aerospace Corp.
Harsco Corp.
Hartford (The)
Hartmarx Corp.
Heller Financial, Inc.
Hercules Inc.
Hewlett-Packard Co.
Hitachi America Ltd.
Home Depot, Inc.
HON Industries Inc.
Houghton Mifflin Co.
HSBC Bank USA
Hubbell Inc.
IKON Office Solutions, Inc.
Industrial Bank of Japan Trust Co. (New York)
Inland Container Corp.

Intel Corp.
International Business Machines Corp.
International Multifoods Corp.
Interpublic Group of Companies, Inc.
Johnson Controls Inc.
Johnson & Johnson
Johnson & Son (S.C.)
Kendall International, Inc.
Kimberly-Clark Corp.
Knight Ridder
KPMG Peat Marwick LLP
Kroger Co.
Lennox International, Inc.
Levi Strauss & Co.
Liberty Mutual Insurance Group
Lilly & Co. (Eli)
Lincoln Electric Co.
Litton Industries, Inc.
Liz Claiborne, Inc.
Lockheed Martin Corp.
Louisiana-Pacific Corp.
LTV Corp.
Lubrizol Corp. (The)
MacMillan Bloedel Inc.
Macy's East Inc.
Masco Corp.
McDonald & Co. Securities, Inc.
McGraw-Hill Companies, Inc.
MCI WorldCom, Inc.
McKesson-HBOC Corp.
Mead Corp.
Mellon Financial Corp.
Menasha Corp.
Merck & Co.
Milliken & Co.
Minnesota Mining & Manufacturing Co.
Mitsubishi Electric America
Motorola Inc.
MTD Products Inc.
Nalco Chemical Co.
National Computer Systems, Inc.
National Service Industries, Inc.
National Starch & Chemical Co.
Nestle U.S.A. Inc.
New York Life Insurance Co.
Nike, Inc.
Nordson Corp.
Norfolk Southern Corp.
Nortel
Northrop Grumman Corp.
Norwest Corp.
Novartis Corporation
Olin Corp.
Outboard Marine Corp.
Owens Corning
Owens-Illinois Inc.
Parker Hannifin Corp.
Pfizer Inc.
Phelps Dodge Corp.
Pheonix Financial Group
Philip Morris Companies Inc.
Philips Electronics North America Corp.
Pioneer Hi-Bred International, Inc.
Polaroid Corp.
Premark International Inc.
Procter & Gamble Co.
Prudential Insurance Co. of America
Quaker Chemical Corp.
Reader's Digest Association, Inc. (The)
REI-Recreational Equipment, Inc.
Reynolds Metals Co.
Rich Products Corp.
Rockwell International Corp.
Rouse Co.
Royal & SunAlliance USA, Inc.
SAFECO Corp.
Salomon Smith Barney
Sara Lee Corp.
Schering-Plough Corp.
Schlumberger Ltd. (USA)
Scientific-Atlanta, Inc.
Scripps Co. (E.W.)
Sears, Roebuck and Co.
Security Life of Denver Insurance Co.
Sharp Electronics Corp.
Shaw Industries Inc.
Shell Oil Co.
Sherwin-Williams Co.
Shoney's Inc.
SmithKline Beecham Corp.
Smurfit-Stone Container Corp.
Sonoco Products Co.
Sony Electronics
Sotheby's Inc.
Springs Industries, Inc.
Sprint Corp.
SPX Corp.
Square D Co.
Standard Products Co.
Stanley Works (The)
State Farm Mutual Automobile Insurance Co.
State Street Bank & Trust Co.
Stone Container Corp.
Stone & Webster Inc.
Sun Microsystems Inc.
SunTrust Bank Atlanta
SuperValu, Inc.
Synovus Financial Corp.
Target Corp.
Temple-Inland Inc.
Tenet Healthcare Corp.
Tenneco Automotive
Texas Instruments Inc.
Textron Inc.
Thompson Co. (J. Walter)
TJX Companies, Inc.
Torchmark Corp.
Tyson Foods Inc.
Union Camp Corp.
Union Carbide Corp.
Unisys Corp.
United Airlines Inc.
United Dominion Industries, Ltd.
United Parcel Service of America Inc.
United Technologies Corp.
USG Corp.
USX Corp.
Vodafone AirTouch Plc
Vulcan Materials Co.
Waffle House Inc.
Wal-Mart Stores, Inc.
Westvaco Corp.
Weyerhaeuser Co.
Whitman Corp.
Williams
Winn-Dixie Stores Inc.
Wrigley Co. (Wm. Jr.)
Xerox Corp.
Zurn Industries, Inc.

Hawaii

Airborne Freight Corp.
Alcon Laboratories, Inc.
Alexander & Baldwin, Inc.
Baxter International Inc.
Butler Manufacturing Co.
Castle & Cooke Properties Inc.
Chevron Corp.
Deloitte & Touche
Delta Air Lines, Inc.
Diebold, Inc.
Eastman Kodak Co.
Ecolab Inc.
Ernst & Young, LLP
FedEx Corp.
Fireman's Fund Insurance Co.
First Hawaiian, Inc.
Fox Entertainment Group
Gannett Co., Inc.
General Mills, Inc.
Gerber Products Co.
Hawaiian Electric Co., Inc.
Hewlett-Packard Co.
International Business Machines Corp.
Kimberly-Clark Corp.
KPMG Peat Marwick LLP
Lee Enterprises
Matsushita Electric Corp. of America
Mead Corp.
Metropolitan Life Insurance Co.
Minnesota Mining & Manufacturing Co.
Morrison Knudsen Corp.
Nalco Chemical Co.
Nissan North America, Inc.
Northrop Grumman Corp.
Oracle Corp.
Pacific Century Financial Corp.
Pioneer Hi-Bred International, Inc.
Reynolds Metals Co.
Sears, Roebuck and Co.
Servco Pacific
Shell Oil Co.
Sotheby's Inc.
Toshiba America Inc.
United Airlines Inc.
United Parcel Service of America Inc.
Unocal Corp.
Wal-Mart Stores, Inc.
Weyerhaeuser Co.

Idaho

Albertson's Inc.
Allstate Insurance Co.
Anheuser-Busch Companies, Inc.
Associated Food Stores
Avista Corporation
Bandag, Inc.
Battelle Memorial Institute
Boeing Co.
Boise Cascade Corp.
Browning-Ferris Industries Inc.
Cargill Inc.
ConAgra, Inc.
Cyprus Amax Minerals Co.
Deloitte & Touche
Delta Air Lines, Inc.
Eastman Kodak Co.
EDS Corp.
Equifax Inc.
Evening Post Publishing Co.
Extendicare Health Services
FedEx Corp.
First Security Bank of Idaho NA
FMC Corp.
Gannett Co., Inc.
General Mills, Inc.
Gerber Products Co.
Heinz Co. (H.J.)
Hewlett-Packard Co.
Idaho Power Co.
Inland Container Corp.
International Business Machines Corp.
Kimball International, Inc.
Kimberly-Clark Corp.
Land O'Lakes, Inc.
Lockheed Martin Corp.
Louisiana-Pacific Corp.
MacMillan Bloedel Inc.
Mead Corp.
Mervyn's California
Morrison Knudsen Corp.
Pillsbury Co.
Pioneer Hi-Bred International, Inc.
Potlatch Corp.
Saint Paul Companies Inc.
Sears, Roebuck and Co.
Simplot Co. (J.R.)
SmithKline Beecham Corp.
Target Corp.
Union Pacific Corp.
U.S. Bancorp Piper Jaffray
Universal Foods Corp.
US West, Inc.

Illinois

7-Eleven, Inc.
Abbott Laboratories
ABC
Advanced Micro Devices, Inc.
Aetna, Inc.
Agrilink Foods, Inc.
Air Products and Chemicals, Inc.
Alcoa Inc.
Alliant Techsystems
AlliedSignal Inc.
AMCORE Bank Rockford
Ameren Corp.
America West Airlines, Inc.
American Electric Power
American Express Co.
American Standard Inc.
American United Life Insurance Co.
Ameritech Corp.
Ameritech Illinois
AMETEK, Inc.
AMP Inc.
Amsted Industries Inc.
Andersons Inc.
Anheuser-Busch Companies, Inc.
Apple Computer, Inc.
Appleton Papers Inc.
Archer-Daniels-Midland Co.
Armstrong World Industries, Inc.
AT&T Corp.
Autodesk Inc.
Avery Dennison Corp.
Avon Products, Inc.
Bank of America
Bard, Inc. (C.R.)
Barnes Group Inc.
Battelle Memorial Institute
Bausch & Lomb Inc.
Baxter International Inc.
Bayer Corp.
Beckman Coulter, Inc.
Bemis Co., Inc.
Ben & Jerry's Homemade Inc.
Bestfoods
BFGoodrich Co.
Blair & Co. (William)
Blount International, Inc.
Boler Co.
Borden, Inc.
Bowater Inc.
BP Amoco Corp.
Bridgestone/Firestone, Inc.
Broderbund Software, Inc.
Browning-Ferris Industries Inc.
Brunswick Corp.
Burlington Industries, Inc.
Butler Manufacturing Co.
Cabot Corp.
Cadence Designs Systems, Inc.
California Bank & Trust
Campbell Soup Co.
Cargill Inc.
Carpenter Technology Corp.
Carrier Corp.
Carter-Wallace, Inc.
Caterpillar Inc.
Central Soya Co.
CertainTeed Corp.
Chase Manhattan Bank, NA
Chicago Board of Trade
Chicago Sun-Times, Inc.
Chicago Tribune Co.
CIBC Oppenheimer
Circuit City Stores, Inc.
CIT Group, Inc. (The)
Citibank Corp.
CLARCOR Inc.
Clark Refining & Marketing
Clorox Co.
CNA
CNF Transportation, Inc.
Coca-Cola Co.
Colgate-Palmolive Co.
Comdisco, Inc.
Comerica Inc.
Commerce Bancshares, Inc.
Commonwealth Edison Co.
Compaq Computer Corp.
Computer Associates International, Inc.
ConAgra, Inc.
Consolidated Papers, Inc.
Cooper Industries, Inc.
Copley Press, Inc.
Cox Enterprises Inc.
Crane Co.
CSX Corp.
Curtis Industries, Inc. (Helene)
DaimlerChrysler Corp.
Dain Bosworth Inc.
Dana Corp.
Dayton Hudson
Deere & Co.
DeKalb Genetics Corp.
Deloitte & Touche
Deluxe Corp.
Dexter Corp.
Dial Corp.
Diebold, Inc.
Donaldson Co., Inc.
Donnelley & Sons Co. (R.R.)
Dow Chemical Co.
Dow Jones & Co., Inc.
DSM Copolymer
du Pont de Nemours & Co. (E.I.)
Duchossois Industries Inc.

Dun & Bradstreet Corp.
Eastman Kodak Co.
Eaton Corp.
Ebsco Industries, Inc.
Ecolab Inc.
EDS Corp.
Emerson Electric Co.
Employers Insurance of Wausau, A Mutual Co.
Employers Mutual Casualty Co.
Equifax Inc.
Ernst & Young, LLP
European American Bank
Exxon Mobil Corp.
Fannie Mae
FedEx Corp.
Fireman's Fund Insurance Co.
First National Bank of Evergreen Park
Firstar Bank Milwaukee NA
Fisher Scientific
Fluor Corp.
FMC Corp.
Fortune Brands, Inc.
Fox Entertainment Group
Frontier Corp.
Fuller Co. (H.B.)
Gannett Co., Inc.
GATX Corp.
General Dynamics Corp.
General Electric Co.
General Mills, Inc.
General Motors Corp.
Gerber Products Co.
Gillette Co.
Goldman Sachs Group
Grace & Co. (W.R.)
Graco, Inc.
Grainger, Inc. (W.W.)
Hamilton Sundstrand Corp.
Hanna Co. (M.A.)
Harcourt General, Inc.
Harland Co. (John H.)
Harrah's Entertainment Inc.
Harris Trust & Savings Bank
Harsco Corp.
Hartford (The)
Hartmarx Corp.
Heller Financial, Inc.
Hercules Inc.
Hewlett-Packard Co.
Hitachi America Ltd.
Hoffer Plastics Corp.
Honeywell International Inc.
Houghton Mifflin Co.
Household International Inc.
IKON Office Solutions, Inc.
Illinois Power Co.
Illinois Tool Works, Inc.
Industrial Bank of Japan Trust Co. (New York)
Inland Container Corp.
International Business Machines Corp.
International Multifoods Corp.
International Paper Co.
Interpublic Group of Companies, Inc.
Johnson Controls Inc.
Johnson & Johnson
Johnson & Son (S.C.)
Jostens, Inc.
Kaman Corp.
Katten, Muchin & Zavis
Kemper National Insurance Companies
Kendall International, Inc.
Kimberly-Clark Corp.
Kirkland & Ellis
KPMG Peat Marwick LLP
Kraft Foods, Inc.
Lee Enterprises
Liberty Mutual Insurance Group
Lincoln Electric Co.
Lincoln Financial Group
Litton Industries, Inc.
Loctite Corp.
Loews Corp.
Louisiana-Pacific Corp.
LTV Corp.
Marcus Corp.
Maritz Inc.
Marshall Field's
Masco Corp.
Matsushita Electric Corp. of America
Mattel Inc.
Maytag Corp.
McCormick & Co. Inc.
McDonald & Co. Securities, Inc.
McDonald's Corp.
McGraw-Hill Companies, Inc.
MCI WorldCom, Inc.
McWane Inc.
Mead Corp.
Medtronic, Inc.
Mellon Financial Corp.
Meredith Corp.
Metropolitan Life Insurance Co.
Microsoft Corp.
MidAmerican Energy Holdings Co.
Milacron, Inc.
Minnesota Mining & Manufacturing Co.
Mitsubishi Electric America
Monsanto Co.
Montgomery Ward & Co., Inc.
Morgan Stanley Dean Witter & Co.
Morton International Inc.
Motorola Inc.
Nalco Chemical Co.
National Starch & Chemical Co.
NEC America, Inc.
Nestle U.S.A. Inc.
New York Times Co.
NICOR Gas Co.
Nissan North America, Inc.
Norfolk Southern Corp.
Nortel
Northern Trust Co.
Northrop Grumman Corp.
Norton Co.
Norwest Corp.
Occidental Petroleum Corp.
Olin Corp.
Oracle Corp.
Outboard Marine Corp.
Owens-Illinois Inc.
Parker Hannifin Corp.
Peoples Energy Corp.
Pfizer Inc.
Philip Morris Companies Inc.
Philips Electronics North America Corp.
Pillsbury Co.
Pioneer Hi-Bred International, Inc.
Pittway Corp.
Playboy Enterprises Inc.
Polaroid Corp.
Premark International Inc.
Premier Industrial Corp.
Promus Hotel Corp.
Prudential Insurance Co. of America
Prudential Securities Inc.
Quanex Corp.
REI-Recreational Equipment, Inc.
Reynolds Metals Co.
Reynolds & Reynolds Co.
Rockwell International Corp.
Rohm & Haas Co.
SAFECO Corp.
Saint Paul Companies Inc.
Sara Lee Corp.
Sara Lee Hosiery, Inc.
Schering-Plough Corp.
Seagram & Sons, Inc. (Joseph E.)
Searle & Co. (G.D.)
Sears, Roebuck and Co.
ServiceMaster Co.
Shaklee Corp.
Sharp Electronics Corp.
Shaw Industries Inc.
Shell Oil Co.
Sherwin-Williams Co.
Smith Corp. (A.O.)
SmithKline Beecham Corp.
Solo Cup Co.
Sony Electronics
Springs Industries, Inc.
Sprint Corp.
SPX Corp.
Square D Co.
Standard Products Co.
Starwood Hotels & Resorts Worldwide, Inc.
State Farm Mutual Automobile Insurance Co.
Stone Container Corp.
Storage Technology Corp.
Sun Microsystems Inc.
SuperValu, Inc.
Target Corp.
Temple-Inland Inc.
Tenneco Automotive
Tenneco Packaging
Texas Instruments Inc.
Textron Inc.
Thompson Co. (J. Walter)
Times Mirror Co.
Timken Co. (The)
Toyota Motor Sales U.S.A., Inc.
Trustmark Insurance Co.
Tyson Foods Inc.
Unilever Home & Personal Care U.S.A.
Unilever United States, Inc.
Union Camp Corp.
Union Carbide Corp.
United Airlines Inc.
United Distillers & Vintners North America
United Parcel Service of America Inc.
Universal Studios
USG Corp.
UST Inc.
USX Corp.
Valmont Industries, Inc.
Valspar Corp.
Vulcan Materials Co.
Wal-Mart Stores, Inc.
Walgreen Co.
Warner-Lambert Co.
Waste Management Inc.
Westvaco Corp.
Weyerhaeuser Co.
Whitman Corp.
Witco Corp.
Woodward Governor Co.
Wrigley Co. (Wm. Jr.)
Xerox Corp.
Zenith Electronics Corp.
Zurn Industries, Inc.

Indiana

7-Eleven, Inc.
ABB Inc.
AEGON U.S.A. Inc.
Aetna, Inc.
Air Products and Chemicals, Inc.
Alcoa Inc.
America West Airlines, Inc.
American Electric Power
American United Life Insurance Co.
Ameritech Corp.
Ameritech Indiana
AMP Inc.
Amsted Industries Inc.
Andersons Inc.
Archer-Daniels-Midland Co.
Arvin Industries, Inc.
Ashland, Inc.
AT&T Corp.
Auburn Foundry
Avery Dennison Corp.
Ball Corp.
Baxter International Inc.
Bayer Corp.
Becton Dickinson & Co.
Ben & Jerry's Homemade Inc.
Bestfoods
Bethlehem Steel Corp.
Blount International, Inc.
Boeing Co.
BP Amoco Corp.
Bridgestone/Firestone, Inc.
Bristol-Myers Squibb Co.
Browning-Ferris Industries Inc.
Campbell Soup Co.
Carrier Corp.
Carris Reels
Caterpillar Inc.
Central Newspapers, Inc.
Central Soya Co.
Chesapeake Corp.
Chevron Corp.
Cinergy Corp.
Circuit City Stores, Inc.
Citibank Corp.
CLARCOR Inc.
CNF Transportation, Inc.
Colgate-Palmolive Co.
Computer Associates International, Inc.
Cooper Industries, Inc.
CSX Corp.
Cummins Engine Co., Inc.
DaimlerChrysler Corp.
Dana Corp.
Dayton Hudson
Deloitte & Touche
Delta Air Lines, Inc.
Dexter Corp.
Diebold, Inc.
Donaldson Co., Inc.
Donnelley & Sons Co. (R.R.)
Dow Jones & Co., Inc.
DSM Copolymer
du Pont de Nemours & Co. (E.I.)
Duracell International
Eaton Corp.
Ecolab Inc.
EDS Corp.
Erb Lumber Co.
Ernst & Young, LLP
Extendicare Health Services
Federal-Mogul Corp.
Ferro Corp.
Fifth Third Bancorp
First Source Corp.
Ford Meter Box Co.
Franklin Electric Co.
Frontier Corp.
Fuller Co. (H.B.)
GATX Corp.
GenCorp
General Electric Co.
General Motors Corp.
Georgia-Pacific Corp.
Gerber Products Co.
Harrah's Entertainment Inc.
Harsco Corp.
Hartford (The)
Hartmarx Corp.
Hewlett-Packard Co.
Hubbell Inc.
Huntington Bancshares Inc.
IKON Office Solutions, Inc.
Inland Container Corp.
International Business Machines Corp.
International Multifoods Corp.
Johnson Controls Inc.
Journal-Gazette Co.
Kimball International, Inc.
Knight Ridder
Koch Enterprises, Inc.
KPMG Peat Marwick LLP
Kraft Foods, Inc.
Kroger Co.
Lehigh Portland Cement Co.
Liberty Corp.
Lilly & Co. (Eli)
Lincoln Electric Co.
Lincoln Financial Group
LTV Corp.
Marcus Corp.
Marshall Field's
Masco Corp.
May Department Stores Co.
Maytag Corp.
McCormick & Co. Inc.
McDonald & Co. Securities, Inc.
McGraw-Hill Companies, Inc.
Mead Corp.
Meijer, Inc.
Mellon Financial Corp.
Microsoft Corp.
Minnesota Mining & Manufacturing Co.
Morton International Inc.
Nalco Chemical Co.
National City Bank of Cleveland
National City Corp.
National Starch & Chemical Co.
Norfolk Southern Corp.
Northern Indiana Public Service Co.
Norton Co.
Norwest Corp.
Old National Bank Evansville
Oracle Corp.
Owens Corning
Owens-Illinois Inc.
Parker Hannifin Corp.
Pfizer Inc.
Phelps Dodge Corp.
Philip Morris Companies Inc.
Philips Electronics North America Corp.
Pillsbury Co.
Pioneer Hi-Bred International, Inc.
PNC Bank
Premier Industrial Corp.
Pulitzer Publishing Co.
Reilly Industries, Inc.

Reynolds Metals Co.
Reynolds & Reynolds Co.
Saint Paul Companies Inc.
Sara Lee Corp.
Schering-Plough Corp.
Scripps Co. (E.W.)
Seagram & Sons, Inc. (Joseph E.)
Sears, Roebuck and Co.
Shell Oil Co.
Sherwin-Williams Co.
Smurfit-Stone Container Corp.
Sony Electronics
South Bend Tribune Corp.
Sprint Corp.
Sprint/United Telephone
SPX Corp.
Square D Co.
Standard Products Co.
Standard Register Co.
Stanley Works (The)
Star Bank NA
Starwood Hotels & Resorts Worldwide, Inc.
State Farm Mutual Automobile Insurance Co.
Stone Container Corp.
Stride Rite Corp.
SuperValu, Inc.
Temple-Inland Inc.
Tenet Healthcare Corp.
Texas Gas Transmission Corp.
Texas Instruments Inc.
Textron Inc.
Tomkins Industries, Inc.
Toshiba America Inc.
Toyota Motor Sales U.S.A., Inc.
Trustmark Insurance Co.
TRW Inc.
Tyson Foods Inc.
Unilever United States, Inc.
Union Camp Corp.
United Parcel Service of America Inc.
United Technologies Corp.
Universal Foods Corp.
USG Corp.
UST Inc.
Valmont Industries, Inc.
Vulcan Materials Co.
Wal-Mart Stores, Inc.
Walgreen Co.
Whirlpool Corp.
Witco Corp.
Zenith Electronics Corp.

Iowa

AEGON U.S.A. Inc.
AFLAC Inc.
Agrilink Foods, Inc.
Air Products and Chemicals, Inc.
Alcoa Inc.
AmerUS Group
Archer-Daniels-Midland Co.
Ball Corp.
Bandag, Inc.
Baxter International Inc.
Blount International, Inc.
Bridgestone/Firestone, Inc.
Browning-Ferris Industries Inc.
Central Soya Co.
CertainTeed Corp.
CGU Insurance
Champion International Corp.
Chesapeake Corp.
Cox Enterprises Inc.
Cummins Engine Co., Inc.
CUNA Mutual Group
Dain Bosworth Inc.
Dana Corp.
Deere & Co.
Deloitte & Touche
Deluxe Corp.
Dial Corp.
Diebold, Inc.
Donaldson Co., Inc.
Dow Corning Corp.
Dow Jones & Co., Inc.
du Pont de Nemours & Co. (E.I.)
Eaton Corp.
Ecolab Inc.
Elf Atochem North America, Inc.
Employers Mutual Casualty Co.
Fannie Mae
FedEx Corp.
Fireman's Fund Insurance Co.
Firstar Bank Milwaukee NA
FMC Corp.
Fortune Brands, Inc.
Gannett Co., Inc.
General Mills, Inc.
General Motors Corp.
Georgia-Pacific Corp.
Grace & Co. (W.R.)
GuideOne Insurance
Harsco Corp.
Heinz Co. (H.J.)
Hickory Tech Corp.
HON Industries Inc.
International Business Machines Corp.
Jeld-wen, Inc.
KPMG Peat Marwick LLP
Kraft Foods, Inc.
Lance, Inc.
Land O'Lakes, Inc.
Lee Enterprises
Lennox International, Inc.
Lilly & Co. (Eli)
Lincoln Electric Co.
Lipton Co.
Litton Industries, Inc.
Marcus Corp.
Masco Corp.
Maytag Corp.
McWane Inc.
Medtronic, Inc.
Menasha Corp.
MidAmerican Energy Holdings Co.
Minnesota Mining & Manufacturing Co.
Motorola Inc.
Nalco Chemical Co.
National Computer Systems, Inc.
Norwest Corp.
Olin Corp.
Parker Hannifin Corp.
Pella Corp.
Pharmacia & Upjohn, Inc.
Philip Morris Companies Inc.
Philips Electronics North America Corp.
Pillsbury Co.
Pioneer Hi-Bred International, Inc.
Principal Financial Group
Procter & Gamble Co.
Quanex Corp.
Rockwell International Corp.
Rouse Co.
Sara Lee Corp.
Sears, Roebuck and Co.
Simpson Investment Co.
Square D Co.
Stone Container Corp.
Sun Microsystems Inc.
SuperValu, Inc.
Tandy Corp.
Target Corp.
Tenet Healthcare Corp.
Tension Envelope Corp.
United Dominion Industries, Ltd.
United Parcel Service of America Inc.
U.S. Bancorp Piper Jaffray
US West, Inc.
USG Corp.
Vulcan Materials Co.
Wal-Mart Stores, Inc.
Weyerhaeuser Co.
Wilbur-Ellis Co. & Connell Brothers Co.
Witco Corp.
Young & Rubicam

Kansas

7-Eleven, Inc.
Abbott Laboratories
Air Products and Chemicals, Inc.
American United Life Insurance Co.
Appleton Papers Inc.
Archer-Daniels-Midland Co.
Avery Dennison Corp.
Baxter International Inc.
Bemis Co., Inc.
Binney & Smith Inc.
Blount International, Inc.
Blue Bell, Inc.
Browning-Ferris Industries Inc.
Burlington Industries, Inc.
Business Men's Assurance Co. of America
CertainTeed Corp.
Cessna Aircraft Co.
Commerce Bancshares, Inc.
Computer Associates International, Inc.
DaimlerChrysler Corp.
Dain Bosworth Inc.
Deere & Co.
Deluxe Corp.
Donaldson Co., Inc.
du Pont de Nemours & Co. (E.I.)
Eastman Kodak Co.
Eaton Corp.
Ecolab Inc.
Emerson Electric Co.
EMI Music Publishing
Equifax Inc.
Excel Corp.
Fireman's Fund Insurance Co.
FMC Corp.
Frontier Corp.
Gannett Co., Inc.
General Electric Co.
General Mills, Inc.
General Motors Corp.
General Reinsurance Corp.
Georgia-Pacific Corp.
Grace & Co. (W.R.)
Harrah's Entertainment Inc.
Hartford (The)
Heinz Co. (H.J.)
Hewlett-Packard Co.
Humana, Inc.
IKON Office Solutions, Inc.
Inland Container Corp.
International Business Machines Corp.
International Multifoods Corp.
INTRUST Financial Corp.
Johnson Controls Inc.
Jostens, Inc.
Knight Ridder
Koch Industries, Inc.
KPMG Peat Marwick LLP
Lee Apparel Co.
Lincoln Electric Co.
Litton Industries, Inc.
Macy's East Inc.
Maritz Inc.
May Department Stores Co.
Maytag Corp.
McCormick & Co. Inc.
Medtronic, Inc.
Merck & Co.
Meredith Corp.
Metropolitan Life Insurance Co.
Morris Communications Corp.
Morton International Inc.
Nalco Chemical Co.
NCR Corp.
Nestle U.S.A. Inc.
Norwest Corp.
Olin Corp.
ONEOK, Inc.
Owens Corning
Parker Hannifin Corp.
PepsiCo, Inc.
Philips Electronics North America Corp.
Pioneer Hi-Bred International, Inc.
Pioneer Natural Resources
PPG Industries, Inc.
Royal & SunAlliance USA, Inc.
Saint Paul Companies Inc.
Sara Lee Corp.
SBC Communications Inc.
Security Benefit Life Insurance Co.
Security Life of Denver Insurance Co.
Sherwin-Williams Co.
Shoney's Inc.
Smith Corp. (A.O.)
Smurfit-Stone Container Corp.
Sprint Corp.
Stanley Works (The)
Sun Microsystems Inc.
SuperValu, Inc.
Target Corp.
Temple-Inland Inc.
Tenneco Automotive
Tension Envelope Corp.
Texas Instruments Inc.
Timken Co. (The)
Tomkins Industries, Inc.
Union Pacific Corp.
United Airlines Inc.
United Parcel Service of America Inc.
U.S. Bancorp Piper Jaffray
Wal-Mart Stores, Inc.
Western Resources Inc.
Williams
Witco Corp.
Yellow Corp.
Zenith Electronics Corp.

Kentucky

AEGON U.S.A. Inc.
Aetna, Inc.
Air Products and Chemicals, Inc.
AK Steel Corp.
American Electric Power
American General Finance
American Standard Inc.
American United Life Insurance Co.
AMETEK, Inc.
Amgen, Inc.
Armstrong World Industries, Inc.
Ashland, Inc.
Becton Dickinson & Co.
BellSouth Telecommunications
Ben & Jerry's Homemade Inc.
Berwind Group
BFGoodrich Co.
Borden, Inc.
Brown & Williamson Tobacco Corp.
Browning-Ferris Industries Inc.
Chesapeake Corp.
Chevron Corp.
Cinergy Corp.
Circuit City Stores, Inc.
CLARCOR Inc.
Commercial Intertech Corp.
ConAgra, Inc.
Cooper Industries, Inc.
Cooper Tire & Rubber Co.
CSX Corp.
Cyprus Amax Minerals Co.
Dana Corp.
Deloitte & Touche
Delta Air Lines, Inc.
Diebold, Inc.
Donnelley & Sons Co. (R.R.)
Dow Corning Corp.
du Pont de Nemours & Co. (E.I.)
Eastman Kodak Co.
Elf Atochem North America, Inc.
Emerson Electric Co.
Equitable Resources, Inc.
Ernst & Young, LLP
FedEx Corp.
Fidelity Investments
Fifth Third Bancorp
Fluor Corp.
Fort James Corp.
Fortune Brands, Inc.
Fuller Co. (H.B.)
Gannett Co., Inc.
General Motors Corp.
Harsco Corp.
Hartmarx Corp.
Hershey Foods Corp.
HON Industries Inc.
Humana, Inc.
Hunt Manufacturing Co.
Huntington Bancshares Inc.
Independent Stave Co.
Inland Container Corp.
International Business Machines Corp.
International Multifoods Corp.
Interpublic Group of Companies, Inc.
Johnson Controls Inc.
Kimball International, Inc.
Knight Ridder
KPMG Peat Marwick LLP
Levi Strauss & Co.
LG&E Energy Corp.
Liberty Corp.
Lilly & Co. (Eli)
Lincoln Electric Co.

Litton Industries, Inc.
Mallinckrodt Chemical, Inc.
Marcus Corp.
Masco Corp.
Mead Corp.
Medtronic, Inc.
Meijer, Inc.
Minnesota Mining & Manufacturing Co.
National City Corp.
New York Times Co.
Norfolk Southern Corp.
Norton Co.
Occidental Petroleum Corp.
Olin Corp.
Oshkosh B'Gosh, Inc.
Owens-Illinois Inc.
PepsiCo, Inc.
Phelps Dodge Corp.
Philip Morris Companies Inc.
PNC Bank
PNC Bank Kentucky Inc.
PNC Financial Services Group
Premark International Inc.
Procter & Gamble Co.
Pulitzer Publishing Co.
Ralston Purina Co.
Reynolds Metals Co.
Rockwell International Corp.
Rohm & Haas Co.
Rouse Co.
Sara Lee Corp.
Seagram & Sons, Inc. (Joseph E.)
Shell Oil Co.
Smith Corp. (A.O.)
Smurfit-Stone Container Corp.
Sprint Corp.
Square D Co.
Standard Products Co.
Star Bank NA
Stone Container Corp.
Stride Rite Corp.
Sun Microsystems Inc.
Target Corp.
Temple-Inland Inc.
Texas Gas Transmission Corp.
Texas Instruments Inc.
Toyota Motor Sales U.S.A., Inc.
TRW Inc.
Union Camp Corp.
United Parcel Service of America Inc.
Vulcan Materials Co.
Wal-Mart Stores, Inc.
Westvaco Corp.
Weyerhaeuser Co.
Winn-Dixie Stores Inc.

Louisiana

Abbott Laboratories
Air Products and Chemicals, Inc.
Alcoa Inc.
AlliedSignal Inc.
American United Life Insurance Co.
Anheuser-Busch Companies, Inc.
Apple Computer, Inc.
Archer-Daniels-Midland Co.
Atlantic Richfield Co.
Baker Hughes Inc.
Bank One Corp.
BankBoston-Connecticut Region
Belo Corp. (A.H.)
Blue Bell, Inc.
Boise Cascade Corp.
Borden, Inc.
BP Amoco Corp.
Browning-Ferris Industries Inc.
Burlington Resources, Inc.
Cabot Corp.
Central & South West Services
CertainTeed Corp.
Chevron Corp.
Circuit City Stores, Inc.
Conoco, Inc.
Consolidated Natural Gas Co.
Cooper Industries, Inc.
Cox Enterprises Inc.
Cranston Print Works Co.
CSX Corp.
Dana Corp.
Deloitte & Touche
Delta Air Lines, Inc.
Deluxe Corp.
Diebold, Inc.
Donaldson Co., Inc.
Dow Chemical Co.
DSM Copolymer
du Pont de Nemours & Co. (E.I.)
Dun & Bradstreet Corp.
Eastman Kodak Co.
Ecolab Inc.
Exxon Mobil Corp.
FedEx Corp.
Ferro Corp.
FINA
Fireman's Fund Insurance Co.
FMC Corp.
Freeport-McMoRan Inc.
Gannett Co., Inc.
GATX Corp.
General Motors Corp.
Georgia-Pacific Corp.
Grace & Co. (W.R.)
Harrah's Entertainment Inc.
Harsco Corp.
Hartford (The)
Hewlett-Packard Co.
Home Depot, Inc.
Inland Container Corp.
International Business Machines Corp.
International Paper Co.
Interpublic Group of Companies, Inc.
Johnson Controls Inc.
KPMG Peat Marwick LLP
Lilly & Co. (Eli)
Litton Industries, Inc.
Lockheed Martin Corp.
Loews Corp.
Louisiana Land & Exploration Co.
Louisiana-Pacific Corp.
Maytag Corp.
McDermott Inc.
Mellon Financial Corp.
Mervyn's California
Morton International Inc.
Murphy Oil Corp.
Nalco Chemical Co.
National Starch & Chemical Co.
Nestle U.S.A. Inc.
New York Times Co.
Norfolk Southern Corp.
Norton Co.
Olin Corp.
Pan-American Life Insurance Co.
Pennzoil-Quaker State Co.
Phelps Dodge Corp.
PPG Industries, Inc.
Premark International Inc.
Procter & Gamble Co.
Promus Hotel Corp.
Prudential Insurance Co. of America
Reily & Co., Inc. (William B.)
Reynolds Metals Co.
Rockwell International Corp.
Rouse Co.
Santa Fe International Corp.
Schering-Plough Corp.
Shell Oil Co.
Sotheby's Inc.
State Farm Mutual Automobile Insurance Co.
Stone Container Corp.
Stone & Webster Inc.
Target Corp.
Temple-Inland Inc.
Tenet Healthcare Corp.
Tenneco Automotive
Texaco Inc.
Texas Gas Transmission Corp.
Ultramar Diamond Shamrock Corp.
Union Carbide Corp.
Union Pacific Corp.
Union Planters Corp.
Unocal Corp.
USG Corp.
Vulcan Materials Co.
Westvaco Corp.
Williams
Winn-Dixie Stores Inc.
Witco Corp.

Maine

ABB Inc.
BankBoston-Connecticut Region
Bausch & Lomb Inc.
Bean, Inc. (L.L.)
Bowater Inc.
Central Maine Power Co.
Champion International Corp.
Cooper Industries, Inc.
Corning Inc.
Delta Air Lines, Inc.
Diebold, Inc.
Donnelley & Sons Co. (R.R.)
Ecolab Inc.
FleetBoston Financial Corp.
Fort James Corp.
Freightliner Corp.
Hannaford Brothers Co.
Kimberly-Clark Corp.
Louisiana-Pacific Corp.
Monsanto Co.
Nalco Chemical Co.
National Starch & Chemical Co.
New York Times Co.
Parker Hannifin Corp.
Philips Electronics North America Corp.
Pillsbury Co.
Reynolds Metals Co.
Royal & SunAlliance USA, Inc.
Shaw's Supermarkets, Inc.
SuperValu, Inc.
Union Camp Corp.
U.S. Bancorp Piper Jaffray
UnumProvident
Wal-Mart Stores, Inc.
Weyerhaeuser Co.
Zurn Industries, Inc.

Maryland

Advanced Micro Devices, Inc.
AEGON U.S.A. Inc.
Air Products and Chemicals, Inc.
Alcon Laboratories, Inc.
Alliant Techsystems
America West Airlines, Inc.
American United Life Insurance Co.
Ameritech Corp.
Amsted Industries Inc.
Aon Corp.
Armstrong World Industries, Inc.
Battelle Memorial Institute
Belk Stores Services Inc.
Bell Atlantic Corp.
Bestfoods
Bethlehem Steel Corp.
Borden, Inc.
Browning-Ferris Industries Inc.
Cadence Designs Systems, Inc.
Chase Manhattan Bank, NA
Chesapeake Corp.
Chevron Corp.
Circuit City Stores, Inc.
Citibank Corp.
Citigroup
Clorox Co.
ConAgra, Inc.
Conectiv
Constellation Energy Group, Inc.
Cooper Industries, Inc.
Country Curtains, Inc.
Crestar Finance Corp.
CSX Corp.
DaimlerChrysler Corp.
Dayton Hudson
Deloitte & Touche
Delta Air Lines, Inc.
Dexter Corp.
Diebold, Inc.
Dow Jones & Co., Inc.
Dun & Bradstreet Corp.
Eastman Kodak Co.
Eaton Corp.
Ebsco Industries, Inc.
Ecolab Inc.
EDS Corp.
Emerson Electric Co.
Equifax Inc.
Ernst & Young, LLP
Extendicare Health Services
FedEx Corp.
First Maryland Bancorp
First Union Corp.
FMC Corp.
Freddie Mac
Fuller Co. (H.B.)
GEICO Corp.
General Electric Co.
General Motors Corp.
Gerber Products Co.
Giant Food Inc.
Goodrich Aerospace - Aerostructures Group (B.F.)
Grace & Co. (W.R.)
Halliburton Co.
Harsco Corp.
Hewlett-Packard Co.
Home Depot, Inc.
IKON Office Solutions, Inc.
International Business Machines Corp.
ISE America
Johnson Controls Inc.
Johnson & Son (S.C.)
Kiewit Sons' Inc. (Peter)
Kimberly-Clark Corp.
Lilly & Co. (Eli)
Litton Industries, Inc.
Lockheed Martin Corp.
Loews Corp.
Lotus Development Corp.
Manor Care Health SVS, Inc.
Marriott International Inc.
May Department Stores Co.
McCormick & Co. Inc.
Mellon Financial Corp.
Meredith Corp.
Mine Safety Appliances Co.
Minnesota Mining & Manufacturing Co.
Morrison Knudsen Corp.
Mutual of Omaha Insurance Co.
Nationwide Insurance Co.
Norfolk Southern Corp.
Northrop Grumman Corp.
Norwest Corp.
Novartis Corporation
Oracle Corp.
Owens Corning
Owens-Illinois Inc.
Paine Webber
Parker Hannifin Corp.
PerkinElmer, Inc.
Philip Morris Companies Inc.
Pillsbury Co.
Pioneer Hi-Bred International, Inc.
Potomac Electric Power Co.
Premark International Inc.
Price Associates (T. Rowe)
Procter & Gamble Co., Cosmetics Division
REI-Recreational Equipment, Inc.
Riggs Bank NA
Rouse Co.
Royal & SunAlliance USA, Inc.
Ruddick Corp.
Scripps Co. (E.W.)
Seagram & Sons, Inc. (Joseph E.)
Sears, Roebuck and Co.
Shell Oil Co.
Sherwin-Williams Co.
Smith Corp. (A.O.)
SmithKline Beecham Corp.
Sotheby's Inc.
SuperValu, Inc.
Target Corp.
Texas Instruments Inc.
Times Mirror Co.
Unilever United States, Inc.
United Parcel Service of America Inc.
USG Corp.
Valspar Corp.
Wal-Mart Stores, Inc.
The Washington Post
Westvaco Corp.
Weyerhaeuser Co.
Williams

Massachusetts

7-Eleven, Inc.
Abbott Laboratories
ABC
Advanced Micro Devices, Inc.
Aetna, Inc.
Air Products and Chemicals, Inc.
Albany International Corp.

Allmerica Financial Corp.
America West Airlines, Inc.
American Express Co.
AMETEK, Inc.
Analog Devices, Inc.
Anheuser-Busch Companies, Inc.
Apple Computer, Inc.
Armstrong World Industries, Inc.
Avery Dennison Corp.
Baker Hughes Inc.
BankBoston-Connecticut Region
BankBoston Corp.
Battelle Memorial Institute
Bausch & Lomb Inc.
Baxter International Inc.
Bayer Corp.
Becton Dickinson & Co.
Bell Atlantic Corp.
Ben & Jerry's Homemade Inc.
Berwind Group
BFGoodrich Co.
Boeing Co.
Boston Edison Co.
Boston Gas Co.
Boston Globe (The)
Bridgestone/Firestone, Inc.
Browning-Ferris Industries Inc.
Cabot Corp.
Cargill Inc.
CertainTeed Corp.
Champion International Corp.
Church & Dwight Co., Inc.
Citizens Financial Group, Inc.
CNF Transportation, Inc.
Compaq Computer Corp.
Computer Associates International, Inc.
ConAgra, Inc.
Corning Inc.
Country Curtains, Inc.
Cox Enterprises Inc.
Crane & Co., Inc.
Cranston Print Works Co.
Cummings Properties Management
Deloitte & Touche
Delta Air Lines, Inc.
Deluxe Corp.
Demoulas Supermarkets Inc.
Dexter Corp.
Diebold, Inc.
Donnelley & Sons Co. (R.R.)
Dow Jones & Co., Inc.
DSM Copolymer
du Pont de Nemours & Co. (E.I.)
Eastern Bank
Eastern Enterprises
Eastman Kodak Co.
Eaton Corp.
Ecolab Inc.
EDS Corp.
Elf Atochem North America, Inc.
Equifax Inc.
Ernst & Young, LLP
Erving Industries
European American Bank
Fannie Mae
FedEx Corp.
Fidelity Investments
Fisher Scientific
FleetBoston Financial Corp.
Fort James Corp.
Fortune Brands, Inc.
Fox Entertainment Group
Frontier Corp.
Fuller Co. (H.B.)
General Dynamics Corp.
General Electric Co.
General Mills, Inc.
General Motors Corp.
General Reinsurance Corp.
Gerber Products Co.
Gillette Co.
Goldman Sachs Group
Golub Corp.
Grace & Co. (W.R.)
GTE Corp.
Hamilton Sundstrand Corp.
Hancock Financial Services (John)
Hannaford Brothers Co.
Hartford (The)
Hercules Inc.
Hewlett-Packard Co.
Hitachi America Ltd.
Home Depot, Inc.
Houghton Mifflin Co.
Housatonic Curtain Co.
Illinois Tool Works, Inc.
Intel Corp.
International Multifoods Corp.
International Paper Co.
Johnson Controls Inc.
Johnson & Johnson
Johnson & Son (S.C.)
Kendall International, Inc.
Kimberly-Clark Corp.
KPMG Peat Marwick LLP
Kraft Foods, Inc.
Levi Strauss & Co.
Liberty Mutual Insurance Group
Lilly & Co. (Eli)
Lincoln Electric Co.
Litton Industries, Inc.
Lockheed Martin Corp.
Lotus Development Corp.
Marcus Corp.
Masco Corp.
Massachusetts Mutual Life Insurance Co.
May Department Stores Co.
Maytag Corp.
McDonald & Co. Securities, Inc.
McGraw-Hill Companies, Inc.
Mead Corp.
Medtronic, Inc.
Mellon Financial Corp.
Menasha Corp.
Microsoft Corp.
Millipore Corp.
Minnesota Mining & Manufacturing Co.
Mitsubishi Electric America
Monsanto Co.
Morrison Knudsen Corp.
Morton International Inc.
Motorola Inc.
Nalco Chemical Co.
NEC America, Inc.
Nestle U.S.A. Inc.
New England Financial
New York Times Co.
Northeast Utilities
Norton Co.
Novartis Corporation
Olin Corp.
Oracle Corp.
Pacific Mutual Life Insurance Co.
Paine Webber
Parker Hannifin Corp.
PerkinElmer, Inc.
Pfizer Inc.
Philip Morris Companies Inc.
Philips Electronics North America Corp.
Phoenix Home Life Mutual Insurance Co.
Pioneer Group
Polaroid Corp.
Procter & Gamble Co.
Providence Journal-Bulletin Co.
Prudential Insurance Co. of America
Prudential Securities Inc.
Putnam Investments
Rayonier Inc.
Reebok International Ltd.
REI-Recreational Equipment, Inc.
Reynolds Metals Co.
Rockwell International Corp.
Rohm & Haas Co.
Roseburg Forest Products Co.
Rouse Co.
Royal & SunAlliance USA, Inc.
Saint Paul Companies Inc.
Salomon Smith Barney
Sears, Roebuck and Co.
Security Life of Denver Insurance Co.
S.G. Cowen
Sharp Electronics Corp.
Shaw Industries Inc.
Shaw's Supermarkets, Inc.
Shell Oil Co.
SmithKline Beecham Corp.
Sotheby's Inc.
Square D Co.
Stanley Works (The)
Starwood Hotels & Resorts Worldwide, Inc.
State Street Bank & Trust Co.
Stone Container Corp.
Stone & Webster Inc.
Stride Rite Corp.
Sun Microsystems Inc.
SuperValu, Inc.
Tenet Healthcare Corp.
Texas Instruments Inc.
Textron Inc.
Thermo Electron Corp.
Times Mirror Co.
TJX Companies, Inc.
Tomkins Industries, Inc.
Unilever United States, Inc.
Union Camp Corp.
Union Carbide Corp.
United Distillers & Vintners North America
United States Trust Co. of New York
United Technologies Corp.
USG Corp.
UST Inc.
Varian Medical Systems, Inc.
Wal-Mart Stores, Inc.
Walgreen Co.
Westvaco Corp.
Whitman Corp.
Wyman-Gordon Co.
Zenith Electronics Corp.

Michigan

7-Eleven, Inc.
ABB Inc.
ABC
Agrilink Foods, Inc.
Air Products and Chemicals, Inc.
Alcoa Inc.
Allegheny Technologies Inc.
AlliedSignal Inc.
Alma Piston Co.
American Electric Power
American United Life Insurance Co.
Ameritech Corp.
Ameritech Michigan
AMP Inc.
Andersons Inc.
Autodesk Inc.
Avery Dennison Corp.
Barnes Group Inc.
Battelle Memorial Institute
Bausch & Lomb Inc.
Baxter International Inc.
Bayer Corp.
Becton Dickinson & Co.
Bemis Co., Inc.
Berwind Group
Blount International, Inc.
Blue Cross & Blue Shield of Michigan
Borman's Inc.
BP Amoco Corp.
Bridgestone/Firestone, Inc.
Briggs & Stratton Corp.
Browning-Ferris Industries Inc.
Campbell Soup Co.
Carpenter Technology Corp.
Carris Reels
CertainTeed Corp.
Champion International Corp.
Citizens Bank-Flint
Cleveland-Cliffs, Inc.
CNF Transportation, Inc.
Colgate-Palmolive Co.
Comerica Inc.
Compaq Computer Corp.
Consumers Energy Co.
Cooper Industries, Inc.
Cox Enterprises Inc.
CSX Corp.
CUNA Mutual Group
DaimlerChrysler Corp.
Dana Corp.
Deloitte & Touche
Delta Air Lines, Inc.
Deluxe Corp.
Detroit Edison Co.
Dexter Corp.
Dial Corp.
Diebold, Inc.
Domino's Pizza Inc.
Donaldson Co., Inc.
Dow Chemical Co.
Dow Corning Corp.
Dow Jones & Co., Inc.
du Pont de Nemours & Co. (E.I.)
Eastman Kodak Co.
Eaton Corp.
Ecolab Inc.
EDS Corp.
Elf Atochem North America, Inc.
EMI Music Publishing
Equifax Inc.
Erb Lumber Co.
Ernst & Young, LLP
Ethyl Corp.
European American Bank
Fannie Mae
Federal-Mogul Corp.
FedEx Corp.
Fisher Scientific
FMC Corp.
Ford Motor Co.
Fort James Corp.
Fox Entertainment Group
Frontier Corp.
Fuller Co. (H.B.)
Gannett Co., Inc.
General Dynamics Corp.
General Motors Corp.
Georgia-Pacific Corp.
Gerber Products Co.
Grace & Co. (W.R.)
Graco, Inc.
Grainger, Inc. (W.W.)
Hanna Co. (M.A.)
Hartford (The)
Heinz Co. (H.J.)
Hercules Inc.
Hewlett-Packard Co.
Hitachi America Ltd.
Household International Inc.
Huntington Bancshares Inc.
IKON Office Solutions, Inc.
Illinois Tool Works, Inc.
Intel Corp.
International Business Machines Corp.
International Multifoods Corp.
Interpublic Group of Companies, Inc.
Johnson Controls Inc.
Journal Communications, Inc.
JSJ Corp.
Kellogg Co.
Kelly Services
Kennametal, Inc.
Kimberly-Clark Corp.
Kmart Corp.
Knight Ridder
KPMG Peat Marwick LLP
Kroger Co.
La-Z-Boy Inc.
Lincoln Electric Co.
Litton Industries, Inc.
Lotus Development Corp.
Louisiana-Pacific Corp.
LTV Corp.
Marcus Corp.
Maritz Inc.
Mark IV Industries
Masco Corp.
Maytag Corp.
Mazda North American Operations
McCormick & Co. Inc.
McKesson-HBOC Corp.
Mead Corp.
Medtronic, Inc.
Meijer, Inc.
Menasha Corp.
Meredith Corp.
Mervyn's California
Metropolitan Life Insurance Co.
Michigan Consolidated Gas Co.
Milacron, Inc.
Minnesota Mining & Manufacturing Co.
Mitsubishi Electric America
Morrison Knudsen Corp.
Morton International Inc.
Nalco Chemical Co.
National Starch & Chemical Co.
Nationwide Insurance Co.
NEC America, Inc.
Nestle U.S.A. Inc.
Nissan North America, Inc.
Norfolk Southern Corp.
Nortel
Norton Co.
Novartis Corporation
Oracle Corp.
Outboard Marine Corp.
Owens-Illinois Inc.
Parker Hannifin Corp.

Pfizer Inc.
Pharmacia & Upjohn, Inc.
Philips Electronics North America Corp.
Pioneer Hi-Bred International, Inc.
Playboy Enterprises Inc.
Prudential Insurance Co. of America
Quaker Chemical Corp.
Quanex Corp.
Reynolds Metals Co.
Rockwell International Corp.
Rouse Co.
Ryder System, Inc.
Sara Lee Corp.
Schlumberger Ltd. (USA)
Scripps Co. (E.W.)
Sears, Roebuck and Co.
Shell Oil Co.
Sherwin-Williams Co.
Simpson Investment Co.
Smith Corp. (A.O.)
Smurfit-Stone Container Corp.
SPX Corp.
Standard Products Co.
Stanley Works (The)
Starwood Hotels & Resorts Worldwide, Inc.
State Farm Mutual Automobile Insurance Co.
Steelcase Inc.
Stone Container Corp.
Sun Microsystems Inc.
Teleflex Inc.
Tenet Healthcare Corp.
Tenneco Automotive
Texas Instruments Inc.
Textron Inc.
Thompson Co. (J. Walter)
Timken Co. (The)
Tomkins Industries, Inc.
Torchmark Corp.
Toyota Motor Sales U.S.A., Inc.
TRW Inc.
Unilever United States, Inc.
Union Camp Corp.
Union Carbide Corp.
Unisys Corp.
United Distillers & Vintners North America
United Technologies Corp.
Universal Studios
Vulcan Materials Co.
Wal-Mart Stores, Inc.
Walgreen Co.
Warner-Lambert Co.
The Washington Post
Westvaco Corp.
Whirlpool Corp.
Witco Corp.
Wolverine World Wide
Zenith Electronics Corp.

Minnesota

Abbott Laboratories
ABC
Advanced Micro Devices, Inc.
Alliant Techsystems
Allianz Life Insurance Co. of North America
AlliedSignal Inc.
America West Airlines, Inc.
American Express Co.
American United Life Insurance Co.
Andersen Corp.
Anheuser-Busch Companies, Inc.
Appleton Papers Inc.
Archer-Daniels-Midland Co.
Ashland, Inc.
AT&T Corp.
Autodesk Inc.
Banta Corp.
Bausch & Lomb Inc.
Baxter International Inc.
Bemis Co., Inc.
Bethlehem Steel Corp.
Blount International, Inc.
Boise Cascade Corp.
Bridgestone/Firestone, Inc.
Browning-Ferris Industries Inc.
Business Improvement
Cargill Inc.
Carlson Companies, Inc.
Cenex Harvest States
CertainTeed Corp.
Champion International Corp.
Church & Dwight Co., Inc.
Citibank Corp.
Clorox Co.
Commercial Intertech Corp.
Compaq Computer Corp.
Computer Associates International, Inc.
ConAgra, Inc.
Cummins Engine Co., Inc.
Curtis Industries, Inc. (Helene)
Cyprus Amax Minerals Co.
DaimlerChrysler Corp.
Dain Bosworth Inc.
Dana Corp.
Dayton Hudson
Deere & Co.
Deloitte & Touche
Deluxe Corp.
Diebold, Inc.
Donnelley & Sons Co. (R.R.)
Eastern Enterprises
Eastman Kodak Co.
Ebsco Industries, Inc.
Ecolab Inc.
Elf Atochem North America, Inc.
Equifax Inc.
Ernst & Young, LLP
Excel Corp.
Extendicare Health Services
Fannie Mae
Farmers Group, Inc.
Federated Mutual Insurance Co.
FedEx Corp.
Firstar Bank Milwaukee NA
FMC Corp.
Forest City Enterprises, Inc.
Fortis, Inc.
Fuller Co. (H.B.)
General Mills, Inc.
Georgia-Pacific Corp.
Gerber Products Co.
Gillette Co.
Grace & Co. (W.R.)
Graco, Inc.
Grainger, Inc. (W.W.)
Harsco Corp.
Hartford (The)
Hartford Steam Boiler Inspection & Insurance Co.
Heinz Co. (H.J.)
Hercules Inc.
Hickory Tech Corp.
Honeywell International Inc.
Hubbard Broadcasting, Inc.
IKON Office Solutions, Inc.
Inland Container Corp.
International Business Machines Corp.
International Multifoods Corp.
Interpublic Group of Companies, Inc.
Jostens, Inc.
Knight Ridder
KPMG Peat Marwick LLP
Land O'Lakes, Inc.
Lee Enterprises
Lehigh Portland Cement Co.
Liberty Diversified Industries
Lilly & Co. (Eli)
Lincoln Electric Co.
Litton Industries, Inc.
LTV Corp.
Marcus Corp.
Masco Corp.
Maytag Corp.
McClatchy Co.
McGraw-Hill Companies, Inc.
Mead Corp.
Medtronic, Inc.
Menasha Corp.
Meredith Corp.
Microsoft Corp.
Minnesota Mining & Manufacturing Co.
Minnesota Mutual Life Insurance Co.
Monsanto Co.
Morris Communications Corp.
MTS Systems Corp.
Nalco Chemical Co.
National Computer Systems, Inc.
National Presto Industries, Inc.
National Starch & Chemical Co.
Nike, Inc.
Northern States Power Co.
Northwest Airlines, Inc.
Norwest Corp.
Oracle Corp.
Owens Corning
Parker Hannifin Corp.
Pentair Inc.
Pfizer Inc.
Pharmacia & Upjohn, Inc.
Philips Electronics North America Corp.
Pillsbury Co.
Potlatch Corp.
Ralston Purina Co.
Red Wing Shoe Co. Inc.
Regis Corp.
REI-Recreational Equipment, Inc.
Reliant Energy Inc.
Reliant Energy Minnegasco
ReliaStar Financial Corp.
Reynolds Metals Co.
Roseburg Forest Products Co.
Rouse Co.
Saint Paul Companies Inc.
Sara Lee Corp.
Sears, Roebuck and Co.
Shaw Industries Inc.
Shell Oil Co.
SIT Investment Associates, Inc.
SmithKline Beecham Corp.
Sotheby's Inc.
Sprint Corp.
Standard Products Co.
Stanley Works (The)
Starwood Hotels & Resorts Worldwide, Inc.
State Farm Mutual Automobile Insurance Co.
State Street Bank & Trust Co.
Stone Container Corp.
Sun Microsystems Inc.
SuperValu, Inc.
Target Corp.
TCF National Bank Minnesota
TENNANT Co.
Tension Envelope Corp.
Texas Instruments Inc.
Textron Inc.
Timken Co. (The)
Transamerica Corp.
Tyson Foods Inc.
Union Carbide Corp.
Unisys Corp.
United Parcel Service of America Inc.
U.S. Bancorp
U.S. Bancorp Piper Jaffray
US West, Inc.
USG Corp.
USX Corp.
Valspar Corp.
The Washington Post
Weyerhaeuser Co.

Mississippi

Air Products and Chemicals, Inc.
Alcoa Inc.
Archer-Daniels-Midland Co.
Armstrong World Industries, Inc.
Avery Dennison Corp.
Barnes Group Inc.
Baxter International Inc.
Bayer Corp.
Belk Stores Services Inc.
BellSouth Telecommunications
Blue Bell, Inc.
Borden, Inc.
BP Amoco Corp.
Browning-Ferris Industries Inc.
Caterpillar Inc.
Chevron Corp.
Clorox Co.
Computer Associates International, Inc.
ConAgra, Inc.
Cooper Industries, Inc.
Cooper Tire & Rubber Co.
Dana Corp.
Deloitte & Touche
Delta Air Lines, Inc.
Deposit Guaranty National Bank
Donnelley & Sons Co. (R.R.)
du Pont de Nemours & Co. (E.I.)
Dun & Bradstreet Corp.
Eastman Kodak Co.
Eckerd Corp.
EDS Corp.
Entergy Corp.
Fannie Mae
FedEx Corp.
FMC Corp.
Fort James Corp.
Fox Entertainment Group
Frontier Corp.
Gannett Co., Inc.
GenCorp
General Motors Corp.
Georgia-Pacific Corp.
Harrah's Entertainment Inc.
Hercules Inc.
IKON Office Solutions, Inc.
Inland Container Corp.
International Business Machines Corp.
International Paper Co.
Kimberly-Clark Corp.
Knight Ridder
KPMG Peat Marwick LLP
La-Z-Boy Inc.
Lilly & Co. (Eli)
Litton Industries, Inc.
Louisiana-Pacific Corp.
Menasha Corp.
Morton International Inc.
Nalco Chemical Co.
National Presto Industries, Inc.
New York Times Co.
Norfolk Southern Corp.
Parker Hannifin Corp.
Pioneer Hi-Bred International, Inc.
Promus Hotel Corp.
Prudential Insurance Co. of America
Quanex Corp.
Sara Lee Corp.
Sara Lee Hosiery, Inc.
Shell Oil Co.
SPX Corp.
Stanley Works (The)
Stone Container Corp.
SuperValu, Inc.
Target Corp.
Temple-Inland Inc.
Texas Gas Transmission Corp.
Thomasville Furniture Industries Inc.
Trustmark National Bank
TRW Inc.
Tyson Foods Inc.
Union Camp Corp.
Union Planters Corp.
United Dominion Industries, Ltd.
United Technologies Corp.
USG Corp.
Wal-Mart Stores, Inc.
Westvaco Corp.
Weyerhaeuser Co.
Witco Corp.

Missouri

7-Eleven, Inc.
ABC
AFLAC Inc.
Air Products and Chemicals, Inc.
Alcoa Inc.
Ameren Corp.
America West Airlines, Inc.
American Express Co.
American United Life Insurance Co.
Ameritech Corp.
Anheuser-Busch Companies, Inc.
Archer-Daniels-Midland Co.
ASARCO Inc.
AT&T Corp.
Autodesk Inc.
Baker Hughes Inc.
Banta Corp.
Battelle Memorial Institute
Bausch & Lomb Inc.
Bayer Corp.
Block, Inc. (H&R)
Briggs & Stratton Corp.
Brown Shoe Co., Inc.

Browning-Ferris Industries Inc.
Business Men's Assurance Co. of America
Butler Manufacturing Co.
CGU Insurance
Champion International Corp.
Chubb Corp.
Church & Dwight Co., Inc.
Circuit City Stores, Inc.
Citibank Corp.
Clark Refining & Marketing
Clorox Co.
CNF Transportation, Inc.
Commerce Bancshares, Inc.
ConAgra, Inc.
Cooper Industries, Inc.
Cooper Tire & Rubber Co.
Cox Enterprises Inc.
CPI Corp.
Crane Co.
DaimlerChrysler Corp.
Dain Bosworth Inc.
Dayton Hudson
Deere & Co.
Deloitte & Touche
Deluxe Corp.
Dexter Corp.
Dial Corp.
Diebold, Inc.
Donaldson Co., Inc.
Dow Chemical Co.
Dow Jones & Co., Inc.
Eastman Kodak Co.
Eaton Corp.
Ecolab Inc.
Edison Brothers Stores, Inc.
EDS Corp.
Elf Atochem North America, Inc.
Emerson Electric Co.
Employers Insurance of Wausau, A Mutual Co.
Enterprise Rent-A-Car Co.
Ernst & Young, LLP
Fannie Mae
Farmers Group, Inc.
Federal-Mogul Corp.
FedEx Corp.
Fireman's Fund Insurance Co.
Fluor Corp.
Fortis, Inc.
Fox Entertainment Group
Gannett Co., Inc.
GenAmerica Corp.
GenCorp
General Dynamics Corp.
General Mills, Inc.
General Motors Corp.
Georgia-Pacific Corp.
Grace & Co. (W.R.)
Grainger, Inc. (W.W.)
Group Health Plan
Hallmark Cards Inc.
Harrah's Entertainment Inc.
Harris Trust & Savings Bank
Hartmarx Corp.
Hercules Inc.
Hewlett-Packard Co.
Hoechst Marion Roussel, Inc.
Hubbell Inc.
Huffy Corp.
Humana, Inc.
IKON Office Solutions, Inc.
Inland Container Corp.
International Business Machines Corp.
International Multifoods Corp.
Johnson Controls Inc.
Johnson & Son (S.C.)
Jones & Co. (Edward D.)
Kimberly-Clark Corp.
KPMG Peat Marwick LLP
Laclede Gas Co.
Levi Strauss & Co.
Lilly & Co. (Eli)
Lincoln Electric Co.
Mallinckrodt Chemical, Inc.
Marcus Corp.
Maritz Inc.
Maytag Corp.
McCormick & Co. Inc.
Mead Corp.
Medtronic, Inc.
Mercantile Bank NA
Meredith Corp.
MFA Inc.
Microsoft Corp.
Minnesota Mining & Manufacturing Co.
Monsanto Co.
Morris Communications Corp.
Nalco Chemical Co.
National Starch & Chemical Co.
Nestle U.S.A. Inc.
Norfolk Southern Corp.
Northrop Grumman Corp.
Olin Corp.
Oracle Corp.
Orscheln Co.
Outboard Marine Corp.
Owens Corning
Owens-Illinois Inc.
Parker Hannifin Corp.
Pentair Inc.
PerkinElmer, Inc.
Pillsbury Co.
Procter & Gamble Co.
Prudential Insurance Co. of America
Pulitzer Publishing Co.
Ralston Purina Co.
Reynolds Metals Co.
Rockwell International Corp.
Rouse Co.
SAFECO Corp.
Sara Lee Corp.
SBC Communications Inc.
Schering-Plough Corp.
Scripps Co. (E.W.)
Shaw Industries Inc.
Shell Oil Co.
Shelter Mutual Insurance Co.
Smurfit-Stone Container Corp.
Sony Electronics
Sprint Corp.
Square D Co.
Stanley Works (The)
Starwood Hotels & Resorts Worldwide, Inc.
State Farm Mutual Automobile Insurance Co.
State Street Bank & Trust Co.
Stone Container Corp.
Stride Rite Corp.
Stupp Brothers Bridge & Iron Co.
Sunmark Capital Corp.
SuperValu, Inc.
Tamko Roofing Products
Tandy Corp.
Target Corp.
Temple-Inland Inc.
Tenet Healthcare Corp.
Tension Envelope Corp.
Texas Instruments Inc.
Thompson Co. (J. Walter)
Times Mirror Co.
Tomkins Industries, Inc.
Torchmark Corp.
Tyson Foods Inc.
Unilever Home & Personal Care U.S.A.
Unilever United States, Inc.
Union Camp Corp.
Union Pacific Corp.
Union Planters Corp.
United Dominion Industries, Ltd.
United Parcel Service of America Inc.
U.S. Bancorp Piper Jaffray
Universal Foods Corp.
USG Corp.
Wal-Mart Stores, Inc.
Walgreen Co.
Weyerhaeuser Co.
Williams
Zenith Electronics Corp.

Montana

American General Finance
ASARCO Inc.
Associated Food Stores
Atlantic Richfield Co.
Boise Cascade Corp.
Browning-Ferris Industries Inc.
Burlington Resources, Inc.
Dain Bosworth Inc.
Delta Air Lines, Inc.
Diebold, Inc.
Equitable Resources, Inc.
Evening Post Publishing Co.
Exxon Mobil Corp.
Gannett Co., Inc.
General Mills, Inc.
International Business Machines Corp.
KPMG Peat Marwick LLP
Land O'Lakes, Inc.
Lee Enterprises
Louisiana-Pacific Corp.
Lubrizol Corp. (The)
Montana Power Co.
Morrison Knudsen Corp.
Mutual of Omaha Insurance Co.
Norwest Corp.
PacifiCorp
Saint Paul Companies Inc.
SuperValu, Inc.
Target Corp.
U.S. Bancorp
U.S. Bancorp Piper Jaffray
Wal-Mart Stores, Inc.

Nebraska

Air Products and Chemicals, Inc.
America West Airlines, Inc.
Ameritas Life Insurance Corp.
Archer-Daniels-Midland Co.
AT&T Corp.
Bausch & Lomb Inc.
Baxter International Inc.
Becton Dickinson & Co.
Bemis Co., Inc.
Blount International, Inc.
Browning-Ferris Industries Inc.
Campbell Soup Co.
Central Soya Co.
CLARCOR Inc.
Commerce Bancshares, Inc.
Commercial Federal Corp.
Computer Associates International, Inc.
ConAgra, Inc.
Cox Enterprises Inc.
Dain Bosworth Inc.
Dana Corp.
Deloitte & Touche
Diebold, Inc.
Eaton Corp.
Ecolab Inc.
EDS Corp.
Fannie Mae
FMC Corp.
Grace & Co. (W.R.)
Hartford (The)
Heinz Co. (H.J.)
Hershey Foods Corp.
Hewlett-Packard Co.
IBP
International Business Machines Corp.
Kellogg Co.
Kiewit Sons' Inc. (Peter)
Kinder Morgn
KPMG Peat Marwick LLP
Land O'Lakes, Inc.
Lee Enterprises
Lilly & Co. (Eli)
Lincoln Electric Co.
Marcus Corp.
Minnesota Mining & Manufacturing Co.
Mutual of Omaha Insurance Co.
National Bank of Commerce Trust & Savings
NEBCO Evans
Northwest Bank Nebraska, NA
Norwest Corp.
Nucor Corp.
Occidental Petroleum Corp.
Oracle Corp.
Parker Hannifin Corp.
Pfizer Inc.
Physicians Mutual Insurance Co.
Pioneer Hi-Bred International, Inc.
Pitney Bowes Inc.
Principal Financial Group
Prudential Insurance Co. of America
Pulitzer Publishing Co.
Reliant Energy Minnegasco
Rockwell International Corp.
Schering-Plough Corp.
SmithKline Beecham Corp.
Sprint Corp.
Square D Co.
State Farm Mutual Automobile Insurance Co.
Target Corp.
Union Pacific Corp.
United Parcel Service of America Inc.
U.S. Bancorp Piper Jaffray
US West, Inc.
Valmont Industries, Inc.
Wal-Mart Stores, Inc.
West Co. Inc.
WICOR, Inc.
Witco Corp.

Nevada

7-Eleven, Inc.
America West Airlines, Inc.
American Express Co.
American Standard Inc.
Armstrong World Industries, Inc.
Bechtel Group, Inc.
Caesar's World, Inc.
California Federal Bank, FSB
Circuit City Stores, Inc.
Citibank Corp.
CSR Rinker Materials Corp.
Cyprus Amax Minerals Co.
Dain Bosworth Inc.
Dana Corp.
Deloitte & Touche
Delta Air Lines, Inc.
Diebold, Inc.
Donnelley & Sons Co. (R.R.)
Eastman Kodak Co.
Ecolab Inc.
Ernst & Young, LLP
Exxon Mobil Corp.
Farmers Group, Inc.
FedEx Corp.
FMC Corp.
Freightliner Corp.
Gannett Co., Inc.
GEICO Corp.
General Mills, Inc.
Hamilton Sundstrand Corp.
Harrah's Entertainment Inc.
Hartford (The)
Hewlett-Packard Co.
Home Depot, Inc.
Idaho Power Co.
IKON Office Solutions, Inc.
International Business Machines Corp.
Journal Communications, Inc.
Kennametal, Inc.
KPMG Peat Marwick LLP
Landmark Communications Inc.
Levi Strauss & Co.
Louisiana-Pacific Corp.
Mead Corp.
Merck & Co.
Meredith Corp.
Potlatch Corp.
Promus Hotel Corp.
Sara Lee Corp.
Sara Lee Hosiery, Inc.
Shell Oil Co.
Sherwin-Williams Co.
Sierra Pacific Resources
Southwest Gas Corp.
Springs Industries, Inc.
Sprint Corp.
Target Corp.
Tenet Healthcare Corp.
Timken Co. (The)
USG Corp.
Witco Corp.
Wyman-Gordon Co.

New Hampshire

7-Eleven, Inc.
Anheuser-Busch Companies, Inc.
Bausch & Lomb Inc.
Baxter International Inc.
Browning-Ferris Industries Inc.
Cadence Designs Systems, Inc.
Circuit City Stores, Inc.
Clorox Co.
Deloitte & Touche
Demoulas Supermarkets Inc.
Dexter Corp.
Diebold, Inc.
Ecolab Inc.
FedEx Corp.
Forest City Enterprises, Inc.
GenCorp
General Motors Corp.
Hannaford Brothers Co.
Hartford (The)
Home Depot, Inc.

IKON Office Solutions, Inc.
Johnson Controls Inc.
Kingsbury Corp.
Kraft Foods, Inc.
Lockheed Martin Corp.
McGraw-Hill Companies, Inc.
Millipore Corp.
Morgan Stanley Dean Witter & Co.
Morton International Inc.
Nortel
Northeast Utilities
Northrop Grumman Corp.
Norton Co.
Oracle Corp.
Owens-Illinois Inc.
Parker Hannifin Corp.
Philip Morris Companies Inc.
Royal & SunAlliance USA, Inc.
Shaw's Supermarkets, Inc.
Stanley Works (The)
State Street Bank & Trust Co.
Teleflex Inc.
Textron Inc.
Timken Co. (The)
United Parcel Service of America Inc.
Wal-Mart Stores, Inc.
Wyman-Gordon Co.

New Jersey

7-Eleven, Inc.
ABB Inc.
Advanced Micro Devices, Inc.
AEGON U.S.A. Inc.
Aetna, Inc.
Agrilink Foods, Inc.
Air Products and Chemicals, Inc.
Alliant Techsystems
AlliedSignal Inc.
American Express Co.
American General Finance
American Standard Inc.
American United Life Insurance Co.
Anheuser-Busch Companies, Inc.
Aon Corp.
Archer-Daniels-Midland Co.
Armstrong World Industries, Inc.
AT&T Corp.
Bard, Inc. (C.R.)
Barnes Group Inc.
Battelle Memorial Institute
Bausch & Lomb Inc.
Bayer Corp.
Bechtel Group, Inc.
Beckman Coulter, Inc.
Bell Atlantic Corp.
Bemis Co., Inc.
Berwind Group
Bestfoods
BFGoodrich Co.
Boeing Co.
Borden, Inc.
BP Amoco Corp.
Bristol-Myers Squibb Co.
Brooklyn Union
Browning-Ferris Industries Inc.
Cadence Designs Systems, Inc.
Caesar's World, Inc.
Campbell Soup Co.
Carillon Importers, Ltd.
Carpenter Technology Corp.
Carter-Wallace, Inc.
Champion International Corp.
Chesapeake Corp.
Circuit City Stores, Inc.
CIT Group, Inc. (The)
CNF Transportation, Inc.
Colgate-Palmolive Co.
Compaq Computer Corp.
Computer Associates International, Inc.
ConAgra, Inc.
Conectiv
Country Curtains, Inc.
CSX Corp.
Curtis Industries, Inc. (Helene)
Deloitte & Touche
Delta Air Lines, Inc.
Deluxe Corp.
Dexter Corp.
Diebold, Inc.
Disney Co. (Walt)
Dow Chemical Co.
Dow Corning Corp.
Dow Jones & Co., Inc.
DSM Copolymer
du Pont de Nemours & Co. (E.I.)
Dun & Bradstreet Corp.
Eastman Kodak Co.
Ebsco Industries, Inc.
EDS Corp.
Equifax Inc.
Ernst & Young, LLP
Exxon Mobil Corp.
Federal-Mogul Corp.
Federated Department Stores, Inc.
FedEx Corp.
Ferro Corp.
Fireman's Fund Insurance Co.
First Union Bank
Fisher Scientific
FleetBoston Financial Corp.
Fluor Corp.
FMC Corp.
Freightliner Corp.
GenCorp
General Motors Corp.
General Reinsurance Corp.
Georgia-Pacific Corp.
Gerber Products Co.
GPU Energy
GPU Inc.
Grace & Co. (W.R.)
Gucci America Inc.
Hanna Co. (M.A.)
Harrah's Entertainment Inc.
Harsco Corp.
Hartford (The)
Hasbro, Inc.
Heinz Co. (H.J.)
Hercules Inc.
Hewlett-Packard Co.
Hitachi America Ltd.
Hoffmann-La Roche Inc.
Home Depot, Inc.
Houghton Mifflin Co.
Illinois Tool Works, Inc.
Inland Container Corp.
International Business Machines Corp.
International Flavors & Fragrances Inc.
International Multifoods Corp.
Interpublic Group of Companies, Inc.
Johnson Controls Inc.
Johnson & Johnson
Johnson & Son (S.C.)
Kellogg Co.
Kimberly-Clark Corp.
Knight Ridder
KPMG Peat Marwick LLP
Kraft Foods, Inc.
Lilly & Co. (Eli)
Lincoln Electric Co.
Lipton Co.
Litton Industries, Inc.
Liz Claiborne, Inc.
Lockheed Martin Corp.
Lotus Development Corp.
Macy's East Inc.
Mamiye Brothers
Masco Corp.
Matsushita Electric Corp. of America
Maybelline, Inc.
Maytag Corp.
McCormick & Co. Inc.
McGraw-Hill Companies, Inc.
MCI WorldCom, Inc.
Mellon Financial Corp.
Menasha Corp.
Merck & Co.
Meredith Corp.
Metropolitan Life Insurance Co.
Minnesota Mining & Manufacturing Co.
MONY Group (The)
Morton International Inc.
Mutual of Omaha Insurance Co.
Nalco Chemical Co.
National Starch & Chemical Co.
NEC America, Inc.
Nestle U.S.A. Inc.
New Jersey Natural Gas Co.
New York Life Insurance Co.
New York Times Co.
Nomura Holding America
Nortel
Norton Co.
Norwest Corp.
Novartis Corporation
Olin Corp.
Oracle Corp.
Orange & Rockland Utilities, Inc.
Owens Corning
Owens-Illinois Inc.
Parker Hannifin Corp.
PECO Energy Co.
PerkinElmer, Inc.
Pharmacia & Upjohn, Inc.
Phelps Dodge Corp.
Philip Morris Companies Inc.
Philips Electronics North America Corp.
Pillsbury Co.
PNC Bank
Polaroid Corp.
Prudential Insurance Co. of America
Prudential Securities Inc.
Public Service Electric & Gas Co.
Rayonier Inc.
Revlon Inc.
Reynolds Metals Co.
Reynolds Tobacco (R.J.)
Rich Products Corp.
Rockwell International Corp.
Rouse Co.
Royal & SunAlliance USA, Inc.
Saint Paul Companies Inc.
Sara Lee Corp.
Schering-Plough Corp.
Sears, Roebuck and Co.
Shaklee Corp.
Sharp Electronics Corp.
Shaw Industries Inc.
Shaw's Supermarkets, Inc.
Shell Oil Co.
Sherwin-Williams Co.
SmithKline Beecham Corp.
Sony Electronics
Sovereign Bank
Sprint Corp.
Square D Co.
Starwood Hotels & Resorts Worldwide, Inc.
State Street Bank & Trust Co.
Stone Container Corp.
Sun Microsystems Inc.
Telcordia Technologies
Temple-Inland Inc.
Tenneco Automotive
Tension Envelope Corp.
Thompson Co. (J. Walter)
Toshiba America Inc.
Unilever United States, Inc.
Union Camp Corp.
Union Carbide Corp.
United Airlines Inc.
United Distillers & Vintners North America
United Parcel Service of America Inc.
U.S. Bancorp Piper Jaffray
Universal Foods Corp.
Universal Studios
USG Corp.
Wal-Mart Stores, Inc.
Walgreen Co.
Warner-Lambert Co.
The Washington Post
Webster Bank
Westvaco Corp.
Weyerhaeuser Co.
Whitman Corp.
Williams
Witco Corp.
Zenith Electronics Corp.

New Mexico

Air Products and Chemicals, Inc.
America West Airlines, Inc.
American Express Co.
Arizona Public Service Co.
Ball Corp.
Battelle Memorial Institute
Borden, Inc.
Burlington Resources, Inc.
Chevron Corp.
Citibank Corp.
Cyprus Amax Minerals Co.
du Pont de Nemours & Co. (E.I.)
Ecolab Inc.
Equifax Inc.
FedEx Corp.
FMC Corp.
GEICO Corp.
GenCorp
Hershey Foods Corp.
Hewlett-Packard Co.
Honeywell International Inc.
Hubbard Broadcasting, Inc.
International Business Machines Corp.
International Multifoods Corp.
KPMG Peat Marwick LLP
Lee Enterprises
Levi Strauss & Co.
Lincoln Electric Co.
Lockheed Martin Corp.
Marcus Corp.
Mark IV Industries
Mervyn's California
Motorola Inc.
Northrop Grumman Corp.
Oracle Corp.
PerkinElmer, Inc.
Phelps Dodge Corp.
Phillips Petroleum Co.
Pulitzer Publishing Co.
REI-Recreational Equipment, Inc.
Sara Lee Corp.
Scripps Co. (E.W.)
Stone Container Corp.
Sun Microsystems Inc.
Target Corp.
Tucson Electric Power Co.
Ultramar Diamond Shamrock Corp.
Union Carbide Corp.
Unocal Corp.
US West, Inc.
Wal-Mart Stores, Inc.

New York

7-Eleven, Inc.
ABB Inc.
Abbott Laboratories
ABC
Advanced Micro Devices, Inc.
Aetna, Inc.
AFLAC Inc.
Agrilink Foods, Inc.
Air Products and Chemicals, Inc.
Albany International Corp.
Alcoa Inc.
Allegheny Technologies Inc.
AlliedSignal Inc.
American Electric Power
American Express Co.
American Stock Exchange, Inc.
Anheuser-Busch Companies, Inc.
Apple Computer, Inc.
Appleton Papers Inc.
Archer-Daniels-Midland Co.
Armstrong World Industries, Inc.
Associated Food Stores
AT&T Corp.
Autodesk Inc.
Avery Dennison Corp.
Avon Products, Inc.
Ball Corp.
Banfi Vintners
Bank of America
Bank of New York Co., Inc.
Barclays Capital
Bard, Inc. (C.R.)
Barnes Group Inc.
Battelle Memorial Institute
Bausch & Lomb Inc.
Baxter International Inc.
Bayer Corp.
Becton Dickinson & Co.
Bell Atlantic Corp.
Bemis Co., Inc.
Ben & Jerry's Homemade Inc.
Bernstein & Co., Inc. (Sanford C.)
Berwind Group
Bethlehem Steel Corp.
Boeing Co.
BP Amoco Corp.
Bridgestone/Firestone, Inc.
Brooklyn Union
Browning-Ferris Industries Inc.

Burlington Industries, Inc.
Burnett Co. (Leo)
Butler Capital Corp.
Cadence Designs Systems, Inc.
California Bank & Trust
Campbell Soup Co.
Cantor, Fitzgerald Securities Corp.
Carrier Corp.
Central National-Gottesman
CertainTeed Corp.
CGU Insurance
Champion International Corp.
Chase Manhattan Bank, NA
Chesapeake Corp.
Chicago Tribune Co.
CIBC Oppenheimer
CIT Group, Inc. (The)
Citibank Corp.
Citigroup
Citizens Financial Group, Inc.
CNF Transportation, Inc.
Collins & Aikman Corp.
Compaq Computer Corp.
Computer Associates International, Inc.
Consolidated Papers, Inc.
Continental Grain Co.
Cooper Industries, Inc.
Corning Inc.
Country Curtains, Inc.
Cox Enterprises Inc.
Crane Co.
Cranston Print Works Co.
Credit Suisse First Boston
CSX Corp.
Cummins Engine Co., Inc.
CUNA Mutual Group
DaimlerChrysler Corp.
Deere & Co.
Deloitte & Touche
Delta Air Lines, Inc.
Deluxe Corp.
Dexter Corp.
Diebold, Inc.
Disney Co. (Walt)
Dixie Group, Inc. (The)
Donaldson Co., Inc.
Dow Jones & Co., Inc.
du Pont de Nemours & Co. (E.I.)
Dun & Bradstreet Corp.
Eastman Chemical Co.
Eastman Kodak Co.
Eaton Corp.
Ecolab Inc.
EDS Corp.
Elf Atochem North America, Inc.
EMI Music Publishing
Equifax Inc.
Ernst & Young, LLP
Ethyl Corp.
European American Bank
Evening Post Publishing Co.
Fannie Mae
Farmers Group, Inc.
Federated Department Stores, Inc.
First Maryland Bancorp
First Union Bank
Fisher Brothers Cleaning Services
Fisher Scientific
FleetBoston Financial Corp.
FMC Corp.
Forbes Inc.
Forest City Enterprises, Inc.
Fortis, Inc.
Fortune Brands, Inc.
Fox Entertainment Group
Freddie Mac
Freightliner Corp.
Frontier Corp.
Fuji Bank & Trust Co.
Fuller Co. (H.B.)
Gannett Co., Inc.
GATX Corp.
GEICO Corp.
GenCorp
General Atlantic Partners II LP
General Electric Co.
General Motors Corp.
General Reinsurance Corp.
Georgia-Pacific Corp.
Gerber Products Co.
Glickenhaus & Co.
Goldman Sachs Group
Golub Corp.
Grace & Co. (W.R.)
Guardian Life Insurance Co. of America
Gucci America Inc.
Hamilton Sundstrand Corp.
Hannaford Brothers Co.
Harcourt General, Inc.
Harris Corp.
Harris Trust & Savings Bank
Harsco Corp.
Hartford (The)
Hartmarx Corp.
Hasbro, Inc.
Heinz Co. (H.J.)
Heller Financial, Inc.
Hercules Inc.
Hewlett-Packard Co.
Hitachi America Ltd.
HON Industries Inc.
Houghton Mifflin Co.
HSBC Bank USA
Hubbell Inc.
IKON Office Solutions, Inc.
Illinois Tool Works, Inc.
Industrial Bank of Japan Trust Co. (New York)
Inland Container Corp.
Intel Corp.
International Business Machines Corp.
International Flavors & Fragrances Inc.
International Multifoods Corp.
International Paper Co.
Interpublic Group of Companies, Inc.
Jacobson & Sons (Benjamin)
Johnson & Johnson
Johnson & Son (S.C.)
Jostens, Inc.
Kaman Corp.
Kimberly-Clark Corp.
KPMG Peat Marwick LLP
Kraft Foods, Inc.
Levi Strauss & Co.
Leviton Manufacturing Co. Inc.
Lilly & Co. (Eli)
Lincoln Electric Co.
Lincoln Financial Group
Little, Inc. (Arthur D.)
Litton Industries, Inc.
Lockheed Martin Corp.
Loctite Corp.
Loews Corp.
Lotus Development Corp.
LTV Corp.
Macy's East Inc.
Mamiye Brothers
Manufacturers & Traders Trust Co.
Maritz Inc.
Mark IV Industries
Masco Corp.
Mattel Inc.
May Department Stores Co.
MBIA Inc.
McGraw-Hill Companies, Inc.
MCI WorldCom, Inc.
McKesson-HBOC Corp.
Medtronic, Inc.
Mellon Financial Corp.
Meredith Corp.
Merrill Lynch & Co., Inc.
Metropolitan Life Insurance Co.
Microsoft Corp.
Minnesota Mining & Manufacturing Co.
Mitsubishi Electric America
Monarch Machine Tool Co.
Monsanto Co.
MONY Group (The)
Morgan & Co. Inc. (J.P.)
Morgan Stanley Dean Witter & Co.
Morrison Knudsen Corp.
Morton International Inc.
Nalco Chemical Co.
National Fuel Gas Distribution Corp.
National Starch & Chemical Co.
Nationwide Insurance Co.
NEC America, Inc.
Nestle U.S.A. Inc.
New York Mercantile Exchange
New York State Electric & Gas Corp.
New York Stock Exchange, Inc.
New York Times Co.
Niagara Mohawk Holdings Inc.
Nike, Inc.
Nissan North America, Inc.
Nomura Holding America
Norfolk Southern Corp.
Northeast Utilities
Northrop Grumman Corp.
Norton Co.
Norwest Corp.
Novartis Corporation
Occidental Petroleum Corp.
Olin Corp.
Oracle Corp.
Orange & Rockland Utilities, Inc.
Oshkosh B'Gosh, Inc.
Overseas Shipholding Group Inc.
Owens Corning
Owens-Illinois Inc.
Paine Webber
Parker Hannifin Corp.
PepsiCo, Inc.
PerkinElmer, Inc.
Pfizer Inc.
Phelps Dodge Corp.
Philip Morris Companies Inc.
Philips Electronics North America Corp.
Phoenix Home Life Mutual Insurance Co.
Pillsbury Co.
Pittway Corp.
Playboy Enterprises Inc.
Premier Industrial Corp.
PricewaterhouseCoopers
Procter & Gamble Co.
Prudential Insurance Co. of America
Prudential Securities Inc.
Ralston Purina Co.
Reader's Digest Association, Inc. (The)
REI-Recreational Equipment, Inc.
ReliaStar Financial Corp.
Revlon Inc.
Reynolds Metals Co.
Reynolds Tobacco (R.J.)
Rich Products Corp.
Rochester Gas & Electric Corp.
Rouse Co.
Royal & SunAlliance USA, Inc.
Russer Foods
Ryder System, Inc.
Saint Paul Companies Inc.
Salomon Smith Barney
Sara Lee Corp.
Schloss & Co. (Marcus)
Schlumberger Ltd. (USA)
Seagram & Sons, Inc. (Joseph E.)
Sears, Roebuck and Co.
S.G. Cowen
Shaklee Corp.
Sharp Electronics Corp.
Shell Oil Co.
Slant/Fin Corp.
SmithKline Beecham Corp.
Smurfit-Stone Container Corp.
Sony Electronics
Sotheby's Inc.
Springs Industries, Inc.
Sprint Corp.
Standard Products Co.
Starwood Hotels & Resorts Worldwide, Inc.
State Farm Mutual Automobile Insurance Co.
Stone & Webster Inc.
Stride Rite Corp.
Sumitomo Bank
Sun Microsystems Inc.
Tai and Co. (J.T.)
TENNANT Co.
Texaco Inc.
Texas Instruments Inc.
Textron Inc.
Thompson Co. (J. Walter)
Times Mirror Co.
Titan Industrial Corp.
TJX Companies, Inc.
Tomkins Industries, Inc.
Torchmark Corp.
Toshiba America Inc.
Toyota Motor Sales U.S.A., Inc.
Trace International Holdings, Inc.
Transamerica Corp.
TRW Inc.
Unilever United States, Inc.
Union Carbide Corp.
Unisys Corp.
United Airlines Inc.
United Distillers & Vintners North America
United Dominion Industries, Ltd.
United Parcel Service of America Inc.
United States Trust Co. of New York
Universal Studios
USG Corp.
Viacom Inc.
Wachtell, Lipton, Rosen & Katz
Wal-Mart Stores, Inc.
Waldbaum's Supermarkets, Inc.
Westvaco Corp.
Wiley & Sons (John)
Williams
Witco Corp.
Wolverine World Wide
Xerox Corp.
Young & Rubicam
Zilkha & Sons

North Carolina

7-Eleven, Inc.
ABB Inc.
Abbott Laboratories
ABC
Advanced Micro Devices, Inc.
AFLAC Inc.
AGL Resources Inc.
Air Products and Chemicals, Inc.
AlliedSignal Inc.
American Honda Motor Co., Inc.
American Standard Inc.
American United Life Insurance Co.
AMETEK, Inc.
AMP Inc.
Apple Computer, Inc.
Archer-Daniels-Midland Co.
Armstrong World Industries, Inc.
AT&T Corp.
Avery Dennison Corp.
Bandag, Inc.
Banta Corp.
Barclays Capital
Battelle Memorial Institute
Bausch & Lomb Inc.
Baxter International Inc.
Bayer Corp.
Bechtel Group, Inc.
Becton Dickinson & Co.
Belk Stores Services Inc.
BellSouth Telecommunications
Bestfoods
Branch Banking & Trust Co.
Bridgestone/Firestone, Inc.
Brown & Williamson Tobacco Corp.
Burlington Industries, Inc.
Burress (J.W.)
Cadence Designs Systems, Inc.
Campbell Soup Co.
Carolina Power & Light Co.
Carris Reels
Caterpillar Inc.
CCB Financial Corp.
Champion International Corp.
Chesapeake Corp.
Circuit City Stores, Inc.
CNF Transportation, Inc.
Collins & Aikman Corp.
Commercial Intertech Corp.
Cone Mills Corp.
Cooper Industries, Inc.
Cox Enterprises Inc.
Crane Co.
Cranston Print Works Co.
CSX Corp.
Cummins Engine Co., Inc.
Cyprus Amax Minerals Co.
DaimlerChrysler Corp.
Dana Corp.
Deloitte & Touche
Delta Air Lines, Inc.
Deluxe Corp.

Deutsch Co.
Dexter Corp.
Diebold, Inc.
Dixie Group, Inc. (The)
Donaldson Co., Inc.
Donnelley & Sons Co. (R.R.)
Dow Corning Corp.
Dow Jones & Co., Inc.
du Pont de Nemours & Co. (E.I.)
Duke Energy
Dun & Bradstreet Corp.
Duracell International
Eastman Kodak Co.
Eaton Corp.
Eckerd Corp.
Ecolab Inc.
EDS Corp.
Emerson Electric Co.
Equifax Inc.
Ernst & Young, LLP
Exxon Mobil Corp.
Fannie Mae
Fisher Scientific
FMC Corp.
Fort James Corp.
Fortune Brands, Inc.
Freightliner Corp.
Fuller Co. (H.B.)
Gannett Co., Inc.
General Electric Co.
General Motors Corp.
Georgia-Pacific Corp.
Gerber Products Co.
Glaxo Wellcome Inc.
Grace & Co. (W.R.)
Hannaford Brothers Co.
Harrah's Entertainment Inc.
Harsco Corp.
Hartford (The)
Heinz Co. (H.J.)
Hercules Inc.
Hewlett-Packard Co.
Hitachi America Ltd.
Hoffmann-La Roche Inc.
Home Depot, Inc.
HON Industries Inc.
HSBC Bank USA
Hubbell Inc.
IKON Office Solutions, Inc.
Inland Container Corp.
International Business Machines Corp.
International Multifoods Corp.
Interpublic Group of Companies, Inc.
Jeld-wen, Inc.
Kendall International, Inc.
Kennametal, Inc.
Kimball International, Inc.
Kimberly-Clark Corp.
Knight Ridder
KPMG Peat Marwick LLP
La-Z-Boy Inc.
Lance, Inc.
Landmark Communications Inc.
Levi Strauss & Co.
Lilly & Co. (Eli)
Lincoln Electric Co.
Litton Industries, Inc.
Loews Corp.
Louisiana-Pacific Corp.
Lowe's Companies
Mallinckrodt Chemical, Inc.
Marcus Corp.
Mark IV Industries
Masco Corp.
MCI WorldCom, Inc.
Mead Corp.
Medtronic, Inc.
Merck & Co.
Microsoft Corp.
Milliken & Co.
Minnesota Mining & Manufacturing Co.
Mitsubishi Electric America
Monsanto Co.
Motorola Inc.
MTS Systems Corp.
National Service Industries, Inc.
National Starch & Chemical Co.
Nationwide Insurance Co.
NEC America, Inc.
New York Times Co.
Newport News Shipbuilding
Nike, Inc.
Nissan North America, Inc.
Norfolk Southern Corp.
Nortel
Norton Co.
Novartis Corporation
Nucor Corp.
Oracle Corp.
Outboard Marine Corp.
Owens Corning
Owens-Illinois Inc.
Pacific Mutual Life Insurance Co.
Parker Hannifin Corp.
Phelps Dodge Corp.
Philip Morris Companies Inc.
Pioneer Hi-Bred International, Inc.
Premark International Inc.
Procter & Gamble Co.
Prudential Insurance Co. of America
Pulitzer Publishing Co.
REI-Recreational Equipment, Inc.
Reilly Industries, Inc.
Reynolds Metals Co.
Reynolds Tobacco (R.J.)
Rockwell International Corp.
Royal & SunAlliance USA, Inc.
Ruddick Corp.
Sara Lee Corp.
Sara Lee Hosiery, Inc.
Sears, Roebuck and Co.
Shaw Industries Inc.
Smith Corp. (A.O.)
SmithKline Beecham Corp.
Smurfit-Stone Container Corp.
Sonoco Products Co.
Sotheby's Inc.
Springs Industries, Inc.
Sprint Corp.
Square D Co.
Standard Products Co.
Stanley Works (The)
State Street Bank & Trust Co.
Steelcase Inc.
Stone Container Corp.
Stonecutter Mills Corp.
Sun Microsystems Inc.
Tenet Healthcare Corp.
Tension Envelope Corp.
Texas Instruments Inc.
Textron Inc.
Thomasville Furniture Industries Inc.
Timken Co. (The)
Trustmark Insurance Co.
Tyson Foods Inc.
Union Camp Corp.
Union Carbide Corp.
United Dominion Industries, Ltd.
United Parcel Service of America Inc.
Universal Leaf Tobacco Co., Inc.
Valspar Corp.
Vulcan Materials Co.
Wachovia Bank of North Carolina NA
Wal-Mart Stores, Inc.
West Co. Inc.
Westvaco Corp.
Weyerhaeuser Co.
Williams
Winn-Dixie Stores Inc.
Young & Rubicam

North Dakota

Bucyrus-Erie Co.
Burlington Resources, Inc.
Diebold, Inc.
Employers Mutual Casualty Co.
Frontier Corp.
Knight Ridder
Lee Enterprises
Meredith Corp.
Monsanto Co.
Northern States Power Co.
Northrop Grumman Corp.
Norwest Corp.
Pioneer Hi-Bred International, Inc.
Pioneer Natural Resources
Saint Paul Companies Inc.
SuperValu, Inc.
Target Corp.
Tenneco Automotive
United Parcel Service of America Inc.
U.S. Bancorp
U.S. Bancorp Piper Jaffray
US West, Inc.

Ohio

7-Eleven, Inc.
ABB Inc.
ABC
Advanced Micro Devices, Inc.
Aetna, Inc.
Agrilink Foods, Inc.
Air Products and Chemicals, Inc.
AK Steel Corp.
Alcoa Inc.
ALLTEL Corp.
American Electric Power
American Express Co.
American Honda Motor Co., Inc.
American Standard Inc.
American United Life Insurance Co.
Ameritech Corp.
Ameritech Ohio
AMETEK, Inc.
Andersons Inc.
Anheuser-Busch Companies, Inc.
Appleton Papers Inc.
Archer-Daniels-Midland Co.
Aristech Chemical Corp.
Ashland, Inc.
AT&T Corp.
Autodesk Inc.
Avery Dennison Corp.
Avon Products, Inc.
Badger Meter, Inc.
Ball Corp.
Bandag, Inc.
Bard, Inc. (C.R.)
Bardes Corp.
Barnes Group Inc.
Barry Corp. (R.G.)
Battelle Memorial Institute
Baxter International Inc.
Bayer Corp.
Beckman Coulter, Inc.
Bemis Co., Inc.
BFGoodrich Co.
Boeing Co.
Borden, Inc.
Bridgestone/Firestone, Inc.
Broderbund Software, Inc.
Browning-Ferris Industries Inc.
Butler Manufacturing Co.
Cadence Designs Systems, Inc.
Campbell Soup Co.
Carpenter Technology Corp.
Carrier Corp.
Central Soya Co.
CertainTeed Corp.
Cessna Aircraft Co.
Champion International Corp.
Chemed Corp.
Chesapeake Corp.
Church & Dwight Co., Inc.
Cincinnati Bell Inc.
Cinergy Corp.
Circuit City Stores, Inc.
CLARCOR Inc.
Cleveland-Cliffs, Inc.
Clorox Co.
CNF Transportation, Inc.
Coca-Cola Co.
Colgate-Palmolive Co.
Collins & Aikman Corp.
Comerica Inc.
Commercial Intertech Corp.
Computer Associates International, Inc.
Consolidated Natural Gas Co.
Cooper Industries, Inc.
Cooper Tire & Rubber Co.
Cox Enterprises Inc.
Crane Co.
CSX Corp.
Cummins Engine Co., Inc.
DaimlerChrysler Corp.
Dana Corp.
Danis Companies
Dayton Hudson
Dayton Power and Light Co.
Deloitte & Touche
Delta Air Lines, Inc.
Deluxe Corp.
Dexter Corp.
Diebold, Inc.
Donaldson Co., Inc.
Donnelley & Sons Co. (R.R.)
Dow Chemical Co.
Dow Jones & Co., Inc.
DSM Copolymer
du Pont de Nemours & Co. (E.I.)
Duriron Co., Inc.
Eastman Kodak Co.
Eaton Corp.
Ecolab Inc.
EDS Corp.
Elf Atochem North America, Inc.
Erb Lumber Co.
Ernst & Young, LLP
Extendicare Health Services
Fannie Mae
Farmers Group, Inc.
Federal-Mogul Corp.
Federated Department Stores, Inc.
FedEx Corp.
Ferro Corp.
Fidelity Investments
Fifth Third Bancorp
Fireman's Fund Insurance Co.
FirstEnergy Corp.
Fisher Scientific
Fluor Corp.
Forest City Enterprises, Inc.
Fort James Corp.
Fortune Brands, Inc.
Fuller Co. (H.B.)
Gannett Co., Inc.
GATX Corp.
GenCorp
General Electric Co.
General Mills, Inc.
General Motors Corp.
Georgia-Pacific Corp.
Gerber Products Co.
Gillette Co.
Grace & Co. (W.R.)
Hanna Co. (M.A.)
Harris Corp.
Harsco Corp.
Hartford (The)
Hasbro, Inc.
Heinz Co. (H.J.)
Hercules Inc.
Hewlett-Packard Co.
Hitachi America Ltd.
Hubbell Inc.
Huffy Corp.
Humana, Inc.
IKON Office Solutions, Inc.
Illinois Tool Works, Inc.
Inland Container Corp.
International Business Machines Corp.
International Multifoods Corp.
International Paper Co.
Invacare Corp.
Jeld-wen, Inc.
Johnson Controls Inc.
Johnson & Johnson
Johnson & Son (S.C.)
Kemper National Insurance Companies
Kendall International, Inc.
Key Bank of Cleveland
Kimberly-Clark Corp.
Knight Ridder
KPMG Peat Marwick LLP
Kroger Co.
Lancaster Lens, Inc.
Lennox International, Inc.
Levi Strauss & Co.
Liberty Corp.
Lilly & Co. (Eli)
Lincoln Electric Co.
Litton Industries, Inc.
Lockheed Martin Corp.
Loctite Corp.
Lotus Development Corp.
Louisiana-Pacific Corp.
LTV Corp.
Lubrizol Corp. (The)
MacMillan Bloedel Inc.
Macy's East Inc.
Marcus Corp.
Mark IV Industries
Marshall Field's
Masco Corp.
May Department Stores Co.
Maytag Corp.
McDermott Inc.
McDonald & Co. Securities, Inc.
McGraw-Hill Companies, Inc.
McWane Inc.
Mead Corp.

Medtronic, Inc.
Meijer, Inc.
Menasha Corp.
Mercantile Bank NA
Microsoft Corp.
Milacron, Inc.
Milliken & Co.
Minnesota Mining & Manufacturing Co.
Mitsubishi Electric America
Monarch Machine Tool Co.
Monsanto Co.
Morrison Knudsen Corp.
Morton International Inc.
MTD Products Inc.
Nalco Chemical Co.
National City Bank of Columbus
National City Corp.
National Machinery Co.
National Starch & Chemical Co.
Nationwide Insurance Co.
NCR Corp.
Nestle U.S.A. Inc.
Newport News Shipbuilding
Nordson Corp.
Northrop Grumman Corp.
Norton Co.
Norwest Corp.
Novartis Corporation
Ohio National Life Insurance Co.
Oracle Corp.
Owens Corning
Owens-Illinois Inc.
PACCAR Inc.
Pacific Mutual Life Insurance Co.
Park National Bank
Parker Hannifin Corp.
Pentair Inc.
PerkinElmer, Inc.
Phelps Dodge Corp.
Philip Morris Companies Inc.
Philips Electronics North America Corp.
Pillsbury Co.
Pioneer Hi-Bred International, Inc.
Pitney Bowes Inc.
Pittway Corp.
PPG Industries, Inc.
Premark International Inc.
Premier Industrial Corp.
Procter & Gamble Co.
Prudential Insurance Co. of America
Ralston Purina Co.
Reynolds Metals Co.
Reynolds & Reynolds Co.
Rich Products Corp.
Rockwell International Corp.
Roseburg Forest Products Co.
Rouse Co.
SAFECO Corp.
Saint Paul Companies Inc.
Sara Lee Corp.
Scripps Co. (E.W.)
Seagram & Sons, Inc. (Joseph E.)
Sears, Roebuck and Co.
Seaway Food Town, Inc.
S.G. Cowen
Shaw Industries Inc.
Shell Oil Co.
Sherwin-Williams Co.
Smith Corp. (A.O.)
Smucker Co. (JM)
Smurfit-Stone Container Corp.
Sprint Corp.
Sprint/United Telephone
SPX Corp.
Square D Co.
Standard Products Co.
Standard Register Co.
Stanley Works (The)
Star Bank NA
Starwood Hotels & Resorts Worldwide, Inc.
State Farm Mutual Automobile Insurance Co.
Stone Container Corp.
Sun Microsystems Inc.
Sunoco Inc.
SuperValu, Inc.
Teleflex Inc.
Temple-Inland Inc.
Tenneco Automotive
Texas Gas Transmission Corp.
Texas Instruments Inc.
Textron Inc.
Thompson Co. (J. Walter)
Timken Co. (The)
Toledo Blade Co.
Tomkins Industries, Inc.
Transamerica Corp.
Trustmark Insurance Co.
TRW Inc.
Unilever United States, Inc.
Union Camp Corp.
Union Carbide Corp.
United Airlines Inc.
United Parcel Service of America Inc.
Unocal Corp.
USG Corp.
USX Corp.
Wal-Mart Stores, Inc.
Walgreen Co.
Western & Southern Life Insurance Co.
Westvaco Corp.
Weyerhaeuser Co.
Whirlpool Corp.
Whitman Corp.
Williams
Winn-Dixie Stores Inc.
Witco Corp.
Young & Rubicam

Oklahoma

Air Products and Chemicals, Inc.
Albertson's Inc.
American Express Co.
Anheuser-Busch Companies, Inc.
Armstrong World Industries, Inc.
Atlantic Richfield Co.
Baker Hughes Inc.
Baxter International Inc.
Belo Corp. (A.H.)
Blount International, Inc.
Blue Bell, Inc.
Boeing Co.
BP Amoco Corp.
Bridgestone/Firestone, Inc.
Burlington Resources, Inc.
Central & South West Services
Circuit City Stores, Inc.
Conoco, Inc.
Cox Enterprises Inc.
DaimlerChrysler Corp.
Dana Corp.
Deloitte & Touche
Delta Air Lines, Inc.
Deluxe Corp.
Diebold, Inc.
Donaldson Co., Inc.
Dow Jones & Co., Inc.
du Pont de Nemours & Co. (E.I.)
Eaton Corp.
Eckerd Corp.
Ecolab Inc.
EDS Corp.
Elf Atochem North America, Inc.
Equifax Inc.
Ernst & Young, LLP
FedEx Corp.
Fluor Corp.
FMC Corp.
Fuller Co. (H.B.)
Gannett Co., Inc.
General Motors Corp.
Georgia-Pacific Corp.
Halliburton Co.
Harsco Corp.
Hartford (The)
Hewlett-Packard Co.
Home Depot, Inc.
International Business Machines Corp.
Johnson Controls Inc.
Kerr-McGee Corp.
Kimberly-Clark Corp.
KPMG Peat Marwick LLP
Lincoln Electric Co.
Louisiana Land & Exploration Co.
Masco Corp.
Mead Corp.
Medtronic, Inc.
Mervyn's California
Metropolitan Life Insurance Co.
Minnesota Mining & Manufacturing Co.
Nalco Chemical Co.
Norfolk Southern Corp.
Northrop Grumman Corp.
Norwest Corp.
Occidental Oil and Gas
OG&E Electric Services
Oklahoma Publishing Co.
ONEOK, Inc.
Owens Corning
PACCAR Inc.
Parker Hannifin Corp.
PerkinElmer, Inc.
Prudential Insurance Co. of America
Public Service Co. of Oklahoma
Quaker Chemical Corp.
Rockwell International Corp.
Santa Fe International Corp.
SBC Communications Inc.
Scripps Co. (E.W.)
Starwood Hotels & Resorts Worldwide, Inc.
State Farm Mutual Automobile Insurance Co.
Stone Container Corp.
Stone & Webster Inc.
Sun Microsystems Inc.
Sunoco Inc.
Target Corp.
Temple-Inland Inc.
Tenneco Automotive
Texaco Inc.
Tyson Foods Inc.
Union Pacific Corp.
United Parcel Service of America Inc.
USG Corp.
Valmont Industries, Inc.
Wal-Mart Stores, Inc.
Western Resources Inc.
Weyerhaeuser Co.
Williams
Witco Corp.
Xerox Corp.

Oregon

ABC
Air Products and Chemicals, Inc.
Albertson's Inc.
American Express Co.
AMP Inc.
Appleton Papers Inc.
Armstrong World Industries, Inc.
Atlantic Richfield Co.
Avista Corporation
Berwind Group
Boeing Co.
Boise Cascade Corp.
Borden, Inc.
Browning-Ferris Industries Inc.
Cadence Designs Systems, Inc.
CGU Insurance
Chevron Corp.
Citibank Corp.
CNF Transportation, Inc.
CSX Corp.
DaimlerChrysler Corp.
Dain Bosworth Inc.
Deere & Co.
Deluxe Corp.
Diebold, Inc.
Donnelley & Sons Co. (R.R.)
Dun & Bradstreet Corp.
Eastman Kodak Co.
Equifax Inc.
Extendicare Health Services
Exxon Mobil Corp.
Fannie Mae
Farmers Group, Inc.
FedEx Corp.
Forest City Enterprises, Inc.
Fort James Corp.
Freightliner Corp.
Fuller Co. (H.B.)
GATX Corp.
General Mills, Inc.
Georgia-Pacific Corp.
Hamilton Sundstrand Corp.
Heinz Co. (H.J.)
Hercules Inc.
Home Depot, Inc.
Idaho Power Co.
IKON Office Solutions, Inc.
Intel Corp.
International Flavors & Fragrances Inc.
International Paper Co.
Johnson Controls Inc.
KPMG Peat Marwick LLP
Land O'Lakes, Inc.
Lee Enterprises
Lincoln Electric Co.
Litton Industries, Inc.
Louisiana-Pacific Corp.
Masco Corp.
May Department Stores Co.
Maytag Corp.
Menasha Corp.
Mervyn's California
Metropolitan Life Insurance Co.
Minnesota Mining & Manufacturing Co.
NEC America, Inc.
Nike, Inc.
Norfolk Southern Corp.
Northwest Natural Gas Co.
Oracle Corp.
Owens Corning
Owens-Illinois Inc.
Pacific Mutual Life Insurance Co.
PacifiCorp
Parker Hannifin Corp.
Philip Morris Companies Inc.
Portland General Electric Co.
Reebok International Ltd.
REI-Recreational Equipment, Inc.
Reynolds Metals Co.
Roseburg Forest Products Co.
Saint Paul Companies Inc.
Schlumberger Ltd. (USA)
Shaklee Corp.
Simpson Investment Co.
Smucker Co. (JM)
Smurfit-Stone Container Corp.
Sprint Corp.
Stanley Works (The)
State Farm Mutual Automobile Insurance Co.
Stone Container Corp.
Sun Microsystems Inc.
SuperValu, Inc.
Target Corp.
Tektronix, Inc.
Tenet Healthcare Corp.
Union Pacific Corp.
United Airlines Inc.
U.S. Bancorp Piper Jaffray
Unocal Corp.
Wal-Mart Stores, Inc.
Weyerhaeuser Co.
Witco Corp.

Pennsylvania

7-Eleven, Inc.
ABB Inc.
ABC
Advanced Micro Devices, Inc.
Agrilink Foods, Inc.
Air Products and Chemicals, Inc.
Alcoa Inc.
Alcon Laboratories, Inc.
Allegheny Technologies Inc.
AlliedSignal Inc.
American Express Co.
American General Finance
American United Life Insurance Co.
AMETEK, Inc.
AMP Inc.
Anheuser-Busch Companies, Inc.
Appleton Papers Inc.
Aristech Chemical Corp.
Armstrong World Industries, Inc.
Ashland, Inc.
AT&T Corp.
Avery Dennison Corp.
Ball Corp.
Barnes Group Inc.
Bausch & Lomb Inc.
Baxter International Inc.
Bayer Corp.
Bechtel Group, Inc.
Beckman Coulter, Inc.
Bell Atlantic Corp.
Bemis Co., Inc.
Berwind Group
Bestfoods
Bethlehem Steel Corp.

Binney & Smith Inc.
Binswanger Companies
Blount International, Inc.
Borden, Inc.
Brunswick Corp.
Butler Manufacturing Co.
Caesar's World, Inc.
Campbell Soup Co.
Carpenter Technology Corp.
Caterpillar Inc.
CertainTeed Corp.
CGU Insurance
Champion International Corp.
Chevron Corp.
CIGNA Corp.
Circuit City Stores, Inc.
CNA
CNF Transportation, Inc.
Coca-Cola Co.
Compaq Computer Corp.
Computer Associates International, Inc.
ConAgra, Inc.
Conectiv
Cooper Industries, Inc.
Cox Enterprises Inc.
Crane Co.
CSS Industries, Inc.
CSX Corp.
CUNA Mutual Group
Cyprus Amax Minerals Co.
DaimlerChrysler Corp.
Dana Corp.
Deloitte & Touche
Delta Air Lines, Inc.
Deluxe Corp.
Dial Corp.
Diebold, Inc.
Donaldson Co., Inc.
Donnelley & Sons Co. (R.R.)
Dow Jones & Co., Inc.
DSM Copolymer
du Pont de Nemours & Co. (E.I.)
Dun & Bradstreet Corp.
Duquesne Light Co.
Dynamet, Inc.
Eastman Kodak Co.
Eaton Corp.
Ebsco Industries, Inc.
Ecolab Inc.
Edison Brothers Stores, Inc.
EDS Corp.
Elf Atochem North America, Inc.
Emerson Electric Co.
Equifax Inc.
Equitable Resources, Inc.
Ernst & Young, LLP
European American Bank
Exxon Mobil Corp.
Fabri-Kal Corp.
Fannie Mae
Federal-Mogul Corp.
FedEx Corp.
Ferro Corp.
First Maryland Bancorp
First Union Bank
First Union National Bank, NA
FirstEnergy Corp.
Fisher Scientific
FMC Corp.
Forest City Enterprises, Inc.
Fort James Corp.
Franklin Mint (The)
Freightliner Corp.
Frontier Corp.
Gannett Co., Inc.
GATX Corp.
GenCorp
General Electric Co.
General Motors Corp.
General Reinsurance Corp.
Georgia-Pacific Corp.
Giant Eagle Inc.
Goldman Sachs Group
Golub Corp.
GPU Energy
GPU Inc.
Grace & Co. (W.R.)
Guardian Life Insurance Co. of America
Halliburton Co.
Hamilton Sundstrand Corp.
Hanna Co. (M.A.)
Harley-Davidson Co.
Harsco Corp.
Hartford (The)
Hartmarx Corp.
Heinz Co. (H.J.)
Hercules Inc.
Hershey Foods Corp.
Hewlett-Packard Co.
Home Depot, Inc.
HON Industries Inc.
Hubbell Inc.
Huffy Corp.
Hunt Manufacturing Co.
IKON Office Solutions, Inc.
Illinois Tool Works, Inc.
Inland Container Corp.
International Business Machines Corp.
International Paper Co.
Jeld-wen, Inc.
Johnson Controls Inc.
Johnson & Johnson
Jostens, Inc.
Kaman Corp.
Kellogg Co.
Kennametal, Inc.
Kimberly-Clark Corp.
Knight Ridder
KPMG Peat Marwick LLP
Kraft Foods, Inc.
Lehigh Portland Cement Co.
Liberty Mutual Insurance Group
Lilly & Co. (Eli)
Lincoln Electric Co.
Lipton Co.
Little, Inc. (Arthur D.)
Litton Industries, Inc.
Lockheed Martin Corp.
Loews Corp.
Lotus Development Corp.
Louisiana-Pacific Corp.
LTV Corp.
Mallinckrodt Chemical, Inc.
Masco Corp.
May Department Stores Co.
McClatchy Co.
McCormick & Co. Inc.
McDonald & Co. Securities, Inc.
McGraw-Hill Companies, Inc.
Mead Corp.
Medtronic, Inc.
Mellon Financial Corp.
Menasha Corp.
Merck & Co.
Metropolitan Life Insurance Co.
Milacron, Inc.
Millipore Corp.
Mine Safety Appliances Co.
Minnesota Mining & Manufacturing Co.
Mitsubishi Electric America
Morton International Inc.
Motorola Inc.
Nalco Chemical Co.
National City Bank of Pennsylvania
National Computer Systems, Inc.
National Fuel Gas Distribution Corp.
Nationwide Insurance Co.
New York Times Co.
Newport News Shipbuilding
Nike, Inc.
Norfolk Southern Corp.
Northrop Grumman Corp.
Norton Co.
Norwest Corp.
Olin Corp.
Oracle Corp.
Orange & Rockland Utilities, Inc.
Owens Corning
Owens-Illinois Inc.
PECO Energy Co.
Penn Mutual Life Insurance Co.
Pennsylvania Power & Light
Pennzoil-Quaker State Co.
PerkinElmer, Inc.
Pfizer Inc.
Philip Morris Companies Inc.
Pillsbury Co.
Pioneer Hi-Bred International, Inc.
PNC Bank
PNC Financial Services Group
Potomac Electric Power Co.
PPG Industries, Inc.
Premier Dental Products Co.
Procter & Gamble Co.
Provident Mutual Life Insurance Co.
Prudential Insurance Co. of America
Quaker Chemical Corp.
REI-Recreational Equipment, Inc.
Reynolds Metals Co.
Rite Aid Corp.
Rockwell International Corp.
Rohm & Haas Co.
Rouse Co.
Royal & SunAlliance USA, Inc.
S&T Bancorp
Sara Lee Corp.
Schlumberger Ltd. (USA)
Sears, Roebuck and Co.
Shaw Industries Inc.
Shell Oil Co.
Sherwin-Williams Co.
Simpson Investment Co.
SmithKline Beecham Corp.
Smucker Co. (JM)
Sony Electronics
Sotheby's Inc.
Sovereign Bank
Sprint Corp.
SPX Corp.
Square D Co.
Standard Products Co.
Standard Register Co.
Stanley Works (The)
Starwood Hotels & Resorts Worldwide, Inc.
State Street Bank & Trust Co.
Stone Container Corp.
Sun Microsystems Inc.
Sunoco Inc.
SuperValu, Inc.
Susquehanna-Pfaltzgraff Co.
Target Corp.
Teleflex Inc.
Temple-Inland Inc.
Tenneco Automotive
Textron Inc.
Times Mirror Co.
Timken Co. (The)
Tomkins Industries, Inc.
True North Communications, Inc.
Trustmark Insurance Co.
Tyson Foods Inc.
Union Camp Corp.
Union Carbide Corp.
Union Pacific Corp.
Unisys Corp.
United Airlines Inc.
United Parcel Service of America Inc.
Universal Studios
USX Corp.
Vanguard Group
Vesper Corp.
Walgreen Co.
West Co. Inc.
Westvaco Corp.
Weyerhaeuser Co.
Whitman Corp.
Witco Corp.
Zurn Industries, Inc.

Puerto Rico

Amgen, Inc.
Avon Products, Inc.
Baxter International Inc.
Bayer Corp.
Bestfoods
Browning-Ferris Industries Inc.
ConAgra, Inc.
Credit Suisse First Boston
Ecolab Inc.
Exxon Mobil Corp.
Gerber Products Co.
Hamilton Sundstrand Corp.
Hanna Co. (M.A.)
Harcourt General, Inc.
Heinz Co. (H.J.)
Hubbell Inc.
Johnson & Johnson
Loctite Corp.
Medtronic, Inc.
Metropolitan Life Insurance Co.
Millipore Corp.
Motorola Inc.
Pharmacia & Upjohn, Inc.
Phillips Petroleum Co.
Polaroid Corp.
Reynolds Tobacco (R.J.)
Schering-Plough Corp.
Sherwin-Williams Co.
Sonoco Products Co.
Sotheby's Inc.
Storage Technology Corp.
Temple-Inland Inc.
Texaco Inc.
True North Communications, Inc.
Unilever Home & Personal Care U.S.A.
Unilever United States, Inc.
Union Carbide Corp.
Wal-Mart Stores, Inc.
West Co. Inc.
Wolverine World Wide

Rhode Island

7-Eleven, Inc.
ABC
American Express Co.
BankBoston-Connecticut Region
Baxter International Inc.
Ben & Jerry's Homemade Inc.
Bestfoods
Borden, Inc.
Circuit City Stores, Inc.
Citizens Financial Group, Inc.
Computer Associates International, Inc.
Country Curtains, Inc.
Cox Enterprises Inc.
Cranston Print Works Co.
Diebold, Inc.
Dow Jones & Co., Inc.
EDS Corp.
Ernst & Young, LLP
FleetBoston Financial Corp.
Hasbro, Inc.
Home Depot, Inc.
KPMG Peat Marwick LLP
Louisiana-Pacific Corp.
Mark IV Industries
McCormick & Co. Inc.
Mellon Financial Corp.
Mine Safety Appliances Co.
NEC America, Inc.
New York Times Co.
PerkinElmer, Inc.
Philips Electronics North America Corp.
Providence Journal-Bulletin Co.
Stanley Works (The)
Textron Inc.
Torchmark Corp.
UST Inc.
Wal-Mart Stores, Inc.

South Carolina

Air Products and Chemicals, Inc.
Albany International Corp.
Alcoa Inc.
American United Life Insurance Co.
Archer-Daniels-Midland Co.
Armstrong World Industries, Inc.
Bard, Inc. (C.R.)
Battelle Memorial Institute
Bausch & Lomb Inc.
Baxter International Inc.
Bayer Corp.
Bechtel Group, Inc.
Becton Dickinson & Co.
Belk-Simpson Department Stores
Belk Stores Services Inc.
BellSouth Telecommunications
Blount International, Inc.
Bowater Inc.
Burlington Industries, Inc.
Carolina Power & Light Co.
Carpenter Technology Corp.
CCB Financial Corp.
Central Soya Co.
CertainTeed Corp.
Champion International Corp.
Church & Dwight Co., Inc.
Citibank Corp.
Colonial Life & Accident Insurance Co.
Computer Associates International, Inc.
ConAgra, Inc.
Cooper Industries, Inc.
Cox Enterprises Inc.
CSX Corp.
Cummins Engine Co., Inc.
DaimlerChrysler Corp.

Dana Corp.
Deere & Co.
Deloitte & Touche
Delta Air Lines, Inc.
Dexter Corp.
Diebold, Inc.
Donnelley & Sons Co. (R.R.)
Dow Corning Corp.
du Pont de Nemours & Co. (E.I.)
Duke Energy
Duracell International
Eastman Kodak Co.
Eaton Corp.
Eckerd Corp.
Ecolab Inc.
Elf Atochem North America, Inc.
Equifax Inc.
Ernst & Young, LLP
Evening Post Publishing Co.
Fabri-Kal Corp.
Federal-Mogul Corp.
First Union Corp.
Fluor Corp.
FMC Corp.
Fort James Corp.
Gannett Co., Inc.
General Electric Co.
Georgia-Pacific Corp.
Grace & Co. (W.R.)
Hasbro, Inc.
Hercules Inc.
Hewlett-Packard Co.
Hubbell Inc.
IKON Office Solutions, Inc.
Inland Container Corp.
Inman Mills
International Business Machines Corp.
International Paper Co.
Johnson Controls Inc.
Jostens, Inc.
Kendall International, Inc.
Kimberly-Clark Corp.
Knight Ridder
Kohler Co.
Kraft Foods, Inc.
La-Z-Boy Inc.
Lance, Inc.
Liberty Corp.
Lincoln Electric Co.
Litton Industries, Inc.
Louisiana-Pacific Corp.
Marcus Corp.
Masco Corp.
Mead Corp.
Medtronic, Inc.
Milacron, Inc.
Milliken & Co.
Minnesota Mining & Manufacturing Co.
Morton International Inc.
Motorola Inc.
Nalco Chemical Co.
Nationwide Insurance Co.
NCR Corp.
Nestle U.S.A. Inc.
New York Times Co.
Norfolk Southern Corp.
Norton Co.
Nucor Corp.
Olin Corp.
Outboard Marine Corp.
Owens Corning
Owens-Illinois Inc.
Parker Hannifin Corp.
Philip Morris Companies Inc.
Phillips Petroleum Co.
Pioneer Hi-Bred International, Inc.
Premark International Inc.
Premier Industrial Corp.
Procter & Gamble Co.
Pulitzer Publishing Co.
Rockwell International Corp.
Sara Lee Corp.
Sara Lee Hosiery, Inc.
SCANA Corp.
Scripps Co. (E.W.)
Shell Oil Co.
Smith Corp. (A.O.)
SmithKline Beecham Corp.
Sonoco Products Co.
Springs Industries, Inc.
Sprint Corp.
Square D Co.
Standard Products Co.
Starwood Hotels & Resorts Worldwide, Inc.
Stone Container Corp.
SuperValu, Inc.
Target Corp.
Temple-Inland Inc.
Tenet Healthcare Corp.
Textron Inc.
Timken Co. (The)
Union Camp Corp.
UnumProvident
Vulcan Materials Co.
Wal-Mart Stores, Inc.
Warner-Lambert Co.
Westvaco Corp.
Whirlpool Corp.
Williams
Winn-Dixie Stores Inc.

South Dakota

American United Life Insurance Co.
Butler Manufacturing Co.
Citibank Corp.
Dain Bosworth Inc.
FMC Corp.
Gannett Co., Inc.
International Business Machines Corp.
Knight Ridder
Land O'Lakes, Inc.
Masco Corp.
Minnesota Mining & Manufacturing Co.
Morris Communications Corp.
Nalco Chemical Co.
Northern States Power Co.
Norwest Corp.
Pioneer Hi-Bred International, Inc.
Reliant Energy Minnegasco
Royal & SunAlliance USA, Inc.
Toshiba America Inc.
U.S. Bancorp
U.S. Bancorp Piper Jaffray
US West, Inc.
Wal-Mart Stores, Inc.

Tennessee

AGL Resources Inc.
Air Products and Chemicals, Inc.
Albertson's Inc.
Alcoa Inc.
American Electric Power
American General Finance
American United Life Insurance Co.
Anheuser-Busch Companies, Inc.
Aon Corp.
Apple Computer, Inc.
Appleton Papers Inc.
Armstrong World Industries, Inc.
ASARCO Inc.
Avery Dennison Corp.
Barnes Group Inc.
Battelle Memorial Institute
Bechtel Group, Inc.
Beckman Coulter, Inc.
BellSouth Telecommunications
Berwind Group
Boeing Co.
Bowater Inc.
Bradford & Co. (J.C.)
Bridgestone/Firestone, Inc.
Browning-Ferris Industries Inc.
Burlington Industries, Inc.
Cargill Inc.
Carolina Power & Light Co.
Carrier Corp.
Champion International Corp.
Circuit City Stores, Inc.
CLARCOR Inc.
CNA
CNF Transportation, Inc.
ConAgra, Inc.
Conwood Co. LP
Cooper Industries, Inc.
CSX Corp.
Cummins Engine Co., Inc.
Dana Corp.
Deloitte & Touche
Delta Air Lines, Inc.
Deluxe Corp.
Diebold, Inc.
Donnelley & Sons Co. (R.R.)
du Pont de Nemours & Co. (E.I.)
Dun & Bradstreet Corp.
Duracell International
Duriron Co., Inc.
Eastman Kodak Co.
Eaton Corp.
Ecolab Inc.
EDS Corp.
Emerson Electric Co.
EMI Music Publishing
Equitable Resources, Inc.
Ernst & Young, LLP
Federal-Mogul Corp.
First Tennessee National Corp.
First Union Corp.
Fisher Scientific
Fluor Corp.
Fuller Co. (H.B.)
Gannett Co., Inc.
GenCorp
General Mills, Inc.
General Motors Corp.
Gerber Products Co.
Grace & Co. (W.R.)
Hanna Co. (M.A.)
Harsco Corp.
Hewlett-Packard Co.
Hitachi America Ltd.
Home Depot, Inc.
Illinois Tool Works, Inc.
Ingram Industries Inc.
Inland Container Corp.
International Business Machines Corp.
International Paper Co.
Johnson Controls Inc.
Johnson & Son (S.C.)
Jostens, Inc.
Kellogg Co.
Kennametal, Inc.
Kimball International, Inc.
Kimberly-Clark Corp.
KPMG Peat Marwick LLP
Kraft Foods, Inc.
Kroger Co.
La-Z-Boy Inc.
Levi Strauss & Co.
Lilly & Co. (Eli)
Lincoln Electric Co.
Lincoln Financial Group
Litton Industries, Inc.
Lockheed Martin Corp.
Loews Corp.
Lotus Development Corp.
Marcus Corp.
Masco Corp.
Mattel Inc.
Maybelline, Inc.
Maytag Corp.
McDonald & Co. Securities, Inc.
McKesson-HBOC Corp.
Mead Corp.
Medtronic, Inc.
Memphis Light Gas & Water Division
Minnesota Mining & Manufacturing Co.
Monsanto Co.
Morton International Inc.
MTD Products Inc.
Nalco Chemical Co.
National Starch & Chemical Co.
Nationwide Insurance Co.
NEC America, Inc.
New York Times Co.
Newport News Shipbuilding
Nike, Inc.
Nissan North America, Inc.
Norfolk Southern Corp.
Nortel
North American Royalties
Norton Co.
Olin Corp.
Oracle Corp.
Osborne Enterprises
Oshkosh B'Gosh, Inc.
Outboard Marine Corp.
Owens Corning
Owens-Illinois Inc.
PACCAR Inc.
Pacific Mutual Life Insurance Co.
Parker Hannifin Corp.
Philip Morris Companies Inc.
Philips Electronics North America Corp.
Pillsbury Co.
Pioneer Hi-Bred International, Inc.
Premark International Inc.
Promus Hotel Corp.
Provident Companies, Inc.
Prudential Insurance Co. of America
Ralston Purina Co.
Reebok International Ltd.
Reynolds Metals Co.
Rich Products Corp.
Rockwell International Corp.
Rohm & Haas Co.
SAFECO Corp.
Sara Lee Corp.
Schering-Plough Corp.
Scripps Co. (E.W.)
Sharp Electronics Corp.
Shaw Industries Inc.
Shell Oil Co.
Shoney's Inc.
Smith Corp. (A.O.)
SmithKline Beecham Corp.
Sony Electronics
Springs Industries, Inc.
Sprint Corp.
Square D Co.
Standard Register Co.
Stanley Works (The)
State Farm Mutual Automobile Insurance Co.
State Street Bank & Trust Co.
Stone Container Corp.
Sun Microsystems Inc.
Target Corp.
Temple-Inland Inc.
Tenet Healthcare Corp.
Tenneco Automotive
Tension Envelope Corp.
Texas Gas Transmission Corp.
Texas Instruments Inc.
Textron Inc.
Thomasville Furniture Industries Inc.
Timken Co. (The)
Tomkins Industries, Inc.
TRW Inc.
Tyson Foods Inc.
Unilever United States, Inc.
Union Planters Corp.
United Distillers & Vintners North America
United Parcel Service of America Inc.
United Technologies Corp.
UST Inc.
Vulcan Materials Co.
Westvaco Corp.
Whirlpool Corp.
Witco Corp.

Texas

7-Eleven, Inc.
ABB Inc.
ABC
Advanced Micro Devices, Inc.
Aetna, Inc.
Agrilink Foods, Inc.
Air Products and Chemicals, Inc.
Albertson's Inc.
Alcoa Inc.
Alcon Laboratories, Inc.
Alliant Techsystems
Allianz Life Insurance Co. of North America
AlliedSignal Inc.
America West Airlines, Inc.
American Express Co.
American General Corp.
American United Life Insurance Co.
Ameritech Corp.
AMR Corp.
Anheuser-Busch Companies, Inc.
Aon Corp.
Apple Computer, Inc.
Appleton Papers Inc.
Archer-Daniels-Midland Co.
Aristech Chemical Corp.
Armstrong World Industries, Inc.
ASARCO Inc.
AT&T Corp.
Atlantic Richfield Co.
Autodesk Inc.
Avery Dennison Corp.
Badger Meter, Inc.
Baker Hughes Inc.
Bandag, Inc.
Bank of America
Bank One, Texas-Houston Office

Bank One, Texas, NA
Barnes Group Inc.
Battelle Memorial Institute
Bausch & Lomb Inc.
Baxter International Inc.
Bayer Corp.
Belk Stores Services Inc.
Belo Corp. (A.H.)
Bemis Co., Inc.
BFGoodrich Co.
Blount International, Inc.
Blue Bell, Inc.
Boeing Co.
Borden, Inc.
BP Amoco Corp.
Bridgestone/Firestone, Inc.
Bristol-Myers Squibb Co.
Broderbund Software, Inc.
Browning-Ferris Industries Inc.
Burlington Resources, Inc.
Cadence Designs Systems, Inc.
California Bank & Trust
Campbell Soup Co.
Carrier Corp.
Caterpillar Inc.
Central & South West Services
CertainTeed Corp.
Champion International Corp.
Chase Bank of Texas
Chase Manhattan Bank, NA
Chevron Corp.
Chicago Tribune Co.
Church & Dwight Co., Inc.
CIBC Oppenheimer
Circuit City Stores, Inc.
CIT Group, Inc. (The)
Citibank Corp.
Citigroup
CLARCOR Inc.
Cleveland-Cliffs, Inc.
Clorox Co.
CNF Transportation, Inc.
Comerica Inc.
Compaq Computer Corp.
Compass Bank
Computer Associates International, Inc.
ConAgra, Inc.
Conoco, Inc.
Contran Corp.
Cooper Industries, Inc.
Cox Enterprises Inc.
CSR Rinker Materials Corp.
Cummins Engine Co., Inc.
CUNA Mutual Group
DaimlerChrysler Corp.
Dana Corp.
Dayton Hudson
Deere & Co.
Deloitte & Touche
Delta Air Lines, Inc.
Deluxe Corp.
Dexter Corp.
Diebold, Inc.
Donaldson Co., Inc.
Donnelley & Sons Co. (R.R.)
Dow Chemical Co.
Dow Jones & Co., Inc.
DSM Copolymer
du Pont de Nemours & Co. (E.I.)
Eastman Chemical Co.
Eastman Kodak Co.
Eaton Corp.
Ebsco Industries, Inc.
Eckerd Corp.
Ecolab Inc.
EDS Corp.
El Paso Energy Co.
Elf Atochem North America, Inc.
Emerson Electric Co.
Entergy Corp.
Equifax Inc.
Ernst & Young, LLP
Ethyl Corp.
European American Bank
Extendicare Health Services
Exxon Mobil Corp.
Fannie Mae
Farmers Group, Inc.
FedEx Corp.
Ferro Corp.
Fidelity Investments
FINA
Fireman's Fund Insurance Co.
Fluor Corp.
FMC Corp.
Fort James Corp.
Fort Worth Star-Telegram Inc.
Fortune Brands, Inc.
Fox Entertainment Group
Freddie Mac
Frito-Lay, Inc.
Frost National Bank
Fuller Co. (H.B.)
GATX Corp.
GEICO Corp.
General Dynamics Corp.
General Mills, Inc.
General Motors Corp.
Georgia-Pacific Corp.
Gerber Products Co.
Goldman Sachs Group
Grace & Co. (W.R.)
Graco, Inc.
GTE Corp.
Gucci America Inc.
Halliburton Co.
Hanna Co. (M.A.)
Harcourt General, Inc.
Harris Trust & Savings Bank
Harsco Corp.
Hartford (The)
Hartford Steam Boiler Inspection & Insurance Co.
Hasbro, Inc.
Heinz Co. (H.J.)
Heller Financial, Inc.
Hercules Inc.
Hewlett-Packard Co.
Hitachi America Ltd.
Home Depot, Inc.
HON Industries Inc.
Humana, Inc.
Hunt Manufacturing Co.
Hunt Oil Co.
IKON Office Solutions, Inc.
Illinois Tool Works, Inc.
Industrial Bank of Japan Trust Co. (New York)
Inland Container Corp.
Intel Corp.
International Business Machines Corp.
International Flavors & Fragrances Inc.
International Multifoods Corp.
International Paper Co.
Interpublic Group of Companies, Inc.
Johnson Controls Inc.
Johnson & Johnson
Johnson & Son (S.C.)
Jostens, Inc.
Kellogg Co.
Kerr-McGee Corp.
Kimball International, Inc.
Kimberly-Clark Corp.
Kohler Co.
KPMG Peat Marwick LLP
Kraft Foods, Inc.
Kroger Co.
Lennox International, Inc.
Levi Strauss & Co.
Liberty Mutual Insurance Group
Lilly & Co. (Eli)
Little, Inc. (Arthur D.)
Litton Industries, Inc.
Liz Claiborne, Inc.
Lockheed Martin Corp.
Loews Corp.
Lotus Development Corp.
Louisiana Land & Exploration Co.
Louisiana-Pacific Corp.
LTV Corp.
Lubrizol Corp. (The)
Lyondell Chemical Co.
Marcus Corp.
Maritz Inc.
Mark IV Industries
Mattel Inc.
Maytag Corp.
Mazda North American Operations
McCormick & Co. Inc.
McDermott Inc.
Medtronic, Inc.
Mellon Financial Corp.
Mervyn's California
Metropolitan Life Insurance Co.
Microsoft Corp.
Minnesota Mining & Manufacturing Co.
Mitsubishi Electric America
Monsanto Co.
Montana Power Co.
Morgan Stanley Dean Witter & Co.
Morrison Knudsen Corp.
Motorola Inc.
MTD Products Inc.
Nalco Chemical Co.
National Starch & Chemical Co.
NEC America, Inc.
Nestle U.S.A. Inc.
New York Life Insurance Co.
Nike, Inc.
Norfolk Southern Corp.
Nortel
Northern Trust Co.
Northrop Grumman Corp.
Norton Co.
Norwest Corp.
Nucor Corp.
Occidental Oil and Gas
Occidental Petroleum Corp.
Olin Corp.
Oracle Corp.
Oshkosh B'Gosh, Inc.
Owens Corning
Owens-Illinois Inc.
PACCAR Inc.
Pacific Mutual Life Insurance Co.
Paine Webber
Parker Hannifin Corp.
Penney Co., Inc. (J.C.)
Pennzoil-Quaker State Co.
PepsiCo, Inc.
PerkinElmer, Inc.
Phelps Dodge Corp.
Philip Morris Companies Inc.
Philips Electronics North America Corp.
Phillips Petroleum Co.
Pioneer Hi-Bred International, Inc.
Pioneer Natural Resources
Pittway Corp.
Potomac Electric Power Co.
Premark International Inc.
Procter & Gamble Co.
Progressive Corp.
Prudential Insurance Co. of America
Public Service Co. of Oklahoma
Quaker Chemical Corp.
Quanex Corp.
REI-Recreational Equipment, Inc.
Reliant Energy Inc.
Reynolds Metals Co.
Rockwell International Corp.
Rohm & Haas Co.
Rouse Co.
Royal & SunAlliance USA, Inc.
Ryder System, Inc.
SAFECO Corp.
Saint Paul Companies Inc.
Salomon Smith Barney
Santa Fe International Corp.
Sara Lee Corp.
Schering-Plough Corp.
Schlumberger Ltd. (USA)
Scripps Co. (E.W.)
Security Life of Denver Insurance Co.
S.G. Cowen
Sharp Electronics Corp.
Shaw Industries Inc.
Shell Oil Co.
Sherwin-Williams Co.
Smith Corp. (A.O.)
SmithKline Beecham Corp.
Smurfit-Stone Container Corp.
Sony Electronics
Sotheby's Inc.
Sprint Corp.
Square D Co.
Standard Products Co.
Standard Register Co.
Stanley Works (The)
State Farm Mutual Automobile Insurance Co.
Stone Container Corp.
Stone & Webster Inc.
Storage Technology Corp.
Stride Rite Corp.
Sun Microsystems Inc.
Tandy Corp.
Target Corp.
Teleflex Inc.
Temple-Inland Inc.
Tenet Healthcare Corp.
Tenneco Automotive
Texaco Inc.
Texas Gas Transmission Corp.
Texas Instruments Inc.
Textron Inc.
Thompson Co. (J. Walter)
Times Mirror Co.
Timken Co. (The)
Tomkins Industries, Inc.
Torchmark Corp.
Toshiba America Inc.
Transamerica Corp.
Trustmark Insurance Co.
TRW Inc.
TU Electric Co.
Tucson Electric Power Co.
Tyson Foods Inc.
Ultramar Diamond Shamrock Corp.
Union Camp Corp.
Union Carbide Corp.
Union Pacific Corp.
Unisys Corp.
United Airlines Inc.
United Dominion Industries, Ltd.
United Parcel Service of America Inc.
Unocal Corp.
USG Corp.
UST Inc.
USX Corp.
Valero Energy Corp.
Valmont Industries, Inc.
Vodafone AirTouch Plc
Vulcan Materials Co.
Wal-Mart Stores, Inc.
Walgreen Co.
The Washington Post
Wells Fargo & Co.
Westvaco Corp.
Weyerhaeuser Co.
Whitman Corp.
Wilbur-Ellis Co. & Connell Brothers Co.
Williams
Winn-Dixie Stores Inc.
Witco Corp.
Xerox Corp.
Zenith Electronics Corp.

Utah

7-Eleven, Inc.
Abbott Laboratories
Air Products and Chemicals, Inc.
Albertson's Inc.
Alliant Techsystems
America West Airlines, Inc.
American Express Co.
ASARCO Inc.
Associated Food Stores
Atlantic Richfield Co.
Baker Hughes Inc.
Barnes Group Inc.
Battelle Memorial Institute
Baxter International Inc.
Boise Cascade Corp.
Browning-Ferris Industries Inc.
Campbell Soup Co.
Chevron Corp.
Computer Associates International, Inc.
Cyprus Amax Minerals Co.
Dain Bosworth Inc.
Dana Corp.
Dayton Hudson
Deloitte & Touche
Delta Air Lines, Inc.
Diebold, Inc.
Dow Jones & Co., Inc.
Dun & Bradstreet Corp.
Duriron Co., Inc.
Ecolab Inc.
Ernst & Young, LLP
FedEx Corp.
Fisher Scientific
GATX Corp.
Georgia-Pacific Corp.
Grace & Co. (W.R.)
IKON Office Solutions, Inc.
Kaman Corp.
Kendall International, Inc.
Kimberly-Clark Corp.
KPMG Peat Marwick LLP
La-Z-Boy Inc.
Land O'Lakes, Inc.
Litton Industries, Inc.
Lockheed Martin Corp.

Mark IV Industries
Mead Corp.
Medtronic, Inc.
Milliken & Co.
Minnesota Mining & Manufacturing Co.
Morton International Inc.
Nalco Chemical Co.
Nestle U.S.A. Inc.
Northrop Grumman Corp.
Norwest Corp.
Nucor Corp.
Oracle Corp.
Pacific Mutual Life Insurance Co.
Parker Hannifin Corp.
PerkinElmer, Inc.
Quanex Corp.
Questar Corp.
REI-Recreational Equipment, Inc.
Royal & SunAlliance USA, Inc.
Smurfit-Stone Container Corp.
Stone Container Corp.
Thompson Co. (J. Walter)
Timken Co. (The)
TRW Inc.
U.S. Bancorp Piper Jaffray
US West, Inc.
USG Corp.
Valmont Industries, Inc.
Varian Medical Systems, Inc.

Vermont

American Express Co.
BankBoston-Connecticut Region
Ben & Jerry's Homemade Inc.
Browning-Ferris Industries Inc.
Carris Reels
Central Vermont Public Service Corp.
ConAgra, Inc.
Diebold, Inc.
FedEx Corp.
Frontier Corp.
Gannett Co., Inc.
General Motors Corp.
Georgia-Pacific Corp.
Golub Corp.
Hannaford Brothers Co.
Hasbro, Inc.
Johnson Controls Inc.
KPMG Peat Marwick LLP
McCormick & Co. Inc.
Mervyn's California
National Life of Vermont
PerkinElmer, Inc.
Simpson Investment Co.
Standard Register Co.
Stanley Works (The)
Textron Inc.
Union Carbide Corp.

Virgin Islands

National Presto Industries, Inc.

Virginia

7-Eleven, Inc.
ABB Inc.
Abbott Laboratories
AFLAC Inc.
Air Products and Chemicals, Inc.
Alcoa Inc.
Allegheny Technologies Inc.
Alliant Techsystems
AlliedSignal Inc.
Allstate Insurance Co.
American Electric Power
American Express Co.
American Standard Inc.
AMP Inc.
Anheuser-Busch Companies, Inc.
Apple Computer, Inc.
Armstrong World Industries, Inc.
Ashland, Inc.
AT&T Corp.
Bausch & Lomb Inc.
Baxter International Inc.
Belk Stores Services Inc.
Bell Atlantic Corp.
Belo Corp. (A.H.)
Ben & Jerry's Homemade Inc.
Boeing Co.
BP Amoco Corp.
Browning-Ferris Industries Inc.
Burlington Industries, Inc.
Butler Manufacturing Co.
Champion International Corp.
Chesapeake Corp.
Circuit City Stores, Inc.
Citibank Corp.
Compaq Computer Corp.
Computer Associates International, Inc.
Conectiv
Consolidated Natural Gas Co.
Cooper Industries, Inc.
Country Curtains, Inc.
Cox Enterprises Inc.
Crestar Finance Corp.
CSX Corp.
Cyprus Amax Minerals Co.
DaimlerChrysler Corp.
Dana Corp.
Deloitte & Touche
Delta Air Lines, Inc.
Deluxe Corp.
Diebold, Inc.
Donnelley & Sons Co. (R.R.)
Dow Jones & Co., Inc.
DSM Copolymer
du Pont de Nemours & Co. (E.I.)
Dun & Bradstreet Corp.
Eastman Kodak Co.
Ecolab Inc.
EDS Corp.
Emerson Electric Co.
Equifax Inc.
Ernst & Young, LLP
Exxon Mobil Corp.
Federal-Mogul Corp.
FedEx Corp.
First Union Corp.
Fisher Scientific
Fluor Corp.
FMC Corp.
Fort James Corp.
Fortune Brands, Inc.
Freddie Mac
Gannett Co., Inc.
GEICO Corp.
General Dynamics Corp.
General Electric Co.
General Motors Corp.
Georgia-Pacific Corp.
Giant Food Inc.
Grace & Co. (W.R.)
Hannaford Brothers Co.
Hartford (The)
Heilig-Meyers Co.
Heinz Co. (H.J.)
Hercules Inc.
Hershey Foods Corp.
Hewlett-Packard Co.
Home Depot, Inc.
HON Industries Inc.
Hubbell Inc.
IKON Office Solutions, Inc.
Illinois Tool Works, Inc.
Inland Container Corp.
International Business Machines Corp.
Interpublic Group of Companies, Inc.
Kaman Corp.
KPMG Peat Marwick LLP
Kraft Foods, Inc.
Kroger Co.
Landmark Communications Inc.
Lehigh Portland Cement Co.
Levi Strauss & Co.
Lincoln Electric Co.
Lipton Co.
Litton Industries, Inc.
Lockheed Martin Corp.
Lotus Development Corp.
Masco Corp.
May Department Stores Co.
McCormick & Co. Inc.
McDermott Inc.
McDonald & Co. Securities, Inc.
Mead Corp.
Medtronic, Inc.
Mellon Financial Corp.
Menasha Corp.
Morton International Inc.
Nalco Chemical Co.
Nationwide Insurance Co.
NEC America, Inc.
Nestle U.S.A. Inc.
Newport News Shipbuilding
Northrop Grumman Corp.
Oracle Corp.
Overnite Transportation Co.
Owens Corning
Owens-Illinois Inc.
PerkinElmer, Inc.
Philip Morris Companies Inc.
Progressive Corp.
Prudential Insurance Co. of America
Reynolds Metals Co.
Riggs Bank NA
Rockwell International Corp.
Royal & SunAlliance USA, Inc.
SAFECO Corp.
Safeway Inc.
Sara Lee Corp.
Scripps Co. (E.W.)
Sharp Electronics Corp.
Shell Oil Co.
Sotheby's Inc.
Sprint Corp.
Stanley Works (The)
Starwood Hotels & Resorts Worldwide, Inc.
State Farm Mutual Automobile Insurance Co.
State Street Bank & Trust Co.
Stone Container Corp.
Sun Microsystems Inc.
Temple-Inland Inc.
Tenneco Automotive
Texas Instruments Inc.
Thomasville Furniture Industries Inc.
Timken Co. (The)
Toshiba America Inc.
TRW Inc.
Ukrop's Super Markets
Union Camp Corp.
Unisys Corp.
United Co.
United Parcel Service of America Inc.
United Technologies Corp.
Universal Leaf Tobacco Co., Inc.
USG Corp.
Vulcan Materials Co.
Wal-Mart Stores, Inc.
The Washington Post
Westvaco Corp.
Weyerhaeuser Co.
Williams
Winn-Dixie Stores Inc.
Xerox Corp.

Washington

Abbott Laboratories
ABC
Aetna, Inc.
Agrilink Foods, Inc.
Air Products and Chemicals, Inc.
Alaska Airlines, Inc.
Albany International Corp.
Albertson's Inc.
Alcoa Inc.
AlliedSignal Inc.
American Express Co.
Ameritech Corp.
AMETEK, Inc.
Atlantic Richfield Co.
Autodesk Inc.
Avista Corporation
Barnes Group Inc.
Battelle Memorial Institute
Baxter International Inc.
Belo Corp. (A.H.)
BFGoodrich Co.
Boeing Co.
Boise Cascade Corp.
Borden, Inc.
Bristol-Myers Squibb Co.
Burlington Industries, Inc.
Cadence Designs Systems, Inc.
California Bank & Trust
Caterpillar Inc.
CertainTeed Corp.
Chevron Corp.
Church & Dwight Co., Inc.
Citibank Corp.
CNF Transportation, Inc.
ConAgra, Inc.
Cooper Tire & Rubber Co.
Cox Enterprises Inc.
CUNA Mutual Group
Dain Bosworth Inc.
Dana Corp.
Dayton Hudson
Deloitte & Touche
Delta Air Lines, Inc.
Deluxe Corp.
Diebold, Inc.
Donaldson Co., Inc.
Donnelley & Sons Co. (R.R.)
Dow Corning Corp.
Dow Jones & Co., Inc.
Eastman Kodak Co.
Eaton Corp.
Ecolab Inc.
Edison Brothers Stores, Inc.
EDS Corp.
Elf Atochem North America, Inc.
Equifax Inc.
European American Bank
Extendicare Health Services
Fannie Mae
Farmers Group, Inc.
Federated Department Stores, Inc.
FMC Corp.
Fort James Corp.
Fortune Brands, Inc.
Fuller Co. (H.B.)
Gannett Co., Inc.
GATX Corp.
General Reinsurance Corp.
Georgia-Pacific Corp.
Goodrich Aerospace - Aerostructures Group (B.F.)
Grace & Co. (W.R.)
Guardian Life Insurance Co. of America
Hamilton Sundstrand Corp.
Hanna Co. (M.A.)
Hartford (The)
Heinz Co. (H.J.)
Heller Financial, Inc.
Hewlett-Packard Co.
Home Depot, Inc.
HON Industries Inc.
Hubbard Broadcasting, Inc.
IKON Office Solutions, Inc.
International Business Machines Corp.
International Multifoods Corp.
Interpublic Group of Companies, Inc.
Johnson Controls Inc.
Johnson & Son (S.C.)
Kimberly-Clark Corp.
KPMG Peat Marwick LLP
Land O'Lakes, Inc.
Leviton Manufacturing Co. Inc.
Lilly & Co. (Eli)
Lincoln Electric Co.
Lotus Development Corp.
Louisiana-Pacific Corp.
MacMillan Bloedel Inc.
Macy's East Inc.
Matsushita Electric Corp. of America
Maytag Corp.
McCormick & Co. Inc.
McGraw-Hill Companies, Inc.
McKesson-HBOC Corp.
Mead Corp.
Medtronic, Inc.
Menasha Corp.
Microsoft Corp.
Minnesota Mining & Manufacturing Co.
Monsanto Co.
Montana Power Co.
Morton International Inc.
Motorola Inc.
Nalco Chemical Co.
NEC America, Inc.
Newport News Shipbuilding
Norfolk Southern Corp.
Northrop Grumman Corp.
Novartis Corporation
Olin Corp.
Oracle Corp.
PACCAR Inc.
Pacific Mutual Life Insurance Co.
PacifiCorp
PEMCO Corp.
Philip Morris Companies Inc.
Phillips Petroleum Co.
Pioneer Hi-Bred International, Inc.
Premark International Inc.
Prudential Insurance Co. of America

Rayonier Inc.
REI-Recreational Equipment, Inc.
ReliaStar Financial Corp.
Reynolds Metals Co.
Rockwell International Corp.
Rouse Co.
SAFECO Corp.
Safeway Inc.
Saint Paul Companies Inc.
Sara Lee Corp.
Sharp Electronics Corp.
Shaw Industries Inc.
Simpson Investment Co.
Smith Corp. (A.O.)
SmithKline Beecham Corp.
Smucker Co. (JM)
Sotheby's Inc.
Sprint Corp.
Square D Co.
Sun Microsystems Inc.
SuperValu, Inc.
Target Corp.
Tektronix, Inc.
Tenneco Automotive
Texas Instruments Inc.
Tyson Foods Inc.
Unilever United States, Inc.
Union Camp Corp.
Union Pacific Corp.
United Airlines Inc.
United Parcel Service of America Inc.
U.S. Bancorp Piper Jaffray
Unocal Corp.
US Bank, Washington
US West, Inc.
USG Corp.
UST Inc.
Wal-Mart Stores, Inc.
Washington Trust Bank
Weyerhaeuser Co.
Zurn Industries, Inc.

West Virginia

7-Eleven, Inc.
ABB Inc.
Air Products and Chemicals, Inc.
American Electric Power
Aristech Chemical Corp.
Ashland, Inc.
AT&T Corp.
Ball Corp.
Belk Stores Services Inc.
Bell Atlantic Corp.
Bell Atlantic Corp.-West Virginia
Berwind Group
Bethlehem Steel Corp.
BFGoodrich Co.
Browning-Ferris Industries Inc.
Chubb Corp.
Circuit City Stores, Inc.
Consolidated Natural Gas Co.
CSX Corp.
Cyprus Amax Minerals Co.
Deloitte & Touche
Diebold, Inc.
du Pont de Nemours & Co. (E.I.)
EDS Corp.
Ernst & Young, LLP
FedEx Corp.
FMC Corp.
General Motors Corp.
Georgia-Pacific Corp.
Harsco Corp.
Heinz Co. (H.J.)
Hewlett-Packard Co.
International Business Machines Corp.
Lee Enterprises
Lilly & Co. (Eli)
Lincoln Electric Co.
Metropolitan Life Insurance Co.
Minnesota Mining & Manufacturing Co.
Monsanto Co.
Montgomery Ward & Co., Inc.
Nalco Chemical Co.
Norfolk Southern Corp.
Northrop Grumman Corp.
Olin Corp.
PacifiCorp
PerkinElmer, Inc.
Phelps Dodge Corp.
PPG Industries, Inc.
Scripps Co. (E.W.)
Union Carbide Corp.
United Parcel Service of America Inc.
USX Corp.
Westvaco Corp.

Wisconsin

7-Eleven, Inc.
ABB Inc.
Air Products and Chemicals, Inc.
Albany International Corp.
America West Airlines, Inc.
American Express Co.
American United Life Insurance Co.
Ameritech Corp.
Ameritech Wisconsin
AMETEK, Inc.
Amsted Industries Inc.
Andersen Corp.
Anheuser-Busch Companies, Inc.
Appleton Papers Inc.
Baird & Co. (Robert W.)
Ball Corp.
BankBoston-Connecticut Region
Banta Corp.
Barnes Group Inc.
Bayer Corp.
Bemis Co., Inc.
Bestfoods
Blount International, Inc.
Briggs & Stratton Corp.
Brown Shoe Co., Inc.
Browning-Ferris Industries Inc.
Bucyrus-Erie Co.
Campbell Soup Co.
Cargill Inc.
Caterpillar Inc.
Charter Manufacturing Co.
Chesapeake Corp.
CNF Transportation, Inc.
Compaq Computer Corp.
Computer Associates International, Inc.
ConAgra, Inc.
Consolidated Papers, Inc.
Cooper Industries, Inc.
Cox Enterprises Inc.
CSX Corp.
DaimlerChrysler Corp.
Dain Bosworth Inc.
Dayton Hudson
Deloitte & Touche
Delta Air Lines, Inc.
Deluxe Corp.
Donaldson Co., Inc.
Dow Jones & Co., Inc.
Eastman Kodak Co.
Eaton Corp.
Ecolab Inc.
EDS Corp.
Elf Atochem North America, Inc.
Employers Insurance of Wausau, A Mutual Co.
Equifax Inc.
Ernst & Young, LLP
Extendicare Health Services
FedEx Corp.
Fireman's Fund Insurance Co.
First Financial Bank
Firstar Bank Milwaukee NA
Fluor Corp.
FMC Corp.
Fort James Corp.
Fortis, Inc.
Fortis Insurance Co.
Fortune Brands, Inc.
Frontier Corp.
Gannett Co., Inc.
General Motors Corp.
Georgia-Pacific Corp.
Gerber Products Co.
Giddings & Lewis
Grainger, Inc. (W.W.)
Grede Foundries
Guardian Life Insurance Co. of America
Harley-Davidson Co.
Harnischfeger Industries
Heinz Co. (H.J.)
Hercules Inc.
Hewlett-Packard Co.
Huffy Corp.
Hunt Manufacturing Co.
IKON Office Solutions, Inc.
International Business Machines Corp.
International Paper Co.
Johnson Controls Inc.
Journal Communications, Inc.
JSJ Corp.
Kemper National Insurance Companies
Kendall International, Inc.
Kimberly-Clark Corp.
Kohler Co.
KPMG Peat Marwick LLP
Kraft Foods, Inc.
Ladish Co., Inc.
Land O'Lakes, Inc.
Lee Enterprises
Lincoln Electric Co.
Lincoln Financial Group
Louisiana-Pacific Corp.
Madison Gas & Electric Co.
Marcus Corp.
Marshall Field's
Marshall & Ilsley Corp.
Maytag Corp.
McDonald & Co. Securities, Inc.
Mead Corp.
Menasha Corp.
MGIC Investment Corp.
Minnesota Mining & Manufacturing Co.
Monsanto Co.
Nalco Chemical Co.
National Presto Industries, Inc.
National Starch & Chemical Co.
Nordson Corp.
Northern States Power Co.
Norwest Corp.
Olin Corp.
Outboard Marine Corp.
Owens Corning
Parker Hannifin Corp.
Pentair Inc.
Pharmacia & Upjohn, Inc.
Philip Morris Companies Inc.
Pieper Power Electric Co.
Pillsbury Co.
Pioneer Hi-Bred International, Inc.
Pittway Corp.
PPG Industries, Inc.
Premark International Inc.
Procter & Gamble Co.
Quanex Corp.
Reinhart Institutional Foods
Reynolds Metals Co.
Reynolds Tobacco (R.J.)
Rockwell International Corp.
Rouse Co.
Ryder System, Inc.
Saint Paul Companies Inc.
Sara Lee Corp.
Sentry Insurance, A Mutual Co.
Smith Corp. (A.O.)
SmithKline Beecham Corp.
Smucker Co. (JM)
Smurfit-Stone Container Corp.
Springs Industries, Inc.
Square D Co.
SuperValu, Inc.
Target Corp.
Tenneco Automotive
Texas Instruments Inc.
Textron Inc.
Timken Co. (The)
Tomkins Industries, Inc.
Transamerica Corp.
Trustmark Insurance Co.
Unilever United States, Inc.
United Dominion Industries, Ltd.
United Parcel Service of America Inc.
U.S. Bancorp
U.S. Bancorp Piper Jaffray
Universal Foods Corp.
Unocal Corp.
USG Corp.
Valspar Corp.
Vulcan Materials Co.
Wal-Mart Stores, Inc.
Walgreen Co.
Wausau Insurance Companies
Westvaco Corp.
Weyerhaeuser Co.
WICOR, Inc.
Wisconsin Energy Corp.
Wisconsin Power & Light Co.
Wisconsin Public Service Corp.
Witco Corp.

Wyoming

American General Finance
Atlantic Richfield Co.
Browning-Ferris Industries Inc.
Burlington Resources, Inc.
Central & South West Services
Chevron Corp.
CNF Transportation, Inc.
Computer Associates International, Inc.
Cyprus Amax Minerals Co.
DaimlerChrysler Corp.
Dain Bosworth Inc.
Delta Air Lines, Inc.
Exxon Mobil Corp.
FMC Corp.
International Business Machines Corp.
Kinder Morgn
Land O'Lakes, Inc.
Litton Industries, Inc.
Montana Power Co.
Nalco Chemical Co.
New Century Energies
Norwest Corp.
Pioneer Natural Resources
Sprint Corp.
Tenet Healthcare Corp.
True Oil Co.
United Parcel Service of America Inc.
U.S. Bancorp Piper Jaffray
Unocal Corp.
US West, Inc.
Wal-Mart Stores, Inc.
Williams

FUNDERS BY LOCATION OF GRANT RECIPIENT

Arranges funders by states in which they have allocated their funds, both within the United States and abroad (generated by the location of grants made by the foundation).

United States

BIRMINGHAM
Blue Cross & Blue Shield of Alabama

CALIFORNIA
Texas Instruments Inc.

CANADA
Disney Co. (Walt)

CEDAR RAPIDS
AEGON U.S.A. Inc.

CENTRAL FLORIDA
Harris Corp.

CHICAGO
Chicago Title Corp.

FALLSCHURCH
Louisiana Land & Exploration Co.

JERSEY CITY
Bard, Inc. (C.R.)

LOS ANGELES
Disney Co. (Walt)

NATIONAL
United Airlines Inc.

NEW YORK
Westvaco Corp.

NORTH HILL
Disney Co. (Walt)

SAN DIEGO
Gap, Inc.

SAN FRANCISCO
APL Ltd.
Gap, Inc.

TUSTIN
Disney Co. (Walt)

Alabama

Alabama Power Co.
Blue Cross & Blue Shield of Alabama
Compass Bank
Olin Corp.
Walter Industries Inc.

ALBERTA
MacMillan Bloedel Inc.

ANNISTON
Alabama Power Co.
Hartmarx Corp.
Walter Industries Inc.

ATHENS
ConAgra, Inc.
Steelcase Inc.

ATTALLA
Alabama Power Co.

AUBURN
Alabama Power Co.
Briggs & Stratton Corp.
Butler Manufacturing Co.
Compass Bank
Danis Companies
Exxon Mobil Corp.
Florida Power & Light Co.
Hamilton Sundstrand Corp.
Jacobs Engineering Group
Louisiana Land & Exploration Co.
Louisiana-Pacific Corp.
MacMillan Bloedel Inc.
State Farm Mutual Automobile Insurance Co.
Temple-Inland Inc.
Union Camp Corp.

AUBURN UNIVERSITY
Coca-Cola Co.
Fluor Corp.
Mead Corp.

AXIS
Elf Atochem North America, Inc.

BIRMINGHAM
Alabama Power Co.
Archer-Daniels-Midland Co.
Arvin Industries, Inc.
Atlantic Investment Co.
Baxter International Inc.
BellSouth Corp.
Blount International, Inc.
Blue Cross & Blue Shield of Alabama
Butler Manufacturing Co.
Cargill Inc.
Coca-Cola Co.
Compass Bank
Dexter Corp.
Eastman Kodak Co.
Enterprise Rent-A-Car Co.
Erb Lumber Co.
Federated Department Stores, Inc.
Lehigh Portland Cement Co.
Liberty Corp.
MacMillan Bloedel Inc.
McWane Inc.
Norfolk Southern Corp.
Reynolds Metals Co.
Sony Electronics
USG Corp.
USX Corp.
Vulcan Materials Co.
Walter Industries Inc.
Winn-Dixie Stores Inc.

CAMDEN
Alabama Power Co.
MacMillan Bloedel Inc.

CHILDRENS HARBOR
Blount International, Inc.

CLANTON
Alabama Power Co.

CLAYTON
Louisiana-Pacific Corp.

CORDOVA
Rayonier Inc.

CULLMAN
Cooper Industries, Inc.

DECATUR
Jacobs Engineering Group
MacMillan Bloedel Inc.
Monsanto Co.

DOTHAN
Alabama Power Co.
Sony Electronics

FAYETTE
Arvin Industries, Inc.
Weyerhaeuser Co.

FLORENCE
Reynolds Metals Co.

FORT PAYNE
Alabama Power Co.

GADSDEN
Blue Cross & Blue Shield of Alabama

GADSEN
Alabama Power Co.

GREENSBORO
Alabama Power Co.

HARTSELLE
Monsanto Co.

HOOVER
Blue Cross & Blue Shield of Alabama

HUNTSVILLE
Cummins Engine Co., Inc.
GenCorp
Johnson & Son (S.C.)
PPG Industries, Inc.
TRW Inc.
Xerox Corp.

JACKSON GAP
Lehigh Portland Cement Co.

JACKSONVILLE
Compass Bank
Parker Hannifin Corp.

LANETT
Tomkins Industries, Inc.

LEEDS
Hubbell Inc.
Lehigh Portland Cement Co.

LIVINGSTON
Alabama Power Co.

MOBILE
Alabama Power Co.
BellSouth Corp.
Blount International, Inc.
Blue Bell, Inc.
Harsco Corp.
International Paper Co.
Kimberly-Clark Corp.
MacMillan Bloedel Inc.

MONTEVALLO
Vulcan Materials Co.

MONTGOMERY
Alabama Power Co.
Blount International, Inc.
Blue Cross & Blue Shield of Alabama
Compass Bank
Liz Claiborne, Inc.
MacMillan Bloedel Inc.
McWane Inc.
Union Camp Corp.
Vulcan Materials Co.
Winn-Dixie Stores Inc.

MOULTON
Alabama Power Co.
Champion International Corp.

PHENIX CITY
Mead Corp.

PINE APPLE
MacMillan Bloedel Inc.

PINE HILL
MacMillan Bloedel Inc.

PRATTVILLE
Union Camp Corp.

SATSUMA
Wal-Mart Stores, Inc.

SELMA
Alabama Power Co.
Blount International, Inc.
Louisiana-Pacific Corp.

SHEFFIELD
Norfolk Southern Corp.

SPRINGVILLE
MacMillan Bloedel Inc.

TALLADEGA
Alabama Power Co.
Blount International, Inc.
Johnson & Son (S.C.)
Regions Bank

TROY
Sony Electronics
Synovus Financial Corp.

TROY STATE UNIVERSITY
Mead Corp.

TUSCALOOSA
Alabama Power Co.
Blount International, Inc.
Blue Cross & Blue Shield of Alabama
Coca-Cola Co.
Louisiana-Pacific Corp.
Tamko Roofing Products
Temple-Inland Inc.

TUSKEGEE
Ford Motor Co.
National Service Industries, Inc.
Polaroid Corp.

UNIVERSITY
Blount International, Inc.
Shell Oil Co.

WAYNEVILLE
Alabama Power Co.

Alaska

Alaska Airlines, Inc.
PacifiCorp

ANCHORAGE
Alaska Airlines, Inc.
Atlantic Richfield Co.
Cook Inlet Region
Forbes Inc.
Hitachi America Ltd.
Unocal Corp.

HAINES
Patagonia Inc.

JUNEAU
American Retail Group
Patagonia Inc.

KENAI
Atlantic Richfield Co.

SOLDOTNA
Cook Inlet Region
Unocal Corp.

VALDEZ
Ben & Jerry's Homemade Inc.

Arizona

Fluor Corp.

ARIZONA CITY
Yellow Corp.

CAREFREE
Orscheln Co.
Solo Cup Co.

CASA GRANDE
Pfizer Inc.

CHANDLER
Shea Co. (John F.)

CONWAY
Central & South West Services

COOLIDGE
Arizona Public Service Co.

FLAGSTAFF
Arizona Public Service Co.
Chesapeake Corp.
Phelps Dodge Corp.
Southwest Gas Corp.

FORT DEFIANCE
American Honda Motor Co., Inc.

GLENDALE
Fluor Corp.
Globe Corp.
Hershey Foods Corp.
Honeywell International Inc.
New England Bio Labs
Phelps Dodge Corp.
Sega of America Inc.

HOTEVILLE
Hitachi America Ltd.

LITCHFIELD PARK
Arizona Public Service Co.
Southwest Gas Corp.

MARICOPA COUNTY
Medtronic, Inc.

MESA
Intel Corp.
TRW Inc.

MEYER
Phelps Dodge Corp.

PARADISE VALLEY
Shea Co. (John F.)

PHOENIX
AlliedSignal Inc.
America West Airlines, Inc.
American Express Co.
AMR Corp.
Arizona Public Service Co.
Bank of America
BFGoodrich Co.
Bucyrus-Erie Co.
Coca-Cola Co.
ConAgra, Inc.
Dial Corp.
Enterprise Rent-A-Car Co.
Federated Mutual Insurance Co.
First National Bank of Evergreen Park
GenCorp
General Electric Co.
Globe Corp.
Honeywell International Inc.
Hubbell Inc.
Intel Corp.
Jacobs Engineering Group
Marshall & Ilsley Corp.
Medtronic, Inc.
Motorola Inc.
Norwest Corp.
Owens Corning
PepsiCo, Inc.
Phelps Dodge Corp.
Pieper Power Electric Co.
Schwab & Co., Inc. (Charles)
Sentry Insurance, A Mutual Co.
Shea Co. (John F.)
Southwest Gas Corp.
State Farm Mutual Automobile Insurance Co.
Trace International Holdings, Inc.
TRW Inc.
US West, Inc.
Walgreen Co.
Wells Fargo & Co.

PRESCOTT
Walgreen Co.

RIO RICO
Badger Meter, Inc.

SCOTTSDALE
Arizona Public Service Co.
Dial Corp.
Gerber Products Co.
Globe Corp.
Phelps Dodge Corp.
Schwab & Co., Inc. (Charles)
Shea Co. (John F.)

SEDONA
Arizona Public Service Co.

SUN CITY
Dial Corp.

TEMPE
AlliedSignal Inc.
Arizona Public Service Co.
Cyprus Amax Minerals Co.
Dial Corp.
FINA
Globe Corp.
Intel Corp.
International Multifoods Corp.
Jacobs Engineering Group
Morris Communications Corp.
Motorola Inc.
Phelps Dodge Corp.
Pulitzer Publishing Co.
Southwest Gas Corp.
United Dominion Industries, Ltd.
US West, Inc.

TUCSON
AlliedSignal Inc.
America West Airlines, Inc.
Archer-Daniels-Midland Co.
Arizona Public Service Co.
Banfi Vintners
Bank of America
Ben & Jerry's Homemade Inc.
Cincinnati Bell Inc.
Coca-Cola Co.
Exxon Mobil Corp.
Globe Corp.
Honeywell International Inc.
Intel Corp.
Kroger Co.
Litton Industries, Inc.
Monarch Machine Tool Co.
Pacific Century Financial Corp.
Patagonia Inc.
Phelps Dodge Corp.
Tucson Electric Power Co.
United Airlines Inc.
Walgreen Co.
Weyerhaeuser Co.

YUMA
Globe Corp.
Southwest Gas Corp.

Arkansas

Bridgestone/Firestone, Inc.

ARKADELPHIA
Levi Strauss & Co.
Regions Bank
Reynolds Metals Co.

ASHDOWN
Georgia-Pacific Corp.

BATESVILLE
Regions Bank

BELLA VISTA
Tamko Roofing Products

BENTONVILLE
Forbes Inc.
MCI WorldCom, Inc.
Wal-Mart Stores, Inc.

BLYTHEVILLE
Harsco Corp.

CLARKSVILLE
Wal-Mart Stores, Inc.

CONWAY
FMC Corp.
Regions Bank

CROSSETT
Bemis Co., Inc.

EL DORADO
Regions Bank
Union Pacific Corp.

ENGLAND
Regions Bank

FAYETTEVILLE
Central & South West Services
Coca-Cola Co.
Franklin Electric Co.
Gerber Products Co.
Huffy Corp.
Phillips Petroleum Co.
Potlatch Corp.
Regions Bank
Tyson Foods Inc.

FORT SMITH
Inland Container Corp.
OG&E Electric Services
Quanex Corp.
SBC Communications Inc.
Tyson Foods Inc.
Whirlpool Corp.

GENTRY
Tyson Foods Inc.

GURDON
International Paper Co.

HENSLEY
Regions Bank

HOPE
Regions Bank

HOT SPRINGS
National Service Industries, Inc.
Regions Bank
Reynolds Metals Co.

JACKSONVILLE
Regions Bank

JASPER
Hitachi America Ltd.

JONESBORO
Liberty Corp.

LIT
Tyson Foods Inc.

LITTLE ROCK
AEGON U.S.A. Inc.
American Retail Group
Ben & Jerry's Homemade Inc.
Cox Enterprises Inc.
Dixie Group, Inc. (The)
Hensel Phelps Construction Co.
Johnson & Son (S.C.)
Levi Strauss & Co.
Regions Bank
Schering-Plough Corp.
Tyson Foods Inc.
Union Pacific Corp.
Wal-Mart Stores, Inc.
Weyerhaeuser Co.

LONOKE
Regions Bank

MAGNOLIA
Tyson Foods Inc.

MONTICELLO
Burlington Industries, Inc.
Potlatch Corp.

MORRILTON
Regions Bank

NORTH LITTLE ROCK
Regions Bank

OSCEOLA
Johnson Controls Inc.

PINE BLUFF
Regions Bank
Tyson Foods Inc.
Union Pacific Corp.

ROGERS
Crane Co.
Tyson Foods Inc.
Wal-Mart Stores, Inc.

SEARCY
Regions Bank
West Co. Inc.

SHERWOOD
Regions Bank

SILOAM SPRINGS
Franklin Electric Co.

SPRINGDALE
Regions Bank
Tyson Foods Inc.

TEXARKANA
Cooper Tire & Rubber Co.

TUCSON
Abbott Laboratories

WASHINGTON
Regions Bank

WEST MEMPHIS
Temple-Inland Inc.

WRIGHTSVILLE
Regions Bank

California

Bank of America
Disney Co. (Walt)
GTE Corp.
Katten, Muchin & Zavis
Manulife Financial
McKesson-HBOC Corp.
MONY Group (The)
Reader's Digest Association, Inc. (The)
Sierra Pacific Resources
Ticketmaster Corp.
United Distillers & Vintners North America
Young & Rubicam

ACTON
Independent Stave Co.

ALBANY
Jeld-wen, Inc.

ALTADENA
Unocal Corp.

ALTHERTON
General Atlantic Partners II LP

ANAHEIM
Disney Co. (Walt)
Indiana Mills & Manufacturing
International Multifoods Corp.
PacifiCare Health Systems
Sega of America Inc.
Vodafone AirTouch Plc

APPLE VALLEY
Southwest Gas Corp.

APTOS
Lipton Co.
Milacron, Inc.

ARCATA
Louisiana-Pacific Corp.
Simpson Investment Co.
Thompson Co. (J. Walter)

ARROYO GRANDE
Citizens Financial Group, Inc.

ATHERTON
Copley Press, Inc.
Wilbur-Ellis Co. & Connell Brothers Co.

AUBURN
Fuller Co. (H.B.)

AVALON
Globe Corp.

BAKERSFIELD
Occidental Oil and Gas
PepsiCo, Inc.
Rutledge Hill Press
Shell Oil Co.
State Farm Mutual Automobile Insurance Co.
Tektronix, Inc.
Texaco Inc.
Wells Fargo & Co.

BANNING
Deutsch Co.

BARSTOW
Wells Fargo & Co.

BEL AIR
Bechtel Group, Inc.

BELLFLOWER
Litton Industries, Inc.

BELMONT
Toshiba America Inc.

BERKELEY
Abbott Laboratories
APL Ltd.
Bechtel Group, Inc.
Chevron Corp.
Clorox Co.
Deloitte & Touche
Exxon Mobil Corp.
Gallo Winery, Inc. (E&J)
General Electric Co.
Industrial Bank of Japan Trust Co. (New York)
Leigh Fibers, Inc.
Louisiana-Pacific Corp.
MCI WorldCom, Inc.
McKesson-HBOC Corp.
Mitsubishi Electric America
Motorola Inc.
Olin Corp.
Patagonia Inc.
PerkinElmer, Inc.
Schlumberger Ltd. (USA)
Schwab & Co., Inc. (Charles)
Sega of America Inc.
Tesoro Hawaii
Vulcan Materials Co.
Wells Fargo & Co.
Wilbur-Ellis Co. & Connell Brothers Co.
Xerox Corp.

BEVERLY HILLS
Calvin Klein
Deutsch Co.
Gap, Inc.
Guess?

BLACKHAWK
Sierra Pacific Industries

BONITA
MCI WorldCom, Inc.

BUENA PARK
PacifiCare Health Systems

BURBANK
Disney Co. (Walt)
Guess?
United States Trust Co. of New York
Universal Studios

BURLINGAME
Sega of America Inc.

BURLINGHAME
Jacobs Engineering Group

CAMARILLO
LandAmerica Financial Services
Minnesota Mining & Manufacturing Co.

CANOGA PARK
PacifiCare Health Systems

CAPILOS
Wrigley Co. (Wm. Jr.)

CAPITOLA
Wells Fargo & Co.

CARLSBAD
Callaway Golf Co.
MCI WorldCom, Inc.

CARMEL
McGraw-Hill Companies, Inc.

CARSON
AlliedSignal Inc.
American Honda Motor Co., Inc.
Mattel Inc.
Ralph's Grocery Co.
TRW Inc.

CASA MESA
PacifiCare Health Systems

CHATSWORTH
Giddings & Lewis
Universal Studios

CHICO
Hensel Phelps Construction Co.
Toshiba America Inc.
Wells Fargo & Co.

CHINO
Mitsubishi Electric America

CLAREMONT
APL Ltd.
Atlantic Richfield Co.
Dreyer's Grand Ice Cream
Gerber Products Co.
Levi Strauss & Co.
Litton Industries, Inc.
Times Mirror Co.
Toyota Motor Sales U.S.A., Inc.
United States Trust Co. of New York
Unocal Corp.

CLOVERDALE
Gallo Winery, Inc. (E&J)

COMMERCE
Kirkland & Ellis

COMPTON
Mattel Inc.

CONCORD
Clorox Co.
Hofmann Co.
Sierra Pacific Industries

CONEJO
Amgen, Inc.

CORONA
Wells Fargo & Co.

COSTA MESA
APL Ltd.
Banfi Vintners
Bourns, Inc.
Burlington Resources, Inc.
Lennox International, Inc.
Pacific Mutual Life Insurance Co.
Ralph's Grocery Co.
Times Mirror Co.
Unocal Corp.

COVINA
Disney Co. (Walt)
Sony Electronics

CRESCENT CITY
Simpson Investment Co.

CROCKETT
Alexander & Baldwin, Inc.

CULVER CITY
AMR Corp.
Manor Care Health SVS, Inc.

CYPRESS
PacifiCare Health Systems

DALY CITY
Stanley Works (The)

DANA POINT
Pacific Mutual Life Insurance Co.

DANVILLE
Pacific Mutual Life Insurance Co.
Sierra Pacific Industries
Witco Corp.

DAVIS
Atlantic Richfield Co.
Chevron Corp.
Hensel Phelps Construction Co.
Metropolitan Life Insurance Co.
Patagonia Inc.

DEATH VALLEY
Ben & Jerry's Homemade Inc.

DEL MAR
Shea Co. (John F.)

DENAIR
Gallo Winery, Inc. (E&J)

DOWNEY
Atlantic Richfield Co.

DUARTE
Bank of America
Emerson Electric Co.
Georgia-Pacific Corp.
Huffy Corp.

Leviton Manufacturing Co. Inc.
Square D Co.
Stanley Works (The)

EAST PALO ALTO
General Atlantic Partners II LP
Sega of America Inc.
Sun Microsystems Inc.

EL CENTRO
Wells Fargo & Co.

EL CERRITO
U.S. Bancorp Piper Jaffray

EL MORRO
Inland Container Corp.

EL SEGUNDO
Hasbro, Inc.
Mattel Inc.

ENCINITAS
Callaway Golf Co.

ENCINO
Aetna, Inc.

ESCONDIDO
Callaway Golf Co.
Copley Press, Inc.
Dreyer's Grand Ice Cream
Fisher Scientific
PacifiCare Health Systems
Schwab & Co., Inc. (Charles)

EUREKA
Simpson Investment Co.
Wells Fargo & Co.

FARMERSVILLE
Griffith Laboratories U.S.A.

FOLSOM
Intel Corp.

FOREST KNOLLS
Patagonia Inc.

FORT DICK
Simpson Investment Co.

FORTUNA
Simpson Investment Co.

FREMONT
APL Ltd.
Quaker Chemical Corp.

FRESNO
Bank of America
FMC Corp.
Gallo Winery, Inc. (E&J)
Gap, Inc.
Hershey Foods Corp.
National Presto Industries, Inc.
State Farm Mutual Automobile Insurance Co.
Wells Fargo & Co.

FULLERTON
Beckman Coulter, Inc.
ConAgra, Inc.
Pacific Mutual Life Insurance Co.

GARBERVILLE
Patagonia Inc.

GARDEN GROVE
Contran Corp.
Disney Co. (Walt)
Johnson Controls Inc.
Pacific Mutual Life Insurance Co.
PepsiCo, Inc.

GARDENA
Deutsch Co.

GLENDALE
Baxter International Inc.
Disney Co. (Walt)
PacifiCare Health Systems

GOLETA
Patagonia Inc.

GRASS VALLEY
Cinergy Corp.
Wells Fargo & Co.

HAWTHORNE
Searle & Co. (G.D.)
Sega of America Inc.

HAYWARD
Clorox Co.
Sun Microsystems Inc.

HEMET
Deutsch Co.

HILLSBOROUGH
S.G. Cowen
Wilbur-Ellis Co. & Connell Brothers Co.

HOLLYWOOD
Gerber Products Co.
PacifiCare Health Systems

HUGHSON
Gallo Winery, Inc. (E&J)

HUNTINGTON
Pacific Mutual Life Insurance Co.
Times Mirror Co.

HUNTINGTON BEACH
Pacific Mutual Life Insurance Co.
PacifiCare Health Systems
Unocal Corp.

INGLEWOOD
Duchossois Industries Inc.
Guess?

IRVINE
Archer-Daniels-Midland Co.
Bank of America
Beckman Coulter, Inc.
Bernstein & Co., Inc. (Sanford C.)
Circuit City Stores, Inc.
Federated Department Stores, Inc.
Fluor Corp.
Pacific Mutual Life Insurance Co.
PacifiCare Health Systems
Parker Hannifin Corp.
Shea Co. (John F.)
Simplot Co. (J.R.)
TENNANT Co.
Texaco Inc.
Times Mirror Co.
Unocal Corp.
Vodafone AirTouch Plc
Wells Fargo & Co.

JULIAN
Gap, Inc.

KENTFIELD
APL Ltd.

LA JOLLA
AT&T Corp.
Bristol-Myers Squibb Co.
Copley Press, Inc.
Fisher Scientific
Fluor Corp.

Gap, Inc.
GEICO Corp.
Lennox International, Inc.
Vodafone AirTouch Plc

LA MIRADA
International Multifoods Corp.

LA VERNE
Mitsubishi Electric America

LAFAYETTE
Hofmann Co.
McKesson-HBOC Corp.

LAGUNA HILLS
PacifiCare Health Systems

LAGUNA NIGUEL
PacifiCare Health Systems

LAKE ARROWHEAD
Witco Corp.

LAKE VIEW TERRACE
Disney Co. (Walt)
Mattel Inc.

LANCASTER
Jostens, Inc.

LARKSPUR
Broderbund Software, Inc.
Fireman's Fund Insurance Co.
Sun Microsystems Inc.

LATTABRA
Portland General Electric Co.

LODI
Gallo Winery, Inc. (E&J)

LOMA LINDA
American Honda Motor Co., Inc.
Bourns, Inc.

LOMPOC
Gap, Inc.
Wells Fargo & Co.

LONG BEACH
Atlantic Richfield Co.
GTE Corp.
Milliken & Co.
Morgan Stanley Dean Witter & Co.
Pacific Mutual Life Insurance Co.
PacifiCare Health Systems
PerkinElmer, Inc.
Square D Co.
Sunmark Capital Corp.
Xerox Corp.

LOS ALTOS
Sega of America Inc.
Sun Microsystems Inc.

LOS ANGELES
ABC
Aetna, Inc.
Alexander & Baldwin, Inc.
AlliedSignal Inc.
Allstate Insurance Co.
American Express Co.
American Honda Motor Co., Inc.
Amgen, Inc.
AMR Corp.
Armstrong World Industries, Inc.
Associated Food Stores
AT&T Corp.
Atlantic Richfield Co.
Avery Dennison Corp.
Bank of America

Barnes Group Inc.
Baxter International Inc.
Bemis Manufacturing Co.
Ben & Jerry's Homemade Inc.
Bernstein & Co., Inc. (Sanford C.)
Binswanger Companies
Boston Globe (The)
Bridgestone/Firestone, Inc.
Broderbund Software, Inc.
Calvin Klein
Carnival Corp.
Carpenter Technology Corp.
CBS Corp.
Chevron Corp.
CIGNA Corp.
Cinergy Corp.
Circuit City Stores, Inc.
Coca-Cola Co.
Collins & Aikman Corp.
Commercial Intertech Corp.
Compaq Computer Corp.
Consolidated Electrical Distributors
Copley Press, Inc.
Crane Co.
Deloitte & Touche
Delta Air Lines, Inc.
Deutsch Co.
Disney Co. (Walt)
Dow Jones & Co., Inc.
Edison International
El Paso Energy Co.
Enterprise Rent-A-Car Co.
Extendicare Health Services
Farmers Group, Inc.
Federated Department Stores, Inc.
Fireman's Fund Insurance Co.
Ford Motor Co.
Gap, Inc.
GATX Corp.
GenCorp
Gerber Products Co.
Goldman Sachs Group
GTE Corp.
Guess?
Harley-Davidson Co.
Harris Corp.
Hartford (The)
Hewlett-Packard Co.
Hitachi America Ltd.
Independent Stave Co.
Inland Container Corp.
Jacobs Engineering Group
Jacobson & Sons (Benjamin)
Katten, Muchin & Zavis
Kirkland & Ellis
Levi Strauss & Co.
Litton Industries, Inc.
Marcus Corp.
Mattel Inc.
May Department Stores Co.
MCI WorldCom, Inc.
Merck & Co.
Monsanto Co.
Nabisco Group Holdings
National Starch & Chemical Co.
Nestle U.S.A. Inc.
New York Life Insurance Co.
Nissan North America, Inc.
Nomura Holding America
Occidental Petroleum Corp.
Owens Corning
Pacific Mutual Life Insurance Co.
PacifiCare Health Systems
PepsiCo, Inc.
PerkinElmer, Inc.
Price Associates (T. Rowe)
Prudential Insurance Co. of America
Ralph's Grocery Co.
Revlon Inc.
Russer Foods
Safeguard Scientifics
Schwab & Co., Inc. (Charles)
Seagram & Sons, Inc. (Joseph E.)
Sega of America Inc.
Shea Co. (John F.)
Shell Oil Co.
Smurfit-Stone Container Corp.
Southwest Gas Corp.
Sprint Corp.
Stone Container Corp.
Sun Microsystems Inc.
SunTrust Bank Atlanta
Tai and Co. (J.T.)
Ticketmaster Corp.
Times Mirror Co.
Timken Co. (The)
Tomkins Industries, Inc.
Toyota Motor Sales U.S.A., Inc.
Transamerica Corp.
True Oil Co.
TRW Inc.
Tyson Foods Inc.
Union Camp Corp.
United Airlines Inc.
United States Trust Co. of New York
Universal Studios
Unocal Corp.
Valspar Corp.
Vodafone AirTouch Plc
Wells Fargo & Co.
Westvaco Corp.
Witco Corp.
Xerox Corp.
Zilkha & Sons

MADERA
Amsted Industries Inc.
CertainTeed Corp.
Wells Fargo & Co.

MALIBU
Deutsch Co.
Hofmann Co.

MARIN CITY
Fireman's Fund Insurance Co.

MARIN COUNTY
Fireman's Fund Insurance Co.

MARINA DEL REY
Guess?

MARTINEZ
Air Products and Chemicals, Inc.
Hofmann Co.

MARYSVILLE
Wells Fargo & Co.

MAYWOOD
Inland Container Corp.

MCKINLEYVILLE
Simpson Investment Co.

MENLO PARK
Barclays Capital
General Atlantic Partners II LP
Owens Corning
Pacific Mutual Life Insurance Co.
Sun Microsystems Inc.
United Distillers & Vintners North America

MERCED
Schwab & Co., Inc. (Charles)
Universal Foods Corp.
Wells Fargo & Co.

MILL VALLEY
Broderbund Software, Inc.
Chevron Corp.
Fireman's Fund Insurance Co.
Paine Webber

MILPITAS
Sun Microsystems Inc.

MISSION HILLS
Anheuser-Busch Companies, Inc.
Universal Studios

MODESTO
Gallo Winery, Inc. (E&J)
Universal Foods Corp.
Wells Fargo & Co.

MONROVIA
Gallo Winery, Inc. (E&J)

MONTCLAIR
Allstate Insurance Co.

MONTEBELLO
Disney Co. (Walt)

MONTEREY
Bank of America
Gallo Winery, Inc. (E&J)
Hewlett-Packard Co.
Lennox International, Inc.
McGraw-Hill Companies, Inc.
Wells Fargo & Co.
Wilbur-Ellis Co. & Connell Brothers Co.

MONTEREY PARK
AMR Corp.
Atlantic Richfield Co.
PacifiCare Health Systems
Unocal Corp.

MORAGA
CIGNA Corp.
Heinz Co. (H.J.)
Hofmann Co.

MOUNT SHASTA
Shea Co. (John F.)

NAPA
Alexander & Baldwin, Inc.
Bank of America
Domino's Pizza Inc.
Hofmann Co.
United Distillers & Vintners North America
Wilbur-Ellis Co. & Connell Brothers Co.

NEWMAN
Patagonia Inc.

NEWPORT BEACH
Bourns, Inc.
Pacific Mutual Life Insurance Co.
PacifiCare Health Systems

NORTH ANDOVER
Sun Microsystems Inc.

NORTH HOLLYWOOD
ABC
Dow Jones & Co., Inc.

NORTHRIDGE
Gallo Winery, Inc. (E&J)
Times Mirror Co.

NOVATO
Arvin Industries, Inc.
Broderbund Software, Inc.
Fireman's Fund Insurance Co.
Revlon Inc.
State Farm Mutual Automobile Insurance Co.
Wrigley Co. (Wm. Jr.)

OAKDALE
Gallo Winery, Inc. (E&J)
Hershey Foods Corp.

OAKLAND
Allstate Insurance Co.
American Retail Group
APL Ltd.
Bechtel Group, Inc.
Ben & Jerry's Homemade Inc.
Broderbund Software, Inc.
Carpenter Technology Corp.
Chevron Corp.
Clorox Co.
Dow Chemical Co.
Dreyer's Grand Ice Cream
Fannie Mae
Freddie Mac
Gap, Inc.
Genentech Inc.
General Atlantic Partners II LP
Gerber Products Co.
Grede Foundries
Hensel Phelps Construction Co.
Hewlett-Packard Co.
Hitachi America Ltd.
Hofmann Co.
McKesson-HBOC Corp.
PACCAR Inc.
PacifiCare Health Systems
Pfizer Inc.
Quaker Chemical Corp.
Schwab & Co., Inc. (Charles)
Sega of America Inc.
Sun Microsystems Inc.
United Airlines Inc.
Vodafone AirTouch Plc
Wilbur-Ellis Co. & Connell Brothers Co.

OCEANSIDE
Callaway Golf Co.
Deutsch Co.
Gap, Inc.

OJAI
Witco Corp.

ONTARIO
Inland Container Corp.

ORANGE
Disney Co. (Walt)
Oklahoma Publishing Co.
Pacific Mutual Life Insurance Co.
PacifiCare Health Systems
PerkinElmer, Inc.
Shea Co. (John F.)

ORICK
Simpson Investment Co.

ORINDA
Hofmann Co.

OROVILLE
Universal Studios

OXNARD
Teleflex Inc.

PA.LO ALTO
Sega of America Inc.

PACIFIC GROVE
Giddings & Lewis

PACIFIC PALISADES
Universal Studios

PACIFICA
Smurfit-Stone Container Corp.

PACOIMA
Universal Studios

PALM DESERT
Deutsch Co.

PALM SPRINGS
Deutsch Co.
Hofmann Co.
Loews Corp.
Marcus Corp.
Nabisco Group Holdings
Wells Fargo & Co.

PALMDALE
Harley-Davidson Co.

PALO ALTO
Bechtel Group, Inc.
General Atlantic Partners II LP
Hewlett-Packard Co.
HON Industries Inc.
Lennox International, Inc.
Liz Claiborne, Inc.
Sega of America Inc.
Sun Microsystems Inc.
Transamerica Corp.
Trustmark Insurance Co.
Universal Studios

PASADENA
AlliedSignal Inc.
Amgen, Inc.
APL Ltd.
Atlantic Richfield Co.
Avery Dennison Corp.
Avon Products, Inc.
Boeing Co.
Butler Manufacturing Co.
Clorox Co.
Disney Co. (Walt)
Dow Chemical Co.
Gap, Inc.
General Motors Corp.
GTE Corp.
Hallmark Cards Inc.
Intel Corp.
Jacobs Engineering Group
Mattel Inc.
PacifiCare Health Systems
Schlumberger Ltd. (USA)
Shea Co. (John F.)
Simpson Investment Co.
TRW Inc.
United States Trust Co. of New York
Van Leer Holding
Xerox Corp.

PENINSULA
United States Trust Co. of New York

PETALUMA
Fireman's Fund Insurance Co.
Sega of America Inc.

PLEASANT HILL
Alexander & Baldwin, Inc.
Dexter Corp.
Kellogg Co.

POMONA
Atlantic Richfield Co.
Fluor Corp.
GenCorp
Morris Communications Corp.
Parker Hannifin Corp.
Simpson Investment Co.
Toshiba America Inc.
Unocal Corp.

QUINCY
Hofmann Co.

RANCHO CORDOVA
PacifiCorp

RANCHO CUCAMONGA
Fannie Mae
Ralph's Grocery Co.

RANCHO MIRAGE
Deutsch Co.
Kimberly-Clark Corp.
Mattel Inc.
Nabisco Group Holdings
NEBCO Evans

REDDING
PacifiCorp
Shea Co. (John F.)
Simpson Investment Co.
Wal-Mart Stores, Inc.
Wells Fargo & Co.

REDLANDS
Borden, Inc.
Wells Fargo & Co.

REDONDO BEACH
TRW Inc.

REDWOOD
Gap, Inc.

REDWOOD CITY
Broderbund Software, Inc.
Sega of America Inc.

RICHMOND
Broderbund Software, Inc.
Chevron Corp.

RICHNERT PARK
Parker Hannifin Corp.

RIVERSIDE
Bourns, Inc.
CUNA Mutual Group
Deutsch Co.
Dow Jones & Co., Inc.
GenCorp
General Motors Corp.
Mattel Inc.
PacifiCare Health Systems
Toshiba America Inc.

ROSEMONT
Litton Industries, Inc.

ROSEVILLE
Fisher Scientific

ROSS
Thompson Co. (J. Walter)

SACRAMENTO
Alaska Airlines, Inc.
American Standard Inc.
Bank of America
CIGNA Corp.
Consolidated Electrical Distributors
Crane Co.
Deutsch Co.
Federated Department Stores, Inc.
Fuller Co. (H.B.)
Gallo Winery, Inc. (E&J)
GenCorp
Goldman Sachs Group
GTE Corp.
Hensel Phelps Construction Co.
Hofmann Co.
Intel Corp.
Kemper National Insurance Companies
Montana Power Co.
Pacific Mutual Life Insurance Co.
Patagonia Inc.
Reynolds Tobacco (R.J.)
Shea Co. (John F.)
Union Pacific Corp.
United Services Automobile Association
Unocal Corp.
USAA Life Insurance Co.
Vodafone AirTouch Plc
Wells Fargo & Co.
Weyerhaeuser Co.

SALINAS
Wells Fargo & Co.

SAN ANSELMO
Broderbund Software, Inc.
Fireman's Fund Insurance Co.

SAN BERNARDINO
Baxter International Inc.
PacifiCare Health Systems
Wells Fargo & Co.

SAN CARLOS
Harris Corp.

SAN CLEMENTE
Mitsubishi Electric America
Shea Co. (John F.)

SAN DIEGO
American Honda Motor Co., Inc.
APL Ltd.
Archer-Daniels-Midland Co.
Baird & Co. (Robert W.)
Bank of America
Baxter International Inc.
Callaway Golf Co.
Carpenter Technology Corp.
Caterpillar Inc.
Copley Press, Inc.
Federated Department Stores, Inc.
Fisher Brothers Cleaning Services
Fisher Scientific
Fortis, Inc.
Gap, Inc.
GATX Corp.
GEICO Corp.
Hamilton Sundstrand Corp.
Hartford (The)
Hoffmann-La Roche Inc.
Huffy Corp.
Indiana Mills & Manufacturing
KPMG Peat Marwick LLP
Mattel Inc.
McGraw-Hill Companies, Inc.
Monsanto Co.
New England Bio Labs
Pacific Mutual Life Insurance Co.
Pieper Power Electric Co.
Pulitzer Publishing Co.
Sega of America Inc.
Shea Co. (John F.)
Sony Electronics
TJX Companies, Inc.
Vodafone AirTouch Plc
Wells Fargo & Co.

SAN DIMAS
ServiceMaster Co.

SAN FRANCISCO
Alcon Laboratories, Inc.
Alexander & Baldwin, Inc.
Allstate Insurance Co.
Alma Piston Co.
American Express Co.
Amgen, Inc.
AMP Inc.
APL Ltd.
AT&T Corp.
Atlantic Richfield Co.
Avon Products, Inc.
Banfi Vintners
Bank of America
Baxter International Inc.
Bechtel Group, Inc.
Bell Atlantic Corp.
BellSouth Corp.
Ben & Jerry's Homemade Inc.
Broderbund Software, Inc.
Burlington Industries, Inc.
CGU Insurance
Chevron Corp.
Circuit City Stores, Inc.
CPI Corp.
Deluxe Corp.
Dow Jones & Co., Inc.
Dreyer's Grand Ice Cream
Enterprise Rent-A-Car Co.
Exxon Mobil Corp.
Federated Department Stores, Inc.
Fireman's Fund Insurance Co.
Fluor Corp.
Freddie Mac
Gallo Winery, Inc. (E&J)
Gap, Inc.
Genentech Inc.
General Atlantic Partners II LP
General Motors Corp.
Guess?
Hallmark Cards Inc.
Hewlett-Packard Co.
Hitachi America Ltd.
Hofmann Co.
IKON Office Solutions, Inc.
Jacobs Engineering Group
Leigh Fibers, Inc.
Lennox International, Inc.
Levi Strauss & Co.
Liberty Diversified Industries
Little, Inc. (Arthur D.)
McGraw-Hill Companies, Inc.
MCI WorldCom, Inc.
McKesson-HBOC Corp.
Mead Corp.
Metropolitan Life Insurance Co.
MidAmerican Energy Holdings Co.
MONY Group (The)
Morgan & Co. Inc. (J.P.)
Nabisco Group Holdings
New York Life Insurance Co.
PacifiCare Health Systems
Patagonia Inc.
Pfizer Inc.
Sara Lee Corp.
Schwab & Co., Inc. (Charles)
Seagram & Sons, Inc. (Joseph E.)
Sega of America Inc.
Shell Oil Co.
Sierra Pacific Industries
Sierra Pacific Resources
Sony Electronics
Southwest Gas Corp.
Standard Products Co.
Stride Rite Corp.
Ticketmaster Corp.
TJX Companies, Inc.
Toshiba America Inc.
Toyota Motor Sales U.S.A., Inc.
Transamerica Corp.
United Airlines Inc.
United Distillers & Vintners North America
US West, Inc.
Vodafone AirTouch Plc
Walter Industries Inc.
Weil, Gotshal & Manges Corp.
Wells Fargo & Co.
Whirlpool Corp.
Wilbur-Ellis Co. & Connell Brothers Co.
Witco Corp.
Wrigley Co. (Wm. Jr.)

SAN GABRIEL
Jacobs Engineering Group
United States Trust Co. of New York

SAN JACINTO
Wells Fargo & Co.

SAN JOSE
Advanced Micro Devices, Inc.
AT&T Corp.
Federated Department Stores, Inc.
Harley-Davidson Co.
Hewlett-Packard Co.
Mitsubishi Electric America
Pacific Mutual Life Insurance Co.
PerkinElmer, Inc.
Sega of America Inc.
Shea Co. (John F.)
Sun Microsystems Inc.

SAN LEANDRO
Hitachi America Ltd.

SAN LUIS OBISPO
Chevron Corp.
Fluor Corp.
Hensel Phelps Construction Co.
Litton Industries, Inc.
Louisiana-Pacific Corp.
Unocal Corp.
Wells Fargo & Co.

SAN LUIS REY
Callaway Golf Co.
Sony Electronics

SAN MARCOS
Callaway Golf Co.
Copley Press, Inc.

SAN MATEO
Sega of America Inc.
Sun Microsystems Inc.

SAN PEDRO
Ben & Jerry's Homemade Inc.

SAN RAFAEL
Alexander & Baldwin, Inc.
Broderbund Software, Inc.
Fireman's Fund Insurance Co.
Forbes Inc.
Hofmann Co.
Mattel Inc.
McKesson-HBOC Corp.
NEC America, Inc.
PEMCO Corp.
Pharmacia & Upjohn, Inc.
Wilbur-Ellis Co. & Connell Brothers Co.

SANFRANCISCO
First Hawaiian, Inc.

SANTA ANA
Baxter International Inc.
Disney Co. (Walt)
Mitsubishi Electric America
Pacific Mutual Life Insurance Co.
PacifiCare Health Systems
Shea Co. (John F.)
Steelcase Inc.
Toshiba America Inc.
Unocal Corp.

SANTA BARBARA
Amgen, Inc.
Contran Corp.
Corning Inc.
Deutsch Co.
LandAmerica Financial Services
NEC America, Inc.
Patagonia Inc.
Quaker Chemical Corp.
Wells Fargo & Co.

SANTA CLARA
Abbott Laboratories
APL Ltd.
Bank of America
Dow Jones & Co., Inc.
Fireman's Fund Insurance Co.
Intel Corp.
Mitsubishi Electric America
Owens Corning
Sony Electronics
Sun Microsystems Inc.
Texas Instruments Inc.
TRW Inc.
Walgreen Co.
Wells Fargo & Co.

SANTA CLARITA
Heinz Co. (H.J.)
Shea Co. (John F.)

SANTA MARIA
Unocal Corp.
Wells Fargo & Co.

SANTA MONICA
Bernstein & Co., Inc. (Sanford C.)

Calvin Klein
Deutsch Co.
Disney Co. (Walt)
Exxon Mobil Corp.
Fisher Brothers Cleaning Services
Fisher Scientific
Fluor Corp.
Gerber Products Co.
GTE Corp.
Hanna Co. (M.A.)
Litton Industries, Inc.
PerkinElmer, Inc.
Ralph's Grocery Co.
Sega of America Inc.
Sunmark Capital Corp.
Ticketmaster Corp.
Trustmark Insurance Co.

SANTA PAULA
Federal-Mogul Corp.

SANTA ROSA
Broderbund Software, Inc.
Fireman's Fund Insurance Co.
Gallo Winery, Inc. (E&J)
Lipton Co.
Shea Co. (John F.)
Waste Management Inc.
Wells Fargo & Co.
Wilbur-Ellis Co. & Connell Brothers Co.

SARATOGA
Bourns, Inc.
PerkinElmer, Inc.
Shea Co. (John F.)

SAUSALITO
Broderbund Software, Inc.

SAUSALLITO
Gap, Inc.

SEBASTOPOL
American Retail Group

SEBASTOPOLA
Broderbund Software, Inc.

SHASTA
Shea Co. (John F.)

SIMI VALLEY
Forbes Inc.

SMITH RIVER
Simpson Investment Co.

SOLANA BEACH
Copley Press, Inc.

SONORA
Wells Fargo & Co.

SOUTH LAGUNA
Pacific Mutual Life Insurance Co.

SOUTH LAKE TAHOE
Sierra Pacific Resources

SOUTH SAN FRANCISCO
Dreyer's Grand Ice Cream
Schwab & Co., Inc. (Charles)
Sega of America Inc.

SOUTHGATE
HON Industries Inc.

SPRING VALLEY
Copley Press, Inc.
Gap, Inc.
Huffy Corp.

STANFORD
Aetna, Inc.
AlliedSignal Inc.
Atlantic Richfield Co.
Bank One Corp.
Bechtel Group, Inc.
Boeing Co.
Briggs & Stratton Corp.
Brown Shoe Co., Inc.
Chevron Corp.
Corning Inc.
Deutsch Co.
DSM Copolymer
Eastern Enterprises
Exxon Mobil Corp.
FMC Corp.
Gap, Inc.
Hewlett-Packard Co.
Industrial Bank of Japan Trust Co. (New York)
Intel Corp.
Litton Industries, Inc.
McKesson-HBOC Corp.
Morgan Stanley Dean Witter & Co.
Nomura Holding America
Price Associates (T. Rowe)
Quaker Chemical Corp.
Reader's Digest Association, Inc. (The)
Rockwell International Corp.
Schering-Plough Corp.
Schwab & Co., Inc. (Charles)
Union Pacific Corp.
Wilbur-Ellis Co. & Connell Brothers Co.
Xerox Corp.

STINSON BEACH
Broderbund Software, Inc.
Wilbur-Ellis Co. & Connell Brothers Co.

STOCKTON
General Mills, Inc.
Inland Container Corp.
Kemper National Insurance Companies
Wells Fargo & Co.

STUDIO CITY
AMR Corp.
Farmers Group, Inc.
Pacific Mutual Life Insurance Co.
Universal Studios

SUN VALLEY
Disney Co. (Walt)
Mitsubishi Electric America

SUNLAND
Nestle U.S.A. Inc.

SUNNYVALE
Arizona Public Service Co.
Sun Microsystems Inc.

TAFT
Occidental Oil and Gas

TAHOE CITY
Sierra Pacific Resources

THOUSAND OAKS
Amgen, Inc.
Griffith Laboratories U.S.A.
GTE Corp.
Litton Industries, Inc.

TORRANCE
Gap, Inc.

TRACY
Inland Container Corp.

TULANE
Wells Fargo & Co.

TUSTIN
Pacific Mutual Life Insurance Co.
PacifiCare Health Systems

UNION CITY
Walter Industries Inc.

UNIVERSAL CITY
Universal Studios

VALENCIA
Disney Co. (Walt)
Occidental Oil and Gas
Times Mirror Co.
Unocal Corp.

VALLEJO
Atlantic Richfield Co.
Chevron Corp.
Wells Fargo & Co.

VAN NUYS
AlliedSignal Inc.
Bernstein & Co., Inc. (Sanford C.)
Cantor, Fitzgerald Securities Corp.
Litton Industries, Inc.
Universal Studios
Waste Management Inc.

VENICE
Deutsch Co.
Pfizer Inc.
Ralph's Grocery Co.

VENTURA
Amgen, Inc.
Rutledge Hill Press
Wells Fargo & Co.

VERNONIA
Sun Microsystems Inc.

VICTORVILLE
Southwest Gas Corp.

VISALIA
Butler Manufacturing Co.
Jostens, Inc.

VISTA
Callaway Golf Co.

WALNUT CREEK
Sega of America Inc.
Sierra Pacific Industries

WATSONVILLE
Metropolitan Life Insurance Co.

WEST HILLS
Disney Co. (Walt)

WEST HOLLYWOOD
Ticketmaster Corp.

WESTMINSTER
Heinz Co. (H.J.)

WILMINGTON
Johnson & Son (S.C.)
Shea Co. (John F.)

WILTON
American Retail Group

WOODAND HILLS
Universal Studios

WOODLAND
Wells Fargo & Co.

WOODLAND HILLS
Freeport-McMoRan Inc.

YREKA
Shea Co. (John F.)

Colorado

Coors Brewing Co.
Cyprus Amax Minerals Co.
Kirkland & Ellis
Woodward Governor Co.

ARVADA
Hamilton Sundstrand Corp.

ASPEN
Banfi Vintners
Ticketmaster Corp.

AURORA
International Multifoods Corp.
Kellwood Co.
Storage Technology Corp.

BOULDER
Baxter International Inc.
Ben & Jerry's Homemade Inc.
El Paso Energy Co.
General Atlantic Partners II LP
Hensel Phelps Construction Co.
Indiana Mills & Manufacturing
Intel Corp.
McClatchy Co.
Morrison Knudsen Corp.
Storage Technology Corp.
Strear Farms Co.
Unilever Home & Personal Care U.S.A.
Xerox Corp.

COLORADO SPRINGS
Bassett Furniture Industries
Bechtel Group, Inc.
BP Amoco Corp.
Carillon Importers, Ltd.
Central National-Gottesman
Deluxe Corp.
Emerson Electric Co.
FINA
Kinder Morgn
McDonald & Co. Securities, Inc.
McGraw-Hill Companies, Inc.
Nomura Holding America
Owens Corning
Phillips Petroleum Co.
Procter & Gamble Co.
Reynolds Tobacco (R.J.)
Shell Oil Co.
Solo Cup Co.
United Services Automobile Association
USAA Life Insurance Co.
Walgreen Co.

DENVER
Alma Piston Co.
AT&T Corp.
Ben & Jerry's Homemade Inc.
BP Amoco Corp.
Bucyrus-Erie Co.
Chase Manhattan Bank, NA
Coors Brewing Co.
Dain Bosworth Inc.
Edwards Enterprise Software (J.D.)
Enterprise Rent-A-Car Co.
Fannie Mae
GTE Corp.
Hamilton Sundstrand Corp.
Hensel Phelps Construction Co.
Huffy Corp.
International Multifoods Corp.
Kinder Morgn
Kirkland & Ellis
Kroger Co.
May Department Stores Co.
McClatchy Co.
McGraw-Hill Companies, Inc.
Metropolitan Life Insurance Co.
Mine Safety Appliances Co.
Morrison Knudsen Corp.
National Presto Industries, Inc.
Norwest Corp.
Ralston Purina Co.
Security Life of Denver Insurance Co.
Southwest Gas Corp.
Storage Technology Corp.
Strear Farms Co.
Texaco Inc.
True Oil Co.
United Airlines Inc.
U.S. Bancorp Piper Jaffray
US West, Inc.
Valmont Industries, Inc.
Walgreen Co.
Wells Fargo & Co.
Weyerhaeuser Co.
Wolverine World Wide

DURANGO
Hensel Phelps Construction Co.
National Presto Industries, Inc.

EDWARDS
Kroger Co.
True North Communications, Inc.

ENGLEWOOD
Edwards Enterprise Software (J.D.)
Heinz Co. (H.J.)
Manor Care Health SVS, Inc.
True Oil Co.

EVERGREEN
Caterpillar Inc.

FORT COLLINS
AK Steel Corp.
Dain Bosworth Inc.
Hensel Phelps Construction Co.
Hewlett-Packard Co.
Masco Corp.
Norwest Corp.
US West, Inc.
Woodward Governor Co.

GLENWOOD SPRINGS
APL Ltd.
Kinder Morgn

GOLDEN
Atlantic Richfield Co.
Bechtel Group, Inc.
Burlington Resources, Inc.
Chevron Corp.
Cyprus Amax Minerals Co.
Deere & Co.
El Paso Energy Co.
Fluor Corp.
National Presto Industries, Inc.
Occidental Petroleum Corp.
Phelps Dodge Corp.
Phillips Petroleum Co.
Schlumberger Ltd. (USA)
True North Communications, Inc.
Unocal Corp.

GRAND JUNCTION
AMETEK, Inc.
Broderbund Software, Inc.
Hamilton Sundstrand Corp.

Hensel Phelps Construction Co.
Kroger Co.
Morrison Knudsen Corp.
Waste Management Inc.

GREELEY
ConAgra, Inc.
Fortis, Inc.
Hensel Phelps Construction Co.
Simplot Co. (J.R.)
Storage Technology Corp.
US West, Inc.
Woodward Governor Co.

HIGHLANDS RANCH
International Multifoods Corp.

KEYSTONE
BP Amoco Corp.
FMC Corp.
Grace & Co. (W.R.)
Little, Inc. (Arthur D.)
Union Carbide Corp.
Waste Management Inc.

KINTER PARK
Tamko Roofing Products

LAKEWOOD
Edwards Enterprise Software (J.D.)
Hensel Phelps Construction Co.
Kinder Morgn
Storage Technology Corp.
Strear Farms Co.

LITTLETON
GEICO Corp.
Hensel Phelps Construction Co.

LONGMONT
Storage Technology Corp.
Strear Farms Co.

LOUISVILLE
Storage Technology Corp.

LOVELAND
Strear Farms Co.
Woodward Governor Co.

PARKER
Carillon Importers, Ltd.

PINE
Red Wing Shoe Co. Inc.

PUEBLO
Cincinnati Bell Inc.

QUINCY
ConAgra, Inc.

SNOWMASS VILLAGE
Glickenhaus & Co.

TELLURIDE
Mattel Inc.

THORNTON
IKON Office Solutions, Inc.

VAIL
Brown Shoe Co., Inc.

WHEAT RIDGE
Inland Container Corp.

Connecticut

Chase Manhattan Bank, NA
Crane Co.
Praxair
Reynolds Tobacco (R.J.)
Union Carbide Corp.
United Distillers & Vintners North America
Wiremold Co.

AVON
Ensign-Bickford Industries
Globe Corp.
Union Carbide Corp.

BLOOMFIELD
Barnes Group Inc.
Hartford Steam Boiler Inspection & Insurance Co.
United Distillers & Vintners North America
Wiremold Co.

BRANFORD
Barden Corp.

BRATTLEBORO
Niagara Mohawk Holdings Inc.

BRIDGEPORT
Barden Corp.
Hubbell Inc.
Shaw's Supermarkets, Inc.
Unilever Home & Personal Care U.S.A.

BRISTOL
Barnes Group Inc.
Dana Corp.
Shaw's Supermarkets, Inc.
Webster Bank

BROOKFIELD
Barden Corp.
Duracell International
Hubbell Inc.
Union Carbide Corp.

CANTON
Barnes Group Inc.

CHESHIRE
Hubbell Inc.
Olin Corp.

CLINTON
Stanley Works (The)

CORNWALL BRIDGE
Crane & Co., Inc.
Duracell International

COS COB
Dun & Bradstreet Corp.
Unilever Home & Personal Care U.S.A.

CROMWELL
Citizens Financial Group, Inc.

DABURY
Barden Corp.

DANBURY
Barden Corp.
Duracell International
First Union Corp.
Jacobson & Sons (Benjamin)
Praxair
Union Carbide Corp.

DARIEN
New York Mercantile Exchange

EAST GRANBY
Norton Co.

EAST HAMPTON
Dexter Corp.

EAST HARTFORD
CIGNA Corp.
Medtronic, Inc.

ENFIELD
Dexter Corp.

ESSEX
Vesper Corp.

FAIRFIELD
Barden Corp.
Forest City Enterprises, Inc.
Hubbell Inc.
Merrill Lynch & Co., Inc.
Olin Corp.
PepsiCo, Inc.
Reader's Digest Association, Inc. (The)
Unilever Home & Personal Care U.S.A.

FAIRHAVEN
Pfizer Inc.

FARMINGTON
Barnes Group Inc.
Hartford Steam Boiler Inspection & Insurance Co.
United States Trust Co. of New York

GALES FERRY
Citizens Financial Group, Inc.
Shaw's Supermarkets, Inc.

GLASTONBURY
Barden Corp.
Hartford Steam Boiler Inspection & Insurance Co.

GREENWICH
Bernstein & Co., Inc. (Sanford C.)
Carter-Wallace, Inc.
Daily News
Heinz Co. (H.J.)
Mattel Inc.
Reilly Industries, Inc.
Unilever Home & Personal Care U.S.A.

GROTON
Citizens Financial Group, Inc.

HAMDEN
Barden Corp.
Barnes Group Inc.
Central National-Gottesman

HARTFORD
Aetna, Inc.
Allegheny Technologies Inc.
Bank One Corp.
BankBoston Corp.
Barnes Group Inc.
Central National-Gottesman
Chase Manhattan Bank, NA
CIGNA Corp.
Citizens Financial Group, Inc.
Crane Co.
Dexter Corp.
Duracell International
Ensign-Bickford Industries
GTE Corp.
Hartford (The)
Hartford Steam Boiler Inspection & Insurance Co.
Hitachi America Ltd.
Hubbell Inc.
IKON Office Solutions, Inc.
Jacobs Engineering Group
LandAmerica Financial Services
Levi Strauss & Co.
Reynolds Metals Co.
Shaw's Supermarkets, Inc.
Stanley Works (The)
Times Mirror Co.
Timken Co. (The)
Unilever United States, Inc.
United Distillers & Vintners North America
Van Leer Holding
Wiremold Co.

LAKEVILLE
Alma Piston Co.

LEE
Crane & Co., Inc.

LYME
Hartford Steam Boiler Inspection & Insurance Co.

MERIDEN
AMETEK, Inc.

MIDDLETOWN
Aetna, Inc.
Binswanger Companies
Citizens Financial Group, Inc.
Hartford Steam Boiler Inspection & Insurance Co.
Olin Corp.
Unilever Home & Personal Care U.S.A.
The Washington Post
Zilkha & Sons

MILFORD
Hubbell Inc.
IKON Office Solutions, Inc.

NEW BRITAIN
Duracell International
Hartford (The)
Hartford Steam Boiler Inspection & Insurance Co.
Stanley Works (The)
United Distillers & Vintners North America
Webster Bank

NEW CANAAN
Bernstein & Co., Inc. (Sanford C.)
BP Amoco Corp.
Millipore Corp.
Putnam Investments
Reader's Digest Association, Inc. (The)
Reynolds Tobacco (R.J.)
Thermo Electron Corp.
Unilever Home & Personal Care U.S.A.

NEW HAVEN
Aetna, Inc.
Allstate Insurance Co.
AMETEK, Inc.
BankBoston Corp.
Barnes Group Inc.
Baxter International Inc.
Bechtel Group, Inc.
Briggs & Stratton Corp.
Calvin Klein
CGU Insurance
Chase Manhattan Bank, NA
Citizens Financial Group, Inc.
Consolidated Electrical Distributors
Continental Grain Co.
Fisher Brothers Cleaning Services
Fisher Scientific
Ford Motor Co.
Freeport-McMoRan Inc.
General Electric Co.
Hartford Steam Boiler Inspection & Insurance Co.
Hubbell Inc.
Humana, Inc.
Independent Stave Co.
Loews Corp.
Masco Corp.
MCI WorldCom, Inc.
Merit Oil Corp.
Nabisco Group Holdings
Pittway Corp.
Prudential Insurance Co. of America
Quaker Chemical Corp.
Shaw's Supermarkets, Inc.
Thompson Co. (J. Walter)
Unilever Home & Personal Care U.S.A.
Unilever United States, Inc.
United States Trust Co. of New York
Vesper Corp.
Waste Management Inc.
Webster Bank
Whitman Corp.
Wilbur-Ellis Co. & Connell Brothers Co.

NEW LONDON
Briggs & Stratton Corp.
Citizens Financial Group, Inc.
Dexter Corp.
Unilever Home & Personal Care U.S.A.
Young & Rubicam

NEW MILFORD
Barden Corp.

NEWINGTON
Barden Corp.

NORWALK
Amsted Industries Inc.
Central National-Gottesman
Champion International Corp.
Dun & Bradstreet Corp.
Hershey Foods Corp.
Kelly Services
Mamiye Brothers
Olin Corp.
Overseas Shipholding Group Inc.
Reader's Digest Association, Inc. (The)
Reynolds Tobacco (R.J.)
Texaco Inc.
Unilever Home & Personal Care U.S.A.

OLD GREENWICK
Young & Rubicam

ORANGE
Hubbell Inc.

PLAINVILLE
Citigroup
Unilever Home & Personal Care U.S.A.

PORTLAND
Unilever Home & Personal Care U.S.A.

RAEFORD
Unilever Home & Personal Care U.S.A.

RIDGEFIELD
Disney Co. (Walt)
Reynolds Tobacco (R.J.)
Union Carbide Corp.

RIVERSIDE
Avon Products, Inc.

SALISBURY
Schloss & Co. (Marcus)

SHELTON
Webster Bank

SIMSBURY
Bernstein & Co., Inc. (Sanford C.)
Bradford & Co. (J.C.)
Dexter Corp.
Ensign-Bickford Industries
Hartford Steam Boiler Inspection & Insurance Co.
Wiremold Co.

SOUTHINGTON
Maytag Corp.
Shaw's Supermarkets, Inc.

STAMFORD
ABC
AMR Corp.
Bethlehem Steel Corp.
Borden, Inc.
Champion International Corp.
Chase Manhattan Bank, NA
Crane Co.
Dun & Bradstreet Corp.
McClatchy Co.
McGraw-Hill Companies, Inc.
PepsiCo, Inc.
Rayonier Inc.
Reynolds Metals Co.
Sun Microsystems Inc.
Unilever Home & Personal Care U.S.A.
Waste Management Inc.
Weil, Gotshal & Manges Corp.
Wrigley Co. (Wm. Jr.)

STONINGTON
Tesoro Hawaii

STORRS
Aetna, Inc.
CIGNA Corp.
First Union Corp.
General Electric Co.
Harcourt General, Inc.
Hartford (The)
MCI WorldCom, Inc.
Merit Oil Corp.
Motorola Inc.
Olin Corp.
Stanley Works (The)
Unilever Home & Personal Care U.S.A.

STRATFORD
La-Z-Boy Inc.

TORRINGTON
Barden Corp.
Golub Corp.

TRUMBULL
Barden Corp.
Unilever Home & Personal Care U.S.A.

WALLINGFORD
Hartford Steam Boiler Inspection & Insurance Co.

WARRINGTON
Crane Co.

WATERBURY
BankBoston Corp.
Bernstein & Co., Inc. (Sanford C.)
Hershey Foods Corp.
Hubbell Inc.
Illinois Tool Works, Inc.
Unilever Home & Personal Care U.S.A.

WATERTOWN
Jacobson & Sons (Benjamin)

WATTERBURY
Shaw's Supermarkets, Inc.

WEST HARTFORD
Cooper Tire & Rubber Co.
Hartford Steam Boiler Inspection & Insurance Co.
Olin Corp.
United Distillers & Vintners North America

WEST HAVEN
Price Associates (T. Rowe)
Unilever Home & Personal Care U.S.A.

WESTPORT
BankBoston Corp.
Barden Corp.
Ford Motor Co.
Texaco Inc.
Unilever Home & Personal Care U.S.A.
Walgreen Co.

WILTON
Barden Corp.
Dun & Bradstreet Corp.

WINDSOR LOCKS
Dexter Corp.

WINSTED
Barden Corp.

Delaware
Avon Products, Inc.

CAMDEN
First Union Securities, Inc.

DAGSBORO
Campbell Soup Co.

GEORGETOWN
First Maryland Bancorp

NEWARK
Air Products and Chemicals, Inc.
Morgan & Co. Inc. (J.P.)
Solo Cup Co.

WILMINGTON
AMETEK, Inc.
Amsted Industries Inc.
Bell Atlantic Corp.
Chase Manhattan Bank, NA
Dreyer's Grand Ice Cream
du Pont de Nemours & Co. (E.I.)
FMC Corp.
Inland Container Corp.
Merit Oil Corp.
Morgan & Co. Inc. (J.P.)
PNC Financial Services Group
Solo Cup Co.
Westvaco Corp.

District of Columbia

WASHINGTON
Abbott Laboratories
ABC
Ace Hardware Corp.
AEGON U.S.A. Inc.
Aetna, Inc.
Alcon Laboratories, Inc.
Allegheny Technologies Inc.
AlliedSignal Inc.
Allstate Insurance Co.
Alma Piston Co.
American Express Co.
American Retail Group
American Standard Inc.
Ameritas Life Insurance Corp.
Ameritech Corp.
AMETEK, Inc.
Amgen, Inc.
AMP Inc.
Amsted Industries Inc.
Andersen Corp.
Anheuser-Busch Companies, Inc.
Aon Corp.
APL Ltd.
Archer-Daniels-Midland Co.
Arizona Public Service Co.
Armstrong World Industries, Inc.
Ashland, Inc.
AT&T Corp.
Atlantic Richfield Co.
Avon Products, Inc.
Banfi Vintners
Bank of America
Barclays Capital
Bard, Inc. (C.R.)
Bardes Corp.
Barry Corp. (R.G.)
Bechtel Group, Inc.
Bell Atlantic Corp.
Bernstein & Co., Inc. (Sanford C.)
Bethlehem Steel Corp.
BFGoodrich Co.
Binswanger Companies
Block, Inc. (H&R)
Blount International, Inc.
Blue Cross & Blue Shield of Minnesota
Borden, Inc.
Borman's Inc.
BP Amoco Corp.
Bridgestone/Firestone, Inc.
Bristol-Myers Squibb Co.
Brown Shoe Co., Inc.
Burlington Industries, Inc.
Burlington Resources, Inc.
Butler Capital Corp.
Calvin Klein
Cantor, Fitzgerald Securities Corp.
Carillon Importers, Ltd.
Carnival Corp.
Carpenter Technology Corp.
Caterpillar Inc.
CBS Corp.
CertainTeed Corp.
CGU Insurance
Champion International Corp.
Chase Manhattan Bank, NA
Chevron Corp.
Chicago Sun-Times, Inc.
Chubb Corp.
CIGNA Corp.
Circuit City Stores, Inc.
CNA
Coca-Cola Co.
Collins & Aikman Corp.
Commercial Intertech Corp.
Compaq Computer Corp.
ConAgra, Inc.
Consolidated Natural Gas Co.
Continental Grain Co.
Conwood Co. LP
Cooper Tire & Rubber Co.
Coors Brewing Co.
Corning Inc.
Crane Co.
Crestar Finance Corp.
Crown Books
CUNA Mutual Group
DaimlerChrysler Corp.
Danis Companies
Dayton Power and Light Co.
Deere & Co.
Delta Air Lines, Inc.
Dial Corp.
Disney Co. (Walt)
Domino's Pizza Inc.
Dow Jones & Co., Inc.
Duchossois Industries Inc.
Dun & Bradstreet Corp.
Duracell International
Eastman Kodak Co.
Eckerd Corp.
El Paso Energy Co.
Emerson Electric Co.
Employers Mutual Casualty Co.
Enterprise Rent-A-Car Co.
Equifax Inc.
Erb Lumber Co.
Erving Industries
Evening Post Publishing Co.
Exxon Mobil Corp.
Fannie Mae
Farmers Group, Inc.
Fidelity Investments
First Maryland Bancorp
First National Bank of Evergreen Park
First Union Securities, Inc.
Fisher Scientific
Florida Power & Light Co.
FMC Corp.
Forbes Inc.
Ford Motor Co.
Forest City Enterprises, Inc.
Freddie Mac
Gallo Winery, Inc. (E&J)
Gap, Inc.
GATX Corp.
GEICO Corp.
GenAmerica Corp.
General Atlantic Partners II LP
General Electric Co.
General Mills, Inc.
General Motors Corp.
Georgia-Pacific Corp.
Gerber Products Co.
Giant Food Inc.
Glickenhaus & Co.
Globe Corp.
Goldman Sachs Group
Grace & Co. (W.R.)
Gulf Power Co.
Halliburton Co.
Hallmark Cards Inc.
Harcourt General, Inc.
Harnischfeger Industries
Harris Corp.
Harsco Corp.
Hasbro, Inc.
Heinz Co. (H.J.)
Hershey Foods Corp.
Hitachi America Ltd.
Hoffmann-La Roche Inc.
Home Depot, Inc.
HON Industries Inc.
Honeywell International Inc.
Humana, Inc.
Independent Stave Co.
Industrial Bank of Japan Trust Co. (New York)
Intel Corp.
International Flavors & Fragrances Inc.
International Paper Co.
Jacobs Engineering Group
Johnson & Johnson
Johnson & Son (S.C.)
Katten, Muchin & Zavis
Kemper National Insurance Companies
Kimberly-Clark Corp.
Kirkland & Ellis
Kmart Corp.
KPMG Peat Marwick LLP
Lance, Inc.
Land O'Lakes, Inc.
LandAmerica Financial Services
Lee Enterprises
Leigh Fibers, Inc.
Lennox International, Inc.
Levi Strauss & Co.
Leviton Manufacturing Co. Inc.
Little, Inc. (Arthur D.)
Litton Industries, Inc.
Loews Corp.
Louisiana-Pacific Corp.
Lubrizol Corp. (The)
Manor Care Health SVS, Inc.
Marcus Corp.
Mark IV Industries
Masco Corp.
Matsushita Electric Corp. of America
Mattel Inc.
Mazda North American Operations
McGraw-Hill Companies, Inc.
MCI WorldCom, Inc.
Medtronic, Inc.
Merck & Co.
Merrill Lynch & Co., Inc.
Metropolitan Life Insurance Co.
Michigan Consolidated Gas Co.
Milliken & Co.
Mine Safety Appliances Co.
Minnesota Mutual Life Insurance Co.
Mitsubishi Electric America
Monsanto Co.
Morgan & Co. Inc. (J.P.)
Motorola Inc.
Nabisco Group Holdings
NASDAQ Stock Market
National Service Industries, Inc.
National Starch & Chemical Co.
Nationwide Insurance Co.
Navcom Systems
Nestle U.S.A. Inc.
New England Bio Labs
New York Life Insurance Co.
New York Stock Exchange, Inc.
Norton Co.
Occidental Petroleum Corp.
Ohio National Life Insurance Co.
Olin Corp.
Owens Corning
PACCAR Inc.
Pacific Mutual Life Insurance Co.
Patagonia Inc.
Penney Co., Inc. (J.C.)
PepsiCo, Inc.
PerkinElmer, Inc.
Pfizer Inc.
Pharmacia & Upjohn, Inc.

Phillips Petroleum Co.
Pittway Corp.
Playboy Enterprises Inc.
PPG Industries, Inc.
Price Associates (T. Rowe)
Principal Financial Group
Procter & Gamble Co.
Providence Journal-Bulletin Co.
Prudential Insurance Co. of America
Prudential Securities Inc.
Pulitzer Publishing Co.
Putnam Investments
Ralph's Grocery Co.
Reader's Digest Association, Inc. (The)
Red Wing Shoe Co. Inc.
Reebok International Ltd.
Reinhart Institutional Foods
Revlon Inc.
Reynolds Metals Co.
Reynolds Tobacco (R.J.)
Rouse Co.
Rutledge Hill Press
Ryder System, Inc.
Sara Lee Corp.
Schering-Plough Corp.
Schloss & Co. (Marcus)
Schlumberger Ltd. (USA)
Seagram & Sons, Inc. (Joseph E.)
Searle & Co. (G.D.)
Sega of America Inc.
S.G. Cowen
Shea Co. (John F.)
Shell Oil Co.
Simplot Co. (J.R.)
Slant/Fin Corp.
Sony Electronics
Sprint Corp.
State Farm Mutual Automobile Insurance Co.
Stone Container Corp.
Sun Microsystems Inc.
Sunmark Capital Corp.
Tai and Co. (J.T.)
Tamko Roofing Products
Teleflex Inc.
Texaco Inc.
Texas Instruments Inc.
Textron Inc.
Thermo Electron Corp.
Thompson Co. (J. Walter)
Times Mirror Co.
Titan Industrial Corp.
TMC Investment Co.
Tomkins Industries, Inc.
Toro Co.
Toshiba America Inc.
Toyota Motor Sales U.S.A., Inc.
Trace International Holdings, Inc.
True North Communications, Inc.
True Oil Co.
Trustmark Insurance Co.
TRW Inc.
Unilever United States, Inc.
Union Camp Corp.
Union Carbide Corp.
United Airlines Inc.
United Parcel Service of America Inc.
United Services Automobile Association
United States Sugar Corp.
Unocal Corp.
UnumProvident
US West, Inc.
USG Corp.
Vodafone AirTouch Plc
Vulcan Materials Co.
Walter Industries Inc.
Warner-Lambert Co.
The Washington Post
Waste Management Inc.
Weil, Gotshal & Manges Corp.
Wells Fargo & Co.
West Co. Inc.
Western & Southern Life Insurance Co.
Westvaco Corp.
Weyerhaeuser Co.
Whirlpool Corp.
Whitman Corp.
Wiley & Sons (John)
Williams
Witco Corp.
Wrigley Co. (Wm. Jr.)
Xerox Corp.
Young & Rubicam
Zilkha & Sons

Florida

Disney Co. (Walt)
Eckerd Corp.
First Union Corp.
Merck & Co.
Publix Supermarkets
Schwab & Co., Inc. (Charles)
Taco Bell Corp.

ALTAMONTE SPRINGS
United States Sugar Corp.

APOPKA
Ben & Jerry's Homemade Inc.
Sentinel Communications Co.

BAYTON BEACH
MTD Products Inc.

BELLE GLADE
United States Sugar Corp.

BOCA RATON
BankAtlantic Bancorp
Cox Enterprises Inc.
Grace & Co. (W.R.)
National Starch & Chemical Co.
Publix Supermarkets
Quanex Corp.

BOYNTON BEACH
BankAtlantic Bancorp
Delta Air Lines, Inc.
Federated Department Stores, Inc.

BOYS RANCH
Carillon Importers, Ltd.

BRADENTON
Florida Power & Light Co.
Publix Supermarkets
Walgreen Co.

CAPE CORAL
United States Sugar Corp.

CHARLOTTESVILLE
Merrill Lynch & Co., Inc.

CLEARWATER
AMETEK, Inc.
Callaway Golf Co.
Demoulas Supermarkets Inc.
Dynamet, Inc.
Eckerd Corp.
GTE Corp.
Honeywell International Inc.

CLEWISTON
United States Sugar Corp.

COCOA
Florida Power & Light Co.
Harris Corp.
Johnson Controls Inc.
Publix Supermarkets
Walgreen Co.

COCOA BEACH
PerkinElmer, Inc.

COCONUT CREEK
BankAtlantic Bancorp

COCONUT GROVE
Ryder System, Inc.
United States Sugar Corp.

CORAL GABLES
BankAtlantic Bancorp
Carnival Corp.
Ryder System, Inc.
Toshiba America Inc.
United States Sugar Corp.

CORAL SPRINGS
BankAtlantic Bancorp
La-Z-Boy Inc.

DAYTONA BEACH
Callaway Golf Co.
Cessna Aircraft Co.
Florida Power & Light Co.
JSJ Corp.
Nabisco Group Holdings
Publix Supermarkets
SunTrust Banks of Florida
Walgreen Co.

DE LAND
Publix Supermarkets
Sentinel Communications Co.

DEIRAY BEACH
BankAtlantic Bancorp

DELRAY
Walgreen Co.

DELRAY BEACH
Grace & Co. (W.R.)

DUNDEE
Russer Foods

EATONVILLE
Sentinel Communications Co.

FERNANDINA BEACH
Rayonier Inc.

FORT LAUDERDALE
American Express Co.
BankAtlantic Bancorp
Baxter International Inc.
Delta Air Lines, Inc.
Enterprise Rent-A-Car Co.
Federated Department Stores, Inc.
First Union Corp.
Florida Power & Light Co.
Motorola Inc.
Publix Supermarkets
Ryder System, Inc.
Walgreen Co.
Waste Management Inc.

FORT MYERS
Boler Co.
Cooper Tire & Rubber Co.
Florida Power & Light Co.
Furniture Brands International, Inc.
United States Sugar Corp.

FORT WALTON BEACH
Gulf Power Co.

FT. MYERS
Sprint Corp.
United States Sugar Corp.

FT. PIERCE
Florida Power & Light Co.

GAINESVILLE
Anheuser-Busch Companies, Inc.
BellSouth Corp.
Crane & Co., Inc.
Dow Chemical Co.
Eckerd Corp.
Elf Atochem North America, Inc.
Florida Power & Light Co.
Florida Rock Industries
Halliburton Co.
Hitachi America Ltd.
Publix Supermarkets
Simplot Co. (J.R.)

GAINSVILLE
Texaco Inc.
United States Sugar Corp.

GREENSVILLE
Fluor Corp.

HAINES CITY
Publix Supermarkets
United States Sugar Corp.

HIGHLAND CITY
AMETEK, Inc.
GEICO Corp.
Publix Supermarkets
State Farm Mutual Automobile Insurance Co.

JACKSONVILLE
Anheuser-Busch Companies, Inc.
AT&T Corp.
Belk Stores Services Inc.
Cincinnati Bell Inc.
Coca-Cola Co.
Emerson Electric Co.
Extendicare Health Services
First Union Corp.
Florida Power & Light Co.
Florida Rock Industries
Hensel Phelps Construction Co.
Merrill Lynch & Co., Inc.
National Presto Industries, Inc.
Prudential Insurance Co. of America
Publix Supermarkets
Rayonier Inc.
Reebok International Ltd.
Reynolds & Reynolds Co.
Ryder System, Inc.
Sega of America Inc.
Star Bank NA
Toshiba America Inc.
Winn-Dixie Stores Inc.

KEY LARGO
TMC Investment Co.

KISSIMMEE
Dynamet, Inc.
Sentinel Communications Co.

LABELLE
United States Sugar Corp.

LAKE CITY
United States Sugar Corp.

LAKE MARY
Mitsubishi Electric America

LAKE WORTH
BankAtlantic Bancorp

LAKELAND
AMETEK, Inc.
Coca-Cola Co.
Eckerd Corp.
Harris Corp.
Publix Supermarkets
Waste Management Inc.

LARGO
AEGON U.S.A. Inc.

LEESBURG
Publix Supermarkets
Sentinel Communications Co.

LONGBOAT KEY
Florida Power & Light Co.

LONGWOOD
Sentinel Communications Co.

MARGATE
Copley Press, Inc.

MELBOURNE
Harris Corp.

MIAMI
AMR Corp.
Anheuser-Busch Companies, Inc.
BankAtlantic Bancorp
BellSouth Corp.
Calvin Klein
Carillon Importers, Ltd.
Carnival Corp.
Carolina Power & Light Co.
CBS Corp.
Circuit City Stores, Inc.
Cooper Tire & Rubber Co.
Deloitte & Touche
Delta Air Lines, Inc.
Fannie Mae
Federated Department Stores, Inc.
First Union Corp.
Florida Power & Light Co.
Fortis, Inc.
General Atlantic Partners II LP
Georgia-Pacific Corp.
Gerber Products Co.
Harris Corp.
Huffy Corp.
Katten, Muchin & Zavis
Loews Corp.
MCI WorldCom, Inc.
Overseas Shipholding Group Inc.
Prudential Securities Inc.
Publix Supermarkets
Russer Foods
Ryder System, Inc.
State Street Bank & Trust Co.
SunTrust Banks of Florida
Taco Bell Corp.
United Airlines Inc.
Walgreen Co.
Weil, Gotshal & Manges Corp.
Winn-Dixie Stores Inc.
Witco Corp.

Funders by Location of Grant Recipient

MIAMI BEACH
BankAtlantic Bancorp
Mattel Inc.
Ryder System, Inc.
Sears, Roebuck and Co.

MIAMI SHORES
American Retail Group
BankAtlantic Bancorp
Ryder System, Inc.

MILTON
Gulf Power Co.

MOORE HAVEN
United States Sugar Corp.

N. MIAMI BEACH
United States Sugar Corp.

NAPLES
Erb Lumber Co.
Florida Power & Light Co.
Manor Care Health SVS, Inc.
Publix Supermarkets
Reinhart Institutional Foods
Russer Foods

NICEVILLE
Gulf Power Co.

NORTH MIAMI
BankAtlantic Bancorp
Extendicare Health Services

NORTH MIAMI BEACH
Century 21

NORTH PALM BEACH
Florida Power & Light Co.
Independent Stave Co.

OAKLAND PARK
BankAtlantic Bancorp

OCALA
Pacific Mutual Life Insurance Co.

ORLANDO
AT&T Corp.
BellSouth Corp.
Brunswick Corp.
Carillon Importers, Ltd.
CGU Insurance
Cincinnati Bell Inc.
Circuit City Stores, Inc.
Cox Enterprises Inc.
Disney Co. (Walt)
Dow Jones & Co., Inc.
Enterprise Rent-A-Car Co.
First Union Corp.
FMC Corp.
General Mills, Inc.
Harcourt General, Inc.
Harris Corp.
Independent Stave Co.
Indiana Mills & Manufacturing
Inland Container Corp.
International Multifoods Corp.
MONY Group (The)
Publix Supermarkets
Schwab & Co., Inc. (Charles)
Sentinel Communications Co.
SunTrust Banks of Florida
United States Sugar Corp.
Walgreen Co.
The Washington Post
Winn-Dixie Stores Inc.

PACE
Air Products and Chemicals, Inc.

PAHOKEE
Toshiba America Inc.

PALM BAY
Harris Corp.

PALM BEACH
Bardes Corp.
Bernstein & Co., Inc. (Sanford C.)
Erving Industries
Florida Power & Light Co.
Jacobson & Sons (Benjamin)
PerkinElmer, Inc.
Publix Supermarkets
Russer Foods
Tyson Foods Inc.

PALM BEACH GARDENS
United States Sugar Corp.

PALM COAST
Brunswick Corp.

PANAMA CITY
Gulf Power Co.

PANAMA CITY BEACH
Toshiba America Inc.

PENSACOLA
Armstrong World Industries, Inc.
Gulf Power Co.
Monsanto Co.
Simplot Co. (J.R.)
Sverdrup Corp.

PINELLAS
West Co. Inc.

PINELLAS PARK
Extendicare Health Services

POMPANO BEACH
Banfi Vintners
BankAtlantic Bancorp
Jacobson & Sons (Benjamin)

PORT CHARLOTTE
Florida Power & Light Co.
Publix Supermarkets

PORT ST. JOHN
Brunswick Corp.

RIVIERA BEACH
BankAtlantic Bancorp
United States Sugar Corp.

ROYAL PALM BEACH
Premier Dental Products Co.

SAINT PETERSBURG
GTE Corp.
Hartford Steam Boiler Inspection & Insurance Co.
Publix Supermarkets
Walgreen Co.

SARASOTA
Banfi Vintners
BP Amoco Corp.
Coca-Cola Co.
Disney Co. (Walt)
Eckerd Corp.
Erving Industries
Florida Power & Light Co.
KPMG Peat Marwick LLP
Lowe's Companies
Mead Corp.
Publix Supermarkets
Schering-Plough Corp.
Walgreen Co.

ST. AUGUSTINE
United States Sugar Corp.

ST. PETERSBURG
AMETEK, Inc.
Eckerd Corp.
Honeywell International Inc.
Waffle House Inc.

STUART
Florida Power & Light Co.
Russer Foods

SUNRISE
BankAtlantic Bancorp

TALLAHASSEE
Blount International, Inc.
Carnival Corp.
Cox Enterprises Inc.
Eckerd Corp.
Extendicare Health Services
Federated Department Stores, Inc.
First Union Corp.
Florida Power & Light Co.
Ford Motor Co.
Fortis, Inc.
Georgia-Pacific Corp.
Grace & Co. (W.R.)
Harris Corp.
Kimberly-Clark Corp.
MONY Group (The)
Parker Hannifin Corp.
PPG Industries, Inc.
Publix Supermarkets
Rayonier Inc.
SBC Communications Inc.
SunTrust Banks of Florida
Textron Inc.
Union Pacific Corp.
United States Sugar Corp.
Wal-Mart Stores, Inc.
The Washington Post
Waste Management Inc.
Xerox Corp.

TAMPA
Alcon Laboratories, Inc.
Baird & Co. (Robert W.)
BankAtlantic Bancorp
BellSouth Corp.
Cox Enterprises Inc.
Eckerd Corp.
Enterprise Rent-A-Car Co.
Federated Department Stores, Inc.
FINA
Florida Power & Light Co.
GTE Corp.
Harris Corp.
Mattel Inc.
MCI WorldCom, Inc.
Medtronic, Inc.
Price Associates (T. Rowe)
Publix Supermarkets
Tai and Co. (J.T.)
United Services Automobile Association
United States Sugar Corp.
Walgreen Co.
Walter Industries Inc.
Winn-Dixie Stores Inc.
Xerox Corp.

TAMPA BAY
Publix Supermarkets

TUTUSVILLE
Brunswick Corp.

UMATILLA
Duchossois Industries Inc.

VALENCIA
Sentinel Communications Co.

VERO BEACH
Florida Power & Light Co.

VIERA
Harris Corp.

WEST PALM BEACH
BankAtlantic Bancorp
Banta Corp.
Bardes Corp.
Bernstein & Co., Inc. (Sanford C.)
Callaway Golf Co.
Cox Enterprises Inc.
Fisher Brothers Cleaning Services
Florida Power & Light Co.
Grace & Co. (W.R.)
Independent Stave Co.
Jacobson & Sons (Benjamin)
Motorola Inc.
Rich Products Corp.
United States Sugar Corp.
United States Trust Co. of New York

WINTER PARK
Bardes Corp.
Carillon Importers, Ltd.
Seagram & Sons, Inc. (Joseph E.)
Sentinel Communications Co.
SunTrust Banks of Florida
Winn-Dixie Stores Inc.

Georgia

Briggs & Stratton Corp.
Delta Air Lines, Inc.
Dixie Group, Inc. (The)
Georgia Power Co.
Hubbell Inc.
Pieper Power Electric Co.

ALBANY
Pieper Power Electric Co.
Procter & Gamble Co.

ALPHARETTA
Atlantic Investment Co.

AMERICUS
AMR Corp.
Cargill Inc.
Cooper Industries, Inc.
Pieper Power Electric Co.
United Airlines Inc.
Weyerhaeuser Co.

ARMSTRONG
Colonial Oil Industries, Inc.

ATHENS
AT&T Corp.
Atlantic Investment Co.
BellSouth Corp.
Bradford & Co. (J.C.)
CertainTeed Corp.
Coca-Cola Co.
Deloitte & Touche
Delta Air Lines, Inc.
Eckerd Corp.
Georgia Power Co.
Harland Co. (John H.)
KPMG Peat Marwick LLP
LandAmerica Financial Services
National Service Industries, Inc.
Patagonia Inc.
Standard Products Co.
State Farm Mutual Automobile Insurance Co.
SunTrust Bank Atlanta
Synovus Financial Corp.
Temple-Inland Inc.

Waffle House Inc.
Waste Management Inc.

ATLANTA
Aetna, Inc.
Alcon Laboratories, Inc.
AlliedSignal Inc.
Allmerica Financial Corp.
Allstate Insurance Co.
American Express Co.
American Standard Inc.
APL Ltd.
Archer-Daniels-Midland Co.
Armstrong World Industries, Inc.
AT&T Corp.
Atlantic Investment Co.
Avon Products, Inc.
BellSouth Corp.
Ben & Jerry's Homemade Inc.
Blount International, Inc.
Blue Bell, Inc.
BP Amoco Corp.
Bristol-Myers Squibb Co.
Butler Manufacturing Co.
CIGNA Corp.
Circuit City Stores, Inc.
Clorox Co.
Coca-Cola Co.
Colonial Oil Industries, Inc.
Consolidated Papers, Inc.
Contran Corp.
Cox Enterprises Inc.
Credit Suisse First Boston
Deloitte & Touche
Delta Air Lines, Inc.
Disney Co. (Walt)
Dixie Group, Inc. (The)
du Pont de Nemours & Co. (E.I.)
Eastman Kodak Co.
Equifax Inc.
Exxon Mobil Corp.
Fannie Mae
Federated Department Stores, Inc.
Federated Mutual Insurance Co.
First Union Corp.
Florida Power & Light Co.
Fluor Corp.
Forbes Inc.
Ford Motor Co.
Fortis, Inc.
Fuller Co. (H.B.)
General Electric Co.
Georgia-Pacific Corp.
Georgia Power Co.
Gerber Products Co.
Goldman Sachs Group
Grace & Co. (W.R.)
Halliburton Co.
Harland Co. (John H.)
Hitachi America Ltd.
HON Industries Inc.
Hubbell Inc.
Intel Corp.
International Multifoods Corp.
International Paper Co.
Johnson & Son (S.C.)
Kimberly-Clark Corp.
KPMG Peat Marwick LLP
Kroger Co.
Landmark Communications Inc.
MCI WorldCom, Inc.
McWane Inc.
Mead Corp.
Medtronic, Inc.
Merrill Lynch & Co., Inc.

Metropolitan Life Insurance Co.
Mitsubishi Electric America
Monsanto Co.
Nabisco Group Holdings
National Service Industries, Inc.
NCR Corp.
New York Life Insurance Co.
Nordson Corp.
Norfolk Southern Corp.
Owens Corning
Pacific Mutual Life Insurance Co.
Pharmacia & Upjohn, Inc.
Phelps Dodge Corp.
Pheonix Financial Group
Phillips Petroleum Co.
Pieper Power Electric Co.
Pillsbury Co.
Potlatch Corp.
Provident Companies, Inc.
Prudential Insurance Co. of America
Publix Supermarkets
Quaker Chemical Corp.
Rayonier Inc.
Reebok International Ltd.
Rich Products Corp.
Royal & SunAlliance USA, Inc.
Schlumberger Ltd. (USA)
Seagram & Sons, Inc. (Joseph E.)
Searle & Co. (G.D.)
Sega of America Inc.
Shell Oil Co.
Sherwin-Williams Co.
Sprint Corp.
State Farm Mutual Automobile Insurance Co.
SunTrust Bank Atlanta
Susquehanna-Pfaltzgraff Co.
Synovus Financial Corp.
TENNANT Co.
Ticketmaster Corp.
Timken Co. (The)
Tomkins Industries, Inc.
Toshiba America Inc.
True North Communications, Inc.
Union Camp Corp.
Union Carbide Corp.
Union Pacific Corp.
United Parcel Service of America Inc.
Vulcan Materials Co.
Wachovia Bank of North Carolina NA
Waffle House Inc.
The Washington Post
Wells Fargo & Co.
Westvaco Corp.
Winn-Dixie Stores Inc.
Xerox Corp.

AUGUSTA
Federated Department Stores, Inc.
Georgia-Pacific Corp.
Georgia Power Co.
International Flavors & Fragrances Inc.
Monsanto Co.
Temple-Inland Inc.

BAXLEY
Rayonier Inc.

BOGART
CertainTeed Corp.

BRUNSWICK
Rayonier Inc.

CALHOUN
Outboard Marine Corp.

CARTERSVILLE
National Service Industries, Inc.
Unilever United States, Inc.

CHAMBLEE
Waffle House Inc.

CHESTNUT MOUNTAIN
Georgia Power Co.
Waffle House Inc.

CLARKSTON
Waffle House Inc.

COCHRAN
National Service Industries, Inc.

COLLEGE PARK
Detroit Edison Co.

COLUMBUS
Hallmark Cards Inc.
Mead Corp.
Synovus Financial Corp.
Vulcan Materials Co.

COMMERCE
Waffle House Inc.

CONYERS
Bard, Inc. (C.R.)

COVINGTON
Bard, Inc. (C.R.)
Fuller Co. (H.B.)
General Mills, Inc.
Harland Co. (John H.)

CUTHBERT
Synovus Financial Corp.

DALTON
Dixie Group, Inc. (The)

DECATUR
Atlantic Investment Co.
Blue Bell, Inc.
Deposit Guaranty National Bank
Harland Co. (John H.)
La-Z-Boy Inc.
PPG Industries, Inc.
Waffle House Inc.
Xerox Corp.

DEKALB
Waffle House Inc.

DUBLIN
Bassett Furniture Industries

DUNWOODY PARK
Equifax Inc.

EAST POINT
Atlantic Investment Co.
Nationwide Insurance Co.
Textron Inc.

EATONTON
Union Camp Corp.

FAYETTE COUNTY
Medtronic, Inc.

FAYETTEVILLE
Delta Air Lines, Inc.

FORT BENNING
Synovus Financial Corp.

FORT VALLEY
Synovus Financial Corp.

GAINESVILLE
Mitsubishi Electric America
Norton Co.
Vulcan Materials Co.
Wachovia Bank of North Carolina NA
Waste Management Inc.
Wrigley Co. (Wm. Jr.)

GRIFFIN
Standard Products Co.

GWINNETT
National Service Industries, Inc.
NCR Corp.

JASPER
Toshiba America Inc.

JEFFERSON
Belk Stores Services Inc.

JESSUP
Rayonier Inc.

JESUP
Rayonier Inc.

JONESBORO
Fuller Co. (H.B.)

KENNESAW
Cox Enterprises Inc.

KEYSVILLE
Hitachi America Ltd.

KINGSLAND
TENNANT Co.

LAGRANGE
Milliken & Co.

LAWRENCEVILE
United Parcel Service of America Inc.

LAWRENCEVILLE
BellSouth Corp.
Georgia Power Co.
Waffle House Inc.

LILBURN
Nordson Corp.
Vodafone AirTouch Plc

LUMBER CITY
Rayonier Inc.

LUMPKIN
Synovus Financial Corp.

MACON
Armstrong World Industries, Inc.
GEICO Corp.
Norfolk Southern Corp.
Pieper Power Electric Co.
SunTrust Bank Atlanta

MARIETTA
Belk-Simpson Department Stores
Deere & Co.
Hitachi America Ltd.
National Service Industries, Inc.
Waffle House Inc.

MEANSVILLE
Synovus Financial Corp.

MONTEZUMA
Agrilink Foods, Inc.

MOUNT BERRY
Florida Rock Industries
Fortis, Inc.
Georgia Power Co.

MOUNT VERNON
Georgia Power Co.

NORCROSS
Nordson Corp.
Vesper Corp.
Waffle House Inc.

NUNEZ
Rayonier Inc.

OXFORD
Bard, Inc. (C.R.)

PEACHTREE
ServiceMaster Co.

PLAINS
Elf Atochem North America, Inc.

ROME
Inland Container Corp.
Nordson Corp.
Temple-Inland Inc.

SAVANNAH
Colonial Oil Industries, Inc.
Hershey Foods Corp.
Kroger Co.
SunTrust Bank Atlanta
Union Camp Corp.
Wachovia Bank of North Carolina NA

SMYRNA
Equifax Inc.

STATESBORO
Briggs & Stratton Corp.
Colonial Oil Industries, Inc.
Tai and Co. (J.T.)
Union Camp Corp.

THOMASVILLE
United Parcel Service of America Inc.

TIFTON
Agrilink Foods, Inc.
Hershey Foods Corp.

TYRONE
Indiana Mills & Manufacturing
Rutledge Hill Press

VALDOSTA
Georgia Power Co.
Levi Strauss & Co.

VIDALIA
Publix Supermarkets

WARM SPRINGS
Equifax Inc.
Synovus Financial Corp.

WATKINSVILLE
Atlantic Investment Co.

WAYCROSS
Cooper Tire & Rubber Co.

WHITE
National Service Industries, Inc.

WINDER
Waffle House Inc.

YOUNG HARRIS
Fortis, Inc.
Harland Co. (John H.)
National Service Industries, Inc.

Hawaii

Hawaiian Electric Co., Inc.
Olin Corp.
Pacific Century Financial Corp.
ServiceMaster Co.

AIEA
Hawaiian Electric Co., Inc.

HAMAKUA
Pacific Century Financial Corp.

HANA
Alexander & Baldwin, Inc.

HILO
First Hawaiian, Inc.
Hawaiian Electric Co., Inc.
Tesoro Hawaii

HONOLULU
Alexander & Baldwin, Inc.
Bank of America
First Hawaiian, Inc.
Goldman Sachs Group
GTE Corp.
Hawaiian Electric Co., Inc.
Old National Bank Evansville
Pacific Century Financial Corp.
Reilly Industries, Inc.
Servco Pacific
Sony Electronics
Tesoro Hawaii
United Airlines Inc.

KAHUKU
Alexander & Baldwin, Inc.

KAILUA
Hawaiian Electric Co., Inc.
Tesoro Hawaii

KAILUA KONA
Hawaiian Electric Co., Inc.

KAILUA-KONA
Tesoro Hawaii

KAMUELA
Pacific Century Financial Corp.

KANEOHE
Contran Corp.
First Hawaiian, Inc.
Pacific Century Financial Corp.

KAUAI
Alexander & Baldwin, Inc.
First Hawaiian, Inc.
Pacific Century Financial Corp.

LAIE
First Hawaiian, Inc.
Hawaiian Electric Co., Inc.
Pacific Century Financial Corp.

LANAI CITY
Hawaiian Electric Co., Inc.

LANIKAI
Pacific Century Financial Corp.

LIHUE
Hawaiian Electric Co., Inc.
Pacific Century Financial Corp.

MANOA
Pacific Century Financial Corp.

MAUI
Alexander & Baldwin, Inc.
First Hawaiian, Inc.
Pacific Century Financial Corp.

NAMAKULI
Pacific Century Financial Corp.

OAHU
Alexander & Baldwin, Inc.
First Hawaiian, Inc.

PAPAIKOU
Tesoro Hawaii

PEARL CITY
Hawaiian Electric Co., Inc.

PEARL HARBOR
Hawaiian Electric Co., Inc.

PRINCEVILLE
First Hawaiian, Inc.

WAIANAE
First Hawaiian, Inc.

WAIKIKI
First Hawaiian, Inc.

WAILUKU
Tesoro Hawaii

Idaho

BOISE
Ben & Jerry's Homemade Inc.
CGU Insurance
Federated Department Stores, Inc.
Heinz Co. (H.J.)
Idaho Power Co.
Louisiana-Pacific Corp.
Morrison Knudsen Corp.
Patagonia Inc.
Portland General Electric Co.
Potlatch Corp.
Simplot Co. (J.R.)
Union Pacific Corp.
U.S. Bancorp

BURLEY
Heinz Co. (H.J.)

CALDWELL
Gallo Winery, Inc. (E&J)
Heinz Co. (H.J.)
Simplot Co. (J.R.)

COEUR D'ALENE
Kimball International, Inc.
Washington Trust Bank

GOODING
Toshiba America Inc.

HERMISTON
Simplot Co. (J.R.)

KETCHUM
Charter Manufacturing Co.

LEWISTON
Blount International, Inc.

MCCALL
Patagonia Inc.
Simplot Co. (J.R.)

MERIDIAN
Land O'Lakes, Inc.
Simplot Co. (J.R.)

MINI-CASSIA
Simplot Co. (J.R.)

MOSCOW
Cenex Harvest States
Heinz Co. (H.J.)
Louisiana-Pacific Corp.
Patagonia Inc.
Simplot Co. (J.R.)

NAMPA
Rayonier Inc.
Simplot Co. (J.R.)

PLUMMER
Rayonier Inc.

POCATELLO
Commercial Intertech Corp.
FMC Corp.
Simplot Co. (J.R.)
Union Pacific Corp.
US West, Inc.

POST FALLS
Kimball International, Inc.

REXBURG
Louisiana-Pacific Corp.
Simplot Co. (J.R.)

TWIN FALLS
Simplot Co. (J.R.)

Illinois

CNA
Comdisco, Inc.
GATX Corp.
Hamilton Sundstrand Corp.
Searle & Co. (G.D.)
USG Corp.
Woodward Governor Co.

ALEDO
HON Industries Inc.

ALTON
Shell Oil Co.

ARLINGTON
Fuller Co. (H.B.)

ARLINGTON HEIGHTS
Allstate Insurance Co.
Chicago Tribune Co.
Hartmarx Corp.

AURORA
Amsted Industries Inc.
Chicago Tribune Co.
Copley Press, Inc.
Evening Post Publishing Co.
Gap, Inc.
Hamilton Sundstrand Corp.
Hitachi America Ltd.
Nalco Chemical Co.
Pittway Corp.

BARRINGTON
Comdisco, Inc.
Duchossois Industries Inc.
Indiana Mills & Manufacturing
Square D Co.
Trustmark Insurance Co.

BARTLETT
Mitsubishi Electric America

BELLEVILLE
Ralston Purina Co.

BELVIDERE
Pillsbury Co.

BENSENVILLE
Nalco Chemical Co.

BERWYN
Chicago Tribune Co.

BLOOMINGTON
Bridgestone/Firestone, Inc.
Commerce Bancshares, Inc.
Deloitte & Touche
Enterprise Rent-A-Car Co.
Johnson & Son (S.C.)
Security Benefit Life Insurance Co.
State Farm Mutual Automobile Insurance Co.
Waste Management Inc.

BROKFIELD
Hartmarx Corp.

BROOKFIELD
AMR Corp.
Chicago Board of Trade
Duchossois Industries Inc.
Globe Corp.
Illinois Tool Works, Inc.
Nalco Chemical Co.
Searle & Co. (G.D.)
USG Corp.

BUFFALO GROVE
Clorox Co.
Trustmark Insurance Co.

CARBONDALE
Laclede Gas Co.
Lee Enterprises
Trustmark Insurance Co.

CENTRALIA
Hubbell Inc.

CHAMPAIGN
Abbott Laboratories
Ameritech Corp.
Butler Manufacturing Co.
Cargill Inc.
Caterpillar Inc.
DeKalb Genetics Corp.
Hartmarx Corp.
Illinois Tool Works, Inc.
Lilly & Co. (Eli)
Lubrizol Corp. (The)
Van Leer Holding
Xerox Corp.

CHATMAN
Eastern Enterprises

CHICAGO
Abbott Laboratories
ABC
Allegheny Technologies Inc.
AlliedSignal Inc.
Allstate Insurance Co.
Alma Piston Co.
American Express Co.
American Standard Inc.
Ameritech Corp.
AMR Corp.
Amsted Industries Inc.
Aon Corp.
Archer-Daniels-Midland Co.
Armstrong World Industries, Inc.
Arvin Industries, Inc.
AT&T Corp.
Baird & Co. (Robert W.)
Bank of America
Bank One Corp.
Bard, Inc. (C.R.)
Baxter International Inc.
Ben & Jerry's Homemade Inc.
Blair & Co. (William)
Blue Cross & Blue Shield of Minnesota
Boler Co.
BP Amoco Corp.
Bridgestone/Firestone, Inc.
Brunswick Corp.
Calvin Klein
Campbell Soup Co.
Carpenter Technology Corp.
CBS Corp.
Charter Manufacturing Co.
Chase Manhattan Bank, NA
Chicago Board of Trade
Chicago Sun-Times, Inc.
Chicago Title Corp.
Chicago Tribune Co.
CIGNA Corp.
Cincinnati Bell Inc.
Clorox Co.
CNA
Coca-Cola Co.
Comdisco, Inc.
ConAgra, Inc.
Cooper Tire & Rubber Co.
Coors Brewing Co.
Credit Suisse First Boston
Deere & Co.
Deloitte & Touche
Deluxe Corp.
Demoulas Supermarkets Inc.
Dial Corp.
Domino's Pizza Inc.
Dow Jones & Co., Inc.
Duchossois Industries Inc.
Ecolab Inc.
Edison Brothers Stores, Inc.
Enterprise Rent-A-Car Co.
Extendicare Health Services
Fannie Mae
Fireman's Fund Insurance Co.
First National Bank of Evergreen Park
FMC Corp.
Forbes Inc.
Forest City Enterprises, Inc.
Freddie Mac
Freeport-McMoRan Inc.
Furniture Brands International, Inc.
Gallo Winery, Inc. (E&J)
Galter Corp.
GATX Corp.
General Mills, Inc.
Gerber Products Co.
Giant Food Inc.
Globe Corp.
Goldman Sachs Group
Grace & Co. (W.R.)
Grede Foundries
Harris Corp.
Harris Trust & Savings Bank
Harsco Corp.
Hartford (The)
Hartmarx Corp.
Heinz Co. (H.J.)
Hoffer Plastics Corp.
Humana, Inc.
IKON Office Solutions, Inc.
Illinois Tool Works, Inc.
Inland Container Corp.
Jacobs Engineering Group
Katten, Muchin & Zavis
Kemper National Insurance Companies
Kimberly-Clark Corp.
Kirkland & Ellis
KPMG Peat Marwick LLP
Land O'Lakes, Inc.
LandAmerica Financial Services
Leviton Manufacturing Co. Inc.
Lipton Co.
Little, Inc. (Arthur D.)
LTV Corp.
Manor Care Health SVS, Inc.
Marshall Field's
Mattel Inc.
McClatchy Co.
MCI WorldCom, Inc.
McWane Inc.
Merrill Lynch & Co., Inc.
Metropolitan Life Insurance Co.
Minnesota Mining & Manufacturing Co.
Mitsubishi Electric America
Montgomery Ward & Co., Inc.
Morgan & Co. Inc. (J.P.)
Morgan Stanley Dean Witter & Co.
Morrison Knudsen Corp.
Morton International Inc.
Motorola Inc.
Nabisco Group Holdings
Nalco Chemical Co.
NASDAQ Stock Market
National Service Industries, Inc.
National Starch & Chemical Co.
Nationwide Insurance Co.
NEC America, Inc.
Nestle U.S.A. Inc.
New York Life Insurance Co.
New York Mercantile Exchange
Northern Trust Co.
Overseas Shipholding Group Inc.
Owens Corning
Paine Webber
Pillsbury Co.
Pittway Corp.
Playboy Enterprises Inc.
Premier Industrial Corp.
Prudential Securities Inc.
Publix Supermarkets
Putnam Investments
Ralston Purina Co.
Russer Foods
Sara Lee Corp.
Searle & Co. (G.D.)
Sega of America Inc.
ServiceMaster Co.
Sherwin-Williams Co.
Sierra Pacific Resources
SIT Investment Associates, Inc.
Solo Cup Co.
Sony Electronics
Southwest Gas Corp.
Sprint Corp.
Square D Co.
State Farm Mutual Automobile Insurance Co.
Stone Container Corp.
Stupp Brothers Bridge & Iron Co.
Tai and Co. (J.T.)
Ticketmaster Corp.
Timken Co. (The)
Tomkins Industries, Inc.

Toshiba America Inc.
Toyota Motor Sales U.S.A., Inc.
Trace International Holdings, Inc.
True North Communications, Inc.
Trustmark Insurance Co.
Union Pacific Corp.
United Airlines Inc.
United Distillers & Vintners North America
Universal Foods Corp.
UPN Channel 50
USG Corp.
Valspar Corp.
Vulcan Materials Co.
Warner-Lambert Co.
Waste Management Inc.
Weil, Gotshal & Manges Corp.
Wells Fargo & Co.
Whirlpool Corp.
Whitman Corp.
Wolverine World Wide
Wrigley Co. (Wm. Jr.)
Xerox Corp.
Young & Rubicam

CICERO
Chicago Tribune Co.

CLINTON
Corning Inc.

CRYSTAL LAKE
Motorola Inc.

DANVILLE
Walgreen Co.

DECATUR
Archer-Daniels-Midland Co.
Bridgestone/Firestone, Inc.
Caterpillar Inc.
Kemper National Insurance Companies
Lee Enterprises
Norfolk Southern Corp.
State Farm Mutual Automobile Insurance Co.
Walgreen Co.

DEERFIELD
Avon Products, Inc.
Bemis Manufacturing Co.
Comdisco, Inc.
Globe Corp.

DEKALB
Blair & Co. (William)
CLARCOR Inc.
DeKalb Genetics Corp.
GTE Corp.
Kemper National Insurance Companies
Square D Co.
USG Corp.

DES PLAINES
Allstate Insurance Co.
Amsted Industries Inc.
Aon Corp.
Auburn Foundry
Blair & Co. (William)
Comdisco, Inc.
Freddie Mac
GEICO Corp.
Heinz Co. (H.J.)
Mine Safety Appliances Co.
National Presto Industries, Inc.
North American Royalties
Northern Trust Co.
Parker Hannifin Corp.

DIXON
Donaldson Co., Inc.
Universal Foods Corp.

DOWNERS GROVE
Nalco Chemical Co.
Waste Management Inc.

DU PAGE
CNA

DUNDEE
Hoffer Plastics Corp.

DUPAGE
Chicago Sun-Times, Inc.

EAST MOLINE
Deere & Co.

EDWARDSVILLE
Amsted Industries Inc.
Andersen Corp.
GenAmerica Corp.

ELGIN
AMCORE Bank Rockford
Amsted Industries Inc.
Chicago Tribune Co.
Hoffer Plastics Corp.
Illinois Tool Works, Inc.

ELK GROVE VILLAGE
Allstate Insurance Co.
Cooper Industries, Inc.
Duchossois Industries Inc.

ELMHURST
Brunswick Corp.
Chicago Tribune Co.
Enterprise Rent-A-Car Co.
Nalco Chemical Co.
Waste Management Inc.

EVANSTON
AlliedSignal Inc.
Ameritech Corp.
AMETEK, Inc.
Amgen, Inc.
AMR Corp.
Amsted Industries Inc.
Aon Corp.
ASARCO Inc.
Atlantic Richfield Co.
Avon Products, Inc.
Bechtel Group, Inc.
BFGoodrich Co.
Blair & Co. (William)
BP Amoco Corp.
Bridgestone/Firestone, Inc.
Bristol-Myers Squibb Co.
Carlson Companies, Inc.
Central Soya Co.
Chicago Title Corp.
CIGNA Corp.
Clorox Co.
ConAgra, Inc.
Consolidated Papers, Inc.
Continental Grain Co.
Cooper Industries, Inc.
Deluxe Corp.
Dow Chemical Co.
Dow Jones & Co., Inc.
Duchossois Industries Inc.
Dun & Bradstreet Corp.
Federal-Mogul Corp.
Federated Department Stores, Inc.
Ferro Corp.
FMC Corp.
GATX Corp.
GenCorp
General Mills, Inc.
Georgia-Pacific Corp.
Hartford (The)
Hartmarx Corp.
Hubbell Inc.
IKON Office Solutions, Inc.
Illinois Tool Works, Inc.
Kennametal, Inc.
Kirkland & Ellis
Lehigh Portland Cement Co.
Lennox International, Inc.
May Department Stores Co.
McClatchy Co.
McGraw-Hill Companies, Inc.
McKesson-HBOC Corp.
McWane Inc.
Metropolitan Life Insurance Co.
Motorola Inc.
Nabisco Group Holdings
Nationwide Insurance Co.
Norfolk Southern Corp.
Northern Trust Co.
Occidental Oil and Gas
Occidental Petroleum Corp.
Olin Corp.
Outboard Marine Corp.
Parker Hannifin Corp.
Pharmacia & Upjohn, Inc.
Phelps Dodge Corp.
Polaroid Corp.
PPG Industries, Inc.
Procter & Gamble Co.
Prudential Securities Inc.
Quanex Corp.
Reynolds Tobacco (R.J.)
Sara Lee Corp.
Schering-Plough Corp.
Searle & Co. (G.D.)
ServiceMaster Co.
Shell Oil Co.
Square D Co.
State Farm Mutual Automobile Insurance Co.
Steelcase Inc.
Storage Technology Corp.
Textron Inc.
Thompson Co. (J. Walter)
TJX Companies, Inc.
Tomkins Industries, Inc.
Trustmark Insurance Co.
Unilever United States, Inc.
United Airlines Inc.
United Parcel Service of America Inc.
USG Corp.
Waste Management Inc.
Weyerhaeuser Co.
Whitman Corp.
Wolverine World Wide

EVANSTOWN
Xerox Corp.

EVERGREEN PARK
First National Bank of Evergreen Park
Nalco Chemical Co.

FAIRFIELD
Standard Products Co.

FREEPORT
Honeywell International Inc.
Trustmark Insurance Co.

GALESBURG
Butler Manufacturing Co.
Caterpillar Inc.
Deere & Co.
Hickory Tech Corp.
Maytag Corp.

GENEVA
Amsted Industries Inc.
Pillsbury Co.

GLEN ELLYN
General Mills, Inc.

GLENCOE
Searle & Co. (G.D.)
United Airlines Inc.

GLENDALE HEIGHTS
Nalco Chemical Co.

GLENVIEW
Chicago Title Corp.
CNA

GLENWOOD
Chicago Board of Trade
Duchossois Industries Inc.
Northern Trust Co.
Smurfit-Stone Container Corp.

GODFREY
Kellwood Co.
Olin Corp.

GOLF
Griffith Laboratories U.S.A.
Sentry Insurance, A Mutual Co.
Smurfit-Stone Container Corp.

GRANITE CITY
Eastern Bank
Ralston Purina Co.
Toshiba America Inc.

GRAYSLAKE
Abbott Laboratories
Baxter International Inc.
Trustmark Insurance Co.

GREEN OAKS
Abbott Laboratories
Allstate Insurance Co.
Baxter International Inc.
Outboard Marine Corp.
Trustmark Insurance Co.

GREENVILLE
Kemper National Insurance Companies
Mercantile Bank NA

GURNEE
Brunswick Corp.
Chicago Tribune Co.
Outboard Marine Corp.
Solo Cup Co.
Trustmark Insurance Co.

HARVEY
Duchossois Industries Inc.

HIGHLAND
Barnes Group Inc.

HIGHLAND PARK
Abbott Laboratories
Amsted Industries Inc.
Aon Corp.
Blair & Co. (William)
Carris Reels
Duchossois Industries Inc.
FMC Corp.
Hartmarx Corp.
Illinois Tool Works, Inc.
Katten, Muchin & Zavis
Marshall Field's
Northern Trust Co.
Searle & Co. (G.D.)
Solo Cup Co.
Trustmark Insurance Co.

HINSDALE
Circuit City Stores, Inc.
GATX Corp.
Waste Management Inc.

HOFFMAN ESTATES
Chicago Tribune Co.
Sara Lee Corp.

HOMEWOOD
Chicago Tribune Co.

INDIANAPOLIS
Lilly & Co. (Eli)

ITASCA
Mine Safety Appliances Co.

JACKSONVILLE
National Starch & Chemical Co.

JOLIET
Crane Co.
Ecolab Inc.
Gap, Inc.
Illinois Tool Works, Inc.
Kemper National Insurance Companies
Nalco Chemical Co.
Unilever United States, Inc.
Walgreen Co.

JOSLIN
IBP

KANE COUNTY
Pittway Corp.

KANKAKEE
Temple-Inland Inc.

LA RABIDA
Square D Co.

LAGRANGE
United Airlines Inc.

LAKE BLUFF
Brunswick Corp.

LAKE CHARLES
Reynolds Metals Co.

LAKE FOREST
Abbott Laboratories
Baxter International Inc.
Blair & Co. (William)
Chemed Corp.
Hartmarx Corp.
Huffy Corp.
Kemper National Insurance Companies
Nomura Holding America
Outboard Marine Corp.
Searle & Co. (G.D.)
Stone Container Corp.
Trustmark Insurance Co.
USG Corp.
Whitman Corp.

LAKE VILLA
Abbott Laboratories
Stone Container Corp.

LAWRENCE
GATX Corp.

LEMONT
Griffith Laboratories U.S.A.

LIBERTYVILLE
Abbott Laboratories
Brunswick Corp.

LISLE
Amsted Industries Inc.
Nalco Chemical Co.

LOVES PARK
Hamilton Sundstrand Corp.

MACOMB
Ameritech Corp.
Archer-Daniels-Midland Co.

MACON
Caterpillar Inc.

MATTESON
Marshall Field's

MAYWOOD
Nalco Chemical Co.

MCCOMB
DSM Copolymer

MCHENRY
Allstate Insurance Co.

MOLINE
Deere & Co.
Lee Enterprises

MONMOUTH
Butler Manufacturing Co.

MORTON
Caterpillar Inc.

MOUNT PROSPECT
Chicago Tribune Co.

MUNCIE
Trustmark Insurance Co.

NAPERVILLE
BP Amoco Corp.
CLARCOR Inc.
Copley Press, Inc.
Dow Jones & Co., Inc.
Kemper National Insurance Companies
LandAmerica Financial Services
Nalco Chemical Co.
USG Corp.
Waste Management Inc.
Wrigley Co. (Wm. Jr.)

NORMAL
Allstate Insurance Co.
CNA
Comdisco, Inc.
Griffith Laboratories U.S.A.
Kemper National Insurance Companies
State Farm Mutual Automobile Insurance Co.

NORTHBROOK
Blair & Co. (William)

NOTRE DAME
Kirkland & Ellis

OAK BROOK
Amgen, Inc.
AMR Corp.
Archer-Daniels-Midland Co.
Griffith Laboratories U.S.A.
Red Wing Shoe Co. Inc.
Shell Oil Co.

OAK FOREST
Whitman Corp.

OAK LAWN
Chicago Tribune Co.
First National Bank of Evergreen Park

OAK PARK
Harris Trust & Savings Bank
Searle & Co. (G.D.)

OLYMPIA FIELDS
Whitman Corp.

PALATINE
Duchossois Industries Inc.
Fuller Co. (H.B.)
Motorola Inc.
Solo Cup Co.
Square D Co.
Unocal Corp.

PALOS HEIGHTS
Waste Management Inc.

PARK RIDGE
Comdisco, Inc.
Fuller Co. (H.B.)
Galter Corp.
Land O'Lakes, Inc.
Morris Communications Corp.
Toledo Blade Co.
Valspar Corp.
Western & Southern Life Insurance Co.

PEKIN
Alcoa Inc.

PEORIA
Archer-Daniels-Midland Co.
Caterpillar Inc.
Commerce Bancshares, Inc.
Copley Press, Inc.
Deere & Co.
First Financial Bank
Gap, Inc.
Hubbell Inc.
Kemper National Insurance Companies
Kroger Co.
Laclede Gas Co.
Merrill Lynch & Co., Inc.
National Presto Industries, Inc.
State Farm Mutual Automobile Insurance Co.
Vesper Corp.
Waste Management Inc.

PRINCETON
Jostens, Inc.

PROSPECT HEIGHTS
Harland Co. (John H.)

QUINCY
Harris Corp.

RIVER FOREST
Chicago Tribune Co.

ROCK ISLAND
Deere & Co.
HON Industries Inc.
Norwest Corp.
PepsiCo, Inc.
Walgreen Co.

ROCKFORD
AMCORE Bank Rockford
CLARCOR Inc.
First Financial Bank
Hamilton Sundstrand Corp.
Valspar Corp.
Woodward Governor Co.

ROLLING MEADOWS
Allstate Insurance Co.
Duchossois Industries Inc.
Mitsubishi Electric America
Motorola Inc.

ROSEMONT
Alma Piston Co.

ROUND LAKE
Abbott Laboratories

SAINT CHARLES
Pittway Corp.

SAVOY
Andersons Inc.

SCHAUMBURG
CNA
Whirlpool Corp.
Whitman Corp.

SCHILLER PARK
Schlumberger Ltd. (USA)
Shell Oil Co.
Warner-Lambert Co.

SKOKIE
Brunswick Corp.
Comdisco, Inc.
Solo Cup Co.
Young & Rubicam

SOUTH ELGIN
Hoffer Plastics Corp.

SPRINGFIELD
Chicago Tribune Co.
CNA
Gap, Inc.
International Multifoods Corp.

ST. CHARLES
Chicago Tribune Co.
Nalco Chemical Co.

ST. LOUIS
Pfizer Inc.

STATEN ISLAND
Jacobson & Sons (Benjamin)
S.G. Cowen

STREAMWOOD
Allstate Insurance Co.

SYCAMORE
DeKalb Genetics Corp.

TAYLOR RIDGE
HON Industries Inc.

UNIVERSITY PARK
Duchossois Industries Inc.
Northern Trust Co.

URBANA
Abbott Laboratories
AlliedSignal Inc.
Amsted Industries Inc.
Deere & Co.
DeKalb Genetics Corp.
Ford Motor Co.
General Electric Co.
General Motors Corp.
International Paper Co.
KPMG Peat Marwick LLP
Microsoft Corp.
Motorola Inc.
Pittway Corp.
Procter & Gamble Co.
Reader's Digest Association, Inc. (The)
Searle & Co. (G.D.)
State Farm Mutual Automobile Insurance Co.
Unocal Corp.
USG Corp.
Waste Management Inc.

VILLA PARK
Nalco Chemical Co.

WASHINGTON
Baxter International Inc.

WAUKEGAN
Abbott Laboratories
Baxter International Inc.
Brunswick Corp.
Chicago Tribune Co.
Dexter Corp.
Marshall Field's
Solo Cup Co.
Trustmark Insurance Co.
Westvaco Corp.

WESTCHESTER
Chicago Tribune Co.
Northern Trust Co.

WHEATON
Indiana Mills & Manufacturing
MTD Products Inc.
Nalco Chemical Co.
ServiceMaster Co.
United States Trust Co. of New York
UPN Channel 50
USG Corp.

WINFIELD
Nalco Chemical Co.

WINNETKA
Solo Cup Co.
Stone Container Corp.

WOODSTOCK
AMCORE Bank Rockford

ZION
Chicago Tribune Co.

Indiana

AK Steel Corp.
Crane Co.
Reilly Industries, Inc.

ANGOLA
Auburn Foundry
Journal-Gazette Co.
SPX Corp.

AUBURN
Auburn Foundry
Cooper Tire & Rubber Co.
Dana Corp.
Journal-Gazette Co.
Reynolds Metals Co.

BEFORD
Lehigh Portland Cement Co.

BLOOMINGTON
American United Life Insurance Co.
Chemed Corp.
CNA
Donaldson Co., Inc.
Inland Container Corp.
Journal-Gazette Co.
Kimball International, Inc.
Lilly & Co. (Eli)
Lubrizol Corp. (The)
Old National Bank Evansville
Procter & Gamble Co.
Reader's Digest Association, Inc. (The)
Temple-Inland Inc.
Waste Management Inc.
Whirlpool Corp.

BLUFFION
Journal-Gazette Co.

BLUFFTON
Andersons Inc.
Franklin Electric Co.

CARMEL
Indiana Mills & Manufacturing
Lilly & Co. (Eli)

COLUMBIA CITY
Journal-Gazette Co.

COLUMBUS
Arvin Industries, Inc.
Cummins Engine Co., Inc.
Kimball International, Inc.
Woodward Governor Co.

CORYDON
Minnesota Mining & Manufacturing Co.

CRAWFORDSVILLE
Inland Container Corp.
Lilly & Co. (Eli)
May Department Stores Co.

CRIFFIN
LTV Corp.

CULVER
Duchossois Industries Inc.

DECATUR
Central Soya Co.

DEKALB
Cooper Tire & Rubber Co.

DONALDSON
First Source Corp.

DUBOIS
Kimball International, Inc.

ECKHART
Cooper Tire & Rubber Co.

ELKHART
First Source Corp.
Journal-Gazette Co.
National Presto Industries, Inc.
Owens Corning

EVANSTON
El Paso Energy Co.

EVANSVILLE
AK Steel Corp.
American General Finance
Kimball International, Inc.
Koch Enterprises, Inc.
Liberty Corp.
Old National Bank Evansville
Temple-Inland Inc.
TJX Companies, Inc.
Walgreen Co.
Whirlpool Corp.

FERDINAND
Kimball International, Inc.

FISHERS
Cinergy Corp.

FORT WAYNE
Auburn Foundry
Central Newspapers, Inc.
Central Soya Co.
Cooper Tire & Rubber Co.
Dana Corp.
Franklin Electric Co.
GTE Corp.
Journal-Gazette Co.
Lincoln Financial Group
Mattel Inc.
New Jersey Natural Gas Co.
Phelps Dodge Corp.
SIT Investment Associates, Inc.
Ticketmaster Corp.
Walgreen Co.

FRANKFORT
PepsiCo, Inc.

FRANKLIN
Arvin Industries, Inc.

FT. WAYNE
Dana Corp.

FT.WAYNE
Ford Meter Box Co.

FULDA
Kimball International, Inc.

GARY
Chicago Tribune Co.
USX Corp.

GOSHEN
First Source Corp.
Huffy Corp.

GREENCASTLE
DeKalb Genetics Corp.
Laclede Gas Co.
Lilly & Co. (Eli)
The Washington Post

GREENFIELD
Arvin Industries, Inc.

GREENVILLE
Parker Hannifin Corp.

GREENWOOD
Indiana Mills & Manufacturing

GRIFFITH
Bethlehem Steel Corp.
BP Amoco Corp.
Lehigh Portland Cement Co.
LTV Corp.
Unilever United States, Inc.
UPN Channel 50
USX Corp.
Walgreen Co.

HAGERSTOWN
Grede Foundries

HAMMOND
Ben & Jerry's Homemade Inc.

HANOVER
Amsted Industries Inc.
Koch Enterprises, Inc.

HENDERSON
Koch Enterprises, Inc.

HOPE
Arvin Industries, Inc.
Cummins Engine Co., Inc.
Susquehanna-Pfaltzgraff Co.

INDIANAPOLIS
Allstate Insurance Co.
American United Life Insurance Co.
Amsted Industries Inc.
Arvin Industries, Inc.
Auburn Foundry
Baxter International Inc.
Bemis Co., Inc.
Bethlehem Steel Corp.
Bridgestone/Firestone, Inc.
Cargill Inc.
Central Newspapers, Inc.
Central Soya Co.
CGU Insurance
Cinergy Corp.
Cooper Tire & Rubber Co.
Cummins Engine Co., Inc.
Donaldson Co., Inc.
Dow Chemical Co.
Federated Department Stores, Inc.
Fifth Third Bancorp
Ford Meter Box Co.
GEICO Corp.
Gerber Products Co.
GTE Corp.
Halliburton Co.
Indiana Mills & Manufacturing
Inland Container Corp.
International Multifoods Corp.
Journal-Gazette Co.
Kemper National Insurance Companies
Kimball International, Inc.
Koch Enterprises, Inc.
Kroger Co.
LandAmerica Financial Services
Lehigh Portland Cement Co.
Lilly & Co. (Eli)
May Department Stores Co.
Maytag Corp.
McDonald & Co. Securities, Inc.
McGraw-Hill Companies, Inc.
Medtronic, Inc.
MONY Group (The)
National City Corp.
National Starch & Chemical Co.
Nationwide Insurance Co.
Old National Bank Evansville
Olin Corp.
Pfizer Inc.
Premier Industrial Corp.
Reilly Industries, Inc.
Sentry Insurance, A Mutual Co.
Sunmark Capital Corp.
Tamko Roofing Products
Temple-Inland Inc.
United Airlines Inc.
Universal Foods Corp.
USAA Life Insurance Co.
USG Corp.
Walgreen Co.
Westvaco Corp.
Wilbur-Ellis Co. & Connell Brothers Co.

JASPER
Kimball International, Inc.

KOKOMO
Ford Meter Box Co.

LA PORTE
Bethlehem Steel Corp.
Whirlpool Corp.

LAFAYETTE
Caterpillar Inc.
Cooper Industries, Inc.
Koch Enterprises, Inc.
Lilly & Co. (Eli)
Shea Co. (John F.)
State Farm Mutual Automobile Insurance Co.
TRW Inc.

LINCOLN CITY
Kimball International, Inc.

LOGANSPORT
Andersons Inc.
First Source Corp.
IBP

LOOGOOTEE
Kimball International, Inc.

MADISON
Cummins Engine Co., Inc.

MANCHESTER
Ford Meter Box Co.

MARION
Dana Corp.
Ford Meter Box Co.
GenCorp

MARTINSVILLE
Lennox International, Inc.
New York Mercantile Exchange

MARTINVILLE
CSS Industries, Inc.

MERRILVILLE
UPN Channel 50

MICHIGAN CITY
Bethlehem Steel Corp.
Hamilton Sundstrand Corp.
Hartmarx Corp.

MISHAWAKA
First Source Corp.

MISHAWKA
First Source Corp.

MITCHELL
Kimball International, Inc.
Lehigh Portland Cement Co.

MONROEVILLE
Koch Enterprises, Inc.

MONTGOMERY
Kimball International, Inc.

MONTPELIER
Franklin Electric Co.

MOUNT VERNON
Cummins Engine Co., Inc.

MUNCIE
Andersons Inc.
CUNA Mutual Group
Elf Atochem North America, Inc.
International Paper Co.
Outboard Marine Corp.
Wisconsin Power & Light Co.

MUNSTER
UPN Channel 50

MURFREESBORO
Fluor Corp.

NEW ALBANY
Chemed Corp.

NEW CASTLE
Agrilink Foods, Inc.

NEWBURGH
AK Steel Corp.
Old National Bank Evansville

NEWPORT
Inland Container Corp.

NORTH MANCHESTER
Ford Meter Box Co.

NORTH VERNON
Lowe's Companies

NOTRE DAME
Abbott Laboratories
ABC
AlliedSignal Inc.
BFGoodrich Co.
Boeing Co.
BP Amoco Corp.
Butler Manufacturing Co.
Deloitte & Touche
Dow Chemical Co.
Dun & Bradstreet Corp.
First Source Corp.
General Motors Corp.
Koch Enterprises, Inc.
Lubrizol Corp. (The)
Motorola Inc.
Olin Corp.
Pheonix Financial Group
Reynolds Tobacco (R.J.)
Texaco Inc.
Union Carbide Corp.
United Parcel Service of America Inc.
Waste Management Inc.

PALASKI
Hubbell Inc.

PENNVILLE
Franklin Electric Co.

PERU
Square D Co.

PLYMOUTH
First Source Corp.
Jeld-wen, Inc.

PORTAGE
Bethlehem Steel Corp.

PORTLAND
Andersons Inc.

REMINGTON
Central Soya Co.

RICHMOND
Dana Corp.
Reilly Industries, Inc.
Standard Products Co.

ROANN
Ford Meter Box Co.

ROCHESTER
Dana Corp.
First Source Corp.
Hartmarx Corp.

ROCKPORT
Kimball International, Inc.

SAINT HENRY
Kimball International, Inc.

SAINT MEINRAD
Kimball International, Inc.

SANTA CLAUS
Kimball International, Inc.
Koch Enterprises, Inc.

SCOTTSBURG
Cummins Engine Co., Inc.
Standard Products Co.

SEYMOUR
Cummins Engine Co., Inc.

SHELBYVILLE
Monarch Machine Tool Co.

SHOALS
Kimball International, Inc.

SIBERIA
Kimball International, Inc.

SOUTH BEND
AlliedSignal Inc.
Cincinnati Bell Inc.
Cooper Tire & Rubber Co.
Federal-Mogul Corp.
First Source Corp.
General Electric Co.
Hubbell Inc.
New York Times Co.
South Bend Tribune Corp.
Trustmark Insurance Co.
Whirlpool Corp.

ST. MEINRAD
Cooper Tire & Rubber Co.

TELL CITY
Kimball International, Inc.

TERRE HAUTE
Banfi Vintners
Bemis Co., Inc.
Cummins Engine Co., Inc.
Dun & Bradstreet Corp.
Kimball International, Inc.
USX Corp.

UPLAND
Cooper Tire & Rubber Co.

VALPARAISO
Bethlehem Steel Corp.
Emerson Electric Co.
Kemper National Insurance Companies
MTD Products Inc.

WABASH
Ford Meter Box Co.

WALKERTON
First Source Corp.

WEST LAFAYETTE
Air Products and Chemicals, Inc.
AlliedSignal Inc.
American United Life Insurance Co.
Ameritech Corp.
Amsted Industries Inc.
Arvin Industries, Inc.
AT&T Corp.
Boeing Co.
BP Amoco Corp.
Caterpillar Inc.
Cooper Tire & Rubber Co.
Dow Chemical Co.
Eastman Kodak Co.
Fluor Corp.
Ford Motor Co.
GTE Corp.
Hoffer Plastics Corp.
Intel Corp.
Koch Enterprises, Inc.
Lilly & Co. (Eli)
Lubrizol Corp. (The)
Merck & Co.
Milacron, Inc.
Procter & Gamble Co.
Temple-Inland Inc.
Trustmark Insurance Co.
Union Carbide Corp.
Whirlpool Corp.

WHITING
UPN Channel 50

WINIMAC
First Source Corp.

Iowa

Blue Cross & Blue Shield of Iowa
Cenex Harvest States

ALBIA
Shelter Mutual Insurance Co.

AMES
Amsted Industries Inc.
Blue Cross & Blue Shield of Iowa
Butler Manufacturing Co.
Cargill Inc.
DeKalb Genetics Corp.
DSM Copolymer
Employers Mutual Casualty Co.
Exxon Mobil Corp.
Fisher Scientific
Fortis, Inc.
Hensel Phelps Construction Co.
HON Industries Inc.
Litton Industries, Inc.
Maytag Corp.
Mercantile Bank NA

Pella Corp.
Phillips Petroleum Co.
Square D Co.
Tension Envelope Corp.

ANKENY
IBP

BETTENDORF
Deere & Co.
Lee Enterprises
Quanex Corp.

BURLINGTON
Cooper Industries, Inc.
Lance, Inc.

CARROLL
Pella Corp.

CEDAR FALLS
AEGON U.S.A. Inc.
Deere & Co.
HON Industries Inc.
Kemper National Insurance Companies
MCI WorldCom, Inc.
Pella Corp.
US West, Inc.

CEDAR RAPIDS
AEGON U.S.A. Inc.
Blue Cross & Blue Shield of Iowa
General Mills, Inc.
Grace & Co. (W.R.)
Land O'Lakes, Inc.
MCI WorldCom, Inc.
Square D Co.

CEDAR RAPIUDS
AEGON U.S.A. Inc.

CLINTON
Ralston Purina Co.

COUNCIL BLUFFS
ConAgra, Inc.
Union Pacific Corp.
Valmont Industries, Inc.

CRESCO
Donaldson Co., Inc.

DAVENPORT
Deere & Co.
Hartmarx Corp.
HON Industries Inc.
Lee Enterprises
Norwest Corp.
Quanex Corp.

DECORAH
Johnson & Son (S.C.)

DENISON
IBP

DES MOINES
Amsted Industries Inc.
Blue Cross & Blue Shield of Iowa
Bridgestone/Firestone, Inc.
Deere & Co.
Donaldson Co., Inc.
Edison Brothers Stores, Inc.
Employers Mutual Casualty Co.
Fortis, Inc.
HON Industries Inc.
IKON Office Solutions, Inc.
Kemper National Insurance Companies
Lance, Inc.
Land O'Lakes, Inc.
Lee Enterprises
Lehigh Portland Cement Co.
Maytag Corp.
Mercantile Bank NA
MidAmerican Energy Holdings Co.
Norwest Corp.
Pella Corp.
Principal Financial Group
Sentry Insurance, A Mutual Co.
Solo Cup Co.
Tension Envelope Corp.
U.S. Bancorp Piper Jaffray
US West, Inc.
Walgreen Co.

DUBUQUE
Deere & Co.
Federal-Mogul Corp.
Hamilton Sundstrand Corp.
Jeld-wen, Inc.

EARLHAM
Nationwide Insurance Co.

EDMUNDSEN
Maytag Corp.

FAIRFIELD
Elf Atochem North America, Inc.

FORT DODGE
IBP
Land O'Lakes, Inc.

GLIDDEN
Pella Corp.

GREENVILLE
Lance, Inc.

GRINNELL
CertainTeed Corp.
Donaldson Co., Inc.
Lennox International, Inc.
Maytag Corp.
Wilbur-Ellis Co. & Connell Brothers Co.

HIAWATHA
American Retail Group

HUDSON
Deere & Co.

INDIANAPOLIS
American Retail Group

INDIANOLA
Amsted Industries Inc.
Principal Financial Group

IOWA CITY
Baxter International Inc.
Employers Mutual Casualty Co.
General Electric Co.
Gerber Products Co.
HON Industries Inc.
Land O'Lakes, Inc.
Maytag Corp.
MidAmerican Energy Holdings Co.
Pella Corp.
Polaroid Corp.
Praxair
Tension Envelope Corp.

JOHNSTON
Principal Financial Group

KNOXVILLE
Pella Corp.

LAMONI
Cooper Tire & Rubber Co.

MARSHALLTOWN
Emerson Electric Co.
Lennox International, Inc.

MASON CITY
Lehigh Portland Cement Co.
Principal Financial Group

MILFORD
MidAmerican Energy Holdings Co.

MOUNT PLEASANT
HON Industries Inc.

MOUNT VERNON
Amsted Industries Inc.
Butler Manufacturing Co.

MUSCATINE
Employers Mutual Casualty Co.
HON Industries Inc.
Lee Enterprises
Monsanto Co.

NEW SHARON
Pella Corp.

NEW TAZWELL
HON Industries Inc.

NEWTON
Maytag Corp.

OELWEIN
Donaldson Co., Inc.

OSKALOOSA
Amsted Industries Inc.
Pella Corp.
Principal Financial Group

OTTUMWA
Deere & Co.
Lee Enterprises
Pella Corp.

PELLA
Amsted Industries Inc.
Deere & Co.
Maytag Corp.
Pella Corp.
Principal Financial Group

PERRY
IBP

PLEASANTVILLE
Pella Corp.

RED OAK
Blue Cross & Blue Shield of Iowa

SHENANDOAH
Pella Corp.

SIOUX CITY
Grace & Co. (W.R.)
IBP
Walgreen Co.

SIOUX FALLS
Norwest Corp.

SULLY
Pella Corp.

URBANDALE
Amsted Industries Inc.
Pella Corp.
Principal Financial Group

WATERLOO
Deere & Co.
Ryder System, Inc.

WAVERLY
CUNA Mutual Group

WEST BRANCH
Maytag Corp.

WEST DES MOINES
Employers Mutual Casualty Co.
Maytag Corp.

Kansas

Cenex Harvest States
Morris Communications Corp.
Rubbermaid Inc.

ATCHISON
Orscheln Co.

BALDWIN
Tension Envelope Corp.

BONNER SPRINGS
International Multifoods Corp.

COFFEYVILLE
Blount International, Inc.
Deere & Co.

DODGE CITY
Morris Communications Corp.

GARDEN CITY
IBP

HAYES
Tension Envelope Corp.

HUTCHINSON
Kroger Co.

INDEPENDENCE
Cessna Aircraft Co.

KANSAS CITY
Butler Manufacturing Co.
Hallmark Cards Inc.
International Multifoods Corp.
Owens Corning
Stanley Works (The)
Tension Envelope Corp.

LACYGNE
Hallmark Cards Inc.
Tension Envelope Corp.

LAWRENCE
Bard, Inc. (C.R.)
Cessna Aircraft Co.
Chesapeake Corp.
Deloitte & Touche
Hallmark Cards Inc.
Koch Industries, Inc.
KPMG Peat Marwick LLP
Kroger Co.
Litton Industries, Inc.
Morris Communications Corp.
Pharmacia & Upjohn, Inc.
Reader's Digest Association, Inc. (The)
Security Benefit Life Insurance Co.
Sverdrup Corp.
Tamko Roofing Products
Tension Envelope Corp.
U.S. Bancorp
U.S. Bancorp Piper Jaffray
Whitman Corp.

LEAVENWORTH
Hallmark Cards Inc.
Orscheln Co.

LIBERAL
DeKalb Genetics Corp.
Occidental Oil and Gas

LINDSBORG
Cooper Tire & Rubber Co.
Federal-Mogul Corp.

LOWRENCE
Deloitte & Touche

MANHATTAN
Anheuser-Busch Companies, Inc.
Cargill Inc.
Commerce Bancshares, Inc.
Hensel Phelps Construction Co.
Morris Communications Corp.
Security Benefit Life Insurance Co.
Tension Envelope Corp.

MCPHERSON
CertainTeed Corp.

MISSION
Cessna Aircraft Co.

OLATHE
Amsted Industries Inc.
Deluxe Corp.

OVERLAND
Security Benefit Life Insurance Co.

OVERLAND PARK
Block, Inc. (H&R)
Tension Envelope Corp.
Transamerica Corp.

PITTSBURG
Central & South West Services
Commerce Bancshares, Inc.
Morris Communications Corp.

SHAWNEE
Security Benefit Life Insurance Co.
Tension Envelope Corp.

SHAWNEE MISSION
General Mills, Inc.
Tension Envelope Corp.

STERLING
Morris Communications Corp.

TOPEKA
Cessna Aircraft Co.
Commerce Bancshares, Inc.
Hallmark Cards Inc.
INTRUST Financial Corp.
Jostens, Inc.
Morris Communications Corp.
SBC Communications Inc.
Security Benefit Life Insurance Co.

UNIONTOWN
Security Benefit Life Insurance Co.

WELLINGTON
INTRUST Financial Corp.

WICHITA
Agrilink Foods, Inc.
Boeing Co.
Cessna Aircraft Co.
Commerce Bancshares, Inc.
Copley Press, Inc.

Employers Mutual Casualty Co.
Grede Foundries
INTRUST Financial Corp.
Koch Industries, Inc.
Kroger Co.
Lee Enterprises
Occidental Oil and Gas
Orscheln Co.
SBC Communications Inc.
Stone Container Corp.
Tamko Roofing Products
Tension Envelope Corp.
Vulcan Materials Co.

WITCHITA
Cessna Aircraft Co.

Kentucky

Equitable Resources, Inc.
Milacron, Inc.
Western & Southern Life Insurance Co.

ASHLAND
Abbott Laboratories
AK Steel Corp.
Aristech Chemical Corp.
Ashland, Inc.

BARBOURVILLE
General Electric Co.
Morrison Knudsen Corp.
United States Trust Co. of New York

BELLEVUE
Fifth Third Bancorp

BEREA
Ashland, Inc.
Hitachi America Ltd.
Humana, Inc.
Sherwin-Williams Co.
Southeastern Mutual Insurance Co.

BOONE
Chesapeake Corp.

BOWLING GREEN
BellSouth Corp.
Mid-America Bank of Louisville

CALVERT CITY
Elf Atochem North America, Inc.

CAMPBELLSVILLE
Southeastern Mutual Insurance Co.

CRESTVIEW HILLS
Chemed Corp.
Cincinnati Bell Inc.
Star Bank NA
Western & Southern Life Insurance Co.

CYNTHIANA
Grede Foundries

DANVILLE
Ashland, Inc.
Red Wing Shoe Co. Inc.
Southeastern Mutual Insurance Co.

EDGEWOOD
Fifth Third Bancorp

ELIZABETHTOWN
CertainTeed Corp.
Dana Corp.

FLORENCE
Mead Corp.

FRANKFORT
Ashland, Inc.
Donaldson Co., Inc.
Humana, Inc.
Southeastern Mutual Insurance Co.

GREEN
Southeastern Mutual Insurance Co.

GREENUP
Ashland, Inc.

HARRODSBURG
Corning Inc.

HENDERSON
American General Finance
Koch Enterprises, Inc.

HIGHLAND HEIGHTS
Ashland, Inc.
Cincinnati Bell Inc.
Fifth Third Bancorp
Milacron, Inc.
Star Bank NA
Western & Southern Life Insurance Co.

HOPKINSVILLE
Dana Corp.
Phelps Dodge Corp.

LA GRANGE
Mid-America Bank of Louisville

LEBANON
Independent Stave Co.

LEXINGTON
AEGON U.S.A. Inc.
AMP Inc.
Ashland, Inc.
Danis Companies
Emerson Electric Co.
Fifth Third Bancorp
GTE Corp.
Humana, Inc.
Inland Container Corp.
Koch Enterprises, Inc.
LandAmerica Financial Services
Mid-America Bank of Louisville
Sherwin-Williams Co.
Southeastern Mutual Insurance Co.
Square D Co.
Standard Products Co.
Texas Instruments Inc.
Textron Inc.
Union Carbide Corp.
United Parcel Service of America Inc.

LIBERTY
Koch Enterprises, Inc.

LOUISVILLE
AEGON U.S.A. Inc.
Arvin Industries, Inc.
Ashland, Inc.
Atlantic Richfield Co.
Belk-Simpson Department Stores
BellSouth Corp.
Borden, Inc.
Brown & Williamson Tobacco Corp.
Clorox Co.
Cooper Industries, Inc.
Enterprise Rent-A-Car Co.
Federated Department Stores, Inc.
Fifth Third Bancorp
Ford Motor Co.
Hartmarx Corp.
Hubbell Inc.
Humana, Inc.
Independent Stave Co.
Kimball International, Inc.
Koch Enterprises, Inc.
Kroger Co.
La-Z-Boy Inc.
LG&E Energy Corp.
Liberty Corp.
Lowe's Companies
Mid-America Bank of Louisville
National City Corp.
Norton Co.
Owens Corning
Penney Co., Inc. (J.C.)
PNC Financial Services Group
Reynolds Metals Co.
Southeastern Mutual Insurance Co.
Toyota Motor Sales U.S.A., Inc.
United Parcel Service of America Inc.
Valmont Industries, Inc.
Walgreen Co.
Winn-Dixie Stores Inc.
Witco Corp.
Young & Rubicam

MARRAY
Southeastern Mutual Insurance Co.

MAYSVILLE
Dayton Power and Light Co.
Grede Foundries
Inland Container Corp.

MIDWAY
Ashland, Inc.
Southeastern Mutual Insurance Co.

MOREHEAD
Ashland, Inc.

MURRAY
Briggs & Stratton Corp.

NICHOLASVILLE
Donaldson Co., Inc.

OWENSBORO
HON Industries Inc.
Kimball International, Inc.
Southeastern Mutual Insurance Co.
Unilever United States, Inc.

PADUCAH
Eastern Enterprises
Elf Atochem North America, Inc.
Fuller Co. (H.B.)
Westvaco Corp.

PIKEVILLE
Ashland, Inc.
Southeastern Mutual Insurance Co.

PIPPA PASSES
Ashland, Inc.

RACELAND
Ashland, Inc.

RICHMOND
Ashland, Inc.
Blue Bell, Inc.

RUSSELL
AK Steel Corp.
Ashland, Inc.

SOMERSET
Hartmarx Corp.

TERRE HAUTE
LG&E Energy Corp.

VERSAILLES
Texas Instruments Inc.

WAVERLY
Koch Enterprises, Inc.

WHITLEY CITY
Calvin Klein

WILLIAMSBURG
Chemed Corp.
Galter Corp.
Lance, Inc.

WILMORE
Ashland, Inc.

Louisiana

Freeport-McMoRan Inc.
Liberty Corp.
Reily & Co., Inc. (William B.)

ALEXANDRIA
Tai and Co. (J.T.)

BASTROP
International Paper Co.

BATON ROGUE
Nalco Chemical Co.

BATON ROUGE
Atlantic Richfield Co.
BellSouth Corp.
Burlington Resources, Inc.
Chevron Corp.
Dow Chemical Co.
DSM Copolymer
Exxon Mobil Corp.
FINA
Fluor Corp.
Freeport-McMoRan Inc.
Halliburton Co.
Jacobs Engineering Group
Louisiana Land & Exploration Co.
Shell Oil Co.
Stupp Brothers Bridge & Iron Co.
Union Carbide Corp.
Vulcan Materials Co.

HAHNVILLE
Monsanto Co.

HAMMOND
Reily & Co., Inc. (William B.)

HOUMA
Consolidated Natural Gas Co.

LAFAYETTE
Louisiana Land & Exploration Co.
Shelter Mutual Insurance Co.
Unocal Corp.
Western & Southern Life Insurance Co.

LAKE CHARLES
Bridgestone/Firestone, Inc.
Grace & Co. (W.R.)
Liberty Corp.
PPG Industries, Inc.
Temple-Inland Inc.
Waste Management Inc.

LULING
Union Carbide Corp.

METAIRIE
Louisiana Land & Exploration Co.
Nalco Chemical Co.
Reily & Co., Inc. (William B.)

MONROE
Louisiana-Pacific Corp.

NATCHITOCHES
International Paper Co.

NEW IBERIA
Fannie Mae

NEW ORLEANS
American Retail Group
Chevron Corp.
Cinergy Corp.
Consolidated Natural Gas Co.
Enterprise Rent-A-Car Co.
Forbes Inc.
Freeport-McMoRan Inc.
Hofmann Co.
Johnson Controls Inc.
Johnson & Son (S.C.)
Louisiana Land & Exploration Co.
Nalco Chemical Co.
National Presto Industries, Inc.
Polaroid Corp.
Reily & Co., Inc. (William B.)
Shell Oil Co.
Tai and Co. (J.T.)
Texaco Inc.
Toshiba America Inc.
USG Corp.
Walgreen Co.
Winn-Dixie Stores Inc.
Xerox Corp.

PALM BEACH GARDENS
American Retail Group

PLAQUEMINE
Jacobs Engineering Group

RUSTON
Central & South West Services
DSM Copolymer
Fluor Corp.

SHREVEPORT
BellSouth Corp.
Deposit Guaranty National Bank
Merrill Lynch & Co., Inc.

ZACHARY
DSM Copolymer

Maine

Crane Co.
UnumProvident

AUGUSTA
Butler Capital Corp.
Hannaford Brothers Co.
Leigh Fibers, Inc.
New England Bio Labs
UnumProvident

BANGOR
Hannaford Brothers Co.
Kimberly-Clark Corp.
Shaw's Supermarkets, Inc.

BAR HARBOR
Hannaford Brothers Co.
Milliken & Co.
S.G. Cowen

BATH
Hannaford Brothers Co.
Susquehanna-Pfaltzgraff Co.
UnumProvident

BELFAST
Leigh Fibers, Inc.

BIDDEFORD
Kingsbury Corp.

BLUE HILL
Consolidated Electrical Distributors

BOOTHBAY HARBOR
Hannaford Brothers Co.

BOWDOIN
Little, Inc. (Arthur D.)

BREWER
Hannaford Brothers Co.

BRISTOL
Schloss & Co. (Marcus)

BROOKSVILLE
Vesper Corp.

BRUNSWICK
Susquehanna-Pfaltzgraff Co.
USG Corp.

CASCO
Bard, Inc. (C.R.)

CUMBERLAND FIRESIDE
Central National-Gottesman

DAMARISCOTTA
Belk Stores Services Inc.
Hannaford Brothers Co.

DOVER FOXCROFT
Lennox International, Inc.

ELLSWORTH
Hannaford Brothers Co.
Shaw's Supermarkets, Inc.
Vesper Corp.

FAIRFIELD
Kimberly-Clark Corp.

FREEPORT
Hannaford Brothers Co.

GORHAM
UnumProvident

HOULTON
Tomkins Industries, Inc.

LEWISTON
American Retail Group
Hannaford Brothers Co.
National Presto Industries, Inc.
United States Trust Co. of New York
West Co. Inc.

LEWISTOWN
Paine Webber

LEWRSTON
Shaw's Supermarkets, Inc.

LIMESTONE
Leigh Fibers, Inc.

LUBEC
Pfizer Inc.

NORTH NEW PORTLAND
Patagonia Inc.

NORWAY
Hannaford Brothers Co.

ORONO
Central National-Gottesman
Crane & Co., Inc.
GenCorp
Simpson Investment Co.
UnumProvident

OWLS HEAD
Fisher Scientific

PORTLAND
American Retail Group
Hannaford Brothers Co.
Leigh Fibers, Inc.
Shaw's Supermarkets, Inc.
UnumProvident

ROCKLAND
Ben & Jerry's Homemade Inc.
Hannaford Brothers Co.

SACO
Hannaford Brothers Co.
UnumProvident

SOUTH BERWICK
Fisher Scientific

SOUTH PORTLAND
Hannaford Brothers Co.
Vesper Corp.

WATERVILLE
Dexter Corp.
Hannaford Brothers Co.
Huffy Corp.

YARMOUTH
Leigh Fibers, Inc.

YORK
BFGoodrich Co.

Maryland

Procter & Gamble Co., Cosmetics Division

ADELPHI
Amsted Industries Inc.
Boeing Co.
Constellation Energy Group, Inc.
First Maryland Bancorp
Freddie Mac
Giant Food Inc.

ANNAPOLIS
Armstrong World Industries, Inc.
Constellation Energy Group, Inc.
Crestar Finance Corp.
First Maryland Bancorp
Hershey Foods Corp.
Hitachi America Ltd.
Landmark Communications Inc.
National Starch & Chemical Co.
Rouse Co.
Rubbermaid Inc.
The Washington Post
Westvaco Corp.
Williams

BALTIMORE
AEGON U.S.A. Inc.
Alcon Laboratories, Inc.
AlliedSignal Inc.
AMP Inc.
Amsted Industries Inc.
Avon Products, Inc.
Bard, Inc. (C.R.)
Bell Atlantic Corp.
Bethlehem Steel Corp.
Bristol-Myers Squibb Co.
Carter-Wallace, Inc.
Clorox Co.
Cone Mills Corp.
Constellation Energy Group, Inc.
Conwood Co. LP
Cranston Print Works Co.
Crestar Finance Corp.
Croft-Leominster
DaimlerChrysler Corp.
Eckerd Corp.
Enterprise Rent-A-Car Co.
Fannie Mae
Fidelity Investments
First Maryland Bancorp
Freddie Mac
Freeport-McMoRan Inc.
GEICO Corp.
Giant Food Inc.
Giddings & Lewis
Grace & Co. (W.R.)
GTE Corp.
Harsco Corp.
Hartford (The)
International Paper Co.
KPMG Peat Marwick LLP
Lehigh Portland Cement Co.
Lubrizol Corp. (The)
Manor Care Health SVS, Inc.
MCI WorldCom, Inc.
Medtronic, Inc.
Merck & Co.
Merit Oil Corp.
Nomura Holding America
Overseas Shipholding Group Inc.
PepsiCo, Inc.
PerkinElmer, Inc.
Pfizer Inc.
Price Associates (T. Rowe)
Procter & Gamble Co.
Procter & Gamble Co., Cosmetics Division
Rouse Co.
Ryder System, Inc.
Schering-Plough Corp.
Seagram & Sons, Inc. (Joseph E.)
Solo Cup Co.
Sony Electronics
Tai and Co. (J.T.)
Teleflex Inc.
Textron Inc.
Times Mirror Co.
Unilever United States, Inc.
United Airlines Inc.
Universal Foods Corp.
Valspar Corp.
Van Leer Holding
Warner-Lambert Co.
The Washington Post
Waste Management Inc.
Westvaco Corp.
Wisconsin Public Service Corp.
Wrigley Co. (Wm. Jr.)

BEL AIR
Clorox Co.
York Federal Savings & Loan Association

BETHESDA
Abbott Laboratories
Alcon Laboratories, Inc.
Andersons Inc.
Bard, Inc. (C.R.)
Cantor, Fitzgerald Securities Corp.
Consumers Energy Co.
Dexter Corp.
Dun & Bradstreet Corp.
Gallo Winery, Inc. (E&J)
Giant Food Inc.
Hoffmann-La Roche Inc.
May Department Stores Co.
Merck & Co.
Motorola Inc.
New York Life Insurance Co.
Pieper Power Electric Co.
Portland General Electric Co.
United States Sugar Corp.

BROOKLANDVILLE
Croft-Leominster
Price Associates (T. Rowe)
Procter & Gamble Co., Cosmetics Division

CATONVILLE
AEGON U.S.A. Inc.

CHARLOTTESVILLE
Crestar Finance Corp.

CHESTERTOWN
Whitman Corp.

CHEVY CHASE
Allstate Insurance Co.
Bridgestone/Firestone, Inc.
Constellation Energy Group, Inc.
Eastman Kodak Co.
Erb Lumber Co.
General Electric Co.
Hallmark Cards Inc.
Rouse Co.
Unocal Corp.

CHURCHVILLE
Brunswick Corp.

COLLEGE PARK
AlliedSignal Inc.
Bechtel Group, Inc.
BFGoodrich Co.
Croft-Leominster
Freddie Mac
Kemper National Insurance Companies
Motorola Inc.
PerkinElmer, Inc.
Pittway Corp.
Rouse Co.
Wiley & Sons (John)
Xerox Corp.

COLUMBIA
ABC
Chase Manhattan Bank, NA
Constellation Energy Group, Inc.
Dow Jones & Co., Inc.
Fannie Mae
First Maryland Bancorp
Freddie Mac
Gerber Products Co.
Giant Food Inc.
Grace & Co. (W.R.)
Metropolitan Life Insurance Co.
MONY Group (The)
Price Associates (T. Rowe)
Prudential Insurance Co. of America
Rouse Co.
Schering-Plough Corp.

CRISFIELD
Sherwin-Williams Co.

CROWNSVILLE
Constellation Energy Group, Inc.

EASTON
Aetna, Inc.
Crestar Finance Corp.
Solo Cup Co.

ELLICOTT CITY
Rouse Co.

EMMITSBURG
AEGON U.S.A. Inc.
LandAmerica Financial Services
Solo Cup Co.
The Washington Post

FOREST HILL
York Federal Savings & Loan Association

FREDERICK
Giant Food Inc.
Lehigh Portland Cement Co.
State Farm Mutual Automobile Insurance Co.
The Washington Post

FROSTBURG
The Washington Post

GAITHERSBURG
Gerber Products Co.
Kimberly-Clark Corp.

GLEN BURNIE
Constellation Energy Group, Inc.
First Maryland Bancorp
Grace & Co. (W.R.)

GREENBELT
KPMG Peat Marwick LLP

HAGERSTOWN
CertainTeed Corp.
First Maryland Bancorp
Reynolds & Reynolds Co.

HANNIBAL
Dexter Corp.

HUNT VALLEY
AEGON U.S.A. Inc.
Crestar Finance Corp.
Lehigh Portland Cement Co.

HUNTINGTON
Constellation Energy Group, Inc.

HYATTSVILLE
Borman's Inc.
Freddie Mac
MidAmerican Energy Holdings Co.

KENSINGTON
Fortis Insurance Co.

LA PLATA
Croft-Leominster
The Washington Post

LANDOVER
Blue Bell, Inc.
Contran Corp.

LARGO
Freddie Mac
Giant Food Inc.

LAUREL
Giant Food Inc.

LEONARDTOWN
The Washington Post

MARYLAND LINE
York Federal Savings & Loan Association

MONKTON
Rouse Co.

MT. RAINIER
American Retail Group

NORTH BETHESDA
GEICO Corp.

OWINGS MILLS
Carillon Importers, Ltd.
Price Associates (T. Rowe)

PORT TOBACCO
Croft-Leominster

PRINCE FREDERICK
The Washington Post

QUEENSTOWN
Dow Jones & Co., Inc.

ROCKVILLE
Abbott Laboratories
Alcon Laboratories, Inc.
Bechtel Group, Inc.
Carter-Wallace, Inc.
Crown Books
Freddie Mac
Galter Corp.
GEICO Corp.
Giant Food Inc.
Hartford (The)
Hoffmann-La Roche Inc.
MidAmerican Energy Holdings Co.
Pharmacia & Upjohn, Inc.
Wyman-Gordon Co.

RUXTON
Croft-Leominster

SALISBURY
Giant Food Inc.
Sherwin-Williams Co.
Standard Products Co.

SILVER SPRING
Abbott Laboratories
ABC
Alma Piston Co.
Bethlehem Steel Corp.
BP Amoco Corp.
Detroit Edison Co.
Eaton Corp.
Fannie Mae
First Maryland Bancorp
GEICO Corp.
Outboard Marine Corp.
PepsiCo, Inc.
ServiceMaster Co.

SPARKS
Croft-Leominster

STEVENSON
AEGON U.S.A. Inc.
Constellation Energy Group, Inc.

SYKESVILLE
AEGON U.S.A. Inc.

TAKOMA PARK
The Washington Post

TOWSON
Constellation Energy Group, Inc.
First Maryland Bancorp
Price Associates (T. Rowe)
Procter & Gamble Co., Cosmetics Division

UNIVERSITY PARK
Coors Brewing Co.

WALDORF
Lehigh Portland Cement Co.

WESTMINSTER
Constellation Energy Group, Inc.
First Maryland Bancorp
Lehigh Portland Cement Co.
Solo Cup Co.

WHEATON
Giant Food Inc.

WHITE PLAINS
Croft-Leominster

Massachusetts

BankBoston Corp.
Crane Co.
Cummings Properties Management
Demoulas Supermarkets Inc.
Housatonic Curtain Co.
Little, Inc. (Arthur D.)
Lotus Development Corp.
State Street Bank & Trust Co.
Wyman-Gordon Co.

ABINGTON
Polaroid Corp.

ACTON
Millipore Corp.
Sun Microsystems Inc.

AMHERST
BankBoston Corp.
Binswanger Companies
Eastern Enterprises
General Electric Co.
Harcourt General, Inc.
Kennametal, Inc.
Kirkland & Ellis
Leigh Fibers, Inc.
Litton Industries, Inc.
Merrill Lynch & Co., Inc.
Millipore Corp.
Polaroid Corp.
Rubbermaid Inc.
Russer Foods
TJX Companies, Inc.
Union Camp Corp.

ANDOVER
Cummings Properties Management
Demoulas Supermarkets Inc.
Putnam Investments
Waste Management Inc.

ATHOL
Erving Industries

ATTLEBORO
Jostens, Inc.
Texas Instruments Inc.

AUGUSTA
Shaw's Supermarkets, Inc.

BABSON PARK
DSM Copolymer

BATH
Shaw's Supermarkets, Inc.

BECKET
Russer Foods

BEDFORD
Millipore Corp.

BELMONT
PerkinElmer, Inc.
Prudential Insurance Co. of America

BEVERLY
Archer-Daniels-Midland Co.
Central National-Gottesman
Crane & Co., Inc.
Cummings Properties Management
Eastern Bank
Housatonic Curtain Co.
Leigh Fibers, Inc.

BIDDEFORD
Shaw's Supermarkets, Inc.

BILLERICA
Bard, Inc. (C.R.)

BORCHESTER
BankBoston Corp.

BOSTON
Abbott Laboratories
Allmerica Financial Corp.
Alma Piston Co.
American Express Co.
AMETEK, Inc.
AMR Corp.
AT&T Corp.
BankBoston Corp.
Barclays Capital
Bardes Corp.
Barry Corp. (R.G.)
Ben & Jerry's Homemade Inc.
Bethlehem Steel Corp.
Binswanger Companies
Borden, Inc.
Boston Edison Co.
Boston Globe (The)
Bristol-Myers Squibb Co.
Brown Shoe Co., Inc.
Burlington Resources, Inc.
Butler Capital Corp.
Cabot Corp.
Carter-Wallace, Inc.
Central National-Gottesman
Circuit City Stores, Inc.
Citizens Financial Group, Inc.
CNA
Comdisco, Inc.
Consolidated Electrical Distributors
Country Curtains, Inc.
CSS Industries, Inc.
Cummings Properties Management
Demoulas Supermarkets Inc.
Deposit Guaranty National Bank
Dexter Corp.
Eastern Bank
Eastern Enterprises
Enterprise Rent-A-Car Co.
Erving Industries
Federated Department Stores, Inc.
Fidelity Investments
Fifth Third Bancorp
Fisher Scientific
Gallo Winery, Inc. (E&J)
General Atlantic Partners II LP
General Electric Co.
General Mills, Inc.
Gerber Products Co.
Gillette Co.
Grace & Co. (W.R.)
GTE Corp.
Hanna Co. (M.A.)
Harcourt General, Inc.
Hartford (The)
Hartmarx Corp.
Hasbro, Inc.
Hewlett-Packard Co.
Housatonic Curtain Co.
Hubbard Broadcasting, Inc.
Hubbell Inc.
IKON Office Solutions, Inc.
Independent Stave Co.
Johnson & Son (S.C.)
Kirkland & Ellis
Leigh Fibers, Inc.
Little, Inc. (Arthur D.)
Lotus Development Corp.
Mamiye Brothers
Mattel Inc.
Mazda North American Operations
MCI WorldCom, Inc.
Medtronic, Inc.
Merck & Co.
Merit Oil Corp.
Merrill Lynch & Co., Inc.
Metropolitan Life Insurance Co.
Millipore Corp.
Mine Safety Appliances Co.
Mitsubishi Electric America
Morgan Stanley Dean Witter & Co.
Motorola Inc.
New England Bio Labs
New England Financial
New York Life Insurance Co.
Overseas Shipholding Group Inc.
Paine Webber
PerkinElmer, Inc.
Pfizer Inc.
Pioneer Group
Polaroid Corp.
Prudential Insurance Co. of America
Prudential Securities Inc.
Putnam Investments
Reebok International Ltd.
Russer Foods
Safeguard Scientifics
Seagram & Sons, Inc. (Joseph E.)
S.G. Cowen
Shaw's Supermarkets, Inc.
Stanley Works (The)
State Street Bank & Trust Co.
Stone Container Corp.
Stride Rite Corp.
Tai and Co. (J.T.)
Textron Inc.
Thermo Electron Corp.
TJX Companies, Inc.
Tomkins Industries, Inc.
Union Carbide Corp.
United Airlines Inc.
United Co.
Universal Studios
UnumProvident
Vesper Corp.
Walgreen Co.
Waste Management Inc.
Wells Fargo & Co.
West Co. Inc.
Wyman-Gordon Co.

BOXFORD
Mitsubishi Electric America

BRADFORD
Demoulas Supermarkets Inc.

BRAINTREE
Bard, Inc. (C.R.)

BRIDGEWATER
Shaw's Supermarkets, Inc.

BRIGHTON
Dow Jones & Co., Inc.
Grace & Co. (W.R.)
Leigh Fibers, Inc.
Millipore Corp.

BROCKPORT
Reebok International Ltd.

BROCKTON
Millipore Corp.
Polaroid Corp.
Reebok International Ltd.
Shaw's Supermarkets, Inc.

BROOKLINE
Millipore Corp.
Pittway Corp.
Polaroid Corp.

BURLINGTON
Bard, Inc. (C.R.)
Leigh Fibers, Inc.
Millipore Corp.
PerkinElmer, Inc.
Thermo Electron Corp.

CAMBRIDGE
Air Products and Chemicals, Inc.
AlliedSignal Inc.
Alma Piston Co.
Amsted Industries Inc.
AT&T Corp.
Bank One Corp.
Bechtel Group, Inc.
Binswanger Companies
Brown Shoe Co., Inc.
Chevron Corp.
Circuit City Stores, Inc.
Cleveland-Cliffs, Inc.
Corning Inc.
Deloitte & Touche
Donaldson Co., Inc.
Eastern Enterprises
Eastman Kodak Co.
Erb Lumber Co.
Exxon Mobil Corp.
Fannie Mae
Fidelity Investments
GEICO Corp.
GenCorp
General Atlantic Partners II LP
General Electric Co.
General Motors Corp.
Goldman Sachs Group
Grace & Co. (W.R.)
Harsco Corp.
Hitachi America Ltd.
Intel Corp.
Kirkland & Ellis
Laclede Gas Co.
Leigh Fibers, Inc.
Leviton Manufacturing Co. Inc.
Little, Inc. (Arthur D.)
Litton Industries, Inc.
Lotus Development Corp.
Manulife Financial
Merck & Co.
Merit Oil Corp.
Millipore Corp.
Morgan Stanley Dean Witter & Co.
Morrison Knudsen Corp.
New England Bio Labs
Nomura Holding America
Olin Corp.
Paine Webber
Patagonia Inc.
Polaroid Corp.
Price Associates (T. Rowe)
Procter & Gamble Co.
Pulitzer Publishing Co.
Putnam Investments
Rubbermaid Inc.

Funders by Location of Grant Recipient

SBC Communications Inc.
Schlumberger Ltd. (USA)
S.G. Cowen
Shaw's Supermarkets, Inc.
Shell Oil Co.
Simplot Co. (J.R.)
Stanley Works (The)
State Street Bank & Trust Co.
Stride Rite Corp.
Sun Microsystems Inc.
Thermo Electron Corp.
Titan Industrial Corp.
TRW Inc.
Unilever United States, Inc.
Union Carbide Corp.
U.S. Bancorp
Vanguard Group
Vesper Corp.
Waste Management Inc.
West Co. Inc.
Westvaco Corp.
Xerox Corp.

CANTON
Leigh Fibers, Inc.

CENTERVILLE
Ameritech Corp.
Georgia-Pacific Corp.
Unilever United States, Inc.

CHELMSFORD
Demoulas Supermarkets Inc.
Sun Microsystems Inc.

CHELSEA
Boston Globe (The)
Lotus Development Corp.

CHESTNUT HILL
Bardes Corp.
Cone Mills Corp.
Eastern Enterprises
General Electric Co.
Kingsbury Corp.
Merrill Lynch & Co., Inc.
Mitsubishi Electric America
Morrison Knudsen Corp.
Price Associates (T. Rowe)
Texaco Inc.
TJX Companies, Inc.
United States Trust Co. of New York

CONCORD
Dexter Corp.
Eastern Enterprises
Fidelity Investments
Millipore Corp.
Patagonia Inc.
Polaroid Corp.
United States Trust Co. of New York

DALTON
Crane & Co., Inc.

DANVERS
Eastern Bank

DARTMOUTH
Deloitte & Touche
Polaroid Corp.

DEDHAM
Polaroid Corp.

DEERFIELD
Binswanger Companies
Central National-Gottesman
Country Curtains, Inc.
Nomura Holding America

DORCHESTER
Boston Globe (The)
Lotus Development Corp.
Millipore Corp.
Polaroid Corp.
Reebok International Ltd.
State Street Bank & Trust Co.
Trace International Holdings, Inc.

DUDLEY
Cranston Print Works Co.
Wyman-Gordon Co.

EAST BOSTON
Fannie Mae
Leigh Fibers, Inc.

EAST BRIDGEWATER
Shaw's Supermarkets, Inc.

EAST LONGMEADOW
Banfi Vintners

EASTHAMPTON
Wiremold Co.

ESSEX
Cummings Properties Management

EVERETT
Monsanto Co.

FAIRHAVEN
Shaw's Supermarkets, Inc.

FALL RIVER
American Retail Group

FITCHBURG
Inland Container Corp.

FRAMINGHAM
Allmerica Financial Corp.
TJX Companies, Inc.
Walgreen Co.

FRANKLIN
Putnam Investments

GLOUCESTER
New England Bio Labs

GREAT BARRINGTON
Country Curtains, Inc.
Crane & Co., Inc.
Lennox International, Inc.

GREENFIELD
Erving Industries

HAMILTON
Demoulas Supermarkets Inc.

HANOVER
Cummings Properties Management

HARVARD
Sun Microsystems Inc.

HATHORNE
Tomkins Industries, Inc.

HINSDALE
Crane & Co., Inc.

HOLYOKE
Leigh Fibers, Inc.

HOUSATONIC
Country Curtains, Inc.

IPSWICH
Cummings Properties Management

JAMAICA PLAIN
Leigh Fibers, Inc.
Lotus Development Corp.
Millipore Corp.
Polaroid Corp.
Sun Microsystems Inc.

JAMAICA PLAINS
Erving Industries
Overseas Shipholding Group Inc.

KENNEBUNK
Shaw's Supermarkets, Inc.

LAWRENCE
AMETEK, Inc.
AT&T Corp.
Borden, Inc.
Demoulas Supermarkets Inc.
GenCorp
Putnam Investments
Sun Microsystems Inc.

LEE
Country Curtains, Inc.
Housatonic Curtain Co.

LEICESTER
Wyman-Gordon Co.

LENOX
Country Curtains, Inc.
Crane & Co., Inc.
Housatonic Curtain Co.

LEOMINSTER
Bard, Inc. (C.R.)
Hoffer Plastics Corp.

LEXINGFON
Stride Rite Corp.

LEXINGTON
Polaroid Corp.
Stride Rite Corp.

LINCOLN
Ben & Jerry's Homemade Inc.
Crane & Co., Inc.
Cranston Print Works Co.
Eastern Enterprises
Merrill Lynch & Co., Inc.
Millipore Corp.
Pacific Mutual Life Insurance Co.
Putnam Investments
Ralph's Grocery Co.
Wyman-Gordon Co.

LOWELL
Cranston Print Works Co.
Demoulas Supermarkets Inc.
Eastern Enterprises
Lotus Development Corp.
Millipore Corp.
Sun Microsystems Inc.
Wal-Mart Stores, Inc.

LYNN
Eastern Bank
General Electric Co.

MAIDEN
Freeport-McMoRan Inc.

MANHASSET
Erving Industries

MARBLEHEAD
Millipore Corp.
NEC America, Inc.

MARION
Vesper Corp.

MARLBOROUGH
State Farm Mutual Automobile Insurance Co.

MEDFORD
Allmerica Financial Corp.
Cummings Properties Management
Erving Industries
Merck & Co.
Schering-Plough Corp.
Searle & Co. (G.D.)
Unilever Home & Personal Care U.S.A.

MIDDLEBORO
Shaw's Supermarkets, Inc.

MILFORD
Anheuser-Busch Companies, Inc.

MILTON
Butler Capital Corp.
Cummings Properties Management
Reynolds Tobacco (R.J.)
S.G. Cowen

NATICK
DaimlerChrysler Corp.

NEEDHAM
Textron Inc.

NEW BEDFORD
Polaroid Corp.
Shaw's Supermarkets, Inc.

NEWBURYPORT
Demoulas Supermarkets Inc.

NEWTON
General Atlantic Partners II LP
S.G. Cowen
Thermo Electron Corp.
TJX Companies, Inc.
Wiley & Sons (John)

NORTH ADAMS
Binswanger Companies
Country Curtains, Inc.
Crane & Co., Inc.
Golub Corp.
Housatonic Curtain Co.

NORTH ANDOVER
Demoulas Supermarkets Inc.
Forbes Inc.

NORTH ATTLEBORO
Shaw's Supermarkets, Inc.

NORTH BROOKFIELD
Alma Piston Co.

NORTH DARTMOUTH
Cranston Print Works Co.

NORTH EASTON
Fidelity Investments
Waste Management Inc.

NORTH HAMPTON
United Parcel Service of America Inc.

NORTHAMPTON
Charter Manufacturing Co.
General Mills, Inc.
Leigh Fibers, Inc.
Merrill Lynch & Co., Inc.
Metropolitan Life Insurance Co.
U.S. Bancorp

PEABODY
Eastern Bank

PEMBROKE
Shaw's Supermarkets, Inc.
United Distillers & Vintners North America

PITTSFIELD
Country Curtains, Inc.
Crane & Co., Inc.
Golub Corp.
Housatonic Curtain Co.
Leigh Fibers, Inc.
Mead Corp.

PLYMOUTH
Shaw's Supermarkets, Inc.

PORTLAND
Shaw's Supermarkets, Inc.

ROXBURY
Ben & Jerry's Homemade Inc.
Fidelity Investments
Lotus Development Corp.
PerkinElmer, Inc.
Polaroid Corp.
Reebok International Ltd.
State Street Bank & Trust Co.
TJX Companies, Inc.

SALEM
Eastern Bank
Merit Oil Corp.
New England Bio Labs

SAUGUS
Grace & Co. (W.R.)

SHEFFIELD
Country Curtains, Inc.

SHELBURNE FALLS
Erving Industries

SHREWSBURY
Allmerica Financial Corp.

SOMERVILLE
International Flavors & Fragrances Inc.
Polaroid Corp.

SOUTH HADLEY
Carter-Wallace, Inc.
Elf Atochem North America, Inc.
Fortis, Inc.
Louisiana-Pacific Corp.
Thompson Co. (J. Walter)
U.S. Bancorp

SOUTHBRIDGE
Shaw's Supermarkets, Inc.

SPRINGFIELD
Boston Globe (The)
Crane & Co., Inc.
Dexter Corp.
Dow Jones & Co., Inc.
Eastern Enterprises
Manulife Financial
Monsanto Co.
Textron Inc.
Tomkins Industries, Inc.
Westvaco Corp.
Wrigley Co. (Wm. Jr.)

ST. WATERTOWN
APL Ltd.

STOCKBRIDGE
Country Curtains, Inc.
Crane & Co., Inc.
Housatonic Curtain Co.

STOUGHTON
Reebok International Ltd.
Russer Foods
Stride Rite Corp.

STURBRIDGE
PerkinElmer, Inc.
Wyman-Gordon Co.

SUDBURY
Cummings Properties Management

MCI WorldCom, Inc.

TRURO
Paine Webber

TURNERS FALLS
Erving Industries

WALTHAM
Bechtel Group, Inc.
Erving Industries
Fidelity Investments
Fisher Brothers Cleaning Services
Millipore Corp.
Nomura Holding America
Sega of America Inc.
Sprint Corp.
Thermo Electron Corp.
Thompson Co. (J. Walter)
TJX Companies, Inc.

WATERTOWN
Barry Corp. (R.G.)
Bell Atlantic Corp.
Brown Shoe Co., Inc.
Demoulas Supermarkets Inc.
Johnson & Son (S.C.)
Reebok International Ltd.
Wolverine World Wide

WATERVILLE
Shaw's Supermarkets, Inc.

WAYLAND
Carris Reels

WEBSTER
Cranston Print Works Co.

WELLESLEY
Cabot Corp.
Central & South West Services
Fidelity Investments
Gillette Co.
GTE Corp.
PerkinElmer, Inc.
Trace International Holdings, Inc.
Whitman Corp.

WELLESLEY HILLS
Central National-Gottesman

WENHAM
Fidelity Investments
Hanna Co. (M.A.)
Rutledge Hill Press

WEST ROXBURY
Demoulas Supermarkets Inc.
Shaw's Supermarkets, Inc.

WEST SOMERVILLE
United Dominion Industries, Ltd.

WESTON
TJX Companies, Inc.
UnumProvident

WESTWOOD
Shaw's Supermarkets, Inc.

WILLIAMSTOWN
Amgen, Inc.
Bank One Corp.
Crane & Co., Inc.
Housatonic Curtain Co.
Rich Products Corp.
Russer Foods

WINCHESTER
Cummings Properties Management
Eastern Bank

WOBURN
Bard, Inc. (C.R.)
Crane & Co., Inc.
Cummings Properties Management
Millipore Corp.
TJX Companies, Inc.
Wiremold Co.

WOLLASTON
Hanna Co. (M.A.)

WOODS HOLE
Colonial Oil Industries, Inc.
Leigh Fibers, Inc.
Little, Inc. (Arthur D.)

WORCESTER
Allmerica Financial Corp.
Alma Piston Co.
Borden, Inc.
Cummings Properties Management
Fidelity Investments
Golub Corp.
Hanna Co. (M.A.)
Huffy Corp.
IKON Office Solutions, Inc.
Mead Corp.
Nomura Holding America
Norton Co.
Pittway Corp.
Polaroid Corp.
Seagram & Sons, Inc. (Joseph E.)
Textron Inc.
TJX Companies, Inc.
Wyman-Gordon Co.

WORCHESTER
Leigh Fibers, Inc.

Michigan

Bridgestone/Firestone, Inc.
Detroit Edison Co.
Elf Atochem North America, Inc.
Erb Lumber Co.
Giddings & Lewis
Huffy Corp.
Masco Corp.
South Bend Tribune Corp.
SPX Corp.
Standard Products Co.
Whirlpool Corp.
Wolverine World Wide

ADA
Michigan Consolidated Gas Co.

ADRIAN
Federal-Mogul Corp.

ALBION
Federal-Mogul Corp.

ALLENDALE
Old Kent Bank
SPX Corp.

ALMA
Alma Piston Co.
Dow Corning Corp.
JSJ Corp.
Pharmacia & Upjohn, Inc.

ANN ARBOR
AlliedSignal Inc.
Blue Cross & Blue Shield of Michigan
Borman's Inc.
Burnett Co. (Leo)
Coca-Cola Co.
Consumers Energy Co.
Deloitte & Touche
Detroit Edison Co.
Domino's Pizza Inc.
Dow Chemical Co.
Federal-Mogul Corp.
Ford Motor Co.
General Electric Co.
General Motors Corp.
Gerber Products Co.
Globe Corp.
Goldman Sachs Group
Heinz Co. (H.J.)
Intel Corp.
Kennametal, Inc.
KPMG Peat Marwick LLP
LandAmerica Financial Services
Lubrizol Corp. (The)
Merck & Co.
Michigan Consolidated Gas Co.
Motorola Inc.
National Starch & Chemical Co.
Pharmacia & Upjohn, Inc.
Procter & Gamble Co.
Rubbermaid Inc.
Schering-Plough Corp.
SPX Corp.
Thompson Co. (J. Walter)
Trustmark Insurance Co.
TRW Inc.
Unilever United States, Inc.
Union Pacific Corp.
Warner-Lambert Co.
Whirlpool Corp.
Whitman Corp.
Witco Corp.
Xerox Corp.

AUBURN HILLS
Borman's Inc.

AUGUSTA
Consumers Energy Co.

BATTLE CREEK
Fabri-Kal Corp.
Kellogg Co.
Pharmacia & Upjohn, Inc.

BAY CITY
Dow Chemical Co.
Dow Corning Corp.

BELOIT
Reynolds Metals Co.

BENTON HARBOR
Agrilink Foods, Inc.
Whirlpool Corp.

BERRIEN SPRINGS
Whirlpool Corp.

BIG RAPIDS
GenCorp
Wolverine World Wide

BINGHAM FARMS
Kelly Services

BIRMINGHAM
Borman's Inc.
Erb Lumber Co.
Federal-Mogul Corp.

BLOOMFIELD
Masco Corp.
TRW Inc.

BLOOMFIELD HILLS
Borman's Inc.
Cone Mills Corp.
DaimlerChrysler Corp.
Detroit Edison Co.
Erb Lumber Co.

BUCHANAN
Mark IV Industries

CADILLAC
Federal-Mogul Corp.
Michigan Consolidated Gas Co.

CENTRAL LAKE
Texas Instruments Inc.

CHARLEVOIX
Consumers Energy Co.

CLINTON
La-Z-Boy Inc.

CLINTON TOWNSHIP
Alma Piston Co.
DaimlerChrysler Corp.

COLDWATER
Ford Meter Box Co.

DEARBORN
Barnes Group Inc.
Borman's Inc.
Commercial Intertech Corp.
DaimlerChrysler Corp.
Detroit Edison Co.
Ford Motor Co.
General Motors Corp.
Giddings & Lewis
Kennametal, Inc.
Masco Corp.
TRW Inc.

DETROIT
Alcon Laboratories, Inc.
AlliedSignal Inc.
Allmerica Financial Corp.
Alma Piston Co.
American Express Co.
Arvin Industries, Inc.
Barnes Group Inc.
Baxter International Inc.
Blue Cross & Blue Shield of Michigan
Borden, Inc.
Borman's Inc.
Boston Globe (The)
Cinergy Corp.
Collins & Aikman Corp.
Consumers Energy Co.
CUNA Mutual Group
DaimlerChrysler Corp.
Dana Corp.
Deloitte & Touche
Delta Air Lines, Inc.
Detroit Edison Co.
Eastman Kodak Co.
Eaton Corp.
Enterprise Rent-A-Car Co.
Erb Lumber Co.
Federal-Mogul Corp.
FMC Corp.
Forbes Inc.
Ford Motor Co.
General Motors Corp.
Giddings & Lewis
Grace & Co. (W.R.)
Hitachi America Ltd.
Johnson Controls Inc.
Kelly Services
Kennametal, Inc.
Manulife Financial
Masco Corp.
Metropolitan Life Insurance Co.
Michigan Consolidated Gas Co.
Milacron, Inc.
Monsanto Co.
National Presto Industries, Inc.
Olin Corp.
Outboard Marine Corp.
Pharmacia & Upjohn, Inc.
Philip Morris Companies Inc.
Polaroid Corp.
Portland General Electric Co.
Premier Industrial Corp.
Quaker Chemical Corp.
Sara Lee Corp.
Schwab & Co., Inc. (Charles)
Seagram & Sons, Inc. (Joseph E.)
Searle & Co. (G.D.)
Solo Cup Co.
SPX Corp.
Standard Products Co.
Stride Rite Corp.
Timken Co. (The)
Tomkins Industries, Inc.
TRW Inc.
United Distillers & Vintners North America
Waste Management Inc.
Young & Rubicam

DOWAGIAC
SPX Corp.

E LANSING
Rubbermaid Inc.

EAST LANSING
Ameritech Corp.
Blue Cross & Blue Shield of Michigan
Consumers Energy Co.
Cox Enterprises Inc.
Dow Chemical Co.
Federal-Mogul Corp.
Gerber Products Co.
Heinz Co. (H.J.)
Kennametal, Inc.
Union Carbide Corp.

ESCANABA
Mead Corp.

FARMINGTON HILLS
Borman's Inc.
JSJ Corp.

FLINT
Arvin Industries, Inc.
Consumers Energy Co.
Eaton Corp.
Federal-Mogul Corp.
Fortis, Inc.
General Motors Corp.
TRW Inc.

FRANKENMUTH
LandAmerica Financial Services

FREEMONT
Gerber Products Co.

FREMONT
Agrilink Foods, Inc.

GAYLORD
Standard Products Co.

GRAND HAVEN
Domino's Pizza Inc.
JSJ Corp.
Kellogg Co.
SPX Corp.

GRAND RAPIDS
Allmerica Financial Corp.
Alma Piston Co.
Banta Corp.
Consumers Energy Co.
Domino's Pizza Inc.
First National Bank of Evergreen Park

Funders by Location of Grant Recipient

Gerber Products Co.
JSJ Corp.
Meijer, Inc.
Michigan Consolidated Gas Co.
New England Financial
Old Kent Bank
Rubbermaid Inc.
ServiceMaster Co.
Steelcase Inc.
Sunmark Capital Corp.
Waste Management Inc.
Wolverine World Wide

GRANDVILLE
Steelcase Inc.

GREENVILLE
Meijer, Inc.
Old Kent Bank

GROSSE POINT WOODS
Masco Corp.

GROSSE POINTE FARMS
Alma Piston Co.
Sverdrup Corp.

GROSSE POINTE WOODS
Alma Piston Co.

HANCOCK
Outboard Marine Corp.

HARBOR SPRINGS
Alma Piston Co.

HIGHLAND PARK
DaimlerChrysler Corp.

HILLSDALE
Bassett Furniture Industries
Dow Chemical Co.
Grace & Co. (W.R.)
Stonecutter Mills Corp.
Sunmark Capital Corp.
True Oil Co.

HOLLAND
Baird & Co. (Robert W.)
Federal-Mogul Corp.
Globe Corp.
JSJ Corp.
Rutledge Hill Press
SPX Corp.
Waste Management Inc.

HOLLY
Alma Piston Co.
DaimlerChrysler Corp.

HOUGHTON
Cleveland-Cliffs, Inc.
Consumers Energy Co.
Detroit Edison Co.
Dow Chemical Co.
Dow Corning Corp.
Ford Motor Co.
Fortis, Inc.
Halliburton Co.
Kimberly-Clark Corp.
Ladish Co., Inc.
Mead Corp.
Whirlpool Corp.
Wisconsin Energy Corp.
Wisconsin Public Service Corp.

HOWELL
Allmerica Financial Corp.

INTERLOCHEN
Consumers Energy Co.
Emerson Electric Co.
Housatonic Curtain Co.

IRON MOUNTAIN
Mead Corp.

ISHPEMING
Cleveland-Cliffs, Inc.

JACKSON
CertainTeed Corp.
Clorox Co.
Consumers Energy Co.
Pacific Mutual Life Insurance Co.
Quanex Corp.
SPX Corp.

KALAMAZOO
Blue Cross & Blue Shield of Michigan
Consumers Energy Co.
Duriron Co., Inc.
Eaton Corp.
Fabri-Kal Corp.
Green Bay Packaging
International Paper Co.
Mead Corp.
Medtronic, Inc.
Old Kent Bank
Parker Hannifin Corp.
Pharmacia & Upjohn, Inc.
SPX Corp.

LAKE CITY
Consumers Energy Co.

LANSING
Allmerica Financial Corp.
Alma Piston Co.
CertainTeed Corp.
Consumers Energy Co.
Dow Chemical Co.
Employers Mutual Casualty Co.
Fannie Mae
General Motors Corp.
Michigan Consolidated Gas Co.
SPX Corp.
Vulcan Materials Co.

LATHRUP VILLAGE
Consumers Energy Co.

LIVONIA
Alma Piston Co.
Consumers Energy Co.

MADISON
Madison Gas & Electric Co.

MADISON HEIGHTS
Milacron, Inc.

MAPLE CITY
Stupp Brothers Bridge & Iron Co.

MARQUETTE
Cleveland-Cliffs, Inc.
Mead Corp.

MARSHALL
State Farm Mutual Automobile Insurance Co.

MENOMINEE
Wisconsin Public Service Corp.

MICHIGAN CENTER
Ford Meter Box Co.

MIDLAND
Bridgestone/Firestone, Inc.
Collins & Aikman Corp.
Conwood Co. LP
Dow Chemical Co.
Dow Corning Corp.
Ford Motor Co.

Milliken & Co.
Tamko Roofing Products
Timken Co. (The)

MISSISSIPPI STATE
Chevron Corp.

MONROE
Andersons Inc.
La-Z-Boy Inc.

MOUNT PLEASANT
Dow Chemical Co.
Michigan Consolidated Gas Co.

MT PLEASANT
Consumers Energy Co.

MUSKEGON
Brunswick Corp.
Dana Corp.
JSJ Corp.
Michigan Consolidated Gas Co.
SPX Corp.
Textron Inc.
Toshiba America Inc.

NEGAUNEE
Cleveland-Cliffs, Inc.

NILES
First Source Corp.
Old Kent Bank
South Bend Tribune Corp.

NORTHVILLE
Mitsubishi Electric America

OAK PARK
Borman's Inc.

OKEMOS
Erb Lumber Co.

OLIVET
Allmerica Financial Corp.

PAW PAW
Agrilink Foods, Inc.

PETOSKEY
Alma Piston Co.

PIGEON
Blue Cross & Blue Shield of Michigan

PLYMOUTH
Detroit Edison Co.
Graco, Inc.
Kennametal, Inc.
Michigan Consolidated Gas Co.

PONTIAC
Borman's Inc.
Erb Lumber Co.

PORT HURON
Detroit Edison Co.

RAPID RIVER
Mead Corp.

REPUBLIC
Cleveland-Cliffs, Inc.
Consolidated Papers, Inc.

RIVER ROUGE
Standard Products Co.

ROCHESTER
DaimlerChrysler Corp.
Warner-Lambert Co.

ROCKFORD
Wolverine World Wide

ROYAL OAK
Alma Piston Co.
Consumers Energy Co.
Michigan Consolidated Gas Co.

SAGINAW
Colonial Oil Industries, Inc.
Consumers Energy Co.
Dow Chemical Co.
Dow Corning Corp.
New England Bio Labs

SAINT JOSEPH
Whirlpool Corp.

SALINE
Barnes Group Inc.

SOUTH LYON
Quanex Corp.

SOUTHFIELD
ABC
Allmerica Financial Corp.
Borman's Inc.
Consumers Energy Co.
DaimlerChrysler Corp.
Erb Lumber Co.
Ford Motor Co.
General Motors Corp.
Kelly Services
Masco Corp.
Michigan Consolidated Gas Co.
Old Kent Bank
Pharmacia & Upjohn, Inc.
Procter & Gamble Co.
Reynolds Tobacco (R.J.)

SPRING ARBOR
Textron Inc.

SPRING LAKE
JSJ Corp.
ServiceMaster Co.

ST. JOSEPH
Agrilink Foods, Inc.

STURGIS
Cooper Industries, Inc.

SWARTZ CREEK
Consumers Energy Co.

TAYLOR
International Paper Co.

THREE RIVERS
Andersons Inc.

TRAVERSE CITY
Michigan Consolidated Gas Co.

TROY
Alma Piston Co.
DaimlerChrysler Corp.
General Motors Corp.
Kelly Services

UNIVERSITY CENTER
Dow Chemical Co.
Dow Corning Corp.

WASHTENAW
Barnes Group Inc.

WATERFORD
DaimlerChrysler Corp.

WAYNE
Detroit Edison Co.

WEST BLOOMFIELD
Borman's Inc.

WYOMING
Steelcase Inc.

YPSILANTI
Sherwin-Williams Co.

Minnesota

Banta Corp.
Caterpillar Inc.
Cenex Harvest States
Donaldson Co., Inc.
Hubbard Broadcasting, Inc.
Minnesota Mining & Manufacturing Co.
TCF National Bank Minnesota

ALEXANDRIA
Andersen Corp.

ANOKA
Blue Cross & Blue Shield of Minnesota
Hickory Tech Corp.

APPLE VALLEY
Bemis Co., Inc.
Dain Bosworth Inc.
Ecolab Inc.
Jostens, Inc.
Northern States Power Co.
Red Wing Shoe Co. Inc.
U.S. Bancorp Piper Jaffray

APPLETON
National Presto Industries, Inc.

ARDEN HILLS
Andersen Corp.
Bemis Co., Inc.
Land O'Lakes, Inc.

ATTLEBORO
Jostens, Inc.

AUSTIN
National Presto Industries, Inc.

AVON
Vesper Corp.

BAYPORT
Andersen Corp.

BEMIDJI
Dain Bosworth Inc.
National Presto Industries, Inc.

BLOOMINGTON
Business Improvement
Dain Bosworth Inc.
Donaldson Co., Inc.
Jostens, Inc.
National City Bank of Minneapolis
U.S. Bancorp Piper Jaffray

BROOKLYN CENTER
Business Improvement
U.S. Bancorp
US West, Inc.

BROOKLYN PARK
Northern States Power Co.

CENTER CITY
ABC
Andersen Corp.
Ecolab Inc.
Solo Cup Co.

CHASKA
Andersen Corp.

CHISHOLM
Cleveland-Cliffs, Inc.
LTV Corp.
USX Corp.

CIRCLE PINES
Northern States Power Co.

CROOKSTON
Blue Cross & Blue Shield of Minnesota

CROSBY
Dain Bosworth Inc.

DULUTH
Bemis Co., Inc.
Blue Cross & Blue Shield of Minnesota
Cleveland-Cliffs, Inc.
Consolidated Papers, Inc.
First Financial Bank
Hubbard Broadcasting, Inc.
Land O'Lakes, Inc.
Pacific Mutual Life Insurance Co.
Potlatch Corp.

EAGAN
Blue Cross & Blue Shield of Minnesota
Minnesota Mutual Life Insurance Co.
Valspar Corp.

EAGLE LAKE
Hickory Tech Corp.

EAST GRAND FORKS
Blue Cross & Blue Shield of Minnesota

EDEN PRAIRIE
MTS Systems Corp.
Rich Products Corp.

EDINA
Blue Cross & Blue Shield of Minnesota
Graco, Inc.
National City Bank of Minneapolis
TENNANT Co.

ELAINE
Fuller Co. (H.B.)

FAIRMONT
Harsco Corp.

FARIBAULT
Land O'Lakes, Inc.
Northern States Power Co.

FINDLEY
Honeywell International Inc.

FRIDLEY
Medtronic, Inc.
U.S. Bancorp

GAYLORD
Andersen Corp.

GOLDEN VALLEY
Cargill Inc.
Dain Bosworth Inc.
Deluxe Corp.
Federated Mutual Insurance Co.
General Mills, Inc.
Graco, Inc.
Minnesota Mining & Manufacturing Co.
National City Bank of Minneapolis
Red Wing Shoe Co. Inc.
SIT Investment Associates, Inc.
TCF National Bank Minnesota
TENNANT Co.
Toro Co.
U.S. Bancorp

GRAND FORKS
Land O'Lakes, Inc.

GRAND RAPIDS
Land O'Lakes, Inc.

HASTINGS
Andersen Corp.
Northern States Power Co.

HOPKINS
Carlson Companies, Inc.
Jostens, Inc.
National City Bank of Minneapolis

INVER GROVE HEIGHTS
Land O'Lakes, Inc.

LAKE CITY
Red Wing Shoe Co. Inc.

LAKE ELMO
Business Improvement

LINDSTROM
Andersen Corp.

MANKATO
Bemis Co., Inc.
Federated Mutual Insurance Co.
Hickory Tech Corp.
Northern States Power Co.
TCF National Bank Minnesota
Tyson Foods Inc.
U.S. Bancorp
US West, Inc.

MAPLEWOOD
Fuller Co. (H.B.)

MARSHALL
Cenex Harvest States

MINNEA POLIS
Blair & Co. (William)

MINNEAPOLI
Cargill Inc.

MINNEAPOLIS
Air Products and Chemicals, Inc.
Alliant Techsystems
Allianz Life Insurance Co. of North America
Andersen Corp.
Ashland, Inc.
Banta Corp.
Baxter International Inc.
Bemis Co., Inc.
Ben & Jerry's Homemade Inc.
Blue Cross & Blue Shield of Minnesota
Business Improvement
Cargill Inc.
Carillon Importers, Ltd.
Carlson Companies, Inc.
Carris Reels
Chesapeake Corp.
Chicago Title Corp.
Circuit City Stores, Inc.
Cleveland-Cliffs, Inc.
Coca-Cola Co.
Consolidated Papers, Inc.
Cummins Engine Co., Inc.
CUNA Mutual Group
Dain Bosworth Inc.
Dana Corp.
Dayton Hudson
Deloitte & Touche
Deluxe Corp.
Donaldson Co., Inc.
Dow Chemical Co.
Ecolab Inc.
Emerson Electric Co.
Fannie Mae
Federated Department Stores, Inc.
Federated Mutual Insurance Co.
Fisher Scientific
Fluor Corp.
Fortis, Inc.
Fuller Co. (H.B.)
General Mills, Inc.
Goldman Sachs Group
Graco, Inc.
Hershey Foods Corp.
Honeywell International Inc.
Hubbard Broadcasting, Inc.
Huffy Corp.
IKON Office Solutions, Inc.
Inland Container Corp.
International Multifoods Corp.
Jostens, Inc.
La-Z-Boy Inc.
Land O'Lakes, Inc.
Liberty Diversified Industries
Louisiana-Pacific Corp.
McClatchy Co.
Medtronic, Inc.
Merck & Co.
Minnesota Mining & Manufacturing Co.
Minnesota Mutual Life Insurance Co.
Mitsubishi Electric America
Morgan Stanley Dean Witter & Co.
MTS Systems Corp.
National City Bank of Minneapolis
New York Life Insurance Co.
Northern States Power Co.
Norwest Corp.
Patagonia Inc.
Pillsbury Co.
Potlatch Corp.
Prudential Insurance Co. of America
Publix Supermarkets
Reader's Digest Association, Inc. (The)
Red Wing Shoe Co. Inc.
Regis Corp.
Rubbermaid Inc.
Saint Paul Companies Inc.
Schering-Plough Corp.
Sentry Insurance, A Mutual Co.
SIT Investment Associates, Inc.
Synovus Financial Corp.
TCF National Bank Minnesota
TENNANT Co.
Tension Envelope Corp.
Toro Co.
Toshiba America Inc.
Union Carbide Corp.
U.S. Bancorp
U.S. Bancorp Piper Jaffray
US West, Inc.
USX Corp.
Valspar Corp.
Walgreen Co.
Warner-Lambert Co.
Wells Fargo & Co.

MINNEPOLIS
U.S. Bancorp Piper Jaffray

MINNETONKA
Bemis Co., Inc.
Donaldson Co., Inc.

MOORHEAD
La-Z-Boy Inc.
Minnesota Mining & Manufacturing Co.
U.S. Bancorp

NEW BRIGHTON
Hershey Foods Corp.
Hubbard Broadcasting, Inc.

NICOLLET
Hickory Tech Corp.

NORTH MANKATO
Hickory Tech Corp.

NORTHFIELD
Donaldson Co., Inc.
Dow Chemical Co.
FINA
General Mills, Inc.
Minnesota Mutual Life Insurance Co.
Norwest Corp.
U.S. Bancorp

OAKDALE
Minnesota Mutual Life Insurance Co.

OLD FRONTENAC
Red Wing Shoe Co. Inc.

ONAMIA
Minnesota Mining & Manufacturing Co.

OWATONNA
Burress (J.W.)
Federated Mutual Insurance Co.
Jostens, Inc.
Red Wing Shoe Co. Inc.
SPX Corp.
U.S. Bancorp Piper Jaffray

PERHAM
Land O'Lakes, Inc.

PILLAGER
Andersen Corp.

PINE ISLAND
Land O'Lakes, Inc.

PLYMOUTH
Johnson Controls Inc.
Saint Paul Companies Inc.
U.S. Bancorp Piper Jaffray

RED WING
Jostens, Inc.
Red Wing Shoe Co. Inc.

RICHFIELD
U.S. Bancorp

ROBBINSDALE
General Mills, Inc.

ROCHESTER
Ameritas Life Insurance Corp.
Blue Cross & Blue Shield of Minnesota
CNA
Cummins Engine Co., Inc.
First Union Corp.
Hubbard Broadcasting, Inc.
Manor Care Health SVS, Inc.
Marshall & Ilsley Corp.
Red Wing Shoe Co. Inc.
Sprint Corp.
Universal Studios
Zilkha & Sons

ROSEAU
Land O'Lakes, Inc.

ROSEVILLE
Red Wing Shoe Co. Inc.
Valspar Corp.

SAINT CLOUD
Vesper Corp.

SAINT CROIX
Hubbard Broadcasting, Inc.

SAINT JOSEPH
Saint Paul Companies Inc.

SAINT LOUIS PARK
Northern States Power Co.

SAINT PAUL
Allianz Life Insurance Co. of North America
Dain Bosworth Inc.
Dayton Hudson
Extendicare Health Services
General Mills, Inc.
Hickory Tech Corp.
HON Industries Inc.
Hubbard Broadcasting, Inc.
Jostens, Inc.
Liberty Diversified Industries
Manulife Financial
Minnesota Mining & Manufacturing Co.
Northern States Power Co.
Norwest Corp.
Saint Paul Companies Inc.
TCF National Bank Minnesota
Valspar Corp.
Walgreen Co.

SAINT PETER
General Mills, Inc.
Hickory Tech Corp.
Hubbard Broadcasting, Inc.
Illinois Tool Works, Inc.
McGraw-Hill Companies, Inc.
McKesson-HBOC Corp.
Metropolitan Life Insurance Co.
Norwest Corp.
Prudential Insurance Co. of America
SBC Communications Inc.
Unocal Corp.

SHAKOPEE
CertainTeed Corp.
Toro Co.

SHOREVIEW
Fuller Co. (H.B.)
Land O'Lakes, Inc.

SOUTH SAINT PAUL
Northern States Power Co.

ST CLOUD
U.S. Bancorp

ST JOSEPH
U.S. Bancorp

ST PAUL
Bemis Co., Inc.
Graco, Inc.
U.S. Bancorp

ST PETER
Bemis Co., Inc.
U.S. Bancorp

ST. ANTHONY
National City Bank of Minneapolis

ST. CLOUD
Blue Cross & Blue Shield of Minnesota
Fortis, Inc.
Grede Foundries
International Multifoods Corp.
Louisiana-Pacific Corp.
Regis Corp.

ST. CROIX
Andersen Corp.

ST. JAMES
ConAgra, Inc.

ST. JOSEPH
Fortis, Inc.

ST. LOUIS PARK
Fuller Co. (H.B.)
Graco, Inc.
National City Bank of Minneapolis

ST. PAUL
Alcon Laboratories, Inc.
Alliant Techsystems
Andersen Corp.
Banta Corp.
Blue Cross & Blue Shield of Minnesota
Business Improvement
Cargill Inc.
Carlson Companies, Inc.
CBS Corp.
CertainTeed Corp.
Cleveland-Cliffs, Inc.
Consolidated Papers, Inc.
Dayton Hudson
DeKalb Genetics Corp.
Deluxe Corp.
Demoulas Supermarkets Inc.
Donaldson Co., Inc.
Ecolab Inc.
Federated Mutual Insurance Co.
Fortis, Inc.
Fuller Co. (H.B.)
Honeywell International Inc.
IKON Office Solutions, Inc.
Land O'Lakes, Inc.
McClatchy Co.
Medtronic, Inc.
Minnesota Mutual Life Insurance Co.
National City Bank of Minneapolis
Pillsbury Co.
Red Wing Shoe Co. Inc.
Regis Corp.
Schwab & Co., Inc. (Charles)
Shea Co. (John F.)
SIT Investment Associates, Inc.
TENNANT Co.
U.S. Bancorp Piper Jaffray
US West, Inc.

ST. PETER
Allstate Insurance Co.
Bank of America
Bardes Corp.
Barnes Group Inc.
Baxter International Inc.
Bethlehem Steel Corp.
Block, Inc. (H&R)
Blue Bell, Inc.
Carlson Companies, Inc.
Chevron Corp.
CIGNA Corp.
Clorox Co.
Compass Bank
DaimlerChrysler Corp.
Dayton Power and Light Co.
Deluxe Corp.
Graco, Inc.
Levi Strauss & Co.
Mazda North American Operations
Millipore Corp.
Red Wing Shoe Co. Inc.
Weyerhaeuser Co.

STILLWATER
Andersen Corp.
Fuller Co. (H.B.)
Northern States Power Co.
U.S. Bancorp Piper Jaffray

TWO HARBORS
Cleveland-Cliffs, Inc.

VADNAIS HEIGHTS
Land O'Lakes, Inc.

VIRGINIA
Andersen Corp.

WAYZATA
TCF National Bank Minnesota

WEST SAINT PAUL
Northern States Power Co.

WEST ST. PAUL
Blue Cross & Blue Shield of Minnesota

WILLMAR
Blue Cross & Blue Shield of Minnesota

WINONA
Federal-Mogul Corp.
Lee Enterprises

WORTHINGTON
Campbell Soup Co.
Land O'Lakes, Inc.

WYOMING
Graco, Inc.

Mississippi

BILOXI
Van Leer Holding

CLEVELAND
Baxter International Inc.
Deposit Guaranty National Bank

CLINTON
Deposit Guaranty National Bank
National Presto Industries, Inc.

FULTON
Toshiba America Inc.

GAUTIER
Litton Industries, Inc.

HATTIESBURG
Cooper Industries, Inc.
Deposit Guaranty National Bank
DSM Copolymer
Inland Container Corp.
Louisiana Land & Exploration Co.
Temple-Inland Inc.

HERNANDO
Deposit Guaranty National Bank

INDIANOLA
MTD Products Inc.

JACKSON
BellSouth Corp.
Clorox Co.
Deposit Guaranty National Bank
General Atlantic Partners II LP
La-Z-Boy Inc.
Levi Strauss & Co.
MTD Products Inc.
National Presto Industries, Inc.
National Service Industries, Inc.
State Farm Mutual Automobile Insurance Co.
Temple-Inland Inc.
Vulcan Materials Co.

LAUREL
MTD Products Inc.

MERIDIAN
Deposit Guaranty National Bank
Gallo Winery, Inc. (E&J)
Waste Management Inc.

MISSISSIPPI STATE
Aristech Chemical Corp.
Deposit Guaranty National Bank
Elf Atochem North America, Inc.
Union Carbide Corp.

MOSS POINT
Litton Industries, Inc.

OCEAN SPRINGS
International Paper Co.
Litton Industries, Inc.

OXFORD
Whirlpool Corp.

PASCAGOULA
Litton Industries, Inc.

PINEY WOODS
Deposit Guaranty National Bank

RAYMOND
Cooper Industries, Inc.
Deposit Guaranty National Bank

SENATOBIA
Conwood Co. LP

STARKVILLE
DSM Copolymer

TOUGALOO
BFGoodrich Co.
Forbes Inc.
Kroger Co.

TUPELO
BellSouth Corp.
Furniture Brands International, Inc.
LandAmerica Financial Services
MTD Products Inc.

UNIVERSITY
Merrill Lynch & Co., Inc.
Reader's Digest Association, Inc. (The)

VANCLEAVE
Litton Industries, Inc.

VICKSBURG
Cooper Industries, Inc.

WALLS
Tension Envelope Corp.

WINONA
United States Sugar Corp.

YAZOO CITY
Deposit Guaranty National Bank

Missouri

Stone Container Corp.

ANNAPOLIS
Chesapeake Corp.

BARNHART
Edwards Enterprise Software (J.D.)

BLUE SPRINGS
Amsted Industries Inc.

BRIDGETON
ABC
Kellwood Co.

CAMDENTON
Ameren Corp.
Orscheln Co.

CANTON
Laclede Gas Co.

CAPE GIRARDEAU
Ameren Corp.
Hartmarx Corp.
Toshiba America Inc.

CARONDELET
Stupp Brothers Bridge & Iron Co.

CHESTERFIELD
Mercantile Bank NA

CHILLICOTHE
Donaldson Co., Inc.

CLAYTON
GenAmerica Corp.

COLUMBIA
ABC
Ameren Corp.
Anheuser-Busch Companies, Inc.
Aristech Chemical Corp.
Coca-Cola Co.
Cooper Tire & Rubber Co.
Fortis, Inc.
Hubbell Inc.
Huffy Corp.
Jacobson & Sons (Benjamin)
Little, Inc. (Arthur D.)
May Department Stores Co.
Mercantile Bank NA
Orscheln Co.
Pulitzer Publishing Co.
Reader's Digest Association, Inc. (The)
Shelter Mutual Insurance Co.
Square D Co.
State Farm Mutual Automobile Insurance Co.

EAST ST. LOUIS
Ralston Purina Co.

EXCELSIOR SPRINGS
Ameren Corp.

FAYETTE
Laclede Gas Co.

FENTON
Stupp Brothers Bridge & Iron Co.

FULTON
Ameren Corp.
Brown Shoe Co., Inc.
Mercantile Bank NA
Orscheln Co.

HANNIBAL
Citizens Financial Group, Inc.
Pillsbury Co.

HAZELWOOD
Commerce Bancshares, Inc.
Edison Brothers Stores, Inc.
Mercantile Bank NA
Monsanto Co.
Sunmark Capital Corp.

HERMITAGE
Shelter Mutual Insurance Co.

INDEPENDENCE
Commerce Bancshares, Inc.
Deere & Co.
International Multifoods Corp.
Olin Corp.

JEFFCTY
Tension Envelope Corp.

JEFFERSON CITY
Ameren Corp.
Commerce Bancshares, Inc.
Edison Brothers Stores, Inc.
Enterprise Rent-A-Car Co.
GenAmerica Corp.
IKON Office Solutions, Inc.
Orscheln Co.
Sverdrup Corp.
Tension Envelope Corp.
Tomkins Industries, Inc.
Unilever Home & Personal Care U.S.A.

JOPLIN
Cessna Aircraft Co.
Pillsbury Co.
Tamko Roofing Products

KANSAS CITY
ABC
AlliedSignal Inc.
Arvin Industries, Inc.
AT&T Corp.
Block, Inc. (H&R)
Brunswick Corp.
Butler Manufacturing Co.
CertainTeed Corp.
Commerce Bancshares, Inc.
Deluxe Corp.
Donaldson Co., Inc.
Federal-Mogul Corp.
Federated Mutual Insurance Co.
Ford Motor Co.
Hallmark Cards Inc.
IKON Office Solutions, Inc.

Inland Container Corp.
International Multifoods Corp.
Lipton Co.
Mercantile Bank NA
MONY Group (The)
Morris Communications Corp.
National Presto Industries, Inc.
National Starch & Chemical Co.
Nationwide Insurance Co.
Orscheln Co.
SBC Communications Inc.
Southwest Gas Corp.
Sprint Corp.
SPX Corp.
State Street Bank & Trust Co.
Tension Envelope Corp.
Union Pacific Corp.
United Parcel Service of America Inc.
Valmont Industries, Inc.
Waste Management Inc.
Western & Southern Life Insurance Co.
Yellow Corp.

KIRKSVILLE
Butler Manufacturing Co.

LAKE OF OZARKS
Orscheln Co.

LEBANON
Commerce Bancshares, Inc.
Independent Stave Co.

LIBERTY
Commerce Bancshares, Inc.
Orscheln Co.
Rubbermaid Inc.
Stupp Brothers Bridge & Iron Co.

LIGUORI
Solo Cup Co.

MARSHALL
ConAgra, Inc.
Orscheln Co.

MEXICO
Commerce Bancshares, Inc.

MOBERLY
Orscheln Co.

MONTGOMERYCITY
Orscheln Co.

NEVADA
Whitman Corp.

POINT LOOKOUT
Laclede Gas Co.

POPLAR BLUFF
Briggs & Stratton Corp.

POTOSI
Ameren Corp.
Red Wing Shoe Co. Inc.

RICHMOND HEIGHTS
GenAmerica Corp.
Sunmark Capital Corp.

RIDGELY
Solo Cup Co.

ROLLA
Ameren Corp.
Atlantic Richfield Co.
Briggs & Stratton Corp.
Emerson Electric Co.
Grace & Co. (W.R.)

Halliburton Co.
Olin Corp.
Smurfit-Stone Container Corp.

SAINT CHARLES
Ameren Corp.

SAINT LOUIS
Ameren Corp.
First Financial Bank
GenAmerica Corp.
Group Health Plan
Hartford (The)
Inland Container Corp.
Kellwood Co.
Kelly Services
Kemper National Insurance Companies
Koch Enterprises, Inc.
May Department Stores Co.
MCI WorldCom, Inc.
Mercantile Bank NA
Morrison Knudsen Corp.
National Presto Industries, Inc.
NEC America, Inc.
Praxair
SBC Communications Inc.
Searle & Co. (G.D.)
Smurfit-Stone Container Corp.
Solo Cup Co.
Sunmark Capital Corp.
Times Mirror Co.
Union Pacific Corp.
USX Corp.
Walgreen Co.
Whirlpool Corp.
Williams
Wrigley Co. (Wm. Jr.)

SALISBURY
Orscheln Co.

SEDALIA
Amsted Industries Inc.
International Multifoods Corp.

SPRINGFIELD
APL Ltd.
Blue Bell, Inc.
Borden, Inc.
Circuit City Stores, Inc.
Commerce Bancshares, Inc.
Cranston Print Works Co.
Fortis, Inc.
Kimberly-Clark Corp.
Kroger Co.
MCI WorldCom, Inc.
Mercantile Bank NA
Nabisco Group Holdings
Reynolds Metals Co.
Rubbermaid Inc.
Shelter Mutual Insurance Co.
Sherwin-Williams Co.
Stupp Brothers Bridge & Iron Co.
Sunmark Capital Corp.
Tyson Foods Inc.
Wal-Mart Stores, Inc.

ST JOSEPH
MidAmerican Energy Holdings Co.

ST LOUIS
Furniture Brands International, Inc.

ST. CHARLES
Laclede Gas Co.

ST. JOSEPH
Commerce Bancshares, Inc.
Johnson Controls Inc.

Mead Corp.

ST. LOUIS
Air Products and Chemicals, Inc.
Anheuser-Busch Companies, Inc.
Archer-Daniels-Midland Co.
Baxter International Inc.
Block, Inc. (H&R)
Briggs & Stratton Corp.
Brown Shoe Co., Inc.
Burlington Resources, Inc.
CGU Insurance
Circuit City Stores, Inc.
Comdisco, Inc.
Commerce Bancshares, Inc.
Cooper Industries, Inc.
CPI Corp.
Crane Co.
DaimlerChrysler Corp.
Edison Brothers Stores, Inc.
Emerson Electric Co.
Enterprise Rent-A-Car Co.
FINA
Fireman's Fund Insurance Co.
Furniture Brands International, Inc.
Gap, Inc.
Gerber Products Co.
Hallmark Cards Inc.
Hartmarx Corp.
Hubbell Inc.
IKON Office Solutions, Inc.
Jones & Co. (Edward D.)
Laclede Gas Co.
Medtronic, Inc.
Monsanto Co.
Nomura Holding America
Orscheln Co.
Pulitzer Publishing Co.
Ralston Purina Co.
Reynolds Tobacco (R.J.)
Ryder System, Inc.
Security Benefit Life Insurance Co.
Sega of America Inc.
Sony Electronics
Stupp Brothers Bridge & Iron Co.
Sverdrup Corp.
Tension Envelope Corp.
Tyson Foods Inc.
Universal Foods Corp.
Warner-Lambert Co.
Weil, Gotshal & Manges Corp.
Whitman Corp.
Wisconsin Energy Corp.
Yellow Corp.

WARRENSBURG
Morris Communications Corp.
Tension Envelope Corp.

WARSAW
Orscheln Co.
Solo Cup Co.

WASHINGTON
Edison Brothers Stores, Inc.

WEBSTER GROVES
Ameren Corp.
Emerson Electric Co.
Kellwood Co.
Mercantile Bank NA
Sverdrup Corp.

Montana

Burlington Resources, Inc.
Cenex Harvest States
MONY Group (The)

BILLINGS
Exxon Mobil Corp.
Lee Enterprises
Montana Power Co.
True Oil Co.

BOZEMAN
Cenex Harvest States
Hensel Phelps Construction Co.
Louisiana-Pacific Corp.
Montana Power Co.
Norwest Corp.
Phillips Petroleum Co.
Rayonier Inc.
True Oil Co.
U.S. Bancorp
US West, Inc.

BROWNING
Orscheln Co.

BUTTE
ASARCO Inc.
Atlantic Richfield Co.
Bechtel Group, Inc.
Burlington Resources, Inc.
Ensign-Bickford Industries
Fisher Brothers Cleaning Services
Halliburton Co.
Lee Enterprises
Montana Power Co.
Phelps Dodge Corp.
USX Corp.

DETROIT
Hanna Co. (M.A.)

DILLON
Montana Power Co.

GREAT FALLS
Alma Piston Co.
Montana Power Co.
Waste Management Inc.

HARDIN
Harland Co. (John H.)

HAVRE
Montana Power Co.

HELENA
Dial Corp.
Lee Enterprises
Montana Power Co.
Orscheln Co.
Patagonia Inc.

LEWISTON
Montana Power Co.

MISSOULA
Evening Post Publishing Co.
Montana Power Co.
Patagonia Inc.

PABLO
Hitachi America Ltd.

POLSON
Lee Enterprises

WHITEFISH
Montana Power Co.
PacifiCorp

Nebraska

Valmont Industries, Inc.

BEATRICE
Ameritas Life Insurance Corp.
Land O'Lakes, Inc.
NEBCO Evans

BELLEVUE
ConAgra, Inc.
Mutual of Omaha Insurance Co.
NEBCO Evans

BERLIN
Shaw's Supermarkets, Inc.

BLAIR
ConAgra, Inc.
Valmont Industries, Inc.

BOYS TOWN
Physicians Mutual Insurance Co.

BROKEN BOW
IBP
Tyson Foods Inc.

CAMBRIDGE
Kinder Morgn

CHADRON
ConAgra, Inc.
True Oil Co.

COLUMBUS
Pieper Power Electric Co.

CRETE
Ameritas Life Insurance Corp.

EMMERSON
IBP

FREMONT
Valmont Industries, Inc.

GENEVA
Crane & Co., Inc.
Wyman-Gordon Co.

GOTHENBURG
CLARCOR Inc.

GRAND ISLAND
NEBCO Evans

HASTINGS
Valmont Industries, Inc.

HEBRON
Kinder Morgn

HOMER
IBP

IMPERIAL
Land O'Lakes, Inc.

KEARNEY
CLARCOR Inc.
Kinder Morgn
West Co. Inc.

LEXINGTON
IBP

LINCOIN
FINA

LINCOLN
Ameritas Life Insurance Corp.
Cenex Harvest States
Deloitte & Touche
General Atlantic Partners II LP
Hensel Phelps Construction Co.
IKON Office Solutions, Inc.
Kemper National Insurance Companies
Kinder Morgn
Lee Enterprises
National Bank of Commerce Trust & Savings

NEBCO Evans
Physicians Mutual Insurance Co.
Shelter Mutual Insurance Co.
US West, Inc.
Valmont Industries, Inc.
West Co. Inc.

MADISON
IBP

NORTH PLATTE
Union Pacific Corp.

OMAHA
Ameritas Life Insurance Corp.
APL Ltd.
ConAgra, Inc.
Dain Bosworth Inc.
Employers Mutual Casualty Co.
Gallo Winery, Inc. (E&J)
Hoffmann-La Roche Inc.
Independent Stave Co.
Kemper National Insurance Companies
Kinder Morgn
Lee Enterprises
Mutual of Omaha Insurance Co.
NEBCO Evans
Norwest Corp.
Orscheln Co.
Physicians Mutual Insurance Co.
Reynolds Tobacco (R.J.)
Tektronix, Inc.
True North Communications, Inc.
Union Pacific Corp.
U.S. Bancorp
US West, Inc.
Valmont Industries, Inc.
West Co. Inc.
Western & Southern Life Insurance Co.

PAMAHA
Valmont Industries, Inc.

PAPILLION
Toshiba America Inc.

SCHRIBNER
IBP

SCOTTSBLUFF
Kinder Morgn

SEWARD
West Co. Inc.

SIDNEY
Kinder Morgn

SOUTH SIOUX CITY
IBP

WAYNE
Ameritas Life Insurance Corp.
Valmont Industries, Inc.

YORK
Ameritas Life Insurance Corp.
Hamilton Sundstrand Corp.

Nevada

Sierra Pacific Resources

CARSON CITY
Farmers Group, Inc.
Pfizer Inc.
Sierra Pacific Resources

ELKO
Sierra Pacific Resources
Simplot Co. (J.R.)
Southwest Gas Corp.

HENDERSON
PerkinElmer, Inc.

INCLINE VILLAGE
Sierra Pacific Resources

LAS VEGAS
America West Airlines, Inc.
Bank of America
Landmark Communications Inc.
Morrison Knudsen Corp.
Southwest Gas Corp.

LOS VEGAS
CSR Rinker Materials Corp.

MESQUITE
Ryder System, Inc.

RENO
Bank of America
Commercial Intertech Corp.
Louisiana-Pacific Corp.
Sierra Pacific Resources
Southwest Gas Corp.
Timken Co. (The)

New Hampshire

BankBoston Corp.
Cummings Properties Management
Kingsbury Corp.
Webster Bank

BERLIN
Shaw's Supermarkets, Inc.

CHARLESTOWN
Champion International Corp.
New York Mercantile Exchange

CONCORD
Fidelity Investments
Fisher Scientific
Shaw's Supermarkets, Inc.
United States Trust Co. of New York

DURHAM
Demoulas Supermarkets Inc.
Fisher Scientific
Kingsbury Corp.

HAMPTON
Fisher Scientific

HANOVER
Ameritech Ohio
Blue Cross & Blue Shield of Minnesota
Croft-Leominster
Eastern Enterprises
Goldman Sachs Group
GTE Corp.
Harsco Corp.
Jacobson & Sons (Benjamin)
Kingsbury Corp.
Mattel Inc.
Nomura Holding America
Quaker Chemical Corp.
Stone Container Corp.
Tai and Co. (J.T.)
U.S. Bancorp

HOLLIS
Barnes Group Inc.

KEENE
Kingsbury Corp.
Shaw's Supermarkets, Inc.

LACONIA
Shaw's Supermarkets, Inc.

LEBANON
Shaw's Supermarkets, Inc.
TJX Companies, Inc.

LISBON
Simpson Investment Co.

MANCHESTER
Cummings Properties Management
DaimlerChrysler Corp.
Fidelity Investments
Fisher Scientific
Hannaford Brothers Co.
Kingsbury Corp.
Merit Oil Corp.

MERRIMACK
Stride Rite Corp.

NASHUA
American Retail Group

NEW IPSWICH
Teleflex Inc.

NEW MARKET
Pfizer Inc.

PETERBOROUGH
Manulife Financial
Minnesota Mining & Manufacturing Co.

PLYMOUTH
Kingsbury Corp.

PORTSMOUTH
Fisher Scientific
Hannaford Brothers Co.

TAMWORTH
Universal Studios

WINDHAM
Carris Reels

New Jersey

Ameritech Corp.
Bard, Inc. (C.R.)
Chase Manhattan Bank, NA
New Jersey Natural Gas Co.
Praxair
Schering-Plough Corp.

AUDUBON
Portland General Electric Co.

BAYONNE
Liz Claiborne, Inc.

BERGEN COUNTY
Medtronic, Inc.

BERNARDSVILLE
Forbes Inc.

BLACKWOOD
CSS Industries, Inc.

BLAIRSTOWN
Schering-Plough Corp.

BLOOMFIELD
Reynolds Tobacco (R.J.)
Schering-Plough Corp.

BOUND BROOK
National Starch & Chemical Co.

BRIDGEWATER
National Starch & Chemical Co.

BROOKDALE
New Jersey Natural Gas Co.

BROWNS MILLS
First Union Corp.
Lipton Co.
New Jersey Natural Gas Co.
Vanguard Group

BRUNSWICK
Tai and Co. (J.T.)

CAMDEN
Bell Atlantic Corp.
Campbell Soup Co.
First Union Bank
First Union Corp.
General Atlantic Partners II LP
Lotus Development Corp.
Merit Oil Corp.
PNC Financial Services Group
Prudential Insurance Co. of America
Rutledge Hill Press
Tai and Co. (J.T.)

CEDAR GROVE
USG Corp.

CEDAR KNOLLS
Nabisco Group Holdings

CHERRY HILL
Campbell Soup Co.
Giant Food Inc.
Merit Oil Corp.

CLARK
Sentry Insurance, A Mutual Co.

CLIFTON
Associated Food Stores

COLLINGSWOOD
Campbell Soup Co.

CRANFORD
Bernstein & Co., Inc. (Sanford C.)
New Jersey Natural Gas Co.

DEAL
Century 21
Mamiye Brothers

DELRAN
Union Carbide Corp.

DENVILLE
AlliedSignal Inc.
Nabisco Group Holdings
Warner-Lambert Co.

EAST BRUNSWICK
International Flavors & Fragrances Inc.

EAST ORANGE
Carter-Wallace, Inc.
Sony Electronics

EDISON
International Flavors & Fragrances Inc.
Revlon Inc.

EGG HARBOR
Universal Studios

ELBERON
Century 21

ELIZABETH
American Retail Group
Bard, Inc. (C.R.)
Cooper Tire & Rubber Co.
Dun & Bradstreet Corp.
Merck & Co.
National Starch & Chemical Co.
Schering-Plough Corp.
Sovereign Bank

ELMER
Campbell Soup Co.

ENGLEWOOD
Barry Corp. (R.G.)
Carillon Importers, Ltd.
Leviton Manufacturing Co. Inc.
Lipton Co.
MONY Group (The)

EWING
West Co. Inc.

FAIR LAWN
Nabisco Group Holdings

FAIRLAWN
Sony Electronics
Wrigley Co. (Wm. Jr.)

FAR HILLS
Forbes Inc.

FARMINGDALE
International Flavors & Fragrances Inc.

FLEMINGTON
Bemis Co., Inc.
National Starch & Chemical Co.

FREEHOLD
New Jersey Natural Gas Co.

GARDEN CITY
Toshiba America Inc.

GILLETTE
Alcon Laboratories, Inc.

GLADSTONE
Duchossois Industries Inc.
Gallo Winery, Inc. (E&J)

GLASSBORO
Merit Oil Corp.

GLEN GARDNER
Bard, Inc. (C.R.)

HACKENSACK
MONY Group (The)
New York Stock Exchange, Inc.
Sovereign Bank

HACKETTSTOWN
Globe Corp.
Louisiana Land & Exploration Co.

HADDONFIELD
Campbell Soup Co.

HAZLET
International Flavors & Fragrances Inc.
New Jersey Natural Gas Co.

HIGH BRIDGE
New England Bio Labs

HIGH RIDGE
Brunswick Corp.

HIGHTSTOWN
Dun & Bradstreet Corp.
Nabisco Group Holdings
Warner-Lambert Co.

HOBOKEN
Exxon Mobil Corp.

HOLMDEL
New Jersey Natural Gas Co.
PNC Financial Services Group

JERSEY CITY
Carillon Importers, Ltd.
Daily News
Dow Jones & Co., Inc.
Liz Claiborne, Inc.
Merit Oil Corp.
Paine Webber
Pfizer Inc.

KEANSBURG
International Flavors & Fragrances Inc.

LAKEWOOD
New Jersey Natural Gas Co.

LAWRENCEVILLE
Bardes Corp.
Dow Jones & Co., Inc.
Globe Corp.
Merit Oil Corp.
Public Service Electric & Gas Co.

LEONARDO
International Flavors & Fragrances Inc.

LIVINGSTON
CIT Group, Inc. (The)

LONG BRANCH
International Flavors & Fragrances Inc.
New Jersey Natural Gas Co.

MADISON
Forbes Inc.
MCI WorldCom, Inc.
Nabisco Group Holdings
Schering-Plough Corp.
Warner-Lambert Co.
West Co. Inc.

MAPLEWOOD
Dun & Bradstreet Corp.
Lipton Co.
Warner-Lambert Co.

MARTINSVILLE
Carter-Wallace, Inc.

MATAWAN
International Flavors & Fragrances Inc.

MERCERVILLE
Pillsbury Co.

METUCHEN
Dun & Bradstreet Corp.

MILBURN
Schering-Plough Corp.

MILLBURN
Dun & Bradstreet Corp.

MILLTOWN
Dow Jones & Co., Inc.
UnumProvident

MILLVILLE
CLARCOR Inc.
Woodward Governor Co.

MONMOUTH
New Jersey Natural Gas Co.

MONMOUTH JUNCTION
International Flavors & Fragrances Inc.

MONTCLAIR
Schering-Plough Corp.

MONTVALE
Texaco Inc.
Union Carbide Corp.

MOORESTOWN
Campbell Soup Co.
Fidelity Investments
Gerber Products Co.
Oshkosh B'Gosh, Inc.

MORRIS PLAINS
Warner-Lambert Co.

MORRISTOWN
Bard, Inc. (C.R.)
Campbell Soup Co.
Nabisco Group Holdings
National Starch & Chemical Co.
New Jersey Natural Gas Co.
New York Mercantile Exchange
Nomura Holding America
Prudential Insurance Co. of America
Schering-Plough Corp.
Warner-Lambert Co.
Witco Corp.

MOUNT HOLLY
CGU Insurance
McGraw-Hill Companies, Inc.

MOUNTAINSIDE
Bard, Inc. (C.R.)
Schering-Plough Corp.

MT. LAUREL
Warner-Lambert Co.

NEPTUNE
Carter-Wallace, Inc.
New Jersey Natural Gas Co.

NEW BRUNSWICK
Avon Products, Inc.
Carillon Importers, Ltd.
Corning Inc.
Elf Atochem North America, Inc.
General Electric Co.
Hartmarx Corp.
Johnson & Johnson
Liz Claiborne, Inc.
McGraw-Hill Companies, Inc.
Merck & Co.
National Starch & Chemical Co.
New Jersey Natural Gas Co.
New York Times Co.
Norton Co.
Schering-Plough Corp.
Tension Envelope Corp.
Warner-Lambert Co.

NEW PROVIDENCE
Bard, Inc. (C.R.)
Dun & Bradstreet Corp.

NEWARK
AlliedSignal Inc.
AT&T Corp.
Avon Products, Inc.
Bard, Inc. (C.R.)
Bernstein & Co., Inc. (Sanford C.)
Carillon Importers, Ltd.
Carter-Wallace, Inc.
Chase Manhattan Bank, NA
CIT Group, Inc. (The)
Colonial Oil Industries, Inc.
Dun & Bradstreet Corp.
First Union Corp.
Fluor Corp.
Forbes Inc.
Ford Motor Co.
Gallo Winery, Inc. (E&J)
Hoffmann-La Roche Inc.
Inland Container Corp.
Merit Oil Corp.
Merrill Lynch & Co., Inc.
Nabisco Group Holdings
National Starch & Chemical Co.
Prudential Insurance Co. of America
Public Service Electric & Gas Co.
Ralph's Grocery Co.
Reynolds Tobacco (R.J.)
Schering-Plough Corp.
True North Communications, Inc.
Union Camp Corp.
Union Carbide Corp.
United Airlines Inc.
Warner-Lambert Co.

NORTH BRANCH
National Starch & Chemical Co.

NORTH BRUNSWICK
International Flavors & Fragrances Inc.

NORTH PLAINFIELD
Merck & Co.
Warner-Lambert Co.

NORTH PLAINSFIELD
Schering-Plough Corp.

OAKHURST
Mamiye Brothers

OCEAN
Century 21
Mamiye Brothers
New Jersey Natural Gas Co.

ORADELL
AlliedSignal Inc.
Federated Department Stores, Inc.
Merit Oil Corp.
Unilever United States, Inc.
Walgreen Co.

PARAMUS
Butler Manufacturing Co.
Federated Department Stores, Inc.
MONY Group (The)

PARSIPPANY
Nabisco Group Holdings

PASSAIC
State Farm Mutual Automobile Insurance Co.

PATERSON
McGraw-Hill Companies, Inc.
State Farm Mutual Automobile Insurance Co.
Union Camp Corp.

PENNINGTON
Freddie Mac

PERTH AMBOY
Sovereign Bank

PISCATAWAY
Dun & Bradstreet Corp.
Warner-Lambert Co.

PLAINFIELD
Dun & Bradstreet Corp.
National Starch & Chemical Co.
Paine Webber
Schering-Plough Corp.
Union Carbide Corp.
Wrigley Co. (Wm. Jr.)

POINT PLEASANT
Eastern Enterprises
New Jersey Natural Gas Co.

POMPTON PLAINS
State Farm Mutual Automobile Insurance Co.

POTTERSVILLE
Forbes Inc.

PRINCETON
AMETEK, Inc.
Barclays Capital
Bard, Inc. (C.R.)
BFGoodrich Co.
Brown Shoe Co., Inc.
Carillon Importers, Ltd.
Carter-Wallace, Inc.
Central National-Gottesman
Citizens Financial Group, Inc.
Cone Mills Corp.
Crane & Co., Inc.
Cyprus Amax Minerals Co.
Dexter Corp.
Dow Jones & Co., Inc.
FMC Corp.
Forbes Inc.
GEICO Corp.
General Motors Corp.
Giant Food Inc.
Hoffmann-La Roche Inc.
Humana, Inc.
Intel Corp.
International Flavors & Fragrances Inc.
Lance, Inc.
Milliken & Co.
Morrison Knudsen Corp.
New York Times Co.
Procter & Gamble Co.
Prudential Insurance Co. of America
Rayonier Inc.
Revlon Inc.
Textron Inc.
Times Mirror Co.
Union Camp Corp.
United Distillers & Vintners North America
United States Trust Co. of New York
Universal Studios
Warner-Lambert Co.
Waste Management Inc.

PRINCETON JUNCTION
FMC Corp.

RAHWAY
Dun & Bradstreet Corp.

RANDOLPH
New Jersey Natural Gas Co.
Warner-Lambert Co.

RED BANK
International Flavors & Fragrances Inc.
New Jersey Natural Gas Co.

RIDGE WOOD
Amgen, Inc.
Comdisco, Inc.

RIDGEWOOD
Bell Atlantic Corp.
Union Camp Corp.

RIGHTSTOWN
Bard, Inc. (C.R.)

RIVER EDGE
Central National-Gottesman
Thompson Co. (J. Walter)

ROCHELLE PARK
Carnival Corp.
Sega of America Inc.

SADDLE BROOK
Masco Corp.

SHORT HILLS
Carter-Wallace, Inc.
Goldman Sachs Group
Prudential Securities Inc.

SOMERSET
Century 21
New York Mercantile Exchange
Schering-Plough Corp.

SOMERVILLE
Merck & Co.
National Starch & Chemical Co.

SOUTH BRUNSWICK
International Flavors & Fragrances Inc.

SOUTH ORANGE
American Retail Group
Elf Atochem North America, Inc.
Reynolds Tobacco (R.J.)

SPOTSWOOD
Bard, Inc. (C.R.)

SPRINGFIELD
Young & Rubicam

STANHOPE
Nabisco Group Holdings

STRATFORD
Campbell Soup Co.

SUMMIT
AlliedSignal Inc.
Barclays Capital
Bard, Inc. (C.R.)
Carter-Wallace, Inc.
Dun & Bradstreet Corp.
Hoffmann-La Roche Inc.
New Jersey Natural Gas Co.
Prudential Insurance Co. of America
Warner-Lambert Co.

TEANECK
Barclays Capital
Bernstein & Co., Inc. (Sanford C.)
Schering-Plough Corp.

TENECK
Merit Oil Corp.

TOMS RIVER
New Jersey Natural Gas Co.
Witco Corp.

TOTOWA
Carillon Importers, Ltd.
Giddings & Lewis

TRENTON
American Standard Inc.
Banfi Vintners
Chase Manhattan Bank, NA

CLARCOR Inc.
Dow Jones & Co., Inc.
International Flavors & Fragrances Inc.
Prudential Insurance Co. of America
Sovereign Bank

UNION
Chase Manhattan Bank, NA

UNION BEACH
International Flavors & Fragrances Inc.

UNION CITY
Bernstein & Co., Inc. (Sanford C.)
Carillon Importers, Ltd.

UNIVERSITY HEIGHTS
National Starch & Chemical Co.

VOORHEES
Campbell Soup Co.

WANAMASSA
Dun & Bradstreet Corp.

WAYNE
Union Camp Corp.

WEEHAWKEN
Carillon Importers, Ltd.

WEST BERGEN
Sony Electronics

WEST LONG BEACH
International Flavors & Fragrances Inc.
New Jersey Natural Gas Co.

WEST ORANGE
Bard, Inc. (C.R.)
Sony Electronics
Warner-Lambert Co.

WESTFIELD
Carillon Importers, Ltd.

WESTWOOD
Lipton Co.
Sony Electronics

WICKATUNK
New Jersey Natural Gas Co.

WOODBURY
International Multifoods Corp.

New Mexico

Intel Corp.

ALAPOGODO
National Presto Industries, Inc.

ALBUQUERQUE
American Honda Motor Co., Inc.
Baxter International Inc.
Bristol-Myers Squibb Co.
Burlington Resources, Inc.
General Atlantic Partners II LP
General Mills, Inc.
Hitachi America Ltd.
Honeywell International Inc.
Hubbard Broadcasting, Inc.
Intel Corp.
Jacobs Engineering Group
Levi Strauss & Co.
Litton Industries, Inc.
Motorola Inc.
Norwest Corp.
PerkinElmer, Inc.
Phelps Dodge Corp.
Sun Microsystems Inc.
US West, Inc.
Walgreen Co.

CLAYTON
Furniture Brands International, Inc.

CROWNPOINT
General Atlantic Partners II LP

FARMINGTON
Burlington Resources, Inc.
El Paso Energy Co.

LAS CRUCES
Burlington Resources, Inc.
National Presto Industries, Inc.
Phelps Dodge Corp.

LAS VEGAS
Phelps Dodge Corp.

MONTEZUMA
Occidental Petroleum Corp.

QUESTA
Unocal Corp.

RIBORN
Oshkosh B'Gosh, Inc.

ROSWELL
Rayonier Inc.

SANTA FE
Carillon Importers, Ltd.
El Paso Energy Co.
Fisher Brothers Cleaning Services
Hitachi America Ltd.
Lipton Co.

SANTA FE SPRINGS
Inland Container Corp.

SILVER CITY
Phelps Dodge Corp.

SIOUX CITY
Norwest Corp.

SOCORRO
Phelps Dodge Corp.

New York

Avon Products, Inc.
Calvin Klein
Chase Manhattan Bank, NA
Chesapeake Corp.
Crane Co.
International Multifoods Corp.
Jacobson & Sons (Benjamin)
Mark IV Industries
Merck & Co.
MONY Group (The)
Overseas Shipholding Group Inc.
Prudential Securities Inc.
Rich Products Corp.
Rubbermaid Inc.
Searle & Co. (G.D.)
Tai and Co. (J.T.)
Toshiba America Inc.

ALBANY
Bard, Inc. (C.R.)
Butler Capital Corp.
Carris Reels
Century 21
CGU Insurance
Champion International Corp.
Chase Manhattan Bank, NA
Corning Inc.
Crane & Co., Inc.
Dun & Bradstreet Corp.
Erb Lumber Co.
Golub Corp.
Hannaford Brothers Co.
Hartford (The)
Hensel Phelps Construction Co.
New York Stock Exchange, Inc.
Niagara Mohawk Holdings Inc.
Pieper Power Electric Co.
Prudential Securities Inc.
S.G. Cowen
Weil, Gotshal & Manges Corp.

ALBERTSON
Merrill Lynch & Co., Inc.
Nomura Holding America
United States Trust Co. of New York

ALBION
Rich Products Corp.

ALFRED
Agrilink Foods, Inc.
Corning Inc.
Dynamet, Inc.
Norton Co.
United States Trust Co. of New York

AMHERST
Russer Foods

AMSTERDAM
Golub Corp.

ANNANDALE-ON-HUDSON
Dow Jones & Co., Inc.

ARLINGTON
Witco Corp.

ARMONK
American Standard Inc.
Commercial Intertech Corp.

ASTORIA
New York Times Co.

BARDONIA
Merck & Co.

BAYSIDE
Schlumberger Ltd. (USA)

BINGHAMTON
AMETEK, Inc.
Corning Inc.
Gerber Products Co.

BLANK
Reader's Digest Association, Inc. (The)

BLAUVELT
American Retail Group

BRENTWOOD
Merit Oil Corp.

BREWSTER
Carillon Importers, Ltd.

BRIARCLIFF MANOR
Searle & Co. (G.D.)

BRIDGEHAMPTON
Trace International Holdings, Inc.

BROADWAY
Century 21

BRONX
American Retail Group
Associated Food Stores
Avon Products, Inc.
Bristol-Myers Squibb Co.
Butler Capital Corp.
Carillon Importers, Ltd.
Carter-Wallace, Inc.
Central National-Gottesman
Chase Manhattan Bank, NA
CIBC Oppenheimer
Deutsch Co.
Fuji Bank & Trust Co.
Glickenhaus & Co.
Grace & Co. (W.R.)
Hitachi America Ltd.
International Flavors & Fragrances Inc.
Loews Corp.
Merrill Lynch & Co., Inc.
Morgan & Co. Inc. (J.P.)
Morgan Stanley Dean Witter & Co.
New York Mercantile Exchange
Overseas Shipholding Group Inc.
Paine Webber
Reynolds Tobacco (R.J.)
Seagram & Sons, Inc. (Joseph E.)
Solo Cup Co.
Texaco Inc.
Thompson Co. (J. Walter)
Toshiba America Inc.
Toyota Motor Sales U.S.A., Inc.
Transamerica Corp.
United States Trust Co. of New York
Vesper Corp.

BRONXVILLE
Titan Industrial Corp.

BROOKLYN
Allstate Insurance Co.
American Retail Group
Associated Food Stores
Avon Products, Inc.
Ben & Jerry's Homemade Inc.
Borden, Inc.
Calvin Klein
Cantor, Fitzgerald Securities Corp.
Century 21
Chase Manhattan Bank, NA
Credit Suisse First Boston
Daily News
Dow Jones & Co., Inc.
Forbes Inc.
Freddie Mac
General Electric Co.
Industrial Bank of Japan Trust Co. (New York)
Jacobs Engineering Group
Litton Industries, Inc.
Liz Claiborne, Inc.
Mamiye Brothers
Mattel Inc.
Merck & Co.
Merit Oil Corp.
Metropolitan Life Insurance Co.
MONY Group (The)
Morgan & Co. Inc. (J.P.)
Morgan Stanley Dean Witter & Co.
New York Life Insurance Co.
New York Mercantile Exchange
New York Times Co.
Pfizer Inc.
Reynolds Tobacco (R.J.)
Schloss & Co. (Marcus)
S.G. Cowen
Tai and Co. (J.T.)
Tension Envelope Corp.
Times Mirror Co.
Toshiba America Inc.
Toyota Motor Sales U.S.A., Inc.
Trace International Holdings, Inc.
Weil, Gotshal & Manges Corp.
Witco Corp.

BROOKVILLE
FINA

BUFFALO
Agrilink Foods, Inc.
Bethlehem Steel Corp.
CertainTeed Corp.
CGU Insurance
Cone Mills Corp.
Duriron Co., Inc.
General Mills, Inc.
Harsco Corp.
Hartmarx Corp.
IKON Office Solutions, Inc.
Manufacturers & Traders Trust Co.
Mark IV Industries
Mattel Inc.
McGraw-Hill Companies, Inc.
Medtronic, Inc.
MONY Group (The)
Nabisco Group Holdings
Niagara Mohawk Holdings Inc.
Norton Co.
Oshkosh B'Gosh, Inc.
Praxair
Rich Products Corp.
Russer Foods

CANANDAIGUA
Eastman Kodak Co.

CANANDAIQUA
Eastman Kodak Co.

CANTON
Corning Inc.
Maytag Corp.

CARMEL
Praxair

CAZENOVIA
Niagara Mohawk Holdings Inc.

CHAPPAGUA
Chicago Title Corp.

CHARLOTTE
AEGON U.S.A. Inc.

CHAUTAUQUA
Russer Foods

CLIFTON SPRINGS
Agrilink Foods, Inc.

CLINTON
Hartmarx Corp.

COBLESKILL
Niagara Mohawk Holdings Inc.

COLD SPRING HARBOR
Schering-Plough Corp.

COMMACK
Associated Food Stores
Reynolds Tobacco (R.J.)

CORNING
Corning Inc.

CORONA PARK
Texaco Inc.

DEER PARK
CGU Insurance
GEICO Corp.
Merit Oil Corp.
Royal & SunAlliance USA, Inc.

DELMAR
Owens Corning

DOBBS FERRY
Central National-Gottesman
Gerber Products Co.

DUNKIRK
Niagara Mohawk Holdings Inc.
Ralston Purina Co.

EAST AURORA
Mattel Inc.

EAST SYRACUSE
Golub Corp.

ELMHURST
United States Trust Co. of New York

ELMIRA
Corning Inc.
Elf Atochem North America, Inc.
Toshiba America Inc.

ELMSFORD
Reader's Digest Association, Inc. (The)

ERIE
International Paper Co.

EVANSTON
PepsiCo, Inc.

FLORIDA
Ben & Jerry's Homemade Inc.

FLUSHING
AMR Corp.
Avon Products, Inc.
CSS Industries, Inc.
Paine Webber
Toshiba America Inc.

FOREST HILLS
AMR Corp.
New York Mercantile Exchange
Schloss & Co. (Marcus)

FREDONIA
Tomkins Industries, Inc.

FRESH MEADOWS
United States Trust Co. of New York

GARDEN CITY
Avon Products, Inc.
Century 21
Daily News
Paine Webber

GARRISON
Aetna, Inc.

GENESEE
Agrilink Foods, Inc.

GENESEO
Pittway Corp.

GLENS FALLS
Bard, Inc. (C.R.)
Golub Corp.
Hartford (The)
Niagara Mohawk Holdings Inc.

GLOVERSVILLE
Niagara Mohawk Holdings Inc.

GREAT NECK
Butler Capital Corp.

HACKENSACK
PNC Financial Services Group

HAMILTON
Banfi Vintners
Heinz Co. (H.J.)
Metropolitan Life Insurance Co.
Paine Webber

HARTSDALE
Reader's Digest Association, Inc. (The)

HAUPPAUGE
Central National-Gottesman

HAWTHORNE
Bernstein & Co., Inc. (Sanford C.)

HEMPSTEAD
General Atlantic Partners II LP
Merrill Lynch & Co., Inc.
Pittway Corp.

HICKSVILLE
Lennox International, Inc.

HORSEHEADS
Corning Inc.

HORSENHEADS
Toshiba America Inc.

HOUGHTON
Florida Power & Light Co.

HOWARD BEACH
Associated Food Stores

HUDSON
AMETEK, Inc.
Carillon Importers, Ltd.
Golub Corp.
Niagara Mohawk Holdings Inc.

HUNTINGTON
Banfi Vintners
Bernstein & Co., Inc. (Sanford C.)
Eastern Enterprises
MONY Group (The)
Reynolds Tobacco (R.J.)
State Street Bank & Trust Co.

HYDE PARK
Avon Products, Inc.
Carillon Importers, Ltd.
Ecolab Inc.
General Mills, Inc.
PepsiCo, Inc.

IRVINGTON
Sunmark Capital Corp.

ITHACA
Agrilink Foods, Inc.
Air Products and Chemicals, Inc.
Anheuser-Busch Companies, Inc.
Banfi Vintners
Ben & Jerry's Homemade Inc.
Chevron Corp.
Corning Inc.
Deloitte & Touche
Eastern Enterprises
Elf Atochem North America, Inc.
Fortis, Inc.
General Electric Co.
General Motors Corp.
GTE Corp.
Johnson & Son (S.C.)
Loews Corp.
Merck & Co.
Merrill Lynch & Co., Inc.
Nestle U.S.A. Inc.
Nomura Holding America
Olin Corp.
PepsiCo, Inc.
Procter & Gamble Co.
SmithKline Beecham Corp.
Tai and Co. (J.T.)
Unilever United States, Inc.
USX Corp.
Xerox Corp.

JAMAICA
ABC
AT&T Corp.
Chase Manhattan Bank, NA
Fuji Bank & Trust Co.
Merrill Lynch & Co., Inc.
Schloss & Co. (Marcus)
Thompson Co. (J. Walter)

KATONAH
Bernstein & Co., Inc. (Sanford C.)
Daily News
Stone Container Corp.

KINGS POINT
Tesoro Hawaii

KINGSTON
AMETEK, Inc.
PerkinElmer, Inc.

LARCHMONT
Jacobson & Sons (Benjamin)
United States Trust Co. of New York

LATHAM
Golub Corp.

LEWISTON
Norton Co.

LIDO BEACH
Associated Food Stores

LITTLE NECK
Leviton Manufacturing Co. Inc.

LIVERPOOL
Cooper Industries, Inc.
Niagara Mohawk Holdings Inc.

LOCKPORT
Harsco Corp.
International Multifoods Corp.

LONG BEACH
Associated Food Stores

LONG ISLAND
Allegheny Technologies Inc.
Pittway Corp.

LONG ISLAND CITY
Ben & Jerry's Homemade Inc.
Morgan Stanley Dean Witter & Co.
Schlumberger Ltd. (USA)

LOUDONVILLE
Golub Corp.

LYONS
Parker Hannifin Corp.

MALONE
Reynolds Metals Co.

MANHASSET
Carter-Wallace, Inc.
S.G. Cowen

MANHATTAN
Glickenhaus & Co.
Royal & SunAlliance USA, Inc.
Tai and Co. (J.T.)

MASSENA
Reynolds Metals Co.

MEDINA
Mattel Inc.

MELVILLE
Bernstein & Co., Inc. (Sanford C.)
NEC America, Inc.
Pittway Corp.
Times Mirror Co.

MERRICK
S.G. Cowen

MILLERTON
Country Curtains, Inc.

MINEOLA
New York Stock Exchange, Inc.

MONSEY
Slant/Fin Corp.

MOUNT KISCO
Fisher Brothers Cleaning Services

NEW HARTFORD
Butler Capital Corp.

NEW HYDE PARK
Bernstein & Co., Inc. (Sanford C.)

NEW ROCHELLE
American Retail Group
Federal-Mogul Corp.
Fisher Brothers Cleaning Services
Reader's Digest Association, Inc. (The)
Texaco Inc.
Witco Corp.

NEW YORK
ABC
Aetna, Inc.
Air Products and Chemicals, Inc.
Alcon Laboratories, Inc.
AlliedSignal Inc.
Allmerica Financial Corp.
Allstate Insurance Co.
Alma Piston Co.
Ameren Corp.
American Express Co.
American Honda Motor Co., Inc.
American Standard Inc.
AMETEK, Inc.
Amgen, Inc.
AMR Corp.
Amsted Industries Inc.
Aon Corp.
Archer-Daniels-Midland Co.
Aristech Chemical Corp.
ASARCO Inc.
Associated Food Stores
AT&T Corp.
Atlantic Richfield Co.
Avon Products, Inc.
Banfi Vintners
Bank of America
BankBoston Corp.
Banta Corp.
Barclays Capital
Bard, Inc. (C.R.)
Bardes Corp.
Barry Corp. (R.G.)
Baxter International Inc.
Bechtel Group, Inc.
Belk-Simpson Department Stores
Belk Stores Services Inc.
Ben & Jerry's Homemade Inc.
Bernstein & Co., Inc. (Sanford C.)
Bethlehem Steel Corp.
BFGoodrich Co.
Binswanger Companies
Blair & Co. (William)
Blount International, Inc.
Borden, Inc.
Borman's Inc.
BP Amoco Corp.
Bristol-Myers Squibb Co.
Brown Shoe Co., Inc.
Butler Capital Corp.
Calvin Klein
Cantor, Fitzgerald Securities Corp.
Carillon Importers, Ltd.
Carlson Companies, Inc.
Carnival Corp.
Carter-Wallace, Inc.
CBS Corp.
Central National-Gottesman
Century 21
CGU Insurance
Chase Manhattan Bank, NA
Chevron Corp.
Chicago Title Corp.
CIBC Oppenheimer
CIGNA Corp.
Circuit City Stores, Inc.
CIT Group, Inc. (The)
CLARCOR Inc.
Cleveland-Cliffs, Inc.
CNA
Coca-Cola Co.
Collins & Aikman Corp.
Colonial Oil Industries, Inc.
Compaq Computer Corp.
Compass Bank
Cone Mills Corp.
Consolidated Electrical Distributors
Consolidated Natural Gas Co.
Consolidated Papers, Inc.
Consumers Energy Co.
Continental Grain Co.
Coors Brewing Co.
Copley Press, Inc.

Corning Inc.
Country Curtains, Inc.
Cox Enterprises Inc.
Crane Co.
Cranston Print Works Co.
Credit Suisse First Boston
Crown Books
CSS Industries, Inc.
Cummins Engine Co., Inc.
Daily News
DaimlerChrysler Corp.
Dayton Hudson
Dayton Power and Light Co.
Deloitte & Touche
Delta Air Lines, Inc.
Demoulas Supermarkets Inc.
Deutsch Co.
Dexter Corp.
Disney Co. (Walt)
Dow Chemical Co.
Dow Jones & Co., Inc.
Dreyer's Grand Ice Cream
Dun & Bradstreet Corp.
Duracell International
Eastman Kodak Co.
Eckerd Corp.
Elf Atochem North America, Inc.
Ensign-Bickford Industries
Enterprise Rent-A-Car Co.
Erb Lumber Co.
Exxon Mobil Corp.
Fannie Mae
Federated Department Stores, Inc.
Ferro Corp.
Fidelity Investments
First Union Corp.
Fisher Brothers Cleaning Services
Fisher Scientific
Florida Rock Industries
FMC Corp.
Forbes Inc.
Ford Motor Co.
Forest City Enterprises, Inc.
Fortis, Inc.
Freddie Mac
Freeport-McMoRan Inc.
Fuji Bank & Trust Co.
Furniture Brands International, Inc.
Gallo Winery, Inc. (E&J)
Galter Corp.
Gap, Inc.
GenCorp
General Atlantic Partners II LP
General Electric Co.
General Mills, Inc.
General Motors Corp.
Georgia-Pacific Corp.
Georgia Power Co.
Gerber Products Co.
Giant Food Inc.
Glickenhaus & Co.
Globe Corp.
Goldman Sachs Group
Grace & Co. (W.R.)
Green Bay Packaging
GTE Corp.
Guess?
Hallmark Cards Inc.
Hanna Co. (M.A.)
Harris Corp.
Harsco Corp.
Hartford Steam Boiler Inspection & Insurance Co.
Hartmarx Corp.
Hasbro, Inc.
Heinz Co. (H.J.)
Hershey Foods Corp.
Hewlett-Packard Co.
Hickory Tech Corp.
Hitachi America Ltd.
Hofmann Co.
Honeywell International Inc.
Housatonic Curtain Co.
Hubbell Inc.
Huffy Corp.
Humana, Inc.
Illinois Tool Works, Inc.
Indiana Mills & Manufacturing
Industrial Bank of Japan Trust Co. (New York)
International Flavors & Fragrances Inc.
International Paper Co.
ISE America
Jacobson & Sons (Benjamin)
Katten, Muchin & Zavis
Kemper National Insurance Companies
Kimberly-Clark Corp.
Kirkland & Ellis
KPMG Peat Marwick LLP
Kraft Foods, Inc.
Lance, Inc.
Lee Enterprises
Leigh Fibers, Inc.
Levi Strauss & Co.
Leviton Manufacturing Co. Inc.
Liberty Corp.
Lipton Co.
Little, Inc. (Arthur D.)
Litton Industries, Inc.
Liz Claiborne, Inc.
Loews Corp.
Lotus Development Corp.
Mamiye Brothers
Manulife Financial
Marcus Corp.
Mark IV Industries
Marshall & Ilsley Corp.
Matsushita Electric Corp. of America
Mattel Inc.
May Department Stores Co.
McDonald & Co. Securities, Inc.
McGraw-Hill Companies, Inc.
Medtronic, Inc.
Menasha Corp.
Merck & Co.
Merit Oil Corp.
Merrill Lynch & Co., Inc.
Metropolitan Life Insurance Co.
MidAmerican Energy Holdings Co.
Milliken & Co.
Mine Safety Appliances Co.
Monsanto Co.
MONY Group (The)
Morgan & Co. Inc. (J.P.)
Morgan Stanley Dean Witter & Co.
Morris Communications Corp.
Morrison Knudsen Corp.
Motorola Inc.
Mutual of Omaha Insurance Co.
Nabisco Group Holdings
NASDAQ Stock Market
National Presto Industries, Inc.
National Service Industries, Inc.
National Starch & Chemical Co.
NEC America, Inc.
Nestle U.S.A. Inc.
New York Life Insurance Co.
New York Mercantile Exchange
New York Stock Exchange, Inc.
New York Times Co.
Niagara Mohawk Holdings Inc.
Nike, Inc.
Nomura Holding America
Norton Co.
Occidental Petroleum Corp.
Old Kent Bank
Olin Corp.
Oshkosh B'Gosh, Inc.
Outboard Marine Corp.
Overseas Shipholding Group Inc.
Owens Corning
PACCAR Inc.
Paine Webber
Patagonia Inc.
Penney Co., Inc. (J.C.)
PepsiCo, Inc.
PerkinElmer, Inc.
Pfizer Inc.
Pharmacia & Upjohn, Inc.
Phelps Dodge Corp.
Phillips Petroleum Co.
Physicians Mutual Insurance Co.
Pieper Power Electric Co.
Pittway Corp.
Playboy Enterprises Inc.
PNC Financial Services Group
Polaroid Corp.
PPG Industries, Inc.
Praxair
Premier Dental Products Co.
Principal Financial Group
Procter & Gamble Co.
Prudential Insurance Co. of America
Prudential Securities Inc.
Pulitzer Publishing Co.
Putnam Investments
Rayonier Inc.
Reader's Digest Association, Inc. (The)
Reebok International Ltd.
Reilly Industries, Inc.
Revlon Inc.
Reynolds Tobacco (R.J.)
Rich Products Corp.
Royal & SunAlliance USA, Inc.
Russer Foods
Ryder System, Inc.
Safeguard Scientifics
Saint Paul Companies Inc.
Sara Lee Corp.
Schering-Plough Corp.
Schloss & Co. (Marcus)
Schlumberger Ltd. (USA)
Schwab & Co., Inc. (Charles)
Seagram & Sons, Inc. (Joseph E.)
Searle & Co. (G.D.)
Sears, Roebuck and Co.
Sega of America Inc.
ServiceMaster Co.
S.G. Cowen
Shell Oil Co.
Sierra Pacific Resources
Slant/Fin Corp.
Solo Cup Co.
Sonoco Products Co.
Sony Electronics
Southwest Gas Corp.
SPX Corp.
Square D Co.
Standard Products Co.
State Farm Mutual Automobile Insurance Co.
Stone Container Corp.
Stonecutter Mills Corp.
SunTrust Bank Atlanta
Sverdrup Corp.
Tai and Co. (J.T.)
Tamko Roofing Products
TCF National Bank Minnesota
Tension Envelope Corp.
Texaco Inc.
Texas Instruments Inc.
Textron Inc.
Thermo Electron Corp.
Thompson Co. (J. Walter)
Ticketmaster Corp.
Times Mirror Co.
Titan Industrial Corp.
TJX Companies, Inc.
Toledo Blade Co.
Toshiba America Inc.
Trace International Holdings, Inc.
True North Communications, Inc.
Unilever Home & Personal Care U.S.A.
Unilever United States, Inc.
Union Camp Corp.
Union Carbide Corp.
United Airlines Inc.
United Distillers & Vintners North America
U.S. Bancorp
United States Sugar Corp.
United States Trust Co. of New York
United Wisconsin Services
Universal Studios
UnumProvident
USG Corp.
Vanguard Group
Vesper Corp.
Wachtell, Lipton, Rosen & Katz
Wal-Mart Stores, Inc.
Walter Industries Inc.
Warner-Lambert Co.
Waste Management Inc.
Weil, Gotshal & Manges Corp.
Wells Fargo & Co.
Westvaco Corp.
Weyerhaeuser Co.
Whirlpool Corp.
Whitman Corp.
Wiley & Sons (John)
Williams
Winn-Dixie Stores Inc.
Witco Corp.
Wrigley Co. (Wm. Jr.)
Yellow Corp.
Young & Rubicam
Zilkha & Sons

NEW YORK CITY
Warner-Lambert Co.

NEWARK
Dun & Bradstreet Corp.

NIAGARA FALLS
Nabisco Group Holdings
Norton Co.
Waste Management Inc.

NORTH BELLMORE
Associated Food Stores

NORTHPORT
Central National-Gottesman

NORWICH
BFGoodrich Co.

NY
American Retail Group

OAKDALE
Jacobson & Sons (Benjamin)

OGDENSBURG
Reynolds Metals Co.

OLEAN
Dexter Corp.
Niagara Mohawk Holdings Inc.

ONEONTA
Central & South West Services

OSSINING
Gerber Products Co.

OSWEGO
Niagara Mohawk Holdings Inc.

OXFORD
PepsiCo, Inc.

PAINTED POST
Corning Inc.

PAUGHKEEPSIE
Hubbell Inc.

PAUL SMITHS
Carillon Importers, Ltd.

PORT WASHINGTON
Liz Claiborne, Inc.

POTSDAM
Eastman Kodak Co.
Niagara Mohawk Holdings Inc.
Reynolds Metals Co.

POUGHKEEPSIE
Country Curtains, Inc.
Demoulas Supermarkets Inc.
Golub Corp.
Hubbell Inc.
Leigh Fibers, Inc.
New York Mercantile Exchange
Reader's Digest Association, Inc. (The)
Toro Co.
United States Trust Co. of New York
Wilbur-Ellis Co. & Connell Brothers Co.

PURCHASE
Alma Piston Co.
Central National-Gottesman
Glickenhaus & Co.
PepsiCo, Inc.

PUTNAM VALLEY
Reader's Digest Association, Inc. (The)

QUEENS
Liz Claiborne, Inc.
Loews Corp.

QUEENSBURY
Bard, Inc. (C.R.)
Chesapeake Corp.
Hannaford Brothers Co.

Niagara Mohawk Holdings Inc.

RAQUETTE LAKE
Niagara Mohawk Holdings Inc.

REGO PARK
Hitachi America Ltd.

RENSSELAER
Westvaco Corp.

RENSSELAERVILLE
Golub Corp.

RIVERDALE
Air Products and Chemicals, Inc.
du Pont de Nemours & Co. (E.I.)
Gap, Inc.

ROCHESTER
Agrilink Foods, Inc.
Bausch & Lomb Inc.
CGU Insurance
Chase Manhattan Bank, NA
Eastman Kodak Co.
Elf Atochem North America, Inc.
Harris Corp.
Hartmarx Corp.
Hubbard Broadcasting, Inc.
Jostens, Inc.
McGraw-Hill Companies, Inc.
Mitsubishi Electric America
MONY Group (The)
Niagara Mohawk Holdings Inc.
Nomura Holding America
PerkinElmer, Inc.
Pharmacia & Upjohn, Inc.
Texaco Inc.

ROME
Butler Capital Corp.
Niagara Mohawk Holdings Inc.

RYE
S.G. Cowen

RYE BROOK
McWane Inc.
Sony Electronics

SARANAC LAKE
National Service Industries, Inc.
Niagara Mohawk Holdings Inc.

SARATOGA SPRINGS
American Retail Group
Calvin Klein
State Farm Mutual Automobile Insurance Co.
Thompson Co. (J. Walter)
United States Trust Co. of New York

SCARSDALE
Bernstein & Co., Inc. (Sanford C.)
Titan Industrial Corp.

SCHENECTADY
General Electric Co.
Golub Corp.
Hubbard Broadcasting, Inc.
National Presto Industries, Inc.
Niagara Mohawk Holdings Inc.
Standard Products Co.

SEA CLIFF
New York Mercantile Exchange

SENECA
United Distillers & Vintners North America

SENECA FALLS
Eastman Kodak Co.

SKANEATELES
Niagara Mohawk Holdings Inc.

SMITHTOWN
Parker Hannifin Corp.

SOUTH BUFFALO
American Retail Group

SOUTHAMPTON
Zilkha & Sons

SPARKILL
Blair & Co. (William)

SPRING VALLEY
Mamiye Brothers

ST. BONAVENTURE
Nomura Holding America

ST. JAMES
Niagara Mohawk Holdings Inc.

STATEN ISLAND
New York Mercantile Exchange
S.G. Cowen

STONE RIDGE
PerkinElmer, Inc.

STONY BROOK
Pittway Corp.

SUNNYSIDE
Carillon Importers, Ltd.

SYOSSET
Schloss & Co. (Marcus)

SYRACUSE
Amgen, Inc.
Central National-Gottesman
CGU Insurance
Chase Manhattan Bank, NA
Consolidated Natural Gas Co.
Cooper Industries, Inc.
Corning Inc.
Crane & Co., Inc.
Fortis, Inc.
General Electric Co.
Glickenhaus & Co.
Golub Corp.
McGraw-Hill Companies, Inc.
Medtronic, Inc.
MONY Group (The)
New York Life Insurance Co.
Niagara Mohawk Holdings Inc.
Reader's Digest Association, Inc. (The)
Royal & SunAlliance USA, Inc.
Sentry Insurance, A Mutual Co.
Thompson Co. (J. Walter)
United Distillers & Vintners North America
United Parcel Service of America Inc.

TARRYTOWN
Bernstein & Co., Inc. (Sanford C.)

International Paper Co.
Prudential Securities Inc.
Texaco Inc.

TONAWANDA
Witco Corp.

TRI-STATE
Unilever United States, Inc.

TROY
AT&T Corp.
Cooper Tire & Rubber Co.
Corning Inc.
Country Curtains, Inc.
Eastman Kodak Co.
GenCorp
General Electric Co.
Golub Corp.
GTE Corp.
Housatonic Curtain Co.
Intel Corp.
Milacron, Inc.
Oshkosh B'Gosh, Inc.
Polaroid Corp.

UNION
Overseas Shipholding Group Inc.

UNION SPRINGS
Textron Inc.

UNIONDALE
Banfi Vintners
Weil, Gotshal & Manges Corp.

UTICA
Barnes Group Inc.
Butler Capital Corp.
Golub Corp.

VALHALIA
Whitman Corp.

VALHALLA
Leigh Fibers, Inc.
Titan Industrial Corp.

WALDEN
Baxter International Inc.

WANTAGH
Banfi Vintners

WARWICK
Star Bank NA

WATERTOWN
Niagara Mohawk Holdings Inc.

WATERVLIET
Norton Co.

WATKINS GLEN
Witco Corp.

WEBSTER
Jostens, Inc.

WEST BRENTWOOD
Banfi Vintners

WEST ISLIP
Paine Webber

WEST POINT
Federal-Mogul Corp.
Pheonix Financial Group
USAA Life Insurance Co.

WESTBURY
Forbes Inc.
Heinz Co. (H.J.)

WESTCHESTER
Glickenhaus & Co.
PepsiCo, Inc.

WESTPORT
Fisher Scientific

WHEATLEY HEIGHTS
Banfi Vintners

WHITE PLAINS
AEGON U.S.A. Inc.
American Express Co.
Avon Products, Inc.
Banfi Vintners
Bernstein & Co., Inc. (Sanford C.)
Central National-Gottesman
Dun & Bradstreet Corp.
Ford Motor Co.
Marcus Corp.
PepsiCo, Inc.
Reader's Digest Association, Inc. (The)
Texaco Inc.
Titan Industrial Corp.
UnumProvident

WHITEVILLE
Hartmarx Corp.

WINONA
Fortis, Inc.

WOODHAVEN
Central National-Gottesman

YONKERS
American Retail Group
Reader's Digest Association, Inc. (The)

North Carolina

Blue Bell, Inc.
Burress (J.W.)
CCB Financial Corp.
Citizens Financial Group, Inc.
Glaxo Wellcome Inc.
Lowe's Companies
Reader's Digest Association, Inc. (The)
Royal & SunAlliance USA, Inc.
Ruddick Corp.
Stanley Works (The)
Transamerica Corp.
United Dominion Industries, Ltd.

ALBEMARLE
Alcoa Inc.

ALBERMARLE
Collins & Aikman Corp.

ARDEN
Belk Stores Services Inc.

ASHBORO
Timken Co. (The)

ASHEBORO
Blue Bell, Inc.
Lance, Inc.
Ralston Purina Co.
Standard Products Co.

ASHERILLE
Carolina Power & Light Co.

ASHEVILLE
Baxter International Inc.
Belk-Simpson Department Stores
Carolina Power & Light Co.
Cooper Industries, Inc.
Norton Co.
Patagonia Inc.
Square D Co.
Steelcase Inc.
Stonecutter Mills Corp.

BELMONT
Belk Stores Services Inc.
Universal Leaf Tobacco Co., Inc.

BLACK MOUNTAIN
Carolina Power & Light Co.
Colonial Oil Industries, Inc.
Cone Mills Corp.
Dixie Group, Inc. (The)
Lance, Inc.
Stonecutter Mills Corp.

BOILING SPRINGS
Cone Mills Corp.
Stonecutter Mills Corp.

BOONE
Belk Stores Services Inc.
Employers Mutual Casualty Co.
Glaxo Wellcome Inc.
Indiana Mills & Manufacturing
Sonoco Products Co.

BREVARD
Belk-Simpson Department Stores
Collins & Aikman Corp.
Stonecutter Mills Corp.

BUIES CREEK
CCB Financial Corp.
Pharmacia & Upjohn, Inc.

BURLINGTON
AMETEK, Inc.
Burlington Industries, Inc.
CCB Financial Corp.
Cone Mills Corp.
Dixie Group, Inc. (The)
Norfolk Southern Corp.

BURNSVILLE
Outboard Marine Corp.

CARRBORO
Burlington Industries, Inc.

CARY
Millipore Corp.

CHAPEL HILL
ABC
Aon Corp.
Burress (J.W.)
Carolina Power & Light Co.
CCB Financial Corp.
Coca-Cola Co.
Cone Mills Corp.
Deloitte & Touche
Duke Energy
First Union Corp.
Fluor Corp.
Fortis, Inc.
Glaxo Wellcome Inc.
Hitachi America Ltd.
Intel Corp.
Kennametal, Inc.
KPMG Peat Marwick LLP
Landmark Communications Inc.
Lilly & Co. (Eli)
Lowe's Companies
Rubbermaid Inc.
Ruddick Corp.
Sonoco Products Co.
Stonecutter Mills Corp.
Wachovia Bank of North Carolina NA

CHARLOTTE
Aetna, Inc.
Belk-Simpson Department Stores
Belk Stores Services Inc.

BellSouth Corp.
Burlington Industries, Inc.
Carolina Power & Light Co.
CCB Financial Corp.
CIGNA Corp.
Collins & Aikman Corp.
Cooper Industries, Inc.
Duke Energy
Fannie Mae
First Union Corp.
Florida Power & Light Co.
Giant Eagle Inc.
Goldman Sachs Group
Harnischfeger Industries
Jeld-wen, Inc.
KPMG Peat Marwick LLP
Lance, Inc.
LandAmerica Financial Services
Lowe's Companies
Manulife Financial
Mitsubishi Electric America
Royal & SunAlliance USA, Inc.
Ruddick Corp.
Sonoco Products Co.
Springs Industries, Inc.
Square D Co.
Stonecutter Mills Corp.
Teleflex Inc.
Transamerica Corp.
Union Camp Corp.
United Dominion Industries, Ltd.
Wachovia Bank of North Carolina NA
The Washington Post
Winn-Dixie Stores Inc.

CLEMMONS
Thomasville Furniture Industries Inc.

CLYDE
Carolina Power & Light Co.

COLFAX
Blue Bell, Inc.

CROSSNORE
Belk Stores Services Inc.

DALLAS
Belk Stores Services Inc.

DAVIDSON
Duke Energy
Ruddick Corp.
Textron Inc.
Ukrop's Super Markets

DENTON
Thomasville Furniture Industries Inc.

DURHAM
AlliedSignal Inc.
Blue Bell, Inc.
Burlington Industries, Inc.
Carter-Wallace, Inc.
CCB Financial Corp.
Coca-Cola Co.
Deloitte & Touche
Duke Energy
Fannie Mae
Ford Motor Co.
General Atlantic Partners II LP
General Electric Co.
Glaxo Wellcome Inc.
Goldman Sachs Group
GTE Corp.
Hannaford Brothers Co.
Hubbell Inc.
Inman Mills
Kennametal, Inc.
KPMG Peat Marwick LLP
Mitsubishi Electric America
New York Times Co.
Rayonier Inc.
Reynolds Tobacco (R.J.)
Schlumberger Ltd. (USA)
Textron Inc.
Unilever United States, Inc.
Wachovia Bank of North Carolina NA
Winn-Dixie Stores Inc.

ELIZABETH CITY
Cox Enterprises Inc.

ELIZABETHTOWN
Carolina Power & Light Co.

ELON
Cone Mills Corp.

FAYETTEVILLE
Belk Stores Services Inc.
Carolina Power & Light Co.

FLAT ROCK
Cranston Print Works Co.

FLETCHER
Cranston Print Works Co.

FOREST CITY
Collins & Aikman Corp.
Stonecutter Mills Corp.

GASTON
Burlington Industries, Inc.

GASTONIA
AMP Inc.
Belk Stores Services Inc.
Bridgestone/Firestone, Inc.
Dana Corp.
Deere & Co.
Dixie Group, Inc. (The)
FMC Corp.
Stonecutter Mills Corp.

GIBSONVILLE
AMETEK, Inc.

GOLDSBORO
Carolina Power & Light Co.
Cooper Industries, Inc.
Weyerhaeuser Co.

GRAHAM
Burlington Industries, Inc.

GREENSBORO
Alliant Techsystems
AlliedSignal Inc.
American Express Co.
AMETEK, Inc.
AMP Inc.
Bechtel Group, Inc.
Belk Stores Services Inc.
Blue Bell, Inc.
Boeing Co.
Burlington Industries, Inc.
CCB Financial Corp.
Coca-Cola Co.
Collins & Aikman Corp.
Cone Mills Corp.
Corning Inc.
Deloitte & Touche
Deluxe Corp.
Duke Energy
Eastman Kodak Co.
Ecolab Inc.
First Union Corp.
Fluor Corp.
Furniture Brands International, Inc.
Glaxo Wellcome Inc.
Johnson & Son (S.C.)
KPMG Peat Marwick LLP
Lance, Inc.
Landmark Communications Inc.
Loews Corp.
Lowe's Companies
Lubrizol Corp. (The)
Polaroid Corp.
Reilly Industries, Inc.
Ruddick Corp.
Stonecutter Mills Corp.
Thomasville Furniture Industries Inc.
Xerox Corp.

GREENVILLE
Collins & Aikman Corp.
Duke Energy
Hanna Co. (M.A.)
West Co. Inc.

GUILFORD
CCB Financial Corp.

HALIFAX
Burlington Industries, Inc.

HAVELOCK
Merrill Lynch & Co., Inc.

HAW RIVER
Cone Mills Corp.

HENDERSON
CertainTeed Corp.
Cranston Print Works Co.

HENDERSONVILLE
Cranston Print Works Co.
Mid-America Bank of Louisville

HICKORY
Collins & Aikman Corp.
Furniture Brands International, Inc.
Lance, Inc.
Owens Corning

HIGH POINT
AMP Inc.
Furniture Brands International, Inc.
La-Z-Boy Inc.
Reinhart Institutional Foods
The Washington Post

HIGHLANDS
Belk-Simpson Department Stores

JAMESTOWN
AMP Inc.
Reilly Industries, Inc.

KINGS MOUNTAIN
Commercial Intertech Corp.

KINSTON
Carolina Power & Light Co.
First Union Corp.
Lowe's Companies

LAKE JUNALUSKA
Indiana Mills & Manufacturing

LAURINBURG
Abbott Laboratories
Butler Manufacturing Co.
Campbell Soup Co.

LENAIR
Furniture Brands International, Inc.

LENOIR
Furniture Brands International, Inc.
La-Z-Boy Inc.
West Co. Inc.

LEXINGTON
Burlington Industries, Inc.
New York Times Co.
PPG Industries, Inc.
Thomasville Furniture Industries Inc.

LINCOLNTON
Timken Co. (The)

MONROE
Cooper Industries, Inc.

MONTREAT
Belk-Simpson Department Stores
Belk Stores Services Inc.
Stonecutter Mills Corp.
Ukrop's Super Markets

MOORESVILLE
Burlington Industries, Inc.

MORGANTON
Borden, Inc.
Dana Corp.
Leviton Manufacturing Co. Inc.

MORGANTOWN
Bradford & Co. (J.C.)
Mazda North American Operations

MORRISVILLE
Cooper Industries, Inc.
Hannaford Brothers Co.
Square D Co.

NEW BERN
Weyerhaeuser Co.

NEWLAND
Belk Stores Services Inc.

NORTH WILKESBORO
First Union Corp.
Lowe's Companies

OXFORD
Burlington Industries, Inc.
CertainTeed Corp.

PEMBROKE
Lance, Inc.

PLEASANT GARDENS
Crane Co.

RALEIGH
Amsted Industries Inc.
AT&T Corp.
Belk-Simpson Department Stores
Belk Stores Services Inc.
Blue Bell, Inc.
Burlington Industries, Inc.
Carolina Power & Light Co.
CCB Financial Corp.
Cone Mills Corp.
Dixie Group, Inc. (The)
Duke Energy
First Union Corp.
Gerber Products Co.
Glaxo Wellcome Inc.
Hitachi America Ltd.
Inland Container Corp.
International Paper Co.
Kennametal, Inc.
KPMG Peat Marwick LLP
Lance, Inc.
Lowe's Companies
Mitsubishi Electric America
Potlatch Corp.
Rubbermaid Inc.
Ruddick Corp.
Rutledge Hill Press
Sonoco Products Co.
Square D Co.
Stonecutter Mills Corp.
Tension Envelope Corp.
Timken Co. (The)
Union Camp Corp.
Union Carbide Corp.
United Dominion Industries, Ltd.
United Parcel Service of America Inc.
Universal Leaf Tobacco Co., Inc.
Wachovia Bank of North Carolina NA
West Co. Inc.
Westvaco Corp.
Winn-Dixie Stores Inc.

REIDSVILLE
Burlington Industries, Inc.

RESEARCH TRIANGLE PARK
Carolina Power & Light Co.
Lance, Inc.
LG&E Energy Corp.

ROANOKE RAPIDS
Kennametal, Inc.

ROCK HILL
Lance, Inc.

ROCKINGHAM
Burlington Industries, Inc.

ROCKY MOUNT
Abbott Laboratories
Cummins Engine Co., Inc.
Standard Products Co.
The Washington Post

ROWAN COUNTY
Cone Mills Corp.

ROXBORO
Eaton Corp.

RUTHERFORD
Burlington Industries, Inc.

RUTHERFORD COUNTY
Cone Mills Corp.

RUTHERFORDTON
Stonecutter Mills Corp.

SALEM
Burlington Industries, Inc.
PepsiCo, Inc.

SALISBURY
Cooper Industries, Inc.
National Starch & Chemical Co.

SANFORD
Wachovia Bank of North Carolina NA

SHELBY
BellSouth Corp.
Lowe's Companies
Stonecutter Mills Corp.

SPINDALE
Collins & Aikman Corp.
Cone Mills Corp.
Rich Products Corp.
Square D Co.
Stonecutter Mills Corp.
Timken Co. (The)

STATESVILLE
Sara Lee Corp.

STOVALL
CertainTeed Corp.

SWANNANOA
Stonecutter Mills Corp.

THOMASVILLE
Cone Mills Corp.
Furniture Brands International, Inc.
Thomasville Furniture Industries Inc.

TRIANGLE PARK
Abbott Laboratories
Wachovia Bank of North Carolina NA

TRYON
Stonecutter Mills Corp.
Timken Co. (The)

WADESBORO
Pfizer Inc.

WALLACE
Carolina Power & Light Co.

WALLBURG
AMP Inc.

WALNUT COVE
Tyson Foods Inc.

WASHINGTON
International Paper Co.

WAXHAW
Rutledge Hill Press

WHITEVILLE
Lance, Inc.

WILMINGTON
Carolina Power & Light Co.
Corning Inc.
General Electric Co.
Glaxo Wellcome Inc.
Hannaford Brothers Co.

WILSON
Bridgestone/Firestone, Inc.
Monarch Machine Tool Co.
Universal Leaf Tobacco Co., Inc.

WINDSOR
Blue Bell, Inc.

WINGATE
Burlington Industries, Inc.
Ruddick Corp.
Stonecutter Mills Corp.

WINSTON - SALEM
Blue Bell, Inc.

WINSTON SALEM
Sara Lee Corp.
Vulcan Materials Co.

WINSTON-SALEM
AMP Inc.
Aon Corp.
Bassett Furniture Industries
Belk Stores Services Inc.
BellSouth Corp.
Blue Bell, Inc.
Burress (J.W.)
Chesapeake Corp.
Coca-Cola Co.
Collins & Aikman Corp.
Compass Bank
Conwood Co. LP
Duke Energy
First Union Securities, Inc.
Furniture Brands International, Inc.
Hitachi America Ltd.
Kemper National Insurance Companies
Lance, Inc.
LandAmerica Financial Services
Lowe's Companies
Merck & Co.
Milliken & Co.
Price Associates (T. Rowe)
Reilly Industries, Inc.
Ruddick Corp.
Sara Lee Corp.
Thomasville Furniture Industries Inc.
Universal Leaf Tobacco Co., Inc.
Wachovia Bank of North Carolina NA
Williams

North Dakota

Cenex Harvest States

BISMARCK
Employers Mutual Casualty Co.
Hickory Tech Corp.
Land O'Lakes, Inc.
Lee Enterprises

FARGO
Cenex Harvest States
Land O'Lakes, Inc.

GRAND FORKS
Cessna Aircraft Co.
Ecolab Inc.
Land O'Lakes, Inc.
Potlatch Corp.
Simplot Co. (J.R.)

MEDORA
True Oil Co.

VALLEY CITY
US West, Inc.

WASHBURN
Lee Enterprises

Ohio

Crane Co.
Huffy Corp.
Rubbermaid Inc.
Sherwin-Williams Co.
Standard Register Co.
Star Bank NA

ADA
Huffy Corp.
Louisiana-Pacific Corp.

AKRON
Bemis Co., Inc.
BFGoodrich Co.
Bridgestone/Firestone, Inc.
Consolidated Natural Gas Co.
Cooper Tire & Rubber Co.
Deloitte & Touche
Eaton Corp.
Fifth Third Bancorp
GenCorp
Hubbell Inc.
Huffy Corp.
Lubrizol Corp. (The)
MONY Group (The)
Morrison Knudsen Corp.
National City Corp.
Sherwin-Williams Co.

ALLIANCE
Amsted Industries Inc.
Lubrizol Corp. (The)
Merit Oil Corp.
Waste Management Inc.

AMHERST
Nordson Corp.

APPLE CREEK
Rubbermaid Inc.

APPLE GREEK
Rubbermaid Inc.

ASHLAND
Aristech Chemical Corp.
Cooper Tire & Rubber Co.
National City Corp.

ASHTABULA
Independent Stave Co.
Kennametal, Inc.

ATHENS
Ben & Jerry's Homemade Inc.
Hanna Co. (M.A.)
Milacron, Inc.
Toyota Motor Sales U.S.A., Inc.
USX Corp.

AVON
Ferro Corp.

BASCOM
National Machinery Co.

BAY VILLAGE
Nordson Corp.

BEACHWOOD
Forest City Enterprises, Inc.

BELLBROOK
Dayton Power and Light Co.

BELLEVUE
Central Soya Co.
Norfolk Southern Corp.

BEREA
Eaton Corp.
Lubrizol Corp. (The)
MTD Products Inc.
Nordson Corp.
Rubbermaid Inc.

BETTSVILLE
National Machinery Co.

BEXLEY
Barry Corp. (R.G.)
Federal-Mogul Corp.

BLUFFTON
Huffy Corp.

BOWLING GREEN
Andersons Inc.
Cooper Tire & Rubber Co.
Tamko Roofing Products
Waste Management Inc.

BUCKHUS
Timken Co. (The)

CANTON
Collins & Aikman Corp.
Consolidated Natural Gas Co.
Diebold, Inc.
Forest City Enterprises, Inc.
Maytag Corp.
McDonald & Co. Securities, Inc.
Timken Co. (The)

CEDARVILLE
Danis Companies
Dayton Power and Light Co.
Huffy Corp.

CELINA
Huffy Corp.
Monarch Machine Tool Co.
Reynolds & Reynolds Co.

CENTERVILLE
Huffy Corp.

CHILLICOTHE
Mead Corp.
PACCAR Inc.

CINCINNATI
Agrilink Foods, Inc.
AK Steel Corp.
Alma Piston Co.
Bardes Corp.
Chemed Corp.
Cincinnati Bell Inc.
Cinergy Corp.
Danis Companies
Dayton Power and Light Co.
Deloitte & Touche
Delta Air Lines, Inc.
Dun & Bradstreet Corp.
Federated Department Stores, Inc.
Fidelity Investments
Fifth Third Bancorp
Freeport-McMoRan Inc.
Hasbro, Inc.
Huffy Corp.
Jacobs Engineering Group
Kroger Co.
Lipton Co.
Lubrizol Corp. (The)
Mead Corp.
Milacron, Inc.
Mitsubishi Electric America
National Presto Industries, Inc.
Norfolk Southern Corp.
Ohio National Life Insurance Co.
PNC Financial Services Group
Procter & Gamble Co.
Rubbermaid Inc.
Star Bank NA
Tomkins Industries, Inc.
USX Corp.
Western & Southern Life Insurance Co.
Winn-Dixie Stores Inc.

CLARKSVILLE
Cincinnati Bell Inc.

CLEVELAND
Alcon Laboratories, Inc.
Ameren Corp.
Ameritech Corp.
Ameritech Ohio
Banfi Vintners
Barnes Group Inc.
Baxter International Inc.
BFGoodrich Co.
Blair & Co. (William)
Boler Co.
Borden, Inc.
Bridgestone/Firestone, Inc.
Callaway Golf Co.
Carnival Corp.
Cleveland-Cliffs, Inc.
Clorox Co.
Collins & Aikman Corp.
Commercial Intertech Corp.
Consolidated Natural Gas Co.
Deloitte & Touche
Demoulas Supermarkets Inc.
Dow Jones & Co., Inc.
Eaton Corp.
Enterprise Rent-A-Car Co.
Fannie Mae
Ferro Corp.
Fifth Third Bancorp
Ford Motor Co.
Forest City Enterprises, Inc.
General Mills, Inc.
General Motors Corp.
Giant Eagle Inc.
Hanna Co. (M.A.)
Huffy Corp.
IKON Office Solutions, Inc.
Invacare Corp.
Ladish Co., Inc.
LandAmerica Financial Services
Lincoln Electric Co.
LTV Corp.
Lubrizol Corp. (The)
Maytag Corp.
McDonald & Co. Securities, Inc.
Morgan Stanley Dean Witter & Co.
Morrison Knudsen Corp.
MTD Products Inc.
National City Corp.
National Presto Industries, Inc.
Nestle U.S.A. Inc.
New York Life Insurance Co.
Nordson Corp.
Norton Co.
Parker Hannifin Corp.
Pfizer Inc.
Pittway Corp.
PPG Industries, Inc.
Premier Industrial Corp.
Rubbermaid Inc.
Schwebel Baking Co.
S.G. Cowen
Sherwin-Williams Co.
Solo Cup Co.
Standard Products Co.
Stanley Works (The)
Star Bank NA
TRW Inc.
Vesper Corp.
Whirlpool Corp.
Xerox Corp.

COLUMBU
Hanna Co. (M.A.)

COLUMBUS
Abbott Laboratories
AK Steel Corp.
America West Airlines, Inc.
American Retail Group
Ameritech Corp.
Ameritech Ohio
Andersons Inc.
Ashland, Inc.
AT&T Corp.
Avon Products, Inc.
Barry Corp. (R.G.)
BFGoodrich Co.
Blair & Co. (William)
Block, Inc. (H&R)
Blue Bell, Inc.
Borden, Inc.
Central National-Gottesman
Central & South West Services
Central Soya Co.
CGU Insurance
CNA
Coca-Cola Co.
Commercial Intertech Corp.

Funders by Location of Grant Recipient

Consolidated Natural Gas Co.
Continental Grain Co.
Cooper Tire & Rubber Co.
Crane Co.
Cummins Engine Co., Inc.
Danis Companies
Dayton Power and Light Co.
Deloitte & Touche
Diebold, Inc.
Disney Co. (Walt)
Emerson Electric Co.
Federated Department Stores, Inc.
Ferro Corp.
Fifth Third Bancorp
Ford Motor Co.
Forest City Enterprises, Inc.
General Electric Co.
Grace & Co. (W.R.)
Hanna Co. (M.A.)
Harsco Corp.
Huffy Corp.
International Flavors & Fragrances Inc.
Invacare Corp.
Kemper National Insurance Companies
Kennametal, Inc.
Kroger Co.
Lancaster Lens, Inc.
Louisiana-Pacific Corp.
Lubrizol Corp. (The)
Marshall Field's
Maytag Corp.
McDonald & Co. Securities, Inc.
McGraw-Hill Companies, Inc.
Mead Corp.
Metropolitan Life Insurance Co.
Milacron, Inc.
MTD Products Inc.
National City Corp.
National Machinery Co.
National Presto Industries, Inc.
Nationwide Insurance Co.
New York Life Insurance Co.
Nordson Corp.
Ohio National Life Insurance Co.
PACCAR Inc.
Park National Bank
Pittway Corp.
Premier Industrial Corp.
Procter & Gamble Co.
Rayonier Inc.
Reilly Industries, Inc.
Reynolds Tobacco (R.J.)
Rubbermaid Inc.
Schwebel Baking Co.
Sherwin-Williams Co.
Standard Products Co.
Standard Register Co.
Star Bank NA
Sun Microsystems Inc.
Timken Co. (The)
Toledo Blade Co.
Tomkins Industries, Inc.
Union Carbide Corp.
The Washington Post
Wolverine World Wide

CUYAHOGA FALLS
GenCorp
Hanna Co. (M.A.)

DAYTON
Ameritech Ohio
AT&T Corp.
Cessna Aircraft Co.
Cincinnati Bell Inc.
Commercial Intertech Corp.
Cooper Industries, Inc.
Cox Enterprises Inc.
Danis Companies
Dayton Power and Light Co.
Duriron Co., Inc.
Federated Department Stores, Inc.
Fifth Third Bancorp
Giddings & Lewis
Gosiger, Inc.
Huffy Corp.
IKON Office Solutions, Inc.
Kroger Co.
Louisiana-Pacific Corp.
Mead Corp.
Monarch Machine Tool Co.
National Presto Industries, Inc.
NCR Corp.
Premier Industrial Corp.
Reynolds & Reynolds Co.
Reynolds Tobacco (R.J.)
Standard Register Co.
Star Bank NA
Tomkins Industries, Inc.

DEFIANCE
Commercial Intertech Corp.
Lubrizol Corp. (The)

DELAWARE
GEICO Corp.
MTD Products Inc.

DELAWARW
The Washington Post

DELTA
Andersons Inc.

DELWARE
The Washington Post

DETROIT
Borman's Inc.

DOVER
Union Camp Corp.

DUBLIN
Danis Companies
Forest City Enterprises, Inc.
Invacare Corp.
LTV Corp.
McDonald & Co. Securities, Inc.
MTD Products Inc.

EATON
Rubbermaid Inc.
Timken Co. (The)

ELYRIA
Invacare Corp.
Nordson Corp.
Parker Hannifin Corp.

EUCLID
Forest City Enterprises, Inc.

EUGENE
Clorox Co.

FAIRBORN
Dayton Power and Light Co.
Mead Corp.

FAIRVIEW PARK
Invacare Corp.

FAYETTE
Andersons Inc.

FILMONT
Timken Co. (The)

FINDLAY
Ameritech Ohio
Cooper Tire & Rubber Co.
Federal-Mogul Corp.
Fifth Third Bancorp
National Machinery Co.
USX Corp.
Whirlpool Corp.

FLAT ROCK
National Machinery Co.

FOSTORIA
Cooper Tire & Rubber Co.
Cummins Engine Co., Inc.
National Machinery Co.

FREMONT
Bemis Co., Inc.
National Machinery Co.
Toledo Blade Co.
Whirlpool Corp.

GAHANNA
LandAmerica Financial Services

GAMBIER
Rayonier Inc.
West Co. Inc.

GARFIELD HEIGHTS
Forest City Enterprises, Inc.

GARFIELD HTS.
Sherwin-Williams Co.

GATE MILLS
BFGoodrich Co.

GIRARD
Commercial Intertech Corp.

GRANVILLE
Heinz Co. (H.J.)

GREENVILLE
Whirlpool Corp.

HAMILTON
Champion International Corp.
Chemed Corp.

HILLSBORO
Milacron, Inc.

HIRAM
BFGoodrich Co.
Ferro Corp.

HUDSON
Cooper Industries, Inc.
Invacare Corp.

HUNTING VALLEY
Cleveland-Cliffs, Inc.

INDEPENDENCE
Ferro Corp.
Invacare Corp.
MTD Products Inc.

JACKSON
Pillsbury Co.

JOHNSTOWN
LandAmerica Financial Services

KENT
AMETEK, Inc.
Commercial Intertech Corp.
Ferro Corp.
GenCorp
Hanna Co. (M.A.)
Lubrizol Corp. (The)
Norton Co.
Schwebel Baking Co.
TRW Inc.

KETTERING
Danis Companies
Huffy Corp.

LAGRANGE
Invacare Corp.

LAKEWOOD
Invacare Corp.
LandAmerica Financial Services

LANCASTER
Ameritech Ohio
Lancaster Lens, Inc.
Park National Bank

LEBANON
AK Steel Corp.
Danis Companies

LEXINGTON
Park National Bank

LIMA
Andersons Inc.
Dana Corp.
Hamilton Sundstrand Corp.

LOGAN
Edwards Enterprise Software (J.D.)

LORAIN
Invacare Corp.
Nordson Corp.

LYNDHURST
Cleveland-Cliffs, Inc.

MANSFIELD
Invacare Corp.
Park National Bank
Timken Co. (The)

MARIETTA
Butler Manufacturing Co.

MARION
Whirlpool Corp.

MARION STEIN
Dayton Power and Light Co.

MATERIALS PARK
Dynamet, Inc.

MAUMEE
Dana Corp.

MCARTHUR
Mead Corp.

MCCUTCHENVILLE
National Machinery Co.

MELMORE
National Machinery Co.

MENTON
Bard, Inc. (C.R.)

MENTOR
Lubrizol Corp. (The)
Motorola Inc.
Walgreen Co.

MIAMI
Deloitte & Touche
Westvaco Corp.

MIDDLETOWN
AK Steel Corp.
Danis Companies
Inland Container Corp.
Mitsubishi Electric America
Square D Co.

MIDLAND
Timken Co. (The)

MILAN
CertainTeed Corp.

MILFORD
Chemed Corp.

MINERAL
Timken Co. (The)

MONTPELIER
SPX Corp.

MOUNT ST. JOSEPH
Cincinnati Bell Inc.

MOUNT VERNON
Hanna Co. (M.A.)
Jeld-wen, Inc.

NEW PHILADELPHIA
Timken Co. (The)

NEWARK
Owens Corning
Park National Bank
Standard Register Co.
State Farm Mutual Automobile Insurance Co.

NILES
Commercial Intertech Corp.

NORTH CANTON
Federal-Mogul Corp.
General Mills, Inc.
Maytag Corp.
Timken Co. (The)

NORTH OLMSTED
Norton Co.

NORWOOD
Star Bank NA
Western & Southern Life Insurance Co.

NOVELTY
Ferro Corp.

OBERLIN
Nordson Corp.

OLD FORT
National Machinery Co.

OREGON
Alma Piston Co.
Andersons Inc.

ORRVILLE
Premier Industrial Corp.
Rubbermaid Inc.

ORWELL
Banta Corp.
Kennametal, Inc.
Menasha Corp.

OXFORD
Consolidated Papers, Inc.
Danis Companies
Dayton Power and Light Co.
Globe Corp.
Huffy Corp.
Jacobs Engineering Group
Milacron, Inc.
Simpson Investment Co.
Square D Co.
Union Camp Corp.

PAINESVILLE
Lubrizol Corp. (The)

PARMA
MTD Products Inc.

PENINSULA
Lubrizol Corp. (The)

PEPPER PIKE
Forest City Enterprises, Inc.
Sherwin-Williams Co.

PERRYSBURG
Andersons Inc.

PIQUA
Fifth Third Bancorp

PIQUAY
Dayton Power and Light Co.

PORTSMOUTH
Aristech Chemical Corp.
Nationwide Insurance Co.
Norfolk Southern Corp.

POWELL
Nationwide Insurance Co.

RAVENNA
Land O'Lakes, Inc.

RICHFIELD
Goldman Sachs Group
Rubbermaid Inc.

RIO GRAND
Danis Companies

RIO GRANDE
Ameritech Ohio

ROCKY RIVER
Cleveland-Cliffs, Inc.
Invacare Corp.
MTD Products Inc.
Nordson Corp.

SANDUSKY
Inland Container Corp.
LandAmerica Financial Services

SIDNEY
Arvin Industries, Inc.
Monarch Machine Tool Co.
Star Bank NA

SMITHVILLE
Rubbermaid Inc.

SOLON
MTD Products Inc.

SPRINGBORO
Huffy Corp.
Standard Register Co.

SPRINGFIELD
Danis Companies
Kemper National Insurance Companies
USX Corp.

ST. MARYS
Monarch Machine Tool Co.

STEUBENVILLE
Domino's Pizza Inc.
Milliken & Co.

THORNTON
Huffy Corp.

TIFFIN
American Standard Inc.
Cooper Tire & Rubber Co.
Fifth Third Bancorp
National Machinery Co.

TIPPECANOE
Rubbermaid Inc.

TOLEDO
American Retail Group
Ameritech Ohio
Andersons Inc.
Barnes Group Inc.
Cooper Tire & Rubber Co.
DaimlerChrysler Corp.
Dana Corp.
Demoulas Supermarkets Inc.
Fifth Third Bancorp
FINA
General Mills, Inc.
Illinois Tool Works, Inc.
Jacobs Engineering Group
Johnson Controls Inc.
Leviton Manufacturing Co. Inc.
Liberty Corp.
National City Corp.
National Machinery Co.
National Presto Industries, Inc.
Owens Corning
PepsiCo, Inc.
Rubbermaid Inc.
Toledo Blade Co.

TROY
Illinois Tool Works, Inc.

UNIVERSITY HEIGHTS
Ameritech Ohio
Eaton Corp.
Parker Hannifin Corp.
Premier Industrial Corp.
Solo Cup Co.
Waste Management Inc.

URBANA
Dayton Power and Light Co.

UTICA
Park National Bank

WADSWORTH
Hubbell Inc.

WAPAKONETA
AMETEK, Inc.

WARREN
Commercial Intertech Corp.
Lubrizol Corp. (The)

WARSAW
Collins & Aikman Corp.

WEST CHESTER
Toshiba America Inc.

WEST SALEM
Rubbermaid Inc.

WESTERVILLE
Nationwide Insurance Co.
Rubbermaid Inc.

WESTLAKE
Commercial Intertech Corp.

WICKLIFFE
Forest City Enterprises, Inc.
Norton Co.

WILBERFORCE
Dayton Power and Light Co.

WILLIARD
MTD Products Inc.

WILMINGTON
Dayton Power and Light Co.

WOOSTER
Premier Industrial Corp.
Rubbermaid Inc.

Timken Co. (The)

WORTHINGTON
Indiana Mills & Manufacturing

YELLOW SPRINGS
International Multifoods Corp.

YOUNGSTOWN
Commercial Intertech Corp.
Giant Eagle Inc.
LTV Corp.
National City Corp.
Schwebel Baking Co.
Trustmark Insurance Co.

Oklahoma

Eckerd Corp.
Williams

ADA
Central & South West Services

ARDMORE
First Union Corp.
United Dominion Industries, Ltd.

BARTLESVILLE
Central & South West Services
Phillips Petroleum Co.

BETHANY
Cooper Tire & Rubber Co.

BRISTOW
Paine Webber

BROKEN ARROW
Williams

CHICKASHA
Arvin Industries, Inc.

DEWEY
Phillips Petroleum Co.

EDMOND
OG&E Electric Services

EL RENO
OG&E Electric Services

GUYMON
Phillips Petroleum Co.

HAWORTH
Tyson Foods Inc.

HODGEN
Shelter Mutual Insurance Co.

HONOBIA
Contran Corp.

LANGSTON
OG&E Electric Services
Sherwin-Williams Co.

MCLOUD
OG&E Electric Services

MUSKOGEE
OG&E Electric Services

NORMAN
AMR Corp.
Atlantic Richfield Co.
BP Amoco Corp.
Burlington Resources, Inc.
Central & South West Services
Coca-Cola Co.
Eckerd Corp.
El Paso Energy Co.
FINA
Halliburton Co.

Morris Communications Corp.
OG&E Electric Services
Phillips Petroleum Co.
Rayonier Inc.

OK CITY
Occidental Oil and Gas

OKLAHOMA CITY
American Fidelity Corp.
AT&T Corp.
Bridgestone/Firestone, Inc.
Brunswick Corp.
Central & South West Services
Cox Enterprises Inc.
Dain Bosworth Inc.
Dana Corp.
McKesson-HBOC Corp.
MONY Group (The)
OG&E Electric Services
Oklahoma Publishing Co.
PacifiCare Health Systems
Phillips Petroleum Co.
Regions Bank
SBC Communications Inc.
True Oil Co.
Waste Management Inc.

OKMULGEE
Central & South West Services

PAULS VALLEY
OG&E Electric Services

PONCA CITY
Tomkins Industries, Inc.

PRYOR
Grede Foundries

SAPULPA
Williams

SEMINOLE
Blue Bell, Inc.
OG&E Electric Services

SHAWNEE
Morris Communications Corp.
OG&E Electric Services
Waste Management Inc.

SPIRO
Shelter Mutual Insurance Co.

STILLWATER
Brunswick Corp.
Central & South West Services
FINA
Halliburton Co.
Hubbard Broadcasting, Inc.
OG&E Electric Services
Oklahoma Publishing Co.
Phillips Petroleum Co.
Whitman Corp.
Williams

TAHLEQUAH
Louisiana-Pacific Corp.

TISHOMINGO
OG&E Electric Services

TULSA
AMR Corp.
Badger Meter, Inc.
BP Amoco Corp.
Brunswick Corp.
Central & South West Services
CLARCOR Inc.
Comdisco, Inc.

Elf Atochem North America, Inc.
Ensign-Bickford Industries
Gerber Products Co.
Morrison Knudsen Corp.
Occidental Oil and Gas
OG&E Electric Services
PACCAR Inc.
PacifiCare Health Systems
Phillips Petroleum Co.
SBC Communications Inc.
Thermo Electron Corp.
Whirlpool Corp.
Whitman Corp.
Williams
Woodward Governor Co.

WESTVILLE
Tyson Foods Inc.

WILBERFORCE
Cincinnati Bell Inc.

WILBURTON
Central & South West Services
Franklin Electric Co.

Oregon

Alaska Airlines, Inc.
Bechtel Group, Inc.
Cenex Harvest States
Idaho Power Co.
Louisiana-Pacific Corp.

ASHLAND
Ben & Jerry's Homemade Inc.
Hitachi America Ltd.

BEAVERTON
Gap, Inc.

BEND
Jeld-wen, Inc.
Shea Co. (John F.)

CENTRAL POINT
Jeld-wen, Inc.

CHILOQUIN
Jeld-wen, Inc.

COOS BAY
Georgia-Pacific Corp.
Weyerhaeuser Co.

CORVALLIS
Burlington Resources, Inc.
Chevron Corp.
Georgia-Pacific Corp.
Jeld-wen, Inc.
PacifiCorp
Simplot Co. (J.R.)
Tektronix, Inc.
Weyerhaeuser Co.

EUGENE
Clorox Co.
Dain Bosworth Inc.
Intel Corp.
Litton Industries, Inc.
U.S. Bancorp
Weyerhaeuser Co.

GRESHAM
Jeld-wen, Inc.

HOOD RIVER
Pfizer Inc.

KLAMATH FALLS
Jeld-wen, Inc.

MARYLHURST
PacifiCorp

MCMINNVILLE
Louisiana-Pacific Corp.

MEDFORD
Jeld-wen, Inc.
LandAmerica Financial Services

PORTLAND
Agrilink Foods, Inc.
Alaska Airlines, Inc.
American Retail Group
Banfi Vintners
Bank of America
Bank One Corp.
Blount International, Inc.
Boeing Co.
CGU Insurance
Chicago Title Corp.
CUNA Mutual Group
Dain Bosworth Inc.
Delta Air Lines, Inc.
Enterprise Rent-A-Car Co.
First Hawaiian, Inc.
Fuller Co. (H.B.)
Heinz Co. (H.J.)
IKON Office Solutions, Inc.
Intel Corp.
International Multifoods Corp.
Jeld-wen, Inc.
LandAmerica Financial Services
Lee Enterprises
Louisiana-Pacific Corp.
Mattel Inc.
MCI WorldCom, Inc.
Mead Corp.
MONY Group (The)
Nabisco Group Holdings
PacifiCare Health Systems
PacifiCorp
Patagonia Inc.
Portland General Electric Co.
Reynolds Metals Co.
Simpson Investment Co.
Solo Cup Co.
Tektronix, Inc.
Union Pacific Corp.
U.S. Bancorp
Universal Foods Corp.
UnumProvident
US West, Inc.
Weyerhaeuser Co.

REDMOND
Jeld-wen, Inc.

SALEM
Cenex Harvest States
PacifiCorp
United Parcel Service of America Inc.

STAYTON
Jeld-wen, Inc.

SWEET HOME
Jeld-wen, Inc.

TROUTDALE
Reynolds Metals Co.

WILLIAMS
Ben & Jerry's Homemade Inc.

Pennsylvania

AMP Inc.
Crane Co.
Elf Atochem North America, Inc.
Nabisco Group Holdings
PPG Industries, Inc.
Safeguard Scientifics
S&T Bancorp

ABINGTON
Binswanger Companies

ALIQUIPPA
Allegheny Technologies Inc.
National City Corp.

ALLENTOWN
Air Products and Chemicals, Inc.
AT&T Corp.
Bard, Inc. (C.R.)
Bethlehem Steel Corp.
Cooper Tire & Rubber Co.
Domino's Pizza Inc.
Dow Jones & Co., Inc.
Lehigh Portland Cement Co.
Sovereign Bank
Times Mirror Co.

ALTOONA
PPG Industries, Inc.
Westvaco Corp.

AMBRIDGE
Gap, Inc.

ANNVILLE
Armstrong World Industries, Inc.
Hershey Foods Corp.
Huffy Corp.
West Co. Inc.

ARDMORE
CGU Insurance

ARNOLD
Valspar Corp.

AUBURN
Quaker Chemical Corp.

AVELLA
Dynamet, Inc.

BADEN
Heinz Co. (H.J.)
Mine Safety Appliances Co.

BALA CYNWYD
Binswanger Companies
CertainTeed Corp.
CSS Industries, Inc.
Levi Strauss & Co.
Premier Dental Products Co.

BEAVER
Leviton Manufacturing Co. Inc.

BERWYN
AMETEK, Inc.
CertainTeed Corp.

BETHLEHEM
Air Products and Chemicals, Inc.
Aristech Chemical Corp.
AT&T Corp.
Bethlehem Steel Corp.
CGU Insurance
CSS Industries, Inc.
Dun & Bradstreet Corp.
Elf Atochem North America, Inc.
First Union Bank
First Union Corp.
Hamilton Sundstrand Corp.
Lehigh Portland Cement Co.
National Presto Industries, Inc.
National Starch & Chemical Co.
New Jersey Natural Gas Co.
Nomura Holding America
Sovereign Bank
Unilever United States, Inc.

BIGLER
National City Corp.

BIGLERVILLE
Inland Container Corp.

BLOOMSBURG
AMP Inc.
Heinz Co. (H.J.)

BLUE BELL
CSS Industries, Inc.
Premier Dental Products Co.

BRADDOCK
USX Corp.

BRADFORD
Glickenhaus & Co.

BREINIGSVILLE
Lehigh Portland Cement Co.

BROOKHAVEN
SmithKline Beecham Corp.

BROOKVILLE
S&T Bancorp

BRYN MAWR
Ameritas Life Insurance Corp.
CertainTeed Corp.
General Mills, Inc.
Louisiana-Pacific Corp.
Manulife Financial
Milliken & Co.
Minnesota Mutual Life Insurance Co.
MONY Group (The)
Ohio National Life Insurance Co.
Quaker Chemical Corp.
Sunmark Capital Corp.
Thompson Co. (J. Walter)

BUTLER
Allegheny Technologies Inc.
Cincinnati Bell Inc.
Harsco Corp.
Mine Safety Appliances Co.
National City Corp.
Star Bank NA

CALIFORNIA
Heinz Co. (H.J.)
National City Corp.

CAMP HILL
AMP Inc.
Harsco Corp.

CANONSBURG
Dynamet, Inc.
S&T Bancorp

CARLISLE
Fortis, Inc.
Merit Oil Corp.
PPG Industries, Inc.

CARNEGIE
Dynamet, Inc.

CENTER VALLEY
Bethlehem Steel Corp.
First Union Securities, Inc.
Lehigh Portland Cement Co.

CHADDS FORD
Duchossois Industries Inc.

CHAMBERSBURG
AMP Inc.

CLAIRTON
Mine Safety Appliances Co.

CLEARFIELD
National City Corp.

COAL CENTER
Dynamet, Inc.

COATESVILLE
West Co. Inc.

COLLEGEVILLE
Air Products and Chemicals, Inc.
Bridgestone/Firestone, Inc.

CONSHOHOCKEN
Aetna, Inc.
Quaker Chemical Corp.

CORAOPOLIS
Aristech Chemical Corp.

CORAOPOLOS
Dynamet, Inc.

CORRY
Barnes Group Inc.

CRANBERRY TOWNSHIP
Mine Safety Appliances Co.

DALLASTOWN
York Federal Savings & Loan Association

DANVILLE
Tomkins Industries, Inc.

DEVON
Binswanger Companies

DOYLESTOWN
International Multifoods Corp.
Lehigh Portland Cement Co.
SmithKline Beecham Corp.
Teleflex Inc.

DUBOIS
S&T Bancorp

EAST LIBERTY
Pfizer Inc.

EASTON
Bethlehem Steel Corp.

ELIZABETH TOWN
Regis Corp.

ELIZABETHTOWN
Armstrong World Industries, Inc.
CLARCOR Inc.
Hershey Foods Corp.

ELKINS PARK
Binswanger Companies
Premier Dental Products Co.

EMMAUS
Air Products and Chemicals, Inc.
Bethlehem Steel Corp.

ENOLA
AMP Inc.
Harsco Corp.

EPHRATA
Harsco Corp.

ERIE
American Retail Group
Carpenter Technology Corp.
Crane Co.
General Electric Co.
Kennametal, Inc.
Mark IV Industries
National City Corp.
National Presto Industries, Inc.
PNC Financial Services Group
Teleflex Inc.

EUFAULA
Teleflex Inc.

EVERETT
Kennametal, Inc.

EXTON
CertainTeed Corp.
SmithKline Beecham Corp.
Teleflex Inc.
West Co. Inc.

FAIRLESS HILLS
USX Corp.

FEASTERVILLE
Donaldson Co., Inc.
Premier Dental Products Co.

FORT WASHINGTON
Binswanger Companies

FOUNTAIN HILL
Bethlehem Steel Corp.

GETTYSBURG
Barnes Group Inc.
West Co. Inc.

GIBSONIA
Mine Safety Appliances Co.

GLADWYNE
Premier Dental Products Co.

GLENSIDE
AMETEK, Inc.

GRANTHAM
Harsco Corp.

GREENSBURG
Consolidated Natural Gas Co.
Kennametal, Inc.
Liz Claiborne, Inc.
Mine Safety Appliances Co.
National City Corp.
Norton Co.
S&T Bancorp
Timken Co. (The)
TMC Investment Co.

GREENVILLE
Aristech Chemical Corp.

GROVE CITY
Aristech Chemical Corp.

GWYNEDD VALLEY
Aetna, Inc.
Teleflex Inc.

HARRISBURG
Air Products and Chemicals, Inc.
AMP Inc.
Aristech Chemical Corp.
Armstrong World Industries, Inc.
Bemis Co., Inc.
Bethlehem Steel Corp.
CGU Insurance
CSS Industries, Inc.
Harsco Corp.
Hershey Foods Corp.
Huffy Corp.
Kennametal, Inc.

Lipton Co.
McClatchy Co.
MCI WorldCom, Inc.
New York Life Insurance Co.
PPG Industries, Inc.
Susquehanna-Pfaltzgraff Co.
TMC Investment Co.
York Federal Savings & Loan Association

HARTSVILLE
CertainTeed Corp.

HAVERFORD
Briggs & Stratton Corp.
Cantor, Fitzgerald Securities Corp.
Tai and Co. (J.T.)
United Parcel Service of America Inc.

HAVERTOWN
Binswanger Companies
CSS Industries, Inc.
First Union Bank

HAZLETON
Bemis Co., Inc.
Fabri-Kal Corp.
Inland Container Corp.

HELLERTOWN
Hanna Co. (M.A.)

HERSHEY
Hershey Foods Corp.
York Federal Savings & Loan Association

HOMESTEAD
National City Corp.
PPG Industries, Inc.

HORSHAM
Alliant Techsystems

HUNTINGDON
Mead Corp.
Owens Corning

HUNTINGTON
Jostens, Inc.

INDIANA
PNC Financial Services Group
S&T Bancorp
West Co. Inc.

IVYLAND
Hamilton Sundstrand Corp.

JENKINTOWN
Binswanger Companies
CSS Industries, Inc.
Premier Dental Products Co.

JOHNSTOWN
Alliant Techsystems
Bethlehem Steel Corp.
S&T Bancorp

KIMBERTON
Credit Suisse First Boston

KUTZTOWN
Carpenter Technology Corp.
Dana Corp.
Lehigh Portland Cement Co.

LA MOTT
Binswanger Companies

LANCASTER
AMP Inc.
Armstrong World Industries, Inc.
CLARCOR Inc.
First Union Securities, Inc.
Harsco Corp.
Hawaiian Electric Co., Inc.
Sovereign Bank
Susquehanna-Pfaltzgraff Co.
Toro Co.
Wisconsin Power & Light Co.
York Federal Savings & Loan Association

LANGHORNE
Louisiana-Pacific Corp.
Southwest Gas Corp.

LANSDALE
Merck & Co.
Teleflex Inc.

LATROBE
Allegheny Technologies Inc.
Dynamet, Inc.
Kennametal, Inc.
TMC Investment Co.

LAYFAYETTE HILL
Quaker Chemical Corp.

LEBANON
Bemis Co., Inc.
Butler Manufacturing Co.
Hershey Foods Corp.

LEHIGH
Bradford & Co. (J.C.)
Deloitte & Touche
GenCorp
Stupp Brothers Bridge & Iron Co.

LEHIGH VALLEY
Air Products and Chemicals, Inc.
Fireman's Fund Insurance Co.
Lehigh Portland Cement Co.
Union Pacific Corp.

LEVITTOWN
Extendicare Health Services

LEWISBURG
Harsco Corp.
Kingsbury Corp.

LIGONIER
TMC Investment Co.

LINCOLN UNIVERSITY
Bell Atlantic Corp.
The Washington Post

LYCOMING
West Co. Inc.

MALVERN
CertainTeed Corp.
CIGNA Corp.
GEICO Corp.
Heinz Co. (H.J.)
IKON Office Solutions, Inc.
West Co. Inc.

MANCHESTER
York Federal Savings & Loan Association

MAYTOWN
Armstrong World Industries, Inc.

MCKEESPORT
Aristech Chemical Corp.
Corning Inc.
National City Corp.
Tai and Co. (J.T.)

MEADOW LANDS
Dynamet, Inc.

MEADVILLE
Federal-Mogul Corp.
LTV Corp.
National City Corp.
PPG Industries, Inc.
TMC Investment Co.

MECHANICSBURG
AMP Inc.
Harsco Corp.
New York Life Insurance Co.
S&T Bancorp
Susquehanna-Pfaltzgraff Co.
West Co. Inc.

MEDIA
Furniture Brands International, Inc.

MELROSE PARK
Premier Dental Products Co.

MERION STATION
Premier Dental Products Co.

MIDDLETOWN
AMP Inc.
Armstrong World Industries, Inc.
Harsco Corp.

MILLERSBURG
Bethlehem Steel Corp.

MILLERSVILLE
AMP Inc.
Armstrong World Industries, Inc.

MONACA
LTV Corp.
Valspar Corp.

MONESSEN
Corning Inc.
PNC Financial Services Group

MOUNTAINTOP
CertainTeed Corp.

NEW WILMINGTON
Heinz Co. (H.J.)

NEWTOWN SQUARE
CSS Industries, Inc.

NORRISTOWN
Aristech Chemical Corp.
CertainTeed Corp.
SmithKline Beecham Corp.
Teleflex Inc.
Union Pacific Corp.
Vesper Corp.

NORTH WALES
Teleflex Inc.

ORANGEBURG
Carpenter Technology Corp.

PAOLI
AMETEK, Inc.
Binswanger Companies
CertainTeed Corp.

PENN VALLEY
Premier Dental Products Co.

PHILADELPHIA
Aetna, Inc.
Air Products and Chemicals, Inc.
Alcon Laboratories, Inc.
AlliedSignal Inc.
Ameren Corp.
American Standard Inc.
Ameritas Life Insurance Corp.
AMETEK, Inc.
AMP Inc.
Aristech Chemical Corp.
AT&T Corp.
Banfi Vintners
Bell Atlantic Corp.
Binswanger Companies
Boeing Co.
Bradford & Co. (J.C.)
Bristol-Myers Squibb Co.
Burlington Industries, Inc.
Campbell Soup Co.
Cantor, Fitzgerald Securities Corp.
Carpenter Technology Corp.
Central National-Gottesman
CertainTeed Corp.
CGU Insurance
CIGNA Corp.
Coca-Cola Co.
Collins & Aikman Corp.
Continental Grain Co.
Coors Brewing Co.
CSS Industries, Inc.
Cummings Properties Management
Domino's Pizza Inc.
du Pont de Nemours & Co. (E.I.)
Dun & Bradstreet Corp.
Elf Atochem North America, Inc.
Enterprise Rent-A-Car Co.
Exxon Mobil Corp.
Fannie Mae
Ferro Corp.
First Union Bank
First Union Corp.
First Union Securities, Inc.
Fluor Corp.
FMC Corp.
Ford Motor Co.
Fortis Insurance Co.
GenAmerica Corp.
General Electric Co.
General Mills, Inc.
Gerber Products Co.
Glickenhaus & Co.
Goldman Sachs Group
Harsco Corp.
Hartmarx Corp.
Hawaiian Electric Co., Inc.
Hershey Foods Corp.
Hitachi America Ltd.
Huffy Corp.
Hunt Manufacturing Co.
IKON Office Solutions, Inc.
Independent Stave Co.
International Flavors & Fragrances Inc.
Johnson & Johnson
Johnson & Son (S.C.)
Katten, Muchin & Zavis
Kemper National Insurance Companies
KPMG Peat Marwick LLP
Leviton Manufacturing Co. Inc.
Manor Care Health SVS, Inc.
Manulife Financial
Matsushita Electric Corp. of America
Mattel Inc.
Merck & Co.
Merit Oil Corp.
Mine Safety Appliances Co.
Minnesota Mining & Manufacturing Co.
Morgan Stanley Dean Witter & Co.
Nabisco Group Holdings
NASDAQ Stock Market
New York Life Insurance Co.
New York Mercantile Exchange
Olin Corp.
Overseas Shipholding Group Inc.
Patagonia Inc.
Pfizer Inc.
Pillsbury Co.
PNC Financial Services Group
PPG Industries, Inc.
Premier Dental Products Co.
Procter & Gamble Co.
Prudential Insurance Co. of America
Putnam Investments
Quaker Chemical Corp.
Rubbermaid Inc.
Safeguard Scientifics
Sara Lee Corp.
Seagram & Sons, Inc. (Joseph E.)
Searle & Co. (G.D.)
S.G. Cowen
Sherwin-Williams Co.
SmithKline Beecham Corp.
Sovereign Bank
Star Bank NA
State Farm Mutual Automobile Insurance Co.
Stonecutter Mills Corp.
Sverdrup Corp.
Tai and Co. (J.T.)
Teleflex Inc.
Timken Co. (The)
Tomkins Industries, Inc.
Toshiba America Inc.
True North Communications, Inc.
Unilever Home & Personal Care U.S.A.
Unilever United States, Inc.
Union Pacific Corp.
United Parcel Service of America Inc.
Vanguard Group
Vesper Corp.
Waste Management Inc.
West Co. Inc.
Westvaco Corp.
Zilkha & Sons

PHILDELPHIA
True North Communications, Inc.

PHILIADELPHIA
The Washington Post

PHOENIXVILLE
Forbes Inc.
Teleflex Inc.
West Co. Inc.

PITTSBURGH
Air Products and Chemicals, Inc.
AK Steel Corp.
Alcoa Inc.
Allegheny Technologies Inc.
AlliedSignal Inc.
AMETEK, Inc.
Aristech Chemical Corp.
BankBoston Corp.
Banta Corp.
Baxter International Inc.
Bemis Manufacturing Co.

Cadence Designs Systems, Inc.
Callaway Golf Co.
CBS Corp.
Consolidated Natural Gas Co.
Crane Co.
DaimlerChrysler Corp.
Deloitte & Touche
Dynamet, Inc.
Enterprise Rent-A-Car Co.
Equitable Resources, Inc.
Federated Department Stores, Inc.
Ford Motor Co.
GenCorp
Giant Eagle Inc.
Globe Corp.
Gosiger, Inc.
Grede Foundries
Heinz Co. (H.J.)
Hitachi America Ltd.
IKON Office Solutions, Inc.
Intel Corp.
Johnson Controls Inc.
Kennametal, Inc.
Leviton Manufacturing Co. Inc.
Lincoln Electric Co.
Litton Industries, Inc.
LTV Corp.
Lubrizol Corp. (The)
May Department Stores Co.
Mine Safety Appliances Co.
Mitsubishi Electric America
Morrison Knudsen Corp.
Nabisco Group Holdings
National City Corp.
National Presto Industries, Inc.
PNC Financial Services Group
PPG Industries, Inc.
Rubbermaid Inc.
S&T Bancorp
Schwebel Baking Co.
Strear Farms Co.
TMC Investment Co.
USX Corp.
Valspar Corp.
The Washington Post

PITTSTON
Air Products and Chemicals, Inc.
National Presto Industries, Inc.

PLYMOUTH MEETING
Quaker Chemical Corp.

POTTSTOWN
Dana Corp.
Teleflex Inc.

PUNXSUTAWNEY
S&T Bancorp

RADNOR
Duchossois Industries Inc.

READING
Carpenter Technology Corp.
Dana Corp.
Grace & Co. (W.R.)
Harsco Corp.
Hershey Foods Corp.
Sovereign Bank
West Co. Inc.

REYNOLDSVILLE
S&T Bancorp

RINGTOWN
Jeld-wen, Inc.

ROSEMONT
Amsted Industries Inc.

SAINT DAVIDS
ServiceMaster Co.

SALTSBURG
S&T Bancorp

SCHUYLKILL
GenCorp

SCRANTON
Air Products and Chemicals, Inc.
Domino's Pizza Inc.
Golub Corp.
PNC Financial Services Group

SEWARD
S&T Bancorp

SEWICKLEY
Aristech Chemical Corp.
Giant Eagle Inc.
Heinz Co. (H.J.)
Mine Safety Appliances Co.

SHARON
National City Corp.

SHENANDOAH
Jeld-wen, Inc.

SHIPPENSBURG
AMP Inc.

SPRING CHURCH
S&T Bancorp

SPRING GROVE
York Federal Savings & Loan Association

ST. DAVIDS
FINA

STATE COLLEGE
Corning Inc.
Jostens, Inc.
PNC Financial Services Group

TARENTUM
Allegheny Technologies Inc.

UNIVERSITY PARK
Agrilink Foods, Inc.
Air Products and Chemicals, Inc.
AlliedSignal Inc.
AMP Inc.
Aristech Chemical Corp.
AT&T Corp.
Bechtel Group, Inc.
Carpenter Technology Corp.
Corning Inc.
Dow Chemical Co.
Eastman Kodak Co.
FINA
General Electric Co.
Harsco Corp.
Hershey Foods Corp.
Kennametal, Inc.
Lubrizol Corp. (The)
Mark IV Industries
National City Corp.
Textron Inc.
Union Carbide Corp.
USX Corp.
Warner-Lambert Co.
West Co. Inc.

UPLAND
Premier Dental Products Co.

VALLEY FORGE
IKON Office Solutions, Inc.
Teleflex Inc.

VANDERGRIFT
Consolidated Natural Gas Co.
S&T Bancorp

VILLANOVA
Air Products and Chemicals, Inc.
Cone Mills Corp.
Deloitte & Touche
Elf Atochem North America, Inc.
Quaker Chemical Corp.
Textron Inc.
West Co. Inc.

WARRENDALE
Bridgestone/Firestone, Inc.
Carpenter Technology Corp.
Deere & Co.
Eaton Corp.
GenCorp
General Motors Corp.
Lubrizol Corp. (The)

WARRINGTON
Premier Dental Products Co.

WASHINGTON
Allegheny Technologies Inc.
Banta Corp.
Dynamet, Inc.
La-Z-Boy Inc.

WAWA
Quaker Chemical Corp.

WAYNE
CIGNA Corp.
Dun & Bradstreet Corp.
First Union Corp.
Florida Power & Light Co.
Honeywell International Inc.
Safeguard Scientifics

WAYNESBURG
Allegheny Technologies Inc.

WEST CHESTER
Boeing Co.
West Co. Inc.

WESTMORELAND COUNTY
Medtronic, Inc.

WHITEHALL
CertainTeed Corp.

WILKES-BARRE
Armstrong World Industries, Inc.
Chicago Title Corp.
Deluxe Corp.
Nabisco Group Holdings
PNC Financial Services Group

WILLIAMSPORT
AMP Inc.
HON Industries Inc.
Kemper National Insurance Companies
Price Associates (T. Rowe)
Susquehanna-Pfaltzgraff Co.
Textron Inc.

WYNCOTE
Toshiba America Inc.

WYNNEWOOD
United States Trust Co. of New York

WYOMISSING
Carpenter Technology Corp.

YORK
AMP Inc.
First Maryland Bancorp
Hannaford Brothers Co.
Harley-Davidson Co.
Lehigh Portland Cement Co.
Olin Corp.
Standard Register Co.
Susquehanna-Pfaltzgraff Co.
Times Mirror Co.
York Federal Savings & Loan Association

YOUNGWOOD
Kennametal, Inc.

Puerto Rico

Reebok International Ltd.
Wal-Mart Stores, Inc.
Walgreen Co.

LAS PIEDRAS
Bard, Inc. (C.R.)

PONCE
American Retail Group
Storage Technology Corp.

SAN JUAN
Amgen, Inc.
Bard, Inc. (C.R.)
Merck & Co.
Pharmacia & Upjohn, Inc.
Storage Technology Corp.

Rhode Island

PPG Industries, Inc.
Providence Journal-Bulletin Co.

BARRINGTON
Providence Journal-Bulletin Co.

BRISTOL
Dexter Corp.

BROWN
Bank One Corp.

CRANSTON
Textron Inc.

CUMBERLAND
General Atlantic Partners II LP
Hasbro, Inc.

KINGSTON
Cranston Print Works Co.
Hasbro, Inc.
Kingsbury Corp.
Providence Journal-Bulletin Co.

MIDDLESEX
Citizens Financial Group, Inc.

NARRAGANSETT
Little, Inc. (Arthur D.)

NEWPORT
APL Ltd.
Bardes Corp.
Dun & Bradstreet Corp.
Milliken & Co.
Prudential Securities Inc.

NORTH PROVIDENCE
Bard, Inc. (C.R.)

PAWTUCKET
Cranston Print Works Co.
Hasbro, Inc.
Providence Journal-Bulletin Co.

PORTSMOUTH
Alma Piston Co.

PROVIDENCE
BankBoston Corp.
Bard, Inc. (C.R.)
Carter-Wallace, Inc.
CGU Insurance
Chesapeake Corp.
Citizens Financial Group, Inc.
Cranston Print Works Co.
Employers Mutual Casualty Co.
Fidelity Investments
Forbes Inc.
Fortis, Inc.
General Atlantic Partners II LP
Harcourt General, Inc.
Hasbro, Inc.
IKON Office Solutions, Inc.
KPMG Peat Marwick LLP
Leviton Manufacturing Co. Inc.
May Department Stores Co.
Merit Oil Corp.
Merrill Lynch & Co., Inc.
Providence Journal-Bulletin Co.
Reebok International Ltd.
Rich Products Corp.
Seagram & Sons, Inc. (Joseph E.)
Stanley Works (The)
Textron Inc.
Thompson Co. (J. Walter)
Trace International Holdings, Inc.
Tyson Foods Inc.
United Distillers & Vintners North America

WAKEFIELD
Stupp Brothers Bridge & Iron Co.

WARWICH
Textron Inc.

WARWICK
Cranston Print Works Co.
Hasbro, Inc.
Textron Inc.

South Carolina

Alcoa Inc.
Milacron, Inc.
Milliken & Co.
Sonoco Products Co.

AIKEN
Hubbell Inc.
Kimberly-Clark Corp.
Owens Corning

ANDERSON
Belk-Simpson Department Stores
Milliken & Co.
Owens Corning
Shea Co. (John F.)

BARNWELL
Waste Management Inc.

CAFFNEY
Timken Co. (The)

CAMDEN
Belk-Simpson Department Stores

CENTRAL
SunTrust Bank Atlanta

CHARLESTON
Belk Stores Services Inc.
BP Amoco Corp.
Carolina Power & Light Co.
Coca-Cola Co.
Cone Mills Corp.
Cummins Engine Co., Inc.
Duke Energy
Evening Post Publishing Co.
Hoffmann-La Roche Inc.
Liberty Corp.
Little, Inc. (Arthur D.)
Wachovia Bank of North Carolina NA
Westvaco Corp.

CHESTER
Springs Industries, Inc.

CLEMSON
Belk-Simpson Department Stores
Carolina Power & Light Co.
Coca-Cola Co.
Cone Mills Corp.
Duke Energy
Grace & Co. (W.R.)
Koch Enterprises, Inc.
Sonoco Products Co.
Springs Industries, Inc.
Temple-Inland Inc.
Toyota Motor Sales U.S.A., Inc.
Union Camp Corp.
Wachovia Bank of North Carolina NA
Waste Management Inc.

CLINTON
Belk-Simpson Department Stores
Jostens, Inc.

COLUMBIA
AlliedSignal Inc.
APL Ltd.
Belk-Simpson Department Stores
BP Amoco Corp.
Carillon Importers, Ltd.
Carolina Power & Light Co.
Cincinnati Bell Inc.
Collins & Aikman Corp.
Cooper Industries, Inc.
Evening Post Publishing Co.
Fluor Corp.
Harsco Corp.
Hubbell Inc.
Inman Mills
Liberty Corp.
Milliken & Co.
NEC America, Inc.
Norfolk Southern Corp.
Sonoco Products Co.
Springs Industries, Inc.
Standard Products Co.
Tai and Co. (J.T.)
Texaco Inc.
Timken Co. (The)
Transamerica Corp.
Union Camp Corp.
Wachovia Bank of North Carolina NA
Waste Management Inc.

CONWAY
Chesapeake Corp.

DARLINGTON
Carolina Power & Light Co.
Sonoco Products Co.

DILLON
Dana Corp.

DUE WEST
Liberty Corp.
Milliken & Co.

ELGIN
Delta Air Lines, Inc.

ENOREE
National Starch & Chemical Co.

FLORENCE
Carolina Power & Light Co.
General Electric Co.
Sonoco Products Co.

FORT MILL
Sonoco Products Co.
Springs Industries, Inc.

GAFFNEY
Collins & Aikman Corp.
Milliken & Co.
Premier Industrial Corp.

GEORGETOWN
Elf Atochem North America, Inc.

GREENSVILLE
Grace & Co. (W.R.)
Leigh Fibers, Inc.

GREENVILLE
Belk-Simpson Department Stores
BellSouth Corp.
Carolina Power & Light Co.
Cone Mills Corp.
Deere & Co.
Duke Energy
Fabri-Kal Corp.
Fluor Corp.
Grace & Co. (W.R.)
Jacobs Engineering Group
Kingsbury Corp.
Liberty Corp.
Milliken & Co.
Ruddick Corp.
SIT Investment Associates, Inc.
Toro Co.
Ukrop's Super Markets
Wachovia Bank of North Carolina NA

GREENWOOD
Cooper Industries, Inc.
Grede Foundries
Inman Mills
Monarch Machine Tool Co.
Monsanto Co.

GREER
Leviton Manufacturing Co. Inc.

HARTSVILLE
Carolina Power & Light Co.
Grace & Co. (W.R.)
Inman Mills
Ruddick Corp.
Sonoco Products Co.

HILTON HEAD
MCI WorldCom, Inc.

INMAN
Inman Mills

JOHNSTON
Milliken & Co.

KERSHAW
Springs Industries, Inc.

LANCASTER
Springs Industries, Inc.

LAURENS
Jostens, Inc.

MARION
Cone Mills Corp.

MCCORMICK
Milliken & Co.

MOUNT PLEASANT
Compass Bank

MURRELLS INLET
Harland Co. (John H.)
Liberty Corp.
Ruddick Corp.

NEWBERRY
Duke Energy
Milliken & Co.
Waste Management Inc.

ORANGEBURG
Carpenter Technology Corp.

PALMETTO
Florida Power & Light Co.

PEMBROKE
Butler Manufacturing Co.

PENDLETON
Owens Corning

ROCK HILL
Cone Mills Corp.
Deere & Co.
Inland Container Corp.
Lance, Inc.
Springs Industries, Inc.

SANFORD
Parker Hannifin Corp.

SPARTANBURG
Bard, Inc. (C.R.)
Burlington Industries, Inc.
Collins & Aikman Corp.
Cone Mills Corp.
Grace & Co. (W.R.)
Inman Mills
Leigh Fibers, Inc.
Milliken & Co.
National Starch & Chemical Co.
Norfolk Southern Corp.
Pfizer Inc.
Sonoco Products Co.
Standard Products Co.
Union Camp Corp.

SUMMERVILLE
Belk Stores Services Inc.

SUMTER
Cooper Industries, Inc.
Sonoco Products Co.

TAYLORS
Cone Mills Corp.
Lance, Inc.
Sonoco Products Co.

UNION
Milliken & Co.

UNION COUNTY
Cone Mills Corp.

WOODRUFF
Standard Products Co.

South Dakota

Blue Cross & Blue Shield of Iowa
Cenex Harvest States

ADERDEEN
American Retail Group

BROOKINGS
Cenex Harvest States
Land O'Lakes, Inc.

CUSTER
Carris Reels

FORT PIERRE
Norwest Corp.

MINOT
Land O'Lakes, Inc.

MITCHELL
Archer-Daniels-Midland Co.
Toshiba America Inc.

RAPID CITY
Domino's Pizza Inc.
Dow Chemical Co.
Dynamet, Inc.
Halliburton Co.
Kroger Co.
Unilever United States, Inc.

SIOUX FALLS
Business Improvement
Graco, Inc.
Jeld-wen, Inc.
Land O'Lakes, Inc.
Norwest Corp.
U.S. Bancorp

SPENCER
Brunswick Corp.

YANKTON
CLARCOR Inc.
Morris Communications Corp.

Tennessee

Alcoa Inc.
Bradford & Co. (J.C.)
Bridgestone/Firestone, Inc.
Calvin Klein
North American Royalties
Provident Companies, Inc.
Rubbermaid Inc.
Tomkins Industries, Inc.

ANTIOCH
First American Corp.

ARLINGTON
Conwood Co. LP

ATHENS
Johnson Controls Inc.

BRENTWOOD
Conwood Co. LP
PACCAR Inc.

BRISTOL
Belk-Simpson Department Stores
First American Corp.
United Co.

CHATTANOOGA
Belk-Simpson Department Stores
Bradford & Co. (J.C.)
Dixie Group, Inc. (The)
First American Corp.
Grace & Co. (W.R.)
National Starch & Chemical Co.
Norfolk Southern Corp.
North American Royalties
Osborne Enterprises
Provident Companies, Inc.
Ruddick Corp.
SunTrust Bank Atlanta
Vulcan Materials Co.
Walter Industries Inc.

CLAKSVILLE
First American Corp.

CLARKSVILLE
First American Corp.

CLEVELAND
First American Corp.
Kroger Co.
Maytag Corp.
Schering-Plough Corp.
Westvaco Corp.

CORDOVA
Kellogg Co.

DAYTON
La-Z-Boy Inc.

DYERSBURG
Dana Corp.

ELIZABETHTON
Winn-Dixie Stores Inc.

FARRAGUT
Brunswick Corp.

FRANKLIN
Indiana Mills & Manufacturing
Rutledge Hill Press

GOODLETTSVILLE
Blue Bell, Inc.

GREENEVILLE
General Atlantic Partners II LP
Parker Hannifin Corp.

GREENFIELD
Parker Hannifin Corp.

HARRIMAN
Waste Management Inc.

HENDERSON
Central & South West Services

HERMITAGE
First American Corp.

HERRMAN
First American Corp.

HIXSON
Osborne Enterprises

JACKSON
Johnson Controls Inc.

JEFFERSON CITY
Brunswick Corp.
First American Corp.

JOHNSON CITY
First American Corp.
General Mills, Inc.
TRW Inc.
United Co.

JONESBOROUGH
First American Corp.

KINGSPORT
First American Corp.

KNOXIVILLE
BellSouth Corp.

KNOXVILLE
Arvin Industries, Inc.
Blue Bell, Inc.
Bradford & Co. (J.C.)
Brunswick Corp.
Deloitte & Touche
Dexter Corp.

Duke Energy
Emerson Electric Co.
First American Corp.
Gerber Products Co.
Levi Strauss & Co.
Nomura Holding America
Norfolk Southern Corp.
Pacific Mutual Life Insurance Co.
Provident Companies, Inc.
Regis Corp.
Sverdrup Corp.
Vulcan Materials Co.
Whirlpool Corp.

LAKE CITY
Ben & Jerry's Homemade Inc.

LAWRENCE
Tomkins Industries, Inc.

LEBANON
Toshiba America Inc.

LOUDON
Arvin Industries, Inc.

MARTIN
Dana Corp.
MTD Products Inc.

MEMPHIS
Baxter International Inc.
BellSouth Corp.
Conwood Co. LP
Cummins Engine Co., Inc.
Dain Bosworth Inc.
Dow Chemical Co.
Federated Department Stores, Inc.
First American Corp.
Hanna Co. (M.A.)
Hofmann Co.
International Paper Co.
Jacobson & Sons (Benjamin)
Jostens, Inc.
Kroger Co.
LandAmerica Financial Services
Memphis Light Gas & Water Division
MTD Products Inc.
NASDAQ Stock Market
National Presto Industries, Inc.
Pfizer Inc.
Rutledge Hill Press
Schering-Plough Corp.
S.G. Cowen
Tension Envelope Corp.
TJX Companies, Inc.
Union Planters Corp.
Waste Management Inc.
Westvaco Corp.

MILLIGAN COLLEGE
United Co.

MURFREESBORO
Pillsbury Co.
State Farm Mutual Automobile Insurance Co.

NASHVILLE
AMR Corp.
Arvin Industries, Inc.
Ashland, Inc.
Banfi Vintners
Blue Bell, Inc.
Bradford & Co. (J.C.)
Bridgestone/Firestone, Inc.
Brown Shoe Co., Inc.
CGU Insurance
Enterprise Rent-A-Car Co.
First American Corp.
Freeport-McMoRan Inc.
Hoffmann-La Roche Inc.
Invacare Corp.
Johnson & Son (S.C.)
Kennametal, Inc.
LandAmerica Financial Services
Landmark Communications Inc.
Levi Strauss & Co.
Louisiana-Pacific Corp.
NEC America, Inc.
North American Royalties
Outboard Marine Corp.
PACCAR Inc.
Pfizer Inc.
Royal & SunAlliance USA, Inc.
Tomkins Industries, Inc.
Toshiba America Inc.
Vanguard Group
Vulcan Materials Co.
The Washington Post
Whirlpool Corp.

NEW MARKET
Hitachi America Ltd.

OAK RIDGE
First American Corp.
Morris Communications Corp.
PerkinElmer, Inc.

PARIS
Dana Corp.

PULASKI
Arvin Industries, Inc.

SEWANEE
North American Royalties

SHELBYVILLE
Bemis Co., Inc.
Jostens, Inc.

SPARTA
Jeld-wen, Inc.

SPRING CITY
La-Z-Boy Inc.

STRAWBERRY PLAINS
Brunswick Corp.

THOMPSONS STATION
Springs Industries, Inc.

TULLAHOMA
Bridgestone/Firestone, Inc.

WASHBURN
Brunswick Corp.

WAVERLY
Inland Container Corp.

Texas

Burlington Resources, Inc.
Fort Worth Star-Telegram Inc.
Freeport-McMoRan Inc.
Milacron, Inc.
Penney Co., Inc. (J.C.)
Stone Container Corp.

ABILENE
Blue Bell, Inc.
Central & South West Services
Extendicare Health Services
United Services Automobile Association

ALAMO
Agrilink Foods, Inc.
Zachry Co. (H.B.)

ALLEN
Millipore Corp.

AMARILLO
Oklahoma Publishing Co.
Owens Corning
Phillips Petroleum Co.
Schlumberger Ltd. (USA)

ANGLETON
Dow Chemical Co.
Monsanto Co.
Phillips Petroleum Co.

ARLINGTON
Alcon Laboratories, Inc.
AMR Corp.
Texas Instruments Inc.

AUSTIN
Allmerica Financial Corp.
Amgen, Inc.
Atlantic Richfield Co.
BP Amoco Corp.
Burlington Resources, Inc.
Callaway Golf Co.
Cargill Inc.
Central & South West Services
Chase Bank of Texas
Chevron Corp.
Compaq Computer Corp.
Cox Enterprises Inc.
Deloitte & Touche
Deluxe Corp.
Dow Chemical Co.
Eckerd Corp.
Exxon Mobil Corp.
FINA
Fluor Corp.
Freeport-McMoRan Inc.
Goldman Sachs Group
Halliburton Co.
Hensel Phelps Construction Co.
KPMG Peat Marwick LLP
Lennox International, Inc.
Louisiana Land & Exploration Co.
Louisiana-Pacific Corp.
Marshall Field's
MCI WorldCom, Inc.
Minnesota Mining & Manufacturing Co.
Motorola Inc.
Orscheln Co.
Paine Webber
Penney Co., Inc. (J.C.)
PerkinElmer, Inc.
Phillips Petroleum Co.
Reader's Digest Association, Inc. (The)
SBC Communications Inc.
Temple-Inland Inc.
Texas Instruments Inc.
Union Carbide Corp.
Westvaco Corp.
Xerox Corp.
Zachry Co. (H.B.)

BAYTOWN
Maytag Corp.

BEAUMONT
Elf Atochem North America, Inc.
FINA
Temple-Inland Inc.

BIG SPRING
FINA

BLOOMINGTON
Union Carbide Corp.

BORGER
Phillips Petroleum Co.

BRADY
Borden, Inc.

BROOKS
SBC Communications Inc.

BROOKSHIRE
Nalco Chemical Co.

BROWNSVILLE
American Retail Group
Norton Co.

BRYAN
Norton Co.

BURLESON
Alcon Laboratories, Inc.

CARTHAGE
HON Industries Inc.

CLEBURNE
Fort Worth Star-Telegram Inc.

COLLEGE STATION
Archer-Daniels-Midland Co.
Aristech Chemical Corp.
Atlantic Richfield Co.
Barry Corp. (R.G.)
BP Amoco Corp.
Burlington Resources, Inc.
Central & South West Services
Chase Bank of Texas
Chevron Corp.
DeKalb Genetics Corp.
Dow Chemical Co.
Eckerd Corp.
FINA
Fluor Corp.
General Electric Co.
Halliburton Co.
Kinder Morgn
Louisiana Land & Exploration Co.
Lubrizol Corp. (The)
Phillips Petroleum Co.
SBC Communications Inc.
Schlumberger Ltd. (USA)
Shell Oil Co.
Temple-Inland Inc.
Texas Instruments Inc.
Union Carbide Corp.
Unocal Corp.

COLLEYVILLE
Alcon Laboratories, Inc.

COMMERCE
HON Industries Inc.

CONROE
Teleflex Inc.

CORPUS CHRISTI
Barnes Group Inc.
Central & South West Services
Jacobs Engineering Group
MONY Group (The)
Occidental Oil and Gas
Reynolds Metals Co.

CYPRESS
Baxter International Inc.

DALLAS
Abbott Laboratories
Aetna, Inc.
AK Steel Corp.
Alcon Laboratories, Inc.
Allstate Insurance Co.
AMR Corp.
AT&T Corp.
Atlantic Richfield Co.
Bank of America
Brunswick Corp.
Campbell Soup Co.
Central & South West Services
CGU Insurance
CIGNA Corp.
Circuit City Stores, Inc.
Compaq Computer Corp.
Contran Corp.
Coors Brewing Co.
Delta Air Lines, Inc.
Dow Jones & Co., Inc.
El Paso Energy Co.
Employers Mutual Casualty Co.
Enterprise Rent-A-Car Co.
Exxon Mobil Corp.
Fannie Mae
Fidelity Investments
FINA
Florida Power & Light Co.
Fort Worth Star-Telegram Inc.
Freddie Mac
GEICO Corp.
General Mills, Inc.
GTE Corp.
Halliburton Co.
Heinz Co. (H.J.)
International Multifoods Corp.
Jacobs Engineering Group
Jeld-wen, Inc.
Kimberly-Clark Corp.
Kroger Co.
LandAmerica Financial Services
Levi Strauss & Co.
Louisiana-Pacific Corp.
Marshall Field's
MCI WorldCom, Inc.
Medtronic, Inc.
Merck & Co.
MONY Group (The)
New York Life Insurance Co.
Oklahoma Publishing Co.
PacifiCare Health Systems
PepsiCo, Inc.
Portland General Electric Co.
Procter & Gamble Co., Cosmetics Division
SBC Communications Inc.
Schlumberger Ltd. (USA)
Sherwin-Williams Co.
Sprint Corp.
Standard Products Co.
State Farm Mutual Automobile Insurance Co.
Susquehanna-Pfaltzgraff Co.
Temple-Inland Inc.
Texas Instruments Inc.
Textron Inc.
Timken Co. (The)
TJX Companies, Inc.
Tomkins Industries, Inc.
Toshiba America Inc.
Transamerica Corp.
Union Pacific Corp.
United Parcel Service of America Inc.

United States Trust Co. of New York
USX Corp.
Vodafone AirTouch Plc
Weil, Gotshal & Manges Corp.
Wells Fargo & Co.
Westvaco Corp.
Wrigley Co. (Wm. Jr.)

DENTON
Atlantic Richfield Co.
Fortis, Inc.
Mattel Inc.
PACCAR Inc.

DIBOLL
Temple-Inland Inc.

EDINBURG
Levi Strauss & Co.
SBC Communications Inc.

EDINBURGH
Wal-Mart Stores, Inc.

EL PASO
Baxter International Inc.
El Paso Energy Co.
Fannie Mae
General Electric Co.
Hasbro, Inc.
Hewlett-Packard Co.
LandAmerica Financial Services
Levi Strauss & Co.
Phelps Dodge Corp.

EVERMAN
Alcon Laboratories, Inc.

FABENS
Blue Bell, Inc.

FORT WORTH
ABC
AMR Corp.
Barry Corp. (R.G.)
Burlington Resources, Inc.
Contran Corp.
Exxon Mobil Corp.
Fort Worth Star-Telegram Inc.
Kimberly-Clark Corp.
Kroger Co.
Lennox International, Inc.
Liberty Diversified Industries
Mitsubishi Electric America
PACCAR Inc.
PepsiCo, Inc.
Reilly Industries, Inc.
SBC Communications Inc.
Stanley Works (The)
Textron Inc.
Union Pacific Corp.
Winn-Dixie Stores Inc.

FT WORTH
Tension Envelope Corp.

FT. WORTH
Alcon Laboratories, Inc.
Sherwin-Williams Co.

GALVESTON
Cooper Industries, Inc.
Freeport-McMoRan Inc.
Gerber Products Co.
Temple-Inland Inc.
Textron Inc.

GARLAND
Texas Instruments Inc.

GEORGETOWN
El Paso Energy Co.
Tai and Co. (J.T.)

GRANBURY
Blue Bell, Inc.

GRAPEVINE
CertainTeed Corp.

HARLINGEN
Central & South West Services

HOUSTON
AMR Corp.
Anheuser-Busch Companies, Inc.
Archer-Daniels-Midland Co.
Aristech Chemical Corp.
Atlantic Richfield Co.
Baker Hughes Inc.
Banfi Vintners
Bank of America
Bard, Inc. (C.R.)
Bechtel Group, Inc.
BP Amoco Corp.
Burlington Resources, Inc.
Chase Bank of Texas
Chevron Corp.
Circuit City Stores, Inc.
Clorox Co.
Collins & Aikman Corp.
Compaq Computer Corp.
Contran Corp.
Cooper Industries, Inc.
Deloitte & Touche
Delta Air Lines, Inc.
Deposit Guaranty National Bank
Dow Jones & Co., Inc.
Eckerd Corp.
El Paso Energy Co.
Elf Atochem North America, Inc.
Enterprise Rent-A-Car Co.
Erving Industries
Exxon Mobil Corp.
Farmers Group, Inc.
Federated Department Stores, Inc.
FINA
Fluor Corp.
FMC Corp.
Goldman Sachs Group
Halliburton Co.
Hasbro, Inc.
Jacobs Engineering Group
Journal-Gazette Co.
Kimberly-Clark Corp.
Kinder Morgn
Kroger Co.
LandAmerica Financial Services
Little, Inc. (Arthur D.)
Louisiana Land & Exploration Co.
Lubrizol Corp. (The)
Marshall Field's
May Department Stores Co.
MCI WorldCom, Inc.
Medtronic, Inc.
Nabisco Group Holdings
Nalco Chemical Co.
Occidental Oil and Gas
PacifiCare Health Systems
Phillips Petroleum Co.
Quanex Corp.
Reilly Industries, Inc.
Royal & SunAlliance USA, Inc.
Safeguard Scientifics
SBC Communications Inc.
Schering-Plough Corp.
Schlumberger Ltd. (USA)
Shell Oil Co.
Simpson Investment Co.
State Street Bank & Trust Co.
Stride Rite Corp.
Temple-Inland Inc.
Texaco Inc.
Texas Instruments Inc.
Textron Inc.
Timken Co. (The)
TJX Companies, Inc.
Toshiba America Inc.
Union Carbide Corp.
Unocal Corp.
USX Corp.
Weil, Gotshal & Manges Corp.
Witco Corp.
Zachry Co. (H.B.)

HUNSTVILLE
Louisiana-Pacific Corp.

INGRAM
LandAmerica Financial Services

IRVING
Allstate Insurance Co.
Fidelity Investments
Halliburton Co.
Kimberly-Clark Corp.
Mitsubishi Electric America
Owens Corning
Physicians Mutual Insurance Co.
Providence Journal-Bulletin Co.
Union Pacific Corp.
Xerox Corp.

KELLER
Exxon Mobil Corp.

KERRVILLE
LandAmerica Financial Services

KILGORE
Occidental Oil and Gas

KOUNTZE
Temple-Inland Inc.

LA FERIA
Norton Co.

LACKLAND
Bard, Inc. (C.R.)

LAKE JACKSON
Nalco Chemical Co.

LANCASTER
AMR Corp.

LAREDO
Central & South West Services

LONGVIEW
Cox Enterprises Inc.
MONY Group (The)
Occidental Oil and Gas

LUBBOCK
American Retail Group
Burlington Resources, Inc.
Cox Enterprises Inc.
Eckerd Corp.
FINA
Halliburton Co.
Hensel Phelps Construction Co.
Louisiana-Pacific Corp.
Phillips Petroleum Co.
SBC Communications Inc.
Texas Instruments Inc.

LUFKIN
Temple-Inland Inc.

MCALLEN
Central & South West Services
Inland Container Corp.
Levi Strauss & Co.
Norton Co.
SBC Communications Inc.

MCKINNEY
Millipore Corp.
Texas Instruments Inc.

MERCEDES
Levi Strauss & Co.

MIDLAND
Atlantic Richfield Co.
Burlington Resources, Inc.
FINA
Occidental Oil and Gas
Texaco Inc.
Texas Instruments Inc.
Wal-Mart Stores, Inc.

MISSION
Norton Co.

NACOGDOCHES
Fisher Scientific
International Paper Co.
Kroger Co.
Louisiana-Pacific Corp.
Temple-Inland Inc.
Waste Management Inc.

NEW BRAUNFELS
Owens Corning

ODESSA
Texas Instruments Inc.

ORANGE
Inland Container Corp.
Temple-Inland Inc.

PALESTINE
Cooper Industries, Inc.

PINELAND
Temple-Inland Inc.

PLANO
FINA
Millipore Corp.

PORT ARTHUR
FINA

PRAIRIE VIEW
Navcom Systems
Xerox Corp.

RICHARDSON
Amsted Industries Inc.
Broderbund Software, Inc.
Schlumberger Ltd. (USA)
Sprint Corp.
Texas Instruments Inc.

RICHMOND
Nalco Chemical Co.
Occidental Oil and Gas

ROSENBERG
Quanex Corp.

SAM RAYBURN
Temple-Inland Inc.

SAN ANGELO
Barry Corp. (R.G.)

SAN ANTONIO
AT&T Corp.
Bradford & Co. (J.C.)
Central & South West Services
Coca-Cola Co.
Exxon Mobil Corp.
Fannie Mae
General Motors Corp.
KPMG Peat Marwick LLP
Lennox International, Inc.
Levi Strauss & Co.
Mattel Inc.
Morrison Knudsen Corp.
Norwest Corp.
PacifiCare Health Systems
Reynolds Metals Co.
SBC Communications Inc.
Schering-Plough Corp.
Sony Electronics
United Services Automobile Association
USAA Life Insurance Co.
Whitman Corp.
Zachry Co. (H.B.)

SAN MARCOS
Amgen, Inc.
Butler Manufacturing Co.
PACCAR Inc.
West Co. Inc.

SHERMAN
Pillsbury Co.
Texas Instruments Inc.

STAFFORD
Nalco Chemical Co.
Unocal Corp.

STEPHENVILLE
FMC Corp.
Hensel Phelps Construction Co.

SUGAR LAND
Unocal Corp.

TEMPLE
Jeld-wen, Inc.
JSJ Corp.
Temple-Inland Inc.

TERRELL
Butler Manufacturing Co.

TEXAS CITY
BP Amoco Corp.
Union Carbide Corp.

TOMBALL
Compaq Computer Corp.
Square D Co.

TYLER
Contran Corp.

WACO
AT&T Corp.
Blue Bell, Inc.
Lehigh Portland Cement Co.
Louisiana-Pacific Corp.
Temple-Inland Inc.
Zachry Co. (H.B.)

WAXAHACHIE
Owens Corning

WEBSTER
Union Carbide Corp.

WICHITA FALLS
CertainTeed Corp.
Grace & Co. (W.R.)
Stanley Works (The)
USG Corp.

WILLIS
Teleflex Inc.

ZAVALLA
Temple-Inland Inc.

Utah
Cincinnati Bell Inc.

CEDAR CITY
Cincinnati Bell Inc.
PacifiCorp

LOGAN
Bourns, Inc.
Simplot Co. (J.R.)

PARK CITY
Schwab & Co., Inc. (Charles)
Witco Corp.

PRICE
PacifiCorp

PROVO
APL Ltd.
GATX Corp.
Hawaiian Electric Co., Inc.
Kemper National Insurance Companies
KPMG Peat Marwick LLP
Litton Industries, Inc.
Louisiana-Pacific Corp.

RICHFIELD
PacifiCorp

SALT LAKE CITY
Abbott Laboratories
American Express Co.
ASARCO Inc.
Bard, Inc. (C.R.)
Broderbund Software, Inc.
Carris Reels
Central & South West Services
Cincinnati Bell Inc.
Delta Air Lines, Inc.
Fidelity Investments
PacifiCorp
Patagonia Inc.
Ryder System, Inc.
Toyota Motor Sales U.S.A., Inc.
Union Pacific Corp.
Witco Corp.

SUNDANCE
Cincinnati Bell Inc.

WEST JORDAN
Fidelity Investments
McKesson-HBOC Corp.

Vermont
Carris Reels

BELLOWS FALLS
Ben & Jerry's Homemade Inc.

BENNINGTON
Stanley Works (The)

BRATTLEBORO
Golub Corp.
Land O'Lakes, Inc.
New England Bio Labs
Patagonia Inc.

BURLINGTON
Carris Reels
Fortis, Inc.
Golub Corp.

DORSET
Warner-Lambert Co.

ESSEX JUNCTION
Carris Reels

GILMAN
Simpson Investment Co.

HAMPTON
Butler Manufacturing Co.

KILLINGTON
Carris Reels

LUNENBURG
Simpson Investment Co.

MIDDLEBURY
Brown Shoe Co., Inc.
Humana, Inc.
International Paper Co.
Leigh Fibers, Inc.
SIT Investment Associates, Inc.

MONTPELIER
Ben & Jerry's Homemade Inc.
Carris Reels
Leigh Fibers, Inc.

POULTNEY
Country Curtains, Inc.
Hewlett-Packard Co.
Housatonic Curtain Co.

PROCTOR
Carris Reels

PUTNEY
Schlumberger Ltd. (USA)

RATLAND
Country Curtains, Inc.

READING
Ben & Jerry's Homemade Inc.

RUTLAND
Carris Reels

SAXTONS RIVER
Ben & Jerry's Homemade Inc.

SOUTH BURLINGTON
Carris Reels

SOUTH STRAFFORD
Ben & Jerry's Homemade Inc.

ST. ALBANS
Ben & Jerry's Homemade Inc.

WALDEN
Patagonia Inc.

WATERBURY
Leigh Fibers, Inc.

WEST RUTLAND
Carris Reels

WILLISTON
Carris Reels

WINDSOR
Jeld-wen, Inc.

WOODSTOCK
Pella Corp.

Virgin Islands

LEXINGTON
FINA

Virginia
Chesapeake Corp.
Crane Co.
DaimlerChrysler Corp.
Dixie Group, Inc. (The)
Fluor Corp.
Georgia-Pacific Corp.
Union Carbide Corp.
Universal Leaf Tobacco Co., Inc.

ABINGDON
Norfolk Southern Corp.
United Co.

ALEXANDRIA
ABC
American Express Co.
Andersons Inc.
Archer-Daniels-Midland Co.
Ashland, Inc.
Avon Products, Inc.
Bechtel Group, Inc.
Bell Atlantic Corp.
Binswanger Companies
Bridgestone/Firestone, Inc.
Briggs & Stratton Corp.
Brown Shoe Co., Inc.
Burress (J.W.)
Campbell Soup Co.
CIGNA Corp.
CNA
Consumers Energy Co.
Deere & Co.
Dow Chemical Co.
Dow Jones & Co., Inc.
Fluor Corp.
FMC Corp.
Fortis, Inc.
Freddie Mac
GenCorp
General Atlantic Partners II LP
General Motors Corp.
Georgia-Pacific Corp.
Hickory Tech Corp.
Honeywell International Inc.
Metropolitan Life Insurance Co.
Minnesota Mutual Life Insurance Co.
NEC America, Inc.
New York Times Co.
Olin Corp.
Owens Corning
Penney Co., Inc. (J.C.)
Phillips Petroleum Co.
Putnam Investments
Rubbermaid Inc.
Schwab & Co., Inc. (Charles)
SmithKline Beecham Corp.
Sony Electronics
Tektronix, Inc.
Tesoro Hawaii
Union Carbide Corp.
United Parcel Service of America Inc.
Vesper Corp.
Wal-Mart Stores, Inc.
Weyerhaeuser Co.
Whirlpool Corp.
Winn-Dixie Stores Inc.

ALTAVISTA
Furniture Brands International, Inc.

ANNANDALE
FMC Corp.
Giant Food Inc.

ARLINGTON
Abbott Laboratories
American Fidelity Corp.
AMR Corp.
Anheuser-Busch Companies, Inc.
Brown Shoe Co., Inc.
Colonial Oil Industries, Inc.
Contran Corp.
Cummins Engine Co., Inc.
Dayton Power and Light Co.
Dow Chemical Co.
Dow Jones & Co., Inc.
Exxon Mobil Corp.
Farmers Group, Inc.
Fisher Scientific
Forbes Inc.
Ford Motor Co.
Freddie Mac
General Atlantic Partners II LP
General Electric Co.
GTE Corp.
Halliburton Co.
Hartmarx Corp.
Hubbell Inc.
Johnson & Son (S.C.)
Kellwood Co.
Litton Industries, Inc.
Milliken & Co.
Morris Communications Corp.
Olin Corp.
Oshkosh B'Gosh, Inc.
Portland General Electric Co.
Procter & Gamble Co.
Prudential Insurance Co. of America
Reilly Industries, Inc.
Ryder System, Inc.
Shell Oil Co.
Sierra Pacific Resources
Sony Electronics
Stone Container Corp.
Sun Microsystems Inc.
Sunmark Capital Corp.
Tamko Roofing Products
True North Communications, Inc.
TRW Inc.
Union Camp Corp.
United Parcel Service of America Inc.
Wal-Mart Stores, Inc.
The Washington Post
Waste Management Inc.
Whirlpool Corp.

ASHLAND
Crestar Finance Corp.
Ukrop's Super Markets
Universal Leaf Tobacco Co., Inc.

BASSETT
Bassett Furniture Industries

BEDFORD
Landmark Communications Inc.

BELLE HAVEN
Gallo Winery, Inc. (E&J)

BIG ISLAND
Lance, Inc.

BLACKSBURG
Bechtel Group, Inc.
Bell Atlantic Corp.
Burlington Industries, Inc.
Corning Inc.
Crestar Finance Corp.
FINA
General Electric Co.
Hubbell Inc.
Kennametal, Inc.
Litton Industries, Inc.
Norfolk Southern Corp.
Wachovia Bank of North Carolina NA

BLACKSTONE
Grace & Co. (W.R.)

BRIDGEWATER
Jacobson & Sons (Benjamin)

BRISTOL
Stanley Works (The)
United Co.

BRISTOW
GEICO Corp.

CHARLOTTESVILLE
AlliedSignal Inc.
Ameritech Ohio
Bardes Corp.
Bassett Furniture Industries
Chesapeake Corp.
Circuit City Stores, Inc.
Collins & Aikman Corp.
Crestar Finance Corp.
Evening Post Publishing Co.
First Union Corp.
FMC Corp.
Giant Food Inc.
Hitachi America Ltd.
Inman Mills
LandAmerica Financial Services
Landmark Communications Inc.
Lehigh Portland Cement Co.
Merrill Lynch & Co., Inc.
Nomura Holding America
Norfolk Southern Corp.
Provident Companies, Inc.
State Farm Mutual Automobile Insurance Co.
Stonecutter Mills Corp.
SunTrust Bank Atlanta
Textron Inc.
Ukrop's Super Markets
Union Camp Corp.

CHESTER
Ukrop's Super Markets

CHESTERFIELD
LandAmerica Financial Services
Ukrop's Super Markets

CHRIST CHURCH
Liberty Corp.

CHRISTIANSBURG
Crestar Finance Corp.
Hubbell Inc.
National Starch & Chemical Co.

COVINGTON
International Paper Co.
Westvaco Corp.

CRITZ
Crestar Finance Corp.

CULPEPER
Ukrop's Super Markets

DANVILLE
AMP Inc.
Crestar Finance Corp.

EMORY
Dexter Corp.
United Co.

EVANSVILLE
United Wisconsin Services

FAIRFAX
Bard, Inc. (C.R.)
Bassett Furniture Industries

Bethlehem Steel Corp.
CBS Corp.
Comdisco, Inc.
Cummins Engine Co., Inc.
DaimlerChrysler Corp.
Exxon Mobil Corp.
Gap, Inc.
General Motors Corp.
Graco, Inc.
Hallmark Cards Inc.
Hoffmann-La Roche Inc.
Honeywell International Inc.
Jostens, Inc.
Kemper National Insurance Companies
Lance, Inc.
McGraw-Hill Companies, Inc.
Merrill Lynch & Co., Inc.
Mine Safety Appliances Co.
National Starch & Chemical Co.
Phelps Dodge Corp.
Procter & Gamble Co.
Pulitzer Publishing Co.
Reynolds Metals Co.
Sunmark Capital Corp.
Tamko Roofing Products
Texaco Inc.
TRW Inc.
Union Pacific Corp.
US West, Inc.
The Washington Post

FALLS CHURCH
Allstate Insurance Co.
Forbes Inc.
Freddie Mac
Leigh Fibers, Inc.

FARMVILLE
Circuit City Stores, Inc.
Universal Leaf Tobacco Co., Inc.

FERRUM
Bassett Furniture Industries
Landmark Communications Inc.

FISHERVILLE
Crestar Finance Corp.

FORT MYER
GEICO Corp.

FRANKLIN
Union Camp Corp.

FREDERICKSBURG
American Honda Motor Co., Inc.
Giant Food Inc.
Independent Stave Co.
Levi Strauss & Co.

FRONT ROYAL
Federal-Mogul Corp.
Laclede Gas Co.

GLEN ALLEN
Circuit City Stores, Inc.
GEICO Corp.
Ukrop's Super Markets

GLOUCHESTER POINT
Norfolk Southern Corp.

GOOCHLAND
Toshiba America Inc.

GRUNDY
Norfolk Southern Corp.
United Co.

HAMPTON
Bell Atlantic Corp.
Jacobson & Sons (Benjamin)
KPMG Peat Marwick LLP
Merit Oil Corp.
PerkinElmer, Inc.
The Washington Post

HANOVER
Ukrop's Super Markets

HARRISBURG
Enterprise Rent-A-Car Co.

HARRISONBURG
Crestar Finance Corp.
Enterprise Rent-A-Car Co.
KPMG Peat Marwick LLP
Universal Leaf Tobacco Co., Inc.

HERNDON
Sonoco Products Co.
Sunmark Capital Corp.
Tamko Roofing Products

HILLSVILLE
Burlington Industries, Inc.

HOLLINS
Norfolk Southern Corp.

JAMESTOWN
Universal Leaf Tobacco Co., Inc.

LEBANON
Grede Foundries
Norfolk Southern Corp.

LEESBURG
GEICO Corp.
Giant Food Inc.

LEXINGTON
Crestar Finance Corp.
Croft-Leominster
First Union Securities, Inc.
Kemper National Insurance Companies
Price Associates (T. Rowe)
Ruddick Corp.

LORTON
Banta Corp.

LURAY
Crestar Finance Corp.
Navcom Systems

LYNCHBURG
Amsted Industries Inc.
Archer-Daniels-Midland Co.
Crestar Finance Corp.
Croft-Leominster
First Union Securities, Inc.
Norfolk Southern Corp.
Timken Co. (The)
Union Camp Corp.

MADISON
United Wisconsin Services

MANASSAS
Crestar Finance Corp.
Crown Books
Navcom Systems
The Washington Post

MARTINSVILLE
Bassett Furniture Industries
Crestar Finance Corp.

MATHEWS
Equifax Inc.

MCLEAN
Fluor Corp.
Hartmarx Corp.
Lee Enterprises
Litton Industries, Inc.
NEC America, Inc.
Union Carbide Corp.

MILLWOOD
Hoffmann-La Roche Inc.
Pharmacia & Upjohn, Inc.
Schering-Plough Corp.

MOUNT VERNON
Kemper National Insurance Companies

NEWPORT NEWS
Circuit City Stores, Inc.
Consolidated Natural Gas Co.
Wachovia Bank of North Carolina NA

NORFOLK
Colonial Oil Industries, Inc.
Consolidated Natural Gas Co.
Cox Enterprises Inc.
Crestar Finance Corp.
First Union Securities, Inc.
Freeport-McMoRan Inc.
Landmark Communications Inc.
Lipton Co.
Norfolk Southern Corp.
Praxair
Safeguard Scientifics
Texaco Inc.
Thompson Co. (J. Walter)

NORTH SPRINGFIELD
Sunmark Capital Corp.

OAKTON
Freddie Mac
Textron Inc.

ORANGE
Crestar Finance Corp.

PARKERSBURG
LandAmerica Financial Services

PEARISBURG
Hubbell Inc.

PETERSBURG
Circuit City Stores, Inc.
Inland Container Corp.
Inman Mills
Reynolds Metals Co.
Xerox Corp.

PIKEVILLE
Norfolk Southern Corp.

PRINCE WILLIAM
Lehigh Portland Cement Co.
Navcom Systems

QUANTICO
Textron Inc.

RADFORD
Crestar Finance Corp.
Federal-Mogul Corp.

RESTON
ABC
Boston Globe (The)
Dow Jones & Co., Inc.
Evening Post Publishing Co.
Exxon Mobil Corp.
GTE Corp.
Landmark Communications Inc.
McClatchy Co.
Merck & Co.
New York Times Co.
Providence Journal-Bulletin Co.
Pulitzer Publishing Co.
Times Mirror Co.
Unocal Corp.
Wiley & Sons (John)

RICHMOND
Bassett Furniture Industries
Belk Stores Services Inc.
Burlington Industries, Inc.
Carpenter Technology Corp.
Chesapeake Corp.
CIGNA Corp.
Circuit City Stores, Inc.
CPI Corp.
Crestar Finance Corp.
Elf Atochem North America, Inc.
First Union Corp.
First Union Securities, Inc.
Freddie Mac
Furniture Brands International, Inc.
Hannaford Brothers Co.
Harris Corp.
Kennametal, Inc.
LandAmerica Financial Services
Landmark Communications Inc.
Lipton Co.
MCI WorldCom, Inc.
Merit Oil Corp.
Nabisco Group Holdings
Navcom Systems
Norfolk Southern Corp.
Price Associates (T. Rowe)
Reynolds Metals Co.
Ruddick Corp.
Sentry Insurance, A Mutual Co.
Ukrop's Super Markets
Universal Leaf Tobacco Co., Inc.
Wachovia Bank of North Carolina NA
The Washington Post
West Co. Inc.
Westvaco Corp.

ROANOKE
Alabama Power Co.
AMP Inc.
APL Ltd.
Bassett Furniture Industries
Belk Stores Services Inc.
Crestar Finance Corp.
First American Corp.
First Union Corp.
Kroger Co.
Landmark Communications Inc.
Norfolk Southern Corp.
Quaker Chemical Corp.
Ruddick Corp.
United Parcel Service of America Inc.

ROCKY MOUNT
Furniture Brands International, Inc.

ROSSLVN
Fluor Corp.

ROSSLYN
Bardes Corp.
Leviton Manufacturing Co. Inc.
Sherwin-Williams Co.
Square D Co.

SALEM
Crestar Finance Corp.
Heinz Co. (H.J.)

SPRINGFIELD
Century 21
Grede Foundries
Publix Supermarkets
Reily & Co., Inc. (William B.)
Stonecutter Mills Corp.
Sunmark Capital Corp.
Tamko Roofing Products

STAUNTON
Burress (J.W.)
Crestar Finance Corp.

SUFFOLK
Lipton Co.

VIENNA
GEICO Corp.
Milliken & Co.
Sun Microsystems Inc.
Toyota Motor Sales U.S.A., Inc.
TRW Inc.

VIRGINIA BEACH
GEICO Corp.
Landmark Communications Inc.
Litton Industries, Inc.
Toshiba America Inc.
United Services Automobile Association
USAA Life Insurance Co.

WAYNESBORO
Hershey Foods Corp.

WEST POINT
Chesapeake Corp.

WILLIAMSBURG
Alabama Power Co.
Bassett Furniture Industries
Blue Bell, Inc.
Circuit City Stores, Inc.
Consolidated Natural Gas Co.
Crestar Finance Corp.
First Union Securities, Inc.
MCI WorldCom, Inc.
New York Life Insurance Co.
Phillips Petroleum Co.
Textron Inc.
Ukrop's Super Markets
United Co.

WINCHESTER
Blair & Co. (William)
Cooper Industries, Inc.
Cummings Properties Management
Rubbermaid Inc.

WINTERGREEN
Air Products and Chemicals, Inc.

WISE
United Co.

WOODBRIDGE
Giant Food Inc.

Washington

Coca-Cola Co.
Crane Co.
Fluor Corp.
Intel Corp.
US Bank, Washington

ABERDEEN
Rayonier Inc.
Simpson Investment Co.
Weyerhaeuser Co.

BAINBRIDGE ISLAND
Boeing Co.

BELFAIR
Simpson Investment Co.

BELLEVUE
Boeing Co.
PACCAR Inc.
PEMCO Corp.
Whirlpool Corp.

BELLINGHAM
Atlantic Richfield Co.
Georgia-Pacific Corp.
Patagonia Inc.
Pfizer Inc.
United States Trust Co. of New York
US Bank, Washington

BOTHELL
Simplot Co. (J.R.)

BREMERTON
Johnson Controls Inc.

CENTRALIA
Citizens Financial Group, Inc.
PacifiCorp

DES MOINES
Tai and Co. (J.T.)

DUBUQUE
Jeld-wen, Inc.

EDMONDS
PEMCO Corp.

EVERETT
Brunswick Corp.
Chicago Title Corp.
Federated Department Stores, Inc.
GTE Corp.
Jeld-wen, Inc.
PACCAR Inc.
PacifiCare Health Systems
Sega of America Inc.

FEDERAL WAY
Weyerhaeuser Co.

FORKS
Rayonier Inc.

FREMONT
Boeing Co.

GIG HARBOR
Walter Industries Inc.

KENNEWICK
Simplot Co. (J.R.)

KIRKLAND
Chicago Title Corp.
Louisiana-Pacific Corp.
PACCAR Inc.
PEMCO Corp.

LONGVIEW
Reynolds Metals Co.
Weyerhaeuser Co.

LYNNWOOD
PEMCO Corp.

MCCLEARY
Simpson Investment Co.

MERCER ISLAND
PEMCO Corp.

MOSSYROCK
Rayonier Inc.

MOUNT VERNON
PACCAR Inc.

OKANOGAN
Boeing Co.

OLYMPIA
Cenex Harvest States
Extendicare Health Services
PEMCO Corp.
Rayonier Inc.
Simpson Investment Co.
US Bank, Washington

PASCO
PEMCO Corp.
US Bank, Washington

PORT ANGELES
Rayonier Inc.

PULLMAN
Boeing Co.
CGU Insurance
Federal-Mogul Corp.
Olin Corp.
PACCAR Inc.
PEMCO Corp.
Rayonier Inc.
Simplot Co. (J.R.)
Washington Trust Bank

REDMOND
Weyerhaeuser Co.

RENTON
PACCAR Inc.

SEATTLE
Agrilink Foods, Inc.
Alaska Airlines, Inc.
Alliant Techsystems
America West Airlines, Inc.
Amgen, Inc.
APL Ltd.
Archer-Daniels-Midland Co.
Baird & Co. (Robert W.)
Banfi Vintners
Banta Corp.
Ben & Jerry's Homemade Inc.
Boeing Co.
Bridgestone/Firestone, Inc.
Bristol-Myers Squibb Co.
Bucyrus-Erie Co.
Burlington Resources, Inc.
Carillon Importers, Ltd.
CGU Insurance
Chevron Corp.
Chicago Title Corp.
Compass Bank
Copley Press, Inc.
Crane Co.
Dain Bosworth Inc.
Deloitte & Touche
Delta Air Lines, Inc.
Dow Chemical Co.
Exxon Mobil Corp.
Fannie Mae
Federated Department Stores, Inc.
Gallo Winery, Inc. (E&J)
Gerber Products Co.
Group Health Plan
Honeywell International Inc.
Intel Corp.
Jeld-wen, Inc.
Liberty Corp.
Manor Care Health SVS, Inc.
Microsoft Corp.
Olin Corp.
PACCAR Inc.
PEMCO Corp.
PepsiCo, Inc.
Potlatch Corp.
Rayonier Inc.
Royal & SunAlliance USA, Inc.
Rutledge Hill Press
Sega of America Inc.
Simpson Investment Co.
Sverdrup Corp.
Texaco Inc.
Toyota Motor Sales U.S.A., Inc.
United Airlines Inc.
U.S. Bancorp
US Bank, Washington
US West, Inc.
Washington Mutual, Inc.
Washington Trust Bank
Wells Fargo & Co.
Weyerhaeuser Co.
Xerox Corp.

SELAH
Jeld-wen, Inc.

SHELTON
Johnson Controls Inc.
Rayonier Inc.
Simpson Investment Co.

SNOQUALMIE
PACCAR Inc.

SOUTH BEND
Patagonia Inc.
Weyerhaeuser Co.

SPOKANE
Barnes Group Inc.
Hensel Phelps Construction Co.
Jacobs Engineering Group
Johnson Controls Inc.
Land O'Lakes, Inc.
Mark IV Industries
Patagonia Inc.
Rayonier Inc.
Simpson Investment Co.
Union Pacific Corp.
U.S. Bancorp
US Bank, Washington
Washington Trust Bank

TACOMA
Agrilink Foods, Inc.
Boeing Co.
Carris Reels
Chicago Title Corp.
Elf Atochem North America, Inc.
Federated Department Stores, Inc.
Glickenhaus & Co.
Intel Corp.
PACCAR Inc.
PEMCO Corp.
Simplot Co. (J.R.)
Simpson Investment Co.
Weyerhaeuser Co.

TOPPENISH
Boeing Co.
Burlington Resources, Inc.
PEMCO Corp.

TRI-CITIES
Bechtel Group, Inc.

VANCOUVER
PacifiCorp
US Bank, Washington

WALLA WALLA
Land O'Lakes, Inc.
Toshiba America Inc.

WENATCHEE
Washington Trust Bank

WOODLAND
PacifiCorp

YAKIMA
Chesapeake Corp.
Jeld-wen, Inc.
PacifiCorp

West Virginia

Equitable Resources, Inc.

BLUEFIELD
Kroger Co.
Norfolk Southern Corp.

BRIDGEPORT
Consolidated Natural Gas Co.

BUCKHANNON
Norton Co.

CABELL COUNTY
Pfizer Inc.

CHARLES TOWN
ASARCO Inc.

CHARLESTON
Ashland, Inc.
Citizens Financial Group, Inc.
First Union Securities, Inc.
IKON Office Solutions, Inc.
Ryder System, Inc.
Tyson Foods Inc.
Union Carbide Corp.

CLARKSBURG
Consolidated Natural Gas Co.
Grede Foundries

FAIRMONT
Consolidated Natural Gas Co.

FRANKLIN
Union Carbide Corp.

GREENVILLE
Hitachi America Ltd.

HUNTINGTON
AK Steel Corp.
Aristech Chemical Corp.
Ashland, Inc.
Lee Enterprises
Patagonia Inc.

HURRICANE
IKON Office Solutions, Inc.

INSTITUTE
Ashland, Inc.

MARTINSBURG
Corning Inc.

MORGANTOWN
Ashland, Inc.
Blue Bell, Inc.
Coca-Cola Co.
Consolidated Natural Gas Co.
Equitable Resources, Inc.
Hubbell Inc.
PerkinElmer, Inc.
TRW Inc.
Union Carbide Corp.
Westvaco Corp.

MUNTINGTON
Fluor Corp.

PARKSBURG
Ashland, Inc.

RIDGELEY
Brunswick Corp.

RIDGEWAY
CertainTeed Corp.

SHEPHERDSTOWN
Monsanto Co.

WHEELING
GenCorp
PerkinElmer, Inc.

WILLIAMSON
Norfolk Southern Corp.

Wisconsin

Bucyrus-Erie Co.
Cenex Harvest States
CUNA Mutual Group
Ecolab Inc.
Fortis Insurance Co.
Huffy Corp.
Louisiana-Pacific Corp.
Madison Gas & Electric Co.
Marcus Corp.
Mead Corp.
Pieper Power Electric Co.
Reader's Digest Association, Inc. (The)
Trustmark Insurance Co.

ALAMEDA
Land O'Lakes, Inc.

AMERY
Andersen Corp.

APPLETON
Baird & Co. (Robert W.)
Banta Corp.
Bemis Co., Inc.
Chesapeake Corp.
Consolidated Papers, Inc.
Kimberly-Clark Corp.
Marshall & Ilsley Corp.
Medtronic, Inc.
Menasha Corp.
Oshkosh B'Gosh, Inc.
Sentry Insurance, A Mutual Co.
Star Bank NA
Thompson Co. (J. Walter)
U.S. Bancorp Piper Jaffray
United Wisconsin Services
Wisconsin Public Service Corp.

ASHLAND
Consolidated Papers, Inc.

BALDWIN
Andersen Corp.

BARABOO
Johnson & Son (S.C.)
Wisconsin Power & Light Co.

BAYSIDE
Harley-Davidson Co.

BEAVER DAM
Deere & Co.
Whitman Corp.

BELOIT
Consolidated Papers, Inc.
Dana Corp.
Ecolab Inc.
Fortis, Inc.
General Mills, Inc.
Harnischfeger Industries
Kemper National Insurance Companies
Outboard Marine Corp.
Wisconsin Power & Light Co.

BLACK EARTH
CUNA Mutual Group
Marcus Corp.

BOULDER JUNCTION
Tai and Co. (J.T.)

BROOKFIELD
Briggs & Stratton Corp.
Grede Foundries
Johnson Controls Inc.
Marshall & Ilsley Corp.

United Wisconsin Services

BROWN DEER
Badger Meter, Inc.

BURLINGTON
Ruddick Corp.

BUTLER
Banta Corp.
Business Improvement

CEDARBURG
Marshall & Ilsley Corp.

CLEVELAND
Bemis Manufacturing Co.

CUDAHY
Ladish Co., Inc.

DE PERE
Bemis Manufacturing Co.
Consolidated Papers, Inc.
Green Bay Packaging

DEPERE
Amsted Industries Inc.
Banta Corp.
Wisconsin Public Service Corp.

DOUGLAS
Ben & Jerry's Homemade Inc.

EAGLE RIVER
Wisconsin Energy Corp.
Wisconsin Public Service Corp.

EAST TROY
Pieper Power Electric Co.
Wisconsin Energy Corp.

EAU CLAIRE
Baird & Co. (Robert W.)
Extendicare Health Services
First Financial Bank
Fortis, Inc.
Louisiana-Pacific Corp.
National Presto Industries, Inc.
Reinhart Institutional Foods
Sentry Insurance, A Mutual Co.
Solo Cup Co.
United Wisconsin Services

ELLSWORTH
Andersen Corp.

ELM GROVE
Wisconsin Energy Corp.

FENNIMORE
Wisconsin Power & Light Co.

FOND DU LAC
Brunswick Corp.
Giddings & Lewis

FOX CITIES
Chesapeake Corp.

FOX CITY
Banta Corp.

FOX VALLEY
Menasha Corp.

GRAFTON
Badger Meter, Inc.
Business Improvement

GREEN BAY
Grace & Co. (W.R.)
Green Bay Packaging
Humana, Inc.
Procter & Gamble Co.
Sentry Insurance, A Mutual Co.
Solo Cup Co.
Wisconsin Public Service Corp.

GREEN LAKE
Oshkosh B'Gosh, Inc.

HARTFORD
Brunswick Corp.

HARTLAND
Consolidated Papers, Inc.

HORICON
Consolidated Papers, Inc.

HUDSON
Andersen Corp.

JAMAICA
Texaco Inc.

JANESVILLE
Giddings & Lewis
United Wisconsin Services
Wisconsin Power & Light Co.

JEFFERSON
Heinz Co. (H.J.)
Ladish Co., Inc.

KAUKAUNA
WICOR, Inc.

KENOSHA
Abbott Laboratories
Amsted Industries Inc.
Consolidated Papers, Inc.
Fortis, Inc.
Johnson & Son (S.C.)
Outboard Marine Corp.
Trustmark Insurance Co.
Wisconsin Energy Corp.

KEWAUNEE
Wisconsin Public Service Corp.

KIMBERLY
Consolidated Papers, Inc.

LA CROSSE
Baird & Co. (Robert W.)
Consolidated Papers, Inc.
First Financial Bank
Grede Foundries
JSJ Corp.
National Presto Industries, Inc.
Reinhart Institutional Foods
Stanley Works (The)

LAC DU FLAMBEAU
Amsted Industries Inc.
Johnson & Son (S.C.)

LADYSMITH
Johnson & Son (S.C.)
Reinhart Institutional Foods

LAKE GENEVA
Griffith Laboratories U.S.A.

MADISCON
Consolidated Papers, Inc.

MADISON
Abbott Laboratories
Ameritech Corp.
Ameritech Wisconsin
Badger Meter, Inc.
Baird & Co. (Robert W.)
Banta Corp.
Bemis Co., Inc.
Bemis Manufacturing Co.
Ben & Jerry's Homemade Inc.
Block, Inc. (H&R)
Bridgestone/Firestone, Inc.
Briggs & Stratton Corp.
Brown Shoe Co., Inc.
Bucyrus-Erie Co.
Butler Manufacturing Co.
Cargill Inc.
Chesapeake Corp.
CNA
ConAgra, Inc.
Consolidated Papers, Inc.
CUNA Mutual Group
Dain Bosworth Inc.
DeKalb Genetics Corp.
Deloitte & Touche
Dow Chemical Co.
Employers Mutual Casualty Co.
Extendicare Health Services
Exxon Mobil Corp.
Firstar Bank Milwaukee NA
FMC Corp.
Fortis, Inc.
General Electric Co.
Grace & Co. (W.R.)
Green Bay Packaging
Harley-Davidson Co.
Hoffmann-La Roche Inc.
Honeywell International Inc.
Huffy Corp.
Intel Corp.
Johnson & Son (S.C.)
Kimberly-Clark Corp.
Kroger Co.
Ladish Co., Inc.
Land O'Lakes, Inc.
Lee Enterprises
Louisiana-Pacific Corp.
Lubrizol Corp. (The)
Madison Gas & Electric Co.
Marcus Corp.
Marshall & Ilsley Corp.
Menasha Corp.
Mitsubishi Electric America
MTD Products Inc.
National Presto Industries, Inc.
Oshkosh B'Gosh, Inc.
Reinhart Institutional Foods
Schering-Plough Corp.
Sentry Insurance, A Mutual Co.
Simplot Co. (J.R.)
Temple-Inland Inc.
True North Communications, Inc.
Trustmark Insurance Co.
Union Camp Corp.
United Wisconsin Services
Wal-Mart Stores, Inc.
Wisconsin Energy Corp.
Wisconsin Power & Light Co.
Wisconsin Public Service Corp.
Woodward Governor Co.

MARINETTE
Giddings & Lewis
Wisconsin Public Service Corp.

MARSHFIELD
First Financial Bank
Land O'Lakes, Inc.
Phillips Petroleum Co.
Sentry Insurance, A Mutual Co.
Weyerhaeuser Co.

MENASHA
Banta Corp.
Chesapeake Corp.
Consolidated Papers, Inc.
Deere & Co.
Menasha Corp.
Oshkosh B'Gosh, Inc.
Wisconsin Energy Corp.
Wisconsin Public Service Corp.

MENOMONEE FALLS
Firstar Bank Milwaukee NA

MENOMONIE
National Presto Industries, Inc.
WICOR, Inc.

MEQUON
Badger Meter, Inc.
Harnischfeger Industries
Ladish Co., Inc.
Marcus Corp.

MERRIMAC
Ben & Jerry's Homemade Inc.

MIDDLETON
CUNA Mutual Group

MILWAUKEE
Aetna, Inc.
Alcon Laboratories, Inc.
American Retail Group
Ameritech Wisconsin
Badger Meter, Inc.
Baird & Co. (Robert W.)
Banta Corp.
Bemis Co., Inc.
Bemis Manufacturing Co.
Briggs & Stratton Corp.
Brunswick Corp.
Bucyrus-Erie Co.
Charter Manufacturing Co.
Commercial Intertech Corp.
Consolidated Papers, Inc.
Cooper Industries, Inc.
CUNA Mutual Group
Danis Companies
Deluxe Corp.
Donaldson Co., Inc.
Eaton Corp.
Employers Mutual Casualty Co.
Extendicare Health Services
First Financial Bank
Firstar Bank Milwaukee NA
Ford Motor Co.
Fortis, Inc.
Fortis Insurance Co.
Giddings & Lewis
Grace & Co. (W.R.)
Grede Foundries
Hamilton Sundstrand Corp.
Harley-Davidson Co.
Harnischfeger Industries
Huffy Corp.
Inland Container Corp.
Johnson Controls Inc.
Johnson & Son (S.C.)
Kennametal, Inc.
Kimberly-Clark Corp.
Ladish Co., Inc.
Land O'Lakes, Inc.
Louisiana-Pacific Corp.
Madison Gas & Electric Co.
Marcus Corp.
Marshall Field's
Marshall & Ilsley Corp.
Menasha Corp.
Metropolitan Life Insurance Co.
National Presto Industries, Inc.
Nationwide Insurance Co.
Oshkosh B'Gosh, Inc.
Outboard Marine Corp.
PerkinElmer, Inc.
Pieper Power Electric Co.
Ralph's Grocery Co.
Reinhart Institutional Foods
Sentry Insurance, A Mutual Co.
Square D Co.
Standard Products Co.
United Parcel Service of America Inc.
U.S. Bancorp
U.S. Bancorp Piper Jaffray
United Wisconsin Services
Universal Foods Corp.
Waste Management Inc.
WICOR, Inc.
Wisconsin Energy Corp.
Wisconsin Power & Light Co.
Wisconsin Public Service Corp.

MILWAUKKE
Charter Manufacturing Co.

NEENAH
Baird & Co. (Robert W.)
Banta Corp.
Bemis Co., Inc.
Chesapeake Corp.
Kimberly-Clark Corp.
Menasha Corp.
Oshkosh B'Gosh, Inc.

NEW LONDON
Banta Corp.
Consolidated Papers, Inc.
Kimberly-Clark Corp.
Menasha Corp.
Oshkosh B'Gosh, Inc.
Sentry Insurance, A Mutual Co.

NEW RICHMOND
Demoulas Supermarkets Inc.

NEWBURG
Badger Meter, Inc.

OAK CREEK
PPG Industries, Inc.

OCONTO
Wisconsin Public Service Corp.

OGEMA
Consolidated Papers, Inc.

ONALASKA
Reinhart Institutional Foods

OSH KOSH
Chesapeake Corp.
Sentry Insurance, A Mutual Co.

OSHKOSH
Banta Corp.
Bemis Co., Inc.
Bemis Manufacturing Co.
Briggs & Stratton Corp.
Brunswick Corp.
Fortis, Inc.
Giddings & Lewis
Menasha Corp.
Oshkosh B'Gosh, Inc.
Wisconsin Power & Light Co.

PEPIN
Red Wing Shoe Co. Inc.

PEWAUKEE
International Multifoods Corp.
National Presto Industries, Inc.

PLATTEVILLE
Deere & Co.
National Presto Industries, Inc.
Sentry Insurance, A Mutual Co.
Wisconsin Power & Light Co.

PLYMOUTH
Borden, Inc.

PRESQUE ISLE
Consolidated Papers, Inc.

RACINE
AMETEK, Inc.
Emerson Electric Co.
Johnson Controls Inc.
Johnson & Son (S.C.)
Marshall & Ilsley Corp.
Menasha Corp.
Wisconsin Energy Corp.

REEDSBURG
Grede Foundries

RHINELANDER
Wisconsin Public Service Corp.

RICE LAKE
Quanex Corp.
Reinhart Institutional Foods

RIPON
Consolidated Papers, Inc.
Employers Mutual Casualty Co.
Fortis, Inc.
Kemper National Insurance Companies
Ladish Co., Inc.
Marcus Corp.
Phillips Petroleum Co.
Wisconsin Power & Light Co.

ROSHELT
Sentry Insurance, A Mutual Co.

ROSHOLD
Wisconsin Public Service Corp.

SAUKVILLE
Charter Manufacturing Co.

SHAWAMO
Kimball International, Inc.

SHEBOYGAN
Banta Corp.
Bemis Manufacturing Co.
Consolidated Papers, Inc.
Grede Foundries
Menasha Corp.
Wisconsin Power & Light Co.

SHEBOYGAN FALLS
Bemis Manufacturing Co.

SHEBOYGAR
Chesapeake Corp.

SHELL LAKE
Reinhart Institutional Foods

SPENCER
Land O'Lakes, Inc.

SPRING GREEN
Briggs & Stratton Corp.
Consolidated Papers, Inc.
CUNA Mutual Group
Sentry Insurance, A Mutual Co.
Wisconsin Power & Light Co.

ST. FRANCIS
Briggs & Stratton Corp.

ST. PT.
Wisconsin Public Service Corp.

STEVENS POINT
AMETEK, Inc.
Champion International Corp.
Consolidated Papers, Inc.
Donaldson Co., Inc.
First Financial Bank
Menasha Corp.
National Presto Industries, Inc.
Potlatch Corp.
Sentry Insurance, A Mutual Co.
United Wisconsin Services
Weyerhaeuser Co.

STOUGHTON
Nabisco Group Holdings

STOUT
Banta Corp.
Minnesota Mining & Manufacturing Co.

STURG BAY
Wisconsin Public Service Corp.

THIENSVILLE
Charter Manufacturing Co.

TOMAH
Wisconsin Power & Light Co.

WASHBURN
Dain Bosworth Inc.

WAUKEGAN
Outboard Marine Corp.

WAUKESHA
Ben & Jerry's Homemade Inc.
Consolidated Papers, Inc.
Cooper Industries, Inc.
First Financial Bank
Huffy Corp.
Johnson & Son (S.C.)
Kemper National Insurance Companies
Marcus Corp.
Pieper Power Electric Co.
Wisconsin Energy Corp.
Wisconsin Public Service Corp.

WAUSAU
Kimberly-Clark Corp.
Nationwide Insurance Co.
Wisconsin Public Service Corp.

WAUWATOSA
Fortis Insurance Co.
Harley-Davidson Co.
Harnischfeger Industries
Ladish Co., Inc.
Loews Corp.
Oshkosh B'Gosh, Inc.
Whitman Corp.

WEST ALLIS
Fortis Insurance Co.

WESTBY
Andersen Corp.

WHITEWATER
Kemper National Insurance Companies
Sentry Insurance, A Mutual Co.
State Farm Mutual Automobile Insurance Co.
Universal Foods Corp.

WILLIAMS BAY
Globe Corp.

WISCONSIN RAPIDS
Consolidated Papers, Inc.
Georgia-Pacific Corp.
Marshall & Ilsley Corp.
Sentry Insurance, A Mutual Co.

Wyoming

BASIN
Walter Industries Inc.

CASPER
PacifiCorp
True Oil Co.

CHEYENNE
Jeld-wen, Inc.
True Oil Co.
Union Pacific Corp.

CODY
Halliburton Co.
Kinder Morgn

DOUGLAS
True Oil Co.

EVANSTON
Union Pacific Corp.

GREEN RIVER
FMC Corp.

JACKSON
Williams

LANDER
Patagonia Inc.

LARAMIE
FMC Corp.
Hensel Phelps Construction Co.
Kinder Morgn
PacifiCorp
True Oil Co.

RAWLINGS
Union Pacific Corp.

ROCK SPRINGS
FMC Corp.

SYRACUSE
Simplot Co. (J.R.)

THERMOPOLIS
True Oil Co.

TORRINGTON
True Oil Co.

International

Argentina

CASILDA
Bristol-Myers Squibb Co.

Australia

Newman's Own Inc.

ADELAIDE
Bristol-Myers Squibb Co.

Austria

STYRIA PROVINCE
Medtronic, Inc.

VIENNA
Baxter International Inc.

Bahamas

NASSAU
Fisher Scientific

Brazil

Cabot Corp.
Goldman Sachs Group

JAGUARINHO
Motorola Inc.

JAGUARINNA
Motorola Inc.

RIO DE JANEIRO
American Express Co.

SAO PAOLO
American Express Co.

SAO PAULO
Motorola Inc.

Bulgaria

Archer-Daniels-Midland Co.

Botswana

GABORONE
Owens Corning

Canada

Cabot Corp.
Dow Chemical Co.
Manulife Financial
Metropolitan Life Insurance Co.

LABRADOR CITY
Cleveland-Cliffs, Inc.

SEPT-ILES
Cleveland-Cliffs, Inc.

VANCOUVER
Goldman Sachs Group

WATERLOO
Cleveland-Cliffs, Inc.

BANFF
American Express Co.
Goldman Sachs Group

CALGARY
Crane Co.
Manulife Financial

COQUITLAM
Patagonia Inc.

KITAMAAT VILLAGE
Patagonia Inc.

NANAIMO
Patagonia Inc.

VANCOUVER
Chevron Corp.
Goldman Sachs Group
Weyerhaeuser Co.

WHITE ROCK
Patagonia Inc.

LAC DU BONNET
Cabot Corp.

WINNIPEG
Manulife Financial
Kimball International, Inc.
Manulife Financial
Wrigley Co. (Wm. Jr.)

GLOUCESTER
Hewlett-Packard Co.

GUELPH
Owens Corning
Xerox Corp.

KINGSTON
Xerox Corp.

KITCHENER
Manulife Financial

LONDON
Goldman Sachs Group

OSHAWA
Manulife Financial

OTTAWA
American Express Co.
Levi Strauss & Co.
Manulife Financial
Medtronic, Inc.
Owens Corning

RICHMOND HILL
Crane Co.

THUNDER BAY
Manulife Financial

TORONTO
AlliedSignal Inc.
American Express Co.
Crane Co.
Equifax Inc.
Goldman Sachs Group
Manulife Financial
Patagonia Inc.
SIT Investment Associates, Inc.
Toshiba America Inc.
Xerox Corp.

VANCOUVER
Manulife Financial

WATERLOO
Manulife Financial

WINDSOR
Milacron, Inc.

MONTREAL
Carter-Wallace, Inc.
Crane Co.
Manulife Financial
Metropolitan Life Insurance Co.
TENNANT Co.

People's Republic of China

Sumitomo Bank

BANGKOK
Sumitomo Bank

BEIJING
Bristol-Myers Squibb Co.
Motorola Inc.
Sumitomo Bank

SHANGHAI
Aetna, Inc.
ISE America

ZHONGSHAN
Sumitomo Bank

Colombia

BOGOTA
Motorola Inc.

Costa Rica

Rutledge Hill Press

SAN JUAN
Abbott Laboratories

Czech Republic

Cabot Corp.
Motorola Inc.

Denmark

COPENHAGEN
Bristol-Myers Squibb Co.

Dominican Republic

HAINA
Baxter International Inc.

Ecuador

QUITO
American Express Co.

Egypt

CAIRO
Bechtel Group, Inc.
Morrison Knudsen Corp.

England

American Express Co.

BRISTOL
American Express Co.

CAMBRIDGE
Little, Inc. (Arthur D.)

LETCHWORTH
Motorola Inc.

LONDON
Bristol-Myers Squibb Co.
Goldman Sachs Group
Medtronic, Inc.

OXFORD
American Standard Inc.

PRINCES RISBOROUGH
American Express Co.

ST. HELENS
Owens Corning

WEST LOTHIAN
Sun Microsystems Inc.

France

Aon Corp.

BESANCON
Patagonia Inc.

CEDEX
Little, Inc. (Arthur D.)

FONTAINEBLEAU
Goldman Sachs Group

LE PUY EN VELAY
Patagonia Inc.

NICE
Bristol-Myers Squibb Co.

PARIS
American Express Co.
Bristol-Myers Squibb Co.
International Flavors & Fragrances Inc.
Levi Strauss & Co.
Zilkha & Sons

Germany

HEIDELBERG
Bristol-Myers Squibb Co.

Hong Kong

American Express Co.
Bechtel Group, Inc.

OCEAN PARK
American Express Co.

QUARRY BAY
American Express Co.

SHATIN
Bristol-Myers Squibb Co.

Honduras

HOLLANO
Sun Microsystems Inc.

SULA
Oshkosh B'Gosh, Inc.

TEGUCIGALPA
Fuller Co. (H.B.)

ZACAPA
Domino's Pizza Inc.

Hungary

BUDAPEST
American Express Co.

India

Cabot Corp.
Medtronic, Inc.

Ireland

CASTLEBAR
Baxter International Inc.

DUBLIN
American Express Co.

KILDARE
Xerox Corp.

Israel

Borman's Inc.
Century 21
Zilkha & Sons

EFRAT
Century 21

RA'ANANA
Giant Eagle Inc.

REHOVOT
Bristol-Myers Squibb Co.

TIBERIAS
Century 21

Italy

BOLOGNA
Bristol-Myers Squibb Co.

FLORENCE
Medtronic, Inc.

MILANO
Bristol-Myers Squibb Co.

ROME
New York Times Co.

Japan

Goldman Sachs Group

NAGOYA
Bristol-Myers Squibb Co.

OSAKA
Medtronic, Inc.

TOKYO
American Express Co.
Bristol-Myers Squibb Co.
Levi Strauss & Co.
Medtronic, Inc.
Texas Instruments Inc.

TOYAMA
ISE America

YAMATO-MACHI
Xerox Corp.

Lebanon

BEIRUT
Bechtel Group, Inc.

Mexico

Toshiba America Inc.

CHIHUAHUA
Baxter International Inc.

CUAUHTEMOC
Baxter International Inc.

CUERNAVACA
Baxter International Inc.

COL DEL VALLE
American Express Co.

MEXICO CITY
American Express Co.

NAUCALPAN
Motorola Inc.

CUERNAVACA
Baxter International Inc.

Mozambique

Coca-Cola Co.

Malaysia

BALIK PULAU
Baxter International Inc.

KUALA LUMPUR
AT&T Corp.
Motorola Inc.

Nigeria

Chevron Corp.

New Zealand

Newman's Own Inc.

Papua New Guinea

PORT MORESBY
Chevron Corp.

Puerto Rico

GUAYAMA
Baxter International Inc.

GUAYNABO
Baxter International Inc.

HATO RAY
Bristol-Myers Squibb Co.

JAYUYA
Baxter International Inc.

MAYAGUEZ
Baxter International Inc.

RIO PIEDRAS
Baxter International Inc.

SAN JUAN
Hewlett-Packard Co.

TRUJILLO ALTO
Baxter International Inc.

Romania

ORADEA
Rutledge Hill Press

Republic of South Africa

Rutledge Hill Press

DURBAN
Nalco Chemical Co.

JOHANNESBURG
Cummins Engine Co., Inc.
Medtronic, Inc.
Nalco Chemical Co.

RONDEBOSCH
Merck & Co.

Scotland

Consolidated Electrical Distributors

ARMADALE
Sun Microsystems Inc.

EDINBURGH
Consolidated Electrical Distributors

Singapore

Bechtel Group, Inc.

Spain

Bristol-Myers Squibb Co.

BARCELONA
Xerox Corp.

SEVILLE
Xerox Corp.

Sri Lanka

COLOMBO
American Express Co.

Sweden

LUND
Bristol-Myers Squibb Co.

STOCKHOLM
Bristol-Myers Squibb Co.

Switzerland

GENEVA
Medtronic, Inc.

LAUSANNE
Bristol-Myers Squibb Co.

POSTFACH
Wachovia Bank of North Carolina NA

Taiwan

Manulife Financial

FUNDERS BY RECIPIENT TYPE

Arranges funders by the types of nonprofit programs and organizations they currently support or have a history of funding.

Arts & Humanities

ART HISTORY

Fidelity Investments
Masco Corp.

ARTS APPRECIATION

Albertson's Inc.
Ameritech Indiana
Atlantic Investment Co.
Bank of America
Bank of New York Co., Inc.
Bemis Co., Inc.
Binney & Smith Inc.
Blair & Co. (William)
Block, Inc. (H&R)
Cabot Corp.
Central Soya Co.
Chase Manhattan Bank, NA
Chicago Title Corp.
Citibank Corp.
Clorox Co.
Colonial Life & Accident Insurance Co.
Cummins Engine Co., Inc.
Dayton Hudson
Delta Air Lines, Inc.
Deluxe Corp.
Deposit Guaranty National Bank
Dixie Group, Inc. (The)
du Pont de Nemours & Co. (E.I.)
Emerson Electric Co.
First Union National Bank, NA
Franklin Mint (The)
Freeport-McMoRan Inc.
Frost National Bank
Hancock Financial Services (John)
Hunt Manufacturing Co.
ISE America
Journal-Gazette Co.
Kimball International, Inc.
Kimberly-Clark Corp.
Kingsbury Corp.
Leviton Manufacturing Co. Inc.
Mallinckrodt Chemical, Inc.
McKesson-HBOC Corp.
National Computer Systems, Inc.
Northern Indiana Public Service Co.
Northwest Natural Gas Co.
Norton Co.
Providence Journal-Bulletin Co.
Pulitzer Publishing Co.
Royal & SunAlliance USA, Inc.
Sara Lee Hosiery, Inc.
SBC Communications Inc.
Seaway Food Town, Inc.
Shaw's Supermarkets, Inc.
Slant/Fin Corp.
Storage Technology Corp.
SunTrust Bank Atlanta
Textron Inc.
Toyota Motor Sales U.S.A., Inc.
United Technologies Corp.
Valero Energy Corp.
Varian Medical Systems, Inc.
Wyman-Gordon Co.

ARTS ASSOCIATIONS & COUNCILS

ABC
Aetna, Inc.
AGL Resources Inc.
Agrilink Foods, Inc.
AK Steel Corp.
Alabama Power Co.
Alcoa Inc.
Alcon Laboratories, Inc.
AlliedSignal Inc.
Allmerica Financial Corp.
AMCORE Bank Rockford
Ameren Corp.
American Fidelity Corp.
American General Finance
American United Life Insurance Co.
Ameritas Life Insurance Corp.
Ameritech Corp.
Ameritech Indiana
Ameritech Michigan
Ameritech Wisconsin
AmerUS Group
Amgen, Inc.
AMP Inc.
AMR Corp.
Amsted Industries Inc.
Andersons Inc.
Anheuser-Busch Companies, Inc.
Aon Corp.
APL Ltd.
Appleton Papers Inc.
Archer-Daniels-Midland Co.
Aristech Chemical Corp.
Arizona Public Service Co.
Arvin Industries, Inc.
Ashland, Inc.
AT&T Corp.
Auburn Foundry
Avon Products, Inc.
Bandag, Inc.
Banfi Vintners
Bank of America
Bank of New York Co., Inc.
Bank One, Texas-Houston Office
BankAtlantic Bancorp
BankBoston Corp.
Barclays Capital
Bardes Corp.
Barnes Group Inc.
Bassett Furniture Industries
Battelle Memorial Institute
Bayer Corp.
Belk Stores Services Inc.
Bell Atlantic Corp.
Bemis Co., Inc.
Bemis Manufacturing Co.
Ben & Jerry's Homemade Inc.
Bernstein & Co., Inc. (Sanford C.)
Bestfoods
Bethlehem Steel Corp.
Binney & Smith Inc.
Binswanger Companies
Block, Inc. (H&R)
Blount International, Inc.
Blue Bell, Inc.
Blue Cross & Blue Shield of Alabama
Borden, Inc.
Borman's Inc.
Boston Globe (The)
Bowater Inc.
Bridgestone/Firestone, Inc.
Bristol-Myers Squibb Co.
Brown Shoe Co., Inc.
Brown & Williamson Tobacco Corp.
Browning-Ferris Industries Inc.
Bucyrus-Erie Co.
Burlington Industries, Inc.
Burlington Resources, Inc.
Burress (J.W.)
Cabot Corp.
Calvin Klein
Carillon Importers, Ltd.
Carnival Corp.
Carolina Power & Light Co.
Carpenter Technology Corp.
Carris Reels
CCB Financial Corp.
Central Maine Power Co.
Central Soya Co.
CertainTeed Corp.
Cessna Aircraft Co.
Chase Bank of Texas
Chase Manhattan Bank, NA
Chesapeake Corp.
Chevron Corp.
CIGNA Corp.
Cinergy Corp.
Circuit City Stores, Inc.
Citibank Corp.
Citigroup
Citizens Bank-Flint
CLARCOR Inc.
Cleveland-Cliffs, Inc.
Clorox Co.
Collins & Aikman Corp.
Colonial Life & Accident Insurance Co.
Commerce Bancshares, Inc.
Commercial Intertech Corp.
Compass Bank
ConAgra, Inc.
Cone Mills Corp.
Consolidated Electrical Distributors
Consolidated Natural Gas Co.
Consolidated Papers, Inc.
Consumers Energy Co.
Conwood Co. LP
Cooper Industries, Inc.
Cooper Tire & Rubber Co.
Coors Brewing Co.
Corning Inc.
Country Curtains, Inc.
Cox Enterprises Inc.
Crane Co.
Crane & Co., Inc.
Credit Suisse First Boston
Crestar Finance Corp.
Cummings Properties Management
Cummins Engine Co., Inc.
CUNA Mutual Group
Daily News
DaimlerChrysler Corp.
Dain Bosworth Inc.
Dana Corp.
Danis Companies
Dayton Hudson
Dayton Power and Light Co.
Deluxe Corp.
Demoulas Supermarkets Inc.
Deposit Guaranty National Bank
Detroit Edison Co.
Deutsch Co.
Dexter Corp.
Dial Corp.
Disney Co. (Walt)
Dixie Group, Inc. (The)
Dominion Resources, Inc.
Dow Corning Corp.
du Pont de Nemours & Co. (E.I.)
Duchossois Industries Inc.
Duke Energy
Dun & Bradstreet Corp.
Duriron Co., Inc.
Eastman Kodak Co.
Eaton Corp.
Ecolab Inc.
Edison International
Emerson Electric Co.
Employers Mutual Casualty Co.
Ensign-Bickford Industries
Entergy Corp.
Enterprise Rent-A-Car Co.
Equifax Inc.
Erving Industries
Ethyl Corp.
Evening Post Publishing Co.
Extendicare Health Services
Exxon Mobil Corp.
Federal-Mogul Corp.
FedEx Corp.
Fidelity Investments
Fifth Third Bancorp
First Hawaiian, Inc.
First Tennessee National Corp.
First Union Corp.
First Union National Bank, NA
First Union Securities, Inc.
Fisher Brothers Cleaning Services
Fisher Scientific
FleetBoston Financial Corp.
Florida Power Corp.
Florida Rock Industries
Fluor Corp.
Forbes Inc.
Ford Meter Box Co.
Ford Motor Co.
Forest City Enterprises, Inc.
Fort James Corp.
Fort Worth Star-Telegram Inc.
Fortis Insurance Co.
Franklin Electric Co.
Franklin Mint (The)
Freeport-McMoRan Inc.
Frost National Bank
Furniture Brands International, Inc.
Gannett Co., Inc.
Gap, Inc.
GATX Corp.
GEICO Corp.
General Dynamics Corp.
General Electric Co.
General Mills, Inc.
General Motors Corp.
Georgia-Pacific Corp.
Georgia Power Co.
Giant Eagle Inc.
Giddings & Lewis
Glaxo Wellcome Inc.
Glickenhaus & Co.
Globe Corp.
Goodrich Aerospace - Aerostructures Group (B.F.)
Gosiger, Inc.
Grede Foundries
GTE Corp.
Gucci America Inc.
Guess?
Gulf Power Co.
Hallmark Cards Inc.
Hamilton Sundstrand Corp.
Hancock Financial Services (John)
Hannaford Brothers Co.
Harcourt General, Inc.
Harnischfeger Industries
Harris Corp.
Harris Trust & Savings Bank
Harsco Corp.
Hartford (The)
Hartford Steam Boiler Inspection & Insurance Co.
Heinz Co. (H.J.)
Hershey Foods Corp.
Hewlett-Packard Co.
HON Industries Inc.
Honeywell International Inc.
Hubbard Broadcasting, Inc.
Huffy Corp.
Humana, Inc.
Hunt Manufacturing Co.
Huntington Bancshares Inc.
IKON Office Solutions, Inc.
Illinois Tool Works, Inc.
Inland Container Corp.
Inman Mills
International Business Machines Corp.
International Paper Co.
Invacare Corp.
ISE America
Jeld-wen, Inc.
Johnson Controls Inc.
Johnson & Son (S.C.)
Jones & Co. (Edward D.)
Jostens, Inc.
Journal-Gazette Co.
JSJ Corp.
Kellogg Co.
Kellwood Co.
Kerr-McGee Corp.
Kiewit Sons' Inc. (Peter)
Kimberly-Clark Corp.
Kinder Morgn
Kingsbury Corp.

Koch Enterprises, Inc.
Koch Industries, Inc.
Kohler Co.
Kroger Co.
La-Z-Boy Inc.
Laclede Gas Co.
Lancaster Lens, Inc.
Lance, Inc.
Land O'Lakes, Inc.
Landmark Communications Inc.
Leigh Fibers, Inc.
Levi Strauss & Co.
Leviton Manufacturing Co. Inc.
LG&E Energy Corp.
Lilly & Co. (Eli)
Lincoln Financial Group
Lipton Co.
Little, Inc. (Arthur D.)
Litton Industries, Inc.
Liz Claiborne, Inc.
Loews Corp.
Lotus Development Corp.
Louisiana Land & Exploration Co.
LTV Corp.
Lubrizol Corp. (The)
Macy's East Inc.
Madison Gas & Electric Co.
Maritz Inc.
Marriott International Inc.
Marshall Field's
Marshall & Ilsley Corp.
Masco Corp.
May Department Stores Co.
MBIA Inc.
McClatchy Co.
McDonald & Co. Securities, Inc.
McWane Inc.
Mead Corp.
Mellon Financial Corp.
Memphis Light Gas & Water Division
Mercantile Bank NA
Mervyn's California
Metropolitan Life Insurance Co.
Michigan Consolidated Gas Co.
Microsoft Corp.
Mid-America Bank of Louisville
Milliken & Co.
Millipore Corp.
Mitsubishi Electric America
Monarch Machine Tool Co.
Monsanto Co.
Morgan & Co. Inc. (J.P.)
Motorola Inc.
Nalco Chemical Co.
National Bank of Commerce Trust & Savings
National City Corp.
National Fuel Gas Distribution Corp.
Nationwide Insurance Co.
NEBCO Evans
New Century Energies
New England Bio Labs
New England Financial
New York Life Insurance Co.
New York Mercantile Exchange
New York Stock Exchange, Inc.
Niagara Mohawk Holdings Inc.
Nike, Inc.
Norfolk Southern Corp.
Northern Indiana Public Service Co.
Northwest Bank Nebraska, NA
Northwest Natural Gas Co.
Norton Co.
Norwest Corp.
Occidental Oil and Gas
OG&E Electric Services
Old Kent Bank
Old National Bank Evansville
Olin Corp.
Oshkosh B'Gosh, Inc.
Overseas Shipholding Group Inc.
Owens Corning
PACCAR Inc.
Pacific Mutual Life Insurance Co.
PacifiCorp
Paine Webber
Pella Corp.
PEMCO Corp.
Penney Co., Inc. (J.C.)
Pennzoil-Quaker State Co.
Peoples Energy Corp.
PepsiCo, Inc.
PerkinElmer, Inc.
Pfizer Inc.
Pharmacia & Upjohn, Inc.
Phelps Dodge Corp.
Philip Morris Companies Inc.
Phillips Petroleum Co.
Physicians Mutual Insurance Co.
Pieper Power Electric Co.
Pittway Corp.
PNC Financial Services Group
Polaroid Corp.
Potomac Electric Power Co.
PPG Industries, Inc.
Premier Dental Products Co.
Premier Industrial Corp.
Procter & Gamble Co.
Providence Journal-Bulletin Co.
Provident Companies, Inc.
Prudential Insurance Co. of America
Publix Supermarkets
Pulitzer Publishing Co.
Quaker Chemical Corp.
Ralston Purina Co.
Rayonier Inc.
Red Wing Shoe Co. Inc.
Reebok International Ltd.
Regis Corp.
Reilly Industries, Inc.
Reily & Co., Inc. (William B.)
Reinhart Institutional Foods
Reliant Energy Inc.
Reynolds Metals Co.
Reynolds & Reynolds Co.
Reynolds Tobacco (R.J.)
Rich Products Corp.
Rockwell International Corp.
Rouse Co.
Royal & SunAlliance USA, Inc.
Rubbermaid Inc.
Ryder System, Inc.
Safeguard Scientifics
Saint Paul Companies Inc.
S&T Bancorp
Sara Lee Corp.
Sara Lee Hosiery, Inc.
SBC Communications Inc.
Schering-Plough Corp.
Schloss & Co. (Marcus)
Schwab & Co., Inc. (Charles)
Schwebel Baking Co.
Seagram & Sons, Inc. (Joseph E.)
Searle & Co. (G.D.)
Seaway Food Town, Inc.
Security Benefit Life Insurance Co.
Security Life of Denver Insurance Co.
Sentry Insurance, A Mutual Co.
S.G. Cowen
Shaw's Supermarkets, Inc.
Sierra Pacific Industries
Sierra Pacific Resources
Simpson Investment Co.
Slant/Fin Corp.
SmithKline Beecham Corp.
Smurfit-Stone Container Corp.
Sonoco Products Co.
Sony Electronics
Southern New England Telephone Co.
Southwest Gas Corp.
Springs Industries, Inc.
Sprint Corp.
Square D Co.
Standard Register Co.
Stanley Works (The)
Starwood Hotels & Resorts Worldwide, Inc.
State Farm Mutual Automobile Insurance Co.
State Street Bank & Trust Co.
Steelcase Inc.
Strear Farms Co.
Stride Rite Corp.
Stupp Brothers Bridge & Iron Co.
Sunoco Inc.
SunTrust Bank Atlanta
Susquehanna-Pfaltzgraff Co.
Sverdrup Corp.
Synovus Financial Corp.
TCF National Bank Minnesota
Tektronix, Inc.
Telcordia Technologies
Temple-Inland Inc.
Tenneco Automotive
Tesoro Hawaii
Texaco Inc.
Texas Gas Transmission Corp.
Textron Inc.
Thomasville Furniture Industries Inc.
Times Mirror Co.
Timken Co. (The)
Titan Industrial Corp.
TJX Companies, Inc.
TMC Investment Co.
Toledo Blade Co.
Tomkins Industries, Inc.
Toro Co.
Toyota Motor Sales U.S.A., Inc.
Trace International Holdings, Inc.
Transamerica Corp.
True North Communications, Inc.
TRW Inc.
Tyson Foods Inc.
Ukrop's Super Markets
Union Camp Corp.
Union Pacific Corp.
United Airlines Inc.
United Distillers & Vintners North America
United Dominion Industries, Ltd.
United Parcel Service of America Inc.
United States Sugar Corp.
United States Trust Co. of New York
United Wisconsin Services
Universal Leaf Tobacco Co., Inc.
Universal Studios
UnumProvident
US Bank, Washington
US West, Inc.
USG Corp.
USX Corp.
Valmont Industries, Inc.
Vodafone AirTouch Plc
Vulcan Materials Co.
Wachovia Bank of North Carolina NA
Waldbaum's Supermarkets, Inc.
Warner-Lambert Co.
Washington Mutual, Inc.
Washington Trust Bank
Waste Management Inc.
Western & Southern Life Insurance Co.
Weyerhaeuser Co.
Whirlpool Corp.
Wilbur-Ellis Co. & Connell Brothers Co.
Williams
Wiremold Co.
Wisconsin Energy Corp.
Witco Corp.
Wolverine World Wide
Xerox Corp.
Yellow Corp.
York Federal Savings & Loan Association
Young & Rubicam

ARTS CENTERS

ABC
Aetna, Inc.
AGL Resources Inc.
Agrilink Foods, Inc.
AK Steel Corp.
Alabama Power Co.
Albertson's Inc.
Alcoa Inc.
Alexander & Baldwin, Inc.
Allegheny Technologies Inc.
AlliedSignal Inc.
Ameren Corp.
American Express Co.
American United Life Insurance Co.
Ameritech Indiana
Ameritech Michigan
Ameritech Wisconsin
AmerUS Group
AMETEK, Inc.
AMP Inc.
AMR Corp.
Amsted Industries Inc.
Andersen Corp.
Andersons Inc.
Anheuser-Busch Companies, Inc.
Aon Corp.
Archer-Daniels-Midland Co.
Aristech Chemical Corp.
Arizona Public Service Co.
Arvin Industries, Inc.
Ashland, Inc.
AT&T Corp.
Atlantic Investment Co.
Atlantic Richfield Co.
Avon Products, Inc.
Banfi Vintners
Bank of America
Bank of New York Co., Inc.
Bank One Corp.
Banta Corp.
Barclays Capital
Barden Corp.
Barnes Group Inc.
Barry Corp. (R.G.)
Bayer Corp.
Belk-Simpson Department Stores
Bemis Co., Inc.
Bemis Manufacturing Co.
Bernstein & Co., Inc. (Sanford C.)
Bestfoods
Bethlehem Steel Corp.
BFGoodrich Co.
Binney & Smith Inc.
Blair & Co. (William)
Block, Inc. (H&R)
Blount International, Inc.
Blue Bell, Inc.
Blue Cross & Blue Shield of Iowa
Boeing Co.
Borden, Inc.
Borman's Inc.
Bowater Inc.
BP Amoco Corp.
Bradford & Co. (J.C.)
Bristol-Myers Squibb Co.
Burnett Co. (Leo)
Cabot Corp.
Calvin Klein
Campbell Soup Co.
Cargill Inc.
Carillon Importers, Ltd.
Carlson Companies, Inc.
Carolina Power & Light Co.
Carrier Corp.
Carris Reels
Carter-Wallace, Inc.
Caterpillar Inc.
Central National-Gottesman
Cessna Aircraft Co.
Chase Bank of Texas
Chase Manhattan Bank, NA
Chevron Corp.
Cincinnati Bell Inc.
Cinergy Corp.
Citibank Corp.
Citigroup
Citizens Bank-Flint
Citizens Financial Group, Inc.
Clorox Co.
Collins & Aikman Corp.
Colonial Life & Accident Insurance Co.
Commerce Bancshares, Inc.
Consolidated Natural Gas Co.
Contran Corp.
Cook Inlet Region
Coors Brewing Co.
Copley Press, Inc.
Country Curtains, Inc.
Cox Enterprises Inc.
Crane Co.
Crane & Co., Inc.
Credit Suisse First Boston
Crestar Finance Corp.
CSR Rinker Materials Corp.
CUNA Mutual Group
Daily News
DaimlerChrysler Corp.
Dain Bosworth Inc.
Dana Corp.

Danis Companies
Dayton Hudson
Deere & Co.
Delta Air Lines, Inc.
Deluxe Corp.
Demoulas Supermarkets Inc.
Deposit Guaranty National Bank
Detroit Edison Co.
Deutsch Co.
Dial Corp.
Disney Co. (Walt)
Dominion Resources, Inc.
Donaldson Co., Inc.
Dow Chemical Co.
Dow Corning Corp.
du Pont de Nemours & Co. (E.I.)
Duke Energy
Dun & Bradstreet Corp.
Dynamet, Inc.
Eastern Bank
Eaton Corp.
Edison International
El Paso Energy Co.
Elf Atochem North America, Inc.
Emerson Electric Co.
Employers Mutual Casualty Co.
Ensign-Bickford Industries
Entergy Corp.
Enterprise Rent-A-Car Co.
Equifax Inc.
Erb Lumber Co.
Ethyl Corp.
Evening Post Publishing Co.
Exxon Mobil Corp.
Federal-Mogul Corp.
Federated Department Stores, Inc.
Federated Mutual Insurance Co.
FedEx Corp.
Fidelity Investments
Fifth Third Bancorp
Fireman's Fund Insurance Co.
First Hawaiian, Inc.
First Maryland Bancorp
First Source Corp.
First Tennessee National Corp.
First Union Corp.
First Union National Bank, NA
First Union Securities, Inc.
Firstar Bank Milwaukee NA
Fisher Brothers Cleaning Services
Fisher Scientific
FleetBoston Financial Corp.
Florida Power Corp.
Florida Power & Light Co.
Fluor Corp.
Forbes Inc.
Ford Motor Co.
Fort James Corp.
Fortune Brands, Inc.
Franklin Electric Co.
Franklin Mint (The)
Freeport-McMoRan Inc.
Fuller Co. (H.B.)
Furniture Brands International, Inc.
Gap, Inc.
GenAmerica Corp.
General Atlantic Partners II LP
General Electric Co.
General Mills, Inc.
General Motors Corp.
Georgia-Pacific Corp.
Georgia Power Co.
Giant Eagle Inc.
Giant Food Inc.
Giddings & Lewis
Gillette Co.
Glaxo Wellcome Inc.
Glickenhaus & Co.
Goldman Sachs Group
Green Bay Packaging
GTE Corp.
Guardian Life Insurance Co. of America
Gucci America Inc.
Gulfstream Aerospace Corp.
Halliburton Co.
Hallmark Cards Inc.
Hamilton Sundstrand Corp.
Hancock Financial Services (John)
Hanna Co. (M.A.)
Hannaford Brothers Co.
Harcourt General, Inc.
Harland Co. (John H.)
Harley-Davidson Co.
Harris Corp.
Harsco Corp.
Hartford (The)
Hartford Steam Boiler Inspection & Insurance Co.
Hasbro, Inc.
Hawaiian Electric Co., Inc.
Heinz Co. (H.J.)
Hewlett-Packard Co.
Hitachi America Ltd.
Hofmann Co.
HON Industries Inc.
Honeywell International Inc.
Hubbard Broadcasting, Inc.
Huffy Corp.
Humana, Inc.
Hunt Manufacturing Co.
Inland Container Corp.
Intel Corp.
International Business Machines Corp.
International Paper Co.
INTRUST Financial Corp.
Jacobs Engineering Group
Jeld-wen, Inc.
Johnson Controls Inc.
Johnson & Johnson
Johnson & Son (S.C.)
Jostens, Inc.
JSJ Corp.
Katten, Muchin & Zavis
Kennametal, Inc.
Kimberly-Clark Corp.
Kinder Morgn
Kingsbury Corp.
Koch Industries, Inc.
Kroger Co.
La-Z-Boy Inc.
Lance, Inc.
Land O'Lakes, Inc.
Landmark Communications Inc.
Lee Enterprises
Leigh Fibers, Inc.
LG&E Energy Corp.
Liberty Corp.
Liberty Diversified Industries
Lipton Co.
Liz Claiborne, Inc.
Lotus Development Corp.
Louisiana Land & Exploration Co.
Louisiana-Pacific Corp.
LTV Corp.
Macy's East Inc.
Madison Gas & Electric Co.
Marcus Corp.
Marshall Field's
Masco Corp.
May Department Stores Co.
Maytag Corp.
McClatchy Co.
McDonald & Co. Securities, Inc.
McGraw-Hill Companies, Inc.
MCI WorldCom, Inc.
Mead Corp.
Medtronic, Inc.
Mercantile Bank NA
Merck & Co.
Meredith Corp.
Merit Oil Corp.
Merrill Lynch & Co., Inc.
Mervyn's California
Metropolitan Life Insurance Co.
Mid-America Bank of Louisville
MidAmerican Energy Holdings Co.
Milacron, Inc.
Milliken & Co.
Millipore Corp.
Mine Safety Appliances Co.
Monsanto Co.
Montana Power Co.
Montgomery Ward & Co., Inc.
MONY Group (The)
Morgan & Co. Inc. (J.P.)
Morrison Knudsen Corp.
Murphy Oil Corp.
National City Bank of Minneapolis
National Computer Systems, Inc.
National Service Industries, Inc.
National Starch & Chemical Co.
Nationwide Insurance Co.
NEBCO Evans
Nestle U.S.A. Inc.
New Century Energies
New England Financial
New York Life Insurance Co.
New York Stock Exchange, Inc.
New York Times Co.
Nordson Corp.
Norfolk Southern Corp.
Nortel
Northern Indiana Public Service Co.
Northern States Power Co.
Northwest Natural Gas Co.
Norton Co.
Norwest Corp.
Ohio National Life Insurance Co.
Olin Corp.
Oshkosh B'Gosh, Inc.
Overseas Shipholding Group Inc.
Owens Corning
Pacific Century Financial Corp.
Pacific Gas and Electric Co.
Pacific Mutual Life Insurance Co.
Paine Webber
Parker Hannifin Corp.
Pella Corp.
Pennzoil-Quaker State Co.
PepsiCo, Inc.
Pfizer Inc.
Phelps Dodge Corp.
Phillips Petroleum Co.
Pieper Power Electric Co.
Pitney Bowes Inc.
Pittway Corp.
PNC Bank Kentucky Inc.
PNC Financial Services Group
Polaroid Corp.
Potomac Electric Power Co.
Premier Industrial Corp.
Principal Financial Group
Procter & Gamble Co.
Procter & Gamble Co., Cosmetics Division
Providence Journal-Bulletin Co.
Prudential Insurance Co. of America
Public Service Electric & Gas Co.
Publix Supermarkets
Pulitzer Publishing Co.
Putnam Investments
Quaker Chemical Corp.
Ralston Purina Co.
Rayonier Inc.
Red Wing Shoe Co. Inc.
Regions Bank
Regis Corp.
Reily & Co., Inc. (William B.)
Reinhart Institutional Foods
Revlon Inc.
Reynolds Metals Co.
Reynolds & Reynolds Co.
Reynolds Tobacco (R.J.)
Rich Products Corp.
Rochester Gas & Electric Corp.
Rockwell International Corp.
Rouse Co.
Royal & SunAlliance USA, Inc.
Rubbermaid Inc.
Russer Foods
Ryder System, Inc.
Saint Paul Companies Inc.
Sara Lee Corp.
SBC Communications Inc.
Schering-Plough Corp.
Schlumberger Ltd. (USA)
Schwab & Co., Inc. (Charles)
Scripps Co. (E.W.)
Seagram & Sons, Inc. (Joseph E.)
Seaway Food Town, Inc.
Security Benefit Life Insurance Co.
Sempra Energy
Shell Oil Co.
Sierra Pacific Industries
Sierra Pacific Resources
Slant/Fin Corp.
Sonoco Products Co.
South Bend Tribune Corp.
Sprint Corp.
Sprint/United Telephone
SPX Corp.
Square D Co.
Standard Register Co.
Star Bank NA
Starwood Hotels & Resorts Worldwide, Inc.
State Street Bank & Trust Co.
Steelcase Inc.
Stone Container Corp.
Stone & Webster Inc.
Storage Technology Corp.
Stride Rite Corp.
Sunoco Inc.
SunTrust Bank Atlanta
Sverdrup Corp.
Synovus Financial Corp.
TCF National Bank Minnesota
TENNANT Co.
Tenneco Automotive
Tension Envelope Corp.
Texas Gas Transmission Corp.
Texas Instruments Inc.
Textron Inc.
Thermo Electron Corp.
Thompson Co. (J. Walter)
Times Mirror Co.
Titan Industrial Corp.
TJX Companies, Inc.
Toledo Blade Co.
Toyota Motor Sales U.S.A., Inc.
Trace International Holdings, Inc.
Tyson Foods Inc.
Unilever Home & Personal Care U.S.A.
Unilever United States, Inc.
Union Carbide Corp.
United Co.
United Dominion Industries, Ltd.
United Parcel Service of America Inc.
U.S. Bancorp
U.S. Bancorp Piper Jaffray
United States Trust Co. of New York
United Technologies Corp.
Universal Leaf Tobacco Co., Inc.
Universal Studios
Unocal Corp.
US Bank, Washington
USX Corp.
Valspar Corp.
Vulcan Materials Co.
Wachovia Bank of North Carolina NA
Waffle House Inc.
Wal-Mart Stores, Inc.
Walter Industries Inc.
Warner-Lambert Co.
Washington Mutual, Inc.
Washington Trust Bank
Weil, Gotshal & Manges Corp.
West Co. Inc.
Westvaco Corp.
Whirlpool Corp.
Williams
Wisconsin Power & Light Co.
Witco Corp.
Xerox Corp.
Yellow Corp.
York Federal Savings & Loan Association
Young & Rubicam

ARTS FESTIVALS

AGL Resources Inc.
Air Products and Chemicals, Inc.
Alabama Power Co.
Alcoa Inc.
Allegheny Technologies Inc.
Allmerica Financial Corp.
Ameren Corp.
American Express Co.
Ameritech Corp.
Ameritech Indiana
Ameritech Wisconsin
Amsted Industries Inc.
Aon Corp.

APL Ltd.
Archer-Daniels-Midland Co.
Armstrong World Industries, Inc.
AT&T Corp.
Atlantic Investment Co.
Avon Products, Inc.
Bank of America
Bank One Corp.
Barnes Group Inc.
Bayer Corp.
Bemis Manufacturing Co.
Bestfoods
Bethlehem Steel Corp.
Binney & Smith Inc.
Binswanger Companies
Blair & Co. (William)
Block, Inc. (H&R)
Blount International, Inc.
Blue Bell, Inc.
Blue Cross & Blue Shield of Alabama
Boler Co.
Boston Globe (The)
Briggs & Stratton Corp.
Brunswick Corp.
Burlington Resources, Inc.
Carnival Corp.
Carpenter Technology Corp.
Central Maine Power Co.
Chase Manhattan Bank, NA
Chevron Corp.
Chicago Board of Trade
Chicago Title Corp.
CIGNA Corp.
Cincinnati Bell Inc.
Cinergy Corp.
Citibank Corp.
Citizens Bank-Flint
Clorox Co.
Coca-Cola Co.
Colonial Life & Accident Insurance Co.
Compass Bank
Consolidated Natural Gas Co.
Constellation Energy Group, Inc.
Country Curtains, Inc.
Cox Enterprises Inc.
Crane & Co., Inc.
Crestar Finance Corp.
Cummins Engine Co., Inc.
CUNA Mutual Group
Deposit Guaranty National Bank
Disney Co. (Walt)
Dominion Resources, Inc.
Dow Corning Corp.
du Pont de Nemours & Co. (E.I.)
Duke Energy
Eaton Corp.
Enterprise Rent-A-Car Co.
Evening Post Publishing Co.
Exxon Mobil Corp.
Federal-Mogul Corp.
Federated Mutual Insurance Co.
First Tennessee National Corp.
First Union Corp.
Fisher Brothers Cleaning Services
Florida Power & Light Co.
FMC Corp.
Ford Motor Co.
Fort Worth Star-Telegram Inc.
Franklin Mint (The)
Freeport-McMoRan Inc.
Frost National Bank
Furniture Brands International, Inc.
General Motors Corp.
Georgia-Pacific Corp.
Georgia Power Co.
Hanna Co. (M.A.)
Harris Trust & Savings Bank
Harsco Corp.
Hartmarx Corp.
Heinz Co. (H.J.)
Humana, Inc.
Illinois Tool Works, Inc.
Inland Container Corp.
Inman Mills
International Paper Co.
Jeld-wen, Inc.
Johnson Controls Inc.
Katten, Muchin & Zavis
Kelly Services
Kemper National Insurance Companies
Kingsbury Corp.
Kroger Co.
Leigh Fibers, Inc.
Liberty Corp.
Lincoln Financial Group
Lipton Co.
Loews Corp.
LTV Corp.
MacMillan Bloedel Inc.
Macy's East Inc.
Marcus Corp.
Marshall Field's
Marshall & Ilsley Corp.
McClatchy Co.
McDonald & Co. Securities, Inc.
McWane Inc.
Mead Corp.
Mellon Financial Corp.
Memphis Light Gas & Water Division
Mervyn's California
Mid-America Bank of Louisville
MidAmerican Energy Holdings Co.
Mine Safety Appliances Co.
Morrison Knudsen Corp.
National Machinery Co.
National Service Industries, Inc.
NEBCO Evans
New Century Energies
New York Times Co.
Nordson Corp.
Northwest Bank Nebraska, NA
Northwest Natural Gas Co.
Ohio National Life Insurance Co.
Oshkosh B'Gosh, Inc.
Pacific Mutual Life Insurance Co.
Pennzoil-Quaker State Co.
Pittway Corp.
PNC Financial Services Group
Portland General Electric Co.
PPG Industries, Inc.
Price Associates (T. Rowe)
Procter & Gamble Co., Cosmetics Division
Provident Companies, Inc.
Publix Supermarkets
Ralph's Grocery Co.
Reynolds Metals Co.
Rockwell International Corp.
Russer Foods
S&T Bancorp
Sara Lee Corp.
SBC Communications Inc.
Schering-Plough Corp.
Schwab & Co., Inc. (Charles)
Scripps Co. (E.W.)
Searle & Co. (G.D.)
Seaway Food Town, Inc.
Sempra Energy
Shell Oil Co.
Shoney's Inc.
Sonoco Products Co.
South Bend Tribune Corp.
Southeastern Mutual Insurance Co.
Sovereign Bank
Springs Industries, Inc.
Sprint Corp.
SPX Corp.
Square D Co.
Star Bank NA
Stride Rite Corp.
SunTrust Bank Atlanta
Synovus Financial Corp.
Target Corp.
Tenneco Automotive
Texaco Inc.
Texas Gas Transmission Corp.
Thomasville Furniture Industries Inc.
Thompson Co. (J. Walter)
Transamerica Corp.
True North Communications, Inc.
Trustmark Insurance Co.
Union Camp Corp.
Union Planters Corp.
United Parcel Service of America Inc.
U.S. Bancorp Piper Jaffray
United Wisconsin Services
Universal Leaf Tobacco Co., Inc.
US Bank, Washington
USX Corp.
Varian Medical Systems, Inc.
Vulcan Materials Co.
Wachovia Bank of North Carolina NA
Wal-Mart Stores, Inc.
Warner-Lambert Co.
Waste Management Inc.
Whitman Corp.
Winn-Dixie Stores Inc.
Wisconsin Power & Light Co.
Wisconsin Public Service Corp.
Witco Corp.
Woodward Governor Co.
York Federal Savings & Loan Association

ARTS FUNDS

ABC
Air Products and Chemicals, Inc.
Alcoa Inc.
Ameren Corp.
American Fidelity Corp.
Ameritech Indiana
AMETEK, Inc.
AMP Inc.
Anheuser-Busch Companies, Inc.
APL Ltd.
Archer-Daniels-Midland Co.
Arizona Public Service Co.
Arvin Industries, Inc.
Ashland, Inc.
Avon Products, Inc.
Bank of America
Bardes Corp.
Barry Corp. (R.G.)
Bestfoods
Binney & Smith Inc.
Block, Inc. (H&R)
Blue Bell, Inc.
Boeing Co.
Boler Co.
Boston Globe (The)
Briggs & Stratton Corp.
Bristol-Myers Squibb Co.
Brunswick Corp.
Bucyrus-Erie Co.
Burlington Industries, Inc.
Burlington Resources, Inc.
Burnett Co. (Leo)
Cabot Corp.
Carlson Companies, Inc.
Carnival Corp.
Central Soya Co.
Charter Manufacturing Co.
Chase Bank of Texas
Chase Manhattan Bank, NA
Chemed Corp.
Chesapeake Corp.
Chevron Corp.
Chicago Tribune Co.
Cincinnati Bell Inc.
Cinergy Corp.
CIT Group, Inc. (The)
Citibank Corp.
Citizens Financial Group, Inc.
Compaq Computer Corp.
ConAgra, Inc.
Cone Mills Corp.
Consolidated Natural Gas Co.
Consumers Energy Co.
Cooper Industries, Inc.
Crane & Co., Inc.
Credit Suisse First Boston
Crestar Finance Corp.
Cummins Engine Co., Inc.
CUNA Mutual Group
Daily News
DaimlerChrysler Corp.
Dain Bosworth Inc.
Danis Companies
Dayton Hudson
Dayton Power and Light Co.
Delta Air Lines, Inc.
Dial Corp.
Disney Co. (Walt)
Dixie Group, Inc. (The)
Donaldson Co., Inc.
DSM Copolymer
du Pont de Nemours & Co. (E.I.)
Duchossois Industries Inc.
Duke Energy
Dynamet, Inc.
Eastman Kodak Co.
Eaton Corp.
Ecolab Inc.
Emerson Electric Co.
Entergy Corp.
Equifax Inc.
Erving Industries
Ethyl Corp.
Federal-Mogul Corp.
Federated Department Stores, Inc.
FedEx Corp.
Fidelity Investments
Fifth Third Bancorp
First Hawaiian, Inc.
First Tennessee National Corp.
First Union Corp.
First Union Securities, Inc.
Fisher Scientific
FleetBoston Financial Corp.
Fluor Corp.
Forbes Inc.
Fort James Corp.
Fortis Insurance Co.
Freeport-McMoRan Inc.
Frost National Bank
Fuller Co. (H.B.)
Furniture Brands International, Inc.
GenAmerica Corp.
General Electric Co.
General Mills, Inc.
General Motors Corp.
Georgia Power Co.
Glaxo Wellcome Inc.
Gucci America Inc.
Harris Corp.
Harris Trust & Savings Bank
Harsco Corp.
Hartford (The)
Hasbro, Inc.
Heinz Co. (H.J.)
Hewlett-Packard Co.
Hubbard Broadcasting, Inc.
Huffy Corp.
Humana, Inc.
Inland Container Corp.
Inman Mills
International Business Machines Corp.
International Paper Co.
ISE America
Johnson Controls Inc.
Johnson & Son (S.C.)
Journal-Gazette Co.
JSJ Corp.
Katten, Muchin & Zavis
Kerr-McGee Corp.
Kimberly-Clark Corp.
Kinder Morgn
Kingsbury Corp.
Kohler Co.
Kroger Co.
Ladish Co., Inc.
Landmark Communications Inc.
Lehigh Portland Cement Co.
LG&E Energy Corp.
Liberty Corp.
Lilly & Co. (Eli)
Lincoln Financial Group
Loews Corp.
LTV Corp.
Lubrizol Corp. (The)
Macy's East Inc.
Maritz Inc.
Mark IV Industries
Marshall Field's
Marshall & Ilsley Corp.
Masco Corp.
May Department Stores Co.
McClatchy Co.
McWane Inc.
Mid-America Bank of Louisville
Milacron, Inc.
Milliken & Co.
Millipore Corp.
Minnesota Mutual Life Insurance Co.
Mitsubishi Electric America
Montana Power Co.
Morgan & Co. Inc. (J.P.)
Morrison Knudsen Corp.
Motorola Inc.
Nabisco Group Holdings
Nalco Chemical Co.
National City Corp.
Nationwide Insurance Co.
NCR Corp.
Norfolk Southern Corp.

Northeast Utilities
Northern States Power Co.
Northwest Bank Nebraska, NA
Northwest Natural Gas Co.
Norton Co.
Norwest Corp.
OG&E Electric Services
Ohio National Life Insurance Co.
Oklahoma Publishing Co.
PACCAR Inc.
Pacific Mutual Life Insurance Co.
PECO Energy Co.
Pfizer Inc.
Pharmacia & Upjohn, Inc.
Phelps Dodge Corp.
Phillips Petroleum Co.
Physicians Mutual Insurance Co.
PNC Bank Kentucky Inc.
PNC Financial Services Group
Polaroid Corp.
Price Associates (T. Rowe)
Procter & Gamble Co.
Promus Hotel Corp.
Provident Companies, Inc.
Prudential Insurance Co. of America
Public Service Electric & Gas Co.
Pulitzer Publishing Co.
Quaker Chemical Corp.
Quanex Corp.
Regions Bank
Reily & Co., Inc. (William B.)
Reinhart Institutional Foods
Reliant Energy Inc.
Reynolds & Reynolds Co.
Rockwell International Corp.
Rouse Co.
Ruddick Corp.
Ryder System, Inc.
SAFECO Corp.
Saint Paul Companies Inc.
Sara Lee Corp.
Sara Lee Hosiery, Inc.
SBC Communications Inc.
Schering-Plough Corp.
Schloss & Co. (Marcus)
Scripps Co. (E.W.)
Seagram & Sons, Inc. (Joseph E.)
Sempra Energy
Shaw's Supermarkets, Inc.
Sierra Pacific Resources
Slant/Fin Corp.
Smith Corp. (A.O.)
Sonoco Products Co.
Southeastern Mutual Insurance Co.
Southwest Gas Corp.
Square D Co.
Standard Register Co.
Star Bank NA
Starwood Hotels & Resorts Worldwide, Inc.
SunTrust Bank Atlanta
TCF National Bank Minnesota
Tenneco Automotive
Texaco Inc.
Texas Gas Transmission Corp.
Texas Instruments Inc.
Textron Inc.
Thompson Co. (J. Walter)
Timken Co. (The)
TJX Companies, Inc.
Torchmark Corp.
True North Communications, Inc.
Ukrop's Super Markets
Union Camp Corp.
Union Pacific Corp.
United Airlines Inc.
United Parcel Service of America Inc.
United States Trust Co. of New York
Universal Studios
Unocal Corp.
US Bank, Washington
US West, Inc.
Valmont Industries, Inc.
Valspar Corp.
Vodafone AirTouch Plc
Vulcan Materials Co.
Wachovia Bank of North Carolina NA
Waste Management Inc.
Western & Southern Life Insurance Co.
Weyerhaeuser Co.
Whirlpool Corp.
Wisconsin Energy Corp.
Xerox Corp.
York Federal Savings & Loan Association
Young & Rubicam

ARTS INSTITUTES

Abbott Laboratories
AEGON U.S.A. Inc.
AGL Resources Inc.
AK Steel Corp.
Alcoa Inc.
AlliedSignal Inc.
Ameren Corp.
American Fidelity Corp.
Ameritech Corp.
Ameritech Indiana
Ameritech Ohio
Amsted Industries Inc.
Andersen Corp.
Aon Corp.
Archer-Daniels-Midland Co.
Aristech Chemical Corp.
Avon Products, Inc.
Baird & Co. (Robert W.)
Bank of America
Bank One Corp.
BankBoston Corp.
Barry Corp. (R.G.)
Baxter International Inc.
Bemis Co., Inc.
Bernstein & Co., Inc. (Sanford C.)
Berwind Group
Binney & Smith Inc.
Blair & Co. (William)
Block, Inc. (H&R)
Blount International, Inc.
Borden, Inc.
Borman's Inc.
Boston Edison Co.
BP Amoco Corp.
Bradford & Co. (J.C.)
Bridgestone/Firestone, Inc.
Briggs & Stratton Corp.
Bristol-Myers Squibb Co.
Brunswick Corp.
Burnett Co. (Leo)
Burress (J.W.)
Butler Manufacturing Co.
Cabot Corp.
Cargill Inc.
Carlson Companies, Inc.
Carpenter Technology Corp.
Carter-Wallace, Inc.
Central Maine Power Co.
Central & South West Services
CertainTeed Corp.
Chicago Board of Trade
Chicago Title Corp.
Chicago Tribune Co.
Cincinnati Bell Inc.
Citibank Corp.
Citizens Financial Group, Inc.
CNA
CNF Transportation, Inc.
Colonial Life & Accident Insurance Co.
Comerica Inc.
Commercial Intertech Corp.
Commonwealth Edison Co.
Consolidated Natural Gas Co.
Consolidated Papers, Inc.
Consumers Energy Co.
Conwood Co. LP
Cox Enterprises Inc.
Crane & Co., Inc.
Credit Suisse First Boston
Cyprus Amax Minerals Co.
Daily News
DaimlerChrysler Corp.
Dain Bosworth Inc.
Dana Corp.
Danis Companies
Dayton Hudson
Dayton Power and Light Co.
Deluxe Corp.
Detroit Edison Co.
Deutsch Co.
Disney Co. (Walt)
Donaldson Co., Inc.
Donnelley & Sons Co. (R.R.)
Dow Corning Corp.
du Pont de Nemours & Co. (E.I.)
Duchossois Industries Inc.
Duriron Co., Inc.
Dynamet, Inc.
Edison International
Emerson Electric Co.
Equitable Resources, Inc.
Erb Lumber Co.
Exxon Mobil Corp.
Fabri-Kal Corp.
Federal-Mogul Corp.
Federated Department Stores, Inc.
Federated Mutual Insurance Co.
Fireman's Fund Insurance Co.
First Maryland Bancorp
First Tennessee National Corp.
First Union Corp.
First Union National Bank, NA
Firstar Bank Milwaukee NA
FleetBoston Financial Corp.
FMC Corp.
Forbes Inc.
Ford Motor Co.
Forest City Enterprises, Inc.
Freeport-McMoRan Inc.
Frost National Bank
GATX Corp.
GenCorp
General Mills, Inc.
General Motors Corp.
Georgia Power Co.
Giant Eagle Inc.
Globe Corp.
Goldman Sachs Group
Golub Corp.
Graco, Inc.
Guess?
Hallmark Cards Inc.
Hancock Financial Services (John)
Hanna Co. (M.A.)
Hannaford Brothers Co.
Harley-Davidson Co.
Harris Trust & Savings Bank
Hartmarx Corp.
Hasbro, Inc.
Hensel Phelps Construction Co.
Honeywell International Inc.
Hubbard Broadcasting, Inc.
Huffy Corp.
Huntington Bancshares Inc.
IKON Office Solutions, Inc.
Illinois Tool Works, Inc.
International Business Machines Corp.
International Multifoods Corp.
Johnson Controls Inc.
Johnson & Son (S.C.)
Jostens, Inc.
JSJ Corp.
Kelly Services
Kmart Corp.
Land O'Lakes, Inc.
Liberty Diversified Industries
Lotus Development Corp.
Lubrizol Corp. (The)
MacMillan Bloedel Inc.
Macy's East Inc.
Marcus Corp.
Maritz Inc.
Marriott International Inc.
Marshall Field's
Marshall & Ilsley Corp.
Masco Corp.
Mattel Inc.
McClatchy Co.
Mead Corp.
Medtronic, Inc.
Metropolitan Life Insurance Co.
Michigan Consolidated Gas Co.
Minnesota Mining & Manufacturing Co.
Minnesota Mutual Life Insurance Co.
Montgomery Ward & Co., Inc.
Morgan Stanley Dean Witter & Co.
Morton International Inc.
Motorola Inc.
Nalco Chemical Co.
National City Bank of Minneapolis
National City Corp.
National Computer Systems, Inc.
NCR Corp.
New England Financial
New York Times Co.
Nordson Corp.
Northern States Power Co.
Northern Trust Co.
Northwest Natural Gas Co.
Norwest Corp.
Occidental Oil and Gas
OG&E Electric Services
Ohio National Life Insurance Co.
Old Kent Bank
Olin Corp.
Outboard Marine Corp.
Pacific Mutual Life Insurance Co.
Parker Hannifin Corp.
Peoples Energy Corp.
PerkinElmer, Inc.
Pharmacia & Upjohn, Inc.
Phillips Petroleum Co.
Pillsbury Co.
Pioneer Group
Pittway Corp.
Polaroid Corp.
Portland General Electric Co.
Premier Industrial Corp.
Price Associates (T. Rowe)
Procter & Gamble Co.
Procter & Gamble Co., Cosmetics Division
Prudential Insurance Co. of America
Pulitzer Publishing Co.
Ralph's Grocery Co.
Red Wing Shoe Co. Inc.
Regis Corp.
Reynolds & Reynolds Co.
Rich Products Corp.
Rockwell International Corp.
Rouse Co.
Saint Paul Companies Inc.
Sara Lee Corp.
SBC Communications Inc.
Searle & Co. (G.D.)
Sempra Energy
Shoney's Inc.
Simpson Investment Co.
SIT Investment Associates, Inc.
Sonoco Products Co.
Sotheby's Inc.
Sprint Corp.
Square D Co.
Standard Register Co.
Star Bank NA
State Street Bank & Trust Co.
Steelcase Inc.
Stone Container Corp.
Stride Rite Corp.
TCF National Bank Minnesota
Tektronix, Inc.
TENNANT Co.
Tension Envelope Corp.
Textron Inc.
Times Mirror Co.
Titan Industrial Corp.
TJX Companies, Inc.
Toyota Motor Sales U.S.A., Inc.
Trace International Holdings, Inc.
Transamerica Corp.
True North Communications, Inc.
Unilever Home & Personal Care U.S.A.
Unilever United States, Inc.
United Airlines Inc.
U.S. Bancorp
U.S. Bancorp Piper Jaffray
Universal Foods Corp.
Universal Studios
Unocal Corp.
USG Corp.
Valspar Corp.
Vulcan Materials Co.
Walgreen Co.
Waste Management Inc.
Western & Southern Life Insurance Co.
Whirlpool Corp.
WICOR, Inc.
Wilbur-Ellis Co. & Connell Brothers Co.
Williams

Witco Corp.
Xerox Corp.
Yellow Corp.

ARTS OUTREACH

Aetna, Inc.
Alcon Laboratories, Inc.
Allmerica Financial Corp.
American Express Co.
Avon Products, Inc.
Block, Inc. (H&R)
Boston Edison Co.
Boston Globe (The)
Bridgestone/Firestone, Inc.
Bristol-Myers Squibb Co.
Brown Shoe Co., Inc.
Cabot Corp.
Cargill Inc.
Carillon Importers, Ltd.
Cessna Aircraft Co.
Chicago Sun-Times, Inc.
Citigroup
Citizens Bank-Flint
Clorox Co.
Consolidated Natural Gas Co.
Contran Corp.
Corning Inc.
Crestar Finance Corp.
Cummins Engine Co., Inc.
Daily News
Dayton Hudson
Dayton Power and Light Co.
Delta Air Lines, Inc.
Duchossois Industries Inc.
Ecolab Inc.
Edwards Enterprise Software (J.D.)
Extendicare Health Services
Ferro Corp.
Fidelity Investments
Fireman's Fund Insurance Co.
Freddie Mac
Fuller Co. (H.B.)
Gap, Inc.
GATX Corp.
GenAmerica Corp.
Golub Corp.
Hallmark Cards Inc.
Heinz Co. (H.J.)
Hickory Tech Corp.
Hitachi America Ltd.
HON Industries Inc.
Honeywell International Inc.
Hubbard Broadcasting, Inc.
Journal-Gazette Co.
Kemper National Insurance Companies
Kraft Foods, Inc.
Levi Strauss & Co.
Lilly & Co. (Eli)
Little, Inc. (Arthur D.)
Loews Corp.
Marshall Field's
McClatchy Co.
MCI WorldCom, Inc.
Medtronic, Inc.
Mercantile Bank NA
Merrill Lynch & Co., Inc.
Minnesota Mining & Manufacturing Co.
Morgan & Co. Inc. (J.P.)
National Service Industries, Inc.
Nestle U.S.A. Inc.
New England Bio Labs
New York Mercantile Exchange
New York Times Co.
Nordson Corp.
Overseas Shipholding Group Inc.
Pharmacia & Upjohn, Inc.
PNC Bank
Polaroid Corp.
Premier Industrial Corp.
Putnam Investments
Quaker Chemical Corp.
Reilly Industries, Inc.
Saint Paul Companies Inc.
Schwab & Co., Inc. (Charles)
Security Life of Denver Insurance Co.
Sega of America Inc.
Shaw's Supermarkets, Inc.
Shell Oil Co.
SmithKline Beecham Corp.
Sony Electronics
Sovereign Bank
State Street Bank & Trust Co.
Stride Rite Corp.
Stupp Brothers Bridge & Iron Co.
Tesoro Hawaii
Toyota Motor Sales U.S.A., Inc.
Union Pacific Corp.
United States Sugar Corp.
US Bank, Washington
Zachry Co. (H.B.)
Zilkha & Sons

BALLET

ABC
Aetna, Inc.
Alcoa Inc.
Alcon Laboratories, Inc.
American Fidelity Corp.
Ameritas Life Insurance Corp.
AMETEK, Inc.
Amsted Industries Inc.
APL Ltd.
Aristech Chemical Corp.
Arizona Public Service Co.
AT&T Corp.
Atlantic Investment Co.
Baird & Co. (Robert W.)
Banfi Vintners
Bank of America
BankAtlantic Bancorp
Barclays Capital
Barry Corp. (R.G.)
BFGoodrich Co.
Block, Inc. (H&R)
Blount International, Inc.
Blue Cross & Blue Shield of Alabama
Borden, Inc.
Boston Edison Co.
Boston Globe (The)
Bradford & Co. (J.C.)
Bridgestone/Firestone, Inc.
Briggs & Stratton Corp.
Bucyrus-Erie Co.
Burnett Co. (Leo)
Butler Manufacturing Co.
Calvin Klein
Central National-Gottesman
CertainTeed Corp.
CGU Insurance
Chase Bank of Texas
Chevron Corp.
Chicago Board of Trade
CIGNA Corp.
Cinergy Corp.
Citigroup
Cleveland-Cliffs, Inc.
Clorox Co.
Coca-Cola Co.
Consolidated Natural Gas Co.
Consolidated Papers, Inc.
Conwood Co. LP
Crane Co.
Crane & Co., Inc.
Credit Suisse First Boston
Crestar Finance Corp.
Daily News
Dain Bosworth Inc.
Dana Corp.
Dayton Power and Light Co.
Delta Air Lines, Inc.
Demoulas Supermarkets Inc.
Deposit Guaranty National Bank
Dexter Corp.
Dial Corp.
Duchossois Industries Inc.
Duriron Co., Inc.
Dynamet, Inc.
Eaton Corp.
El Paso Energy Co.
Elf Atochem North America, Inc.
Emerson Electric Co.
Employers Mutual Casualty Co.
Ferro Corp.
Fireman's Fund Insurance Co.
First American Corp.
First Union Securities, Inc.
Firstar Bank Milwaukee NA
Florida Power & Light Co.
Forest City Enterprises, Inc.
Fort Worth Star-Telegram Inc.
Freeport-McMoRan Inc.
GenCorp
Giant Eagle Inc.
Giant Food Inc.
Globe Corp.
Hallmark Cards Inc.
Hanna Co. (M.A.)
Harcourt General, Inc.
Hartford Steam Boiler Inspection & Insurance Co.
Heinz Co. (H.J.)
Hofmann Co.
Hubbard Broadcasting, Inc.
Huffy Corp.
Humana, Inc.
Hunt Manufacturing Co.
Huntington Bancshares Inc.
International Flavors & Fragrances Inc.
Johnson Controls Inc.
Katten, Muchin & Zavis
Kingsbury Corp.
Koch Industries, Inc.
Kroger Co.
Lancaster Lens, Inc.
LG&E Energy Corp.
Lilly & Co. (Eli)
Lincoln Electric Co.
Little, Inc. (Arthur D.)
Litton Industries, Inc.
Louisiana Land & Exploration Co.
Louisiana-Pacific Corp.
LTV Corp.
Mattel Inc.
May Department Stores Co.
McDonald & Co. Securities, Inc.
McWane Inc.
Metropolitan Life Insurance Co.
Mid-America Bank of Louisville
MidAmerican Energy Holdings Co.
Millipore Corp.
Mine Safety Appliances Co.
Morgan & Co. Inc. (J.P.)
Morgan Stanley Dean Witter & Co.
National City Corp.
Nationwide Insurance Co.
NCR Corp.
NEBCO Evans
New England Bio Labs
New England Financial
New York Life Insurance Co.
New York Times Co.
Norton Co.
Occidental Oil and Gas
OG&E Electric Services
Pacific Mutual Life Insurance Co.
PacifiCorp
Park National Bank
Parker Hannifin Corp.
PEMCO Corp.
PerkinElmer, Inc.
Phelps Dodge Corp.
Physicians Mutual Insurance Co.
Pieper Power Electric Co.
Pioneer Group
PNC Bank Kentucky Inc.
PNC Financial Services Group
Polaroid Corp.
PPG Industries, Inc.
Premier Industrial Corp.
Principal Financial Group
Procter & Gamble Co.
Providence Journal-Bulletin Co.
Putnam Investments
Quaker Chemical Corp.
Reilly Industries, Inc.
Reynolds & Reynolds Co.
Russer Foods
Ryder System, Inc.
Safeguard Scientifics
Salomon Smith Barney
S&T Bancorp
Schlumberger Ltd. (USA)
Schwab & Co., Inc. (Charles)
Schwebel Baking Co.
Security Benefit Life Insurance Co.
Security Life of Denver Insurance Co.
Servco Pacific
S.G. Cowen
Shea Co. (John F.)
Shell Oil Co.
Sherwin-Williams Co.
SmithKline Beecham Corp.
Smurfit-Stone Container Corp.
Southeastern Mutual Insurance Co.
Southwest Gas Corp.
Sprint Corp.
Sprint/United Telephone
State Street Bank & Trust Co.
Steelcase Inc.
Stride Rite Corp.
SunTrust Bank Atlanta
Tektronix, Inc.
Teleflex Inc.
Texaco Inc.
Thermo Electron Corp.
Thompson Co. (J. Walter)
TMC Investment Co.
Toledo Blade Co.
Trace International Holdings, Inc.
Transamerica Corp.
TRW Inc.
Union Pacific Corp.
United Airlines Inc.
United Distillers & Vintners North America
United Parcel Service of America Inc.
United States Trust Co. of New York
Universal Leaf Tobacco Co., Inc.
Universal Studios
UPN Channel 50
US Bank, Washington
US West, Inc.
USX Corp.
Valmont Industries, Inc.
Vanguard Group
Vodafone AirTouch Plc
Vulcan Materials Co.
Waffle House Inc.
Walter Industries Inc.
Warner-Lambert Co.
Washington Mutual, Inc.
Washington Trust Bank
Whirlpool Corp.
Wiley & Sons (John)
Wiremold Co.
Witco Corp.
Yellow Corp.
Zilkha & Sons

COMMUNITY ARTS

Abbott Laboratories
AEGON U.S.A. Inc.
AFLAC Inc.
AGL Resources Inc.
Agrilink Foods, Inc.
Air Products and Chemicals, Inc.
AK Steel Corp.
Alabama Power Co.
Albany International Corp.
Albertson's Inc.
Alcoa Inc.
AlliedSignal Inc.
America West Airlines, Inc.
Ameritech Illinois
Ameritech Indiana
Ameritech Michigan
AmerUS Group
AMR Corp.
Anheuser-Busch Companies, Inc.
Apple Computer, Inc.
Ashland, Inc.
Atlantic Investment Co.
Atlantic Richfield Co.
Avon Products, Inc.
Bandag, Inc.
Bank of America
Bank One Corp.
BankBoston Corp.
Bardes Corp.
Barnes Group Inc.
Barry Corp. (R.G.)
Battelle Memorial Institute
Bayer Corp.
Bernstein & Co., Inc. (Sanford C.)
Bestfoods
Bethlehem Steel Corp.
BFGoodrich Co.
Binney & Smith Inc.
Binswanger Companies
Block, Inc. (H&R)
Blue Bell, Inc.
Boeing Co.
Boise Cascade Corp.

Borden, Inc.
Borman's Inc.
Bowater Inc.
Bridgestone/Firestone, Inc.
Briggs & Stratton Corp.
Brunswick Corp.
Burlington Resources, Inc.
Cabot Corp.
California Bank & Trust
Campbell Soup Co.
Cantor, Fitzgerald Securities Corp.
Carlson Companies, Inc.
Carpenter Technology Corp.
Carrier Corp.
Caterpillar Inc.
Central Maine Power Co.
Central Vermont Public Service Corp.
CertainTeed Corp.
Charter Manufacturing Co.
Chase Bank of Texas
Chase Manhattan Bank, NA
Chesapeake Corp.
Chevron Corp.
Chicago Board of Trade
Chicago Sun-Times, Inc.
Chicago Title Corp.
Church & Dwight Co., Inc.
Cinergy Corp.
CIT Group, Inc. (The)
Citigroup
Citizens Bank-Flint
Clorox Co.
Colonial Life & Accident Insurance Co.
Commerce Bancshares, Inc.
Commonwealth Edison Co.
Consolidated Papers, Inc.
Consumers Energy Co.
Coors Brewing Co.
Corning Inc.
Crane & Co., Inc.
Crestar Finance Corp.
CSS Industries, Inc.
Cummins Engine Co., Inc.
CUNA Mutual Group
Daily News
DaimlerChrysler Corp.
Danis Companies
Dayton Hudson
Deere & Co.
Deposit Guaranty National Bank
Dixie Group, Inc. (The)
Dominion Resources, Inc.
Donaldson Co., Inc.
Dow Corning Corp.
DSM Copolymer
du Pont de Nemours & Co. (E.I.)
Duchossois Industries Inc.
Duke Energy
Duriron Co., Inc.
Eastern Bank
Eaton Corp.
Eckerd Corp.
Edison International
Elf Atochem North America, Inc.
Emerson Electric Co.
Erb Lumber Co.
Ethyl Corp.
Exxon Mobil Corp.
Federal-Mogul Corp.
Federated Mutual Insurance Co.
Fifth Third Bancorp
Fireman's Fund Insurance Co.
First Tennessee National Corp.
First Union Bank
First Union Corp.
First Union National Bank, NA
Fisher Scientific
FleetBoston Financial Corp.
FMC Corp.
Ford Meter Box Co.
Ford Motor Co.
Fort James Corp.
Fortune Brands, Inc.
Fox Entertainment Group
Franklin Mint (The)
Freeport-McMoRan Inc.
Freightliner Corp.
Frost National Bank
GATX Corp.
GEICO Corp.
GenAmerica Corp.
Georgia Power Co.
Giant Eagle Inc.
Giant Food Inc.
Giddings & Lewis
Glaxo Wellcome Inc.
Grace & Co. (W.R.)
Green Bay Packaging
Guardian Life Insurance Co. of America
Gucci America Inc.
Hamilton Sundstrand Corp.
Hancock Financial Services (John)
Harcourt General, Inc.
Harris Corp.
Harsco Corp.
Hartford (The)
Hawaiian Electric Co., Inc.
Honeywell International Inc.
Hubbard Broadcasting, Inc.
Huffy Corp.
Humana, Inc.
Hunt Manufacturing Co.
Idaho Power Co.
Inman Mills
Intel Corp.
International Business Machines Corp.
International Multifoods Corp.
Johnson & Johnson
Johnson & Son (S.C.)
JSJ Corp.
Kennametal, Inc.
Kimball International, Inc.
Kimberly-Clark Corp.
Kingsbury Corp.
La-Z-Boy Inc.
Land O'Lakes, Inc.
Liberty Corp.
Lilly & Co. (Eli)
Lincoln Financial Group
Liz Claiborne, Inc.
Louisiana Land & Exploration Co.
LTV Corp.
Macy's East Inc.
Madison Gas & Electric Co.
Marcus Corp.
Maritz Inc.
Marshall Field's
May Department Stores Co.
McClatchy Co.
McDonald & Co. Securities, Inc.
Mead Corp.
Mellon Financial Corp.
Menasha Corp.
Morgan Stanley Dean Witter & Co.
Morris Communications Corp.
Morrison Knudsen Corp.
Mutual of Omaha Insurance Co.
Nabisco Group Holdings
Nalco Chemical Co.
National City Bank of Minneapolis
National Computer Systems, Inc.
New Century Energies
New England Bio Labs
New England Financial
New York Mercantile Exchange
New York Stock Exchange, Inc.
New York Times Co.
Newman's Own Inc.
Nordson Corp.
Nortel
Northern States Power Co.
Northwest Bank Nebraska, NA
Northwest Natural Gas Co.
Norton Co.
Occidental Oil and Gas
Old National Bank Evansville
Olin Corp.
Oshkosh B'Gosh, Inc.
Owens Corning
Park National Bank
Pennzoil-Quaker State Co.
Pharmacia & Upjohn, Inc.
Phelps Dodge Corp.
Phillips Petroleum Co.
Pillsbury Co.
Pioneer Group
Pioneer Hi-Bred International, Inc.
Pitney Bowes Inc.
Playboy Enterprises Inc.
PNC Financial Services Group
Polaroid Corp.
PPG Industries, Inc.
Price Associates (T. Rowe)
Principal Financial Group
Prudential Insurance Co. of America
Publix Supermarkets
Quaker Chemical Corp.
Reliant Energy Inc.
Reynolds & Reynolds Co.
Reynolds Tobacco (R.J.)
Rockwell International Corp.
Rouse Co.
Royal & SunAlliance USA, Inc.
Ruddick Corp.
SAFECO Corp.
Saint Paul Companies Inc.
Sara Lee Corp.
Sara Lee Hosiery, Inc.
SBC Communications Inc.
Schering-Plough Corp.
Schwab & Co., Inc. (Charles)
Seaway Food Town, Inc.
Sempra Energy
Sentry Insurance, A Mutual Co.
Shoney's Inc.
Sierra Pacific Resources
SIT Investment Associates, Inc.
Sonoco Products Co.
Southwest Gas Corp.
Sovereign Bank
Springs Industries, Inc.
Standard Register Co.
Stanley Works (The)
State Street Bank & Trust Co.
Stride Rite Corp.
SunTrust Bank Atlanta
SuperValu, Inc.
Susquehanna-Pfaltzgraff Co.
Target Corp.
Tenneco Automotive
Tenneco Packaging
Tension Envelope Corp.
Texaco Inc.
Texas Gas Transmission Corp.
Textron Inc.
Thomasville Furniture Industries Inc.
TJX Companies, Inc.
Toledo Blade Co.
Tomkins Industries, Inc.
Torchmark Corp.
True North Communications, Inc.
Trustmark Insurance Co.
TRW Inc.
TU Electric Co.
Tyson Foods Inc.
Ukrop's Super Markets
Union Camp Corp.
United Services Automobile Association
United States Trust Co. of New York
United Technologies Corp.
United Wisconsin Services
Universal Leaf Tobacco Co., Inc.
Unocal Corp.
US Bank, Washington
Valspar Corp.
Vulcan Materials Co.
Wachovia Bank of North Carolina NA
Wal-Mart Stores, Inc.
Waldbaum's Supermarkets, Inc.
Washington Mutual, Inc.
Washington Trust Bank
Webster Bank
West Co. Inc.
Weyerhaeuser Co.
Whirlpool Corp.
Williams
Wisconsin Energy Corp.
Wisconsin Power & Light Co.
Yellow Corp.
York Federal Savings & Loan Association

DANCE

Abbott Laboratories
ABC
AEGON U.S.A. Inc.
Air Products and Chemicals, Inc.
AK Steel Corp.
Alabama Power Co.
Albany International Corp.
Alcoa Inc.
Allegheny Technologies Inc.
AlliedSignal Inc.
AMCORE Bank Rockford
Ameren Corp.
American Express Co.
American General Finance
American Standard Inc.
Ameritas Life Insurance Corp.
Ameritech Illinois
Ameritech Indiana
AMETEK, Inc.
Aon Corp.
APL Ltd.
Aristech Chemical Corp.
Arizona Public Service Co.
Ashland, Inc.
AT&T Corp.
Atlantic Richfield Co.
Bank One Corp.
BankAtlantic Bancorp
Barclays Capital
Barnes Group Inc.
Barry Corp. (R.G.)
Battelle Memorial Institute
Bestfoods
BFGoodrich Co.
Binney & Smith Inc.
Blair & Co. (William)
Block, Inc. (H&R)
Blount International, Inc.
Boeing Co.
Boise Cascade Corp.
Boler Co.
Borden, Inc.
Borman's Inc.
Boston Edison Co.
Boston Globe (The)
Bradford & Co. (J.C.)
Bridgestone/Firestone, Inc.
Briggs & Stratton Corp.
Brown Shoe Co., Inc.
Brown & Williamson Tobacco Corp.
Brunswick Corp.
Bucyrus-Erie Co.
Burlington Resources, Inc.
Butler Manufacturing Co.
Cabot Corp.
Calvin Klein
Carillon Importers, Ltd.
Central Maine Power Co.
Central National-Gottesman
CGU Insurance
Chase Manhattan Bank, NA
Chevron Corp.
Citibank Corp.
Citigroup
CLARCOR Inc.
Clorox Co.
CNA
Colonial Life & Accident Insurance Co.
Commonwealth Edison Co.
ConAgra, Inc.
Consolidated Natural Gas Co.
Constellation Energy Group, Inc.
Contran Corp.
Cooper Industries, Inc.
Coors Brewing Co.
Copley Press, Inc.
Country Curtains, Inc.
CPI Corp.
Crane & Co., Inc.
Credit Suisse First Boston
CSS Industries, Inc.
Cummins Engine Co., Inc.
CUNA Mutual Group
Daily News
Danis Companies
Dayton Hudson
Dayton Power and Light Co.
Deluxe Corp.
Demoulas Supermarkets Inc.
Deutsch Co.
Dexter Corp.
Dial Corp.
Dominion Resources, Inc.
Donaldson Co., Inc.
Dow Corning Corp.
du Pont de Nemours & Co. (E.I.)

Duchossois Industries Inc.
Duke Energy
Dun & Bradstreet Corp.
Eaton Corp.
Edison International
Elf Atochem North America, Inc.
Emerson Electric Co.
Enterprise Rent-A-Car Co.
Exxon Mobil Corp.
Fannie Mae
Fireman's Fund Insurance Co.
First Maryland Bancorp
First Tennessee National Corp.
First Union Bank
First Union Corp.
First Union National Bank, NA
Firstar Bank Milwaukee NA
Fisher Brothers Cleaning Services
FleetBoston Financial Corp.
Fluor Corp.
Forbes Inc.
Ford Meter Box Co.
Freeport-McMoRan Inc.
Fuller Co. (H.B.)
Furniture Brands International, Inc.
Gap, Inc.
GATX Corp.
GenAmerica Corp.
GenCorp
General Electric Co.
General Mills, Inc.
General Motors Corp.
Georgia-Pacific Corp.
Georgia Power Co.
Giant Eagle Inc.
Giant Food Inc.
Gillette Co.
Globe Corp.
GTE Corp.
Gucci America Inc.
Hallmark Cards Inc.
Hamilton Sundstrand Corp.
Hancock Financial Services (John)
Harris Trust & Savings Bank
Harsco Corp.
Hartford (The)
Hartmarx Corp.
Heinz Co. (H.J.)
Honeywell International Inc.
Huffy Corp.
Humana, Inc.
Hunt Manufacturing Co.
Illinois Tool Works, Inc.
International Business Machines Corp.
International Flavors & Fragrances Inc.
International Paper Co.
ISE America
Johnson Controls Inc.
Johnson & Johnson
Katten, Muchin & Zavis
Kiewit Sons' Inc. (Peter)
Kimberly-Clark Corp.
Kingsbury Corp.
Koch Industries, Inc.
Kraft Foods, Inc.
Kroger Co.
Laclede Gas Co.
Leviton Manufacturing Co. Inc.
Lilly & Co. (Eli)
Lincoln Electric Co.
Lincoln Financial Group
Lipton Co.
Loews Corp.
Louisiana Land & Exploration Co.
LTV Corp.
Lubrizol Corp. (The)
Macy's East Inc.
Marcus Corp.
Maritz Inc.
Marshall Field's
Maytag Corp.
McClatchy Co.
McGraw-Hill Companies, Inc.
McKesson-HBOC Corp.
McWane Inc.
Mead Corp.
Mellon Financial Corp.
Mercantile Bank NA
Mervyn's California
Metropolitan Life Insurance Co.
Mid-America Bank of Louisville
Mine Safety Appliances Co.
Monarch Machine Tool Co.
Monsanto Co.
MONY Group (The)
Morgan & Co. Inc. (J.P.)
Morgan Stanley Dean Witter & Co.
Motorola Inc.
Nabisco Group Holdings
Nalco Chemical Co.
National City Corp.
National Starch & Chemical Co.
NCR Corp.
New Century Energies
New England Bio Labs
New England Financial
New York Times Co.
Northern Trust Co.
Northwest Bank Nebraska, NA
Northwest Natural Gas Co.
Norton Co.
Old National Bank Evansville
Olin Corp.
Oshkosh B'Gosh, Inc.
Overseas Shipholding Group Inc.
Pacific Mutual Life Insurance Co.
PECO Energy Co.
Penney Co., Inc. (J.C.)
Pennzoil-Quaker State Co.
Peoples Energy Corp.
Pfizer Inc.
Philip Morris Companies Inc.
Phillips Petroleum Co.
Pioneer Hi-Bred International, Inc.
Polaroid Corp.
Portland General Electric Co.
Potlatch Corp.
Potomac Electric Power Co.
PPG Industries, Inc.
Premier Industrial Corp.
Principal Financial Group
Procter & Gamble Co., Cosmetics Division
Pulitzer Publishing Co.
Reliant Energy Inc.
Reynolds & Reynolds Co.
Reynolds Tobacco (R.J.)
Rockwell International Corp.
Rouse Co.
Royal & SunAlliance USA, Inc.
Russer Foods
Ryder System, Inc.
SAFECO Corp.
Saint Paul Companies Inc.
Sara Lee Corp.
SBC Communications Inc.
Schering-Plough Corp.
Schloss & Co. (Marcus)
Schlumberger Ltd. (USA)
Seagram & Sons, Inc. (Joseph E.)
Security Benefit Life Insurance Co.
Sempra Energy
Shell Oil Co.
Smith Corp. (A.O.)
Smurfit-Stone Container Corp.
Sonoco Products Co.
Southern New England Telephone Co.
Southwest Gas Corp.
Square D Co.
Stanley Works (The)
Starwood Hotels & Resorts Worldwide, Inc.
State Street Bank & Trust Co.
Steelcase Inc.
Storage Technology Corp.
Stride Rite Corp.
Sunoco Inc.
SunTrust Bank Atlanta
Sverdrup Corp.
Target Corp.
TENNANT Co.
Tenneco Automotive
Tension Envelope Corp.
Texaco Inc.
Texas Gas Transmission Corp.
Textron Inc.
Thermo Electron Corp.
Thompson Co. (J. Walter)
Times Mirror Co.
Titan Industrial Corp.
TJX Companies, Inc.
Tomkins Industries, Inc.
Torchmark Corp.
Trace International Holdings, Inc.
Transamerica Corp.
True North Communications, Inc.
Union Pacific Corp.
United Airlines Inc.
United States Trust Co. of New York
United Wisconsin Services
Universal Leaf Tobacco Co., Inc.
Universal Studios
Unocal Corp.
UnumProvident
UPN Channel 50
US Bank, Washington
USX Corp.
Vulcan Materials Co.
Wachovia Bank of North Carolina NA
Wal-Mart Stores, Inc.
Weil, Gotshal & Manges Corp.
Weyerhaeuser Co.
Whirlpool Corp.
Wiley & Sons (John)
Williams
Wisconsin Public Service Corp.
Witco Corp.
Xerox Corp.
Yellow Corp.
Young & Rubicam
Zilkha & Sons

ETHNIC & FOLK ARTS

ABC
AEGON U.S.A. Inc.
AGL Resources Inc.
American United Life Insurance Co.
Ameritech Indiana
AMETEK, Inc.
Archer-Daniels-Midland Co.
Arizona Public Service Co.
Atlantic Richfield Co.
Avon Products, Inc.
Banfi Vintners
Bank of America
Bank One Corp.
Bank One, Texas-Houston Office
BankBoston Corp.
Barry Corp. (R.G.)
Bechtel Group, Inc.
Belo Corp. (A.H.)
Ben & Jerry's Homemade Inc.
Bestfoods
Block, Inc. (H&R)
Blount International, Inc.
Boeing Co.
Borman's Inc.
Boston Globe (The)
BP Amoco Corp.
Broderbund Software, Inc.
Brown Shoe Co., Inc.
Brown & Williamson Tobacco Corp.
Cabot Corp.
Carillon Importers, Ltd.
Central Maine Power Co.
Central & South West Services
Chase Manhattan Bank, NA
Chicago Tribune Co.
Circuit City Stores, Inc.
Citibank Corp.
CLARCOR Inc.
Clorox Co.
Colonial Life & Accident Insurance Co.
Commonwealth Edison Co.
Cook Inlet Region
Coors Brewing Co.
Copley Press, Inc.
Cranston Print Works Co.
Crestar Finance Corp.
Daily News
DaimlerChrysler Corp.
Dayton Hudson
Dayton Power and Light Co.
Disney Co. (Walt)
du Pont de Nemours & Co. (E.I.)
Duchossois Industries Inc.
Duke Energy
Edison International
Equifax Inc.
Exxon Mobil Corp.
Federated Department Stores, Inc.
Fireman's Fund Insurance Co.
First Tennessee National Corp.
First Union Corp.
First Union National Bank, NA
First Union Securities, Inc.
Fisher Scientific
FleetBoston Financial Corp.
Forbes Inc.
Ford Motor Co.
Freeport-McMoRan Inc.
Frost National Bank
GATX Corp.
General Electric Co.
Georgia-Pacific Corp.
Georgia Power Co.
Glickenhaus & Co.
Golub Corp.
Gucci America Inc.
Hallmark Cards Inc.
Hancock Financial Services (John)
Harris Trust & Savings Bank
Honeywell International Inc.
Huntington Bancshares Inc.
International Business Machines Corp.
International Multifoods Corp.
ISE America
Johnson & Son (S.C.)
Jostens, Inc.
Kingsbury Corp.
Koch Industries, Inc.
Land O'Lakes, Inc.
Landmark Communications Inc.
LG&E Energy Corp.
Lilly & Co. (Eli)
Liz Claiborne, Inc.
Louisiana Land & Exploration Co.
Maritz Inc.
Marshall Field's
May Department Stores Co.
Mazda North American Operations
McClatchy Co.
McDonald & Co. Securities, Inc.
Mercantile Bank NA
Merit Oil Corp.
Merrill Lynch & Co., Inc.
Mervyn's California
Metropolitan Life Insurance Co.
Mid-America Bank of Louisville
Minnesota Mining & Manufacturing Co.
Monsanto Co.
Morrison Knudsen Corp.
Motorola Inc.
New Century Energies
New England Bio Labs
New England Financial
New York Times Co.
Nordson Corp.
Northern States Power Co.
Northwest Natural Gas Co.
Norton Co.
Norwest Corp.
OG&E Electric Services
Overseas Shipholding Group Inc.
Pacific Century Financial Corp.
Pacific Gas and Electric Co.
Pacific Mutual Life Insurance Co.
PECO Energy Co.
Peoples Energy Corp.
Pharmacia & Upjohn, Inc.
Playboy Enterprises Inc.
Polaroid Corp.
Portland General Electric Co.
Prudential Securities Inc.
Pulitzer Publishing Co.
Ralph's Grocery Co.
Reliant Energy Inc.
Reynolds & Reynolds Co.
Reynolds Tobacco (R.J.)
Rouse Co.

Royal & SunAlliance USA, Inc.
Saint Paul Companies Inc.
Sara Lee Corp.
SBC Communications Inc.
Schering-Plough Corp.
Schlumberger Ltd. (USA)
Schwab & Co., Inc. (Charles)
Seagram & Sons, Inc. (Joseph E.)
Seaway Food Town, Inc.
Sempra Energy
Servco Pacific
Shoney's Inc.
Sierra Pacific Resources
SmithKline Beecham Corp.
State Street Bank & Trust Co.
Steelcase Inc.
SunTrust Bank Atlanta
Target Corp.
Temple-Inland Inc.
Times Mirror Co.
Titan Industrial Corp.
Trace International Holdings, Inc.
Transamerica Corp.
TRW Inc.
Ukrop's Super Markets
Union Camp Corp.
United Airlines Inc.
US Bank, Washington
US West, Inc.
Valmont Industries, Inc.
Vodafone AirTouch Plc
Vulcan Materials Co.
Washington Mutual, Inc.
Whirlpool Corp.
Wilbur-Ellis Co. & Connell Brothers Co.
Williams
Wyman-Gordon Co.
York Federal Savings & Loan Association
Zachry Co. (H.B.)

FILM & VIDEO

ABC
AK Steel Corp.
BankAtlantic Bancorp
Ben & Jerry's Homemade Inc.
Binney & Smith Inc.
Blount International, Inc.
Burnett Co. (Leo)
Calvin Klein
Carillon Importers, Ltd.
CBS Corp.
CertainTeed Corp.
Chevron Corp.
Clorox Co.
Daily News
Dayton Hudson
Disney Co. (Walt)
Dynamet, Inc.
Entergy Corp.
First Hawaiian, Inc.
Ford Meter Box Co.
General Mills, Inc.
Glickenhaus & Co.
Hallmark Cards Inc.
Heinz Co. (H.J.)
Independent Stave Co.
Intel Corp.
Leigh Fibers, Inc.
Levi Strauss & Co.
Marcus Corp.
Marshall & Ilsley Corp.
MCI WorldCom, Inc.
Metropolitan Life Insurance Co.
Mitsubishi Electric America
National City Bank of Minneapolis
New York Times Co.
Ohio National Life Insurance Co.
Overseas Shipholding Group Inc.
Pacific Mutual Life Insurance Co.
PepsiCo, Inc.
Ralph's Grocery Co.
Sara Lee Corp.
Sara Lee Hosiery, Inc.
Sega of America Inc.
Southwest Gas Corp.
Sunmark Capital Corp.
Tesoro Hawaii
Titan Industrial Corp.
Toyota Motor Sales U.S.A., Inc.
Trace International Holdings, Inc.
U.S. Bancorp Piper Jaffray
Universal Studios
US West, Inc.
Western & Southern Life Insurance Co.

ARTS & HUMANITIES-GENERAL

7-Eleven, Inc.
Abbott Laboratories
ABC
Aetna, Inc.
Airborne Freight Corp.
Alaska Airlines, Inc.
Alcoa Inc.
Allmerica Financial Corp.
Alma Piston Co.
Alyeska Pipeline Service Co.
AMCORE Bank Rockford
American General Corp.
American Retail Group
Ameritech Ohio
AmerUS Group
Amgen, Inc.
Andersen Corp.
APL Ltd.
Aristech Chemical Corp.
Arvin Industries, Inc.
Autodesk Inc.
Avery Dennison Corp.
Avista Corporation
Badger Meter, Inc.
Baird & Co. (Robert W.)
Ball Corp.
Bank One Corp.
Bank One, Texas-Houston Office
Bank One, Texas, NA
BankBoston-Connecticut Region
BankBoston Corp.
Banta Corp.
Barry Corp. (R.G.)
Bell Atlantic Corp.
Bell Atlantic Corp.-West Virginia
Bell Atlantic-Delaware, Inc.
Bernstein & Co., Inc. (Sanford C.)
Berwind Group
Binswanger Companies
Blair & Co. (William)
Boston Gas Co.
Boston Globe (The)
Bourns, Inc.
Bradford & Co. (J.C.)
Branch Banking & Trust Co.
Bridgestone/Firestone, Inc.
Briggs & Stratton Corp.
Brooklyn Union
Burnett Co. (Leo)
Business Men's Assurance Co. of America
Cadence Designs Systems, Inc.
Caesar's World, Inc.
Calvin Klein
Campbell Soup Co.
Cantor, Fitzgerald Securities Corp.
Cargill Inc.
Carillon Importers, Ltd.
Castle & Cooke Properties Inc.
Caterpillar Inc.
CCB Financial Corp.
Cenex Harvest States
Centex Corp.
Central Maine Power Co.
CertainTeed Corp.
Chemed Corp.
Chicago Sun-Times, Inc.
Chicago Title Corp.
Cinergy Corp.
Citizens Bank-Flint
CLARCOR Inc.
Clorox Co.
Coachmen Industries, Inc.
Colgate-Palmolive Co.
Collins & Aikman Corp.
Colonial Oil Industries, Inc.
Commercial Federal Corp.
Commercial Intertech Corp.
Compaq Computer Corp.
Computer Associates International, Inc.
Conectiv
Consumers Energy Co.
Conwood Co. LP
Cook Inlet Region
Cooper Tire & Rubber Co.
Copley Press, Inc.
Country Curtains, Inc.
Crane & Co., Inc.
Credit Suisse First Boston
Croft-Leominster
CSX Corp.
CUNA Mutual Group
Curtis Industries, Inc. (Helene)
Daily News
DaimlerChrysler Corp.
Dain Bosworth Inc.
Dayton Hudson
Deere & Co.
Deluxe Corp.
Demoulas Supermarkets Inc.
Deutsch Co.
Diebold, Inc.
Disney Co. (Walt)
Dreyer's Grand Ice Cream
Duchossois Industries Inc.
Dun & Bradstreet Corp.
Duracell International
Duriron Co., Inc.
Eastern Bank
Eastman Chemical Co.
Ebsco Industries, Inc.
EDS Corp.
Employers Insurance of Wausau, A Mutual Co.
Employers Mutual Casualty Co.
Ensign-Bickford Industries
Enterprise Rent-A-Car Co.
Equitable Resources, Inc.
Erving Industries
Evening Post Publishing Co.
Fabri-Kal Corp.
Farmers Group, Inc.
Ferro Corp.
Fidelity Investments
First Financial Bank
First Security Bank of Idaho NA
FirstEnergy Corp.
Florida Power & Light Co.
Forbes Inc.
Ford Motor Co.
Forest City Enterprises, Inc.
Frito-Lay, Inc.
Frontier Corp.
Furniture Brands International, Inc.
Gap, Inc.
Gates Rubber Corp.
GEICO Corp.
General Mills, Inc.
Giant Eagle Inc.
Globe Corp.
GPU Energy
Graco, Inc.
Grainger, Inc. (W.W.)
Guess?
Gulf Power Co.
Hallmark Cards Inc.
Hamilton Sundstrand Corp.
Harcourt General, Inc.
Hartford (The)
Hartford Steam Boiler Inspection & Insurance Co.
Hartmarx Corp.
Heinz Co. (H.J.)
Hercules Inc.
Hickory Tech Corp.
Hitachi America Ltd.
Hoffer Plastics Corp.
HON Industries Inc.
Housatonic Curtain Co.
HSBC Bank USA
Huffy Corp.
Hunt Manufacturing Co.
Hunt Oil Co.
Huntington Bancshares Inc.
Idaho Power Co.
Independent Stave Co.
Ingram Industries Inc.
Interpublic Group of Companies, Inc.
INTRUST Financial Corp.
ISE America
Jacobs Engineering Group
Jostens, Inc.
Journal Communications, Inc.
JSJ Corp.
Kaman Corp.
Kellwood Co.
Kelly Services
Kendall International, Inc.
Kimball International, Inc.
Kimberly-Clark Corp.
Kinder Morgn
Kingsbury Corp.
Lee Enterprises
Levi Strauss & Co.
Liberty Corp.
Liberty Mutual Insurance Group
Loctite Corp.
Lowe's Companies
LTV Corp.
Lyondell Chemical Co.
Madison Gas & Electric Co.
Manulife Financial
Masco Corp.
Massachusetts Mutual Life Insurance Co.
MBIA Inc.
Medtronic, Inc.
Menasha Corp.
Merit Oil Corp.
Mid-America Bank of Louisville
Milliken & Co.
Minnesota Mutual Life Insurance Co.
Monsanto Co.
Morgan & Co. Inc. (J.P.)
Mutual of Omaha Insurance Co.
National City Bank of Cleveland
National City Bank of Columbus
National City Bank of Minneapolis
National City Bank of Pennsylvania
National Computer Systems, Inc.
National Life of Vermont
Nationwide Insurance Co.
NCR Corp.
NEBCO Evans
New England Bio Labs
New Jersey Natural Gas Co.
New York Mercantile Exchange
New York State Electric & Gas Corp.
Niagara Mohawk Holdings Inc.
Nike, Inc.
Nomura Holding America
Nordson Corp.
Northrop Grumman Corp.
Northwest Natural Gas Co.
Norton Co.
Norwest Corp.
OG&E Electric Services
Ohio National Life Insurance Co.
Old National Bank Evansville
ONEOK, Inc.
Owens-Illinois Inc.
Pacific Century Financial Corp.
Pacific Mutual Life Insurance Co.
Penn Mutual Life Insurance Co.
Pennsylvania Power & Light
Pentair Inc.
Philip Morris Companies Inc.
Pioneer Group
Pioneer Natural Resources
PNC Bank
PNC Financial Services Group
Provident Mutual Life Insurance Co.
Public Service Co. of Oklahoma
Pulitzer Publishing Co.
Red Wing Shoe Co. Inc.
Regions Bank
Regions Financial Corp.
Regis Corp.
Riggs Bank NA
Rochester Gas & Electric Corp.
Rohm & Haas Co.
Royal & SunAlliance USA, Inc.
Ruddick Corp.
Safeguard Scientifics
Santa Fe International Corp.
SCANA Corp.
Schering-Plough Corp.
Scientific-Atlanta, Inc.
Security Life of Denver Insurance Co.

Servco Pacific
ServiceMaster Co.
Shaw Industries Inc.
Sherwin-Williams Co.
Sierra Pacific Resources
Simplot Co. (J.R.)
Simpson Investment Co.
Smurfit-Stone Container Corp.
Solo Cup Co.
Sonoco Products Co.
Sprint Corp.
Sprint/United Telephone
SPX Corp.
Stanley Works (The)
Storage Technology Corp.
Stride Rite Corp.
Student Loan Marketing Association
Stupp Brothers Bridge & Iron Co.
Susquehanna-Pfaltzgraff Co.
Tampa Electric Co.
TCF National Bank Minnesota
Teleflex Inc.
Tenneco Packaging
Tesoro Hawaii
Texas Instruments Inc.
Thompson Co. (J. Walter)
Ticketmaster Corp.
Times Mirror Co.
Timken Co. (The)
Titan Industrial Corp.
Toyota Motor Sales U.S.A., Inc.
True North Communications, Inc.
Trustmark Insurance Co.
Trustmark National Bank
TRW Inc.
Tyson Foods Inc.
Ultramar Diamond Shamrock Corp.
Union Planters Corp.
United Distillers & Vintners North America
U.S. Bancorp Piper Jaffray
US Bank, Washington
Valero Energy Corp.
Valmont Industries, Inc.
Vanguard Group
Vesper Corp.
Waffle House Inc.
Washington Mutual, Inc.
Wausau Insurance Companies
West Co. Inc.
Whirlpool Corp.
Wilbur-Ellis Co. & Connell Brothers Co.
Wiremold Co.
Wisconsin Public Service Corp.
Witco Corp.
Wolverine World Wide
Woodward Governor Co.
Wyman-Gordon Co.
Yellow Corp.
Young & Rubicam
Zachry Co. (H.B.)
Zurn Industries, Inc.

HISTORIC PRESERVATION

Abbott Laboratories
ABC
AEGON U.S.A. Inc.
Aetna, Inc.
AFLAC Inc.
AGL Resources Inc.
Air Products and Chemicals, Inc.
Alabama Power Co.
Albertson's Inc.
Alcoa Inc.
Alexander & Baldwin, Inc.
Allegheny Technologies Inc.
AlliedSignal Inc.
AMCORE Bank Rockford
Ameren Corp.
American Express Co.
American Fidelity Corp.
American General Finance
Ameritech Indiana
Ameritech Michigan
Ameritech Wisconsin
AMETEK, Inc.
Amgen, Inc.
AMR Corp.
Amsted Industries Inc.
Andersen Corp.
Andersons Inc.
Anheuser-Busch Companies, Inc.
Aon Corp.
APL Ltd.
Archer-Daniels-Midland Co.
Armstrong World Industries, Inc.
Ashland, Inc.
Atlantic Richfield Co.
Banfi Vintners
Bank of America
Bank of New York Co., Inc.
Bank One Corp.
BankBoston Corp.
Bardes Corp.
Barnes Group Inc.
Belo Corp. (A.H.)
Ben & Jerry's Homemade Inc.
Bestfoods
Bethlehem Steel Corp.
BFGoodrich Co.
Binney & Smith Inc.
Binswanger Companies
Blount International, Inc.
Blue Bell, Inc.
Blue Cross & Blue Shield of Alabama
Borden, Inc.
Borman's Inc.
Boston Edison Co.
Bridgestone/Firestone, Inc.
Briggs & Stratton Corp.
Bristol-Myers Squibb Co.
Brown & Williamson Tobacco Corp.
Brunswick Corp.
Bucyrus-Erie Co.
Burlington Industries, Inc.
Burnett Co. (Leo)
Butler Capital Corp.
Cabot Corp.
Campbell Soup Co.
Cantor, Fitzgerald Securities Corp.
Carolina Power & Light Co.
Carrier Corp.
Carter-Wallace, Inc.
Caterpillar Inc.
Central Maine Power Co.
CertainTeed Corp.
Chase Bank of Texas
Chesapeake Corp.
Chevron Corp.
Church & Dwight Co., Inc.
Cinergy Corp.
Citibank Corp.
Cleveland-Cliffs, Inc.
Clorox Co.
CNA
Coca-Cola Co.
Colonial Life & Accident Insurance Co.
Colonial Oil Industries, Inc.
Commerce Bancshares, Inc.
Consolidated Natural Gas Co.
Consolidated Papers, Inc.
Constellation Energy Group, Inc.
Consumers Energy Co.
Continental Grain Co.
Contran Corp.
Cook Inlet Region
Cooper Industries, Inc.
Coors Brewing Co.
Corning Inc.
Country Curtains, Inc.
Cox Enterprises Inc.
Crane Co.
Crane & Co., Inc.
Crestar Finance Corp.
Cummins Engine Co., Inc.
CUNA Mutual Group
Daily News
DaimlerChrysler Corp.
Dana Corp.
Dayton Power and Light Co.
Deere & Co.
Deluxe Corp.
Demoulas Supermarkets Inc.
Deposit Guaranty National Bank
Detroit Edison Co.
Dexter Corp.
Dixie Group, Inc. (The)
Donaldson Co., Inc.
Donnelley & Sons Co. (R.R.)
Dow Corning Corp.
du Pont de Nemours & Co. (E.I.)
Duke Energy
Dun & Bradstreet Corp.
Dynamet, Inc.
Eastern Bank
Eaton Corp.
Edison International
Elf Atochem North America, Inc.
Emerson Electric Co.
Employers Mutual Casualty Co.
Ensign-Bickford Industries
Equifax Inc.
Ethyl Corp.
Evening Post Publishing Co.
Exxon Mobil Corp.
Federal-Mogul Corp.
Ferro Corp.
Fidelity Investments
Fifth Third Bancorp
Fireman's Fund Insurance Co.
First American Corp.
First Hawaiian, Inc.
First Maryland Bancorp
First Source Corp.
First Tennessee National Corp.
First Union Bank
First Union Corp.
First Union Securities, Inc.
Firstar Bank Milwaukee NA
Fisher Brothers Cleaning Services
FleetBoston Financial Corp.
Florida Rock Industries
Forbes Inc.
Ford Meter Box Co.
Ford Motor Co.
Fort Worth Star-Telegram Inc.
Fortune Brands, Inc.
Freeport-McMoRan Inc.
Frost National Bank
Furniture Brands International, Inc.
Gap, Inc.
GATX Corp.
GEICO Corp.
GenCorp
General Electric Co.
General Mills, Inc.
General Motors Corp.
Georgia-Pacific Corp.
Georgia Power Co.
Glaxo Wellcome Inc.
Golub Corp.
Guardian Life Insurance Co. of America
Gulf Power Co.
Gulfstream Aerospace Corp.
Hallmark Cards Inc.
Hancock Financial Services (John)
Hanna Co. (M.A.)
Harcourt General, Inc.
Harland Co. (John H.)
Harris Trust & Savings Bank
Harsco Corp.
Hartmarx Corp.
Hawaiian Electric Co., Inc.
Heinz Co. (H.J.)
Hensel Phelps Construction Co.
Hickory Tech Corp.
Hitachi America Ltd.
Hoffer Plastics Corp.
Housatonic Curtain Co.
Hubbard Broadcasting, Inc.
Hubbell Inc.
Huffy Corp.
Humana, Inc.
Illinois Tool Works, Inc.
Inland Container Corp.
International Business Machines Corp.
International Paper Co.
INTRUST Financial Corp.
Jacobs Engineering Group
Johnson Controls Inc.
Johnson & Son (S.C.)
Journal-Gazette Co.
Kennametal, Inc.
Kerr-McGee Corp.
Kiewit Sons' Inc. (Peter)
Kimberly-Clark Corp.
Kinder Morgn
Kingsbury Corp.
Koch Industries, Inc.
Kohler Co.
Kroger Co.
La-Z-Boy Inc.
Laclede Gas Co.
LandAmerica Financial Services
Lee Enterprises
Lehigh Portland Cement Co.
Leigh Fibers, Inc.
Lilly & Co. (Eli)
Lincoln Electric Co.
Lincoln Financial Group
Lipton Co.
Loews Corp.
Louisiana Land & Exploration Co.
LTV Corp.
Lubrizol Corp. (The)
Macy's East Inc.
Mallinckrodt Chemical, Inc.
Marcus Corp.
Maritz Inc.
Marshall & Ilsley Corp.
Masco Corp.
May Department Stores Co.
MBIA Inc.
McClatchy Co.
McCormick & Co. Inc.
McDonald & Co. Securities, Inc.
Mead Corp.
Menasha Corp.
Meredith Corp.
Merrill Lynch & Co., Inc.
Metropolitan Life Insurance Co.
Minnesota Mining & Manufacturing Co.
Minnesota Mutual Life Insurance Co.
Monsanto Co.
Montana Power Co.
Morgan Stanley Dean Witter & Co.
Nalco Chemical Co.
National Computer Systems, Inc.
National Fuel Gas Distribution Corp.
National Service Industries, Inc.
Nationwide Insurance Co.
New Century Energies
New England Bio Labs
New England Financial
New York Life Insurance Co.
New York Times Co.
Niagara Mohawk Holdings Inc.
Nordson Corp.
Norfolk Southern Corp.
North American Royalties
Northern Indiana Public Service Co.
Northwest Natural Gas Co.
Norton Co.
Norwest Corp.
OG&E Electric Services
Oklahoma Publishing Co.
Old National Bank Evansville
Olin Corp.
Overseas Shipholding Group Inc.
PACCAR Inc.
Pacific Century Financial Corp.
Pacific Mutual Life Insurance Co.
PacifiCorp
Park National Bank
Parker Hannifin Corp.
Pella Corp.
Pennzoil-Quaker State Co.
Peoples Energy Corp.
PepsiCo, Inc.
PerkinElmer, Inc.
Pfizer Inc.
Pharmacia & Upjohn, Inc.
Phillips Petroleum Co.
Pieper Power Electric Co.
Pittway Corp.
PNC Financial Services Group
Polaroid Corp.
Potomac Electric Power Co.
PPG Industries, Inc.
Premier Dental Products Co.
Premier Industrial Corp.
Price Associates (T. Rowe)
Procter & Gamble Co.
Procter & Gamble Co., Cosmetics Division
Providence Journal-Bulletin Co.

Prudential Insurance Co. of America
Public Service Electric & Gas Co.
Pulitzer Publishing Co.
Putnam Investments
Quaker Chemical Corp.
Ralph's Grocery Co.
Ralston Purina Co.
Rayonier Inc.
Red Wing Shoe Co. Inc.
Reily & Co., Inc. (William B.)
Reinhart Institutional Foods
Reliant Energy Inc.
Reynolds Tobacco (R.J.)
Rich Products Corp.
Rockwell International Corp.
Rouse Co.
Royal & SunAlliance USA, Inc.
Rubbermaid Inc.
SAFECO Corp.
Salomon Smith Barney
Sara Lee Corp.
Sara Lee Hosiery, Inc.
SBC Communications Inc.
Schering-Plough Corp.
Schlumberger Ltd. (USA)
Security Life of Denver Insurance Co.
Sempra Energy
Shaw's Supermarkets, Inc.
Shell Oil Co.
Sherwin-Williams Co.
Simpson Investment Co.
Slant/Fin Corp.
Smith Corp. (A.O.)
Sonoco Products Co.
Sony Electronics
South Bend Tribune Corp.
Southwest Gas Corp.
Sovereign Bank
Sprint Corp.
Star Bank NA
State Street Bank & Trust Co.
Steelcase Inc.
Stone Container Corp.
SunTrust Bank Atlanta
SunTrust Banks of Florida
Susquehanna-Pfaltzgraff Co.
Synovus Financial Corp.
Tenneco Automotive
Textron Inc.
Thermo Electron Corp.
Thompson Co. (J. Walter)
Times Mirror Co.
Timken Co. (The)
Titan Industrial Corp.
TJX Companies, Inc.
Torchmark Corp.
Trace International Holdings, Inc.
Transamerica Corp.
True Oil Co.
Ukrop's Super Markets
Unilever United States, Inc.
Union Camp Corp.
Union Pacific Corp.
United Distillers & Vintners North America
United Parcel Service of America Inc.
United States Trust Co. of New York
United Technologies Corp.
Universal Foods Corp.
Universal Leaf Tobacco Co., Inc.
Universal Studios
Unocal Corp.
UnumProvident
US Bank, Washington
US West, Inc.
USG Corp.
USX Corp.
Valspar Corp.
Varian Medical Systems, Inc.
Vesper Corp.
Vulcan Materials Co.
Wachovia Bank of North Carolina NA
Wal-Mart Stores, Inc.
Waste Management Inc.
West Co. Inc.
Western & Southern Life Insurance Co.
Westvaco Corp.
Weyerhaeuser Co.
Whirlpool Corp.
Wilbur-Ellis Co. & Connell Brothers Co.
Williams
Wiremold Co.
Wisconsin Energy Corp.
Wisconsin Power & Light Co.
Woodward Governor Co.
Wyman-Gordon Co.
Xerox Corp.
Yellow Corp.
York Federal Savings & Loan Association
Zachry Co. (H.B.)
Zilkha & Sons

HISTORY & ARCHAEOLOGY

ABC
AEGON U.S.A. Inc.
Aetna, Inc.
AK Steel Corp.
Alabama Power Co.
Alcoa Inc.
Alexander & Baldwin, Inc.
Allegheny Technologies Inc.
Alliant Techsystems
Allmerica Financial Corp.
Alma Piston Co.
Ameren Corp.
American Fidelity Corp.
American Retail Group
Ameritas Life Insurance Corp.
Ameritech Corp.
AMETEK, Inc.
AMR Corp.
Amsted Industries Inc.
Andersen Corp.
Andersons Inc.
Anheuser-Busch Companies, Inc.
Aon Corp.
APL Ltd.
Archer-Daniels-Midland Co.
Aristech Chemical Corp.
Arizona Public Service Co.
Arvin Industries, Inc.
ASARCO Inc.
Ashland, Inc.
Associated Food Stores
Baird & Co. (Robert W.)
Bank One Corp.
BankAtlantic Bancorp
BankBoston Corp.
Banta Corp.
Bardes Corp.
Barry Corp. (R.G.)
Bassett Furniture Industries
Belk-Simpson Department Stores
Bell Atlantic Corp.
Bemis Co., Inc.
Bemis Manufacturing Co.
Bernstein & Co., Inc. (Sanford C.)
Bethlehem Steel Corp.
BFGoodrich Co.
Binswanger Companies
Blair & Co. (William)
Blount International, Inc.
Blue Cross & Blue Shield of Alabama
Boeing Co.
Bradford & Co. (J.C.)
Burnett Co. (Leo)
Burress (J.W.)
Butler Capital Corp.
Calvin Klein
Cantor, Fitzgerald Securities Corp.
Cargill Inc.
Carillon Importers, Ltd.
Carnival Corp.
Carolina Power & Light Co.
Carpenter Technology Corp.
Central National-Gottesman
Central & South West Services
Central Soya Co.
Century 21
CertainTeed Corp.
CGU Insurance
Chesapeake Corp.
Chicago Board of Trade
Chicago Tribune Co.
CIGNA Corp.
Cinergy Corp.
Circuit City Stores, Inc.
Citigroup
Citizens Financial Group, Inc.
CLARCOR Inc.
Cleveland-Cliffs, Inc.
Coca-Cola Co.
Colonial Oil Industries, Inc.
Commerce Bancshares, Inc.
Commercial Intertech Corp.
Compaq Computer Corp.
ConAgra, Inc.
Consolidated Natural Gas Co.
Consolidated Papers, Inc.
Constellation Energy Group, Inc.
Consumers Energy Co.
Country Curtains, Inc.
Cox Enterprises Inc.
Crane Co.
Crane & Co., Inc.
Cranston Print Works Co.
Crestar Finance Corp.
CSS Industries, Inc.
Cummings Properties Management
Cummins Engine Co., Inc.
CUNA Mutual Group
DaimlerChrysler Corp.
Dayton Hudson
Dayton Power and Light Co.
Deere & Co.
Deluxe Corp.
Demoulas Supermarkets Inc.
Dexter Corp.
Dixie Group, Inc. (The)
Donaldson Co., Inc.
Dow Chemical Co.
Dow Jones & Co., Inc.
Duchossois Industries Inc.
Dynamet, Inc.
Eastern Bank
Eastman Kodak Co.
Eckerd Corp.
Ecolab Inc.
Edison Brothers Stores, Inc.
El Paso Energy Co.
Elf Atochem North America, Inc.
Emerson Electric Co.
Employers Mutual Casualty Co.
Ensign-Bickford Industries
Enterprise Rent-A-Car Co.
Erb Lumber Co.
Evening Post Publishing Co.
Fabri-Kal Corp.
Federal-Mogul Corp.
Ferro Corp.
Fidelity Investments
Fireman's Fund Insurance Co.
First Hawaiian, Inc.
First Source Corp.
First Union Bank
First Union Securities, Inc.
Firstar Bank Milwaukee NA
Fisher Scientific
FleetBoston Financial Corp.
Florida Power Corp.
Florida Rock Industries
Fluor Corp.
Forbes Inc.
Ford Meter Box Co.
Ford Motor Co.
Fort Worth Star-Telegram Inc.
Freeport-McMoRan Inc.
Furniture Brands International, Inc.
Gallo Winery, Inc. (E&J)
GenAmerica Corp.
General Mills, Inc.
Giant Eagle Inc.
Giant Food Inc.
Globe Corp.
Gosiger, Inc.
Graco, Inc.
Green Bay Packaging
GTE Corp.
Gulf Power Co.
Halliburton Co.
Hallmark Cards Inc.
Hamilton Sundstrand Corp.
Hanna Co. (M.A.)
Hannaford Brothers Co.
Harcourt General, Inc.
Harland Co. (John H.)
Harley-Davidson Co.
Harris Trust & Savings Bank
Harsco Corp.
Hartford (The)
Hartmarx Corp.
Hawaiian Electric Co., Inc.
Heinz Co. (H.J.)
Hewlett-Packard Co.
Hitachi America Ltd.
Hoffer Plastics Corp.
Honeywell International Inc.
Housatonic Curtain Co.
Hubbard Broadcasting, Inc.
Hubbell Inc.
Huffy Corp.
Humana, Inc.
Illinois Tool Works, Inc.
INTRUST Financial Corp.
Invacare Corp.
Jacobs Engineering Group
Jeld-wen, Inc.
Johnson & Son (S.C.)
Journal-Gazette Co.
Kellogg Co.
Kennametal, Inc.
Kimberly-Clark Corp.
Kinder Morgn
Kingsbury Corp.
Koch Enterprises, Inc.
La-Z-Boy Inc.
Lancaster Lens, Inc.
Landmark Communications Inc.
Lee Enterprises
Lehigh Portland Cement Co.
Leigh Fibers, Inc.
LG&E Energy Corp.
Lilly & Co. (Eli)
Lincoln Electric Co.
Liz Claiborne, Inc.
Lotus Development Corp.
Louisiana-Pacific Corp.
LTV Corp.
Lubrizol Corp. (The)
Madison Gas & Electric Co.
Marcus Corp.
Masco Corp.
Mead Corp.
Meijer, Inc.
Menasha Corp.
Mercantile Bank NA
Merit Oil Corp.
Merrill Lynch & Co., Inc.
Michigan Consolidated Gas Co.
Mid-America Bank of Louisville
MidAmerican Energy Holdings Co.
Milacron, Inc.
Milliken & Co.
Minnesota Mutual Life Insurance Co.
Monsanto Co.
Montana Power Co.
Morgan & Co. Inc. (J.P.)
Morgan Stanley Dean Witter & Co.
Morris Communications Corp.
Morrison Knudsen Corp.
Nalco Chemical Co.
National City Corp.
National Machinery Co.
National Service Industries, Inc.
Nationwide Insurance Co.
NEBCO Evans
Nestle U.S.A. Inc.
New England Bio Labs
New York Times Co.
Niagara Mohawk Holdings Inc.
Nordson Corp.
Norfolk Southern Corp.
North American Royalties
Northern States Power Co.
Norton Co.
Norwest Corp.
OG&E Electric Services
Oklahoma Publishing Co.
Old Kent Bank
Old National Bank Evansville
Orscheln Co.
PACCAR Inc.
Pacific Century Financial Corp.
Park National Bank
Pella Corp.
PEMCO Corp.
PepsiCo, Inc.
PerkinElmer, Inc.
Pfizer Inc.
Pharmacia & Upjohn, Inc.
Phelps Dodge Corp.
Physicians Mutual Insurance Co.
Pieper Power Electric Co.
Pittway Corp.
PNC Financial Services Group

Polaroid Corp.
PPG Industries, Inc.
Premier Industrial Corp.
Price Associates (T. Rowe)
Principal Financial Group
Providence Journal-Bulletin Co.
Prudential Insurance Co. of America
Prudential Securities Inc.
Pulitzer Publishing Co.
Putnam Investments
Quaker Chemical Corp.
Ralph's Grocery Co.
Ralston Purina Co.
Rayonier Inc.
Red Wing Shoe Co. Inc.
Reinhart Institutional Foods
Revlon Inc.
Reynolds Metals Co.
Reynolds & Reynolds Co.
Reynolds Tobacco (R.J.)
Rich Products Corp.
Rockwell International Corp.
Rubbermaid Inc.
Ruddick Corp.
Russer Foods
Ryder System, Inc.
Saint Paul Companies Inc.
S&T Bancorp
Sara Lee Corp.
SBC Communications Inc.
Scripps Co. (E.W.)
Security Benefit Life Insurance Co.
Security Life of Denver Insurance Co.
Sentinel Communications Co.
Sentry Insurance, A Mutual Co.
Shaw's Supermarkets, Inc.
Shell Oil Co.
Shelter Mutual Insurance Co.
Sherwin-Williams Co.
Simpson Investment Co.
SIT Investment Associates, Inc.
SmithKline Beecham Corp.
Sonoco Products Co.
South Bend Tribune Corp.
Southeastern Mutual Insurance Co.
Star Bank NA
State Farm Mutual Automobile Insurance Co.
State Street Bank & Trust Co.
Steelcase Inc.
Stone Container Corp.
Stupp Brothers Bridge & Iron Co.
SunTrust Bank Atlanta
Susquehanna-Pfaltzgraff Co.
Sverdrup Corp.
Synovus Financial Corp.
Tektronix, Inc.
Teleflex Inc.
TENNANT Co.
Texaco Inc.
TJX Companies, Inc.
TMC Investment Co.
Toledo Blade Co.
Tomkins Industries, Inc.
Toro Co.
Trace International Holdings, Inc.
True North Communications, Inc.
True Oil Co.
TRW Inc.
Ukrop's Super Markets
Unilever Home & Personal Care U.S.A.
Union Pacific Corp.
Union Planters Corp.
United Distillers & Vintners North America
United Wisconsin Services
Universal Leaf Tobacco Co., Inc.
UnumProvident
US West, Inc.
USG Corp.
USX Corp.
Valmont Industries, Inc.
Vanguard Group
Vesper Corp.
Vodafone AirTouch Plc
Vulcan Materials Co.
Wachovia Bank of North Carolina NA
Waffle House Inc.
Washington Trust Bank
Weil, Gotshal & Manges Corp.
Wells Fargo & Co.
West Co. Inc.
Westvaco Corp.
Weyerhaeuser Co.
Whirlpool Corp.
WICOR, Inc.
Williams
Winn-Dixie Stores Inc.
Wisconsin Power & Light Co.
Wisconsin Public Service Corp.
Wyman-Gordon Co.
York Federal Savings & Loan Association
Young & Rubicam
Zilkha & Sons

LIBRARIES

Abbott Laboratories
ABC
AEGON U.S.A. Inc.
Aetna, Inc.
Agrilink Foods, Inc.
Air Products and Chemicals, Inc.
Alabama Power Co.
Albertson's Inc.
Alcoa Inc.
Alcon Laboratories, Inc.
Allegheny Technologies Inc.
Allianz Life Insurance Co. of North America
AlliedSignal Inc.
Allmerica Financial Corp.
Alma Piston Co.
AMCORE Bank Rockford
Ameren Corp.
American Fidelity Corp.
American General Finance
American Standard Inc.
American United Life Insurance Co.
Ameritas Life Insurance Corp.
Ameritech Corp.
AMETEK, Inc.
Amgen, Inc.
AMP Inc.
AMR Corp.
Andersen Corp.
Andersons Inc.
Anheuser-Busch Companies, Inc.
Aon Corp.
APL Ltd.
Appleton Papers Inc.
Archer-Daniels-Midland Co.
Aristech Chemical Corp.
Arizona Public Service Co.
Armstrong World Industries, Inc.
Arvin Industries, Inc.
AT&T Corp.
Atlantic Richfield Co.
Auburn Foundry
Avista Corporation
Avon Products, Inc.
Badger Meter, Inc.
Baird & Co. (Robert W.)
Bank of America
Bank of New York Co., Inc.
Bank One Corp.
Bank One, Texas-Houston Office
BankAtlantic Bancorp
BankBoston Corp.
Banta Corp.
Bardes Corp.
Barnes Group Inc.
Barry Corp. (R.G.)
Battelle Memorial Institute
Bausch & Lomb Inc.
Bechtel Group, Inc.
Belk Stores Services Inc.
Bell Atlantic Corp.
BellSouth Corp.
Bemis Co., Inc.
Bemis Manufacturing Co.
Ben & Jerry's Homemade Inc.
Bernstein & Co., Inc. (Sanford C.)
Berwind Group
Bestfoods
Bethlehem Steel Corp.
BFGoodrich Co.
Binney & Smith Inc.
Binswanger Companies
Blair & Co. (William)
Block, Inc. (H&R)
Blount International, Inc.
Blue Bell, Inc.
Blue Cross & Blue Shield of Iowa
Boeing Co.
Boise Cascade Corp.
Borden, Inc.
Borman's Inc.
Boston Edison Co.
Boston Globe (The)
Bowater Inc.
BP Amoco Corp.
Bradford & Co. (J.C.)
Bridgestone/Firestone, Inc.
Bristol-Myers Squibb Co.
Broderbund Software, Inc.
Brown & Williamson Tobacco Corp.
Brunswick Corp.
Bucyrus-Erie Co.
Burlington Industries, Inc.
Burlington Resources, Inc.
Burnett Co. (Leo)
Butler Capital Corp.
Cabot Corp.
California Bank & Trust
Cargill Inc.
Carillon Importers, Ltd.
Carlson Companies, Inc.
Carolina Power & Light Co.
Carpenter Technology Corp.
Carris Reels
Carter-Wallace, Inc.
CBS Corp.
CCB Financial Corp.
Central Maine Power Co.
Central Newspapers, Inc.
Central & South West Services
Central Vermont Public Service Corp.
CertainTeed Corp.
Cessna Aircraft Co.
CGU Insurance
Champion International Corp.
Chase Bank of Texas
Chase Manhattan Bank, NA
Chesapeake Corp.
Chevron Corp.
Chicago Board of Trade
Chicago Title Corp.
Church & Dwight Co., Inc.
CIBC Oppenheimer
CIGNA Corp.
Cinergy Corp.
CIT Group, Inc. (The)
Citibank Corp.
Citigroup
Citizens Financial Group, Inc.
CLARCOR Inc.
Cleveland-Cliffs, Inc.
Clorox Co.
CNA
Coca-Cola Co.
Collins & Aikman Corp.
Colonial Life & Accident Insurance Co.
Comerica Inc.
Commerce Bancshares, Inc.
Commercial Intertech Corp.
Commonwealth Edison Co.
Consolidated Natural Gas Co.
Consolidated Papers, Inc.
Constellation Energy Group, Inc.
Consumers Energy Co.
Contran Corp.
Cooper Industries, Inc.
Cooper Tire & Rubber Co.
Copley Press, Inc.
Corning Inc.
Country Curtains, Inc.
Cox Enterprises Inc.
Crane Co.
Cranston Print Works Co.
Credit Suisse First Boston
Crestar Finance Corp.
Cummings Properties Management
Cummins Engine Co., Inc.
CUNA Mutual Group
Daily News
DaimlerChrysler Corp.
Dayton Hudson
Dayton Power and Light Co.
Deere & Co.
DeKalb Genetics Corp.
Demoulas Supermarkets Inc.
Detroit Edison Co.
Dexter Corp.
Dial Corp.
Disney Co. (Walt)
Dominion Resources, Inc.
Domino's Pizza Inc.
Donaldson Co., Inc.
Donnelley & Sons Co. (R.R.)
Dow Corning Corp.
Dow Jones & Co., Inc.
du Pont de Nemours & Co. (E.I.)
Duchossois Industries Inc.
Duke Energy
Dun & Bradstreet Corp.
Dynamet, Inc.
Eastern Bank
Eastman Kodak Co.
Eaton Corp.
Ebsco Industries, Inc.
Edison Brothers Stores, Inc.
Edison International
El Paso Energy Co.
Elf Atochem North America, Inc.
Employers Mutual Casualty Co.
Ensign-Bickford Industries
Erving Industries
Ethyl Corp.
Evening Post Publishing Co.
Excel Corp.
Exxon Mobil Corp.
Federal-Mogul Corp.
Federated Mutual Insurance Co.
Fidelity Investments
Fireman's Fund Insurance Co.
First American Corp.
First Financial Bank
First Hawaiian, Inc.
First Maryland Bancorp
First Source Corp.
First Tennessee National Corp.
First Union Corp.
First Union National Bank, NA
First Union Securities, Inc.
Firstar Bank Milwaukee NA
Fisher Brothers Cleaning Services
FleetBoston Financial Corp.
Forbes Inc.
Ford Meter Box Co.
Ford Motor Co.
Fort James Corp.
Fort Worth Star-Telegram Inc.
Fortis Insurance Co.
Fortune Brands, Inc.
Freeport-McMoRan Inc.
Frost National Bank
Fuller Co. (H.B.)
Gallo Winery, Inc. (E&J)
Galter Corp.
Gap, Inc.
GATX Corp.
GenAmerica Corp.
GenCorp
General Electric Co.
General Mills, Inc.
General Motors Corp.
Georgia-Pacific Corp.
Georgia Power Co.
Giant Eagle Inc.
Giant Food Inc.
Giddings & Lewis
Gillette Co.
Grede Foundries
GTE Corp.
Guardian Life Insurance Co. of America
Gulf Power Co.
Halliburton Co.
Hamilton Sundstrand Corp.
Hancock Financial Services (John)
Hannaford Brothers Co.
Harcourt General, Inc.
Harley-Davidson Co.
Harnischfeger Industries
Harsco Corp.
Hartford (The)
Hartmarx Corp.
Hasbro, Inc.
Heinz Co. (H.J.)
Heller Financial, Inc.
Hershey Foods Corp.
Hickory Tech Corp.
Hoffmann-La Roche Inc.

HON Industries Inc.
Housatonic Curtain Co.
Hubbard Broadcasting, Inc.
Humana, Inc.
Hunt Manufacturing Co.
Huntington Bancshares Inc.
IBP
Illinois Tool Works, Inc.
Inland Container Corp.
Inman Mills
International Business Machines Corp.
International Flavors & Fragrances Inc.
International Multifoods Corp.
International Paper Co.
Jeld-wen, Inc.
Johnson Controls Inc.
Johnson & Son (S.C.)
Jostens, Inc.
Journal-Gazette Co.
Kemper National Insurance Companies
Kennametal, Inc.
Kimberly-Clark Corp.
Kinder Morgn
Kingsbury Corp.
Kmart Corp.
Kroger Co.
La-Z-Boy Inc.
Ladish Co., Inc.
Lee Enterprises
Lehigh Portland Cement Co.
Leigh Fibers, Inc.
LG&E Energy Corp.
Liberty Corp.
Lilly & Co. (Eli)
Lipton Co.
Little, Inc. (Arthur D.)
Liz Claiborne, Inc.
Loews Corp.
Louisiana-Pacific Corp.
Lowe's Companies
LTV Corp.
MacMillan Bloedel Inc.
Macy's East Inc.
Madison Gas & Electric Co.
Marcus Corp.
Maritz Inc.
Marshall & Ilsley Corp.
Massachusetts Mutual Life Insurance Co.
Mattel Inc.
May Department Stores Co.
MBIA Inc.
McClatchy Co.
McCormick & Co. Inc.
McDonald & Co. Securities, Inc.
McGraw-Hill Companies, Inc.
MCI WorldCom, Inc.
Mead Corp.
Medtronic, Inc.
Merck & Co.
Merit Oil Corp.
Merrill Lynch & Co., Inc.
Metropolitan Life Insurance Co.
MidAmerican Energy Holdings Co.
Milliken & Co.
Millipore Corp.
Mine Safety Appliances Co.
Minnesota Mining & Manufacturing Co.
Minnesota Mutual Life Insurance Co.
Monarch Machine Tool Co.
Monsanto Co.
Montana Power Co.
MONY Group (The)
Morgan & Co. Inc. (J.P.)
Morgan Stanley Dean Witter & Co.
Morris Communications Corp.
Morrison Knudsen Corp.
MTD Products Inc.
Nabisco Group Holdings
Nalco Chemical Co.
National City Corp.
National Machinery Co.
National Service Industries, Inc.
NEBCO Evans
Nestle U.S.A. Inc.
New Jersey Natural Gas Co.
New York Life Insurance Co.
New York Mercantile Exchange
New York Stock Exchange, Inc.
New York Times Co.
Newman's Own Inc.
Niagara Mohawk Holdings Inc.
North American Royalties
Northern States Power Co.
Northwest Bank Nebraska, NA
Northwest Natural Gas Co.
Norton Co.
Norwest Corp.
Occidental Oil and Gas
OG&E Electric Services
Ohio National Life Insurance Co.
Old Kent Bank
Old National Bank Evansville
Olin Corp.
Oshkosh B'Gosh, Inc.
Outboard Marine Corp.
Overseas Shipholding Group Inc.
PACCAR Inc.
Pacific Mutual Life Insurance Co.
PacifiCorp
Paine Webber
Parker Hannifin Corp.
PECO Energy Co.
Pella Corp.
Pennzoil-Quaker State Co.
Peoples Energy Corp.
PepsiCo, Inc.
Pfizer Inc.
Phelps Dodge Corp.
Physicians Mutual Insurance Co.
PNC Financial Services Group
Polaroid Corp.
Potomac Electric Power Co.
PPG Industries, Inc.
Premier Industrial Corp.
Price Associates (T. Rowe)
Principal Financial Group
Procter & Gamble Co., Cosmetics Division
Providence Journal-Bulletin Co.
Provident Companies, Inc.
Prudential Insurance Co. of America
Prudential Securities Inc.
Public Service Electric & Gas Co.
Pulitzer Publishing Co.
Putnam Investments
Quaker Chemical Corp.
Ralph's Grocery Co.
Ralston Purina Co.
Reader's Digest Association, Inc. (The)
Red Wing Shoe Co. Inc.
Reinhart Institutional Foods
Reliant Energy Inc.
Revlon Inc.
Reynolds Metals Co.
Reynolds Tobacco (R.J.)
Rich Products Corp.
Rockwell International Corp.
Rouse Co.
Royal & SunAlliance USA, Inc.
Russer Foods
Rutledge Hill Press
SAFECO Corp.
Saint Paul Companies Inc.
Salomon Smith Barney
S&T Bancorp
Sara Lee Corp.
Sara Lee Hosiery, Inc.
SBC Communications Inc.
Schering-Plough Corp.
Schloss & Co. (Marcus)
Schlumberger Ltd. (USA)
Schwab & Co., Inc. (Charles)
Scripps Co. (E.W.)
Seagram & Sons, Inc. (Joseph E.)
Seaway Food Town, Inc.
Security Life of Denver Insurance Co.
Sega of America Inc.
Sempra Energy
Sentry Insurance, A Mutual Co.
Shaw's Supermarkets, Inc.
Shea Co. (John F.)
Shell Oil Co.
Sherwin-Williams Co.
Sierra Pacific Industries
Sierra Pacific Resources
Simplot Co. (J.R.)
Simpson Investment Co.
Slant/Fin Corp.
Smith Corp. (A.O.)
SmithKline Beecham Corp.
Sonoco Products Co.
South Bend Tribune Corp.
Southeastern Mutual Insurance Co.
Southern New England Telephone Co.
Sovereign Bank
SPX Corp.
Square D Co.
Standard Register Co.
Stanley Works (The)
Star Bank NA
State Street Bank & Trust Co.
Steelcase Inc.
Stone Container Corp.
Stonecutter Mills Corp.
Storage Technology Corp.
Stupp Brothers Bridge & Iron Co.
SunTrust Bank Atlanta
SunTrust Banks of Florida
TCF National Bank Minnesota
Tektronix, Inc.
Teleflex Inc.
Temple-Inland Inc.
Tenneco Automotive
Tenneco Packaging
Texaco Inc.
Texas Instruments Inc.
Textron Inc.
Thermo Electron Corp.
Thomasville Furniture Industries Inc.
Thompson Co. (J. Walter)
Ticketmaster Corp.
Times Mirror Co.
Titan Industrial Corp.
TMC Investment Co.
Toledo Blade Co.
Tomkins Industries, Inc.
Trace International Holdings, Inc.
Transamerica Corp.
Ultramar Diamond Shamrock Corp.
Unilever Home & Personal Care U.S.A.
Unilever United States, Inc.
Union Camp Corp.
Union Carbide Corp.
Union Pacific Corp.
United Airlines Inc.
United Distillers & Vintners North America
United Dominion Industries, Ltd.
United Services Automobile Association
U.S. Bancorp Piper Jaffray
United States Sugar Corp.
United Wisconsin Services
Universal Studios
Unocal Corp.
US Bank, Washington
USAA Life Insurance Co.
USG Corp.
USX Corp.
Valmont Industries, Inc.
Vanguard Group
Vesper Corp.
Vodafone AirTouch Plc
Vulcan Materials Co.
Wachovia Bank of North Carolina NA
Wachtell, Lipton, Rosen & Katz
Wal-Mart Stores, Inc.
Washington Mutual, Inc.
Weil, Gotshal & Manges Corp.
West Co. Inc.
Western & Southern Life Insurance Co.
Westvaco Corp.
Weyerhaeuser Co.
Whirlpool Corp.
WICOR, Inc.
Wilbur-Ellis Co. & Connell Brothers Co.
Wiley & Sons (John)
Williams
Winn-Dixie Stores Inc.
Wiremold Co.
Wisconsin Power & Light Co.
Wisconsin Public Service Corp.
Witco Corp.
Wolverine World Wide
Wyman-Gordon Co.
Xerox Corp.
Yellow Corp.
York Federal Savings & Loan Association
Young & Rubicam
Zachry Co. (H.B.)
Zilkha & Sons

LITERARY ARTS

Alcoa Inc.
AMCORE Bank Rockford
Ameritech Indiana
Bank of New York Co., Inc.
Binney & Smith Inc.
Block, Inc. (H&R)
Blount International, Inc.
Borman's Inc.
Cabot Corp.
Calvin Klein
Central Maine Power Co.
Chase Manhattan Bank, NA
Chicago Tribune Co.
Citizens Financial Group, Inc.
Clorox Co.
CNA
Copley Press, Inc.
Dayton Hudson
Deluxe Corp.
Demoulas Supermarkets Inc.
Dexter Corp.
Dominion Resources, Inc.
Donnelley & Sons Co. (R.R.)
du Pont de Nemours & Co. (E.I.)
Duchossois Industries Inc.
Excel Corp.
First American Corp.
First Union Corp.
First Union National Bank, NA
Forbes Inc.
Fuller Co. (H.B.)
General Atlantic Partners II LP
General Mills, Inc.
Goldman Sachs Group
Golub Corp.
Hartford (The)
Hartford Steam Boiler Inspection & Insurance Co.
Heinz Co. (H.J.)
Hitachi America Ltd.
Honeywell International Inc.
Lee Enterprises
Macy's East Inc.
Marshall Field's
McClatchy Co.
MONY Group (The)
Morris Communications Corp.
MTD Products Inc.
NEBCO Evans
New England Financial
New York Times Co.
Niagara Mohawk Holdings Inc.
Norton Co.
Old National Bank Evansville
Pella Corp.
PNC Financial Services Group
PPG Industries, Inc.
Reynolds Tobacco (R.J.)
Rouse Co.
Rubbermaid Inc.
Ryder System, Inc.
Saint Paul Companies Inc.
Sara Lee Hosiery, Inc.
Schloss & Co. (Marcus)
Schlumberger Ltd. (USA)
Scripps Co. (E.W.)
Slant/Fin Corp.
Steelcase Inc.
TENNANT Co.
Texaco Inc.
Toledo Blade Co.
Tomkins Industries, Inc.
Trace International Holdings, Inc.
Transamerica Corp.
Union Camp Corp.
United Parcel Service of America Inc.
Universal Studios
Vesper Corp.

Vulcan Materials Co.
Whirlpool Corp.
Wiremold Co.

MUSEUMS/GALLERIES

Abbott Laboratories
ABC
AEGON U.S.A. Inc.
AFLAC Inc.
AGL Resources Inc.
Agrilink Foods, Inc.
Air Products and Chemicals, Inc.
AK Steel Corp.
Alabama Power Co.
Albany International Corp.
Alcoa Inc.
Alcon Laboratories, Inc.
Alexander & Baldwin, Inc.
Allegheny Technologies Inc.
Alliant Techsystems
Allianz Life Insurance Co. of North America
AlliedSignal Inc.
Allmerica Financial Corp.
Allstate Insurance Co.
AMCORE Bank Rockford
Ameren Corp.
American Express Co.
American Fidelity Corp.
American General Finance
American Stock Exchange, Inc.
American United Life Insurance Co.
Ameritas Life Insurance Corp.
Ameritech Corp.
Ameritech Illinois
Ameritech Indiana
Ameritech Michigan
Ameritech Ohio
Ameritech Wisconsin
AMETEK, Inc.
Amgen, Inc.
AMP Inc.
AMR Corp.
Amsted Industries Inc.
Analog Devices, Inc.
Andersen Corp.
Andersons Inc.
Anheuser-Busch Companies, Inc.
Aon Corp.
APL Ltd.
Apple Computer, Inc.
Appleton Papers Inc.
Archer-Daniels-Midland Co.
Aristech Chemical Corp.
Arizona Public Service Co.
Arvin Industries, Inc.
Ashland, Inc.
AT&T Corp.
Atlantic Investment Co.
Avery Dennison Corp.
Avista Corporation
Avon Products, Inc.
Badger Meter, Inc.
Baird & Co. (Robert W.)
Baker Hughes Inc.
Banfi Vintners
Bank of America
Bank of New York Co., Inc.
Bank One Corp.
Bank One, Texas-Houston Office
BankAtlantic Bancorp
BankBoston Corp.
Banta Corp.
Barclays Capital
Bard, Inc. (C.R.)
Barden Corp.
Bardes Corp.
Barnes Group Inc.
Barry Corp. (R.G.)
Bassett Furniture Industries
Battelle Memorial Institute
Bausch & Lomb Inc.
Baxter International Inc.
Bayer Corp.
Bean, Inc. (L.L.)
Bechtel Group, Inc.
Belk-Simpson Department Stores
Belk Stores Services Inc.
Bell Atlantic Corp.
BellSouth Corp.
Belo Corp. (A.H.)
Bemis Co., Inc.
Bemis Manufacturing Co.
Bernstein & Co., Inc. (Sanford C.)
Berwind Group
Bestfoods
Bethlehem Steel Corp.
BFGoodrich Co.
Binney & Smith Inc.
Binswanger Companies
Blair & Co. (William)
Block, Inc. (H&R)
Blount International, Inc.
Blue Bell, Inc.
Blue Cross & Blue Shield of Minnesota
Boeing Co.
Boise Cascade Corp.
Borden, Inc.
Borman's Inc.
Boston Edison Co.
Boston Globe (The)
Bourns, Inc.
BP Amoco Corp.
Bradford & Co. (J.C.)
Bridgestone/Firestone, Inc.
Briggs & Stratton Corp.
Bristol-Myers Squibb Co.
Brown Shoe Co., Inc.
Brown & Williamson Tobacco Corp.
Browning-Ferris Industries Inc.
Brunswick Corp.
Bucyrus-Erie Co.
Burlington Industries, Inc.
Burlington Resources, Inc.
Burnett Co. (Leo)
Burress (J.W.)
Butler Capital Corp.
Butler Manufacturing Co.
Cabot Corp.
California Bank & Trust
Callaway Golf Co.
Calvin Klein
Campbell Soup Co.
Cantor, Fitzgerald Securities Corp.
Cargill Inc.
Carillon Importers, Ltd.
Carlson Companies, Inc.
Carnival Corp.
Carolina Power & Light Co.
Carpenter Technology Corp.
Carrier Corp.
Carter-Wallace, Inc.
Caterpillar Inc.
CBS Corp.
Central Maine Power Co.
Central National-Gottesman
Central & South West Services
Central Soya Co.
Central Vermont Public Service Corp.
CertainTeed Corp.
Cessna Aircraft Co.
CGU Insurance
Champion International Corp.
Charter Manufacturing Co.
Chase Bank of Texas
Chase Manhattan Bank, NA
Chemed Corp.
Chesapeake Corp.
Chevron Corp.
Chicago Board of Trade
Chicago Sun-Times, Inc.
Chicago Title Corp.
Chicago Tribune Co.
Chubb Corp.
Church & Dwight Co., Inc.
CIGNA Corp.
Cincinnati Bell Inc.
Cinergy Corp.
Circuit City Stores, Inc.
CIT Group, Inc. (The)
Citibank Corp.
Citigroup
Citizens Financial Group, Inc.
CLARCOR Inc.
Clark Refining & Marketing
Cleveland-Cliffs, Inc.
Clorox Co.
CNA
CNF Transportation, Inc.
Coca-Cola Co.
Collins & Aikman Corp.
Colonial Life & Accident Insurance Co.
Colonial Oil Industries, Inc.
Comdisco, Inc.
Commerce Bancshares, Inc.
Commonwealth Edison Co.
Compaq Computer Corp.
Compass Bank
ConAgra, Inc.
Consolidated Natural Gas Co.
Consolidated Papers, Inc.
Constellation Energy Group, Inc.
Consumers Energy Co.
Continental Grain Co.
Contran Corp.
Conwood Co. LP
Cook Inlet Region
Cooper Industries, Inc.
Cooper Tire & Rubber Co.
Coors Brewing Co.
Copley Press, Inc.
Corning Inc.
Country Curtains, Inc.
Cox Enterprises Inc.
CPI Corp.
Crane Co.
Crane & Co., Inc.
Cranston Print Works Co.
Credit Suisse First Boston
Crestar Finance Corp.
Croft-Leominster
CSS Industries, Inc.
Cummings Properties Management
Cummins Engine Co., Inc.
CUNA Mutual Group
Cyprus Amax Minerals Co.
Daily News
DaimlerChrysler Corp.
Dain Bosworth Inc.
Dana Corp.
Danis Companies
Dayton Hudson
Dayton Power and Light Co.
Deere & Co.
DeKalb Genetics Corp.
Deluxe Corp.
Demoulas Supermarkets Inc.
Deposit Guaranty National Bank
Detroit Edison Co.
Deutsch Co.
Dexter Corp.
Dial Corp.
Disney Co. (Walt)
Dixie Group, Inc. (The)
Dominion Resources, Inc.
Donaldson Co., Inc.
Donnelley & Sons Co. (R.R.)
Dow Chemical Co.
Dow Corning Corp.
Dow Jones & Co., Inc.
du Pont de Nemours & Co. (E.I.)
Duchossois Industries Inc.
Duke Energy
Dun & Bradstreet Corp.
Dynamet, Inc.
Eastern Bank
Eastern Enterprises
Eastman Kodak Co.
Eaton Corp.
Eckerd Corp.
Ecolab Inc.
Edison International
El Paso Energy Co.
Elf Atochem North America, Inc.
Emerson Electric Co.
Employers Mutual Casualty Co.
Ensign-Bickford Industries
Entergy Corp.
Enterprise Rent-A-Car Co.
Erb Lumber Co.
Ethyl Corp.
Evening Post Publishing Co.
Exxon Mobil Corp.
Fabri-Kal Corp.
Fannie Mae
Federal-Mogul Corp.
Federated Department Stores, Inc.
FedEx Corp.
Ferro Corp.
Fidelity Investments
Fifth Third Bancorp
FINA
Fireman's Fund Insurance Co.
First Financial Bank
First Hawaiian, Inc.
First Maryland Bancorp
First Source Corp.
First Tennessee National Corp.
First Union Bank
First Union Corp.
First Union National Bank, NA
First Union Securities, Inc.
Firstar Bank Milwaukee NA
Fisher Brothers Cleaning Services
Fisher Scientific
FleetBoston Financial Corp.
Florida Power & Light Co.
Florida Rock Industries
Fluor Corp.
FMC Corp.
Forbes Inc.
Ford Meter Box Co.
Ford Motor Co.
Forest City Enterprises, Inc.
Fort James Corp.
Fort Worth Star-Telegram Inc.
Fortis, Inc.
Fortis Insurance Co.
Fortune Brands, Inc.
Franklin Mint (The)
Freeport-McMoRan Inc.
Frost National Bank
Fuller Co. (H.B.)
Furniture Brands International, Inc.
Gallo Winery, Inc. (E&J)
Gap, Inc.
GATX Corp.
GEICO Corp.
GenAmerica Corp.
GenCorp
General Mills, Inc.
General Motors Corp.
Georgia-Pacific Corp.
Georgia Power Co.
Giant Eagle Inc.
Giant Food Inc.
Giddings & Lewis
Gillette Co.
Glaxo Wellcome Inc.
Glickenhaus & Co.
Globe Corp.
Goldman Sachs Group
Golub Corp.
Grede Foundries
Green Bay Packaging
GTE Corp.
Guardian Life Insurance Co. of America
Gucci America Inc.
Gulf Power Co.
Halliburton Co.
Hallmark Cards Inc.
Hamilton Sundstrand Corp.
Hancock Financial Services (John)
Hanna Co. (M.A.)
Hannaford Brothers Co.
Harcourt General, Inc.
Harland Co. (John H.)
Harley-Davidson Co.
Harnischfeger Industries
Harris Corp.
Harris Trust & Savings Bank
Harsco Corp.
Hartford (The)
Hartford Steam Boiler Inspection & Insurance Co.
Hartmarx Corp.
Hasbro, Inc.
Hawaiian Electric Co., Inc.
Heinz Co. (H.J.)
Hensel Phelps Construction Co.
Hershey Foods Corp.
Hewlett-Packard Co.
Hitachi America Ltd.
Hoffer Plastics Corp.
Hoffmann-La Roche Inc.
Hofmann Co.
Home Depot, Inc.
HON Industries Inc.
Honeywell International Inc.
Housatonic Curtain Co.
Household International Inc.
Hubbard Broadcasting, Inc.
Hubbell Inc.
Huffy Corp.
Humana, Inc.
Hunt Manufacturing Co.
Huntington Bancshares Inc.
IKON Office Solutions, Inc.
Illinois Tool Works, Inc.
Industrial Bank of Japan Trust Co. (New York)
Inland Container Corp.
Intel Corp.

International Business Machines Corp.
International Flavors & Fragrances Inc.
International Multifoods Corp.
International Paper Co.
INTRUST Financial Corp.
ISE America
Jacobs Engineering Group
Jacobson & Sons (Benjamin)
Jeld-wen, Inc.
Johnson Controls Inc.
Johnson & Johnson
Johnson & Son (S.C.)
Jones & Co. (Edward D.)
Jostens, Inc.
Journal-Gazette Co.
JSJ Corp.
Katten, Muchin & Zavis
Kellwood Co.
Kelly Services
Kemper National Insurance Companies
Kennametal, Inc.
Kerr-McGee Corp.
Kiewit Sons' Inc. (Peter)
Kimball International, Inc.
Kimberly-Clark Corp.
Kinder Morgn
Kingsbury Corp.
Kirkland & Ellis
Kmart Corp.
Koch Enterprises, Inc.
Kohler Co.
Kroger Co.
La-Z-Boy Inc.
Laclede Gas Co.
Ladish Co., Inc.
Lancaster Lens, Inc.
Lance, Inc.
Landmark Communications Inc.
Lee Enterprises
Lehigh Portland Cement Co.
Leigh Fibers, Inc.
Levi Strauss & Co.
Leviton Manufacturing Co. Inc.
LG&E Energy Corp.
Liberty Corp.
Lilly & Co. (Eli)
Lincoln Electric Co.
Lincoln Financial Group
Lipton Co.
Little, Inc. (Arthur D.)
Litton Industries, Inc.
Liz Claiborne, Inc.
Loews Corp.
Lotus Development Corp.
Louisiana Land & Exploration Co.
Louisiana-Pacific Corp.
LTV Corp.
Lubrizol Corp. (The)
Macy's East Inc.
Madison Gas & Electric Co.
Marcus Corp.
Maritz Inc.
Mark IV Industries
Marriott International Inc.
Marshall Field's
Marshall & Ilsley Corp.
Masco Corp.
Massachusetts Mutual Life Insurance Co.
May Department Stores Co.
Maytag Corp.
MBIA Inc.
McClatchy Co.
McCormick & Co. Inc.
McDonald & Co. Securities, Inc.
McDonald's Corp.
McGraw-Hill Companies, Inc.
MCI WorldCom, Inc.
McKesson-HBOC Corp.
McWane Inc.
Mead Corp.
Medtronic, Inc.
Mellon Financial Corp.
Menasha Corp.
Mercantile Bank NA
Merck & Co.
Meredith Corp.
Merit Oil Corp.
Merrill Lynch & Co., Inc.
Mervyn's California
Metropolitan Life Insurance Co.
Michigan Consolidated Gas Co.
Mid-America Bank of Louisville
Milacron, Inc.
Milliken & Co.
Millipore Corp.
Mine Safety Appliances Co.
Minnesota Mining & Manufacturing Co.
Minnesota Mutual Life Insurance Co.
Monsanto Co.
Montana Power Co.
Montgomery Ward & Co., Inc.
MONY Group (The)
Morgan & Co. Inc. (J.P.)
Morgan Stanley Dean Witter & Co.
Morrison Knudsen Corp.
Morton International Inc.
Motorola Inc.
MTD Products Inc.
Mutual of Omaha Insurance Co.
Nabisco Group Holdings
Nalco Chemical Co.
National Bank of Commerce Trust & Savings
National City Bank of Minneapolis
National City Corp.
National Computer Systems, Inc.
National Fuel Gas Distribution Corp.
National Presto Industries, Inc.
National Service Industries, Inc.
National Starch & Chemical Co.
Nationwide Insurance Co.
NEBCO Evans
Nestle U.S.A. Inc.
New Century Energies
New England Financial
New York Life Insurance Co.
New York Mercantile Exchange
New York Stock Exchange, Inc.
New York Times Co.
Newman's Own Inc.
Niagara Mohawk Holdings Inc.
Nordson Corp.
Norfolk Southern Corp.
Nortel
North American Royalties
Northern Indiana Public Service Co.
Northern States Power Co.
Northern Trust Co.
Northwest Natural Gas Co.
Norton Co.
Norwest Corp.
Occidental Oil and Gas
Occidental Petroleum Corp.
OG&E Electric Services
Ohio National Life Insurance Co.
Oklahoma Publishing Co.
Old Kent Bank
Old National Bank Evansville
Olin Corp.
Oshkosh B'Gosh, Inc.
Outboard Marine Corp.
Overnite Transportation Co.
Overseas Shipholding Group Inc.
Owens Corning
PACCAR Inc.
Pacific Century Financial Corp.
Pacific Gas and Electric Co.
Pacific Mutual Life Insurance Co.
PacifiCare Health Systems
PacifiCorp
Paine Webber
Pan-American Life Insurance Co.
Parker Hannifin Corp.
Pella Corp.
PEMCO Corp.
Penney Co., Inc. (J.C.)
Pennzoil-Quaker State Co.
Peoples Bank
Peoples Energy Corp.
PepsiCo, Inc.
PerkinElmer, Inc.
Pfizer Inc.
Pharmacia & Upjohn, Inc.
Phelps Dodge Corp.
Philip Morris Companies Inc.
Philips Electronics North America Corp.
Phillips Petroleum Co.
Physicians Mutual Insurance Co.
Pieper Power Electric Co.
Pillsbury Co.
Pioneer Group
Pittway Corp.
PNC Bank Kentucky Inc.
PNC Financial Services Group
Polaroid Corp.
Potlatch Corp.
Potomac Electric Power Co.
PPG Industries, Inc.
Premier Dental Products Co.
Premier Industrial Corp.
Price Associates (T. Rowe)
Procter & Gamble Co.
Procter & Gamble Co., Cosmetics Division
Promus Hotel Corp.
Providence Journal-Bulletin Co.
Provident Companies, Inc.
Prudential Insurance Co. of America
Prudential Securities Inc.
Public Service Electric & Gas Co.
Publix Supermarkets
Pulitzer Publishing Co.
Putnam Investments
Quaker Chemical Corp.
Quanex Corp.
Questar Corp.
Ralph's Grocery Co.
Ralston Purina Co.
Rayonier Inc.
Reader's Digest Association, Inc. (The)
Red Wing Shoe Co. Inc.
Reebok International Ltd.
Regions Bank
Regis Corp.
Reilly Industries, Inc.
Reily & Co., Inc. (William B.)
Reliant Energy Inc.
ReliaStar Financial Corp.
Revlon Inc.
Reynolds Metals Co.
Reynolds & Reynolds Co.
Reynolds Tobacco (R.J.)
Rich Products Corp.
Rochester Gas & Electric Corp.
Rockwell International Corp.
Rouse Co.
Royal & SunAlliance USA, Inc.
Rubbermaid Inc.
Ruddick Corp.
Russer Foods
Ryder System, Inc.
SAFECO Corp.
Safeguard Scientifics
Saint Paul Companies Inc.
Salomon Smith Barney
S&T Bancorp
Sara Lee Corp.
Sara Lee Hosiery, Inc.
SBC Communications Inc.
Schering-Plough Corp.
Schloss & Co. (Marcus)
Schlumberger Ltd. (USA)
Schwab & Co., Inc. (Charles)
Scripps Co. (E.W.)
Seagram & Sons, Inc. (Joseph E.)
Searle & Co. (G.D.)
Seaway Food Town, Inc.
Security Benefit Life Insurance Co.
Security Life of Denver Insurance Co.
Sempra Energy
Servco Pacific
S.G. Cowen
Shaklee Corp.
Shaw's Supermarkets, Inc.
Shea Co. (John F.)
Shell Oil Co.
Sherwin-Williams Co.
Sierra Pacific Industries
Sierra Pacific Resources
Simplot Co. (J.R.)
Simpson Investment Co.
SIT Investment Associates, Inc.
Slant/Fin Corp.
Smith Corp. (A.O.)
SmithKline Beecham Corp.
Smurfit-Stone Container Corp.
Sonoco Products Co.
Sony Electronics
South Bend Tribune Corp.
Southeastern Mutual Insurance Co.
Southwest Gas Corp.
Sovereign Bank
Springs Industries, Inc.
Sprint Corp.
Sprint/United Telephone
SPX Corp.
Square D Co.
Stanley Works (The)
Star Bank NA
Starwood Hotels & Resorts Worldwide, Inc.
State Street Bank & Trust Co.
Steelcase Inc.
Stone Container Corp.
Stonecutter Mills Corp.
Storage Technology Corp.
Strear Farms Co.
Stride Rite Corp.
Stupp Brothers Bridge & Iron Co.
Sun Microsystems Inc.
Sunoco Inc.
SunTrust Bank Atlanta
SunTrust Banks of Florida
Sverdrup Corp.
Synovus Financial Corp.
Target Corp.
TCF National Bank Minnesota
Tektronix, Inc.
Teleflex Inc.
Temple-Inland Inc.
TENNANT Co.
Tenneco Automotive
Tenneco Packaging
Tension Envelope Corp.
Tesoro Hawaii
Texaco Inc.
Texas Gas Transmission Corp.
Texas Instruments Inc.
Textron Inc.
Thermo Electron Corp.
Thomasville Furniture Industries Inc.
Thompson Co. (J. Walter)
Times Mirror Co.
Timken Co. (The)
Titan Industrial Corp.
TJX Companies, Inc.
TMC Investment Co.
Toledo Blade Co.
Torchmark Corp.
Toro Co.
Toyota Motor Sales U.S.A., Inc.
Trace International Holdings, Inc.
Transamerica Corp.
True North Communications, Inc.
True Oil Co.
Trustmark Insurance Co.
TRW Inc.
TU Electric Co.
Tyson Foods Inc.
Ukrop's Super Markets
Unilever Home & Personal Care U.S.A.
Unilever United States, Inc.
Union Camp Corp.
Union Carbide Corp.
Union Pacific Corp.
Union Planters Corp.
Unisys Corp.
United Airlines Inc.
United Co.
United Distillers & Vintners North America
United Dominion Industries, Ltd.
United Parcel Service of America Inc.
United Services Automobile Association
U.S. Bancorp

U.S. Bancorp Piper Jaffray
United States Sugar Corp.
United States Trust Co. of New York
United Technologies Corp.
United Wisconsin Services
Universal Foods Corp.
Universal Leaf Tobacco Co., Inc.
Universal Studios
Unocal Corp.
UnumProvident
UPN Channel 50
US Bank, Washington
US West, Inc.
USAA Life Insurance Co.
USG Corp.
USX Corp.
Valmont Industries, Inc.
Varian Medical Systems, Inc.
Vesper Corp.
Vodafone AirTouch Plc
Vulcan Materials Co.
Wachovia Bank of North Carolina NA
Wachtell, Lipton, Rosen & Katz
Wal-Mart Stores, Inc.
Waldbaum's Supermarkets, Inc.
Walgreen Co.
Walter Industries Inc.
Warner-Lambert Co.
Washington Mutual, Inc.
The Washington Post
Washington Trust Bank
Waste Management Inc.
Webster Bank
Weil, Gotshal & Manges Corp.
West Co. Inc.
Western & Southern Life Insurance Co.
Westvaco Corp.
Weyerhaeuser Co.
Whirlpool Corp.
Whitman Corp.
WICOR, Inc.
Wilbur-Ellis Co. & Connell Brothers Co.
Wiley & Sons (John)
Williams
Wiremold Co.
Wisconsin Energy Corp.
Wisconsin Power & Light Co.
Wisconsin Public Service Corp.
Witco Corp.
Woodward Governor Co.
Wrigley Co. (Wm. Jr.)
Wyman-Gordon Co.
Xerox Corp.
Yellow Corp.
York Federal Savings & Loan Association
Young & Rubicam
Zachry Co. (H.B.)
Zilkha & Sons

MUSIC

Abbott Laboratories
AEGON U.S.A. Inc.
AGL Resources Inc.
Agrilink Foods, Inc.
Air Products and Chemicals, Inc.
AK Steel Corp.
Alabama Power Co.
Albany International Corp.
Albertson's Inc.
Alcoa Inc.
Alcon Laboratories, Inc.
Alexander & Baldwin, Inc.
Allegheny Technologies Inc.
Alliant Techsystems
Allianz Life Insurance Co. of North America
AlliedSignal Inc.
Allmerica Financial Corp.
AMCORE Bank Rockford
Ameren Corp.
American Express Co.
American Fidelity Corp.
American General Finance
American United Life Insurance Co.
Ameritas Life Insurance Corp.
Ameritech Corp.
Ameritech Illinois
Ameritech Indiana
Ameritech Michigan
Ameritech Ohio
Ameritech Wisconsin
AmerUS Group
AMETEK, Inc.
Amgen, Inc.
AMP Inc.
AMR Corp.
Amsted Industries Inc.
Andersen Corp.
Andersons Inc.
Anheuser-Busch Companies, Inc.
Aon Corp.
APL Ltd.
Apple Computer, Inc.
Appleton Papers Inc.
Archer-Daniels-Midland Co.
Aristech Chemical Corp.
Arizona Public Service Co.
Arvin Industries, Inc.
Ashland, Inc.
AT&T Corp.
Atlantic Investment Co.
Atlantic Richfield Co.
Auburn Foundry
Avery Dennison Corp.
Avon Products, Inc.
Badger Meter, Inc.
Baird & Co. (Robert W.)
Banfi Vintners
Bank of America
Bank of New York Co., Inc.
Bank One Corp.
BankAtlantic Bancorp
BankBoston Corp.
Banta Corp.
Barclays Capital
Bard, Inc. (C.R.)
Barden Corp.
Bardes Corp.
Barnes Group Inc.
Barry Corp. (R.G.)
Battelle Memorial Institute
Bausch & Lomb Inc.
Baxter International Inc.
Bayer Corp.
Belk-Simpson Department Stores
Bell Atlantic Corp.
Bemis Co., Inc.
Bemis Manufacturing Co.
Ben & Jerry's Homemade Inc.
Bernstein & Co., Inc. (Sanford C.)
Berwind Group
Bestfoods
Bethlehem Steel Corp.
BFGoodrich Co.
Binney & Smith Inc.
Binswanger Companies
Blair & Co. (William)
Block, Inc. (H&R)
Blount International, Inc.
Blue Bell, Inc.
Blue Cross & Blue Shield of Alabama
Blue Cross & Blue Shield of Iowa
Boeing Co.
Boise Cascade Corp.
Borden, Inc.
Borman's Inc.
Boston Edison Co.
Boston Globe (The)
Bowater Inc.
BP Amoco Corp.
Bradford & Co. (J.C.)
Bridgestone/Firestone, Inc.
Briggs & Stratton Corp.
Bristol-Myers Squibb Co.
Broderbund Software, Inc.
Brown Shoe Co., Inc.
Browning-Ferris Industries Inc.
Brunswick Corp.
Bucyrus-Erie Co.
Burlington Resources, Inc.
Burnett Co. (Leo)
Butler Capital Corp.
Butler Manufacturing Co.
Cabot Corp.
California Bank & Trust
Calvin Klein
Campbell Soup Co.
Cantor, Fitzgerald Securities Corp.
Cargill Inc.
Carillon Importers, Ltd.
Carlson Companies, Inc.
Carnival Corp.
Carolina Power & Light Co.
Carpenter Technology Corp.
Carrier Corp.
Carris Reels
Carter-Wallace, Inc.
Caterpillar Inc.
Central Maine Power Co.
Central Soya Co.
Central Vermont Public Service Corp.
CertainTeed Corp.
Cessna Aircraft Co.
CGU Insurance
Charter Manufacturing Co.
Chase Bank of Texas
Chase Manhattan Bank, NA
Chemed Corp.
Chesapeake Corp.
Chevron Corp.
Chicago Board of Trade
Chicago Sun-Times, Inc.
Chicago Title Corp.
Chicago Tribune Co.
Church & Dwight Co., Inc.
CIGNA Corp.
Cincinnati Bell Inc.
Cinergy Corp.
Circuit City Stores, Inc.
CIT Group, Inc. (The)
Citibank Corp.
Citigroup
Citizens Financial Group, Inc.
CLARCOR Inc.
Cleveland-Cliffs, Inc.
Clorox Co.
CNA
Collins & Aikman Corp.
Colonial Life & Accident Insurance Co.
Colonial Oil Industries, Inc.
Comerica Inc.
Commerce Bancshares, Inc.
Commercial Intertech Corp.
Compaq Computer Corp.
Compass Bank
ConAgra, Inc.
Consolidated Natural Gas Co.
Consolidated Papers, Inc.
Constellation Energy Group, Inc.
Consumers Energy Co.
Continental Grain Co.
Contran Corp.
Cooper Industries, Inc.
Coors Brewing Co.
Copley Press, Inc.
Corning Inc.
Country Curtains, Inc.
Crane Co.
Crane & Co., Inc.
Credit Suisse First Boston
Crestar Finance Corp.
CSR Rinker Materials Corp.
CSS Industries, Inc.
Cummings Properties Management
Cummins Engine Co., Inc.
CUNA Mutual Group
Daily News
DaimlerChrysler Corp.
Dain Bosworth Inc.
Dana Corp.
Danis Companies
Dayton Hudson
Dayton Power and Light Co.
Deere & Co.
Delta Air Lines, Inc.
Deluxe Corp.
Demoulas Supermarkets Inc.
Deposit Guaranty National Bank
Detroit Edison Co.
Deutsch Co.
Dexter Corp.
Dial Corp.
Disney Co. (Walt)
Dixie Group, Inc. (The)
Dominion Resources, Inc.
Donaldson Co., Inc.
Dow Chemical Co.
Dow Corning Corp.
Dow Jones & Co., Inc.
DSM Copolymer
du Pont de Nemours & Co. (E.I.)
Duchossois Industries Inc.
Duke Energy
Duriron Co., Inc.
Dynamet, Inc.
Eastman Kodak Co.
Eaton Corp.
Eckerd Corp.
Ecolab Inc.
Edison International
El Paso Energy Co.
Elf Atochem North America, Inc.
Emerson Electric Co.
EMI Music Publishing
Employers Mutual Casualty Co.
Ensign-Bickford Industries
Enterprise Rent-A-Car Co.
Equitable Resources, Inc.
Erb Lumber Co.
Erving Industries
Ethyl Corp.
Evening Post Publishing Co.
Exxon Mobil Corp.
Fabri-Kal Corp.
Fannie Mae
Federal-Mogul Corp.
Federated Department Stores, Inc.
Federated Mutual Insurance Co.
Ferro Corp.
Fidelity Investments
Fifth Third Bancorp
FINA
Fireman's Fund Insurance Co.
First Financial Bank
First Hawaiian, Inc.
First Maryland Bancorp
First Source Corp.
First Tennessee National Corp.
First Union Bank
First Union Corp.
First Union National Bank, NA
First Union Securities, Inc.
Firstar Bank Milwaukee NA
Fisher Scientific
FleetBoston Financial Corp.
Florida Power Corp.
Florida Power & Light Co.
Florida Rock Industries
Fluor Corp.
FMC Corp.
Forbes Inc.
Ford Meter Box Co.
Ford Motor Co.
Forest City Enterprises, Inc.
Fort Worth Star-Telegram Inc.
Fortis, Inc.
Fortis Insurance Co.
Fortune Brands, Inc.
Franklin Mint (The)
Freeport-McMoRan Inc.
Frost National Bank
Fuller Co. (H.B.)
Furniture Brands International, Inc.
Gallo Winery, Inc. (E&J)
Galter Corp.
Gap, Inc.
GATX Corp.
GEICO Corp.
GenAmerica Corp.
GenCorp
General Electric Co.
General Mills, Inc.
General Motors Corp.
Georgia-Pacific Corp.
Georgia Power Co.
Giant Eagle Inc.
Giant Food Inc.
Giddings & Lewis
Gillette Co.
Glaxo Wellcome Inc.
Glickenhaus & Co.
Globe Corp.
Goldman Sachs Group
Golub Corp.
Goodrich Aerospace - Aerostructures Group (B.F.)
Gosiger, Inc.
Graco, Inc.
Green Bay Packaging
GTE Corp.
Guardian Life Insurance Co. of America
Guess?
Gulf Power Co.
Halliburton Co.
Hallmark Cards Inc.
Hamilton Sundstrand Corp.
Hancock Financial Services (John)

Hanna Co. (M.A.)
Hannaford Brothers Co.
Harcourt General, Inc.
Harley-Davidson Co.
Harnischfeger Industries
Harris Corp.
Harris Trust & Savings Bank
Harsco Corp.
Hartford (The)
Hartford Steam Boiler Inspection & Insurance Co.
Hartmarx Corp.
Hasbro, Inc.
Hawaiian Electric Co., Inc.
Heinz Co. (H.J.)
Heller Financial, Inc.
Hewlett-Packard Co.
Hickory Tech Corp.
Hitachi America Ltd.
Hoffer Plastics Corp.
Hoffmann-La Roche Inc.
Hofmann Co.
HON Industries Inc.
Honeywell International Inc.
Housatonic Curtain Co.
Household International Inc.
Hubbard Broadcasting, Inc.
Hubbell Inc.
Huffy Corp.
Humana, Inc.
Hunt Manufacturing Co.
Idaho Power Co.
IKON Office Solutions, Inc.
Illinois Tool Works, Inc.
Independent Stave Co.
Inland Container Corp.
Inman Mills
Intel Corp.
International Business Machines Corp.
International Flavors & Fragrances Inc.
International Multifoods Corp.
International Paper Co.
INTRUST Financial Corp.
Invacare Corp.
Jacobs Engineering Group
Jacobson & Sons (Benjamin)
Jeld-wen, Inc.
Johnson Controls Inc.
Johnson & Johnson
Johnson & Son (S.C.)
Jones & Co. (Edward D.)
Jostens, Inc.
Journal-Gazette Co.
JSJ Corp.
Katten, Muchin & Zavis
Kelly Services
Kemper National Insurance Companies
Kennametal, Inc.
Kerr-McGee Corp.
Kiewit Sons' Inc. (Peter)
Kimball International, Inc.
Kimberly-Clark Corp.
Kinder Morgn
Kingsbury Corp.
Kirkland & Ellis
Kmart Corp.
Koch Enterprises, Inc.
Koch Industries, Inc.
Kohler Co.
Kraft Foods, Inc.
Kroger Co.
La-Z-Boy Inc.
Laclede Gas Co.
Lancaster Lens, Inc.
Lance, Inc.
Landmark Communications Inc.
Lee Enterprises
Lehigh Portland Cement Co.
Leigh Fibers, Inc.
LG&E Energy Corp.
Liberty Corp.
Liberty Diversified Industries
Lilly & Co. (Eli)
Lincoln Electric Co.
Lincoln Financial Group
Lipton Co.
Little, Inc. (Arthur D.)
Litton Industries, Inc.
Liz Claiborne, Inc.
Loews Corp.
Louisiana Land & Exploration Co.
Louisiana-Pacific Corp.
LTV Corp.
Lubrizol Corp. (The)
Macy's East Inc.
Madison Gas & Electric Co.
Mallinckrodt Chemical, Inc.
Mamiye Brothers
Manufacturers & Traders Trust Co.
Marcus Corp.
Maritz Inc.
Mark IV Industries
Marshall Field's
Marshall & Ilsley Corp.
Masco Corp.
Massachusetts Mutual Life Insurance Co.
Mattel Inc.
May Department Stores Co.
Maytag Corp.
McClatchy Co.
McCormick & Co. Inc.
McDonald & Co. Securities, Inc.
McGraw-Hill Companies, Inc.
MCI WorldCom, Inc.
McKesson-HBOC Corp.
McWane Inc.
Mead Corp.
Medtronic, Inc.
Mellon Financial Corp.
Menasha Corp.
Mercantile Bank NA
Merck & Co.
Merit Oil Corp.
Merrill Lynch & Co., Inc.
Mervyn's California
Metropolitan Life Insurance Co.
Michigan Consolidated Gas Co.
Mid-America Bank of Louisville
MidAmerican Energy Holdings Co.
Milacron, Inc.
Milliken & Co.
Millipore Corp.
Mine Safety Appliances Co.
Minnesota Mining & Manufacturing Co.
Minnesota Mutual Life Insurance Co.
Monarch Machine Tool Co.
Monsanto Co.
Montana Power Co.
Montgomery Ward & Co., Inc.
Morgan & Co. Inc. (J.P.)
Morgan Stanley Dean Witter & Co.
Morrison Knudsen Corp.
Motorola Inc.
MTD Products Inc.
Nabisco Group Holdings
Nalco Chemical Co.
National Bank of Commerce Trust & Savings
National City Bank of Minneapolis
National City Corp.
National Computer Systems, Inc.
National Fuel Gas Distribution Corp.
National Service Industries, Inc.
National Starch & Chemical Co.
Nationwide Insurance Co.
Navcom Systems
NEBCO Evans
Nestle U.S.A. Inc.
New Century Energies
New England Bio Labs
New England Financial
New York Life Insurance Co.
New York Mercantile Exchange
New York Stock Exchange, Inc.
New York Times Co.
Niagara Mohawk Holdings Inc.
Nomura Holding America
Nordson Corp.
Norfolk Southern Corp.
Nortel
Northern Indiana Public Service Co.
Northern States Power Co.
Northern Trust Co.
Northwest Bank Nebraska, NA
Northwest Natural Gas Co.
Norton Co.
Norwest Corp.
Occidental Oil and Gas
Occidental Petroleum Corp.
OG&E Electric Services
Ohio National Life Insurance Co.
Old Kent Bank
Old National Bank Evansville
Olin Corp.
Oshkosh B'Gosh, Inc.
Overseas Shipholding Group Inc.
Owens Corning
PACCAR Inc.
Pacific Century Financial Corp.
Pacific Gas and Electric Co.
Pacific Mutual Life Insurance Co.
PacifiCorp
Paine Webber
Park National Bank
Parker Hannifin Corp.
PECO Energy Co.
Pella Corp.
PEMCO Corp.
Penney Co., Inc. (J.C.)
Pennzoil-Quaker State Co.
PepsiCo, Inc.
PerkinElmer, Inc.
Pfizer Inc.
Pharmacia & Upjohn, Inc.
Phelps Dodge Corp.
Phillips Petroleum Co.
Physicians Mutual Insurance Co.
Pieper Power Electric Co.
Pillsbury Co.
Pioneer Group
Pittway Corp.
PNC Financial Services Group
Polaroid Corp.
Portland General Electric Co.
Potlatch Corp.
Potomac Electric Power Co.
PPG Industries, Inc.
Premier Dental Products Co.
Premier Industrial Corp.
Price Associates (T. Rowe)
Principal Financial Group
Procter & Gamble Co.
Procter & Gamble Co., Cosmetics Division
Promus Hotel Corp.
Providence Journal-Bulletin Co.
Provident Companies, Inc.
Prudential Insurance Co. of America
Prudential Securities Inc.
Pulitzer Publishing Co.
Putnam Investments
Quaker Chemical Corp.
Quanex Corp.
Questar Corp.
Ralph's Grocery Co.
Ralston Purina Co.
Rayonier Inc.
Red Wing Shoe Co. Inc.
Regions Bank
Regis Corp.
Reilly Industries, Inc.
Reily & Co., Inc. (William B.)
Reinhart Institutional Foods
Reliant Energy Inc.
ReliaStar Financial Corp.
Revlon Inc.
Reynolds Metals Co.
Reynolds & Reynolds Co.
Reynolds Tobacco (R.J.)
Rich Products Corp.
Riggs Bank NA
Rochester Gas & Electric Corp.
Rockwell International Corp.
Rouse Co.
Royal & SunAlliance USA, Inc.
Russer Foods
Ryder System, Inc.
Safeguard Scientifics
Saint Paul Companies Inc.
Salomon Smith Barney
S&T Bancorp
Sara Lee Corp.
Sara Lee Hosiery, Inc.
SBC Communications Inc.
Schering-Plough Corp.
Schloss & Co. (Marcus)
Schlumberger Ltd. (USA)
Schwab & Co., Inc. (Charles)
Schwebel Baking Co.
Scripps Co. (E.W.)
Seagram & Sons, Inc. (Joseph E.)
Searle & Co. (G.D.)
Security Benefit Life Insurance Co.
Security Life of Denver Insurance Co.
Sempra Energy
Sentry Insurance, A Mutual Co.
S.G. Cowen
Shaklee Corp.
Shaw's Supermarkets, Inc.
Shea Co. (John F.)
Shell Oil Co.
Shelter Mutual Insurance Co.
Sherwin-Williams Co.
Shoney's Inc.
Sierra Pacific Industries
Sierra Pacific Resources
Simplot Co. (J.R.)
Simpson Investment Co.
SIT Investment Associates, Inc.
Slant/Fin Corp.
Smith Corp. (A.O.)
SmithKline Beecham Corp.
Smurfit-Stone Container Corp.
Sonoco Products Co.
Sony Electronics
South Bend Tribune Corp.
Southeastern Mutual Insurance Co.
Southern New England Telephone Co.
Southwest Gas Corp.
Sovereign Bank
Sprint Corp.
Sprint/United Telephone
SPX Corp.
Square D Co.
Standard Products Co.
Standard Register Co.
Stanley Works (The)
Star Bank NA
Starwood Hotels & Resorts Worldwide, Inc.
State Street Bank & Trust Co.
Steelcase Inc.
Stone Container Corp.
Storage Technology Corp.
Stride Rite Corp.
Sunoco Inc.
SunTrust Bank Atlanta
Susquehanna-Pfaltzgraff Co.
Sverdrup Corp.
Synovus Financial Corp.
Tamko Roofing Products
Target Corp.
TCF National Bank Minnesota
Tektronix, Inc.
Teleflex Inc.
TENNANT Co.
Tenneco Automotive
Tesoro Hawaii
Texaco Inc.
Texas Gas Transmission Corp.
Texas Instruments Inc.
Textron Inc.
Thermo Electron Corp.
Thomasville Furniture Industries Inc.
Thompson Co. (J. Walter)
Ticketmaster Corp.
Times Mirror Co.
Titan Industrial Corp.
TMC Investment Co.
Toledo Blade Co.
Tomkins Industries, Inc.
Torchmark Corp.
Toro Co.
Toyota Motor Sales U.S.A., Inc.
Trace International Holdings, Inc.
Transamerica Corp.
True North Communications, Inc.
True Oil Co.
Trustmark Insurance Co.
TRW Inc.
Tyson Foods Inc.
Unilever Home & Personal Care U.S.A.

Funders by Recipient Type

Unilever United States, Inc.
Union Camp Corp.
Union Pacific Corp.
United Airlines Inc.
United Distillers & Vintners North America
United Dominion Industries, Ltd.
United Parcel Service of America Inc.
United Services Automobile Association
U.S. Bancorp
U.S. Bancorp Piper Jaffray
United States Trust Co. of New York
United Technologies Corp.
United Wisconsin Services
Universal Foods Corp.
Universal Leaf Tobacco Co., Inc.
Universal Studios
Unocal Corp.
UnumProvident
UPN Channel 50
US Bank, Washington
US West, Inc.
USAA Life Insurance Co.
USG Corp.
USX Corp.
Valmont Industries, Inc.
Valspar Corp.
Vodafone AirTouch Plc
Vulcan Materials Co.
Wachovia Bank of North Carolina NA
Wal-Mart Stores, Inc.
Waldbaum's Supermarkets, Inc.
Walter Industries Inc.
Warner-Lambert Co.
Washington Mutual, Inc.
The Washington Post
Washington Trust Bank
Waste Management Inc.
Webster Bank
Weil, Gotshal & Manges Corp.
Wells Fargo & Co.
West Co. Inc.
Western & Southern Life Insurance Co.
Westvaco Corp.
Weyerhaeuser Co.
Whirlpool Corp.
Whitman Corp.
WICOR, Inc.
Wilbur-Ellis Co. & Connell Brothers Co.
Williams
Winn-Dixie Stores Inc.
Wiremold Co.
Wisconsin Energy Corp.
Wisconsin Power & Light Co.
Wisconsin Public Service Corp.
Witco Corp.
Wolverine World Wide
Wrigley Co. (Wm. Jr.)
Wyman-Gordon Co.
Xerox Corp.
Yellow Corp.
York Federal Savings & Loan Association
Young & Rubicam
Zachry Co. (H.B.)
Zilkha & Sons

OPERA

Abbott Laboratories
Aetna, Inc.
AGL Resources Inc.
Air Products and Chemicals, Inc.
AK Steel Corp.
Albertson's Inc.
Alcoa Inc.
Alcon Laboratories, Inc.
Alexander & Baldwin, Inc.
Allegheny Technologies Inc.
AlliedSignal Inc.
Ameren Corp.
American Express Co.
American United Life Insurance Co.
Ameritech Corp.
Ameritech Illinois
Ameritech Indiana
Ameritech Michigan
Ameritech Ohio
AmerUS Group
AMR Corp.
Amsted Industries Inc.
Andersons Inc.
Aon Corp.
APL Ltd.
Archer-Daniels-Midland Co.
Aristech Chemical Corp.
Arizona Public Service Co.
Armstrong World Industries, Inc.
Ashland, Inc.
AT&T Corp.
Avon Products, Inc.
Badger Meter, Inc.
Baird & Co. (Robert W.)
Banfi Vintners
Bank of America
Bank of New York Co., Inc.
Bank One Corp.
BankAtlantic Bancorp
Barnes Group Inc.
Barry Corp. (R.G.)
Battelle Memorial Institute
Baxter International Inc.
Bayer Corp.
Belk Stores Services Inc.
Bemis Co., Inc.
Bernstein & Co., Inc. (Sanford C.)
BFGoodrich Co.
Binney & Smith Inc.
Blair & Co. (William)
Block, Inc. (H&R)
Blount International, Inc.
Blue Cross & Blue Shield of Alabama
Blue Cross & Blue Shield of Iowa
Boeing Co.
Boise Cascade Corp.
Boler Co.
Borden, Inc.
Bradford & Co. (J.C.)
Bridgestone/Firestone, Inc.
Bristol-Myers Squibb Co.
Brown Shoe Co., Inc.
Bucyrus-Erie Co.
Burlington Resources, Inc.
Burnett Co. (Leo)
Butler Manufacturing Co.
Cabot Corp.
Cargill Inc.
Carlson Companies, Inc.
Carrier Corp.
Carter-Wallace, Inc.
Central Soya Co.
Chase Bank of Texas
Chase Manhattan Bank, NA
Chemed Corp.
Chevron Corp.
Chicago Board of Trade
Chicago Title Corp.
Chicago Tribune Co.
CIGNA Corp.
Cincinnati Bell Inc.
Cinergy Corp.
Citibank Corp.
Citigroup
CLARCOR Inc.
Cleveland-Cliffs, Inc.
Clorox Co.
CNA
Colonial Life & Accident Insurance Co.
Comerica Inc.
Commerce Bancshares, Inc.
Commonwealth Edison Co.
Compaq Computer Corp.
ConAgra, Inc.
Consolidated Natural Gas Co.
Consumers Energy Co.
Continental Grain Co.
Cooper Industries, Inc.
Coors Brewing Co.
Copley Press, Inc.
Country Curtains, Inc.
Cox Enterprises Inc.
Credit Suisse First Boston
Crestar Finance Corp.
CUNA Mutual Group
DaimlerChrysler Corp.
Dain Bosworth Inc.
Dana Corp.
Dayton Hudson
Dayton Power and Light Co.
Deere & Co.
Delta Air Lines, Inc.
Deluxe Corp.
Demoulas Supermarkets Inc.
Deposit Guaranty National Bank
Detroit Edison Co.
Dexter Corp.
Dial Corp.
Dominion Resources, Inc.
Donaldson Co., Inc.
du Pont de Nemours & Co. (E.I.)
Duchossois Industries Inc.
Duke Energy
Dynamet, Inc.
Eaton Corp.
Ecolab Inc.
Edison International
El Paso Energy Co.
Elf Atochem North America, Inc.
Emerson Electric Co.
Employers Mutual Casualty Co.
Ensign-Bickford Industries
Ethyl Corp.
Exxon Mobil Corp.
Fannie Mae
Federal-Mogul Corp.
Federated Department Stores, Inc.
Ferro Corp.
Fidelity Investments
FINA
Fireman's Fund Insurance Co.
First Maryland Bancorp
First Tennessee National Corp.
First Union Bank
First Union Corp.
First Union National Bank, NA
First Union Securities, Inc.
Firstar Bank Milwaukee NA
Fisher Brothers Cleaning Services
Fisher Scientific
FleetBoston Financial Corp.
Florida Rock Industries
Fluor Corp.
FMC Corp.
Forbes Inc.
Ford Meter Box Co.
Ford Motor Co.
Forest City Enterprises, Inc.
Fort Worth Star-Telegram Inc.
Fortune Brands, Inc.
Freeport-McMoRan Inc.
Fuller Co. (H.B.)
Furniture Brands International, Inc.
Gallo Winery, Inc. (E&J)
Gap, Inc.
GATX Corp.
GEICO Corp.
GenAmerica Corp.
General Electric Co.
General Mills, Inc.
General Motors Corp.
Georgia-Pacific Corp.
Giant Eagle Inc.
Giant Food Inc.
Glickenhaus & Co.
GTE Corp.
Guardian Life Insurance Co. of America
Halliburton Co.
Hallmark Cards Inc.
Hamilton Sundstrand Corp.
Hancock Financial Services (John)
Hanna Co. (M.A.)
Hannaford Brothers Co.
Harley-Davidson Co.
Harnischfeger Industries
Harris Trust & Savings Bank
Harsco Corp.
Hartford (The)
Hartmarx Corp.
Heinz Co. (H.J.)
Hoffmann-La Roche Inc.
Honeywell International Inc.
Housatonic Curtain Co.
Household International Inc.
Hubbard Broadcasting, Inc.
Huffy Corp.
Humana, Inc.
Hunt Manufacturing Co.
Huntington Bancshares Inc.
IKON Office Solutions, Inc.
Illinois Tool Works, Inc.
International Business Machines Corp.
International Flavors & Fragrances Inc.
International Multifoods Corp.
International Paper Co.
Invacare Corp.
Jacobson & Sons (Benjamin)
Jeld-wen, Inc.
Johnson Controls Inc.
Jones & Co. (Edward D.)
Jostens, Inc.
JSJ Corp.
Katten, Muchin & Zavis
Kelly Services
Kemper National Insurance Companies
Kiewit Sons' Inc. (Peter)
Kimberly-Clark Corp.
Kingsbury Corp.
Kirkland & Ellis
Kmart Corp.
Koch Industries, Inc.
Kroger Co.
Laclede Gas Co.
Landmark Communications Inc.
Lilly & Co. (Eli)
Lincoln Electric Co.
Litton Industries, Inc.
Liz Claiborne, Inc.
Louisiana Land & Exploration Co.
Louisiana-Pacific Corp.
LTV Corp.
Lubrizol Corp. (The)
Macy's East Inc.
Mallinckrodt Chemical, Inc.
Manufacturers & Traders Trust Co.
Marcus Corp.
Maritz Inc.
Marshall Field's
Masco Corp.
Maytag Corp.
McClatchy Co.
McDonald & Co. Securities, Inc.
McKesson-HBOC Corp.
Mead Corp.
Medtronic, Inc.
Mellon Financial Corp.
Merrill Lynch & Co., Inc.
Mervyn's California
Metropolitan Life Insurance Co.
Michigan Consolidated Gas Co.
Mid-America Bank of Louisville
Mine Safety Appliances Co.
Minnesota Mining & Manufacturing Co.
Minnesota Mutual Life Insurance Co.
Monsanto Co.
MONY Group (The)
Morgan & Co. Inc. (J.P.)
Morrison Knudsen Corp.
Morton International Inc.
Motorola Inc.
Mutual of Omaha Insurance Co.
Nalco Chemical Co.
National City Bank of Minneapolis
National City Corp.
National Computer Systems, Inc.
National Service Industries, Inc.
National Starch & Chemical Co.
Nationwide Insurance Co.
New Century Energies
New England Financial
New York Times Co.
Nomura Holding America
Nordson Corp.
Norfolk Southern Corp.
Nortel
Northern States Power Co.
Northern Trust Co.
Northwest Natural Gas Co.
Norton Co.
Norwest Corp.
Occidental Oil and Gas
Old Kent Bank
Olin Corp.
Oshkosh B'Gosh, Inc.
Owens Corning
PACCAR Inc.
Pacific Century Financial Corp.

Pacific Mutual Life Insurance Co.
PacifiCorp
Parker Hannifin Corp.
PECO Energy Co.
Pella Corp.
Penney Co., Inc. (J.C.)
Pennzoil-Quaker State Co.
Peoples Energy Corp.
PepsiCo, Inc.
Pfizer Inc.
Phelps Dodge Corp.
Phillips Petroleum Co.
Physicians Mutual Insurance Co.
Pieper Power Electric Co.
Pioneer Group
Pioneer Hi-Bred International, Inc.
Pittway Corp.
PNC Bank Kentucky Inc.
PNC Financial Services Group
Polaroid Corp.
Portland General Electric Co.
Potlatch Corp.
Potomac Electric Power Co.
PPG Industries, Inc.
Premier Industrial Corp.
Price Associates (T. Rowe)
Principal Financial Group
Procter & Gamble Co.
Procter & Gamble Co., Cosmetics Division
Promus Hotel Corp.
Provident Companies, Inc.
Prudential Insurance Co. of America
Pulitzer Publishing Co.
Quaker Chemical Corp.
Questar Corp.
Regis Corp.
Reilly Industries, Inc.
Reily & Co., Inc. (William B.)
Reynolds Metals Co.
Reynolds & Reynolds Co.
Reynolds Tobacco (R.J.)
Rockwell International Corp.
Rouse Co.
Royal & SunAlliance USA, Inc.
Ryder System, Inc.
SAFECO Corp.
Salomon Smith Barney
Sara Lee Corp.
SBC Communications Inc.
Schlumberger Ltd. (USA)
Schwab & Co., Inc. (Charles)
Searle & Co. (G.D.)
Seaway Food Town, Inc.
Security Life of Denver Insurance Co.
Sempra Energy
S.G. Cowen
Shaklee Corp.
Shell Oil Co.
Sherwin-Williams Co.
Shoney's Inc.
Sierra Pacific Industries
Sierra Pacific Resources
Simplot Co. (J.R.)
Simpson Investment Co.
SIT Investment Associates, Inc.
Slant/Fin Corp.
SmithKline Beecham Corp.
Sonoco Products Co.
Sony Electronics
Southeastern Mutual Insurance Co.
Southwest Gas Corp.
Sovereign Bank
Sprint Corp.
Sprint/United Telephone
Square D Co.
Stanley Works (The)
Star Bank NA
Starwood Hotels & Resorts Worldwide, Inc.
State Street Bank & Trust Co.
Steelcase Inc.
Stone Container Corp.
Stride Rite Corp.
Sun Microsystems Inc.
SunTrust Bank Atlanta
Susquehanna-Pfaltzgraff Co.
Sverdrup Corp.
Synovus Financial Corp.
Target Corp.
TCF National Bank Minnesota
Tektronix, Inc.
TENNANT Co.
Tenneco Automotive
Tesoro Hawaii
Texaco Inc.
Texas Instruments Inc.
Textron Inc.
Titan Industrial Corp.
Toledo Blade Co.
Torchmark Corp.
Toyota Motor Sales U.S.A., Inc.
Trace International Holdings, Inc.
Transamerica Corp.
True North Communications, Inc.
True Oil Co.
TRW Inc.
Ukrop's Super Markets
Unilever Home & Personal Care U.S.A.
Union Pacific Corp.
United Airlines Inc.
U.S. Bancorp
U.S. Bancorp Piper Jaffray
United States Trust Co. of New York
United Technologies Corp.
United Wisconsin Services
Universal Foods Corp.
Unocal Corp.
US Bank, Washington
US West, Inc.
USAA Life Insurance Co.
USG Corp.
USX Corp.
Valspar Corp.
Vodafone AirTouch Plc
Vulcan Materials Co.
Wachovia Bank of North Carolina NA
Walgreen Co.
Walter Industries Inc.
Warner-Lambert Co.
The Washington Post
Washington Trust Bank
Waste Management Inc.
Weil, Gotshal & Manges Corp.
Westvaco Corp.
Weyerhaeuser Co.
Whirlpool Corp.
Whitman Corp.
WICOR, Inc.
Wilbur-Ellis Co. & Connell Brothers Co.
Wiley & Sons (John)
Williams
Wisconsin Energy Corp.
Wisconsin Public Service Corp.
Witco Corp.
Wolverine World Wide
Xerox Corp.
Yellow Corp.
Young & Rubicam
Zilkha & Sons

PERFORMING ARTS

Abbott Laboratories
ABC
AGL Resources Inc.
Agrilink Foods, Inc.
Air Products and Chemicals, Inc.
AK Steel Corp.
Alabama Power Co.
Albany International Corp.
Albertson's Inc.
Alcoa Inc.
Alcon Laboratories, Inc.
Alexander & Baldwin, Inc.
Allegheny Technologies Inc.
AlliedSignal Inc.
Allmerica Financial Corp.
AMCORE Bank Rockford
Ameren Corp.
America West Airlines, Inc.
American Express Co.
American Stock Exchange, Inc.
American United Life Insurance Co.
Ameritas Life Insurance Corp.
Ameritech Corp.
Ameritech Michigan
Ameritech Ohio
Ameritech Wisconsin
AmerUS Group
AMR Corp.
Anheuser-Busch Companies, Inc.
Aon Corp.
APL Ltd.
Apple Computer, Inc.
Appleton Papers Inc.
Archer-Daniels-Midland Co.
Arizona Public Service Co.
ASARCO Inc.
Ashland, Inc.
AT&T Corp.
Atlantic Investment Co.
Atlantic Richfield Co.
Avista Corporation
Avon Products, Inc.
Badger Meter, Inc.
Baird & Co. (Robert W.)
Baker Hughes Inc.
Bandag, Inc.
Banfi Vintners
Bank of America
Bank of New York Co., Inc.
Bank One Corp.
Bank One, Texas-Houston Office
BankAtlantic Bancorp
BankBoston Corp.
Banta Corp.
Barclays Capital
Bard, Inc. (C.R.)
Bardes Corp.
Barry Corp. (R.G.)
Battelle Memorial Institute
Bausch & Lomb Inc.
Bayer Corp.
Bean, Inc. (L.L.)
Belk-Simpson Department Stores
Bemis Co., Inc.
Bemis Manufacturing Co.
Bernstein & Co., Inc. (Sanford C.)
Berwind Group
Bestfoods
Bethlehem Steel Corp.
BFGoodrich Co.
Binney & Smith Inc.
Blair & Co. (William)
Block, Inc. (H&R)
Blount International, Inc.
Boeing Co.
Boise Cascade Corp.
Borden, Inc.
Borman's Inc.
Boston Edison Co.
Boston Globe (The)
Bowater Inc.
BP Amoco Corp.
Bradford & Co. (J.C.)
Briggs & Stratton Corp.
Bristol-Myers Squibb Co.
Brown Shoe Co., Inc.
Browning-Ferris Industries Inc.
Brunswick Corp.
Bucyrus-Erie Co.
Burnett Co. (Leo)
Butler Manufacturing Co.
Cabot Corp.
Calvin Klein
Campbell Soup Co.
Cantor, Fitzgerald Securities Corp.
Carillon Importers, Ltd.
Carpenter Technology Corp.
Carrier Corp.
Carter-Wallace, Inc.
Caterpillar Inc.
CBS Corp.
CCB Financial Corp.
Central Maine Power Co.
Central & South West Services
CertainTeed Corp.
CGU Insurance
Charter Manufacturing Co.
Chase Bank of Texas
Chase Manhattan Bank, NA
Chevron Corp.
Chicago Sun-Times, Inc.
Chicago Title Corp.
Chicago Tribune Co.
Cincinnati Bell Inc.
Cinergy Corp.
Circuit City Stores, Inc.
CIT Group, Inc. (The)
Citibank Corp.
Citigroup
Citizens Financial Group, Inc.
Clark Refining & Marketing
Cleveland-Cliffs, Inc.
Clorox Co.
CNA
CNF Transportation, Inc.
Colonial Life & Accident Insurance Co.
Colonial Oil Industries, Inc.
Commercial Intertech Corp.
Commonwealth Edison Co.
Compaq Computer Corp.
Compass Bank
ConAgra, Inc.
Consolidated Natural Gas Co.
Consolidated Papers, Inc.
Constellation Energy Group, Inc.
Consumers Energy Co.
Continental Grain Co.
Contran Corp.
Cooper Industries, Inc.
Coors Brewing Co.
Copley Press, Inc.
Corning Inc.
Country Curtains, Inc.
Cox Enterprises Inc.
CPI Corp.
Crane Co.
Crane & Co., Inc.
Credit Suisse First Boston
CSR Rinker Materials Corp.
CSS Industries, Inc.
Cummins Engine Co., Inc.
CUNA Mutual Group
Daily News
DaimlerChrysler Corp.
Dain Bosworth Inc.
Danis Companies
Dayton Hudson
Dayton Power and Light Co.
Delta Air Lines, Inc.
Deluxe Corp.
Deposit Guaranty National Bank
Detroit Edison Co.
Dial Corp.
Disney Co. (Walt)
Dominion Resources, Inc.
Donaldson Co., Inc.
Donnelley & Sons Co. (R.R.)
Dow Corning Corp.
du Pont de Nemours & Co. (E.I.)
Duchossois Industries Inc.
Duke Energy
Dun & Bradstreet Corp.
Dynamet, Inc.
Eastern Bank
Eastman Kodak Co.
Eaton Corp.
Eckerd Corp.
Ecolab Inc.
Edison International
El Paso Energy Co.
Elf Atochem North America, Inc.
Emerson Electric Co.
EMI Music Publishing
Employers Mutual Casualty Co.
Ensign-Bickford Industries
Equifax Inc.
Erb Lumber Co.
Erving Industries
Ethyl Corp.
Evening Post Publishing Co.
Exxon Mobil Corp.
Fannie Mae
Federal-Mogul Corp.
Federated Department Stores, Inc.
Federated Mutual Insurance Co.
Ferro Corp.
Fidelity Investments
Fifth Third Bancorp
Fireman's Fund Insurance Co.
First American Corp.
First Financial Bank
First Maryland Bancorp
First Tennessee National Corp.
First Union Corp.
First Union National Bank, NA
First Union Securities, Inc.
Firstar Bank Milwaukee NA
Fisher Brothers Cleaning Services
Fisher Scientific
FleetBoston Financial Corp.

Florida Power & Light Co.
Florida Rock Industries
Fluor Corp.
Forbes Inc.
Ford Meter Box Co.
Ford Motor Co.
Forest City Enterprises, Inc.
Fort James Corp.
Fort Worth Star-Telegram Inc.
Fortis Insurance Co.
Fortune Brands, Inc.
Freeport-McMoRan Inc.
Frost National Bank
Fuller Co. (H.B.)
Furniture Brands International, Inc.
Gannett Co., Inc.
Gap, Inc.
GATX Corp.
GEICO Corp.
GenAmerica Corp.
GenCorp
General Dynamics Corp.
General Electric Co.
General Mills, Inc.
General Motors Corp.
Georgia Power Co.
Giant Eagle Inc.
Giant Food Inc.
Giddings & Lewis
Glaxo Wellcome Inc.
Glickenhaus & Co.
Golub Corp.
Goodrich Aerospace - Aerostructures Group (B.F.)
Grace & Co. (W.R.)
Grede Foundries
Green Bay Packaging
GTE Corp.
Guardian Life Insurance Co. of America
Gucci America Inc.
Halliburton Co.
Hallmark Cards Inc.
Hamilton Sundstrand Corp.
Hancock Financial Services (John)
Hanna Co. (M.A.)
Hannaford Brothers Co.
Harcourt General, Inc.
Harley-Davidson Co.
Harnischfeger Industries
Harris Corp.
Harsco Corp.
Hartford (The)
Hartford Steam Boiler Inspection & Insurance Co.
Hartmarx Corp.
Hasbro, Inc.
Hawaiian Electric Co., Inc.
Heinz Co. (H.J.)
Hickory Tech Corp.
Hoffer Plastics Corp.
Hoffmann-La Roche Inc.
Honeywell International Inc.
Housatonic Curtain Co.
Hubbard Broadcasting, Inc.
Hubbell Inc.
Humana, Inc.
Hunt Manufacturing Co.
Huntington Bancshares Inc.
Idaho Power Co.
Illinois Power Co.
Illinois Tool Works, Inc.
Inland Container Corp.
International Business Machines Corp.
International Flavors & Fragrances Inc.
INTRUST Financial Corp.
Jacobson & Sons (Benjamin)
Johnson Controls Inc.
Johnson & Johnson
Johnson & Son (S.C.)
Jostens, Inc.
Journal-Gazette Co.
JSJ Corp.
Kellwood Co.
Kerr-McGee Corp.
Key Bank of Cleveland
Kimberly-Clark Corp.
Kinder Morgn
Kingsbury Corp.
Kmart Corp.
Kraft Foods, Inc.
Kroger Co.
Laclede Gas Co.
Ladish Co., Inc.
Lance, Inc.
Land O'Lakes, Inc.
Lehigh Portland Cement Co.
Leviton Manufacturing Co. Inc.
Liberty Corp.
Lilly & Co. (Eli)
Lincoln Electric Co.
Lincoln Financial Group
Lipton Co.
Little, Inc. (Arthur D.)
Litton Industries, Inc.
Loews Corp.
Louisiana-Pacific Corp.
LTV Corp.
Lubrizol Corp. (The)
Macy's East Inc.
Mallinckrodt Chemical, Inc.
Manufacturers & Traders Trust Co.
Marcus Corp.
Maritz Inc.
Marriott International Inc.
Marshall Field's
Marshall & Ilsley Corp.
Masco Corp.
Mattel Inc.
May Department Stores Co.
Mazda North American Operations
MBIA Inc.
McClatchy Co.
McDonald & Co. Securities, Inc.
McGraw-Hill Companies, Inc.
MCI WorldCom, Inc.
McKesson-HBOC Corp.
McWane Inc.
Mead Corp.
Medtronic, Inc.
Mellon Financial Corp.
Menasha Corp.
Mercantile Bank NA
Merck & Co.
Meredith Corp.
Merit Oil Corp.
Merrill Lynch & Co., Inc.
Mervyn's California
Metropolitan Life Insurance Co.
MGIC Investment Corp.
Michigan Consolidated Gas Co.
Mid-America Bank of Louisville
MidAmerican Energy Holdings Co.
Milacron, Inc.
Milliken & Co.
Millipore Corp.
Mine Safety Appliances Co.
Minnesota Mining & Manufacturing Co.
Monsanto Co.
Montana Power Co.
MONY Group (The)
Morgan & Co. Inc. (J.P.)
Morgan Stanley Dean Witter & Co.
Morrison Knudsen Corp.
Morton International Inc.
Motorola Inc.
MTD Products Inc.
Mutual of Omaha Insurance Co.
Nabisco Group Holdings
Nalco Chemical Co.
National Bank of Commerce Trust & Savings
National City Corp.
National Computer Systems, Inc.
National Machinery Co.
National Presto Industries, Inc.
National Starch & Chemical Co.
Nationwide Insurance Co.
NCR Corp.
NEBCO Evans
Nestle U.S.A. Inc.
New Century Energies
New England Bio Labs
New England Financial
New York Life Insurance Co.
New York Stock Exchange, Inc.
New York Times Co.
Niagara Mohawk Holdings Inc.
Nomura Holding America
Nordson Corp.
Norfolk Southern Corp.
Nortel
Northern Indiana Public Service Co.
Northern States Power Co.
Northern Trust Co.
Northwest Bank Nebraska, NA
Northwest Natural Gas Co.
Norton Co.
Occidental Petroleum Corp.
Ohio National Life Insurance Co.
Old National Bank Evansville
Olin Corp.
Oshkosh B'Gosh, Inc.
Outboard Marine Corp.
Overnite Transportation Co.
Overseas Shipholding Group Inc.
PACCAR Inc.
Pacific Century Financial Corp.
Pacific Gas and Electric Co.
Pacific Mutual Life Insurance Co.
PacifiCorp
Park National Bank
Parker Hannifin Corp.
Pella Corp.
Penney Co., Inc. (J.C.)
Pennzoil-Quaker State Co.
Peoples Bank
Peoples Energy Corp.
PepsiCo, Inc.
PerkinElmer, Inc.
Pfizer Inc.
Pharmacia & Upjohn, Inc.
Phelps Dodge Corp.
Philip Morris Companies Inc.
Phillips Petroleum Co.
Pieper Power Electric Co.
Pioneer Group
Pioneer Hi-Bred International, Inc.
Pittway Corp.
PNC Financial Services Group
Polaroid Corp.
Portland General Electric Co.
Potlatch Corp.
Potomac Electric Power Co.
PPG Industries, Inc.
Premier Dental Products Co.
Premier Industrial Corp.
Principal Financial Group
Procter & Gamble Co.
Procter & Gamble Co., Cosmetics Division
Providence Journal-Bulletin Co.
Provident Companies, Inc.
Prudential Insurance Co. of America
Prudential Securities Inc.
Public Service Electric & Gas Co.
Publix Supermarkets
Pulitzer Publishing Co.
Putnam Investments
Quaker Chemical Corp.
Quanex Corp.
Ralph's Grocery Co.
Ralston Purina Co.
Reader's Digest Association, Inc. (The)
Red Wing Shoe Co. Inc.
Reilly Industries, Inc.
Reliant Energy Inc.
ReliaStar Financial Corp.
Revlon Inc.
Reynolds Metals Co.
Reynolds & Reynolds Co.
Reynolds Tobacco (R.J.)
Rich Products Corp.
Riggs Bank NA
Rockwell International Corp.
Rouse Co.
Royal & SunAlliance USA, Inc.
Ruddick Corp.
Russer Foods
Ryder System, Inc.
SAFECO Corp.
Safeguard Scientifics
Saint Paul Companies Inc.
Salomon Smith Barney
Sara Lee Corp.
Sara Lee Hosiery, Inc.
SBC Communications Inc.
Schering-Plough Corp.
Schloss & Co. (Marcus)
Schlumberger Ltd. (USA)
Schwab & Co., Inc. (Charles)
Schwebel Baking Co.
Scripps Co. (E.W.)
Seagram & Sons, Inc. (Joseph E.)
Searle & Co. (G.D.)
Seaway Food Town, Inc.
Security Benefit Life Insurance Co.
Sempra Energy
S.G. Cowen
Shaklee Corp.
Shell Oil Co.
Sherwin-Williams Co.
Shoney's Inc.
Simpson Investment Co.
SIT Investment Associates, Inc.
Slant/Fin Corp.
Smith Corp. (A.O.)
Smucker Co. (JM)
Solo Cup Co.
Sonoco Products Co.
Sony Electronics
South Bend Tribune Corp.
Southern New England Telephone Co.
Southwest Gas Corp.
Sprint Corp.
SPX Corp.
Stanley Works (The)
State Street Bank & Trust Co.
Steelcase Inc.
Stone Container Corp.
Storage Technology Corp.
Stride Rite Corp.
Stupp Brothers Bridge & Iron Co.
Sunoco Inc.
SunTrust Bank Atlanta
Tandy Corp.
Target Corp.
TCF National Bank Minnesota
Tektronix, Inc.
TENNANT Co.
Tenneco Automotive
Tesoro Hawaii
Texaco Inc.
Texas Instruments Inc.
Textron Inc.
Thermo Electron Corp.
Thomasville Furniture Industries Inc.
Thompson Co. (J. Walter)
Ticketmaster Corp.
Times Mirror Co.
Titan Industrial Corp.
TJX Companies, Inc.
Tomkins Industries, Inc.
Torchmark Corp.
Toyota Motor Sales U.S.A., Inc.
Trace International Holdings, Inc.
Transamerica Corp.
True North Communications, Inc.
True Oil Co.
Trustmark Insurance Co.
TRW Inc.
TU Electric Co.
Tucson Electric Power Co.
Unilever Home & Personal Care U.S.A.
Unilever United States, Inc.
Union Carbide Corp.
Union Pacific Corp.
United Distillers & Vintners North America
United Dominion Industries, Ltd.
United Services Automobile Association
U.S. Bancorp
U.S. Bancorp Piper Jaffray
United States Trust Co. of New York
United Technologies Corp.
United Wisconsin Services
Universal Foods Corp.
Universal Leaf Tobacco Co., Inc.
Universal Studios
Unocal Corp.
UnumProvident
US Bank, Washington
USX Corp.
Valmont Industries, Inc.
Valspar Corp.

Vesper Corp.
Vodafone AirTouch Plc
Vulcan Materials Co.
Wachovia Bank of North Carolina NA
Waffle House Inc.
Walter Industries Inc.
Warner-Lambert Co.
Washington Mutual, Inc.
The Washington Post
Washington Trust Bank
Waste Management Inc.
Webster Bank
Weil, Gotshal & Manges Corp.
Wells Fargo & Co.
West Co. Inc.
Western & Southern Life Insurance Co.
Westvaco Corp.
Whirlpool Corp.
Whitman Corp.
WICOR, Inc.
Wilbur-Ellis Co. & Connell Brothers Co.
Wiley & Sons (John)
Williams
Wiremold Co.
Wisconsin Energy Corp.
Wisconsin Power & Light Co.
Wisconsin Public Service Corp.
Witco Corp.
Woodward Governor Co.
Wrigley Co. (Wm. Jr.)
Yellow Corp.
York Federal Savings & Loan Association
Young & Rubicam
Zachry Co. (H.B.)
Zilkha & Sons

PUBLIC BROADCASTING

ABB Inc.
Abbott Laboratories
ABC
AEGON U.S.A. Inc.
AGL Resources Inc.
Agrilink Foods, Inc.
Air Products and Chemicals, Inc.
AK Steel Corp.
Albertson's Inc.
Alcoa Inc.
Alcon Laboratories, Inc.
Alexander & Baldwin, Inc.
Allegheny Technologies Inc.
Alliant Techsystems
AlliedSignal Inc.
AMCORE Bank Rockford
Ameren Corp.
American General Finance
American United Life Insurance Co.
Ameritas Life Insurance Corp.
Ameritech Michigan
Ameritech Ohio
Ameritech Wisconsin
AMP Inc.
AMR Corp.
Amsted Industries Inc.
Analog Devices, Inc.
Andersen Corp.
Andersons Inc.
Anheuser-Busch Companies, Inc.
Aon Corp.
Archer-Daniels-Midland Co.
Aristech Chemical Corp.
Arizona Public Service Co.
Ashland, Inc.
Atlantic Richfield Co.
Avista Corporation
Avon Products, Inc.
Baird & Co. (Robert W.)
Banfi Vintners
Bank of America
Bank of New York Co., Inc.
Bank One Corp.
Bank One, Texas-Houston Office
BankAtlantic Bancorp
BankBoston Corp.
Banta Corp.
Bard, Inc. (C.R.)
Bardes Corp.
Barnes Group Inc.
Barry Corp. (R.G.)
Battelle Memorial Institute
Bayer Corp.
Bean, Inc. (L.L.)
Belk Stores Services Inc.
Bell Atlantic Corp.
Bemis Co., Inc.
Bemis Manufacturing Co.
Ben & Jerry's Homemade Inc.
Bernstein & Co., Inc. (Sanford C.)
Berwind Group
Bestfoods
Bethlehem Steel Corp.
BFGoodrich Co.
Binney & Smith Inc.
Blair & Co. (William)
Block, Inc. (H&R)
Blount International, Inc.
Blue Cross & Blue Shield of Alabama
Boston Globe (The)
Bowater Inc.
Bridgestone/Firestone, Inc.
Briggs & Stratton Corp.
Bristol-Myers Squibb Co.
Brown Shoe Co., Inc.
Brown & Williamson Tobacco Corp.
Bucyrus-Erie Co.
Burlington Resources, Inc.
Burnett Co. (Leo)
Burress (J.W.)
Cargill Inc.
Carillon Importers, Ltd.
Carlson Companies, Inc.
Carolina Power & Light Co.
Carpenter Technology Corp.
Carrier Corp.
Carris Reels
Carter-Wallace, Inc.
Caterpillar Inc.
CBS Corp.
Central Maine Power Co.
Central Soya Co.
Central Vermont Public Service Corp.
Chase Bank of Texas
Chase Manhattan Bank, NA
Chemed Corp.
Chevron Corp.
Chicago Board of Trade
Chicago Title Corp.
Church & Dwight Co., Inc.
CIGNA Corp.
Cincinnati Bell Inc.
Cinergy Corp.
Circuit City Stores, Inc.
CIT Group, Inc. (The)
Citibank Corp.
Citigroup
Clorox Co.
CNF Transportation, Inc.
Colonial Oil Industries, Inc.
Comerica Inc.
Commerce Bancshares, Inc.
Commercial Intertech Corp.
Commonwealth Edison Co.
Compaq Computer Corp.
Compass Bank
Consolidated Natural Gas Co.
Consolidated Papers, Inc.
Consumers Energy Co.
Contran Corp.
Conwood Co. LP
Cook Inlet Region
Cooper Industries, Inc.
Cooper Tire & Rubber Co.
Coors Brewing Co.
Copley Press, Inc.
Corning Inc.
Country Curtains, Inc.
Crane Co.
Crane & Co., Inc.
Credit Suisse First Boston
CSS Industries, Inc.
Cummings Properties Management
Cummins Engine Co., Inc.
CUNA Mutual Group
Daily News
DaimlerChrysler Corp.
Dain Bosworth Inc.
Dana Corp.
Danis Companies
Dayton Hudson
Dayton Power and Light Co.
Deere & Co.
DeKalb Genetics Corp.
Deluxe Corp.
Deposit Guaranty National Bank
Detroit Edison Co.
Deutsch Co.
Dexter Corp.
Dial Corp.
Disney Co. (Walt)
Dixie Group, Inc. (The)
Dominion Resources, Inc.
Donaldson Co., Inc.
Dow Corning Corp.
DSM Copolymer
du Pont de Nemours & Co. (E.I.)
Duchossois Industries Inc.
Dun & Bradstreet Corp.
Duriron Co., Inc.
Dynamet, Inc.
Eastern Enterprises
Eaton Corp.
Ecolab Inc.
Edison International
El Paso Energy Co.
Elf Atochem North America, Inc.
Emerson Electric Co.
Employers Mutual Casualty Co.
Enterprise Rent-A-Car Co.
Erb Lumber Co.
Ethyl Corp.
Excel Corp.
Exxon Mobil Corp.
Fannie Mae
Federal-Mogul Corp.
Federated Department Stores, Inc.
FedEx Corp.
Ferro Corp.
Fifth Third Bancorp
FINA
Fireman's Fund Insurance Co.
First Financial Bank
First Hawaiian, Inc.
First Source Corp.
First Tennessee National Corp.
First Union Bank
First Union Corp.
First Union National Bank, NA
First Union Securities, Inc.
Fisher Scientific
FleetBoston Financial Corp.
Florida Power Corp.
Florida Power & Light Co.
Florida Rock Industries
Fluor Corp.
Forbes Inc.
Ford Motor Co.
Fort James Corp.
Fortis Insurance Co.
Fortune Brands, Inc.
Freddie Mac
Freeport-McMoRan Inc.
Frost National Bank
Fuller Co. (H.B.)
Gallo Winery, Inc. (E&J)
Galter Corp.
Gap, Inc.
GATX Corp.
GEICO Corp.
GenAmerica Corp.
GenCorp
General Electric Co.
General Mills, Inc.
General Motors Corp.
Georgia-Pacific Corp.
Gerber Products Co.
Giant Eagle Inc.
Giant Food Inc.
Gillette Co.
Glaxo Wellcome Inc.
Glickenhaus & Co.
Globe Corp.
Goodrich Aerospace - Aerostructures Group (B.F.)
Graco, Inc.
GTE Corp.
Guardian Life Insurance Co. of America
Gucci America Inc.
Guess?
Hallmark Cards Inc.
Hamilton Sundstrand Corp.
Hancock Financial Services (John)
Hanna Co. (M.A.)
Harley-Davidson Co.
Harsco Corp.
Hartford (The)
Hartford Steam Boiler Inspection & Insurance Co.
Hartmarx Corp.
Hawaiian Electric Co., Inc.
Heinz Co. (H.J.)
Heller Financial, Inc.
Hickory Tech Corp.
Hoffer Plastics Corp.
Hofmann Co.
Honeywell International Inc.
HSBC Bank USA
Hubbard Broadcasting, Inc.
Huffy Corp.
Humana, Inc.
Hunt Manufacturing Co.
IBP
Idaho Power Co.
IKON Office Solutions, Inc.
Illinois Power Co.
Illinois Tool Works, Inc.
Inland Container Corp.
Intel Corp.
International Business Machines Corp.
International Flavors & Fragrances Inc.
International Paper Co.
Jacobs Engineering Group
Jacobson & Sons (Benjamin)
Johnson Controls Inc.
Johnson & Johnson
Johnson & Son (S.C.)
Jostens, Inc.
Journal-Gazette Co.
JSJ Corp.
Katten, Muchin & Zavis
Kemper National Insurance Companies
Kennametal, Inc.
Kimball International, Inc.
Kimberly-Clark Corp.
Kingsbury Corp.
Kmart Corp.
Koch Enterprises, Inc.
Kroger Co.
La-Z-Boy Inc.
Ladish Co., Inc.
Lance, Inc.
Land O'Lakes, Inc.
Lee Enterprises
Lehigh Portland Cement Co.
Leigh Fibers, Inc.
Levi Strauss & Co.
LG&E Energy Corp.
Lilly & Co. (Eli)
Lincoln Financial Group
Lipton Co.
Little, Inc. (Arthur D.)
Litton Industries, Inc.
Liz Claiborne, Inc.
Loews Corp.
Lotus Development Corp.
Louisiana Land & Exploration Co.
LTV Corp.
Lubrizol Corp. (The)
Macy's East Inc.
Madison Gas & Electric Co.
Manulife Financial
Maritz Inc.
Mark IV Industries
Marriott International Inc.
Marshall & Ilsley Corp.
Masco Corp.
Massachusetts Mutual Life Insurance Co.
May Department Stores Co.
Maytag Corp.
McClatchy Co.
McCormick & Co. Inc.
McDermott Inc.
McDonald & Co. Securities, Inc.
McGraw-Hill Companies, Inc.
MCI WorldCom, Inc.
McKesson-HBOC Corp.
McWane Inc.
Mead Corp.
Medtronic, Inc.
Menasha Corp.
Merck & Co.
Merrill Lynch & Co., Inc.
Metropolitan Life Insurance Co.
Michigan Consolidated Gas Co.
Mid-America Bank of Louisville
Milacron, Inc.
Milliken & Co.
Millipore Corp.
Mine Safety Appliances Co.

Minnesota Mining & Manufacturing Co.
Minnesota Mutual Life Insurance Co.
Monarch Machine Tool Co.
Monsanto Co.
Montana Power Co.
Montgomery Ward & Co., Inc.
MONY Group (The)
Morgan & Co. Inc. (J.P.)
Morgan Stanley Dean Witter & Co.
Morris Communications Corp.
Morrison Knudsen Corp.
Morton International Inc.
Motorola Inc.
Nabisco Group Holdings
Nalco Chemical Co.
National City Bank of Minneapolis
National Computer Systems, Inc.
National Fuel Gas Distribution Corp.
National Machinery Co.
National Presto Industries, Inc.
Nationwide Insurance Co.
Navcom Systems
NCR Corp.
NEBCO Evans
New Century Energies
New York Life Insurance Co.
New York Mercantile Exchange
New York Stock Exchange, Inc.
New York Times Co.
Newman's Own Inc.
Niagara Mohawk Holdings Inc.
Nordson Corp.
Norfolk Southern Corp.
Nortel
North American Royalties
Northern Indiana Public Service Co.
Northern States Power Co.
Northern Trust Co.
Northwest Natural Gas Co.
Norton Co.
Norwest Corp.
Ohio National Life Insurance Co.
Old National Bank Evansville
Olin Corp.
Oshkosh B'Gosh, Inc.
Outboard Marine Corp.
Overseas Shipholding Group Inc.
Owens Corning
PACCAR Inc.
Pacific Century Financial Corp.
Pacific Mutual Life Insurance Co.
PacifiCare Health Systems
PacifiCorp
Pan-American Life Insurance Co.
Pella Corp.
PEMCO Corp.
Penney Co., Inc. (J.C.)
Pennzoil-Quaker State Co.
Peoples Bank
Peoples Energy Corp.
PepsiCo, Inc.
PerkinElmer, Inc.
Pfizer Inc.
Phelps Dodge Corp.
Phillips Petroleum Co.
Physicians Mutual Insurance Co.
Pillsbury Co.
Pittway Corp.
Playboy Enterprises Inc.
PNC Financial Services Group
Polaroid Corp.
Portland General Electric Co.
Potomac Electric Power Co.
PPG Industries, Inc.
Premier Industrial Corp.
Price Associates (T. Rowe)
Principal Financial Group
Procter & Gamble Co., Cosmetics Division
Promus Hotel Corp.
Providence Journal-Bulletin Co.
Prudential Insurance Co. of America
Prudential Securities Inc.
Public Service Electric & Gas Co.
Publix Supermarkets
Pulitzer Publishing Co.
Putnam Investments
Quanex Corp.
Ralston Purina Co.
Rayonier Inc.
Red Wing Shoe Co. Inc.
Reebok International Ltd.
Regions Bank
Reily & Co., Inc. (William B.)
Reinhart Institutional Foods
Reliant Energy Inc.
ReliaStar Financial Corp.
Revlon Inc.
Reynolds Metals Co.
Reynolds & Reynolds Co.
Reynolds Tobacco (R.J.)
Rich Products Corp.
Rochester Gas & Electric Corp.
Rockwell International Corp.
Rouse Co.
Royal & SunAlliance USA, Inc.
Russer Foods
SAFECO Corp.
Saint Paul Companies Inc.
Salomon Smith Barney
Sara Lee Corp.
Sara Lee Hosiery, Inc.
SBC Communications Inc.
Schlumberger Ltd. (USA)
Schwab & Co., Inc. (Charles)
Schwebel Baking Co.
Scripps Co. (E.W.)
Seagram & Sons, Inc. (Joseph E.)
Seaway Food Town, Inc.
Security Benefit Life Insurance Co.
Security Life of Denver Insurance Co.
Sentry Insurance, A Mutual Co.
Shaw's Supermarkets, Inc.
Shea Co. (John F.)
Shoney's Inc.
Sierra Pacific Industries
Sierra Pacific Resources
Simplot Co. (J.R.)
Smucker Co. (JM)
Sonoco Products Co.
Sony Electronics
South Bend Tribune Corp.
Southeastern Mutual Insurance Co.
Southwest Gas Corp.
Sovereign Bank
Sprint Corp.
Sprint/United Telephone
SPX Corp.
Square D Co.
Standard Products Co.
Stanley Works (The)
Star Bank NA
Starwood Hotels & Resorts Worldwide, Inc.
State Farm Mutual Automobile Insurance Co.
Steelcase Inc.
Stone Container Corp.
Storage Technology Corp.
Strear Farms Co.
Stride Rite Corp.
Sunmark Capital Corp.
SunTrust Bank Atlanta
Susquehanna-Pfaltzgraff Co.
TCF National Bank Minnesota
Tektronix, Inc.
TENNANT Co.
Tenneco Automotive
Tenneco Packaging
Tension Envelope Corp.
Tesoro Hawaii
Texas Instruments Inc.
Textron Inc.
Thermo Electron Corp.
Times Mirror Co.
TJX Companies, Inc.
TMC Investment Co.
Toledo Blade Co.
Tomkins Industries, Inc.
Toro Co.
Toyota Motor Sales U.S.A., Inc.
Trace International Holdings, Inc.
Transamerica Corp.
True Oil Co.
TRW Inc.
TU Electric Co.
Unilever Home & Personal Care U.S.A.
Unilever United States, Inc.
Union Camp Corp.
Union Carbide Corp.
Union Pacific Corp.
Union Planters Corp.
United Distillers & Vintners North America
United Dominion Industries, Ltd.
United Parcel Service of America Inc.
U.S. Bancorp
U.S. Bancorp Piper Jaffray
United States Trust Co. of New York
United Wisconsin Services
Universal Foods Corp.
Universal Leaf Tobacco Co., Inc.
Universal Studios
UnumProvident
UPN Channel 50
US West, Inc.
USAA Life Insurance Co.
USG Corp.
UST Inc.
USX Corp.
Valmont Industries, Inc.
Valspar Corp.
Vulcan Materials Co.
Wachovia Bank of North Carolina NA
Wachtell, Lipton, Rosen & Katz
Wal-Mart Stores, Inc.
Washington Mutual, Inc.
The Washington Post
Waste Management Inc.
Weil, Gotshal & Manges Corp.
Western & Southern Life Insurance Co.
Westvaco Corp.
Weyerhaeuser Co.
Whirlpool Corp.
Wiley & Sons (John)
Williams
Winn-Dixie Stores Inc.
Wiremold Co.
Wisconsin Energy Corp.
Wisconsin Power & Light Co.
Woodward Governor Co.
Wrigley Co. (Wm. Jr.)
Wyman-Gordon Co.
Yellow Corp.
Young & Rubicam
Zachry Co. (H.B.)
Zenith Electronics Corp.
Zilkha & Sons

THEATER

Abbott Laboratories
ABC
AEGON U.S.A. Inc.
AGL Resources Inc.
Agrilink Foods, Inc.
Air Products and Chemicals, Inc.
AK Steel Corp.
Alabama Power Co.
Albany International Corp.
Alcoa Inc.
Alcon Laboratories, Inc.
Alexander & Baldwin, Inc.
Allegheny Technologies Inc.
AlliedSignal Inc.
Allmerica Financial Corp.
AMCORE Bank Rockford
Ameren Corp.
American Express Co.
American Fidelity Corp.
American General Finance
American United Life Insurance Co.
Ameritas Life Insurance Corp.
Ameritech Illinois
Ameritech Indiana
Ameritech Michigan
Ameritech Ohio
AMP Inc.
Andersen Corp.
Andersons Inc.
Anheuser-Busch Companies, Inc.
Aon Corp.
APL Ltd.
Apple Computer, Inc.
Archer-Daniels-Midland Co.
Aristech Chemical Corp.
Arizona Public Service Co.
Ashland, Inc.
AT&T Corp.
Atlantic Richfield Co.
Avista Corporation
Avon Products, Inc.
Badger Meter, Inc.
Baird & Co. (Robert W.)
Banfi Vintners
Bank of America
Bank One Corp.
BankAtlantic Bancorp
BankBoston Corp.
Banta Corp.
Barclays Capital
Bard, Inc. (C.R.)
Barden Corp.
Bardes Corp.
Barnes Group Inc.
Barry Corp. (R.G.)
Bassett Furniture Industries
Battelle Memorial Institute
Bausch & Lomb Inc.
Bean, Inc. (L.L.)
Bell Atlantic Corp.
Bemis Co., Inc.
Bemis Manufacturing Co.
Bernstein & Co., Inc. (Sanford C.)
Berwind Group
Bestfoods
Bethlehem Steel Corp.
BFGoodrich Co.
Binney & Smith Inc.
Binswanger Companies
Blair & Co. (William)
Block, Inc. (H&R)
Blount International, Inc.
Blue Bell, Inc.
Blue Cross & Blue Shield of Alabama
Blue Cross & Blue Shield of Iowa
Blue Cross & Blue Shield of Minnesota
Boeing Co.
Boise Cascade Corp.
Borden, Inc.
Borman's Inc.
Boston Globe (The)
Bradford & Co. (J.C.)
Bridgestone/Firestone, Inc.
Briggs & Stratton Corp.
Bristol-Myers Squibb Co.
Broderbund Software, Inc.
Brown Shoe Co., Inc.
Brunswick Corp.
Bucyrus-Erie Co.
Burlington Resources, Inc.
Burnett Co. (Leo)
Burress (J.W.)
Butler Manufacturing Co.
Cabot Corp.
Calvin Klein
Cantor, Fitzgerald Securities Corp.
Cargill Inc.
Carillon Importers, Ltd.
Carlson Companies, Inc.
Carrier Corp.
Carris Reels
Carter-Wallace, Inc.
Caterpillar Inc.
CBS Corp.
CCB Financial Corp.
Central Maine Power Co.
Central Soya Co.
CertainTeed Corp.
Cessna Aircraft Co.
CGU Insurance
Charter Manufacturing Co.
Chase Bank of Texas
Chase Manhattan Bank, NA
Chemed Corp.
Chesapeake Corp.
Chevron Corp.
Chicago Sun-Times, Inc.
Chicago Title Corp.
Chicago Tribune Co.
CIGNA Corp.
Cincinnati Bell Inc.
Cinergy Corp.
Circuit City Stores, Inc.

CIT Group, Inc. (The)
Citibank Corp.
Citigroup
Citizens Financial Group, Inc.
CLARCOR Inc.
Cleveland-Cliffs, Inc.
Clorox Co.
CNA
Coca-Cola Co.
Colonial Life & Accident Insurance Co.
Colonial Oil Industries, Inc.
Commerce Bancshares, Inc.
Commonwealth Edison Co.
Compaq Computer Corp.
Compass Bank
Consolidated Natural Gas Co.
Consolidated Papers, Inc.
Constellation Energy Group, Inc.
Consumers Energy Co.
Contran Corp.
Cooper Industries, Inc.
Coors Brewing Co.
Copley Press, Inc.
Corning Inc.
Country Curtains, Inc.
Cox Enterprises Inc.
CPI Corp.
Crane Co.
Crane & Co., Inc.
Credit Suisse First Boston
Crestar Finance Corp.
CUNA Mutual Group
Daily News
DaimlerChrysler Corp.
Dain Bosworth Inc.
Danis Companies
Dayton Hudson
Dayton Power and Light Co.
Deere & Co.
Delta Air Lines, Inc.
Deluxe Corp.
Deposit Guaranty National Bank
Detroit Edison Co.
Deutsch Co.
Dexter Corp.
Dial Corp.
Dominion Resources, Inc.
Donaldson Co., Inc.
Donnelley & Sons Co. (R.R.)
Dow Corning Corp.
Dow Jones & Co., Inc.
du Pont de Nemours & Co. (E.I.)
Duchossois Industries Inc.
Duke Energy
Dun & Bradstreet Corp.
Duriron Co., Inc.
Dynamet, Inc.
Eastern Enterprises
Eaton Corp.
Eckerd Corp.
Ecolab Inc.
Edison International
El Paso Energy Co.
Elf Atochem North America, Inc.
Emerson Electric Co.
Ensign-Bickford Industries
Enterprise Rent-A-Car Co.
Equitable Resources, Inc.
Evening Post Publishing Co.
Exxon Mobil Corp.
Fannie Mae
Federal-Mogul Corp.
Federated Mutual Insurance Co.
Ferro Corp.
Fifth Third Bancorp
Fireman's Fund Insurance Co.
First Financial Bank
First Hawaiian, Inc.
First Maryland Bancorp
First Tennessee National Corp.
First Union Bank
First Union Corp.
First Union National Bank, NA
First Union Securities, Inc.
Firstar Bank Milwaukee NA
Fisher Brothers Cleaning Services
Fisher Scientific
FleetBoston Financial Corp.
Florida Rock Industries
Fluor Corp.
Forbes Inc.
Ford Meter Box Co.
Ford Motor Co.
Forest City Enterprises, Inc.
Fort James Corp.
Fort Worth Star-Telegram Inc.
Fortune Brands, Inc.
Freeport-McMoRan Inc.
Frost National Bank
Fuller Co. (H.B.)
Furniture Brands International, Inc.
Gallo Winery, Inc. (E&J)
Galter Corp.
Gap, Inc.
GATX Corp.
GEICO Corp.
GenAmerica Corp.
GenCorp
General Atlantic Partners II LP
General Dynamics Corp.
General Electric Co.
General Mills, Inc.
General Motors Corp.
Georgia-Pacific Corp.
Georgia Power Co.
Giant Eagle Inc.
Giant Food Inc.
Giddings & Lewis
Glaxo Wellcome Inc.
Glickenhaus & Co.
Golub Corp.
Goodrich Aerospace - Aerostructures Group (B.F.)
Grace & Co. (W.R.)
Graco, Inc.
Green Bay Packaging
GTE Corp.
Guardian Life Insurance Co. of America
Gucci America Inc.
Hallmark Cards Inc.
Hamilton Sundstrand Corp.
Hancock Financial Services (John)
Hanna Co. (M.A.)
Hannaford Brothers Co.
Harcourt General, Inc.
Harland Co. (John H.)
Harley-Davidson Co.
Harris Corp.
Harris Trust & Savings Bank
Harsco Corp.
Hartford (The)
Hartmarx Corp.
Hasbro, Inc.
Hawaiian Electric Co., Inc.
Heinz Co. (H.J.)
Hensel Phelps Construction Co.
Hershey Foods Corp.
Hickory Tech Corp.
Hofmann Co.
Honeywell International Inc.
Housatonic Curtain Co.
Hubbard Broadcasting, Inc.
Huffy Corp.
Humana, Inc.
Hunt Manufacturing Co.
Huntington Bancshares Inc.
IKON Office Solutions, Inc.
Illinois Tool Works, Inc.
Inland Container Corp.
International Business Machines Corp.
International Flavors & Fragrances Inc.
International Multifoods Corp.
International Paper Co.
INTRUST Financial Corp.
Invacare Corp.
Jacobs Engineering Group
Johnson Controls Inc.
Johnson & Son (S.C.)
Jostens, Inc.
Journal-Gazette Co.
JSJ Corp.
Katten, Muchin & Zavis
Kellwood Co.
Kemper National Insurance Companies
Kennametal, Inc.
Kerr-McGee Corp.
Kiewit Sons' Inc. (Peter)
Kimball International, Inc.
Kimberly-Clark Corp.
Kinder Morgn
Kingsbury Corp.
Kmart Corp.
Koch Enterprises, Inc.
Kohler Co.
Kraft Foods, Inc.
Kroger Co.
La-Z-Boy Inc.
Land O'Lakes, Inc.
Landmark Communications Inc.
Lee Enterprises
Lehigh Portland Cement Co.
Levi Strauss & Co.
Leviton Manufacturing Co. Inc.
Liberty Corp.
Lilly & Co. (Eli)
Lincoln Electric Co.
Lincoln Financial Group
Lipton Co.
Little, Inc. (Arthur D.)
Liz Claiborne, Inc.
Loews Corp.
Lotus Development Corp.
Louisiana Land & Exploration Co.
Louisiana-Pacific Corp.
LTV Corp.
Lubrizol Corp. (The)
MacMillan Bloedel Inc.
Madison Gas & Electric Co.
Mallinckrodt Chemical, Inc.
Manufacturers & Traders Trust Co.
Marcus Corp.
Maritz Inc.
Mark IV Industries
Marriott International Inc.
Marshall Field's
Marshall & Ilsley Corp.
Massachusetts Mutual Life Insurance Co.
Mattel Inc.
May Department Stores Co.
McClatchy Co.
McCormick & Co. Inc.
McDonald & Co. Securities, Inc.
McKesson-HBOC Corp.
Mead Corp.
Medtronic, Inc.
Mellon Financial Corp.
Menasha Corp.
Merck & Co.
Merrill Lynch & Co., Inc.
Mervyn's California
Metropolitan Life Insurance Co.
Michigan Consolidated Gas Co.
Mid-America Bank of Louisville
Milliken & Co.
Mine Safety Appliances Co.
Minnesota Mining & Manufacturing Co.
Minnesota Mutual Life Insurance Co.
Monsanto Co.
Montana Power Co.
Morgan & Co. Inc. (J.P.)
Morris Communications Corp.
Morrison Knudsen Corp.
Motorola Inc.
MTD Products Inc.
Mutual of Omaha Insurance Co.
Nabisco Group Holdings
National City Bank of Minneapolis
National City Corp.
National Computer Systems, Inc.
National Fuel Gas Distribution Corp.
National Machinery Co.
National Service Industries, Inc.
National Starch & Chemical Co.
Nationwide Insurance Co.
NEBCO Evans
NEC America, Inc.
Nestle U.S.A. Inc.
New England Bio Labs
New England Financial
New York Stock Exchange, Inc.
New York Times Co.
Newman's Own Inc.
Niagara Mohawk Holdings Inc.
Nordson Corp.
Norfolk Southern Corp.
Nortel
Northern States Power Co.
Northern Trust Co.
Northwest Bank Nebraska, NA
Northwest Natural Gas Co.
Norton Co.
Norwest Corp.
Occidental Oil and Gas
OG&E Electric Services
Ohio National Life Insurance Co.
Old National Bank Evansville
Olin Corp.
Orscheln Co.
Overnite Transportation Co.
Overseas Shipholding Group Inc.
PACCAR Inc.
Pacific Century Financial Corp.
Pacific Mutual Life Insurance Co.
PacifiCorp
Paine Webber
Park National Bank
Parker Hannifin Corp.
Pella Corp.
PEMCO Corp.
Penney Co., Inc. (J.C.)
Pennzoil-Quaker State Co.
Peoples Bank
Peoples Energy Corp.
PepsiCo, Inc.
PerkinElmer, Inc.
Pfizer Inc.
Pharmacia & Upjohn, Inc.
Phelps Dodge Corp.
Philip Morris Companies Inc.
Phillips Petroleum Co.
Physicians Mutual Insurance Co.
Pieper Power Electric Co.
Pillsbury Co.
Pittway Corp.
PNC Financial Services Group
Polaroid Corp.
Potomac Electric Power Co.
Premier Dental Products Co.
Premier Industrial Corp.
Price Associates (T. Rowe)
Principal Financial Group
Procter & Gamble Co.
Procter & Gamble Co., Cosmetics Division
Promus Hotel Corp.
Providence Journal-Bulletin Co.
Prudential Securities Inc.
Public Service Electric & Gas Co.
Publix Supermarkets
Pulitzer Publishing Co.
Putnam Investments
Quanex Corp.
Questar Corp.
Ralph's Grocery Co.
Ralston Purina Co.
Reader's Digest Association, Inc. (The)
Red Wing Shoe Co. Inc.
Regions Bank
Regis Corp.
Reilly Industries, Inc.
Reliant Energy Inc.
Revlon Inc.
Reynolds Metals Co.
Reynolds & Reynolds Co.
Reynolds Tobacco (R.J.)
Rich Products Corp.
Rochester Gas & Electric Corp.
Rockwell International Corp.
Rouse Co.
Royal & SunAlliance USA, Inc.
Ruddick Corp.
Russer Foods
Ryder System, Inc.
Safeguard Scientifics
Saint Paul Companies Inc.
Salomon Smith Barney
Sara Lee Corp.
SBC Communications Inc.
Schering-Plough Corp.
Schloss & Co. (Marcus)
Schlumberger Ltd. (USA)
Scripps Co. (E.W.)

Seagram & Sons, Inc. (Joseph E.)
Searle & Co. (G.D.)
Seaway Food Town, Inc.
Security Benefit Life Insurance Co.
Sempra Energy
Sentry Insurance, A Mutual Co.
Servco Pacific
S.G. Cowen
Shaw's Supermarkets, Inc.
Shell Oil Co.
Sherwin-Williams Co.
Shoney's Inc.
Sierra Pacific Resources
Simpson Investment Co.
Slant/Fin Corp.
SmithKline Beecham Corp.
Smurfit-Stone Container Corp.
Solo Cup Co.
Sonoco Products Co.
Sony Electronics
Southeastern Mutual Insurance Co.
Southern New England Telephone Co.
Southwest Gas Corp.
Sprint Corp.
Sprint/United Telephone
SPX Corp.
Square D Co.
Standard Products Co.
Stanley Works (The)
Star Bank NA
State Farm Mutual Automobile Insurance Co.
State Street Bank & Trust Co.
Steelcase Inc.
Stone Container Corp.
Storage Technology Corp.
Strear Farms Co.
Stride Rite Corp.
SunTrust Bank Atlanta
Susquehanna-Pfaltzgraff Co.
Sverdrup Corp.
Synovus Financial Corp.
Tamko Roofing Products
Target Corp.
TCF National Bank Minnesota
Tektronix, Inc.
Temple-Inland Inc.
TENNANT Co.
Tenneco Automotive
Tension Envelope Corp.
Tesoro Hawaii
Texas Gas Transmission Corp.
Texas Instruments Inc.
Textron Inc.
Thermo Electron Corp.
Thomasville Furniture Industries Inc.
Thompson Co. (J. Walter)
Times Mirror Co.
Timken Co. (The)
Titan Industrial Corp.
TJX Companies, Inc.
TMC Investment Co.
Toledo Blade Co.
Tomkins Industries, Inc.
Toro Co.
Toyota Motor Sales U.S.A., Inc.
Trace International Holdings, Inc.
Transamerica Corp.
True North Communications, Inc.
True Oil Co.
Trustmark Insurance Co.
TRW Inc.
TU Electric Co.
Tucson Electric Power Co.
Ukrop's Super Markets
Unilever Home & Personal Care U.S.A.
Unilever United States, Inc.
Union Camp Corp.
Union Pacific Corp.
Union Planters Corp.
United Airlines Inc.
United Co.
United Distillers & Vintners North America
United Dominion Industries, Ltd.
United Services Automobile Association
U.S. Bancorp
U.S. Bancorp Piper Jaffray
United States Trust Co. of New York
United Wisconsin Services
Universal Foods Corp.
Universal Leaf Tobacco Co., Inc.
Universal Studios
Unocal Corp.
UPN Channel 50
US Bank, Washington
US West, Inc.
USAA Life Insurance Co.
USG Corp.
UST Inc.
USX Corp.
Valmont Industries, Inc.
Valspar Corp.
Vanguard Group
Vulcan Materials Co.
Wal-Mart Stores, Inc.
Washington Mutual, Inc.
Washington Trust Bank
Waste Management Inc.
West Co. Inc.
Westvaco Corp.
Weyerhaeuser Co.
Whirlpool Corp.
Whitman Corp.
WICOR, Inc.
Wilbur-Ellis Co. & Connell Brothers Co.
Wiley & Sons (John)
Williams
Wisconsin Energy Corp.
Wisconsin Power & Light Co.
Wisconsin Public Service Corp.
Witco Corp.
Woodward Governor Co.
Wyman-Gordon Co.
Yellow Corp.
York Federal Savings & Loan Association
Young & Rubicam
Zachry Co. (H.B.)
Zilkha & Sons

VISUAL ARTS

Alabama Power Co.
Alcoa Inc.
Ameren Corp.
American Express Co.
American United Life Insurance Co.
Ameritech Indiana
Appleton Papers Inc.
AT&T Corp.
BankBoston Corp.
Banta Corp.
Bard, Inc. (C.R.)
Bemis Co., Inc.
Bethlehem Steel Corp.
BFGoodrich Co.
Binney & Smith Inc.
Block, Inc. (H&R)
Blount International, Inc.
Boston Globe (The)
Campbell Soup Co.
Carris Reels
Central Maine Power Co.
Central Soya Co.
Century 21
Champion International Corp.
Chase Manhattan Bank, NA
Citigroup
Clorox Co.
CNF Transportation, Inc.
Colonial Life & Accident Insurance Co.
Consolidated Papers, Inc.
Copley Press, Inc.
Corning Inc.
Daily News
Dayton Hudson
Dayton Power and Light Co.
Deposit Guaranty National Bank
Dominion Resources, Inc.
Dow Corning Corp.
du Pont de Nemours & Co. (E.I.)
Duchossois Industries Inc.
Eaton Corp.
Erb Lumber Co.
Fireman's Fund Insurance Co.
First Hawaiian, Inc.
First Maryland Bancorp
First Tennessee National Corp.
First Union Corp.
FleetBoston Financial Corp.
Forest City Enterprises, Inc.
Fort James Corp.
Franklin Mint (The)
Gannett Co., Inc.
Gap, Inc.
GATX Corp.
General Electric Co.
General Motors Corp.
Glaxo Wellcome Inc.
Graco, Inc.
GTE Corp.
Hallmark Cards Inc.
Hubbard Broadcasting, Inc.
Huffy Corp.
Hunt Manufacturing Co.
Huntington Bancshares Inc.
International Business Machines Corp.
INTRUST Financial Corp.
ISE America
Jacobs Engineering Group
Kingsbury Corp.
Kraft Foods, Inc.
Kroger Co.
Lee Enterprises
Macy's East Inc.
Maritz Inc.
Marshall Field's
Marshall & Ilsley Corp.
McClatchy Co.
McDonald & Co. Securities, Inc.
Medtronic, Inc.
Mercantile Bank NA
Meredith Corp.
Mervyn's California
Metropolitan Life Insurance Co.
Mid-America Bank of Louisville
Morgan & Co. Inc. (J.P.)
Morgan Stanley Dean Witter & Co.
National Computer Systems, Inc.
National Starch & Chemical Co.
New England Financial
Nortel
Northern Indiana Public Service Co.
Northwest Bank Nebraska, NA
Northwest Natural Gas Co.
Norton Co.
Occidental Petroleum Corp.
Olin Corp.
Overseas Shipholding Group Inc.
PACCAR Inc.
Pacific Century Financial Corp.
Pella Corp.
Pharmacia & Upjohn, Inc.
Philip Morris Companies Inc.
Pittway Corp.
PNC Bank Kentucky Inc.
Polaroid Corp.
Procter & Gamble Co., Cosmetics Division
Provident Companies, Inc.
Pulitzer Publishing Co.
Reynolds & Reynolds Co.
Reynolds Tobacco (R.J.)
Rouse Co.
Royal & SunAlliance USA, Inc.
SAFECO Corp.
Salomon Smith Barney
Sara Lee Corp.
Sara Lee Hosiery, Inc.
Seaway Food Town, Inc.
Sega of America Inc.
Sempra Energy
S.G. Cowen
Slant/Fin Corp.
Sony Electronics
Springs Industries, Inc.
Target Corp.
Tenneco Automotive
Tesoro Hawaii
Union Camp Corp.
United Distillers & Vintners North America
United States Trust Co. of New York
US Bank, Washington
US West, Inc.
Vulcan Materials Co.
Walter Industries Inc.
Whirlpool Corp.
Wilbur-Ellis Co. & Connell Brothers Co.
Williams
Witco Corp.
Yellow Corp.
Young & Rubicam

Civic & Public Affairs

AFRICAN AMERICAN AFFAIRS

ABC
Aetna, Inc.
Agrilink Foods, Inc.
Alabama Power Co.
Alcoa Inc.
Alcon Laboratories, Inc.
Alliant Techsystems
AlliedSignal Inc.
Allstate Insurance Co.
AMCORE Bank Rockford
Ameren Corp.
American Express Co.
Ameritech Corp.
Ameritech Ohio
Ameritech Wisconsin
AMP Inc.
AMR Corp.
Andersons Inc.
Anheuser-Busch Companies, Inc.
APL Ltd.
Archer-Daniels-Midland Co.
Arizona Public Service Co.
Armstrong World Industries, Inc.
Ashland, Inc.
AT&T Corp.
Avon Products, Inc.
Bandag, Inc.
Bank One Corp.
BankAtlantic Bancorp
Barden Corp.
Barnes Group Inc.
Bechtel Group, Inc.
Belk-Simpson Department Stores
Bell Atlantic Corp.
Bemis Co., Inc.
Ben & Jerry's Homemade Inc.
Bethlehem Steel Corp.
Binswanger Companies
Blue Cross & Blue Shield of Minnesota
Borden, Inc.
BP Amoco Corp.
Bridgestone/Firestone, Inc.
Briggs & Stratton Corp.
Bristol-Myers Squibb Co.
Brown Shoe Co., Inc.
Bucyrus-Erie Co.
Burnett Co. (Leo)
Cabot Corp.
Campbell Soup Co.
Cargill Inc.
Carpenter Technology Corp.
Caterpillar Inc.
Central Soya Co.
Cessna Aircraft Co.
Chase Bank of Texas
Chase Manhattan Bank, NA
Chesapeake Corp.
Chevron Corp.
Chicago Title Corp.
Chicago Tribune Co.
CIGNA Corp.
Cincinnati Bell Inc.
Cinergy Corp.
CIT Group, Inc. (The)
Citigroup
Citizens Bank-Flint
Citizens Financial Group, Inc.
Clark Refining & Marketing
Clorox Co.
Coca-Cola Co.
Commerce Bancshares, Inc.
Continental Grain Co.
Coors Brewing Co.
Cox Enterprises Inc.
Credit Suisse First Boston
Cummins Engine Co., Inc.
CUNA Mutual Group
Daily News
DaimlerChrysler Corp.
Danis Companies

Dayton Hudson
Dayton Power and Light Co.
Deluxe Corp.
Deposit Guaranty National Bank
Detroit Edison Co.
Dial Corp.
Disney Co. (Walt)
Dixie Group, Inc. (The)
Dow Chemical Co.
Dow Jones & Co., Inc.
Dun & Bradstreet Corp.
Duriron Co., Inc.
Eastern Bank
Eastman Kodak Co.
Eckerd Corp.
Emerson Electric Co.
Equitable Resources, Inc.
Exxon Mobil Corp.
Federal-Mogul Corp.
Ferro Corp.
Fidelity Investments
Fifth Third Bancorp
FINA
Firstar Bank Milwaukee NA
Fisher Brothers Cleaning Services
FleetBoston Financial Corp.
Florida Power & Light Co.
Florida Rock Industries
FMC Corp.
Forbes Inc.
Ford Motor Co.
Forest City Enterprises, Inc.
Fortis Insurance Co.
Freeport-McMoRan Inc.
Fuller Co. (H.B.)
Furniture Brands International, Inc.
Gallo Winery, Inc. (E&J)
Gap, Inc.
GEICO Corp.
GenAmerica Corp.
General Atlantic Partners II LP
General Electric Co.
General Mills, Inc.
General Motors Corp.
Georgia-Pacific Corp.
Georgia Power Co.
Gerber Products Co.
Giant Eagle Inc.
Giant Food Inc.
Goldman Sachs Group
Golub Corp.
GTE Corp.
Gulf Power Co.
Hallmark Cards Inc.
Hanna Co. (M.A.)
Harcourt General, Inc.
Harley-Davidson Co.
Harsco Corp.
Hartford (The)
Hartford Steam Boiler Inspection & Insurance Co.
Hartmarx Corp.
Hasbro, Inc.
Heinz Co. (H.J.)
Hitachi America Ltd.
Honeywell International Inc.
Hubbard Broadcasting, Inc.
Huffy Corp.
Humana, Inc.
Huntington Bancshares Inc.
IKON Office Solutions, Inc.
Jacobs Engineering Group
Journal-Gazette Co.
Katten, Muchin & Zavis
Kimball International, Inc.
Kimberly-Clark Corp.
KPMG Peat Marwick LLP
Lancaster Lens, Inc.
LandAmerica Financial Services
Landmark Communications Inc.
Levi Strauss & Co.
LG&E Energy Corp.
Liberty Corp.
Lilly & Co. (Eli)
Lincoln Financial Group
Loews Corp.
Lotus Development Corp.
LTV Corp.
Lubrizol Corp. (The)
Madison Gas & Electric Co.
Marcus Corp.
Mattel Inc.
May Department Stores Co.
McDonald & Co. Securities, Inc.
McGraw-Hill Companies, Inc.
MCI WorldCom, Inc.
Mead Corp.
Medtronic, Inc.
Mercantile Bank NA
Merrill Lynch & Co., Inc.
Metropolitan Life Insurance Co.
Michigan Consolidated Gas Co.
Mid-America Bank of Louisville
Milacron, Inc.
Millipore Corp.
Minnesota Mining & Manufacturing Co.
Monarch Machine Tool Co.
Monsanto Co.
MONY Group (The)
Morgan & Co. Inc. (J.P.)
Morrison Knudsen Corp.
Motorola Inc.
National City Bank of Minneapolis
National City Corp.
National Starch & Chemical Co.
Nationwide Insurance Co.
New Jersey Natural Gas Co.
New York Life Insurance Co.
Nissan North America, Inc.
Nordson Corp.
Northern Trust Co.
Norwest Corp.
Occidental Petroleum Corp.
Ohio National Life Insurance Co.
Old National Bank Evansville
Olin Corp.
Owens Corning
PacifiCorp
PepsiCo, Inc.
PerkinElmer, Inc.
Pharmacia & Upjohn, Inc.
Physicians Mutual Insurance Co.
Pillsbury Co.
PNC Financial Services Group
Polaroid Corp.
Premier Industrial Corp.
Procter & Gamble Co.
Procter & Gamble Co., Cosmetics Division
Providence Journal-Bulletin Co.
Prudential Insurance Co. of America
Prudential Securities Inc.
Publix Supermarkets
Pulitzer Publishing Co.
Ralph's Grocery Co.
Ralston Purina Co.
Reebok International Ltd.
Regions Bank
Revlon Inc.
Reynolds Metals Co.
Reynolds & Reynolds Co.
Reynolds Tobacco (R.J.)
Rockwell International Corp.
Royal & SunAlliance USA, Inc.
Rubbermaid Inc.
Ryder System, Inc.
Saint Paul Companies Inc.
Sara Lee Corp.
SBC Communications Inc.
Schwab & Co., Inc. (Charles)
Scripps Co. (E.W.)
Seagram & Sons, Inc. (Joseph E.)
Security Benefit Life Insurance Co.
Sentinel Communications Co.
Servco Pacific
Shell Oil Co.
Sierra Pacific Resources
Simpson Investment Co.
SIT Investment Associates, Inc.
Slant/Fin Corp.
Sonoco Products Co.
Sony Electronics
Southeastern Mutual Insurance Co.
Southwest Gas Corp.
Sovereign Bank
Stanley Works (The)
Star Bank NA
State Farm Mutual Automobile Insurance Co.
State Street Bank & Trust Co.
Steelcase Inc.
Synovus Financial Corp.
TCF National Bank Minnesota
Temple-Inland Inc.
Texaco Inc.
Texas Instruments Inc.
Thompson Co. (J. Walter)
Times Mirror Co.
Timken Co. (The)
TJX Companies, Inc.
Toledo Blade Co.
Tomkins Industries, Inc.
Transamerica Corp.
True North Communications, Inc.
TRW Inc.
Ukrop's Super Markets
Unilever Home & Personal Care U.S.A.
Unilever United States, Inc.
Union Carbide Corp.
United Airlines Inc.
United Parcel Service of America Inc.
United States Sugar Corp.
United Wisconsin Services
Universal Studios
Unocal Corp.
US Bank, Washington
USG Corp.
Vulcan Materials Co.
Wachovia Bank of North Carolina NA
Waffle House Inc.
Wal-Mart Stores, Inc.
Walter Industries Inc.
Warner-Lambert Co.
Weil, Gotshal & Manges Corp.
Western & Southern Life Insurance Co.
Westvaco Corp.
Weyerhaeuser Co.
Wilbur-Ellis Co. & Connell Brothers Co.
Williams
Winn-Dixie Stores Inc.
Wiremold Co.
Wisconsin Power & Light Co.
Woodward Governor Co.
Wrigley Co. (Wm. Jr.)
Young & Rubicam

ASIAN AMERICAN AFFAIRS

Alexander & Baldwin, Inc.
Allstate Insurance Co.
Amgen, Inc.
Amsted Industries Inc.
Atlantic Richfield Co.
Avon Products, Inc.
Bank of America
Bank One Corp.
Baxter International Inc.
Ben & Jerry's Homemade Inc.
Blue Cross & Blue Shield of Minnesota
Boeing Co.
BP Amoco Corp.
Brunswick Corp.
Chase Manhattan Bank, NA
Chesapeake Corp.
Chicago Title Corp.
Chicago Tribune Co.
Citizens Bank-Flint
Clorox Co.
Dow Jones & Co., Inc.
Eastern Bank
Fannie Mae
First Hawaiian, Inc.
First Union Bank
FleetBoston Financial Corp.
Fuller Co. (H.B.)
Gap, Inc.
General Atlantic Partners II LP
General Mills, Inc.
Harris Trust & Savings Bank
Hitachi America Ltd.
Humana, Inc.
Huntington Bancshares Inc.
ISE America
Landmark Communications Inc.
Levi Strauss & Co.
Liz Claiborne, Inc.
Lotus Development Corp.
Madison Gas & Electric Co.
McDonald & Co. Securities, Inc.
Minnesota Mutual Life Insurance Co.
National City Bank of Minneapolis
Nestle U.S.A. Inc.
New York Life Insurance Co.
New York Mercantile Exchange
Nissan North America, Inc.
Norwest Corp.
Owens Corning
Pacific Century Financial Corp.
Pacific Mutual Life Insurance Co.
Pfizer Inc.
Pillsbury Co.
Polaroid Corp.
Pulitzer Publishing Co.
Reebok International Ltd.
Reynolds Tobacco (R.J.)
Rockwell International Corp.
Saint Paul Companies Inc.
Sara Lee Corp.
Schwab & Co., Inc. (Charles)
Sega of America Inc.
Servco Pacific
Sony Electronics
Sovereign Bank
State Street Bank & Trust Co.
Sun Microsystems Inc.
Tesoro Hawaii
Times Mirror Co.
Transamerica Corp.
US Bank, Washington
USX Corp.
Walter Industries Inc.
Washington Mutual, Inc.
Whitman Corp.
WICOR, Inc.

BOTANICAL GARDENS/ PARKS

Abbott Laboratories
ABC
Alabama Power Co.
Alcoa Inc.
AMCORE Bank Rockford
Ameren Corp.
American Express Co.
American General Finance
Ameritech Ohio
AMETEK, Inc.
Amgen, Inc.
AMR Corp.
Amsted Industries Inc.
Andersons Inc.
Anheuser-Busch Companies, Inc.
Arizona Public Service Co.
Arvin Industries, Inc.
Ashland, Inc.
Atlantic Investment Co.
Badger Meter, Inc.
Bank of America
Bank One Corp.
BankBoston Corp.
Banta Corp.
Bardes Corp.
Bausch & Lomb Inc.
Belk Stores Services Inc.
Belo Corp. (A.H.)
Bethlehem Steel Corp.
BFGoodrich Co.
Binswanger Companies
Block, Inc. (H&R)
Blue Bell, Inc.
Boeing Co.
Borden, Inc.
Boston Globe (The)
Bradford & Co. (J.C.)
Bristol-Myers Squibb Co.
Brown Shoe Co., Inc.
Brunswick Corp.
Burlington Industries, Inc.
Burress (J.W.)
Cabot Corp.
Calvin Klein
Campbell Soup Co.
Cantor, Fitzgerald Securities Corp.
Cargill Inc.
Carter-Wallace, Inc.
Caterpillar Inc.
Charter Manufacturing Co.
Chase Bank of Texas
Chase Manhattan Bank, NA
Chemed Corp.
Chesapeake Corp.

Funders by Recipient Type

Chicago Title Corp.
Cinergy Corp.
Citigroup
Citizens Bank-Flint
Citizens Financial Group, Inc.
CLARCOR Inc.
Cleveland-Cliffs, Inc.
Commerce Bancshares, Inc.
Commercial Intertech Corp.
Compaq Computer Corp.
Compass Bank
Consolidated Papers, Inc.
Consumers Energy Co.
Contran Corp.
Conwood Co. LP
Coors Brewing Co.
Country Curtains, Inc.
Cox Enterprises Inc.
Crane Co.
Crane & Co., Inc.
Credit Suisse First Boston
Crestar Finance Corp.
Croft-Leominster
Cummins Engine Co., Inc.
CUNA Mutual Group
Daily News
Dana Corp.
Dayton Hudson
Deere & Co.
DeKalb Genetics Corp.
Demoulas Supermarkets Inc.
Deutsch Co.
DSM Copolymer
Duriron Co., Inc.
Eastman Kodak Co.
Emerson Electric Co.
Employers Mutual Casualty Co.
Ensign-Bickford Industries
Enterprise Rent-A-Car Co.
Equifax Inc.
Erb Lumber Co.
Exxon Mobil Corp.
Fabri-Kal Corp.
Ferro Corp.
FINA
First American Corp.
First Financial Bank
First Maryland Bancorp
First Source Corp.
Fisher Brothers Cleaning Services
Fisher Scientific
Florida Power & Light Co.
Florida Rock Industries
Fluor Corp.
Forbes Inc.
Ford Meter Box Co.
Ford Motor Co.
Franklin Electric Co.
Freeport-McMoRan Inc.
Furniture Brands International, Inc.
Gap, Inc.
GATX Corp.
GenAmerica Corp.
Georgia-Pacific Corp.
Georgia Power Co.
Glickenhaus & Co.
Goldman Sachs Group
Gosiger, Inc.
Graco, Inc.
Green Bay Packaging
Hallmark Cards Inc.
Hamilton Sundstrand Corp.
Harland Co. (John H.)
Harnischfeger Industries
Harris Trust & Savings Bank
Hartford (The)
Hartmarx Corp.
Hawaiian Electric Co., Inc.
Heinz Co. (H.J.)
Hickory Tech Corp.
Hofmann Co.
Hubbell Inc.
Huffy Corp.
Humana, Inc.
Inland Container Corp.
International Flavors & Fragrances Inc.
International Multifoods Corp.
International Paper Co.
INTRUST Financial Corp.
Invacare Corp.
Jacobson & Sons (Benjamin)
Jeld-wen, Inc.
Journal-Gazette Co.
Kellogg Co.
Kellwood Co.
Kimberly-Clark Corp.
Kingsbury Corp.
Koch Enterprises, Inc.
Kroger Co.
Liberty Corp.
Lilly & Co. (Eli)
Lincoln Electric Co.
Liz Claiborne, Inc.
Loews Corp.
Louisiana Land & Exploration Co.
Louisiana-Pacific Corp.
Lubrizol Corp. (The)
MacMillan Bloedel Inc.
Madison Gas & Electric Co.
Mark IV Industries
Mattel Inc.
May Department Stores Co.
Mead Corp.
Medtronic, Inc.
Meijer, Inc.
Menasha Corp.
Mercantile Bank NA
Merck & Co.
Merrill Lynch & Co., Inc.
Metropolitan Life Insurance Co.
Mid-America Bank of Louisville
Mine Safety Appliances Co.
Mitsubishi Electric America
Monarch Machine Tool Co.
Monsanto Co.
Montgomery Ward & Co., Inc.
Morgan & Co. Inc. (J.P.)
Morgan Stanley Dean Witter & Co.
Morris Communications Corp.
MTD Products Inc.
National City Corp.
National Machinery Co.
National Presto Industries, Inc.
National Service Industries, Inc.
Nationwide Insurance Co.
NEBCO Evans
Nestle U.S.A. Inc.
New England Bio Labs
New Jersey Natural Gas Co.
New York Mercantile Exchange
New York Stock Exchange, Inc.
New York Times Co.
Nomura Holding America
Norfolk Southern Corp.
Northern States Power Co.
Norton Co.
Norwest Corp.
Occidental Oil and Gas
OG&E Electric Services
Ohio National Life Insurance Co.
Oklahoma Publishing Co.
Old Kent Bank
Orscheln Co.
Oshkosh B'Gosh, Inc.
Overseas Shipholding Group Inc.
PACCAR Inc.
Pacific Century Financial Corp.
Pacific Mutual Life Insurance Co.
Paine Webber
Park National Bank
Pella Corp.
PepsiCo, Inc.
Pfizer Inc.
Phelps Dodge Corp.
Pillsbury Co.
PPG Industries, Inc.
Praxair
Price Associates (T. Rowe)
Principal Financial Group
Prudential Insurance Co. of America
Prudential Securities Inc.
Pulitzer Publishing Co.
Putnam Investments
Ralston Purina Co.
Red Wing Shoe Co. Inc.
Regions Bank
Reily & Co., Inc. (William B.)
Reynolds Metals Co.
Reynolds & Reynolds Co.
Reynolds Tobacco (R.J.)
Rich Products Corp.
Rouse Co.
Ruddick Corp.
Russer Foods
Ryder System, Inc.
Safeguard Scientifics
SBC Communications Inc.
Schloss & Co. (Marcus)
Schlumberger Ltd. (USA)
Schwab & Co., Inc. (Charles)
Schwebel Baking Co.
Scripps Co. (E.W.)
Security Life of Denver Insurance Co.
Shell Oil Co.
Sierra Pacific Industries
Simpson Investment Co.
Sonoco Products Co.
South Bend Tribune Corp.
Southeastern Mutual Insurance Co.
Southwest Gas Corp.
Square D Co.
Standard Register Co.
Star Bank NA
Steelcase Inc.
Stone Container Corp.
Strear Farms Co.
Stride Rite Corp.
Stupp Brothers Bridge & Iron Co.
SunTrust Bank Atlanta
Sverdrup Corp.
Tension Envelope Corp.
Tesoro Hawaii
Texaco Inc.
Thompson Co. (J. Walter)
Times Mirror Co.
Toledo Blade Co.
Toshiba America Inc.
Toyota Motor Sales U.S.A., Inc.
Trace International Holdings, Inc.
Transamerica Corp.
True Oil Co.
Unilever United States, Inc.
Union Pacific Corp.
United Airlines Inc.
United Distillers & Vintners North America
United Parcel Service of America Inc.
Universal Leaf Tobacco Co., Inc.
Universal Studios
Unocal Corp.
UPN Channel 50
Valmont Industries, Inc.
Vesper Corp.
Vulcan Materials Co.
Wachovia Bank of North Carolina NA
Wachtell, Lipton, Rosen & Katz
Waffle House Inc.
Walter Industries Inc.
Weil, Gotshal & Manges Corp.
Western & Southern Life Insurance Co.
Westvaco Corp.
Whirlpool Corp.
WICOR, Inc.
Wilbur-Ellis Co. & Connell Brothers Co.
Wiley & Sons (John)
Williams
Wisconsin Energy Corp.
Wisconsin Power & Light Co.
Wisconsin Public Service Corp.
Wolverine World Wide
Woodward Governor Co.
Young & Rubicam
Zachry Co. (H.B.)
Zilkha & Sons

BUSINESS/FREE ENTERPRISE

ABC
Aetna, Inc.
Agrilink Foods, Inc.
Air Products and Chemicals, Inc.
AK Steel Corp.
Alabama Power Co.
Alcoa Inc.
Alcon Laboratories, Inc.
Allegheny Technologies Inc.
Alliant Techsystems
Allmerica Financial Corp.
Allstate Insurance Co.
AMCORE Bank Rockford
America West Airlines, Inc.
American General Finance
American Retail Group
American Standard Inc.
American United Life Insurance Co.
Ameritech Corp.
Ameritech Indiana
Ameritech Michigan
AmerUS Group
AMP Inc.
AMR Corp.
Amsted Industries Inc.
Andersen Corp.
Aon Corp.
Appleton Papers Inc.
Archer-Daniels-Midland Co.
Aristech Chemical Corp.
Armstrong World Industries, Inc.
Arvin Industries, Inc.
Ashland, Inc.
Atlantic Investment Co.
Avon Products, Inc.
Baird & Co. (Robert W.)
Bandag, Inc.
Bank of America
Bank of New York Co., Inc.
Bank One Corp.
Bank One, Texas-Houston Office
BankAtlantic Bancorp
BankBoston Corp.
Banta Corp.
Barry Corp. (R.G.)
Battelle Memorial Institute
Bausch & Lomb Inc.
Baxter International Inc.
Bechtel Group, Inc.
Belk Stores Services Inc.
Bemis Co., Inc.
Bemis Manufacturing Co.
Ben & Jerry's Homemade Inc.
Bernstein & Co., Inc. (Sanford C.)
Bestfoods
Bethlehem Steel Corp.
BFGoodrich Co.
Binney & Smith Inc.
Binswanger Companies
Blair & Co. (William)
Block, Inc. (H&R)
Blue Cross & Blue Shield of Alabama
Boeing Co.
Boise Cascade Corp.
Borden, Inc.
Boston Globe (The)
BP Amoco Corp.
Bridgestone/Firestone, Inc.
Bristol-Myers Squibb Co.
Broderbund Software, Inc.
Brown & Williamson Tobacco Corp.
Bucyrus-Erie Co.
Burlington Industries, Inc.
Burnett Co. (Leo)
Cabot Corp.
Campbell Soup Co.
Carlson Companies, Inc.
Carolina Power & Light Co.
Carpenter Technology Corp.
Carrier Corp.
Caterpillar Inc.
CCB Financial Corp.
CertainTeed Corp.
CGU Insurance
Chase Manhattan Bank, NA
Chevron Corp.
Chicago Title Corp.
CIGNA Corp.
Cincinnati Bell Inc.
Circuit City Stores, Inc.
CIT Group, Inc. (The)
Citibank Corp.
Citigroup
Citizens Bank-Flint
Cleveland-Cliffs, Inc.
CNA
Colonial Life & Accident Insurance Co.
Colonial Oil Industries, Inc.
Comerica Inc.
Commercial Intertech Corp.
Compass Bank
Cone Mills Corp.
Consolidated Natural Gas Co.
Constellation Energy Group, Inc.
Cooper Industries, Inc.
Coors Brewing Co.

Country Curtains, Inc.
CPI Corp.
Crane Co.
Crane & Co., Inc.
Credit Suisse First Boston
Crestar Finance Corp.
Cummings Properties Management
CUNA Mutual Group
DaimlerChrysler Corp.
Dana Corp.
Dayton Hudson
Deere & Co.
Deposit Guaranty National Bank
Detroit Edison Co.
Dial Corp.
Disney Co. (Walt)
du Pont de Nemours & Co. (E.I.)
Duchossois Industries Inc.
Duke Energy
Dun & Bradstreet Corp.
Duriron Co., Inc.
Eastman Kodak Co.
Eaton Corp.
Ecolab Inc.
Edison International
Elf Atochem North America, Inc.
Emerson Electric Co.
Employers Mutual Casualty Co.
Enterprise Rent-A-Car Co.
Equifax Inc.
Ethyl Corp.
European American Bank
Evening Post Publishing Co.
Federal-Mogul Corp.
Federated Department Stores, Inc.
FedEx Corp.
Fifth Third Bancorp
FINA
First Hawaiian, Inc.
First Source Corp.
First Tennessee National Corp.
First Union Bank
First Union Corp.
First Union National Bank, NA
First Union Securities, Inc.
Firstar Bank Milwaukee NA
Fisher Brothers Cleaning Services
FleetBoston Financial Corp.
Florida Power & Light Co.
FMC Corp.
Ford Meter Box Co.
Ford Motor Co.
Forest City Enterprises, Inc.
Fort James Corp.
Fort Worth Star-Telegram Inc.
Freddie Mac
Freeport-McMoRan Inc.
Frost National Bank
Furniture Brands International, Inc.
Gallo Winery, Inc. (E&J)
Gap, Inc.
GEICO Corp.
GenCorp
General Electric Co.
General Mills, Inc.
General Motors Corp.
Georgia-Pacific Corp.
Giant Food Inc.
Giddings & Lewis
Glaxo Wellcome Inc.
Glickenhaus & Co.
Goldman Sachs Group
Grace & Co. (W.R.)
Graco, Inc.
Guardian Life Insurance Co. of America
Halliburton Co.
Hallmark Cards Inc.
Hancock Financial Services (John)
Harcourt General, Inc.
Harland Co. (John H.)
Harley-Davidson Co.
Harris Corp.
Harsco Corp.
Hartford (The)
Hartmarx Corp.
Hasbro, Inc.
Hawaiian Electric Co., Inc.
Heinz Co. (H.J.)
Heller Financial, Inc.
Hershey Foods Corp.
Hewlett-Packard Co.
Hickory Tech Corp.
Hitachi America Ltd.
HON Industries Inc.
Honeywell International Inc.
Household International Inc.
Hubbell Inc.
Huffy Corp.
Humana, Inc.
Huntington Bancshares Inc.
Illinois Tool Works, Inc.
Inland Container Corp.
Inman Mills
Invacare Corp.
Jacobs Engineering Group
Jeld-wen, Inc.
Johnson Controls Inc.
Johnson & Son (S.C.)
Jones & Co. (Edward D.)
Katten, Muchin & Zavis
Kellwood Co.
Kemper National Insurance Companies
Kennametal, Inc.
Key Bank of Cleveland
Kiewit Sons' Inc. (Peter)
Kimball International, Inc.
Kimberly-Clark Corp.
Kinder Morgn
Kroger Co.
La-Z-Boy Inc.
Ladish Co., Inc.
Land O'Lakes, Inc.
LandAmerica Financial Services
Lee Enterprises
Lehigh Portland Cement Co.
Levi Strauss & Co.
Liberty Corp.
Liberty Diversified Industries
Lilly & Co. (Eli)
Lincoln Electric Co.
Lipton Co.
Little, Inc. (Arthur D.)
Loews Corp.
Lotus Development Corp.
Louisiana-Pacific Corp.
LTV Corp.
Lubrizol Corp. (The)
Macy's East Inc.
Madison Gas & Electric Co.
Maritz Inc.
Mark IV Industries
Matsushita Electric Corp. of America
Mattel Inc.
Maytag Corp.
McCormick & Co. Inc.
McDermott Inc.
McDonald & Co. Securities, Inc.
McGraw-Hill Companies, Inc.
MCI WorldCom, Inc.
Mead Corp.
Mellon Financial Corp.
Merrill Lynch & Co., Inc.
Metropolitan Life Insurance Co.
Michigan Consolidated Gas Co.
MidAmerican Energy Holdings Co.
Milacron, Inc.
Minnesota Mining & Manufacturing Co.
Montana Power Co.
MONY Group (The)
Morgan & Co. Inc. (J.P.)
Morrison Knudsen Corp.
Motorola Inc.
Nabisco Group Holdings
Nalco Chemical Co.
National City Bank of Minneapolis
National City Corp.
National Service Industries, Inc.
National Starch & Chemical Co.
Nestle U.S.A. Inc.
New York Life Insurance Co.
Nordson Corp.
Norfolk Southern Corp.
North American Royalties
Northern Trust Co.
Norton Co.
Occidental Petroleum Corp.
Old National Bank Evansville
Olin Corp.
Orscheln Co.
Osborne Enterprises
Oshkosh B'Gosh, Inc.
PACCAR Inc.
Pacific Century Financial Corp.
Pan-American Life Insurance Co.
Park National Bank
Pella Corp.
PEMCO Corp.
Penney Co., Inc. (J.C.)
PepsiCo, Inc.
PerkinElmer, Inc.
Pfizer Inc.
Pharmacia & Upjohn, Inc.
Phelps Dodge Corp.
Phillips Petroleum Co.
PNC Bank
PNC Financial Services Group
Potomac Electric Power Co.
PPG Industries, Inc.
Praxair
Principal Financial Group
Procter & Gamble Co.
Procter & Gamble Co., Cosmetics Division
Providence Journal-Bulletin Co.
Prudential Insurance Co. of America
Prudential Securities Inc.
Pulitzer Publishing Co.
Ralston Purina Co.
Rayonier Inc.
Red Wing Shoe Co. Inc.
Reebok International Ltd.
Regions Bank
Reily & Co., Inc. (William B.)
Reliant Energy Inc.
Reynolds Metals Co.
Reynolds & Reynolds Co.
Reynolds Tobacco (R.J.)
Rich Products Corp.
Rockwell International Corp.
Royal & SunAlliance USA, Inc.
Rubbermaid Inc.
Safeguard Scientifics
Saint Paul Companies Inc.
S&T Bancorp
Sara Lee Hosiery, Inc.
Schloss & Co. (Marcus)
Schwab & Co., Inc. (Charles)
Scripps Co. (E.W.)
Seagram & Sons, Inc. (Joseph E.)
Searle & Co. (G.D.)
Sentry Insurance, A Mutual Co.
ServiceMaster Co.
S.G. Cowen
Shaklee Corp.
Shaw's Supermarkets, Inc.
Shea Co. (John F.)
Shell Oil Co.
Sierra Pacific Industries
Sierra Pacific Resources
SIT Investment Associates, Inc.
Smith Corp. (A.O.)
Sonoco Products Co.
Sony Electronics
Southeastern Mutual Insurance Co.
Sovereign Bank
Springs Industries, Inc.
Sprint Corp.
Sprint/United Telephone
SPX Corp.
Square D Co.
Stanley Works (The)
Star Bank NA
Starwood Hotels & Resorts Worldwide, Inc.
State Street Bank & Trust Co.
Steelcase Inc.
Stone Container Corp.
Stone & Webster Inc.
Stonecutter Mills Corp.
Storage Technology Corp.
Sun Microsystems Inc.
Sunmark Capital Corp.
Sunoco Inc.
SunTrust Bank Atlanta
Tamko Roofing Products
TCF National Bank Minnesota
Tektronix, Inc.
Teleflex Inc.
Tenneco Automotive
Tension Envelope Corp.
Texaco Inc.
Textron Inc.
Thermo Electron Corp.
Thompson Co. (J. Walter)
Ticketmaster Corp.
Timken Co. (The)
TJX Companies, Inc.
Toledo Blade Co.
Tomkins Industries, Inc.
Torchmark Corp.
Trace International Holdings, Inc.
Transamerica Corp.
True Oil Co.
TRW Inc.
TU Electric Co.
Tyson Foods Inc.
Ukrop's Super Markets
Unilever Home & Personal Care U.S.A.
Unilever United States, Inc.
Union Camp Corp.
Union Carbide Corp.
Union Pacific Corp.
United Airlines Inc.
United Distillers & Vintners North America
United Parcel Service of America Inc.
U.S. Bancorp Piper Jaffray
United States Sugar Corp.
United States Trust Co. of New York
United Technologies Corp.
United Wisconsin Services
Universal Leaf Tobacco Co., Inc.
Universal Studios
Unocal Corp.
UnumProvident
US Bank, Washington
US West, Inc.
USX Corp.
Valmont Industries, Inc.
Vulcan Materials Co.
Wachovia Bank of North Carolina NA
Waffle House Inc.
Wal-Mart Stores, Inc.
Walgreen Co.
Walter Industries Inc.
Warner-Lambert Co.
Washington Mutual, Inc.
Washington Trust Bank
Weil, Gotshal & Manges Corp.
Western & Southern Life Insurance Co.
Westvaco Corp.
Weyerhaeuser Co.
Whirlpool Corp.
WICOR, Inc.
Williams
Winn-Dixie Stores Inc.
Wisconsin Energy Corp.
Wisconsin Power & Light Co.
Wisconsin Public Service Corp.
Woodward Governor Co.
Wyman-Gordon Co.
York Federal Savings & Loan Association
Young & Rubicam

CHAMBERS OF COMMERCE

ABC
AEGON U.S.A. Inc.
Aetna, Inc.
AK Steel Corp.
Allegheny Technologies Inc.
AlliedSignal Inc.
Allstate Insurance Co.
AMCORE Bank Rockford
Ameren Corp.
Armstrong World Industries, Inc.
Arvin Industries, Inc.
Atlantic Investment Co.
Avon Products, Inc.
Bandag, Inc.
Banfi Vintners
BankBoston Corp.
Banta Corp.
Barclays Capital
Bassett Furniture Industries
Bechtel Group, Inc.
Belk-Simpson Department Stores
BellSouth Corp.

BFGoodrich Co.
Blue Bell, Inc.
Borden, Inc.
BP Amoco Corp.
Burnett Co. (Leo)
Campbell Soup Co.
Cargill Inc.
Carolina Power & Light Co.
Carpenter Technology Corp.
CBS Corp.
Central & South West Services
CIBC Oppenheimer
CIGNA Corp.
Cincinnati Bell Inc.
Cinergy Corp.
Citizens Bank-Flint
Cleveland-Cliffs, Inc.
Clorox Co.
Colonial Oil Industries, Inc.
Compass Bank
ConAgra, Inc.
Consumers Energy Co.
Continental Grain Co.
Coors Brewing Co.
CPI Corp.
Crane & Co., Inc.
Crestar Finance Corp.
CSS Industries, Inc.
Cummins Engine Co., Inc.
DaimlerChrysler Corp.
Dain Bosworth Inc.
Dana Corp.
Deere & Co.
Detroit Edison Co.
Dial Corp.
Dixie Group, Inc. (The)
Dow Chemical Co.
Dow Corning Corp.
Duchossois Industries Inc.
Duke Energy
El Paso Energy Co.
Elf Atochem North America, Inc.
Equifax Inc.
Evening Post Publishing Co.
Excel Corp.
Fabri-Kal Corp.
Federated Mutual Insurance Co.
Fifth Third Bancorp
FINA
First American Corp.
First Financial Bank
First Union Bank
First Union Corp.
FleetBoston Financial Corp.
Florida Power & Light Co.
Ford Motor Co.
Franklin Electric Co.
Gallo Winery, Inc. (E&J)
GenAmerica Corp.
General Motors Corp.
Georgia Power Co.
Giant Food Inc.
Graco, Inc.
Guess?
Hannaford Brothers Co.
Harley-Davidson Co.
Harnischfeger Industries
Harsco Corp.
Hickory Tech Corp.
HON Industries Inc.
Huntington Bancshares Inc.
Idaho Power Co.
IKON Office Solutions, Inc.
Inland Container Corp.
Intel Corp.
Jacobs Engineering Group
Jeld-wen, Inc.
Journal-Gazette Co.
Kennametal, Inc.
Kimball International, Inc.
Kimberly-Clark Corp.
Kinder Morgn
Kingsbury Corp.
Koch Enterprises, Inc.
Kroger Co.
Liberty Corp.
Lilly & Co. (Eli)
Loews Corp.
Madison Gas & Electric Co.
McClatchy Co.
Mead Corp.
Memphis Light Gas & Water Division
Michigan Consolidated Gas Co.
Milliken & Co.
Minnesota Mining & Manufacturing Co.
Monarch Machine Tool Co.
Morris Communications Corp.
Mutual of Omaha Insurance Co.
NCR Corp.
North American Royalties
Norwest Corp.
Occidental Oil and Gas
Occidental Petroleum Corp.
Ohio National Life Insurance Co.
Old Kent Bank
Olin Corp.
Orange & Rockland Utilities, Inc.
Oshkosh B'Gosh, Inc.
Park National Bank
Pella Corp.
Physicians Mutual Insurance Co.
Pillsbury Co.
Premier Dental Products Co.
Procter & Gamble Co.
Procter & Gamble Co., Cosmetics Division
Publix Supermarkets
Quanex Corp.
Ralston Purina Co.
Red Wing Shoe Co. Inc.
Regions Bank
Reynolds Tobacco (R.J.)
Rockwell International Corp.
Saint Paul Companies Inc.
Scripps Co. (E.W.)
Security Life of Denver Insurance Co.
Sentry Insurance, A Mutual Co.
Sierra Pacific Industries
Sony Electronics
Southwest Gas Corp.
Sprint Corp.
Star Bank NA
Stone Container Corp.
Sun Microsystems Inc.
SunTrust Bank Atlanta
Susquehanna-Pfaltzgraff Co.
TCF National Bank Minnesota
Textron Inc.
Times Mirror Co.
Timken Co. (The)
True North Communications, Inc.
Ukrop's Super Markets
United Dominion Industries, Ltd.
United Parcel Service of America Inc.
U.S. Bancorp Piper Jaffray
United States Sugar Corp.
United Wisconsin Services
Universal Leaf Tobacco Co., Inc.
US Bank, Washington
US West, Inc.
USG Corp.
Valmont Industries, Inc.
Wachovia Bank of North Carolina NA
Waffle House Inc.
Warner-Lambert Co.
Washington Trust Bank
Webster Bank
Western & Southern Life Insurance Co.
Wisconsin Public Service Corp.
Wrigley Co. (Wm. Jr.)
Wyman-Gordon Co.
Young & Rubicam

CIVIL RIGHTS

AGL Resources Inc.
Agrilink Foods, Inc.
Air Products and Chemicals, Inc.
Alabama Power Co.
Alcoa Inc.
American Express Co.
Ameritech Corp.
Ameritech Illinois
Ameritech Michigan
AMP Inc.
AMR Corp.
Andersen Corp.
Anheuser-Busch Companies, Inc.
Aon Corp.
APL Ltd.
Archer-Daniels-Midland Co.
Aristech Chemical Corp.
Arizona Public Service Co.
AT&T Corp.
Atlantic Richfield Co.
Avon Products, Inc.
Bank of America
Bank of New York Co., Inc.
Bank One Corp.
Bank One, Texas-Houston Office
BankAtlantic Bancorp
Barclays Capital
Barden Corp.
Ben & Jerry's Homemade Inc.
Bernstein & Co., Inc. (Sanford C.)
Bestfoods
Bethlehem Steel Corp.
Binney & Smith Inc.
Block, Inc. (H&R)
Boise Cascade Corp.
Borden, Inc.
Borman's Inc.
Bridgestone/Firestone, Inc.
Browning-Ferris Industries Inc.
Brunswick Corp.
Burnett Co. (Leo)
Burress (J.W.)
Calvin Klein
Carnival Corp.
Carrier Corp.
Carris Reels
Caterpillar Inc.
Central Maine Power Co.
Chase Manhattan Bank, NA
Chicago Tribune Co.
Citibank Corp.
Clorox Co.
Commonwealth Edison Co.
Compass Bank
Coors Brewing Co.
Credit Suisse First Boston
CSS Industries, Inc.
Cummins Engine Co., Inc.
Dana Corp.
Dayton Hudson
Deposit Guaranty National Bank
Detroit Edison Co.
Deutsch Co.
Dial Corp.
du Pont de Nemours & Co. (E.I.)
Duke Energy
Dun & Bradstreet Corp.
Eastern Bank
Edison International
Emerson Electric Co.
Equifax Inc.
European American Bank
Federal-Mogul Corp.
Federated Department Stores, Inc.
FedEx Corp.
Fifth Third Bancorp
First Maryland Bancorp
First Tennessee National Corp.
First Union National Bank, NA
Firstar Bank Milwaukee NA
Fisher Brothers Cleaning Services
FleetBoston Financial Corp.
Forbes Inc.
Ford Motor Co.
Forest City Enterprises, Inc.
Fortune Brands, Inc.
Fox Entertainment Group
Furniture Brands International, Inc.
Gallo Winery, Inc. (E&J)
Gap, Inc.
GATX Corp.
General Atlantic Partners II LP
General Electric Co.
General Mills, Inc.
General Motors Corp.
Georgia-Pacific Corp.
Georgia Power Co.
Giant Eagle Inc.
Grace & Co. (W.R.)
Guess?
Hancock Financial Services (John)
Harcourt General, Inc.
Harley-Davidson Co.
Harsco Corp.
Hartford (The)
Heinz Co. (H.J.)
Hofmann Co.
Household International Inc.
Humana, Inc.
IKON Office Solutions, Inc.
Illinois Tool Works, Inc.
Inland Container Corp.
International Business Machines Corp.
Jacobs Engineering Group
Johnson Controls Inc.
Johnson & Son (S.C.)
Katten, Muchin & Zavis
Kimberly-Clark Corp.
Kirkland & Ellis
Kroger Co.
Levi Strauss & Co.
Liberty Diversified Industries
Lilly & Co. (Eli)
Lipton Co.
Lotus Development Corp.
Macy's East Inc.
Maritz Inc.
Mattel Inc.
May Department Stores Co.
Mazda North American Operations
McClatchy Co.
McDonald & Co. Securities, Inc.
McGraw-Hill Companies, Inc.
McWane Inc.
Memphis Light Gas & Water Division
Merrill Lynch & Co., Inc.
Metropolitan Life Insurance Co.
Morris Communications Corp.
Morrison Knudsen Corp.
Motorola Inc.
National Fuel Gas Distribution Corp.
Nationwide Insurance Co.
New England Financial
New York Life Insurance Co.
Nordson Corp.
Norfolk Southern Corp.
Northern Trust Co.
Norton Co.
Olin Corp.
Pacific Mutual Life Insurance Co.
Penney Co., Inc. (J.C.)
Peoples Energy Corp.
PerkinElmer, Inc.
Pfizer Inc.
Pharmacia & Upjohn, Inc.
Phelps Dodge Corp.
Philip Morris Companies Inc.
Phillips Petroleum Co.
Pillsbury Co.
Pitney Bowes Inc.
Pittway Corp.
Playboy Enterprises Inc.
Polaroid Corp.
Potomac Electric Power Co.
PPG Industries, Inc.
Principal Financial Group
Procter & Gamble Co., Cosmetics Division
Provident Companies, Inc.
Prudential Insurance Co. of America
Prudential Securities Inc.
Pulitzer Publishing Co.
Ralston Purina Co.
Reebok International Ltd.
Rockwell International Corp.
Royal & SunAlliance USA, Inc.
Russer Foods
Sara Lee Corp.
Sara Lee Hosiery, Inc.
Schering-Plough Corp.
Schwab & Co., Inc. (Charles)
Seagram & Sons, Inc. (Joseph E.)
Shell Oil Co.
Slant/Fin Corp.
Smith Corp. (A.O.)
Sovereign Bank
Starwood Hotels & Resorts Worldwide, Inc.
State Street Bank & Trust Co.
Stonecutter Mills Corp.
Strear Farms Co.
Sunmark Capital Corp.
SunTrust Bank Atlanta
Tamko Roofing Products

Texaco Inc.
Textron Inc.
Thermo Electron Corp.
Times Mirror Co.
TJX Companies, Inc.
Torchmark Corp.
Trace International Holdings, Inc.
Unilever Home & Personal Care U.S.A.
Unilever United States, Inc.
United Airlines Inc.
Universal Studios
Unocal Corp.
UnumProvident
US Bank, Washington
USG Corp.
Vulcan Materials Co.
Wachovia Bank of North Carolina NA
Washington Trust Bank
Weil, Gotshal & Manges Corp.
Western & Southern Life Insurance Co.
Westvaco Corp.
Whirlpool Corp.
Wiley & Sons (John)
Wisconsin Energy Corp.
Witco Corp.
Wrigley Co. (Wm. Jr.)
Xerox Corp.
Zenith Electronics Corp.

CLUBS

Abbott Laboratories
AEGON U.S.A. Inc.
Agrilink Foods, Inc.
AK Steel Corp.
Alcon Laboratories, Inc.
Allmerica Financial Corp.
Allstate Insurance Co.
Alma Piston Co.
AMCORE Bank Rockford
American Fidelity Corp.
American General Finance
Ameritas Life Insurance Corp.
AMP Inc.
AMR Corp.
Amsted Industries Inc.
Andersen Corp.
Andersons Inc.
Anheuser-Busch Companies, Inc.
APL Ltd.
Archer-Daniels-Midland Co.
Arvin Industries, Inc.
Avon Products, Inc.
Baird & Co. (Robert W.)
Bandag, Inc.
Banfi Vintners
Bank One Corp.
Barclays Capital
Barden Corp.
Bardes Corp.
Barnes Group Inc.
Barry Corp. (R.G.)
Baxter International Inc.
Bechtel Group, Inc.
Bemis Manufacturing Co.
Bernstein & Co., Inc. (Sanford C.)
Binswanger Companies
Blair & Co. (William)
Block, Inc. (H&R)
Blue Bell, Inc.
Blue Cross & Blue Shield of Alabama
Blue Cross & Blue Shield of Iowa
Borden, Inc.
Bourns, Inc.
Bradford & Co. (J.C.)
Brown Shoe Co., Inc.
Brunswick Corp.
Burlington Industries, Inc.
Burlington Resources, Inc.
Burress (J.W.)
Carillon Importers, Ltd.
Carris Reels
Central & South West Services
Central Soya Co.
CertainTeed Corp.
CGU Insurance
Chase Bank of Texas
Chicago Title Corp.
Chicago Tribune Co.
Cleveland-Cliffs, Inc.
Clorox Co.
CNA
Colonial Oil Industries, Inc.
Cone Mills Corp.
Conwood Co. LP
Credit Suisse First Boston
Croft-Leominster
Cummings Properties Management
Dayton Hudson
Demoulas Supermarkets Inc.
Duchossois Industries Inc.
Dun & Bradstreet Corp.
Duriron Co., Inc.
Eastern Bank
Eastman Kodak Co.
Edison Brothers Stores, Inc.
El Paso Energy Co.
Emerson Electric Co.
Employers Mutual Casualty Co.
Ensign-Bickford Industries
Enterprise Rent-A-Car Co.
Erb Lumber Co.
Erving Industries
Federated Mutual Insurance Co.
Fifth Third Bancorp
First Financial Bank
First Union Corp.
FMC Corp.
Ford Meter Box Co.
Forest City Enterprises, Inc.
Fort Worth Star-Telegram Inc.
Freeport-McMoRan Inc.
Furniture Brands International, Inc.
Gallo Winery, Inc. (E&J)
Galter Corp.
Gerber Products Co.
Giant Eagle Inc.
Giddings & Lewis
Globe Corp.
Hamilton Sundstrand Corp.
Harnischfeger Industries
Hartmarx Corp.
Hawaiian Electric Co., Inc.
Hewlett-Packard Co.
Hickory Tech Corp.
Hoffer Plastics Corp.
Hofmann Co.
Hubbard Broadcasting, Inc.
Hubbell Inc.
Hunt Manufacturing Co.
Illinois Tool Works, Inc.
Inman Mills
International Flavors & Fragrances Inc.
International Multifoods Corp.
Invacare Corp.
Jacobs Engineering Group
Jacobson & Sons (Benjamin)
Journal-Gazette Co.
Kimberly-Clark Corp.
Kinder Morgn
Kingsbury Corp.
Koch Industries, Inc.
KPMG Peat Marwick LLP
Lance, Inc.
Land O'Lakes, Inc.
Loews Corp.
Madison Gas & Electric Co.
Marcus Corp.
Mark IV Industries
May Department Stores Co.
McWane Inc.
Meijer, Inc.
Memphis Light Gas & Water Division
Mercantile Bank NA
Mid-America Bank of Louisville
MidAmerican Energy Holdings Co.
Milliken & Co.
Millipore Corp.
Minnesota Mutual Life Insurance Co.
Monsanto Co.
Montana Power Co.
Motorola Inc.
Nabisco Group Holdings
National City Bank of Minneapolis
National Service Industries, Inc.
Norton Co.
Old National Bank Evansville
Osborne Enterprises
Owens Corning
Pacific Mutual Life Insurance Co.
Paine Webber
Pella Corp.
PEMCO Corp.
PNC Financial Services Group
Premier Dental Products Co.
Premier Industrial Corp.
Procter & Gamble Co., Cosmetics Division
Provident Companies, Inc.
Pulitzer Publishing Co.
Putnam Investments
Quanex Corp.
Ralston Purina Co.
Red Wing Shoe Co. Inc.
Regions Bank
Reinhart Institutional Foods
Reynolds & Reynolds Co.
Reynolds Tobacco (R.J.)
Rich Products Corp.
Saint Paul Companies Inc.
S&T Bancorp
SBC Communications Inc.
Schwab & Co., Inc. (Charles)
Security Benefit Life Insurance Co.
Sentry Insurance, A Mutual Co.
ServiceMaster Co.
Shea Co. (John F.)
Shell Oil Co.
Shelter Mutual Insurance Co.
Sierra Pacific Industries
Sierra Pacific Resources
Sonoco Products Co.
Southwest Gas Corp.
SPX Corp.
Standard Register Co.
State Street Bank & Trust Co.
Stone Container Corp.
Stride Rite Corp.
Stupp Brothers Bridge & Iron Co.
Sunmark Capital Corp.
Sverdrup Corp.
Temple-Inland Inc.
Tesoro Hawaii
Timken Co. (The)
Toledo Blade Co.
Toro Co.
True Oil Co.
Trustmark Insurance Co.
Ukrop's Super Markets
United Airlines Inc.
United Parcel Service of America Inc.
United States Sugar Corp.
Unocal Corp.
Valmont Industries, Inc.
Vesper Corp.
Vulcan Materials Co.
Wachovia Bank of North Carolina NA
Waffle House Inc.
Walter Industries Inc.
Whirlpool Corp.
Whitman Corp.
Wilbur-Ellis Co. & Connell Brothers Co.
Williams
Winn-Dixie Stores Inc.
Wisconsin Public Service Corp.
Witco Corp.
Wyman-Gordon Co.
Young & Rubicam

COMMUNITY FOUNDATIONS

Abbott Laboratories
ABC
AEGON U.S.A. Inc.
Agrilink Foods, Inc.
AK Steel Corp.
Alabama Power Co.
Alcoa Inc.
Allmerica Financial Corp.
Allstate Insurance Co.
American Fidelity Corp.
American General Finance
American Standard Inc.
Ameritas Life Insurance Corp.
Ameritech Corp.
Amgen, Inc.
AMR Corp.
Amsted Industries Inc.
Andersen Corp.
APL Ltd.
Archer-Daniels-Midland Co.
Arvin Industries, Inc.
Ashland, Inc.
AT&T Corp.
Atlantic Investment Co.
Atlantic Richfield Co.
Bandag, Inc.
Banfi Vintners
Bank of America
BankAtlantic Bancorp
Bard, Inc. (C.R.)
Barnes Group Inc.
Barry Corp. (R.G.)
Baxter International Inc.
Bemis Co., Inc.
Ben & Jerry's Homemade Inc.
Bethlehem Steel Corp.
Binney & Smith Inc.
Block, Inc. (H&R)
Blount International, Inc.
Blue Cross & Blue Shield of Minnesota
Borden, Inc.
BP Amoco Corp.
Bradford & Co. (J.C.)
Bridgestone/Firestone, Inc.
Briggs & Stratton Corp.
Bristol-Myers Squibb Co.
Brown Shoe Co., Inc.
Brunswick Corp.
Burlington Industries, Inc.
Cabot Corp.
Carpenter Technology Corp.
Caterpillar Inc.
Central & South West Services
Central Soya Co.
CertainTeed Corp.
CGU Insurance
Champion International Corp.
Charter Manufacturing Co.
Chase Bank of Texas
Chesapeake Corp.
Cincinnati Bell Inc.
Cinergy Corp.
Citizens Bank-Flint
Cleveland-Cliffs, Inc.
Clorox Co.
Colonial Oil Industries, Inc.
Commerce Bancshares, Inc.
Cone Mills Corp.
Consolidated Papers, Inc.
Consumers Energy Co.
Contran Corp.
Cooper Tire & Rubber Co.
Copley Press, Inc.
Corning Inc.
Country Curtains, Inc.
Cox Enterprises Inc.
CPI Corp.
Credit Suisse First Boston
CSR Rinker Materials Corp.
Cummins Engine Co., Inc.
CUNA Mutual Group
DaimlerChrysler Corp.
Dain Bosworth Inc.
Dana Corp.
Danis Companies
Dayton Hudson
Dayton Power and Light Co.
Deere & Co.
DeKalb Genetics Corp.
Delta Air Lines, Inc.
Deluxe Corp.
Deposit Guaranty National Bank
Detroit Edison Co.
Disney Co. (Walt)
Dixie Group, Inc. (The)
Dow Chemical Co.
Dow Corning Corp.
DSM Copolymer
Duchossois Industries Inc.
Duriron Co., Inc.
Eastern Bank
Eaton Corp.
El Paso Energy Co.
Emerson Electric Co.
Employers Mutual Casualty Co.
Enterprise Rent-A-Car Co.
Equitable Resources, Inc.
Erb Lumber Co.
Erving Industries
Excel Corp.
Exxon Mobil Corp.
Fannie Mae
Federal-Mogul Corp.
Federated Mutual Insurance Co.
Fidelity Investments
Fifth Third Bancorp
First Financial Bank

First Hawaiian, Inc.
First Maryland Bancorp
First Source Corp.
First Union Securities, Inc.
Florida Power & Light Co.
Fluor Corp.
Forbes Inc.
Ford Meter Box Co.
Ford Motor Co.
Gap, Inc.
GenCorp
General Atlantic Partners II LP
General Electric Co.
General Motors Corp.
Georgia-Pacific Corp.
Georgia Power Co.
Gerber Products Co.
Giddings & Lewis
Globe Corp.
Graco, Inc.
Grede Foundries
Green Bay Packaging
Gulf Power Co.
Hallmark Cards Inc.
Hamilton Sundstrand Corp.
Hanna Co. (M.A.)
Harley-Davidson Co.
Hartmarx Corp.
Hasbro, Inc.
Hawaiian Electric Co., Inc.
Heinz Co. (H.J.)
Hershey Foods Corp.
Hewlett-Packard Co.
Hickory Tech Corp.
Hitachi America Ltd.
Hoffmann-La Roche Inc.
Hofmann Co.
HON Industries Inc.
Huffy Corp.
Humana, Inc.
Huntington Bancshares Inc.
IKON Office Solutions, Inc.
Independent Stave Co.
Inman Mills
Invacare Corp.
Jacobs Engineering Group
Jacobson & Sons (Benjamin)
Journal-Gazette Co.
JSJ Corp.
Kellogg Co.
Kennametal, Inc.
Kimball International, Inc.
Kimberly-Clark Corp.
Kinder Morgn
Koch Enterprises, Inc.
Kroger Co.
La-Z-Boy Inc.
Lee Enterprises
Lehigh Portland Cement Co.
Leigh Fibers, Inc.
Levi Strauss & Co.
Liberty Corp.
Lilly & Co. (Eli)
Lincoln Electric Co.
Little, Inc. (Arthur D.)
Madison Gas & Electric Co.
Mark IV Industries
Masco Corp.
Mattel Inc.
McClatchy Co.
McDonald & Co. Securities, Inc.
Mead Corp.
Medtronic, Inc.
Memphis Light Gas & Water Division
Mercantile Bank NA
Merit Oil Corp.
Merrill Lynch & Co., Inc.
Michigan Consolidated Gas Co.
Mid-America Bank of Louisville
MidAmerican Energy Holdings Co.
Milacron, Inc.
Milliken & Co.
Minnesota Mining & Manufacturing Co.
MONY Group (The)
Morgan & Co. Inc. (J.P.)
Morgan Stanley Dean Witter & Co.
Morris Communications Corp.
Morrison Knudsen Corp.
MTD Products Inc.
National Presto Industries, Inc.
National Service Industries, Inc.
NEBCO Evans
New England Bio Labs
New Jersey Natural Gas Co.
New York Mercantile Exchange
Nissan North America, Inc.
Nordson Corp.
Norfolk Southern Corp.
Norton Co.
OG&E Electric Services
Ohio National Life Insurance Co.
Old Kent Bank
Old National Bank Evansville
Oshkosh B'Gosh, Inc.
Outboard Marine Corp.
Pacific Century Financial Corp.
Pacific Mutual Life Insurance Co.
PacifiCare Health Systems
PacifiCorp
Paine Webber
Park National Bank
Parker Hannifin Corp.
PEMCO Corp.
Pharmacia & Upjohn, Inc.
Physicians Mutual Insurance Co.
Pillsbury Co.
Pittway Corp.
PNC Financial Services Group
Polaroid Corp.
Premier Industrial Corp.
Price Associates (T. Rowe)
Principal Financial Group
Procter & Gamble Co.
Procter & Gamble Co., Cosmetics Division
Providence Journal-Bulletin Co.
Putnam Investments
Quanex Corp.
Ralston Purina Co.
Regions Bank
Regis Corp.
Reily & Co., Inc. (William B.)
Reynolds & Reynolds Co.
Rubbermaid Inc.
Ruddick Corp.
Russer Foods
Ryder System, Inc.
Safeguard Scientifics
SBC Communications Inc.
Schering-Plough Corp.
Schloss & Co. (Marcus)
Schwab & Co., Inc. (Charles)
Sega of America Inc.
Sentry Insurance, A Mutual Co.
Shaw's Supermarkets, Inc.
Shell Oil Co.
Sherwin-Williams Co.
Simpson Investment Co.
Slant/Fin Corp.
Sony Electronics
South Bend Tribune Corp.
Sprint Corp.
Sprint/United Telephone
Standard Products Co.
Stanley Works (The)
Star Bank NA
Steelcase Inc.
Storage Technology Corp.
Stride Rite Corp.
Sun Microsystems Inc.
SunTrust Bank Atlanta
Susquehanna-Pfaltzgraff Co.
Synovus Financial Corp.
Temple-Inland Inc.
Tension Envelope Corp.
Texas Instruments Inc.
TJX Companies, Inc.
Transamerica Corp.
Trustmark Insurance Co.
TRW Inc.
United Airlines Inc.
United Parcel Service of America Inc.
U.S. Bancorp
U.S. Bancorp Piper Jaffray
United States Sugar Corp.
United Wisconsin Services
Universal Studios
US West, Inc.
USX Corp.
Valmont Industries, Inc.
Van Leer Holding
Wachovia Bank of North Carolina NA
Waffle House Inc.
Walter Industries Inc.
Warner-Lambert Co.
Washington Trust Bank
Webster Bank
Western & Southern Life Insurance Co.
Whirlpool Corp.
WICOR, Inc.
Wisconsin Energy Corp.
Wisconsin Power & Light Co.
Wisconsin Public Service Corp.
York Federal Savings & Loan Association

ECONOMIC DEVELOPMENT

Abbott Laboratories
ABC
Aetna, Inc.
AFLAC Inc.
AGL Resources Inc.
Agrilink Foods, Inc.
Air Products and Chemicals, Inc.
Alabama Power Co.
Alcoa Inc.
Alexander & Baldwin, Inc.
Allegheny Technologies Inc.
Alliant Techsystems
Allianz Life Insurance Co. of North America
AlliedSignal Inc.
Allmerica Financial Corp.
Allstate Insurance Co.
Alyeska Pipeline Service Co.
AMCORE Bank Rockford
Ameren Corp.
America West Airlines, Inc.
American Express Co.
American Fidelity Corp.
American General Finance
American United Life Insurance Co.
Ameritas Life Insurance Corp.
Ameritech Corp.
Ameritech Illinois
Ameritech Indiana
Ameritech Michigan
AmerUS Group
AMP Inc.
Andersons Inc.
Aon Corp.
APL Ltd.
Archer-Daniels-Midland Co.
Aristech Chemical Corp.
Arizona Public Service Co.
Armstrong World Industries, Inc.
Arvin Industries, Inc.
Ashland, Inc.
AT&T Corp.
Atlantic Richfield Co.
Avon Products, Inc.
Badger Meter, Inc.
Baird & Co. (Robert W.)
Banfi Vintners
Bank of America
Bank of New York Co., Inc.
Bank One Corp.
Bank One, Texas-Houston Office
BankAtlantic Bancorp
BankBoston Corp.
Banta Corp.
Barry Corp. (R.G.)
Bassett Furniture Industries
Battelle Memorial Institute
Bausch & Lomb Inc.
Baxter International Inc.
Bechtel Group, Inc.
Bemis Co., Inc.
Ben & Jerry's Homemade Inc.
Bernstein & Co., Inc. (Sanford C.)
Bestfoods
Bethlehem Steel Corp.
BFGoodrich Co.
Binney & Smith Inc.
Blair & Co. (William)
Block, Inc. (H&R)
Blount International, Inc.
Blue Cross & Blue Shield of Minnesota
Boeing Co.
Boise Cascade Corp.
Borden, Inc.
Boston Edison Co.
Boston Globe (The)
Bourns, Inc.
Bowater Inc.
BP Amoco Corp.
Bradford & Co. (J.C.)
Bridgestone/Firestone, Inc.
Briggs & Stratton Corp.
Bristol-Myers Squibb Co.
Brown & Williamson Tobacco Corp.
Brunswick Corp.
Bucyrus-Erie Co.
Burnett Co. (Leo)
Cabot Corp.
California Bank & Trust
Calvin Klein
Campbell Soup Co.
Cargill Inc.
Carolina Power & Light Co.
Carpenter Technology Corp.
Caterpillar Inc.
Central Maine Power Co.
Central National-Gottesman
Central Soya Co.
Central Vermont Public Service Corp.
CertainTeed Corp.
CGU Insurance
Chase Bank of Texas
Chase Manhattan Bank, NA
Chesapeake Corp.
Chevron Corp.
Chicago Sun-Times, Inc.
Chicago Title Corp.
Chicago Tribune Co.
CIBC Oppenheimer
CIGNA Corp.
Cincinnati Bell Inc.
Cinergy Corp.
Circuit City Stores, Inc.
CIT Group, Inc. (The)
Citibank Corp.
Citigroup
Citizens Bank-Flint
Citizens Financial Group, Inc.
CLARCOR Inc.
Cleveland-Cliffs, Inc.
Clorox Co.
Coachmen Industries, Inc.
Collins & Aikman Corp.
Colonial Life & Accident Insurance Co.
Comerica Inc.
Commerce Bancshares, Inc.
Commercial Intertech Corp.
Commonwealth Edison Co.
Compass Bank
ConAgra, Inc.
Conoco, Inc.
Consolidated Natural Gas Co.
Consolidated Papers, Inc.
Constellation Energy Group, Inc.
Consumers Energy Co.
Contran Corp.
Cooper Industries, Inc.
Corning Inc.
Country Curtains, Inc.
Cox Enterprises Inc.
Crane Co.
Crane & Co., Inc.
Credit Suisse First Boston
Crestar Finance Corp.
Crown Books
CSR Rinker Materials Corp.
Cummins Engine Co., Inc.
CUNA Mutual Group
Daily News
DaimlerChrysler Corp.
Dain Bosworth Inc.
Dana Corp.
Danis Companies
Dayton Hudson
Dayton Power and Light Co.
Deere & Co.
DeKalb Genetics Corp.
Delta Air Lines, Inc.
Deluxe Corp.
Detroit Edison Co.
Dexter Corp.
Dial Corp.
Disney Co. (Walt)
Dixie Group, Inc. (The)
Donaldson Co., Inc.
Dow Corning Corp.
du Pont de Nemours & Co. (E.I.)
Duchossois Industries Inc.
Duke Energy
Dun & Bradstreet Corp.

Dynamet, Inc.
Eastern Bank
Eastman Kodak Co.
Eaton Corp.
Ecolab Inc.
Edison International
Edwards Enterprise Software (J.D.)
El Paso Energy Co.
Elf Atochem North America, Inc.
Emerson Electric Co.
Ensign-Bickford Industries
Entergy Corp.
Enterprise Rent-A-Car Co.
Equifax Inc.
Equitable Resources, Inc.
Ethyl Corp.
European American Bank
Evening Post Publishing Co.
Exxon Mobil Corp.
Fannie Mae
Federal-Mogul Corp.
Federated Department Stores, Inc.
Ferro Corp.
Fidelity Investments
Fifth Third Bancorp
FINA
Fireman's Fund Insurance Co.
First American Corp.
First Financial Bank
First Maryland Bancorp
First Source Corp.
First Tennessee National Corp.
First Union Bank
First Union Corp.
First Union National Bank, NA
First Union Securities, Inc.
Firstar Bank Milwaukee NA
Fisher Brothers Cleaning Services
FleetBoston Financial Corp.
Florida Power Corp.
Florida Power & Light Co.
Fluor Corp.
FMC Corp.
Forbes Inc.
Ford Meter Box Co.
Ford Motor Co.
Forest City Enterprises, Inc.
Fort James Corp.
Fortis Insurance Co.
Fortune Brands, Inc.
Freddie Mac
Freeport-McMoRan Inc.
Frontier Corp.
Frost National Bank
Fuller Co. (H.B.)
Furniture Brands International, Inc.
Gallo Winery, Inc. (E&J)
Gannett Co., Inc.
Gap, Inc.
GATX Corp.
GEICO Corp.
GenCorp
General Atlantic Partners II LP
General Electric Co.
General Mills, Inc.
General Motors Corp.
General Reinsurance Corp.
Georgia-Pacific Corp.
Georgia Power Co.
Giant Eagle Inc.
Giddings & Lewis
Glaxo Wellcome Inc.
Glickenhaus & Co.
Goldman Sachs Group
Goodrich Aerospace - Aerostructures Group (B.F.)
Grace & Co. (W.R.)
Graco, Inc.
Grede Foundries
Green Bay Packaging
GTE Corp.
Guardian Life Insurance Co. of America
Hallmark Cards Inc.
Hancock Financial Services (John)
Hanna Co. (M.A.)
Harcourt General, Inc.
Harley-Davidson Co.
Harnischfeger Industries
Harris Corp.
Harris Trust & Savings Bank
Harsco Corp.
Hartford (The)
Hartford Steam Boiler Inspection & Insurance Co.
Hartmarx Corp.
Hasbro, Inc.
Heinz Co. (H.J.)
Hershey Foods Corp.
Hewlett-Packard Co.
Hickory Tech Corp.
Hitachi America Ltd.
HON Industries Inc.
Honeywell International Inc.
Household International Inc.
Hubbard Broadcasting, Inc.
Hubbell Inc.
Huffy Corp.
Hughes Electronics Corp.
Humana, Inc.
Hunt Manufacturing Co.
Huntington Bancshares Inc.
IKON Office Solutions, Inc.
Illinois Power Co.
Illinois Tool Works, Inc.
Industrial Bank of Japan Trust Co. (New York)
Inland Container Corp.
INTRUST Financial Corp.
Invacare Corp.
Jacobs Engineering Group
Jeld-wen, Inc.
Johnson Controls Inc.
Johnson & Son (S.C.)
Jostens, Inc.
Katten, Muchin & Zavis
Kennametal, Inc.
Kerr-McGee Corp.
Key Bank of Cleveland
Kiewit Sons' Inc. (Peter)
Kimball International, Inc.
Kimberly-Clark Corp.
Kinder Morgn
Kingsbury Corp.
Koch Enterprises, Inc.
Koch Industries, Inc.
Kroger Co.
La-Z-Boy Inc.
Laclede Gas Co.
Lance, Inc.
LandAmerica Financial Services
Leigh Fibers, Inc.
Levi Strauss & Co.
Leviton Manufacturing Co. Inc.
LG&E Energy Corp.
Liberty Corp.
Lilly & Co. (Eli)
Lincoln Electric Co.
Lincoln Financial Group
Lipton Co.
Little, Inc. (Arthur D.)
Loews Corp.
Lotus Development Corp.
Lowe's Companies
LTV Corp.
Lubrizol Corp. (The)
Madison Gas & Electric Co.
Marcus Corp.
Maritz Inc.
Mark IV Industries
Marshall & Ilsley Corp.
Masco Corp.
Mattel Inc.
May Department Stores Co.
McClatchy Co.
McCormick & Co. Inc.
McDonald & Co. Securities, Inc.
McGraw-Hill Companies, Inc.
MCI WorldCom, Inc.
McWane Inc.
Mead Corp.
Mellon Financial Corp.
Memphis Light Gas & Water Division
Menasha Corp.
Mercantile Bank NA
Merrill Lynch & Co., Inc.
Metropolitan Life Insurance Co.
Michigan Consolidated Gas Co.
Mid-America Bank of Louisville
Milliken & Co.
Mine Safety Appliances Co.
Minnesota Mining & Manufacturing Co.
Minnesota Mutual Life Insurance Co.
Montgomery Ward & Co., Inc.
MONY Group (The)
Morgan & Co. Inc. (J.P.)
Morgan Stanley Dean Witter & Co.
Morris Communications Corp.
Morrison Knudsen Corp.
Motorola Inc.
Mutual of Omaha Insurance Co.
Nabisco Group Holdings
National City Bank of Minneapolis
National City Corp.
National Computer Systems, Inc.
National Machinery Co.
National Service Industries, Inc.
National Starch & Chemical Co.
Nationwide Insurance Co.
NEBCO Evans
Nestle U.S.A. Inc.
New Century Energies
New England Bio Labs
New England Financial
New Jersey Natural Gas Co.
New York Life Insurance Co.
New York Stock Exchange, Inc.
New York Times Co.
Niagara Mohawk Holdings Inc.
Nissan North America, Inc.
Nordson Corp.
Norfolk Southern Corp.
North American Royalties
Northeast Utilities
Northern Indiana Public Service Co.
Northern Trust Co.
Northwest Bank Nebraska, NA
Northwest Natural Gas Co.
Norton Co.
Norwest Corp.
OG&E Electric Services
Oklahoma Publishing Co.
Old Kent Bank
Old National Bank Evansville
Osborne Enterprises
Outboard Marine Corp.
Overnite Transportation Co.
Pacific Gas and Electric Co.
Pacific Mutual Life Insurance Co.
PacifiCare Health Systems
PacifiCorp
Park National Bank
Parker Hannifin Corp.
Pella Corp.
Penney Co., Inc. (J.C.)
Peoples Bank
Peoples Energy Corp.
PepsiCo, Inc.
PerkinElmer, Inc.
Pfizer Inc.
Pharmacia & Upjohn, Inc.
Phelps Dodge Corp.
Philips Electronics North America Corp.
Phillips Petroleum Co.
Pieper Power Electric Co.
Pillsbury Co.
Pioneer Hi-Bred International, Inc.
Pittway Corp.
PNC Bank
PNC Bank Kentucky Inc.
PNC Financial Services Group
Polaroid Corp.
Portland General Electric Co.
Potlatch Corp.
PPG Industries, Inc.
Praxair
Premier Dental Products Co.
Premier Industrial Corp.
Price Associates (T. Rowe)
Principal Financial Group
Procter & Gamble Co.
Procter & Gamble Co., Cosmetics Division
Promus Hotel Corp.
Providence Journal-Bulletin Co.
Provident Companies, Inc.
Prudential Insurance Co. of America
Prudential Securities Inc.
Public Service Electric & Gas Co.
Pulitzer Publishing Co.
Quaker Chemical Corp.
Quanex Corp.
Ralph's Grocery Co.
Ralston Purina Co.
Rayonier Inc.
Red Wing Shoe Co. Inc.
Regions Bank
Reily & Co., Inc. (William B.)
Reliant Energy Inc.
ReliaStar Financial Corp.
Reynolds Metals Co.
Reynolds & Reynolds Co.
Reynolds Tobacco (R.J.)
Rich Products Corp.
Rochester Gas & Electric Corp.
Rockwell International Corp.
Rouse Co.
Royal & SunAlliance USA, Inc.
Rubbermaid Inc.
Ryder System, Inc.
SAFECO Corp.
Safeguard Scientifics
Saint Paul Companies Inc.
Salomon Smith Barney
S&T Bancorp
Sara Lee Corp.
Sara Lee Hosiery, Inc.
SBC Communications Inc.
Schering-Plough Corp.
Schlumberger Ltd. (USA)
Schwab & Co., Inc. (Charles)
Scripps Co. (E.W.)
Searle & Co. (G.D.)
Sempra Energy
Shaw's Supermarkets, Inc.
Shea Co. (John F.)
Shell Oil Co.
Sherwin-Williams Co.
Sierra Pacific Resources
Simplot Co. (J.R.)
Simpson Investment Co.
Slant/Fin Corp.
Smith Corp. (A.O.)
Smurfit-Stone Container Corp.
Sonoco Products Co.
Sony Electronics
South Bend Tribune Corp.
Southeastern Mutual Insurance Co.
Southern New England Telephone Co.
Sovereign Bank
Springs Industries, Inc.
Sprint Corp.
SPX Corp.
Standard Products Co.
Standard Register Co.
Star Bank NA
Starwood Hotels & Resorts Worldwide, Inc.
State Street Bank & Trust Co.
Steelcase Inc.
Stone Container Corp.
Stride Rite Corp.
Stupp Brothers Bridge & Iron Co.
Sun Microsystems Inc.
Sunmark Capital Corp.
Sunoco Inc.
SunTrust Bank Atlanta
Synovus Financial Corp.
TCF National Bank Minnesota
Tektronix, Inc.
TENNANT Co.
Texaco Inc.
Texas Gas Transmission Corp.
Textron Inc.
Thermo Electron Corp.
Thomasville Furniture Industries Inc.
Thompson Co. (J. Walter)
Times Mirror Co.
Timken Co. (The)
Toledo Blade Co.
Trace International Holdings, Inc.
Transamerica Corp.
True Oil Co.
Trustmark Insurance Co.
TRW Inc.
TU Electric Co.

Tyson Foods Inc.
Ukrop's Super Markets
Ultramar Diamond Shamrock Corp.
Unilever Home & Personal Care U.S.A.
Unilever United States, Inc.
Union Camp Corp.
Union Pacific Corp.
United Airlines Inc.
United Distillers & Vintners North America
United Dominion Industries, Ltd.
United Parcel Service of America Inc.
U.S. Bancorp
U.S. Bancorp Piper Jaffray
United States Sugar Corp.
United States Trust Co. of New York
United Wisconsin Services
Universal Foods Corp.
Universal Leaf Tobacco Co., Inc.
Universal Studios
Unocal Corp.
UnumProvident
US Bank, Washington
US West, Inc.
USG Corp.
Valmont Industries, Inc.
Valspar Corp.
Vulcan Materials Co.
Wachovia Bank of North Carolina NA
Waffle House Inc.
Wal-Mart Stores, Inc.
Walter Industries Inc.
Warner-Lambert Co.
Washington Mutual, Inc.
Weil, Gotshal & Manges Corp.
Wells Fargo & Co.
Western & Southern Life Insurance Co.
Westvaco Corp.
Weyerhaeuser Co.
Whirlpool Corp.
Whitman Corp.
WICOR, Inc.
Wilbur-Ellis Co. & Connell Brothers Co.
Williams
Wisconsin Energy Corp.
Wisconsin Power & Light Co.
Woodward Governor Co.
Wyman-Gordon Co.
Xerox Corp.
Yellow Corp.
Young & Rubicam
Zachry Co. (H.B.)

ECONOMIC POLICY

Abbott Laboratories
Air Products and Chemicals, Inc.
Alcoa Inc.
Alexander & Baldwin, Inc.
Allegheny Technologies Inc.
Alliant Techsystems
American Standard Inc.
Ameritas Life Insurance Corp.
Ameritech Corp.
Ameritech Indiana
Andersen Corp.
Andersons Inc.
Aon Corp.
Archer-Daniels-Midland Co.
Aristech Chemical Corp.
Armstrong World Industries, Inc.
AT&T Corp.
Avon Products, Inc.
Baird & Co. (Robert W.)
Bechtel Group, Inc.
Ben & Jerry's Homemade Inc.
Bethlehem Steel Corp.
BFGoodrich Co.
Binney & Smith Inc.
Blount International, Inc.
Boise Cascade Corp.
Borden, Inc.
BP Amoco Corp.
Bucyrus-Erie Co.
Burlington Resources, Inc.
Cabot Corp.
Campbell Soup Co.
Caterpillar Inc.
Central Maine Power Co.
CertainTeed Corp.
CGU Insurance
Chase Bank of Texas
Chase Manhattan Bank, NA
Chevron Corp.
CIGNA Corp.
CIT Group, Inc. (The)
Citibank Corp.
Colonial Life & Accident Insurance Co.
Cone Mills Corp.
Cooper Industries, Inc.
Coors Brewing Co.
Crane Co.
Credit Suisse First Boston
Crestar Finance Corp.
CSS Industries, Inc.
Cummins Engine Co., Inc.
DaimlerChrysler Corp.
Dayton Power and Light Co.
Detroit Edison Co.
Dial Corp.
Dow Jones & Co., Inc.
du Pont de Nemours & Co. (E.I.)
Dun & Bradstreet Corp.
Eastman Kodak Co.
Eaton Corp.
Edison International
El Paso Energy Co.
Elf Atochem North America, Inc.
Emerson Electric Co.
Equifax Inc.
Exxon Mobil Corp.
Federal-Mogul Corp.
Fidelity Investments
First Source Corp.
First Union Bank
First Union Corp.
First Union Securities, Inc.
Fisher Scientific
FleetBoston Financial Corp.
FMC Corp.
Forbes Inc.
Ford Meter Box Co.
Ford Motor Co.
GenCorp
General Atlantic Partners II LP
General Electric Co.
General Motors Corp.
Georgia Power Co.
Giant Eagle Inc.
Goldman Sachs Group
Goodrich Aerospace - Aerostructures Group (B.F.)
Grace & Co. (W.R.)
Grede Foundries
Guardian Life Insurance Co. of America
Hamilton Sundstrand Corp.
Hancock Financial Services (John)
Harcourt General, Inc.
Harley-Davidson Co.
Harris Corp.
Harsco Corp.
Heinz Co. (H.J.)
Hickory Tech Corp.
HON Industries Inc.
Hubbell Inc.
Hunt Manufacturing Co.
Jacobs Engineering Group
Kennametal, Inc.
Kerr-McGee Corp.
Kimball International, Inc.
Kimberly-Clark Corp.
KPMG Peat Marwick LLP
Lance, Inc.
Land O'Lakes, Inc.
Leigh Fibers, Inc.
Levi Strauss & Co.
Lilly & Co. (Eli)
Louisiana Land & Exploration Co.
Macy's East Inc.
Mamiye Brothers
Mattel Inc.
McDonald & Co. Securities, Inc.
Metropolitan Life Insurance Co.
Motorola Inc.
National City Corp.
National Computer Systems, Inc.
National Service Industries, Inc.
Nationwide Insurance Co.
NEBCO Evans
New York Life Insurance Co.
New York Stock Exchange, Inc.
Norton Co.
Occidental Oil and Gas
PACCAR Inc.
Pacific Mutual Life Insurance Co.
PEMCO Corp.
Peoples Energy Corp.
Pfizer Inc.
Phelps Dodge Corp.
Phillips Petroleum Co.
Pioneer Group
PNC Financial Services Group
PPG Industries, Inc.
Procter & Gamble Co.
Promus Hotel Corp.
Provident Companies, Inc.
Prudential Insurance Co. of America
Publix Supermarkets
Putnam Investments
Rayonier Inc.
Reynolds Metals Co.
Reynolds Tobacco (R.J.)
Rockwell International Corp.
Rubbermaid Inc.
Schlumberger Ltd. (USA)
Searle & Co. (G.D.)
Shell Oil Co.
Sherwin-Williams Co.
SmithKline Beecham Corp.
Southwest Gas Corp.
SPX Corp.
Stanley Works (The)
Starwood Hotels & Resorts Worldwide, Inc.
State Farm Mutual Automobile Insurance Co.
State Street Bank & Trust Co.
Storage Technology Corp.
Sunmark Capital Corp.
SunTrust Bank Atlanta
Tamko Roofing Products
Tektronix, Inc.
Texaco Inc.
Texas Gas Transmission Corp.
Texas Instruments Inc.
Textron Inc.
Thermo Electron Corp.
Times Mirror Co.
Timken Co. (The)
True Oil Co.
TRW Inc.
Tyson Foods Inc.
Unilever United States, Inc.
Union Camp Corp.
United States Sugar Corp.
United Wisconsin Services
Universal Leaf Tobacco Co., Inc.
Unocal Corp.
USX Corp.
Vulcan Materials Co.
Wal-Mart Stores, Inc.
Warner-Lambert Co.
Weil, Gotshal & Manges Corp.
Western & Southern Life Insurance Co.
Westvaco Corp.
Whirlpool Corp.
Whitman Corp.
Williams
Winn-Dixie Stores Inc.
Wisconsin Power & Light Co.
Xerox Corp.
Young & Rubicam

EMPLOYMENT/JOB TRAINING

ABC
Advanced Micro Devices, Inc.
Aetna, Inc.
AGL Resources Inc.
Agrilink Foods, Inc.
Alcoa Inc.
Allegheny Technologies Inc.
Alliant Techsystems
AlliedSignal Inc.
Allstate Insurance Co.
AMCORE Bank Rockford
American Express Co.
American Honda Motor Co., Inc.
American Retail Group
American Standard Inc.
American United Life Insurance Co.
Ameritas Life Insurance Corp.
Ameritech Corp.
Ameritech Indiana
Ameritech Wisconsin
AMP Inc.
Anheuser-Busch Companies, Inc.
Aon Corp.
APL Ltd.
Aristech Chemical Corp.
Arvin Industries, Inc.
Associated Food Stores
AT&T Corp.
Atlantic Investment Co.
Atlantic Richfield Co.
Avon Products, Inc.
Badger Meter, Inc.
Baird & Co. (Robert W.)
Bank of America
BankBoston-Connecticut Region
BankBoston Corp.
Bard, Inc. (C.R.)
Bassett Furniture Industries
Battelle Memorial Institute
Bausch & Lomb Inc.
Baxter International Inc.
Belk Stores Services Inc.
Bemis Co., Inc.
Bemis Manufacturing Co.
Ben & Jerry's Homemade Inc.
Bernstein & Co., Inc. (Sanford C.)
Bestfoods
Bethlehem Steel Corp.
BFGoodrich Co.
Binswanger Companies
Blair & Co. (William)
Block, Inc. (H&R)
Blue Bell, Inc.
Boston Edison Co.
Boston Globe (The)
BP Amoco Corp.
Bridgestone/Firestone, Inc.
Bristol-Myers Squibb Co.
Broderbund Software, Inc.
Brown & Williamson Tobacco Corp.
Bucyrus-Erie Co.
Burlington Industries, Inc.
Butler Manufacturing Co.
Cabot Corp.
California Bank & Trust
Callaway Golf Co.
Campbell Soup Co.
Cargill Inc.
Carillon Importers, Ltd.
Carpenter Technology Corp.
Carris Reels
Central Maine Power Co.
CertainTeed Corp.
Cessna Aircraft Co.
Chase Bank of Texas
Chase Manhattan Bank, NA
Chesapeake Corp.
Chevron Corp.
Chicago Board of Trade
Chicago Sun-Times, Inc.
Chicago Title Corp.
Chicago Tribune Co.
CIBC Oppenheimer
Cincinnati Bell Inc.
Citibank Corp.
Citigroup
Citizens Financial Group, Inc.
CLARCOR Inc.
Cleveland-Cliffs, Inc.
Clorox Co.
CNA
Colonial Life & Accident Insurance Co.
Compaq Computer Corp.
Consolidated Papers, Inc.
Consumers Energy Co.
Contran Corp.
Conwood Co. LP
Cooper Industries, Inc.
Cooper Tire & Rubber Co.
Corning Inc.
Crane & Co., Inc.
Credit Suisse First Boston
Crestar Finance Corp.
Croft-Leominster
Cummings Properties Management
Cummins Engine Co., Inc.

DaimlerChrysler Corp.
Dain Bosworth Inc.
Dayton Hudson
Dayton Power and Light Co.
Delta Air Lines, Inc.
Deluxe Corp.
Dexter Corp.
Dominion Resources, Inc.
Donaldson Co., Inc.
Donnelley & Sons Co. (R.R.)
Dow Chemical Co.
Dow Corning Corp.
du Pont de Nemours & Co. (E.I.)
Duriron Co., Inc.
Dynamet, Inc.
Eastern Bank
Eastman Kodak Co.
Eaton Corp.
Ecolab Inc.
EDS Corp.
Edwards Enterprise Software (J.D.)
Elf Atochem North America, Inc.
Emerson Electric Co.
Ensign-Bickford Industries
Equifax Inc.
Exxon Mobil Corp.
Fabri-Kal Corp.
Fannie Mae
Federal-Mogul Corp.
Federated Department Stores, Inc.
Ferro Corp.
Fidelity Investments
Fifth Third Bancorp
Fireman's Fund Insurance Co.
First Union Bank
First Union Corp.
First Union National Bank, NA
Firstar Bank Milwaukee NA
Fisher Brothers Cleaning Services
Fisher Scientific
FleetBoston Financial Corp.
Florida Rock Industries
Fluor Corp.
FMC Corp.
Forbes Inc.
Ford Meter Box Co.
Ford Motor Co.
Fort James Corp.
Fortis Insurance Co.
Fortune Brands, Inc.
Freeport-McMoRan Inc.
Frost National Bank
Fuller Co. (H.B.)
Furniture Brands International, Inc.
Gallo Winery, Inc. (E&J)
Gannett Co., Inc.
Gap, Inc.
GATX Corp.
GEICO Corp.
GenAmerica Corp.
GenCorp
General Atlantic Partners II LP
General Electric Co.
General Mills, Inc.
General Motors Corp.
General Reinsurance Corp.
Georgia-Pacific Corp.
Georgia Power Co.
Gerber Products Co.
Giant Food Inc.
Gillette Co.
Glaxo Wellcome Inc.
Glickenhaus & Co.
Grace & Co. (W.R.)
Graco, Inc.
GTE Corp.
Halliburton Co.
Hallmark Cards Inc.
Hamilton Sundstrand Corp.
Hancock Financial Services (John)
Hanna Co. (M.A.)
Harcourt General, Inc.
Harley-Davidson Co.
Harris Trust & Savings Bank
Harsco Corp.
Hartford (The)
Hartford Steam Boiler Inspection & Insurance Co.
Heinz Co. (H.J.)
Hensel Phelps Construction Co.
Hershey Foods Corp.
Hewlett-Packard Co.
Hitachi America Ltd.
Hoffmann-La Roche Inc.
Home Depot, Inc.
Honeywell International Inc.
Housatonic Curtain Co.
Household International Inc.
Hunt Manufacturing Co.
Huntington Bancshares Inc.
Idaho Power Co.
IKON Office Solutions, Inc.
Illinois Tool Works, Inc.
Industrial Bank of Japan Trust Co. (New York)
Inman Mills
International Business Machines Corp.
International Flavors & Fragrances Inc.
INTRUST Financial Corp.
Invacare Corp.
Jeld-wen, Inc.
Johnson Controls Inc.
Johnson & Johnson
Johnson & Son (S.C.)
Jostens, Inc.
Journal-Gazette Co.
Kelly Services
Kroger Co.
Land O'Lakes, Inc.
Lee Enterprises
Lehigh Portland Cement Co.
Leigh Fibers, Inc.
Levi Strauss & Co.
Liberty Corp.
Lilly & Co. (Eli)
Lincoln Electric Co.
Lincoln Financial Group
Little, Inc. (Arthur D.)
Liz Claiborne, Inc.
Loews Corp.
Lotus Development Corp.
LTV Corp.
Lubrizol Corp. (The)
Macy's East Inc.
Mamiye Brothers
Marcus Corp.
Maritz Inc.
Marriott International Inc.
Marshall Field's
Marshall & Ilsley Corp.
Mattel Inc.
May Department Stores Co.
MBIA Inc.
McClatchy Co.
McDonald & Co. Securities, Inc.
McDonald's Corp.
McGraw-Hill Companies, Inc.
MCI WorldCom, Inc.
Medtronic, Inc.
Memphis Light Gas & Water Division
Merit Oil Corp.
Merrill Lynch & Co., Inc.
Metropolitan Life Insurance Co.
MGIC Investment Corp.
Michigan Consolidated Gas Co.
Mid-America Bank of Louisville
Milacron, Inc.
Millipore Corp.
Minnesota Mining & Manufacturing Co.
Minnesota Mutual Life Insurance Co.
Mitsubishi Electric America
Montana Power Co.
MONY Group (The)
Morgan & Co. Inc. (J.P.)
Morgan Stanley Dean Witter & Co.
Morris Communications Corp.
Motorola Inc.
MTD Products Inc.
Nalco Chemical Co.
NASDAQ Stock Market
National Bank of Commerce Trust & Savings
National City Bank of Minneapolis
National Computer Systems, Inc.
National Fuel Gas Distribution Corp.
National Machinery Co.
National Presto Industries, Inc.
Nationwide Insurance Co.
NEBCO Evans
NEC America, Inc.
Nestle U.S.A. Inc.
New England Financial
New York Life Insurance Co.
New York Mercantile Exchange
New York Times Co.
Niagara Mohawk Holdings Inc.
Nissan North America, Inc.
Nomura Holding America
Nordson Corp.
Northern Indiana Public Service Co.
Northern States Power Co.
Northern Trust Co.
Norton Co.
Norwest Corp.
Orange & Rockland Utilities, Inc.
PACCAR Inc.
Pacific Century Financial Corp.
Pacific Gas and Electric Co.
Pacific Mutual Life Insurance Co.
PacifiCorp
Paine Webber
Parker Hannifin Corp.
Penney Co., Inc. (J.C.)
Peoples Energy Corp.
PerkinElmer, Inc.
Pfizer Inc.
Pharmacia & Upjohn, Inc.
Philip Morris Companies Inc.
Phillips Petroleum Co.
Pillsbury Co.
Pioneer Hi-Bred International, Inc.
Pitney Bowes Inc.
PNC Bank
PNC Financial Services Group
Polaroid Corp.
Potomac Electric Power Co.
PPG Industries, Inc.
Premier Dental Products Co.
Premier Industrial Corp.
Principal Financial Group
Procter & Gamble Co.
Procter & Gamble Co., Cosmetics Division
Prudential Insurance Co. of America
Public Service Electric & Gas Co.
Pulitzer Publishing Co.
Putnam Investments
Quaker Chemical Corp.
Ralston Purina Co.
Rayonier Inc.
Regions Bank
Reily & Co., Inc. (William B.)
ReliaStar Financial Corp.
Reynolds & Reynolds Co.
Reynolds Tobacco (R.J.)
Rockwell International Corp.
Rouse Co.
Rubbermaid Inc.
Russer Foods
SAFECO Corp.
Safeway Inc.
Saint Paul Companies Inc.
Salomon Smith Barney
Sara Lee Corp.
SBC Communications Inc.
Schwab & Co., Inc. (Charles)
Scripps Co. (E.W.)
Searle & Co. (G.D.)
Sears, Roebuck and Co.
Security Benefit Life Insurance Co.
Sempra Energy
Sentry Insurance, A Mutual Co.
ServiceMaster Co.
Shea Co. (John F.)
Shell Oil Co.
Sherwin-Williams Co.
Shoney's Inc.
SmithKline Beecham Corp.
Solo Cup Co.
Sony Electronics
Southwest Gas Corp.
Springs Industries, Inc.
Sprint Corp.
Standard Products Co.
Standard Register Co.
Stanley Works (The)
Star Bank NA
Starwood Hotels & Resorts Worldwide, Inc.
State Farm Mutual Automobile Insurance Co.
State Street Bank & Trust Co.
Stone Container Corp.
Stonecutter Mills Corp.
Stride Rite Corp.
Sun Microsystems Inc.
Sunoco Inc.
SunTrust Bank Atlanta
SuperValu, Inc.
Synovus Financial Corp.
TCF National Bank Minnesota
Temple-Inland Inc.
TENNANT Co.
Tenneco Automotive
Tesoro Hawaii
Texaco Inc.
Texas Instruments Inc.
Textron Inc.
Thermo Electron Corp.
Times Mirror Co.
TJX Companies, Inc.
Toledo Blade Co.
Tomkins Industries, Inc.
Transamerica Corp.
TRW Inc.
Unilever Home & Personal Care U.S.A.
Unilever United States, Inc.
Union Camp Corp.
Union Carbide Corp.
United Airlines Inc.
United Distillers & Vintners North America
United Parcel Service of America Inc.
U.S. Bancorp
U.S. Bancorp Piper Jaffray
United States Trust Co. of New York
United Wisconsin Services
Universal Foods Corp.
Universal Leaf Tobacco Co., Inc.
Universal Studios
Unocal Corp.
UnumProvident
UPN Channel 50
US Bank, Washington
US West, Inc.
USG Corp.
USX Corp.
Valspar Corp.
Vodafone AirTouch Plc
Waffle House Inc.
Walter Industries Inc.
Warner-Lambert Co.
Washington Mutual, Inc.
Washington Trust Bank
Weil, Gotshal & Manges Corp.
Wells Fargo & Co.
Western Resources Inc.
Western & Southern Life Insurance Co.
Westvaco Corp.
Weyerhaeuser Co.
Whirlpool Corp.
WICOR, Inc.
Williams
Wiremold Co.
Wisconsin Energy Corp.
Wisconsin Power & Light Co.
Woodward Governor Co.
Wrigley Co. (Wm. Jr.)
Xerox Corp.
York Federal Savings & Loan Association
Young & Rubicam

ENVIRONMENTAL AFFAIRS (GENERAL)

Excel Corp.
Federated Mutual Insurance Co.
New England Bio Labs
Reliant Energy Minnegasco

ENVIRONMENTAL AFFAIRS (AIR/WATER QUALITY)

Donaldson Co., Inc.
Federated Mutual Insurance Co.
New England Bio Labs

ENVIRONMENTAL AFFAIRS (CONSERVATION)

Donaldson Co., Inc.
Huntington Bancshares Inc.
New England Bio Labs
Security Life of Denver Insurance Co.

ENVIRONMENTAL AFFAIRS (WILDLIFE PROTECTION)

Federated Mutual Insurance Co.

ETHNIC ORGANIZATIONS

Alliant Techsystems
APL Ltd.
Armstrong World Industries, Inc.
Arvin Industries, Inc.
Atlantic Richfield Co.
Bandag, Inc.
Banfi Vintners
Bechtel Group, Inc.
Ben & Jerry's Homemade Inc.
Borden, Inc.
Brown Shoe Co., Inc.
Calvin Klein
Carlson Companies, Inc.
Caterpillar Inc.
CertainTeed Corp.
Chicago Sun-Times, Inc.
Cox Enterprises Inc.
Cummings Properties Management
Daily News
DaimlerChrysler Corp.
Dow Chemical Co.
Eastern Bank
Eastman Kodak Co.
Ecolab Inc.
Erving Industries
Fisher Brothers Cleaning Services
Forest City Enterprises, Inc.
Gallo Winery, Inc. (E&J)
General Motors Corp.
Graco, Inc.
Harcourt General, Inc.
Harsco Corp.
Hasbro, Inc.
Housatonic Curtain Co.
Huntington Bancshares Inc.
International Flavors & Fragrances Inc.
Jacobson & Sons (Benjamin)
Lincoln Financial Group
Lotus Development Corp.
Masco Corp.
McDonald & Co. Securities, Inc.
Nationwide Insurance Co.
New York Mercantile Exchange
Occidental Petroleum Corp.
Overseas Shipholding Group Inc.
PepsiCo, Inc.
Physicians Mutual Insurance Co.
Polaroid Corp.
Premier Dental Products Co.
Regions Bank
SBC Communications Inc.
Seagram & Sons, Inc. (Joseph E.)
Slant/Fin Corp.
Sony Electronics
Sovereign Bank
US Bank, Washington
Valmont Industries, Inc.
Weil, Gotshal & Manges Corp.
Whitman Corp.
Young & Rubicam
Zilkha & Sons

FIRST AMENDMENT ISSUES

ABC
Binney & Smith Inc.
Dow Jones & Co., Inc.
General Motors Corp.
Knight Ridder
McClatchy Co.
McGraw-Hill Companies, Inc.
National Computer Systems, Inc.
New York Times Co.
Playboy Enterprises Inc.
Pulitzer Publishing Co.
Scripps Co. (E.W.)
Times Mirror Co.
Toledo Blade Co.
Whirlpool Corp.
Wiley & Sons (John)

GAY/LESBIAN ISSUES

Amgen, Inc.
Ben & Jerry's Homemade Inc.
Bernstein & Co., Inc. (Sanford C.)
Dow Jones & Co., Inc.
Fireman's Fund Insurance Co.
Gap, Inc.
Levi Strauss & Co.
Liz Claiborne, Inc.
MONY Group (The)
Morgan & Co. Inc. (J.P.)
Overseas Shipholding Group Inc.
Sovereign Bank
US Bank, Washington

CIVIC & PUBLIC AFFAIRS-GENERAL

7-Eleven, Inc.
Abbott Laboratories
ABC
Advanced Micro Devices, Inc.
AEGON U.S.A. Inc.
Agrilink Foods, Inc.
Air Products and Chemicals, Inc.
Airborne Freight Corp.
AK Steel Corp.
Alabama Power Co.
Alaska Airlines, Inc.
Alcon Laboratories, Inc.
Alexander & Baldwin, Inc.
Allegheny Technologies Inc.
Alliant Techsystems
AlliedSignal Inc.
Allmerica Financial Corp.
Allstate Insurance Co.
Alma Piston Co.
Alyeska Pipeline Service Co.
AMCORE Bank Rockford
American Fidelity Corp.
American General Corp.
American General Finance
American Retail Group
American Stock Exchange, Inc.
Ameritas Life Insurance Corp.
Ameritech Corp.
Ameritech Ohio
Ameritech Wisconsin
AMETEK, Inc.
Amgen, Inc.
AMR Corp.
Amsted Industries Inc.
Andersen Corp.
Aristech Chemical Corp.
Arizona Public Service Co.
Ashland, Inc.
Associated Food Stores
Atlantic Investment Co.
Atlantic Richfield Co.
Autodesk Inc.
Avery Dennison Corp.
Avista Corporation
Badger Meter, Inc.
Baird & Co. (Robert W.)
Ball Corp.
Banfi Vintners
Bank One, Texas-Houston Office
Bank One, Texas, NA
BankAtlantic Bancorp
BankBoston-Connecticut Region
BankBoston Corp.
Banta Corp.
Barclays Capital
Bard, Inc. (C.R.)
Barden Corp.
Bardes Corp.
Barnes Group Inc.
Barry Corp. (R.G.)
Baxter International Inc.
Belk-Simpson Department Stores
Belk Stores Services Inc.
Bell Atlantic Corp.
Bell Atlantic Corp.-West Virginia
Bell Atlantic-Delaware, Inc.
Bemis Manufacturing Co.
Ben & Jerry's Homemade Inc.
Bernstein & Co., Inc. (Sanford C.)
Berwind Group
Bethlehem Steel Corp.
BFGoodrich Co.
Binney & Smith Inc.
Binswanger Companies
Blair & Co. (William)
Blue Bell, Inc.
Blue Cross & Blue Shield of Alabama
Blue Cross & Blue Shield of Iowa
Blue Cross & Blue Shield of Minnesota
Boeing Co.
Boler Co.
Borman's Inc.
Boston Gas Co.
Bourns, Inc.
Bradford & Co. (J.C.)
Branch Banking & Trust Co.
Bridgestone/Firestone, Inc.
Briggs & Stratton Corp.
Bristol-Myers Squibb Co.
Broderbund Software, Inc.
Brooklyn Union
Burlington Industries, Inc.
Burnett Co. (Leo)
Burress (J.W.)
Business Improvement
Business Men's Assurance Co. of America
Cadence Designs Systems, Inc.
Caesar's World, Inc.
Calvin Klein
Cantor, Fitzgerald Securities Corp.
Cargill Inc.
Carillon Importers, Ltd.
Carlson Companies, Inc.
Carris Reels
Castle & Cooke Properties Inc.
Caterpillar Inc.
CCB Financial Corp.
Cenex Harvest States
Centex Corp.
Central National-Gottesman
Central & South West Services
Century 21
CertainTeed Corp.
CGU Insurance
Charter Manufacturing Co.
Chase Bank of Texas
Chase Manhattan Bank, NA
Chemed Corp.
Chicago Board of Trade
Chicago Title Corp.
Chicago Tribune Co.
CIGNA Corp.
Cincinnati Bell Inc.
Cinergy Corp.
CIT Group, Inc. (The)
Citizens Bank-Flint
Citizens Financial Group, Inc.
CLARCOR Inc.
Cleveland-Cliffs, Inc.
Clorox Co.
CNA
Coachmen Industries, Inc.
Colgate-Palmolive Co.
Colonial Oil Industries, Inc.
Commerce Bancshares, Inc.
Commercial Federal Corp.
Commercial Intertech Corp.
Compass Bank
Computer Associates International, Inc.
Conectiv
Consolidated Natural Gas Co.
Consolidated Papers, Inc.
Consumers Energy Co.
Contran Corp.
Conwood Co. LP
Cook Inlet Region
Cooper Tire & Rubber Co.
Copley Press, Inc.
Cox Enterprises Inc.
Crane Co.
Crane & Co., Inc.
Credit Suisse First Boston
Crestar Finance Corp.
Croft-Leominster
CSS Industries, Inc.
CSX Corp.
Cummings Properties Management
CUNA Mutual Group
Curtis Industries, Inc. (Helene)
Daily News
DaimlerChrysler Corp.
Dain Bosworth Inc.
Danis Companies
Deere & Co.
DeKalb Genetics Corp.
Delta Air Lines, Inc.
Deluxe Corp.
Demoulas Supermarkets Inc.
Deposit Guaranty National Bank
Deutsch Co.
Dial Corp.
Diebold, Inc.
Disney Co. (Walt)
Dixie Group, Inc. (The)
Dow Chemical Co.
Dow Jones & Co., Inc.
DSM Copolymer
Duchossois Industries Inc.
Duracell International
Duriron Co., Inc.
Eastern Bank
Eastman Chemical Co.
Eastman Kodak Co.
Eaton Corp.
Ebsco Industries, Inc.
Ecolab Inc.
EDS Corp.
Edwards Enterprise Software (J.D.)
El Paso Energy Co.
Elf Atochem North America, Inc.
Emerson Electric Co.
EMI Music Publishing
Employers Insurance of Wausau, A Mutual Co.
Employers Mutual Casualty Co.
Ensign-Bickford Industries
Enterprise Rent-A-Car Co.
Equitable Resources, Inc.
Erb Lumber Co.
Erving Industries
Evening Post Publishing Co.
Excel Corp.
Extendicare Health Services
Fabri-Kal Corp.
Farmers Group, Inc.
Federated Mutual Insurance Co.
Ferro Corp.
Fidelity Investments
Fifth Third Bancorp
Fireman's Fund Insurance Co.
First American Corp.
First Financial Bank
First Hawaiian, Inc.
First Maryland Bancorp
First National Bank of Evergreen Park
First Security Bank of Idaho NA
First Source Corp.
First Union Bank
First Union Securities, Inc.
FirstEnergy Corp.
Fisher Brothers Cleaning Services
FleetBoston Financial Corp.
Florida Power & Light Co.
Florida Rock Industries
Fluor Corp.
Forbes Inc.
Ford Meter Box Co.
Ford Motor Co.
Forest City Enterprises, Inc.
Fortis, Inc.
Frito-Lay, Inc.
Frontier Corp.
Fuji Bank & Trust Co.
Fuller Co. (H.B.)
Furniture Brands International, Inc.
Gallo Winery, Inc. (E&J)
Galter Corp.
Gap, Inc.
Gates Rubber Corp.
GEICO Corp.
GenAmerica Corp.
GenCorp
Genentech Inc.
General Atlantic Partners II LP
General Electric Co.

General Mills, Inc.
General Motors Corp.
Georgia-Pacific Corp.
Georgia Power Co.
Gerber Products Co.
Giant Eagle Inc.
Giddings & Lewis
Glickenhaus & Co.
Globe Corp.
Goldman Sachs Group
Golub Corp.
Gosiger, Inc.
GPU Energy
Graco, Inc.
Grainger, Inc. (W.W.)
Grede Foundries
Green Bay Packaging
Griffith Laboratories U.S.A.
Group Health Plan
GTE Corp.
Guess?
Gulf Power Co.
Halliburton Co.
Hallmark Cards Inc.
Hamilton Sundstrand Corp.
Hanna Co. (M.A.)
Hannaford Brothers Co.
Harcourt General, Inc.
Harland Co. (John H.)
Harley-Davidson Co.
Harnischfeger Industries
Harris Corp.
Harris Trust & Savings Bank
Harsco Corp.
Hartford (The)
Hartford Steam Boiler Inspection & Insurance Co.
Hartmarx Corp.
Hasbro, Inc.
Hawaiian Electric Co., Inc.
Heinz Co. (H.J.)
Hensel Phelps Construction Co.
Hercules Inc.
Hershey Foods Corp.
Hickory Tech Corp.
Hitachi America Ltd.
Hoffer Plastics Corp.
Hoffmann-La Roche Inc.
Hofmann Co.
HON Industries Inc.
Honeywell International Inc.
Housatonic Curtain Co.
HSBC Bank USA
Hubbard Broadcasting, Inc.
Hubbell Inc.
Huffy Corp.
Humana, Inc.
Hunt Oil Co.
Huntington Bancshares Inc.
Idaho Power Co.
Independent Stave Co.
Indiana Mills & Manufacturing
Industrial Bank of Japan Trust Co. (New York)
Ingram Industries Inc.
Inman Mills
International Flavors & Fragrances Inc.
International Multifoods Corp.
International Paper Co.
Interpublic Group of Companies, Inc.
INTRUST Financial Corp.
Invacare Corp.
ISE America
Jacobs Engineering Group
Jacobson & Sons (Benjamin)
Johnson Controls Inc.
Jostens, Inc.
Journal Communications, Inc.
Journal-Gazette Co.
JSJ Corp.
Kaman Corp.
Katten, Muchin & Zavis
Kellwood Co.
Kendall International, Inc.
Kennametal, Inc.
Key Bank of Cleveland
Kimberly-Clark Corp.
Kinder Morgn
Kingsbury Corp.
Koch Enterprises, Inc.
Kraft Foods, Inc.
Lancaster Lens, Inc.
Lance, Inc.
LandAmerica Financial Services
Landmark Communications Inc.
Lee Enterprises
Lehigh Portland Cement Co.
Leigh Fibers, Inc.
Lennox International, Inc.
Levi Strauss & Co.
Leviton Manufacturing Co. Inc.
Liberty Diversified Industries
Liberty Mutual Insurance Group
Lilly & Co. (Eli)
Lipton Co.
Little, Inc. (Arthur D.)
Litton Industries, Inc.
Liz Claiborne, Inc.
Loctite Corp.
Loews Corp.
Louisiana-Pacific Corp.
Lowe's Companies
Lubrizol Corp. (The)
Madison Gas & Electric Co.
Mamiye Brothers
Manor Care Health SVS, Inc.
Marcus Corp.
Mark IV Industries
Masco Corp.
Massachusetts Mutual Life Insurance Co.
Mattel Inc.
May Department Stores Co.
Mazda North American Operations
MBIA Inc.
McClatchy Co.
McDonald & Co. Securities, Inc.
MCI WorldCom, Inc.
McKesson-HBOC Corp.
McWane Inc.
Mead Corp.
Meijer, Inc.
Memphis Light Gas & Water Division
Mercantile Bank NA
Merck & Co.
Merit Oil Corp.
Merrill Lynch & Co., Inc.
Metropolitan Life Insurance Co.
Michigan Consolidated Gas Co.
Microsoft Corp.
Mid-America Bank of Louisville
MidAmerican Energy Holdings Co.
Milacron, Inc.
Milliken & Co.
Minnesota Mining & Manufacturing Co.
Monarch Machine Tool Co.
Monsanto Co.
Montana Power Co.
Montgomery Ward & Co., Inc.
MONY Group (The)
Morris Communications Corp.
Morrison Knudsen Corp.
MTS Systems Corp.
Mutual of Omaha Insurance Co.
Nabisco Group Holdings
Nalco Chemical Co.
National Bank of Commerce Trust & Savings
National City Bank of Cleveland
National City Bank of Columbus
National City Bank of Minneapolis
National City Bank of Pennsylvania
National City Corp.
National Computer Systems, Inc.
National Life of Vermont
National Service Industries, Inc.
National Starch & Chemical Co.
Nationwide Insurance Co.
Navcom Systems
NCR Corp.
NEBCO Evans
New England Bio Labs
New Jersey Natural Gas Co.
New United Motor Manufacturing Inc.
New York Mercantile Exchange
New York State Electric & Gas Corp.
New York Stock Exchange, Inc.
Niagara Mohawk Holdings Inc.
Nike, Inc.
Nomura Holding America
Nordson Corp.
Norfolk Southern Corp.
Nortel
North American Royalties
Northrop Grumman Corp.
Northwest Natural Gas Co.
Norton Co.
Occidental Oil and Gas
OG&E Electric Services
Ohio National Life Insurance Co.
Old National Bank Evansville
Orange & Rockland Utilities, Inc.
Orscheln Co.
Oshkosh B'Gosh, Inc.
Outboard Marine Corp.
Overseas Shipholding Group Inc.
Owens-Illinois Inc.
Pacific Century Financial Corp.
Pacific Mutual Life Insurance Co.
PacifiCare Health Systems
PacifiCorp
Paine Webber
Parker Hannifin Corp.
PEMCO Corp.
Penn Mutual Life Insurance Co.
Penney Co., Inc. (J.C.)
Pennsylvania Power & Light
Pentair Inc.
PepsiCo, Inc.
Pieper Power Electric Co.
Pioneer Group
Pioneer Natural Resources
Pittway Corp.
PNC Bank
PNC Financial Services Group
Praxair
Premier Dental Products Co.
Premier Industrial Corp.
Price Associates (T. Rowe)
Procter & Gamble Co., Cosmetics Division
Providence Journal-Bulletin Co.
Provident Mutual Life Insurance Co.
Prudential Securities Inc.
Public Service Co. of Oklahoma
Pulitzer Publishing Co.
Putnam Investments
Quanex Corp.
Ralph's Grocery Co.
Red Wing Shoe Co. Inc.
Reebok International Ltd.
Regions Bank
Regions Financial Corp.
Regis Corp.
Reilly Industries, Inc.
Reily & Co., Inc. (William B.)
Reinhart Institutional Foods
Revlon Inc.
Reynolds Metals Co.
Reynolds & Reynolds Co.
Reynolds Tobacco (R.J.)
Rich Products Corp.
Riggs Bank NA
Rohm & Haas Co.
Rouse Co.
Royal & SunAlliance USA, Inc.
Rubbermaid Inc.
Ruddick Corp.
Russer Foods
Ryder System, Inc.
Safeguard Scientifics
Saint Paul Companies Inc.
S&T Bancorp
Santa Fe International Corp.
Sara Lee Corp.
Sara Lee Hosiery, Inc.
SBC Communications Inc.
SCANA Corp.
Schloss & Co. (Marcus)
Schwab & Co., Inc. (Charles)
Schwebel Baking Co.
Scientific-Atlanta, Inc.
Scripps Co. (E.W.)
Seagram & Sons, Inc. (Joseph E.)
Searle & Co. (G.D.)
Security Benefit Life Insurance Co.
Sentry Insurance, A Mutual Co.
Servco Pacific
ServiceMaster Co.
S.G. Cowen
Shaw Industries Inc.
Shaw's Supermarkets, Inc.
Shea Co. (John F.)
Shelter Mutual Insurance Co.
Sherwin-Williams Co.
Shoney's Inc.
Sierra Pacific Industries
Sierra Pacific Resources
Simplot Co. (J.R.)
Simpson Investment Co.
SIT Investment Associates, Inc.
Slant/Fin Corp.
Smurfit-Stone Container Corp.
Solo Cup Co.
Sonoco Products Co.
Sony Electronics
Sotheby's Inc.
South Bend Tribune Corp.
Southeastern Mutual Insurance Co.
Southern Co. Services Inc.
Southwest Gas Corp.
Sprint Corp.
Sprint/United Telephone
SPX Corp.
Standard Products Co.
Standard Register Co.
Stanley Works (The)
Starwood Hotels & Resorts Worldwide, Inc.
Steelcase Inc.
Stone Container Corp.
Stonecutter Mills Corp.
Storage Technology Corp.
Strear Farms Co.
Stride Rite Corp.
Student Loan Marketing Association
Sun Microsystems Inc.
SunTrust Bank Atlanta
Susquehanna-Pfaltzgraff Co.
Sverdrup Corp.
Synovus Financial Corp.
Tai and Co. (J.T.)
Tamko Roofing Products
Tampa Electric Co.
TCF National Bank Minnesota
Tektronix, Inc.
Teleflex Inc.
TENNANT Co.
Tenneco Packaging
Tension Envelope Corp.
Tesoro Hawaii
Textron Inc.
Thermo Electron Corp.
Thomasville Furniture Industries Inc.
Thompson Co. (J. Walter)
Ticketmaster Corp.
Times Mirror Co.
Timken Co. (The)
Titan Industrial Corp.
TJX Companies, Inc.
TMC Investment Co.
Toledo Blade Co.
Tomkins Industries, Inc.
Toro Co.
Trace International Holdings, Inc.
Transamerica Corp.
True North Communications, Inc.
True Oil Co.
Trustmark Insurance Co.
Trustmark National Bank
TRW Inc.
Tucson Electric Power Co.
Ukrop's Super Markets
Ultramar Diamond Shamrock Corp.
Unilever Home & Personal Care U.S.A.
Unilever United States, Inc.
Union Camp Corp.
Union Planters Corp.
United Distillers & Vintners North America

Funders by Recipient Type

United Dominion Industries, Ltd.
United Parcel Service of America Inc.
U.S. Bancorp
U.S. Bancorp Piper Jaffray
United States Sugar Corp.
Universal Foods Corp.
Universal Leaf Tobacco Co., Inc.
Universal Studios
UnumProvident
UPN Channel 50
US Bank, Washington
US West, Inc.
USG Corp.
USX Corp.
Valmont Industries, Inc.
Vesper Corp.
Vulcan Materials Co.
Wachovia Bank of North Carolina NA
Waffle House Inc.
Walter Industries Inc.
Warner-Lambert Co.
Washington Mutual, Inc.
Washington Trust Bank
Wausau Insurance Companies
Weil, Gotshal & Manges Corp.
Western & Southern Life Insurance Co.
Whirlpool Corp.
Whitman Corp.
WICOR, Inc.
Wilbur-Ellis Co. & Connell Brothers Co.
Winn-Dixie Stores Inc.
Wiremold Co.
Wisconsin Power & Light Co.
Wisconsin Public Service Corp.
Witco Corp.
Wolverine World Wide
Wrigley Co. (Wm. Jr.)
Wyman-Gordon Co.
York Federal Savings & Loan Association
Young & Rubicam
Zachry Co. (H.B.)
Zilkha & Sons
Zurn Industries, Inc.

HISPANIC AFFAIRS

Abbott Laboratories
Aetna, Inc.
Alcoa Inc.
Alcon Laboratories, Inc.
Allmerica Financial Corp.
Allstate Insurance Co.
AMCORE Bank Rockford
American Express Co.
American Retail Group
Ameritech Corp.
Amgen, Inc.
AMP Inc.
AMR Corp.
Anheuser-Busch Companies, Inc.
Archer-Daniels-Midland Co.
Arizona Public Service Co.
Arvin Industries, Inc.
AT&T Corp.
Atlantic Richfield Co.
Avon Products, Inc.
Badger Meter, Inc.
Bandag, Inc.
Banfi Vintners
Bank of America
Bank One Corp.
BankBoston Corp.
Bard, Inc. (C.R.)
Baxter International Inc.
Bechtel Group, Inc.
Ben & Jerry's Homemade Inc.
Bethlehem Steel Corp.
Binney & Smith Inc.
Borden, Inc.
Boston Globe (The)
BP Amoco Corp.
Broderbund Software, Inc.
Bucyrus-Erie Co.
Burlington Resources, Inc.
Burnett Co. (Leo)
Calvin Klein
Campbell Soup Co.
Carillon Importers, Ltd.
Carpenter Technology Corp.
CertainTeed Corp.
Charter Manufacturing Co.
Chase Bank of Texas
Chevron Corp.
Chicago Tribune Co.
CIGNA Corp.
Citigroup
Citizens Financial Group, Inc.
CLARCOR Inc.
Clorox Co.
Coca-Cola Co.
Compaq Computer Corp.
Coors Brewing Co.
Crane Co.
Daily News
Dayton Hudson
Delta Air Lines, Inc.
Deluxe Corp.
Disney Co. (Walt)
Dow Jones & Co., Inc.
Duchossois Industries Inc.
Eastern Bank
Ecolab Inc.
El Paso Energy Co.
Exxon Mobil Corp.
Fannie Mae
Ferro Corp.
First Union Bank
First Union Corp.
Firstar Bank Milwaukee NA
Fisher Brothers Cleaning Services
FleetBoston Financial Corp.
Fluor Corp.
Ford Motor Co.
Fortis Insurance Co.
Freddie Mac
Gallo Winery, Inc. (E&J)
Gap, Inc.
General Mills, Inc.
General Motors Corp.
Gerber Products Co.
Grede Foundries
GTE Corp.
Hallmark Cards Inc.
Hamilton Sundstrand Corp.
Harcourt General, Inc.
Harley-Davidson Co.
Harris Trust & Savings Bank
Harsco Corp.
Hartford (The)
Hartford Steam Boiler Inspection & Insurance Co.
Hitachi America Ltd.
Honeywell International Inc.
Humana, Inc.
International Multifoods Corp.
INTRUST Financial Corp.
Invacare Corp.
Jacobs Engineering Group
Johnson & Son (S.C.)
Journal-Gazette Co.
KPMG Peat Marwick LLP
Ladish Co., Inc.
Leigh Fibers, Inc.
Levi Strauss & Co.
Lilly & Co. (Eli)
Little, Inc. (Arthur D.)
Lotus Development Corp.
Marcus Corp.
Marshall Field's
Marshall & Ilsley Corp.
McDonald & Co. Securities, Inc.
McGraw-Hill Companies, Inc.
Medtronic, Inc.
Menasha Corp.
Merck & Co.
Metropolitan Life Insurance Co.
Millipore Corp.
Minnesota Mining & Manufacturing Co.
Montgomery Ward & Co., Inc.
MONY Group (The)
Morgan & Co. Inc. (J.P.)
Morgan Stanley Dean Witter & Co.
Morrison Knudsen Corp.
Nestle U.S.A. Inc.
New England Financial
New York Mercantile Exchange
Nordson Corp.
Northern States Power Co.
Northern Trust Co.
Norton Co.
Old National Bank Evansville
Pacific Mutual Life Insurance Co.
PacifiCare Health Systems
PEMCO Corp.
Penney Co., Inc. (J.C.)
PepsiCo, Inc.
PerkinElmer, Inc.
Pfizer Inc.
Physicians Mutual Insurance Co.
Pieper Power Electric Co.
Pillsbury Co.
Praxair
Prudential Insurance Co. of America
Ralph's Grocery Co.
Reebok International Ltd.
Reynolds Tobacco (R.J.)
Rockwell International Corp.
Saint Paul Companies Inc.
Sara Lee Corp.
SBC Communications Inc.
Schering-Plough Corp.
Schwab & Co., Inc. (Charles)
Schwebel Baking Co.
Security Benefit Life Insurance Co.
Shea Co. (John F.)
Shell Oil Co.
Sierra Pacific Resources
Simplot Co. (J.R.)
Southwest Gas Corp.
Sovereign Bank
Sprint Corp.
State Street Bank & Trust Co.
Steelcase Inc.
Stone Container Corp.
Stride Rite Corp.
Tektronix, Inc.
Texas Instruments Inc.
Times Mirror Co.
TJX Companies, Inc.
Toyota Motor Sales U.S.A., Inc.
Unilever Home & Personal Care U.S.A.
Union Carbide Corp.
United Parcel Service of America Inc.
Unocal Corp.
US Bank, Washington
US West, Inc.
USG Corp.
Waffle House Inc.
Warner-Lambert Co.
Washington Mutual, Inc.
Whirlpool Corp.
Whitman Corp.
WICOR, Inc.
Wisconsin Energy Corp.
Wrigley Co. (Wm. Jr.)
York Federal Savings & Loan Association
Young & Rubicam

HOUSING

Abbott Laboratories
ABC
AEGON U.S.A. Inc.
AGL Resources Inc.
Agrilink Foods, Inc.
Air Products and Chemicals, Inc.
AK Steel Corp.
Alcoa Inc.
Alexander & Baldwin, Inc.
Allianz Life Insurance Co. of North America
AlliedSignal Inc.
Allmerica Financial Corp.
Allstate Insurance Co.
AMCORE Bank Rockford
Ameren Corp.
American Express Co.
American General Finance
American Retail Group
American Standard Inc.
Ameritas Life Insurance Corp.
Ameritech Corp.
Ameritech Illinois
AmerUS Group
Amgen, Inc.
AMP Inc.
Amsted Industries Inc.
Andersen Corp.
Andersons Inc.
Anheuser-Busch Companies, Inc.
Arizona Public Service Co.
Armstrong World Industries, Inc.
Arvin Industries, Inc.
AT&T Corp.
Atlantic Investment Co.
Atlantic Richfield Co.
Auburn Foundry
Badger Meter, Inc.
Bandag, Inc.
Bank of America
Bank of New York Co., Inc.
Bank One Corp.
Bank One, Texas-Houston Office
BankAtlantic Bancorp
BankBoston-Connecticut Region
BankBoston Corp.
Barclays Capital
Bard, Inc. (C.R.)
Barnes Group Inc.
Bausch & Lomb Inc.
Baxter International Inc.
Belk Stores Services Inc.
Ben & Jerry's Homemade Inc.
Bernstein & Co., Inc. (Sanford C.)
Bethlehem Steel Corp.
Block, Inc. (H&R)
Blue Bell, Inc.
Blue Cross & Blue Shield of Alabama
Blue Cross & Blue Shield of Minnesota
Boeing Co.
Borman's Inc.
Boston Edison Co.
Boston Globe (The)
BP Amoco Corp.
Bradford & Co. (J.C.)
Bridgestone/Firestone, Inc.
Bristol-Myers Squibb Co.
Brown Shoe Co., Inc.
Bucyrus-Erie Co.
Burlington Industries, Inc.
Burlington Resources, Inc.
Burnett Co. (Leo)
California Bank & Trust
Calvin Klein
Campbell Soup Co.
Cargill Inc.
Carolina Power & Light Co.
Carpenter Technology Corp.
Carter-Wallace, Inc.
Caterpillar Inc.
CCB Financial Corp.
Central Maine Power Co.
Central & South West Services
CertainTeed Corp.
Cessna Aircraft Co.
CGU Insurance
Chase Bank of Texas
Chase Manhattan Bank, NA
Chemed Corp.
Chesapeake Corp.
Chevron Corp.
Chicago Title Corp.
Chicago Tribune Co.
CIBC Oppenheimer
Cincinnati Bell Inc.
Circuit City Stores, Inc.
CIT Group, Inc. (The)
Citigroup
Citizens Bank-Flint
Citizens Financial Group, Inc.
CLARCOR Inc.
CNA
Colonial Life & Accident Insurance Co.
Colonial Oil Industries, Inc.
Commerce Bancshares, Inc.
Commonwealth Edison Co.
ConAgra, Inc.
Cone Mills Corp.
Consolidated Natural Gas Co.
Consolidated Papers, Inc.
Constellation Energy Group, Inc.
Consumers Energy Co.
Contran Corp.
Conwood Co. LP
Cooper Industries, Inc.
Cox Enterprises Inc.
CPI Corp.
Crane Co.
Crestar Finance Corp.
Croft-Leominster
Cummings Properties Management
Cummins Engine Co., Inc.
CUNA Mutual Group
Daily News
DaimlerChrysler Corp.
Dain Bosworth Inc.

Dana Corp.
Dayton Hudson
Dayton Power and Light Co.
Demoulas Supermarkets Inc.
Deposit Guaranty National Bank
Detroit Edison Co.
Dial Corp.
Dixie Group, Inc. (The)
Dominion Resources, Inc.
Donaldson Co., Inc.
du Pont de Nemours & Co. (E.I.)
Duchossois Industries Inc.
Duke Energy
Duriron Co., Inc.
Dynamet, Inc.
Eastern Bank
Eastman Kodak Co.
Eaton Corp.
Ecolab Inc.
Edison International
Edwards Enterprise Software (J.D.)
Employers Mutual Casualty Co.
Enterprise Rent-A-Car Co.
Equifax Inc.
Equitable Resources, Inc.
Erb Lumber Co.
Erving Industries
Exxon Mobil Corp.
Fannie Mae
Federal-Mogul Corp.
Federated Mutual Insurance Co.
Fidelity Investments
Fifth Third Bancorp
Fireman's Fund Insurance Co.
First American Corp.
First Financial Bank
First Hawaiian, Inc.
First Maryland Bancorp
First Source Corp.
First Union Bank
First Union Corp.
First Union National Bank, NA
First Union Securities, Inc.
Firstar Bank Milwaukee NA
Fisher Brothers Cleaning Services
Fisher Scientific
FleetBoston Financial Corp.
Florida Power Corp.
Fluor Corp.
Forbes Inc.
Ford Meter Box Co.
Ford Motor Co.
Forest City Enterprises, Inc.
Fort James Corp.
Fort Worth Star-Telegram Inc.
Fortis Insurance Co.
Freddie Mac
Freeport-McMoRan Inc.
Fuji Bank & Trust Co.
Fuller Co. (H.B.)
Furniture Brands International, Inc.
Gap, Inc.
GATX Corp.
GEICO Corp.
GenCorp
General Electric Co.
General Mills, Inc.
General Motors Corp.
General Reinsurance Corp.
Georgia Power Co.
Gerber Products Co.
Giant Food Inc.
Giddings & Lewis
Glickenhaus & Co.
Globe Corp.
Golub Corp.
Grace & Co. (W.R.)
Graco, Inc.
Grede Foundries
Gulf Power Co.
Hallmark Cards Inc.
Hamilton Sundstrand Corp.
Harley-Davidson Co.
Harnischfeger Industries
Harris Corp.
Harris Trust & Savings Bank
Harsco Corp.
Hartford (The)
Hartford Steam Boiler Inspection & Insurance Co.
Hartmarx Corp.
Hasbro, Inc.
Hawaiian Electric Co., Inc.
Heinz Co. (H.J.)
Hensel Phelps Construction Co.
Hickory Tech Corp.
Hitachi America Ltd.
Hoffer Plastics Corp.
Home Depot, Inc.
Honeywell International Inc.
Household International Inc.
Hubbard Broadcasting, Inc.
Hubbell Inc.
Huffy Corp.
Humana, Inc.
Huntington Bancshares Inc.
Illinois Tool Works, Inc.
Independent Stave Co.
Industrial Bank of Japan Trust Co. (New York)
INTRUST Financial Corp.
Jacobs Engineering Group
Jacobson & Sons (Benjamin)
Jeld-wen, Inc.
Johnson Controls Inc.
Johnson & Son (S.C.)
Jones & Co. (Edward D.)
Jostens, Inc.
Kimball International, Inc.
Koch Enterprises, Inc.
Kroger Co.
La-Z-Boy Inc.
Ladish Co., Inc.
Lance, Inc.
Land O'Lakes, Inc.
LandAmerica Financial Services
Landmark Communications Inc.
Lennox International, Inc.
Levi Strauss & Co.
LG&E Energy Corp.
Liberty Corp.
Lilly & Co. (Eli)
Lincoln Financial Group
Little, Inc. (Arthur D.)
Liz Claiborne, Inc.
Lotus Development Corp.
Louisiana-Pacific Corp.
Madison Gas & Electric Co.
Marcus Corp.
Marshall & Ilsley Corp.
Mattel Inc.
May Department Stores Co.
MBIA Inc.
McClatchy Co.
McGraw-Hill Companies, Inc.
MCI WorldCom, Inc.
Medtronic, Inc.
Mellon Financial Corp.
Memphis Light Gas & Water Division
Menasha Corp.
Meredith Corp.
Merrill Lynch & Co., Inc.
Metropolitan Life Insurance Co.
Michigan Consolidated Gas Co.
Mid-America Bank of Louisville
MidAmerican Energy Holdings Co.
Minnesota Mutual Life Insurance Co.
Mitsubishi Electric America
Monsanto Co.
Montana Power Co.
Montgomery Ward & Co., Inc.
MONY Group (The)
Morgan & Co. Inc. (J.P.)
Morgan Stanley Dean Witter & Co.
Morrison Knudsen Corp.
Motorola Inc.
MTD Products Inc.
Nalco Chemical Co.
National Bank of Commerce Trust & Savings
National City Bank of Minneapolis
National City Corp.
National Machinery Co.
National Presto Industries, Inc.
National Starch & Chemical Co.
Nationwide Insurance Co.
NEBCO Evans
Nestle U.S.A. Inc.
New England Financial
New York Mercantile Exchange
New York Times Co.
Newman's Own Inc.
Niagara Mohawk Holdings Inc.
Nissan North America, Inc.
Nordson Corp.
Norfolk Southern Corp.
Northeast Utilities
Northern States Power Co.
Northern Trust Co.
Northwest Bank Nebraska, NA
Northwest Natural Gas Co.
Norwest Corp.
Occidental Oil and Gas
Ohio National Life Insurance Co.
Old Kent Bank
Old National Bank Evansville
Oshkosh B'Gosh, Inc.
Outboard Marine Corp.
Owens Corning
PACCAR Inc.
Pacific Century Financial Corp.
Pacific Mutual Life Insurance Co.
PacifiCorp
Park National Bank
PECO Energy Co.
Pella Corp.
PEMCO Corp.
Peoples Bank
Peoples Energy Corp.
PepsiCo, Inc.
PerkinElmer, Inc.
Pfizer Inc.
Pharmacia & Upjohn, Inc.
Phoenix Home Life Mutual Insurance Co.
Physicians Mutual Insurance Co.
Pieper Power Electric Co.
Pillsbury Co.
Pitney Bowes Inc.
Pittway Corp.
PNC Bank
PNC Bank Kentucky Inc.
PNC Financial Services Group
Polaroid Corp.
Portland General Electric Co.
PPG Industries, Inc.
Price Associates (T. Rowe)
Principal Financial Group
Procter & Gamble Co.
Procter & Gamble Co., Cosmetics Division
Providence Journal-Bulletin Co.
Provident Companies, Inc.
Prudential Insurance Co. of America
Prudential Securities Inc.
Public Service Electric & Gas Co.
Putnam Investments
Ralph's Grocery Co.
Ralston Purina Co.
Red Wing Shoe Co. Inc.
Regions Bank
Regis Corp.
Reilly Industries, Inc.
Reily & Co., Inc. (William B.)
Reliant Energy Minnegasco
Reynolds Metals Co.
Reynolds Tobacco (R.J.)
Rockwell International Corp.
Rouse Co.
Royal & SunAlliance USA, Inc.
Rubbermaid Inc.
Ruddick Corp.
Ryder System, Inc.
SAFECO Corp.
Safeguard Scientifics
Saint Paul Companies Inc.
Sara Lee Corp.
Schering-Plough Corp.
Schwab & Co., Inc. (Charles)
Scripps Co. (E.W.)
Security Benefit Life Insurance Co.
Sentinel Communications Co.
Sentry Insurance, A Mutual Co.
Shea Co. (John F.)
Shell Oil Co.
Shelter Mutual Insurance Co.
SIT Investment Associates, Inc.
Slant/Fin Corp.
Sonoco Products Co.
Southwest Gas Corp.
Sovereign Bank
SPX Corp.
Standard Products Co.
Stanley Works (The)
Star Bank NA
Starwood Hotels & Resorts Worldwide, Inc.
State Street Bank & Trust Co.
Steelcase Inc.
Stonecutter Mills Corp.
Storage Technology Corp.
Sun Microsystems Inc.
SunTrust Bank Atlanta
Synovus Financial Corp.
Tamko Roofing Products
TCF National Bank Minnesota
Teleflex Inc.
Temple-Inland Inc.
TENNANT Co.
Tenneco Automotive
Tension Envelope Corp.
Tesoro Hawaii
Texaco Inc.
Texas Gas Transmission Corp.
Textron Inc.
Thomasville Furniture Industries Inc.
Times Mirror Co.
Timken Co. (The)
TJX Companies, Inc.
Toledo Blade Co.
Tomkins Industries, Inc.
Transamerica Corp.
True Oil Co.
Ukrop's Super Markets
Unilever Home & Personal Care U.S.A.
United Airlines Inc.
United Distillers & Vintners North America
United Dominion Industries, Ltd.
United Parcel Service of America Inc.
U.S. Bancorp
U.S. Bancorp Piper Jaffray
United States Sugar Corp.
United States Trust Co. of New York
Universal Leaf Tobacco Co., Inc.
Universal Studios
Unocal Corp.
US Bank, Washington
USG Corp.
Valspar Corp.
Van Leer Holding
Vodafone AirTouch Plc
Wachovia Bank of North Carolina NA
Waffle House Inc.
Wal-Mart Stores, Inc.
Washington Mutual, Inc.
Washington Trust Bank
Webster Bank
Wells Fargo & Co.
Western & Southern Life Insurance Co.
Westvaco Corp.
Weyerhaeuser Co.
Whirlpool Corp.
WICOR, Inc.
Williams
Wiremold Co.
Wisconsin Energy Corp.
Wisconsin Public Service Corp.
Woodward Governor Co.
Wrigley Co. (Wm. Jr.)
Wyman-Gordon Co.
Xerox Corp.
York Federal Savings & Loan Association
Zachry Co. (H.B.)

INNER-CITY DEVELOPMENT

Allstate Insurance Co.
Atlantic Investment Co.
Bandag, Inc.
CIBC Oppenheimer
Citizens Bank-Flint
Equitable Resources, Inc.

Fuji Bank & Trust Co.
Harley-Davidson Co.
Huntington Bancshares Inc.
McDonald & Co. Securities, Inc.
New England Bio Labs
New York Mercantile Exchange
Nissan North America, Inc.
Ohio National Life Insurance Co.
Old National Bank Evansville
Regions Bank
ServiceMaster Co.
Sovereign Bank
US Bank, Washington

LAW & JUSTICE

Abbott Laboratories
Aetna, Inc.
AGL Resources Inc.
Alcoa Inc.
Allegheny Technologies Inc.
AlliedSignal Inc.
Allstate Insurance Co.
Ameritech Illinois
Ameritech Michigan
Ameritech Wisconsin
Amsted Industries Inc.
Anheuser-Busch Companies, Inc.
Aon Corp.
Archer-Daniels-Midland Co.
Aristech Chemical Corp.
Ashland, Inc.
Atlantic Investment Co.
Avon Products, Inc.
Badger Meter, Inc.
Baird & Co. (Robert W.)
Bank One Corp.
Bank One, Texas-Houston Office
Ben & Jerry's Homemade Inc.
Bestfoods
Bethlehem Steel Corp.
BFGoodrich Co.
Blair & Co. (William)
Block, Inc. (H&R)
Blue Bell, Inc.
Borden, Inc.
Boston Edison Co.
BP Amoco Corp.
Bridgestone/Firestone, Inc.
Bristol-Myers Squibb Co.
Brown & Williamson Tobacco Corp.
Burlington Industries, Inc.
Burnett Co. (Leo)
Business Improvement
Cabot Corp.
Campbell Soup Co.
Cantor, Fitzgerald Securities Corp.
Cargill Inc.
Carter-Wallace, Inc.
Caterpillar Inc.
CertainTeed Corp.
Chase Manhattan Bank, NA
Chevron Corp.
Chicago Title Corp.
CIGNA Corp.
Citizens Financial Group, Inc.
Clorox Co.
CNA
Colonial Life & Accident Insurance Co.
Colonial Oil Industries, Inc.
Constellation Energy Group, Inc.
Cooper Industries, Inc.
Copley Press, Inc.
Crane Co.
Credit Suisse First Boston
Deposit Guaranty National Bank
Deutsch Co.
Dial Corp.
Disney Co. (Walt)
du Pont de Nemours & Co. (E.I.)
Dun & Bradstreet Corp.
Eaton Corp.
Ecolab Inc.
Edison International
Elf Atochem North America, Inc.
Emerson Electric Co.
Exxon Mobil Corp.
Federal-Mogul Corp.
Fifth Third Bancorp
First Hawaiian, Inc.
First Union Bank
First Union National Bank, NA
Fisher Scientific
FleetBoston Financial Corp.
FMC Corp.
Ford Meter Box Co.
Ford Motor Co.
Fort Worth Star-Telegram Inc.
Freddie Mac
GEICO Corp.
General Atlantic Partners II LP
General Electric Co.
General Mills, Inc.
General Motors Corp.
General Reinsurance Corp.
Georgia-Pacific Corp.
Giant Eagle Inc.
Giant Food Inc.
Glickenhaus & Co.
Goodrich Aerospace - Aerostructures Group (B.F.)
Grace & Co. (W.R.)
GTE Corp.
Guardian Life Insurance Co. of America
Hancock Financial Services (John)
Hanna Co. (M.A.)
Harsco Corp.
Hartford (The)
Hartmarx Corp.
Hasbro, Inc.
Heinz Co. (H.J.)
Hensel Phelps Construction Co.
Hewlett-Packard Co.
Hitachi America Ltd.
Hofmann Co.
Illinois Tool Works, Inc.
Johnson & Son (S.C.)
Katten, Muchin & Zavis
Kerr-McGee Corp.
Kimberly-Clark Corp.
Kirkland & Ellis
Lee Enterprises
LG&E Energy Corp.
Liberty Diversified Industries
Lilly & Co. (Eli)
Lincoln Electric Co.
Lipton Co.
Litton Industries, Inc.
Liz Claiborne, Inc.
Louisiana Land & Exploration Co.
LTV Corp.
Macy's East Inc.
McCormick & Co. Inc.
McDonald & Co. Securities, Inc.
McGraw-Hill Companies, Inc.
McWane Inc.
Metropolitan Life Insurance Co.
Milliken & Co.
MONY Group (The)
Morgan & Co. Inc. (J.P.)
Morris Communications Corp.
Motorola Inc.
MTD Products Inc.
Nalco Chemical Co.
National City Bank of Minneapolis
National Computer Systems, Inc.
National Machinery Co.
Nationwide Insurance Co.
New York Life Insurance Co.
New York Times Co.
Norfolk Southern Corp.
Northeast Utilities
Northern Trust Co.
Norwest Corp.
Ohio National Life Insurance Co.
Overseas Shipholding Group Inc.
PACCAR Inc.
Pacific Mutual Life Insurance Co.
PECO Energy Co.
Peoples Energy Corp.
PerkinElmer, Inc.
Pfizer Inc.
Phelps Dodge Corp.
Phillips Petroleum Co.
Pittway Corp.
Playboy Enterprises Inc.
Polaroid Corp.
PPG Industries, Inc.
Procter & Gamble Co., Cosmetics Division
Prudential Insurance Co. of America
Prudential Securities Inc.
Public Service Electric & Gas Co.
Quanex Corp.
Red Wing Shoe Co. Inc.
Regions Bank
Reliant Energy Inc.
Reynolds Tobacco (R.J.)
Rockwell International Corp.
Rubbermaid Inc.
Salomon Smith Barney
Sara Lee Corp.
Searle & Co. (G.D.)
Shea Co. (John F.)
Shell Oil Co.
Slant/Fin Corp.
Southwest Gas Corp.
Sprint Corp.
State Farm Mutual Automobile Insurance Co.
State Street Bank & Trust Co.
Stone Container Corp.
Stride Rite Corp.
Sun Microsystems Inc.
Sunmark Capital Corp.
SunTrust Bank Atlanta
SuperValu, Inc.
Tamko Roofing Products
TCF National Bank Minnesota
Temple-Inland Inc.
Tenneco Automotive
Texaco Inc.
Textron Inc.
Timken Co. (The)
TJX Companies, Inc.
True Oil Co.
Union Camp Corp.
Union Carbide Corp.
United Dominion Industries, Ltd.
United States Sugar Corp.
United Technologies Corp.
Universal Studios
Unocal Corp.
UnumProvident
US West, Inc.
USG Corp.
UST Inc.
USX Corp.
Wachtell, Lipton, Rosen & Katz
Wal-Mart Stores, Inc.
Weil, Gotshal & Manges Corp.
Whirlpool Corp.
Williams
Winn-Dixie Stores Inc.
Witco Corp.
Woodward Governor Co.

LEGAL AID

Alcoa Inc.
Allegheny Technologies Inc.
American Standard Inc.
American United Life Insurance Co.
Amsted Industries Inc.
Andersen Corp.
Archer-Daniels-Midland Co.
Avon Products, Inc.
Bank of America
Barnes Group Inc.
Bechtel Group, Inc.
Bernstein & Co., Inc. (Sanford C.)
Bethlehem Steel Corp.
Block, Inc. (H&R)
Brunswick Corp.
Cabot Corp.
Calvin Klein
Cargill Inc.
Carpenter Technology Corp.
CertainTeed Corp.
Chase Manhattan Bank, NA
Chevron Corp.
Chicago Title Corp.
CIBC Oppenheimer
Clark Refining & Marketing
Clorox Co.
Colonial Life & Accident Insurance Co.
Colonial Oil Industries, Inc.
Commerce Bancshares, Inc.
Compass Bank
Continental Grain Co.
Crane Co.
Cummins Engine Co., Inc.
Dayton Hudson
Deutsch Co.
Dexter Corp.
Disney Co. (Walt)
du Pont de Nemours & Co. (E.I.)
Duke Energy
Eaton Corp.
Ensign-Bickford Industries
Equifax Inc.
Fidelity Investments
Fireman's Fund Insurance Co.
First National Bank of Evergreen Park
First Union Bank
First Union National Bank, NA
Florida Power Corp.
Forbes Inc.
Fortis Insurance Co.
Fortune Brands, Inc.
Freddie Mac
Freeport-McMoRan Inc.
Fuller Co. (H.B.)
Gap, Inc.
GenCorp
General Atlantic Partners II LP
General Mills, Inc.
Georgia Power Co.
Gerber Products Co.
Giant Eagle Inc.
Glickenhaus & Co.
Grede Foundries
Harcourt General, Inc.
Harsco Corp.
Hartmarx Corp.
Hasbro, Inc.
Hawaiian Electric Co., Inc.
Heinz Co. (H.J.)
Hensel Phelps Construction Co.
Hofmann Co.
HON Industries Inc.
Humana, Inc.
Hunt Manufacturing Co.
Illinois Tool Works, Inc.
Jostens, Inc.
Katten, Muchin & Zavis
Kerr-McGee Corp.
Kimball International, Inc.
Kimberly-Clark Corp.
Levi Strauss & Co.
Liberty Corp.
Lipton Co.
Little, Inc. (Arthur D.)
Litton Industries, Inc.
Loews Corp.
Macy's East Inc.
Masco Corp.
McKesson-HBOC Corp.
Millipore Corp.
Minnesota Mining & Manufacturing Co.
Minnesota Mutual Life Insurance Co.
Montgomery Ward & Co., Inc.
Morgan & Co. Inc. (J.P.)
Morris Communications Corp.
Morrison Knudsen Corp.
Motorola Inc.
Nalco Chemical Co.
National City Bank of Minneapolis
National Machinery Co.
New England Bio Labs
New York Life Insurance Co.
Nordson Corp.
Northeast Utilities
Northern States Power Co.
Norton Co.
Norwest Corp.
Occidental Oil and Gas
Pacific Mutual Life Insurance Co.
PerkinElmer, Inc.
Pfizer Inc.
Philip Morris Companies Inc.
Phillips Petroleum Co.
Playboy Enterprises Inc.
PNC Financial Services Group
Praxair

Providence Journal-Bulletin Co.
Prudential Insurance Co. of America
Questar Corp.
Ralph's Grocery Co.
Reebok International Ltd.
Reynolds Tobacco (R.J.)
Rockwell International Corp.
Salomon Smith Barney
Sara Lee Corp.
Schlumberger Ltd. (USA)
Seagram & Sons, Inc. (Joseph E.)
Searle & Co. (G.D.)
Sempra Energy
Shea Co. (John F.)
Simplot Co. (J.R.)
Southwest Gas Corp.
Sprint Corp.
Sprint/United Telephone
Square D Co.
Stone Container Corp.
Sunmark Capital Corp.
SunTrust Bank Atlanta
Texaco Inc.
Textron Inc.
Thermo Electron Corp.
Times Mirror Co.
Titan Industrial Corp.
Toro Co.
Trace International Holdings, Inc.
Transamerica Corp.
True Oil Co.
Union Camp Corp.
Union Carbide Corp.
United States Sugar Corp.
United States Trust Co. of New York
Unocal Corp.
UnumProvident
USG Corp.
Washington Trust Bank
Weil, Gotshal & Manges Corp.
Weyerhaeuser Co.
WICOR, Inc.
Williams
Winn-Dixie Stores Inc.
Woodward Governor Co.
Wyman-Gordon Co.

MINORITY BUSINESS

ABC
Aetna, Inc.
AMCORE Bank Rockford
American Express Co.
AMP Inc.
AMR Corp.
Atlantic Richfield Co.
Barnes Group Inc.
Bechtel Group, Inc.
Bethlehem Steel Corp.
Burlington Industries, Inc.
Campbell Soup Co.
Cargill Inc.
Chicago Tribune Co.
CLARCOR Inc.
Clark Refining & Marketing
Crane Co.
CUNA Mutual Group
DaimlerChrysler Corp.
Dayton Hudson
Dexter Corp.
Edison Brothers Stores, Inc.
Exxon Mobil Corp.
Fifth Third Bancorp
First Source Corp.
First Union Bank
Freddie Mac
Freeport-McMoRan Inc.
General Motors Corp.
Hasbro, Inc.
Hofmann Co.
HON Industries Inc.
Huntington Bancshares Inc.
Levi Strauss & Co.
Minnesota Mutual Life Insurance Co.
Mutual of Omaha Insurance Co.
Nestle U.S.A. Inc.
Norton Co.
Old National Bank Evansville
Olin Corp.
PepsiCo, Inc.
Polaroid Corp.
Praxair
Putnam Investments
Schlumberger Ltd. (USA)
Scripps Co. (E.W.)
Square D Co.
Times Mirror Co.
Unilever Home & Personal Care U.S.A.
Union Carbide Corp.
United States Trust Co. of New York
Unocal Corp.
Wal-Mart Stores, Inc.
Washington Trust Bank
York Federal Savings & Loan Association

MUNICIPALITIES/TOWNS

ABC
Air Products and Chemicals, Inc.
Alcoa Inc.
American Fidelity Corp.
American General Finance
AMETEK, Inc.
AMP Inc.
AMR Corp.
Andersen Corp.
Andersons Inc.
APL Ltd.
Arizona Public Service Co.
Arvin Industries, Inc.
Ashland, Inc.
Badger Meter, Inc.
Baird & Co. (Robert W.)
Bandag, Inc.
Bank One, Texas-Houston Office
BankBoston Corp.
Bard, Inc. (C.R.)
Barden Corp.
Barnes Group Inc.
Baxter International Inc.
Belo Corp. (A.H.)
Ben & Jerry's Homemade Inc.
Bestfoods
Bethlehem Steel Corp.
BFGoodrich Co.
Blair & Co. (William)
Blount International, Inc.
Blue Bell, Inc.
Borden, Inc.
Boston Edison Co.
Briggs & Stratton Corp.
Bristol-Myers Squibb Co.
Browning-Ferris Industries Inc.
Bucyrus-Erie Co.
Burlington Industries, Inc.
Burnett Co. (Leo)
Cabot Corp.
Carnival Corp.
Carolina Power & Light Co.
Caterpillar Inc.
Central Soya Co.
CertainTeed Corp.
Chase Bank of Texas
Chase Manhattan Bank, NA
Chesapeake Corp.
Chevron Corp.
Chicago Tribune Co.
CIBC Oppenheimer
Cincinnati Bell Inc.
Cinergy Corp.
CIT Group, Inc. (The)
Citigroup
Cleveland-Cliffs, Inc.
Clorox Co.
Collins & Aikman Corp.
Commerce Bancshares, Inc.
Commercial Intertech Corp.
Compass Bank
ConAgra, Inc.
Cone Mills Corp.
Consolidated Natural Gas Co.
Consolidated Papers, Inc.
Cooper Industries, Inc.
Corning Inc.
Credit Suisse First Boston
Cummings Properties Management
Cummins Engine Co., Inc.
CUNA Mutual Group
Daily News
DaimlerChrysler Corp.
Dain Bosworth Inc.
Dana Corp.
Dayton Power and Light Co.
Deere & Co.
DeKalb Genetics Corp.
Delta Air Lines, Inc.
Demoulas Supermarkets Inc.
Detroit Edison Co.
Deutsch Co.
Dexter Corp.
Dow Corning Corp.
du Pont de Nemours & Co. (E.I.)
Duke Energy
Dun & Bradstreet Corp.
Eaton Corp.
Elf Atochem North America, Inc.
Employers Mutual Casualty Co.
Ensign-Bickford Industries
Equifax Inc.
Equitable Resources, Inc.
Erb Lumber Co.
Erving Industries
Federated Mutual Insurance Co.
Ferro Corp.
Fifth Third Bancorp
Fireman's Fund Insurance Co.
First Financial Bank
First Source Corp.
First Union Bank
First Union Corp.
First Union Securities, Inc.
Fisher Brothers Cleaning Services
Florida Power & Light Co.
Ford Meter Box Co.
Forest City Enterprises, Inc.
Fort Worth Star-Telegram Inc.
Freeport-McMoRan Inc.
Furniture Brands International, Inc.
Gallo Winery, Inc. (E&J)
Gap, Inc.
GenAmerica Corp.
GenCorp
General Atlantic Partners II LP
General Mills, Inc.
General Motors Corp.
Georgia-Pacific Corp.
Georgia Power Co.
Giant Eagle Inc.
Giddings & Lewis
Glickenhaus & Co.
Goldman Sachs Group
Hallmark Cards Inc.
Hanna Co. (M.A.)
Harcourt General, Inc.
Harnischfeger Industries
Harris Trust & Savings Bank
Hasbro, Inc.
Hewlett-Packard Co.
Hitachi America Ltd.
Hoffer Plastics Corp.
Hofmann Co.
HON Industries Inc.
Hubbard Broadcasting, Inc.
Huffy Corp.
IKON Office Solutions, Inc.
International Multifoods Corp.
International Paper Co.
Invacare Corp.
Jacobson & Sons (Benjamin)
Jeld-wen, Inc.
Johnson & Son (S.C.)
Journal-Gazette Co.
JSJ Corp.
Kellogg Co.
Kimberly-Clark Corp.
Kinder Morgn
Koch Enterprises, Inc.
Kroger Co.
La-Z-Boy Inc.
Lancaster Lens, Inc.
Lance, Inc.
LandAmerica Financial Services
Lee Enterprises
Lehigh Portland Cement Co.
Lennox International, Inc.
Levi Strauss & Co.
Liberty Corp.
Liberty Diversified Industries
Lilly & Co. (Eli)
Lincoln Electric Co.
Lincoln Financial Group
Little, Inc. (Arthur D.)
Loews Corp.
Louisiana Land & Exploration Co.
Louisiana-Pacific Corp.
LTV Corp.
Mallinckrodt Chemical, Inc.
Marcus Corp.
Maritz Inc.
May Department Stores Co.
MBIA Inc.
McDonald & Co. Securities, Inc.
Mead Corp.
Medtronic, Inc.
Meijer, Inc.
Mercantile Bank NA
Merrill Lynch & Co., Inc.
Metropolitan Life Insurance Co.
Mid-America Bank of Louisville
Milliken & Co.
Millipore Corp.
Minnesota Mining & Manufacturing Co.
Monsanto Co.
Morgan & Co. Inc. (J.P.)
Morris Communications Corp.
National City Bank of Minneapolis
National City Corp.
National Machinery Co.
National Presto Industries, Inc.
National Service Industries, Inc.
New York Life Insurance Co.
New York Stock Exchange, Inc.
Northern States Power Co.
Norton Co.
Norwest Corp.
OG&E Electric Services
Old National Bank Evansville
PACCAR Inc.
Pacific Mutual Life Insurance Co.
Paine Webber
Park National Bank
Parker Hannifin Corp.
Pella Corp.
Pfizer Inc.
Pharmacia & Upjohn, Inc.
Phillips Petroleum Co.
Pillsbury Co.
PNC Financial Services Group
Polaroid Corp.
Potomac Electric Power Co.
PPG Industries, Inc.
Premier Dental Products Co.
Premier Industrial Corp.
Procter & Gamble Co.
Procter & Gamble Co., Cosmetics Division
Providence Journal-Bulletin Co.
Prudential Insurance Co. of America
Prudential Securities Inc.
Publix Supermarkets
Quanex Corp.
Ralston Purina Co.
Rayonier Inc.
Reader's Digest Association, Inc. (The)
Red Wing Shoe Co. Inc.
Reebok International Ltd.
Reily & Co., Inc. (William B.)
Reliant Energy Inc.
Reynolds Metals Co.
Reynolds & Reynolds Co.
Reynolds Tobacco (R.J.)
Rockwell International Corp.
Russer Foods
Safeguard Scientifics
S&T Bancorp
SBC Communications Inc.
Seagram & Sons, Inc. (Joseph E.)
Sherwin-Williams Co.
Sierra Pacific Resources
Simpson Investment Co.
SmithKline Beecham Corp.
Smurfit-Stone Container Corp.
Sonoco Products Co.
South Bend Tribune Corp.
Southeastern Mutual Insurance Co.
Sovereign Bank
SPX Corp.
Standard Products Co.
Star Bank NA
State Street Bank & Trust Co.
Stonecutter Mills Corp.
Stupp Brothers Bridge & Iron Co.

Sun Microsystems Inc.
SunTrust Bank Atlanta
Synovus Financial Corp.
TCF National Bank Minnesota
Temple-Inland Inc.
Tenneco Packaging
Texaco Inc.
Textron Inc.
Thermo Electron Corp.
Thompson Co. (J. Walter)
Times Mirror Co.
Timken Co. (The)
TJX Companies, Inc.
TMC Investment Co.
Toledo Blade Co.
Tomkins Industries, Inc.
Trace International Holdings, Inc.
TRW Inc.
Tyson Foods Inc.
Ukrop's Super Markets
Unilever Home & Personal Care U.S.A.
Unilever United States, Inc.
Union Camp Corp.
United States Sugar Corp.
Universal Leaf Tobacco Co., Inc.
UnumProvident
Vesper Corp.
Vulcan Materials Co.
Wachovia Bank of North Carolina NA
Wachtell, Lipton, Rosen & Katz
Wal-Mart Stores, Inc.
Walgreen Co.
Washington Trust Bank
Waste Management Inc.
Weil, Gotshal & Manges Corp.
Weyerhaeuser Co.
Whirlpool Corp.
Wilbur-Ellis Co. & Connell Brothers Co.
Wisconsin Power & Light Co.
Wisconsin Public Service Corp.
Young & Rubicam
Zachry Co. (H.B.)

NATIVE AMERICAN AFFAIRS

American Fidelity Corp.
Archer-Daniels-Midland Co.
Arizona Public Service Co.
Avon Products, Inc.
Bandag, Inc.
Bank of America
Baxter International Inc.
Ben & Jerry's Homemade Inc.
Broderbund Software, Inc.
Bucyrus-Erie Co.
Burlington Resources, Inc.
Cargill Inc.
Carillon Importers, Ltd.
Carris Reels
Chicago Tribune Co.
Coca-Cola Co.
Cook Inlet Region
Coors Brewing Co.
Country Curtains, Inc.
Crane & Co., Inc.
Dain Bosworth Inc.
Dayton Hudson
Deluxe Corp.
Dial Corp.
Disney Co. (Walt)
Dow Jones & Co., Inc.
Eastern Bank
Edwards Enterprise Software (J.D.)
El Paso Energy Co.
Fidelity Investments
FleetBoston Financial Corp.
General Atlantic Partners II LP
General Mills, Inc.
Graco, Inc.
Harris Trust & Savings Bank
Hitachi America Ltd.
Honeywell International Inc.
Housatonic Curtain Co.
IBP
IKON Office Solutions, Inc.
Intel Corp.
Invacare Corp.
Lehigh Portland Cement Co.
Leigh Fibers, Inc.
Levi Strauss & Co.
McClatchy Co.
Mead Corp.
Millipore Corp.
Minnesota Mining & Manufacturing Co.
Morrison Knudsen Corp.
National City Bank of Minneapolis
Nordson Corp.
Northern States Power Co.
Norwest Corp.
Physicians Mutual Insurance Co.
Pillsbury Co.
Rutledge Hill Press
Saint Paul Companies Inc.
Sierra Pacific Resources
SIT Investment Associates, Inc.
Southwest Gas Corp.
Sovereign Bank
Standard Register Co.
State Farm Mutual Automobile Insurance Co.
Steelcase Inc.
Storage Technology Corp.
Tektronix, Inc.
Thermo Electron Corp.
Times Mirror Co.
Toyota Motor Sales U.S.A., Inc.
Unilever Home & Personal Care U.S.A.
U.S. Bancorp Piper Jaffray
US Bank, Washington
US West, Inc.
Van Leer Holding
Washington Mutual, Inc.
Washington Trust Bank
Weyerhaeuser Co.
Witco Corp.

NONPROFIT MANAGEMENT

American Express Co.
American Fidelity Corp.
AT&T Corp.
Atlantic Investment Co.
Atlantic Richfield Co.
Avon Products, Inc.
Bank of America
BankAtlantic Bancorp
Baxter International Inc.
Bechtel Group, Inc.
Block, Inc. (H&R)
Blue Cross & Blue Shield of Minnesota
Borden, Inc.
Boston Globe (The)
BP Amoco Corp.
Burlington Industries, Inc.
Business Improvement
Cargill Inc.
Carolina Power & Light Co.
Caterpillar Inc.
Central Vermont Public Service Corp.
Charter Manufacturing Co.
Chase Bank of Texas
Chase Manhattan Bank, NA
Chesapeake Corp.
Chevron Corp.
Chicago Title Corp.
CIGNA Corp.
Cinergy Corp.
Citibank Corp.
Citizens Bank-Flint
Clorox Co.
Colonial Life & Accident Insurance Co.
Contran Corp.
Coors Brewing Co.
CPI Corp.
CSS Industries, Inc.
Cummins Engine Co., Inc.
DaimlerChrysler Corp.
Dain Bosworth Inc.
Dayton Hudson
Deloitte & Touche
Delta Air Lines, Inc.
Deluxe Corp.
Deposit Guaranty National Bank
Deutsch Co.
Domino's Pizza Inc.
Donaldson Co., Inc.
du Pont de Nemours & Co. (E.I.)
Eastern Bank
Ecolab Inc.
Edwards Enterprise Software (J.D.)
El Paso Energy Co.
Exxon Mobil Corp.
Fidelity Investments
Fireman's Fund Insurance Co.
Firstar Bank Milwaukee NA
FleetBoston Financial Corp.
Fluor Corp.
Forbes Inc.
Ford Meter Box Co.
Fortis Insurance Co.
Fuller Co. (H.B.)
Gap, Inc.
GEICO Corp.
General Electric Co.
General Motors Corp.
Graco, Inc.
Hallmark Cards Inc.
Hannaford Brothers Co.
Harnischfeger Industries
Harris Trust & Savings Bank
Hartford (The)
Hartford Steam Boiler Inspection & Insurance Co.
Hartmarx Corp.
Hewlett-Packard Co.
Hitachi America Ltd.
Honeywell International Inc.
Household International Inc.
Hubbard Broadcasting, Inc.
Humana, Inc.
Huntington Bancshares Inc.
Illinois Tool Works, Inc.
Industrial Bank of Japan Trust Co. (New York)
Johnson Controls Inc.
Jostens, Inc.
Kellogg Co.
Kellwood Co.
Lance, Inc.
Landmark Communications Inc.
Levi Strauss & Co.
Little, Inc. (Arthur D.)
Litton Industries, Inc.
Lotus Development Corp.
Louisiana Land & Exploration Co.
Matsushita Electric Corp. of America
McClatchy Co.
MCI WorldCom, Inc.
McKesson-HBOC Corp.
Mellon Financial Corp.
Millipore Corp.
Minnesota Mining & Manufacturing Co.
Minnesota Mutual Life Insurance Co.
Mitsubishi Electric America
Monsanto Co.
Montgomery Ward & Co., Inc.
MONY Group (The)
Morgan & Co. Inc. (J.P.)
Motorola Inc.
Nabisco Group Holdings
Nalco Chemical Co.
National City Bank of Minneapolis
National Computer Systems, Inc.
National Starch & Chemical Co.
Nationwide Insurance Co.
New England Bio Labs
New England Financial
New York Life Insurance Co.
Nordson Corp.
Northern States Power Co.
Norton Co.
Norwest Corp.
Occidental Oil and Gas
Pacific Mutual Life Insurance Co.
Penney Co., Inc. (J.C.)
Pieper Power Electric Co.
Polaroid Corp.
Premier Industrial Corp.
Procter & Gamble Co., Cosmetics Division
Prudential Insurance Co. of America
Ralston Purina Co.
Red Wing Shoe Co. Inc.
Reily & Co., Inc. (William B.)
Rockwell International Corp.
SAFECO Corp.
Saint Paul Companies Inc.
Schering-Plough Corp.
Schlumberger Ltd. (USA)
Schwab & Co., Inc. (Charles)
Sega of America Inc.
SIT Investment Associates, Inc.
Smith Corp. (A.O.)
SmithKline Beecham Corp.
Sony Electronics
Sovereign Bank
SPX Corp.
State Street Bank & Trust Co.
Sunmark Capital Corp.
SunTrust Bank Atlanta
Susquehanna-Pfaltzgraff Co.
Tamko Roofing Products
TCF National Bank Minnesota
Tenet Healthcare Corp.
Tesoro Hawaii
Texas Instruments Inc.
Times Mirror Co.
Transamerica Corp.
Unilever United States, Inc.
Union Carbide Corp.
United Dominion Industries, Ltd.
United Parcel Service of America Inc.
U.S. Bancorp Piper Jaffray
United States Sugar Corp.
United States Trust Co. of New York
Unocal Corp.
US West, Inc.
Varian Medical Systems, Inc.
Vodafone AirTouch Plc
Westvaco Corp.
Whirlpool Corp.
WICOR, Inc.
Wrigley Co. (Wm. Jr.)
Zachry Co. (H.B.)

PARADES/FESTIVALS

AK Steel Corp.
Alcoa Inc.
Allmerica Financial Corp.
AMCORE Bank Rockford
American General Finance
Ameritas Life Insurance Corp.
Ameritech Ohio
Ameritech Wisconsin
AMR Corp.
Amsted Industries Inc.
Andersons Inc.
Aon Corp.
APL Ltd.
Armstrong World Industries, Inc.
Arvin Industries, Inc.
Badger Meter, Inc.
Baird & Co. (Robert W.)
Bandag, Inc.
Banfi Vintners
Banta Corp.
Barden Corp.
Belk-Simpson Department Stores
Belk Stores Services Inc.
BFGoodrich Co.
Blair & Co. (William)
Blount International, Inc.
Blue Cross & Blue Shield of Alabama
Borden, Inc.
Borman's Inc.
Briggs & Stratton Corp.
Broderbund Software, Inc.
Brown Shoe Co., Inc.
Bucyrus-Erie Co.
Business Improvement
Cantor, Fitzgerald Securities Corp.
Carillon Importers, Ltd.
Carpenter Technology Corp.
Carris Reels
Central Soya Co.
Century 21
Chicago Board of Trade
Citigroup
CLARCOR Inc.
Cleveland-Cliffs, Inc.
Commerce Bancshares, Inc.
Compaq Computer Corp.
ConAgra, Inc.
Consumers Energy Co.
Country Curtains, Inc.
CPI Corp.
Crane Co.
Crestar Finance Corp.
CUNA Mutual Group
DaimlerChrysler Corp.

Dain Bosworth Inc.
Danis Companies
Dayton Power and Light Co.
Deere & Co.
Demoulas Supermarkets Inc.
Detroit Edison Co.
Dow Chemical Co.
DSM Copolymer
Duchossois Industries Inc.
Dynamet, Inc.
Eastern Bank
Eastman Kodak Co.
Eaton Corp.
Ecolab Inc.
Emerson Electric Co.
Employers Mutual Casualty Co.
Ensign-Bickford Industries
Enterprise Rent-A-Car Co.
Equitable Resources, Inc.
Evening Post Publishing Co.
Federated Mutual Insurance Co.
Ferro Corp.
Fidelity Investments
Fifth Third Bancorp
Fireman's Fund Insurance Co.
First American Corp.
First Hawaiian, Inc.
First Source Corp.
Firstar Bank Milwaukee NA
Ford Meter Box Co.
Forest City Enterprises, Inc.
Fort Worth Star-Telegram Inc.
Furniture Brands International, Inc.
Gallo Winery, Inc. (E&J)
GEICO Corp.
GenAmerica Corp.
GenCorp
Gerber Products Co.
Guess?
Gulf Power Co.
Hamilton Sundstrand Corp.
Hanna Co. (M.A.)
Hannaford Brothers Co.
Harnischfeger Industries
Hartford (The)
Hawaiian Electric Co., Inc.
Hickory Tech Corp.
Housatonic Curtain Co.
Hubbell Inc.
Huffy Corp.
Huntington Bancshares Inc.
Jacobson & Sons (Benjamin)
Johnson Controls Inc.
Journal-Gazette Co.
Kelly Services
Kimball International, Inc.
Kimberly-Clark Corp.
Kinder Morgn
Kingsbury Corp.
Koch Enterprises, Inc.
Kroger Co.
Land O'Lakes, Inc.
Lee Enterprises
Leviton Manufacturing Co. Inc.
Lilly & Co. (Eli)
Lincoln Electric Co.
Lincoln Financial Group
Loews Corp.
LTV Corp.
Lubrizol Corp. (The)
Madison Gas & Electric Co.
Marcus Corp.
Mark IV Industries
May Department Stores Co.
McDonald & Co. Securities, Inc.
Meijer, Inc.
Michigan Consolidated Gas Co.
Mid-America Bank of Louisville
Minnesota Mining & Manufacturing Co.
Minnesota Mutual Life Insurance Co.
Morrison Knudsen Corp.
Nabisco Group Holdings
National City Corp.
National Machinery Co.
Niagara Mohawk Holdings Inc.
Norfolk Southern Corp.
North American Royalties
Northern States Power Co.
Norton Co.
Old National Bank Evansville
Oshkosh B'Gosh, Inc.
Owens Corning
Pacific Century Financial Corp.
Park National Bank
Parker Hannifin Corp.
Pella Corp.
Pharmacia & Upjohn, Inc.
Physicians Mutual Insurance Co.
Pieper Power Electric Co.
PNC Financial Services Group
Premier Industrial Corp.
Principal Financial Group
Procter & Gamble Co.
Providence Journal-Bulletin Co.
Provident Companies, Inc.
Quanex Corp.
Ralston Purina Co.
Regions Bank
Reily & Co., Inc. (William B.)
Reinhart Institutional Foods
Reynolds & Reynolds Co.
Reynolds Tobacco (R.J.)
Ruddick Corp.
Russer Foods
S&T Bancorp
SBC Communications Inc.
Security Benefit Life Insurance Co.
Servco Pacific
Shell Oil Co.
Shelter Mutual Insurance Co.
Sherwin-Williams Co.
Sierra Pacific Industries
Sierra Pacific Resources
Smurfit-Stone Container Corp.
Sonoco Products Co.
South Bend Tribune Corp.
Southwest Gas Corp.
Sovereign Bank
Sprint Corp.
SPX Corp.
Square D Co.
Standard Products Co.
Star Bank NA
Stupp Brothers Bridge & Iron Co.
Sverdrup Corp.
Synovus Financial Corp.
Times Mirror Co.
Toledo Blade Co.
Toro Co.
True North Communications, Inc.
Trustmark Insurance Co.
TRW Inc.
Union Carbide Corp.
United Wisconsin Services
Unocal Corp.
Valmont Industries, Inc.
Warner-Lambert Co.
Washington Trust Bank
Weil, Gotshal & Manges Corp.
Wisconsin Power & Light Co.
Wolverine World Wide
Wyman-Gordon Co.
York Federal Savings & Loan Association
Zilkha & Sons

PHILANTHROPIC ORGANIZATIONS

ABC
AEGON U.S.A. Inc.
Alcoa Inc.
Alcon Laboratories, Inc.
Alexander & Baldwin, Inc.
Allegheny Technologies Inc.
Alliant Techsystems
Allmerica Financial Corp.
AMCORE Bank Rockford
American Express Co.
Ameritech Indiana
AMR Corp.
Amsted Industries Inc.
Aon Corp.
Armstrong World Industries, Inc.
Arvin Industries, Inc.
Ashland, Inc.
Atlantic Investment Co.
Avon Products, Inc.
Bandag, Inc.
BankBoston Corp.
Bard, Inc. (C.R.)
Baxter International Inc.
Bechtel Group, Inc.
Bethlehem Steel Corp.
Binney & Smith Inc.
Blair & Co. (William)
Blount International, Inc.
Borden, Inc.
Borman's Inc.
Boston Edison Co.
Boston Globe (The)
Briggs & Stratton Corp.
Brown Shoe Co., Inc.
Burlington Industries, Inc.
Burlington Resources, Inc.
Burress (J.W.)
Calvin Klein
Central Newspapers, Inc.
Central & South West Services
Central Soya Co.
CGU Insurance
Chase Manhattan Bank, NA
Chesapeake Corp.
Chicago Board of Trade
CIGNA Corp.
CIT Group, Inc. (The)
Citizens Financial Group, Inc.
Cleveland-Cliffs, Inc.
CNA
Colonial Life & Accident Insurance Co.
Comdisco, Inc.
Commercial Intertech Corp.
Compaq Computer Corp.
Consumers Energy Co.
Contran Corp.
Crestar Finance Corp.
CSS Industries, Inc.
Cummings Properties Management
CUNA Mutual Group
Dayton Power and Light Co.
Demoulas Supermarkets Inc.
Deposit Guaranty National Bank
Deutsch Co.
Disney Co. (Walt)
Dixie Group, Inc. (The)
Domino's Pizza Inc.
Dow Corning Corp.
DSM Copolymer
du Pont de Nemours & Co. (E.I.)
Duchossois Industries Inc.
Dynamet, Inc.
Elf Atochem North America, Inc.
Erb Lumber Co.
Erving Industries
Fidelity Investments
FINA
Fireman's Fund Insurance Co.
First Hawaiian, Inc.
First Maryland Bancorp
First Union Corp.
Fisher Scientific
FleetBoston Financial Corp.
Forbes Inc.
Ford Meter Box Co.
Ford Motor Co.
Forest City Enterprises, Inc.
Fortis Insurance Co.
Franklin Mint (The)
Furniture Brands International, Inc.
Gap, Inc.
GEICO Corp.
GenAmerica Corp.
Georgia Power Co.
Giant Eagle Inc.
Globe Corp.
Graco, Inc.
Gulfstream Aerospace Corp.
Halliburton Co.
Harcourt General, Inc.
Harnischfeger Industries
Harsco Corp.
Heinz Co. (H.J.)
Hoffer Plastics Corp.
Hoffmann-La Roche Inc.
Honeywell International Inc.
Household International Inc.
Hubbard Broadcasting, Inc.
Hubbell Inc.
Humana, Inc.
Huntington Bancshares Inc.
IBP
IKON Office Solutions, Inc.
International Flavors & Fragrances Inc.
Jacobs Engineering Group
Jacobson & Sons (Benjamin)
Kellogg Co.
Kennametal, Inc.
Kimberly-Clark Corp.
Koch Industries, Inc.
Kohler Co.
Kroger Co.
Lancaster Lens, Inc.
Lance, Inc.
Landmark Communications Inc.
Leigh Fibers, Inc.
Liberty Corp.
Lipton Co.
Little, Inc. (Arthur D.)
Loews Corp.
Lowe's Companies
Mallinckrodt Chemical, Inc.
Marcus Corp.
Maritz Inc.
Mark IV Industries
Masco Corp.
Mattel Inc.
McDonald & Co. Securities, Inc.
McWane Inc.
Mead Corp.
Michigan Consolidated Gas Co.
Mid-America Bank of Louisville
Millipore Corp.
Montgomery Ward & Co., Inc.
Morgan & Co. Inc. (J.P.)
Morris Communications Corp.
Morrison Knudsen Corp.
Motorola Inc.
National City Bank of Minneapolis
National Computer Systems, Inc.
National Presto Industries, Inc.
National Service Industries, Inc.
National Starch & Chemical Co.
Nationwide Insurance Co.
New Jersey Natural Gas Co.
New York Life Insurance Co.
Northwest Bank Nebraska, NA
Norwest Corp.
Old National Bank Evansville
Oshkosh B'Gosh, Inc.
Overseas Shipholding Group Inc.
Owens Corning
Pacific Century Financial Corp.
Penney Co., Inc. (J.C.)
PerkinElmer, Inc.
Philip Morris Companies Inc.
Physicians Mutual Insurance Co.
Pittway Corp.
Playboy Enterprises Inc.
PNC Financial Services Group
Polaroid Corp.
Premier Industrial Corp.
Procter & Gamble Co., Cosmetics Division
Putnam Investments
Rayonier Inc.
Reebok International Ltd.
Revlon Inc.
Reynolds Metals Co.
Reynolds & Reynolds Co.
Reynolds Tobacco (R.J.)
Rubbermaid Inc.
Ruddick Corp.
Safeguard Scientifics
Sara Lee Corp.
Sara Lee Hosiery, Inc.
Schering-Plough Corp.
Schwab & Co., Inc. (Charles)
Seaway Food Town, Inc.
Sega of America Inc.
SIT Investment Associates, Inc.
Slant/Fin Corp.
SmithKline Beecham Corp.
Solo Cup Co.
Sony Electronics
Southwest Gas Corp.
Sovereign Bank
Star Bank NA
Stone Container Corp.

Stride Rite Corp.
Stupp Brothers Bridge & Iron Co.
Sunmark Capital Corp.
Synovus Financial Corp.
TENNANT Co.
Texaco Inc.
Thermo Electron Corp.
Timken Co. (The)
TJX Companies, Inc.
Tomkins Industries, Inc.
Transamerica Corp.
United Distillers & Vintners North America
United Parcel Service of America Inc.
United States Sugar Corp.
Universal Leaf Tobacco Co., Inc.
Universal Studios
Unocal Corp.
Vesper Corp.
Wachovia Bank of North Carolina NA
Wachtell, Lipton, Rosen & Katz
Waffle House Inc.
Wal-Mart Stores, Inc.
Walter Industries Inc.
Warner-Lambert Co.
Williams
Wisconsin Public Service Corp.
Woodward Governor Co.
Wrigley Co. (Wm. Jr.)
Zachry Co. (H.B.)
Zilkha & Sons

PROFESSIONAL & TRADE ASSOCIATIONS

Abbott Laboratories
ABC
AFLAC Inc.
AGL Resources Inc.
Alcoa Inc.
Allegheny Technologies Inc.
Alliant Techsystems
AlliedSignal Inc.
Allstate Insurance Co.
America West Airlines, Inc.
American United Life Insurance Co.
Ameritas Life Insurance Corp.
AMETEK, Inc.
AMP Inc.
AMR Corp.
Amsted Industries Inc.
APL Ltd.
Archer-Daniels-Midland Co.
Aristech Chemical Corp.
Arizona Public Service Co.
Armstrong World Industries, Inc.
AT&T Corp.
Bandag, Inc.
Banfi Vintners
Bank of America
Battelle Memorial Institute
Baxter International Inc.
Bayer Corp.
Bechtel Group, Inc.
Ben & Jerry's Homemade Inc.
Bestfoods
Bethlehem Steel Corp.
BFGoodrich Co.
Blair & Co. (William)
Boeing Co.
Borden, Inc.
Boston Edison Co.
Boston Globe (The)
BP Amoco Corp.
Bridgestone/Firestone, Inc.
Briggs & Stratton Corp.
Bristol-Myers Squibb Co.
Brown Shoe Co., Inc.
Brunswick Corp.
Bucyrus-Erie Co.
Burnett Co. (Leo)
Butler Manufacturing Co.
Campbell Soup Co.
Carillon Importers, Ltd.
Carolina Power & Light Co.
Carpenter Technology Corp.
Carter-Wallace, Inc.
Central Maine Power Co.
Central Soya Co.
CertainTeed Corp.
Cessna Aircraft Co.
CGU Insurance
Chase Bank of Texas
Chase Manhattan Bank, NA
Chesapeake Corp.
Chevron Corp.
Chicago Tribune Co.
CIGNA Corp.
Cincinnati Bell Inc.
CIT Group, Inc. (The)
CNA
Collins & Aikman Corp.
Colonial Life & Accident Insurance Co.
Commercial Intertech Corp.
Compass Bank
Consolidated Natural Gas Co.
Consolidated Papers, Inc.
Constellation Energy Group, Inc.
Consumers Energy Co.
Contran Corp.
Copley Press, Inc.
Corning Inc.
Country Curtains, Inc.
Crane & Co., Inc.
Credit Suisse First Boston
CSR Rinker Materials Corp.
DaimlerChrysler Corp.
Dana Corp.
Dayton Hudson
Deere & Co.
DeKalb Genetics Corp.
Deloitte & Touche
Delta Air Lines, Inc.
Detroit Edison Co.
Dow Chemical Co.
Dow Corning Corp.
Dow Jones & Co., Inc.
du Pont de Nemours & Co. (E.I.)
Duke Energy
Dun & Bradstreet Corp.
Eastman Kodak Co.
Eaton Corp.
Eckerd Corp.
Edison International
Elf Atochem North America, Inc.
Emerson Electric Co.
Ensign-Bickford Industries
Evening Post Publishing Co.
Extendicare Health Services
Exxon Mobil Corp.
Fannie Mae
Federal-Mogul Corp.
Federated Mutual Insurance Co.
First Maryland Bancorp
First Tennessee National Corp.
Fisher Brothers Cleaning Services
Fisher Scientific
Fluor Corp.
FMC Corp.
Forbes Inc.
Ford Meter Box Co.
Ford Motor Co.
Fort James Corp.
Fox Entertainment Group
Franklin Mint (The)
Frost National Bank
Furniture Brands International, Inc.
Gallo Winery, Inc. (E&J)
GEICO Corp.
GenAmerica Corp.
GenCorp
General Electric Co.
General Mills, Inc.
General Motors Corp.
Georgia Power Co.
Gerber Products Co.
Giddings & Lewis
Glickenhaus & Co.
Goldman Sachs Group
Golub Corp.
Grede Foundries
Green Bay Packaging
GTE Corp.
Hancock Financial Services (John)
Hanna Co. (M.A.)
Harris Corp.
Harsco Corp.
Hartford (The)
Hartmarx Corp.
Heinz Co. (H.J.)
Heller Financial, Inc.
Hewlett-Packard Co.
Hoffmann-La Roche Inc.
Hubbard Broadcasting, Inc.
Hubbell Inc.
Huffy Corp.
Humana, Inc.
IBP
IKON Office Solutions, Inc.
Illinois Tool Works, Inc.
Inman Mills
International Flavors & Fragrances Inc.
International Paper Co.
Johnson Controls Inc.
Johnson & Son (S.C.)
Kellwood Co.
Kerr-McGee Corp.
Knight Ridder
KPMG Peat Marwick LLP
Kroger Co.
Ladish Co., Inc.
Lancaster Lens, Inc.
Lance, Inc.
Land O'Lakes, Inc.
Landmark Communications Inc.
Lee Enterprises
Lehigh Portland Cement Co.
Levi Strauss & Co.
Liberty Corp.
Lilly & Co. (Eli)
Lincoln Electric Co.
Little, Inc. (Arthur D.)
Litton Industries, Inc.
Loews Corp.
Louisiana Land & Exploration Co.
MacMillan Bloedel Inc.
Macy's East Inc.
Mamiye Brothers
Marcus Corp.
Marshall & Ilsley Corp.
Masco Corp.
McClatchy Co.
McCormick & Co. Inc.
McDermott Inc.
McDonald & Co. Securities, Inc.
McGraw-Hill Companies, Inc.
MCI WorldCom, Inc.
Menasha Corp.
Mercantile Bank NA
Merck & Co.
Metropolitan Life Insurance Co.
Michigan Consolidated Gas Co.
Milliken & Co.
Millipore Corp.
Mine Safety Appliances Co.
Minnesota Mining & Manufacturing Co.
Minnesota Mutual Life Insurance Co.
Monsanto Co.
Montana Power Co.
Montgomery Ward & Co., Inc.
Morris Communications Corp.
Morrison Knudsen Corp.
Motorola Inc.
Nabisco Group Holdings
National City Bank of Minneapolis
National Computer Systems, Inc.
National Starch & Chemical Co.
Nationwide Insurance Co.
New England Financial
New York Life Insurance Co.
New York Mercantile Exchange
New York Times Co.
Nordson Corp.
Northwest Natural Gas Co.
Norton Co.
OG&E Electric Services
Oklahoma Publishing Co.
Old National Bank Evansville
Olin Corp.
Orange & Rockland Utilities, Inc.
Oshkosh B'Gosh, Inc.
Overseas Shipholding Group Inc.
Pacific Mutual Life Insurance Co.
PEMCO Corp.
Peoples Energy Corp.
PepsiCo, Inc.
Pfizer Inc.
Pharmacia & Upjohn, Inc.
Phillips Petroleum Co.
Pieper Power Electric Co.
Pittway Corp.
PNC Financial Services Group
Portland General Electric Co.
PPG Industries, Inc.
Praxair
Premier Industrial Corp.
Price Associates (T. Rowe)
Procter & Gamble Co.
Procter & Gamble Co., Cosmetics Division
Providence Journal-Bulletin Co.
Prudential Insurance Co. of America
Public Service Electric & Gas Co.
Pulitzer Publishing Co.
Putnam Investments
Quanex Corp.
Ralston Purina Co.
Reebok International Ltd.
Regions Bank
Reily & Co., Inc. (William B.)
Reliant Energy Inc.
Reynolds Metals Co.
Reynolds Tobacco (R.J.)
Rich Products Corp.
Rockwell International Corp.
Rubbermaid Inc.
Ryder System, Inc.
S&T Bancorp
Sara Lee Corp.
Schering-Plough Corp.
Schlumberger Ltd. (USA)
Schwab & Co., Inc. (Charles)
Scripps Co. (E.W.)
Searle & Co. (G.D.)
Sears, Roebuck and Co.
Security Benefit Life Insurance Co.
Sega of America Inc.
Sempra Energy
Shea Co. (John F.)
Sherwin-Williams Co.
Sierra Pacific Resources
Simplot Co. (J.R.)
Simpson Investment Co.
Slant/Fin Corp.
SmithKline Beecham Corp.
Smurfit-Stone Container Corp.
Sonoco Products Co.
Sony Electronics
Southeastern Mutual Insurance Co.
Springs Industries, Inc.
Sprint/United Telephone
SPX Corp.
Star Bank NA
State Farm Mutual Automobile Insurance Co.
Storage Technology Corp.
Stupp Brothers Bridge & Iron Co.
Sunmark Capital Corp.
Sverdrup Corp.
TCF National Bank Minnesota
Telcordia Technologies
Tenneco Automotive
Tension Envelope Corp.
Textron Inc.
Thermo Electron Corp.
Thompson Co. (J. Walter)
Times Mirror Co.
Toledo Blade Co.
Tomkins Industries, Inc.
Trace International Holdings, Inc.
True North Communications, Inc.
True Oil Co.
TRW Inc.
TU Electric Co.
Tyson Foods Inc.
Unilever United States, Inc.
Union Camp Corp.
Union Carbide Corp.
Union Pacific Corp.
United States Sugar Corp.
United Wisconsin Services
Universal Leaf Tobacco Co., Inc.
Universal Studios
Unocal Corp.
US Bank, Washington
USX Corp.
Valmont Industries, Inc.
Vodafone AirTouch Plc

Wachovia Bank of North Carolina NA
Wal-Mart Stores, Inc.
Warner-Lambert Co.
Waste Management Inc.
Western & Southern Life Insurance Co.
Westvaco Corp.
Whirlpool Corp.
Wiley & Sons (John)
Williams
Wisconsin Power & Light Co.
Wyman-Gordon Co.
Xerox Corp.
Young & Rubicam

PUBLIC POLICY

Abbott Laboratories
ABC
AEGON U.S.A. Inc.
Aetna, Inc.
AFLAC Inc.
Air Products and Chemicals, Inc.
AK Steel Corp.
Alcoa Inc.
Alexander & Baldwin, Inc.
Alliant Techsystems
AlliedSignal Inc.
Allmerica Financial Corp.
Allstate Insurance Co.
Alma Piston Co.
AMCORE Bank Rockford
American Express Co.
American Fidelity Corp.
American Retail Group
American Stock Exchange, Inc.
American United Life Insurance Co.
Ameritech Corp.
Ameritech Illinois
Ameritech Ohio
Amgen, Inc.
AMR Corp.
Andersen Corp.
Andersons Inc.
Anheuser-Busch Companies, Inc.
Aon Corp.
Archer-Daniels-Midland Co.
Armstrong World Industries, Inc.
ASARCO Inc.
Ashland, Inc.
AT&T Corp.
Atlantic Investment Co.
Atlantic Richfield Co.
Avon Products, Inc.
Badger Meter, Inc.
Baird & Co. (Robert W.)
Banfi Vintners
Bank of America
Bank One Corp.
BankBoston Corp.
Barclays Capital
Bardes Corp.
Barnes Group Inc.
Bausch & Lomb Inc.
Bayer Corp.
Bechtel Group, Inc.
Becton Dickinson & Co.
BellSouth Corp.
Bemis Co., Inc.
Ben & Jerry's Homemade Inc.
Bernstein & Co., Inc. (Sanford C.)
Bestfoods
Bethlehem Steel Corp.
BFGoodrich Co.
Binswanger Companies
Blair & Co. (William)
Block, Inc. (H&R)
Blount International, Inc.
Blue Bell, Inc.
Blue Cross & Blue Shield of Iowa
Blue Cross & Blue Shield of Minnesota
Boise Cascade Corp.
Borden, Inc.
Borman's Inc.
BP Amoco Corp.
Bridgestone/Firestone, Inc.
Bristol-Myers Squibb Co.
Brown Shoe Co., Inc.
Brown & Williamson Tobacco Corp.
Browning-Ferris Industries Inc.
Bucyrus-Erie Co.
Burlington Industries, Inc.
Burnett Co. (Leo)
Cabot Corp.
Calvin Klein
Cargill Inc.
Carnival Corp.
Carpenter Technology Corp.
Caterpillar Inc.
Central Maine Power Co.
CertainTeed Corp.
CGU Insurance
Champion International Corp.
Chase Manhattan Bank, NA
Chesapeake Corp.
Chevron Corp.
Chicago Tribune Co.
CIGNA Corp.
Cincinnati Bell Inc.
Cinergy Corp.
Citibank Corp.
Citigroup
Cleveland-Cliffs, Inc.
CNA
Coca-Cola Co.
Commercial Intertech Corp.
Compass Bank
ConAgra, Inc.
Cone Mills Corp.
Consolidated Natural Gas Co.
Consolidated Papers, Inc.
Consumers Energy Co.
Contran Corp.
Cooper Industries, Inc.
Copley Press, Inc.
Corning Inc.
Country Curtains, Inc.
Crane Co.
Credit Suisse First Boston
Crestar Finance Corp.
Croft-Leominster
Cummings Properties Management
Cummins Engine Co., Inc.
CUNA Mutual Group
Daily News
DaimlerChrysler Corp.
Dain Bosworth Inc.
Dana Corp.
Dayton Hudson
Dayton Power and Light Co.
Deere & Co.
DeKalb Genetics Corp.
Deposit Guaranty National Bank
Detroit Edison Co.
Deutsch Co.
Dial Corp.
Disney Co. (Walt)
Dixie Group, Inc. (The)
Domino's Pizza Inc.
Donnelley & Sons Co. (R.R.)
Dow Chemical Co.
Dow Jones & Co., Inc.
du Pont de Nemours & Co. (E.I.)
Duchossois Industries Inc.
Duke Energy
Dun & Bradstreet Corp.
Dynamet, Inc.
Eastman Kodak Co.
Eaton Corp.
Eckerd Corp.
Edison International
Edwards Enterprise Software (J.D.)
Elf Atochem North America, Inc.
Emerson Electric Co.
Employers Mutual Casualty Co.
Ensign-Bickford Industries
Erb Lumber Co.
European American Bank
Exxon Mobil Corp.
Fannie Mae
Federal-Mogul Corp.
Fidelity Investments
First Tennessee National Corp.
First Union Bank
First Union Securities, Inc.
Fisher Scientific
FleetBoston Financial Corp.
Florida Power & Light Co.
Fluor Corp.
FMC Corp.
Forbes Inc.
Ford Meter Box Co.
Ford Motor Co.
Forest City Enterprises, Inc.
Fortis Insurance Co.
Freeport-McMoRan Inc.
Fuller Co. (H.B.)
Furniture Brands International, Inc.
Gallo Winery, Inc. (E&J)
GATX Corp.
GEICO Corp.
GenAmerica Corp.
GenCorp
General Atlantic Partners II LP
General Electric Co.
General Mills, Inc.
General Motors Corp.
General Reinsurance Corp.
Georgia-Pacific Corp.
Gerber Products Co.
Giant Eagle Inc.
Glickenhaus & Co.
Globe Corp.
Goldman Sachs Group
Golub Corp.
GPU Inc.
Grace & Co. (W.R.)
Graco, Inc.
Grede Foundries
GTE Corp.
Guess?
Halliburton Co.
Hallmark Cards Inc.
Hancock Financial Services (John)
Harcourt General, Inc.
Harnischfeger Industries
Harris Trust & Savings Bank
Harsco Corp.
Hartford (The)
Hartmarx Corp.
Hasbro, Inc.
Heinz Co. (H.J.)
Heller Financial, Inc.
Hitachi America Ltd.
HON Industries Inc.
Honeywell International Inc.
Housatonic Curtain Co.
Household International Inc.
HSBC Bank USA
Hubbard Broadcasting, Inc.
Hubbell Inc.
Idaho Power Co.
IKON Office Solutions, Inc.
Illinois Tool Works, Inc.
Inland Container Corp.
International Business Machines Corp.
Jacobs Engineering Group
Jeld-wen, Inc.
Johnson & Son (S.C.)
Jostens, Inc.
Journal-Gazette Co.
JSJ Corp.
Katten, Muchin & Zavis
Kellogg Co.
Kelly Services
Kemper National Insurance Companies
Kennametal, Inc.
Kerr-McGee Corp.
Kimberly-Clark Corp.
Koch Enterprises, Inc.
Kroger Co.
Laclede Gas Co.
Ladish Co., Inc.
Land O'Lakes, Inc.
Landmark Communications Inc.
Lee Enterprises
Leigh Fibers, Inc.
Levi Strauss & Co.
Leviton Manufacturing Co. Inc.
Lilly & Co. (Eli)
Lincoln Financial Group
Lipton Co.
Litton Industries, Inc.
Loews Corp.
Lotus Development Corp.
Louisiana Land & Exploration Co.
Louisiana-Pacific Corp.
Lowe's Companies
Macy's East Inc.
Marcus Corp.
Maritz Inc.
Mattel Inc.
May Department Stores Co.
McClatchy Co.
McDonald & Co. Securities, Inc.
McGraw-Hill Companies, Inc.
MCI WorldCom, Inc.
McKesson-HBOC Corp.
Merck & Co.
Merrill Lynch & Co., Inc.
Metropolitan Life Insurance Co.
Michigan Consolidated Gas Co.
Mid-America Bank of Louisville
MidAmerican Energy Holdings Co.
Milacron, Inc.
Milliken & Co.
Millipore Corp.
Mine Safety Appliances Co.
Minnesota Mutual Life Insurance Co.
Monarch Machine Tool Co.
Monsanto Co.
Montana Power Co.
Morris Communications Corp.
Morrison Knudsen Corp.
Motorola Inc.
Nabisco Group Holdings
National City Bank of Minneapolis
National Computer Systems, Inc.
National Service Industries, Inc.
National Starch & Chemical Co.
Nestle U.S.A. Inc.
New Jersey Natural Gas Co.
New York Life Insurance Co.
New York Mercantile Exchange
New York Stock Exchange, Inc.
Newman's Own Inc.
Nordson Corp.
Norfolk Southern Corp.
Northern Trust Co.
Norton Co.
Norwest Corp.
Occidental Oil and Gas
Occidental Petroleum Corp.
Oklahoma Publishing Co.
Olin Corp.
Oshkosh B'Gosh, Inc.
Outboard Marine Corp.
PACCAR Inc.
Pacific Century Financial Corp.
Pacific Mutual Life Insurance Co.
Parker Hannifin Corp.
Patagonia Inc.
Penney Co., Inc. (J.C.)
Pennzoil-Quaker State Co.
PepsiCo, Inc.
PerkinElmer, Inc.
Pfizer Inc.
Pharmacia & Upjohn, Inc.
Phelps Dodge Corp.
Philip Morris Companies Inc.
Phillips Petroleum Co.
Physicians Mutual Insurance Co.
Pillsbury Co.
Pittway Corp.
Playboy Enterprises Inc.
PNC Financial Services Group
Polaroid Corp.
PPG Industries, Inc.
Price Associates (T. Rowe)
Procter & Gamble Co.
Prudential Insurance Co. of America
Prudential Securities Inc.
Public Service Electric & Gas Co.
Publix Supermarkets
Pulitzer Publishing Co.
Ralph's Grocery Co.
Ralston Purina Co.
Red Wing Shoe Co. Inc.
Reilly Industries, Inc.
Reily & Co., Inc. (William B.)
Reinhart Institutional Foods
Reliant Energy Inc.
Revlon Inc.
Reynolds Metals Co.
Reynolds Tobacco (R.J.)
Rockwell International Corp.
Rouse Co.
Royal & SunAlliance USA, Inc.
Ryder System, Inc.

SAFECO Corp.
Sara Lee Corp.
SBC Communications Inc.
Schering-Plough Corp.
Scripps Co. (E.W.)
Seagram & Sons, Inc. (Joseph E.)
Searle & Co. (G.D.)
Security Benefit Life Insurance Co.
Sega of America Inc.
Sentry Insurance, A Mutual Co.
ServiceMaster Co.
S.G. Cowen
Shell Oil Co.
Shelter Mutual Insurance Co.
Sherwin-Williams Co.
SIT Investment Associates, Inc.
Slant/Fin Corp.
SmithKline Beecham Corp.
Smurfit-Stone Container Corp.
Sonoco Products Co.
Sony Electronics
Southeastern Mutual Insurance Co.
Southern New England Telephone Co.
Southwest Gas Corp.
Springs Industries, Inc.
State Farm Mutual Automobile Insurance Co.
State Street Bank & Trust Co.
Stonecutter Mills Corp.
Stride Rite Corp.
Sun Microsystems Inc.
Sunmark Capital Corp.
Sunoco Inc.
SunTrust Bank Atlanta
Synovus Financial Corp.
Tamko Roofing Products
Temple-Inland Inc.
Tenneco Automotive
Texaco Inc.
Textron Inc.
Thermo Electron Corp.
Thompson Co. (J. Walter)
Times Mirror Co.
Titan Industrial Corp.
TJX Companies, Inc.
TMC Investment Co.
Toledo Blade Co.
Toyota Motor Sales U.S.A., Inc.
Trace International Holdings, Inc.
Transamerica Corp.
True North Communications, Inc.
True Oil Co.
TRW Inc.
Ukrop's Super Markets
Unilever United States, Inc.
Union Camp Corp.
Union Carbide Corp.
Union Pacific Corp.
Unisys Corp.
United Distillers & Vintners North America
United Dominion Industries, Ltd.
United Parcel Service of America Inc.
United States Sugar Corp.
United States Trust Co. of New York
United Technologies Corp.
United Wisconsin Services
Universal Leaf Tobacco Co., Inc.
Universal Studios
Unocal Corp.
UnumProvident
UPN Channel 50
US Bank, Washington
US West, Inc.
USG Corp.
USX Corp.
Varian Medical Systems, Inc.
Vodafone AirTouch Plc
Vulcan Materials Co.
Wachovia Bank of North Carolina NA
Wal-Mart Stores, Inc.
Walgreen Co.
Walter Industries Inc.
Warner-Lambert Co.
Washington Mutual, Inc.
The Washington Post
Weil, Gotshal & Manges Corp.
West Co. Inc.
Westvaco Corp.
Weyerhaeuser Co.
Whirlpool Corp.
WICOR, Inc.
Williams
Winn-Dixie Stores Inc.
Wiremold Co.
Woodward Governor Co.
Wrigley Co. (Wm. Jr.)
Wyman-Gordon Co.
Xerox Corp.
Young & Rubicam
Zilkha & Sons

RURAL AFFAIRS

AGL Resources Inc.
Agrilink Foods, Inc.
Alyeska Pipeline Service Co.
Andersons Inc.
Anheuser-Busch Companies, Inc.
Archer-Daniels-Midland Co.
Bank of America
Ben & Jerry's Homemade Inc.
Blue Cross & Blue Shield of Iowa
Bridgestone/Firestone, Inc.
Briggs & Stratton Corp.
Bristol-Myers Squibb Co.
Broderbund Software, Inc.
Brunswick Corp.
Burnett Co. (Leo)
Cenex Harvest States
Central Maine Power Co.
Central Soya Co.
Chase Bank of Texas
Chase Manhattan Bank, NA
Chevron Corp.
Compass Bank
ConAgra, Inc.
Cummins Engine Co., Inc.
DaimlerChrysler Corp.
Deere & Co.
DeKalb Genetics Corp.
Duke Energy
Eaton Corp.
Enterprise Rent-A-Car Co.
Federal-Mogul Corp.
FMC Corp.
Freeport-McMoRan Inc.
General Atlantic Partners II LP
General Motors Corp.
Georgia Power Co.
Hallmark Cards Inc.
Heinz Co. (H.J.)
Hitachi America Ltd.
IBP
International Flavors & Fragrances Inc.
Journal-Gazette Co.
Kinder Morgn
Kroger Co.
Land O'Lakes, Inc.
Lee Enterprises
Levi Strauss & Co.
Metropolitan Life Insurance Co.
Morgan & Co. Inc. (J.P.)
Morris Communications Corp.
Nabisco Group Holdings
Nationwide Insurance Co.
New England Bio Labs
Niagara Mohawk Holdings Inc.
Norton Co.
Occidental Oil and Gas
Pacific Century Financial Corp.
PacifiCorp
Pioneer Hi-Bred International, Inc.
Publix Supermarkets
Quanex Corp.
Regions Bank
Reynolds Tobacco (R.J.)
Shell Oil Co.
Sierra Pacific Industries
Simplot Co. (J.R.)
Square D Co.
Sunmark Capital Corp.
United States Sugar Corp.
United States Trust Co. of New York
US West, Inc.
Valmont Industries, Inc.
Valspar Corp.
Weyerhaeuser Co.
Williams
Wisconsin Public Service Corp.
Young & Rubicam

SAFETY

Abbott Laboratories
ABC
AGL Resources Inc.
Agrilink Foods, Inc.
Air Products and Chemicals, Inc.
AK Steel Corp.
Alcoa Inc.
AlliedSignal Inc.
Allmerica Financial Corp.
Allstate Insurance Co.
AMCORE Bank Rockford
Ameren Corp.
American General Finance
Ameritech Michigan
AMETEK, Inc.
AMP Inc.
AMR Corp.
Amsted Industries Inc.
Andersen Corp.
Andersons Inc.
Aon Corp.
Archer-Daniels-Midland Co.
Armstrong World Industries, Inc.
Avista Corporation
Bandag, Inc.
Banfi Vintners
Bard, Inc. (C.R.)
Barden Corp.
Barnes Group Inc.
Bassett Furniture Industries
Bayer Corp.
Bemis Co., Inc.
Ben & Jerry's Homemade Inc.
Bestfoods
Bethlehem Steel Corp.
Blair & Co. (William)
Block, Inc. (H&R)
Blount International, Inc.
Blue Bell, Inc.
Blue Cross & Blue Shield of Alabama
Blue Cross & Blue Shield of Iowa
Boston Edison Co.
Boston Globe (The)
Briggs & Stratton Corp.
Bristol-Myers Squibb Co.
Bucyrus-Erie Co.
Burlington Industries, Inc.
Cabot Corp.
Carpenter Technology Corp.
Caterpillar Inc.
Cenex Harvest States
Central Maine Power Co.
Central Soya Co.
CertainTeed Corp.
Cessna Aircraft Co.
CGU Insurance
Chase Manhattan Bank, NA
Chesapeake Corp.
Chevron Corp.
CIGNA Corp.
Citigroup
Clark Refining & Marketing
Clorox Co.
CNA
Colonial Life & Accident Insurance Co.
Colonial Oil Industries, Inc.
Compass Bank
Conoco, Inc.
Consolidated Papers, Inc.
Conwood Co. LP
Cooper Industries, Inc.
Crane Co.
Crane & Co., Inc.
Cranston Print Works Co.
Croft-Leominster
CSR Rinker Materials Corp.
Cummings Properties Management
CUNA Mutual Group
DaimlerChrysler Corp.
Danis Companies
Demoulas Supermarkets Inc.
Detroit Edison Co.
Deutsch Co.
Dial Corp.
Dominion Resources, Inc.
Donaldson Co., Inc.
DSM Copolymer
du Pont de Nemours & Co. (E.I.)
Duchossois Industries Inc.
Duke Energy
Duriron Co., Inc.
Eastern Bank
Eastman Kodak Co.
Eaton Corp.
Edison International
Edwards Enterprise Software (J.D.)
Elf Atochem North America, Inc.
Employers Mutual Casualty Co.
Ensign-Bickford Industries
Equitable Resources, Inc.
Erb Lumber Co.
Exxon Mobil Corp.
Farmers Group, Inc.
Federal-Mogul Corp.
Federated Mutual Insurance Co.
Ferro Corp.
Fireman's Fund Insurance Co.
First Union Corp.
Fisher Brothers Cleaning Services
FleetBoston Financial Corp.
Fluor Corp.
Forbes Inc.
Ford Meter Box Co.
Ford Motor Co.
Forest City Enterprises, Inc.
Fort James Corp.
Fort Worth Star-Telegram Inc.
Fortis Insurance Co.
Franklin Electric Co.
Freeport-McMoRan Inc.
GEICO Corp.
General Motors Corp.
General Reinsurance Corp.
Georgia-Pacific Corp.
Gerber Products Co.
Giddings & Lewis
Glaxo Wellcome Inc.
Globe Corp.
Guardian Life Insurance Co. of America
Gulf Power Co.
Hallmark Cards Inc.
Hanna Co. (M.A.)
Harsco Corp.
Hartford (The)
Hartmarx Corp.
Heinz Co. (H.J.)
Hubbard Broadcasting, Inc.
Hubbell Inc.
Huffy Corp.
Hunt Manufacturing Co.
IBP
International Flavors & Fragrances Inc.
Invacare Corp.
Jacobs Engineering Group
Jeld-wen, Inc.
Johnson & Johnson
Johnson & Son (S.C.)
Kerr-McGee Corp.
Kimball International, Inc.
Kimberly-Clark Corp.
Kingsbury Corp.
Kmart Corp.
Koch Enterprises, Inc.
Kroger Co.
La-Z-Boy Inc.
Lancaster Lens, Inc.
Lance, Inc.
Land O'Lakes, Inc.
Leviton Manufacturing Co. Inc.
Lincoln Electric Co.
Lipton Co.
Loews Corp.
Louisiana Land & Exploration Co.
Lowe's Companies
LTV Corp.
MacMillan Bloedel Inc.
Macy's East Inc.
Madison Gas & Electric Co.
Mallinckrodt Chemical, Inc.
May Department Stores Co.
McDermott Inc.
McWane Inc.
Mead Corp.
Medtronic, Inc.
Memphis Light Gas & Water Division
Menasha Corp.

Merck & Co.
Metropolitan Life Insurance Co.
Milacron, Inc.
Milliken & Co.
Mine Safety Appliances Co.
Minnesota Mining & Manufacturing Co.
Monsanto Co.
Morrison Knudsen Corp.
Motorola Inc.
Mutual of Omaha Insurance Co.
Nalco Chemical Co.
National City Corp.
National Machinery Co.
Nationwide Insurance Co.
New Jersey Natural Gas Co.
New York Stock Exchange, Inc.
New York Times Co.
Niagara Mohawk Holdings Inc.
Norfolk Southern Corp.
Northeast Utilities
Northern States Power Co.
Norton Co.
Old National Bank Evansville
Overseas Shipholding Group Inc.
PACCAR Inc.
Pacific Mutual Life Insurance Co.
Parker Hannifin Corp.
Pella Corp.
Penney Co., Inc. (J.C.)
Pennzoil-Quaker State Co.
Pfizer Inc.
Pharmacia & Upjohn, Inc.
Phelps Dodge Corp.
Phillips Petroleum Co.
Physicians Mutual Insurance Co.
Pillsbury Co.
Pittway Corp.
PNC Financial Services Group
Polaroid Corp.
PPG Industries, Inc.
Premier Industrial Corp.
Procter & Gamble Co.
Procter & Gamble Co., Cosmetics Division
Prudential Insurance Co. of America
Public Service Electric & Gas Co.
Quanex Corp.
Rayonier Inc.
Red Wing Shoe Co. Inc.
Reily & Co., Inc. (William B.)
Reinhart Institutional Foods
Reliant Energy Inc.
Reynolds Metals Co.
Reynolds Tobacco (R.J.)
Rockwell International Corp.
Royal & SunAlliance USA, Inc.
Ryder System, Inc.
SAFECO Corp.
S&T Bancorp
Sempra Energy
Sentinel Communications Co.
Shaw's Supermarkets, Inc.
Shell Oil Co.
Shelter Mutual Insurance Co.
Sherwin-Williams Co.
Sierra Pacific Industries
Sierra Pacific Resources
Simpson Investment Co.
Slant/Fin Corp.
Smith Corp. (A.O.)
Sonoco Products Co.
Square D Co.
Standard Register Co.
State Farm Mutual Automobile Insurance Co.
State Street Bank & Trust Co.
Stonecutter Mills Corp.
SunTrust Bank Atlanta
TCF National Bank Minnesota
Temple-Inland Inc.
Tenneco Automotive
Tesoro Hawaii
Texaco Inc.
Textron Inc.
Thompson Co. (J. Walter)
TMC Investment Co.
Tomkins Industries, Inc.
Torchmark Corp.
TRW Inc.
TU Electric Co.
Tyson Foods Inc.
Unilever United States, Inc.
Union Camp Corp.
Union Carbide Corp.
United Airlines Inc.
United Parcel Service of America Inc.
United States Sugar Corp.
United Wisconsin Services
Unocal Corp.
USG Corp.
Valspar Corp.
Waffle House Inc.
Wal-Mart Stores, Inc.
Washington Trust Bank
Waste Management Inc.
West Co. Inc.
Westvaco Corp.
Weyerhaeuser Co.
Whirlpool Corp.
Williams
Wisconsin Power & Light Co.
Witco Corp.
Woodward Governor Co.

URBAN & COMMUNITY AFFAIRS

Abbott Laboratories
ABC
Aetna, Inc.
Agrilink Foods, Inc.
Air Products and Chemicals, Inc.
AK Steel Corp.
Alabama Power Co.
Alcoa Inc.
Alcon Laboratories, Inc.
Alexander & Baldwin, Inc.
Allegheny Technologies Inc.
Allianz Life Insurance Co. of North America
AlliedSignal Inc.
Allmerica Financial Corp.
Allstate Insurance Co.
Alyeska Pipeline Service Co.
AMCORE Bank Rockford
Ameren Corp.
America West Airlines, Inc.
American Express Co.
American Fidelity Corp.
American General Finance
American Retail Group
American Stock Exchange, Inc.
American United Life Insurance Co.
Ameritas Life Insurance Corp.
Ameritech Corp.
Ameritech Illinois
Ameritech Indiana
Ameritech Michigan
Ameritech Ohio
Ameritech Wisconsin
AMETEK, Inc.
AMP Inc.
AMR Corp.
Amsted Industries Inc.
Andersen Corp.
Andersons Inc.
Anheuser-Busch Companies, Inc.
Aon Corp.
APL Ltd.
Archer-Daniels-Midland Co.
Aristech Chemical Corp.
Arizona Public Service Co.
Armstrong World Industries, Inc.
Arvin Industries, Inc.
Ashland, Inc.
AT&T Corp.
Atlantic Investment Co.
Atlantic Richfield Co.
Avon Products, Inc.
Badger Meter, Inc.
Baird & Co. (Robert W.)
Bandag, Inc.
Bank of America
Bank One Corp.
Bank One, Texas-Houston Office
BankAtlantic Bancorp
BankBoston Corp.
Banta Corp.
Barclays Capital
Bard, Inc. (C.R.)
Barden Corp.
Bardes Corp.
Barnes Group Inc.
Barry Corp. (R.G.)
Bassett Furniture Industries
Bausch & Lomb Inc.
Baxter International Inc.
Bayer Corp.
Bechtel Group, Inc.
Belk Stores Services Inc.
BellSouth Corp.
Belo Corp. (A.H.)
Bemis Co., Inc.
Bemis Manufacturing Co.
Ben & Jerry's Homemade Inc.
Bernstein & Co., Inc. (Sanford C.)
Bestfoods
Bethlehem Steel Corp.
BFGoodrich Co.
Binswanger Companies
Blair & Co. (William)
Block, Inc. (H&R)
Blount International, Inc.
Blue Bell, Inc.
Blue Cross & Blue Shield of Alabama
Blue Cross & Blue Shield of Minnesota
Boeing Co.
Borden, Inc.
Borman's Inc.
Boston Edison Co.
Boston Globe (The)
Bowater Inc.
BP Amoco Corp.
Bradford & Co. (J.C.)
Bridgestone/Firestone, Inc.
Briggs & Stratton Corp.
Bristol-Myers Squibb Co.
Brown Shoe Co., Inc.
Brown & Williamson Tobacco Corp.
Brunswick Corp.
Bucyrus-Erie Co.
Burlington Industries, Inc.
Burlington Resources, Inc.
Burnett Co. (Leo)
Butler Manufacturing Co.
Cabot Corp.
California Bank & Trust
Calvin Klein
Campbell Soup Co.
Cargill Inc.
Carlson Companies, Inc.
Carnival Corp.
Carolina Power & Light Co.
Carter-Wallace, Inc.
Caterpillar Inc.
CCB Financial Corp.
Cenex Harvest States
Central Maine Power Co.
Central National-Gottesman
Central & South West Services
Central Soya Co.
CertainTeed Corp.
Cessna Aircraft Co.
CGU Insurance
Champion International Corp.
Charter Manufacturing Co.
Chase Bank of Texas
Chase Manhattan Bank, NA
Chesapeake Corp.
Chevron Corp.
Chicago Sun-Times, Inc.
Chicago Title Corp.
Chicago Tribune Co.
Church & Dwight Co., Inc.
CIBC Oppenheimer
CIGNA Corp.
Cincinnati Bell Inc.
Cinergy Corp.
Circuit City Stores, Inc.
CIT Group, Inc. (The)
Citibank Corp.
Citizens Bank-Flint
Citizens Financial Group, Inc.
Clark Refining & Marketing
Cleveland-Cliffs, Inc.
Clorox Co.
CNA
Collins & Aikman Corp.
Colonial Oil Industries, Inc.
Comdisco, Inc.
Comerica Inc.
Commerce Bancshares, Inc.
Commercial Intertech Corp.
Commonwealth Edison Co.
Compass Bank
ConAgra, Inc.
Cone Mills Corp.
Conoco, Inc.
Consolidated Natural Gas Co.
Constellation Energy Group, Inc.
Consumers Energy Co.
Continental Grain Co.
Contran Corp.
Conwood Co. LP
Cooper Industries, Inc.
Coors Brewing Co.
Copley Press, Inc.
Corning Inc.
Country Curtains, Inc.
Cox Enterprises Inc.
CPI Corp.
Crane Co.
Crane & Co., Inc.
Credit Suisse First Boston
Crestar Finance Corp.
Croft-Leominster
CSR Rinker Materials Corp.
CSS Industries, Inc.
Cummings Properties Management
Cummins Engine Co., Inc.
CUNA Mutual Group
DaimlerChrysler Corp.
Dain Bosworth Inc.
Dana Corp.
Danis Companies
Dayton Hudson
Dayton Power and Light Co.
Deere & Co.
DeKalb Genetics Corp.
Delta Air Lines, Inc.
Deluxe Corp.
Demoulas Supermarkets Inc.
Deposit Guaranty National Bank
Detroit Edison Co.
Deutsch Co.
Dexter Corp.
Dial Corp.
Disney Co. (Walt)
Dominion Resources, Inc.
Donnelley & Sons Co. (R.R.)
Dow Corning Corp.
Dow Jones & Co., Inc.
DSM Copolymer
du Pont de Nemours & Co. (E.I.)
Duchossois Industries Inc.
Duke Energy
Dun & Bradstreet Corp.
Duriron Co., Inc.
Dynamet, Inc.
Eastern Bank
Eastman Kodak Co.
Eaton Corp.
Eckerd Corp.
Ecolab Inc.
Edison International
EDS Corp.
Edwards Enterprise Software (J.D.)
El Paso Energy Co.
Elf Atochem North America, Inc.
Emerson Electric Co.
Employers Mutual Casualty Co.
Ensign-Bickford Industries
Enterprise Rent-A-Car Co.
Equifax Inc.
Erb Lumber Co.
Ethyl Corp.
European American Bank
Evening Post Publishing Co.
Extendicare Health Services
Exxon Mobil Corp.
Fannie Mae
Farmers Group, Inc.
Federal-Mogul Corp.
Federated Department Stores, Inc.
Federated Mutual Insurance Co.
FedEx Corp.
Ferro Corp.
Fidelity Investments
Fifth Third Bancorp
FINA
Fireman's Fund Insurance Co.
First American Corp.
First Financial Bank
First Hawaiian, Inc.
First National Bank of Evergreen Park
First Source Corp.

Funders by Recipient Type

First Tennessee National Corp.
First Union Bank
First Union Corp.
First Union National Bank, NA
First Union Securities, Inc.
Firstar Bank Milwaukee NA
Fisher Brothers Cleaning Services
FleetBoston Financial Corp.
Florida Power Corp.
Florida Power & Light Co.
Florida Rock Industries
Fluor Corp.
FMC Corp.
Forbes Inc.
Ford Meter Box Co.
Ford Motor Co.
Forest City Enterprises, Inc.
Fort Worth Star-Telegram Inc.
Fortis Insurance Co.
Fortune Brands, Inc.
Franklin Electric Co.
Freddie Mac
Freeport-McMoRan Inc.
Freightliner Corp.
Fuji Bank & Trust Co.
Fuller Co. (H.B.)
Furniture Brands International, Inc.
Gallo Winery, Inc. (E&J)
Gap, Inc.
GATX Corp.
GEICO Corp.
GenAmerica Corp.
GenCorp
General Atlantic Partners II LP
General Electric Co.
General Mills, Inc.
General Motors Corp.
Georgia-Pacific Corp.
Georgia Power Co.
Giant Eagle Inc.
Giant Food Inc.
Giddings & Lewis
Gillette Co.
Glaxo Wellcome Inc.
Glickenhaus & Co.
Globe Corp.
Goldman Sachs Group
Golub Corp.
Grace & Co. (W.R.)
Graco, Inc.
Grede Foundries
GTE Corp.
Guardian Life Insurance Co. of America
Guess?
Gulf Power Co.
Halliburton Co.
Hallmark Cards Inc.
Hamilton Sundstrand Corp.
Hancock Financial Services (John)
Hanna Co. (M.A.)
Hannaford Brothers Co.
Harcourt General, Inc.
Harland Co. (John H.)
Harley-Davidson Co.
Harnischfeger Industries
Harris Corp.
Harris Trust & Savings Bank
Harsco Corp.
Hartford (The)
Hartford Steam Boiler Inspection & Insurance Co.
Hartmarx Corp.
Hasbro, Inc.
Hawaiian Electric Co., Inc.
Heinz Co. (H.J.)
Hickory Tech Corp.
Hitachi America Ltd.
Hoffmann-La Roche Inc.
Hofmann Co.
Home Depot, Inc.
HON Industries Inc.
Honeywell International Inc.
Household International Inc.
Hubbell Inc.
Huffy Corp.
Humana, Inc.
Hunt Manufacturing Co.
Huntington Bancshares Inc.
IBP
IKON Office Solutions, Inc.
Illinois Power Co.
Illinois Tool Works, Inc.
Industrial Bank of Japan Trust Co. (New York)
Inland Container Corp.
Inman Mills
International Business Machines Corp.
International Paper Co.
INTRUST Financial Corp.
Invacare Corp.
Jacobs Engineering Group
Jacobson & Sons (Benjamin)
Jeld-wen, Inc.
Johnson Controls Inc.
Johnson & Son (S.C.)
Jones & Co. (Edward D.)
Journal-Gazette Co.
JSJ Corp.
Katten, Muchin & Zavis
Kellogg Co.
Kellwood Co.
Kelly Services
Kennametal, Inc.
Kerr-McGee Corp.
Key Bank of Cleveland
Kimball International, Inc.
Kimberly-Clark Corp.
Kinder Morgn
Kingsbury Corp.
Kmart Corp.
Koch Enterprises, Inc.
Kroger Co.
Laclede Gas Co.
Lance, Inc.
Land O'Lakes, Inc.
Landmark Communications Inc.
Lee Enterprises
Lehigh Portland Cement Co.
Levi Strauss & Co.
LG&E Energy Corp.
Liberty Corp.
Lilly & Co. (Eli)
Lincoln Financial Group
Lipton Co.
Little, Inc. (Arthur D.)
Liz Claiborne, Inc.
Loews Corp.
Lotus Development Corp.
Louisiana Land & Exploration Co.
Louisiana-Pacific Corp.
Lowe's Companies
LTV Corp.
Macy's East Inc.
Madison Gas & Electric Co.
Mallinckrodt Chemical, Inc.
Marcus Corp.
Mark IV Industries
Marriott International Inc.
Marshall Field's
Marshall & Ilsley Corp.
Mattel Inc.
May Department Stores Co.
McClatchy Co.
McCormick & Co. Inc.
McDonald & Co. Securities, Inc.
MCI WorldCom, Inc.
McKesson-HBOC Corp.
McWane Inc.
Mead Corp.
Medtronic, Inc.
Mellon Financial Corp.
Menasha Corp.
Mercantile Bank NA
Merck & Co.
Merit Oil Corp.
Metropolitan Life Insurance Co.
Michigan Consolidated Gas Co.
Mid-America Bank of Louisville
MidAmerican Energy Holdings Co.
Milacron, Inc.
Milliken & Co.
Millipore Corp.
Mine Safety Appliances Co.
Minnesota Mining & Manufacturing Co.
Minnesota Mutual Life Insurance Co.
Monarch Machine Tool Co.
Monsanto Co.
Montana Power Co.
Montgomery Ward & Co., Inc.
MONY Group (The)
Morgan & Co. Inc. (J.P.)
Morris Communications Corp.
Morrison Knudsen Corp.
Motorola Inc.
MTD Products Inc.
Nabisco Group Holdings
Nalco Chemical Co.
National Bank of Commerce Trust & Savings
National City Bank of Minneapolis
National City Corp.
National Computer Systems, Inc.
National Machinery Co.
National Starch & Chemical Co.
Nationwide Insurance Co.
NEBCO Evans
Nestle U.S.A. Inc.
New England Bio Labs
New England Financial
New Jersey Natural Gas Co.
New York Life Insurance Co.
New York Mercantile Exchange
New York Stock Exchange, Inc.
New York Times Co.
Niagara Mohawk Holdings Inc.
Nike, Inc.
Nissan North America, Inc.
Nordson Corp.
Norfolk Southern Corp.
North American Royalties
Northeast Utilities
Northern States Power Co.
Northern Trust Co.
Northwest Natural Gas Co.
Norton Co.
Norwest Corp.
Occidental Oil and Gas
Occidental Petroleum Corp.
OG&E Electric Services
Ohio National Life Insurance Co.
Old National Bank Evansville
Olin Corp.
Orscheln Co.
Osborne Enterprises
Oshkosh B'Gosh, Inc.
Outboard Marine Corp.
Overnite Transportation Co.
Overseas Shipholding Group Inc.
Owens Corning
PACCAR Inc.
Pacific Century Financial Corp.
Pacific Gas and Electric Co.
Pacific Mutual Life Insurance Co.
PacifiCorp
Parker Hannifin Corp.
PECO Energy Co.
Pella Corp.
PEMCO Corp.
Penney Co., Inc. (J.C.)
Pennzoil-Quaker State Co.
Peoples Energy Corp.
PepsiCo, Inc.
PerkinElmer, Inc.
Pfizer Inc.
Pharmacia & Upjohn, Inc.
Phelps Dodge Corp.
Phillips Petroleum Co.
Physicians Mutual Insurance Co.
Pieper Power Electric Co.
Pillsbury Co.
Pitney Bowes Inc.
Pittway Corp.
PNC Bank Kentucky Inc.
PNC Financial Services Group
Polaroid Corp.
Portland General Electric Co.
Potomac Electric Power Co.
PPG Industries, Inc.
Praxair
Premier Industrial Corp.
Price Associates (T. Rowe)
Principal Financial Group
Procter & Gamble Co.
Procter & Gamble Co., Cosmetics Division
Promus Hotel Corp.
Providence Journal-Bulletin Co.
Provident Companies, Inc.
Prudential Insurance Co. of America
Prudential Securities Inc.
Public Service Electric & Gas Co.
Pulitzer Publishing Co.
Putnam Investments
Quaker Chemical Corp.
Quanex Corp.
Ralph's Grocery Co.
Ralston Purina Co.
Rayonier Inc.
Red Wing Shoe Co. Inc.
Reebok International Ltd.
Regions Bank
Regis Corp.
Reily & Co., Inc. (William B.)
Reinhart Institutional Foods
Reliant Energy Inc.
Reliant Energy Minnegasco
ReliaStar Financial Corp.
Revlon Inc.
Reynolds Metals Co.
Reynolds & Reynolds Co.
Reynolds Tobacco (R.J.)
Rich Products Corp.
Rochester Gas & Electric Corp.
Rockwell International Corp.
Ruddick Corp.
Russer Foods
Rutledge Hill Press
Ryder System, Inc.
SAFECO Corp.
Safeguard Scientifics
Saint Paul Companies Inc.
S&T Bancorp
Sara Lee Corp.
Sara Lee Hosiery, Inc.
SBC Communications Inc.
Schloss & Co. (Marcus)
Schwab & Co., Inc. (Charles)
Schwebel Baking Co.
Scripps Co. (E.W.)
Seagram & Sons, Inc. (Joseph E.)
Searle & Co. (G.D.)
Security Benefit Life Insurance Co.
Security Life of Denver Insurance Co.
Sentinel Communications Co.
Sentry Insurance, A Mutual Co.
ServiceMaster Co.
Shaw's Supermarkets, Inc.
Shea Co. (John F.)
Shell Oil Co.
Shelter Mutual Insurance Co.
Sherwin-Williams Co.
Sierra Pacific Industries
Sierra Pacific Resources
Simplot Co. (J.R.)
Simpson Investment Co.
SIT Investment Associates, Inc.
Slant/Fin Corp.
Smith Corp. (A.O.)
SmithKline Beecham Corp.
Smucker Co. (JM)
Smurfit-Stone Container Corp.
Solo Cup Co.
Sonoco Products Co.
Sony Electronics
South Bend Tribune Corp.
Southeastern Mutual Insurance Co.
Southern California Gas Co.
Southwest Gas Corp.
Sovereign Bank
Sprint Corp.
Sprint/United Telephone
SPX Corp.
Square D Co.
Standard Products Co.
Stanley Works (The)
Star Bank NA
Starwood Hotels & Resorts Worldwide, Inc.
State Street Bank & Trust Co.
Steelcase Inc.
Stone Container Corp.
Storage Technology Corp.
Stride Rite Corp.
Stupp Brothers Bridge & Iron Co.
Sun Microsystems Inc.
Sunoco Inc.
SunTrust Bank Atlanta
Susquehanna-Pfaltzgraff Co.
Synovus Financial Corp.
Tai and Co. (J.T.)

Tamko Roofing Products
TCF National Bank Minnesota
Tektronix, Inc.
Temple-Inland Inc.
TENNANT Co.
Tenneco Automotive
Tension Envelope Corp.
Tesoro Hawaii
Texaco Inc.
Texas Gas Transmission Corp.
Textron Inc.
Thermo Electron Corp.
Ticketmaster Corp.
Times Mirror Co.
Timken Co. (The)
Titan Industrial Corp.
TJX Companies, Inc.
TMC Investment Co.
Toledo Blade Co.
Tomkins Industries, Inc.
Toro Co.
Trace International Holdings, Inc.
Transamerica Corp.
True North Communications, Inc.
Trustmark Insurance Co.
TRW Inc.
TU Electric Co.
Tyson Foods Inc.
Ukrop's Super Markets
Unilever Home & Personal Care U.S.A.
Unilever United States, Inc.
Union Camp Corp.
Union Carbide Corp.
Union Pacific Corp.
United Airlines Inc.
United Distillers & Vintners North America
United Dominion Industries, Ltd.
United Parcel Service of America Inc.
U.S. Bancorp Piper Jaffray
United States Sugar Corp.
United States Trust Co. of New York
United Technologies Corp.
United Wisconsin Services
Universal Foods Corp.
Universal Leaf Tobacco Co., Inc.
Universal Studios
Unocal Corp.
UnumProvident
UPN Channel 50
US Bank, Washington
US West, Inc.
USG Corp.
UST Inc.
USX Corp.
Valmont Industries, Inc.
Valspar Corp.
Vanguard Group
Vesper Corp.
Vulcan Materials Co.
Wachovia Bank of North Carolina NA
Waffle House Inc.
Wal-Mart Stores, Inc.
Walgreen Co.
Walter Industries Inc.
Warner-Lambert Co.
Washington Mutual, Inc.
Washington Trust Bank
Waste Management Inc.
Webster Bank
Weil, Gotshal & Manges Corp.
Wells Fargo & Co.
West Co. Inc.
Western & Southern Life Insurance Co.
Westvaco Corp.
Weyerhaeuser Co.
Whirlpool Corp.
Whitman Corp.
WICOR, Inc.
Wilbur-Ellis Co. & Connell Brothers Co.
Williams
Winn-Dixie Stores Inc.
Wiremold Co.
Wisconsin Energy Corp.
Wisconsin Power & Light Co.
Wisconsin Public Service Corp.
Witco Corp.
Wolverine World Wide
Woodward Governor Co.
Wrigley Co. (Wm. Jr.)
Wyman-Gordon Co.
Xerox Corp.
Yellow Corp.
York Federal Savings & Loan Association
Young & Rubicam
Zachry Co. (H.B.)
Zilkha & Sons

WOMEN'S AFFAIRS

Abbott Laboratories
ABC
AGL Resources Inc.
Agrilink Foods, Inc.
Air Products and Chemicals, Inc.
Alcoa Inc.
Alcon Laboratories, Inc.
Alexander & Baldwin, Inc.
Allegheny Technologies Inc.
Alliant Techsystems
AlliedSignal Inc.
Allmerica Financial Corp.
Allstate Insurance Co.
AMCORE Bank Rockford
American Express Co.
American Fidelity Corp.
American Retail Group
American Stock Exchange, Inc.
Ameritech Corp.
Ameritech Indiana
AMETEK, Inc.
AMR Corp.
Amsted Industries Inc.
Aon Corp.
Archer-Daniels-Midland Co.
Aristech Chemical Corp.
Arizona Public Service Co.
AT&T Corp.
Atlantic Richfield Co.
Avery Dennison Corp.
Avista Corporation
Avon Products, Inc.
Bandag, Inc.
Bank of America
BankBoston Corp.
Barclays Capital
Bausch & Lomb Inc.
Belk Stores Services Inc.
Bemis Co., Inc.
Ben & Jerry's Homemade Inc.
Bernstein & Co., Inc. (Sanford C.)
Berwind Group
BFGoodrich Co.
Block, Inc. (H&R)
Blount International, Inc.
Blue Cross & Blue Shield of Alabama
Boise Cascade Corp.
Borden, Inc.
Boston Globe (The)
BP Amoco Corp.
Brown & Williamson Tobacco Corp.
Brunswick Corp.
Business Improvement
Cabot Corp.
Calvin Klein
Cargill Inc.
Carillon Importers, Ltd.
Central Maine Power Co.
Central Soya Co.
CertainTeed Corp.
Champion International Corp.
Chase Bank of Texas
Chase Manhattan Bank, NA
Chevron Corp.
Chicago Title Corp.
CIGNA Corp.
Cincinnati Bell Inc.
CIT Group, Inc. (The)
Citibank Corp.
Citigroup
Citizens Financial Group, Inc.
CLARCOR Inc.
Clorox Co.
CNA
Comdisco, Inc.
Compaq Computer Corp.
Consolidated Natural Gas Co.
Continental Grain Co.
Contran Corp.
Cooper Industries, Inc.
Coors Brewing Co.
Corning Inc.
Country Curtains, Inc.
Cox Enterprises Inc.
CPI Corp.
Crane Co.
Crane & Co., Inc.
Credit Suisse First Boston
CSS Industries, Inc.
Cummins Engine Co., Inc.
Daily News
DaimlerChrysler Corp.
Dain Bosworth Inc.
Dana Corp.
Danis Companies
Dayton Hudson
Dayton Power and Light Co.
Deluxe Corp.
Demoulas Supermarkets Inc.
Detroit Edison Co.
Deutsch Co.
Dexter Corp.
Dominion Resources, Inc.
Dow Jones & Co., Inc.
du Pont de Nemours & Co. (E.I.)
Duchossois Industries Inc.
Duke Energy
Duriron Co., Inc.
Eastern Bank
Ecolab Inc.
Edison International
El Paso Energy Co.
Employers Mutual Casualty Co.
Ensign-Bickford Industries
Equifax Inc.
Equitable Resources, Inc.
Erb Lumber Co.
Evening Post Publishing Co.
Exxon Mobil Corp.
Fabri-Kal Corp.
Fannie Mae
Federal-Mogul Corp.
Federated Department Stores, Inc.
Fidelity Investments
Fireman's Fund Insurance Co.
First Maryland Bancorp
First Union Bank
First Union Corp.
First Union National Bank, NA
First Union Securities, Inc.
Firstar Bank Milwaukee NA
FleetBoston Financial Corp.
Fluor Corp.
Forest City Enterprises, Inc.
Fort Worth Star-Telegram Inc.
Fortis Insurance Co.
Fortune Brands, Inc.
Freddie Mac
Freeport-McMoRan Inc.
Furniture Brands International, Inc.
Gallo Winery, Inc. (E&J)
GATX Corp.
GenAmerica Corp.
GenCorp
General Atlantic Partners II LP
General Electric Co.
General Mills, Inc.
General Motors Corp.
General Reinsurance Corp.
Georgia Power Co.
Giant Eagle Inc.
Giant Food Inc.
Glaxo Wellcome Inc.
Glickenhaus & Co.
Globe Corp.
Goldman Sachs Group
Graco, Inc.
Group Health Plan
Gulf Power Co.
Halliburton Co.
Hallmark Cards Inc.
Hancock Financial Services (John)
Harnischfeger Industries
Harris Corp.
Harris Trust & Savings Bank
Hartford (The)
Hartford Steam Boiler Inspection & Insurance Co.
Hartmarx Corp.
Hasbro, Inc.
Hawaiian Electric Co., Inc.
Heinz Co. (H.J.)
Hickory Tech Corp.
Hitachi America Ltd.
Honeywell International Inc.
Household International Inc.
Huffy Corp.
Humana, Inc.
Huntington Bancshares Inc.
IKON Office Solutions, Inc.
Illinois Tool Works, Inc.
Industrial Bank of Japan Trust Co. (New York)
Intel Corp.
International Business Machines Corp.
International Flavors & Fragrances Inc.
Jacobs Engineering Group
Jeld-wen, Inc.
Johnson Controls Inc.
Johnson & Johnson
Johnson & Son (S.C.)
Jostens, Inc.
Journal-Gazette Co.
JSJ Corp.
Katten, Muchin & Zavis
Kellwood Co.
Kelly Services
Kennametal, Inc.
Kimball International, Inc.
Kimberly-Clark Corp.
Kingsbury Corp.
Kmart Corp.
Kraft Foods, Inc.
Kroger Co.
La-Z-Boy Inc.
Lance, Inc.
LandAmerica Financial Services
Lee Enterprises
Leigh Fibers, Inc.
Levi Strauss & Co.
Leviton Manufacturing Co. Inc.
LG&E Energy Corp.
Liberty Corp.
Lincoln Financial Group
Lipton Co.
Little, Inc. (Arthur D.)
Litton Industries, Inc.
Liz Claiborne, Inc.
Loews Corp.
Lotus Development Corp.
Lowe's Companies
LTV Corp.
Macy's East Inc.
Madison Gas & Electric Co.
Mallinckrodt Chemical, Inc.
Maritz Inc.
Mark IV Industries
Marriott International Inc.
Marshall Field's
Marshall & Ilsley Corp.
Mattel Inc.
Maybelline, Inc.
MBIA Inc.
McClatchy Co.
McDonald & Co. Securities, Inc.
McGraw-Hill Companies, Inc.
McKesson-HBOC Corp.
Mead Corp.
Mellon Financial Corp.
Menasha Corp.
Merck & Co.
Merrill Lynch & Co., Inc.
Metropolitan Life Insurance Co.
Mid-America Bank of Louisville
MONY Group (The)
Morgan & Co. Inc. (J.P.)
Morgan Stanley Dean Witter & Co.
Morrison Knudsen Corp.
Morton International Inc.
Motorola Inc.
Nalco Chemical Co.
National City Bank of Minneapolis
National Computer Systems, Inc.
National Service Industries, Inc.
Nestle U.S.A. Inc.
New Century Energies
New England Bio Labs
New England Financial
New Jersey Natural Gas Co.
New York Life Insurance Co.
New York Times Co.
Nomura Holding America
Northern States Power Co.
Northern Trust Co.

Northwest Natural Gas Co.
Norton Co.
Norwest Corp.
Occidental Petroleum Corp.
Ohio National Life Insurance Co.
Overseas Shipholding Group Inc.
Owens Corning
Pacific Gas and Electric Co.
Pacific Mutual Life Insurance Co.
PacifiCare Health Systems
Paine Webber
Penney Co., Inc. (J.C.)
Peoples Energy Corp.
Pfizer Inc.
Pharmacia & Upjohn, Inc.
Philip Morris Companies Inc.
Physicians Mutual Insurance Co.
Pillsbury Co.
Pitney Bowes Inc.
Pittway Corp.
Playboy Enterprises Inc.
Polaroid Corp.
Potomac Electric Power Co.
PPG Industries, Inc.
Praxair
Premier Industrial Corp.
Principal Financial Group
Procter & Gamble Co.
Procter & Gamble Co., Cosmetics Division
Providence Journal-Bulletin Co.
Prudential Insurance Co. of America
Prudential Securities Inc.
Public Service Electric & Gas Co.
Pulitzer Publishing Co.
Putnam Investments
Quaker Chemical Corp.
Red Wing Shoe Co. Inc.
Reebok International Ltd.
Regions Bank
Reliant Energy Inc.
ReliaStar Financial Corp.
Revlon Inc.
Reynolds & Reynolds Co.
Reynolds Tobacco (R.J.)
Rockwell International Corp.
Rubbermaid Inc.
Safeguard Scientifics
Saint Paul Companies Inc.
Salomon Smith Barney
Sara Lee Corp.
Schlumberger Ltd. (USA)
Schwab & Co., Inc. (Charles)
Scripps Co. (E.W.)
Seagram & Sons, Inc. (Joseph E.)
Searle & Co. (G.D.)
Security Benefit Life Insurance Co.
Sentinel Communications Co.
ServiceMaster Co.
S.G. Cowen
Shea Co. (John F.)
Shell Oil Co.
Sierra Pacific Industries
Sierra Pacific Resources
SIT Investment Associates, Inc.
SmithKline Beecham Corp.
Sonoco Products Co.
Southeastern Mutual Insurance Co.
Southern California Gas Co.
Sovereign Bank
SPX Corp.
Standard Products Co.
Standard Register Co.
Starwood Hotels & Resorts Worldwide, Inc.
State Street Bank & Trust Co.
Steelcase Inc.
Stone Container Corp.
Storage Technology Corp.
Stride Rite Corp.
Sun Microsystems Inc.
Sunmark Capital Corp.
SunTrust Bank Atlanta
Synovus Financial Corp.
TCF National Bank Minnesota
TENNANT Co.
Tenneco Automotive
Tension Envelope Corp.
Tesoro Hawaii
Texaco Inc.
Textron Inc.
Thompson Co. (J. Walter)
Times Mirror Co.
Titan Industrial Corp.
TJX Companies, Inc.
TMC Investment Co.
Toledo Blade Co.
Tomkins Industries, Inc.
Trace International Holdings, Inc.
True North Communications, Inc.
TRW Inc.
Union Camp Corp.
Union Carbide Corp.
United Airlines Inc.
United Parcel Service of America Inc.
U.S. Bancorp Piper Jaffray
United Technologies Corp.
United Wisconsin Services
Universal Studios
Unocal Corp.
US Bank, Washington
US West, Inc.
USG Corp.
Valmont Industries, Inc.
Varian Medical Systems, Inc.
Wachovia Bank of North Carolina NA
Waffle House Inc.
Wal-Mart Stores, Inc.
Walgreen Co.
Walter Industries Inc.
Warner-Lambert Co.
Washington Mutual, Inc.
Washington Trust Bank
Weil, Gotshal & Manges Corp.
Western & Southern Life Insurance Co.
Westvaco Corp.
Whirlpool Corp.
Whitman Corp.
WICOR, Inc.
Wilbur-Ellis Co. & Connell Brothers Co.
Williams
Winn-Dixie Stores Inc.
Wiremold Co.
Wisconsin Public Service Corp.
Witco Corp.
Woodward Governor Co.
Xerox Corp.
Young & Rubicam
Zilkha & Sons

ZOOS/AQUARIUMS

Abbott Laboratories
AEGON U.S.A. Inc.
Alabama Power Co.
Alcoa Inc.
Alcon Laboratories, Inc.
Allegheny Technologies Inc.
America West Airlines, Inc.
American Express Co.
American Fidelity Corp.
American United Life Insurance Co.
Ameritech Illinois
Ameritech Indiana
Ameritech Michigan
Ameritech Ohio
Ameritech Wisconsin
AMETEK, Inc.
AMR Corp.
Amsted Industries Inc.
Analog Devices, Inc.
Andersen Corp.
Andersons Inc.
Anheuser-Busch Companies, Inc.
Aon Corp.
Archer-Daniels-Midland Co.
Aristech Chemical Corp.
Arizona Public Service Co.
Atlantic Investment Co.
Atlantic Richfield Co.
Avon Products, Inc.
Badger Meter, Inc.
Baird & Co. (Robert W.)
Bank of America
Bank of New York Co., Inc.
Bank One Corp.
Barclays Capital
Barden Corp.
Bardes Corp.
Barnes Group Inc.
Battelle Memorial Institute
Bausch & Lomb Inc.
Baxter International Inc.
Bechtel Group, Inc.
Bemis Co., Inc.
Berwind Group
Bestfoods
Binswanger Companies
Blair & Co. (William)
Block, Inc. (H&R)
Blount International, Inc.
Blue Bell, Inc.
Blue Cross & Blue Shield of Alabama
Blue Cross & Blue Shield of Iowa
Boeing Co.
Boise Cascade Corp.
Borman's Inc.
Boston Edison Co.
Boston Globe (The)
BP Amoco Corp.
Bridgestone/Firestone, Inc.
Bristol-Myers Squibb Co.
Broderbund Software, Inc.
Brown Shoe Co., Inc.
Brown & Williamson Tobacco Corp.
Brunswick Corp.
Bucyrus-Erie Co.
Burlington Resources, Inc.
Burnett Co. (Leo)
Cabot Corp.
Campbell Soup Co.
Cargill Inc.
Carter-Wallace, Inc.
Central & South West Services
Central Soya Co.
CertainTeed Corp.
Cessna Aircraft Co.
CGU Insurance
Chase Bank of Texas
Chemed Corp.
Chevron Corp.
Chicago Board of Trade
Chicago Title Corp.
Chicago Tribune Co.
CIGNA Corp.
Cincinnati Bell Inc.
Cinergy Corp.
Citibank Corp.
Citizens Financial Group, Inc.
Cleveland-Cliffs, Inc.
Clorox Co.
CNA
Collins & Aikman Corp.
Colonial Life & Accident Insurance Co.
Commerce Bancshares, Inc.
Commonwealth Edison Co.
Compaq Computer Corp.
Compass Bank
ConAgra, Inc.
Consolidated Natural Gas Co.
Consolidated Papers, Inc.
Constellation Energy Group, Inc.
Consumers Energy Co.
Contran Corp.
Cooper Industries, Inc.
Copley Press, Inc.
Country Curtains, Inc.
Cox Enterprises Inc.
Crane Co.
Crestar Finance Corp.
Cummings Properties Management
CUNA Mutual Group
Cyprus Amax Minerals Co.
Daily News
DaimlerChrysler Corp.
Dain Bosworth Inc.
Dana Corp.
Deere & Co.
DeKalb Genetics Corp.
Deposit Guaranty National Bank
Detroit Edison Co.
Deutsch Co.
Dial Corp.
Disney Co. (Walt)
Dixie Group, Inc. (The)
Donaldson Co., Inc.
Donnelley & Sons Co. (R.R.)
Dow Corning Corp.
du Pont de Nemours & Co. (E.I.)
Duchossois Industries Inc.
Duke Energy
Dynamet, Inc.
Eastern Enterprises
Ecolab Inc.
Edison International
El Paso Energy Co.
Elf Atochem North America, Inc.
Emerson Electric Co.
Employers Mutual Casualty Co.
Enterprise Rent-A-Car Co.
Equifax Inc.
Erb Lumber Co.
Evening Post Publishing Co.
Excel Corp.
Extendicare Health Services
Exxon Mobil Corp.
Federal-Mogul Corp.
Federated Mutual Insurance Co.
Ferro Corp.
Fidelity Investments
Fifth Third Bancorp
FINA
Fireman's Fund Insurance Co.
First Maryland Bancorp
First Tennessee National Corp.
First Union Bank
First Union Corp.
First Union National Bank, NA
Firstar Bank Milwaukee NA
Fisher Scientific
FleetBoston Financial Corp.
FMC Corp.
Forbes Inc.
Ford Meter Box Co.
Ford Motor Co.
Forest City Enterprises, Inc.
Fortis Insurance Co.
Fortune Brands, Inc.
Freeport-McMoRan Inc.
Frost National Bank
Furniture Brands International, Inc.
Gap, Inc.
GATX Corp.
GenAmerica Corp.
GenCorp
General Electric Co.
General Mills, Inc.
General Motors Corp.
Georgia-Pacific Corp.
Georgia Power Co.
Gerber Products Co.
Giant Eagle Inc.
Giant Food Inc.
Glaxo Wellcome Inc.
Globe Corp.
Goodrich Aerospace - Aerostructures Group (B.F.)
Grace & Co. (W.R.)
GTE Corp.
Guardian Life Insurance Co. of America
Halliburton Co.
Hallmark Cards Inc.
Hanna Co. (M.A.)
Hannaford Brothers Co.
Harcourt General, Inc.
Harley-Davidson Co.
Harnischfeger Industries
Harris Corp.
Harris Trust & Savings Bank
Hartmarx Corp.
Hasbro, Inc.
Heinz Co. (H.J.)
Hewlett-Packard Co.
Hoffmann-La Roche Inc.
Honeywell International Inc.
Hubbard Broadcasting, Inc.
Humana, Inc.
Huntington Bancshares Inc.
IKON Office Solutions, Inc.
Illinois Tool Works, Inc.
Independent Stave Co.
Inland Container Corp.
Intel Corp.
International Business Machines Corp.
International Flavors & Fragrances Inc.
International Paper Co.
INTRUST Financial Corp.
Jacobson & Sons (Benjamin)
Johnson Controls Inc.
Johnson & Son (S.C.)
Jones & Co. (Edward D.)
Jostens, Inc.

Journal-Gazette Co.
JSJ Corp.
Katten, Muchin & Zavis
Kellogg Co.
Kellwood Co.
Kelly Services
Kerr-McGee Corp.
Kiewit Sons' Inc. (Peter)
Kimberly-Clark Corp.
Kmart Corp.
Koch Enterprises, Inc.
Kraft Foods, Inc.
Kroger Co.
Laclede Gas Co.
Ladish Co., Inc.
Lancaster Lens, Inc.
Lance, Inc.
Land O'Lakes, Inc.
Landmark Communications Inc.
Lee Enterprises
Lehigh Portland Cement Co.
Lennox International, Inc.
Liberty Corp.
Liberty Diversified Industries
Lilly & Co. (Eli)
Lincoln Electric Co.
Lincoln Financial Group
Lipton Co.
Little, Inc. (Arthur D.)
Liz Claiborne, Inc.
Loews Corp.
Louisiana Land & Exploration Co.
Louisiana-Pacific Corp.
LTV Corp.
Lubrizol Corp. (The)
Macy's East Inc.
Madison Gas & Electric Co.
Mallinckrodt Chemical, Inc.
Manufacturers & Traders Trust Co.
Maritz Inc.
Mark IV Industries
Marshall & Ilsley Corp.
Masco Corp.
May Department Stores Co.
Maytag Corp.
McClatchy Co.
McDonald & Co. Securities, Inc.
McKesson-HBOC Corp.
McWane Inc.
Mead Corp.
Medtronic, Inc.
Meijer, Inc.
Menasha Corp.
Mercantile Bank NA
Merrill Lynch & Co., Inc.
Metropolitan Life Insurance Co.
Michigan Consolidated Gas Co.
Mid-America Bank of Louisville
MidAmerican Energy Holdings Co.
Milacron, Inc.
Millipore Corp.
Mine Safety Appliances Co.
Minnesota Mutual Life Insurance Co.
Monsanto Co.
Montgomery Ward & Co., Inc.
Morgan & Co. Inc. (J.P.)
Morgan Stanley Dean Witter & Co.
Morrison Knudsen Corp.
Morton International Inc.
Motorola Inc.
MTD Products Inc.
Mutual of Omaha Insurance Co.
Nalco Chemical Co.
National Bank of Commerce Trust & Savings
National City Bank of Minneapolis
National City Corp.
National Computer Systems, Inc.
National Fuel Gas Distribution Corp.
National Service Industries, Inc.
Nationwide Insurance Co.
NEBCO Evans
Nestle U.S.A. Inc.
New Century Energies
New York Life Insurance Co.
Nordson Corp.
Norfolk Southern Corp.
North American Royalties
Northern States Power Co.
Northern Trust Co.
Northwest Bank Nebraska, NA
Northwest Natural Gas Co.
Norton Co.
Norwest Corp.
Occidental Oil and Gas
OG&E Electric Services
Ohio National Life Insurance Co.
Old Kent Bank
Old National Bank Evansville
Olin Corp.
Oshkosh B'Gosh, Inc.
Outboard Marine Corp.
PACCAR Inc.
Pacific Mutual Life Insurance Co.
Parker Hannifin Corp.
Pella Corp.
Penney Co., Inc. (J.C.)
Pennzoil-Quaker State Co.
Peoples Energy Corp.
PerkinElmer, Inc.
Pfizer Inc.
Pharmacia & Upjohn, Inc.
Phelps Dodge Corp.
Physicians Mutual Insurance Co.
Pieper Power Electric Co.
Pittway Corp.
PNC Financial Services Group
PPG Industries, Inc.
Premier Industrial Corp.
Price Associates (T. Rowe)
Principal Financial Group
Procter & Gamble Co.
Procter & Gamble Co., Cosmetics Division
Providence Journal-Bulletin Co.
Provident Companies, Inc.
Prudential Securities Inc.
Publix Supermarkets
Pulitzer Publishing Co.
Putnam Investments
Quaker Chemical Corp.
Questar Corp.
Ralston Purina Co.
Red Wing Shoe Co. Inc.
Reilly Industries, Inc.
Reliant Energy Inc.
Reynolds Metals Co.
Rich Products Corp.
Rockwell International Corp.
Rouse Co.
Russer Foods
SAFECO Corp.
Salomon Smith Barney
Sara Lee Corp.
SBC Communications Inc.
Schering-Plough Corp.
Schwab & Co., Inc. (Charles)
Searle & Co. (G.D.)
Seaway Food Town, Inc.
Security Benefit Life Insurance Co.
Security Life of Denver Insurance Co.
Sempra Energy
Shaklee Corp.
Shaw's Supermarkets, Inc.
Shell Oil Co.
Simpson Investment Co.
Slant/Fin Corp.
SmithKline Beecham Corp.
Smurfit-Stone Container Corp.
Sprint Corp.
Sprint/United Telephone
Star Bank NA
Starwood Hotels & Resorts Worldwide, Inc.
State Farm Mutual Automobile Insurance Co.
State Street Bank & Trust Co.
Steelcase Inc.
Stone Container Corp.
Strear Farms Co.
Stride Rite Corp.
Stupp Brothers Bridge & Iron Co.
Sun Microsystems Inc.
SunTrust Bank Atlanta
SunTrust Banks of Florida
Synovus Financial Corp.
Tektronix, Inc.
Teleflex Inc.
Temple-Inland Inc.
TENNANT Co.
Tenneco Automotive
Tension Envelope Corp.
Tesoro Hawaii
Texaco Inc.
Texas Instruments Inc.
Textron Inc.
Times Mirror Co.
Timken Co. (The)
Toledo Blade Co.
Toyota Motor Sales U.S.A., Inc.
Transamerica Corp.
True North Communications, Inc.
Trustmark Insurance Co.
TU Electric Co.
Ukrop's Super Markets
Unilever United States, Inc.
Union Camp Corp.
Union Pacific Corp.
United Airlines Inc.
United Dominion Industries, Ltd.
United Parcel Service of America Inc.
U.S. Bancorp Piper Jaffray
United States Trust Co. of New York
Universal Foods Corp.
Universal Leaf Tobacco Co., Inc.
UnumProvident
US Bank, Washington
USG Corp.
Valmont Industries, Inc.
Vanguard Group
Vulcan Materials Co.
Wachovia Bank of North Carolina NA
Wal-Mart Stores, Inc.
Walgreen Co.
Walter Industries Inc.
Washington Trust Bank
Waste Management Inc.
Wells Fargo & Co.
West Co. Inc.
Western & Southern Life Insurance Co.
Westvaco Corp.
Weyerhaeuser Co.
Whitman Corp.
WICOR, Inc.
Wilbur-Ellis Co. & Connell Brothers Co.
Wiley & Sons (John)
Williams
Winn-Dixie Stores Inc.
Wisconsin Energy Corp.
Wisconsin Public Service Corp.
Young & Rubicam

Education

AFTERSCHOOL/ ENRICHMENT PROGRAMS

Aetna, Inc.
American Retail Group
Armstrong World Industries, Inc.
Bank of America
Barnes Group Inc.
Beckman Coulter, Inc.
Belk Stores Services Inc.
BFGoodrich Co.
Binney & Smith Inc.
Block, Inc. (H&R)
Blue Cross & Blue Shield of Iowa
Boston Edison Co.
Boston Globe (The)
Campbell Soup Co.
Chicago Sun-Times, Inc.
Citigroup
Citizens Bank-Flint
Citizens Financial Group, Inc.
Coca-Cola Co.
Comdisco, Inc.
Consolidated Papers, Inc.
Cook Inlet Region
Corning Inc.
CPI Corp.
Cummins Engine Co., Inc.
Daily News
Dain Bosworth Inc.
Deere & Co.
Delta Air Lines, Inc.
Dreyer's Grand Ice Cream
Eastern Bank
Edwards Enterprise Software (J.D.)
El Paso Energy Co.
Equitable Resources, Inc.
Fannie Mae
Federated Mutual Insurance Co.
Fort Worth Star-Telegram Inc.
Freddie Mac
Fuller Co. (H.B.)
Gallo Winery, Inc. (E&J)
Gap, Inc.
GATX Corp.
General Atlantic Partners II LP
Graco, Inc.
Harris Trust & Savings Bank
Hoffer Plastics Corp.
HON Industries Inc.
Hunt Manufacturing Co.
Intel Corp.
JSJ Corp.
Lee Enterprises
Levi Strauss & Co.
Little, Inc. (Arthur D.)
Lotus Development Corp.
Louisiana Land & Exploration Co.
Louisiana-Pacific Corp.
MacMillan Bloedel Inc.
McDonald & Co. Securities, Inc.
Mercantile Bank NA
Millipore Corp.
Monsanto Co.
Morgan & Co. Inc. (J.P.)
National Service Industries, Inc.
New England Bio Labs
New York Mercantile Exchange
Nissan North America, Inc.
Northern States Power Co.
Old National Bank Evansville
Owens Corning
PacifiCorp
Pharmacia & Upjohn, Inc.
Pillsbury Co.
Premier Industrial Corp.
Prudential Insurance Co. of America
Ralph's Grocery Co.
Reader's Digest Association, Inc. (The)
Ruddick Corp.
Schwab & Co., Inc. (Charles)
Security Life of Denver Insurance Co.
Sega of America Inc.
Sovereign Bank
State Street Bank & Trust Co.
Stride Rite Corp.
Toyota Motor Sales U.S.A., Inc.
Ukrop's Super Markets
Union Pacific Corp.
United Airlines Inc.
United Distillers & Vintners North America
United Parcel Service of America Inc.
United States Sugar Corp.
US Bank, Washington
US West, Inc.
Whirlpool Corp.
Williams
Zachry Co. (H.B.)

AGRICULTURAL EDUCATION

AGL Resources Inc.
Agrilink Foods, Inc.
Alcoa Inc.
American General Finance
American Standard Inc.
Andersons Inc.
Anheuser-Busch Companies, Inc.
Archer-Daniels-Midland Co.
Arizona Public Service Co.
Atlantic Richfield Co.
Bank of America
Block, Inc. (H&R)
Blue Bell, Inc.
Blue Cross & Blue Shield of Iowa
BP Amoco Corp.
Bridgestone/Firestone, Inc.
Briggs & Stratton Corp.

Burlington Industries, Inc.
Burnett Co. (Leo)
Butler Manufacturing Co.
Cargill Inc.
Carolina Power & Light Co.
Cenex Harvest States
Central Soya Co.
Cessna Aircraft Co.
CGU Insurance
Chesapeake Corp.
Chevron Corp.
Church & Dwight Co., Inc.
Colonial Life & Accident Insurance Co.
Commerce Bancshares, Inc.
ConAgra, Inc.
Consumers Energy Co.
Continental Grain Co.
Country Curtains, Inc.
Crane & Co., Inc.
DaimlerChrysler Corp.
Dana Corp.
Deere & Co.
DeKalb Genetics Corp.
Detroit Edison Co.
Dixie Group, Inc. (The)
Donaldson Co., Inc.
Dow Chemical Co.
du Pont de Nemours & Co. (E.I.)
Duke Energy
El Paso Energy Co.
Excel Corp.
First Financial Bank
First Union Corp.
FMC Corp.
Ford Meter Box Co.
Ford Motor Co.
Freeport-McMoRan Inc.
Frost National Bank
Gallo Winery, Inc. (E&J)
General Mills, Inc.
General Motors Corp.
Georgia Power Co.
Gerber Products Co.
Gulf Power Co.
Halliburton Co.
Hallmark Cards Inc.
Hartford (The)
Heinz Co. (H.J.)
HON Industries Inc.
Huntington Bancshares Inc.
International Multifoods Corp.
International Paper Co.
Jacobs Engineering Group
Johnson Controls Inc.
Journal-Gazette Co.
Kimball International, Inc.
Kinder Morgn
Koch Enterprises, Inc.
Kroger Co.
Lance, Inc.
Land O'Lakes, Inc.
Liberty Diversified Industries
May Department Stores Co.
Metropolitan Life Insurance Co.
MFA Inc.
Monarch Machine Tool Co.
Montana Power Co.
Montgomery Ward & Co., Inc.
Motorola Inc.
MTD Products Inc.
National Machinery Co.
Nationwide Insurance Co.
NEBCO Evans
Nestle U.S.A. Inc.
New England Bio Labs
Niagara Mohawk Holdings Inc.
Northwest Bank Nebraska, NA
Norwest Corp.
Novartis Corporation
Orscheln Co.
Oshkosh B'Gosh, Inc.
Pacific Century Financial Corp.
Phillips Petroleum Co.
Physicians Mutual Insurance Co.
Pioneer Hi-Bred International, Inc.
Principal Financial Group
Quanex Corp.
Reynolds Tobacco (R.J.)
Rubbermaid Inc.
S&T Bancorp
Searle & Co. (G.D.)
Servco Pacific
Sierra Pacific Industries
Sierra Pacific Resources
Simplot Co. (J.R.)
Simpson Investment Co.
Smurfit-Stone Container Corp.
Standard Products Co.
Stonecutter Mills Corp.
Susquehanna-Pfaltzgraff Co.
Tesoro Hawaii
Tomkins Industries, Inc.
Toshiba America Inc.
True Oil Co.
Tyson Foods Inc.
Unilever United States, Inc.
Union Camp Corp.
Union Pacific Corp.
United States Sugar Corp.
Unocal Corp.
UnumProvident
Valero Energy Corp.
Valmont Industries, Inc.
Wachovia Bank of North Carolina NA
Wal-Mart Stores, Inc.
Washington Mutual, Inc.
Williams
Wisconsin Public Service Corp.
Yellow Corp.

ARTS/HUMANITIES EDUCATION

Aetna, Inc.
Air Products and Chemicals, Inc.
Alcoa Inc.
Alexander & Baldwin, Inc.
Allegheny Technologies Inc.
AlliedSignal Inc.
Ameren Corp.
American Express Co.
Ameritech Corp.
Ameritech Indiana
Ameritech Michigan
AMR Corp.
Andersen Corp.
Anheuser-Busch Companies, Inc.
Aon Corp.
APL Ltd.
Archer-Daniels-Midland Co.
Armstrong World Industries, Inc.
AT&T Corp.
Avon Products, Inc.
Badger Meter, Inc.
Bandag, Inc.
Bank One Corp.
BankAtlantic Bancorp
Banta Corp.
Barclays Capital
Barry Corp. (R.G.)
Bassett Furniture Industries
Belk-Simpson Department Stores
Bell Atlantic Corp.
BellSouth Corp.
Bernstein & Co., Inc. (Sanford C.)
Bethlehem Steel Corp.
Binney & Smith Inc.
Binswanger Companies
Block, Inc. (H&R)
Blount International, Inc.
Blue Bell, Inc.
Blue Cross & Blue Shield of Alabama
Bourns, Inc.
Bradford & Co. (J.C.)
Bridgestone/Firestone, Inc.
Bristol-Myers Squibb Co.
Broderbund Software, Inc.
Burlington Resources, Inc.
Burnett Co. (Leo)
Burress (J.W.)
Calvin Klein
Cargill Inc.
Carillon Importers, Ltd.
Carpenter Technology Corp.
CCB Financial Corp.
Central Maine Power Co.
Central National-Gottesman
CertainTeed Corp.
Chemed Corp.
Chevron Corp.
Chicago Sun-Times, Inc.
Church & Dwight Co., Inc.
CIGNA Corp.
Cinergy Corp.
Citibank Corp.
Citigroup
Citizens Bank-Flint
Citizens Financial Group, Inc.
Clorox Co.
CNA
Coca-Cola Co.
Colonial Life & Accident Insurance Co.
Commerce Bancshares, Inc.
Commercial Intertech Corp.
Compass Bank
Consolidated Electrical Distributors
Consolidated Papers, Inc.
Constellation Energy Group, Inc.
Consumers Energy Co.
Contran Corp.
Cooper Industries, Inc.
Copley Press, Inc.
Country Curtains, Inc.
Crane Co.
Crane & Co., Inc.
Cranston Print Works Co.
Credit Suisse First Boston
Crestar Finance Corp.
Cummings Properties Management
Cummins Engine Co., Inc.
Daily News
DaimlerChrysler Corp.
Dayton Hudson
Deere & Co.
Deluxe Corp.
Detroit Edison Co.
Deutsch Co.
Dexter Corp.
Disney Co. (Walt)
Dixie Group, Inc. (The)
Dow Corning Corp.
Dow Jones & Co., Inc.
Dreyer's Grand Ice Cream
Duchossois Industries Inc.
Duke Energy
Eastern Bank
El Paso Energy Co.
Elf Atochem North America, Inc.
Emerson Electric Co.
Ensign-Bickford Industries
Enterprise Rent-A-Car Co.
Equifax Inc.
Equitable Resources, Inc.
Erb Lumber Co.
Evening Post Publishing Co.
Federated Department Stores, Inc.
Ferro Corp.
Fidelity Investments
Fifth Third Bancorp
First American Corp.
First Hawaiian, Inc.
First Maryland Bancorp
First Source Corp.
First Union Corp.
First Union National Bank, NA
First Union Securities, Inc.
FleetBoston Financial Corp.
Forbes Inc.
Ford Meter Box Co.
Ford Motor Co.
Forest City Enterprises, Inc.
Fortis, Inc.
Fortune Brands, Inc.
Franklin Mint (The)
Frost National Bank
Fuller Co. (H.B.)
Furniture Brands International, Inc.
Gap, Inc.
GATX Corp.
GenAmerica Corp.
General Electric Co.
General Mills, Inc.
General Motors Corp.
Georgia Power Co.
Gerber Products Co.
Giant Food Inc.
Grace & Co. (W.R.)
Grede Foundries
Guardian Life Insurance Co. of America
Guess?
Hallmark Cards Inc.
Hanna Co. (M.A.)
Hannaford Brothers Co.
Harley-Davidson Co.
Harnischfeger Industries
Harris Trust & Savings Bank
Harsco Corp.
Hartford (The)
Hartmarx Corp.
Hasbro, Inc.
Hawaiian Electric Co., Inc.
Heinz Co. (H.J.)
Hickory Tech Corp.
Hitachi America Ltd.
Housatonic Curtain Co.
Hubbard Broadcasting, Inc.
Huffy Corp.
Hunt Manufacturing Co.
IKON Office Solutions, Inc.
International Flavors & Fragrances Inc.
Invacare Corp.
ISE America
Jacobs Engineering Group
Johnson Controls Inc.
Johnson & Son (S.C.)
JSJ Corp.
Kemper National Insurance Companies
Kimball International, Inc.
Kimberly-Clark Corp.
Kingsbury Corp.
Koch Industries, Inc.
Kraft Foods, Inc.
Lancaster Lens, Inc.
Leigh Fibers, Inc.
Leviton Manufacturing Co. Inc.
Liberty Corp.
Lincoln Electric Co.
Lincoln Financial Group
Little, Inc. (Arthur D.)
Liz Claiborne, Inc.
Loews Corp.
Lubrizol Corp. (The)
MacMillan Bloedel Inc.
Mark IV Industries
Marshall Field's
Marshall & Ilsley Corp.
Masco Corp.
May Department Stores Co.
McClatchy Co.
McDonald's Corp.
McWane Inc.
Mead Corp.
Medtronic, Inc.
Menasha Corp.
Merck & Co.
Merit Oil Corp.
Metropolitan Life Insurance Co.
Milacron, Inc.
Milliken & Co.
Mitsubishi Electric America
Monsanto Co.
Montgomery Ward & Co., Inc.
Morgan & Co. Inc. (J.P.)
Morgan Stanley Dean Witter & Co.
Morrison Knudsen Corp.
National City Bank of Minneapolis
National City Corp.
National Computer Systems, Inc.
National Service Industries, Inc.
Nationwide Insurance Co.
Navcom Systems
NEBCO Evans
Nestle U.S.A. Inc.
New England Bio Labs
New England Financial
New York Life Insurance Co.
New York Times Co.
Nomura Holding America
Nordson Corp.
Norfolk Southern Corp.
Northern Indiana Public Service Co.
Northern Trust Co.
Norton Co.
Ohio National Life Insurance Co.
Old National Bank Evansville
PACCAR Inc.
Pacific Century Financial Corp.
Park National Bank
Philip Morris Companies Inc.
Pieper Power Electric Co.
Pittway Corp.
PNC Financial Services Group
Polaroid Corp.
Price Associates (T. Rowe)
Procter & Gamble Co., Cosmetics Division

Providence Journal-Bulletin Co.
Prudential Insurance Co. of America
Pulitzer Publishing Co.
Putnam Investments
Quaker Chemical Corp.
Ralston Purina Co.
Red Wing Shoe Co. Inc.
Reynolds Tobacco (R.J.)
Rich Products Corp.
Rouse Co.
Russer Foods
Ryder System, Inc.
SAFECO Corp.
Safeguard Scientifics
Saint Paul Companies Inc.
Salomon Smith Barney
Sara Lee Corp.
SBC Communications Inc.
Schering-Plough Corp.
Schloss & Co. (Marcus)
Schlumberger Ltd. (USA)
Scripps Co. (E.W.)
Seagram & Sons, Inc. (Joseph E.)
Sears, Roebuck and Co.
Security Life of Denver Insurance Co.
Sega of America Inc.
Sempra Energy
Servco Pacific
S.G. Cowen
Shelter Mutual Insurance Co.
Simplot Co. (J.R.)
SIT Investment Associates, Inc.
SmithKline Beecham Corp.
Sonoco Products Co.
Sony Electronics
Sotheby's Inc.
Southeastern Mutual Insurance Co.
Southwest Gas Corp.
Square D Co.
Star Bank NA
Starwood Hotels & Resorts Worldwide, Inc.
State Farm Mutual Automobile Insurance Co.
State Street Bank & Trust Co.
Steelcase Inc.
Stone Container Corp.
Stonecutter Mills Corp.
Storage Technology Corp.
Strear Farms Co.
Stride Rite Corp.
Stupp Brothers Bridge & Iron Co.
SunTrust Bank Atlanta
Tektronix, Inc.
Teleflex Inc.
Tenneco Packaging
Tesoro Hawaii
Texaco Inc.
Textron Inc.
Thomasville Furniture Industries Inc.
Times Mirror Co.
Tomkins Industries, Inc.
Toyota Motor Sales U.S.A., Inc.
Trace International Holdings, Inc.
True North Communications, Inc.
TRW Inc.
Tyson Foods Inc.
Unilever Home & Personal Care U.S.A.
Union Pacific Corp.
United Airlines Inc.
United Co.
United Distillers & Vintners North America
U.S. Bancorp Piper Jaffray
United States Sugar Corp.
United States Trust Co. of New York
Universal Foods Corp.
Universal Studios
Unocal Corp.
UPN Channel 50
USX Corp.
Vesper Corp.
Vodafone AirTouch Plc
Vulcan Materials Co.
Wachovia Bank of North Carolina NA
Walter Industries Inc.
Warner-Lambert Co.
Washington Mutual, Inc.
Washington Trust Bank
Weil, Gotshal & Manges Corp.
West Co. Inc.
Whirlpool Corp.
Whitman Corp.
Wilbur-Ellis Co. & Connell Brothers Co.
Wiley & Sons (John)
Williams
Wisconsin Energy Corp.
Witco Corp.
Wolverine World Wide
Wyman-Gordon Co.
Yellow Corp.
Young & Rubicam
Zachry Co. (H.B.)
Zilkha & Sons

BUSINESS EDUCATION

Abbott Laboratories
ABC
AEGON U.S.A. Inc.
Aetna, Inc.
AFLAC Inc.
AGL Resources Inc.
Agrilink Foods, Inc.
Air Products and Chemicals, Inc.
AK Steel Corp.
Alabama Power Co.
Alaska Airlines, Inc.
Albertson's Inc.
Alcoa Inc.
Alcon Laboratories, Inc.
Allegheny Technologies Inc.
Alliant Techsystems
AlliedSignal Inc.
Allmerica Financial Corp.
Allstate Insurance Co.
AMCORE Bank Rockford
Ameren Corp.
America West Airlines, Inc.
American Express Co.
American Fidelity Corp.
American General Finance
American Standard Inc.
American United Life Insurance Co.
Ameritas Life Insurance Corp.
Ameritech Corp.
Ameritech Indiana
Ameritech Michigan
Ameritech Ohio
Ameritech Wisconsin
AMETEK, Inc.
Amgen, Inc.
AMR Corp.
Andersons Inc.
Anheuser-Busch Companies, Inc.
Aon Corp.
APL Ltd.
Archer-Daniels-Midland Co.
Aristech Chemical Corp.
Arizona Public Service Co.
Armstrong World Industries, Inc.
Arvin Industries, Inc.
Ashland, Inc.
Associated Food Stores
AT&T Corp.
Atlantic Investment Co.
Atlantic Richfield Co.
Auburn Foundry
Avon Products, Inc.
Badger Meter, Inc.
Baird & Co. (Robert W.)
Bandag, Inc.
Banfi Vintners
Bank of America
Bank One Corp.
BankAtlantic Bancorp
BankBoston Corp.
Barclays Capital
Barden Corp.
Bardes Corp.
Barnes Group Inc.
Barry Corp. (R.G.)
Bassett Furniture Industries
Battelle Memorial Institute
Baxter International Inc.
Bayer Corp.
Belk Stores Services Inc.
Bell Atlantic Corp.
BellSouth Corp.
Bemis Co., Inc.
Bemis Manufacturing Co.
Bernstein & Co., Inc. (Sanford C.)
Berwind Group
Bestfoods
Bethlehem Steel Corp.
BFGoodrich Co.
Binney & Smith Inc.
Blair & Co. (William)
Block, Inc. (H&R)
Blount International, Inc.
Blue Bell, Inc.
Blue Cross & Blue Shield of Alabama
Blue Cross & Blue Shield of Iowa
Blue Cross & Blue Shield of Minnesota
Boeing Co.
Boise Cascade Corp.
Boler Co.
Borden, Inc.
Bourns, Inc.
Bowater Inc.
BP Amoco Corp.
Bradford & Co. (J.C.)
Bridgestone/Firestone, Inc.
Briggs & Stratton Corp.
Bristol-Myers Squibb Co.
Brown Shoe Co., Inc.
Browning-Ferris Industries Inc.
Brunswick Corp.
Bucyrus-Erie Co.
Burlington Industries, Inc.
Burlington Resources, Inc.
Burnett Co. (Leo)
Burress (J.W.)
Business Improvement
Cabot Corp.
Calvin Klein
Campbell Soup Co.
Cargill Inc.
Carillon Importers, Ltd.
Carolina Power & Light Co.
Carpenter Technology Corp.
Caterpillar Inc.
Central Maine Power Co.
Central National-Gottesman
Central & South West Services
Central Soya Co.
Cessna Aircraft Co.
CGU Insurance
Charter Manufacturing Co.
Chase Bank of Texas
Chase Manhattan Bank, NA
Chemed Corp.
Chesapeake Corp.
Chevron Corp.
Chicago Sun-Times, Inc.
Chicago Title Corp.
Church & Dwight Co., Inc.
CIBC Oppenheimer
CIGNA Corp.
Cincinnati Bell Inc.
Cinergy Corp.
Circuit City Stores, Inc.
CIT Group, Inc. (The)
Citibank Corp.
Citigroup
Citizens Bank-Flint
Citizens Financial Group, Inc.
CLARCOR Inc.
Cleveland-Cliffs, Inc.
Clorox Co.
CNA
Coca-Cola Co.
Collins & Aikman Corp.
Colonial Life & Accident Insurance Co.
Colonial Oil Industries, Inc.
Comdisco, Inc.
Commerce Bancshares, Inc.
Commercial Intertech Corp.
Compaq Computer Corp.
Compass Bank
ConAgra, Inc.
Cone Mills Corp.
Conoco, Inc.
Consolidated Natural Gas Co.
Consolidated Papers, Inc.
Consumers Energy Co.
Continental Grain Co.
Contran Corp.
Conwood Co. LP
Cooper Industries, Inc.
Cooper Tire & Rubber Co.
Coors Brewing Co.
Corning Inc.
Crane Co.
Crane & Co., Inc.
Cranston Print Works Co.
Credit Suisse First Boston
Crestar Finance Corp.
CSR Rinker Materials Corp.
CSS Industries, Inc.
Cummings Properties Management
Cummins Engine Co., Inc.
CUNA Mutual Group
DaimlerChrysler Corp.
Dain Bosworth Inc.
Dana Corp.
Danis Companies
Dayton Power and Light Co.
Deere & Co.
DeKalb Genetics Corp.
Deloitte & Touche
Deluxe Corp.
Demoulas Supermarkets Inc.
Deposit Guaranty National Bank
Detroit Edison Co.
Deutsch Co.
Dexter Corp.
Dial Corp.
Disney Co. (Walt)
Dixie Group, Inc. (The)
Donaldson Co., Inc.
Dreyer's Grand Ice Cream
DSM Copolymer
du Pont de Nemours & Co. (E.I.)
Duchossois Industries Inc.
Duke Energy
Dun & Bradstreet Corp.
Duriron Co., Inc.
Eastman Kodak Co.
Eaton Corp.
Eckerd Corp.
Ecolab Inc.
Edison Brothers Stores, Inc.
Edison International
Elf Atochem North America, Inc.
Emerson Electric Co.
Employers Mutual Casualty Co.
Ensign-Bickford Industries
Equifax Inc.
Erb Lumber Co.
Ernst & Young, LLP
Evening Post Publishing Co.
Exxon Mobil Corp.
Federal-Mogul Corp.
Federated Department Stores, Inc.
Federated Mutual Insurance Co.
Ferro Corp.
Fidelity Investments
Fifth Third Bancorp
FINA
Fireman's Fund Insurance Co.
First American Corp.
First Hawaiian, Inc.
First Maryland Bancorp
First Source Corp.
First Union Corp.
First Union National Bank, NA
First Union Securities, Inc.
Firstar Bank Milwaukee NA
Fisher Brothers Cleaning Services
Fisher Scientific
FleetBoston Financial Corp.
Florida Power Corp.
Florida Rock Industries
Fluor Corp.
FMC Corp.
Ford Meter Box Co.
Ford Motor Co.
Fortis, Inc.
Fortis Insurance Co.
Fortune Brands, Inc.
Franklin Electric Co.
Freeport-McMoRan Inc.
Frost National Bank
Furniture Brands International, Inc.
Gallo Winery, Inc. (E&J)
Gap, Inc.
GEICO Corp.
GenAmerica Corp.
GenCorp
General Electric Co.
General Mills, Inc.
General Motors Corp.
Georgia-Pacific Corp.
Georgia Power Co.
Gerber Products Co.

Giant Eagle Inc.
Giddings & Lewis
Gillette Co.
Glaxo Wellcome Inc.
Globe Corp.
Goldman Sachs Group
Golub Corp.
Goodrich Aerospace - Aerostructures Group (B.F.)
Grace & Co. (W.R.)
Graco, Inc.
GTE Corp.
Guardian Life Insurance Co. of America
Gulf Power Co.
Halliburton Co.
Hallmark Cards Inc.
Hamilton Sundstrand Corp.
Hancock Financial Services (John)
Hanna Co. (M.A.)
Hannaford Brothers Co.
Harcourt General, Inc.
Harley-Davidson Co.
Harnischfeger Industries
Harris Trust & Savings Bank
Harsco Corp.
Hartford (The)
Hartford Steam Boiler Inspection & Insurance Co.
Hartmarx Corp.
Hasbro, Inc.
Heinz Co. (H.J.)
Hewlett-Packard Co.
Hickory Tech Corp.
Hoffer Plastics Corp.
HON Industries Inc.
Honeywell International Inc.
Household International Inc.
Hubbard Broadcasting, Inc.
Hubbell Inc.
Huffy Corp.
Humana, Inc.
Huntington Bancshares Inc.
Illinois Tool Works, Inc.
Independent Stave Co.
Inland Container Corp.
Inman Mills
Intel Corp.
International Flavors & Fragrances Inc.
International Multifoods Corp.
International Paper Co.
INTRUST Financial Corp.
Jacobs Engineering Group
Johnson Controls Inc.
Johnson & Johnson
Johnson & Son (S.C.)
Jones & Co. (Edward D.)
Jostens, Inc.
Journal-Gazette Co.
JSJ Corp.
Katten, Muchin & Zavis
Kellwood Co.
Kelly Services
Kemper National Insurance Companies
Key Bank of Cleveland
Kimball International, Inc.
Kimberly-Clark Corp.
Kinder Morgn
Kingsbury Corp.
KPMG Peat Marwick LLP
Kroger Co.
Laclede Gas Co.
Ladish Co., Inc.
Lancaster Lens, Inc.
Lance, Inc.
Land O'Lakes, Inc.
LandAmerica Financial Services
Landmark Communications Inc.
Lee Enterprises
Lehigh Portland Cement Co.
Leigh Fibers, Inc.
Leviton Manufacturing Co. Inc.
LG&E Energy Corp.
Liberty Corp.
Liberty Diversified Industries
Lilly & Co. (Eli)
Lincoln Electric Co.
Lincoln Financial Group
Lipton Co.
Little, Inc. (Arthur D.)
Litton Industries, Inc.
Loews Corp.
Louisiana Land & Exploration Co.
Louisiana-Pacific Corp.
LTV Corp.
Lubrizol Corp. (The)
Macy's East Inc.
Marcus Corp.
Mark IV Industries
Marshall & Ilsley Corp.
Mattel Inc.
May Department Stores Co.
Maytag Corp.
MBIA Inc.
McClatchy Co.
McCormick & Co. Inc.
McDonald & Co. Securities, Inc.
McGraw-Hill Companies, Inc.
MCI WorldCom, Inc.
McWane Inc.
Medtronic, Inc.
Mellon Financial Corp.
Memphis Light Gas & Water Division
Menasha Corp.
Mercantile Bank NA
Merck & Co.
Merrill Lynch & Co., Inc.
Metropolitan Life Insurance Co.
Michigan Consolidated Gas Co.
Mid-America Bank of Louisville
MidAmerican Energy Holdings Co.
Milacron, Inc.
Milliken & Co.
Millipore Corp.
Mine Safety Appliances Co.
Minnesota Mining & Manufacturing Co.
Minnesota Mutual Life Insurance Co.
Monsanto Co.
MONY Group (The)
Morgan & Co. Inc. (J.P.)
Morgan Stanley Dean Witter & Co.
Morris Communications Corp.
Morrison Knudsen Corp.
Motorola Inc.
MTD Products Inc.
MTS Systems Corp.
Nabisco Group Holdings
Nalco Chemical Co.
NASDAQ Stock Market
National City Bank of Minneapolis
National City Corp.
National Computer Systems, Inc.
National Machinery Co.
National Service Industries, Inc.
National Starch & Chemical Co.
Nationwide Insurance Co.
NEBCO Evans
Nestle U.S.A. Inc.
New Century Energies
New England Financial
New York Life Insurance Co.
New York Stock Exchange, Inc.
Niagara Mohawk Holdings Inc.
Nissan North America, Inc.
Nomura Holding America
Nordson Corp.
Norfolk Southern Corp.
Northern Indiana Public Service Co.
Northern States Power Co.
Northwest Natural Gas Co.
Norton Co.
Norwest Corp.
Occidental Oil and Gas
OG&E Electric Services
Ohio National Life Insurance Co.
Old Kent Bank
Old National Bank Evansville
Olin Corp.
Orange & Rockland Utilities, Inc.
Oshkosh B'Gosh, Inc.
Overnite Transportation Co.
Overseas Shipholding Group Inc.
Owens Corning
PACCAR Inc.
Pacific Century Financial Corp.
Pacific Mutual Life Insurance Co.
PacifiCorp
Paine Webber
Pan-American Life Insurance Co.
Park National Bank
Parker Hannifin Corp.
PECO Energy Co.
Pella Corp.
PEMCO Corp.
Penney Co., Inc. (J.C.)
Pennzoil-Quaker State Co.
PepsiCo, Inc.
PerkinElmer, Inc.
Pfizer Inc.
Pharmacia & Upjohn, Inc.
Phelps Dodge Corp.
Phillips Petroleum Co.
Physicians Mutual Insurance Co.
Pieper Power Electric Co.
Pillsbury Co.
Pittway Corp.
PNC Financial Services Group
Polaroid Corp.
Portland General Electric Co.
Potlatch Corp.
PPG Industries, Inc.
Praxair
Premier Industrial Corp.
Price Associates (T. Rowe)
PricewaterhouseCoopers
Principal Financial Group
Procter & Gamble Co.
Procter & Gamble Co., Cosmetics Division
Providence Journal-Bulletin Co.
Provident Companies, Inc.
Prudential Insurance Co. of America
Prudential Securities Inc.
Public Service Electric & Gas Co.
Pulitzer Publishing Co.
Putnam Investments
Quanex Corp.
Questar Corp.
Ralph's Grocery Co.
Ralston Purina Co.
Rayonier Inc.
Red Wing Shoe Co. Inc.
Regis Corp.
Reilly Industries, Inc.
Reily & Co., Inc. (William B.)
ReliaStar Financial Corp.
Revlon Inc.
Reynolds Metals Co.
Reynolds & Reynolds Co.
Reynolds Tobacco (R.J.)
Rich Products Corp.
Rockwell International Corp.
Rouse Co.
Royal & SunAlliance USA, Inc.
Rubbermaid Inc.
Ruddick Corp.
Ryder System, Inc.
SAFECO Corp.
Saint Paul Companies Inc.
Salomon Smith Barney
S&T Bancorp
Sara Lee Corp.
Sara Lee Hosiery, Inc.
SBC Communications Inc.
Schering-Plough Corp.
Schloss & Co. (Marcus)
Schwab & Co., Inc. (Charles)
Schwebel Baking Co.
Scripps Co. (E.W.)
Seagram & Sons, Inc. (Joseph E.)
Searle & Co. (G.D.)
Sears, Roebuck and Co.
Security Benefit Life Insurance Co.
Security Life of Denver Insurance Co.
Sempra Energy
Sentry Insurance, A Mutual Co.
Servco Pacific
S.G. Cowen
Shea Co. (John F.)
Shell Oil Co.
Shelter Mutual Insurance Co.
Sherwin-Williams Co.
Shoney's Inc.
Sierra Pacific Resources
Simplot Co. (J.R.)
Simpson Investment Co.
SIT Investment Associates, Inc.
Smith Corp. (A.O.)
SmithKline Beecham Corp.
Smurfit-Stone Container Corp.
Solo Cup Co.
Sonoco Products Co.
Sony Electronics
South Bend Tribune Corp.
Southeastern Mutual Insurance Co.
Southwest Gas Corp.
Springs Industries, Inc.
Sprint Corp.
Sprint/United Telephone
SPX Corp.
Square D Co.
Standard Products Co.
Standard Register Co.
Stanley Works (The)
Star Bank NA
Starwood Hotels & Resorts Worldwide, Inc.
State Farm Mutual Automobile Insurance Co.
State Street Bank & Trust Co.
Steelcase Inc.
Stone Container Corp.
Stone & Webster Inc.
Storage Technology Corp.
Stupp Brothers Bridge & Iron Co.
Sun Microsystems Inc.
Sunmark Capital Corp.
Sunoco Inc.
SunTrust Bank Atlanta
TCF National Bank Minnesota
Tektronix, Inc.
Teleflex Inc.
Temple-Inland Inc.
TENNANT Co.
Tenneco Automotive
Tenneco Packaging
Tension Envelope Corp.
Tesoro Hawaii
Texaco Inc.
Texas Gas Transmission Corp.
Texas Instruments Inc.
Textron Inc.
Thermo Electron Corp.
Thompson Co. (J. Walter)
Times Mirror Co.
Timken Co. (The)
Titan Industrial Corp.
TJX Companies, Inc.
TMC Investment Co.
Toledo Blade Co.
Tomkins Industries, Inc.
Toro Co.
Trace International Holdings, Inc.
Transamerica Corp.
True North Communications, Inc.
Trustmark Insurance Co.
TRW Inc.
Tyson Foods Inc.
Ukrop's Super Markets
Ultramar Diamond Shamrock Corp.
Unilever Home & Personal Care U.S.A.
Unilever United States, Inc.
Union Camp Corp.
Union Carbide Corp.
Union Pacific Corp.
United Airlines Inc.
United Distillers & Vintners North America
United Dominion Industries, Ltd.
United Parcel Service of America Inc.
U.S. Bancorp
U.S. Bancorp Piper Jaffray
United States Sugar Corp.
United States Trust Co. of New York
United Technologies Corp.
United Wisconsin Services
Universal Foods Corp.
Universal Leaf Tobacco Co., Inc.
Universal Studios
Unocal Corp.

UnumProvident
US Bank, Washington
US West, Inc.
USAA Life Insurance Co.
USG Corp.
USX Corp.
Valmont Industries, Inc.
Valspar Corp.
Varian Medical Systems, Inc.
Vodafone AirTouch Plc
Vulcan Materials Co.
Wachovia Bank of North Carolina NA
Wachtell, Lipton, Rosen & Katz
Waffle House Inc.
Wal-Mart Stores, Inc.
Walter Industries Inc.
Warner-Lambert Co.
Washington Mutual, Inc.
Washington Trust Bank
Wells Fargo & Co.
Western & Southern Life Insurance Co.
Westvaco Corp.
Weyerhaeuser Co.
Whirlpool Corp.
Whitman Corp.
WICOR, Inc.
Wiley & Sons (John)
Williams
Winn-Dixie Stores Inc.
Wiremold Co.
Wisconsin Energy Corp.
Wisconsin Power & Light Co.
Wisconsin Public Service Corp.
Witco Corp.
Wolverine World Wide
Woodward Governor Co.
Wrigley Co. (Wm. Jr.)
Wyman-Gordon Co.
Xerox Corp.
Yellow Corp.
York Federal Savings & Loan Association
Young & Rubicam
Zachry Co. (H.B.)

BUSINESS-SCHOOL PARTNERSHIPS

Aetna, Inc.
AlliedSignal Inc.
Allmerica Financial Corp.
Amsted Industries Inc.
Aon Corp.
Arvin Industries, Inc.
Badger Meter, Inc.
Baird & Co. (Robert W.)
Bandag, Inc.
BankAtlantic Bancorp
Bechtel Group, Inc.
Beckman Coulter, Inc.
BellSouth Corp.
Bethlehem Steel Corp.
Binswanger Companies
Boston Edison Co.
Boston Globe (The)
Carolina Power & Light Co.
Carpenter Technology Corp.
Chase Manhattan Bank, NA
Chicago Board of Trade
Chicago Sun-Times, Inc.
Cinergy Corp.
Citigroup
Citizens Bank-Flint
Collins & Aikman Corp.
Commerce Bancshares, Inc.
Cone Mills Corp.
Consumers Energy Co.
Corning Inc.
Crane & Co., Inc.
Cummins Engine Co., Inc.
CUNA Mutual Group
Detroit Edison Co.
Dial Corp.
Eastern Bank
Ecolab Inc.
Emerson Electric Co.
Equitable Resources, Inc.
Erb Lumber Co.
Erving Industries
Exxon Mobil Corp.
Federal-Mogul Corp.
Federated Mutual Insurance Co.
Fluor Corp.
Freddie Mac
GenCorp
General Mills, Inc.
GTE Corp.
Halliburton Co.
Hallmark Cards Inc.
Hickory Tech Corp.
Honeywell International Inc.
Hunt Manufacturing Co.
Huntington Bancshares Inc.
Intel Corp.
Ladish Co., Inc.
Lehigh Portland Cement Co.
Lilly & Co. (Eli)
Little, Inc. (Arthur D.)
Madison Gas & Electric Co.
Masco Corp.
Memphis Light Gas & Water Division
Merrill Lynch & Co., Inc.
Michigan Consolidated Gas Co.
Millipore Corp.
Minnesota Mutual Life Insurance Co.
Nabisco Group Holdings
New England Financial
New York Stock Exchange, Inc.
Olin Corp.
Pacific Mutual Life Insurance Co.
Parker Hannifin Corp.
Penney Co., Inc. (J.C.)
PepsiCo, Inc.
Pfizer Inc.
Phillips Petroleum Co.
Physicians Mutual Insurance Co.
Pieper Power Electric Co.
PNC Bank Kentucky Inc.
PPG Industries, Inc.
Principal Financial Group
Procter & Gamble Co.
Procter & Gamble Co., Cosmetics Division
Reynolds Tobacco (R.J.)
Ryder System, Inc.
Sherwin-Williams Co.
Sonoco Products Co.
State Street Bank & Trust Co.
Subway Sandwich Shops, Inc.
TCF National Bank Minnesota
Tension Envelope Corp.
Times Mirror Co.
True North Communications, Inc.
Unilever Home & Personal Care U.S.A.
Unilever United States, Inc.
Union Camp Corp.
Union Carbide Corp.
United Airlines Inc.
Universal Leaf Tobacco Co., Inc.
US Bank, Washington
US West, Inc.
Wachovia Bank of North Carolina NA
Waffle House Inc.
West Co. Inc.
Wyman-Gordon Co.
Zachry Co. (H.B.)

COLLEGES & UNIVERSITIES

ABB Inc.
Abbott Laboratories
ABC
Advanced Micro Devices, Inc.
AEGON U.S.A. Inc.
Aetna, Inc.
AFLAC Inc.
AGL Resources Inc.
Agrilink Foods, Inc.
Air Products and Chemicals, Inc.
AK Steel Corp.
Alabama Power Co.
Albertson's Inc.
Alcoa Inc.
Alcon Laboratories, Inc.
Alexander & Baldwin, Inc.
Allegheny Technologies Inc.
Alliant Techsystems
Allianz Life Insurance Co. of North America
AlliedSignal Inc.
Allmerica Financial Corp.
Allstate Insurance Co.
Alma Piston Co.
AMCORE Bank Rockford
Ameren Corp.
America West Airlines, Inc.
American Express Co.
American Fidelity Corp.
American General Corp.
American General Finance
American Honda Motor Co., Inc.
American Retail Group
American Standard Inc.
American United Life Insurance Co.
Ameritas Life Insurance Corp.
Ameritech Corp.
Ameritech Illinois
Ameritech Indiana
Ameritech Michigan
Ameritech Ohio
Ameritech Wisconsin
AMETEK, Inc.
Amgen, Inc.
AMP Inc.
AMR Corp.
Amsted Industries Inc.
Analog Devices, Inc.
Andersen Corp.
Andersons Inc.
Anheuser-Busch Companies, Inc.
Aon Corp.
APL Ltd.
Appleton Papers Inc.
Archer-Daniels-Midland Co.
Aristech Chemical Corp.
Arizona Public Service Co.
Armstrong World Industries, Inc.
Arvin Industries, Inc.
ASARCO Inc.
Ashland, Inc.
Associated Food Stores
AT&T Corp.
Atlantic Investment Co.
Atlantic Richfield Co.
Auburn Foundry
Avery Dennison Corp.
Avista Corporation
Avon Products, Inc.
Badger Meter, Inc.
Baird & Co. (Robert W.)
Bandag, Inc.
Banfi Vintners
Bank of America
Bank One Corp.
Bank One, Texas-Houston Office
Bank One, Texas, NA
BankAtlantic Bancorp
BankBoston-Connecticut Region
BankBoston Corp.
Banta Corp.
Barclays Capital
Bard, Inc. (C.R.)
Barden Corp.
Bardes Corp.
Barnes Group Inc.
Barry Corp. (R.G.)
Bassett Furniture Industries
Battelle Memorial Institute
Bausch & Lomb Inc.
Baxter International Inc.
Bayer Corp.
Bechtel Group, Inc.
Beckman Coulter, Inc.
Becton Dickinson & Co.
Belk-Simpson Department Stores
Belk Stores Services Inc.
Bell Atlantic Corp.
BellSouth Corp.
Bemis Co., Inc.
Bemis Manufacturing Co.
Bernstein & Co., Inc. (Sanford C.)
Berwind Group
Bestfoods
Bethlehem Steel Corp.
BFGoodrich Co.
Binney & Smith Inc.
Binswanger Companies
Blair & Co. (William)
Block, Inc. (H&R)
Blount International, Inc.
Blue Bell, Inc.
Blue Cross & Blue Shield of Alabama
Blue Cross & Blue Shield of Iowa
Blue Cross & Blue Shield of Minnesota
Boeing Co.
Boise Cascade Corp.
Boler Co.
Borden, Inc.
Borman's Inc.
Boston Edison Co.
Boston Globe (The)
Bourns, Inc.
Bowater Inc.
BP Amoco Corp.
Bradford & Co. (J.C.)
Bridgestone/Firestone, Inc.
Briggs & Stratton Corp.
Bristol-Myers Squibb Co.
Brown Shoe Co., Inc.
Brown & Williamson Tobacco Corp.
Browning-Ferris Industries Inc.
Brunswick Corp.
Bucyrus-Erie Co.
Burlington Industries, Inc.
Burlington Resources, Inc.
Burnett Co. (Leo)
Burress (J.W.)
Business Improvement
Butler Manufacturing Co.
Cabot Corp.
Cadence Designs Systems, Inc.
California Bank & Trust
Calvin Klein
Campbell Soup Co.
Cantor, Fitzgerald Securities Corp.
Cargill Inc.
Carillon Importers, Ltd.
Carlson Companies, Inc.
Carolina Power & Light Co.
Carpenter Technology Corp.
Carrier Corp.
Carris Reels
Carter-Wallace, Inc.
Caterpillar Inc.
CCB Financial Corp.
Cenex Harvest States
Central Maine Power Co.
Central National-Gottesman
Central Newspapers, Inc.
Central & South West Services
Central Soya Co.
Central Vermont Public Service Corp.
CertainTeed Corp.
Cessna Aircraft Co.
CGU Insurance
Champion International Corp.
Charter Manufacturing Co.
Chase Bank of Texas
Chase Manhattan Bank, NA
Chemed Corp.
Chesapeake Corp.
Chevron Corp.
Chicago Title Corp.
Chicago Tribune Co.
Chubb Corp.
Church & Dwight Co., Inc.
CIGNA Corp.
Cincinnati Bell Inc.
Cinergy Corp.
Circuit City Stores, Inc.
CIT Group, Inc. (The)
Citibank Corp.
Citigroup
Citizens Bank-Flint
Citizens Financial Group, Inc.
CLARCOR Inc.
Cleveland-Cliffs, Inc.
Clorox Co.
CNA
CNF Transportation, Inc.
Coca-Cola Co.
Collins & Aikman Corp.
Colonial Life & Accident Insurance Co.
Colonial Oil Industries, Inc.
Comerica Inc.
Commerce Bancshares, Inc.
Commercial Intertech Corp.
Commonwealth Edison Co.
Compass Bank
ConAgra, Inc.
Cone Mills Corp.
Conoco, Inc.
Consolidated Electrical Distributors
Consolidated Natural Gas Co.
Consolidated Papers, Inc.
Constellation Energy Group, Inc.

Consumers Energy Co.
Continental Grain Co.
Contran Corp.
Conwood Co. LP
Cooper Industries, Inc.
Cooper Tire & Rubber Co.
Coors Brewing Co.
Copley Press, Inc.
Corning Inc.
Country Curtains, Inc.
Cox Enterprises Inc.
CPI Corp.
Crane Co.
Crane & Co., Inc.
Cranston Print Works Co.
Credit Suisse First Boston
Crestar Finance Corp.
Croft-Leominster
CSR Rinker Materials Corp.
CSS Industries, Inc.
Cummings Properties Management
Cummins Engine Co., Inc.
CUNA Mutual Group
Cyprus Amax Minerals Co.
Daily News
DaimlerChrysler Corp.
Dain Bosworth Inc.
Dana Corp.
Danis Companies
Dayton Hudson
Dayton Power and Light Co.
Deere & Co.
DeKalb Genetics Corp.
Deloitte & Touche
Delta Air Lines, Inc.
Deluxe Corp.
Demoulas Supermarkets Inc.
Deposit Guaranty National Bank
Detroit Edison Co.
Deutsch Co.
Dexter Corp.
Dial Corp.
Disney Co. (Walt)
Dixie Group, Inc. (The)
Dollar General Corp.
Dominion Resources, Inc.
Domino's Pizza Inc.
Donaldson Co., Inc.
Donnelley & Sons Co. (R.R.)
Dow Chemical Co.
Dow Corning Corp.
Dow Jones & Co., Inc.
Dreyer's Grand Ice Cream
DSM Copolymer
du Pont de Nemours & Co. (E.I.)
Duchossois Industries Inc.
Duke Energy
Dun & Bradstreet Corp.
Duriron Co., Inc.
Dynamet, Inc.
Eastern Bank
Eastern Enterprises
Eastman Kodak Co.
Eaton Corp.
Eckerd Corp.
Ecolab Inc.
Edison International
Edwards Enterprise Software (J.D.)
El Paso Energy Co.
Elf Atochem North America, Inc.
Emerson Electric Co.
Employers Mutual Casualty Co.
Ensign-Bickford Industries
Enterprise Rent-A-Car Co.
Equifax Inc.
Equitable Resources, Inc.
Erb Lumber Co.
Ernst & Young, LLP
Erving Industries
Ethyl Corp.
European American Bank
Evening Post Publishing Co.
Excel Corp.
Extendicare Health Services
Exxon Mobil Corp.
Farmers Group, Inc.
Federal-Mogul Corp.
Federated Department Stores, Inc.
Federated Mutual Insurance Co.
FedEx Corp.
Ferro Corp.
Fidelity Investments
Fifth Third Bancorp
FINA
Fireman's Fund Insurance Co.
First American Corp.
First Financial Bank
First Hawaiian, Inc.
First Maryland Bancorp
First National Bank of Evergreen Park
First Source Corp.
First Tennessee National Corp.
First Union Bank
First Union Corp.
First Union National Bank, NA
First Union Securities, Inc.
Firstar Bank Milwaukee NA
Fisher Brothers Cleaning Services
Fisher Scientific
FleetBoston Financial Corp.
Florida Power Corp.
Florida Power & Light Co.
Florida Rock Industries
Fluor Corp.
FMC Corp.
Forbes Inc.
Ford Meter Box Co.
Ford Motor Co.
Forest City Enterprises, Inc.
Fort James Corp.
Fort Worth Star-Telegram Inc.
Fortis, Inc.
Fortune Brands, Inc.
Fox Entertainment Group
Franklin Electric Co.
Freeport-McMoRan Inc.
Frontier Corp.
Frost National Bank
Fuller Co. (H.B.)
Furniture Brands International, Inc.
Gallo Winery, Inc. (E&J)
Galter Corp.
Gap, Inc.
GATX Corp.
GEICO Corp.
GenAmerica Corp.
GenCorp
Genentech Inc.
General Atlantic Partners II LP
General Dynamics Corp.
General Electric Co.
General Mills, Inc.
General Motors Corp.
General Reinsurance Corp.
Georgia-Pacific Corp.
Georgia Power Co.
Gerber Products Co.
Giant Eagle Inc.
Giant Food Inc.
Giddings & Lewis
Gillette Co.
Glaxo Wellcome Inc.
Glickenhaus & Co.
Globe Corp.
Goldman Sachs Group
Golub Corp.
Goodrich Aerospace - Aerostructures Group (B.F.)
Gosiger, Inc.
Grace & Co. (W.R.)
Graco, Inc.
Grede Foundries
Green Bay Packaging
Group Health Plan
GTE Corp.
Guardian Life Insurance Co. of America
Guess?
GuideOne Insurance
Gulf Power Co.
Gulfstream Aerospace Corp.
Halliburton Co.
Hallmark Cards Inc.
Hamilton Sundstrand Corp.
Hanna Co. (M.A.)
Hannaford Brothers Co.
Harcourt General, Inc.
Harland Co. (John H.)
Harley-Davidson Co.
Harnischfeger Industries
Harris Corp.
Harris Trust & Savings Bank
Harsco Corp.
Hartford (The)
Hartford Steam Boiler Inspection & Insurance Co.
Hartmarx Corp.
Hasbro, Inc.
Hawaiian Electric Co., Inc.
Heinz Co. (H.J.)
Heller Financial, Inc.
Hensel Phelps Construction Co.
Hershey Foods Corp.
Hewlett-Packard Co.
Hickory Tech Corp.
Hitachi America Ltd.
Hoffer Plastics Corp.
Hoffmann-La Roche Inc.
Hofmann Co.
HON Industries Inc.
Honeywell International Inc.
Housatonic Curtain Co.
Household International Inc.
HSBC Bank USA
Hubbard Broadcasting, Inc.
Hubbell Inc.
Huffy Corp.
Hughes Electronics Corp.
Humana, Inc.
Hunt Manufacturing Co.
Huntington Bancshares Inc.
Idaho Power Co.
IKON Office Solutions, Inc.
Illinois Power Co.
Illinois Tool Works, Inc.
Industrial Bank of Japan Trust Co. (New York)
Inland Container Corp.
Inman Mills
Intel Corp.
International Business Machines Corp.
International Flavors & Fragrances Inc.
International Multifoods Corp.
International Paper Co.
INTRUST Financial Corp.
ISE America
Jacobs Engineering Group
Jacobson & Sons (Benjamin)
Jeld-wen, Inc.
Johnson Controls Inc.
Johnson & Johnson
Johnson & Son (S.C.)
Jones & Co. (Edward D.)
Jostens, Inc.
Journal-Gazette Co.
JSJ Corp.
Katten, Muchin & Zavis
Kellwood Co.
Kelly Services
Kemper National Insurance Companies
Kennametal, Inc.
Kerr-McGee Corp.
Key Bank of Cleveland
Kiewit Sons' Inc. (Peter)
Kimball International, Inc.
Kimberly-Clark Corp.
Kinder Morgn
Kingsbury Corp.
Kmart Corp.
Koch Enterprises, Inc.
Koch Industries, Inc.
Kohler Co.
KPMG Peat Marwick LLP
Kroger Co.
La-Z-Boy Inc.
Laclede Gas Co.
Ladish Co., Inc.
Lancaster Lens, Inc.
Lance, Inc.
Land O'Lakes, Inc.
LandAmerica Financial Services
Landmark Communications Inc.
Lee Enterprises
Lehigh Portland Cement Co.
Leigh Fibers, Inc.
Lennox International, Inc.
Levi Strauss & Co.
Leviton Manufacturing Co. Inc.
LG&E Energy Corp.
Liberty Corp.
Liberty Diversified Industries
Lilly & Co. (Eli)
Lincoln Electric Co.
Lincoln Financial Group
Lipton Co.
Little, Inc. (Arthur D.)
Litton Industries, Inc.
Liz Claiborne, Inc.
Loews Corp.
Louisiana Land & Exploration Co.
Louisiana-Pacific Corp.
Lowe's Companies
LTV Corp.
Lubrizol Corp. (The)
MacMillan Bloedel Inc.
Macy's East Inc.
Madison Gas & Electric Co.
Mallinckrodt Chemical, Inc.
Manor Care Health SVS, Inc.
Manulife Financial
Marcus Corp.
Maritz Inc.
Mark IV Industries
Marriott International Inc.
Marshall & Ilsley Corp.
Masco Corp.
Massachusetts Mutual Life Insurance Co.
Mattel Inc.
May Department Stores Co.
Maytag Corp.
MBIA Inc.
McClatchy Co.
McCormick & Co. Inc.
McDermott Inc.
McDonald & Co. Securities, Inc.
McDonald's Corp.
McGraw-Hill Companies, Inc.
MCI WorldCom, Inc.
McKesson-HBOC Corp.
McWane Inc.
Mead Corp.
Medtronic, Inc.
Memphis Light Gas & Water Division
Menasha Corp.
Mercantile Bank NA
Merck & Co.
Meredith Corp.
Merit Oil Corp.
Merrill Lynch & Co., Inc.
Metropolitan Life Insurance Co.
MFA Inc.
MGIC Investment Corp.
Michigan Consolidated Gas Co.
Microsoft Corp.
Mid-America Bank of Louisville
MidAmerican Energy Holdings Co.
Milacron, Inc.
Milliken & Co.
Millipore Corp.
Mine Safety Appliances Co.
Minnesota Mining & Manufacturing Co.
Minnesota Mutual Life Insurance Co.
Monarch Machine Tool Co.
Monsanto Co.
Montana Power Co.
Montgomery Ward & Co., Inc.
MONY Group (The)
Morgan & Co. Inc. (J.P.)
Morgan Stanley Dean Witter & Co.
Morris Communications Corp.
Morrison Knudsen Corp.
Morton International Inc.
Motorola Inc.
MTD Products Inc.
MTS Systems Corp.
Murphy Oil Corp.
Mutual of Omaha Insurance Co.
Nabisco Group Holdings
Nalco Chemical Co.
NASDAQ Stock Market
National Bank of Commerce Trust & Savings
National City Bank of Minneapolis
National City Corp.
National Computer Systems, Inc.
National Fuel Gas Distribution Corp.
National Machinery Co.
National Presto Industries, Inc.
National Service Industries, Inc.
Nationwide Insurance Co.
Navcom Systems
NCR Corp.
NEBCO Evans

Nestle U.S.A. Inc.
New Century Energies
New England Bio Labs
New England Financial
New Jersey Natural Gas Co.
New York Life Insurance Co.
New York Mercantile Exchange
New York Stock Exchange, Inc.
New York Times Co.
Niagara Mohawk Holdings Inc.
Nike, Inc.
Nomura Holding America
Nordson Corp.
Norfolk Southern Corp.
Nortel
North American Royalties
Northeast Utilities
Northern Indiana Public Service Co.
Northern States Power Co.
Northern Trust Co.
Northwest Bank Nebraska, NA
Northwest Natural Gas Co.
Norton Co.
Norwest Corp.
Novartis Corporation
Occidental Oil and Gas
Occidental Petroleum Corp.
OG&E Electric Services
Ohio National Life Insurance Co.
Oklahoma Publishing Co.
Old Kent Bank
Old National Bank Evansville
Olin Corp.
ONEOK, Inc.
Orscheln Co.
Oshkosh B'Gosh, Inc.
Outboard Marine Corp.
Overseas Shipholding Group Inc.
Owens Corning
PACCAR Inc.
Pacific Century Financial Corp.
Pacific Gas and Electric Co.
Pacific Mutual Life Insurance Co.
PacifiCorp
Paine Webber
Pan-American Life Insurance Co.
Park National Bank
Parker Hannifin Corp.
PECO Energy Co.
Pella Corp.
PEMCO Corp.
Penney Co., Inc. (J.C.)
Pennzoil-Quaker State Co.
Peoples Bank
Peoples Energy Corp.
PepsiCo, Inc.
PerkinElmer, Inc.
Pfizer Inc.
Pharmacia & Upjohn, Inc.
Phelps Dodge Corp.
Pheonix Financial Group
Philip Morris Companies Inc.
Philips Electronics North America Corp.
Phillips Petroleum Co.
Physicians Mutual Insurance Co.
Pieper Power Electric Co.
Pillsbury Co.
Pioneer Hi-Bred International, Inc.
Pitney Bowes Inc.
Pittway Corp.
PNC Bank
PNC Financial Services Group
Polaroid Corp.
Portland General Electric Co.
Potlatch Corp.
Potomac Electric Power Co.
PPG Industries, Inc.
Praxair
Premier Dental Products Co.
Premier Industrial Corp.
Price Associates (T. Rowe)
PricewaterhouseCoopers
Principal Financial Group
Procter & Gamble Co.
Procter & Gamble Co., Cosmetics Division
Promus Hotel Corp.
Providence Journal-Bulletin Co.
Provident Companies, Inc.
Prudential Insurance Co. of America
Prudential Securities Inc.
Public Service Electric & Gas Co.
Publix Supermarkets
Pulitzer Publishing Co.
Putnam Investments
Quaker Chemical Corp.
Quanex Corp.
Questar Corp.
Ralph's Grocery Co.
Ralston Purina Co.
Rayonier Inc.
Reader's Digest Association, Inc. (The)
Red Wing Shoe Co. Inc.
Regions Bank
Regis Corp.
Reilly Industries, Inc.
Reily & Co., Inc. (William B.)
Reinhart Institutional Foods
Reliant Energy Inc.
ReliaStar Financial Corp.
Revlon Inc.
Reynolds Metals Co.
Reynolds & Reynolds Co.
Reynolds Tobacco (R.J.)
Rich Products Corp.
Rochester Gas & Electric Corp.
Rockwell International Corp.
Rouse Co.
Royal & SunAlliance USA, Inc.
Rubbermaid Inc.
Ruddick Corp.
Russer Foods
Rutledge Hill Press
Ryder System, Inc.
SAFECO Corp.
Safeguard Scientifics
Saint Paul Companies Inc.
S&T Bancorp
Sara Lee Corp.
SBC Communications Inc.
Schering-Plough Corp.
Schloss & Co. (Marcus)
Schlumberger Ltd. (USA)
Schwab & Co., Inc. (Charles)
Schwebel Baking Co.
Scripps Co. (E.W.)
Seagram & Sons, Inc. (Joseph E.)
Searle & Co. (G.D.)
Sears, Roebuck and Co.
Seaway Food Town, Inc.
Security Benefit Life Insurance Co.
Sega of America Inc.
Sempra Energy
Sentinel Communications Co.
Sentry Insurance, A Mutual Co.
Servco Pacific
ServiceMaster Co.
S.G. Cowen
Shaklee Corp.
Sharp Electronics Corp.
Shaw's Supermarkets, Inc.
Shea Co. (John F.)
Shell Oil Co.
Shelter Mutual Insurance Co.
Sherwin-Williams Co.
Shoney's Inc.
Sierra Pacific Industries
Sierra Pacific Resources
Simplot Co. (J.R.)
Simpson Investment Co.
SIT Investment Associates, Inc.
Slant/Fin Corp.
Smith Corp. (A.O.)
SmithKline Beecham Corp.
Smucker Co. (JM)
Smurfit-Stone Container Corp.
Sonoco Products Co.
Sony Electronics
South Bend Tribune Corp.
Southeastern Mutual Insurance Co.
Southern New England Telephone Co.
Southwest Gas Corp.
Sovereign Bank
Springs Industries, Inc.
Sprint Corp.
Sprint/United Telephone
SPX Corp.
Square D Co.
Standard Products Co.
Standard Register Co.
Stanley Works (The)
Star Bank NA
Starwood Hotels & Resorts Worldwide, Inc.
State Farm Mutual Automobile Insurance Co.
State Street Bank & Trust Co.
Steelcase Inc.
Stone Container Corp.
Stonecutter Mills Corp.
Storage Technology Corp.
Strear Farms Co.
Stride Rite Corp.
Stupp Brothers Bridge & Iron Co.
Subway Sandwich Shops, Inc.
Sun Microsystems Inc.
Sunmark Capital Corp.
Sunoco Inc.
SunTrust Bank Atlanta
SunTrust Banks of Florida
SuperValu, Inc.
Susquehanna-Pfaltzgraff Co.
Sverdrup Corp.
Synovus Financial Corp.
Tai and Co. (J.T.)
Tamko Roofing Products
TCF National Bank Minnesota
Tektronix, Inc.
Telcordia Technologies
Teleflex Inc.
Temple-Inland Inc.
Tenet Healthcare Corp.
TENNANT Co.
Tenneco Automotive
Tenneco Packaging
Tension Envelope Corp.
Tesoro Hawaii
Texaco Inc.
Texas Gas Transmission Corp.
Texas Instruments Inc.
Textron Inc.
Thermo Electron Corp.
Thomasville Furniture Industries Inc.
Thompson Co. (J. Walter)
Ticketmaster Corp.
Times Mirror Co.
Timken Co. (The)
Titan Industrial Corp.
TJX Companies, Inc.
TMC Investment Co.
Toledo Blade Co.
Tomkins Industries, Inc.
Torchmark Corp.
Toro Co.
Toyota Motor Sales U.S.A., Inc.
Trace International Holdings, Inc.
Transamerica Corp.
True North Communications, Inc.
True Oil Co.
Trustmark Insurance Co.
TRW Inc.
TU Electric Co.
Tyson Foods Inc.
Ukrop's Super Markets
Unilever Home & Personal Care U.S.A.
Unilever United States, Inc.
Union Camp Corp.
Union Carbide Corp.
Union Pacific Corp.
United Airlines Inc.
United Co.
United Distillers & Vintners North America
United Dominion Industries, Ltd.
United Parcel Service of America Inc.
United Services Automobile Association
U.S. Bancorp
U.S. Bancorp Piper Jaffray
United States Sugar Corp.
United States Trust Co. of New York
United Technologies Corp.
United Wisconsin Services
Universal Foods Corp.
Universal Leaf Tobacco Co., Inc.
Universal Studios
Unocal Corp.
UnumProvident
US Bank, Washington
US West, Inc.
USAA Life Insurance Co.
USG Corp.
UST Inc.
USX Corp.
Valmont Industries, Inc.
Valspar Corp.
Van Leer Holding
Vanguard Group
Varian Medical Systems, Inc.
Vesper Corp.
Vulcan Materials Co.
Wachovia Bank of North Carolina NA
Wachtell, Lipton, Rosen & Katz
Waffle House Inc.
Wal-Mart Stores, Inc.
Waldbaum's Supermarkets, Inc.
Walgreen Co.
Walter Industries Inc.
Warner-Lambert Co.
Washington Mutual, Inc.
The Washington Post
Washington Trust Bank
Waste Management Inc.
Webster Bank
Weil, Gotshal & Manges Corp.
Wells Fargo & Co.
West Co. Inc.
Western Resources Inc.
Western & Southern Life Insurance Co.
Westvaco Corp.
Weyerhaeuser Co.
Whirlpool Corp.
Whitman Corp.
WICOR, Inc.
Wilbur-Ellis Co. & Connell Brothers Co.
Wiley & Sons (John)
Williams
Winn-Dixie Stores Inc.
Wiremold Co.
Wisconsin Energy Corp.
Wisconsin Power & Light Co.
Wisconsin Public Service Corp.
Witco Corp.
Wolverine World Wide
Woodward Governor Co.
Wrigley Co. (Wm. Jr.)
Wyman-Gordon Co.
Xerox Corp.
Yellow Corp.
York Federal Savings & Loan Association
Young & Rubicam
Zachry Co. (H.B.)
Zenith Electronics Corp.
Zilkha & Sons
Zurn Industries, Inc.

COMMUNITY & JUNIOR COLLEGES

ABB Inc.
Abbott Laboratories
AEGON U.S.A. Inc.
AFLAC Inc.
AGL Resources Inc.
Agrilink Foods, Inc.
Alabama Power Co.
Albertson's Inc.
Alcoa Inc.
Alcon Laboratories, Inc.
Allegheny Technologies Inc.
AlliedSignal Inc.
Allmerica Financial Corp.
Allstate Insurance Co.
AMCORE Bank Rockford
Ameren Corp.
American Express Co.
American Fidelity Corp.
AmerUS Group
AMP Inc.
Amsted Industries Inc.
Archer-Daniels-Midland Co.
Arizona Public Service Co.
Arvin Industries, Inc.
Ashland, Inc.
Avista Corporation
Avon Products, Inc.

Bandag, Inc.
Bank of America
BankAtlantic Bancorp
BankBoston Corp.
Barclays Capital
Barden Corp.
Barnes Group Inc.
Barry Corp. (R.G.)
Bassett Furniture Industries
Battelle Memorial Institute
Bausch & Lomb Inc.
Beckman Coulter, Inc.
Belk Stores Services Inc.
BellSouth Corp.
Bemis Co., Inc.
Bestfoods
BFGoodrich Co.
Binney & Smith Inc.
Block, Inc. (H&R)
Blue Bell, Inc.
Boeing Co.
Boise Cascade Corp.
Bowater Inc.
BP Amoco Corp.
Bridgestone/Firestone, Inc.
Briggs & Stratton Corp.
Brunswick Corp.
Burlington Industries, Inc.
Burnett Co. (Leo)
Cabot Corp.
Campbell Soup Co.
Cargill Inc.
Carolina Power & Light Co.
Carpenter Technology Corp.
Caterpillar Inc.
Cenex Harvest States
Central Maine Power Co.
Central & South West Services
CertainTeed Corp.
Chase Bank of Texas
Chesapeake Corp.
Cincinnati Bell Inc.
Circuit City Stores, Inc.
Citibank Corp.
Citizens Bank-Flint
Citizens Financial Group, Inc.
Cleveland-Cliffs, Inc.
Clorox Co.
Collins & Aikman Corp.
Colonial Life & Accident Insurance Co.
Compass Bank
ConAgra, Inc.
Consolidated Natural Gas Co.
Consumers Energy Co.
Cooper Industries, Inc.
Coors Brewing Co.
Corning Inc.
Country Curtains, Inc.
Crane Co.
Crane & Co., Inc.
Cranston Print Works Co.
Crestar Finance Corp.
Croft-Leominster
CSR Rinker Materials Corp.
Cummins Engine Co., Inc.
DaimlerChrysler Corp.
Dain Bosworth Inc.
Dana Corp.
Dayton Power and Light Co.
Deere & Co.
DeKalb Genetics Corp.
Deposit Guaranty National Bank
Detroit Edison Co.
Dexter Corp.
Dial Corp.
Dixie Group, Inc. (The)
Donaldson Co., Inc.
Dow Corning Corp.
du Pont de Nemours & Co. (E.I.)
Dun & Bradstreet Corp.
Eastern Bank
Eastman Kodak Co.
Eaton Corp.
El Paso Energy Co.
Elf Atochem North America, Inc.
Emerson Electric Co.
Equitable Resources, Inc.
Erving Industries
Ferro Corp.
Fireman's Fund Insurance Co.
First Union Corp.
First Union National Bank, NA
First Union Securities, Inc.
FleetBoston Financial Corp.
Florida Power Corp.
Florida Power & Light Co.
FMC Corp.
Forest City Enterprises, Inc.
Fortune Brands, Inc.
Freeport-McMoRan Inc.
Furniture Brands International, Inc.
Gallo Winery, Inc. (E&J)
Gap, Inc.
GEICO Corp.
GenCorp
Genentech Inc.
General Mills, Inc.
General Motors Corp.
General Reinsurance Corp.
Georgia Power Co.
Gerber Products Co.
Giant Food Inc.
Glaxo Wellcome Inc.
Golub Corp.
Goodrich Aerospace - Aerostructures Group (B.F.)
Grede Foundries
GTE Corp.
Guardian Life Insurance Co. of America
Guess?
Gulf Power Co.
Halliburton Co.
Hamilton Sundstrand Corp.
Hanna Co. (M.A.)
Harris Corp.
Harsco Corp.
Hartford (The)
Hartmarx Corp.
Heinz Co. (H.J.)
Hensel Phelps Construction Co.
Hershey Foods Corp.
Hickory Tech Corp.
Hitachi America Ltd.
HON Industries Inc.
Honeywell International Inc.
Housatonic Curtain Co.
Huffy Corp.
Humana, Inc.
Hunt Manufacturing Co.
Huntington Bancshares Inc.
IBP
Illinois Tool Works, Inc.
Intel Corp.
International Business Machines Corp.
INTRUST Financial Corp.
Invacare Corp.
Jeld-wen, Inc.
Johnson Controls Inc.
JSJ Corp.
Kelly Services
Kemper National Insurance Companies
Kennametal, Inc.
Kimberly-Clark Corp.
Kinder Morgn
Kingsbury Corp.
Koch Enterprises, Inc.
Kroger Co.
La-Z-Boy Inc.
Lance, Inc.
Landmark Communications Inc.
Lee Enterprises
Lehigh Portland Cement Co.
Leigh Fibers, Inc.
Levi Strauss & Co.
Leviton Manufacturing Co. Inc.
Lipton Co.
Louisiana-Pacific Corp.
LTV Corp.
Lubrizol Corp. (The)
MacMillan Bloedel Inc.
Macy's East Inc.
Maritz Inc.
Mark IV Industries
Marshall & Ilsley Corp.
Massachusetts Mutual Life Insurance Co.
McClatchy Co.
McDonald & Co. Securities, Inc.
Mead Corp.
Medtronic, Inc.
Merck & Co.
Merit Oil Corp.
Metropolitan Life Insurance Co.
Michigan Consolidated Gas Co.
Milacron, Inc.
Millipore Corp.
Mine Safety Appliances Co.
Monarch Machine Tool Co.
Monsanto Co.
Montana Power Co.
Morris Communications Corp.
Motorola Inc.
Mutual of Omaha Insurance Co.
National Computer Systems, Inc.
National Presto Industries, Inc.
National Starch & Chemical Co.
Navcom Systems
Nestle U.S.A. Inc.
New England Financial
New Jersey Natural Gas Co.
New York Life Insurance Co.
New York Times Co.
Niagara Mohawk Holdings Inc.
Nordson Corp.
Northeast Utilities
Northern States Power Co.
Northwest Bank Nebraska, NA
Norton Co.
Norwest Corp.
Occidental Oil and Gas
Occidental Petroleum Corp.
OG&E Electric Services
Old Kent Bank
Olin Corp.
ONEOK, Inc.
Orange & Rockland Utilities, Inc.
Orscheln Co.
Outboard Marine Corp.
Owens Corning
PACCAR Inc.
Parker Hannifin Corp.
PECO Energy Co.
Pella Corp.
PEMCO Corp.
Penney Co., Inc. (J.C.)
Peoples Energy Corp.
PerkinElmer, Inc.
Pfizer Inc.
Pharmacia & Upjohn, Inc.
Phelps Dodge Corp.
Philip Morris Companies Inc.
Phillips Petroleum Co.
Physicians Mutual Insurance Co.
Pillsbury Co.
PNC Financial Services Group
Polaroid Corp.
Portland General Electric Co.
PPG Industries, Inc.
Principal Financial Group
Provident Companies, Inc.
Prudential Insurance Co. of America
Public Service Electric & Gas Co.
Publix Supermarkets
Quaker Chemical Corp.
Quanex Corp.
Reebok International Ltd.
Reilly Industries, Inc.
Reily & Co., Inc. (William B.)
Reliant Energy Inc.
ReliaStar Financial Corp.
Reynolds Metals Co.
Rockwell International Corp.
Rouse Co.
Royal & SunAlliance USA, Inc.
Rubbermaid Inc.
Ruddick Corp.
Ryder System, Inc.
Saint Paul Companies Inc.
S&T Bancorp
Sara Lee Hosiery, Inc.
SBC Communications Inc.
Searle & Co. (G.D.)
Sentinel Communications Co.
Sentry Insurance, A Mutual Co.
Servco Pacific
Shoney's Inc.
Sierra Pacific Resources
Simpson Investment Co.
Slant/Fin Corp.
Smith Corp. (A.O.)
Sonoco Products Co.
Sony Electronics
Southeastern Mutual Insurance Co.
Southern New England Telephone Co.
Southwest Gas Corp.
Sovereign Bank
Sprint Corp.
SPX Corp.
Square D Co.
Standard Products Co.
Standard Register Co.
State Farm Mutual Automobile Insurance Co.
Steelcase Inc.
Stonecutter Mills Corp.
Stride Rite Corp.
Sun Microsystems Inc.
Sverdrup Corp.
Tai and Co. (J.T.)
TCF National Bank Minnesota
Tektronix, Inc.
Tenneco Automotive
Tension Envelope Corp.
Texaco Inc.
Texas Gas Transmission Corp.
Texas Instruments Inc.
Textron Inc.
Thermo Electron Corp.
Thomasville Furniture Industries Inc.
Titan Industrial Corp.
Toro Co.
Toyota Motor Sales U.S.A., Inc.
True Oil Co.
Trustmark Insurance Co.
TRW Inc.
TU Electric Co.
Ukrop's Super Markets
Union Camp Corp.
Union Pacific Corp.
United Parcel Service of America Inc.
United Services Automobile Association
United States Sugar Corp.
United Technologies Corp.
Universal Leaf Tobacco Co., Inc.
Universal Studios
US West, Inc.
USX Corp.
Valmont Industries, Inc.
Wal-Mart Stores, Inc.
Washington Mutual, Inc.
Washington Trust Bank
Webster Bank
West Co. Inc.
Westvaco Corp.
Weyerhaeuser Co.
Whirlpool Corp.
Whitman Corp.
Wilbur-Ellis Co. & Connell Brothers Co.
Wiley & Sons (John)
Williams
Wrigley Co. (Wm. Jr.)
Wyman-Gordon Co.
Yellow Corp.
Zachry Co. (H.B.)

CONTINUING EDUCATION

Abbott Laboratories
AGL Resources Inc.
AlliedSignal Inc.
American Express Co.
Ameritas Life Insurance Corp.
Ameritech Indiana
Anheuser-Busch Companies, Inc.
APL Ltd.
Atlantic Richfield Co.
Bandag, Inc.
Banfi Vintners
Bank One, Texas-Houston Office
BankBoston-Connecticut Region
Binney & Smith Inc.
Block, Inc. (H&R)
Boeing Co.
Borden, Inc.
Bowater Inc.
BP Amoco Corp.
Bradford & Co. (J.C.)
Carillon Importers, Ltd.
Central Maine Power Co.
Chase Bank of Texas

Chesapeake Corp.
Cincinnati Bell Inc.
CIT Group, Inc. (The)
Citibank Corp.
Clark Refining & Marketing
Cleveland-Cliffs, Inc.
Clorox Co.
CNA
Consolidated Papers, Inc.
Constellation Energy Group, Inc.
Credit Suisse First Boston
DaimlerChrysler Corp.
Deloitte & Touche
Dexter Corp.
Dollar General Corp.
Dow Chemical Co.
Ecolab Inc.
Federated Department Stores, Inc.
FedEx Corp.
Fireman's Fund Insurance Co.
First Hawaiian, Inc.
First Union Corp.
FleetBoston Financial Corp.
Florida Rock Industries
Fortune Brands, Inc.
General Electric Co.
General Mills, Inc.
General Motors Corp.
Goldman Sachs Group
Goodrich Aerospace - Aerostructures Group (B.F.)
Hallmark Cards Inc.
Hancock Financial Services (John)
Harcourt General, Inc.
Harland Co. (John H.)
Harris Corp.
Hartford (The)
Heinz Co. (H.J.)
Hubbell Inc.
Humana, Inc.
Inman Mills
Intel Corp.
Johnson Controls Inc.
Journal-Gazette Co.
JSJ Corp.
Kingsbury Corp.
KPMG Peat Marwick LLP
Land O'Lakes, Inc.
Lehigh Portland Cement Co.
Little, Inc. (Arthur D.)
Louisiana Land & Exploration Co.
MacMillan Bloedel Inc.
Macy's East Inc.
May Department Stores Co.
McClatchy Co.
Mead Corp.
Motorola Inc.
National Computer Systems, Inc.
NCR Corp.
New England Financial
Norwest Corp.
Ohio National Life Insurance Co.
Overseas Shipholding Group Inc.
Pacific Mutual Life Insurance Co.
Parker Hannifin Corp.
PepsiCo, Inc.
Physicians Mutual Insurance Co.
Polaroid Corp.
Portland General Electric Co.
Prudential Insurance Co. of America
Rich Products Corp.
Rockwell International Corp.
Royal & SunAlliance USA, Inc.
SAFECO Corp.
Simpson Investment Co.
State Street Bank & Trust Co.
Storage Technology Corp.
Tension Envelope Corp.
Timken Co. (The)
Toyota Motor Sales U.S.A., Inc.
Trace International Holdings, Inc.
Trustmark Insurance Co.
Union Camp Corp.
Union Carbide Corp.
United Distillers & Vintners North America
United Parcel Service of America Inc.
United Wisconsin Services
Unocal Corp.
Vesper Corp.
Wal-Mart Stores, Inc.
Warner-Lambert Co.
Wells Fargo & Co.
Westvaco Corp.
Whitman Corp.
Wiley & Sons (John)
Zachry Co. (H.B.)

ECONOMIC EDUCATION

AGL Resources Inc.
Air Products and Chemicals, Inc.
AK Steel Corp.
Albany International Corp.
Albertson's Inc.
Alcoa Inc.
Allegheny Technologies Inc.
Alliant Techsystems
Allianz Life Insurance Co. of North America
Allstate Insurance Co.
AMCORE Bank Rockford
Ameren Corp.
America West Airlines, Inc.
American Express Co.
American Fidelity Corp.
American Honda Motor Co., Inc.
American United Life Insurance Co.
Ameritas Life Insurance Corp.
Ameritech Corp.
Ameritech Illinois
Ameritech Indiana
Ameritech Ohio
Ameritech Wisconsin
Andersen Corp.
Appleton Papers Inc.
Archer-Daniels-Midland Co.
Aristech Chemical Corp.
Arvin Industries, Inc.
ASARCO Inc.
Ashland, Inc.
Atlantic Richfield Co.
Avista Corporation
Avon Products, Inc.
Baird & Co. (Robert W.)
Bank of America
Bank One Corp.
BankAtlantic Bancorp
Barclays Capital
Bard, Inc. (C.R.)
Battelle Memorial Institute
Belk Stores Services Inc.
Bernstein & Co., Inc. (Sanford C.)
Bestfoods
Bethlehem Steel Corp.
BFGoodrich Co.
Binney & Smith Inc.
Blair & Co. (William)
Block, Inc. (H&R)
Blount International, Inc.
Blue Bell, Inc.
Blue Cross & Blue Shield of Alabama
Blue Cross & Blue Shield of Minnesota
Boeing Co.
Boise Cascade Corp.
Bowater Inc.
Bradford & Co. (J.C.)
Bridgestone/Firestone, Inc.
Brown Shoe Co., Inc.
Bucyrus-Erie Co.
Business Improvement
Cabot Corp.
Cargill Inc.
Carpenter Technology Corp.
Carrier Corp.
Caterpillar Inc.
Central Maine Power Co.
Central National-Gottesman
Cessna Aircraft Co.
Chase Manhattan Bank, NA
Chevron Corp.
Chicago Title Corp.
Cincinnati Bell Inc.
Citibank Corp.
Citigroup
Citizens Financial Group, Inc.
CLARCOR Inc.
Cleveland-Cliffs, Inc.
Clorox Co.
CNA
CNF Transportation, Inc.
Coachmen Industries, Inc.
Colonial Life & Accident Insurance Co.
Colonial Oil Industries, Inc.
Commercial Intertech Corp.
Cone Mills Corp.
Conoco, Inc.
Consolidated Natural Gas Co.
Consolidated Papers, Inc.
Consumers Energy Co.
Cooper Industries, Inc.
Coors Brewing Co.
Crane Co.
Credit Suisse First Boston
Crestar Finance Corp.
DaimlerChrysler Corp.
Dain Bosworth Inc.
Dana Corp.
Deere & Co.
DeKalb Genetics Corp.
Deluxe Corp.
Deposit Guaranty National Bank
Detroit Edison Co.
Donaldson Co., Inc.
Dreyer's Grand Ice Cream
DSM Copolymer
du Pont de Nemours & Co. (E.I.)
Duke Energy
Dynamet, Inc.
Eaton Corp.
Eckerd Corp.
Ecolab Inc.
Edison International
Edwards Enterprise Software (J.D.)
Elf Atochem North America, Inc.
Emerson Electric Co.
Equifax Inc.
Erb Lumber Co.
Ethyl Corp.
Exxon Mobil Corp.
Federal-Mogul Corp.
Federated Department Stores, Inc.
First Financial Bank
First Hawaiian, Inc.
First Source Corp.
First Tennessee National Corp.
First Union Corp.
First Union National Bank, NA
Firstar Bank Milwaukee NA
FleetBoston Financial Corp.
FMC Corp.
Forbes Inc.
Ford Motor Co.
Fort James Corp.
Fortis Insurance Co.
Fortune Brands, Inc.
Freeport-McMoRan Inc.
Fuller Co. (H.B.)
Furniture Brands International, Inc.
GenAmerica Corp.
General Electric Co.
General Mills, Inc.
General Motors Corp.
Georgia-Pacific Corp.
Georgia Power Co.
Goldman Sachs Group
Grace & Co. (W.R.)
Graco, Inc.
GTE Corp.
Guardian Life Insurance Co. of America
Hamilton Sundstrand Corp.
Hancock Financial Services (John)
Hanna Co. (M.A.)
Harsco Corp.
Hartmarx Corp.
Hasbro, Inc.
Heinz Co. (H.J.)
Hensel Phelps Construction Co.
Hershey Foods Corp.
Hickory Tech Corp.
Hoffmann-La Roche Inc.
Honeywell International Inc.
Household International Inc.
Hubbard Broadcasting, Inc.
Huntington Bancshares Inc.
Illinois Tool Works, Inc.
International Multifoods Corp.
International Paper Co.
Invacare Corp.
Johnson Controls Inc.
Johnson & Son (S.C.)
Jostens, Inc.
JSJ Corp.
Kemper National Insurance Companies
Kennametal, Inc.
Kerr-McGee Corp.
Kiewit Sons' Inc. (Peter)
Kimberly-Clark Corp.
Koch Enterprises, Inc.
Kroger Co.
Laclede Gas Co.
Lance, Inc.
Lee Enterprises
Lehigh Portland Cement Co.
Liberty Diversified Industries
Lincoln Financial Group
Lipton Co.
Louisiana Land & Exploration Co.
LTV Corp.
Lubrizol Corp. (The)
Macy's East Inc.
Maritz Inc.
Mattel Inc.
McClatchy Co.
McCormick & Co. Inc.
McDonald & Co. Securities, Inc.
MCI WorldCom, Inc.
Mead Corp.
Merck & Co.
Merrill Lynch & Co., Inc.
Metropolitan Life Insurance Co.
Milliken & Co.
Mine Safety Appliances Co.
Minnesota Mining & Manufacturing Co.
Minnesota Mutual Life Insurance Co.
MONY Group (The)
Motorola Inc.
MTS Systems Corp.
Nalco Chemical Co.
NASDAQ Stock Market
National City Corp.
National Computer Systems, Inc.
National Service Industries, Inc.
Nationwide Insurance Co.
NEBCO Evans
New Century Energies
New York Stock Exchange, Inc.
Nomura Holding America
Norfolk Southern Corp.
Northeast Utilities
Norton Co.
OG&E Electric Services
Overnite Transportation Co.
PACCAR Inc.
Pacific Mutual Life Insurance Co.
Penney Co., Inc. (J.C.)
PepsiCo, Inc.
Pfizer Inc.
Pharmacia & Upjohn, Inc.
Phelps Dodge Corp.
Pheonix Financial Group
Phillips Petroleum Co.
Physicians Mutual Insurance Co.
Pillsbury Co.
Pittway Corp.
PPG Industries, Inc.
Premier Industrial Corp.
Procter & Gamble Co.
Procter & Gamble Co., Cosmetics Division
Provident Companies, Inc.
Prudential Insurance Co. of America
Prudential Securities Inc.
Publix Supermarkets
Rayonier Inc.
Red Wing Shoe Co. Inc.
Regions Bank
Reilly Industries, Inc.
Reliant Energy Inc.
ReliaStar Financial Corp.
Reynolds Metals Co.
Rockwell International Corp.
Rubbermaid Inc.
SAFECO Corp.
Safeguard Scientifics
Salomon Smith Barney
Schlumberger Ltd. (USA)
Schwab & Co., Inc. (Charles)
Scripps Co. (E.W.)

Searle & Co. (G.D.)
Security Benefit Life Insurance Co.
Sempra Energy
Sentry Insurance, A Mutual Co.
S.G. Cowen
Shell Oil Co.
Sherwin-Williams Co.
Simplot Co. (J.R.)
Simpson Investment Co.
SIT Investment Associates, Inc.
Smith Corp. (A.O.)
Sonoco Products Co.
Southeastern Mutual Insurance Co.
Springs Industries, Inc.
Square D Co.
Standard Products Co.
Stanley Works (The)
Star Bank NA
Starwood Hotels & Resorts Worldwide, Inc.
State Farm Mutual Automobile Insurance Co.
State Street Bank & Trust Co.
Stone Container Corp.
Sunmark Capital Corp.
SunTrust Bank Atlanta
Synovus Financial Corp.
Tamko Roofing Products
Tektronix, Inc.
Teleflex Inc.
Tenneco Automotive
Tenneco Packaging
Tension Envelope Corp.
Tesoro Hawaii
Texas Instruments Inc.
Textron Inc.
Thermo Electron Corp.
TMC Investment Co.
Toyota Motor Sales U.S.A., Inc.
Transamerica Corp.
True Oil Co.
Tyson Foods Inc.
Unilever Home & Personal Care U.S.A.
Unilever United States, Inc.
Union Camp Corp.
Union Carbide Corp.
Union Pacific Corp.
United Distillers & Vintners North America
United Parcel Service of America Inc.
U.S. Bancorp
U.S. Bancorp Piper Jaffray
United States Sugar Corp.
Universal Leaf Tobacco Co., Inc.
Unocal Corp.
UnumProvident
US Bank, Washington
US West, Inc.
USG Corp.
USX Corp.
Valmont Industries, Inc.
Valspar Corp.
Vanguard Group
Vulcan Materials Co.
Wachovia Bank of North Carolina NA
Waffle House Inc.
Wal-Mart Stores, Inc.
Walgreen Co.
Walter Industries Inc.
Warner-Lambert Co.
Washington Mutual, Inc.
Wells Fargo & Co.
Western & Southern Life Insurance Co.
Weyerhaeuser Co.
Whirlpool Corp.
WICOR, Inc.
Williams
Wisconsin Energy Corp.
Wolverine World Wide
Wyman-Gordon Co.
Xerox Corp.
Yellow Corp.
York Federal Savings & Loan Association
Young & Rubicam
Zachry Co. (H.B.)

EDUCATION ASSOCIATIONS

Abbott Laboratories
Aetna, Inc.
AGL Resources Inc.
Air Products and Chemicals, Inc.
Alcoa Inc.
Alcon Laboratories, Inc.
Allegheny Technologies Inc.
Alliant Techsystems
Allstate Insurance Co.
Ameritech Corp.
Ameritech Michigan
AMETEK, Inc.
AMP Inc.
Andersen Corp.
Andersons Inc.
Aon Corp.
APL Ltd.
Archer-Daniels-Midland Co.
Arvin Industries, Inc.
Ashland, Inc.
AT&T Corp.
Banfi Vintners
Bank of New York Co., Inc.
Bank One Corp.
Barry Corp. (R.G.)
Baxter International Inc.
Becton Dickinson & Co.
Belk Stores Services Inc.
BellSouth Corp.
Bemis Co., Inc.
Bestfoods
BFGoodrich Co.
Binney & Smith Inc.
Blount International, Inc.
Blue Bell, Inc.
Boler Co.
Borden, Inc.
BP Amoco Corp.
Bradford & Co. (J.C.)
Briggs & Stratton Corp.
Brown Shoe Co., Inc.
Brown & Williamson Tobacco Corp.
Brunswick Corp.
Burlington Industries, Inc.
Burlington Resources, Inc.
Butler Manufacturing Co.
Carnival Corp.
Carpenter Technology Corp.
Carrier Corp.
Carter-Wallace, Inc.
Central Maine Power Co.
Central & South West Services
Central Soya Co.
Chase Manhattan Bank, NA
Chesapeake Corp.
Chevron Corp.
Chicago Board of Trade
Citibank Corp.
Citizens Financial Group, Inc.
Cleveland-Cliffs, Inc.
Clorox Co.
CNA
Coca-Cola Co.
Colonial Oil Industries, Inc.
ConAgra, Inc.
Cooper Industries, Inc.
Corning Inc.
Country Curtains, Inc.
CUNA Mutual Group
DaimlerChrysler Corp.
DeKalb Genetics Corp.
Deloitte & Touche
Deluxe Corp.
Detroit Edison Co.
Deutsch Co.
Dexter Corp.
Dixie Group, Inc. (The)
Donnelley & Sons Co. (R.R.)
Dow Chemical Co.
Dow Jones & Co., Inc.
du Pont de Nemours & Co. (E.I.)
Duke Energy
Dun & Bradstreet Corp.
Eaton Corp.
Ecolab Inc.
Emerson Electric Co.
Entergy Corp.
Equifax Inc.
Ernst & Young, LLP
Exxon Mobil Corp.
Federal-Mogul Corp.
Federated Department Stores, Inc.
FINA
First Source Corp.
First Union Bank
First Union Corp.
First Union Securities, Inc.
FleetBoston Financial Corp.
Fluor Corp.
Forbes Inc.
Ford Meter Box Co.
Ford Motor Co.
Fortune Brands, Inc.
Freddie Mac
Freeport-McMoRan Inc.
Freightliner Corp.
Furniture Brands International, Inc.
Gallo Winery, Inc. (E&J)
GATX Corp.
GEICO Corp.
GenAmerica Corp.
GenCorp
General Atlantic Partners II LP
General Electric Co.
General Mills, Inc.
General Motors Corp.
Georgia-Pacific Corp.
Georgia Power Co.
Glaxo Wellcome Inc.
Glickenhaus & Co.
GTE Corp.
Gulf Power Co.
Harcourt General, Inc.
Harsco Corp.
Hartford (The)
Hartmarx Corp.
Heinz Co. (H.J.)
Hensel Phelps Construction Co.
Hitachi America Ltd.
Honeywell International Inc.
Household International Inc.
HSBC Bank USA
Hubbell Inc.
Humana, Inc.
Illinois Tool Works, Inc.
Inland Container Corp.
International Business Machines Corp.
International Flavors & Fragrances Inc.
Jacobson & Sons (Benjamin)
Johnson Controls Inc.
Jostens, Inc.
Journal-Gazette Co.
JSJ Corp.
Kennametal, Inc.
Kerr-McGee Corp.
Kimberly-Clark Corp.
Koch Enterprises, Inc.
Kroger Co.
Ladish Co., Inc.
Lance, Inc.
LandAmerica Financial Services
Lehigh Portland Cement Co.
Lennox International, Inc.
Liberty Corp.
Lilly & Co. (Eli)
Lincoln Electric Co.
Lincoln Financial Group
Lipton Co.
Litton Industries, Inc.
Marcus Corp.
Marshall & Ilsley Corp.
Masco Corp.
May Department Stores Co.
Maytag Corp.
McClatchy Co.
McGraw-Hill Companies, Inc.
MCI WorldCom, Inc.
Mead Corp.
Merck & Co.
Metropolitan Life Insurance Co.
Michigan Consolidated Gas Co.
Mid-America Bank of Louisville
Milliken & Co.
Mine Safety Appliances Co.
Minnesota Mining & Manufacturing Co.
Montgomery Ward & Co., Inc.
Morgan Stanley Dean Witter & Co.
Morris Communications Corp.
Motorola Inc.
MTD Products Inc.
MTS Systems Corp.
Nalco Chemical Co.
National Computer Systems, Inc.
National Starch & Chemical Co.
Navcom Systems
New York Life Insurance Co.
Nordson Corp.
Norfolk Southern Corp.
Norton Co.
Occidental Petroleum Corp.
PACCAR Inc.
Paine Webber
Park National Bank
PEMCO Corp.
PepsiCo, Inc.
PerkinElmer, Inc.
Pfizer Inc.
Phelps Dodge Corp.
Philip Morris Companies Inc.
Phillips Petroleum Co.
Pittway Corp.
PNC Financial Services Group
Potlatch Corp.
Potomac Electric Power Co.
PPG Industries, Inc.
Premier Industrial Corp.
PricewaterhouseCoopers
Procter & Gamble Co., Cosmetics Division
Prudential Insurance Co. of America
Prudential Securities Inc.
Rayonier Inc.
Reader's Digest Association, Inc. (The)
Red Wing Shoe Co. Inc.
Regions Bank
Regis Corp.
Reilly Industries, Inc.
Reily & Co., Inc. (William B.)
Reynolds Metals Co.
Rockwell International Corp.
Rubbermaid Inc.
SAFECO Corp.
Sara Lee Corp.
SBC Communications Inc.
Schering-Plough Corp.
Schlumberger Ltd. (USA)
Security Benefit Life Insurance Co.
Sega of America Inc.
Shell Oil Co.
Shelter Mutual Insurance Co.
Southern New England Telephone Co.
Springs Industries, Inc.
Sprint Corp.
Standard Register Co.
Star Bank NA
State Farm Mutual Automobile Insurance Co.
Stone Container Corp.
Stonecutter Mills Corp.
Storage Technology Corp.
Sun Microsystems Inc.
Sunmark Capital Corp.
Sunoco Inc.
Synovus Financial Corp.
TCF National Bank Minnesota
Tenneco Automotive
Texaco Inc.
Texas Instruments Inc.
Textron Inc.
Timken Co. (The)
TJX Companies, Inc.
Tomkins Industries, Inc.
Transamerica Corp.
Unilever Home & Personal Care U.S.A.
Unilever United States, Inc.
Union Camp Corp.
Union Carbide Corp.
United Parcel Service of America Inc.
United States Sugar Corp.
Universal Studios
Unocal Corp.
UnumProvident
US West, Inc.
USG Corp.
USX Corp.
Wal-Mart Stores, Inc.
Warner-Lambert Co.
Westvaco Corp.
Weyerhaeuser Co.
Whirlpool Corp.
Wiley & Sons (John)
Williams
Wisconsin Energy Corp.
Wrigley Co. (Wm. Jr.)
Wyman-Gordon Co.
Xerox Corp.

EDUCATION FUNDS

AEGON U.S.A. Inc.
Aetna, Inc.
AGL Resources Inc.
Agrilink Foods, Inc.
Air Products and Chemicals, Inc.
AK Steel Corp.
Alabama Power Co.
Alaska Airlines, Inc.
Alcoa Inc.
Allegheny Technologies Inc.
Allianz Life Insurance Co. of North America
AlliedSignal Inc.
Allstate Insurance Co.
Ameren Corp.
American Express Co.
American Fidelity Corp.
American General Finance
American Standard Inc.
American United Life Insurance Co.
Ameritas Life Insurance Corp.
Ameritech Corp.
Ameritech Michigan
Ameritech Ohio
AMETEK, Inc.
Amgen, Inc.
Amsted Industries Inc.
Andersen Corp.
Andersons Inc.
Anheuser-Busch Companies, Inc.
Aon Corp.
APL Ltd.
Archer-Daniels-Midland Co.
Aristech Chemical Corp.
Armstrong World Industries, Inc.
Arvin Industries, Inc.
Ashland, Inc.
AT&T Corp.
Atlantic Richfield Co.
Auburn Foundry
Avon Products, Inc.
Badger Meter, Inc.
Banfi Vintners
Bank of America
Bank One Corp.
BankBoston-Connecticut Region
Banta Corp.
Bard, Inc. (C.R.)
Barden Corp.
Bardes Corp.
Barnes Group Inc.
Barry Corp. (R.G.)
Bassett Furniture Industries
Baxter International Inc.
Bechtel Group, Inc.
Belk Stores Services Inc.
Belo Corp. (A.H.)
Bemis Co., Inc.
Bernstein & Co., Inc. (Sanford C.)
BFGoodrich Co.
Binney & Smith Inc.
Blair & Co. (William)
Block, Inc. (H&R)
Blount International, Inc.
Blue Bell, Inc.
Blue Cross & Blue Shield of Alabama
Boeing Co.
Boler Co.
Borden, Inc.
Bourns, Inc.
BP Amoco Corp.
Bradford & Co. (J.C.)
Bridgestone/Firestone, Inc.
Bristol-Myers Squibb Co.
Brooklyn Union
Bucyrus-Erie Co.
Burlington Industries, Inc.
Burlington Resources, Inc.
Burnett Co. (Leo)
Burress (J.W.)
Cabot Corp.
Calvin Klein
Cargill Inc.
Carlson Companies, Inc.
Carnival Corp.
Carolina Power & Light Co.
Carpenter Technology Corp.
Carter-Wallace, Inc.
Caterpillar Inc.
Central Maine Power Co.
Central & South West Services
Central Soya Co.
CertainTeed Corp.
Cessna Aircraft Co.
CGU Insurance
Chase Bank of Texas
Chase Manhattan Bank, NA
Chesapeake Corp.
Chevron Corp.
Cincinnati Bell Inc.
Cinergy Corp.
CIT Group, Inc. (The)
Citibank Corp.
Citigroup
Citizens Financial Group, Inc.
Cleveland-Cliffs, Inc.
Clorox Co.
CNA
Coca-Cola Co.
Collins & Aikman Corp.
Colonial Oil Industries, Inc.
Comdisco, Inc.
Commerce Bancshares, Inc.
Commercial Intertech Corp.
Compass Bank
Cone Mills Corp.
Consolidated Natural Gas Co.
Consolidated Papers, Inc.
Constellation Energy Group, Inc.
Continental Grain Co.
Conwood Co. LP
Cooper Industries, Inc.
Cooper Tire & Rubber Co.
Copley Press, Inc.
Country Curtains, Inc.
CPI Corp.
Crane Co.
Crane & Co., Inc.
Credit Suisse First Boston
Crestar Finance Corp.
Croft-Leominster
CSS Industries, Inc.
Cummins Engine Co., Inc.
CUNA Mutual Group
Daily News
DaimlerChrysler Corp.
Dain Bosworth Inc.
Dana Corp.
Danis Companies
Deloitte & Touche
Delta Air Lines, Inc.
Deluxe Corp.
Demoulas Supermarkets Inc.
Deposit Guaranty National Bank
Detroit Edison Co.
Disney Co. (Walt)
Dixie Group, Inc. (The)
Dominion Resources, Inc.
Donaldson Co., Inc.
DSM Copolymer
du Pont de Nemours & Co. (E.I.)
Duchossois Industries Inc.
Duke Energy
Dun & Bradstreet Corp.
Duriron Co., Inc.
Eastman Kodak Co.
Eaton Corp.
Eckerd Corp.
Ecolab Inc.
Edison Brothers Stores, Inc.
Edwards Enterprise Software (J.D.)
Emerson Electric Co.
Enterprise Rent-A-Car Co.
Equifax Inc.
Erving Industries
Evening Post Publishing Co.
Exxon Mobil Corp.
Federal-Mogul Corp.
Federated Department Stores, Inc.
Ferro Corp.
Fifth Third Bancorp
FINA
Fireman's Fund Insurance Co.
First Hawaiian, Inc.
First Maryland Bancorp
First Source Corp.
First Union Bank
First Union Corp.
First Union Securities, Inc.
Firstar Bank Milwaukee NA
Fluor Corp.
FMC Corp.
Ford Meter Box Co.
Forest City Enterprises, Inc.
Fortis, Inc.
Frost National Bank
Fuller Co. (H.B.)
Furniture Brands International, Inc.
Gallo Winery, Inc. (E&J)
Gap, Inc.
GEICO Corp.
GenAmerica Corp.
GenCorp
General Mills, Inc.
General Motors Corp.
Georgia-Pacific Corp.
Georgia Power Co.
Gerber Products Co.
Giant Eagle Inc.
Giant Food Inc.
Giddings & Lewis
Glickenhaus & Co.
Grace & Co. (W.R.)
Graco, Inc.
Grede Foundries
GTE Corp.
Guardian Life Insurance Co. of America
Guess?
Gulf Power Co.
Hancock Financial Services (John)
Hanna Co. (M.A.)
Harcourt General, Inc.
Harland Co. (John H.)
Harnischfeger Industries
Harris Corp.
Harsco Corp.
Hartford (The)
Hartford Steam Boiler Inspection & Insurance Co.
Hartmarx Corp.
Hasbro, Inc.
Heinz Co. (H.J.)
Hickory Tech Corp.
Hoffmann-La Roche Inc.
Honeywell International Inc.
Houghton Mifflin Co.
Hubbard Broadcasting, Inc.
Hubbell Inc.
Huffy Corp.
Humana, Inc.
IKON Office Solutions, Inc.
Illinois Tool Works, Inc.
Industrial Bank of Japan Trust Co. (New York)
Inland Container Corp.
Inman Mills
International Multifoods Corp.
INTRUST Financial Corp.
Invacare Corp.
Johnson Controls Inc.
Johnson & Son (S.C.)
Jostens, Inc.
Journal-Gazette Co.
JSJ Corp.
Kellwood Co.
Kelly Services
Kennametal, Inc.
Kimball International, Inc.
Kimberly-Clark Corp.
Kingsbury Corp.
Koch Enterprises, Inc.
Kroger Co.
La-Z-Boy Inc.
Ladish Co., Inc.
Lancaster Lens, Inc.
Lance, Inc.
LandAmerica Financial Services
Landmark Communications Inc.
Lee Enterprises
Lehigh Portland Cement Co.
Leigh Fibers, Inc.
Lennox International, Inc.
Levi Strauss & Co.
Liberty Corp.
Lilly & Co. (Eli)
Lincoln Electric Co.
Lincoln Financial Group
Lipton Co.
Little, Inc. (Arthur D.)
Litton Industries, Inc.
Liz Claiborne, Inc.
Loews Corp.
Louisiana Land & Exploration Co.
Louisiana-Pacific Corp.
LTV Corp.
Lubrizol Corp. (The)
Macy's East Inc.
Madison Gas & Electric Co.
Marcus Corp.
Marshall & Ilsley Corp.
Masco Corp.
Massachusetts Mutual Life Insurance Co.
Mattel Inc.
May Department Stores Co.
Maytag Corp.
McClatchy Co.
McDonald & Co. Securities, Inc.
McGraw-Hill Companies, Inc.
MCI WorldCom, Inc.
McKesson-HBOC Corp.
Mead Corp.
Merck & Co.
Michigan Consolidated Gas Co.
Mid-America Bank of Louisville
Milacron, Inc.
Milliken & Co.
Mine Safety Appliances Co.
Minnesota Mining & Manufacturing Co.
Minnesota Mutual Life Insurance Co.
Monarch Machine Tool Co.
Montgomery Ward & Co., Inc.
Morris Communications Corp.
Morrison Knudsen Corp.
Motorola Inc.
MTD Products Inc.
Nabisco Group Holdings
National City Bank of Minneapolis
National Computer Systems, Inc.
National Machinery Co.
National Service Industries, Inc.
National Starch & Chemical Co.
Nationwide Insurance Co.
NEBCO Evans
New Jersey Natural Gas Co.
New York Life Insurance Co.
Nike, Inc.
Nomura Holding America
Nordson Corp.
Norfolk Southern Corp.
Nortel
North American Royalties
Northern Indiana Public Service Co.
Northwest Bank Nebraska, NA
Norton Co.
Norwest Corp.
Occidental Oil and Gas
Ohio National Life Insurance Co.
Old National Bank Evansville
Osborne Enterprises
Oshkosh B'Gosh, Inc.
Owens Corning
PACCAR Inc.
Pacific Mutual Life Insurance Co.
PacifiCorp
Park National Bank
Parker Hannifin Corp.
PECO Energy Co.
Pella Corp.
PEMCO Corp.
Pfizer Inc.
Pharmacia & Upjohn, Inc.
Phelps Dodge Corp.
Philip Morris Companies Inc.
Phillips Petroleum Co.
Physicians Mutual Insurance Co.
Pitney Bowes Inc.
Pittway Corp.
PNC Financial Services Group
Portland General Electric Co.
Potomac Electric Power Co.
PPG Industries, Inc.
Praxair
Premier Industrial Corp.
Price Associates (T. Rowe)
Principal Financial Group
Procter & Gamble Co.
Procter & Gamble Co., Cosmetics Division
Providence Journal-Bulletin Co.
Prudential Insurance Co. of America
Prudential Securities Inc.
Pulitzer Publishing Co.

Quanex Corp.
Ralston Purina Co.
Rayonier Inc.
Red Wing Shoe Co. Inc.
Reebok International Ltd.
Regions Bank
Reilly Industries, Inc.
Reily & Co., Inc. (William B.)
Revlon Inc.
Reynolds Metals Co.
Reynolds & Reynolds Co.
Reynolds Tobacco (R.J.)
Rockwell International Corp.
Rouse Co.
Royal & SunAlliance USA, Inc.
Rubbermaid Inc.
Ryder System, Inc.
Sara Lee Hosiery, Inc.
SBC Communications Inc.
Schering-Plough Corp.
Schwebel Baking Co.
Scripps Co. (E.W.)
Seagram & Sons, Inc. (Joseph E.)
Security Benefit Life Insurance Co.
Sempra Energy
Sentry Insurance, A Mutual Co.
Shaklee Corp.
Shaw's Supermarkets, Inc.
Shell Oil Co.
Sherwin-Williams Co.
Shoney's Inc.
Simpson Investment Co.
Slant/Fin Corp.
Smith Corp. (A.O.)
SmithKline Beecham Corp.
Smurfit-Stone Container Corp.
Sonoco Products Co.
Sony Electronics
South Bend Tribune Corp.
Southeastern Mutual Insurance Co.
SPX Corp.
Square D Co.
Standard Products Co.
Standard Register Co.
Star Bank NA
State Farm Mutual Automobile Insurance Co.
State Street Bank & Trust Co.
Steelcase Inc.
Stone Container Corp.
Stonecutter Mills Corp.
Storage Technology Corp.
Stride Rite Corp.
Stupp Brothers Bridge & Iron Co.
Sunmark Capital Corp.
SunTrust Bank Atlanta
Susquehanna-Pfaltzgraff Co.
Synovus Financial Corp.
TCF National Bank Minnesota
Tektronix, Inc.
TENNANT Co.
Tenneco Automotive
Tension Envelope Corp.
Texaco Inc.
Texas Instruments Inc.
Textron Inc.
Thomasville Furniture Industries Inc.
Thompson Co. (J. Walter)
Times Mirror Co.
Timken Co. (The)
TJX Companies, Inc.
TMC Investment Co.
Toledo Blade Co.
Tomkins Industries, Inc.
Toyota Motor Sales U.S.A., Inc.
Transamerica Corp.
True Oil Co.
TRW Inc.
Tyson Foods Inc.
Ukrop's Super Markets
Unilever Home & Personal Care U.S.A.
Union Camp Corp.
Union Carbide Corp.
Union Pacific Corp.
United Airlines Inc.
United Dominion Industries, Ltd.
United Parcel Service of America Inc.
U.S. Bancorp Piper Jaffray
United States Sugar Corp.
United Wisconsin Services
Universal Foods Corp.
Universal Leaf Tobacco Co., Inc.
Universal Studios
Unocal Corp.
US West, Inc.
Valmont Industries, Inc.
Valspar Corp.
Vodafone AirTouch Plc
Vulcan Materials Co.
Wachovia Bank of North Carolina NA
Wal-Mart Stores, Inc.
Warner-Lambert Co.
Washington Mutual, Inc.
Washington Trust Bank
Waste Management Inc.
Wells Fargo & Co.
West Co. Inc.
Western & Southern Life Insurance Co.
Westvaco Corp.
Weyerhaeuser Co.
Whirlpool Corp.
Whitman Corp.
Wilbur-Ellis Co. & Connell Brothers Co.
Wiley & Sons (John)
Williams
Wiremold Co.
Wisconsin Energy Corp.
Wisconsin Power & Light Co.
Wisconsin Public Service Corp.
Wrigley Co. (Wm. Jr.)
Xerox Corp.
Young & Rubicam

EDUCATION REFORM

ABC
Aetna, Inc.
Air Products and Chemicals, Inc.
Alabama Power Co.
Alcoa Inc.
AlliedSignal Inc.
Allmerica Financial Corp.
Ameren Corp.
American Express Co.
American Honda Motor Co., Inc.
American Standard Inc.
American United Life Insurance Co.
Ameritech Corp.
Amgen, Inc.
AMR Corp.
Andersons Inc.
Anheuser-Busch Companies, Inc.
APL Ltd.
Aristech Chemical Corp.
Arizona Public Service Co.
Arvin Industries, Inc.
Ashland, Inc.
AT&T Corp.
Atlantic Richfield Co.
Baird & Co. (Robert W.)
Bank of America
BankAtlantic Bancorp
Baxter International Inc.
Bean, Inc. (L.L.)
Bechtel Group, Inc.
Bell Atlantic Corp.
BellSouth Corp.
Bemis Co., Inc.
Bernstein & Co., Inc. (Sanford C.)
BFGoodrich Co.
Block, Inc. (H&R)
Blount International, Inc.
Boston Edison Co.
Boston Globe (The)
Briggs & Stratton Corp.
Bristol-Myers Squibb Co.
Burlington Industries, Inc.
Burnett Co. (Leo)
Campbell Soup Co.
Cargill Inc.
Caterpillar Inc.
CertainTeed Corp.
Cessna Aircraft Co.
CGU Insurance
Chase Manhattan Bank, NA
Chevron Corp.
CIGNA Corp.
Cincinnati Bell Inc.
Cinergy Corp.
Circuit City Stores, Inc.
CIT Group, Inc. (The)
Citigroup
Cleveland-Cliffs, Inc.
Clorox Co.
Coca-Cola Co.
Collins & Aikman Corp.
Colonial Oil Industries, Inc.
Continental Grain Co.
Contran Corp.
Corning Inc.
Cox Enterprises Inc.
Crane Co.
Credit Suisse First Boston
Croft-Leominster
Cummins Engine Co., Inc.
DaimlerChrysler Corp.
Dayton Hudson
Dayton Power and Light Co.
Deloitte & Touche
Delta Air Lines, Inc.
Deutsch Co.
Disney Co. (Walt)
Donaldson Co., Inc.
Dreyer's Grand Ice Cream
Duchossois Industries Inc.
Duriron Co., Inc.
Dynamet, Inc.
Eastman Kodak Co.
Eaton Corp.
Ecolab Inc.
El Paso Energy Co.
Elf Atochem North America, Inc.
Evening Post Publishing Co.
Exxon Mobil Corp.
Fabri-Kal Corp.
Federal-Mogul Corp.
Ferro Corp.
Fidelity Investments
First Financial Bank
First Maryland Bancorp
First Union Corp.
First Union Securities, Inc.
Firstar Bank Milwaukee NA
Fisher Brothers Cleaning Services
Fisher Scientific
Florida Power & Light Co.
Fluor Corp.
Forbes Inc.
Ford Motor Co.
Forest City Enterprises, Inc.
Fort Worth Star-Telegram Inc.
Freddie Mac
Freeport-McMoRan Inc.
Fuller Co. (H.B.)
Furniture Brands International, Inc.
Gallo Winery, Inc. (E&J)
GATX Corp.
GenCorp
General Atlantic Partners II LP
General Electric Co.
General Mills, Inc.
General Motors Corp.
Georgia Power Co.
Glickenhaus & Co.
Goldman Sachs Group
Graco, Inc.
GTE Corp.
Hallmark Cards Inc.
Hanna Co. (M.A.)
Harcourt General, Inc.
Harley-Davidson Co.
Harnischfeger Industries
Harris Trust & Savings Bank
Hartmarx Corp.
Hasbro, Inc.
Hewlett-Packard Co.
Hitachi America Ltd.
Hoffer Plastics Corp.
HON Industries Inc.
Honeywell International Inc.
Huffy Corp.
Hughes Electronics Corp.
Humana, Inc.
Industrial Bank of Japan Trust Co. (New York)
International Flavors & Fragrances Inc.
International Paper Co.
Invacare Corp.
Jacobs Engineering Group
Jeld-wen, Inc.
Johnson Controls Inc.
Jostens, Inc.
Katten, Muchin & Zavis
Koch Enterprises, Inc.
KPMG Peat Marwick LLP
LG&E Energy Corp.
Liberty Corp.
Lilly & Co. (Eli)
Lincoln Electric Co.
Lipton Co.
Litton Industries, Inc.
Liz Claiborne, Inc.
Loews Corp.
Lotus Development Corp.
LTV Corp.
Marshall Field's
Marshall & Ilsley Corp.
Mattel Inc.
May Department Stores Co.
McClatchy Co.
McDonald & Co. Securities, Inc.
McGraw-Hill Companies, Inc.
MCI WorldCom, Inc.
McKesson-HBOC Corp.
McWane Inc.
Mead Corp.
Medtronic, Inc.
Menasha Corp.
Merrill Lynch & Co., Inc.
Metropolitan Life Insurance Co.
Microsoft Corp.
Milliken & Co.
Millipore Corp.
Minnesota Mutual Life Insurance Co.
Monsanto Co.
Morgan & Co. Inc. (J.P.)
Morrison Knudsen Corp.
National City Corp.
Nationwide Insurance Co.
Nestle U.S.A. Inc.
New England Financial
New Jersey Natural Gas Co.
New York Mercantile Exchange
Nordson Corp.
Northern States Power Co.
Northern Trust Co.
Norton Co.
Overseas Shipholding Group Inc.
Owens Corning
Pacific Mutual Life Insurance Co.
Paine Webber
Park National Bank
Parker Hannifin Corp.
Pella Corp.
PEMCO Corp.
Penney Co., Inc. (J.C.)
PepsiCo, Inc.
PerkinElmer, Inc.
Pfizer Inc.
Pharmacia & Upjohn, Inc.
Philip Morris Companies Inc.
Phillips Petroleum Co.
Pillsbury Co.
Polaroid Corp.
Premier Industrial Corp.
Procter & Gamble Co.
Provident Companies, Inc.
Prudential Insurance Co. of America
Ralph's Grocery Co.
Red Wing Shoe Co. Inc.
Regions Bank
Reily & Co., Inc. (William B.)
Reynolds Metals Co.
Reynolds & Reynolds Co.
Reynolds Tobacco (R.J.)
Rockwell International Corp.
Rouse Co.
Royal & SunAlliance USA, Inc.
Rubbermaid Inc.
Ryder System, Inc.
Saint Paul Companies Inc.
S&T Bancorp
SBC Communications Inc.
Seagram & Sons, Inc. (Joseph E.)
Sega of America Inc.
Shell Oil Co.
Sierra Pacific Resources
Simpson Investment Co.
Sonoco Products Co.
Sony Electronics
Southeastern Mutual Insurance Co.
Sprint Corp.
Sprint/United Telephone
State Street Bank & Trust Co.
Storage Technology Corp.

Strear Farms Co.
Stride Rite Corp.
Sunmark Capital Corp.
Synovus Financial Corp.
TENNANT Co.
Tension Envelope Corp.
Texaco Inc.
Texas Instruments Inc.
Textron Inc.
Thompson Co. (J. Walter)
Times Mirror Co.
Timken Co. (The)
Toro Co.
Toyota Motor Sales U.S.A., Inc.
TRW Inc.
Ukrop's Super Markets
Union Carbide Corp.
United Airlines Inc.
United Dominion Industries, Ltd.
United Parcel Service of America Inc.
U.S. Bancorp Piper Jaffray
United States Sugar Corp.
United Wisconsin Services
Universal Foods Corp.
Universal Studios
Unocal Corp.
UnumProvident
US Bank, Washington
USX Corp.
Vulcan Materials Co.
Waffle House Inc.
Washington Mutual, Inc.
Washington Trust Bank
Weil, Gotshal & Manges Corp.
Whirlpool Corp.
WICOR, Inc.
Wisconsin Energy Corp.
Wyman-Gordon Co.
York Federal Savings & Loan Association

ELEMENTARY EDUCATION (PRIVATE)

AFLAC Inc.
AGL Resources Inc.
Alabama Power Co.
Albertson's Inc.
Alcoa Inc.
Alexander & Baldwin, Inc.
Ameren Corp.
America West Airlines, Inc.
American Honda Motor Co., Inc.
American Retail Group
Ameritech Indiana
AMETEK, Inc.
Andersen Corp.
Aon Corp.
APL Ltd.
Apple Computer, Inc.
Arvin Industries, Inc.
Atlantic Investment Co.
Avista Corporation
Bank of America
Bank of New York Co., Inc.
Bank One, Texas-Houston Office
Barclays Capital
Bard, Inc. (C.R.)
Battelle Memorial Institute
BellSouth Corp.
Bemis Co., Inc.
Binney & Smith Inc.
Blair & Co. (William)
Boeing Co.
Boler Co.
Boston Globe (The)
Bradford & Co. (J.C.)
Bucyrus-Erie Co.
Cabot Corp.
Cargill Inc.
Carpenter Technology Corp.
Central Maine Power Co.
CertainTeed Corp.
Chase Manhattan Bank, NA
Chevron Corp.
CIGNA Corp.
Cincinnati Bell Inc.
Cinergy Corp.
Citibank Corp.
Clorox Co.
Coca-Cola Co.
Consolidated Natural Gas Co.
Cummings Properties Management
Cummins Engine Co., Inc.
DeKalb Genetics Corp.
Deluxe Corp.
Duchossois Industries Inc.
Duke Energy
Eastern Enterprises
Federal-Mogul Corp.
First Source Corp.
First Tennessee National Corp.
Fortune Brands, Inc.
Freeport-McMoRan Inc.
Frontier Corp.
Fuller Co. (H.B.)
GATX Corp.
GenCorp
Genentech Inc.
General Motors Corp.
Georgia Power Co.
Giant Eagle Inc.
Glaxo Wellcome Inc.
Goodrich Aerospace - Aerostructures Group (B.F.)
Graco, Inc.
Hallmark Cards Inc.
Hartford Steam Boiler Inspection & Insurance Co.
Heinz Co. (H.J.)
Heller Financial, Inc.
Hewlett-Packard Co.
Hitachi America Ltd.
Honeywell International Inc.
Hubbell Inc.
Humana, Inc.
Hunt Manufacturing Co.
Huntington Bancshares Inc.
Intel Corp.
International Paper Co.
Johnson Controls Inc.
Kroger Co.
Litton Industries, Inc.
Lotus Development Corp.
LTV Corp.
Maritz Inc.
Marshall & Ilsley Corp.
Matsushita Electric Corp. of America
Mattel Inc.
MBIA Inc.
McClatchy Co.
Medtronic, Inc.
Minnesota Mutual Life Insurance Co.
Nabisco Group Holdings
National Computer Systems, Inc.
National Fuel Gas Distribution Corp.
National Starch & Chemical Co.
New England Financial
Nortel
Northwest Bank Nebraska, NA
Northwest Natural Gas Co.
Old National Bank Evansville
Osborne Enterprises
Oshkosh B'Gosh, Inc.
Pella Corp.
Penney Co., Inc. (J.C.)
Peoples Bank
Peoples Energy Corp.
Pfizer Inc.
Phillips Petroleum Co.
Physicians Mutual Insurance Co.
Pillsbury Co.
Pitney Bowes Inc.
Pittway Corp.
Polaroid Corp.
Price Associates (T. Rowe)
Prudential Insurance Co. of America
Public Service Electric & Gas Co.
Quanex Corp.
Reily & Co., Inc. (William B.)
ReliaStar Financial Corp.
Reynolds Metals Co.
Reynolds Tobacco (R.J.)
Royal & SunAlliance USA, Inc.
SAFECO Corp.
Salomon Smith Barney
Sara Lee Hosiery, Inc.
Seaway Food Town, Inc.
Security Life of Denver Insurance Co.
Sempra Energy
Shell Oil Co.
Shoney's Inc.
Simpson Investment Co.
Smucker Co. (JM)
Sonoco Products Co.
Stanley Works (The)
State Street Bank & Trust Co.
Stonecutter Mills Corp.
Strear Farms Co.
Temple-Inland Inc.
Tenneco Packaging
TJX Companies, Inc.
Toyota Motor Sales U.S.A., Inc.
Transamerica Corp.
Unilever United States, Inc.
Union Camp Corp.
U.S. Bancorp
U.S. Bancorp Piper Jaffray
United States Sugar Corp.
Universal Leaf Tobacco Co., Inc.
Varian Medical Systems, Inc.
Vulcan Materials Co.
Wachovia Bank of North Carolina NA
Wal-Mart Stores, Inc.
Waste Management Inc.
Wells Fargo & Co.
Westvaco Corp.
Weyerhaeuser Co.
Whirlpool Corp.
WICOR, Inc.
Wiley & Sons (John)
Williams
Woodward Governor Co.
Zilkha & Sons
Zurn Industries, Inc.

ELEMENTARY EDUCATION (PUBLIC)

Alliant Techsystems
AlliedSignal Inc.
Allstate Insurance Co.
American Honda Motor Co., Inc.
AMP Inc.
Andersen Corp.
Arvin Industries, Inc.
AT&T Corp.
Atlantic Richfield Co.
Bandag, Inc.
Baxter International Inc.
Bean, Inc. (L.L.)
Bechtel Group, Inc.
Beckman Coulter, Inc.
Belk Stores Services Inc.
Ben & Jerry's Homemade Inc.
Blue Bell, Inc.
Boston Edison Co.
Bradford & Co. (J.C.)
Burlington Industries, Inc.
Burlington Resources, Inc.
CertainTeed Corp.
Clorox Co.
Compaq Computer Corp.
Compass Bank
Consolidated Natural Gas Co.
Crane Co.
DeKalb Genetics Corp.
Delta Air Lines, Inc.
Deposit Guaranty National Bank
Donaldson Co., Inc.
Eastman Kodak Co.
Erving Industries
Excel Corp.
First Hawaiian, Inc.
Ford Meter Box Co.
Freddie Mac
Freeport-McMoRan Inc.
GenCorp
General Mills, Inc.
Halliburton Co.
Harcourt General, Inc.
Hasbro, Inc.
Hewlett-Packard Co.
Hoffer Plastics Corp.
Honeywell International Inc.
Hughes Electronics Corp.
IBP
Industrial Bank of Japan Trust Co. (New York)
Inland Container Corp.
International Multifoods Corp.
International Paper Co.
Invacare Corp.
Jacobs Engineering Group
Jeld-wen, Inc.
Kimball International, Inc.
Kingsbury Corp.
La-Z-Boy Inc.
Land O'Lakes, Inc.
Lehigh Portland Cement Co.
Leviton Manufacturing Co. Inc.
Litton Industries, Inc.
Liz Claiborne, Inc.
MacMillan Bloedel Inc.
Madison Gas & Electric Co.
Marshall Field's
Matsushita Electric Corp. of America
Mattel Inc.
McDonald & Co. Securities, Inc.
Millipore Corp.
National Life of Vermont
National Machinery Co.
NEBCO Evans
New England Bio Labs
New York Mercantile Exchange
Nissan North America, Inc.
North American Royalties
Northern States Power Co.
Occidental Oil and Gas
Olin Corp.
Orange & Rockland Utilities, Inc.
Pfizer Inc.
Physicians Mutual Insurance Co.
Principal Financial Group
Procter & Gamble Co., Cosmetics Division
Prudential Insurance Co. of America
Rayonier Inc.
Regions Bank
Reilly Industries, Inc.
Reily & Co., Inc. (William B.)
Reinhart Institutional Foods
Reynolds Tobacco (R.J.)
Rubbermaid Inc.
Schwab & Co., Inc. (Charles)
Scripps Co. (E.W.)
Security Life of Denver Insurance Co.
Sega of America Inc.
Shea Co. (John F.)
Sierra Pacific Industries
Sierra Pacific Resources
Sonoco Products Co.
Square D Co.
Stanley Works (The)
Stonecutter Mills Corp.
Sun Microsystems Inc.
Tesoro Hawaii
Texas Instruments Inc.
Thomasville Furniture Industries Inc.
Toshiba America Inc.
Union Camp Corp.
United Parcel Service of America Inc.
United States Sugar Corp.
USX Corp.
Vesper Corp.
Vodafone AirTouch Plc
Waffle House Inc.
Washington Mutual, Inc.
The Washington Post
Weyerhaeuser Co.
WICOR, Inc.
Wiley & Sons (John)
Zachry Co. (H.B.)

ENGINEERING/ TECHNOLOGICAL EDUCATION

Abbott Laboratories
ABC
AGL Resources Inc.
Air Products and Chemicals, Inc.
AK Steel Corp.
Alabama Power Co.
Alcoa Inc.
Allegheny Technologies Inc.
Alliant Techsystems
AlliedSignal Inc.
Allmerica Financial Corp.
Ameren Corp.
American Honda Motor Co., Inc.
Ameritech Illinois
Ameritech Indiana
Ameritech Michigan
AMETEK, Inc.
AMP Inc.
Amsted Industries Inc.
Andersen Corp.
Anheuser-Busch Companies, Inc.

Appleton Papers Inc.
Aristech Chemical Corp.
Armstrong World Industries, Inc.
Arvin Industries, Inc.
ASARCO Inc.
Ashland, Inc.
AT&T Corp.
Atlantic Investment Co.
Atlantic Richfield Co.
Avista Corporation
Badger Meter, Inc.
Baird & Co. (Robert W.)
Baker Hughes Inc.
Bandag, Inc.
Bank of America
Bank One Corp.
BankBoston Corp.
Banta Corp.
Barden Corp.
Barnes Group Inc.
Battelle Memorial Institute
Bechtel Group, Inc.
Beckman Coulter, Inc.
Becton Dickinson & Co.
Bell Atlantic Corp.
BellSouth Corp.
Bemis Co., Inc.
Bethlehem Steel Corp.
BFGoodrich Co.
Blount International, Inc.
Blue Bell, Inc.
Boeing Co.
Boise Cascade Corp.
Borden, Inc.
Boston Edison Co.
Bourns, Inc.
Bowater Inc.
BP Amoco Corp.
Bridgestone/Firestone, Inc.
Briggs & Stratton Corp.
Brunswick Corp.
Bucyrus-Erie Co.
Burlington Industries, Inc.
Burlington Resources, Inc.
Burnett Co. (Leo)
Butler Manufacturing Co.
Cabot Corp.
Cargill Inc.
Carolina Power & Light Co.
Carrier Corp.
Caterpillar Inc.
Central Maine Power Co.
Central National-Gottesman
Central Newspapers, Inc.
Central & South West Services
CertainTeed Corp.
Cessna Aircraft Co.
Champion International Corp.
Charter Manufacturing Co.
Chase Bank of Texas
Chase Manhattan Bank, NA
Chesapeake Corp.
Chevron Corp.
Cincinnati Bell Inc.
Cinergy Corp.
CIT Group, Inc. (The)
Cleveland-Cliffs, Inc.
Coca-Cola Co.
Colonial Oil Industries, Inc.
Commercial Intertech Corp.
ConAgra, Inc.
Cone Mills Corp.
Conoco, Inc.
Consolidated Natural Gas Co.
Consolidated Papers, Inc.
Consumers Energy Co.
Cooper Industries, Inc.
Cooper Tire & Rubber Co.
Corning Inc.
Cox Enterprises Inc.
Crane & Co., Inc.
Cranston Print Works Co.
Credit Suisse First Boston
Crestar Finance Corp.
Cummins Engine Co., Inc.
DaimlerChrysler Corp.
Dana Corp.
Danis Companies
Dayton Hudson
Dayton Power and Light Co.
Deere & Co.
DeKalb Genetics Corp.
Deloitte & Touche
Delta Air Lines, Inc.
Detroit Edison Co.
Deutsch Co.
Dexter Corp.
Disney Co. (Walt)
Dixie Group, Inc. (The)
Dominion Resources, Inc.
Donaldson Co., Inc.
Dow Chemical Co.
Dow Corning Corp.
DSM Copolymer
du Pont de Nemours & Co. (E.I.)
Duchossois Industries Inc.
Duke Energy
Duriron Co., Inc.
Dynamet, Inc.
Eastman Kodak Co.
Eaton Corp.
Eckerd Corp.
Edison International
El Paso Energy Co.
Elf Atochem North America, Inc.
Emerson Electric Co.
Ensign-Bickford Industries
Erb Lumber Co.
Erving Industries
Exxon Mobil Corp.
Federal-Mogul Corp.
Fifth Third Bancorp
FINA
First Source Corp.
First Union Corp.
First Union Securities, Inc.
Firstar Bank Milwaukee NA
FleetBoston Financial Corp.
Florida Power & Light Co.
Fluor Corp.
FMC Corp.
Ford Motor Co.
Forest City Enterprises, Inc.
Fortis, Inc.
Franklin Electric Co.
Freeport-McMoRan Inc.
Frost National Bank
GenCorp
General Electric Co.
General Mills, Inc.
General Motors Corp.
Georgia-Pacific Corp.
Georgia Power Co.
Gerber Products Co.
Giddings & Lewis
Goodrich Aerospace - Aerostructures Group (B.F.)
Grace & Co. (W.R.)
Grede Foundries
GTE Corp.
Gulf Power Co.
Halliburton Co.
Hamilton Sundstrand Corp.
Harcourt General, Inc.
Harland Co. (John H.)
Harley-Davidson Co.
Harnischfeger Industries
Harris Corp.
Harris Trust & Savings Bank
Harsco Corp.
Hartmarx Corp.
Hensel Phelps Construction Co.
Hershey Foods Corp.
Hewlett-Packard Co.
Hickory Tech Corp.
HON Industries Inc.
Honeywell International Inc.
Hubbard Broadcasting, Inc.
Hubbell Inc.
Huffy Corp.
Hughes Electronics Corp.
Illinois Tool Works, Inc.
Inland Container Corp.
Inman Mills
Intel Corp.
International Business Machines Corp.
International Flavors & Fragrances Inc.
International Paper Co.
Jacobs Engineering Group
Jeld-wen, Inc.
Johnson Controls Inc.
Johnson & Son (S.C.)
JSJ Corp.
Katten, Muchin & Zavis
Kemper National Insurance Companies
Kennametal, Inc.
Kerr-McGee Corp.
Kiewit Sons' Inc. (Peter)
Kimberly-Clark Corp.
Kinder Morgn
Kingsbury Corp.
Koch Enterprises, Inc.
KPMG Peat Marwick LLP
Ladish Co., Inc.
Lehigh Portland Cement Co.
Leigh Fibers, Inc.
Lennox International, Inc.
Leviton Manufacturing Co. Inc.
LG&E Energy Corp.
Liberty Corp.
Lilly & Co. (Eli)
Lincoln Electric Co.
Little, Inc. (Arthur D.)
Litton Industries, Inc.
Lotus Development Corp.
Louisiana Land & Exploration Co.
Lowe's Companies
LTV Corp.
Lubrizol Corp. (The)
Mallinckrodt Chemical, Inc.
Marcus Corp.
Marshall & Ilsley Corp.
Mattel Inc.
May Department Stores Co.
Maytag Corp.
McClatchy Co.
McGraw-Hill Companies, Inc.
McWane Inc.
Mead Corp.
Medtronic, Inc.
Menasha Corp.
Mercantile Bank NA
Merck & Co.
Metropolitan Life Insurance Co.
Michigan Consolidated Gas Co.
Milacron, Inc.
Milliken & Co.
Millipore Corp.
Mine Safety Appliances Co.
Minnesota Mining & Manufacturing Co.
Monsanto Co.
Montana Power Co.
Morgan Stanley Dean Witter & Co.
Morris Communications Corp.
Morrison Knudsen Corp.
Motorola Inc.
MTD Products Inc.
MTS Systems Corp.
Nalco Chemical Co.
National Computer Systems, Inc.
National Presto Industries, Inc.
National Service Industries, Inc.
National Starch & Chemical Co.
Navcom Systems
Nestle U.S.A. Inc.
New York Times Co.
Norfolk Southern Corp.
North American Royalties
Northeast Utilities
Northern Indiana Public Service Co.
Norton Co.
Norwest Corp.
Novartis Corporation
Occidental Oil and Gas
Occidental Petroleum Corp.
Old National Bank Evansville
Olin Corp.
Orange & Rockland Utilities, Inc.
Outboard Marine Corp.
Overseas Shipholding Group Inc.
PACCAR Inc.
Pacific Gas and Electric Co.
Parker Hannifin Corp.
Pella Corp.
Pennzoil-Quaker State Co.
PepsiCo, Inc.
PerkinElmer, Inc.
Pfizer Inc.
Pharmacia & Upjohn, Inc.
Phelps Dodge Corp.
Pheonix Financial Group
Philip Morris Companies Inc.
Philips Electronics North America Corp.
Phillips Petroleum Co.
Pieper Power Electric Co.
Pittway Corp.
Polaroid Corp.
Potlatch Corp.
PPG Industries, Inc.
Praxair
Procter & Gamble Co.
Procter & Gamble Co., Cosmetics Division
Prudential Insurance Co. of America
Public Service Electric & Gas Co.
Putnam Investments
Quaker Chemical Corp.
Quanex Corp.
Rayonier Inc.
Reilly Industries, Inc.
Reliant Energy Minnegasco
Reynolds Metals Co.
Reynolds Tobacco (R.J.)
Rockwell International Corp.
Rubbermaid Inc.
Ryder System, Inc.
SBC Communications Inc.
Schering-Plough Corp.
Schlumberger Ltd. (USA)
Scripps Co. (E.W.)
Sempra Energy
Sentry Insurance, A Mutual Co.
Shell Oil Co.
Sierra Pacific Resources
Simpson Investment Co.
Slant/Fin Corp.
Smith Corp. (A.O.)
Sonoco Products Co.
Sony Electronics
Southern California Gas Co.
Southern New England Telephone Co.
Sprint Corp.
SPX Corp.
Square D Co.
Stanley Works (The)
Starwood Hotels & Resorts Worldwide, Inc.
State Street Bank & Trust Co.
Stonecutter Mills Corp.
Storage Technology Corp.
Sun Microsystems Inc.
Sunoco Inc.
SunTrust Bank Atlanta
Sverdrup Corp.
Synovus Financial Corp.
Tai and Co. (J.T.)
Tektronix, Inc.
Temple-Inland Inc.
Tenneco Automotive
Tenneco Packaging
Tesoro Hawaii
Texaco Inc.
Texas Instruments Inc.
Textron Inc.
Thermo Electron Corp.
Thompson Co. (J. Walter)
Times Mirror Co.
Timken Co. (The)
TMC Investment Co.
Tomkins Industries, Inc.
Toshiba America Inc.
Toyota Motor Sales U.S.A., Inc.
TRW Inc.
Unilever Home & Personal Care U.S.A.
Unilever United States, Inc.
Union Camp Corp.
Union Carbide Corp.
Union Pacific Corp.
United Distillers & Vintners North America
United Parcel Service of America Inc.
United Technologies Corp.
Universal Foods Corp.
Unocal Corp.
US West, Inc.
USX Corp.
Valmont Industries, Inc.
Varian Medical Systems, Inc.
Vesper Corp.
Vulcan Materials Co.
Wachovia Bank of North Carolina NA
Waffle House Inc.
Wal-Mart Stores, Inc.
Warner-Lambert Co.
The Washington Post
Washington Trust Bank
Waste Management Inc.
West Co. Inc.
Westvaco Corp.
Weyerhaeuser Co.
Whirlpool Corp.

WICOR, Inc.
Williams
Wisconsin Energy Corp.
Wisconsin Power & Light Co.
Wisconsin Public Service Corp.
Witco Corp.
Woodward Governor Co.
Wrigley Co. (Wm. Jr.)
Wyman-Gordon Co.
Xerox Corp.
Young & Rubicam
Zachry Co. (H.B.)

ENVIRONMENTAL EDUCATION

AlliedSignal Inc.
American Honda Motor Co., Inc.
American Standard Inc.
AMP Inc.
Aristech Chemical Corp.
Bank of America
Block, Inc. (H&R)
Boston Globe (The)
Brunswick Corp.
Chesapeake Corp.
Clorox Co.
Coca-Cola Co.
Corning Inc.
Crestar Finance Corp.
Cyprus Amax Minerals Co.
Detroit Edison Co.
Deutsch Co.
Ecolab Inc.
Exxon Mobil Corp.
Georgia-Pacific Corp.
Globe Corp.
Hannaford Brothers Co.
Heinz Co. (H.J.)
Honeywell International Inc.
IKON Office Solutions, Inc.
Industrial Bank of Japan Trust Co. (New York)
Lee Enterprises
Leigh Fibers, Inc.
LG&E Energy Corp.
Little, Inc. (Arthur D.)
Michigan Consolidated Gas Co.
Overseas Shipholding Group Inc.
Patagonia Inc.
Phillips Petroleum Co.
Pillsbury Co.
Potlatch Corp.
PPG Industries, Inc.
Quaker Chemical Corp.
Rayonier Inc.
Red Wing Shoe Co. Inc.
Reliant Energy Minnegasco
Ruddick Corp.
Scripps Co. (E.W.)
Security Benefit Life Insurance Co.
Shaw's Supermarkets, Inc.
Simplot Co. (J.R.)
Simpson Investment Co.
Sony Electronics
Steelcase Inc.
Tektronix, Inc.
Texaco Inc.
Thomasville Furniture Industries Inc.
Toro Co.
Toshiba America Inc.
Toyota Motor Sales U.S.A., Inc.
Union Camp Corp.
Union Carbide Corp.
United States Sugar Corp.
USX Corp.
Weyerhaeuser Co.
Yellow Corp.

FACULTY DEVELOPMENT

Alcoa Inc.
Alliant Techsystems
AlliedSignal Inc.
Allmerica Financial Corp.
America West Airlines, Inc.
American Express Co.
American Fidelity Corp.
American United Life Insurance Co.
Ameritas Life Insurance Corp.
Ameritech Corp.
Ameritech Indiana
Aon Corp.
Appleton Papers Inc.
Archer-Daniels-Midland Co.
Arvin Industries, Inc.
AT&T Corp.
Atlantic Investment Co.
Atlantic Richfield Co.
Avista Corporation
Badger Meter, Inc.
Bandag, Inc.
Bank of America
Battelle Memorial Institute
Beckman Coulter, Inc.
BellSouth Corp.
Bestfoods
Blair & Co. (William)
Blue Cross & Blue Shield of Minnesota
Boeing Co.
Boler Co.
Boston Globe (The)
Burlington Industries, Inc.
Cabot Corp.
Campbell Soup Co.
Cargill Inc.
Carpenter Technology Corp.
Caterpillar Inc.
Central Maine Power Co.
Chase Manhattan Bank, NA
Chevron Corp.
CIGNA Corp.
Cincinnati Bell Inc.
Cinergy Corp.
CLARCOR Inc.
Clorox Co.
CNA
Coca-Cola Co.
Constellation Energy Group, Inc.
Contran Corp.
Cooper Tire & Rubber Co.
Corning Inc.
Crane Co.
Crestar Finance Corp.
DaimlerChrysler Corp.
Dayton Power and Light Co.
Deloitte & Touche
Deposit Guaranty National Bank
Dial Corp.
Donaldson Co., Inc.
Dow Corning Corp.
du Pont de Nemours & Co. (E.I.)
Duchossois Industries Inc.
Ecolab Inc.
Edison International
Exxon Mobil Corp.
Federated Department Stores, Inc.
First Tennessee National Corp.
First Union Corp.
First Union Securities, Inc.
Fisher Scientific
Ford Motor Co.
Frost National Bank
GATX Corp.
General Electric Co.
General Mills, Inc.
General Motors Corp.
Georgia Power Co.
Giant Eagle Inc.
Glaxo Wellcome Inc.
GTE Corp.
Halliburton Co.
Harris Trust & Savings Bank
Hartmarx Corp.
Hickory Tech Corp.
Hitachi America Ltd.
Honeywell International Inc.
Hughes Electronics Corp.
Illinois Power Co.
International Business Machines Corp.
INTRUST Financial Corp.
Kemper National Insurance Companies
Kimberly-Clark Corp.
KPMG Peat Marwick LLP
Land O'Lakes, Inc.
Landmark Communications Inc.
Levi Strauss & Co.
Lilly & Co. (Eli)
Little, Inc. (Arthur D.)
Lotus Development Corp.
LTV Corp.
Mallinckrodt Chemical, Inc.
Marcus Corp.
Masco Corp.
McClatchy Co.
MCI WorldCom, Inc.
Medtronic, Inc.
Merck & Co.
Metropolitan Life Insurance Co.
Monarch Machine Tool Co.
Morgan & Co. Inc. (J.P.)
Nalco Chemical Co.
National City Corp.
National Computer Systems, Inc.
New York Mercantile Exchange
New York Times Co.
Nomura Holding America
Norfolk Southern Corp.
Norton Co.
Pacific Century Financial Corp.
Pella Corp.
PEMCO Corp.
Pfizer Inc.
Pharmacia & Upjohn, Inc.
Phillips Petroleum Co.
Physicians Mutual Insurance Co.
PNC Financial Services Group
Polaroid Corp.
PPG Industries, Inc.
Principal Financial Group
Procter & Gamble Co.
Prudential Insurance Co. of America
Regions Bank
Reily & Co., Inc. (William B.)
Reynolds Tobacco (R.J.)
Rockwell International Corp.
Ruddick Corp.
Ryder System, Inc.
Saint Paul Companies Inc.
SBC Communications Inc.
Schering-Plough Corp.
Schlumberger Ltd. (USA)
Schwab & Co., Inc. (Charles)
Seagram & Sons, Inc. (Joseph E.)
Security Benefit Life Insurance Co.
Sega of America Inc.
Shell Oil Co.
Sonoco Products Co.
Springs Industries, Inc.
Standard Products Co.
State Street Bank & Trust Co.
TCF National Bank Minnesota
Tenneco Automotive
Texas Instruments Inc.
Times Mirror Co.
Toshiba America Inc.
Toyota Motor Sales U.S.A., Inc.
TRW Inc.
Tyson Foods Inc.
Union Camp Corp.
Union Carbide Corp.
Union Pacific Corp.
United Parcel Service of America Inc.
United Wisconsin Services
Unocal Corp.
US West, Inc.
Varian Medical Systems, Inc.
Washington Mutual, Inc.
The Washington Post
Whitman Corp.
Zachry Co. (H.B.)

EDUCATION-GENERAL

7-Eleven, Inc.
AEGON U.S.A. Inc.
Aetna, Inc.
Air Products and Chemicals, Inc.
Airborne Freight Corp.
AK Steel Corp.
Alabama Power Co.
Alaska Airlines, Inc.
Alcoa Inc.
AlliedSignal Inc.
Allmerica Financial Corp.
Allstate Insurance Co.
Alma Piston Co.
Alyeska Pipeline Service Co.
AMCORE Bank Rockford
Ameren Corp.
American Express Co.
American Fidelity Corp.
American General Corp.
American General Finance
American Retail Group
American Standard Inc.
American United Life Insurance Co.
Ameritas Life Insurance Corp.
Ameritech Corp.
Ameritech Wisconsin
AmerUS Group
AMETEK, Inc.
Amgen, Inc.
AMP Inc.
AMR Corp.
Andersen Corp.
Andersons Inc.
Anheuser-Busch Companies, Inc.
Aon Corp.
APL Ltd.
Archer-Daniels-Midland Co.
Aristech Chemical Corp.
Arizona Public Service Co.
Arvin Industries, Inc.
Ashland, Inc.
Associated Food Stores
AT&T Corp.
Atlantic Investment Co.
Atlantic Richfield Co.
Autodesk Inc.
Avery Dennison Corp.
Badger Meter, Inc.
Baird & Co. (Robert W.)
Ball Corp.
Bandag, Inc.
Bank of America
Bank One, Texas-Houston Office
BankBoston-Connecticut Region
Banta Corp.
Bard, Inc. (C.R.)
Barden Corp.
Bardes Corp.
Barnes Group Inc.
Barry Corp. (R.G.)
Baxter International Inc.
Bayer Corp.
Bean, Inc. (L.L.)
Bechtel Group, Inc.
Beckman Coulter, Inc.
Bell Atlantic Corp.
Bell Atlantic Corp.-West Virginia
Bell Atlantic-Delaware, Inc.
BellSouth Corp.
Bemis Co., Inc.
Ben & Jerry's Homemade Inc.
Bernstein & Co., Inc. (Sanford C.)
Berwind Group
Bethlehem Steel Corp.
BFGoodrich Co.
Binney & Smith Inc.
Binswanger Companies
Blair & Co. (William)
Block, Inc. (H&R)
Blount International, Inc.
Blue Cross & Blue Shield of Alabama
Blue Cross & Blue Shield of Iowa
Boeing Co.
Boler Co.
Borden, Inc.
Boston Gas Co.
Boston Globe (The)
Bourns, Inc.
BP Amoco Corp.
Bradford & Co. (J.C.)
Branch Banking & Trust Co.
Briggs & Stratton Corp.
Brooklyn Union
Bucyrus-Erie Co.
Burlington Industries, Inc.
Burress (J.W.)
Business Improvement
Business Men's Assurance Co. of America
Butler Manufacturing Co.
Cabot Corp.
Cadence Designs Systems, Inc.
Caesar's World, Inc.
Calvin Klein
Campbell Soup Co.
Cargill Inc.
Carillon Importers, Ltd.
Carlson Companies, Inc.
Carpenter Technology Corp.
Carris Reels
Castle & Cooke Properties Inc.
Caterpillar Inc.
CCB Financial Corp.

Cenex Harvest States
Centex Corp.
Central National-Gottesman
Central Newspapers, Inc.
Central Soya Co.
Century 21
CGU Insurance
Chase Bank of Texas
Chase Manhattan Bank, NA
Chemed Corp.
Chesapeake Corp.
Chevron Corp.
Chicago Sun-Times, Inc.
Chicago Title Corp.
Chicago Tribune Co.
CIGNA Corp.
Cincinnati Bell Inc.
Cinergy Corp.
Circuit City Stores, Inc.
CIT Group, Inc. (The)
Citigroup
Citizens Bank-Flint
CLARCOR Inc.
Cleveland-Cliffs, Inc.
Clorox Co.
CNA
Coachmen Industries, Inc.
Coca-Cola Co.
Colgate-Palmolive Co.
Collins & Aikman Corp.
Colonial Oil Industries, Inc.
Comdisco, Inc.
Commerce Bancshares, Inc.
Commercial Federal Corp.
Commercial Intertech Corp.
Compass Bank
Computer Associates International, Inc.
ConAgra, Inc.
Cone Mills Corp.
Conectiv
Consolidated Natural Gas Co.
Consolidated Papers, Inc.
Constellation Energy Group, Inc.
Contran Corp.
Conwood Co. LP
Cook Inlet Region
Cooper Tire & Rubber Co.
Country Curtains, Inc.
Cox Enterprises Inc.
CPI Corp.
Crane Co.
Crane & Co., Inc.
Credit Suisse First Boston
Crown Books
CSR Rinker Materials Corp.
CSS Industries, Inc.
CSX Corp.
Cummings Properties Management
Cummins Engine Co., Inc.
CUNA Mutual Group
Curtis Industries, Inc. (Helene)
DaimlerChrysler Corp.
Dain Bosworth Inc.
Deere & Co.
DeKalb Genetics Corp.
Deloitte & Touche
Deluxe Corp.
Demoulas Supermarkets Inc.
Detroit Edison Co.
Deutsch Co.
Dexter Corp.
Dial Corp.
Diebold, Inc.
Disney Co. (Walt)
Dixie Group, Inc. (The)
Dollar General Corp.
Dow Chemical Co.
Dreyer's Grand Ice Cream
Duchossois Industries Inc.
Duke Energy
Dun & Bradstreet Corp.
Duquesne Light Co.
Duracell International
Duriron Co., Inc.
Dynamet, Inc.
Eastern Bank
Eastman Chemical Co.
Eastman Kodak Co.
Eaton Corp.
Ebsco Industries, Inc.
Eckerd Corp.
Edison International
EDS Corp.
El Paso Energy Co.
Elf Atochem North America, Inc.
Emerson Electric Co.
Employers Insurance of Wausau, A Mutual Co.
Employers Mutual Casualty Co.
Equitable Resources, Inc.
Erb Lumber Co.
Erving Industries
Evening Post Publishing Co.
Excel Corp.
Exxon Mobil Corp.
Fabri-Kal Corp.
Farmers Group, Inc.
Federal-Mogul Corp.
Ferro Corp.
Fidelity Investments
Fifth Third Bancorp
FINA
Fireman's Fund Insurance Co.
First American Corp.
First Hawaiian, Inc.
First Security Bank of Idaho NA
First Source Corp.
First Union Bank
First Union Securities, Inc.
Firstar Bank Milwaukee NA
FirstEnergy Corp.
Fisher Brothers Cleaning Services
Fisher Scientific
FleetBoston Financial Corp.
Florida Power & Light Co.
Florida Rock Industries
Fluor Corp.
Forbes Inc.
Ford Meter Box Co.
Ford Motor Co.
Forest City Enterprises, Inc.
Fort Worth Star-Telegram Inc.
Fortis, Inc.
Franklin Electric Co.
Freeport-McMoRan Inc.
Frito-Lay, Inc.
Frontier Corp.
Fuller Co. (H.B.)
Furniture Brands International, Inc.
Gallo Winery, Inc. (E&J)
Gates Rubber Corp.
GATX Corp.
GEICO Corp.
GenCorp
General Atlantic Partners II LP
General Mills, Inc.
General Motors Corp.
Georgia-Pacific Corp.
Gerber Products Co.
Giddings & Lewis
Glickenhaus & Co.
Globe Corp.
Goldman Sachs Group
Golub Corp.
Gosiger, Inc.
GPU Energy
Grace & Co. (W.R.)
Graco, Inc.
Grainger, Inc. (W.W.)
Grede Foundries
Green Bay Packaging
Group Health Plan
GTE Corp.
Guess?
Gulf Power Co.
Halliburton Co.
Hallmark Cards Inc.
Hannaford Brothers Co.
Harcourt General, Inc.
Harley-Davidson Co.
Harnischfeger Industries
Harris Corp.
Harsco Corp.
Hartford (The)
Hartford Steam Boiler Inspection & Insurance Co.
Hasbro, Inc.
Heinz Co. (H.J.)
Hensel Phelps Construction Co.
Hercules Inc.
Hewlett-Packard Co.
Hickory Tech Corp.
Hitachi America Ltd.
Hoffer Plastics Corp.
Hoffmann-La Roche Inc.
Hofmann Co.
Honeywell International Inc.
Housatonic Curtain Co.
HSBC Bank USA
Hubbard Broadcasting, Inc.
Hubbell Inc.
Huffy Corp.
Humana, Inc.
Hunt Oil Co.
Huntington Bancshares Inc.
IBP
Idaho Power Co.
IKON Office Solutions, Inc.
Illinois Power Co.
Illinois Tool Works, Inc.
Independent Stave Co.
Industrial Bank of Japan Trust Co. (New York)
Ingram Industries Inc.
Inland Container Corp.
Inman Mills
Intel Corp.
International Flavors & Fragrances Inc.
International Multifoods Corp.
International Paper Co.
Interpublic Group of Companies, Inc.
INTRUST Financial Corp.
ISE America
Jacobs Engineering Group
Jeld-wen, Inc.
Johnson Controls Inc.
Johnson & Son (S.C.)
Jostens, Inc.
Journal Communications, Inc.
Journal-Gazette Co.
JSJ Corp.
Kaman Corp.
Katten, Muchin & Zavis
Kellwood Co.
Kelly Services
Kemper National Insurance Companies
Kendall International, Inc.
Kennametal, Inc.
Kimball International, Inc.
Kimberly-Clark Corp.
Kinder Morgn
Kingsbury Corp.
Knight Ridder
Koch Enterprises, Inc.
Kohler Co.
KPMG Peat Marwick LLP
La-Z-Boy Inc.
Ladish Co., Inc.
LandAmerica Financial Services
Landmark Communications Inc.
Lee Enterprises
Lehigh Portland Cement Co.
Lennox International, Inc.
Levi Strauss & Co.
Liberty Corp.
Liberty Mutual Insurance Group
Little, Inc. (Arthur D.)
Liz Claiborne, Inc.
Loctite Corp.
Loews Corp.
Lotus Development Corp.
Louisiana Land & Exploration Co.
Louisiana-Pacific Corp.
Lowe's Companies
LTV Corp.
Lubrizol Corp. (The)
MacMillan Bloedel Inc.
Mamiye Brothers
Manulife Financial
Marcus Corp.
Masco Corp.
Matsushita Electric Corp. of America
Mattel Inc.
May Department Stores Co.
MBIA Inc.
McDonald & Co. Securities, Inc.
McGraw-Hill Companies, Inc.
MCI WorldCom, Inc.
McWane Inc.
Medtronic, Inc.
Memphis Light Gas & Water Division
Menasha Corp.
Merck & Co.
Merit Oil Corp.
Metropolitan Life Insurance Co.
Michigan Consolidated Gas Co.
Mid-America Bank of Louisville
MidAmerican Energy Holdings Co.
Milacron, Inc.
Milliken & Co.
Millipore Corp.
Mitsubishi Electric America
Monarch Machine Tool Co.
Monsanto Co.
Montana Power Co.
Montgomery Ward & Co., Inc.
MONY Group (The)
Morgan & Co. Inc. (J.P.)
Morgan Stanley Dean Witter & Co.
Morris Communications Corp.
Morrison Knudsen Corp.
Motorola Inc.
MTD Products Inc.
Mutual of Omaha Insurance Co.
Nabisco Group Holdings
Nalco Chemical Co.
National City Bank of Cleveland
National City Bank of Columbus
National City Bank of Minneapolis
National City Bank of Pennsylvania
National City Corp.
National Computer Systems, Inc.
National Machinery Co.
National Service Industries, Inc.
National Starch & Chemical Co.
Nationwide Insurance Co.
NCR Corp.
NEBCO Evans
Nestle U.S.A. Inc.
New England Bio Labs
New Jersey Natural Gas Co.
New United Motor Manufacturing Inc.
New York Mercantile Exchange
New York State Electric & Gas Corp.
Niagara Mohawk Holdings Inc.
Nordson Corp.
Nortel
North American Royalties
Northern Trust Co.
Northrop Grumman Corp.
Northwest Natural Gas Co.
Norwest Corp.
Occidental Oil and Gas
OG&E Electric Services
Ohio National Life Insurance Co.
Old Kent Bank
Old National Bank Evansville
Olin Corp.
ONEOK, Inc.
Orange & Rockland Utilities, Inc.
Oshkosh B'Gosh, Inc.
Overseas Shipholding Group Inc.
Owens-Illinois Inc.
PACCAR Inc.
Pacific Century Financial Corp.
Pacific Mutual Life Insurance Co.
PacifiCare Health Systems
PacifiCorp
Park National Bank
Parker Hannifin Corp.
PECO Energy Co.
Pella Corp.
PEMCO Corp.
Penn Mutual Life Insurance Co.
Penney Co., Inc. (J.C.)
Pennsylvania Power & Light
Pentair Inc.
PepsiCo, Inc.
PerkinElmer, Inc.
Pfizer Inc.
Pharmacia & Upjohn, Inc.
Pheonix Financial Group
Phillips Petroleum Co.
Phoenix Home Life Mutual Insurance Co.

Physicians Mutual Insurance Co.
Pieper Power Electric Co.
Pillsbury Co.
Pioneer Group
Pioneer Natural Resources
PNC Bank
PNC Financial Services Group
Polaroid Corp.
Praxair
Premark International Inc.
Premier Dental Products Co.
Premier Industrial Corp.
Price Associates (T. Rowe)
Procter & Gamble Co.
Procter & Gamble Co., Cosmetics Division
Providence Journal-Bulletin Co.
Provident Companies, Inc.
Provident Mutual Life Insurance Co.
Prudential Insurance Co. of America
Prudential Securities Inc.
Public Service Co. of Oklahoma
Pulitzer Publishing Co.
Putnam Investments
Ralph's Grocery Co.
Ralston Purina Co.
Rayonier Inc.
Reader's Digest Association, Inc. (The)
Red Wing Shoe Co. Inc.
Reebok International Ltd.
Regions Bank
Regions Financial Corp.
Reily & Co., Inc. (William B.)
Reinhart Institutional Foods
Reynolds & Reynolds Co.
Reynolds Tobacco (R.J.)
Riggs Bank NA
Rockwell International Corp.
Rohm & Haas Co.
Rouse Co.
Royal & SunAlliance USA, Inc.
Rubbermaid Inc.
Ryder System, Inc.
S&T Bancorp
Santa Fe International Corp.
Sara Lee Hosiery, Inc.
SBC Communications Inc.
SCANA Corp.
Schering-Plough Corp.
Schwebel Baking Co.
Scientific-Atlanta, Inc.
Seagram & Sons, Inc. (Joseph E.)
Sears, Roebuck and Co.
Security Benefit Life Insurance Co.
Security Life of Denver Insurance Co.
Sega of America Inc.
Sentry Insurance, A Mutual Co.
Servco Pacific
ServiceMaster Co.
Shaw Industries Inc.
Shea Co. (John F.)
Shell Oil Co.
Shelter Mutual Insurance Co.
Sherwin-Williams Co.
Sierra Pacific Industries
Sierra Pacific Resources
Simplot Co. (J.R.)
Simpson Investment Co.
Slant/Fin Corp.
SmithKline Beecham Corp.
Smurfit-Stone Container Corp.
Sonoco Products Co.
Sony Electronics
Southeastern Mutual Insurance Co.
Southern Co. Services Inc.
Sprint Corp.
Sprint/United Telephone
SPX Corp.
Square D Co.
Standard Register Co.
Star Bank NA
Starwood Hotels & Resorts Worldwide, Inc.
State Street Bank & Trust Co.
Stone Container Corp.
Stonecutter Mills Corp.
Storage Technology Corp.
Stride Rite Corp.
Student Loan Marketing Association
Stupp Brothers Bridge & Iron Co.
Subway Sandwich Shops, Inc.
Sun Microsystems Inc.
Sunmark Capital Corp.
Susquehanna-Pfaltzgraff Co.
Synovus Financial Corp.
Taco Bell Corp.
Tai and Co. (J.T.)
Tamko Roofing Products
Tampa Electric Co.
Tandy Corp.
TCF National Bank Minnesota
Tektronix, Inc.
Teleflex Inc.
Temple-Inland Inc.
TENNANT Co.
Tenneco Packaging
Tension Envelope Corp.
Tesoro Hawaii
Texaco Inc.
Texas Instruments Inc.
Textron Inc.
Thermo Electron Corp.
Thomasville Furniture Industries Inc.
Thompson Co. (J. Walter)
Times Mirror Co.
Timken Co. (The)
Titan Industrial Corp.
TJX Companies, Inc.
TMC Investment Co.
Tomkins Industries, Inc.
Toro Co.
Toyota Motor Sales U.S.A., Inc.
Trace International Holdings, Inc.
True North Communications, Inc.
True Oil Co.
Trustmark Insurance Co.
Trustmark National Bank
TRW Inc.
Tucson Electric Power Co.
Tyson Foods Inc.
Ukrop's Super Markets
Ultramar Diamond Shamrock Corp.
Unilever Home & Personal Care U.S.A.
Union Carbide Corp.
Union Planters Corp.
United Airlines Inc.
United Distillers & Vintners North America
United Parcel Service of America Inc.
U.S. Bancorp Piper Jaffray
United States Trust Co. of New York
United Wisconsin Services
Universal Foods Corp.
Universal Leaf Tobacco Co., Inc.
Universal Studios
Unocal Corp.
UnumProvident
US Bank, Washington
US West, Inc.
USAA Life Insurance Co.
USG Corp.
Valmont Industries, Inc.
Valspar Corp.
Vodafone AirTouch Plc
Vulcan Materials Co.
Waffle House Inc.
Wal-Mart Stores, Inc.
Warner-Lambert Co.
Washington Mutual, Inc.
Washington Trust Bank
Wausau Insurance Companies
Western & Southern Life Insurance Co.
Weyerhaeuser Co.
Whirlpool Corp.
Whitman Corp.
WICOR, Inc.
Wilbur-Ellis Co. & Connell Brothers Co.
Wiley & Sons (John)
Williams
Wiremold Co.
Wisconsin Power & Light Co.
Wisconsin Public Service Corp.
Witco Corp.
Wolverine World Wide
Woodward Governor Co.
Wyman-Gordon Co.
York Federal Savings & Loan Association
Young & Rubicam
Zachry Co. (H.B.)
Zilkha & Sons
Zurn Industries, Inc.

GIFTED & TALENTED PROGRAMS

Alcoa Inc.
Alexander & Baldwin, Inc.
Alma Piston Co.
American Honda Motor Co., Inc.
Banfi Vintners
Banta Corp.
Bard, Inc. (C.R.)
Consolidated Papers, Inc.
CUNA Mutual Group
Delta Air Lines, Inc.
First Hawaiian, Inc.
General Mills, Inc.
GTE Corp.
Hensel Phelps Construction Co.
Jostens, Inc.
Lennox International, Inc.
Owens Corning
Rockwell International Corp.
Sentry Insurance, A Mutual Co.
Servco Pacific
Slant/Fin Corp.
Solo Cup Co.
Tesoro Hawaii
U.S. Bancorp Piper Jaffray
United Wisconsin Services
Warner-Lambert Co.

HEALTH & PHYSICAL EDUCATION

Abbott Laboratories
Aetna, Inc.
AFLAC Inc.
Alcon Laboratories, Inc.
AlliedSignal Inc.
AMCORE Bank Rockford
American Honda Motor Co., Inc.
Ameritas Life Insurance Corp.
Anheuser-Busch Companies, Inc.
Aon Corp.
Archer-Daniels-Midland Co.
Badger Meter, Inc.
Bandag, Inc.
Bank of America
BankBoston Corp.
Baxter International Inc.
BellSouth Corp.
Bemis Co., Inc.
Blue Cross & Blue Shield of Minnesota
Cabot Corp.
Central Soya Co.
Chase Bank of Texas
Chase Manhattan Bank, NA
CIGNA Corp.
Citizens Bank-Flint
Coca-Cola Co.
Constellation Energy Group, Inc.
CSS Industries, Inc.
DaimlerChrysler Corp.
Dana Corp.
Disney Co. (Walt)
Donaldson Co., Inc.
Eastman Kodak Co.
Entergy Corp.
Erving Industries
Evening Post Publishing Co.
Exxon Mobil Corp.
Firstar Bank Milwaukee NA
FleetBoston Financial Corp.
Ford Motor Co.
Fortis Insurance Co.
Frost National Bank
General Motors Corp.
Georgia Power Co.
Glickenhaus & Co.
Group Health Plan
Harcourt General, Inc.
Harley-Davidson Co.
Hartford (The)
Heinz Co. (H.J.)
Huntington Bancshares Inc.
Johnson & Son (S.C.)
Lance, Inc.
Lilly & Co. (Eli)
Lipton Co.
McDonald's Corp.
Mead Corp.
Medtronic, Inc.
Memphis Light Gas & Water Division
Merck & Co.
Merrill Lynch & Co., Inc.
Metropolitan Life Insurance Co.
National Computer Systems, Inc.
NEBCO Evans
New England Financial
New York Life Insurance Co.
New York Stock Exchange, Inc.
Norton Co.
Osborne Enterprises
Pacific Mutual Life Insurance Co.
Pharmacia & Upjohn, Inc.
Phelps Dodge Corp.
Phillips Petroleum Co.
Polaroid Corp.
Procter & Gamble Co., Cosmetics Division
Provident Companies, Inc.
Prudential Insurance Co. of America
Schering-Plough Corp.
Sempra Energy
Shaklee Corp.
Shell Oil Co.
Sonoco Products Co.
Standard Register Co.
Susquehanna-Pfaltzgraff Co.
Tai and Co. (J.T.)
Texaco Inc.
Thermo Electron Corp.
United Co.
United Services Automobile Association

INTERNATIONAL EXCHANGE

Alcoa Inc.
AlliedSignal Inc.
American Express Co.
American Standard Inc.
AMETEK, Inc.
Anheuser-Busch Companies, Inc.
APL Ltd.
Archer-Daniels-Midland Co.
Arvin Industries, Inc.
AT&T Corp.
Bank of America
BellSouth Corp.
Bernstein & Co., Inc. (Sanford C.)
Bestfoods
Borman's Inc.
BP Amoco Corp.
Cabot Corp.
CertainTeed Corp.
CIGNA Corp.
Citibank Corp.
Clark Refining & Marketing
Coca-Cola Co.
Colonial Life & Accident Insurance Co.
Cummins Engine Co., Inc.
Dayton Hudson
Delta Air Lines, Inc.
du Pont de Nemours & Co. (E.I.)
Ecolab Inc.
Emerson Electric Co.
Erb Lumber Co.
First Source Corp.
First Union Bank
First Union National Bank, NA
FMC Corp.
Frost National Bank
General Electric Co.
General Mills, Inc.
General Motors Corp.
Hallmark Cards Inc.
Harsco Corp.
Heinz Co. (H.J.)
Hitachi America Ltd.
Hoffmann-La Roche Inc.
Honeywell International Inc.
Huntington Bancshares Inc.
Inland Container Corp.
Johnson & Son (S.C.)
Merck & Co.

Minnesota Mining & Manufacturing Co.
National Computer Systems, Inc.
Nestle U.S.A. Inc.
PerkinElmer, Inc.
Pfizer Inc.
Phelps Dodge Corp.
Phillips Petroleum Co.
Pulitzer Publishing Co.
Reynolds Tobacco (R.J.)
Sara Lee Corp.
Seagram & Sons, Inc. (Joseph E.)
SmithKline Beecham Corp.
Sony Electronics
SunTrust Bank Atlanta
Tai and Co. (J.T.)
Thompson Co. (J. Walter)
Titan Industrial Corp.
Union Carbide Corp.
Unocal Corp.
Warner-Lambert Co.
Wiremold Co.
Wrigley Co. (Wm. Jr.)

INTERNATIONAL STUDIES

Aetna, Inc.
AK Steel Corp.
Alcoa Inc.
Alliant Techsystems
American Express Co.
Amsted Industries Inc.
APL Ltd.
Archer-Daniels-Midland Co.
Ashland, Inc.
AT&T Corp.
Bank of America
Bank One Corp.
Banta Corp.
Bechtel Group, Inc.
Bemis Co., Inc.
Bestfoods
Bridgestone/Firestone, Inc.
Burlington Resources, Inc.
Cabot Corp.
Carillon Importers, Ltd.
Carlson Companies, Inc.
Carnival Corp.
Caterpillar Inc.
CertainTeed Corp.
Chase Manhattan Bank, NA
Chevron Corp.
Citibank Corp.
Coca-Cola Co.
Colonial Life & Accident Insurance Co.
Continental Grain Co.
Country Curtains, Inc.
Crane Co.
DeKalb Genetics Corp.
Demoulas Supermarkets Inc.
Deutsch Co.
Dial Corp.
Dixie Group, Inc. (The)
Dow Chemical Co.
du Pont de Nemours & Co. (E.I.)
Dun & Bradstreet Corp.
El Paso Energy Co.
Employers Mutual Casualty Co.
First Hawaiian, Inc.
Ford Meter Box Co.
Furniture Brands International, Inc.
General Electric Co.
General Mills, Inc.
General Motors Corp.
General Reinsurance Corp.
Globe Corp.
GTE Corp.
Hamilton Sundstrand Corp.
Harcourt General, Inc.
Hartford (The)
Heinz Co. (H.J.)
Hickory Tech Corp.
Hitachi America Ltd.
Huntington Bancshares Inc.
Industrial Bank of Japan Trust Co. (New York)
International Flavors & Fragrances Inc.
Kellwood Co.
Kemper National Insurance Companies
Kerr-McGee Corp.
Kimberly-Clark Corp.
Kingsbury Corp.
KPMG Peat Marwick LLP
Lee Enterprises
Leigh Fibers, Inc.
Levi Strauss & Co.
Lilly & Co. (Eli)
Loews Corp.
MCI WorldCom, Inc.
Mitsubishi Electric America
National Computer Systems, Inc.
Nomura Holding America
Nordson Corp.
Overseas Shipholding Group Inc.
PerkinElmer, Inc.
Pfizer Inc.
Phillips Petroleum Co.
Pittway Corp.
Procter & Gamble Co.
Ralph's Grocery Co.
Rockwell International Corp.
Saint Paul Companies Inc.
Schlumberger Ltd. (USA)
Seagram & Sons, Inc. (Joseph E.)
Servco Pacific
Shell Oil Co.
Sony Electronics
Stone Container Corp.
SunTrust Bank Atlanta
TENNANT Co.
Texaco Inc.
Textron Inc.
Thomasville Furniture Industries Inc.
Times Mirror Co.
True North Communications, Inc.
Unilever United States, Inc.
Union Carbide Corp.
United Parcel Service of America Inc.
United States Trust Co. of New York
Universal Studios
Unocal Corp.
US West, Inc.
USG Corp.
Vodafone AirTouch Plc
Weil, Gotshal & Manges Corp.
Westvaco Corp.
Whirlpool Corp.
Wilbur-Ellis Co. & Connell Brothers Co.
Young & Rubicam
Zilkha & Sons

JOURNALISM/MEDIA EDUCATION

ABC
AGL Resources Inc.
Alcoa Inc.
Ameritech Indiana
Belo Corp. (A.H.)
Boston Globe (The)
CBS Corp.
Central National-Gottesman
Central Newspapers, Inc.
Chevron Corp.
Chicago Sun-Times, Inc.
Chicago Title Corp.
Chicago Tribune Co.
CIT Group, Inc. (The)
Clorox Co.
Cox Enterprises Inc.
Daily News
Dow Jones & Co., Inc.
du Pont de Nemours & Co. (E.I.)
Ford Motor Co.
Georgia Power Co.
Hartford (The)
Heinz Co. (H.J.)
Hubbard Broadcasting, Inc.
Journal-Gazette Co.
Lancaster Lens, Inc.
Landmark Communications Inc.
Lee Enterprises
McClatchy Co.
McGraw-Hill Companies, Inc.
Merck & Co.
Meredith Corp.
Merrill Lynch & Co., Inc.
Milliken & Co.
Minnesota Mining & Manufacturing Co.
Monsanto Co.
Morris Communications Corp.
MTS Systems Corp.
New York Times Co.
Playboy Enterprises Inc.
Prudential Insurance Co. of America
Pulitzer Publishing Co.
Reader's Digest Association, Inc. (The)
Regions Bank
Scripps Co. (E.W.)
Sentinel Communications Co.
Shell Oil Co.
Stone Container Corp.
Sunmark Capital Corp.
Times Mirror Co.
Whirlpool Corp.
Young & Rubicam

LEADERSHIP TRAINING

Aetna, Inc.
American Honda Motor Co., Inc.
American Retail Group
American United Life Insurance Co.
Ameritas Life Insurance Corp.
APL Ltd.
Avon Products, Inc.
Bank of America
Bard, Inc. (C.R.)
BellSouth Corp.
Blue Cross & Blue Shield of Minnesota
Boston Edison Co.
Bradford & Co. (J.C.)
Briggs & Stratton Corp.
Broderbund Software, Inc.
Brown Shoe Co., Inc.
Brunswick Corp.
Cargill Inc.
Carillon Importers, Ltd.
Chase Manhattan Bank, NA
Cinergy Corp.
Coca-Cola Co.
Contran Corp.
Cox Enterprises Inc.
Dain Bosworth Inc.
Danis Companies
Demoulas Supermarkets Inc.
Deposit Guaranty National Bank
Emerson Electric Co.
Exxon Mobil Corp.
Fidelity Investments
First Union Bank
Firstar Bank Milwaukee NA
Forbes Inc.
Ford Meter Box Co.
Freddie Mac
Freeport-McMoRan Inc.
Gap, Inc.
Georgia-Pacific Corp.
Georgia Power Co.
Globe Corp.
Hanna Co. (M.A.)
Hannaford Brothers Co.
Harland Co. (John H.)
Harsco Corp.
Hickory Tech Corp.
Hitachi America Ltd.
Humana, Inc.
Johnson & Son (S.C.)
Kinder Morgn
KPMG Peat Marwick LLP
Levi Strauss & Co.
Lilly & Co. (Eli)
Little, Inc. (Arthur D.)
Louisiana Land & Exploration Co.
Louisiana-Pacific Corp.
Marcus Corp.
Mark IV Industries
Marshall & Ilsley Corp.
Mattel Inc.
Mazda North American Operations
McClatchy Co.
MidAmerican Energy Holdings Co.
Millipore Corp.
Minnesota Mutual Life Insurance Co.
MONY Group (The)
Morgan & Co. Inc. (J.P.)
Morgan Stanley Dean Witter & Co.
National Service Industries, Inc.
Navcom Systems
NEBCO Evans
New York Times Co.
Nordson Corp.
ONEOK, Inc.
Osborne Enterprises
Pacific Mutual Life Insurance Co.
Pfizer Inc.
Pheonix Financial Group
Polaroid Corp.
Prudential Insurance Co. of America
Regions Bank
Reynolds Tobacco (R.J.)
Rich Products Corp.
Ruddick Corp.
Saint Paul Companies Inc.
Schwab & Co., Inc. (Charles)
Southeastern Mutual Insurance Co.
State Street Bank & Trust Co.
Steelcase Inc.
Storage Technology Corp.
Stride Rite Corp.
Toyota Motor Sales U.S.A., Inc.
True North Communications, Inc.
United Parcel Service of America Inc.
U.S. Bancorp Piper Jaffray
Unocal Corp.
UnumProvident
US West, Inc.
Washington Mutual, Inc.
Washington Trust Bank
WICOR, Inc.
Wisconsin Energy Corp.
Young & Rubicam
Zachry Co. (H.B.)

LEGAL EDUCATION

Abbott Laboratories
ABC
Air Products and Chemicals, Inc.
Alcoa Inc.
AlliedSignal Inc.
American Retail Group
American United Life Insurance Co.
Ameritech Indiana
AMETEK, Inc.
Aon Corp.
APL Ltd.
Archer-Daniels-Midland Co.
ASARCO Inc.
Banfi Vintners
BankAtlantic Bancorp
Bechtel Group, Inc.
BellSouth Corp.
Bemis Co., Inc.
Berwind Group
Bethlehem Steel Corp.
Block, Inc. (H&R)
Boeing Co.
Bradford & Co. (J.C.)
Bristol-Myers Squibb Co.
Business Improvement
Central & South West Services
CertainTeed Corp.
Chase Bank of Texas
Chicago Title Corp.
CIGNA Corp.
CIT Group, Inc. (The)
CLARCOR Inc.
Compass Bank
Consumers Energy Co.
Continental Grain Co.
Country Curtains, Inc.
Crane Co.
CSS Industries, Inc.
CUNA Mutual Group
Daily News
Danis Companies
Delta Air Lines, Inc.
Disney Co. (Walt)
Donaldson Co., Inc.
du Pont de Nemours & Co. (E.I.)
El Paso Energy Co.
Emerson Electric Co.
Equitable Resources, Inc.
Federal-Mogul Corp.
First Union Corp.
First Union Securities, Inc.
Fortis, Inc.
Freddie Mac
Freeport-McMoRan Inc.
Furniture Brands International, Inc.
Gallo Winery, Inc. (E&J)
General Atlantic Partners II LP
General Electric Co.
General Mills, Inc.
General Motors Corp.

Glickenhaus & Co.
Globe Corp.
Halliburton Co.
Hanna Co. (M.A.)
Harcourt General, Inc.
Hartford (The)
Heinz Co. (H.J.)
Huffy Corp.
Katten, Muchin & Zavis
Kemper National Insurance Companies
Kerr-McGee Corp.
Kirkland & Ellis
Koch Industries, Inc.
KPMG Peat Marwick LLP
LandAmerica Financial Services
Lipton Co.
Loews Corp.
Macy's East Inc.
MBIA Inc.
MCI WorldCom, Inc.
Merrill Lynch & Co., Inc.
Mid-America Bank of Louisville
Mitsubishi Electric America
Morris Communications Corp.
National Service Industries, Inc.
Nationwide Insurance Co.
New York Life Insurance Co.
New York Stock Exchange, Inc.
New York Times Co.
Nomura Holding America
Norfolk Southern Corp.
Northern States Power Co.
Occidental Petroleum Corp.
Ohio National Life Insurance Co.
Overseas Shipholding Group Inc.
Paine Webber
Pfizer Inc.
Procter & Gamble Co.
Prudential Insurance Co. of America
Pulitzer Publishing Co.
Rayonier Inc.
Rich Products Corp.
Rouse Co.
Ryder System, Inc.
Scripps Co. (E.W.)
Shell Oil Co.
Shelter Mutual Insurance Co.
Sierra Pacific Resources
Southwest Gas Corp.
Stone Container Corp.
Sunmark Capital Corp.
SunTrust Bank Atlanta
Synovus Financial Corp.
Tamko Roofing Products
Texaco Inc.
Textron Inc.
TJX Companies, Inc.
Transamerica Corp.
Union Camp Corp.
Union Pacific Corp.
United Co.
Universal Studios
Unocal Corp.
USX Corp.
Wachtell, Lipton, Rosen & Katz
Walter Industries Inc.
Warner-Lambert Co.
Webster Bank
Weil, Gotshal & Manges Corp.
Whitman Corp.
Wilbur-Ellis Co. & Connell Brothers Co.
Wiley & Sons (John)
Witco Corp.

LITERACY

7-Eleven, Inc.
ABC
AGL Resources Inc.
Agrilink Foods, Inc.
Air Products and Chemicals, Inc.
Alabama Power Co.
Alcoa Inc.
AlliedSignal Inc.
AMCORE Bank Rockford
America West Airlines, Inc.
American Express Co.
American General Finance
American Honda Motor Co., Inc.
American Retail Group
Ameritech Corp.
Ameritech Indiana
Ameritech Ohio
AMETEK, Inc.
Amgen, Inc.
AMP Inc.
Amsted Industries Inc.
Andersons Inc.
Anheuser-Busch Companies, Inc.
Arvin Industries, Inc.
Ashland, Inc.
Atlantic Richfield Co.
Avon Products, Inc.
Badger Meter, Inc.
Bandag, Inc.
BankBoston-Connecticut Region
BankBoston Corp.
Barclays Capital
Battelle Memorial Institute
Belk Stores Services Inc.
Bell Atlantic Corp.
Belo Corp. (A.H.)
Bestfoods
Bethlehem Steel Corp.
Binney & Smith Inc.
Blair & Co. (William)
Block, Inc. (H&R)
Blount International, Inc.
Blue Bell, Inc.
Blue Cross & Blue Shield of Alabama
Boeing Co.
Boise Cascade Corp.
Borden, Inc.
Boston Globe (The)
Broderbund Software, Inc.
Browning-Ferris Industries Inc.
Brunswick Corp.
Bucyrus-Erie Co.
Burlington Industries, Inc.
Burlington Resources, Inc.
Cabot Corp.
Callaway Golf Co.
Calvin Klein
Campbell Soup Co.
Carpenter Technology Corp.
Carrier Corp.
Central Maine Power Co.
Central National-Gottesman
CertainTeed Corp.
Champion International Corp.
Chase Bank of Texas
Chase Manhattan Bank, NA
Chesapeake Corp.
Chevron Corp.
Chicago Sun-Times, Inc.
Chicago Title Corp.
Chicago Tribune Co.
CIGNA Corp.
Cincinnati Bell Inc.
Cinergy Corp.
Citibank Corp.
Citigroup
CLARCOR Inc.
Clark Refining & Marketing
Clorox Co.
CNA
Coca-Cola Co.
Collins & Aikman Corp.
Colonial Oil Industries, Inc.
Commerce Bancshares, Inc.
Compaq Computer Corp.
Compass Bank
Cone Mills Corp.
Consolidated Natural Gas Co.
Consolidated Papers, Inc.
Constellation Energy Group, Inc.
Contran Corp.
Conwood Co. LP
Cooper Industries, Inc.
Coors Brewing Co.
Copley Press, Inc.
Cox Enterprises Inc.
Crane Co.
Crane & Co., Inc.
Crown Books
CSR Rinker Materials Corp.
DaimlerChrysler Corp.
Danis Companies
Dayton Hudson
Delta Air Lines, Inc.
Deposit Guaranty National Bank
Detroit Edison Co.
Dial Corp.
Dollar General Corp.
Donaldson Co., Inc.
Donnelley & Sons Co. (R.R.)
DSM Copolymer
du Pont de Nemours & Co. (E.I.)
Duke Energy
Dun & Bradstreet Corp.
Edison International
Emerson Electric Co.
Entergy Corp.
Equifax Inc.
Erving Industries
Evening Post Publishing Co.
Excel Corp.
Federated Department Stores, Inc.
Fidelity Investments
Fireman's Fund Insurance Co.
First Hawaiian, Inc.
First Union Corp.
First Union National Bank, NA
Firstar Bank Milwaukee NA
FleetBoston Financial Corp.
Forbes Inc.
Fortis Insurance Co.
Fortune Brands, Inc.
Franklin Mint (The)
Freeport-McMoRan Inc.
Frost National Bank
Gannett Co., Inc.
GATX Corp.
GenCorp
General Dynamics Corp.
General Electric Co.
General Mills, Inc.
General Motors Corp.
General Reinsurance Corp.
Georgia-Pacific Corp.
Georgia Power Co.
Glickenhaus & Co.
Globe Corp.
Golub Corp.
Graco, Inc.
GTE Corp.
Guardian Life Insurance Co. of America
Gulf Power Co.
Gulfstream Aerospace Corp.
Halliburton Co.
Hallmark Cards Inc.
Hamilton Sundstrand Corp.
Harland Co. (John H.)
Harris Trust & Savings Bank
Hartford (The)
Hartford Steam Boiler Inspection & Insurance Co.
Hartmarx Corp.
Hasbro, Inc.
Heinz Co. (H.J.)
Heller Financial, Inc.
Hensel Phelps Construction Co.
Hershey Foods Corp.
Hitachi America Ltd.
Honeywell International Inc.
Household International Inc.
Humana, Inc.
Hunt Manufacturing Co.
Illinois Tool Works, Inc.
International Business Machines Corp.
International Paper Co.
Johnson Controls Inc.
Johnson & Son (S.C.)
Jostens, Inc.
Journal-Gazette Co.
Katten, Muchin & Zavis
Kelly Services
Kimberly-Clark Corp.
Kmart Corp.
Kroger Co.
Ladish Co., Inc.
Landmark Communications Inc.
Lehigh Portland Cement Co.
Levi Strauss & Co.
LG&E Energy Corp.
Lincoln Financial Group
Lipton Co.
Liz Claiborne, Inc.
Loews Corp.
Louisiana-Pacific Corp.
LTV Corp.
MacMillan Bloedel Inc.
Maritz Inc.
Marshall Field's
Marshall & Ilsley Corp.
Mattel Inc.
May Department Stores Co.
Mazda North American Operations
McClatchy Co.
McDonald & Co. Securities, Inc.
McDonald's Corp.
McGraw-Hill Companies, Inc.
McWane Inc.
Mead Corp.
Mellon Financial Corp.
Merrill Lynch & Co., Inc.
Metropolitan Life Insurance Co.
Millipore Corp.
Minnesota Mutual Life Insurance Co.
MONY Group (The)
Morgan & Co. Inc. (J.P.)
Morgan Stanley Dean Witter & Co.
Motorola Inc.
Nalco Chemical Co.
National City Bank of Minneapolis
National City Corp.
National Service Industries, Inc.
Nationwide Insurance Co.
NEBCO Evans
Nestle U.S.A. Inc.
New England Financial
New York Life Insurance Co.
New York Times Co.
Newman's Own Inc.
Nissan North America, Inc.
Nordson Corp.
Norfolk Southern Corp.
North American Royalties
Northeast Utilities
Northern Indiana Public Service Co.
Northern Trust Co.
Norton Co.
Occidental Oil and Gas
Ohio National Life Insurance Co.
Olin Corp.
Oshkosh B'Gosh, Inc.
Pacific Century Financial Corp.
PEMCO Corp.
Penney Co., Inc. (J.C.)
Peoples Energy Corp.
Pfizer Inc.
Philip Morris Companies Inc.
Phillips Petroleum Co.
Physicians Mutual Insurance Co.
Pillsbury Co.
Pitney Bowes Inc.
Pittway Corp.
PNC Bank
PNC Financial Services Group
Polaroid Corp.
Potlatch Corp.
Potomac Electric Power Co.
Price Associates (T. Rowe)
Principal Financial Group
Procter & Gamble Co., Cosmetics Division
Providence Journal-Bulletin Co.
Provident Companies, Inc.
Prudential Insurance Co. of America
Prudential Securities Inc.
Putnam Investments
Quaker Chemical Corp.
Quanex Corp.
Ralston Purina Co.
Reader's Digest Association, Inc. (The)
Reily & Co., Inc. (William B.)
Reliant Energy Inc.
ReliaStar Financial Corp.
Reynolds & Reynolds Co.
Rich Products Corp.
Rockwell International Corp.
Royal & SunAlliance USA, Inc.
SAFECO Corp.
Saint Paul Companies Inc.
Salomon Smith Barney
Sara Lee Corp.
Sara Lee Hosiery, Inc.
SBC Communications Inc.
Schering-Plough Corp.
Schloss & Co. (Marcus)
Scripps Co. (E.W.)
Seaway Food Town, Inc.

Security Life of Denver Insurance Co.
Sega of America Inc.
Sempra Energy
Sentinel Communications Co.
Smith Corp. (A.O.)
SmithKline Beecham Corp.
Sony Electronics
Southern California Gas Co.
Southern New England Telephone Co.
Southwest Gas Corp.
Sovereign Bank
Sprint Corp.
Stanley Works (The)
Starwood Hotels & Resorts Worldwide, Inc.
State Street Bank & Trust Co.
Storage Technology Corp.
Stride Rite Corp.
Sunoco Inc.
SunTrust Banks of Florida
Synovus Financial Corp.
Tenneco Automotive
Texaco Inc.
Textron Inc.
Thermo Electron Corp.
Thomasville Furniture Industries Inc.
Times Mirror Co.
Titan Industrial Corp.
Toledo Blade Co.
Tomkins Industries, Inc.
Toyota Motor Sales U.S.A., Inc.
Tyson Foods Inc.
Ukrop's Super Markets
Unilever United States, Inc.
Union Camp Corp.
Union Carbide Corp.
Union Pacific Corp.
United Airlines Inc.
United Distillers & Vintners North America
United Parcel Service of America Inc.
United States Sugar Corp.
United States Trust Co. of New York
United Technologies Corp.
United Wisconsin Services
Universal Foods Corp.
Universal Studios
US Bank, Washington
Valmont Industries, Inc.
Vodafone AirTouch Plc
Vulcan Materials Co.
Waffle House Inc.
Wal-Mart Stores, Inc.
Washington Mutual, Inc.
The Washington Post
Westvaco Corp.
Whirlpool Corp.
WICOR, Inc.
Wiley & Sons (John)
Williams
Wiremold Co.
Woodward Governor Co.
Xerox Corp.
York Federal Savings & Loan Association
Young & Rubicam
Zachry Co. (H.B.)

MEDICAL EDUCATION

Abbott Laboratories
ABC
Aetna, Inc.
Alcoa Inc.
Alcon Laboratories, Inc.
Alliant Techsystems
AlliedSignal Inc.
Allmerica Financial Corp.
Allstate Insurance Co.
AMCORE Bank Rockford
American Retail Group
American United Life Insurance Co.
Ameritas Life Insurance Corp.
AMETEK, Inc.
Amgen, Inc.
Anheuser-Busch Companies, Inc.
Archer-Daniels-Midland Co.
Arizona Public Service Co.
Armstrong World Industries, Inc.
AT&T Corp.
Avon Products, Inc.
Badger Meter, Inc.
Baird & Co. (Robert W.)
Bank of America
Banta Corp.
Bard, Inc. (C.R.)
Battelle Memorial Institute
Baxter International Inc.
Bayer Corp.
Becton Dickinson & Co.
Belk-Simpson Department Stores
Belk Stores Services Inc.
BellSouth Corp.
Bemis Co., Inc.
Blount International, Inc.
Blue Cross & Blue Shield of Iowa
Blue Cross & Blue Shield of Minnesota
Boston Globe (The)
Bridgestone/Firestone, Inc.
Briggs & Stratton Corp.
Bristol-Myers Squibb Co.
Broderbund Software, Inc.
Bucyrus-Erie Co.
Campbell Soup Co.
Cargill Inc.
Carillon Importers, Ltd.
Carter-Wallace, Inc.
Caterpillar Inc.
Central National-Gottesman
Central & South West Services
CertainTeed Corp.
Cessna Aircraft Co.
Charter Manufacturing Co.
Chase Bank of Texas
Chicago Title Corp.
CIGNA Corp.
Cincinnati Bell Inc.
Citigroup
Citizens Bank-Flint
Citizens Financial Group, Inc.
Coca-Cola Co.
Consolidated Papers, Inc.
Constellation Energy Group, Inc.
Contran Corp.
Cooper Industries, Inc.
Copley Press, Inc.
Cox Enterprises Inc.
Cranston Print Works Co.
Crestar Finance Corp.
Dana Corp.
Delta Air Lines, Inc.
Demoulas Supermarkets Inc.
Disney Co. (Walt)
Duke Energy
Eastern Bank
Eckerd Corp.
Emerson Electric Co.
Ensign-Bickford Industries
Equifax Inc.
Equitable Resources, Inc.
Erving Industries
Exxon Mobil Corp.
Fabri-Kal Corp.
Federated Department Stores, Inc.
Fifth Third Bancorp
First Maryland Bancorp
First Source Corp.
First Union Corp.
First Union Securities, Inc.
Firstar Bank Milwaukee NA
Fisher Brothers Cleaning Services
Fisher Scientific
Florida Power Corp.
Fluor Corp.
Forbes Inc.
Frost National Bank
Galter Corp.
GenAmerica Corp.
Genentech Inc.
General Atlantic Partners II LP
General Dynamics Corp.
General Electric Co.
General Mills, Inc.
Georgia Power Co.
Gerber Products Co.
Giant Food Inc.
Glaxo Wellcome Inc.
Glickenhaus & Co.
Globe Corp.
Goldman Sachs Group
Golub Corp.
Grace & Co. (W.R.)
Graco, Inc.
Grede Foundries
Green Bay Packaging
Group Health Plan
Guess?
Halliburton Co.
Hamilton Sundstrand Corp.
Hancock Financial Services (John)
Harcourt General, Inc.
Harnischfeger Industries
Harsco Corp.
Hartford (The)
Heinz Co. (H.J.)
Hensel Phelps Construction Co.
Hewlett-Packard Co.
Hitachi America Ltd.
Hoffmann-La Roche Inc.
Hofmann Co.
Hubbard Broadcasting, Inc.
Hubbell Inc.
Humana, Inc.
Independent Stave Co.
Invacare Corp.
Jacobson & Sons (Benjamin)
Johnson Controls Inc.
Johnson & Son (S.C.)
Journal-Gazette Co.
Kemper National Insurance Companies
Kimball International, Inc.
Kimberly-Clark Corp.
Kroger Co.
Lee Enterprises
Leigh Fibers, Inc.
Leviton Manufacturing Co. Inc.
Lilly & Co. (Eli)
Lipton Co.
Liz Claiborne, Inc.
Loews Corp.
Lowe's Companies
Macy's East Inc.
Manor Care Health SVS, Inc.
Marcus Corp.
Mark IV Industries
Marshall & Ilsley Corp.
Masco Corp.
Mattel Inc.
May Department Stores Co.
MCI WorldCom, Inc.
Medtronic, Inc.
Mercantile Bank NA
Merck & Co.
Merit Oil Corp.
Metropolitan Life Insurance Co.
Milliken & Co.
Millipore Corp.
Minnesota Mining & Manufacturing Co.
Morgan & Co. Inc. (J.P.)
Morris Communications Corp.
Nabisco Group Holdings
Nalco Chemical Co.
National Bank of Commerce Trust & Savings
National Service Industries, Inc.
New York Life Insurance Co.
New York Mercantile Exchange
New York Stock Exchange, Inc.
Nomura Holding America
Nordson Corp.
Norfolk Southern Corp.
Occidental Petroleum Corp.
Old National Bank Evansville
Olin Corp.
Orscheln Co.
Oshkosh B'Gosh, Inc.
Overseas Shipholding Group Inc.
Pacific Mutual Life Insurance Co.
PepsiCo, Inc.
Pfizer Inc.
Pharmacia & Upjohn, Inc.
Phelps Dodge Corp.
Philips Electronics North America Corp.
Phillips Petroleum Co.
Pittway Corp.
Polaroid Corp.
Praxair
Premier Dental Products Co.
Premier Industrial Corp.
Procter & Gamble Co., Cosmetics Division
Prudential Insurance Co. of America
Pulitzer Publishing Co.
Ralph's Grocery Co.
Ralston Purina Co.
Reinhart Institutional Foods
Revlon Inc.
Reynolds Tobacco (R.J.)
Ruddick Corp.
SBC Communications Inc.
Schering-Plough Corp.
Schlumberger Ltd. (USA)
Seagram & Sons, Inc. (Joseph E.)
Searle & Co. (G.D.)
Sempra Energy
Shell Oil Co.
Sherwin-Williams Co.
Slant/Fin Corp.
Smith Corp. (A.O.)
SmithKline Beecham Corp.
Southeastern Mutual Insurance Co.
Star Bank NA
State Farm Mutual Automobile Insurance Co.
State Street Bank & Trust Co.
SunTrust Bank Atlanta
Synovus Financial Corp.
Tai and Co. (J.T.)
Tenet Healthcare Corp.
Texaco Inc.
Texas Instruments Inc.
Textron Inc.
Thompson Co. (J. Walter)
TJX Companies, Inc.
Toledo Blade Co.
Trace International Holdings, Inc.
True North Communications, Inc.
Tyson Foods Inc.
Ukrop's Super Markets
Unilever Home & Personal Care U.S.A.
Unilever United States, Inc.
Union Camp Corp.
Union Carbide Corp.
United Parcel Service of America Inc.
United Wisconsin Services
Universal Foods Corp.
Universal Studios
Unocal Corp.
Wachtell, Lipton, Rosen & Katz
Wal-Mart Stores, Inc.
Warner-Lambert Co.
West Co. Inc.
Westvaco Corp.
Whirlpool Corp.
WICOR, Inc.
Wiley & Sons (John)
Winn-Dixie Stores Inc.
Wisconsin Energy Corp.
Wisconsin Public Service Corp.
Witco Corp.
Wrigley Co. (Wm. Jr.)
Zachry Co. (H.B.)
Zilkha & Sons

MINORITY EDUCATION

Abbott Laboratories
ABC
Aetna, Inc.
AGL Resources Inc.
Agrilink Foods, Inc.
Air Products and Chemicals, Inc.
Alabama Power Co.
Albertson's Inc.
Alcoa Inc.
Alcon Laboratories, Inc.
Allegheny Technologies Inc.
Alliant Techsystems
AlliedSignal Inc.
Allstate Insurance Co.
Alma Piston Co.
AMCORE Bank Rockford
Ameren Corp.
America West Airlines, Inc.
American Express Co.
American Honda Motor Co., Inc.
American United Life Insurance Co.
Ameritas Life Insurance Corp.
Ameritech Corp.
Ameritech Indiana
AMP Inc.
AMR Corp.
Amsted Industries Inc.

Analog Devices, Inc.
Andersen Corp.
Andersons Inc.
Anheuser-Busch Companies, Inc.
APL Ltd.
Apple Computer, Inc.
Appleton Papers Inc.
Archer-Daniels-Midland Co.
Armstrong World Industries, Inc.
Arvin Industries, Inc.
AT&T Corp.
Atlantic Richfield Co.
Avista Corporation
Avon Products, Inc.
Badger Meter, Inc.
Baird & Co. (Robert W.)
Bandag, Inc.
Banfi Vintners
Bank of America
Bank of New York Co., Inc.
Bank One Corp.
BankAtlantic Bancorp
Banta Corp.
Barclays Capital
Bard, Inc. (C.R.)
Barnes Group Inc.
Bassett Furniture Industries
Battelle Memorial Institute
Bausch & Lomb Inc.
Baxter International Inc.
Bayer Corp.
Bechtel Group, Inc.
Belk Stores Services Inc.
Bell Atlantic Corp.
BellSouth Corp.
Bemis Co., Inc.
Bernstein & Co., Inc. (Sanford C.)
Berwind Group
Bestfoods
Bethlehem Steel Corp.
BFGoodrich Co.
Binswanger Companies
Block, Inc. (H&R)
Blount International, Inc.
Blue Bell, Inc.
Blue Cross & Blue Shield of Alabama
Blue Cross & Blue Shield of Minnesota
Boeing Co.
Boise Cascade Corp.
Borden, Inc.
Borman's Inc.
Boston Edison Co.
Boston Globe (The)
Bowater Inc.
BP Amoco Corp.
Bridgestone/Firestone, Inc.
Briggs & Stratton Corp.
Bristol-Myers Squibb Co.
Broderbund Software, Inc.
Brown Shoe Co., Inc.
Brown & Williamson Tobacco Corp.
Brunswick Corp.
Bucyrus-Erie Co.
Burlington Industries, Inc.
Burlington Resources, Inc.
Burnett Co. (Leo)
Butler Manufacturing Co.
Cabot Corp.
Campbell Soup Co.
Cargill Inc.
Carlson Companies, Inc.
Carpenter Technology Corp.
Carrier Corp.
Carter-Wallace, Inc.
Caterpillar Inc.
CBS Corp.
Central Maine Power Co.
Central National-Gottesman
Central Newspapers, Inc.
Central & South West Services
Central Soya Co.
CertainTeed Corp.
CGU Insurance
Champion International Corp.
Chase Bank of Texas
Chase Manhattan Bank, NA
Chesapeake Corp.
Chevron Corp.
Chicago Title Corp.
Cincinnati Bell Inc.
Circuit City Stores, Inc.
CIT Group, Inc. (The)
Citibank Corp.
Citigroup
Citizens Bank-Flint
Cleveland-Cliffs, Inc.
Clorox Co.
CNA
Coca-Cola Co.
Colonial Oil Industries, Inc.
Comerica Inc.
Commercial Intertech Corp.
ConAgra, Inc.
Cone Mills Corp.
Conoco, Inc.
Consolidated Natural Gas Co.
Consolidated Papers, Inc.
Constellation Energy Group, Inc.
Consumers Energy Co.
Continental Grain Co.
Cook Inlet Region
Coors Brewing Co.
Corning Inc.
Country Curtains, Inc.
Crane Co.
Cranston Print Works Co.
Credit Suisse First Boston
Crestar Finance Corp.
Cummings Properties Management
Cummins Engine Co., Inc.
CUNA Mutual Group
Daily News
DaimlerChrysler Corp.
Dain Bosworth Inc.
Dana Corp.
Deere & Co.
Deloitte & Touche
Delta Air Lines, Inc.
Deluxe Corp.
Detroit Edison Co.
Dexter Corp.
Dial Corp.
Disney Co. (Walt)
Dixie Group, Inc. (The)
Donaldson Co., Inc.
Dow Chemical Co.
Dow Corning Corp.
Dow Jones & Co., Inc.
du Pont de Nemours & Co. (E.I.)
Duchossois Industries Inc.
Duke Energy
Dun & Bradstreet Corp.
Duriron Co., Inc.
Eastman Kodak Co.
Eaton Corp.
Eckerd Corp.
Ecolab Inc.
Edison International
Elf Atochem North America, Inc.
Emerson Electric Co.
Employers Mutual Casualty Co.
Enterprise Rent-A-Car Co.
Equifax Inc.
Erb Lumber Co.
Ernst & Young, LLP
European American Bank
Exxon Mobil Corp.
Fannie Mae
Federal-Mogul Corp.
Federated Department Stores, Inc.
FedEx Corp.
Ferro Corp.
FINA
First Union Corp.
First Union National Bank, NA
First Union Securities, Inc.
Firstar Bank Milwaukee NA
Fisher Brothers Cleaning Services
Fisher Scientific
FleetBoston Financial Corp.
Florida Power Corp.
Florida Power & Light Co.
Florida Rock Industries
Fluor Corp.
FMC Corp.
Forbes Inc.
Ford Motor Co.
Fortis Insurance Co.
Fortune Brands, Inc.
Freeport-McMoRan Inc.
Frontier Corp.
Fuller Co. (H.B.)
Furniture Brands International, Inc.
Gallo Winery, Inc. (E&J)
Gap, Inc.
GATX Corp.
GEICO Corp.
GenAmerica Corp.
GenCorp
General Electric Co.
General Mills, Inc.
General Motors Corp.
Georgia-Pacific Corp.
Georgia Power Co.
Gerber Products Co.
Giant Eagle Inc.
Giant Food Inc.
Glickenhaus & Co.
Goldman Sachs Group
Goodrich Aerospace - Aerostructures Group (B.F.)
Grace & Co. (W.R.)
Graco, Inc.
GTE Corp.
Halliburton Co.
Hallmark Cards Inc.
Hamilton Sundstrand Corp.
Hancock Financial Services (John)
Hanna Co. (M.A.)
Harley-Davidson Co.
Harnischfeger Industries
Harris Corp.
Harris Trust & Savings Bank
Harsco Corp.
Hartford (The)
Hartford Steam Boiler Inspection & Insurance Co.
Hartmarx Corp.
Hasbro, Inc.
Heinz Co. (H.J.)
Heller Financial, Inc.
Hewlett-Packard Co.
Hickory Tech Corp.
Hitachi America Ltd.
Hoffmann-La Roche Inc.
Honeywell International Inc.
Household International Inc.
Hubbard Broadcasting, Inc.
Huffy Corp.
Humana, Inc.
Huntington Bancshares Inc.
Illinois Power Co.
Illinois Tool Works, Inc.
Inland Container Corp.
Intel Corp.
International Business Machines Corp.
International Multifoods Corp.
International Paper Co.
Johnson Controls Inc.
Johnson & Johnson
Johnson & Son (S.C.)
Jostens, Inc.
JSJ Corp.
Kellwood Co.
Kelly Services
Kemper National Insurance Companies
Kerr-McGee Corp.
Kiewit Sons' Inc. (Peter)
Kimball International, Inc.
Kimberly-Clark Corp.
Kmart Corp.
KPMG Peat Marwick LLP
Kraft Foods, Inc.
Kroger Co.
Lancaster Lens, Inc.
Lance, Inc.
Land O'Lakes, Inc.
LandAmerica Financial Services
Landmark Communications Inc.
Lee Enterprises
LG&E Energy Corp.
Lilly & Co. (Eli)
Lincoln Financial Group
Lipton Co.
Little, Inc. (Arthur D.)
Litton Industries, Inc.
Liz Claiborne, Inc.
Loews Corp.
Lotus Development Corp.
Louisiana Land & Exploration Co.
LTV Corp.
Lubrizol Corp. (The)
Macy's East Inc.
Madison Gas & Electric Co.
Mallinckrodt Chemical, Inc.
Maritz Inc.
Marshall & Ilsley Corp.
Masco Corp.
Mattel Inc.
May Department Stores Co.
Maytag Corp.
McClatchy Co.
McCormick & Co. Inc.
McDonald & Co. Securities, Inc.
McDonald's Corp.
McGraw-Hill Companies, Inc.
Mead Corp.
Medtronic, Inc.
Mellon Financial Corp.
Memphis Light Gas & Water Division
Merck & Co.
Merrill Lynch & Co., Inc.
Metropolitan Life Insurance Co.
Michigan Consolidated Gas Co.
Mid-America Bank of Louisville
Milliken & Co.
Millipore Corp.
Mine Safety Appliances Co.
Minnesota Mining & Manufacturing Co.
Minnesota Mutual Life Insurance Co.
Monsanto Co.
Morgan & Co. Inc. (J.P.)
Morgan Stanley Dean Witter & Co.
Morrison Knudsen Corp.
Morton International Inc.
Motorola Inc.
MTD Products Inc.
Nalco Chemical Co.
National City Bank of Minneapolis
National City Corp.
National Computer Systems, Inc.
National Machinery Co.
National Service Industries, Inc.
National Starch & Chemical Co.
Nationwide Insurance Co.
NCR Corp.
Nestle U.S.A. Inc.
New Century Energies
New England Financial
New Jersey Natural Gas Co.
New York Life Insurance Co.
New York Times Co.
Niagara Mohawk Holdings Inc.
Nike, Inc.
Nissan North America, Inc.
Nordson Corp.
Norfolk Southern Corp.
Nortel
Northeast Utilities
Northern States Power Co.
Northern Trust Co.
Northwest Natural Gas Co.
Norton Co.
Norwest Corp.
Occidental Petroleum Corp.
Ohio National Life Insurance Co.
Olin Corp.
Oshkosh B'Gosh, Inc.
Outboard Marine Corp.
Owens Corning
Owens-Illinois Inc.
PACCAR Inc.
Pacific Gas and Electric Co.
Pacific Mutual Life Insurance Co.
Paine Webber
Park National Bank
Parker Hannifin Corp.
Penney Co., Inc. (J.C.)
PepsiCo, Inc.
Pfizer Inc.
Pharmacia & Upjohn, Inc.
Phelps Dodge Corp.
Pheonix Financial Group
Philip Morris Companies Inc.
Phillips Petroleum Co.
Physicians Mutual Insurance Co.
Pillsbury Co.
Pitney Bowes Inc.
Pittway Corp.
PNC Bank Kentucky Inc.
Polaroid Corp.
Potomac Electric Power Co.
PPG Industries, Inc.
Premier Dental Products Co.
Premier Industrial Corp.
Price Associates (T. Rowe)

Principal Financial Group
Procter & Gamble Co.
Procter & Gamble Co., Cosmetics Division
Promus Hotel Corp.
Prudential Insurance Co. of America
Prudential Securities Inc.
Public Service Electric & Gas Co.
Publix Supermarkets
Pulitzer Publishing Co.
Putnam Investments
Quanex Corp.
Ralston Purina Co.
Rayonier Inc.
Reader's Digest Association, Inc. (The)
Reebok International Ltd.
Regions Bank
Reily & Co., Inc. (William B.)
Reliant Energy Inc.
ReliaStar Financial Corp.
Revlon Inc.
Reynolds Metals Co.
Reynolds Tobacco (R.J.)
Rockwell International Corp.
Rouse Co.
Royal & SunAlliance USA, Inc.
Rubbermaid Inc.
Rutledge Hill Press
Ryder System, Inc.
SAFECO Corp.
Saint Paul Companies Inc.
Salomon Smith Barney
Sara Lee Corp.
Sara Lee Hosiery, Inc.
SBC Communications Inc.
Schering-Plough Corp.
Schloss & Co. (Marcus)
Schlumberger Ltd. (USA)
Schwab & Co., Inc. (Charles)
Scripps Co. (E.W.)
Seagram & Sons, Inc. (Joseph E.)
Sears, Roebuck and Co.
Security Benefit Life Insurance Co.
Sega of America Inc.
Sempra Energy
Sentry Insurance, A Mutual Co.
S.G. Cowen
Shell Oil Co.
Sherwin-Williams Co.
Slant/Fin Corp.
Smith Corp. (A.O.)
Smurfit-Stone Container Corp.
Sonoco Products Co.
Sony Electronics
Southeastern Mutual Insurance Co.
Southern California Gas Co.
Southern New England Telephone Co.
Sovereign Bank
Springs Industries, Inc.
Sprint Corp.
Sprint/United Telephone
SPX Corp.
Square D Co.
Standard Products Co.
Standard Register Co.
Stanley Works (The)
Starwood Hotels & Resorts Worldwide, Inc.
State Farm Mutual Automobile Insurance Co.
State Street Bank & Trust Co.
Stone Container Corp.
Storage Technology Corp.
Stupp Brothers Bridge & Iron Co.
Sun Microsystems Inc.
Sunoco Inc.
SunTrust Bank Atlanta
Susquehanna-Pfaltzgraff Co.
Synovus Financial Corp.
Tektronix, Inc.
Tenet Healthcare Corp.
TENNANT Co.
Tenneco Automotive
Tenneco Packaging
Tension Envelope Corp.
Texaco Inc.
Texas Instruments Inc.
Textron Inc.
Thomasville Furniture Industries Inc.
Thompson Co. (J. Walter)
Times Mirror Co.
Timken Co. (The)
TJX Companies, Inc.
TMC Investment Co.
Toledo Blade Co.
Tomkins Industries, Inc.
Toyota Motor Sales U.S.A., Inc.
Trace International Holdings, Inc.
Transamerica Corp.
True North Communications, Inc.
Trustmark Insurance Co.
TRW Inc.
Tyson Foods Inc.
Ukrop's Super Markets
Unilever Home & Personal Care U.S.A.
Unilever United States, Inc.
Union Camp Corp.
Union Carbide Corp.
Union Pacific Corp.
United Airlines Inc.
United Distillers & Vintners North America
United Parcel Service of America Inc.
U.S. Bancorp
U.S. Bancorp Piper Jaffray
United States Trust Co. of New York
United Technologies Corp.
United Wisconsin Services
Universal Leaf Tobacco Co., Inc.
Universal Studios
Unocal Corp.
US Bank, Washington
US West, Inc.
USG Corp.
UST Inc.
USX Corp.
Valmont Industries, Inc.
Varian Medical Systems, Inc.
Vulcan Materials Co.
Wachovia Bank of North Carolina NA
Wachtell, Lipton, Rosen & Katz
Wal-Mart Stores, Inc.
Warner-Lambert Co.
Washington Mutual, Inc.
Waste Management Inc.
Wells Fargo & Co.
West Co. Inc.
Western & Southern Life Insurance Co.
Westvaco Corp.
Weyerhaeuser Co.
Whirlpool Corp.
Whitman Corp.
WICOR, Inc.
Wiley & Sons (John)
Williams
Winn-Dixie Stores Inc.
Wiremold Co.
Wisconsin Energy Corp.
Wisconsin Public Service Corp.
Witco Corp.
Wolverine World Wide
Wrigley Co. (Wm. Jr.)
Xerox Corp.
Young & Rubicam

PRESCHOOL EDUCATION

Alcoa Inc.
Allmerica Financial Corp.
AMCORE Bank Rockford
America West Airlines, Inc.
American Express Co.
American Honda Motor Co., Inc.
Andersen Corp.
Aon Corp.
AT&T Corp.
Atlantic Richfield Co.
BankBoston Corp.
Banta Corp.
Baxter International Inc.
Belk Stores Services Inc.
BellSouth Corp.
Bemis Co., Inc.
Binney & Smith Inc.
Block, Inc. (H&R)
Blount International, Inc.
Blue Cross & Blue Shield of Iowa
Boeing Co.
Boston Edison Co.
Boston Globe (The)
Broderbund Software, Inc.
Burnett Co. (Leo)
Cabot Corp.
Cargill Inc.
Carpenter Technology Corp.
Central Maine Power Co.
Chase Manhattan Bank, NA
Citigroup
Clorox Co.
CNA
Comdisco, Inc.
Consolidated Natural Gas Co.
Constellation Energy Group, Inc.
Credit Suisse First Boston
CSR Rinker Materials Corp.
Dain Bosworth Inc.
Delta Air Lines, Inc.
Dial Corp.
du Pont de Nemours & Co. (E.I.)
Dynamet, Inc.
Eastman Kodak Co.
Employers Mutual Casualty Co.
Equifax Inc.
Fidelity Investments
FINA
Fireman's Fund Insurance Co.
First American Corp.
First Hawaiian, Inc.
First Tennessee National Corp.
First Union Corp.
FleetBoston Financial Corp.
Ford Meter Box Co.
Freddie Mac
Freeport-McMoRan Inc.
Frost National Bank
Fuller Co. (H.B.)
GATX Corp.
General Atlantic Partners II LP
General Mills, Inc.
Golub Corp.
Hallmark Cards Inc.
Harcourt General, Inc.
Harris Trust & Savings Bank
Hasbro, Inc.
Home Depot, Inc.
Honeywell International Inc.
Hubbell Inc.
Humana, Inc.
IBP
Intel Corp.
Jeld-wen, Inc.
Lehigh Portland Cement Co.
Leviton Manufacturing Co. Inc.
Lincoln Financial Group
Liz Claiborne, Inc.
Lotus Development Corp.
Louisiana Land & Exploration Co.
Madison Gas & Electric Co.
Maritz Inc.
Meredith Corp.
MidAmerican Energy Holdings Co.
Millipore Corp.
Mine Safety Appliances Co.
Mitsubishi Electric America
Monarch Machine Tool Co.
Montana Power Co.
Montgomery Ward & Co., Inc.
MTD Products Inc.
National City Bank of Minneapolis
National Computer Systems, Inc.
National Machinery Co.
National Starch & Chemical Co.
New England Bio Labs
New England Financial
Niagara Mohawk Holdings Inc.
Nordson Corp.
Northern States Power Co.
Northern Trust Co.
Norton Co.
Old Kent Bank
Old National Bank Evansville
Pella Corp.
Penney Co., Inc. (J.C.)
Peoples Bank
Pillsbury Co.
PNC Financial Services Group
Polaroid Corp.
Principal Financial Group
Prudential Insurance Co. of America
Putnam Investments
Quanex Corp.
Rayonier Inc.
Reinhart Institutional Foods
Reynolds Tobacco (R.J.)
Royal & SunAlliance USA, Inc.
S&T Bancorp
Sara Lee Hosiery, Inc.
Schering-Plough Corp.
Scripps Co. (E.W.)
Searle & Co. (G.D.)
Sempra Energy
Sherwin-Williams Co.
Shoney's Inc.
Slant/Fin Corp.
Solo Cup Co.
Springs Industries, Inc.
Starwood Hotels & Resorts Worldwide, Inc.
State Street Bank & Trust Co.
Steelcase Inc.
Storage Technology Corp.
Temple-Inland Inc.
Tesoro Hawaii
Texas Instruments Inc.
Ticketmaster Corp.
Transamerica Corp.
True North Communications, Inc.
TRW Inc.
Union Camp Corp.
United Dominion Industries, Ltd.
United States Sugar Corp.
United States Trust Co. of New York
US Bank, Washington
US West, Inc.
Wal-Mart Stores, Inc.
Washington Mutual, Inc.
The Washington Post
Wiley & Sons (John)
Williams
Wisconsin Power & Light Co.
Witco Corp.
Woodward Governor Co.
York Federal Savings & Loan Association

PRIVATE EDUCATION (PRECOLLEGE)

Abbott Laboratories
ABC
Advanced Micro Devices, Inc.
AEGON U.S.A. Inc.
Agrilink Foods, Inc.
Alcoa Inc.
Alcon Laboratories, Inc.
Alexander & Baldwin, Inc.
Alliant Techsystems
AlliedSignal Inc.
Allmerica Financial Corp.
Alma Piston Co.
AMCORE Bank Rockford
Ameren Corp.
America West Airlines, Inc.
American Fidelity Corp.
American General Finance
American Honda Motor Co., Inc.
American Retail Group
American Standard Inc.
American United Life Insurance Co.
Ameritas Life Insurance Corp.
Ameritech Indiana
Ameritech Ohio
AMETEK, Inc.
Amgen, Inc.
AMP Inc.
AMR Corp.
Amsted Industries Inc.
Andersen Corp.
Andersons Inc.
Anheuser-Busch Companies, Inc.
Aon Corp.
APL Ltd.
Archer-Daniels-Midland Co.
Armstrong World Industries, Inc.

Arvin Industries, Inc.
ASARCO Inc.
Ashland, Inc.
Associated Food Stores
Atlantic Investment Co.
Atlantic Richfield Co.
Auburn Foundry
Badger Meter, Inc.
Baird & Co. (Robert W.)
Banfi Vintners
Bank of New York Co., Inc.
Bank One Corp.
Bank One, Texas-Houston Office
BankBoston Corp.
Bard, Inc. (C.R.)
Barden Corp.
Bardes Corp.
Barnes Group Inc.
Barry Corp. (R.G.)
Bassett Furniture Industries
Bayer Corp.
Bechtel Group, Inc.
Belk-Simpson Department Stores
Belk Stores Services Inc.
Bemis Co., Inc.
Bemis Manufacturing Co.
Ben & Jerry's Homemade Inc.
Bernstein & Co., Inc. (Sanford C.)
Bestfoods
Bethlehem Steel Corp.
Binney & Smith Inc.
Binswanger Companies
Blair & Co. (William)
Block, Inc. (H&R)
Blount International, Inc.
Blue Bell, Inc.
Blue Cross & Blue Shield of Alabama
Boeing Co.
Boler Co.
Borden, Inc.
Borman's Inc.
Boston Edison Co.
Boston Globe (The)
Bourns, Inc.
Bradford & Co. (J.C.)
Briggs & Stratton Corp.
Bristol-Myers Squibb Co.
Brunswick Corp.
Bucyrus-Erie Co.
Burlington Industries, Inc.
Burlington Resources, Inc.
Burnett Co. (Leo)
Burress (J.W.)
Business Improvement
Butler Capital Corp.
Butler Manufacturing Co.
Cabot Corp.
Calvin Klein
Campbell Soup Co.
Cantor, Fitzgerald Securities Corp.
Cargill Inc.
Carillon Importers, Ltd.
Carlson Companies, Inc.
Carris Reels
Carter-Wallace, Inc.
Central National-Gottesman
Century 21
CertainTeed Corp.
Cessna Aircraft Co.
CGU Insurance
Charter Manufacturing Co.
Chase Manhattan Bank, NA
Chemed Corp.
Chesapeake Corp.
Chicago Board of Trade
CIGNA Corp.
Cincinnati Bell Inc.
Cinergy Corp.
Circuit City Stores, Inc.
CIT Group, Inc. (The)
Citibank Corp.
Citigroup
Citizens Financial Group, Inc.
CLARCOR Inc.
Cleveland-Cliffs, Inc.
Clorox Co.
CNA
Coca-Cola Co.
Colonial Life & Accident Insurance Co.
Colonial Oil Industries, Inc.
Commerce Bancshares, Inc.
Compass Bank
Consolidated Papers, Inc.
Contran Corp.
Cooper Industries, Inc.
Cooper Tire & Rubber Co.
Copley Press, Inc.
Country Curtains, Inc.
CPI Corp.
Crane Co.
Credit Suisse First Boston
Crestar Finance Corp.
Croft-Leominster
CSR Rinker Materials Corp.
Cummings Properties Management
Cummins Engine Co., Inc.
Daily News
DaimlerChrysler Corp.
Dain Bosworth Inc.
Dana Corp.
Danis Companies
Dayton Hudson
Deere & Co.
Deluxe Corp.
Demoulas Supermarkets Inc.
Deposit Guaranty National Bank
Detroit Edison Co.
Deutsch Co.
Dexter Corp.
Dial Corp.
Dixie Group, Inc. (The)
Domino's Pizza Inc.
Donaldson Co., Inc.
Dow Jones & Co., Inc.
Dreyer's Grand Ice Cream
du Pont de Nemours & Co. (E.I.)
Duchossois Industries Inc.
Duke Energy
Eastern Bank
Eastman Kodak Co.
Eaton Corp.
Edison International
Edwards Enterprise Software (J.D.)
Elf Atochem North America, Inc.
Emerson Electric Co.
EMI Music Publishing
Ensign-Bickford Industries
Enterprise Rent-A-Car Co.
Erb Lumber Co.
Erving Industries
Evening Post Publishing Co.
Federal-Mogul Corp.
Federated Department Stores, Inc.
Fidelity Investments
FINA
Fireman's Fund Insurance Co.
First Hawaiian, Inc.
First Maryland Bancorp
First National Bank of Evergreen Park
First Source Corp.
First Union Bank
First Union Corp.
First Union Securities, Inc.
Fisher Brothers Cleaning Services
Fisher Scientific
Florida Power & Light Co.
Forbes Inc.
Ford Meter Box Co.
Forest City Enterprises, Inc.
Fort Worth Star-Telegram Inc.
Fortune Brands, Inc.
Franklin Electric Co.
Freeport-McMoRan Inc.
Frost National Bank
Furniture Brands International, Inc.
Gallo Winery, Inc. (E&J)
Galter Corp.
Gap, Inc.
GATX Corp.
GenCorp
General Mills, Inc.
General Reinsurance Corp.
Georgia-Pacific Corp.
Georgia Power Co.
Gerber Products Co.
Giant Eagle Inc.
Giddings & Lewis
Glaxo Wellcome Inc.
Glickenhaus & Co.
Globe Corp.
Goldman Sachs Group
Gosiger, Inc.
Grace & Co. (W.R.)
Graco, Inc.
Grede Foundries
Group Health Plan
GTE Corp.
Guess?
Hallmark Cards Inc.
Hamilton Sundstrand Corp.
Hanna Co. (M.A.)
Harland Co. (John H.)
Harley-Davidson Co.
Harnischfeger Industries
Harris Trust & Savings Bank
Hartford (The)
Hartford Steam Boiler Inspection & Insurance Co.
Hartmarx Corp.
Hasbro, Inc.
Hawaiian Electric Co., Inc.
Heinz Co. (H.J.)
Heller Financial, Inc.
Hensel Phelps Construction Co.
Hickory Tech Corp.
Hoffer Plastics Corp.
Hoffmann-La Roche Inc.
Hofmann Co.
Honeywell International Inc.
Housatonic Curtain Co.
HSBC Bank USA
Hubbard Broadcasting, Inc.
Hubbell Inc.
Huffy Corp.
Humana, Inc.
IKON Office Solutions, Inc.
Illinois Tool Works, Inc.
Independent Stave Co.
Inland Container Corp.
Inman Mills
Intel Corp.
International Business Machines Corp.
International Multifoods Corp.
International Paper Co.
Jacobson & Sons (Benjamin)
Jeld-wen, Inc.
Johnson Controls Inc.
Johnson & Son (S.C.)
Journal-Gazette Co.
JSJ Corp.
Katten, Muchin & Zavis
Kellwood Co.
Kimball International, Inc.
Kimberly-Clark Corp.
Kinder Morgn
Kingsbury Corp.
Koch Enterprises, Inc.
Kroger Co.
Laclede Gas Co.
Ladish Co., Inc.
Lancaster Lens, Inc.
Land O'Lakes, Inc.
LandAmerica Financial Services
Lee Enterprises
Lehigh Portland Cement Co.
Leigh Fibers, Inc.
Lennox International, Inc.
Liberty Corp.
Lilly & Co. (Eli)
Lipton Co.
Little, Inc. (Arthur D.)
Litton Industries, Inc.
Liz Claiborne, Inc.
Louisiana Land & Exploration Co.
Louisiana-Pacific Corp.
LTV Corp.
Lubrizol Corp. (The)
Macy's East Inc.
Mamiye Brothers
Manufacturers & Traders Trust Co.
Marshall & Ilsley Corp.
Mattel Inc.
McClatchy Co.
McGraw-Hill Companies, Inc.
MCI WorldCom, Inc.
McKesson-HBOC Corp.
McWane Inc.
Medtronic, Inc.
Merit Oil Corp.
Mid-America Bank of Louisville
MidAmerican Energy Holdings Co.
Milacron, Inc.
Milliken & Co.
Millipore Corp.
Mitsubishi Electric America
Monarch Machine Tool Co.
Monsanto Co.
Montana Power Co.
Montgomery Ward & Co., Inc.
MONY Group (The)
Morris Communications Corp.
Morrison Knudsen Corp.
Motorola Inc.
MTD Products Inc.
Mutual of Omaha Insurance Co.
Nabisco Group Holdings
National Bank of Commerce Trust & Savings
National City Corp.
National Computer Systems, Inc.
National Machinery Co.
National Service Industries, Inc.
National Starch & Chemical Co.
NEBCO Evans
New York Mercantile Exchange
New York Stock Exchange, Inc.
New York Times Co.
Nomura Holding America
Nordson Corp.
Norfolk Southern Corp.
North American Royalties
Northern Trust Co.
Norton Co.
Occidental Oil and Gas
Occidental Petroleum Corp.
OG&E Electric Services
Old Kent Bank
Old National Bank Evansville
Olin Corp.
Orscheln Co.
Osborne Enterprises
Oshkosh B'Gosh, Inc.
Outboard Marine Corp.
Overseas Shipholding Group Inc.
PACCAR Inc.
Pacific Century Financial Corp.
Pacific Mutual Life Insurance Co.
Paine Webber
Park National Bank
Pella Corp.
PEMCO Corp.
Peoples Energy Corp.
PepsiCo, Inc.
PerkinElmer, Inc.
Pfizer Inc.
Phelps Dodge Corp.
Physicians Mutual Insurance Co.
Pieper Power Electric Co.
Pillsbury Co.
Pittway Corp.
PNC Financial Services Group
Polaroid Corp.
PPG Industries, Inc.
Premier Dental Products Co.
Price Associates (T. Rowe)
Principal Financial Group
Procter & Gamble Co., Cosmetics Division
Providence Journal-Bulletin Co.
Provident Companies, Inc.
Prudential Insurance Co. of America
Public Service Electric & Gas Co.
Publix Supermarkets
Pulitzer Publishing Co.
Putnam Investments
Quaker Chemical Corp.
Quanex Corp.
Ralph's Grocery Co.
Ralston Purina Co.
Rayonier Inc.
Reilly Industries, Inc.
Reily & Co., Inc. (William B.)
Reinhart Institutional Foods
Revlon Inc.
Reynolds Metals Co.
Reynolds Tobacco (R.J.)
Rich Products Corp.
Rockwell International Corp.
Royal & SunAlliance USA, Inc.
Rubbermaid Inc.
Ruddick Corp.
Russer Foods
SAFECO Corp.

Funders by Recipient Type

Saint Paul Companies Inc.
Sara Lee Hosiery, Inc.
Schering-Plough Corp.
Schloss & Co. (Marcus)
Schlumberger Ltd. (USA)
Schwab & Co., Inc. (Charles)
Scripps Co. (E.W.)
Seagram & Sons, Inc. (Joseph E.)
Sega of America Inc.
Sentry Insurance, A Mutual Co.
Servco Pacific
ServiceMaster Co.
S.G. Cowen
Shea Co. (John F.)
Shell Oil Co.
Sherwin-Williams Co.
Shoney's Inc.
Sierra Pacific Industries
Simpson Investment Co.
SmithKline Beecham Corp.
Smurfit-Stone Container Corp.
Solo Cup Co.
Sonoco Products Co.
Sony Electronics
South Bend Tribune Corp.
Southeastern Mutual Insurance Co.
Southern New England Telephone Co.
Southwest Gas Corp.
Sprint Corp.
Standard Products Co.
Star Bank NA
Starwood Hotels & Resorts Worldwide, Inc.
State Farm Mutual Automobile Insurance Co.
State Street Bank & Trust Co.
Steelcase Inc.
Stone Container Corp.
Stonecutter Mills Corp.
Storage Technology Corp.
Strear Farms Co.
Stride Rite Corp.
Stupp Brothers Bridge & Iron Co.
Sun Microsystems Inc.
SunTrust Bank Atlanta
Susquehanna-Pfaltzgraff Co.
Sverdrup Corp.
Synovus Financial Corp.
Tamko Roofing Products
Tandy Corp.
TCF National Bank Minnesota
Tektronix, Inc.
Teleflex Inc.
Temple-Inland Inc.
Tension Envelope Corp.
Tesoro Hawaii
Texaco Inc.
Texas Instruments Inc.
Textron Inc.
Thermo Electron Corp.
Thomasville Furniture Industries Inc.
Thompson Co. (J. Walter)
TJX Companies, Inc.
TMC Investment Co.
Toledo Blade Co.
Tomkins Industries, Inc.
Toro Co.
Toshiba America Inc.
Toyota Motor Sales U.S.A., Inc.
Trace International Holdings, Inc.
Transamerica Corp.
True Oil Co.
Trustmark Insurance Co.
Tyson Foods Inc.
Ukrop's Super Markets
Unilever Home & Personal Care U.S.A.
Unilever United States, Inc.
Union Camp Corp.
Union Carbide Corp.
United Airlines Inc.
United Co.
United Dominion Industries, Ltd.
United Parcel Service of America Inc.
U.S. Bancorp
U.S. Bancorp Piper Jaffray
United States Sugar Corp.
United States Trust Co. of New York
Universal Foods Corp.
Universal Leaf Tobacco Co., Inc.
Unocal Corp.
UnumProvident
USAA Life Insurance Co.
Valmont Industries, Inc.
Valspar Corp.
Vanguard Group
Vesper Corp.
Wachovia Bank of North Carolina NA
Wachtell, Lipton, Rosen & Katz
Waffle House Inc.
Waldbaum's Supermarkets, Inc.
Walter Industries Inc.
Warner-Lambert Co.
Washington Mutual, Inc.
The Washington Post
Washington Trust Bank
Webster Bank
Weil, Gotshal & Manges Corp.
West Co. Inc.
Western & Southern Life Insurance Co.
Westvaco Corp.
Weyerhaeuser Co.
Whirlpool Corp.
Whitman Corp.
WICOR, Inc.
Wilbur-Ellis Co. & Connell Brothers Co.
Wiley & Sons (John)
Williams
Wisconsin Energy Corp.
Wisconsin Power & Light Co.
Witco Corp.
Woodward Governor Co.
Wyman-Gordon Co.
York Federal Savings & Loan Association
Young & Rubicam
Zachry Co. (H.B.)
Zilkha & Sons

PUBLIC EDUCATION (PRECOLLEGE)

Abbott Laboratories
ABC
Advanced Micro Devices, Inc.
AEGON U.S.A. Inc.
Aetna, Inc.
AK Steel Corp.
Alabama Power Co.
Alcoa Inc.
Alcon Laboratories, Inc.
Alexander & Baldwin, Inc.
Allegheny Technologies Inc.
Alliant Techsystems
AlliedSignal Inc.
Allmerica Financial Corp.
AMCORE Bank Rockford
Ameren Corp.
America West Airlines, Inc.
American Express Co.
American Fidelity Corp.
American General Finance
American Honda Motor Co., Inc.
American Standard Inc.
Ameritas Life Insurance Corp.
Ameritech Corp.
Ameritech Indiana
Ameritech Ohio
Ameritech Wisconsin
AmerUS Group
AMETEK, Inc.
Amgen, Inc.
AMP Inc.
AMR Corp.
Andersen Corp.
Andersons Inc.
Anheuser-Busch Companies, Inc.
Aon Corp.
APL Ltd.
Apple Computer, Inc.
Arizona Public Service Co.
Armstrong World Industries, Inc.
Arvin Industries, Inc.
ASARCO Inc.
Ashland, Inc.
AT&T Corp.
Atlantic Richfield Co.
Auburn Foundry
Avista Corporation
Badger Meter, Inc.
Bank One, Texas-Houston Office
BankBoston-Connecticut Region
BankBoston Corp.
Barden Corp.
Barnes Group Inc.
Battelle Memorial Institute
Baxter International Inc.
Bayer Corp.
Bechtel Group, Inc.
Belk Stores Services Inc.
Bell Atlantic Corp.
BellSouth Corp.
Bemis Co., Inc.
Bemis Manufacturing Co.
Bernstein & Co., Inc. (Sanford C.)
Bestfoods
Bethlehem Steel Corp.
BFGoodrich Co.
Binney & Smith Inc.
Blair & Co. (William)
Block, Inc. (H&R)
Blount International, Inc.
Blue Bell, Inc.
Blue Cross & Blue Shield of Alabama
Blue Cross & Blue Shield of Iowa
Boeing Co.
Borden, Inc.
Boston Globe (The)
Bourns, Inc.
BP Amoco Corp.
Bridgestone/Firestone, Inc.
Briggs & Stratton Corp.
Broderbund Software, Inc.
Bucyrus-Erie Co.
Burlington Industries, Inc.
Burlington Resources, Inc.
Burnett Co. (Leo)
Burress (J.W.)
Butler Manufacturing Co.
Cabot Corp.
California Bank & Trust
Campbell Soup Co.
Cargill Inc.
Carillon Importers, Ltd.
Caterpillar Inc.
CCB Financial Corp.
Central Maine Power Co.
Central Soya Co.
CertainTeed Corp.
Cessna Aircraft Co.
CGU Insurance
Champion International Corp.
Chase Bank of Texas
Chase Manhattan Bank, NA
Chemed Corp.
Chesapeake Corp.
Chevron Corp.
Chicago Sun-Times, Inc.
Chicago Title Corp.
Chicago Tribune Co.
CIGNA Corp.
Cincinnati Bell Inc.
Cinergy Corp.
Circuit City Stores, Inc.
CIT Group, Inc. (The)
Citibank Corp.
Citigroup
CLARCOR Inc.
Cleveland-Cliffs, Inc.
Clorox Co.
CNA
Coca-Cola Co.
Colonial Life & Accident Insurance Co.
Colonial Oil Industries, Inc.
Comerica Inc.
Commerce Bancshares, Inc.
Commercial Intertech Corp.
Compass Bank
ConAgra, Inc.
Cone Mills Corp.
Conoco, Inc.
Consolidated Natural Gas Co.
Consumers Energy Co.
Contran Corp.
Conwood Co. LP
Cooper Industries, Inc.
Coors Brewing Co.
Corning Inc.
Country Curtains, Inc.
Cox Enterprises Inc.
Crane Co.
Crane & Co., Inc.
Credit Suisse First Boston
Crestar Finance Corp.
Cummins Engine Co., Inc.
CUNA Mutual Group
DaimlerChrysler Corp.
Dain Bosworth Inc.
Dana Corp.
Dayton Hudson
Dayton Power and Light Co.
Deere & Co.
DeKalb Genetics Corp.
Deposit Guaranty National Bank
Detroit Edison Co.
Dexter Corp.
Dial Corp.
Dixie Group, Inc. (The)
Donaldson Co., Inc.
Dow Chemical Co.
Dreyer's Grand Ice Cream
du Pont de Nemours & Co. (E.I.)
Duchossois Industries Inc.
Duke Energy
Duriron Co., Inc.
Eastman Kodak Co.
Eaton Corp.
Eckerd Corp.
Ecolab Inc.
Edwards Enterprise Software (J.D.)
El Paso Energy Co.
Emerson Electric Co.
EMI Music Publishing
Employers Mutual Casualty Co.
Ensign-Bickford Industries
Erving Industries
Evening Post Publishing Co.
Exxon Mobil Corp.
Fabri-Kal Corp.
Farmers Group, Inc.
Federal-Mogul Corp.
Federated Department Stores, Inc.
Federated Mutual Insurance Co.
Ferro Corp.
Fifth Third Bancorp
FINA
Fireman's Fund Insurance Co.
First Hawaiian, Inc.
First Source Corp.
First Tennessee National Corp.
First Union Corp.
Fisher Brothers Cleaning Services
FleetBoston Financial Corp.
Florida Power & Light Co.
Fluor Corp.
Forbes Inc.
Ford Meter Box Co.
Ford Motor Co.
Fort Worth Star-Telegram Inc.
Fortis Insurance Co.
Fortune Brands, Inc.
Freeport-McMoRan Inc.
Frontier Corp.
Frost National Bank
Furniture Brands International, Inc.
Gallo Winery, Inc. (E&J)
Gap, Inc.
GenAmerica Corp.
GenCorp
Genentech Inc.
General Atlantic Partners II LP
General Electric Co.
General Mills, Inc.
General Motors Corp.
Georgia Power Co.
Gerber Products Co.
Giddings & Lewis
Glaxo Wellcome Inc.
Globe Corp.
Goldman Sachs Group
Golub Corp.
Grace & Co. (W.R.)
Graco, Inc.
Grede Foundries
Gulfstream Aerospace Corp.
Hallmark Cards Inc.
Harcourt General, Inc.
Harley-Davidson Co.
Harnischfeger Industries
Harris Corp.
Harris Trust & Savings Bank

Harsco Corp.
Hartford (The)
Hartmarx Corp.
Hasbro, Inc.
Hawaiian Electric Co., Inc.
Heinz Co. (H.J.)
Heller Financial, Inc.
Hewlett-Packard Co.
Hickory Tech Corp.
Hitachi America Ltd.
Hoffer Plastics Corp.
Honeywell International Inc.
HSBC Bank USA
Hubbard Broadcasting, Inc.
Hubbell Inc.
Huffy Corp.
Humana, Inc.
Hunt Manufacturing Co.
IBP
IKON Office Solutions, Inc.
Illinois Power Co.
Independent Stave Co.
Industrial Bank of Japan Trust Co. (New York)
Inland Container Corp.
Inman Mills
Intel Corp.
International Business Machines Corp.
International Flavors & Fragrances Inc.
International Multifoods Corp.
International Paper Co.
INTRUST Financial Corp.
Invacare Corp.
Jacobson & Sons (Benjamin)
Jeld-wen, Inc.
Johnson Controls Inc.
Johnson & Son (S.C.)
Jostens, Inc.
Journal-Gazette Co.
Kellwood Co.
Kennametal, Inc.
Kimball International, Inc.
Kingsbury Corp.
Koch Enterprises, Inc.
Kraft Foods, Inc.
Kroger Co.
La-Z-Boy Inc.
Lance, Inc.
Land O'Lakes, Inc.
Landmark Communications Inc.
Lee Enterprises
Lehigh Portland Cement Co.
Leigh Fibers, Inc.
Levi Strauss & Co.
Leviton Manufacturing Co. Inc.
Liberty Corp.
Lilly & Co. (Eli)
Lincoln Electric Co.
Lipton Co.
Little, Inc. (Arthur D.)
Litton Industries, Inc.
Liz Claiborne, Inc.
Loews Corp.
Louisiana-Pacific Corp.
LTV Corp.
Lubrizol Corp. (The)
Lyondell Chemical Co.
MacMillan Bloedel Inc.
Madison Gas & Electric Co.
Maritz Inc.
Masco Corp.
Massachusetts Mutual Life Insurance Co.
Matsushita Electric Corp. of America
Mattel Inc.
May Department Stores Co.
Maytag Corp.
McClatchy Co.
McDonald & Co. Securities, Inc.
MCI WorldCom, Inc.
McWane Inc.
Mead Corp.
Medtronic, Inc.
Merck & Co.
Michigan Consolidated Gas Co.
Mid-America Bank of Louisville
Milliken & Co.
Millipore Corp.
Monsanto Co.
Montana Power Co.
Montgomery Ward & Co., Inc.
MONY Group (The)
Morgan & Co. Inc. (J.P.)
Morgan Stanley Dean Witter & Co.
Morrison Knudsen Corp.
Motorola Inc.
Mutual of Omaha Insurance Co.
Nabisco Group Holdings
Nalco Chemical Co.
National Bank of Commerce Trust & Savings
National City Bank of Minneapolis
National City Corp.
National Computer Systems, Inc.
National Machinery Co.
National Presto Industries, Inc.
Nationwide Insurance Co.
NEBCO Evans
Nestle U.S.A. Inc.
New England Financial
New Jersey Natural Gas Co.
New York Mercantile Exchange
New York Times Co.
Newman's Own Inc.
Nissan North America, Inc.
Nordson Corp.
Nortel
North American Royalties
Northeast Utilities
Northern Trust Co.
Northwest Bank Nebraska, NA
Norton Co.
Norwest Corp.
Occidental Oil and Gas
OG&E Electric Services
Old National Bank Evansville
Olin Corp.
Orscheln Co.
Osborne Enterprises
Oshkosh B'Gosh, Inc.
Owens Corning
Pacific Century Financial Corp.
Pacific Mutual Life Insurance Co.
PacifiCare Health Systems
PacifiCorp
Park National Bank
PECO Energy Co.
Pella Corp.
PEMCO Corp.
Penney Co., Inc. (J.C.)
Peoples Bank
Peoples Energy Corp.
Pfizer Inc.
Pharmacia & Upjohn, Inc.
Phillips Petroleum Co.
Pieper Power Electric Co.
Pillsbury Co.
PNC Bank Kentucky Inc.
Polaroid Corp.
Potomac Electric Power Co.
PPG Industries, Inc.
Price Associates (T. Rowe)
Principal Financial Group
Procter & Gamble Co.
Providence Journal-Bulletin Co.
Provident Companies, Inc.
Prudential Insurance Co. of America
Public Service Electric & Gas Co.
Publix Supermarkets
Pulitzer Publishing Co.
Putnam Investments
Quanex Corp.
Ralston Purina Co.
Rayonier Inc.
Reader's Digest Association, Inc. (The)
Red Wing Shoe Co. Inc.
Reebok International Ltd.
Reilly Industries, Inc.
Reily & Co., Inc. (William B.)
ReliaStar Financial Corp.
Reynolds Metals Co.
Reynolds & Reynolds Co.
Reynolds Tobacco (R.J.)
Rockwell International Corp.
Royal & SunAlliance USA, Inc.
Rubbermaid Inc.
Ryder System, Inc.
SAFECO Corp.
Saint Paul Companies Inc.
Salomon Smith Barney
S&T Bancorp
SBC Communications Inc.
Schloss & Co. (Marcus)
Schlumberger Ltd. (USA)
Schwab & Co., Inc. (Charles)
Schwebel Baking Co.
Seagram & Sons, Inc. (Joseph E.)
Searle & Co. (G.D.)
Security Benefit Life Insurance Co.
Sega of America Inc.
Sentinel Communications Co.
Sentry Insurance, A Mutual Co.
Servco Pacific
Shea Co. (John F.)
Shell Oil Co.
Shelter Mutual Insurance Co.
Shoney's Inc.
Sierra Pacific Industries
Sierra Pacific Resources
Simpson Investment Co.
Sonoco Products Co.
Sony Electronics
Southeastern Mutual Insurance Co.
Southern California Gas Co.
Southwest Gas Corp.
Springs Industries, Inc.
Sprint Corp.
Sprint/United Telephone
SPX Corp.
Square D Co.
Standard Products Co.
Stanley Works (The)
Star Bank NA
State Street Bank & Trust Co.
Steelcase Inc.
Stonecutter Mills Corp.
Storage Technology Corp.
Stride Rite Corp.
Sun Microsystems Inc.
Sunoco Inc.
SunTrust Bank Atlanta
Susquehanna-Pfaltzgraff Co.
Synovus Financial Corp.
Tandy Corp.
Tektronix, Inc.
Teleflex Inc.
Temple-Inland Inc.
TENNANT Co.
Tenneco Automotive
Tenneco Packaging
Tension Envelope Corp.
Tesoro Hawaii
Texaco Inc.
Texas Instruments Inc.
Textron Inc.
Thomasville Furniture Industries Inc.
Times Mirror Co.
Timken Co. (The)
TJX Companies, Inc.
Toledo Blade Co.
Tomkins Industries, Inc.
Toro Co.
Toshiba America Inc.
Toyota Motor Sales U.S.A., Inc.
True Oil Co.
TRW Inc.
Tyson Foods Inc.
Ukrop's Super Markets
Unilever United States, Inc.
Union Camp Corp.
Union Carbide Corp.
United Airlines Inc.
United Distillers & Vintners North America
United Dominion Industries, Ltd.
United Parcel Service of America Inc.
U.S. Bancorp
U.S. Bancorp Piper Jaffray
United States Sugar Corp.
United States Trust Co. of New York
United Technologies Corp.
Universal Foods Corp.
Universal Leaf Tobacco Co., Inc.
Unocal Corp.
UnumProvident
USG Corp.
USX Corp.
Varian Medical Systems, Inc.
Vulcan Materials Co.
Wachovia Bank of North Carolina NA
Waffle House Inc.
Wal-Mart Stores, Inc.
Washington Mutual, Inc.
The Washington Post
Waste Management Inc.
Webster Bank
Wells Fargo & Co.
West Co. Inc.
Weyerhaeuser Co.
Whirlpool Corp.
WICOR, Inc.
Wilbur-Ellis Co. & Connell Brothers Co.
Wiley & Sons (John)
Williams
Wisconsin Energy Corp.
Wisconsin Public Service Corp.
Witco Corp.
Wolverine World Wide
York Federal Savings & Loan Association
Young & Rubicam
Zachry Co. (H.B.)
Zilkha & Sons

RELIGIOUS EDUCATION

Abbott Laboratories
Allmerica Financial Corp.
American Retail Group
Ameritas Life Insurance Corp.
Amsted Industries Inc.
Andersen Corp.
Aon Corp.
APL Ltd.
Archer-Daniels-Midland Co.
ASARCO Inc.
Atlantic Investment Co.
Badger Meter, Inc.
Barnes Group Inc.
Barry Corp. (R.G.)
Belk-Simpson Department Stores
Bemis Co., Inc.
Bernstein & Co., Inc. (Sanford C.)
Blair & Co. (William)
Blount International, Inc.
Borman's Inc.
Boston Edison Co.
Bourns, Inc.
Bridgestone/Firestone, Inc.
Bristol-Myers Squibb Co.
Bucyrus-Erie Co.
Burress (J.W.)
Cargill Inc.
Carnival Corp.
Central National-Gottesman
Central & South West Services
Central Soya Co.
Century 21
CertainTeed Corp.
CGU Insurance
Cincinnati Bell Inc.
Compass Bank
Constellation Energy Group, Inc.
Contran Corp.
CUNA Mutual Group
Danis Companies
Delta Air Lines, Inc.
Deluxe Corp.
Demoulas Supermarkets Inc.
Deposit Guaranty National Bank
Dexter Corp.
Domino's Pizza Inc.
Duke Energy
Dynamet, Inc.
Eastman Kodak Co.
Eaton Corp.
Federal-Mogul Corp.
Federated Department Stores, Inc.
Fifth Third Bancorp
Fireman's Fund Insurance Co.
First Hawaiian, Inc.
First Maryland Bancorp
First National Bank of Evergreen Park
First Union Securities, Inc.
Ford Meter Box Co.
Forest City Enterprises, Inc.
Fuller Co. (H.B.)
Gallo Winery, Inc. (E&J)
Galter Corp.
Gap, Inc.
GEICO Corp.

General Mills, Inc.
Giant Eagle Inc.
Giant Food Inc.
Green Bay Packaging
Halliburton Co.
Harsco Corp.
Hartford (The)
Heinz Co. (H.J.)
Hensel Phelps Construction Co.
Hickory Tech Corp.
Hofmann Co.
International Multifoods Corp.
Jacobson & Sons (Benjamin)
Johnson & Son (S.C.)
Kennametal, Inc.
Kimball International, Inc.
Koch Enterprises, Inc.
La-Z-Boy Inc.
Lance, Inc.
Lilly & Co. (Eli)
Louisiana Land & Exploration Co.
Louisiana-Pacific Corp.
Mamiye Brothers
Masco Corp.
Millipore Corp.
Monarch Machine Tool Co.
Morris Communications Corp.
MTD Products Inc.
National Machinery Co.
New York Life Insurance Co.
Northwest Bank Nebraska, NA
Occidental Petroleum Corp.
Ohio National Life Insurance Co.
Old National Bank Evansville
Orscheln Co.
Osborne Enterprises
Overseas Shipholding Group Inc.
Pacific Century Financial Corp.
Paine Webber
Physicians Mutual Insurance Co.
Premier Dental Products Co.
Procter & Gamble Co.
Procter & Gamble Co., Cosmetics Division
Prudential Insurance Co. of America
Ralph's Grocery Co.
Reily & Co., Inc. (William B.)
Revlon Inc.
Rich Products Corp.
Russer Foods
Rutledge Hill Press
Scripps Co. (E.W.)
Seagram & Sons, Inc. (Joseph E.)
Sentry Insurance, A Mutual Co.
ServiceMaster Co.
S.G. Cowen
Sierra Pacific Resources
Slant/Fin Corp.
Solo Cup Co.
Southeastern Mutual Insurance Co.
Star Bank NA
Stonecutter Mills Corp.
Strear Farms Co.
Stride Rite Corp.
SunTrust Bank Atlanta
Temple-Inland Inc.
Texaco Inc.
Thermo Electron Corp.
TJX Companies, Inc.
Tomkins Industries, Inc.
Trace International Holdings, Inc.
True North Communications, Inc.
Ukrop's Super Markets
Union Camp Corp.
Union Pacific Corp.
Universal Leaf Tobacco Co., Inc.
Valmont Industries, Inc.
Wal-Mart Stores, Inc.
Westvaco Corp.
Wilbur-Ellis Co. & Connell Brothers Co.
Young & Rubicam

SCHOOL VOLUNTEERISM

Allmerica Financial Corp.
Allstate Insurance Co.
American Retail Group
AMP Inc.
AMR Corp.
APL Ltd.
BellSouth Corp.
Blair & Co. (William)
Carolina Power & Light Co.
Chesapeake Corp.
Chicago Title Corp.
Clorox Co.
Cox Enterprises Inc.
Credit Suisse First Boston
Cummings Properties Management
Daily News
Dayton Hudson
Deposit Guaranty National Bank
Detroit Edison Co.
Dreyer's Grand Ice Cream
Eastman Kodak Co.
Ecolab Inc.
Edwards Enterprise Software (J.D.)
El Paso Energy Co.
FINA
Freddie Mac
Furniture Brands International, Inc.
Gap, Inc.
Hasbro, Inc.
International Flavors & Fragrances Inc.
Kimberly-Clark Corp.
Kingsbury Corp.
Levi Strauss & Co.
Little, Inc. (Arthur D.)
Mitsubishi Electric America
Montgomery Ward & Co., Inc.
Morgan Stanley Dean Witter & Co.
National City Bank of Minneapolis
National Machinery Co.
New England Bio Labs
New York Times Co.
Pacific Mutual Life Insurance Co.
Prudential Insurance Co. of America
Prudential Securities Inc.
Reinhart Institutional Foods
Reynolds Tobacco (R.J.)
SBC Communications Inc.
Schwab & Co., Inc. (Charles)
Sega of America Inc.
Simpson Investment Co.
State Street Bank & Trust Co.
Stride Rite Corp.
Titan Industrial Corp.
Tomkins Industries, Inc.
Ukrop's Super Markets
Union Carbide Corp.
United Airlines Inc.
Vesper Corp.
Waffle House Inc.
Wal-Mart Stores, Inc.
Witco Corp.

SCIENCE/MATHEMATICS EDUCATION

ABB Inc.
Abbott Laboratories
Advanced Micro Devices, Inc.
Aetna, Inc.
Air Products and Chemicals, Inc.
Alabama Power Co.
Alcoa Inc.
Alcon Laboratories, Inc.
Allegheny Technologies Inc.
Alliant Techsystems
AlliedSignal Inc.
AMCORE Bank Rockford
Ameren Corp.
American Fidelity Corp.
American Honda Motor Co., Inc.
Ameritas Life Insurance Corp.
Ameritech Corp.
Ameritech Illinois
Ameritech Indiana
Ameritech Michigan
Ameritech Ohio
Ameritech Wisconsin
AMETEK, Inc.
Amgen, Inc.
AMP Inc.
AMR Corp.
Amsted Industries Inc.
Analog Devices, Inc.
Andersen Corp.
Andersons Inc.
Anheuser-Busch Companies, Inc.
Aon Corp.
Appleton Papers Inc.
Archer-Daniels-Midland Co.
Aristech Chemical Corp.
Arizona Public Service Co.
Armstrong World Industries, Inc.
Arvin Industries, Inc.
ASARCO Inc.
AT&T Corp.
Atlantic Investment Co.
Atlantic Richfield Co.
Auburn Foundry
Avon Products, Inc.
Badger Meter, Inc.
Bank of America
Bank One Corp.
Banta Corp.
Barnes Group Inc.
Battelle Memorial Institute
Bausch & Lomb Inc.
Baxter International Inc.
Bayer Corp.
Bean, Inc. (L.L.)
Bechtel Group, Inc.
Beckman Coulter, Inc.
Becton Dickinson & Co.
Belk Stores Services Inc.
Bell Atlantic Corp.
BellSouth Corp.
Bernstein & Co., Inc. (Sanford C.)
Bestfoods
Bethlehem Steel Corp.
BFGoodrich Co.
Block, Inc. (H&R)
Blount International, Inc.
Boeing Co.
Borden, Inc.
Borman's Inc.
Boston Edison Co.
Boston Globe (The)
Bourns, Inc.
BP Amoco Corp.
Bridgestone/Firestone, Inc.
Briggs & Stratton Corp.
Broderbund Software, Inc.
Brown & Williamson Tobacco Corp.
Brunswick Corp.
Bucyrus-Erie Co.
Burlington Industries, Inc.
Burlington Resources, Inc.
Burnett Co. (Leo)
Cabot Corp.
Cadence Designs Systems, Inc.
Campbell Soup Co.
Carillon Importers, Ltd.
Carpenter Technology Corp.
Carrier Corp.
Carris Reels
Caterpillar Inc.
Cenex Harvest States
Central Maine Power Co.
Central National-Gottesman
Central & South West Services
Central Soya Co.
Cessna Aircraft Co.
CGU Insurance
Chase Manhattan Bank, NA
Chesapeake Corp.
Chevron Corp.
Citibank Corp.
Citigroup
Cleveland-Cliffs, Inc.
Clorox Co.
CNA
Coca-Cola Co.
Collins & Aikman Corp.
Comdisco, Inc.
Compaq Computer Corp.
Compass Bank
Conoco, Inc.
Consolidated Natural Gas Co.
Consolidated Papers, Inc.
Constellation Energy Group, Inc.
Consumers Energy Co.
Cooper Industries, Inc.
Coors Brewing Co.
Corning Inc.
Crane Co.
Crane & Co., Inc.
Cranston Print Works Co.
CSR Rinker Materials Corp.
Cummins Engine Co., Inc.
CUNA Mutual Group
Cyprus Amax Minerals Co.
DaimlerChrysler Corp.
Dana Corp.
Danis Companies
Dayton Power and Light Co.
Deere & Co.
DeKalb Genetics Corp.
Deloitte & Touche
Delta Air Lines, Inc.
Deposit Guaranty National Bank
Detroit Edison Co.
Disney Co. (Walt)
Donaldson Co., Inc.
Dow Chemical Co.
Dow Corning Corp.
DSM Copolymer
du Pont de Nemours & Co. (E.I.)
Duke Energy
Dynamet, Inc.
Eastern Bank
Eastman Kodak Co.
Eaton Corp.
Ecolab Inc.
Edison International
El Paso Energy Co.
Elf Atochem North America, Inc.
Emerson Electric Co.
Equitable Resources, Inc.
Erb Lumber Co.
Erving Industries
Ethyl Corp.
Exxon Mobil Corp.
Federal-Mogul Corp.
Federated Department Stores, Inc.
Fireman's Fund Insurance Co.
First American Corp.
First Hawaiian, Inc.
First Union Bank
First Union Corp.
Florida Power & Light Co.
Fluor Corp.
FMC Corp.
Forbes Inc.
Ford Meter Box Co.
Ford Motor Co.
Fortis Insurance Co.
Freddie Mac
Freeport-McMoRan Inc.
Frontier Corp.
Frost National Bank
Furniture Brands International, Inc.
Gap, Inc.
GATX Corp.
GEICO Corp.
GenAmerica Corp.
GenCorp
Genentech Inc.
General Electric Co.
General Mills, Inc.
General Motors Corp.
Georgia-Pacific Corp.
Georgia Power Co.
Gerber Products Co.
Giant Food Inc.
Glaxo Wellcome Inc.
Golub Corp.
Grace & Co. (W.R.)
Graco, Inc.
Grede Foundries
Green Bay Packaging
GTE Corp.
Gulfstream Aerospace Corp.
Halliburton Co.
Hallmark Cards Inc.
Hamilton Sundstrand Corp.
Hancock Financial Services (John)
Hanna Co. (M.A.)
Harnischfeger Industries
Harris Trust & Savings Bank
Harsco Corp.
Hartford (The)
Hartmarx Corp.
Hawaiian Electric Co., Inc.
Heinz Co. (H.J.)
Hensel Phelps Construction Co.
Hershey Foods Corp.
Hewlett-Packard Co.
Hickory Tech Corp.
Hitachi America Ltd.

Hoffer Plastics Corp.
Hoffmann-La Roche Inc.
HON Industries Inc.
Honeywell International Inc.
Hughes Electronics Corp.
Huntington Bancshares Inc.
Illinois Power Co.
Illinois Tool Works, Inc.
Industrial Bank of Japan Trust Co. (New York)
Inland Container Corp.
Intel Corp.
International Business Machines Corp.
International Flavors & Fragrances Inc.
International Multifoods Corp.
International Paper Co.
Jeld-wen, Inc.
Johnson Controls Inc.
Johnson & Son (S.C.)
Kemper National Insurance Companies
Kerr-McGee Corp.
Kimball International, Inc.
Kimberly-Clark Corp.
Kingsbury Corp.
KPMG Peat Marwick LLP
Kroger Co.
Ladish Co., Inc.
Landmark Communications Inc.
Lee Enterprises
Lehigh Portland Cement Co.
Leigh Fibers, Inc.
Lennox International, Inc.
Levi Strauss & Co.
Leviton Manufacturing Co. Inc.
LG&E Energy Corp.
Liberty Corp.
Liberty Diversified Industries
Lilly & Co. (Eli)
Lipton Co.
Little, Inc. (Arthur D.)
Litton Industries, Inc.
Liz Claiborne, Inc.
Lotus Development Corp.
Louisiana Land & Exploration Co.
Louisiana-Pacific Corp.
LTV Corp.
Lubrizol Corp. (The)
MacMillan Bloedel Inc.
Mallinckrodt Chemical, Inc.
Mark IV Industries
Masco Corp.
Mattel Inc.
May Department Stores Co.
McCormick & Co. Inc.
MCI WorldCom, Inc.
Mead Corp.
Medtronic, Inc.
Mercantile Bank NA
Merck & Co.
Merrill Lynch & Co., Inc.
Metropolitan Life Insurance Co.
Milacron, Inc.
Milliken & Co.
Millipore Corp.
Mine Safety Appliances Co.
Minnesota Mining & Manufacturing Co.
Minnesota Mutual Life Insurance Co.
Mitsubishi Electric America
Monsanto Co.
Montana Power Co.
Morgan & Co. Inc. (J.P.)
Morris Communications Corp.
Motorola Inc.
MTS Systems Corp.
Nalco Chemical Co.
National Computer Systems, Inc.
National Machinery Co.
National Presto Industries, Inc.
National Starch & Chemical Co.
NEBCO Evans
NEC America, Inc.
Nestle U.S.A. Inc.
New Century Energies
New England Bio Labs
New York Times Co.
Nissan North America, Inc.
Nordson Corp.
Norfolk Southern Corp.
North American Royalties
Northeast Utilities
Norton Co.
Novartis Corporation
Occidental Oil and Gas
Occidental Petroleum Corp.
OG&E Electric Services
Oklahoma Publishing Co.
Olin Corp.
Orange & Rockland Utilities, Inc.
Oshkosh B'Gosh, Inc.
PACCAR Inc.
Pacific Century Financial Corp.
Pacific Gas and Electric Co.
PacifiCorp
Pella Corp.
Pennzoil-Quaker State Co.
PerkinElmer, Inc.
Pfizer Inc.
Pharmacia & Upjohn, Inc.
Phelps Dodge Corp.
Pheonix Financial Group
Phillips Petroleum Co.
Pioneer Hi-Bred International, Inc.
Pitney Bowes Inc.
Pittway Corp.
Polaroid Corp.
Portland General Electric Co.
Potlatch Corp.
Potomac Electric Power Co.
PPG Industries, Inc.
Premier Dental Products Co.
Premier Industrial Corp.
Principal Financial Group
Procter & Gamble Co.
Procter & Gamble Co., Cosmetics Division
Provident Companies, Inc.
Prudential Insurance Co. of America
Public Service Electric & Gas Co.
Pulitzer Publishing Co.
Ralph's Grocery Co.
Ralston Purina Co.
Rayonier Inc.
Red Wing Shoe Co. Inc.
Reily & Co., Inc. (William B.)
Revlon Inc.
Reynolds Metals Co.
Reynolds Tobacco (R.J.)
Rockwell International Corp.
Royal & SunAlliance USA, Inc.
Rubbermaid Inc.
Ruddick Corp.
Ryder System, Inc.
SBC Communications Inc.
Schering-Plough Corp.
Schlumberger Ltd. (USA)
Schwab & Co., Inc. (Charles)
Scripps Co. (E.W.)
Seagram & Sons, Inc. (Joseph E.)
Searle & Co. (G.D.)
Sega of America Inc.
Sempra Energy
Sentry Insurance, A Mutual Co.
Shea Co. (John F.)
Shell Oil Co.
Sherwin-Williams Co.
Sierra Pacific Resources
Simplot Co. (J.R.)
Simpson Investment Co.
Slant/Fin Corp.
SmithKline Beecham Corp.
Solo Cup Co.
Sonoco Products Co.
Sony Electronics
Southern California Gas Co.
Southern New England Telephone Co.
Sprint Corp.
SPX Corp.
Stanley Works (The)
Starwood Hotels & Resorts Worldwide, Inc.
State Farm Mutual Automobile Insurance Co.
State Street Bank & Trust Co.
Stone Container Corp.
Stonecutter Mills Corp.
Storage Technology Corp.
Stride Rite Corp.
Stupp Brothers Bridge & Iron Co.
Sun Microsystems Inc.
Sunoco Inc.
SunTrust Bank Atlanta
Tamko Roofing Products
TCF National Bank Minnesota
Tektronix, Inc.
Tenneco Automotive
Tenneco Packaging
Tesoro Hawaii
Texaco Inc.
Texas Instruments Inc.
Textron Inc.
Thermo Electron Corp.
Thomasville Furniture Industries Inc.
Timken Co. (The)
Tomkins Industries, Inc.
Toshiba America Inc.
Toyota Motor Sales U.S.A., Inc.
Transamerica Corp.
True North Communications, Inc.
TRW Inc.
Tyson Foods Inc.
Ukrop's Super Markets
Unilever Home & Personal Care U.S.A.
Unilever United States, Inc.
Union Camp Corp.
Union Carbide Corp.
Union Pacific Corp.
Unisys Corp.
United Airlines Inc.
United Distillers & Vintners North America
United Parcel Service of America Inc.
United States Sugar Corp.
United Technologies Corp.
Universal Foods Corp.
Universal Leaf Tobacco Co., Inc.
Unocal Corp.
UnumProvident
US West, Inc.
USX Corp.
Valspar Corp.
Varian Medical Systems, Inc.
Vodafone AirTouch Plc
Vulcan Materials Co.
Wachovia Bank of North Carolina NA
Wal-Mart Stores, Inc.
Warner-Lambert Co.
Washington Mutual, Inc.
The Washington Post
Waste Management Inc.
Western & Southern Life Insurance Co.
Westvaco Corp.
Weyerhaeuser Co.
Whirlpool Corp.
Whitman Corp.
Wilbur-Ellis Co. & Connell Brothers Co.
Wiley & Sons (John)
Williams
Wisconsin Energy Corp.
Wisconsin Public Service Corp.
Wyman-Gordon Co.
Xerox Corp.

SECONDARY EDUCATION (PRIVATE)

Aetna, Inc.
Alcon Laboratories, Inc.
Alexander & Baldwin, Inc.
Allegheny Technologies Inc.
Alma Piston Co.
AMCORE Bank Rockford
American Retail Group
American Standard Inc.
Ameritas Life Insurance Corp.
AMP Inc.
Andersons Inc.
Anheuser-Busch Companies, Inc.
APL Ltd.
Archer-Daniels-Midland Co.
ASARCO Inc.
Atlantic Investment Co.
Badger Meter, Inc.
Banta Corp.
Barnes Group Inc.
Baxter International Inc.
Binney & Smith Inc.
Blair & Co. (William)
Blount International, Inc.
Blue Cross & Blue Shield of Alabama
Boler Co.
Bradford & Co. (J.C.)
Broderbund Software, Inc.
Brunswick Corp.
Burress (J.W.)
Butler Capital Corp.
Carpenter Technology Corp.
Central National-Gottesman
Century 21
CertainTeed Corp.
CGU Insurance
Chesapeake Corp.
CIT Group, Inc. (The)
Cleveland-Cliffs, Inc.
Commerce Bancshares, Inc.
Consolidated Papers, Inc.
Cooper Tire & Rubber Co.
Copley Press, Inc.
Crane Co.
Croft-Leominster
Cummings Properties Management
Dain Bosworth Inc.
Danis Companies
Deere & Co.
DeKalb Genetics Corp.
Demoulas Supermarkets Inc.
Dixie Group, Inc. (The)
Dreyer's Grand Ice Cream
Eastman Kodak Co.
Edwards Enterprise Software (J.D.)
Evening Post Publishing Co.
Ferro Corp.
First Hawaiian, Inc.
First National Bank of Evergreen Park
First Source Corp.
Fisher Scientific
Gallo Winery, Inc. (E&J)
Giddings & Lewis
Globe Corp.
Goldman Sachs Group
Graco, Inc.
Hanna Co. (M.A.)
Harnischfeger Industries
Hawaiian Electric Co., Inc.
Heinz Co. (H.J.)
Hickory Tech Corp.
Hofmann Co.
Hubbard Broadcasting, Inc.
Hubbell Inc.
Humana, Inc.
Invacare Corp.
Jacobson & Sons (Benjamin)
Johnson & Son (S.C.)
Journal-Gazette Co.
Katten, Muchin & Zavis
Kinder Morgn
Koch Enterprises, Inc.
LandAmerica Financial Services
Leigh Fibers, Inc.
Lilly & Co. (Eli)
Liz Claiborne, Inc.
Loews Corp.
Marshall & Ilsley Corp.
Menasha Corp.
Mid-America Bank of Louisville
Millipore Corp.
Montana Power Co.
Montgomery Ward & Co., Inc.
Morrison Knudsen Corp.
MTD Products Inc.
National Bank of Commerce Trust & Savings
National City Corp.
National Starch & Chemical Co.
Nestle U.S.A. Inc.
Nomura Holding America
Norton Co.
Old National Bank Evansville
ONEOK, Inc.
Orscheln Co.
Osborne Enterprises
Overseas Shipholding Group Inc.
PACCAR Inc.
Pacific Century Financial Corp.
Pella Corp.
Physicians Mutual Insurance Co.
Pittway Corp.
Price Associates (T. Rowe)

Procter & Gamble Co., Cosmetics Division
Providence Journal-Bulletin Co.
Prudential Insurance Co. of America
Publix Supermarkets
Quanex Corp.
Reynolds & Reynolds Co.
Reynolds Tobacco (R.J.)
Ruddick Corp.
Schloss & Co. (Marcus)
Schwab & Co., Inc. (Charles)
Security Benefit Life Insurance Co.
Sentry Insurance, A Mutual Co.
S.G. Cowen
Shea Co. (John F.)
Solo Cup Co.
Sprint Corp.
Stone Container Corp.
Strear Farms Co.
Stupp Brothers Bridge & Iron Co.
Sun Microsystems Inc.
Susquehanna-Pfaltzgraff Co.
Sverdrup Corp.
Temple-Inland Inc.
Tesoro Hawaii
Transamerica Corp.
Union Camp Corp.
United States Trust Co. of New York
Universal Leaf Tobacco Co., Inc.
Vesper Corp.
Wachovia Bank of North Carolina NA
Wachtell, Lipton, Rosen & Katz
Waffle House Inc.
Walter Industries Inc.
Washington Trust Bank
Webster Bank
Weil, Gotshal & Manges Corp.
West Co. Inc.
Whirlpool Corp.
Whitman Corp.
Wilbur-Ellis Co. & Connell Brothers Co.
Wiley & Sons (John)
Williams
Wisconsin Energy Corp.
Woodward Governor Co.
Young & Rubicam

SECONDARY EDUCATION (PUBLIC)

AEGON U.S.A. Inc.
Aetna, Inc.
Alcon Laboratories, Inc.
Alexander & Baldwin, Inc.
AMCORE Bank Rockford
American General Finance
American Honda Motor Co., Inc.
American Retail Group
American Standard Inc.
Amgen, Inc.
AMR Corp.
Andersons Inc.
Anheuser-Busch Companies, Inc.
Arizona Public Service Co.
Arvin Industries, Inc.
AT&T Corp.
Badger Meter, Inc.
Banfi Vintners
Bassett Furniture Industries
Bayer Corp.
Bechtel Group, Inc.
Binney & Smith Inc.
Blue Bell, Inc.
Borman's Inc.
Carris Reels
Central National-Gottesman
CertainTeed Corp.
CGU Insurance
Chicago Tribune Co.
CIGNA Corp.
CIT Group, Inc. (The)
Citigroup
Citizens Financial Group, Inc.
Cleveland-Cliffs, Inc.
Clorox Co.
Colonial Oil Industries, Inc.
Commerce Bancshares, Inc.
Consolidated Papers, Inc.
Consumers Energy Co.
Contran Corp.
Cooper Industries, Inc.
CPI Corp.
Crane Co.
Crestar Finance Corp.
Cummings Properties Management
CUNA Mutual Group
Dain Bosworth Inc.
Dana Corp.
Danis Companies
DeKalb Genetics Corp.
Dexter Corp.
Domino's Pizza Inc.
Donaldson Co., Inc.
Dreyer's Grand Ice Cream
Duchossois Industries Inc.
Dynamet, Inc.
Eastman Kodak Co.
Eaton Corp.
Ecolab Inc.
Ensign-Bickford Industries
Erving Industries
Exxon Mobil Corp.
Fifth Third Bancorp
Fireman's Fund Insurance Co.
First Hawaiian, Inc.
First Source Corp.
Firstar Bank Milwaukee NA
Ford Meter Box Co.
Ford Motor Co.
Freddie Mac
Fuller Co. (H.B.)
Gallo Winery, Inc. (E&J)
GEICO Corp.
GenAmerica Corp.
GenCorp
General Mills, Inc.
Georgia Power Co.
Giddings & Lewis
Graco, Inc.
Grede Foundries
Harley-Davidson Co.
Harris Corp.
Hewlett-Packard Co.
Hickory Tech Corp.
Hoffer Plastics Corp.
Hoffmann-La Roche Inc.
Hofmann Co.
HON Industries Inc.
Honeywell International Inc.
Hubbard Broadcasting, Inc.
Hubbell Inc.
Huffy Corp.
Hunt Manufacturing Co.
IBP
Illinois Power Co.
Industrial Bank of Japan Trust Co. (New York)
International Paper Co.
Invacare Corp.
ISE America
Journal-Gazette Co.
Kimball International, Inc.
Kinder Morgn
Koch Enterprises, Inc.
La-Z-Boy Inc.
Ladish Co., Inc.
Lance, Inc.
Land O'Lakes, Inc.
Lee Enterprises
Lehigh Portland Cement Co.
Litton Industries, Inc.
Louisiana-Pacific Corp.
Lowe's Companies
LTV Corp.
MacMillan Bloedel Inc.
Madison Gas & Electric Co.
Masco Corp.
Mattel Inc.
McKesson-HBOC Corp.
Mead Corp.
Mid-America Bank of Louisville
Milacron, Inc.
Millipore Corp.
Monsanto Co.
Montana Power Co.
Morris Communications Corp.
National Life of Vermont
National Machinery Co.
National Presto Industries, Inc.
National Starch & Chemical Co.
NEBCO Evans
New England Financial
New Jersey Natural Gas Co.
Nomura Holding America
Nordson Corp.
Norton Co.
Occidental Oil and Gas
OG&E Electric Services
ONEOK, Inc.
Orscheln Co.
Osborne Enterprises
PACCAR Inc.
Pacific Mutual Life Insurance Co.
Parker Hannifin Corp.
Pella Corp.
PEMCO Corp.
PepsiCo, Inc.
Pfizer Inc.
Phillips Petroleum Co.
Polaroid Corp.
PPG Industries, Inc.
Procter & Gamble Co.
Procter & Gamble Co., Cosmetics Division
Putnam Investments
Quanex Corp.
Ralston Purina Co.
Rayonier Inc.
Regions Bank
Reynolds Metals Co.
Reynolds Tobacco (R.J.)
Rubbermaid Inc.
Rutledge Hill Press
Safeguard Scientifics
Schwab & Co., Inc. (Charles)
Scripps Co. (E.W.)
Security Benefit Life Insurance Co.
Sega of America Inc.
Sentry Insurance, A Mutual Co.
ServiceMaster Co.
Shaw's Supermarkets, Inc.
Shea Co. (John F.)
Shell Oil Co.
Shelter Mutual Insurance Co.
Sierra Pacific Industries
Slant/Fin Corp.
Sonoco Products Co.
Sony Electronics
Southeastern Mutual Insurance Co.
Star Bank NA
Starwood Hotels & Resorts Worldwide, Inc.
State Street Bank & Trust Co.
Stonecutter Mills Corp.
Sun Microsystems Inc.
Tamko Roofing Products
TCF National Bank Minnesota
Temple-Inland Inc.
Tesoro Hawaii
Texaco Inc.
Thomasville Furniture Industries Inc.
Timken Co. (The)
Toro Co.
Toshiba America Inc.
Transamerica Corp.
Tyson Foods Inc.
Union Camp Corp.
Union Pacific Corp.
United States Sugar Corp.
Universal Foods Corp.
Unocal Corp.
Vesper Corp.
Wal-Mart Stores, Inc.
The Washington Post
Whitman Corp.
Wiley & Sons (John)
Winn-Dixie Stores Inc.
Wisconsin Energy Corp.
Woodward Governor Co.
Zachry Co. (H.B.)

SOCIAL SCIENCES EDUCATION

AlliedSignal Inc.
American Express Co.
Ameritech Corp.
Ameritech Indiana
AT&T Corp.
Binney & Smith Inc.
Block, Inc. (H&R)
Briggs & Stratton Corp.
Bristol-Myers Squibb Co.
Cargill Inc.
Carpenter Technology Corp.
CBS Corp.
Central Maine Power Co.
Circuit City Stores, Inc.
Coca-Cola Co.
Commercial Intertech Corp.
Compaq Computer Corp.
Compass Bank
Constellation Energy Group, Inc.
du Pont de Nemours & Co. (E.I.)
Duke Energy
Erving Industries
Extendicare Health Services
Farmers Group, Inc.
First Hawaiian, Inc.
First Union Corp.
Firstar Bank Milwaukee NA
FleetBoston Financial Corp.
Forbes Inc.
Fuller Co. (H.B.)
General Atlantic Partners II LP
General Mills, Inc.
Glickenhaus & Co.
Goldman Sachs Group
Halliburton Co.
Hickory Tech Corp.
Hitachi America Ltd.
Industrial Bank of Japan Trust Co. (New York)
Jacobs Engineering Group
Johnson & Son (S.C.)
Lance, Inc.
Lee Enterprises
Levi Strauss & Co.
Litton Industries, Inc.
Loews Corp.
Macy's East Inc.
McClatchy Co.
Mid-America Bank of Louisville
Minnesota Mining & Manufacturing Co.
Mitsubishi Electric America
MONY Group (The)
Morgan & Co. Inc. (J.P.)
Nalco Chemical Co.
Niagara Mohawk Holdings Inc.
Nordson Corp.
Pittway Corp.
Prudential Insurance Co. of America
Red Wing Shoe Co. Inc.
Revlon Inc.
Rouse Co.
Saint Paul Companies Inc.
Schwebel Baking Co.
Seagram & Sons, Inc. (Joseph E.)
Sunmark Capital Corp.
Tamko Roofing Products
Texas Instruments Inc.
Thompson Co. (J. Walter)
Trace International Holdings, Inc.
Union Camp Corp.
Union Pacific Corp.
United Distillers & Vintners North America
United Wisconsin Services
Unocal Corp.
US West, Inc.
Whirlpool Corp.
Wisconsin Energy Corp.
Zilkha & Sons

SPECIAL EDUCATION

AFLAC Inc.
AGL Resources Inc.
Agrilink Foods, Inc.
AlliedSignal Inc.
AMCORE Bank Rockford
Andersen Corp.
Anheuser-Busch Companies, Inc.
Associated Food Stores
Atlantic Investment Co.
Avon Products, Inc.
Banfi Vintners
Bard, Inc. (C.R.)
Barnes Group Inc.
BellSouth Corp.
Bernstein & Co., Inc. (Sanford C.)
Binney & Smith Inc.
Blair & Co. (William)
Block, Inc. (H&R)
Blount International, Inc.
Blue Cross & Blue Shield of Alabama
Boeing Co.
Boise Cascade Corp.
Borden, Inc.
Boston Globe (The)
Bridgestone/Firestone, Inc.
Bristol-Myers Squibb Co.
Brown Shoe Co., Inc.

Burress (J.W.)
Cabot Corp.
Cargill Inc.
CBS Corp.
Central National-Gottesman
Central Newspapers, Inc.
Central Soya Co.
Cessna Aircraft Co.
Chase Manhattan Bank, NA
Chesapeake Corp.
Chicago Board of Trade
CIGNA Corp.
Cincinnati Bell Inc.
CIT Group, Inc. (The)
Citibank Corp.
Clorox Co.
Colonial Oil Industries, Inc.
Commercial Intertech Corp.
Compass Bank
Constellation Energy Group, Inc.
Cox Enterprises Inc.
CPI Corp.
Credit Suisse First Boston
Crestar Finance Corp.
CSS Industries, Inc.
Daily News
Dain Bosworth Inc.
Dana Corp.
Dayton Hudson
DeKalb Genetics Corp.
Delta Air Lines, Inc.
Deluxe Corp.
Demoulas Supermarkets Inc.
Deposit Guaranty National Bank
Disney Co. (Walt)
Donaldson Co., Inc.
Duchossois Industries Inc.
Dynamet, Inc.
Eastman Kodak Co.
Ecolab Inc.
Edison International
Edwards Enterprise Software (J.D.)
Enterprise Rent-A-Car Co.
Equifax Inc.
Equitable Resources, Inc.
Exxon Mobil Corp.
Federated Department Stores, Inc.
Fifth Third Bancorp
First Hawaiian, Inc.
First Union Bank
First Union Corp.
Forbes Inc.
Fort Worth Star-Telegram Inc.
Fortune Brands, Inc.
Freddie Mac
Freeport-McMoRan Inc.
Fuller Co. (H.B.)
Furniture Brands International, Inc.
GATX Corp.
GEICO Corp.
General Mills, Inc.
Georgia-Pacific Corp.
Giant Eagle Inc.
Giant Food Inc.
Glickenhaus & Co.
Globe Corp.
Grace & Co. (W.R.)
Graco, Inc.
Hallmark Cards Inc.
Hancock Financial Services (John)
Hannaford Brothers Co.
Harcourt General, Inc.
Hartford (The)
Hartford Steam Boiler Inspection & Insurance Co.
Hasbro, Inc.
Heinz Co. (H.J.)
Hitachi America Ltd.
Honeywell International Inc.
Hubbard Broadcasting, Inc.
Humana, Inc.
IKON Office Solutions, Inc.
International Business Machines Corp.
International Multifoods Corp.
Johnson & Son (S.C.)
Journal-Gazette Co.
Kellwood Co.
Kimberly-Clark Corp.
Koch Industries, Inc.
La-Z-Boy Inc.
Ladish Co., Inc.
Lehigh Portland Cement Co.
Liberty Corp.
Little, Inc. (Arthur D.)
Lotus Development Corp.
Macy's East Inc.
Madison Gas & Electric Co.
Mattel Inc.
McDonald's Corp.
MCI WorldCom, Inc.
McKesson-HBOC Corp.
Mercantile Bank NA
Merrill Lynch & Co., Inc.
Milacron, Inc.
Milliken & Co.
Mine Safety Appliances Co.
Mitsubishi Electric America
Montgomery Ward & Co., Inc.
Morgan Stanley Dean Witter & Co.
Nabisco Group Holdings
Nalco Chemical Co.
National Computer Systems, Inc.
NEC America, Inc.
New England Financial
New York Mercantile Exchange
New York Times Co.
Norfolk Southern Corp.
Northern Trust Co.
OG&E Electric Services
Old National Bank Evansville
Pacific Mutual Life Insurance Co.
PacifiCare Health Systems
Pella Corp.
Penney Co., Inc. (J.C.)
Phillips Petroleum Co.
Physicians Mutual Insurance Co.
Polaroid Corp.
Premier Dental Products Co.
Procter & Gamble Co.
Providence Journal-Bulletin Co.
Prudential Insurance Co. of America
Pulitzer Publishing Co.
Quaker Chemical Corp.
Ralph's Grocery Co.
Ralston Purina Co.
Rayonier Inc.
Red Wing Shoe Co. Inc.
Regions Bank
Reynolds Tobacco (R.J.)
Rich Products Corp.
Rockwell International Corp.
Safeguard Scientifics
Schloss & Co. (Marcus)
Schlumberger Ltd. (USA)
Schwab & Co., Inc. (Charles)
Schwebel Baking Co.
Scripps Co. (E.W.)
Sega of America Inc.
Shelter Mutual Insurance Co.
Smurfit-Stone Container Corp.
Sony Electronics
Southeastern Mutual Insurance Co.
Sprint Corp.
Star Bank NA
Stone Container Corp.
Storage Technology Corp.
SunTrust Bank Atlanta
Synovus Financial Corp.
TENNANT Co.
Tenneco Packaging
Texaco Inc.
Texas Instruments Inc.
TJX Companies, Inc.
TMC Investment Co.
Transamerica Corp.
True North Communications, Inc.
Trustmark Insurance Co.
Tyson Foods Inc.
Union Camp Corp.
Union Carbide Corp.
Union Pacific Corp.
United Parcel Service of America Inc.
United States Sugar Corp.
United States Trust Co. of New York
US Bank, Washington
USX Corp.
Vulcan Materials Co.
Waffle House Inc.
Wal-Mart Stores, Inc.
Washington Mutual, Inc.
Washington Trust Bank
Webster Bank
Western & Southern Life Insurance Co.
Wilbur-Ellis Co. & Connell Brothers Co.
Young & Rubicam

STUDENT AID

Abbott Laboratories
ABC
AEGON U.S.A. Inc.
Aetna, Inc.
Agrilink Foods, Inc.
AK Steel Corp.
Alcoa Inc.
Alcon Laboratories, Inc.
Allegheny Technologies Inc.
Alliant Techsystems
AlliedSignal Inc.
Allmerica Financial Corp.
Allstate Insurance Co.
Alma Piston Co.
Ameren Corp.
American General Finance
American Honda Motor Co., Inc.
American Retail Group
American Standard Inc.
American United Life Insurance Co.
Ameritech Ohio
AMETEK, Inc.
Amgen, Inc.
AMR Corp.
Andersen Corp.
Anheuser-Busch Companies, Inc.
Aon Corp.
Appleton Papers Inc.
Archer-Daniels-Midland Co.
Aristech Chemical Corp.
Armstrong World Industries, Inc.
Arvin Industries, Inc.
ASARCO Inc.
Ashland, Inc.
Associated Food Stores
AT&T Corp.
Atlantic Investment Co.
Atlantic Richfield Co.
Avon Products, Inc.
Badger Meter, Inc.
Bandag, Inc.
Banfi Vintners
Bank of America
Bank One, Texas-Houston Office
Banta Corp.
Barclays Capital
Bard, Inc. (C.R.)
Barden Corp.
Bardes Corp.
Barnes Group Inc.
Barry Corp. (R.G.)
Baxter International Inc.
Bechtel Group, Inc.
Bell Atlantic Corp.
Bemis Co., Inc.
Bernstein & Co., Inc. (Sanford C.)
Bestfoods
Bethlehem Steel Corp.
BFGoodrich Co.
Binney & Smith Inc.
Blair & Co. (William)
Block, Inc. (H&R)
Blount International, Inc.
Blue Bell, Inc.
Blue Cross & Blue Shield of Alabama
Blue Cross & Blue Shield of Iowa
Blue Cross & Blue Shield of Minnesota
Boeing Co.
Boler Co.
Borden, Inc.
Boston Edison Co.
Boston Globe (The)
Bourns, Inc.
BP Amoco Corp.
Bradford & Co. (J.C.)
Bridgestone/Firestone, Inc.
Briggs & Stratton Corp.
Bristol-Myers Squibb Co.
Broderbund Software, Inc.
Brown Shoe Co., Inc.
Brunswick Corp.
Bucyrus-Erie Co.
Burlington Industries, Inc.
Burlington Resources, Inc.
Burnett Co. (Leo)
Butler Manufacturing Co.
Cabot Corp.
Cargill Inc.
Carillon Importers, Ltd.
Carlson Companies, Inc.
Carpenter Technology Corp.
Carter-Wallace, Inc.
Caterpillar Inc.
CBS Corp.
Cenex Harvest States
Central Maine Power Co.
Central National-Gottesman
Central Newspapers, Inc.
Central & South West Services
Central Soya Co.
Century 21
Cessna Aircraft Co.
CGU Insurance
Chase Manhattan Bank, NA
Chemed Corp.
Chesapeake Corp.
Chevron Corp.
Chicago Board of Trade
Chicago Title Corp.
Chubb Corp.
CIGNA Corp.
Cincinnati Bell Inc.
Cinergy Corp.
Circuit City Stores, Inc.
CIT Group, Inc. (The)
Citigroup
Citizens Financial Group, Inc.
Cleveland-Cliffs, Inc.
Clorox Co.
CNA
CNF Transportation, Inc.
Coca-Cola Co.
Colonial Life & Accident Insurance Co.
Comdisco, Inc.
Compaq Computer Corp.
Compass Bank
ConAgra, Inc.
Cone Mills Corp.
Consolidated Papers, Inc.
Constellation Energy Group, Inc.
Continental Grain Co.
Cooper Industries, Inc.
Copley Press, Inc.
Corning Inc.
Country Curtains, Inc.
Cox Enterprises Inc.
Crane Co.
Crane & Co., Inc.
Cranston Print Works Co.
Credit Suisse First Boston
Croft-Leominster
Crown Books
CSR Rinker Materials Corp.
CSS Industries, Inc.
Cummings Properties Management
Cummins Engine Co., Inc.
CUNA Mutual Group
Cyprus Amax Minerals Co.
DaimlerChrysler Corp.
Dain Bosworth Inc.
Dana Corp.
Danis Companies
Dayton Power and Light Co.
Deloitte & Touche
Deluxe Corp.
Demoulas Supermarkets Inc.
Detroit Edison Co.
Dexter Corp.
Dixie Group, Inc. (The)
Domino's Pizza Inc.
Donaldson Co., Inc.
Dow Chemical Co.
Dow Jones & Co., Inc.
Dreyer's Grand Ice Cream
DSM Copolymer
du Pont de Nemours & Co. (E.I.)
Duchossois Industries Inc.
Duke Energy
Dun & Bradstreet Corp.
Duriron Co., Inc.
Eastern Bank
Eastman Kodak Co.
Eaton Corp.
Ecolab Inc.
El Paso Energy Co.
Elf Atochem North America, Inc.
Emerson Electric Co.
Employers Mutual Casualty Co.
Ensign-Bickford Industries

Erving Industries
Exxon Mobil Corp.
Fannie Mae
Federal-Mogul Corp.
Federated Department Stores, Inc.
Ferro Corp.
Fifth Third Bancorp
FINA
First American Corp.
First Financial Bank
First Hawaiian, Inc.
First Maryland Bancorp
First Source Corp.
First Union Securities, Inc.
Firstar Bank Milwaukee NA
Fisher Brothers Cleaning Services
Florida Power & Light Co.
Florida Rock Industries
Fluor Corp.
FMC Corp.
Forbes Inc.
Ford Meter Box Co.
Forest City Enterprises, Inc.
Fortis, Inc.
Franklin Electric Co.
Freddie Mac
Freeport-McMoRan Inc.
Furniture Brands International, Inc.
Gallo Winery, Inc. (E&J)
GATX Corp.
GEICO Corp.
GenAmerica Corp.
GenCorp
Genentech Inc.
General Atlantic Partners II LP
General Electric Co.
General Mills, Inc.
General Motors Corp.
Georgia-Pacific Corp.
Georgia Power Co.
Gerber Products Co.
Giant Eagle Inc.
Giant Food Inc.
Giddings & Lewis
Glickenhaus & Co.
Globe Corp.
Goldman Sachs Group
Golub Corp.
Gosiger, Inc.
Grace & Co. (W.R.)
Graco, Inc.
Grede Foundries
Griffith Laboratories U.S.A.
GTE Corp.
Guess?
Gulf Power Co.
Hallmark Cards Inc.
Hamilton Sundstrand Corp.
Hanna Co. (M.A.)
Hannaford Brothers Co.
Harcourt General, Inc.
Harsco Corp.
Hartford (The)
Hartmarx Corp.
Hawaiian Electric Co., Inc.
Heinz Co. (H.J.)
Hensel Phelps Construction Co.
Hickory Tech Corp.
Hofmann Co.
HON Industries Inc.
Honeywell International Inc.
Hubbard Broadcasting, Inc.
Hubbell Inc.
Huffy Corp.
Humana, Inc.
Hunt Manufacturing Co.
Huntington Bancshares Inc.
IKON Office Solutions, Inc.
Illinois Tool Works, Inc.
Inland Container Corp.
Inman Mills
Intel Corp.
International Flavors & Fragrances Inc.
INTRUST Financial Corp.
Invacare Corp.
Jacobs Engineering Group
Jacobson & Sons (Benjamin)
Jeld-wen, Inc.
Johnson Controls Inc.
Johnson & Son (S.C.)
Journal-Gazette Co.
Kemper National Insurance Companies
Kennametal, Inc.
Kerr-McGee Corp.
Kimberly-Clark Corp.
Kingsbury Corp.
Koch Enterprises, Inc.
Koch Industries, Inc.
KPMG Peat Marwick LLP
Kroger Co.
Laclede Gas Co.
Ladish Co., Inc.
Lance, Inc.
Land O'Lakes, Inc.
LandAmerica Financial Services
Landmark Communications Inc.
Lehigh Portland Cement Co.
Lennox International, Inc.
Levi Strauss & Co.
Leviton Manufacturing Co. Inc.
LG&E Energy Corp.
Liberty Corp.
Lincoln Electric Co.
Lipton Co.
Little, Inc. (Arthur D.)
Litton Industries, Inc.
Loews Corp.
Louisiana Land & Exploration Co.
Louisiana-Pacific Corp.
LTV Corp.
Lubrizol Corp. (The)
MacMillan Bloedel Inc.
Madison Gas & Electric Co.
Mamiye Brothers
Mark IV Industries
Marshall Field's
Marshall & Ilsley Corp.
Mattel Inc.
May Department Stores Co.
Mazda North American Operations
McCormick & Co. Inc.
McDonald & Co. Securities, Inc.
McGraw-Hill Companies, Inc.
MCI WorldCom, Inc.
McKesson-HBOC Corp.
McWane Inc.
Medtronic, Inc.
Memphis Light Gas & Water Division
Merrill Lynch & Co., Inc.
Metropolitan Life Insurance Co.
MFA Inc.
Michigan Consolidated Gas Co.
MidAmerican Energy Holdings Co.
Milacron, Inc.
Millipore Corp.
Minnesota Mining & Manufacturing Co.
Mitsubishi Electric America
Monarch Machine Tool Co.
Montana Power Co.
Montgomery Ward & Co., Inc.
Morgan & Co. Inc. (J.P.)
Morris Communications Corp.
Morrison Knudsen Corp.
Motorola Inc.
Nabisco Group Holdings
Nalco Chemical Co.
National Bank of Commerce Trust & Savings
National City Bank of Minneapolis
National Computer Systems, Inc.
National Presto Industries, Inc.
National Starch & Chemical Co.
Nationwide Insurance Co.
NCR Corp.
NEBCO Evans
Nestle U.S.A. Inc.
New England Financial
New Jersey Natural Gas Co.
New York Stock Exchange, Inc.
New York Times Co.
Nomura Holding America
Nordson Corp.
Norfolk Southern Corp.
North American Royalties
Northern States Power Co.
Northern Trust Co.
Norton Co.
Norwest Corp.
Occidental Oil and Gas
Occidental Petroleum Corp.
Ohio National Life Insurance Co.
Old Kent Bank
Old National Bank Evansville
Olin Corp.
Orscheln Co.
Osborne Enterprises
Oshkosh B'Gosh, Inc.
Owens Corning
Pacific Century Financial Corp.
Pacific Mutual Life Insurance Co.
Paine Webber
Parker Hannifin Corp.
Pella Corp.
PEMCO Corp.
Pennzoil-Quaker State Co.
PepsiCo, Inc.
Pfizer Inc.
Pharmacia & Upjohn, Inc.
Phelps Dodge Corp.
Pheonix Financial Group
Philips Electronics North America Corp.
Phillips Petroleum Co.
Pillsbury Co.
Pittway Corp.
PNC Bank Kentucky Inc.
PNC Financial Services Group
Polaroid Corp.
Portland General Electric Co.
Potomac Electric Power Co.
PPG Industries, Inc.
Praxair
Premier Dental Products Co.
Premier Industrial Corp.
Price Associates (T. Rowe)
Principal Financial Group
Procter & Gamble Co.
Procter & Gamble Co., Cosmetics Division
Providence Journal-Bulletin Co.
Provident Companies, Inc.
Prudential Insurance Co. of America
Prudential Securities Inc.
Publix Supermarkets
Pulitzer Publishing Co.
Putnam Investments
Quaker Chemical Corp.
Quanex Corp.
Ralph's Grocery Co.
Ralston Purina Co.
Rayonier Inc.
Reader's Digest Association, Inc. (The)
Regions Bank
Regis Corp.
Reilly Industries, Inc.
Reinhart Institutional Foods
Revlon Inc.
Reynolds Metals Co.
Reynolds & Reynolds Co.
Reynolds Tobacco (R.J.)
Rich Products Corp.
Rockwell International Corp.
Rouse Co.
Ruddick Corp.
Russer Foods
Ryder System, Inc.
Saint Paul Companies Inc.
S&T Bancorp
Sara Lee Corp.
SBC Communications Inc.
Schering-Plough Corp.
Schlumberger Ltd. (USA)
Schwab & Co., Inc. (Charles)
Schwebel Baking Co.
Scripps Co. (E.W.)
Seagram & Sons, Inc. (Joseph E.)
Sega of America Inc.
Sentry Insurance, A Mutual Co.
S.G. Cowen
Shaklee Corp.
Shell Oil Co.
Shelter Mutual Insurance Co.
Sherwin-Williams Co.
Shoney's Inc.
Sierra Pacific Industries
Simplot Co. (J.R.)
Simpson Investment Co.
Smith Corp. (A.O.)
SmithKline Beecham Corp.
Smurfit-Stone Container Corp.
Solo Cup Co.
Sonoco Products Co.
Sony Electronics
Southeastern Mutual Insurance Co.
Sovereign Bank
Square D Co.
Standard Products Co.
Star Bank NA
Starwood Hotels & Resorts Worldwide, Inc.
State Farm Mutual Automobile Insurance Co.
State Street Bank & Trust Co.
Steelcase Inc.
Stone Container Corp.
Storage Technology Corp.
Stride Rite Corp.
Sumitomo Bank
Sun Microsystems Inc.
Sunoco Inc.
SunTrust Banks of Florida
Susquehanna-Pfaltzgraff Co.
Synovus Financial Corp.
TCF National Bank Minnesota
Tektronix, Inc.
TENNANT Co.
Tenneco Automotive
Texaco Inc.
Texas Instruments Inc.
Textron Inc.
Thomasville Furniture Industries Inc.
Thompson Co. (J. Walter)
Times Mirror Co.
TJX Companies, Inc.
Toledo Blade Co.
Tomkins Industries, Inc.
Toro Co.
True North Communications, Inc.
Trustmark Insurance Co.
TRW Inc.
Tyson Foods Inc.
Ukrop's Super Markets
Unilever Home & Personal Care U.S.A.
Unilever United States, Inc.
Union Camp Corp.
Union Carbide Corp.
Union Pacific Corp.
United Airlines Inc.
United Co.
United Distillers & Vintners North America
United Parcel Service of America Inc.
U.S. Bancorp Piper Jaffray
United States Sugar Corp.
United States Trust Co. of New York
United Wisconsin Services
Universal Foods Corp.
Universal Leaf Tobacco Co., Inc.
Universal Studios
Unocal Corp.
UnumProvident
US West, Inc.
USG Corp.
USX Corp.
Valmont Industries, Inc.
Varian Medical Systems, Inc.
Vodafone AirTouch Plc
Vulcan Materials Co.
Wachovia Bank of North Carolina NA
Wal-Mart Stores, Inc.
Waldbaum's Supermarkets, Inc.
Warner-Lambert Co.
The Washington Post
West Co. Inc.
Western & Southern Life Insurance Co.
Weyerhaeuser Co.
Whirlpool Corp.
Whitman Corp.
WICOR, Inc.
Williams
Winn-Dixie Stores Inc.
Wiremold Co.
Wisconsin Power & Light Co.
Wisconsin Public Service Corp.
Witco Corp.
Wolverine World Wide
Wrigley Co. (Wm. Jr.)

Wyman-Gordon Co.
Xerox Corp.
York Federal Savings & Loan Association
Young & Rubicam
Zachry Co. (H.B.)
Zilkha & Sons

VOCATIONAL & TECHNICAL EDUCATION

Aetna, Inc.
American Express Co.
AMETEK, Inc.
Amgen, Inc.
AMP Inc.
Amsted Industries Inc.
Andersen Corp.
Andersons Inc.
Anheuser-Busch Companies, Inc.
Atlantic Richfield Co.
Baird & Co. (Robert W.)
Bandag, Inc.
BankBoston Corp.
Banta Corp.
Barden Corp.
Bardes Corp.
Barnes Group Inc.
Bean, Inc. (L.L.)
Bechtel Group, Inc.
Bell Atlantic Corp.
BellSouth Corp.
Bemis Co., Inc.
Bemis Manufacturing Co.
Bethlehem Steel Corp.
Bradford & Co. (J.C.)
Bridgestone/Firestone, Inc.
Briggs & Stratton Corp.
Burlington Industries, Inc.
Campbell Soup Co.
Cargill Inc.
Carpenter Technology Corp.
Caterpillar Inc.
Cenex Harvest States
Cessna Aircraft Co.
Chase Manhattan Bank, NA
Chesapeake Corp.
Chicago Tribune Co.
Cincinnati Bell Inc.
Coca-Cola Co.
Collins & Aikman Corp.
ConAgra, Inc.
Cone Mills Corp.
Consolidated Papers, Inc.
Cooper Industries, Inc.
Cooper Tire & Rubber Co.
Cranston Print Works Co.
Credit Suisse First Boston
CUNA Mutual Group
Dain Bosworth Inc.
Deere & Co.
Delta Air Lines, Inc.
Deluxe Corp.
Donaldson Co., Inc.
Duriron Co., Inc.
Emerson Electric Co.
Enterprise Rent-A-Car Co.
Equitable Resources, Inc.
Erving Industries
Fannie Mae
Ferro Corp.
First Financial Bank
Florida Power & Light Co.
Florida Rock Industries
Fortis Insurance Co.
Franklin Electric Co.
Furniture Brands International, Inc.
Georgia Power Co.
Gerber Products Co.
Graco, Inc.
Grede Foundries
Green Bay Packaging
GTE Corp.
Hamilton Sundstrand Corp.
Hartford (The)
Hartmarx Corp.
Hawaiian Electric Co., Inc.
Hickory Tech Corp.
Hoffmann-La Roche Inc.
Honeywell International Inc.
Hubbard Broadcasting, Inc.
Hubbell Inc.
Hunt Manufacturing Co.
Huntington Bancshares Inc.
Inman Mills
Jeld-wen, Inc.
Kingsbury Corp.
Laclede Gas Co.
Ladish Co., Inc.
Lee Enterprises
Lehigh Portland Cement Co.
Leigh Fibers, Inc.
Lincoln Electric Co.
Little, Inc. (Arthur D.)
McClatchy Co.
Mead Corp.
Menasha Corp.
Mercantile Bank NA
Merit Oil Corp.
Milacron, Inc.
Millipore Corp.
Minnesota Mining & Manufacturing Co.
Monsanto Co.
Montana Power Co.
Morgan & Co. Inc. (J.P.)
Morris Communications Corp.
MTS Systems Corp.
National Presto Industries, Inc.
National Service Industries, Inc.
New England Bio Labs
Nissan North America, Inc.
Nordson Corp.
North American Royalties
Novartis Corporation
Oshkosh B'Gosh, Inc.
Outboard Marine Corp.
PACCAR Inc.
Pella Corp.
PEMCO Corp.
PerkinElmer, Inc.
Phillips Petroleum Co.
Pieper Power Electric Co.
Pillsbury Co.
Polaroid Corp.
Praxair
Prudential Insurance Co. of America
Pulitzer Publishing Co.
Putnam Investments
Quaker Chemical Corp.
Ralston Purina Co.
Rayonier Inc.
Reilly Industries, Inc.
Reinhart Institutional Foods
Reynolds Tobacco (R.J.)
Rockwell International Corp.
SBC Communications Inc.
Schwab & Co., Inc. (Charles)
Scripps Co. (E.W.)
Sega of America Inc.
Sherwin-Williams Co.
Simplot Co. (J.R.)
Smurfit-Stone Container Corp.
Sprint Corp.
Standard Products Co.
Starwood Hotels & Resorts Worldwide, Inc.
State Street Bank & Trust Co.
Sun Microsystems Inc.
SunTrust Bank Atlanta
Susquehanna-Pfaltzgraff Co.
Sverdrup Corp.
Tai and Co. (J.T.)
Temple-Inland Inc.
TENNANT Co.
Tension Envelope Corp.
Textron Inc.
Times Mirror Co.
Tomkins Industries, Inc.
Transamerica Corp.
Unilever Home & Personal Care U.S.A.
Union Camp Corp.
Union Carbide Corp.
United Parcel Service of America Inc.
U.S. Bancorp Piper Jaffray
United States Trust Co. of New York
United Wisconsin Services
Universal Foods Corp.
UnumProvident
US West, Inc.
USX Corp.
Vesper Corp.
Warner-Lambert Co.
Washington Trust Bank
Western & Southern Life Insurance Co.
Weyerhaeuser Co.
Whirlpool Corp.
Wisconsin Power & Light Co.
Woodward Governor Co.
Xerox Corp.
York Federal Savings & Loan Association
Zachry Co. (H.B.)

Environment

AIR/WATER QUALITY

Air Products and Chemicals, Inc.
Anheuser-Busch Companies, Inc.
Bandag, Inc.
BankBoston Corp.
Barnes Group Inc.
Ben & Jerry's Homemade Inc.
Bethlehem Steel Corp.
BP Amoco Corp.
Bristol-Myers Squibb Co.
Butler Capital Corp.
Cabot Corp.
Calvin Klein
Carillon Importers, Ltd.
Carpenter Technology Corp.
Chesapeake Corp.
Clark Refining & Marketing
Consolidated Natural Gas Co.
Consolidated Papers, Inc.
Constellation Energy Group, Inc.
Crane & Co., Inc.
Credit Suisse First Boston
Crestar Finance Corp.
Dana Corp.
Exxon Mobil Corp.
First Union Securities, Inc.
Fisher Brothers Cleaning Services
FMC Corp.
Franklin Electric Co.
Fuller Co. (H.B.)
Gap, Inc.
Georgia-Pacific Corp.
Globe Corp.
GPU Inc.
Grace & Co. (W.R.)
GTE Corp.
Guess?
Harnischfeger Industries
Hasbro, Inc.
Hubbard Broadcasting, Inc.
Hughes Electronics Corp.
Johnson & Son (S.C.)
Journal-Gazette Co.
Kimberly-Clark Corp.
Kinder Morgn
Kingsbury Corp.
Leigh Fibers, Inc.
Liz Claiborne, Inc.
Mattel Inc.
McGraw-Hill Companies, Inc.
Memphis Light Gas & Water Division
Michigan Consolidated Gas Co.
Morgan & Co. Inc. (J.P.)
Morgan Stanley Dean Witter & Co.
New England Bio Labs
New York Mercantile Exchange
New York Times Co.
Norfolk Southern Corp.
North American Royalties
Norwest Corp.
Occidental Oil and Gas
Olin Corp.
Outboard Marine Corp.
Patagonia Inc.
Red Wing Shoe Co. Inc.
Reinhart Institutional Foods
Simplot Co. (J.R.)
Stone Container Corp.
Synovus Financial Corp.
TENNANT Co.
Texaco Inc.
Textron Inc.
TMC Investment Co.
Unilever Home & Personal Care U.S.A.
Union Camp Corp.
Union Pacific Corp.
Wilbur-Ellis Co. & Connell Brothers Co.
Witco Corp.

ENERGY

Bucyrus-Erie Co.
CIGNA Corp.
Clark Refining & Marketing
Commercial Intertech Corp.
Consolidated Natural Gas Co.
Consumers Energy Co.
CUNA Mutual Group
Dayton Power and Light Co.
Exxon Mobil Corp.
General Electric Co.
Halliburton Co.
Harnischfeger Industries
Honeywell International Inc.
Johnson Controls Inc.
Louisiana Land & Exploration Co.
ONEOK, Inc.
Overseas Shipholding Group Inc.
PacifiCorp
Standard Products Co.
Texaco Inc.
Toyota Motor Sales U.S.A., Inc.
True Oil Co.
Unocal Corp.
Webster Bank

FORESTRY

Abbott Laboratories
Ameren Corp.
Archer-Daniels-Midland Co.
Ben & Jerry's Homemade Inc.
Blount International, Inc.
Broderbund Software, Inc.
Carlson Companies, Inc.
Chesapeake Corp.
Duchossois Industries Inc.
Forest City Enterprises, Inc.
Fuller Co. (H.B.)
Furniture Brands International, Inc.
Gap, Inc.
Graco, Inc.
Guess?
Harland Co. (John H.)
Hasbro, Inc.
Hitachi America Ltd.
Kellwood Co.
Leigh Fibers, Inc.
Loews Corp.
Louisiana-Pacific Corp.
Morgan & Co. Inc. (J.P.)
New England Bio Labs
Norfolk Southern Corp.
Patagonia Inc.
Pella Corp.
PepsiCo, Inc.
Rayonier Inc.
Regions Bank
Sierra Pacific Resources
Simpson Investment Co.
Sonoco Products Co.
Stone Container Corp.
Temple-Inland Inc.
Texaco Inc.
Ticketmaster Corp.
True North Communications, Inc.
UnumProvident
Waffle House Inc.
Westvaco Corp.
Weyerhaeuser Co.

ENVIRONMENT-GENERAL

Abbott Laboratories
ABC
AGL Resources Inc.
Agrilink Foods, Inc.
Air Products and Chemicals, Inc.
Alabama Power Co.
Alaska Airlines, Inc.
Alcoa Inc.
Alexander & Baldwin, Inc.
Allegheny Technologies Inc.
AlliedSignal Inc.
Allmerica Financial Corp.
Alyeska Pipeline Service Co.
AMCORE Bank Rockford
Ameren Corp.
America West Airlines, Inc.
American Fidelity Corp.
American Honda Motor Co., Inc.
Ameritas Life Insurance Corp.
Ameritech Corp.
Ameritech Michigan
Ameritech Wisconsin
AMETEK, Inc.
Amgen, Inc.
AMP Inc.
Analog Devices, Inc.
Andersen Corp.
Andersons Inc.
Anheuser-Busch Companies, Inc.
Aon Corp.

APL Ltd.
Apple Computer, Inc.
Appleton Papers Inc.
Archer-Daniels-Midland Co.
Aristech Chemical Corp.
Arizona Public Service Co.
ASARCO Inc.
Ashland, Inc.
AT&T Corp.
Atlantic Investment Co.
Atlantic Richfield Co.
Autodesk Inc.
Avista Corporation
Avon Products, Inc.
Badger Meter, Inc.
Bank of America
Bank of New York Co., Inc.
Bank One Corp.
Bank One, Texas-Houston Office
BankBoston-Connecticut Region
BankBoston Corp.
Bardes Corp.
Barnes Group Inc.
Bausch & Lomb Inc.
Bean, Inc. (L.L.)
Belk-Simpson Department Stores
Belk Stores Services Inc.
Bell Atlantic Corp.-West Virginia
Bemis Co., Inc.
Bemis Manufacturing Co.
Ben & Jerry's Homemade Inc.
Berwind Group
Bestfoods
Bethlehem Steel Corp.
Binney & Smith Inc.
Block, Inc. (H&R)
Blount International, Inc.
Blue Cross & Blue Shield of Minnesota
Boeing Co.
Boise Cascade Corp.
Borden, Inc.
Borman's Inc.
Boston Globe (The)
Bowater Inc.
BP Amoco Corp.
Bridgestone/Firestone, Inc.
Briggs & Stratton Corp.
Bristol-Myers Squibb Co.
Broderbund Software, Inc.
Brooklyn Union
Brown Shoe Co., Inc.
Brown & Williamson Tobacco Corp.
Browning-Ferris Industries Inc.
Brunswick Corp.
Burlington Industries, Inc.
Burlington Resources, Inc.
Burnett Co. (Leo)
Butler Capital Corp.
Cabot Corp.
Calvin Klein
Cantor, Fitzgerald Securities Corp.
Cargill Inc.
Carolina Power & Light Co.
Carpenter Technology Corp.
Carris Reels
Carter-Wallace, Inc.
Caterpillar Inc.
Central Maine Power Co.
Central & South West Services
Central Soya Co.
Central Vermont Public Service Corp.
CertainTeed Corp.
Champion International Corp.
Charter Manufacturing Co.
Chase Manhattan Bank, NA
Chemed Corp.
Chesapeake Corp.
Chevron Corp.
Chicago Tribune Co.
Church & Dwight Co., Inc.
Cinergy Corp.
Circuit City Stores, Inc.
Citibank Corp.
Citigroup
Citizens Financial Group, Inc.
Clark Refining & Marketing
Cleveland-Cliffs, Inc.
Clorox Co.
Collins & Aikman Corp.
Colonial Life & Accident Insurance Co.
Commerce Bancshares, Inc.
ConAgra, Inc.
Conoco, Inc.
Consolidated Natural Gas Co.
Consolidated Papers, Inc.
Constellation Energy Group, Inc.
Consumers Energy Co.
Contran Corp.
Cooper Industries, Inc.
Coors Brewing Co.
Corning Inc.
Cox Enterprises Inc.
Crane Co.
Crane & Co., Inc.
Cranston Print Works Co.
Crestar Finance Corp.
Cummins Engine Co., Inc.
Cyprus Amax Minerals Co.
Dain Bosworth Inc.
Dana Corp.
Danis Companies
Deere & Co.
Deluxe Corp.
Demoulas Supermarkets Inc.
Deposit Guaranty National Bank
Detroit Edison Co.
Deutsch Co.
Dexter Corp.
Dial Corp.
Disney Co. (Walt)
Dixie Group, Inc. (The)
Dominion Resources, Inc.
Donaldson Co., Inc.
Dow Chemical Co.
Dow Corning Corp.
Dreyer's Grand Ice Cream
DSM Copolymer
du Pont de Nemours & Co. (E.I.)
Duchossois Industries Inc.
Duke Energy
Eastman Kodak Co.
Eaton Corp.
Ecolab Inc.
Edison International
Elf Atochem North America, Inc.
Emerson Electric Co.
Employers Mutual Casualty Co.
Ensign-Bickford Industries
Ethyl Corp.
Evening Post Publishing Co.
Exxon Mobil Corp.
Fabri-Kal Corp.
Federated Mutual Insurance Co.
FedEx Corp.
Ferro Corp.
Fidelity Investments
FINA
Fireman's Fund Insurance Co.
First Financial Bank
First Hawaiian, Inc.
First Tennessee National Corp.
First Union Corp.
First Union Securities, Inc.
Fisher Brothers Cleaning Services
Fisher Scientific
FleetBoston Financial Corp.
Florida Power Corp.
Florida Power & Light Co.
Florida Rock Industries
Fluor Corp.
FMC Corp.
Forbes Inc.
Ford Motor Co.
Fort James Corp.
Fort Worth Star-Telegram Inc.
Fortis Insurance Co.
Fortune Brands, Inc.
Franklin Mint (The)
Freeport-McMoRan Inc.
Frost National Bank
Fuller Co. (H.B.)
Gap, Inc.
GEICO Corp.
GenCorp
General Atlantic Partners II LP
General Electric Co.
General Mills, Inc.
General Motors Corp.
General Reinsurance Corp.
Georgia-Pacific Corp.
Georgia Power Co.
Gerber Products Co.
Giant Eagle Inc.
Globe Corp.
Goldman Sachs Group
Goodrich Aerospace - Aerostructures Group (B.F.)
GPU Inc.
Grace & Co. (W.R.)
Graco, Inc.
Green Bay Packaging
Griffith Laboratories U.S.A.
GTE Corp.
Gulf Power Co.
Gulfstream Aerospace Corp.
Halliburton Co.
Hallmark Cards Inc.
Hancock Financial Services (John)
Hanna Co. (M.A.)
Hannaford Brothers Co.
Harley-Davidson Co.
Harris Corp.
Harsco Corp.
Hartford (The)
Hartford Steam Boiler Inspection & Insurance Co.
Hasbro, Inc.
Hawaiian Electric Co., Inc.
Heinz Co. (H.J.)
Hewlett-Packard Co.
Hickory Tech Corp.
Hitachi America Ltd.
Hoffer Plastics Corp.
Hoffmann-La Roche Inc.
Hofmann Co.
Home Depot, Inc.
HON Industries Inc.
Honeywell International Inc.
Housatonic Curtain Co.
HSBC Bank USA
Hubbard Broadcasting, Inc.
Hubbell Inc.
Huffy Corp.
Humana, Inc.
IKON Office Solutions, Inc.
Illinois Power Co.
Ingram Industries Inc.
Inland Container Corp.
International Business Machines Corp.
International Flavors & Fragrances Inc.
International Multifoods Corp.
International Paper Co.
Jacobs Engineering Group
Jeld-wen, Inc.
Johnson Controls Inc.
Johnson & Son (S.C.)
Jones & Co. (Edward D.)
Jostens, Inc.
Kennametal, Inc.
Kimberly-Clark Corp.
Kinder Morgn
Kingsbury Corp.
Koch Enterprises, Inc.
Kraft Foods, Inc.
Kroger Co.
Land O'Lakes, Inc.
Lee Enterprises
Lehigh Portland Cement Co.
Leigh Fibers, Inc.
Lennox International, Inc.
Levi Strauss & Co.
Liberty Corp.
Lilly & Co. (Eli)
Lincoln Electric Co.
Lincoln Financial Group
Lipton Co.
Little, Inc. (Arthur D.)
Liz Claiborne, Inc.
Loews Corp.
Lotus Development Corp.
Louisiana Land & Exploration Co.
Louisiana-Pacific Corp.
LTV Corp.
Lubrizol Corp. (The)
Madison Gas & Electric Co.
Mallinckrodt Chemical, Inc.
Maritz Inc.
Marshall & Ilsley Corp.
Masco Corp.
Mattel Inc.
May Department Stores Co.
Maytag Corp.
McCormick & Co. Inc.
McDonald & Co. Securities, Inc.
MCI WorldCom, Inc.
McWane Inc.
Meijer, Inc.
Memphis Light Gas & Water Division
Menasha Corp.
Merck & Co.
Merit Oil Corp.
Metropolitan Life Insurance Co.
Michigan Consolidated Gas Co.
Microsoft Corp.
MidAmerican Energy Holdings Co.
Milliken & Co.
Millipore Corp.
Mine Safety Appliances Co.
Minnesota Mining & Manufacturing Co.
Mitsubishi Electric America
Montana Power Co.
MONY Group (The)
Morgan & Co. Inc. (J.P.)
Morgan Stanley Dean Witter & Co.
Morrison Knudsen Corp.
Motorola Inc.
MTD Products Inc.
Nabisco Group Holdings
Nalco Chemical Co.
National Computer Systems, Inc.
National Presto Industries, Inc.
National Service Industries, Inc.
National Starch & Chemical Co.
Nationwide Insurance Co.
NEBCO Evans
New Century Energies
New England Bio Labs
New England Financial
New Jersey Natural Gas Co.
New York Mercantile Exchange
New York Stock Exchange, Inc.
New York Times Co.
Newman's Own Inc.
Niagara Mohawk Holdings Inc.
Nike, Inc.
Nordson Corp.
Norfolk Southern Corp.
North American Royalties
Northeast Utilities
Northern States Power Co.
Norton Co.
Occidental Oil and Gas
Occidental Petroleum Corp.
Old National Bank Evansville
Olin Corp.
ONEOK, Inc.
Oshkosh B'Gosh, Inc.
Outboard Marine Corp.
Overnite Transportation Co.
Overseas Shipholding Group Inc.
Pacific Century Financial Corp.
Pacific Gas and Electric Co.
Pacific Mutual Life Insurance Co.
PacifiCorp
Paine Webber
Patagonia Inc.
PECO Energy Co.
Pella Corp.
PerkinElmer, Inc.
Pfizer Inc.
Pharmacia & Upjohn, Inc.
Phelps Dodge Corp.
Philip Morris Companies Inc.
Phillips Petroleum Co.
Physicians Mutual Insurance Co.
Pillsbury Co.
Pioneer Group
PNC Financial Services Group
Polaroid Corp.
Portland General Electric Co.
Potlatch Corp.
Potomac Electric Power Co.
PPG Industries, Inc.
Praxair
Premier Industrial Corp.

Price Associates (T. Rowe)
Principal Financial Group
Procter & Gamble Co.
Promus Hotel Corp.
Providence Journal-Bulletin Co.
Provident Companies, Inc.
Prudential Insurance Co. of America
Prudential Securities Inc.
Public Service Electric & Gas Co.
Publix Supermarkets
Pulitzer Publishing Co.
Putnam Investments
Quaker Chemical Corp.
Questar Corp.
Ralph's Grocery Co.
Ralston Purina Co.
Rayonier Inc.
Red Wing Shoe Co. Inc.
REI-Recreational Equipment, Inc.
Reily & Co., Inc. (William B.)
Reliant Energy Inc.
Reliant Energy Minnegasco
Reynolds Metals Co.
Rockwell International Corp.
Rohm & Haas Co.
Royal & SunAlliance USA, Inc.
Ruddick Corp.
SAFECO Corp.
Safeguard Scientifics
Sara Lee Hosiery, Inc.
Schloss & Co. (Marcus)
Schlumberger Ltd. (USA)
Schwab & Co., Inc. (Charles)
Scripps Co. (E.W.)
Searle & Co. (G.D.)
Sempra Energy
Sentinel Communications Co.
Sentry Insurance, A Mutual Co.
ServiceMaster Co.
Shaklee Corp.
Shaw's Supermarkets, Inc.
Shea Co. (John F.)
Shell Oil Co.
Sierra Pacific Industries
Sierra Pacific Resources
Simplot Co. (J.R.)
Simpson Investment Co.
Slant/Fin Corp.
Smith Corp. (A.O.)
SmithKline Beecham Corp.
Smurfit-Stone Container Corp.
Sonoco Products Co.
Sony Electronics
Southeastern Mutual Insurance Co.
Southern California Gas Co.
Southwest Gas Corp.
Sovereign Bank
Springs Industries, Inc.
Standard Products Co.
Stanley Works (The)
Starwood Hotels & Resorts Worldwide, Inc.
Stone Container Corp.
Stonecutter Mills Corp.
Strear Farms Co.
Sun Microsystems Inc.
SunTrust Bank Atlanta
SuperValu, Inc.
Tektronix, Inc.
Temple-Inland Inc.
TENNANT Co.
Tenneco Automotive
Tension Envelope Corp.
Tesoro Hawaii
Texaco Inc.
Texas Instruments Inc.
Textron Inc.
Thermo Electron Corp.
Thompson Co. (J. Walter)
Times Mirror Co.
Timken Co. (The)
Toro Co.
Toshiba America Inc.
Toyota Motor Sales U.S.A., Inc.
Transamerica Corp.
True North Communications, Inc.
True Oil Co.
TRW Inc.
TU Electric Co.
Tyson Foods Inc.
Ukrop's Super Markets
Unilever Home & Personal Care U.S.A.
Unilever United States, Inc.
Union Camp Corp.
Union Carbide Corp.
Union Pacific Corp.
United Airlines Inc.
United Distillers & Vintners North America
U.S. Bancorp Piper Jaffray
United States Sugar Corp.
United States Trust Co. of New York
United Technologies Corp.
United Wisconsin Services
Universal Leaf Tobacco Co., Inc.
Universal Studios
Unocal Corp.
UnumProvident
US West, Inc.
USX Corp.
Valero Energy Corp.
Varian Medical Systems, Inc.
Vesper Corp.
Vodafone AirTouch Plc
Vulcan Materials Co.
Wachovia Bank of North Carolina NA
Wal-Mart Stores, Inc.
Walter Industries Inc.
Washington Trust Bank
Waste Management Inc.
Weil, Gotshal & Manges Corp.
Western Resources Inc.
Westvaco Corp.
Weyerhaeuser Co.
Whirlpool Corp.
WICOR, Inc.
Wilbur-Ellis Co. & Connell Brothers Co.
Williams
Wiremold Co.
Wisconsin Energy Corp.
Wisconsin Power & Light Co.
Wisconsin Public Service Corp.
Witco Corp.
Woodward Governor Co.
Wrigley Co. (Wm. Jr.)
Wyman-Gordon Co.
Xerox Corp.
York Federal Savings & Loan Association

PROTECTION

Ben & Jerry's Homemade Inc.
Blue Cross & Blue Shield of Alabama
Boston Globe (The)
Clark Refining & Marketing
Consolidated Natural Gas Co.
Dexter Corp.
El Paso Energy Co.
Emerson Electric Co.
Florida Power & Light Co.
Freddie Mac
Gap, Inc.
Leigh Fibers, Inc.
Lotus Development Corp.
Olin Corp.
Patagonia Inc.
Ralph's Grocery Co.
Reynolds & Reynolds Co.
Synovus Financial Corp.
Washington Trust Bank

RESEARCH

Deere & Co.
Erb Lumber Co.
Hubbard Broadcasting, Inc.
Menasha Corp.
Patagonia Inc.
Phillips Petroleum Co.
Southwest Gas Corp.
Union Pacific Corp.

RESOURCE CONSERVATION

AEGON U.S.A. Inc.
Agrilink Foods, Inc.
Air Products and Chemicals, Inc.
Alcoa Inc.
Alexander & Baldwin, Inc.
American Express Co.
American Fidelity Corp.
American Honda Motor Co., Inc.
Ameritas Life Insurance Corp.
AMETEK, Inc.
Amgen, Inc.
AMR Corp.
Andersen Corp.
Anheuser-Busch Companies, Inc.
Aon Corp.
APL Ltd.
Archer-Daniels-Midland Co.
Aristech Chemical Corp.
Arizona Public Service Co.
Armstrong World Industries, Inc.
Arvin Industries, Inc.
Ashland, Inc.
Atlantic Richfield Co.
Badger Meter, Inc.
Bandag, Inc.
Bank of America
BankBoston Corp.
Banta Corp.
Bassett Furniture Industries
Bean, Inc. (L.L.)
Belk-Simpson Department Stores
Belk Stores Services Inc.
BellSouth Corp.
Ben & Jerry's Homemade Inc.
Bethlehem Steel Corp.
Blair & Co. (William)
Blue Bell, Inc.
Blue Cross & Blue Shield of Iowa
BP Amoco Corp.
Bradford & Co. (J.C.)
Briggs & Stratton Corp.
Broderbund Software, Inc.
Bucyrus-Erie Co.
Burlington Resources, Inc.
Butler Capital Corp.
Calvin Klein
Cargill Inc.
Carpenter Technology Corp.
Caterpillar Inc.
CertainTeed Corp.
Champion International Corp.
Chase Bank of Texas
Chesapeake Corp.
Chevron Corp.
CIGNA Corp.
Cinergy Corp.
Citigroup
Cleveland-Cliffs, Inc.
Clorox Co.
Colonial Oil Industries, Inc.
Commerce Bancshares, Inc.
Compass Bank
Cone Mills Corp.
Consolidated Natural Gas Co.
Constellation Energy Group, Inc.
Consumers Energy Co.
Copley Press, Inc.
Corning Inc.
Country Curtains, Inc.
Crane & Co., Inc.
Cranston Print Works Co.
Crestar Finance Corp.
Cummins Engine Co., Inc.
CUNA Mutual Group
Daily News
Dayton Power and Light Co.
Deere & Co.
DeKalb Genetics Corp.
Deutsch Co.
Dexter Corp.
Disney Co. (Walt)
Dixie Group, Inc. (The)
Donaldson Co., Inc.
Dow Chemical Co.
DSM Copolymer
Duchossois Industries Inc.
Dynamet, Inc.
Eastman Kodak Co.
El Paso Energy Co.
Employers Mutual Casualty Co.
Erb Lumber Co.
Evening Post Publishing Co.
Exxon Mobil Corp.
Fireman's Fund Insurance Co.
First Hawaiian, Inc.
Fisher Scientific
Freeport-McMoRan Inc.
Gallo Winery, Inc. (E&J)
Gap, Inc.
General Atlantic Partners II LP
General Electric Co.
General Motors Corp.
Georgia-Pacific Corp.
Georgia Power Co.
Giant Eagle Inc.
Globe Corp.
GPU Inc.
Hanna Co. (M.A.)
Hannaford Brothers Co.
Harland Co. (John H.)
Hawaiian Electric Co., Inc.
Hershey Foods Corp.
Hickory Tech Corp.
Hitachi America Ltd.
HON Industries Inc.
Honeywell International Inc.
Housatonic Curtain Co.
Huffy Corp.
Humana, Inc.
IKON Office Solutions, Inc.
International Paper Co.
Jacobson & Sons (Benjamin)
Johnson Controls Inc.
Johnson & Son (S.C.)
Journal-Gazette Co.
Kennametal, Inc.
Kimball International, Inc.
Kimberly-Clark Corp.
Kingsbury Corp.
Koch Enterprises, Inc.
Landmark Communications Inc.
Lee Enterprises
Leigh Fibers, Inc.
Lennox International, Inc.
Levi Strauss & Co.
LG&E Energy Corp.
Liberty Corp.
Liberty Diversified Industries
Little, Inc. (Arthur D.)
Loews Corp.
Lowe's Companies
McClatchy Co.
Mead Corp.
Memphis Light Gas & Water Division
Menasha Corp.
Merck & Co.
Merit Oil Corp.
MidAmerican Energy Holdings Co.
Milliken & Co.
Mitsubishi Electric America
Monsanto Co.
Montana Power Co.
Morris Communications Corp.
Morrison Knudsen Corp.
National Starch & Chemical Co.
Nationwide Insurance Co.
NEBCO Evans
Nestle U.S.A. Inc.
New England Bio Labs
New York Mercantile Exchange
Niagara Mohawk Holdings Inc.
Norfolk Southern Corp.
Norton Co.
Occidental Petroleum Corp.
OG&E Electric Services
Old National Bank Evansville
Olin Corp.
Outboard Marine Corp.
Pacific Century Financial Corp.
PacifiCorp
Patagonia Inc.
PepsiCo, Inc.
Pfizer Inc.
Pharmacia & Upjohn, Inc.
Phillips Petroleum Co.
PNC Financial Services Group
Praxair
Premier Industrial Corp.
Price Associates (T. Rowe)
Procter & Gamble Co.
Providence Journal-Bulletin Co.
Provident Companies, Inc.
Putnam Investments
Red Wing Shoe Co. Inc.
Reilly Industries, Inc.
Rouse Co.
Ruddick Corp.
Schloss & Co. (Marcus)
Schlumberger Ltd. (USA)
Schwab & Co., Inc. (Charles)

Security Benefit Life Insurance Co.
Shell Oil Co.
Sierra Pacific Industries
Sierra Pacific Resources
Simplot Co. (J.R.)
Simpson Investment Co.
Sony Electronics
Southeastern Mutual Insurance Co.
Southwest Gas Corp.
Stanley Works (The)
Stone Container Corp.
Stonecutter Mills Corp.
Stride Rite Corp.
Sun Microsystems Inc.
SunTrust Bank Atlanta
Susquehanna-Pfaltzgraff Co.
Tektronix, Inc.
Temple-Inland Inc.
Tesoro Hawaii
Texaco Inc.
Thermo Electron Corp.
Thompson Co. (J. Walter)
Timken Co. (The)
Toledo Blade Co.
Transamerica Corp.
True Oil Co.
Union Camp Corp.
Union Carbide Corp.
Union Pacific Corp.
United Airlines Inc.
United Distillers & Vintners North America
United Dominion Industries, Ltd.
U.S. Bancorp Piper Jaffray
United States Sugar Corp.
Universal Studios
Unocal Corp.
Valmont Industries, Inc.
Vanguard Group
Vesper Corp.
Vulcan Materials Co.
Wachovia Bank of North Carolina NA
Waffle House Inc.
Wal-Mart Stores, Inc.
Washington Mutual, Inc.
Washington Trust Bank
Webster Bank
Westvaco Corp.
Weyerhaeuser Co.
Wilbur-Ellis Co. & Connell Brothers Co.
Wiley & Sons (John)
Williams
Wisconsin Energy Corp.
Wrigley Co. (Wm. Jr.)
York Federal Savings & Loan Association

SANITARY SYSTEMS

Crane & Co., Inc.
Ensign-Bickford Industries
Fisher Brothers Cleaning Services
Orscheln Co.
Vulcan Materials Co.

WATERSHED

Block, Inc. (H&R)
Consumers Energy Co.
Delta Air Lines, Inc.
Dexter Corp.
Gap, Inc.
General Electric Co.
Leigh Fibers, Inc.
Menasha Corp.
Oshkosh B'Gosh, Inc.
Patagonia Inc.
Providence Journal-Bulletin Co.
TMC Investment Co.
Union Carbide Corp.
Wiremold Co.

WILDLIFE PROTECTION

AK Steel Corp.
Andersons Inc.
Anheuser-Busch Companies, Inc.
Aristech Chemical Corp.
Associated Food Stores
Atlantic Richfield Co.
Banfi Vintners
Bean, Inc. (L.L.)
Ben & Jerry's Homemade Inc.
Bethlehem Steel Corp.
Binney & Smith Inc.
Blount International, Inc.
Blue Bell, Inc.
BP Amoco Corp.
Broderbund Software, Inc.
Brunswick Corp.
Burnett Co. (Leo)
Butler Capital Corp.
Cabot Corp.
Carlson Companies, Inc.
CertainTeed Corp.
Charter Manufacturing Co.
Chase Manhattan Bank, NA
Chevron Corp.
Cleveland-Cliffs, Inc.
Clorox Co.
Consolidated Papers, Inc.
Consumers Energy Co.
Cox Enterprises Inc.
Crane Co.
Crane & Co., Inc.
CSR Rinker Materials Corp.
Cummins Engine Co., Inc.
Daily News
Detroit Edison Co.
Disney Co. (Walt)
Donaldson Co., Inc.
Dow Chemical Co.
Evening Post Publishing Co.
Exxon Mobil Corp.
Federated Mutual Insurance Co.
FMC Corp.
Forbes Inc.
Freeport-McMoRan Inc.
Gallo Winery, Inc. (E&J)
Gap, Inc.
General Electric Co.
Georgia-Pacific Corp.
Georgia Power Co.
Giant Eagle Inc.
Globe Corp.
Green Bay Packaging
Gulf Power Co.
Hartmarx Corp.
Hawaiian Electric Co., Inc.
Hickory Tech Corp.
Hoffer Plastics Corp.
Hoffmann-La Roche Inc.
Hofmann Co.
Idaho Power Co.
Independent Stave Co.
Jacobs Engineering Group
Jeld-wen, Inc.
Johnson & Son (S.C.)
Land O'Lakes, Inc.
Lee Enterprises
Leigh Fibers, Inc.
Liberty Corp.
Loews Corp.
Louisiana-Pacific Corp.
Marcus Corp.
McDonald & Co. Securities, Inc.
Memphis Light Gas & Water Division
Menasha Corp.
Merrill Lynch & Co., Inc.
Millipore Corp.
Montana Power Co.
Morgan Stanley Dean Witter & Co.
Morrison Knudsen Corp.
National Presto Industries, Inc.
Nationwide Insurance Co.
Nestle U.S.A. Inc.
New England Bio Labs
New York Times Co.
Niagara Mohawk Holdings Inc.
Northern States Power Co.
Occidental Oil and Gas
Pacific Mutual Life Insurance Co.
PacifiCorp
Patagonia Inc.
Phillips Petroleum Co.
Pieper Power Electric Co.
Principal Financial Group
Red Wing Shoe Co. Inc.
Reily & Co., Inc. (William B.)
Reynolds Metals Co.
Rich Products Corp.
Russer Foods
Schloss & Co. (Marcus)
Schlumberger Ltd. (USA)
Schwab & Co., Inc. (Charles)
Sentry Insurance, A Mutual Co.
Sierra Pacific Industries
Sierra Pacific Resources
Simpson Investment Co.
Smurfit-Stone Container Corp.
Sony Electronics
Southwest Gas Corp.
Susquehanna-Pfaltzgraff Co.
Temple-Inland Inc.
Tesoro Hawaii
Texaco Inc.
Titan Industrial Corp.
Toyota Motor Sales U.S.A., Inc.
Transamerica Corp.
True Oil Co.
Tyson Foods Inc.
Union Carbide Corp.
Union Pacific Corp.
Union Planters Corp.
Universal Foods Corp.
US West, Inc.
Valmont Industries, Inc.
Wachovia Bank of North Carolina NA
Wachtell, Lipton, Rosen & Katz
Westvaco Corp.
Weyerhaeuser Co.
Wilbur-Ellis Co. & Connell Brothers Co.
Wiley & Sons (John)
Williams
Wisconsin Public Service Corp.

Health

ADOLESCENT HEALTH ISSUES

Bandag, Inc.
CIGNA Corp.
Citizens Bank-Flint
Group Health Plan
Honeywell International Inc.
Kimberly-Clark Corp.
Lance, Inc.
Little, Inc. (Arthur D.)
Medtronic, Inc.
Nissan North America, Inc.
Northern Trust Co.
Old National Bank Evansville
PacifiCare Health Systems
Pfizer Inc.
PNC Bank
Providence Journal-Bulletin Co.
Royal & SunAlliance USA, Inc.
Saint Paul Companies Inc.
State Street Bank & Trust Co.
Trustmark Insurance Co.
Unilever Home & Personal Care U.S.A.
US Bank, Washington

AIDS/HIV

Aetna, Inc.
Alcoa Inc.
Alexander & Baldwin, Inc.
Allmerica Financial Corp.
AMCORE Bank Rockford
American Express Co.
American Fidelity Corp.
American General Finance
American Retail Group
American United Life Insurance Co.
Ameritas Life Insurance Corp.
Ameritech Wisconsin
Amgen, Inc.
AMR Corp.
Anheuser-Busch Companies, Inc.
Aon Corp.
APL Ltd.
BankBoston Corp.
Banta Corp.
Barclays Capital
Bard, Inc. (C.R.)
Bardes Corp.
Barry Corp. (R.G.)
Baxter International Inc.
Beckman Coulter, Inc.
Ben & Jerry's Homemade Inc.
Bernstein & Co., Inc. (Sanford C.)
Block, Inc. (H&R)
Blue Cross & Blue Shield of Alabama
Blue Cross & Blue Shield of Minnesota
Borden, Inc.
Borman's Inc.
Boston Edison Co.
Boston Globe (The)
Bristol-Myers Squibb Co.
Broderbund Software, Inc.
Burlington Industries, Inc.
Calvin Klein
Cargill Inc.
Carillon Importers, Ltd.
Carpenter Technology Corp.
Carris Reels
Cessna Aircraft Co.
Chevron Corp.
Chicago Tribune Co.
CIT Group, Inc. (The)
Citigroup
Citizens Financial Group, Inc.
Clark Refining & Marketing
CNA
Collins & Aikman Corp.
Compaq Computer Corp.
Contran Corp.
Coors Brewing Co.
Copley Press, Inc.
Country Curtains, Inc.
Crestar Finance Corp.
CUNA Mutual Group
Dain Bosworth Inc.
Dana Corp.
Dayton Hudson
Delta Air Lines, Inc.
Deluxe Corp.
Duchossois Industries Inc.
Dun & Bradstreet Corp.
Eastern Bank
Ecolab Inc.
Emerson Electric Co.
Fireman's Fund Insurance Co.
First Financial Bank
First Union Bank
Fisher Brothers Cleaning Services
FleetBoston Financial Corp.
Forbes Inc.
Forest City Enterprises, Inc.
Fort Worth Star-Telegram Inc.
Fortis, Inc.
Fortis Insurance Co.
Freddie Mac
Freeport-McMoRan Inc.
Furniture Brands International, Inc.
Galter Corp.
Gap, Inc.
GATX Corp.
GenAmerica Corp.
Gerber Products Co.
Giant Eagle Inc.
Glickenhaus & Co.
Globe Corp.
Group Health Plan
Guess?
Hallmark Cards Inc.
Hamilton Sundstrand Corp.
Hannaford Brothers Co.
Harnischfeger Industries
Hartford (The)
Hartford Steam Boiler Inspection & Insurance Co.
Hartmarx Corp.
Hasbro, Inc.
Heinz Co. (H.J.)
Hoffmann-La Roche Inc.
Hofmann Co.
Hunt Manufacturing Co.
IKON Office Solutions, Inc.
Journal-Gazette Co.
Katten, Muchin & Zavis
Leigh Fibers, Inc.
Levi Strauss & Co.
Lilly & Co. (Eli)
Lincoln Financial Group
Little, Inc. (Arthur D.)
Liz Claiborne, Inc.
Loews Corp.
Lotus Development Corp.
Madison Gas & Electric Co.
Marshall Field's
Mattel Inc.
May Department Stores Co.
McDonald & Co. Securities, Inc.
McGraw-Hill Companies, Inc.
McKesson-HBOC Corp.
Merrill Lynch & Co., Inc.
Metropolitan Life Insurance Co.
Millipore Corp.

Minnesota Mutual Life Insurance Co.
Monsanto Co.
Montgomery Ward & Co., Inc.
MONY Group (The)
Morgan Stanley Dean Witter & Co.
Mutual of Omaha Insurance Co.
Nalco Chemical Co.
National City Bank of Minneapolis
National Machinery Co.
Nationwide Insurance Co.
Navcom Systems
New England Financial
New York Life Insurance Co.
New York Mercantile Exchange
Northern States Power Co.
Northern Trust Co.
Norton Co.
Occidental Petroleum Corp.
Ohio National Life Insurance Co.
Overseas Shipholding Group Inc.
PACCAR Inc.
Pacific Mutual Life Insurance Co.
PacifiCare Health Systems
Paine Webber
Pella Corp.
Pfizer Inc.
Pharmacia & Upjohn, Inc.
Polaroid Corp.
Praxair
Premier Industrial Corp.
Principal Financial Group
Procter & Gamble Co., Cosmetics Division
Providence Journal-Bulletin Co.
Prudential Insurance Co. of America
Pulitzer Publishing Co.
Putnam Investments
Quanex Corp.
Ralph's Grocery Co.
Regions Bank
Reily & Co., Inc. (William B.)
Revlon Inc.
Reynolds Tobacco (R.J.)
Safeguard Scientifics
Saint Paul Companies Inc.
Schwab & Co., Inc. (Charles)
Seagram & Sons, Inc. (Joseph E.)
Searle & Co. (G.D.)
Security Life of Denver Insurance Co.
Sega of America Inc.
SmithKline Beecham Corp.
Southeastern Mutual Insurance Co.
Sovereign Bank
Sun Microsystems Inc.
Thermo Electron Corp.
Ticketmaster Corp.
Titan Industrial Corp.
TJX Companies, Inc.
Transamerica Corp.
Trustmark Insurance Co.
United Distillers & Vintners North America
United Parcel Service of America Inc.
U.S. Bancorp
United States Trust Co. of New York
UnumProvident
US Bank, Washington
USG Corp.
Valmont Industries, Inc.
Vodafone AirTouch Plc
Washington Mutual, Inc.
Washington Trust Bank
Weil, Gotshal & Manges Corp.
Wiley & Sons (John)
Williams
Wiremold Co.
Witco Corp.
Wyman-Gordon Co.
Young & Rubicam
Zilkha & Sons

ALZHEIMERS DISEASE

AEGON U.S.A. Inc.
AlliedSignal Inc.
AMCORE Bank Rockford
American General Finance
Amgen, Inc.
Amsted Industries Inc.
Anheuser-Busch Companies, Inc.
Aon Corp.
Beckman Coulter, Inc.
Blue Cross & Blue Shield of Alabama
Blue Cross & Blue Shield of Iowa
Borman's Inc.
Boston Edison Co.
Brown Shoe Co., Inc.
Business Improvement
Callaway Golf Co.
Calvin Klein
CertainTeed Corp.
Clark Refining & Marketing
Consumers Energy Co.
Copley Press, Inc.
Croft-Leominster
CSS Industries, Inc.
Dana Corp.
Danis Companies
Dial Corp.
El Paso Energy Co.
Emerson Electric Co.
Enterprise Rent-A-Car Co.
Extendicare Health Services
Ferro Corp.
Fireman's Fund Insurance Co.
Florida Rock Industries
Forest City Enterprises, Inc.
Fortis Insurance Co.
Gallo Winery, Inc. (E&J)
GenAmerica Corp.
General Motors Corp.
Group Health Plan
Hanna Co. (M.A.)
Hannaford Brothers Co.
Hasbro, Inc.
Huffy Corp.
Huntington Bancshares Inc.
IKON Office Solutions, Inc.
Invacare Corp.
Jacobs Engineering Group
Katten, Muchin & Zavis
Kelly Services
Ladish Co., Inc.
Leigh Fibers, Inc.
Liberty Diversified Industries
LTV Corp.
Lubrizol Corp. (The)
Manor Care Health SVS, Inc.
Marcus Corp.
McDonald & Co. Securities, Inc.
Monsanto Co.
Morris Communications Corp.
Nalco Chemical Co.
Nationwide Insurance Co.
Ohio National Life Insurance Co.
Orscheln Co.
Pacific Mutual Life Insurance Co.
PacifiCare Health Systems
Physicians Mutual Insurance Co.
Pittway Corp.
Premier Dental Products Co.
Ralston Purina Co.
Rich Products Corp.
Schlumberger Ltd. (USA)
Shelter Mutual Insurance Co.
Smurfit-Stone Container Corp.
Stone Container Corp.
SunTrust Bank Atlanta
Synovus Financial Corp.
TMC Investment Co.
Tomkins Industries, Inc.
Trace International Holdings, Inc.
True Oil Co.
TRW Inc.
Union Pacific Corp.
United Airlines Inc.
United States Sugar Corp.
United Wisconsin Services
UnumProvident
US West, Inc.
Waffle House Inc.
Warner-Lambert Co.
Winn-Dixie Stores Inc.
Woodward Governor Co.
Wrigley Co. (Wm. Jr.)
Zilkha & Sons

ARTHRITIS

AEGON U.S.A. Inc.
American Fidelity Corp.
American General Finance
Badger Meter, Inc.
Beckman Coulter, Inc.
Bernstein & Co., Inc. (Sanford C.)
Blount International, Inc.
Blue Cross & Blue Shield of Alabama
Borden, Inc.
Bradford & Co. (J.C.)
Carter-Wallace, Inc.
CIT Group, Inc. (The)
Clark Refining & Marketing
Colonial Oil Industries, Inc.
CSS Industries, Inc.
Danis Companies
Deutsch Co.
Dial Corp.
DSM Copolymer
Equitable Resources, Inc.
Forbes Inc.
Galter Corp.
Globe Corp.
Golub Corp.
Group Health Plan
Hensel Phelps Construction Co.
Hubbard Broadcasting, Inc.
Huntington Bancshares Inc.
Independent Stave Co.
Invacare Corp.
Jacobson & Sons (Benjamin)
Jostens, Inc.
Kroger Co.
Ladish Co., Inc.
Leigh Fibers, Inc.
Manulife Financial
Marcus Corp.
MCI WorldCom, Inc.
Merit Oil Corp.
National Service Industries, Inc.
Newman's Own Inc.
Nomura Holding America
Orscheln Co.
Paine Webber
Physicians Mutual Insurance Co.
Prudential Securities Inc.
Putnam Investments
Regions Bank
Reynolds & Reynolds Co.
Russer Foods
Shea Co. (John F.)
Southwest Gas Corp.
Storage Technology Corp.
Timken Co. (The)
TMC Investment Co.
Toledo Blade Co.
United Wisconsin Services
Unocal Corp.
Valmont Industries, Inc.

CANCER

ABC
Aetna, Inc.
Agrilink Foods, Inc.
Air Products and Chemicals, Inc.
AK Steel Corp.
Alabama Power Co.
Alcoa Inc.
Alcon Laboratories, Inc.
Alliant Techsystems
AlliedSignal Inc.
Allmerica Financial Corp.
Alma Piston Co.
AMCORE Bank Rockford
American General Finance
American United Life Insurance Co.
Ameritech Wisconsin
AMETEK, Inc.
Amgen, Inc.
AMP Inc.
AMR Corp.
Andersen Corp.
Anheuser-Busch Companies, Inc.
APL Ltd.
Archer-Daniels-Midland Co.
Arizona Public Service Co.
Armstrong World Industries, Inc.
Arvin Industries, Inc.
Ashland, Inc.
Associated Food Stores
Atlantic Investment Co.
Avon Products, Inc.
Badger Meter, Inc.
Baird & Co. (Robert W.)
Banfi Vintners
BankBoston Corp.
Banta Corp.
Barclays Capital
Bard, Inc. (C.R.)
Barden Corp.
Bardes Corp.
Barnes Group Inc.
Barry Corp. (R.G.)
Bassett Furniture Industries
Bechtel Group, Inc.
Beckman Coulter, Inc.
Belk-Simpson Department Stores
Bemis Manufacturing Co.
Ben & Jerry's Homemade Inc.
Bernstein & Co., Inc. (Sanford C.)
Binswanger Companies
Block, Inc. (H&R)
Blount International, Inc.
Blue Bell, Inc.
Blue Cross & Blue Shield of Alabama
Blue Cross & Blue Shield of Iowa
Blue Cross & Blue Shield of Michigan
Blue Cross & Blue Shield of Minnesota
Boler Co.
Borden, Inc.
Borman's Inc.
Boston Edison Co.
Bourns, Inc.
Bradford & Co. (J.C.)
Bristol-Myers Squibb Co.
Broderbund Software, Inc.
Burnett Co. (Leo)
Burress (J.W.)
Business Improvement
Butler Capital Corp.
Cabot Corp.
Callaway Golf Co.
Calvin Klein
Campbell Soup Co.
Cantor, Fitzgerald Securities Corp.
Cargill Inc.
Carillon Importers, Ltd.
Carlson Companies, Inc.
Carpenter Technology Corp.
Carris Reels
Carter-Wallace, Inc.
Caterpillar Inc.
Central National-Gottesman
Central Newspapers, Inc.
Century 21
CertainTeed Corp.
Cessna Aircraft Co.
CGU Insurance
Charter Manufacturing Co.
Chase Bank of Texas
Chemed Corp.
Chicago Board of Trade
Chicago Title Corp.
CIGNA Corp.
Cincinnati Bell Inc.
CIT Group, Inc. (The)
Citigroup
CLARCOR Inc.
Clark Refining & Marketing
Cleveland-Cliffs, Inc.
Collins & Aikman Corp.
Colonial Oil Industries, Inc.
Commerce Bancshares, Inc.
Commercial Intertech Corp.
Compaq Computer Corp.
Compass Bank
Consolidated Natural Gas Co.
Consumers Energy Co.
Continental Grain Co.
Contran Corp.
Cooper Industries, Inc.
Cox Enterprises Inc.
Crane Co.
Crane & Co., Inc.
Credit Suisse First Boston
Crestar Finance Corp.
CSR Rinker Materials Corp.
CSS Industries, Inc.
Cummings Properties Management
CUNA Mutual Group
Daily News
DaimlerChrysler Corp.

Dain Bosworth Inc.
Danis Companies
Dayton Power and Light Co.
DeKalb Genetics Corp.
Deluxe Corp.
Demoulas Supermarkets Inc.
Deutsch Co.
Dial Corp.
Disney Co. (Walt)
Domino's Pizza Inc.
Dreyer's Grand Ice Cream
DSM Copolymer
Duchossois Industries Inc.
Dun & Bradstreet Corp.
Dynamet, Inc.
Eaton Corp.
Eckerd Corp.
Ecolab Inc.
Edwards Enterprise Software (J.D.)
El Paso Energy Co.
Ensign-Bickford Industries
Enterprise Rent-A-Car Co.
Erb Lumber Co.
Erving Industries
Evening Post Publishing Co.
Exxon Mobil Corp.
Federal-Mogul Corp.
Federated Mutual Insurance Co.
Ferro Corp.
Fidelity Investments
FINA
First Hawaiian, Inc.
First Union Bank
First Union Securities, Inc.
Fisher Brothers Cleaning Services
Fisher Scientific
Florida Power Corp.
Florida Power & Light Co.
Florida Rock Industries
Fluor Corp.
Forbes Inc.
Ford Meter Box Co.
Forest City Enterprises, Inc.
Fort Worth Star-Telegram Inc.
Fortis, Inc.
Freeport-McMoRan Inc.
Gallo Winery, Inc. (E&J)
Galter Corp.
Gap, Inc.
GATX Corp.
GEICO Corp.
GenAmerica Corp.
GenCorp
General Mills, Inc.
General Motors Corp.
Georgia Power Co.
Gerber Products Co.
Giant Eagle Inc.
Giant Food Inc.
Glaxo Wellcome Inc.
Glickenhaus & Co.
Golub Corp.
Graco, Inc.
Grede Foundries
Group Health Plan
Guess?
Gulf Power Co.
Halliburton Co.
Hallmark Cards Inc.
Hanna Co. (M.A.)
Hannaford Brothers Co.
Harcourt General, Inc.
Harland Co. (John H.)
Harley-Davidson Co.
Harnischfeger Industries
Harris Corp.
Harsco Corp.
Hartmarx Corp.
Hasbro, Inc.
Hawaiian Electric Co., Inc.
Heinz Co. (H.J.)
Hensel Phelps Construction Co.
Hoffmann-La Roche Inc.
Hofmann Co.
Honeywell International Inc.
Hubbard Broadcasting, Inc.
Hubbell Inc.
Huffy Corp.
Humana, Inc.
Huntington Bancshares Inc.
IKON Office Solutions, Inc.
Independent Stave Co.
International Flavors & Fragrances Inc.
INTRUST Financial Corp.
Invacare Corp.
Jacobs Engineering Group
Jacobson & Sons (Benjamin)
Johnson Controls Inc.
Johnson & Johnson
Johnson & Son (S.C.)
Jostens, Inc.
Journal-Gazette Co.
Katten, Muchin & Zavis
Kellwood Co.
Kelly Services
Kennametal, Inc.
Kimberly-Clark Corp.
Kingsbury Corp.
Koch Enterprises, Inc.
Koch Industries, Inc.
Kroger Co.
Ladish Co., Inc.
Lancaster Lens, Inc.
Lance, Inc.
LandAmerica Financial Services
Lehigh Portland Cement Co.
Levi Strauss & Co.
Leviton Manufacturing Co. Inc.
Liberty Corp.
Lilly & Co. (Eli)
Lincoln Electric Co.
Lipton Co.
Liz Claiborne, Inc.
Loews Corp.
Louisiana-Pacific Corp.
LTV Corp.
Manulife Financial
Marcus Corp.
Mark IV Industries
Marshall & Ilsley Corp.
Mattel Inc.
May Department Stores Co.
McDonald & Co. Securities, Inc.
MCI WorldCom, Inc.
McWane Inc.
Medtronic, Inc.
Memphis Light Gas & Water Division
Mercantile Bank NA
Merck & Co.
Merrill Lynch & Co., Inc.
Metropolitan Life Insurance Co.
Mid-America Bank of Louisville
MidAmerican Energy Holdings Co.
Milacron, Inc.
Millipore Corp.
Mitsubishi Electric America
Monarch Machine Tool Co.
Monsanto Co.
Montana Power Co.
Montgomery Ward & Co., Inc.
MONY Group (The)
Morgan & Co. Inc. (J.P.)
Morgan Stanley Dean Witter & Co.
Morris Communications Corp.
MTD Products Inc.
Nalco Chemical Co.
National Machinery Co.
National Presto Industries, Inc.
National Service Industries, Inc.
Nationwide Insurance Co.
New England Financial
New Jersey Natural Gas Co.
New York Mercantile Exchange
New York Stock Exchange, Inc.
Niagara Mohawk Holdings Inc.
Nomura Holding America
Norfolk Southern Corp.
Northern States Power Co.
Norton Co.
Norwest Corp.
Occidental Oil and Gas
Occidental Petroleum Corp.
Ohio National Life Insurance Co.
Orange & Rockland Utilities, Inc.
Oshkosh B'Gosh, Inc.
Outboard Marine Corp.
Overseas Shipholding Group Inc.
Owens Corning
PACCAR Inc.
Pacific Mutual Life Insurance Co.
PacifiCare Health Systems
Paine Webber
Park National Bank
PEMCO Corp.
PepsiCo, Inc.
PerkinElmer, Inc.
Pharmacia & Upjohn, Inc.
Phelps Dodge Corp.
Physicians Mutual Insurance Co.
Pittway Corp.
PNC Financial Services Group
Praxair
Principal Financial Group
Procter & Gamble Co.
Procter & Gamble Co., Cosmetics Division
Providence Journal-Bulletin Co.
Publix Supermarkets
Pulitzer Publishing Co.
Putnam Investments
Quanex Corp.
Ralph's Grocery Co.
Red Wing Shoe Co. Inc.
Regions Bank
Regis Corp.
Reilly Industries, Inc.
Reinhart Institutional Foods
Revlon Inc.
Reynolds & Reynolds Co.
Reynolds Tobacco (R.J.)
Rich Products Corp.
Rockwell International Corp.
Royal & SunAlliance USA, Inc.
Rubbermaid Inc.
Russer Foods
Saint Paul Companies Inc.
S&T Bancorp
Sara Lee Corp.
SBC Communications Inc.
Schering-Plough Corp.
Schloss & Co. (Marcus)
Schlumberger Ltd. (USA)
Schwab & Co., Inc. (Charles)
Schwebel Baking Co.
Seagram & Sons, Inc. (Joseph E.)
Searle & Co. (G.D.)
Security Benefit Life Insurance Co.
Security Life of Denver Insurance Co.
Sega of America Inc.
Sentry Insurance, A Mutual Co.
Servco Pacific
S.G. Cowen
Shea Co. (John F.)
Sherwin-Williams Co.
Sierra Pacific Industries
Simplot Co. (J.R.)
Slant/Fin Corp.
SmithKline Beecham Corp.
Smurfit-Stone Container Corp.
Solo Cup Co.
Sonoco Products Co.
Southeastern Mutual Insurance Co.
Southwest Gas Corp.
Sprint Corp.
Square D Co.
Standard Register Co.
Stanley Works (The)
Star Bank NA
State Farm Mutual Automobile Insurance Co.
State Street Bank & Trust Co.
Stone Container Corp.
Storage Technology Corp.
Strear Farms Co.
Stupp Brothers Bridge & Iron Co.
Sun Microsystems Inc.
SunTrust Banks of Florida
Sverdrup Corp.
Synovus Financial Corp.
Tai and Co. (J.T.)
Tamko Roofing Products
Tesoro Hawaii
Texaco Inc.
Textron Inc.
Thompson Co. (J. Walter)
Times Mirror Co.
Titan Industrial Corp.
TJX Companies, Inc.
TMC Investment Co.
Tomkins Industries, Inc.
Toro Co.
Trace International Holdings, Inc.
Transamerica Corp.
True North Communications, Inc.
True Oil Co.
Ukrop's Super Markets
Unilever Home & Personal Care U.S.A.
Union Pacific Corp.
United Airlines Inc.
United Co.
United Dominion Industries, Ltd.
United Services Automobile Association
U.S. Bancorp Piper Jaffray
United States Sugar Corp.
United States Trust Co. of New York
United Wisconsin Services
Universal Foods Corp.
Universal Studios
US Bank, Washington
USAA Life Insurance Co.
USG Corp.
Valspar Corp.
Vesper Corp.
Vulcan Materials Co.
Waffle House Inc.
Wal-Mart Stores, Inc.
Warner-Lambert Co.
Washington Mutual, Inc.
Washington Trust Bank
Weil, Gotshal & Manges Corp.
West Co. Inc.
Western & Southern Life Insurance Co.
Westvaco Corp.
Winn-Dixie Stores Inc.
Wisconsin Power & Light Co.
Witco Corp.
Woodward Governor Co.
Wyman-Gordon Co.
Yellow Corp.
Young & Rubicam
Zachry Co. (H.B.)
Zilkha & Sons

CHILDREN'S HEALTH/ HOSPITALS

Abbott Laboratories
ABC
Ace Hardware Corp.
AEGON U.S.A. Inc.
Aetna, Inc.
Agrilink Foods, Inc.
Air Products and Chemicals, Inc.
Alcoa Inc.
Alcon Laboratories, Inc.
Alexander & Baldwin, Inc.
Allegheny Technologies Inc.
Alliant Techsystems
AlliedSignal Inc.
Allmerica Financial Corp.
Allstate Insurance Co.
Alma Piston Co.
Ameren Corp.
American Express Co.
American Fidelity Corp.
American General Finance
American Retail Group
Ameritas Life Insurance Corp.
Amgen, Inc.
AMP Inc.
AMR Corp.
Andersen Corp.
Anheuser-Busch Companies, Inc.
Aon Corp.
APL Ltd.
Archer-Daniels-Midland Co.
Arizona Public Service Co.
Arvin Industries, Inc.
Associated Food Stores
AT&T Corp.
Atlantic Investment Co.
Atlantic Richfield Co.
Avery Dennison Corp.
Avon Products, Inc.
Baird & Co. (Robert W.)
Bandag, Inc.
Bank of America
Bank One Corp.
Banta Corp.

Barclays Capital
Bard, Inc. (C.R.)
Barden Corp.
Barnes Group Inc.
Baxter International Inc.
Belk Stores Services Inc.
Bemis Manufacturing Co.
Bernstein & Co., Inc. (Sanford C.)
BFGoodrich Co.
Binney & Smith Inc.
Binswanger Companies
Blair & Co. (William)
Block, Inc. (H&R)
Blue Bell, Inc.
Blue Cross & Blue Shield of Alabama
Blue Cross & Blue Shield of Iowa
Blue Cross & Blue Shield of Minnesota
Boler Co.
Borden, Inc.
Borman's Inc.
Boston Globe (The)
Bourns, Inc.
BP Amoco Corp.
Bradford & Co. (J.C.)
Bridgestone/Firestone, Inc.
Briggs & Stratton Corp.
Bristol-Myers Squibb Co.
Broderbund Software, Inc.
Brown Shoe Co., Inc.
Brunswick Corp.
Bucyrus-Erie Co.
Burlington Industries, Inc.
Burlington Resources, Inc.
Burnett Co. (Leo)
Business Improvement
Butler Manufacturing Co.
Callaway Golf Co.
Calvin Klein
Campbell Soup Co.
Cargill Inc.
Carillon Importers, Ltd.
Carlson Companies, Inc.
Carris Reels
Central National-Gottesman
Central Soya Co.
CertainTeed Corp.
Cessna Aircraft Co.
CGU Insurance
Charter Manufacturing Co.
Chase Bank of Texas
Chase Manhattan Bank, NA
Chemed Corp.
Chesapeake Corp.
Chicago Sun-Times, Inc.
Chicago Title Corp.
Chicago Tribune Co.
CIGNA Corp.
Cinergy Corp.
CIT Group, Inc. (The)
Citigroup
Citizens Bank-Flint
Clark Refining & Marketing
Cleveland-Cliffs, Inc.
Clorox Co.
CNA
Colonial Oil Industries, Inc.
Comdisco, Inc.
Commerce Bancshares, Inc.
Commercial Intertech Corp.
Compaq Computer Corp.
Compass Bank
Consolidated Natural Gas Co.
Consumers Energy Co.
Continental Grain Co.
Contran Corp.
Conwood Co. LP
Copley Press, Inc.
Country Curtains, Inc.
Cox Enterprises Inc.
CPI Corp.
Crane & Co., Inc.
Credit Suisse First Boston
Crestar Finance Corp.
Crown Books
CSR Rinker Materials Corp.
CSS Industries, Inc.
Cummings Properties Management
Cummins Engine Co., Inc.
CUNA Mutual Group
Dain Bosworth Inc.
Danis Companies
Dayton Power and Light Co.
Delta Air Lines, Inc.
Deluxe Corp.
Demoulas Supermarkets Inc.
Deposit Guaranty National Bank
Detroit Edison Co.
Deutsch Co.
Dexter Corp.
Dial Corp.
Disney Co. (Walt)
Dixie Group, Inc. (The)
Donaldson Co., Inc.
Duchossois Industries Inc.
Duriron Co., Inc.
Dynamet, Inc.
Eastern Bank
Ecolab Inc.
Edwards Enterprise Software (J.D.)
Emerson Electric Co.
Employers Mutual Casualty Co.
Ensign-Bickford Industries
Enterprise Rent-A-Car Co.
Equifax Inc.
Equitable Resources, Inc.
Farmers Group, Inc.
Federal-Mogul Corp.
Federated Mutual Insurance Co.
Ferro Corp.
Fidelity Investments
Fifth Third Bancorp
First Financial Bank
First Hawaiian, Inc.
First Union Bank
First Union Corp.
First Union Securities, Inc.
Firstar Bank Milwaukee NA
Fisher Brothers Cleaning Services
FleetBoston Financial Corp.
Florida Rock Industries
Fluor Corp.
Ford Meter Box Co.
Forest City Enterprises, Inc.
Fort Worth Star-Telegram Inc.
Fortis, Inc.
Fortis Insurance Co.
Franklin Electric Co.
Freddie Mac
Freeport-McMoRan Inc.
Furniture Brands International, Inc.
Gallo Winery, Inc. (E&J)
Galter Corp.
GEICO Corp.
GenAmerica Corp.
GenCorp
General Mills, Inc.
Georgia-Pacific Corp.
Georgia Power Co.
Gerber Products Co.
Giant Eagle Inc.
Giant Food Inc.
Glickenhaus & Co.
Globe Corp.
Golub Corp.
Graco, Inc.
Green Bay Packaging
Griffith Laboratories U.S.A.
Group Health Plan
Gulf Power Co.
Hallmark Cards Inc.
Hamilton Sundstrand Corp.
Hannaford Brothers Co.
Harcourt General, Inc.
Harley-Davidson Co.
Harnischfeger Industries
Harris Corp.
Harsco Corp.
Hartford (The)
Hartmarx Corp.
Hasbro, Inc.
Hawaiian Electric Co., Inc.
Heinz Co. (H.J.)
Hoffer Plastics Corp.
Hoffmann-La Roche Inc.
Hofmann Co.
HON Industries Inc.
Honeywell International Inc.
Hubbard Broadcasting, Inc.
Hubbell Inc.
Huffy Corp.
Humana, Inc.
Hunt Manufacturing Co.
Huntington Bancshares Inc.
IKON Office Solutions, Inc.
Illinois Tool Works, Inc.
Inland Container Corp.
INTRUST Financial Corp.
Invacare Corp.
Jacobs Engineering Group
Jacobson & Sons (Benjamin)
Johnson Controls Inc.
Johnson & Son (S.C.)
Jostens, Inc.
Journal-Gazette Co.
Katten, Muchin & Zavis
Kellwood Co.
Kelly Services
Kimberly-Clark Corp.
Kinder Morgn
Kingsbury Corp.
Koch Enterprises, Inc.
Koch Industries, Inc.
Kroger Co.
Laclede Gas Co.
Ladish Co., Inc.
Land O'Lakes, Inc.
Lehigh Portland Cement Co.
Leigh Fibers, Inc.
Leviton Manufacturing Co. Inc.
LG&E Energy Corp.
Liberty Corp.
Liberty Diversified Industries
Lilly & Co. (Eli)
Lincoln Electric Co.
Lipton Co.
Little, Inc. (Arthur D.)
Loews Corp.
Louisiana-Pacific Corp.
LTV Corp.
Lubrizol Corp. (The)
Madison Gas & Electric Co.
Mamiye Brothers
Marcus Corp.
Mark IV Industries
Marshall & Ilsley Corp.
Mattel Inc.
May Department Stores Co.
McDonald & Co. Securities, Inc.
McKesson-HBOC Corp.
McWane Inc.
Medtronic, Inc.
Memphis Light Gas & Water Division
Menasha Corp.
Mercantile Bank NA
Merck & Co.
Merit Oil Corp.
Merrill Lynch & Co., Inc.
Metropolitan Life Insurance Co.
Mid-America Bank of Louisville
MidAmerican Energy Holdings Co.
Milliken & Co.
Millipore Corp.
Mine Safety Appliances Co.
Mitsubishi Electric America
Monarch Machine Tool Co.
Monsanto Co.
Montana Power Co.
Montgomery Ward & Co., Inc.
Morgan Stanley Dean Witter & Co.
Morris Communications Corp.
Morrison Knudsen Corp.
Nalco Chemical Co.
National City Bank of Minneapolis
National City Corp.
National Machinery Co.
National Presto Industries, Inc.
Nationwide Insurance Co.
NEBCO Evans
NEC America, Inc.
New England Financial
New Jersey Natural Gas Co.
New York Mercantile Exchange
Newman's Own Inc.
Niagara Mohawk Holdings Inc.
Nissan North America, Inc.
Norfolk Southern Corp.
Northern Trust Co.
Norton Co.
Occidental Oil and Gas
OG&E Electric Services
Ohio National Life Insurance Co.
Oklahoma Publishing Co.
Old National Bank Evansville
Oshkosh B'Gosh, Inc.
Overseas Shipholding Group Inc.
PACCAR Inc.
Pacific Century Financial Corp.
Pacific Mutual Life Insurance Co.
PacifiCare Health Systems
PacifiCorp
Paine Webber
Parker Hannifin Corp.
PEMCO Corp.
PepsiCo, Inc.
PerkinElmer, Inc.
Pfizer Inc.
Phelps Dodge Corp.
Physicians Mutual Insurance Co.
Pieper Power Electric Co.
Pillsbury Co.
PNC Financial Services Group
Praxair
Premier Dental Products Co.
Principal Financial Group
Procter & Gamble Co., Cosmetics Division
Prudential Insurance Co. of America
Prudential Securities Inc.
Pulitzer Publishing Co.
Putnam Investments
Quanex Corp.
Ralph's Grocery Co.
Ralston Purina Co.
Red Wing Shoe Co. Inc.
Reebok International Ltd.
Regions Bank
Reilly Industries, Inc.
Reinhart Institutional Foods
Reynolds Metals Co.
Reynolds & Reynolds Co.
Reynolds Tobacco (R.J.)
Rich Products Corp.
Rockwell International Corp.
Royal & SunAlliance USA, Inc.
Rubbermaid Inc.
Russer Foods
Ryder System, Inc.
Safeguard Scientifics
S&T Bancorp
SBC Communications Inc.
Schering-Plough Corp.
Schwab & Co., Inc. (Charles)
Schwebel Baking Co.
Security Benefit Life Insurance Co.
Sega of America Inc.
S.G. Cowen
Shaw's Supermarkets, Inc.
Shea Co. (John F.)
Shell Oil Co.
Shelter Mutual Insurance Co.
Sierra Pacific Resources
Simpson Investment Co.
SIT Investment Associates, Inc.
Slant/Fin Corp.
Smurfit-Stone Container Corp.
Solo Cup Co.
Sonoco Products Co.
Sony Electronics
Southeastern Mutual Insurance Co.
Southwest Gas Corp.
Sprint Corp.
Sprint/United Telephone
Square D Co.
Standard Products Co.
Standard Register Co.
Stanley Works (The)
Star Bank NA
State Farm Mutual Automobile Insurance Co.
State Street Bank & Trust Co.
Steelcase Inc.
Stone Container Corp.
Storage Technology Corp.
Strear Farms Co.
Stride Rite Corp.
Stupp Brothers Bridge & Iron Co.
Sun Microsystems Inc.
SunTrust Bank Atlanta
Susquehanna-Pfaltzgraff Co.
Sverdrup Corp.
Synovus Financial Corp.
Tai and Co. (J.T.)
Temple-Inland Inc.
Tesoro Hawaii
Texaco Inc.

Textron Inc.
Ticketmaster Corp.
TJX Companies, Inc.
TMC Investment Co.
Toledo Blade Co.
Tomkins Industries, Inc.
Trace International Holdings, Inc.
True Oil Co.
TRW Inc.
Tyson Foods Inc.
Unilever United States, Inc.
Union Camp Corp.
Union Pacific Corp.
United Airlines Inc.
United Distillers & Vintners North America
United Dominion Industries, Ltd.
United Services Automobile Association
U.S. Bancorp
U.S. Bancorp Piper Jaffray
United States Sugar Corp.
United States Trust Co. of New York
United Wisconsin Services
Universal Foods Corp.
Universal Leaf Tobacco Co., Inc.
Universal Studios
Unocal Corp.
US Bank, Washington
USAA Life Insurance Co.
Valmont Industries, Inc.
Vulcan Materials Co.
Waffle House Inc.
Wal-Mart Stores, Inc.
Walter Industries Inc.
Warner-Lambert Co.
Washington Mutual, Inc.
Washington Trust Bank
Webster Bank
West Co. Inc.
Weyerhaeuser Co.
WICOR, Inc.
Williams
Winn-Dixie Stores Inc.
Wiremold Co.
Wisconsin Energy Corp.
Wisconsin Power & Light Co.
Wisconsin Public Service Corp.
Witco Corp.
Woodward Governor Co.
Wyman-Gordon Co.
Yellow Corp.
York Federal Savings & Loan Association
Young & Rubicam
Zachry Co. (H.B.)

CLINICS/MEDICAL CENTERS

Abbott Laboratories
ABC
Advanced Micro Devices, Inc.
Aetna, Inc.
Agrilink Foods, Inc.
AK Steel Corp.
Alcon Laboratories, Inc.
Alexander & Baldwin, Inc.
AlliedSignal Inc.
Allmerica Financial Corp.
Allstate Insurance Co.
AMCORE Bank Rockford
American Fidelity Corp.
Ameritas Life Insurance Corp.
Ameritech Ohio
Ameritech Wisconsin
AMETEK, Inc.
Amgen, Inc.
AMP Inc.
AMR Corp.
Amsted Industries Inc.
Andersen Corp.
Andersons Inc.
Aon Corp.
APL Ltd.
Aristech Chemical Corp.
Armstrong World Industries, Inc.
Arvin Industries, Inc.
Ashland, Inc.
Associated Food Stores
Atlantic Investment Co.
Bandag, Inc.
Bank of America
BankBoston Corp.
Banta Corp.
Bard, Inc. (C.R.)
Bausch & Lomb Inc.
Baxter International Inc.
Bayer Corp.
Belk-Simpson Department Stores
Bemis Co., Inc.
Bernstein & Co., Inc. (Sanford C.)
Blair & Co. (William)
Block, Inc. (H&R)
Blue Cross & Blue Shield of Iowa
Blue Cross & Blue Shield of Minnesota
Boeing Co.
Boston Edison Co.
Boston Globe (The)
BP Amoco Corp.
Bristol-Myers Squibb Co.
Brunswick Corp.
Bucyrus-Erie Co.
Burlington Industries, Inc.
Burnett Co. (Leo)
Butler Manufacturing Co.
Cabot Corp.
Calvin Klein
Cargill Inc.
Carillon Importers, Ltd.
Carlson Companies, Inc.
Carnival Corp.
Carpenter Technology Corp.
Carter-Wallace, Inc.
Central & South West Services
CertainTeed Corp.
Cessna Aircraft Co.
CGU Insurance
Chase Bank of Texas
Chase Manhattan Bank, NA
Chevron Corp.
Chicago Board of Trade
CIGNA Corp.
Cincinnati Bell Inc.
CIT Group, Inc. (The)
Citigroup
Citizens Bank-Flint
Citizens Financial Group, Inc.
CLARCOR Inc.
Clark Refining & Marketing
Cleveland-Cliffs, Inc.
Clorox Co.
Collins & Aikman Corp.
Comdisco, Inc.
Commerce Bancshares, Inc.
Commercial Intertech Corp.
Compass Bank
ConAgra, Inc.
Consolidated Natural Gas Co.
Constellation Energy Group, Inc.
Contran Corp.
Conwood Co. LP
Copley Press, Inc.
Corning Inc.
Country Curtains, Inc.
Crane & Co., Inc.
Credit Suisse First Boston
Crestar Finance Corp.
Cummings Properties Management
CUNA Mutual Group
Dain Bosworth Inc.
Danis Companies
DeKalb Genetics Corp.
Delta Air Lines, Inc.
Deluxe Corp.
Deutsch Co.
Dexter Corp.
Disney Co. (Walt)
Dixie Group, Inc. (The)
Dow Jones & Co., Inc.
Duchossois Industries Inc.
Dynamet, Inc.
Eastern Bank
Eastman Kodak Co.
Eaton Corp.
Eckerd Corp.
Ecolab Inc.
Edwards Enterprise Software (J.D.)
Elf Atochem North America, Inc.
Enterprise Rent-A-Car Co.
Erving Industries
Exxon Mobil Corp.
Federal-Mogul Corp.
Ferro Corp.
Fidelity Investments
FINA
First American Corp.
First Financial Bank
First Hawaiian, Inc.
First Maryland Bancorp
First National Bank of Evergreen Park
First Union Bank
First Union Securities, Inc.
Firstar Bank Milwaukee NA
Fisher Scientific
FleetBoston Financial Corp.
Florida Power Corp.
Florida Rock Industries
Fluor Corp.
Forbes Inc.
Forest City Enterprises, Inc.
Fortis Insurance Co.
Freeport-McMoRan Inc.
Gallo Winery, Inc. (E&J)
Galter Corp.
Gap, Inc.
GATX Corp.
GenAmerica Corp.
General Electric Co.
General Mills, Inc.
Georgia Power Co.
Gerber Products Co.
Gillette Co.
Glaxo Wellcome Inc.
Glickenhaus & Co.
Globe Corp.
Golub Corp.
Graco, Inc.
Grede Foundries
Group Health Plan
Guess?
Hamilton Sundstrand Corp.
Hanna Co. (M.A.)
Hannaford Brothers Co.
Harcourt General, Inc.
Harland Co. (John H.)
Harley-Davidson Co.
Harnischfeger Industries
Harris Corp.
Harris Trust & Savings Bank
Harsco Corp.
Hartford (The)
Hartmarx Corp.
Hasbro, Inc.
Hawaiian Electric Co., Inc.
Heinz Co. (H.J.)
Hensel Phelps Construction Co.
Hershey Foods Corp.
Hofmann Co.
Humana, Inc.
IBP
Illinois Tool Works, Inc.
Inman Mills
International Flavors & Fragrances Inc.
International Paper Co.
Invacare Corp.
Jacobs Engineering Group
Jacobson & Sons (Benjamin)
Johnson Controls Inc.
Johnson & Son (S.C.)
Journal-Gazette Co.
Katten, Muchin & Zavis
Kellogg Co.
Kelly Services
Kimberly-Clark Corp.
Kingsbury Corp.
Koch Enterprises, Inc.
La-Z-Boy Inc.
Ladish Co., Inc.
Lee Enterprises
Leigh Fibers, Inc.
Levi Strauss & Co.
Liberty Corp.
Lincoln Electric Co.
Lipton Co.
Liz Claiborne, Inc.
Loews Corp.
LTV Corp.
Lubrizol Corp. (The)
Marcus Corp.
Marshall & Ilsley Corp.
Mattel Inc.
McGraw-Hill Companies, Inc.
McKesson-HBOC Corp.
Medtronic, Inc.
Menasha Corp.
Mercantile Bank NA
Merck & Co.
Merit Oil Corp.
Merrill Lynch & Co., Inc.
Metropolitan Life Insurance Co.
Milliken & Co.
Millipore Corp.
Minnesota Mining & Manufacturing Co.
Monarch Machine Tool Co.
Monsanto Co.
Montana Power Co.
Morgan & Co. Inc. (J.P.)
Morris Communications Corp.
Morton International Inc.
MTD Products Inc.
Nabisco Group Holdings
Nalco Chemical Co.
National City Corp.
National Machinery Co.
National Starch & Chemical Co.
Nestle U.S.A. Inc.
New England Bio Labs
New England Financial
New Jersey Natural Gas Co.
New York Life Insurance Co.
New York Mercantile Exchange
Nissan North America, Inc.
Nordson Corp.
North American Royalties
Northern States Power Co.
Northern Trust Co.
Norton Co.
Norwest Corp.
Occidental Oil and Gas
OG&E Electric Services
Ohio National Life Insurance Co.
Oklahoma Publishing Co.
Old National Bank Evansville
Oshkosh B'Gosh, Inc.
Outboard Marine Corp.
Overseas Shipholding Group Inc.
PACCAR Inc.
Pacific Century Financial Corp.
PacifiCare Health Systems
Pella Corp.
PEMCO Corp.
PerkinElmer, Inc.
Pfizer Inc.
Phelps Dodge Corp.
Phillips Petroleum Co.
Pieper Power Electric Co.
Pillsbury Co.
Pioneer Group
Pittway Corp.
Polaroid Corp.
PPG Industries, Inc.
Praxair
Premier Industrial Corp.
Procter & Gamble Co., Cosmetics Division
Prudential Insurance Co. of America
Putnam Investments
Quanex Corp.
Ralph's Grocery Co.
Reader's Digest Association, Inc. (The)
Red Wing Shoe Co. Inc.
Reebok International Ltd.
Regions Bank
Reilly Industries, Inc.
Reily & Co., Inc. (William B.)
Reinhart Institutional Foods
Revlon Inc.
Reynolds Tobacco (R.J.)
Rich Products Corp.
Riggs Bank NA
Rouse Co.
Rubbermaid Inc.
Ruddick Corp.
Saint Paul Companies Inc.
S&T Bancorp
Schering-Plough Corp.
Schloss & Co. (Marcus)
Schwab & Co., Inc. (Charles)
Seagram & Sons, Inc. (Joseph E.)
Searle & Co. (G.D.)
Sega of America Inc.
Servco Pacific
Shaw's Supermarkets, Inc.
Shell Oil Co.
Simplot Co. (J.R.)
Simpson Investment Co.
Slant/Fin Corp.
Southeastern Mutual Insurance Co.
Southwest Gas Corp.
Sovereign Bank
Square D Co.
Standard Products Co.

Standard Register Co.
Star Bank NA
State Farm Mutual Automobile Insurance Co.
State Street Bank & Trust Co.
Steelcase Inc.
Stone Container Corp.
Storage Technology Corp.
SunTrust Bank Atlanta
SunTrust Banks of Florida
Synovus Financial Corp.
Tai and Co. (J.T.)
TCF National Bank Minnesota
Temple-Inland Inc.
TENNANT Co.
Tension Envelope Corp.
Tesoro Hawaii
Texaco Inc.
Texas Instruments Inc.
Thermo Electron Corp.
Thompson Co. (J. Walter)
Ticketmaster Corp.
Titan Industrial Corp.
TJX Companies, Inc.
TMC Investment Co.
Toledo Blade Co.
Tomkins Industries, Inc.
Trace International Holdings, Inc.
Transamerica Corp.
True Oil Co.
Trustmark Insurance Co.
TRW Inc.
Unilever Home & Personal Care U.S.A.
Union Camp Corp.
Union Carbide Corp.
Union Pacific Corp.
United Co.
U.S. Bancorp
United States Sugar Corp.
United Wisconsin Services
Universal Foods Corp.
Universal Studios
Unocal Corp.
UnumProvident
USG Corp.
Vulcan Materials Co.
Walter Industries Inc.
Warner-Lambert Co.
Washington Mutual, Inc.
Washington Trust Bank
Webster Bank
Weyerhaeuser Co.
Whirlpool Corp.
WICOR, Inc.
Wilbur-Ellis Co. & Connell Brothers Co.
Williams
Winn-Dixie Stores Inc.
Wisconsin Energy Corp.
Wisconsin Power & Light Co.
Witco Corp.
Wolverine World Wide
Woodward Governor Co.
Wrigley Co. (Wm. Jr.)
York Federal Savings & Loan Association
Young & Rubicam
Zachry Co. (H.B.)
Zilkha & Sons

DIABETES

AEGON U.S.A. Inc.
Alabama Power Co.
AlliedSignal Inc.
American General Finance
AMETEK, Inc.
AMR Corp.
Associated Food Stores
Atlantic Investment Co.
Barclays Capital
Barry Corp. (R.G.)
Beckman Coulter, Inc.
Bernstein & Co., Inc. (Sanford C.)
Blue Bell, Inc.
Blue Cross & Blue Shield of Michigan
Blue Cross & Blue Shield of Minnesota
Bourns, Inc.
Bristol-Myers Squibb Co.
Business Improvement
Cabot Corp.
Campbell Soup Co.
Cantor, Fitzgerald Securities Corp.
Central National-Gottesman
Century 21
CGU Insurance
Chase Bank of Texas
Chesapeake Corp.
Chicago Title Corp.
Citigroup
Clark Refining & Marketing
Colonial Oil Industries, Inc.
Commercial Intertech Corp.
Compaq Computer Corp.
Compass Bank
Crane Co.
Crane & Co., Inc.
CSS Industries, Inc.
Cummings Properties Management
DaimlerChrysler Corp.
Dain Bosworth Inc.
Demoulas Supermarkets Inc.
Deposit Guaranty National Bank
Dial Corp.
Disney Co. (Walt)
Dynamet, Inc.
Eckerd Corp.
Enterprise Rent-A-Car Co.
Federal-Mogul Corp.
Ferro Corp.
Fisher Brothers Cleaning Services
Fisher Scientific
Fluor Corp.
Forbes Inc.
Forest City Enterprises, Inc.
Gallo Winery, Inc. (E&J)
Galter Corp.
GenAmerica Corp.
GenCorp
Gerber Products Co.
Giant Eagle Inc.
Globe Corp.
Graco, Inc.
Group Health Plan
Guess?
Harcourt General, Inc.
Harley-Davidson Co.
Harris Corp.
Harsco Corp.
Hartmarx Corp.
Hasbro, Inc.
Hofmann Co.
International Flavors & Fragrances Inc.
International Multifoods Corp.
Invacare Corp.
Jacobson & Sons (Benjamin)
Katten, Muchin & Zavis
Kellwood Co.
Kennametal, Inc.
Kimberly-Clark Corp.
Kroger Co.
La-Z-Boy Inc.
LandAmerica Financial Services
Liberty Diversified Industries
Lilly & Co. (Eli)
Lipton Co.
Loews Corp.
Louisiana Land & Exploration Co.
Mark IV Industries
Mattel Inc.
McDonald & Co. Securities, Inc.
McWane Inc.
Mead Corp.
MidAmerican Energy Holdings Co.
Millipore Corp.
Mitsubishi Electric America
Montana Power Co.
MTD Products Inc.
National Service Industries, Inc.
New Jersey Natural Gas Co.
New York Mercantile Exchange
Occidental Oil and Gas
Ohio National Life Insurance Co.
Oshkosh B'Gosh, Inc.
Overseas Shipholding Group Inc.
Paine Webber
PerkinElmer, Inc.
Physicians Mutual Insurance Co.
Polaroid Corp.
Premier Dental Products Co.
Procter & Gamble Co., Cosmetics Division
Putnam Investments
Quanex Corp.
Ralph's Grocery Co.
Reinhart Institutional Foods
Rich Products Corp.
Russer Foods
Safeguard Scientifics
S&T Bancorp
Schwab & Co., Inc. (Charles)
Schwebel Baking Co.
Security Benefit Life Insurance Co.
Sega of America Inc.
Servco Pacific
S.G. Cowen
Sierra Pacific Resources
Simplot Co. (J.R.)
Southwest Gas Corp.
SPX Corp.
State Street Bank & Trust Co.
Stone Container Corp.
Strear Farms Co.
Texaco Inc.
Thompson Co. (J. Walter)
Ticketmaster Corp.
Times Mirror Co.
TJX Companies, Inc.
TMC Investment Co.
Tomkins Industries, Inc.
True North Communications, Inc.
True Oil Co.
Trustmark Insurance Co.
U.S. Bancorp
United States Sugar Corp.
Universal Studios
USG Corp.
Western & Southern Life Insurance Co.
Whitman Corp.
Wiley & Sons (John)
Winn-Dixie Stores Inc.
Wrigley Co. (Wm. Jr.)
Young & Rubicam
Zachry Co. (H.B.)

EMERGENCY/ AMBULANCE SERVICES

Abbott Laboratories
Ace Hardware Corp.
Aetna, Inc.
Agrilink Foods, Inc.
Air Products and Chemicals, Inc.
AK Steel Corp.
Albertson's Inc.
Alcoa Inc.
Alcon Laboratories, Inc.
Alexander & Baldwin, Inc.
Allegheny Technologies Inc.
Alliant Techsystems
Allmerica Financial Corp.
Allstate Insurance Co.
Alma Piston Co.
AMCORE Bank Rockford
Ameren Corp.
American Express Co.
American Fidelity Corp.
American General Finance
American Standard Inc.
Ameritas Life Insurance Corp.
Ameritech Corp.
AMETEK, Inc.
Amgen, Inc.
AMP Inc.
AMR Corp.
Andersen Corp.
Andersons Inc.
Anheuser-Busch Companies, Inc.
Aon Corp.
Aristech Chemical Corp.
Arizona Public Service Co.
Armstrong World Industries, Inc.
Arvin Industries, Inc.
AT&T Corp.
Atlantic Investment Co.
Avon Products, Inc.
Baird & Co. (Robert W.)
Bank of America
BankAtlantic Bancorp
Banta Corp.
Bard, Inc. (C.R.)
Barden Corp.
Bardes Corp.
Barnes Group Inc.
Bassett Furniture Industries
Baxter International Inc.
Bechtel Group, Inc.
Belk-Simpson Department Stores
Belk Stores Services Inc.
Bemis Co., Inc.
Bethlehem Steel Corp.
BFGoodrich Co.
Binney & Smith Inc.
Blue Bell, Inc.
Blue Cross & Blue Shield of Alabama
Blue Cross & Blue Shield of Iowa
Blue Cross & Blue Shield of Minnesota
Boeing Co.
Boise Cascade Corp.
Borden, Inc.
Borman's Inc.
Boston Edison Co.
BP Amoco Corp.
Bridgestone/Firestone, Inc.
Bristol-Myers Squibb Co.
Broderbund Software, Inc.
Brown Shoe Co., Inc.
Brunswick Corp.
Burlington Industries, Inc.
Burlington Resources, Inc.
Business Improvement
Butler Manufacturing Co.
Campbell Soup Co.
Cargill Inc.
Carillon Importers, Ltd.
Carpenter Technology Corp.
Carris Reels
Caterpillar Inc.
CCB Financial Corp.
Central Maine Power Co.
Central & South West Services
Central Soya Co.
CertainTeed Corp.
Cessna Aircraft Co.
CGU Insurance
Chase Bank of Texas
Chemed Corp.
Chesapeake Corp.
Chevron Corp.
Chicago Title Corp.
Church & Dwight Co., Inc.
Cincinnati Bell Inc.
Cinergy Corp.
Circuit City Stores, Inc.
CIT Group, Inc. (The)
Citibank Corp.
Citizens Financial Group, Inc.
CLARCOR Inc.
Cleveland-Cliffs, Inc.
Clorox Co.
Colonial Life & Accident Insurance Co.
Colonial Oil Industries, Inc.
Commerce Bancshares, Inc.
Commercial Intertech Corp.
ConAgra, Inc.
Cone Mills Corp.
Consolidated Natural Gas Co.
Consolidated Papers, Inc.
Consumers Energy Co.
Continental Grain Co.
Cooper Industries, Inc.
Coors Brewing Co.
Corning Inc.
Country Curtains, Inc.
Cox Enterprises Inc.
Crane Co.
Crane & Co., Inc.
Cranston Print Works Co.
Credit Suisse First Boston
Crestar Finance Corp.
Croft-Leominster
CSS Industries, Inc.
CUNA Mutual Group
Cyprus Amax Minerals Co.
DaimlerChrysler Corp.
Dain Bosworth Inc.
Dana Corp.
Deere & Co.
DeKalb Genetics Corp.
Delta Air Lines, Inc.
Deluxe Corp.
Detroit Edison Co.
Dexter Corp.
Dial Corp.
Dominion Resources, Inc.
Donaldson Co., Inc.
Dreyer's Grand Ice Cream
du Pont de Nemours & Co. (E.I.)
Duke Energy
Dun & Bradstreet Corp.
Duriron Co., Inc.
Dynamet, Inc.

Eastman Kodak Co.
Eaton Corp.
Ecolab Inc.
Elf Atochem North America, Inc.
Employers Mutual Casualty Co.
Enterprise Rent-A-Car Co.
Erving Industries
Ethyl Corp.
Exxon Mobil Corp.
Farmers Group, Inc.
Federated Mutual Insurance Co.
Ferro Corp.
Fifth Third Bancorp
First Hawaiian, Inc.
First Union Bank
First Union Corp.
First Union Securities, Inc.
Firstar Bank Milwaukee NA
Fisher Scientific
FleetBoston Financial Corp.
Florida Power Corp.
Florida Power & Light Co.
Fluor Corp.
FMC Corp.
Forbes Inc.
Ford Meter Box Co.
Ford Motor Co.
Forest City Enterprises, Inc.
Fort James Corp.
Fortis, Inc.
Fortune Brands, Inc.
Freeport-McMoRan Inc.
Fuller Co. (H.B.)
Furniture Brands International, Inc.
Gallo Winery, Inc. (E&J)
Gap, Inc.
GEICO Corp.
GenAmerica Corp.
GenCorp
General Atlantic Partners II LP
General Electric Co.
General Mills, Inc.
General Motors Corp.
General Reinsurance Corp.
Georgia-Pacific Corp.
Georgia Power Co.
Giant Eagle Inc.
Giddings & Lewis
Gillette Co.
Glickenhaus & Co.
Goldman Sachs Group
Green Bay Packaging
Group Health Plan
GTE Corp.
Hallmark Cards Inc.
Hamilton Sundstrand Corp.
Hanna Co. (M.A.)
Hannaford Brothers Co.
Harley-Davidson Co.
Harnischfeger Industries
Harris Corp.
Harsco Corp.
Hartford Steam Boiler Inspection & Insurance Co.
Hasbro, Inc.
Hawaiian Electric Co., Inc.
Hewlett-Packard Co.
Hoffmann-La Roche Inc.
Hofmann Co.
Hubbell Inc.
Humana, Inc.
IBP
IKON Office Solutions, Inc.
International Flavors & Fragrances Inc.
International Paper Co.
Jacobson & Sons (Benjamin)
Jeld-wen, Inc.
Jones & Co. (Edward D.)
Jostens, Inc.
Journal-Gazette Co.
Katten, Muchin & Zavis
Kellogg Co.
Kellwood Co.
Kemper National Insurance Companies
Kimberly-Clark Corp.
Kinder Morgn
Koch Enterprises, Inc.
La-Z-Boy Inc.
Ladish Co., Inc.
Lance, Inc.
Land O'Lakes, Inc.
LandAmerica Financial Services
Landmark Communications Inc.
Lee Enterprises
Lehigh Portland Cement Co.
Lennox International, Inc.
Levi Strauss & Co.
LG&E Energy Corp.
Liberty Corp.
Lilly & Co. (Eli)
Lincoln Electric Co.
Little, Inc. (Arthur D.)
Loews Corp.
Louisiana Land & Exploration Co.
Louisiana-Pacific Corp.
Lubrizol Corp. (The)
MacMillan Bloedel Inc.
Macy's East Inc.
Mark IV Industries
May Department Stores Co.
McDonald & Co. Securities, Inc.
MCI WorldCom, Inc.
McKesson-HBOC Corp.
McWane Inc.
Mead Corp.
Medtronic, Inc.
Menasha Corp.
Mercantile Bank NA
Merck & Co.
Merit Oil Corp.
Merrill Lynch & Co., Inc.
Mid-America Bank of Louisville
MidAmerican Energy Holdings Co.
Milacron, Inc.
Milliken & Co.
Millipore Corp.
Mine Safety Appliances Co.
Minnesota Mining & Manufacturing Co.
Minnesota Mutual Life Insurance Co.
Monsanto Co.
Montana Power Co.
Montgomery Ward & Co., Inc.
MONY Group (The)
Morgan & Co. Inc. (J.P.)
Morris Communications Corp.
Morrison Knudsen Corp.
Motorola Inc.
Nalco Chemical Co.
National City Bank of Minneapolis
National Machinery Co.
National Presto Industries, Inc.
National Starch & Chemical Co.
Nationwide Insurance Co.
Nestle U.S.A. Inc.
New Jersey Natural Gas Co.
New York Life Insurance Co.
New York Mercantile Exchange
Niagara Mohawk Holdings Inc.
Nomura Holding America
Nordson Corp.
Norfolk Southern Corp.
Northeast Utilities
Norton Co.
Norwest Corp.
Occidental Oil and Gas
Occidental Petroleum Corp.
OG&E Electric Services
Old National Bank Evansville
Olin Corp.
Oshkosh B'Gosh, Inc.
PACCAR Inc.
Pacific Century Financial Corp.
Pacific Mutual Life Insurance Co.
PacifiCorp
Paine Webber
Park National Bank
Parker Hannifin Corp.
Pella Corp.
PEMCO Corp.
Penney Co., Inc. (J.C.)
Pennzoil-Quaker State Co.
PerkinElmer, Inc.
Pfizer Inc.
Pharmacia & Upjohn, Inc.
Physicians Mutual Insurance Co.
PPG Industries, Inc.
Praxair
Premier Industrial Corp.
Price Associates (T. Rowe)
Principal Financial Group
Procter & Gamble Co.
Procter & Gamble Co., Cosmetics Division
Providence Journal-Bulletin Co.
Prudential Insurance Co. of America
Public Service Electric & Gas Co.
Publix Supermarkets
Pulitzer Publishing Co.
Quanex Corp.
Red Wing Shoe Co. Inc.
Reinhart Institutional Foods
Reynolds Metals Co.
Reynolds & Reynolds Co.
Reynolds Tobacco (R.J.)
Rich Products Corp.
Rockwell International Corp.
Royal & SunAlliance USA, Inc.
Rubbermaid Inc.
Safeguard Scientifics
Sara Lee Hosiery, Inc.
SBC Communications Inc.
Schering-Plough Corp.
Schloss & Co. (Marcus)
Schwab & Co., Inc. (Charles)
Scripps Co. (E.W.)
Security Benefit Life Insurance Co.
Servco Pacific
Shaw's Supermarkets, Inc.
Shea Co. (John F.)
Sherwin-Williams Co.
Sierra Pacific Resources
Simpson Investment Co.
SIT Investment Associates, Inc.
Smith Corp. (A.O.)
SmithKline Beecham Corp.
Sonoco Products Co.
Sony Electronics
Southeastern Mutual Insurance Co.
Southwest Gas Corp.
Sprint/United Telephone
SPX Corp.
Square D Co.
Standard Products Co.
Standard Register Co.
Stanley Works (The)
Starwood Hotels & Resorts Worldwide, Inc.
Steelcase Inc.
Stone Container Corp.
Storage Technology Corp.
Sun Microsystems Inc.
SunTrust Bank Atlanta
Synovus Financial Corp.
Taco Bell Corp.
Tai and Co. (J.T.)
Tektronix, Inc.
Telcordia Technologies
Tenneco Automotive
Tenneco Packaging
Tesoro Hawaii
Texaco Inc.
Thermo Electron Corp.
Thomasville Furniture Industries Inc.
Times Mirror Co.
Timken Co. (The)
TJX Companies, Inc.
TMC Investment Co.
Tomkins Industries, Inc.
Toro Co.
Trace International Holdings, Inc.
Transamerica Corp.
True Oil Co.
TRW Inc.
Tyson Foods Inc.
Ukrop's Super Markets
Ultramar Diamond Shamrock Corp.
Unilever Home & Personal Care U.S.A.
Union Camp Corp.
Union Pacific Corp.
United Services Automobile Association
U.S. Bancorp
U.S. Bancorp Piper Jaffray
United States Sugar Corp.
Universal Leaf Tobacco Co., Inc.
Universal Studios
Unocal Corp.
UnumProvident
US West, Inc.
Valero Energy Corp.
Valmont Industries, Inc.
Wachovia Bank of North Carolina NA
Waffle House Inc.
Wal-Mart Stores, Inc.
Washington Mutual, Inc.
Webster Bank
Weil, Gotshal & Manges Corp.
West Co. Inc.
Western & Southern Life Insurance Co.
Weyerhaeuser Co.
Whirlpool Corp.
Whitman Corp.
WICOR, Inc.
Wilbur-Ellis Co. & Connell Brothers Co.
Winn-Dixie Stores Inc.
Wiremold Co.
Wisconsin Power & Light Co.
Wisconsin Public Service Corp.
Witco Corp.
Wolverine World Wide
Woodward Governor Co.
Wyman-Gordon Co.
York Federal Savings & Loan Association
Young & Rubicam
Zilkha & Sons

EYES/BLINDNESS

Alabama Power Co.
Alcon Laboratories, Inc.
Allmerica Financial Corp.
AMR Corp.
Andersen Corp.
Arizona Public Service Co.
Armstrong World Industries, Inc.
Arvin Industries, Inc.
Associated Food Stores
Atlantic Investment Co.
Bandag, Inc.
Banfi Vintners
Bardes Corp.
Baxter International Inc.
Bernstein & Co., Inc. (Sanford C.)
Blue Cross & Blue Shield of Alabama
Borden, Inc.
Borman's Inc.
Brown Shoe Co., Inc.
Burress (J.W.)
Butler Capital Corp.
Callaway Golf Co.
Campbell Soup Co.
Cantor, Fitzgerald Securities Corp.
Cargill Inc.
Carlson Companies, Inc.
Carter-Wallace, Inc.
Central Newspapers, Inc.
Chase Manhattan Bank, NA
Chemed Corp.
Chicago Title Corp.
Clark Refining & Marketing
Collins & Aikman Corp.
Compaq Computer Corp.
Consolidated Papers, Inc.
CPI Corp.
Crane Co.
Crane & Co., Inc.
Crestar Finance Corp.
Cummins Engine Co., Inc.
Deluxe Corp.
Deutsch Co.
Dial Corp.
Disney Co. (Walt)
Dynamet, Inc.
Erb Lumber Co.
Federated Department Stores, Inc.
First Union Securities, Inc.
Ford Meter Box Co.
Fort Worth Star-Telegram Inc.
Freeport-McMoRan Inc.
Georgia-Pacific Corp.
Gerber Products Co.
Glaxo Wellcome Inc.
Golub Corp.
Group Health Plan
Hanna Co. (M.A.)
Harcourt General, Inc.
Hartford (The)

Hewlett-Packard Co.
Huntington Bancshares Inc.
International Flavors & Fragrances Inc.
Jostens, Inc.
Kellwood Co.
Kelly Services
Kroger Co.
Ladish Co., Inc.
Liz Claiborne, Inc.
LTV Corp.
Lubrizol Corp. (The)
McDonald & Co. Securities, Inc.
McGraw-Hill Companies, Inc.
Nationwide Insurance Co.
NEC America, Inc.
New England Bio Labs
Ohio National Life Insurance Co.
Oshkosh B'Gosh, Inc.
Pacific Mutual Life Insurance Co.
Polaroid Corp.
Premier Dental Products Co.
Premier Industrial Corp.
Ralph's Grocery Co.
Reinhart Institutional Foods
Schlumberger Ltd. (USA)
Security Life of Denver Insurance Co.
S.G. Cowen
Shea Co. (John F.)
Shell Oil Co.
Sonoco Products Co.
Sony Electronics
Southwest Gas Corp.
Star Bank NA
Stone Container Corp.
Susquehanna-Pfaltzgraff Co.
Synovus Financial Corp.
Tesoro Hawaii
Times Mirror Co.
Titan Industrial Corp.
Trace International Holdings, Inc.
United States Sugar Corp.
United Wisconsin Services
Universal Leaf Tobacco Co., Inc.
Universal Studios
USG Corp.
Vodafone AirTouch Plc
Waffle House Inc.
Whitman Corp.
Wolverine World Wide

HEALTH-GENERAL

Airborne Freight Corp.
Alaska Airlines, Inc.
Allmerica Financial Corp.
AMCORE Bank Rockford
American General Corp.
American Retail Group
American Stock Exchange, Inc.
Ameritech Wisconsin
AmerUS Group
Avery Dennison Corp.
Baird & Co. (Robert W.)
Ball Corp.
Bandag, Inc.
Bank One, Texas-Houston Office
BankBoston-Connecticut Region
Bard, Inc. (C.R.)
Barry Corp. (R.G.)
Bell Atlantic Corp.-West Virginia
Bell Atlantic-Delaware, Inc.
Berwind Group
Binney & Smith Inc.
Blair & Co. (William)
Blue Cross & Blue Shield of Michigan
Blue Cross & Blue Shield of Minnesota
Boston Gas Co.
Bourns, Inc.
Branch Banking & Trust Co.
Briggs & Stratton Corp.
Brooklyn Union
Business Men's Assurance Co. of America
Caesar's World, Inc.
Castle & Cooke Properties Inc.
CCB Financial Corp.
Cenex Harvest States
Centex Corp.
Central Maine Power Co.
Chemed Corp.
Chicago Sun-Times, Inc.
Cinergy Corp.
Citizens Bank-Flint
Clark Refining & Marketing
CNA
Coachmen Industries, Inc.
Colgate-Palmolive Co.
Colonial Oil Industries, Inc.
Commercial Intertech Corp.
Computer Associates International, Inc.
Conectiv
Conwood Co. LP
Cooper Tire & Rubber Co.
Crane & Co., Inc.
CSX Corp.
Curtis Industries, Inc. (Helene)
DeKalb Genetics Corp.
Diebold, Inc.
Disney Co. (Walt)
Duquesne Light Co.
Duracell International
Duriron Co., Inc.
Eastern Bank
Eastman Chemical Co.
Ebsco Industries, Inc.
Employers Insurance of Wausau, A Mutual Co.
Employers Mutual Casualty Co.
Entergy Corp.
Equitable Resources, Inc.
Erving Industries
Evening Post Publishing Co.
Excel Corp.
Fabri-Kal Corp.
Farmers Group, Inc.
Federated Mutual Insurance Co.
Ferro Corp.
Firstar Bank Milwaukee NA
FirstEnergy Corp.
Fox Entertainment Group
Frito-Lay, Inc.
Gates Rubber Corp.
Gerber Products Co.
Group Health Plan
Hercules Inc.
Hewlett-Packard Co.
HSBC Bank USA
Huffy Corp.
Hunt Oil Co.
Huntington Bancshares Inc.
Idaho Power Co.
Ingram Industries Inc.
Interpublic Group of Companies, Inc.
INTRUST Financial Corp.
Invacare Corp.
Jacobs Engineering Group
Kaman Corp.
Kellwood Co.
Kelly Services
Kendall International, Inc.
Kimberly-Clark Corp.
Kinder Morgn
Lehigh Portland Cement Co.
Liberty Mutual Insurance Group
Loctite Corp.
Lowe's Companies
Manulife Financial
Maritz Inc.
MBIA Inc.
McDonald & Co. Securities, Inc.
Memphis Light Gas & Water Division
Merit Oil Corp.
Mid-America Bank of Louisville
Mutual of Omaha Insurance Co.
National City Bank of Cleveland
National City Bank of Columbus
National City Bank of Pennsylvania
National Computer Systems, Inc.
National Life of Vermont
New England Bio Labs
New Jersey Natural Gas Co.
New York Mercantile Exchange
New York State Electric & Gas Corp.
Niagara Mohawk Holdings Inc.
Northrop Grumman Corp.
Northwest Natural Gas Co.
Ohio National Life Insurance Co.
Old National Bank Evansville
ONEOK, Inc.
Orange & Rockland Utilities, Inc.
Owens-Illinois Inc.
PEMCO Corp.
Penn Mutual Life Insurance Co.
Pennsylvania Power & Light
Pentair Inc.
Phoenix Home Life Mutual Insurance Co.
Physicians Mutual Insurance Co.
Pioneer Group
Pioneer Natural Resources
PNC Bank
Provident Mutual Life Insurance Co.
Public Service Co. of Oklahoma
Regions Financial Corp.
Rohm & Haas Co.
Royal & SunAlliance USA, Inc.
Santa Fe International Corp.
Sara Lee Hosiery, Inc.
SCANA Corp.
Scientific-Atlanta, Inc.
Security Life of Denver Insurance Co.
Servco Pacific
ServiceMaster Co.
Shaw Industries Inc.
Sonoco Products Co.
Southern Co. Services Inc.
Sprint/United Telephone
SPX Corp.
Storage Technology Corp.
Susquehanna-Pfaltzgraff Co.
Tampa Electric Co.
TCF National Bank Minnesota
Teleflex Inc.
Tenneco Packaging
Texas Gas Transmission Corp.
Times Mirror Co.
Trustmark Insurance Co.
Trustmark National Bank
Ultramar Diamond Shamrock Corp.
US Bank, Washington
Washington Mutual, Inc.
Wausau Insurance Companies
WICOR, Inc.
Wilbur-Ellis Co. & Connell Brothers Co.
Wiremold Co.
Wolverine World Wide
Wyman-Gordon Co.
Zachry Co. (H.B.)
Zurn Industries, Inc.

GERIATRIC HEALTH

Abbott Laboratories
Agrilink Foods, Inc.
Albertson's Inc.
Alcoa Inc.
AlliedSignal Inc.
American Retail Group
Ameritech Michigan
Associated Food Stores
Bard, Inc. (C.R.)
Battelle Memorial Institute
Bausch & Lomb Inc.
Bernstein & Co., Inc. (Sanford C.)
Bethlehem Steel Corp.
BFGoodrich Co.
Block, Inc. (H&R)
Blue Cross & Blue Shield of Michigan
Borman's Inc.
Bristol-Myers Squibb Co.
Carnival Corp.
Central Maine Power Co.
Chase Manhattan Bank, NA
Citigroup
Citizens Financial Group, Inc.
Clorox Co.
Colonial Life & Accident Insurance Co.
CPI Corp.
Deutsch Co.
du Pont de Nemours & Co. (E.I.)
Edison International
Extendicare Health Services
Federated Mutual Insurance Co.
First Union Corp.
First Union National Bank, NA
Fisher Brothers Cleaning Services
Florida Power & Light Co.
Florida Rock Industries
Ford Meter Box Co.
Fortis Insurance Co.
Gallo Winery, Inc. (E&J)
GATX Corp.
General Mills, Inc.
Georgia Power Co.
Giant Eagle Inc.
Giant Food Inc.
Glickenhaus & Co.
Group Health Plan
GTE Corp.
Harland Co. (John H.)
Hartford (The)
Hasbro, Inc.
Huntington Bancshares Inc.
Johnson & Johnson
Journal-Gazette Co.
Kimberly-Clark Corp.
Land O'Lakes, Inc.
Lee Enterprises
Loews Corp.
Lubrizol Corp. (The)
Mamiye Brothers
Manor Care Health SVS, Inc.
MBIA Inc.
Medtronic, Inc.
Merck & Co.
Merrill Lynch & Co., Inc.
Minnesota Mining & Manufacturing Co.
Morgan & Co. Inc. (J.P.)
Nalco Chemical Co.
National City Corp.
National Machinery Co.
New England Financial
New York Life Insurance Co.
Norton Co.
Overseas Shipholding Group Inc.
Pacific Mutual Life Insurance Co.
PacifiCare Health Systems
PEMCO Corp.
Pfizer Inc.
Phelps Dodge Corp.
Phillips Petroleum Co.
Premier Dental Products Co.
Prudential Insurance Co. of America
Publix Supermarkets
Reynolds Tobacco (R.J.)
Royal & SunAlliance USA, Inc.
Russer Foods
Seaway Food Town, Inc.
Sempra Energy
Shaw's Supermarkets, Inc.
Simpson Investment Co.
Slant/Fin Corp.
Starwood Hotels & Resorts Worldwide, Inc.
State Street Bank & Trust Co.
Steelcase Inc.
SunTrust Bank Atlanta
Synovus Financial Corp.
Trace International Holdings, Inc.
Union Camp Corp.
United States Trust Co. of New York
United Wisconsin Services
Wachtell, Lipton, Rosen & Katz
Wal-Mart Stores, Inc.
Warner-Lambert Co.
Witco Corp.
Woodward Governor Co.
Young & Rubicam
Zilkha & Sons

HEALTH POLICY/COST CONTAINMENT

Alcoa Inc.
Allstate Insurance Co.
Ameritech Illinois
Ameritech Indiana
Ameritech Ohio
Anheuser-Busch Companies, Inc.
AT&T Corp.

Bandag, Inc.
Battelle Memorial Institute
Baxter International Inc.
Bemis Co., Inc.
Bestfoods
Bethlehem Steel Corp.
Blue Cross & Blue Shield of Michigan
Blue Cross & Blue Shield of Minnesota
Butler Manufacturing Co.
Chase Manhattan Bank, NA
Chevron Corp.
Citibank Corp.
Colonial Life & Accident Insurance Co.
Consolidated Natural Gas Co.
Cox Enterprises Inc.
Crestar Finance Corp.
CSS Industries, Inc.
CUNA Mutual Group
Deere & Co.
DeKalb Genetics Corp.
du Pont de Nemours & Co. (E.I.)
Duke Energy
Eaton Corp.
Employers Mutual Casualty Co.
Extendicare Health Services
Federated Mutual Insurance Co.
FMC Corp.
Ford Motor Co.
Fortis Insurance Co.
General Electric Co.
General Mills, Inc.
General Reinsurance Corp.
Gerber Products Co.
Glaxo Wellcome Inc.
Group Health Plan
GTE Corp.
Guardian Life Insurance Co. of America
Hancock Financial Services (John)
Hartford (The)
International Business Machines Corp.
International Flavors & Fragrances Inc.
Jeld-wen, Inc.
JSJ Corp.
Lilly & Co. (Eli)
LTV Corp.
Medtronic, Inc.
Merck & Co.
Metropolitan Life Insurance Co.
Minnesota Mining & Manufacturing Co.
Monsanto Co.
Morgan & Co. Inc. (J.P.)
Nalco Chemical Co.
National Computer Systems, Inc.
Norton Co.
Ohio National Life Insurance Co.
Pacific Mutual Life Insurance Co.
Physicians Mutual Insurance Co.
PPG Industries, Inc.
Principal Financial Group
Prudential Insurance Co. of America
Ralston Purina Co.
Rockwell International Corp.
SAFECO Corp.
Schering-Plough Corp.
State Street Bank & Trust Co.
Steelcase Inc.
TENNANT Co.
Tesoro Hawaii
Textron Inc.
TRW Inc.
United States Trust Co. of New York
United Technologies Corp.
United Wisconsin Services
UnumProvident
Whitman Corp.
WICOR, Inc.
Xerox Corp.

HEALTH FUNDS

Alcoa Inc.
Alcon Laboratories, Inc.
Allstate Insurance Co.
AMETEK, Inc.
AMR Corp.
Andersen Corp.
Aon Corp.
Arizona Public Service Co.
Avon Products, Inc.
Bandag, Inc.
Bard, Inc. (C.R.)
Barry Corp. (R.G.)
Bayer Corp.
Belk Stores Services Inc.
Bemis Co., Inc.
Bestfoods
Block, Inc. (H&R)
Blue Cross & Blue Shield of Minnesota
Bradford & Co. (J.C.)
Briggs & Stratton Corp.
Browning-Ferris Industries Inc.
Carpenter Technology Corp.
Central National-Gottesman
Central Soya Co.
Cessna Aircraft Co.
Chevron Corp.
Church & Dwight Co., Inc.
CLARCOR Inc.
Clorox Co.
Compass Bank
Cooper Industries, Inc.
Coors Brewing Co.
Crane & Co., Inc.
Crestar Finance Corp.
Danis Companies
Detroit Edison Co.
Dexter Corp.
Dial Corp.
Donaldson Co., Inc.
Duchossois Industries Inc.
Duriron Co., Inc.
Eaton Corp.
Eckerd Corp.
Federal-Mogul Corp.
Federated Department Stores, Inc.
Fifth Third Bancorp
First Financial Bank
First Source Corp.
First Union Corp.
FMC Corp.
Forbes Inc.
Gap, Inc.
Georgia-Pacific Corp.
Globe Corp.
Grace & Co. (W.R.)
Harcourt General, Inc.
Hubbard Broadcasting, Inc.
Huffy Corp.
IKON Office Solutions, Inc.
Invacare Corp.
Kerr-McGee Corp.
Kimberly-Clark Corp.
Leigh Fibers, Inc.
Lennox International, Inc.
Lipton Co.
LTV Corp.
Macy's East Inc.
Marriott International Inc.
May Department Stores Co.
Metropolitan Life Insurance Co.
Mine Safety Appliances Co.
Minnesota Mutual Life Insurance Co.
National Presto Industries, Inc.
National Starch & Chemical Co.
Newman's Own Inc.
Nissan North America, Inc.
Nomura Holding America
Orscheln Co.
Parker Hannifin Corp.
PEMCO Corp.
Pfizer Inc.
Phelps Dodge Corp.
Pittway Corp.
ReliaStar Financial Corp.
Royal & SunAlliance USA, Inc.
Shell Oil Co.
Shoney's Inc.
SmithKline Beecham Corp.
Southern California Gas Co.
Square D Co.
Standard Register Co.
Storage Technology Corp.
TCF National Bank Minnesota
Transamerica Corp.
True Oil Co.
Union Camp Corp.
United Distillers & Vintners North America
United States Trust Co. of New York
Universal Leaf Tobacco Co., Inc.
Wachovia Bank of North Carolina NA
Wal-Mart Stores, Inc.
Warner-Lambert Co.
Waste Management Inc.
Westvaco Corp.
Williams
Wrigley Co. (Wm. Jr.)

HEALTH ORGANIZATIONS

Abbott Laboratories
ABC
Aetna, Inc.
AFLAC Inc.
AGL Resources Inc.
Agrilink Foods, Inc.
Air Products and Chemicals, Inc.
Alabama Power Co.
Alcoa Inc.
Alcon Laboratories, Inc.
Alexander & Baldwin, Inc.
Allianz Life Insurance Co. of North America
AlliedSignal Inc.
Allmerica Financial Corp.
Allstate Insurance Co.
AMCORE Bank Rockford
Ameren Corp.
America West Airlines, Inc.
American Express Co.
American Fidelity Corp.
American Retail Group
American United Life Insurance Co.
Ameritas Life Insurance Corp.
Ameritech Illinois
AMETEK, Inc.
Amgen, Inc.
AMP Inc.
AMR Corp.
Amsted Industries Inc.
Andersen Corp.
Anheuser-Busch Companies, Inc.
Archer-Daniels-Midland Co.
Armstrong World Industries, Inc.
Arvin Industries, Inc.
Ashland, Inc.
Atlantic Investment Co.
Avon Products, Inc.
Badger Meter, Inc.
Baird & Co. (Robert W.)
Bandag, Inc.
Banfi Vintners
Bank of America
Bank of New York Co., Inc.
Bank One, Texas-Houston Office
BankBoston Corp.
Bard, Inc. (C.R.)
Barden Corp.
Barry Corp. (R.G.)
Baxter International Inc.
Bayer Corp.
Belk-Simpson Department Stores
Belk Stores Services Inc.
Belo Corp. (A.H.)
Bemis Co., Inc.
Bernstein & Co., Inc. (Sanford C.)
Bestfoods
Bethlehem Steel Corp.
BFGoodrich Co.
Binswanger Companies
Blair & Co. (William)
Block, Inc. (H&R)
Blount International, Inc.
Blue Cross & Blue Shield of Alabama
Blue Cross & Blue Shield of Iowa
Blue Cross & Blue Shield of Minnesota
Borman's Inc.
Boston Edison Co.
Boston Globe (The)
Bowater Inc.
Bridgestone/Firestone, Inc.
Briggs & Stratton Corp.
Bristol-Myers Squibb Co.
Browning-Ferris Industries Inc.
Brunswick Corp.
Bucyrus-Erie Co.
Burlington Industries, Inc.
Burnett Co. (Leo)
Business Improvement
Butler Manufacturing Co.
Cabot Corp.
California Bank & Trust
Callaway Golf Co.
Calvin Klein
Cargill Inc.
Carillon Importers, Ltd.
Carnival Corp.
Carpenter Technology Corp.
Carrier Corp.
Carris Reels
Carter-Wallace, Inc.
Caterpillar Inc.
Central Maine Power Co.
Central & South West Services
Central Soya Co.
CertainTeed Corp.
Cessna Aircraft Co.
Charter Manufacturing Co.
Chase Bank of Texas
Chase Manhattan Bank, NA
Chesapeake Corp.
Chevron Corp.
Chicago Title Corp.
Chicago Tribune Co.
Church & Dwight Co., Inc.
CIGNA Corp.
CIT Group, Inc. (The)
Citibank Corp.
Citigroup
Citizens Financial Group, Inc.
CLARCOR Inc.
Cleveland-Cliffs, Inc.
Clorox Co.
CNA
Collins & Aikman Corp.
Colonial Oil Industries, Inc.
Commerce Bancshares, Inc.
Commercial Intertech Corp.
Commonwealth Edison Co.
Compass Bank
ConAgra, Inc.
Cone Mills Corp.
Consolidated Natural Gas Co.
Consolidated Papers, Inc.
Contran Corp.
Cooper Industries, Inc.
Coors Brewing Co.
Crane Co.
Crane & Co., Inc.
Crestar Finance Corp.
CUNA Mutual Group
DaimlerChrysler Corp.
Dain Bosworth Inc.
Dana Corp.
Danis Companies
Dayton Hudson
Deere & Co.
Delta Air Lines, Inc.
Deluxe Corp.
Demoulas Supermarkets Inc.
Deposit Guaranty National Bank
Detroit Edison Co.
Deutsch Co.
Dexter Corp.
Dial Corp.
Disney Co. (Walt)
Dixie Group, Inc. (The)
Dominion Resources, Inc.
Donaldson Co., Inc.
Dreyer's Grand Ice Cream
du Pont de Nemours & Co. (E.I.)
Duchossois Industries Inc.
Duke Energy
Dun & Bradstreet Corp.
Duriron Co., Inc.
Dynamet, Inc.
Eastern Bank
Eastman Kodak Co.
Eaton Corp.
Eckerd Corp.
Edison International
Emerson Electric Co.
Ensign-Bickford Industries
Enterprise Rent-A-Car Co.
Equifax Inc.
Ethyl Corp.
Extendicare Health Services
Exxon Mobil Corp.
Federal-Mogul Corp.

Federated Mutual Insurance Co.
FedEx Corp.
Fidelity Investments
FINA
Fireman's Fund Insurance Co.
First Hawaiian, Inc.
First Source Corp.
First Union Corp.
First Union Securities, Inc.
Firstar Bank Milwaukee NA
Fisher Scientific
Florida Power & Light Co.
Florida Rock Industries
FMC Corp.
Forbes Inc.
Ford Meter Box Co.
Ford Motor Co.
Forest City Enterprises, Inc.
Fort Worth Star-Telegram Inc.
Fortis Insurance Co.
Fortune Brands, Inc.
Freddie Mac
Freeport-McMoRan Inc.
Fuller Co. (H.B.)
Gallo Winery, Inc. (E&J)
Galter Corp.
Gap, Inc.
GATX Corp.
General Atlantic Partners II LP
General Electric Co.
General Mills, Inc.
General Motors Corp.
General Reinsurance Corp.
Georgia-Pacific Corp.
Georgia Power Co.
Gerber Products Co.
Giant Eagle Inc.
Glaxo Wellcome Inc.
Glickenhaus & Co.
Globe Corp.
Golub Corp.
Goodrich Aerospace - Aerostructures Group (B.F.)
Grace & Co. (W.R.)
Graco, Inc.
Green Bay Packaging
Group Health Plan
Guess?
Gulf Power Co.
Hallmark Cards Inc.
Hannaford Brothers Co.
Harley-Davidson Co.
Harris Corp.
Harris Trust & Savings Bank
Harsco Corp.
Hartford (The)
Hartford Steam Boiler Inspection & Insurance Co.
Hartmarx Corp.
Hawaiian Electric Co., Inc.
Heinz Co. (H.J.)
Hoffmann-La Roche Inc.
Hofmann Co.
Honeywell International Inc.
Household International Inc.
Hubbard Broadcasting, Inc.
Hubbell Inc.
Huffy Corp.
Humana, Inc.
IKON Office Solutions, Inc.
Inland Container Corp.
Inman Mills
International Business Machines Corp.
International Paper Co.
INTRUST Financial Corp.
Jacobs Engineering Group
Jacobson & Sons (Benjamin)
Jeld-wen, Inc.
Johnson Controls Inc.
Johnson & Johnson
Johnson & Son (S.C.)
Journal-Gazette Co.
JSJ Corp.
Katten, Muchin & Zavis
Kellogg Co.
Kennametal, Inc.
Kerr-McGee Corp.
Kimberly-Clark Corp.
Kinder Morgn
Kingsbury Corp.
Kraft Foods, Inc.
Kroger Co.
Ladish Co., Inc.
Lance, Inc.
Lehigh Portland Cement Co.
Lennox International, Inc.
Levi Strauss & Co.
Liberty Corp.
Lilly & Co. (Eli)
Lincoln Electric Co.
Lipton Co.
Liz Claiborne, Inc.
Loews Corp.
Lotus Development Corp.
Louisiana Land & Exploration Co.
Louisiana-Pacific Corp.
LTV Corp.
Lubrizol Corp. (The)
Macy's East Inc.
Madison Gas & Electric Co.
Mamiye Brothers
Manulife Financial
Marcus Corp.
Marriott International Inc.
Marshall & Ilsley Corp.
Masco Corp.
Mattel Inc.
May Department Stores Co.
MBIA Inc.
McCormick & Co. Inc.
McDonald & Co. Securities, Inc.
McGraw-Hill Companies, Inc.
MCI WorldCom, Inc.
Medtronic, Inc.
Mellon Financial Corp.
Merck & Co.
Merit Oil Corp.
Merrill Lynch & Co., Inc.
Metropolitan Life Insurance Co.
MFA Inc.
Michigan Consolidated Gas Co.
Milacron, Inc.
Millipore Corp.
Mine Safety Appliances Co.
Minnesota Mining & Manufacturing Co.
Monsanto Co.
Montana Power Co.
MONY Group (The)
Morgan & Co. Inc. (J.P.)
Morris Communications Corp.
Morrison Knudsen Corp.
MTD Products Inc.
Nabisco Group Holdings
Nalco Chemical Co.
National Bank of Commerce Trust & Savings
National City Bank of Columbus
National City Bank of Minneapolis
National Machinery Co.
National Starch & Chemical Co.
Nationwide Insurance Co.
NCR Corp.
NEBCO Evans
New England Bio Labs
New England Financial
New Jersey Natural Gas Co.
New York Life Insurance Co.
Nissan North America, Inc.
Norfolk Southern Corp.
Northern States Power Co.
Northern Trust Co.
Northwest Bank Nebraska, NA
Northwest Natural Gas Co.
Norton Co.
Occidental Petroleum Corp.
OG&E Electric Services
Old National Bank Evansville
Olin Corp.
Orscheln Co.
Oshkosh B'Gosh, Inc.
PACCAR Inc.
Pacific Century Financial Corp.
Pacific Mutual Life Insurance Co.
PacifiCare Health Systems
PacifiCorp
Parker Hannifin Corp.
Penney Co., Inc. (J.C.)
Pennzoil-Quaker State Co.
Peoples Energy Corp.
PepsiCo, Inc.
PerkinElmer, Inc.
Pfizer Inc.
Pharmacia & Upjohn, Inc.
Phelps Dodge Corp.
Phillips Petroleum Co.
Physicians Mutual Insurance Co.
PNC Financial Services Group
Potomac Electric Power Co.
PPG Industries, Inc.
Premier Dental Products Co.
Premier Industrial Corp.
Price Associates (T. Rowe)
Principal Financial Group
Procter & Gamble Co.
Procter & Gamble Co., Cosmetics Division
Providence Journal-Bulletin Co.
Provident Companies, Inc.
Prudential Insurance Co. of America
Prudential Securities Inc.
Quaker Chemical Corp.
Quanex Corp.
Questar Corp.
Ralph's Grocery Co.
Ralston Purina Co.
Red Wing Shoe Co. Inc.
Regions Bank
Reilly Industries, Inc.
Reily & Co., Inc. (William B.)
Reliant Energy Inc.
Reynolds & Reynolds Co.
Rich Products Corp.
Rockwell International Corp.
Royal & SunAlliance USA, Inc.
Rubbermaid Inc.
Ruddick Corp.
Russer Foods
SAFECO Corp.
Safeguard Scientifics
Sara Lee Corp.
Sara Lee Hosiery, Inc.
SBC Communications Inc.
Schloss & Co. (Marcus)
Schwebel Baking Co.
Searle & Co. (G.D.)
Seaway Food Town, Inc.
Security Benefit Life Insurance Co.
Sega of America Inc.
Sempra Energy
Sentinel Communications Co.
Sentry Insurance, A Mutual Co.
S.G. Cowen
Shaw's Supermarkets, Inc.
Shell Oil Co.
Shoney's Inc.
Sierra Pacific Industries
Simplot Co. (J.R.)
Simpson Investment Co.
SIT Investment Associates, Inc.
SmithKline Beecham Corp.
Smucker Co. (JM)
Sonoco Products Co.
Sony Electronics
Southeastern Mutual Insurance Co.
SPX Corp.
Standard Products Co.
Star Bank NA
State Street Bank & Trust Co.
Steelcase Inc.
Stone & Webster Inc.
Storage Technology Corp.
Stupp Brothers Bridge & Iron Co.
SunTrust Bank Atlanta
Synovus Financial Corp.
Taco Bell Corp.
Tai and Co. (J.T.)
TCF National Bank Minnesota
Temple-Inland Inc.
Tenet Healthcare Corp.
TENNANT Co.
Tenneco Automotive
Tension Envelope Corp.
Texaco Inc.
Textron Inc.
Timken Co. (The)
Titan Industrial Corp.
TJX Companies, Inc.
TMC Investment Co.
Tomkins Industries, Inc.
Torchmark Corp.
Toyota Motor Sales U.S.A., Inc.
Trace International Holdings, Inc.
Transamerica Corp.
TRW Inc.
Tyson Foods Inc.
Unilever Home & Personal Care U.S.A.
Unilever United States, Inc.
Union Camp Corp.
Union Pacific Corp.
United Distillers & Vintners North America
United States Sugar Corp.
United States Trust Co. of New York
United Technologies Corp.
United Wisconsin Services
Universal Leaf Tobacco Co., Inc.
Universal Studios
Unocal Corp.
USG Corp.
UST Inc.
USX Corp.
Varian Medical Systems, Inc.
Vulcan Materials Co.
Wachovia Bank of North Carolina NA
Waffle House Inc.
Wal-Mart Stores, Inc.
Walter Industries Inc.
Warner-Lambert Co.
Webster Bank
West Co. Inc.
Western & Southern Life Insurance Co.
Westvaco Corp.
Whirlpool Corp.
Wilbur-Ellis Co. & Connell Brothers Co.
Williams
Wiremold Co.
Wisconsin Energy Corp.
Wisconsin Power & Light Co.
Wisconsin Public Service Corp.
Woodward Governor Co.
Wrigley Co. (Wm. Jr.)
Wyman-Gordon Co.
Yellow Corp.
York Federal Savings & Loan Association
Zachry Co. (H.B.)

HEART

Abbott Laboratories
ABC
AEGON U.S.A. Inc.
Aetna, Inc.
Agrilink Foods, Inc.
Air Products and Chemicals, Inc.
AK Steel Corp.
Alabama Power Co.
Alaska Airlines, Inc.
Alexander & Baldwin, Inc.
Allianz Life Insurance Co. of North America
AlliedSignal Inc.
Allmerica Financial Corp.
Alma Piston Co.
American Fidelity Corp.
American General Finance
Amgen, Inc.
Anheuser-Busch Companies, Inc.
APL Ltd.
Arizona Public Service Co.
Badger Meter, Inc.
Baird & Co. (Robert W.)
Banta Corp.
Bard, Inc. (C.R.)
Bardes Corp.
Baxter International Inc.
Beckman Coulter, Inc.
Bernstein & Co., Inc. (Sanford C.)
Block, Inc. (H&R)
Blue Bell, Inc.
Blue Cross & Blue Shield of Alabama
Blue Cross & Blue Shield of Michigan
Blue Cross & Blue Shield of Minnesota
Bradford & Co. (J.C.)
Briggs & Stratton Corp.
Bristol-Myers Squibb Co.
Business Improvement
Cabot Corp.
Campbell Soup Co.
Carlson Companies, Inc.
Carpenter Technology Corp.
Central National-Gottesman
CertainTeed Corp.

Cessna Aircraft Co.
Chase Bank of Texas
Circuit City Stores, Inc.
CIT Group, Inc. (The)
Cleveland-Cliffs, Inc.
Commercial Intertech Corp.
Compaq Computer Corp.
Compass Bank
Cooper Industries, Inc.
Crane & Co., Inc.
Crestar Finance Corp.
Croft-Leominster
Cummings Properties Management
Dain Bosworth Inc.
Danis Companies
Dial Corp.
Eastern Bank
Erving Industries
Federated Mutual Insurance Co.
First Union Securities, Inc.
Firstar Bank Milwaukee NA
FleetBoston Financial Corp.
Ford Meter Box Co.
Freddie Mac
Freeport-McMoRan Inc.
Gallo Winery, Inc. (E&J)
Galter Corp.
GEICO Corp.
GenAmerica Corp.
Gerber Products Co.
Giant Eagle Inc.
Giant Food Inc.
Giddings & Lewis
Globe Corp.
Group Health Plan
Hanna Co. (M.A.)
Hannaford Brothers Co.
Harnischfeger Industries
Hasbro, Inc.
Hawaiian Electric Co., Inc.
Hensel Phelps Construction Co.
Hofmann Co.
Humana, Inc.
Huntington Bancshares Inc.
IKON Office Solutions, Inc.
Illinois Tool Works, Inc.
Inman Mills
International Flavors & Fragrances Inc.
Invacare Corp.
Jacobs Engineering Group
Kelly Services
Kennametal, Inc.
Kingsbury Corp.
Ladish Co., Inc.
Lancaster Lens, Inc.
LandAmerica Financial Services
Lehigh Portland Cement Co.
Leviton Manufacturing Co. Inc.
Lilly & Co. (Eli)
Lipton Co.
Louisiana-Pacific Corp.
LTV Corp.
Madison Gas & Electric Co.
Manor Care Health SVS, Inc.
Manulife Financial
Marcus Corp.
Mark IV Industries
May Department Stores Co.
McWane Inc.
Medtronic, Inc.
Merck & Co.
Merrill Lynch & Co., Inc.
Metropolitan Life Insurance Co.
Mid-America Bank of Louisville
MidAmerican Energy Holdings Co.
Mutual of Omaha Insurance Co.
Nalco Chemical Co.
National Machinery Co.
National Presto Industries, Inc.
National Service Industries, Inc.
Nationwide Insurance Co.
NEBCO Evans
Niagara Mohawk Holdings Inc.
Norfolk Southern Corp.
Occidental Oil and Gas
OG&E Electric Services
Ohio National Life Insurance Co.
Orange & Rockland Utilities, Inc.
Oshkosh B'Gosh, Inc.
Overseas Shipholding Group Inc.
Pacific Mutual Life Insurance Co.
PacifiCare Health Systems
PEMCO Corp.
Physicians Mutual Insurance Co.
Price Associates (T. Rowe)
Provident Companies, Inc.
Prudential Securities Inc.
Putnam Investments
Quanex Corp.
Regions Bank
Reinhart Institutional Foods
Rich Products Corp.
Royal & SunAlliance USA, Inc.
Ruddick Corp.
Russer Foods
Safeguard Scientifics
S&T Bancorp
Schwebel Baking Co.
Searle & Co. (G.D.)
Sega of America Inc.
Sentry Insurance, A Mutual Co.
Servco Pacific
S.G. Cowen
Shell Oil Co.
Sierra Pacific Industries
Sierra Pacific Resources
SIT Investment Associates, Inc.
Southeastern Mutual Insurance Co.
Southwest Gas Corp.
Star Bank NA
Storage Technology Corp.
Sun Microsystems Inc.
Synovus Financial Corp.
Tai and Co. (J.T.)
TCF National Bank Minnesota
Thompson Co. (J. Walter)
TJX Companies, Inc.
TMC Investment Co.
Transamerica Corp.
Tyson Foods Inc.
United Airlines Inc.
United States Sugar Corp.
United Wisconsin Services
Universal Foods Corp.
USG Corp.
Valmont Industries, Inc.
Waffle House Inc.
Walter Industries Inc.
Warner-Lambert Co.
Washington Trust Bank
Weil, Gotshal & Manges Corp.
Winn-Dixie Stores Inc.
York Federal Savings & Loan Association
Young & Rubicam

HOME-CARE SERVICES

Baxter International Inc.
Citigroup
Commercial Intertech Corp.
Erving Industries
Federated Mutual Insurance Co.
Fireman's Fund Insurance Co.
Galter Corp.
Heinz Co. (H.J.)
Industrial Bank of Japan Trust Co. (New York)
Kelly Services
Manor Care Health SVS, Inc.
Millipore Corp.
Morgan Stanley Dean Witter & Co.
Nalco Chemical Co.
Old National Bank Evansville
PEMCO Corp.
Pulitzer Publishing Co.
Royal & SunAlliance USA, Inc.
Schwab & Co., Inc. (Charles)
Union Carbide Corp.
Witco Corp.

HOSPICES

Abbott Laboratories
AFLAC Inc.
AGL Resources Inc.
Agrilink Foods, Inc.
AK Steel Corp.
Albany International Corp.
Alcoa Inc.
AMCORE Bank Rockford
American General Finance
AmerUS Group
Amgen, Inc.
AMP Inc.
Andersons Inc.
Aristech Chemical Corp.
Arizona Public Service Co.
Armstrong World Industries, Inc.
Arvin Industries, Inc.
ASARCO Inc.
Atlantic Investment Co.
Avon Products, Inc.
Bandag, Inc.
Barclays Capital
Bard, Inc. (C.R.)
Barden Corp.
Bardes Corp.
BFGoodrich Co.
Block, Inc. (H&R)
Blount International, Inc.
Blue Bell, Inc.
Blue Cross & Blue Shield of Iowa
Boeing Co.
Boler Co.
Borman's Inc.
Boston Edison Co.
Bourns, Inc.
Bridgestone/Firestone, Inc.
Broderbund Software, Inc.
Browning-Ferris Industries Inc.
Brunswick Corp.
Burnett Co. (Leo)
Business Improvement
Carnival Corp.
Caterpillar Inc.
Central Maine Power Co.
Central National-Gottesman
CertainTeed Corp.
Cessna Aircraft Co.
Champion International Corp.
Chase Bank of Texas
Chevron Corp.
Cincinnati Bell Inc.
Citibank Corp.
Citizens Financial Group, Inc.
CLARCOR Inc.
Clorox Co.
Collins & Aikman Corp.
Colonial Life & Accident Insurance Co.
Colonial Oil Industries, Inc.
Comdisco, Inc.
Commercial Intertech Corp.
Compass Bank
ConAgra, Inc.
Cone Mills Corp.
Consolidated Papers, Inc.
Constellation Energy Group, Inc.
Cooper Industries, Inc.
Coors Brewing Co.
Copley Press, Inc.
Corning Inc.
Country Curtains, Inc.
Cox Enterprises Inc.
Crane & Co., Inc.
Crestar Finance Corp.
Cummings Properties Management
Cummins Engine Co., Inc.
DaimlerChrysler Corp.
Dain Bosworth Inc.
Dana Corp.
Danis Companies
Deere & Co.
DeKalb Genetics Corp.
Demoulas Supermarkets Inc.
Dial Corp.
Dominion Resources, Inc.
Donaldson Co., Inc.
DSM Copolymer
du Pont de Nemours & Co. (E.I.)
Duchossois Industries Inc.
Duke Energy
Dynamet, Inc.
Eastern Bank
Eaton Corp.
Eckerd Corp.
Edison International
El Paso Energy Co.
Employers Mutual Casualty Co.
Equifax Inc.
Erb Lumber Co.
Erving Industries
Evening Post Publishing Co.
Federal-Mogul Corp.
Federated Department Stores, Inc.
Fidelity Investments
Fifth Third Bancorp
First Maryland Bancorp
First Source Corp.
First Union Corp.
First Union National Bank, NA
Firstar Bank Milwaukee NA
Fisher Scientific
FleetBoston Financial Corp.
Forbes Inc.
Ford Meter Box Co.
Ford Motor Co.
Forest City Enterprises, Inc.
Freddie Mac
Frost National Bank
Furniture Brands International, Inc.
Gallo Winery, Inc. (E&J)
Gap, Inc.
GATX Corp.
GEICO Corp.
General Motors Corp.
General Reinsurance Corp.
Georgia Power Co.
Gerber Products Co.
Giant Food Inc.
Giddings & Lewis
Globe Corp.
Golub Corp.
Goodrich Aerospace - Aerostructures Group (B.F.)
Grace & Co. (W.R.)
Group Health Plan
Guardian Life Insurance Co. of America
Gulf Power Co.
Gulfstream Aerospace Corp.
Hallmark Cards Inc.
Hamilton Sundstrand Corp.
Hannaford Brothers Co.
Harcourt General, Inc.
Harris Trust & Savings Bank
Harsco Corp.
Hartford (The)
Hasbro, Inc.
Hawaiian Electric Co., Inc.
Heinz Co. (H.J.)
Hoffmann-La Roche Inc.
Hofmann Co.
Hubbell Inc.
Huffy Corp.
Huntington Bancshares Inc.
Inman Mills
INTRUST Financial Corp.
Invacare Corp.
Jacobs Engineering Group
Jeld-wen, Inc.
Jostens, Inc.
JSJ Corp.
Kellogg Co.
Kerr-McGee Corp.
Kimball International, Inc.
Kingsbury Corp.
Koch Industries, Inc.
Kroger Co.
La-Z-Boy Inc.
Lehigh Portland Cement Co.
Leigh Fibers, Inc.
Leviton Manufacturing Co. Inc.
Lipton Co.
Little, Inc. (Arthur D.)
Louisiana Land & Exploration Co.
Louisiana-Pacific Corp.
Lowe's Companies
Lubrizol Corp. (The)
Manor Care Health SVS, Inc.
Mark IV Industries
McDonald & Co. Securities, Inc.
Mead Corp.
Milacron, Inc.
Minnesota Mining & Manufacturing Co.
MONY Group (The)
Motorola Inc.
Mutual of Omaha Insurance Co.
Nalco Chemical Co.
National Computer Systems, Inc.
National Fuel Gas Distribution Corp.

National Machinery Co.
Newman's Own Inc.
Niagara Mohawk Holdings Inc.
Nordson Corp.
Northern Indiana Public Service Co.
Northern Trust Co.
Northwest Natural Gas Co.
Norton Co.
Occidental Oil and Gas
Ohio National Life Insurance Co.
Old Kent Bank
Olin Corp.
Pacific Mutual Life Insurance Co.
Paine Webber
PEMCO Corp.
Pennzoil-Quaker State Co.
Pfizer Inc.
Pharmacia & Upjohn, Inc.
Physicians Mutual Insurance Co.
Pittway Corp.
PNC Financial Services Group
Polaroid Corp.
Potomac Electric Power Co.
Praxair
Premier Industrial Corp.
Principal Financial Group
Providence Journal-Bulletin Co.
Publix Supermarkets
Pulitzer Publishing Co.
Putnam Investments
Quaker Chemical Corp.
Quanex Corp.
Ralston Purina Co.
Rayonier Inc.
Red Wing Shoe Co. Inc.
Reynolds & Reynolds Co.
Reynolds Tobacco (R.J.)
Rockwell International Corp.
Rouse Co.
Royal & SunAlliance USA, Inc.
Rubbermaid Inc.
Ruddick Corp.
Russer Foods
Sara Lee Hosiery, Inc.
Schering-Plough Corp.
Schloss & Co. (Marcus)
Schlumberger Ltd. (USA)
Schwab & Co., Inc. (Charles)
Schwebel Baking Co.
Security Benefit Life Insurance Co.
Sempra Energy
Sentinel Communications Co.
Shell Oil Co.
Sherwin-Williams Co.
Sierra Pacific Industries
Simpson Investment Co.
SIT Investment Associates, Inc.
Slant/Fin Corp.
South Bend Tribune Corp.
Southwest Gas Corp.
Springs Industries, Inc.
Standard Register Co.
Starwood Hotels & Resorts Worldwide, Inc.
Steelcase Inc.
Stonecutter Mills Corp.
Storage Technology Corp.
Stupp Brothers Bridge & Iron Co.
Synovus Financial Corp.
Teleflex Inc.
Temple-Inland Inc.
Tenneco Automotive
Tenneco Packaging
Tension Envelope Corp.
Tesoro Hawaii
Texaco Inc.
Textron Inc.
Thermo Electron Corp.
TJX Companies, Inc.
Tomkins Industries, Inc.
Transamerica Corp.
True North Communications, Inc.
Trustmark Insurance Co.
TRW Inc.
Union Camp Corp.
Union Carbide Corp.
Union Pacific Corp.
United Dominion Industries, Ltd.
United States Sugar Corp.
US Bank, Washington
USG Corp.
Wachovia Bank of North Carolina NA
Waffle House Inc.
Wal-Mart Stores, Inc.
Walter Industries Inc.
Warner-Lambert Co.
Western & Southern Life Insurance Co.
Weyerhaeuser Co.
Wilbur-Ellis Co. & Connell Brothers Co.
Williams
Winn-Dixie Stores Inc.
Woodward Governor Co.
York Federal Savings & Loan Association

HOSPITALS

ABB Inc.
Abbott Laboratories
ABC
Advanced Micro Devices, Inc.
AEGON U.S.A. Inc.
Aetna, Inc.
Agrilink Foods, Inc.
AK Steel Corp.
Albertson's Inc.
Alcoa Inc.
Alcon Laboratories, Inc.
Alexander & Baldwin, Inc.
Allegheny Technologies Inc.
Allianz Life Insurance Co. of North America
AlliedSignal Inc.
Allmerica Financial Corp.
Allstate Insurance Co.
Alma Piston Co.
AMCORE Bank Rockford
America West Airlines, Inc.
American Express Co.
American Fidelity Corp.
American General Finance
American United Life Insurance Co.
Ameritas Life Insurance Corp.
Ameritech Michigan
Ameritech Wisconsin
AMETEK, Inc.
Amgen, Inc.
AMP Inc.
AMR Corp.
Amsted Industries Inc.
Analog Devices, Inc.
Andersen Corp.
Andersons Inc.
Anheuser-Busch Companies, Inc.
Aon Corp.
APL Ltd.
Archer-Daniels-Midland Co.
Arizona Public Service Co.
Armstrong World Industries, Inc.
Arvin Industries, Inc.
Ashland, Inc.
Associated Food Stores
AT&T Corp.
Atlantic Investment Co.
Avon Products, Inc.
Badger Meter, Inc.
Baird & Co. (Robert W.)
Bandag, Inc.
Banfi Vintners
Bank of America
Bank of New York Co., Inc.
Bank One Corp.
Bank One, Texas-Houston Office
BankBoston-Connecticut Region
BankBoston Corp.
Banta Corp.
Barclays Capital
Bard, Inc. (C.R.)
Barden Corp.
Bardes Corp.
Barnes Group Inc.
Battelle Memorial Institute
Baxter International Inc.
Bayer Corp.
Bean, Inc. (L.L.)
Bechtel Group, Inc.
Becton Dickinson & Co.
Belk-Simpson Department Stores
Belk Stores Services Inc.
Belo Corp. (A.H.)
Bemis Co., Inc.
Bemis Manufacturing Co.
Bernstein & Co., Inc. (Sanford C.)
Berwind Group
Bestfoods
Bethlehem Steel Corp.
BFGoodrich Co.
Binswanger Companies
Blair & Co. (William)
Block, Inc. (H&R)
Blount International, Inc.
Blue Bell, Inc.
Blue Cross & Blue Shield of Alabama
Blue Cross & Blue Shield of Iowa
Blue Cross & Blue Shield of Michigan
Blue Cross & Blue Shield of Minnesota
Boise Cascade Corp.
Boler Co.
Borden, Inc.
Borman's Inc.
Boston Edison Co.
Boston Globe (The)
Bourns, Inc.
Bowater Inc.
BP Amoco Corp.
Bradford & Co. (J.C.)
Bridgestone/Firestone, Inc.
Bristol-Myers Squibb Co.
Broderbund Software, Inc.
Brown Shoe Co., Inc.
Brunswick Corp.
Bucyrus-Erie Co.
Burlington Industries, Inc.
Burnett Co. (Leo)
Business Improvement
Butler Manufacturing Co.
Cabot Corp.
Calvin Klein
Campbell Soup Co.
Cantor, Fitzgerald Securities Corp.
Cargill Inc.
Carillon Importers, Ltd.
Carlson Companies, Inc.
Carolina Power & Light Co.
Carpenter Technology Corp.
Carrier Corp.
Carter-Wallace, Inc.
Caterpillar Inc.
CCB Financial Corp.
Central Maine Power Co.
Central National-Gottesman
Central Soya Co.
Century 21
CertainTeed Corp.
Cessna Aircraft Co.
CGU Insurance
Champion International Corp.
Chase Bank of Texas
Chase Manhattan Bank, NA
Chesapeake Corp.
Chevron Corp.
Chicago Title Corp.
Church & Dwight Co., Inc.
Cincinnati Bell Inc.
Cinergy Corp.
CIT Group, Inc. (The)
Citibank Corp.
Citigroup
Citizens Financial Group, Inc.
CLARCOR Inc.
Cleveland-Cliffs, Inc.
Clorox Co.
CNA
Collins & Aikman Corp.
Colonial Life & Accident Insurance Co.
Comerica Inc.
Commerce Bancshares, Inc.
Commercial Intertech Corp.
Commonwealth Edison Co.
Compass Bank
Consolidated Natural Gas Co.
Consolidated Papers, Inc.
Constellation Energy Group, Inc.
Consumers Energy Co.
Continental Grain Co.
Contran Corp.
Cooper Industries, Inc.
Coors Brewing Co.
Copley Press, Inc.
Country Curtains, Inc.
Cox Enterprises Inc.
CPI Corp.
Crane Co.
Crane & Co., Inc.
Cranston Print Works Co.
Credit Suisse First Boston
Crestar Finance Corp.
Croft-Leominster
CSS Industries, Inc.
Cummings Properties Management
Cummins Engine Co., Inc.
Daily News
DaimlerChrysler Corp.
Dain Bosworth Inc.
Dana Corp.
Danis Companies
DeKalb Genetics Corp.
Demoulas Supermarkets Inc.
Deposit Guaranty National Bank
Detroit Edison Co.
Deutsch Co.
Dexter Corp.
Dial Corp.
Disney Co. (Walt)
Dixie Group, Inc. (The)
Dominion Resources, Inc.
Donaldson Co., Inc.
Donnelley & Sons Co. (R.R.)
Dow Jones & Co., Inc.
du Pont de Nemours & Co. (E.I.)
Duchossois Industries Inc.
Duke Energy
Dun & Bradstreet Corp.
Duquesne Light Co.
Dynamet, Inc.
Eastern Bank
Eaton Corp.
Eckerd Corp.
Edison International
Elf Atochem North America, Inc.
Emerson Electric Co.
Employers Mutual Casualty Co.
Ensign-Bickford Industries
Enterprise Rent-A-Car Co.
Equitable Resources, Inc.
Erb Lumber Co.
Erving Industries
Ethyl Corp.
European American Bank
Exxon Mobil Corp.
Federal-Mogul Corp.
Ferro Corp.
Fidelity Investments
Fifth Third Bancorp
FINA
Fireman's Fund Insurance Co.
First Financial Bank
First Hawaiian, Inc.
First Maryland Bancorp
First National Bank of Evergreen Park
First Source Corp.
First Tennessee National Corp.
First Union Bank
First Union Corp.
First Union Securities, Inc.
Firstar Bank Milwaukee NA
Fisher Brothers Cleaning Services
Fisher Scientific
FleetBoston Financial Corp.
Florida Power Corp.
Fluor Corp.
FMC Corp.
Forbes Inc.
Ford Meter Box Co.
Ford Motor Co.
Forest City Enterprises, Inc.
Fort Worth Star-Telegram Inc.
Fortis Insurance Co.
Fortune Brands, Inc.
Fox Entertainment Group
Franklin Electric Co.
Franklin Mint (The)
Freeport-McMoRan Inc.
Frost National Bank
Furniture Brands International, Inc.
Gallo Winery, Inc. (E&J)
Galter Corp.
Gap, Inc.
GATX Corp.
GEICO Corp.
GenAmerica Corp.
GenCorp
General Electric Co.

General Mills, Inc.
General Motors Corp.
General Reinsurance Corp.
Georgia-Pacific Corp.
Georgia Power Co.
Gerber Products Co.
Giant Eagle Inc.
Giant Food Inc.
Giddings & Lewis
Gillette Co.
Glaxo Wellcome Inc.
Glickenhaus & Co.
Globe Corp.
Goldman Sachs Group
Golub Corp.
Goodrich Aerospace - Aerostructures Group (B.F.)
GPU Energy
Grace & Co. (W.R.)
Graco, Inc.
Grede Foundries
Green Bay Packaging
Group Health Plan
GTE Corp.
Gucci America Inc.
Gulf Power Co.
Halliburton Co.
Hallmark Cards Inc.
Hamilton Sundstrand Corp.
Hancock Financial Services (John)
Hanna Co. (M.A.)
Hannaford Brothers Co.
Harcourt General, Inc.
Harland Co. (John H.)
Harris Corp.
Harsco Corp.
Hartford (The)
Hartford Steam Boiler Inspection & Insurance Co.
Hartmarx Corp.
Hasbro, Inc.
Hawaiian Electric Co., Inc.
Heinz Co. (H.J.)
Hensel Phelps Construction Co.
Hershey Foods Corp.
Hewlett-Packard Co.
Hickory Tech Corp.
Hoffer Plastics Corp.
Hoffmann-La Roche Inc.
Hofmann Co.
HON Industries Inc.
Honeywell International Inc.
Housatonic Curtain Co.
Hubbard Broadcasting, Inc.
Hubbell Inc.
Huffy Corp.
Humana, Inc.
Huntington Bancshares Inc.
IBP
IKON Office Solutions, Inc.
Illinois Tool Works, Inc.
Inland Container Corp.
International Business Machines Corp.
International Flavors & Fragrances Inc.
International Paper Co.
INTRUST Financial Corp.
Invacare Corp.
Jacobs Engineering Group
Jacobson & Sons (Benjamin)
Jeld-wen, Inc.
Johnson Controls Inc.
Johnson & Johnson
Johnson & Son (S.C.)
Jostens, Inc.
Journal-Gazette Co.
Katten, Muchin & Zavis
Kellogg Co.
Kelly Services
Kemper National Insurance Companies
Kennametal, Inc.
Kerr-McGee Corp.
Key Bank of Cleveland
Kimball International, Inc.
Kimberly-Clark Corp.
Kinder Morgn
Koch Enterprises, Inc.
Kroger Co.
La-Z-Boy Inc.
Laclede Gas Co.
Ladish Co., Inc.
LandAmerica Financial Services
Landmark Communications Inc.
Lee Enterprises
Lehigh Portland Cement Co.
Leigh Fibers, Inc.
Leviton Manufacturing Co. Inc.
Liberty Corp.
Lincoln Electric Co.
Lipton Co.
Little, Inc. (Arthur D.)
Liz Claiborne, Inc.
Loews Corp.
Louisiana-Pacific Corp.
Lowe's Companies
LTV Corp.
Lubrizol Corp. (The)
Macy's East Inc.
Madison Gas & Electric Co.
Mallinckrodt Chemical, Inc.
Mamiye Brothers
Manulife Financial
Marcus Corp.
Maritz Inc.
Mark IV Industries
Marshall & Ilsley Corp.
Masco Corp.
Mattel Inc.
May Department Stores Co.
McDermott Inc.
McDonald & Co. Securities, Inc.
McDonald's Corp.
McGraw-Hill Companies, Inc.
MCI WorldCom, Inc.
McKesson-HBOC Corp.
McWane Inc.
Medtronic, Inc.
Menasha Corp.
Mercantile Bank NA
Merck & Co.
Merit Oil Corp.
Merrill Lynch & Co., Inc.
Metropolitan Life Insurance Co.
MGIC Investment Corp.
Michigan Consolidated Gas Co.
Mid-America Bank of Louisville
Milliken & Co.
Millipore Corp.
Mine Safety Appliances Co.
Minnesota Mining & Manufacturing Co.
Monarch Machine Tool Co.
Monsanto Co.
Montana Power Co.
Morgan & Co. Inc. (J.P.)
Morgan Stanley Dean Witter & Co.
Morris Communications Corp.
Morton International Inc.
Motorola Inc.
MTD Products Inc.
Murphy Oil Corp.
Nabisco Group Holdings
Nalco Chemical Co.
National Bank of Commerce Trust & Savings
National City Bank of Columbus
National City Corp.
National Computer Systems, Inc.
National Fuel Gas Distribution Corp.
National Machinery Co.
National Presto Industries, Inc.
National Service Industries, Inc.
National Starch & Chemical Co.
Nationwide Insurance Co.
NEBCO Evans
Nestle U.S.A. Inc.
New England Financial
New Jersey Natural Gas Co.
New York Life Insurance Co.
New York Mercantile Exchange
New York Stock Exchange, Inc.
Newman's Own Inc.
Niagara Mohawk Holdings Inc.
Norfolk Southern Corp.
Northeast Utilities
Northern Indiana Public Service Co.
Northern States Power Co.
Northern Trust Co.
Northwest Natural Gas Co.
Norton Co.
Norwest Corp.
Occidental Oil and Gas
Occidental Petroleum Corp.
OG&E Electric Services
Ohio National Life Insurance Co.
Old National Bank Evansville
Olin Corp.
Orange & Rockland Utilities, Inc.
Orscheln Co.
Osborne Enterprises
Outboard Marine Corp.
Overseas Shipholding Group Inc.
PACCAR Inc.
Pacific Century Financial Corp.
Pacific Mutual Life Insurance Co.
PacifiCare Health Systems
PacifiCorp
Paine Webber
Park National Bank
Parker Hannifin Corp.
PECO Energy Co.
Pella Corp.
PEMCO Corp.
Penney Co., Inc. (J.C.)
Pennzoil-Quaker State Co.
Peoples Energy Corp.
PepsiCo, Inc.
PerkinElmer, Inc.
Pfizer Inc.
Pharmacia & Upjohn, Inc.
Phelps Dodge Corp.
Philips Electronics North America Corp.
Phillips Petroleum Co.
Physicians Mutual Insurance Co.
Pillsbury Co.
Pitney Bowes Inc.
Pittway Corp.
PNC Bank
PNC Financial Services Group
Polaroid Corp.
Potlatch Corp.
Potomac Electric Power Co.
PPG Industries, Inc.
Praxair
Premier Industrial Corp.
Price Associates (T. Rowe)
Procter & Gamble Co.
Procter & Gamble Co., Cosmetics Division
Providence Journal-Bulletin Co.
Prudential Insurance Co. of America
Prudential Securities Inc.
Public Service Electric & Gas Co.
Publix Supermarkets
Pulitzer Publishing Co.
Putnam Investments
Quaker Chemical Corp.
Quanex Corp.
Questar Corp.
Ralston Purina Co.
Rayonier Inc.
Reilly Industries, Inc.
Reily & Co., Inc. (William B.)
Reinhart Institutional Foods
Reliant Energy Inc.
Revlon Inc.
Reynolds Metals Co.
Reynolds Tobacco (R.J.)
Rich Products Corp.
Rochester Gas & Electric Corp.
Rockwell International Corp.
Rouse Co.
Royal & SunAlliance USA, Inc.
Rubbermaid Inc.
Ruddick Corp.
Russer Foods
Ryder System, Inc.
Salomon Smith Barney
S&T Bancorp
Sara Lee Corp.
Sara Lee Hosiery, Inc.
SBC Communications Inc.
Schering-Plough Corp.
Schloss & Co. (Marcus)
Schlumberger Ltd. (USA)
Schwebel Baking Co.
Seaway Food Town, Inc.
Sega of America Inc.
Sempra Energy
Sentry Insurance, A Mutual Co.
Servco Pacific
S.G. Cowen
Shaw's Supermarkets, Inc.
Shea Co. (John F.)
Shell Oil Co.
Sherwin-Williams Co.
Shoney's Inc.
Sierra Pacific Resources
Simpson Investment Co.
Slant/Fin Corp.
Smith Corp. (A.O.)
Solo Cup Co.
Sonoco Products Co.
Sony Electronics
Southeastern Mutual Insurance Co.
Southern New England Telephone Co.
Southwest Gas Corp.
Sovereign Bank
Springs Industries, Inc.
SPX Corp.
Square D Co.
Standard Products Co.
Standard Register Co.
Stanley Works (The)
Star Bank NA
Starwood Hotels & Resorts Worldwide, Inc.
State Farm Mutual Automobile Insurance Co.
State Street Bank & Trust Co.
Stone Container Corp.
Stonecutter Mills Corp.
Storage Technology Corp.
Strear Farms Co.
Stride Rite Corp.
Stupp Brothers Bridge & Iron Co.
Sun Microsystems Inc.
Sunoco Inc.
SunTrust Bank Atlanta
Susquehanna-Pfaltzgraff Co.
Synovus Financial Corp.
Tai and Co. (J.T.)
Tamko Roofing Products
TCF National Bank Minnesota
Tektronix, Inc.
Telcordia Technologies
Temple-Inland Inc.
Tenneco Automotive
Tenneco Packaging
Tension Envelope Corp.
Tesoro Hawaii
Texaco Inc.
Texas Instruments Inc.
Textron Inc.
Thermo Electron Corp.
Thomasville Furniture Industries Inc.
Thompson Co. (J. Walter)
Titan Industrial Corp.
TJX Companies, Inc.
TMC Investment Co.
Tomkins Industries, Inc.
Torchmark Corp.
Trace International Holdings, Inc.
Transamerica Corp.
True North Communications, Inc.
True Oil Co.
Trustmark Insurance Co.
TRW Inc.
TU Electric Co.
Ukrop's Super Markets
Unilever Home & Personal Care U.S.A.
Unilever United States, Inc.
Union Camp Corp.
Union Carbide Corp.
Union Pacific Corp.
United Airlines Inc.
United Distillers & Vintners North America
United Dominion Industries, Ltd.
United Services Automobile Association
U.S. Bancorp Piper Jaffray
United States Sugar Corp.
United States Trust Co. of New York
United Technologies Corp.
Universal Foods Corp.

Universal Studios
Unocal Corp.
USG Corp.
Valmont Industries, Inc.
Valspar Corp.
Vesper Corp.
Wachovia Bank of North Carolina NA
Waffle House Inc.
Wal-Mart Stores, Inc.
Walgreen Co.
Walter Industries Inc.
Warner-Lambert Co.
Washington Trust Bank
Waste Management Inc.
Webster Bank
West Co. Inc.
Western & Southern Life Insurance Co.
Westvaco Corp.
Weyerhaeuser Co.
Whirlpool Corp.
Whitman Corp.
WICOR, Inc.
Wilbur-Ellis Co. & Connell Brothers Co.
Williams
Winn-Dixie Stores Inc.
Wiremold Co.
Wisconsin Energy Corp.
Wisconsin Power & Light Co.
Wisconsin Public Service Corp.
Witco Corp.
Woodward Governor Co.
Wrigley Co. (Wm. Jr.)
Wyman-Gordon Co.
York Federal Savings & Loan Association
Young & Rubicam
Zachry Co. (H.B.)
Zenith Electronics Corp.
Zilkha & Sons

HOSPITALS (UNIVERSITY AFFILIATED)

Abbott Laboratories
ABC
Allmerica Financial Corp.
Allstate Insurance Co.
American Express Co.
American Fidelity Corp.
AMR Corp.
Bandag, Inc.
Bard, Inc. (C.R.)
Baxter International Inc.
Belk Stores Services Inc.
Binswanger Companies
Blair & Co. (William)
Blue Cross & Blue Shield of Iowa
Carter-Wallace, Inc.
Citigroup
Contran Corp.
Corning Inc.
Crane & Co., Inc.
Deutsch Co.
Duchossois Industries Inc.
Eaton Corp.
El Paso Energy Co.
Equitable Resources, Inc.
Erving Industries
Ferro Corp.
FINA
First Union Bank
FleetBoston Financial Corp.
Galter Corp.
GenAmerica Corp.
GenCorp
General Electric Co.
Goldman Sachs Group
Green Bay Packaging
Group Health Plan
Hannaford Brothers Co.
Harcourt General, Inc.
Hasbro, Inc.
Honeywell International Inc.
Hubbell Inc.
Huntington Bancshares Inc.
Kimberly-Clark Corp.
LTV Corp.
Masco Corp.
McGraw-Hill Companies, Inc.
Merck & Co.
Morgan Stanley Dean Witter & Co.
Nalco Chemical Co.
National City Corp.
Premier Dental Products Co.
S.G. Cowen
Shea Co. (John F.)
Shell Oil Co.
Sherwin-Williams Co.
Texaco Inc.
Texas Instruments Inc.
Trace International Holdings, Inc.
TRW Inc.
Vesper Corp.
Wachtell, Lipton, Rosen & Katz
Whitman Corp.
Zachry Co. (H.B.)
Zilkha & Sons

KIDNEY

Abbott Laboratories
AMR Corp.
Andersen Corp.
Beckman Coulter, Inc.
Blue Cross & Blue Shield of Minnesota
Campbell Soup Co.
Contran Corp.
Conwood Co. LP
Crane & Co., Inc.
Cranston Print Works Co.
CSS Industries, Inc.
Dain Bosworth Inc.
Dial Corp.
Dynamet, Inc.
Equifax Inc.
Ford Motor Co.
Galter Corp.
Genentech Inc.
Giant Eagle Inc.
Glickenhaus & Co.
Group Health Plan
Hasbro, Inc.
Hubbard Broadcasting, Inc.
Leviton Manufacturing Co. Inc.
LTV Corp.
Mine Safety Appliances Co.
National City Bank of Minneapolis
PEMCO Corp.
Phelps Dodge Corp.
Quanex Corp.
Regions Bank
Riggs Bank NA
Schwab & Co., Inc. (Charles)
Shea Co. (John F.)
TMC Investment Co.
Universal Leaf Tobacco Co., Inc.
Valmont Industries, Inc.

LONG-TERM CARE

Alma Piston Co.
AMCORE Bank Rockford
American Retail Group
Associated Food Stores
BankBoston Corp.
Baxter International Inc.
Bernstein & Co., Inc. (Sanford C.)
Boler Co.
Borman's Inc.
Boston Edison Co.
Briggs & Stratton Corp.
Century 21
CGU Insurance
CLARCOR Inc.
Colonial Oil Industries, Inc.
Comdisco, Inc.
Commercial Intertech Corp.
CSS Industries, Inc.
Daily News
Demoulas Supermarkets Inc.
Ecolab Inc.
First Union Securities, Inc.
Group Health Plan
Hallmark Cards Inc.
Hamilton Sundstrand Corp.
Huntington Bancshares Inc.
Indiana Mills & Manufacturing
Kelly Services
Levi Strauss & Co.
Liberty Diversified Industries
Lincoln Electric Co.
Liz Claiborne, Inc.
Lubrizol Corp. (The)
Manor Care Health SVS, Inc.
Marshall & Ilsley Corp.
Medtronic, Inc.
Minnesota Mutual Life Insurance Co.
Monarch Machine Tool Co.
Morrison Knudsen Corp.
National Bank of Commerce Trust & Savings
Nationwide Insurance Co.
PacifiCare Health Systems
Physicians Mutual Insurance Co.
PNC Financial Services Group
PPG Industries, Inc.
Pulitzer Publishing Co.
Reilly Industries, Inc.
Schering-Plough Corp.
Sherwin-Williams Co.
SmithKline Beecham Corp.
Square D Co.
Stone Container Corp.
Synovus Financial Corp.
Union Pacific Corp.
U.S. Bancorp Piper Jaffray
United States Trust Co. of New York
USG Corp.
Wachtell, Lipton, Rosen & Katz
Washington Mutual, Inc.
Western & Southern Life Insurance Co.

MEDICAL REHABILITATION

Abbott Laboratories
Agrilink Foods, Inc.
Albertson's Inc.
Alcoa Inc.
Alexander & Baldwin, Inc.
Allegheny Technologies Inc.
AlliedSignal Inc.
American General Finance
Ameritech Corp.
AMETEK, Inc.
Amsted Industries Inc.
Andersen Corp.
Aon Corp.
Avon Products, Inc.
Baird & Co. (Robert W.)
Bard, Inc. (C.R.)
Barden Corp.
Bardes Corp.
Baxter International Inc.
Belk Stores Services Inc.
Blair & Co. (William)
Block, Inc. (H&R)
Blue Bell, Inc.
Blue Cross & Blue Shield of Minnesota
Bristol-Myers Squibb Co.
Bucyrus-Erie Co.
Callaway Golf Co.
Carrier Corp.
Central Maine Power Co.
Central Soya Co.
Chase Manhattan Bank, NA
Chesapeake Corp.
Chevron Corp.
Citigroup
Citizens Financial Group, Inc.
Compaq Computer Corp.
Consolidated Papers, Inc.
Cooper Tire & Rubber Co.
Coors Brewing Co.
Cox Enterprises Inc.
CSS Industries, Inc.
CUNA Mutual Group
Dain Bosworth Inc.
Deluxe Corp.
Demoulas Supermarkets Inc.
Deutsch Co.
Dial Corp.
Disney Co. (Walt)
Donaldson Co., Inc.
du Pont de Nemours & Co. (E.I.)
Duchossois Industries Inc.
Dynamet, Inc.
Eastman Kodak Co.
Ecolab Inc.
El Paso Energy Co.
Elf Atochem North America, Inc.
Equifax Inc.
Excel Corp.
Exxon Mobil Corp.
Ferro Corp.
Fifth Third Bancorp
Fireman's Fund Insurance Co.
First Hawaiian, Inc.
First National Bank of Evergreen Park
First Union Bank
First Union Corp.
Florida Power & Light Co.
FMC Corp.
Fortis Insurance Co.
Frost National Bank
Galter Corp.
GATX Corp.
GEICO Corp.
GenAmerica Corp.
General Mills, Inc.
General Motors Corp.
General Reinsurance Corp.
Georgia-Pacific Corp.
Georgia Power Co.
Gerber Products Co.
Giant Eagle Inc.
Golub Corp.
Grace & Co. (W.R.)
Graco, Inc.
Group Health Plan
Harris Trust & Savings Bank
Hartford (The)
Hartford Steam Boiler Inspection & Insurance Co.
Hasbro, Inc.
Hawaiian Electric Co., Inc.
Heinz Co. (H.J.)
Hickory Tech Corp.
Household International Inc.
Hubbard Broadcasting, Inc.
Hubbell Inc.
Illinois Tool Works, Inc.
Invacare Corp.
Kemper National Insurance Companies
Koch Enterprises, Inc.
Kroger Co.
Lipton Co.
Loews Corp.
Lubrizol Corp. (The)
Macy's East Inc.
Mattel Inc.
McClatchy Co.
Mid-America Bank of Louisville
Milliken & Co.
Mine Safety Appliances Co.
Minnesota Mining & Manufacturing Co.
Minnesota Mutual Life Insurance Co.
Mitsubishi Electric America
Morgan Stanley Dean Witter & Co.
Morrison Knudsen Corp.
Nalco Chemical Co.
National City Bank of Minneapolis
National Machinery Co.
National Service Industries, Inc.
National Starch & Chemical Co.
NEC America, Inc.
New England Financial
New York Life Insurance Co.
New York Mercantile Exchange
Newman's Own Inc.
Northern Trust Co.
Northwest Natural Gas Co.
Norton Co.
Norwest Corp.
Occidental Oil and Gas
Ohio National Life Insurance Co.
Old National Bank Evansville
Olin Corp.
Oshkosh B'Gosh, Inc.
Pacific Century Financial Corp.
Pan-American Life Insurance Co.
PEMCO Corp.
Pennzoil-Quaker State Co.
PerkinElmer, Inc.
Pfizer Inc.
Phillips Petroleum Co.
Pillsbury Co.
Pittway Corp.
PNC Financial Services Group
PPG Industries, Inc.
Praxair
Premier Dental Products Co.
Procter & Gamble Co., Cosmetics Division
Prudential Insurance Co. of America
Red Wing Shoe Co. Inc.
Reilly Industries, Inc.
Reynolds Metals Co.
Rich Products Corp.
Rockwell International Corp.
Safeguard Scientifics
Schering-Plough Corp.
Servco Pacific
Shell Oil Co.

Sherwin-Williams Co.
SIT Investment Associates, Inc.
Slant/Fin Corp.
Smith Corp. (A.O.)
Sonoco Products Co.
Sony Electronics
Southeastern Mutual Insurance Co.
State Farm Mutual Automobile Insurance Co.
State Street Bank & Trust Co.
Steelcase Inc.
Stone Container Corp.
Storage Technology Corp.
SunTrust Bank Atlanta
Synovus Financial Corp.
TCF National Bank Minnesota
TENNANT Co.
Texaco Inc.
Textron Inc.
TJX Companies, Inc.
TMC Investment Co.
Torchmark Corp.
True Oil Co.
TRW Inc.
Union Camp Corp.
Union Carbide Corp.
Union Pacific Corp.
United Parcel Service of America Inc.
U.S. Bancorp Piper Jaffray
United States Sugar Corp.
United States Trust Co. of New York
Unocal Corp.
UnumProvident
USX Corp.
Valmont Industries, Inc.
Waffle House Inc.
Wal-Mart Stores, Inc.
Warner-Lambert Co.
West Co. Inc.
Westvaco Corp.
Whitman Corp.
Wisconsin Energy Corp.
Wisconsin Public Service Corp.
Woodward Governor Co.
Zachry Co. (H.B.)

MEDICAL RESEARCH

Abbott Laboratories
ABC
AFLAC Inc.
AGL Resources Inc.
Alcoa Inc.
Alcon Laboratories, Inc.
Alliant Techsystems
AlliedSignal Inc.
Allmerica Financial Corp.
Allstate Insurance Co.
Alma Piston Co.
American United Life Insurance Co.
Ameritas Life Insurance Corp.
AMETEK, Inc.
Amgen, Inc.
Andersen Corp.
Andersons Inc.
Anheuser-Busch Companies, Inc.
Aon Corp.
APL Ltd.
Arizona Public Service Co.
Armstrong World Industries, Inc.
Associated Food Stores
Avon Products, Inc.
Badger Meter, Inc.
Baird & Co. (Robert W.)
Baker Hughes Inc.
Banfi Vintners
Bank of America
Bank One, Texas-Houston Office
Barclays Capital
Bard, Inc. (C.R.)
Bardes Corp.
Barnes Group Inc.
Barry Corp. (R.G.)
Battelle Memorial Institute
Baxter International Inc.
Beckman Coulter, Inc.
Becton Dickinson & Co.
Belk-Simpson Department Stores
Bemis Manufacturing Co.
Bernstein & Co., Inc. (Sanford C.)
Bestfoods
Binswanger Companies
Blair & Co. (William)
Blue Bell, Inc.
Blue Cross & Blue Shield of Michigan
Blue Cross & Blue Shield of Minnesota
Borden, Inc.
Boston Globe (The)
Bridgestone/Firestone, Inc.
Bristol-Myers Squibb Co.
Bucyrus-Erie Co.
Calvin Klein
Campbell Soup Co.
Cantor, Fitzgerald Securities Corp.
Carillon Importers, Ltd.
Carlson Companies, Inc.
Carnival Corp.
Carter-Wallace, Inc.
Cenex Harvest States
Central & South West Services
CertainTeed Corp.
CGU Insurance
Charter Manufacturing Co.
Chase Bank of Texas
Church & Dwight Co., Inc.
CIT Group, Inc. (The)
Citibank Corp.
Citigroup
Citizens Financial Group, Inc.
CNA
Collins & Aikman Corp.
Colonial Life & Accident Insurance Co.
Compaq Computer Corp.
Contran Corp.
Crane Co.
Credit Suisse First Boston
CSS Industries, Inc.
Cummings Properties Management
CUNA Mutual Group
Daily News
Dain Bosworth Inc.
Danis Companies
Demoulas Supermarkets Inc.
Deutsch Co.
Dixie Group, Inc. (The)
Dow Corning Corp.
DSM Copolymer
du Pont de Nemours & Co. (E.I.)
Duchossois Industries Inc.
Dynamet, Inc.
El Paso Energy Co.
Elf Atochem North America, Inc.
Emerson Electric Co.
EMI Music Publishing
Erb Lumber Co.
Exxon Mobil Corp.
Federal-Mogul Corp.
Federated Mutual Insurance Co.
Fidelity Investments
First Financial Bank
First Union Bank
First Union Securities, Inc.
Fisher Scientific
FleetBoston Financial Corp.
Florida Rock Industries
Forbes Inc.
Ford Meter Box Co.
Fort Worth Star-Telegram Inc.
Fortis Insurance Co.
Fortune Brands, Inc.
Freeport-McMoRan Inc.
Frost National Bank
Furniture Brands International, Inc.
Gallo Winery, Inc. (E&J)
Galter Corp.
Gap, Inc.
GEICO Corp.
GenAmerica Corp.
General Mills, Inc.
General Reinsurance Corp.
Georgia-Pacific Corp.
Georgia Power Co.
Gerber Products Co.
Giant Eagle Inc.
Glaxo Wellcome Inc.
Glickenhaus & Co.
Globe Corp.
Grace & Co. (W.R.)
Grede Foundries
Group Health Plan
Guardian Life Insurance Co. of America
Gucci America Inc.
Guess?
Hamilton Sundstrand Corp.
Hancock Financial Services (John)
Hannaford Brothers Co.
Harcourt General, Inc.
Harnischfeger Industries
Harsco Corp.
Hartford (The)
Hasbro, Inc.
Heinz Co. (H.J.)
Hoffmann-La Roche Inc.
Hofmann Co.
Hubbard Broadcasting, Inc.
Huffy Corp.
Humana, Inc.
Huntington Bancshares Inc.
Illinois Tool Works, Inc.
Inman Mills
International Flavors & Fragrances Inc.
Jacobs Engineering Group
Jacobson & Sons (Benjamin)
Johnson Controls Inc.
Johnson & Johnson
Johnson & Son (S.C.)
Katten, Muchin & Zavis
Kemper National Insurance Companies
Kennametal, Inc.
Kerr-McGee Corp.
Kimberly-Clark Corp.
Kingsbury Corp.
Kraft Foods, Inc.
Kroger Co.
Ladish Co., Inc.
Lancaster Lens, Inc.
Lance, Inc.
Leigh Fibers, Inc.
Leviton Manufacturing Co. Inc.
Liberty Diversified Industries
Lilly & Co. (Eli)
Lincoln Financial Group
Lipton Co.
Little, Inc. (Arthur D.)
Loews Corp.
Louisiana Land & Exploration Co.
Louisiana-Pacific Corp.
LTV Corp.
Macy's East Inc.
Madison Gas & Electric Co.
Mamiye Brothers
Manulife Financial
Marcus Corp.
Marshall & Ilsley Corp.
Masco Corp.
Massachusetts Mutual Life Insurance Co.
Mazda North American Operations
MBIA Inc.
McCormick & Co. Inc.
McDonald & Co. Securities, Inc.
Merck & Co.
Merrill Lynch & Co., Inc.
Metropolitan Life Insurance Co.
Millipore Corp.
Minnesota Mutual Life Insurance Co.
Monsanto Co.
MONY Group (The)
Nalco Chemical Co.
National Life of Vermont
National Presto Industries, Inc.
National Service Industries, Inc.
Nationwide Insurance Co.
New England Financial
New York Life Insurance Co.
Nordson Corp.
Norfolk Southern Corp.
Norton Co.
OG&E Electric Services
Ohio National Life Insurance Co.
Orange & Rockland Utilities, Inc.
Overseas Shipholding Group Inc.
Owens Corning
PACCAR Inc.
Pacific Mutual Life Insurance Co.
Paine Webber
Pan-American Life Insurance Co.
Parker Hannifin Corp.
Pennzoil-Quaker State Co.
PerkinElmer, Inc.
Pfizer Inc.
Pharmacia & Upjohn, Inc.
Phelps Dodge Corp.
Phillips Petroleum Co.
Physicians Mutual Insurance Co.
Pittway Corp.
Playboy Enterprises Inc.
Polaroid Corp.
Potomac Electric Power Co.
Premier Dental Products Co.
Principal Financial Group
Prudential Securities Inc.
Putnam Investments
Quaker Chemical Corp.
Quanex Corp.
Ralston Purina Co.
Regions Bank
Reilly Industries, Inc.
Reinhart Institutional Foods
Reliant Energy Inc.
Reynolds Metals Co.
Reynolds Tobacco (R.J.)
Ruddick Corp.
Russer Foods
Salomon Smith Barney
SBC Communications Inc.
Schering-Plough Corp.
Schlumberger Ltd. (USA)
Schwab & Co., Inc. (Charles)
Seagram & Sons, Inc. (Joseph E.)
Searle & Co. (G.D.)
Sempra Energy
Sentry Insurance, A Mutual Co.
Shell Oil Co.
Shelter Mutual Insurance Co.
Sierra Pacific Industries
Slant/Fin Corp.
SmithKline Beecham Corp.
Sonoco Products Co.
Southwest Gas Corp.
Square D Co.
Standard Products Co.
Stanley Works (The)
Star Bank NA
Starwood Hotels & Resorts Worldwide, Inc.
Stone Container Corp.
Stonecutter Mills Corp.
Strear Farms Co.
Stupp Brothers Bridge & Iron Co.
Tai and Co. (J.T.)
Temple-Inland Inc.
Tenet Healthcare Corp.
Tenneco Automotive
Texaco Inc.
Texas Instruments Inc.
Thomasville Furniture Industries Inc.
Thompson Co. (J. Walter)
Ticketmaster Corp.
Tomkins Industries, Inc.
Trace International Holdings, Inc.
Transamerica Corp.
True Oil Co.
Trustmark Insurance Co.
Ukrop's Super Markets
Union Camp Corp.
Union Pacific Corp.
United Airlines Inc.
United Dominion Industries, Ltd.
United Wisconsin Services
Universal Foods Corp.
Universal Studios
Unocal Corp.
UnumProvident
USAA Life Insurance Co.
USG Corp.
UST Inc.
Valspar Corp.
Van Leer Holding
Wal-Mart Stores, Inc.
Walter Industries Inc.
Warner-Lambert Co.
Washington Mutual, Inc.
Waste Management Inc.
Weil, Gotshal & Manges Corp.
West Co. Inc.
Westvaco Corp.

Williams
Wisconsin Energy Corp.
Witco Corp.
Woodward Governor Co.
Wyman-Gordon Co.
Young & Rubicam
Zachry Co. (H.B.)
Zilkha & Sons

MEDICAL TRAINING

Abbott Laboratories
ABC
Alcoa Inc.
American United Life Insurance Co.
Becton Dickinson & Co.
Blue Cross & Blue Shield of Minnesota
Bristol-Myers Squibb Co.
Chase Bank of Texas
Colonial Life & Accident Insurance Co.
du Pont de Nemours & Co. (E.I.)
Exxon Mobil Corp.
General Motors Corp.
General Reinsurance Corp.
Gerber Products Co.
Group Health Plan
Hoffmann-La Roche Inc.
Johnson & Son (S.C.)
Kerr-McGee Corp.
Lipton Co.
Macy's East Inc.
Marshall & Ilsley Corp.
MCI WorldCom, Inc.
Mercantile Bank NA
Merck & Co.
Metropolitan Life Insurance Co.
Millipore Corp.
National Starch & Chemical Co.
New York Life Insurance Co.
Pacific Mutual Life Insurance Co.
Phelps Dodge Corp.
Prudential Insurance Co. of America
Schering-Plough Corp.
SunTrust Bank Atlanta
Tenet Healthcare Corp.
Texaco Inc.
Union Camp Corp.
Unocal Corp.

MENTAL HEALTH

AGL Resources Inc.
Agrilink Foods, Inc.
Alabama Power Co.
Albertson's Inc.
Alcoa Inc.
Alcon Laboratories, Inc.
Allegheny Technologies Inc.
AMCORE Bank Rockford
American General Finance
American United Life Insurance Co.
AMETEK, Inc.
AMP Inc.
Andersons Inc.
Atlantic Investment Co.
Avon Products, Inc.
Badger Meter, Inc.
Ben & Jerry's Homemade Inc.
Bestfoods
Binswanger Companies
Block, Inc. (H&R)
Blount International, Inc.
Blue Cross & Blue Shield of Michigan
Blue Cross & Blue Shield of Minnesota
Boeing Co.
Borden, Inc.
Borman's Inc.
Boston Globe (The)
Broderbund Software, Inc.
Brunswick Corp.
Butler Capital Corp.
Calvin Klein
Carrier Corp.
Carter-Wallace, Inc.
Caterpillar Inc.
Central Maine Power Co.
Central National-Gottesman
Central Vermont Public Service Corp.
Chase Bank of Texas
Chesapeake Corp.
Chevron Corp.
Church & Dwight Co., Inc.
Cinergy Corp.
CIT Group, Inc. (The)
Citizens Financial Group, Inc.
CLARCOR Inc.
Clorox Co.
Colonial Life & Accident Insurance Co.
Comerica Inc.
Compaq Computer Corp.
Compass Bank
Contran Corp.
Cooper Industries, Inc.
Coors Brewing Co.
Copley Press, Inc.
Crane Co.
Credit Suisse First Boston
Crestar Finance Corp.
Cummins Engine Co., Inc.
CUNA Mutual Group
DeKalb Genetics Corp.
Detroit Edison Co.
Deutsch Co.
Dexter Corp.
Disney Co. (Walt)
Dixie Group, Inc. (The)
Dominion Resources, Inc.
Donaldson Co., Inc.
Donnelley & Sons Co. (R.R.)
du Pont de Nemours & Co. (E.I.)
Duchossois Industries Inc.
Duke Energy
Dun & Bradstreet Corp.
Dynamet, Inc.
Eastman Kodak Co.
Enterprise Rent-A-Car Co.
Erb Lumber Co.
Extendicare Health Services
Ferro Corp.
Fidelity Investments
Fireman's Fund Insurance Co.
First National Bank of Evergreen Park
First Source Corp.
First Union Corp.
Forbes Inc.
Ford Meter Box Co.
Fortis Insurance Co.
Franklin Mint (The)
Freddie Mac
Freeport-McMoRan Inc.
Frost National Bank
Fuller Co. (H.B.)
Furniture Brands International, Inc.
Gannett Co., Inc.
GATX Corp.
GEICO Corp.
GenCorp
General Atlantic Partners II LP
General Mills, Inc.
General Motors Corp.
General Reinsurance Corp.
Georgia Power Co.
Giant Eagle Inc.
Giant Food Inc.
Glickenhaus & Co.
Group Health Plan
Hallmark Cards Inc.
Hamilton Sundstrand Corp.
Harley-Davidson Co.
Harnischfeger Industries
Harris Trust & Savings Bank
Harsco Corp.
Hasbro, Inc.
Hawaiian Electric Co., Inc.
Heller Financial, Inc.
Hoffmann-La Roche Inc.
Honeywell International Inc.
Household International Inc.
Hubbard Broadcasting, Inc.
Hubbell Inc.
Humana, Inc.
Illinois Tool Works, Inc.
International Business Machines Corp.
International Flavors & Fragrances Inc.
INTRUST Financial Corp.
Journal-Gazette Co.
Katten, Muchin & Zavis
Kennametal, Inc.
Kimball International, Inc.
Koch Enterprises, Inc.
Laclede Gas Co.
Lilly & Co. (Eli)
Lincoln Electric Co.
Lincoln Financial Group
Lipton Co.
Little, Inc. (Arthur D.)
Lotus Development Corp.
LTV Corp.
Macy's East Inc.
Maritz Inc.
Marshall & Ilsley Corp.
McDonald & Co. Securities, Inc.
McWane Inc.
Memphis Light Gas & Water Division
Michigan Consolidated Gas Co.
Millipore Corp.
Mine Safety Appliances Co.
Minnesota Mining & Manufacturing Co.
MONY Group (The)
Nalco Chemical Co.
National City Corp.
National Fuel Gas Distribution Corp.
National Life of Vermont
Nationwide Insurance Co.
NEBCO Evans
New England Financial
New York Life Insurance Co.
Nordson Corp.
Northeast Utilities
Northern States Power Co.
Northern Trust Co.
Northwest Bank Nebraska, NA
Northwest Natural Gas Co.
Norton Co.
Occidental Oil and Gas
Olin Corp.
Oshkosh B'Gosh, Inc.
Overseas Shipholding Group Inc.
Owens Corning
PACCAR Inc.
Pacific Century Financial Corp.
Pacific Mutual Life Insurance Co.
Park National Bank
Parker Hannifin Corp.
Pfizer Inc.
Pharmacia & Upjohn, Inc.
Phillips Petroleum Co.
Pittway Corp.
Polaroid Corp.
PPG Industries, Inc.
Principal Financial Group
Procter & Gamble Co., Cosmetics Division
Prudential Insurance Co. of America
Prudential Securities Inc.
Pulitzer Publishing Co.
Rayonier Inc.
Regions Bank
Reliant Energy Inc.
Rockwell International Corp.
Royal & SunAlliance USA, Inc.
SAFECO Corp.
SBC Communications Inc.
Schering-Plough Corp.
Schloss & Co. (Marcus)
Seagram & Sons, Inc. (Joseph E.)
Sempra Energy
Shell Oil Co.
Sierra Pacific Resources
Smith Corp. (A.O.)
Smurfit-Stone Container Corp.
Sonoco Products Co.
Sony Electronics
Square D Co.
State Street Bank & Trust Co.
Steelcase Inc.
Stone Container Corp.
Storage Technology Corp.
SunTrust Bank Atlanta
Synovus Financial Corp.
Tenet Healthcare Corp.
TENNANT Co.
Tenneco Automotive
Tension Envelope Corp.
Tesoro Hawaii
TJX Companies, Inc.
Transamerica Corp.
TRW Inc.
Union Camp Corp.
Union Pacific Corp.
United States Sugar Corp.
United Wisconsin Services
Universal Studios
Unocal Corp.
US Bank, Washington
USG Corp.
USX Corp.
Varian Medical Systems, Inc.
Vulcan Materials Co.
Wal-Mart Stores, Inc.
Walgreen Co.
Washington Mutual, Inc.
Waste Management Inc.
Western & Southern Life Insurance Co.
Wiley & Sons (John)
Williams
Winn-Dixie Stores Inc.
Wisconsin Energy Corp.
Woodward Governor Co.

MULTIPLE SCLEROSIS

Air Products and Chemicals, Inc.
AlliedSignal Inc.
AMR Corp.
APL Ltd.
Banfi Vintners
Beckman Coulter, Inc.
Block, Inc. (H&R)
Blue Cross & Blue Shield of Alabama
Blue Cross & Blue Shield of Iowa
Blue Cross & Blue Shield of Minnesota
Borman's Inc.
Brown Shoe Co., Inc.
Burlington Industries, Inc.
Burnett Co. (Leo)
Business Improvement
Calvin Klein
Central National-Gottesman
CertainTeed Corp.
Cessna Aircraft Co.
CGU Insurance
Chicago Board of Trade
Chicago Title Corp.
Clark Refining & Marketing
Commercial Intertech Corp.
Compaq Computer Corp.
Cone Mills Corp.
Continental Grain Co.
Contran Corp.
Cox Enterprises Inc.
CPI Corp.
Crane Co.
Crestar Finance Corp.
CSS Industries, Inc.
Eckerd Corp.
Employers Mutual Casualty Co.
Ensign-Bickford Industries
Ferro Corp.
Forest City Enterprises, Inc.
Fortis, Inc.
Gallo Winery, Inc. (E&J)
Galter Corp.
Giddings & Lewis
Group Health Plan
Guess?
Hickory Tech Corp.
Huntington Bancshares Inc.
IKON Office Solutions, Inc.
Invacare Corp.
Jacobs Engineering Group
Katten, Muchin & Zavis
Kimberly-Clark Corp.
Ladish Co., Inc.
Leigh Fibers, Inc.
Lipton Co.
Loews Corp.
Mark IV Industries
Mattel Inc.
May Department Stores Co.
McDonald & Co. Securities, Inc.
McWane Inc.
Merit Oil Corp.
Mid-America Bank of Louisville
MidAmerican Energy Holdings Co.
Mine Safety Appliances Co.
Morrison Knudsen Corp.
National Presto Industries, Inc.
National Service Industries, Inc.
New York Mercantile Exchange
Nomura Holding America

Occidental Oil and Gas
Ohio National Life Insurance Co.
Pacific Century Financial Corp.
Pacific Mutual Life Insurance Co.
PEMCO Corp.
PepsiCo, Inc.
Physicians Mutual Insurance Co.
Pieper Power Electric Co.
Putnam Investments
Ralph's Grocery Co.
Rich Products Corp.
Russer Foods
Schloss & Co. (Marcus)
Schwab & Co., Inc. (Charles)
Schwebel Baking Co.
Shea Co. (John F.)
Smurfit-Stone Container Corp.
Sonoco Products Co.
Sony Electronics
Southeastern Mutual Insurance Co.
Stone Container Corp.
Storage Technology Corp.
Subway Sandwich Shops, Inc.
Synovus Financial Corp.
Ticketmaster Corp.
Toledo Blade Co.
True North Communications, Inc.
U.S. Bancorp
U.S. Bancorp Piper Jaffray
Universal Leaf Tobacco Co., Inc.
Universal Studios
Waffle House Inc.
Washington Trust Bank
Western & Southern Life Insurance Co.
Witco Corp.
Wyman-Gordon Co.
York Federal Savings & Loan Association
Young & Rubicam

NURSING SERVICES

Abbott Laboratories
Aetna, Inc.
Agrilink Foods, Inc.
Allegheny Technologies Inc.
AlliedSignal Inc.
Allmerica Financial Corp.
AMCORE Bank Rockford
American United Life Insurance Co.
Andersons Inc.
Armstrong World Industries, Inc.
Associated Food Stores
Bank of New York Co., Inc.
Banta Corp.
Barden Corp.
Battelle Memorial Institute
Bausch & Lomb Inc.
Baxter International Inc.
Becton Dickinson & Co.
Bemis Co., Inc.
Bernstein & Co., Inc. (Sanford C.)
Bestfoods
Bethlehem Steel Corp.
BFGoodrich Co.
Boston Edison Co.
Bridgestone/Firestone, Inc.
Briggs & Stratton Corp.
Brunswick Corp.
Burlington Resources, Inc.
Carris Reels
Central & South West Services
Citizens Financial Group, Inc.
CLARCOR Inc.
Collins & Aikman Corp.
Colonial Life & Accident Insurance Co.
Continental Grain Co.
Contran Corp.
Country Curtains, Inc.
Cummings Properties Management
CUNA Mutual Group
Dexter Corp.
Eastman Kodak Co.
Eaton Corp.
Edison International
El Paso Energy Co.
Ensign-Bickford Industries
Equifax Inc.
Exxon Mobil Corp.
Fabri-Kal Corp.
Ferro Corp.
Firstar Bank Milwaukee NA
Forbes Inc.
Fort Worth Star-Telegram Inc.
GenCorp
Gerber Products Co.
Giddings & Lewis
Globe Corp.
Group Health Plan
Hamilton Sundstrand Corp.
Hartmarx Corp.
Hubbell Inc.
Humana, Inc.
IKON Office Solutions, Inc.
Illinois Tool Works, Inc.
Invacare Corp.
Kimberly-Clark Corp.
Ladish Co., Inc.
Leigh Fibers, Inc.
Lincoln Electric Co.
Lubrizol Corp. (The)
Manor Care Health SVS, Inc.
Marshall & Ilsley Corp.
McDonald & Co. Securities, Inc.
Medtronic, Inc.
Menasha Corp.
Metropolitan Life Insurance Co.
Michigan Consolidated Gas Co.
Mid-America Bank of Louisville
Minnesota Mutual Life Insurance Co.
National Machinery Co.
National Starch & Chemical Co.
Nationwide Insurance Co.
New York Life Insurance Co.
Nordson Corp.
Northern Indiana Public Service Co.
Northern States Power Co.
Norton Co.
Olin Corp.
Parker Hannifin Corp.
Pharmacia & Upjohn, Inc.
Physicians Mutual Insurance Co.
Pittway Corp.
Polaroid Corp.
PPG Industries, Inc.
Premier Dental Products Co.
Premier Industrial Corp.
Procter & Gamble Co., Cosmetics Division
Providence Journal-Bulletin Co.
Quaker Chemical Corp.
Ralston Purina Co.
S&T Bancorp
Schwab & Co., Inc. (Charles)
Searle & Co. (G.D.)
Shaw's Supermarkets, Inc.
Simpson Investment Co.
Southeastern Mutual Insurance Co.
Stride Rite Corp.
SunTrust Bank Atlanta
Teleflex Inc.
Tenet Healthcare Corp.
Tenneco Packaging
Texas Instruments Inc.
TJX Companies, Inc.
Union Camp Corp.
United Parcel Service of America Inc.
United States Trust Co. of New York
Waffle House Inc.
Washington Trust Bank
Webster Bank
West Co. Inc.
Wisconsin Power & Light Co.
Wrigley Co. (Wm. Jr.)
Wyman-Gordon Co.
Young & Rubicam

NUTRITION

Abbott Laboratories
Aetna, Inc.
AGL Resources Inc.
Air Products and Chemicals, Inc.
Alexander & Baldwin, Inc.
AMCORE Bank Rockford
Battelle Memorial Institute
Bethlehem Steel Corp.
Blue Cross & Blue Shield of Minnesota
Boston Globe (The)
Bristol-Myers Squibb Co.
Campbell Soup Co.
Carillon Importers, Ltd.
Central Maine Power Co.
ConAgra, Inc.
Conoco, Inc.
Duke Energy
Ecolab Inc.
FleetBoston Financial Corp.
Fortis Insurance Co.
GATX Corp.
General Mills, Inc.
Gerber Products Co.
Group Health Plan
Hancock Financial Services (John)
Hasbro, Inc.
Heinz Co. (H.J.)
Hershey Foods Corp.
Johnson & Son (S.C.)
Kroger Co.
Lance, Inc.
Lipton Co.
Loews Corp.
Lotus Development Corp.
McCormick & Co. Inc.
McDonald's Corp.
Metropolitan Life Insurance Co.
Nabisco Group Holdings
National Computer Systems, Inc.
Nestle U.S.A. Inc.
New England Bio Labs
New England Financial
Northeast Utilities
Northern Trust Co.
Norton Co.
Novartis Corporation
Pacific Mutual Life Insurance Co.
Pharmacia & Upjohn, Inc.
Phillips Petroleum Co.
Pillsbury Co.
Procter & Gamble Co.
Quaker Chemical Corp.
Quanex Corp.
SAFECO Corp.
Sara Lee Corp.
Seaway Food Town, Inc.
Shaklee Corp.
Shea Co. (John F.)
Sierra Pacific Industries
Starwood Hotels & Resorts Worldwide, Inc.
Steelcase Inc.
Storage Technology Corp.
Tenneco Automotive
Tesoro Hawaii
Toyota Motor Sales U.S.A., Inc.
United States Trust Co. of New York
Valmont Industries, Inc.
Wal-Mart Stores, Inc.

OUTPATIENT HEALTH CARE

American Retail Group
Avon Products, Inc.
Burlington Industries, Inc.
Deere & Co.
Ford Meter Box Co.
Leigh Fibers, Inc.
Parker Hannifin Corp.
Pella Corp.
Synovus Financial Corp.

PRENATAL HEALTH ISSUES

Aetna, Inc.
Alcoa Inc.
Alcon Laboratories, Inc.
Allstate Insurance Co.
Alma Piston Co.
American Fidelity Corp.
American General Finance
American Retail Group
APL Ltd.
Arizona Public Service Co.
Auburn Foundry
Avon Products, Inc.
Bandag, Inc.
Bank of America
Bemis Co., Inc.
Bernstein & Co., Inc. (Sanford C.)
Block, Inc. (H&R)
Blue Bell, Inc.
Blue Cross & Blue Shield of Alabama
Blue Cross & Blue Shield of Iowa
Blue Cross & Blue Shield of Michigan
Blue Cross & Blue Shield of Minnesota
Borden, Inc.
Brunswick Corp.
Burlington Resources, Inc.
Cabot Corp.
Callaway Golf Co.
Central Soya Co.
CertainTeed Corp.
CGU Insurance
Chase Bank of Texas
Chicago Tribune Co.
CIGNA Corp.
Cinergy Corp.
Citigroup
Clorox Co.
Colonial Oil Industries, Inc.
Contran Corp.
Cranston Print Works Co.
Credit Suisse First Boston
CUNA Mutual Group
Dain Bosworth Inc.
Dial Corp.
Duchossois Industries Inc.
Edwards Enterprise Software (J.D.)
Equifax Inc.
Federal-Mogul Corp.
First Union Securities, Inc.
FleetBoston Financial Corp.
Ford Meter Box Co.
Ford Motor Co.
Forest City Enterprises, Inc.
Freddie Mac
Freeport-McMoRan Inc.
Gallo Winery, Inc. (E&J)
Galter Corp.
Gap, Inc.
Gerber Products Co.
Giant Eagle Inc.
Giant Food Inc.
Giddings & Lewis
Golub Corp.
Group Health Plan
Guess?
Gulf Power Co.
Harcourt General, Inc.
Harnischfeger Industries
Hartford (The)
Hartmarx Corp.
Hasbro, Inc.
Honeywell International Inc.
Housatonic Curtain Co.
IBP
IKON Office Solutions, Inc.
Invacare Corp.
Jostens, Inc.
Kroger Co.
Ladish Co., Inc.
Lehigh Portland Cement Co.
Lilly & Co. (Eli)
Lipton Co.
Liz Claiborne, Inc.
Loews Corp.
Lotus Development Corp.
Louisiana-Pacific Corp.
Marcus Corp.
Mark IV Industries
Memphis Light Gas & Water Division
Metropolitan Life Insurance Co.
Mid-America Bank of Louisville
Milliken & Co.
Minnesota Mutual Life Insurance Co.
MONY Group (The)
Morgan Stanley Dean Witter & Co.
Nalco Chemical Co.
National Service Industries, Inc.
New England Bio Labs
New England Financial
New Jersey Natural Gas Co.
Niagara Mohawk Holdings Inc.
Norton Co.
Orscheln Co.
Park National Bank
Pharmacia & Upjohn, Inc.
Pillsbury Co.
Pittway Corp.
Putnam Investments

Ralph's Grocery Co.
Reinhart Institutional Foods
Rich Products Corp.
Rouse Co.
Russer Foods
Rutledge Hill Press
Sara Lee Corp.
Schwab & Co., Inc. (Charles)
Sega of America Inc.
Simplot Co. (J.R.)
Solo Cup Co.
Sony Electronics
Southeastern Mutual Insurance Co.
Southwest Gas Corp.
Standard Products Co.
Steelcase Inc.
Textron Inc.
TJX Companies, Inc.
Tomkins Industries, Inc.
Trustmark Insurance Co.
Union Pacific Corp.
United Distillers & Vintners North America
U.S. Bancorp
United Wisconsin Services
US Bank, Washington
Waffle House Inc.
Warner-Lambert Co.
Weil, Gotshal & Manges Corp.
West Co. Inc.
Whitman Corp.
Williams
Winn-Dixie Stores Inc.
Wisconsin Public Service Corp.
Wrigley Co. (Wm. Jr.)
York Federal Savings & Loan Association
Young & Rubicam

PREVENTIVE MEDICINE/ WELLNESS ORGANIZATIONS

AMETEK, Inc.
Amgen, Inc.
Andersons Inc.
Badger Meter, Inc.
Bandag, Inc.
Bard, Inc. (C.R.)
Bardes Corp.
Baxter International Inc.
Bernstein & Co., Inc. (Sanford C.)
Blue Cross & Blue Shield of Michigan
Blue Cross & Blue Shield of Minnesota
Broderbund Software, Inc.
Brown Shoe Co., Inc.
Burlington Industries, Inc.
Burlington Resources, Inc.
Central Newspapers, Inc.
Cessna Aircraft Co.
Citigroup
Cleveland-Cliffs, Inc.
Consolidated Papers, Inc.
Copley Press, Inc.
Cox Enterprises Inc.
Cummins Engine Co., Inc.
Dana Corp.
DeKalb Genetics Corp.
Dial Corp.
Donaldson Co., Inc.
Eastern Bank
Enterprise Rent-A-Car Co.
Erving Industries
Evening Post Publishing Co.
Fireman's Fund Insurance Co.
First Source Corp.
Gap, Inc.
GenAmerica Corp.
Gerber Products Co.
Glaxo Wellcome Inc.
Group Health Plan
Hartford (The)
Hofmann Co.
Hubbard Broadcasting, Inc.
INTRUST Financial Corp.
Jacobs Engineering Group
Lincoln Electric Co.
Medtronic, Inc.
Nalco Chemical Co.
Nestle U.S.A. Inc.
New England Bio Labs
Owens Corning
PacifiCare Health Systems
PerkinElmer, Inc.
Red Wing Shoe Co. Inc.
Rouse Co.
Rutledge Hill Press
Scripps Co. (E.W.)
Sony Electronics
Southeastern Mutual Insurance Co.
Toledo Blade Co.
Trustmark Insurance Co.
Waffle House Inc.

PUBLIC HEALTH

Abbott Laboratories
AEGON U.S.A. Inc.
Aetna, Inc.
AGL Resources Inc.
Agrilink Foods, Inc.
AK Steel Corp.
Albertson's Inc.
Alcoa Inc.
Alcon Laboratories, Inc.
AlliedSignal Inc.
Allmerica Financial Corp.
Allstate Insurance Co.
AMCORE Bank Rockford
American Retail Group
American United Life Insurance Co.
Ameritas Life Insurance Corp.
AMETEK, Inc.
AMR Corp.
Andersen Corp.
Anheuser-Busch Companies, Inc.
APL Ltd.
Arizona Public Service Co.
Armstrong World Industries, Inc.
Arvin Industries, Inc.
Baird & Co. (Robert W.)
Bandag, Inc.
BankBoston-Connecticut Region
BankBoston Corp.
Bard, Inc. (C.R.)
Bardes Corp.
Baxter International Inc.
Bemis Co., Inc.
Bethlehem Steel Corp.
Binswanger Companies
Block, Inc. (H&R)
Blue Bell, Inc.
Blue Cross & Blue Shield of Iowa
Blue Cross & Blue Shield of Minnesota
Borden, Inc.
BP Amoco Corp.
Broderbund Software, Inc.
Burlington Resources, Inc.
Carlson Companies, Inc.
Carnival Corp.
Carris Reels
Carter-Wallace, Inc.
Central Maine Power Co.
Central & South West Services
Central Soya Co.
CertainTeed Corp.
Chase Manhattan Bank, NA
Chevron Corp.
CIGNA Corp.
Cincinnati Bell Inc.
Citigroup
Citizens Financial Group, Inc.
CLARCOR Inc.
Cleveland-Cliffs, Inc.
Clorox Co.
Collins & Aikman Corp.
Colonial Life & Accident Insurance Co.
Commerce Bancshares, Inc.
Commercial Intertech Corp.
Constellation Energy Group, Inc.
Contran Corp.
Cooper Tire & Rubber Co.
Copley Press, Inc.
Country Curtains, Inc.
Cox Enterprises Inc.
Cummins Engine Co., Inc.
CUNA Mutual Group
Dain Bosworth Inc.
Danis Companies
Deere & Co.
Detroit Edison Co.
Deutsch Co.
Dexter Corp.
Disney Co. (Walt)
Donaldson Co., Inc.
Eaton Corp.
Eckerd Corp.
Ecolab Inc.
Edison Brothers Stores, Inc.
El Paso Energy Co.
Equifax Inc.
Extendicare Health Services
Exxon Mobil Corp.
FINA
First Financial Bank
First Source Corp.
FMC Corp.
Ford Motor Co.
Forest City Enterprises, Inc.
Fort Worth Star-Telegram Inc.
Fortis Insurance Co.
Fortune Brands, Inc.
Frost National Bank
Gallo Winery, Inc. (E&J)
Galter Corp.
Gap, Inc.
GATX Corp.
GEICO Corp.
GenAmerica Corp.
General Atlantic Partners II LP
General Motors Corp.
General Reinsurance Corp.
Georgia Power Co.
Gerber Products Co.
Globe Corp.
Green Bay Packaging
Group Health Plan
Hallmark Cards Inc.
Hancock Financial Services (John)
Harley-Davidson Co.
Harsco Corp.
Hartford (The)
Hartmarx Corp.
Hasbro, Inc.
Hawaiian Electric Co., Inc.
Heinz Co. (H.J.)
Hewlett-Packard Co.
Hoffmann-La Roche Inc.
Hofmann Co.
Honeywell International Inc.
Hubbell Inc.
Humana, Inc.
Independent Stave Co.
Jacobs Engineering Group
Jeld-wen, Inc.
Johnson Controls Inc.
Jostens, Inc.
Katten, Muchin & Zavis
Kimberly-Clark Corp.
Kinder Morgn
Koch Enterprises, Inc.
Lee Enterprises
Lennox International, Inc.
Levi Strauss & Co.
Lilly & Co. (Eli)
Lincoln Electric Co.
Little, Inc. (Arthur D.)
Liz Claiborne, Inc.
Loews Corp.
Lotus Development Corp.
Louisiana-Pacific Corp.
LTV Corp.
Lubrizol Corp. (The)
Macy's East Inc.
Madison Gas & Electric Co.
Manor Care Health SVS, Inc.
Manulife Financial
Marcus Corp.
Masco Corp.
Mattel Inc.
McKesson-HBOC Corp.
Mead Corp.
Medtronic, Inc.
Menasha Corp.
Merck & Co.
Merit Oil Corp.
Metropolitan Life Insurance Co.
Milliken & Co.
Millipore Corp.
Minnesota Mutual Life Insurance Co.
MONY Group (The)
Morgan & Co. Inc. (J.P.)
Morrison Knudsen Corp.
Nalco Chemical Co.
National Bank of Commerce Trust & Savings
National City Corp.
National Computer Systems, Inc.
National Starch & Chemical Co.
New England Bio Labs
New England Financial
New Jersey Natural Gas Co.
New York Mercantile Exchange
Northern Trust Co.
Northwest Bank Nebraska, NA
Norton Co.
OG&E Electric Services
Ohio National Life Insurance Co.
Orscheln Co.
Pacific Mutual Life Insurance Co.
PacifiCare Health Systems
PacifiCorp
Paine Webber
Park National Bank
Pfizer Inc.
Pharmacia & Upjohn, Inc.
Phillips Petroleum Co.
Physicians Mutual Insurance Co.
Polaroid Corp.
Portland General Electric Co.
PPG Industries, Inc.
Premier Dental Products Co.
Premier Industrial Corp.
Procter & Gamble Co., Cosmetics Division
Prudential Insurance Co. of America
Quanex Corp.
Reebok International Ltd.
Reinhart Institutional Foods
Reynolds Metals Co.
Rich Products Corp.
Rockwell International Corp.
Royal & SunAlliance USA, Inc.
SAFECO Corp.
S&T Bancorp
Sara Lee Hosiery, Inc.
Schering-Plough Corp.
Schloss & Co. (Marcus)
Searle & Co. (G.D.)
Sentinel Communications Co.
Sentry Insurance, A Mutual Co.
Shaw's Supermarkets, Inc.
Sherwin-Williams Co.
Shoney's Inc.
Smith Corp. (A.O.)
Solo Cup Co.
Sony Electronics
Southeastern Mutual Insurance Co.
Sovereign Bank
Sprint Corp.
Standard Register Co.
State Farm Mutual Automobile Insurance Co.
Steelcase Inc.
Storage Technology Corp.
Stupp Brothers Bridge & Iron Co.
Sunoco Inc.
SunTrust Bank Atlanta
Susquehanna-Pfaltzgraff Co.
Tai and Co. (J.T.)
Tamko Roofing Products
TCF National Bank Minnesota
Teleflex Inc.
Tension Envelope Corp.
Texaco Inc.
TJX Companies, Inc.
TMC Investment Co.
Tomkins Industries, Inc.
Toro Co.
True North Communications, Inc.
True Oil Co.
Ukrop's Super Markets
U.S. Bancorp Piper Jaffray
United States Sugar Corp.
United Wisconsin Services
USG Corp.
Van Leer Holding
Varian Medical Systems, Inc.
Vodafone AirTouch Plc
Wal-Mart Stores, Inc.
Warner-Lambert Co.
Washington Mutual, Inc.
Webster Bank
West Co. Inc.
Western Resources Inc.
Weyerhaeuser Co.
Winn-Dixie Stores Inc.
Wiremold Co.
Wisconsin Energy Corp.
Wisconsin Power & Light Co.
Woodward Governor Co.
Wrigley Co. (Wm. Jr.)

Wyman-Gordon Co.
Yellow Corp.
York Federal Savings & Loan Association
Young & Rubicam

RESEARCH/STUDIES INSTITUTES

Abbott Laboratories
Ameritas Life Insurance Corp.
Arizona Public Service Co.
Arvin Industries, Inc.
Atlantic Richfield Co.
Baxter International Inc.
Bechtel Group, Inc.
Block, Inc. (H&R)
BP Amoco Corp.
Bristol-Myers Squibb Co.
Central National-Gottesman
Chesapeake Corp.
Clorox Co.
Copley Press, Inc.
Cummins Engine Co., Inc.
Dain Bosworth Inc.
Dayton Hudson
Deutsch Co.
Duchossois Industries Inc.
Equifax Inc.
First Hawaiian, Inc.
First Union Corp.
Fisher Scientific
Fort Worth Star-Telegram Inc.
Fuller Co. (H.B.)
Gap, Inc.
Glaxo Wellcome Inc.
Globe Corp.
Graco, Inc.
Hannaford Brothers Co.
Harcourt General, Inc.
Hasbro, Inc.
Honeywell International Inc.
Hubbard Broadcasting, Inc.
Inman Mills
Jacobs Engineering Group
Journal-Gazette Co.
Landmark Communications Inc.
Levi Strauss & Co.
Liberty Corp.
Loews Corp.
Manor Care Health SVS, Inc.
Marshall & Ilsley Corp.
Merck & Co.
Metropolitan Life Insurance Co.
Minnesota Mutual Life Insurance Co.
Monsanto Co.
MONY Group (The)
MTD Products Inc.
National City Bank of Minneapolis
NEBCO Evans
New York Mercantile Exchange
Norfolk Southern Corp.
Northern Trust Co.
PACCAR Inc.
PEMCO Corp.
Pharmacia & Upjohn, Inc.
Pieper Power Electric Co.
Prudential Insurance Co. of America
Russer Foods
Ryder System, Inc.
Schering-Plough Corp.
Sonoco Products Co.
Texaco Inc.
Texas Instruments Inc.
Titan Industrial Corp.
TRW Inc.
U.S. Bancorp
Washington Trust Bank
Woodward Governor Co.
Zilkha & Sons

RESPIRATORY

Aetna, Inc.
Arvin Industries, Inc.
Baxter International Inc.
Beckman Coulter, Inc.
Blue Bell, Inc.
Blue Cross & Blue Shield of Alabama
Blue Cross & Blue Shield of Iowa
Blue Cross & Blue Shield of Minnesota
Broderbund Software, Inc.
Burlington Industries, Inc.
Business Improvement
Chicago Title Corp.
CLARCOR Inc.
Colonial Oil Industries, Inc.
Coors Brewing Co.
CPI Corp.
Crane & Co., Inc.
Cummings Properties Management
Demoulas Supermarkets Inc.
Dial Corp.
Fortis Insurance Co.
Galter Corp.
Group Health Plan
Hartmarx Corp.
Hensel Phelps Construction Co.
Hofmann Co.
Hubbell Inc.
Huntington Bancshares Inc.
Invacare Corp.
Ladish Co., Inc.
Lancaster Lens, Inc.
Levi Strauss & Co.
Leviton Manufacturing Co. Inc.
Lincoln Electric Co.
May Department Stores Co.
Old National Bank Evansville
Orange & Rockland Utilities, Inc.
Oshkosh B'Gosh, Inc.
Overseas Shipholding Group Inc.
Owens Corning
PEMCO Corp.
Physicians Mutual Insurance Co.
Principal Financial Group
Procter & Gamble Co., Cosmetics Division
Pulitzer Publishing Co.
Regions Bank
Russer Foods
Sega of America Inc.
Sierra Pacific Resources
Southeastern Mutual Insurance Co.
Southwest Gas Corp.
Texaco Inc.
Ticketmaster Corp.
Times Mirror Co.
Toledo Blade Co.
True Oil Co.
United Wisconsin Services
Wachovia Bank of North Carolina NA
Walter Industries Inc.
Wisconsin Energy Corp.
Young & Rubicam

SINGLE-DISEASE HEALTH ASSOCIATIONS

Abbott Laboratories
ABC
AEGON U.S.A. Inc.
AFLAC Inc.
Agrilink Foods, Inc.
Air Products and Chemicals, Inc.
AK Steel Corp.
Alabama Power Co.
Alcoa Inc.
Alcon Laboratories, Inc.
Alexander & Baldwin, Inc.
Allegheny Technologies Inc.
Alliant Techsystems
AlliedSignal Inc.
Allmerica Financial Corp.
Alma Piston Co.
AMCORE Bank Rockford
America West Airlines, Inc.
American Express Co.
American Fidelity Corp.
American General Finance
American United Life Insurance Co.
Ameritas Life Insurance Corp.
Amgen, Inc.
AMP Inc.
AMR Corp.
Andersen Corp.
Andersons Inc.
Anheuser-Busch Companies, Inc.
Aon Corp.
APL Ltd.
Apple Computer, Inc.
Appleton Papers Inc.
Aristech Chemical Corp.
Armstrong World Industries, Inc.
Arvin Industries, Inc.
Ashland, Inc.
Associated Food Stores
Avon Products, Inc.
Badger Meter, Inc.
Banfi Vintners
Bank of New York Co., Inc.
Barclays Capital
Bard, Inc. (C.R.)
Barden Corp.
Bardes Corp.
Barnes Group Inc.
Barry Corp. (R.G.)
Bassett Furniture Industries
Battelle Memorial Institute
Bayer Corp.
Belk-Simpson Department Stores
Bemis Co., Inc.
Bernstein & Co., Inc. (Sanford C.)
Bestfoods
Binswanger Companies
Blair & Co. (William)
Block, Inc. (H&R)
Blount International, Inc.
Blue Bell, Inc.
Blue Cross & Blue Shield of Alabama
Blue Cross & Blue Shield of Michigan
Blue Cross & Blue Shield of Minnesota
Borden, Inc.
Borman's Inc.
Boston Edison Co.
BP Amoco Corp.
Bradford & Co. (J.C.)
Bridgestone/Firestone, Inc.
Broderbund Software, Inc.
Browning-Ferris Industries Inc.
Brunswick Corp.
Bucyrus-Erie Co.
Burlington Industries, Inc.
Burlington Resources, Inc.
Burnett Co. (Leo)
Burress (J.W.)
Business Improvement
Calvin Klein
Campbell Soup Co.
Cantor, Fitzgerald Securities Corp.
Carillon Importers, Ltd.
Carlson Companies, Inc.
Carnival Corp.
Carolina Power & Light Co.
Carris Reels
Carter-Wallace, Inc.
Caterpillar Inc.
Central Maine Power Co.
Central National-Gottesman
Central Soya Co.
CertainTeed Corp.
Cessna Aircraft Co.
CGU Insurance
Charter Manufacturing Co.
Chase Bank of Texas
Chemed Corp.
Chevron Corp.
Chicago Board of Trade
Chicago Title Corp.
Cincinnati Bell Inc.
Circuit City Stores, Inc.
CIT Group, Inc. (The)
Citibank Corp.
Citizens Financial Group, Inc.
Clorox Co.
Collins & Aikman Corp.
Colonial Life & Accident Insurance Co.
Comdisco, Inc.
Comerica Inc.
Commerce Bancshares, Inc.
Commercial Intertech Corp.
Commonwealth Edison Co.
Compaq Computer Corp.
Continental Grain Co.
Contran Corp.
Conwood Co. LP
Cooper Industries, Inc.
Coors Brewing Co.
Copley Press, Inc.
Cox Enterprises Inc.
Crane Co.
Crane & Co., Inc.
Credit Suisse First Boston
CSS Industries, Inc.
Cummings Properties Management
CUNA Mutual Group
Cyprus Amax Minerals Co.
Dain Bosworth Inc.
Dana Corp.
Danis Companies
Deluxe Corp.
Demoulas Supermarkets Inc.
Deposit Guaranty National Bank
Detroit Edison Co.
Deutsch Co.
Dexter Corp.
Dial Corp.
Disney Co. (Walt)
DSM Copolymer
du Pont de Nemours & Co. (E.I.)
Duchossois Industries Inc.
Duke Energy
Dun & Bradstreet Corp.
Dynamet, Inc.
Eastman Kodak Co.
Eaton Corp.
Emerson Electric Co.
Ensign-Bickford Industries
Enterprise Rent-A-Car Co.
Equifax Inc.
European American Bank
Fannie Mae
Federal-Mogul Corp.
Federated Department Stores, Inc.
FedEx Corp.
Fifth Third Bancorp
First Hawaiian, Inc.
First Union Bank
First Union Corp.
First Union Securities, Inc.
Firstar Bank Milwaukee NA
Fisher Brothers Cleaning Services
Fisher Scientific
Florida Rock Industries
Forbes Inc.
Ford Meter Box Co.
Forest City Enterprises, Inc.
Fort Worth Star-Telegram Inc.
Fortis, Inc.
Fortis Insurance Co.
Fortune Brands, Inc.
Franklin Mint (The)
Freeport-McMoRan Inc.
Frost National Bank
Furniture Brands International, Inc.
Gallo Winery, Inc. (E&J)
Galter Corp.
Gap, Inc.
GATX Corp.
GEICO Corp.
GenAmerica Corp.
General Motors Corp.
Georgia-Pacific Corp.
Georgia Power Co.
Giant Eagle Inc.
Giant Food Inc.
Giddings & Lewis
Glaxo Wellcome Inc.
Glickenhaus & Co.
Globe Corp.
Golub Corp.
Goodrich Aerospace - Aerostructures Group (B.F.)
Grede Foundries
Green Bay Packaging
Griffith Laboratories U.S.A.
Group Health Plan
Guardian Life Insurance Co. of America
Gucci America Inc.
Gulf Power Co.
Hancock Financial Services (John)
Harland Co. (John H.)
Harley-Davidson Co.
Harnischfeger Industries
Harsco Corp.
Hartmarx Corp.
Hasbro, Inc.
Hawaiian Electric Co., Inc.
Heinz Co. (H.J.)
Hoffmann-La Roche Inc.
Hofmann Co.
Hubbard Broadcasting, Inc.
Hubbell Inc.
Huffy Corp.
Humana, Inc.
IKON Office Solutions, Inc.
Independent Stave Co.
Inland Container Corp.

Inman Mills
International Business Machines Corp.
International Flavors & Fragrances Inc.
INTRUST Financial Corp.
Invacare Corp.
Jacobs Engineering Group
Jacobson & Sons (Benjamin)
Johnson Controls Inc.
Johnson & Johnson
Johnson & Son (S.C.)
Journal-Gazette Co.
Katten, Muchin & Zavis
Kellwood Co.
Kemper National Insurance Companies
Kennametal, Inc.
Kerr-McGee Corp.
Kimberly-Clark Corp.
Koch Enterprises, Inc.
Koch Industries, Inc.
Kroger Co.
La-Z-Boy Inc.
Ladish Co., Inc.
Lancaster Lens, Inc.
Lance, Inc.
LandAmerica Financial Services
Lee Enterprises
Lennox International, Inc.
Leviton Manufacturing Co. Inc.
Liberty Corp.
Lilly & Co. (Eli)
Lincoln Electric Co.
Lincoln Financial Group
Lipton Co.
Liz Claiborne, Inc.
Loews Corp.
Louisiana Land & Exploration Co.
Louisiana-Pacific Corp.
LTV Corp.
Lubrizol Corp. (The)
Madison Gas & Electric Co.
Mamiye Brothers
Manulife Financial
Marcus Corp.
Mark IV Industries
Marriott International Inc.
Marshall & Ilsley Corp.
Mattel Inc.
MBIA Inc.
McDonald & Co. Securities, Inc.
McDonald's Corp.
MCI WorldCom, Inc.
McWane Inc.
Merck & Co.
Merit Oil Corp.
Merrill Lynch & Co., Inc.
MGIC Investment Corp.
Milliken & Co.
Millipore Corp.
Mine Safety Appliances Co.
Mitsubishi Electric America
MONY Group (The)
Morrison Knudsen Corp.
Motorola Inc.
Nalco Chemical Co.
National Computer Systems, Inc.
National Life of Vermont
National Machinery Co.
National Presto Industries, Inc.
Nationwide Insurance Co.
New Jersey Natural Gas Co.
New York Life Insurance Co.
New York Mercantile Exchange
Newman's Own Inc.
Nomura Holding America
Nordson Corp.
Norfolk Southern Corp.
Northern Indiana Public Service Co.
Northern States Power Co.
Northwest Bank Nebraska, NA
Northwest Natural Gas Co.
Norton Co.
Occidental Oil and Gas
Occidental Petroleum Corp.
Old National Bank Evansville
Olin Corp.
Orscheln Co.
Oshkosh B'Gosh, Inc.
Overseas Shipholding Group Inc.
Pacific Mutual Life Insurance Co.
PacifiCare Health Systems
Paine Webber
PEMCO Corp.
Pennzoil-Quaker State Co.
PerkinElmer, Inc.
Pfizer Inc.
Pharmacia & Upjohn, Inc.
Physicians Mutual Insurance Co.
Pittway Corp.
Playboy Enterprises Inc.
PNC Financial Services Group
Potomac Electric Power Co.
PPG Industries, Inc.
Praxair
Premier Dental Products Co.
Price Associates (T. Rowe)
Principal Financial Group
Procter & Gamble Co., Cosmetics Division
Providence Journal-Bulletin Co.
Prudential Securities Inc.
Publix Supermarkets
Pulitzer Publishing Co.
Putnam Investments
Quaker Chemical Corp.
Quanex Corp.
Ralph's Grocery Co.
Ralston Purina Co.
Red Wing Shoe Co. Inc.
Reily & Co., Inc. (William B.)
Reinhart Institutional Foods
Reliant Energy Inc.
Revlon Inc.
Reynolds Metals Co.
Rich Products Corp.
Riggs Bank NA
Rockwell International Corp.
Royal & SunAlliance USA, Inc.
Ruddick Corp.
Russer Foods
Ryder System, Inc.
SAFECO Corp.
Safeguard Scientifics
Salomon Smith Barney
Schering-Plough Corp.
Schloss & Co. (Marcus)
Schlumberger Ltd. (USA)
Schwab & Co., Inc. (Charles)
Schwebel Baking Co.
Searle & Co. (G.D.)
Security Benefit Life Insurance Co.
Security Life of Denver Insurance Co.
Sega of America Inc.
Sempra Energy
Servco Pacific
S.G. Cowen
Shaw's Supermarkets, Inc.
Shea Co. (John F.)
Shell Oil Co.
Shelter Mutual Insurance Co.
Sherwin-Williams Co.
Sierra Pacific Industries
Sierra Pacific Resources
SIT Investment Associates, Inc.
Slant/Fin Corp.
SmithKline Beecham Corp.
Smurfit-Stone Container Corp.
Solo Cup Co.
Sonoco Products Co.
Southeastern Mutual Insurance Co.
Southwest Gas Corp.
Springs Industries, Inc.
Square D Co.
Standard Products Co.
Star Bank NA
Starwood Hotels & Resorts Worldwide, Inc.
Steelcase Inc.
Stone Container Corp.
Storage Technology Corp.
Stupp Brothers Bridge & Iron Co.
SunTrust Bank Atlanta
Susquehanna-Pfaltzgraff Co.
Sverdrup Corp.
Synovus Financial Corp.
Tamko Roofing Products
Tenet Healthcare Corp.
TENNANT Co.
Tenneco Automotive
Tenneco Packaging
Textron Inc.
Titan Industrial Corp.
TJX Companies, Inc.
TMC Investment Co.
Toledo Blade Co.
Tomkins Industries, Inc.
Torchmark Corp.
Trace International Holdings, Inc.
Transamerica Corp.
True North Communications, Inc.
True Oil Co.
Trustmark Insurance Co.
Tyson Foods Inc.
Ukrop's Super Markets
Unilever United States, Inc.
Union Camp Corp.
United Airlines Inc.
United Dominion Industries, Ltd.
United Parcel Service of America Inc.
United States Sugar Corp.
United Wisconsin Services
Universal Leaf Tobacco Co., Inc.
Universal Studios
Unocal Corp.
USG Corp.
USX Corp.
Valmont Industries, Inc.
Valspar Corp.
Vesper Corp.
Waffle House Inc.
Wal-Mart Stores, Inc.
Walgreen Co.
Walter Industries Inc.
Warner-Lambert Co.
Washington Mutual, Inc.
Waste Management Inc.
Weil, Gotshal & Manges Corp.
Wells Fargo & Co.
Western & Southern Life Insurance Co.
Westvaco Corp.
Whitman Corp.
Wilbur-Ellis Co. & Connell Brothers Co.
Williams
Winn-Dixie Stores Inc.
Wisconsin Energy Corp.
Wisconsin Power & Light Co.
Wisconsin Public Service Corp.
Witco Corp.
Woodward Governor Co.
Wrigley Co. (Wm. Jr.)
York Federal Savings & Loan Association
Young & Rubicam

SPEECH & HEARING

Alcoa Inc.
Ameritech Ohio
Andersen Corp.
Ashland, Inc.
AT&T Corp.
Badger Meter, Inc.
Bandag, Inc.
Bard, Inc. (C.R.)
Barry Corp. (R.G.)
Bemis Co., Inc.
Bernstein & Co., Inc. (Sanford C.)
Binney & Smith Inc.
Blue Cross & Blue Shield of Alabama
Briggs & Stratton Corp.
Carter-Wallace, Inc.
Chemed Corp.
Cincinnati Bell Inc.
Commercial Intertech Corp.
Crestar Finance Corp.
DaimlerChrysler Corp.
Duchossois Industries Inc.
Dun & Bradstreet Corp.
Ecolab Inc.
Fifth Third Bancorp
Fisher Scientific
Furniture Brands International, Inc.
Gerber Products Co.
Grede Foundries
Group Health Plan
Hensel Phelps Construction Co.
HON Industries Inc.
Hubbard Broadcasting, Inc.
Huntington Bancshares Inc.
Ladish Co., Inc.
Loews Corp.
McDonald & Co. Securities, Inc.
Nationwide Insurance Co.
Nordson Corp.
Occidental Oil and Gas
Oshkosh B'Gosh, Inc.
Pacific Mutual Life Insurance Co.
Pieper Power Electric Co.
Polaroid Corp.
Shea Co. (John F.)
Strear Farms Co.
Thompson Co. (J. Walter)
Wachtell, Lipton, Rosen & Katz
Woodward Governor Co.

TRANSPLANT NETWORKS/ DONOR BANKS

ABC
AlliedSignal Inc.
Badger Meter, Inc.
Bristol-Myers Squibb Co.
Burress (J.W.)
Charter Manufacturing Co.
Chase Manhattan Bank, NA
Chicago Tribune Co.
Circuit City Stores, Inc.
CIT Group, Inc. (The)
Compass Bank
Contran Corp.
Crane Co.
Credit Suisse First Boston
Dayton Power and Light Co.
Deere & Co.
Deposit Guaranty National Bank
Firstar Bank Milwaukee NA
Fisher Brothers Cleaning Services
Fisher Scientific
Florida Power Corp.
Fort Worth Star-Telegram Inc.
Gallo Winery, Inc. (E&J)
Gap, Inc.
Giddings & Lewis
Grede Foundries
Group Health Plan
Hamilton Sundstrand Corp.
Hoffmann-La Roche Inc.
Johnson Controls Inc.
Kellwood Co.
Ladish Co., Inc.
Lehigh Portland Cement Co.
Marshall & Ilsley Corp.
McGraw-Hill Companies, Inc.
Memphis Light Gas & Water Division
Merrill Lynch & Co., Inc.
Metropolitan Life Insurance Co.
Minnesota Mining & Manufacturing Co.
Morgan & Co. Inc. (J.P.)
Nomura Holding America
Overseas Shipholding Group Inc.
Paine Webber
Pella Corp.
Pfizer Inc.
Pharmacia & Upjohn, Inc.
Praxair
Prudential Securities Inc.
Publix Supermarkets
Reilly Industries, Inc.
Reynolds Metals Co.
Schering-Plough Corp.
Schwab & Co., Inc. (Charles)
S.G. Cowen
Shea Co. (John F.)
Sierra Pacific Industries
Standard Products Co.
Storage Technology Corp.
Texaco Inc.
Universal Foods Corp.
Universal Leaf Tobacco Co., Inc.
Weil, Gotshal & Manges Corp.
WICOR, Inc.
Young & Rubicam
Zilkha & Sons

TRAUMA TREATMENT

Banfi Vintners
Barnes Group Inc.
Blue Cross & Blue Shield of Alabama

Blue Cross & Blue Shield of Minnesota
Briggs & Stratton Corp.
Chicago Title Corp.
CIT Group, Inc. (The)
Collins & Aikman Corp.
Consolidated Papers, Inc.
Demoulas Supermarkets Inc.
Deutsch Co.
Gap, Inc.
Group Health Plan
Hickory Tech Corp.
International Flavors & Fragrances Inc.
Jostens, Inc.
Lance, Inc.
Lilly & Co. (Eli)
Marcus Corp.
Marshall & Ilsley Corp.
Medtronic, Inc.
Nalco Chemical Co.
New York Mercantile Exchange
PEMCO Corp.
Reynolds & Reynolds Co.
Simpson Investment Co.
Southeastern Mutual Insurance Co.
Unilever United States, Inc.
USX Corp.
Waffle House Inc.
West Co. Inc.
Wisconsin Energy Corp.

International

FOREIGN ARTS ORGANIZATIONS

ABC
AK Steel Corp.
Alcoa Inc.
American Express Co.
AT&T Corp.
Banfi Vintners
Bardes Corp.
Bernstein & Co., Inc. (Sanford C.)
Boston Globe (The)
Brown Shoe Co., Inc.
Bucyrus-Erie Co.
Burnett Co. (Leo)
Cabot Corp.
Cantor, Fitzgerald Securities Corp.
Carillon Importers, Ltd.
Central National-Gottesman
CertainTeed Corp.
Consolidated Electrical Distributors
Country Curtains, Inc.
Cummins Engine Co., Inc.
Daily News
Deposit Guaranty National Bank
Deutsch Co.
Eastman Kodak Co.
El Paso Energy Co.
Equifax Inc.
Federated Department Stores, Inc.
Fidelity Investments
Florida Power & Light Co.
Forbes Inc.
Ford Meter Box Co.
Fort Worth Star-Telegram Inc.
Glaxo Wellcome Inc.
Glickenhaus & Co.
Goldman Sachs Group
Harsco Corp.
Hartmarx Corp.
Hawaiian Electric Co., Inc.
Hewlett-Packard Co.
International Flavors & Fragrances Inc.
ISE America
Kimball International, Inc.
Kroger Co.
Loews Corp.
Manulife Financial
Marcus Corp.
Metropolitan Life Insurance Co.
Morgan & Co. Inc. (J.P.)
Morris Communications Corp.
New York Times Co.
Newman's Own Inc.
Norton Co.
Overseas Shipholding Group Inc.
Pacific Century Financial Corp.
PerkinElmer, Inc.
Pfizer Inc.
Pharmacia & Upjohn, Inc.
Publix Supermarkets
Reilly Industries, Inc.
Schloss & Co. (Marcus)
Scripps Co. (E.W.)
Seagram & Sons, Inc. (Joseph E.)
Sony Electronics
Sprint Corp.
SunTrust Banks of Florida
Tesoro Hawaii
Times Mirror Co.
Titan Industrial Corp.
Toshiba America Inc.
Trace International Holdings, Inc.
United Wisconsin Services
Wachovia Bank of North Carolina NA
Westvaco Corp.
Wilbur-Ellis Co. & Connell Brothers Co.
Young & Rubicam
Zachry Co. (H.B.)
Zilkha & Sons

FOREIGN EDUCATIONAL INSTITUTIONS

Aetna, Inc.
Alcoa Inc.
Alcon Laboratories, Inc.
AlliedSignal Inc.
American Express Co.
American Retail Group
American Standard Inc.
Ameritech Corp.
AMR Corp.
Aon Corp.
Archer-Daniels-Midland Co.
Arvin Industries, Inc.
AT&T Corp.
Avon Products, Inc.
BankBoston Corp.
Baxter International Inc.
Bechtel Group, Inc.
Bemis Manufacturing Co.
Bernstein & Co., Inc. (Sanford C.)
Binswanger Companies
Blount International, Inc.
Borman's Inc.
BP Amoco Corp.
Bristol-Myers Squibb Co.
Butler Capital Corp.
Cabot Corp.
Carillon Importers, Ltd.
Carnival Corp.
Carpenter Technology Corp.
Carter-Wallace, Inc.
Central National-Gottesman
Century 21
CertainTeed Corp.
Chase Manhattan Bank, NA
Chevron Corp.
Citibank Corp.
Coca-Cola Co.
Copley Press, Inc.
Corning Inc.
Cummins Engine Co., Inc.
Deere & Co.
Deposit Guaranty National Bank
Deutsch Co.
Dixie Group, Inc. (The)
Domino's Pizza Inc.
Dow Chemical Co.
du Pont de Nemours & Co. (E.I.)
Duriron Co., Inc.
Eastman Kodak Co.
Elf Atochem North America, Inc.
Fidelity Investments
First Hawaiian, Inc.
Forbes Inc.
Fuller Co. (H.B.)
General Atlantic Partners II LP
General Electric Co.
Goldman Sachs Group
Graco, Inc.
GTE Corp.
Halliburton Co.
Heinz Co. (H.J.)
Hewlett-Packard Co.
Hitachi America Ltd.
Humana, Inc.
Industrial Bank of Japan Trust Co. (New York)
Intel Corp.
International Business Machines Corp.
Katten, Muchin & Zavis
Lennox International, Inc.
Levi Strauss & Co.
Liberty Corp.
Little, Inc. (Arthur D.)
Litton Industries, Inc.
Louisiana-Pacific Corp.
Manulife Financial
Marcus Corp.
Mark IV Industries
McClatchy Co.
Medtronic, Inc.
Merck & Co.
Merrill Lynch & Co., Inc.
Metropolitan Life Insurance Co.
MidAmerican Energy Holdings Co.
Millipore Corp.
Minnesota Mining & Manufacturing Co.
Montana Power Co.
Morgan & Co. Inc. (J.P.)
Morrison Knudsen Corp.
Motorola Inc.
Nabisco Group Holdings
Nalco Chemical Co.
New England Bio Labs
New York Times Co.
Newman's Own Inc.
Norton Co.
Olin Corp.
Overseas Shipholding Group Inc.
Owens Corning
Pacific Century Financial Corp.
Paine Webber
PepsiCo, Inc.
Pfizer Inc.
Pharmacia & Upjohn, Inc.
Premier Dental Products Co.
Revlon Inc.
Reynolds Tobacco (R.J.)
Rutledge Hill Press
SBC Communications Inc.
Schloss & Co. (Marcus)
Schlumberger Ltd. (USA)
Seagram & Sons, Inc. (Joseph E.)
Sega of America Inc.
Servco Pacific
ServiceMaster Co.
SIT Investment Associates, Inc.
Slant/Fin Corp.
SmithKline Beecham Corp.
Sprint/United Telephone
Stone Container Corp.
Sumitomo Bank
Sun Microsystems Inc.
Tai and Co. (J.T.)
Texaco Inc.
Texas Instruments Inc.
Textron Inc.
Toro Co.
Toshiba America Inc.
Trace International Holdings, Inc.
United Distillers & Vintners North America
Wachtell, Lipton, Rosen & Katz
Weil, Gotshal & Manges Corp.
Weyerhaeuser Co.
Whirlpool Corp.
Witco Corp.
Wrigley Co. (Wm. Jr.)
Xerox Corp.
Zilkha & Sons

INTERNATIONAL-GENERAL

APL Ltd.
Baxter International Inc.
Bell Atlantic Corp.-West Virginia
Cabot Corp.
Cenex Harvest States
Crane Co.
Eastman Chemical Co.
Intel Corp.
International Flavors & Fragrances Inc.
Medtronic, Inc.
New England Bio Labs
Oshkosh B'Gosh, Inc.
PepsiCo, Inc.
Regions Bank
Rutledge Hill Press
Servco Pacific

HEALTH CARE/HOSPITALS

Abbott Laboratories
AEGON U.S.A. Inc.
Aetna, Inc.
Alcoa Inc.
Alcon Laboratories, Inc.
Alma Piston Co.
American Express Co.
American Retail Group
American United Life Insurance Co.
Ameritech Michigan
Amgen, Inc.
APL Ltd.
Archer-Daniels-Midland Co.
Armstrong World Industries, Inc.
Arvin Industries, Inc.
Associated Food Stores
Avon Products, Inc.
Bard, Inc. (C.R.)
Baxter International Inc.
Becton Dickinson & Co.
Blue Bell, Inc.
Borman's Inc.
BP Amoco Corp.
Bristol-Myers Squibb Co.
Burnett Co. (Leo)
Cabot Corp.
Carlson Companies, Inc.
Carnival Corp.
Carter-Wallace, Inc.
CertainTeed Corp.
CGU Insurance
Chase Manhattan Bank, NA
Chesapeake Corp.
Chevron Corp.
Citibank Corp.
Citizens Financial Group, Inc.
Cleveland-Cliffs, Inc.
Coca-Cola Co.
Comdisco, Inc.
Compass Bank
Continental Grain Co.
Contran Corp.
Cooper Industries, Inc.
Cox Enterprises Inc.
Crane Co.
Credit Suisse First Boston
Crestar Finance Corp.
Croft-Leominster
CSS Industries, Inc.
Cummings Properties Management
Delta Air Lines, Inc.
Deutsch Co.
Dow Chemical Co.
du Pont de Nemours & Co. (E.I.)
Duchossois Industries Inc.
Dynamet, Inc.
Eastman Kodak Co.
Ensign-Bickford Industries
Erb Lumber Co.
Exxon Mobil Corp.
Federal-Mogul Corp.
First Hawaiian, Inc.
First Union Bank
Fisher Brothers Cleaning Services
Fisher Scientific
Ford Meter Box Co.
Fortis, Inc.
Fortis Insurance Co.
Fortune Brands, Inc.
Freddie Mac
Fuller Co. (H.B.)
General Electric Co.
Gerber Products Co.
Giant Eagle Inc.
Group Health Plan
Guess?
Hamilton Sundstrand Corp.
Hasbro, Inc.
Hawaiian Electric Co., Inc.
Heinz Co. (H.J.)
Hewlett-Packard Co.
Hoffmann-La Roche Inc.
International Business Machines Corp.
International Flavors & Fragrances Inc.
Lance, Inc.
Leigh Fibers, Inc.
Levi Strauss & Co.
Lilly & Co. (Eli)
Litton Industries, Inc.
Loews Corp.

Louisiana-Pacific Corp.
LTV Corp.
Manulife Financial
Mattel Inc.
Medtronic, Inc.
Merck & Co.
Merrill Lynch & Co., Inc.
Metropolitan Life Insurance Co.
Motorola Inc.
National Service Industries, Inc.
Nationwide Insurance Co.
New England Bio Labs
Newman's Own Inc.
Nomura Holding America
Norton Co.
Overseas Shipholding Group Inc.
Owens Corning
Pacific Mutual Life Insurance Co.
PepsiCo, Inc.
Pfizer Inc.
Pharmacia & Upjohn, Inc.
Phelps Dodge Corp.
Praxair
Premier Dental Products Co.
Putnam Investments
Quaker Chemical Corp.
Reebok International Ltd.
Reynolds Metals Co.
Reynolds Tobacco (R.J.)
Safeguard Scientifics
Schering-Plough Corp.
Schwab & Co., Inc. (Charles)
Seagram & Sons, Inc. (Joseph E.)
Searle & Co. (G.D.)
Sentry Insurance, A Mutual Co.
ServiceMaster Co.
SIT Investment Associates, Inc.
Slant/Fin Corp.
SmithKline Beecham Corp.
Sprint Corp.
State Street Bank & Trust Co.
Strear Farms Co.
Texaco Inc.
Unilever United States, Inc.
United Parcel Service of America Inc.
U.S. Bancorp Piper Jaffray
Van Leer Holding
Warner-Lambert Co.
West Co. Inc.
Whirlpool Corp.
Wilbur-Ellis Co. & Connell Brothers Co.
Witco Corp.
Xerox Corp.
Young & Rubicam
Zilkha & Sons

HUMAN RIGHTS

AMR Corp.
Archer-Daniels-Midland Co.
Bard, Inc. (C.R.)
Ben & Jerry's Homemade Inc.
Boston Globe (The)
Chicago Tribune Co.
CIGNA Corp.
Continental Grain Co.
Cummins Engine Co., Inc.
Dial Corp.
Dow Jones & Co., Inc.
Forbes Inc.
Fuller Co. (H.B.)
GATX Corp.
General Atlantic Partners II LP
Glickenhaus & Co.
Goldman Sachs Group
Hasbro, Inc.
Heinz Co. (H.J.)
Hitachi America Ltd.
Hoffmann-La Roche Inc.
Humana, Inc.
Lee Enterprises
Liz Claiborne, Inc.
Loews Corp.
Lotus Development Corp.
Manulife Financial
McClatchy Co.
MCI WorldCom, Inc.
Merck & Co.
Minnesota Mutual Life Insurance Co.
Morgan & Co. Inc. (J.P.)
Morris Communications Corp.
National City Bank of Minneapolis
Overseas Shipholding Group Inc.
PepsiCo, Inc.
Polaroid Corp.
Prudential Insurance Co. of America
Pulitzer Publishing Co.
Reebok International Ltd.
Sara Lee Corp.
Scripps Co. (E.W.)
Seagram & Sons, Inc. (Joseph E.)
Tamko Roofing Products
TENNANT Co.
Textron Inc.
Titan Industrial Corp.
TJX Companies, Inc.
Trace International Holdings, Inc.
Unilever United States, Inc.
United Parcel Service of America Inc.
Universal Leaf Tobacco Co., Inc.
Weil, Gotshal & Manges Corp.
Wiley & Sons (John)
Wrigley Co. (Wm. Jr.)
Young & Rubicam
Zilkha & Sons

INTERNATIONAL AFFAIRS

ABC
Allegheny Technologies Inc.
AlliedSignal Inc.
Alma Piston Co.
American Express Co.
American Standard Inc.
AMETEK, Inc.
Amsted Industries Inc.
Aon Corp.
Archer-Daniels-Midland Co.
Arvin Industries, Inc.
AT&T Corp.
Bard, Inc. (C.R.)
Bardes Corp.
Barry Corp. (R.G.)
Bechtel Group, Inc.
Binswanger Companies
Blair & Co. (William)
Borman's Inc.
BP Amoco Corp.
Bristol-Myers Squibb Co.
Brunswick Corp.
Burlington Industries, Inc.
Burnett Co. (Leo)
Chase Manhattan Bank, NA
Chevron Corp.
Cincinnati Bell Inc.
Clorox Co.
Coca-Cola Co.
Commerce Bancshares, Inc.
Commercial Intertech Corp.
Compaq Computer Corp.
Cooper Industries, Inc.
CSS Industries, Inc.
Delta Air Lines, Inc.
Duchossois Industries Inc.
Duriron Co., Inc.
Dynamet, Inc.
Exxon Mobil Corp.
Ferro Corp.
First Union Bank
Fluor Corp.
FMC Corp.
Forbes Inc.
Freeport-McMoRan Inc.
GenCorp
General Electric Co.
General Motors Corp.
Georgia Power Co.
Glickenhaus & Co.
Goldman Sachs Group
Hasbro, Inc.
Heinz Co. (H.J.)
Hewlett-Packard Co.
Hitachi America Ltd.
Hoffmann-La Roche Inc.
Huffy Corp.
Hunt Manufacturing Co.
Huntington Bancshares Inc.
IKON Office Solutions, Inc.
Indiana Mills & Manufacturing
Industrial Bank of Japan Trust Co. (New York)
Jacobs Engineering Group
Kellwood Co.
Kennametal, Inc.
Levi Strauss & Co.
Lilly & Co. (Eli)
Lincoln Electric Co.
Litton Industries, Inc.
Lubrizol Corp. (The)
Mark IV Industries
Medtronic, Inc.
Merck & Co.
Merrill Lynch & Co., Inc.
Montana Power Co.
Morgan & Co. Inc. (J.P.)
Motorola Inc.
National Service Industries, Inc.
Nationwide Insurance Co.
Occidental Oil and Gas
OG&E Electric Services
Olin Corp.
PepsiCo, Inc.
PerkinElmer, Inc.
Pittway Corp.
Premier Industrial Corp.
Principal Financial Group
Procter & Gamble Co.
Procter & Gamble Co., Cosmetics Division
Providence Journal-Bulletin Co.
Publix Supermarkets
Putnam Investments
Reebok International Ltd.
Reynolds Tobacco (R.J.)
Rockwell International Corp.
Saint Paul Companies Inc.
Scripps Co. (E.W.)
Seagram & Sons, Inc. (Joseph E.)
Slant/Fin Corp.
Sony Electronics
Sprint Corp.
Sprint/United Telephone
Star Bank NA
State Street Bank & Trust Co.
Stone Container Corp.
Sun Microsystems Inc.
Synovus Financial Corp.
Teleflex Inc.
Tension Envelope Corp.
Tesoro Hawaii
Texaco Inc.
Textron Inc.
Times Mirror Co.
Toledo Blade Co.
Trace International Holdings, Inc.
True North Communications, Inc.
TRW Inc.
Unilever United States, Inc.
United Dominion Industries, Ltd.
United Parcel Service of America Inc.
Unocal Corp.
Warner-Lambert Co.
Weil, Gotshal & Manges Corp.
Weyerhaeuser Co.
Whitman Corp.
Wilbur-Ellis Co. & Connell Brothers Co.
Wolverine World Wide
Young & Rubicam
Zachry Co. (H.B.)
Zilkha & Sons

INTERNATIONAL DEVELOPMENT

Abbott Laboratories
Aetna, Inc.
Alcoa Inc.
Allstate Insurance Co.
American Express Co.
American Retail Group
American Standard Inc.
Archer-Daniels-Midland Co.
ASARCO Inc.
Ashland, Inc.
Avon Products, Inc.
BankBoston Corp.
Barry Corp. (R.G.)
Bechtel Group, Inc.
Ben & Jerry's Homemade Inc.
Blue Bell, Inc.
Cabot Corp.
Campbell Soup Co.
Carillon Importers, Ltd.
CertainTeed Corp.
Chase Bank of Texas
Chase Manhattan Bank, NA
Clorox Co.
Coca-Cola Co.
Continental Grain Co.
Contran Corp.
Crane Co.
Dow Chemical Co.
Duke Energy
El Paso Energy Co.
Equifax Inc.
Fluor Corp.
Ford Motor Co.
General Atlantic Partners II LP
General Electric Co.
Guess?
Heinz Co. (H.J.)
Huffy Corp.
Huntington Bancshares Inc.
International Flavors & Fragrances Inc.
Kimball International, Inc.
KPMG Peat Marwick LLP
Land O'Lakes, Inc.
Leigh Fibers, Inc.
Levi Strauss & Co.
Little, Inc. (Arthur D.)
Louisiana-Pacific Corp.
Marcus Corp.
Mattel Inc.
McGraw-Hill Companies, Inc.
Mead Corp.
Merrill Lynch & Co., Inc.
MONY Group (The)
Morgan & Co. Inc. (J.P.)
Nalco Chemical Co.
Nationwide Insurance Co.
New England Bio Labs
Norton Co.
Paine Webber
PepsiCo, Inc.
Pfizer Inc.
Pharmacia & Upjohn, Inc.
Phillips Petroleum Co.
Pillsbury Co.
PNC Financial Services Group
Putnam Investments
Red Wing Shoe Co. Inc.
Reebok International Ltd.
Revlon Inc.
Rutledge Hill Press
SIT Investment Associates, Inc.
Sony Electronics
Stanley Works (The)
Sunmark Capital Corp.
Texaco Inc.
Thermo Electron Corp.
Ticketmaster Corp.
United Airlines Inc.
Westvaco Corp.
Weyerhaeuser Co.
Whirlpool Corp.
Young & Rubicam

INTERNATIONAL ENVIRONMENTAL ISSUES

Alcoa Inc.
American Express Co.
Archer-Daniels-Midland Co.
Bank of America
Bell Atlantic Corp.
Bemis Co., Inc.
Ben & Jerry's Homemade Inc.
Bernstein & Co., Inc. (Sanford C.)
BP Amoco Corp.
Broderbund Software, Inc.
Burnett Co. (Leo)
Calvin Klein
Cargill Inc.
Chevron Corp.
Coca-Cola Co.
Compaq Computer Corp.
Consolidated Electrical Distributors
Crane Co.
Disney Co. (Walt)
Duchossois Industries Inc.
Eastman Kodak Co.
Ecolab Inc.
Erb Lumber Co.
Exxon Mobil Corp.
Fidelity Investments
Florida Rock Industries
FMC Corp.
Ford Motor Co.
Fuller Co. (H.B.)
General Atlantic Partners II LP
General Electric Co.
General Motors Corp.

Graco, Inc.
Hawaiian Electric Co., Inc.
Hitachi America Ltd.
Hoffmann-La Roche Inc.
Hofmann Co.
Hubbard Broadcasting, Inc.
Independent Stave Co.
Johnson & Son (S.C.)
Leigh Fibers, Inc.
Lennox International, Inc.
Levi Strauss & Co.
Little, Inc. (Arthur D.)
Louisiana-Pacific Corp.
Medtronic, Inc.
Nalco Chemical Co.
Nationwide Insurance Co.
New England Bio Labs
Olin Corp.
Oshkosh B'Gosh, Inc.
Pacific Mutual Life Insurance Co.
Patagonia Inc.
Red Wing Shoe Co. Inc.
Schwab & Co., Inc. (Charles)
Slant/Fin Corp.
Stone Container Corp.
Stupp Brothers Bridge & Iron Co.
Sun Microsystems Inc.
Tesoro Hawaii
Texaco Inc.
Thermo Electron Corp.
Ticketmaster Corp.
Toro Co.
Toshiba America Inc.
Tyson Foods Inc.
Union Carbide Corp.
United Airlines Inc.
United Wisconsin Services
Wachovia Bank of North Carolina NA
Weyerhaeuser Co.
Wilbur-Ellis Co. & Connell Brothers Co.

INTERNATIONAL ORGANIZATIONS

Aetna, Inc.
Alcoa Inc.
Allstate Insurance Co.
Alma Piston Co.
American Express Co.
American Retail Group
Archer-Daniels-Midland Co.
Arvin Industries, Inc.
Avon Products, Inc.
Banfi Vintners
Barclays Capital
Baxter International Inc.
Bayer Corp.
Bechtel Group, Inc.
Bernstein & Co., Inc. (Sanford C.)
Binswanger Companies
Borman's Inc.
BP Amoco Corp.
Bristol-Myers Squibb Co.
Brown Shoe Co., Inc.
Burlington Resources, Inc.
Burnett Co. (Leo)
Cabot Corp.
Calvin Klein
Carillon Importers, Ltd.
Carlson Companies, Inc.
CertainTeed Corp.
Chase Manhattan Bank, NA
Cone Mills Corp.
Consolidated Electrical Distributors
Continental Grain Co.
Copley Press, Inc.
Crane Co.
CUNA Mutual Group
Dain Bosworth Inc.
Dixie Group, Inc. (The)
Dow Chemical Co.
Dow Jones & Co., Inc.
Dynamet, Inc.
Eastman Kodak Co.
Edwards Enterprise Software (J.D.)
El Paso Energy Co.
Equifax Inc.
Erb Lumber Co.
First Union Bank
Fisher Scientific
Forbes Inc.
Ford Motor Co.
Fuller Co. (H.B.)
Gallo Winery, Inc. (E&J)
General Atlantic Partners II LP
General Electric Co.
Giant Eagle Inc.
Goldman Sachs Group
Guess?
Harland Co. (John H.)
Hasbro, Inc.
Heinz Co. (H.J.)
Hewlett-Packard Co.
Hitachi America Ltd.
Hofmann Co.
Honeywell International Inc.
Hubbard Broadcasting, Inc.
Hubbell Inc.
Indiana Mills & Manufacturing
Inland Container Corp.
ISE America
Katten, Muchin & Zavis
LandAmerica Financial Services
Leigh Fibers, Inc.
Levi Strauss & Co.
Lipton Co.
Loews Corp.
Louisiana-Pacific Corp.
Manulife Financial
Mark IV Industries
Mead Corp.
Metropolitan Life Insurance Co.
MidAmerican Energy Holdings Co.
Minnesota Mutual Life Insurance Co.
Monsanto Co.
Motorola Inc.
National Service Industries, Inc.
Nationwide Insurance Co.
Newman's Own Inc.
Norton Co.
Oshkosh B'Gosh, Inc.
Overseas Shipholding Group Inc.
Owens Corning
PacifiCorp
Park National Bank
Patagonia Inc.
PepsiCo, Inc.
Pioneer Hi-Bred International, Inc.
Premier Dental Products Co.
Pulitzer Publishing Co.
Putnam Investments
Quaker Chemical Corp.
Red Wing Shoe Co. Inc.
Reebok International Ltd.
Regions Bank
Revlon Inc.
Rutledge Hill Press
Schwab & Co., Inc. (Charles)
Seagram & Sons, Inc. (Joseph E.)
Sentinel Communications Co.
ServiceMaster Co.
Shell Oil Co.
SIT Investment Associates, Inc.
Slant/Fin Corp.
SmithKline Beecham Corp.
Stride Rite Corp.
Susquehanna-Pfaltzgraff Co.
TCF National Bank Minnesota
Teleflex Inc.
TENNANT Co.
Textron Inc.
Thermo Electron Corp.
Thompson Co. (J. Walter)
Times Mirror Co.
Titan Industrial Corp.
Toro Co.
Trace International Holdings, Inc.
Ukrop's Super Markets
Unocal Corp.
USG Corp.
Vulcan Materials Co.
West Co. Inc.
Whirlpool Corp.
Wilbur-Ellis Co. & Connell Brothers Co.
Xerox Corp.
Zilkha & Sons

INTERNATIONAL PEACE & SECURITY ISSUES

Air Products and Chemicals, Inc.
Alcoa Inc.
Alcon Laboratories, Inc.
Alexander & Baldwin, Inc.
American Express Co.
Andersen Corp.
Archer-Daniels-Midland Co.
ASARCO Inc.
Bechtel Group, Inc.
Bemis Co., Inc.
Ben & Jerry's Homemade Inc.
Bernstein & Co., Inc. (Sanford C.)
Bestfoods
Briggs & Stratton Corp.
Broderbund Software, Inc.
Calvin Klein
Cantor, Fitzgerald Securities Corp.
Carillon Importers, Ltd.
Carnival Corp.
Caterpillar Inc.
Chase Manhattan Bank, NA
Chevron Corp.
CIT Group, Inc. (The)
Citibank Corp.
Continental Grain Co.
Crane Co.
Cummins Engine Co., Inc.
Dain Bosworth Inc.
du Pont de Nemours & Co. (E.I.)
Duke Energy
Equifax Inc.
Erving Industries
Exxon Mobil Corp.
Federal-Mogul Corp.
Fisher Brothers Cleaning Services
FMC Corp.
Forbes Inc.
Ford Motor Co.
Fortune Brands, Inc.
General Electric Co.
General Motors Corp.
Glickenhaus & Co.
Goldman Sachs Group
Grace & Co. (W.R.)
Guess?
Hasbro, Inc.
Heinz Co. (H.J.)
Hitachi America Ltd.
IKON Office Solutions, Inc.
International Business Machines Corp.
LandAmerica Financial Services
Loews Corp.
Lotus Development Corp.
Merrill Lynch & Co., Inc.
Metropolitan Life Insurance Co.
Mine Safety Appliances Co.
Morgan & Co. Inc. (J.P.)
Newman's Own Inc.
PepsiCo, Inc.
Pfizer Inc.
Phelps Dodge Corp.
Phillips Petroleum Co.
Potomac Electric Power Co.
Principal Financial Group
Prudential Securities Inc.
Reebok International Ltd.
Reynolds Tobacco (R.J.)
Rockwell International Corp.
Ryder System, Inc.
Sara Lee Corp.
Schering-Plough Corp.
Schloss & Co. (Marcus)
Seagram & Sons, Inc. (Joseph E.)
Shell Oil Co.
Slant/Fin Corp.
Starwood Hotels & Resorts Worldwide, Inc.
Sunmark Capital Corp.
Textron Inc.
Titan Industrial Corp.
Trace International Holdings, Inc.
Transamerica Corp.
United Parcel Service of America Inc.
UnumProvident
Wachovia Bank of North Carolina NA
Weil, Gotshal & Manges Corp.
Western & Southern Life Insurance Co.
Wilbur-Ellis Co. & Connell Brothers Co.
Witco Corp.
Young & Rubicam

INTERNATIONAL RELATIONS

Alcoa Inc.
Allegheny Technologies Inc.
American Express Co.
American Standard Inc.
AMP Inc.
AMR Corp.
Amsted Industries Inc.
Aon Corp.
Archer-Daniels-Midland Co.
Armstrong World Industries, Inc.
AT&T Corp.
Banfi Vintners
Bank of America
Bechtel Group, Inc.
Bernstein & Co., Inc. (Sanford C.)
Bestfoods
Binney & Smith Inc.
Blair & Co. (William)
Block, Inc. (H&R)
Borden, Inc.
BP Amoco Corp.
Briggs & Stratton Corp.
Bristol-Myers Squibb Co.
Brown Shoe Co., Inc.
Brunswick Corp.
Burlington Industries, Inc.
Burnett Co. (Leo)
Cabot Corp.
Carillon Importers, Ltd.
Carlson Companies, Inc.
Carnival Corp.
Central National-Gottesman
CertainTeed Corp.
Chase Manhattan Bank, NA
Chevron Corp.
CIT Group, Inc. (The)
Citibank Corp.
Commercial Intertech Corp.
Consolidated Electrical Distributors
Consolidated Papers, Inc.
Consumers Energy Co.
Continental Grain Co.
Credit Suisse First Boston
Crestar Finance Corp.
Cummins Engine Co., Inc.
Deutsch Co.
Dial Corp.
Disney Co. (Walt)
Dow Jones & Co., Inc.
du Pont de Nemours & Co. (E.I.)
Duke Energy
Dynamet, Inc.
Eastman Kodak Co.
Eaton Corp.
Emerson Electric Co.
Employers Mutual Casualty Co.
Entergy Corp.
Equifax Inc.
Exxon Mobil Corp.
Fidelity Investments
FINA
First Union Bank
First Union National Bank, NA
Forbes Inc.
Ford Motor Co.
Forest City Enterprises, Inc.
Fortune Brands, Inc.
Frost National Bank
General Atlantic Partners II LP
General Dynamics Corp.
General Electric Co.
General Motors Corp.
Georgia Power Co.
Glickenhaus & Co.
Goldman Sachs Group
Harsco Corp.
Hasbro, Inc.
Hawaiian Electric Co., Inc.
Heinz Co. (H.J.)
Hewlett-Packard Co.
Hitachi America Ltd.
Hoffmann-La Roche Inc.
Hughes Electronics Corp.
Industrial Bank of Japan Trust Co. (New York)
International Flavors & Fragrances Inc.
Jacobs Engineering Group
Johnson Controls Inc.
Johnson & Son (S.C.)
Kennametal, Inc.
Kerr-McGee Corp.
Kimberly-Clark Corp.

Kroger Co.
Lance, Inc.
Liberty Corp.
Lincoln Electric Co.
Lipton Co.
Loews Corp.
Marshall & Ilsley Corp.
Merck & Co.
Merrill Lynch & Co., Inc.
Milliken & Co.
Mine Safety Appliances Co.
Morgan & Co. Inc. (J.P.)
Morrison Knudsen Corp.
Newman's Own Inc.
Nordson Corp.
Overseas Shipholding Group Inc.
Owens Corning
PACCAR Inc.
PepsiCo, Inc.
Pfizer Inc.
Phelps Dodge Corp.
Phillips Petroleum Co.
Physicians Mutual Insurance Co.
Pittway Corp.
PPG Industries, Inc.
Principal Financial Group
Procter & Gamble Co., Cosmetics Division
Prudential Insurance Co. of America
Pulitzer Publishing Co.
Quaker Chemical Corp.
Ralston Purina Co.
Reinhart Institutional Foods
Reynolds Tobacco (R.J.)
Rockwell International Corp.
Rouse Co.
Rutledge Hill Press
Sara Lee Corp.
Schering-Plough Corp.
Scripps Co. (E.W.)
Seagram & Sons, Inc. (Joseph E.)
Servco Pacific
Shell Oil Co.
Slant/Fin Corp.
SmithKline Beecham Corp.
Sony Electronics
Stone Container Corp.
Strear Farms Co.
Sunmark Capital Corp.
Tai and Co. (J.T.)
Tamko Roofing Products
Tension Envelope Corp.
Tesoro Hawaii
Texaco Inc.
Textron Inc.
Thermo Electron Corp.
Thompson Co. (J. Walter)
Times Mirror Co.
Titan Industrial Corp.
Trace International Holdings, Inc.
True North Communications, Inc.
Unilever United States, Inc.
United Dominion Industries, Ltd.
United States Sugar Corp.
Unocal Corp.
USG Corp.
Vodafone AirTouch Plc
Weil, Gotshal & Manges Corp.
Westvaco Corp.
Whirlpool Corp.
Whitman Corp.
Wilbur-Ellis Co. & Connell Brothers Co.
Williams
Witco Corp.
Xerox Corp.
Young & Rubicam
Zilkha & Sons

INTERNATIONAL RELIEF EFFORTS

ABC
Aetna, Inc.
Alcoa Inc.
Alma Piston Co.
American Express Co.
American Fidelity Corp.
AMR Corp.
APL Ltd.
Archer-Daniels-Midland Co.
Associated Food Stores
Avon Products, Inc.
Banfi Vintners
Barclays Capital
Bard, Inc. (C.R.)
Barnes Group Inc.
Barry Corp. (R.G.)
Baxter International Inc.
Ben & Jerry's Homemade Inc.
Boeing Co.
Borden, Inc.
Borman's Inc.
Brown Shoe Co., Inc.
Burnett Co. (Leo)
Cabot Corp.
Calvin Klein
Campbell Soup Co.
Carter-Wallace, Inc.
CGU Insurance
Chesapeake Corp.
Chevron Corp.
Coca-Cola Co.
Continental Grain Co.
Contran Corp.
Crane Co.
CSR Rinker Materials Corp.
Erb Lumber Co.
Fidelity Investments
Forbes Inc.
Forest City Enterprises, Inc.
Freeport-McMoRan Inc.
Fuller Co. (H.B.)
Gallo Winery, Inc. (E&J)
Gap, Inc.
GEICO Corp.
General Atlantic Partners II LP
General Electric Co.
Gerber Products Co.
Giant Eagle Inc.
Glickenhaus & Co.
Goldman Sachs Group
Graco, Inc.
Hasbro, Inc.
Heinz Co. (H.J.)
Hewlett-Packard Co.
Hitachi America Ltd.
Hubbell Inc.
Indiana Mills & Manufacturing
Inland Container Corp.
International Flavors & Fragrances Inc.
Jacobson & Sons (Benjamin)
Katten, Muchin & Zavis
Kimberly-Clark Corp.
Koch Enterprises, Inc.
LandAmerica Financial Services
Leigh Fibers, Inc.
Levi Strauss & Co.
Little, Inc. (Arthur D.)
Loews Corp.
Louisiana-Pacific Corp.
Masco Corp.
Mattel Inc.
Medtronic, Inc.
Merrill Lynch & Co., Inc.
Metropolitan Life Insurance Co.
Milacron, Inc.
Millipore Corp.
Morgan & Co. Inc. (J.P.)
Morrison Knudsen Corp.
Motorola Inc.
MTD Products Inc.
National City Corp.
New England Bio Labs
Newman's Own Inc.
Norton Co.
Oshkosh B'Gosh, Inc.
Overseas Shipholding Group Inc.
Owens Corning
Paine Webber
PepsiCo, Inc.
Phelps Dodge Corp.
Physicians Mutual Insurance Co.
Premier Dental Products Co.
Putnam Investments
Reebok International Ltd.
Reinhart Institutional Foods
Reynolds Tobacco (R.J.)
Rutledge Hill Press
Sega of America Inc.
ServiceMaster Co.
Shaklee Corp.
Sierra Pacific Industries
Simpson Investment Co.
State Street Bank & Trust Co.
Stride Rite Corp.
Tai and Co. (J.T.)
TENNANT Co.
Tension Envelope Corp.
Texaco Inc.
Thermo Electron Corp.
TJX Companies, Inc.
Toledo Blade Co.
True North Communications, Inc.
Unilever Home & Personal Care U.S.A.
Unilever United States, Inc.
United Airlines Inc.
Van Leer Holding
Vodafone AirTouch Plc
Weyerhaeuser Co.
Wolverine World Wide
Young & Rubicam
Zilkha & Sons

MISSIONARY/RELIGIOUS ACTIVITIES

Alcoa Inc.
Alma Piston Co.
American Express Co.
American Retail Group
Archer-Daniels-Midland Co.
Associated Food Stores
Barry Corp. (R.G.)
Baxter International Inc.
Bechtel Group, Inc.
Bernstein & Co., Inc. (Sanford C.)
Binswanger Companies
Blair & Co. (William)
Borden, Inc.
Borman's Inc.
BP Amoco Corp.
Bristol-Myers Squibb Co.
Burnett Co. (Leo)
Calvin Klein
Carillon Importers, Ltd.
Carnival Corp.
Century 21
Cessna Aircraft Co.
CGU Insurance
Circuit City Stores, Inc.
CIT Group, Inc. (The)
Citigroup
CPI Corp.
Croft-Leominster
CSS Industries, Inc.
Cummings Properties Management
Delta Air Lines, Inc.
Deutsch Co.
Domino's Pizza Inc.
Duchossois Industries Inc.
Eastman Kodak Co.
Edwards Enterprise Software (J.D.)
Equifax Inc.
Erb Lumber Co.
Erving Industries
Federated Department Stores, Inc.
First Hawaiian, Inc.
Fisher Scientific
Ford Meter Box Co.
Forest City Enterprises, Inc.
Fort Worth Star-Telegram Inc.
Galter Corp.
Gap, Inc.
General Electric Co.
Giant Eagle Inc.
Glickenhaus & Co.
Goldman Sachs Group
Griffith Laboratories U.S.A.
Guess?
Hewlett-Packard Co.
Hofmann Co.
Indiana Mills & Manufacturing
Jacobson & Sons (Benjamin)
Katten, Muchin & Zavis
Leviton Manufacturing Co. Inc.
Loews Corp.
Mamiye Brothers
MidAmerican Energy Holdings Co.
MTD Products Inc.
Newman's Own Inc.
Overseas Shipholding Group Inc.
Pacific Mutual Life Insurance Co.
PacifiCare Health Systems
Premier Dental Products Co.
Prudential Securities Inc.
Putnam Investments
Reebok International Ltd.
Rich Products Corp.
Russer Foods
Rutledge Hill Press
Seagram & Sons, Inc. (Joseph E.)
ServiceMaster Co.
S.G. Cowen
Slant/Fin Corp.
Solo Cup Co.
Stone Container Corp.
Strear Farms Co.
Tension Envelope Corp.
Texaco Inc.
Titan Industrial Corp.
Trace International Holdings, Inc.
USG Corp.
Vesper Corp.
Wachtell, Lipton, Rosen & Katz
Weil, Gotshal & Manges Corp.
Wilbur-Ellis Co. & Connell Brothers Co.
Witco Corp.
Zachry Co. (H.B.)
Zilkha & Sons

TRADE

APL Ltd.
Archer-Daniels-Midland Co.
Caterpillar Inc.
Dayton Hudson
Evening Post Publishing Co.
General Electric Co.
Huntington Bancshares Inc.
McDonald & Co. Securities, Inc.
Occidental Petroleum Corp.
PepsiCo, Inc.
Thompson Co. (J. Walter)

Religion

BIBLE STUDY/ TRANSLATION

Crane Co.
First National Bank of Evergreen Park
First Source Corp.
Montgomery Ward & Co., Inc.
MTD Products Inc.
National Bank of Commerce Trust & Savings
Outboard Marine Corp.
Rockwell International Corp.
Rubbermaid Inc.
Rutledge Hill Press
Wiley & Sons (John)

CHURCHES

Allegheny Technologies Inc.
Allianz Life Insurance Co. of North America
AlliedSignal Inc.
Alma Piston Co.
American Fidelity Corp.
American Retail Group
Andersen Corp.
Andersons Inc.
Aon Corp.
Archer-Daniels-Midland Co.
Atlantic Investment Co.
Banfi Vintners
Bardes Corp.
Barry Corp. (R.G.)
Belk-Simpson Department Stores
Belk Stores Services Inc.
Bemis Manufacturing Co.
Blue Bell, Inc.
Blue Cross & Blue Shield of Minnesota
Borden, Inc.
Borman's Inc.
Bradford & Co. (J.C.)
Burress (J.W.)
Business Improvement
Campbell Soup Co.
Carillon Importers, Ltd.
Carlson Companies, Inc.
Carpenter Technology Corp.
Carris Reels
Central Soya Co.
CertainTeed Corp.
Cessna Aircraft Co.
CGU Insurance
Chase Manhattan Bank, NA
Chemed Corp.
Citigroup
Citizens Financial Group, Inc.
CLARCOR Inc.
Colonial Oil Industries, Inc.

Comdisco, Inc.
Continental Grain Co.
Contran Corp.
Country Curtains, Inc.
Crane & Co., Inc.
Croft-Leominster
Cummings Properties Management
Danis Companies
Dayton Power and Light Co.
Deluxe Corp.
Demoulas Supermarkets Inc.
Domino's Pizza Inc.
Duchossois Industries Inc.
Duke Energy
Duriron Co., Inc.
Edwards Enterprise Software (J.D.)
Ensign-Bickford Industries
Enterprise Rent-A-Car Co.
Erb Lumber Co.
Erving Industries
Ferro Corp.
Fidelity Investments
First Hawaiian, Inc.
First Union Bank
First Union Corp.
Forbes Inc.
Ford Meter Box Co.
Forest City Enterprises, Inc.
Freddie Mac
Frost National Bank
Furniture Brands International, Inc.
Gallo Winery, Inc. (E&J)
Galter Corp.
Gap, Inc.
GenAmerica Corp.
Glickenhaus & Co.
Globe Corp.
Green Bay Packaging
Griffith Laboratories U.S.A.
Harland Co. (John H.)
Hitachi America Ltd.
Hoffer Plastics Corp.
Hoffmann-La Roche Inc.
Hofmann Co.
HON Industries Inc.
Housatonic Curtain Co.
Hubbard Broadcasting, Inc.
Humana, Inc.
IBP
IKON Office Solutions, Inc.
Independent Stave Co.
Indiana Mills & Manufacturing
Inman Mills
International Multifoods Corp.
Jacobs Engineering Group
Jacobson & Sons (Benjamin)
Journal-Gazette Co.
Katten, Muchin & Zavis
Kimball International, Inc.
Koch Enterprises, Inc.
Kroger Co.
La-Z-Boy Inc.
Lancaster Lens, Inc.
Lehigh Portland Cement Co.
Leigh Fibers, Inc.
Leviton Manufacturing Co. Inc.
Liberty Corp.
Louisiana Land & Exploration Co.
MacMillan Bloedel Inc.
May Department Stores Co.
McClatchy Co.
McWane Inc.
Michigan Consolidated Gas Co.
Mid-America Bank of Louisville
Milliken & Co.
MONY Group (The)
MTD Products Inc.
National Presto Industries, Inc.
Navcom Systems
NEBCO Evans
New England Financial
New York Mercantile Exchange
Nordson Corp.
Norton Co.
Old National Bank Evansville
Orscheln Co.
Overseas Shipholding Group Inc.
Pacific Century Financial Corp.
PacifiCare Health Systems
Paine Webber
Pan-American Life Insurance Co.
Park National Bank
Pella Corp.
PEMCO Corp.
PepsiCo, Inc.
Physicians Mutual Insurance Co.
Pillsbury Co.
Potomac Electric Power Co.
Providence Journal-Bulletin Co.
Prudential Securities Inc.
Publix Supermarkets
Pulitzer Publishing Co.
Ralph's Grocery Co.
Regions Bank
Reily & Co., Inc. (William B.)
Reinhart Institutional Foods
Rich Products Corp.
Rockwell International Corp.
Ruddick Corp.
Rutledge Hill Press
Safeway Inc.
Sara Lee Hosiery, Inc.
Schering-Plough Corp.
Schloss & Co. (Marcus)
Seaway Food Town, Inc.
Servco Pacific
ServiceMaster Co.
S.G. Cowen
Shea Co. (John F.)
Sherwin-Williams Co.
Shoney's Inc.
Sierra Pacific Industries
Simpson Investment Co.
Solo Cup Co.
Sony Electronics
SPX Corp.
Stanley Works (The)
Steelcase Inc.
Stonecutter Mills Corp.
Stride Rite Corp.
Stupp Brothers Bridge & Iron Co.
Susquehanna-Pfaltzgraff Co.
Synovus Financial Corp.
Tai and Co. (J.T.)
Tamko Roofing Products
TMC Investment Co.
Transamerica Corp.
True North Communications, Inc.
True Oil Co.
TRW Inc.
Ukrop's Super Markets
Union Camp Corp.
United Distillers & Vintners North America
United Parcel Service of America Inc.
U.S. Bancorp Piper Jaffray
United States Sugar Corp.
Vesper Corp.
Wal-Mart Stores, Inc.
Walter Industries Inc.
Washington Trust Bank
Western & Southern Life Insurance Co.
Weyerhaeuser Co.
Wilbur-Ellis Co. & Connell Brothers Co.
Witco Corp.
Wyman-Gordon Co.
York Federal Savings & Loan Association
Young & Rubicam

DIOCESES

AEGON U.S.A. Inc.
AlliedSignal Inc.
Ameren Corp.
American Retail Group
BankBoston Corp.
Borden, Inc.
Chase Manhattan Bank, NA
Cincinnati Bell Inc.
CIT Group, Inc. (The)
Citizens Financial Group, Inc.
Commerce Bancshares, Inc.
ConAgra, Inc.
Coors Brewing Co.
Copley Press, Inc.
First Maryland Bancorp
Forest City Enterprises, Inc.
Gallo Winery, Inc. (E&J)
Humana, Inc.
International Paper Co.
Kellwood Co.
Koch Enterprises, Inc.
Leigh Fibers, Inc.
May Department Stores Co.
McDonald & Co. Securities, Inc.
Mercantile Bank NA
Mid-America Bank of Louisville
Mine Safety Appliances Co.
Monsanto Co.
National City Corp.
Occidental Petroleum Corp.
Orscheln Co.
PACCAR Inc.
Pacific Century Financial Corp.
Paine Webber
Physicians Mutual Insurance Co.
Pulitzer Publishing Co.
Reinhart Institutional Foods
Rich Products Corp.
Scripps Co. (E.W.)
Shea Co. (John F.)
Sherwin-Williams Co.
Simpson Investment Co.
Solo Cup Co.
Southeastern Mutual Insurance Co.
Stonecutter Mills Corp.
True North Communications, Inc.
United Airlines Inc.
U.S. Bancorp Piper Jaffray
Weil, Gotshal & Manges Corp.
Western & Southern Life Insurance Co.

RELIGION-GENERAL

Atlantic Investment Co.
Brown Shoe Co., Inc.
Cenex Harvest States
Chemed Corp.
CLARCOR Inc.
Erving Industries
Ingram Industries Inc.
National City Bank of Pennsylvania
NEBCO Evans
New York Mercantile Exchange
Ohio National Life Insurance Co.
Old National Bank Evansville
Pillsbury Co.
Rutledge Hill Press
Servco Pacific

JEWISH CAUSES

ABC
Alabama Power Co.
Alcoa Inc.
Allegheny Technologies Inc.
AlliedSignal Inc.
AMCORE Bank Rockford
Ameren Corp.
American United Life Insurance Co.
AMETEK, Inc.
AMR Corp.
Anheuser-Busch Companies, Inc.
Aon Corp.
Archer-Daniels-Midland Co.
ASARCO Inc.
Associated Food Stores
Baird & Co. (Robert W.)
BankBoston Corp.
Barclays Capital
Barry Corp. (R.G.)
Baxter International Inc.
Bechtel Group, Inc.
Bernstein & Co., Inc. (Sanford C.)
Binswanger Companies
Blair & Co. (William)
Block, Inc. (H&R)
Blue Bell, Inc.
Blue Cross & Blue Shield of Alabama
Boeing Co.
Borman's Inc.
Bristol-Myers Squibb Co.
Brown Shoe Co., Inc.
Burlington Industries, Inc.
Burnett Co. (Leo)
Calvin Klein
Cantor, Fitzgerald Securities Corp.
Carillon Importers, Ltd.
Carnival Corp.
Carpenter Technology Corp.
Carris Reels
Central National-Gottesman
Century 21
CGU Insurance
Chase Bank of Texas
Chase Manhattan Bank, NA
Chicago Tribune Co.
Circuit City Stores, Inc.
CIT Group, Inc. (The)
Citigroup
Citizens Financial Group, Inc.
Collins & Aikman Corp.
Compaq Computer Corp.
Constellation Energy Group, Inc.
Continental Grain Co.
Contran Corp.
Conwood Co. LP
Coors Brewing Co.
Corning Inc.
Cox Enterprises Inc.
Cranston Print Works Co.
Crown Books
CSS Industries, Inc.
Cummings Properties Management
DaimlerChrysler Corp.
Delta Air Lines, Inc.
Deutsch Co.
Dial Corp.
Duchossois Industries Inc.
Duke Energy
Eastern Bank
Eastman Kodak Co.
Eckerd Corp.
Edison Brothers Stores, Inc.
Employers Mutual Casualty Co.
Enterprise Rent-A-Car Co.
Equifax Inc.
Erb Lumber Co.
Erving Industries
Evening Post Publishing Co.
Fannie Mae
Fifth Third Bancorp
First Maryland Bancorp
First Union Securities, Inc.
Firstar Bank Milwaukee NA
Fisher Brothers Cleaning Services
Florida Rock Industries
Forbes Inc.
Ford Motor Co.
Forest City Enterprises, Inc.
Fort Worth Star-Telegram Inc.
Freddie Mac
Furniture Brands International, Inc.
Gallo Winery, Inc. (E&J)
Galter Corp.
GenAmerica Corp.
Georgia-Pacific Corp.
Giant Eagle Inc.
Giant Food Inc.
Gillette Co.
Glickenhaus & Co.
Goldman Sachs Group
Golub Corp.
Group Health Plan
Guess?
Harcourt General, Inc.
Harris Trust & Savings Bank
Hartmarx Corp.
Hasbro, Inc.
Hofmann Co.
Hubbard Broadcasting, Inc.
Huntington Bancshares Inc.
IKON Office Solutions, Inc.
Independent Stave Co.
Indiana Mills & Manufacturing
International Flavors & Fragrances Inc.
Jacobs Engineering Group
Jacobson & Sons (Benjamin)
Journal-Gazette Co.
Katten, Muchin & Zavis
Laclede Gas Co.
Lancaster Lens, Inc.
Lee Enterprises
Levi Strauss & Co.
Leviton Manufacturing Co. Inc.
Liberty Diversified Industries
Liz Claiborne, Inc.
Loews Corp.
Lotus Development Corp.
Lubrizol Corp. (The)
Mamiye Brothers
Manor Care Health SVS, Inc.
Manufacturers & Traders Trust Co.
Marcus Corp.
Mark IV Industries

May Department Stores Co.
McDonald & Co. Securities, Inc.
McWane Inc.
Mercantile Bank NA
Merit Oil Corp.
Merrill Lynch & Co., Inc.
Mid-America Bank of Louisville
MidAmerican Energy Holdings Co.
Milliken & Co.
Monsanto Co.
Montgomery Ward & Co., Inc.
Morrison Knudsen Corp.
Nabisco Group Holdings
National City Bank of Minneapolis
National City Corp.
National Service Industries, Inc.
Nationwide Insurance Co.
New Jersey Natural Gas Co.
New York Mercantile Exchange
New York Times Co.
Nomura Holding America
Northern Trust Co.
Occidental Petroleum Corp.
Ohio National Life Insurance Co.
Oshkosh B'Gosh, Inc.
Overseas Shipholding Group Inc.
Paine Webber
Physicians Mutual Insurance Co.
Pittway Corp.
PNC Financial Services Group
PPG Industries, Inc.
Praxair
Premier Dental Products Co.
Premier Industrial Corp.
Price Associates (T. Rowe)
Prudential Securities Inc.
Pulitzer Publishing Co.
Putnam Investments
Ralph's Grocery Co.
Ralston Purina Co.
Reader's Digest Association, Inc. (The)
Reebok International Ltd.
Regis Corp.
Revlon Inc.
Reynolds Tobacco (R.J.)
Rich Products Corp.
Russer Foods
Schloss & Co. (Marcus)
Schwab & Co., Inc. (Charles)
Schwebel Baking Co.
Seagram & Sons, Inc. (Joseph E.)
Security Life of Denver Insurance Co.
Sentinel Communications Co.
S.G. Cowen
Sherwin-Williams Co.
Slant/Fin Corp.
Smurfit-Stone Container Corp.
Solo Cup Co.
Sony Electronics
Southwest Gas Corp.
Star Bank NA
State Street Bank & Trust Co.
Stone Container Corp.
Storage Technology Corp.
Strear Farms Co.
Stupp Brothers Bridge & Iron Co.
SunTrust Bank Atlanta
Tension Envelope Corp.
Thermo Electron Corp.
Thompson Co. (J. Walter)
Ticketmaster Corp.
Titan Industrial Corp.
TJX Companies, Inc.
Toledo Blade Co.
Trace International Holdings, Inc.
Transamerica Corp.
True North Communications, Inc.
Trustmark Insurance Co.
United Services Automobile Association
U.S. Bancorp Piper Jaffray
United States Trust Co. of New York
Universal Studios
USG Corp.
Van Leer Holding
Vulcan Materials Co.
Wachovia Bank of North Carolina NA
Wachtell, Lipton, Rosen & Katz
Waffle House Inc.
Weil, Gotshal & Manges Corp.
WICOR, Inc.
Witco Corp.
York Federal Savings & Loan Association
Young & Rubicam
Zachry Co. (H.B.)
Zilkha & Sons

MINISTRIES

Alcon Laboratories, Inc.
Allegheny Technologies Inc.
AlliedSignal Inc.
Ameren Corp.
American Fidelity Corp.
American Retail Group
AMETEK, Inc.
AMP Inc.
Andersons Inc.
Atlantic Investment Co.
Barclays Capital
Belk Stores Services Inc.
Blair & Co. (William)
Blue Bell, Inc.
BP Amoco Corp.
Bradford & Co. (J.C.)
Bridgestone/Firestone, Inc.
Broderbund Software, Inc.
Brunswick Corp.
Burlington Industries, Inc.
Burress (J.W.)
Business Improvement
Cabot Corp.
Calvin Klein
Carlson Companies, Inc.
Central Soya Co.
Cessna Aircraft Co.
Chase Bank of Texas
Chase Manhattan Bank, NA
Citizens Financial Group, Inc.
Clorox Co.
Commercial Intertech Corp.
Compaq Computer Corp.
Compass Bank
Cone Mills Corp.
Contran Corp.
Dial Corp.
Domino's Pizza Inc.
Duke Energy
Eckerd Corp.
Edwards Enterprise Software (J.D.)
El Paso Energy Co.
Fireman's Fund Insurance Co.
First National Bank of Evergreen Park
Fortis Insurance Co.
Freddie Mac
GenAmerica Corp.
General Electric Co.
Gulf Power Co.
Hallmark Cards Inc.
Hartford (The)
Hunt Manufacturing Co.
Independent Stave Co.
Indiana Mills & Manufacturing
Inland Container Corp.
INTRUST Financial Corp.
Jeld-wen, Inc.
Journal-Gazette Co.
JSJ Corp.
Kimball International, Inc.
Koch Enterprises, Inc.
La-Z-Boy Inc.
LandAmerica Financial Services
Landmark Communications Inc.
Levi Strauss & Co.
Lilly & Co. (Eli)
Louisiana-Pacific Corp.
May Department Stores Co.
Milliken & Co.
Nalco Chemical Co.
National City Corp.
Nordson Corp.
Occidental Oil and Gas
Occidental Petroleum Corp.
Ohio National Life Insurance Co.
Oklahoma Publishing Co.
Old Kent Bank
Old National Bank Evansville
Osborne Enterprises
Paine Webber
Pella Corp.
Pharmacia & Upjohn, Inc.
PNC Financial Services Group
Publix Supermarkets
Quanex Corp.
Reilly Industries, Inc.
Rouse Co.
Royal & SunAlliance USA, Inc.
Rubbermaid Inc.
Rutledge Hill Press
Ryder System, Inc.
Schwab & Co., Inc. (Charles)
ServiceMaster Co.
Shell Oil Co.
Simpson Investment Co.
SIT Investment Associates, Inc.
Solo Cup Co.
Steelcase Inc.
Stride Rite Corp.
Sun Microsystems Inc.
Tamko Roofing Products
TCF National Bank Minnesota
Texas Instruments Inc.
TJX Companies, Inc.
Toledo Blade Co.
Ukrop's Super Markets
United Parcel Service of America Inc.
U.S. Bancorp Piper Jaffray
US West, Inc.
USG Corp.
Waffle House Inc.
Walter Industries Inc.

MISSIONARY ACTIVITIES (DOMESTIC)

Alabama Power Co.
Alma Piston Co.
Archer-Daniels-Midland Co.
Bristol-Myers Squibb Co.
Cessna Aircraft Co.
CGU Insurance
Citizens Financial Group, Inc.
Collins & Aikman Corp.
Colonial Oil Industries, Inc.
Commerce Bancshares, Inc.
Disney Co. (Walt)
Galter Corp.
Indiana Mills & Manufacturing
Lipton Co.
McClatchy Co.
Mead Corp.
Navcom Systems
Ralph's Grocery Co.
Shea Co. (John F.)
Solo Cup Co.
Textron Inc.
Waffle House Inc.

RELIGIOUS ORGANIZATIONS

Alcoa Inc.
Alexander & Baldwin, Inc.
Allegheny Technologies Inc.
Allianz Life Insurance Co. of North America
Alma Piston Co.
Ameren Corp.
American General Finance
American Retail Group
American Standard Inc.
Ameritas Life Insurance Corp.
Ameritech Michigan
AMR Corp.
Andersen Corp.
Andersons Inc.
Aon Corp.
Archer-Daniels-Midland Co.
ASARCO Inc.
Associated Food Stores
Atlantic Investment Co.
Baird & Co. (Robert W.)
Banfi Vintners
Banta Corp.
Barden Corp.
Bardes Corp.
Barry Corp. (R.G.)
Belk-Simpson Department Stores
Belk Stores Services Inc.
Bernstein & Co., Inc. (Sanford C.)
BFGoodrich Co.
Binswanger Companies
Blair & Co. (William)
Block, Inc. (H&R)
Blount International, Inc.
Blue Bell, Inc.
Blue Cross & Blue Shield of Alabama
Borden, Inc.
Borman's Inc.
Burress (J.W.)
Business Improvement
Calvin Klein
Cantor, Fitzgerald Securities Corp.
Carlson Companies, Inc.
Central National-Gottesman
Central & South West Services
Central Soya Co.
Century 21
CertainTeed Corp.
Cessna Aircraft Co.
CGU Insurance
Chase Manhattan Bank, NA
Chemed Corp.
Chicago Tribune Co.
CIT Group, Inc. (The)
Citigroup
Citizens Financial Group, Inc.
Clorox Co.
Comdisco, Inc.
Commerce Bancshares, Inc.
Compass Bank
Conwood Co. LP
Cox Enterprises Inc.
CPI Corp.
Crestar Finance Corp.
Croft-Leominster
CSS Industries, Inc.
Cummings Properties Management
Daily News
Dana Corp.
Danis Companies
Delta Air Lines, Inc.
Demoulas Supermarkets Inc.
Deutsch Co.
Dexter Corp.
Dial Corp.
Domino's Pizza Inc.
Duchossois Industries Inc.
Dynamet, Inc.
Edwards Enterprise Software (J.D.)
Emerson Electric Co.
Ensign-Bickford Industries
Erb Lumber Co.
Fabri-Kal Corp.
Fidelity Investments
Fifth Third Bancorp
Fireman's Fund Insurance Co.
First Financial Bank
First National Bank of Evergreen Park
First Source Corp.
First Union Securities, Inc.
Fisher Scientific
Florida Rock Industries
Forbes Inc.
Forest City Enterprises, Inc.
Fort Worth Star-Telegram Inc.
Frost National Bank
Fuller Co. (H.B.)
Furniture Brands International, Inc.
Gallo Winery, Inc. (E&J)
Galter Corp.
GenAmerica Corp.
Giant Eagle Inc.
Giant Food Inc.
Giddings & Lewis
Glickenhaus & Co.
Golub Corp.
Graco, Inc.
Green Bay Packaging
Group Health Plan
Gucci America Inc.
Gulf Power Co.
Hanna Co. (M.A.)
Harland Co. (John H.)
Harnischfeger Industries
Harris Trust & Savings Bank
Hartmarx Corp.
Hasbro, Inc.
Heinz Co. (H.J.)
Hoffmann-La Roche Inc.
Hofmann Co.
HON Industries Inc.

Funders by Recipient Type

Hubbell Inc.
Humana, Inc.
IKON Office Solutions, Inc.
Inman Mills
International Paper Co.
INTRUST Financial Corp.
Jacobson & Sons (Benjamin)
Journal-Gazette Co.
JSJ Corp.
Katten, Muchin & Zavis
Kellogg Co.
Kellwood Co.
Kerr-McGee Corp.
Kimball International, Inc.
Kirkland & Ellis
Koch Enterprises, Inc.
Lance, Inc.
LandAmerica Financial Services
Leigh Fibers, Inc.
Levi Strauss & Co.
Leviton Manufacturing Co. Inc.
LG&E Energy Corp.
Liberty Diversified Industries
Lipton Co.
Litton Industries, Inc.
Louisiana Land & Exploration Co.
Louisiana-Pacific Corp.
LTV Corp.
Madison Gas & Electric Co.
Mamiye Brothers
Marcus Corp.
Mark IV Industries
Marshall & Ilsley Corp.
Masco Corp.
May Department Stores Co.
McDonald & Co. Securities, Inc.
Merit Oil Corp.
Michigan Consolidated Gas Co.
Mid-America Bank of Louisville
MidAmerican Energy Holdings Co.
Milacron, Inc.
Mine Safety Appliances Co.
Minnesota Mutual Life Insurance Co.
Monarch Machine Tool Co.
Montgomery Ward & Co., Inc.
Morris Communications Corp.
Morrison Knudsen Corp.
MTD Products Inc.
National Bank of Commerce Trust & Savings
National City Bank of Minneapolis
National Presto Industries, Inc.
National Service Industries, Inc.
Nationwide Insurance Co.
Navcom Systems
NEBCO Evans
New York Stock Exchange, Inc.
Nomura Holding America
Old National Bank Evansville
Orscheln Co.
Overseas Shipholding Group Inc.
PACCAR Inc.
Paine Webber
Pella Corp.
PEMCO Corp.
Phelps Dodge Corp.
Physicians Mutual Insurance Co.
Potomac Electric Power Co.
Premier Dental Products Co.
Premier Industrial Corp.
Prudential Securities Inc.
Publix Supermarkets
Pulitzer Publishing Co.
Ralph's Grocery Co.
Ralston Purina Co.
Regions Bank
Regis Corp.
Reilly Industries, Inc.
Reinhart Institutional Foods
Revlon Inc.
Reynolds Metals Co.
Rich Products Corp.
Rubbermaid Inc.
Ruddick Corp.
Schloss & Co. (Marcus)
Seagram & Sons, Inc. (Joseph E.)
Sentry Insurance, A Mutual Co.
S.G. Cowen
Shea Co. (John F.)
Slant/Fin Corp.
Smurfit-Stone Container Corp.
Solo Cup Co.
Southeastern Mutual Insurance Co.
Southwest Gas Corp.
SPX Corp.
Standard Register Co.
Star Bank NA
Steelcase Inc.
Stone Container Corp.
Stonecutter Mills Corp.
Strear Farms Co.
Stupp Brothers Bridge & Iron Co.
Sunmark Capital Corp.
Synovus Financial Corp.
Tai and Co. (J.T.)
TCF National Bank Minnesota
Tension Envelope Corp.
Thompson Co. (J. Walter)
Titan Industrial Corp.
Toledo Blade Co.
Tomkins Industries, Inc.
True North Communications, Inc.
True Oil Co.
Ukrop's Super Markets
Unilever Home & Personal Care U.S.A.
Union Camp Corp.
Union Pacific Corp.
Universal Leaf Tobacco Co., Inc.
USX Corp.
Valmont Industries, Inc.
Vesper Corp.
Wachovia Bank of North Carolina NA
Waffle House Inc.
Waldbaum's Supermarkets, Inc.
Washington Trust Bank
Weil, Gotshal & Manges Corp.
Western & Southern Life Insurance Co.
Whitman Corp.
WICOR, Inc.
Wilbur-Ellis Co. & Connell Brothers Co.
Winn-Dixie Stores Inc.
Wisconsin Energy Corp.
Witco Corp.
Young & Rubicam
Zilkha & Sons

RELIGIOUS WELFARE

Abbott Laboratories
ABC
AEGON U.S.A. Inc.
Agrilink Foods, Inc.
Air Products and Chemicals, Inc.
AK Steel Corp.
Alcoa Inc.
Alcon Laboratories, Inc.
Alexander & Baldwin, Inc.
Allegheny Technologies Inc.
AlliedSignal Inc.
Allmerica Financial Corp.
Allstate Insurance Co.
Alma Piston Co.
AMCORE Bank Rockford
Ameren Corp.
American Fidelity Corp.
American General Finance
American Retail Group
American Standard Inc.
Ameritas Life Insurance Corp.
Ameritech Corp.
Ameritech Michigan
Ameritech Wisconsin
Amgen, Inc.
AMR Corp.
Amsted Industries Inc.
Andersen Corp.
Andersons Inc.
Anheuser-Busch Companies, Inc.
Aon Corp.
APL Ltd.
Archer-Daniels-Midland Co.
Aristech Chemical Corp.
Arizona Public Service Co.
Armstrong World Industries, Inc.
Ashland, Inc.
Associated Food Stores
Atlantic Investment Co.
Auburn Foundry
Avon Products, Inc.
Badger Meter, Inc.
Baird & Co. (Robert W.)
Banfi Vintners
Banta Corp.
Barclays Capital
Bard, Inc. (C.R.)
Barden Corp.
Bardes Corp.
Barry Corp. (R.G.)
Baxter International Inc.
Bayer Corp.
Bechtel Group, Inc.
Belk-Simpson Department Stores
Belk Stores Services Inc.
Bemis Co., Inc.
Bemis Manufacturing Co.
Ben & Jerry's Homemade Inc.
Bernstein & Co., Inc. (Sanford C.)
Binswanger Companies
Blair & Co. (William)
Block, Inc. (H&R)
Blount International, Inc.
Blue Bell, Inc.
Blue Cross & Blue Shield of Alabama
Blue Cross & Blue Shield of Iowa
Blue Cross & Blue Shield of Minnesota
Boeing Co.
Borden, Inc.
Borman's Inc.
Boston Edison Co.
Boston Globe (The)
Bourns, Inc.
BP Amoco Corp.
Bradford & Co. (J.C.)
Bristol-Myers Squibb Co.
Broderbund Software, Inc.
Brown Shoe Co., Inc.
Brunswick Corp.
Bucyrus-Erie Co.
Burlington Industries, Inc.
Burlington Resources, Inc.
Burnett Co. (Leo)
Burress (J.W.)
Business Improvement
Butler Manufacturing Co.
Callaway Golf Co.
Calvin Klein
Campbell Soup Co.
Cargill Inc.
Carillon Importers, Ltd.
Carlson Companies, Inc.
Carnival Corp.
Carpenter Technology Corp.
Carris Reels
Caterpillar Inc.
CBS Corp.
Cenex Harvest States
Central & South West Services
Central Soya Co.
CertainTeed Corp.
Cessna Aircraft Co.
CGU Insurance
Chase Bank of Texas
Chase Manhattan Bank, NA
Chemed Corp.
Chesapeake Corp.
Chicago Board of Trade
Chicago Tribune Co.
CIGNA Corp.
Cincinnati Bell Inc.
Cinergy Corp.
Circuit City Stores, Inc.
CIT Group, Inc. (The)
Citigroup
Citizens Financial Group, Inc.
CLARCOR Inc.
Cleveland-Cliffs, Inc.
Clorox Co.
CNA
Collins & Aikman Corp.
Colonial Oil Industries, Inc.
Comdisco, Inc.
Commerce Bancshares, Inc.
Commercial Intertech Corp.
Compaq Computer Corp.
Compass Bank
Cone Mills Corp.
Consolidated Natural Gas Co.
Consolidated Papers, Inc.
Constellation Energy Group, Inc.
Consumers Energy Co.
Contran Corp.
Conwood Co. LP
Cooper Industries, Inc.
Cooper Tire & Rubber Co.
Copley Press, Inc.
Country Curtains, Inc.
Cox Enterprises Inc.
CPI Corp.
Crane Co.
Crane & Co., Inc.
Cranston Print Works Co.
Credit Suisse First Boston
Crestar Finance Corp.
Croft-Leominster
CSS Industries, Inc.
Cummings Properties Management
Cummins Engine Co., Inc.
CUNA Mutual Group
Daily News
DaimlerChrysler Corp.
Dain Bosworth Inc.
Dana Corp.
Danis Companies
Dayton Hudson
Deere & Co.
Delta Air Lines, Inc.
Deluxe Corp.
Demoulas Supermarkets Inc.
Deposit Guaranty National Bank
Detroit Edison Co.
Deutsch Co.
Dexter Corp.
Dial Corp.
Disney Co. (Walt)
Dixie Group, Inc. (The)
Domino's Pizza Inc.
Donaldson Co., Inc.
Dreyer's Grand Ice Cream
DSM Copolymer
Duchossois Industries Inc.
Duke Energy
Dun & Bradstreet Corp.
Dynamet, Inc.
Eastern Bank
Eastman Kodak Co.
Eaton Corp.
Eckerd Corp.
Ecolab Inc.
Edwards Enterprise Software (J.D.)
El Paso Energy Co.
Employers Mutual Casualty Co.
Ensign-Bickford Industries
Enterprise Rent-A-Car Co.
Equifax Inc.
Erb Lumber Co.
Evening Post Publishing Co.
Extendicare Health Services
Fabri-Kal Corp.
Fannie Mae
Federal-Mogul Corp.
Federated Department Stores, Inc.
Federated Mutual Insurance Co.
Ferro Corp.
Fidelity Investments
Fifth Third Bancorp
FINA
Fireman's Fund Insurance Co.
First Financial Bank
First Hawaiian, Inc.
First Maryland Bancorp
First Source Corp.
First Union Bank
First Union Securities, Inc.
Firstar Bank Milwaukee NA
Fisher Brothers Cleaning Services
Florida Power & Light Co.
Florida Rock Industries
Fluor Corp.
Forbes Inc.
Ford Meter Box Co.
Forest City Enterprises, Inc.
Fort Worth Star-Telegram Inc.
Fortis Insurance Co.
Freddie Mac
Fuller Co. (H.B.)

Furniture Brands International, Inc.
Gallo Winery, Inc. (E&J)
Galter Corp.
Gap, Inc.
GATX Corp.
GenAmerica Corp.
General Atlantic Partners II LP
General Electric Co.
General Mills, Inc.
General Motors Corp.
Georgia-Pacific Corp.
Georgia Power Co.
Gerber Products Co.
Giant Eagle Inc.
Giant Food Inc.
Giddings & Lewis
Glickenhaus & Co.
Globe Corp.
Golub Corp.
Grace & Co. (W.R.)
Graco, Inc.
Grede Foundries
Green Bay Packaging
Group Health Plan
Guess?
Gulf Power Co.
Halliburton Co.
Hallmark Cards Inc.
Hamilton Sundstrand Corp.
Hanna Co. (M.A.)
Hannaford Brothers Co.
Harland Co. (John H.)
Harris Corp.
Harris Trust & Savings Bank
Harsco Corp.
Hartford (The)
Hartford Steam Boiler Inspection & Insurance Co.
Hartmarx Corp.
Hasbro, Inc.
Hawaiian Electric Co., Inc.
Heinz Co. (H.J.)
Hickory Tech Corp.
Hofmann Co.
HON Industries Inc.
Honeywell International Inc.
Hubbard Broadcasting, Inc.
Hubbell Inc.
Humana, Inc.
IBP
IKON Office Solutions, Inc.
Illinois Tool Works, Inc.
Independent Stave Co.
Indiana Mills & Manufacturing
Inland Container Corp.
Inman Mills
Intel Corp.
International Paper Co.
INTRUST Financial Corp.
Invacare Corp.
Jacobs Engineering Group
Jacobson & Sons (Benjamin)
Johnson Controls Inc.
Johnson & Son (S.C.)
Jones & Co. (Edward D.)
Journal-Gazette Co.
JSJ Corp.
Kellwood Co.
Kerr-McGee Corp.
Kimball International, Inc.
Kimberly-Clark Corp.
Kinder Morgn
Kingsbury Corp.
Koch Enterprises, Inc.
Kroger Co.
La-Z-Boy Inc.
Ladish Co., Inc.
Land O'Lakes, Inc.
LandAmerica Financial Services
Landmark Communications Inc.
Lee Enterprises
Leigh Fibers, Inc.
Levi Strauss & Co.
Leviton Manufacturing Co. Inc.
LG&E Energy Corp.
Liberty Corp.
Liberty Diversified Industries
Lilly & Co. (Eli)
Lincoln Electric Co.
Lincoln Financial Group
Lipton Co.
Litton Industries, Inc.
Liz Claiborne, Inc.
Lotus Development Corp.
Louisiana Land & Exploration Co.
Louisiana-Pacific Corp.
Lowe's Companies
LTV Corp.
Lubrizol Corp. (The)
Madison Gas & Electric Co.
Manor Care Health SVS, Inc.
Manufacturers & Traders Trust Co.
Manulife Financial
Marcus Corp.
Mark IV Industries
Marshall & Ilsley Corp.
Masco Corp.
Mattel Inc.
May Department Stores Co.
McClatchy Co.
McDonald & Co. Securities, Inc.
McGraw-Hill Companies, Inc.
McKesson-HBOC Corp.
McWane Inc.
Mead Corp.
Medtronic, Inc.
Memphis Light Gas & Water Division
Mercantile Bank NA
Merck & Co.
Merit Oil Corp.
Merrill Lynch & Co., Inc.
Metropolitan Life Insurance Co.
Michigan Consolidated Gas Co.
Mid-America Bank of Louisville
MidAmerican Energy Holdings Co.
Milacron, Inc.
Milliken & Co.
Mine Safety Appliances Co.
Minnesota Mining & Manufacturing Co.
Minnesota Mutual Life Insurance Co.
Mitsubishi Electric America
Monarch Machine Tool Co.
Monsanto Co.
Montgomery Ward & Co., Inc.
MONY Group (The)
Morgan & Co. Inc. (J.P.)
Morgan Stanley Dean Witter & Co.
Morris Communications Corp.
Morrison Knudsen Corp.
Motorola Inc.
MTD Products Inc.
Nabisco Group Holdings
Nalco Chemical Co.
National Bank of Commerce Trust & Savings
National City Bank of Minneapolis
National Machinery Co.
National Presto Industries, Inc.
National Service Industries, Inc.
Nationwide Insurance Co.
Navcom Systems
NEBCO Evans
New England Financial
New Jersey Natural Gas Co.
New York Mercantile Exchange
New York Stock Exchange, Inc.
Newman's Own Inc.
Niagara Mohawk Holdings Inc.
Nomura Holding America
Nordson Corp.
Northern States Power Co.
Northern Trust Co.
Northwest Bank Nebraska, NA
Norton Co.
Norwest Corp.
Occidental Oil and Gas
OG&E Electric Services
Ohio National Life Insurance Co.
Oklahoma Publishing Co.
Old Kent Bank
Old National Bank Evansville
Orscheln Co.
Osborne Enterprises
Overseas Shipholding Group Inc.
PACCAR Inc.
Pacific Century Financial Corp.
Pacific Mutual Life Insurance Co.
PacifiCare Health Systems
Paine Webber
Pella Corp.
PEMCO Corp.
PepsiCo, Inc.
PerkinElmer, Inc.
Pharmacia & Upjohn, Inc.
Phelps Dodge Corp.
Phillips Petroleum Co.
Physicians Mutual Insurance Co.
Pieper Power Electric Co.
Pillsbury Co.
Pittway Corp.
PNC Financial Services Group
Polaroid Corp.
PPG Industries, Inc.
Praxair
Premier Dental Products Co.
Premier Industrial Corp.
Price Associates (T. Rowe)
Principal Financial Group
Providence Journal-Bulletin Co.
Prudential Insurance Co. of America
Prudential Securities Inc.
Publix Supermarkets
Pulitzer Publishing Co.
Putnam Investments
Quaker Chemical Corp.
Quanex Corp.
Ralph's Grocery Co.
Ralston Purina Co.
Rayonier Inc.
Red Wing Shoe Co. Inc.
Reebok International Ltd.
Reilly Industries, Inc.
Reily & Co., Inc. (William B.)
Reinhart Institutional Foods
Revlon Inc.
Reynolds Metals Co.
Reynolds Tobacco (R.J.)
Rich Products Corp.
Rockwell International Corp.
Rouse Co.
Royal & SunAlliance USA, Inc.
Rubbermaid Inc.
Ruddick Corp.
Russer Foods
Rutledge Hill Press
Ryder System, Inc.
Safeguard Scientifics
Saint Paul Companies Inc.
S&T Bancorp
Sara Lee Corp.
SBC Communications Inc.
Schering-Plough Corp.
Schloss & Co. (Marcus)
Schwab & Co., Inc. (Charles)
Schwebel Baking Co.
Scripps Co. (E.W.)
Seagram & Sons, Inc. (Joseph E.)
Sega of America Inc.
Sentinel Communications Co.
Sentry Insurance, A Mutual Co.
Servco Pacific
ServiceMaster Co.
S.G. Cowen
Shea Co. (John F.)
Shell Oil Co.
Shelter Mutual Insurance Co.
Sherwin-Williams Co.
Sierra Pacific Industries
Simplot Co. (J.R.)
Simpson Investment Co.
SIT Investment Associates, Inc.
Slant/Fin Corp.
Smurfit-Stone Container Corp.
Solo Cup Co.
Sony Electronics
Southeastern Mutual Insurance Co.
Southwest Gas Corp.
Sovereign Bank
SPX Corp.
Standard Products Co.
Standard Register Co.
Stanley Works (The)
Star Bank NA
State Farm Mutual Automobile Insurance Co.
Steelcase Inc.
Stone Container Corp.
Strear Farms Co.
Stride Rite Corp.
Stupp Brothers Bridge & Iron Co.
Sun Microsystems Inc.
Sunmark Capital Corp.
Susquehanna-Pfaltzgraff Co.
Sverdrup Corp.
Synovus Financial Corp.
Taco Bell Corp.
Tamko Roofing Products
TCF National Bank Minnesota
TENNANT Co.
Tension Envelope Corp.
Tesoro Hawaii
Texas Instruments Inc.
Textron Inc.
Thermo Electron Corp.
Thomasville Furniture Industries Inc.
Ticketmaster Corp.
Titan Industrial Corp.
TJX Companies, Inc.
TMC Investment Co.
Toledo Blade Co.
Tomkins Industries, Inc.
Trace International Holdings, Inc.
Transamerica Corp.
True North Communications, Inc.
True Oil Co.
Trustmark Insurance Co.
TRW Inc.
Ukrop's Super Markets
Unilever Home & Personal Care U.S.A.
Unilever United States, Inc.
Union Camp Corp.
Union Pacific Corp.
United Airlines Inc.
United Distillers & Vintners North America
United Parcel Service of America Inc.
United Services Automobile Association
U.S. Bancorp
U.S. Bancorp Piper Jaffray
United States Sugar Corp.
United States Trust Co. of New York
United Wisconsin Services
Universal Foods Corp.
Universal Leaf Tobacco Co., Inc.
Unocal Corp.
US West, Inc.
USAA Life Insurance Co.
USG Corp.
USX Corp.
Valmont Industries, Inc.
Vesper Corp.
Vodafone AirTouch Plc
Vulcan Materials Co.
Wachovia Bank of North Carolina NA
Wachtell, Lipton, Rosen & Katz
Waffle House Inc.
Wal-Mart Stores, Inc.
Walter Industries Inc.
Warner-Lambert Co.
Washington Mutual, Inc.
Washington Trust Bank
Webster Bank
Weil, Gotshal & Manges Corp.
Western & Southern Life Insurance Co.
Westvaco Corp.
Whirlpool Corp.
Whitman Corp.
WICOR, Inc.
Wilbur-Ellis Co. & Connell Brothers Co.
Winn-Dixie Stores Inc.
Wiremold Co.
Wisconsin Energy Corp.
Wisconsin Power & Light Co.
Wisconsin Public Service Corp.
Witco Corp.
Woodward Governor Co.
Wrigley Co. (Wm. Jr.)
Wyman-Gordon Co.
Yellow Corp.

York Federal Savings & Loan Association
Young & Rubicam
Zachry Co. (H.B.)
Zilkha & Sons

SEMINARIES

Aetna, Inc.
Alcoa Inc.
Alcon Laboratories, Inc.
Alma Piston Co.
American United Life Insurance Co.
Anheuser-Busch Companies, Inc.
Associated Food Stores
Atlantic Investment Co.
Banfi Vintners
Belk-Simpson Department Stores
Belk Stores Services Inc.
Borman's Inc.
Brown Shoe Co., Inc.
Burlington Resources, Inc.
Calvin Klein
Carlson Companies, Inc.
Central & South West Services
CertainTeed Corp.
Citigroup
Constellation Energy Group, Inc.
Continental Grain Co.
Cooper Tire & Rubber Co.
Deposit Guaranty National Bank
Dynamet, Inc.
Federal-Mogul Corp.
First Maryland Bancorp
Forest City Enterprises, Inc.
Galter Corp.
Halliburton Co.
Hofmann Co.
Kellwood Co.
Kennametal, Inc.
Kimball International, Inc.
Laclede Gas Co.
Montgomery Ward & Co., Inc.
National City Corp.
Navcom Systems
Orscheln Co.
Premier Dental Products Co.
Reilly Industries, Inc.
Rubbermaid Inc.
Sentry Insurance, A Mutual Co.
Slant/Fin Corp.
Susquehanna-Pfaltzgraff Co.
Temple-Inland Inc.
Tesoro Hawaii
United Distillers & Vintners North America
U.S. Bancorp
United States Trust Co. of New York
Vesper Corp.
Wachtell, Lipton, Rosen & Katz
Young & Rubicam
Zilkha & Sons

SOCIAL/POLICY ISSUES

Alma Piston Co.
American Retail Group
Armstrong World Industries, Inc.
Banfi Vintners
BankBoston Corp.
Binswanger Companies
Block, Inc. (H&R)
Blue Bell, Inc.
Blue Cross & Blue Shield of Alabama
Boston Edison Co.
Brown Shoe Co., Inc.
Calvin Klein
Carnival Corp.
Cessna Aircraft Co.
Chemed Corp.
Contran Corp.
CPI Corp.
Crestar Finance Corp.
CSS Industries, Inc.
Danis Companies
Dayton Power and Light Co.
Deutsch Co.
Dial Corp.
Dixie Group, Inc. (The)
Domino's Pizza Inc.
Fireman's Fund Insurance Co.
Forest City Enterprises, Inc.
Gallo Winery, Inc. (E&J)
GEICO Corp.
General Mills, Inc.
Giant Eagle Inc.
Giant Food Inc.
Gulf Power Co.
Harris Corp.
Harsco Corp.
Independent Stave Co.
Jacobson & Sons (Benjamin)
Katten, Muchin & Zavis
Koch Enterprises, Inc.
Lance, Inc.
Levi Strauss & Co.
Liberty Diversified Industries
Mark IV Industries
McDonald & Co. Securities, Inc.
McWane Inc.
Mid-America Bank of Louisville
MidAmerican Energy Holdings Co.
Milliken & Co.
Minnesota Mining & Manufacturing Co.
Monsanto Co.
National Service Industries, Inc.
New Jersey Natural Gas Co.
Ohio National Life Insurance Co.
Orscheln Co.
Polaroid Corp.
Premier Dental Products Co.
Premier Industrial Corp.
Quanex Corp.
Ralston Purina Co.
Reinhart Institutional Foods
Rich Products Corp.
Smurfit-Stone Container Corp.
Sovereign Bank
Sprint Corp.
Star Bank NA
Strear Farms Co.
Sunmark Capital Corp.
Tension Envelope Corp.
United Parcel Service of America Inc.
U.S. Bancorp Piper Jaffray
Universal Leaf Tobacco Co., Inc.
USG Corp.
Valmont Industries, Inc.
Waffle House Inc.
Williams
Young & Rubicam

SYNAGOGUES/TEMPLES

Barclays Capital
Barry Corp. (R.G.)
Bernstein & Co., Inc. (Sanford C.)
Borman's Inc.
Cantor, Fitzgerald Securities Corp.
Carnival Corp.
Central National-Gottesman
Century 21
Cincinnati Bell Inc.
Deutsch Co.
Erving Industries
Fisher Brothers Cleaning Services
Galter Corp.
Giant Eagle Inc.
Golub Corp.
Guess?
Hofmann Co.
Jacobson & Sons (Benjamin)
LandAmerica Financial Services
Mamiye Brothers
May Department Stores Co.
MidAmerican Energy Holdings Co.
National Presto Industries, Inc.
New York Mercantile Exchange
Premier Dental Products Co.
Prudential Securities Inc.
Regis Corp.
Revlon Inc.
Russer Foods
Schloss & Co. (Marcus)
Seaway Food Town, Inc.
Servco Pacific
Shea Co. (John F.)
Slant/Fin Corp.
Star Bank NA
Strear Farms Co.
Tension Envelope Corp.
Titan Industrial Corp.
Trace International Holdings, Inc.
Union Camp Corp.
Witco Corp.
Zilkha & Sons

Science

SCIENCE-GENERAL

Alcon Laboratories, Inc.
Archer-Daniels-Midland Co.
Beckman Coulter, Inc.
Bell Atlantic Corp.-West Virginia
Cenex Harvest States
Duracell International
Eastman Chemical Co.
Gap, Inc.
Group Health Plan
Huntington Bancshares Inc.
New England Bio Labs
Orange & Rockland Utilities, Inc.
Penn Mutual Life Insurance Co.
Regions Bank
Susquehanna-Pfaltzgraff Co.
Wolverine World Wide
Zachry Co. (H.B.)

OBSERVATORIES & PLANETARIUMS

Abbott Laboratories
AGL Resources Inc.
Ameritech Corp.
Amsted Industries Inc.
Arizona Public Service Co.
Bank One Corp.
Baxter International Inc.
Beckman Coulter, Inc.
Blair & Co. (William)
Chesapeake Corp.
Chevron Corp.
Chicago Board of Trade
Deposit Guaranty National Bank
Donaldson Co., Inc.
Dreyer's Grand Ice Cream
Equifax Inc.
Ethyl Corp.
Fireman's Fund Insurance Co.
First Union Corp.
Genentech Inc.
Harris Trust & Savings Bank
Hickory Tech Corp.
Illinois Tool Works, Inc.
Kellwood Co.
Kingsbury Corp.
Laclede Gas Co.
Mallinckrodt Chemical, Inc.
Mine Safety Appliances Co.
Motorola Inc.
Nalco Chemical Co.
Northern Trust Co.
Norton Co.
Peoples Energy Corp.
Pittway Corp.
PPG Industries, Inc.
Publix Supermarkets
Sara Lee Corp.
Sempra Energy
TCF National Bank Minnesota
Texaco Inc.
Thermo Electron Corp.
Toyota Motor Sales U.S.A., Inc.
Transamerica Corp.
United Airlines Inc.
US West, Inc.
West Co. Inc.
Zachry Co. (H.B.)

SCIENCE EXHIBITS & FAIRS

ABB Inc.
AGL Resources Inc.
Air Products and Chemicals, Inc.
Alabama Power Co.
Alcoa Inc.
Ameritech Indiana
Ameritech Michigan
Ameritech Ohio
Barden Corp.
Bechtel Group, Inc.
Beckman Coulter, Inc.
BFGoodrich Co.
Block, Inc. (H&R)
Briggs & Stratton Corp.
Cabot Corp.
Carpenter Technology Corp.
Central Maine Power Co.
Central Vermont Public Service Corp.
Chase Bank of Texas
Chevron Corp.
Clorox Co.
Commerce Bancshares, Inc.
Crestar Finance Corp.
Dayton Power and Light Co.
Dow Corning Corp.
DSM Copolymer
du Pont de Nemours & Co. (E.I.)
Duke Energy
Edison International
Equitable Resources, Inc.
Ethyl Corp.
Federal-Mogul Corp.
Fireman's Fund Insurance Co.
First Union Corp.
Fluor Corp.
Freeport-McMoRan Inc.
Genentech Inc.
General Motors Corp.
Glaxo Wellcome Inc.
Goodrich Aerospace - Aerostructures Group (B.F.)
Grace & Co. (W.R.)
Griffith Laboratories U.S.A.
Gulfstream Aerospace Corp.
Hickory Tech Corp.
HON Industries Inc.
Illinois Tool Works, Inc.
Intel Corp.
International Business Machines Corp.
Kroger Co.
LG&E Energy Corp.
Lincoln Financial Group
Little, Inc. (Arthur D.)
Louisiana Land & Exploration Co.
Louisiana-Pacific Corp.
Lubrizol Corp. (The)
McClatchy Co.
Medtronic, Inc.
Merck & Co.
Millipore Corp.
Motorola Inc.
MTS Systems Corp.
National Computer Systems, Inc.
Nortel
Northern Indiana Public Service Co.
Northwest Natural Gas Co.
Norton Co.
Portland General Electric Co.
PPG Industries, Inc.
Praxair
Provident Companies, Inc.
Public Service Electric & Gas Co.
Questar Corp.
Rockwell International Corp.
Seaway Food Town, Inc.
Sempra Energy
Shell Oil Co.
Shoney's Inc.
Simplot Co. (J.R.)
Simpson Investment Co.
Sonoco Products Co.
Southern California Gas Co.
Springs Industries, Inc.
Stanley Works (The)
Tektronix, Inc.
Tenneco Automotive
Textron Inc.
Thermo Electron Corp.
Torchmark Corp.
Union Camp Corp.
Union Carbide Corp.
Unisys Corp.
United Airlines Inc.
United States Sugar Corp.
United Technologies Corp.
Unocal Corp.
Valmont Industries, Inc.
Varian Medical Systems, Inc.
Vulcan Materials Co.
Whirlpool Corp.
Williams
Wyman-Gordon Co.

SCIENCE MUSEUMS

Abbott Laboratories
ABC
Agrilink Foods, Inc.
Alabama Power Co.
Alcoa Inc.
Alcon Laboratories, Inc.
Alexander & Baldwin, Inc.
Allstate Insurance Co.
AMCORE Bank Rockford
American Fidelity Corp.
American General Finance
American Honda Motor Co., Inc.
Ameritech Corp.
Ameritech Ohio
AMETEK, Inc.
Amgen, Inc.
AMP Inc.
AMR Corp.
Amsted Industries Inc.
Andersen Corp.
Aon Corp.
APL Ltd.
Arizona Public Service Co.
Arvin Industries, Inc.
AT&T Corp.
Atlantic Richfield Co.
Avon Products, Inc.
Baird & Co. (Robert W.)
Bank of America
Bank One Corp.
BankAtlantic Bancorp
BankBoston Corp.
Barden Corp.
Barnes Group Inc.
Baxter International Inc.
Bechtel Group, Inc.
Beckman Coulter, Inc.
BellSouth Corp.
Bemis Co., Inc.
BFGoodrich Co.
Binswanger Companies
Blair & Co. (William)
Boeing Co.
Borden, Inc.
Boston Edison Co.
Boston Globe (The)
BP Amoco Corp.
Briggs & Stratton Corp.
Bristol-Myers Squibb Co.
Broderbund Software, Inc.
Brown Shoe Co., Inc.
Burlington Industries, Inc.
Burlington Resources, Inc.
Burnett Co. (Leo)
Cabot Corp.
Campbell Soup Co.
Cargill Inc.
Carter-Wallace, Inc.
CCB Financial Corp.
CertainTeed Corp.
Cessna Aircraft Co.
Charter Manufacturing Co.
Chase Bank of Texas
Chase Manhattan Bank, NA
Chesapeake Corp.
Chicago Board of Trade
Chicago Tribune Co.
CIGNA Corp.
Circuit City Stores, Inc.
Citizens Financial Group, Inc.
CLARCOR Inc.
Cleveland-Cliffs, Inc.
Coca-Cola Co.
Colonial Oil Industries, Inc.
Commerce Bancshares, Inc.
Compass Bank
Consolidated Natural Gas Co.
Consolidated Papers, Inc.
Constellation Energy Group, Inc.
Continental Grain Co.
Contran Corp.
Cooper Industries, Inc.
Corning Inc.
Cox Enterprises Inc.
Crestar Finance Corp.
CSS Industries, Inc.
Cummings Properties Management
Danis Companies
Dayton Power and Light Co.
Deere & Co.
Deluxe Corp.
Demoulas Supermarkets Inc.
Deutsch Co.
Dexter Corp.
Donaldson Co., Inc.
Duke Energy
Duriron Co., Inc.
Eastman Kodak Co.
Eaton Corp.
Ecolab Inc.
Elf Atochem North America, Inc.
Enterprise Rent-A-Car Co.
Equifax Inc.
Erving Industries
Exxon Mobil Corp.
Ferro Corp.
FINA
Fireman's Fund Insurance Co.
First Hawaiian, Inc.
First Union Corp.
First Union Securities, Inc.
Fisher Brothers Cleaning Services
Fisher Scientific
Florida Power Corp.
Florida Rock Industries
FMC Corp.
Forbes Inc.
Ford Motor Co.
Fort Worth Star-Telegram Inc.
Freeport-McMoRan Inc.
Fuller Co. (H.B.)
Gap, Inc.
GATX Corp.
GenCorp
Genentech Inc.
General Mills, Inc.
Georgia-Pacific Corp.
Georgia Power Co.
Giddings & Lewis
Glaxo Wellcome Inc.
Golub Corp.
Graco, Inc.
GTE Corp.
Halliburton Co.
Hamilton Sundstrand Corp.
Hanna Co. (M.A.)
Harcourt General, Inc.
Harley-Davidson Co.
Harnischfeger Industries
Harris Corp.
Harris Trust & Savings Bank
Harsco Corp.
Hartmarx Corp.
Hasbro, Inc.
Hawaiian Electric Co., Inc.
Hewlett-Packard Co.
Hitachi America Ltd.
Hoffer Plastics Corp.
Hoffmann-La Roche Inc.
Hofmann Co.
Honeywell International Inc.
Hubbard Broadcasting, Inc.
Hubbell Inc.
Huffy Corp.
Humana, Inc.
Huntington Bancshares Inc.
IKON Office Solutions, Inc.
Illinois Tool Works, Inc.
Independent Stave Co.
Industrial Bank of Japan Trust Co. (New York)
Intel Corp.
International Multifoods Corp.
Invacare Corp.
Jeld-wen, Inc.
Johnson Controls Inc.
Jostens, Inc.
Journal-Gazette Co.
Kemper National Insurance Companies
Kinder Morgn
Koch Enterprises, Inc.
Koch Industries, Inc.
Lance, Inc.
Land O'Lakes, Inc.
Landmark Communications Inc.
Lee Enterprises
Lennox International, Inc.
Liberty Diversified Industries
Lincoln Electric Co.
Little, Inc. (Arthur D.)
Litton Industries, Inc.
Liz Claiborne, Inc.
Loews Corp.
Lotus Development Corp.
Louisiana-Pacific Corp.
LTV Corp.
Lubrizol Corp. (The)
Marshall & Ilsley Corp.
McClatchy Co.
McDonald & Co. Securities, Inc.
MCI WorldCom, Inc.
McWane Inc.
Mead Corp.
Medtronic, Inc.
Merrill Lynch & Co., Inc.
Metropolitan Life Insurance Co.
Michigan Consolidated Gas Co.
Mid-America Bank of Louisville
Milacron, Inc.
Millipore Corp.
Minnesota Mining & Manufacturing Co.
Minnesota Mutual Life Insurance Co.
Monsanto Co.
Morgan & Co. Inc. (J.P.)
Morgan Stanley Dean Witter & Co.
Morrison Knudsen Corp.
Motorola Inc.
MTD Products Inc.
Nalco Chemical Co.
National City Bank of Minneapolis
National City Corp.
Nationwide Insurance Co.
NCR Corp.
NEC America, Inc.
Nestle U.S.A. Inc.
New York Life Insurance Co.
New York Times Co.
Niagara Mohawk Holdings Inc.
Nordson Corp.
Norfolk Southern Corp.
Northern Trust Co.
Norton Co.
Norwest Corp.
Occidental Oil and Gas
OG&E Electric Services
Oklahoma Publishing Co.
Old National Bank Evansville
Olin Corp.
Orange & Rockland Utilities, Inc.
Oshkosh B'Gosh, Inc.
PACCAR Inc.
Pacific Century Financial Corp.
Pacific Mutual Life Insurance Co.
PacifiCorp
Parker Hannifin Corp.
PepsiCo, Inc.
PerkinElmer, Inc.
Pfizer Inc.
Phelps Dodge Corp.
Pillsbury Co.
Pioneer Group
PNC Financial Services Group
Praxair
Premier Industrial Corp.
Price Associates (T. Rowe)
Procter & Gamble Co.
Procter & Gamble Co., Cosmetics Division
Provident Companies, Inc.
Publix Supermarkets
Putnam Investments
Quaker Chemical Corp.
Quanex Corp.
Red Wing Shoe Co. Inc.
Reebok International Ltd.
Reynolds Metals Co.
Reynolds & Reynolds Co.
Rockwell International Corp.
Royal & SunAlliance USA, Inc.
Ruddick Corp.
Russer Foods
Safeguard Scientifics
Saint Paul Companies Inc.
Sara Lee Corp.
Schlumberger Ltd. (USA)
Schwab & Co., Inc. (Charles)
Scripps Co. (E.W.)
Searle & Co. (G.D.)
S.G. Cowen
Shaw's Supermarkets, Inc.
Shell Oil Co.
Sherwin-Williams Co.
Sierra Pacific Industries
Sony Electronics
Southwest Gas Corp.
Standard Register Co.
State Street Bank & Trust Co.
Stone Container Corp.
Stonecutter Mills Corp.
Storage Technology Corp.
Strear Farms Co.
Stride Rite Corp.
Stupp Brothers Bridge & Iron Co.
Sun Microsystems Inc.
Susquehanna-Pfaltzgraff Co.
Synovus Financial Corp.
TCF National Bank Minnesota
Tektronix, Inc.
Temple-Inland Inc.
TENNANT Co.
Tesoro Hawaii
Texaco Inc.
Texas Instruments Inc.
Thermo Electron Corp.
Thompson Co. (J. Walter)
Times Mirror Co.
Timken Co. (The)
Tomkins Industries, Inc.
Toshiba America Inc.
Toyota Motor Sales U.S.A., Inc.
Trace International Holdings, Inc.
Transamerica Corp.
True North Communications, Inc.
TRW Inc.
Ukrop's Super Markets
Unilever Home & Personal Care U.S.A.
Unilever United States, Inc.
Union Carbide Corp.
Union Planters Corp.
United Airlines Inc.
United Parcel Service of America Inc.
U.S. Bancorp Piper Jaffray
Universal Foods Corp.
Universal Leaf Tobacco Co., Inc.
Unocal Corp.
US Bank, Washington
US West, Inc.
USG Corp.
USX Corp.
Valspar Corp.
Vulcan Materials Co.
Waffle House Inc.
Warner-Lambert Co.
West Co. Inc.
Weyerhaeuser Co.
Whitman Corp.
WICOR, Inc.
Wiley & Sons (John)
Wiremold Co.
Wisconsin Energy Corp.
Wisconsin Public Service Corp.
Woodward Governor Co.
York Federal Savings & Loan Association
Young & Rubicam
Zachry Co. (H.B.)

SCIENTIFIC CENTERS & INSTITUTES

Abbott Laboratories
AEGON U.S.A. Inc.
Aetna, Inc.
Allegheny Technologies Inc.
AlliedSignal Inc.
Allmerica Financial Corp.
Ameren Corp.
American Honda Motor Co., Inc.
American Standard Inc.
Ameritech Corp.
Ameritech Ohio
AMETEK, Inc.
Amgen, Inc.
AMP Inc.
Amsted Industries Inc.
Andersons Inc.
Anheuser-Busch Companies, Inc.
Aon Corp.
Archer-Daniels-Midland Co.
Aristech Chemical Corp.
Arizona Public Service Co.
Armstrong World Industries, Inc.
Arvin Industries, Inc.
Avon Products, Inc.
Bandag, Inc.
Bank of America
Bank One Corp.
Bard, Inc. (C.R.)
Bausch & Lomb Inc.

Bechtel Group, Inc.
Beckman Coulter, Inc.
Berwind Group
Bethlehem Steel Corp.
BFGoodrich Co.
Binswanger Companies
Blue Bell, Inc.
Boeing Co.
Borden, Inc.
Borman's Inc.
Bridgestone/Firestone, Inc.
Briggs & Stratton Corp.
Bristol-Myers Squibb Co.
Broderbund Software, Inc.
Brown Shoe Co., Inc.
Burlington Industries, Inc.
Cargill Inc.
Carris Reels
Central Maine Power Co.
Central Soya Co.
Cessna Aircraft Co.
CGU Insurance
Champion International Corp.
Chase Manhattan Bank, NA
Chesapeake Corp.
Chevron Corp.
CIGNA Corp.
Circuit City Stores, Inc.
Citizens Financial Group, Inc.
Cleveland-Cliffs, Inc.
Coca-Cola Co.
Collins & Aikman Corp.
Commerce Bancshares, Inc.
ConAgra, Inc.
Consolidated Natural Gas Co.
Consolidated Papers, Inc.
Constellation Energy Group, Inc.
Consumers Energy Co.
Cooper Industries, Inc.
Corning Inc.
Cox Enterprises Inc.
CPI Corp.
Crane Co.
Crestar Finance Corp.
Daily News
DaimlerChrysler Corp.
Dana Corp.
DeKalb Genetics Corp.
Delta Air Lines, Inc.
Detroit Edison Co.
Dexter Corp.
Disney Co. (Walt)
Dixie Group, Inc. (The)
Dow Chemical Co.
Dow Corning Corp.
du Pont de Nemours & Co. (E.I.)
Duke Energy
Dun & Bradstreet Corp.
Dynamet, Inc.
Eastman Kodak Co.
Eaton Corp.
Edison International
El Paso Energy Co.
Elf Atochem North America, Inc.
Emerson Electric Co.
Employers Mutual Casualty Co.
Enterprise Rent-A-Car Co.
Equitable Resources, Inc.
Erb Lumber Co.
Ethyl Corp.
Exxon Mobil Corp.
Federal-Mogul Corp.
Federated Department Stores, Inc.
Ferro Corp.
Fidelity Investments
First Hawaiian, Inc.
First Maryland Bancorp
First Union Corp.
Fluor Corp.
FMC Corp.
Ford Motor Co.
Forest City Enterprises, Inc.
Franklin Electric Co.
Freeport-McMoRan Inc.
Furniture Brands International, Inc.
Galter Corp.
Gap, Inc.
GEICO Corp.
GenAmerica Corp.
GenCorp
Genentech Inc.
General Dynamics Corp.
General Electric Co.
General Motors Corp.
Georgia Power Co.
Gerber Products Co.
Giant Eagle Inc.
Globe Corp.
Grede Foundries
Green Bay Packaging
Group Health Plan
GTE Corp.
Hanna Co. (M.A.)
Harcourt General, Inc.
Harley-Davidson Co.
Harnischfeger Industries
Harris Corp.
Harris Trust & Savings Bank
Harsco Corp.
Heinz Co. (H.J.)
Hershey Foods Corp.
Hitachi America Ltd.
Hoffmann-La Roche Inc.
Hofmann Co.
HON Industries Inc.
Hubbell Inc.
Humana, Inc.
Hunt Manufacturing Co.
IKON Office Solutions, Inc.
Illinois Tool Works, Inc.
Intel Corp.
International Flavors & Fragrances Inc.
Johnson Controls Inc.
Journal-Gazette Co.
Kennametal, Inc.
Land O'Lakes, Inc.
Landmark Communications Inc.
Leigh Fibers, Inc.
LG&E Energy Corp.
Liberty Corp.
Little, Inc. (Arthur D.)
Litton Industries, Inc.
Lotus Development Corp.
Louisiana Land & Exploration Co.
LTV Corp.
Lubrizol Corp. (The)
Mallinckrodt Chemical, Inc.
Masco Corp.
Mattel Inc.
May Department Stores Co.
McDonald & Co. Securities, Inc.
MCI WorldCom, Inc.
Mead Corp.
Medtronic, Inc.
Mercantile Bank NA
Merck & Co.
Merrill Lynch & Co., Inc.
Metropolitan Life Insurance Co.
Michigan Consolidated Gas Co.
Microsoft Corp.
Mid-America Bank of Louisville
Milliken & Co.
Millipore Corp.
Mine Safety Appliances Co.
Monsanto Co.
Motorola Inc.
MTD Products Inc.
Nabisco Group Holdings
Nalco Chemical Co.
National City Corp.
National Computer Systems, Inc.
National Fuel Gas Distribution Corp.
National Starch & Chemical Co.
Nationwide Insurance Co.
NEC America, Inc.
New England Bio Labs
Nordson Corp.
Norfolk Southern Corp.
Norton Co.
Occidental Oil and Gas
Olin Corp.
Overseas Shipholding Group Inc.
Owens Corning
PACCAR Inc.
Pacific Mutual Life Insurance Co.
Parker Hannifin Corp.
Pella Corp.
PEMCO Corp.
Pfizer Inc.
Pharmacia & Upjohn, Inc.
Phelps Dodge Corp.
Phillips Petroleum Co.
PNC Financial Services Group
Potlatch Corp.
PPG Industries, Inc.
Premier Dental Products Co.
Premier Industrial Corp.
Principal Financial Group
Procter & Gamble Co., Cosmetics Division
Public Service Electric & Gas Co.
Publix Supermarkets
Pulitzer Publishing Co.
Quaker Chemical Corp.
Ralston Purina Co.
Red Wing Shoe Co. Inc.
Reilly Industries, Inc.
Reynolds Metals Co.
Rockwell International Corp.
Rouse Co.
Rubbermaid Inc.
Safeguard Scientifics
Salomon Smith Barney
SBC Communications Inc.
Schering-Plough Corp.
Schlumberger Ltd. (USA)
Schwab & Co., Inc. (Charles)
Searle & Co. (G.D.)
Sega of America Inc.
Shell Oil Co.
Sherwin-Williams Co.
Simpson Investment Co.
SmithKline Beecham Corp.
Smurfit-Stone Container Corp.
Sony Electronics
Southeastern Mutual Insurance Co.
Southwest Gas Corp.
Sprint Corp.
Sprint/United Telephone
SPX Corp.
Stride Rite Corp.
Stupp Brothers Bridge & Iron Co.
SunTrust Bank Atlanta
SunTrust Banks of Florida
Sverdrup Corp.
Teleflex Inc.
Texaco Inc.
Textron Inc.
Thomasville Furniture Industries Inc.
TJX Companies, Inc.
Tomkins Industries, Inc.
Toshiba America Inc.
Toyota Motor Sales U.S.A., Inc.
Transamerica Corp.
True North Communications, Inc.
TRW Inc.
Ukrop's Super Markets
Union Carbide Corp.
Union Pacific Corp.
United Airlines Inc.
United Distillers & Vintners North America
United Parcel Service of America Inc.
United States Sugar Corp.
Universal Studios
Unocal Corp.
US West, Inc.
USX Corp.
Wachovia Bank of North Carolina NA
Waffle House Inc.
Warner-Lambert Co.
Washington Mutual, Inc.
Washington Trust Bank
West Co. Inc.
Weyerhaeuser Co.
Whirlpool Corp.
Wilbur-Ellis Co. & Connell Brothers Co.
Wiley & Sons (John)
Wiremold Co.
Witco Corp.
Wyman-Gordon Co.
Zachry Co. (H.B.)
Zilkha & Sons

SCIENTIFIC LABS

Alabama Power Co.
Amsted Industries Inc.
Beckman Coulter, Inc.
DeKalb Genetics Corp.
Disney Co. (Walt)
Exxon Mobil Corp.
Fidelity Investments
Hannaford Brothers Co.
Hoffmann-La Roche Inc.
International Paper Co.
Merck & Co.
Merrill Lynch & Co., Inc.
MidAmerican Energy Holdings Co.
Monarch Machine Tool Co.
New England Bio Labs
Pfizer Inc.
Pittway Corp.
Polaroid Corp.
Schering-Plough Corp.
S.G. Cowen
SmithKline Beecham Corp.
Southwest Gas Corp.
Texaco Inc.
Westvaco Corp.

SCIENTIFIC ORGANIZATIONS

AGL Resources Inc.
Alcoa Inc.
Ameritech Indiana
Andersons Inc.
Anheuser-Busch Companies, Inc.
Aristech Chemical Corp.
Banfi Vintners
Barden Corp.
Bechtel Group, Inc.
Beckman Coulter, Inc.
Becton Dickinson & Co.
Bell Atlantic Corp.
BFGoodrich Co.
Blair & Co. (William)
Borden, Inc.
Borman's Inc.
BP Amoco Corp.
Bridgestone/Firestone, Inc.
Briggs & Stratton Corp.
Bristol-Myers Squibb Co.
Brown & Williamson Tobacco Corp.
Cabot Corp.
Champion International Corp.
Chase Manhattan Bank, NA
Chevron Corp.
Church & Dwight Co., Inc.
Cincinnati Bell Inc.
Colonial Oil Industries, Inc.
ConAgra, Inc.
Corning Inc.
DeKalb Genetics Corp.
Deposit Guaranty National Bank
Detroit Edison Co.
du Pont de Nemours & Co. (E.I.)
Duchossois Industries Inc.
Duke Energy
Dynamet, Inc.
Eastman Kodak Co.
Edison International
Elf Atochem North America, Inc.
Ensign-Bickford Industries
Equitable Resources, Inc.
Ethyl Corp.
First Union Corp.
FMC Corp.
Freeport-McMoRan Inc.
Freightliner Corp.
Frost National Bank
Gallo Winery, Inc. (E&J)
GenCorp
General Electric Co.
General Motors Corp.
Gerber Products Co.
Grace & Co. (W.R.)
Harris Corp.
Heinz Co. (H.J.)
Hershey Foods Corp.
Hewlett-Packard Co.
Hoffmann-La Roche Inc.
Humana, Inc.
IKON Office Solutions, Inc.
Industrial Bank of Japan Trust Co. (New York)
Intel Corp.
International Business Machines Corp.
International Flavors & Fragrances Inc.
Lehigh Portland Cement Co.
Lipton Co.
Litton Industries, Inc.
Mattel Inc.
McCormick & Co. Inc.
Merck & Co.
Michigan Consolidated Gas Co.
Milacron, Inc.
Millipore Corp.

National Computer Systems, Inc.
National Starch & Chemical Co.
Nestle U.S.A. Inc.
New York Life Insurance Co.
Norton Co.
Occidental Oil and Gas
PACCAR Inc.
PepsiCo, Inc.
Pharmacia & Upjohn, Inc.
Phillips Petroleum Co.
Pittway Corp.
Polaroid Corp.
Portland General Electric Co.
PPG Industries, Inc.
Reily & Co., Inc. (William B.)
Reliant Energy Inc.
Rockwell International Corp.
Searle & Co. (G.D.)
Sega of America Inc.
Sempra Energy
Shell Oil Co.
SmithKline Beecham Corp.
Sprint/United Telephone
SPX Corp.
Starwood Hotels & Resorts Worldwide, Inc.
Texaco Inc.
TRW Inc.
TU Electric Co.
Ukrop's Super Markets
Unilever United States, Inc.
Union Camp Corp.
Union Carbide Corp.
United Parcel Service of America Inc.
United States Sugar Corp.
Unocal Corp.
USX Corp.
Varian Medical Systems, Inc.
West Co. Inc.
Whirlpool Corp.
Wiley & Sons (John)
Williams
Wisconsin Energy Corp.
Witco Corp.
Xerox Corp.

SCIENTIFIC RESEARCH

Abbott Laboratories
Agrilink Foods, Inc.
Andersons Inc.
Anheuser-Busch Companies, Inc.
Baxter International Inc.
Bechtel Group, Inc.
Beckman Coulter, Inc.
Bristol-Myers Squibb Co.
Constellation Energy Group, Inc.
Crane & Co., Inc.
Crestar Finance Corp.
DSM Copolymer
Dynamet, Inc.
Exxon Mobil Corp.
First Hawaiian, Inc.
First Maryland Bancorp
First Union Securities, Inc.
Gerber Products Co.
Giant Eagle Inc.
Group Health Plan
Hoffmann-La Roche Inc.
HON Industries Inc.
International Flavors & Fragrances Inc.
Jacobson & Sons (Benjamin)
Kimberly-Clark Corp.
Leigh Fibers, Inc.
Milliken & Co.
Millipore Corp.
Minnesota Mining & Manufacturing Co.
MTD Products Inc.
New England Bio Labs
Norton Co.
Norwest Corp.
Ohio National Life Insurance Co.
Pfizer Inc.
Phillips Petroleum Co.
Procter & Gamble Co., Cosmetics Division
Regions Bank
Schering-Plough Corp.
Security Benefit Life Insurance Co.
Sierra Pacific Resources
Texaco Inc.
Thermo Electron Corp.
Thompson Co. (J. Walter)
Toshiba America Inc.
Ukrop's Super Markets
Union Carbide Corp.
Universal Leaf Tobacco Co., Inc.
USAA Life Insurance Co.
Warner-Lambert Co.
Wyman-Gordon Co.
Zachry Co. (H.B.)

Social Services

ANIMAL PROTECTION

Agrilink Foods, Inc.
American United Life Insurance Co.
Ameritas Life Insurance Corp.
Ameritech Ohio
Andersen Corp.
Andersons Inc.
Arvin Industries, Inc.
Atlantic Investment Co.
Avon Products, Inc.
Barclays Capital
Bassett Furniture Industries
Ben & Jerry's Homemade Inc.
Blount International, Inc.
Borman's Inc.
Briggs & Stratton Corp.
Broderbund Software, Inc.
Carris Reels
Church & Dwight Co., Inc.
Collins & Aikman Corp.
Colonial Life & Accident Insurance Co.
Colonial Oil Industries, Inc.
Compaq Computer Corp.
Consolidated Papers, Inc.
Cooper Industries, Inc.
Copley Press, Inc.
Cox Enterprises Inc.
Cummings Properties Management
DaimlerChrysler Corp.
Deutsch Co.
Dial Corp.
Disney Co. (Walt)
du Pont de Nemours & Co. (E.I.)
Duke Energy
El Paso Energy Co.
Emerson Electric Co.
Evening Post Publishing Co.
Federal-Mogul Corp.
First Source Corp.
Florida Rock Industries
Ford Meter Box Co.
Franklin Mint (The)
Gallo Winery, Inc. (E&J)
Galter Corp.
GEICO Corp.
Green Bay Packaging
Hannaford Brothers Co.
Hartmarx Corp.
Heinz Co. (H.J.)
Hoffmann-La Roche Inc.
Hofmann Co.
HON Industries Inc.
Humana, Inc.
Huntington Bancshares Inc.
Idaho Power Co.
IKON Office Solutions, Inc.
Independent Stave Co.
Invacare Corp.
Jeld-wen, Inc.
Johnson & Son (S.C.)
Jones & Co. (Edward D.)
Kellwood Co.
Kingsbury Corp.
Kroger Co.
La-Z-Boy Inc.
Laclede Gas Co.
Ladish Co., Inc.
Loews Corp.
Louisiana Land & Exploration Co.
Marshall & Ilsley Corp.
Mattel Inc.
McDonald & Co. Securities, Inc.
McWane Inc.
Menasha Corp.
Morris Communications Corp.
Morrison Knudsen Corp.
Murphy Oil Corp.
National Bank of Commerce Trust & Savings
National City Bank of Minneapolis
National City Corp.
National Fuel Gas Distribution Corp.
National Service Industries, Inc.
Nationwide Insurance Co.
NEBCO Evans
New England Financial
Northern Indiana Public Service Co.
Northwest Natural Gas Co.
Oklahoma Publishing Co.
Old Kent Bank
Old National Bank Evansville
PacifiCare Health Systems
Paine Webber
Pharmacia & Upjohn, Inc.
Potomac Electric Power Co.
Ralston Purina Co.
Regions Bank
Rich Products Corp.
Sara Lee Hosiery, Inc.
Schwab & Co., Inc. (Charles)
Security Benefit Life Insurance Co.
Sentry Insurance, A Mutual Co.
Shea Co. (John F.)
Slant/Fin Corp.
State Street Bank & Trust Co.
Steelcase Inc.
Stride Rite Corp.
Stupp Brothers Bridge & Iron Co.
Sunmark Capital Corp.
Susquehanna-Pfaltzgraff Co.
Synovus Financial Corp.
Tenneco Automotive
Tesoro Hawaii
Thomasville Furniture Industries Inc.
Timken Co. (The)
TMC Investment Co.
Tomkins Industries, Inc.
Trace International Holdings, Inc.
U.S. Bancorp
Universal Leaf Tobacco Co., Inc.
Vesper Corp.
Vulcan Materials Co.
Waffle House Inc.
Wal-Mart Stores, Inc.
Westvaco Corp.
Whirlpool Corp.
Wilbur-Ellis Co. & Connell Brothers Co.
Wisconsin Public Service Corp.
Witco Corp.

AT-RISK YOUTH

ABC
Aetna, Inc.
Alcoa Inc.
AlliedSignal Inc.
Alma Piston Co.
American Express Co.
American Retail Group
Ameritas Life Insurance Corp.
Ameritech Wisconsin
Amgen, Inc.
AMR Corp.
Anheuser-Busch Companies, Inc.
Aon Corp.
Atlantic Richfield Co.
Avon Products, Inc.
Bandag, Inc.
Bank One Corp.
BankAtlantic Bancorp
Baxter International Inc.
Binney & Smith Inc.
Block, Inc. (H&R)
Blue Bell, Inc.
Blue Cross & Blue Shield of Minnesota
Borden, Inc.
BP Amoco Corp.
Bridgestone/Firestone, Inc.
Broderbund Software, Inc.
Brown Shoe Co., Inc.
Brunswick Corp.
Burlington Resources, Inc.
Burnett Co. (Leo)
Butler Manufacturing Co.
Cabot Corp.
Callaway Golf Co.
Cargill Inc.
CertainTeed Corp.
Chase Manhattan Bank, NA
Chicago Board of Trade
Chicago Sun-Times, Inc.
Chicago Title Corp.
Citigroup
Citizens Bank-Flint
CLARCOR Inc.
Clorox Co.
Constellation Energy Group, Inc.
Contran Corp.
Corning Inc.
CPI Corp.
Crane Co.
Credit Suisse First Boston
Crestar Finance Corp.
Cummings Properties Management
CUNA Mutual Group
Daily News
Dain Bosworth Inc.
Danis Companies
Dayton Hudson
Delta Air Lines, Inc.
Deluxe Corp.
Dreyer's Grand Ice Cream
Duchossois Industries Inc.
Dun & Bradstreet Corp.
Ecolab Inc.
Edwards Enterprise Software (J.D.)
El Paso Energy Co.
Emerson Electric Co.
Erb Lumber Co.
Erving Industries
Excel Corp.
Federated Department Stores, Inc.
Federated Mutual Insurance Co.
Fidelity Investments
Fireman's Fund Insurance Co.
First Union Bank
FleetBoston Financial Corp.
Florida Rock Industries
Ford Meter Box Co.
Freddie Mac
Freeport-McMoRan Inc.
Gallo Winery, Inc. (E&J)
GATX Corp.
GenAmerica Corp.
General Mills, Inc.
Georgia Power Co.
Gerber Products Co.
Giant Eagle Inc.
Goldman Sachs Group
Grace & Co. (W.R.)
Graco, Inc.
Group Health Plan
Hamilton Sundstrand Corp.
Hanna Co. (M.A.)
Harcourt General, Inc.
Hartmarx Corp.
Hickory Tech Corp.
Hofmann Co.
Honeywell International Inc.
Hubbell Inc.
International Multifoods Corp.
Jostens, Inc.
Journal-Gazette Co.
Katten, Muchin & Zavis
Kellogg Co.
Kellwood Co.
Kennametal, Inc.
La-Z-Boy Inc.
LandAmerica Financial Services
Lehigh Portland Cement Co.
Levi Strauss & Co.
Leviton Manufacturing Co. Inc.
LG&E Energy Corp.
Lipton Co.
Lotus Development Corp.
Louisiana Land & Exploration Co.
Louisiana-Pacific Corp.
Madison Gas & Electric Co.
Mamiye Brothers
Marshall Field's
Massachusetts Mutual Life Insurance Co.
McClatchy Co.
McDonald & Co. Securities, Inc.
McWane Inc.
Medtronic, Inc.
Mercantile Bank NA
Merrill Lynch & Co., Inc.

Metropolitan Life Insurance Co.
Millipore Corp.
Monarch Machine Tool Co.
Morgan & Co. Inc. (J.P.)
Morgan Stanley Dean Witter & Co.
Morrison Knudsen Corp.
Mutual of Omaha Insurance Co.
Nalco Chemical Co.
National City Bank of Minneapolis
National City Corp.
National Machinery Co.
New York Stock Exchange, Inc.
Nissan North America, Inc.
Nordson Corp.
Norwest Corp.
Old National Bank Evansville
Oshkosh B'Gosh, Inc.
Outboard Marine Corp.
Pacific Century Financial Corp.
Pacific Mutual Life Insurance Co.
PacifiCare Health Systems
PacifiCorp
Paine Webber
Pharmacia & Upjohn, Inc.
Physicians Mutual Insurance Co.
Pillsbury Co.
Pittway Corp.
Polaroid Corp.
Praxair
Principal Financial Group
Procter & Gamble Co., Cosmetics Division
Prudential Insurance Co. of America
Publix Supermarkets
Putnam Investments
Quaker Chemical Corp.
Ralston Purina Co.
Reebok International Ltd.
Reilly Industries, Inc.
Reily & Co., Inc. (William B.)
Rubbermaid Inc.
Saint Paul Companies Inc.
Seagram & Sons, Inc. (Joseph E.)
Searle & Co. (G.D.)
Security Life of Denver Insurance Co.
Sentry Insurance, A Mutual Co.
Simpson Investment Co.
SIT Investment Associates, Inc.
Smurfit-Stone Container Corp.
Solo Cup Co.
Southeastern Mutual Insurance Co.
Southwest Gas Corp.
Square D Co.
Storage Technology Corp.
Stride Rite Corp.
Stupp Brothers Bridge & Iron Co.
Sverdrup Corp.
Taco Bell Corp.
Tai and Co. (J.T.)
TENNANT Co.
Thompson Co. (J. Walter)
Trace International Holdings, Inc.
Transamerica Corp.
True North Communications, Inc.
Union Carbide Corp.
United Parcel Service of America Inc.
United Services Automobile Association
U.S. Bancorp Piper Jaffray
Unocal Corp.
US Bank, Washington
USX Corp.
Valmont Industries, Inc.
Vesper Corp.
Waffle House Inc.
Washington Trust Bank
Weil, Gotshal & Manges Corp.
Whitman Corp.
Williams
Winn-Dixie Stores Inc.
Wisconsin Public Service Corp.
Woodward Governor Co.
Zachry Co. (H.B.)

BIG BROTHER/BIG SISTER

Alcoa Inc.
Alexander & Baldwin, Inc.
Allmerica Financial Corp.
American Express Co.
American Fidelity Corp.
American General Finance
AMP Inc.
AMR Corp.
Amsted Industries Inc.
Atlantic Investment Co.
Barnes Group Inc.
Bernstein & Co., Inc. (Sanford C.)
Borden, Inc.
Briggs & Stratton Corp.
Broderbund Software, Inc.
Brunswick Corp.
Bucyrus-Erie Co.
Butler Manufacturing Co.
Callaway Golf Co.
Cargill Inc.
CertainTeed Corp.
Cessna Aircraft Co.
Chase Bank of Texas
Chicago Title Corp.
CLARCOR Inc.
Clorox Co.
Comdisco, Inc.
ConAgra, Inc.
Corning Inc.
Cranston Print Works Co.
Croft-Leominster
CUNA Mutual Group
Dain Bosworth Inc.
Danis Companies
Dayton Power and Light Co.
Deutsch Co.
Donaldson Co., Inc.
Dreyer's Grand Ice Cream
Duriron Co., Inc.
Ecolab Inc.
Elf Atochem North America, Inc.
Emerson Electric Co.
Fabri-Kal Corp.
Federated Mutual Insurance Co.
Fireman's Fund Insurance Co.
First Hawaiian, Inc.
First Source Corp.
First Union Bank
First Union Securities, Inc.
Fisher Brothers Cleaning Services
Ford Meter Box Co.
Fort Worth Star-Telegram Inc.
Freeport-McMoRan Inc.
Fuller Co. (H.B.)
Gallo Winery, Inc. (E&J)
General Mills, Inc.
Georgia-Pacific Corp.
Georgia Power Co.
Giant Eagle Inc.
Giant Food Inc.
Giddings & Lewis
Globe Corp.
Green Bay Packaging
Hannaford Brothers Co.
Harcourt General, Inc.
Hartford (The)
Hasbro, Inc.
Hawaiian Electric Co., Inc.
Honeywell International Inc.
Huffy Corp.
Hunt Manufacturing Co.
IKON Office Solutions, Inc.
International Multifoods Corp.
INTRUST Financial Corp.
Jacobs Engineering Group
Jostens, Inc.
Katten, Muchin & Zavis
Kellogg Co.
Kroger Co.
Leviton Manufacturing Co. Inc.
Lipton Co.
Liz Claiborne, Inc.
Mattel Inc.
McWane Inc.
Monarch Machine Tool Co.
Montana Power Co.
MONY Group (The)
National Machinery Co.
New England Financial
New Jersey Natural Gas Co.
Occidental Oil and Gas
Osborne Enterprises
Oshkosh B'Gosh, Inc.
PacifiCare Health Systems
PEMCO Corp.
Physicians Mutual Insurance Co.
Pillsbury Co.
Provident Companies, Inc.
Prudential Securities Inc.
Putnam Investments
Quanex Corp.
Regions Bank
Reinhart Institutional Foods
S&T Bancorp
Schwab & Co., Inc. (Charles)
Scripps Co. (E.W.)
Security Benefit Life Insurance Co.
Servco Pacific
Shea Co. (John F.)
Sherwin-Williams Co.
Southwest Gas Corp.
Standard Register Co.
Storage Technology Corp.
Stride Rite Corp.
Sun Microsystems Inc.
Titan Industrial Corp.
Unilever Home & Personal Care U.S.A.
United Distillers & Vintners North America
United Parcel Service of America Inc.
U.S. Bancorp Piper Jaffray
United States Sugar Corp.
Universal Studios
Unocal Corp.
Valspar Corp.
Waffle House Inc.
Walter Industries Inc.
Weil, Gotshal & Manges Corp.
West Co. Inc.
Whirlpool Corp.
Winn-Dixie Stores Inc.
Wisconsin Public Service Corp.
Zachry Co. (H.B.)

CAMPS

Alcon Laboratories, Inc.
Andersen Corp.
Andersons Inc.
Arvin Industries, Inc.
Atlantic Investment Co.
Bandag, Inc.
Bassett Furniture Industries
Baxter International Inc.
Bemis Manufacturing Co.
Block, Inc. (H&R)
Blue Cross & Blue Shield of Alabama
Boston Globe (The)
Cabot Corp.
Central National-Gottesman
Citizens Bank-Flint
Citizens Financial Group, Inc.
Commercial Intertech Corp.
Consolidated Papers, Inc.
Consumers Energy Co.
Contran Corp.
Cox Enterprises Inc.
CPI Corp.
Cummings Properties Management
CUNA Mutual Group
Dana Corp.
Delta Air Lines, Inc.
Deluxe Corp.
Demoulas Supermarkets Inc.
Deutsch Co.
Disney Co. (Walt)
Dow Chemical Co.
Dynamet, Inc.
Eastern Bank
Ensign-Bickford Industries
Equifax Inc.
Erb Lumber Co.
Fabri-Kal Corp.
Federated Mutual Insurance Co.
Fidelity Investments
Ford Motor Co.
Forest City Enterprises, Inc.
Fortis Insurance Co.
Freddie Mac
Freeport-McMoRan Inc.
Fuller Co. (H.B.)
Gap, Inc.
Georgia-Pacific Corp.
Georgia Power Co.
Green Bay Packaging
Hanna Co. (M.A.)
Hannaford Brothers Co.
Harnischfeger Industries
Hartford (The)
Hartmarx Corp.
Hensel Phelps Construction Co.
Hickory Tech Corp.
Hofmann Co.
Hubbard Broadcasting, Inc.
Huntington Bancshares Inc.
IKON Office Solutions, Inc.
Invacare Corp.
Jacobs Engineering Group
Jacobson & Sons (Benjamin)
Jostens, Inc.
Journal-Gazette Co.
Kellwood Co.
Kennametal, Inc.
Kingsbury Corp.
Lehigh Portland Cement Co.
Leigh Fibers, Inc.
Lilly & Co. (Eli)
Lincoln Electric Co.
Little, Inc. (Arthur D.)
Liz Claiborne, Inc.
Loews Corp.
Lotus Development Corp.
Mattel Inc.
McDonald & Co. Securities, Inc.
McKesson-HBOC Corp.
National Service Industries, Inc.
Nationwide Insurance Co.
New England Financial
New York Mercantile Exchange
New York Stock Exchange, Inc.
Newman's Own Inc.
Norton Co.
Occidental Oil and Gas
OG&E Electric Services
Oshkosh B'Gosh, Inc.
Overseas Shipholding Group Inc.
Park National Bank
Pella Corp.
PEMCO Corp.
Pharmacia & Upjohn, Inc.
Pheonix Financial Group
Physicians Mutual Insurance Co.
Polaroid Corp.
Premier Dental Products Co.
Putnam Investments
Rayonier Inc.
Regions Bank
Reilly Industries, Inc.
Reynolds Tobacco (R.J.)
Russer Foods
Seagram & Sons, Inc. (Joseph E.)
Sega of America Inc.
Sentry Insurance, A Mutual Co.
Sierra Pacific Resources
SmithKline Beecham Corp.
Sonoco Products Co.
Southeastern Mutual Insurance Co.
Sprint Corp.
Star Bank NA
Steelcase Inc.
Stride Rite Corp.
Stupp Brothers Bridge & Iron Co.
Temple-Inland Inc.
Times Mirror Co.
Titan Industrial Corp.
TJX Companies, Inc.
Trace International Holdings, Inc.
Transamerica Corp.
United Distillers & Vintners North America
United Dominion Industries, Ltd.
Unocal Corp.
US Bank, Washington
USG Corp.
Waffle House Inc.
Washington Mutual, Inc.
Weil, Gotshal & Manges Corp.
Wiremold Co.
Witco Corp.
Yellow Corp.

York Federal Savings & Loan Association
Zachry Co. (H.B.)

CHILD ABUSE

Aetna, Inc.
Alma Piston Co.
American Fidelity Corp.
Amgen, Inc.
AMP Inc.
APL Ltd.
Avon Products, Inc.
Bank of America
BankBoston Corp.
Baxter International Inc.
Bernstein & Co., Inc. (Sanford C.)
Blue Bell, Inc.
Blue Cross & Blue Shield of Iowa
Broderbund Software, Inc.
Callaway Golf Co.
Carillon Importers, Ltd.
Carris Reels
CertainTeed Corp.
Chicago Sun-Times, Inc.
Chicago Tribune Co.
Citigroup
CNA
Comdisco, Inc.
Constellation Energy Group, Inc.
Copley Press, Inc.
Crane Co.
Crane & Co., Inc.
Dial Corp.
Dreyer's Grand Ice Cream
DSM Copolymer
El Paso Energy Co.
Erving Industries
Fidelity Investments
First Maryland Bancorp
First Source Corp.
Ford Meter Box Co.
Freddie Mac
Fuller Co. (H.B.)
Gallo Winery, Inc. (E&J)
GATX Corp.
Georgia Power Co.
Gerber Products Co.
Hunt Manufacturing Co.
International Flavors & Fragrances Inc.
Jostens, Inc.
Journal-Gazette Co.
Katten, Muchin & Zavis
Leigh Fibers, Inc.
Little, Inc. (Arthur D.)
Liz Claiborne, Inc.
Marcus Corp.
Menasha Corp.
Michigan Consolidated Gas Co.
Minnesota Mutual Life Insurance Co.
Montgomery Ward & Co., Inc.
Morris Communications Corp.
National Service Industries, Inc.
Nationwide Insurance Co.
Newman's Own Inc.
Oklahoma Publishing Co.
Oshkosh B'Gosh, Inc.
Pacific Mutual Life Insurance Co.
PacifiCare Health Systems
Pella Corp.
Price Associates (T. Rowe)
Prudential Insurance Co. of America
Putnam Investments
Ralph's Grocery Co.
Rayonier Inc.
Royal & SunAlliance USA, Inc.
Sega of America Inc.
Servco Pacific
Simpson Investment Co.
Sony Electronics
Southeastern Mutual Insurance Co.
SPX Corp.
State Street Bank & Trust Co.
Steelcase Inc.
Stride Rite Corp.
Synovus Financial Corp.
Tomkins Industries, Inc.
United Distillers & Vintners North America
United Parcel Service of America Inc.
Waffle House Inc.
Whitman Corp.
WICOR, Inc.
Wrigley Co. (Wm. Jr.)

CHILD WELFARE

ABB Inc.
Abbott Laboratories
ABC
Advanced Micro Devices, Inc.
AEGON U.S.A. Inc.
Aetna, Inc.
AFLAC Inc.
AGL Resources Inc.
Agrilink Foods, Inc.
Air Products and Chemicals, Inc.
AK Steel Corp.
Alabama Power Co.
Albertson's Inc.
Alcoa Inc.
Alcon Laboratories, Inc.
Alexander & Baldwin, Inc.
Allegheny Technologies Inc.
Alliant Techsystems
AlliedSignal Inc.
Allmerica Financial Corp.
Alma Piston Co.
AMCORE Bank Rockford
Ameren Corp.
American Express Co.
American Fidelity Corp.
American Stock Exchange, Inc.
American United Life Insurance Co.
AMETEK, Inc.
Amgen, Inc.
AMP Inc.
AMR Corp.
Amsted Industries Inc.
Andersen Corp.
Andersons Inc.
Anheuser-Busch Companies, Inc.
Aon Corp.
APL Ltd.
Appleton Papers Inc.
Archer-Daniels-Midland Co.
Arizona Public Service Co.
Armstrong World Industries, Inc.
Ashland, Inc.
AT&T Corp.
Atlantic Investment Co.
Atlantic Richfield Co.
Avon Products, Inc.
Badger Meter, Inc.
Baird & Co. (Robert W.)
Bandag, Inc.
Banfi Vintners
Bank of America
Bank of New York Co., Inc.
Bank One Corp.
BankAtlantic Bancorp
BankBoston Corp.
Banta Corp.
Barclays Capital
Barden Corp.
Bardes Corp.
Barnes Group Inc.
Barry Corp. (R.G.)
Battelle Memorial Institute
Bausch & Lomb Inc.
Baxter International Inc.
Bechtel Group, Inc.
Belk-Simpson Department Stores
Belk Stores Services Inc.
Bell Atlantic Corp.
Bemis Co., Inc.
Bemis Manufacturing Co.
Ben & Jerry's Homemade Inc.
Bernstein & Co., Inc. (Sanford C.)
Berwind Group
Bestfoods
Bethlehem Steel Corp.
Binney & Smith Inc.
Binswanger Companies
Blair & Co. (William)
Block, Inc. (H&R)
Blount International, Inc.
Blue Bell, Inc.
Blue Cross & Blue Shield of Alabama
Blue Cross & Blue Shield of Iowa
Blue Cross & Blue Shield of Minnesota
Boeing Co.
Borden, Inc.
Borman's Inc.
Boston Globe (The)
BP Amoco Corp.
Bridgestone/Firestone, Inc.
Briggs & Stratton Corp.
Broderbund Software, Inc.
Brown & Williamson Tobacco Corp.
Brunswick Corp.
Bucyrus-Erie Co.
Burlington Resources, Inc.
Burnett Co. (Leo)
Burress (J.W.)
Butler Manufacturing Co.
Cabot Corp.
Callaway Golf Co.
Calvin Klein
Cargill Inc.
Carillon Importers, Ltd.
Carlson Companies, Inc.
Carolina Power & Light Co.
Carpenter Technology Corp.
Carrier Corp.
Carris Reels
Caterpillar Inc.
CCB Financial Corp.
Central Maine Power Co.
Central National-Gottesman
Central Soya Co.
Century 21
CertainTeed Corp.
Cessna Aircraft Co.
CGU Insurance
Chase Bank of Texas
Chase Manhattan Bank, NA
Chemed Corp.
Chevron Corp.
Chicago Board of Trade
Chicago Sun-Times, Inc.
Chicago Title Corp.
Chicago Tribune Co.
CIGNA Corp.
Cincinnati Bell Inc.
Cinergy Corp.
Circuit City Stores, Inc.
CIT Group, Inc. (The)
Citibank Corp.
Citigroup
Citizens Bank-Flint
Citizens Financial Group, Inc.
CLARCOR Inc.
Cleveland-Cliffs, Inc.
Clorox Co.
CNA
Colonial Life & Accident Insurance Co.
Colonial Oil Industries, Inc.
Comdisco, Inc.
Commerce Bancshares, Inc.
Commercial Intertech Corp.
Compaq Computer Corp.
Compass Bank
ConAgra, Inc.
Cone Mills Corp.
Consolidated Electrical Distributors
Consolidated Natural Gas Co.
Constellation Energy Group, Inc.
Continental Grain Co.
Contran Corp.
Conwood Co. LP
Cooper Industries, Inc.
Copley Press, Inc.
Country Curtains, Inc.
CPI Corp.
Crane Co.
Crane & Co., Inc.
Credit Suisse First Boston
Crestar Finance Corp.
Cummings Properties Management
Cummins Engine Co., Inc.
CUNA Mutual Group
Daily News
DaimlerChrysler Corp.
Dain Bosworth Inc.
Dana Corp.
Danis Companies
Dayton Hudson
Dayton Power and Light Co.
Deere & Co.
Delta Air Lines, Inc.
Deluxe Corp.
Deposit Guaranty National Bank
Detroit Edison Co.
Deutsch Co.
Dexter Corp.
Dial Corp.
Disney Co. (Walt)
Dixie Group, Inc. (The)
Dominion Resources, Inc.
Donaldson Co., Inc.
Dow Jones & Co., Inc.
du Pont de Nemours & Co. (E.I.)
Duchossois Industries Inc.
Duke Energy
Dun & Bradstreet Corp.
Dynamet, Inc.
Eastern Bank
Eastman Kodak Co.
Eaton Corp.
Eckerd Corp.
Ecolab Inc.
Edison International
Edwards Enterprise Software (J.D.)
El Paso Energy Co.
Emerson Electric Co.
Employers Mutual Casualty Co.
Ensign-Bickford Industries
Entergy Corp.
Enterprise Rent-A-Car Co.
Equifax Inc.
Erb Lumber Co.
Erving Industries
European American Bank
Extendicare Health Services
Exxon Mobil Corp.
Fabri-Kal Corp.
Federal-Mogul Corp.
Federated Department Stores, Inc.
Ferro Corp.
Fidelity Investments
Fifth Third Bancorp
FINA
Fireman's Fund Insurance Co.
First Hawaiian, Inc.
First Union Bank
First Union Corp.
First Union National Bank, NA
First Union Securities, Inc.
Firstar Bank Milwaukee NA
FleetBoston Financial Corp.
Florida Power & Light Co.
Florida Rock Industries
Fluor Corp.
FMC Corp.
Forbes Inc.
Ford Meter Box Co.
Ford Motor Co.
Forest City Enterprises, Inc.
Fort Worth Star-Telegram Inc.
Fortis, Inc.
Fortis Insurance Co.
Fortune Brands, Inc.
Fox Entertainment Group
Franklin Electric Co.
Franklin Mint (The)
Freddie Mac
Freeport-McMoRan Inc.
Frost National Bank
Fuller Co. (H.B.)
Furniture Brands International, Inc.
Gallo Winery, Inc. (E&J)
Galter Corp.
Gap, Inc.
GATX Corp.
GEICO Corp.
GenAmerica Corp.
General Atlantic Partners II LP
General Dynamics Corp.
General Electric Co.
General Mills, Inc.
General Motors Corp.
Georgia-Pacific Corp.
Georgia Power Co.
Gerber Products Co.
Giant Eagle Inc.
Giant Food Inc.
Giddings & Lewis
Glaxo Wellcome Inc.
Glickenhaus & Co.
Goldman Sachs Group
Grace & Co. (W.R.)
Graco, Inc.
Grede Foundries
Green Bay Packaging
GTE Corp.

Funders by Recipient Type

Gucci America Inc.
Guess?
Gulf Power Co.
Gulfstream Aerospace Corp.
Hamilton Sundstrand Corp.
Hancock Financial Services (John)
Hanna Co. (M.A.)
Hannaford Brothers Co.
Harcourt General, Inc.
Harley-Davidson Co.
Harnischfeger Industries
Harris Corp.
Harris Trust & Savings Bank
Harsco Corp.
Hartford (The)
Hartmarx Corp.
Hasbro, Inc.
Heinz Co. (H.J.)
Hitachi America Ltd.
Hofmann Co.
Home Depot, Inc.
Honeywell International Inc.
Housatonic Curtain Co.
Household International Inc.
Hubbard Broadcasting, Inc.
Hubbell Inc.
Huffy Corp.
Humana, Inc.
Hunt Manufacturing Co.
Idaho Power Co.
Illinois Tool Works, Inc.
Independent Stave Co.
Inland Container Corp.
International Business Machines Corp.
International Flavors & Fragrances Inc.
International Multifoods Corp.
International Paper Co.
INTRUST Financial Corp.
Invacare Corp.
Jacobs Engineering Group
Jacobson & Sons (Benjamin)
Jeld-wen, Inc.
Johnson Controls Inc.
Johnson & Son (S.C.)
Jostens, Inc.
Journal-Gazette Co.
Katten, Muchin & Zavis
Kellwood Co.
Kelly Services
Kimberly-Clark Corp.
Kinder Morgn
Koch Industries, Inc.
Kraft Foods, Inc.
Kroger Co.
Laclede Gas Co.
Ladish Co., Inc.
Lancaster Lens, Inc.
Lance, Inc.
Land O'Lakes, Inc.
Landmark Communications Inc.
Lee Enterprises
Lehigh Portland Cement Co.
Leigh Fibers, Inc.
Levi Strauss & Co.
LG&E Energy Corp.
Liberty Corp.
Liberty Diversified Industries
Lilly & Co. (Eli)
Lincoln Electric Co.
Lincoln Financial Group
Little, Inc. (Arthur D.)
Litton Industries, Inc.
Liz Claiborne, Inc.
Loews Corp.
Lotus Development Corp.
Louisiana Land & Exploration Co.
Louisiana-Pacific Corp.
LTV Corp.
MacMillan Bloedel Inc.
Macy's East Inc.
Madison Gas & Electric Co.
Mamiye Brothers
Marcus Corp.
Maritz Inc.
Mark IV Industries
Marshall & Ilsley Corp.
Mattel Inc.
May Department Stores Co.
Mazda North American Operations
McClatchy Co.
McDonald & Co. Securities, Inc.
McDonald's Corp.
MCI WorldCom, Inc.
McKesson-HBOC Corp.
Mead Corp.
Menasha Corp.
Mercantile Bank NA
Merck & Co.
Merit Oil Corp.
Merrill Lynch & Co., Inc.
Metropolitan Life Insurance Co.
MidAmerican Energy Holdings Co.
Milacron, Inc.
Milliken & Co.
Mine Safety Appliances Co.
Minnesota Mining & Manufacturing Co.
Mitsubishi Electric America
Monarch Machine Tool Co.
Monsanto Co.
Montana Power Co.
Montgomery Ward & Co., Inc.
MONY Group (The)
Morgan & Co. Inc. (J.P.)
Morgan Stanley Dean Witter & Co.
Morris Communications Corp.
Morrison Knudsen Corp.
Motorola Inc.
MTD Products Inc.
Nabisco Group Holdings
Nalco Chemical Co.
National City Bank of Minneapolis
National Computer Systems, Inc.
National Machinery Co.
National Service Industries, Inc.
National Starch & Chemical Co.
Nationwide Insurance Co.
NEBCO Evans
Nestle U.S.A. Inc.
New Century Energies
New England Bio Labs
New Jersey Natural Gas Co.
New York Life Insurance Co.
New York Mercantile Exchange
New York Stock Exchange, Inc.
Newman's Own Inc.
Niagara Mohawk Holdings Inc.
Nike, Inc.
Nordson Corp.
Norfolk Southern Corp.
Northeast Utilities
Northern States Power Co.
Northern Trust Co.
Northwest Bank Nebraska, NA
Northwest Natural Gas Co.
Norton Co.
Norwest Corp.
Occidental Oil and Gas
Oklahoma Publishing Co.
Orscheln Co.
Oshkosh B'Gosh, Inc.
Overseas Shipholding Group Inc.
PACCAR Inc.
Pacific Century Financial Corp.
Pacific Mutual Life Insurance Co.
PacifiCare Health Systems
PacifiCorp
Paine Webber
PECO Energy Co.
Pella Corp.
PEMCO Corp.
Pennzoil-Quaker State Co.
Peoples Energy Corp.
PepsiCo, Inc.
Pfizer Inc.
Phillips Petroleum Co.
Physicians Mutual Insurance Co.
Pieper Power Electric Co.
Pillsbury Co.
Pittway Corp.
PNC Financial Services Group
Polaroid Corp.
Portland General Electric Co.
Potlatch Corp.
Potomac Electric Power Co.
PPG Industries, Inc.
Premier Industrial Corp.
Price Associates (T. Rowe)
Principal Financial Group
Procter & Gamble Co.
Procter & Gamble Co., Cosmetics Division
Providence Journal-Bulletin Co.
Prudential Insurance Co. of America
Public Service Electric & Gas Co.
Publix Supermarkets
Pulitzer Publishing Co.
Putnam Investments
Quaker Chemical Corp.
Questar Corp.
Ralph's Grocery Co.
Ralston Purina Co.
Rayonier Inc.
Red Wing Shoe Co. Inc.
Reebok International Ltd.
Regis Corp.
Reilly Industries, Inc.
Reily & Co., Inc. (William B.)
Reliant Energy Inc.
Reynolds Metals Co.
Reynolds Tobacco (R.J.)
Rich Products Corp.
Rockwell International Corp.
Rouse Co.
Royal & SunAlliance USA, Inc.
Rubbermaid Inc.
Ruddick Corp.
Russer Foods
Ryder System, Inc.
Saint Paul Companies Inc.
S&T Bancorp
Sara Lee Corp.
Sara Lee Hosiery, Inc.
SBC Communications Inc.
Schering-Plough Corp.
Schloss & Co. (Marcus)
Schwab & Co., Inc. (Charles)
Schwebel Baking Co.
Scripps Co. (E.W.)
Seagram & Sons, Inc. (Joseph E.)
Searle & Co. (G.D.)
Seaway Food Town, Inc.
Security Benefit Life Insurance Co.
Sega of America Inc.
Sempra Energy
Sentinel Communications Co.
S.G. Cowen
Shaw's Supermarkets, Inc.
Shea Co. (John F.)
Shell Oil Co.
Shelter Mutual Insurance Co.
Shoney's Inc.
Sierra Pacific Industries
Simpson Investment Co.
SIT Investment Associates, Inc.
Slant/Fin Corp.
Smith Corp. (A.O.)
Smurfit-Stone Container Corp.
Sonoco Products Co.
Sony Electronics
South Bend Tribune Corp.
Southeastern Mutual Insurance Co.
Southern New England Telephone Co.
Southwest Gas Corp.
Sovereign Bank
Sprint Corp.
Sprint/United Telephone
Square D Co.
Star Bank NA
Starwood Hotels & Resorts Worldwide, Inc.
State Farm Mutual Automobile Insurance Co.
State Street Bank & Trust Co.
Steelcase Inc.
Stone Container Corp.
Stonecutter Mills Corp.
Storage Technology Corp.
Strear Farms Co.
Stride Rite Corp.
Stupp Brothers Bridge & Iron Co.
SunTrust Bank Atlanta
SunTrust Banks of Florida
Sverdrup Corp.
Synovus Financial Corp.
Taco Bell Corp.
Tandy Corp.
TCF National Bank Minnesota
Tektronix, Inc.
Teleflex Inc.
Temple-Inland Inc.
Tenet Healthcare Corp.
TENNANT Co.
Tension Envelope Corp.
Tesoro Hawaii
Texaco Inc.
Texas Gas Transmission Corp.
Textron Inc.
Thermo Electron Corp.
Thomasville Furniture Industries Inc.
Times Mirror Co.
Titan Industrial Corp.
TJX Companies, Inc.
Toledo Blade Co.
Tomkins Industries, Inc.
Toyota Motor Sales U.S.A., Inc.
Trace International Holdings, Inc.
Transamerica Corp.
True North Communications, Inc.
True Oil Co.
Trustmark Insurance Co.
TRW Inc.
Ukrop's Super Markets
Unilever Home & Personal Care U.S.A.
Union Camp Corp.
Union Carbide Corp.
Union Pacific Corp.
United Airlines Inc.
United Co.
United Distillers & Vintners North America
United Dominion Industries, Ltd.
United Parcel Service of America Inc.
U.S. Bancorp
U.S. Bancorp Piper Jaffray
United States Sugar Corp.
United States Trust Co. of New York
United Technologies Corp.
Universal Leaf Tobacco Co., Inc.
Universal Studios
Unocal Corp.
UnumProvident
US Bank, Washington
US West, Inc.
Valmont Industries, Inc.
Valspar Corp.
Varian Medical Systems, Inc.
Vulcan Materials Co.
Wachovia Bank of North Carolina NA
Waffle House Inc.
Wal-Mart Stores, Inc.
Waldbaum's Supermarkets, Inc.
Walgreen Co.
Walter Industries Inc.
Warner-Lambert Co.
Washington Mutual, Inc.
The Washington Post
Washington Trust Bank
Weil, Gotshal & Manges Corp.
Wells Fargo & Co.
Western & Southern Life Insurance Co.
Weyerhaeuser Co.
Whirlpool Corp.
Whitman Corp.
WICOR, Inc.
Williams
Winn-Dixie Stores Inc.
Wiremold Co.
Wisconsin Energy Corp.
Wisconsin Power & Light Co.
Witco Corp.
Wolverine World Wide
Woodward Governor Co.
Wrigley Co. (Wm. Jr.)
Wyman-Gordon Co.
Xerox Corp.
York Federal Savings & Loan Association
Young & Rubicam
Zachry Co. (H.B.)
Zilkha & Sons

COMMUNITY CENTERS

Abbott Laboratories
Advanced Micro Devices, Inc.
AGL Resources Inc.
Agrilink Foods, Inc.
Alabama Power Co.
Albertson's Inc.
Alcoa Inc.
Alcon Laboratories, Inc.
Alexander & Baldwin, Inc.
Allegheny Technologies Inc.
AlliedSignal Inc.
Allmerica Financial Corp.
AMCORE Bank Rockford
Ameren Corp.
American Express Co.
American Retail Group
American United Life Insurance Co.
Ameritech Indiana
Ameritech Wisconsin
AmerUS Group
AMP Inc.
Andersen Corp.
Andersons Inc.
Aon Corp.
APL Ltd.
Avon Products, Inc.
Badger Meter, Inc.
Baird & Co. (Robert W.)
Bandag, Inc.
Banfi Vintners
BankBoston Corp.
Barden Corp.
Barry Corp. (R.G.)
Bassett Furniture Industries
Bausch & Lomb Inc.
Bemis Co., Inc.
Ben & Jerry's Homemade Inc.
Bernstein & Co., Inc. (Sanford C.)
Berwind Group
Bestfoods
Bethlehem Steel Corp.
BFGoodrich Co.
Binney & Smith Inc.
Blair & Co. (William)
Block, Inc. (H&R)
Blount International, Inc.
Blue Bell, Inc.
Boeing Co.
Boise Cascade Corp.
Borman's Inc.
Boston Edison Co.
Boston Globe (The)
BP Amoco Corp.
Bradford & Co. (J.C.)
Bridgestone/Firestone, Inc.
Briggs & Stratton Corp.
Brown & Williamson Tobacco Corp.
Brunswick Corp.
Bucyrus-Erie Co.
Burlington Industries, Inc.
Burnett Co. (Leo)
Burress (J.W.)
Business Improvement
Cabot Corp.
Campbell Soup Co.
Cargill Inc.
Carrier Corp.
Caterpillar Inc.
Central Maine Power Co.
Century 21
CertainTeed Corp.
Chase Bank of Texas
Chase Manhattan Bank, NA
Chevron Corp.
Cincinnati Bell Inc.
Circuit City Stores, Inc.
CIT Group, Inc. (The)
Citibank Corp.
Citigroup
Citizens Financial Group, Inc.
CLARCOR Inc.
Clark Refining & Marketing
Clorox Co.
Colonial Life & Accident Insurance Co.
Commerce Bancshares, Inc.
Compass Bank
Consolidated Natural Gas Co.
Consumers Energy Co.
Cooper Industries, Inc.
Copley Press, Inc.
Corning Inc.
Country Curtains, Inc.
Crane & Co., Inc.
Credit Suisse First Boston
Cummins Engine Co., Inc.
CUNA Mutual Group
DaimlerChrysler Corp.
Dana Corp.
Dayton Hudson
Deere & Co.
DeKalb Genetics Corp.
Demoulas Supermarkets Inc.
Deposit Guaranty National Bank
Detroit Edison Co.
Deutsch Co.
Disney Co. (Walt)
Dixie Group, Inc. (The)
Donaldson Co., Inc.
Dow Chemical Co.
Dow Corning Corp.
du Pont de Nemours & Co. (E.I.)
Duke Energy
Dun & Bradstreet Corp.
Dynamet, Inc.
Eastern Bank
Eaton Corp.
Edison International
EDS Corp.
Emerson Electric Co.
Employers Mutual Casualty Co.
Ensign-Bickford Industries
Equifax Inc.
Extendicare Health Services
Federal-Mogul Corp.
Ferro Corp.
Fifth Third Bancorp
Fireman's Fund Insurance Co.
First American Corp.
First Financial Bank
First Hawaiian, Inc.
First Union Corp.
First Union National Bank, NA
First Union Securities, Inc.
Firstar Bank Milwaukee NA
FleetBoston Financial Corp.
Florida Rock Industries
Forbes Inc.
Fortis Insurance Co.
Fortune Brands, Inc.
Franklin Electric Co.
Frost National Bank
Fuller Co. (H.B.)
Furniture Brands International, Inc.
Gap, Inc.
GATX Corp.
GEICO Corp.
GenAmerica Corp.
GenCorp
General Electric Co.
General Mills, Inc.
General Motors Corp.
Georgia-Pacific Corp.
Georgia Power Co.
Giant Eagle Inc.
Giant Food Inc.
Glaxo Wellcome Inc.
Globe Corp.
Golub Corp.
Goodrich Aerospace - Aerostructures Group (B.F.)
Grace & Co. (W.R.)
Graco, Inc.
Grede Foundries
Green Bay Packaging
GTE Corp.
Hamilton Sundstrand Corp.
Hancock Financial Services (John)
Hanna Co. (M.A.)
Harley-Davidson Co.
Harnischfeger Industries
Harsco Corp.
Hartmarx Corp.
Hasbro, Inc.
Hawaiian Electric Co., Inc.
Heinz Co. (H.J.)
Hensel Phelps Construction Co.
Hitachi America Ltd.
Hoffer Plastics Corp.
Home Depot, Inc.
HON Industries Inc.
Honeywell International Inc.
Household International Inc.
Hubbell Inc.
Humana, Inc.
IKON Office Solutions, Inc.
Inland Container Corp.
Inman Mills
Intel Corp.
International Paper Co.
INTRUST Financial Corp.
Jacobs Engineering Group
Jeld-wen, Inc.
Johnson Controls Inc.
Jostens, Inc.
Kelly Services
Kerr-McGee Corp.
Key Bank of Cleveland
Kimberly-Clark Corp.
Kinder Morgn
Kingsbury Corp.
Kroger Co.
La-Z-Boy Inc.
Land O'Lakes, Inc.
Lee Enterprises
Leigh Fibers, Inc.
Lennox International, Inc.
Leviton Manufacturing Co. Inc.
Liberty Corp.
Lincoln Financial Group
Lipton Co.
Little, Inc. (Arthur D.)
Lotus Development Corp.
LTV Corp.
Lubrizol Corp. (The)
MacMillan Bloedel Inc.
Macy's East Inc.
Madison Gas & Electric Co.
Mallinckrodt Chemical, Inc.
Marcus Corp.
Marshall & Ilsley Corp.
Mattel Inc.
May Department Stores Co.
MBIA Inc.
McClatchy Co.
McDonald & Co. Securities, Inc.
McDonald's Corp.
McKesson-HBOC Corp.
Medtronic, Inc.
Mellon Financial Corp.
Mercantile Bank NA
Merrill Lynch & Co., Inc.
Michigan Consolidated Gas Co.
Mid-America Bank of Louisville
Milacron, Inc.
Milliken & Co.
Minnesota Mining & Manufacturing Co.
Monarch Machine Tool Co.
Montana Power Co.
MONY Group (The)
Morgan & Co. Inc. (J.P.)
Morris Communications Corp.
Morrison Knudsen Corp.
Nalco Chemical Co.
National City Bank of Minneapolis
National City Corp.
National Computer Systems, Inc.
National Fuel Gas Distribution Corp.
National Life of Vermont
National Machinery Co.
National Presto Industries, Inc.
National Service Industries, Inc.
National Starch & Chemical Co.
NEBCO Evans
Nestle U.S.A. Inc.
New England Bio Labs
New England Financial
New Jersey Natural Gas Co.
New York Life Insurance Co.
New York Mercantile Exchange
Newman's Own Inc.
Nissan North America, Inc.
Nordson Corp.
Northeast Utilities
Northern Indiana Public Service Co.
Northern States Power Co.
Northwest Bank Nebraska, NA
Northwest Natural Gas Co.
Norton Co.
Norwest Corp.
Occidental Oil and Gas
Ohio National Life Insurance Co.
Old Kent Bank
Olin Corp.
Owens Corning
PACCAR Inc.
Pacific Century Financial Corp.
PacifiCorp
Parker Hannifin Corp.
Pella Corp.
Peoples Energy Corp.
PerkinElmer, Inc.
Pfizer Inc.
Phillips Petroleum Co.
Pieper Power Electric Co.
Pillsbury Co.
PNC Financial Services Group
Portland General Electric Co.
PPG Industries, Inc.
Praxair
Premier Dental Products Co.
Premier Industrial Corp.
Procter & Gamble Co.
Providence Journal-Bulletin Co.
Prudential Insurance Co. of America
Rayonier Inc.
Red Wing Shoe Co. Inc.
Reebok International Ltd.
Regions Bank
Reilly Industries, Inc.
Reinhart Institutional Foods
Reliant Energy Inc.
Reynolds Tobacco (R.J.)
Rich Products Corp.
Royal & SunAlliance USA, Inc.
Rubbermaid Inc.
Saint Paul Companies Inc.
S&T Bancorp
Sara Lee Corp.
SBC Communications Inc.
Schwebel Baking Co.
Seaway Food Town, Inc.
Sempra Energy
Servco Pacific
Shell Oil Co.
Sherwin-Williams Co.
Shoney's Inc.
Simplot Co. (J.R.)
Simpson Investment Co.
SIT Investment Associates, Inc.
Slant/Fin Corp.
Smith Corp. (A.O.)
Solo Cup Co.
Sonoco Products Co.
Sovereign Bank
Springs Industries, Inc.
Square D Co.
Standard Products Co.
Star Bank NA
State Street Bank & Trust Co.
Steelcase Inc.
Stone Container Corp.
Stone & Webster Inc.
Stride Rite Corp.
Sun Microsystems Inc.
SunTrust Bank Atlanta
Synovus Financial Corp.
TCF National Bank Minnesota
Tenet Healthcare Corp.
TENNANT Co.
Tenneco Automotive
Tesoro Hawaii
Texas Instruments Inc.
Textron Inc.
Thomasville Furniture Industries Inc.
Thompson Co. (J. Walter)
Times Mirror Co.
TJX Companies, Inc.
Toledo Blade Co.
Tomkins Industries, Inc.
Trace International Holdings, Inc.
Transamerica Corp.
Trustmark Insurance Co.
Tyson Foods Inc.
Ultramar Diamond Shamrock Corp.
Unilever United States, Inc.
Union Camp Corp.
Union Carbide Corp.
Union Pacific Corp.
United Airlines Inc.
United Distillers & Vintners North America

United Parcel Service of America Inc.
U.S. Bancorp Piper Jaffray
United States Sugar Corp.
United States Trust Co. of New York
United Wisconsin Services
Universal Leaf Tobacco Co., Inc.
Universal Studios
US Bank, Washington
US West, Inc.
USX Corp.
Vulcan Materials Co.
Wachovia Bank of North Carolina NA
Wal-Mart Stores, Inc.
Warner-Lambert Co.
Washington Mutual, Inc.
Washington Trust Bank
West Co. Inc.
Weyerhaeuser Co.
Whirlpool Corp.
WICOR, Inc.
Wisconsin Energy Corp.
Wisconsin Power & Light Co.
Wisconsin Public Service Corp.
Woodward Governor Co.
York Federal Savings & Loan Association
Zachry Co. (H.B.)

COMMUNITY SERVICE ORGANIZATIONS

Abbott Laboratories
ABC
Advanced Micro Devices, Inc.
AEGON U.S.A. Inc.
AGL Resources Inc.
Agrilink Foods, Inc.
Air Products and Chemicals, Inc.
AK Steel Corp.
Alabama Power Co.
Albertson's Inc.
Alcoa Inc.
Alcon Laboratories, Inc.
Allegheny Technologies Inc.
AlliedSignal Inc.
Allmerica Financial Corp.
Allstate Insurance Co.
Alma Piston Co.
AMCORE Bank Rockford
Ameren Corp.
America West Airlines, Inc.
American Express Co.
American Fidelity Corp.
American General Finance
American Retail Group
American Standard Inc.
American United Life Insurance Co.
Ameritas Life Insurance Corp.
Ameritech Illinois
Ameritech Indiana
Ameritech Michigan
Ameritech Ohio
Ameritech Wisconsin
AMETEK, Inc.
Amgen, Inc.
AMP Inc.
AMR Corp.
Analog Devices, Inc.
Andersen Corp.
Andersons Inc.
Anheuser-Busch Companies, Inc.
Aon Corp.
APL Ltd.
Appleton Papers Inc.
Archer-Daniels-Midland Co.
Aristech Chemical Corp.
Arizona Public Service Co.
Armstrong World Industries, Inc.
Arvin Industries, Inc.
Associated Food Stores
AT&T Corp.
Atlantic Investment Co.
Atlantic Richfield Co.
Avista Corporation
Avon Products, Inc.
Badger Meter, Inc.
Baird & Co. (Robert W.)
Bandag, Inc.
Banfi Vintners
Bank of America
Bank of New York Co., Inc.
Bank One Corp.
Bank One, Texas-Houston Office
BankAtlantic Bancorp
BankBoston Corp.
Banta Corp.
Barclays Capital
Bard, Inc. (C.R.)
Barden Corp.
Bardes Corp.
Barnes Group Inc.
Barry Corp. (R.G.)
Bausch & Lomb Inc.
Baxter International Inc.
Bayer Corp.
Bean, Inc. (L.L.)
Belk-Simpson Department Stores
Bemis Co., Inc.
Bemis Manufacturing Co.
Ben & Jerry's Homemade Inc.
Bernstein & Co., Inc. (Sanford C.)
Bestfoods
Bethlehem Steel Corp.
BFGoodrich Co.
Binswanger Companies
Blair & Co. (William)
Block, Inc. (H&R)
Blount International, Inc.
Blue Bell, Inc.
Blue Cross & Blue Shield of Alabama
Blue Cross & Blue Shield of Iowa
Blue Cross & Blue Shield of Minnesota
Boeing Co.
Boler Co.
Borden, Inc.
Borman's Inc.
Boston Edison Co.
Boston Globe (The)
Bourns, Inc.
BP Amoco Corp.
Bradford & Co. (J.C.)
Bridgestone/Firestone, Inc.
Briggs & Stratton Corp.
Bristol-Myers Squibb Co.
Broderbund Software, Inc.
Brown Shoe Co., Inc.
Brown & Williamson Tobacco Corp.
Browning-Ferris Industries Inc.
Brunswick Corp.
Bucyrus-Erie Co.
Burlington Industries, Inc.
Burnett Co. (Leo)
Business Improvement
Butler Manufacturing Co.
Cabot Corp.
California Bank & Trust
Callaway Golf Co.
Calvin Klein
Campbell Soup Co.
Cantor, Fitzgerald Securities Corp.
Cargill Inc.
Carillon Importers, Ltd.
Carlson Companies, Inc.
Carnival Corp.
Carolina Power & Light Co.
Carpenter Technology Corp.
Carris Reels
Caterpillar Inc.
CBS Corp.
Central Maine Power Co.
Central National-Gottesman
Central Newspapers, Inc.
Central & South West Services
Central Soya Co.
Central Vermont Public Service Corp.
Century 21
CertainTeed Corp.
Cessna Aircraft Co.
CGU Insurance
Champion International Corp.
Chase Bank of Texas
Chase Manhattan Bank, NA
Chesapeake Corp.
Chevron Corp.
Chicago Board of Trade
Chicago Sun-Times, Inc.
Chicago Title Corp.
Chicago Tribune Co.
Church & Dwight Co., Inc.
CIGNA Corp.
Cincinnati Bell Inc.
CIT Group, Inc. (The)
Citibank Corp.
Citigroup
Citizens Bank-Flint
Citizens Financial Group, Inc.
CLARCOR Inc.
Clark Refining & Marketing
Cleveland-Cliffs, Inc.
Clorox Co.
CNA
CNF Transportation, Inc.
Colonial Life & Accident Insurance Co.
Colonial Oil Industries, Inc.
Comdisco, Inc.
Commerce Bancshares, Inc.
Commonwealth Edison Co.
Compaq Computer Corp.
Compass Bank
Consolidated Natural Gas Co.
Consolidated Papers, Inc.
Constellation Energy Group, Inc.
Consumers Energy Co.
Continental Grain Co.
Contran Corp.
Conwood Co. LP
Cooper Industries, Inc.
Copley Press, Inc.
Corning Inc.
Country Curtains, Inc.
Cox Enterprises Inc.
CPI Corp.
Crane Co.
Crane & Co., Inc.
Cranston Print Works Co.
Credit Suisse First Boston
Crestar Finance Corp.
Croft-Leominster
CSS Industries, Inc.
Cummings Properties Management
Cummins Engine Co., Inc.
CUNA Mutual Group
Curtis Industries, Inc. (Helene)
Daily News
DaimlerChrysler Corp.
Dain Bosworth Inc.
Dana Corp.
Danis Companies
Dayton Hudson
Dayton Power and Light Co.
Deere & Co.
Delta Air Lines, Inc.
Deluxe Corp.
Demoulas Supermarkets Inc.
Detroit Edison Co.
Deutsch Co.
Dexter Corp.
Dial Corp.
Disney Co. (Walt)
Dixie Group, Inc. (The)
Donaldson Co., Inc.
Dow Corning Corp.
Dow Jones & Co., Inc.
Dreyer's Grand Ice Cream
DSM Copolymer
du Pont de Nemours & Co. (E.I.)
Duchossois Industries Inc.
Duke Energy
Dun & Bradstreet Corp.
Duriron Co., Inc.
Dynamet, Inc.
Eastern Bank
Eastman Kodak Co.
Eaton Corp.
Eckerd Corp.
Ecolab Inc.
Edison Brothers Stores, Inc.
Edison International
EDS Corp.
Edwards Enterprise Software (J.D.)
El Paso Energy Co.
Elf Atochem North America, Inc.
Emerson Electric Co.
Employers Mutual Casualty Co.
Ensign-Bickford Industries
Enterprise Rent-A-Car Co.
Equifax Inc.
Equitable Resources, Inc.
Erb Lumber Co.
Ethyl Corp.
Evening Post Publishing Co.
Exxon Mobil Corp.
Fabri-Kal Corp.
Farmers Group, Inc.
Federal-Mogul Corp.
Federated Department Stores, Inc.
Federated Mutual Insurance Co.
FedEx Corp.
Ferro Corp.
Fidelity Investments
Fifth Third Bancorp
FINA
Fireman's Fund Insurance Co.
First American Corp.
First Financial Bank
First Hawaiian, Inc.
First Maryland Bancorp
First Source Corp.
First Tennessee National Corp.
First Union Bank
First Union Corp.
First Union National Bank, NA
First Union Securities, Inc.
Firstar Bank Milwaukee NA
Fisher Brothers Cleaning Services
Fisher Scientific
FleetBoston Financial Corp.
Florida Power Corp.
Florida Power & Light Co.
Florida Rock Industries
Fluor Corp.
FMC Corp.
Forbes Inc.
Ford Meter Box Co.
Ford Motor Co.
Forest City Enterprises, Inc.
Fort Worth Star-Telegram Inc.
Fortis, Inc.
Fortis Insurance Co.
Fortune Brands, Inc.
Freddie Mac
Freeport-McMoRan Inc.
Freightliner Corp.
Frost National Bank
Fuller Co. (H.B.)
Furniture Brands International, Inc.
Gallo Winery, Inc. (E&J)
Galter Corp.
Gannett Co., Inc.
Gap, Inc.
GATX Corp.
GEICO Corp.
GenAmerica Corp.
General Atlantic Partners II LP
General Electric Co.
General Mills, Inc.
General Motors Corp.
General Reinsurance Corp.
Georgia-Pacific Corp.
Georgia Power Co.
Gerber Products Co.
Giant Eagle Inc.
Giant Food Inc.
Giddings & Lewis
Glaxo Wellcome Inc.
Glickenhaus & Co.
Globe Corp.
Golub Corp.
Goodrich Aerospace - Aerostructures Group (B.F.)
Grace & Co. (W.R.)
Graco, Inc.
Grede Foundries
Green Bay Packaging
Group Health Plan
GTE Corp.
Guess?
Gulf Power Co.
Hallmark Cards Inc.
Hancock Financial Services (John)
Hanna Co. (M.A.)
Harcourt General, Inc.
Harland Co. (John H.)
Harley-Davidson Co.
Harris Corp.
Harris Trust & Savings Bank
Harsco Corp.
Hartford (The)
Hartmarx Corp.
Hasbro, Inc.
Hawaiian Electric Co., Inc.
Heinz Co. (H.J.)
Hensel Phelps Construction Co.
Hershey Foods Corp.

Hewlett-Packard Co.
Hickory Tech Corp.
Hitachi America Ltd.
Hoffer Plastics Corp.
Hoffmann-La Roche Inc.
Hofmann Co.
HON Industries Inc.
Honeywell International Inc.
Housatonic Curtain Co.
Household International Inc.
Hubbard Broadcasting, Inc.
Hubbell Inc.
Huffy Corp.
Hughes Electronics Corp.
Humana, Inc.
IBP
Idaho Power Co.
IKON Office Solutions, Inc.
Illinois Power Co.
Independent Stave Co.
Indiana Mills & Manufacturing
Inman Mills
Intel Corp.
International Business Machines Corp.
International Flavors & Fragrances Inc.
International Multifoods Corp.
International Paper Co.
INTRUST Financial Corp.
Invacare Corp.
Jacobs Engineering Group
Jacobson & Sons (Benjamin)
Johnson Controls Inc.
Johnson & Son (S.C.)
Jostens, Inc.
Journal-Gazette Co.
JSJ Corp.
Katten, Muchin & Zavis
Kellogg Co.
Kellwood Co.
Kelly Services
Kennametal, Inc.
Kerr-McGee Corp.
Kiewit Sons' Inc. (Peter)
Kimball International, Inc.
Kimberly-Clark Corp.
Kingsbury Corp.
Kmart Corp.
Koch Enterprises, Inc.
Koch Industries, Inc.
Kroger Co.
La-Z-Boy Inc.
Laclede Gas Co.
Ladish Co., Inc.
Lancaster Lens, Inc.
Lance, Inc.
LandAmerica Financial Services
Landmark Communications Inc.
Lee Enterprises
Lehigh Portland Cement Co.
Leigh Fibers, Inc.
Lennox International, Inc.
Levi Strauss & Co.
Leviton Manufacturing Co. Inc.
LG&E Energy Corp.
Liberty Corp.
Liberty Diversified Industries
Lilly & Co. (Eli)
Lincoln Electric Co.
Lincoln Financial Group
Lipton Co.
Little, Inc. (Arthur D.)
Litton Industries, Inc.
Liz Claiborne, Inc.
Loews Corp.
Lotus Development Corp.
Louisiana Land & Exploration Co.
Louisiana-Pacific Corp.
Lowe's Companies
LTV Corp.
Lubrizol Corp. (The)
Macy's East Inc.
Madison Gas & Electric Co.
Mallinckrodt Chemical, Inc.
Mamiye Brothers
Manulife Financial
Marcus Corp.
Mark IV Industries
Marriott International Inc.
Marshall Field's
Marshall & Ilsley Corp.
Masco Corp.
Mattel Inc.
May Department Stores Co.
MBIA Inc.
McClatchy Co.
McCormick & Co. Inc.
McDermott Inc.
McDonald & Co. Securities, Inc.
McGraw-Hill Companies, Inc.
McKesson-HBOC Corp.
McWane Inc.
Mead Corp.
Medtronic, Inc.
Menasha Corp.
Mercantile Bank NA
Merck & Co.
Meredith Corp.
Merit Oil Corp.
Metropolitan Life Insurance Co.
MGIC Investment Corp.
Michigan Consolidated Gas Co.
Microsoft Corp.
Mid-America Bank of Louisville
MidAmerican Energy Holdings Co.
Milliken & Co.
Millipore Corp.
Mine Safety Appliances Co.
Minnesota Mining & Manufacturing Co.
Minnesota Mutual Life Insurance Co.
Mitsubishi Electric America
Monarch Machine Tool Co.
Monsanto Co.
Montana Power Co.
Montgomery Ward & Co., Inc.
MONY Group (The)
Morgan & Co. Inc. (J.P.)
Morgan Stanley Dean Witter & Co.
Morris Communications Corp.
Morrison Knudsen Corp.
Motorola Inc.
MTD Products Inc.
Murphy Oil Corp.
Nalco Chemical Co.
National City Bank of Minneapolis
National City Corp.
National Machinery Co.
National Presto Industries, Inc.
National Service Industries, Inc.
National Starch & Chemical Co.
Nationwide Insurance Co.
NCR Corp.
NEBCO Evans
NEC America, Inc.
Nestle U.S.A. Inc.
New Century Energies
New England Bio Labs
New England Financial
New Jersey Natural Gas Co.
New York Life Insurance Co.
New York Mercantile Exchange
New York Stock Exchange, Inc.
New York Times Co.
Newman's Own Inc.
Niagara Mohawk Holdings Inc.
Nissan North America, Inc.
Nordson Corp.
Northeast Utilities
Northern Indiana Public Service Co.
Northern States Power Co.
Northern Trust Co.
Norton Co.
Norwest Corp.
Occidental Oil and Gas
OG&E Electric Services
Oklahoma Publishing Co.
Old Kent Bank
Old National Bank Evansville
Olin Corp.
Orscheln Co.
Osborne Enterprises
Oshkosh B'Gosh, Inc.
Outboard Marine Corp.
Overseas Shipholding Group Inc.
PACCAR Inc.
Pacific Century Financial Corp.
Pacific Mutual Life Insurance Co.
PacifiCare Health Systems
PacifiCorp
Paine Webber
Pan-American Life Insurance Co.
Park National Bank
Pella Corp.
PEMCO Corp.
Pennzoil-Quaker State Co.
Peoples Energy Corp.
PepsiCo, Inc.
PerkinElmer, Inc.
Pfizer Inc.
Phelps Dodge Corp.
Phillips Petroleum Co.
Physicians Mutual Insurance Co.
Pieper Power Electric Co.
Pillsbury Co.
Pitney Bowes Inc.
Pittway Corp.
Playboy Enterprises Inc.
PNC Bank
PNC Financial Services Group
Polaroid Corp.
Portland General Electric Co.
Potomac Electric Power Co.
PPG Industries, Inc.
Praxair
Premier Dental Products Co.
Premier Industrial Corp.
Price Associates (T. Rowe)
Principal Financial Group
Procter & Gamble Co.
Procter & Gamble Co., Cosmetics Division
Providence Journal-Bulletin Co.
Provident Companies, Inc.
Prudential Insurance Co. of America
Prudential Securities Inc.
Public Service Electric & Gas Co.
Publix Supermarkets
Pulitzer Publishing Co.
Putnam Investments
Quaker Chemical Corp.
Quanex Corp.
Ralph's Grocery Co.
Ralston Purina Co.
Rayonier Inc.
Red Wing Shoe Co. Inc.
Regions Bank
Regis Corp.
REI-Recreational Equipment, Inc.
Reilly Industries, Inc.
Reily & Co., Inc. (William B.)
Reinhart Institutional Foods
Reliant Energy Inc.
Reliant Energy Minnegasco
Revlon Inc.
Reynolds Metals Co.
Reynolds & Reynolds Co.
Reynolds Tobacco (R.J.)
Rich Products Corp.
Rockwell International Corp.
Rouse Co.
Royal & SunAlliance USA, Inc.
Rubbermaid Inc.
Ruddick Corp.
Russer Foods
Rutledge Hill Press
SAFECO Corp.
Safeguard Scientifics
Saint Paul Companies Inc.
S&T Bancorp
Sara Lee Corp.
Sara Lee Hosiery, Inc.
SBC Communications Inc.
Schloss & Co. (Marcus)
Schlumberger Ltd. (USA)
Schwab & Co., Inc. (Charles)
Schwebel Baking Co.
Scripps Co. (E.W.)
Seagram & Sons, Inc. (Joseph E.)
Sears, Roebuck and Co.
Seaway Food Town, Inc.
Security Benefit Life Insurance Co.
Sega of America Inc.
Sempra Energy
Sentinel Communications Co.
Sentry Insurance, A Mutual Co.
Servco Pacific
ServiceMaster Co.
S.G. Cowen
Sharp Electronics Corp.
Shaw's Supermarkets, Inc.
Shea Co. (John F.)
Shell Oil Co.
Shelter Mutual Insurance Co.
Shoney's Inc.
Sierra Pacific Industries
Sierra Pacific Resources
Simplot Co. (J.R.)
Simpson Investment Co.
SIT Investment Associates, Inc.
Slant/Fin Corp.
Smith Corp. (A.O.)
Smucker Co. (JM)
Smurfit-Stone Container Corp.
Solo Cup Co.
Sonoco Products Co.
Sony Electronics
Southeastern Mutual Insurance Co.
Southern New England Telephone Co.
Southwest Gas Corp.
Sovereign Bank
Sprint Corp.
SPX Corp.
Square D Co.
Standard Products Co.
Standard Register Co.
Stanley Works (The)
Star Bank NA
Starwood Hotels & Resorts Worldwide, Inc.
State Farm Mutual Automobile Insurance Co.
State Street Bank & Trust Co.
Steelcase Inc.
Stone Container Corp.
Stonecutter Mills Corp.
Storage Technology Corp.
Stride Rite Corp.
Stupp Brothers Bridge & Iron Co.
Sun Microsystems Inc.
Sunmark Capital Corp.
Sunoco Inc.
SunTrust Bank Atlanta
Susquehanna-Pfaltzgraff Co.
Synovus Financial Corp.
Taco Bell Corp.
Tai and Co. (J.T.)
Tamko Roofing Products
TCF National Bank Minnesota
Tektronix, Inc.
Teleflex Inc.
Temple-Inland Inc.
TENNANT Co.
Tenneco Automotive
Tenneco Packaging
Tension Envelope Corp.
Tesoro Hawaii
Texaco Inc.
Texas Gas Transmission Corp.
Texas Instruments Inc.
Textron Inc.
Thermo Electron Corp.
Thomasville Furniture Industries Inc.
Ticketmaster Corp.
Times Mirror Co.
Timken Co. (The)
Titan Industrial Corp.
TJX Companies, Inc.
TMC Investment Co.
Toledo Blade Co.
Tomkins Industries, Inc.
Torchmark Corp.
Toro Co.
Trace International Holdings, Inc.
Transamerica Corp.
True North Communications, Inc.
True Oil Co.
Trustmark Insurance Co.
TRW Inc.
Tyson Foods Inc.
Ukrop's Super Markets
Unilever Home & Personal Care U.S.A.
Unilever United States, Inc.
Union Camp Corp.
Union Carbide Corp.
Union Pacific Corp.

United Airlines Inc.
United Co.
United Distillers & Vintners North America
United Dominion Industries, Ltd.
United Parcel Service of America Inc.
U.S. Bancorp
U.S. Bancorp Piper Jaffray
United States Sugar Corp.
United States Trust Co. of New York
United Technologies Corp.
United Wisconsin Services
Universal Foods Corp.
Universal Leaf Tobacco Co., Inc.
Universal Studios
Unocal Corp.
UnumProvident
US Bank, Washington
US West, Inc.
USG Corp.
UST Inc.
USX Corp.
Valspar Corp.
Varian Medical Systems, Inc.
Vulcan Materials Co.
Wachovia Bank of North Carolina NA
Wachtell, Lipton, Rosen & Katz
Waffle House Inc.
Wal-Mart Stores, Inc.
Waldbaum's Supermarkets, Inc.
Walter Industries Inc.
Washington Mutual, Inc.
The Washington Post
Washington Trust Bank
Webster Bank
Weil, Gotshal & Manges Corp.
Wells Fargo & Co.
West Co. Inc.
Western Resources Inc.
Western & Southern Life Insurance Co.
Westvaco Corp.
Weyerhaeuser Co.
Whirlpool Corp.
Whitman Corp.
WICOR, Inc.
Wilbur-Ellis Co. & Connell Brothers Co.
Williams
Winn-Dixie Stores Inc.
Wiremold Co.
Wisconsin Energy Corp.
Wisconsin Power & Light Co.
Wisconsin Public Service Corp.
Witco Corp.
Wolverine World Wide
Woodward Governor Co.
Wrigley Co. (Wm. Jr.)
Wyman-Gordon Co.
Xerox Corp.
York Federal Savings & Loan Association
Young & Rubicam
Zachry Co. (H.B.)

COUNSELING

ABB Inc.
Air Products and Chemicals, Inc.
Alcoa Inc.
Alcon Laboratories, Inc.
Allegheny Technologies Inc.
Alliant Techsystems
AlliedSignal Inc.
Allstate Insurance Co.
AMCORE Bank Rockford
Ameren Corp.
American Express Co.
American Retail Group
American United Life Insurance Co.
AmerUS Group
AMR Corp.
Anheuser-Busch Companies, Inc.
Aon Corp.
Appleton Papers Inc.
Bandag, Inc.
Banta Corp.
Baxter International Inc.
Bemis Co., Inc.
Bernstein & Co., Inc. (Sanford C.)
Bethlehem Steel Corp.
Blair & Co. (William)
Block, Inc. (H&R)
Blue Bell, Inc.
Boston Edison Co.
Boston Globe (The)
Briggs & Stratton Corp.
Broderbund Software, Inc.
Cabot Corp.
Carter-Wallace, Inc.
Central Maine Power Co.
Chase Manhattan Bank, NA
Chemed Corp.
Cleveland-Cliffs, Inc.
Clorox Co.
CNA
Colonial Life & Accident Insurance Co.
Commerce Bancshares, Inc.
Compaq Computer Corp.
Consolidated Natural Gas Co.
Contran Corp.
Country Curtains, Inc.
Cox Enterprises Inc.
CPI Corp.
Cummins Engine Co., Inc.
Delta Air Lines, Inc.
Deluxe Corp.
Deutsch Co.
Donaldson Co., Inc.
du Pont de Nemours & Co. (E.I.)
Duke Energy
Eaton Corp.
Edison International
EDS Corp.
Edwards Enterprise Software (J.D.)
Exxon Mobil Corp.
First Union Corp.
FleetBoston Financial Corp.
Fort Worth Star-Telegram Inc.
Freddie Mac
Freeport-McMoRan Inc.
Frost National Bank
Gannett Co., Inc.
GATX Corp.
GEICO Corp.
GenAmerica Corp.
General Mills, Inc.
Giant Eagle Inc.
Glickenhaus & Co.
Golub Corp.
Goodrich Aerospace - Aerostructures Group (B.F.)
GTE Corp.
Gulf Power Co.
Hancock Financial Services (John)
Harcourt General, Inc.
Hawaiian Electric Co., Inc.
Heinz Co. (H.J.)
Hoffer Plastics Corp.
Hofmann Co.
Home Depot, Inc.
Household International Inc.
Hubbard Broadcasting, Inc.
Hunt Manufacturing Co.
Intel Corp.
Jacobs Engineering Group
Jacobson & Sons (Benjamin)
Johnson Controls Inc.
JSJ Corp.
Kimberly-Clark Corp.
Laclede Gas Co.
Lehigh Portland Cement Co.
Leigh Fibers, Inc.
Lennox International, Inc.
Little, Inc. (Arthur D.)
Louisiana Land & Exploration Co.
LTV Corp.
Macy's East Inc.
Mallinckrodt Chemical, Inc.
May Department Stores Co.
MBIA Inc.
McDonald & Co. Securities, Inc.
McKesson-HBOC Corp.
Metropolitan Life Insurance Co.
Minnesota Mining & Manufacturing Co.
Morgan & Co. Inc. (J.P.)
Motorola Inc.
Nalco Chemical Co.
National City Bank of Minneapolis
Nationwide Insurance Co.
NEBCO Evans
New England Financial
New York Life Insurance Co.
New York Mercantile Exchange
Nordson Corp.
Northeast Utilities
Northern Indiana Public Service Co.
Northern States Power Co.
Northwest Bank Nebraska, NA
Northwest Natural Gas Co.
Norton Co.
Pacific Mutual Life Insurance Co.
Paine Webber
Pfizer Inc.
Physicians Mutual Insurance Co.
Polaroid Corp.
Prudential Insurance Co. of America
Public Service Electric & Gas Co.
Putnam Investments
Quaker Chemical Corp.
Rayonier Inc.
Regions Bank
Reynolds Tobacco (R.J.)
Rockwell International Corp.
Royal & SunAlliance USA, Inc.
Sara Lee Corp.
Sara Lee Hosiery, Inc.
Schwebel Baking Co.
Sempra Energy
Shoney's Inc.
SIT Investment Associates, Inc.
Standard Register Co.
Star Bank NA
State Street Bank & Trust Co.
Steelcase Inc.
Stride Rite Corp.
Sun Microsystems Inc.
SunTrust Bank Atlanta
Synovus Financial Corp.
Tesoro Hawaii
Texas Gas Transmission Corp.
Texas Instruments Inc.
Textron Inc.
Thermo Electron Corp.
TJX Companies, Inc.
TMC Investment Co.
Transamerica Corp.
Unilever Home & Personal Care U.S.A.
Union Camp Corp.
United Distillers & Vintners North America
Universal Studios
US Bank, Washington
Varian Medical Systems, Inc.
Vulcan Materials Co.
Waffle House Inc.
Wal-Mart Stores, Inc.
Walter Industries Inc.
Washington Trust Bank
Westvaco Corp.
Whirlpool Corp.
Wisconsin Energy Corp.
Woodward Governor Co.

CRIME PREVENTION

AK Steel Corp.
Allstate Insurance Co.
AMCORE Bank Rockford
AMR Corp.
Barnes Group Inc.
Ben & Jerry's Homemade Inc.
Binswanger Companies
Block, Inc. (H&R)
Blue Cross & Blue Shield of Minnesota
Boston Globe (The)
Bradford & Co. (J.C.)
Bristol-Myers Squibb Co.
Butler Manufacturing Co.
Campbell Soup Co.
Cargill Inc.
Carillon Importers, Ltd.
Carter-Wallace, Inc.
CCB Financial Corp.
Central & South West Services
CGU Insurance
Chevron Corp.
Chicago Sun-Times, Inc.
Chicago Title Corp.
CIGNA Corp.
CLARCOR Inc.
Compaq Computer Corp.
Consolidated Papers, Inc.
Contran Corp.
CSS Industries, Inc.
Cummings Properties Management
Danis Companies
Deutsch Co.
Dial Corp.
DSM Copolymer
Ensign-Bickford Industries
Erving Industries
Ferro Corp.
First Source Corp.
Fisher Brothers Cleaning Services
Ford Meter Box Co.
Forest City Enterprises, Inc.
Fort Worth Star-Telegram Inc.
Fortis Insurance Co.
Freeport-McMoRan Inc.
Gallo Winery, Inc. (E&J)
Goldman Sachs Group
Guess?
Hallmark Cards Inc.
Hanna Co. (M.A.)
Harcourt General, Inc.
Harley-Davidson Co.
Harnischfeger Industries
Hartford (The)
Hartmarx Corp.
Hitachi America Ltd.
Honeywell International Inc.
Huffy Corp.
IKON Office Solutions, Inc.
International Multifoods Corp.
Invacare Corp.
Jeld-wen, Inc.
Johnson & Son (S.C.)
Journal-Gazette Co.
Kingsbury Corp.
La-Z-Boy Inc.
Lancaster Lens, Inc.
Lance, Inc.
Leigh Fibers, Inc.
Lincoln Electric Co.
Liz Claiborne, Inc.
Louisiana Land & Exploration Co.
LTV Corp.
Marcus Corp.
Mark IV Industries
McClatchy Co.
McWane Inc.
Merrill Lynch & Co., Inc.
Metropolitan Life Insurance Co.
Minnesota Mining & Manufacturing Co.
Minnesota Mutual Life Insurance Co.
Monsanto Co.
Morgan & Co. Inc. (J.P.)
Morgan Stanley Dean Witter & Co.
Motorola Inc.
National Machinery Co.
New York Life Insurance Co.
New York Mercantile Exchange
New York Stock Exchange, Inc.
New York Times Co.
Occidental Oil and Gas
Osborne Enterprises
PacifiCare Health Systems
Pella Corp.
PEMCO Corp.
Phillips Petroleum Co.
Pillsbury Co.
Polaroid Corp.
Praxair
Premier Industrial Corp.
Prudential Insurance Co. of America
Prudential Securities Inc.
Quanex Corp.
Ralph's Grocery Co.
Ralston Purina Co.
Red Wing Shoe Co. Inc.
Reily & Co., Inc. (William B.)
Reinhart Institutional Foods
Reynolds Tobacco (R.J.)
Royal & SunAlliance USA, Inc.
Safeguard Scientifics
S.G. Cowen
Shelter Mutual Insurance Co.

Sherwin-Williams Co.
Sierra Pacific Industries
Sierra Pacific Resources
SmithKline Beecham Corp.
Sovereign Bank
Sprint/United Telephone
SPX Corp.
Stonecutter Mills Corp.
Tamko Roofing Products
Temple-Inland Inc.
Tension Envelope Corp.
Thomasville Furniture Industries Inc.
Thompson Co. (J. Walter)
Timken Co. (The)
TJX Companies, Inc.
True North Communications, Inc.
True Oil Co.
United Airlines Inc.
Unocal Corp.
USG Corp.
Valmont Industries, Inc.
Van Leer Holding
Weil, Gotshal & Manges Corp.
Williams
Witco Corp.
Woodward Governor Co.
Yellow Corp.
York Federal Savings & Loan Association

DAY CARE

Air Products and Chemicals, Inc.
Alcoa Inc.
Allmerica Financial Corp.
AMCORE Bank Rockford
American Express Co.
American General Finance
American Retail Group
American United Life Insurance Co.
Ameritech Corp.
AmerUS Group
Amgen, Inc.
Archer-Daniels-Midland Co.
Arvin Industries, Inc.
AT&T Corp.
Badger Meter, Inc.
BankAtlantic Bancorp
Barden Corp.
Baxter International Inc.
BellSouth Corp.
Bemis Co., Inc.
Bethlehem Steel Corp.
Binswanger Companies
Blair & Co. (William)
Block, Inc. (H&R)
Blue Bell, Inc.
Blue Cross & Blue Shield of Alabama
Blue Cross & Blue Shield of Iowa
Blue Cross & Blue Shield of Minnesota
Borman's Inc.
Boston Globe (The)
Briggs & Stratton Corp.
Broderbund Software, Inc.
Brunswick Corp.
Bucyrus-Erie Co.
Business Improvement
Cabot Corp.
Calvin Klein
Cargill Inc.
Central Maine Power Co.
Central Soya Co.
Chase Manhattan Bank, NA
Chemed Corp.
Chevron Corp.
Citibank Corp.
Citigroup
Citizens Bank-Flint
Citizens Financial Group, Inc.
CLARCOR Inc.
Clorox Co.
Colonial Life & Accident Insurance Co.
Commercial Intertech Corp.
Compaq Computer Corp.
CPI Corp.
Crane & Co., Inc.
Cummins Engine Co., Inc.
CUNA Mutual Group
Dain Bosworth Inc.
Deere & Co.
DeKalb Genetics Corp.
Deluxe Corp.
Deutsch Co.
Dial Corp.
Donaldson Co., Inc.
Dow Chemical Co.
du Pont de Nemours & Co. (E.I.)
Eastman Kodak Co.
Ecolab Inc.
El Paso Energy Co.
Equifax Inc.
Exxon Mobil Corp.
Fireman's Fund Insurance Co.
First Hawaiian, Inc.
First Union Corp.
FleetBoston Financial Corp.
Fort Worth Star-Telegram Inc.
Fortis Insurance Co.
Fortune Brands, Inc.
Freddie Mac
Gap, Inc.
General Mills, Inc.
Georgia Power Co.
Glaxo Wellcome Inc.
Glickenhaus & Co.
Globe Corp.
Graco, Inc.
Green Bay Packaging
Group Health Plan
Hallmark Cards Inc.
Hamilton Sundstrand Corp.
Hannaford Brothers Co.
Harsco Corp.
Hartford (The)
Hasbro, Inc.
Hofmann Co.
Home Depot, Inc.
Hubbard Broadcasting, Inc.
Huffy Corp.
Industrial Bank of Japan Trust Co. (New York)
International Flavors & Fragrances Inc.
International Paper Co.
Invacare Corp.
Johnson & Son (S.C.)
Jostens, Inc.
Journal-Gazette Co.
JSJ Corp.
Kellwood Co.
Kingsbury Corp.
Kroger Co.
Ladish Co., Inc.
Land O'Lakes, Inc.
Lee Enterprises
Lehigh Portland Cement Co.
Levi Strauss & Co.
LG&E Energy Corp.
Lincoln Financial Group
Liz Claiborne, Inc.
Lotus Development Corp.
Louisiana Land & Exploration Co.
LTV Corp.
MacMillan Bloedel Inc.
Madison Gas & Electric Co.
Marcus Corp.
Marshall & Ilsley Corp.
MBIA Inc.
McClatchy Co.
McDonald & Co. Securities, Inc.
Merck & Co.
Mervyn's California
Minnesota Mining & Manufacturing Co.
Monsanto Co.
MONY Group (The)
Morgan & Co. Inc. (J.P.)
Morrison Knudsen Corp.
MTD Products Inc.
National City Bank of Minneapolis
National Computer Systems, Inc.
National Life of Vermont
Nationwide Insurance Co.
New England Financial
New Jersey Natural Gas Co.
New York Life Insurance Co.
New York Mercantile Exchange
New York Stock Exchange, Inc.
Nordson Corp.
Northern States Power Co.
Northern Trust Co.
Northwest Natural Gas Co.
Old National Bank Evansville
Orscheln Co.
Oshkosh B'Gosh, Inc.
PACCAR Inc.
Pacific Century Financial Corp.
Pacific Mutual Life Insurance Co.
Paine Webber
Pella Corp.
PEMCO Corp.
Penney Co., Inc. (J.C.)
Peoples Bank
Pillsbury Co.
Pitney Bowes Inc.
Pittway Corp.
Polaroid Corp.
PPG Industries, Inc.
Praxair
Principal Financial Group
Prudential Insurance Co. of America
Rayonier Inc.
Reilly Industries, Inc.
Reily & Co., Inc. (William B.)
Reynolds Metals Co.
Rubbermaid Inc.
SAFECO Corp.
Saint Paul Companies Inc.
Sara Lee Corp.
Sara Lee Hosiery, Inc.
Schloss & Co. (Marcus)
Schlumberger Ltd. (USA)
Schwab & Co., Inc. (Charles)
Seagram & Sons, Inc. (Joseph E.)
Sempra Energy
Shoney's Inc.
SIT Investment Associates, Inc.
Starwood Hotels & Resorts Worldwide, Inc.
Stride Rite Corp.
Sun Microsystems Inc.
Tesoro Hawaii
Texas Gas Transmission Corp.
Texas Instruments Inc.
Titan Industrial Corp.
True North Communications, Inc.
TRW Inc.
Unilever United States, Inc.
Union Camp Corp.
United Dominion Industries, Ltd.
United Parcel Service of America Inc.
U.S. Bancorp
United States Sugar Corp.
US Bank, Washington
Van Leer Holding
Wachovia Bank of North Carolina NA
Wal-Mart Stores, Inc.
Washington Mutual, Inc.
Whirlpool Corp.
Wisconsin Public Service Corp.
Young & Rubicam

DELINQUENCY & CRIMINAL REHABILITATION

Abbott Laboratories
AGL Resources Inc.
Agrilink Foods, Inc.
Air Products and Chemicals, Inc.
Alabama Power Co.
Alcoa Inc.
AlliedSignal Inc.
AMCORE Bank Rockford
Ameren Corp.
American Express Co.
American United Life Insurance Co.
Amsted Industries Inc.
Anheuser-Busch Companies, Inc.
Avon Products, Inc.
Baird & Co. (Robert W.)
Berwind Group
Bethlehem Steel Corp.
Binswanger Companies
Blair & Co. (William)
Block, Inc. (H&R)
Boeing Co.
Borman's Inc.
BP Amoco Corp.
Brunswick Corp.
Burlington Industries, Inc.
Carris Reels
Central Maine Power Co.
CGU Insurance
Chase Bank of Texas
Chase Manhattan Bank, NA
Chevron Corp.
Chicago Title Corp.
Chicago Tribune Co.
Cleveland-Cliffs, Inc.
Clorox Co.
CNA
Colonial Life & Accident Insurance Co.
CSS Industries, Inc.
Dana Corp.
Deposit Guaranty National Bank
Detroit Edison Co.
Dexter Corp.
Dial Corp.
Donaldson Co., Inc.
du Pont de Nemours & Co. (E.I.)
Eastern Bank
Eaton Corp.
Ecolab Inc.
Equifax Inc.
Erb Lumber Co.
Exxon Mobil Corp.
Federal-Mogul Corp.
FedEx Corp.
First Source Corp.
First Union Corp.
First Union National Bank, NA
Firstar Bank Milwaukee NA
FleetBoston Financial Corp.
Ford Motor Co.
Forest City Enterprises, Inc.
Fort James Corp.
Freddie Mac
Freeport-McMoRan Inc.
Frost National Bank
Furniture Brands International, Inc.
Gap, Inc.
GATX Corp.
General Mills, Inc.
Georgia Power Co.
Giant Eagle Inc.
Goodrich Aerospace - Aerostructures Group (B.F.)
Grace & Co. (W.R.)
Hallmark Cards Inc.
Hancock Financial Services (John)
Hartford (The)
Heinz Co. (H.J.)
Honeywell International Inc.
Household International Inc.
International Business Machines Corp.
Johnson & Son (S.C.)
Kimberly-Clark Corp.
Kinder Morgn
Kroger Co.
Levi Strauss & Co.
Lincoln Financial Group
Little, Inc. (Arthur D.)
Liz Claiborne, Inc.
Louisiana Land & Exploration Co.
LTV Corp.
Macy's East Inc.
Maritz Inc.
Mattel Inc.
McClatchy Co.
McDonald & Co. Securities, Inc.
McKesson-HBOC Corp.
Metropolitan Life Insurance Co.
Millipore Corp.
Minnesota Mining & Manufacturing Co.
Nalco Chemical Co.
National Computer Systems, Inc.
New England Financial
New York Mercantile Exchange
New York Times Co.
Newman's Own Inc.
Niagara Mohawk Holdings Inc.
Nordson Corp.
Northeast Utilities
Northern Indiana Public Service Co.
Northern States Power Co.
Northwest Natural Gas Co.
Norton Co.
Occidental Oil and Gas
Old National Bank Evansville
Osborne Enterprises

Outboard Marine Corp.
Pacific Mutual Life Insurance Co.
Pennzoil-Quaker State Co.
Pfizer Inc.
Physicians Mutual Insurance Co.
Pillsbury Co.
Pittway Corp.
Playboy Enterprises Inc.
PNC Financial Services Group
Portland General Electric Co.
Prudential Insurance Co. of America
Public Service Electric & Gas Co.
Ralston Purina Co.
Rayonier Inc.
Reily & Co., Inc. (William B.)
Reliant Energy Inc.
Rockwell International Corp.
SAFECO Corp.
Salomon Smith Barney
Searle & Co. (G.D.)
Sempra Energy
Sentry Insurance, A Mutual Co.
Shell Oil Co.
Shoney's Inc.
Sierra Pacific Resources
SIT Investment Associates, Inc.
Solo Cup Co.
Starwood Hotels & Resorts Worldwide, Inc.
State Street Bank & Trust Co.
Steelcase Inc.
Stride Rite Corp.
Sun Microsystems Inc.
SunTrust Bank Atlanta
Tenneco Automotive
Texaco Inc.
Texas Gas Transmission Corp.
TMC Investment Co.
Trustmark Insurance Co.
Ukrop's Super Markets
Union Camp Corp.
United Airlines Inc.
United States Trust Co. of New York
Universal Studios
USG Corp.
USX Corp.
Varian Medical Systems, Inc.
Vulcan Materials Co.
Wachovia Bank of North Carolina NA
Waffle House Inc.
Whirlpool Corp.
Williams
Wrigley Co. (Wm. Jr.)
Zachry Co. (H.B.)

DOMESTIC VIOLENCE

AEGON U.S.A. Inc.
Agrilink Foods, Inc.
Air Products and Chemicals, Inc.
Alcoa Inc.
AlliedSignal Inc.
Allmerica Financial Corp.
Allstate Insurance Co.
AMCORE Bank Rockford
American Express Co.
American General Finance
American Retail Group
American United Life Insurance Co.
APL Ltd.
Appleton Papers Inc.
Arizona Public Service Co.
Atlantic Richfield Co.
Avon Products, Inc.
Baird & Co. (Robert W.)
Bandag, Inc.
BankAtlantic Bancorp
Banta Corp.
Bard, Inc. (C.R.)
Baxter International Inc.
Bemis Co., Inc.
Bestfoods
Bethlehem Steel Corp.
Binney & Smith Inc.
Block, Inc. (H&R)
Blount International, Inc.
Blue Bell, Inc.
Blue Cross & Blue Shield of Iowa
Blue Cross & Blue Shield of Minnesota
Boeing Co.
Borden, Inc.
Borman's Inc.
Boston Globe (The)
Broderbund Software, Inc.
Brown Shoe Co., Inc.
Bucyrus-Erie Co.
Cabot Corp.
Callaway Golf Co.
Cargill Inc.
Central Maine Power Co.
CertainTeed Corp.
Charter Manufacturing Co.
Chase Manhattan Bank, NA
Chesapeake Corp.
Chevron Corp.
Chicago Sun-Times, Inc.
Chicago Tribune Co.
Citigroup
Clorox Co.
Colonial Life & Accident Insurance Co.
Commerce Bancshares, Inc.
Commercial Intertech Corp.
Consolidated Natural Gas Co.
Contran Corp.
Coors Brewing Co.
CPI Corp.
Crane Co.
Crestar Finance Corp.
Cummins Engine Co., Inc.
Dain Bosworth Inc.
Dayton Power and Light Co.
Deluxe Corp.
Dexter Corp.
Dial Corp.
Disney Co. (Walt)
Donaldson Co., Inc.
Donnelley & Sons Co. (R.R.)
Dow Chemical Co.
DSM Copolymer
du Pont de Nemours & Co. (E.I.)
Eastern Bank
El Paso Energy Co.
EMI Music Publishing
Enterprise Rent-A-Car Co.
Equitable Resources, Inc.
Erving Industries
Federated Department Stores, Inc.
Fireman's Fund Insurance Co.
First Hawaiian, Inc.
First Union Corp.
First Union National Bank, NA
FleetBoston Financial Corp.
Ford Meter Box Co.
Fort Worth Star-Telegram Inc.
Fortis Insurance Co.
Freddie Mac
Freeport-McMoRan Inc.
Frost National Bank
Fuller Co. (H.B.)
Furniture Brands International, Inc.
Gallo Winery, Inc. (E&J)
Gap, Inc.
GATX Corp.
GenAmerica Corp.
General Atlantic Partners II LP
General Mills, Inc.
Gerber Products Co.
Giant Eagle Inc.
Globe Corp.
Goodrich Aerospace - Aerostructures Group (B.F.)
Graco, Inc.
GTE Corp.
Gulfstream Aerospace Corp.
Hallmark Cards Inc.
Harcourt General, Inc.
Harnischfeger Industries
Harris Corp.
Harris Trust & Savings Bank
Hartford (The)
Hartmarx Corp.
Hofmann Co.
Honeywell International Inc.
Hubbell Inc.
Hunt Manufacturing Co.
International Flavors & Fragrances Inc.
Kimberly-Clark Corp.
Land O'Lakes, Inc.
Lehigh Portland Cement Co.
Leigh Fibers, Inc.
Levi Strauss & Co.
Lincoln Financial Group
Liz Claiborne, Inc.
Lotus Development Corp.
LTV Corp.
Madison Gas & Electric Co.
Marcus Corp.
Maritz Inc.
McClatchy Co.
McDonald & Co. Securities, Inc.
Mead Corp.
Menasha Corp.
Merit Oil Corp.
MGIC Investment Corp.
Mid-America Bank of Louisville
Minnesota Mining & Manufacturing Co.
Minnesota Mutual Life Insurance Co.
Monsanto Co.
Montana Power Co.
Morgan & Co. Inc. (J.P.)
Morrison Knudsen Corp.
Mutual of Omaha Insurance Co.
Nalco Chemical Co.
National Computer Systems, Inc.
National Life of Vermont
National Machinery Co.
National Service Industries, Inc.
NEBCO Evans
New England Financial
New York Life Insurance Co.
New York Mercantile Exchange
Newman's Own Inc.
Nordson Corp.
Northeast Utilities
Northern States Power Co.
Northern Trust Co.
Norton Co.
Occidental Oil and Gas
Oshkosh B'Gosh, Inc.
Pacific Century Financial Corp.
Pacific Mutual Life Insurance Co.
PacifiCare Health Systems
Park National Bank
PEMCO Corp.
Phillips Petroleum Co.
Pieper Power Electric Co.
Playboy Enterprises Inc.
PNC Financial Services Group
Polaroid Corp.
Premier Industrial Corp.
Procter & Gamble Co., Cosmetics Division
Ralph's Grocery Co.
Ralston Purina Co.
Rayonier Inc.
Reebok International Ltd.
Regions Bank
Reynolds Metals Co.
Rockwell International Corp.
Rouse Co.
Russer Foods
Sara Lee Corp.
Sara Lee Hosiery, Inc.
Schwab & Co., Inc. (Charles)
Seaway Food Town, Inc.
Security Life of Denver Insurance Co.
Shea Co. (John F.)
Shoney's Inc.
Sonoco Products Co.
Southwest Gas Corp.
Sovereign Bank
Starwood Hotels & Resorts Worldwide, Inc.
State Street Bank & Trust Co.
Steelcase Inc.
Stonecutter Mills Corp.
Storage Technology Corp.
SunTrust Bank Atlanta
Synovus Financial Corp.
Target Corp.
TENNANT Co.
Tension Envelope Corp.
Texas Gas Transmission Corp.
Times Mirror Co.
TJX Companies, Inc.
Trustmark Insurance Co.
Union Camp Corp.
Union Pacific Corp.
United Dominion Industries, Ltd.
United Parcel Service of America Inc.
U.S. Bancorp Piper Jaffray
UnumProvident
US Bank, Washington
UST Inc.
Waffle House Inc.
Wal-Mart Stores, Inc.
Waldbaum's Supermarkets, Inc.
Warner-Lambert Co.
Washington Mutual, Inc.
Whirlpool Corp.
WICOR, Inc.
Williams
Wisconsin Public Service Corp.
Wrigley Co. (Wm. Jr.)
Xerox Corp.
Zachry Co. (H.B.)

EMERGENCY RELIEF

Abbott Laboratories
Agrilink Foods, Inc.
Air Products and Chemicals, Inc.
Albertson's Inc.
Alcoa Inc.
Allstate Insurance Co.
Alyeska Pipeline Service Co.
AMCORE Bank Rockford
Ameren Corp.
America West Airlines, Inc.
American General Finance
American United Life Insurance Co.
Amsted Industries Inc.
Andersen Corp.
Anheuser-Busch Companies, Inc.
Appleton Papers Inc.
Archer-Daniels-Midland Co.
AT&T Corp.
Atlantic Investment Co.
Bandag, Inc.
Barden Corp.
Bechtel Group, Inc.
Belk Stores Services Inc.
Bemis Co., Inc.
Ben & Jerry's Homemade Inc.
Bethlehem Steel Corp.
BFGoodrich Co.
Block, Inc. (H&R)
Blue Bell, Inc.
Borden, Inc.
Borman's Inc.
Boston Edison Co.
Bridgestone/Firestone, Inc.
Brunswick Corp.
Business Improvement
Cabot Corp.
Carillon Importers, Ltd.
Carpenter Technology Corp.
Central Maine Power Co.
CGU Insurance
Chase Manhattan Bank, NA
Chemed Corp.
Chevron Corp.
Chicago Board of Trade
Church & Dwight Co., Inc.
Citibank Corp.
CLARCOR Inc.
Cleveland-Cliffs, Inc.
Collins & Aikman Corp.
Colonial Life & Accident Insurance Co.
Commercial Intertech Corp.
Cooper Industries, Inc.
Coors Brewing Co.
CSS Industries, Inc.
Cummins Engine Co., Inc.
CUNA Mutual Group
DaimlerChrysler Corp.
Dana Corp.
Deluxe Corp.
Donaldson Co., Inc.
du Pont de Nemours & Co. (E.I.)
Duke Energy
Eaton Corp.
Ecolab Inc.
Edison International
Equifax Inc.
Excel Corp.
Fannie Mae
Farmers Group, Inc.
Federated Mutual Insurance Co.

Fireman's Fund Insurance Co.
First Union Bank
First Union Corp.
First Union National Bank, NA
Ford Meter Box Co.
Fortis, Inc.
Freeport-McMoRan Inc.
Frost National Bank
Furniture Brands International, Inc.
Gallo Winery, Inc. (E&J)
GEICO Corp.
GenAmerica Corp.
General Mills, Inc.
Goodrich Aerospace - Aerostructures Group (B.F.)
Graco, Inc.
GTE Corp.
Hallmark Cards Inc.
Harsco Corp.
Hartford (The)
Hasbro, Inc.
Hewlett-Packard Co.
Hofmann Co.
Home Depot, Inc.
Honeywell International Inc.
Hubbard Broadcasting, Inc.
Hubbell Inc.
Hughes Electronics Corp.
Humana, Inc.
IKON Office Solutions, Inc.
Inland Container Corp.
International Business Machines Corp.
Johnson & Son (S.C.)
Katten, Muchin & Zavis
Kerr-McGee Corp.
Kimball International, Inc.
Kingsbury Corp.
Kroger Co.
Lee Enterprises
Lehigh Portland Cement Co.
Leviton Manufacturing Co. Inc.
Liberty Corp.
Lincoln Financial Group
Lipton Co.
Little, Inc. (Arthur D.)
Liz Claiborne, Inc.
Louisiana Land & Exploration Co.
Louisiana-Pacific Corp.
LTV Corp.
Macy's East Inc.
Maritz Inc.
McClatchy Co.
McDonald & Co. Securities, Inc.
MCI WorldCom, Inc.
Mercantile Bank NA
Merrill Lynch & Co., Inc.
Mine Safety Appliances Co.
Minnesota Mining & Manufacturing Co.
Minnesota Mutual Life Insurance Co.
Montgomery Ward & Co., Inc.
Morgan Stanley Dean Witter & Co.
Morton International Inc.
National Computer Systems, Inc.
National Machinery Co.
National Service Industries, Inc.
National Starch & Chemical Co.
Nationwide Insurance Co.
New England Financial
New York Mercantile Exchange
Northern Indiana Public Service Co.
Northern States Power Co.
Norton Co.
Occidental Oil and Gas
OG&E Electric Services
Owens Corning
Pacific Mutual Life Insurance Co.
Pennzoil-Quaker State Co.
Pfizer Inc.
Pharmacia & Upjohn, Inc.
Philip Morris Companies Inc.
Phillips Petroleum Co.
Physicians Mutual Insurance Co.
Pillsbury Co.
Portland General Electric Co.
Premier Industrial Corp.
Prudential Insurance Co. of America
Publix Supermarkets
Pulitzer Publishing Co.
Ralph's Grocery Co.
Rayonier Inc.
Red Wing Shoe Co. Inc.
Regions Bank
Rockwell International Corp.
SAFECO Corp.
Saint Paul Companies Inc.
Salomon Smith Barney
Sara Lee Hosiery, Inc.
Schwab & Co., Inc. (Charles)
Seagram & Sons, Inc. (Joseph E.)
Security Life of Denver Insurance Co.
Sega of America Inc.
Sempra Energy
Shaklee Corp.
Shell Oil Co.
Shoney's Inc.
Sonoco Products Co.
Sovereign Bank
Springs Industries, Inc.
Square D Co.
Starwood Hotels & Resorts Worldwide, Inc.
Steelcase Inc.
Stone Container Corp.
Storage Technology Corp.
Sunoco Inc.
SunTrust Bank Atlanta
Taco Bell Corp.
Tenneco Automotive
Tenneco Packaging
Tesoro Hawaii
Texaco Inc.
Textron Inc.
Thermo Electron Corp.
Torchmark Corp.
Trace International Holdings, Inc.
Unilever Home & Personal Care U.S.A.
Union Camp Corp.
Union Carbide Corp.
United Airlines Inc.
United Distillers & Vintners North America
United Parcel Service of America Inc.
U.S. Bancorp Piper Jaffray
Universal Studios
US Bank, Washington
USG Corp.
Vodafone AirTouch Plc
Vulcan Materials Co.
Wal-Mart Stores, Inc.
Washington Trust Bank
Weil, Gotshal & Manges Corp.
Wiley & Sons (John)
Williams
Wisconsin Power & Light Co.
Woodward Governor Co.

FAMILY PLANNING

Agrilink Foods, Inc.
Alcoa Inc.
American Retail Group
Ameritech Michigan
Amsted Industries Inc.
Andersen Corp.
Archer-Daniels-Midland Co.
Armstrong World Industries, Inc.
Bardes Corp.
Barry Corp. (R.G.)
Battelle Memorial Institute
Belk Stores Services Inc.
Bemis Co., Inc.
Bernstein & Co., Inc. (Sanford C.)
Berwind Group
Block, Inc. (H&R)
Borman's Inc.
Bridgestone/Firestone, Inc.
Brunswick Corp.
Cargill Inc.
Carter-Wallace, Inc.
Central Maine Power Co.
Charter Manufacturing Co.
Chase Bank of Texas
Chase Manhattan Bank, NA
Chicago Title Corp.
Citizens Bank-Flint
Clorox Co.
Colonial Life & Accident Insurance Co.
Commerce Bancshares, Inc.
Commercial Intertech Corp.
Consolidated Papers, Inc.
Contran Corp.
Corning Inc.
Country Curtains, Inc.
Cummins Engine Co., Inc.
Dain Bosworth Inc.
Dana Corp.
Dayton Hudson
Deutsch Co.
Dial Corp.
Donaldson Co., Inc.
Duke Energy
Ecolab Inc.
Edwards Enterprise Software (J.D.)
Enterprise Rent-A-Car Co.
Erb Lumber Co.
Federated Department Stores, Inc.
First Union Corp.
First Union National Bank, NA
FleetBoston Financial Corp.
Forbes Inc.
Fort Worth Star-Telegram Inc.
Fortis, Inc.
Fortis Insurance Co.
Freddie Mac
GenAmerica Corp.
General Mills, Inc.
Georgia Power Co.
Glickenhaus & Co.
Globe Corp.
Goodrich Aerospace - Aerostructures Group (B.F.)
Harley-Davidson Co.
Harsco Corp.
Hartmarx Corp.
Hasbro, Inc.
Heinz Co. (H.J.)
Honeywell International Inc.
Hubbard Broadcasting, Inc.
Huffy Corp.
Humana, Inc.
Illinois Tool Works, Inc.
Independent Stave Co.
International Flavors & Fragrances Inc.
Journal-Gazette Co.
Kinder Morgn
Lance, Inc.
Lee Enterprises
Leigh Fibers, Inc.
Lennox International, Inc.
Lincoln Electric Co.
Lipton Co.
Loews Corp.
Lotus Development Corp.
Marshall & Ilsley Corp.
MBIA Inc.
McClatchy Co.
McCormick & Co. Inc.
McDonald & Co. Securities, Inc.
MCI WorldCom, Inc.
MidAmerican Energy Holdings Co.
Milliken & Co.
Montana Power Co.
MONY Group (The)
Morgan & Co. Inc. (J.P.)
Morgan Stanley Dean Witter & Co.
National City Bank of Minneapolis
National Computer Systems, Inc.
Nationwide Insurance Co.
NEBCO Evans
New England Financial
Northern Trust Co.
Northwest Bank Nebraska, NA
Norton Co.
OG&E Electric Services
Old National Bank Evansville
Pacific Mutual Life Insurance Co.
PacifiCorp
Patagonia Inc.
PepsiCo, Inc.
PerkinElmer, Inc.
Pharmacia & Upjohn, Inc.
Phelps Dodge Corp.
Pieper Power Electric Co.
Pillsbury Co.
Pittway Corp.
Playboy Enterprises Inc.
Premier Dental Products Co.
Principal Financial Group
Providence Journal-Bulletin Co.
Prudential Insurance Co. of America
Publix Supermarkets
Pulitzer Publishing Co.
Ralph's Grocery Co.
Ralston Purina Co.
Regions Bank
Reilly Industries, Inc.
Reily & Co., Inc. (William B.)
Salomon Smith Barney
Sara Lee Corp.
Schloss & Co. (Marcus)
Schlumberger Ltd. (USA)
Schwab & Co., Inc. (Charles)
Security Benefit Life Insurance Co.
Sega of America Inc.
Sierra Pacific Resources
Sovereign Bank
SPX Corp.
Steelcase Inc.
Stone Container Corp.
Stupp Brothers Bridge & Iron Co.
TENNANT Co.
Tension Envelope Corp.
Textron Inc.
Toledo Blade Co.
Union Camp Corp.
United Dominion Industries, Ltd.
U.S. Bancorp Piper Jaffray
Universal Leaf Tobacco Co., Inc.
Universal Studios
Van Leer Holding
Vodafone AirTouch Plc
Wachovia Bank of North Carolina NA
Weil, Gotshal & Manges Corp.
West Co. Inc.
Whirlpool Corp.
Wilbur-Ellis Co. & Connell Brothers Co.
Williams
Witco Corp.
Young & Rubicam

FAMILY SERVICES

ABB Inc.
Abbott Laboratories
ABC
AEGON U.S.A. Inc.
Aetna, Inc.
AGL Resources Inc.
Agrilink Foods, Inc.
Air Products and Chemicals, Inc.
AK Steel Corp.
Alabama Power Co.
Alcoa Inc.
Alcon Laboratories, Inc.
Allegheny Technologies Inc.
Alliant Techsystems
AlliedSignal Inc.
Allmerica Financial Corp.
Allstate Insurance Co.
AMCORE Bank Rockford
Ameren Corp.
American Express Co.
American Fidelity Corp.
American General Finance
American Retail Group
American United Life Insurance Co.
Ameritas Life Insurance Corp.
Ameritech Michigan
AmerUS Group
Amgen, Inc.
AMP Inc.
AMR Corp.
Amsted Industries Inc.
Andersen Corp.
Andersons Inc.
APL Ltd.
Aristech Chemical Corp.
Arizona Public Service Co.
Arvin Industries, Inc.
AT&T Corp.
Atlantic Investment Co.
Atlantic Richfield Co.
Avon Products, Inc.
Banfi Vintners
Bank of America
Bank of New York Co., Inc.
Bank One Corp.

BankAtlantic Bancorp
BankBoston Corp.
Barclays Capital
Bard, Inc. (C.R.)
Barden Corp.
Bardes Corp.
Barnes Group Inc.
Barry Corp. (R.G.)
Battelle Memorial Institute
Baxter International Inc.
Becton Dickinson & Co.
Belk Stores Services Inc.
BellSouth Corp.
Bemis Co., Inc.
Bernstein & Co., Inc. (Sanford C.)
Bestfoods
Bethlehem Steel Corp.
Binney & Smith Inc.
Binswanger Companies
Blair & Co. (William)
Block, Inc. (H&R)
Blount International, Inc.
Blue Cross & Blue Shield of Iowa
Blue Cross & Blue Shield of Minnesota
Borden, Inc.
Borman's Inc.
Boston Edison Co.
Boston Globe (The)
BP Amoco Corp.
Bradford & Co. (J.C.)
Bridgestone/Firestone, Inc.
Broderbund Software, Inc.
Brown Shoe Co., Inc.
Brown & Williamson Tobacco Corp.
Brunswick Corp.
Bucyrus-Erie Co.
Burlington Industries, Inc.
Burlington Resources, Inc.
Burnett Co. (Leo)
Burress (J.W.)
Butler Manufacturing Co.
California Bank & Trust
Calvin Klein
Campbell Soup Co.
Cantor, Fitzgerald Securities Corp.
Cargill Inc.
Carillon Importers, Ltd.
Carpenter Technology Corp.
Carris Reels
Caterpillar Inc.
Central Maine Power Co.
Central Newspapers, Inc.
Cessna Aircraft Co.
Chase Manhattan Bank, NA
Chemed Corp.
Chesapeake Corp.
Chevron Corp.
Chicago Tribune Co.
Citibank Corp.
Citigroup
Citizens Financial Group, Inc.
CLARCOR Inc.
Cleveland-Cliffs, Inc.
Clorox Co.
CNA
Colonial Life & Accident Insurance Co.
Colonial Oil Industries, Inc.
Comdisco, Inc.
Commerce Bancshares, Inc.
Compass Bank
ConAgra, Inc.
Constellation Energy Group, Inc.
Consumers Energy Co.
Continental Grain Co.
Contran Corp.
Country Curtains, Inc.
Cox Enterprises Inc.
CPI Corp.
Crane & Co., Inc.
Crestar Finance Corp.
CSS Industries, Inc.
Cummins Engine Co., Inc.
CUNA Mutual Group
Daily News
Dain Bosworth Inc.
Dana Corp.
Dayton Hudson
Deere & Co.
DeKalb Genetics Corp.
Delta Air Lines, Inc.
Deluxe Corp.
Deposit Guaranty National Bank
Detroit Edison Co.
Deutsch Co.
Dial Corp.
Disney Co. (Walt)
Domino's Pizza Inc.
Donaldson Co., Inc.
Donnelley & Sons Co. (R.R.)
Dow Jones & Co., Inc.
Dreyer's Grand Ice Cream
du Pont de Nemours & Co. (E.I.)
Duchossois Industries Inc.
Duke Energy
Dun & Bradstreet Corp.
Duriron Co., Inc.
Eastern Bank
Eastman Kodak Co.
Eaton Corp.
Ecolab Inc.
Edison International
EDS Corp.
El Paso Energy Co.
Emerson Electric Co.
Employers Mutual Casualty Co.
Equifax Inc.
Erb Lumber Co.
Extendicare Health Services
Exxon Mobil Corp.
Fabri-Kal Corp.
Federal-Mogul Corp.
Federated Department Stores, Inc.
Federated Mutual Insurance Co.
Fidelity Investments
Fifth Third Bancorp
Fireman's Fund Insurance Co.
First Hawaiian, Inc.
First Maryland Bancorp
First Source Corp.
First Union Corp.
First Union National Bank, NA
Firstar Bank Milwaukee NA
Fisher Scientific
FleetBoston Financial Corp.
Florida Power Corp.
Florida Power & Light Co.
Florida Rock Industries
Forbes Inc.
Ford Meter Box Co.
Fortis Insurance Co.
Freddie Mac
Freeport-McMoRan Inc.
Frost National Bank
Fuller Co. (H.B.)
Gallo Winery, Inc. (E&J)
Gap, Inc.
GATX Corp.
GEICO Corp.
GenCorp
General Atlantic Partners II LP
General Dynamics Corp.
General Electric Co.
General Mills, Inc.
General Motors Corp.
Georgia-Pacific Corp.
Georgia Power Co.
Gerber Products Co.
Giant Eagle Inc.
Giant Food Inc.
Glaxo Wellcome Inc.
Glickenhaus & Co.
Globe Corp.
Golub Corp.
Goodrich Aerospace - Aerostructures Group (B.F.)
Graco, Inc.
Grede Foundries
Green Bay Packaging
GTE Corp.
Hallmark Cards Inc.
Hamilton Sundstrand Corp.
Hancock Financial Services (John)
Hanna Co. (M.A.)
Hannaford Brothers Co.
Harcourt General, Inc.
Harley-Davidson Co.
Harris Trust & Savings Bank
Hartford (The)
Hartmarx Corp.
Hasbro, Inc.
Hawaiian Electric Co., Inc.
Heinz Co. (H.J.)
Hoffer Plastics Corp.
Hofmann Co.
HON Industries Inc.
Honeywell International Inc.
Household International Inc.
Hubbard Broadcasting, Inc.
Hubbell Inc.
Huffy Corp.
Humana, Inc.
Hunt Manufacturing Co.
Illinois Tool Works, Inc.
Independent Stave Co.
Indiana Mills & Manufacturing
International Business Machines Corp.
International Flavors & Fragrances Inc.
International Multifoods Corp.
International Paper Co.
INTRUST Financial Corp.
Jacobs Engineering Group
Jacobson & Sons (Benjamin)
Johnson Controls Inc.
Johnson & Son (S.C.)
Jostens, Inc.
Journal-Gazette Co.
JSJ Corp.
Katten, Muchin & Zavis
Kellwood Co.
Kimberly-Clark Corp.
Kinder Morgn
Kingsbury Corp.
Kmart Corp.
Koch Enterprises, Inc.
Koch Industries, Inc.
Kraft Foods, Inc.
La-Z-Boy Inc.
Ladish Co., Inc.
Lance, Inc.
Land O'Lakes, Inc.
Lee Enterprises
Lehigh Portland Cement Co.
Leigh Fibers, Inc.
Lennox International, Inc.
Levi Strauss & Co.
Leviton Manufacturing Co. Inc.
LG&E Energy Corp.
Liberty Corp.
Lincoln Financial Group
Little, Inc. (Arthur D.)
Liz Claiborne, Inc.
Lotus Development Corp.
Louisiana-Pacific Corp.
LTV Corp.
MacMillan Bloedel Inc.
Madison Gas & Electric Co.
Marcus Corp.
Mark IV Industries
Marshall & Ilsley Corp.
Mattel Inc.
Maytag Corp.
MBIA Inc.
McClatchy Co.
McCormick & Co. Inc.
McDonald & Co. Securities, Inc.
McDonald's Corp.
McGraw-Hill Companies, Inc.
McKesson-HBOC Corp.
McWane Inc.
Mead Corp.
Medtronic, Inc.
Mellon Financial Corp.
Mercantile Bank NA
Merck & Co.
Meredith Corp.
Merit Oil Corp.
Merrill Lynch & Co., Inc.
Mervyn's California
Metropolitan Life Insurance Co.
MGIC Investment Corp.
Mid-America Bank of Louisville
MidAmerican Energy Holdings Co.
Milacron, Inc.
Millipore Corp.
Mine Safety Appliances Co.
Minnesota Mining & Manufacturing Co.
Minnesota Mutual Life Insurance Co.
Mitsubishi Electric America
Monsanto Co.
Montgomery Ward & Co., Inc.
MONY Group (The)
Morgan & Co. Inc. (J.P.)
Morgan Stanley Dean Witter & Co.
Morrison Knudsen Corp.
Nalco Chemical Co.
National City Bank of Minneapolis
National Machinery Co.
National Starch & Chemical Co.
Nationwide Insurance Co.
NEBCO Evans
New Century Energies
New England Financial
New Jersey Natural Gas Co.
New York Life Insurance Co.
New York Mercantile Exchange
Newman's Own Inc.
Nordson Corp.
Northeast Utilities
Northern States Power Co.
Northern Trust Co.
Norton Co.
Occidental Oil and Gas
OG&E Electric Services
Old Kent Bank
Old National Bank Evansville
Olin Corp.
Oshkosh B'Gosh, Inc.
PACCAR Inc.
Pacific Century Financial Corp.
Pacific Mutual Life Insurance Co.
Paine Webber
Park National Bank
Pella Corp.
Peoples Energy Corp.
Pfizer Inc.
Pharmacia & Upjohn, Inc.
Pheonix Financial Group
Phillips Petroleum Co.
Physicians Mutual Insurance Co.
Pieper Power Electric Co.
Pillsbury Co.
Pittway Corp.
PNC Financial Services Group
Polaroid Corp.
Potomac Electric Power Co.
PPG Industries, Inc.
Praxair
Price Associates (T. Rowe)
Principal Financial Group
Procter & Gamble Co., Cosmetics Division
Prudential Insurance Co. of America
Publix Supermarkets
Pulitzer Publishing Co.
Putnam Investments
Ralston Purina Co.
Reebok International Ltd.
Regions Bank
Reilly Industries, Inc.
Reily & Co., Inc. (William B.)
Reliant Energy Inc.
Rich Products Corp.
Rockwell International Corp.
Rouse Co.
Royal & SunAlliance USA, Inc.
Russer Foods
Ryder System, Inc.
Saint Paul Companies Inc.
Sara Lee Corp.
Sara Lee Hosiery, Inc.
SBC Communications Inc.
Schering-Plough Corp.
Schloss & Co. (Marcus)
Schlumberger Ltd. (USA)
Schwab & Co., Inc. (Charles)
Schwebel Baking Co.
Seagram & Sons, Inc. (Joseph E.)
Security Benefit Life Insurance Co.
Sega of America Inc.
Sempra Energy
Sentinel Communications Co.
Servco Pacific
ServiceMaster Co.
S.G. Cowen
Shell Oil Co.
Sherwin-Williams Co.
Shoney's Inc.
Simpson Investment Co.
SIT Investment Associates, Inc.
Smith Corp. (A.O.)
Solo Cup Co.
Sonoco Products Co.
Sony Electronics
Southwest Gas Corp.
Sovereign Bank
Springs Industries, Inc.

SPX Corp.
Stanley Works (The)
State Farm Mutual Automobile Insurance Co.
State Street Bank & Trust Co.
Steelcase Inc.
Storage Technology Corp.
Stride Rite Corp.
Stupp Brothers Bridge & Iron Co.
Sun Microsystems Inc.
SunTrust Bank Atlanta
SunTrust Banks of Florida
Sverdrup Corp.
Synovus Financial Corp.
Target Corp.
Temple-Inland Inc.
TENNANT Co.
Tension Envelope Corp.
Thomasville Furniture Industries Inc.
Times Mirror Co.
Titan Industrial Corp.
TJX Companies, Inc.
TMC Investment Co.
Tomkins Industries, Inc.
Trace International Holdings, Inc.
Transamerica Corp.
True North Communications, Inc.
Trustmark Insurance Co.
TRW Inc.
Tyson Foods Inc.
Ukrop's Super Markets
Union Camp Corp.
Union Carbide Corp.
Union Pacific Corp.
United Distillers & Vintners North America
United Dominion Industries, Ltd.
United Parcel Service of America Inc.
U.S. Bancorp Piper Jaffray
United States Sugar Corp.
United States Trust Co. of New York
United Technologies Corp.
United Wisconsin Services
Universal Leaf Tobacco Co., Inc.
Universal Studios
Unocal Corp.
UnumProvident
US Bank, Washington
US West, Inc.
USG Corp.
UST Inc.
USX Corp.
Valmont Industries, Inc.
Van Leer Holding
Varian Medical Systems, Inc.
Vodafone AirTouch Plc
Vulcan Materials Co.
Wachovia Bank of North Carolina NA
Waffle House Inc.
Wal-Mart Stores, Inc.
Waldbaum's Supermarkets, Inc.
Washington Mutual, Inc.
Weil, Gotshal & Manges Corp.
Wells Fargo & Co.
Weyerhaeuser Co.
Whirlpool Corp.
WICOR, Inc.
Williams
Winn-Dixie Stores Inc.
Wiremold Co.
Wisconsin Energy Corp.
Wisconsin Power & Light Co.
Wisconsin Public Service Corp.
Witco Corp.
Wolverine World Wide
Woodward Governor Co.
Wyman-Gordon Co.
York Federal Savings & Loan Association
Young & Rubicam
Zachry Co. (H.B.)

FOOD/CLOTHING DISTRIBUTION

ABC
Advanced Micro Devices, Inc.
AGL Resources Inc.
Agrilink Foods, Inc.
Air Products and Chemicals, Inc.
Alabama Power Co.
Albertson's Inc.
Alcoa Inc.
Alcon Laboratories, Inc.
Alexander & Baldwin, Inc.
Allegheny Technologies Inc.
Alliant Techsystems
AlliedSignal Inc.
Allmerica Financial Corp.
Alma Piston Co.
AMCORE Bank Rockford
Ameren Corp.
American Express Co.
American Fidelity Corp.
American General Finance
American United Life Insurance Co.
Ameritas Life Insurance Corp.
Ameritech Michigan
AmerUS Group
AMETEK, Inc.
AMP Inc.
AMR Corp.
Andersen Corp.
Andersons Inc.
Anheuser-Busch Companies, Inc.
Aon Corp.
APL Ltd.
Appleton Papers Inc.
Archer-Daniels-Midland Co.
Aristech Chemical Corp.
Arizona Public Service Co.
Armstrong World Industries, Inc.
Arvin Industries, Inc.
Atlantic Richfield Co.
Auburn Foundry
Avon Products, Inc.
Badger Meter, Inc.
Banfi Vintners
Bank of America
BankBoston-Connecticut Region
BankBoston Corp.
Banta Corp.
Barclays Capital
Baxter International Inc.
Bechtel Group, Inc.
Beckman Coulter, Inc.
Belk-Simpson Department Stores
Bemis Co., Inc.
Ben & Jerry's Homemade Inc.
Berwind Group
Bethlehem Steel Corp.
Blair & Co. (William)
Block, Inc. (H&R)
Blount International, Inc.
Blue Bell, Inc.
Blue Cross & Blue Shield of Iowa
Blue Cross & Blue Shield of Minnesota
Boeing Co.
Borden, Inc.
Borman's Inc.
Boston Edison Co.
Boston Globe (The)
Bradford & Co. (J.C.)
Briggs & Stratton Corp.
Bristol-Myers Squibb Co.
Broderbund Software, Inc.
Brunswick Corp.
Bucyrus-Erie Co.
Burlington Resources, Inc.
Burnett Co. (Leo)
Business Improvement
Cabot Corp.
Calvin Klein
Campbell Soup Co.
Cantor, Fitzgerald Securities Corp.
Cargill Inc.
Carillon Importers, Ltd.
Carpenter Technology Corp.
Carris Reels
Central Maine Power Co.
Central Soya Co.
CertainTeed Corp.
Cessna Aircraft Co.
Chase Bank of Texas
Chase Manhattan Bank, NA
Chemed Corp.
Chevron Corp.
Chicago Board of Trade
Chicago Title Corp.
Chicago Tribune Co.
Church & Dwight Co., Inc.
CIGNA Corp.
Cincinnati Bell Inc.
CIT Group, Inc. (The)
Citibank Corp.
Citigroup
Citizens Financial Group, Inc.
CLARCOR Inc.
Cleveland-Cliffs, Inc.
Clorox Co.
CNA
Collins & Aikman Corp.
Colonial Life & Accident Insurance Co.
Colonial Oil Industries, Inc.
Commerce Bancshares, Inc.
Compaq Computer Corp.
ConAgra, Inc.
Consolidated Natural Gas Co.
Consumers Energy Co.
Contran Corp.
Conwood Co. LP
Cooper Industries, Inc.
Copley Press, Inc.
Cox Enterprises Inc.
CPI Corp.
Crane Co.
Crane & Co., Inc.
Credit Suisse First Boston
Crestar Finance Corp.
Croft-Leominster
Cummings Properties Management
Cummins Engine Co., Inc.
CUNA Mutual Group
Daily News
DaimlerChrysler Corp.
Dain Bosworth Inc.
Dana Corp.
Dayton Power and Light Co.
DeKalb Genetics Corp.
Deluxe Corp.
Demoulas Supermarkets Inc.
Deposit Guaranty National Bank
Detroit Edison Co.
Deutsch Co.
Dexter Corp.
Dial Corp.
Disney Co. (Walt)
Dixie Group, Inc. (The)
Dominion Resources, Inc.
Donaldson Co., Inc.
Dreyer's Grand Ice Cream
DSM Copolymer
du Pont de Nemours & Co. (E.I.)
Duke Energy
Dun & Bradstreet Corp.
Dynamet, Inc.
Eastern Bank
Eaton Corp.
Ecolab Inc.
Edwards Enterprise Software (J.D.)
El Paso Energy Co.
Enterprise Rent-A-Car Co.
Equifax Inc.
Erb Lumber Co.
Erving Industries
Fabri-Kal Corp.
Federal-Mogul Corp.
Federated Department Stores, Inc.
Federated Mutual Insurance Co.
Fidelity Investments
Fifth Third Bancorp
Fireman's Fund Insurance Co.
First Hawaiian, Inc.
First Source Corp.
First Union Corp.
First Union National Bank, NA
First Union Securities, Inc.
FleetBoston Financial Corp.
Forbes Inc.
Ford Meter Box Co.
Forest City Enterprises, Inc.
Fort Worth Star-Telegram Inc.
Fortis, Inc.
Fortis Insurance Co.
Fortune Brands, Inc.
Franklin Mint (The)
Freeport-McMoRan Inc.
Frost National Bank
Furniture Brands International, Inc.
Gallo Winery, Inc. (E&J)
Gap, Inc.
GATX Corp.
GEICO Corp.
GenAmerica Corp.
General Atlantic Partners II LP
General Electric Co.
General Mills, Inc.
General Motors Corp.
General Reinsurance Corp.
Georgia-Pacific Corp.
Georgia Power Co.
Gerber Products Co.
Giant Eagle Inc.
Giant Food Inc.
Golub Corp.
Goodrich Aerospace - Aerostructures Group (B.F.)
Graco, Inc.
Guardian Life Insurance Co. of America
Guess?
Gulf Power Co.
Hallmark Cards Inc.
Hamilton Sundstrand Corp.
Hancock Financial Services (John)
Hanna Co. (M.A.)
Hannaford Brothers Co.
Harley-Davidson Co.
Harris Corp.
Harsco Corp.
Hartford (The)
Hartmarx Corp.
Hasbro, Inc.
Hawaiian Electric Co., Inc.
Heinz Co. (H.J.)
Hershey Foods Corp.
Hickory Tech Corp.
Hofmann Co.
Honeywell International Inc.
Household International Inc.
Hubbard Broadcasting, Inc.
Hubbell Inc.
Humana, Inc.
Hunt Manufacturing Co.
Inman Mills
International Flavors & Fragrances Inc.
International Multifoods Corp.
International Paper Co.
Jacobson & Sons (Benjamin)
Johnson Controls Inc.
Journal-Gazette Co.
Katten, Muchin & Zavis
Kellogg Co.
Kellwood Co.
Kimberly-Clark Corp.
Kingsbury Corp.
Kmart Corp.
Koch Enterprises, Inc.
Koch Industries, Inc.
Kroger Co.
Ladish Co., Inc.
Land O'Lakes, Inc.
LandAmerica Financial Services
Landmark Communications Inc.
Lee Enterprises
Levi Strauss & Co.
LG&E Energy Corp.
Liberty Diversified Industries
Lincoln Electric Co.
Lincoln Financial Group
Lipton Co.
Liz Claiborne, Inc.
Louisiana-Pacific Corp.
LTV Corp.
Madison Gas & Electric Co.
Manulife Financial
Maritz Inc.
Marshall & Ilsley Corp.
May Department Stores Co.
MBIA Inc.
McClatchy Co.
McCormick & Co. Inc.
McDonald & Co. Securities, Inc.
McKesson-HBOC Corp.
Mead Corp.
Memphis Light Gas & Water Division
Menasha Corp.
Merit Oil Corp.
Merrill Lynch & Co., Inc.
Metropolitan Life Insurance Co.
MGIC Investment Corp.

Michigan Consolidated Gas Co.
Milliken & Co.
Millipore Corp.
Minnesota Mining & Manufacturing Co.
Minnesota Mutual Life Insurance Co.
Monsanto Co.
Montana Power Co.
Montgomery Ward & Co., Inc.
MONY Group (The)
Morgan & Co. Inc. (J.P.)
Morgan Stanley Dean Witter & Co.
Motorola Inc.
MTD Products Inc.
Nabisco Group Holdings
Nalco Chemical Co.
National City Corp.
National Presto Industries, Inc.
National Service Industries, Inc.
National Starch & Chemical Co.
Nationwide Insurance Co.
NEBCO Evans
Nestle U.S.A. Inc.
New England Financial
New Jersey Natural Gas Co.
New York Life Insurance Co.
New York Mercantile Exchange
New York Stock Exchange, Inc.
New York Times Co.
Newman's Own Inc.
Niagara Mohawk Holdings Inc.
Nike, Inc.
Nissan North America, Inc.
Nordson Corp.
North American Royalties
Northeast Utilities
Northern Indiana Public Service Co.
Northern States Power Co.
Northern Trust Co.
Northwest Bank Nebraska, NA
Northwest Natural Gas Co.
Norton Co.
Occidental Oil and Gas
Ohio National Life Insurance Co.
Old National Bank Evansville
Olin Corp.
Orscheln Co.
Osborne Enterprises
PACCAR Inc.
Pacific Century Financial Corp.
Pacific Mutual Life Insurance Co.
PacifiCare Health Systems
Paine Webber
Pella Corp.
PEMCO Corp.
Penney Co., Inc. (J.C.)
PerkinElmer, Inc.
Pfizer Inc.
Pharmacia & Upjohn, Inc.
Philip Morris Companies Inc.
Phillips Petroleum Co.
Physicians Mutual Insurance Co.
Pieper Power Electric Co.
Pillsbury Co.
Pittway Corp.
PNC Bank Kentucky Inc.
PNC Financial Services Group
Polaroid Corp.
Portland General Electric Co.
Potomac Electric Power Co.
PPG Industries, Inc.
Premier Dental Products Co.
Premier Industrial Corp.
Price Associates (T. Rowe)
Principal Financial Group
Procter & Gamble Co.
Procter & Gamble Co., Cosmetics Division
Providence Journal-Bulletin Co.
Provident Companies, Inc.
Prudential Insurance Co. of America
Prudential Securities Inc.
Public Service Electric & Gas Co.
Publix Supermarkets
Pulitzer Publishing Co.
Putnam Investments
Quaker Chemical Corp.
Questar Corp.
Ralph's Grocery Co.
Ralston Purina Co.
Rayonier Inc.
Reebok International Ltd.
Regions Bank
Reilly Industries, Inc.
Reily & Co., Inc. (William B.)
Reynolds Metals Co.
Rich Products Corp.
Rouse Co.
Ruddick Corp.
Russer Foods
Safeway Inc.
Salomon Smith Barney
Sara Lee Corp.
Sara Lee Hosiery, Inc.
Schloss & Co. (Marcus)
Schlumberger Ltd. (USA)
Schwab & Co., Inc. (Charles)
Schwebel Baking Co.
Scripps Co. (E.W.)
Seagram & Sons, Inc. (Joseph E.)
Seaway Food Town, Inc.
Security Life of Denver Insurance Co.
Sega of America Inc.
Sempra Energy
Sentinel Communications Co.
Servco Pacific
S.G. Cowen
Shaklee Corp.
Shaw's Supermarkets, Inc.
Shell Oil Co.
Shoney's Inc.
Sierra Pacific Industries
Sierra Pacific Resources
Simpson Investment Co.
SIT Investment Associates, Inc.
Slant/Fin Corp.
Solo Cup Co.
Southeastern Mutual Insurance Co.
Southwest Gas Corp.
Sovereign Bank
Sprint Corp.
SPX Corp.
Square D Co.
Standard Products Co.
Star Bank NA
Starwood Hotels & Resorts Worldwide, Inc.
Steelcase Inc.
Stone Container Corp.
Storage Technology Corp.
Strear Farms Co.
Subway Sandwich Shops, Inc.
Sun Microsystems Inc.
SunTrust Bank Atlanta
Temple-Inland Inc.
Tenneco Automotive
Tenneco Packaging
Tesoro Hawaii
Texas Gas Transmission Corp.
Textron Inc.
Thermo Electron Corp.
Times Mirror Co.
Timken Co. (The)
Titan Industrial Corp.
TJX Companies, Inc.
Toledo Blade Co.
Tomkins Industries, Inc.
Toro Co.
Trace International Holdings, Inc.
Transamerica Corp.
True North Communications, Inc.
True Oil Co.
TRW Inc.
Tyson Foods Inc.
Ukrop's Super Markets
Unilever Home & Personal Care U.S.A.
Unilever United States, Inc.
Union Pacific Corp.
United Distillers & Vintners North America
United Parcel Service of America Inc.
U.S. Bancorp
U.S. Bancorp Piper Jaffray
United States Trust Co. of New York
United Technologies Corp.
United Wisconsin Services
Universal Leaf Tobacco Co., Inc.
Universal Studios
Unocal Corp.
UnumProvident
US Bank, Washington
USG Corp.
Valero Energy Corp.
Vulcan Materials Co.
Wachovia Bank of North Carolina NA
Waffle House Inc.
Wal-Mart Stores, Inc.
Washington Mutual, Inc.
Washington Trust Bank
Wells Fargo & Co.
Whirlpool Corp.
WICOR, Inc.
Williams
Winn-Dixie Stores Inc.
Wiremold Co.
Wisconsin Power & Light Co.
Woodward Governor Co.
Wrigley Co. (Wm. Jr.)
Young & Rubicam

HOMES

ABB Inc.
ABC
AFLAC Inc.
AGL Resources Inc.
Agrilink Foods, Inc.
Air Products and Chemicals, Inc.
AK Steel Corp.
Alcoa Inc.
Alcon Laboratories, Inc.
Alexander & Baldwin, Inc.
Allegheny Technologies Inc.
Alliant Techsystems
AlliedSignal Inc.
AMCORE Bank Rockford
Ameren Corp.
Ameritas Life Insurance Corp.
AmerUS Group
AMETEK, Inc.
Andersen Corp.
Aon Corp.
Badger Meter, Inc.
Barclays Capital
Barnes Group Inc.
Bausch & Lomb Inc.
Belk-Simpson Department Stores
Bemis Co., Inc.
Bernstein & Co., Inc. (Sanford C.)
Block, Inc. (H&R)
Blount International, Inc.
Blue Bell, Inc.
Boeing Co.
Boise Cascade Corp.
Borden, Inc.
Boston Globe (The)
BP Amoco Corp.
Bradford & Co. (J.C.)
Bucyrus-Erie Co.
Burlington Resources, Inc.
Burress (J.W.)
Business Improvement
Cabot Corp.
Carpenter Technology Corp.
Caterpillar Inc.
Century 21
CertainTeed Corp.
CGU Insurance
Chase Bank of Texas
Chase Manhattan Bank, NA
Chesapeake Corp.
Chevron Corp.
Chicago Board of Trade
Cincinnati Bell Inc.
CIT Group, Inc. (The)
Citibank Corp.
Citizens Financial Group, Inc.
CLARCOR Inc.
Colonial Life & Accident Insurance Co.
Comdisco, Inc.
Compass Bank
Consolidated Natural Gas Co.
Conwood Co. LP
Copley Press, Inc.
Cox Enterprises Inc.
Crane Co.
Dana Corp.
Deere & Co.
Deluxe Corp.
Demoulas Supermarkets Inc.
Deposit Guaranty National Bank
Dial Corp.
Dominion Resources, Inc.
Donaldson Co., Inc.
du Pont de Nemours & Co. (E.I.)
Duchossois Industries Inc.
Duriron Co., Inc.
Dynamet, Inc.
Eastman Kodak Co.
Eaton Corp.
EDS Corp.
Emerson Electric Co.
Entergy Corp.
Erb Lumber Co.
Fireman's Fund Insurance Co.
First Hawaiian, Inc.
First Source Corp.
First Union Corp.
First Union National Bank, NA
FleetBoston Financial Corp.
Florida Rock Industries
Forbes Inc.
Ford Meter Box Co.
Furniture Brands International, Inc.
Gallo Winery, Inc. (E&J)
GEICO Corp.
GenAmerica Corp.
General Mills, Inc.
General Motors Corp.
Georgia Power Co.
Grace & Co. (W.R.)
Group Health Plan
Gulf Power Co.
Hamilton Sundstrand Corp.
Hancock Financial Services (John)
Harland Co. (John H.)
Harsco Corp.
Hartford (The)
Heinz Co. (H.J.)
Home Depot, Inc.
Household International Inc.
Hubbard Broadcasting, Inc.
Humana, Inc.
Huntington Bancshares Inc.
Illinois Tool Works, Inc.
International Paper Co.
INTRUST Financial Corp.
Johnson & Son (S.C.)
JSJ Corp.
Kiewit Sons' Inc. (Peter)
Kingsbury Corp.
Kroger Co.
Ladish Co., Inc.
Lancaster Lens, Inc.
Lee Enterprises
Levi Strauss & Co.
Liberty Diversified Industries
Lilly & Co. (Eli)
Little, Inc. (Arthur D.)
Louisiana-Pacific Corp.
Macy's East Inc.
Madison Gas & Electric Co.
MBIA Inc.
McDonald's Corp.
MCI WorldCom, Inc.
Metropolitan Life Insurance Co.
Milliken & Co.
Millipore Corp.
Minnesota Mining & Manufacturing Co.
Monarch Machine Tool Co.
Morgan Stanley Dean Witter & Co.
Mutual of Omaha Insurance Co.
National Bank of Commerce Trust & Savings
National City Bank of Minneapolis
National Machinery Co.
National Presto Industries, Inc.
Nationwide Insurance Co.
NEBCO Evans
Nestle U.S.A. Inc.
New England Financial
New York Times Co.
Newman's Own Inc.
Nordson Corp.
Northeast Utilities

Northern States Power Co.
Northwest Bank Nebraska, NA
Northwest Natural Gas Co.
Norton Co.
Pacific Mutual Life Insurance Co.
Peoples Bank
Peoples Energy Corp.
PPG Industries, Inc.
Premier Industrial Corp.
Prudential Insurance Co. of America
Publix Supermarkets
Pulitzer Publishing Co.
Quaker Chemical Corp.
Ralston Purina Co.
Regions Bank
Reilly Industries, Inc.
Reily & Co., Inc. (William B.)
Rouse Co.
Royal & SunAlliance USA, Inc.
Rubbermaid Inc.
Sara Lee Corp.
Sentinel Communications Co.
Shoney's Inc.
SIT Investment Associates, Inc.
Slant/Fin Corp.
Smith Corp. (A.O.)
Sonoco Products Co.
Sovereign Bank
Sprint/United Telephone
Square D Co.
Stanley Works (The)
State Street Bank & Trust Co.
Steelcase Inc.
Stonecutter Mills Corp.
Storage Technology Corp.
Stride Rite Corp.
Stupp Brothers Bridge & Iron Co.
SunTrust Bank Atlanta
Synovus Financial Corp.
Times Mirror Co.
TJX Companies, Inc.
Trustmark Insurance Co.
Tyson Foods Inc.
Ukrop's Super Markets
Union Camp Corp.
Union Pacific Corp.
United States Trust Co. of New York
Universal Leaf Tobacco Co., Inc.
Unocal Corp.
US Bank, Washington
USX Corp.
Wal-Mart Stores, Inc.
Western & Southern Life Insurance Co.
Whirlpool Corp.
Whitman Corp.
WICOR, Inc.
Williams
Wisconsin Energy Corp.
Wisconsin Public Service Corp.
Witco Corp.
Woodward Governor Co.

PEOPLE WITH DISABILITIES

Abbott Laboratories
ABC
Advanced Micro Devices, Inc.
Aetna, Inc.
AGL Resources Inc.
Agrilink Foods, Inc.
Air Products and Chemicals, Inc.
AK Steel Corp.
Alabama Power Co.
Alcoa Inc.
Alcon Laboratories, Inc.
Allegheny Technologies Inc.
Alliant Techsystems
Allianz Life Insurance Co. of North America
AlliedSignal Inc.
Alma Piston Co.
AMCORE Bank Rockford
Ameren Corp.
American Express Co.
American Fidelity Corp.
American General Finance
American United Life Insurance Co.
Ameritas Life Insurance Corp.
Ameritech Illinois
Ameritech Indiana
Ameritech Wisconsin
AMETEK, Inc.
Amgen, Inc.
AMP Inc.
Andersen Corp.
Andersons Inc.
Anheuser-Busch Companies, Inc.
Aon Corp.
APL Ltd.
Appleton Papers Inc.
Archer-Daniels-Midland Co.
Aristech Chemical Corp.
Arizona Public Service Co.
Armstrong World Industries, Inc.
Arvin Industries, Inc.
ASARCO Inc.
Ashland, Inc.
Associated Food Stores
AT&T Corp.
Atlantic Investment Co.
Auburn Foundry
Avon Products, Inc.
Badger Meter, Inc.
Baird & Co. (Robert W.)
Banfi Vintners
Bank of America
Bank One Corp.
BankAtlantic Bancorp
BankBoston Corp.
Banta Corp.
Barden Corp.
Barnes Group Inc.
Barry Corp. (R.G.)
Battelle Memorial Institute
Bausch & Lomb Inc.
Baxter International Inc.
Bayer Corp.
Bemis Co., Inc.
Ben & Jerry's Homemade Inc.
Bernstein & Co., Inc. (Sanford C.)
Bestfoods
Bethlehem Steel Corp.
BFGoodrich Co.
Binswanger Companies
Blair & Co. (William)
Block, Inc. (H&R)
Blue Bell, Inc.
Blue Cross & Blue Shield of Alabama
Blue Cross & Blue Shield of Iowa
Blue Cross & Blue Shield of Minnesota
Boeing Co.
Borden, Inc.
Borman's Inc.
Boston Edison Co.
Boston Globe (The)
BP Amoco Corp.
Bridgestone/Firestone, Inc.
Bristol-Myers Squibb Co.
Broderbund Software, Inc.
Brown Shoe Co., Inc.
Brunswick Corp.
Bucyrus-Erie Co.
Burlington Industries, Inc.
Burlington Resources, Inc.
Cabot Corp.
California Bank & Trust
Callaway Golf Co.
Calvin Klein
Cantor, Fitzgerald Securities Corp.
Cargill Inc.
Carlson Companies, Inc.
Carnival Corp.
Carpenter Technology Corp.
Carrier Corp.
Carter-Wallace, Inc.
Caterpillar Inc.
Central Maine Power Co.
Central National-Gottesman
Central Newspapers, Inc.
Central Soya Co.
CertainTeed Corp.
Cessna Aircraft Co.
CGU Insurance
Charter Manufacturing Co.
Chase Bank of Texas
Chase Manhattan Bank, NA
Chemed Corp.
Chesapeake Corp.
Chevron Corp.
Chicago Board of Trade
Chicago Sun-Times, Inc.
Chicago Tribune Co.
CIGNA Corp.
Cincinnati Bell Inc.
Cinergy Corp.
CIT Group, Inc. (The)
Citibank Corp.
Citizens Bank-Flint
Citizens Financial Group, Inc.
CLARCOR Inc.
Cleveland-Cliffs, Inc.
Clorox Co.
CNA
CNF Transportation, Inc.
Collins & Aikman Corp.
Colonial Life & Accident Insurance Co.
Colonial Oil Industries, Inc.
Comdisco, Inc.
Commercial Intertech Corp.
Compaq Computer Corp.
Compass Bank
ConAgra, Inc.
Cone Mills Corp.
Consolidated Natural Gas Co.
Consolidated Papers, Inc.
Constellation Energy Group, Inc.
Consumers Energy Co.
Continental Grain Co.
Cooper Industries, Inc.
Coors Brewing Co.
Copley Press, Inc.
Country Curtains, Inc.
CPI Corp.
Crane Co.
Crane & Co., Inc.
Credit Suisse First Boston
Crestar Finance Corp.
CSS Industries, Inc.
Cummings Properties Management
CUNA Mutual Group
Daily News
DaimlerChrysler Corp.
Dain Bosworth Inc.
Dana Corp.
Danis Companies
Dayton Hudson
Dayton Power and Light Co.
Deere & Co.
Delta Air Lines, Inc.
Deluxe Corp.
Demoulas Supermarkets Inc.
Deposit Guaranty National Bank
Deutsch Co.
Dexter Corp.
Dial Corp.
Disney Co. (Walt)
Dominion Resources, Inc.
Domino's Pizza Inc.
Donaldson Co., Inc.
Donnelley & Sons Co. (R.R.)
Dow Jones & Co., Inc.
Dreyer's Grand Ice Cream
du Pont de Nemours & Co. (E.I.)
Duchossois Industries Inc.
Duke Energy
Dun & Bradstreet Corp.
Duriron Co., Inc.
Dynamet, Inc.
Eastern Bank
Eastman Kodak Co.
Eaton Corp.
Eckerd Corp.
Ecolab Inc.
Edison International
EDS Corp.
Edwards Enterprise Software (J.D.)
El Paso Energy Co.
Elf Atochem North America, Inc.
Emerson Electric Co.
EMI Music Publishing
Employers Mutual Casualty Co.
Ensign-Bickford Industries
Equifax Inc.
Equitable Resources, Inc.
Erb Lumber Co.
Evening Post Publishing Co.
Fabri-Kal Corp.
Federal-Mogul Corp.
Federated Department Stores, Inc.
Federated Mutual Insurance Co.
FedEx Corp.
Ferro Corp.
Fidelity Investments
Fifth Third Bancorp
Fireman's Fund Insurance Co.
First Financial Bank
First Hawaiian, Inc.
First Source Corp.
First Union Bank
First Union Corp.
First Union Securities, Inc.
Firstar Bank Milwaukee NA
Fisher Brothers Cleaning Services
Fisher Scientific
FleetBoston Financial Corp.
Florida Power Corp.
Florida Power & Light Co.
Florida Rock Industries
Fort Worth Star-Telegram Inc.
Fortis Insurance Co.
Fortune Brands, Inc.
Franklin Mint (The)
Freddie Mac
Freeport-McMoRan Inc.
Frontier Corp.
Frost National Bank
Fuller Co. (H.B.)
Furniture Brands International, Inc.
Gallo Winery, Inc. (E&J)
Galter Corp.
Gannett Co., Inc.
GATX Corp.
GEICO Corp.
GenAmerica Corp.
General Dynamics Corp.
General Electric Co.
General Mills, Inc.
General Motors Corp.
General Reinsurance Corp.
Georgia-Pacific Corp.
Georgia Power Co.
Gerber Products Co.
Giant Eagle Inc.
Giant Food Inc.
Giddings & Lewis
Glaxo Wellcome Inc.
Glickenhaus & Co.
Globe Corp.
Golub Corp.
Goodrich Aerospace - Aerostructures Group (B.F.)
Grace & Co. (W.R.)
Graco, Inc.
Grede Foundries
Green Bay Packaging
Group Health Plan
GTE Corp.
Gulf Power Co.
Hallmark Cards Inc.
Hamilton Sundstrand Corp.
Hancock Financial Services (John)
Hanna Co. (M.A.)
Harcourt General, Inc.
Harnischfeger Industries
Harris Trust & Savings Bank
Harsco Corp.
Hartford (The)
Hartford Steam Boiler Inspection & Insurance Co.
Hartmarx Corp.
Hasbro, Inc.
Hawaiian Electric Co., Inc.
Heinz Co. (H.J.)
Hensel Phelps Construction Co.
Hershey Foods Corp.
Hoffmann-La Roche Inc.
Hofmann Co.
Honeywell International Inc.
Housatonic Curtain Co.
Household International Inc.
Hubbard Broadcasting, Inc.
Hubbell Inc.
Huffy Corp.
Humana, Inc.
Illinois Tool Works, Inc.
Inland Container Corp.
Inman Mills
International Business Machines Corp.
International Flavors & Fragrances Inc.
International Multifoods Corp.
INTRUST Financial Corp.
Invacare Corp.
Jacobson & Sons (Benjamin)

Jeld-wen, Inc.
Johnson Controls Inc.
Johnson & Johnson
Jostens, Inc.
Journal-Gazette Co.
Kaman Corp.
Katten, Muchin & Zavis
Kellogg Co.
Kellwood Co.
Kelly Services
Kemper National Insurance Companies
Kennametal, Inc.
Kerr-McGee Corp.
Kiewit Sons' Inc. (Peter)
Kimberly-Clark Corp.
Kinder Morgn
Koch Enterprises, Inc.
Koch Industries, Inc.
Kroger Co.
Laclede Gas Co.
Ladish Co., Inc.
Lance, Inc.
Land O'Lakes, Inc.
Lehigh Portland Cement Co.
Leigh Fibers, Inc.
Levi Strauss & Co.
Liberty Corp.
Liberty Diversified Industries
Lilly & Co. (Eli)
Lincoln Electric Co.
Lipton Co.
Little, Inc. (Arthur D.)
Litton Industries, Inc.
Loews Corp.
Lotus Development Corp.
Louisiana-Pacific Corp.
LTV Corp.
Lubrizol Corp. (The)
Macy's East Inc.
Madison Gas & Electric Co.
Mallinckrodt Chemical, Inc.
Maritz Inc.
Mark IV Industries
Marriott International Inc.
Marshall Field's
Marshall & Ilsley Corp.
Mattel Inc.
May Department Stores Co.
Maytag Corp.
Mazda North American Operations
MBIA Inc.
McClatchy Co.
McDonald & Co. Securities, Inc.
McDonald's Corp.
McGraw-Hill Companies, Inc.
MCI WorldCom, Inc.
McKesson-HBOC Corp.
Mellon Financial Corp.
Menasha Corp.
Mercantile Bank NA
Merrill Lynch & Co., Inc.
Michigan Consolidated Gas Co.
Mid-America Bank of Louisville
MidAmerican Energy Holdings Co.
Milliken & Co.
Millipore Corp.
Mine Safety Appliances Co.
Minnesota Mining & Manufacturing Co.
Minnesota Mutual Life Insurance Co.
Mitsubishi Electric America
Monarch Machine Tool Co.
Montgomery Ward & Co., Inc.
MONY Group (The)
Morgan & Co. Inc. (J.P.)
Morris Communications Corp.
Morrison Knudsen Corp.
Morton International Inc.
Motorola Inc.
MTD Products Inc.
Mutual of Omaha Insurance Co.
Nabisco Group Holdings
Nalco Chemical Co.
National Computer Systems, Inc.
National Fuel Gas Distribution Corp.
National Presto Industries, Inc.
National Service Industries, Inc.
Nationwide Insurance Co.
NEBCO Evans
NEC America, Inc.
Nestle U.S.A. Inc.
New England Financial
New Jersey Natural Gas Co.
New York Life Insurance Co.
New York Mercantile Exchange
New York Stock Exchange, Inc.
Newman's Own Inc.
Niagara Mohawk Holdings Inc.
Nordson Corp.
North American Royalties
Northeast Utilities
Northern Indiana Public Service Co.
Northern States Power Co.
Northern Trust Co.
Northwest Bank Nebraska, NA
Northwest Natural Gas Co.
Norton Co.
Norwest Corp.
Occidental Oil and Gas
OG&E Electric Services
Oklahoma Publishing Co.
Old National Bank Evansville
Orange & Rockland Utilities, Inc.
Oshkosh B'Gosh, Inc.
Overseas Shipholding Group Inc.
PACCAR Inc.
Pacific Century Financial Corp.
Pacific Mutual Life Insurance Co.
PacifiCare Health Systems
PacifiCorp
Paine Webber
Pella Corp.
PEMCO Corp.
Penney Co., Inc. (J.C.)
Pennzoil-Quaker State Co.
PepsiCo, Inc.
PerkinElmer, Inc.
Pfizer Inc.
Pharmacia & Upjohn, Inc.
Phillips Petroleum Co.
Physicians Mutual Insurance Co.
Pittway Corp.
Playboy Enterprises Inc.
PNC Bank Kentucky Inc.
PNC Financial Services Group
Polaroid Corp.
Portland General Electric Co.
Potomac Electric Power Co.
PPG Industries, Inc.
Premier Dental Products Co.
Price Associates (T. Rowe)
Principal Financial Group
Procter & Gamble Co.
Procter & Gamble Co., Cosmetics Division
Providence Journal-Bulletin Co.
Prudential Insurance Co. of America
Prudential Securities Inc.
Public Service Electric & Gas Co.
Publix Supermarkets
Putnam Investments
Quaker Chemical Corp.
Quanex Corp.
Questar Corp.
Ralph's Grocery Co.
Ralston Purina Co.
Rayonier Inc.
Red Wing Shoe Co. Inc.
Reilly Industries, Inc.
Reily & Co., Inc. (William B.)
Reinhart Institutional Foods
Reliant Energy Inc.
Revlon Inc.
Reynolds Metals Co.
Reynolds Tobacco (R.J.)
Rockwell International Corp.
Rouse Co.
Royal & SunAlliance USA, Inc.
Rubbermaid Inc.
Russer Foods
SAFECO Corp.
S&T Bancorp
Sara Lee Corp.
Sara Lee Hosiery, Inc.
SBC Communications Inc.
Schloss & Co. (Marcus)
Schlumberger Ltd. (USA)
Schwab & Co., Inc. (Charles)
Schwebel Baking Co.
Scripps Co. (E.W.)
Security Benefit Life Insurance Co.
Security Life of Denver Insurance Co.
Sempra Energy
Sentinel Communications Co.
Sentry Insurance, A Mutual Co.
S.G. Cowen
Shea Co. (John F.)
Shell Oil Co.
Shelter Mutual Insurance Co.
Sherwin-Williams Co.
Sierra Pacific Resources
SIT Investment Associates, Inc.
Slant/Fin Corp.
Smith Corp. (A.O.)
SmithKline Beecham Corp.
Solo Cup Co.
Sony Electronics
Southern New England Telephone Co.
Southwest Gas Corp.
Sovereign Bank
SPX Corp.
Square D Co.
Standard Products Co.
Stanley Works (The)
Star Bank NA
Starwood Hotels & Resorts Worldwide, Inc.
State Street Bank & Trust Co.
Steelcase Inc.
Stone Container Corp.
Storage Technology Corp.
Stride Rite Corp.
Stupp Brothers Bridge & Iron Co.
Subway Sandwich Shops, Inc.
Sun Microsystems Inc.
Sunoco Inc.
SunTrust Bank Atlanta
SuperValu, Inc.
Tai and Co. (J.T.)
Tamko Roofing Products
Temple-Inland Inc.
Tenet Healthcare Corp.
TENNANT Co.
Tenneco Automotive
Tension Envelope Corp.
Tesoro Hawaii
Texaco Inc.
Texas Gas Transmission Corp.
Texas Instruments Inc.
Textron Inc.
Thermo Electron Corp.
Times Mirror Co.
Titan Industrial Corp.
TJX Companies, Inc.
TMC Investment Co.
Tomkins Industries, Inc.
Torchmark Corp.
Toro Co.
Toyota Motor Sales U.S.A., Inc.
Trace International Holdings, Inc.
Transamerica Corp.
True North Communications, Inc.
Trustmark Insurance Co.
TRW Inc.
Unilever United States, Inc.
Union Camp Corp.
Union Carbide Corp.
Union Pacific Corp.
United Distillers & Vintners North America
United Dominion Industries, Ltd.
United Parcel Service of America Inc.
U.S. Bancorp
U.S. Bancorp Piper Jaffray
United States Sugar Corp.
United States Trust Co. of New York
United Technologies Corp.
Universal Foods Corp.
Universal Leaf Tobacco Co., Inc.
Universal Studios
Unocal Corp.
UnumProvident
US Bank, Washington
USG Corp.
USX Corp.
Valmont Industries, Inc.
Valspar Corp.
Varian Medical Systems, Inc.
Vulcan Materials Co.
Wachovia Bank of North Carolina NA
Waffle House Inc.
Wal-Mart Stores, Inc.
Waldbaum's Supermarkets, Inc.
Walgreen Co.
Warner-Lambert Co.
Washington Trust Bank
Wells Fargo & Co.
West Co. Inc.
Western & Southern Life Insurance Co.
Westvaco Corp.
Weyerhaeuser Co.
Whirlpool Corp.
Whitman Corp.
WICOR, Inc.
Wilbur-Ellis Co. & Connell Brothers Co.
Williams
Winn-Dixie Stores Inc.
Wiremold Co.
Wisconsin Energy Corp.
Wisconsin Power & Light Co.
Wisconsin Public Service Corp.
Witco Corp.
Woodward Governor Co.
Wrigley Co. (Wm. Jr.)
Wyman-Gordon Co.
Xerox Corp.
York Federal Savings & Loan Association
Young & Rubicam
Zachry Co. (H.B.)
Zenith Electronics Corp.
Zilkha & Sons

RECREATION & ATHLETICS

AEGON U.S.A. Inc.
Agrilink Foods, Inc.
Air Products and Chemicals, Inc.
AK Steel Corp.
Alcoa Inc.
Allegheny Technologies Inc.
Alliant Techsystems
AlliedSignal Inc.
Allmerica Financial Corp.
Allstate Insurance Co.
Alma Piston Co.
AMCORE Bank Rockford
Ameren Corp.
America West Airlines, Inc.
American Fidelity Corp.
American General Finance
American United Life Insurance Co.
Ameritech Michigan
Ameritech Ohio
Ameritech Wisconsin
Amgen, Inc.
AMP Inc.
AMR Corp.
Amsted Industries Inc.
Andersen Corp.
Andersons Inc.
Anheuser-Busch Companies, Inc.
Aon Corp.
APL Ltd.
Appleton Papers Inc.
Archer-Daniels-Midland Co.
Aristech Chemical Corp.
Arizona Public Service Co.
Armstrong World Industries, Inc.
Arvin Industries, Inc.
Associated Food Stores
Atlantic Richfield Co.
Avery Dennison Corp.
Avon Products, Inc.
Badger Meter, Inc.
Bandag, Inc.
Banfi Vintners
BankBoston Corp.
Banta Corp.
Bard, Inc. (C.R.)
Barden Corp.
Bardes Corp.

Barnes Group Inc.
Bassett Furniture Industries
Battelle Memorial Institute
Bausch & Lomb Inc.
Baxter International Inc.
Bean, Inc. (L.L.)
Bechtel Group, Inc.
Belk Stores Services Inc.
Bemis Co., Inc.
Bemis Manufacturing Co.
Ben & Jerry's Homemade Inc.
Bernstein & Co., Inc. (Sanford C.)
Bethlehem Steel Corp.
BFGoodrich Co.
Binswanger Companies
Blair & Co. (William)
Block, Inc. (H&R)
Blount International, Inc.
Blue Bell, Inc.
Blue Cross & Blue Shield of Alabama
Blue Cross & Blue Shield of Iowa
Boeing Co.
Boise Cascade Corp.
Borden, Inc.
Borman's Inc.
Boston Edison Co.
Boston Globe (The)
Bourns, Inc.
BP Amoco Corp.
Bridgestone/Firestone, Inc.
Bristol-Myers Squibb Co.
Brunswick Corp.
Bucyrus-Erie Co.
Burlington Industries, Inc.
Burlington Resources, Inc.
Burnett Co. (Leo)
Cabot Corp.
Callaway Golf Co.
Calvin Klein
Campbell Soup Co.
Cargill Inc.
Carillon Importers, Ltd.
Carolina Power & Light Co.
Carpenter Technology Corp.
Carris Reels
Carter-Wallace, Inc.
Central Maine Power Co.
Central National-Gottesman
Central Soya Co.
CertainTeed Corp.
Cessna Aircraft Co.
Chase Bank of Texas
Chase Manhattan Bank, NA
Chesapeake Corp.
Cincinnati Bell Inc.
Cinergy Corp.
Circuit City Stores, Inc.
CIT Group, Inc. (The)
Citigroup
Citizens Financial Group, Inc.
CLARCOR Inc.
Cleveland-Cliffs, Inc.
Clorox Co.
Coca-Cola Co.
Collins & Aikman Corp.
Colonial Life & Accident Insurance Co.
Colonial Oil Industries, Inc.
Comdisco, Inc.
Commercial Intertech Corp.
Compass Bank
Cone Mills Corp.
Consolidated Natural Gas Co.
Consolidated Papers, Inc.
Consumers Energy Co.
Cooper Industries, Inc.
Coors Brewing Co.
Copley Press, Inc.
Corning Inc.
Country Curtains, Inc.
CPI Corp.
Crane Co.
Crane & Co., Inc.
Credit Suisse First Boston
Crestar Finance Corp.
Croft-Leominster
CSS Industries, Inc.
Cummings Properties Management
Cummins Engine Co., Inc.
CUNA Mutual Group
Daily News
DaimlerChrysler Corp.
Dain Bosworth Inc.
Dana Corp.
Deere & Co.
DeKalb Genetics Corp.
Demoulas Supermarkets Inc.
Deposit Guaranty National Bank
Detroit Edison Co.
Deutsch Co.
Dial Corp.
Disney Co. (Walt)
Dixie Group, Inc. (The)
Dreyer's Grand Ice Cream
du Pont de Nemours & Co. (E.I.)
Duchossois Industries Inc.
Duke Energy
Dun & Bradstreet Corp.
Dynamet, Inc.
Eastern Bank
Eastman Kodak Co.
Eaton Corp.
Eckerd Corp.
Edison International
EDS Corp.
Edwards Enterprise Software (J.D.)
El Paso Energy Co.
Emerson Electric Co.
Employers Mutual Casualty Co.
Ensign-Bickford Industries
Enterprise Rent-A-Car Co.
Erving Industries
Evening Post Publishing Co.
Federal-Mogul Corp.
Federated Department Stores, Inc.
Fidelity Investments
Fifth Third Bancorp
FINA
First American Corp.
First Financial Bank
First Hawaiian, Inc.
First Maryland Bancorp
First Source Corp.
First Union National Bank, NA
First Union Securities, Inc.
Firstar Bank Milwaukee NA
Fisher Brothers Cleaning Services
FleetBoston Financial Corp.
Florida Power Corp.
Florida Rock Industries
Forbes Inc.
Ford Meter Box Co.
Ford Motor Co.
Fort Worth Star-Telegram Inc.
Fortis, Inc.
Fortune Brands, Inc.
Franklin Electric Co.
Freddie Mac
Freeport-McMoRan Inc.
Frost National Bank
Fuller Co. (H.B.)
Furniture Brands International, Inc.
Gallo Winery, Inc. (E&J)
Gannett Co., Inc.
Gap, Inc.
GEICO Corp.
GenAmerica Corp.
General Mills, Inc.
General Reinsurance Corp.
Georgia-Pacific Corp.
Georgia Power Co.
Gerber Products Co.
Giant Eagle Inc.
Giant Food Inc.
Giddings & Lewis
Golub Corp.
Grace & Co. (W.R.)
Graco, Inc.
Hallmark Cards Inc.
Hamilton Sundstrand Corp.
Hancock Financial Services (John)
Hanna Co. (M.A.)
Harnischfeger Industries
Harris Corp.
Harsco Corp.
Hartford (The)
Hartmarx Corp.
Hasbro, Inc.
Hawaiian Electric Co., Inc.
Heinz Co. (H.J.)
Hensel Phelps Construction Co.
Hickory Tech Corp.
Hoffer Plastics Corp.
Hofmann Co.
HON Industries Inc.
Hubbard Broadcasting, Inc.
Hubbell Inc.
Huffy Corp.
Humana, Inc.
IBP
IKON Office Solutions, Inc.
Independent Stave Co.
Inman Mills
International Flavors & Fragrances Inc.
International Multifoods Corp.
INTRUST Financial Corp.
Invacare Corp.
Jacobs Engineering Group
Jacobson & Sons (Benjamin)
Jeld-wen, Inc.
Johnson Controls Inc.
Johnson & Son (S.C.)
Journal-Gazette Co.
JSJ Corp.
Kennametal, Inc.
Kerr-McGee Corp.
Kiewit Sons' Inc. (Peter)
Kimberly-Clark Corp.
Kinder Morgn
Kingsbury Corp.
Kroger Co.
Ladish Co., Inc.
Lancaster Lens, Inc.
Lance, Inc.
Land O'Lakes, Inc.
Lee Enterprises
Lehigh Portland Cement Co.
Lennox International, Inc.
Liberty Diversified Industries
Lilly & Co. (Eli)
Lincoln Financial Group
Lipton Co.
Litton Industries, Inc.
Liz Claiborne, Inc.
Loews Corp.
Louisiana Land & Exploration Co.
Louisiana-Pacific Corp.
LTV Corp.
Lubrizol Corp. (The)
MacMillan Bloedel Inc.
Macy's East Inc.
Madison Gas & Electric Co.
Marcus Corp.
Mark IV Industries
Marshall & Ilsley Corp.
Masco Corp.
Mattel Inc.
Maytag Corp.
MBIA Inc.
McClatchy Co.
McDonald & Co. Securities, Inc.
MCI WorldCom, Inc.
McWane Inc.
Menasha Corp.
Merit Oil Corp.
Merrill Lynch & Co., Inc.
Michigan Consolidated Gas Co.
Mid-America Bank of Louisville
MidAmerican Energy Holdings Co.
Milliken & Co.
Millipore Corp.
Mine Safety Appliances Co.
Minnesota Mining & Manufacturing Co.
Mitsubishi Electric America
Montana Power Co.
Montgomery Ward & Co., Inc.
Morgan & Co. Inc. (J.P.)
Morgan Stanley Dean Witter & Co.
Morris Communications Corp.
Morrison Knudsen Corp.
Motorola Inc.
MTD Products Inc.
Nabisco Group Holdings
National Bank of Commerce Trust & Savings
National City Bank of Minneapolis
National City Corp.
National Computer Systems, Inc.
National Life of Vermont
National Presto Industries, Inc.
National Service Industries, Inc.
National Starch & Chemical Co.
Nationwide Insurance Co.
Navcom Systems
NEBCO Evans
New England Financial
New York Life Insurance Co.
New York Mercantile Exchange
New York Stock Exchange, Inc.
New York Times Co.
Nike, Inc.
Nordson Corp.
Northern Indiana Public Service Co.
Northern Trust Co.
Northwest Bank Nebraska, NA
Norton Co.
Norwest Corp.
OG&E Electric Services
Ohio National Life Insurance Co.
Oklahoma Publishing Co.
Old National Bank Evansville
Osborne Enterprises
Oshkosh B'Gosh, Inc.
Outboard Marine Corp.
Overseas Shipholding Group Inc.
Pacific Century Financial Corp.
Pacific Mutual Life Insurance Co.
PacifiCare Health Systems
PacifiCorp
Paine Webber
Park National Bank
Pella Corp.
Penney Co., Inc. (J.C.)
Pfizer Inc.
Pharmacia & Upjohn, Inc.
Phelps Dodge Corp.
Phillips Petroleum Co.
Physicians Mutual Insurance Co.
Pieper Power Electric Co.
Pillsbury Co.
PNC Financial Services Group
Polaroid Corp.
Potomac Electric Power Co.
Premier Dental Products Co.
Premier Industrial Corp.
Price Associates (T. Rowe)
Principal Financial Group
Procter & Gamble Co.
Procter & Gamble Co., Cosmetics Division
Provident Companies, Inc.
Prudential Insurance Co. of America
Public Service Electric & Gas Co.
Pulitzer Publishing Co.
Putnam Investments
Quaker Chemical Corp.
Quanex Corp.
Ralph's Grocery Co.
Ralston Purina Co.
Rayonier Inc.
Red Wing Shoe Co. Inc.
Reebok International Ltd.
Regions Bank
REI-Recreational Equipment, Inc.
Reinhart Institutional Foods
Reynolds Metals Co.
Reynolds Tobacco (R.J.)
Rich Products Corp.
Rockwell International Corp.
Royal & SunAlliance USA, Inc.
Russer Foods
Ryder System, Inc.
Safeguard Scientifics
Saint Paul Companies Inc.
Salomon Smith Barney
S&T Bancorp
Schwab & Co., Inc. (Charles)
Schwebel Baking Co.
Seaway Food Town, Inc.
Security Life of Denver Insurance Co.
Sega of America Inc.
Sempra Energy
Sentry Insurance, A Mutual Co.
S.G. Cowen
Shaklee Corp.
Shaw's Supermarkets, Inc.
Shea Co. (John F.)

Funders by Recipient Type

Shell Oil Co.
Sherwin-Williams Co.
Sierra Pacific Industries
Sierra Pacific Resources
Simplot Co. (J.R.)
Simpson Investment Co.
SIT Investment Associates, Inc.
Slant/Fin Corp.
Smith Corp. (A.O.)
Sonoco Products Co.
Sony Electronics
Southwest Gas Corp.
Square D Co.
Standard Register Co.
Star Bank NA
Starwood Hotels & Resorts Worldwide, Inc.
State Street Bank & Trust Co.
Steelcase Inc.
Stonecutter Mills Corp.
Storage Technology Corp.
Stride Rite Corp.
Stupp Brothers Bridge & Iron Co.
Sun Microsystems Inc.
SunTrust Bank Atlanta
Susquehanna-Pfaltzgraff Co.
Synovus Financial Corp.
TCF National Bank Minnesota
Tenneco Packaging
Tesoro Hawaii
Texaco Inc.
Texas Gas Transmission Corp.
Textron Inc.
Thomasville Furniture Industries Inc.
Thompson Co. (J. Walter)
Ticketmaster Corp.
Times Mirror Co.
TMC Investment Co.
Toledo Blade Co.
Tomkins Industries, Inc.
Toro Co.
Trace International Holdings, Inc.
Transamerica Corp.
True North Communications, Inc.
True Oil Co.
Trustmark Insurance Co.
TRW Inc.
Tyson Foods Inc.
Ukrop's Super Markets
Unilever Home & Personal Care U.S.A.
Unilever United States, Inc.
Union Camp Corp.
Union Pacific Corp.
United Airlines Inc.
United Distillers & Vintners North America
United Dominion Industries, Ltd.
U.S. Bancorp Piper Jaffray
United States Sugar Corp.
United Wisconsin Services
Universal Leaf Tobacco Co., Inc.
Universal Studios
Unocal Corp.
UnumProvident
Valmont Industries, Inc.
Varian Medical Systems, Inc.
Vesper Corp.
Vodafone AirTouch Plc
Vulcan Materials Co.
Wachovia Bank of North Carolina NA
Waffle House Inc.
Wal-Mart Stores, Inc.
Walter Industries Inc.
Washington Trust Bank
Webster Bank
Weil, Gotshal & Manges Corp.
Westvaco Corp.
Weyerhaeuser Co.
Whirlpool Corp.
Whitman Corp.
WICOR, Inc.
Wilbur-Ellis Co. & Connell Brothers Co.
Williams
Winn-Dixie Stores Inc.
Wiremold Co.
Wisconsin Energy Corp.
Wisconsin Public Service Corp.
Witco Corp.
Wolverine World Wide
Woodward Governor Co.
Wyman-Gordon Co.
York Federal Savings & Loan Association
Young & Rubicam
Zilkha & Sons

REFUGEE ASSISTANCE

American Retail Group
Andersen Corp.
Andersons Inc.
Aon Corp.
APL Ltd.
Avon Products, Inc.
Baxter International Inc.
Bernstein & Co., Inc. (Sanford C.)
Bestfoods
Blair & Co. (William)
Block, Inc. (H&R)
Chevron Corp.
Colonial Life & Accident Insurance Co.
Dayton Hudson
FleetBoston Financial Corp.
Fuller Co. (H.B.)
General Mills, Inc.
Hasbro, Inc.
Honeywell International Inc.
Levi Strauss & Co.
Lotus Development Corp.
McClatchy Co.
Minnesota Mutual Life Insurance Co.
MONY Group (The)
National City Bank of Minneapolis
New England Financial
Northern States Power Co.
Physicians Mutual Insurance Co.
Playboy Enterprises Inc.
Reebok International Ltd.
Reliant Energy Inc.
Royal & SunAlliance USA, Inc.
Sara Lee Corp.
Sara Lee Hosiery, Inc.
Slant/Fin Corp.
State Street Bank & Trust Co.
TENNANT Co.
Textron Inc.
Trace International Holdings, Inc.
US Bank, Washington

SCOUTS

Abbott Laboratories
ABC
Aetna, Inc.
Agrilink Foods, Inc.
Air Products and Chemicals, Inc.
AK Steel Corp.
Alabama Power Co.
Alexander & Baldwin, Inc.
Allegheny Technologies Inc.
Allianz Life Insurance Co. of North America
Allmerica Financial Corp.
Allstate Insurance Co.
AMCORE Bank Rockford
Ameren Corp.
American Fidelity Corp.
American General Finance
American United Life Insurance Co.
Ameritas Life Insurance Corp.
Ameritech Ohio
AMETEK, Inc.
AMP Inc.
AMR Corp.
Andersen Corp.
Andersons Inc.
Anheuser-Busch Companies, Inc.
APL Ltd.
Archer-Daniels-Midland Co.
Aristech Chemical Corp.
Arizona Public Service Co.
Armstrong World Industries, Inc.
Arvin Industries, Inc.
Associated Food Stores
Atlantic Investment Co.
Atlantic Richfield Co.
Auburn Foundry
Badger Meter, Inc.
Baird & Co. (Robert W.)
BankAtlantic Bancorp
Banta Corp.
Barclays Capital
Bard, Inc. (C.R.)
Barden Corp.
Barnes Group Inc.
Barry Corp. (R.G.)
Bassett Furniture Industries
Bechtel Group, Inc.
Belk Stores Services Inc.
Bemis Co., Inc.
Bemis Manufacturing Co.
BFGoodrich Co.
Binswanger Companies
Blair & Co. (William)
Block, Inc. (H&R)
Blount International, Inc.
Blue Bell, Inc.
Blue Cross & Blue Shield of Alabama
Blue Cross & Blue Shield of Iowa
Blue Cross & Blue Shield of Minnesota
Borden, Inc.
Bourns, Inc.
Bradford & Co. (J.C.)
Bridgestone/Firestone, Inc.
Briggs & Stratton Corp.
Brown Shoe Co., Inc.
Brunswick Corp.
Bucyrus-Erie Co.
Burlington Industries, Inc.
Burnett Co. (Leo)
Butler Manufacturing Co.
Calvin Klein
Campbell Soup Co.
Cargill Inc.
Carlson Companies, Inc.
Carpenter Technology Corp.
Carris Reels
Central National-Gottesman
Central Soya Co.
Century 21
CertainTeed Corp.
Cessna Aircraft Co.
CGU Insurance
Charter Manufacturing Co.
Chase Bank of Texas
Chase Manhattan Bank, NA
Chesapeake Corp.
Chicago Board of Trade
Chicago Title Corp.
Cincinnati Bell Inc.
Cinergy Corp.
CIT Group, Inc. (The)
Citigroup
Citizens Financial Group, Inc.
CLARCOR Inc.
Cleveland-Cliffs, Inc.
Clorox Co.
CNA
Collins & Aikman Corp.
Colonial Oil Industries, Inc.
Comdisco, Inc.
Commerce Bancshares, Inc.
Commercial Intertech Corp.
Compaq Computer Corp.
Compass Bank
ConAgra, Inc.
Consolidated Papers, Inc.
Constellation Energy Group, Inc.
Consumers Energy Co.
Conwood Co. LP
Corning Inc.
CPI Corp.
Cranston Print Works Co.
Credit Suisse First Boston
Crestar Finance Corp.
CSR Rinker Materials Corp.
CSS Industries, Inc.
Cummings Properties Management
Cummins Engine Co., Inc.
CUNA Mutual Group
DaimlerChrysler Corp.
Dain Bosworth Inc.
Dana Corp.
Danis Companies
Dayton Power and Light Co.
Deere & Co.
Deluxe Corp.
Demoulas Supermarkets Inc.
Deposit Guaranty National Bank
Dexter Corp.
Dial Corp.
Disney Co. (Walt)
Dixie Group, Inc. (The)
Dow Corning Corp.
Dreyer's Grand Ice Cream
Duchossois Industries Inc.
Duke Energy
Duriron Co., Inc.
Dynamet, Inc.
Eastman Kodak Co.
Edwards Enterprise Software (J.D.)
El Paso Energy Co.
Emerson Electric Co.
Employers Mutual Casualty Co.
Ensign-Bickford Industries
Enterprise Rent-A-Car Co.
Erving Industries
Exxon Mobil Corp.
Federal-Mogul Corp.
Federated Mutual Insurance Co.
Fidelity Investments
Fifth Third Bancorp
FINA
First American Corp.
First Financial Bank
First Hawaiian, Inc.
First Maryland Bancorp
Fisher Brothers Cleaning Services
Fisher Scientific
Florida Power & Light Co.
Florida Rock Industries
Fluor Corp.
Forbes Inc.
Ford Meter Box Co.
Fort Worth Star-Telegram Inc.
Fortis Insurance Co.
Franklin Electric Co.
Freeport-McMoRan Inc.
Fuller Co. (H.B.)
Furniture Brands International, Inc.
Gallo Winery, Inc. (E&J)
Galter Corp.
GEICO Corp.
GenAmerica Corp.
GenCorp
General Mills, Inc.
Georgia-Pacific Corp.
Georgia Power Co.
Giant Eagle Inc.
Giant Food Inc.
Giddings & Lewis
Golub Corp.
Grace & Co. (W.R.)
Graco, Inc.
Guess?
Gulf Power Co.
Halliburton Co.
Hallmark Cards Inc.
Hamilton Sundstrand Corp.
Hannaford Brothers Co.
Harcourt General, Inc.
Harley-Davidson Co.
Harris Corp.
Harris Trust & Savings Bank
Harsco Corp.
Hartmarx Corp.
Hasbro, Inc.
Hawaiian Electric Co., Inc.
Hickory Tech Corp.
Hoffer Plastics Corp.
Hofmann Co.
HON Industries Inc.
Honeywell International Inc.
Hubbard Broadcasting, Inc.
Hubbell Inc.
Huffy Corp.
Humana, Inc.
Idaho Power Co.
IKON Office Solutions, Inc.
Illinois Tool Works, Inc.
Independent Stave Co.
Inland Container Corp.
Inman Mills
International Flavors & Fragrances Inc.
International Multifoods Corp.
INTRUST Financial Corp.
Invacare Corp.
Jacobs Engineering Group
Jacobson & Sons (Benjamin)
Jeld-wen, Inc.
Johnson & Son (S.C.)
Jostens, Inc.
Journal-Gazette Co.
JSJ Corp.
Katten, Muchin & Zavis

Kellwood Co.
Kelly Services
Kennametal, Inc.
Kimball International, Inc.
Kingsbury Corp.
Koch Enterprises, Inc.
Kroger Co.
Laclede Gas Co.
Lance, Inc.
Lee Enterprises
Lehigh Portland Cement Co.
Levi Strauss & Co.
Leviton Manufacturing Co. Inc.
LG&E Energy Corp.
Liberty Corp.
Lincoln Electric Co.
Lipton Co.
Litton Industries, Inc.
Loews Corp.
Louisiana Land & Exploration Co.
Louisiana-Pacific Corp.
LTV Corp.
Lubrizol Corp. (The)
Madison Gas & Electric Co.
Marcus Corp.
May Department Stores Co.
McWane Inc.
Mead Corp.
Mercantile Bank NA
Merit Oil Corp.
Merrill Lynch & Co., Inc.
Metropolitan Life Insurance Co.
Mid-America Bank of Louisville
MidAmerican Energy Holdings Co.
Milliken & Co.
Mine Safety Appliances Co.
Minnesota Mining & Manufacturing Co.
Minnesota Mutual Life Insurance Co.
Mitsubishi Electric America
Monarch Machine Tool Co.
Monsanto Co.
Montana Power Co.
Montgomery Ward & Co., Inc.
MONY Group (The)
Morgan Stanley Dean Witter & Co.
Morris Communications Corp.
Morrison Knudsen Corp.
MTD Products Inc.
National Bank of Commerce Trust & Savings
National City Bank of Minneapolis
National City Corp.
National Machinery Co.
National Service Industries, Inc.
National Starch & Chemical Co.
NEBCO Evans
New Jersey Natural Gas Co.
New York Stock Exchange, Inc.
Niagara Mohawk Holdings Inc.
Nomura Holding America
Nordson Corp.
Norton Co.
Occidental Oil and Gas
OG&E Electric Services
Oklahoma Publishing Co.
Old Kent Bank
Old National Bank Evansville
Orscheln Co.
Osborne Enterprises
Oshkosh B'Gosh, Inc.
Outboard Marine Corp.
Owens Corning
PACCAR Inc.
Pacific Century Financial Corp.
PacifiCorp
Park National Bank
Parker Hannifin Corp.
Pella Corp.
PEMCO Corp.
PepsiCo, Inc.
Phelps Dodge Corp.
Pheonix Financial Group
Phillips Petroleum Co.
Physicians Mutual Insurance Co.
Pieper Power Electric Co.
Pillsbury Co.
PNC Financial Services Group
PPG Industries, Inc.
Praxair
Premier Industrial Corp.
Price Associates (T. Rowe)
Principal Financial Group
Procter & Gamble Co.
Providence Journal-Bulletin Co.
Provident Companies, Inc.
Prudential Insurance Co. of America
Prudential Securities Inc.
Publix Supermarkets
Pulitzer Publishing Co.
Putnam Investments
Quaker Chemical Corp.
Quanex Corp.
Ralph's Grocery Co.
Ralston Purina Co.
Rayonier Inc.
Red Wing Shoe Co. Inc.
Regions Bank
Reilly Industries, Inc.
Reily & Co., Inc. (William B.)
Reinhart Institutional Foods
Reynolds Metals Co.
Reynolds & Reynolds Co.
Reynolds Tobacco (R.J.)
Rockwell International Corp.
Ruddick Corp.
Russer Foods
Ryder System, Inc.
Safeguard Scientifics
S&T Bancorp
SBC Communications Inc.
Schloss & Co. (Marcus)
Scripps Co. (E.W.)
Security Benefit Life Insurance Co.
Sega of America Inc.
Sentry Insurance, A Mutual Co.
Servco Pacific
Shea Co. (John F.)
Shell Oil Co.
Shelter Mutual Insurance Co.
Sierra Pacific Industries
Sierra Pacific Resources
Simpson Investment Co.
Smurfit-Stone Container Corp.
Solo Cup Co.
Sonoco Products Co.
Sony Electronics
Southeastern Mutual Insurance Co.
Southwest Gas Corp.
Sprint Corp.
SPX Corp.
Standard Products Co.
Standard Register Co.
Star Bank NA
State Street Bank & Trust Co.
Steelcase Inc.
Stone Container Corp.
Stonecutter Mills Corp.
Storage Technology Corp.
Stride Rite Corp.
Stupp Brothers Bridge & Iron Co.
Susquehanna-Pfaltzgraff Co.
Sverdrup Corp.
Synovus Financial Corp.
Tamko Roofing Products
TCF National Bank Minnesota
Teleflex Inc.
Tesoro Hawaii
Texas Instruments Inc.
Textron Inc.
Thermo Electron Corp.
Thompson Co. (J. Walter)
Times Mirror Co.
Timken Co. (The)
TJX Companies, Inc.
TMC Investment Co.
Toledo Blade Co.
Tomkins Industries, Inc.
Trace International Holdings, Inc.
Transamerica Corp.
True North Communications, Inc.
TRW Inc.
Tyson Foods Inc.
Unilever Home & Personal Care U.S.A.
Union Camp Corp.
Union Pacific Corp.
Union Planters Corp.
United Co.
United Distillers & Vintners North America
United Dominion Industries, Ltd.
United Services Automobile Association
U.S. Bancorp
U.S. Bancorp Piper Jaffray
United States Sugar Corp.
United Wisconsin Services
Universal Foods Corp.
Universal Leaf Tobacco Co., Inc.
Universal Studios
Unocal Corp.
UnumProvident
USG Corp.
USX Corp.
Valmont Industries, Inc.
Vodafone AirTouch Plc
Vulcan Materials Co.
Wachovia Bank of North Carolina NA
Waffle House Inc.
Walter Industries Inc.
Washington Mutual, Inc.
Washington Trust Bank
Weil, Gotshal & Manges Corp.
West Co. Inc.
Western & Southern Life Insurance Co.
Weyerhaeuser Co.
Whitman Corp.
WICOR, Inc.
Winn-Dixie Stores Inc.
Wisconsin Energy Corp.
Wisconsin Public Service Corp.
Witco Corp.
Wolverine World Wide
Woodward Governor Co.
Wyman-Gordon Co.
Yellow Corp.
York Federal Savings & Loan Association
Young & Rubicam
Zachry Co. (H.B.)
Zilkha & Sons

SENIOR SERVICES

ABC
AGL Resources Inc.
Agrilink Foods, Inc.
Air Products and Chemicals, Inc.
AK Steel Corp.
Alabama Power Co.
Albertson's Inc.
Alcoa Inc.
Allegheny Technologies Inc.
AlliedSignal Inc.
Alma Piston Co.
AMCORE Bank Rockford
Ameren Corp.
American Express Co.
American General Finance
American Retail Group
American United Life Insurance Co.
Ameritas Life Insurance Corp.
Ameritech Corp.
Ameritech Indiana
Ameritech Michigan
AMETEK, Inc.
Amgen, Inc.
AMR Corp.
Andersons Inc.
Anheuser-Busch Companies, Inc.
Aon Corp.
Appleton Papers Inc.
Archer-Daniels-Midland Co.
Ashland, Inc.
Atlantic Richfield Co.
Avista Corporation
Avon Products, Inc.
Banfi Vintners
BankAtlantic Bancorp
BankBoston Corp.
Barnes Group Inc.
Barry Corp. (R.G.)
Battelle Memorial Institute
Baxter International Inc.
Belk-Simpson Department Stores
Belk Stores Services Inc.
Bemis Co., Inc.
Ben & Jerry's Homemade Inc.
Bernstein & Co., Inc. (Sanford C.)
Berwind Group
Bestfoods
Bethlehem Steel Corp.
BFGoodrich Co.
Blair & Co. (William)
Block, Inc. (H&R)
Blount International, Inc.
Blue Cross & Blue Shield of Iowa
Blue Cross & Blue Shield of Minnesota
Boeing Co.
Boise Cascade Corp.
Borman's Inc.
Boston Edison Co.
Bridgestone/Firestone, Inc.
Broderbund Software, Inc.
Brown & Williamson Tobacco Corp.
Brunswick Corp.
Bucyrus-Erie Co.
Burress (J.W.)
Cabot Corp.
Cargill Inc.
Carrier Corp.
Carris Reels
Central Maine Power Co.
CGU Insurance
Chase Bank of Texas
Chase Manhattan Bank, NA
Chevron Corp.
Chicago Title Corp.
Chicago Tribune Co.
Citizens Financial Group, Inc.
Cleveland-Cliffs, Inc.
Clorox Co.
CNF Transportation, Inc.
Colonial Life & Accident Insurance Co.
Commercial Intertech Corp.
Consolidated Natural Gas Co.
Consolidated Papers, Inc.
Constellation Energy Group, Inc.
Consumers Energy Co.
Cooper Industries, Inc.
Cooper Tire & Rubber Co.
Coors Brewing Co.
Copley Press, Inc.
Corning Inc.
Crestar Finance Corp.
Cummings Properties Management
Cummins Engine Co., Inc.
CUNA Mutual Group
DaimlerChrysler Corp.
Dain Bosworth Inc.
Dayton Power and Light Co.
Deere & Co.
Deluxe Corp.
Demoulas Supermarkets Inc.
Deposit Guaranty National Bank
Deutsch Co.
Dominion Resources, Inc.
Domino's Pizza Inc.
Donaldson Co., Inc.
du Pont de Nemours & Co. (E.I.)
Duke Energy
Duriron Co., Inc.
Dynamet, Inc.
Eaton Corp.
Ecolab Inc.
Edison International
El Paso Energy Co.
Emerson Electric Co.
EMI Music Publishing
Employers Mutual Casualty Co.
Ensign-Bickford Industries
Equifax Inc.
Equitable Resources, Inc.
Erb Lumber Co.
European American Bank
Extendicare Health Services
Fabri-Kal Corp.
Federated Department Stores, Inc.
Federated Mutual Insurance Co.
FedEx Corp.
Fidelity Investments
Fifth Third Bancorp

Funders by Recipient Type

Fireman's Fund Insurance Co.
First Financial Bank
First Hawaiian, Inc.
First Union Corp.
First Union National Bank, NA
First Union Securities, Inc.
Firstar Bank Milwaukee NA
Fisher Brothers Cleaning Services
FleetBoston Financial Corp.
Florida Power Corp.
Florida Power & Light Co.
Florida Rock Industries
Forbes Inc.
Ford Meter Box Co.
Fort Worth Star-Telegram Inc.
Fox Entertainment Group
Freddie Mac
Freeport-McMoRan Inc.
Frontier Corp.
Frost National Bank
Furniture Brands International, Inc.
Gallo Winery, Inc. (E&J)
Galter Corp.
Gannett Co., Inc.
Gap, Inc.
GATX Corp.
GEICO Corp.
GenAmerica Corp.
General Electric Co.
General Mills, Inc.
General Motors Corp.
Georgia Power Co.
Giant Eagle Inc.
Giant Food Inc.
Glaxo Wellcome Inc.
Glickenhaus & Co.
Golub Corp.
Goodrich Aerospace - Aerostructures Group (B.F.)
Grace & Co. (W.R.)
Graco, Inc.
Grede Foundries
GTE Corp.
Gucci America Inc.
Gulf Power Co.
Hallmark Cards Inc.
Hancock Financial Services (John)
Hanna Co. (M.A.)
Hannaford Brothers Co.
Hartford (The)
Hartmarx Corp.
Hasbro, Inc.
Heinz Co. (H.J.)
Hickory Tech Corp.
Hofmann Co.
Honeywell International Inc.
Household International Inc.
Humana, Inc.
Hunt Manufacturing Co.
Illinois Tool Works, Inc.
Inland Container Corp.
International Business Machines Corp.
International Flavors & Fragrances Inc.
International Paper Co.
Invacare Corp.
Jacobs Engineering Group
Jeld-wen, Inc.
Johnson Controls Inc.
Jostens, Inc.
Journal-Gazette Co.
Katten, Muchin & Zavis
Kellogg Co.
Kelly Services
Kimball International, Inc.
Kimberly-Clark Corp.
Kinder Morgn
Kingsbury Corp.
Koch Industries, Inc.
Kroger Co.
La-Z-Boy Inc.
Ladish Co., Inc.
Lance, Inc.
Land O'Lakes, Inc.
Lee Enterprises
Leigh Fibers, Inc.
Levi Strauss & Co.
Leviton Manufacturing Co. Inc.
Lincoln Financial Group
Little, Inc. (Arthur D.)
Liz Claiborne, Inc.
LTV Corp.
Macy's East Inc.
Madison Gas & Electric Co.
Manor Care Health SVS, Inc.
Mazda North American Operations
MBIA Inc.
McDonald & Co. Securities, Inc.
Medtronic, Inc.
Menasha Corp.
Merck & Co.
Merrill Lynch & Co., Inc.
MGIC Investment Corp.
Michigan Consolidated Gas Co.
Minnesota Mining & Manufacturing Co.
MONY Group (The)
Morgan & Co. Inc. (J.P.)
Motorola Inc.
National City Bank of Minneapolis
National City Corp.
National Machinery Co.
Nationwide Insurance Co.
NEBCO Evans
New Century Energies
New England Financial
New York Life Insurance Co.
New York Mercantile Exchange
New York Times Co.
Newman's Own Inc.
Nordson Corp.
Northeast Utilities
Northern Indiana Public Service Co.
Northern States Power Co.
Northwest Natural Gas Co.
Norton Co.
Occidental Oil and Gas
OG&E Electric Services
Old Kent Bank
Old National Bank Evansville
Oshkosh B'Gosh, Inc.
PACCAR Inc.
Pacific Century Financial Corp.
Pacific Mutual Life Insurance Co.
PacifiCare Health Systems
Park National Bank
Parker Hannifin Corp.
Pella Corp.
PEMCO Corp.
Peoples Energy Corp.
Pfizer Inc.
Pharmacia & Upjohn, Inc.
Phelps Dodge Corp.
Philip Morris Companies Inc.
Phillips Petroleum Co.
Physicians Mutual Insurance Co.
Playboy Enterprises Inc.
PNC Financial Services Group
Portland General Electric Co.
Potomac Electric Power Co.
PPG Industries, Inc.
Principal Financial Group
Procter & Gamble Co., Cosmetics Division
Providence Journal-Bulletin Co.
Prudential Insurance Co. of America
Prudential Securities Inc.
Public Service Electric & Gas Co.
Pulitzer Publishing Co.
Quanex Corp.
Ralston Purina Co.
Rayonier Inc.
Reader's Digest Association, Inc. (The)
Reilly Industries, Inc.
Reliant Energy Inc.
Reynolds & Reynolds Co.
Reynolds Tobacco (R.J.)
Rouse Co.
Royal & SunAlliance USA, Inc.
Ruddick Corp.
Russer Foods
SAFECO Corp.
Saint Paul Companies Inc.
S&T Bancorp
Sara Lee Corp.
Sara Lee Hosiery, Inc.
SBC Communications Inc.
Schwab & Co., Inc. (Charles)
Searle & Co. (G.D.)
Security Life of Denver Insurance Co.
Sempra Energy
Sentinel Communications Co.
Shaw's Supermarkets, Inc.
Shea Co. (John F.)
Shell Oil Co.
Shelter Mutual Insurance Co.
Sierra Pacific Industries
Sierra Pacific Resources
Simpson Investment Co.
Slant/Fin Corp.
Smith Corp. (A.O.)
Solo Cup Co.
Southeastern Mutual Insurance Co.
Southern New England Telephone Co.
Square D Co.
Standard Register Co.
Star Bank NA
Starwood Hotels & Resorts Worldwide, Inc.
Steelcase Inc.
Stride Rite Corp.
Stupp Brothers Bridge & Iron Co.
Subway Sandwich Shops, Inc.
Sunoco Inc.
SunTrust Bank Atlanta
Synovus Financial Corp.
Tamko Roofing Products
TCF National Bank Minnesota
Teleflex Inc.
Tenet Healthcare Corp.
Tenneco Automotive
Texaco Inc.
Texas Gas Transmission Corp.
Textron Inc.
Thermo Electron Corp.
Times Mirror Co.
Transamerica Corp.
True North Communications, Inc.
TRW Inc.
Unilever Home & Personal Care U.S.A.
Unilever United States, Inc.
Union Camp Corp.
Union Pacific Corp.
United Airlines Inc.
United Dominion Industries, Ltd.
United Parcel Service of America Inc.
United States Trust Co. of New York
United Technologies Corp.
United Wisconsin Services
Universal Studios
UnumProvident
US Bank, Washington
UST Inc.
USX Corp.
Valero Energy Corp.
Valmont Industries, Inc.
Varian Medical Systems, Inc.
Vulcan Materials Co.
Wachovia Bank of North Carolina NA
Waffle House Inc.
Wal-Mart Stores, Inc.
Waldbaum's Supermarkets, Inc.
Warner-Lambert Co.
Washington Mutual, Inc.
Washington Trust Bank
Wells Fargo & Co.
West Co. Inc.
Western Resources Inc.
Western & Southern Life Insurance Co.
Whirlpool Corp.
Wiremold Co.
Wisconsin Energy Corp.
Wisconsin Public Service Corp.
Woodward Governor Co.
Wrigley Co. (Wm. Jr.)
Wyman-Gordon Co.
Xerox Corp.
Zachry Co. (H.B.)

SEXUAL ABUSE

Abbott Laboratories
Allegheny Technologies Inc.
AlliedSignal Inc.
Allmerica Financial Corp.
Baxter International Inc.
Binney & Smith Inc.
Bradford & Co. (J.C.)
Broderbund Software, Inc.
Caterpillar Inc.
Chase Manhattan Bank, NA
Citizens Financial Group, Inc.
Colonial Oil Industries, Inc.
Dain Bosworth Inc.
Deutsch Co.
Dial Corp.
Forest City Enterprises, Inc.
Giant Eagle Inc.
Hallmark Cards Inc.
Harsco Corp.
Hartmarx Corp.
Hasbro, Inc.
Lehigh Portland Cement Co.
Levi Strauss & Co.
Little, Inc. (Arthur D.)
McDonald & Co. Securities, Inc.
Mid-America Bank of Louisville
Morgan & Co. Inc. (J.P.)
Northern Trust Co.
Norton Co.
Occidental Oil and Gas
Oshkosh B'Gosh, Inc.
Providence Journal-Bulletin Co.
Quaker Chemical Corp.
Rouse Co.
Simpson Investment Co.
Sovereign Bank
Trustmark Insurance Co.
Tyson Foods Inc.
US Bank, Washington
Waffle House Inc.
York Federal Savings & Loan Association

SHELTERS/ HOMELESSNESS

Abbott Laboratories
Advanced Micro Devices, Inc.
AFLAC Inc.
AGL Resources Inc.
Agrilink Foods, Inc.
Air Products and Chemicals, Inc.
Alabama Power Co.
Albertson's Inc.
Alcoa Inc.
Alcon Laboratories, Inc.
AlliedSignal Inc.
Allmerica Financial Corp.
AMCORE Bank Rockford
Ameren Corp.
American Express Co.
American General Finance
American Retail Group
American United Life Insurance Co.
AmerUS Group
AMETEK, Inc.
AMP Inc.
Anheuser-Busch Companies, Inc.
Appleton Papers Inc.
Archer-Daniels-Midland Co.
Aristech Chemical Corp.
Arizona Public Service Co.
Armstrong World Industries, Inc.
Atlantic Investment Co.
Avon Products, Inc.
Badger Meter, Inc.
Bank of New York Co., Inc.
BankAtlantic Bancorp
BankBoston-Connecticut Region
BankBoston Corp.
Barry Corp. (R.G.)
Baxter International Inc.
Belk-Simpson Department Stores
Belk Stores Services Inc.
Bemis Co., Inc.
Ben & Jerry's Homemade Inc.
Bernstein & Co., Inc. (Sanford C.)
Bethlehem Steel Corp.
Binney & Smith Inc.
Blair & Co. (William)
Block, Inc. (H&R)
Blue Cross & Blue Shield of Alabama
Blue Cross & Blue Shield of Minnesota

Boeing Co.
Borden, Inc.
Borman's Inc.
Boston Edison Co.
Boston Globe (The)
Bourns, Inc.
Bristol-Myers Squibb Co.
Broderbund Software, Inc.
Browning-Ferris Industries Inc.
Brunswick Corp.
Bucyrus-Erie Co.
Burlington Industries, Inc.
Callaway Golf Co.
Calvin Klein
Campbell Soup Co.
Carillon Importers, Ltd.
Carnival Corp.
Carpenter Technology Corp.
Central Maine Power Co.
Central National-Gottesman
CertainTeed Corp.
CGU Insurance
Chase Bank of Texas
Chase Manhattan Bank, NA
Chemed Corp.
Chevron Corp.
Chicago Board of Trade
Chicago Title Corp.
Chicago Tribune Co.
Circuit City Stores, Inc.
CIT Group, Inc. (The)
Citibank Corp.
Citigroup
Citizens Bank-Flint
Citizens Financial Group, Inc.
Clorox Co.
CNA
Collins & Aikman Corp.
Comdisco, Inc.
Commerce Bancshares, Inc.
Compaq Computer Corp.
ConAgra, Inc.
Consolidated Papers, Inc.
Consumers Energy Co.
Contran Corp.
Coors Brewing Co.
Copley Press, Inc.
Country Curtains, Inc.
Cox Enterprises Inc.
CPI Corp.
Credit Suisse First Boston
Crestar Finance Corp.
Croft-Leominster
Cummins Engine Co., Inc.
CUNA Mutual Group
Dain Bosworth Inc.
Dana Corp.
Dayton Hudson
Delta Air Lines, Inc.
Deluxe Corp.
Deposit Guaranty National Bank
Deutsch Co.
Dexter Corp.
Dial Corp.
Dixie Group, Inc. (The)
Dominion Resources, Inc.
Donaldson Co., Inc.
Donnelley & Sons Co. (R.R.)
Dreyer's Grand Ice Cream
du Pont de Nemours & Co. (E.I.)
Duchossois Industries Inc.
Dynamet, Inc.
Eastern Bank
Eaton Corp.
Ecolab Inc.
EDS Corp.
Edwards Enterprise Software (J.D.)
Employers Mutual Casualty Co.
Equifax Inc.
Erving Industries
Ethyl Corp.
Exxon Mobil Corp.
Fannie Mae
Federated Department Stores, Inc.
Federated Mutual Insurance Co.
Fidelity Investments
Fireman's Fund Insurance Co.
First Hawaiian, Inc.
First Source Corp.
First Union Corp.
First Union National Bank, NA
First Union Securities, Inc.
Firstar Bank Milwaukee NA
Fisher Brothers Cleaning Services
Fisher Scientific
FleetBoston Financial Corp.
Florida Power & Light Co.
Florida Rock Industries
Fort James Corp.
Fort Worth Star-Telegram Inc.
Fortis, Inc.
Fortune Brands, Inc.
Freddie Mac
Fuller Co. (H.B.)
Gannett Co., Inc.
Gap, Inc.
GATX Corp.
General Atlantic Partners II LP
General Dynamics Corp.
General Electric Co.
General Mills, Inc.
General Motors Corp.
Georgia Power Co.
Giant Eagle Inc.
Giant Food Inc.
Glickenhaus & Co.
Graco, Inc.
GTE Corp.
Gulf Power Co.
Gulfstream Aerospace Corp.
Hallmark Cards Inc.
Hancock Financial Services (John)
Harcourt General, Inc.
Harris Trust & Savings Bank
Harsco Corp.
Hartford (The)
Hartmarx Corp.
Hasbro, Inc.
Hitachi America Ltd.
Hofmann Co.
Home Depot, Inc.
Honeywell International Inc.
Household International Inc.
Huntington Bancshares Inc.
Inland Container Corp.
International Paper Co.
Jacobs Engineering Group
Johnson & Johnson
Journal-Gazette Co.
JSJ Corp.
Kimberly-Clark Corp.
Kraft Foods, Inc.
Kroger Co.
Ladish Co., Inc.
Lancaster Lens, Inc.
Land O'Lakes, Inc.
LandAmerica Financial Services
Landmark Communications Inc.
Lehigh Portland Cement Co.
Leigh Fibers, Inc.
Levi Strauss & Co.
Lincoln Financial Group
Little, Inc. (Arthur D.)
Lotus Development Corp.
Louisiana-Pacific Corp.
LTV Corp.
Mallinckrodt Chemical, Inc.
Marcus Corp.
Maritz Inc.
Marshall & Ilsley Corp.
Masco Corp.
MBIA Inc.
McClatchy Co.
McDonald & Co. Securities, Inc.
McKesson-HBOC Corp.
Mead Corp.
Mellon Financial Corp.
Menasha Corp.
Merck & Co.
Merit Oil Corp.
Merrill Lynch & Co., Inc.
Metropolitan Life Insurance Co.
MGIC Investment Corp.
Mid-America Bank of Louisville
MidAmerican Energy Holdings Co.
Milliken & Co.
Minnesota Mining & Manufacturing Co.
Minnesota Mutual Life Insurance Co.
Monsanto Co.
Montgomery Ward & Co., Inc.
MONY Group (The)
Morgan & Co. Inc. (J.P.)
Morgan Stanley Dean Witter & Co.
Morris Communications Corp.
Motorola Inc.
MTD Products Inc.
Mutual of Omaha Insurance Co.
National Computer Systems, Inc.
National Life of Vermont
National Presto Industries, Inc.
Nationwide Insurance Co.
New England Financial
New York Life Insurance Co.
New York Mercantile Exchange
New York Stock Exchange, Inc.
New York Times Co.
Newman's Own Inc.
Nike, Inc.
Northeast Utilities
Northern Indiana Public Service Co.
Northern States Power Co.
Northern Trust Co.
Northwest Natural Gas Co.
Norton Co.
Occidental Oil and Gas
Ohio National Life Insurance Co.
Old National Bank Evansville
Olin Corp.
Overseas Shipholding Group Inc.
Pacific Century Financial Corp.
Pacific Gas and Electric Co.
Pacific Mutual Life Insurance Co.
PacifiCorp
Paine Webber
Pan-American Life Insurance Co.
Parker Hannifin Corp.
Patagonia Inc.
Penney Co., Inc. (J.C.)
Pennzoil-Quaker State Co.
Peoples Bank
Peoples Energy Corp.
Pfizer Inc.
Phelps Dodge Corp.
Pheonix Financial Group
Physicians Mutual Insurance Co.
Pioneer Group
Pitney Bowes Inc.
Playboy Enterprises Inc.
PNC Bank
PNC Financial Services Group
Polaroid Corp.
Portland General Electric Co.
Potomac Electric Power Co.
PPG Industries, Inc.
Price Associates (T. Rowe)
Principal Financial Group
Procter & Gamble Co.
Procter & Gamble Co., Cosmetics Division
Provident Companies, Inc.
Prudential Insurance Co. of America
Prudential Securities Inc.
Publix Supermarkets
Putnam Investments
Quanex Corp.
Questar Corp.
Ralston Purina Co.
Rayonier Inc.
Reilly Industries, Inc.
Revlon Inc.
Reynolds Metals Co.
Reynolds Tobacco (R.J.)
Rockwell International Corp.
Rouse Co.
Royal & SunAlliance USA, Inc.
SAFECO Corp.
Safeway Inc.
Sara Lee Corp.
Sara Lee Hosiery, Inc.
SBC Communications Inc.
Schloss & Co. (Marcus)
Schlumberger Ltd. (USA)
Schwab & Co., Inc. (Charles)
Schwebel Baking Co.
Seaway Food Town, Inc.
Sega of America Inc.
Sempra Energy
Sentinel Communications Co.
Shea Co. (John F.)
Shell Oil Co.
Sherwin-Williams Co.
Sierra Pacific Industries
Simpson Investment Co.
SIT Investment Associates, Inc.
Slant/Fin Corp.
Smith Corp. (A.O.)
Sonoco Products Co.
Sovereign Bank
Stanley Works (The)
Starwood Hotels & Resorts Worldwide, Inc.
State Street Bank & Trust Co.
Steelcase Inc.
Stone Container Corp.
Storage Technology Corp.
Stride Rite Corp.
SunTrust Bank Atlanta
Synovus Financial Corp.
TCF National Bank Minnesota
Temple-Inland Inc.
TENNANT Co.
Tenneco Automotive
Tenneco Packaging
Tension Envelope Corp.
Tesoro Hawaii
Texaco Inc.
Texas Gas Transmission Corp.
Texas Instruments Inc.
Textron Inc.
Thermo Electron Corp.
TJX Companies, Inc.
TMC Investment Co.
Trace International Holdings, Inc.
Transamerica Corp.
True North Communications, Inc.
Trustmark Insurance Co.
TRW Inc.
Ukrop's Super Markets
Unilever Home & Personal Care U.S.A.
Unilever United States, Inc.
Union Camp Corp.
Union Pacific Corp.
United Distillers & Vintners North America
United Parcel Service of America Inc.
U.S. Bancorp Piper Jaffray
United States Sugar Corp.
United States Trust Co. of New York
US Bank, Washington
Valspar Corp.
Varian Medical Systems, Inc.
Vulcan Materials Co.
Wachtell, Lipton, Rosen & Katz
Waffle House Inc.
Wal-Mart Stores, Inc.
Walter Industries Inc.
Warner-Lambert Co.
Washington Trust Bank
Weil, Gotshal & Manges Corp.
Western & Southern Life Insurance Co.
Weyerhaeuser Co.
Whirlpool Corp.
Whitman Corp.
Wilbur-Ellis Co. & Connell Brothers Co.
Wiley & Sons (John)
Williams
Winn-Dixie Stores Inc.
Wisconsin Energy Corp.
Wisconsin Power & Light Co.
Witco Corp.
Woodward Governor Co.
Xerox Corp.

SOCIAL SERVICES-GENERAL

7-Eleven, Inc.
Airborne Freight Corp.
Alaska Airlines, Inc.
Alcoa Inc.
Alcon Laboratories, Inc.
Allmerica Financial Corp.

Alyeska Pipeline Service Co.
AMCORE Bank Rockford
American General Corp.
Ameritech Wisconsin
AmerUS Group
Amgen, Inc.
AMR Corp.
APL Ltd.
Associated Food Stores
Autodesk Inc.
Avery Dennison Corp.
Baird & Co. (Robert W.)
Ball Corp.
Bandag, Inc.
Bank One, Texas-Houston Office
Bank One, Texas, NA
BankBoston-Connecticut Region
Barry Corp. (R.G.)
Bell Atlantic Corp.-West Virginia
Bell Atlantic-Delaware, Inc.
Binney & Smith Inc.
Blair & Co. (William)
Bourns, Inc.
BP Amoco Corp.
Branch Banking & Trust Co.
Briggs & Stratton Corp.
Brooklyn Union
Business Men's Assurance Co. of America
Caesar's World, Inc.
Campbell Soup Co.
Castle & Cooke Properties Inc.
CCB Financial Corp.
Cenex Harvest States
Centex Corp.
Central Maine Power Co.
CGU Insurance
Chemed Corp.
Cinergy Corp.
Citizens Bank-Flint
CNA
Coachmen Industries, Inc.
Colgate-Palmolive Co.
Commercial Federal Corp.
Commercial Intertech Corp.
Computer Associates International, Inc.
Conectiv
Conwood Co. LP
Cooper Tire & Rubber Co.
Crane & Co., Inc.
Crestar Finance Corp.
CSS Industries, Inc.
CSX Corp.
CUNA Mutual Group
Curtis Industries, Inc. (Helene)
Diebold, Inc.
Duquesne Light Co.
Duracell International
Duriron Co., Inc.
Eastern Bank
Eastman Chemical Co.
Ebsco Industries, Inc.
EDS Corp.
Employers Insurance of Wausau, A Mutual Co.
Employers Mutual Casualty Co.
Entergy Corp.
Equitable Resources, Inc.
Erving Industries
Evening Post Publishing Co.
Excel Corp.
Fabri-Kal Corp.
Farmers Group, Inc.
Federated Mutual Insurance Co.
Ferro Corp.
First Security Bank of Idaho NA
FirstEnergy Corp.
Fisher Brothers Cleaning Services
Fisher Scientific
Fortis, Inc.
Frito-Lay, Inc.
Frontier Corp.
Fuller Co. (H.B.)
Gates Rubber Corp.
Graco, Inc.
Grainger, Inc. (W.W.)
Hanna Co. (M.A.)
Hannaford Brothers Co.
Harcourt General, Inc.
Harris Trust & Savings Bank
Hartford (The)
Hartford Steam Boiler Inspection & Insurance Co.
Hercules Inc.
Hickory Tech Corp.
HSBC Bank USA
Hubbard Broadcasting, Inc.
Hubbell Inc.
Huffy Corp.
Hunt Oil Co.
Huntington Bancshares Inc.
Idaho Power Co.
Ingram Industries Inc.
International Paper Co.
Interpublic Group of Companies, Inc.
INTRUST Financial Corp.
Jacobs Engineering Group
Journal Communications, Inc.
JSJ Corp.
Kaman Corp.
Kellwood Co.
Kelly Services
Kendall International, Inc.
Kinder Morgn
Kingsbury Corp.
Lehigh Portland Cement Co.
Liberty Mutual Insurance Group
Lotus Development Corp.
Lowe's Companies
Lubrizol Corp. (The)
Manulife Financial
Maritz Inc.
MBIA Inc.
McDonald & Co. Securities, Inc.
Memphis Light Gas & Water Division
Merit Oil Corp.
Microsoft Corp.
Mid-America Bank of Louisville
Morgan & Co. Inc. (J.P.)
Mutual of Omaha Insurance Co.
National City Bank of Cleveland
National City Bank of Columbus
National City Bank of Minneapolis
National City Bank of Pennsylvania
National Computer Systems, Inc.
New England Bio Labs
New Jersey Natural Gas Co.
New York Mercantile Exchange
New York State Electric & Gas Corp.
New York Times Co.
Niagara Mohawk Holdings Inc.
Northrop Grumman Corp.
Northwest Natural Gas Co.
Norton Co.
Occidental Oil and Gas
Old National Bank Evansville
ONEOK, Inc.
Orange & Rockland Utilities, Inc.
Owens-Illinois Inc.
Pacific Century Financial Corp.
Pacific Mutual Life Insurance Co.
Paine Webber
Penn Mutual Life Insurance Co.
Penney Co., Inc. (J.C.)
Pennsylvania Power & Light
Pentair Inc.
Physicians Mutual Insurance Co.
Pioneer Group
Pioneer Natural Resources
PNC Bank
Premier Dental Products Co.
Provident Mutual Life Insurance Co.
Public Service Co. of Oklahoma
Putnam Investments
Reebok International Ltd.
Regions Bank
Regions Financial Corp.
Riggs Bank NA
Rohm & Haas Co.
Royal & SunAlliance USA, Inc.
Ryder System, Inc.
Santa Fe International Corp.
Sara Lee Hosiery, Inc.
SCANA Corp.
Security Life of Denver Insurance Co.
Sentinel Communications Co.
Servco Pacific
ServiceMaster Co.
Shaw Industries Inc.
Sierra Pacific Resources
Solo Cup Co.
Sonoco Products Co.
Southern Co. Services Inc.
Sprint/United Telephone
SPX Corp.
State Street Bank & Trust Co.
Storage Technology Corp.
Student Loan Marketing Association
Susquehanna-Pfaltzgraff Co.
TCF National Bank Minnesota
Teleflex Inc.
Tenneco Packaging
Thompson Co. (J. Walter)
Titan Industrial Corp.
TMC Investment Co.
True North Communications, Inc.
Trustmark Insurance Co.
Trustmark National Bank
Tucson Electric Power Co.
Ultramar Diamond Shamrock Corp.
U.S. Bancorp Piper Jaffray
Unocal Corp.
US Bank, Washington
Washington Mutual, Inc.
Wausau Insurance Companies
West Co. Inc.
Whirlpool Corp.
WICOR, Inc.
Wilbur-Ellis Co. & Connell Brothers Co.
Wiremold Co.
Wisconsin Power & Light Co.
Witco Corp.
Wolverine World Wide
Young & Rubicam
Zachry Co. (H.B.)
Zurn Industries, Inc.

SPECIAL OLYMPICS

Alcoa Inc.
Alexander & Baldwin, Inc.
Allmerica Financial Corp.
American General Finance
American United Life Insurance Co.
Ameritech Corp.
Aristech Chemical Corp.
Avon Products, Inc.
Barclays Capital
Bard, Inc. (C.R.)
Barden Corp.
Barnes Group Inc.
Block, Inc. (H&R)
Blue Bell, Inc.
Broderbund Software, Inc.
Brunswick Corp.
Burlington Industries, Inc.
Calvin Klein
Campbell Soup Co.
Carpenter Technology Corp.
Carris Reels
Cessna Aircraft Co.
Cinergy Corp.
Clark Refining & Marketing
Comdisco, Inc.
Compaq Computer Corp.
Constellation Energy Group, Inc.
Crane Co.
Credit Suisse First Boston
Cummings Properties Management
CUNA Mutual Group
Dain Bosworth Inc.
Dreyer's Grand Ice Cream
Dun & Bradstreet Corp.
Duriron Co., Inc.
Dynamet, Inc.
Employers Mutual Casualty Co.
Enterprise Rent-A-Car Co.
Equifax Inc.
Federated Mutual Insurance Co.
Fortis, Inc.
Fuller Co. (H.B.)
Galter Corp.
GEICO Corp.
Georgia Power Co.
Gerber Products Co.
Griffith Laboratories U.S.A.
Hasbro, Inc.
Hawaiian Electric Co., Inc.
Hofmann Co.
Hubbell Inc.
IKON Office Solutions, Inc.
Independent Stave Co.
Invacare Corp.
Jostens, Inc.
Kingsbury Corp.
Kroger Co.
Ladish Co., Inc.
Lance, Inc.
Land O'Lakes, Inc.
Lee Enterprises
Lipton Co.
Louisiana-Pacific Corp.
Madison Gas & Electric Co.
Mark IV Industries
McKesson-HBOC Corp.
Mead Corp.
Mercantile Bank NA
Mid-America Bank of Louisville
Milliken & Co.
Mitsubishi Electric America
Niagara Mohawk Holdings Inc.
Occidental Oil and Gas
OG&E Electric Services
Osborne Enterprises
Oshkosh B'Gosh, Inc.
PEMCO Corp.
PerkinElmer, Inc.
Procter & Gamble Co.
Quanex Corp.
Reilly Industries, Inc.
Reinhart Institutional Foods
Royal & SunAlliance USA, Inc.
Russer Foods
SBC Communications Inc.
Searle & Co. (G.D.)
Sentry Insurance, A Mutual Co.
Shea Co. (John F.)
Sonoco Products Co.
Southeastern Mutual Insurance Co.
Southwest Gas Corp.
SPX Corp.
Standard Products Co.
Storage Technology Corp.
Stupp Brothers Bridge & Iron Co.
Synovus Financial Corp.
Tamko Roofing Products
Teleflex Inc.
Tesoro Hawaii
Textron Inc.
Tomkins Industries, Inc.
True North Communications, Inc.
Ukrop's Super Markets
Unilever Home & Personal Care U.S.A.
United Distillers & Vintners North America
United Parcel Service of America Inc.
Unocal Corp.
Vesper Corp.
Waffle House Inc.
Warner-Lambert Co.
Washington Trust Bank
Winn-Dixie Stores Inc.
Wiremold Co.
Wisconsin Public Service Corp.
Woodward Governor Co.

SUBSTANCE ABUSE

ABB Inc.
Abbott Laboratories
ABC
AFLAC Inc.
AGL Resources Inc.
Agrilink Foods, Inc.
Air Products and Chemicals, Inc.
Alabama Power Co.
Albertson's Inc.
Alcoa Inc.
Alexander & Baldwin, Inc.
AlliedSignal Inc.
Allmerica Financial Corp.

Allstate Insurance Co.
AMCORE Bank Rockford
American Express Co.
American Fidelity Corp.
American General Finance
American United Life Insurance Co.
Ameritas Life Insurance Corp.
Ameritech Illinois
Ameritech Indiana
Ameritech Wisconsin
AmerUS Group
AMP Inc.
AMR Corp.
Andersen Corp.
Anheuser-Busch Companies, Inc.
Appleton Papers Inc.
Archer-Daniels-Midland Co.
Armstrong World Industries, Inc.
AT&T Corp.
Avon Products, Inc.
Badger Meter, Inc.
Bandag, Inc.
Banfi Vintners
Bank of America
Bank of New York Co., Inc.
Bank One, Texas-Houston Office
Banta Corp.
Bard, Inc. (C.R.)
Barnes Group Inc.
Barry Corp. (R.G.)
Battelle Memorial Institute
Baxter International Inc.
Bechtel Group, Inc.
Belk Stores Services Inc.
Bemis Co., Inc.
Bestfoods
Bethlehem Steel Corp.
BFGoodrich Co.
Binswanger Companies
Blair & Co. (William)
Block, Inc. (H&R)
Blount International, Inc.
Blue Bell, Inc.
Blue Cross & Blue Shield of Alabama
Blue Cross & Blue Shield of Iowa
Boeing Co.
Boise Cascade Corp.
Borman's Inc.
Boston Globe (The)
Bridgestone/Firestone, Inc.
Briggs & Stratton Corp.
Bristol-Myers Squibb Co.
Broderbund Software, Inc.
Brown & Williamson Tobacco Corp.
Brunswick Corp.
Bucyrus-Erie Co.
Burlington Industries, Inc.
Cabot Corp.
Calvin Klein
Cargill Inc.
Carpenter Technology Corp.
Carris Reels
Carter-Wallace, Inc.
Caterpillar Inc.
Central Maine Power Co.
Central & South West Services
CertainTeed Corp.
Cessna Aircraft Co.
CGU Insurance
Champion International Corp.
Chase Bank of Texas
Chase Manhattan Bank, NA
Chevron Corp.
Chicago Tribune Co.
Cinergy Corp.
CIT Group, Inc. (The)
Citigroup
Citizens Financial Group, Inc.
Clorox Co.
Collins & Aikman Corp.
Colonial Life & Accident Insurance Co.
Commerce Bancshares, Inc.
Commercial Intertech Corp.
Commonwealth Edison Co.
Compaq Computer Corp.
ConAgra, Inc.
Cone Mills Corp.
Consolidated Natural Gas Co.
Consumers Energy Co.
Contran Corp.
Coors Brewing Co.
Copley Press, Inc.
Crane Co.
Croft-Leominster
CSR Rinker Materials Corp.
CSS Industries, Inc.
Cummings Properties Management
Cummins Engine Co., Inc.
DaimlerChrysler Corp.
Dain Bosworth Inc.
Dana Corp.
Dayton Power and Light Co.
Deere & Co.
DeKalb Genetics Corp.
Deluxe Corp.
Demoulas Supermarkets Inc.
Deposit Guaranty National Bank
Detroit Edison Co.
Deutsch Co.
Dexter Corp.
Dial Corp.
Dixie Group, Inc. (The)
Dominion Resources, Inc.
Donaldson Co., Inc.
du Pont de Nemours & Co. (E.I.)
Duchossois Industries Inc.
Duke Energy
Dun & Bradstreet Corp.
Dynamet, Inc.
Ecolab Inc.
Edison Brothers Stores, Inc.
Edison International
EDS Corp.
Edwards Enterprise Software (J.D.)
Emerson Electric Co.
EMI Music Publishing
Equifax Inc.
Erb Lumber Co.
European American Bank
Exxon Mobil Corp.
Fabri-Kal Corp.
Farmers Group, Inc.
Federal-Mogul Corp.
Federated Department Stores, Inc.
Federated Mutual Insurance Co.
Ferro Corp.
Fireman's Fund Insurance Co.
First Hawaiian, Inc.
First Source Corp.
First Union Bank
First Union Corp.
First Union National Bank, NA
Firstar Bank Milwaukee NA
FleetBoston Financial Corp.
Fluor Corp.
Forbes Inc.
Ford Meter Box Co.
Ford Motor Co.
Forest City Enterprises, Inc.
Fort James Corp.
Fort Worth Star-Telegram Inc.
Fortis Insurance Co.
Fortune Brands, Inc.
Freddie Mac
Freeport-McMoRan Inc.
Frost National Bank
Fuller Co. (H.B.)
Gallo Winery, Inc. (E&J)
GATX Corp.
GEICO Corp.
GenAmerica Corp.
General Atlantic Partners II LP
General Electric Co.
General Mills, Inc.
General Motors Corp.
General Reinsurance Corp.
Georgia-Pacific Corp.
Georgia Power Co.
Giant Eagle Inc.
Giant Food Inc.
Giddings & Lewis
Glaxo Wellcome Inc.
Goodrich Aerospace - Aerostructures Group (B.F.)
Grace & Co. (W.R.)
Group Health Plan
GTE Corp.
Guardian Life Insurance Co. of America
Gucci America Inc.
Guess?
GuideOne Insurance
Halliburton Co.
Hallmark Cards Inc.
Hamilton Sundstrand Corp.
Hancock Financial Services (John)
Hanna Co. (M.A.)
Harley-Davidson Co.
Harris Corp.
Harsco Corp.
Hartford (The)
Hartford Steam Boiler Inspection & Insurance Co.
Heinz Co. (H.J.)
Hershey Foods Corp.
Hewlett-Packard Co.
Hoffmann-La Roche Inc.
Honeywell International Inc.
Household International Inc.
Hubbard Broadcasting, Inc.
Huffy Corp.
IKON Office Solutions, Inc.
Illinois Tool Works, Inc.
Inland Container Corp.
International Business Machines Corp.
International Flavors & Fragrances Inc.
International Multifoods Corp.
International Paper Co.
Jacobs Engineering Group
Jacobson & Sons (Benjamin)
Johnson Controls Inc.
Johnson & Johnson
Johnson & Son (S.C.)
Jostens, Inc.
Journal-Gazette Co.
JSJ Corp.
Katten, Muchin & Zavis
Kellogg Co.
Kellwood Co.
Kemper National Insurance Companies
Kimberly-Clark Corp.
Kingsbury Corp.
Kirkland & Ellis
Koch Enterprises, Inc.
Kroger Co.
Lancaster Lens, Inc.
Lehigh Portland Cement Co.
Liberty Diversified Industries
Lincoln Electric Co.
Lincoln Financial Group
Lipton Co.
Louisiana Land & Exploration Co.
Louisiana-Pacific Corp.
LTV Corp.
Macy's East Inc.
Mallinckrodt Chemical, Inc.
Maritz Inc.
Mark IV Industries
Mattel Inc.
May Department Stores Co.
Mazda North American Operations
MBIA Inc.
McClatchy Co.
McDonald & Co. Securities, Inc.
McDonald's Corp.
McGraw-Hill Companies, Inc.
McKesson-HBOC Corp.
McWane Inc.
Menasha Corp.
Merck & Co.
Merit Oil Corp.
Merrill Lynch & Co., Inc.
Metropolitan Life Insurance Co.
MGIC Investment Corp.
Michigan Consolidated Gas Co.
Milliken & Co.
Millipore Corp.
Minnesota Mining & Manufacturing Co.
Minnesota Mutual Life Insurance Co.
Monsanto Co.
MONY Group (The)
Motorola Inc.
Nalco Chemical Co.
National City Bank of Minneapolis
National City Corp.
National Computer Systems, Inc.
National Fuel Gas Distribution Corp.
National Life of Vermont
National Machinery Co.
National Starch & Chemical Co.
Nationwide Insurance Co.
New England Financial
New Jersey Natural Gas Co.
New York Life Insurance Co.
New York Mercantile Exchange
New York Times Co.
Nordson Corp.
Northeast Utilities
Northern States Power Co.
Northern Trust Co.
Northwest Natural Gas Co.
Norton Co.
Norwest Corp.
Occidental Oil and Gas
Ohio National Life Insurance Co.
Old National Bank Evansville
Olin Corp.
Outboard Marine Corp.
Overseas Shipholding Group Inc.
Owens Corning
PACCAR Inc.
Pacific Mutual Life Insurance Co.
Paine Webber
Parker Hannifin Corp.
Pella Corp.
Penney Co., Inc. (J.C.)
Pennzoil-Quaker State Co.
PepsiCo, Inc.
PerkinElmer, Inc.
Pfizer Inc.
Pharmacia & Upjohn, Inc.
Phillips Petroleum Co.
Physicians Mutual Insurance Co.
Pittway Corp.
Portland General Electric Co.
Potomac Electric Power Co.
Premier Industrial Corp.
Principal Financial Group
Procter & Gamble Co.
Procter & Gamble Co., Cosmetics Division
Providence Journal-Bulletin Co.
Provident Companies, Inc.
Prudential Insurance Co. of America
Prudential Securities Inc.
Public Service Electric & Gas Co.
Publix Supermarkets
Ralph's Grocery Co.
Ralston Purina Co.
Rayonier Inc.
Red Wing Shoe Co. Inc.
Reinhart Institutional Foods
Reliant Energy Inc.
Reynolds Metals Co.
Reynolds Tobacco (R.J.)
Rich Products Corp.
Rockwell International Corp.
Rouse Co.
Royal & SunAlliance USA, Inc.
Rubbermaid Inc.
Ruddick Corp.
Russer Foods
Ryder System, Inc.
SAFECO Corp.
Salomon Smith Barney
Sara Lee Corp.
Sara Lee Hosiery, Inc.
Schering-Plough Corp.
Schloss & Co. (Marcus)
Schlumberger Ltd. (USA)
Scripps Co. (E.W.)
Seagram & Sons, Inc. (Joseph E.)
Seaway Food Town, Inc.
Sega of America Inc.
Sempra Energy
Sentry Insurance, A Mutual Co.
Servco Pacific
Shell Oil Co.
Shoney's Inc.
Simpson Investment Co.
SIT Investment Associates, Inc.
Smith Corp. (A.O.)
SmithKline Beecham Corp.
Solo Cup Co.
Sonoco Products Co.
Southeastern Mutual Insurance Co.

Southern New England Telephone Co.
Springs Industries, Inc.
SPX Corp.
Standard Products Co.
Stanley Works (The)
Starwood Hotels & Resorts Worldwide, Inc.
State Farm Mutual Automobile Insurance Co.
Steelcase Inc.
Stone Container Corp.
Storage Technology Corp.
Strear Farms Co.
Stride Rite Corp.
Stupp Brothers Bridge & Iron Co.
Sunoco Inc.
SunTrust Bank Atlanta
SunTrust Banks of Florida
SuperValu, Inc.
Synovus Financial Corp.
TCF National Bank Minnesota
Temple-Inland Inc.
TENNANT Co.
Tenneco Automotive
Tension Envelope Corp.
Tesoro Hawaii
Texaco Inc.
Texas Gas Transmission Corp.
Texas Instruments Inc.
Textron Inc.
Thermo Electron Corp.
Thompson Co. (J. Walter)
Timken Co. (The)
TJX Companies, Inc.
Tomkins Industries, Inc.
Toro Co.
Toyota Motor Sales U.S.A., Inc.
Trustmark Insurance Co.
Tyson Foods Inc.
Unilever Home & Personal Care U.S.A.
Unilever United States, Inc.
Union Camp Corp.
Union Pacific Corp.
United Distillers & Vintners North America
United Dominion Industries, Ltd.
United States Sugar Corp.
United States Trust Co. of New York
United Technologies Corp.
United Wisconsin Services
Universal Studios
Unocal Corp.
US Bank, Washington
USG Corp.
UST Inc.
USX Corp.
Valmont Industries, Inc.
Vulcan Materials Co.
Wachovia Bank of North Carolina NA
Wal-Mart Stores, Inc.
Walgreen Co.
Walter Industries Inc.
Warner-Lambert Co.
West Co. Inc.
Westvaco Corp.
Weyerhaeuser Co.
Whirlpool Corp.
WICOR, Inc.
Williams
Winn-Dixie Stores Inc.
Wisconsin Public Service Corp.
Woodward Governor Co.
Wrigley Co. (Wm. Jr.)
Xerox Corp.
York Federal Savings & Loan Association
Young & Rubicam
Zachry Co. (H.B.)
Zilkha & Sons

UNITED FUNDS/UNITED WAYS

ABB Inc.
Abbott Laboratories
Advanced Micro Devices, Inc.
AEGON U.S.A. Inc.
Aetna, Inc.
AFLAC Inc.
AGL Resources Inc.
Agrilink Foods, Inc.
Air Products and Chemicals, Inc.
AK Steel Corp.
Alabama Power Co.
Albertson's Inc.
Alcoa Inc.
Alexander & Baldwin, Inc.
Allegheny Technologies Inc.
Alliant Techsystems
Allianz Life Insurance Co. of North America
AlliedSignal Inc.
Allmerica Financial Corp.
Allstate Insurance Co.
Alma Piston Co.
Alyeska Pipeline Service Co.
AMCORE Bank Rockford
Ameren Corp.
American Express Co.
American Fidelity Corp.
American General Corp.
American General Finance
American Standard Inc.
American United Life Insurance Co.
Ameritas Life Insurance Corp.
Ameritech Corp.
Ameritech Illinois
Ameritech Indiana
Ameritech Michigan
Ameritech Ohio
Ameritech Wisconsin
AmerUS Group
AMETEK, Inc.
Amgen, Inc.
AMP Inc.
AMR Corp.
Amsted Industries Inc.
Analog Devices, Inc.
Andersen Corp.
Andersons Inc.
Anheuser-Busch Companies, Inc.
Aon Corp.
APL Ltd.
Appleton Papers Inc.
Archer-Daniels-Midland Co.
Aristech Chemical Corp.
Arizona Public Service Co.
Armstrong World Industries, Inc.
Arvin Industries, Inc.
ASARCO Inc.
Ashland, Inc.
AT&T Corp.
Atlantic Investment Co.
Atlantic Richfield Co.
Auburn Foundry
Avery Dennison Corp.
Avista Corporation
Avon Products, Inc.
Badger Meter, Inc.
Baird & Co. (Robert W.)
Bandag, Inc.
Banfi Vintners
Bank of America
Bank of New York Co., Inc.
Bank One Corp.
Bank One, Texas-Houston Office
Bank One, Texas, NA
BankAtlantic Bancorp
BankBoston-Connecticut Region
BankBoston Corp.
Banta Corp.
Barclays Capital
Bard, Inc. (C.R.)
Barden Corp.
Bardes Corp.
Barnes Group Inc.
Barry Corp. (R.G.)
Battelle Memorial Institute
Bausch & Lomb Inc.
Baxter International Inc.
Bayer Corp.
Bechtel Group, Inc.
Beckman Coulter, Inc.
Becton Dickinson & Co.
Belk-Simpson Department Stores
Belk Stores Services Inc.
Bell Atlantic Corp.
Bemis Co., Inc.
Bemis Manufacturing Co.
Bernstein & Co., Inc. (Sanford C.)
Berwind Group
Bestfoods
Bethlehem Steel Corp.
BFGoodrich Co.
Binney & Smith Inc.
Binswanger Companies
Block, Inc. (H&R)
Blount International, Inc.
Blue Bell, Inc.
Blue Cross & Blue Shield of Alabama
Blue Cross & Blue Shield of Iowa
Blue Cross & Blue Shield of Minnesota
Boeing Co.
Boise Cascade Corp.
Borden, Inc.
Borman's Inc.
Boston Edison Co.
Boston Gas Co.
Boston Globe (The)
Bourns, Inc.
Bowater Inc.
BP Amoco Corp.
Bradford & Co. (J.C.)
Bridgestone/Firestone, Inc.
Briggs & Stratton Corp.
Bristol-Myers Squibb Co.
Broderbund Software, Inc.
Brown Shoe Co., Inc.
Brown & Williamson Tobacco Corp.
Browning-Ferris Industries Inc.
Brunswick Corp.
Bucyrus-Erie Co.
Burlington Industries, Inc.
Burlington Resources, Inc.
Burnett Co. (Leo)
Business Improvement
Butler Capital Corp.
Butler Manufacturing Co.
Cabot Corp.
California Bank & Trust
Calvin Klein
Campbell Soup Co.
Cantor, Fitzgerald Securities Corp.
Cargill Inc.
Carlson Companies, Inc.
Carolina Power & Light Co.
Carpenter Technology Corp.
Carrier Corp.
Carris Reels
Carter-Wallace, Inc.
Caterpillar Inc.
CBS Corp.
CCB Financial Corp.
Centex Corp.
Central Maine Power Co.
Central National-Gottesman
Central & South West Services
Central Soya Co.
Century 21
CertainTeed Corp.
Cessna Aircraft Co.
CGU Insurance
Champion International Corp.
Charter Manufacturing Co.
Chase Bank of Texas
Chase Manhattan Bank, NA
Chemed Corp.
Chesapeake Corp.
Chevron Corp.
Chicago Board of Trade
Chicago Title Corp.
Chicago Tribune Co.
Church & Dwight Co., Inc.
CIBC Oppenheimer
CIGNA Corp.
Cincinnati Bell Inc.
Cinergy Corp.
Circuit City Stores, Inc.
CIT Group, Inc. (The)
Citibank Corp.
Citigroup
Citizens Bank-Flint
Citizens Financial Group, Inc.
CLARCOR Inc.
Clark Refining & Marketing
Cleveland-Cliffs, Inc.
Clorox Co.
CNA
CNF Transportation, Inc.
Collins & Aikman Corp.
Colonial Life & Accident Insurance Co.
Colonial Oil Industries, Inc.
Comerica Inc.
Commerce Bancshares, Inc.
Commercial Intertech Corp.
Commonwealth Edison Co.
Compaq Computer Corp.
Compass Bank
ConAgra, Inc.
Cone Mills Corp.
Conoco, Inc.
Consolidated Natural Gas Co.
Consolidated Papers, Inc.
Constellation Energy Group, Inc.
Consumers Energy Co.
Continental Grain Co.
Contran Corp.
Conwood Co. LP
Cooper Industries, Inc.
Cooper Tire & Rubber Co.
Copley Press, Inc.
Corning Inc.
Country Curtains, Inc.
CPI Corp.
Crane Co.
Crane & Co., Inc.
Cranston Print Works Co.
Credit Suisse First Boston
Crestar Finance Corp.
CSR Rinker Materials Corp.
CSS Industries, Inc.
Cummings Properties Management
Cummins Engine Co., Inc.
CUNA Mutual Group
Cyprus Amax Minerals Co.
Daily News
DaimlerChrysler Corp.
Dain Bosworth Inc.
Dana Corp.
Danis Companies
Dayton Hudson
Dayton Power and Light Co.
Deere & Co.
DeKalb Genetics Corp.
Delta Air Lines, Inc.
Deluxe Corp.
Deposit Guaranty National Bank
Detroit Edison Co.
Deutsch Co.
Dexter Corp.
Disney Co. (Walt)
Dixie Group, Inc. (The)
Donaldson Co., Inc.
Donnelley & Sons Co. (R.R.)
Dow Chemical Co.
Dow Corning Corp.
Dow Jones & Co., Inc.
DSM Copolymer
du Pont de Nemours & Co. (E.I.)
Duchossois Industries Inc.
Duke Energy
Dun & Bradstreet Corp.
Duquesne Light Co.
Duriron Co., Inc.
Dynamet, Inc.
Eastern Bank
Eastman Kodak Co.
Eaton Corp.
Eckerd Corp.
Ecolab Inc.
Edison Brothers Stores, Inc.
Edison International
El Paso Energy Co.
Elf Atochem North America, Inc.
Emerson Electric Co.
EMI Music Publishing
Employers Insurance of Wausau, A Mutual Co.
Employers Mutual Casualty Co.
Ensign-Bickford Industries
Enterprise Rent-A-Car Co.
Equifax Inc.
Equitable Resources, Inc.
Erb Lumber Co.
Erving Industries
Ethyl Corp.
European American Bank
Evening Post Publishing Co.
Excel Corp.
Exxon Mobil Corp.
Fabri-Kal Corp.
Fannie Mae
Federal-Mogul Corp.
Federated Department Stores, Inc.
Federated Mutual Insurance Co.
FedEx Corp.
Ferro Corp.
Fidelity Investments
Fifth Third Bancorp
FINA

Fireman's Fund Insurance Co.
First American Corp.
First Financial Bank
First Hawaiian, Inc.
First Maryland Bancorp
First Source Corp.
First Tennessee National Corp.
First Union Bank
First Union Corp.
First Union National Bank, NA
First Union Securities, Inc.
Firstar Bank Milwaukee NA
Fisher Brothers Cleaning Services
Fisher Scientific
FleetBoston Financial Corp.
Florida Power Corp.
Florida Power & Light Co.
Florida Rock Industries
Fluor Corp.
FMC Corp.
Forbes Inc.
Ford Meter Box Co.
Ford Motor Co.
Forest City Enterprises, Inc.
Fort James Corp.
Fort Worth Star-Telegram Inc.
Fortis, Inc.
Fortis Insurance Co.
Fortune Brands, Inc.
Franklin Electric Co.
Franklin Mint (The)
Freeport-McMoRan Inc.
Freightliner Corp.
Fuller Co. (H.B.)
Furniture Brands International, Inc.
Gallo Winery, Inc. (E&J)
Galter Corp.
Gap, Inc.
GATX Corp.
GEICO Corp.
GenAmerica Corp.
GenCorp
General Electric Co.
General Mills, Inc.
General Motors Corp.
General Reinsurance Corp.
Georgia-Pacific Corp.
Georgia Power Co.
Gerber Products Co.
Giant Eagle Inc.
Giant Food Inc.
Giddings & Lewis
Gillette Co.
Glaxo Wellcome Inc.
Glickenhaus & Co.
Globe Corp.
Goldman Sachs Group
Golub Corp.
Goodrich Aerospace - Aerostructures Group (B.F.)
GPU Energy
Grace & Co. (W.R.)
Graco, Inc.
Grede Foundries
Green Bay Packaging
GTE Corp.
Guardian Life Insurance Co. of America
Gucci America Inc.
GuideOne Insurance
Gulf Power Co.
Gulfstream Aerospace Corp.
Hallmark Cards Inc.
Hamilton Sundstrand Corp.
Hancock Financial Services (John)
Hanna Co. (M.A.)
Hannaford Brothers Co.
Harland Co. (John H.)
Harley-Davidson Co.
Harnischfeger Industries
Harris Corp.
Harris Trust & Savings Bank
Harsco Corp.
Hartford (The)
Hartford Steam Boiler Inspection & Insurance Co.
Hartmarx Corp.
Hasbro, Inc.
Hawaiian Electric Co., Inc.
Heinz Co. (H.J.)
Heller Financial, Inc.
Hensel Phelps Construction Co.
Hershey Foods Corp.
Hickory Tech Corp.
Hoffer Plastics Corp.
Hoffmann-La Roche Inc.
Hofmann Co.
HON Industries Inc.
Honeywell International Inc.
Houghton Mifflin Co.
Housatonic Curtain Co.
Household International Inc.
HSBC Bank USA
Hubbard Broadcasting, Inc.
Hubbell Inc.
Huffy Corp.
Hughes Electronics Corp.
Humana, Inc.
Hunt Manufacturing Co.
Huntington Bancshares Inc.
IBP
Idaho Power Co.
IKON Office Solutions, Inc.
Illinois Power Co.
Illinois Tool Works, Inc.
Inland Container Corp.
Inman Mills
Intel Corp.
International Business Machines Corp.
International Flavors & Fragrances Inc.
International Multifoods Corp.
INTRUST Financial Corp.
Invacare Corp.
Jacobs Engineering Group
Jacobson & Sons (Benjamin)
Jeld-wen, Inc.
Johnson Controls Inc.
Johnson & Johnson
Johnson & Son (S.C.)
Jones & Co. (Edward D.)
Jostens, Inc.
Journal-Gazette Co.
JSJ Corp.
Katten, Muchin & Zavis
Kellwood Co.
Kelly Services
Kennametal, Inc.
Kerr-McGee Corp.
Key Bank of Cleveland
Kiewit Sons' Inc. (Peter)
Kimball International, Inc.
Kimberly-Clark Corp.
Kingsbury Corp.
Kirkland & Ellis
Kmart Corp.
Knight Ridder
Koch Enterprises, Inc.
Koch Industries, Inc.
Kraft Foods, Inc.
Kroger Co.
La-Z-Boy Inc.
Laclede Gas Co.
Ladish Co., Inc.
Lancaster Lens, Inc.
Lance, Inc.
Land O'Lakes, Inc.
LandAmerica Financial Services
Landmark Communications Inc.
Lee Enterprises
Lehigh Portland Cement Co.
Lennox International, Inc.
Levi Strauss & Co.
Leviton Manufacturing Co. Inc.
LG&E Energy Corp.
Liberty Corp.
Liberty Diversified Industries
Lilly & Co. (Eli)
Lincoln Electric Co.
Lincoln Financial Group
Lipton Co.
Little, Inc. (Arthur D.)
Litton Industries, Inc.
Loews Corp.
Louisiana Land & Exploration Co.
Louisiana-Pacific Corp.
LTV Corp.
Lubrizol Corp. (The)
Lyondell Chemical Co.
Macy's East Inc.
Madison Gas & Electric Co.
Mallinckrodt Chemical, Inc.
Mamiye Brothers
Manufacturers & Traders Trust Co.
Manulife Financial
Marcus Corp.
Maritz Inc.
Mark IV Industries
Marshall Field's
Marshall & Ilsley Corp.
Masco Corp.
Mattel Inc.
May Department Stores Co.
Maytag Corp.
McClatchy Co.
McCormick & Co. Inc.
McDermott Inc.
McDonald & Co. Securities, Inc.
McGraw-Hill Companies, Inc.
MCI WorldCom, Inc.
McKesson-HBOC Corp.
Mead Corp.
Medtronic, Inc.
Mellon Financial Corp.
Memphis Light Gas & Water Division
Menasha Corp.
Mercantile Bank NA
Merck & Co.
Meredith Corp.
Merit Oil Corp.
Merrill Lynch & Co., Inc.
Mervyn's California
Metropolitan Life Insurance Co.
MGIC Investment Corp.
Michigan Consolidated Gas Co.
Mid-America Bank of Louisville
MidAmerican Energy Holdings Co.
Milacron, Inc.
Milliken & Co.
Millipore Corp.
Mine Safety Appliances Co.
Minnesota Mining & Manufacturing Co.
Minnesota Mutual Life Insurance Co.
Mitsubishi Electric America
Monarch Machine Tool Co.
Monsanto Co.
Montana Power Co.
Montgomery Ward & Co., Inc.
MONY Group (The)
Morgan Stanley Dean Witter & Co.
Morris Communications Corp.
Morrison Knudsen Corp.
Morton International Inc.
Motorola Inc.
MTD Products Inc.
MTS Systems Corp.
Mutual of Omaha Insurance Co.
Nabisco Group Holdings
National Bank of Commerce Trust & Savings
National City Bank of Minneapolis
National City Corp.
National Computer Systems, Inc.
National Fuel Gas Distribution Corp.
National Life of Vermont
National Machinery Co.
National Presto Industries, Inc.
National Service Industries, Inc.
National Starch & Chemical Co.
Nationwide Insurance Co.
NCR Corp.
NEBCO Evans
Nestle U.S.A. Inc.
New Century Energies
New England Financial
New Jersey Natural Gas Co.
New York Life Insurance Co.
New York Stock Exchange, Inc.
New York Times Co.
Niagara Mohawk Holdings Inc.
Nike, Inc.
Nordson Corp.
Norfolk Southern Corp.
Nortel
North American Royalties
Northeast Utilities
Northern Indiana Public Service Co.
Northern States Power Co.
Northern Trust Co.
Northwest Bank Nebraska, NA
Northwest Natural Gas Co.
Norton Co.
Norwest Corp.
Occidental Oil and Gas
Occidental Petroleum Corp.
Ohio National Life Insurance Co.
Oklahoma Publishing Co.
Old Kent Bank
Old National Bank Evansville
Olin Corp.
Orange & Rockland Utilities, Inc.
Orscheln Co.
Osborne Enterprises
Oshkosh B'Gosh, Inc.
Outboard Marine Corp.
Overnite Transportation Co.
Overseas Shipholding Group Inc.
Owens Corning
PACCAR Inc.
Pacific Century Financial Corp.
Pacific Gas and Electric Co.
Pacific Mutual Life Insurance Co.
PacifiCare Health Systems
PacifiCorp
Pan-American Life Insurance Co.
Park National Bank
Parker Hannifin Corp.
PECO Energy Co.
Pella Corp.
PEMCO Corp.
Penney Co., Inc. (J.C.)
Pennzoil-Quaker State Co.
Peoples Bank
Peoples Energy Corp.
PepsiCo, Inc.
PerkinElmer, Inc.
Pfizer Inc.
Pharmacia & Upjohn, Inc.
Phelps Dodge Corp.
Pheonix Financial Group
Philips Electronics North America Corp.
Phillips Petroleum Co.
Phoenix Home Life Mutual Insurance Co.
Physicians Mutual Insurance Co.
Pieper Power Electric Co.
Pillsbury Co.
Pioneer Group
Pioneer Hi-Bred International, Inc.
Pitney Bowes Inc.
Pittway Corp.
PNC Bank Kentucky Inc.
PNC Financial Services Group
Polaroid Corp.
Portland General Electric Co.
Potlatch Corp.
Potomac Electric Power Co.
PPG Industries, Inc.
Praxair
Premier Industrial Corp.
Price Associates (T. Rowe)
Principal Financial Group
Procter & Gamble Co.
Procter & Gamble Co., Cosmetics Division
Progressive Corp.
Promus Hotel Corp.
Providence Journal-Bulletin Co.
Provident Companies, Inc.
Prudential Insurance Co. of America
Prudential Securities Inc.
Public Service Electric & Gas Co.
Publix Supermarkets
Pulitzer Publishing Co.
Putnam Investments
Quaker Chemical Corp.
Quanex Corp.
Questar Corp.
Ralph's Grocery Co.
Ralston Purina Co.
Rayonier Inc.
Red Wing Shoe Co. Inc.
Reebok International Ltd.
Regions Bank

Regis Corp.
Reilly Industries, Inc.
Reily & Co., Inc. (William B.)
Reinhart Institutional Foods
Reliant Energy Inc.
Reliant Energy Minnegasco
ReliaStar Financial Corp.
Revlon Inc.
Reynolds Metals Co.
Reynolds & Reynolds Co.
Reynolds Tobacco (R.J.)
Rich Products Corp.
Rochester Gas & Electric Corp.
Rockwell International Corp.
Rouse Co.
Royal & SunAlliance USA, Inc.
Rubbermaid Inc.
Ruddick Corp.
Russer Foods
Ryder System, Inc.
SAFECO Corp.
Safeguard Scientifics
Saint Paul Companies Inc.
S&T Bancorp
Sara Lee Corp.
Sara Lee Hosiery, Inc.
SBC Communications Inc.
Schering-Plough Corp.
Schloss & Co. (Marcus)
Schwab & Co., Inc. (Charles)
Schwebel Baking Co.
Scripps Co. (E.W.)
Searle & Co. (G.D.)
Sears, Roebuck and Co.
Security Benefit Life Insurance Co.
Security Life of Denver Insurance Co.
Sega of America Inc.
Sempra Energy
Sentinel Communications Co.
Sentry Insurance, A Mutual Co.
Servco Pacific
S.G. Cowen
Shaklee Corp.
Sharp Electronics Corp.
Shaw's Supermarkets, Inc.
Shea Co. (John F.)
Shell Oil Co.
Sherwin-Williams Co.
Shoney's Inc.
Sierra Pacific Resources
Simplot Co. (J.R.)
Simpson Investment Co.
SIT Investment Associates, Inc.
Slant/Fin Corp.
Smith Corp. (A.O.)
SmithKline Beecham Corp.
Smurfit-Stone Container Corp.
Solo Cup Co.
Sonoco Products Co.
Sony Electronics
South Bend Tribune Corp.
Southeastern Mutual Insurance Co.
Southern New England Telephone Co.
Southwest Gas Corp.
Sovereign Bank
Springs Industries, Inc.
Sprint Corp.
Sprint/United Telephone
SPX Corp.
Square D Co.
Standard Products Co.
Standard Register Co.
Stanley Works (The)
Star Bank NA
Starwood Hotels & Resorts Worldwide, Inc.
State Farm Mutual Automobile Insurance Co.
State Street Bank & Trust Co.
Steelcase Inc.
Stone Container Corp.
Stonecutter Mills Corp.
Storage Technology Corp.
Strear Farms Co.
Stride Rite Corp.
Stupp Brothers Bridge & Iron Co.
Sun Microsystems Inc.
Sunoco Inc.
SunTrust Bank Atlanta
Susquehanna-Pfaltzgraff Co.
Sverdrup Corp.
Synovus Financial Corp.
TCF National Bank Minnesota
Tektronix, Inc.
Telcordia Technologies
Temple-Inland Inc.
TENNANT Co.
Tenneco Automotive
Tenneco Packaging
Tension Envelope Corp.
Tesoro Hawaii
Texaco Inc.
Texas Gas Transmission Corp.
Texas Instruments Inc.
Textron Inc.
Thermo Electron Corp.
Thomasville Furniture Industries Inc.
Thompson Co. (J. Walter)
Times Mirror Co.
Timken Co. (The)
Titan Industrial Corp.
TJX Companies, Inc.
TMC Investment Co.
Toledo Blade Co.
Tomkins Industries, Inc.
Torchmark Corp.
Toro Co.
Trace International Holdings, Inc.
Transamerica Corp.
True North Communications, Inc.
True Oil Co.
Trustmark Insurance Co.
TRW Inc.
TU Electric Co.
Tyson Foods Inc.
Ukrop's Super Markets
Unilever Home & Personal Care U.S.A.
Unilever United States, Inc.
Union Camp Corp.
Union Carbide Corp.
Union Pacific Corp.
Union Planters Corp.
Unisys Corp.
United Airlines Inc.
United Distillers & Vintners North America
United Dominion Industries, Ltd.
United Parcel Service of America Inc.
United Services Automobile Association
U.S. Bancorp
U.S. Bancorp Piper Jaffray
United States Sugar Corp.
United States Trust Co. of New York
United Wisconsin Services
Universal Foods Corp.
Universal Leaf Tobacco Co., Inc.
Universal Studios
Unocal Corp.
UnumProvident
US Bank, Washington
US West, Inc.
USAA Life Insurance Co.
USG Corp.
USX Corp.
Valmont Industries, Inc.
Valspar Corp.
Vanguard Group
Varian Medical Systems, Inc.
Vesper Corp.
Vodafone AirTouch Plc
Vulcan Materials Co.
Wachovia Bank of North Carolina NA
Wachtell, Lipton, Rosen & Katz
Wal-Mart Stores, Inc.
Waldbaum's Supermarkets, Inc.
Walgreen Co.
Walter Industries Inc.
Warner-Lambert Co.
Washington Mutual, Inc.
The Washington Post
Washington Trust Bank
Webster Bank
Weil, Gotshal & Manges Corp.
Wells Fargo & Co.
West Co. Inc.
Western Resources Inc.
Western & Southern Life Insurance Co.
Westvaco Corp.
Weyerhaeuser Co.
Whirlpool Corp.
Whitman Corp.
WICOR, Inc.
Wilbur-Ellis Co. & Connell Brothers Co.
Williams
Winn-Dixie Stores Inc.
Wiremold Co.
Wisconsin Energy Corp.
Wisconsin Power & Light Co.
Wisconsin Public Service Corp.
Witco Corp.
Wolverine World Wide
Woodward Governor Co.
Wrigley Co. (Wm. Jr.)
Wyman-Gordon Co.
Xerox Corp.
Yellow Corp.
York Federal Savings & Loan Association
Young & Rubicam
Zachry Co. (H.B.)
Zenith Electronics Corp.
Zilkha & Sons

VETERANS

Agrilink Foods, Inc.
AMCORE Bank Rockford
Carris Reels
CIT Group, Inc. (The)
Compass Bank
Dain Bosworth Inc.
Demoulas Supermarkets Inc.
Erving Industries
Extendicare Health Services
Fortis Insurance Co.
Galter Corp.
GEICO Corp.
Johnson & Son (S.C.)
La-Z-Boy Inc.
Little, Inc. (Arthur D.)
Madison Gas & Electric Co.
Mark IV Industries
Merrill Lynch & Co., Inc.
Occidental Oil and Gas
Osborne Enterprises
Pacific Mutual Life Insurance Co.
Prudential Insurance Co. of America
S&T Bancorp
Sentry Insurance, A Mutual Co.
Servco Pacific
Universal Studios
Witco Corp.

VOLUNTEER SERVICES

ABB Inc.
Abbott Laboratories
ABC
Aetna, Inc.
AGL Resources Inc.
Agrilink Foods, Inc.
Air Products and Chemicals, Inc.
Alcoa Inc.
Alliant Techsystems
AlliedSignal Inc.
Allmerica Financial Corp.
Allstate Insurance Co.
AMCORE Bank Rockford
Ameren Corp.
America West Airlines, Inc.
American Express Co.
American General Finance
American United Life Insurance Co.
Ameritech Ohio
AmerUS Group
AMR Corp.
Andersen Corp.
Anheuser-Busch Companies, Inc.
Aon Corp.
APL Ltd.
Archer-Daniels-Midland Co.
Arizona Public Service Co.
Atlantic Richfield Co.
Avon Products, Inc.
Bandag, Inc.
Bank of New York Co., Inc.
BankAtlantic Bancorp
BankBoston-Connecticut Region
BankBoston Corp.
Barden Corp.
Bean, Inc. (L.L.)
Beckman Coulter, Inc.
Becton Dickinson & Co.
Bell Atlantic Corp.
Bernstein & Co., Inc. (Sanford C.)
Bethlehem Steel Corp.
Binney & Smith Inc.
Block, Inc. (H&R)
Blue Cross & Blue Shield of Alabama
Boeing Co.
Borden, Inc.
BP Amoco Corp.
Bridgestone/Firestone, Inc.
Bristol-Myers Squibb Co.
Broderbund Software, Inc.
Brunswick Corp.
Burlington Resources, Inc.
Business Improvement
Cabot Corp.
Carrier Corp.
Central Maine Power Co.
CertainTeed Corp.
CGU Insurance
Chase Bank of Texas
Chase Manhattan Bank, NA
Chevron Corp.
CIGNA Corp.
CIT Group, Inc. (The)
Citibank Corp.
Citizens Bank-Flint
Clorox Co.
Colonial Life & Accident Insurance Co.
Colonial Oil Industries, Inc.
Commercial Intertech Corp.
Compaq Computer Corp.
Constellation Energy Group, Inc.
Consumers Energy Co.
Continental Grain Co.
Contran Corp.
Conwood Co. LP
Coors Brewing Co.
Cox Enterprises Inc.
Crane Co.
Crane & Co., Inc.
Credit Suisse First Boston
Cummins Engine Co., Inc.
Daily News
DaimlerChrysler Corp.
Dana Corp.
Deluxe Corp.
Deposit Guaranty National Bank
Deutsch Co.
Disney Co. (Walt)
Donaldson Co., Inc.
Dow Jones & Co., Inc.
DSM Copolymer
du Pont de Nemours & Co. (E.I.)
Duchossois Industries Inc.
Dynamet, Inc.
Eaton Corp.
Ecolab Inc.
Edison International
EDS Corp.
Edwards Enterprise Software (J.D.)
Elf Atochem North America, Inc.
Employers Mutual Casualty Co.
Ensign-Bickford Industries
Equitable Resources, Inc.
Exxon Mobil Corp.
Fabri-Kal Corp.
Federal-Mogul Corp.
Federated Department Stores, Inc.
Fidelity Investments
Fireman's Fund Insurance Co.
First Hawaiian, Inc.
First Tennessee National Corp.
First Union Corp.
First Union National Bank, NA
Firstar Bank Milwaukee NA
Fisher Brothers Cleaning Services
FleetBoston Financial Corp.
Fluor Corp.
Forbes Inc.
Ford Motor Co.
Forest City Enterprises, Inc.
Fort James Corp.
Fortis Insurance Co.
Fortune Brands, Inc.
Freeport-McMoRan Inc.

Frontier Corp.
Frost National Bank
Fuller Co. (H.B.)
Gap, Inc.
GenAmerica Corp.
GenCorp
General Electric Co.
General Mills, Inc.
General Motors Corp.
Gerber Products Co.
Globe Corp.
Goldman Sachs Group
Green Bay Packaging
GTE Corp.
Hallmark Cards Inc.
Hancock Financial Services (John)
Harcourt General, Inc.
Harris Trust & Savings Bank
Harsco Corp.
Hartford Steam Boiler Inspection & Insurance Co.
Hartmarx Corp.
Hasbro, Inc.
Heinz Co. (H.J.)
Hensel Phelps Construction Co.
Hershey Foods Corp.
Hewlett-Packard Co.
Hickory Tech Corp.
Hitachi America Ltd.
Hofmann Co.
HON Industries Inc.
Household International Inc.
Hubbard Broadcasting, Inc.
Huntington Bancshares Inc.
Illinois Power Co.
Illinois Tool Works, Inc.
International Business Machines Corp.
International Multifoods Corp.
International Paper Co.
Jacobs Engineering Group
Jeld-wen, Inc.
Journal-Gazette Co.
JSJ Corp.
Kellogg Co.
Kimball International, Inc.
Kimberly-Clark Corp.
Kingsbury Corp.
Knight Ridder
Kraft Foods, Inc.
Ladish Co., Inc.
Land O'Lakes, Inc.
Levi Strauss & Co.
Lincoln Electric Co.
Lipton Co.
Little, Inc. (Arthur D.)
Litton Industries, Inc.
Loews Corp.
LTV Corp.
Macy's East Inc.
Mallinckrodt Chemical, Inc.
Marcus Corp.
Marshall & Ilsley Corp.
MBIA Inc.
McClatchy Co.
McCormick & Co. Inc.
McDonald & Co. Securities, Inc.
McGraw-Hill Companies, Inc.
McKesson-HBOC Corp.
Medtronic, Inc.
Memphis Light Gas & Water Division
Menasha Corp.
Metropolitan Life Insurance Co.
MGIC Investment Corp.
Mid-America Bank of Louisville
Minnesota Mining & Manufacturing Co.
Mitsubishi Electric America
Montgomery Ward & Co., Inc.
MONY Group (The)
Morgan & Co. Inc. (J.P.)
Morgan Stanley Dean Witter & Co.
Motorola Inc.
National Computer Systems, Inc.
National Service Industries, Inc.
New Century Energies
New England Financial
New York Life Insurance Co.
New York Stock Exchange, Inc.
New York Times Co.
Nordson Corp.
Nortel
Northeast Utilities
Northern Indiana Public Service Co.
Northern States Power Co.
Northern Trust Co.
Northwest Natural Gas Co.
Norton Co.
Olin Corp.
Orange & Rockland Utilities, Inc.
Pacific Mutual Life Insurance Co.
PacifiCare Health Systems
Parker Hannifin Corp.
Pella Corp.
PEMCO Corp.
Penney Co., Inc. (J.C.)
Peoples Bank
Peoples Energy Corp.
PerkinElmer, Inc.
Pfizer Inc.
Pharmacia & Upjohn, Inc.
Pheonix Financial Group
Physicians Mutual Insurance Co.
Pillsbury Co.
Portland General Electric Co.
PPG Industries, Inc.
Premier Industrial Corp.
Principal Financial Group
Procter & Gamble Co.
Procter & Gamble Co., Cosmetics Division
Prudential Insurance Co. of America
Quaker Chemical Corp.
Questar Corp.
Ralston Purina Co.
Rayonier Inc.
Regions Bank
Reliant Energy Inc.
Revlon Inc.
Reynolds Tobacco (R.J.)
Rockwell International Corp.
Rouse Co.
Royal & SunAlliance USA, Inc.
Ryder System, Inc.
SAFECO Corp.
Saint Paul Companies Inc.
Sara Lee Corp.
Sara Lee Hosiery, Inc.
SBC Communications Inc.
Schwab & Co., Inc. (Charles)
Searle & Co. (G.D.)
Security Benefit Life Insurance Co.
Sega of America Inc.
Sempra Energy
Shell Oil Co.
Sherwin-Williams Co.
Shoney's Inc.
SmithKline Beecham Corp.
Solo Cup Co.
Sonoco Products Co.
Sony Electronics
Southwest Gas Corp.
Sovereign Bank
Springs Industries, Inc.
Sprint Corp.
Starwood Hotels & Resorts Worldwide, Inc.
Steelcase Inc.
Stone Container Corp.
Storage Technology Corp.
Stride Rite Corp.
TCF National Bank Minnesota
Temple-Inland Inc.
Tenneco Automotive
Tension Envelope Corp.
Texaco Inc.
Texas Gas Transmission Corp.
Texas Instruments Inc.
Textron Inc.
Thermo Electron Corp.
Times Mirror Co.
TJX Companies, Inc.
Toledo Blade Co.
True North Communications, Inc.
Trustmark Insurance Co.
TRW Inc.
Unilever Home & Personal Care U.S.A.
Union Camp Corp.
Union Carbide Corp.
United Airlines Inc.
United Parcel Service of America Inc.
U.S. Bancorp Piper Jaffray
United States Trust Co. of New York
United Technologies Corp.
United Wisconsin Services
Universal Studios
Unocal Corp.
US Bank, Washington
USG Corp.
Vodafone AirTouch Plc
Wal-Mart Stores, Inc.
Washington Mutual, Inc.
Weil, Gotshal & Manges Corp.
Wells Fargo & Co.
Weyerhaeuser Co.
Whirlpool Corp.
WICOR, Inc.
Wisconsin Public Service Corp.
Woodward Governor Co.

YMCA/YWCA/YMHA/YWHA

Abbott Laboratories
ABC
AEGON U.S.A. Inc.
Agrilink Foods, Inc.
AK Steel Corp.
Alcoa Inc.
Alcon Laboratories, Inc.
Alexander & Baldwin, Inc.
Allegheny Technologies Inc.
Allianz Life Insurance Co. of North America
Allmerica Financial Corp.
Allstate Insurance Co.
AMCORE Bank Rockford
Ameren Corp.
American Fidelity Corp.
American General Finance
American United Life Insurance Co.
Ameritas Life Insurance Corp.
Ameritech Ohio
AMETEK, Inc.
Amgen, Inc.
AMP Inc.
AMR Corp.
Amsted Industries Inc.
Andersen Corp.
Andersons Inc.
Anheuser-Busch Companies, Inc.
APL Ltd.
Archer-Daniels-Midland Co.
Arizona Public Service Co.
Armstrong World Industries, Inc.
Associated Food Stores
Atlantic Investment Co.
Atlantic Richfield Co.
Auburn Foundry
Avon Products, Inc.
Badger Meter, Inc.
Baird & Co. (Robert W.)
Bank of America
Bank One Corp.
BankAtlantic Bancorp
Banta Corp.
Barclays Capital
Bard, Inc. (C.R.)
Barden Corp.
Barnes Group Inc.
Barry Corp. (R.G.)
Bassett Furniture Industries
Baxter International Inc.
Belk-Simpson Department Stores
Belk Stores Services Inc.
Bemis Co., Inc.
Bemis Manufacturing Co.
Ben & Jerry's Homemade Inc.
Bernstein & Co., Inc. (Sanford C.)
Block, Inc. (H&R)
Blount International, Inc.
Blue Bell, Inc.
Blue Cross & Blue Shield of Alabama
Blue Cross & Blue Shield of Iowa
Boeing Co.
Borden, Inc.
Bourns, Inc.
BP Amoco Corp.
Bradford & Co. (J.C.)
Briggs & Stratton Corp.
Brown Shoe Co., Inc.
Brunswick Corp.
Bucyrus-Erie Co.
Burlington Industries, Inc.
Burlington Resources, Inc.
Burress (J.W.)
Butler Manufacturing Co.
Cabot Corp.
Campbell Soup Co.
Cargill Inc.
Carolina Power & Light Co.
Carpenter Technology Corp.
Caterpillar Inc.
Central & South West Services
Central Soya Co.
CertainTeed Corp.
Cessna Aircraft Co.
Charter Manufacturing Co.
Chase Bank of Texas
Chase Manhattan Bank, NA
Chemed Corp.
Chesapeake Corp.
Chicago Title Corp.
CIBC Oppenheimer
Cinergy Corp.
Circuit City Stores, Inc.
CIT Group, Inc. (The)
Citigroup
Citizens Financial Group, Inc.
CLARCOR Inc.
Cleveland-Cliffs, Inc.
Clorox Co.
Coca-Cola Co.
Collins & Aikman Corp.
Colonial Oil Industries, Inc.
Comdisco, Inc.
Commerce Bancshares, Inc.
Commercial Intertech Corp.
Compaq Computer Corp.
Compass Bank
ConAgra, Inc.
Cone Mills Corp.
Consolidated Natural Gas Co.
Consolidated Papers, Inc.
Constellation Energy Group, Inc.
Consumers Energy Co.
Continental Grain Co.
Contran Corp.
Cooper Industries, Inc.
Copley Press, Inc.
Corning Inc.
Cox Enterprises Inc.
CPI Corp.
Crane Co.
Crane & Co., Inc.
Cranston Print Works Co.
Credit Suisse First Boston
Crestar Finance Corp.
CSR Rinker Materials Corp.
Cummings Properties Management
Cummins Engine Co., Inc.
CUNA Mutual Group
DaimlerChrysler Corp.
Dain Bosworth Inc.
Dana Corp.
Danis Companies
Dayton Hudson
Dayton Power and Light Co.
Deere & Co.
DeKalb Genetics Corp.
Deluxe Corp.
Demoulas Supermarkets Inc.
Deutsch Co.
Dial Corp.
Disney Co. (Walt)
Dixie Group, Inc. (The)
Donaldson Co., Inc.
Dow Corning Corp.
Duke Energy
Dun & Bradstreet Corp.
Duriron Co., Inc.
Dynamet, Inc.
Eastern Bank
Eaton Corp.
Ecolab Inc.
El Paso Energy Co.
Elf Atochem North America, Inc.
Emerson Electric Co.
Employers Mutual Casualty Co.
Enterprise Rent-A-Car Co.
Erb Lumber Co.
Erving Industries
Evening Post Publishing Co.
Exxon Mobil Corp.
Fabri-Kal Corp.
Ferro Corp.
Fidelity Investments

Fifth Third Bancorp
FINA
Fireman's Fund Insurance Co.
First American Corp.
First Financial Bank
First Hawaiian, Inc.
First Maryland Bancorp
First Source Corp.
First Union Bank
First Union Corp.
Firstar Bank Milwaukee NA
Fisher Scientific
FleetBoston Financial Corp.
Florida Power & Light Co.
Florida Rock Industries
Fluor Corp.
FMC Corp.
Ford Motor Co.
Forest City Enterprises, Inc.
Fort Worth Star-Telegram Inc.
Fortis Insurance Co.
Franklin Electric Co.
Freddie Mac
Freeport-McMoRan Inc.
Fuller Co. (H.B.)
Furniture Brands International, Inc.
Gallo Winery, Inc. (E&J)
Gap, Inc.
GenAmerica Corp.
GenCorp
General Mills, Inc.
Georgia-Pacific Corp.
Georgia Power Co.
Gerber Products Co.
Giant Eagle Inc.
Giddings & Lewis
Glickenhaus & Co.
Globe Corp.
Goldman Sachs Group
Golub Corp.
Grace & Co. (W.R.)
Graco, Inc.
Grede Foundries
Green Bay Packaging
GTE Corp.
Gulf Power Co.
Halliburton Co.
Hallmark Cards Inc.
Hamilton Sundstrand Corp.
Hanna Co. (M.A.)
Hannaford Brothers Co.
Harcourt General, Inc.
Harley-Davidson Co.
Harnischfeger Industries
Harris Trust & Savings Bank
Harsco Corp.
Hartford (The)
Hartmarx Corp.
Hasbro, Inc.
Hawaiian Electric Co., Inc.
Heinz Co. (H.J.)
Hensel Phelps Construction Co.
Hewlett-Packard Co.
Hickory Tech Corp.
Hoffer Plastics Corp.
Hoffmann-La Roche Inc.
HON Industries Inc.
Honeywell International Inc.
Hubbard Broadcasting, Inc.
Huffy Corp.
Humana, Inc.
Hunt Manufacturing Co.
Idaho Power Co.
IKON Office Solutions, Inc.
Illinois Tool Works, Inc.
Inman Mills
International Multifoods Corp.
INTRUST Financial Corp.
Invacare Corp.
Jacobs Engineering Group
Jacobson & Sons (Benjamin)
Jeld-wen, Inc.
Johnson Controls Inc.
Johnson & Son (S.C.)
Jones & Co. (Edward D.)
Jostens, Inc.
Journal-Gazette Co.
JSJ Corp.
Katten, Muchin & Zavis
Kellogg Co.
Kellwood Co.
Kelly Services
Kennametal, Inc.
Kimberly-Clark Corp.
Kinder Morgn
Kingsbury Corp.
Koch Enterprises, Inc.
Kroger Co.
La-Z-Boy Inc.
Ladish Co., Inc.
Lancaster Lens, Inc.
Lance, Inc.
Land O'Lakes, Inc.
Landmark Communications Inc.
Lee Enterprises
Lehigh Portland Cement Co.
Lennox International, Inc.
Levi Strauss & Co.
Leviton Manufacturing Co. Inc.
Liberty Corp.
Liberty Diversified Industries
Lilly & Co. (Eli)
Litton Industries, Inc.
Liz Claiborne, Inc.
Loews Corp.
Lotus Development Corp.
Louisiana-Pacific Corp.
LTV Corp.
Madison Gas & Electric Co.
Mamiye Brothers
Marcus Corp.
Mark IV Industries
Marshall & Ilsley Corp.
Masco Corp.
Mattel Inc.
May Department Stores Co.
McClatchy Co.
McDonald & Co. Securities, Inc.
McGraw-Hill Companies, Inc.
McWane Inc.
Mead Corp.
Medtronic, Inc.
Menasha Corp.
Mercantile Bank NA
Merrill Lynch & Co., Inc.
Metropolitan Life Insurance Co.
Mid-America Bank of Louisville
MidAmerican Energy Holdings Co.
Milacron, Inc.
Milliken & Co.
Minnesota Mining & Manufacturing Co.
Minnesota Mutual Life Insurance Co.
Mitsubishi Electric America
Monarch Machine Tool Co.
Monsanto Co.
Montana Power Co.
Montgomery Ward & Co., Inc.
MONY Group (The)
Morgan & Co. Inc. (J.P.)
Morgan Stanley Dean Witter & Co.
Morris Communications Corp.
Morrison Knudsen Corp.
Motorola Inc.
MTD Products Inc.
Nabisco Group Holdings
Nalco Chemical Co.
National City Bank of Minneapolis
National City Corp.
National Machinery Co.
National Service Industries, Inc.
National Starch & Chemical Co.
Nationwide Insurance Co.
NCR Corp.
NEBCO Evans
New Jersey Natural Gas Co.
New York Mercantile Exchange
New York Stock Exchange, Inc.
New York Times Co.
Niagara Mohawk Holdings Inc.
Nordson Corp.
Norfolk Southern Corp.
North American Royalties
Northern Trust Co.
Norton Co.
Norwest Corp.
Occidental Oil and Gas
OG&E Electric Services
Ohio National Life Insurance Co.
Oklahoma Publishing Co.
Old Kent Bank
Old National Bank Evansville
Orscheln Co.
Oshkosh B'Gosh, Inc.
Outboard Marine Corp.
Owens Corning
PACCAR Inc.
Pacific Century Financial Corp.
Pacific Mutual Life Insurance Co.
Paine Webber
Park National Bank
Parker Hannifin Corp.
Pella Corp.
Pharmacia & Upjohn, Inc.
Pheonix Financial Group
Phillips Petroleum Co.
Physicians Mutual Insurance Co.
Pillsbury Co.
Pittway Corp.
Polaroid Corp.
PPG Industries, Inc.
Praxair
Premier Industrial Corp.
Principal Financial Group
Procter & Gamble Co.
Procter & Gamble Co., Cosmetics Division
Prudential Securities Inc.
Publix Supermarkets
Pulitzer Publishing Co.
Putnam Investments
Quanex Corp.
Ralph's Grocery Co.
Ralston Purina Co.
Rayonier Inc.
Red Wing Shoe Co. Inc.
Reebok International Ltd.
Regions Bank
Regis Corp.
Reilly Industries, Inc.
Reily & Co., Inc. (William B.)
Reinhart Institutional Foods
Revlon Inc.
Reynolds Metals Co.
Reynolds & Reynolds Co.
Reynolds Tobacco (R.J.)
Rockwell International Corp.
Rouse Co.
Royal & SunAlliance USA, Inc.
Rubbermaid Inc.
Ruddick Corp.
Russer Foods
Ryder System, Inc.
Saint Paul Companies Inc.
S&T Bancorp
Sara Lee Corp.
SBC Communications Inc.
Schering-Plough Corp.
Schloss & Co. (Marcus)
Schwab & Co., Inc. (Charles)
Schwebel Baking Co.
Scripps Co. (E.W.)
Security Benefit Life Insurance Co.
Sega of America Inc.
Sentry Insurance, A Mutual Co.
Servco Pacific
Shaw's Supermarkets, Inc.
Shea Co. (John F.)
Sherwin-Williams Co.
Sierra Pacific Resources
Simplot Co. (J.R.)
SIT Investment Associates, Inc.
Slant/Fin Corp.
Smurfit-Stone Container Corp.
Solo Cup Co.
Sonoco Products Co.
South Bend Tribune Corp.
Southeastern Mutual Insurance Co.
Southwest Gas Corp.
Sovereign Bank
SPX Corp.
Square D Co.
Standard Products Co.
Standard Register Co.
Star Bank NA
State Farm Mutual Automobile Insurance Co.
State Street Bank & Trust Co.
Steelcase Inc.
Stone Container Corp.
Storage Technology Corp.
Strear Farms Co.
Stride Rite Corp.
Stupp Brothers Bridge & Iron Co.
Sun Microsystems Inc.
Susquehanna-Pfaltzgraff Co.
Sverdrup Corp.
Synovus Financial Corp.
TCF National Bank Minnesota
Teleflex Inc.
Temple-Inland Inc.
TENNANT Co.
Tension Envelope Corp.
Tesoro Hawaii
Texas Instruments Inc.
Thomasville Furniture Industries Inc.
Times Mirror Co.
Titan Industrial Corp.
TMC Investment Co.
Toledo Blade Co.
Tomkins Industries, Inc.
Toro Co.
Toshiba America Inc.
Trace International Holdings, Inc.
Transamerica Corp.
True North Communications, Inc.
True Oil Co.
TRW Inc.
Ukrop's Super Markets
Unilever Home & Personal Care U.S.A.
Unilever United States, Inc.
Union Camp Corp.
Union Carbide Corp.
Union Pacific Corp.
United Airlines Inc.
United Co.
United Dominion Industries, Ltd.
United Parcel Service of America Inc.
United Services Automobile Association
U.S. Bancorp
U.S. Bancorp Piper Jaffray
United States Sugar Corp.
United Wisconsin Services
Universal Foods Corp.
Universal Leaf Tobacco Co., Inc.
Universal Studios
Unocal Corp.
UnumProvident
US Bank, Washington
USAA Life Insurance Co.
USG Corp.
USX Corp.
Valmont Industries, Inc.
Valspar Corp.
Vulcan Materials Co.
Wachovia Bank of North Carolina NA
Waffle House Inc.
Walter Industries Inc.
Warner-Lambert Co.
Washington Mutual, Inc.
Washington Trust Bank
Webster Bank
Weil, Gotshal & Manges Corp.
Wells Fargo & Co.
West Co. Inc.
Westvaco Corp.
Weyerhaeuser Co.
Whirlpool Corp.
Whitman Corp.
WICOR, Inc.
Williams
Winn-Dixie Stores Inc.
Wisconsin Energy Corp.
Wisconsin Power & Light Co.
Wisconsin Public Service Corp.
Woodward Governor Co.
Wyman-Gordon Co.
York Federal Savings & Loan Association
Young & Rubicam
Zachry Co. (H.B.)
Zilkha & Sons

YOUTH ORGANIZATIONS

ABB Inc.
Abbott Laboratories
ABC
Advanced Micro Devices, Inc.
Aetna, Inc.
AGL Resources Inc.
Agrilink Foods, Inc.

Air Products and Chemicals, Inc.
AK Steel Corp.
Alabama Power Co.
Albertson's Inc.
Alcoa Inc.
Alcon Laboratories, Inc.
Alexander & Baldwin, Inc.
Allegheny Technologies Inc.
Allianz Life Insurance Co. of North America
AlliedSignal Inc.
Allmerica Financial Corp.
Allstate Insurance Co.
Alma Piston Co.
Alyeska Pipeline Service Co.
AMCORE Bank Rockford
Ameren Corp.
America West Airlines, Inc.
American Express Co.
American Fidelity Corp.
American General Finance
American Retail Group
American Stock Exchange, Inc.
American United Life Insurance Co.
Ameritas Life Insurance Corp.
Ameritech Illinois
Ameritech Indiana
Ameritech Michigan
Ameritech Wisconsin
AMETEK, Inc.
Amgen, Inc.
AMP Inc.
AMR Corp.
Amsted Industries Inc.
Andersen Corp.
Andersons Inc.
Anheuser-Busch Companies, Inc.
Aon Corp.
APL Ltd.
Appleton Papers Inc.
Archer-Daniels-Midland Co.
Aristech Chemical Corp.
Arizona Public Service Co.
Armstrong World Industries, Inc.
Arvin Industries, Inc.
ASARCO Inc.
Ashland, Inc.
Associated Food Stores
AT&T Corp.
Atlantic Investment Co.
Atlantic Richfield Co.
Avista Corporation
Avon Products, Inc.
Badger Meter, Inc.
Baird & Co. (Robert W.)
Bandag, Inc.
Banfi Vintners
Bank of America
Bank of New York Co., Inc.
Bank One Corp.
Bank One, Texas-Houston Office
BankAtlantic Bancorp
BankBoston Corp.
Banta Corp.
Barclays Capital
Bard, Inc. (C.R.)
Barden Corp.
Bardes Corp.
Barnes Group Inc.
Barry Corp. (R.G.)
Battelle Memorial Institute
Bausch & Lomb Inc.
Baxter International Inc.
Bayer Corp.
Bechtel Group, Inc.
Becton Dickinson & Co.
Belk-Simpson Department Stores
Belk Stores Services Inc.
Bell Atlantic Corp.
Bemis Co., Inc.
Ben & Jerry's Homemade Inc.
Bernstein & Co., Inc. (Sanford C.)
Bestfoods
Bethlehem Steel Corp.
BFGoodrich Co.
Binney & Smith Inc.
Binswanger Companies
Blair & Co. (William)
Block, Inc. (H&R)
Blount International, Inc.
Blue Bell, Inc.
Blue Cross & Blue Shield of Alabama
Blue Cross & Blue Shield of Iowa
Boeing Co.
Boise Cascade Corp.
Borden, Inc.
Borman's Inc.
Boston Edison Co.
Boston Globe (The)
Bourns, Inc.
Bowater Inc.
BP Amoco Corp.
Bradford & Co. (J.C.)
Bridgestone/Firestone, Inc.
Briggs & Stratton Corp.
Bristol-Myers Squibb Co.
Broderbund Software, Inc.
Brooklyn Union
Brown Shoe Co., Inc.
Browning-Ferris Industries Inc.
Brunswick Corp.
Bucyrus-Erie Co.
Burlington Industries, Inc.
Burlington Resources, Inc.
Burnett Co. (Leo)
Burress (J.W.)
Business Improvement
Butler Manufacturing Co.
Cabot Corp.
Cadence Designs Systems, Inc.
California Bank & Trust
Callaway Golf Co.
Campbell Soup Co.
Cargill Inc.
Carlson Companies, Inc.
Carnival Corp.
Carpenter Technology Corp.
Carrier Corp.
Carter-Wallace, Inc.
Caterpillar Inc.
Centex Corp.
Central Maine Power Co.
Central National-Gottesman
Central & South West Services
Central Soya Co.
Century 21
CertainTeed Corp.
Cessna Aircraft Co.
CGU Insurance
Charter Manufacturing Co.
Chase Bank of Texas
Chase Manhattan Bank, NA
Chesapeake Corp.
Chevron Corp.
Chicago Board of Trade
Chicago Sun-Times, Inc.
Chicago Title Corp.
Chicago Tribune Co.
Church & Dwight Co., Inc.
Cincinnati Bell Inc.
Cinergy Corp.
Circuit City Stores, Inc.
CIT Group, Inc. (The)
Citibank Corp.
Citigroup
Citizens Bank-Flint
Citizens Financial Group, Inc.
CLARCOR Inc.
Clark Refining & Marketing
Cleveland-Cliffs, Inc.
Clorox Co.
CNA
CNF Transportation, Inc.
Coca-Cola Co.
Collins & Aikman Corp.
Colonial Life & Accident Insurance Co.
Colonial Oil Industries, Inc.
Comdisco, Inc.
Comerica Inc.
Commerce Bancshares, Inc.
Commercial Intertech Corp.
Commonwealth Edison Co.
Compaq Computer Corp.
Compass Bank
ConAgra, Inc.
Cone Mills Corp.
Consolidated Natural Gas Co.
Consolidated Papers, Inc.
Constellation Energy Group, Inc.
Consumers Energy Co.
Continental Grain Co.
Contran Corp.
Conwood Co. LP
Cooper Industries, Inc.
Copley Press, Inc.
Corning Inc.
Country Curtains, Inc.
Cox Enterprises Inc.
CPI Corp.
Crane Co.
Crane & Co., Inc.
Cranston Print Works Co.
Credit Suisse First Boston
Crestar Finance Corp.
Croft-Leominster
CSR Rinker Materials Corp.
CSS Industries, Inc.
Cummings Properties Management
Cummins Engine Co., Inc.
CUNA Mutual Group
Daily News
DaimlerChrysler Corp.
Dain Bosworth Inc.
Dana Corp.
Danis Companies
Dayton Hudson
Dayton Power and Light Co.
Deere & Co.
Delta Air Lines, Inc.
Deluxe Corp.
Demoulas Supermarkets Inc.
Deposit Guaranty National Bank
Detroit Edison Co.
Deutsch Co.
Dexter Corp.
Dial Corp.
Disney Co. (Walt)
Dixie Group, Inc. (The)
Domino's Pizza Inc.
Donaldson Co., Inc.
Donnelley & Sons Co. (R.R.)
Dow Corning Corp.
Dreyer's Grand Ice Cream
DSM Copolymer
du Pont de Nemours & Co. (E.I.)
Duchossois Industries Inc.
Duke Energy
Dun & Bradstreet Corp.
Duquesne Light Co.
Duriron Co., Inc.
Dynamet, Inc.
Eastern Bank
Eastern Enterprises
Eastman Kodak Co.
Eaton Corp.
Eckerd Corp.
Ecolab Inc.
Edison International
EDS Corp.
Edwards Enterprise Software (J.D.)
El Paso Energy Co.
Elf Atochem North America, Inc.
Emerson Electric Co.
EMI Music Publishing
Employers Mutual Casualty Co.
Ensign-Bickford Industries
Enterprise Rent-A-Car Co.
Equifax Inc.
Equitable Resources, Inc.
Erb Lumber Co.
Erving Industries
Ethyl Corp.
European American Bank
Evening Post Publishing Co.
Exxon Mobil Corp.
Fabri-Kal Corp.
Fannie Mae
Federal-Mogul Corp.
Federated Department Stores, Inc.
FedEx Corp.
Fidelity Investments
Fifth Third Bancorp
Fireman's Fund Insurance Co.
First American Corp.
First Financial Bank
First Hawaiian, Inc.
First Maryland Bancorp
First Source Corp.
First Tennessee National Corp.
First Union Bank
First Union Corp.
First Union National Bank, NA
First Union Securities, Inc.
Firstar Bank Milwaukee NA
Fisher Brothers Cleaning Services
Fisher Scientific
FleetBoston Financial Corp.
Florida Power Corp.
Florida Rock Industries
Fluor Corp.
FMC Corp.
Forbes Inc.
Ford Meter Box Co.
Ford Motor Co.
Forest City Enterprises, Inc.
Fort James Corp.
Fort Worth Star-Telegram Inc.
Fortis, Inc.
Fortis Insurance Co.
Fortune Brands, Inc.
Fox Entertainment Group
Freddie Mac
Freeport-McMoRan Inc.
Freightliner Corp.
Frost National Bank
Fuller Co. (H.B.)
Furniture Brands International, Inc.
Gallo Winery, Inc. (E&J)
Galter Corp.
Gannett Co., Inc.
Gap, Inc.
GATX Corp.
GEICO Corp.
GenAmerica Corp.
GenCorp
General Atlantic Partners II LP
General Dynamics Corp.
General Electric Co.
General Mills, Inc.
General Motors Corp.
Georgia-Pacific Corp.
Georgia Power Co.
Gerber Products Co.
Giant Eagle Inc.
Giant Food Inc.
Giddings & Lewis
Gillette Co.
Glaxo Wellcome Inc.
Globe Corp.
Golub Corp.
Goodrich Aerospace - Aerostructures Group (B.F.)
Grace & Co. (W.R.)
Graco, Inc.
Grede Foundries
Green Bay Packaging
Group Health Plan
GTE Corp.
Guardian Life Insurance Co. of America
Gucci America Inc.
Gulf Power Co.
Halliburton Co.
Hallmark Cards Inc.
Hamilton Sundstrand Corp.
Hancock Financial Services (John)
Hanna Co. (M.A.)
Hannaford Brothers Co.
Harcourt General, Inc.
Harland Co. (John H.)
Harley-Davidson Co.
Harnischfeger Industries
Harris Corp.
Harris Trust & Savings Bank
Harsco Corp.
Hartford (The)
Hartford Steam Boiler Inspection & Insurance Co.
Hartmarx Corp.
Hasbro, Inc.
Hawaiian Electric Co., Inc.
Heinz Co. (H.J.)
Heller Financial, Inc.
Hensel Phelps Construction Co.
Hewlett-Packard Co.
Hickory Tech Corp.
Hitachi America Ltd.
Hoffer Plastics Corp.
Hofmann Co.
Home Depot, Inc.
HON Industries Inc.
Honeywell International Inc.
Housatonic Curtain Co.
Household International Inc.
HSBC Bank USA
Hubbard Broadcasting, Inc.
Hubbell Inc.
Huffy Corp.
Hughes Electronics Corp.
Humana, Inc.
Hunt Manufacturing Co.

Huntington Bancshares Inc.
IBP
Idaho Power Co.
IKON Office Solutions, Inc.
Illinois Tool Works, Inc.
Independent Stave Co.
Inland Container Corp.
Inman Mills
Intel Corp.
International Business Machines Corp.
International Flavors & Fragrances Inc.
International Multifoods Corp.
International Paper Co.
INTRUST Financial Corp.
Invacare Corp.
Jacobs Engineering Group
Jacobson & Sons (Benjamin)
Jeld-wen, Inc.
Johnson Controls Inc.
Johnson & Johnson
Johnson & Son (S.C.)
Jostens, Inc.
Journal-Gazette Co.
JSJ Corp.
Katten, Muchin & Zavis
Kellogg Co.
Kellwood Co.
Kelly Services
Kemper National Insurance Companies
Kennametal, Inc.
Kerr-McGee Corp.
Kiewit Sons' Inc. (Peter)
Kimball International, Inc.
Kimberly-Clark Corp.
Kinder Morgn
Kingsbury Corp.
Kmart Corp.
Koch Enterprises, Inc.
Koch Industries, Inc.
Kraft Foods, Inc.
Kroger Co.
La-Z-Boy Inc.
Laclede Gas Co.
Ladish Co., Inc.
Lancaster Lens, Inc.
Lance, Inc.
Land O'Lakes, Inc.
LandAmerica Financial Services
Landmark Communications Inc.
Lee Enterprises
Lehigh Portland Cement Co.
Leigh Fibers, Inc.
Levi Strauss & Co.
Leviton Manufacturing Co. Inc.
Liberty Corp.
Liberty Diversified Industries
Lilly & Co. (Eli)
Lincoln Electric Co.
Lincoln Financial Group
Lipton Co.
Little, Inc. (Arthur D.)
Litton Industries, Inc.
Liz Claiborne, Inc.
Loews Corp.
Lotus Development Corp.
Louisiana Land & Exploration Co.
Louisiana-Pacific Corp.
LTV Corp.
Lubrizol Corp. (The)
Macy's East Inc.
Madison Gas & Electric Co.
Mallinckrodt Chemical, Inc.
Mamiye Brothers
Marcus Corp.
Maritz Inc.
Marriott International Inc.
Marshall Field's
Marshall & Ilsley Corp.
Masco Corp.
Mattel Inc.
May Department Stores Co.
Mazda North American Operations
MBIA Inc.
McClatchy Co.
McCormick & Co. Inc.
McDermott Inc.
McDonald & Co. Securities, Inc.
McDonald's Corp.
MCI WorldCom, Inc.
McKesson-HBOC Corp.
McWane Inc.
Mead Corp.
Medtronic, Inc.
Mellon Financial Corp.
Menasha Corp.
Mercantile Bank NA
Merck & Co.
Meredith Corp.
Merit Oil Corp.
Merrill Lynch & Co., Inc.
Metropolitan Life Insurance Co.
MFA Inc.
MGIC Investment Corp.
Michigan Consolidated Gas Co.
Mid-America Bank of Louisville
Milacron, Inc.
Milliken & Co.
Millipore Corp.
Mine Safety Appliances Co.
Minnesota Mining & Manufacturing Co.
Minnesota Mutual Life Insurance Co.
Mitsubishi Electric America
Monarch Machine Tool Co.
Monsanto Co.
Montana Power Co.
Montgomery Ward & Co., Inc.
MONY Group (The)
Morgan & Co. Inc. (J.P.)
Morgan Stanley Dean Witter & Co.
Morris Communications Corp.
Morrison Knudsen Corp.
Morton International Inc.
Motorola Inc.
MTD Products Inc.
Mutual of Omaha Insurance Co.
Nabisco Group Holdings
Nalco Chemical Co.
National City Bank of Minneapolis
National City Corp.
National Computer Systems, Inc.
National Life of Vermont
National Machinery Co.
National Presto Industries, Inc.
National Service Industries, Inc.
National Starch & Chemical Co.
Nationwide Insurance Co.
NCR Corp.
NEBCO Evans
Nestle U.S.A. Inc.
New Century Energies
New England Bio Labs
New England Financial
New Jersey Natural Gas Co.
New York Life Insurance Co.
New York Mercantile Exchange
New York Stock Exchange, Inc.
New York Times Co.
Newman's Own Inc.
Niagara Mohawk Holdings Inc.
Nike, Inc.
Nordson Corp.
Norfolk Southern Corp.
North American Royalties
Northeast Utilities
Northern Indiana Public Service Co.
Northern States Power Co.
Northern Trust Co.
Northwest Bank Nebraska, NA
Northwest Natural Gas Co.
Norton Co.
Norwest Corp.
Occidental Oil and Gas
Occidental Petroleum Corp.
OG&E Electric Services
Ohio National Life Insurance Co.
Old National Bank Evansville
Olin Corp.
Orscheln Co.
Oshkosh B'Gosh, Inc.
Overseas Shipholding Group Inc.
Owens Corning
PACCAR Inc.
Pacific Century Financial Corp.
Pacific Gas and Electric Co.
Pacific Mutual Life Insurance Co.
PacifiCare Health Systems
PacifiCorp
Paine Webber
Pan-American Life Insurance Co.
Parker Hannifin Corp.
Pella Corp.
PEMCO Corp.
Penney Co., Inc. (J.C.)
Pennzoil-Quaker State Co.
Peoples Energy Corp.
PerkinElmer, Inc.
Pfizer Inc.
Pharmacia & Upjohn, Inc.
Phelps Dodge Corp.
Pheonix Financial Group
Philips Electronics North America Corp.
Phillips Petroleum Co.
Physicians Mutual Insurance Co.
Pieper Power Electric Co.
Pillsbury Co.
Pittway Corp.
Playboy Enterprises Inc.
PNC Financial Services Group
Polaroid Corp.
Portland General Electric Co.
Potlatch Corp.
Potomac Electric Power Co.
PPG Industries, Inc.
Praxair
Premier Dental Products Co.
Premier Industrial Corp.
Price Associates (T. Rowe)
Principal Financial Group
Procter & Gamble Co.
Procter & Gamble Co., Cosmetics Division
Providence Journal-Bulletin Co.
Provident Companies, Inc.
Prudential Insurance Co. of America
Prudential Securities Inc.
Public Service Electric & Gas Co.
Publix Supermarkets
Pulitzer Publishing Co.
Putnam Investments
Quaker Chemical Corp.
Quanex Corp.
Questar Corp.
Ralph's Grocery Co.
Ralston Purina Co.
Rayonier Inc.
Red Wing Shoe Co. Inc.
Reebok International Ltd.
Regions Bank
Regis Corp.
Reilly Industries, Inc.
Reily & Co., Inc. (William B.)
Reinhart Institutional Foods
Reliant Energy Inc.
Reynolds Metals Co.
Reynolds & Reynolds Co.
Reynolds Tobacco (R.J.)
Rich Products Corp.
Rockwell International Corp.
Rouse Co.
Royal & SunAlliance USA, Inc.
Rubbermaid Inc.
Ruddick Corp.
Ryder System, Inc.
SAFECO Corp.
Safeguard Scientifics
Saint Paul Companies Inc.
Salomon Smith Barney
Sara Lee Corp.
Sara Lee Hosiery, Inc.
SBC Communications Inc.
Schering-Plough Corp.
Schloss & Co. (Marcus)
Schlumberger Ltd. (USA)
Schwab & Co., Inc. (Charles)
Schwebel Baking Co.
Seagram & Sons, Inc. (Joseph E.)
Searle & Co. (G.D.)
Seaway Food Town, Inc.
Security Benefit Life Insurance Co.
Security Life of Denver Insurance Co.
Sega of America Inc.
Sempra Energy
Sentinel Communications Co.
Sentry Insurance, A Mutual Co.
Servco Pacific
ServiceMaster Co.
S.G. Cowen
Shaklee Corp.
Sharp Electronics Corp.
Shaw's Supermarkets, Inc.
Shea Co. (John F.)
Shell Oil Co.
Shelter Mutual Insurance Co.
Sherwin-Williams Co.
Shoney's Inc.
Sierra Pacific Industries
Sierra Pacific Resources
Simplot Co. (J.R.)
Simpson Investment Co.
SIT Investment Associates, Inc.
Slant/Fin Corp.
Smith Corp. (A.O.)
SmithKline Beecham Corp.
Smurfit-Stone Container Corp.
Solo Cup Co.
Sonoco Products Co.
Sony Electronics
South Bend Tribune Corp.
Southern New England Telephone Co.
Southwest Gas Corp.
Springs Industries, Inc.
Sprint Corp.
SPX Corp.
Square D Co.
Standard Products Co.
Standard Register Co.
Stanley Works (The)
Star Bank NA
Starwood Hotels & Resorts Worldwide, Inc.
State Street Bank & Trust Co.
Steelcase Inc.
Stone Container Corp.
Stonecutter Mills Corp.
Storage Technology Corp.
Stride Rite Corp.
Stupp Brothers Bridge & Iron Co.
Sun Microsystems Inc.
Sunmark Capital Corp.
Sunoco Inc.
SunTrust Bank Atlanta
SuperValu, Inc.
Sverdrup Corp.
Synovus Financial Corp.
Taco Bell Corp.
Tamko Roofing Products
TCF National Bank Minnesota
Tektronix, Inc.
Teleflex Inc.
Temple-Inland Inc.
Tenet Healthcare Corp.
TENNANT Co.
Tenneco Automotive
Tenneco Packaging
Tension Envelope Corp.
Tesoro Hawaii
Texaco Inc.
Texas Gas Transmission Corp.
Texas Instruments Inc.
Textron Inc.
Thomasville Furniture Industries Inc.
Thompson Co. (J. Walter)
Times Mirror Co.
Timken Co. (The)
Titan Industrial Corp.
TJX Companies, Inc.
Toledo Blade Co.
Tomkins Industries, Inc.
Torchmark Corp.
Toro Co.
Toshiba America Inc.
Trace International Holdings, Inc.
Transamerica Corp.
True North Communications, Inc.
True Oil Co.
Trustmark Insurance Co.
TRW Inc.
Tucson Electric Power Co.
Tyson Foods Inc.
Ukrop's Super Markets

Unilever Home & Personal Care U.S.A.
Unilever United States, Inc.
Union Camp Corp.
Union Carbide Corp.
Union Pacific Corp.
United Airlines Inc.
United Co.
United Distillers & Vintners North America
United Dominion Industries, Ltd.
United Parcel Service of America Inc.
U.S. Bancorp
U.S. Bancorp Piper Jaffray
United States Sugar Corp.
United States Trust Co. of New York
United Technologies Corp.
United Wisconsin Services
Universal Foods Corp.
Universal Leaf Tobacco Co., Inc.
Universal Studios
Unocal Corp.
UnumProvident
US Bank, Washington
US West, Inc.
USG Corp.
USX Corp.
Valmont Industries, Inc.
Valspar Corp.
Varian Medical Systems, Inc.
Vesper Corp.
Vulcan Materials Co.
Wachovia Bank of North Carolina NA
Waffle House Inc.
Wal-Mart Stores, Inc.
Waldbaum's Supermarkets, Inc.
Walgreen Co.
Walter Industries Inc.
Warner-Lambert Co.
Washington Mutual, Inc.
The Washington Post
Washington Trust Bank
Webster Bank
Weil, Gotshal & Manges Corp.
Wells Fargo & Co.
Western Resources Inc.
Western & Southern Life Insurance Co.
Westvaco Corp.
Weyerhaeuser Co.
Whirlpool Corp.
Whitman Corp.
WICOR, Inc.
Williams
Winn-Dixie Stores Inc.
Wiremold Co.
Wisconsin Energy Corp.
Wisconsin Power & Light Co.
Wisconsin Public Service Corp.
Witco Corp.
Woodward Governor Co.
Wrigley Co. (Wm. Jr.)
Wyman-Gordon Co.
Xerox Corp.
Yellow Corp.
York Federal Savings & Loan Association
Young & Rubicam
Zachry Co. (H.B.)
Zenith Electronics Corp.
Zilkha & Sons

FUNDERS BY GRANT TYPE

Lists funders by the types of support they generally prefer or are required by their charters to endorse.

Award

Airborne Freight Corp.
AK Steel Corp.
Albany International Corp.
Albertson's Inc.
Alcoa Inc.
Allstate Insurance Co.
Ameritech Michigan
Aon Corp.
Appleton Papers Inc.
AT&T Corp.
Bandag, Inc.
Bank of New York Co., Inc.
Banta Corp.
Bean, Inc. (L.L.)
Bell Atlantic Corp.-West Virginia
Bemis Co., Inc.
Bernstein & Co., Inc. (Sanford C.)
BFGoodrich Co.
Blair & Co. (William)
Blue Cross & Blue Shield of Michigan
Borman's Inc.
Brooklyn Union
Brown & Williamson Tobacco Corp.
Burger King Corp.
Burlington Industries, Inc.
Butler Manufacturing Co.
Central Maine Power Co.
CertainTeed Corp.
Chase Manhattan Bank, NA
Chevron Corp.
Chicago Title Corp.
Clark Refining & Marketing
Commercial Intertech Corp.
Consolidated Natural Gas Co.
CPI Corp.
Dana Corp.
DeKalb Genetics Corp.
Donaldson Co., Inc.
Duke Energy
Duriron Co., Inc.
Eastman Kodak Co.
Eaton Corp.
Eckerd Corp.
EDS Corp.
El Paso Energy Co.
Erving Industries
Evening Post Publishing Co.
Fannie Mae
Fortis, Inc.
Franklin Mint (The)
GenAmerica Corp.
Group Health Plan
GTE Corp.
Gulfstream Aerospace Corp.
Harris Trust & Savings Bank
Hitachi America Ltd.
Home Depot, Inc.
Hughes Electronics Corp.
Huntington Bancshares Inc.
IBP
Illinois Power Co.
Intel Corp.
INTRUST Financial Corp.
Invacare Corp.
Kemper National Insurance Companies
Laclede Gas Co.
Leigh Fibers, Inc.
Liberty Corp.
Lincoln Electric Co.
Lincoln Financial Group
Little, Inc. (Arthur D.)
Lubrizol Corp. (The)
Maritz Inc.
Mark IV Industries
Marshall Field's
McDonald & Co. Securities, Inc.
Mitsubishi Electric America
Montgomery Ward & Co., Inc.
MONY Group (The)
National City Bank of Columbus
National Computer Systems, Inc.
National Life of Vermont
New England Financial
Norfolk Southern Corp.
Nortel
North American Royalties
Novartis Corporation
Olin Corp.
Orange & Rockland Utilities, Inc.
Pacific Mutual Life Insurance Co.
Penn Mutual Life Insurance Co.
Peoples Energy Corp.
Pfizer Inc.
Phillips Petroleum Co.
Pioneer Hi-Bred International, Inc.
Promus Hotel Corp.
REI-Recreational Equipment, Inc.
Reynolds Metals Co.
Rochester Gas & Electric Corp.
SAFECO Corp.
Sara Lee Corp.
Sara Lee Hosiery, Inc.
SBC Communications Inc.
Scientific-Atlanta, Inc.
Scripps Co. (E.W.)
Shaklee Corp.
SmithKline Beecham Corp.
Sonoco Products Co.
Steelcase Inc.
Student Loan Marketing Association
Tenet Healthcare Corp.
Tenneco Packaging
Thomasville Furniture Industries Inc.
Toshiba America Inc.
Trustmark Insurance Co.
TRW Inc.
Unilever Home & Personal Care U.S.A.
Union Camp Corp.
Union Pacific Corp.
Universal Foods Corp.
Universal Studios
UnumProvident
Weyerhaeuser Co.
Wolverine World Wide
Xerox Corp.

Capital

AEGON U.S.A. Inc.
AGL Resources Inc.
Agrilink Foods, Inc.
Air Products and Chemicals, Inc.
Airborne Freight Corp.
Alabama Power Co.
Albany International Corp.
Albertson's Inc.
Alcoa Inc.
Alexander & Baldwin, Inc.
Allegheny Technologies Inc.
Allianz Life Insurance Co. of North America
AlliedSignal Inc.
AMCORE Bank Rockford
Ameren Corp.
American Electric Power
American United Life Insurance Co.
Ameritas Life Insurance Corp.
AmerUS Group
AMP Inc.
Andersen Corp.
Andersons Inc.
Anheuser-Busch Companies, Inc.
Aon Corp.
Appleton Papers Inc.
Aristech Chemical Corp.
Arizona Public Service Co.
Arvin Industries, Inc.
Atlantic Investment Co.
Avon Products, Inc.
Baird & Co. (Robert W.)
Bandag, Inc.
Bank of America
Bank of New York Co., Inc.
Bank One Corp.
Bank One, Texas-Houston Office
Bank One, Texas, NA
Banta Corp.
Battelle Memorial Institute
Bayer Corp.
Bean, Inc. (L.L.)
Becton Dickinson & Co.
Belk Stores Services Inc.
BellSouth Corp.
Belo Corp. (A.H.)
Bemis Co., Inc.
Bernstein & Co., Inc. (Sanford C.)
Berwind Group
Bethlehem Steel Corp.
BFGoodrich Co.
Binney & Smith Inc.
Block, Inc. (H&R)
Blount International, Inc.
Boeing Co.
Boise Cascade Corp.
Boston Edison Co.
Boston Globe (The)
Bourns, Inc.
Bowater Inc.
BP Amoco Corp.
Bridgestone/Firestone, Inc.
Briggs & Stratton Corp.
Brown Shoe Co., Inc.
Brown & Williamson Tobacco Corp.
Browning-Ferris Industries Inc.
Bucyrus-Erie Co.
Burlington Industries, Inc.
Burlington Northern Santa Fe Corp.
Burlington Resources, Inc.
Butler Manufacturing Co.
Cabot Corp.
California Bank & Trust
Cargill Inc.
Carolina Power & Light Co.
Carpenter Technology Corp.
Carrier Corp.
Caterpillar Inc.
Central Maine Power Co.
Central Soya Co.
Cessna Aircraft Co.
CGU Insurance
Chase Bank of Texas
Chase Manhattan Bank, NA
Chemed Corp.
Chesapeake Corp.
Cincinnati Bell Inc.
CLARCOR Inc.
Cleveland-Cliffs, Inc.
Clorox Co.
Coca-Cola Co.
Comerica Inc.
Commonwealth Edison Co.
Compass Bank
ConAgra, Inc.
Cone Mills Corp.
Conectiv
Consolidated Natural Gas Co.
Consolidated Papers, Inc.
Constellation Energy Group, Inc.
Consumers Energy Co.
Contran Corp.
Cooper Industries, Inc.
Copley Press, Inc.
Country Curtains, Inc.
Cox Enterprises Inc.
CPI Corp.
Crane & Co., Inc.
CUNA Mutual Group
Dain Bosworth Inc.
Dana Corp.
Danis Companies
Dayton Power and Light Co.
Deere & Co.
DeKalb Genetics Corp.
Delta Air Lines, Inc.
Deluxe Corp.
Detroit Edison Co.
Diebold, Inc.
Disney Co. (Walt)
Dixie Group, Inc. (The)
Dollar General Corp.
Dominion Resources, Inc.
Donaldson Co., Inc.
Donnelley & Sons Co. (R.R.)
Dow Corning Corp.
du Pont de Nemours & Co. (E.I.)
Duke Energy
Duriron Co., Inc.
Eastern Bank
Eastman Kodak Co.
Eaton Corp.
Eckerd Corp.
Ecolab Inc.
Elf Atochem North America, Inc.
Ensign-Bickford Industries
Equifax Inc.
Equitable Resources, Inc.
Erving Industries
Ethyl Corp.
Evening Post Publishing Co.
Fabri-Kal Corp.
Fannie Mae
Federated Department Stores, Inc.
FedEx Corp.
Fidelity Investments
Fifth Third Bancorp
First Financial Bank
First Hawaiian, Inc.
First Maryland Bancorp
First Security Bank of Idaho NA
First Tennessee National Corp.
First Union Corp.
First Union National Bank, NA
First Union Securities, Inc.
Firstar Bank Milwaukee NA
FirstEnergy Corp.
Fisher Scientific
FleetBoston Financial Corp.
Florida Power Corp.
Florida Power & Light Co.
Fluor Corp.
FMC Corp.
Forbes Inc.
Ford Motor Co.
Fort James Corp.
Fort Worth Star-Telegram Inc.
Franklin Mint (The)
Freddie Mac
Freeport-McMoRan Inc.
Frost National Bank
Fuji Bank & Trust Co.
Furniture Brands International, Inc.
Gannett Co., Inc.
GenAmerica Corp.
General Dynamics Corp.
General Mills, Inc.
General Reinsurance Corp.
Georgia-Pacific Corp.
Georgia Power Co.
Gillette Co.
Globe Corp.
Grace & Co. (W.R.)
Graco, Inc.
GTE Corp.
Gulfstream Aerospace Corp.
Hallmark Cards Inc.
Hamilton Sundstrand Corp.
Hancock Financial Services (John)
Harcourt General, Inc.
Harsco Corp.
Hartford (The)
Hartmarx Corp.

Hawaiian Electric Co., Inc.
Heinz Co. (H.J.)
Hercules Inc.
Hershey Foods Corp.
Hickory Tech Corp.
Hofmann Co.
HON Industries Inc.
Honeywell International Inc.
Houghton Mifflin Co.
Household International Inc.
Hubbard Broadcasting, Inc.
Hubbell Inc.
Humana, Inc.
Hunt Manufacturing Co.
Huntington Bancshares Inc.
IBP
Idaho Power Co.
Illinois Tool Works, Inc.
Independent Stave Co.
International Business Machines Corp.
International Multifoods Corp.
INTRUST Financial Corp.
Jacobs Engineering Group
Jeld-wen, Inc.
Johnson Controls Inc.
Journal-Gazette Co.
JSJ Corp.
Kaman Corp.
Kellwood Co.
Key Bank of Cleveland
Kiewit Sons' Inc. (Peter)
Kimball International, Inc.
Kimberly-Clark Corp.
Koch Industries, Inc.
Kohler Co.
Kroger Co.
Laclede Gas Co.
Land O'Lakes, Inc.
Landmark Communications Inc.
Lee Enterprises
LG&E Energy Corp.
Liberty Corp.
Liberty Mutual Insurance Group
Lilly & Co. (Eli)
Lincoln Electric Co.
Lincoln Financial Group
Louisiana Land & Exploration Co.
Louisiana-Pacific Corp.
LTV Corp.
Lubrizol Corp. (The)
MacMillan Bloedel Inc.
Mallinckrodt Chemical, Inc.
Maritz Inc.
Mark IV Industries
Marshall & Ilsley Corp.
Masco Corp.
Mattel Inc.
May Department Stores Co.
Maytag Corp.
McClatchy Co.
McCormick & Co. Inc.
McDermott Inc.
McDonald & Co. Securities, Inc.
McKesson-HBOC Corp.
McWane Inc.
Mead Corp.
Mellon Financial Corp.
Mercantile Bank NA
Meredith Corp.
Merrill Lynch & Co., Inc.
Michigan Consolidated Gas Co.
Microsoft Corp.
Mid-America Bank of Louisville
MidAmerican Energy Holdings Co.
Milacron, Inc.
Milliken & Co.
Millipore Corp.
Mine Safety Appliances Co.
Minnesota Mutual Life Insurance Co.
Montana Power Co.
Morgan & Co. Inc. (J.P.)
Motorola Inc.
Murphy Oil Corp.
Nabisco Group Holdings
Nalco Chemical Co.
National City Bank of Columbus
National City Corp.
National Computer Systems, Inc.
National Fuel Gas Distribution Corp.
National Life of Vermont
National Starch & Chemical Co.
Nationwide Insurance Co.
New Century Energies
New England Financial
New York Life Insurance Co.
Niagara Mohawk Holdings Inc.
Nordson Corp.
Norfolk Southern Corp.
Northeast Utilities
Northern Indiana Public Service Co.
Northern States Power Co.
Northern Trust Co.
Northrop Grumman Corp.
Northwest Natural Gas Co.
Norton Co.
Norwest Corp.
OG&E Electric Services
Ohio National Life Insurance Co.
Old National Bank Evansville
Olin Corp.
ONEOK, Inc.
PACCAR Inc.
Pacific Century Financial Corp.
Pacific Gas and Electric Co.
Pacific Mutual Life Insurance Co.
PacifiCorp
Pan-American Life Insurance Co.
Parker Hannifin Corp.
PECO Energy Co.
Pella Corp.
Penn Mutual Life Insurance Co.
Pentair Inc.
Peoples Energy Corp.
Pharmacia & Upjohn, Inc.
Physicians Mutual Insurance Co.
Pioneer Hi-Bred International, Inc.
Pitney Bowes Inc.
Pittway Corp.
PNC Bank
PNC Bank Kentucky Inc.
PNC Financial Services Group
Portland General Electric Co.
Potomac Electric Power Co.
PPG Industries, Inc.
Premier Industrial Corp.
Price Associates (T. Rowe)
Principal Financial Group
Procter & Gamble Co.
Procter & Gamble Co., Cosmetics Division
Providence Journal-Bulletin Co.
Public Service Electric & Gas Co.
Publix Supermarkets
Pulitzer Publishing Co.
Questar Corp.
Ralston Purina Co.
Red Wing Shoe Co. Inc.
Reily & Co., Inc. (William B.)
Reliant Energy Inc.
ReliaStar Financial Corp.
Reynolds Tobacco (R.J.)
Rockwell International Corp.
Rohm & Haas Co.
Rouse Co.
Rubbermaid Inc.
SAFECO Corp.
Saint Paul Companies Inc.
S&T Bancorp
Sara Lee Hosiery, Inc.
SBC Communications Inc.
SCANA Corp.
Schering-Plough Corp.
Schlumberger Ltd. (USA)
Schwab & Co., Inc. (Charles)
Scientific-Atlanta, Inc.
Scripps Co. (E.W.)
Security Life of Denver Insurance Co.
Sentinel Communications Co.
Shaw's Supermarkets, Inc.
Shell Oil Co.
Sherwin-Williams Co.
Simpson Investment Co.
Smith Corp. (A.O.)
Solo Cup Co.
Southern New England Telephone Co.
Southwest Gas Corp.
Sovereign Bank
Springs Industries, Inc.
Sprint Corp.
SPX Corp.
Square D Co.
Standard Products Co.
Stanley Works (The)
Star Bank NA
State Farm Mutual Automobile Insurance Co.
State Street Bank & Trust Co.
Steelcase Inc.
Stone Container Corp.
Stride Rite Corp.
SunTrust Bank Atlanta
SunTrust Banks of Florida
Susquehanna-Pfaltzgraff Co.
Synovus Financial Corp.
Telcordia Technologies
Tenet Healthcare Corp.
TENNANT Co.
Tenneco Automotive
Tesoro Hawaii
Texas Instruments Inc.
Textron Inc.
Thermo Electron Corp.
Times Mirror Co.
Timken Co. (The)
TJX Companies, Inc.
Torchmark Corp.
TRW Inc.
Tucson Electric Power Co.
Unilever Home & Personal Care U.S.A.
Union Camp Corp.
Union Pacific Corp.
United Dominion Industries, Ltd.
U.S. Bancorp
U.S. Bancorp Piper Jaffray
United States Sugar Corp.
United Technologies Corp.
Universal Foods Corp.
Universal Studios
UnumProvident
US Bank, Washington
USG Corp.
UST Inc.
USX Corp.
Valero Energy Corp.
Valmont Industries, Inc.
Vulcan Materials Co.
Wachovia Bank of North Carolina NA
Waste Management Inc.
West Co. Inc.
Western Resources Inc.
Westvaco Corp.
Weyerhaeuser Co.
WICOR, Inc.
Williams
Wisconsin Energy Corp.
Wisconsin Power & Light Co.
Wisconsin Public Service Corp.
Wolverine World Wide
Woodward Governor Co.
Yellow Corp.
Zachry Co. (H.B.)
Zenith Electronics Corp.
Zurn Industries, Inc.

Challenge

Alcoa Inc.
American Honda Motor Co., Inc.
Aon Corp.
Atlantic Investment Co.
Bandag, Inc.
Battelle Memorial Institute
Beckman Coulter, Inc.
Becton Dickinson & Co.
Borden, Inc.
Boston Edison Co.
Bridgestone/Firestone, Inc.
Browning-Ferris Industries Inc.
Cabot Corp.
Campbell Soup Co.
Central Maine Power Co.
Chase Manhattan Bank, NA
Circuit City Stores, Inc.
Citizens Bank-Flint
Coca-Cola Co.
Cooper Industries, Inc.
Cummins Engine Co., Inc.
Dana Corp.
Detroit Edison Co.
Disney Co. (Walt)
Duke Energy
Duriron Co., Inc.
El Paso Energy Co.
Ethyl Corp.
Evening Post Publishing Co.
FedEx Corp.
First Tennessee National Corp.
GATX Corp.
Hallmark Cards Inc.
Harcourt General, Inc.
Hartford (The)
Heinz Co. (H.J.)
Huntington Bancshares Inc.
IBP
Jeld-wen, Inc.
Liz Claiborne, Inc.
LTV Corp.
Mercantile Bank NA
Minnesota Mining & Manufacturing Co.
National Computer Systems, Inc.
National Life of Vermont
Norfolk Southern Corp.
Northern Trust Co.
Old National Bank Evansville
Olin Corp.
Orange & Rockland Utilities, Inc.
Pharmacia & Upjohn, Inc.
Procter & Gamble Co., Cosmetics Division
Public Service Electric & Gas Co.
Publix Supermarkets
Reynolds Tobacco (R.J.)
Rohm & Haas Co.
Rouse Co.
SAFECO Corp.
Scientific-Atlanta, Inc.
Seagram & Sons, Inc. (Joseph E.)
Shaw's Supermarkets, Inc.
Stanley Works (The)
State Street Bank & Trust Co.
Susquehanna-Pfaltzgraff Co.
Texas Instruments Inc.
TJX Companies, Inc.
Union Pacific Corp.
Unocal Corp.
UnumProvident
UST Inc.
Valero Energy Corp.
Varian Medical Systems, Inc.
Wachovia Bank of North Carolina NA
Wells Fargo & Co.
Whitman Corp.
Wolverine World Wide
Zachry Co. (H.B.)

Conference/ Seminar

AGL Resources Inc.
Albertson's Inc.
Alcoa Inc.
American Retail Group
Aristech Chemical Corp.
Arizona Public Service Co.
AT&T Corp.
Atlantic Investment Co.
Baird & Co. (Robert W.)
Bank of New York Co., Inc.
Battelle Memorial Institute
Beckman Coulter, Inc.
BellSouth Corp.
Bethlehem Steel Corp.
Blue Cross & Blue Shield of Michigan
Blue Cross & Blue Shield of Minnesota
Branch Banking & Trust Co.
Burger King Corp.
Burlington Industries, Inc.
California Bank & Trust
Central Maine Power Co.
CIGNA Corp.
Cinergy Corp.
Commercial Intertech Corp.
Constellation Energy Group, Inc.
Coors Brewing Co.
Deloitte & Touche
Detroit Edison Co.
du Pont de Nemours & Co. (E.I.)
Duke Energy
Eaton Corp.
EDS Corp.
Ensign-Bickford Industries
Ernst & Young, LLP
Fannie Mae

Federated Department Stores, Inc.
Fidelity Investments
Fifth Third Bancorp
Ford Motor Co.
Freddie Mac
Freeport-McMoRan Inc.
Georgia Power Co.
Glaxo Wellcome Inc.
Heinz Co. (H.J.)
Humana, Inc.
Kemper National Insurance Companies
Key Bank of Cleveland
Landmark Communications Inc.
Lincoln Financial Group
Maritz Inc.
Matsushita Electric Corp. of America
Mine Safety Appliances Co.
Monsanto Co.
Montana Power Co.
National City Bank of Columbus
Old National Bank Evansville
Olin Corp.
Pan-American Life Insurance Co.
Pella Corp.
Penn Mutual Life Insurance Co.
Pieper Power Electric Co.
ReliaStar Financial Corp.
SBC Communications Inc.
Schwab & Co., Inc. (Charles)
Scripps Co. (E.W.)
Sempra Energy
Southern New England Telephone Co.
Stone & Webster Inc.
Student Loan Marketing Association
Tenneco Automotive
Texas Instruments Inc.
Universal Foods Corp.
US West, Inc.
UST Inc.
Wachovia Bank of North Carolina NA
Waste Management Inc.
WICOR, Inc.
Witco Corp.

Department

AlliedSignal Inc.
Aon Corp.
Blount International, Inc.
Borden, Inc.
Caterpillar Inc.
CertainTeed Corp.
Chase Manhattan Bank, NA
Deere & Co.
Eastman Kodak Co.
El Paso Energy Co.
Ford Motor Co.
Freeport-McMoRan Inc.
Harsco Corp.
Humana, Inc.
Johnson Controls Inc.
Merck & Co.
Olin Corp.
PACCAR Inc.
PPG Industries, Inc.
PricewaterhouseCoopers
Reynolds Tobacco (R.J.)
Rohm & Haas Co.
Rouse Co.
Shell Oil Co.
Sotheby's Inc.
Star Bank NA
TCF National Bank Minnesota
Tenneco Automotive
Texaco Inc.
United Airlines Inc.
Universal Foods Corp.
Unocal Corp.
US West, Inc.
Vulcan Materials Co.
Weyerhaeuser Co.
Xerox Corp.

Emergency

Advanced Micro Devices, Inc.
Agrilink Foods, Inc.
Airborne Freight Corp.
Alaska Airlines, Inc.
Albertson's Inc.
Alcoa Inc.
American Retail Group
Aristech Chemical Corp.
AT&T Corp.
Bandag, Inc.
Bank of New York Co., Inc.
Battelle Memorial Institute
BellSouth Corp.
BP Amoco Corp.
Branch Banking & Trust Co.
Butler Manufacturing Co.
Cargill Inc.
Cenex Harvest States
Central Maine Power Co.
Central Vermont Public Service Corp.
CIGNA Corp.
Comerica Inc.
Cooper Industries, Inc.
Crane Co.
CUNA Mutual Group
DaimlerChrysler Corp.
Dana Corp.
Dixie Group, Inc. (The)
Donnelley & Sons Co. (R.R.)
du Pont de Nemours & Co. (E.I.)
Eastman Kodak Co.
Eaton Corp.
EDS Corp.
Edwards Enterprise Software (J.D.)
Erving Industries
Fannie Mae
Ferro Corp.
First Union Corp.
Fisher Scientific
Georgia Power Co.
Glickenhaus & Co.
GTE Corp.
Harcourt General, Inc.
Hawaiian Electric Co., Inc.
Hofmann Co.
Hughes Electronics Corp.
Huntington Bancshares Inc.
Johnson & Johnson
Jostens, Inc.
Kmart Corp.
Landmark Communications Inc.
Liberty Mutual Insurance Group
Lincoln Financial Group
Louisiana-Pacific Corp.
Mallinckrodt Chemical, Inc.
Maritz Inc.
MBIA Inc.
McDonald's Corp.
Menasha Corp.
Meredith Corp.
Morton International Inc.
Nabisco Group Holdings
National City Bank of Columbus
National Life of Vermont
Nationwide Insurance Co.
New York Mercantile Exchange
Northeast Utilities
Olin Corp.
PacifiCorp
Physicians Mutual Insurance Co.
Pitney Bowes Inc.
PPG Industries, Inc.
Prudential Securities Inc.
Questar Corp.
Reebok International Ltd.
Sara Lee Hosiery, Inc.
SBC Communications Inc.
Schwab & Co., Inc. (Charles)
Sempra Energy
Simpson Investment Co.
Sonoco Products Co.
Springs Industries, Inc.
Stone & Webster Inc.
Student Loan Marketing Association
Sun Microsystems Inc.
Susquehanna-Pfaltzgraff Co.
TENNANT Co.
Tenneco Packaging
Timken Co. (The)
Toyota Motor Sales U.S.A., Inc.
Unilever United States, Inc.
United Dominion Industries, Ltd.
United States Sugar Corp.
Universal Foods Corp.
Universal Studios
UST Inc.
Valero Energy Corp.
Vulcan Materials Co.
Wachovia Bank of North Carolina NA
West Co. Inc.
Western Resources Inc.
Westvaco Corp.
Wisconsin Public Service Corp.
Woodward Governor Co.
Zachry Co. (H.B.)
Zurn Industries, Inc.

Employee Matching Gifts

ABB Inc.
Abbott Laboratories
ABC
Advanced Micro Devices, Inc.
AEGON U.S.A. Inc.
Aetna, Inc.
AGL Resources Inc.
Air Products and Chemicals, Inc.
Airborne Freight Corp.
AK Steel Corp.
Alabama Power Co.
Albany International Corp.
Albertson's Inc.
Alcoa Inc.
Alexander & Baldwin, Inc.
Allegheny Technologies Inc.
Alliant Techsystems
AlliedSignal Inc.
Allmerica Financial Corp.
Allstate Insurance Co.
Alyeska Pipeline Service Co.
Ameren Corp.
American Electric Power
American Express Co.
American General Corp.
American Standard Inc.
American United Life Insurance Co.
Ameritech Corp.
Ameritech Illinois
Ameritech Indiana
Ameritech Michigan
Ameritech Ohio
Ameritech Wisconsin
AmerUS Group
Amgen, Inc.
AMP Inc.
Amsted Industries Inc.
Analog Devices, Inc.
Andersons Inc.
Anheuser-Busch Companies, Inc.
Aon Corp.
APL Ltd.
Apple Computer, Inc.
Appleton Papers Inc.
Archer-Daniels-Midland Co.
Aristech Chemical Corp.
Arizona Public Service Co.
Armstrong World Industries, Inc.
Ashland, Inc.
AT&T Corp.
Atlantic Richfield Co.
Avon Products, Inc.
Ball Corp.
Bandag, Inc.
Bank of New York Co., Inc.
Bank One Corp.
Bank One, Texas-Houston Office
BankBoston-Connecticut Region
BankBoston Corp.
Banta Corp.
Barclays Capital
Bard, Inc. (C.R.)
Baxter International Inc.
Bechtel Group, Inc.
Beckman Coulter, Inc.
Becton Dickinson & Co.
Bell Atlantic Corp.
Bell Atlantic-Delaware, Inc.
BellSouth Corp.
Bemis Co., Inc.
Berwind Group
Bestfoods
Bethlehem Steel Corp.
BFGoodrich Co.
Binney & Smith Inc.
Block, Inc. (H&R)
Blount International, Inc.
Blue Bell, Inc.
Blue Cross & Blue Shield of Minnesota
Boeing Co.
Boise Cascade Corp.
Borden, Inc.
Boston Edison Co.
Boston Globe (The)
Bowater Inc.
BP Amoco Corp.
Bridgestone/Firestone, Inc.
Bristol-Myers Squibb Co.
Brooklyn Union
Brown Shoe Co., Inc.
Brown & Williamson Tobacco Corp.
Bucyrus-Erie Co.
Burlington Industries, Inc.
Burlington Northern Santa Fe Corp.
Burlington Resources, Inc.
Burnett Co. (Leo)
Business Men's Assurance Co. of America
Butler Manufacturing Co.
Cabot Corp.
California Bank & Trust
California Federal Bank, FSB
Campbell Soup Co.
Cargill Inc.
Carolina Power & Light Co.
Carpenter Technology Corp.
Carrier Corp.
Carter-Wallace, Inc.
Castle & Cooke Properties Inc.
Caterpillar Inc.
CBS Corp.
Central Maine Power Co.
Central & South West Services
CertainTeed Corp.
Cessna Aircraft Co.
CGU Insurance
Champion International Corp.
Chase Manhattan Bank, NA
Chesapeake Corp.
Chevron Corp.
Chicago Title Corp.
Chicago Tribune Co.
Church & Dwight Co., Inc.
CIGNA Corp.
Cincinnati Bell Inc.
Cinergy Corp.
Circuit City Stores, Inc.
Citibank Corp.
Citizens Bank-Flint
CLARCOR Inc.
Clark Refining & Marketing
Cleveland-Cliffs, Inc.
Clorox Co.
CNA
CNF Transportation, Inc.
Coca-Cola Co.
Colgate-Palmolive Co.
Collins & Aikman Corp.
Comerica Inc.
Commercial Intertech Corp.
Commonwealth Edison Co.
Compaq Computer Corp.
Computer Associates International, Inc.
Conoco, Inc.
Consolidated Natural Gas Co.
Consolidated Papers, Inc.
Constellation Energy Group, Inc.
Consumers Energy Co.
Cooper Industries, Inc.
Cooper Tire & Rubber Co.
Copley Press, Inc.
Corning Inc.
CPI Corp.
Crane Co.
Cranston Print Works Co.
Crestar Finance Corp.
CSX Corp.
Cummins Engine Co., Inc.
CUNA Mutual Group
Curtis Industries, Inc. (Helene)
DaimlerChrysler Corp.
Dain Bosworth Inc.
Dayton Hudson
DeKalb Genetics Corp.
Deloitte & Touche
Delta Air Lines, Inc.
Deluxe Corp.
Deposit Guaranty National Bank
Detroit Edison Co.
Dexter Corp.
Dominion Resources, Inc.
Donnelley & Sons Co. (R.R.)
Dow Chemical Co.

DSM Copolymer
Duke Energy
Dun & Bradstreet Corp.
Duquesne Light Co.
Duracell International
Eaton Corp.
Eckerd Corp.
Ecolab Inc.
Edison International
El Paso Energy Co.
Elf Atochem North America, Inc.
Emerson Electric Co.
Ensign-Bickford Industries
Equifax Inc.
Equitable Resources, Inc.
Ernst & Young, LLP
Erving Industries
Ethyl Corp.
European American Bank
Excel Corp.
Exxon Mobil Corp.
Fannie Mae
Federated Department Stores, Inc.
FedEx Corp.
Ferro Corp.
Fidelity Investments
Fifth Third Bancorp
FINA
Fireman's Fund Insurance Co.
First Financial Bank
First Hawaiian, Inc.
First Maryland Bancorp
First Union Bank
First Union Corp.
First Union National Bank, NA
First Union Securities, Inc.
FirstEnergy Corp.
FleetBoston Financial Corp.
Florida Power & Light Co.
Fluor Corp.
FMC Corp.
Ford Motor Co.
Fort James Corp.
Fortis, Inc.
Fortis Insurance Co.
Fortune Brands, Inc.
Fox Entertainment Group
Freddie Mac
Freeport-McMoRan Inc.
Frito-Lay, Inc.
Fuji Bank & Trust Co.
Fuller Co. (H.B.)
Gannett Co., Inc.
Gap, Inc.
Gates Rubber Corp.
GATX Corp.
GEICO Corp.
GenCorp
General Dynamics Corp.
General Electric Co.
General Mills, Inc.
General Reinsurance Corp.
Georgia-Pacific Corp.
Georgia Power Co.
Gerber Products Co.
Glaxo Wellcome Inc.
Globe Corp.
Goldman Sachs Group
Golub Corp.
Goodrich Aerospace - Aerostructures Group (B.F.)
GPU Energy
Grace & Co. (W.R.)
Graco, Inc.
Grainger, Inc. (W.W.)
GTE Corp.
Guardian Life Insurance Co. of America
GuideOne Insurance
Gulf Power Co.
Halliburton Co.
Hallmark Cards Inc.
Hamilton Sundstrand Corp.
Hancock Financial Services (John)
Hanna Co. (M.A.)
Harcourt General, Inc.
Harrah's Entertainment Inc.
Harris Corp.
Harris Trust & Savings Bank
Harsco Corp.
Hartford (The)
Hartford Steam Boiler Inspection & Insurance Co.
Hartmarx Corp.
Hasbro, Inc.
Hawaiian Electric Co., Inc.
Heinz Co. (H.J.)
Heller Financial, Inc.
Hershey Foods Corp.
Hewlett-Packard Co.
Hickory Tech Corp.
Hitachi America Ltd.
Hoffmann-La Roche Inc.
Home Depot, Inc.
Honeywell International Inc.
Houghton Mifflin Co.
Household International Inc.
HSBC Bank USA
Hubbell Inc.
Huffy Corp.
Hughes Electronics Corp.
Humana, Inc.
Hunt Manufacturing Co.
IKON Office Solutions, Inc.
Illinois Tool Works, Inc.
Industrial Bank of Japan Trust Co. (New York)
Intel Corp.
International Business Machines Corp.
International Flavors & Fragrances Inc.
International Multifoods Corp.
International Paper Co.
Johnson Controls Inc.
Johnson & Johnson
Johnson & Son (S.C.)
Jostens, Inc.
JSJ Corp.
Kellogg Co.
Kellwood Co.
Kennametal, Inc.
Kerr-McGee Corp.
Key Bank of Cleveland
Kimberly-Clark Corp.
Kinder Morgn
Kingsbury Corp.
Kirkland & Ellis
Kmart Corp.
Knight Ridder
Koch Enterprises, Inc.
KPMG Peat Marwick LLP
Laclede Gas Co.
Land O'Lakes, Inc.
Lehigh Portland Cement Co.
Levi Strauss & Co.
LG&E Energy Corp.
Lilly & Co. (Eli)
Lincoln Financial Group
Lipton Co.
Liz Claiborne, Inc.
Loctite Corp.
Loews Corp.
Lotus Development Corp.
Louisiana Land & Exploration Co.
Lubrizol Corp. (The)
Lyondell Chemical Co.
Macy's East Inc.
Manulife Financial
Maritz Inc.
Mark IV Industries
Massachusetts Mutual Life Insurance Co.
Mattel Inc.
May Department Stores Co.
Maytag Corp.
MBIA Inc.
McClatchy Co.
McCormick & Co. Inc.
McDonald's Corp.
McGraw-Hill Companies, Inc.
McKesson-HBOC Corp.
Mead Corp.
Medtronic, Inc.
Mellon Financial Corp.
Menasha Corp.
Merck & Co.
Meredith Corp.
Merit Oil Corp.
Merrill Lynch & Co., Inc.
Metropolitan Life Insurance Co.
Michigan Consolidated Gas Co.
Microsoft Corp.
Milliken & Co.
Millipore Corp.
Minnesota Mining & Manufacturing Co.
Minnesota Mutual Life Insurance Co.
Mitsubishi Electric America
Monsanto Co.
Montana Power Co.
Montgomery Ward & Co., Inc.
MONY Group (The)
Morgan & Co. Inc. (J.P.)
Morgan Stanley Dean Witter & Co.
Morris Communications Corp.
Morrison Knudsen Corp.
Morton International Inc.
Motorola Inc.
MTS Systems Corp.
Murphy Oil Corp.
Nabisco Group Holdings
National City Bank of Columbus
National City Bank of Pennsylvania
National City Corp.
National Computer Systems, Inc.
National Starch & Chemical Co.
Nationwide Insurance Co.
NCR Corp.
New Century Energies
New England Financial
New York Life Insurance Co.
New York State Electric & Gas Corp.
New York Stock Exchange, Inc.
New York Times Co.
Newport News Shipbuilding
Niagara Mohawk Holdings Inc.
NICOR Gas Co.
Nike, Inc.
Nordson Corp.
Norfolk Southern Corp.
Nortel
Northeast Utilities
Northern Indiana Public Service Co.
Northern States Power Co.
Northern Trust Co.
Northwest Natural Gas Co.
Norton Co.
Norwest Corp.
Novartis Corporation
Occidental Oil and Gas
Occidental Petroleum Corp.
OG&E Electric Services
Ohio National Life Insurance Co.
Olin Corp.
ONEOK, Inc.
Orange & Rockland Utilities, Inc.
Outboard Marine Corp.
Owens Corning
Owens-Illinois Inc.
PACCAR Inc.
Pacific Century Financial Corp.
Pacific Enterprises
Pacific Gas and Electric Co.
Pacific Mutual Life Insurance Co.
Parker Hannifin Corp.
Patagonia Inc.
Pella Corp.
Penn Mutual Life Insurance Co.
Penney Co., Inc. (J.C.)
Pennsylvania Power & Light
Pentair Inc.
Peoples Bank
Peoples Energy Corp.
PepsiCo, Inc.
Pfizer Inc.
Pharmacia & Upjohn, Inc.
Phelps Dodge Corp.
Philip Morris Companies Inc.
Philips Electronics North America Corp.
Phillips Petroleum Co.
Phoenix Home Life Mutual Insurance Co.
Pieper Power Electric Co.
Pioneer Group
Pioneer Hi-Bred International, Inc.
Pitney Bowes Inc.
Pittway Corp.
Playboy Enterprises Inc.
PNC Bank
PNC Financial Services Group
Polaroid Corp.
Potlatch Corp.
PPG Industries, Inc.
Premark International Inc.
Price Associates (T. Rowe)
Principal Financial Group
Procter & Gamble Co.
Procter & Gamble Co., Cosmetics Division
Promus Hotel Corp.
Provident Companies, Inc.
Provident Mutual Life Insurance Co.
Prudential Insurance Co. of America
Public Service Electric & Gas Co.
Publix Supermarkets
Quaker Chemical Corp.
Ralston Purina Co.
Rayonier Inc.
Reader's Digest Association, Inc. (The)
Reebok International Ltd.
Reilly Industries, Inc.
Reliant Energy Minnegasco
ReliaStar Financial Corp.
Revlon Inc.
Reynolds Tobacco (R.J.)
Rockwell International Corp.
Rohm & Haas Co.
Rouse Co.
Royal & SunAlliance USA, Inc.
Rubbermaid Inc.
Ryder System, Inc.
SAFECO Corp.
Saint Paul Companies Inc.
Salomon Smith Barney
Sara Lee Corp.
Sara Lee Hosiery, Inc.
SBC Communications Inc.
Schering-Plough Corp.
Schwab & Co., Inc. (Charles)
Scientific-Atlanta, Inc.
Scripps Co. (E.W.)
Seagram & Sons, Inc. (Joseph E.)
Searle & Co. (G.D.)
Security Life of Denver Insurance Co.
Sega of America Inc.
Sempra Energy
Sentinel Communications Co.
Sentry Insurance, A Mutual Co.
Shaklee Corp.
Shell Oil Co.
Sherwin-Williams Co.
Sierra Pacific Resources
Simpson Investment Co.
Smith Corp. (A.O.)
SmithKline Beecham Corp.
Sonoco Products Co.
Sony Electronics
Southeastern Mutual Insurance Co.
Southern Co. Services Inc.
Southern New England Telephone Co.
Southwest Gas Corp.
Springs Industries, Inc.
Sprint Corp.
Sprint/United Telephone
SPX Corp.
Square D Co.
Standard Products Co.
Stanley Works (The)
Starwood Hotels & Resorts Worldwide, Inc.
State Farm Mutual Automobile Insurance Co.
State Street Bank & Trust Co.
Steelcase Inc.
Stone & Webster Inc.
Storage Technology Corp.
Stride Rite Corp.
Student Loan Marketing Association
Sun Microsystems Inc.
Sunoco Inc.
SunTrust Bank Atlanta
SuperValu, Inc.
Tandy Corp.
TCF National Bank Minnesota
Tektronix, Inc.
Teleflex Inc.
Temple-Inland Inc.
Tenet Healthcare Corp.
TENNANT Co.
Tenneco Automotive
Tenneco Packaging
Tesoro Hawaii
Texaco Inc.
Texas Gas Transmission Corp.
Texas Instruments Inc.
Textron Inc.
Thompson Co. (J. Walter)

Times Mirror Co.
Tomkins Industries, Inc.
Torchmark Corp.
Toro Co.
Toyota Motor Sales U.S.A., Inc.
Transamerica Corp.
Trustmark Insurance Co.
TRW Inc.
Unilever Home & Personal Care U.S.A.
Unilever United States, Inc.
Union Camp Corp.
Union Pacific Corp.
United Airlines Inc.
United Distillers & Vintners North America
United Parcel Service of America Inc.
U.S. Bancorp
U.S. Bancorp Piper Jaffray
United States Trust Co. of New York
United Technologies Corp.
Universal Foods Corp.
Universal Studios
Unocal Corp.
UnumProvident
US Bank, Washington
US West, Inc.
USG Corp.
UST Inc.
USX Corp.
Valero Energy Corp.
Varian Medical Systems, Inc.
Vulcan Materials Co.
Wal-Mart Stores, Inc.
Warner-Lambert Co.
Washington Mutual, Inc.
The Washington Post
Waste Management Inc.
Wausau Insurance Companies
Webster Bank
Wells Fargo & Co.
West Co. Inc.
Western Resources Inc.
Westvaco Corp.
Weyerhaeuser Co.
Whirlpool Corp.
Whitman Corp.
WICOR, Inc.
Williams
Winn-Dixie Stores Inc.
Wiremold Co.
Wisconsin Energy Corp.
Wisconsin Power & Light Co.
Wolverine World Wide
Wyman-Gordon Co.
Xerox Corp.
Yellow Corp.
York Federal Savings & Loan Association
Zurn Industries, Inc.

Endowment

Agrilink Foods, Inc.
Alabama Power Co.
Albertson's Inc.
American United Life Insurance Co.
Aon Corp.
Aristech Chemical Corp.
Atlantic Investment Co.
Baird & Co. (Robert W.)
Bank of New York Co., Inc.
Bank One Corp.
Bayer Corp.
Belk Stores Services Inc.
BellSouth Corp.
Belo Corp. (A.H.)
Blount International, Inc.
Bourns, Inc.
Brooklyn Union
Central Vermont Public Service Corp.
CertainTeed Corp.
Clorox Co.
Coca-Cola Co.
Consolidated Papers, Inc.
Copley Press, Inc.
CSX Corp.
Cyprus Amax Minerals Co.
Danis Companies
DeKalb Genetics Corp.
Demoulas Supermarkets Inc.
Detroit Edison Co.
Dixie Group, Inc. (The)
Eastman Kodak Co.
Equitable Resources, Inc.
Erving Industries
Ethyl Corp.
Fabri-Kal Corp.
Fannie Mae
Federated Department Stores, Inc.
Fidelity Investments
First Maryland Bancorp
First Security Bank of Idaho NA
First Tennessee National Corp.
First Union Corp.
Florida Power & Light Co.
Fluor Corp.
Forbes Inc.
Freeport-McMoRan Inc.
GenCorp
Georgia-Pacific Corp.
Georgia Power Co.
Glickenhaus & Co.
Globe Corp.
Gulfstream Aerospace Corp.
Halliburton Co.
Harcourt General, Inc.
Hartford (The)
Heinz Co. (H.J.)
Hershey Foods Corp.
Honeywell International Inc.
Houghton Mifflin Co.
Household International Inc.
Humana, Inc.
Huntington Bancshares Inc.
Koch Industries, Inc.
KPMG Peat Marwick LLP
Landmark Communications Inc.
Lee Enterprises
Liberty Mutual Insurance Group
Lincoln Electric Co.
Litton Industries, Inc.
Louisiana Land & Exploration Co.
Mallinckrodt Chemical, Inc.
MBIA Inc.
McClatchy Co.
Morgan & Co. Inc. (J.P.)
National City Bank of Columbus
Nationwide Insurance Co.
New England Financial
Olin Corp.
Overseas Shipholding Group Inc.
PACCAR Inc.
Pacific Century Financial Corp.
Pan-American Life Insurance Co.
Pella Corp.
Physicians Mutual Insurance Co.
PNC Bank Kentucky Inc.
Procter & Gamble Co., Cosmetics Division
Pulitzer Publishing Co.
Ralston Purina Co.
ReliaStar Financial Corp.
Rouse Co.
Saint Paul Companies Inc.
SBC Communications Inc.
Schering-Plough Corp.
Scripps Co. (E.W.)
Sonoco Products Co.
Springs Industries, Inc.
Star Bank NA
State Farm Mutual Automobile Insurance Co.
SunTrust Banks of Florida
Susquehanna-Pfaltzgraff Co.
Tenet Healthcare Corp.
Tenneco Automotive
Thomasville Furniture Industries Inc.
Titan Industrial Corp.
TJX Companies, Inc.
Union Camp Corp.
U.S. Bancorp Piper Jaffray
Universal Foods Corp.
UST Inc.
Valero Energy Corp.
Varian Medical Systems, Inc.
Vulcan Materials Co.
Wachovia Bank of North Carolina NA
Waste Management Inc.
Westvaco Corp.
WICOR, Inc.
Wilbur-Ellis Co. & Connell Brothers Co.
Williams
Wisconsin Energy Corp.
Witco Corp.
Wolverine World Wide
Zurn Industries, Inc.

Fellowship

Airborne Freight Corp.
Alcoa Inc.
American Honda Motor Co., Inc.
ASARCO Inc.
AT&T Corp.
Bank of New York Co., Inc.
Bank One Corp.
Battelle Memorial Institute
BellSouth Corp.
Blount International, Inc.
BP Amoco Corp.
Brooklyn Union
Brunswick Corp.
Cabot Corp.
CertainTeed Corp.
Chase Manhattan Bank, NA
CIGNA Corp.
Citibank Corp.
Coca-Cola Co.
Commercial Intertech Corp.
Corning Inc.
CPI Corp.
Deloitte & Touche
Dow Chemical Co.
du Pont de Nemours & Co. (E.I.)
Eastman Kodak Co.
Eaton Corp.
Eckerd Corp.
Equitable Resources, Inc.
Erving Industries
Fidelity Investments
First Union Corp.
Freeport-McMoRan Inc.
General Atlantic Partners II LP
General Electric Co.
GTE Corp.
Harcourt General, Inc.
Heinz Co. (H.J.)
Hoffmann-La Roche Inc.
Indiana Mills & Manufacturing
Intel Corp.
International Business Machines Corp.
Johnson & Son (S.C.)
Kemper National Insurance Companies
KPMG Peat Marwick LLP
Landmark Communications Inc.
Liberty Mutual Insurance Group
Little, Inc. (Arthur D.)
Loctite Corp.
Lubrizol Corp. (The)
Mallinckrodt Chemical, Inc.
Mercantile Bank NA
Merck & Co.
Microsoft Corp.
Minnesota Mining & Manufacturing Co.
MTS Systems Corp.
Olin Corp.
Phillips Petroleum Co.
Premark International Inc.
PricewaterhouseCoopers
Reliant Energy Minnegasco
Reynolds Tobacco (R.J.)
Rohm & Haas Co.
Saint Paul Companies Inc.
Schering-Plough Corp.
Schlumberger Ltd. (USA)
Scripps Co. (E.W.)
Seagram & Sons, Inc. (Joseph E.)
State Farm Mutual Automobile Insurance Co.
Texaco Inc.
Toyota Motor Sales U.S.A., Inc.
TRW Inc.
Union Camp Corp.
United Parcel Service of America Inc.
United States Sugar Corp.
Unocal Corp.
Valero Energy Corp.
Varian Medical Systems, Inc.
Vulcan Materials Co.
Wachovia Bank of North Carolina NA
Westvaco Corp.
Witco Corp.
Wyman-Gordon Co.
Xerox Corp.
Zenith Electronics Corp.

General Support

7-Eleven, Inc.
ABB Inc.
Abbott Laboratories
ABC
Advanced Micro Devices, Inc.
AEGON U.S.A. Inc.
Aetna, Inc.
AFLAC Inc.
Agrilink Foods, Inc.
Air Products and Chemicals, Inc.
Airborne Freight Corp.
Alabama Power Co.
Alaska Airlines, Inc.
Albertson's Inc.
Alcoa Inc.
Alcon Laboratories, Inc.
Alexander & Baldwin, Inc.
Allegheny Technologies Inc.
Alliant Techsystems
Allianz Life Insurance Co. of North America
AlliedSignal Inc.
Allmerica Financial Corp.
Allstate Insurance Co.
Alma Piston Co.
Alyeska Pipeline Service Co.
AMCORE Bank Rockford
Ameren Corp.
America West Airlines, Inc.
American Electric Power
American Fidelity Corp.
American General Finance
American Honda Motor Co., Inc.
American Standard Inc.
American Stock Exchange, Inc.
American United Life Insurance Co.
Ameritas Life Insurance Corp.
Ameritech Illinois
AmerUS Group
AMETEK, Inc.
Amgen, Inc.
AMR Corp.
Amsted Industries Inc.
Analog Devices, Inc.
Andersen Corp.
Andersons Inc.
Anheuser-Busch Companies, Inc.
Aon Corp.
Apple Computer, Inc.
Appleton Papers Inc.
Archer-Daniels-Midland Co.
Aristech Chemical Corp.
Armstrong World Industries, Inc.
Arvin Industries, Inc.
ASARCO Inc.
Ashland, Inc.
Associated Food Stores
Atlantic Investment Co.
Atlantic Richfield Co.
Auburn Foundry
Autodesk Inc.
Avery Dennison Corp.
Avista Corporation
Badger Meter, Inc.
Baird & Co. (Robert W.)
Ball Corp.
Bandag, Inc.
Banfi Vintners
Bank of America
Bank of New York Co., Inc.
Bank One Corp.
Bank One, Texas-Houston Office
Bank One, Texas, NA
BankBoston-Connecticut Region
BankBoston Corp.
Banta Corp.
Barclays Capital
Bard, Inc. (C.R.)
Barden Corp.
Bardes Corp.
Barnes Group Inc.
Barry Corp. (R.G.)
Bassett Furniture Industries
Battelle Memorial Institute
Bausch & Lomb Inc.
Baxter International Inc.
Bayer Corp.
Bean, Inc. (L.L.)

Bechtel Group, Inc.
Belk-Simpson Department Stores
Belk Stores Services Inc.
Bell Atlantic Corp.
Bell Atlantic Corp.-West Virginia
Bell Atlantic-Delaware, Inc.
BellSouth Corp.
Bemis Co., Inc.
Bemis Manufacturing Co.
Ben & Jerry's Homemade Inc.
Bernstein & Co., Inc. (Sanford C.)
Berwind Group
Bestfoods
Bethlehem Steel Corp.
BFGoodrich Co.
Binswanger Companies
Blair & Co. (William)
Block, Inc. (H&R)
Blount International, Inc.
Blue Bell, Inc.
Blue Cross & Blue Shield of Alabama
Blue Cross & Blue Shield of Iowa
Blue Cross & Blue Shield of Minnesota
Boler Co.
Borden, Inc.
Borman's Inc.
Boston Edison Co.
Boston Gas Co.
Boston Globe (The)
Bowater Inc.
BP Amoco Corp.
Bradford & Co. (J.C.)
Branch Banking & Trust Co.
Bridgestone/Firestone, Inc.
Briggs & Stratton Corp.
Bristol-Myers Squibb Co.
Broderbund Software, Inc.
Brooklyn Union
Brown Shoe Co., Inc.
Brown & Williamson Tobacco Corp.
Browning-Ferris Industries Inc.
Bucyrus-Erie Co.
Burger King Corp.
Burlington Industries, Inc.
Burlington Northern Santa Fe Corp.
Burlington Resources, Inc.
Burnett Co. (Leo)
Burress (J.W.)
Business Improvement
Business Men's Assurance Co. of America
Butler Capital Corp.
Butler Manufacturing Co.
Cabot Corp.
Cadence Designs Systems, Inc.
Caesar's World, Inc.
California Bank & Trust
California Federal Bank, FSB
Callaway Golf Co.
Calvin Klein
Campbell Soup Co.
Cantor, Fitzgerald Securities Corp.
Cargill Inc.
Carillon Importers, Ltd.
Carlson Companies, Inc.
Carnival Corp.
Carolina Power & Light Co.
Carpenter Technology Corp.
Carrier Corp.
Carris Reels
Carter-Wallace, Inc.
Castle & Cooke Properties Inc.
Caterpillar Inc.
CBS Corp.
CCB Financial Corp.
Centex Corp.
Central Maine Power Co.
Central National-Gottesman
Central & South West Services
Central Soya Co.
Central Vermont Public Service Corp.
Century 21
CertainTeed Corp.
CGU Insurance
Champion International Corp.
Charter Manufacturing Co.
Chase Bank of Texas
Chase Manhattan Bank, NA
Chemed Corp.
Chevron Corp.
Chicago Board of Trade
Chicago Title Corp.
Chicago Tribune Co.
CIBC Oppenheimer
CIGNA Corp.
Cincinnati Bell Inc.
Circuit City Stores, Inc.
CIT Group, Inc. (The)
Citibank Corp.
Citigroup
Citizens Bank-Flint
Citizens Financial Group, Inc.
CLARCOR Inc.
Cleveland-Cliffs, Inc.
Clorox Co.
CNA
CNF Transportation, Inc.
Coachmen Industries, Inc.
Coca-Cola Co.
Colgate-Palmolive Co.
Collins & Aikman Corp.
Colonial Life & Accident Insurance Co.
Colonial Oil Industries, Inc.
Comdisco, Inc.
Comerica Inc.
Commerce Bancshares, Inc.
Commercial Federal Corp.
Commercial Intertech Corp.
Commonwealth Edison Co.
Compaq Computer Corp.
Compass Bank
ConAgra, Inc.
Conectiv
Consolidated Natural Gas Co.
Consolidated Papers, Inc.
Constellation Energy Group, Inc.
Consumers Energy Co.
Continental Grain Co.
Contran Corp.
Conwood Co. LP
Cooper Industries, Inc.
Cooper Tire & Rubber Co.
Coors Brewing Co.
Country Curtains, Inc.
CPI Corp.
Crane Co.
Crane & Co., Inc.
Cranston Print Works Co.
Credit Suisse First Boston
Crestar Finance Corp.
Croft-Leominster
Crown Books
CSR Rinker Materials Corp.
CSS Industries, Inc.
CSX Corp.
Cummings Properties Management
Cummins Engine Co., Inc.
Curtis Industries, Inc. (Helene)
Cyprus Amax Minerals Co.
Daily News
DaimlerChrysler Corp.
Dana Corp.
Danis Companies
Dayton Hudson
Dayton Power and Light Co.
Deere & Co.
Deluxe Corp.
Demoulas Supermarkets Inc.
Deposit Guaranty National Bank
Detroit Edison Co.
Deutsch Co.
Dexter Corp.
Dial Corp.
Diebold, Inc.
Disney Co. (Walt)
Dixie Group, Inc. (The)
Dollar General Corp.
Dominion Resources, Inc.
Donaldson Co., Inc.
Donnelley & Sons Co. (R.R.)
Dow Chemical Co.
Dow Jones & Co., Inc.
Dreyer's Grand Ice Cream
DSM Copolymer
du Pont de Nemours & Co. (E.I.)
Duchossois Industries Inc.
Duke Energy
Dun & Bradstreet Corp.
Duquesne Light Co.
Duriron Co., Inc.
Dynamet, Inc.
Eastern Bank
Eastman Chemical Co.
Eastman Kodak Co.
Eaton Corp.
Ebsco Industries, Inc.
Ecolab Inc.
Edison Brothers Stores, Inc.
Edison International
EDS Corp.
Edwards Enterprise Software (J.D.)
El Paso Energy Co.
Elf Atochem North America, Inc.
Emerson Electric Co.
EMI Music Publishing
Employers Insurance of Wausau, A Mutual Co.
Employers Mutual Casualty Co.
Ensign-Bickford Industries
Entergy Corp.
Enterprise Rent-A-Car Co.
Equifax Inc.
Erb Lumber Co.
Erving Industries
Ethyl Corp.
European American Bank
Evening Post Publishing Co.
Exxon Mobil Corp.
Fannie Mae
Farmers Group, Inc.
Federal-Mogul Corp.
Federated Department Stores, Inc.
Federated Mutual Insurance Co.
FedEx Corp.
Ferro Corp.
Fifth Third Bancorp
FINA
First Financial Bank
First Hawaiian, Inc.
First Maryland Bancorp
First National Bank of Evergreen Park
First Security Bank of Idaho NA
First Source Corp.
First Tennessee National Corp.
First Union Bank
First Union Corp.
First Union National Bank, NA
First Union Securities, Inc.
Firstar Bank Milwaukee NA
FirstEnergy Corp.
Fisher Brothers Cleaning Services
Fisher Scientific
FleetBoston Financial Corp.
Florida Power Corp.
Florida Power & Light Co.
Florida Rock Industries
Fluor Corp.
FMC Corp.
Forbes Inc.
Ford Meter Box Co.
Ford Motor Co.
Forest City Enterprises, Inc.
Fort James Corp.
Fort Worth Star-Telegram Inc.
Fortis Insurance Co.
Fortune Brands, Inc.
Fox Entertainment Group
Franklin Mint (The)
Freddie Mac
Freeport-McMoRan Inc.
Freightliner Corp.
Frito-Lay, Inc.
Frontier Corp.
Frost National Bank
Fuji Bank & Trust Co.
Fuller Co. (H.B.)
Furniture Brands International, Inc.
Gallo Winery, Inc. (E&J)
Galter Corp.
Gannett Co., Inc.
Gap, Inc.
Gates Rubber Corp.
GATX Corp.
GEICO Corp.
GenAmerica Corp.
GenCorp
General Dynamics Corp.
General Electric Co.
General Mills, Inc.
General Motors Corp.
General Reinsurance Corp.
Georgia-Pacific Corp.
Georgia Power Co.
Gerber Products Co.
Giant Eagle Inc.
Giant Food Inc.
Giddings & Lewis
Gillette Co.
Globe Corp.
Golub Corp.
Goodrich Aerospace - Aerostructures Group (B.F.)
GPU Energy
Grace & Co. (W.R.)
Graco, Inc.
Grainger, Inc. (W.W.)
Grede Foundries
Green Bay Packaging
Griffith Laboratories U.S.A.
Group Health Plan
GTE Corp.
Guardian Life Insurance Co. of America
Gucci America Inc.
Gulf Power Co.
Gulfstream Aerospace Corp.
Halliburton Co.
Hallmark Cards Inc.
Hamilton Sundstrand Corp.
Hancock Financial Services (John)
Hanna Co. (M.A.)
Hannaford Brothers Co.
Harcourt General, Inc.
Harland Co. (John H.)
Harnischfeger Industries
Harrah's Entertainment Inc.
Harris Corp.
Harris Trust & Savings Bank
Harsco Corp.
Hartford (The)
Hartford Steam Boiler Inspection & Insurance Co.
Hartmarx Corp.
Hawaiian Electric Co., Inc.
Heinz Co. (H.J.)
Heller Financial, Inc.
Hensel Phelps Construction Co.
Hercules Inc.
Hershey Foods Corp.
Hickory Tech Corp.
Hoechst Marion Roussel, Inc.
Hoffer Plastics Corp.
Home Depot, Inc.
HON Industries Inc.
Honeywell International Inc.
Houghton Mifflin Co.
Housatonic Curtain Co.
Household International Inc.
HSBC Bank USA
Hubbell Inc.
Huffy Corp.
Hughes Electronics Corp.
Humana, Inc.
Hunt Manufacturing Co.
Hunt Oil Co.
IBP
Idaho Power Co.
IKON Office Solutions, Inc.
Illinois Power Co.
Illinois Tool Works, Inc.
Independent Stave Co.
Indiana Mills & Manufacturing
Ingram Industries Inc.
Inland Container Corp.
Inman Mills
International Business Machines Corp.
International Flavors & Fragrances Inc.
International Multifoods Corp.
International Paper Co.
Interpublic Group of Companies, Inc.
INTRUST Financial Corp.
Invacare Corp.
Jacobs Engineering Group
Jacobson & Sons (Benjamin)
Jeld-wen, Inc.
Johnson Controls Inc.
Johnson & Johnson
Johnson & Son (S.C.)
Jones & Co. (Edward D.)
Jostens, Inc.
Journal Communications, Inc.
JSJ Corp.
Kaman Corp.
Katten, Muchin & Zavis
Kellogg Co.
Kellwood Co.
Kelly Services
Kendall International, Inc.
Kennametal, Inc.
Kerr-McGee Corp.

Key Bank of Cleveland
Kiewit Sons' Inc. (Peter)
Kimball International, Inc.
Kimberly-Clark Corp.
Kinder Morgn
Kingsbury Corp.
Kmart Corp.
Knight Ridder
Koch Enterprises, Inc.
Kohler Co.
Kroger Co.
La-Z-Boy Inc.
Laclede Gas Co.
Ladish Co., Inc.
Lancaster Lens, Inc.
Lance, Inc.
Land O'Lakes, Inc.
LandAmerica Financial Services
Lee Enterprises
Lehigh Portland Cement Co.
Leigh Fibers, Inc.
Lennox International, Inc.
Levi Strauss & Co.
Leviton Manufacturing Co. Inc.
LG&E Energy Corp.
Liberty Corp.
Liberty Diversified Industries
Liberty Mutual Insurance Group
Lilly & Co. (Eli)
Lincoln Electric Co.
Lincoln Financial Group
Lipton Co.
Little, Inc. (Arthur D.)
Litton Industries, Inc.
Liz Claiborne, Inc.
Loctite Corp.
Loews Corp.
Louisiana Land & Exploration Co.
Louisiana-Pacific Corp.
Lowe's Companies
LTV Corp.
Lubrizol Corp. (The)
Lyondell Chemical Co.
MacMillan Bloedel Inc.
Macy's East Inc.
Madison Gas & Electric Co.
Mallinckrodt Chemical, Inc.
Mamiye Brothers
Manor Care Health SVS, Inc.
Manufacturers & Traders Trust Co.
Manulife Financial
Marcus Corp.
Maritz Inc.
Mark IV Industries
Marriott International Inc.
Marshall Field's
Marshall & Ilsley Corp.
Masco Corp.
Massachusetts Mutual Life Insurance Co.
Matsushita Electric Corp. of America
Mattel Inc.
Maybelline, Inc.
Maytag Corp.
Mazda North American Operations
McClatchy Co.
McDermott Inc.
McDonald & Co. Securities, Inc.
McDonald's Corp.
McGraw-Hill Companies, Inc.
McKesson-HBOC Corp.
McWane Inc.
Mead Corp.
Meijer, Inc.
Mellon Financial Corp.
Memphis Light Gas & Water Division
Menasha Corp.
Meredith Corp.
Merit Oil Corp.
Merrill Lynch & Co., Inc.
Metropolitan Life Insurance Co.
MGIC Investment Corp.
Michigan Consolidated Gas Co.
Microsoft Corp.
Mid-America Bank of Louisville
MidAmerican Energy Holdings Co.
Milacron, Inc.
Milliken & Co.
Millipore Corp.
Mine Safety Appliances Co.
Minnesota Mining & Manufacturing Co.
Minnesota Mutual Life Insurance Co.
Mitsubishi Electric America
Monarch Machine Tool Co.
Montana Power Co.
Montgomery Ward & Co., Inc.
Morgan & Co. Inc. (J.P.)
Morgan Stanley Dean Witter & Co.
Morris Communications Corp.
Morton International Inc.
Motorola Inc.
MTD Products Inc.
MTS Systems Corp.
Mutual of Omaha Insurance Co.
Nabisco Group Holdings
Nalco Chemical Co.
NASDAQ Stock Market
National Bank of Commerce Trust & Savings
National City Bank of Cleveland
National City Bank of Columbus
National City Bank of Minneapolis
National City Bank of Pennsylvania
National City Corp.
National Life of Vermont
National Machinery Co.
National Presto Industries, Inc.
National Service Industries, Inc.
National Starch & Chemical Co.
Nationwide Insurance Co.
NEBCO Evans
NEC America, Inc.
Nestle U.S.A. Inc.
New England Bio Labs
New England Financial
New Jersey Natural Gas Co.
New United Motor Manufacturing Inc.
New York Life Insurance Co.
New York Mercantile Exchange
New York State Electric & Gas Corp.
New York Stock Exchange, Inc.
New York Times Co.
Newman's Own Inc.
Newport News Shipbuilding
Nike, Inc.
Nissan North America, Inc.
Nordson Corp.
Norfolk Southern Corp.
Nortel
Northeast Utilities
Northern Indiana Public Service Co.
Northern States Power Co.
Northern Trust Co.
Northrop Grumman Corp.
Northwest Bank Nebraska, NA
Northwest Natural Gas Co.
Norton Co.
Norwest Corp.
Novartis Corporation
Nucor Corp.
Occidental Oil and Gas
Occidental Petroleum Corp.
OG&E Electric Services
Ohio National Life Insurance Co.
Oklahoma Publishing Co.
Old Kent Bank
Old National Bank Evansville
ONEOK, Inc.
Orange & Rockland Utilities, Inc.
Orscheln Co.
Osborne Enterprises
Oshkosh B'Gosh, Inc.
Overnite Transportation Co.
Overseas Shipholding Group Inc.
Owens-Illinois Inc.
PACCAR Inc.
Pacific Century Financial Corp.
Pacific Gas and Electric Co.
Pacific Mutual Life Insurance Co.
PacifiCorp
Paine Webber
Pan-American Life Insurance Co.
Park National Bank
Parker Hannifin Corp.
Patagonia Inc.
PECO Energy Co.
Pella Corp.
PEMCO Corp.
Penn Mutual Life Insurance Co.
Penney Co., Inc. (J.C.)
Pennsylvania Power & Light
Pennzoil-Quaker State Co.
Pentair Inc.
Peoples Bank
Peoples Energy Corp.
PepsiCo, Inc.
PerkinElmer, Inc.
Pfizer Inc.
Pharmacia & Upjohn, Inc.
Phelps Dodge Corp.
Philip Morris Companies Inc.
Phillips Petroleum Co.
Phoenix Home Life Mutual Insurance Co.
Physicians Mutual Insurance Co.
Pieper Power Electric Co.
Pillsbury Co.
Pioneer Group
Pioneer Natural Resources
Pitney Bowes Inc.
Pittway Corp.
Playboy Enterprises Inc.
PNC Bank
PNC Financial Services Group
Polaroid Corp.
Portland General Electric Co.
Potlatch Corp.
PPG Industries, Inc.
Premark International Inc.
Premier Dental Products Co.
Premier Industrial Corp.
Price Associates (T. Rowe)
Principal Financial Group
Procter & Gamble Co.
Procter & Gamble Co., Cosmetics Division
Progressive Corp.
Promus Hotel Corp.
Providence Journal-Bulletin Co.
Prudential Insurance Co. of America
Prudential Securities Inc.
Public Service Co. of Oklahoma
Public Service Electric & Gas Co.
Publix Supermarkets
Puget Sound Energy (PSE) Inc.
Pulitzer Publishing Co.
Putnam Investments
Quaker Chemical Corp.
Quanex Corp.
Questar Corp.
Ralph's Grocery Co.
Ralston Purina Co.
Rayonier Inc.
Red Wing Shoe Co. Inc.
Reebok International Ltd.
Regions Financial Corp.
Regis Corp.
REI-Recreational Equipment, Inc.
Reilly Industries, Inc.
Reily & Co., Inc. (William B.)
Reinhart Institutional Foods
Reliant Energy Inc.
Reliant Energy Minnegasco
ReliaStar Financial Corp.
Revlon Inc.
Reynolds Metals Co.
Reynolds & Reynolds Co.
Reynolds Tobacco (R.J.)
Rich Products Corp.
Riggs Bank NA
Rite Aid Corp.
Rochester Gas & Electric Corp.
Rockwell International Corp.
Rohm & Haas Co.
Roseburg Forest Products Co.
Rouse Co.
Royal & SunAlliance USA, Inc.
Ruddick Corp.
Russer Foods
Ryder System, Inc.
SAFECO Corp.
Safeguard Scientifics
Safeway Inc.
Saint Paul Companies Inc.
Salomon Smith Barney
S&T Bancorp
Santa Fe International Corp.
Sara Lee Corp.
Sara Lee Hosiery, Inc.
SBC Communications Inc.
Schering-Plough Corp.
Schlumberger Ltd. (USA)
Schwab & Co., Inc. (Charles)
Schwebel Baking Co.
Scientific-Atlanta, Inc.
Scripps Co. (E.W.)
Seagram & Sons, Inc. (Joseph E.)
Searle & Co. (G.D.)
Sears, Roebuck and Co.
Seaway Food Town, Inc.
Security Benefit Life Insurance Co.
Security Life of Denver Insurance Co.
Sentinel Communications Co.
Sentry Insurance, A Mutual Co.
ServiceMaster Co.
S.G. Cowen
Shaklee Corp.
Shaw Industries Inc.
Shaw's Supermarkets, Inc.
Shea Co. (John F.)
Shell Oil Co.
Shelter Mutual Insurance Co.
Sherwin-Williams Co.
Shoney's Inc.
Sierra Pacific Industries
Sierra Pacific Resources
Simplot Co. (J.R.)
Simpson Investment Co.
SIT Investment Associates, Inc.
Slant/Fin Corp.
Smith Corp. (A.O.)
SmithKline Beecham Corp.
Smucker Co. (JM)
Smurfit-Stone Container Corp.
Solo Cup Co.
Sonoco Products Co.
Sony Electronics
Sotheby's Inc.
South Bend Tribune Corp.
Southern California Gas Co.
Southern Co. Services Inc.
Southwest Gas Corp.
Sovereign Bank
Springs Industries, Inc.
Sprint Corp.
Sprint/United Telephone
SPX Corp.
Square D Co.
Standard Products Co.
Standard Register Co.
Stanley Works (The)
Star Bank NA
Starwood Hotels & Resorts Worldwide, Inc.
State Street Bank & Trust Co.
Steelcase Inc.
Stone Container Corp.
Stone & Webster Inc.
Stonecutter Mills Corp.
Storage Technology Corp.
Strear Farms Co.
Student Loan Marketing Association
Stupp Brothers Bridge & Iron Co.
Subway Sandwich Shops, Inc.
Sunmark Capital Corp.
Sunoco Inc.
SunTrust Bank Atlanta
SunTrust Banks of Florida
SuperValu, Inc.
Susquehanna-Pfaltzgraff Co.
Sverdrup Corp.
Synovus Financial Corp.
Tai and Co. (J.T.)
Tampa Electric Co.
Tandy Corp.
TCF National Bank Minnesota
Tektronix, Inc.
Telcordia Technologies
Teleflex Inc.

Temple-Inland Inc.
Tenet Healthcare Corp.
TENNANT Co.
Tenneco Packaging
Tension Envelope Corp.
Tesoro Hawaii
Texas Gas Transmission Corp.
Texas Instruments Inc.
Textron Inc.
Thermo Electron Corp.
Thomasville Furniture Industries Inc.
Thompson Co. (J. Walter)
Times Mirror Co.
Timken Co. (The)
Titan Industrial Corp.
TJX Companies, Inc.
TMC Investment Co.
Toledo Blade Co.
Tomkins Industries, Inc.
Torchmark Corp.
Toro Co.
Toyota Motor Sales U.S.A., Inc.
Trace International Holdings, Inc.
Transamerica Corp.
True North Communications, Inc.
True Oil Co.
Trustmark Insurance Co.
Trustmark National Bank
TRW Inc.
TU Electric Co.
Tucson Electric Power Co.
Tyson Foods Inc.
Ukrop's Super Markets
Ultramar Diamond Shamrock Corp.
Unilever Home & Personal Care U.S.A.
Unilever United States, Inc.
Union Camp Corp.
Union Carbide Corp.
Union Pacific Corp.
Union Planters Corp.
Unisys Corp.
United Airlines Inc.
United Co.
United Distillers & Vintners North America
United Dominion Industries, Ltd.
U.S. Bancorp
U.S. Bancorp Piper Jaffray
United States Sugar Corp.
United States Trust Co. of New York
United Wisconsin Services
Universal Foods Corp.
Universal Leaf Tobacco Co., Inc.
Universal Studios
Unocal Corp.
US Bank, Washington
US West, Inc.
USAA Life Insurance Co.
USG Corp.
UST Inc.
USX Corp.
Valero Energy Corp.
Valmont Industries, Inc.
Valspar Corp.
Varian Medical Systems, Inc.
Vesper Corp.
Vulcan Materials Co.
Wachovia Bank of North Carolina NA
Wachtell, Lipton, Rosen & Katz
Waldbaum's Supermarkets, Inc.
Walgreen Co.
Walter Industries Inc.
Warner-Lambert Co.
Washington Mutual, Inc.
The Washington Post
Washington Trust Bank
Waste Management Inc.
Wausau Insurance Companies
Webster Bank
Weil, Gotshal & Manges Corp.
Wells Fargo & Co.
West Co. Inc.
Western Resources Inc.
Western & Southern Life Insurance Co.
Westvaco Corp.
Weyerhaeuser Co.
Whitman Corp.
WICOR, Inc.
Wilbur-Ellis Co. & Connell Brothers Co.
Williams
Winn-Dixie Stores Inc.
Wiremold Co.
Wisconsin Energy Corp.
Wisconsin Power & Light Co.
Wisconsin Public Service Corp.
Witco Corp.
Wolverine World Wide
Wrigley Co. (Wm. Jr.)
Wyman-Gordon Co.
Xerox Corp.
Yellow Corp.
York Federal Savings & Loan Association
Young & Rubicam
Zenith Electronics Corp.
Zilkha & Sons
Zurn Industries, Inc.

Loan

BP Amoco Corp.
California Bank & Trust
CIBC Oppenheimer
EDS Corp.
Fannie Mae
Fuji Bank & Trust Co.
Gulfstream Aerospace Corp.
Harris Trust & Savings Bank
INTRUST Financial Corp.
Lincoln Financial Group
Meredith Corp.
Metropolitan Life Insurance Co.
MidAmerican Energy Holdings Co.
Pitney Bowes Inc.
UST Inc.

Matching

Aetna, Inc.
AK Steel Corp.
Alabama Power Co.
Albertson's Inc.
Alcoa Inc.
Allianz Life Insurance Co. of North America
American General Finance
American Honda Motor Co., Inc.
APL Ltd.
Arizona Public Service Co.
ASARCO Inc.
AT&T Corp.
Avista Corporation
Baker Hughes Inc.
Bank One, Texas, NA
Battelle Memorial Institute
BellSouth Corp.
Bemis Co., Inc.
Binney & Smith Inc.
Blue Cross & Blue Shield of Michigan
Boston Edison Co.
Brooklyn Union
Burlington Northern Santa Fe Corp.
Callaway Golf Co.
Central Maine Power Co.
Central Soya Co.
Chicago Title Corp.
Cincinnati Bell Inc.
Clark Refining & Marketing
Cleveland-Cliffs, Inc.
Comerica Inc.
Commonwealth Edison Co.
Computer Associates International, Inc.
Cooper Industries, Inc.
CPI Corp.
CSX Corp.
CUNA Mutual Group
Dain Bosworth Inc.
Dana Corp.
Duracell International
Eastern Enterprises
Eastman Kodak Co.
Eaton Corp.
EDS Corp.
El Paso Energy Co.
Entergy Corp.
Equifax Inc.
Ernst & Young, LLP
Exxon Mobil Corp.
Fannie Mae
Federated Department Stores, Inc.
Fidelity Investments
First Union Corp.
Fluor Corp.
Fortis, Inc.
Freddie Mac
Freightliner Corp.
Frost National Bank
Gallo Winery, Inc. (E&J)
GATX Corp.
GTE Corp.
Household International Inc.
International Business Machines Corp.
INTRUST Financial Corp.
Key Bank of Cleveland
Laclede Gas Co.
Land O'Lakes, Inc.
LandAmerica Financial Services
Landmark Communications Inc.
LG&E Energy Corp.
Lincoln Financial Group
Loctite Corp.
Loews Corp.
Mallinckrodt Chemical, Inc.
Manor Care Health SVS, Inc.
Maritz Inc.
Massachusetts Mutual Life Insurance Co.
Mattel Inc.
McDonald & Co. Securities, Inc.
Michigan Consolidated Gas Co.
Mid-America Bank of Louisville
Millipore Corp.
Mitsubishi Electric America
Montana Power Co.
Nabisco Group Holdings
National City Bank of Pennsylvania
Nationwide Insurance Co.
NEBCO Evans
New Jersey Natural Gas Co.
Niagara Mohawk Holdings Inc.
Nortel
Northern Indiana Public Service Co.
Oklahoma Publishing Co.
Osborne Enterprises
PacifiCorp
Penn Mutual Life Insurance Co.
Penney Co., Inc. (J.C.)
Pioneer Hi-Bred International, Inc.
Pitney Bowes Inc.
Playboy Enterprises Inc.
PNC Bank Kentucky Inc.
Puget Sound Energy (PSE) Inc.
ReliaStar Financial Corp.
Rouse Co.
Saint Paul Companies Inc.
Scientific-Atlanta, Inc.
Security Benefit Life Insurance Co.
Shaklee Corp.
Sonoco Products Co.
Springs Industries, Inc.
Star Bank NA
State Farm Mutual Automobile Insurance Co.
Steelcase Inc.
Stone Container Corp.
Student Loan Marketing Association
Telcordia Technologies
Tenet Healthcare Corp.
Toyota Motor Sales U.S.A., Inc.
Ultramar Diamond Shamrock Corp.
Union Camp Corp.
Universal Foods Corp.
Universal Leaf Tobacco Co., Inc.
USX Corp.
Wachovia Bank of North Carolina NA
Wal-Mart Stores, Inc.
Waldbaum's Supermarkets, Inc.
Western & Southern Life Insurance Co.
Winn-Dixie Stores Inc.
Wisconsin Energy Corp.
Wolverine World Wide
Xerox Corp.
Young & Rubicam
Zurn Industries, Inc.

Multiyear/ Continuing Support

Aetna, Inc.
Air Products and Chemicals, Inc.
Airborne Freight Corp.
Alabama Power Co.
Albany International Corp.
Albertson's Inc.
Alcoa Inc.
AlliedSignal Inc.
Ameren Corp.
American Electric Power
American Honda Motor Co., Inc.
American Retail Group
Ameritas Life Insurance Corp.
AMP Inc.
AMR Corp.
Andersen Corp.
Appleton Papers Inc.
Aristech Chemical Corp.
Arizona Public Service Co.
ASARCO Inc.
AT&T Corp.
Avista Corporation
Ball Corp.
Bandag, Inc.
Bank of New York Co., Inc.
Bank One, Texas-Houston Office
Bank One, Texas, NA
Banta Corp.
Battelle Memorial Institute
Bean, Inc. (L.L.)
Bell Atlantic Corp.-West Virginia
BellSouth Corp.
Bemis Co., Inc.
Bethlehem Steel Corp.
Block, Inc. (H&R)
Boeing Co.
Borden, Inc.
Boston Globe (The)
Bourns, Inc.
Brooklyn Union
Browning-Ferris Industries Inc.
Burger King Corp.
Burlington Northern Santa Fe Corp.
Cargill Inc.
CBS Corp.
Central Maine Power Co.
Central Vermont Public Service Corp.
Chase Bank of Texas
Chase Manhattan Bank, NA
Cincinnati Bell Inc.
Citibank Corp.
CLARCOR Inc.
Cleveland-Cliffs, Inc.
CNA
Colgate-Palmolive Co.
Comerica Inc.
Commonwealth Edison Co.
ConAgra, Inc.
Constellation Energy Group, Inc.
Cooper Industries, Inc.
Copley Press, Inc.
CSR Rinker Materials Corp.
CUNA Mutual Group
Dana Corp.
Dayton Hudson
Dayton Power and Light Co.
DeKalb Genetics Corp.
Dollar General Corp.
Donaldson Co., Inc.
Donnelley & Sons Co. (R.R.)
Dow Corning Corp.
du Pont de Nemours & Co. (E.I.)
Duchossois Industries Inc.
Duke Energy
Duracell International
Eastern Enterprises
Eastman Kodak Co.
Eaton Corp.
El Paso Energy Co.
Ensign-Bickford Industries
Enterprise Rent-A-Car Co.
Equifax Inc.
Ernst & Young, LLP
Erving Industries
Excel Corp.
Exxon Mobil Corp.

Fannie Mae
Federated Department Stores, Inc.
Ferro Corp.
FINA
First Maryland Bancorp
First Union Bank
First Union Corp.
First Union National Bank, NA
Firstar Bank Milwaukee NA
Florida Power & Light Co.
Ford Motor Co.
Fort James Corp.
Fortune Brands, Inc.
Franklin Mint (The)
Freddie Mac
Frost National Bank
GATX Corp.
GenAmerica Corp.
GenCorp
General Electric Co.
General Mills, Inc.
Georgia Power Co.
Gerber Products Co.
Glaxo Wellcome Inc.
Grace & Co. (W.R.)
Graco, Inc.
GTE Corp.
Harcourt General, Inc.
Harris Trust & Savings Bank
Hawaiian Electric Co., Inc.
Hercules Inc.
Hickory Tech Corp.
Hitachi America Ltd.
Household International Inc.
Huntington Bancshares Inc.
Idaho Power Co.
Illinois Power Co.
Illinois Tool Works, Inc.
Inland Container Corp.
International Business Machines Corp.
International Multifoods Corp.
Invacare Corp.
Johnson Controls Inc.
Jostens, Inc.
JSJ Corp.
Kelly Services
Kemper National Insurance Companies
Key Bank of Cleveland
Kiewit Sons' Inc. (Peter)
Kingsbury Corp.
KPMG Peat Marwick LLP
Laclede Gas Co.
Land O'Lakes, Inc.
Landmark Communications Inc.
Leigh Fibers, Inc.
Levi Strauss & Co.
Liberty Corp.
Liberty Mutual Insurance Group
Lilly & Co. (Eli)
Lincoln Electric Co.
Lincoln Financial Group
Little, Inc. (Arthur D.)
Loctite Corp.
Louisiana Land & Exploration Co.
LTV Corp.
Lubrizol Corp. (The)
Mallinckrodt Chemical, Inc.
Maritz Inc.
Massachusetts Mutual Life Insurance Co.
Maytag Corp.
McDonald & Co. Securities, Inc.
Mead Corp.
Memphis Light Gas & Water Division
Menasha Corp.
Merrill Lynch & Co., Inc.
Metropolitan Life Insurance Co.
Michigan Consolidated Gas Co.
Microsoft Corp.
Mid-America Bank of Louisville
MidAmerican Energy Holdings Co.
Milacron, Inc.
Millipore Corp.
Minnesota Mutual Life Insurance Co.
Montana Power Co.
Montgomery Ward & Co., Inc.
Morgan & Co. Inc. (J.P.)
Motorola Inc.
MTS Systems Corp.
National Life of Vermont
National Starch & Chemical Co.
Nationwide Insurance Co.
NEBCO Evans
New England Financial
New York Times Co.
Niagara Mohawk Holdings Inc.
Nike, Inc.
Nissan North America, Inc.
Northern Indiana Public Service Co.
Northwest Natural Gas Co.
Norton Co.
Norwest Corp.
Novartis Corporation
Occidental Petroleum Corp.
Ohio National Life Insurance Co.
Olin Corp.
ONEOK, Inc.
Orange & Rockland Utilities, Inc.
Pacific Mutual Life Insurance Co.
PacifiCorp
Pan-American Life Insurance Co.
Penn Mutual Life Insurance Co.
Peoples Energy Corp.
Pfizer Inc.
Pharmacia & Upjohn, Inc.
Phelps Dodge Corp.
Pitney Bowes Inc.
Pittway Corp.
Playboy Enterprises Inc.
PNC Financial Services Group
Portland General Electric Co.
PPG Industries, Inc.
Price Associates (T. Rowe)
PricewaterhouseCoopers
Providence Journal-Bulletin Co.
Prudential Insurance Co. of America
Publix Supermarkets
Reader's Digest Association, Inc. (The)
ReliaStar Financial Corp.
Reynolds Metals Co.
Rockwell International Corp.
Rouse Co.
Royal & SunAlliance USA, Inc.
Saint Paul Companies Inc.
SBC Communications Inc.
Schering-Plough Corp.
Schwab & Co., Inc. (Charles)
Scientific-Atlanta, Inc.
Scripps Co. (E.W.)
Seaway Food Town, Inc.
Security Life of Denver Insurance Co.
Shaklee Corp.
Sonoco Products Co.
Southwest Gas Corp.
Sovereign Bank
Springs Industries, Inc.
State Farm Mutual Automobile Insurance Co.
Steelcase Inc.
Stone & Webster Inc.
Stride Rite Corp.
Student Loan Marketing Association
Sun Microsystems Inc.
SunTrust Banks of Florida
Susquehanna-Pfaltzgraff Co.
Telcordia Technologies
Texas Gas Transmission Corp.
Times Mirror Co.
Timken Co. (The)
True North Communications, Inc.
Trustmark Insurance Co.
Ultramar Diamond Shamrock Corp.
Union Pacific Corp.
United Airlines Inc.
United Parcel Service of America Inc.
United Wisconsin Services
Universal Foods Corp.
Universal Studios
UnumProvident
US West, Inc.
Valero Energy Corp.
Varian Medical Systems, Inc.
Vulcan Materials Co.
Warner-Lambert Co.
Waste Management Inc.
West Co. Inc.
Western Resources Inc.
Westvaco Corp.
WICOR, Inc.
Wisconsin Energy Corp.
Woodward Governor Co.
Xerox Corp.
Yellow Corp.
Zachry Co. (H.B.)

Operating Expenses

Air Products and Chemicals, Inc.
Alexander & Baldwin, Inc.
American Honda Motor Co., Inc.
American Retail Group
Aon Corp.
AT&T Corp.
Atlantic Investment Co.
Banfi Vintners
Bank One Corp.
Belk Stores Services Inc.
Bell Atlantic Corp.-West Virginia
Blue Cross & Blue Shield of Minnesota
Bridgestone/Firestone, Inc.
Brown & Williamson Tobacco Corp.
Burnett Co. (Leo)
Carpenter Technology Corp.
Caterpillar Inc.
CBS Corp.
Central Soya Co.
Chase Manhattan Bank, NA
Chemed Corp.
CIBC Oppenheimer
Clorox Co.
CNA
Consumers Energy Co.
Dain Bosworth Inc.
Deluxe Corp.
Disney Co. (Walt)
Dollar General Corp.
Dreyer's Grand Ice Cream
Enterprise Rent-A-Car Co.
Erving Industries
Ferro Corp.
First Union National Bank, NA
Firstar Bank Milwaukee NA
FleetBoston Financial Corp.
Fluor Corp.
Fuji Bank & Trust Co.
Fuller Co. (H.B.)
GATX Corp.
General Dynamics Corp.
General Mills, Inc.
Gillette Co.
Hershey Foods Corp.
Houghton Mifflin Co.
Hubbard Broadcasting, Inc.
Huntington Bancshares Inc.
Idaho Power Co.
Illinois Power Co.
Journal-Gazette Co.
Kaman Corp.
Kelly Services
Key Bank of Cleveland
Kimberly-Clark Corp.
Kingsbury Corp.
Kroger Co.
Leigh Fibers, Inc.
Lincoln Electric Co.
LTV Corp.
Manor Care Health SVS, Inc.
Marriott International Inc.
May Department Stores Co.
McDonald & Co. Securities, Inc.
Mercantile Bank NA
Merit Oil Corp.
MidAmerican Energy Holdings Co.
Minnesota Mining & Manufacturing Co.
National Computer Systems, Inc.
National Life of Vermont
National Starch & Chemical Co.
New England Bio Labs
New England Financial
Nissan North America, Inc.
Northeast Utilities
Northwest Natural Gas Co.
Norwest Corp.
Old National Bank Evansville
PECO Energy Co.
Penn Mutual Life Insurance Co.
Physicians Mutual Insurance Co.
PNC Bank
Polaroid Corp.
PPG Industries, Inc.
Publix Supermarkets
Putnam Investments
Reynolds Tobacco (R.J.)
Rohm & Haas Co.
Rouse Co.
SAFECO Corp.
Security Life of Denver Insurance Co.
Shell Oil Co.
Smith Corp. (A.O.)
Solo Cup Co.
Stanley Works (The)
Stride Rite Corp.
SunTrust Bank Atlanta
SuperValu, Inc.
Susquehanna-Pfaltzgraff Co.
TCF National Bank Minnesota
TENNANT Co.
Tesoro Hawaii
Texas Gas Transmission Corp.
Texas Instruments Inc.
True North Communications, Inc.
TRW Inc.
U.S. Bancorp Piper Jaffray
United Wisconsin Services
Woodward Governor Co.
Yellow Corp.

Professorship

Ameritas Life Insurance Corp.
Atlantic Investment Co.
Belk Stores Services Inc.
Cabot Corp.
Chase Manhattan Bank, NA
Duriron Co., Inc.
Ethyl Corp.
First Tennessee National Corp.
GenAmerica Corp.
Georgia Power Co.
Huntington Bancshares Inc.
KPMG Peat Marwick LLP
MTS Systems Corp.
National Computer Systems, Inc.
Overseas Shipholding Group Inc.
Schering-Plough Corp.
Schlumberger Ltd. (USA)
Seagram & Sons, Inc. (Joseph E.)
Torchmark Corp.
TRW Inc.
United Parcel Service of America Inc.
United States Sugar Corp.
Unocal Corp.
Varian Medical Systems, Inc.

Project

7-Eleven, Inc.
ABB Inc.
Advanced Micro Devices, Inc.
AEGON U.S.A. Inc.
Air Products and Chemicals, Inc.
Alabama Power Co.
Alexander & Baldwin, Inc.
Allstate Insurance Co.
Ameren Corp.
American Express Co.
American Honda Motor Co., Inc.
American Retail Group
American Stock Exchange, Inc.
Ameritas Life Insurance Corp.
Ameritech Corp.
Ameritech Illinois
Ameritech Indiana
Ameritech Michigan
Ameritech Ohio
Ameritech Wisconsin
AMR Corp.
Analog Devices, Inc.

Andersons Inc.
Apple Computer, Inc.
Appleton Papers Inc.
AT&T Corp.
Atlantic Investment Co.
Avista Corporation
Ball Corp.
Bandag, Inc.
Bank of America
Bank One Corp.
BankBoston-Connecticut Region
BankBoston Corp.
Beckman Coulter, Inc.
Becton Dickinson & Co.
Bell Atlantic Corp.-West Virginia
Ben & Jerry's Homemade Inc.
Blount International, Inc.
Boeing Co.
Boise Cascade Corp.
Borman's Inc.
Boston Edison Co.
Bridgestone/Firestone, Inc.
Bristol-Myers Squibb Co.
Browning-Ferris Industries Inc.
Brunswick Corp.
Bucyrus-Erie Co.
Burnett Co. (Leo)
Cabot Corp.
California Bank & Trust
Campbell Soup Co.
Cargill Inc.
Carrier Corp.
Caterpillar Inc.
CBS Corp.
Central Maine Power Co.
Central Newspapers, Inc.
CertainTeed Corp.
Chase Manhattan Bank, NA
Chemed Corp.
Chicago Sun-Times, Inc.
Chicago Tribune Co.
CIBC Oppenheimer
Cincinnati Bell Inc.
Cinergy Corp.
Citibank Corp.
Citigroup
Citizens Bank-Flint
Clorox Co.
Coca-Cola Co.
ConAgra, Inc.
Conoco, Inc.
Consolidated Natural Gas Co.
Consolidated Papers, Inc.
Consumers Energy Co.
Corning Inc.
Cox Enterprises Inc.
Cummins Engine Co., Inc.
DaimlerChrysler Corp.
Dain Bosworth Inc.
Dayton Hudson
Dayton Power and Light Co.
Deere & Co.
Deluxe Corp.
Detroit Edison Co.
Dexter Corp.
Disney Co. (Walt)
Domino's Pizza Inc.
Dow Chemical Co.
Dow Corning Corp.
Dreyer's Grand Ice Cream
Duke Energy
Eastern Enterprises
Eaton Corp.
Emerson Electric Co.
Ensign-Bickford Industries
Enterprise Rent-A-Car Co.
Equitable Resources, Inc.
Erving Industries
Farmers Group, Inc.
Federated Mutual Insurance Co.
FedEx Corp.
Fifth Third Bancorp
Fireman's Fund Insurance Co.
First Hawaiian, Inc.
First Tennessee National Corp.
First Union Bank
First Union National Bank, NA
Fluor Corp.
Ford Meter Box Co.
Freightliner Corp.
Fuller Co. (H.B.)
Gannett Co., Inc.
GATX Corp.
GEICO Corp.
GenAmerica Corp.
General Electric Co.
General Motors Corp.
Georgia Power Co.
Gerber Products Co.
Glaxo Wellcome Inc.
Group Health Plan
Hallmark Cards Inc.
Hancock Financial Services (John)
Harley-Davidson Co.
Hartford (The)
Hasbro, Inc.
Heinz Co. (H.J.)
Hershey Foods Corp.
Hewlett-Packard Co.
Hitachi America Ltd.
Hofmann Co.
Household International Inc.
Hunt Manufacturing Co.
Huntington Bancshares Inc.
Industrial Bank of Japan Trust Co. (New York)
International Business Machines Corp.
International Flavors & Fragrances Inc.
ISE America
Jeld-wen, Inc.
Johnson & Johnson
Johnson & Son (S.C.)
Jostens, Inc.
Kemper National Insurance Companies
Kerr-McGee Corp.
Kiewit Sons' Inc. (Peter)
Kimberly-Clark Corp.
Kingsbury Corp.
Koch Industries, Inc.
Kraft Foods, Inc.
Lincoln Electric Co.
Little, Inc. (Arthur D.)
Liz Claiborne, Inc.
Lotus Development Corp.
Louisiana-Pacific Corp.
Macy's East Inc.
Manor Care Health SVS, Inc.
Marriott International Inc.
Marshall Field's
McDonald & Co. Securities, Inc.
MCI WorldCom, Inc.
Mead Corp.
Medtronic, Inc.
Memphis Light Gas & Water Division
Menasha Corp.
Mercantile Bank NA
Merck & Co.
Meredith Corp.
Mervyn's California
Metropolitan Life Insurance Co.
Mine Safety Appliances Co.
Minnesota Mining & Manufacturing Co.
Mitsubishi Electric America
Monsanto Co.
MONY Group (The)
Morgan & Co. Inc. (J.P.)
Motorola Inc.
MTS Systems Corp.
Murphy Oil Corp.
Mutual of Omaha Insurance Co.
Nalco Chemical Co.
National Computer Systems, Inc.
NEC America, Inc.
New Century Energies
New England Bio Labs
New England Financial
New York Life Insurance Co.
New York Mercantile Exchange
Nomura Holding America
Nordson Corp.
Nortel
Northeast Utilities
Northern States Power Co.
Northern Trust Co.
Northwest Natural Gas Co.
Norton Co.
Norwest Corp.
Old National Bank Evansville
Olin Corp.
ONEOK, Inc.
Outboard Marine Corp.
Patagonia Inc.
PepsiCo, Inc.
Philip Morris Companies Inc.
Pillsbury Co.
Pitney Bowes Inc.
PNC Bank Kentucky Inc.
Polaroid Corp.
Portland General Electric Co.
Potomac Electric Power Co.
PPG Industries, Inc.
Premier Industrial Corp.
Principal Financial Group
Public Service Electric & Gas Co.
Publix Supermarkets
Pulitzer Publishing Co.
Putnam Investments
Ralston Purina Co.
Reliant Energy Minnegasco
Revlon Inc.
Reynolds Metals Co.
Reynolds & Reynolds Co.
Reynolds Tobacco (R.J.)
Rohm & Haas Co.
Rouse Co.
Saint Paul Companies Inc.
SBC Communications Inc.
Schlumberger Ltd. (USA)
Schwab & Co., Inc. (Charles)
Sears, Roebuck and Co.
Security Life of Denver Insurance Co.
Sega of America Inc.
Sempra Energy
Sentinel Communications Co.
Shaklee Corp.
Shell Oil Co.
Smith Corp. (A.O.)
SmithKline Beecham Corp.
Solo Cup Co.
Sonoco Products Co.
Sotheby's Inc.
Southeastern Mutual Insurance Co.
Southern California Gas Co.
Star Bank NA
State Street Bank & Trust Co.
Steelcase Inc.
Stone Container Corp.
SunTrust Bank Atlanta
SuperValu, Inc.
Susquehanna-Pfaltzgraff Co.
Taco Bell Corp.
Target Corp.
Tektronix, Inc.
Tesoro Hawaii
Texaco Inc.
Times Mirror Co.
Timken Co. (The)
TJX Companies, Inc.
Torchmark Corp.
Toshiba America Inc.
Toyota Motor Sales U.S.A., Inc.
TRW Inc.
Union Pacific Corp.
United Airlines Inc.
United Dominion Industries, Ltd.
United Parcel Service of America Inc.
United States Sugar Corp.
United States Trust Co. of New York
Universal Studios
Unocal Corp.
UnumProvident
US West, Inc.
UST Inc.
Valero Energy Corp.
Vulcan Materials Co.
Waffle House Inc.
Waldbaum's Supermarkets, Inc.
Warner-Lambert Co.
Wells Fargo & Co.
Weyerhaeuser Co.
Whirlpool Corp.
Williams
Winn-Dixie Stores Inc.
Wolverine World Wide
Yellow Corp.

Research

ABB Inc.
Abbott Laboratories
Alcoa Inc.
Ameritas Life Insurance Corp.
AMETEK, Inc.
Aon Corp.
Bandag, Inc.
Beckman Coulter, Inc.
Blount International, Inc.
Blue Cross & Blue Shield of Michigan
Blue Cross & Blue Shield of Minnesota
Bristol-Myers Squibb Co.
Brown & Williamson Tobacco Corp.
Browning-Ferris Industries Inc.
Brunswick Corp.
Cabot Corp.
Central Maine Power Co.
Central Soya Co.
Church & Dwight Co., Inc.
Dexter Corp.
Disney Co. (Walt)
Dow Chemical Co.
Duriron Co., Inc.
Eastman Kodak Co.
Ensign-Bickford Industries
Extendicare Health Services
Franklin Electric Co.
Freightliner Corp.
Gallo Winery, Inc. (E&J)
GEICO Corp.
GenAmerica Corp.
Genentech Inc.
General Electric Co.
Georgia Power Co.
Giant Eagle Inc.
Glickenhaus & Co.
Harsco Corp.
Hartford (The)
Hartmarx Corp.
Hershey Foods Corp.
Hoechst Marion Roussel, Inc.
Hoffmann-La Roche Inc.
Hofmann Co.
Humana, Inc.
Huntington Bancshares Inc.
Independent Stave Co.
International Business Machines Corp.
KPMG Peat Marwick LLP
LTV Corp.
Manor Care Health SVS, Inc.
Metropolitan Life Insurance Co.
National Life of Vermont
National Starch & Chemical Co.
New England Bio Labs
New England Financial
New York Mercantile Exchange
Nordson Corp.
Nortel
Northwest Natural Gas Co.
Ohio National Life Insurance Co.
Paine Webber
Pennzoil-Quaker State Co.
Procter & Gamble Co., Cosmetics Division
Reliant Energy Inc.
Reynolds Tobacco (R.J.)
Schering-Plough Corp.
Schlumberger Ltd. (USA)
Seagram & Sons, Inc. (Joseph E.)
Shell Oil Co.
Shelter Mutual Insurance Co.
Solo Cup Co.
Sonoco Products Co.
SunTrust Bank Atlanta
Tamko Roofing Products
Tektronix, Inc.
Telcordia Technologies
Texaco Inc.
Texas Instruments Inc.
Timken Co. (The)
Trustmark Insurance Co.
TRW Inc.
United Dominion Industries, Ltd.
United Parcel Service of America Inc.
Unocal Corp.
Valero Energy Corp.
Varian Medical Systems, Inc.
Vulcan Materials Co.
Winn-Dixie Stores Inc.
Witco Corp.
Wolverine World Wide
Zachry Co. (H.B.)
Zenith Electronics Corp.

Scholarship

AEGON U.S.A. Inc.
AGL Resources Inc.
AK Steel Corp.
Alabama Power Co.

Alcoa Inc.
Allstate Insurance Co.
Ameren Corp.
American Electric Power
American General Finance
American Honda Motor Co., Inc.
American Standard Inc.
AMR Corp.
Appleton Papers Inc.
Armstrong World Industries, Inc.
ASARCO Inc.
Ashland, Inc.
Avon Products, Inc.
Bandag, Inc.
Barden Corp.
Becton Dickinson & Co.
Bemis Manufacturing Co.
Blount International, Inc.
Blue Cross & Blue Shield of Iowa
Blue Cross & Blue Shield of Minnesota
Boeing Co.
Bourns, Inc.
BP Amoco Corp.
Bridgestone/Firestone, Inc.
Briggs & Stratton Corp.
Brown & Williamson Tobacco Corp.
Brunswick Corp.
Butler Manufacturing Co.
Cabot Corp.
Carolina Power & Light Co.
Carpenter Technology Corp.
Carrier Corp.
CBS Corp.
Cenex Harvest States
Central Maine Power Co.
Central National-Gottesman
Central Newspapers, Inc.
Central Soya Co.
Chemed Corp.
Chesapeake Corp.
Chubb Corp.
Cinergy Corp.
Circuit City Stores, Inc.
CIT Group, Inc. (The)
Citizens Bank-Flint
Clark Refining & Marketing
Clorox Co.
CNA
Coca-Cola Co.
Compass Bank
Consolidated Papers, Inc.
Continental Grain Co.
Cook Inlet Region
Copley Press, Inc.
Cummins Engine Co., Inc.
Danis Companies
Dayton Hudson
Dayton Power and Light Co.
DeKalb Genetics Corp.
Disney Co. (Walt)
Dixie Group, Inc. (The)
Donaldson Co., Inc.
Donnelley & Sons Co. (R.R.)
Dow Chemical Co.
DSM Copolymer
Duke Energy
Duriron Co., Inc.
Eastern Bank
Eastman Kodak Co.
Eckerd Corp.
Ensign-Bickford Industries
Equitable Resources, Inc.
Erving Industries
Ethyl Corp.
Excel Corp.
Farmers Group, Inc.
Fluor Corp.
Forest City Enterprises, Inc.
Fort Worth Star-Telegram Inc.
Fortis, Inc.
Fortune Brands, Inc.
Frontier Corp.
Gallo Winery, Inc. (E&J)
GEICO Corp.
GenAmerica Corp.
Genentech Inc.
Georgia-Pacific Corp.
Gerber Products Co.
Gillette Co.
Glaxo Wellcome Inc.
Goldman Sachs Group
Golub Corp.
Grace & Co. (W.R.)
Grede Foundries
Green Bay Packaging
Group Health Plan
Gulf Power Co.
Hannaford Brothers Co.
Harrah's Entertainment Inc.
Harsco Corp.
Hartford (The)
Hartmarx Corp.
Hawaiian Electric Co., Inc.
Heinz Co. (H.J.)
Hickory Tech Corp.
HON Industries Inc.
Housatonic Curtain Co.
Huffy Corp.
Humana, Inc.
Huntington Bancshares Inc.
Illinois Power Co.
Illinois Tool Works, Inc.
Intel Corp.
INTRUST Financial Corp.
Jeld-wen, Inc.
Johnson Controls Inc.
Johnson & Son (S.C.)
Kemper National Insurance Companies
Kerr-McGee Corp.
Kimball International, Inc.
Kingsbury Corp.
Koch Enterprises, Inc.
Koch Industries, Inc.
KPMG Peat Marwick LLP
Lehigh Portland Cement Co.
Lennox International, Inc.
LG&E Energy Corp.
Liberty Corp.
Litton Industries, Inc.
Loews Corp.
Louisiana Land & Exploration Co.
Louisiana-Pacific Corp.
LTV Corp.
Lubrizol Corp. (The)
Mallinckrodt Chemical, Inc.
Marshall & Ilsley Corp.
Mattel Inc.
McCormick & Co. Inc.
McDonald & Co. Securities, Inc.
McWane Inc.
Menasha Corp.
Mercantile Bank NA
Metropolitan Life Insurance Co.
MFA Inc.
Microsoft Corp.
Milacron, Inc.
Minnesota Mining & Manufacturing Co.
Motorola Inc.
MTS Systems Corp.
National Computer Systems, Inc.
National Presto Industries, Inc.
National Starch & Chemical Co.
New England Financial
New York Life Insurance Co.
New York Mercantile Exchange
New York Times Co.
Nike, Inc.
Northwest Natural Gas Co.
Nucor Corp.
Occidental Oil and Gas
Occidental Petroleum Corp.
OG&E Electric Services
Ohio National Life Insurance Co.
Orange & Rockland Utilities, Inc.
Orscheln Co.
Osborne Enterprises
Oshkosh B'Gosh, Inc.
Outboard Marine Corp.
Pacific Gas and Electric Co.
Parker Hannifin Corp.
PEMCO Corp.
Penn Mutual Life Insurance Co.
PepsiCo, Inc.
Phelps Dodge Corp.
Philips Electronics North America Corp.
Physicians Mutual Insurance Co.
Pieper Power Electric Co.
Pillsbury Co.
Portland General Electric Co.
Potlatch Corp.
Premark International Inc.
Premier Industrial Corp.
Procter & Gamble Co., Cosmetics Division
Providence Journal-Bulletin Co.
Public Service Electric & Gas Co.
Publix Supermarkets
Pulitzer Publishing Co.
Questar Corp.
Rayonier Inc.
Reader's Digest Association, Inc. (The)
Regis Corp.
Reilly Industries, Inc.
ReliaStar Financial Corp.
Reynolds Tobacco (R.J.)
Rohm & Haas Co.
Rouse Co.
Rubbermaid Inc.
Salomon Smith Barney
S&T Bancorp
SBC Communications Inc.
Schering-Plough Corp.
Schlumberger Ltd. (USA)
Schwebel Baking Co.
Sentry Insurance, A Mutual Co.
Shaklee Corp.
Shelter Mutual Insurance Co.
Shoney's Inc.
Sierra Pacific Industries
Simplot Co. (J.R.)
Smith Corp. (A.O.)
Solo Cup Co.
Sonoco Products Co.
Sony Electronics
State Farm Mutual Automobile Insurance Co.
Stone Container Corp.
Stonecutter Mills Corp.
Storage Technology Corp.
Stride Rite Corp.
Sverdrup Corp.
Tektronix, Inc.
Telcordia Technologies
Temple-Inland Inc.
TENNANT Co.
Tenneco Packaging
Texaco Inc.
Textron Inc.
Times Mirror Co.
Timken Co. (The)
TJX Companies, Inc.
Toledo Blade Co.
True Oil Co.
TRW Inc.
Ukrop's Super Markets
Union Camp Corp.
United Distillers & Vintners North America
United Parcel Service of America Inc.
United Wisconsin Services
Unocal Corp.
UnumProvident
USAA Life Insurance Co.
USG Corp.
UST Inc.
Valspar Corp.
Varian Medical Systems, Inc.
Vulcan Materials Co.
Waffle House Inc.
Wal-Mart Stores, Inc.
Waldbaum's Supermarkets, Inc.
West Co. Inc.
Western & Southern Life Insurance Co.
Whirlpool Corp.
Williams
Winn-Dixie Stores Inc.
Wisconsin Public Service Corp.
Witco Corp.
Wolverine World Wide
Wyman-Gordon Co.
York Federal Savings & Loan Association
Zenith Electronics Corp.

Seed Money

AGL Resources Inc.
Alabama Power Co.
Alcoa Inc.
American Honda Motor Co., Inc.
American Retail Group
Andersons Inc.
Bandag, Inc.
Bank of America
Beckman Coulter, Inc.
Becton Dickinson & Co.
Boeing Co.
Boston Edison Co.
Bridgestone/Firestone, Inc.
Cabot Corp.
Central Maine Power Co.
Chemed Corp.
Chicago Sun-Times, Inc.
CIBC Oppenheimer
Cinergy Corp.
Citizens Bank-Flint
Cummins Engine Co., Inc.
Dain Bosworth Inc.
Dollar General Corp.
Donnelley & Sons Co. (R.R.)
Ensign-Bickford Industries
FedEx Corp.
Freightliner Corp.
GATX Corp.
General Atlantic Partners II LP
Glaxo Wellcome Inc.
Group Health Plan
Hallmark Cards Inc.
Hasbro, Inc.
Hitachi America Ltd.
Hoffmann-La Roche Inc.
Hunt Manufacturing Co.
Huntington Bancshares Inc.
Jeld-wen, Inc.
Johnson & Son (S.C.)
Kingsbury Corp.
Kroger Co.
Leigh Fibers, Inc.
Lincoln Electric Co.
Lotus Development Corp.
Manor Care Health SVS, Inc.
Metropolitan Life Insurance Co.
New England Bio Labs
New York Mercantile Exchange
Northern Trust Co.
Northwest Natural Gas Co.
Orange & Rockland Utilities, Inc.
PNC Bank Kentucky Inc.
Polaroid Corp.
Providence Journal-Bulletin Co.
Public Service Electric & Gas Co.
Reliant Energy Inc.
Rohm & Haas Co.
Rouse Co.
Schering-Plough Corp.
Simpson Investment Co.
Stanley Works (The)
SunTrust Bank Atlanta
Telcordia Technologies
Tesoro Hawaii
UnumProvident
Valero Energy Corp.
Varian Medical Systems, Inc.
Vulcan Materials Co.
Woodward Governor Co.
Wyman-Gordon Co.

FUNDERS BY NONMONETARY SUPPORT TYPE

The following index classifies companies by the type of non-financial support they generally fund. Within each nonmonetary type of support, company names are listed in alphabetical order.

Cause-related Marketing & Promotion

Loaned Employees

Loaned Executives

BankBoston-Connecticut Region
BankBoston Corp.
Bell Atlantic Corp.
BellSouth Corp.
Blue Cross & Blue Shield of Minnesota
Brown Shoe Co., Inc.
Browning-Ferris Industries Inc.
Burger King Corp.
Burlington Industries, Inc.
Cabot Corp.
Cargill Inc.
Carrier Corp.
Caterpillar Inc.
Central & South West Services
CGU Insurance
Church & Dwight Co., Inc.
Cincinnati Bell Inc.
Citizens Bank-Flint
CLARCOR Inc.
Cleveland-Cliffs, Inc.
Colonial Life & Accident Insurance Co.
Comerica Inc.
Commercial Intertech Corp.
Conectiv
Corning Inc.
Cummins Engine Co., Inc.
Dana Corp.
Deere & Co.
Detroit Edison Co.
Dexter Corp.
Diebold, Inc.
Dominion Resources, Inc.
Donnelley & Sons Co. (R.R.)
Dow Chemical Co.
Duquesne Light Co.
Duracell International
Eckerd Corp.
Edison International
EDS Corp.
Employers Mutual Casualty Co.
Equifax Inc.
Fabri-Kal Corp.
FedEx Corp.
Ferro Corp.
First Security Bank of Idaho NA
First Tennessee National Corp.
Florida Power Corp.
Forest City Enterprises, Inc.
Fortis Insurance Co.
Freeport-McMoRan Inc.
Frito-Lay, Inc.
Frost National Bank
GenCorp
General Mills, Inc.
Georgia Power Co.
Gillette Co.
Glaxo Wellcome Inc.
Grace & Co. (W.R.)
Gulfstream Aerospace Corp.
Hancock Financial Services (John)
Hartford (The)
Hawaiian Electric Co., Inc.
Hensel Phelps Construction Co.
Hershey Foods Corp.
Huntington Bancshares Inc.
IBP
Industrial Bank of Japan Trust Co. (New York)
International Business Machines Corp.
INTRUST Financial Corp.
Johnson & Son (S.C.)
Jostens, Inc.
Journal Communications, Inc.
Kiewit Sons' Inc. (Peter)
Kmart Corp.
Knight Ridder
Land O'Lakes, Inc.
Liberty Corp.
Lincoln Financial Group
LTV Corp.
Lubrizol Corp. (The)
Manufacturers & Traders Trust Co.
Maritz Inc.
Massachusetts Mutual Life Insurance Co.
McDonald & Co. Securities, Inc.
Mellon Financial Corp.
Memphis Light Gas & Water Division
Mercantile Bank NA
Metropolitan Life Insurance Co.
Mid-America Bank of Louisville
Minnesota Mutual Life Insurance Co.
Mitsubishi Electric America
Morrison Knudsen Corp.
Murphy Oil Corp.
Nalco Chemical Co.
National City Bank of Columbus
National Computer Systems, Inc.
National Fuel Gas Distribution Corp.
Nationwide Insurance Co.
New England Financial
Newport News Shipbuilding
NICOR Gas Co.
Nortel
Northern Indiana Public Service Co.
Northern States Power Co.
Northern Trust Co.
Northwest Bank Nebraska, NA
Northwest Natural Gas Co.
Novartis Corporation
Nucor Corp.
OG&E Electric Services
Old National Bank Evansville
Pacific Gas and Electric Co.
Patagonia Inc.
PECO Energy Co.
Penn Mutual Life Insurance Co.
Peoples Energy Corp.
Pharmacia & Upjohn, Inc.
Physicians Mutual Insurance Co.
Pioneer Natural Resources
Portland General Electric Co.
Procter & Gamble Co.
Promus Hotel Corp.
Provident Companies, Inc.
Prudential Insurance Co. of America
Public Service Electric & Gas Co.
Quaker Chemical Corp.
Questar Corp.
Ralston Purina Co.
Regions Financial Corp.
Reliant Energy Inc.
Reliant Energy Minnegasco
ReliaStar Financial Corp.
Reynolds & Reynolds Co.
Rochester Gas & Electric Corp.
Rohm & Haas Co.
SCANA Corp.
Scientific-Atlanta, Inc.
Shell Oil Co.
Southern New England Telephone Co.
Southwest Gas Corp.
Sprint Corp.
State Street Bank & Trust Co.
Student Loan Marketing Association
SunTrust Bank Atlanta
Susquehanna-Pfaltzgraff Co.
Tenneco Automotive
Texaco Inc.
Texas Instruments Inc.
Thomasville Furniture Industries Inc.
Thompson Co. (J. Walter)
Trustmark Insurance Co.
Trustmark National Bank
TRW Inc.
United Parcel Service of America Inc.
Valero Energy Corp.
Varian Medical Systems, Inc.
Vulcan Materials Co.
Wachovia Bank of North Carolina NA
Washington Mutual, Inc.
Weyerhaeuser Co.
WICOR, Inc.
Williams
Wyman-Gordon Co.

In-kind Services

Advanced Micro Devices, Inc.
AEGON U.S.A. Inc.
Aetna, Inc.
AGL Resources Inc.
Air Products and Chemicals, Inc.
Alabama Power Co.
Alaska Airlines, Inc.
Albertson's Inc.
Allmerica Financial Corp.
Allstate Insurance Co.
Alyeska Pipeline Service Co.
America West Airlines, Inc.
American Electric Power
American General Corp.
American Stock Exchange, Inc.
Ameritech Illinois
Ameritech Michigan
AmerUS Group
AMP Inc.
AMR Corp.
Arizona Public Service Co.
ASARCO Inc.
Ashland, Inc.
AT&T Corp.
Atlantic Richfield Co.
Avista Corporation
Avon Products, Inc.
Bank One Corp.
BankBoston-Connecticut Region
BankBoston Corp.
Bausch & Lomb Inc.
Bechtel Group, Inc.
Becton Dickinson & Co.
Bell Atlantic Corp.-West Virginia
BellSouth Telecommunications
Bestfoods
Bethlehem Steel Corp.
Blue Cross & Blue Shield of Minnesota
Boeing Co.
Borden, Inc.
Boston Globe (The)
Branch Banking & Trust Co.
Brooklyn Union
Brown Shoe Co., Inc.
Browning-Ferris Industries Inc.
Burger King Corp.
Business Men's Assurance Co. of America
Cabot Corp.
California Bank & Trust
Campbell Soup Co.
Carolina Power & Light Co.
Carpenter Technology Corp.
Carrier Corp.
Caterpillar Inc.
CBS Corp.
Cenex Harvest States
Central Maine Power Co.
CertainTeed Corp.
Chase Manhattan Bank, NA
Chemed Corp.
Chicago Sun-Times, Inc.
Church & Dwight Co., Inc.
Cincinnati Bell Inc.
Cinergy Corp.
Citizens Bank-Flint
Clorox Co.
CNA
Colgate-Palmolive Co.
Colonial Life & Accident Insurance Co.
Comerica Inc.
Commercial Federal Corp.
Commonwealth Edison Co.
Compaq Computer Corp.
Conectiv
Conoco, Inc.
Constellation Energy Group, Inc.
Consumers Energy Co.
Cook Inlet Region
Cooper Industries, Inc.
Coors Brewing Co.
Cox Enterprises Inc.
CPI Corp.
Cyprus Amax Minerals Co.
Dana Corp.
Dayton Power and Light Co.
Deere & Co.
DeKalb Genetics Corp.
Detroit Edison Co.
Dominion Resources, Inc.
Dow Chemical Co.
Duke Energy
Duquesne Light Co.
Duracell International
Ecolab Inc.
Edison International
EDS Corp.
Equitable Resources, Inc.
European American Bank
Federated Department Stores, Inc.
FedEx Corp.
Ferro Corp.
Fireman's Fund Insurance Co.
First Security Bank of Idaho NA
First Tennessee National Corp.
First Union Bank
First Union National Bank, NA
FirstEnergy Corp.
Fluor Corp.
Fortis Insurance Co.
Fortune Brands, Inc.
Freeport-McMoRan Inc.
Freightliner Corp.
Frontier Corp.
Frost National Bank
Fuji Bank & Trust Co.
Fuller Co. (H.B.)
Gannett Co., Inc.
Gap, Inc.
Gates Rubber Corp.
GATX Corp.
GEICO Corp.
GenCorp
General Motors Corp.
Georgia Power Co.
Giant Food Inc.
Gillette Co.
Glaxo Wellcome Inc.
GPU Inc.
Grace & Co. (W.R.)
Hallmark Cards Inc.
Hancock Financial Services (John)
Harris Trust & Savings Bank
Hartford (The)
Hensel Phelps Construction Co.
Hitachi America Ltd.
Hoechst Marion Roussel, Inc.
Hoffmann-La Roche Inc.
Home Depot, Inc.
Honeywell International Inc.
Hunt Oil Co.
Huntington Bancshares Inc.
Illinois Power Co.
Illinois Tool Works, Inc.
Industrial Bank of Japan Trust Co. (New York)
Informix Software, Inc.
International Business Machines Corp.
International Paper Co.
Invacare Corp.
Johnson Controls Inc.
Johnson & Son (S.C.)
Jostens, Inc.
Journal Communications, Inc.
Kelly Services
Kemper National Insurance Companies
Kerr-McGee Corp.
Key Bank of Cleveland
Kingsbury Corp.
Kmart Corp.
Kohler Co.
Kroger Co.
Landmark Communications Inc.
Little, Inc. (Arthur D.)
Lotus Development Corp.
LTV Corp.
Mallinckrodt Chemical, Inc.
Manufacturers & Traders Trust Co.
Maritz Inc.
Marriott International Inc.
Massachusetts Mutual Life Insurance Co.
MBIA Inc.
McDonald & Co. Securities, Inc.
MCI WorldCom, Inc.
Mead Corp.
Mellon Financial Corp.
Memphis Light Gas & Water Division
Merrill Lynch & Co., Inc.
Metropolitan Life Insurance Co.
Michigan Consolidated Gas Co.
Minnesota Mining & Manufacturing Co.

Minnesota Mutual Life Insurance Co.
Mitsubishi Electric America
MONY Group (The)
Morrison Knudsen Corp.
Nabisco Group Holdings
National City Bank of Cleveland
National City Bank of Columbus
National City Bank of Pennsylvania
National Life of Vermont
Nationwide Insurance Co.
NCR Corp.
NEC America, Inc.
New Century Energies
New England Financial
New York State Electric & Gas Corp.
Newport News Shipbuilding
NICOR Gas Co.
Nortel
Northeast Utilities
Northern Indiana Public Service Co.
Northern States Power Co.
Northern Trust Co.
Northwest Airlines, Inc.
Northwest Bank Nebraska, NA
Northwest Natural Gas Co.
Novartis Corporation
Nucor Corp.
Occidental Oil and Gas
Old National Bank Evansville
Owens Corning
Owens-Illinois Inc.
Pacific Gas and Electric Co.
Pacific Mutual Life Insurance Co.
Pan-American Life Insurance Co.
Patagonia Inc.
PECO Energy Co.
Penn Mutual Life Insurance Co.
Penney Co., Inc. (J.C.)
Peoples Bank
Peoples Energy Corp.
Pharmacia & Upjohn, Inc.
Phelps Dodge Corp.
Philip Morris Companies Inc.
Physicians Mutual Insurance Co.
Pillsbury Co.
Pioneer Hi-Bred International, Inc.
Pitney Bowes Inc.
PNC Bank
Portland General Electric Co.
PPG Industries, Inc.
Promus Hotel Corp.
Providence Journal-Bulletin Co.
Provident Mutual Life Insurance Co.
Prudential Insurance Co. of America
Prudential Securities Inc.
Public Service Electric & Gas Co.
Questar Corp.
Ralph's Grocery Co.
Ralston Purina Co.
Rayonier Inc.
Regions Financial Corp.
Reliant Energy Inc.
Reliant Energy Minnegasco
ReliaStar Financial Corp.
Reynolds & Reynolds Co.
Reynolds Tobacco (R.J.)
Rockwell International Corp.
Rohm & Haas Co.
Rouse Co.
Royal & SunAlliance USA, Inc.
Ryder System, Inc.
Schering-Plough Corp.
Schwab & Co., Inc. (Charles)
Scientific-Atlanta, Inc.
Seaway Food Town, Inc.
Security Benefit Life Insurance Co.
Sempra Energy
Sentinel Communications Co.
Shaklee Corp.
Shoney's Inc.
Sierra Pacific Resources
Sotheby's Inc.
Southern Co. Services Inc.
Southern New England Telephone Co.
Southwest Gas Corp.
Sovereign Bank
Springs Industries, Inc.
Sprint Corp.
Star Bank NA
State Farm Mutual Automobile Insurance Co.
State Street Bank & Trust Co.
Steelcase Inc.
Storage Technology Corp.
Student Loan Marketing Association
Sun Microsystems Inc.
SuperValu, Inc.
Susquehanna-Pfaltzgraff Co.
Telcordia Technologies
Tenneco Automotive
Texaco Inc.
Texas Gas Transmission Corp.
Thompson Co. (J. Walter)
Times Mirror Co.
TJX Companies, Inc.
Torchmark Corp.
Toro Co.
Transamerica Corp.
Trustmark Insurance Co.
Trustmark National Bank
TRW Inc.
Tucson Electric Power Co.
Union Carbide Corp.
Union Planters Corp.
Unisys Corp.
U.S. Bancorp Piper Jaffray
United States Trust Co. of New York
United Technologies Corp.
Universal Foods Corp.
Universal Studios
UnumProvident
Valero Energy Corp.
Varian Medical Systems, Inc.
Vulcan Materials Co.
Wal-Mart Stores, Inc.
Walgreen Co.
Warner-Lambert Co.
Washington Mutual, Inc.
Washington Trust Bank
Waste Management Inc.
Wausau Insurance Companies
Wells Fargo & Co.
WICOR, Inc.
Williams
Yellow Corp.
Zenith Electronics Corp.

Workplace Solicitation

7-Eleven, Inc.
ABB Inc.
AGL Resources Inc.
AK Steel Corp.
Alabama Power Co.
Allianz Life Insurance Co. of North America
Allmerica Financial Corp.
AMP Inc.
Ball Corp.
Bandag, Inc.
Bank One, Texas, NA
BankBoston-Connecticut Region
Boston Edison Co.
Brown Shoe Co., Inc.
Brown & Williamson Tobacco Corp.
Burger King Corp.
Business Men's Assurance Co. of America
Campbell Soup Co.
CertainTeed Corp.
Cincinnati Bell Inc.
Cinergy Corp.
Cleveland-Cliffs, Inc.
Clorox Co.
Conectiv
Dayton Hudson
Detroit Edison Co.
Diebold, Inc.
Duriron Co., Inc.
Ebsco Industries, Inc.
EDS Corp.
First Tennessee National Corp.
Fortis Insurance Co.
GATX Corp.
Gillette Co.
Hawaiian Electric Co., Inc.
Kiewit Sons' Inc. (Peter)
Liberty Mutual Insurance Group
LTV Corp.
Mid-America Bank of Louisville
Minnesota Mutual Life Insurance Co.
MONY Group (The)
National City Bank of Columbus
National Computer Systems, Inc.
National Fuel Gas Distribution Corp.
New England Financial
NICOR Gas Co.
Nike, Inc.
Northeast Utilities
Novartis Corporation
Ohio National Life Insurance Co.
PACCAR Inc.
PacifiCorp
Patagonia Inc.
Penn Mutual Life Insurance Co.
Physicians Mutual Insurance Co.
Pitney Bowes Inc.
Promus Hotel Corp.
Ralston Purina Co.
Regions Financial Corp.
Reliant Energy Minnegasco
Reynolds & Reynolds Co.
Reynolds Tobacco (R.J.)
Ryder System, Inc.
Saint Paul Companies Inc.
Scientific-Atlanta, Inc.
Security Life of Denver Insurance Co.
Sempra Energy
Sovereign Bank
Stanley Works (The)
Stone & Webster Inc.
Sun Microsystems Inc.
Sunoco Inc.
SunTrust Bank Atlanta
Susquehanna-Pfaltzgraff Co.
Thompson Co. (J. Walter)
TJX Companies, Inc.
Union Carbide Corp.
Union Planters Corp.
United Parcel Service of America Inc.
UnumProvident
US Bank, Washington
Vulcan Materials Co.
Wal-Mart Stores, Inc.
Waste Management Inc.
Weyerhaeuser Co.
Wiley & Sons (John)
Williams
Xerox Corp.
Yellow Corp.

Donated Equipment

Advanced Micro Devices, Inc.
AFLAC Inc.
AGL Resources Inc.
Air Products and Chemicals, Inc.
Alexander & Baldwin, Inc.
AlliedSignal Inc.
Allmerica Financial Corp.
Allstate Insurance Co.
Alyeska Pipeline Service Co.
Ameren Corp.
American Electric Power
American General Corp.
American United Life Insurance Co.
Ameritech Illinois
Ameritech Ohio
AmerUS Group
Amgen, Inc.
Analog Devices, Inc.
APL Ltd.
Apple Computer, Inc.
Appleton Papers Inc.
Archer-Daniels-Midland Co.
Arizona Public Service Co.
ASARCO Inc.
Ashland, Inc.
Atlantic Richfield Co.
Avista Corporation
Avon Products, Inc.
Ball Corp.
Bank of America
Bank One Corp.
Bank One, Texas-Houston Office
BankBoston-Connecticut Region
BankBoston Corp.
Battelle Memorial Institute
Beckman Coulter, Inc.
Becton Dickinson & Co.
Bell Atlantic Corp.
BellSouth Telecommunications
Berwind Group
Bestfoods
Bethlehem Steel Corp.
Blue Cross & Blue Shield of Minnesota
Boeing Co.
Boise Cascade Corp.
Boston Edison Co.
Bourns, Inc.
BP Amoco Corp.
Branch Banking & Trust Co.
Brooklyn Union
Brown Shoe Co., Inc.
Brown & Williamson Tobacco Corp.
Burger King Corp.
Burlington Northern Santa Fe Corp.
Cabot Corp.
Caesar's World, Inc.
California Bank & Trust
California Federal Bank, FSB
Campbell Soup Co.
Cargill Inc.
Carolina Power & Light Co.
Caterpillar Inc.
Central Maine Power Co.
CertainTeed Corp.
Chase Bank of Texas
Chase Manhattan Bank, NA
Chemed Corp.
Chevron Corp.
Church & Dwight Co., Inc.
CIBC Oppenheimer
CIGNA Corp.
Cincinnati Bell Inc.
Cinergy Corp.
Citibank Corp.
Citizens Bank-Flint
Citizens Financial Group, Inc.
Clorox Co.
CNA
Coachmen Industries, Inc.
Coca-Cola Co.
Colgate-Palmolive Co.
Colonial Life & Accident Insurance Co.
Comerica Inc.
Commercial Federal Corp.
Commonwealth Edison Co.
Compaq Computer Corp.
Cone Mills Corp.
Conoco, Inc.
Consolidated Natural Gas Co.
Constellation Energy Group, Inc.
Cooper Industries, Inc.
Cooper Tire & Rubber Co.
Coors Brewing Co.
Cox Enterprises Inc.
Cummins Engine Co., Inc.
CUNA Mutual Group
Cyprus Amax Minerals Co.
DaimlerChrysler Corp.
Dana Corp.
Dayton Power and Light Co.
Detroit Edison Co.
Diebold, Inc.
Dominion Resources, Inc.
Domino's Pizza Inc.
Donnelley & Sons Co. (R.R.)
Dow Chemical Co.
du Pont de Nemours & Co. (E.I.)
Duke Energy
Duquesne Light Co.
Duracell International
Eastman Kodak Co.
Edison International
EDS Corp.
Edwards Enterprise Software (J.D.)
Employers Mutual Casualty Co.
Ensign-Bickford Industries
Equitable Resources, Inc.
Ernst & Young, LLP
Ethyl Corp.

European American Bank
Federated Department Stores, Inc.
FedEx Corp.
Fireman's Fund Insurance Co.
First Maryland Bancorp
First Security Bank of Idaho NA
First Tennessee National Corp.
First Union National Bank, NA
First Union Securities, Inc.
FirstEnergy Corp.
Florida Power Corp.
Fluor Corp.
Ford Motor Co.
Fortis Insurance Co.
Fortune Brands, Inc.
Fox Entertainment Group
Franklin Electric Co.
Freddie Mac
Freeport-McMoRan Inc.
Freightliner Corp.
Frost National Bank
Fuji Bank & Trust Co.
Fuller Co. (H.B.)
Gap, Inc.
GATX Corp.
GEICO Corp.
GenCorp
General Electric Co.
General Motors Corp.
General Reinsurance Corp.
Georgia-Pacific Corp.
Georgia Power Co.
Giant Food Inc.
Gillette Co.
Glaxo Wellcome Inc.
Goodrich Aerospace - Aerostructures Group (B.F.)
GPU Inc.
Grace & Co. (W.R.)
Graco, Inc.
GTE Corp.
Halliburton Co.
Hallmark Cards Inc.
Harrah's Entertainment Inc.
Harris Corp.
Harris Trust & Savings Bank
Hartford (The)
Heller Financial, Inc.
Hercules Inc.
Hewlett-Packard Co.
Hitachi America Ltd.
Home Depot, Inc.
Honeywell International Inc.
Household International Inc.
Hughes Electronics Corp.
Hunt Oil Co.
Huntington Bancshares Inc.
IBP
Idaho Power Co.
Illinois Power Co.
Illinois Tool Works, Inc.
Industrial Bank of Japan Trust Co. (New York)
Intel Corp.
International Business Machines Corp.
INTRUST Financial Corp.
Invacare Corp.
Johnson Controls Inc.
Johnson & Son (S.C.)
Journal Communications, Inc.
JSJ Corp.
Kelly Services
Kerr-McGee Corp.
Kingsbury Corp.
Kohler Co.
KPMG Peat Marwick LLP
Laclede Gas Co.
Liberty Corp.
Liberty Mutual Insurance Group
Lincoln Electric Co.
Lincoln Financial Group
Louisiana-Pacific Corp.
LTV Corp.
Lubrizol Corp. (The)
Mallinckrodt Chemical, Inc.
Manufacturers & Traders Trust Co.
Manulife Financial
Maritz Inc.
Marriott International Inc.
Massachusetts Mutual Life Insurance Co.
Mazda North American Operations
MBIA Inc.
McDonald & Co. Securities, Inc.
MCI WorldCom, Inc.
Mead Corp.
Medtronic, Inc.
Mellon Financial Corp.
Memphis Light Gas & Water Division
Merrill Lynch & Co., Inc.
Metropolitan Life Insurance Co.
Michigan Consolidated Gas Co.
Mid-America Bank of Louisville
Milacron, Inc.
Millipore Corp.
Minnesota Mining & Manufacturing Co.
Mitsubishi Electric America
Monsanto Co.
Montana Power Co.
Montgomery Ward & Co., Inc.
MONY Group (The)
Morgan & Co. Inc. (J.P.)
Morgan Stanley Dean Witter & Co.
Morrison Knudsen Corp.
Morton International Inc.
MTS Systems Corp.
Mutual of Omaha Insurance Co.
Nabisco Group Holdings
Nalco Chemical Co.
National City Bank of Columbus
National City Bank of Pennsylvania
National City Corp.
National Computer Systems, Inc.
National Life of Vermont
Nationwide Insurance Co.
New Century Energies
New England Bio Labs
New England Financial
New Jersey Natural Gas Co.
New York Mercantile Exchange
New York State Electric & Gas Corp.
Niagara Mohawk Holdings Inc.
NICOR Gas Co.
Nordson Corp.
Norfolk Southern Corp.
Nortel
Northern States Power Co.
Northern Trust Co.
Northrop Grumman Corp.
Northwest Bank Nebraska, NA
Northwest Natural Gas Co.
Novartis Corporation
Nucor Corp.
Occidental Oil and Gas
Ohio National Life Insurance Co.
Old National Bank Evansville
Orange & Rockland Utilities, Inc.
Overnite Transportation Co.
Owens-Illinois Inc.
Pacific Gas and Electric Co.
Pacific Mutual Life Insurance Co.
PacifiCorp
Pan-American Life Insurance Co.
PECO Energy Co.
Penn Mutual Life Insurance Co.
Penney Co., Inc. (J.C.)
Peoples Bank
Peoples Energy Corp.
Philip Morris Companies Inc.
Physicians Mutual Insurance Co.
Pillsbury Co.
Pioneer Group
Pioneer Natural Resources
PNC Bank
Portland General Electric Co.
Premark International Inc.
Principal Financial Group
Procter & Gamble Co.
Promus Hotel Corp.
Providence Journal-Bulletin Co.
Provident Companies, Inc.
Prudential Insurance Co. of America
Public Service Electric & Gas Co.
Quanex Corp.
Questar Corp.
Ralph's Grocery Co.
Ralston Purina Co.
Reebok International Ltd.
Regions Financial Corp.
REI-Recreational Equipment, Inc.
Reliant Energy Inc.
Reliant Energy Minnegasco
ReliaStar Financial Corp.
Reynolds Metals Co.
Reynolds & Reynolds Co.
Reynolds Tobacco (R.J.)
Rockwell International Corp.
Rohm & Haas Co.
Rouse Co.
Royal & SunAlliance USA, Inc.
Ryder System, Inc.
SAFECO Corp.
Saint Paul Companies Inc.
SCANA Corp.
Schering-Plough Corp.
Schwab & Co., Inc. (Charles)
Scientific-Atlanta, Inc.
Seaway Food Town, Inc.
Security Benefit Life Insurance Co.
Security Life of Denver Insurance Co.
Sega of America Inc.
Sempra Energy
Sentinel Communications Co.
Shaklee Corp.
Shaw Industries Inc.
SmithKline Beecham Corp.
Sonoco Products Co.
Southern Co. Services Inc.
Southern New England Telephone Co.
Sovereign Bank
Springs Industries, Inc.
Sprint Corp.
Square D Co.
Star Bank NA
State Farm Mutual Automobile Insurance Co.
State Street Bank & Trust Co.
Storage Technology Corp.
Stride Rite Corp.
Student Loan Marketing Association
SunTrust Bank Atlanta
Susquehanna-Pfaltzgraff Co.
Target Corp.
Tektronix, Inc.
Telcordia Technologies
TENNANT Co.
Tenneco Automotive
Tesoro Hawaii
Texaco Inc.
Texas Gas Transmission Corp.
Texas Instruments Inc.
Thomasville Furniture Industries Inc.
Times Mirror Co.
TJX Companies, Inc.
Torchmark Corp.
Toro Co.
Toyota Motor Sales U.S.A., Inc.
Transamerica Corp.
Trustmark Insurance Co.
Trustmark National Bank
Tucson Electric Power Co.
Unilever United States, Inc.
Union Carbide Corp.
Union Planters Corp.
U.S. Bancorp
U.S. Bancorp Piper Jaffray
United States Trust Co. of New York
Universal Foods Corp.
Universal Studios
UnumProvident
US Bank, Washington
Valero Energy Corp.
Varian Medical Systems, Inc.
Vulcan Materials Co.
Wal-Mart Stores, Inc.
Warner-Lambert Co.
Washington Mutual, Inc.
Wausau Insurance Companies
Wells Fargo & Co.
Western Resources Inc.
Weyerhaeuser Co.
WICOR, Inc.
Wisconsin Public Service Corp.
Xerox Corp.
Zenith Electronics Corp.

Donated Products

7-Eleven, Inc.
Abbott Laboratories
Advanced Micro Devices, Inc.
AFLAC Inc.
Agrilink Foods, Inc.
Albany International Corp.
Albertson's Inc.
Alcon Laboratories, Inc.
Alexander & Baldwin, Inc.
AlliedSignal Inc.
America West Airlines, Inc.
Ameritech Michigan
Amgen, Inc.
AMP Inc.
AMR Corp.
Analog Devices, Inc.
Anheuser-Busch Companies, Inc.
Appleton Papers Inc.
Ashland, Inc.
AT&T Corp.
Autodesk Inc.
Avery Dennison Corp.
Avon Products, Inc.
Ball Corp.
Bank One, Texas-Houston Office
Bank One, Texas, NA
BankBoston-Connecticut Region
Bard, Inc. (C.R.)
Barry Corp. (R.G.)
Baxter International Inc.
Bayer Corp.
Bean, Inc. (L.L.)
Becton Dickinson & Co.
BellSouth Telecommunications
Ben & Jerry's Homemade Inc.
Bestfoods
Bethlehem Steel Corp.
Binney & Smith Inc.
Boeing Co.
Boise Cascade Corp.
Borden, Inc.
Bowater Inc.
BP Amoco Corp.
Branch Banking & Trust Co.
Briggs & Stratton Corp.
Bristol-Myers Squibb Co.
Brooklyn Union
Brown Shoe Co., Inc.
Burger King Corp.
Burlington Industries, Inc.
Business Men's Assurance Co. of America
Butler Manufacturing Co.
Cabot Corp.
Cadence Designs Systems, Inc.
Caesar's World, Inc.
Campbell Soup Co.
Cargill Inc.
Castle & Cooke Properties Inc.
Centex Corp.
Central Maine Power Co.
CertainTeed Corp.
Champion International Corp.
Church & Dwight Co., Inc.
Circuit City Stores, Inc.
Clark Refining & Marketing
Clorox Co.
Coachmen Industries, Inc.
Colgate-Palmolive Co.
Constellation Energy Group, Inc.
Cooper Industries, Inc.
Cooper Tire & Rubber Co.
Coors Brewing Co.
CPI Corp.
Crane & Co., Inc.
Cummins Engine Co., Inc.
Curtis Industries, Inc. (Helene)
DaimlerChrysler Corp.
Delta Air Lines, Inc.
Deluxe Corp.
Diebold, Inc.
Dollar General Corp.
Dow Chemical Co.
Dreyer's Grand Ice Cream

Duracell International
Eastman Kodak Co.
Eaton Corp.
Ebsco Industries, Inc.
EDS Corp.
EMI Music Publishing
Ernst & Young, LLP
Excel Corp.
FedEx Corp.
First Tennessee National Corp.
Ford Motor Co.
Fort James Corp.
Fortune Brands, Inc.
Fox Entertainment Group
Franklin Electric Co.
Franklin Mint (The)
Freightliner Corp.
Frito-Lay, Inc.
Frost National Bank
Fuller Co. (H.B.)
Gap, Inc.
GenCorp
General Electric Co.
General Mills, Inc.
General Motors Corp.
Georgia-Pacific Corp.
Georgia Power Co.
Gerber Products Co.
Giant Food Inc.
Gillette Co.
Glaxo Wellcome Inc.
Grace & Co. (W.R.)
Gucci America Inc.
Gulfstream Aerospace Corp.
Halliburton Co.
Hallmark Cards Inc.
Hancock Financial Services (John)
Hannaford Brothers Co.
Harcourt General, Inc.
Harley-Davidson Co.
Harrah's Entertainment Inc.
Harris Trust & Savings Bank
Hasbro, Inc.
Hershey Foods Corp.
Hewlett-Packard Co.
Hoechst Marion Roussel, Inc.
Home Depot, Inc.
Honeywell International Inc.
Houghton Mifflin Co.
Huffy Corp.
Hunt Manufacturing Co.
IBP
Informix Software, Inc.
International Business Machines Corp.
International Multifoods Corp.
International Paper Co.
Invacare Corp.
Johnson & Johnson
Johnson & Son (S.C.)
Jostens, Inc.
Kelly Services
Kendall International, Inc.
Kimberly-Clark Corp.
Kingsbury Corp.
Kmart Corp.
Kohler Co.
Kraft Foods, Inc.
Kroger Co.
Laclede Gas Co.
Land O'Lakes, Inc.
Lilly & Co. (Eli)
Lincoln Electric Co.
Liz Claiborne, Inc.
Loews Corp.
Lotus Development Corp.
Louisiana-Pacific Corp.
Maritz Inc.
Marriott International Inc.
Matsushita Electric Corp. of America
Mattel Inc.
Maybelline, Inc.
Maytag Corp.
Mazda North American Operations
McCormick & Co. Inc.
McDonald & Co. Securities, Inc.
McGraw-Hill Companies, Inc.
MCI WorldCom, Inc.
McKesson-HBOC Corp.
Mead Corp.
Medtronic, Inc.
Meijer, Inc.
Merck & Co.
Mervyn's California
Microsoft Corp.
Mid-America Bank of Louisville
Millipore Corp.
Minnesota Mining & Manufacturing Co.
Mitsubishi Electric America
Monsanto Co.
Montgomery Ward & Co., Inc.
Nabisco Group Holdings
National Computer Systems, Inc.
National Fuel Gas Distribution Corp.
Nestle U.S.A. Inc.
Newport News Shipbuilding
Nike, Inc.
Nordson Corp.
Norfolk Southern Corp.
Northwest Airlines, Inc.
Northwest Natural Gas Co.
Norton Co.
Novartis Corporation
Nucor Corp.
Owens Corning
Pacific Gas and Electric Co.
Patagonia Inc.
Penney Co., Inc. (J.C.)
Pentair Inc.
PepsiCo, Inc.
Pfizer Inc.
Pharmacia & Upjohn, Inc.
Phelps Dodge Corp.
Philip Morris Companies Inc.
Philips Electronics North America Corp.
Pillsbury Co.
Pioneer Hi-Bred International, Inc.
Playboy Enterprises Inc.
PNC Bank
Polaroid Corp.
Portland General Electric Co.
Procter & Gamble Co.
Promus Hotel Corp.
Public Service Electric & Gas Co.
Quanex Corp.
Ralston Purina Co.
Reebok International Ltd.
REI-Recreational Equipment, Inc.
Revlon Inc.
Reynolds Tobacco (R.J.)
Rockwell International Corp.
Rohm & Haas Co.
Roseburg Forest Products Co.
Rubbermaid Inc.
Safeway Inc.
Sara Lee Corp.
Schering-Plough Corp.
Scientific-Atlanta, Inc.
Seagram & Sons, Inc. (Joseph E.)
Searle & Co. (G.D.)
Seaway Food Town, Inc.
Sega of America Inc.
Sentinel Communications Co.
ServiceMaster Co.
Shaklee Corp.
Shaw's Supermarkets, Inc.
Shoney's Inc.
Simpson Investment Co.
SmithKline Beecham Corp.
Smucker Co. (JM)
Sonoco Products Co.
Sony Electronics
Southwest Gas Corp.
Sovereign Bank
Springs Industries, Inc.
Stanley Works (The)
State Farm Mutual Automobile Insurance Co.
Steelcase Inc.
Stride Rite Corp.
Subway Sandwich Shops, Inc.
Sun Microsystems Inc.
SuperValu, Inc.
Susquehanna-Pfaltzgraff Co.
Target Corp.
Tektronix, Inc.
Tenneco Packaging
Tesoro Hawaii
Thomasville Furniture Industries Inc.
Times Mirror Co.
TJX Companies, Inc.
Toro Co.
Toyota Motor Sales U.S.A., Inc.
Unilever Home & Personal Care U.S.A.
Unilever United States, Inc.
Union Camp Corp.
United Distillers & Vintners North America
Universal Foods Corp.
Universal Studios
UnumProvident
US Bank, Washington
UST Inc.
Valspar Corp.
Vulcan Materials Co.
Wal-Mart Stores, Inc.
Waldbaum's Supermarkets, Inc.
Warner-Lambert Co.
Washington Trust Bank
Weyerhaeuser Co.
WICOR, Inc.
Wiley & Sons (John)
Wisconsin Public Service Corp.
Wolverine World Wide
Zenith Electronics Corp.

FUNDERS BY APPLICATION DEADLINE

Arranged by month, this index alphabetically lists the funders according to their application deadlines.

Newman's Own Inc.
Norfolk Southern Corp.
Occidental Oil and Gas
Pacific Mutual Life Insurance Co.
PacifiCorp
Phoenix Home Life Mutual Insurance Co.
Pioneer Hi-Bred International, Inc.
Principal Financial Group
Saint Paul Companies Inc.
Sara Lee Corp.
Sega of America Inc.
Tampa Electric Co.
United Parcel Service of America Inc.
United States Trust Co. of New York
The Washington Post
Weyerhaeuser Co.
Wisconsin Power & Light Co.

October

AMETEK, Inc.
BankBoston Corp.
Borden, Inc.
Boston Edison Co.
Briggs & Stratton Corp.
Bristol-Myers Squibb Co.
Chase Manhattan Bank, NA
Clorox Co.
ConAgra, Inc.
Cox Enterprises Inc.
Crestar Finance Corp.
Deloitte & Touche
Disney Co. (Walt)
Dreyer's Grand Ice Cream
Dun & Bradstreet Corp.
First Tennessee National Corp.
Fuller Co. (H.B.)
GATX Corp.
GenAmerica Corp.
Georgia-Pacific Corp.
Glaxo Wellcome Inc.
Gucci America Inc.
Harcourt General, Inc.
Harley-Davidson Co.
Hewlett-Packard Co.
Inland Container Corp.
Kerr-McGee Corp.
LandAmerica Financial Services
LG&E Energy Corp.
Mallinckrodt Chemical, Inc.
Medtronic, Inc.
Michigan Consolidated Gas Co.
Microsoft Corp.
National Starch & Chemical Co.
Northern Trust Co.
Pacific Gas and Electric Co.
Pan-American Life Insurance Co.
Pentair Inc.
Providence Journal-Bulletin Co.
Reynolds Metals Co.
Smith Corp. (A.O.)
Tandy Corp.
Times Mirror Co.
U.S. Bancorp Piper Jaffray
US West, Inc.
Valspar Corp.
Washington Mutual, Inc.
Whirlpool Corp.
WICOR, Inc.
Wrigley Co. (Wm. Jr.)

November

ABC
American Electric Power
American Honda Motor Co., Inc.
Banta Corp.
Belk-Simpson Department Stores
Ben & Jerry's Homemade Inc.
Berwind Group
Cadence Designs Systems, Inc.
Carolina Power & Light Co.
Chevron Corp.
Dain Bosworth Inc.
Deposit Guaranty National Bank
Donnelley & Sons Co. (R.R.)
Eastern Bank
Fannie Mae
Freeport-McMoRan Inc.
Hickory Tech Corp.
Johnson & Son (S.C.)
Kellwood Co.
Kemper National Insurance Companies
La-Z-Boy Inc.
Menasha Corp.
Minnesota Mutual Life Insurance Co.
Montgomery Ward & Co., Inc.
National Starch & Chemical Co.
Nordson Corp.
Northrop Grumman Corp.
Rayonier Inc.
Reliant Energy Minnegasco
Schwebel Baking Co.
Sun Microsystems Inc.
SunTrust Bank Atlanta
SuperValu, Inc.
Target Corp.
Ukrop's Super Markets
Weil, Gotshal & Manges Corp.

December

Ace Hardware Corp.
Advanced Micro Devices, Inc.
AMP Inc.
Aon Corp.
Atlantic Investment Co.
Barden Corp.
Chesapeake Corp.
Chubb Corp.
Cook Inlet Region
Delta Air Lines, Inc.
Detroit Edison Co.
Disney Co. (Walt)
Donaldson Co., Inc.
Graco, Inc.
Grede Foundries
Kmart Corp.
Lipton Co.
National Starch & Chemical Co.
New Century Energies
New England Financial
New York Times Co.
Northern Trust Co.
Occidental Petroleum Corp.
Oracle Corp.
PacifiCorp
Paine Webber
Pioneer Hi-Bred International, Inc.
Pittway Corp.
Principal Financial Group
Reader's Digest Association, Inc. (The)
Saint Paul Companies Inc.
The Washington Post
Williams

No Application Deadline

Wachovia Bank of North Carolina NA
Wachovia Bank of North Carolina NA
Sun Microsystems Inc.
Wachovia Bank of North Carolina NA
7-Eleven, Inc.
ABB Inc.
Abbott Laboratories
AEGON U.S.A. Inc.
AFLAC Inc.
AGL Resources Inc.
Agrilink Foods, Inc.
Air Products and Chemicals, Inc.
Airborne Freight Corp.
AK Steel Corp.
Alabama Power Co.
Alaska Airlines, Inc.
Albertson's Inc.
Alcoa Inc.
Alcon Laboratories, Inc.
Allegheny Technologies Inc.
Alliant Techsystems
Allmerica Financial Corp.
Allstate Insurance Co.
Alyeska Pipeline Service Co.
AMCORE Bank Rockford
Ameren Corp.
American Express Co.
American General Corp.
American Standard Inc.
American Stock Exchange, Inc.
Ameritas Life Insurance Corp.
Ameritech Corp.
Ameritech Illinois
Ameritech Indiana
Ameritech Michigan
Ameritech Ohio
Ameritech Wisconsin
AmerUS Group
Amgen, Inc.
AMR Corp.
Analog Devices, Inc.
Andersen Corp.
Anheuser-Busch Companies, Inc.
Appleton Papers Inc.
Archer-Daniels-Midland Co.
Arizona Public Service Co.
Arvin Industries, Inc.
ASARCO Inc.
Ashland, Inc.
AT&T Corp.
Atlantic Richfield Co.
Auburn Foundry
Avery Dennison Corp.
Avista Corporation
Avon Products, Inc.
Badger Meter, Inc.
Banfi Vintners
Bank of America
Bank of New York Co., Inc.
Bank One Corp.
BankAtlantic Bancorp
BankBoston-Connecticut Region
Bard, Inc. (C.R.)
Bardes Corp.
Barry Corp. (R.G.)
Battelle Memorial Institute
Bausch & Lomb Inc.
Baxter International Inc.
Bechtel Group, Inc.
Belk Stores Services Inc.
Bell Atlantic Corp.
Bell Atlantic-Delaware, Inc.
Belo Corp. (A.H.)
Bemis Co., Inc.
Bemis Manufacturing Co.
Ben & Jerry's Homemade Inc.
Bestfoods
Binswanger Companies
Blair & Co. (William)
Block, Inc. (H&R)
Blount International, Inc.
Blue Bell, Inc.
Blue Cross & Blue Shield of Alabama
Blue Cross & Blue Shield of Iowa
Blue Cross & Blue Shield of Minnesota
Boeing Co.
Boise Cascade Corp.
Borman's Inc.
Boston Globe (The)
Bourns, Inc.
Bowater Inc.
Branch Banking & Trust Co.
Bridgestone/Firestone, Inc.
Broderbund Software, Inc.
Brooklyn Union
Brown Shoe Co., Inc.
Browning-Ferris Industries Inc.
Brunswick Corp.
Bucyrus-Erie Co.
Burger King Corp.
Burlington Industries, Inc.
Burlington Northern Santa Fe Corp.
Burlington Resources, Inc.
Burnett Co. (Leo)
Burress (J.W.)
Business Men's Assurance Co. of America
Butler Manufacturing Co.
California Bank & Trust
California Federal Bank, FSB
Calvin Klein
Campbell Soup Co.
Cargill Inc.
Carillon Importers, Ltd.
Carnival Corp.
Carpenter Technology Corp.
Carrier Corp.
Castle & Cooke Properties Inc.
Caterpillar Inc.
CCB Financial Corp.
Cenex Harvest States
Central Maine Power Co.
Central & South West Services
Central Soya Co.
CertainTeed Corp.
Cessna Aircraft Co.
Champion International Corp.
Chemed Corp.
Chevron Corp.
Chicago Board of Trade
Church & Dwight Co., Inc.
CIGNA Corp.
Cincinnati Bell Inc.
Circuit City Stores, Inc.
CIT Group, Inc. (The)
Citigroup
Citizens Financial Group, Inc.
CLARCOR Inc.
Cleveland-Cliffs, Inc.
CNA
CNF Transportation, Inc.
Coachmen Industries, Inc.
Coca-Cola Co.
Colgate-Palmolive Co.
Colonial Oil Industries, Inc.
Comdisco, Inc.
Comerica Inc.
Commerce Bancshares, Inc.
Commercial Federal Corp.
Commercial Intertech Corp.
Commonwealth Edison Co.
Compaq Computer Corp.
Compass Bank
Cone Mills Corp.
Conectiv
Conoco, Inc.
Consolidated Electrical Distributors
Consolidated Natural Gas Co.
Constellation Energy Group, Inc.
Consumers Energy Co.
Contran Corp.
Conwood Co. LP
Cooper Industries, Inc.
Cooper Tire & Rubber Co.
Coors Brewing Co.
Corning Inc.
Country Curtains, Inc.
CPI Corp.
Crane Co.
Credit Suisse First Boston
Croft-Leominster
Crown Books
CSX Corp.
Cummins Engine Co., Inc.
CUNA Mutual Group
Curtis Industries, Inc. (Helene)
Cyprus Amax Minerals Co.
Daily News
DaimlerChrysler Corp.
Dana Corp.
Dayton Hudson
Dayton Power and Light Co.
Deere & Co.
DeKalb Genetics Corp.
Deluxe Corp.
Demoulas Supermarkets Inc.
Deutsch Co.
Dexter Corp.
Dixie Group, Inc. (The)
Dollar General Corp.
Dominion Resources, Inc.
Dow Chemical Co.
Dow Corning Corp.
DSM Copolymer
du Pont de Nemours & Co. (E.I.)
Duchossois Industries Inc.
Duke Energy
Duquesne Light Co.
Duriron Co., Inc.
Eastern Bank
Eaton Corp.
Ebsco Industries, Inc.
Eckerd Corp.
Edison International
EDS Corp.
Edwards Enterprise Software (J.D.)
El Paso Energy Co.
Elf Atochem North America, Inc.
Emerson Electric Co.
EMI Music Publishing
Employers Insurance of Wausau, A Mutual Co.
Employers Mutual Casualty Co.

Ensign-Bickford Industries
Enterprise Rent-A-Car Co.
Equitable Resources, Inc.
Ernst & Young, LLP
European American Bank
Evening Post Publishing Co.
Exxon Mobil Corp.
Fabri-Kal Corp.
Farmers Group, Inc.
Federated Department Stores, Inc.
Federated Mutual Insurance Co.
Ferro Corp.
Fifth Third Bancorp
FINA
Fireman's Fund Insurance Co.
First American Corp.
First Hawaiian, Inc.
First Maryland Bancorp
First National Bank of Evergreen Park
First Source Corp.
First Union Bank
First Union Corp.
First Union Securities, Inc.
Firstar Bank Milwaukee NA
FirstEnergy Corp.
FleetBoston Financial Corp.
Florida Power Corp.
Florida Power & Light Co.
Florida Rock Industries
Fluor Corp.
FMC Corp.
Ford Meter Box Co.
Ford Motor Co.
Forest City Enterprises, Inc.
Fort James Corp.
Fort Worth Star-Telegram Inc.
Fortis, Inc.
Fortune Brands, Inc.
Fox Entertainment Group
Franklin Mint (The)
Freightliner Corp.
Furniture Brands International, Inc.
Gallo Winery, Inc. (E&J)
Gannett Co., Inc.
Gap, Inc.
Gates Rubber Corp.
GEICO Corp.
GenCorp
General Atlantic Partners II LP
General Electric Co.
General Mills, Inc.
Georgia Power Co.
Giant Eagle Inc.
Giant Food Inc.
Gillette Co.
Glaxo Wellcome Inc.
Glickenhaus & Co.
Golub Corp.
Goodrich Aerospace - Aerostructures Group (B.F.)
GPU Energy
GPU Inc.
Grace & Co. (W.R.)
Grainger, Inc. (W.W.)
Green Bay Packaging
Group Health Plan
GTE Corp.
Guardian Life Insurance Co. of America
Guess?
Gulfstream Aerospace Corp.
Halliburton Co.
Hallmark Cards Inc.
Hamilton Sundstrand Corp.
Hancock Financial Services (John)
Hanna Co. (M.A.)
Hannaford Brothers Co.
Harland Co. (John H.)
Harrah's Entertainment Inc.
Harris Corp.
Harris Trust & Savings Bank
Harsco Corp.
Hartford Steam Boiler Inspection & Insurance Co.
Hartmarx Corp.
Hasbro, Inc.
Heinz Co. (H.J.)
Heller Financial, Inc.
Hensel Phelps Construction Co.
Hershey Foods Corp.
Hoechst Marion Roussel, Inc.
Hoffer Plastics Corp.
Hoffmann-La Roche Inc.
Hofmann Co.
Home Depot, Inc.
Honeywell International Inc.
Houghton Mifflin Co.
Housatonic Curtain Co.
Household International Inc.
HSBC Bank USA
Huffy Corp.
Hughes Electronics Corp.
Humana, Inc.
Hunt Oil Co.
Huntington Bancshares Inc.
IBP
Idaho Power Co.
IKON Office Solutions, Inc.
Illinois Power Co.
Illinois Tool Works, Inc.
Independent Stave Co.
Indiana Mills & Manufacturing
Informix Software, Inc.
Ingram Industries Inc.
Intel Corp.
International Business Machines Corp.
International Multifoods Corp.
Interpublic Group of Companies, Inc.
Invacare Corp.
Johnson Controls Inc.
Johnson & Johnson
Journal Communications, Inc.
Journal-Gazette Co.
Kaman Corp.
Katten, Muchin & Zavis
Kellogg Co.
Kelly Services
Kendall International, Inc.
Key Bank of Cleveland
Kiewit Sons' Inc. (Peter)
Kimball International, Inc.
Kimberly-Clark Corp.
Kinder Morgn
Kmart Corp.
Knight Ridder
Koch Enterprises, Inc.
Koch Industries, Inc.
Kohler Co.
Kraft Foods, Inc.
Kroger Co.
Lance, Inc.
Land O'Lakes, Inc.
Landmark Communications Inc.
Lee Enterprises
Lehigh Portland Cement Co.
Levi Strauss & Co.
Liberty Corp.
Liberty Diversified Industries
Liberty Mutual Insurance Group
Little, Inc. (Arthur D.)
Litton Industries, Inc.
Liz Claiborne, Inc.
Lockheed Martin Corp.
Loctite Corp.
Loews Corp.
Louisiana Land & Exploration Co.
Louisiana-Pacific Corp.
Lowe's Companies
LTV Corp.
Lubrizol Corp. (The)
Lyondell Chemical Co.
Macy's East Inc.
Madison Gas & Electric Co.
Mamiye Brothers
Manufacturers & Traders Trust Co.
Manulife Financial
Maritz Inc.
Mark IV Industries
Marriott International Inc.
Marshall & Ilsley Corp.
Masco Corp.
Matsushita Electric Corp. of America
Mattel Inc.
May Department Stores Co.
Maytag Corp.
MBIA Inc.
McClatchy Co.
McCormick & Co. Inc.
McDermott Inc.
McDonald & Co. Securities, Inc.
McDonald's Corp.
McGraw-Hill Companies, Inc.
MCI WorldCom, Inc.
McKesson-HBOC Corp.
McWane Inc.
Mead Corp.
Medtronic, Inc.
Mellon Financial Corp.
Mercantile Bank NA
Merck & Co.
Meredith Corp.
Merit Oil Corp.
Merrill Lynch & Co., Inc.
Mervyn's California
Metropolitan Life Insurance Co.
MGIC Investment Corp.
Mid-America Bank of Louisville
MidAmerican Energy Holdings Co.
Milacron, Inc.
Millipore Corp.
Mine Safety Appliances Co.
Monsanto Co.
Montana Power Co.
MONY Group (The)
Morgan Stanley Dean Witter & Co.
Morris Communications Corp.
Morrison Knudsen Corp.
Morton International Inc.
Murphy Oil Corp.
Nabisco Group Holdings
Nalco Chemical Co.
National Bank of Commerce Trust & Savings
National City Bank of Cleveland
National City Bank of Columbus
National City Bank of Minneapolis
National City Corp.
National Computer Systems, Inc.
National Life of Vermont
National Machinery Co.
National Presto Industries, Inc.
National Service Industries, Inc.
NCR Corp.
NEBCO Evans
New Jersey Natural Gas Co.
New United Motor Manufacturing Inc.
New York Life Insurance Co.
New York Mercantile Exchange
New York State Electric & Gas Corp.
New York Stock Exchange, Inc.
Niagara Mohawk Holdings Inc.
Nike, Inc.
Northern Indiana Public Service Co.
Northern States Power Co.
Northwest Bank Nebraska, NA
Northwest Natural Gas Co.
Norton Co.
Norwest Corp.
OG&E Electric Services
Ohio National Life Insurance Co.
Old National Bank Evansville
Olin Corp.
Orscheln Co.
Oshkosh B'Gosh, Inc.
Owens-Illinois Inc.
PACCAR Inc.
PECO Energy Co.
Pella Corp.
PEMCO Corp.
Penney Co., Inc. (J.C.)
Pennsylvania Power & Light
Peoples Bank
Peoples Energy Corp.
PepsiCo, Inc.
PerkinElmer, Inc.
Pfizer Inc.
Pharmacia & Upjohn, Inc.
Philip Morris Companies Inc.
Philips Electronics North America Corp.
Physicians Mutual Insurance Co.
Pitney Bowes Inc.
Playboy Enterprises Inc.
PNC Bank
PNC Financial Services Group
Polaroid Corp.
Portland General Electric Co.
Potlatch Corp.
Potomac Electric Power Co.
PPG Industries, Inc.
Praxair
Premark International Inc.
Premier Industrial Corp.
Price Associates (T. Rowe)
PricewaterhouseCoopers
Procter & Gamble Co.
Procter & Gamble Co., Cosmetics Division
Promus Hotel Corp.
Prudential Insurance Co. of America
Prudential Securities Inc.
Public Service Electric & Gas Co.
Publix Supermarkets
Puget Sound Energy (PSE) Inc.
Pulitzer Publishing Co.
Questar Corp.
Ralph's Grocery Co.
Ralston Purina Co.
Red Wing Shoe Co. Inc.
Reebok International Ltd.
Regions Financial Corp.
Regis Corp.
Reilly Industries, Inc.
Reily & Co., Inc. (William B.)
ReliaStar Financial Corp.
Reynolds & Reynolds Co.
Reynolds Tobacco (R.J.)
Rich Products Corp.
Riggs Bank NA
Rochester Gas & Electric Corp.
Rockwell International Corp.
Rohm & Haas Co.
Roseburg Forest Products Co.
Rouse Co.
Royal & SunAlliance USA, Inc.
Rubbermaid Inc.
Ruddick Corp.
Russer Foods
Rutledge Hill Press
Ryder System, Inc.
SAFECO Corp.
Salomon Smith Barney
S&T Bancorp
Santa Fe International Corp.
SBC Communications Inc.
Schlumberger Ltd. (USA)
Schwab & Co., Inc. (Charles)
Scientific-Atlanta, Inc.
Scripps Co. (E.W.)
Seagram & Sons, Inc. (Joseph E.)
Searle & Co. (G.D.)
Sears, Roebuck and Co.
Security Benefit Life Insurance Co.
Sempra Energy
Sentry Insurance, A Mutual Co.
Servco Pacific
Shaklee Corp.
Shaw Industries Inc.
Shell Oil Co.
Shelter Mutual Insurance Co.
Sherwin-Williams Co.
Shoney's Inc.
Sierra Pacific Resources
SmithKline Beecham Corp.
Smucker Co. (JM)
Smurfit-Stone Container Corp.
Solo Cup Co.
Sonoco Products Co.
Sony Electronics
Sotheby's Inc.
South Bend Tribune Corp.
Southeastern Mutual Insurance Co.
Southern California Gas Co.
Southern Co. Services Inc.
Southern New England Telephone Co.
Southwest Gas Corp.
Sovereign Bank
Springs Industries, Inc.
Sprint Corp.
Sprint/United Telephone
SPX Corp.
Standard Products Co.
Star Bank NA
Starwood Hotels & Resorts Worldwide, Inc.
State Farm Mutual Automobile Insurance Co.
State Street Bank & Trust Co.

Stone Container Corp.
Stone & Webster Inc.
Stonecutter Mills Corp.
Storage Technology Corp.
Stride Rite Corp.
Student Loan Marketing Association
Subway Sandwich Shops, Inc.
Sunoco Inc.
SunTrust Banks of Florida
Susquehanna-Pfaltzgraff Co.
Sverdrup Corp.
Synovus Financial Corp.
Tai and Co. (J.T.)
TCF National Bank Minnesota
Tektronix, Inc.
Telcordia Technologies
Temple-Inland Inc.
Tenet Healthcare Corp.
Tenneco Packaging
Tension Envelope Corp.
Tesoro Hawaii
Texaco Inc.
Texas Gas Transmission Corp.
Texas Instruments Inc.
Textron Inc.
Thermo Electron Corp.
Thomasville Furniture Industries Inc.
Thompson Co. (J. Walter)
Timken Co. (The)
TJX Companies, Inc.
TMC Investment Co.
Torchmark Corp.
Toro Co.
Toyota Motor Sales U.S.A., Inc.
Transamerica Corp.
True North Communications, Inc.
Trustmark National Bank
TU Electric Co.
Ultramar Diamond Shamrock Corp.
Unilever United States, Inc.
Union Camp Corp.
United Airlines Inc.
United Distillers & Vintners North America
United Dominion Industries, Ltd.
United States Sugar Corp.
United Wisconsin Services
Universal Leaf Tobacco Co., Inc.
Universal Studios
UnumProvident
USAA Life Insurance Co.
USG Corp.
UST Inc.
Valero Energy Corp.
Valmont Industries, Inc.
Vodafone AirTouch Plc
Vulcan Materials Co.
Waffle House Inc.
Wal-Mart Stores, Inc.
Waldbaum's Supermarkets, Inc.
Walgreen Co.
Walter Industries Inc.
Warner-Lambert Co.
Washington Mutual, Inc.
Washington Trust Bank
Waste Management Inc.
Wausau Insurance Companies
Wells Fargo & Co.
West Co. Inc.
Western Resources Inc.
Western & Southern Life Insurance Co.
Westvaco Corp.
Wiley & Sons (John)
Williams
Winn-Dixie Stores Inc.
Wiremold Co.
Wisconsin Energy Corp.
Wisconsin Public Service Corp.
Witco Corp.
Woodward Governor Co.
Wyman-Gordon Co.
Xerox Corp.
Yellow Corp.
York Federal Savings & Loan Association
Wachovia Bank of North Carolina NA
Hubbard Broadcasting, Inc.
Cook Inlet Region

Officers And Directors By Name

Arranges officers, trustees, directors, managers, staff, and contact people in alphabetical order with the name of the funder.

A

Aaronson, Morton C.: vice president, Kinder Morgn; director, KN Energy Foundation

Abbett, Barbara A.: vice president communications, Mallinckrodt Chemical, Inc.

Abdoo, Richard A.: chairman, president, chief executive officer, Wisconsin Energy Corp.; president, director, Wisconsin Energy Corp. Foundation, Inc.

Abel, Alice: director, Abel Foundation

Abel, Elizabeth N.: director, Abel Foundation

Abel, James P.: president, Abel Foundation; president, director, NEBCO Evans

Abel, John C.: president, Abel Foundation

Abel, Mary C.: director, Abel Foundation

Abercrombie, George: director, Glaxo Wellcome Foundation

Abrams, A. R.: vice president, director, Pheonix Foundation

Abrams, B. W.: president, Pheonix Foundation

Abrams, E. M.: president, Pheonix Foundation

Abrams, J. A.: director, Pheonix Foundation

Abrams, Thomas: chairman, president, chief executive officer, chief financial officer, Pheonix Financial Group; founder, Pheonix Foundation

Abrew, Frederick H.: chairman, president, chief executive officer, director, Equitable Resources, Inc.

Ackerman, F. Duane: president, chief executive officer, BellSouth Corp.

Ackerman, Philip Charles: senior vice president, director, National Fuel Gas Distribution Corp.

Ackerman, Roger G.: trustee, Corning Inc. Foundation

Acomb, Joanne: president, director, Wisconsin Power & Light Foundation, Inc.

Acquaviva, Theresa: foundation administrator, Hasbro Children's Foundation

Adam, J. Marc: president, director, 3M Foundation; vice president marketing, Minnesota Mining & Manufacturing Co.

Adam, Ronald: director, Consolidated Natural Gas System Foundation

Adams, John B., Junior: chairman, president, chief executive officer, Dominion Resources, Inc.

Adams, Richard M.: director, TENNANT Co. Foundation

Adderley, Mary E.: president, director, Kelly Services Foundation

Adderley, Terence E.: chairman, president, chief executive officer, director, Kelly Services; president, director, Kelly Services Foundation

Adelson, Andrew: trustee, Bernstein & Co. Foundation, Inc. (Sanford C.)

Adisek, Valerie: admin secretary, Johnson Controls Foundation

Adler, Ira R.: executive vice president, chief financial officer, Tucson Electric Power Co.

Adler, Michelle: director community service, Tampa Electric Co.

Agger, James Harrington: senior vice president, secretary, general counsel, Air Products and Chemicals, Inc.; director, Air Products Foundation

Aghababian, Robert V.: committee member, Thermo Electron Foundation

Agness, Terry D.: president, director, Ford Meter Box Co.; director, Honeywell Foundation

Agnich, Richard John: director, Texas Instruments Foundation; senior vice president, secretary, general counsel, Texas Instruments Inc.

Ahlers, Linda: president, department store division, Dayton Hudson; trustee, Target Foundation

Ahnert, Edward F.: president, Exxon Mobil Education Foundation

Ahuja, Sanjiv: president, chief operating officer, director, Telcordia Technologies

Akers, Bruce H.: chairman, Key Foundation

Akers, John Fellows: director, New York Times Co.

Albaugh, Jim F.: senior vice president, president space and communications systems, Boeing Co.

Albert, David: trustee, Citizens Bank-Flint

Alberts, Bruce Michael, PhD: director, Genentech Foundation for Biomedical Sciences

Albertson, Paula M.: trustee, Dow Corning Foundation

Albrecht, Richard Raymond: chairman, chief executive officer, director, Boeing Co.

Albright, David L.: president, Campbell Soup Co.

Albstein, Carollyn: treasurer, Unilever Foundation

Alden, Alison: senior vice president sales, service, human resources, Boston Edison Co.; trustee, Boston Edison Foundation

Aldinger, William F., III: chairman, chief executive officer, director, Household International Inc.

Alegi, August Paul: director, GEICO Philanthropic Foundation

Alex, Deonne: senior vice president auto forms, Reynolds & Reynolds Co.

Alexander, Anthony J.: executive vice president, general counsel, FirstEnergy Corp.

Alexander, Arthur W.: secretary-treasurer, Schlumberger Foundation

Alexander, John F.: trustee, PerkinElmer Foundation; senior vice president, chief financial officer, PerkinElmer, Inc.

Alexander, Stuart: director, Deluxe Corp. Foundation

Aley, Paul Nathaniel: president, director, National Machinery Co.; president, National Machinery Foundation, Inc.

Alfiero, Salvatore Harry: founder, chairman, chief executive officer, director, Mark IV Industries; chairman, Mark IV Industries Foundation

Alfonso, Marilda G.: president, executive director, Aetna Foundation

Allaire, Paul Arthur: chairman, chief executive officer, chairman executive committee, Xerox Corp.; president, Xerox Foundation

Allardyce, Fred A.: director, American Standard Foundation; senior vice president medical products sector, American Standard Inc.

Allbritton, Joe Lewis: chairman, chief executive officer, Riggs Bank NA

Allen, Barry K.: president regulatory & wholesale operation, Ameritech Corp.

Allen, James R.: treasurer, NASDAQ Stock Market Educational Foundation

Allen, Jay: vice president corporate affairs, Wal-Mart Stores, Inc.

Allen, Lloyd: vice chairman, Cenex Harvest States; vchairman, Cenex Harvest States Foundation

Allen, Richard E.: vice president finance, chief financial officer, Edwards Enterprise Software (J.D.)

Allen, W. Wayne: chairman, chief executive officer, director, Phillips Petroleum Co.

Allex, Kenneth R.: vice president, treasurer, Humanitas Foundation

Allison, Herbert Monroe, Jr.: vice president, trustee, Merrill Lynch & Co. Foundation Inc.; president, chief operating officer, Merrill Lynch & Co., Inc.

Allison, John Andrew, IV: chairman, chief executive officer, director, Branch Banking & Trust Co.

Allison, Judith N.: director, First Union Foundation

Alm, John Richard: director, Coca-Cola Foundation

Alm, Robert: director, First Hawaiian Foundation

Almeida, Richard: chairman, chief executive officer, Heller Financial, Inc.

Almy, Richard E.: executive vice president, chief operating officer, director, Walter Industries Inc.

Alpert, Janet A.: president, chief operating officer, director, LandAmerica Financial Services; trustee, LandAmerica Foundation

Altenbaumer, Larry F.: senior vice president, chief financial officer, Illinois Power Co.

Alter, Francie: corp. relations manager, Nortel

Altman, David R.: vice president corporate communications, Southern Co. Services Inc.

Altmansburger, D. Chris: vice president, director, CertainTeed Corp. Foundation

Alton, Robert D., Jr.: chairman, president, chief executive officer, Hickory Tech Corp.; trustee, Hickory Tech Corp. Foundation

Alvarez, Ramon A.: director, Honeywell Foundation

Alveres, Kenneth M.: president, Sun Microsystems Foundation, Inc.

Amato, Anthony J.: senior vice president, Wisconsin Power & Light Co.; president, director, Wisconsin Power & Light Foundation, Inc.

Ambler, John Doss: vice president, Texaco Inc.

Ambler, Lloyd: vice president, director, CertainTeed Corp.

Ambler, Michael N.: general tax counsel, Texaco Inc.

Amemiya, Koichi: president, chief executive officer, director, American Honda Motor Co., Inc.

Amick, Michael: executive vice president forest products & industrial packaging, International Paper Co.

Amos, Daniel P.: president, chief executive officer, director, AFLAC Inc.

Amos, Paul Shelby: cofounder, chairman, director, AFLAC Inc.

Amoss, George B.: vice president finance, chief financial officer, CertainTeed Corp.; chief financial officer, CertainTeed Corp. Foundation

Amsterdam, Jack: secretary, treasurer, Leviton Foundation New York; chairman, treasurer, director, Leviton Manufacturing Co. Inc.

Andersen, Anthony Lee: director, Fuller Co. Foundation (H.B.); chairman, director, Fuller Co. (H.B.)

Andersen, Kathy: administrator corporate contributions, AMR/American Airlines Foundation

Anderson, Basil L.: executive vice president, chief financial officer, Campbell Soup Co.

Anderson, Bruce: vchairman, Cenex Harvest States Foundation
Anderson, Charles D.: trustee, Anderson Foundation
Anderson, Darius: executive director, Ralph's-Food 4 Less Foundation
Anderson, David H.: vice chairman, trustee, Lennox Foundation
Anderson, David J.: senior vice president, chief financial officer, Newport News Shipbuilding
Anderson, Deb: manager, Saint Paul Companies Inc.
Anderson, Eugene Karl: vice president, Contran Corp.; treasurer, Simmons Foundation, Inc. (Harold)
Anderson, F. G.: assistant secretary-treasurer, Copolymer Foundation; treasurer, DSM Copolymer
Anderson, Girard F.: chairman, chief executive officer, president, Tampa Electric Co.
Anderson, Gordon M.: chairman, Santa Fe International Corp.
Anderson, Ivan Verner, Jr.: president, chief executive officer, Evening Post Publishing Co.; vice president, Post and Courier Foundation
Anderson, J. C.: vice president, Whirlpool Corp.; trustee, Whirlpool Foundation
Anderson, Jeffrey W.: chairman, trustee, Anderson Foundation
Anderson, Jennifer A.: director, Deluxe Corp. Foundation
Anderson, John: secretary, Toshiba America Foundation
Anderson, Judy M.: vice president, corporate secretary, Georgia Power Co.; executive director, secretary, assistant treasurer, Georgia Power Foundation
Anderson, Kevin: trustee, Anderson Foundation
Anderson, Kjestine M.: director, Texaco Foundation; general tax counsel, Texaco Inc.
Anderson, Kristin: secretary, contact, Burnett Co. Charitable Foundation (Leo); vice president, director community affairs, Burnett Co. (Leo)
Anderson, Lowell Carlton: chairman, director, Allianz Life Insurance Co. of North America
Anderson, Mark Bo: senior vice president, European American Bank
Anderson, Mary: trustee, Anderson Foundation
Anderson, Norris, MD: director, Blue Cross & Blue Shield of Minnesota Foundation Inc.
Anderson, Rich: chief financial officer, Blue Cross & Blue Shield of Iowa
Anderson, Sherwood L.: director, Smith Foundation Inc. (Harold Webster)
Anderson, Thomas Harold: chairman, trustee, Anderson Foundation; chairman, director, Andersons Inc.
Anderson, William J.: assistant secretary, Pella Corp.; secretary, Pella Rolscreen Foundation
Ando, Tetsuo: chief financial officer, executive vice president, treasurer, Bridgestone/Firestone, Inc.
Andreas, David Lowell: chairman, director, National City Bank Foundation; chairman, chief executive officer, National City Bank of Minneapolis
Andreas, Dwayne Orville: chairman, chief executive officer, Archer-Daniels-Midland Co.
Andreas, Lowell Willard: chairman audit committee, member executive & finance committee, Archer-Daniels-Midland Co.
Andrews, Barry S.: secretary, Unocal Foundation
Andrews, Harry C.: executive vice president, Minnesota Mining & Manufacturing Co.
Anello, John A.: treasurer, Praxair Foundation
Angelastro, Linda W.: executive director, Ensign-Bickford Foundation
Angelica, Robert: chairman, chief executive officer, AT&T Corp.; treasurer, AT&T Foundation
Angelo, Robert A.: president, chief operating officer, York Federal Savings & Loan Association; secretary, York Federal Savings & Loan Foundation
Anglebeck, Eleanor: assistant secretary, Hallmark Corporate Foundation
Anicetti, Richard A.: director, Hannaford Charitable Foundation
Anthony, Barbara Cox: chairman, Cox Foundation (James M.)
Anthony, Beverly S.: secretary, Indiana Mills & Manufacturing
Anthony, James R.: president, IMMI Word and Deed Foundation; chairman, Indiana Mills & Manufacturing
Anthony, James T.: director, IMMI Word and Deed Foundation; secretary, Indiana Mills & Manufacturing
Apatoff, Rub: president, executive director, Aetna Foundation
Apodaca, Clara: trustee, Hitachi Foundation
Apostolides, William: assistant treasurer, RJR Nabisco Foundation
Appel, John C.: director, Dain Bosworth Foundation; vice chairman, president fixed income group, Dain Bosworth Inc.
Appell, George N.: treasurer, Susquehanna-Pfaltzgraff Co.; vice president, Susquehanna-Pfaltzgraff Foundation
Appell, Louis J., Jr.: president, Susquehanna-Pfaltzgraff Co.
Appelman, Joe: vice president, chief financial officer, Erb Lumber Co.
Araki, Nobuo: president, chief operating officer, Nissan North America, Inc.
Arbor, Patrick H.: chairman, Chicago Board of Trade
Archer, W. C., III: senior vice president external affairs, Georgia Power Co.; director, Georgia Power Foundation
Archinaco, Frank A.: director, PPG Industries Foundation; executive vice president, PPG Industries, Inc.
Arditti, Elliot: director, Crown Books Foundation
Argentine, Peter Dominic: executive vice president, chief financial officer, Nestle U.S.A. Inc.
Argyris, Marcia M.: president, McKesson Foundation
Arison, M. Micky: trustee, Arison Foundation; chairman, president, chief executive officer, Carnival Corp.
Arison, Marilyn: trustee, Arison Foundation
Arison, Shari: president, Arison Foundation; director, Carnival Corp.
Aristides, George: president, chief executive officer, director, Graco, Inc.
Armstrong, C. Michael: chairman, chief executive officer, AT&T Corp.
Armstrong, Malcolm: executive vice president operations, Delta Air Lines, Inc.
Armstrong, Neil A.: trustee, Milacron Foundation; director, Milacron, Inc.
Arnold, Neil E., Sr.: vice president, chief financial officer, treasurer, Fifth Third Bancorp
Arth, Lawrence Joseph: vice president, director, Ameritas Charitable Foundation; chairman, chief executive officer, director, Ameritas Life Insurance Corp.
Aschelman, Steven J.: president, Pharmacia & Upjohn Foundation
Ashe, Carol: secretary, general counsel, SmithKline Beecham Foundation
Ashley, James Wheeler: director, Globe Foundation
Ashton, Deborah: secretary, Medtronic Foundation
Ashwill, Terry M.: vice president, director, True North Foundation
Ashworth, Brenda K.: program director, Price Associates Foundation (T. Rowe)
Atkins, Sarah Humphreys: vice president, Craig Foundation (E.L.)
Atkiss, Anthony W.: president, Exxon Mobil Education Foundation
Atwater, Horace Brewster, Jr.: trustee, Merck Co. Foundation
Atwood, Robert T.: executive vice president, chief financial officer, First Union Corp.; director, First Union Foundation
Auguste, MacDonald: treasurer, Rayonier Foundation
Austin, H. Brent: executive vice president, chief financial officer, El Paso Energy Co.; vice president, treasurer, director, El Paso Energy Foundation
Austin, Patrick J.: assistant secretary, treasurer, director, Tribune New York Foundation
Autry, Rebecca: chief financial officer, Bardes Corp.; secretary, Bardes Fund
Axelrod, Janet: director, Lotus Development Philanthropy Program
Ayer, Ramani: chairman, president, chief executive officer, Hartford (The)
Ayer, William S.: president, Alaska Airlines, Inc.
Aylesworth, William Andrew: treasurer, Texas Instruments Foundation; chief financial officer, treasurer, Texas Instruments Inc.
Aylward, Rayna: executive director, Mitsubishi Electric America Foundation
Ayotte, Robert C.: executive vice president, director, CertainTeed Corp.; vice president, director, Norton Co. Foundation
Azoulay, Bernard: president, chief executive officer, Elf Atochem North America, Inc.

B

Babs, Douglas: director, Burlington Northern Santa Fe Foundation
Bach, Tom: vice president revenue management and area marketing, Northwest Airlines, Inc.
Bachhuber, Richard A., Jr.: vice president, trustee, Procter & Gamble Fund
Bachman, Brian R.: senior vice president, member contributions committee, Eaton Charitable Fund; senior vice president semiconductor & specialty systems, Eaton Corp.
Bachman, Mark: trustee, National Service Foundation
Bachmann, John W.: managing partner, Jones & Co. (Edward D.); chairman, Jones & Co. Foundation (Edward D.)
Bachmann, Richard Arthur: vice president, secretary, treasurer, director, Louisiana Land & Exploration Co. Foundation
Bachner, Robert L.: director, Wishnick Foundation (Robert I.)
Bacon, Kenneth J.: senior vice president, Fannie Mae; director, Fannie Mae Foundation
Baer, Timothy: trustee, Target Foundation
Bailey, Janice M.: vice president, Reynolds Metals Co. Foundation
Bailey, Keith E.: chairman, president, director, chief executive officer, Texas Gas Transmission Corp.; president, director, Williams Companies Foundation (The)
Bains, Harrison MacKellar, Jr.: vice president, treasurer, Bristol-Myers Squibb Co.; treasurer, Bristol-Myers Squibb Foundation Inc.
Bainum, Stewart William, Jr.: chairman, Manor Care Health SVS, Inc.
Baird, Dugald Euan: chairman, president, chief executive officer, Schlumberger Ltd. (USA)
Baird, Patrick S.: chief operating officer, chief financial officer, AEGON U.S.A. Inc.
Baird, Richard A.: president, chief executive officer, Giant Food Inc.
Baish, Richard Owen: vice president, treasurer, director, El Paso Energy Foundation
Bakane, John L.: president, chief executive officer, director, Cone Mills Corp.
Baker, Ann: trustee, Cranston Foundation
Baker, Anne: manager corporate contributions

Baker, C. Allen: trustee, Alcon Foundation; executive vice president, Alcon Laboratories, Inc.
Baker, Calvin H.: vice president finance, chief financial officer, Wisconsin Energy Corp.; treasurer, director, Wisconsin Energy Corp. Foundation, Inc.
Baker, David: trust, Cenex Harvest States Foundation
Baker, Dennis J.: vice president, director, CertainTeed Corp.; director, CertainTeed Corp. Foundation; vice president, director, Norton Co. Foundation
Baker, Edward L.: chairman, director, Florida Rock Industries; president, Florida Rock Industries Foundation
Baker, James Kendrick: chairman, director, Arvin Foundation; vice chairman, director, Arvin Industries, Inc.
Baker, John Daniel, II: president, chief executive officer, director, Florida Rock Industries; vice president, Florida Rock Industries Foundation
Baker, Larry: assistant secretary, treasurer, National Machinery Foundation, Inc.
Baker, Leslie Mayo, Jr.: president, chief executive officer, chairman, Wachovia Bank of North Carolina NA; chairman, Wachovia Foundation, Inc. (The)
Baker, Paula W.: vice president, IBM International Foundation
Baker, Reginald W.: trustee, Gerber Foundation
Baker, Richard C.: director, Fuller Co. Foundation (H.B.)
Baker, Robert Woodward: executive vice president, AMR Corp.
Baker, Tracy A.: secretary, trustee, Gerber Foundation
Baker, W. A., Jr.: vice president, treasurer, Colonial Foundation
Baker, W. Kendall: trustee, Walter Foundation; executive vice president, chief operating officer, director, Walter Industries Inc.
Baker-Stokes, Maxine: director, Freddie Mac Foundation
Baldassari, Dennis P.: president, chief operating officer, GPU Energy
Baldwin, Christopher: manager, Gannett Foundation
Baldwin, Ron: vice chairman, INTRUST Bank Charitable Trust
Ball, James Herington: senior vice president, general counsel, director, Nestle U.S.A. Inc.
Ballantyne, Richard Lee: vice president, general counsel, secretary, Harris Corp.; secretary, treasurer, Harris Foundation
Ballengee, Jerry Hunter: president, chief operating officer, director, Union Camp Corp.
Ballentine, Richard O.: vice president, secretary, general counsel, Butler Manufacturing Co.; secretary, Butler Manufacturing Co. Foundation
Ballmer, Steven Anthony: president, chief executive officer, director, Microsoft Corp.
Balloun, James S.: chairman, chief executive officer, president, National Service Industries, Inc.
Ballway, Joseph H., Jr.: vice president, general counsel, Cleveland-Cliffs, Inc.
Balousek, John B.: president, director, True North Communications, Inc.; vice president, director, True North Foundation
Balzer, Giorgio: chairman, chief executive officer, Business Men's Assurance Co. of America
Bame, Tracy L.: vice president, treasurer, Phelps Dodge Corp.; manager community affairs, Phelps Dodge Foundation
Bangs, Lawrence N.: group executive, Household International Inc.
Bank, Adrienne: member scholarship committee, Circuit City Foundation
Bankowski, Elizabeth: secretary, Ben & Jerry's Foundation
Banks, Marie, MD: president, Blue Cross & Blue Shield of Minnesota
Banks, Paula: director, BP Amoco Foundation
Banks, Peter L.: vice president external affairs, AGL Resources Inc.
Banks, Sandy: vice president corporate affairs, Masco Corp.
Bankston, Ralph: director community affairs, AGL Resources Inc.
Bannell, Scott: advertising and brand manager, Stanley Works (The)
Baptie, Tilly J.: executive director, Disney Co. Foundation (Walt)
Barad, Jill Elikann: director, Mattel Foundation; chairman, chief executive officer, director, Mattel Inc.
Barbakow, Jeffrey C.: chairman, chief executive officer, director, Tenet Healthcare Corp.
Barbera, Rosalie N.: vice president, director, Banta Corp. Foundation
Bardes, Merrilyn B.: president, Bardes Corp.
Bares, William G.: chairman, president, chief executive officer, Lubrizol Corp. (The); trustee, Lubrizol Foundation (The)
Barker, Dixie: executive director, administrator, Federated Department Stores Foundation
Barlament, Patricia L.: trustee, Johnson Wax Fund (S.C.)
Barna, Roger: executive director, Mitsubishi Electric America Foundation
Barnes, Jennifer: senior program officer, IBJ Foundation
Barnes, Margo: senior vice president, Bayer Corp.; vice president, Bayer Foundation
Barnes, Thomas O.: director, Barnes Group Foundation Inc.
Barnes, W. Michael: senior vice president finance & planning, chief financial officer, Rockwell International Corp.; member trust committee, Rockwell International Corp. Trust
Barnes, Wallace W.: director, Barnes Group Foundation Inc.
Barnett, Hoyt R.: executive vice president, director, Publix Supermarkets
Barnett, Robert L.: director, Ameritech Foundation
Barnette, Curtis Handley: chairman, chief executive officer, director, Bethlehem Steel Corp.
Barrett, Allen M., Jr.: chairman, McCormick & Co. Inc.
Barrett, Craig R.: president, chief operating officer, director, Intel Corp.
Barrett, John F.: trustee, Western-Southern Foundation, Inc.; president, chief executive officer, director, Western & Southern Life Insurance Co.
Barrett, M. Patricia: vice president corporate communications, Ameren Corp.
Barrett, Robert E.: executive vice president, UST Inc.
Barris, Mary: trustee, Donaldson Foundation
Barron, Donald Ray: president, director, Atlantic Investment Co.
Barry, Richard Francis, III: director, Landmark Communications Foundation; vice chairman, Landmark Communications Inc.
Barry, Tina S.: president, director, Kimberly-Clark Foundation
Barth, Lynn: director corporate contributions, Monsanto Co.
Bartz, Carol A.: director, Autodesk Foundation; chairman, chief executive officer, Autodesk Inc.
Barun, Kenneth Lee: president, director, McDonald's Corp. Charitable Foundation
Bass, Robert: executive vice president, Cenex Harvest States Foundation
Bassett, Robert: treasurer, Praxair Foundation
Batauick, George: comptroller, Texaco Foundation; chairman, chief executive officer, Texaco Inc.
Bates, George E.: treasurer
Bates, Janice W.: director
Bates, Jeanne M.: assistant secretary, Hallmark Corporate Foundation
Bath, Charles S.: vice president, Nationwide Insurance Enterprise Foundation
Battaglia, Thomas S.: director, American Standard Foundation
Batten, Frank, Junior: executive vice president, Landmark Communications Inc.
Batten, Frank, Sr.: chairman, director, Landmark Communications Foundation; chairman, Landmark Communications Inc.
Batten, Richard D.: trustee, Trustmark Foundation
Bauder, Lillian: vice president corporate affairs, Masco Corp.
Bauer, Chris Michael: president, Firstar Milwaukee Foundation
Bauer, Douglas: director community partnership, SmithKline Beecham Corp.; executive director, SmithKline Beecham Foundation
Bauernfeind, George G.: vice president, Humana Foundation
Bauge, Bernard L. Henges: chairman, CNA
Baukol, Ronald O.: director, executive vice president, Minnesota Mining & Manufacturing Co.
Baumann, Lawra: executive vice president, chief financial officer, Fifth Third Bancorp; assistant vice president, Fifth Third Foundation
Baumblatt, Stanley: trustee, Merrill Lynch & Co. Foundation Inc.
Baumgardner, Anita A.: secretary, trustee, Copley Foundation (James S.)
Baumgarner, John C., Jr.: senior vice president corporate development, Williams; director, Williams Companies Foundation (The)
Bava, John: treasurer, secretary, Deloitte & Touche Foundation
Baxter, James G.: vice president, treasurer, Farber Foundation
Bay, Mogens C.: chairman, chief executive officer, Valmont Industries, Inc.
Bayless, Charles Edward: chairman, president, chief executive officer, director, Illinois Power Co.
Beach, Roger C.: chairman, chief executive officer, director, Unocal Corp.
Beadle, Robert Sheldon: senior vice president corporate development, Ultramar Diamond Shamrock Corp.
Beale, Michelle: director, Coca-Cola Foundation
Beale, Susan M.: director, Detroit Edison Foundation
Beall, Donald Ray: director, Rockwell International Corp.
Beard, Anson McCook, Jr.: treasurer, NASDAQ Stock Market Educational Foundation
Beard, Etonya M.: director, Fort James Foundation (The)
Beard, Peter: director, Fannie Mae Foundation
Beargie, William T.: trustee, Lubrizol Foundation (The)
Bearman, David: senior vice president, chief financial officer, NCR Corp.; director, NCR Foundation
Beath, Donna: executive vice president, chief financial officer, Penn Mutual Life Insurance Co.
Beatt, Bruce H.: secretary, Dexter Corp. Foundation
Beattie, Art P.: vice president, secretary, treasurer, Alabama Power Co.; treasurer, Alabama Power Foundation
Beatty, Richard: president, chief executive officer, Mazda North American Operations
Beaudet, Debra K.: officer, SIT Investment Associates Foundation
Beaver, William S.: treasurer, vice president, Westvaco Corp.; trustee, Westvaco Foundation Trust
Beaz, Marianne: vice president client service & pension investments, Pacific Mutual Life Insurance Co.
Becherer, Hans Walter: chairman, chief executive officer, director, Deere & Co.; director, Deere Foundation (John)
Bechtel, Riley Peart: chairman, Bechtel Foundation; chairman, chief executive

officer, director, Bechtel Group, Inc.
Bechtold, Ned W.: vice chairman, Firstar Milwaukee Foundation
Beck, Edward W.: senior vice president, general counsel, secretary, director, Shaklee Corp.
Becker, Howard C.: trustee, Ohio National Foundation
Becker, John A.: president, chief operating officer, director, Firstar Bank Milwaukee NA; vice chairman, Firstar Milwaukee Foundation
Becket, MacDonald G.: secretary, Unocal Foundation
Becraft, F. Joseph: president, chief financial officer, Valero Energy Corp.
Beddia, Paul J.: vice president government & community affairs, Lincoln Electric Co.
Beebe, Lydia I.: corporate secretary, Chevron Corp.
Beebe, Stephen A.: president, chief executive officer, director, Simplot Co. (J.R.)
Beemer, K. Larry: trustee, Gerber Foundation
Beer, William M.: treasurer, Maytag Corp. Foundation
Beetle, Vivian: admin director, Hoffmann-La Roche Foundation
Beghini, Victor Gene: trustee, USX Foundation, Inc.
Begley, Roy W., Jr.: treasurer, Sherman-Standard Register Foundation
Beideck, Edward L.: vice president, M&T Charitable Foundation
Belanger, Keith M.: vice president, M&T Charitable Foundation
Belcher, Donald D.: chairman, president, chief executive officer, director, Banta Corp.; vice president, director, Banta Corp. Foundation
Belk, Claudia: member board advisors, Belk Foundation
Belk, John Montgomery: member board advisors, Belk Foundation; chairman, Belk-Simpson Department Stores
Belk, Judy: vice president, secretary, Levi Strauss Foundation
Belk, Katherine McKay: member board advisors, Belk Foundation
Bell, Bradley John: vice president, treasurer, Whirlpool Corp.; treasurer, Whirlpool Foundation
Bell, Charles: director, Extendicare Foundation
Bell, James D.: trustee, Baird & Co. Foundation (Robert W.); executive vice president, Baird & Co. (Robert W.)
Bell, Lawrence T.: vice president law, general counsel, assistant secretary, Ecolab Inc.
Bell, Peter: president, TCF Foundation
Bell, Susan M.: senior supervisor-corporate communications, Ameren Corp.
Bell, Vance D.: executive vice president operations, Shaw Industries Inc.
Bell, Wayne: secretary, Ralph's-Food 4 Less Foundation; senior counsel, assistant secretary, Ralph's Grocery Co.
Bell, Wayne L.: secretary, United Coal Co. Charitable Foundation
Bell-Rose, Stephanie: chairman, president, director, Goldman Sachs Foundation
Bemis, Peter F.: president, Bemis Family Foundation (F.K.)
Bemis, Richard A.: president, Bemis Family Foundation (F.K.); president, chief executive officer, director, Bemis Manufacturing Co.
Benenson, James, Jr.: chairman, president, director, Vesper Corp.; trustee, Vesper Foundation
Benhase, Daniel B.: executive vice president, Star Bank NA; treasurer, Star Bank NA, Cincinnati Foundation
Benjamin, John D.: director, Smith Foundation Inc. (Harold Webster)
Bennet, James: secretary, Maytag Corp. Foundation
Bennett, Harry S.: trustee, AT&T Foundation
Bennett, Kathleen M.: director, Fort James Foundation (The)
Benninger, Edward Charles, Jr.: president, chief financial officer, Valero Energy Corp.
Bennyhoff, George R.: senior vice president human resources, West Co. Inc.; chairman, trustee, West Foundation (Herman O.)
Benson, Bill R.: executive vice president, chief financial officer, Physicians Mutual Insurance Co.; vice president, Physicians Mutual Insurance Co. Foundation
Benson, James M.: chief executive officer, Metropolitan Life Insurance Co.; chairman, chief executive officer, New England Financial
Benson, Jeanne: chairman, president, chief executive officer, director, Pentair Inc.
Benson, John W.: executive vice president health care, Minnesota Mining & Manufacturing Co.
Berens, Martha L.: trustee, Lubrizol Foundation (The)
Berey, Mark H.: senior vice president, chief financial officer, treasurer, Giant Food Inc.
Berg, Harvey: director, Associated Food Stores Charitable Foundation
Berg, Sue M.: secretary, CLARCOR Foundation
Berg, Thomas C.: vice president, general counsel, secretary, Amsted Industries Inc.
Bergeman, Richard P.: chairman contributions committee, Bestfoods
Berger, Bruce K.: vice president corporate affairs, Whirlpool Corp.; president, trustee, Whirlpool Foundation
Berger, Hans G.: managing director, Butler Manufacturing Co.
Bergerac, Michel Christian: director, CBS Foundation
Bergquist, Renee: vice president public affairs, Albertson's Inc.
Bergsteinsson, Paul: assistant treasurer, CIGNA Foundation
Berkeley, Vincent L., Jr: senior vice president, Burger King Corp.
Berkley, Eliot S.: president, Tension Envelope Foundation
Berkley, Eugene Bertram: chairman, director, Tension Envelope Corp.; treasurer, Tension Envelope Foundation
Berkley, Richard L.: treasurer, secretary, director, Tension Envelope Corp.; president, Tension Envelope Foundation
Berkley, William S.: president, chief executive officer, director, Tension Envelope Corp.; director, Tension Envelope Foundation
Berkowitz, Martin A.: comptroller, Prudential Foundation; trustee, Prudential Insurance Co. of America
Berlik, Leonard J.: vice president, National Starch & Chemical Co.
Bernadotte, Christian C.: vice president, Nordson Corp.
Bernard, Betsy J.: executive vice president retail mkts, US West, Inc.
Bernard, Bruce E.: director, Shell Oil Co. Foundation
Bernard, Robert: member grantmaking committee, Claiborne Foundation (Liz); senior vice president international sales, Liz Claiborne, Inc.
Bernauer, David W.: president, chief operating officer, Walgreen Co.
Bernhard, Don: manager economic development & community affairs
Bero, Donald B.: president, National Machinery Foundation, Inc.
Bero, Robert D.: president, chief executive officer, Menasha Corp.
Berrier, Ronald G.: vice president, treasurer, assistant secretary, Thomasville Furniture Industries Inc.
Berry, Ilona M.: secretary, First National Bank of Chicago Foundation
Berry, Roger D.: vice president, chief information officer, Campbell Soup Co.
Berry, William S.: treasurer, Rayonier Foundation
Bersticker, Albert C.: chairman, director, chief executive officer, Ferro Corp.; president, trustee, Ferro Foundation
Bertran, David R.: senior vice president manufacturing & logistics, Nalco Chemical Co.; director, Nalco Foundation
Bertrand, Frederic Howard: chairman, Central Vermont Public Service Corp.
Berwind, C. Graham, Jr.: chairman, president, chief executive officer, Berwind Group
Bescherer, Edwin A., Jr.: assistant secretary, Dun & Bradstreet Corp. Foundation, Inc.
Besser, John Edward: director, Barnes Group Foundation Inc.; senior vice president finance & law, Barnes Group Inc.
Betlejewski, Tina L.: manager corporate communications, SPX Corp.; secretary, trustee, SPX Foundation
Bettacchi, Robert J.: senior vice president, Grace & Co. (W.R.)
Beumer, Richard Eugene: president, Sverdrup Corp.
Beversdorf, William R.: vice president, Sentry Insurance Foundation Inc.
Bewley, Peter D.: vice president, secretary, Clorox Co. Foundation
Beyer, Jeffrey C.: president, Farmers Group Safety Foundation
Bezik, Cynthia B.: senior vice president, finance, Cleveland-Cliffs, Inc.
Biale, Patricia: chairman contributions committee, Bestfoods
Bibart, Charles H.: vice president, treasurer, Pharmacia & Upjohn Foundation
Bible, Geoffrey Cyril: secretary, New York Stock Exchange Foundation, Inc.; chairman, chief executive officer, director, Philip Morris Companies Inc.
Bicket, Pat: vice president, assistant secretary, Bank of New York Co., Inc.
Bickner, Bruce P.: chairman, chief executive officer, director, DeKalb Genetics Corp.
Biddy, Ralph L., MD: director, Group Health Foundation
Biehl, George C.: senior vice president, chief financial officer, corporate secretary, director, Southwest Gas Corp.; trustee, Southwest Gas Corp. Foundation
Bienz, Walt: trustee, Auburn Foundry Foundation
Bifuco, Frank, Junior: director, Coca-Cola Foundation
Biggs, James: president, Peoples Bank
Bigham, James John: executive vice president, chief financial officer, director, Continental Grain Co.
Bihary, Kristen: director public affairs, member contributions committee, Eaton Charitable Fund; vice president corporate affairs, Eaton Corp.
Bijur, Peter I.: chairman, chief executive officer, Texaco Inc.
Bilton, Stuart Douglas: president, chief executive officer, Chicago Title Corp.; trustee, Chicago Title and Trust Co. Foundation
Binder, Gordon M.: chairman, chief executive officer, director, Amgen, Inc.
Bindley, Thomas L.: executive vice president finance & administration, Whitman Corp.; vice president, treasurer, Whitman Corp. Foundation
Binswanger, David R.: president, chief executive officer, Binswanger Companies; treasurer, Binswanger Foundation
Binswanger, Frank G., III: chief financial officer, senior vice president, Binswanger Companies; secretary, Binswanger Foundation
Binswanger, Frank G., Jr.: co-chairman, director, Binswanger Companies
Binswanger, John K.: co-chairman, director, Binswanger Companies; chairman, Binswanger Foundation
Binswanger, Robert B.: chairman, Binswanger Foundation
Binyon, Bryan A.: treasurer, American General Finance Foundation

Bires, G. Nicholas: president, Guess? Foundation
Bishop, Kim: director, Matlock Foundation
Bissonette, Paul A.: assistant secretary, treasurer, director, Tribune New York Foundation
Bittner, D. P.: treasurer, assistant secretary, Wisconsin Public Service Foundation, Inc.
Biver, John P.: director, Badger Meter Foundation
Black, Daniel James: treasurer, Carter-Wallace Foundation; president, chief operating officer, director, Carter-Wallace, Inc.
Black, Gary E.: president, director, Fireman's Fund Foundation; president claims division, director, Fireman's Fund Insurance Co.
Black, Lennox K.: president, Teleflex Foundation; chairman, director, Teleflex Inc.
Black, Natalie A.: group vice president interiors, general counsel, director, Kohler Co.
Black, Sherry Salway: trustee, Hitachi Foundation
Blackburn, Deirdre: secretary, Safeguard Scientifics Foundation
Blaine, Gregory W.: chief operating officer, True North Communications, Inc.; president, director, True North Foundation
Blair, Gary J.: vice president, trustee, Blade Foundation
Blair, James Burton: trustee, Tyson Foundation, Inc.
Blake, Ronald L.: president general business services, Ameritech Corp.; director, Ameritech Foundation
Blakely, Robert T.: executive vice president, chief financial officer, Lyondell Chemical Co.
Blamer, Bob: secretary, Fuller Co. Foundation (H.B.)
Blanchard, J. A., III: president, chief executive officer, director, Deluxe Corp.
Blanchard, James Hubert: chairman, chief executive officer, Synovus Financial Corp.
Blanchard, Larry: assistant secretary, treasurer, CUNA Mutual Group Foundation, Inc.
Blank, Arthur M.: president, chief executive officer, director, Home Depot, Inc.
Blanke, Gail Ann: vice president, Avon Products Foundation, Inc.
Blankley, Walter Elwood: president, director, AMETEK Foundation; chairman, director, AMETEK, Inc.
Blaquiere, Ray: controller, Slant/Fin Corp.
Blaufuss, William, Jr.: trustee, KPMG Peat Marwick Foundation
Bleeker, Alfred E.: trustee, First Evergreen Foundation
Bleustein, Jeffrey L.: president, chief executive officer, director, Harley-Davidson Co.
Bloch, Henry Wollman: chairman, Block Foundation (H&R); chairman, director, Block, Inc. (H&R)
Bloch, Robert L.: chairman, Block Foundation (H&R)
Block, Allan James: vice president, trustee, Blade Foundation; director, Toledo Blade Co.
Block, John Robinson: vice president, trustee, Blade Foundation
Block, Stephen A.: secretary, IFF Foundation Inc.
Block, William: vice president, trustee, Blade Foundation; chairman, director, Toledo Blade Co.
Block, William, Jr.: president, trustee, Blade Foundation; president, director, Toledo Blade Co.
Blohm, Donald E.: administrator, La-Z-Boy Foundation
Bloodworth, Carolyn A.: secretary-trs, Consumers Energy Co.
Bloom, Geoffrey B.: chairman, chief executive officer, director, Wolverine World Wide
Bloom, Larry L.: chief financial officer, Lee Enterprises
Blouch, Gerald B.: president, chief operating officer, Invacare Corp.; trustee, Invacare Foundation
Blount, Winton Malcolm, Jr.: chairman, Blount International, Inc.
Blurton, Jerry Halbert: chairman, director, Halliburton Co.; treasurer, Halliburton Foundation, Inc.
Blystone, John B.: chairman, president, chief executive officer, director, SPX Corp.
Bodalski, Gerard: director, Extendicare Foundation
Boddie-Neal, Lydia: chairman, president, chief executive officer, Rochester Gas & Electric Corp.
Bodman, Samuel Wright, III: chairman, chief executive officer, director, Cabot Corp.; president, director, Cabot Corp. Foundation
Bodnar, J. Michael: president, chief executive officer, Shoney's Inc.
Boeckmann, Alan: trustee, Fluor Foundation
Boehne, Dean: trustee, Presto Foundation
Boesel, Stephen W.: program director, Price Associates Foundation (T. Rowe)
Bogle, John C.: senior chairman, Vanguard Group; chairman, Vanguard Group Foundation
Bogomolny, Robert Lee: director, Searle Charitable Trust; senior vice president, general counsel, secretary, Searle & Co. (G.D.)
Bohling, John A.: senior vice president, PacifiCorp; board member, PacifiCorp Foundation
Bohman, Michael J.: senior vice president, director community outreach, Star Bank NA; trustee, Star Bank NA, Cincinnati Foundation
Bohn, Karen M.: president, Piper Jaffray Companies Foundation; chief executive officer, U.S. Bancorp Piper Jaffray
Boisture, Bill: president, chief executive officer, Gulfstream Aerospace Corp.
Boitano, Caroline O.: president, executive director, Bank of America Foundation
Boland, Jack: vice president, director, True North Foundation
Boler, John M.: chairman, president, chief executive officer, owner, director, Boler Co.; trustee, Boler Co. Foundation
Bolling, Carol: chairman, chief executive officer, director, Hancock Financial Services (John)
Bolton, John Roger: senior vice president, Aetna Foundation; senior vice president corporate communications, Aetna, Inc.
Bonachi, Edward J.: senior vice president, treasurer, chief financial officer, Allianz Life Insurance Co. of North America
Bone, Dennis M.: president, chief executive officer, Bell Atlantic Corp.-West Virginia
Bonkoski, Kenneth John: controller, Menasha Corp.; treasurer, Menasha Corp. Foundation
Bonner, Teresa: vice president, Piper Jaffray Companies Foundation; media relations manager, U.S. Bancorp Piper Jaffray
Bonno, Anthony J.: senior vice president human resources, Pacific Mutual Life Insurance Co.
Bono, Joseph C.: vice president, First Union Regional Foundation
Bonsignore, Michael Robert: director, Honeywell Foundation; chairman, chief executive officer, director, Honeywell International Inc.
Bonvino, Frank W.: vice president, secretary, general counsel, International Multifoods Corp.
Booher, Pamela K.: secretary, Huffy Foundation, Inc.
Booker, Harris T., Junior: director, AMP Foundation
Bookman, Arlene: administrator, Collins & Aikman Foundation
Bookshester, Dennis S.: chairman, chief executive officer, Playboy Enterprises Inc.
Booth, Chesleu Peter Washburn: senior vice president development, Corning Inc.; trustee, Corning Inc. Foundation
Booth, Cynthia: senior vice president, director community outreach, Star Bank NA; treasurer, Star Bank NA, Cincinnati Foundation
Booth, Gwyneth Gamble: chairman, PGE-Enron Foundation; vice president public affairs, Portland General Electric Co.
Booth, Richard W.: chairman, treasurer, trustee, Lennox Foundation; chairman, Lennox International, Inc.
Borman, Gilbert: secretary, treasurer, director, Borman Fund (The)
Borman, Marlene: secretary, treasurer, director, Borman Fund (The)
Borman, Paul: president, director, Borman Fund (The); chairman, Borman's Inc.
Borsheim, Evelyn M: director, Fuller Co. Foundation (H.B.)
Borst, Stephen L.: assistant secretary, CertainTeed Corp.
Bosacker, Lyle T.: director, Hickory Tech Corp.; trustee, Hickory Tech Corp. Foundation
Bossidy, Lawrence Arthur: chairman, director, AlliedSignal Foundation Inc.; chairman, chief executive officer, director, AlliedSignal Inc.
Boswell, John Joseph: president, Boswell Foundation, Inc.; chairman, Independent Stave Co.
Boswell, Tiffany R.: president, Boswell Foundation, Inc.
Botham, Lydia: vice chairman, secretary, Land O'Lakes Foundation
Bottorff, Dennis C.: chairman, president, chief executive officer, director, First American Corp.
Bottorff, Mary Kay: president, Brunswick Foundation
Boudreau, Donald L.: vice president, trustee, Chase Manhattan Foundation
Boudreaux, Bernard: community relations manager, Mervyn's California
Bourgois, Nicole: president, chief operating officer, director, Dow Jones & Co., Inc.; member advisory committee, Dow Jones Foundation
Bourns, Gordon L.: president, trustee, Bourns Foundation; chairman, Bourns, Inc.
Bowden, Travis J.: chairman, president, chief executive officer, director, Gulf Power Co.
Bowdoin, William R., Jr.: first vice president, SunTrust Bank Atlanta; secretary, SunTrust Bank Atlanta Foundation
Bowen, William Gordon, PhD: trustee, Merck Co. Foundation
Bowerman, Charles L.: executive vice president, director, Phillips Petroleum Co.
Bowers, Betty H.: trustee, Fluor Foundation
Bowers, David C.: senior vice president, chief financial officer, Park National Bank
Bowles, Crandall Close: president, chief executive officer, chairman, director, Springs Industries, Inc.
Bowlin, Michael Ray: chairman, director, ARCO Foundation; chairman, chief executive officer, director, Atlantic Richfield Co.
Bowlus, Brad A.: member, PacifiCare Health System Foundation
Bowman, George A., Jr.: vice president community affairs, State Street Bank & Trust Co.; foundation manager, vice president, State Street Foundation
Bowman, Harold W.: president, OMC Foundation; chairman, president, chief executive officer, director, Outboard Marine Corp.
Bowman, Robert A.: president, chief operating officer, Starwood Hotels & Resorts Worldwide, Inc.
Bowne, Garrett D., IV: director, Hannaford Charitable Foundation
Boyajian, James E.: director, BP Amoco Foundation

Boyce, Donna J.: treasurer, Hannaford Charitable Foundation
Boyd, Madeline: chairman, New York Mercantile Exchange Charitable Foundation
Boyer, David Scott: president, chief executive officer, director, Teleflex Inc.
Boyer, Herbert Wayne, PhD: chairman, president, director, Genentech Foundation for Biomedical Sciences; co-founder, director, Genentech Inc.
Boyette, John G.: chairman, Cox Foundation (James M.)
Boyle, Donald C.: director, IMMI Word and Deed Foundation
Boyle, Francis J.: vice president, chief financial officer, Central Vermont Public Service Corp.
Boyle, Judy: secretary, AUL Foundation Inc.
Boyle, Richard James: vice chairman, director, Chase Manhattan Bank, NA; trustee, Chase Manhattan Foundation
Boze, Buck: corporate relations manager
Bozzone, Robert P.: vice chairman, director, Allegheny Technologies Inc.; trustee, Allegheny Technologies Inc. Charitable Trust
Brademas, John: director, Texaco Foundation
Braden, Jane: coordinator, Northwest Bank Nebraska, NA
Bradford, James C., Jr.: president, Bradford and Co. Foundation (J.C.); senior partner, Bradford & Co. (J.C.)
Bradford, Pamela: executive director, PacifiCorp Foundation
Bradford, William Edward: chairman, director, Halliburton Co.
Bradish, Mary E.: secretary, MichCon Foundation
Brady, Martha: administrator public affairs, Kerr-McGee Corp.
Bragin, David H.: treasurer, assistant secretary, director, Winn-Dixie Stores Foundation
Braham, W. Martin: trustee, Delta Air Lines Foundation; executive vice president operations, Delta Air Lines, Inc.
Bramble, Frank P.: president, chief executive officer, director, First Maryland Bancorp; president, trustee, First Maryland Foundation
Brammer, Billy M.: treasurer, director, Bassett Furniture Industries Fdn.
Brand, Susan F., Esq.: officer, Cummings Properties Foundation
Brandmahl, John C.: trustee, Standard Products Co. Charitable Foundation
Brandt, Dora: vice president corporate communications,
Brandt, Gerard: director, Georgia-Pacific Foundation
Brannon, Marguerite: president, Chicago Tribune Foundation
Brashear, Albert R.: director public affairs, Motorola Foundation; corp. vice president, director corporate communications, Motorola Inc.
Bratton, W. Tal: treasurer, American General Finance Foundation
Braun, Jan: program manager, Reader's Digest Foundation
Brazier, Robert George: president, chief operating officer, director, Airborne Freight Corp.
Breen, John Gerald: chairman, chief executive officer, director, Sherwin-Williams Co.; president, trustee, Sherwin-Williams Foundation
Brei, Linda: director, Wisconsin Power & Light Foundation, Inc.
Breisinger, James R.: vice president, controller, Kennametal Foundation; vice president, controller, chief financial officer, Kennametal, Inc.
Brendsel, Leland C.: chairman, chief executive officer, director, Freddie Mac; director, Freddie Mac Foundation
Brenizer, Bruce R.: director, Mitsubishi Electric America Foundation
Brennan, Alice C.: vice president, secretary, Bristol-Myers Squibb Co.; secretary, Bristol-Myers Squibb Foundation Inc.
Brennan, David P.: chairman, Chicago Board of Trade
Brennan, John J.: chairman, chief executive officer, Vanguard Group; president, Vanguard Group Foundation
Brennan, John V.: treasurer, Smith Foundation Inc. (Harold Webster); executive vice president, chief financial officer, Webster Bank
Brennan, Leo Joseph, Jr.: vice president, executive director, Ford Motor Co. Fund
Brennan, Michael J.: chief financial officer, senior vice president, Binswanger Companies
Brenninkmeyer, Anthony: vice president, treasurer, Humanitas Foundation
Brenninkmeyer, Louis: president, director, Humanitas Foundation
Brenninkmeyer, Roland M.: president, chief executive officer, director, American Retail Group; president, director, Humanitas Foundation
Breslawsky, Marc C.: president, chief operating officer, Pitney Bowes Inc.
Brewer, Oliver Gordon, Jr.: vice president finance, treasurer, IKON Office Solutions Foundation, Inc.
Brian, Pierre Leonce Thibaut: director, Air Products Foundation
Bridgeland, James Ralph, Jr.: trustee, Star Bank NA, Cincinnati Foundation
Bridgewater, Bernard Adolphus, Jr.: member board control, Brown Shoe Co. Charitable Trust; chairman, president, chief executive officer, director, Brown Shoe Co., Inc.
Briesch, John: president consumer products group, Sony Electronics
Brigham, S.T. Jack, III: senior vice president corporate affairs, general counsel, Hewlett-Packard Co.
Bright, Stanley J.: chairman, president, chief executive officer, director, MidAmerican Energy Holdings Co.
Brill, Ronald M.: executive vice president, chief administrative officer, director, Home Depot, Inc.
Brimner, David: chairman, Shaw's Supermarkets, Inc.
Brinberg, Simeon: director, Wishnick Foundation (Robert I.)
Brine, Kevin R.: trustee, Bernstein & Co. Foundation, Inc. (Sanford C.)
Brinegar, Claude Stout: trustee, Unocal Foundation
Brinzo, John S.: trustee, Cleveland-Cliffs Foundation (The); president, chief executive officer, Cleveland-Cliffs, Inc.
Britt, Wayne: trustee, Tyson Foundation, Inc.
Britton, Robert A.: secretary, manager, AMR/American Airlines Foundation; executive vice president, AMR Corp.
Broadhead, James Lowell: chairman, president, chief executive officer, director, Florida Power & Light Co.; chief executive officer, director, FPL Group Foundation, Inc.
Broderick, Bryan: vice president human resources, Goodrich Aerospace - Aerostructures Group (B.F.)
Broderick, Terry: director, Royal & SunAlliance Insurance Foundation, Inc.; president, Royal & SunAlliance USA, Inc.
Brodie, Nancy S.: executive vice president, chief financial officer, Penn Mutual Life Insurance Co.
Broffman, Peter: program officer, Intel Foundation
Brohn, Karen: director, Blue Cross & Blue Shield of Minnesota Foundation Inc.
Brom, Joseph P.: trustee, Ohio National Foundation
Broman, Susan: executive director, Steelcase Foundation
Bronfman, Charles Rosner: trustee, Bronfman Foundation/Joseph E. Seagram & Sons, Inc. Fund (Samuel)
Bronfman, Edgar Miles: chairman, trustee, Bronfman Foundation/Joseph E. Seagram & Sons, Inc. Fund (Samuel); chairman, Seagram & Sons, Inc. (Joseph E.)
Bronfman, Edgar Miles, Jr.: trustee, Bronfman Foundation/Joseph E. Seagram & Sons, Inc. Fund (Samuel); president, chief executive officer, Seagram & Sons, Inc. (Joseph E.)
Bronfman, Samuel, II: president, trustee, Bronfman Foundation/Joseph E. Seagram & Sons, Inc. Fund (Samuel)
Brookes, Nick: chairman, president, chief executive officer, Brown & Williamson Tobacco Corp.
Brooklier, John: chairman, chief executive officer, Heller Financial, Inc.
Brookman, Ann: president, Piper Jaffray Companies Foundation
Brooks, Bruce M.: director community affairs, Microsoft Corp.
Brooks, Delcy: secretary, director, Slant/Fin Foundation
Brooks, E. Richard 'Dick': chairman, chief executive officer, director, Central & South West Services
Brooks, Rand: trustee, Reilly Foundation
Brooks, Roger Kay: chairman, AmerUS Group
Broome, Burton Edward: vice president, controller, Transamerica Corp.; vice president, treasurer, Transamerica Foundation
Broomfield, Michael W.: chief executive officer, Giant Food Inc.
Brostowitz, James M.: president, chief executive officer, director, Harley-Davidson Co.; treasurer, Harley-Davidson Foundation
Brothers, John Alfred 'Fred': trustee, Ashland Inc. Foundation
Browman, Brett: assistant vice president, American Fidelity Corp.; member, American Fidelity Corp. Founders Fund
Brown, Craig J.: treasurer, Sherman-Standard Register Foundation; senior vice president administration, treasurer, chief financial officer, Standard Register Co.
Brown, David V.: chairman, treasurer, trustee, Lennox Foundation
Brown, Donald P.: executive vice president, treasurer, director, Slant/Fin Corp.; treasurer, director, Slant/Fin Foundation
Brown, Francis A.: vice president, treasurer, Colonial Foundation; vice president finance, treasurer, director, Colonial Oil Industries, Inc.
Brown, Harold, PhD: chairman, Mattel Foundation
Brown, James M.: vice president, Blue Cross & Blue Shield of Alabama; secretary, Caring Foundation
Brown, JoAnn Fitzpatrick: president, High Meadow Foundation
Brown, JoBeth Goode: trustee, Anheuser-Busch Companies, Inc.
Brown, Joseph Warner, Jr.: chairman, chief executive officer, MBIA Inc.
Brown, Julian E.: community relations director, NICOR Gas Co.
Brown, Lindsay W.: trustee, Corning Inc. Foundation
Brown, Margaret S.: director, CIRI Foundation
Brown, Mary Rose: vice president corporate communications, Valero Energy Corp.
Brown, Michael: president, Foundation of the Litton Industries; president, chief operating officer, Litton Industries, Inc.
Brown, Michele Courton: director, BankBoston Charitable Foundation; director corporate contributions, BankBoston Corp.
Brown, Morgan: senior community affairs officer, TCF Foundation; executive vice president, chief financial officer, treasurer, TCF National Bank Minnesota
Brown, Richard A.: chairman, chief executive officer, director, Philip Morris Companies Inc.

Brown, Richard Harris: chairman, chief executive officer, director, EDS Corp.

Brown, Robert: director, PricewaterhouseCoopers Foundation

Brown, Ronald C.: executive vice president, chief financial officer, Starwood Hotels & Resorts Worldwide, Inc.

Brown, Ronald D.: trustee, Milacron Foundation

Brown, Russ: vice president human resources, Analog Devices, Inc.

Brown, Stephen Lee: chairman, chief executive officer, director, Hancock Financial Services (John)

Brown, Tammy: manager community relations, Carolina Power & Light Co.; secretary, CP&L Foundation

Browne, John: chief executive officer, BP Amoco Corp.

Browning, Laurance LeWright, Jr.: member public policy committee, Emerson Charitable Trust; director, Emerson Electric Co.

Browning, Peter C.: chief executive officer, president, director, Sonoco Products Co.

Brozowski, Patricia D.: vice president communications, FMC Corp.; president, director, FMC Foundation

Brozyna, Jeffry H.: trustee

Bruce, Peter Wayne: director, Badger Meter Foundation

Brukardt, David: vice president, Harnischfeger Industries Foundation

Brumm, Paul Michael: executive vice president, chief financial officer, Fifth Third Bancorp

Brummett, Larry W.: chairman, chief executive officer, director, ONEOK, Inc.

Brune, David A.: secretary, treasurer, Baltimore Gas & Electric Foundation

Brunelle, Paul E.: director, TENNANT Co. Foundation

Brunetti, Wayne H.: vice chairman, president, chief operating officer, director, New Century Energies; president, chief executive officer, New Century Energies Foundation

Brunner, Betty: treasurer, Extendicare Foundation

Brunner, Vernon A.: executive vice president marketing, Walgreen Co.

Bryan, John Henry: chairman, Sara Lee Corp.; director, Sara Lee Foundation

Bryant, Andy D.: senior vice president, chief financial & enterprise services officer, Intel Corp.

Bryne, Patricia R.: assistant treasurer, grants manager, Citigroup Foundation

Bryson, John E.: chairman, chief executive officer, Edison International

Buccieri, Shirley H.: senior vice president, Transamerica Corp.; vice president, secretary, Transamerica Foundation

Buccy, Kathleen: director external relations, Southern New England Telephone Co.

Buchan, Ray: chief executive officer, National Starch & Chemical Co.

Buchanan, William Hobart, Jr.: assistant secretary, Dun & Bradstreet Corp. Foundation, Inc.

Buchholz, William E.: vice president, chief financial officer, Nalco Chemical Co.

Buchman, Joel: secretary, director, Grand Marnier Foundation

Buck, James E.: secretary, New York Stock Exchange Foundation, Inc.

Buckler, Robert J.: director, Detroit Edison Foundation

Buckley, Jerry S.: executive vice president, chief financial officer, Campbell Soup Co.; vice chairman, Campbell Soup Foundation

Buckley, John: director, Fannie Mae Foundation

Buckwalter, Alan Roland, III: chief executive officer, Chase Bank of Texas; president, Chase Bank of Texas Foundation, Inc.

Budney, Albert J., Jr.: president, director, Niagara Mohawk Holdings Inc.

Budzik, Ronald F.: executive director, Mead Corp. Foundation

Bueche, Wendell Francis: director, Marshall & Ilsley Foundation, Inc.

Buechel, Kathleen W.: president, treasurer, Alcoa Foundation

Buechner, Thomas Scharman: trustee, Corning Inc. Foundation

Buesman, Jon: president, chief executive officer, Battelle Memorial Institute

Buhrmaster, Robert C.: president, chief executive officer, director, chairman, Jostens, Inc.

Buker, Margaret R.: vice president, Piedmont Charitable Foundation

Bukowick, Peter A.: president, chief operating officer, director, Alliant Techsystems

Bullard, M. L.: vice president, director, United Dominion Foundation

Bundschuh, George August William: director, New York Life Foundation

Buntin, Nancy: vice president finance, Synovus Charitable Trust; chairman, chief executive officer, Synovus Financial Corp.

Bunton, Mary Anne: vice president, Liberty Corp.

Burak, Howard Paul: president consumer products group, Sony Electronics; secretary, director, Sony U.S.A. Foundation Inc.

Burchfield, Edward: chairman, chief executive officer, Valmont Industries, Inc.

Burd, Steven A.: president, chief executive officer, chairman, director, Safeway Inc.

Burdett, Kathleen: vice president, chief financial officer, Dexter Corp.; vice president, Dexter Corp. Foundation

Burenga, Kenneth L.: president, chief operating officer, director, Dow Jones & Co., Inc.

Burg, H. Peter: president, chief operating officer, FirstEnergy Corp.

Burgess, Christopher R.: assistant vice president, Chesapeake Corp.

Burgess, Ron: chief financial officer, Roseburg Forest Products Co.

Burke, Daniel Barnett: vice president, treasurer, director, ABC Foundation

Burke, Kathleen J.: president, executive director, Bank of America Foundation

Burke, Pamela: trustee, McDonald & Co. Securities Foundation

Burke, Robert W.: president, chief executive officer, Putnam Investors Fund

Burke, William L.: vice president, trustee, Merrill Lynch & Co. Foundation Inc.

Burkett, Bob: president, Guess? Foundation

Burkle, Ron: chairman, Ralph's Grocery Co.

Burleigh, William Robert: president, chief executive officer, director, Scripps Co. (E.W.); member, Scripps Howard Foundation

Burlingame, Harold W.: executive vice president wireless group, AT&T Corp.; trustee, AT&T Foundation

Burlingame, John Hunter: executive partner, Scripps Co. (E.W.)

Burner, David L.: chairman, president, chief executive officer, director, BFGoodrich Co.

Burnett, Gene: chief financial officer, Osborne Enterprises

Burnham, Duane Lee: chairman, chief executive officer, director, Abbott Laboratories

Burns, B. B., Jr.: vice president, director, United Dominion Foundation

Burns, Mitchell Anthony: president, director, Ryder System Charitable Foundation; chairman, president, chief executive officer, Ryder System, Inc.

Burns, Ron: chief financial officer, Grede Foundries

Burns, Sara: president, CMP, Central Maine Power Co.

Burrell, Richard L.: senator vice president finance, secretary, treasurer, Barry Corp. (R.G.); treasurer, Barry Foundation

Burress, John W., III: president, treasurer, Burress Foundation (J.W.); chairman, president, chief executive officer, Burress (J.W.)

Burroughs, Linda Kendrix: president, Mervyn's California

Burrus, Clark D.: secretary, First National Bank of Chicago Foundation

Burrus, Robert Lewis, Jr.: member scholarship committee, Circuit City Foundation

Burson, Glenda: vice president, treasurer, McWane Inc.

Burt, Robert Norcross: chairman, chief executive officer, director, FMC Corp.; director, FMC Foundation

Burton, Carl: director marketing communication department, Deloitte & Touche

Burton, Mike: director-at-large, Deloitte & Touche Foundation

Burts, Stephen L., Jr.: president, treasurer, chief financial officer, Synovus Financial Corp.

Busby, Gail: vice president, director, Tribune New York Foundation

Busch, August Adolphus, III: chairman, president, chief executive officer, Anheuser-Busch Companies, Inc.

Bush, Antoinette Cook: partner, CNA

Bush, Michael J.: vice president real estate, Giant Food Inc.

Bush, Norman: vice president, Fort James Corp.

Bushyeager, Peter: vice president, Prudential Foundation

Buss, Dennis: director, Analog Devices, Inc.

Butcher, Robert M.: chief financial officer, HSBC Bank USA

Butler, Andrew J.: trustee, Dow Chemical Co.

Butler, Gilbert: president, Butler Capital Corp.; president, treasurer, director, Butler Foundation

Butler, James R.: vice president, Montgomery Ward Foundation

Butler, John D.: executive vice president, chief human resources officer, Textron Inc.

Butts, David Wayne: senior vice president, Illinois Power Co.

Butzer, Bart: president, Mervyn's California

Buxton, Charles Ingraham, II: chairman, Federated Mutual Insurance Co.; president, Federated Mutual Insurance Foundation

Buxton, Winslow Hurlbert: chairman, president, chief executive officer, director, Pentair Inc.

Byck, Joseph S.: vice president, Union Carbide Foundation

Byers, Raymond Lester, Jr.: vice president, executive director, Ford Motor Co.

Byrd, Arthur A.: trustee, Kellogg Co. Twenty-Five Year Employees' Fund Inc.

Byrd, Edward R.: chief financial officer, Pacific Mutual Charitable Foundation

Byrd, Richard Hays: treasurer, Borden Foundation, Inc.

Byrne, Arthur P.: chairman, president, chief executive officer, director, Wiremold Co.; treasurer, Wiremold Foundation

Bzdak, Michael J.: director corporate contributions, Johnson & Johnson Family of Companies Contribution Fund

C

Cabot, John G. L.: vice chairman, Kinder Morgn

Cabral, Mary L.: trustee, Weyerhaeuser Co. Foundation

Caccamo, Aldo M.: vice president public affairs, Chevron Corp.

Caccini, Gianpaolo: chairman, chief executive officer, director, CertainTeed Corp.; chairman, CertainTeed Corp. Foundation; chairman, chief executive officer, director,

Norton Co.; president, director, Norton Co. Foundation
Cahalan, Joseph M.: president, Xerox Foundation
Cahn, Becky: trustee, Donaldson Foundation
Cahn, Charles C.: trustee, Bernstein & Co. Foundation, Inc. (Sanford C.)
Cain, Alan F.: director, Montana Power Foundation
Cain, William D.: director corporate & community relations, Montana Power Co.; executive director, Montana Power Foundation
Cal Kin, Joy: president, chief executive officer, Extendicare Health Services
Calderone, Phillip D.: treasurer, Banfi Vintners Foundation
Calderoni, Robert M.: chief financial officer, senior vice president finance, Avery Dennison Corp.
Caldwell, Barry: trustee, Alcon Foundation
Caldwell, Donald R.: president, chief operating officer, director, Safeguard Scientifics; vice president, Safeguard Scientifics Foundation
Caldwell, Robin: director community relations, Penney Co., Inc. (J.C.)
Caldwell, Royce S.: director, SBC Foundation
Calfee, William Rushton: trustee, Cleveland-Cliffs Foundation (The); executive vice president, commercial, Cleveland-Cliffs, Inc.
Calhoun, Essie L.: president, Eastman Kodak Charitable Trust; president, chief operating officer, director, Eastman Kodak Co.
Calise, Nicholas James: vice president, associate general counsel, secretary, BFGoodrich Co.; secretary, Goodrich Foundation, Inc. (B.F.)
Calise, William Joseph, Junior: senior vice president, secretary, general counsel, Rockwell International Corp.
Call, Robert V., Jr.: chairman, trustee, Agrilink Foods/Pro-Fac Foundation
Callahan, James C., Jr.: trustee, Eastern Bank Charitable Foundation
Callaway, Ely Reeves, Jr.: chairman, Callaway Golf Co.
Callaway, Lee: vice president public relations, Pacific Gas and Electric Co.
Cambell, Lewis B.: chairman, chief executive officer, director, Textron Inc.
Cambrom, Joe Carroll: member, American Fidelity Corp. Founders Fund
Cambrom, Laura: member, American Fidelity Corp. Founders Fund
Cambrom, William M.: member, American Fidelity Corp. Founders Fund
Camden, Carl T.: vice president, director, Kelly Services Foundation
Cameron, Gerry B.: chairman, director, U.S. Bancorp
Camilleri, Louis C.: chief financial officer, senior vice president, Philip Morris Companies Inc.
Cammarata, Bernard: president, chief executive officer, director, TJX Companies, Inc.; president, TJX Foundation, Inc.
Campanaro, Leonard A.: treasurer, Harsco Corp. Fund
Campbell, Cheryl Nichols: operation service advisory group, Cincinnati Bell Inc.
Campbell, Cole C.: editor, Pulitzer Publishing Co.; director, Pulitzer Publishing Co. Foundation
Campbell, Donald G.: executive vice president, chief financial officer, TJX Companies, Inc.; treasurer, director, TJX Foundation, Inc.
Campbell, Duane M.: vice president, Nationwide Insurance Enterprise Foundation
Campbell, Edward Patrick: president, chief operating officer, drc, Nordson Corp.; trustee, Nordson Corp. Foundation
Campbell, George Leroy: vice president public affairs, Florida Power Corp.
Campbell, Keith M.: vice president, director, Minnesota Mutual Foundation
Campbell, Phyllis J.: president private financial services, US Bank, Washington
Campbell, Robert Henderson: chairman, chief executive officer, Sunoco Inc.
Campbell, Stephen: vice president, Blair & Co. Foundation (William)
Campbell, Van C.: vice chairman, chief financial officer, chief administrative officer, director, Corning Inc.; trustee, Corning Inc. Foundation
Campbell, W. Patrick: executive vice president corporate strategy & business development, Ameritech Corp.
Cannata, Phyllis F.: manager community relations, Peoples Bank
Cannefax, Amy D.: trust representative, USAA Foundation, A Charitable Trust
Cannellos, Peter C.: assistant vice president, Wachtell, Lipton, Rosen & Katz Foundation
Canning, John Beckman: director, Rayonier Foundation
Cantalupo, James R.: vice chairman, McDonald's Corp.
Cantor, Bernard Gerald: president, director, Cantor, Fitzgerald Foundation; chairman, director, Cantor, Fitzgerald Securities Corp.
Cantor, Iris: president, director, Cantor, Fitzgerald Foundation
Cantu, Carlos H.: president, chief executive officer, director, ServiceMaster Co.
Cantwell, R. W.: secretary, Franklin Electric, Edward J. Schaefer, and T. W. KehoeCharitable and Educational Foundation
Capasso, Bob: chief financial officer, CSR Rinker Materials Corp.
Capell, Robert L., III: president, chief executive officer, BellSouth Corp.
Capizzi, Tom: president, McKesson Foundation
Capo, Thomas Patrick: senior vice president, treasurer, DaimlerChrysler Corp.
Capri, Tricia L.: vice president public relations, Pacific Gas and Electric Co.
Carbone, Anthony J.: vice chairman, director, Dow Chemical Co.
Cardello, Ann L.: trustee, Boston Edison Foundation
Cardoza, Christina: treasurer, Unocal Foundation
Cardy, Robert Willard: chairman, president, chief executive officer, director, Carpenter Technology Corp.; president, Carpenter Technology Corp. Foundation
Carey, Chase: chief executive officer, chairman, Fox Entertainment Group
Carey, Kathryn Ann: foundation manager, American Honda Foundation; president, chief executive officer, director, American Honda Motor Co., Inc.
Carl, John L.: executive vice president, chief financial officer, BP Amoco Corp.; director, BP Amoco Foundation
Carlin, E. Taylor: director, AMCORE Foundation
Carlson, Arleen M.: president, treasurer, Carlson Family Foundation (Curtis L.)
Carlson, Curtis Leroy: chairman, director, Carlson Companies, Inc.; president, treasurer, Carlson Family Foundation (Curtis L.)
Carlson, Glenn: trustee, Cranston Foundation
Carlson, Ruggles B.: vice president, Florida Rock Industries Foundation
Carlson, Susan E.: manager, Eastern Enterprises Foundation
Carlston, Douglas G.: president, director, Broderbund Foundation; chairman, Broderbund Software, Inc.
Carlston, Erin G.: president, director, Broderbund Foundation
Carmichael, Barbara S.: trustee, Dow Corning Foundation
Carmichael, David R.: senior vice president, general counsel, director, Pacific Mutual Life Insurance Co.
Carmichael, John A.: vice president, M&T Charitable Foundation
Carney, Richard: vice president, Universal Foods Foundation
Carol, Mary Beth: president, chief operating officer, FirstEnergy Corp.
Carp, Daniel A.: president, chief operating officer, director, Eastman Kodak Co.
Carpenter, Marshall L.: vice president, chief financial officer, MTS Systems Corp.
Carpenter, William M.: chief executive officer, director, chairman, Bausch & Lomb Inc.
Carpin, John: director, Illinois Tool Works Foundation
Carr, Cassandra Colvin: director, SBC Foundation
Carr, James: vice president national & neighborhood initiatives, Fannie Mae Foundation
Carr, Robert, MD: executive director, SmithKline Beecham Foundation
Carra, Phillip C.: director, Pharmacia & Upjohn Foundation; vice president public relations, Pharmacia & Upjohn, Inc.
Carrico, Stephen J.: director, Hensel Phelps Foundation
Carris, Barbara T.: president, Carris Corp. Foundation
Carris, William H.: president, Carris Corp. Foundation; chairman, president, chief executive officer, Carris Reels
Carroll, Charles A.: president, chief operating officer, director, Rubbermaid Inc.
Carroll, Philip Joseph: chairman, chief executive officer, Fluor Corp.; chairman, trustee, Fluor Foundation
Carson, David Ellis Adams: chairman, chief executive officer, Peoples Bank
Carter, Clayton R.: director, Graco Foundation; vice president industrial equipment division, Graco, Inc.
Carter, George: director, Carter Star Telegram Employees Fund (Amon G.); president, publisher, Fort Worth Star-Telegram Inc.
Carter, George Kent: vice president, treasurer, Chevron Corp.
Carter, J. Wesley: chief executive officer, Extendicare Foundation; chief operating officer, Extendicare Health Services
Carter, Jerry N.: trustee, Union Camp Charitable Trust; president, chief operating officer, director, Union Camp Corp.
Carter, Jill H.: director, Baxter Allegiance Foundation; president, chief executive officer, chairman, Baxter International Inc.
Carter, John Douglas: executive vice president, director, Bechtel Group, Inc.
Carter, Marshall Nichols: chairman, chief executive officer, State Street Bank & Trust Co.
Carter, Paul R.: executive vice president, Wal-Mart Stores, Inc.
Carter, Theresa: director, GenCorp Foundation
Cartmill, Molly: director corporate contributions, Sempra Energy
Carty, Donald J.: vice president, treasurer, AMR/American Airlines Foundation; president, chairman, chief executive officer, director, AMR Corp.
Carver, Martin Gregory: chairman, president, chief executive officer, Bandag, Inc.
Case, John J.: administrator, La-Z-Boy Foundation
Casey, Jeremiah E.: chairman, First Maryland Bancorp; chairman, trustee, First Maryland Foundation
Casey, Noreen: vice chairman, First Union Regional Foundation
Cash, R. D.: chairman, president, chief executive officer, director, Questar Corp.
Caspall, Ken: director, MFA Foundation
Cassidy, M. Sharon: trustee, USX Foundation, Inc.
Cassidy, Samuel M.: director, Star Bank NA

Castellani, John: executive vice president, Tenneco Automotive
Castellano, Joseph: director, CBS Foundation
Castellini, Clateo: chairman, president, chief executive officer, Becton Dickinson & Co.
Castellini, Daniel J.: senior vice president finance & administration, chief financial officer, Scripps Co. (E.W.); treasurer, Scripps Howard Foundation
Catell, Robert Barry: chairman, chief executive officer, Brooklyn Union
Catlow, Walter S.: executive vice president, Ameritech Corp.
Caulfield, Gary: director, First Hawaiian Foundation
Causey, Jerry L.: director, Consolidated Natural Gas System Foundation
Causey, John Paul, Jr.: senior vice president, secretary, general counsel, Chesapeake Corp.; chairman, trustee, Chesapeake Corp. Foundation
Cavanaugh, William, III: chairman, president, chief executive officer, Carolina Power & Light Co.; president, CP&L Foundation
Cawley, Michael J.: vice president risk management, Eastern Enterprises
Cerulli, Robert F.: assistant treasurer, director, May Department Stores Computer Foundation (The)
Cerza, James F., Jr.: executive vice president operations, Heilig-Meyers Co.
Cesan, Paul: president, chief operating officer, Schering-Plough Corp.
Cescau, Patrick: president, chief executive officer, Lipton Co.
Chabraja, Nicholas D.: chairman, chief executive officer, director, General Dynamics Corp.
Chain, John T., Junior: trustee, Kemper Foundation (James S.); president, Kemper National Insurance Companies
Chain, Mark: chairman, Deloitte & Touche Foundation
Chait, Gerald: trustee, Giant Eagle Foundation
Chambers, Anne Cox: treasurer, Cox Foundation (James M.)
Chambers, Caroline Solomon: secretary, Comerica Foundation; chairman, chief executive officer, Comerica Inc.
Chan, Iris S: director, Wells Fargo Foundation
Chandler, Charles Q.: co-trustee, INTRUST Bank Charitable Trust; chairman, INTRUST Financial Corp.
Chandler, Charles Quarles, IV: co-trustee, INTRUST Bank Charitable Trust; president, director, INTRUST Financial Corp.
Chandler, George N., II: vice president, reduced iron, Cleveland-Cliffs, Inc.
Chandler, J. Harold: chairman, president, chief executive officer, Provident Companies, Inc.
Chandler, John T.: trustee, Equifax Foundation; corporate vice president, chief administrative officer, Equifax Inc.
Chandler, Wallace Lee: member, Universal Leaf Foundation
Chandler, William Everett: senior vice president finance, secretary, chief financial officer, Hunt Manufacturing Co.
Chang, David: employee representative, Mitsubishi Electric America Foundation
Chapman, Max, Jr.: chairman, chief executive officer, director, Nomura America Foundation
Chapman, Norman H.: chairman, Inman-Riverdale Foundation
Chapman, Robert H., III: president, Inman Mills; chairman, Inman-Riverdale Foundation
Chappell, Robert E.: chairman, chief executive officer, Penn Mutual Life Insurance Co.
Chappell, Stephen: corporate vice president, Telcordia Technologies
Chappell, Thomas E.: treasurer, Alabama Power Foundation
Chapple, Thomas Leslie: senior vice president, general counsel, secretary, Gannett Co., Inc.; secretary, Gannett Foundation
Charlestein, Morton: president, Charlestein Foundation (Julius and Ray)
Chavez, Annette: administrator, Amgen Foundation; chairman, chief executive officer, director, Amgen, Inc.
Chavez, Sandra: treasurer, trustee, Blade Foundation
Chawla, Ashok: president global business group, Mallinckrodt Chemical, Inc.
Chazen, Jerome A.: trustee, Claiborne Foundation (Liz); co-founder, chairman, director, Liz Claiborne, Inc.
Chelberg, Bruce Stanley: chairman, chief executive officer, director, Whitman Corp.; director, Whitman Corp. Foundation
Chellgren, Paul Wilbur: chief executive officer, chairman, director, Ashland, Inc.; member, Ashland Inc. Foundation
Chemerow, David I.: executive vice president, chief financial officer, Playboy Enterprises Inc.
Chen, Y. C.: assistant secretary, Tai and Co. Foundation, Inc. (J.T.)
Chenault, Kenneth Irvine: president, chief operating officer, director, American Express Co.; trustee, American Express Foundation
Cheney, Jeffrey P.: senior vice president, finance, Kohler Co.
Cheney, Richard B.: chief executive officer, Halliburton Co.; president, Halliburton Foundation, Inc.
Chernin, Peter: chairman, chief executive officer, Fox Entertainment Group
Cherrington, R.G.: trustee, Air Products Foundation
Chessum, Darrell D.: chairman, chief executive officer, director, Unocal Corp.; treasurer, Unocal Foundation
Chiafari, Anthony: director, Chesebrough Foundation
Chiappetta, Robert A.: trustee, Amsted Industries Foundation; vice president, chief financial officer, Amsted Industries Inc.
Chiba, Takashi: trustee, Hitachi Foundation
Childress, Jan C.: vice president, Brooklyn Union
Childs, Kay: vice president human resources, Shaklee Corp.
Ching, Meredith J.: senior vice president, director, chairman HI committee, Alexander & Baldwin Foundation; vice president government & community relations, Alexander & Baldwin, Inc.
Ching, Patrick D.: treasurer, Servco Foundation
Choate, Jerry D.: chairman, chief executive officer, director, Allstate Foundation
Chokey, James A.: treasurer, Harnischfeger Industries Foundation
Chookaszian, Dennis Haig: chairman, chief executive officer, CNA
Chouinard, Yvon: owner, principal, Patagonia Inc.
Chow, Myra: director, Gap Foundation/Gap Inc. Community Relations
Christensen, Gary M.: president, Pella Corp.; president, director, Pella Rolscreen Foundation
Christopher, Stephen: president, chief operating officer, Security Life of Denver Insurance Co.
Chung, H. Young: trustee, Donaldson Foundation
Churchill, Charlie: vice president, North America industrial group, Matsushita Electric Corp. of America
Churchwell, Pete: president, Public Service Co. of Oklahoma
Cianciola, Charles Sal: chairman, trustee, Chesapeake Corp. Foundation
Cich, Brenda M.: director, Piper Jaffray Companies Foundation
Ciconte, Thomas: vice president, Hercules Inc.
Ciraulo, Jerry: secretary, director, Grand Marnier Foundation
Cismoski, Jerome J.: trustee, First Evergreen Foundation
Citrone, Neil: chairman, New York Mercantile Exchange Charitable Foundation
Civello, Nelson D.: director, Dain Bosworth Foundation
Civgin, Don: vice president, treasurer, Montgomery Ward & Co., Inc.
Clabes, Judy G.: president, chief executive officer, Scripps Co. (E.W.); president, chief executive officer, trustee, member, Scripps Howard Foundation
Clanin, Robert J.: senior vice president, chief financial officer, treasurer, director, United Parcel Service of America Inc.
Clapham, Clarence D.: secretary, Lancaster Lens Foundation
Clarey, Patricia T.: vice president, Transamerica Corp.; president, Transamerica Foundation
Clarity, Barbara A.: director, TENNANT Co. Foundation
Clark, Howard Longstreth, Jr.: vice chairman, Walter Industries Inc.
Clark, John W.: secretary-trs, Consumers Energy Co.; president, Consumers Energy Foundation
Clark, Kathy: trustee, Fortis Insurance Foundation
Clark, L. Hill: president, chief operating officer, Crane Co.
Clark, Maura: chief financial officer, Clark Refining & Marketing
Clark, Patricia: director professional development, Autodesk Foundation
Clark, Richard: manager corporate communication, McDonald & Co. Securities, Inc.
Clark, Richard McCourt: senior vice president, general counsel, secretary, Kellogg Co.; vice president, trustee, Kellogg Co. Twenty-Five Year Employees' Fund Inc.
Clark, Sylvia: executive director, NEC Foundation of America
Clark, Thomas A.: treasurer
Clark, Wade: vice president government affairs, Deere & Co.
Clarke, Glenn S.: vice president, Avon Products Foundation, Inc.
Clarke, Lois A.: treasurer, United Coal Co. Charitable Foundation; executive vice president finance, chief financial officer, United Co.
Clarke, Robert F.: chairman, president, chief executive officer, director, Hawaiian Electric Co., Inc.; president, director, Hawaiian Electric Industries Charitable Foundation
Clarke, Thomas E.: president, chief operating officer, Nike, Inc.
Clarke, Wendolyn C.: assistant secretary, UNUM Foundation
Clayton, Jon Kerry: trustee, Fortis Foundation; executive vice president, Fortis, Inc.
Clayton, Joseph P.: president, chief executive officer, director, Frontier Corp.
Clayton, Paul: president, Burger King Corp.
Cleary, Joan: administrator, Blue Cross & Blue Shield of Minnesota
Cleary, William C.: director, AMETEK Foundation
Clemens, Richard: president, chief executive officer, Monarch Machine Tool Co.
Clemente, Constantine Louis: chairman, Pfizer Foundation; executive vice president corporate affairs, secretary, corporate counsel, Pfizer Inc.
Clemins, Reter J., III: trustee, Vulcan Materials Co. Foundation
Clerico, John A.: chief financial officer, Praxair; secretary, Praxair Foundation
Clevidence, Thomas G.: secretary, McDonald & Co. Securities Foundation; executive, McDonald & Co. Securities, Inc.
Click, Dennis W.: vice president, treasurer, Nationwide Insurance Enterprise Foundation
Clifford, Cliff: vice president, IBM International Foundation
Clifton, Paul Hoot, Jr.: president, Colonial Life & Accident Insurance Co.

Cline, Robert Stanley: chairman, chief executive officer, director, Airborne Freight Corp.

Cloninger, Kriss, III: executive vice president, chief financial officer, treasurer, AFLAC Inc.

Cloud, Bruce Benjamin, Sr.: vice chairman, director, Zachry Co. (H.B.)

Clouser, Christopher E.: vice president revenue management and area marketing, Northwest Airlines, Inc.

Clutterbuck, Robert T.: president, McDonald & Co. Securities, Inc.

Cochran, Travis L.: member, Anthem Foundation, Inc.

Cockerham, Haven E.: senior vice president human resources, Donnelley & Sons Co. (R.R.)

Cocklin, Kim Roland: senior vice president, Texas Gas Transmission Corp.

Codey, Lawrence R.: president, chief operating officer, Public Service Electric & Gas Co.

Cody, Thomas Gerald: executive vice president legal & human resources, Federated Department Stores, Inc.

Coen, Beverly J.: trustee, Nordson Corp. Foundation

Coffey, John: vice president programs, State Farm Companies Foundation; senior vice president, State Farm Mutual Automobile Insurance Co.

Coffey, Robin S.: director, Harris Bank Foundation

Coffin, Dwight C.: vice president human resources, Continental Grain Co.; vice president, secretary, director, Continental Grain Foundation

Coffin, Sarah R.: director, Fuller Co. Foundation (H.B.); vice president specialty group, Fuller Co. (H.B.)

Coffman, Vance: vice president, Lockheed Martin Corp.

Cogan, John Francis, Jr.: president, chief executive officer, director, Pioneer Group

Cogan, Marshall Stuart: chairman, president, chief executive officer, director, Trace International Holdings, Inc.; director, Trace International Holdings, Inc. Foundation

Cogswell, Lourdes: executive director, NEC America, Inc.

Cohen, Edwin C.: chairman, Echoing Green Foundation

Cohen, Eileen Phillips: chairman, president, trustee, Presto Foundation

Cohen, Jonathan L.: secretary, director, Goldman Sachs Foundation

Cohen, Joseph M.: president, director, Cowen Foundation; chairman, chief executive officer, S.G. Cowen

Cohen, Maryjo Rose: president, chief executive officer, director, National Presto Industries, Inc.; vice president, treasurer, trustee, Presto Foundation

Cohen, Melvin Samuel: chairman, National Presto Industries, Inc.; chairman, president, trustee, Presto Foundation

Cohen, Sandra: trustee, Bank of America Foundation

Cohen, Sharon: executive director, trustee, Reebok Human Rights Foundation (The)

Coker, Charles Westfield: trustee, Sonoco Foundation; vice president, Sonoco Products Co.

Coker-Nelson, Marg: vice president, Sentry Insurance Foundation Inc.

Colatrella, Brenda D.: trustee, Merck Co. Foundation

Colburn, Keith W.: chairman, chief executive officer, Consolidated Electrical Distributors

Cole, Franklin Alan: chairman, Aon Foundation

Cole, John T.: corporate controller, Butler Manufacturing Co.

Cole, Ken: chairman, director, AlliedSignal Foundation Inc.

Cole, Kenneth O.: vice president customer service, Memphis Light Gas & Water Division

Cole, Lewis George: president, director, AMETEK Foundation

Cole, Robert A.: chief financial officer, senior vice president, American General Finance; senior vice president, chief financial officer, director, American General Finance Foundation

Coleman, J. Reed: trustee, Kemper Foundation (James S.)

Coleman, John A.: senior vice president, secretary, general counsel, Rockwell International Corp. Trust

Coleman, Lester Earl: trustee, Lubrizol Foundation (The)

Coles, Jann: manager corporate education, Colgate-Palmolive Co.

Colgan, Celeste: president, Halliburton Foundation, Inc.

Collamore, Tom: chief financial officer, senior vice president, Philip Morris Companies Inc.

Collins, Arthur D.: chief operating officer, Medtronic, Inc.

Collins, Duane E.: president, chief executive officer, director, Parker Hannifin Corp.; vice president, trustee, Parker Hannifin Foundation

Collins, Michael J.: president pharmaceuticals group, Mallinckrodt Chemical, Inc.

Collins, Paul John: vice chairman, director, Citibank Corp.

Collins, Theodore J.: senior vice president law and contracts, Boeing Co.

Collins, William F., Jr.: trustee, Eastern Bank Charitable Foundation

Collison, Mary E.: vice president finance, chief financial officer, Edwards Enterprise Software (J.D.); vice chairman, Edwards Foundation (J.D.)

Colman, Robert L.: executive vice president human resources, Delta Air Lines, Inc.

Coltman, Charles L., III: vice president, First Union Regional Foundation

Coltman, David A.: senior vice president marketing, United Airlines Inc.

Colton, S. David: senior vice president, general counsel, Phelps Dodge Corp.

Comb, Donald G.: president, New England Bio Labs; trustee, New England Bio Labs Foundation

Combs, Esther: secretary, treasurer, CIRI Foundation

Commes, Thomas Allen: president, chief operating officer, director, Sherwin-Williams Co.; assistant secretary, trustee, Sherwin-Williams Foundation

Compton, Ronald E.: senior vice president, Aetna Foundation

Conant, Colleen Christner: branch manager, Scripps Co. (E.W.); trustee, Scripps Howard Foundation

Conaty, William J.: treasurer, GE Fund

Condit, Philip Murray: chairman, chief executive officer, director, Boeing Co.

Condon, James Edward: treasurer, Hartmarx Charitable Foundation; vice president, treasurer, Hartmarx Corp.

Conklin, Thomas J.: senior vice president, secretary, MONY Group (The); director, MONY Life Insurance of New York (The)

Conley, E. Renae: president, Cinergy Corp.

Conley, Michael L.: executive vice president, chief executive officer, McDonald's Corp.

Connelly, James F.: manager regional relations, Detroit Edison Co.; director, Detroit Edison Foundation

Connolly, Charles H.: senior vice president corporate affairs & investor relations, Whitman Corp.; president, Whitman Corp. Foundation

Connolly, Edward M., Jr.: president, Hoechst Marion Roussel, Inc.

Connolly, Eugene Bernard, Jr.: chairman emeritus, USG Corp.

Connolly, Gerald Edward: trustee, Reinhart Family Foundation (D. B. and Marjorie)

Connolly, John: manager community relations, Sears, Roebuck and Co.; vice president, Sears, Roebuck and Co. Foundation

Connolly, John J.: director corporate relations, Boston Edison Co.; director, Boston Edison Foundation

Connor, James Richard: trustee, Kemper Foundation (James S.)

Connor, Richard L.: president, publisher, Fort Worth Star-Telegram Inc.

Connor, Walter Robert: director, Glaxo Wellcome Foundation

Connors, John: senior vice president finance and administration, chief financial officer, Microsoft Corp.

Conroy, James T.: senior vice president, Revlon Foundation Inc.

Conroy, Patrick F.: chief financial officer, New York Mercantile Exchange

Contino, Francis A.: executive vice president, chief financial officer, McCormick & Co. Inc.

Convisser, Theodora S.: trustee, Boston Edison Foundation

Cook, J. Michael: chairman, chief executive officer, Deloitte & Touche; chairman, Deloitte & Touche Foundation

Cook, Jane Bancroft: member advisory committee, Dow Jones Foundation

Cook, John Rowland: trustee, Harcourt General Charitable Foundation; senior vice president, chief financial officer, Harcourt General, Inc.

Cook, Susan J.: vice president, member contributions committee, Eaton Charitable Fund; vice president human resources, Eaton Corp.

Cook, Timothy D.: senior vice president worldwide operations, Apple Computer, Inc.

Cooke, Anne R.: vice president marketing, sales, Michigan Consolidated Gas Co.

Cookson, John Simmons: vice president finance, treasurer, assistant secretary, Kingsbury Corp.; trustee, Kingsbury Fund

Cool, Judd R.: senior vice president human resources, Allegheny Technologies Inc.

Cooley, Karin: administrator corp. contributions, Loctite Corp.

Coolidge, E. David, III: vice president, Blair & Co. Foundation (William); chief executive officer, Blair & Co. (William); vice president, Pittway Corp. Charitable Foundation

Coon, Jerome J.: vice president, Physicians Mutual Insurance Co. Foundation

Cooper, Adrian R. T.: trustee, Credit Suisse First Boston Foundation Trust

Cooper, Aldrage B.: vice president community relations, Johnson & Johnson; member corporate contributions committee, Johnson & Johnson Family of Companies Contribution Fund

Cooper, Deborah: trustee, Scripps Howard Foundation

Cooper, Janis Campbell: secretary, Maytag Corp. Foundation

Cooper, Robert N.: president, Ameritech Michigan

Cooper, William Allen: chairman, director, TCF National Bank Minnesota

Coors, Peter Hanson: vice president, director, Coors Brewing Co.

Coors, William K.: chairman, president, director, Coors Brewing Co.

Copeland, Frederick C., Jr.: chairman, president, Aetna Foundation

Copeland, James E.: managing partner, Deloitte & Touche

Copenhaver, Don: director, MFA Foundation; president, chief executive officer, MFA Inc.

Copes, Ronald A.: executive director, Massachusetts Mutual Life Insurance Co.

Copley, David C.: president, trustee, Copley Foundation (James S.); president, chief executive officer, director, senior management board, Copley Press, Inc.
Copley, Helen K.: chairman, trustee, Copley Foundation (James S.); chairman, director, senior management board, Copley Press, Inc.
Coppinger, John J., Jr.: comptroller, Texaco Foundation
Coppola, Joseph R.: chairman, president, chief executive officer, director, Giddings & Lewis
Corbin, William R.: executive vice president timberlands & distribution, Weyerhaeuser Co.; trustee, Weyerhaeuser Co. Foundation
Corbitt, Luke: chairman, chief executive officer, director, Kerr-McGee Corp.
Corbo, Vincent J.: president, chief executive officer, director, Hercules Inc.
Corby, Francis Michael, Jr.: executive vice president finance & administration, chief financial officer, Harnischfeger Industries; treasurer, Harnischfeger Industries Foundation
Corcoran, John J.: assistant treasurer, CIGNA Foundation
Corcoran, Martha: trustee, Anderson Foundation
Cordaro, C. Roberto: director, Cummins Engine Foundation
Cordes, Donald L.: secretary, Koch Foundation, Inc. (Fred C. and Mary R.)
Corley, Robin: chief executive officer, chairman, Fox Entertainment Group
Cornelius, James M.: secretary, AUL Foundation Inc.
Cornish, Cathy: executive vice president, chief financial officer, Starwood Hotels & Resorts Worldwide, Inc.
Correll, Alston Dayton 'Pete', Jr.: chairman, president, chief executive officer, director, Georgia-Pacific Corp.; director, Georgia-Pacific Foundation
Correnti, John D.: president, chief executive officer, director, Nucor Corp.
Corson, Keith Daniel: president, chief operating officer, Coachmen Industries, Inc.
Corti, Mario A.: senior vice president, chief administrative officer, Nestle U.S.A. Inc.
Corwin, Laura J.: director, New York Times Co. Foundation
Cosgrove, Michael J.: treasurer, GE Fund
Cosse, Steven Anthony: senior vice president, general counsel, Murphy Oil Corp.
Costa, Jo-Ann G.: director public affairs & administration, Hughes Electronics Corp.
Costa, Paulo F.: group chairman, Johnson & Johnson; member corporate contributions committee, Johnson & Johnson Family of Companies Contribution Fund
Costello, John T.: vice president corporate relations, Commonwealth Edison Co.
Costley, Gary E.: chairman, president, chief executive officer, director, International Multifoods Corp.
Cotter, Robert F.: chief operating officer, Starwood Hotels & Resorts Worldwide, Inc.
Cottingham, Patty: administrator, Scripps Howard Foundation
Cottrell, G. Walton: senior vice president, chief financial officer, Carpenter Technology Corp.
Coughenour, Katherine N.: trustee, Quaker Chemical Foundation
Coughlan, Gary Patrick: chief financial officer, senior vice president finance, Abbott Laboratories; director, Abbott Laboratories Fund
Coughlin, Thomas Martin: member, Wal-Mart Foundation; executive vice president, Wal-Mart Stores, Inc.
Coughlin, Timothy C.: president, Riggs Bank NA
Coulter, David A.: president, director, Bank of America
Coulter, Joan: secretary, treasurer, Reily Foundation
Coulter, Patrick C. G.: president, Bell Atlantic Foundation; senior vice president corporate communications, Gulfstream Aerospace Corp.
Countryman, Gary Lee: chairman, Liberty Mutual Insurance Group
Counts, Wil: vice president, scholarships and grants committee, America West Airlines Foundation
Courts, Richard Winn, II: chairman, director, Atlantic Investment Co.
Coury, Maxime: treasurer, director, Grand Marnier Foundation
Cowan, James R.: vice president, director, Stonecutter Foundation; chairman, president, chief executive officer, director, Stonecutter Mills Corp.
Cowan, Keith O.: vice president corporate development, BellSouth Corp.
Cowan, Mark: director, Extendicare Foundation
Cowell, Marion Aubrey, Jr.: senior vice president, director corporate contributions, First Union Foundation
Cowgill, Bruce H.: president, CertainTeed Corp.; director, CertainTeed Corp. Foundation
Cox, Daniel T.: executive vice president, Aon Corp.
Cox, Phillip R.: president, Cinergy Corp.; director, Cinergy Foundation
Cox, Robert T.: director, Shelter Insurance Foundation
Cox, William Coburn, Jr.: director, Dow Jones & Co., Inc.
Coyle, Dennis Patrick: chief executive officer, director, FPL Group Foundation, Inc.
Coyne, William E.: senior vice president, Minnesota Mining & Manufacturing Co.
Craig, Mary Ellen: senior manager, American Express Foundation
Crandall, Robert Lloyd: director, AMR Corp.
Crandall, Steven D.: senior vice president, secretary, Old Kent Foundation
Crane, David W.: trustee, Crane & Co. Fund; chief financial officer, Crane & Co., Inc.
Crane, Lansing E.: chairman, president, Crane & Co., Inc.
Crane, Russell L.: director, PPG Industries Foundation; senior vice president, PPG Industries, Inc.
Crawford, James D.: president, chief executive officer, director, Simplot Co. (J.R.); treasurer, Simplot Foundation (J.R.)
Crawford, Lisa: president, chief operating officer, Nike, Inc.
Crawford, William G.: vice president, Ecolab Inc.
Creach, Dale H.: director, MFA Foundation
Creach, Ormal C.: director, MFA Foundation
Creek, Wallace W.: secretary, General Motors Foundation
Crenshaw, Gordon Lee, II: member, Universal Leaf Foundation; chairman emeritus, Universal Leaf Tobacco Co., Inc.
Cristallo, Peter P.: associate senior vice president human resources & administration, NEC America, Inc.
Critchlow, Paul W.: president, trustee, Merrill Lynch & Co. Foundation Inc.; senior vice president marketing & communications, Merrill Lynch & Co., Inc.
Critelli, Michael J.: vice president, secretary, general counsel, chairman, Pitney Bowes Inc.
Critser, Gary P.: senior executive vice president, secretary, treasurer, director, Habig Foundation
Croce, Robert W.: group chairman, Johnson & Johnson
Croft, Jane A.: vice president, Croft-Leominster Foundation
Croft, Kent G.: president, chief executive officer, Croft-Leominster; president, Croft-Leominster Foundation
Croft, L. Gordon: chairman, Croft-Leominster; vice president, Croft-Leominster Foundation
Croll, Alan D.: director, Katten, Muchin & Zavis Foundation
Cromer, Richard F.: executive vice president, chief operating officer energy supply division, Montana Power Co.; director, Montana Power Foundation
Cromwell, Carol: manager, IBM International Foundation; program manager, International Business Machines Corp.
Cron, James: vice president planning & scheduling, Northwest Airlines, Inc.
Cronk, William F., III: president, director, Dreyer's Grand Ice Cream
Crook, Donald Martin: president, director, Kimberly-Clark Foundation
Crooke, Edward A.: president, Baltimore Gas & Electric Foundation
Crosbie, Stewart: treasurer, Physicians Mutual Insurance Co. Foundation
Crosley, Britton E.: secretary, treasurer, CIRI Foundation
Crossman, Elizabeth A.: vice president, Weyerhaeuser Co. Foundation
Crouch, Robert F.: chairman, trustee, Copley Foundation (James S.)
Crull, Timm F.: retired chairman, Nestle U.S.A. Inc.
Csaszar, Bernice: chief financial officer, executive vice president, treasurer, Bridgestone/Firestone, Inc.; administrator, Bridgestone/Firestone Trust Fund (The)
Cudlip, Brittain B.: chairman, Bardes Corp.
Cullen, Claire: trustee, Bronfman Foundation/Joseph E. Seagram & Sons, Inc. Fund (Samuel)
Cullen, Pat: trustee, Fortis Insurance Foundation
Cullers, Jeanne E.: director, FINA Foundation
Culp, E. Ronald: vice president public affairs, Sears, Roebuck and Co.; president, Sears, Roebuck and Co. Foundation
Cumming, Marilee J.: president, Penney Co., Inc. (J.C.)
Cummings, Daniel W.: trustee, Cummings Properties Foundation
Cummings, Fred: trustee, McDonald & Co. Securities Foundation; manager corporate communication, McDonald & Co. Securities, Inc.
Cummings, Marilyn D., MD: trustee, Cummings Properties Foundation; chairman, Cummings Properties Management
Cummings, William S.: chairman, Cummings Properties Management
Cummiskey, Elizabeth: director, Chesebrough Foundation
Cunningham, James: vice president, director, MFA Foundation
Cunningham, Thomas P.: chairman, Chicago Board of Trade Foundation
Curci, John V.: chief financial officer, Vesper Corp.; trustee, Vesper Foundation
Curley, John J.: chairman, chief executive officer, director, Gannett Co., Inc.; chairman, Gannett Foundation
Curran, Bill: executive vice president, chief financial officer, Philips Electronics North America Corp.
Curran, Charles E.: secretary, program officer, Block Foundation (H&R)
Curry, David R.: vice president corporate contributions, Unisys Corp.
Curry, Faith: director, Dana Corp. Foundation
Curtis, Barron W.: vice president government affairs, Deere & Co.; assistant treasurer, Deere Foundation (John)
Curtis, Donna Streibich: director, Harris Bank Foundation
Cushwa, Charles Benton, III: trustee, Commercial Intertech Foundation
Cushwa, William Wallace: director, Commercial Intertech Corp.; trustee, Commercial Intertech Foundation
Cusick, Thomas A.: chairman, TCF National Bank Minnesota

Cusumano, James C.: chief financial officer, Schloss & Co. (Marcus)

Cutchins, Clifford Armstrong, IV: president, Fort James Corp.; chairman, director, Fort James Foundation (The)

Cutler, Alexander MacDonald: senior vice president, member contributions committee, Eaton Charitable Fund

Cutler, Richard M.: vice chairman, director, Putnam Investments

Czajkowski, Andrew P.: chief executive officer, Blue Cross & Blue Shield of Minnesota; chairman, director, Blue Cross & Blue Shield of Minnesota Foundation Inc.

D

D'Alessandro, David F.: president, chief operating officer, Hancock Financial Services (John)

D'Alessandro, Dominic: president, chief executive officer, director, Manulife Financial

d'Alessio, Jon W.: trustee, McKesson Foundation

D'Almada, Peter: senior vice president, Ecolab Inc.

D'Amato, Anthony S.: secretary, Borden Foundation, Inc.

D'Andrade, Hugh Alfred: president, chief operating officer, Schering-Plough Corp.; trustee, member, Schering-Plough Foundation

Daberko, David A.: chairman, chief executive officer, National City Corp.

Dabney, Donna C.: vice president, Reynolds Metals Co. Foundation

Dabney, Fred E., II: executive director, Royal & SunAlliance Insurance Foundation, Inc.; vice president corporate communications, Royal & SunAlliance USA, Inc.

Daddario, Richard M.: director, MONY Life Insurance of New York (The)

Daft, Douglas: chairman, chief executive officer, Coca-Cola Co.

Dagley, Larry J.: senior vice president, chief financial officer, Pacific Enterprises

Dagnon, James B.: senior vice president people, Boeing Co.

Dahan, Rene: senior vice president, Exxon Mobil Corp.

Dahl, Anna: vice president, scholarships and grants committee, America West Airlines Foundation

Dahl, Richard J.: president, Pacific Century Financial Corp.

Dahlberg, Alfred William, III: chairman, president, chief executive officer, Southern Co. Services Inc.

Dahle, Johannes: vice president, treasurer, trustee, Presto Foundation

Dahm, Anthony Edward: controller, Giant Food Inc.

Dale, Clayton: vice president, trustee, Procter & Gamble Fund

Daley, Leo J.: vice president, treasurer, Air Products and Chemicals, Inc.

Dalle, Jean-Paul: vice president, CertainTeed Corp.

Dalton, James F.: chairman, trustee, Tektronix Foundation; vice president, general counsel, secretary, Tektronix, Inc.

Damas, Mary D.: assistant secretary, Winthrop Foundation

Damico, Joseph F.: director, Baxter Allegiance Foundation

Dammerman, Dennis Dean: vice chairman, director, General Electric Co.

Damonti, John L.: secretary, Bristol-Myers Squibb Foundation Inc.

Dana, Charles H.: president, chairman, Owens Corning Foundation, Inc.

Danford, Philip C.: trustee, Dun & Bradstreet Corp. Foundation, Inc.

Daniels, John Hancock: chairman audit committee, member executive & finance committee, Archer-Daniels-Midland Co.; chairman, Archer-Daniels-Midland Foundation

Daniels, Mitchell E., Jr.: chairman, treasurer, Lilly Foundation (Eli)

Danielson, John G.: vice president, treasurer, Albertson's Inc.

Danielson, John R.: senior vice president investor & corporate relations, U.S. Bancorp

Dardess, Margaret: president, director, Glaxo Wellcome Foundation; senior vice president, Glaxo Wellcome Inc.

Darehshori, Nader Farhang: chairman, president, chief executive officer, Houghton Mifflin Co.

Dargene, Carl J.: director, AMCORE Foundation

Darling, Michele S.: comptroller, Prudential Foundation

Darling, Robert Edward, Jr.: executive director, Ensign-Bickford Foundation

Dascoli, D. Paul: chief financial officer, vice president, Thomasville Furniture Industries Inc.

Daugherty, Robert B.: president, Valmont Foundation; director, Valmont Industries, Inc.

Dauska, Walter J.: treasurer, Green Bay Packaging

Davenport, Margaret: trustee, Golub Foundation

David, George A. L.: chairman, president, chief executive officer, chief operating officer, United Technologies Corp.

Davidson, George A., Jr.: chairman, chief executive officer, director, Consolidated Natural Gas Co.

Davidson, Park R.: trustee, Burlington Industries Foundation

Davidson, Sheila C.: director, Chicago Tribune Foundation

Davies, Charles R.: director, GEICO Philanthropic Foundation

Davies, Richard Warren: trustee, Hubbell Foundation (Harvey)

Davies, Samantha: vice president corporate communications, Washington Mutual, Inc.

Davis, Andrew Dano: vice president, director, Winn-Dixie Stores Foundation; vice president, Winn-Dixie Stores Inc.

Davis, Betty G.: director, Grede Foundation; chief financial officer, Grede Foundries

Davis, Carolyne Kahle, PhD: assistant secretary, Merck Co. Foundation; president, Prudential Foundation

Davis, Donald H., Jr.: president, chief executive officer, chairman, Rockwell International Corp.; chairman trust committee, Rockwell International Corp. Trust

Davis, Dwight D.: president, chief operating officer

Davis, Edward J.: chief financial officer, vice president, treasurer, Wyman-Gordon Co.

Davis, Erroll Brown, Jr.: president, chief executive officer, director, Wisconsin Power & Light Co.

Davis, James K.: senior vice president corporate relations, Georgia Power Co.; director, Georgia Power Foundation

Davis, John B., MD: secretary, Physicians Mutual Insurance Co. Foundation

Davis, Joseph E.: program director

Davis, Karen: director, Hasbro Charitable Trust Inc.

Davis, Karyll A.: trustee, Heinz Co. Foundation (H.J.)

Davis, Mike: chief financial officer, DSM Copolymer

Davis, R. Steven: trustee, AT&T Foundation

Davis, Robert M.: trustee, Barden Foundation, Inc.

Davis, Ruth Margaret: secretary, Air Products Foundation

Davis, Sonya M.: director corporate contributions, Monsanto Co.; secretary, Monsanto Fund

Davis, Ted C.: trustee, Gerber Foundation

Davis, W. Derek: trustee, Dixie Yarns Foundation, Inc.

Davis, Walter Stewart: director, Grede Foundation

Davis, William E.: chairman, chief executive officer, Niagara Mohawk Holdings Inc.

Davis, William L.: chairman, chief executive officer, director, Donnelley & Sons Co. (R.R.)

Davisson, Ralph M.: trustee, Potlatch Foundation II

Dawson, Angela: communications administration, Reliant Energy Minnegasco

Dawson, Edwin H.: chairman, director, Arvin Foundation

Dawson-White, Gail: mgr, Sovereign Bank Foundation

Day, Carolyn C.: assistant secretary, Publix Supermarkets

Day, Frank R.: chairman, Trustmark National Bank

De Bakcsy, Alex: vice president, trustee, Copley Foundation (James S.)

de Chalendar, Pierre-Andre: president abrasives branch, Norton Co.

de Garne, Lilo Navales: chairman, chief executive officer, State Street Bank & Trust Co.; foundation officer, State Street Foundation

de Gasperis, Francois: director, Grand Marnier Foundation

de la Garza, Luis Adolpho: president, chief financial officer, Valero Energy Corp.

De Nicola, Paul J.: president, chief executive officer, Southern Co. Services Inc.

de Ocejo, Luis J.: senior vice president human resources, Pillsbury Co.; president, director, Pillsbury Co. Foundation

De Raismes, Ann D.: chairman, president, chief executive officer, Hartford (The)

De Schutter, Richard U.: director, Searle Charitable Trust; chairman, chief executive officer, Searle & Co. (G.D.)

de Vink, Lodewijk J. R.: director, Warner-Lambert Charitable Foundation; president, chief operating officer, director, Warner-Lambert Co.

de Vlugt, William: chairman, Van Leer Holding

Dean, John W., III: vice president, treasurer, Rubbermaid Inc.

Dean, Roger W.: controller, chief administrative officer, Fifth Third Bancorp

Dearstyne, William D., Jr.: group chairman, Johnson & Johnson; member corporate contributions committee, Johnson & Johnson Family of Companies Contribution Fund

Deavenport, Earnest W., Jr.: chairman, chief executive officer, director, Eastman Chemical Co.

DeBoer, Anne M.: trustee, Dow Corning Foundation

deBuhr, Dean: vice president, general manager professional products, Ecolab Inc.

DeCarlo, Sue: vice president, Union Carbide Foundation

DeCaro, Angelo: secretary, director, Goldman Sachs Foundation

Decherd, Robert William: chairman, president, chief executive officer, director, Belo Corp. (A.H.); chairman, trustee, Belo Corp. Foundation (A.H.)

Dechman, David: managing director, Goldman Sachs Group

Decker, Don M.: director, Dana Corp. Foundation

Deddens, Carl J.: vice president, Revlon Foundation Inc.

Dee, Steve: director, Montana Power Foundation

Deeney, Gerald D.: vice president, chief financial officer, Hubbard Broadcasting, Inc.; secretary, Hubbard Foundation

Deering, Anthony W.: chairman, chief executive officer, Rouse Co.; chairman, president, trustee, Rouse Co. Foundation

DeGraan, Edward F.: president, Duracell International

Deig, Mary R.: community relations coordinator, American General Finance; assistant secretary, American General Finance Foundation

Deitch, Sande: vice president, Bayer Foundation

del Sol, Carlos: vice chairman, director, Campbell Soup Co.; trustee, Campbell Soup Foundation

Delacote, Goery, PhD: chairman, president, director, Genentech Foundation for Biomedical Sciences
Delattre, Edwin J.: trustee, Quaker Chemical Foundation
DeLawder, C. Daniel: president, director, Park National Bank; president, Park National Corp. Foundation
Delgado, Gloria: director, SBC Foundation
DeLissio, Janet: chairman, Ensign-Bickford Foundation
Dellafave, Anna Marie: vice president, treasurer, Revlon Foundation Inc.
Delo, Robert Paul: president, Chicago Tribune Foundation
DeLoach, Harris E., Junior: executive vice president, director, Sonoco Products Co.
DeLuca, Fred: vice president, Subway Sandwich Shops, Inc.
Demere, Robert H.: president, Colonial Foundation; chairman, Colonial Oil Industries, Inc.
Demere, Robert H., Jr.: vice president, secretary, Colonial Foundation; president, chief executive officer, Colonial Oil Industries, Inc.
Demeritt, Stephen R.: vice chairman, General Mills, Inc.
Deming, Claiborne P.: president, chief executive officer, director, Murphy Oil Corp.
Demoulas, Arthur T.: trustee, Demoulas Foundation
Demoulas, Telemachus A.: trustee, Demoulas Foundation; president, chief executive officer, treasurer, Demoulas Supermarkets Inc.
Denlea, Leo Edward, Jr.: retired chairman, president, chief executive officer, director, Farmers Group, Inc.; vice president, Farmers Group Safety Foundation
Denning, Steven A.: vice president, General Atlantic Partners II LP
Dennis, Donna: secretary, Bard Foundation (C.R.)
Denny, Charles W.: president, chief executive officer, director, Square D Co.
Denny, Dwight D.: president, director, Ryder System Charitable Foundation
Denson, William Frank, III: trustee, Vulcan Materials Co. Foundation
Dent, William F.: president, chairman, Owens Corning Foundation, Inc.
Dero, Dan: chairman, Eckerd Corp. Foundation
Derr, Kenneth Tindall: vice president, treasurer, Chevron Corp.
Derry, R. Michael: vice president, HON Industries Charitable Foundation
DeRusha, William Charles: chairman, chief executive officer, Heilig-Meyers Co.
Deshotel, Adrian B.: secretary, treasurer, American Standard Foundation; vice president human resources, American Standard Inc.
DeSimone, Livio Diego: chairman, chief executive officer, Minnesota Mining & Manufacturing Co.
DeSole, Domenico: president, chief executive officer, Gucci America Inc.
Detlefs, Suzanne H.: vice president corporate development, BellSouth Corp.; trustee, BellSouth Foundation
Deutfa, Hunt: secretary, SunTrust Banks Foundation
Deutsch, Carl: president, Deutsch Foundation
Deutsch, Lester: president, Deutsch Foundation
DeValle, Terry: community relations representative, Arizona Public Service Co.
Dever, Robert M.: vice president public affairs, Land O'Lakes, Inc.
DeVito, Mathias Joseph: senior vice president, chief financial officer, Rouse Co.
Devlin, James Richard: director, Sprint Foundation
Devries, Robert K.: member administration committee, Nabisco Foundation Trust
Dewane, John Richard: director, Honeywell Foundation
DeWitt, Larry: member contributions committee, Cargill Inc.
DeWolfe, Lawrence Donald: vice president, Farmers Group Safety Foundation
DiBiase, Stephen A.: vice president research & development, Lubrizol Corp. (The); trustee, Lubrizol Foundation (The)
DiCamillo, Gary Thomas: chairman, chief executive officer, director, Polaroid Corp.
Dickemper, Robert A.: director, SBC Foundation
Dickey, Boh A.: president, chief operating officer, SAFECO Corp.
Dickey, Gloria: chairman, chief executive officer, Fox Entertainment Group
Dickoff, Gil A.: president, chief operating officer, Crane Co.; treasurer, Crane Foundation
Dickson, Alan Thomas: president, Dickson Foundation; chairman, Ruddick Corp.
Dickson, Rush S., III: vice president, Dickson Foundation
Dickson, Rush Stuart: vice president, Dickson Foundation
Dickson, Thomas W.: vice president, Dickson Foundation
Diekman, Susan: executive director, AirTouch Communications Foundation
Diersen, Carmen: secretary, Medtronic Foundation
Dietz, Carolyn Emmerson: chairman, president, Sierra Pacific Foundation
DiGirolamo, Vincent A.: executive vice president, vice chairman, National City Bank of Cleveland
Dillion, Cynthia: director, Pacific Mutual Charitable Foundation; senior vice president, general counsel, director, Pacific Mutual Life Insurance Co.
Dillon, Adrian T.: executive vice president, chief financial officer, planning officer, Eaton Corp.
Dillon, Carol L.: secretary, Reynolds Metals Co. Foundation
Dillon, John T.: chairman, chief executive officer, director, International Paper Co.
Dills, Max J.: director, Shelter Mutual Insurance Co.
DiMarco, James F.: senior vice president, Johnson & Son (S.C.)
Dimon, James R.: assistant treasurer, grants manager, Citigroup Foundation; president, chief operating officer, chief financial officer, Salomon Smith Barney
Dineley, Steve: vice president, chief financial officer, Extendicare Health Services
Dinerstein, Martha L.: managing director, head marketing & corporate communications, United States Trust Co. of New York
Dingell, Deborah I.: secretary, General Motors Foundation
Dingfield, Barbara J.: director community affairs, Microsoft Corp.
Dingman, Michael David: assistant secretary, Winthrop Foundation
Dinsmore, Anne: senior vice president, UnumProvident
DiPaola, Ricard: secretary, Calvin Klein; trustee, Calvin Klein Foundation
Disbrow, Cliff: president, director, Glaxo Wellcome Foundation
Disher, J. William: director, Lance Foundation; chairman, Lance, Inc.
DiSilvestro, Anthony P.: vice president, treasurer, Campbell Soup Co.; treasurer, Campbell Soup Foundation
Disney, Roy Edward: trustee, Disney Co. Foundation (Walt); vice chairman, director, Disney Co. (Walt)
Disser, Dan: vice president, Tomkins Corp. Foundation; chief financial officer, Tomkins Industries, Inc.
Dix, Ronald H.: director, Badger Meter Foundation; vice president administration & human resources, Badger Meter, Inc.
Dixon, Allan: executive director, Royal & SunAlliance Insurance Foundation, Inc.
Dixon, Greg A.: vice chairman, Edwards Foundation (J.D.)
Dixon, Judith: vice president, director, Winn-Dixie Stores Foundation
Dixon, Michelle: community relations coordinator, American General Finance
do Carmo, Winston G.: vice president human resources, Giant Food Inc.
Doane, W. Allen: president, chief executive officer, director, Alexander & Baldwin, Inc.
Dobbins, Ken: chief financial officer L'Eggs, Sara Lee Hosiery, Inc.
Dobbins, Z. E.: vice president, director, Stonecutter Foundation
Dobson, Debbie: director, GATX Corp.
Dodd, Cliff: executive vice president systems integration, US West, Inc.
Dods, Walter Arthur, Jr.: president, director, First Hawaiian Foundation; chairman, chief executive officer, director, First Hawaiian, Inc.
Dodson, Paulette: director, Chicago Tribune Foundation
Doerfler, Ronald J.: senior vice president, chief financial officer, ABC; vice president, director, ABC Foundation
Doherty, Jack N.: director, Shell Oil Co. Foundation
Doherty, Leonard Edward: director, Dow Jones & Co., Inc.; member advisory committee, admin officer, Dow Jones Foundation
Dolan, Regina A.: chief financial officer, vice president, Paine Webber; trustee, Paine Webber Foundation
Dolan, Ronald J.: trustee, Ohio National Foundation; senior vice president, chief financial officer, director, Ohio National Life Insurance Co.
Dolanski, A. P.: trustee, KPMG Peat Marwick Foundation
Doll, Mary Ellen: president, Pieper Power Electric Co.; vice president, Pieper Power Electric Foundation
Doll, Norman R.: president, Pieper Power Electric Co.
Dollar, William Michael: vice president, treasurer, chief financial officer, Harland Co. (John H.)
Donahue, Jeffrey H.: senior vice president, chief financial officer, Rouse Co.
Donahue, Richard King: vice chairman, Nike, Inc.
Donald, Odie C.: trustee, BellSouth Foundation
Donald, Robert E.: assistant secretary, Owens Corning Foundation, Inc.
Donaldson, Randal W.: vice president, Coca-Cola Co.; director, Coca-Cola Foundation
Donches, Steven G.: vice president public affairs, Bethlehem Steel Corp.; president, Bethlehem Steel Foundation
Donehue, J. Douglas: vice president, Post and Courier Foundation
Donnelley, James R.: vice chairman, Donnelley & Sons Co. (R.R.)
Donnelly, James Charles: vice president, director, WICOR Foundation; vice president, WICOR, Inc.
Donofrio, Nicholas M.: senior vice president technology manufacturing, International Business Machines Corp.
Donovan, Dianne Francys: secretary, Chicago Tribune Foundation
Donovan, Pat: director, Norwest Foundation
Donovan, Thomas Roy: president, chief executive officer, Chicago Board of Trade
Dora, James E.: director, AUL Foundation Inc.
Dorn, Gail: vice president, communications, Dayton Hudson; trustee, Target Foundation
Dorrance, Bennett: vice chairman, director, Campbell Soup Co.
Dorsey, Jerry E.: executive vice president, chief operating officer, West Co. Inc.
Dossman, Curley M., Junior: director, Georgia-Pacific Foundation
Dotzel, Cynthia A., CPA: secretary, York Federal

Savings & Loan Foundation

Doucette, James Willard: vice president, Humana Foundation

Doughty, H. C., Jr.: treasurer, Borden Foundation, Inc.

Douglas, Paul W.: director, Phelps Dodge Foundation

Douglass, Robert Royal: trustee, Chase Manhattan Foundation

Dow, Howard L., III: senior vice president, chief financial officer, treasurer, Michigan Consolidated Gas Co.

Dowd, William: vice president, ASARCO Foundation; controller, ASARCO Inc.

Dowdy, Sue G.: member, Ashland Inc. Foundation

Dowling, Anne T.: assistant comptroller, Texaco Foundation; executive director, Texaco Inc.

Dowling, Edward C.: senior vice president, operations, Cleveland-Cliffs, Inc.

Dowling, Thomas: vice president, Carris Corp. Foundation

Downes, Laurence M.: president, chief executive officer, director, chairman, New Jersey Natural Gas Co.; trustee, New Jersey Natural Gas Foundation

Downey, Joseph L.: vice chairman, director, Dow Chemical Co.

Downing, Kathryn M.: executive vice president, Times Mirror Co.; vice chairman, Times Mirror Foundation

Downs, Sue: president, chief executive officer, Shoney's Inc.

Doyle, Robert A.: director, AMCORE Foundation

Dozier, Ollin Kemp: vice president, director, Universal Leaf Foundation

Dragomier, Lynne: vice president, Maytag Corp. Foundation

Draher, Donna: trustee, McKesson Foundation

Drake, Shelley C.: chairman, president, M&T Charitable Foundation; chairman, president, chief executive officer, Manufacturers & Traders Trust Co.

Draper, Ernest Linn, Jr.: chairman, president, chief executive officer, director, American Electric Power

Drasner, Fred: co-founder, president, chief executive officer, co-publisher, director, Daily News

Drew, William J.: corporate secretary, Kohler Co.

Drexler, Millard S.: trustee, Gap Foundation/Gap Inc. Community Relations; president, chief executive officer, director, Gap, Inc.

Dreyer, William E.: director, SBC Foundation

Dreyfus, Branton B.: director, Alexander & Baldwin Foundation; president, chief executive officer, director, Alexander & Baldwin, Inc.

Dries, William: president, director, United Dominion Foundation

Driscoll, Jane: vice president, Phoenix Foundation

Driscoll, William P., Junior: vice president, officer, General Electric Co.

Droege, Mark E.: president, BellSouth Foundation

Drosdick, Don: president, Sunoco Inc.

Drought, David W.: treasurer, First Financial Foundation

Druen, W. Sidney: vice president, assistant secretary, Nationwide Insurance Enterprise Foundation

Drury, David J.: chief executive officer, chairman, Principal Financial Group

Drury, Robert E.: secretary, director, United Dominion Foundation

Duberstein, Kenneth: director, Cinergy Foundation

Dubes, Michael: membership, ReliaStar Foundation

Dubin, Melvin: chairman, Slant/Fin Corp.; president, director, Slant/Fin Foundation

Dubin, Stephen Victor: vice president, treasurer, Farber Foundation

Dubois, Everett D.: treasurer, Burlington Resources Foundation; senior vice president, treasurer, Burlington Resources, Inc.

DuBose, Suzanne A.: president, Bell Atlantic Foundation

Duchak, Susan: president, Sears, Roebuck and Co. Foundation

Duchossois, Craig J.: director, Duchossois Foundation; president, director, Duchossois Industries Inc.

Duchossois, Dayle Paige: secretary, Duchossois Foundation

Duchossois, Kimberly: director, Duchossois Foundation

Duchossois, R. Bruce: director, Duchossois Foundation

Duchossois, Richard Louis: secretary, Duchossois Foundation; chairman, chief executive officer, director, Duchossois Industries Inc.

Dudek, Patricia L.: vice president, trustee, Chicago Sun-Times Charity Trust

Duello, J. Donald: director, Shelter Insurance Foundation

Duer, Walter: trustee, KPMG Peat Marwick Foundation

Duff, Andrew S.: president, U.S. Bancorp Piper Jaffray

Duff-Bloom, Gale: president co. communications & corporate image, Penney Co., Inc. (J.C.)

Duffy, J. Kevin: associate manager, Reebok Human Rights Foundation (The)

Duffy, John: president, chief executive officer, Callaway Golf Co. Foundation

Duffy, Lois West: senior vice president, chief technology & environment officer, Ecolab Inc.

Dugan, Allan E.: senior vice president corporate strategic service, Xerox Corp.; trustee, Xerox Foundation

Dugan, Brendan J.: president, European American Bank

Duggan, Robert D.: chairman, chief executive officer, S&T Bancorp; chairman, S&T Bancorp Charitable Foundation

Duim, Gary T.: vice chairman commercial banking & private financial service, U.S. Bancorp

Dulle, Mary: trustee, Alcon Foundation

Dumas, Betty A.: senior vice president, chief administrative officer, Nestle U.S.A. Inc.

Dunbar, Ronald H.: vice president, Revlon Foundation Inc.; senior vice president human resources, director, Revlon Inc.

Duncan, Ian: trustee, Tomkins Corp. Foundation; deputy chairman, managing director finance, Tomkins Industries, Inc.

Duncan, Paul R.: executive director, trustee, Reebok Human Rights Foundation (The)

Duncan, Sam: president, Ralph's Grocery Co.

Dunham, Archie W.: president, chief executive officer, Conoco, Inc.

Dunham, Duane R.: president, Sparrows Point Division, Bethlehem Steel Corp.; director, Bethlehem Steel Foundation

Dunlap, F. Thomas, Jr.: president, chief operating officer, director, Intel Corp.; secretary, director, Intel Foundation

Dunn, Leo R.: director, Minnesota Mining & Manufacturing Co.

Dunn, Norma F.: vice president investor & public relations, El Paso Energy Co.; prs, El Paso Energy Foundation

Dunning, Richard E.: trustee, Gerber Foundation; assistant treasurer, Gerber Products Co.

DuPont, Augustus I.: treasurer, Crane Foundation

Durham, Lofton: treasurer, Hitachi Foundation

Durham, Shirley: vice president, executive director, Ford Motor Co.; contributions manager, Ford Motor Co. Fund

Durney, Michael: director, Lotus Development Philanthropy Program

Durrett, Joseph P.: chief executive officer, Broderbund Software, Inc.

Durrett, William E.: senior chairman, American Fidelity Corp.; president, American Fidelity Corp. Founders Fund

Dwyer, Carol: trustee, Standard Products Co. Charitable Foundation

Dwyer, Dean P.: vice president finance, treasurer, senior management board, Copley Press, Inc.

Dye, Donald H.: president, chief executive officer, Callaway Golf Co.

Dye, Edward R.: assistant general counsel & secretary, GenCorp; financial secretary, GenCorp Foundation

Dzwonkowski, David: treasurer, Niagara Mohawk Foundation; chairman, chief executive officer, Niagara Mohawk Holdings Inc.

E

Eads, Roger: administrator, Collins & Aikman Foundation

Earley, Anthony Francis, Jr.: president, chief operating officer, Detroit Edison Co.; director, Detroit Edison Foundation

Early, William Bernard: trustee, Jeld-wen Foundation; senior vice president, assistant secretary, director, Jeld-wen, Inc.

Easley, William K.: senior vice president, Springs Industries, Inc.

Eason, Donald: vice president, Diebold, Inc.

Eason, William Everette, Jr.: senior vice president, corporate secretary, general counsel, Scientific-Atlanta, Inc.

Easterly, David E.: president, chief operating officer, Cox Enterprises Inc.

Eastlund, Jane (Nachtigl): vice president planning & scheduling, Northwest Airlines, Inc.

Eaton, Geraldine: vice president, trustee, Presto Foundation

Eaton, Robert James: cochairman, president, chief executive officer, DaimlerChrysler Corp.

Ebbers, Bernard J.: president, chief executive officer, director, MCI WorldCom, Inc.

Ebert, Michael G.: trustee, Gerber Foundation

Ebrom, Charles E.: director, vice president, Zachry Co. (H.B.); treasurer, trustee, Zachry Foundation (The)

Eccles, Spencer Fox: chairman, chief executive officer, director, First Security Bank of Idaho NA

Ecker, H. Allen: president subscriber systems, Scientific-Atlanta, Inc.

Eckert, Constance L.: secretary, Hubbard Foundation

Eckert, Ralph John: trustee, Trustmark Foundation

Eckstein, Marie N.: trustee, Dow Corning Foundation

Edelson, Ruth C.: director special projects, Johnson & Johnson; member corporate contributions committee, Johnson & Johnson Family of Companies Contribution Fund

Edgerley, Edward, Jr,PhD: director, Group Health Foundation

Edgerton, Brenda Evans: vice president business development, Campbell Soup Co.; treasurer, trustee, Campbell Soup Foundation

Edison, Bernard Alan: member, Edison Family Foundation

Edison, Donna Furlong: chairman, chief executive officer, director, Polaroid Corp.; executive director, Polaroid Foundation

Edmundson, Kathryn L.: secretary, CBS Foundation

Edwards, Charles: director, Galter Foundation

Edwards, Claudia L.: program manager, Reader's Digest Foundation

Edwards, David M.: vice president finance, chief financial officer, GATX Corp.

Edwards, Earnest Jonathan: president, treasurer, Alcoa Foundation

Edwards, John Kenneth: executive president, group president power generation, Cummins Engine Co., Inc.; director, Cummins Engine Foundation

Edwards, Neil: chief financial officer, Patagonia Inc.

Edwards, Susan: treasurer, director, Wisconsin Energy Corp. Foundation, Inc.

Egan, Thomas P., Jr.: president, Valmont Foundation

Egge, Teresa K.: director community relations, ReliaStar Financial Corp.; director, ReliaStar Foundation

Egger, Terrance C.Z.: director, Pulitzer Publishing Co. Foundation

Ehrlich, M. Gordon: trustee, Orchard Foundation

Eidson, Julian W.: vice president, controller, Scientific-Atlanta, Inc.

Eigner, Michael: co-founder, president, chief executive officer, co-publisher, director, Daily News; president, director, Tribune New York Foundation

Eigsti, Roger Harry: chairman, chief executive officer, SAFECO Corp.

Einhorn, David M.: assistant vice president, Wachtell, Lipton, Rosen & Katz Foundation

Eischens, Curt: president, chief executive officer, Cenex Harvest States; trustee, Cenex Harvest States Foundation

Eisenman, Bill: director, NCR Foundation

Eisenstein, Joshua J.: treasurer, Central National-Gottesman

Eisman, Paul: senior vice president refining Southwest, Ultramar Diamond Shamrock Corp.

Eisner, Michael Dammann: president, trustee, Disney Co. Foundation (Walt); chairman, chief executive officer, director, Disney Co. (Walt)

Eiter, Craig: member, Star Tribune Foundation

Elam, Lloyd Charles, MD: trustee, Merck Co. Foundation

Elbert, Paul A.: president, chief executive officer natural gas, Consumers Energy Co.

Eleazer, Carol A.: vice president, trustee, UNUM Foundation; vice president corporate communications, UnumProvident

Elias, Janet L.: executive director, Dow Corning Foundation

Elkes, Linda I.: executive director, Reynolds Tobacco (R.J.); assistant treasurer, RJR Nabisco Foundation

Elkins, Lloyd Edwin, Junior: vice president, Chevron Corp.

Ellenberger, Richard G.: president, chief executive officer, director, Cincinnati Bell Inc.

Ellerbrake, Richard P.: president, director, Group Health Foundation

Ellers, Steven A.: chief financial officer, West Co. Inc.

Elliot, Steven G.: chief financial officer, Mellon Financial Corp.

Elliott, Anson Wright: trustee, Chase Manhattan Foundation

Elliott, David Holland: consultant, chairman executive committee, MBIA Inc.

Elliott, Erma B.: secretary, treasurer, Oklahoma Gas & Electric Co. Foundation

Elliott, Harry: senior vice president finance, administration, Bestfoods

Elliott, R. Keith: chief executive officer, president, Hercules Inc.

Elliott, Robert: trustee, KPMG Peat Marwick Foundation

Ellis, Darlene S.: chairman, director, Deere Foundation (John)

Ellis, David B.: director, Sara Lee Foundation

Ellis, James D.: president, SBC Foundation

Ellis, William Edward, Jr.: treasurer, Barry Foundation

Ellis, William H.: director, Piper Jaffray Companies Foundation; president, U.S. Bancorp Piper Jaffray

Ellison, Lawrence J.: chairman, chief executive officer, director, president, Oracle Corp.

Else, Robert K.: director, Hickory Tech Corp.; secretary, Hickory Tech Corp. Foundation

Emerson, Frederick George: vice president, secretary, director, Viad Corp. Fund

Emery, Sidney W., Jr.: president, chief executive officer, MTS Systems Corp.

Emling, John: vice president, Barden Corp.; trustee, Barden Foundation, Inc.

Emmerson, A. A.: president, Sierra Pacific Industries

Emmerson, George: director, Sierra Pacific Foundation; vice president, Sierra Pacific Industries

Emmerson, Mark D.: treasurer, Sierra Pacific Foundation; chief financial officer, Sierra Pacific Industries

Emmet, Robert: vice president financial planning, treasurer, Cleveland-Cliffs, Inc.

Emmett, Denis L.: chief financial officer, Erving Industries

Emmett, Mike: trustee, Cranston Foundation

Emro, Todd: vice president business development, GATX Corp.

Endicott, Cheryl: vice president, director, GenAmerican Foundation

Engel, Joel Stanley: vice president technology, Ameritech Corp.

Engh, Rolf: senior vice president, general counsel, secretary, Valspar Corp.; secretary, Valspar Foundation

Engibous, Thomas James: director, Texas Instruments Foundation; president, chief executive officer, chairman, director, Texas Instruments Inc.

England, Fredrick, Junior: trustee, Eastern Bank Charitable Foundation

England, Joseph Walker: assistant treasurer, Deere Foundation (John)

English, William D.: director, CIRI Foundation

Engoran, Frances: director, PricewaterhouseCoopers

Ennest, John William: chief financial officer, Citizens Bank-Flint

Enrico, Roger A.: chairman, PepsiCo Foundation, Inc.; chairman, chief executive officer, director, PepsiCo, Inc.

Epstein, Lisa K. Simmons: assistant secretary, Simmons Foundation, Inc. (Harold)

Erb, Frederick A.: president, Erb Foundation; vice president, chief financial officer, Erb Lumber Co.

Erb, John M.: president, Erb Foundation

Erdahl, Rebecca: executive director, Pillsbury Co.; president, director, Pillsbury Co. Foundation

Erdos, Robert W.: trustee, York Federal Savings & Loan Foundation

Ernst, Fred V.: president, director, MacMillan Bloedel Inc.

Ervanian, Armen: vice president, secretary, director, Viad Corp. Fund

Esber, Suzanne Huffmon: chairman, trustee, Fluor Foundation

Escalante, Rebecca: community affairs officer, TCF Foundation; chairman, TCF National Bank Minnesota

Escarra, Vicki: executive vice president customer service, Delta Air Lines, Inc.

Esposito, Anthony G.: trustee, Ohio National Foundation

Esposito, Michael Patrick, Jr.: trustee, Chase Manhattan Foundation

Esrey, William Todd: chairman, chief executive officer, Sprint Corp.

Essex, Kathleen: vice president-human resources, Hunt Manufacturing Co.

Essman, Alyn V.: chairman, chief executive officer, CPI Corp.

Esstman, Michael B.: trustee, GTE Foundation

Estenson, Noel Keith: president, chief executive officer, Cenex Harvest States

Evangelist, Frank E.: secretary, Regis Foundation

Evans, Cynthia: president, chief executive officer, New Century Energies Foundation

Evans, Gorton M., Jr.: president, chief executive officer, director, Consolidated Papers, Inc.

Evans, Jennifer L.: manager, secretary, Cooper Industries, Inc.

Evans, John B.: vice president, trustee, Chase Manhattan Foundation

Evans, Richard W., Jr.: chairman, chief executive officer, Frost National Bank

Evans, Robert Sheldon: chairman, chief executive officer, Crane Co.; chairman, president, director, Crane Foundation

Evanson, Paul John: secretary, director, FPL Group Foundation, Inc.

Everest, Christine Gaylord: trustee, Oklahoman Foundation (The)

Everett, Malcolm E., III: senior vice president, director corporate contributions, First Union Foundation

Everingham, Lyle J.: assistant treasurer, Milacron Foundation

Ewing, Stephen E.: president, chief executive officer, director, Michigan Consolidated Gas Co.

Exley, Charles Errol, Jr.: trustee, Merck Co. Foundation

F

Fadden, Paula: director, Piper Jaffray Companies Foundation

Fahey, Christine: trustee, member, Schering-Plough Foundation

Failing, Barbara M.: trustee, Potlatch Foundation II

Fair, Russell B.: vice president pharmacy operations, Giant Food Inc.

Fairbanks, J. Nelson: president, chief executive officer, director, United States Sugar Corp.

Falberg, Kathryn E.: senior vice president finance, chief financial officer, Amgen, Inc.

Falcon, Rick: president, Burger King Corp.; director community affairs, Burger King Foundation

Falk, Harvey L.: member grantmaking committee, Claiborne Foundation (Liz); president, vice chairman, Liz Claiborne, Inc.

Falla, Enrique Crabb: senior consult, director, Dow Chemical Co.

Fani, Robert J.: senior vice president, Brooklyn Union

Farber, Jack: chairman, president, director, CSS Industries, Inc.; president, Farber Foundation

Farinas, Suzanne: assistant to chief executive officer, assistant corporate secretary, Southwest Gas Corp.

Farley, James Bernard: chairman emeritus, trustee, Walter Industries Inc.

Farman, Richard Donald: chairman, chief executive officer, Pacific Enterprises

Farmer, Kenneth W.: director, Abbott Laboratories Fund

Farmer, Phillip W.: chairman, president, chief executive officer, Harris Corp.; president, trustee, Harris Foundation

Farnsworth, Philip Richeson: secretary, ABC

Farrell, W. James: chairman, chief executive officer, Illinois Tool Works, Inc.

Farrington, Ann: secretary, Little Foundation (Arthur D.)

Farrington, Hugh G.: president, chief executive officer, director, Hannaford Brothers Co.

Farris, Banks H.: executive vice president, director, Alabama Power Foundation

Farver, Charles: director, Pella Rolscreen Foundation

Farver, Joan Kuyper: chairman emeritus, director, Pella Corp.; director, Pella Rolscreen Foundation

Fast, Robert B.: trustee, UNUM Foundation

Faust, F. Lee: vice president, CertainTeed Corp.

Faust, Michael L.: administrator, Kiewit Companies Foundation

Fay, Barbara Lee: corporate controller, Butler Manufacturing Co.; foundation administrator, Butler Manufacturing Co. Foundation

Feaster, Joyce: director, Wisconsin Energy Corp. Foundation, Inc.

Feidler, Mark L.: trustee, BellSouth Foundation

Feinman, Alfred: general partner, Glickenhaus & Co.; secretary-treasurer, Glickenhaus Foundation

Feinstein, Martin D.: chairman, chief executive officer, Farmers Group, Inc.

Feith, Susan: vice president, executive director, Consolidated Papers Foundation, Inc.; president, chief executive officer, director, Consolidated Papers, Inc.

Felch, Lisa: director, Extendicare Foundation; vice president, chief financial officer, Extendicare Health Services

Feldhouse, Lynn Alexandra: co-chairman, president, chief executive officer, DaimlerChrysler Corp.; vice president, secretary, DaimlerChrysler Corp. Fund

Feller, Mimi A.: senior vice president public affairs & government relations, Gannett Co., Inc.; vice president, Gannett Foundation

Feller, Robert J.: vice president, Shelter Mutual Insurance Co.

Felsinger, Donald E.: president, chief executive officer, Sempra Energy

Fenton, Robert W.: vice president, controller, CertainTeed Corp.

Fercho, Brad: president imaging group, Mallinckrodt Chemical, Inc.

Ferguson, Ronald Eugene: chairman, president, chief executive officer, director, General Reinsurance Corp.

Fering, Thomas: assistant treasurer, assistant secretary, Wisconsin Energy Corp. Foundation, Inc.

Ferland, E. James: chairman, president, chief executive officer, Public Service Electric & Gas Co.

Ferrari, Giannantonio A.: director, Honeywell Foundation; president, chief operating officer, director, Honeywell International Inc.

Ferry, Richard Michael: chairman, Pacific Mutual Life Insurance Co.

Fesenmyer, Bob: general manager, vice president, Dana Corp.; director, Dana Corp. Foundation

Fessler, Dianne: chairman, chief executive officer, director, Airborne Freight Corp.

Fessler, Kathryn M.: member contributions committee, Dominion Resources, Inc.

Fetterer, Peter: corporate secretary, Kohler Co.

Field, Benjamin R., III: senior vice president, chief financial officer, treasurer, Bemis Co., Inc.

Fields, Michael D.: president, Commerce Bancshares Foundation

Fierce, Hughlyn F.: vice president, director, Chase Manhattan Foundation

Fiez, Terri: manager community relations, CUNA Mutual Group; executive director, CUNA Mutual Group Foundation, Inc.

Findlay, Mary A.: vice president, MichCon Foundation; vice president customer operations, Michigan Consolidated Gas Co.

Fine, Roger Seth: vice president, general counsel, Johnson & Johnson; president, Johnson & Johnson Family of Companies Contribution Fund

Fink, David: president, Auburn Foundry

Fink, Richard H.: secretary, Koch Foundation, Inc. (Fred C. and Mary R.)

Fink, William E.: chairman, Auburn Foundry; trustee, Auburn Foundry Foundation

Finkelstein, Hilary: president, IBJ Foundation

Finlayson, John L.: vice president finance & administration, Susquehanna-Pfaltzgraff Co.

Finnegan, John P.: chief financial officer, Rutledge Hill Press

Finney, Elisha M.: vice president finance, chief financial officer, Varian Medical Systems, Inc.

Fino, Raymond M.: second vice president, Warner-Lambert Charitable Foundation; vice president human resources, Warner-Lambert Co.

Finto, Don: chief financial officer, Rutledge Hill Press; director, Rutledge Hill Press Foundation

Fiola, Janet S.: senior vice president human resources, Medtronic, Inc.

Fiondella, Robert William: chairman, president, chief executive officer, Phoenix Home Life Mutual Insurance Co.

Fiorani, R. P.: president, chief executive officer, director, Square D Co.; vice president, director, Square D Foundation

Fiorina, Carleton S.: president, chief executive officer, director, Hewlett-Packard Co.

Fireman, Paul B.: executive director, trustee, Reebok Human Rights Foundation (The)

Fischer, Don R.: senior vice president, chief financial officer, treasurer, director, United Parcel Service of America Inc.; trustee, UPS Foundation

Fischer, Jorge: manager corporate contributions, National Computer Systems, Inc.

Fischer, Miles P.: president, chief executive officer, director, Humanitas Foundation

Fischer, Patrick: chairman, president, chief executive officer, director, Donaldson Co., Inc.; trustee, Donaldson Foundation

Fischer, Richard Lawrence: director, Alcoa Foundation; executive vice president, chairman counsel, Alcoa Inc.

Fish, Lawrence K.: trustee, Citizens Charitable Foundation; chairman, chief executive officer, Citizens Financial Group, Inc.

Fisher, Arnold: director, Fisher Brothers Foundation, Inc.

Fisher, David J.: president, chief executive officer, Chicago Board of Trade; director, Chicago Board of Trade Foundation

Fisher, Donald George: president, Gap Foundation/Gap Inc. Community Relations; founder, chairman, director, Gap, Inc.

Fisher, Doris F.: vice president, Gap Foundation/ Gap Inc. Community Relations

Fisher, Francis M., Jr.: chairman, president, chief executive officer, director, Gulf Power Co.; trustee, Gulf Power Foundation

Fisher, George Myles Cordell: chairman, president, chief executive officer, director, Eastman Kodak Co.

Fisher, Lawrence: partner, Fisher Brothers Cleaning Services; director, Fisher Brothers Foundation, Inc.

Fisher, M. Anthony: director, Fisher Brothers Foundation, Inc.

Fisher, Nancy: director public relations, Putnam Investments

Fisher, Richard: director, Fisher Brothers Foundation, Inc.

Fisher, Robert J.: president, Gap Foundation/Gap Inc. Community Relations

Fisher, Walter B.: treasurer, Tracy Fund (Emmet and Frances)

Fisher, Zachary: partner, Fisher Brothers Cleaning Services; director, Fisher Brothers Foundation, Inc.

Fishman, Jerald G.: president, chief executive officer, director, Analog Devices, Inc.

Fiterman, Ben: secretary, director, Fiterman Foundation (Jack and Bessie); chairman, Liberty Diversified Industries

Fiterman, Linda: secretary, director, Fiterman Foundation (Jack and Bessie)

Fiterman, Michael: president, director, Fiterman Foundation (Jack and Bessie); president, chief executive officer, Liberty Diversified Industries

Fites, Donald Vester: trustee, Caterpillar Foundation

Fitz-Gerald, David: treasurer, Carris Corp. Foundation; chief financial officer, Carris Reels

Fitzgerald, William Allingham: chairman, director, Commercial Federal Corp.

FitzGibbon, David J.: president, chief executive officer, Bardes Corp.

Fitzpatrick, Jane P.: chairman, treasurer; chairman, chief executive officer, treasurer, Country Curtains, Inc.; chairman, High Meadow Foundation

Fitzpatrick, John H.: chairman, High Meadow Foundation; president, director, Housatonic Curtain Co.

Fitzpatrick, Nancy J.: clerk, trustee, High Meadow Foundation; president, director, Housatonic Curtain Co.

Fitzsimmons, Thomas D.: chairman, trustee, First Maryland Foundation

Fitzsimonds, Roger Leon: secretary, treasurer, Firstar Milwaukee Foundation

Fiume, Orest J.: vice president finance, chief financial officer, Wiremold Co.

Fix, James H.: assistant comptroller, USX Corp.

Fizdale, Richard B.: chairman, chief executive officer, director, Burnett Co. (Leo)

Fjelstul, Dean M.: senior vice president, chief financial officer, Walter Industries Inc.

Flaherty, Gerald S.: trustee, Caterpillar Foundation; group president, Caterpillar Inc.

Flaherty, Walter J.: chief financial officer, senior vice president, Eastern Enterprises; trustee, Eastern Enterprises Foundation

Flake, Floyd Harold: senior vice president, Fannie Mae Foundation

Flanagan, David T.: president, chief executive officer, director, Central Maine Power Co.

Flaws, James B.: senior vice president, chief financial officer, treasurer, Corning Inc.; trustee, Corning Inc. Foundation

Fleming, Richard Harrison: chief financial officer, senior vice president, USG Corp.; treasurer, trustee, USG Foundation

Fleshman, Betty R.: secretary, Potlatch Corp.

Fligg, James E.: executive vice president, BP Amoco Corp.

Flinn, Timothy: trustee, KPMG Peat Marwick Foundation

Flint, Mark: co-chief operating officer, Crown Books

Floerchinger, Craig A.: director, CIRI Foundation; vice president, Cook Inlet Region

Flood, Al: chairman, chief executive officer, CIBC Oppenheimer

Flood, Joan Moore: director, Trace International Holdings, Inc. Foundation

Florio, Fred: committee member, Thermo Electron Foundation

Fluno, Jere David: vice chairman, Grainger, Inc. (W.W.)

Fluor, John Robert, II: president, trustee, Fluor Corp.; manager, community relationss, Fluor Foundation

Flury, L. Richard: executive vice president, BP Amoco Corp.

Fogg, Eric P.: manager community investments, Pioneer Hi-Bred International, Inc.

Foley, Cheryl M.: vice president, secretary, general counsel, Cinergy Corp.; vice president, secretary, director, Cinergy Foundation

Foley, Patricia A.: assistant secretary, Inland Container Corp.; secretary, treasurer, director, Inland Foundation, Inc.

Folick, Jeffrey M.: member, PacifiCare Health System Foundation

Foltz, Sharon B.: executive vice president, chief financial officer, Tucson Electric Power Co.

Fonstad, Eric: secretary, Harnischfeger Industries Foundation

Fonteyne, Herman J.: president, chief executive officer, director, Ensign-Bickford Industries

Foote-Hudson, Marilyn: president, director, Glaxo Wellcome Foundation

Forbes, Christopher 'Kip': vice president, Forbes Foundation; vice chairman, corporate secretary, director, Forbes Inc.

Forbes, Dorothy L.: president, director, Cabot Corp. Foundation

Forbes, Malcolm Stevenson, Jr.: president, Forbes Foundation
Ford, Alfred B.: chairman, Ford Motor Co.; trustee, Ford Motor Co. Fund
Ford, David S.: assistant secretary, assistant treasurer, Chase Manhattan Foundation
Ford, Jess B.: chief financial officer, vice president, Franklin Electric Co.
Ford, Joanne C.: vice president, chief financial officer, Nalco Chemical Co.; president, director, Nalco Foundation
Ford, Joseph 'Joe': chairman, chief executive officer, president, ALLTEL Corp.
Ford, Kenneth W.: chairman, Roseburg Forest Products Co.
Ford, Richard E.: president, director, Ford Meter Box Co.; president, Ford Meter Box Foundation
Ford, Steven R.: secretary, treasurer, Ford Meter Box Co.; treasurer, Ford Meter Box Foundation
Ford, Tom: vice president association relations, CGU Insurance
Ford, Virginia: chairman, trustee, Agrilink Foods/ Pro-Fac Foundation
Ford, W. Douglas: executive vice president, BP Amoco Corp.
Ford, William Clay, Jr.: chairman, Ford Motor Co.
Forkner, Thomas F.: vice chairman, director, Waffle House Inc.
Formica, Mark J.: trustee, Citizens Charitable Foundation; president, Citizens Financial Group, Inc.
Formisano, Roger: vice president, United Wisconsin Services Foundation
Forsgren, John: senior vice president, chief financial officer, Northeast Utilities
Forster, Peter Hans: chairman, director, Dayton Power and Light Co.
Forstmann, Theodore J.: chairman, Gulfstream Aerospace Corp.
Forsyth, John A.: trustee, Cummings Properties Foundation
Forsyth, John D.: president, chief executive officer, Blue Cross & Blue Shield of Iowa
Forsyth, Marian E.: trustee, Cummings Properties Foundation
Forsythe, Donald George: vice president corporate relations, Sprint Corp.; executive director, Sprint Foundation
Forsythe, John G.: vice president tax and public affairs, Ecolab Inc.
Forte, Gabriella: president, chief operating officer, Calvin Klein
Foster, Charles E.: director, SBC Foundation
Foster, Charles H., Jr.: chairman, chief executive officer, director, LandAmerica Financial Services; trustee, LandAmerica Foundation
Foster, Karen: secretary, administrator, Sierra Pacific Resources Charitable Foundation
Foster, Kent B.: president, director, GTE Corp.; trustee, GTE Foundation
Foti, Samuel J.: president, chief operating officer, director, MONY Group (The); director, MONY Life Insurance of New York (The)
Fotopolous, Camille: chairman contributions committee, Northern Trust Co. Charitable Trust
Fountain, W. Frank, Jr.: senior vice president government affairs, DaimlerChrysler Corp.; president, DaimlerChrysler Corp. Fund
Fowler, June: director community affairs, Mallinckrodt Chemical, Inc.
Fowler, William A.: chief financial officer, national managing director finance, Deloitte & Touche
Fowlkes, J. Thomas: president, United Coal Co. Charitable Foundation
Fox, Bill: chairman, chief executive officer, director, Consolidated Natural Gas Co.; director, Consolidated Natural Gas System Foundation
Fox, Gary: chairman, Edwards Foundation (J.D.)
Fox, Jerome E., Jr.: trustee, Invacare Foundation
Fox, Jerry D.: secretary, treasurer, director, Journal-Gazette Foundation, Inc.
Fox, Joseph Carter: chairman, president, chief executive officer, Chesapeake Corp.
Fox, William J.: senior vice president, Revlon Foundation Inc.; executive vice president, chief financial officer, Revlon Inc.
Foxworthy, James C.: secretary, treasurer, director, Inland Foundation, Inc.
Foy, Douglas: trustee, New England Bio Labs Foundation
Foy, J. Thomas: president, chief executive officer, Furniture Brands International, Inc.
Francis, Cheryl A.: executive vice president, chief financial officer, Donnelley & Sons Co. (R.R.)
Francis, John: manager human resources, Analog Devices, Inc.
Francis-Dickerson, Dierdre: foundation administrator, Nissan Foundation; manager strategic relations, Nissan North America, Inc.
Franck, C. Duffy: chairman, president, chief executive officer, Osborne Enterprises; assistant secretary, Osborne Foundation (Weldon F.)
Frank, Stephen E.: president, chief operating officer, director, Edison International
Franke, William Augustus: chairman, president, chief executive officer, America West Airlines, Inc.; director, Phelps Dodge Foundation
Franklin, Barbara Hackman: director, Dow Chemical Co.
Franklin, Carroll R.: president, general counsel, director, GEICO Philanthropic Foundation
Franklin, H. Allen: president, chief executive officer, Georgia Power Co.
Franklin, Marc Scott: senior vice president strategic planning, Pacific Mutual Life Insurance Co.
Franklin, Nick: member, PacifiCare Health System Foundation
Fraumann, Willard George: president, director, partner, Kirkland & Ellis; president, Kirkland & Ellis Foundation
Frazier, Kenneth C.: vice president, deputy general counsel, Merck & Co.
Fredericksen, Jay A.: secretary, Rayonier Foundation
Fredrickson, Dennis: director, Firstar Milwaukee Foundation
Freedman, Allen Royal: trustee, Fortis Foundation; chairman, chief executive officer, president, Fortis, Inc.
Freeman, David: chairman, president, chief executive officer, director, Loctite Corp.
Freeman, James D.: vp, Schurz Communications Foundation
Freeman, Jim: vice president, chairman corporate contributions committee, American United Life Insurance Co.
French, David: director, Novartis Corporation; chairman, Novartis US Foundation
French, Jerry: director, Shelter Insurance Foundation
French, Stephanie: vice president, Philip Morris Companies Inc.
Frenchman, Gerald: president, director, Continental Grain Foundation
Fretheim, Inge B.: executive vice president, BP Amoco Corp.; director, BP Amoco Foundation
Fretthold, Timothy Jon: executive vice president, general counsel, director, Ultramar Diamond Shamrock Corp.
Frew, Burdette L.: director, MFA Foundation
Frey, Roger: trustee, Woodward Governor Co. Charitable Trust
Fribourg, Michel: chairman emeritus, director, Continental Grain Co.; president, director, Continental Grain Foundation
Frick, David R.: member, Anthem Foundation, Inc.
Fricke, Howard R.: president, director, Security Benefit Life Insurance Co.; trustee, Security Benefit Life Insurance Co. Charitable Trust
Fricks, William Peavy: chairman, chief executive officer, Newport News Shipbuilding
Fried, Eliot M.: managing director, Walter Industries Inc.
Friede, Barbara: president, director, Fireman's Fund Foundation
Friedewald, William Thomas, MD: director, MetLife Foundation; chief executive officer, Metropolitan Life Insurance Co.
Friedlaender, Helmut N.: director, AMETEK Foundation
Friedman, Louis: treasurer, Gallo Foundation
Friedman, Stephen James: senior advisor, Goldman Sachs Group
Frierson, Daniel K.: chairman, chief executive officer, Dixie Group, Inc. (The); president, trustee, Dixie Yarns Foundation, Inc.
Frisch, Maureen: president, director, Matlock Foundation; vice president public affairs, Simpson Investment Co.
Fritze, Steven L.: vice president, treasurer, Ecolab Inc.
Fritzson, Paul A.: president, chief executive officer, director, Hannaford Brothers Co.; president, director, Hannaford Charitable Foundation
Frohlich, William O.: treasurer, Dun & Bradstreet Corp. Foundation, Inc.
Fromm, Ronald A.: vice president, Brown Shoe Co., Inc.
Frost, Thomas C., Senior: chairman, Frost National Bank
Fry, Jana: grant administration, Grand Victoria Foundation
Frydryk, Karl S.: president, chief executive officer, Monarch Machine Tool Co.; trustee, Monarch Machine Tool Co. Foundation
Frye, Shirley T.: executive director, Glaxo Wellcome Foundation
Fryling, Victor J.: president, chief executive officer natural gas, Consumers Energy Co.; director, Consumers Energy Foundation
Fuellgraf, Charles Louis, Jr.: director, Nationwide Insurance Enterprise Foundation
Fuhrman, Gary R.: president, Baltimore Gas & Electric Foundation
Fukunaga, Eric S.: chairman, director, Servco Foundation
Fukunaga, Mark H.: chairman, director, Servco Foundation; chief executive officer, chairman, Servco Pacific
Fuller, Harry Laurance: co-chairman, director, BP Amoco Corp.
Fuller, Jim: chief financial officer, vice president finance, Danis Companies
Fumagalli, John: member, Northern Trust Co. Charitable Trust
Funaro, Patricia P.: assistant comptroller, USX Corp.; program administrator, USX Foundation, Inc.
Funk, Donna M.: group executive, Household International Inc.
Furey, John J.: corporate secretary, corporate counsel, Campbell Soup Co.
Furlaud, Richard Mortimer: interim chief executive officer, International Flavors & Fragrances Inc.
Furlong, James P.: director civic affairs
Furman, Jeffrey: secretary, Ben & Jerry's Foundation

G

Gaard, Tom: contributions coordinator, Principal Financial Group Foundation, Inc.
Gabel, Ivan H.: trustee, Merit Gasoline Foundation; president, chief executive officer, Merit Oil Corp.
Gadosik, Barbara: assistant secretary, trustee, Sherwin-Williams Foundation
Gaffney, Leslie: community affairs representative, Sony Electronics; secretary, director, Sony U.S.A. Foundation Inc.

Gage, Barbara C: director, Carlson Companies, Inc.; president, Carlson Family Foundation (Curtis L.)
Gagliardi, Mary: vice president, National Starch & Chemical Co.
Gagnier, Charles E.: chairman, AMCORE Bank Rockford; president, director, AMCORE Foundation
Gagnon, Lee A.: vice president, Smith Foundation Inc. (Harold Webster); executive vice president, chief operating officer, secretary, Webster Bank
Gagnon, Sharon: director, CIRI Foundation
Gailey, John Robert, III: vice president, general counsel, secretary, West Co. Inc.
Gaiswinkler, Robert Sigfried: chairman, director, First Financial Bank; director, First Financial Foundation
Gajewski, Edward: vice president, director, M&T Charitable Foundation
Galia, Gary C.: vice president finance, treasurer, Fabri-Kal Corp.; vice president finance, Fabri-Kal Foundation
Gallagher, Donald J.: vice president, sales, Cleveland-Cliffs, Inc.
Gallagher, Jim: manager corporate giving, Starwood Hotels & Resorts Worldwide, Inc.
Gallagher, Richard S.: director, Badger Meter Foundation
Gallagher, Terence Joseph: chairman, Pfizer Foundation
Gallant, Robert E.: vice president investor relations, public affairs, Hercules Inc.
Gallo, Ernest: director, Gallo Foundation; co-founder, chairman, Gallo Winery, Inc. (E&J)
Gallo, Joseph E.: director, Gallo Foundation
Gallo, Robert J.: co-president, Gallo Foundation
Gallucci, Michael A., Jr.: director, Glaxo Wellcome Foundation
Galter, Dollie: president, chief executive officer, Galter Corp.; director, Galter Foundation
Galter, William: director, Galter Foundation
Galvin, Christopher B.: director, Motorola Foundation; president, chief executive officer, director, Motorola Inc.
Galvin, John: trustee, Commercial Intertech Foundation
Galvin, Raymond E.: vice president, Chevron Corp.
Gambill, Malcolm W.: treasurer, Harsco Corp. Fund
Gammill, Lee Morgan, Jr.: director, New York Life Foundation; vice chairman, director, New York Life Insurance Co.
Gamper, Albert R., Jr.: president, chief executive officer, director, CIT Group Foundation; president, chief executive officer, chairman, CIT Group, Inc. (The)
Gamron, W. Anthony: secretary, Kimberly-Clark Foundation
Gandolfo, Joseph C.: director, Mattel Foundation
Gannon, Laurie: manager public affairs, Taco Bell Foundation
Gannon, Robert P.: chairman, president, director, chief executive officer, Montana Power Co.; president, director, Montana Power Foundation
Gans, Terry Alexander: vice president, advertising, Giant Food Inc.
Garber, Bart: director, CIRI Foundation
Garber, Sted: president, chief executive officer, Santa Fe International Corp.
Garberding, Larry Gailbert: chief financial officer, executive vice president, Detroit Edison Co.; director, Detroit Edison Foundation
Gardner, D. L.: vice president, assistant treasurer, Cleveland-Cliffs Foundation (The); vice president financial planning, treasurer, Cleveland-Cliffs, Inc.
Gardner, Frank: senior vice president, Scripps Co. (E.W.)
Gardner, Gary E.: vice president human resources & public affairs, Valspar Corp.; vice president, assistant treasurer, Valspar Foundation
Gardner, James L.: president, trustee, Fluor Corp.; trustee, Fluor Foundation
Gardner, James Richard: secretary, director, Pfizer Foundation
Gardner, Jeff: chief financial officer, ALLTEL Corp.
Gareau, Joseph H.: executive vice president, chief investment officer, Hartford (The)
Garneau, Robert M.: chief financial officer, Kaman Corp.
Garner, Andre F.: manager communication affairs, Peoples Energy Corp.
Garnett, David E.: trustee, Xerox Foundation
Garrett, Joseph H., Junior: vice president government & international operations, Rockwell International Corp.
Garrett, Judith M.: chairman, trustee, Belo Corp. Foundation (A.H.)
Garrett, Michael D.: chairman, Alabama Power Foundation
Garrity, Norman E.: executive vice president, director, Corning Inc.; trustee, Corning Inc. Foundation
Garron, Dynell: senior director, Gap Foundation/Gap Inc. Community Relations; director, Gap, Inc.
Gary, Robert W.: chairman, chief executive officer, director, Allstate Foundation
Gary, William: vice president operations, Navcom Systems
Gasich, Anthony F.: vice president administration, Farmers Group, Inc.; contributions officer, Farmers Group Safety Foundation
Gaston, Karen H.: vice president corporate affairs, Equifax Inc.
Gates, William Henry, III: co-founder, chairman, chief software architect, Microsoft Corp.
Gauvreau, Paul Richard: vice chairman, director, Pittway Corp.; treasurer, Pittway Corp. Charitable Foundation
Gaylord, Edward K., II: trustee, Oklahoman Foundation (The)
Gaylord, Edward Lewis: chairman, chief executive officer, director, publisher, Oklahoma Publishing Co.; trustee, Oklahoman Foundation (The)
Gaynor, John M.: chief financial officer, treasurer, assistant secretary, controller, Boler Co.; trustee, Boler Co. Foundation
Gebel, Riva: member, PacifiCare Health System Foundation
Gecowets, Jerry: executive vice president, Gosiger Foundation
Geevarghese, Salin: executive director, BellSouth Foundation
Geier, Peter E.: vice chairman, Huntington Bancshares Inc.
Geier, Philip Henry, Jr.: chairman, president, chief executive officer, Interpublic Group of Companies, Inc.
Geissinger, Frederick: chairman, chief executive officer, prs, American General Finance
Geissinger, Frederick Wallace: chairman, chief executive officer, prs, American General Finance; chairman, chief executive officer, president, director, American General Finance Foundation
Gelb, Arthur: secretary, New York Times Co. Foundation
Gelb, Morris: executive vice president, chief operating officer, Lyondell Chemical Co.
Gelb, Richard Lee: secretary, New York Times Co. Foundation
Gelbman, Ronald G.: chairman diagnostics group, Johnson & Johnson; member corporate contributions committee, Johnson & Johnson Family of Companies Contribution Fund
Geller, Eric P.: trustee, Harcourt General Charitable Foundation; senior vice president, general counsel, secretary, Harcourt General, Inc.
Gelston, Steven: trustee, Chase Manhattan Bank, NA
Gentry, Barbara B.: trustee rep, USAA Foundation, A Charitable Trust
George, A. Fred: corporate secretary, corporate counsel, Campbell Soup Co.; trustee, Campbell Soup Foundation
George, Tom: trustee, McKesson Foundation
George, William Wallace: chief executive officer, chairman, Medtronic, Inc.
Georges, John A.: director, International Paper Co.
Georgius, John R.: director, First Union Foundation
Gerard, Jamie K.: attorney, Newman's Own Foundation
Gerber, Harry: director, First Source Foundation
Gerber, Mary E.: president, director, AMCORE Foundation
Gerber, William: executive vice president finance, chief financial officer, Kelly Services
Gerke, Marie: secretary, PricewaterhouseCoopers
Gerlach, Jay, Jr.: chairman, president, chief executive officer, chief operating officer, director, Lancaster Lens, Inc.
Gersh, Gary: president, chief executive officer, EMI Music Publishing
Gerstle, Mark R.: director, Cummins Engine Foundation
Gerstner, Louis Vincent, Jr.: chairman, chief executive officer, director, International Business Machines Corp.
Gesiriech, Mary: contributions coordinator, Principal Financial Group
Getz, Barbara: trustee, Gerber Foundation
Getz, Bert A.: chairman, Globe Corp.; president, director, Globe Foundation
Getz, Bert A., Jr.: executive vice president, Globe Corp.; vice president, Globe Foundation
Getz, George F.: president, Globe Corp.; secretary, director, Globe Foundation
Getz, Herbert A.: senior vice president, secretary, general counsel, Waste Management Inc.
Getz, Sandra Lynn: director, Globe Foundation
Gherlein, Gerald Lee: member contributions committee, Eaton Charitable Fund; executive vice president, chief financial officer, planning officer, Eaton Corp.
Gherty, John E.: president, chief executive officer, Land O'Lakes, Inc.
Giaramita, Phillip S.: vice president corporate communications, International Paper Co.; president, director, International Paper Co. Foundation
Gibbs, Patricia E.: committee member, Thermo Electron Foundation
Gibson, Dan: chief operating officer, Starwood Hotels & Resorts Worldwide, Inc.
Gibson, Richard P.: vice president, controller, Kennametal Foundation
Gibson, Tim: trustee, Monarch Machine Tool Co. Foundation
Gidley, Marta D.: treasurer, Ford Meter Box Foundation
Gidwitz, Gerald S.: chairman, Curtis Industries, Inc. (Helene)
Gidwitz, Ronald J.: president, chief executive officer, Curtis Industries, Inc. (Helene)
Gierer, Vincent A., Jr.: chairman, president, chief executive officer, director, UST Inc.
Giering, John L.: senior vice president finance & administration, chief financial officer, NCR Corp.
Giertz, James R.: senior vice president, chief financial officer, Donaldson Co., Inc.; chief financial officer, vice president, Donaldson Foundation
Gieszl, Yale: executive vice president, Toyota Motor Sales U.S.A., Inc.
Gifford, Charles Kilvert: trustee, BankBoston Charitable Foundation; chairman, chief executive officer, BankBoston Corp.
Gilbert, Glen S.: vice president advertising & social responsibility, GTE Corp.
Gilbert, Wayne E: president, chief operating officer, director, Alliant Techsystems; secretary-treasurer,

director, Alliant Techsystems Community Investment Foundation

Gildersleeve, Elizabeth T.: chairman, Chubb Foundation

Giles, Julie: president, chief executive officer, Mazda North American Operations

Gill, John A.: senior vice president, FirstEnergy Corp.

Gill, Juliann: vice president, Dun & Bradstreet Corp. Foundation, Inc.

Gill, Margaret G.: senior vice president legal and external affairs, Vodafone AirTouch Plc

Gillan, George M.: secretary, Humanitas Foundation

Gillespie, Ann: secretary, Little Foundation (Arthur D.)

Gillfillan, Michael J.: vice chairman, Wells Fargo & Co.

Gilligan, Matthew: trustee, UNUM Foundation; vice president, UnumProvident

Gillis, Edwin J.: president, Lotus Development Corp.

Gillivray, Thomas K.: treasurer, Central Newspapers, Inc.

Gilmar, Leonard E.: trustee, Merit Gasoline Foundation

Gilmartin, Raymond V.: chairman, president, chief executive officer, Merck & Co.; chairman, Merck Co. Foundation

Gilmer, Gary D.: group executive, Household International Inc.

Gilpin, Jerry L.: chairman, chief executive officer, president, director, American General Finance Foundation

Gilpin, Larry: executive vice president, Target Corp.; trustee, Target Foundation

Gilvar, Barry S.: secretary, Liberty Mutual Insurance Group

Gindi, Abraham: trustee, Century 21 Associates Foundation

Gindi, Sam: trustee, Century 21 Associates Foundation

Gingrich, James: director, Sundstrand Corp. Foundation

Ginn, Samuel L.: chairman, director, AirTouch Communications Foundation; chairman, chief executive officer, director, Vodafone AirTouch Plc

Giresi, Mark: senior vice president, Burger King Corp.

Girvan, Daniel J.: senior vice president, director, Fort James Corp.; director, Fort James Foundation (The)

Girvin, Larry M.: senior vice president commercial operations, Dominion Resources, Inc.

Gittis, Howard: senior vice president, Revlon Foundation Inc.

Givan, Boyd Eugene: chairman, chief executive officer, director, Boeing Co.

Glancy, John E.: corporate executive vice president, chairman, Telcordia Technologies

Glanzer, Aaron: trustee, Cenex Harvest States Foundation

Glaser, Gary A.: president, chief executive officer, National City Bank of Columbus

Glass, David Dayne: trustee, Wal-Mart Foundation; director, Wal-Mart Stores, Inc.

Glass, Deborah: chairman, director, Blue Cross & Blue Shield of Minnesota Foundation Inc.

Glazer, Patricia: secretary, Bronfman Foundation/Joseph E. Seagram & Sons, Inc. Fund (Samuel)

Glazerman, Ellen J.: director, Ernst & Young Foundation

Gleaves, James Leslie: assistant secretary, American General Finance Foundation

Glickenhaus, James M.: ltd. partner, Glickenhaus & Co.; vice president, Glickenhaus Foundation

Glickenhaus, Seth M.: general partner, Glickenhaus & Co.

Gloyd, Lawrence Eugene: trustee, CLARCOR Foundation; chairman, chief executive officer, director, CLARCOR Inc.

Glynn, Gary Allen: president, USX Corp.; vice president, USX Foundation, Inc.

Gober, Ira: chairman, chief financial officer, partner, director, Associated Food Stores; director, Associated Food Stores Charitable Foundation

Gochenaur, Jack A.: senior vice president administration & services, chief financial officer, Fortis Insurance Co.; president, trustee, Fortis Insurance Foundation

Goddu, Roger V.: chairman, chief executive officer, director, Montgomery Ward & Co., Inc.

Godfrey, Cullen Michael: director, FINA Foundation

Godlasky, Tom: executive vice president, chief investment officer, AmerUS Group

Goeltz, Richard Karl: vice chairman, chief financial officer, American Express Co.

Goetschel, Arthur W.: chairman, president, chief executive officer, Amsted Industries Inc.

Goggin, Joseph P.: treasurer, Red Wing Shoe Co. Foundation

Goin, Wanda: manager community affairs, Kraft Foods, Inc.

Goings, Laneta: secretary, trustee, Blade Foundation

Goldberg, Edward Jay: president, chief operating officer, Macy's East Inc.

Golden, Charles E.: executive vice president, chief financial officer, Lilly & Co. (Eli)

Golden, Rebecca: director, Ben & Jerry's Foundation; co-founder, vice chairman, Ben & Jerry's Homemade Inc.

Goldman, Ruth E.: assistant treasurer, Merck & Co.; program officer, Merck Co. Foundation

Goldstein, Ned S.: secretary, Ticketmaster Foundation

Goldstein, Richard A.: president, chief executive officer, director, Lipton Co.

Goldstone, Steven F.: chairman, chief executive officer, director, Reynolds Tobacco (R.J.); chairman, RJR Nabisco Foundation

Golkin, Perry: member, Walter Industries Inc.

Golleher, George C: president, Ralph's-Food 4 Less Foundation; chief executive officer, Ralph's Grocery Co.

Golonski, Thomas W.: president, chairman, chief executive officer, National City Bank of Pennsylvania

Golub, Harvey: chairman, chief executive officer, director, American Express Co.; trustee, American Express Foundation

Golub, Lewis: chairman, chief executive officer, director, Golub Corp.

Golub, Mona: chairman, chief executive officer, director, Golub Corp.; trustee, Golub Foundation

Gonnason, Jeff: director, CIRI Foundation

Gonring, Matthew P.: treasurer, trustee, USG Foundation

Gonzalez, Carmen D.: vice president, ASARCO Foundation

Goode, David Ronald: chairman, president, chief executive officer, director, Norfolk Southern Corp.

Goode, R. Ray: director, Ryder System Charitable Foundation

Goodes, Melvin Russell: chairman, chief executive officer, director, Ameritech Corp.

Goodman, Helen G.: investment officer, Hartford (The)

Goodman, Roy: executive vice president, chief financial officer, Heilig-Meyers Co.

Goodwin, James E.: president, chief operating officer, director, United Airlines Inc.

Goodwin, Mark B.: vice president, general counsel, Overnite Transportation Co.

Goodwin, Morris, Jr.: president, chief executive officer, director, Deluxe Corp.; director, Deluxe Corp. Foundation

Goodyear, William M.: president, director, Bank of America; trustee, Bank of America Foundation

Goossen, Dawn: trustee, Stauffer Communications Foundation

Gore, Carol: director, CIRI Foundation

Gore, Dee: director, Piper Jaffray Companies Foundation

Gorelick, Jamie Shona: vice chairman, Fannie Mae

Gorman, Joseph T.: chairman, chief executive officer, TRW Inc.

Gorman, Leon A.: president, chief executive officer, Bean, Inc. (L.L.)

Gorman, Maureen V.: trustee, GTE Foundation

Gosnell, M. Ann: trustee, Corning Inc. Foundation

Gottlieb, Richard Douglas: president, chief executive officer, director, Lee Enterprises

Gottstein, Robert: director, CIRI Foundation

Gottwald, Bruce Cobb: chairman, chief executive officer, director, Ethyl Corp.

Gottwald, Thomas E.: president, chief operating officer, director, Ethyl Corp.

Gould, Holly: director, Extendicare Foundation

Gould, John T., Jr.: vice president, Unilever Foundation; director corporate affairs, Unilever United States, Inc.

Gowdy, Robert: president, chief executive officer, CGU Insurance

Gozon, Richard C.: executive vice president pulp paper & packaging, Weyerhaeuser Co.; trustee, Weyerhaeuser Co. Foundation

Graber, Don R.: chairman, president, chief executive officer, director, Huffy Corp.; trustee, Huffy Foundation, Inc.

Grade, Jeffery T.: chairman, chief executive officer, director, Harnischfeger Industries; president, Harnischfeger Industries Foundation

Graf, Alan B., Jr.: executive vice president, chief financial officer, FedEx Corp.

Graf, Thomas J.: chief actuary, Principal Financial Group

Grafe, Tim: trustee, Donaldson Foundation

Graff, Stephen Ney: director, Bucyrus-Erie Foundation

Graham, Donald Edward: chairman, chief executive officer, director, publisher, The Washington Post

Graham, John Gourlay: chief financial officer, senior vice president, GPU Energy

Graham, Katharine Meyer: chairman executive committee, director, The Washington Post

Graham, Patricia Albjerg, PhD: executive & program assistant, Hitachi Foundation

Graham, Richard William: president, chief executive officer, chief operating officer, director, Smurfit-Stone Container Corp.

Graham, Thomas Carlisle: trustee, AK Steel Foundation

Graham, William B.: chairman, director, Baxter Allegiance Foundation; chairman emeritus, Baxter International Inc.

Grainger, David William: senior chairman, Grainger, Inc. (W.W.)

Graitcer, Leslie: trustee, BellSouth Foundation

Gramm, Frank G., III: trustee, Trustmark Foundation

Grandstrand, David P.: senior vice president, treasurer, U.S. Bancorp

Graner, James: vice president, controller, Graco, Inc.

Grano, Joseph J., Jr.: president, Paine Webber

Granoff, Mark Howard: vice president, United Wisconsin Services Foundation

Granzow, Paul H.: chairman, director, Standard Register Co.

Grasley, Michael Howard: senior vice president, Shell Oil Co.; member executive committee, director, Shell Oil Co. Foundation

Grass, Martin Lehrman: chairman, chief executive officer, director, Rite Aid Corp.

Grasso, Richard A.: chairman, chief executive officer, New York Stock Exchange, Inc.
Graves, Earl Gilbert: director, Aetna Foundation
Graves, Eric: vice president corporate communications, Browning-Ferris Industries Inc.
Graves, Ronald Norman: treasurer, Simplot Foundation (J.R.)
Gray, C. William: treasurer, Harley-Davidson Foundation
Gray, Carol M.: vice president, controller, CertainTeed Corp.; assistant secretary, CertainTeed Corp. Foundation
Gray, Charles Agustus: vice president technology, Cabot Corp.; director, Cabot Corp. Foundation
Gray, James E.: president, chief operating officer, Macy's East Inc.
Gray, Janet: member, Northern Trust Co. Charitable Trust
Grealis, William J.: vice president, Cinergy Corp.; director, Cinergy Foundation
Greanias, Michelle: director, Fannie Mae
Greco, Jerome D.: director, First Union Foundation
Greehey, William Eugene: chairman, chief executive officer, director, Valero Energy Corp.
Green, Margaret H: associate director, grant maker, BellSouth Foundation
Greenberg, Jack M.: chairman, chief executive officer, McDonald's Corp.
Greenberg, Martin S., DDS: director, Group Health Foundation
Greenberger, Robert M.: president, director, Cowen Foundation
Greene, Donald Ray: assistant vice president, Coca-Cola Co.; president, director, Coca-Cola Foundation
Greene, John Frederick: executive vice president exploration & production, director, Louisiana Land & Exploration Co.
Greene, Virginia Arana: vice chairman, Wells Fargo & Co.; director, Wells Fargo Foundation
Greenfield, Hope: vice president human resources, Bard, Inc. (C.R.)
Greenfield, Jerry: co-founder, vice chairman, Ben & Jerry's Homemade Inc.
Greenwald, Gerald: chairman, chief executive officer, director, United Airlines Inc.
Greenwood, Fred M.: manager, Ashland Inc. Foundation
Greenwood, Greg: vice president, treasurer, Western Resources Foundation; executive vice president, general counsel, corp. secretary, Western Resources Inc.
Gregg, Walter Emmor, Junior: senior executive vice president finance & administration, PNC Financial Services Group
Grennan, Thomas L.: executive vice president electric operations, Western Resources Inc.
Grenz, M. Kay: director, 3M Foundation; vice president human resources, Minnesota Mining & Manufacturing Co.
Griebel, R. Nelson: vice chairman, BankBoston Charitable Foundation; president, chief executive officer, director, BankBoston-Connecticut Region
Gries, Lynn Ann: trustee, McDonald & Co. Securities Foundation
Griffin, Donald Wayne: chairman, president, chief executive officer, director, Olin Corp.; trustee, Olin Corp. Charitable Trust
Griffin, James B.: director, Ryder System Charitable Foundation
Griffin, Leslie: director, Boston Globe Foundation
Griffin, Terry: senior vice president, TU Electric Co.
Griffith, Alan Richard: vice chairman, Bank of New York Co., Inc.
Griffith, Beverly H.: general counsel, Texas Gas Transmission Corp.
Griffith, Dean L.: chairman, president, chief executive officer, director, Griffith Laboratories U.S.A.
Griffith, J. Brian: president, director, MFA Foundation
Grigal, Dennis: trustee, Donaldson Foundation
Grigg, Richard R.: vice president, Wisconsin Energy Corp.; director, Wisconsin Energy Corp. Foundation, Inc.
Grijalva, Norbert R.: prs, El Paso Energy Foundation
Grinstein, Gerald: director, PACCAR Inc.
Grisanti, Eugene P.: interim chief executive officer, International Flavors & Fragrances Inc.
Grise, Cheryl W.: senior vice president, chief administrative officer, Northeast Utilities
Griswell, Barry: president, Principal Financial Group
Griswold, Benjamin Howell, IV: director, New York Stock Exchange Foundation, Inc.
Groman, Arthur: president, Occidental Petroleum Charitable Foundation
Gross, Bert M.: secretary, Regis Foundation
Gross, Liza: director, Chicago Tribune Foundation
Gross, Murray: trustee, PerkinElmer Foundation; senior vice president, general counsel, clerk, PerkinElmer, Inc.
Gross, Randall A.: trustee, York Federal Savings & Loan Foundation
Gross, Ronald Martin: chairman, president, director, Rayonier Foundation; chairman, president, chief executive officer, director, Rayonier Inc.
Grove, Andrew S.: chairman, Intel Corp.
Grove, Wade: president, trustee, Fortis Insurance Foundation
Groves, N. Michael: vice president, general counsel, Telcordia Technologies
Grubb, Edgar Harold: executive vice president, chief financial officer, Transamerica Corp.; director, Transamerica Foundation
Gruber, David P.: president, chief executive officer, director, Wyman-Gordon Co.; chairman, vice president, director, Wyman-Gordon Foundation
Grubman, Stanley D.: secretary, Warner-Lambert Charitable Foundation; chairman, chief executive officer, director, Warner-Lambert Co.
Grum, Clifford J.: director, Temple-Inland Foundation; director, chairman, chief executive officer, Temple-Inland Inc.
Grundhofer, John Francis: president, chief executive officer, director, U.S. Bancorp
Gubert, Walter: vice chairman, Morgan & Co. Inc. (J.P.)
Guedry, James Walter: chairman, chief executive officer, director, International Paper Co.; president, International Paper Co. Foundation
Guempel, Scot R.: trustee, KPMG Peat Marwick Foundation
Guerrero, Anthony R., Jr.: president, director, First Hawaiian Foundation
Guertin, Timothy E.: vice president, Varian Medical Systems, Inc.
Guethle, K. R.: director, Group Health Foundation
Guillaume, Raymond Kendrick: vice chairman, chief executive officer, Mid-America Bank of Louisville
Guin, James M.: vice president human resources & public relations, Burlington Industries, Inc.
Guinn, Donald Eugene: chairman emeritus, Pacific Mutual Life Insurance Co.
Guiterrez, Stigfredo: director, Bucyrus-Erie Foundation
Gulis, Stephen L., Jr.: executive vice president, treasurer, chief financial officer, Wolverine World Wide
Gullotti, Russell A.: chairman, president, chief executive officer, National Computer Systems, Inc.
Gumprecht, Pamela (Howard): senior vice president, Scripps Co. (E.W.); trustee, Scripps Howard Foundation
Gundhofer, Jerry A.: chairman, director, Star Bank NA; vice president, Star Bank NA, Cincinnati Foundation
Gunter, Jana: manager community relations, Chase Bank of Texas; secretary, Chase Bank of Texas Foundation, Inc.
Gunther, Donald J.: director, Bechtel Group, Inc.
Gura, Jerry W.: contact, Amsted Industries Foundation; director, public affairs, Amsted Industries Inc.
Gurney, Peter: executive director, Franklin Mint Foundation for the Arts (The)
Gushing, N. V.: trustee, Monarch Machine Tool Co. Foundation
Gussin, Robert Zalmon, PhD: vice president science & technology, Johnson & Johnson; member corporate contributions committee, Johnson & Johnson Family of Companies Contribution Fund
Gust, Anne: executive vice president human resources, legal, administration, Gap, Inc.
Gust, Anne B.: executive vice president, chief administrative officer, Gap, Inc.
Gustafson, James E.: president, chief operating officer, Saint Paul Companies Inc.
Gustafson, Judy: vice president, treasurer, Montgomery Ward Foundation
Gustin, Lester Carl: director, Boston Edison Foundation
Guthart, Leo A.: vice chairman, director, Pittway Corp.
Guthrie, Paul: senior vice president auto forms, Reynolds & Reynolds Co.
Gutman, Roberta: director, Motorola Foundation

H

Haas, Peter Edgar, Sr.: chairman executive committee, director, Levi Strauss & Co.
Haas, Robert Douglas: chairman, chief executive officer, director, Levi Strauss & Co.; president, Levi Strauss Foundation
Haase, Bronson J.: president, chief executive officer, Ameritech Wisconsin
Haase, Maurice R.: trustee, Trustmark Foundation
Habegger, Gary L.: vice president human resources, BFGoodrich Co.; president, Goodrich Foundation, Inc. (B.F.)
Haber, Thomas R.: assistant treasurer, Glaxo Wellcome Foundation
Habig, Brian K.: chairman, chief executive officer, director, Habig Foundation
Habig, Douglas A.: chairman, chief executive officer, director, Habig Foundation
Habig, John B.: chairman, chief executive officer, director, Habig Foundation
Habig, Thomas L.: vice chairman, director, Habig Foundation
Hackborn, Richard A.: chairman, Hewlett-Packard Co.
Hacker, Douglas A.: senior vice president finance, chief financial officer, United Airlines Inc.
Hackett, James P.: trustee, Steelcase Foundation; president, chief executive officer, Steelcase Inc.
Haddock, John R.: board member, Ryder System Charitable Foundation; senior vice president marketing, Ryder System, Inc.
Haddock, Ronald Wayne: president, chief executive officer, director, FINA; president, FINA Foundation
Hadfield, Judi A.: vice president corporate relations, Marriott International Inc.
Hadley, Claudette: director, Chicago Tribune Foundation
Hadley, Leonard Anson: chairman, chief executive officer, director, Maytag Corp.; president, trustee, Maytag Corp. Foundation
Hadley-Devine, Mary: director-at-large, Deloitte & Touche Foundation
Hafer, Fred Douglass: chairman, president, chief executive officer, GPU Inc.
Haffey, Jack: assistant secretary, Montana Power Foundation
Hagale, John E.: vice president, Burlington Resources Foundation

Hagar, George L.: executive secretary, Elf Atochem North America Foundation; president, chief executive officer, Elf Atochem North America, Inc.
Hageman, Andrew F.: assistant secretary, Schering-Plough Foundation
Hagen, Garnis W.: vice president, UST Inc.
Haggerty, Gretchen R.: vice president, treasurer, USX Corp.
Haines, Jordan L.: trustee, Cessna Foundation, Inc.
Haislip, Wallace G.: senior vice president finance, chief financial officer, treasurer, Scientific-Atlanta, Inc.
Halbrook, John A.: chief executive officer, chairman, Woodward Governor Co.
Hale, Christine W.: secretary, Fort James Corp.; executive administrator, Fort James Foundation (The)
Hale, J. Joseph, Jr.: director, Cinergy Foundation
Hale, James Thomas: senior vice president, general counsel, secretary, Dayton Hudson; trustee, Target Foundation
Hale, Roger Loucks: chairman, TENNANT Co.; president, TENNANT Co. Foundation
Hale, Roger W.: chairman, chief executive officer, director, LG&E Energy Corp.; president, LG&E Energy Foundation
Haley, Carrie L.: vice president, Gosiger Foundation
Haley, Jane Gosiger: president, Gosiger Foundation
Haley, John: president, Gosiger Foundation
Haley, Pete: vice president, Gosiger Foundation
Hall, Donald Joyce: chairman board, director, Hallmark Cards Inc.; chairman, Hallmark Corporate Foundation
Hall, Floyd: chairman, president, chief executive officer, director, Kmart Corp.
Hall, Karla: administrator corporate contributions, Detroit Edison Co.; secretary, director, Detroit Edison Foundation
Hall, Katrinka: program officer, Hitachi Foundation
Hall, Larry D.: chairman, president, chief executive officer, director, Kinder Morgn; president, director, KN Energy Foundation
Hall, Thomas J.: vice president, Butler Manufacturing Co.
Hall, William Austin: vice president, secretary, Hallmark Corporate Foundation
Hallenbeck, Stephen M.: trustee, First Evergreen Foundation
Hallett, Mia: manager, PNC Bank Foundation; senior executive vice president finance & administration, PNC Financial Services Group
Halperin, Richard E.: director, Revlon Foundation Inc.
Haltiwanter, Jo Ann: trustee, Hitachi Foundation
Hamblett, Stephen: chairman, chief executive officer, publisher, Providence Journal-Bulletin Co.; trustee, Providence Journal Charitable Foundation
Hamilton, Gordon C.: vice president public relations, SAFECO Corp.
Hamilton, James L., III: general manager, USX Corp.
Hamilton, Lexanne: manager corporate education, Colgate-Palmolive Co.
Hamilton, Peter Bannerman: president, Brunswick Foundation; trustee, Kemper Foundation (James S.)
Hammerman, Stephen Lawrence: vice president, trustee, Merrill Lynch & Co. Foundation Inc.; vice chairman, general counsel, Merrill Lynch & Co., Inc.
Hammond, Darrell: chief financial officer, vice president finance, Danis Companies; treasurer, Danis Foundation
Hammond, Donna: foundation manager, American Honda Foundation
Hamp, Sheila F.: trustee, Ford Motor Co. Fund
Hampton, Alisa: program officer, Intel Foundation
Hamsa, William R., MD: director, Physicians Mutual Insurance Co. Foundation
Hamway, Lisa: director corporate contributions, Ameritech Michigan
Hand, Elbert O.: chairman, chief executive officer, director, Hartmarx Corp.
Haney, R. Lee: senior vice president, chief financial officer, Orange & Rockland Utilities, Inc.
Hanks, Stephen G.: president, Morrison Knudsen Corp. Foundation, Inc.
Hanley, Philip M.: senior vice president, chief financial officer, American General Finance; senior vice president, American General Finance Foundation
Hanlon, Tim: director, Wells Fargo Foundation
Hanna, William W.: president, chief operating officer, director, Koch Industries, Inc.
Hannity, Vincent Thomas: vice president corporate communications & investor relations, Boise Cascade Corp.
Hanower, L. David: vice president finance, Burlington Resources Foundation
Hanrahan, Michael: trustee, Kingsbury Fund
Hansen, Andrew: trustee, Cenex Harvest States Foundation
Hansen, Christopher W.: senior vice president operations, Boeing Co.
Hansen, Darryl: chairman, president, chief executive officer, GuideOne Insurance
Hansen, Kenneth N.: president, chief executive officer, director, ServiceMaster Co.; director, ServiceMaster Foundation
Hansestein, Heidi: trustee, Fortis Insurance Foundation
Hansmeyer, Herbert F.: chairman, Fireman's Fund Insurance Co.
Hanson, Clyde: vice president human resources, Graco, Inc.
Hanson, John N.: president, Harnischfeger Industries Foundation
Hanson, Jon F.: trustee, Prudential Foundation
Hanson, Richard E.: director, 3M Foundation; vice president, director, Minnesota Mining & Manufacturing Co.
Hanson, Terry: chief financial officer, Madison Gas & Electric Co.
Hanway, H. Edward: president, chief executive officer, CIGNA Corp.
Haqq, Constance T.: assistant controller, director, Nordson Corp. Foundation
Harad, George Jay: chairman, chief executive officer, director, Boise Cascade Corp.
Harden, Glen: executive vice president, chief financial officer, Carolina Power & Light Co.; treasurer, CP& L Foundation
Harden, Oleta J.: trustee, New Jersey Natural Gas Foundation
Hardiman, Joseph R.: director, NASDAQ Stock Market Educational Foundation
Harding, Jack R.: president, chief executive officer, Cadence Designs Systems, Inc.
Hardis, Stephen Roger: chairman, chief executive officer, director, Eaton Corp.
Hardison, Roy L.: senior vice president, American General Finance Foundation
Hardwick, Charles: chief operating officer, Pfizer Foundation; vice chairman, Pfizer Inc.
Hardy, Gene M.: director, La-Z-Boy Foundation
Haren, Mary Ellen: director public relations, Providence Journal-Bulletin Co.
Harkey, Robert Shelton: trustee, Delta Air Lines Foundation; senior vice president, general counsel, secretary, Delta Air Lines, Inc.
Harkins, James F., Jr.: assistant secretary, CertainTeed Corp. Foundation
Harless, Sandra K.: executive director, Central Newspapers Foundation; treasurer, Central Newspapers, Inc.
Harmon, Jo Ann: senior vice president, Emerson Charitable Trust; senior vice president administration, Emerson Electric Co.
Harmon, Sam W.: senior vice president human resources, GenCorp; trustee, GenCorp Foundation
Harms, Carol J.: vice president, treasurer, Montgomery Ward & Co., Inc.; senior vice president, Montgomery Ward Foundation
Harness, R. Randall: chief financial officer, Bradford & Co. (J.C.)
Harper, James J.: vice president, controller, Eastern Enterprises
Harreld, Michael Neal: president, chief executive officer, PNC Bank Kentucky Inc.
Harrell, Henry Howze: director, Universal Leaf Foundation; chairman, chief executive officer, director, Universal Leaf Tobacco Co., Inc.
Harrigan, Wendy: director, Royal & SunAlliance Insurance Foundation, Inc.; information technology executive, Royal & SunAlliance USA, Inc.
Harrington, Margaret Ann: president, director, Dreyer's Grand Ice Cream; director, Dreyer's Grand Ice Cream Charitable Foundation
Harris, Bronal Z.: senior vice president, First Union Regional Foundation
Harris, E. Lee, Jr.: senior vice president human resources, Compass Bank; contact, Compass Bank Foundation
Harris, Edward D., Jr.: director, Genentech Foundation for Biomedical Sciences
Harris, Elmer Beseler: president, chief executive officer, director, Alabama Power Co.
Harris, Fred: trustee, Cenex Harvest States Foundation
Harris, Grace: trustee, Circuit City Foundation
Harris, Ike: controller, BellSouth Telecommunications
Harris, Irving Brooks: chairman executive committee, director, Pittway Corp.; chairman, director, Pittway Corp. Charitable Foundation
Harris, Judith C.: trustee, Little Foundation (Arthur D.); vice president, Little, Inc. (Arthur D.)
Harris, King William: president, chief executive officer, Pittway Corp.; vice president, director, Pittway Corp. Charitable Foundation
Harris, Marilyn A.: assistant secretary, USX Foundation, Inc.
Harris, Ralph A.: vice president corporate development, Campbell Soup Co.
Harris, Richard Nelson: chairman, director, Pittway Corp.; president, director, Pittway Corp. Charitable Foundation
Harris, Susan: assistant treasurer, Grace Foundation Inc.
Harris, T. G.: chairman, president, chief executive officer, Chesapeake Corp.; trustee, Chesapeake Corp. Foundation
Harris, William W.: treasurer, Pittway Corp. Charitable Foundation
Harris Palmer, Lesley: director, IBJ Foundation
Harrison, Sandra L.: senior vice president, Hughes Electronics Corp.
Hart, Steve: trustee, Fortis Insurance Foundation
Harting, Robert M.: trustee, Merit Gasoline Foundation
Hartman, Donna Ellenga: president, Alaska Airlines, Inc.
Hartman, Lauren M.: assistant secretary, CIGNA Foundation
Hartshorn, Terry O'Dell: director, PacifiCare Health System Foundation
Harvey, A. Mosby, Jr.: secretary, HON Industries Charitable Foundation; vice president, secretary,

general counsel, HON Industries Inc.
Harvey, Robert W.: vice chairman, Reliant Energy Inc.
Hasch, J. Bruce: president, chief operating officer, director, Peoples Energy Corp.
Haskell, Robert G.: president, director, Pacific Mutual Charitable Foundation; senior vice president public affairs, Pacific Mutual Life Insurance Co.
Haskin, Donald Lee: vice president, PNC Bank
Hasler, James A.: member contributions committee, Clorox Co.; vice president, secretary, Clorox Co. Foundation
Hassenfeld, Alan Geoffrey: president, Hasbro Charitable Trust Inc.; chairman, chief executive officer, Hasbro, Inc.
Hatcher, Dottie: treasurer, Gap Foundation/Gap Inc. Community Relations
Hathaway, Derek C.: chairman, chief executive officer, Harsco Corp.; vice president, trustee, Harsco Corp. Fund
Hatsopoulos, George Nicholas: founder, chairman, chief executive officer, director, Thermo Electron Corp.; committee member, Thermo Electron Foundation
Hatsopoulos, John Nicholas: retired president, Thermo Electron Corp.; committee member, Thermo Electron Foundation
Hattendorf, William C.: trustee, Cooper Tire & Rubber Foundation
Hattox, Brock Alan: director, National Service Foundation; executive vice president, chief financial officer, National Service Industries, Inc.
Haubein, Robert H., Jr.: director, Georgia Power Foundation
Hausmann, Carl L.: chairman, president, chief executive officer, Central Soya Co.
Havens, Christopher: senior vice president, Ultramar Diamond Shamrock Corp.
Haw, C. L. William: trustee, Butler Manufacturing Co. Foundation
Hawes, Alexander Boyd, Jr.: president, Boston Globe Foundation
Hawkins, David B.: trustee, Mid-American Foundation; chairman, president, chief executive officer, director, MidAmerican Energy Holdings Co.
Hay, Gary W.: vice chairman, Cessna Aircraft Co.; trustee, Cessna Foundation, Inc.
Hayashi, Beverly: secretary, Castle & Cooke Properties Inc.
Hayashida, Joel J.: member contributions committee, Clorox Co.
Hayden, Joseph Page, Jr.: vice president, Star Bank NA, Cincinnati Foundation
Hayes, John Edward, Jr.: trustee, Western Resources Foundation
Haynes, Michael: director, Callaway Golf Co. Foundation
Hays, Lydia L.: president, CIRI Foundation
Hays, Thomas Chandler: chairman, chief executive officer, director, Fortune Brands, Inc.
Hazelton, Warren: director, Tenneco Packaging
Hazen, Paul Mandeville: chairman, chief executive officer, director, Wells Fargo & Co.
Heagney, Lawrence: member advisory committee, contact, Milliken Foundation
Healy, Jo Ann: president, chief executive officer, director, Wisconsin Power & Light Co.; administrator, Wisconsin Power & Light Foundation, Inc.
Hearn, Kathleen: manager, Boston Gas Co.
Heartman, Mary: vice president, Ultramar Diamond Shamrock Corp.
Heasley, Philip G.: president, chief operating officer, U.S. Bancorp
Hebe, James L.: chairman, president, chief executive officer, Freightliner Corp.
Hebert, William L.: assistant secretary, treasurer, Louisiana-Pacific Foundation
Hecht, John: chief financial officer, AMCORE Bank Rockford
Hecht, William F.: chairman, president, chief executive officer, Pennsylvania Power & Light
Hecker, Robert: trustee, UNUM Foundation; second vice president human resources, Unum-Provident
Heffner, Jane E.: president, chief operating officer, chief financial officer, Salomon Smith Barney
Hefner, Christie Ann: chairman, chief executive officer, Playboy Enterprises Inc.; director, Playboy Foundation
Hefner, Hugh Marston: founder, chairman emeritus, Playboy Enterprises Inc.
Hefty, Thomas R.: chairman, president, chief executive officer, United Wisconsin Services
Hegel, Garrett R.: chief financial officer, Compass Bank; president, Compass Bank Foundation
Hegel, Henry H.: president, OMC Foundation
Heggie, Colin: chief financial officer, Burger King Corp.; director, Burger King Foundation
Hehl, David K.: director, La-Z-Boy Inc.
Heidt, Julia Scripps: senior vice president newspapers, Scripps Co. (E.W.); trustee, Scripps Howard Foundation
Heilala, John A.: president, Vulcan Materials Co. Foundation
Heim, Ed: secretary advisory committee, Blue Bell Foundation
Heimbold, Charles Andreas, Jr.: chairman, president, chief executive officer, Bristol-Myers Squibb Co.
Heine, Spencer H.: executive vice president, secretary, Montgomery Ward & Co., Inc.; president, Montgomery Ward Foundation
Heinecke, James O.: director, First Financial Foundation
Heineman, Benjamin Walter, Jr.: director, GE Fund; vice president, officer, General Electric Co.
Heinen, Nancy R.: senior vice president, general counsel, Apple Computer, Inc.
Heiner, Clyde Mont: executive vice president, Questar Corp.
Heisen, JoAnn Heffernan: vice president, chief information officer, Johnson & Johnson; treasurer, Johnson & Johnson Family of Companies Contribution Fund
Held, Valerie T.: chairman, president, chief executive officer, director, UST Inc.
Heldreth, Nick E.: vice president human resources corporate relations, Harris Corp.
Helewicz, Joseph S.: vice president public affairs, Brown & Williamson Tobacco Corp.
Helfrecht, Donald J.: chairman, Madison Gas & Electric Foundation
Helland, Diane: senior legal counsel, Fuller Co. (H.B.)
Heller, Carol: manager government affairs & community investments, BankBoston-Connecticut Region
Heller, John: vice president Asia, Pacific, Latin America development marketing, Graco, Inc.
Hellman, Anne: president, chairman, chief executive officer, National City Bank of Pennsylvania
Hellman, Daryl A.: trustee, Eastern Bank Charitable Foundation
Helmig, Albert: chief financial officer, New York Mercantile Exchange; director, New York Mercantile Exchange Charitable Foundation
Helms, William E.: executive vice president, Puerto Rico, Heilig-Meyers Co.
Helmstetter, Richard: director, Callaway Golf Co. Foundation
Helsby, Keith R.: treasurer, New York Stock Exchange Foundation, Inc.; chairman, chief executive officer, New York Stock Exchange, Inc.
Helton, Bill D.: chairman, New Century Energies
Hemelt, William J.: treasurer, director, APS Foundation, Inc.; controller, Arizona Public Service Co.
Hemminghaus, Roger Roy: chairman, director, Ultramar Diamond Shamrock Corp.
Henderson, George W., III: trustee, Burlington Industries Foundation; president, chief executive officer, director, Burlington Industries, Inc.
Henderson, James Alan: vice chairman, chief executive officer, director, Ameritech Corp.; chairman, director, Cummins Engine Foundation
Henderson, Kathy: director, Piper Jaffray Companies Foundation
Hendler, Donald: secretary, treasurer, Leviton Foundation New York
Hendrickson, Brenda: manager corporate affairs and corporate giving, Advanced Micro Devices, Inc.
Hendrix, Bennie D.: senior vice president, American General Finance Foundation
Hengel, Nancy: trustee, Reinhart Family Foundation (D. B. and Marjorie)
Henley, Jeffrey O.: executive vice president, chief financial officer, director, Oracle Corp.
Henn, Catherine Emily Campbell: director, Boston Globe Foundation
Hennah, Adrian: director, Glaxo Wellcome Foundation
Henningsen, Arthur E., Jr.: senior vice president, controller, Ecolab Inc.
Henry, Michael E.: executive vice president, chief financial officer, treasurer, AFLAC Inc.
Henry, Robert A., MD: secretary, AMCORE Foundation
Henry, Taylor H., Jr.: president, chief executive officer, Shoney's Inc.
Henry-Williams, Dee: arts senior program officer, Dayton Hudson; grants program assistant, Target Foundation
Henseler, Gerald A.: executive vice president, chief financial officer, director, Banta Corp.; president, Banta Corp. Foundation
Herald, James E.: vice president finance, Mine Safety Appliances Co.; secretary, Mine Safety Appliances Co. Charitable Foundation
Herbert, Bart, Jr.: executive vice president, chief marketing officer, AEGON U.S.A. Inc.
Herbold, Robert J.: executive vice president, chief operating officer, Microsoft Corp.
Hergenhan, Joyce: director, GE Fund
Herman, William A., III: secretary, treasurer, director, Morris Communications Corp.
Hermance, Frank S.: president, chief executive officer, director, AMETEK, Inc.
Hernandez, Colleen: vice chairman, Fannie Mae; director, Fannie Mae Foundation
Hernandez, Robert M.: vice chairman, chief financial officer, director, USX Corp.; trustee, USX Foundation, Inc.
Hernandez, William H.: director, PPG Industries Foundation; senior vice president, PPG Industries, Inc.
Herowitz, Janet: director community affairs, CIT Group, Inc. (The)
Herr, Eric B.: president, chief operating officer, Autodesk Inc.
Herres, Robert T.: chairman, chief executive officer, United Services Automobile Association
Herriman, M. Davis, Junior: senior vice president, chief merchandising officer, Giant Food Inc.
Herring, Leonard Gray: vice president, Lowe's Charitable and Educational Foundation
Herring, T. Andrew: vice president, SuperValu, Inc.
Herringer, Frank Casper: president, chief executive

officer, director, chairman, Transamerica Corp.; vice chairman, director, Transamerica Foundation
Herrmann, Harold M.: chief financial officer, Reily & Co., Inc. (William B.)
Herron, James Michael: vice president, director, Ryder System Charitable Foundation
Hershman, Linda D.: director, Southern New England Telephone Co.
Hershon, Judith G.: assistant treasurer, Trace International Holdings, Inc. Foundation
Hertog, Roger: trustee, Bernstein & Co. Foundation, Inc. (Sanford C.)
Herweg, Darlynn: director, Union Pacific Corp.
Hessler, David J.: secretary, trustee, Jochum-Moll Foundation (The); president, partner, MTD Products Inc.
Hester, Stephen A. M.: chief financial officer, Credit Suisse First Boston
Heuchling, Theodore Paul: trustee, Little Foundation (Arthur D.)
Heumann, Stephen Michael: vice president, treasurer, West Co. Inc.
Hewes, Philip A.: secretary, director, Comdisco Foundation
Hewitt, James Watt: director, Abel Foundation
Hewitt, Steven J.: senior vice president, chief financial officer, Commercial Intertech Corp.
Heyer, Gloria A.: officer, SIT Investment Associates Foundation
Hiatt, Arnold Selig: chairman, director, Stride Rite Foundation
Hickey, J. Gregory: vice president, Smith Foundation Inc. (Harold Webster)
Hickey, M.: president, director, AirTouch Communications Foundation; senior vice president legal and external affairs, Vodafone AirTouch Plc
Hicks, Carole: president, Public Service Co. of Oklahoma
Hicks, Michael E.: trustee, GenCorp
Hickson, Richard G.: chief executive officer, Trustmark National Bank
Hiddeman, J.: chairman, Alcon Foundation
Hield, James S.: executive director, Cargill Foundation; member contributions committee, Cargill Inc.
Hiersteiner, Walter L.: vice chairman, Tension Envelope Corp.; vice president, Tension Envelope Foundation
Higbee, David M.: secretary, Williams; secretary, treasurer, Williams Companies Foundation (The)
Higginbotham, A. Leon, Jr.: director, New York Times Co. Foundation
Higgins, Patricia L.: director, Alcoa Foundation
Higgins, Thomas: vice president corporate contributions, Edison International
Higginson, Cornelia W.: trustee, American Express Foundation
Higgs, John H.: director, IBJ Foundation
Hijikata, Koji: foundation administrator, Nissan Foundation
Hilbrich, Jerry: trustee, KPMG Peat Marwick Foundation
Hill, Allen M.: president, chief executive officer, Dayton Power and Light Co.
Hill, Anita H.: administration assistant, CSX Corp.
Hill, Bonnie Guiton: vice president, Times Mirror Co.; president, chief executive officer, Times Mirror Foundation
Hill, Frank Trent, Jr.: trustee, Sonoco Foundation; vice president, chief financial officer, Sonoco Products Co.
Hill, George Richard: trustee, Lubrizol Foundation (The)
Hill, James: senior vice president corporate affairs, SmithKline Beecham Corp.
Hill, James M.: president, trustee, Ferro Foundation
Hill, Kenneth D.: vice president, Sunoco Inc.
Hill, Linda Bourns: president, trustee, Bourns Foundation
Hill, Richard: trustee, Commercial Intertech Foundation
Hill, Steven Richard: senior vice president human resources, Weyerhaeuser Co.; trustee, Weyerhaeuser Co. Foundation
Hill, Trizia L.: director, Sega Foundation
Hillenbrand, John A., II: director, Cinergy Foundation
Hillmer, Patricia: secretary, treasurer, trustee, National Machinery Foundation, Inc.
Hilyard, James E.: president, CertainTeed Corp.; director, CertainTeed Corp. Foundation
Himle, Karen: vice president corporate committee, Saint Paul Companies Inc.
Hine, Emily: executive vice president, chief operating officer, Microsoft Corp.
Hiner, Glen Harold, Jr.: chairman, chief executive officer, director, Owens Corning
Hines, B. E.: secretary, Duriron Foundation
Hines, J. Susan: vice president medical programs, HCR ManorCare Foundation; chairman, Manor Care Health SVS, Inc.
Hinrichs, Horst: vice chairman, director, American Standard Inc.
Hinshaw, Juanita H.: vice president, treasurer, Monsanto Co.; treasurer, Monsanto Fund
Hinson, Ronnie T.: president, Pieper Power Electric Co.
Hinton, John R.: executive vice president administration, chief financial officer, Kellogg Co.; president, trustee, Kellogg Co. Twenty-Five Year Employees' Fund Inc.
Hinton, Michael R.: president, chief operating officer, director, Old National Bank Evansville
Hipp, William Hayne: president, chief executive officer, director, Liberty Corp.; chairman, president, director, Liberty Corp. Foundation
Hird, Steve: treasurer, Piper Jaffray Companies Foundation
Hirose, Yutaka: chairman, trustee, Mazda Foundation (USA), Inc.; president, chief executive officer, Mazda North American Operations
Hirsch, Laurence E.: chairman, chief executive officer, director, Centex Corp.
Hirschman, Frank Frederick: secretary, treasurer, director, Inland Foundation, Inc.
Hjerpe, William M.: president, Honeywell Foundation
Hoag, Betty: executive vice president exploration & production, director, Louisiana Land & Exploration Co.; contributions coordinator, Louisiana Land & Exploration Co. Foundation
Hoag, David H.: chairman, president, chief executive officer, director, LTV Corp.; trustee, LTV Foundation
Hoak, Jon: senior vice president finance & administration, chief financial officer, NCR Corp.; trustee, NCR Foundation
Hobbes, Julius: director community service, Tampa Electric Co.
Hobbs, Richard F.: vice president administration, Universal Foods Corp.; vice president, director, Universal Foods Foundation
Hobgood, William P.: senior vice president, human resources, United Airlines Inc.
Hobor, Nancy A.: vice president communications & investor relations, Morton International Inc.
Hock, Delwin D.: chairman, New Century Energies
Hockaday, Irvine O., Jr.: president, chief executive officer, director, Hallmark Cards Inc.
Hocker, Mark: chief financial officer, controller, South Bend Tribune Corp.
Hodge, Joseph E.: vice president operations, Lubrizol Corp. (The); trustee, Lubrizol Foundation (The)
Hodge, Linda J.: administrator, Amgen Foundation
Hodge, Ronald C.: president, director, Hannaford Brothers Co.; director, Hannaford Charitable Foundation
Hodges, Gene R.: president, chief executive officer, Georgia Power Co.; director, Georgia Power Foundation
Hodges, John E., Jr.: trustee, Gulf Power Foundation
Hodgson, Thomas Richard: president, chief operating officer, director, Abbott Laboratories
Hodnik, David F.: president, chief executive officer, Ace Hardware Corp.
Hoff, Ted: executive vice president sales & marketing, director, Sega of America Inc.; trustee, Sega Foundation
Hoffer, Helen C.: trustee, Hoffer Foundation
Hoffer, Robert A.: trustee, Hoffer Foundation; president, Hoffer Plastics Corp.
Hoffer, Robert A., Jr.: trustee, Hoffer Foundation; vice president, Hoffer Plastics Corp.
Hoffman, David W.: secretary, Liberty Mutual Insurance Group
Hoffman, Lee R.: president, chief executive officer, CIGNA Corp.; assistant secretary, CIGNA Foundation
Hoffman, Marion: manager government & community affairs, Burger King Corp.
Hoffmann, J. Robert: executive vice president, chief credit officer, U.S. Bancorp
Hoffmann, Richard W.: general counsel, Employers Mutual Casualty Co.
Hofmann, Kenneth H.: president, director, Hofmann Co.; president, Hofmann Foundation
Hofmann, Vita Lori: president, Hofmann Foundation
Hofmann-Seeno, Lisa Ann: general counsel, Hofmann Foundation
Hogan, Cathy: director change management, Smucker Co. (JM)
Hogan, Lee W.: vice chairman, executive vice president, Reliant Energy Inc.
Hogans, Mack L.: trustee, Weyerhaeuser Co. Foundation
Hogarty, Mary: vice president community relations, California Federal Bank, FSB
Hogel, Carol C.: chairman, chief executive officer, Consolidated Electrical Distributors; president, director, Dunard Fund U.S.A., Ltd.
Hogel, Jens C.: president, director, Dunard Fund U.S.A., Ltd.
Hohn, Harry George, Jr.: director, New York Life Foundation
Holaday, G. Stephen: senior vice president, Alexander & Baldwin, Inc.
Holcombe, Paul A., Jr.: treasurer, Glaxo Wellcome Foundation
Holder, Vickie: general manager, administrator operations, Thomasville Furniture Industries Foundation; chief financial officer, vice president, Thomasville Furniture Industries Inc.
Holderness, Craig J.: president, director, Nalco Foundation
Holdrege, James H.: director, Hickory Tech Corp.; trustee, Hickory Tech Corp. Foundation
Holewa, Jack: assistant secretary, Regis Foundation
Holkemp, William: executive vice president, Enterprise Rent-A-Car Co.
Holland, John J.: president, chief executive officer, director, Butler Manufacturing Co.
Holland, Willard R.: chairman, chief executive officer, FirstEnergy Corp.
Holland, William Ray: vice president, director, United Dominion Foundation; chairman, chief executive officer, director, United Dominion Industries, Ltd.
Holler, William: treasurer, Deutsch Co.
Holliday, Charles O., Jr.: chairman, chief executive officer, director, du Pont de Nemours & Co. (E.I.)
Holliman, Vonda: treasurer, Koch Foundation, Inc. (Fred C. and Mary R.); president, chief operating

officer, director, Koch Industries, Inc.

Holliman, Wilbert G. 'Mickey': chairman, president, chief executive officer, director, Furniture Brands International, Inc.

Holling, Henry W.: director, Caterpillar Foundation

Hollingsworth, John Mark: treasurer, Simmons Foundation, Inc. (Harold)

Holman, Carl Ray: chairman, chief executive officer, director, Mallinckrodt Chemical, Inc.

Holmes, David Richard: chief executive officer, chief operating officer, director, Reynolds & Reynolds Co.

Holmes, Reva A.: senior vice president, Johnson & Son (S.C.); vice president, executive director, trustee, Johnson Wax Fund (S.C.)

Holt, Ron: trustee, Western Resources Foundation

Holtzberg, Celia: chairman, director, New York Life Foundation

Hood, Vickie: president, Kirkland & Ellis Foundation

Hoolihan, Thomas J.: vice president, Unilever Foundation

Hoops, Alan R.: chairman, PacifiCare Health System Foundation

Hoover, R. David: executive vice president, chief financial officer, Ball Corp.

Hopkins, Deborah C.: senior vice president, chief financial officer, Boeing Co.

Hopkins, Thomas E.: vice president human resources, Sherwin-Williams Co.; assistant secretary, trustee, Sherwin-Williams Foundation

Hopkins, Wayne W.: vice president corporate communications, Tampa Electric Co.

Hopson, Kathy: administrative assistant, Provident Mutual Life Insurance Co.

Horack, Thomas Borland: director, Lance Foundation

Horan, Douglas S.: senior vice president, general counsel, Boston Edison Co.; trustee, Boston Edison Foundation

Hornbeck, Daniel L.: assistant secretary, Yellow Corp. Foundation

Horner, Donald G.: director, First Hawaiian Foundation

Horner, H. B.: treasurer, Florida Rock Industries Foundation

Horsley, Richard David: vice chairman, executive financial officer, director, Regions Financial Corp.

Horton, Alan M.: senior vice president newspapers, Scripps Co. (E.W.)

Horton, Joan: corporate events, Revlon Inc.

Hosaka, Hiroshi: chairman, trustee, Mazda Foundation (USA), Inc.

Hostutler, Thomas C.: chairman, president, chief executive officer, director, Norfolk Southern Corp.

Hotard, Edgar G.: president, Praxair

Hotchner, Aaron Edward: vice president, director, executive, Newman's Own Foundation; vice president, treasurer, Newman's Own Inc.

Hough, G. Thomas: director, Ernst & Young Foundation

Hough, Lawrence Alan: president, chief executive officer, Student Loan Marketing Association

Houghton, James Richardson: director, Corning Inc.; trustee, Corning Inc. Foundation

House, Arthur H.: senior vice president corporate affairs, Tenneco Automotive

Householder, Steven L.: vice president, assistant secretary, general counsel, Inland Container Corp.; vice president, director, Inland Foundation, Inc.

Housen, Charles B.: chairman, president, chief executive officer, director, Erving Industries; president, director, Housen Foundation

Housen, Morris: president, director, Housen Foundation

Hoven, M. Patricia: director, Honeywell Foundation

Hovind, David J.: president, director, PACCAR Inc.

Howard, David P.: vice president, chief financial officer, treasurer, Furniture Brands International, Inc.

Howard, James Joseph, III: chairman, president, chief executive officer, director, Northern States Power Co.

Howat, Bruce Bradshaw, Jr.: secretary, corporate counsel, Ameritech Corp.

Howe, Linda: director, Alexander & Baldwin Foundation

Howe, Stanley M.: president, HON Industries Charitable Foundation; chairman emeritus, director, HON Industries Inc.

Howe, Wesley Jackson: chairman emeritus, director, Becton Dickinson & Co.

Howell, Doug: chief financial officer, GuideOne Insurance

Hower, Frank Beard, Jr.: chairman, Anthem Foundation, Inc.

Hower, Matthew J.: treasurer, Amsted Industries Inc.

Howes, William B.: chairman, chief executive officer, Inland Container Corp.; vice president, director, Inland Foundation, Inc.

Howison, George Everett: treasurer, Burlington Resources Foundation

Howlett, C. A.: senior vice president public affairs, America West Airlines, Inc.

Howliski, Bill: administrator, Wisconsin Power & Light Foundation, Inc.

Howze, Patricia: president, Wells Fargo Foundation

Hoy, Lee Ann: director corporate contributions, Ameritech Indiana

Hoyt, Charles Orcutt: director, Carter-Wallace Foundation; chairman executive committee, director, Carter-Wallace, Inc.

Hoyt, Henry Hamilton, Jr.: president, Carter-Wallace Foundation; chairman, chief executive officer, director, Carter-Wallace, Inc.

Hrabowski, Jacquelin: chairman, president, Price Associates Foundation (T. Rowe)

Hrevnack, Linda A.: vice president human resources, Bard, Inc. (C.R.)

Hron, Renata D.: program assistant, Hitachi Foundation

Hsu, F. Richard: assistant secretary, Tai and Co. Foundation, Inc. (J.T.)

Huang, Shuang R.: chairman, Merck Co. Foundation

Hubbard, Albert C., Jr.: vice president, secretary, treasurer, Price Associates Foundation (T. Rowe)

Hubbard, Karen H.: assistant secretary, Hubbard Foundation

Hubbard, Stanley S.: chairman, president, chief executive officer, Hubbard Broadcasting, Inc.; president, Hubbard Foundation

Hubbard Rominski, Kathryn: corporate secretary, Hubbard Broadcasting, Inc.; director, Hubbard Foundation

Huber, Dianne: assistant secretary, Enterprise Rent-A-Car Foundation

Huber, Richard Leslie: chairman, president, chief executive officer, director, Aetna, Inc.

Hubschman, Henry A.: director, president, GE Fund

Hudnut, Stewart Skinner: director, Illinois Tool Works Foundation; chairman, chief executive officer, Illinois Tool Works, Inc.

Hudson, C. B.: chairman, chief executive officer, Torchmark Corp.

Hudson, Timothy D.: trustee, Kennametal Foundation; vice president, director human resources, Kennametal, Inc.

Huerter, M. Jane: executive vice president, corporate secretary, Mutual of Omaha Insurance Co.

Huey, John W.: vice president administration, Butler Manufacturing Co.; trustee, Butler Manufacturing Co. Foundation

Huey, Ward L., Jr.: president broadcast division, vice chairman, director, Belo Corp. (A.H.); vice president, trustee, Belo Corp. Foundation (A.H.)

Hughes, Helen M.: treasurer, Johnson & Johnson Family of Companies Contribution Fund

Hughes, Robert: director, Autodesk Foundation; president, chief operating officer, Autodesk Inc.

Hughes, Timothy W.: senior vice president, Cox Enterprises Inc.; trustee, Cox Foundation (James M.)

Hughes, Victoria: treasurer, Koch Foundation, Inc. (Fred C. and Mary R.)

Huhndorf, Roy M.: director, CIRI Foundation

Hulings, Mary Andersen: vice president, Bayport Foundation

Hulseman, John F.: vice president manufacturing, secretary, director, Solo Cup Co.; vice president, Solo Cup Foundation

Hulseman, Robert L.: president, chief executive officer, director, Solo Cup Co.; president, Solo Cup Foundation

Hult, Frank A.: vice president, controller, chief accounting officer, Walter Industries Inc.

Hultgren, Dennis N.: director, Appleton Papers Inc.

Humann, L. Phillip: secretary, SunTrust Bank Atlanta Foundation

Humleker, Margaret Banta: president, Banta Corp. Foundation

Humphrey, Deborah L.: director, Bowater Inc.

Humphrey, Neil Darwin: trustee, Commercial Intertech Foundation

Humphreys, David Craig: secretary-treasurer, Craig Foundation (E.L.); president, chief operating officer, director, Tamko Roofing Products

Humphreys, Ethel Mae Craig: president, Craig Foundation (E.L.); chairman, chief executive officer, Tamko Roofing Products

Hunkin, John: president, CIBC Oppenheimer

Hunsucker, Glenn A.: president, chief operating officer, Bassett Furniture Industries; president, director, Bassett Furniture Industries Fdn.

Hunt, Penny: executive director staff, Medtronic Foundation; chief executive officer, chairman, Medtronic, Inc.

Hunt, Ray Lee: chairman, chief executive officer, director, Hunt Oil Co.

Hunt, V. William: director, Arvin Foundation; chief executive officer, chairman, president, director, Arvin Industries, Inc.

Hunter, Robert D.: trustee, Chase Manhattan Bank, NA

Hunting, David Dyer, Jr.: trustee, Steelcase Foundation; director, Steelcase Inc.

Huot, Paul: director, Fuller Co. Foundation (H.B.)

Hupfer, Charles J.: trustee, Sonoco Foundation

Hurford, Gary Thomas: president, director, Hunt Oil Co.

Hurley, Rose: member, SAFECO Corp.

Hursh, Judy K.: president, director, Montana Power Foundation

Hurt, Douglas M.: director, Glaxo Wellcome Foundation

Hushen, John Wallace: chairman, chief executive officer, director, Eaton Corp.

Huston, Edwin Allen: vice president, director, Ryder System Charitable Foundation; vice chairman, director, Ryder System, Inc.

Huston, Steve: secretary, Wrigley Co. Foundation (Wm. Jr.)

Hutchings, Gregory: vice president, Tomkins Corp. Foundation

Hutchings, Peter Lounsbery: president, Guardian Life Insurance Co. of America

Hutchins, H. R.: member executive committee, director, Shell Oil Co. Foundation

Hutchins, William Bruce, III: president, chief executive officer, director, Alabama Power Co.; director, Alabama Power Foundation

Hutta, Jane: general counsel, assistant treasurer, staff attorney, Sumitomo

Bank; secretary, Sumitomo Bank Global Foundation
Hutton, Edward L.: chairman, chief executive officer, director, Chemed Corp.
Hutton, Thomas C., Esq.: chairman, chief executive officer, director, Chemed Corp.; director, Chemed Foundation
Hyatt, Kenneth Ernest: chairman, president, chief executive officer, director, Walter Industries Inc.
Hyatt, Linda S.: vice president, executive director, Landmark Communications Foundation; executive vice president, Landmark Communications Inc.
Hyde, Douglas W.: chairman, president, chief executive officer, Oshkosh B'Gosh, Inc.
Hyman, Morton Peter: vice president, director, OSG Foundation; president, director, Overseas Shipholding Group Inc.
Hynes, Maryanne: director, Hamilton Sundstrand Corp.

I

Imeson, Tom: board member, PacifiCorp Foundation
Ingersoll, Robert Stephen: vice president, North America industrial group, Matsushita Electric Corp. of America; chairman, director, Panasonic Foundation
Ingham, Dewey: membership, ReliaStar Foundation
Ingle, Donald B., Jr.: president energy services business unit, vice president, Cinergy Corp.
Ingram, Martha R.: chairman, director, Ingram Industries Inc.
Ingram, Robert A.: chairman, director, Glaxo Wellcome Foundation; president, chief executive officer, director, Glaxo Wellcome Inc.
Ingram, W. E.: president, chief executive officer, Conwood Co. LP
Inone, Masa: executive vice president, Shaklee Corp.
Inskeep, Harriet J.: president, director, Journal-Gazette Foundation, Inc.
Inskeep, Richard G.: owner, Journal-Gazette Co.; president, director, Journal-Gazette Foundation, Inc.
Iott, Richard B.: president, chief executive officer, director, Seaway Food Town, Inc.
Iott, Wallace D.: chairman, director, Seaway Food Town, Inc.
Irani, Raymond Reza: director, Occidental Petroleum Charitable Foundation; chairman, director, chief executive officer, Occidental Petroleum Corp.
Iraola, Manuel J.: senior vice president, director, Phelps Dodge Corp.
Ireland, R. A., II: vice president, consultant, Bell Atlantic Corp.-West Virginia
Irimajri, Shoichiro: trustee, Sega Foundation
Ise, Hikonobu: president, trustee, Ise Cultural Foundation
Ishii, Katsumi: vice president finance, chief financial officer, Nissan North America, Inc.
Ishizaka, Yoshio: president, chief executive officer, Toyota Motor Sales U.S.A., Inc.; president, Toyota U.S.A. Foundation
Ishkenian, Mark: director corporate communications, Central Maine Power Co.
Ito, Hideo: secretary, Toshiba America Foundation
Itoh, Iwao: chairman, president, chief executive officer, New United Motor Manufacturing Inc.
Ivens, Barbara J.: executive director, Gerber Foundation
Iverson, Francis Kenneth: chairman, director, Nucor Corp.; director, Nucor Foundation
Iverson, Kenneth A.: vice president, corporate secretary, Ecolab Inc.
Ives, J. Atwood: chairman, chief executive officer, Boston Gas Co.; chairman, chief executive officer, trustee, Eastern Enterprises; trustee, Eastern Enterprises Foundation
Ivester, Melvin Douglas: president, director, Coca-Cola Foundation
Ivey, Ray N.: director, Consolidated Natural Gas System Foundation
Iwamoto, Yasul: director, Mitsubishi Electric America Foundation
Iwanicki, John: member, Northern Trust Co. Charitable Trust
Iwasaki, Itsumi: associate senior vice president human resources & administration, NEC America, Inc.; treasurer, NEC Foundation of America
Iwashita, Kenneth M.: trustee, Lubrizol Foundation (The)

J

Jack, Patrick: president, chief operating officer, Aristech Chemical Corp.
Jackson, Andrew: secretary, ABC Foundation
Jackson, Anita M.: vice president, Baltimore Gas & Electric Foundation
Jackson, Elijah: president, Navcom Charities Foundation; president, chief executive officer, Navcom Systems
Jackson, Frederick H.: executive vice president finance, director, La-Z-Boy Inc.
Jackson, Ira A.: trustee, BankBoston Charitable Foundation
Jackson, John E.: executive director, Nordson Corp. Foundation
Jackson, Kenneth G.: executive vice president, chief financial officer, Shaw Industries Inc.
Jackson, Mary: vice president, Navcom Charities Foundation; executive vice president, Navcom Systems
Jackson, Sonya: vice president, Sears, Roebuck and Co. Foundation
Jackson, Yvonne: senior vice president, Burger King Corp.; director, Burger King Foundation
Jacobi, Peter A.: president, Levi Strauss & Co.; vice president, Levi Strauss Foundation
Jacobs, Bruce E.: vice president, director, Grede Foundation; president, director, Grede Foundries
Jacobs, Burleigh Edmund: president, director, Grede Foundation; chairman, Grede Foundries; director, Marshall & Ilsley Foundation, Inc.
Jacobs, Joseph J.: president, director, Jacobs Engineering Foundation; chairman, director, Jacobs Engineering Group
Jacobs, Libby: president, Principal Financial Group; secretary, Principal Financial Group Foundation, Inc.
Jacobs, Rodney L.: chairman, chief executive officer, director, Wells Fargo & Co.; chief financial officer, Wells Fargo Foundation
Jacobs, Susan A.: senior vice president, deputy general counsel, secretary, American General Corp.
Jacobsen, James C.: vice chairman, Kellwood Co.; vice president, director, Kellwood Foundation
Jacobsen, Lowell: chairman, Medtronic Foundation; executive director staff, Medtronic, Inc.
Jacobsen, Thomas Herbert: chairman, president, chief executive officer, Mercantile Bank NA
Jacobson, Arthur L.: secretary, director, Jacobson & Sons Foundation (Benjamin)
Jacobson, James A.: treasurer, director, Jacobson & Sons Foundation (Benjamin)
Jacobson, Lyle Gordon: trustee, Hickory Tech Corp. Foundation
Jacobson, Richard J.: vice president, treasurer, Cox Enterprises Inc.
Jacobson, Robert J., Jr.: partner, Jacobson & Sons (Benjamin); secretary, director, Jacobson & Sons Foundation (Benjamin)
Jacobson, Robert J., Sr.: president, director, Jacobson & Sons Foundation (Benjamin)
Jacobson, Sibyl C.: director, MetLife Foundation
Jacoby, A. James: treasurer, New York Stock Exchange Foundation, Inc.
Jacono, Vince: manager public affairs, Conectiv
Jaeger, Joseph: vice president finance, Maybelline, Inc.
Jaenke, Norma: secretary, trustee, Presto Foundation
Jaffe, Ira J.: treasurer, Erb Foundation
Jager, Durk I.: chairman, president, chief executive, Procter & Gamble Co.
Jahn, Gloria: corporate manager philanthropy, Toyota Motor Sales U.S.A., Inc.; senior vice president, coordinating officer, Toyota U.S.A. Foundation
James, Argentina: vice president corporate communications, Browning-Ferris Industries Inc.
James, Donald M.: trustee, Vulcan Materials Co. Foundation
James, George Barker, II: senior vice president, chief financial officer, Levi Strauss & Co.
James, John D.: senior vice president, Pioneer Hi-Bred International, Inc.
James, John J.: president, trustee, Gerber Foundation
James, Stacy J.: tax officer, El Paso Energy Foundation
Jamison, Zean, Jr.: director, Lance Foundation; director human resources, Lance, Inc.
Jander, Steve: vice president corporate development, Campbell Soup Co.; trustee, Campbell Soup Foundation
Janitz, John A.: president, chief executive officer, chairman, Textron Inc.
Jannotta, Edgar D.: president, Blair & Co. Foundation (William); senior director, Blair & Co. (William)
Janson, Peter S.: president, chief executive officer, ABB Inc.
Jao, C. S. Daisy: trustee, Boston Edison Foundation
Jarman, Richard Sinclair: executive vice president, Butler Manufacturing Co.; trustee, Butler Manufacturing Co. Foundation
Jarvela, Dennis: director, Owens Corning Foundation, Inc.
Jasse, Andre C., Jr.: trustee, Eastern Bank Charitable Foundation
Jastrow, Kenneth M., II: director, Temple-Inland Foundation
Jaudes, Robert Christian: chairman, trustee, Laclede Gas Charitable Trust
Jayne, Bill: president, Rutledge Hill Press
Jayo, David: grants administrator, REI-Recreational Equipment, Inc.
Jean, Raymond A.: corporate vice president, Amsted Industries Inc.
Jeannero, Jane: trustee, Gerber Foundation
Jeffries, April: trustee, Campbell Soup Foundation
Jenest, Jeffrey M.: senior vice president new business development, Playboy Enterprises Inc.; director, Playboy Foundation
Jenifer, Franklyn Green: trustee, Texaco Foundation; executive director, Texaco Inc.
Jenkins, A. H.: director, Dow Chemical Co.; secretary, Dow Chemical Co. Foundation
Jenkins, Benjamin P., III: vice chairman general bank, First Union Corp.; member, First Union Foundation
Jenkins, Bob: director, Hamilton Sundstrand Corp.
Jenkins, James Robert: trustee, Dow Corning Foundation
Jenkins, Thomas A.: president, chief executive officer, Dayton Power and Light Co.; treasurer, trustee, Dayton Power and Light Co. Foundation

Jenney, Suzanne: assistant secretary, Reynolds Tobacco (R.J.)

Jennings, James Burnett: president, Hunt Oil Co.

Jennings, Karen E.: chairman, director, chief executive officer, SBC Communications Inc.; director, SBC Foundation

Jeray, Jackie: trustee, Fortis Insurance Foundation

Jeremiah, Barbara S.: director, Alcoa Foundation

Jernigan, Donna: manager, Ameritech Illinois

Jerome, Joseph M.: executive director, trustee, Merit Gasoline Foundation

Jerrold, Douglas M.: vice president, director, Reynolds Metals Co. Foundation

Jewell, George Hiram: director, Schlumberger Foundation; chairman, president, chief executive officer, Schlumberger Ltd. (USA)

Jewell, Robert: vice president communications, BFGoodrich Co.

Jewett, George Frederick, Jr.: secretary, Potlatch Foundation II

Jobe, G. David: director, MFA Foundation; senior vice president, MFA Inc.

Jobe, Warren Yancey: executive vice president, Georgia Power Co.; president, director, Georgia Power Foundation

Jobs, Steven Paul: interim chief executive officer, Apple Computer, Inc.

Jochum, Emil: secretary, trustee, Jochum-Moll Foundation (The)

John, Sharon: executive director, CIRI Foundation

Johns, William: manager, PNC Bank Foundation

Johnsmeyer, William L.: trustee, Butler Manufacturing Co. Foundation

Johnson, Alice: president, Waffle House Foundation, Inc.; vice chairman, director, Waffle House Inc.

Johnson, Amy: chairman, chief executive officer, director, Rite Aid Corp.

Johnson, B. Kristine: chief operating officer, Medtronic, Inc.

Johnson, Carmella J.: manager, Clorox Co.; trustee, Clorox Co. Foundation

Johnson, Charleen: executive director, Millipore Foundation (The)

Johnson, Charles B.: executive vice president operation, Cessna Aircraft Co.; trustee, Cessna Foundation, Inc.; director, NASDAQ Stock Market Educational Foundation

Johnson, Charles M.: vice chairman, Wells Fargo & Co.

Johnson, Charles S.: president, chief executive officer, chairman, Pioneer Hi-Bred International, Inc.

Johnson, Clark Hughes: director corporate contributions, Johnson & Johnson Family of Companies Contribution Fund

Johnson, Daniel: director, Blue Cross & Blue Shield of Minnesota Foundation Inc.

Johnson, David Willis: chairman, director, Campbell Soup Co.

Johnson, Don R.: director, First Union Foundation

Johnson, Donald A.: chairman, secretary, JSJ Foundation

Johnson, Douglas: assistant secretary-treasurer, Cenex Harvest States Foundation

Johnson, Edward Crosby, III: president, Fidelity Foundation; chairman, president, chief executive officer, director, Fidelity Investments

Johnson, F. Martin: chairman, chief executive officer, director, JSJ Corp.; trustee, JSJ Foundation

Johnson, Glen M.: director, Chicago Board of Trade Foundation

Johnson, Gwen A.: treasurer, trustee, Fortis Insurance Foundation

Johnson, Hansford Tillman: trustee, USAA Foundation, A Charitable Trust; chairman, chief executive officer, USAA Life Insurance Co.

Johnson, James A.: chairman, chief executive officer, director, Fannie Mae; chairman, Fannie Mae Foundation

Johnson, James L.: secretary, director, Globe Foundation

Johnson, James Lawrence: chairman emeritus, Walter Industries Inc.

Johnson, Joan L.: vice president finance, chief financial officer, Wiremold Co.; secretary, Wiremold Foundation

Johnson, Kenneth James: vice president, controller, director, Motorola Inc.

Johnson, Laura L.: manager, TRW Foundation; chairman, chief executive officer, TRW Inc.

Johnson, Lawrence M.: president, Pacific Century Financial Corp.

Johnson, Mark L.: director, Carter Star Telegram Employees Fund (Amon G.)

Johnson, Mary J.: manager, Lincoln Financial Group

Johnson, Murray Lloyd, Jr.: treasurer, trustee, Zachry Foundation (The)

Johnson, Norman E.: trustee, CLARCOR Foundation; senior vice president technology, Weyerhaeuser Co.; trustee, Weyerhaeuser Co. Foundation

Johnson, Owen C., Jr.: vice president human resources, Northern Indiana Public Service Co.

Johnson, P. J.: chairman, chief executive officer, director, Nomura America Foundation; vice president, Nomura Holding America

Johnson, Robbin S.: vice president, Cargill Foundation; corporate vice president public affairs, Cargill Inc.

Johnson, Samuel Curtis: chairman, director, president, Johnson & Son (S.C.); chairman, trustee, Johnson Wax Fund (S.C.)

Johnson, Sandra: chief financial officer, vice president, Donaldson Foundation

Johnson, Scott W.: senior vice president, secretary, general counsel, Bemis Co., Inc.

Johnson, Suzanne: human resources consultant, American Stock Exchange, Inc.

Johnson, Tina: treasurer, director, Publix Supermarkets

Johnson, William R.: president, chief executive officer, Heinz Co. (H.J.)

Johnson-Bly, Ann: senior vice president, chief administrative officer, Northeast Utilities

Johnston, Gerald E.: member contributions committee, Clorox Co.; trustee, Clorox Co. Foundation

Johnston, James W.: director, La-Z-Boy Inc.

Johnston, William E., Junior: president, chief operating officer, director, Morton International Inc.

Johnston, William R.: treasurer, New York Stock Exchange Foundation, Inc.

Jokiel, Peter E.: senior vice president, chief financial officer, CNA

Jonakin, Lynn: president, MacMillan Bloedel Foundation; president, director, MacMillan Bloedel Inc.

Jones, Carl E., Jr.: president, chief executive officer, Regions Financial Corp.

Jones, Christine G.: chairman, chief executive officer, director, Boeing Co.

Jones, Christopher: program manager, Microsoft Corp.; chief executive officer, Thompson Co. (J. Walter)

Jones, D. Michael: senior vice president, general counsel, Reynolds Metals Co.; vice president, director, Reynolds Metals Co. Foundation

Jones, D. Paul, Jr.: chairman, chief executive officer, Compass Bank; trustee, Compass Bank Foundation

Jones, Dale P.: vice president, secretary, Halliburton Foundation, Inc.

Jones, David Allen: chairman, chief executive officer, director, Humana Foundation; co-founder, chairman, director, Humana, Inc.

Jones, David L. E.: vice president, National Starch & Chemical Co.

Jones, David R.: principal, AGL Resources Inc.

Jones, Dennis H.: chief information officer, FedEx Corp.

Jones, Edward L.: vice chairman, Morgan & Co. Inc. (J.P.)

Jones, H. L.: vice president, Caring Foundation

Jones, Ingrid Saunders: secretary, director, Coca-Cola Foundation

Jones, James: vice president, director, Reebok Human Rights Foundation (The)

Jones, Jill: treasurer, State Farm Companies Foundation

Jones, Joseph A.: trustee, Eastern Bank Charitable Foundation

Jones, Joseph West: president, director, Coca-Cola Foundation

Jones, Kenneth W.: controller, Liberty Corp.; controller, treasurer, Liberty Corp. Foundation

Jones, Lewis B.: vice president, partner, USX Corp.

Jones, M. William: vice president, director, Armstrong Foundation

Jones, Marilyn: manager, Matsushita Electric Corp. of America; chairman, director, Panasonic Foundation

Jones, Patrick A.: director, Badger Meter Foundation

Jones, Raymond E.: secretary, director, Shelter Insurance Foundation; executive vice president, secretary, Shelter Mutual Insurance Co.

Jones, Ross: senior vice president, chief financial officer, Knight Ridder

Jones, Russell H.: chief financial officer, Kaman Corp.

Jones, Sumner: executive vice president, Eastern Bank

Joos, David W.: president, chief executive officer electric, executive vice president, Consumers Energy Co.

Jordan, Anne: senior vice president, Brooklyn Union

Jordan, William M.: president, chief executive officer, chairman, director, Duriron Co., Inc.; president, Duriron Foundation

Jordin, John N.: vice president, director, Armstrong Foundation

Jorndt, Louis Daniel: president, chief executive officer, director, Walgreen Co.

Joseph, Burton: director, Playboy Foundation

Joslin, David C.: trustee, Gerber Foundation

Joslin, Roger Scott: vice president programs, State Farm Companies Foundation

Joyce, William H.: chairman, president, chief executive officer, chief operating officer, Union Carbide Corp.

Judge, James J.: senior vice president corporate service business unit, treasurer, Boston Edison Co.; trustee, Boston Edison Foundation

Juilfs, George C.: president energy services business unit, vice president, Cinergy Corp.; director, Cinergy Foundation

Juliber, Lois: chief operating officer, Colgate-Palmolive Co.

Julsrud, Christopher K.: vice president human resources, Morton International Inc.

Jung, Howard J.: chairman, director, Ace Hardware Corp.

Jursch, Eve: chief executive officer, Patagonia Inc.

K

Kabat, Kevin T.: vice chairman, president, Old Kent Bank; trustee, Old Kent Foundation

Kaden, Ellen O.: chairman, director, Campbell Soup Co.; trustee, Campbell Soup Foundation

Kahle, Shawn M.: chairman, president, chief executive officer, director, Kmart Corp.

Kahler, Judy: director, Land O'Lakes Foundation; president, chief executive officer, Land O'Lakes, Inc.

Kaitz, Patricia M.: chief financial officer, secretary, Genentech Inc.

Kalaher, Richard A.: president, American Standard Foundation; vice president, secretary, general counsel, American Standard Inc.

Kalainov, Sam Charles: chairman, president, chief executive officer, AmerUS Group

Kalaris, Thomas: chief executive americas, Barclays Capital

Kalis, David B.: vice president communications, International Business Machines Corp.

Kalnow, A. H.: trustee, National Machinery Foundation, Inc.

Kalnow, Carl F.: trustee, National Machinery Foundation, Inc.

Kaman, Charles Huron: chairman, president, chief executive officer, director, Kaman Corp.

Kamen, Harry Paul: chairman, president, chief executive officer, Metropolitan Life Insurance Co.

Kamphuis, Robert D.: vice president financial, chief financial officer, director, Giddings & Lewis; president, Giddings & Lewis Foundation

Kampouris, Emmanuel Andrew: chairman, president, chief executive officer, director, American Standard Inc.

Kanai, Tsutomu: chairman, trustee, Hitachi Foundation

Kangas, Edward A.: chairman, chief executive officer, Deloitte & Touche

Kanitz, Betsy: program director

Kann, Peter Robert: chairman, chief executive officer, publisher, director, Dow Jones & Co., Inc.; member advisory committee, Dow Jones Foundation

Kantor, Gregg: vice president, Northwest Natural Gas Co.

Kaplinsky, Raymond J.: chairman, Vanguard Group Foundation

Karabelnikoff, Don: director, CIRI Foundation

Karibjanian, S. A.: president, trustee, Kellogg Co. Twenty-Five Year Employees' Fund Inc.

Kariya, Akio: treasurer, IBJ Foundation; senior vice president, Industrial Bank of Japan Trust Co. (New York)

Karmel, Roberta S.: trustee, Kemper Foundation (James S.); partner, Kemper National Insurance Companies

Karow, Barbara: director, Wisconsin Energy Corp. Foundation, Inc.

Karr, Howard Henry: vice president, director, First Hawaiian Foundation

Karr, Mary: vice president, NCR Corp.; trustee, NCR Foundation

Karvellas, Steven: director, New York Mercantile Exchange Charitable Foundation

Kasenter, Robert Albert: executive vice president human resources, Montgomery Ward & Co., Inc.; executive vice president, Montgomery Ward Foundation

Kasputys, Joseph Edward: program assistant, Hitachi Foundation

Kast, Howard C.: treasurer, Edwards Foundation (J.D.)

Kaste, Mary: trustee, Cenex Harvest States Foundation

Kasten, G. Frederick, Jr.: trustee, Baird & Co. Foundation (Robert W.); chairman, chief executive officer, director, Baird & Co. (Robert W.)

Kasting, Barbara Glenn: assistant secretary, Milacron Foundation; vice president human resources, Milacron, Inc.

Katayama, Akira: chairman, chief executive officer, Mitsubishi Electric America; director, Mitsubishi Electric America Foundation

Kato, Harumi: director human resources, NEC America, Inc.; general manager corporate planning, NEC Foundation of America

Kato, Masahiro: director, NEC America, Inc.; chairman, executive vice president, NEC Foundation of America

Kato, Robert: director, Harris Bank Foundation

Katsurada, Masamichi: director, Toshiba America Foundation

Kaufman, Frank Joseph: senior vice president taxes, McGraw-Hill Companies, Inc.

Kaufmann, Barbara W.: vice president, director, Minnesota Mining & Manufacturing Co.

Kavetas, Harry L.: chief financial officer, executive vice president, director, Eastman Kodak Co.

Kawai, Tadasu: community affairs representative, Sony Electronics; director, Sony U.S.A. Foundation Inc.

Kay, Barry: chief financial officer, Sharp Electronics Corp.

Kaye, Diane L.: vice president, secretary, general counsel, Federal-Mogul Corp.

Kayser, John P.: chief financial officer, secretary, Blair & Co. Foundation (William); chief financial officer, Blair & Co. (William)

Kean, Stewart B.: mgr, Sovereign Bank Foundation

Keane, John: president retail business group, Northeast Utilities

Kearney, Christopher J.: chairman, president, chief executive officer, director, SPX Foundation

Kearney, R. Wynn, Jr.: director, Hickory Tech Corp.; trustee, Hickory Tech Corp. Foundation

Kearns, Richard P.: partner, partner affairs, PricewaterhouseCoopers; vice president, Pricewaterhouse-Coopers Foundation

Keating, Kevin: vice president, Pfizer Foundation

Keating, Michael K.: executive vice president, counsel, secretary, Fifth Third Bancorp

Kebayashi, Tadao: senior program officer, American Honda Foundation

Keegan, Peter: secretary, treasurer, trustee, Loews Foundation

Keelty, Richard W.: senior vice president public affairs, Warner-Lambert Charitable Foundation

Keen, J. LaMont: vice president, chief financial officer, Idaho Power Co.

Keenan, Jack: chief executive officer, United Distillers & Vintners North America

Keene, Donald: president, trustee, Ise Cultural Foundation

Keith, Robert F.: director, ServiceMaster Foundation

Keith, Susan Stewart: vice president, secretary, Halliburton Foundation, Inc.

Kelbley, Stephen Paul: executive vice president, Springs Industries, Inc.

Kelleher, L. J.: president, treasurer, director, FPL Group Foundation, Inc.

Kelleher, Paul F.: committee member, Thermo Electron Foundation

Keller, Celeste: chairman, chief executive officer, director, First Security Bank of Idaho NA

Keller, Roger A.: vice president, secretary, general counsel, Mallinckrodt Chemical, Inc.

Keller, Thomas M.: president, Fortis Insurance Co.

Kellett, Martine: trustee, New England Bio Labs Foundation

Kelley, Barbara M.: vice president, Bausch & Lomb Foundation, Inc.; chief executive officer, director, chairman, Bausch & Lomb Inc.

Kelley, Bruce Gunn: general counsel, Employers Mutual Casualty Co.; vice president, director, Employers Mutual Charitable Foundation

Kelley, John B.: vice president investor relations, Alexander & Baldwin, Inc.

Kelley, John C., Jr.: president Memphis Banking Group, First Tennessee National Corp.

Kelley, John J.: trustee, UPS Foundation

Kelliher, Eileen V.: treasurer, Niagara Mohawk Foundation; director, Niagara Mohawk Holdings Inc.

Kellner, Jack F.: president, Marshall & Ilsley Corp.; director, board member, Marshall & Ilsley Foundation, Inc.

Kellogg, Terry: vice president, Caring Foundation

Kelly, Anastasia: chairman, Fannie Mae Foundation

Kelly, Burnett S.: vice president, Dow Corning Corp.

Kelly, Colin P.: senior vice president human resources, Household International Inc.

Kelly, Edmund F.: president, chief executive officer, Liberty Mutual Insurance Group

Kelly, Edward W.: chairman, Eckerd Corp. Foundation

Kelly, J. Peter: president, chief operating officer, director, LTV Corp.; trustee, LTV Foundation

Kelly, Janet L.: executive vice president corporate development, general counsel, secretary, Kellogg Co.

Kelly, John F.: chairman, chief executive officer, director, Alaska Airlines, Inc.

Kelly, Richard C.: executive vice president, chief financial officer, New Century Energies; treasurer, New Century Energies Foundation

Kelly, Warren: director, Piper Jaffray Companies Foundation

Kelly, Wilhelmena: president, chairman, chief executive officer, National City Bank of Pennsylvania

Kelly-Judd, Virginia: chairman, chief executive officer, director, Humana Foundation

Kelson, Richard B.: director, Alcoa Foundation

Kemper, David Woods: chairman, president, chief executive officer, director, Commerce Bancshares, Inc.

Kemper, James M., Jr.: director, Commerce Bancshares Foundation; chairman, president, director, Commerce Bancshares, Inc.

Kemper, James Scott, Jr.: trustee, Kemper Foundation (James S.)

Kemper, Jonathan McBride: director, Commerce Bancshares Foundation; vice chairman, Commerce Bancshares, Inc.

Kemper, Michele: member contributions committee, SAFECO Corp.

Kendall, J. William: director, Arvin Foundation

Kendall, Janet: associate vice president, SBC Communications Inc.; chairman, SBC Foundation

Kendall, Richard C.: trustee, Crane & Co. Fund

Kendrick, William J.: vice president public affairs, Air Products and Chemicals, Inc.; chairman, Air Products Foundation

Kennedy, Bernard Joseph: chairman, president, chief executive officer, director, National Fuel Gas Distribution Corp.

Kennedy, George Danner: honorary chairman, Kemper Foundation (James S.)

Kennedy, James Andrew: vice president, National Starch & Chemical Co.

Kennedy, James Cox: chairman, chief executive officer, director, Cox Enterprises Inc.; trustee, Cox Foundation (James M.)

Kennel, Russel R.: president, chief executive officer, director, Lee Foundation

Kenney, Richard John: director, Consolidated Papers Foundation, Inc.; senior vice president finance, Consolidated Papers, Inc.

Kenny, John J.: treasurer, Loews Corp.; secretary, treasurer, trustee, Loews Foundation

Kenny, Siobann: corporate contributions, Apple Computer, Inc.

Keno, Marcy: director, Chicago Tribune Foundation

Kentz, Frederick C., III: trustee, Hoffmann-La Roche Foundation; vice president, secretary, general counsel, Hoffmann-La Roche Inc.

Keough, William H.: senior vice president, chief financial officer, Pioneer Group

Kercher, Idella: board member, Edwards Foundation (J.D.)

Kerckhove, George H.: vice president, chief financial officer, American Standard Inc.

Kerr, Steven: director, GE Fund; vice president corporate leadership development, General Electric Co.

Kerr, Thomas: executive director, Bayer Foundation

Kerr, William T.: chairman, chief executive officer, director, Meredith Corp.

Kerridge, Isaac C.: executive director, Baker Hughes Foundation

Kersten, Katherine: vice president, Cargill Foundation

Kessel, Gerry Roth: vice president, secretary, Revlon Foundation Inc.

Kesseler, Roger L.: secretary, Dow Chemical Co. Foundation

Keuthen, Catherine J.: trustee, Boston Edison Foundation

Keyes, James Henry: advisor, Johnson Controls Foundation; president, Johnson Controls Inc.

Keyes, James W.: executive vice president, chief operating officer, 7-Eleven, Inc.

Keyser, Alan J.: trustee, Quaker Chemical Foundation

Keyser, F. Ray, Jr.: chairman, director, Central Vermont Public Service Corp.

Keyser, Richard Lee: chairman, chief executive officer, president, Grainger, Inc. (W.W.)

Khoury, Kenneth F.: president, Georgia-Pacific Foundation

Khristie, Robert: director public affairs, FMC Corp.

Kicfer, Francs: treasurer, assistant secretary, Wisconsin Public Service Foundation, Inc.

Kidder, C. Robert: chairman, president, chief executive officer, director, Borden, Inc.

Kiely, W. Leo, III: president, chief operating officer, Coors Brewing Co.

Kiemle, George E.: chairman, chief executive officer, director, Owens Corning; director, Owens Corning Foundation, Inc.

Kiener, Dan W.: director, PPG Industries Foundation

Kienker, James: chief financial officer, Maritz Inc.

Kiernan, Donald E., Sr.: senior vice president, chief financial officer, treasurer, SBC Communications Inc.; director, SBC Foundation

Kiker, John D.: vice president corporate communications, United Airlines Inc.

Kile, James: mgr, assistant secretary-treasurer, Cenex Harvest States Foundation

Killian, John: assistant secretary, State Farm Companies Foundation

Killinger, Kerry Kent: chairman, president, chief executive officer, director, Washington Mutual, Inc.

Kilpatrick, Kay M.: trustee, Harcourt General Charitable Foundation

Kim, John Y.: director, Aetna Foundation

Kimbrell, Curtis C.: executive vice president merchandising, Heilig-Meyers Co.

Kincaid, Brent B.: president, chief executive officer, Furniture Brands International, Inc.

Kindle, JoAnn Taylor: executive vice president public relations, Enterprise Rent-A-Car Co.; president, Enterprise Rent-A-Car Foundation

Kindler, Jeffrey B.: executive vice president, corporate general counsel, McDonald's Corp.

King, D. E.: trustee, National Machinery Foundation, Inc.

King, Lawrence J.: executive vice president, Eastern Bank

King, Miles B.: vice president investor relations, Alexander & Baldwin, Inc.

King, Reatha Clark: director, Fuller Co. Foundation (H.B.); president, executive director, General Mills Foundation

King, Richard L.: president, chief operating officer, Albertson's Inc.

King, Roger Leo: vice president, officer, Graco, Inc.

King, Thomas A.: chairman, treasurer, Lilly Foundation (Eli)

King, Tom: director, Autodesk Foundation

Kingsbury, Brigitte L.: trustee, Orchard Foundation

Kinisky, Thomas G.: vice president, director, CertainTeed Corp.

Kinley, Don: chief financial officer, National Bank of Commerce Trust & Savings

Kinney, Richard J.: trustee, member, Schering-Plough Foundation

Kinosh, Diana: chairman, president, chief executive officer, director, Aetna, Inc.

Kinsolving, Augustus Blagden: assistant secretary, ASARCO Foundation

Kipnis, Mark: vice president, trustee, Chicago Sun-Times Charity Trust

Kirby, John L.: chief financial officer, United States Trust Co. of New York

Kirby, William Joseph: president, director, FMC Foundation

Kirchhof, Anton Conrad: corporate secretary, general counsel, Louisiana-Pacific Corp.; secretary, Louisiana-Pacific Foundation

Kirchhoff, Greg: trustee, Tomkins Corp. Foundation

Kirchner, Audrey: secretary, Bemis Co. Foundation; senior vice president, secretary, general counsel, Bemis Co., Inc.

Kirk, Jill Powers: chairman, trustee, Tektronix Foundation

Kirklin, Starr J.: director, Hickory Tech Corp.; trustee, Hickory Tech Corp. Foundation

Kirsch, Nancy: general counsel, Cranston Print Works Co.

Kiser, Gerald L.: president, chief operating officer, director, La-Z-Boy Inc.

Kiskis, Ronald C.: vice president, Chevron Corp.

Kissinger, Henry Alfred: president, CBS Foundation

Kissling, Walter: director, Fuller Co. (H.B.)

Kissner, Naida: program assistant, Fuller Co. Foundation (H.B.); senior legal counsel, Fuller Co. (H.B.)

Kita, John J.: vice president, treasurer, controller, Smith Corp. (A.O.); treasurer, Smith Foundation, Inc. (A.O.)

Kitchen, Michael B.: president, chief executive officer, director, CUNA Mutual Group; secretary, treasurer, executive officer, CUNA Mutual Group Foundation, Inc.

Kitchen, Steven L.: trustee, Western Resources Foundation

Kitchens, John L.: vice president, FPL Group Foundation, Inc.

Kittelberger, Larry E.: senior vice president, chief information officer, AlliedSignal Inc.

Kittredge, Robert P.: chairman, chief executive officer, director, Fabri-Kal Corp.; president, Fabri-Kal Foundation

Klatman, Michael: president, StorageTek Foundation

Klein, Barbara A.: vice president, comptroller, Ameritech Corp.

Klein, Bertram W.: chairman, director, Bank of Louisville Charities

Klein, Beth Paxton: director, Bank of Louisville Charities; senior vice president community relations, Mid-America Bank of Louisville

Klein, Bruce A.: trustee, CLARCOR Foundation; chief financial officer, CLARCOR Inc.

Klein, Calvin Richard: president, Calvin Klein

Klein, David: director, Bank of Louisville Charities

Klein, David M.: senior vice president, Hartford (The)

Klein, Martin: chief financial officer, executive vice president, National Life of Vermont

Klein, Starr T.: president, trustee, Dixie Yarns Foundation, Inc.

Kleinfeldt, Richard C.: vice president financial, chief financial officer, director, Giddings & Lewis

Klesse, William R.: executive vice president operations, Ultramar Diamond Shamrock Corp.

Kleven, Cynthia F.: secretary, director, 3M Foundation; director community affairs, Minnesota Mining & Manufacturing Co.

Kline, Cheryl: director, Dana Corp. Foundation

Kline, Philip E.: director, Royal & SunAlliance Insurance Foundation, Inc.

Kline, Richard: president, Lehigh Portland Cement Co.

Klinedinst, Thomas John, Jr.: trustee, Star Bank NA, Cincinnati Foundation

Klitten, Martin R.: vice president, chief financial officer, Chevron Corp.

Kloenhammer, Janet S.: director, Fireman's Fund Foundation; chairman, Fireman's Fund Insurance Co.

Kloff, Robert: president, chief executive officer, Provident Mutual Life Insurance Co.

Klotz-Collins, Marlene: vice president community rels, America West Airlines Foundation; senior vice president public affairs, America West Airlines, Inc.

Klotzer, Michele: vice president, Subway Sandwich Shops, Inc.

Kluge, Robert H.: president, Varian Medical Systems, Inc.

Klugman, Craig: editor, Journal-Gazette Co.

Klyczek, John: chairman, president, chief executive officer, chief operating officer, GATX Corp.

Knaup, Marianne: president, Enterprise Rent-A-Car Foundation

Knauss, Dalton L.: trustee, Kemper Foundation (James S.)

Kneale, James C.: chief financial officer, ONEOK, Inc.

Knepper, Peter B.: senior vice president, chief financial officer, Ticketmaster Corp.; chief financial officer, Ticketmaster Foundation

Knese, William F.: chairman, trustee, CLARCOR Foundation; vice president, treasurer, CLARCOR Inc.

Knez, Brian J.: trustee, Harcourt General Charitable Foundation

Knicely, Howard V.: manager, TRW Foundation

Kniffen, Jan Rogers: senior vice president, treasurer, May Department Stores Co.; vice president, secretary, treasurer, director, May Department Stores Computer Foundation (The)

Knight, Charles Field: chairman, chief executive officer, Emerson Electric Co.

Knight, Lester B.: chairman, director, Baxter Allegiance Foundation

Knight, Merrill Donaldson, III: director, GEICO Philanthropic Foundation

Knight, Philip Hampson: chairman, chief executive officer, Nike, Inc.

Knight, Robert E.: assistant secretary, Osborne Foundation (Weldon F.)

Knight, Stacy: director, MFA Foundation

Knittle, Charles H.: executive vice president, Montgomery Ward Foundation

Knowles, Marie L.: executive vice president, chief financial officer, Atlantic Richfield Co.

Knox, Wendell J.: trustee, Eastern Bank Charitable Foundation

Knue, Paul Frederick: trustee, Scripps Howard Foundation

Kobe, Yoshinori: chairman, president, chief executive officer, Matsushita Electric Corp. of America

Kober, Roger W.: chairman, chief executive officer, director, Rochester Gas & Electric Corp.

Koch, Charles de Ganahl: chairman, chief executive officer, director, president, Koch Industries, Inc.

Koch, David Andrew: president, Graco Foundation;

chairman, director, Graco, Inc.

Koch, David Hamilton: president, director, Koch Foundation, Inc. (Fred C. and Mary R.)

Koch, Elizabeth B.: vice president, Koch Foundation, Inc. (Fred C. and Mary R.)

Koch, George: director, Land O'Lakes Foundation

Koch, Robert E.: trustee, Texaco Foundation

Koch, Robert Louis, II: president, chief executive officer, director, Koch Enterprises, Inc.; president, director, Koch Foundation

Kodama, Ryuzo: director, head Americas Division, Sumitomo Bank; director, Sumitomo Bank Global Foundation

Koenemann, Carl F.: chief financial officer, executive vice president, Motorola Inc.

Koenig, Brian C.: senior vice president human resources, Scientific-Atlanta, Inc.

Koenig, Fred: director, MFA Foundation

Koeppe, Alfred C.: chairman, president, chief executive officer, Public Service Electric & Gas Co.; senior vice president corporate services & external affairs, Public Service Electric & Gas Foundation

Kofol, Milan: vice president, treasurer, Reader's Digest Association, Inc. (The); treasurer, Reader's Digest Foundation

Kogan, Richard Jay: chairman, chief executive officer, Schering-Plough Corp.; trustee, member, Schering-Plough Foundation

Kohet, Carl F.: executive vice president, assistant chief operating officer, Eastman Kodak Co.

Kohler, Herbert Vollrath, Jr.: chairman, president, director, Kohler Co.

Kohm, Amelia: administrator, Sears, Roebuck and Co.; president, Sears, Roebuck and Co. Foundation

Kolsrud, Douglas C.: executive vice president, chief investment officer, AEGON U.S.A. Inc.

Komansky, David H.: trustee, vice president, Merrill Lynch & Co. Foundation Inc.; chairman, chief executive officer, Merrill Lynch & Co., Inc.

Kometer, Clyde W.: corporate controller, Kohler Co.

Kononowitz, Thomas J.: secretary, New Jersey Natural Gas Foundation

Konrad, Jean: manager, First Union National Bank, NA

Koonce, Joel: chief financial officer, group vice president financial, Cenex Harvest States

Koontz, James L.: president, chief executive officer, director, Kingsbury Corp.; trustee, Kingsbury Fund

Koosmann, Gerhard: division controller, Fuller Co. (H.B.)

Kopp, David C.: director civic affairs, CIGNA Foundation

Korba, Judy: chairman, chief executive officer, Heller Financial, Inc.

Kordus, Lynn: president, chief operating officer; coordinator, Employers Insurance of Wausau, A Mutual Co.

Korell, Brad: president, National Bank of Commerce Trust & Savings

Kornegay, S. Dock: director, secretary, Duke Energy Foundation

Kosche, Peter C.: senior vice president corporate affairs, Olin Corp.; trustee, Olin Corp. Charitable Trust

Kosminsky, Jay: treasurer, Pfizer Foundation

Kostecky, James Frank: executive director, Bethlehem Steel Corp.; president, Bethlehem Steel Foundation

Koster, Sherry: director, Dain Bosworth Foundation

Kostmayer, Rosmary: executive vice president, chief marketing officer, AEGON U.S.A. Inc.

Kota, Leslie: vice president, Kmart Corp.

Koupal, Carl M., Jr.: trustee, Western Resources Foundation; executive vice president, chief administrative officer, Western Resources Inc.

Koutsky, Lori J.: vice president, director, Minnesota Mutual Foundation

Kovacevich, Richard M.: chairman, president, chief executive officer, Norwest Corp.; director, Norwest Foundation

Kowalke, Stephen C.: trustee, Target Foundation

Koziar, Stephen F., Jr.: treasurer, trustee, Dayton Power and Light Co. Foundation

Kozlowski, J. A.: president, DaimlerChrysler Corp. Fund

Kraemer, Harry M. Jansen, Jr.: president, chief executive officer, chairman, Baxter International Inc.

Kraft, Richard A.: manager, Matsushita Electric Corp. of America; president, director, Panasonic Foundation

Kraiss, Glenn S.: executive vice president store operations, Walgreen Co.

Kramer, Mary Elizabeth: president, chief executive officer, Blue Cross & Blue Shield of Iowa; vice president, Wellmark Foundation

Kraus, John P.: trustee, Anderson Foundation

Kraus, Rick: president, Federated Mutual Insurance Foundation

Krause, Steve: member, Northern Trust Co. Charitable Trust

Kreh, Gordon W.: president, chief executive officer, director, Hartford Steam Boiler Inspection & Insurance Co.

Kreindler, Peter Michael: president, director, AlliedSignal Foundation Inc.; senior vice president, general counsel, secretary, AlliedSignal Inc.

Kremna, Larry: director human resources, NEC America, Inc.

Kresa, Kent: chairman, president, chief executive officer, director, Northrop Grumman Corp.

Kress, George F.: honorary chairman, director, Green Bay Packaging; president, Kress Foundation (George)

Kress, James F.: chairman, director, Green Bay Packaging

Kress, John: chairman, director, Green Bay Packaging; secretary, treasurer, Kress Foundation (George)

Kress, William F.: president, director, Green Bay Packaging

Kretschmar, Lanie: vice president, Dexter Corp. Foundation

Kretzman, Robert K.: president, Revlon Foundation Inc.

Krieger, John J.: director, GEICO Philanthropic Foundation

Kroeber, C. Kent: chairman, president, chief executive officer, Interpublic Group of Companies, Inc.

Kromholz, Steven S.: treasurer, Menasha Corp. Foundation

Krommenacker, David A.: director, Consolidated Papers Foundation, Inc.

Krueger, Harvey M.: secretary, Barry Foundation

Krulak, Allan C.: vice president, Forest City Enterprises Charitable Foundation, Inc.; vice president corporate & public affairs, director, Forest City Enterprises, Inc.

Krutzman, Ronald L.: chairman, trustee, Laclede Gas Charitable Trust

Krzos, Joseph T.: chief financial officer, Madison Gas & Electric Co.; treasurer, Madison Gas & Electric Foundation

Kucharski, John Michael: trustee, PerkinElmer Foundation; chairman, chief executive officer, director, PerkinElmer, Inc.

Kuchs, Michael: assistant secretary, CIGNA Foundation

Kuechle, Scott E.: vice president treasurer, BFGoodrich Co.; treasurer, Goodrich Foundation, Inc. (B.F.)

Kuester, Dennis J.: president, Marshall & Ilsley Corp.

Kufeldt, James: vice president, director, Winn-Dixie Stores Foundation; president, director, Winn-Dixie Stores Inc.

Kuhlin, Michael E.: vice chairman, chief executive officer, director, Ameritech Corp.

Kuhne, John A.: director, Belk-Simpson Foundation

Kuhne, Lucy S.: chairman, Belk-Simpson Department Stores; director, Belk-Simpson Foundation

Kulczak, Michael J.: director, NASDAQ Stock Market Educational Foundation

Kullman, Mary C.: treasurer, Laclede Gas Charitable Trust

Kulynych, Petro: vice president, Lowe's Charitable and Educational Foundation

Kuni, Paige: chairman, Intel Corp.; program officer, Intel Foundation

Kunin, Myron: chairman, director, Regis Corp.; president, Regis Foundation

Kunkel, David M.: senior vice president, director, Ford Meter Box Co.; vice president, Ford Meter Box Foundation

Kunz, Heidi: executive vice president, chief financial officer, Gap, Inc.

Kupferschmidt, Walter: president, chairman, chief executive officer, National City Bank of Pennsylvania

Kurack, Sandra: vice president, trustee, PEMCO Foundation

Kurczewski, Walter W.: vice president, secretary, general counsel, Square D Co.; president, director, Square D Foundation

Kurren, Faye Watanabe: president, Tesoro Hawaii

Kurtz, Larry: trustee, McKesson Foundation

Kurtz, Melvin H.: foundation contact, Chesebrough Foundation

Kwasniak, George: chief financial officer, Excel Corp.

Kyle, David L.: president, ONEOK, Inc.

Kyte, Dennis: president, Ralph's-Food 4 Less Foundation

L

Labahn, Mary Ann W.: secretary, manager, trustee, Bucyrus-Erie Foundation

Labik, Nancy: trustee, Chicago Title and Trust Co. Foundation

Labrato, Ronnie R.: chairman, Gulf Power Foundation

Labrecque, Thomas Goulet: president, chief operating officer, director, Chase Manhattan Bank, NA; president, Chase Manhattan Foundation

Labutka, Carolyn E.: executive vice president, Aon Corp.; executive director, Aon Foundation

Lacey, David C.: executive vice president, chief financial officer, Storage Technology Corp.; chief financial officer, director, StorageTek Foundation

Lachman, Marguerite Leanne: trustee, Chicago Title and Trust Co. Foundation

Lackey, S. Allen: vice president, director, Shell Oil Co. Foundation

Lacy, Alan J.: president credit, Sears, Roebuck and Co.

Lacy, William Howard: president, MGIC Investment Corp.

Ladish, John: trustee, Ladish Co. Foundation

Laffon, Polk, IV: vice president corporate relations, corporate secretary, Knight Ridder

Lagomasino, Maria Elena: president, Chase Manhattan Foundation

Lake, Carolyn: administrator, Cranston Foundation

Lake, Douglas T.: executive vice president, chief strategic officer, Western Resources Inc.

Lakey, Ronald L.: secretary, Shea Co. Foundation (J. F.)

Lakin, Thomas J.: regional chairman, Star Bank NA; president, Star Bank NA, Cincinnati Foundation

Laksh, Eileen A.: chief executive officer, SmithKline Beecham Corp.; treasurer, director, SmithKline Beecham Foundation

LaMacchia, John Thomas: trustee, Cincinnati Bell Foundation, Inc.; president, chief executive officer, director, Cincinnati Bell Inc.

LaMantia, Charles Robert: president, chief executive officer, director, Little, Inc. (Arthur D.)

Lambe, James F.: senior vice president human resources, Nalco Chemical Co.; director, Nalco Foundation

Lambert, James K.: senior vice president operations and quality, GenCorp

Lambert, William: assistant secretary, Mitsubishi Electric America Foundation

Lambrix, Thomas G.: senior vice president communications & public affairs, Union Camp Corp.

Lamme, Kathryn A.: trustee, Standard Register Co.

Lammert, Richard A.: vice president, M&T Charitable Foundation

Lancaster, J. Thomas: assistant treasurer, Western-Southern Foundation, Inc.; vice president, treasurer, Western & Southern Life Insurance Co.

Landes, Robert Nathan: senior vice president taxes, McGraw-Hill Companies, Inc.

Landin, Thomas Milton: vice president, director, CertainTeed Corp.; president abrasives branch, Norton Co.; vice president, Norton Co. Foundation

Lane, Lynn L.: treasurer, Burlington Industries, Inc.

Lane, Thomas H.: vice president, Dow Corning Corp.; trustee, Dow Corning Foundation

Lane, William: president, Rutledge Hill Press; director, Rutledge Hill Press Foundation

Laney, Sandra E.: director, Chemed Foundation

Lang, Paul Louis: vice president, Illinois Power Co.

Lang, Robert Todd: chairman, director, Weil, Gotshal & Manges Foundation

Lang, Rudolph E., Jr.: senior vice president, chief financial officer, Litton Industries, Inc.

Lang, Sherry: vice president & director investor relations, TJX Companies, Inc.; director, TJX Foundation, Inc.

Langbo, Arnold Gordon: chairman, chief executive officer, director, Kellogg Co.

Lange, Beverly J.: trustee, Anderson Foundation

Lanier, Elizabeth K.: vice president, chief financial officer, Cinergy Corp.; director, Cinergy Foundation

Lanning, Donald R.: vice president grocery operations, Campbell Soup Co.

Lansaw, Judy W.: president, trustee, Dayton Power and Light Co. Foundation

Laone, Joseph: executive vice president, CIT Group, Inc. (The)

LaPlaca, Frank: chief financial officer, CSR Rinker Materials Corp.

Lapp, Robert J.: vice president public affairs, Timken Co. (The)

Larance, Charles L.: vice president corporate relations, GenAmerica Corp.; president, GenAmerican Foundation

Larini, Ernest J.: chief financial officer, Warner-Lambert Charitable Foundation; vice president, chief financial officer, Warner-Lambert Co.

Larman, Barry W.: tax director, UNUM Foundation; vice president tax, Unum-Provident

Larmay, Jerry: senior vice president, TU Electric Co.

Larsen, Marianne: president, director, International Paper Co.; manager contributions program, International Paper Co. Foundation

Larsen, Ralph Stanley: chairman, president, chief executive officer, director, Johnson & Johnson

Larsen, Terrence A.: chairman, chief executive officer, First Union Bank; chairman, First Union Regional Foundation

Larson, David A.: senior vice president, chief merchandising officer, Giant Food Inc.

Larson, Jan: secretary, Dow Chemical Co. Foundation

Larson, Mark: chief executive officer, United Distillers & Vintners North America

Larson, Peggy: president, chief executive officer, Ameritech Wisconsin

Larson, Peter N.: chairman, chief executive officer, director, Brunswick Corp.

Larson, Wayne E.: trustee, Ladish Co. Foundation

LaRue, Mary A.: chairman, president, chief executive officer, Berwind Group

Lasell, Raymond E.: secretary, HON Industries Charitable Foundation; secretary, director, HON Industries Inc.

Laskawy, Philip A.: chairman, chief executive officer, director, Ernst & Young, LLP

Lasota, Kathleen: trustee, Quaker Chemical Foundation

Lasser, Lawrence Jay: president, chief executive officer, director, Putnam Investments; president, chief executive officer, Putnam Investors Fund

Latzer, Richard Neal: vice chairman, director, Transamerica Foundation

Laubach, David A.: trustee, Merit Gasoline Foundation

Lauchert, F. H.: executive secretary, Elf Atochem North America Foundation

Lauderdale, Gary D.: senior vice president, general manager, Texas Gas Transmission Corp.

Lauer, J. Michael: executive vice president, chief financial officer, MGIC Investment Corp.

Lauer, Len J.: executive director, Sprint Foundation

Laufer, Harry: president, chief executive officer, partner, director, Associated Food Stores; director, Associated Food Stores Charitable Foundation

Launius, Leigh Ann (Korns): trustee, Cox Foundation (James M.)

Laurance, Dale R.: director, Occidental Petroleum Charitable Foundation; president, senior operations officer, director, Occidental Petroleum Corp.

Laurent, Carol: executive director, Blue Cross & Blue Shield of Minnesota Foundation Inc.

Lautenbach, Terry Robert: assistant secretary, Air Products Foundation

Lavigne, Louis J., Jr.: executive vice president, chief financial officer, Genentech Inc.

Law, L. William, Jr.: senior vice president, general counsel, secretary, Eastern Enterprises

Lawless, Robert J.: chairman, president, chief executive officer, chief operating officer, director, McCormick & Co. Inc.

Lawrence, James A.: chief financial officer, executive vice president, General Mills, Inc.

Lawrence, Robert Ashton: director, New York Times Co. Foundation

Lawrence-Stofer, Janice: vice president human resources, Northern Indiana Public Service Co.

Laws, Donald P.: secretary advisory committee, Blue Bell Foundation

Lawson, John K.: senior vice president, Deere & Co.; director, Deere Foundation (John)

Lawson, William Hogan, III: chairman, chief executive officer, director, Franklin Electric Co.; president, Franklin Electric, Edward J. Schaefer, and T. W. KehoeCharitable and Educational Foundation

Lay, Terry: president, Lee, Lee Apparel Co.

Lay, Wanda: director, First Financial Foundation

Leahy, Eileen: senior vice president corporate services & external affairs, Public Service Electric & Gas Foundation

Leander, Henry A.: chairman, Ford Meter Box Co.

Leask, Janie: director, CIRI Foundation

Leatherdale, Douglas West: chairman, chief executive officer, president, Saint Paul Companies Inc.

Lebedoff, Randy Miller: vice president, general counsel, McClatchy Co.; secretary, Star Tribune Foundation

Lebedun, Barbara: president, Block Foundation (H&R)

Lebherz, Kent A.: president, Ameritech Indiana

LeBoeuf, Raymond W.: director, PPG Industries Foundation; director, chairman, chief executive officer, PPG Industries, Inc.

LeBrescu, Betty: president, chief executive officer, director, Murphy Oil Corp.

Ledgett, Ronald A.: executive vice president, Boston Edison Co.; trustee, Boston Edison Foundation

Lee, Charles Robert: chairman, chief executive officer, director, GTE Corp.; chief executive officer, trustee, GTE Foundation

Lee, Kimary: executive vice president store operations, Walgreen Co.

Lee, Lillie: chairman, chief executive officer, director, publisher, The Washington Post

Lee, Stephanie: trustee, Sunmark Foundation

Lee, Wanda: member, PacifiCare Health System Foundation

Lefevre, John H.: director, Deluxe Corp. Foundation

Leggett, Richard B.: director, PPG Industries Foundation

Lehman, Michael E.: president, Sun Microsystems Foundation, Inc.

Lehner, Carl P.: president, chief executive officer, Leigh Fibers, Inc.; trustee, Orchard Foundation

Lehner, Heidi: trustee, Orchard Foundation

Lehner, Peter: trustee, Orchard Foundation

Lehner, Philip: chairman, Leigh Fibers, Inc.; trustee, Orchard Foundation

Lehr, Gustav J.: vice president, director, Shelter Insurance Foundation; chairman, director, Shelter Mutual Insurance Co.

Lehrkind, Carl, III: director, Montana Power Foundation

Leibensperger, Robert L.: secretary, treasurer, trustee, Timken Co. Educational Fund

Leighton, Wayne: executive vice president, Koch Foundation, Inc. (Fred C. and Mary R.); chairman, chief executive officer, director, president, Koch Industries, Inc.

Leininger, Jeffrey L.: vice chairman specialized commercial banking, Mellon Financial Corp.

Leising, Cindy Scripps: director, Scripps Co. (E.W.); member, Scripps Howard Foundation

Leland, Leslie S.: assistant secretary, Burlington Resources Foundation

Lemaster, James: vice chairman, Anthem Foundation, Inc.

Lemberg, Thomas Michael: treasurer, director, Lotus Development Corp.; clerk, Lotus Development Philanthropy Program; executive director, Polaroid Foundation

Lemeiux, Richard: chairman, chief executive officer, director, Ernst & Young, LLP

Lemieux, Joseph Henry: chairman, chief executive officer, director, Owens-Illinois Inc.

Lemke, Carl R.: director, Consolidated Papers Foundation, Inc.

Lempka, Arnold W., MD: chairman, director, Physicians Mutual Insurance Co.; director, Physicians Mutual Insurance Co. Foundation

Lenhard, John E.: secretary, associate general counsel, Cleveland-Cliffs, Inc.

Lenox, John W.: director, Shelter Insurance Foundation; president, chief executive officer, director, Shelter Mutual Insurance Co.

Leonard, Laurence B., Jr.: trustee, Eastern Bank Charitable Foundation

Leonard, Terry: treasurer, Goodrich Foundation, Inc. (B.F.)

Leonis, John Michael: chairman, director, Litton Industries, Inc.

Leroux, Robert J.: controller, Cleveland-Cliffs, Inc.

Lervett, Wayne: chief executive officer, Entergy Corp.

Lesar, David J.: president, chief operating officer, Halliburton Co.; trustee, Halliburton Foundation, Inc.

Leschly, Jan: chief executive officer, SmithKline Beecham Corp.

Leser, Lawrence Arthur: chairman, director, Scripps Co. (E.W.); member, Scripps Howard Foundation

Leshin, Arthur: senior vice president, chief financial officer, Gucci America Inc.

Lesser, Richard G.: executive vice president, chief operating officer, director, TJX Companies, Inc.; chief operating officer, director, TJX Foundation, Inc.

Lester, Susan E.: executive vice president, chief financial officer, U.S. Bancorp

LeSuer, Ken R.: assistant secretary, assistant treasurer, Halliburton Foundation, Inc.

LeSuer, William Monroe: president, Lubrizol Foundation (The)

Letbetter, R. Steve: chairman, president, chief executive officer, Reliant Energy Inc.

Leube, Helmut: president, Lehigh Portland Cement Co.

Levan, Alan: chairman, president, chief executive officer, BankAtlantic Bancorp; president, trustee, BankAtlantic Foundation

Levan, B. W.: secretary, Shell Oil Co. Foundation

Levin, Jerry Wayne: assistant treasurer, Revlon Foundation Inc.

Levin, Michael Stuart: president, chief executive officer, Titan Industrial Corp.

Levine, Kenneth M.: executive vice president, chief investment officer, director, MONY Group (The); director, MONY Life Insurance of New York (The)

Levine, Lawrence E.: chairman, president, chief executive officer, Matsushita Electric Corp. of America; secretary, Panasonic Foundation

Levine, Ralph: president, chief operating officer, director, Carter-Wallace, Inc.

Levinson, Arthur David: president, chief executive officer, director, Genentech Inc.

Levinson, Donald M.: director, CIGNA Corp.; assistant secretary, CIGNA Foundation

Leviton, Harold: president, Leviton Foundation New York; president, chief executive officer, Leviton Manufacturing Co. Inc.

Leviton, Shirley: president, Leviton Foundation New York

Levy, David: director, National Service Foundation

Levy, H. George: director, La-Z-Boy Inc.

Levy, Richard M.: president, chief executive officer, Varian Medical Systems, Inc.

Levy, Susan M.: executive vice president, chief financial officer, Donnelley & Sons Co. (R.R.)

Lew, Yung: vice chairman, Wells Fargo & Co.; director, Wells Fargo Foundation

LeWinter, Sharon: director, Novartis Corporation

Lewis, Andre: director, Honeywell Foundation

Lewis, Arlyce K.: president, StorageTek Foundation

Lewis, C. Stephen: trustee, Weyerhaeuser Co. Foundation

Lewis, Diana D.: vice president human resources, Ecolab Inc.

Lewis, E. Lavonne: trustee, PerkinElmer Foundation; vice president human resources, PerkinElmer, Inc.

Lewis, Frances Aaronson: member scholarship committee, Circuit City Foundation

Lewis, George Ralph: trustee, Kemper Foundation (James S.)

Lewis, John D.: vice chairman, Comerica Inc.

Lewis, Peter Benjamin: chairman, president, chief executive officer, director, Progressive Corp.

Lewis, Peter C.: director, Hawaiian Electric Industries Charitable Foundation

Lewis, Roger: chairman, director, Commercial Federal Corp.

Lewis, Russell T.: president, chief operating officer, New York Times Co.

Lhota, William J.: executive vice president, American Electric Power

Li, Victor Hao: president, director, Hawaiian Electric Industries Charitable Foundation

Lichtenberger, Horst William: chairman, chief executive officer, Praxair

Liddy, Edward M.: vice president, trustee, Allstate Foundation; president, chief operating officer, director, Allstate Insurance Co.

Liddy, Richard A.: chairman, president, chief executive officer, GenAmerica Corp.

Liebler, Arthur C.: vice president communications, DaimlerChrysler Corp.; trustee, DaimlerChrysler Corp. Fund

Liggett, Jerry W.: vice president human resources, Cinergy Corp.

Light, Walter Frederick: chairman, Air Products Foundation

Liljebeck, Roy C.: executive vice president, chief financial officer, Airborne Freight Corp.

Lilly, Diane P.: vice president, Norwest Corp.; president, director, Norwest Foundation

Lindblom, Marjorie P.: director, Kirkland & Ellis Foundation

Lindeman, David: director, Extendicare Foundation

Lindeman, Stuart: director, Extendicare Foundation

Lindenauer, Arthur: executive vice president, chief financial officer, Schlumberger Ltd. (USA)

Lindsay, David J.: trustee, CLARCOR Foundation; vice president, CLARCOR Inc.

Lindsay, John B.: president, Franklin Electric Co.

Linehan, John Charles: chairman, chief executive officer, director, Kerr-McGee Corp.

Linen, Jonathan S.: vice chairman, American Express Co.; trustee, American Express Foundation

Link, James F.: vice president, Texaco Foundation

Linnell, Norman C.: general counsel, secretary, Donaldson Co., Inc.; trustee, Donaldson Foundation

Lintell, J. V.: co-trustee, INTRUST Bank Charitable Trust

Lione, Gail: vice president, Harley-Davidson Foundation

Lipetz, Marcia: secretary-treasurer, WPWR-TV Channel 50 Foundation

Lipp, Robert Irving: chief executive officer, Citigroup; vice president, treasurer, trustee, Citigroup Foundation

Lippes, Gerald Sanford: chairman, Mark IV Industries Foundation

Lippman, Scott: president, Hitachi Foundation

Lipton, Martin: partner, Wachtell, Lipton, Rosen & Katz; president, Wachtell, Lipton, Rosen & Katz Foundation

Liska, Paul J.: executive vice president, chief financial officer, Saint Paul Companies Inc.

Lison, Stephen A.: trustee, SPX Foundation

Litow, Stanley S.: president, IBM International Foundation; vice president communications, International Business Machines Corp.

Little, Gene E.: trustee, advisor, Timken Co. Charitable Trust (The); secretary, treasurer, trustee, Timken Co. Educational Fund

Little, William G.: chairman, president, chief executive officer, director, West Co. Inc.

Little, William Norris: vice chairman, director, Shaw Industries Inc.

Litvack, Sanford M.: senior executive vice president, chief corporate operations, director, Disney Co. (Walt)

Lloyd, Robert: member, PacifiCare Health System Foundation

Lobman, Helaine F., Esq.: director, Mitsubishi Electric America Foundation

Locher, John J.: treasurer, Barnes Group Foundation Inc.; vice president, treasurer, Barnes Group Inc.

Lockard, Jamie: director community affairs, Lee Apparel Co.

Lockett, Walter: secretary, director, Chesebrough Foundation

Lockwood, Glenn C.: senior vice president, chief financial officer, New Jersey Natural Gas Co.; treasurer, New Jersey Natural Gas Foundation

Lodge, John: chairman, president, chief executive officer, Bandag, Inc.

Lodge, Robert W.: senior vice president, chief financial officer, Carpenter Technology Corp.; vice president, Carpenter Technology Corp. Foundation

Loeb, Jerome Thomas: chairman, director, May Department Stores Co.; president, director, May Department Stores Computer Foundation (The)

Loflin, Clyatt E., Jr.: trustee officer, Wachovia Bank of North Carolina NA

Loflin, Ed: assistant treasurer, Wachovia Bank of North Carolina NA

Loftin, Nancy Carol: secretary, director, APS Foundation, Inc.; vice president, general counsel, Arizona Public Service Co.

Logan, Wendy B.: chairman, president, chief executive officer, director, Johnson & Johnson; member corporate contributions committee, Johnson & Johnson Family of Companies Contribution Fund

Lohbeck, David J.: president, Chemed Foundation

Lohman, Gordon Russell: trustee, Amsted Industries Foundation; director, Amsted Industries Inc.

Lohmann, Walter H.: director, Kirkland & Ellis Foundation

Lohr, William J. (Bill): vice president finance, Sentry Insurance, A Mutual Co.; treasurer, Sentry Insurance Foundation Inc.

Lombardi, Thomas J.: trustee, vice president, Merrill Lynch & Co. Foundation Inc.

London, Kenneth: board member, Edwards Foundation (J.D.)

Londra, Kathryn E.: director, AMETEK Foundation

Long, Francis A.: executive vice president, chief operating officer, director, Pennsylvania Power & Light

Long, Gail: assistant to vice chairman, Ukrop's Super Markets

Long, L. G.: trustee, Air Products Foundation

Long, Michael Thomas: director, Ensign-Bickford Foundation; chairman, director, Ensign-Bickford Industries

Long, Robert R.: chairman, SunTrust Bank Atlanta

Longa, Angie J.: vice president public affairs, National City Bank of Pennsylvania

Longfield, William H.: president, Bard Foundation (C.R.); chairman, chief executive officer, director, Bard, Inc. (C.R.)

Longford, Bernadette Williams: vice president, director, ABC Foundation

Longley, Elizabeth A.: vice president corporate affairs, Prudential Securities Foundation; 1st vice president, Prudential Securities Inc.

Longwell, Harry J.: senior vice president, Exxon Mobil Corp.

Lonon, Van H.: president, director, Stonecutter Foundation

Loomans, Leslie Louis: secretary, director, Detroit Edison Foundation

Loos, Henry J.: secretary, Charter Manufacturing Co. Foundation

Loose, John W.: trustee, Corning Inc. Foundation

Lopiano, John A.: senior vice president, Xerox Corp.; trustee, Xerox Foundation
Lorch, George A.: chairman, chief executive officer, director, Armstrong World Industries, Inc.
Lord, Gerald S.: vice president, controller, Campbell Soup Co.
Loughman, Thomas F.: trustee, Barden Foundation, Inc.
Loughrey, F. Joseph: group president worldwide operations & technology, vice president, Cummins Engine Co., Inc.; director, Cummins Engine Foundation
Louis, Kenneth C.: president, chief operating officer, director, Ameritas Life Insurance Corp.
Louras, Peter N.: manager, Clorox Co.; vice president, Clorox Co. Foundation
Love, Sherwood L.: director, secretary, Duke Energy Foundation
Lovejoy, David R.: vice chairman-financial markets & corporate development, Mellon Financial Corp.
Lovejoy, Joseph Ensign: chairman, director, Ensign-Bickford Industries
Lovett, John Robert: trustee, Air Products Foundation
Lowden, Francis V., III: director, Universal Leaf Foundation
Lowe, David M.: vice president lubrication equip division, Graco, Inc.
Lower, H. Louis Gordon, II: vice president, trustee, Allstate Foundation
Lowrie, William G.: president, deputy chief executive officer, director, BP Amoco Corp.
Lowry, David B.: executive director, Freeport-McMoRan Foundation
Lowry, Robert L.: executive director, Central Newspapers Foundation
Loye, Linda: trustee, Chicago Sun-Times Charity Trust
Lozano, Ignacio Eugenio, Jr.: chairman, Pacific Mutual Life Insurance Co.
Lubar, Sheldon B.: chairman, Ameritech Corp.
Lucas, Donald Leo: chairman, Cadence Designs Systems, Inc.
Lucas, Wilfred J.: chairman, director, Baxter Allegiance Foundation
Luck, Mary Jo: president, chief executive officer, National City Bank of Columbus
Lucky, Robert Wendell: corporate vice president, Telcordia Technologies
Ludden, Timothy Wayne: vice president, treasurer, cash manager, Unum-Provident
Ludes, John T.: chairman, chief executive officer, director, Fortune Brands, Inc.
Ludlow, Madaleine W.: vice president, chief financial officer, Cinergy Corp.
Ludwick, John D.: president, MGIC Investment Corp.
Luff, Paula: president, Pfizer Foundation; senior program officer, Pfizer Inc.
Luftglass, Rick: senior program officer, Pfizer Inc.
Lukaszewicz, Peter: treasurer, Bemis Family Foundation (F.K.); treasurer, director, Bemis Manufacturing Co.
Luke, John A., Jr.: chairman, president, chief executive officer, director, Westvaco Corp.
Luke, Kathleen Allen: chairman, PepsiCo Foundation, Inc.
Lukens, Max L.: president, chairman, chief executive officer, chief operating officer, Baker Hughes Inc.
Lukowski, Stanley J.: president, Eastern Bank
Luljak, Tom: chairman, president, chief executive officer, United Wisconsin Services Foundation
Luloo, Tom: chief financial officer, Consolidated Electrical Distributors
Lumar-Johnson, Eileen: vice president, Pan-American Life Insurance Co.
Lundgren, H. David: director, Fireman's Fund Foundation
Lundhagen, E. Wayne: president, director, KN Energy Foundation
Lundy, Marjorie W.: secretary contributions committee, Northern Trust Co. Charitable Trust
Lunger, Francis: chief financial officer, corporate vice president, Millipore Corp.
Luongo, Frank: president, trustee, Whirlpool Foundation
Luthy, Thomas M.: senior vice president wood products, Weyerhaeuser Co.
Lutnick, Howard W.: trustee, Cantor, Fitzgerald Foundation
Luton, Barbara B.: chairman, chief executive officer, director, Tenet Healthcare Corp.; executive director, Tenet Healthcare Foundation
Lux, Clifton L.: treasurer, assistant secretary, Globe Foundation
Lyall, Katharine Culbert: trustee, Kemper Foundation (James S.)
Lynch, Charles Allen: chairman, director, Pacific Mutual Life Insurance Co.
Lynch, Christopher P.: assistant treasurer, Merck & Co.
Lynch, David A.: vice president, partner, USX Corp.; assistant secretary, USX Foundation, Inc.
Lynch, Marie: director, Hamilton Sundstrand Corp.; secretary, Sundstrand Corp. Foundation
Lynch, Michael: director, Illinois Tool Works Foundation
Lynch, Thomas C.: trustee, Chase Manhattan Foundation
Lyon, Marina: director, Piper Jaffray Companies Foundation; director public affairs, U.S. Bancorp Piper Jaffray
Lyon, Wayne Barton: president, chief operating officer, director, Masco Corp.
Lyons, Bernard E.: vice president, director, Dunard Fund U.S.A., Ltd.
Lyons, Melanie: member grantmaking committee, Claiborne Foundation (Liz)
Lytle, Gary R.: vice president federal relations, Ameritech Corp.

M

Maas, Suzanne W.: assistant treasurer, Boston Globe Foundation
Maatman, Gerald Leonard: chairman, president, trustee, Kemper Foundation (James S.); director, Kemper National Insurance Companies
Mac Kimm, Margaret (Pontius) 'Mardie': foundation coord, Chicago Title and Trust Co. Foundation
MacBeth, Anita L.: vice president, trustee, Bourns Foundation
MacDonald, J. Randall: senior vice president human resources administration, GTE Corp.; trustee, GTE Foundation
MacDonald, John: secretary, Union Carbide Foundation
MacDonald, John A.: chairman, Hallmark Corporate Foundation
MacElree, Jane Cox: member advisory committee, Dow Jones Foundation
Mack, Raymond Phillip: director, Arvin Foundation; vice president human resources, Arvin Industries, Inc.
MacKay, William L.: vice president public affairs, Alaska Airlines, Inc.
MacKenzie, Hugh C.: president retail business group, Northeast Utilities
Mackey, Howard D.: director, Sovereign Bank Foundation
Mackin, Carroll: trustee, Fortis Foundation
Mackin, James Stanley: chairman, chief executive officer, Regions Financial Corp.
MacLeay, Thomas H.: president, chief operating officer, National Life of Vermont
MacMillan, Whitney: director, Cargill Foundation; member contributions committee, Cargill Inc.
Macrie, Sari: vice president investor relations, Ameritech Corp.
Madding, Claudia: secretary, Archer-Daniels-Midland Foundation
Madia, William J.: executive vice president, manager, Battelle Memorial Institute
Madsen, Dennis: chief executive officer, REI-Recreational Equipment, Inc.
Maffie, Michael O.: president, chief executive officer, director, Southwest Gas Corp.; trustee, Southwest Gas Corp. Foundation
Maffucci, David G.: senior vice president, chief financial officer, Bowater Inc.
Magee, John Francis: chairman, director, Little, Inc. (Arthur D.)
Magee, R. L.: vice president, director, United Dominion Foundation
Magidsohn, Karen: vice president, Citizens Bank-Flint
Magill, Donna: member screening committee, PPG Industries Foundation
Magliochetti, Joseph M.: president, chief executive officer, director, Dana Corp.; president, director, Dana Corp. Foundation
Magowan, Peter Alden: president, managing general partner, Safeway Inc.
Maher, Francesca M.: senior vice president, general counsel, secretary, United Airlines Inc.
Mahoney, David L.: co-chief executive officer, McKesson-HBOC Corp.
Mahoney, Robert W.: chairman, president, chief executive officer, director, Diebold, Inc.
Main, David M.: president, Arvin Foundation
Maio, Nathalie P.: vice president corporate affairs, Prudential Securities Foundation
Maitland, Peter K.: vice president, trustee, USG Foundation
Maitland, William T.: secretary, Nomura America Foundation; vice president, Nomura Holding America
Maki, David J.: treasurer, Fuller Co. Foundation (H.B.); vice president, corporate controller, Fuller Co. (H.B.)
Malaff, P. C.: vice president, National Starch & Chemical Co.; secretary, National Starch & Chemical Foundation
Malamatinas, Dennis: chief executive officer, Burger King Corp.
Mallardi, Michael Patrick: senior vice president, ABC; vice president, director, ABC Foundation
Mallick, Craig D.: trustee, USX Foundation, Inc.
Malloy, Elen: chairman, president, chief executive officer, chief operating officer, Union Carbide Corp.; secretary, Union Carbide Foundation
Malloy, Julie: director, Callaway Golf Co. Foundation
Malmberg, David Curtis: director, National City Bank of Minneapolis
Malmloff, Cheryl: community relations administrator, Donnelley & Sons Co. (R.R.)
Malone, R.: president, Alyeska Pipeline Service Co.
Malone, Thomas J.: president, chief operating officer, Milliken & Co.; member advisory committee, Milliken Foundation
Maloni, William R.: senior vice president policy & public affairs, Fannie Mae; director, Fannie Mae Foundation
Malott, C. Taxon: secretary, treasurer, Bradford and Co. Foundation (J.C.); part owner, Bradford & Co. (J.C.)
Malquist, Malyn K.: chairman, Sierra Pacific Resources
Malt, R. Bradford: treasurer, Butler Foundation
Malvasio, Joseph: chief financial officer, Cantor, Fitzgerald Securities Corp.
Mamiye, Charles D.: president, Mamiye Foundation
Mamiye, David: vice president, Mamiye Foundation
Mamiye, Jack C.: chairman, president, chief executive officer, director, Mamiye Brothers; president, Mamiye Foundation
Manalo, Beth: director search selection, Echoing

Green Foundation; vice president, General Atlantic Partners II LP
Manchester, Gilbert Mott: senior vice president, chief financial officer, Commercial Intertech Corp.; assistant secretary, Commercial Intertech Foundation
Mandel, Jack N.: director, Premier Industrial Corp.
Mandel, Joseph C.: director, Premier Industrial Corp.
Mandel, Morton Leon: deputy chairman, Premier Industrial Corp.; trustee, Premier Industrial Foundation
Mandeville, Robert: trustee, Cranston Foundation; chief financial officer, secretary, treasurer, Cranston Print Works Co.
Mandich, Mitch: senior vice president, Apple Computer, Inc.
Manfredi, John Frederick: member administration committee, Nabisco Foundation Trust
Manigault, Peter: chairman, Evening Post Publishing Co.; president, Post and Courier Foundation
Manlove, Benson: vice president, Michigan Consolidated Gas Co.
Manning, James D.: trustee, Crane & Co. Fund
Manning, Janine M.: vice president, trustee, UNUM Foundation
Manning, Kenneth Paul: president, Universal Foods Corp.; president, director, Universal Foods Foundation
Manoogian, Richard Alexander: chairman, chief executive officer, director, Masco Corp.
Mansour, N. Ned: president, director, Mattel Inc.
Manz, Richard W.: assistant vice president, General Reinsurance Corp.
Manzi, James Paul: clerk, Lotus Development Corp.
Marcantonio, Richard L.: senior vice president industrial, Ecolab Inc.
Marcela, Paul A.: trustee, Dow Corning Foundation
Marchesi, Michele Potter: trustee, Tektronix Foundation; vice president corporate communications & human resources, Tektronix, Inc.
Marciano, Armand: director, Guess? Foundation
Marciano, Maurice: chairman, chief executive officer, Guess?; director, Guess? Foundation
Marciano, Paul: president, director advtg, Guess?; director, Guess? Foundation
Marciniak, Jere D.: secretary, Dow Corning Foundation
Marcum, Kenneth William: assistant secretary, Commercial Intertech Foundation
Marcus, Bernard: chairman, director, Home Depot, Inc.
Marcus, Stephen Howard: chairman, chief executive officer, Marcus Corp.; president, director, Marcus Corp. Foundation
Margenthaler, Donald R.: president, director, Deere & Co.; director, Deere Foundation (John)
Margolin, Abraham E.: vice president, Tension Envelope Foundation
Margolis, Jay M.: director, member grant committee, Claiborne Foundation (Liz)
Margolis, Phil: manager external affairs, BankBoston-Connecticut Region
Margonine, Doris A.: president, chairman, chief executive officer, National City Bank of Pennsylvania
Mariani, Harry F.: president, treasurer, director, Banfi Vintners; director, Banfi Vintners Foundation
Mariani, John J.: chairman, chief executive officer, director, Banfi Vintners; director, Banfi Vintners Foundation
Maritz, W. Stephen: president, chief operating officer, Maritz Inc.
Maritz, William Edward: chairman, chief executive officer, president, Maritz Inc.
Mark, Reuben: chairman, chief executive officer, Colgate-Palmolive Co.
Markel, Charles A., III: vice president finance, treasurer, LG&E Energy Corp.; vice president, treasurer, LG&E Energy Foundation
Markey, Carol S.: manager community involvement, Eaton Charitable Fund; chairman, chief executive officer, director, Eaton Corp.
Markkula, Armas Clifford, Jr.: chairman, director, Apple Computer, Inc.
Markley, William C., III: president, director, Jacobs Engineering Foundation
Marks, Michael J.: vice president, general counsel, secretary, Alexander & Baldwin, Inc.
Marlin, Ray C.: treasurer, Osborne Foundation (Weldon F.)
Marmer, Lynn: president, The Kroger Co. Foundation
Marnier, Jacques: director, Grand Marnier Foundation
Marohn, William D.: vice chairman, director, Whirlpool Corp.
Marr, K. J.: trustee, Lubrizol Foundation (The)
Marriott, J. Willard, Jr.: chairman, chief executive officer, Marriott International Inc.
Marron, Donald Baird: chairman, chief executive officer, director, Paine Webber; trustee, Paine Webber Foundation
Marrs, Carl H.: director, CIRI Foundation; president, chief executive officer, Cook Inlet Region
Marsh, David E.: chief financial officer, Central Maine Power Co.
Marsh, Harold N., III: director, Fireman's Fund Foundation
Marsh, R. Bruce: general tax counsel, Chevron Corp.
Marshall, Betty J.: senior vice president, Shoney's Inc.
Marshall, Joseph W.: chairman, chief executive officer, Idaho Power Co.
Marshall, Siri M.: trustee, General Mills Foundation; senior vice president, general counsel, General Mills, Inc.
Marston, Ted Leroy: director, Cummins Engine Foundation
Martello, M. E.: assistant treasurer, Bechtel Foundation; director, Bechtel Group, Inc.
Martin, Bobby L.: trustee, Wal-Mart Foundation
Martin, Dezora M.: corporate secretary, Norfolk Southern Corp.; secretary, Norfolk Southern Foundation
Martin, George: president, Anthem Foundation, Inc.
Martin, James W.: president, Evening Post Publishing Co.
Martin, Jim: trustee, Donaldson Foundation
Martin, JoAnn M.: controller, Ameritas Charitable Foundation; senior vice president, partner, chief financial officer, Ameritas Life Insurance Corp.
Martin, John E.: chairman, chief executive officer, Taco Bell Corp.; chairman, Taco Bell Foundation
Martin, John William, Jr.: trustee, Ford Motor Co. Fund
Martin, Karen C.: trustee, Corning Inc. Foundation
Martin, Lauralee: chief financial officer, Heller Financial, Inc.
Martin, Lenore: assistant secretary, PacifiCorp Foundation
Martin, Lois: vice president, controller, Deluxe Corp.; director, Deluxe Corp. Foundation
Martin, Lynn M.: vice president investor relations, Ameritech Corp.; director, Ameritech Foundation
Martin, Mary Ann: treasurer, New Jersey Natural Gas Foundation
Martin, Richard: president finance & administration, Calvin Klein; trustee, Calvin Klein Foundation
Martin, Richard J.: executive vice president public relations employee communications, AT&T Corp.; chairman, trustee, AT&T Foundation
Martin, Theodore E.: treasurer, Barnes Group Foundation Inc.
Martin, William A.: treasurer, Analog Devices, Inc.
Martinez, Arthur C.: chairman, chief executive officer, president, Sears, Roebuck and Co.
Martiny, Mary Ann: secretary, Harley-Davidson Foundation
Martore, Gracia C.: vice president investor relations, treasurer, Gannett Co., Inc.; assistant treasurer, Gannett Foundation
Marty, Mary: treasurer, Boston Globe Foundation
Masin, Michael Terry: vice chairman, president international, director, GTE Corp.; trustee, GTE Foundation
Maslick, Joseph R.: trustee, Griffith Laboratories Foundation; executive vice president, secretary, chief financial officer, Griffith Laboratories U.S.A.
Mason, James L.: manager community involvement, Eaton Charitable Fund
Mason, John L.: treasurer, Monsanto Fund
Mason, W. Bruce: chairman, chief executive officer, director, True North Communications, Inc.
Mason, William: trustee, Cranston Foundation
Mass, Nathaniel J.: senior vice president strategic growth, GenCorp; trustee, GenCorp Foundation
Massaro, Anthony A.: president, chief executive officer, chairman, chief operating officer, Lincoln Electric Co.
Matheny, Edward Taylor, Junior: director, Block Foundation (H&R)
Matherne, Louis K.: treasurer, Chesapeake Corp.
Mathews, Odonna: vice president consumer affairs, Giant Food Inc.
Mathies, Allen Wray, Jr.: vice president, Pacific Mutual Charitable Foundation
Mathis, David B.: chairman, president, trustee, Kemper Foundation (James S.)
Mathison, William A.: member corporate contributions committee, Ecolab Inc.
Mathruni, Arjun K.: executive vice president, chief financial officer, Chase Manhattan Bank, NA; trustee, Chase Manhattan Foundation
Matikan, Ann L.: secretary, treasurer, Hitachi Foundation
Matis, Nina B.: director, Katten, Muchin & Zavis Foundation
Matlin, Howard A.: president, treasurer, director, Butler Foundation
Matsch, J. Richard: secretary, Consolidated Papers Foundation, Inc.
Matschullat, Robert W.: trustee, Bronfman Foundation/Joseph E. Seagram & Sons, Inc. Fund (Samuel); vice chairman, chief financial officer, Seagram & Sons, Inc. (Joseph E.)
Matsue, Shigeki: general manager corporate planning, NEC Foundation of America
Matteo, Donna: vice president, director, Thompson Co. Fund (J. Walter)
Matthews, B. Frank, II: member board advisors, Belk Foundation
Matthews, Clark J., II: president, chief executive officer, director, 7-Eleven, Inc.
Matthews, Craig Gerard: president, chief operating officer, Brooklyn Union
Matthews, Robert F.: executive vice president, chief financial officer, Philips Electronics North America Corp.
Matthews, Westina Lomax: secretary, trustee, Merrill Lynch & Co. Foundation Inc.; senior director, first vice president corporate respons, Merrill Lynch & Co., Inc.
Mattison, Robert Mayer: director, Graco Foundation; vice president, general counsel, secretary, Graco, Inc.
Mattson, Bradford C.: executive vice president exterior building products, CertainTeed Corp.
Mattson, David C.: director, Shelter Mutual Insurance Co.

Mattson, Eric Leonard: senior vice president, chief financial officer, Baker Hughes Inc.
Matzke, Richard H.: vice chairman, Chevron Corp.
Maughan, Deryck C.: director, New York Stock Exchange Foundation, Inc.; co-chairman, co-chief executive officer, Salomon Smith Barney
Maurer, Jeffrey Stuart: president, chief operating officer, director, United States Trust Co. of New York
Maurer, John S.: senior vice president, general counsel, secretary, Aristech Chemical Corp.; executive director, Aristech Foundation
Mauro, Margaret: trustee, Rouse Co. Foundation
Maxwell, Harold C.: director, Temple-Inland Foundation
May, Larry H.: president, director, Winn-Dixie Stores Foundation; vice president, director associate relations & human resources, Winn-Dixie Stores Inc.
May, T. Michael: president, Hawaiian Electric Co., Inc.; director, Hawaiian Electric Industries Charitable Foundation
May, Thomas J.: trustee, Boston Edison Foundation
Maybee, Terri R.: treasurer, Hallmark Corporate Foundation
Maynard, Priscilla K.: trustee, Kingsbury Fund
Mayrl, Robin Bieger: director, Extendicare Foundation
Mays, Alfred T.: member corporate contributions committee, Johnson & Johnson Family of Companies Contribution Fund
McAllister, Francis R.: vice president, director, ASARCO Foundation; president, chief executive officer, ASARCO Inc.
McAloon, Brian: vice president sales, Analog Devices, Inc.
McCahon, Jane W.: vice president corporate relations, Eastern Enterprises
McCall, James W.: manager corporate contributions, Chesebrough Foundation
McCall, Jeffrey G.: chairman, president, chief executive officer, Provident Companies, Inc.
McCall, John: president, LG&E Energy Foundation
McCallister, Beth: director, Badger Meter Foundation
McCammon, David Noel: trustee, Ford Motor Co. Fund
McCann, Gregory L.: treasurer, Danis Foundation
McCargo, Bill: senior vice president, chairman, corp. operating committee, Scientific-Atlanta, Inc.
McCarragher, Bernard John: chairman, director, Menasha Corp.; chairman, Menasha Corp. Foundation
McCarthy, Gerald P.: president, director, Tribune New York Foundation
McCarthy, Helen D.: secretary, Chicago Sun-Times Charity Trust
McCarthy, John Michael: president, Waffle House Foundation, Inc.
McCarthy, Michael D.: director, Goldman Sachs Foundation; senior advisor, Goldman Sachs Group
McCarthy, Peter John: trustee, Elf Atochem North America Foundation; vice president public affairs, Elf Atochem North America, Inc.
McCarty, James L.: senior executive vice president, Ecolab Inc.
McCaskill, Beverly H.: secretary, Chase Bank of Texas; vice president, treasurer, Chase Bank of Texas Foundation, Inc.
McCausland, Edwin P., Jr.: executive vice president, chief investment officer, Nationwide Insurance Enterprise Foundation
McClain, Terry James: director, Valmont Foundation; senior vice president, chief financial officer, Valmont Industries, Inc.
McClelland, William Craig: trustee, Union Camp Charitable Trust; chairman, chief executive officer, director, Union Camp Corp.
McClimon, Timothy J.: chairman, trustee, AT&T Foundation
McClung, James Allen: director public affairs, FMC Corp.; vice president, director, FMC Foundation
McConnell, Richard Lynn: senior vice president, director research, Pioneer Hi-Bred International, Inc.
McConnell, William Thompson: chairman, ceo, Park National Bank; chairman, Park National Corp. Foundation
McCook, Richard P.: vice president, Winn-Dixie Stores Foundation; vice president finance, chief financial officer, Winn-Dixie Stores Inc.
McCorkindale, Douglas H.: vice chairman, president, Gannett Co., Inc.; president, Gannett Foundation
McCormick, William Thomas, Jr.: chairman, chief executive officer, director, Consumers Energy Co.; chairman, Consumers Energy Foundation
McCown, J. Ross: vice president, treasurer, Abel Foundation
McCoy, John Bonnet: president, chief executive officer, Ameritech Corp.
McCracken, Steve: director, Callaway Golf Co. Foundation
McCullough, Ouida: co-president, Gallo Foundation
McDade, Sandy D.: secretary, Weyerhaeuser Co.; assistant secretary legal affairs, Weyerhaeuser Co. Foundation
McDaniel, Tom J.: vice chairman, director, Kerr-McGee Corp.
McDevitt, Amy: vice president, First Security Bank of Idaho NA
McDivitt, Norris E.: vice president operations & engineering, Texas Gas Transmission Corp.
McDonagh, William M.: director, Broderbund Foundation; president, chief operating officer, Broderbund Software, Inc.
McDonald, James F.: president, chief executive officer, Scientific-Atlanta, Inc.
McDonald, James P.: chairman, chief executive officer, Mellon Financial Corp.
McDonald, Thomas: trustee, McDonald & Co. Securities Foundation
McDonough, Gerald C.: treasurer, Commercial Intertech Foundation
McDonough, Joseph E.: vice president finance, chief financial officer, Analog Devices, Inc.
McDougal, Mark: foundation coordinator, GuideOne Foundation; chief financial officer, GuideOne Insurance
McDowell, J. Walter: president, chief executive officer, director, Wachovia Bank of North Carolina NA; director, Wachovia Foundation, Inc. (The)
McEvoy, Timothy G.: secretary, director, M&T Charitable Foundation
McFadden, Harry W., Jr. MD: director, Physicians Mutual Insurance Co. Foundation
McFerson, Dimon Richard: chairman, chief executive officer, Nationwide Insurance Co.; chairman, chief executive officer, trustee, Nationwide Insurance Enterprise Foundation; chairman, chief executive officer, Wausau Insurance Companies
McGahen, Graham: credit risk manager, Barclays Capital
McGeehan, Robert L.: trustee, Kennametal Foundation
McGehee, Robert B.: executive vice president, general counsel, Carolina Power & Light Co.; trustee, CP&L Foundation
McGinley, Jack L.: president, director, Baxter Allegiance Foundation; group vice president, Baxter International Inc.
McGinnis, W. Patrick: co-chief executive officer, Ralston Purina Co.
McGlothlin, James W.: chief executive officer, United Coal Co. Charitable Foundation; chairman, chief executive officer, United Co.
McGovern, John Francis: chief financial officer, executive vice president, Georgia-Pacific Corp.; chairman, Georgia-Pacific Foundation
McGowan, John: director civic affairs
McGowan, W. Brian: assistant treasurer, Grace Foundation Inc.
McGrath, Donald: director community affairs, Textron Inc.
McGrath, Joan S.: president, chief operating officer, Fortune Brands, Inc.
McGrath, Lee Upton: treasurer, Fuller Co. Foundation (H.B.); vice president, treasurer, Fuller Co. (H.B.); treasurer, Jostens Foundation Inc. (The); president, chief executive officer, director, chairman, Jostens, Inc.
McGraw, Harold Whittlesey 'Terry', III: chairman, president, chief executive officer, McGraw-Hill Companies, Inc.
McGraw, Michael J.: senior vice president law & human resources, Brown & Williamson Tobacco Corp.
McGreevy, Stephen R.: vice president accounting & financial control, Consolidated Natural Gas Co.; director, Consolidated Natural Gas System Foundation
McGregor, Douglas A.: senior vice president, chief financial officer, Rouse Co.; trustee, Rouse Co. Foundation
McGregor, Douglas J.: president, chief operating officer, director, Hanna Co. (M.A.)
McGregor, Mark: vice president, treasurer, Storage Technology Corp.
McGuinn, Martin Gregory: chairman, chief executive officer, Mellon Financial Corp.
McHale, Dave: president,
McInnes, Duncan Joseph: executive vice president administration, chief administrative officer, Blount International, Inc.
McIntosh, David H.: co-president, Toro Co.; director, Toro Foundation
McIntyre, Diane: director, Dreyer's Grand Ice Cream Charitable Foundation
McIntyre, Larry: director, Toro Foundation
McKamey, William: general manager, director, Public Service Co. of Oklahoma
McKay, Emily B.: president, director, Consolidated Papers Foundation, Inc.
McKay, Irene: admin assistant
McKee, E. Marie: senior vice president, Corning Inc.; chairman, trustee, Corning Inc. Foundation
McKee, Raymond M.: chairman, Bank of America Foundation
McKee, Robert E., III: executive vice president corporate strategy & development, du Pont de Nemours & Co. (E.I.)
McKellar, Charles H.: vice president, director, Winn-Dixie Stores Foundation; executive vice president, director, Winn-Dixie Stores Inc.
McKenna, Andrew James: treasurer, Aon Foundation
McKenna, Matthew M.: treasurer, PepsiCo Foundation, Inc.; senior vice president, treasurer, PepsiCo, Inc.
McKenna, William John: director, chairman, Kellwood Co.; chairman, president, director, Kellwood Foundation
McKenna, William P.: vice president finance, chief financial officer, treasurer, Bourns, Inc.
McKennon, Keith Robert: chairman, president, PacifiCorp; member, PacifiCorp Foundation
McKeown, James L.: president, trustee, Cummings Properties Foundation; president, director, Cummings Properties Management

McKinley, Ron: executive vice president, chief financial officer, Saint Paul Companies Inc.
McKinley, Terry L.: secretary, Ashland Inc. Foundation
McKinnell, Henry A., PhD: president, chief operating officer, Pfizer Inc.
McKinney, R. P.: assistant secretary, United Dominion Foundation
McKinnon, Thomas E.: director, Ryder System Charitable Foundation; executive vice president human resources, Ryder System, Inc.
McKone, Francis L.: president, chief executive officer, director, Albany International Corp.
McLaren, Ross: chief executive officer, Shaw's Supermarkets, Inc.
McLaughlin, Ann D.: director, Fannie Mae Foundation
McLaughlin, Elizabeth: chairman, Royal & SunAlliance Insurance Foundation, Inc.
McLaughlin, Joe: trustee, Credit Suisse First Boston Foundation Trust
McLaughlin, Loretta: executive director, Boston Globe Foundation
McLaughlin, Michael John: secretary, New York Life Foundation; senior vice president, deputy general counsel, New York Life Insurance Co.
McLaughlin, Michael T.: secretary, Pacific Mutual Charitable Foundation
McLaughlin, Sandra J.: membership corporate review committee, Mellon Financial Corp.
McLaughlin, Sue A.: trustee, BellSouth Foundation
McLean, James: president, Meijer, Inc.
McLendon, Charles A.: trustee, Burlington Industries Foundation
McLeod, Kaye A.: trustee, Gerber Foundation
McMahon, John J., Jr.: trustee, McWane Foundation; chairman, president, chief executive officer, treasurer, McWane Inc.
McMahon, Steve: program director, School-to-Career, Autodesk Foundation
McMahon, Tracy: vice president, Student Loan Marketing Association
McManigal, David M.: executive vice president, American General Finance Foundation
McMicken, Artist: chairman, chief executive officer, Regions Financial Corp.
McMillan, C. Steven: president, chief executive officer, Sara Lee Corp.
McMillan, Cary D.: executive vice president, chief financial officer, chief administrative officer, Sara Lee Corp.
McMillan, Howard Lamar, Jr.: president, chief operating officer, director, Deposit Guaranty National Bank
McMorrow, William J.: director civic affairs
McMullan, James M.: chief financial officer, secretary, Blair & Co. Foundation (William)
McMullin, Anne: interim chief executive officer, Apple Computer, Inc.
McMurray, J. Patrick: president, First Security Bank of Idaho NA
McNally, Alan G.: chairman, chief executive officer, Harris Trust & Savings Bank
McNally, Mark K.: senior vice president, general counsel, secretary, Aristech Chemical Corp.
McNamara, Anne H.: senior vice president, general counsel, AMR Corp.
McNamara, Kevin J.: president, director, Chemed Corp.; secretary, trustee, Chemed Foundation
McNaughton, Stanley W., Junior: president, trustee, PEMCO Foundation
McNealy, Scott G.: chairman, chief executive officer, director, Sun Microsystems Inc.
McNeary, Joseph Allen: member grantmaking committee, Claiborne Foundation (Liz); senior vice president, Liz Claiborne, Inc.
McNeel, Richard L.: president, deputy chief executive officer, director, BP Amoco Corp.; director, BP Amoco Foundation
McNeeley, Robert D.: president, director, Reilly Industries, Inc.
McNeill, Corbin Asahel, Jr.: president, chief executive officer, director, chairman, PECO Energy Co.
McNeive, Jerald T.: chairman, trustee, Laclede Gas Charitable Trust
McPeak, Brian: manager corporate community affairs, Rohm & Haas Co.
McPhail, Gary: president emeritus, AmerUS Group
McQuade, Kathryn B.: vice president financial planning, Norfolk Southern Corp.; vice president, chief officer, Norfolk Southern Foundation
McSweeney, Eileen: director contributions community support program
McVaney, C. Edward: founder, president, Edwards Enterprise Software (J.D.)
McWilliams, D. Bradley: vice president, Cooper Industries Foundation; chief financial officer, senior vice president finance, Cooper Industries, Inc.
Meacham, William B.: director, Lance Foundation; vice president acquisitions & subsidiaries, director, Lance, Inc.
Mead, Dana George: chairman, chief executive officer, director, Tenneco Automotive
Mead, George Wilson, II: president, director, Consolidated Papers Foundation, Inc.; chairman, director, Consolidated Papers, Inc.
Mead, Susan W. A.: vice president, ReliaStar Financial Corp.; director, ReliaStar Foundation
Meadows, John: president, chief operating officer, Coors Brewing Co.
Mebane, David Cummins: chairman, president, chief executive officer, director, Madison Gas & Electric Co.; vice president, Madison Gas & Electric Foundation
Medford, Dale L.: vice president corporate finance, chief financial officer, Reynolds & Reynolds Co.
Medland, Richard H.: director, OMC Foundation
Medvin, Harvey Norman: executive vice president, treasurer, chief financial officer, Aon Corp.; treasurer, Aon Foundation
Mee, Michael F.: senior vice president, chief financial officer, Bristol-Myers Squibb Co.
Meelia, Richard J.: president, chief executive officer, Kendall International, Inc.
Meers, Robert: director, Reebok Human Rights Foundation (The)
Meeusen, Richard A.: vice president, chief financial officer, treasurer, Badger Meter, Inc.
Meidinger, J.: president, Alyeska Pipeline Service Co.
Meier, Deborah: director, Panasonic Foundation
Meier, Stephen Charles: vice chairman, Times Mirror Co.; president, chief executive officer, Times Mirror Foundation
Meijer, Douglas: co-chairman, director, chief executive officer, Meijer, Inc.
Meijer, Frederik G. H.: trustee, Meijer Foundation; chairman executive committee, director, Meijer, Inc.
Meijer, Hendrik G.: co-chairman, director, Meijer, Inc.
Meilahn, J. E.: administrator, Federated Mutual Insurance Foundation
Meirelles, Henrique de-Campos: president, chief operating officer, BankBoston Corp.
Meissner, Harold C.: vice president, Bayport Foundation
Meister, Mark W.: vice president, Lubrizol Corp. (The); trustee, Lubrizol Foundation (The)
Meister, Paul M.: partner, director, Winthrop Foundation
Mekesson, Wilbur: senior vice president, director communication development, Washington Mutual, Inc.
Melampy, Gary: vice president, AK Steel Corp.
Melancon, Pat: chief information officer, FedEx Corp.
Melican, James Patrick, Jr.: executive vice president legal & external affairs, International Paper Co.; director, International Paper Co. Foundation
Mellowes, John A.: chairman, chief executive officer, director, Charter Manufacturing Co.; vice president, treasurer, Charter Manufacturing Co. Foundation
Mellowes, Linda T.: vice president, treasurer, Charter Manufacturing Co. Foundation
Melnuk, Paul D.: president, chief executive officer, Clark Refining & Marketing
Melrose, Kendrick B.: chairman, co-president, chief executive officer, director, Toro Co.; director, Toro Foundation
Melton, Elinor: senior vice president human resources, Scientific-Atlanta, Inc.
Melton, Florence: trustee, Barry Foundation
Melton, Joseph N., Jr.: treasurer, director, Ukrop Foundation; assistant to vice chairman, Ukrop's Super Markets
Mendoza, Roberto G.: vice president, Morgan & Co. Inc. (J.P.)
Mentesana, Carolyn: treasurer, director, Kimberly-Clark Foundation
Menzer, John: executive vice president, Wal-Mart Stores, Inc.
Merdek, Andrew Austin: vice president legal affairs, secretary, Cox Enterprises Inc.; secretary, Cox Foundation (James M.)
Meredith, Edwin Thomas, III: chairman executive committee, Meredith Corp.
Meredith, Lois: director, MFA Foundation
Meriage, Larry: president, Occidental Oil and Gas Foundation
Merlotti, Frank Henry: trustee, Steelcase Foundation; director, Steelcase Inc.
Merrell, Pamela K.: secretary, Montana Power Co.; vice president, secretary, Montana Power Foundation
Merritt, Raymond W.: secretary, treasurer, Cowen Foundation
Mersereau, Susan M.: assistant secretary legal affairs, Weyerhaeuser Co. Foundation
Mesher, John R.: vice president, director, CertainTeed Corp.; assistant secretary, CertainTeed Corp. Foundation
Mesloh, Jim: director, Consolidated Natural Gas System Foundation
Messer, Chester R.: president, chief operating officer, Boston Gas Co.; senior vice president, general counsel, secretary, Eastern Enterprises; trustee, Eastern Enterprises Foundation
Messey, R. J.: senior vice president, chief financial officer, Sverdrup Corp.
Metts, James A.: treasurer, Fuller Co. Foundation (H.B.)
Metzger, Michael D.: vice president, chief financial officer, JSJ Corp.
Meuleman, Robert Joseph: chief financial officer, AMCORE Bank Rockford; director, AMCORE Foundation
Meurer, Thomas E.: senior vice president administration, Hunt Oil Co.
Meyer, Daniel Joseph: president, Milacron Foundation; chairman, president, chief executive officer, director, Milacron, Inc.
Meyer, Jerome J.: chairman, chief executive officer, Tektronix, Inc.
Meyer, Karen: director, Toro Foundation
Meyer, Ronald: president, director, Universal Studios
Meyer, Russell William, Jr.: chairman, chief executive officer, Cessna Aircraft Co.; president, Cessna Foundation, Inc.

Meyer, Sarah: senior program officer, Microsoft Corp.

Meyer, W. Frederick: director, Arvin Foundation

Meyers, Hyman: trustee, Circuit City Foundation

Meyers, Scott: vice president, treasurer, chief financial officer, Alliant Techsystems

Meyerson, Ivan D.: vice president, general counsel, McKesson-HBOC Corp.

Meyerson, Martin: secretary, Panasonic Foundation

Micek, Ernest S.: member contributions committee, Cargill Inc.

Michael, Gary Glenn: chairman, chief executive officer, director, Albertson's Inc.

Michael, John D.: president, director, Fabri-Kal Corp.

Michael, Robert W.: senior vice president, group executive, Walter Industries Inc.

Michaels, Jack D.: secretary, HON Industries Charitable Foundation; chairman, president, chief executive officer, director, HON Industries Inc.

Micheletti, Tom: vice president public & government affairs, Northern States Power Co.

Miglio, Daniel Joseph: chairman, president, director, chief executive officer, Southern New England Telephone Co.

Mika, John J.: president, chief executive officer, Santa Fe International Corp.

Mikulak, John P.: vice president, director, CertainTeed Corp.

Milano, Bernard J.: trustee, KPMG Peat Marwick Foundation; executive director, KPMG Peat Marwick LLP

Milfs, Audrey L.: secretary, Pacific Mutual Charitable Foundation; vice president, corporate secretary, director, Pacific Mutual Life Insurance Co.

Millan, Jacqueline R.: vice president, manager corporate contributions, PepsiCo Foundation, Inc.; manager corporate contributions, PepsiCo, Inc.

Millard, Elisabeth: trustee, Credit Suisse First Boston Foundation Trust

Millenbruch, Gary Lee: executive vice president, chief financial officer, director, trustee, Bethlehem Steel Corp.

Miller, Charles Daly: chairman, director, Avery Dennison Corp.; treasurer, Whirlpool Foundation

Miller, Daniel S.: vice president tax financial planning, Dun & Bradstreet Corp.; assistant treasurer, Dun & Bradstreet Corp. Foundation, Inc.

Miller, David O.: chairman, Employers Insurance of Wausau, A Mutual Co.; chairman, chief executive officer, trustee, Nationwide Insurance Enterprise Foundation; chairman, Wausau Insurance Companies

Miller, Diane Disney: director, Wells Fargo Foundation

Miller, Donn Biddle: president, chief executive officer, Pacific Mutual Life Insurance Co.

Miller, Edwin W.: vice president, treasurer, Lilly & Co. (Eli)

Miller, Eugene A.: chairman, chief executive officer, Comerica Inc.

Miller, Fred D.: vice president public affairs, Portland General Electric Co.

Miller, Harvey R.: president, director, Weil, Gotshal & Manges Foundation

Miller, James A.: vice president marketing, Ecolab Inc.

Miller, James C.: president, director, S&T Bancorp; president, S&T Bancorp Charitable Foundation

Miller, James H., III: senior vice president, Alabama Power Co.; director, Alabama Power Foundation

Miller, Joseph Irwin: director associate, Cummins Engine Co., Inc.; director, Cummins Engine Foundation

Miller, Ken: chief financial officer, Credit Suisse First Boston; trustee, Credit Suisse First Boston Foundation Trust

Miller, Kimberly Ann: secretary, Louisiana-Pacific Foundation

Miller, Larry C.: vice president finance, chief financial officer, Butler Manufacturing Co.; treasurer, Butler Manufacturing Co. Foundation

Miller, Lisa R.: director, Hannaford Charitable Foundation

Miller, Loren: member, Northern Trust Co. Charitable Trust

Miller, Mary J.: vice president, trustee, Price Associates Foundation (T. Rowe)

Miller, Steve: chief executive officer, Waste Management Inc.

Miller, Ty: president, Bank One, Texas, NA

Miller, William Irwin: director, Cummins Engine Foundation

Milliken, Gerrish H., Jr.: member advisory committee, Milliken Foundation

Milliken, Minot King: member advisory committee, Milliken Foundation

Milliken, Roger: chairman, chief executive officer, Milliken & Co.; member advisory committee, Milliken Foundation

Millman, Paul: director, Mattel Foundation

Mills, John T.: vice president, tax counsel, USX Corp.

Mills, Linda S.: director, SBC Foundation

Mills, Paul D.: treasurer, York Federal Savings & Loan Foundation

Millstein, Ira M.: partner, Weil, Gotshal & Manges Corp.; president, director, Weil, Gotshal & Manges Foundation

Milne, Garth Leroy: senior vice president, treasurer, Motorola Inc.

Milulak, John P.: vice president, Norton Co. Foundation

Minami, Wayne K.: director, Hawaiian Electric Industries Charitable Foundation

Minnis, Ann: director, Texas Instruments Foundation

Minor, Annette: director, Piper Jaffray Companies Foundation; director public affairs, U.S. Bancorp Piper Jaffray

Minton, Dwight Church: chairman, director, Church & Dwight Co., Inc.

Mirsky, Susan: vice president, director, Thompson Co. Fund (J. Walter); chief executive officer, Thompson Co. (J. Walter)

Misner, J. W.: chairman, chief executive officer, director, Kellogg Co.; trustee, Kellogg Co. Twenty-Five Year Employees' Fund Inc.

Mita, Katsushige: executive secretary, Hitachi Foundation

Mitau, Lee R.: executive vice president, general counsel, secretary, U.S. Bancorp

Mitchell, David E.: vice chairman, director, Whirlpool Corp.; trustee, Whirlpool Foundation

Mitchell, James: grants administrator, director, Texas Instruments Foundation

Mitchell, John Francis: vice chairman, director, Motorola Inc.

Mitchell, Susan: senior vice president, CIT Group Foundation; executive vice president, CIT Group, Inc. (The)

Mitchell, Warren I.: president, director, Southern California Gas Co.

Mitchelson, Peter L.: director, SIT Investment Associates Foundation; president, director, SIT Investment Associates, Inc.

Mitrisin, Eldon J.: secretary, El Paso Energy Foundation

Mitropoulis, Iris: chairman, Kingsbury Corp.

Mittendorf, George: chief executive officer, chairman, Woodward Governor Co.; trustee, Woodward Governor Co. Charitable Trust

Mixon, A. Malachi, III: chairman, chief executive officer, Invacare Corp.; trustee, Invacare Foundation

Miyahara, Wally: president, chief executive officer, director, Castle & Cooke Properties Inc.

Mock, Steve: chief financial officer, Warner-Lambert Charitable Foundation

Moe, James D.: corporate vice president, general counsel, secretary, Cargill Inc.

Moe, Thomas O.: member contributions committee, Cargill Inc.

Moffitt, A. E., Junior: senior vice president, chief administrative officer, Bethlehem Steel Corp.; director, Bethlehem Steel Foundation

Moffitt, Donald Eugene: chairman, director, CNF Transportation, Inc.

Mogensen, Dennis: chief financial officer, Simplot Co. (J.R.)

Mohn, Richard E.: chairman, director, Sovereign Bank; director, Sovereign Bank Foundation

Moland, Bruce: president, director, Norwest Foundation

Molen, Richard L.: chairman, chief executive officer, director, Huffy Corp.; trustee, Huffy Foundation, Inc.

Moll, Curtis E.: trustee, Jochum-Moll Foundation (The)

Moll, Darrell: treasurer, trustee, Jochum-Moll Foundation (The)

Molloy, Elen: president, Union Carbide Foundation

Monaghan, Thomas Stephen: assistant secretary

Monahan, Michael J.: vice president external relations, Ecolab Inc.

Monahan, Michael T.: chairman, chief executive officer, Comerica Inc.

Monfor, John: director, CIRI Foundation

Monis, Antonio, Jr.: president, Consolidated Electrical Distributors

Monroe, Ellen: treasurer, Anthem Foundation, Inc.

Montague, William Patrick: president, chief operating officer, director, Mark IV Industries; president, Mark IV Industries Foundation

Monte, Constance: president, Wachtell, Lipton, Rosen & Katz Foundation

Montgomery, Deborah: secretary, director, Blue Cross & Blue Shield of Minnesota Foundation Inc.

Montgomery, Paul: chairman, chief executive officer, director, Eastman Chemical Co.

Montoya, Maria: president, director, Avon Products Foundation, Inc.

Montrone, Paul Michael: vice president, treasurer, Winthrop Foundation

Mooney, Edward J., Jr.: chairman, president, chief executive officer, director, Nalco Chemical Co.

Mooney, J. Robert: senior vice president, chief financial officer, Ethyl Corp.

Moore, E. Kevin: president, Schering-Plough Foundation

Moore, Gordon E., PhD: cofounder, chairman emeritus, director, Intel Corp.; trustee, Intel Foundation

Moore, Jackson W.: president, director, Union Planters Corp.

Moore, James L.: senior vice president public affairs, Deposit Guaranty Foundation; president, chief operating officer, director, Deposit Guaranty National Bank

Moore, John E.: executive vice president human resources, Cessna Aircraft Co.; vice president, Cessna Foundation, Inc.

Moore, John S.: vice president, director, Lance, Inc.

Moore, M. Thomas: secretary, associate general counsel, Cleveland-Cliffs, Inc.

Moore, Patrick J.: vice president, Smurfit-Stone Container Corp.

Moore, Robert: secretary, Gulf Power Foundation

Moore, Robert P.: treasurer, trustee, Barden Foundation, Inc.

Moore, Steven: secretary, treasurer, Oklahoma Gas & Electric Co. Foundation

Moore, Thomas R.: treasurer, secretary distribution committee, PNC Bank Foundation

Moore, Virlyn B., Jr.: founder, Pheonix Foundation

Moore, William B.: director, Western Resources Foundation; executive vice president, chief financial officer, treasurer, Western Resources Inc.; senior vice president, secretary, general counsel, Whitman Corp.; secretary, Whitman Corp. Foundation

Moorer, Creola: president, MacMillan Bloedel Foundation

Moorhead, Thomas Leib, Esq.: vice president law, assistant secretary, Nordson Corp.; trustee, Nordson Corp. Foundation

Moran, Harry J.: executive vice president, Sonoco Products Co.

Moran, Raymond K.: chief operating officer, managing director, S.G. Cowen

Moran, Tina: secretary, Niagara Mohawk Foundation; director, Niagara Mohawk Holdings Inc.

Moravitz, Edward: trustee, Giant Eagle Foundation

Morby, Carolyn R.: vice president, trustee, Gerber Foundation

Morby, Jacqueline C.: managing partner, Pacific Mutual Life Insurance Co.

Morcott, Southwood J.: president, director, Dana Corp. Foundation

Morel, Donald E.: president, West Co. Inc.

Moreland, Jeffrey: director, Burlington Northern Santa Fe Foundation

Morgan, Barbara J.: treasurer, Reader's Digest Foundation

Morgan, Carol: director, National Service Foundation

Morgan, Edward L.: group senior vice president, Hartford (The)

Morgan, Geraldine K.: vice president,

Morgan, Glenn R.: executive vice president, chief financial officer, Hartmarx Corp.

Morgan, James McClay: director, Shell Oil Co. Foundation

Morgan, Judy: director, Autodesk Foundation

Morgan, Patricia A.: director, Baxter Allegiance Foundation

Morgensen, Jerry L.: president, chief executive officer, director, Hensel Phelps Construction Co.; director, Hensel Phelps Foundation

Mori, Ron: vice president, trustee, Allstate Foundation; executive director, Allstate Insurance Co.

Morie, G. Glen: secretary, treasurer, PACCAR Foundation; president, director, PACCAR Inc.

Morita, Masaaki: director, Sony Electronics; chairman, director, Sony U.S.A. Foundation Inc.

Morito, Yoshio: vice president, trustee, Ise Cultural Foundation

Moritz, Charles Worthington: chairman, director, Dun & Bradstreet Corp.

Moroney, James McQueen, Jr.: vice president, trustee, Belo Corp. Foundation (A.H.)

Morressey, Karen M.: director, Cabot Corp. Foundation

Morris, Gabriella: vice president, Prudential Foundation

Morris, Herman, Jr.: president, chief executive officer, Memphis Light Gas & Water Division

Morris, James Thomas: treasurer, AUL Foundation Inc.

Morris, Michael H.: secretary, director, Sun Microsystems Foundation, Inc.; chairman, chief executive officer, director, Sun Microsystems Inc.

Morris, Robert S.: chief executive officer, Kraft Foods, Inc.

Morris, William Shivers, III: founder, chairman, chief executive officer, director, Morris Communications Corp.; trustee, Stauffer Communications Foundation

Morris, William Shivers, IV: president, director, Morris Communications Corp.; trustee, Stauffer Communications Foundation

Morrison, A. F.: senior vice president, secretary, Sverdrup Corp.; mem, Sverdrup Corp. Charitable Trust

Morrow, George J.: chairman, director, Glaxo Wellcome Foundation

Morrow, Roy L.: director corporate relations, Lincoln Electric Co.; vice president government & community affairs, Lincoln Electric Foundation

Morse, Carole: chairman, PGE-Enron Foundation

Morton, Judith: chief executive officer, president, Hercules Inc.

Morton, Margaret H.: president, Fidelity Foundation

Morua, Andrew: director, Harris Bank Foundation; chairman, chief executive officer, Harris Trust & Savings Bank

Moseley, Colin: director, Matlock Foundation; chairman, chief executive officer, Simpson Investment Co.

Moseley, Joe: director, Shelter Insurance Foundation

Moseley, Susan R.: administrator, Matlock Foundation

Moser, Robert W.: executive vice president, Springs Industries, Inc.

Mosner, Lawrence: director, Deluxe Corp. Foundation

Moss, Bonnie: director corporate affairs, Browning-Ferris Industries Inc.

Moss, James H.: trustee, York Federal Savings & Loan Foundation

Moten, John, Junior: vice president community relations, Laclede Gas Co.

Mox, Greg: vice president human resources, Sentry Insurance, A Mutual Co.; president, director, Sentry Insurance Foundation Inc.

Moyer, Paul W.: trustee, York Federal Savings & Loan Foundation

Moyles, Denise L.: trustee, Bourns Foundation

Mrlik, Robert D.: senior vice president, deputy general counsel, secretary, American General Corp.

Mrozek, Ernest J.: executive vice president, chief financial officer, ServiceMaster Co.

Muchin, Allan B.: chairman, Katten, Muchin & Zavis; director, Katten, Muchin & Zavis Foundation

Muehlbauer, James Herman: president, director, Koch Foundation

Mueller, Charles William: chairman, president, chief executive officer, Ameren Corp.; trustee, Ameren Corp. Charitable Trust

Mueller, Gerd Dieter: executive vice president, chief financial officer, director, chief administrative officer, Bayer Corp.; president, Bayer Foundation

Mueller, Marvin A.: director, Group Health Foundation

Muir, Nigel D.: chairman, chief executive officer, Praxair; president, director, Praxair Foundation

Mulcahy, J. Patrick: co-chief executive officer, Ralston Purina Co.

Mulford, David: chairman, Credit Suisse First Boston

Mulhern, Mark: trustee, CP& L Foundation

Mulholland, Charles Bradley: executive vice president, director, Alexander & Baldwin Foundation; executive vice president, Alexander & Baldwin, Inc.

Mulkey, Larry S.: board member, Ryder System Charitable Foundation

Mullane, Donald A.: executive vice president, Bank of America; chairman, Bank of America Foundation

Mullen, Dennis M.: president, chief executive officer, director, Agrilink Foods, Inc.

Mullen, John R.: member corporate contributions committee, Johnson & Johnson Family of Companies Contribution Fund

Mullen, Tim: member, SAFECO Corp.

Muller, Karen P.: executive director, Fuller Co. Foundation (H.B.); division controller, Fuller Co. (H.B.)

Mullin, Kathleen: director, Autodesk Foundation

Mullin, Leo Francis: chairman, president, chief executive officer, Delta Air Lines, Inc.

Mulva, James J.: president, chief operating officer, director, Phillips Petroleum Co.

Munder, Barbara A.: senior vice president new initiatives, McGraw-Hill Companies, Inc.

Mundy, Donna T.: vice president, trustee, UNUM Foundation; senior vice president, UnumProvident

Munn, David: assistant secretary, Pella Corp.

Munro, J. Richard: president, chief executive officer, director, Genentech Inc.

Murdoch, Rupert P.: chairman, Fox Entertainment Group

Murdy, James L.: executive vice president finance and administration, chief financial officer, Allegheny Technologies Inc.; trustee, Allegheny Technologies Inc. Charitable Trust

Murphy, Christopher J., III: president, chief executive officer, director, First Source Corp.; director, First Source Foundation

Murphy, Eugene F.: director, GE Fund

Murphy, James W.: senior vice president corporate finance, American United Life Insurance Co.; treasurer, AUL Foundation Inc.

Murphy, John Davis: secretary, Wiremold Foundation

Murphy, John M., Jr.: chairman, chief investment officer, U.S. Bancorp

Murphy, Michael Emmett: assistant treasurer, Sara Lee Foundation

Murphy, Patsy: director, Broderbund Foundation

Murphy, R. Madison: chairman, director, Murphy Oil Corp.

Murphy, Robert H.: president, Wiremold Foundation

Murphy, Thomas Sawyer: vice president, ABC

Murray, James E.: executive director, Humana Foundation

Murray, Kieran: treasurer, Texaco Foundation

Murray, Malcolm T., Jr.: director, First Union Foundation

Murray, Patricia: vice president, director human resources, Intel Corp.; chairman, Intel Foundation

Murtagh, Frank: vice president, Trace International Holdings, Inc. Foundation

Musgrave, Colleen: president, director, Matlock Foundation

Music, Rick E.: assistant secretary, Ashland Inc. Foundation

Musser, Warren Van Dyke: chairman, chief executive officer, director, Safeguard Scientifics; president, director, Safeguard Scientifics Foundation

Muth, Robert James: director, ASARCO Foundation

Mutz, John M.: vice president, Cinergy Corp.; director, Cinergy Foundation

Myers, Mark B.: senior vice president corporate research & technology, Xerox Corp.; trustee, Xerox Foundation

Myers, Susan: president, chief executive officer, Bardes Corp.

Myhers, Richard: executive director, Presto Foundation

Myrum, Stanton D.: chairman, Medtronic Foundation

Myszka, Michele: vice president, Pacific Mutual Charitable Foundation; chairman, director, Pacific Mutual Life Insurance Co.

N

Naeve, Stephen W.: vice chairman, executive vice president, chief financial officer, Reliant Energy Inc.

Nagai, Michio: treasurer, Ise Cultural Foundation

Nagler, Barry: director, Reebok Human Rights Foundation (The)

Nagorske, Lynn A.: executive vice president, chief

financial officer, treasurer, TCF National Bank Minnesota
Nagy, Charles F.: treasurer, Standard Products Co.; trustee, Standard Products Co. Charitable Foundation
Nahl, Michael C.: chief financial officer, Albany International Corp.
Najim, Harry: executive vice president, Koch Foundation, Inc. (Fred C. and Mary R.)
Nakagawa, Jean H.: president, director, Servco Foundation
Nakai, Hajime: president, IBJ Foundation
Nakamura, Alyson J.: secretary, Alexander & Baldwin Foundation
Nakamura, Hidetake: president, chief executive officer, Fuji Bank & Trust Co.
Nakatogawa, H.: director, NEC Foundation of America
Nalbach, Kay C.: president, Hartmarx Charitable Foundation; executive vice president, chief financial officer, Hartmarx Corp.
Naples, Ronald James: president, chief executive officer, director, Quaker Chemical Corp.
Naravjo, Arthur: director, Ameritech Foundation
Nasby, David Asher: trustee, General Mills Foundation
Nash, Laurence J.: director, US West Foundation
Nasser, Jacques A.: president, chief executive officer, Ford Motor Co.
Natale, James: president, Bard Foundation (C.R.)
Nation, Robert F.: former president, director, Harsco Corp.; trustee, Harsco Corp. Fund
Nayak, P. Ranganath: trustee, Little Foundation (Arthur D.); senior vice president, Little, Inc. (Arthur D.)
Naylor, L. K.: trustee, Lubrizol Foundation (The)
Naylor, Michael E.: senior vice president operations, Rubbermaid Inc.
Neal, Jerry D.: president, ONEOK, Inc.
Neal, Monica: vice president, Morgan & Co. Inc. (J.P.)
Neal, Philip Mark: president, chief executive officer, director, Avery Dennison Corp.
Neal, Sharon: president, chief executive officer, director, 7-Eleven, Inc.
Neale, Gary L.: chairman, president, chief executive officer, Northern Indiana Public Service Co.
Nearon, Barbara: vice president, Sunoco Inc.
Necessary, Steven K.: senior vice president marketing, Scientific-Atlanta, Inc.
Needleman, Harry: secretary, Cantor, Fitzgerald Foundation; executive vice president, general counsel, Cantor, Fitzgerald Securities Corp.
Neel, Curtis Dean, Jr.: trustee, Eckerd Corp. Foundation
Neels, J.: president, director, AirTouch Communications Foundation
Neely, Walter Emerson: chief operating officer, senior vice president, Humana Foundation
Nees, Kenneth L.: senior vice president, secretary, Sony Electronics; president, assistant secretary, director, Sony U.S.A. Foundation Inc.
Negron, Edna: member contributions committee, Hartford (The)
Neiger, John: vice president financial, Auburn Foundry
Nelson, Glen David, MD: vice chairman, Medtronic, Inc.
Nelson, John Martin: chairman, director, TJX Companies, Inc.
Nelson, Joyce: director, International Paper Co. Foundation
Nelson, Katherine: director, Toro Foundation
Nelson, Kirk N.: president, chief executive officer, Federated Mutual Insurance Co.; vice president, Federated Mutual Insurance Foundation
Nelson, Kristen C.: assistant secretary, Graco, Inc.
Nelson, Marilyn Carlson: chairman, chief executive officer, president, Carlson Companies, Inc.
Nelson, Merlin Edward: treasurer, IBJ Foundation
Nelson, Robert N.: assistant treasurer, Trace International Holdings, Inc. Foundation
Nelson, Scott F.: director, du Pont de Nemours & Co. (E.I.)
Nelson, Virginia: corporate communications manager, TJX Companies, Inc.
Nelson, William O.: director, AMCORE Foundation
Nemecek, Nancy: president, director, Universal Studios; manager corporate communications, public affairs, Universal Studios Foundation
Nern, Christopher C.: vice president, general counsel, Detroit Edison Co.; director, Detroit Edison Foundation
Nero, Vivian: executive director, AT&T Foundation
Nerren, Evonne: director, Temple-Inland Foundation
Netzky, Theodore: director, Galter Foundation
Neuenfeldt, Bonnie: director, Land O'Lakes Foundation
Neville, James Morton: co-chief executive officer, Ralston Purina Co.; member board control, Ralston Purina Trust Fund
Newbold, Claudia: trustee, McKesson Foundation; co-chief executive officer, McKesson-HBOC Corp.
Newbold, W. H.: senior vice president, Alyeska Pipeline Service Co.
Newell, David: manager, First Union National Bank, NA
Newland, Thomas D.: director, Consolidated Natural Gas System Foundation
Newlin, William Rankin: trustee, Kennametal Foundation
Newman, Andrew E.: member, Edison Family Foundation
Newman, Joseph W.: controller, Amsted Industries Inc.
Newman, Paul L.: president, Newman's Own Foundation; vice president, director, executive, Newman's Own Inc.
Newschaffer, Tom: executive vice president, chief financial officer, First Financial Bank
Newsted, Richard E.: executive vice president, AK Steel Corp.
Niblack, John F., PhD: vice chairman, Pfizer Inc.
Nicholas, Jon O.: president, trustee, Maytag Corp. Foundation
Nichols, Kenwood C.: vice chairman, executive officer, Champion International Corp.
Nichols, Mack G.: president, chief executive officer, director, Mallinckrodt Chemical, Inc.
Nichols, Wade Hampton, III: vice president, Revlon Foundation Inc.; executive vice president, general counsel, Revlon Inc.
Nicholson, Debi: chairman, president, chief executive officer, Freightliner Corp.
Nicholson, Jayne: trustee, Anheuser-Busch Companies, Inc.
Nickerson, Lucille M.: secretary, Aetna Foundation; vice president, corporate secretary, Aetna, Inc.
Nicolet, Jules: director, Wisconsin Power & Light Foundation, Inc.
Nides, Tom: director, Fannie Mae Foundation
Niebla, J. Fernando: chairman, chief executive officer, Pacific Mutual Life Insurance Co.
Nielsen, Willard D.: vice president public affairs, Johnson & Johnson; member corporate contributions committee, Johnson & Johnson Family of Companies Contribution Fund
Niemiec, Richard M.: director, Blue Cross & Blue Shield of Minnesota Foundation Inc.
Nikka, Joanne: chairman, Millipore Foundation (The)
Nisbett, Janet S.: senior vice president, controller, Old Kent Bank; treasurer, trustee, Old Kent Foundation
Nishida, Atsutoshi: director, Toshiba America Foundation
Nishimura, Takao: director, Mitsubishi Electric America Foundation
Nishiyama, Tom: senior vice president, treasurer, Toyota Motor Sales U.S.A., Inc.
Nisita, Maurizio: senior vice president global operations, Ecolab Inc.
Noel, Alfred C.: treasurer, Sentry Insurance Foundation Inc.
Noetzelman, Gloria: secretary, director, National City Bank Foundation; director, National City Bank of Minneapolis
Nofziger, Sally Alene: member, PacifiCorp Foundation
Noguchi, Shoji: director, IBJ Foundation; general manager, Industrial Bank of Japan Trust Co. (New York)
Noha, Edward J.: senior vice president, chief financial officer, CNA; director, CNA Foundation
Nomura, Katsufumi: treasurer, Toshiba America Foundation
Noonan, Geri: executive director, trustee, Reebok Human Rights Foundation (The)
Noonan, Timothy J.: president, chief operating officer, director, Rite Aid Corp.
Norberg, Jaron B.: vice president, director, APS Foundation, Inc.; director, Arizona Public Service Co.
Nordberg, Linda C.: committee member, Thermo Electron Foundation
Norman, Paul R.: controller, Boston Globe (The); comptroller, Boston Globe Foundation
Norris, Paul J.: chairman, president, chief executive officer, director, Grace & Co. (W.R.); director, Grace Foundation Inc.
North, Donald K.: secretary, Burlington Resources Foundation
Norton, Helen A.: vice president finance & administration, Susquehanna-Pfaltzgraff Co.; vice president, Susquehanna-Pfaltzgraff Foundation
Norton, Patrick H.: chairman, director, La-Z-Boy Inc.
Norwood, Ralph M.: secretary, Polaroid Foundation
Noski, Charles H.: senior executive vice president, chief financial officer, AT&T Corp.
Noss, Stanley: trustee, Barden Foundation, Inc.
Notebaert, Richard C.: chairman, chief executive officer, Ameritech Corp.; director, Ameritech Foundation
Novak, Richard F.: vice president, human resources, Cleveland-Cliffs, Inc.
Novello, Robert J.: chairman, Butler Manufacturing Co.; member, Butler Manufacturing Co. Foundation
Nowak, Pat: president, chief executive officer, director, Seaway Food Town, Inc.
Nowakowski, David R.: treasurer, director, MichCon Foundation; vice president human resources, Michigan Consolidated Gas Co.
Nowell, Lionell: executive director, Pillsbury Co.; secretary-treasurer, Pillsbury Co. Foundation
Nowell, Tommy Lynn: vice president finance, controller, Occidental Oil and Gas; treasurer, Occidental Oil and Gas Foundation
Nowland, Frankie: president, director social responsibilities, Borden Foundation, Inc.; chairman, president, chief executive officer, director, Borden, Inc.
Noyes, Don M.: vice president, director, ASARCO Foundation
Nozaki, Roger H.: honorary chairman, Hitachi Foundation
Nozari, Mohamed S.: executive vice president, Minnesota Mining & Manufacturing Co.
Nunes, Geoffrey: chief financial officer, corporate vice president, Millipore Corp.; chairman, Millipore Foundation (The)

Nutter, Wallace L.: chairman, president, director, Rayonier Foundation
Nye, Erle Allen: chairman, chief executive officer, director, TU Electric Co.
Nyquist, L. K.: vice president, NCR Corp.; secretary, NCR Foundation

O

O'Brien, James E.: director, Schoeneckers Foundation
O'Brien, John F.: trustee, McDonald & Co. Securities Foundation
O'Brien, John Francis, Jr.: president, chief executive officer, Allmerica Financial Corp.
O'Brien, Polly: vice president, secretary, general counsel, chairman, Pitney Bowes Inc.
O'Brien, Richard A.: director, Smith Foundation Inc. (Harold Webster)
O'Brien, Richard T.: executive vice president, chief operating officer, PacifiCorp; member, PacifiCorp Foundation
O'Brien, Thomas H., Jr.: chairman, chief executive officer, PNC Financial Services Group
O'Brien, William J., III: trustee, DaimlerChrysler Corp. Fund
O'Connell, John T.: chief financial officer, Enterprise Rent-A-Car Co.; vice president, treasurer, Enterprise Rent-A-Car Foundation
O'Connor, Edward J.: treasurer, Smith Foundation, Inc. (A.O.)
O'Connor, Pamela: secretary, trustee, Zachry Foundation (The)
O'Connor, Thomas P.: executive vice president, Springs Industries, Inc.
O'Donnell, Francis X.: treasurer, Chicago Board of Trade Foundation
O'Donnell, James P.: treasurer, ConAgra Foundation
O'Donovan, Timothy: president, Wolverine World Wide
O'Hare, Dean Raymond: chairman, Chubb Corp.
O'Hare, Don R.: director, Hamilton Sundstrand Corp.; president, director, Sundstrand Corp. Foundation
O'Laughlin, Jan: headquarters director, Mervyn's California
O'Leary, David C.: chairman, Credit Suisse First Boston; chairman, trustee, Credit Suisse First Boston Foundation Trust
O'Leary, Ellen: chairman, president, chief executive officer, Houghton Mifflin Co.
O'Leary, Patrick J.: vice president finance, treasurer, chief financial officer, SPX Corp.; secretary, treasurer, SPX Foundation
O'Leary, Thomas Howard: president, Burlington Resources Foundation
O'Maley, David B.: president, trustee, Ohio National Foundation; chairman, president, chief executive officer, director, Ohio National Life Insurance Co.
O'Mea, Elizabeth: senior vice president, Callaway Golf Co.; director, Callaway Golf Co. Foundation
O'Neil, James E.: vice president technology, Kingsbury Corp.; executive trustee, Kingsbury Fund
O'Neil, Thomas J.: trustee, Cleveland-Cliffs Foundation (The); executive vice president, operations, Cleveland-Cliffs, Inc.
O'Neill, Brian Edward: vice president operations & engineering, Texas Gas Transmission Corp.
O'Neill, Emilie F.: trustee, Boston Edison Foundation
O'Neill, Mike: senior vice president public affairs, American Express Co.
O'Neill, Paul Henry: director, Alcoa Foundation
O'Reilly, Bill: treasurer, Sentry Insurance Foundation Inc.
O'Reilly, David J.: chairman, chief executive officer, Chevron Corp.
O'Reilly, F. Anthony John: chairman, trustee, Heinz Co. Foundation (H.J.); chairman, director, Heinz Co. (H.J.)
O'Rourke, Thomas J.: senior vice president, CIT Group, Inc. (The)
O'Shanna, Dick: president, director, Square D Foundation
O'Toole, Robert Joseph: director, Firstar Milwaukee Foundation; chairman, president, chief executive officer, director, Smith Corp. (A.O.); director, Smith Foundation, Inc. (A.O.)
O'Toole, Timothy S.: executive vice president, treasurer, director, Chemed Corp.
Oakley, Robert Alan: vice president fixed income securities, Nationwide Insurance Enterprise Foundation
Oates, Warren T., Jr.: president, Philips Electronics North America Corp.
Oberwetter, Jim: senior vice president administration, Hunt Oil Co.
Oechsle, Vernon E.: president, chief executive officer, Quanex Corp.; vice president, director, Quanex Foundation
Oehm, Ronald: trustee, KPMG Peat Marwick Foundation
Oelkers, Robert C.: president, Texaco Foundation
Oesterreicher, James E.: chairman, chief executive officer, director, Penney Co., Inc. (J.C.)
Offutt, James A.: director, Shelter Insurance Foundation
Ohlgart, Thomas: secretary, Pieper Power Electric Co.; treasurer, Pieper Power Electric Foundation
Okada, Alan: president, Citibank Corp.
Okada, Natsuo: president, Sumitomo Bank; president, director, Sumitomo Bank Global Foundation
Oken, Loretta M.: trustee, Heinz Co. Foundation (H.J.)
Olan, Patty: president, director, Lotus Development Corp.; manager philanthropy program, Lotus Development Philanthropy Program
Oldenburg, Richard Erik: chairman, Sotheby's Inc.
Olesen, Douglas Eugene, PhD: president, chief executive officer, Battelle Memorial Institute
Oliver, Charles R.: trustee, Fluor Foundation
Oliver, John: director public affairs, Bean, Inc. (L.L.)
Oliver, Orson: president, director, Mid-America Bank of Louisville
Oliver, Walter Maurice: senior vice president human resources, Ameritech Corp.
Oliver, William H.: secretary, AT&T Foundation
Olivier, Leon J.: Chief nuclear office, Boston Edison Co.; trustee, Boston Edison Foundation
Olschwang, Alan P., Esq.: director, Mitsubishi Electric America Foundation
Olsen, Dave: chief financial officer, Patagonia Inc.
Olson, A. Craig: senior vice president finance, chief financial officer, Albertson's Inc.
Olson, Gaylord: chief financial officer, group vice president financial, Cenex Harvest States; secretary-treasurer, Cenex Harvest States Foundation
Olson, Jim: senior vice president external affairs, Toyota Motor Sales U.S.A., Inc.
Olson, Keith D.: vice president, Bayport Foundation
Olson, Richard E.: chairman, chief executive officer, director, Champion International Corp.
Olson, Roger D.: senior vice president human resources, Giant Food Inc.
Olukotun, Oye: vice president medical affairs, Mallinckrodt Chemical, Inc.
Omachinski, David L.: chief financial officer, treasurer, vice president, Oshkosh B'Gosh Foundation Inc.
Ong, John Doyle: chairman board, director, Ameritech Corp.
Ono, Masatoshi: chairman, chief executive officer, Bridgestone/Firestone, Inc.
Opie, John D.: vice chairman, executive officer, director, General Electric Co.
Oran, Stuart I.: director, United Airlines Foundation; senior vice president international, United Airlines Inc.
Orlando, Robert: president, director, Chesebrough Foundation
Orman, Traci: president, chief executive officer, PNC Bank Kentucky Inc.
Orme, Tony: senior vice president auto forms, Reynolds & Reynolds Co.; trustee, Reynolds & Reynolds Co. Foundation
Ormond, Paul: vice president medical programs, HCR ManorCare Foundation
Ornelas, Maria: director, Pheonix Foundation
Orr, Charles Lee: president, chief executive officer, Shaklee Corp.
Orr, James F., III: president, trustee, UNUM Foundation; chairman, Unum-Provident
Orscheln, Donald W.: director, chairman, Orscheln Co.; secretary, Orscheln Industries Foundation, Inc.
Orscheln, Gerald A.: director, Orscheln Industries Foundation, Inc.
Orscheln, Phillip A.: secretary, Orscheln Industries Foundation, Inc.
Orscheln, William L.: treasurer, Orscheln Industries Foundation, Inc.
Orser, William Stanley: executive vice president energy supply, Carolina Power & Light Co.
Ortino, Hector R.: president, chief executive officer, director, Ferro Corp.; vice president, trustee, Ferro Foundation
Osborne, Burl: president publishing division, director, Belo Corp. (A.H.); president, trustee, Belo Corp. Foundation (A.H.)
Osborne, Richard de Jongh: director, ASARCO Foundation; chairman, chief executive officer, director, ASARCO Inc.
Oseroff, Stephen L.: vice president real estate, Giant Food Inc.
Osler, Randy W.: president, Sprint/United Telephone
Ostergard, Paul Michael: vice president, director corporate contributions, Citibank Corp.; president, Citigroup Foundation; president, chairman, chief executive officer, National City Bank of Pennsylvania
Ostler, Clyde W.: vice chairman, Wells Fargo & Co.
Ostrov, Gerlad M.: member corporate contributions committee, Johnson & Johnson Family of Companies Contribution Fund
Oswald, Kathleen M.: vice president human resources, DaimlerChrysler Corp.; trustee, DaimlerChrysler Corp. Fund
Otake, Yoshiki: chairman, AFLAC Inc.
Otani, Tim: vice president community relations department, Washington Mutual Bank Foundation; chairman, president, chief executive officer, director, Washington Mutual, Inc.
Ott, Betty: vice president, treasurer, Western Resources Foundation
Ottaway, James Haller, Jr.: senior vice president, director, Dow Jones & Co., Inc.; member advisory committee, Dow Jones Foundation
Otto, Charlotte R.: trustee, Procter & Gamble Fund
Otto, Peter: president, Lehigh Portland Cement Co.
Overbaugh, Joseph C.: director, AMP Foundation
Owens, Jack Byron: executive vice president, general counsel, Gallo Winery, Inc. (E&J)
Ozark, Edward L.: vice president, chief financial officer, JSJ Corp.; trustee, JSJ Foundation
Ozinga, Kenneth J.: principal mgr, trustee, First Evergreen Foundation; chairman, president, chief executive officer, director, First National Bank of Evergreen Park

P

Pace, James C., Jr.: controller, Inman Mills; trustee, Inman-Riverdale Foundation

Pachtner, John: director corporate communications, APL Ltd.

Packard, Ralph K.: chairman, chief financial officer, Vanguard Group; treasurer, Vanguard Group Foundation

Packwood, Jan: president, chief operating officer, Idaho Power Co.

Pagano, Ralph J.: director, Panasonic Foundation

Page, Barbara B.: trustee, Golub Foundation

Page, Gregory R.: president, chief executive officer, Excel Corp.

Page, Henry C., Jr.: senior vice president, chief financial officer, Ethyl Corp.

Page, Robert A.: chief financial officer, Tenneco Packaging

Painter, Alan Sproul: vice president, executive director, AlliedSignal Foundation Inc.; senior vice president, chief information officer, AlliedSignal Inc.

Pajak, John Joseph: president, chief operating officer, Massachusetts Mutual Life Insurance Co.

Paladino, Daniel R.: trustee, Bronfman Foundation/Joseph E. Seagram & Sons, Inc. Fund (Samuel); executive vice president, general counsel, secretary, Seagram & Sons, Inc. (Joseph E.)

Palmer, Denise: vice president, strategy & finance, Chicago Tribune Co.; treasurer, Chicago Tribune Foundation

Palmieri, Peter C.: vice chairman, chief credit officer, First Union National Bank, NA

Panettiere, John Michael: president, chief executive officer, director, chairman, Blount International, Inc.

Pang, Gerald M.: treasurer, director, First Hawaiian Foundation

Pannetta, Leon: director, New York Stock Exchange, Inc.

Pappert, E. Thomas: vice president sales & service, DaimlerChrysler Corp.; trustee, DaimlerChrysler Corp. Fund

Papso, Anna Mae: vice president, controller, West Co. Inc.

Paquette, Robert H.: director, Tribune New York Foundation

Parent, Mary: treasurer, Bemis Family Foundation (F.K.)

Parfet, Donald R.: president, Pharmacia & Upjohn Foundation; senior vice president associated business, Pharmacia & Upjohn, Inc.

Parham, Joseph G., Jr.: senior vice president, human resources, Polaroid Corp.; president, Polaroid Foundation

Parish, Jim: founder, president, Edwards Enterprise Software (J.D.); board member, Edwards Foundation (J.D.)

Parisi, Franklin Joseph: secretary, Star Tribune Foundation

Park, Christine: senior program officer, social action, Dayton Hudson; director, trustee, Target Foundation

Parker, Bruce: director, Callaway Golf Co. Foundation

Parker, John: vice president information services, Northwest Airlines, Inc.

Parker, John W.: executive vice president, chief financial officer, Union Planters Corp.

Parker, Michael D.: president, chief executive officer, director, Dow Chemical Co.

Parker, Patrick Streeter: chairman, director, Parker Hannifin Corp.; president, trustee, Parker Hannifin Foundation

Parks, Stephen E.: vice president, treasurer, chief financial officer, Questar Corp.

Parnell, Dale Paul: director, Autodesk Foundation

Parrillo, Douglas: secretary, NASDAQ Stock Market Educational Foundation

Parrin, David J.: senior vice president, controller, U.S. Bancorp

Parrish, Jere Paul: member executive committee, director, Shell Oil Co. Foundation

Parrs, Marianne M.: executive vice president, International Paper Co.

Parry, William E.: vice president, general counsel, Nalco Chemical Co.

Parsons, Earl B., Jr.: director, Alabama Power Foundation

Parsons, Stuart N.: chairman, Park National Corp. Foundation

Parsons, Susan E.: secretary, treasurer, Koch Enterprises, Inc.; secretary, treasurer, director, Koch Foundation

Pasquale, Michael: chief operating officer, Hershey Foods Corp.

Pastrana, Glenn M.: chairman, director, ARCO Foundation

Pate, James Leonard: chairman, chief executive officer, director, Pennzoil-Quaker State Co.

Pate, William C.: trustee, BellSouth Foundation

Patel, Homi Burjor: president, chief operating officer, director, Hartmarx Corp.

Patel, Kiran M.: director, Cummins Engine Foundation

Paton, Leland B.: president capital marketings, director, member executive committee, Prudential Securities Inc.

Patrick, Charles F.: treasurer, trustee, Copley Foundation (James S.); executive vice president, chief operating officer, senior management board, Copley Press, Inc.

Patterson, Debra: manager, Lincoln Financial Group

Patterson, James F.: executive vice president, chief financial officer, Nationwide Insurance Enterprise Foundation

Patterson, Kin: chairman, BellSouth Foundation

Patterson, Michael E.: vice chairman, Morgan & Co. Inc. (J.P.)

Patterson, Thomas J., Jr.: chairman, First Union Regional Foundation

Patton, Stephen R.: director, Kirkland & Ellis Foundation

Paul, Douglas L.: chairman, trustee, Credit Suisse First Boston Foundation Trust

Paul, Gary S.: executive vice president, chief financial officer, Manufacturers & Traders Trust Co.

Pauli, William: senior vice president external affairs, Toyota Motor Sales U.S.A., Inc.

Paulson, Henry M., Jr.: chairman, chief executive officer, Goldman Sachs Group

Paulus, Henry P.: executive director, New England Bio Labs Foundation

Paumgarten, Nicholas Biddle: managing director, Scripps Co. (E.W.); member, Scripps Howard Foundation

Pavletich, Kristi: chairman, Menasha Corp. Foundation

Pawley, Dennis K.: executive vice president manufacturing, DaimlerChrysler Corp.

Payne, J. Stanley: president, director, Bassett Furniture Industries Fdn.

Payton, Sylvia: comptroller, Boston Globe Foundation

Payzant, Thomas: member, Goldman Sachs Foundation; chairman, chief executive officer, Goldman Sachs Group

Pearce, Harry J.: vice chairman, General Motors Corp.

Pearl, Melvin E.: director, Katten, Muchin & Zavis Foundation

Pearle, M.J.: contact, Allmerica Financial Charitable Foundation, Inc.; second vice president public relations, Allmerica Financial Corp.

Pearlman, Bob: director, Autodesk Foundation

Pease, Kendall: chairman, chief executive officer, director, General Dynamics Corp.

Peck, Arthur John, Jr.: secretary, vice president, Corning Inc.; secretary, Corning Inc. Foundation

Peconi, Maurice V.: member screening committee, PPG Industries Foundation

Pederson, Jerrold P.: vice president, chief financial officer, director, Montana Power Co.; director, Montana Power Foundation

Peel, Michael A.: trustee, General Mills Foundation; senior vice president human resources, General Mills, Inc.

Peery, J. K.: vice president, director, Quanex Foundation

Peery, Troy A., Jr.: executive vice president, chief financial officer, Heilig-Meyers Co.

Peet, Creighton Houck: vice president, director, Cowen Foundation; chief financial officer, managing director, S.G. Cowen

Pehlke, Richard W.: vice president, treasurer, Ameritech Corp.

Pellegrino, Allison G.: vice president, partner, Winthrop Foundation

Pendergraft, Jeffrey R.: executive vice president, chief administrative officer, Lyondell Chemical Co.

Pendexter, Harold E., Jr.: senior vice president, chief administrative officer, USG Corp.; president, director, USG Foundation

Penglase, Frank Dennis: chairman, president, chief executive officer, McGraw-Hill Companies, Inc.

Pennington, Hilliary: director, Autodesk Foundation

Penny, Roger Pratt: president, chief operating officer, director, Bethlehem Steel Corp.

Peoples, D. Louis: vice chairman, chief executive officer, director, Orange & Rockland Utilities, Inc.

Pepper, John E., Jr.: chairman executive committee, Procter & Gamble Co.

Perabo, Fred H.: member board control, Ralston Purina Trust Fund

Perelman, Ronald Owen: vice president, Revlon Foundation Inc.

Peressinni, William E.: senior vice president, chief financial officer, PacifiCorp; treasurer, PacifiCorp Foundation

Perez, Arnaldo: assistant vice president, secretary, Arison Foundation; vice president, general counsel, secretary, Carnival Corp.

Perez, Mario: director, Fuller Co. Foundation (H.B.); vice president, Fuller Co. (H.B.)

Perkins, Phil: secretary, treasurer, MFA Foundation

Perkins, Shirley L.: treasurer, Red Wing Shoe Co. Foundation

Perlman, Ira: treasurer, Panasonic Foundation

Pero, Perry R.: senior executive vice president, chief financial officer, Northern Trust Co.

Perona, Dale F.: chairman, chief executive officer, director, True North Communications, Inc.; secretary, treasurer, True North Foundation

Perry, James M.: vice chairman, Stonecutter Mills Corp.

Person, Conrad: member corporate contributions committee, Johnson & Johnson Family of Companies Contribution Fund

Peru, Ramiro G.: senior vice president, chief financial officer, Phelps Dodge Corp.

Pesce, William J.: president, chief executive officer, Wiley & Sons (John)

Pestillo, Peter John: executive chairman, Ford Motor Co.; trustee, Ford Motor Co. Fund

Petas, John: president, American Honda Foundation

Petersen, Gary N.: communications administration, Reliant Energy Minnegasco

Petersen, James R.: senior staff writer, Playboy Magazine, Playboy Enterprises Inc.

Peterson, Adaire C.: director, ReliaStar Foundation

Peterson, Charles T.: chief financial officer, managing director, S.G. Cowen

Peterson, Donald Matthew: trustee, Trustmark Foundation; president, chief executive officer, director, Trustmark Insurance Co.

Peterson, Edward M.: member corporate responsibility committee, Commonwealth Edison Co.

Peterson, James: director, Playboy Enterprises Inc.

Peterson, Nills: president, Eastern Bank; trustee, Eastern Bank Charitable Foundation

Peterson, Patty: communications administration, Reliant Energy Minnegasco

Peterson, Robert L.: chairman, chief executive officer, director, IBP

Peterson, Thomas E.: trustee, Bank of America Foundation

Peterson, William E.: general counsel, Sierra Pacific Resources

Petrovich, Dushan: treasurer, Wrigley Co. Foundation (Wm. Jr.); vice president, Wrigley Co. (Wm. Jr.)

Pettinato, Fred: trustee, Alcon Foundation

Petzoad, Arthur: trustee, Presto Foundation

Pew, Robert Cunningham, II: trustee, Steelcase Foundation

Pfaff, Christian J.: chairman, president, chief executive officer, director, Thomasville Furniture Industries Inc.

Pfeiffer, Eckhard A.: president, chief executive officer, director, Compaq Computer Corp.

Pfund, William H.: trustee, Rubbermaid Foundation; senior vice president operations, Rubbermaid Inc.

Phair, Joseph Baschon: corporate secretary, general counsel, vice president, Varian Medical Systems, Inc.

Phares, Lynn Levisay: treasurer, ConAgra Foundation

Philipp, Michel: director, Western Resources Foundation

Phillips, David E.: manager corporate philanthropy, Lockheed Martin Corp.

Phillips, Derwyn Fraser: director

Phillips, Ellyn C.: president, Charlestein Foundation (Julius and Ray)

Phillips, Larry: assistant treasurer, State Farm Companies Foundation

Phillips, Ped Wesley: president, trustee, Hanna Co. Foundation (M.A.)

Phillips, Richard B.: chairman, president, director, Crane Foundation

Phillips, Robert M.: president, Unilever Home & Personal Care U.S.A.

Phillips, Rosalind Ann: assistant secretary, GEICO Philanthropic Foundation

Phillips, W. Thomas: senior vice president, director research, Pioneer Hi-Bred International, Inc.

Philp, Lisa: chairman, president, chief executive officer, director, Morgan & Co. Inc. (J.P.)

Phin, Sydney N.: director human resources, Union Camp Corp.

Piacentini, Carmella V.: trustee, Olin Corp. Charitable Trust

Piano, Evelyn: chairman, Star Tribune Foundation

Piano, Phyllis J.: president, Cooper Industries Foundation; vice president public affairs, Cooper Industries, Inc.

Pickard, Mary: community affairs officer, Saint Paul Companies Inc.

Pidherny, Dennis N.: chairman, director, Dun & Bradstreet Corp.; assistant treasurer, Dun & Bradstreet Corp. Foundation, Inc.

Piedra, Ling J.: executive vice president manufacturing, DaimlerChrysler Corp.; trustee, DaimlerChrysler Corp. Fund

Pieper, Richard R.: chairman, chief executive officer, director, Pieper Power Electric Co.; secretary, Pieper Power Electric Foundation

Pieper, Suzanne: secretary, Pieper Power Electric Foundation

Pier, Nancy G.: general partner, Glickenhaus & Co.; president, Glickenhaus Foundation

Piergallini, Alfred A.: trustee, Gerber Foundation

Pierre, Percy A.: senior program officer, Hitachi Foundation

Piet, William M.: vice president, director, Wrigley Co. Foundation (Wm. Jr.); vice president corporate affairs, secretary, assistant to president, Wrigley Co. (Wm. Jr.)

Pietrafitta, Clifford E.: vice president finance, treasurer, CSS Industries, Inc.

Pigott, Charles McGee: president, director, PACCAR Foundation; chairman emeritus, director, PACCAR Inc.

Pike, Robert William: vice president, secretary, Allstate Foundation; senior vice president, secretary, general counsel, director, Allstate Insurance Co.

Pilch, Donald: chief financial officer, Crown Books

Pilon, Lawrence James: senior vice president human resources, Whitman Corp.

Pilot, Kenneth S.: president Gap brand, Gap, Inc.

Pinho, Maria B.: general manager corporate responsibility, Public Service Electric & Gas Co.

Pinover, Bruce M.: treasurer, Chesapeake Corp.; trustee, Chesapeake Corp. Foundation

Pinto, Michael P.: executive vice president, chief financial officer, Manufacturers & Traders Trust Co.

Piper, Addison Lewis: director, Piper Jaffray Companies Foundation; chairman, chief executive officer, director, U.S. Bancorp Piper Jaffray

Pitkin, Ronald: president, Rutledge Hill Press Foundation

Pitofsky, Jim: director search selection, Echoing Green Foundation

Pitorak, Larry John: senior vice president finance, treasurer, chief financial officer, Sherwin-Williams Co.; secretary, treasurer, trustee, Sherwin-Williams Foundation

Pitsenbarger, Myrtle N.: director, GEICO Philanthropic Foundation

Pitts, Brenda S.: director, Cummins Engine Foundation

Pitts, John Wilson: secretary, treasurer, PACCAR Foundation

Pitts, Rod: co-trustee, INTRUST Bank Charitable Trust

Platania, Lynn M.: director community relations, Tandy Corp.

Platt, Lewis Emmett: chairman, Hewlett-Packard Co.

Plazak, Kathryn F.: second vice president, New England Financial

Plourde, William: corporate manager philanthropy, Toyota Motor Sales U.S.A., Inc.; senior vice president, Toyota U.S.A. Foundation

Plumeri, Joseph James, II: president, Citigroup

Plung, Donald: trustee, Giant Eagle Foundation

Poindexter, Christian Herndon: chairman, Baltimore Gas & Electric Foundation; chairman, chief executive officer, director, Constellation Energy Group, Inc.

Poirier, Rie: director, United Distillers & Vintners North America

Polark, Roger L.: senior vice president, chief financial officer, Walgreen Co.

Polin, Jane Louise: manager, comptroller, GE Fund; vice chairman, executive officer, director, General Electric Co.

Pollard, Charles William, Jr.: chairman, director, ServiceMaster Co.; president, director, ServiceMaster Foundation

Pollard, David R.: director, Fireman's Fund Foundation; officer, Fireman's Fund Insurance Co.

Pollay, Richard L.: vice chairman, director, Chicago Title Corp.; trustee, Chicago Title and Trust Co. Foundation

Polley, Brooke: senior communication relations specialist, BankBoston Charitable Foundation; manager external affairs, BankBoston-Connecticut Region

Pollicino, Joseph Anthony: executive vice chairman, CIT Group Foundation; vice chairman, director, CIT Group, Inc. (The)

Pollnow, Charles F., Jr.: treasurer, director, Matlock Foundation; chief financial officer, Simpson Investment Co.

Pollock, E. Kears: director, PPG Industries Foundation; executive vice president, PPG Industries, Inc.

Pomerantz, Marvin Alvin: trustee, Mid-American Foundation

Pond, Byron O.: chairman, chief executive officer, director, Arvin Industries, Inc.

Ponitz, Cathy: trustee, Reynolds & Reynolds Co. Foundation

Pontikes, Lynne: president, director, Comdisco Foundation

Pontikes, Nicholas K.: secretary, director, Comdisco Foundation

Pontz, Curtis M.: vice president, director, CertainTeed Corp.; assistant secretary, CertainTeed Corp. Foundation

Pope, G. Phillip: chief financial officer, Blue Cross & Blue Shield of Alabama; vice president, Caring Foundation

Port, Frederick R.: executive vice president, Callaway Golf Co.; director, Callaway Golf Co. Foundation

Porter, Charles W.: trustee, Giant Eagle Foundation

Porter, Donald E.: director, Bucyrus-Erie Foundation

Porter, Edward A.: vice president, general counsel, secretary, Walter Industries Inc.

Porter, James T.: director, Honeywell Foundation; vice president, chief administrative officer, Honeywell International Inc.

Porter, Sue: chairman, president, chief executive officer, director, Scripps Co. (E.W.); trustee, Scripps Howard Foundation

Portney, David: second vice president public relations, Allmerica Financial Corp.

Poses, Frederick M.: director, AlliedSignal Foundation Inc.; president, chief operating officer, AlliedSignal Inc.

Posey, Warren M., Jr.: treasurer, Armstrong Foundation; chairman, chief executive officer, director, Armstrong World Industries, Inc.

Post, David A.: vice president, Equifax Foundation; corporate vice president, chief financial officer, Equifax Inc.

Post, Jeffery H.: executive vice president, chief financial officer, chief actuary, Fireman's Fund Insurance Co.

Post, William J.: vice president, director, APS Foundation, Inc.; president, chief executive officer, Arizona Public Service Co.

Pottenger, Charles R.: group vice president pulp & paperboard group, Potlatch Corp.; trustee, Potlatch Foundation II

Pottruck, David Steven: president, chief executive officer, director, Schwab & Co., Inc. (Charles)

Powell, Cornelius Patrick: director, Air Products Foundation

Powell, George Everett, III: president, chief executive officer, director, Yellow Corp.; trustee, Yellow Corp. Foundation

Powell, George Everett, Jr.: assistant secretary, Yellow Corp. Foundation

Powell, James R.: director, Rutledge Hill Press Foundation

Powell, Jerry W.: secretary, general counsel, Compass Bank; secretary, Compass Bank Foundation

Powell, Larry R.: president, Copolymer Foundation; chairman, president, chief executive officer, DSM Copolymer

Powell, Nancy G.: secretary, Universal Leaf Foundation

Powell, Sandra Theresa: trustee, Potlatch Foundation II

Powell, William H.: secretary, National Starch & Chemical Foundation

Powers, Betty Jean: chairman, president, chief executive officer, director, Progressive Corp.

Powers, Paul Joseph: chairman, president, chief executive officer, director, Commercial Intertech Corp.; president, trustee, Commercial Intertech Foundation

Powis, Richard R.: trustee, Eckerd Corp. Foundation

Prager, Susan Westerberg: chairman, chief executive officer, Pacific Mutual Life Insurance Co.

Prancan, Jane: director, US West Foundation

Pratt, Donald Henry: chairman, Butler Manufacturing Co.; vice president, trustee, Butler Manufacturing Co. Foundation

Preheim, Randall F.: executive vice president, AK Steel Corp.; president, trustee, AK Steel Foundation

Preleski, David J.: director, Smith Foundation Inc. (Harold Webster)

Prendergast, G. Joseph: director, Wachovia Foundation, Inc. (The)

Prendergast, Michael J.: vice president, chief financial officer, Aristech Chemical Corp.

Prendergast, Suzanne: secretary, National Starch & Chemical Foundation

Prentis, John: trustee, Sunmark Foundation

Preston, James Edward: vice president, director, Avon Products Foundation, Inc.; chairman, chief executive officer, director, Avon Products, Inc.

Preston, Kasandra K.: secretary, treasurer, director, Briggs & Stratton Corp. Foundation

Previte, Richard: president, chief operating officer, director, Advanced Micro Devices, Inc.

Pribanic, Gerald J.: executive vice president, chief financial officer, Maytag Corp.; trustee, Maytag Corp. Foundation

Price, Carry: director public relations, Liberty Corp.

Price, Charles H., II: president, chief operating officer, New York Times Co.; director, New York Times Co. Foundation

Price, Clarence L.: director, Foundation of the Litton Industries; chairman, director, Litton Industries, Inc.

Price, David B., Jr.: vice president, Goodrich Foundation, Inc. (B.F.)

Price, Timothy: president, chief executive officer, director, MCI WorldCom, Inc.

Prillaman, L. I.: vice chairman, chief marketing officer, Norfolk Southern Corp.

Prince, Charles O., III: senior vice president, general counsel, secretary, Citigroup; secretary, trustee, Citigroup Foundation

Prior, Michael: managing director, Barclays Capital

Pritchard, Marc S.: president, Procter & Gamble Cosmetics Foundation

Proctor, Georgeanne: assistant treasurer, Bechtel Foundation

Proctor, Timothy D.: director, Glaxo Wellcome Foundation

Procyk, Nicholas P.: assistant treasurer, Merck & Co.

Proffitt, G. E.: vice chairman, INTRUST Bank Charitable Trust

Prohofsky, Dennis E.: secretary, Minnesota Mutual Foundation; senior vice president, general counsel, secretary, Minnesota Mutual Life Insurance Co.

Prokop, Rodney A.: senior vice president, chief financial officer, Phelps Dodge Corp.; assistant treasurer, Phelps Dodge Foundation

Prosser, John Warren, Jr.: treasurer, director, Jacobs Engineering Foundation; senior vice president finance & administration, treasurer, Jacobs Engineering Group

Proto, Chris: trustee, Jochum-Moll Foundation (The)

Ptacek, P. J.: vice president human resources, Alyeska Pipeline Service Co.

Puckett, Marlene: president, Morrison Knudsen Corp. Foundation, Inc.

Puelicher, John A.: director, board member, Marshall & Ilsley Foundation, Inc.

Puerner, John: president, chief executive officer, Sentinel Communications Co.

Puerto, Mariella: executive secretary, Boston Globe Foundation

Puff, Randy: trustee, Gerber Foundation

Pugh, Lawrence R.: chairman, director, Blue Bell, Inc.

Pugnetti, Wendy: director, Rayonier Foundation

Pulatie, David L.: senior vice president human resources, Phelps Dodge Corp.

Pulido, Mark A.: president, chief executive officer, director, chairman, McKesson-HBOC Corp.

Pulitzer, Michael Edgar: chairman, president, chief executive officer, director, Pulitzer Publishing Co.; chairman, president, chief executive officer, Pulitzer Publishing Co. Foundation

Pulliam, Eugene Smith: assistant treasurer, Central Newspapers Foundation

Pullo, Robert W.: chairman, chief executive officer, director, York Federal Savings & Loan Association; president, trustee, York Federal Savings & Loan Foundation

Purcell, Nancy L.: assistant secretary, Anthem Foundation, Inc.

Purcell, Paul E.: president, Baird & Co. (Robert W.)

Purcell, W. Riker: trustee, LandAmerica Foundation

Purser, Charles A.: treasurer, Occidental Oil and Gas Foundation

Purvis, George Frank, Jr.: chairman, president, chief executive officer, director, Pan-American Life Insurance Co.

Puryear, Mary: trustee, Prudential Foundation

Putman, Jerry: senior vice president, Novartis Corporation

Putnam, George, Jr.: chairman, president, chief executive officer, Putnam Investments

Pyke, John Secrest, Jr.: president, trustee, Hanna Co. Foundation (M.A.); vice president, secretary, general counsel, Hanna Co. (M.A.)

Pyrcik, Paul: chief executive officer, Waste Management Inc.

Q

Qualls, T. L.: vice president, Winn-Dixie Stores Foundation

Quass, Susan J.: program officer, Merck Co. Foundation

Queenan, Charles J., Jr.: trustee, Tippins Foundation

Quesnel, Gregory L.: president, chief executive officer, director, CNF Transportation, Inc.

Quin, Joseph Marvin: trustee, Ashland Inc. Foundation

Quinlan, Kathleen: assistant secretary, Zilkha Foundation, Inc.

Quinlan, Michael Robert: chairman executive committee, McDonald's Corp.; director, McDonald's Corp. Charitable Foundation

Quinn, David W.: executive vice president, chief financial officer, director, Centex Corp.

Quinn, Mary: vice president, director, Avon Products Foundation, Inc.

R

Rabbe, Fred M.: president, chairman executive committee, director, Shell Oil Co. Foundation

Rabbino, Robert A., Jr.: joint general manager, Sumitomo Bank; director, Sumitomo Bank Global Foundation

Raclin, Ernestine Morris: chairman emeritus, director, First Source Corp.; chairman, director, First Source Foundation

Radcliffe, R. Stephen: executive vice president, American United Life Insurance Co.

Radler, F. David: chairman, publisher, Chicago Sun-Times, Inc.

Radler, Rona: president, trustee, Chicago Sun-Times Charity Trust; chairman, publisher, Chicago Sun-Times, Inc.

Rafferty, Emily Kernan: director, Butler Foundation

Rahill, Richard E.: secretary, Corning Inc. Foundation

Rainbolt, Harold E.: chairman, SBC Foundation

Raines, Franklin Delano: chairman, chief executive officer, Fannie Mae; director, Fannie Mae Foundation

Rakowitz, Cindy: vice president public relations, Playboy Enterprises Inc.; director, Playboy Foundation

Ralph, E. Jack: vice president finance, controller, Texas Gas Transmission Corp.

Ramsay, Scott W.: trustee, Shaw's Supermarkets Charitable Foundation; executive vice president administration, treasurer, director, Shaw's Supermarkets, Inc.

Ramsey, JoElla: treasurer, American Fidelity Corp. Founders Fund

Ramsey, John D.: president, chief executive officer, director, CCB Financial Corp.; president, CCB Foundation

Ranck, Bruce E.: president, chief executive officer, director, Browning-Ferris Industries Inc.

Rand, Addison Barry: executive vice president operations, Xerox Corp.; trustee, Xerox Foundation

Randaccio, Sharon D.: executive vice president, chief financial officer, Manufacturers & Traders Trust Co.

Randall, James R.: president, director, Archer-Daniels-Midland Co.

Randall, Kenneth A.: trustee, Kemper Foundation (James S.)

Randell-Ellis, Marilyn: senior community affairs representative, Peoples Energy Corp.

Randolph, Jackson Harold: chairman, Cinergy Corp.; chairman, director, Cinergy Foundation

Randolph, Sanna: director, Autodesk Foundation

Rane, David A.: executive vice president, chief financial officer, Callaway Golf Co.; chief financial officer, Callaway Golf Co. Foundation

Rappaport, Daniel: chairman, director, New York Mercantile Exchange; president, director, New York Mercantile Exchange Charitable Foundation

Rash, Janet: vice president, US West Foundation

Raskin, Fred C.: president, chief operating officer, Eastern Enterprises; trustee, Eastern Enterprises Foundation

Rasmuson, Edward B.: director, CIRI Foundation

Rasmussen, Paul E.: officer, SIT Investment Associates Foundation; chief financial officer, SIT Investment Associates, Inc.

Raspino, Louis A., Jr.: senior vice president, chief financial officer, Louisiana Land & Exploration Co.; director, Louisiana Land & Exploration Co. Foundation

Rassi, Alan J.: vice president, Caterpillar Foundation

Ratchford, Mike: director corporate communications, Conectiv

Ratcliffe, David M.: chief financial officer, treasurer, director, Georgia Power Co.

Ratcliffe, George Jackson, Jr.: trustee, Hubbell Foundation (Harvey); chairman, president, chief executive officer, Hubbell Inc.

Ratner, Albert Benjamin: trustee, Forest City Enterprises Charitable Foundation, Inc.; co-chairman, director, Forest City Enterprises, Inc.

Rau, John E.: trustee, Chicago Title and Trust Co. Foundation

Rauchenberger, Louis J., Jr.: director, CBS Foundation
Rauman, Thomas R.: chief financial officer, DeKalb Genetics Corp.; treasurer, director, DeKalb Genetics Foundation
Rawlings, Cathy: project director, Boston Globe Foundation
Rawlins, Benjamin W., Jr.: chairman, chief executive officer, director, Union Planters Corp.
Rawlins, Charles O.: chief financial officer, treasurer, director, Georgia Power Co.; treasurer, assistant secretary, Georgia Power Foundation
Ray, John Thomas, Jr.: director, Fuller Co. Foundation (H.B.)
Ray, Terry D.: vice president business development, Eastern Enterprises
Raymond, Charles V.: president, Citigroup
Raymond, Lee R.: chairman, president, chief executive officer, Exxon Mobil Corp.
Raymond, Louise: director corporate contributions, McGraw-Hill Companies, Inc.
Read, Michael: vice president public affairs, Albertson's Inc.
Reading, Anthony John: president, trustee, Tomkins Corp. Foundation; president, chief executive officer, Tomkins Industries, Inc.
Ream, Byron A.: president, trustee, York Federal Savings & Loan Foundation
Reardon, Edward J., II: director, Commerce Bancshares Foundation
Recanati, Michael A.: vice president, director, OSG Foundation
Recanati, Raphael: executive vice president, director, OSG Foundation
Redding, Peter Stoddard: trustee, Sherman-Standard Register Foundation; president, chief executive officer, director, Standard Register Co.
Reddy, Lata: chairman, Prudential Foundation
Redgrave, Martyn R.: executive vice president, chief financial officer, Carlson Companies, Inc.
Redlinger, Donald J.: director, AlliedSignal Foundation Inc.; senior vice president human resources & communications, AlliedSignal Inc.
Redman, Charles E.: treasurer, Bechtel Foundation
Redmond, Daniel: trustee, UNUM Foundation; vice president, UnumProvident
Redmond, Paul Anthony: chairman, chief executive officer, director, Avista Corporation
Redstone, Sumner Murray: chairman, Viacom Inc.
Reed, Cynthia: assistant secretary, Hasbro Charitable Trust Inc.; senior vice president, general counsel, Hasbro, Inc.
Reed, James M.: trustee, Union Camp Charitable Trust; vice chairman, chief financial officer, director, Union Camp Corp.
Reed, John: trustee, Sunmark Foundation
Reed, John Shepard: co-chairman, Citibank Corp.
Reed, Nancy: president, Dreyer's Grand Ice Cream Charitable Foundation
Reed, Robert A.: president, chief executive officer, Physicians Mutual Insurance Co.; president, director, Physicians Mutual Insurance Co. Foundation
Reed, Scott Eldridge: senior executive vice president, chief financial officer, Branch Banking & Trust Co.
Reed, Ward: corporate vice president, chief financial officer, Telcordia Technologies
Reed, William Garrard, Jr.: director, Matlock Foundation
Reese, Ronald W.: trustee, North American Royalties Foundation
Reese, Terry W.: secretary, treasurer, Vulcan Materials Co.; assistant treasurer, Vulcan Materials Co. Foundation
Reeves, Ken: secretary, International Paper Co. Foundation
Regelbrugge, Laurie A.: director emeritus, Hitachi Foundation
Rehm, Jack Daniel: chairman emeritus, director, Meredith Corp.
Reich, Charles: executive vice president, Minnesota Mining & Manufacturing Co.
Reichardt, Carl E.: vice chairman, Wells Fargo & Co.
Reid, Frederick W.: executive vice president, chief marketing officer, Delta Air Lines, Inc.
Reid, James Sims, Jr.: chairman, director, Standard Products Co.; chairman, president, Standard Products Co. Charitable Foundation
Reid, Joyce M.: president, chief executive officer, director, Avery Dennison Corp.
Reilly, Elizabeth C.: trustee, Reilly Foundation
Reilly, Thomas E., Jr.: trustee, Reilly Foundation; chairman, chief executive officer, director, Reilly Industries, Inc.
Reily, H. Eustis: secretary, director, Reily & Co., Inc. (William B.); director, Reily Foundation
Reily, Robert D.: vice president, director, Reily & Co., Inc. (William B.); president, director, Reily Foundation
Reily, William Boatner, III: president, chief executive officer, director, Reily & Co., Inc. (William B.); director, Reily Foundation
Reiman, Thomas Jay: senior vice president public policy, Ameritech Corp.
Rein, Catherine Amelia: director, MetLife Foundation; vice president, Metropolitan Life Insurance Co.
Reinemund, Steve S.: chairman, chief executive officer, Frito-Lay, Inc.
Reinhard, J. Pedro: executive vice president, chief financial officer, director, Dow Chemical Co.
Reinhart, Marjorie A.: director, Reinhart Family Foundation (D. B. and Marjorie)
Reintjes, Robert J., Sr.: director, Butler Manufacturing Co.; member, Butler Manufacturing Co. Foundation
Reising, Richard P.: senior vice president, general counsel, secretary, Archer-Daniels-Midland Co.; secretary, Archer-Daniels-Midland Foundation
Reiter, Robin: president, trustee, BankAtlantic Foundation
Remmel, Jerry G.: chief financial officer, vice president, treasurer, Wisconsin Energy Corp.
Renfro, John F., Jr.: vice president, Inman Mills; treasurer, trustee, Inman-Riverdale Foundation
Renyi, Thomas A.: president, chief executive officer, director, Bank of New York Co., Inc.
Rescorla, Charles L.: director, Graco Foundation
Resnick, Alan H.: treasurer, Bausch & Lomb Foundation, Inc.; vice president, treasurer, Bausch & Lomb Inc.
Resnick, Lynda Rae: vice chairman, co-owner, Franklin Mint (The)
Resnick, Myron J.: vice president, secretary, Allstate Foundation
Resnick, Stewart A.: chairman, chief executive officer, Franklin Mint (The)
Retzke, Ronald E., PhD: director, Extendicare Foundation
Reusing, Vincent P.: director, MetLife Foundation; chairman, president, chief executive officer, Metropolitan Life Insurance Co.
Reuter, Carol Joan: chief executive officer, director, New York Life Foundation; vice president, New York Life Insurance Co.
Reuterfors, Robert: trustee, Woodward Governor Co. Charitable Trust
Rex, John: president, American Fidelity Corp.; treasurer, American Fidelity Corp. Founders Fund
Reyelts, Paul C.: vice president finance, chief financial officer, Valspar Corp.; vice president, assistant secretary, Valspar Foundation
Reynolds, Donna L.: vice president communications, Inland Container Corp.; vice president, director, Inland Foundation, Inc.
Reynolds, Randolph Nicklas: vice chairman, executive officer, director, Reynolds Metals Co.; director, Reynolds Metals Co. Foundation
Reynolds, William Gray, Jr.: vice president government relations & public affairs, Reynolds Metals Co.; director, Reynolds Metals Co. Foundation
Reznick, Marilyn: trustee, AT&T Foundation
Rhein, Timothy James: president, chief executive officer, APL Ltd.
Rhodes, James Thomas: president, chief executive officer, director, Dominion Resources, Inc.
Rhodes, Skip: chairman, chief executive officer, Chevron Corp.
Rhodes, William Reginald: vice chairman, Citibank Corp.
Rice, Liston Michael, Jr.: director, Texas Instruments Foundation
Rice, Nell M.: director, Belk-Simpson Foundation
Rice, William D.: senior vice president, chief financial officer, secretary, Agrilink Foods, Inc.; trustee, Agrilink Foods/Pro-Fac Foundation
Rich, David A.: executive director, Rich Family Foundation; vice president, secretary, director, Rich Products Corp.
Rich, Janet W.: assistant secretary, Rich Family Foundation; vice president, director, Rich Products Corp.
Rich, Robert E., Jr.: secretary, Rich Family Foundation; president, director, Rich Products Corp.
Rich, Robert E., Sr.: president, treasurer, Rich Family Foundation; founder, chairman, director, Rich Products Corp.
Richard, Shirley A.: vice president, director, APS Foundation, Inc.; executive vice president customer service marketing & corporate relations, Arizona Public Service Co.
Richards, E. D.: secretary board control, Ralston Purina Trust Fund
Richards, Joel, III: assistant secretary, El Paso Energy Foundation
Richards, John M.: chairman, chief executive officer, director, Potlatch Corp.; trustee, Potlatch Foundation II
Richards, Maureen: vice president, controller, West Co. Inc.; administrator, West Foundation (Herman O.)
Richards, Steve, MD: director, Blue Cross & Blue Shield of Minnesota Foundation Inc.
Richards, Thomas E.: executive vice president communications information products sector, Ameritech Corp.
Richards, Thomas S.: chairman, president, chief executive officer, Rochester Gas & Electric Corp.
Richardson, Alan: board member, PacifiCorp Foundation
Richardson, George E., Jr.: chairman contributions, Northwest Natural Gas Co.
Richardson, John P.: trustee, JSJ Foundation
Richardson, Joseph H.: vice president public affairs, Florida Power Corp.
Richelsen, Raymond C.: director, 3M Foundation; executive vice president, Minnesota Mining & Manufacturing Co.
Richie, Leroy C.: trustee, DaimlerChrysler Corp. Fund
Richie, Shawnelle: chairman, chief executive officer, president, Sears, Roebuck and Co.
Richman, M. David, PhD: secretary, Giant Food Foundation
Richmond, John L.: assistant treasurer, USX Corp.
Richter, Alice: trustee, KPMG Peat Marwick Foundation
Richter, Linda: treasurer, CBS Foundation

Richwine, Marilyn: president, Cessna Foundation, Inc.
Rickard, David: chief financial officer, Reynolds Tobacco (R.J.)
Rickettes, Carl A.: president, Western Resources Foundation
Rickman, Ronald L.: secretary, director, Lee Foundation
Ridder, Paul Anthony: chairman, chief executive officer, director, Knight Ridder
Riddick, Frank A., III: senior vice president, chief financial officer, Armstrong World Industries, Inc.
Rider, D. Brickford: vice president, Reynolds Metals Co. Foundation
Ridgley, Robert Louis: chairman, director, Northwest Natural Gas Co.
Ridgway, Ronald H.: senior vice president, Pulitzer Publishing Co.; secretary, treasurer, director, Pulitzer Publishing Co. Foundation
Riehmann, Ron: manager corporate contributions, Telcordia Technologies
Riess, John M.: chairman, Gates Rubber Corp.
Riethman, Robert B.: chief financial officer, Monarch Machine Tool Co.; treasurer, secretary, Monarch Machine Tool Co. Foundation
Riggs, William R.: executive vice president, American United Life Insurance Co.; director, AUL Foundation Inc.
Riley, Ann Marie: president, director, Dana Corp. Foundation
Riley, H. John, Jr.: chairman, president, chief executive officer, Cooper Industries Foundation; chairman, president, chief executive officer, director, Cooper Industries, Inc.
Riley, J. Michael: treasurer, First Maryland Foundation
Riley, Pat: secretary, treasurer, Bayport Foundation; director, Consolidated Natural Gas System Foundation
Rinaldi, Joseph T.: trustee, Dow Corning Foundation
Rinehart, Charles Robert: chairman, chief executive officer, director, Washington Mutual, Inc.
Ringel, Grant: vice president, treasurer, LG&E Energy Foundation
Ringler, James M.: chairman, president, chief executive officer, director, Premark International Inc.
Rinisky, Thomas G.: vice president, director, Norton Co. Foundation
Rintamaki, John M.: group vice president, chief of staff, Ford Motor Co.; secretary, Ford Motor Co. Fund
Riordan, Gerald R.: executive director, Ryder System Charitable Foundation
Riordan, Kathleen: giving coord, Phoenix Foundation; chairman, president, chief executive officer, Phoenix Home Life Mutual Insurance Co.
Ripley, Sidney Dillon, II: trustee, Hitachi Foundation
Ripp, Robert M.: chairman, chief executive officer, director, AMP Inc.
Rish, Stephen A.: vice president, corporate public involvement, Nationwide Insurance Co.; president, Nationwide Insurance Enterprise Foundation
Risinger, James A.: chairman, chief executive officer, Old National Bank Evansville
Ritondaro, G. H.: vice president, trustee, Ferro Foundation
Ritter, Cheryl: trustee, Maytag Corp. Foundation
Rittler, Jennifer: president, director, Extendicare Foundation
Roach, John Vinson, II: chairman, director, Tandy Corp.
Roadman, Ross: assistant secretary, Ryder System Charitable Foundation
Robbins, Patricia H.: secretary, Inman Mills
Robers, Ignatius H.: executive vice president, chief financial officer, First Financial Bank; director, First Financial Foundation
Roberto, Jerry: president, Telcordia Technologies
Roberts, Bert C., Jr.: chairman, MCI WorldCom, Inc.
Roberts, John Kenneth, Jr.: president, chief executive officer, director, Pan-American Life Insurance Co.
Robertson, David L.: senior vice president human resources, Rubbermaid Inc.
Robertson, E. S.: vice president, chief financial officer, Conwood Co. LP
Robin, Kenneth H.: senior vice president, general counsel, Household International Inc.
Robinette, Gary: president, Erb Lumber Co.
Robinson, Danita: assistant treasurer, Hallmark Corporate Foundation
Robinson, E. B., Jr.: chairman, chief executive officer, director, Deposit Guaranty National Bank
Robinson, Edward Joseph: president, chief operating officer, director, Avon Products, Inc.
Robinson, J. William: vice president, Piedmont Charitable Foundation
Robinson, Jack: chairman, chief executive officer, Deloitte & Touche; director, Deloitte & Touche Foundation
Robinson, John H.: director, Carter Star Telegram Employees Fund (Amon G.)
Robinson, John W., IV: vice president, treasurer, chief financial officer, Harland Co. (John H.); vice president, Piedmont Charitable Foundation
Robinson, Leroy: member board advisors, Belk Foundation
Robinson, Peter S.: assistant treasurer, Humanitas Foundation
Robinson, R. Lee: president, director, Piedmont Charitable Foundation
Robinson, Randy: first vice president, Washington Mutual, Inc.
Roblee, Martha: trustee, Rubbermaid Foundation; senior vice president human resources, Rubbermaid Inc.
Robles, Josue: chief financial officer, United Services Automobile Association
Robling, Sally G.: vice president, controller, Campbell Soup Co.; trustee, Campbell Soup Foundation
Roby, Carolyn H.: director, Norwest Foundation
Rocca, Michael A.: senior vice president, chief financial officer, Mallinckrodt Chemical, Inc.
Roche, George A.: chairman, president, Price Associates (T. Rowe)
Rock, Arthur: co-founder, chairman executive committee, director, Intel Corp.
Rockefeller, Frederic Lincoln: trustee, Cranston Foundation
Rockey, Travis O.: vice president, director, Evening Post Publishing Co.
Rodriguez, Ana R.: director, Foundation of the Litton Industries
Roe, John H.: chairman, director, Bemis Co., Inc.
Roellig, Mark D.: executive vice president, general counsel, secretary, US West, Inc.
Roesler, Deborah K.: chief financial officer, U.S. Bancorp Piper Jaffray
Roessler-Alsoa, Ernest C.: president, chief executive officer, director, CCB Financial Corp.
Rogala, Judith A.: vice president, trustee, Butler Manufacturing Co. Foundation
Roger, Brian C.: vice president, trustee, Price Associates Foundation (T. Rowe); chairman, president, Price Associates (T. Rowe)
Rogers, C. B., Jr.: chairman, Equifax Foundation; chairman, director, Equifax Inc.
Rogers, Desiree Glapion: vice president community affairs, Peoples Energy Corp.
Rogers, Glenn Robert: secretary, Alexander & Baldwin Foundation
Rogers, James E., Jr.: vice chairman, president, chief executive officer, Cinergy Corp.; vice chairman, director, Cinergy Foundation
Rogers, Joe W., Jr.: president, director, Waffle House Inc.
Rogers, Joe W., Sr.: founder, chairman, director, Waffle House Inc.
Rogers, Nancy: member grantmaking committee, Claiborne Foundation (Liz)
Rogers, T. Gary: chairman, chief executive officer, director, Dreyer's Grand Ice Cream
Rohach, Catherine: director, Graco Foundation; assistant secretary, Graco, Inc.
Rohde, Bruce: vice chairman, chief executive officer, ConAgra, Inc.
Rohr, Daniel C.: executive vice president commercial & business banking, U.S. Bancorp
Rohr, James Edward: chief executive officer, president, director, PNC Financial Services Group
Rohrkemper, Paul H.: treasurer, CIGNA Corp.; vice president, treasurer, CIGNA Foundation
Rollans, James Ora: senior vice president, chief administrative officer, chief financial officer, Fluor Corp.; trustee, Fluor Foundation
Roller, Donald E.: executive vice president, USG Corp.; vice president, USG Foundation
Rollins, Carl P.: chairman, chief executive officer, Shaw Industries Inc.
Romeril, Barry D.: executive vice president, chief financial officer, Xerox Corp.
Rompala, Richard M.: president, chief executive officer, director, chairman, Valspar Corp.; vice president, Valspar Foundation
Rooney, Patrick W.: chairman, president, chief executive officer, director, Cooper Tire & Rubber Co.
Root, Charles A.: president, director, Safeguard Scientifics Foundation
Rosa, Bruce L.: president, Lancaster Lens Foundation; chairman, president, chief executive officer, chief operating officer, director, Lancaster Lens, Inc.
Rosane, Edwin L.: president, USAA Life Insurance Co.
Rose, Karen M.: vice president, treasurer, Clorox Co.
Rose, Matthew K.: senior vice president, chief executive officer, Burlington Northern Santa Fe Corp.
Rose, Wayne Myron: president, director, Quanex Foundation
Rosen, David: trustee, Sega Foundation
Rosen, Fredric D.: president, chief executive officer, Ticketmaster Corp.; president, Ticketmaster Foundation
Rosen, Leonard M.: senior partner, Wachtell, Lipton, Rosen & Katz; vice president, secretary, Wachtell, Lipton, Rosen & Katz Foundation
Rosenberg, John K.: president, Western Resources Foundation
Rosenberg, Richard Morris: chairman, chief executive officer (retired), Bank of America
Rosenberger, David M.: treasurer, Tracy Fund (Emmet and Frances)
Rosenblatt, Roslyn: director, PPG Industries Foundation
Rosenthal, Sol: counsel, Playboy Enterprises Inc.
Rosenzweig, Richard Stuart: executive vice president, director, Playboy Enterprises Inc.
Rosett, Richard Nathaniel: chairman, Kemper Foundation (James S.)
Rosi, Frances: trustee, Circuit City Foundation
Rosilier, Glenn D.: executive vice president, chief financial officer, Central & South West Services
Ross, Arthur: senior vice president, Central National-Gottesman; director, Central National-Gottesman Foundation
Ross, Donald L.: vice president, treasurer, Enterprise Rent-A-Car Co.
Ross, Emerson J.: treasurer, Owens Corning; director, Owens Corning Foundation, Inc.

Ross, Frank K.: trustee, KPMG Peat Marwick Foundation
Ross, Katherine: chairman, Sotheby's Inc.
Ross, Tom: vice president, director, American Honda Foundation
Rossi, Endvar: vice president, Dow Corning Corp.; trustee, Dow Corning Foundation
Rossi, Nick: director, Hofmann Foundation
Rossin, Alan: materials director, Dynamet, Inc.
Rosson, William Mimms: chairman, Conwood Co. LP
Roth, John: president, chief executive officer, chief operating officer, director, Nortel
Roth, Michael I.: chairman, chief executive officer, director, MONY Group (The); director, MONY Life Insurance of New York (The)
Rothberg, Robert: vice president, general counsel, Cabot Corp.; director, Cabot Corp. Foundation
Rothermel, Elizabeth B.: director, Sovereign Bank Foundation
Rothstein, Joel: secretary, Cantor, Fitzgerald Foundation
Roub, Bryan Roger: vice president human resources corporate relations, Harris Corp.; trustee, Harris Foundation
Roundtree, Kimberly Dyslin: chairman, Georgia-Pacific Foundation
Rout, Robert E.: senior vice president, chief financial officer, S&T Bancorp
Routt, J. Robert: vice president, controller, Scripps Co. (E.W.); trustee, Scripps Howard Foundation
Roux, Michel: president, chief executive officer, director, Carillon Importers, Ltd.; president, director, Grand Marnier Foundation
Rowe, John W.: chairman, chief executive officer, Commonwealth Edison Co.
Rowe, Thomas E.: chairman, director, Fireman's Fund Foundation; director, Fireman's Fund Insurance Co.
Rowe-Adler, Susan: director community affairs, Washington Trust Bank
Rowell, Harry Brown, Jr.: trustee, Hubbell Foundation (Harvey)
Rowland, T. Keith: secretary, Unilever Foundation
Royall, Kenneth C., Jr.: director, Glaxo Wellcome Foundation
Rozelle, Mark A.: vice president, UST Inc.
Rubenstein, Jon: senior vice president, Apple Computer, Inc.
Rubenstein, Leonard Mark: executive vice president investment, director, GenAmerica Corp.; vice president, director, GenAmerican Foundation
Rubin, Donald S.: senior vice president investor relations, McGraw-Hill Companies, Inc.
Rubin, Joseph H.: director, Pheonix Foundation
Rubino, John A.: senior vice president human resources, Walgreen Co.
Ruckelshaus, William Doyle: chairman, director, Browning-Ferris Industries Inc.
Rudin, Jeffrey: vice president, general counsel, Millipore Corp.; trustee, Millipore Foundation (The)
Ruding, Herman Onno: vice chairman, director, Citibank Corp.
Rudnick, Alan A.: vice president, general counsel, corporate secretary, CSX Corp.
Ruelle, Mark A.: senior vice president, chief financial officer, Sierra Pacific Resources
Ruggiero, Anthony W.: executive vice president, chief financial officer, Olin Corp.
Rukeyser, Robert James: senior vice president corporate affairs, Fortune Brands, Inc.
Rulle, Michael: chief executive officer, CIBC Oppenheimer
Runcis, Veronica: vice president corporate affairs, Eaton Corp.
Rupley, Theodore J.: president, chief executive officer, director, Allmerica Financial Corp.
Rupple, Brenton H.: director, Bucyrus-Erie Foundation
Ruprecht, William: chief executive officer, president, Sotheby's Inc.
Russ, Gina S.: director, Ryder System Charitable Foundation
Russack, Richard A.: director, Burlington Northern Santa Fe Foundation
Russell, Frank Eli: president, Central Newspapers Foundation; chairman, Central Newspapers, Inc.
Russell, Richard C.: president, chief operating officer, director, Danis Companies; vice president, Danis Foundation
Russom, Mary S.: secretary, treasurer, Vulcan Materials Co.; chairman, Vulcan Materials Co. Foundation
Rust, Edward Barry, Jr.: chairman, president, director, State Farm Companies Foundation; chairman, president, chief executive officer, director, State Farm Mutual Automobile Insurance Co.
Ruszin, Thomas E., Jr.: assistant secretary, assistant treasurer, Baltimore Gas & Electric Foundation; treasurer, Constellation Energy Group, Inc.
Rutherford, Winthrop, Jr.: vice president, clerk, director, Butler Foundation
Rutigliano, Mary: treasurer, trustee, BankAtlantic Foundation
Rutledge, Ronald E.: executive, Butler Manufacturing Co.
Rutstein, David W.: secretary, Giant Food Foundation; senior vice president, general counsel, chief administrative officer, Giant Food Inc.
Ruvane, Joseph J., Jr.: secretary, director, Glaxo Wellcome Foundation
Ryan, Ann Marie: executive vice president, International Paper Co.; secretary, International Paper Co. Foundation
Ryan, Arthur Frederick: trustee, Chase Manhattan Foundation; chairman, chief executive officer, Prudential Insurance Co. of America
Ryan, Bob: vice chairman, Medtronic Foundation
Ryan, John Thomas, III: chairman, chief executive officer, Mine Safety Appliances Co.
Ryan, Joseph: executive vice president, general counsel, Marriott International Inc.
Ryan, Patrick G.: chairman, president, chief executive officer, Aon Corp.; president, Aon Foundation
Ryan, Richard O.: president, director, DeKalb Genetics Corp.; president, chief operating officer, DeKalb Genetics Foundation
Ryan, Thomas: president, chief operating officer, American Stock Exchange, Inc.
Rydin, Craig: trustee, Campbell Soup Foundation
Rynders, Linnea: executive vice president, Target Corp.

S

Sa, Sophie: director, Panasonic Foundation
Sabbag, Allen L.: president, Meredith Corp.
Sabin, Darryl R.: member, SAFECO Corp.
Sacks, David G.: trustee, Bronfman Foundation/Joseph E. Seagram & Sons, Inc. Fund (Samuel)
Sadler, Robert E., Jr.: chief executive officer, M&T Charitable Foundation; executive vice president, Manufacturers & Traders Trust Co.
Sadler, Robert L.: president, vice chairman, director, Old Kent Bank
Sager, Mark: director, Extendicare Foundation
Sahl, Ellen: chairman, director, Stride Rite Foundation
Sakaguchi, Russell G.: research assistant, matching gifts coordinator, ARCO Foundation
Sakurai, George S.: vice president, director, Servco Foundation
Salarantis, Pete: secretary, Mitsubishi Electric America Foundation
Sale, Alvin T.: director, First Union Foundation
Salerno, Mary Beth: director, American Express Foundation
Sales, A. R.: director, Arvin Foundation; treasurer, Arvin Industries, Inc.
Salinger, Robert M.: director, First Financial Foundation
Salizzoni, Frank L.: vice chairman, Block Foundation (H&R); president, chief executive officer, director, Block, Inc. (H&R)
Salley, Kim: trustee, McKesson Foundation; president, chief executive officer, director, chairman, McKesson-HBOC Corp.
Salome, Bruce W.: senior vice president, chief financial officer, S&T Bancorp; vice president, S&T Bancorp Charitable Foundation
Salomon, Mary: trustee, Lubrizol Foundation (The)
Salvi, Walter E.: trustee, Boston Edison Foundation
Samuels, Ethel: chairman, chief executive officer, director, Tenneco Automotive
Sand, Morton: trustee, Merit Gasoline Foundation
Sandbach, Henry A.: member administration committee, Nabisco Foundation Trust
Sanders, D. Faye: trustee, Citizens Charitable Foundation
Sanders, John W.: trustee, Cleveland-Cliffs Foundation (The); senior vice president, international development, Cleveland-Cliffs, Inc.
Sanders, Lewis A.: trustee, Bernstein & Co. Foundation, Inc. (Sanford C.); chairman, chief executive officer, Bernstein & Co., Inc. (Sanford C.)
Sanders, Walter Jeremiah, III: chairman, chief executive officer, director, Advanced Micro Devices, Inc.
Sanders, Wayne R.: chairman, chief executive officer, director, Kimberly-Clark Corp.
Sandman, Dan D.: senior vice president human resources, secretary, general counsel, USX Corp.; trustee, USX Foundation, Inc.
Saneishi-Kim, Sherelee: president,
Sanger, Carol A.: executive vice president, Federated Department Stores, Inc.
Sanger, Stephen W.: chairman, trustee, General Mills Foundation; chairman, chief executive officer, director, General Mills, Inc.
Sansone, Thomas M.: chief financial officer, Reynolds Tobacco (R.J.); assistant treasurer, RJR Nabisco Foundation
Santiago, Ken: director, Chicago Tribune Foundation
Santiga, Ken: treasurer, Chicago Tribune Foundation
Santucci, Diani: vice president health & safety, Bestfoods
Sargent, Joseph Dudley: president, chief executive officer, director, Guardian Life Insurance Co. of America
Saricea, Lew: program officer, BankAtlantic Foundation
Sarin, Arun: director, AirTouch Communications Foundation; president, chief operating officer, vice chairman, vice president, Vodafone AirTouch Plc
Sasaki, Robert K.: secretary, Alexander & Baldwin Foundation
Sasso, John: director, Fannie Mae Foundation
Sather, (H.) Dennis: president, director, PACCAR Foundation
Sato, Suzanne M.: president, trustee, AT&T Foundation
Satre, Philip Glen: chairman, president, chief executive officer, director, Promus Hotel Corp.
Saul, Bernard: secretary-treasurer, Cenex Harvest States Foundation
Saul, Julian D.: president, Shaw Industries Inc.

Savage, John: assistant secretary, assistant treasurer, Mitsubishi Electric America Foundation
Savage, Terry: senior vice president public affairs, American Express Co.; director, American Express Foundation
Savedge, Henry S., Jr.: executive vice president, chief financial officer, director, Reynolds Metals Co.; executive vice president, director, Reynolds Metals Co. Foundation
Sawai, Mary: vice president, director, Transamerica Foundation
Sawchuck, Arthur: chairman, director, Manulife Financial
Sawyer, Bo: secretary, NCR Foundation
Saxelby, William E.: president, director, Baxter Allegiance Foundation
Sayre, Robert H.: executive vice president human resources, U.S. Bancorp
Scanlon, Jean: member contributions committee, Clorox Co.; chairman, Clorox Co. Foundation
Scarbrough, Arlan Earl: vice president financial, Gulf Power Co.; trustee, Gulf Power Foundation
Schacht, Henry Brewer: director, Cummins Engine Foundation
Schadt, James Phillip: chairman, president, chief executive officer, director, Reader's Digest Association, Inc. (The); chairman, director, Reader's Digest Foundation
Schaefer, George A., Jr.: president, Fifth Third Bancorp
Schaefer, Judy E.: chairman, chief executive officer, director, Morton International Inc.
Schaeffer, Richard: president, director, New York Mercantile Exchange Charitable Foundation
Schaeffer, Wayne G.: community president, Citizens Bank-Flint
Schafer, Glenn Stanley: president, director, Pacific Mutual Life Insurance Co.
Schaffer, Donald J.: vice president finance, chief financial officer, GATX Corp.
Schamberger, John P.: member advisory board, Blue Bell Foundation; president, chairman jeanswear coalition, Blue Bell, Inc.
Schara, Charles Gerard: treasurer, GEICO Corp.; assistant treasurer, director, GEICO Philanthropic Foundation
Schechter, Loren: president capital marketings, director, member executive committee, Prudential Securities Inc.
Scheid, Steven L.: executive vice president, chief financial officer, Schwab & Co., Inc. (Charles)
Scheper, Fran: chairman, chief executive officer, CPI Corp.
Scher, Barry F.: vice president public affairs, Giant Food Inc.
Schermer, Lloyd G.: chairman, director, Lee Enterprises
Scheurer, Charles B.: chairman, president, chief executive officer, director, Diebold, Inc.
Schick, Thomas E.: executive vice president corporate affairs & communications, American Express Co.; trustee, American Express Foundation
Schiek, Fredrick A.: executive vice president, chief operating officer, Employers Mutual Casualty Co.
Schiek, Lisa: senior vice president, chief financial officer, Gucci America Inc.
Schievelbein, Thomas C.: executive vice president, Newport News Shipbuilding
Schilmoeller, Denis: trustee, Cenex Harvest States Foundation
Schimpf, Glenn P.: chairman, Danis Companies; vice president, Danis Foundation
Schiro, James J.: chairman, senior partner, PricewaterhouseCoopers
Schlag, Darwin W., Jr.: vice president, chairman of planning committee, Group Health Foundation
Schlauch, Walter F.: group vice president, National Starch & Chemical Co.
Schlinker, Margie L.: president, chief executive officer, director, Mallinckrodt Chemical, Inc.
Schloss, Douglas: secretary, Rexford Fund; chairman, chief executive officer, Schloss & Co. (Marcus)
Schloss, Richard: treasurer, Rexford Fund; president, Schloss & Co. (Marcus)
Schlumberger, Pierre Marcel: director, Schlumberger Foundation; executive vice president, chief financial officer, Schlumberger Ltd. (USA)
Schmedding, Gary N.: chairman, director, Lee Enterprises; vice president, director, Lee Foundation
Schmidhammer, Joseph E.: president, Lancaster Lens Foundation
Schmidt, George W.: controller, assistant secretary, American General Finance
Schmidt, Jill W.: vice president communications, International Multifoods Corp.
Schmidt, Peter W.: vice president, director, Cowen Foundation
Schmidt, Sylvia: director community relations, Williams
Schmitt, Henry A.: vice president,
Schmitt, Jerry: director, First Union Foundation
Schmitt, Wolfgang Rudolph: chairman, chief executive officer, director, Rubbermaid Inc.
Schmitz, Michael D.: chairman, chief executive officer, director, Brunswick Corp.; secretary, Brunswick Foundation
Schneider, Bonnie: trustee, Donaldson Foundation
Schneider, Robert F.: officer, Habig Foundation; executive vice president, chief financial officer, assistant treasurer, Kimball International, Inc.
Schoch, Steven J.: vice president, treasurer, Times Mirror Co.; treasurer, chief financial officer, Times Mirror Foundation
Schoellkopf, Wolfgang: vice chairman, chief credit officer, First Union National Bank, NA
Schoenecker, Guy: president, chief executive officer, Business Improvement; president, Schoeneckers Foundation
Schoenecker, Larry: president, Schoeneckers Foundation
Schoenholz, David A.: executive vice president, chief financial officer, Household International Inc.
Schoening, Robert Walters: senior vice president information systems, Giant Food Inc.
Schoenwetter, L. James: director, Minnesota Mining & Manufacturing Co.
Scholtens, Jean A.: vice president, treasurer, Eastern Enterprises
Schoon, Susan Wylie: trustee, Chase Manhattan Foundation
Schrader, Thomas F.: vice president, director, WICOR Foundation
Schrekengost, Kim: chairman, director, Home Depot, Inc.
Schrempp, Jurgen E.: chairman, DaimlerChrysler Corp.
Schrickel, Patrick D.: secretary, assistant treasurer, Wisconsin Public Service Foundation, Inc.
Schroeder, John M.: senior vice president, advisor, Johnson & Son (S.C.); treasurer, Johnson Wax Fund (S.C.)
Schroeder, Lorraine D.: trustee, Reilly Foundation
Schubach, John J.: senior vice president strategic management, Timken Co. (The); trustee, advisor, Timken Co. Charitable Trust (The)
Schubert, Rolf B.: president, director, Fuller Co. Foundation (H.B.)
Schuchardt, Daniel Norman: vice president, director, FMC Foundation
Schuchinski, Luis: vice president taxes, Bestfoods
Schueler, John R.: publisher, president, McClatchy Co.
Schuenke, Donald John: director, Freddie Mac; executive director, Freddie Mac Foundation
Schueppert, George Louis: chief financial officer, executive vice president, Outboard Marine Corp.
Schuh, Dale R.: president, chief executive officer, Sentry Insurance, A Mutual Co.
Schuit, Alexander J.: president, chief executive officer, chief financial officer, Van Leer Holding
Schulman, David R.: treasurer, director, Katten, Muchin & Zavis Foundation
Schulter, Linda M.: trustee,
Schultz, Christopher F.: director, ASARCO Foundation
Schumacher, Mary J.: vice president, chief technical officer, Ecolab Inc.
Schuman, Allan L.: president, chief executive officer, director, chairman, Ecolab Inc.
Schuneman, Chris: employee representative, Mitsubishi Electric America Foundation
Schurz, James Montgomery: president, Schurz Communications Foundation; chief financial officer, controller, South Bend Tribune Corp.
Schurz, Todd F.: vice president, Schurz Communications Foundation; president, publisher, editor, director, South Bend Tribune Corp.
Schwab, Charles R.: chairman, co-chief executive officer, director, Schwab & Co., Inc. (Charles); chairman, Schwab Corp. Foundation (Charles)
Schwab, Cindy A.: president, chief operating officer, director, Abbott Laboratories; vice president, Abbott Laboratories Fund
Schwanke, Lawrence E.: trustee, Bemis Co. Foundation; chairman, director, Bemis Co., Inc.
Schwartz, Andy: trustee, Fluor Foundation
Schwartz, Barry K.: chairman, chief executive officer, director, Calvin Klein
Schwartz, H. G., Jr.: mem, Sverdrup Corp. Charitable Trust
Schwartz, Peter A.: chief financial officer, consultant, Computer Associates International, Inc.
Schwartz, Richard: chairman, president, chief executive officer, director, Alliant Techsystems
Schwartz, Ronald M.: executive vice president, director, Paine Webber; trustee, Paine Webber Foundation
Schwarz, H. Marshall: chairman, chief executive officer, United States Trust Co. of New York
Schwebel, Joseph M.: president, director, Schwebel Baking Co.; trustee, Schwebel Family Foundation
Schweitzer, Peter A.: president, Thompson Co. (J. Walter)
Scicutella, John Vincent: trustee, Chase Manhattan Foundation
Scott, Alison: president, Dickson Foundation
Scott, David J.: president, United Distillers & Vintners North America
Scott, David William: secretary, Ford Motor Co. Fund
Scott, Elizabeth: chairman emeritus, director, Becton Dickinson & Co.
Scott, Jan: director, Wisconsin Power & Light Foundation, Inc.
Scott, Larry P.: vice president, Pricewaterhouse-Coopers
Scott, Michael L.: secretary, treasurer, Alabama Power Foundation
Scott, Taylor C., CPA: director, Group Health Foundation
Scott, Walter, Jr.: administrator, Kiewit Companies Foundation
Scripps, Charles Edward: chairman executive committee, director, vice president, Scripps Co. (E.W.); member, Scripps Howard Foundation
Scripps, Edward Wyllis, II: trustee, Scripps Howard Foundation

Scripps, Maggie: member, Scripps Howard Foundation

Scripps, Paul K.: vice president, director, Scripps Co. (E.W.); trustee, Scripps Howard Foundation

Scripps, Robert P., Jr.: trustee, Scripps Co. (E.W.)

Sear, Timothy R. G.: trustee, Alcon Foundation; president, chief executive officer, Alcon Laboratories, Inc.

Sease, Gene Elwood: director, Central Newspapers Foundation

Seay, Thomas Patrick: trustee, Wal-Mart Foundation

Sebesta, Carol A.: vice president, Abbott Laboratories Fund

Seiffert, Ron J.: vice chairman, Huntington Bancshares Inc.

Seita, Pat: vice president, trust officer, SunTrust Banks of Florida; contact, SunTrust Banks Foundation

Seitz, Crystal A.: executive vice president corporate affairs, GPU Inc.

Self, Evelyn: director, Warner-Lambert Charitable Foundation

Seltzer, Maryanne: contributions officer, Farmers Group Safety Foundation

Semler, Jerry D.: chairman, president, chief executive officer, director, American United Life Insurance Co.; chairman, director, AUL Foundation Inc.

Sempier, Philip J.: vice president, treasurer, Chubb Corp.; president, treasurer, Chubb Foundation

Senechal, Ellen M.: treasurer, Montana Power Co.

Senger, Alan F.: president, TRW Foundation

Senkler, Robert L.: president, director, Minnesota Mutual Foundation; chairman, president, chief executive officer, Minnesota Mutual Life Insurance Co.

Seramur, John C.: president, chief executive officer, director, First Financial Bank

Serda, Gary F.: secretary, director, Sun Microsystems Foundation, Inc.

Seremet, Peter M.: treasurer, United Distillers & Vintners North America

Sergi, Vincent A. F.: director, Katten, Muchin & Zavis Foundation

Setterstrom, William N.: senior executive vice president, chief financial officer, Northern Trust Co.; chairman contributions committee, Northern Trust Co. Charitable Trust

Setzner, Leah Manning: vice president, general counsel, corporate secretary, Illinois Power Co.

Sexter, Alan S.: president, Rexford Fund; chief financial officer, Schloss & Co. (Marcus)

Seymour, S. Mark: president, director, Praxair Foundation

Shafer, Douglas C.: trustee, Tektronix Foundation; president, America operations, Tektronix, Inc.

Shaffer, Donald S.: president, chief operating officer, Heilig-Meyers Co.

Shaffer, Oren G.: executive vice president, chief financial officer, Ameritech Corp.

Shaffer, Robert L.: vice president, director, United Dominion Foundation; vice president, United Dominion Industries, Ltd.

Shafran, Nathan P.: vice chairman, director, Forest City Enterprises, Inc.

Shaia, Jacquelyn S.: director, Alabama Power Foundation

Shanahan, William: president, Colgate-Palmolive Co.

Shane, John A.: trustee, Eastern Bank Charitable Foundation

Shaner, John: vice president corporate relations, Dana Corp.

Shanks, David C.: trustee, Little Foundation (Arthur D.); vice president human resources, Little, Inc. (Arthur D.)

Shannon, Michael E.: chairman, chief financial officer, chief administration officer, director, Ecolab Inc.

Shapira, David S.: trustee, Giant Eagle Foundation; chairman, chief executive officer, director, Giant Eagle Inc.

Shapiro, Howard: executive vice president, general counsel, Playboy Enterprises Inc.; director, Playboy Foundation

Shapiro, Isaac: vice president, trustee, Ise Cultural Foundation

Shapiro, Robert B.: chairman, president, chief executive officer, director, Monsanto Co.

Share, Elizabeth: president, Autodesk Foundation

Sharkey, William Henry, Jr.: director, CNA Foundation

Sharp, Richard L.: trustee, Circuit City Foundation; chairman, chief executive officer, director, Circuit City Stores, Inc.

Sharpe, James G.: treasurer, Dow Corning Foundation

Sharpe, Robert Francis, Jr.: senior vice president public affairs, general counsel, PepsiCo, Inc.; assistant treasurer, RJR Nabisco Foundation

Shaw, Albert T.: president, Hofmann Co.; director, Hofmann Foundation

Shaw, Joseph A.: president, TENNANT Co. Foundation

Shaw, Julius C., Jr.: executive vice president corporate communications, Shaw Industries Inc.

Shaw, Klare E.: bookkeeper, Boston Globe Foundation

Shaw, L. Edward, Jr.: general counsel, Aetna, Inc.; trustee, Chase Manhattan Foundation

Shaw, Robert E.: chairman, chief executive officer, Shaw Industries Inc.

Shaw, William J.: president, chief operating officer, Marriott International Inc.

Shea, Edmund H., Jr.: secretary, Shea Co. Foundation (J. F.); executive vice president, Shea Co. (John F.)

Shea, John F.: president, Shea Co. Foundation (J. F.); chief executive officer, director, Shea Co. (John F.)

Shea, Peter O.: secretary, Shea Co. Foundation (J. F.)

Shea, Tom: president, Western Resources Foundation

Sheafer, William L.: vice president, treasurer, Cinergy Corp.; treasurer, director, Cinergy Foundation

Sheahan, Mark: treasurer, Graco Foundation

Sheahan, Patrick M.: assistant treasurer, Sara Lee Foundation

Sheehan, Jeremiah J.: executive vice president, director, Reynolds Metals Co. Foundation

Sheets, Thomas R.: vice president, general counsel, Southwest Gas Corp.; trustee, Southwest Gas Corp. Foundation

Sheft, Hope Grittis: vice president, Revlon Foundation Inc.; president, director, Revlon Inc.

Shehan, Dave: director, Piper Jaffray Companies Foundation; chief financial officer, U.S. Bancorp Piper Jaffray

Sheley, Donald R., Junior: vice president finance, chief financial officer, Standard Products Co.; treasurer, trustee, Standard Products Co. Charitable Foundation

Shell, Fred: vice president public policy, Michigan Consolidated Gas Co.

Shelley, James Herbert: chairman, Sonoco Foundation; executive vice president, Sonoco Products Co.

Sheneman, Celia: vice president, director corporate relations, Coors Brewing Co.

Shepard, Donald James: chairman, president, chief executive officer, AEGON U.S.A. Inc.

Shepherd, Kathleen Shearen Maynard: director, Tribune New York Foundation

Sherbrooke, Ross E.: program officer, Fidelity Foundation

Sherin, Keith S.: manager, comptroller, GE Fund

Sherman, Charles F.: vice president, Sherman-Standard Register Foundation

Sherman, James L.: trustee, Sherman-Standard Register Foundation

Sherman, John Q., II: president, Sherman-Standard Register Foundation

Sherman, Joseph: trustee, Chicago Sun-Times Charity Trust; vice president, assistant publisher, Chicago Sun-Times, Inc.

Sherman, Saul S.: vice chairman, director, Trace International Holdings, Inc.

Sherwood, Lynne: trust, JSJ Foundation

Shewbridge, Chuck: treasurer, BellSouth Foundation

Shibata, Kenji: president, Bridgestone/Firestone, Inc.

Shideler, Shirley Ann Williams: president, Central Newspapers Foundation

Shiel, William A.: senior vice president facilities development, Walgreen Co.

Shields, Shirley M.: trustee, Commercial Intertech Foundation

Shiely, John Stephen: president, chief operating officer, director, Briggs & Stratton Corp.; vice president, director, Briggs & Stratton Corp. Foundation

Shiffman, Joellen M.: chief financial officer, Reynolds Tobacco (R.J.)

Shigley, John: executive vice president, Caesar's World, Inc.

Shimayama, Tomoharu: president, Hitachi America Ltd.

Shinkel, Donald: executive vice president, Wal-Mart Stores, Inc.

Shinn, George Latimer: director, New York Times Co. Foundation

Shipley, Larry: chief financial officer, IBP

Shisler, Arden L.: president, Nationwide Insurance Enterprise Foundation

Shoemate, Charles Richard: chairman, president, chief executive officer, Bestfoods

Sholty, Paul: director, GATX Corp.

Shore, Sue S.: vice president, Piedmont Charitable Foundation

Shortal, Vicki: secretary, trustee, Dayton Power and Light Co. Foundation

Shourd, Roy Ray: director, Schlumberger Foundation

Shuster, George Whitcomb: trustee, Cranston Foundation; president, chief executive officer, director, Cranston Print Works Co.

Shyrock, Larry: vice president, treasurer, Chase Bank of Texas Foundation, Inc.

Sibol, Mike: director, Susquehanna-Pfaltzgraff Co.

Sidgmore, John W.: vice chairman, MCI WorldCom, Inc.

Sidhu, Jay S.: president, chief executive officer, Sovereign Bank; director, Sovereign Bank Foundation

Siegel, Jeannette: chairman, chief executive officer, director, Penney Co., Inc. (J.C.)

Siegel, Jerome A.: chairman, treasurer, director, Titan Industrial Corp.; president, treasurer, Titan Industrial Foundation

Siegel, Louis Pendelton: chairman, president, chief executive officer, chief operating officer, Potlatch Corp.; vice president, trustee, Potlatch Foundation II

Siegel, Samuel: vice chairman, secretary, treasurer, chief financial officer, director, Nucor Corp.; director, Nucor Foundation

Siegle, Helen: president, chief executive officer, director, Lipton Co.; administrator, Lipton Foundation

Siewert, Penny: vice president regional services, United Wisconsin Services; vice president, secretary, treasurer, United Wisconsin Services Foundation

Sikkema, Karen Ann: administrator, Unocal Foundation

Sills, R. A.: assistant secretary, Armstrong Foundation; senior vice president, chief financial officer, Armstrong World Industries, Inc.

Silver-Parker, Esther: vice president education program, AT&T Foundation

Silverman, Fred: chairman, director, Apple Computer, Inc.

Simmons, Glenn Reuben: vice chairman, Contran Corp.

Simmons, Hardwick: president, chief executive officer, director, Prudential Securities Inc.

Simmons, Harold Clark: vice chairman, Contran Corp.; chairman, director, Simmons Foundation, Inc. (Harold)

Simmons, Hildy J.: managing director, Morgan Charitable Trust (J.P.); vice chairman, Morgan & Co. Inc. (J.P.)

Simmons, Richard Paul: chairman, president, chief executive officer, Allegheny Technologies Inc.

Simock, Debbie: chairman, chief executive officer, director, Avista Corporation

Simone, Virginia: assistant treasurer, Dun & Bradstreet Corp. Foundation, Inc.

Simons, Doyle: president, Temple-Inland Foundation; director investor relations, Temple-Inland Inc.

Simons, W. Lucas: secretary, treasurer, Bradford and Co. Foundation (J.C.)

Simplot, Donald J.: chief financial officer, Simplot Co. (J.R.); vice president, Simplot Foundation (J.R.)

Simplot, John Richard: chairman, founder, Simplot Co. (J.R.); president, Simplot Foundation (J.R.)

Simpson, Andrea Lynn: president, Tesoro Hawaii

Simpson, Carolyn: vice president, director, WICOR Foundation

Simpson, David Louis, III: vice president, chief financial officer, Conwood Co. LP

Simpson, Irma E.: assistant treasurer, Gannett Foundation

Simpson, Kate M.: director, Belk-Simpson Foundation

Simpson, Louis Allen: president, chief executive officer capital operations, director, GEICO Corp.

Simpson, Phyllis T.: secretary, Duke Energy; assistant secretary, Duke Energy Foundation

Simpson, Robert L.: trustee, York Federal Savings & Loan Foundation

Simpson, William H.: president, Susquehanna-Pfaltzgraff Co.; secretary, Susquehanna-Pfaltzgraff Foundation

Sims, Frank: director, Cargill Foundation; member contributions committee, Cargill Inc.

Sims, Philip Stuart: vice chairman, treasurer, Premier Industrial Corp.

Sims, Raymond J.: controller, assistant secretary, American General Finance Foundation

Sindoni, Linda: chairman contributions committee, Interpublic Group of Companies, Inc.

Singh, Manoj: director-at-large, Deloitte & Touche Foundation

Singleton, Matt: managing director, CIBC Oppenheimer

Singsank, Robert J.: corporate vice president, Telcordia Technologies

Sink, Ronald E.: secretary, Norfolk Southern Foundation

Siska, Nancy P.: director, Cargill Foundation; member contributions committee, Cargill Inc.

Sislak, G. G.: vice president, trustee, Ferro Foundation

Sissel, George A.: chairman, president, chief executive officer, director, Ball Corp.

Sit, Debra A.: director, SIT Investment Associates Foundation

Sit, Eugene C.: director, SIT Investment Associates Foundation; chairman, chief executive officer, director, SIT Investment Associates, Inc.

Sittinger, Tammy: vice president, director, Square D Foundation

Siverts, Mary Sylvia: vice president, Brown Shoe Co., Inc.

Skelly, Thomas Francis: director

Skidmore, Brenda L.: trustee, Chesapeake Corp. Foundation; secretary, treasurer, Crestar Foundation

Skiles, Win: vice president, Texas Instruments Foundation; senior vice president, Texas Instruments Inc.

Skilling, Raymond Inwood: executive vice president, chief counsel, director, Aon Corp.; director, Aon Foundation

Skillrud, Diane: assistant to chairman, Ultramar Diamond Shamrock Corp.

Skinner, Claire Corson: chairman, chief executive officer, Coachmen Industries, Inc.

Skoda, Daniel: president, Marshall Field's

Skovholt, G. J.: director, Honeywell Foundation

Skule, John L., III: senior vice president corporate environmental affairs, Bristol-Myers Squibb Co.; director, Bristol-Myers Squibb Foundation Inc.

Skurek, John C.: vice president, treasurer, LTV Corp.; trustee, LTV Foundation

Skurlock, J. M.: president, Osborne Foundation (Weldon F.)

Slagle, Robert F.: director, Alcoa Foundation; executive vice president human resources and communications, Alcoa Inc.

Slaughter, William L., Jr.: vice president finance, Synovus Charitable Trust

Slavin, Morton A.: secretary, director, Housen Foundation

Slizewski, Bea B.: vice president corporate communications, Agrilink Foods, Inc.

Sloan, Albert Frazier: director, Lance Foundation

Sloan, Sue: chairman, executive director, PPG Industries Foundation

Slovin, Bruce: president, director, Revlon Inc.

Small, Lawrence Malcolm: president, chief operating officer, Fannie Mae; director, Fannie Mae Foundation

Smart, George M.: president, trustee, Commercial Intertech Foundation

Smart, Roger B.: secretary, treasurer, Temple-Inland Foundation

Smelkinson, Karen: chief financial officer, Callaway Golf Co. Foundation

Smiekar, Thomas J.: vice president, trustee, Potlatch Foundation II

Smillie, Carolyn: chairman, director, Home Depot, Inc.

Smith, Arthur O.: director, Smith Foundation, Inc. (A.O.)

Smith, Claibourne D.: executive vice president corporate strategy & development, du Pont de Nemours & Co. (E.I.)

Smith, D. Scarborough, III: joint general manager, Sumitomo Bank; director, Sumitomo Bank Global Foundation

Smith, Dan F.: president, chief executive officer, director, Lyondell Chemical Co.

Smith, David S.: vice president finance, chief financial officer, Crane Co.; executive vice president, controller, Crane Foundation

Smith, Diane M.: vice president, director, First National Bank of Chicago Foundation

Smith, Donald Kaye: senior vice president, general counsel, director, GEICO Corp.

Smith, E. Berry: president, Schurz Communications Foundation

Smith, Elizabeth Patience: director, Texaco Foundation; vice president investor relations & shareholder service, Texaco Inc.

Smith, Estella W.: manager community relations

Smith, Frederick C.: trustee, Huffy Foundation, Inc.

Smith, Frederick Wallace: chairman, president, chief executive officer, director, FedEx Corp.

Smith, Geoffrey: secretary, Brunswick Foundation

Smith, Gilbert H., Jr.: director, Bell Atlantic-Delaware, Inc.

Smith, Gordon: senior program manager, Pacific Gas and Electric Co.

Smith, Gordon L., Jr.: trustee, North American Royalties Foundation

Smith, Grace: director, Alcoa Foundation

Smith, Gregory L.: chief financial officer, treasurer, Duriron Co., Inc.; treasurer, Duriron Foundation

Smith, J.: treasurer, Abbott Laboratories Fund

Smith, Jack A.: senior vice president, Reader's Digest Association, Inc. (The)

Smith, James C.: president, Smith Foundation Inc. (Harold Webster); chairman, chief executive officer, Webster Bank

Smith, John Francis, Jr.: chairman, General Motors Corp.

Smith, Kendra: vice president, treasurer, Lilly & Co. (Eli); secretary, Lilly Foundation (Eli)

Smith, LaDonna: chairman, chief executive officer, director, Owens-Illinois Inc.

Smith, Menlo F.: trustee, Sunmark Foundation

Smith, Nancy Z.: vice president, Sumitomo Bank; treasurer, Sumitomo Bank Global Foundation

Smith, Oliver C.: secretary, Menasha Corp. Foundation

Smith, Philip N., Jr.: treasurer, Trace International Holdings, Inc. Foundation

Smith, Raymond W.: chairman, chief executive officer, director, Bell Atlantic Corp.

Smith, Richard Alan: treasurer, director, Arvin Foundation; chairman, chief executive officer, director, Arvin Industries, Inc.; chairman, director, chief executive officer, Harcourt General, Inc.

Smith, Richard C.: chief executive officer, director, Telcordia Technologies

Smith, Richard Donald: president, director, Chubb Corp.

Smith, Robert A.: trustee, Harcourt General Charitable Foundation; co-chief executive officer, director, president, Harcourt General, Inc.

Smith, Robert N.: secretary, Philips Electronics North America Corp.

Smith, Sylvia: director community relations, Williams; managing director, Williams Companies Foundation (The)

Smith, W. Keith: senior vice chairman, member corporate review committee, director, Mellon Financial Corp.

Smith, W. Read: assistant treasurer, RJR Nabisco Foundation

Smith, William C.: controller, Ameritas Charitable Foundation

Smith, William D.: secretary, treasurer, trustee, Kemper Foundation (James S.)

Smithies, Dave: president, director, Waldbaum's Supermarkets, Inc.

Smoot, Richard Leonard: chairman, PNC Bank

Smucker, Timothy Paul: chairman, director, Smucker Co. (JM)

Smurfit, Michael William J.: chairman, Smurfit-Stone Container Corp.

Snedeker, William: vice president, general manager pest elimination, Ecolab Inc.

Snell, Richard: chairman, president, chief executive officer, director, Arizona Public Service Co.

Snider, Timothy R.: senior vice president, Phelps Dodge Corp.

Snow, John William: chairman, president, chief executive officer, CSX Corp.

Snyder, Bill: president, chief executive officer, CSR Rinker Materials Corp.

Snyder, Carole B.: executive vice president corporate affairs, GPU Foundation; chairman, president, chief executive officer, GPU Inc.

Snyder, Dale E.: senior vice president, technical services, Kohler Co.

Snyder, Donna D.: executive vice president, chief financial officer, Carlson Companies, Inc.; secretary, Carlson Family Foundation (Curtis L.)

Snyder, Frank Ronald, II: president, Lehigh Portland Cement Co.

Snyder, Mary Ann: director, High Meadow Foundation
Snyder, Nancy T.: trustee, Whirlpool Foundation
Snyder, Richard A.: treasurer, director, TENNANT Co. Foundation
Soden, Paul A.: senior vice president, secretary, general counsel, Reader's Digest Association, Inc. (The)
Soderquist, Donald G.: trustee, Wal-Mart Foundation; senior vice chairman, director, Wal-Mart Stores, Inc.
Sodhani, Arvind: corp. vice president, treasurer, Intel Corp.; treasurer, Intel Foundation
Solipante, Robert C.: senior vice president, ReliaStar Financial Corp.
Solomon, Frances: chairman, director, Schwebel Baking Co.; trustee, Schwebel Family Foundation
Solso, Theodore Matthew: president, chief operating officer, director, Cummins Engine Co., Inc.; director, Cummins Engine Foundation
Somers, Daniel E.: senior executive vice president, chief financial officer, AT&T Corp.
Sommer, Charles S.: member board control, Ralston Purina Trust Fund
Sonstegard, David A.: director, Minnesota Mining & Manufacturing Co.
Sopranos, Orpheus Javaras: corporate vice president, Amsted Industries Inc.
Sorenson, Arne M.: executive vice president, chief financial officer, Marriott International Inc.
Sosa, Enrique J.: executive vice president, chief financial officer, director, Dow Chemical Co.; trustee, Dow Chemical Co. Foundation
Sosland, Morton Irvin: director, Block Foundation (H&R)
Soulliere, Anne-Marie: trustee, Fidelity Foundation
Southerland, Pat L.: director, Alabama Power Foundation
Spaeth, Karl Henry: president, chief executive officer, director, Quaker Chemical Corp.; chairman, trustee, Quaker Chemical Foundation
Spangler, Phillip A.: vice president, treasurer, Yellow Corp.; treasurer, secretary, Yellow Corp. Foundation
Sparks, Walter Alvon, Jr.: senior vice president, general counsel, director, GEICO Corp.; director, GEICO Philanthropic Foundation
Speice, Byron D.: corporate vice president, Amsted Industries Inc.
Spence, Bryan K.: contributions administrator, New England Financial
Spence, Will B.: director, Wachovia Foundation, Inc. (The)
Spencer, Gina: president, chief executive officer, Kendall International, Inc.
Spencer, JoLeen: secretary, treasurer, Harris Bank Foundation
Spiegel, Jeff: senior community relations representative, Mervyn's California
Spiegel, John William: chairman, SunTrust Bank Atlanta Foundation
Spies, Allan R.: executive vice president, chief financial officer, US West, Inc.
Spies, John: assistant treasurer, Harnischfeger Industries Foundation
Spilman, Robert H.: chairman, chief executive officer, Bassett Furniture Industries; chairman, director, Bassett Furniture Industries Fdn.
Spina, David Anthony: president, chief operating officer, State Street Bank & Trust Co.
Spindler, George S.: senior vice president law & corporate affairs, BP Amoco Corp.; chairman, director, BP Amoco Foundation
Splinter, Betty Ann M.: director, Hawaiian Electric Industries Charitable Foundation
Spoon, Alan Gary: president, chief operating officer, director, The Washington Post
Spooner, Don: vice president, GATX Corp.
Spooner, John P.: senior vice president international, Ecolab Inc.
Spradlin, Diane: chairman, chief executive officer, director, EDS Corp.
Spraker, Cindy: president, chief executive officer, Sentinel Communications Co.
Sprieser, Judith A.: deputy director, Sara Lee Foundation
Springer, Denis E.: senior vice president, chief financial officer, Burlington Northern Santa Fe Corp.; director, Burlington Northern Santa Fe Foundation
Springer, Neil A.: secretary, treasurer, executive officer, CUNA Mutual Group Foundation, Inc.
Sproule, Michael E.: chief financial officer, director, AmerUS Group
Spurgeon, Larry D.: director, Koch Foundation, Inc. (Fred C. and Mary R.)
Squires, Vernon T.: president, director, ServiceMaster Foundation
St. Dennis, Donald: secretary, Toro Foundation
Stacko, Laura: trustee, LTV Foundation
Staffieri, Victor A.: vice president, LG&E Energy Foundation
Staheli, Donald L.: chairman, director, Continental Grain Co.; vice president, director, Continental Grain Foundation
Stahl, Jack L.: president, Coca-Cola Co.
Stair, Charles W.: vice chairman international, director, ServiceMaster Co.
Stalder, Ruedi: trustee, Credit Suisse First Boston Foundation Trust
Staley, Robert Wayne: vice chairman Asia Pacific, Emerson Electric Co.
Staley, Warren R.: president, chief executive officer, Cargill Inc.; chairman, Excel Corp.
Stallkamp, William J.: senior vice chairman, member corporate review committee, director, Mellon Financial Corp.
Stamm, Doug: chairman, chief executive officer, Nike, Inc.
Stancato, Kenneth J.: vice president, controller, Weyerhaeuser Co.; controller, Weyerhaeuser Co. Foundation
Stancaxi, Joe: vice president corporate relations, Dana Corp.; director, Dana Corp. Foundation
Standen, Craig Clayton: senior vice president corporate development, Scripps Co. (E.W.)
Standish, J. Spencer: chairman, director, Albany International Corp.
Stanley, Brian C.: director, Valmont Foundation
Stanley, John: senior vice president, chief financial officer, Ralph's Grocery Co.
Stanley, Peter William: vice president, Hitachi Foundation
Stanton, Peter F.: chairman, president, chief executive officer, Washington Trust Bank
Stanton, Philip H.: chief executive officer, director, Washington Trust Bank
Stark, Kenneth: vice president, Harnischfeger Industries Foundation
Starkweather, Kendall: director, Autodesk Foundation
Starkweather, Kendall N.: vice president, chief financial officer, Autodesk Foundation
Starr, Joe F.: trustee, Tyson Foundation, Inc.
Starrett, Cam: executive vice president human resources & corporate relations, Nestle U.S.A. Inc.
Starzel, Robert F.: director, Union Pacific Corp.; president, Union Pacific Foundation
Stata, Ray S.: chairman, chief executive officer, director, Analog Devices, Inc.
Staton, Robert Emmett: president, Colonial Life & Accident Insurance Co.
Staubitz, Arthur Frederick: president, director, Baxter Allegiance Foundation
Stauffer, John H.: chairman, Stauffer Communications Foundation
Stauffer, Stanley Howard: trustee, Stauffer Communications Foundation
Staven, Ralph R.: president, chief executive officer, director, First Financial Bank; chairman, president, mgr, director, First Financial Foundation
Stavropoulos, William S.: president, chief executive officer, director, Dow Chemical Co.
Stawarz, Raymond R.: chief financial officer, Federated Mutual Insurance Co.; treasurer, Federated Mutual Insurance Foundation
Stebbins, Joan: director, Extendicare Foundation
Stecher, Esta: member, Goldman Sachs Foundation; tax director, managing director, Goldman Sachs Group
Stecko, Paul T.: president, director, Tenneco Packaging
Steele, Elizabeth R.: member advisory committee, Dow Jones Foundation
Steere, William Campbell, Jr.: chairman, chief executive officer, director, Pfizer Inc.
Steffens, John Laundon: executive vice president, Merrill Lynch & Co., Inc.
Stein, James C.: president, chief operating officer, Fluor Corp.; trustee, Fluor Foundation
Steinberg, Dennis P.: treasurer, PacifiCorp Foundation
Steinberg, Norman: director, Katten, Muchin & Zavis Foundation
Steiner, Jennifer: vice president medical programs, HCR ManorCare Foundation
Steinhause, Mitchell: director, New York Mercantile Exchange Charitable Foundation
Steinhauser, Carolyn E.: trustee, York Federal Savings & Loan Foundation
Stekas, Lynn: director, MONY Life Insurance of New York (The)
Stender, Oswald K.: director, Hawaiian Electric Industries Charitable Foundation
Stenmark, Lizbeth: vice president, treasurer, StorageTek Foundation
Stephan, Richard C.: vice president, Viad Corp. Fund
Stephens, Elton Bryson: founder, chairman, Ebsco Industries, Inc.
Stephens, James T.: president, director, Ebsco Industries, Inc.
Sterling, John: chief financial officer, Patagonia Inc.
Sterling, Mary K.: assistant treasurer, Phelps Dodge Foundation
Sterling, Sonja J.: president, director, Deere & Co.; secretary, Deere Foundation (John)
Sternlicht, Barry S.: chairman, chief executive officer, Starwood Hotels & Resorts Worldwide, Inc.
Steuert, D. Michael: trustee, GenCorp Foundation
Stevens, Gregory W.: vice president, treasurer, Phelps Dodge Corp.
Stevens, Lorne G.: director, La-Z-Boy Inc.
Stevens, Martha: president, director, Mitsubishi Electric America Foundation
Stevens, Paul E.: director, Alexander & Baldwin Foundation
Stevens, Philip Ashworth: trustee, National Machinery Foundation, Inc.
Stevens, Tamara: director, High Meadow Foundation
Steward, H. Leighton: chairman, chief executive officer, president, Louisiana Land & Exploration Co.; director, Louisiana Land & Exploration Co. Foundation
Steward, Larry: trustee, Invacare Foundation
Stewart, Cynthia: vice president, Texas Instruments Foundation
Stewart, Donald M.: director, New York Times Co. Foundation
Stewart, James Gathings: executive vice president, chief financial officer, CIGNA Corp.
Stewart, Joseph Melvin: senior vice president corporate affairs, Kellogg Co.; trustee, Kellogg Co. Twenty-Five Year Employees' Fund Inc.

Stewart, S. Jay: chairman, chief executive officer, director, Morton International Inc.
Stilwill, Gail: president, Meredith Corp.
Stinnett, J. Daniel: director, Commerce Bancshares Foundation
Stinnette, Joe L., Jr.: director, Fireman's Fund Foundation; president, chief executive officer, director, Fireman's Fund Insurance Co.
Stinson, Kenneth E.: member contributions committee, Kiewit Companies Foundation; chairman, chief executive officer, director, Kiewit Sons' Inc. (Peter)
Stitle, Stephen A.: chairman, National City Bank of Cleveland
Stivers, William Charles: senior vice president, chief financial officer, treasurer, Weyerhaeuser Co.; treasurer, trustee, Weyerhaeuser Co. Foundation
Stockman, David A.: co-chairman, director, Collins & Aikman Corp.; president, director, Collins & Aikman Foundation
Stoddart, Cassandra: trustee, Circuit City Foundation
Stokes, Spencer: secretary, Winthrop Foundation
Stokstad, Kathryn L.: president, director, Sundstrand Corp. Foundation
Stolar, Bernie: trustee, Sega Foundation
Stone, Andy: trustee, Credit Suisse First Boston Foundation Trust
Stone, Jerome H.: director, Stone Foundation
Stone, Lawrence Mynatt: chairman, publisher, Rutledge Hill Press; secretary, treasurer, Rutledge Hill Press Foundation
Stone, Marvin N.: president, Stone Foundation
Stone, Richard: director, Tribune New York Foundation
Stone, Roger Warren: chairman, president, chief executive officer, director, Stone Container Corp.; president, Stone Foundation
Stonebraker, Barbara J.: executive vice president, Cincinnati Bell Foundation, Inc.; senior vice president, Cincinnati Bell Inc.
Stonecipher, Harry C.: president, chief operating officer, director, Boeing Co.
Stoner, Richard Burkett, Jr.: director, Cummins Engine Foundation
Storch, Gerald L.: senior vice president strategic business, Dayton Hudson
Stovall, James: vice president, director, Farmers Group, Inc.
Stoveken, James E., Jr.: senior vice president, Westvaco Corp.; trustee, Westvaco Foundation Trust
Strah, David: chairman, chief executive officer, Nike, Inc.
Straine, James J.: secretary, Prudential Foundation
Strandjord, Mary Jeannine: president, Sprint Foundation
Strang, William: treasurer, director, TENNANT Co. Foundation
Stranghoener, Larry W.: director, Honeywell Foundation; chief financial officer, vice president, Honeywell International Inc.
Strasser, Doug: trustee, Reynolds & Reynolds Co. Foundation
Stratton, Frederick Prescott, Jr.: chairman, chief executive officer, director, Briggs & Stratton Corp.; president, director, Briggs & Stratton Corp. Foundation
Straw, Jack: member administration committee, Jefferson Smurfit Corp. Charitable Trust; chairman, Smurfit-Stone Container Corp.
Strawn, Kathryn: executive director, Mead Corp. Foundation
Strayer, Jacqueline: chairman, president, chief executive officer, chief operating officer, United Technologies Corp.
Strear, Leonard: president, Strear Family Foundation; chairman, president, chief executive officer, Strear Farms Co.
Strear, Michael: president, Strear Family Foundation
Strecker, A. M.: president, Oklahoma Gas & Electric Co. Foundation
Street, Gordon P., Jr.: chairman, president, chief executive officer, director, North American Royalties; trustee, North American Royalties Foundation
Streeter, Bill: senior vice president, MFA Inc.
Strickland, Carol A.: chairman, chief executive officer, United States Trust Co. of New York; chairman corporate contributions committee, U.S. Trust Corp. Foundation
Strickland, Robert Louis: chairman, treasurer, Lowe's Charitable and Educational Foundation
Strickling, Lawrence E.: vice president, president public policy, Ameritech Corp.
Strobel, Pamela B.: senior vice president, general counsel, Commonwealth Edison Co.
Strong, Gregory S.: treasurer, Minnesota Mutual Foundation; vice president actuary, Minnesota Mutual Life Insurance Co.
Strongin, Linda: vice president public relations, European American Bank
Stroup, Paul A., III: director, Lance Foundation; president, chief executive officer, director, Lance, Inc.
Stroup, Stanley Stephenson: executive vice president, general counsel, Norwest Corp.
Strouse, Pat: trustee, Cranston Foundation
Strumwasser, Ira, PhD.: executive director, Blue Cross & Blue Shield of Michigan Foundation
Stryker, Linda: senior vice president, HSBC Bank USA
Stryker, Steven Charles: senior admin representative, Shell Oil Co. Foundation
Stuart, James, III: vice president, NBC Foundation
Stuart, James, Jr.: chairman, chief executive officer, National Bank of Commerce Trust & Savings; president, NBC Foundation
Stuart, Scott: president, NBC Foundation
Stuebgen, William J.: vice president, controller, chief acct officer, APL Ltd.
Stump, Maryann: treasurer, director, Blue Cross & Blue Shield of Minnesota Foundation Inc.
Stupp, Erwin P., Jr.: chairman, Stupp Brothers Bridge & Iron Co.; trustee, Stupp Brothers Bridge & Iron Co. Foundation
Stupp, John P., Jr.: executive vice president, chief operating officer, director, Stupp Brothers Bridge & Iron Co.; trustee, Stupp Brothers Bridge & Iron Co. Foundation
Stupp, Robert P.: president, director, Stupp Brothers Bridge & Iron Co.; trustee, Stupp Brothers Bridge & Iron Co. Foundation
Stupski, Lawrence J.: president, vice chairman, chief operating officer, director, Schwab & Co., Inc. (Charles); chief financial officer, secretary, Schwab Corp. Foundation (Charles)
Sturgeon, John: president, chief operating officer, Mutual of Omaha Insurance Co.
Sturges, Robert: assistant vice president, secretary, Arison Foundation
Subin, Robert: senior vice president, Campbell Soup Co.
Suggs, Leo H.: director, chairman, chief executive officer, Overnite Transportation Co.
Sugiyama, Mineo: assistant secretary, NEC Foundation of America
Sugizaki, Teruyuki: president, Toshiba America Foundation
Sullivan, Austin Padraic, Junior: trustee, General Mills Foundation; senior vice president corporate relations, General Mills, Inc.
Sullivan, D. Harold: vice president finance, treasurer, director, Demoulas Supermarkets Inc.
Sullivan, Donald M.: chairman, director, MTS Systems Corp.
Sullivan, Frank P.: vice president sales & marketing, Square D Co.; vice president, director, Square D Foundation
Sullivan, G. Craig: chairman, president, chief executive officer, director, Clorox Co.; chairman, Clorox Co. Foundation
Sullivan, James Norman: vice chairman, director, Chevron Corp.
Sullivan, Jeremiah M.: treasurer, Owens Corning; director, Owens Corning Foundation, Inc.
Sullivan, Kevin F.: program officer, PPG Industries Foundation
Sullivan, Laura P.: vice president, secretary, director, State Farm Companies Foundation; vice president, secretary, counsel, State Farm Mutual Automobile Insurance Co.
Sullivan, Thomas John: senior vice president investor relations, McGraw-Hill Companies, Inc.
Sulzberger, Arthur Ochs, Junior: director, chairman emeritus, New York Times Co.
Sulzberger, Arthur Ochs, Sr.: director, New York Times Co.; chairman, director, New York Times Co. Foundation
Sulzberger, Judith P., MD: director, New York Times Co. Foundation
Sumansky, John: treasurer, Toshiba America Foundation
Sumegi, Lois: vice president, Goodrich Foundation, Inc. (B.F.)
Summers, Stuart G.: president, trustee, Ohio National Foundation
Summers, William B., Jr.: trustee, McDonald & Co. Securities Foundation; chairman, chief executive officer, president, McDonald & Co. Securities, Inc.
Summey, Mark L.: director, Stonecutter Foundation; vice chairman, Stonecutter Mills Corp.
Surat, Deborah: secretary, Union Carbide Foundation
Surges, Meg: president, director, Marshall & Ilsley Foundation, Inc.
Suter, Albert E.: senior vice chairman, chief administrative officer, director, Emerson Electric Co.
Suttmiller, Tom: senior vice president auto forms, Reynolds & Reynolds Co.
Sutton, Howard: director public relations, Providence Journal-Bulletin Co.; president, Providence Journal Charitable Foundation; trustee, Steelcase Foundation
Sutton, Thomas C.: chairman, director, Pacific Mutual Charitable Foundation; chairman, chief executive officer, director, Pacific Mutual Life Insurance Co.
Suwyn, Mark A.: vice president, Louisiana-Pacific Foundation
Svitek, John: vice president finance, Slant/Fin Corp.; vice president, director, Slant/Fin Foundation
Swain, Kristin A.: trustee, Corning Inc. Foundation
Swan, Robert C.: vice president, secretary, Phelps Dodge Corp.; president, Phelps Dodge Foundation
Swanson, Robert A.: director, Genentech Foundation for Biomedical Sciences; president, chief executive officer, director, Genentech Inc.
Swanson, Robert M., Ph.D.: treasurer, director, Group Health Foundation
Swartwout, Shirley Doss: secretary, treasurer, Crestar Foundation
Swartz, Thomas: chairman, chief executive officer, director, Rochester Gas & Electric Corp.
Sweasy, William J.: secretary, Red Wing Shoe Co. Foundation
Sweeney, Eileen A.: director, United Airlines Foundation; manager, United Airlines Inc.
Sweeney, John J., III: vice president, CertainTeed Corp.
Sweeny, Jack C.: president, Temple-Inland Foundation

Swigon, Catherine: secretary, treasurer, FMC Foundation
Swihart, Susannah: trustee, BankBoston Charitable Foundation
Swinney, Jo Ann: chairman, chief executive officer, director, Tenneco Automotive
Sykora, Donald D.: director, Reliant Energy Inc.
Sylla, Casey J.: senior vice president, chief investment officer, Allstate Insurance Co.
Symington, Charles, Jr.: vice president, NASDAQ Stock Market Educational Foundation
Syron, Richard F.: chairman, chief executive officer, director, American Stock Exchange, Inc.
Sznewajs, Robert D.: vice chairman retail banking, U.S. Bancorp

T

Tai, Ping Y.: co-president, co-treasurer, Tai and Co. Foundation, Inc. (J.T.); co-president, Tai and Co. (J.T.)
Tai, Yuan: co-president, co-treasurer, Tai and Co. Foundation, Inc. (J.T.)
Tait, Peter B.: trustee,
Takahashi, Ted: vice president, finance, Matsushita Electric Corp. of America; vice president, Panasonic Foundation
Talbot, Carol G.: chairman executive committee, Procter & Gamble Co.; vice president, secretary, Procter & Gamble Fund
Talbot, Deborah L.: trustee, Chase Manhattan Foundation
Talen, Polly M.: senior program officer, social action, Dayton Hudson; treasurer, Target Foundation
Talleriso, Joseph: director, Autodesk Foundation
Tambakakis, Barbara: chairman, chief executive officer, director, Pennzoil-Quaker State Co.
Tambakeras, Markos I.: director, Honeywell Foundation
Tamke, George W.: president, chief operating officer, director, Emerson Electric Co.
Tanabe, Takeshi: chief financial officer, Fuji Bank & Trust Co.
Tanaka, Hidetoshi: trustee, Mazda Foundation (USA), Inc.
Taniguchi, Ichiro: president, Mitsubishi Electric America; director, Mitsubishi Electric America Foundation
Tanner, K. S., Jr.: director, Stonecutter Foundation
Taplin, Linda: director, Wisconsin Power & Light Foundation, Inc.
Tarasovich, Barbara: treasurer, Chesebrough Foundation; president, Unilever Home & Personal Care U.S.A.
Tarlow, Eric: chairman, director, IBJ Foundation
Tarola, Robert M.: senior vice president, chief financial officer, Grace & Co. (W.R.)
Tarpey, Michael: treasurer, NCR Foundation
Tart, Maureen: vice president arts & culture program, AT&T Foundation
Tasaka, Diane: director corporate communications, Farmers Group, Inc.; vice president, Farmers Group Safety Foundation
Tatar, Jerome F.: chairman, chief executive officer, president, Mead Corp.
Tate, Warren E.: trustee, Gulf Power Foundation
Tatum, Nenetta Carter: treasurer, secretary, Carter Star Telegram Employees Fund (Amon G.)
Taulbee, Richard: assistant treasurer, Western-Southern Foundation, Inc.; vice president, Western & Southern Life Insurance Co.
Taurel, Sidney: chairman, president, chief executive officer, Lilly & Co. (Eli)
Taylor, Albert P.: vice president, executive assistant to chief executive officer, Comerica Inc.
Taylor, Andrew C.: president, chief executive officer, director, Enterprise Rent-A-Car Co.
Taylor, Benjamin B.: assistant director, Boston Globe Foundation
Taylor, Brett M., Junior: director, Hickory Tech Corp.; president, Hickory Tech Corp. Foundation
Taylor, Frederick B.: vice chairman, chief investment officer, United States Trust Co. of New York
Taylor, John I.: director, Zenith Electronics Corp.
Taylor, John R.: senior director public construction, Merck & Co.; executive vice president, Merck Co. Foundation
Taylor, Julian Howard: chairman, director, Reynolds Metals Co. Foundation
Taylor, Mary E.: vice president, trustee, Merrill Lynch & Co. Foundation Inc.; executive vice president, Merrill Lynch & Co., Inc.
Taylor, Philip E.: president, JSJ Corp.
Taylor, S. Martin: senior vice president, Detroit Edison Co.; president, director, Detroit Edison Foundation
Taylor, Terrence J.: vice president, general counsel, Nalco Chemical Co.; treasurer, Nalco Foundation
Taylor, William Osgood: chairman, chief executive officer, director, Boston Globe (The); chairman, director, Boston Globe Foundation
Taylor, Wilson H.: executive vice president, chief financial officer, CIGNA Corp.
Tedeschi, Frederick: treasurer, MONY Life Insurance of New York (The)
Teets, John William: vice president, controller, director, Dial Corp.; president, chief executive officer, director, Viad Corp. Fund
Teig, Eva S.: member contributions committee, Dominion Resources, Inc.
Tello, Elia E.: grant administrator, Target Corp.
Temple, Arthur, III: director, Temple-Inland Foundation
Tenniman, Nicholas G., IV: vice president newspaper operations, Pulitzer Publishing Co.; director, Pulitzer Publishing Co. Foundation
Tennison, Raymond P.: director, Matlock Foundation
Teramura, Soji: president, Hitachi America Ltd.; secretary, director, Hitachi Foundation
Ternlieb, David: assistant secretary, RJR Nabisco Foundation
Terracciano, Anthony Patrick: director, First Union Foundation; vice chairman, chief credit officer, First Union National Bank, NA
Terrien, Linda L.: controller, Weyerhaeuser Co. Foundation
Terrill, James E.: executive vice president, United States Sugar Corp.
Terrill, Richard D.: executive vice president, general counsel, corp. secretary, Western Resources Inc.
Terry, Mary: senior vice president, secretary, general counsel, Reader's Digest Association, Inc. (The); assistant secretary, Reader's Digest Foundation
Terry, Richard Edward: chairman, chief executive officer, director, Peoples Energy Corp.
Tetrault, Roger E.: chairman, chief executive officer, director, McDermott Inc.
Tevanian, Avadis, Jr.: senior vice president, Apple Computer, Inc.
Thacher, Carter Pomeroy: chairman, director, Wilbur-Ellis Co. & Connell Brothers Co.; vice president, Wilbur Foundation (Brayton)
Thacher, Michael: general manager public relations & communications, Unocal Corp.
Thawerbhoy, Nazim G.: treasurer, director, Jacobs Engineering Foundation
Thayer, Tyrone K.: corp. vice president, Cargill Inc.
Thelen, Cynthia A.: trustee, General Mills Foundation
Thiele, Randy: trustee, Donaldson Foundation
Thies, Richard Henry: vice president, Madison Gas & Electric Foundation
Thoman, G. Richard: president, chief operating officer, Xerox Corp.
Thomas, Franklin Augustine: chairman, co-chief executive officer, CBS Corp.; director, CBS Foundation
Thomas, Grover: trustee, Fortis Foundation
Thomas, J. G.: trustee, Fortis Foundation
Thomas, Larry: president delivery business unit, Cinergy Corp.
Thomas, Nancy: chairman, Hewlett-Packard Co.
Thomas, Ray J.: director, AMP Foundation; chairman, chief executive officer, director, AMP Inc.
Thomas, Richard Lee: vice president, director, First National Bank of Chicago Foundation
Thomason, Donald W.: executive vice president service & technology, Kellogg Co.; trustee, Kellogg Co. Twenty-Five Year Employees' Fund Inc.
Thomasson, Dan King: senior vice president corporate development, Scripps Co. (E.W.); vice president, trustee, Scripps Howard Foundation
Thompson, Astrid I.: vice president, trustee, PEMCO Foundation
Thompson, Charles P.: vice president community rels, America West Airlines Foundation; manager, APS Foundation, Inc.; chairman, president, chief executive officer, director, Arizona Public Service Co.
Thompson, Donald L.: chairman, chief executive officer, Hunt Manufacturing Co.
Thompson, G. Kennedy: president, chief operating officer, First Union Corp.; member, First Union Foundation
Thompson, Johanna: vice president, Revlon Foundation Inc.
Thompson, John D.: coordinator, Dexter Corp. Foundation
Thompson, Lawrence M., Jr.: director, Sovereign Bank Foundation
Thompson, Robert L.: vice president public affairs, Springs Industries, Inc.
Thompson, Sheldon Lee: senior vice president, chief administrative officer, Sunoco Inc.
Thomson, Gregory M.: director, Owens Corning Foundation, Inc.
Thomson, Jim: director, Consolidated Natural Gas System Foundation
Thomson, R. Patrick: president, director, New York Mercantile Exchange
Thomson, Todd: chief financial officer, Citigroup
Thornton, John L.: board member, Goldman Sachs Foundation; president, chief operating officer, Goldman Sachs Group
Thornton, John T.: executive vice president, chief financial officer, Norwest Corp.; treasurer, Norwest Foundation
Thorp, Peter C.: co-chairman, Citibank Corp.
Thorstenson, T.: trustee, Caterpillar Foundation
Thrasher, F. Martin: senior vice president, Campbell Soup Co.
Thurman, Charles W.: director, Baxter Allegiance Foundation
Thurston, Samuel E.: senior vice president distribution, Giant Food Inc.
Thyen, James C.: president, director, Habig Foundation
Thyen, John T.: senior executive vice president, director, Habig Foundation; senior executive vice president marketing & sales, director, Kimball International, Inc.
Thyen, Ronald J.: senior executive vice president, director, Habig Foundation; senior executive vice president, chief operating officer director, Kimball International, Inc.
Tiedens, George R.: group president power systems, Kohler Co.
Tiefel, William R.: vice chairman, director, Marriott International Inc.

Tierney, Diane: manager corporate contributions, Dial Corp.; president, chief executive officer, director, Viad Corp. Fund

Tierno, David: vice president, Ernst & Young Foundation

Tignatelli, Jim: chairman, president, chief executive officer, director, Tucson Electric Power Co.

Tilghman, Richard Granville: principal, Crestar Foundation

Till, A. Grey, Jr.: vice president, Caring Foundation

Tillman, Robert L.: chairman, president, chief executive officer, Lowe's Companies

Timken, Ward Jackson: vice president, director, officer, Timken Co. (The); vice president, Timken Co. Charitable Trust (The); trustee, Timken Co. Educational Fund

Timken, William Robert, Jr.: chairman, president, chief executive officer, director, Timken Co. (The)

Tippins, Carolyn H.: trustee, Tippins Foundation

Tippins, George W.: trustee, Tippins Foundation

Tisch, James S.: president, chief executive officer, director, CNA

Tisch, Laurence Alan: chairman, co-chief executive officer, CBS Corp.; trustee, Loews Foundation

Tisch, Preston Robert: assistant treasurer, CBS Foundation; co-chairman, co-chief executive officer, director, CNA; trustee, Loews Foundation

Titas, Frank G.: vice president, Hanna Co. Foundation (M.A.)

Tobias, Randall L.: chairman emeritus, Lilly & Co. (Eli)

Tobias, Steven C.: vice chairman, chief operating officer, Norfolk Southern Corp.; director, Norfolk Southern Foundation

Toelle, Michael: trustee, Cenex Harvest States Foundation

Toffolon, John E., Jr.: treasurer, executive managing director, director, Nomura America Foundation; chief financial officer, Nomura Holding America

Toft, Richard Paul: chairman, Chicago Title Corp.; trustee, Chicago Title and Trust Co. Foundation

Tokarz, Michael T.: founding partner, Walter Industries Inc.

Toler, William D.: senior vice president, Campbell Soup Co.; trustee, Campbell Soup Foundation

Toll, Daniel Roger: trustee, Kemper Foundation (James S.)

Tomber, Barbara: director, First Hawaiian Foundation

Tomich, Rosemary: director, Occidental Petroleum Charitable Foundation

Tomlinson, Joseph Ernest: vice president, treasurer, controller, Inland Container Corp.; vice president, director, Inland Foundation, Inc.

Toner, Jeffrey M.: executive trustee, Kingsbury Fund

Tooker, Eric S.: secretary, Central Newspapers Foundation; corporate secretary, vice president, general counsel, Central Newspapers, Inc.

Topham, Verl Reed: board member, PacifiCorp Foundation

Topping, Karin: president, chief executive officer, Shaklee Corp.

Toran, Daniel: president, Penn Mutual Life Insurance Co.

Torbert, Martin: group vice president, National Starch & Chemical Co.; chairman, National Starch & Chemical Foundation

Torcolini, Bob: president, Dynamet, Inc.

Torgerson, William T.: managing, Potomac Electric Power Co.

Torgeson, Aileen: trustee, Donaldson Foundation

Torrey, Susan K.: vice president, USG Foundation

Tortorella, Albert J.: vice president,

Tosh, Dennis A.: secretary, Ford Motor Co. Fund

Towers, Thomas R.: vice president, director, Universal Leaf Foundation

Townsend, David L.: vice president administration, Walter Industries Inc.

Toyama, Yoji: trustee, Mazda Foundation (USA), Inc.

Toyoda, Shinobu: trustee, Sega Foundation

Tracy, Emmet E., Jr.: president, chief executive officer, director, Alma Piston Co.; president, Tracy Fund (Emmet and Frances)

Trainer, Francis H., Jr.: trustee, Bernstein & Co. Foundation, Inc. (Sanford C.)

Tran, Khanh T.: senior vice president, chief financial officer, director, Pacific Mutual Life Insurance Co.

Traphagen, Richard: trustee, Cenex Harvest States Foundation

Trask, Robert B.: president, chief operating officer, director, Country Curtains, Inc.; clerk, trustee, High Meadow Foundation; director,

Travaglianti, Edward: chairman, chief executive officer, European American Bank

Travaille, Hubert Duane: trustee, Potlatch Foundation II

Travinsky, Kathleen B.: president, treasurer, Chubb Foundation

Treanor, Mark C.: senior vice president, general counsel, First Union Corp.; member, First Union Foundation

Trencher, Lewis J.: chairman, director, Thompson Co. Fund (J. Walter); chief operating officer, director, Thompson Co. (J. Walter)

Trethewey, James A.: senior vice president, operations services, Cleveland-Cliffs, Inc.

Trogdon, Dewey Leonard, Jr.: director, ABC Foundation; chairman, Cone Mills Corp.

Troiano, John G.: director, Banfi Vintners Foundation

Trosino, Vincent Joseph: assistant secretary, State Farm Companies Foundation; executive vice president, vice chairman, chief operating officer, director, State Farm Mutual Automobile Insurance Co.

Trotman, Alexander James: assistant treasurer, Ford Motor Co. Fund

Trotter, Lloyd G.: director, GE Fund

Troy, Joseph J.: vice president, treasurer, Walter Industries Inc.

True, Connie: community relations coordinator, Central & South West Foundation; executive vice president, chief financial officer, Central & South West Services

True, David: partner, True Oil Co.

True, Diemer: partner, True Oil Co.

True, Jean Durland: trustee, True Foundation; partner, True Oil Co.

Trujillo, Solomon D.: president, US West Foundation; president, chief executive officer, US West, Inc.

Tryloff, Robin: director community relations, Sara Lee Corp.; executive director, Sara Lee Foundation

Tsang, Terrence: chief financial officer, Guess?

Tschetter, John: board member, grants coordinator, Dain Bosworth Foundation

Tsui, Diana: European communication affairs manager, Nike, Inc.

Tsui, John K.: director, First Hawaiian Foundation

Tsutsumi, Senji: chairman, secretary, trustee, Ise Cultural Foundation

Tucker, Don Eugene: secretary, Commercial Intertech Foundation

Tuerff, James R.: president, director, American General Finance

Tufo, Judy: chairman, chief executive officer (retired), Bank of America; finance officer, Bank of America Foundation

Tulley, Herbert B.: vice president, chief financial officer, treasurer, Wilbur-Ellis Co. & Connell Brothers Co.; secretary, treasurer, Wilbur Foundation (Brayton)

Tully, Amy C.: vice president, Morgan & Co. Inc. (J.P.)

Tumminello, Stephen C.: president, chief executive officer, director, Philips Electronics North America Corp.

Tuohy, John E.: director, Texaco Foundation

Tuominen, William: senior vice president, chief technology & environment officer, Ecolab Inc.

Turberville, P. G.: director, Shell Oil Co. Foundation

Turner, Cal, Jr.: chairman, chief executive officer, director, Dollar General Corp.

Turner, Elizabeth 'Betty' M.: senior vice president, Springs Industries, Inc.

Turner, Fred L.: senior chairman, director, McDonald's Corp.

Turner, John Gosney: chairman, chief executive officer, director, ReliaStar Financial Corp.; director, ReliaStar Foundation

Turner, Lawrence: president, The Kroger Co. Foundation

Turner, Robert W.: vice president public affairs, Champion International Corp.

Tusa, J. C.: president, Copolymer Foundation

Tyler, Kenneth Scott, Jr.: president, chief executive officer, Furniture Brands International, Inc.

Tyner, Neal Edward: president, director, Ameritas Charitable Foundation

Typermass, Arthur G.: senior vice president, treasurer, Metropolitan Life Insurance Co.

Tysoe, Ronald W.: vice chairman, director, Federated Department Stores, Inc.; member, Scripps Howard Foundation

Tyson, Cheryl F.: senior chairman, Tyson Foods Inc.; trustee, Tyson Foundation, Inc.

Tyson, Donald John: senior chairman, Tyson Foods Inc.

Tyson, John H.: chairman, chief executive officer, president, director, Tyson Foods Inc.; trustee, Tyson Foundation, Inc.

Tyson, Laura D'Andrea: vice president, president public policy, Ameritech Corp.; director, Ameritech Foundation

U

Ughetta, William Casper: president, Corning Inc. Foundation

Ukrop, Jacqueline L.: director, Ukrop Foundation

Ukrop, James E.: vice chairman, chief executive officer, director, Ukrop Foundation; vice chairman, chief executive officer, Ukrop's Super Markets

Ukrop, Joseph Edward: director, Ukrop Foundation; chairman, Ukrop's Super Markets

Ukrop, Robert S.: president, chief operating officer, director, Ukrop Foundation; president, chief operating officer, Ukrop's Super Markets

Ukropina, James R.: partner, Pacific Mutual Life Insurance Co.

Ulrich, Robert J.: chairman, chief executive officer, director, Dayton Hudson; chairman, trustee, Target Foundation

Ungerland, Thomas J.: executive vice president, controller, Crane Foundation

Unruh, James Arlen: director, Ameritech Foundation

Upbin, Hal Jay: president, chief executive officer, director, Kellwood Co.

Urkowitz, Michael: senior vice president, Chase Manhattan Bank, NA; trustee, Chase Manhattan Foundation

Ursu, John Joseph: director, 3M Foundation; general counsel, senior vice president legal affairs, Minnesota Mining & Manufacturing Co.

Urushisako, Toshiahi: chairman, president, chief executive officer, Sharp Electronics Corp.

Usher, Thomas J.: chairman, chief executive officer, USX Corp.; chairman board trustees, USX Foundation, Inc.

Utley, Edward Harold: vice chairman, president,

GEICO Corp.; chairman, director, GEICO Philanthropic Foundation

Utter, Nancy M.: director public affairs, member contributions committee, Eaton Charitable Fund

V

Vadasz, Leslie L.: executive vice president, director, Intel Corp.

Vagelos, Pindaros Roy: trustee, Prudential Foundation

Vaimberg, Mitzi: trustee, AT&T Foundation

Valade, Gary C.: executive vice president, chief financial officer, DaimlerChrysler Corp.; trustee, DaimlerChrysler Corp. Fund

Valdez, Joanie: chairman, chief executive officer, president, Sears, Roebuck and Co.

Valentine, E. Massey: trustee, Chesapeake Corp. Foundation

Valentine, J. E.: chief financial officer, Bardes Corp.

Van Benschoten, David: coordinator, General Mills Foundation

Van Cleve, William Moore: member public policy committee, Emerson Charitable Trust; partner, Emerson Electric Co.

Van Den Berg, Jay: trustee, Whirlpool Foundation

Van Dyke, William Grant: chairman, president, chief executive officer, director, Donaldson Co., Inc.

Van Himbergen, Thomas: director, Deluxe Corp. Foundation

Van Mieghem, Dennis: trustee, KPMG Peat Marwick Foundation

Van Nort, Peter S.: president, Zachry Co. (H.B.)

Van Zante, Mary: corporate communications, Pella Corp.; director, Pella Rolscreen Foundation

Vance, Robert L.: trustee, Tektronix Foundation

Vanderhoef, H. Kent: chairman, director, Orange & Rockland Utilities, Inc.

VanderRoest, Stan: trustee, treasurer, Gerber Foundation; vice president, comptroller, controller, Gerber Products Co.

Vandevoort, Gerald C.: director, Honeywell Foundation

Vannoni, Leo: director, Reebok Human Rights Foundation (The)

Varet, Elizabeth Rosenwald: vice president, director, AMETEK Foundation; director, AMETEK, Inc.

Vargas, Jimmy: president, chairman, chief executive officer, National City Bank of Pennsylvania

Vaughn, Donald C.: vice chairman, Halliburton Co.

Vaughn, John: vice president unit development & strategy, Ameritech Corp.

Vaughn, R. C.: president, treasurer, Burress Foundation (J.W.)

Veitenhans, Karen L.: assistant treasurer, Weyerhaeuser Co. Foundation

Vemlyak, James M.: chief financial officer, Baird & Co. (Robert W.)

Vencent, Peter: treasurer, Occidental Oil and Gas Foundation

Ver Hagen, Jan Karol: president, United Dominion Industries, Ltd.

Vergas, Sophia: director public relations, Liberty Corp.; secretary, administrator, Liberty Corp. Foundation

Verheij, Richard H.: executive vice president, general counsel, UST Inc.

Verley, Roy: chairman, Hewlett-Packard Co.; executive director, Hewlett-Packard Co. Foundation

Vermilion, Mark: manager corporate affairs, Sun Microsystems Foundation, Inc.

Verrecchia, Alfred J.: treasurer, trustee, Hasbro Charitable Trust Inc.; executive, director, Hasbro, Inc.

Verven, Maria: media relations manager, U.S. Bancorp Piper Jaffray

Verville, Norbert J.: vice president, chief financial officer, treasurer, director, Bucyrus-Erie Co.; treasurer, Bucyrus-Erie Foundation

Vezeris, David J.: director, Humanitas Foundation

Viault, Raymond: vice chairman, director, General Mills, Inc.

Vickers, Julie: president, chief executive officer, director, Compaq Computer Corp.

Victor, Lois B.: trustee, Merit Gasoline Foundation

Vigrass, Kristen: chairman, chief executive officer, director, Calvin Klein; coordinator, Calvin Klein Foundation

Villanueva, Edward: executive director, Circuit City Foundation

Vinney, Les C.: senior vice president, chief financial officer, BFGoodrich Co.

Vipond, J. Robert: director, Praxair Foundation

Vitale, David J.: vice chairman, Bank One Corp.; vice president, director, First National Bank of Chicago Foundation

Viviano, Joseph P.: president, court, Hershey Foods Corp.

Voet, Paul C.: executive vice president, treasurer, director, Chemed Corp.; trustee, Chemed Foundation

Vogel, Howard Stanley: general counsel, Texaco Foundation

von Glahn, William G.: senior vice president, general counsel, Williams; director, Williams Companies Foundation (The)

Vondrasek, Frank Charles, Jr.: assistant treasurer, Madison Gas & Electric Foundation

Voorhees, Vernon W., II: chairman, chief executive officer, Business Men's Assurance Co. of America

Vorgard, Carrie: president, Fortis Insurance Co.; vice president, trustee, Fortis Insurance Foundation

Vosicky, John J.: treasurer, director, Comdisco Foundation; executive vice president finance, chief financial officer, Comdisco, Inc.

Vry, Ann: manager community relations, America West Airlines Foundation

Vujovich, Christine M.: senior executive vice president, director, Habig Foundation

W

Wachtel, Michael D.: president, Oshkosh B'Gosh Foundation Inc.; chief operating officer, Oshkosh B'Gosh, Inc.

Wachtell, Herbert M.: senior partner, Wachtell, Lipton, Rosen & Katz; vice president, treasurer, Wachtell, Lipton, Rosen & Katz Foundation

Wackerman, Dorothy C.: vice president, CertainTeed Corp.; vice president, secretary, director, CertainTeed Corp. Foundation; vice president, director, Norton Co. Foundation

Waddle, Allen C.: senior vice president, National City Corp.; administrator, National City Corp. Charitable Foundation

Wade, Nigel: trustee, Chicago Sun-Times Charity Trust

Wadlington, Cuba, Jr.: vice president, Williams

Wagar, James Lee: manager, Carter-Wallace Foundation; president, chief operating officer, director, Carter-Wallace, Inc.

Wagele, James: finance officer, Bank of America Foundation

Wagley, Dave: treasurer, director, DeKalb Genetics Foundation

Wagner, David J.: chairman, president, chief executive officer, Old Kent Bank; treasurer, Old Kent Foundation

Wagner, Harold A.: chairman, president, chief executive officer, director, Air Products and Chemicals, Inc.

Wagner, J. Wilt: vice president, treasurer, director, Reynolds Metals Co. Foundation

Wagner, Martin S.: president, chief operating officer, Xerox Corp.; secretary, general counsel, Xerox Foundation

Wagner, Thomas Joseph: president, CIGNA Foundation

Wagnon, Kenneth J.: secretary, treasurer, Cessna Foundation, Inc.

Wagoner, G. Richard, Jr.: president, chief executive officer, director, General Motors Corp.

Wahlig, George C.: vice president, director, Lee Foundation

Wahlig, Michael J.: chairman, trustee, Target Foundation

Wahner, Jim: director, Extendicare Foundation

Wake, Roffe: trustee, West Foundation (Herman O.)

Wakefield, Mary Lou: trustee, Ralph's-Food 4 Less Foundation; senior vice president, chief financial officer, Ralph's Grocery Co.

Walburn, Jackie: president, MacMillan Bloedel Foundation

Walda, Julie Inskeep: editor, Journal-Gazette Co.; director, Journal-Gazette Foundation, Inc.

Walker, David: editorial director, international publishing, Playboy Enterprises Inc.

Walker, G. P.: assistant secretary, Armstrong Foundation

Walker, Grahame: chairman, chief executive officer, Dexter Corp.; president, Dexter Corp. Foundation

Walker, Jack, Jr.: president, director, Alabama Power Foundation

Walker, Joan H.: senior vice president corporate communications, Ameritech Corp.

Walker, Martin Dean: chairman, chief executive officer, director, Hanna Co. (M.A.)

Walker, Norman: chairman, senior partner, PricewaterhouseCoopers; president, PricewaterhouseCoopers Foundation

Walker, Thomas P.: director, Stonecutter Foundation

Walker, W. Paul: secretary, Boswell Foundation, Inc.; chief financial officer, secretary, treasurer, Independent Stave Co.

Wall, Hugh E., III: treasurer, Gosiger Foundation

Wall, Jim: director, Deloitte & Touche Foundation

Wall, Robert C.: executive vice president finance, First National Bank of Evergreen Park

Wallace, Carl J.: chief financial officer, Navcom Systems

Wallach, Ira D.: chairman, Central National-Gottesman; executive vice president, Central National-Gottesman Foundation

Wallach, Kenneth L.: executive vice president, Central National-Gottesman Foundation

Wallman, Susan A.: manager corporate contributions, McGraw-Hill Companies, Inc.

Walmsley, Cheryl M.: chairman, chief executive officer, Hunt Manufacturing Co.

Walsh, Edward F.: vice president human resources, Campbell Soup Co.

Walsh, Michael J.: vice president, CertainTeed Corp.

Walsh, Paul S.: chairman, president, chief executive officer, Pillsbury Co.; director, Pillsbury Co. Foundation

Walsh, Steve: manager community affairs, GATX Corp.

Walter, James W.: trustee, Walter Foundation; chairman emeritus, founder, director, Walter Industries Inc.

Walter, Robert A.: trustee, Walter Foundation

Walters, John Alexander: trustee, Alcon Foundation

Walters, Peter: chairman, SmithKline Beecham Corp.

Walther, Larry: director, SBC Foundation

Walton, Jon David: chairman, president, chief executive officer, Allegheny Technologies Inc.; trustee, Allegheny Technologies Inc. Charitable Trust

Walton, S. Robson: member, Wal-Mart Foundation; chairman, director, Wal-Mart Stores, Inc.
Waltrip, William H.: chairman, director, Bausch & Lomb Inc.
Walvoord, Ellen M.: secretary, Abbott Laboratories Fund
Wander, Herbert S.: secretary, Katten, Muchin & Zavis Foundation
Wangstad, Kristi Rollag: vice president public affairs, Alliant Techsystems; president, Alliant Techsystems Community Investment Foundation
Ward, Carol J.: secretary, compliance officer, CIGNA Corp.; secretary, CIGNA Foundation
Ward, Lloyd D.: trustee, Maytag Corp. Foundation
Wardeberg, George E.: president, WICOR Foundation; president, chief executive officer, director, WICOR, Inc.
Warden, Debra: vice president, Invacare Foundation
Warden, William C., Jr.: secretary, Lowe's Charitable and Educational Foundation; chairman, president, chief executive officer, Lowe's Companies
Wardrop, Richard M., Jr.: chairman, chief executive officer, director, AK Steel Corp.
Wareham, James Lyman: president, AK Steel Corp.
Wareham, John P.: president, chief executive officer, director, Beckman Coulter, Inc.
Warner, Douglas Alexander, III: chairman, president, chief executive officer, director, Morgan & Co. Inc. (J.P.)
Warner, John Andrew, III: director, Telcordia Technologies
Warner, M. Richard: director, Temple-Inland Foundation
Warner, Tim: trustee, McKesson Foundation
Warsaw, James: president, chief executive officer, director, AMCORE Bank Rockford
Washington, Don: director communications & investor relations, McDermott Inc.
Washington, Earl S.: senior vice president communications, Rockwell International Corp.; secretary, Rockwell International Corp. Trust
Wasserman, David Sherman: vice president, treasurer, Harris Corp.; trustee, Harris Foundation
Watanabe, Jeffrey N.: director, Hawaiian Electric Industries Charitable Foundation
Watcher, Paul S.: vice president financial, Atlantic Investment Co.
Watjen, Thomas R.: vice chairman, chief financial officer, Provident Companies, Inc.
Watson, Charles H.: director, Arvin Foundation
Watson, Douglas G.: chairman, Novartis US Foundation
Watson, Karen: chairman, director, GEICO Philanthropic Foundation
Watson, Noel G.: vice president, director, Jacobs Engineering Foundation; president, chief executive officer, director, Jacobs Engineering Group
Watson, Raymond L.: vice chairman, Pacific Mutual Life Insurance Co.
Watson, Solomon Brown, IV: director, New York Times Co. Foundation
Watson, Steven L.: vice president, secretary, Contran Corp.; vice president, secretary, director, Simmons Foundation, Inc. (Harold)
Wayman, Robert P.: executive vice president finance & administration, chief financial officer, Hewlett-Packard Co.
Weafee, Robert J., Jr.: vice president, controller, Boston Edison Co.
Weatherstone, Dennis: executive vice president, Merck Co. Foundation
Weaver, Connie: vice president corporate communications & investor relations, Boise Cascade Corp.
Weaver, John F.: director, La-Z-Boy Inc.
Weaver, Patricia A.: vice president, Carpenter Technology Corp.
Weaver, Philip G.: executive vice president, chief financial officer, trustee, Cooper Tire & Rubber Co.; trustee, Cooper Tire & Rubber Foundation
Weaver, Warren W.: chairman, Commerce Bancshares, Inc.
Webb, Charles B., Jr.: vice chairman, United States Sugar Corp.
Weber, Carol: chairman, chief executive officer, director, Knight Ridder
Weber, Stephen Robert: assistant treasurer, Cowen Foundation
Weber-Kelley, Ruth: director, ReliaStar Foundation
Webster, Elroy: chairman, director, Cenex Harvest States; chairman, Cenex Harvest States Foundation
Weeden, Curtis G.: manager international programs & product giving, Johnson & Johnson Family of Companies Contribution Fund
Weedman, Sidney: chairman, National City Bank of Cleveland
Weekly, John William: chairman, chief executive officer, Mutual of Omaha Insurance Co.
Wege, Peter M.: trustee, Steelcase Foundation; vice chairman, director, Steelcase Inc.
Wege, Peter M., II: trustee, Steelcase Foundation
Wegmann, Karen: vice chairman, Wells Fargo & Co.; president, director, Wells Fargo Foundation
Wegner, Pamela J.: director, Wisconsin Power & Light Foundation, Inc.
Wehling, Robert Louis: global marketing, government relations officer, Procter & Gamble Co.; president, trustee, Procter & Gamble Fund
Wehmeier, Helge H.: president, chief executive officer, director, Bayer Corp.
Wehrle, Thomas E.: treasurer, Sverdrup Corp.; mem, Sverdrup Corp. Charitable Trust
Weidemeyer, Thomas H.: senior vice president, director, United Parcel Service of America Inc.; trustee, UPS Foundation
Weigand, George C.: vice president, trustee, Rubbermaid Foundation; chief financial officer, senior vice president, Rubbermaid Inc.
Weigel, David V.: president, MONY Life Insurance of New York (The)
Weil, Robert J.: vice president operations, McClatchy Co.; member, Star Tribune Foundation
Weill, Richard L.: president, MBIA Inc.
Weill, Sanford I.: chairman, chief executive officer, Citibank Corp.; chairman, Citigroup Foundation
Weinberg, John Livingston: chairman board, Goldman Sachs Foundation
Weinberger, Caspar Willard: chairman, Forbes Inc.
Weinman, Connie: secretary, director, National City Bank Foundation
Weirs, Geol L.: arts senior program officer, Dayton Hudson; assistant secretary, Target Foundation
Weisenbeck, Arnold: chairman, Cenex Harvest States Foundation
Weiser, Irving: chairman, president, chief executive officer, Dain Bosworth Inc.
Weiss, David E.: chairman, president, chief executive officer, director, Storage Technology Corp.
Weiss, Deborah D.: vice president, treasurer, Valspar Corp.; treasurer, Valspar Foundation
Weiss, Neil: chief financial officer, Butler Capital Corp.
Weissman, Robert Evan: secretary, Dun & Bradstreet Corp. Foundation, Inc.
Weizenbaum, Norman: trustee, Giant Eagle Foundation
Welch, John Francis, Jr.: chairman, chief executive officer, director, General Electric Co.
Welch, Kim: vice president corporate affairs, Federal-Mogul Corp.
Welch, Patrick: chief executive officer, National Life of Vermont
Weldon, Virginia V., MD: chairman, president, chief executive officer, director, Monsanto Co.
Wellborn, Sam M.: vice president, Synovus Charitable Trust
Weller, Joseph M.: officer,-director, Nestle U.S.A. Inc.
Wellman, Thomas A.: controller, assistant treasurer, Alexander & Baldwin, Inc.
Wellman, W. Arvid: director, Bayport Foundation
Wells, Henry G.: vice president, director, Banta Corp. Foundation
Wells, James M., III: president, Crestar Finance Corp.
Wells, Richard Arthur: group president power systems, Kohler Co.
Welsh, Kelly Raymond: executive vice president, general counsel, Ameritech Corp.
Welty, John Rider: vice president, Carpenter Technology Corp.; secretary, Carpenter Technology Corp. Foundation
Wendlandt, Gary Edward: executive vice president, chief investment officer, Massachusetts Mutual Life Insurance Co.
Wendt, John R.: president, Maybelline, Inc.
Wendt, Nancy: trustee, Jeld-wen Foundation
Wendt, Richard L.: trustee, Jeld-wen Foundation; chief executive officer, chairman, Jeld-wen, Inc.
Wendt, Roderick C.: trustee, Jeld-wen Foundation; president, director, Jeld-wen, Inc.
Wentworth, Jack Roberts, Ph.D.: director, Habig Foundation
Wenzel, Fred William: chairman emeritus, Kellwood Co.
Wenzler, Joseph P.: secretary, treasurer, WICOR Foundation; senior vice president, chief financial officer, WICOR, Inc.
Weppler, Lawrence G.: treasurer, Continental Grain Foundation
Werner, Lea: senior vice president, Washington Trust Bank
Wesley, Norman H.: president, chief operating officer, Fortune Brands, Inc.
Wessel, Larry K.: trustee, Ashland Inc. Foundation
Wessels, Kenneth J.: director, Dain Bosworth Foundation; chairman, president, chief executive officer, Dain Bosworth Inc.
West, A. Stanley: trustee, Cleveland-Cliffs Foundation (The); senior vice president, sales & commercial planning, Cleveland-Cliffs, Inc.
West, Arnold B.: counsel, Aetna Foundation; assistant secretary counsel, Aetna, Inc.
West, Doug: senior vice president external affairs, Toyota Motor Sales U.S.A., Inc.; senior vice president, coordinating officer, Toyota U.S.A. Foundation
West, Edward H.: chief financial officer, Delta Air Lines, Inc.
West, Franklin: administrator, West Foundation (Herman O.)
West, Gillis: trustee, Reynolds & Reynolds Co. Foundation
West, Jean M.: director, Fuller Co. Foundation (H.B.)
West, Randall E.: director, Ryder System Charitable Foundation
West, Rhonda K.: vice president corporate communications, May Department Stores Co.
West, Robert H.: executive, Butler Manufacturing Co.
Westerman, Ted G.: director public affairs & administration, Hughes Electronics Corp.
Westfall, David M.: senior vice president, chief financial officer, Consolidated Natural Gas Co.
Westin, David: manager corporate giving, ABC Foundation
Westover, Frank Thomas: senior vice president, Whitman Corp.; director, Whitman Corp. Foundation

Wetter, Larry V.: trustee, Jeld-wen Foundation; vice chairman, director, Jeld-wen, Inc.
Weyerhaeuser, George Hunt: director, Weyerhaeuser Co.; trustee, Weyerhaeuser Co. Foundation
Weyers, James A.: president, AK Steel Corp.; executive secretary, AK Steel Foundation
Weyers, Larry Lee: chief executive officer, chairman, director, Wisconsin Public Service Corp.; president, chief executive officer, Wisconsin Public Service Foundation, Inc.
Weyhing, R. L., III: president, director, Fabri-Kal Corp.; secretary, Fabri-Kal Foundation
Whalen, Kevin: treasurer, Jostens Foundation Inc. (The)
Whaley, Ronald L.: vice president, Solo Cup Foundation
Wheat, Allen D.: president, chairman, Credit Suisse First Boston
Wheat, Ted W.: chief financial officer, director, AmerUS Group
Wheatley, Bruce C.: trustee, Commercial Intertech Foundation
Wheeler, Joyce W.: secretary, Royal & SunAlliance Insurance Foundation, Inc.; vice president, corporate secretary, Royal & SunAlliance USA, Inc.
Wheeler, Kathryn Lillard: chairman, Cadence Designs Systems, Inc.
Wheeler, Thomas Beardsley: chairman, chief executive officer, Massachusetts Mutual Life Insurance Co.
Wheelock, Ann Marie: director, Fannie Mae Foundation
Whelan, Jay: secretary, treasurer, Wyman-Gordon Foundation
Whelpley, Kathy: director, Freddie Mac; associates director, Freddie Mac Foundation
Whisler, J. Steven: chairman, president, chief executive officer, Phelps Dodge Corp.
Whitacre, Edward E., Jr.: chairman, director, chief executive officer, SBC Communications Inc.
White, Bernard Joseph: director, Cummins Engine Foundation
White, Britton, Jr.: chairman, director, El Paso Energy Foundation
White, Eileen: chairman, president, chief executive officer, director, Cooper Tire & Rubber Co.; trustee, Cooper Tire & Rubber Foundation
White, Eugene A.: vice president, secretary, Collins & Aikman Corp.; president, director, Collins & Aikman Foundation
White, Gerald Andrew: chairman, president, chief executive officer, director, Air Products and Chemicals, Inc.; director, Air Products Foundation
White, James M., III: general counsel, Universal Leaf Foundation; senior vice president, general counsel, assistant secretary, Universal Leaf Tobacco Co., Inc.
White, James R.: coord, Square D Foundation
White, Kathy B.: director, Baxter Allegiance Foundation
White, Michael: senior vice president, Shoney's Inc.
White, Patricia: assistant vice president public relations, Maybelline, Inc.
White, Thomas A. H.: vice president corporate relations, Provident Companies, Inc.
White, Tommi A.: executive vice president finance, chief financial officer, Kelly Services; director, Kelly Services Foundation
White, Walter Lucas: trustee, Kemper Foundation (James S.)
Whitehead, Charles: assistant treasurer, Ashland Inc. Foundation
Whitehead, John Cunningham: board member, Goldman Sachs Foundation
Whitehurst, David B.: corporate vice president, Amsted Industries Inc.
Whitelaw, Essie M.: president, chief operating officer, United Wisconsin Services; vice president, United Wisconsin Services Foundation
Whitfield, J. D.: vice chairman, Sverdrup Corp.
Whitman, Tracy: secretary, Anthem Foundation, Inc.
Whitney, Wallace F., Jr.: chairman, vice president, director, Wyman-Gordon Foundation
Whittam, James H.: executive vice president, Shaklee Companies, Shaklee Corp.
Whitwam, David Ray: chairman, president, chief executive officer, director, Whirlpool Corp.
Wiborg, James Hooker: corporate service manager, PACCAR Foundation
Wiengarten, Tom: president, chief executive officer, Sentry Insurance, A Mutual Co.
Wiens, Harold J.: executive vice president, Minnesota Mining & Manufacturing Co.
Wiese, Ronald O.: trustee, Ladish Co. Foundation
Wiesner, Carol A.: secretary, Foundation of the Litton Industries
Wiest, Hiram L.: trustee, York Federal Savings & Loan Foundation
Wigdale, James B.: vice president, Marshall & Ilsley Corp.; vice president, director, Marshall & Ilsley Foundation, Inc.
Wiksten, Barry Frank: vice president, executive director, CIGNA Foundation
Wilbur, Brayton, Jr.: president, chief executive officer, Wilbur-Ellis Co. & Connell Brothers Co.; president, Wilbur Foundation (Brayton)
Wilczura, Christiane S.: member contributions committee, GATX Corp.
Wild, Heidi Karin: secretary,
Wilder, Michael Stephen: member contributions committee, Hartford (The)
Wilder, Robert D.: executive vice president, chief financial officer, Wiley & Sons (John)
Wiley, Barbara M.: president, director, Badger Meter Foundation
Wiley, Bradford, II: chairman, director, Wiley & Sons (John)
Wiley, Deborah: vice chairman, Wiley & Sons (John)
Wiley, Michael E.: president, ARCO Foundation
Wiley, S. Donald: chairman, trustee, Heinz Co. Foundation (H.J.)
Wilhelm, Clarke L.: trustee, Reilly Foundation
Wilhelm, Paul J.: chairman board trustees, USX Foundation, Inc.
Wilhelm, Robert E.: senior vice president, Exxon Mobil Corp.
Wilhelm, Suzanne Anthony: director, IMMI Word and Deed Foundation
Wilks, David M.: treasurer, New Century Energies Foundation
Willes, Mark Hinckley: chairman, president, chief executive officer, Times Mirror Co.; chairman, Times Mirror Foundation
Willet, Daniel J.: vice president, director, Continental Grain Foundation
Williams, Barbara Coull: vice president human resources, Pacific Gas and Electric Co.
Williams, Carolyn R.: president, director, Southern California Gas Co.
Williams, Charles, Jr.: senior vice president auto forms, Reynolds & Reynolds Co.
Williams, David: chief financial officer, North American Royalties
Williams, David R.: trustee, Heinz Co. Foundation (H.J.); executive vice president, director, Heinz Co. (H.J.)
Williams, David T.: president, trustee, Invacare Foundation
Williams, Edward Joseph: director, Harris Bank Foundation
Williams, Elynor Alberta: executive director, Sara Lee Foundation
Williams, Eugene Flewellyn, Jr.: member public policy committee, Emerson Charitable Trust
Williams, Jane: chairman, trustee, Quaker Chemical Foundation
Williams, John A.: president, chief executive officer, Louisiana Land & Exploration Co.; director, Louisiana Land & Exploration Co. Foundation
Williams, Karen Hastie: director, Fannie Mae Foundation
Williams, Lynn M.: chairman, president, chief executive officer, Southern Co. Services Inc.
Williams, Martha G.: secretary, administrator, Liberty Corp. Foundation
Williams, R. M.: president, director, Riggs Bank NA
Williams, Robert: secretary, treasurer, MacMillan Bloedel Foundation
Williams, Sarah: chairman, chief executive officer, director, Pfizer Inc.
Williams, Stephen E.: senior vice president, general counsel, Consolidated Natural Gas Co.; president, Consolidated Natural Gas System Foundation
Williams, William Joseph: trustee, Western-Southern Foundation, Inc.; chairman, director, Western & Southern Life Insurance Co.
Williamson, Henry Gaston, Jr.: chief operating officer, Branch Banking & Trust Co.
Willis, Bertram C.: trustee, Campbell Soup Foundation
Willis, Gordon A.: chief financial officer, vice president, treasurer, Wisconsin Energy Corp.; assistant treasurer, assistant secretary, Wisconsin Energy Corp. Foundation, Inc.
Willis, Jo Ellyn: secretary, director, Square D Foundation
Willis, Patricia: vice president, BellSouth Foundation
Willner, Robin: president, IBM International Foundation
Willoughby, Donald E.: chief financial officer, IBP; executive director, IBP Foundation
Wills, Dianna K.: director, AMP Foundation; assistant chairman contributions committee, AMP Inc.
Wilmers, Robert George: chairman, president, chief executive officer, Manufacturers & Traders Trust Co.
Wilson, Bonita: co-chief operating officer, Crown Books
Wilson, Bruce A.: senior vice president, BankBoston-Connecticut Region
Wilson, Charles D.: vice president, Fort James Corp.; director, Fort James Foundation (The)
Wilson, Cleo Francine: director, Playboy Enterprises Inc.; executive director, Playboy Foundation
Wilson, Dennis K.: vice president finance, chief financial officer, Beckman Coulter, Inc.
Wilson, Eric L.: director, Hensel Phelps Foundation
Wilson, Gary Lee: chairman, director, Northwest Airlines, Inc.
Wilson, Harold S.: vice president, Osborne Foundation (Weldon F.)
Wilson, Jackie: president, chief executive officer, director, Lyondell Chemical Co.
Wilson, James Lawrence: chairman, chief executive officer, director, Rohm & Haas Co.
Wilson, Larry: vice president, director, CUNA Mutual Group Foundation, Inc.
Wilson, Mary Jane: treasurer, Nalco Foundation
Wilson, Rita P.: chairman, chief executive officer, president, Sears, Roebuck and Co.; director, Sears, Roebuck and Co. Foundation
Wilson, Robert B.: secretary, Weyerhaeuser Co. Foundation
Wilson, Sandra C.: vice president, administrator, director, International Paper Co. Foundation
Wilson, Stephen R.: executive vice president, chief financial officer, Reader's Digest Association, Inc. (The)

Windham, Dick: executive director, Burlington Industries Foundation; director public relations, Burlington Industries, Inc.
Windle, Timothy J.: vice president, controller, chief acct officer, APL Ltd.
Windsor, Francis: director, Blue Cross & Blue Shield of Minnesota Foundation Inc.
Winger, Charles Joseph (Chuck): vice president, chief financial officer, Cinergy Corp.
Winick, Alyson: trustee, Schwebel Family Foundation
Winiger, Leonard J.: president, director, American General Finance; assistant treasurer, assistant controller, American General Finance Foundation
Winking, Thomas: trustee, Woodward Governor Co. Charitable Trust
Winter, William Bergford: president, Bucyrus-Erie Co.; chairman, president, director, Bucyrus-Erie Foundation
Winterton, Joyce: director, Autodesk Foundation
Wise, Terri: president, chief executive officer, director, Kellwood Co.; secretary, treasurer, director, Kellwood Foundation
Wise, William Allen: chairman, president, chief executive officer, director, El Paso Energy Co.; chairman, director, El Paso Energy Foundation
Wishart, Steven William: director, ReliaStar Foundation
Wishnick, Lisa: president, director, Wishnick Foundation (Robert I.)
Wishnick, William: director, Wishnick Foundation (Robert I.)
Wiskowski, Carol A.: assistant vice president administration, Madison Gas & Electric Co.; secretary, Madison Gas & Electric Foundation
Witham, Marvin: president, chief executive officer, chief financial officer, Van Leer Holding; treasurer, Van Leer U.S. Foundation
Witmer, Cathy R.: assistant treasurer, Armstrong Foundation
Wittig, David C.: chairman, president, chief executive officer, Western Resources Inc.
Wobst, Frank: chairman, chief executive officer, director, Huntington Bancshares Inc.
Wohlert, Roger W.: vice president, secretary, SBC Foundation
Woischke, Rody: executive vice president, American Electric Power
Wojchik, Larry: executive director, Land O'Lakes Foundation
Wolf, Gregory H.: president, chief operating officer, director, Humana, Inc.
Wolf, Henry C.: vice chairman, chief financial officer, Norfolk Southern Corp.; vice president finance, Norfolk Southern Foundation
Wolf, Janet: vice president, secretary, director, CertainTeed Corp. Foundation
Wolf, Philip C.: senior vice president, general counsel, secretary, Cyprus Amax Minerals Co.
Wolf, Thomas W.: trustee, York Federal Savings & Loan Foundation
Wolf, William T.: trustee, York Federal Savings & Loan Foundation
Wolfe, Dan: member, SAFECO Corp.
Wolfe, Kenneth L.: chairman, chief executive officer, director, Hershey Foods Corp.
Wolfert, Rick: president, chief operating officer, Heller Financial, Inc.
Wolff, Herbert Eric: director, First Hawaiian Foundation
Wolff, Jesse David: secretary, director, Weil, Gotshal & Manges Foundation
Wolter, Gary J.: senior vice president administration, Madison Gas & Electric Co.; vice president, Madison Gas & Electric Foundation
Wolters, Kate Pew: trustee, Steelcase Foundation
Womack, C. Suzanne: manager, Lincoln Financial Group
Womack, Robert R.: chairman, chief executive officer, director, Zurn Industries, Inc.
Wong, Evelyn S.: director, Occidental Petroleum Charitable Foundation
Wong, Sandra C. H.: vice president, director, Servco Foundation
Woo, Richard A.: vice president, Levi Strauss Foundation
Wood, Bill: member, PacifiCare Health System Foundation
Wood, Edward Jenner: member, SunTrust Bank Atlanta Foundation
Wood, Paul W.: director, Unilever Foundation
Wood, Stephen R.: president, LG&E Energy Corp.; vice president, LG&E Energy Foundation
Wood, Willis B., Jr.: chairman, chief executive officer, director, Pacific Enterprises
Woodbury, John D., MD: president, director, Physicians Mutual Insurance Co. Foundation
Woods, F. E.: secretary, treasurer, Copolymer Foundation
Woods, Jacqueline F.: president, Ameritech Ohio
Woodward, Joanne Gignilliat: president, Newman's Own Foundation
Woodward, Robert J., Jr.: trustee, Nationwide Insurance Enterprise Foundation
Woolard, Edgar Smith, Jr.: director, du Pont de Nemours & Co. (E.I.)
Woolbert, Richard E.: chairman, chief executive officer, director, McDermott Inc.
Woolsey, J. R.: executive vice president, chief administrative officer, director corporate compliance, McDermott Inc.
Work, David F.: senior vice president shared service, BP Amoco Corp.; director, BP Amoco Foundation
Workman, John L.: executive vice president, Montgomery Ward & Co., Inc.; executive vice president, director, Montgomery Ward Foundation
Worley, Kenneth: secretary, director, Group Health Foundation
Wraith, William: chief executive officer, Nomura Holding America
Wray, Donald E.: president, chief operating officer, director, Tyson Foods Inc.
Wredberg, Conrad J., Junior: senior vice president, chairman, corp. operating committee, Scientific-Atlanta, Inc.
Wright, Arnold W., Jr.: executive vice president, chief financial officer, CIGNA Corp.; vice president, executive director, CIGNA Foundation
Wright, Donald Franklin: treasurer, chief financial officer, Times Mirror Foundation
Wright, Elease E.: counsel, Aetna Foundation
Wright, James O.: president, director, Badger Meter Foundation; chairman, director, Badger Meter, Inc.; secretary, Marshall & Ilsley Foundation, Inc.
Wright, Jason H.: senior vice president worldwide communications, Reynolds Tobacco (R.J.); president, RJR Nabisco Foundation
Wright, Michael William: chairman, president, chief executive officer, director, SuperValu, Inc.
Wright, Samuel G.: trustee, Eckerd Corp. Foundation
Wright, Victor R.: director, NASDAQ Stock Market Educational Foundation
Wrigley, Julie Ann: director, Scripps Co. (E.W.)
Wrigley, William: chairman, director, Wrigley Co. Foundation (Wm. Jr.); president, chief executive officer, director, Wrigley Co. (Wm. Jr.)
Wrigley, William, Jr.: vice president, director, Wrigley Co. Foundation (Wm. Jr.)
Wulf, Gene C.: trustee, Bemis Co. Foundation
Wurtele, C. Angus: vice president, Valspar Foundation
Wurtzel, Alan Leon: chairman, Circuit City Foundation; chairman, trustee, Circuit City Stores, Inc.
Wyld, Deborah: vice president finance, Norfolk Southern Foundation
Wyman, William: president, Oshkosh B'Gosh Foundation Inc.
Wyne, Jon R.: senior vice president, treasurer, Bayer Corp.; treasurer, Bayer Foundation
Wynia, Ann: director, Fuller Co. Foundation (H.B.)
Wynn, Pat: treasurer, Sundstrand Corp. Foundation
Wynne, John Oliver: president, director, Landmark Communications Foundation; president, chief executive officer, Landmark Communications Inc.
Wyper, Janet: director public affairs, Bean, Inc. (L.L.)
Wyrsch, Martha B.: treasurer, KN Energy Foundation
Wyse, J. Christopher: trustee, Whirlpool Foundation
Wyszomierski, Jack L.: treasurer, Schering-Plough Foundation

Y

Yablon, Leonard Harold: secretary-treasurer, Forbes Foundation; chairman, Forbes Inc.
Yaeger, Douglas H.: chairman, trustee, Laclede Gas Charitable Trust; vice president community relations, Laclede Gas Co.
Yamaguchi, C.: senior vice president, treasurer, Toyota Motor Sales U.S.A., Inc.
Yamashita, Shunichi: president, chief executive officer, Toshiba America Inc.
Yancey, James D.: vice chairman, director, president, chief operating officer, Synovus Financial Corp.
Yao, Lily K.: director, First Hawaiian, Inc.
Yasinsky, John B.: chairman, president, chief executive officer, GenCorp
Yasui, Toshihide: director, Toshiba America Foundation; president, chief executive officer, Toshiba America Inc.
Yates, Jim R.: trustee,
Yeager, Jane Meseck: senior program officer, Microsoft Corp.
Yeomans, Janet L.: treasurer, director, 3M Foundation; director, Minnesota Mining & Manufacturing Co.
Yezbak, Mona: trustee, Reynolds & Reynolds Co. Foundation
Yocum, Robert G.: trustee, Harsco Corp. Fund
Yohe, Merrill A., Jr.: director, AMP Foundation; chairman contributions committee, AMP Inc.
Yoshimatsu, Hiroki: director, Mitsubishi Electric America Foundation
Yoshiyama, Hirokichi: secretary, director, Hitachi Foundation
Young, Gerald T.: secretary, treasurer, trustee, Bourns Foundation; vice president finance, chief financial officer, treasurer, Bourns, Inc.
Young, Mike: vice president community affairs, Delta Air Lines Foundation; chairman, president, chief executive officer, Delta Air Lines, Inc.
Young, Robert Harris: president, chief executive officer, Central Vermont Public Service Corp.
Young, William D.: chief operating officer, Genentech Inc.
Younglove, Eileen M.: secretary, United Airlines Foundation; contributions manager, United Airlines Inc.
Younts, Rosemary: senior vice president communications, GenCorp

Z

Zaar, Carl L.: president, director, Universal Foods Foundation
Zabala, John: administrator, secretary, director, Morrison Knudsen Corp. Foundation, Inc.
Zaccaria, Adrian: president, chief operating officer, director, Bechtel Group, Inc.

Zachem, Harry M.: president, Ashland Inc. Foundation
Zachry, Henry Bartell, Jr.: chairman, Zachry Co. (H.B.); trustee, Zachry Foundation (The)
Zachry, J. P.: trustee, Zachry Foundation (The)
Zachry, Mollie Steves: trustee, Zachry Foundation (The)
Zackrison, Jack: director, Kirkland & Ellis Foundation
Zacks, Gordon Benjamin: chairman, president, chief executive officer, director, Barry Corp. (R.G.); president, Barry Foundation
Zadel, C. William: chairman, president, chief executive officer, Millipore Corp.; trustee, Millipore Foundation (The)
Zahara, Ellis: assistant secretary, Winn-Dixie Stores Foundation
Zamora, Gloria: chairman, president, chief executive officer, director, Whirlpool Corp.; trustee, Whirlpool Foundation
Zampetis, Theodore K.: president, chief operating officer, director, Standard Products Co.
Zapf, Tom: president, chief operating officer, Macy's East Inc.
Zatta, Robert J.: vice president finance, Campbell Soup Co.
Zavis, Michael W.: managing partner, Katten, Muchin & Zavis; president, director, Katten, Muchin & Zavis Foundation
Zech, Ronald H.: chairman, president, chief executive officer, chief operating officer, GATX Corp.
Zeffren, Eugene: chairman, Curtis Industries, Inc. (Helene)
Zeglis, John D.: chairman and chief executive officer wireless group, AT&T Corp.
Zeien, Alfred Michael: director
Zeigler, Kenneth B.: treasurer, Brunswick Foundation
Zeigon, James W.: executive vice president, Chase Manhattan Bank, NA; trustee, Chase Manhattan Foundation
Zemelman, David: director, CBS Foundation
Zemsky, Howard: president, Russer Foods; trustee, Russer Foods/Zemsky Family Trust
Zemsky, Sam: chairman, director, Russer Foods; trustee, Russer Foods/ Zemsky Family Trust
Zemsky, Shirley: trustee, Russer Foods/Zemsky Family Trust
Zenner, Patrick J.: trustee, Hoffmann-La Roche Foundation; president, chief executive officer, director, Hoffmann-La Roche Inc.
Zermuehlen, William: president, director, Pittway Corp. Charitable Foundation
Ziegler, Juliet Joy: community relations manager, US Bank, Washington
Ziegler, R. Douglas: advisor, Johnson Controls Foundation
Ziemer, James L.: assistant secretary, Harley-Davidson Foundation
Zigas, Barry: senior vice president, Fannie Mae; director, Fannie Mae Foundation
Zilkha, Cecile E.: president, treasurer, Zilkha Foundation, Inc.
Zilkha, Ezra Khedouri: president, treasurer, Zilkha Foundation, Inc.; president, Zilkha & Sons
Zilligen, Jil: chief financial officer, Patagonia Inc.
Zimmerman, James M.: chairman, chief executive officer, director, Federated Department Stores, Inc.
Zimmerman, Michael E.: vice president, general counsel, Montana Power Co.
Zimmerman, S. LaNette: senior vice president human resources, Chicago Title Corp.; trustee, Chicago Title and Trust Co. Foundation
Zimmerman, Wayne M.: vice president, Caterpillar Foundation
Zlotnik, Ronald: trustee, Sherman-Standard Register Foundation; chairman, director, Standard Register Co.
ZoBell, Karl: treasurer, trustee, Copley Foundation (James S.)
Zoffmann, Beth Clark: assistant secretary, Georgia-Pacific Foundation
Zona, Richard A.: vice chairman commercial banking & institutional finance, U.S. Bancorp
Zuber, Harold L., Jr.: vice president, chief financial officer, Teleflex Inc.
Zuckerman, Mortimer Benjamin: co-founder, chairman, co-publisher, director, Daily News
Zuehlke, Gerald L.: treasurer, Potlatch Corp.
Zuendt, William F.: president, chief executive officer, Wells Fargo & Co.
Zukrou, Susan: director, Chicago Tribune Foundation
Zumbach, Steve: trustee, Mid-American Foundation
Zumbrun, Maria: director public affairs & administration, Hughes Electronics Corp.
Zunker, Richard E.: member, SAFECO Corp.
Zurn, James A.: chairman, chief executive officer, director, Zurn Industries, Inc.
Zutz, Denise M.: admin secretary, Johnson Controls Foundation
Zwemer, Andy: member contributions committee, Clorox Co.
Zylstra, Stanley James: chairman, director, Land O'Lakes, Inc.

Officers And Directors By Place Of Birth

Lists individuals by the state or country in which they were born.

United States

Alabama

Amos, Paul Shelby: co-founder, chairman, director, AFLAC Inc.

Bakane, John L.: president, chief executive officer, director, Cone Mills Corp.

Blount, Winton Malcolm, Jr.: chairman, Blount International, Inc.

Bowden, Travis J.: chairman, president, chief executive officer, director, Gulf Power Co.

Bowdoin, William R., Jr.: first vice president, SunTrust Bank Atlanta; secretary, SunTrust Bank Atlanta Foundation

Callaway, Lee: vice president public relations, Pacific Gas and Electric Co.

Denson, William Frank, III: president, Vulcan Materials Co. Foundation

Dollar, William Michael: vice president, treasurer, chief financial officer, Harland Co. (John H.)

Fountain, W. Frank, Jr.: senior vice president government affairs, DaimlerChrysler Corp.; president, DaimlerChrysler Corp. Fund

Ginn, Samuel L.: chairman, director, AirTouch Communications Foundation; chairman, chief executive officer, director, Vodafone AirTouch Plc

Hardy, Gene M.: director, La-Z-Boy Foundation

Harris, Elmer Beseler: president, chief executive officer, director, Alabama Power Co.

Hogans, Mack L.: chairman, president, trustee, Weyerhaeuser Co. Foundation

Horsley, Richard David: vice chairman, executive financial officer, director, Regions Financial Corp.

Hutchins, William Bruce, III: director, Alabama Power Foundation

Jones, D. Paul, Jr.: chairman, chief executive officer, Compass Bank; trustee, Compass Bank Foundation

Leggett, Richard B.: member screening committee, PPG Industries Foundation

Mackin, James Stanley: chairman, chief executive officer, Regions Financial Corp.

McInnes, Duncan Joseph: executive vice president administration, chief administrative officer, Blount International, Inc.

Moore, Jackson W.: president, director, Union Planters Corp.

Nichols, Mack G.: president, chief executive officer, director, Mallinckrodt Chemical, Inc.

Powell, Jerry W.: secretary, general counsel, Compass Bank; secretary, Compass Bank Foundation

Reese, Terry W.: assistant treasurer, Vulcan Materials Co. Foundation

Rogers, C. B., Jr.: chairman, Equifax Foundation; chairman, director, Equifax Inc.

Rogers, James E., Jr.: vice chairman, president, chief executive officer, Cinergy Corp.; vice chairman, director, Cinergy Foundation

Sheafer, William L.: vice president, treasurer, Cinergy Corp.; treasurer, director, Cinergy Foundation

Stephens, Elton Bryson: founder, chairman, Ebsco Industries, Inc.

Thoman, G. Richard: president, chief operating officer, Xerox Corp.

Alaska

Knauss, Dalton L.: trustee, Kemper Foundation (James S.)

Arizona

Bush, Michael J.: vice president real estate, Giant Food Inc.

Campbell, George Leroy: vice president public affairs, Florida Power Corp.

Felsinger, Donald E.: president, chief executive officer, Sempra Energy

Henley, Jeffrey O.: executive vice president, chief financial officer, director, Oracle Corp.

Loftin, Nancy Carol: secretary, director, APS Foundation, Inc.; vice president, general counsel, Arizona Public Service Co.

Peru, Ramiro G.: senior vice president, chief financial officer, Phelps Dodge Corp.

Snell, Richard: chairman, president, chief executive officer, director, Arizona Public Service Co.

Arkansas

Blair, James Burton: trustee, Tyson Foundation, Inc.

Carter, Paul R.: executive vice president, Wal-Mart Stores, Inc.

Davis, Andrew Dano: vice president, director, Winn-Dixie Stores Foundation; vice president, Winn-Dixie Stores Inc.

Elam, Lloyd Charles, MD: trustee, Merck Co. Foundation

Ford, Joseph 'Joe': chairman, chief executive officer, president, ALLTEL Corp.

Holman, Carl Ray: chairman, chief executive officer, director, Mallinckrodt Chemical, Inc.

Temple, Arthur, III: director, Temple-Inland Foundation

Zimmerman, S. LaNette: senior vice president human resources, Chicago Title Corp.; trustee, Chicago Title and Trust Co. Foundation

California

Anderson, Gordon M.: chairman, Santa Fe International Corp.

Bains, Harrison MacKellar, Jr.: vice president, treasurer, Bristol-Myers Squibb Co.; treasurer, Bristol-Myers Squibb Foundation Inc.

Barbakow, Jeffrey C.: chairman, chief executive officer, director, Tenet Healthcare Corp.

Barrett, Craig R.: president, chief operating officer, director, Intel Corp.

Beall, Donald Ray: director, Rockwell International Corp.

Bell, Wayne: secretary, Ralph's-Food 4 Less Foundation; senior counsel, assistant secretary, Ralph's Grocery Co.

Berry, William S.: director, Rayonier Foundation

Binyon, Bryan A.: treasurer, American General Finance Foundation

Black, Natalie A.: group vice president interiors, general counsel, director, Kohler Co.

Brinegar, Claude Stout: trustee, Unocal Foundation

Carey, Kathryn Ann: foundation manager, American Honda Foundation

Clarke, Robert F.: chairman, president, chief executive officer, director, Hawaiian Electric Co., Inc.; president, director, Hawaiian Electric Industries Charitable Foundation

Condit, Philip Murray: chairman, chief executive officer, director, Boeing Co.

Coughlan, Gary Patrick: chief financial officer, senior vice president finance, Abbott Laboratories; director, Abbott Laboratories Fund

Darling, Robert Edward, Jr.: chairman, Ensign-Bickford Foundation

Disney, Roy Edward: trustee, Disney Co. Foundation (Walt); vice chairman, director, Disney Co. (Walt)

Dreyfus, Branton B.: director, Alexander & Baldwin Foundation

Dye, Donald H.: president, chief executive officer, Callaway Golf Co.

Edwards, David M.: vice president finance, chief financial officer, GATX Corp.

Farman, Richard Donald: chairman, chief executive officer, Pacific Enterprises

Flake, Floyd Harold: director, Fannie Mae Foundation

Fluor, John Robert, II: president, trustee, Fluor Corp.

Fraumann, Willard George: president, director, partner, Kirkland & Ellis; president, Kirkland & Ellis Foundation

Gallo, Ernest: director, Gallo Foundation; co-founder, chairman, Gallo Winery, Inc. (E&J)

Groman, Arthur: president, Occidental Petroleum Charitable Foundation

Grundhofer, John Francis: president, chief executive officer, director, U.S. Bancorp

Haas, Peter Edgar, Sr.: chairman executive committee, director, Levi Strauss & Co.

Haas, Robert Douglas: chairman, chief executive officer, director, Levi Strauss & Co.; president, Levi Strauss Foundation

Haskell, Robert G.: president, director, Pacific Mutual Charitable Foundation; senior vice president public affairs, Pacific Mutual Life Insurance Co.

Hill, Steven Richard: senior vice president human resources, Weyerhaeuser Co.; trustee, Weyerhaeuser Co. Foundation

Howat, Bruce Bradshaw, Jr.: secretary, corporate counsel, Ameritech Corp.

Jordan, William M.: president, chief executive officer, chairman, director, Duriron Co., Inc.; president, Duriron Foundation

Klitten, Martin R.: vice president, chief financial officer, Chevron Corp.

Lacey, David C.: executive vice president, chief financial officer, Storage Technology Corp.; chief financial officer, director, StorageTek Foundation

Larson, Peter N.: chairman, chief executive officer, director, Brunswick Corp.

Leonis, John Michael: chairman, director, Litton Industries, Inc.

Lucas, Donald Leo: chairman, Cadence Designs Systems, Inc.

Maffie, Michael O.: president, chief executive officer, director, Southwest Gas Corp.; trustee, Southwest Gas Corp. Foundation

Malquist, Malyn K.: chairman, Sierra Pacific Resources

McCracken, Steve: director, secretary, Callaway Golf Co. Foundation

McFerson, Dimon Richard: chairman, chief executive officer, Nationwide Insurance Co.; chairman, chief executive officer, trustee, Nationwide Insurance Enterprise Foundation; chairman, chief executive officer, Wausau Insurance Companies

Meier, Stephen Charles: vice chairman, Times Mirror Co.

Mitchell, Warren I.: president, director, Southern California Gas Co.

Moore, Gordon E., PhD: cofounder, chairman emeritus, director, Intel Corp.; trustee, Intel Foundation

Moran, Harry J.: executive vice president, Sonoco Products Co.

Morby, Jacqueline C.: managing partner, Pacific Mutual Life Insurance Co.

Mulholland, Charles Bradley: executive vice president, director, Alexander & Baldwin Foundation; executive vice president, Alexander & Baldwin, Inc.

Mullane, Donald A.: executive vice president, Bank of America; chairman, Bank of America Foundation

Neal, Philip Mark: president, chief executive officer, director, Avery Dennison Corp.

Owens, Jack Byron: executive vice president, general counsel, Gallo Winery, Inc. (E&J)

Prosser, John Warren, Jr.: treasurer, director, Jacobs Engineering Foundation; senior vice president finance & administration, treasurer, Jacobs Engineering Group

Reid, Frederick W.: executive vice president, chief marketing officer, Delta Air Lines, Inc.

Rhein, Timothy James: president, chief executive officer, APL Ltd.

Rinehart, Charles Robert: chairman, chief executive officer, director, Washington Mutual, Inc.

Rollans, James Ora: senior vice president, chief administrative officer, chief financial officer, Fluor Corp.; trustee, Fluor Foundation

Rupley, Theodore J.: president, chief executive officer, director, Allmerica Financial Corp.

Satre, Philip Glen: chairman, president, chief executive officer, director, Promus Hotel Corp.

Schwab, Charles R.: chairman, co-chief executive officer, director, Schwab & Co., Inc. (Charles); chairman, Schwab Corp. Foundation (Charles)

Scripps, Charles Edward: chairman executive committee, director, vice president, Scripps Co. (E.W.); member, Scripps Howard Foundation

Scripps, Edward Wyllis, II: member, Scripps Howard Foundation

Simpson, Andrea Lynn: president,

Stivers, William Charles: senior vice president, chief financial officer, treasurer, Weyerhaeuser Co.; treasurer, trustee, Weyerhaeuser Co. Foundation

Stroup, Stanley Stephenson: executive vice president, general counsel, Norwest Corp.

Sullivan, James Norman: vice chairman, director, Chevron Corp.

Ukropina, James R.: partner, Pacific Mutual Life Insurance Co.

Wagner, Harold A.: chairman, president, chief executive officer, director, Air Products and Chemicals, Inc.

Washington, Earl S.: senior vice president communications, Rockwell International Corp.; secretary, Rockwell International Corp. Trust

Weinberger, Caspar Willard: chairman, Forbes Inc.

Wilbur, Brayton, Jr.: president, chief executive officer, Wilbur-Ellis Co. & Connell Brothers Co.; president, Wilbur Foundation (Brayton)

ZoBell, Karl: vice president, trustee, Copley Foundation (James S.)

d'Alessio, Jon W.: trustee, McKesson Foundation

Colorado

Coors, Peter Hanson: vice president, director, Coors Brewing Co.

Coors, William K.: chairman, president, director, Coors Brewing Co.

Eaton, Robert James: cochairman, president, chief executive officer, DaimlerChrysler Corp.

Gaylord, Edward Lewis: chairman, chief executive officer, director, publisher, Oklahoma Publishing Co.; trustee, Oklahoman Foundation (The)

Hay, Gary W.: vice chairman, Cessna Aircraft Co.; trustee, Cessna Foundation, Inc.

Herres, Robert T.: chairman, chief executive officer, United Services Automobile Association

Hock, Delwin D.: chairman, New Century Energies

Lynch, Charles Allen: chairman, director, Pacific Mutual Life Insurance Co.

McConnell, Richard Lynn: senior vice president, director research, Pioneer Hi-Bred International, Inc.

Stuebgen, William J.: vice president, controller, chief acct officer, APL Ltd.

Suwyn, Mark A.: chairman, president, Louisiana-Pacific Foundation

Toll, Daniel Roger: trustee, Kemper Foundation (James S.)

Connecticut

Barnes, Wallace W.: director, Barnes Group Foundation Inc.

Bigham, James John: executive vice president, chief financial officer, director, Continental Grain Co.

Block, William, Jr.: president, trustee, Blade Foundation; president, director, Toledo Blade Co.

Byck, Joseph S.: vice president, Union Carbide Foundation

Cookson, John Simmons: vice president finance, treasurer, assistant secretary, Kingsbury Corp.; trustee, Kingsbury Fund

Cowan, Keith O.: vice president corporate development, BellSouth Corp.

Daddario, Richard M.: chief financial officer, MONY Life Insurance of New York (The)

DiSilvestro, Anthony P.: vice president, treasurer, Campbell Soup Co.; treasurer, Campbell Soup Foundation

Dingman, Michael David: partner, director, Winthrop Foundation

Elliott, David Holland: consultant, chairman executive committee, MBIA Inc.

Field, Benjamin R., III: senior vice president, chief financial officer, treasurer, Bemis Co., Inc.

Fiondella, Robert William: chairman, president, chief executive officer, Phoenix Home Life Mutual Insurance Co.

Forstmann, Theodore J.: chairman, Gulfstream Aerospace Corp.

Franklin, Marc Scott: senior vice president strategic planning, Pacific Mutual Life Insurance Co.

Goodman, Helen G.: senior vice president, Hartford (The)

Gorman, Maureen V.: vice president, GTE Foundation

Grano, Joseph J., Jr.: president, Paine Webber

Howison, George Everett: vice president, Burlington Resources Foundation

Jones, Russell H.: officer, Kaman Corp.

Kiernan, Donald E., Sr.: senior vice president, chief financial officer, treasurer, SBC Communications Inc.; director, SBC Foundation

Long, Michael Thomas: director, Ensign-Bickford Foundation

Loose, John W.: trustee, Corning Inc. Foundation

Maffucci, David G.: senior vice president, chief financial officer, Bowater Inc.

Miller, Charles Daly: chairman, director, Avery Dennison Corp.; trustee, Whirlpool Foundation

Nickerson, Lucille M.: secretary, Aetna Foundation; vice president, corporate secretary, Aetna, Inc.

Orser, William Stanley: executive vice president energy supply, Carolina Power & Light Co.

Pestillo, Peter John: executive chairman, Ford Motor Co.; trustee, Ford Motor Co. Fund

Phillips, Richard B.: vice president, Crane Foundation

Rubenstein, Leonard Mark: executive vice president investment, director, GenAmerica Corp.; vice president, director, GenAmerican Foundation

Simmons, Richard Paul: chairman, president, chief executive officer, Allegheny Technologies Inc.

Tetrault, Roger E.: chairman, chief executive officer, director, McDermott Inc.

Thurston, Samuel E.: senior vice president distribution, Giant Food Inc.

Warner, John Andrew, III: director, Telcordia Technologies

Weigel, David V.: treasurer, MONY Life Insurance of New York (The)

Delaware

Haskin, Donald Lee: vice president, PNC Bank

Jones, Joseph West: secretary, director, Coca-Cola Foundation

Sparks, Walter Alvon, Jr.: director, GEICO Philanthropic Foundation

Townsend, David L.: vice president administration, Walter Industries Inc.

Wagoner, G. Richard, Jr.: president, chief executive officer, director, General Motors Corp.

Walter, James W.: trustee, Walter Foundation; chairman emeritus, founder, director, Walter Industries Inc.

District of Columbia

Anderson, Mark Bo: senior vice president, European American Bank

Chemerow, David I.: executive vice president, chief financial officer, Playboy Enterprises Inc.

Gans, Terry Alexander: vice president, advertising, Giant Food Inc.

Gilmartin, Raymond V.: chairman, president, chief executive officer, Merck & Co.; chairman, Merck Co. Foundation

Gray, Charles Agustus: vice president technology, Cabot Corp.; director, Cabot Corp. Foundation

Hawes, Alexander Boyd, Jr.: treasurer, Boston Globe Foundation

Heisen, JoAnn Heffernan: vice president, chief information officer, Johnson & Johnson; treasurer, Johnson & Johnson Family of Companies Contribution Fund

Herriman, M. Davis, Junior: senior vice president, chief merchandising officer, Giant Food Inc.

Howes, William B.: chairman, chief executive officer, Inland Container Corp.; vice president, director, Inland Foundation, Inc.

Huey, John W.: vice president administration, Butler Manufacturing Co.; trustee, Butler Manufacturing Co. Foundation

Hunt, V. William: director, Arvin Foundation; chief executive officer, chairman, president, director, Arvin Industries, Inc.

Kaman, Charles Huron: chairman, president, chief executive officer, director, Kaman Corp.

LaMacchia, John Thomas: trustee, Cincinnati Bell Foundation, Inc.; president, chief executive officer, director, Cincinnati Bell Inc.

Lebedoff, Randy Miller: vice president, general counsel, McClatchy Co.; secretary, Star Tribune Foundation

Marriott, J. Willard, Jr.: chairman, chief executive officer, Marriott International Inc.

Mathews, Odonna: vice president consumer affairs, Giant Food Inc.

McCormick, William Thomas, Jr.: chairman, chief executive officer, director, Consumers Energy Co.; chairman, Consumers Energy Foundation

McKenna, Matthew M.: treasurer, PepsiCo Foundation, Inc.; senior vice president, treasurer, PepsiCo, Inc.

Moritz, Charles Worthington: chairman, director, Dun & Bradstreet Corp.

Murphy, Christopher J., III: president, chief executive officer, director, First Source Corp.; director, First Source Foundation

Rand, Addison Barry: executive vice president operations, Xerox Corp.; trustee, Xerox Foundation

Rose, Wayne Myron: treasurer, director, Quanex Foundation

Sharp, Richard L.: trustee, Circuit City Foundation; chairman, chief executive officer, director, Circuit City Stores, Inc.

Sullivan, Austin Padraic, Junior: trustee, General Mills Foundation; senior vice president corporate relations, General Mills, Inc.

Williams, Karen Hastie: director, Fannie Mae Foundation

Yeomans, Janet L.: treasurer, director, 3M Foundation

Florida

Ackerman, F. Duane: president, chief executive officer, BellSouth Corp.

Amos, Daniel P.: president, chief executive officer, director, AFLAC Inc.

Anderson, Judy M.: vice president, corporate secretary, Georgia Power Co.; executive director, secretary, assistant treasurer, Georgia Power Foundation

Baker, John Daniel, II: president, chief executive officer, director, Florida Rock Industries; vice president, Florida Rock Industries Foundation

Buxton, Winslow Hurlbert: chairman, president, chief executive officer, director, Pentair Inc.

Campbell, Cheryl Nichols: operation service advisory group, Cincinnati Bell Inc.

Labrato, Ronnie R.: secretary, Gulf Power Foundation

McCook, Richard P.: vice president, Winn-Dixie Stores Foundation; vice president finance, chief financial officer, Winn-Dixie Stores Inc.

Melrose, Kendrick B.: chairman, co-president, chief executive officer, director, Toro Co.; director, Toro Foundation

West, Edward H.: chief financial officer, Delta Air Lines, Inc.

Georgia

Banks, Peter L.: vice president external affairs, AGL Resources Inc.

Barron, Donald Ray: president, director, Atlantic Investment Co.

Benenson, James, Jr.: chairman, president, director, Vesper Corp.; trustee, Vesper Foundation

Blanchard, James Hubert: chairman, chief executive officer, Synovus Financial Corp.

Burts, Stephen L., Jr.: president, treasurer, chief financial officer, Synovus Financial Corp.

Callaway, Ely Reeves, Jr.: chairman, Callaway Golf Co.

Correll, Alston Dayton 'Pete', Jr.: chairman, president, chief executive officer, director, Georgia-Pacific Corp.; director, Georgia-Pacific Foundation

Courts, Richard Winn, II: chairman, director, Atlantic Investment Co.

Dahlberg, Alfred William, III: chairman, president, chief executive officer, Southern Co. Services Inc.

Demere, Robert H.: president, Colonial Foundation; chairman, Colonial Oil Industries, Inc.

Ecker, H. Allen: president subscriber systems, Scientific-Atlanta, Inc.

Edison, Bernard Alan: member, Edison Family Foundation

Escarra, Vicki: executive vice president customer service, Delta Air Lines, Inc.

Fricks, William Peavy: chairman, chief executive officer, Newport News Shipbuilding

Greene, Donald Ray: assistant vice president, Coca-Cola Co.; president, director, Coca-Cola Foundation

Herman, William A., III: secretary, treasurer, director, Morris Communications Corp.

Hopkins, Wayne W.: vice president corporate communications, Tampa Electric Co.

Hyatt, Kenneth Ernest: chairman, president, chief executive officer, director, Walter Industries Inc.

Ives, J. Atwood: chairman, chief executive officer, Boston Gas Co.; chairman, chief executive officer, trustee, Eastern Enterprises; trustee, Eastern Enterprises Foundation

Jones, David R.: principal, AGL Resources Inc.

Levy, David: trustee, National Service Foundation

Mathis, David B.: chairman, Kemper Foundation (James S.)

Morris, William Shivers, III: founder, chairman, chief executive officer, director, Morris Communications Corp.; trustee, Stauffer Communications Foundation

Ratcliffe, David M.: chief financial officer, treasurer, director, Georgia Power Co.

Rowell, Harry Brown, Jr.: trustee, Hubbell Foundation (Harvey)

Shaw, Robert E.: chairman, chief executive officer, Shaw Industries Inc.

Sutton, Thomas C.: chairman, director, Pacific Mutual Charitable Foundation; chairman, chief executive officer, director, Pacific Mutual Life Insurance Co.

Thompson, Robert L.: vice president public affairs, Springs Industries, Inc.

Woodward, Joanne Gignilliat: director, Newman's Own Foundation

Zoffmann, Beth Clark: vice president, director, Georgia-Pacific Foundation

Hawaii

Anthony, Barbara Cox: chairman, Cox Foundation (James M.)

Ching, Meredith J.: senior vice president, director, chairman HI committee, Alexander & Baldwin Foundation; vice president government & community relations, Alexander & Baldwin, Inc.

Dods, Walter Arthur, Jr.: president, director, First Hawaiian Foundation; chairman, chief executive officer, director, First Hawaiian, Inc.

Fukunaga, Mark H.: chairman, director, Servco Foundation; chief executive officer, chairman, Servco Pacific

Guerrero, Anthony R., Jr.: director, First Hawaiian Foundation

Johnson, Lawrence M.: president, Pacific Century Financial Corp.

Karr, Howard Henry: treasurer, director, First Hawaiian Foundation

Nakagawa, Jean H.: vice president, director, Servco Foundation

Nakamura, Alyson J.: secretary, Alexander & Baldwin Foundation

Pang, Gerald M.: director, First Hawaiian Foundation

Sasaki, Robert K.: director, Alexander & Baldwin Foundation

Watanabe, Jeffrey N.: director, Hawaiian Electric Industries Charitable Foundation

Idaho

Crawford, James D.: treasurer, Simplot Foundation (J.R.)

Graves, Ronald Norman: secretary, Simplot Foundation (J.R.)

Heiner, Clyde Mont: executive vice president, Questar Corp.

Humphrey, Neil Darwin: trustee, Commercial Intertech Foundation

Keen, J. LaMont: vice president, chief financial officer, Idaho Power Co.

Marshall, Joseph W.: chairman, chief executive officer, Idaho Power Co.

Olson, A. Craig: senior vice president finance, chief financial officer, Albertson's Inc.

Powell, Sandra Theresa: trustee, Potlatch Foundation II

Illinois

Alberts, Bruce Michael, PhD: director, Genentech Foundation for Biomedical Sciences

Alpert, Janet A.: president, chief operating officer, director, LandAmerica Financial Services; trustee, LandAmerica Foundation

Altenbaumer, Larry F.: senior vice president, chief financial officer, Illinois Power Co.

Ashley, James Wheeler: director, Globe Foundation

Bachmann, John W.: managing partner, Jones & Co. (Edward D.); chairman, Jones & Co. Foundation (Edward D.)

Ballantyne, Richard Lee: vice president, general counsel, secretary, Harris Corp.; secretary, treasurer, Harris Foundation

Baukol, Ronald O.: director, executive vice president, Minnesota Mining & Manufacturing Co.

Bell, Bradley John: vice president, treasurer, Whirlpool Corp.; treasurer, Whirlpool Foundation

Benninger, Edward Charles, Jr.: president, chief financial officer, Valero Energy Corp.

Berlik, Leonard J.: vice president, National Starch & Chemical Co.

Bickner, Bruce P.: chairman, chief executive officer, director, DeKalb Genetics Corp.

Bodman, Samuel Wright, III: chairman, chief executive officer, director, Cabot Corp.; president, director, Cabot Corp. Foundation

Boswell, John Joseph: president, Boswell Foundation, Inc.; chairman, Independent Stave Co.

Braham, W. Martin: trustee, Delta Air Lines Foundation

Brazier, Robert George: president, chief operating officer, director, Airborne Freight Corp.

Brown, Joseph Warner, Jr.: chairman, chief executive officer, MBIA Inc.

Brunner, Vernon A.: executive vice president marketing, Walgreen Co.

Burrus, Clark D.: vice president, director, First National Bank of Chicago Foundation

Butts, David Wayne: senior vice president, Illinois Power Co.

Canning, John Beckman: secretary, Rayonier Foundation

Carpenter, Marshall L.: vice president, chief financial officer, MTS Systems Corp.

Carr, Cassandra Colvin: director, SBC Foundation

Chelberg, Bruce Stanley: chairman, chief executive officer, director, Whitman Corp.; director, Whitman Corp. Foundation

Chookaszian, Dennis Haig: chairman, chief executive officer, CNA

Clanin, Robert J.: senior vice president, chief financial officer, treasurer, director, United Parcel Service of America Inc.

Cline, Robert Stanley: chairman, chief executive officer, director, Airborne Freight Corp.

Coffey, John: vice president programs, State Farm Companies Foundation; senior vice president, State Farm Mutual Automobile Insurance Co.

Commes, Thomas Allen: president, chief operating officer, director, Sherwin-Williams Co.; assistant secretary, trustee, Sherwin-Williams Foundation

Condon, James Edward: treasurer, Hartmarx Charitable Foundation; vice president, treasurer, Hartmarx Corp.

Corby, Francis Michael, Jr.: executive vice president finance & administration, chief financial officer, Harnischfeger Industries; treasurer, Harnischfeger Industries Foundation

Creek, Wallace W.: secretary, General Motors Foundation

Dabney, Donna C.: secretary, Reynolds Metals Co. Foundation

Dabney, Fred E., II: executive director, Royal & SunAlliance Insurance Foundation, Inc.; vice president corporate communications, Royal & SunAlliance USA, Inc.

Dahm, Anthony Edward: controller, Giant Food Inc.

Dargene, Carl J.: director, AMCORE Foundation

Davis, Walter Stewart: secretary, treasurer, Grede Foundation

Donnelley, James R.: vice chairman, Donnelley & Sons Co. (R.R.)

Donovan, Thomas Roy: president, chief executive officer, Chicago Board of Trade

Duchossois, Richard Louis: secretary, Duchossois Foundation; chairman, chief executive officer, director, Duchossois Industries Inc.

England, Joseph Walker: chairman, director, Deere Foundation (John)

Ervanian, Armen: vice president, Viad Corp. Fund

Feller, Robert J.: vice president, Shelter Mutual Insurance Co.

Ferguson, Ronald Eugene: chairman, president, chief executive officer, director, General Reinsurance Corp.

Fish, Lawrence K.: trustee, Citizens Charitable Foundation; chairman, chief executive officer, Citizens Financial Group, Inc.

Fisher, George Myles Cordell: chairman, president, chief executive officer, director, Eastman Kodak Co.

Flaherty, Gerald S.: trustee, Caterpillar Foundation; group president, Caterpillar Inc.

Forsythe, John G.: vice president tax and public affairs, Ecolab Inc.

Fuller, Harry Laurance: co-chairman, director, BP Amoco Corp.

Gaiswinkler, Robert Sigfried: chairman, director, First Financial Bank; director, First Financial Foundation

Gauvreau, Paul Richard: treasurer, Pittway Corp. Charitable Foundation

Getz, Bert A.: chairman, Globe Corp.; president, director, Globe Foundation

Getz, Bert A., Jr.: executive vice president, Globe Corp.; vice president, Globe Foundation

Gidwitz, Ronald J.: president, chief executive officer, Curtis Industries, Inc. (Helene)

Gilpin, Larry: executive vice president, Target Corp.; trustee, Target Foundation

Goeltz, Richard Karl: vice chairman, chief financial officer, American Express Co.

Grade, Jeffery T.: chairman, chief executive officer, director, Harnischfeger Industries; president, Harnischfeger Industries Foundation

Graham, William B.: chairman, director, Baxter Allegiance Foundation; chairman emeritus, Baxter International Inc.

Grainger, David William: senior chairman, Grainger, Inc. (W.W.)

Grigg, Richard R.: vice president, Wisconsin Energy Corp.; director, Wisconsin Energy Corp. Foundation, Inc.

Haddock, Ronald Wayne: president, chief executive officer, director, FINA; president, FINA Foundation

Hanley, Philip M.: senior vice president, chief financial officer, American General Finance; senior vice president, American General Finance Foundation

Harms, Carol J.: vice president, treasurer, Montgomery Ward & Co., Inc.; senior vice president, Montgomery Ward Foundation

Hays, Thomas Chandler: chairman, chief executive officer, director, Fortune Brands, Inc.

Hefner, Christie Ann: chairman, chief executive officer, Playboy Enterprises Inc.; director, Playboy Foundation

Hefner, Hugh Marston: founder, chairman emeritus, Playboy Enterprises Inc.

Hegel, Garrett R.: chief financial officer, Compass Bank; president, Compass Bank Foundation

Heineman, Benjamin Walter, Jr.: director, GE Fund

Herron, James Michael: secretary, director, Ryder System Charitable Foundation

Heuchling, Theodore Paul: trustee, Little Foundation (Arthur D.)

Hill, Bonnie Guiton: vice president, Times Mirror Co.; president, chief executive officer, Times Mirror Foundation

Hobor, Nancy A.: vice president communications & investor relations, Morton International Inc.

Hodnik, David F.: president, chief executive officer, Ace Hardware Corp.

Howard, David P.: vice president, chief financial officer, treasurer, Furniture Brands International, Inc.

Hult, Frank A.: vice president, controller, chief accounting officer, Walter Industries Inc.

Huston, Steve: secretary, Wrigley Co. Foundation (Wm. Jr.)

Ingersoll, Robert Stephen: chairman, director, Panasonic Foundation

Iverson, Francis Kenneth: chairman, director, Nucor Corp.; director, Nucor Foundation

Jacobsen, James C.: vice chairman, Kellwood Co.; vice president, director, Kellwood Foundation

Jacobsen, Thomas Herbert: chairman, president, chief executive officer, Mercantile Bank NA

Jannotta, Edgar D.: president, Blair & Co. Foundation (William); senior director, Blair & Co. (William)

Jenkins, James Robert: trustee, Dow Corning Foundation

Johnson, Kenneth James: vice president, controller, director, Motorola Inc.

Jorndt, Louis Daniel: president, chief executive officer, director, Walgreen Co.

Joslin, Roger Scott: treasurer, State Farm Companies Foundation

Julsrud, Christopher K.: vice president human resources, Morton International Inc.

Karmel, Roberta S.: trustee, Kemper Foundation (James S.); partner, Kemper National Insurance Companies

Kemper, James Scott, Jr.: honorary chairman, Kemper Foundation (James S.)

Kenney, Richard John: director, Consolidated Papers Foundation, Inc.; senior vice president finance, Consolidated Papers, Inc.

King, Roger Leo: vice president, officer, Graco, Inc.

Kniffen, Jan Rogers: senior vice president, treasurer, May Department Stores Co.; vice president, secretary, treasurer, director, May Department Stores Computer Foundation (The)

Knight, Charles Field: chairman, chief executive officer, Emerson Electric Co.

Kopp, David C.: assistant secretary, CIGNA Foundation

Kraiss, Glenn S.: executive vice president store operations, Walgreen Co.

Krzos, Joseph T.: treasurer, Madison Gas & Electric Foundation

Lacy, William Howard: president, MGIC Investment Corp.

Larsen, Terrence A.: chairman, chief executive officer, First Union Bank; chairman, First Union Regional Foundation

Lawson, John K.: senior vice president, Deere & Co.; director, Deere Foundation (John)

LeBoeuf, Raymond W.: director, PPG Industries Foundation; director, chairman, chief executive officer, PPG Industries, Inc.

Lester, Susan E.: executive vice president, chief financial officer, U.S. Bancorp

Levan, B. W.: vice president, director, Shell Oil Co. Foundation

Lohman, Gordon Russell: trustee, Amsted Industries Foundation; director, Amsted Industries Inc.

Longfield, William H.: president, Bard Foundation (C.R.); chairman, chief executive officer, director, Bard, Inc. (C.R.)

Lux, Clifton L.: director, Globe Foundation

Maatman, Gerald Leonard: chairman, president, trustee, Kemper Foundation (James S.); director, Kemper National Insurance Companies

Mac Kimm, Margaret (Pontius) 'Mardie': trustee, Chicago Title and Trust Co. Foundation

Mack, Raymond Phillip: director, Arvin Foundation; vice president human resources, Arvin Industries, Inc.

Maher, Francesca M.: senior vice president, general counsel, secretary, United Airlines Inc.

Mason, James L.: director public affairs, member contributions committee, Eaton Charitable Fund

Mason, W. Bruce: chairman, chief executive officer, director, True North Communications, Inc.

Matheny, Edward Taylor, Junior: director, Block Foundation (H&R)

McKenna, Andrew James: director, Aon Foundation

Medvin, Harvey Norman: executive vice president, treasurer, chief financial officer, Aon Corp.; treasurer, Aon Foundation

Menzer, John: executive vice president, Wal-Mart Stores, Inc.

Meredith, Edwin Thomas, III: chairman executive committee, Meredith Corp.

Merlotti, Frank Henry: trustee, Steelcase Foundation; director, Steelcase Inc.

Mitchell, John Francis: vice chairman, director, Motorola Inc.

Morgan, Glenn R.: executive vice president, chief financial officer, Hartmarx Corp.

Mrozek, Ernest J.: executive vice president, chief financial officer, ServiceMaster Co.

Mueller, Charles William: chairman, president, chief executive officer, Ameren Corp.; trustee, Ameren Corp. Charitable Trust

Mulford, David: chairman, Credit Suisse First Boston

Nalbach, Kay C.: president, Hartmarx Charitable Foundation

O'Hare, Don R.: director, Hamilton Sundstrand Corp.; president, director, Sundstrand Corp. Foundation

O'Toole, Robert Joseph: director, Firstar Milwaukee Foundation; chairman, president, chief executive officer, director, Smith Corp. (A.O.); director, Smith Foundation, Inc. (A.O.)

Oliver, Walter Maurice: senior vice president human resources, Ameritech Corp.

Olschwang, Alan P., Esq.: secretary, Mitsubishi Electric America Foundation

Pate, James Leonard: chairman, chief executive officer, director, Pennzoil-Quaker State Co.

Pearl, Melvin E.: treasurer, director, Katten, Muchin & Zavis Foundation

Pehlke, Richard W.: vice president, treasurer, Ameritech Corp.

Piet, William M.: vice president, director, Wrigley Co. Foundation (Wm. Jr.); vice president corporate affairs, secretary, assistant to president, Wrigley Co. (Wm. Jr.)

Pollard, Charles William, Jr.: chairman, director, ServiceMaster Co.; president, director, ServiceMaster Foundation

Quinlan, Michael Robert: chairman executive committee, McDonald's

Corp.; director, McDonald's Corp. Charitable Foundation

Rauman, Thomas R.: chief financial officer, DeKalb Genetics Corp.; treasurer, director, DeKalb Genetics Foundation

Reed, John Shepard: co-chairman, Citibank Corp.

Reed, Scott Eldridge: senior executive vice president, chief financial officer, Branch Banking & Trust Co.

Reiman, Thomas Jay: senior vice president public policy, Ameritech Corp.

Rubin, Donald S.: senior vice president investor relations, McGraw-Hill Companies, Inc.

Rust, Edward Barry, Jr.: chairman, president, director, State Farm Companies Foundation; chairman, president, chief executive officer, director, State Farm Mutual Automobile Insurance Co.

Sanders, Walter Jeremiah, III: chairman, chief executive officer, director, Advanced Micro Devices, Inc.

Sanders, Wayne R.: chairman, chief executive officer, director, Kimberly-Clark Corp.

Schoenholz, David A.: executive vice president, chief financial officer, Household International Inc.

Schweitzer, Peter A.: president, Thompson Co. (J. Walter)

Shannon, Michael E.: chairman, chief financial officer, chief administration officer, director, Ecolab Inc.

Shapiro, Howard: executive vice president, general counsel, Playboy Enterprises Inc.; director, Playboy Foundation

Shiel, William A.: senior vice president facilities development, Walgreen Co.

Shoemate, Charles Richard: chairman, president, chief executive officer, Bestfoods

Shourd, Roy Ray: president, Schlumberger Foundation

Simpson, Louis Allen: president, chief executive officer capital operations, director, GEICO Corp.

Sissel, George A.: chairman, president, chief executive officer, director, Ball Corp.

Soderquist, Donald G.: trustee, Wal-Mart Foundation; senior vice chairman, director, Wal-Mart Stores, Inc.

Sopranos, Orpheus Javaras: corporate vice president, Amsted Industries Inc.

Staley, Robert Wayne: vice chairman Asia Pacific, Emerson Electric Co.

Stephan, Richard C.: vice president, controller, director, Viad Corp. Fund

Stone, Jerome H.: vice president, secretary, treasurer, Stone Foundation

Stone, Marvin N.: director, Stone Foundation

Stone, Roger Warren: chairman, president, chief executive officer, director, Stone Container Corp.; president, Stone Foundation

Strobel, Pamela B.: senior vice president, general counsel, Commonwealth Edison Co.

Sutton, Howard: trustee, Steelcase Foundation

Teets, John William: president, chief executive officer, director, Viad Corp. Fund

Tomlinson, Joseph Ernest: vice president, treasurer, controller, Inland Container Corp.; vice president, director, Inland Foundation, Inc.

True, Jean Durland: trustee, True Foundation; partner, True Oil Co.

Wehling, Robert Louis: global marketing, government relations officer, Procter & Gamble Co.; president, trustee, Procter & Gamble Fund

Welsh, Kelly Raymond: executive vice president, general counsel, Ameritech Corp.

Wentworth, Jack Roberts, Ph.D.: director, Habig Foundation

Wheatley, Bruce C.: vice president, Commercial Intertech Foundation

Whitehead, John Cunningham: chairman board, Goldman Sachs Foundation

Williams, Edward Joseph: president, director, Harris Bank Foundation

Wilson, Cleo Francine: executive director, Playboy Foundation

Wrigley, William: chairman, director, Wrigley Co. Foundation (Wm. Jr.); president, chief executive officer, director, Wrigley Co. (Wm. Jr.)

Zadel, C. William: chairman, president, chief executive officer, Millipore Corp.; trustee, Millipore Foundation (The)

Zavis, Michael W.: managing partner, Katten, Muchin & Zavis; president, director, Katten, Muchin & Zavis Foundation

Zona, Richard A.: vice chairman commercial banking & institutional finance, U.S. Bancorp

Indiana

Alexander, Stuart: president, director, Deluxe Corp. Foundation

Allen, Barry K.: president regulatory & wholesale operation, Ameritech Corp.

Aylesworth, William Andrew: treasurer, Texas Instruments Foundation; chief financial officer, treasurer, Texas Instruments Inc.

Baker, James Kendrick: chairman, director, Arvin Foundation; vice chairman, director, Arvin Industries, Inc.

Beale, Susan M.: director, Detroit Edison Foundation

Bindley, Thomas L.: executive vice president finance & administration, Whitman Corp.; vice president, treasurer, Whitman Corp. Foundation

Bottorff, Dennis C.: chairman, president, chief executive officer, director, First American Corp.

Bowerman, Charles L.: executive vice president, director, Phillips Petroleum Co.

Brademas, John: chairman, Texaco Foundation

Burleigh, William Robert: president, chief executive officer, director, Scripps Co. (E.W.); member, Scripps Howard Foundation

Burns, Ron: chief financial officer, Grede Foundries

Carl, John L.: executive vice president, chief financial officer, BP Amoco Corp.; director, BP Amoco Foundation

Chabraja, Nicholas D.: chairman, chief executive officer, director, General Dynamics Corp.

Clifton, Paul Hoot, Jr.: president, Colonial Life & Accident Insurance Co.

Conley, E. Renae: president, Cinergy Corp.

Connor, James Richard: executive director, Kemper Foundation (James S.)

Corson, Keith Daniel: president, chief operating officer, Coachmen Industries, Inc.

Fites, Donald Vester: director, Caterpillar Foundation

Gamron, W. Anthony: treasurer, director, Kimberly-Clark Foundation

Geier, Peter E.: vice chairman, Huntington Bancshares Inc.

Gloyd, Lawrence Eugene: trustee, CLARCOR Foundation; chairman, chief executive officer, director, CLARCOR Inc.

Gorman, Joseph T.: chairman, chief executive officer, TRW Inc.

Graf, Alan B., Jr.: executive vice president, chief financial officer, FedEx Corp.

Graham, Patricia Albjerg, PhD: trustee, Hitachi Foundation

Griffin, Donald Wayne: chairman, president, chief executive officer, director, Olin Corp.; trustee, Olin Corp. Charitable Trust

Habegger, Gary L.: vice president human resources, BFGoodrich Co.; president, Goodrich Foundation, Inc. (B.F.)

Habig, Thomas L.: vice chairman, director, Habig Foundation

Hattendorf, William C.: trustee, Cooper Tire & Rubber Foundation

Henderson, James Alan: vice chairman, chief executive officer, director, Ameritech Corp.; chairman, director, Cummins Engine Foundation

Hinton, Michael R.: president, chief operating officer, director, Old National Bank Evansville

Hutton, Edward L.: chairman, chief executive officer, director, Chemed Corp.

Johnston, William E., Junior: president, chief operating officer, director, Morton International Inc.

Knue, Paul Frederick: trustee, Scripps Howard Foundation

Koch, Robert Louis, II: president, chief executive officer, director, Koch Enterprises, Inc.; president, director, Koch Foundation

Larson, Wayne E.: trustee, Ladish Co. Foundation

Lauderdale, Gary D.: senior vice president, general manager, Texas Gas Transmission Corp.

McKee, E. Marie: senior vice president, Corning Inc.; chairman, trustee, Corning Inc. Foundation

McNealy, Scott G.: chairman, chief executive officer, director, Sun Microsystems Inc.

Meuleman, Robert Joseph: director, AMCORE Foundation

Miller, Joseph Irwin: director associate, Cummins Engine Co., Inc.; director, Cummins Engine Foundation

Miller, William Irwin: director, Cummins Engine Foundation

Moffitt, Donald Eugene: chairman, director, CNF Transportation, Inc.

Morris, James Thomas: director, AUL Foundation Inc.

Muehlbauer, James Herman: vice president, director, Koch Foundation

Mutz, John M.: vice president, Cinergy Corp.; director, Cinergy Foundation

Myers, Mark B.: senior vice president corporate research & technology, Xerox Corp.; trustee, Xerox Foundation

Parsons, Susan E.: secretary, treasurer, Koch Enterprises, Inc.; secretary, treasurer, director, Koch Foundation

Pitts, Brenda S.: director, Cummins Engine Foundation

Poindexter, Christian Herndon: chairman, Baltimore Gas & Electric Foundation; chairman, chief executive officer, director, Constellation Energy Group, Inc.

Raclin, Ernestine Morris: chairman emeritus, director, First Source Corp.; chairman, director, First Source Foundation

Radcliffe, R. Stephen: executive vice president, American United Life Insurance Co.

Ralph, E. Jack: vice president finance, controller, Texas Gas Transmission Corp.

Ridgley, Robert Louis: chairman, director, Northwest Natural Gas Co.

Risinger, James A.: chairman, chief executive officer, Old National Bank Evansville

Ruckelshaus, William Doyle: chairman, director, Browning-Ferris Industries Inc.

Russell, Frank Eli: president, Central Newspapers Foundation; chairman, Central Newspapers, Inc.

Schrader, Thomas F.: vice president, director, WICOR Foundation

Schurz, James Montgomery: president, Schurz Communications Foundation

Semler, Jerry D.: chairman, president, chief executive officer, director, American United Life Insurance Co.; chairman, director, AUL Foundation Inc.

Shanks, David C.: trustee, Little Foundation (Arthur D.); vice president human resources, Little, Inc. (Arthur D.)

Sheley, Donald R., Junior: vice president finance, chief financial officer,

Standard Products Co.; treasurer, trustee, Standard Products Co. Charitable Foundation
Shideler, Shirley Ann Williams: director, Central Newspapers Foundation
Spiegel, John William: member, SunTrust Bank Atlanta Foundation
Springer, Denis E.: senior vice president, chief financial officer, Burlington Northern Santa Fe Corp.; director, Burlington Northern Santa Fe Foundation
Stewart, James Gathings: executive vice president, chief financial officer, CIGNA Corp.
Stoner, Richard Burkett, Jr.: director, Cummins Engine Foundation
Taylor, John I.: director, Zenith Electronics Corp.
Thomasson, Dan King: vice president, trustee, Scripps Howard Foundation
Thyen, James C.: president, director, Habig Foundation
Thyen, Ronald J.: senior executive vice president, director, Habig Foundation; senior executive vice president, chief operating officer director, Kimball International, Inc.
Tobias, Randall L.: chairman emeritus, Lilly & Co. (Eli)
Tuerff, James R.: president, director, American General Finance
Walker, Martin Dean: chairman, chief executive officer, director, Hanna Co. (M.A.)
Winger, Charles Joseph (Chuck): vice president, chief financial officer, Cinergy Corp.
Zacks, Gordon Benjamin: chairman, president, chief executive officer, director, Barry Corp. (R.G.); president, Barry Foundation

Iowa

Anderson, William J.: assistant secretary, Pella Corp.; secretary, Pella Rolscreen Foundation
Andreas, Lowell Willard: chairman audit committee, member executive & finance committee, Archer-Daniels-Midland Co.
Besser, John Edward: director, Barnes Group Foundation Inc.; senior vice president finance & law, Barnes Group Inc.
Brooks, Roger Kay: chairman, AmerUS Group
Carver, Martin Gregory: chairman, president, chief executive officer, Bandag, Inc.
Copley, Helen K.: chairman, trustee, Copley Foundation (James S.); chairman, director, senior management board, Copley Press, Inc.
Coughlin, Timothy C.: president, Riggs Bank NA
Dammerman, Dennis Dean: vice chairman, director, General Electric Co.
Davidson, Park R.: trustee, Burlington Industries Foundation
Dubes, Michael: membership, ReliaStar Foundation
Fjelstul, Dean M.: senior vice president, chief financial officer, Walter Industries Inc.
Forsythe, Donald George: vice president corporate relations, Sprint Corp.; executive director, Sprint Foundation
Garberding, Larry Gailbert: chief financial officer, executive vice president, Detroit Edison Co.; director, Detroit Edison Foundation
Getz, Herbert A.: senior vice president, secretary, general counsel, Waste Management Inc.
Gottlieb, Richard Douglas: president, chief executive officer, director, Lee Enterprises
Graff, Stephen Ney: director, Bucyrus-Erie Foundation
Greehey, William Eugene: chairman, chief executive officer, director, Valero Energy Corp.
Grum, Clifford J.: director, Temple-Inland Foundation; director, chairman, chief executive officer, Temple-Inland Inc.
Hadley, Leonard Anson: chairman, chief executive officer, director, Maytag Corp.; president, trustee, Maytag Corp. Foundation
Hiersteiner, Walter L.: vice chairman, Tension Envelope Corp.; vice president, Tension Envelope Foundation
Hoffmann, Richard W.: general counsel, Employers Mutual Casualty Co.
Howe, Stanley M.: president, HON Industries Charitable Foundation; chairman emeritus, director, HON Industries Inc.
Johnson, Norman E.: trustee, CLARCOR Foundation
Killinger, Kerry Kent: chairman, president, chief executive officer, director, Washington Mutual, Inc.
Kramer, Mary Elizabeth: vice president, Wellmark Foundation
Lasell, Raymond E.: secretary, director, HON Industries Charitable Foundation
McClimon, Timothy J.: executive director, AT&T Foundation
Mead, Dana George: chairman, chief executive officer, director, Tenneco Automotive
Meyer, Russell William, Jr.: chairman, chief executive officer, Cessna Aircraft Co.; president, Cessna Foundation, Inc.
Pomerantz, Marvin Alvin: trustee, Mid-American Foundation
Reed, James M.: trustee, Union Camp Charitable Trust; vice chairman, chief financial officer, director, Union Camp Corp.
Reyelts, Paul C.: vice president finance, chief financial officer, Valspar Corp.; vice president, assistant secretary, Valspar Foundation
Schaffer, Donald J.: member contributions committee, GATX Corp.
Schiek, Fredrick A.: executive vice president, chief operating officer, Employers Mutual Casualty Co.
Schoon, Susan Wylie: trustee, Chase Manhattan Foundation
Shepard, Donald James: chairman, president, chief executive officer, AEGON U.S.A. Inc.
Simplot, John Richard: chairman, founder, Simplot Co. (J.R.); president, Simplot Foundation (J.R.)
Sullivan, Laura P.: vice president, secretary, director, State Farm Companies Foundation; vice president, secretary, counsel, State Farm Mutual Automobile Insurance Co.
Turner, Fred L.: senior chairman, director, McDonald's Corp.
Wareham, James Lyman: president, AK Steel Corp.
Weekly, John William: chairman, chief executive officer, Mutual of Omaha Insurance Co.
Wetter, Larry V.: trustee, Jeld-wen Foundation; vice chairman, director, Jeld-wen, Inc.
White, Walter Lucas: secretary, treasurer, trustee, Kemper Foundation (James S.)
Wise, William Allen: chairman, president, chief executive officer, director, El Paso Energy Co.; chairman, director, El Paso Energy Foundation
Zylstra, Stanley James: chairman, director, Land O'Lakes, Inc.

Kansas

Beard, Etonya M.: director, Fort James Foundation (The)
Beck, Edward W.: senior vice president, general counsel, secretary, director, Shaklee Corp.
Beebe, Lydia I.: corporate secretary, Chevron Corp.
Chandler, Charles Q.: co-trustee, INTRUST Bank Charitable Trust; chairman, INTRUST Financial Corp.
Chandler, Charles Quarles, IV: co-trustee, INTRUST Bank Charitable Trust; president, director, INTRUST Financial Corp.
Crane, Russell L.: director, PPG Industries Foundation; senior vice president, PPG Industries, Inc.
Crook, Donald Martin: secretary, Kimberly-Clark Foundation
Guinn, Donald Eugene: chairman emeritus, Pacific Mutual Life Insurance Co.
Koch, Charles de Ganahl: chairman, chief executive officer, director, president, Koch Industries, Inc.
Koch, David Hamilton: director, Koch Foundation, Inc. (Fred C. and Mary R.)
Matthews, Clark J., II: president, chief executive officer, director, 7-Eleven, Inc.
Millenbruch, Gary Lee: executive vice president, chief financial officer, director, trustee, Bethlehem Steel Corp.
Pratt, Donald Henry: chairman, Butler Manufacturing Co.; vice president, trustee, Butler Manufacturing Co. Foundation
Pulliam, Eugene Smith: vice president, director, Central Newspapers Foundation
Richard, Shirley A.: vice president, director, APS Foundation, Inc.; executive vice president customer service marketing & corporate relations, Arizona Public Service Co.
Sadler, Robert L.: president, vice chairman, director, Old Kent Bank
Stauffer, John H.: trustee, Stauffer Communications Foundation
Stauffer, Stanley Howard: chairman, Stauffer Communications Foundation
Taylor, Julian Howard: vice president, treasurer, director, Reynolds Metals Co. Foundation
Tyson, Donald John: senior chairman, Tyson Foods Inc.

Kentucky

Browning, Laurance LeWright, Jr.: member public policy committee, Emerson Charitable Trust; director, Emerson Electric Co.
Cassidy, Samuel M.: director, Star Bank NA
Clabes, Judy G.: president, chief executive officer, Scripps Co. (E.W.); president, chief executive officer, trustee, member, Scripps Howard Foundation
Doucette, James Willard: vice president, treasurer, Humana Foundation
Griffith, Beverly H.: general counsel, Texas Gas Transmission Corp.
Guillaume, Raymond Kendrick: vice chairman, chief executive officer, Mid-America Bank of Louisville
Habig, Douglas A.: chairman, chief executive officer, director, Habig Foundation
Harreld, Michael Neal: president, chief executive officer, PNC Bank Kentucky Inc.
Hower, Frank Beard, Jr.: vice chairman, Anthem Foundation, Inc.
Jones, David Allen: chairman, chief executive officer, director, Humana Foundation; co-founder, chairman, director, Humana, Inc.
Kendall, J. William: chairman, director, Arvin Foundation
Klein, Bertram W.: chairman, director, Bank of Louisville Charities
Klein, Bruce A.: trustee, CLARCOR Foundation; chief financial officer, CLARCOR Inc.
Lawson, William Hogan, III: chairman, chief executive officer, director, Franklin Electric Co.; president, Franklin Electric, Edward J. Schaefer, and T. W. KehoeCharitable and Educational Foundation
McDonald, James F.: president, chief executive officer, Scientific-Atlanta, Inc.
Oliver, Orson: president, director, Mid-America Bank of Louisville
Osborne, Burl: president publishing division, director, Belo Corp. (A.H.); president, trustee, Belo Corp. Foundation (A.H.)
Resnick, Myron J.: vice president, treasurer,

trustee, Allstate Foundation

Reynolds, Randolph Nicklas: vice chairman, executive officer, director, Reynolds Metals Co.; director, Reynolds Metals Co. Foundation

Skiles, Win: vice president, Texas Instruments Foundation; senior vice president, Texas Instruments Inc.

Smoot, Richard Leonard: chairman, PNC Bank

Turner, Cal, Jr.: chairman, chief executive officer, director, Dollar General Corp.

Viviano, Joseph P.: president, court, Hershey Foods Corp.

Louisiana

Armstrong, Malcolm: executive vice president operations, Delta Air Lines, Inc.

Brian, Pierre Leonce Thibaut: trustee, Air Products Foundation

Brown, JoBeth Goode: trustee, Anheuser-Busch Companies, Inc.

Carroll, Philip Joseph: chairman, chief executive officer, Fluor Corp.; chairman, trustee, Fluor Foundation

Cavanaugh, William, III: chairman, president, chief executive officer, Carolina Power & Light Co.; president, CP&L Foundation

Cosse, Steven Anthony: senior vice president, general counsel, Murphy Oil Corp.

Deming, Claiborne P.: president, chief executive officer, director, Murphy Oil Corp.

Elliott, Anson Wright: vice president, trustee, Chase Manhattan Foundation

Farnsworth, Philip Richeson: secretary, ABC

Faust, F. Lee: vice president, CertainTeed Corp.

Guedry, James Walter: president, International Paper Co. Foundation

Johnson, Murray Lloyd, Jr.: secretary, trustee, Zachry Foundation (The)

Larance, Charles L.: vice president corporate relations, GenAmerica Corp.; president, GenAmerican Foundation

Longwell, Harry J.: senior vice president, Exxon Mobil Corp.

Marsh, R. Bruce: general tax counsel, Chevron Corp.

Pierre, Percy A.: trustee, Hitachi Foundation

Posey, Warren M., Jr.: treasurer, Armstrong Foundation

Purvis, George Frank, Jr.: chairman, president, chief executive officer, director, Pan-American Life Insurance Co.

Raspino, Louis A., Jr.: senior vice president, chief financial officer, Louisiana Land & Exploration Co.; director, Louisiana Land & Exploration Co. Foundation

Rogers, Desiree Glapion: vice president community affairs, Peoples Energy Corp.

Stewart, Joseph Melvin: senior vice president corporate affairs, Kellogg Co.; trustee, Kellogg Co. Twenty-Five Year Employees' Fund Inc.

Maine

Chouinard, Yvon: owner, principal, Patagonia Inc.

Connor, Richard L.: president, publisher, Fort Worth Star-Telegram Inc.

Flanagan, David T.: president, chief executive officer, director, Central Maine Power Co.

Gould, John T., Jr.: vice president, Unilever Foundation; director corporate affairs, Unilever United States, Inc.

Koenig, Brian C.: senior vice president human resources, Scientific-Atlanta, Inc.

Ludden, Timothy Wayne: vice president, treasurer, cash manager, Unum-Provident

Magee, John Francis: chairman, director, Little, Inc. (Arthur D.)

Merdek, Andrew Austin: vice president legal affairs, secretary, Cox Enterprises Inc.; secretary, Cox Foundation (James M.)

Mundy, Donna T.: vice president, trustee, UNUM Foundation; senior vice president, UnumProvident

Pendexter, Harold E., Jr.: senior vice president, chief administrative officer, USG Corp.; president, director, USG Foundation

Maryland

Bainum, Stewart William, Jr.: chairman, Manor Care Health SVS, Inc.

Baker, Leslie Mayo, Jr.: president, chief executive officer, chairman, Wachovia Bank of North Carolina NA; chairman, Wachovia Foundation, Inc. (The)

Barrett, Allen M., Jr.: chairman, McCormick & Co. Inc.

Causey, John Paul, Jr.: senior vice president, secretary, general counsel, Chesapeake Corp.; chairman, trustee, Chesapeake Corp. Foundation

Golleher, George C: president, Ralph's-Food 4 Less Foundation; chief executive officer, Ralph's Grocery Co.

Graham, Donald Edward: chairman, chief executive officer, director, publisher, The Washington Post

Hale, Roger W.: chairman, chief executive officer, director, LG&E Energy Corp.; president, LG&E Energy Foundation

Hemelt, William J.: treasurer, director, APS Foundation, Inc.; controller, Arizona Public Service Co.

Higgs, John H.: director, IBJ Foundation

Kirby, William Joseph: vice president, director, FMC Foundation

Murphy, James W.: senior vice president corporate finance, American United Life Insurance Co.; treasurer, AUL Foundation Inc.

Oseroff, Stephen L.: vice president real estate, Giant Food Inc.

Prendergast, Michael J.: vice president, chief financial officer, Aristech Chemical Corp.

Rosenthal, Sol: counsel, Playboy Enterprises Inc.

Rosett, Richard Nathaniel: trustee, Kemper Foundation (James S.)

Simmons, Hardwick: president, chief executive officer, director, Prudential Securities Inc.

Stone, Lawrence Mynatt: chairman, publisher, Rutledge Hill Press; secretary, treasurer, Rutledge Hill Press Foundation

Sullivan, Kevin F.: member screening committee, PPG Industries Foundation

Torgerson, William T.: managing, Potomac Electric Power Co.

Massachusetts

Akers, John Fellows: director, New York Times Co.

Allaire, Paul Arthur: chairman, chief executive officer, chairman executive committee, Xerox Corp.; president, Xerox Foundation

Bankowski, Elizabeth: secretary, Ben & Jerry's Foundation

Bloom, Geoffrey B.: chairman, chief executive officer, director, Wolverine World Wide

Bossidy, Lawrence Arthur: chairman, director, AlliedSignal Foundation Inc.; chairman, chief executive officer, director, AlliedSignal Inc.

Brennan, John J.: chairman, chief executive officer, Vanguard Group; president, Vanguard Group Foundation

Cawley, Michael J.: vice president risk management, Eastern Enterprises

Clark, Richard McCourt: senior vice president, general counsel, secretary, Kellogg Co.; vice president, trustee, Kellogg Co. Twenty-Five Year Employees' Fund Inc.

Cogan, John Francis, Jr.: president, chief executive officer, director, Pioneer Group

Cogan, Marshall Stuart: chairman, president, chief executive officer, director, Trace International Holdings, Inc.; director, Trace International Holdings, Inc. Foundation

Connolly, Gerald Edward: trustee, Reinhart Family Foundation (D. B. and Marjorie)

Connor, Walter Robert: director, Glaxo Wellcome Foundation

Corwin, Laura J.: secretary, New York Times Co. Foundation

Cutler, Richard M.: vice chairman, director, Putnam Investments

Davies, Richard Warren: trustee, Hubbell Foundation (Harvey)

Davis, Edward J.: chief financial officer, vice president, treasurer, Wyman-Gordon Co.

Doherty, Leonard Edward: member advisory committee, admin officer, Dow Jones Foundation

Donahue, Richard King: vice chairman, Nike, Inc.

Donnelly, James Charles: vice president, director, WICOR Foundation; vice president, WICOR, Inc.

Douglas, Paul W.: director, Phelps Dodge Foundation

Ehrlich, M. Gordon: trustee, Orchard Foundation

Emerson, Frederick George: vice president, secretary, director, Viad Corp. Fund

Ferland, E. James: chairman, president, chief executive officer, Public Service Electric & Gas Co.

Gareau, Joseph H.: executive vice president, chief investment officer, Hartford (The)

Goldstein, Richard A.: president, chief executive officer, director, Lipton Co.

Gullotti, Russell A.: chairman, president, chief executive officer, National Computer Systems, Inc.

Hiatt, Arnold Selig: chairman, director, Stride Rite Foundation

James, George Barker, II: senior vice president, chief financial officer, Levi Strauss & Co.

Jenest, Jeffrey M.: senior vice president new business development, Playboy Enterprises Inc.; director, Playboy Foundation

Johnson, Edward Crosby, III: president, Fidelity Foundation; chairman, president, chief executive officer, director, Fidelity Investments

Kelleher, Paul F.: committee member, Thermo Electron Foundation

Kendrick, William J.: vice president public affairs, Air Products and Chemicals, Inc.; chairman, Air Products Foundation

Keough, William H.: senior vice president, chief financial officer, Pioneer Group

Kinsolving, Augustus Blagden: director, ASARCO Foundation

Koch, David Andrew: president, Graco Foundation; chairman, director, Graco, Inc.

Koziar, Stephen F., Jr.: president, trustee, Dayton Power and Light Co. Foundation

Lawrence, Robert Ashton: director, New York Times Co. Foundation

Lesser, Richard G.: executive vice president, chief operating officer, director, TJX Companies, Inc.; chief operating officer, director, TJX Foundation, Inc.

Loughrey, F. Joseph: group president worldwide operations & technology, vice president, Cummins Engine Co., Inc.; director, Cummins Engine Foundation

Lovejoy, Joseph Ensign: chairman, director, Ensign-Bickford Industries

Mahoney, David L.: co-chief executive officer, McKesson-HBOC Corp.

Martore, Gracia C.: vice president investor relations, treasurer, Gannett Co., Inc.; assistant treasurer, Gannett Foundation

McKone, Francis L.: president, chief executive officer, director, Albany International Corp.

McLaughlin, Michael John: secretary, New York Life Foundation; senior vice president, deputy general counsel, New York Life Insurance Co.

Mee, Michael F.: senior vice president, chief financial officer, Bristol-Myers Squibb Co.

Melican, James Patrick, Jr.: executive vice president legal & external affairs, International Paper Co.; director, International Paper Co. Foundation

Mullin, Leo Francis: chairman, president, chief executive officer, Delta Air Lines, Inc.

Neely, Walter Emerson: vice president, Humana Foundation

O'Brien, John Francis, Jr.: president, chief executive officer, Allmerica Financial Corp.

Pajak, John Joseph: president, chief operating officer, Massachusetts Mutual Life Insurance Co.

Paton, Leland B.: president capital marketings, director, member executive committee, Prudential Securities Inc.

Powers, Paul Joseph: chairman, president, chief executive officer, director, Commercial Intertech Corp.; president, trustee, Commercial Intertech Foundation

Previte, Richard: president, chief operating officer, director, Advanced Micro Devices, Inc.

Price, Timothy: president, chief executive officer, director, MCI WorldCom, Inc.

Pullo, Robert W.: chairman, chief executive officer, director, York Federal Savings & Loan Association; president, trustee, York Federal Savings & Loan Foundation

Putnam, George, Jr.: chairman, president, chief executive officer, Putnam Investments

Redstone, Sumner Murray: chairman, Viacom Inc.

Resnick, Alan H.: treasurer, Bausch & Lomb Foundation, Inc.; vice president, treasurer, Bausch & Lomb Inc.

Rosenberg, Richard Morris: chairman, chief executive officer (retired), Bank of America

Smith, John Francis, Jr.: chairman, General Motors Corp.

Smith, Richard Alan: treasurer, director, Arvin Foundation; chairman, director, chief executive officer, Harcourt General, Inc.

Stallkamp, William J.: member corporate review committee, Mellon Financial Corp.

Syron, Richard F.: chairman, chief executive officer, director, American Stock Exchange, Inc.

Taylor, William Osgood: chairman, chief executive officer, director, Boston Globe (The); chairman, director, Boston Globe Foundation; director, New York Times Co. Foundation

Trask, Robert B.: president, chief operating officer, director, Country Curtains, Inc.; clerk, trustee, High Meadow Foundation; clerk,

Turner, John Gosney: chairman, chief executive officer, director, ReliaStar Financial Corp.; director, ReliaStar Foundation

Vitale, David J.: vice chairman, Bank One Corp.; vice president, director, First National Bank of Chicago Foundation

Welch, John Francis, Jr.: chairman, chief executive officer, director, General Electric Co.

Michigan

Abdoo, Richard A.: chairman, president, chief executive officer, Wisconsin Energy Corp.; president, director, Wisconsin Energy Corp. Foundation, Inc.

Adderley, Terence E.: chairman, president, chief executive officer, director, Kelly Services; president, director, Kelly Services Foundation

Anderson, Charles D.: trustee, Anderson Foundation

Anderson, Girard F.: chairman, chief executive officer, president, Tampa Electric Co.

Armstrong, C. Michael: chairman, chief executive officer, AT&T Corp.

Ballmer, Steven Anthony: president, chief executive officer, director, Microsoft Corp.

Becherer, Hans Walter: chairman, chief executive officer, director, Deere & Co.; director, Deere Foundation (John)

Borman, Paul: president, director, Borman Fund (The); chairman, Borman's Inc.

Boyer, David Scott: president, chief executive officer, director, Teleflex Inc.

Brennan, Leo Joseph, Jr.: vice president, executive director, Ford Motor Co. Fund

Buckler, Robert J.: director, Detroit Edison Foundation

Bueche, Wendell Francis: director, Marshall & Ilsley Foundation, Inc.

Capo, Thomas Patrick: senior vice president, treasurer, DaimlerChrysler Corp.

Cardy, Robert Willard: chairman, president, chief executive officer, director, Carpenter Technology Corp.; president, Carpenter Technology Corp. Foundation

Cooper, William Allen: chairman, director, TCF National Bank Minnesota

Cornelius, James M.: director, AUL Foundation Inc.

Coyle, Dennis Patrick: secretary, director, FPL Group Foundation, Inc.

Cusick, Thomas A.: chairman, TCF National Bank Minnesota

De Schutter, Richard U.: director, Searle Charitable Trust; chairman, chief executive officer, Searle & Co. (G.D.)

Delo, Robert Paul: director, Chicago Tribune Foundation

Derry, R. Michael: vice president, HON Industries Charitable Foundation

Ennest, John William: chief financial officer, Citizens Bank-Flint

Erb, Frederick A.: president, Erb Foundation

Everingham, Lyle J.: trustee, Milacron Foundation

Exley, Charles Errol, Jr.: trustee, Merck Co. Foundation

Feldhouse, Lynn Alexandra: vice president, secretary, DaimlerChrysler Corp. Fund

Geier, Philip Henry, Jr.: chairman, president, chief executive officer, Interpublic Group of Companies, Inc.

George, William Wallace: chief executive officer, chairman, Medtronic, Inc.

Gochenaur, Jack A.: senior vice president administration & services, chief financial officer, Fortis Insurance Co.; president, trustee, Fortis Insurance Foundation

Greene, John Frederick: executive vice president exploration & production, director, Louisiana Land & Exploration Co.

Hazen, Paul Mandeville: chairman, chief executive officer, director, Wells Fargo & Co.

Heilala, John A.: trustee, Vulcan Materials Co. Foundation

Hockaday, Irvine O., Jr.: president, chief executive officer, director, Hallmark Cards Inc.

Holler, William: treasurer, Deutsch Co.

Hunting, David Dyer, Jr.: trustee, Steelcase Foundation; director, Steelcase Inc.

Jones, Ingrid Saunders: chairman, director, Coca-Cola Foundation

Lavigne, Louis J., Jr.: executive vice president, chief financial officer, Genentech Inc.

Lemberg, Thomas Michael: clerk, Lotus Development Corp.; secretary, Polaroid Foundation

Loomans, Leslie Louis: treasurer, director, Detroit Edison Foundation

Lytle, Gary R.: vice president federal relations, Ameritech Corp.

Marcum, Kenneth William: treasurer, Commercial Intertech Foundation

McGregor, Douglas J.: president, chief operating officer, director, Hanna Co. (M.A.)

Meister, Paul M.: vice president, treasurer, Winthrop Foundation

Metzger, Michael D.: vice president, chief financial officer, JSJ Corp.

Meyer, Daniel Joseph: president, Milacron Foundation; chairman, president, chief executive officer, director, Milacron, Inc.

Miller, Eugene A.: chairman, chief executive officer, Comerica Inc.

Oesterreicher, James E.: chairman, chief executive officer, director, Penney Co., Inc. (J.C.)

Parfet, Donald R.: president, Pharmacia & Upjohn Foundation; senior vice president associated business, Pharmacia & Upjohn, Inc.

Pilon, Lawrence James: senior vice president human resources, Whitman Corp.

Pond, Byron O.: chairman, chief executive officer, director, Arvin Industries, Inc.

Porter, Edward A.: vice president, general counsel, secretary, Walter Industries Inc.

Schadt, James Phillip: chairman, president, chief executive officer, director, Reader's Digest Association, Inc. (The); chairman, director, Reader's Digest Foundation

Schaeffer, Wayne G.: community president, Citizens Bank-Flint

Schafer, Glenn Stanley: president, director, Pacific Mutual Life Insurance Co.

Sikkema, Karen Ann: president, trustee, Unocal Foundation

Spoon, Alan Gary: president, chief operating officer, director, The Washington Post

Steere, William Campbell, Jr.: chairman, chief executive officer, director, Pfizer Inc.

Ursu, John Joseph: director, 3M Foundation; general counsel, senior vice president legal affairs, Minnesota Mining & Manufacturing Co.

Valade, Gary C.: executive vice president, chief financial officer, DaimlerChrysler Corp.; trustee, DaimlerChrysler Corp. Fund

VanderRoest, Stan: trustee, treasurer, Gerber Foundation; vice president, comptroller, controller, Gerber Products Co.

Wagner, Thomas Joseph: chairman, CIGNA Foundation

Watjen, Thomas R.: vice chairman, chief financial officer, Provident Companies, Inc.

Wege, Peter M.: trustee, Steelcase Foundation; vice chairman, director, Steelcase Inc.

Westin, David: vice president, director, ABC Foundation

Westover, Frank Thomas: senior vice president, Whitman Corp.; director, Whitman Corp. Foundation

Wild, Heidi Karin: trustee,

Minnesota

Agnich, Richard John: director, Texas Instruments Foundation; senior vice president, secretary, general counsel, Texas Instruments Inc.

Anderson, Lowell Carlton: chairman, director, Allianz Life Insurance Co. of North America

Andreas, David Lowell: chairman, director, National City Bank Foundation; chairman, chief executive officer, National City Bank of Minneapolis

Andreas, Dwayne Orville: chairman, chief executive officer, Archer-Daniels-Midland Co.

Atwater, Horace Brewster, Jr.: trustee, Merck Co. Foundation

Beatt, Bruce H.: secretary, Dexter Corp. Foundation

Benson, John W.: executive vice president health

care, Minnesota Mining & Manufacturing Co.
Bernauer, David W.: president, chief operating officer, Walgreen Co.
Burnham, Duane Lee: chairman, chief executive officer, director, Abbott Laboratories
Buxton, Charles Ingraham, II: chairman, Federated Mutual Insurance Co.; president, Federated Mutual Insurance Foundation
Carlson, Curtis Leroy: chairman, director, Carlson Companies, Inc.; president, treasurer, Carlson Family Foundation (Curtis L.)
Cohen, Melvin Samuel: chairman, National Presto Industries, Inc.; chairman, president, trustee, Presto Foundation
Daniels, John Hancock: chairman, Archer-Daniels-Midland Foundation
Duff, Andrew S.: president, U.S. Bancorp Piper Jaffray
Estenson, Noel Keith: president, chief executive officer, Cenex Harvest States
Fritze, Steven L.: vice president, treasurer, Ecolab Inc.
Grenz, M. Kay: director, 3M Foundation; vice president human resources, Minnesota Mining & Manufacturing Co.
Hale, James Thomas: senior vice president, general counsel, secretary, Dayton Hudson; trustee, Target Foundation
Harris, Irving Brooks: chairman executive committee, director, Pittway Corp.; chairman, director, Pittway Corp. Charitable Foundation
Harris, King William: president, chief executive officer, Pittway Corp.; vice president, director, Pittway Corp. Charitable Foundation
Harris, Richard Neison: chairman, director, Pittway Corp.; president, director, Pittway Corp. Charitable Foundation
Harris, William W.: director, Pittway Corp. Charitable Foundation
Hubbard, Stanley S.: chairman, president, chief executive officer, Hubbard Broadcasting, Inc.; president, Hubbard Foundation
Jacobson, Lyle Gordon: treasurer, Hickory Tech Corp. Foundation
Johnson, James A.: chairman, chief executive officer, director, Fannie Mae; chairman, Fannie Mae Foundation
Johnson, Scott W.: senior vice president, secretary, general counsel, Bemis Co., Inc.
Kunin, Myron: chairman, director, Regis Corp.; president, Regis Foundation
Malmberg, David Curtis: director, National City Bank of Minneapolis
Marcus, Stephen Howard: chairman, chief executive officer, Marcus Corp.; president, director, Marcus Corp. Foundation
Martin, Lauralee: chief financial officer, Heller Financial, Inc.
Mattison, Robert Mayer: director, Graco Foundation; vice president, general counsel, secretary, Graco, Inc.
Mattson, Bradford C.: executive vice president exterior building products, CertainTeed Corp.
Meyer, Jerome J.: chairman, chief executive officer, Tektronix, Inc.
Mitau, Lee R.: executive vice president, general counsel, secretary, U.S. Bancorp
Nagorske, Lynn A.: executive vice president, chief financial officer, treasurer, TCF National Bank Minnesota
Nelson, Marilyn Carlson: chairman, chief executive officer, president, Carlson Companies, Inc.
Neville, James Morton: member board control, Ralston Purina Trust Fund
North, Donald K.: president, Burlington Resources Foundation
Orr, James F., III: president, trustee, UNUM Foundation; chairman, Unum-Provident
Piper, Addison Lewis: director, Piper Jaffray Companies Foundation; chairman, chief executive officer, director, U.S. Bancorp Piper Jaffray
Powell, Cornelius Patrick: president, Air Products Foundation
Prohofsky, Dennis E.: secretary, Minnesota Mutual Foundation; senior vice president, general counsel, secretary, Minnesota Mutual Life Insurance Co.
Rice, William D.: senior vice president, chief financial officer, secretary, Agrilink Foods, Inc.; trustee, Agrilink Foods/Pro-Fac Foundation
Ridder, Paul Anthony: chairman, chief executive officer, director, Knight Ridder
Roe, John H.: chairman, director, Bemis Co., Inc.
Senkler, Robert L.: president, director, Minnesota Mutual Foundation; chairman, president, chief executive officer, Minnesota Mutual Life Insurance Co.
Sheahan, Mark: treasurer, Graco Foundation
Shiely, John Stephen: president, chief operating officer, director, Briggs & Stratton Corp.; vice president, director, Briggs & Stratton Corp. Foundation
Thompson, Sheldon Lee: senior vice president, chief administrative officer, Sunoco Inc.
Tuominen, William: senior vice president, chief technology & environment officer, Ecolab Inc.
Ulrich, Robert J.: chairman, chief executive officer, director, Dayton Hudson; chairman, trustee, Target Foundation
Van Dyke, William Grant: chairman, president, chief executive officer, director, Donaldson Co., Inc.
Wardeberg, George E.: president, WICOR Foundation; president, chief executive officer, director, WICOR, Inc.
Wolff, Jesse David: treasurer, director, Weil, Gotshal & Manges Foundation
Wright, Donald Franklin: director, Times Mirror Foundation
Wright, Michael William: chairman, president, chief executive officer, director, SuperValu, Inc.
Wurtele, C. Angus: president, Valspar Foundation

Mississippi

Allbritton, Joe Lewis: chairman, chief executive officer, Riggs Bank NA
Bryan, John Henry: chairman, Sara Lee Corp.; director, Sara Lee Foundation
Cooper, Janis Campbell: vice president, Maytag Corp. Foundation
Deavenport, Earnest W., Jr.: chairman, chief executive officer, director, Eastman Chemical Co.
Hattox, Brock Alan: director, National Service Foundation; executive vice president, chief financial officer, National Service Industries, Inc.
Lackey, S. Allen: director, Shell Oil Co. Foundation
McGehee, Robert B.: executive vice president, general counsel, Carolina Power & Light Co.; trustee, CP&L Foundation
McMillan, Howard Lamar, Jr.: president, chief operating officer, director, Deposit Guaranty National Bank
Quin, Joseph Marvin: trustee, Ashland Inc. Foundation
Ray, John Thomas, Jr.: president, director, Fuller Co. Foundation (H.B.)
Robinson, E. B., Jr.: chairman, chief executive officer, director, Deposit Guaranty National Bank
Scarbrough, Arlan Earl: vice president financial, Gulf Power Co.; trustee, Gulf Power Foundation
Smith, Frederick Wallace: chairman, president, chief executive officer, director, FedEx Corp.
Wilson, James Lawrence: chairman, chief executive officer, director, Rohm & Haas Co.

Missouri

Bailey, Keith E.: chairman, president, director, chief executive officer, Texas Gas Transmission Corp.; president, director, Williams Companies Foundation (The)
Ball, James Herington: senior vice president, general counsel, director, Nestle U.S.A. Inc.
Bangs, Lawrence N.: group executive, Household International Inc.
Barrett, M. Patricia: vice president corporate communications, Ameren Corp.
Belcher, Donald D.: chairman, president, chief executive officer, director, Banta Corp.; vice president, director, Banta Corp. Foundation
Berkley, Eugene Bertram: chairman, director, Tension Envelope Corp.; treasurer, Tension Envelope Foundation
Berkley, William S.: president, chief executive officer, director, Tension Envelope Corp.; director, Tension Envelope Foundation
Binder, Gordon M.: chairman, chief executive officer, director, Amgen, Inc.
Bloch, Henry Wollman: chairman, Block Foundation (H&R); chairman, director, Block, Inc. (H&R)
Bolton, John Roger: senior vice president, Aetna Foundation; senior vice president corporate communications, Aetna, Inc.
Busch, August Adolphus, III: chairman, president, chief executive officer, Anheuser-Busch Companies, Inc.
Cool, Judd R.: senior vice president human resources, Allegheny Technologies Inc.
Early, William Bernard: trustee, Jeld-wen Foundation; senior vice president, assistant secretary, director, Jeld-wen, Inc.
Engibous, Thomas James: director, Texas Instruments Foundation; president, chief executive officer, chairman, director, Texas Instruments Inc.
Essman, Alyn V.: chairman, chief executive officer, CPI Corp.
Gasich, Anthony F.: vice president administration, Farmers Group, Inc.; contributions officer, Farmers Group Safety Foundation
Glass, David Dayne: trustee, Wal-Mart Foundation; director, Wal-Mart Stores, Inc.
Greenwald, Gerald: chairman, chief executive officer, director, United Airlines Inc.
Hagale, John E.: vice president finance, Burlington Resources Foundation
Hall, Donald Joyce: chairman board, director, Hallmark Cards Inc.; chairman, Hallmark Corporate Foundation
Hall, William Austin: president, Hallmark Corporate Foundation
Hemminghaus, Roger Roy: chairman, director, Ultramar Diamond Shamrock Corp.
Henn, Catherine Emily Campbell: president, Boston Globe Foundation
Hotchner, Aaron Edward: vice president, director, executive, Newman's Own Foundation; vice president, treasurer, Newman's Own Inc.
Jaudes, Robert Christian: chairman, trustee, Laclede Gas Charitable Trust
Jobe, G. David: director, MFA Foundation; senior vice president, MFA Inc.
Jones, Raymond E.: secretary, director, Shelter Insurance Foundation; executive vice president, secretary, Shelter Mutual Insurance Co.
Kemper, David Woods: chairman, president, chief executive officer, director, Commerce Bancshares, Inc.
Kemper, James M., Jr.: director, Commerce Bancshares Foundation; chairman, president, director, Commerce Bancshares, Inc.

Kemper, Jonathan McBride: director, Commerce Bancshares Foundation; vice chairman, Commerce Bancshares, Inc.

Koupal, Carl M., Jr.: trustee, Western Resources Foundation; executive vice president, chief administrative officer, Western Resources Inc.

Loeb, Jerome Thomas: chairman, director, May Department Stores Co.; president, director, May Department Stores Computer Foundation (The)

Margolin, Abraham E.: director, Tension Envelope Foundation

Maritz, William Edward: chairman, chief executive officer, president, Maritz Inc.

Martin, Bobby L.: member, Wal-Mart Foundation

Moore, William B.: director, Western Resources Foundation; executive vice president, chief financial officer, treasurer, Western Resources Inc.

Moten, John, Junior: vice president community relations, Laclede Gas Co.

Necessary, Steven K.: senior vice president marketing, Scientific-Atlanta, Inc.

Neel, Curtis Dean, Jr.: trustee, Eckerd Corp. Foundation

Newman, Andrew E.: member, Edison Family Foundation

O'Connor, Edward J.: secretary, director, Smith Foundation, Inc. (A.O.)

Offutt, James A.: director, Shelter Insurance Foundation

Panettiere, John Michael: president, chief executive officer, director, chairman, Blount International, Inc.

Peoples, D. Louis: vice chairman, chief executive officer, director, Orange & Rockland Utilities, Inc.

Phillips, Rosalind Ann: secretary, GEICO Philanthropic Foundation

Powell, George Everett, III: president, chief executive officer, director, Yellow Corp.; trustee, Yellow Corp. Foundation

Powell, George Everett, Jr.: trustee, Yellow Corp. Foundation

Price, Charles H., II: director, New York Times Co. Foundation

Pulitzer, Michael Edgar: chairman, president, chief executive officer, director, Pulitzer Publishing Co.; chairman, president, chief executive officer, Pulitzer Publishing Co. Foundation

Schermer, Lloyd G.: chairman, director, Lee Enterprises

Schoch, Steven J.: vice president, treasurer, Times Mirror Co.; treasurer, chief financial officer, Times Mirror Foundation

Schoening, Robert Walters: senior vice president information systems, Giant Food Inc.

Schuchardt, Daniel Norman: secretary, treasurer, FMC Foundation

Sosland, Morton Irvin: director, Block Foundation (H&R)

Strandjord, Mary Jeannine: director, Sprint Foundation

Stupp, Robert P.: president, director, Stupp Brothers Bridge & Iron Co.; trustee, Stupp Brothers Bridge & Iron Co. Foundation

Toft, Richard Paul: chairman, Chicago Title Corp.; trustee, Chicago Title and Trust Co. Foundation

Wadlington, Cuba, Jr.: vice president, Williams

Weber, Stephen Robert: director, Cowen Foundation

Wenzel, Fred William: chairman emeritus, Kellwood Co.

Williams, Eugene Flewellyn, Jr.: member public policy committee, Emerson Charitable Trust

Wood, Willis B., Jr.: chairman, chief executive officer, director, Pacific Enterprises

Zeffren, Eugene: executive vice president, Curtis Industries, Inc. (Helene)

Montana

Dickey, Boh A.: president, chief operating officer, SAFECO Corp.

Michael, Gary Glenn: chairman, chief executive officer, director, Albertson's Inc.

Pederson, Jerrold P.: vice president, chief financial officer, director, Montana Power Co.; director, Montana Power Foundation

Peressinni, William E.: senior vice president, chief financial officer, PacifiCorp; treasurer, PacifiCorp Foundation

Stinnett, J. Daniel: director, Commerce Bancshares Foundation

Nebraska

Anderson, Eugene Karl: vice president, Contran Corp.; treasurer, Simmons Foundation, Inc. (Harold)

Arth, Lawrence Joseph: vice president, director, Ameritas Charitable Foundation; chairman, chief executive officer, director, Ameritas Life Insurance Corp.

Beach, Roger C.: chairman, chief executive officer, director, Unocal Corp.

Cheney, Richard B.: chief executive officer, Halliburton Co.; president, Halliburton Foundation, Inc.

Davis, John B., MD: director, Physicians Mutual Insurance Co. Foundation

Feller, Mimi A.: senior vice president public affairs & government relations, Gannett Co., Inc.; vice president, Gannett Foundation

Fitzgerald, William Allingham: chairman, director, Commercial Federal Corp.

Hall, Larry D.: chairman, president, chief executive officer, director, Kinder Morgn; president, director, KN Energy Foundation

Hewitt, James Watt: vice president, treasurer, Abel Foundation

Huerter, M. Jane: executive vice president, corporate secretary, Mutual of Omaha Insurance Co.

Jarman, Richard Sinclair: executive vice president, Butler Manufacturing Co.; trustee, Butler Manufacturing Co. Foundation

Lempka, Arnold W., MD: chairman, director, Physicians Mutual Insurance Co.; director, Physicians Mutual Insurance Co. Foundation

Martin, JoAnn M.: controller, Ameritas Charitable Foundation; senior vice president, partner, chief financial officer, Ameritas Life Insurance Corp.

McClain, Terry James: director, Valmont Foundation; senior vice president, chief financial officer, Valmont Industries, Inc.

McVaney, C. Edward: founder, president, Edwards Enterprise Software (J.D.)

Peterson, Robert L.: chairman, chief executive officer, director, IBP

Roberts, John Kenneth, Jr.: president, chief executive officer, director, Pan-American Life Insurance Co.

Scott, Walter, Jr.: member contributions committee, Kiewit Companies Foundation

Spindler, George S.: senior vice president law & corporate affairs, BP Amoco Corp.; chairman, director, BP Amoco Foundation

Stryker, Steven Charles: director, Shell Oil Co. Foundation

Sturgeon, John: president, chief operating officer, Mutual of Omaha Insurance Co.

Tyner, Neal Edward: treasurer, director, Ameritas Charitable Foundation

Vondrasek, Frank Charles, Jr.: president, Madison Gas & Electric Foundation

Weill, Richard L.: president, MBIA Inc.

Weyers, Larry Lee: chief executive officer, chairman, director, Wisconsin Public Service Corp.; president, chief executive officer, Wisconsin Public Service Foundation, Inc.

Nevada

Burns, Mitchell Anthony: president, director, Ryder System Charitable Foundation; chairman, president, chief executive officer, Ryder System, Inc.

New Hampshire

Fair, Russell B.: vice president pharmacy operations, Giant Food Inc.

Gorman, Leon A.: president, chief executive officer, Bean, Inc. (L.L.)

Hamblett, Stephen: chairman, chief executive officer, publisher, Providence Journal-Bulletin Co.; trustee, Providence Journal Charitable Foundation

Messer, Chester R.: president, chief operating officer, Boston Gas Co.; trustee, Eastern Enterprises Foundation

Norwood, Ralph M.: treasurer, Polaroid Foundation

New Jersey

Ackerman, Roger G.: trustee, Corning Inc. Foundation

Allardyce, Fred A.: director, American Standard Foundation; senior vice president medical products sector, American Standard Inc.

Baxter, James G.: vice president, treasurer, Farber Foundation

Beadle, Robert Sheldon: senior vice president corporate development, Ultramar Diamond Shamrock Corp.

Bewley, Peter D.: vice president, secretary, Clorox Co. Foundation

Black, Daniel James: treasurer, Carter-Wallace Foundation; president, chief operating officer, director, Carter-Wallace, Inc.

Brown, Richard Harris: chairman, chief executive officer, director, EDS Corp.

Buchanan, William Hobart, Jr.: assistant secretary, Dun & Bradstreet Corp. Foundation, Inc.

Burenga, Kenneth L.: president, chief operating officer, director, Dow Jones & Co., Inc.

Codey, Lawrence R.: president, chief operating officer, Public Service Electric & Gas Co.

Colman, Robert L.: executive vice president human resources, Delta Air Lines, Inc.

Critelli, Michael J.: vice president, secretary, general counsel, chairman, Pitney Bowes Inc.

D'Andrade, Hugh Alfred: trustee, member, Schering-Plough Foundation

Devlin, James Richard: director, Sprint Foundation

Doerfler, Ronald J.: senior vice president, chief financial officer, ABC; vice president, director, ABC Foundation

Downes, Laurence M.: president, chief executive officer, director, chairman, New Jersey Natural Gas Co.; trustee, New Jersey Natural Gas Foundation

Esposito, Michael Patrick, Jr.: trustee, Chase Manhattan Foundation

Fino, Raymond M.: second vice president, Warner-Lambert Charitable Foundation; vice president human resources, Warner-Lambert Co.

Forbes, Christopher 'Kip': vice president, Forbes Foundation; vice chairman, corporate secretary, director, Forbes Inc.

Forbes, Malcolm Stevenson, Jr.: president, Forbes Foundation

Graham, John Gourlay: chief financial officer, senior vice president, GPU Energy

Hale, Roger Loucks: chairman, TENNANT Co.; president, TENNANT Co. Foundation

Harad, George Jay: chairman, chief executive officer, director, Boise Cascade Corp.

Heimbold, Charles Andreas, Jr.: chairman, president, chief executive officer, Bristol-Myers Squibb Co.

Higginbotham, A. Leon, Jr.: director, New York Times Co. Foundation

Howe, Wesley Jackson: chairman emeritus, director, Becton Dickinson & Co.

Hoyt, Charles Orcutt: director, Carter-Wallace Foundation; chairman executive committee, director, Carter-Wallace, Inc.

Hoyt, Henry Hamilton, Jr.: president, Carter-Wallace Foundation; chairman, chief executive officer, director, Carter-Wallace, Inc.

Hubschman, Henry A.: director, GE Fund

Kenny, John J.: treasurer, Loews Corp.; secretary, treasurer, trustee, Loews Foundation

Kentz, Frederick C., III: trustee, Hoffmann-La Roche Foundation; vice president, secretary, general counsel, Hoffmann-La Roche Inc.

Keyes, James W.: executive vice president, chief operating officer, 7-Eleven, Inc.

Klesse, William R.: executive vice president operations, Ultramar Diamond Shamrock Corp.

Krueger, Harvey M.: trustee, Barry Foundation

Labrecque, Thomas Goulet: president, chief operating officer, director, Chase Manhattan Bank, NA; president, Chase Manhattan Foundation

Lipton, Martin: partner, Wachtell, Lipton, Rosen & Katz; president, Wachtell, Lipton, Rosen & Katz Foundation

Lorch, George A.: chairman, chief executive officer, director, Armstrong World Industries, Inc.

Manoogian, Richard Alexander: chairman, chief executive officer, director, Masco Corp.

Marcus, Bernard: chairman, director, Home Depot, Inc.

Mark, Reuben: chairman, chief executive officer, Colgate-Palmolive Co.

McClelland, William Craig: trustee, Union Camp Charitable Trust; chairman, chief executive officer, director, Union Camp Corp.

McGraw, Harold Whittlesey 'Terry', III: chairman, president, chief executive officer, McGraw-Hill Companies, Inc.

Morie, G. Glen: secretary, treasurer, PACCAR Foundation

Mullen, Dennis M.: president, chief executive officer, director, Agrilink Foods, Inc.

Naples, Ronald James: president, chief executive officer, director, Quaker Chemical Corp.

O'Hare, Dean Raymond: chairman, Chubb Corp.

Painter, Alan Sproul: vice president, executive director, AlliedSignal Foundation Inc.

Palmieri, Peter C.: vice chairman, chief credit officer, First Union National Bank, NA

Peck, Arthur John, Jr.: secretary, vice president, Corning Inc.; secretary, Corning Inc. Foundation

Plumeri, Joseph James, II: president, Citigroup

Renyi, Thomas A.: president, chief executive officer, director, Bank of New York Co., Inc.

Resnick, Stewart A.: chairman, chief executive officer, Franklin Mint (The)

Sharpe, Robert Francis, Jr.: senior vice president public affairs, general counsel, PepsiCo, Inc.

Shuster, George Whitcomb: trustee, Cranston Foundation; president, chief executive officer, director, Cranston Print Works Co.

Siegel, Samuel: vice chairman, secretary, treasurer, chief financial officer, director, Nucor Corp.; director, Nucor Foundation

Slagle, Robert F.: director, Alcoa Foundation; executive vice president human resources and communications, Alcoa Inc.

Smith, Frederick C.: chairman, trustee, Huffy Foundation, Inc.

Standen, Craig Clayton: senior vice president corporate development, Scripps Co. (E.W.)

Sullivan, Thomas John: vice president, director,

Suter, Albert E.: senior vice chairman, chief administrative officer, director, Emerson Electric Co.

Sutton, Howard: president, Providence Journal Charitable Foundation

Tisch, James S.: president, chief executive officer, director, CNA

Tumminello, Stephen C.: president, chief executive officer, director, Philips Electronics North America Corp.

Tyson, Laura D'Andrea: director, Ameritech Foundation

Vagelos, Pindaros Roy: trustee, Prudential Insurance Co. of America

Watson, Solomon Brown, IV: vice president, New York Times Co. Foundation

Wiley, Bradford, II: chairman, director, Wiley & Sons (John)

New Mexico

Apodaca, Clara: trustee, Hitachi Foundation

Law, L. William, Jr.: senior vice president, general counsel, secretary, Eastern Enterprises

McNeill, Corbin Asahel, Jr.: president, chief executive officer, director, chairman, PECO Energy Co.

Parrish, Jere Paul: president, chairman executive committee, director, Shell Oil Co. Foundation

New York

Ackerman, Philip Charles: senior vice president, director, National Fuel Gas Distribution Corp.

Adler, Ira R.: executive vice president, chief financial officer, Tucson Electric Power Co.

Aldinger, William F., III: chairman, chief executive officer, director, Household International Inc.

Alegi, August Paul: director, GEICO Philanthropic Foundation

Alm, John Richard: director, Coca-Cola Foundation

Almeida, Richard: chairman, chief executive officer, Heller Financial, Inc.

Baker, Robert Woodward: executive vice president, AMR Corp.

Barad, Jill Elikann: director, Mattel Foundation; chairman, chief executive officer, director, Mattel Inc.

Barrett, Robert E.: executive vice president, UST Inc.

Barun, Kenneth Lee: president, director, McDonald's Corp. Charitable Foundation

Beard, Anson McCook, Jr.: director, NASDAQ Stock Market Educational Foundation

Bescherer, Edwin A., Jr.: trustee, Dun & Bradstreet Corp. Foundation, Inc.

Bijur, Peter I.: chairman, chief executive officer, Texaco Inc.

Blank, Arthur M.: president, chief executive officer, director, Home Depot, Inc.

Block, William: vice president, trustee, Blade Foundation; chairman, director, Toledo Blade Co.

Bonsignore, Michael Robert: director, Honeywell Foundation; chairman, chief executive officer, director, Honeywell International Inc.

Bonvino, Frank W.: vice president, secretary, general counsel, International Multifoods Corp.

Booth, Chesleu Peter Washburn: senior vice president development, Corning Inc.; trustee, Corning Inc. Foundation

Boudreau, Donald L.: vice president, trustee, Chase Manhattan Foundation

Boyle, Richard James: vice chairman, director, Chase Manhattan Bank, NA; trustee, Chase Manhattan Foundation

Bozzone, Robert P.: vice chairman, director, Allegheny Technologies Inc.; trustee, Allegheny Technologies Inc. Charitable Trust

Brennan, Alice C.: vice president, secretary, Bristol-Myers Squibb Co.; secretary, Bristol-Myers Squibb Foundation Inc.

Breslawsky, Marc C.: president, chief operating officer, Pitney Bowes Inc.

Bright, Stanley J.: chairman, president, chief executive officer, director, MidAmerican Energy Holdings Co.

Brine, Kevin R.: trustee, Bernstein & Co. Foundation, Inc. (Sanford C.)

Broadhead, James Lowell: chairman, president, chief executive officer, director, Florida Power & Light Co.; chief executive officer, director, FPL Group Foundation Inc.

Broome, Burton Edward: vice president, controller, Transamerica Corp.; vice president, treasurer, Transamerica Foundation

Brown, Harold, PhD: chairman, Mattel Foundation

Brozyna, Jeffry H.: trustee

Bruce, Peter Wayne: director, Badger Meter Foundation

Bryson, John E.: chairman, chief executive officer, Edison International

Buckwalter, Alan Roland, III: chief executive officer, Chase Bank of Texas; president, Chase Bank of Texas Foundation, Inc.

Buechner, Thomas Scharman: trustee, Corning Inc. Foundation

Buhrmaster, Robert C.: president, chief executive officer, director, chairman, Jostens, Inc.

Bundschuh, George August William: director, New York Life Foundation

Burak, Howard Paul: secretary, director, Sony U.S.A. Foundation Inc.

Burke, Daniel Barnett: vice president, treasurer, director, ABC Foundation

Bush, Norman: vice president, Fort James Corp.

Calise, Nicholas James: vice president, associate general counsel, secretary, BFGoodrich Co.; secretary, Goodrich Foundation, Inc. (B.F.)

Calise, William Joseph, Junior: senior vice president, secretary, general counsel, Rockwell International Corp.

Call, Robert V., Jr.: chairman, trustee, Agrilink Foods/Pro-Fac Foundation

Cammarata, Bernard: president, chief executive officer, director, TJX Companies, Inc.; president, TJX Foundation, Inc.

Cantor, Bernard Gerald: president, director, Cantor, Fitzgerald Foundation; chairman, director, Cantor, Fitzgerald Securities Corp.

Castellani, John: executive vice president, Tenneco Automotive

Catell, Robert Barry: chairman, chief executive officer, Brooklyn Union

Chapple, Thomas Leslie: senior vice president, general counsel, secretary, Gannett Co., Inc.; secretary, Gannett Foundation

Chazen, Jerome A.: trustee, Claiborne Foundation (Liz); co-founder, chairman, director, Liz Claiborne, Inc.

Chenault, Kenneth Irvine: president, chief operating officer, director, American Express Co.; trustee, American Express Foundation

Civello, Nelson D.: director, Dain Bosworth Foundation

Clark, Howard Longstreth, Jr.: vice chairman, Walter Industries Inc.

Clarke, Thomas E.: president, chief operating officer, Nike, Inc.

Clemente, Constantine Louis: chairman, Pfizer Foundation; executive vice president corporate affairs, secretary, corporate counsel, Pfizer Inc.

Cody, Thomas Gerald: executive vice president legal & human resources, Federated Department Stores, Inc.

Cohen, Jonathan L.: secretary, director, Goldman Sachs Foundation

Cohen, Joseph M.: president, director, Cowen Foundation; chairman, chief executive officer, S.G. Cowen

Cole, Lewis George: director, AMETEK Foundation

Conaty, William J.: director, GE Fund

Conklin, Thomas J.: senior vice president, secretary, MONY Group (The); director, MONY Life Insurance of New York (The)
Connolly, Charles H.: senior vice president corporate affairs & investor relations, Whitman Corp.; president, Whitman Corp. Foundation
Connolly, Eugene Bernard, Jr.: chairman emeritus, USG Corp.
Convisser, Theodora S.: trustee, Boston Edison Foundation
Cook, J. Michael: chairman, chief executive officer, Deloitte & Touche; chairman, Deloitte & Touche Foundation
Cook, John Rowland: trustee, Harcourt General Charitable Foundation; senior vice president, chief financial officer, Harcourt General, Inc.
Correnti, John D.: president, chief executive officer, director, Nucor Corp.
Cottrell, G. Walton: senior vice president, chief financial officer, Carpenter Technology Corp.
Cristallo, Peter P.: associate senior vice president human resources & administration, NEC America, Inc.
D'Amato, Anthony S.: chairman, Borden Foundation, Inc.
Davis, Carolyne Kahle, PhD: trustee, Merck Co. Foundation
Davis, William E.: chairman, chief executive officer, Niagara Mohawk Holdings Inc.
DeCaro, Angelo: treasurer, director, Goldman Sachs Foundation
Denlea, Leo Edward, Jr.: retired chairman, president, chief executive officer, director, Farmers Group, Inc.; vice president, Farmers Group Safety Foundation
DiCamillo, Gary Thomas: chairman, chief executive officer, director, Polaroid Corp.
Dickoff, Gil A.: treasurer, Crane Foundation
Dillon, John T.: chairman, chief executive officer, director, International Paper Co.
Dimon, James R.: trustee, Citigroup Foundation; president, chief operating officer, chief financial officer, Salomon Smith Barney
Douglass, Robert Royal: trustee, Chase Manhattan Foundation
Drexler, Millard S.: trustee, Gap Foundation/Gap Inc. Community Relations; president, chief executive officer, director, Gap, Inc.
Dubin, Melvin: chairman, Slant/Fin Corp.; president, director, Slant/Fin Foundation
Dubin, Stephen Victor: vice president, secretary, Farber Foundation
Dugan, Allan E.: senior vice president corporate strategic service, Xerox Corp.; trustee, Xerox Foundation
Earley, Anthony Francis, Jr.: president, chief operating officer, Detroit Edison Co.; director, Detroit Edison Foundation
Eckstein, Marie N.: trustee, Dow Corning Foundation
Eisner, Michael Dammann: president, trustee, Disney Co. Foundation (Walt); chairman, chief executive officer, director, Disney Co. (Walt)
Ellison, Lawrence J.: chairman, chief executive officer, director, president, Oracle Corp.
Engel, Joel Stanley: vice president technology, Ameritech Corp.
Evanson, Paul John: president, treasurer, director, FPL Group Foundation, Inc.
Farrell, W. James: chairman, chief executive officer, Illinois Tool Works, Inc.
Fierce, Hughlyn F.: trustee, Chase Manhattan Foundation
Fine, Roger Seth: vice president, general counsel, Johnson & Johnson; president, Johnson & Johnson Family of Companies Contribution Fund
Foley, Patricia A.: assistant secretary, Inland Container Corp.; secretary, treasurer, director, Inland Foundation, Inc.
Freedman, Allen Royal: trustee, Fortis Foundation; chairman, chief executive officer, president, Fortis, Inc.
Friedewald, William Thomas, MD: director, MetLife Foundation
Friedman, Stephen James: senior advisor, Goldman Sachs Group
Furlaud, Richard Mortimer: interim chief executive officer, International Flavors & Fragrances Inc.
Gallagher, Terence Joseph: secretary, director, Pfizer Foundation
Gammill, Lee Morgan, Jr.: director, New York Life Foundation; vice chairman, director, New York Life Insurance Co.
Gardner, James Richard: vice president, Pfizer Foundation
Gelb, Richard Lee: director, New York Times Co. Foundation
Gerstner, Louis Vincent, Jr.: chairman, chief executive officer, director, International Business Machines Corp.
Giaramita, Phillip S.: vice president corporate communications, International Paper Co.; president, director, International Paper Co. Foundation
Gierer, Vincent A., Jr.: chairman, president, chief executive officer, director, UST Inc.
Gilbert, Glen S.: vice president advertising & social responsibility, GTE Corp.
Golub, Harvey: chairman, chief executive officer, director, American Express Co.; trustee, American Express Foundation
Gorelick, Jamie Shona: vice chairman, Fannie Mae
Graham, Katharine Meyer: chairman executive committee, director, The Washington Post
Granoff, Mark Howard: vice president, United Wisconsin Services Foundation
Graves, Earl Gilbert: director, Aetna Foundation
Greenfield, Jerry: cofounder, vice chairman, Ben & Jerry's Homemade Inc.
Gregg, Walter Emmor, Junior: senior executive vice president finance & administration, PNC Financial Services Group
Griffith, Alan Richard: vice chairman, Bank of New York Co., Inc.
Gross, Murray: trustee, PerkinElmer Foundation; senior vice president, general counsel, clerk, PerkinElmer, Inc.
Guthart, Leo A.: vice chairman, director, Pittway Corp.
Halperin, Richard E.: president, Revlon Foundation Inc.
Hammerman, Stephen Lawrence: vice president, trustee, Merrill Lynch & Co. Foundation Inc.; vice chairman, general counsel, Merrill Lynch & Co., Inc.
Hanower, L. David: assistant secretary, Burlington Resources Foundation
Hardis, Stephen Roger: chairman, chief executive officer, director, Eaton Corp.
Harris, Ralph A.: vice president corporate development, Campbell Soup Co.
Hecht, William F.: chairman, president, chief executive officer, Pennsylvania Power & Light
Hergenhan, Joyce: director, president, GE Fund
Herringer, Frank Casper: president, chief executive officer, director, chairman, Transamerica Corp.; vice chairman, director, Transamerica Foundation
Hirsch, Laurence E.: chairman, chief executive officer, director, Centex Corp.
Hohn, Harry George, Jr.: chairman, director, New York Life Foundation
Houghton, James Richardson: director, Corning Inc.; trustee, Corning Inc. Foundation
Hunt, Ray Lee: chairman, chief executive officer, director, Hunt Oil Co.
Hutchings, Peter Lounsbery: president, Guardian Life Insurance Co. of America
Hyman, Morton Peter: vice president, director, OSG Foundation; president, director, Overseas Shipholding Group Inc.
Jacobs, Joseph J.: president, director, Jacobs Engineering Foundation; chairman, director, Jacobs Engineering Group
Jerrold, Douglas M.: vice president, Reynolds Metals Co. Foundation
Jones, Ross: senior vice president, chief financial officer, Knight Ridder
Kaden, Ellen O.: trustee, Campbell Soup Foundation
Kann, Peter Robert: chairman, chief executive officer, publisher, director, Dow Jones & Co., Inc.; member advisory committee, Dow Jones Foundation
Kasputys, Joseph Edward: chairman, trustee, Hitachi Foundation
Kaufman, Frank Joseph: senior vice president taxes, McGraw-Hill Companies, Inc.
Kennedy, Bernard Joseph: chairman, president, chief executive officer, director, National Fuel Gas Distribution Corp.
Khoury, Kenneth F.: secretary, Georgia-Pacific Foundation
Kidder, C. Robert: chairman, president, chief executive officer, director, Borden, Inc.
Klein, Calvin Richard: president, Calvin Klein
Klein, David M.: vice president, Hartford (The)
Kober, Roger W.: chairman, chief executive officer, director, Rochester Gas & Electric Corp.
Kogan, Richard Jay: chairman, chief executive officer, Schering-Plough Corp.; trustee, member, Schering-Plough Foundation
Komansky, David H.: trustee, vice president, Merrill Lynch & Co. Foundation Inc.; chairman, chief executive officer, Merrill Lynch & Co., Inc.
Kreindler, Peter Michael: president, director, AlliedSignal Foundation Inc.; senior vice president, general counsel, secretary, AlliedSignal Inc.
Kresa, Kent: chairman, president, chief executive officer, director, Northrop Grumman Corp.
Kroeber, C. Kent: chairman contributions committee, Interpublic Group of Companies, Inc.
Kurtz, Melvin H.: secretary, director, Chesebrough Foundation
LaMantia, Charles Robert: president, chief executive officer, director, Little, Inc. (Arthur D.)
Lang, Robert Todd: chairman, director, Weil, Gotshal & Manges Foundation
Larsen, Ralph Stanley: chairman, president, chief executive officer, director, Johnson & Johnson
Latzer, Richard Neal: vice president, director, Transamerica Foundation
Levin, Michael Stuart: president, chief executive officer, Titan Industrial Corp.
Levine, Kenneth M.: executive vice president, chief investment officer, director, MONY Group (The); director, MONY Life Insurance of New York (The)
Levine, Lawrence E.: secretary, Panasonic Foundation
Levine, Ralph: president, chief operating officer, director, Carter-Wallace, Inc.
Lewis, Frances Aaronson: trustee, Circuit City Foundation
Lindenauer, Arthur: executive vice president, chief financial officer, Schlumberger Ltd. (USA)
Lippes, Gerald Sanford: secretary, Mark IV Industries Foundation
Litvack, Sanford M.: senior executive vice president, chief corporate operations, director, Disney Co. (Walt)
Lower, H. Louis Gordon, II: vice president, trustee, Allstate Foundation
Luke, John A., Jr.: chairman, president, chief executive officer, director, Westvaco Corp.

MacDonald, J. Randall: senior vice president human resources administration, GTE Corp.; trustee, GTE Foundation

Magowan, Peter Alden: president, managing general partner, Safeway Inc.

Mahoney, Robert W.: chairman, president, chief executive officer, director, Diebold, Inc.

Mallardi, Michael Patrick: senior vice president, ABC; vice president, director, ABC Foundation

Manfredi, John Frederick: member administration committee, Nabisco Foundation Trust

Manning, Kenneth Paul: president, Universal Foods Corp.; president, director, Universal Foods Foundation

Manzi, James Paul: president, director, Lotus Development Corp.

Margolis, Jay M.: member grantmaking committee, Claiborne Foundation (Liz)

Marron, Donald Baird: chairman, chief executive officer, director, Paine Webber; trustee, Paine Webber Foundation

Martinez, Arthur C.: chairman, chief executive officer, president, Sears, Roebuck and Co.

Matis, Nina B.: director, Katten, Muchin & Zavis Foundation

Matthews, Craig Gerard: president, chief operating officer, Brooklyn Union

Maurer, Jeffrey Stuart: president, chief operating officer, director, United States Trust Co. of New York

McCorkindale, Douglas H.: vice chairman, president, Gannett Co., Inc.; president, Gannett Foundation

McGovern, John Francis: chief financial officer, executive vice president, Georgia-Pacific Corp.; chairman, Georgia-Pacific Foundation

McGrath, Lee Upton: treasurer, Fuller Co. Foundation (H.B.); vice president, treasurer, Fuller Co. (H.B.); treasurer, Jostens Foundation Inc. (The)

McKenna, William John: director, chairman, Kellwood Co.; chairman, president, director, Kellwood Foundation

McNeary, Joseph Allen: member grantmaking committee, Claiborne Foundation (Liz); senior vice president, Liz Claiborne, Inc.

Mead, Susan W. A.: vice president, ReliaStar Financial Corp.; director, ReliaStar Foundation

Meyerson, Martin: director, Panasonic Foundation

Miller, Harvey R.: secretary, director, Weil, Gotshal & Manges Foundation

Milliken, Gerrish H., Jr.: member advisory committee, Milliken Foundation

Milliken, Minot King: member advisory committee, Milliken Foundation

Milliken, Roger: chairman, chief executive officer, Milliken & Co.; member advisory committee, Milliken Foundation

Millstein, Ira M.: partner, Weil, Gotshal & Manges Corp.; president, director, Weil, Gotshal & Manges Foundation

Minton, Dwight Church: chairman, director, Church & Dwight Co., Inc.

Mirsky, Susan: vice president, director, Thompson Co. Fund (J. Walter)

Munder, Barbara A.: senior vice president new initiatives, McGraw-Hill Companies, Inc.

Needleman, Harry: secretary, Cantor, Fitzgerald Foundation; executive vice president, general counsel, Cantor, Fitzgerald Securities Corp.

Nelson, John Martin: chairman, director, TJX Companies, Inc.

Nern, Christopher C.: vice president, general counsel, Detroit Edison Co.; director, Detroit Edison Foundation

Nicholas, Jon O.: vice president, trustee, Maytag Corp. Foundation

Nichols, Wade Hampton, III: vice president, Revlon Foundation Inc.; executive vice president, general counsel, Revlon Inc.

Noha, Edward J.: director, CNA Foundation

Nunes, Geoffrey: chairman, Millipore Foundation (The)

O'Leary, Thomas Howard: chairman, Burlington Resources Foundation

Osborne, Richard de Jongh: director, ASARCO Foundation; chairman, chief executive officer, director, ASARCO Inc.

Ottaway, James Haller, Jr.: senior vice president, director, Dow Jones & Co., Inc.; member advisory committee, Dow Jones Foundation

Ozark, Edward L.: trustee, JSJ Foundation

Paladino, Daniel R.: trustee, Bronfman Foundation/Joseph E. Seagram & Sons, Inc. Fund (Samuel); executive vice president, general counsel, secretary, Seagram & Sons, Inc. (Joseph E.)

Parisi, Franklin Joseph: chairman, Star Tribune Foundation

Parry, William E.: vice president, general counsel, Nalco Chemical Co.

Patterson, Michael E.: vice chairman, Morgan & Co. Inc. (J.P.)

Peet, Creighton Houck: vice president, director, Cowen Foundation

Penny, Roger Pratt: president, chief operating officer, director, Bethlehem Steel Corp.

Peterson, Charles T.: chief financial officer, managing director, S.G. Cowen

Peterson, Donald Matthew: trustee, Trustmark Foundation; president, chief executive officer, director, Trustmark Insurance Co.

Pew, Robert Cunningham, II: trustee, Steelcase Foundation

Phair, Joseph Baschon: corporate secretary, general counsel, vice president, Varian Medical Systems, Inc.

Platt, Lewis Emmett: chairman, Hewlett-Packard Co.

Polin, Jane Louise: manager, comptroller, GE Fund

Pollicino, Joseph Anthony: executive vice chairman, CIT Group Foundation; vice chairman, director, CIT Group, Inc. (The)

Poses, Frederick M.: director, AlliedSignal Foundation Inc.; president, chief operating officer, AlliedSignal Inc.

Raskin, Fred C.: president, chief operating officer, Eastern Enterprises; trustee, Eastern Enterprises Foundation

Ray, Terry D.: vice president business development, Eastern Enterprises

Recanati, Michael A.: executive vice president, director, OSG Foundation

Redding, Peter Stoddard: trustee, Sherman-Standard Register Foundation; president, chief executive officer, director, Standard Register Co.

Rehm, Jack Daniel: chairman emeritus, director, Meredith Corp.

Reinemund, Steve S.: chairman, chief executive officer, Frito-Lay, Inc.

Reuter, Carol Joan: chief executive officer, director, New York Life Foundation; vice president, New York Life Insurance Co.

Reynolds, William Gray, Jr.: vice president government relations & public affairs, Reynolds Metals Co.; director, Reynolds Metals Co. Foundation

Rhodes, William Reginald: vice chairman, Citibank Corp.

Rich, David A.: executive director, Rich Family Foundation; vice president, secretary, director, Rich Products Corp.

Rich, Robert E., Jr.: secretary, Rich Family Foundation; president, director, Rich Products Corp.

Rich, Robert E., Sr.: president, treasurer, Rich Family Foundation; founder, chairman, director, Rich Products Corp.

Riley, H. John, Jr.: chairman, president, chief executive officer, Cooper Industries Foundation; chairman, president, chief executive officer, director, Cooper Industries, Inc.

Ripley, Sidney Dillon, II: director emeritus, Hitachi Foundation

Ripp, Robert M.: chairman, chief executive officer, director, AMP Inc.

Robinson, Edward Joseph: president, chief operating officer, director, Avon Products, Inc.

Roche, George A.: chairman, president, Price Associates (T. Rowe)

Rock, Arthur: co-founder, chairman executive committee, director, Intel Corp.

Rockefeller, Frederic Lincoln: trustee, Cranston Foundation

Ross, Arthur: senior vice president, Central National-Gottesman; director, Central National-Gottesman Foundation

Roth, Michael I.: chairman, chief executive officer, director, MONY Group (The); director, MONY Life Insurance of New York (The)

Rukeyser, Robert James: senior vice president corporate affairs, Fortune Brands, Inc.

Rutstein, David W.: secretary, Giant Food Foundation; senior vice president, general counsel, chief administrative officer, Giant Food Inc.

Ryan, Arthur Frederick: trustee, Chase Manhattan Foundation; chairman, chief executive officer, Prudential Insurance Co. of America

Sacks, David G.: trustee, Bronfman Foundation/Joseph E. Seagram & Sons, Inc. Fund (Samuel)

Sanders, Lewis A.: trustee, Bernstein & Co. Foundation, Inc. (Sanford C.); chairman, chief executive officer, Bernstein & Co., Inc. (Sanford C.)

Schara, Charles Gerard: treasurer, GEICO Corp.; assistant treasurer, director, GEICO Philanthropic Foundation

Schlauch, Walter F.: group vice president, National Starch & Chemical Co.

Schwartz, Barry K.: chairman, chief executive officer, director, Calvin Klein

Schwarz, H. Marshall: chairman, chief executive officer, United States Trust Co. of New York

Scicutella, John Vincent: trustee, Chase Manhattan Foundation

Setterstrom, William N.: chairman contributions committee, Northern Trust Co. Charitable Trust

Shapiro, Robert B.: chairman, president, chief executive officer, director, Monsanto Co.

Shaw, L. Edward, Jr.: general counsel, Aetna, Inc.; trustee, Chase Manhattan Foundation

Sheehan, Jeremiah J.: chairman, director, Reynolds Metals Co. Foundation

Shepherd, Kathleen Shearen Maynard: director, Tribune New York Foundation

Simpson, William H.: president, Susquehanna-Pfaltzgraff Co.; secretary, Susquehanna-Pfaltzgraff Foundation

Skoda, Daniel: president, Marshall Field's

Slizewski, Bea B.: vice president corporate communications, Agrilink Foods, Inc.

Slovin, Bruce: president, director, Revlon Inc.

Smith, Elizabeth Patience: director, Texaco Foundation; vice president investor relations & shareholder service, Texaco Inc.

Soden, Paul A.: senior vice president, secretary, general counsel, Reader's Digest Association, Inc. (The)

Spina, David Anthony: president, chief operating officer, State Street Bank & Trust Co.

Standish, J. Spencer: chairman, director, Albany International Corp.

Stanley, Peter William: trustee, Hitachi Foundation

Stavropoulos, William S.: president, chief executive officer, director, Dow Chemical Co.

Strickland, Carol A.: chairman corporate contributions committee, U.S. Trust Corp. Foundation

Sulzberger, Arthur Ochs, Junior: director, chairman emeritus, New York Times Co.

Sulzberger, Arthur Ochs, Sr.: director, New York Times Co.; chairman, director, New York Times Co. Foundation

Swanson, Robert A.: director, Genentech Foundation for Biomedical Sciences

Taylor, Frederick B.: vice chairman, chief investment officer, United States Trust Co. of New York

Thomas, Franklin Augustine: director, CBS Foundation

Thornton, John T.: executive vice president, chief financial officer, Norwest Corp.; treasurer, Norwest Foundation

Tisch, Laurence Alan: chairman, co-chief executive officer, CBS Corp.; trustee, Loews Foundation

Tisch, Preston Robert: chairman, director, CBS Foundation; co-chairman, co-chief executive officer, director, CNA; trustee, Loews Foundation

Typermass, Arthur G.: senior vice president, treasurer, Metropolitan Life Insurance Co.

Ughetta, William Casper: trustee, Corning Inc. Foundation

Upbin, Hal Jay: president, chief executive officer, director, Kellwood Co.

Urkowitz, Michael: senior vice president, Chase Manhattan Bank, NA; trustee, Chase Manhattan Foundation

Viault, Raymond: vice chairman, director, General Mills, Inc.

Villanueva, Edward: trustee, Circuit City Foundation

Wagar, James Lee: manager, Carter-Wallace Foundation

Wallach, Ira D.: chairman, Central National-Gottesman; executive vice president, Central National-Gottesman Foundation

Wasserman, David Sherman: vice president, treasurer, Harris Corp.; trustee, Harris Foundation

Weidemeyer, Thomas H.: senior vice president, director, United Parcel Service of America Inc.; trustee, UPS Foundation

Weill, Sanford I.: chairman, chief executive officer, Citibank Corp.; chairman, Citigroup Foundation

Weinberg, John Livingston: chairman, president, director, Goldman Sachs Foundation

Wheeler, Thomas Beardsley: chairman, chief executive officer, Massachusetts Mutual Life Insurance Co.

White, Gerald Andrew: director, Air Products Foundation

Wilmers, Robert George: chairman, president, chief executive officer, Manufacturers & Traders Trust Co.

Wishnick, William: president, director, Wishnick Foundation (Robert I.)

Wright, Elease E.: director, Aetna Foundation

Wurtzel, Alan Leon: chairman, Circuit City Foundation; chairman, trustee, Circuit City Stores, Inc.

Yablon, Leonard Harold: secretary-treasurer, Forbes Foundation

Young, Robert Harris: president, chief executive officer, Central Vermont Public Service Corp.

Zigas, Barry: senior vice president, Fannie Mae; director, Fannie Mae Foundation

von Glahn, William G.: senior vice president, general counsel, Williams; director, Williams Companies Foundation (The)

North Carolina

Allison, John Andrew, IV: chairman, chief executive officer, director, Branch Banking & Trust Co.

Barnett, Hoyt R.: executive vice president, director, Publix Supermarkets

Belk, John Montgomery: member board advisors, Belk Foundation; chairman, Belk-Simpson Department Stores

Berrier, Ronald G.: vice president, treasurer, assistant secretary, Thomasville Furniture Industries Inc.

Brewer, Oliver Gordon, Jr.: vice president finance, treasurer, IKON Office Solutions Foundation, Inc.

Denny, Dwight D.: director, Ryder System Charitable Foundation

Dickson, Alan Thomas: president, Dickson Foundation; chairman, Ruddick Corp.

Dickson, Rush Stuart: chairman, Dickson Foundation

Disher, J. William: director, Lance Foundation; chairman, Lance, Inc.

Donehue, J. Douglas: managing director, Post and Courier Foundation

Dozier, Ollin Kemp: treasurer, Universal Leaf Foundation

Eason, William Everette, Jr.: senior vice president, corporate secretary, general counsel, Scientific-Atlanta, Inc.

Ellis, William Edward, Jr.: secretary, Barry Foundation

Farmer, Phillip W.: chairman, president, chief executive officer, Harris Corp.; president, trustee, Harris Foundation

Gambill, Malcolm W.: president, trustee, Harsco Corp. Fund

Grise, Cheryl W.: senior vice president, chief administrative officer, Northeast Utilities

Harkey, Robert Shelton: trustee, Delta Air Lines Foundation; senior vice president, general counsel, secretary, Delta Air Lines, Inc.

Herring, Leonard Gray: vice president, Lowe's Charitable and Educational Foundation

Hill, Frank Trent, Jr.: trustee, Sonoco Foundation; vice president, chief financial officer, Sonoco Products Co.

Hinshaw, Juanita H.: vice president, treasurer, Monsanto Co.; treasurer, Monsanto Fund

Horack, Thomas Borland: vice president, director, Lance Foundation

Horner, Donald G.: vice president, director, First Hawaiian Foundation

Huber, Richard Leslie: chairman, president, chief executive officer, director, Aetna, Inc.

Jamison, Zean, Jr.: director, Lance Foundation; director human resources, Lance, Inc.

Jobe, Warren Yancey: executive vice president, Georgia Power Co.; president, director, Georgia Power Foundation

Jones, D. Michael: senior vice president, general counsel, Reynolds Metals Co.; vice president, director, Reynolds Metals Co. Foundation

Lay, Terry: president, Lee, Lee Apparel Co.

Little, William Norris: vice chairman, director, Shaw Industries Inc.

Perelman, Ronald Owen: director, Revlon Foundation Inc.

Rhodes, James Thomas: president, chief executive officer, director, Dominion Resources, Inc.

Sloan, Albert Frazier: director, Lance Foundation

Trogdon, Dewey Leonard, Jr.: director, ABC Foundation; chairman, Cone Mills Corp.

Wheeler, Joyce W.: secretary, Royal & SunAlliance Insurance Foundation, Inc.; vice president, corporate secretary, Royal & SunAlliance USA, Inc.

Williamson, Henry Gaston, Jr.: chief operating officer, Branch Banking & Trust Co.

Womack, Robert R.: chairman, chief executive officer, director, Zurn Industries, Inc.

Woolard, Edgar Smith, Jr.: director, du Pont de Nemours & Co. (E.I.)

North Dakota

Bohn, Karen M.: president, Piper Jaffray Companies Foundation; chief executive officer, U.S. Bancorp Piper Jaffray

Borman, Marlene: vice president, director, Borman Fund (The)

Burd, Steven A.: president, chief executive officer, chairman, director, Safeway Inc.

Gallagher, Richard S.: director, Badger Meter Foundation

Joos, David W.: president, chief executive officer electric, executive vice president, Consumers Energy Co.

Kalainov, Sam Charles: chairman, president, chief executive officer, AmerUS Group

Klugman, Craig: editor, Journal-Gazette Co.

Nelson, Merlin Edward: chairman, director, IBJ Foundation

Setzner, Leah Manning: vice president, general counsel, corporate secretary, Illinois Power Co.

Unruh, James Arlen: director, Ameritech Foundation

Ohio

Aley, Paul Nathaniel: president, director, National Machinery Co.; president, National Machinery Foundation, Inc.

Altman, David R.: vice president corporate communications, Southern Co. Services Inc.

Anderson, Ivan Verner, Jr.: president, chief executive officer, Evening Post Publishing Co.; vice president, Post and Courier Foundation

Anderson, Thomas Harold: chairman, trustee, Anderson Foundation; chairman, director, Andersons Inc.

Armstrong, Neil A.: trustee, Milacron Foundation; director, Milacron, Inc.

Ballentine, Richard O.: vice president, secretary, general counsel, Butler Manufacturing Co.; secretary, Butler Manufacturing Co. Foundation

Beargie, William T.: trustee, Lubrizol Foundation (The)

Bersticker, Albert C.: chairman, director, chief executive officer, Ferro Corp.; president, trustee, Ferro Foundation

Bezik, Cynthia B.: senior vice president, finance, Cleveland-Cliffs, Inc.

Blanke, Gail Ann: vice president, Avon Products Foundation, Inc.

Block, Allan James: vice president, trustee, Blade Foundation; director, Toledo Blade Co.

Block, John Robinson: vice president, trustee, Blade Foundation

Boesel, Stephen W.: vice president, secretary, treasurer, Price Associates Foundation (T. Rowe)

Bogomolny, Robert Lee: director, Searle Charitable Trust; senior vice president, general counsel, secretary, Searle & Co. (G.D.)

Bowen, William Gordon, PhD: trustee, Merck Co. Foundation

Breen, John Gerald: chairman, chief executive officer, director, Sherwin-Williams Co.; president, trustee, Sherwin-Williams Foundation

Bridgeland, James Ralph, Jr.: trustee, Star Bank NA, Cincinnati Foundation

Brinzo, John S.: trustee, Cleveland-Cliffs Foundation (The); president, chief executive officer, Cleveland-Cliffs, Inc.

Brodie, Nancy S.: executive vice president, chief financial officer, Penn Mutual Life Insurance Co.

Brown, Craig J.: treasurer, Sherman-Standard Register Foundation; senior

vice president administration, treasurer, chief financial officer, Standard Register Co.

Brown, Ronald D.: assistant treasurer, Milacron Foundation

Brumm, Paul Michael: executive vice president, chief financial officer, Fifth Third Bancorp

Brunetti, Wayne H.: vice chairman, president, chief operating officer, director, New Century Energies; president, chief executive officer, New Century Energies Foundation

Burlingame, Harold W.: executive vice president wireless group, AT&T Corp.; trustee, AT&T Foundation

Burner, David L.: chairman, president, chief executive officer, director, BFGoodrich Co.

Burrell, Richard L.: senator vice president finance, secretary, treasurer, Barry Corp. (R.G.); treasurer, Barry Foundation

Burt, Robert Norcross: chairman, chief executive officer, director, FMC Corp.; director, FMC Foundation

Calfee, William Rushton: trustee, Cleveland-Cliffs Foundation (The); executive vice president, commercial, Cleveland-Cliffs, Inc.

Carter, George Kent: vice president, treasurer, Chevron Corp.

Chambers, Anne Cox: chairman, trustee, Cox Foundation (James M.)

Clayton, Jon Kerry: trustee, Fortis Foundation; executive vice president, Fortis, Inc.

Cocklin, Kim Roland: senior vice president, Texas Gas Transmission Corp.

Cole, Robert A.: chief financial officer, senior vice president, American General Finance; senior vice president, chief financial officer, director, American General Finance Foundation

Coughlin, Thomas Martin: member, Wal-Mart Foundation; executive vice president, Wal-Mart Stores, Inc.

Cushwa, Charles Benton, III: trustee, Commercial Intertech Foundation

Cushwa, William Wallace: director, Commercial Intertech Corp.; trustee, Commercial Intertech Foundation

Daberko, David A.: chairman, chief executive officer, National City Corp.

Danford, Philip C.: treasurer, Dun & Bradstreet Corp. Foundation, Inc.

Dolan, Ronald J.: trustee, Ohio National Foundation; senior vice president, chief financial officer, director, Ohio National Life Insurance Co.

Ferry, Richard Michael: chairman, Pacific Mutual Life Insurance Co.

Foley, Cheryl M.: vice president, secretary, general counsel, Cinergy Corp.; vice president, secretary, director, Cinergy Foundation

Francis, Cheryl A.: executive vice president, chief financial officer, Donnelley & Sons Co. (R.R.)

Fretthold, Timothy Jon: executive vice president, general counsel, director, Ultramar Diamond Shamrock Corp.

Gherlein, Gerald Lee: member contributions committee, Eaton Charitable Fund

Giering, John L.: senior vice president finance & administration, chief financial officer, NCR Corp.

Glaser, Gary A.: president, chief executive officer, National City Bank of Columbus

Graber, Don R.: chairman, president, chief executive officer, director, Huffy Corp.; trustee, Huffy Foundation, Inc.

Grasley, Michael Howard: senior vice president, Shell Oil Co.; member executive committee, director, Shell Oil Co. Foundation

Grealis, William J.: vice president, Cinergy Corp.; director, Cinergy Foundation

Gross, Ronald Martin: chairman, president, director, Rayonier Foundation; chairman, president, chief executive officer, director, Rayonier Inc.

Hayden, Joseph Page, Jr.: trustee, Star Bank NA, Cincinnati Foundation

Hill, Allen M.: president, chief executive officer, Dayton Power and Light Co.

Hines, B. E.: secretary, Duriron Foundation

Hodgson, Thomas Richard: president, chief operating officer, director, Abbott Laboratories

Hudnut, Stewart Skinner: director, Illinois Tool Works Foundation

Huston, Edwin Allen: vice president, director, Ryder System Charitable Foundation; vice chairman, director, Ryder System, Inc.

Iott, Richard B.: president, chief executive officer, director, Seaway Food Town, Inc.

Jackson, Frederick H.: executive vice president finance, director, La-Z-Boy Inc.

Jenkins, Thomas A.: treasurer, trustee, Dayton Power and Light Co. Foundation

Kelbley, Stephen Paul: executive vice president, Springs Industries, Inc.

Kiener, Dan W.: member screening committee, PPG Industries Foundation

Kline, Philip E.: treasurer, director, Royal & SunAlliance Insurance Foundation, Inc.

Klinedinst, Thomas John, Jr.: trustee, Star Bank NA, Cincinnati Foundation

Koontz, James L.: president, chief executive officer, director, Kingsbury Corp.; trustee, Kingsbury Fund

Lakin, Thomas J.: regional chairman, Star Bank NA; president, Star Bank NA, Cincinnati Foundation

Lansaw, Judy W.: secretary, trustee, Dayton Power and Light Co. Foundation

Lautenbach, Terry Robert: trustee, Air Products Foundation

Leser, Lawrence Arthur: chairman, director, Scripps Co. (E.W.); member, Scripps Howard Foundation

Levy, Richard M.: president, chief executive officer, Varian Medical Systems, Inc.

Lewis, Peter Benjamin: chairman, president, chief executive officer, director, Progressive Corp.

Lowrie, William G.: president, deputy chief executive officer, director, BP Amoco Corp.

Ludwick, John D.: vice president human resources, MGIC Investment Corp.

Lyon, Wayne Barton: president, chief operating officer, director, Masco Corp.

Manchester, Gilbert Mott: assistant secretary, Commercial Intertech Foundation

Mandel, Morton Leon: deputy chairman, Premier Industrial Corp.; trustee, Premier Industrial Foundation

Marohn, William D.: vice chairman, director, Whirlpool Corp.

Marshall, Betty J.: senior vice president, Shoney's Inc.

Matthews, Westina Lomax: secretary, trustee, Merrill Lynch & Co. Foundation Inc.; senior director, first vice president corporate respons, Merrill Lynch & Co., Inc.

McClung, James Allen: vice president, director, FMC Foundation

McConnell, William Thompson: chairman, ceo, Park National Bank; chairman, Park National Corp. Foundation

McCoy, John Bonnet: president, chief executive officer, Ameritech Corp.

McDonough, Gerald C.: trustee, Commercial Intertech Foundation

McNamara, Kevin J.: president, director, Chemed Corp.; secretary, trustee, Chemed Foundation

Mebane, David Cummins: chairman, president, chief executive officer, director, Madison Gas & Electric Co.; vice president, Madison Gas & Electric Foundation

Medford, Dale L.: vice president corporate finance, chief financial officer, Reynolds & Reynolds Co.

Miller, Donn Biddle: president, chief executive officer, Pacific Mutual Life Insurance Co.

Molen, Richard L.: chairman, chief executive officer, director, Huffy Corp.; trustee, Huffy Foundation, Inc.

Moorhead, Thomas Leib, Esq.: vice president law, assistant secretary, Nordson Corp.; trustee, Nordson Corp. Foundation

Nagy, Charles F.: treasurer, Standard Products Co.; trustee, Standard Products Co. Charitable Foundation

Newman, Paul L.: president, Newman's Own Foundation

O'Brien, John F.: trustee, McDonald & Co. Securities Foundation

Oakley, Robert Alan: executive vice president, chief financial officer, Nationwide Insurance Enterprise Foundation

Ong, John Doyle: chairman board, director, Ameritech Corp.

Ostergard, Paul Michael: vice president, director corporate contributions, Citibank Corp.; president, Citigroup Foundation

Parker, Patrick Streeter: chairman, director, Parker Hannifin Corp.; president, trustee, Parker Hannifin Foundation

Parsons, Stuart N.: secretary, treasurer, director, Park National Corp. Foundation

Pike, Robert William: vice president, secretary, Allstate Foundation; senior vice president, secretary, general counsel, director, Allstate Insurance Co.

Pitorak, Larry John: senior vice president finance, treasurer, chief financial officer, Sherwin-Williams Co.; secretary, treasurer, trustee, Sherwin-Williams Foundation

Post, David A.: vice president, Equifax Foundation; corporate vice president, chief financial officer, Equifax Inc.

Post, William J.: vice president, director, APS Foundation, Inc.; president, chief executive officer, Arizona Public Service Co.

Preston, James Edward: vice president, director, Avon Products Foundation, Inc.; chairman, chief executive officer, director, Avon Products, Inc.

Pyke, John Secrest, Jr.: president, trustee, Hanna Co. Foundation (M.A.); vice president, secretary, general counsel, Hanna Co. (M.A.)

Randolph, Jackson Harold: chairman, Cinergy Corp.; chairman, director, Cinergy Foundation

Ratner, Albert Benjamin: trustee, Forest City Enterprises Charitable Foundation, Inc.; co-chairman, director, Forest City Enterprises, Inc.

Reid, James Sims, Jr.: chairman, director, Standard Products Co.; chairman, president, Standard Products Co. Charitable Foundation

Riethman, Robert B.: chief financial officer, Monarch Machine Tool Co.; treasurer, secretary, Monarch Machine Tool Co. Foundation

Rish, Stephen A.: vice president, corporate public involvement, Nationwide Insurance Co.; president, Nationwide Insurance Enterprise Foundation

Rohr, James Edward: chief executive officer, president, director, PNC Financial Services Group

Roub, Bryan Roger: trustee, Harris Foundation

Rudnick, Alan A.: vice president, general counsel, corporate secretary, CSX Corp.

Schaefer, George A., Jr.: president, Fifth Third Bancorp

Scheurer, Charles B.: director, Diebold, Inc.

Schwebel, Joseph M.: president, director, Schwebel Baking Co.; trustee, Schwebel Family Foundation

Seiffert, Ron J.: vice chairman, Huntington Bancshares Inc.

Shinn, George Latimer: director, New York Times Co. Foundation

Sims, Philip Stuart: vice chairman, treasurer, Premier Industrial Corp.

Smart, George M.: trustee, Commercial Intertech Foundation

Smith, Donald Kaye: senior vice president, general counsel, director, GEICO Corp.

Smucker, Timothy Paul: chairman, director, Smucker Co. (JM)

Snow, John William: chairman, president, chief executive officer, CSX Corp.

Steffens, John Laundon: executive vice president, Merrill Lynch & Co., Inc.

Stein, James C.: president, chief operating officer, Fluor Corp.; trustee, Fluor Foundation

Stevens, Philip Ashworth: vice president, trustee, National Machinery Foundation, Inc.

Stonebraker, Barbara J.: executive vice president, Cincinnati Bell Foundation, Inc.; senior vice president, Cincinnati Bell Inc.

Taulbee, Richard: assistant treasurer, Western-Southern Foundation, Inc.; vice president, Western & Southern Life Insurance Co.

Thomas, Richard Lee: vice president, First National Bank of Chicago Foundation

Timken, Ward Jackson: vice president, director, officer, Timken Co. (The); vice president, Timken Co. Charitable Trust (The); president, Timken Co. Educational Fund

Timken, William Robert, Jr.: chairman, president, chief executive officer, director, Timken Co. (The)

Tucker, Don Eugene: trustee, Commercial Intertech Foundation

Vinney, Les C.: senior vice president, chief financial officer, BFGoodrich Co.

Voet, Paul C.: trustee, Chemed Foundation

Wagner, David J.: chairman, president, chief executive officer, Old Kent Bank; treasurer, Old Kent Foundation

Wander, Herbert S.: secretary, director, Katten, Muchin & Zavis Foundation

Warner, Douglas Alexander, III: chairman, president, chief executive officer, director, Morgan & Co. Inc. (J.P.)

Williams, William Joseph: trustee, Western-Southern Foundation, Inc.; chairman, director, Western & Southern Life Insurance Co.

Wilson, Gary Lee: chairman, director, Northwest Airlines, Inc.

Zachem, Harry M.: chairman, trustee, Ashland Inc. Foundation

Oklahoma

Bridgewater, Bernard Adolphus, Jr.: member board control, Brown Shoe Co. Charitable Trust; chairman, president, chief executive officer, director, Brown Shoe Co., Inc.

Choate, Jerry D.: chairman, chief executive officer, director, Allstate Foundation

Cloud, Bruce Benjamin, Sr.: vice chairman, director, Zachry Co. (H.B.)

Conant, Colleen Christner: branch manager, Scripps Co. (E.W.); trustee, Scripps Howard Foundation

Dunham, Archie W.: president, chief executive officer, Conoco, Inc.

Elkins, Lloyd Edwin, Junior: vice president, Chevron Corp.

Fleshman, Betty R.: secretary, Potlatch Corp.

Hall, Floyd: chairman, president, chief executive officer, director, Kmart Corp.

Holland, William Ray: vice president, director, United Dominion Foundation; chairman, chief executive officer, director, United Dominion Industries, Ltd.

McDaniel, Tom J.: vice chairman, director, Kerr-McGee Corp.

Mixon, A. Malachi, III: chairman, chief executive officer, Invacare Corp.; trustee, Invacare Foundation

Moore, Steven: president, Oklahoma Gas & Electric Co. Foundation

Rainbolt, Harold E.: vice president, secretary, SBC Foundation

Strecker, A. M.: vice president, director, Oklahoma Gas & Electric Co. Foundation

Oregon

Carter, John Douglas: executive vice president, director, Bechtel Group, Inc.

Davisson, Ralph M.: trustee, Potlatch Foundation II

Hoak, Jon: trustee, NCR Foundation

Kirchhof, Anton Conrad: corporate secretary, general counsel, Louisiana-Pacific Corp.; secretary, Louisiana-Pacific Foundation

Knight, Philip Hampson: chairman, chief executive officer, Nike, Inc.

McKennon, Keith Robert: chairman, president, PacifiCorp; member, PacifiCorp Foundation

Mersereau, Susan M.: trustee, Weyerhaeuser Co. Foundation

Nutter, Wallace L.: director, Rayonier Foundation

Quesnel, Gregory L.: president, chief executive officer, director, CNF Transportation, Inc.

Redmond, Paul Anthony: chairman, chief executive officer, director, Avista Corporation

Shafer, Douglas C.: trustee, Tektronix Foundation; president, America operations, Tektronix, Inc.

Walsh, Michael J.: vice president, CertainTeed Corp.

Pennsylvania

Agger, James Harrington: senior vice president, secretary, general counsel, Air Products and Chemicals, Inc.; director, Air Products Foundation

Alexander, John F.: trustee, PerkinElmer Foundation; senior vice president, chief financial officer, PerkinElmer, Inc.

Allison, Herbert Monroe, Jr.: vice president, trustee, Merrill Lynch & Co. Foundation Inc.; president, chief operating officer, Merrill Lynch & Co., Inc.

Argentine, Peter Dominic: executive vice president, chief financial officer, Nestle U.S.A. Inc.

Baldassari, Dennis P.: president, chief operating officer, GPU Energy

Beattie, Art P.: vice president, secretary, treasurer, Alabama Power Co.; treasurer, Alabama Power Foundation

Beaver, William S.: treasurer, vice president, Westvaco Corp.; trustee, Westvaco Foundation Trust

Beghini, Victor Gene: trustee, USX Foundation, Inc.

Berwind, C. Graham, Jr.: chairman, president, chief executive officer, Berwind Group

Binswanger, David R.: president, chief executive officer, Binswanger Companies; treasurer, Binswanger Foundation

Binswanger, Frank G., Jr.: co-chairman, director, Binswanger Companies

Binswanger, John K.: co-chairman, director, Binswanger Companies; chairman, Binswanger Foundation

Blankley, Walter Elwood: president, director, AMETEK Foundation; chairman, director, AMETEK, Inc.

Block, Stephen A.: secretary, IFF Foundation Inc.

Blystone, John B.: chairman, president, chief executive officer, director, SPX Corp.

Boyer, Herbert Wayne, PhD: chairman, president, director, Genentech Foundation for Biomedical Sciences; co-founder, director, Genentech Inc.

Breisinger, James R.: vice president, controller, Kennametal Foundation; vice president, controller, chief financial officer, Kennametal, Inc.

Brennan, Michael J.: chief financial officer, senior vice president, Binswanger Companies

Campanaro, Leonard A.: treasurer, Harsco Corp. Fund

Campbell, Robert Henderson: chairman, chief executive officer, Sunoco Inc.

Cassidy, M. Sharon: assistant secretary, USX Foundation, Inc.

Coulter, David A.: president, director, Bank of America

Curley, John J.: chairman, chief executive officer, director, Gannett Co., Inc.; chairman, Gannett Foundation

Daley, Leo J.: vice president, treasurer, Air Products and Chemicals, Inc.

David, George A. L.: chairman, president, chief executive officer, chief operating officer, United Technologies Corp.

Davidson, George A., Jr.: chairman, chief executive officer, director, Consolidated Natural Gas Co.

Davies, Charles R.: president, general counsel, director, GEICO Philanthropic Foundation

Davis, Erroll Brown, Jr.: president, chief executive officer, director, Wisconsin Power & Light Co.

Davis, Ruth Margaret: trustee, Air Products Foundation

Dean, John W., III: vice president, treasurer, Rubbermaid Inc.

Donches, Steven G.: vice president public affairs, Bethlehem Steel Corp.; president, Bethlehem Steel Foundation

Drury, David J.: chief executive officer, chairman, Principal Financial Group

Dunlap, F. Thomas, Jr.: secretary, director, Intel Foundation

Edwards, John Kenneth: executive president, group president power generation, Cummins Engine Co., Inc.; director, Cummins Engine Foundation

Esrey, William Todd: chairman, chief executive officer, Sprint Corp.

Evans, Robert Sheldon: chairman, chief executive officer, Crane Co.; chairman, president, director, Crane Foundation

Farley, James Bernard: chairman emeritus, trustee, Walter Industries Inc.

Fischer, Richard Lawrence: director, Alcoa Foundation; executive vice president, chairman counsel, Alcoa Inc.

Franklin, Barbara Hackman: director, Dow Chemical Co.

Fuellgraf, Charles Louis, Jr.: trustee, Nationwide Insurance Enterprise Foundation

Furey, John J.: corporate secretary, corporate counsel, Campbell Soup Co.

Gailey, John Robert, III: vice president, general counsel, secretary, West Co. Inc.

Garrity, Norman E.: executive vice president, director, Corning Inc.; trustee, Corning Inc. Foundation

Geissinger, Frederick: chairman, chief executive officer, prs, American General Finance

Geissinger, Frederick Wallace: chairman, chief executive officer, president, director, American General Finance Foundation

Gill, John A.: senior vice president, FirstEnergy Corp.

Gittis, Howard: director, Revlon Foundation Inc.

Godlasky, Tom: executive vice president, chief investment officer, AmerUS Group

Graham, Richard William: president, chief executive officer, chief operating officer, director, Smurfit-Stone Container Corp.

Graham, Thomas Carlisle: trustee, AK Steel Foundation

Grass, Martin Lehrman: chairman, chief executive officer, director, Rite Aid Corp.

Grubb, Edgar Harold: executive vice president, chief financial officer, Transamerica Corp.; director, Transamerica Foundation

Gussin, Robert Zalmon, PhD: vice president science & technology, Johnson & Johnson; member corporate contributions committee, Johnson & Johnson Family of Companies Contribution Fund

Hafer, Fred Douglass: chairman, president, chief executive officer, GPU Inc.

Hamilton, Peter Bannerman: director, Brunswick Foundation; trustee, Kemper Foundation (James S.)

Hanway, H. Edward: president, chief executive officer, CIGNA Corp.

Harris, Edward D., Jr.: director, Genentech Foundation for Biomedical Sciences

Helsby, Keith R.: treasurer, New York Stock Exchange Foundation, Inc.

Hernandez, Robert M.: vice chairman, chief financial officer, director, USX Corp.; trustee, USX Foundation, Inc.

Hernandez, William H.: director, PPG Industries Foundation; senior vice president, PPG Industries, Inc.

Hershman, Linda D.: vice president, Southern New England Telephone Co.

Heumann, Stephen Michael: vice president, treasurer, West Co. Inc.

Hill, Kenneth D.: vice president, Sunoco Inc.

Hilyard, James E.: president, CertainTeed Corp.; director, CertainTeed Corp. Foundation

Howard, James Joseph, III: chairman, president, chief executive officer, director, Northern States Power Co.

Hudson, Timothy D.: trustee, Kennametal Foundation; vice president, director human resources, Kennametal, Inc.

Jeremiah, Barbara S.: director, Alcoa Foundation

Joyce, William H.: chairman, president, chief executive officer, chief operating officer, Union Carbide Corp.

Kasenter, Robert Albert: executive vice president human resources, Montgomery Ward & Co., Inc.; executive vice president, Montgomery Ward Foundation

Kelley, Bruce Gunn: vice president, director, Employers Mutual Charitable Foundation

Kelson, Richard B.: director, Alcoa Foundation

Kennedy, George Danner: trustee, Kemper Foundation (James S.)

Keyser, Richard Lee: chairman, chief executive officer, president, Grainger, Inc. (W.W.)

Kittredge, Robert P.: chairman, chief executive officer, director, Fabri-Kal Corp.; president, Fabri-Kal Foundation

Klein, Barbara A.: vice president, comptroller, Ameritech Corp.

Kostecky, James Frank: executive director, Bethlehem Steel Corp.

Kulynych, Petro: chairman, treasurer, Lowe's Charitable and Educational Foundation

Landin, Thomas Milton: vice president, director, CertainTeed Corp.; vice president, Norton Co. Foundation

Lang, Paul Louis: vice president, Illinois Power Co.

Lee, Charles Robert: chairman, chief executive officer, director, GTE Corp.; chief executive officer, trustee, GTE Foundation

Liebler, Arthur C.: vice president communications, DaimlerChrysler Corp.; trustee, DaimlerChrysler Corp. Fund

Lison, Stephen A.: vice president, trustee, SPX Foundation

Louis, Kenneth C.: president, chief operating officer, director, Ameritas Life Insurance Corp.

Lovett, John Robert: director, Air Products Foundation

Lucky, Robert Wendell: corporate vice president, Telcordia Technologies

Lunger, Francis: chief financial officer, corporate vice president, Millipore Corp.

Lyall, Katharine Culbert: trustee, Kemper Foundation (James S.)

Madia, William J.: executive vice president, manager, Battelle Memorial Institute

Maloni, William R.: senior vice president policy & public affairs, Fannie Mae; director, Fannie Mae Foundation

Mattson, Eric Leonard: senior vice president, chief financial officer, Baker Hughes Inc.

McCarthy, Peter John: trustee, Elf Atochem North America Foundation; vice president public affairs, Elf Atochem North America, Inc.

McGuinn, Martin Gregory: chairman, chief executive officer, Mellon Financial Corp.

McNally, Mark K.: senior vice president, general counsel, secretary, Aristech Chemical Corp.

Miglio, Daniel Joseph: chairman, president, director, chief executive officer, Southern New England Telephone Co.

Montague, William Patrick: president, chief operating officer, director, Mark IV Industries; president, Mark IV Industries Foundation

Montrone, Paul Michael: vice president, partner, Winthrop Foundation

Morgan, Edward L.: group senior vice president, Hartford (The)

Morgan, James McClay: member executive committee, director, Shell Oil Co. Foundation

Moss, James H.: treasurer, York Federal Savings & Loan Foundation

Musser, Warren Van Dyke: chairman, chief executive officer, director, Safeguard Scientifics; president, director, Safeguard Scientifics Foundation

Muth, Robert James: president, director, ASARCO Foundation

Newlin, William Rankin: trustee, Kennametal Foundation

Orr, Charles Lee: president, chief executive officer, Shaklee Corp.

Overbaugh, Joseph C.: director, AMP Foundation

Paumgarten, Nicholas Biddle: managing director, Scripps Co. (E.W.); member, Scripps Howard Foundation

Peconi, Maurice V.: member screening committee, PPG Industries Foundation

Pepper, John E., Jr.: chairman executive committee, Procter & Gamble Co.

Phillips, Ped Wesley: vice president, Hanna Co. Foundation (M.A.)

Piergallini, Alfred A.: trustee, Gerber Foundation

Pietrafitta, Clifford E.: vice president finance, treasurer, CSS Industries, Inc.

Pollock, E. Kears: director, PPG Industries Foundation; executive vice president, PPG Industries, Inc.

Rein, Catherine Amelia: director, MetLife Foundation; vice president, Metropolitan Life Insurance Co.

Robin, Kenneth H.: senior vice president, general counsel, Household International, Inc.

Roessler-Alsoa, Ernest C.: president, chief executive officer, director, CCB Financial Corp.

Rompala, Richard M.: president, chief executive officer, director, chairman, Valspar Corp.; vice president, Valspar Foundation

Ryan, John Thomas, III: chairman, chief executive officer, Mine Safety Appliances Co.

Sargent, Joseph Dudley: president, chief executive officer, director, Guardian Life Insurance Co. of America

Schacht, Henry Brewer: director, Cummins Engine Foundation

Sease, Gene Elwood: director, Central Newspapers Foundation

Shaffer, Oren G.: executive vice president, chief financial officer, Ameritech Corp.

Smith, Raymond W.: chairman, chief executive officer, director, Bell Atlantic Corp.

Snyder, Frank Ronald, II: trustee,

Spaeth, Karl Henry: chairman, trustee, Quaker Chemical Foundation

Stata, Ray S.: chairman, chief executive officer, director, Analog Devices, Inc.

Sweeney, John J., III: vice president, CertainTeed Corp.

Trosino, Vincent Joseph: assistant secretary, State Farm Companies Foundation; executive vice president, vice chairman, chief operating officer, director, State Farm Mutual Automobile Insurance Co.

Usher, Thomas J.: chairman, chief executive officer, USX Corp.; chairman board trustees, USX Foundation, Inc.

Walters, John Alexander: trustee, Alcon Foundation

Walton, Jon David: trustee, Allegheny Technologies Inc. Charitable Trust

Wardrop, Richard M., Jr.: chairman, chief executive officer, director, AK Steel Corp.

Welty, John Rider: secretary, Carpenter Technology Corp. Foundation

Wiesner, Carol A.: treasurer, director, Foundation of the Litton Industries

Wiley, S. Donald: vice chairman, trustee, Heinz Co. Foundation (H.J.)

Wilson, Rita P.: director, Sears, Roebuck and Co. Foundation

Yasinsky, John B.: chairman, president, chief executive officer, GenCorp

Yohe, Merrill A., Jr.: chairman contributions committee, AMP Inc.

Rhode Island

Alfiero, Salvatore Harry: founder, chairman, chief executive officer, director, Mark IV Industries; chairman, Mark IV Industries Foundation

Brown, Stephen Lee: chairman, chief executive officer, director, Hancock Financial Services (John)

Crandall, Robert Lloyd: director, AMR Corp.

Dascoli, D. Paul: chief financial officer, vice president, Thomasville Furniture Industries Inc.

Gifford, Charles Kilvert: trustee, BankBoston Charitable Foundation; chairman, chief executive officer, BankBoston Corp.

Hassenfeld, Alan Geoffrey: president, Hasbro Charitable Trust Inc.; chairman, chief executive officer, Hasbro, Inc.

Keegan, Peter: senior vice president, Loews Foundation

Lemieux, Joseph Henry: chairman, chief executive officer, director, Owens-Illinois Inc.

Mandeville, Robert: trustee, Cranston Foundation; chief financial officer, secretary, treasurer, Cranston Print Works Co.

Verrecchia, Alfred J.: treasurer, trustee, Hasbro Charitable Trust Inc.; executive, director, Hasbro, Inc.

South Carolina

Chandler, J. Harold: chairman, president, chief executive officer, Provident Companies, Inc.

Coker, Charles Westfield: trustee, Sonoco Foundation; vice president, Sonoco Products Co.

DeLoach, Harris E., Junior: executive vice president, director, Sonoco Products Co.

Elliott, R. Keith: chief executive officer, president, Hercules Inc.

Harmon, Sam W.: senior vice president human resources, GenCorp; trustee, GenCorp Foundation

Hipp, William Hayne: president, chief executive officer, director, Liberty

Corp.; chairman, president, director, Liberty Corp. Foundation

Ingram, Martha R.: chairman, director, Ingram Industries Inc.

Johnson, Hansford Tillman: trustee, USAA Foundation, A Charitable Trust

Manigault, Peter: chairman, Evening Post Publishing Co.; president, Post and Courier Foundation

Moser, Robert W.: executive vice president, Springs Industries, Inc.

Shelley, James Herbert: chairman, Sonoco Foundation

Strickland, Robert Louis: vice president, Lowe's Charitable and Educational Foundation

South Dakota

Brendsel, Leland C.: chairman, chief executive officer, director, Freddie Mac; director, Freddie Mac Foundation

Murdy, James L.: executive vice president finance and administration, chief financial officer, Allegheny Technologies Inc.; trustee, Allegheny Technologies Inc. Charitable Trust

Neale, Gary L.: chairman, president, chief executive officer, Northern Indiana Public Service Co.

Raymond, Lee R.: chairman, president, chief executive officer, Exxon Mobil Corp.

Wangstad, Kristi Rollag: vice president public affairs, Alliant Techsystems; president, Alliant Techsystems Community Investment Foundation

Tennessee

Bradford, James C., Jr.: president, Bradford and Co. Foundation (J.C.); senior partner, Bradford & Co. (J.C)

Chandler, William Everett: senior vice president finance, secretary, chief financial officer, Hunt Manufacturing Co.

Chellgren, Paul Wilbur: chief executive officer, chairman, director, Ashland, Inc.; member, Ashland Inc. Foundation

Cole, Kenneth O.: vice president customer service, Memphis Light Gas & Water Division

Gidwitz, Gerald S.: chairman, Curtis Industries, Inc. (Helene)

Harvey, A. Mosby, Jr.: secretary, HON Industries Charitable Foundation; vice president, secretary, general counsel, HON Industries Inc.

Holland, Willard R.: chairman, chief executive officer, FirstEnergy Corp.

Matherne, Louis K.: treasurer, Chesapeake Corp.

McCarthy, John Michael: vice president, Waffle House Foundation, Inc.

Morris, Herman, Jr.: president, chief executive officer, Memphis Light Gas & Water Division

Oliver, Charles R.: trustee, Fluor Foundation

Rosson, William Mimms: chairman, Conwood Co. LP

Spilman, Robert H.: chairman, chief executive officer, Bassett Furniture Industries; chairman, director, Bassett Furniture Industries Fdn.

Stonecipher, Harry C.: president, chief operating officer, director, Boeing Co.

Street, Gordon P., Jr.: chairman, president, chief executive officer, director, North American Royalties; trustee, North American Royalties Foundation

White, Thomas A. H.: vice president corporate relations, Provident Companies, Inc.

Texas

Bacon, Kenneth J.: senior vice president, Fannie Mae; director, Fannie Mae Foundation

Baish, Richard Owen: senior vice president, director, El Paso Energy Foundation

Bowlin, Michael Ray: chairman, director, ARCO Foundation; chairman, chief executive officer, director, Atlantic Richfield Co.

Bradford, William Edward: chairman, director, Halliburton Co.

Brooks, E. Richard 'Dick': chairman, chief executive officer, director, Central & South West Services

Campbell, Edward Patrick: president, chief operating officer, drc, Nordson Corp.; trustee, Nordson Corp. Foundation

Cash, R. D.: chairman, president, chief executive officer, director, Questar Corp.

Cloninger, Kriss, III: executive vice president, chief financial officer, treasurer, AFLAC Inc.

Dagley, Larry J.: senior vice president, chief financial officer, Pacific Enterprises

Decherd, Robert William: chairman, president, chief executive officer, director, Belo Corp. (A.H.); chairman, trustee, Belo Corp. Foundation (A.H.)

Donovan, Dianne Francys: director, Chicago Tribune Foundation

Draper, Ernest Linn, Jr.: chairman, president, chief executive officer, director, American Electric Power

Easterly, David E.: president, chief operating officer, Cox Enterprises Inc.

Franke, William Augustus: chairman, president, chief executive officer, America West Airlines, Inc.; director, Phelps Dodge Foundation

Frost, Thomas C., Senior: chairman, Frost National Bank

Georges, John A.: director, International Paper Co.

Gleaves, James Leslie: assistant treasurer, American General Finance Foundation

Godfrey, Cullen Michael: vice president, FINA Foundation

Harden, Glen: executive vice president, chief financial officer, Carolina Power & Light Co.; treasurer, CP& L Foundation

Helton, Bill D.: chairman, New Century Energies Foundation

Hollingsworth, John Mark: assistant secretary, Simmons Foundation, Inc. (Harold)

Huey, Ward L., Jr.: president broadcast division, vice chairman, director, Belo Corp. (A.H.); vice president, trustee, Belo Corp. Foundation (A.H.)

Hurford, Gary Thomas: president, director, Hunt Oil Co.

Jackson, John E.: trustee, Nordson Corp. Foundation

Jennings, James Burnett: president, Hunt Oil Co.

Jewell, George Hiram: director, Schlumberger Foundation

Johnson, James Lawrence: chairman emeritus, Walter Industries Inc.

Keith, Susan Stewart: assistant secretary, assistant treasurer, Halliburton Foundation, Inc.

Lozano, Ignacio Eugenio, Jr.: chairman, Pacific Mutual Life Insurance Co.

Morgensen, Jerry L.: president, chief executive officer, director, Hensel Phelps Construction Co.; director, Hensel Phelps Foundation

Moroney, James McQueen, Jr.: trustee, Belo Corp. Foundation (A.H.)

Nowell, Tommy Lynn: vice president finance, controller, Occidental Oil and Gas; treasurer, Occidental Oil and Gas Foundation

Nye, Erle Allen: chairman, chief executive officer, director, TU Electric Co.

Page, Barbara B.: trustee, Golub Foundation

Penglase, Frank Dennis: vice president, treasurer,

Phares, Lynn Levisay: president, fund manager, director, ConAgra Foundation

Quinn, David W.: executive vice president, chief financial officer, director, Centex Corp.

Rasmuson, Edward B.: director, CIRI Foundation

Rice, Liston Michael, Jr.: president, director public affairs, Texas Instruments Foundation

Roach, John Vinson, II: chairman, director, Tandy Corp.

Rosilier, Glenn D.: executive vice president, chief financial officer, Central & South West Services

Simmons, Glenn Reuben: vice chairman, Contran Corp.

Simmons, Harold Clark: chairman, director, Simmons Foundation, Inc. (Harold)

Skinner, Claire Corson: chairman, chief executive officer, Coachmen Industries, Inc.

Skurek, John C.: vice president, treasurer, LTV Corp.; trustee, LTV Foundation

Steward, H. Leighton: chairman, chief executive officer, president, Louisiana Land & Exploration Co.; director, Louisiana Land & Exploration Co. Foundation

Stockman, David A.: co-chairman, director, Collins & Aikman Corp.; president, director, Collins & Aikman Foundation

Sykora, Donald D.: director, Reliant Energy Inc.

Terrill, James E.: executive vice president, United States Sugar Corp.

Warner, M. Richard: director, Temple-Inland Foundation

Whitacre, Edward E., Jr.: chairman, director, chief executive officer, SBC Communications Inc.

Wilks, David M.: vice president, New Century Energies Foundation

Wynia, Ann: director, Fuller Co. Foundation (H.B.)

Younts, Rosemary: senior vice president communications, GenCorp

Zachry, Henry Bartell, Jr.: chairman, Zachry Co. (H.B.); trustee, Zachry Foundation (The)

Utah

Bohling, John A.: senior vice president, PacifiCorp; board member, PacifiCorp Foundation

Eccles, Spencer Fox: chairman, chief executive officer, director, First Security Bank of Idaho NA

Herbert, Bart, Jr.: executive vice president, chief marketing officer, AEGON U.S.A. Inc.

Higbee, David M.: secretary, Williams; secretary, treasurer, Williams Companies Foundation (The)

Hill, George Richard: president, trustee, Lubrizol Foundation (The)

Holmes, David Richard: chief executive officer, chief operating officer, director, Reynolds & Reynolds Co.

McAllister, Francis R.: vice president, director, ASARCO Foundation; president, chief executive officer, ASARCO Inc.

Merrell, Pamela K.: secretary, Montana Power Co.; vice president, secretary, Montana Power Foundation

Milne, Garth Leroy: senior vice president, treasurer, Motorola Inc.

Richards, Joel, III: vice president, El Paso Energy Foundation

Staheli, Donald L.: chairman, director, Continental Grain Co.; vice president, director, Continental Grain Foundation

Willes, Mark Hinckley: chairman, president, chief executive officer, Times Mirror Co.; chairman, Times Mirror Foundation

Vermont

Bertrand, Frederic Howard: chairman, Central Vermont Public Service Corp.

Garneau, Robert M.: chief financial officer, Kaman Corp.

Glynn, Gary Allen: president, USX Corp.; vice president, USX Foundation, Inc.

Keyser, F. Ray, Jr.: chairman, director, Central Vermont Public Service Corp.

MacLeay, Thomas H.: president, chief operating officer, National Life of Vermont

Virginia

Ambler, John Doss: vice president, Texaco Inc.

Ballengee, Jerry Hunter: president, chief operating

officer, director, Union Camp Corp.

Barry, Richard Francis, III: director, Landmark Communications Foundation; vice chairman, Landmark Communications Inc.

Batten, Frank, Sr.: chairman, director, Landmark Communications Foundation; chairman, Landmark Communications Inc.

Burrus, Robert Lewis, Jr.: trustee, Circuit City Foundation

Campbell, Cole C.: editor, Pulitzer Publishing Co.; director, Pulitzer Publishing Co. Foundation

Carter, Marshall Nichols: chairman, chief executive officer, State Street Bank & Trust Co.

Chandler, Wallace Lee: vice president, director, Universal Leaf Foundation

Crenshaw, Gordon Lee, II: member, Universal Leaf Foundation; chairman emeritus, Universal Leaf Tobacco Co., Inc.

Cutchins, Clifford Armstrong, IV: president, Fort James Corp.; chairman, director, Fort James Foundation (The)

DeRusha, William Charles: chairman, chief executive officer, Heilig-Meyers Co.

Druen, W. Sidney: director, Nationwide Insurance Enterprise Foundation

Edgerton, Brenda Evans: vice president business development, Campbell Soup Co.; treasurer, trustee, Campbell Soup Foundation

Edwards, Earnest Jonathan: director, Alcoa Foundation

Flood, Joan Moore: assistant treasurer, Trace International Holdings, Inc. Foundation

Fox, Joseph Carter: chairman, president, chief executive officer, Chesapeake Corp.

Goode, David Ronald: chairman, president, chief executive officer, director, Norfolk Southern Corp.

Gottwald, Bruce Cobb: chairman, chief executive officer, director, Ethyl Corp.

Harrell, Henry Howze: director, Universal Leaf Foundation; chairman, chief executive officer, director, Universal Leaf Tobacco Co., Inc.

Henderson, George W., III: trustee, Burlington Industries Foundation; president, chief executive officer, director, Burlington Industries, Inc.

Knight, Merrill Donaldson, III: director, GEICO Philanthropic Foundation

Lewis, George Ralph: trustee, Kemper Foundation (James S.)

Lowden, Francis V., III: secretary, Universal Leaf Foundation

McKamey, William: general manager, director, Public Service Co. of Oklahoma

Savedge, Henry S., Jr.: executive vice president, chief financial officer, director, Reynolds Metals Co.; executive vice president, director, Reynolds Metals Co. Foundation

Scher, Barry F.: vice president public affairs, Giant Food Inc.

Siegel, Louis Pendelton: chairman, president, chief executive officer, chief operating officer, Potlatch Corp.; vice president, trustee, Potlatch Foundation II

Staton, Robert Emmett: president, Colonial Life & Accident Insurance Co.

Tilghman, Richard Granville: chairman, chief executive officer, Crestar Foundation

Tyler, Kenneth Scott, Jr.: president, chief executive officer, Furniture Brands International, Inc.

Warden, William C., Jr.: secretary, Lowe's Charitable and Educational Foundation

Wood, Edward Jenner: member, SunTrust Bank Atlanta Foundation

Wynne, John Oliver: president, director, Landmark Communications Foundation; president, chief executive officer, Landmark Communications Inc.

Washington

Almy, Richard E.: executive vice president, chief operating officer, director, Walter Industries Inc.

Cameron, Gerry B.: chairman, director, U.S. Bancorp

Campbell, Phyllis J.: president private financial services, US Bank, Washington

Coulter, Patrick C. G.: president, Bell Atlantic Foundation; senior vice president corporate communications, Gulfstream Aerospace Corp.

Countryman, Gary Lee: chairman, Liberty Mutual Insurance Group

Eigsti, Roger Harry: chairman, chief executive officer, SAFECO Corp.

Gates, William Henry, III: co-founder, chairman, chief software architect, Microsoft Corp.

Grinstein, Gerald: director, PACCAR Inc.

Hannity, Vincent Thomas: vice president corporate communications & investor relations, Boise Cascade Corp.

Jewett, George Frederick, Jr.: trustee, Potlatch Foundation II

Kerr, William T.: chairman, chief executive officer, director, Meredith Corp.

Kovacevich, Richard M.: chairman, president, chief executive officer, Norwest Corp.; director, Norwest Foundation

Levinson, Arthur David: president, chief executive officer, director, Genentech Inc.

Liljebeck, Roy C.: executive vice president, chief financial officer, Airborne Freight Corp.

McDade, Sandy D.: secretary, Weyerhaeuser Co.; assistant secretary legal affairs, Weyerhaeuser Co. Foundation

Olesen, Douglas Eugene, PhD: president, chief executive officer, Battelle Memorial Institute

Pigott, Charles McGee: president, director, PACCAR Foundation; chairman emeritus, director, PACCAR Inc.

Raines, Franklin Delano: chairman, chief executive officer, Fannie Mae; director, Fannie Mae Foundation

Schievelbein, Thomas C.: executive vice president, Newport News Shipbuilding

Solso, Theodore Matthew: president, chief operating officer, director, Cummins Engine Co., Inc.; director, Cummins Engine Foundation

Weyerhaeuser, George Hunt: director, Weyerhaeuser Co.; trustee, Weyerhaeuser Co. Foundation

Wiborg, James Hooker: director, PACCAR Foundation

Wiksten, Barry Frank: president, CIGNA Foundation

West Virginia

Barnette, Curtis Handley: chairman, chief executive officer, director, Bethlehem Steel Corp.

Bayless, Charles Edward: chairman, president, chief executive officer, director, Illinois Power Co.

Brothers, John Alfred 'Fred': trustee, Ashland Inc. Foundation

Byrd, Richard Hays: treasurer, Borden Foundation, Inc.

Campbell, Van C.: vice chairman, chief financial officer, chief administrative officer, director, Corning Inc.; trustee, Corning Inc. Foundation

Hiner, Glen Harold, Jr.: chairman, chief executive officer, director, Owens Corning

Knicely, Howard V.: president, TRW Foundation

Martin, Dezora M.: corporate secretary, Norfolk Southern Corp.; secretary, Norfolk Southern Foundation

Mooney, Edward J., Jr.: chairman, president, chief executive officer, director, Nalco Chemical Co.

Moore, John E.: executive vice president human resources, Cessna Aircraft Co.; vice president, Cessna Foundation, Inc.

Ratcliffe, George Jackson, Jr.: trustee, Hubbell Foundation (Harvey); chairman, president, chief executive officer, Hubbell Inc.

Stewart, S. Jay: chairman, chief executive officer, director, Morton International Inc.

Wisconsin

Amato, Anthony J.: senior vice president, Wisconsin Power & Light Co.; president, director, Wisconsin Power & Light Foundation, Inc.

Bachmann, Richard Arthur: vice president, secretary, treasurer, director, Louisiana Land & Exploration Co. Foundation

Bartz, Carol A.: director, Autodesk Foundation; chairman, chief executive officer, Autodesk Inc.

Bauer, Chris Michael: president, Firstar Milwaukee Foundation

Becker, John A.: president, chief operating officer, director, Firstar Bank Milwaukee NA; vice chairman, Firstar Milwaukee Foundation

Beyer, Jeffrey C.: president, Farmers Group Safety Foundation

Bonkoski, Kenneth John: controller, Menasha Corp.; treasurer, Menasha Corp. Foundation

Brostowitz, James M.: treasurer, Harley-Davidson Foundation

Burlingame, John Hunter: executive partner, Scripps Co. (E.W.)

Cianciola, Charles Sal: trustee, Chesapeake Corp. Foundation

Cohen, Maryjo Rose: president, chief executive officer, director, National Presto Industries, Inc.; vice president, treasurer, trustee, Presto Foundation

Cole, Franklin Alan: chairman, Aon Foundation

Collins, Paul John: vice chairman, director, Citibank Corp.

Dewane, John Richard: director, Honeywell Foundation

Eckert, Ralph John: trustee, Trustmark Foundation

Fitzsimonds, Roger Leon: chairman, Firstar Milwaukee Foundation

Fleming, Richard Harrison: chief financial officer, senior vice president, USG Corp.; treasurer, trustee, USG Foundation

Fluno, Jere David: vice chairman, Grainger, Inc. (W.W.)

Gherty, John E.: president, chief executive officer, Land O'Lakes, Inc.

Gonring, Matthew P.: vice president, trustee, USG Foundation

Henseler, Gerald A.: executive vice president, chief financial officer, director, Banta Corp.; president, Banta Corp. Foundation

Hobbs, Richard F.: vice president administration, Universal Foods Corp.; vice president, director, Universal Foods Foundation

Hough, Lawrence Alan: president, chief executive officer, Student Loan Marketing Association

Hultgren, Dennis N.: director, Appleton Papers Inc.

Jacobs, Bruce E.: vice president, director, Grede Foundation; president, director, Grede Foundries

Jacobs, Burleigh Edmund: president, director, Grede Foundation; chairman, Grede Foundries; director, Marshall & Ilsley Foundation, Inc.

Johnson, Samuel Curtis: chairman, director, president, Johnson & Son (S.C.); chairman, trustee, Johnson Wax Fund (S.C.)

Kalaher, Richard A.: president, American Standard Foundation; vice president, secretary, general counsel, American Standard Inc.

Keyes, James Henry: advisor, Johnson Controls Foundation; president, Johnson Controls Inc.

Kleinfeldt, Richard C.: vice president financial, chief financial officer, director, Giddings & Lewis

Kohler, Herbert Vollrath, Jr.: chairman, president, director, Kohler Co.
Kress, George F.: honorary chairman, director, Green Bay Packaging; president, Kress Foundation (George)
Kucharski, John Michael: trustee, PerkinElmer Foundation; chairman, chief executive officer, director, PerkinElmer, Inc.
Ladish, John: trustee, Ladish Co. Foundation
Lubar, Sheldon B.: chairman, Ameritech Corp.; director, Firstar Milwaukee Foundation
McCarragher, Bernard John: chairman, director, Menasha Corp.; chairman, Menasha Corp. Foundation
Mead, George Wilson, II: president, director, Consolidated Papers Foundation, Inc.; chairman, director, Consolidated Papers, Inc.
Muchin, Allan B.: chairman, Katten, Muchin & Zavis; director, Katten, Muchin & Zavis Foundation
Mulva, James J.: president, chief operating officer, director, Phillips Petroleum Co.
Omachinski, David L.: chief financial officer, treasurer, vice president, Oshkosh B'Gosh Foundation Inc.
Pfund, William H.: trustee, Rubbermaid Foundation
Piano, Phyllis J.: president, Cooper Industries Foundation; vice president public affairs, Cooper Industries, Inc.
Puelicher, John A.: president, director, Marshall & Ilsley Foundation, Inc.
Rau, John E.: trustee, Chicago Title and Trust Co. Foundation
Rosenzweig, Richard Stuart: executive vice president, director, Playboy Enterprises Inc.
Rupple, Brenton H.: director, Bucyrus-Erie Foundation
Ryan, Patrick G.: chairman, president, chief executive officer, Aon Corp.; president, Aon Foundation
Salinger, Robert M.: secretary, First Financial Foundation
Scholtens, Jean A.: vice president, treasurer, Eastern Enterprises
Schrickel, Patrick D.: vice president, Wisconsin Public Service Foundation, Inc.
Schuenke, Donald John: director, Freddie Mac
Schueppert, George Louis: chief financial officer, executive vice president, Outboard Marine Corp.
Stratton, Frederick Prescott, Jr.: chairman, chief executive officer, director, Briggs & Stratton Corp.; president, director, Briggs & Stratton Corp. Foundation
Terry, Richard Edward: chairman, chief executive officer, director, Peoples Energy Corp.
Thies, Richard Henry: assistant treasurer, Madison Gas & Electric Foundation
Ver Hagen, Jan Karol: president, United Dominion Industries, Ltd.
Wendlandt, Gary Edward: executive vice president, chief investment officer, Massachusetts Mutual Life Insurance Co.
Wenzler, Joseph P.: secretary, treasurer, WICOR Foundation; senior vice president, chief financial officer, WICOR, Inc.
Whitwam, David Ray: chairman, president, chief executive officer, director, Whirlpool Corp.
Willis, Gordon A.: assistant treasurer, assistant secretary, Wisconsin Energy Corp. Foundation, Inc.
Winter, William Bergford: president, Bucyrus-Erie Co.; chairman, president, director, Bucyrus-Erie Foundation
Wright, James O.: president, director, Badger Meter Foundation; chairman, director, Badger Meter, Inc.; director, Marshall & Ilsley Foundation, Inc.
Zech, Ronald H.: chairman, president, chief executive officer, chief operating officer, GATX Corp.
Ziegler, R. Douglas: advisor, Johnson Controls Foundation
Zutz, Denise M.: member advisory board, Johnson Controls Foundation

Wyoming

Colgan, Celeste: vice president, secretary, Halliburton Foundation, Inc.
Schuman, Allan L.: president, chief executive officer, director, chairman, Ecolab Inc.
Wellman, Thomas A.: controller, assistant treasurer, Alexander & Baldwin, Inc.

International

Argentina

Ortino, Hector R.: president, chief executive officer, director, Ferro Corp.; vice president, trustee, Ferro Foundation

Australia

Bible, Geoffrey Cyril: director, New York Stock Exchange Foundation, Inc.; chairman, chief executive officer, director, Philip Morris Companies Inc.
Fligg, James E.: executive vice president, BP Amoco Corp.
Johnson, David Willis: chairman, director, Campbell Soup Co.
Murdoch, Rupert P.: chairman, Fox Entertainment Group

Austria

Mandel, Jack N.: director, Premier Industrial Corp.
Leube, Helmut: trustee,

Belgium

Fonteyne, Herman J.: president, chief executive officer, director, Ensign-Bickford Industries

Brazil

Cabot, John G. L.: vice chairman, Kinder Morgn
do Carmo, Winston G.: vice president human resources, Giant Food Inc.
Reinhard, J. Pedro: executive vice president, chief financial officer, director, Dow Chemical Co.

Canada

Ebbers, Bernard J.: president, chief executive officer, director, MCI WorldCom, Inc.
Lachman, Marguerite Leanne: trustee, Chicago Title and Trust Co. Foundation
Langbo, Arnold Gordon: chairman, chief executive officer, director, Kellogg Co.
Pitts, John Wilson: director, PACCAR Foundation
Leatherdale, Douglas West: chairman, chief executive officer, president, Saint Paul Companies Inc.
Melnuk, Paul D.: president, chief executive officer, Clark Refining & Marketing
Adam, J. Marc: president, director, 3M Foundation; vice president marketing, Minnesota Mining & Manufacturing Co.
Coyne, William E.: senior vice president, Minnesota Mining & Manufacturing Co.
Flood, Al: chairman, chief executive officer, CIBC Oppenheimer
Goodes, Melvin Russell: chairman, chief executive officer, director, Ameritech Corp.
Hunkin, John: president, CIBC Oppenheimer
Kitchen, Michael B.: president, chief executive officer, director, CUNA Mutual Group; secretary, treasurer, executive officer, CUNA Mutual Group Foundation, Inc.
Kreh, Gordon W.: president, chief executive officer, director, Hartford Steam Boiler Inspection & Insurance Co.
Laurance, Dale R.: director, Occidental Petroleum Charitable Foundation; president, senior operations officer, director, Occidental Petroleum Corp.
Lawless, Robert J.: chairman, president, chief executive officer, chief operating officer, director, McCormick & Co. Inc.
Light, Walter Frederick: trustee, Air Products Foundation
Ranck, Bruce E.: president, chief executive officer, director, Browning-Ferris Industries Inc.
Black, Lennox K.: president, Teleflex Foundation; chairman, director, Teleflex Inc.
Bronfman, Charles Rosner: trustee, Bronfman Foundation/Joseph E. Seagram & Sons, Inc. Fund (Samuel)
Bronfman, Edgar Miles: chairman, trustee, Bronfman Foundation/Joseph E. Seagram & Sons, Inc. Fund (Samuel); chairman, Seagram & Sons, Inc. (Joseph E.)
DeSimone, Livio Diego: chairman, chief executive officer, Minnesota Mining & Manufacturing Co.
Kamen, Harry Paul: chairman, president, chief executive officer, Metropolitan Life Insurance Co.
Masin, Michael Terry: vice chairman, president international, director, GTE Corp.; trustee, GTE Foundation
McNally, Alan G.: chairman, chief executive officer, Harris Trust & Savings Bank
Notebaert, Richard C.: chairman, chief executive officer, Ameritech Corp.; director, Ameritech Foundation
Zuckerman, Mortimer Benjamin: co-founder, chairman, co-publisher, director, Daily News

Colombia

Tobias, Steven C.: vice chairman, chief operating officer, Norfolk Southern Corp.; director, Norfolk Southern Foundation

Costa Rica

Kissling, Walter: director, Fuller Co. (H.B.)

Cuba

Falla, Enrique Crabb: senior consult, director, Dow Chemical Co.
Sales, A. R.: director, Arvin Foundation; treasurer, Arvin Industries, Inc.

Egypt

Kampouris, Emmanuel Andrew: chairman, president, chief executive officer, director, American Standard Inc.
Tambakeras, Markos I.: director, Honeywell Foundation

England

Bilton, Stuart Douglas: president, chief executive officer, Chicago Title Corp.; trustee, Chicago Title and Trust Co. Foundation
Carson, David Ellis Adams: chairman, chief executive officer, Peoples Bank
Coltman, David A.: senior vice president marketing, United Airlines Inc.
Reading, Anthony John: president, trustee, Tomkins Corp. Foundation; president, chief executive officer, Tomkins Industries, Inc.
Walters, Peter: chairman, SmithKline Beecham Corp.
Romeril, Barry D.: executive vice president, chief financial officer, Xerox Corp.
Weatherstone, Dennis: trustee, Merck Co. Foundation
Walker, Grahame: chairman, chief executive officer, Dexter Corp.; president, Dexter Corp. Foundation
Maughan, Deryck C.: director, New York Stock Exchange Foundation, Inc.; co-chairman, co-chief executive officer, Salomon Smith Barney
Naylor, Michael E.: senior vice president operations, Rubbermaid Inc.
Williams, David R.: trustee, Heinz Co. Foundation (H.J.); executive vice president, director, Heinz Co. (H.J.)
Skilling, Raymond Inwood: executive vice president, chief counsel, director, Aon Corp.; director, Aon Foundation

France

Bergerac, Michel Christian: director, CBS Foundation

Germany

Forster, Peter Hans: chairman, director, Dayton Power and Light Co.

Kissinger, Henry Alfred: director, CBS Foundation

Mueller, Gerd Dieter: executive vice president, chief financial officer, director, chief administrative officer, Bayer Corp.; president, Bayer Foundation

Pfeiffer, Eckhard A.: president, chief executive officer, director, Compaq Computer Corp.

Stolar, Bernie: trustee, Sega Foundation

Wehmeier, Helge H.: president, chief executive officer, director, Bayer Corp.

Wolff, Herbert Eric: secretary, director, First Hawaiian Foundation

Schubert, Rolf B.: director, Fuller Co. Foundation (H.B.)

Eisman, Paul: senior vice president refining Southwest, Ultramar Diamond Shamrock Corp.

Otto, Peter: president, Lehigh Portland Cement Co.

Schrempp, Jurgen E.: chairman, DaimlerChrysler Corp.

Weiser, Irving: chairman, president, chief executive officer, Dain Bosworth Inc.

Wobst, Frank: chairman, chief executive officer, director, Huntington Bancshares Inc.

Schmitt, Wolfgang Rudolph: chairman, chief executive officer, director, Rubbermaid Inc.

Greece

Hatsopoulos, George Nicholas: founder, chairman, chief executive officer, director, Thermo Electron Corp.; committee member, Thermo Electron Foundation

Hatsopoulos, John Nicholas: retired president, Thermo Electron Corp.; committee member, Thermo Electron Foundation

Zampetis, Theodore K.: president, chief operating officer, director, Standard Products Co.

Recanati, Raphael: president, director, OSG Foundation

Hungary

Grove, Andrew S.: chairman, Intel Corp.

India

Nayak, P. Ranganath: trustee, Little Foundation (Arthur D.); senior vice president, Little, Inc. (Arthur D.)

Pinto, Michael P.: executive vice president, chief financial officer, Manufacturers & Traders Trust Co.

Ayer, Ramani: chairman, president, chief executive officer, Hartford (The)

Patel, Homi Burjor: president, chief operating officer, director, Hartmarx Corp.

Thawerbhoy, Nazim G.: controller, Jacobs Engineering Foundation

Iran

Darehshori, Nader Farhang: chairman, president, chief executive officer, Houghton Mifflin Co.

Iraq

Zilkha, Ezra Khedouri: president, treasurer, Zilkha Foundation, Inc.; president, Zilkha & Sons

Ireland

O'Reilly, F. Anthony John: chairman, trustee, Heinz Co. Foundation (H.J.); chairman, director, Heinz Co. (H.J.)

Nikka, Joanne: trustee, Millipore Foundation (The)

Israel

Arison, M. Micky: trustee, Arison Foundation; chairman, president, chief executive officer, Carnival Corp.

Italy

Castellini, Clateo: chairman, president, chief executive officer, Becton Dickinson & Co.

D'Alessandro, Dominic: president, chief executive officer, director, Manulife Financial

Japan

Ando, Tetsuo: chief financial officer, executive vice president, treasurer, Bridgestone/Firestone, Inc.

Shapiro, Isaac: chairman, secretary, trustee, Ise Cultural Foundation

Tsutsumi, Senji: vice president, trustee, Ise Cultural Foundation

Mita, Katsushige: honorary chairman, Hitachi Foundation

Lebanon

Irani, Raymond Reza: director, Occidental Petroleum Charitable Foundation; chairman, director, chief executive officer, Occidental Petroleum Corp.

Mexico

Niebla, J. Fernando: chairman, chief executive officer, Pacific Mutual Life Insurance Co.

Morocco

Dahan, Rene: senior vice president, Exxon Mobil Corp.

Netherlands

Ruding, Herman Onno: vice chairman, director, Citibank Corp.

People's Republic of China

McNamara, Anne H.: senior vice president, general counsel, AMR Corp.

Republic of South Africa

Ernst, Fred V.: president, director, MacMillan Bloedel Inc.

Scotland

Baird, Dugald Euan: chairman, president, chief executive officer, Schlumberger Ltd. (USA)

Sweden

Oldenburg, Richard Erik: chairman, Sotheby's Inc.

Switzerland

Stalder, Ruedi: trustee, Credit Suisse First Boston Foundation Trust

Thailand

Travaille, Hubert Duane: president, trustee, Potlatch Foundation II

United Kingdom

Butler, Andrew J.: trustee, Dow Chemical Co.

Vietnam

Tran, Khanh T.: senior vice president, chief financial officer, director, Pacific Mutual Life Insurance Co.

Yugoslavia

Lichtenberger, Horst William: chairman, chief executive officer, Praxair

Officers and Directors by Alma Mater

Lists individuals by the colleges or universities that they attended or received a degree.

Aberdeen University

Baird, Dugald Euan: chairman, president, chief executive officer, Schlumberger Ltd. (USA)

Turberville, P. G.: vice president, director, Shell Oil Co. Foundation

Abilene Christian University

Caldwell, Royce S.: director, SBC Foundation

Air Force Institute Technology

Herres, Robert T.: chairman, chief executive officer, United Services Automobile Association

Akron University

Burg, H. Peter: president, chief operating officer, FirstEnergy Corp.

Albany Law School

Brozyna, Jeffry H.: trustee

Chapple, Thomas Leslie: senior vice president, general counsel, secretary, Gannett Co., Inc.; secretary, Gannett Foundation

Albany Medical College

Noonan, Timothy J.: president, chief operating officer, director, Rite Aid Corp.

Albright College

Wheeler, Joyce W.: secretary, Royal & SunAlliance Insurance Foundation, Inc.; vice president, corporate secretary, Royal & SunAlliance USA, Inc.

Alfred University

Maurer, Jeffrey Stuart: president, chief operating officer, director, United States Trust Co. of New York

Allegheny College

Hoag, David H.: chairman, president, chief executive officer, director, LTV Corp.; trustee, LTV Foundation

Alvernia College

Hafer, Fred Douglass: chairman, president, chief executive officer, GPU Inc.

American College

Dubes, Michael: membership, ReliaStar Foundation

American College Life Underwriters

Kalainov, Sam Charles: chairman, president, chief executive officer, AmerUS Group

American International University

Garneau, Robert M.: chief financial officer, Kaman Corp.

American University

Alegi, August Paul: director, GEICO Philanthropic Foundation

Davis, Ruth Margaret: trustee, Air Products Foundation

Gonring, Matthew P.: vice president, trustee, USG Foundation

Labrecque, Thomas Goulet: president, chief operating officer, director, Chase Manhattan Bank, NA; president, Chase Manhattan Foundation

Larance, Charles L.: vice president corporate relations, GenAmerica Corp.; president, GenAmerican Foundation

Manning, Kenneth Paul: president, Universal Foods Corp.; president, director, Universal Foods Foundation

Rand, Addison Barry: executive vice president operations, Xerox Corp.; trustee, Xerox Foundation

Scher, Barry F.: vice president public affairs, Giant Food Inc.

Welty, John Rider: secretary, Carpenter Technology Corp. Foundation

de Vink, Lodewijk J. R.: director, Warner-Lambert Charitable Foundation; president, chief operating officer, director, Warner-Lambert Co.

American University Beirut

Irani, Raymond Reza: director, Occidental Petroleum Charitable Foundation; chairman, director, chief executive officer, Occidental Petroleum Corp.

Amherst College

Dillon, Adrian T.: executive vice president, chief financial officer, planning officer, Eaton Corp.

Huston, Edwin Allen: vice president, director, Ryder System Charitable Foundation; vice chairman, director, Ryder System, Inc.

Lehner, Carl P.: president, chief executive officer, Leigh Fibers, Inc.; trustee, Orchard Foundation

Schermer, Lloyd G.: chairman, director, Lee Enterprises

Shinn, George Latimer: director, New York Times Co. Foundation

Sommer, Charles S.: member board control, Ralston Purina Trust Fund

Turner, John Gosney: chairman, chief executive officer, director, ReliaStar Financial Corp.; director, ReliaStar Foundation

Anderson College

Kufeldt, James: vice president, director, Winn-Dixie Stores Foundation; president, director, Winn-Dixie Stores Inc.

Andrews University

Bainum, Stewart William, Jr.: chairman, Manor Care Health SVS, Inc.

Antioch College

Higginbotham, A. Leon, Jr.: director, New York Times Co. Foundation

Lasser, Lawrence Jay: president, chief executive officer, director, Putnam Investments; president, chief executive officer, Putnam Investors Fund

Mersereau, Susan M.: trustee, Weyerhaeuser Co. Foundation

Aquinas College

Ozark, Edward L.: trustee, JSJ Foundation

Arizona State College

Pulatie, David L.: senior vice president human resources, Phelps Dodge Corp.

Arizona State University

Knez, Brian J.: trustee, Harcourt General Charitable Foundation

Loftin, Nancy Carol: secretary, director, APS Foundation, Inc.; vice president, general counsel, Arizona Public Service Co.

Macrie, Sari: vice president investor relations, Ameritech Corp.

Mebane, David Cummins: chairman, president, chief executive officer, director, Madison Gas & Electric Co.; vice president, Madison Gas & Electric Foundation

Post, William J.: vice president, director, APS Foundation, Inc.; president, chief executive officer, Arizona Public Service Co.

Ashland College

Sheets, Thomas R.: vice president, general counsel, Southwest Gas Corp.; trustee, Southwest Gas Corp. Foundation

Assumption College

Dorsey, Jerry E.: executive vice president, chief operating officer, West Co. Inc.

Aston University

Hathaway, Derek C.: chairman, chief executive officer, Harsco Corp.; vice president, trustee, Harsco Corp. Fund

Athens College

Hatsopoulos, John Nicholas: retired president, Thermo Electron Corp.; committee member, Thermo Electron Foundation

Atlanta Law School

Anderson, Judy M.: vice president, corporate secretary, Georgia Power Co.; executive director, secretary, assistant treasurer, Georgia Power Foundation

Barron, Donald Ray: president, director, Atlantic Investment Co.

Atlantic Christian College

Horack, Thomas Borland: vice president, director, Lance Foundation

Auburn University

Armstrong, Malcolm: executive vice president operations, Delta Air Lines, Inc.

Davis, W. Derek: trustee, Dixie Yarns Foundation, Inc.

Dollar, William Michael: vice president, treasurer, chief financial officer, Harland Co. (John H.)

Farris, Banks H.: chairman, Alabama Power Foundation

Fricks, William Peavy: chairman, chief executive officer, Newport News Shipbuilding

Ginn, Samuel L.: chairman, director, AirTouch Communications Foundation; chairman, chief executive officer, director, Vodafone AirTouch Plc

Harris, Elmer Beseler: president, chief executive officer, director, Alabama Power Co.

Hemminghaus, Roger Roy: chairman, director, Ultramar Diamond Shamrock Corp.

Leggett, Richard B.: member screening committee, PPG Industries Foundation

Long, Robert R.: chairman, SunTrust Bank Atlanta

Mackin, James Stanley: chairman, chief executive officer, Regions Financial Corp.

Nichols, Kenwood C.: vice chairman, executive officer, Champion International Corp.

Nichols, Mack G.: president, chief executive officer, director, Mallinckrodt Chemical, Inc.

Oliver, Charles R.: trustee, Fluor Foundation

Augusta College

Boyette, John G.: treasurer, Cox Foundation (James M.)

Augustana College

Carpenter, Marshall L.: vice president, chief financial officer, MTS Systems Corp.

Egger, Terrance C.Z.: director, Pulitzer Publishing Co. Foundation

Martin, Lois: vice president, controller, Deluxe Corp.; director, Deluxe Corp. Foundation

Aurora College

Tucker, Don Eugene: trustee, Commercial Intertech Foundation

Austin College

Easterly, David E.: president, chief operating officer, Cox Enterprises Inc.

Grum, Clifford J.: director, Temple-Inland Foundation; director, chairman, chief executive officer, Temple-Inland Inc.

Johnson, Murray Lloyd, Jr.: secretary, trustee, Zachry Foundation (The)

Austin Peay State College

Mass, Nathaniel J.: senior vice president strategic growth, GenCorp; trustee, GenCorp Foundation

Austin University

Frost, Thomas C., Senior: chairman, Frost National Bank

Babson College

Blank, Arthur M.: president, chief executive officer, director, Home Depot, Inc.

Cawley, Michael J.: vice president risk management, Eastern Enterprises

Cookson, John Simmons: vice president finance, treasurer, assistant secretary, Kingsbury Corp.; trustee, Kingsbury Fund

Enrico, Roger A.: chairman, PepsiCo Foundation, Inc.; chairman, chief executive officer, director, PepsiCo, Inc.

Flaherty, Walter J.: chief financial officer, senior vice president, Eastern Enterprises; trustee, Eastern Enterprises Foundation

Judge, James J.: senior vice president corporate service business unit, treasurer, Boston Edison Co.; trustee, Boston Edison Foundation

Lavigne, Louis J., Jr.: executive vice president, chief financial officer, Genentech Inc.

Baker University

Sadler, Robert L.: president, vice chairman, director, Old Kent Bank

Bakersfield Junior College

Hall, Floyd: chairman, president, chief executive officer, director, Kmart Corp.

Baldwin-Wallace College

Boesel, Stephen W.: vice president, secretary, treasurer, Price Associates Foundation (T. Rowe)

Glaser, Gary A.: president, chief executive officer, National City Bank of Columbus

Skurek, John C.: vice president, treasurer, LTV Corp.; trustee, LTV Foundation

Ball State University

Catlow, Walter S.: executive vice president, Ameritech Corp.

Conley, E. Renae: president, Cinergy Corp.

Greene, Donald Ray: assistant vice president, Coca-Cola Co.; president, director, Coca-Cola Foundation

Taylor, Philip E.: president, JSJ Corp.

Bard College

Sulzberger, Arthur Ochs, Sr.: director, New York Times Co.; chairman, director, New York Times Co. Foundation

Barnard College

Goodman, Helen G.: senior vice president, Hartford (The)

Baruch College

Heasley, Philip G.: president, chief operating officer, U.S. Bancorp

Bates College

Colman, Robert L.: executive vice president human resources, Delta Air Lines, Inc.

Williams, Karen Hastie: director, Fannie Mae Foundation

Baylor University

Allbritton, Joe Lewis: chairman, chief executive officer, Riggs Bank NA

Dagley, Larry J.: senior vice president, chief financial officer, Pacific Enterprises

Keith, Susan Stewart: assistant secretary, assistant treasurer, Halliburton Foundation, Inc.

Skiles, Win: vice president, Texas Instruments Foundation; senior vice president, Texas Instruments Inc.

Warner, M. Richard: director, Temple-Inland Foundation

Beacom College

Jones, Joseph West: secretary, director, Coca-Cola Foundation

Bellarmine College

Clayton, Joseph P.: president, chief executive officer, director, Frontier Corp.

Hughes, Timothy W.: senior vice president, Cox Enterprises Inc.; trustee, Cox Foundation (James M.)

Reynolds, Randolph Nicklas: vice chairman, executive officer, director, Reynolds Metals Co.; director, Reynolds Metals Co. Foundation

Belmont Abbey College

Jamison, Zean, Jr.: director, Lance Foundation; director human resources, Lance, Inc.

Beloit College

Young, Robert Harris: president, chief executive officer, Central Vermont Public Service Corp.

Bentley College

Demoulas, Arthur T.: trustee, Demoulas Foundation

Flaherty, Walter J.: chief financial officer, senior vice president, Eastern Enterprises; trustee, Eastern Enterprises Foundation

Kelleher, Paul F.: committee member, Thermo Electron Foundation

Ludden, Timothy Wayne: vice president, treasurer, cash manager, Unum-Provident

McCahon, Jane W.: vice president corporate relations, Eastern Enterprises

Mee, Michael F.: senior vice president, chief financial officer, Bristol-Myers Squibb Co.

Berea College

Walker, Thomas P.: secretary, Stonecutter Foundation

Bernard Baruch School

Gober, Ira: chairman, chief financial officer, partner, director, Associated Food Stores; director, Associated Food Stores Charitable Foundation

Bethel College

Van Benschoten, David: treasurer, General Mills Foundation

Biltmore College

Suggs, Leo H.: director, chairman, chief executive officer, Overnite Transportation Co.

Birmingham-Southern College

Powell, Jerry W.: secretary, general counsel, Compass Bank; secretary, Compass Bank Foundation

Stephens, Elton Bryson: founder, chairman, Ebsco Industries, Inc.

Blackburn College

Ferguson, Ronald Eugene: chairman, president, chief executive officer, director, General Reinsurance Corp.

Bocconi University

Castellini, Clateo: chairman, president, chief executive officer, Becton Dickinson & Co.

Boston College

Allen, Barry K.: president regulatory & wholesale operation, Ameritech Corp.

Bankowski, Elizabeth: secretary, Ben & Jerry's Foundation

Dalton, James F.: chairman, trustee, Tektronix Foundation; vice president, general counsel, secretary, Tektronix, Inc.

Hausmann, Carl L.: chairman, president, chief executive officer, Central Soya Co.

Jasse, Andre C., Jr.: trustee, Eastern Bank Charitable Foundation

Kelleher, Paul F.: committee member, Thermo Electron Foundation

Kendrick, William J.: vice president public affairs, Air Products and Chemicals, Inc.; chairman, Air Products Foundation

Keough, William H.: senior vice president, chief financial officer, Pioneer Group

Kiernan, Donald E., Sr.: senior vice president, chief financial officer, treasurer, SBC Communications Inc.; director, SBC Foundation

Knez, Brian J.: trustee, Harcourt General Charitable Foundation

McLaughlin, Michael John: secretary, New York Life Foundation; senior vice president, deputy general counsel, New York Life Insurance Co.

Rau, John E.: trustee, Chicago Title and Trust Co. Foundation

Sullivan, G. Craig: chairman, president, chief executive officer, director, Clorox Co.; chairman, Clorox Co. Foundation

Syron, Richard F.: chairman, chief executive officer, director, American Stock Exchange, Inc.

Boston College Law School

Flanagan, David T.: president, chief executive officer, director, Central Maine Power Co.

Boston University

Clark, Howard Longstreth, Jr.: vice chairman, Walter Industries Inc.

Convisser, Theodora S.: trustee, Boston Edison Foundation

Crane, Lansing E.: chairman, president, Crane & Co., Inc.

Davies, Richard Warren: trustee, Hubbell Foundation (Harvey)

Donahue, Richard King: vice chairman, Nike, Inc.

Drexler, Millard S.: trustee, Gap Foundation/Gap Inc. Community Relations; president, chief executive officer, director, Gap, Inc.

Dubin, Stephen Victor: vice president, secretary, Farber Foundation

Elliott, David Holland: consultant, chairman executive committee, MBIA Inc.

Fishman, Jerald G.: president, chief executive officer, director, Analog Devices, Inc.

Goldstein, Richard A.: president, chief executive officer, director, Lipton Co.

Gullotti, Russell A.: chairman, president, chief executive officer, National Computer Systems, Inc.

Gustin, Lester Carl: trustee, Boston Edison Foundation

Halperin, Richard E.: president, Revlon Foundation Inc.

Mulford, David: chairman, Credit Suisse First Boston

Orr, James F., III: president, trustee, UNUM Foundation; chairman, Unum-Provident

Roth, Michael I.: chairman, chief executive officer, director, MONY Group (The); director, MONY Life Insurance of New York (The)
Smith, John Francis, Jr.: chairman, General Motors Corp.
Wangstad, Kristi Rollag: vice president public affairs, Alliant Techsystems; president, Alliant Techsystems Community Investment Foundation
Wiley, Deborah: vice chairman, Wiley & Sons (John)

Boston University Law School

Keyser, F. Ray, Jr.: chairman, director, Central Vermont Public Service Corp.

Bowdoin College

Binswanger, David R.: president, chief executive officer, Binswanger Companies; treasurer, Binswanger Foundation
Chenault, Kenneth Irvine: president, chief operating officer, director, American Express Co.; trustee, American Express Foundation
Gorman, Leon A.: president, chief executive officer, Bean, Inc. (L.L.)
Gould, John T., Jr.: vice president, Unilever Foundation; director corporate affairs, Unilever United States, Inc.
Magee, John Francis: chairman, director, Little, Inc. (Arthur D.)
Morie, G. Glen: secretary, treasurer, PACCAR Foundation
Pendexter, Harold E., Jr.: senior vice president, chief administrative officer, USG Corp.; president, director, USG Foundation

Bowling Green State University

Blouch, Gerald B.: president, chief operating officer, Invacare Corp.; trustee, Invacare Foundation
Brown, Craig J.: treasurer, Sherman-Standard Register Foundation; senior vice president administration, treasurer, chief financial officer, Standard Register Co.
Civello, Nelson D.: director, Dain Bosworth Foundation
Hattendorf, William C.: trustee, Cooper Tire & Rubber Foundation
Jackson, Frederick H.: executive vice president finance, director, La-Z-Boy Inc.
Pike, Robert William: vice president, secretary, Allstate Foundation; senior vice president, secretary, general counsel, director, Allstate Insurance Co.
Wardeberg, George E.: president, WICOR Foundation; president, chief executive officer, director, WICOR, Inc.

Bradley University

Berry, Ilona M.: secretary, First National Bank of Chicago Foundation
Clanin, Robert J.: senior vice president, chief financial officer, treasurer, director, United Parcel Service of America Inc.
Frew, Burdette L.: president, director, MFA Foundation
Johnson, Lawrence M.: president, Pacific Century Financial Corp.
Rich, David A.: executive director, Rich Family Foundation; vice president, secretary, director, Rich Products Corp.

Brandeis University

Convisser, Theodora S.: trustee, Boston Edison Foundation
Hefner, Christie Ann: chairman, chief executive officer, Playboy Enterprises Inc.; director, Playboy Foundation

Brigham Young University

Burns, Mitchell Anthony: president, director, Ryder System Charitable Foundation; chairman, president, chief executive officer, Ryder System, Inc.
Colton, S. David: senior vice president, general counsel, Phelps Dodge Corp.
Doane, W. Allen: president, chief executive officer, director, Alexander & Baldwin, Inc.
Haney, R. Lee: senior vice president, chief financial officer, Orange & Rockland Utilities, Inc.
Hanks, Stephen G.: president, Morrison Knudsen Corp. Foundation, Inc.
Higbee, David M.: secretary, Williams; secretary, treasurer, Williams Companies Foundation (The)
Humphrey, Neil Darwin: trustee, Commercial Intertech Foundation
Lang, Rudolph E., Jr.: senior vice president, chief financial officer, Litton Industries, Inc.
Malquist, Malyn K.: chairman, Sierra Pacific Resources
Norberg, Jaron B.: vice president, director, APS Foundation, Inc.; director, Arizona Public Service Co.
Rane, David A.: executive vice president, chief financial officer, Callaway Golf Co.; chief financial officer, Callaway Golf Co. Foundation
Richards, Joel, III: vice president, El Paso Energy Foundation
Wellman, Thomas A.: controller, assistant treasurer, Alexander & Baldwin, Inc.

Brigham Young University J. Reuben Clark College of Law

Colton, S. David: senior vice president, general counsel, Phelps Dodge Corp.

Britannia Royal Naval College

Walker, Grahame: chairman, chief executive officer, Dexter Corp.; president, Dexter Corp. Foundation

Brooklyn Law School

Aldinger, William F., III: chairman, chief executive officer, director, Household International Inc.
Forster, Peter Hans: chairman, director, Dayton Power and Light Co.
Gross, Murray: trustee, PerkinElmer Foundation; senior vice president, general counsel, clerk, PerkinElmer, Inc.
Weiser, Irving: chairman, president, chief executive officer, Dain Bosworth Inc.

Brown University

Corwin, Laura J.: secretary, New York Times Co. Foundation
Fisher, George Myles Cordell: chairman, president, chief executive officer, director, Eastman Kodak Co.
Gidwitz, Ronald J.: president, chief executive officer, Curtis Industries, Inc. (Helene)
Goeltz, Richard Karl: vice chairman, chief financial officer, American Express Co.
Hale, Roger Loucks: chairman, TENNANT Co.; president, TENNANT Co. Foundation
Harris, Ralph A.: vice president corporate development, Campbell Soup Co.
Jones, Ross: senior vice president, chief financial officer, Knight Ridder
Keegan, Peter: senior vice president, Loews Foundation
Parrs, Marianne M.: executive vice president, International Paper Co.
Rhodes, William Reginald: vice chairman, Citibank Corp.
Small, Lawrence Malcolm: president, chief operating officer, Fannie Mae; director, Fannie Mae Foundation
Viault, Raymond: vice chairman, director, General Mills, Inc.

Bryant College

Conaty, William J.: director, GE Fund
Lemieux, Joseph Henry: chairman, chief executive officer, director, Owens-Illinois Inc.
Mandeville, Robert: trustee, Cranston Foundation; chief financial officer, secretary, treasurer, Cranston Print Works Co.
Wilson, Bruce A.: senior vice president, BankBoston-Connecticut Region

Bucknell University

Calise, William Joseph, Junior: senior vice president, secretary, general counsel, Rockwell International Corp.
Garrity, Norman E.: executive vice president, director, Corning Inc.; trustee, Corning Inc. Foundation
Smith, Elizabeth Patience: director, Texaco Foundation; vice president investor relations & shareholder service, Texaco Inc.
Tisch, Preston Robert: chairman, director, CBS Foundation; co-chairman, co-chief executive officer, director, CNA; trustee, Loews Foundation

Buenos Aires University

Ortino, Hector R.: president, chief executive officer, director, Ferro Corp.; vice president, trustee, Ferro Foundation

Butler University

Geier, Peter E.: vice chairman, Huntington Bancshares Inc.
Morris, James Thomas: director, AUL Foundation Inc.

C. W. Post University

Barrett, Robert E.: executive vice president, UST Inc.

California Institute of Technology

Hays, Thomas Chandler: chairman, chief executive officer, director, Fortune Brands, Inc.
Moore, Gordon E., PhD: cofounder, chairman emeritus, director, Intel Corp.; trustee, Intel Foundation

California State Polytechnic University, Pomona

Oliver, Charles R.: trustee, Fluor Foundation

California State University

Carey, Kathryn Ann: foundation manager, American Honda Foundation
Coughlin, Thomas Martin: member, Wal-Mart Foundation; executive vice president, Wal-Mart Stores, Inc.
Feinstein, Martin D.: chairman, chief executive officer, Farmers Group, Inc.
Kelly, Colin P.: senior vice president human resources, Household International Inc.
Rollans, James Ora: senior vice president, chief administrative officer, chief financial officer, Fluor Corp.; trustee, Fluor Foundation
Washington, Earl S.: senior vice president communications, Rockwell International Corp.; secretary, Rockwell International Corp. Trust
Weidemeyer, Thomas H.: senior vice president, director, United Parcel Service of America Inc.; trustee, UPS Foundation
Younts, Rosemary: senior vice president communications, GenCorp

California State University, Fullerton

Golleher, George C: president, Ralph's-Food 4 Less Foundation; chief executive officer, Ralph's Grocery Co.
Grubb, Edgar Harold: executive vice president, chief financial officer, Transamerica Corp.; director, Transamerica Foundation

California State University, Hayward

Hill, Bonnie Guiton: vice president, Times Mirror Co.; president, chief executive officer, Times Mirror Foundation

California State University, Long Beach

Campbell, George Leroy: vice president public affairs, Florida Power Corp.

California State University, Northridge

Coulter, Patrick C. G.: president, Bell Atlantic Foundation; senior vice president corporate communications, Gulfstream Aerospace Corp.

Prosser, John Warren, Jr.: treasurer, director, Jacobs Engineering Foundation; senior vice president finance & administration, treasurer, Jacobs Engineering Group

Calvin College

VanderRoest, Stan: trustee, treasurer, Gerber Foundation; vice president, comptroller, controller, Gerber Products Co.

Cambridge University

Baird, Dugald Euan: chairman, president, chief executive officer, Schlumberger Ltd. (USA)

Butler, Andrew J.: trustee, Dow Chemical Co.

Canisius College

Civello, Nelson D.: director, Dain Bosworth Foundation

Ozark, Edward L.: trustee, JSJ Foundation

Capital University

Woodward, Robert J., Jr.: executive vice president, chief investment officer, Nationwide Insurance Enterprise Foundation

Capital University Law School

Foley, Cheryl M.: vice president, secretary, general counsel, Cinergy Corp.; vice president, secretary, director, Cinergy Foundation

Carleton College

Buxton, Charles Ingraham, II: chairman, Federated Mutual Insurance Co.; president, Federated Mutual Insurance Foundation

Wentworth, Jack Roberts, Ph.D.: director, Habig Foundation

Carnegie Institute of Technology

Wishnick, William: president, director, Wishnick Foundation (Robert I.)

Carnegie Mellon University

Allaire, Paul Arthur: chairman, chief executive officer, chairman executive committee, Xerox Corp.; president, Xerox Foundation

Aylesworth, William Andrew: treasurer, Texas Instruments Foundation; chief financial officer, treasurer, Texas Instruments Inc.

Bertrand, Frederic Howard: chairman, Central Vermont Public Service Corp.

Campbell, Robert Henderson: chairman, chief executive officer, Sunoco Inc.

Coulter, David A.: president, director, Bank of America

Davis, Erroll Brown, Jr.: president, chief executive officer, director, Wisconsin Power & Light Co.

Fuellgraf, Charles Louis, Jr.: trustee, Nationwide Insurance Enterprise Foundation

Hill, George Richard: president, trustee, Lubrizol Foundation (The)

Hilyard, James E.: president, CertainTeed Corp.; director, CertainTeed Corp. Foundation

Kostecky, James Frank: executive director, Bethlehem Steel Corp.

Lang, Paul Louis: vice president, Illinois Power Co.

Pollock, E. Kears: director, PPG Industries Foundation; executive vice president, PPG Industries, Inc.

Smith, Raymond W.: chairman, chief executive officer, director, Bell Atlantic Corp.

Stallkamp, William J.: member corporate review committee, Mellon Financial Corp.

Wilhelm, Paul J.: trustee, USX Foundation, Inc.

Wyszomierski, Jack L.: trustee, member, Schering-Plough Foundation

Yasinsky, John B.: chairman, president, chief executive officer, GenCorp

Carroll College

Bemis, Peter F.: vice president, Bemis Family Foundation (F.K.)

Burd, Steven A.: president, chief executive officer, chairman, director, Safeway Inc.

Harms, Carol J.: vice president, treasurer, Montgomery Ward & Co., Inc.; senior vice president, Montgomery Ward Foundation

Carthage College

Graham, William B.: chairman, director, Baxter Allegiance Foundation; chairman emeritus, Baxter International Inc.

Case Western Reserve University

Bares, William G.: chairman, president, chief executive officer, Lubrizol Corp. (The); trustee, Lubrizol Foundation (The)

Barnett, Robert L.: director, Ameritech Foundation

Bezik, Cynthia B.: senior vice president, finance, Cleveland-Cliffs, Inc.

Breen, John Gerald: chairman, chief executive officer, director, Sherwin-Williams Co.; president, trustee, Sherwin-Williams Foundation

Brinzo, John S.: trustee, Cleveland-Cliffs Foundation (The); president, chief executive officer, Cleveland-Cliffs, Inc.

Cushwa, William Wallace: director, Commercial Intertech Corp.; trustee, Commercial Intertech Foundation

Daberko, David A.: chairman, chief executive officer, National City Corp.

Farley, James Bernard: chairman emeritus, trustee, Walter Industries Inc.

Fretthold, Timothy Jon: executive vice president, general counsel, director, Ultramar Diamond Shamrock Corp.

Glaser, Gary A.: president, chief executive officer, National City Bank of Columbus

Haggerty, Gretchen R.: vice president, treasurer, USX Corp.

Herbold, Robert J.: executive vice president, chief operating officer, Microsoft Corp.

Hilyard, James E.: president, CertainTeed Corp.; director, CertainTeed Corp. Foundation

Horan, Douglas S.: senior vice president, general counsel, Boston Edison Co.; trustee, Boston Edison Foundation

Jackson, Frederick H.: executive vice president finance, director, La-Z-Boy Inc.

Manchester, Gilbert Mott: assistant secretary, Commercial Intertech Foundation

Mandel, Morton Leon: deputy chairman, Premier Industrial Corp.; trustee, Premier Industrial Foundation

Mason, James L.: director public affairs, member contributions committee, Eaton Charitable Fund

McDonough, Gerald C.: trustee, Commercial Intertech Foundation

McGregor, Douglas A.: trustee, Rouse Co. Foundation

Morgan, James McClay: member executive committee, director, Shell Oil Co. Foundation

Ostergard, Paul Michael: vice president, director corporate contributions, Citibank Corp.; president, Citigroup Foundation

Rudnick, Alan A.: vice president, general counsel, corporate secretary, CSX Corp.

Schubach, John J.: senior vice president strategic management, Timken Co. (The); trustee, advisor, Timken Co. Charitable Trust (The)

Sims, Philip Stuart: vice chairman, treasurer, Premier Industrial Corp.

Sullivan, Kevin F.: member screening committee, PPG Industries Foundation

Verheij, Richard H.: executive vice president, general counsel, UST Inc.

Catholic University America

Kaman, Charles Huron: chairman, president, chief executive officer, director, Kaman Corp.

LaMacchia, John Thomas: trustee, Cincinnati Bell Foundation, Inc.; president, chief executive officer, director, Cincinnati Bell Inc.

Rhodes, James Thomas: president, chief executive officer, director, Dominion Resources, Inc.

Williams, Karen Hastie: director, Fannie Mae Foundation

Catholic University of Milan

Ferrari, Giannantonio A.: director, Honeywell Foundation; president, chief operating officer, director, Honeywell International Inc.

Centenary College

Bradford, William Edward: chairman, director, Halliburton Co.

Central Methodist College

Orscheln, William L.: treasurer, Orscheln Industries Foundation, Inc.

Central Michigan University

Carbone, Anthony J.: vice chairman, director, Dow Chemical Co.

Wolf, Gregory H.: president, chief operating officer, director, Humana, Inc.

Central Missouri State University

Jobe, G. David: director, MFA Foundation; senior vice president, MFA Inc.

Centre College of Kentucky

Hower, Frank Beard, Jr.: vice chairman, Anthem Foundation, Inc.

Chartered Institute Management Accountants UK

Bible, Geoffrey Cyril: director, New York Stock Exchange Foundation, Inc.; chairman, chief executive officer, director, Philip Morris Companies Inc.

Chicago State University

Kaden, Ellen O.: trustee, Campbell Soup Foundation

O'Brien, Richard T.: executive vice president, chief operating officer, PacifiCorp; member, PacifiCorp Foundation

Chittagong University

Thawerbhoy, Nazim G.: controller, Jacobs Engineering Foundation

Choate School

Kohler, Herbert Vollrath, Jr.: chairman, president, director, Kohler Co.

Citadel

Tobias, Steven C.: vice chairman, chief operating officer, Norfolk Southern Corp.; director, Norfolk Southern Foundation

City College of New York

Fishman, Jerald G.: president, chief executive officer, director, Analog Devices, Inc.

Gober, Ira: chairman, chief financial officer, partner, director, Associated Food Stores; director, Associated Food Stores Charitable Foundation

Grove, Andrew S.: chairman, Intel Corp.

Roth, Michael I.: chairman, chief executive officer, director, MONY Group (The); director, MONY Life Insurance of New York (The)

City University of New York

Auguste, MacDonald: treasurer, Rayonier Foundation

Bush, Norman: vice president, Fort James Corp.

Catell, Robert Barry: chairman, chief executive officer, Brooklyn Union

Dubin, Stephen Victor: vice president, secretary, Farber Foundation

Granoff, Mark Howard: vice president, United Wisconsin Services Foundation

Griffith, Alan Richard: vice chairman, Bank of New York Co., Inc.

Joseph, Burton: chairman, director, Playboy Foundation

Kerr, Steven: director, GE Fund; vice president corporate leadership development, General Electric Co.

Kogan, Richard Jay: chairman, chief executive officer, Schering-Plough Corp.; trustee, member, Schering-Plough Foundation

Kurtz, Melvin H.: secretary, director, Chesebrough Foundation

Levine, Kenneth M.: executive vice president, chief investment officer, director, MONY Group (The); director, MONY Life Insurance of New York (The)

Levine, Ralph: president, chief operating officer, director, Carter-Wallace, Inc.

Needleman, Harry: secretary, Cantor, Fitzgerald Foundation; executive vice president, general counsel, Cantor, Fitzgerald Securities Corp.

Schlauch, Walter F.: group vice president, National Starch & Chemical Co.

Siegel, Samuel: vice chairman, secretary, treasurer, chief financial officer, director, Nucor Corp.; director, Nucor Foundation

Urkowitz, Michael: senior vice president, Chase Manhattan Bank, NA; trustee, Chase Manhattan Foundation

Yablon, Leonard Harold: secretary-treasurer, Forbes Foundation

City University of New York Bernard M. Baruch College

Aldinger, William F., III: chairman, chief executive officer, director, Household International Inc.

Marron, Donald Baird: chairman, chief executive officer, director, Paine Webber; trustee, Paine Webber Foundation

City University of New York Brooklyn College

Kasputys, Joseph Edward: chairman, trustee, Hitachi Foundation

City University of New York City College

Engel, Joel Stanley: vice president technology, Ameritech Corp.

Claremont Graduate School

Lachman, Marguerite Leanne: trustee, Chicago Title and Trust Co. Foundation

Claremont McKenna College

Edwards, John Kenneth: executive president, group president power generation, Cummins Engine Co., Inc.; director, Cummins Engine Foundation

Franklin, Marc Scott: senior vice president strategic planning, Pacific Mutual Life Insurance Co.

Clarion University of Pennsylvania

Dean, John W., III: vice president, treasurer, Rubbermaid Inc.

Clark College

King, Reatha Clark: director, Fuller Co. Foundation (H.B.); president, executive director, General Mills Foundation

McKamey, William: general manager, director, Public Service Co. of Oklahoma

Clark University

Gillis, Edwin J.: president, Lotus Development Corp.

Pero, Perry R.: senior executive vice president, chief financial officer, Northern Trust Co.

Clarkson University

Correnti, John D.: president, chief executive officer, director, Nucor Corp.

Kober, Roger W.: chairman, chief executive officer, director, Rochester Gas & Electric Corp.

Clemson University

Moser, Robert W.: executive vice president, Springs Industries, Inc.

Perry, James M.: vice chairman, Stonecutter Mills Corp.

Cleveland College

Mandel, Jack N.: director, Premier Industrial Corp.

Cleveland Institute of Technology

Borman, Marlene: vice president, director, Borman Fund (The)

Cleveland State University

Brodie, Nancy S.: executive vice president, chief financial officer, Penn Mutual Life Insurance Co.

Hopkins, Thomas E.: vice president human resources, Sherwin-Williams Co.; assistant secretary, trustee, Sherwin-Williams Foundation

Hughes, Timothy W.: senior vice president, Cox Enterprises Inc.; trustee, Cox Foundation (James M.)

Thompson, John D.: treasurer, Dexter Corp. Foundation

Cleveland-Marshall College of Law

Pitorak, Larry John: senior vice president finance, treasurer, chief financial officer, Sherwin-Williams Co.; secretary, treasurer, trustee, Sherwin-Williams Foundation

Coe College

Bonvino, Frank W.: vice president, secretary, general counsel, International Multifoods Corp.

White, Walter Lucas: secretary, treasurer, trustee, Kemper Foundation (James S.)

Colby College

Cookson, John Simmons: vice president finance, treasurer, assistant secretary, Kingsbury Corp.; trustee, Kingsbury Fund

Colgate University

Bossidy, Lawrence Arthur: chairman, director, AlliedSignal Foundation Inc.; chairman, chief executive officer, director, AlliedSignal Inc.

Browning, Peter C.: chief executive officer, president, director, Sonoco Products Co.

Geier, Philip Henry, Jr.: chairman, president, chief executive officer, Interpublic Group of Companies, Inc.

King, Roger Leo: vice president, officer, Graco, Inc.

Loos, Henry J.: secretary, Charter Manufacturing Co. Foundation

Manzi, James Paul: president, director, Lotus Development Corp.

Mariani, Harry F.: president, treasurer, director, Banfi Vintners; director, Banfi Vintners Foundation

Colgate University Darden School of Business Administration

Dickson, Thomas W.: vice president, Dickson Foundation

College William & Mary

Gardner, Jeff: chief financial officer, ALLTEL Corp.

College of Idaho

Graves, Ronald Norman: secretary, Simplot Foundation (J.R.)

Keen, J. LaMont: vice president, chief financial officer, Idaho Power Co.

College of Notre Dame

Koch, David Andrew: president, Graco Foundation; chairman, director, Graco, Inc.

College of Saint Thomas

Iverson, Kenneth A.: vice president, corporate secretary, Ecolab Inc.

Koch, David Andrew: president, Graco Foundation; chairman, director, Graco, Inc.

Mead, Susan W. A.: vice president, ReliaStar Financial Corp.; director, ReliaStar Foundation

College of William & Mary

Bertrand, Frederic Howard: chairman, Central Vermont Public Service Corp.

Crandall, Robert Lloyd: director, AMR Corp.

Fricks, William Peavy: chairman, chief executive officer, Newport News Shipbuilding

Mac Kimm, Margaret (Pontius) 'Mardie': trustee, Chicago Title and Trust Co. Foundation

May, T. Michael: president, Hawaiian Electric Co., Inc.; director, Hawaiian Electric Industries Charitable Foundation

McGlothlin, James W.: chief executive officer, United Coal Co. Charitable Foundation; chairman, chief executive officer, United Co.

Plumeri, Joseph James, II: president, Citigroup

Scher, Barry F.: vice president public affairs, Giant Food Inc.

Scripps, Charles Edward: chairman executive committee, director, vice president, Scripps Co. (E.W.); member, Scripps Howard Foundation

Sharp, Richard L.: trustee, Circuit City Foundation; chairman, chief executive officer, director, Circuit City Stores, Inc.

Wolf, Henry C.: vice chairman, chief financial officer, Norfolk Southern Corp.; vice president finance, Norfolk Southern Foundation

College of William & Mary Marshall-Wythe School & Law College

White, James M., III: general counsel, Universal Leaf Foundation; senior vice president, general counsel, assistant secretary, Universal Leaf Tobacco Co., Inc.

College of William and Mary

Mooney, J. Robert: senior vice president, chief financial officer, Ethyl Corp.

College of Wooster

McClung, James Allen: vice president, director, FMC Foundation

Smucker, Timothy Paul: chairman, director, Smucker Co. (JM)

College of the Holy Cross

Anderson, John: secretary, Toshiba America Foundation
Boyle, Richard James: vice chairman, director, Chase Manhattan Bank, NA; trustee, Chase Manhattan Foundation
Cawley, Michael J.: vice president risk management, Eastern Enterprises
Clark, Richard McCourt: senior vice president, general counsel, secretary, Kellogg Co.; vice president, trustee, Kellogg Co. Twenty-Five Year Employees' Fund Inc.
Clemente, Constantine Louis: chairman, Pfizer Foundation; executive vice president corporate affairs, secretary, corporate counsel, Pfizer Inc.
Connolly, Gerald Edward: trustee, Reinhart Family Foundation (D. B. and Marjorie)
Fino, Raymond M.: second vice president, Warner-Lambert Charitable Foundation; vice president human resources, Warner-Lambert Co.
McKenna, William P.: vice president finance, chief financial officer, treasurer, Bourns, Inc.
O'Brien, William J., III: trustee, DaimlerChrysler Corp. Fund
O'Leary, Thomas Howard: chairman, Burlington Resources Foundation
Pajak, John Joseph: president, chief operating officer, Massachusetts Mutual Life Insurance Co.
Peterson, William E.: general counsel, Sierra Pacific Resources
Rehm, Jack Daniel: chairman emeritus, director, Meredith Corp.
Schara, Charles Gerard: treasurer, GEICO Corp.; assistant treasurer, director, GEICO Philanthropic Foundation
Spina, David Anthony: president, chief operating officer, State Street Bank & Trust Co.
Tracy, Emmet E., Jr.: president, chief executive officer, director, Alma Piston Co.; president, Tracy Fund (Emmet and Frances)
White, Britton, Jr.: vice president, El Paso Energy Foundation

Colorado School of Mines

Beach, Roger C.: chairman, chief executive officer, director, Unocal Corp.
Elkins, Lloyd Edwin, Junior: vice president, Chevron Corp.
McKee, Robert E., III: executive vice president corporate strategy & development, du Pont de Nemours & Co. (E.I.)
Whisler, J. Steven: chairman, president, chief executive officer, Phelps Dodge Corp.

Colorado State University

Martin, JoAnn M.: controller, Ameritas Charitable Foundation; senior vice president, partner, chief financial officer, Ameritas Life Insurance Corp.
McConnell, Richard Lynn: senior vice president, director research, Pioneer Hi-Bred International, Inc.
Scott, Walter, Jr.: member contributions committee, Kiewit Companies Foundation
Stancato, Kenneth J.: vice president, controller, Weyerhaeuser Co.; controller, Weyerhaeuser Co. Foundation
Stuebgen, William J.: vice president, controller, chief acct officer, APL Ltd.
Thomasson, Dan King: vice president, trustee, Scripps Howard Foundation

Columbia College

Fine, Roger Seth: vice president, general counsel, Johnson & Johnson; president, Johnson & Johnson Family of Companies Contribution Fund
Heine, Spencer H.: executive vice president, secretary, Montgomery Ward & Co., Inc.; president, Montgomery Ward Foundation
Krueger, Harvey M.: trustee, Barry Foundation
Pyke, John Secrest, Jr.: president, trustee, Hanna Co. Foundation (M.A.); vice president, secretary, general counsel, Hanna Co. (M.A.)
Villanueva, Edward: trustee, Circuit City Foundation

Colorado College

Berkley, William S.: president, chief executive officer, director, Tension Envelope Corp.; director, Tension Envelope Foundation

Columbia College School Graduate Faculties

Pyke, John Secrest, Jr.: president, trustee, Hanna Co. Foundation (M.A.); vice president, secretary, general counsel, Hanna Co. (M.A.)

Columbia University

Biehl, George C.: senior vice president, chief financial officer, corporate secretary, director, Southwest Gas Corp.; trustee, Southwest Gas Corp. Foundation
Biggs, James: president, Peoples Bank
Bigham, James John: executive vice president, chief financial officer, director, Continental Grain Co.
Bijur, Peter I.: chairman, chief executive officer, Texaco Inc.
Bleustein, Jeffrey L.: president, chief executive officer, director, Harley-Davidson Co.
Bowles, Crandall Close: president, chief executive officer, chairman, director, Springs Industries, Inc.
Brennan, Alice C.: vice president, secretary, Bristol-Myers Squibb Co.; secretary, Bristol-Myers Squibb Foundation Inc.
Broadhead, James Lowell: chairman, president, chief executive officer, director, Florida Power & Light Co.; chief executive officer, director, FPL Group Foundation, Inc.
Brown, Harold, PhD: chairman, Mattel Foundation
Burak, Howard Paul: secretary, director, Sony U.S.A. Foundation Inc.
Byck, Joseph S.: vice president, Union Carbide Foundation
Calise, Nicholas James: vice president, associate general counsel, secretary, BFGoodrich Co.; secretary, Goodrich Foundation, Inc. (B.F.)
Calise, William Joseph, Junior: senior vice president, secretary, general counsel, Rockwell International Corp.
Canning, John Beckman: secretary, Rayonier Foundation
Chazen, Jerome A.: trustee, Claiborne Foundation (Liz); co-founder, chairman, director, Liz Claiborne, Inc.
Clark, Howard Longstreth, Jr.: vice chairman, Walter Industries Inc.
Clemente, Constantine Louis: chairman, Pfizer Foundation; executive vice president corporate affairs, secretary, corporate counsel, Pfizer Inc.
Cohen, Joseph M.: president, director, Cowen Foundation; chairman, chief executive officer, S.G. Cowen
Connolly, Charles H.: senior vice president corporate affairs & investor relations, Whitman Corp.; president, Whitman Corp. Foundation
Copeland, Frederick C., Jr.: director, Aetna Foundation
Corby, Francis Michael, Jr.: executive vice president finance & administration, chief financial officer, Harnischfeger Industries; treasurer, Harnischfeger Industries Foundation
Coyle, Dennis Patrick: secretary, director, FPL Group Foundation, Inc.
Curley, John J.: chairman, chief executive officer, director, Gannett Co., Inc.; chairman, Gannett Foundation
D'Andrade, Hugh Alfred: trustee, member, Schering-Plough Foundation
Dillon, John T.: chairman, chief executive officer, director, International Paper Co.
Donehue, J. Douglas: managing director, Post and Courier Foundation
Eccles, Spencer Fox: chairman, chief executive officer, director, First Security Bank of Idaho NA
Evans, Robert Sheldon: chairman, chief executive officer, Crane Co.; chairman, president, director, Crane Foundation
Evanson, Paul John: president, treasurer, director, FPL Group Foundation, Inc.
Exley, Charles Errol, Jr.: trustee, Merck Co. Foundation
Fjelstul, Dean M.: senior vice president, chief financial officer, Walter Industries Inc.
Forstmann, Theodore J.: chairman, Gulfstream Aerospace Corp.
Friedman, Stephen James: senior advisor, Goldman Sachs Group
Geier, Philip Henry, Jr.: chairman, president, chief executive officer, Interpublic Group of Companies, Inc.
Goeltz, Richard Karl: vice chairman, chief financial officer, American Express Co.
Goodman, Helen G.: senior vice president, Hartford (The)
Gorman, Maureen V.: vice president, GTE Foundation
Graham, Patricia Albjerg, PhD: trustee, Hitachi Foundation
Heiner, Clyde Mont: executive vice president, Questar Corp.
Hergenhan, Joyce: director, president, GE Fund
Hoyt, Charles Orcutt: director, Carter-Wallace Foundation; chairman executive committee, director, Carter-Wallace, Inc.
Hunter, Robert D.: trustee, Chase Manhattan Foundation
Jones, Ross: senior vice president, chief financial officer, Knight Ridder
Kaden, Ellen O.: trustee, Campbell Soup Foundation
Keegan, Peter: senior vice president, Loews Foundation
Kiener, Dan W.: member screening committee, PPG Industries Foundation
Krueger, Harvey M.: trustee, Barry Foundation
LaMantia, Charles Robert: president, chief executive officer, director, Little, Inc. (Arthur D.)
Levinson, Donald M.: director, CIGNA Corp.
Manfredi, John Frederick: member administration committee, Nabisco Foundation Trust
McCorkindale, Douglas H.: vice chairman, president, Gannett Co., Inc.; president, Gannett Foundation
Meyerson, Martin: director, Panasonic Foundation
Millstein, Ira M.: partner, Weil, Gotshal & Manges Corp.; president, director, Weil, Gotshal & Manges Foundation
Montrone, Paul Michael: vice president, partner, Winthrop Foundation
Muth, Robert James: president, director, ASARCO Foundation
Neely, Walter Emerson: vice president, Humana Foundation
Nichols, Wade Hampton, III: vice president, Revlon Foundation Inc.; executive vice president, general counsel, Revlon Inc.
Patel, Homi Burjor: president, chief operating officer, director, Hartmarx Corp.
Patterson, Michael E.: vice chairman, Morgan & Co. Inc. (J.P.)
Paumgarten, Nicholas Biddle: managing director, Scripps Co. (E.W.); member, Scripps Howard Foundation
Penglase, Frank Dennis: vice president, treasurer,
Perez, Arnaldo: assistant vice president, secretary,

Arison Foundation; vice president, general counsel, secretary, Carnival Corp.

Polin, Jane Louise: manager, comptroller, GE Fund

Resnick, Alan H.: treasurer, Bausch & Lomb Foundation, Inc.; vice president, treasurer, Bausch & Lomb Inc.

Rompala, Richard M.: president, chief executive officer, director, chairman, Valspar Corp.; vice president, Valspar Foundation

Rosett, Richard Nathaniel: trustee, Kemper Foundation (James S.)

Ross, Arthur: senior vice president, Central National-Gottesman; director, Central National-Gottesman Foundation

Rubin, Donald S.: senior vice president investor relations, McGraw-Hill Companies, Inc.

Ruggiero, Anthony W.: executive vice president, chief financial officer, Olin Corp.

Sacks, David G.: trustee, Bronfman Foundation/Joseph E. Seagram & Sons, Inc. Fund (Samuel)

Sanders, Lewis A.: trustee, Bernstein & Co. Foundation, Inc. (Sanford C.); chairman, chief executive officer, Bernstein & Co., Inc. (Sanford C.)

Scicutella, John Vincent: trustee, Chase Manhattan Foundation

Shapiro, Isaac: chairman, secretary, trustee, Ise Cultural Foundation

Shapiro, Robert B.: chairman, president, chief executive officer, director, Monsanto Co.

Sulzberger, Arthur Ochs, Sr.: director, New York Times Co.; chairman, director, New York Times Co. Foundation

Taurel, Sidney: chairman, president, chief executive officer, Lilly & Co. (Eli)

Thomas, Franklin Augustine: director, CBS Foundation

Typermass, Arthur G.: senior vice president, treasurer, Metropolitan Life Insurance Co.

Vagelos, Pindaros Roy: trustee, Prudential Insurance Co. of America

Viault, Raymond: vice chairman, director, General Mills, Inc.

Wallach, Ira D.: chairman, Central National-Gottesman; executive vice president, Central National-Gottesman Foundation

Walton, S. Robson: member, Wal-Mart Foundation; chairman, director, Wal-Mart Stores, Inc.

Weyers, Larry Lee: chief executive officer, chairman, director, Wisconsin Public Service Corp.; president, chief executive officer, Wisconsin Public Service Foundation, Inc.

Wiley, Bradford, II: chairman, director, Wiley & Sons (John)

Willes, Mark Hinckley: chairman, president, chief executive officer, Times Mirror Co.; chairman, Times Mirror Foundation

ZoBell, Karl: vice president, trustee, Copley Foundation (James S.)

Columbia University Executive Management Program

Escarra, Vicki: executive vice president customer service, Delta Air Lines, Inc.

Columbia University Graduate Executive Program in Business Administration

Quesnel, Gregory L.: president, chief executive officer, director, CNF Transportation, Inc.

Columbia University School of Business Administration

Bundschuh, George August William: director, New York Life Foundation

Mulholland, Charles Bradley: executive vice president, director, Alexander & Baldwin Foundation; executive vice president, Alexander & Baldwin, Inc.

Columbia University School of Law

Miller, Harvey R.: secretary, director, Weil, Gotshal & Manges Foundation

Pyke, John Secrest, Jr.: president, trustee, Hanna Co. Foundation (M.A.); vice president, secretary, general counsel, Hanna Co. (M.A.)

Columbus College

Burts, Stephen L., Jr.: president, treasurer, chief financial officer, Synovus Financial Corp.

Commonwealth College

Harrell, Henry Howze: director, Universal Leaf Foundation; chairman, chief executive officer, director, Universal Leaf Tobacco Co., Inc.

Concord College

Martin, Dezora M.: corporate secretary, Norfolk Southern Corp.; secretary, Norfolk Southern Foundation

Concordia College

Lundhagen, E. Wayne: treasurer, KN Energy Foundation

Connecticut College

Nickerson, Lucille M.: secretary, Aetna Foundation; vice president, corporate secretary, Aetna, Inc.

Yeomans, Janet L.: treasurer, director, 3M Foundation

Cooper Union

Schwartz, Richard: chairman, president, chief executive officer, director, Alliant Techsystems

Cornell University

Aylesworth, William Andrew: treasurer, Texas Instruments Foundation; chief financial officer, treasurer, Texas Instruments Inc.

Beadle, Robert Sheldon: senior vice president corporate development, Ultramar Diamond Shamrock Corp.

Bleustein, Jeffrey L.: president, chief executive officer, director, Harley-Davidson Co.

Bodman, Samuel Wright, III: chairman, chief executive officer, director, Cabot Corp.; president, director, Cabot Corp. Foundation

Broadhead, James Lowell: chairman, president, chief executive officer, director, Florida Power & Light Co.; chief executive officer, director, FPL Group Foundation, Inc.

Browning, Laurance LeWright, Jr.: member public policy committee, Emerson Charitable Trust; director, Emerson Electric Co.

Burak, Howard Paul: secretary, director, Sony U.S.A. Foundation Inc.

Call, Robert V., Jr.: chairman, trustee, Agrilink Foods/Pro-Fac Foundation

Campbell, Van C.: vice chairman, chief financial officer, chief administrative officer, director, Corning Inc.; trustee, Corning Inc. Foundation

Chapple, Thomas Leslie: senior vice president, general counsel, secretary, Gannett Co., Inc.; secretary, Gannett Foundation

Clark, Richard McCourt: senior vice president, general counsel, secretary, Kellogg Co.; vice president, trustee, Kellogg Co. Twenty-Five Year Employees' Fund Inc.

Coors, Peter Hanson: vice president, director, Coors Brewing Co.

Cottrell, G. Walton: senior vice president, chief financial officer, Carpenter Technology Corp.

Donahue, Jeffrey H.: senior vice president, chief financial officer, Rouse Co.

Douglass, Robert Royal: trustee, Chase Manhattan Foundation

Draper, Ernest Linn, Jr.: chairman, president, chief executive officer, director, American Electric Power

Elliott, Anson Wright: vice president, trustee, Chase Manhattan Foundation

Francis, Cheryl A.: executive vice president, chief financial officer, Donnelley & Sons Co. (R.R.)

Friedman, Stephen James: senior advisor, Goldman Sachs Group

Fuller, Harry Laurance: co-chairman, director, BP Amoco Corp.

Glancy, John E.: corporate executive vice president, chairman, Telcordia Technologies

Golub, Harvey: chairman, chief executive officer, director, American Express Co.; trustee, American Express Foundation

Grass, Martin Lehrman: chairman, chief executive officer, director, Rite Aid Corp.

Gray, Charles Agustus: vice president technology, Cabot Corp.; director, Cabot Corp. Foundation

Hardis, Stephen Roger: chairman, chief executive officer, director, Eaton Corp.

Hyman, Morton Peter: vice president, director, OSG Foundation; president, director, Overseas Shipholding Group Inc.

Iverson, Francis Kenneth: chairman, director, Nucor Corp.; director, Nucor Foundation

Jennings, James Burnett: president, Hunt Oil Co.

Johnson, Samuel Curtis: chairman, director, president, Johnson & Son (S.C.); chairman, trustee, Johnson Wax Fund (S.C.)

Kaden, Ellen O.: trustee, Campbell Soup Foundation

Kirby, William Joseph: vice president, director, FMC Foundation

Knight, Charles Field: chairman, chief executive officer, Emerson Electric Co.

Lee, Charles Robert: chairman, chief executive officer, director, GTE Corp.; chief executive officer, trustee, GTE Foundation

Lyall, Katharine Culbert: trustee, Kemper Foundation (James S.)

Mariani, John J.: chairman, chief executive officer, director, Banfi Vintners; director, Banfi Vintners Foundation

Marks, Michael J.: vice president, general counsel, secretary, Alexander & Baldwin, Inc.

McCormick, William Thomas, Jr.: chairman, chief executive officer, director, Consumers Energy Co.; chairman, Consumers Energy Foundation

McNally, Alan G.: chairman, chief executive officer, Harris Trust & Savings Bank

McNamara, Anne H.: senior vice president, general counsel, AMR Corp.

McNamara, Kevin J.: president, director, Chemed Corp.; secretary, trustee, Chemed Foundation

Mellowes, John A.: chairman, chief executive officer, director, Charter Manufacturing Co.; vice president, treasurer, Charter Manufacturing Co. Foundation

Mulcahy, J. Patrick: co-chief executive officer, Ralston Purina Co.

Oran, Stuart I.: director, United Airlines Foundation; senior vice president international, United Airlines Inc.

Platt, Lewis Emmett: chairman, Hewlett-Packard Co.

Ridgley, Robert Louis: chairman, director, Northwest Natural Gas Co.

Rothberg, Robert: vice president, general counsel, Cabot Corp.; director, Cabot Corp. Foundation

Rukeyser, Robert James: senior vice president corporate affairs, Fortune Brands, Inc.
Shanks, David C.: trustee, Little Foundation (Arthur D.); vice president human resources, Little, Inc. (Arthur D.)
Slagle, Robert F.: director, Alcoa Foundation; executive vice president human resources and communications, Alcoa Inc.
Slovin, Bruce: president, director, Revlon Inc.
Smith, Frederick C.: chairman, trustee, Huffy Foundation, Inc.
Staley, Robert Wayne: vice chairman Asia Pacific, Emerson Electric Co.
Staley, Warren R.: president, chief executive officer, Cargill Inc.; chairman, Excel Corp.
Sullivan, Laura P.: vice president, secretary, director, State Farm Companies Foundation; vice president, secretary, counsel, State Farm Mutual Automobile Insurance Co.
Suter, Albert E.: senior vice chairman, chief administrative officer, director, Emerson Electric Co.
Tisch, James S.: president, chief executive officer, director, CNA
Vinney, Les C.: senior vice president, chief financial officer, BFGoodrich Co.
Weill, Sanford I.: chairman, chief executive officer, Citibank Corp.; chairman, Citigroup Foundation

Cornell University Graduate School Business & Public Administration

Weill, Sanford I.: chairman, chief executive officer, Citibank Corp.; chairman, Citigroup Foundation

Cornell University Law School

Scott, David J.: secretary, United Distillers & Vintners North America

Creighton University

Egan, Thomas P., Jr.: officer, Valmont Foundation
Feller, Mimi A.: senior vice president public affairs & government relations, Gannett Co., Inc.; vice president, Gannett Foundation
Fitzgerald, William Allingham: chairman, director, Commercial Federal Corp.
Huerter, M. Jane: executive vice president, corporate secretary, Mutual of Omaha Insurance Co.
Lempka, Arnold W., MD: chairman, director, Physicians Mutual Insurance Co.; director, Physicians Mutual Insurance Co. Foundation
Reed, Robert A.: president, chief executive officer, Physicians Mutual Insurance Co.; president, director, Physicians Mutual Insurance Co. Foundation
Rohde, Bruce: vice chairman, chief executive officer, ConAgra, Inc.
Vondrasek, Frank Charles, Jr.: president, Madison Gas & Electric Foundation
Zenner, Patrick J.: trustee, Hoffmann-La Roche Foundation; president, chief executive officer, director, Hoffmann-La Roche Inc.

Dartmouth College

Armstrong, C. Michael: chairman, chief executive officer, AT&T Corp.
Barrett, Allen M., Jr.: chairman, McCormick & Co. Inc.
Belcher, Donald D.: chairman, president, chief executive officer, director, Banta Corp.; vice president, director, Banta Corp. Foundation
Biggs, James: president, Peoples Bank
Brennan, John J.: chairman, chief executive officer, Vanguard Group; president, Vanguard Group Foundation
Buhrmaster, Robert C.: president, chief executive officer, director, chairman, Jostens, Inc.
Burdett, Kathleen: vice president, chief financial officer, Dexter Corp.; vice president, Dexter Corp. Foundation
Campbell, Cheryl Nichols: operation service advisory group, Cincinnati Bell Inc.
Carpenter, William M.: chief executive officer, director, chairman, Bausch & Lomb Inc.
Chemerow, David I.: executive vice president, chief financial officer, Playboy Enterprises Inc.
Cline, Robert Stanley: chairman, chief executive officer, director, Airborne Freight Corp.
Cohen, Jonathan L.: secretary, director, Goldman Sachs Foundation
Coyle, Dennis Patrick: secretary, director, FPL Group Foundation, Inc.
Crane, David W.: trustee, Crane & Co. Fund; chief financial officer, Crane & Co., Inc.
DiSilvestro, Anthony P.: vice president, treasurer, Campbell Soup Co.; treasurer, Campbell Soup Foundation
Donahue, Richard King: vice chairman, Nike, Inc.
Donnelley, James R.: vice chairman, Donnelley & Sons Co. (R.R.)
Douglass, Robert Royal: trustee, Chase Manhattan Foundation
Farrington, Hugh G.: president, chief executive officer, director, Hannaford Brothers Co.
Fjelstul, Dean M.: senior vice president, chief financial officer, Walter Industries Inc.
Flaws, James B.: senior vice president, chief financial officer, treasurer, Corning Inc.; trustee, Corning Inc. Foundation
Fleming, Richard Harrison: chief financial officer, senior vice president, USG Corp.; treasurer, trustee, USG Foundation
Gammill, Lee Morgan, Jr.: director, New York Life Foundation; vice chairman, director, New York Life Insurance Co.
Geissinger, Frederick: chairman, chief executive officer, prs, American General Finance
Geissinger, Frederick Wallace: chairman, chief executive officer, president, director, American General Finance Foundation
Gerstner, Louis Vincent, Jr.: chairman, chief executive officer, director, International Business Machines Corp.
Goodyear, William M.: trustee, Bank of America Foundation
Hale, James Thomas: senior vice president, general counsel, secretary, Dayton Hudson; trustee, Target Foundation
Hall, Donald Joyce: chairman board, director, Hallmark Cards Inc.; chairman, Hallmark Corporate Foundation
Harris, Edward D., Jr.: director, Genentech Foundation for Biomedical Sciences
Harvey, A. Mosby, Jr.: secretary, HON Industries Charitable Foundation; vice president, secretary, general counsel, HON Industries Inc.
Herringer, Frank Casper: president, chief executive officer, director, chairman, Transamerica Corp.; vice chairman, director, Transamerica Foundation
Higgs, John H.: director, IBJ Foundation
Hoffmann, Richard W.: general counsel, Employers Mutual Casualty Co.
Howison, George Everett: vice president, Burlington Resources Foundation
Jewett, George Frederick, Jr.: trustee, Potlatch Foundation II
Kelley, Bruce Gunn: vice president, director, Employers Mutual Charitable Foundation
Levy, Richard M.: president, chief executive officer, Varian Medical Systems, Inc.
Lindenauer, Arthur: executive vice president, chief financial officer, Schlumberger Ltd. (USA)
Little, Gene E.: trustee, advisor, Timken Co. Charitable Trust (The); secretary, treasurer, trustee, Timken Co. Educational Fund
Masin, Michael Terry: vice chairman, president international, director, GTE Corp.; trustee, GTE Foundation
Mitau, Lee R.: executive vice president, general counsel, secretary, U.S. Bancorp
Roessler-Alsoa, Ernest C.: president, chief executive officer, director, CCB Financial Corp.
Schoch, Steven J.: vice president, treasurer, Times Mirror Co.; treasurer, chief financial officer, Times Mirror Foundation
Scholtens, Jean A.: vice president, treasurer, Eastern Enterprises
Siegel, Louis Pendelton: chairman, president, chief executive officer, chief operating officer, Potlatch Corp.; vice president, trustee, Potlatch Foundation II
Steffens, John Laundon: executive vice president, Merrill Lynch & Co., Inc.
Sulzberger, Arthur Ochs, Sr.: director, New York Times Co.; chairman, director, New York Times Co. Foundation
Wolf, Thomas W.: trustee, York Federal Savings & Loan Foundation
Wolff, Jesse David: treasurer, director, Weil, Gotshal & Manges Foundation

Dartmouth College Amos Tuck Graduate School of Business Administration

Berkley, William S.: president, chief executive officer, director, Tension Envelope Corp.; director, Tension Envelope Foundation
Chemerow, David I.: executive vice president, chief financial officer, Playboy Enterprises Inc.
Lindenauer, Arthur: executive vice president, chief financial officer, Schlumberger Ltd. (USA)
Roessler-Alsoa, Ernest C.: president, chief executive officer, director, CCB Financial Corp.

Dartmouth College Amos Tuck School Executive Program

Schiro, James J.: chairman, senior partner, PricewaterhouseCoopers

Dartmouth College Graduate School of Credit & Finance Management

Pollicino, Joseph Anthony: executive vice chairman, CIT Group Foundation; vice chairman, director, CIT Group, Inc. (The)

Davidson College

Belk, John Montgomery: member board advisors, Belk Foundation; chairman, Belk-Simpson Department Stores
Causey, John Paul, Jr.: senior vice president, secretary, general counsel, Chesapeake Corp.; chairman, trustee, Chesapeake Corp. Foundation
Dickson, Rush Stuart: chairman, Dickson Foundation
Robinson, E. B., Jr.: chairman, chief executive officer, director, Deposit Guaranty National Bank

Dayton

Murray, James E.: chief operating officer, senior vice president, Humana Foundation

DeFiance College

Smart, George M.: trustee, Commercial Intertech Foundation

DePaul University

Berg, Thomas C.: vice president, general counsel, secretary, Amsted Industries Inc.
Bloom, Larry L.: chief financial officer, Lee Enterprises
Cole, Robert A.: chief financial officer, senior vice president, American General Finance; senior vice president, chief financial officer, director, American General Finance Foundation

Delo, Robert Paul: director, Chicago Tribune Foundation
Fuller, Harry Laurance: co-chairman, director, BP Amoco Corp.
Grade, Jeffery T.: chairman, chief executive officer, director, Harnischfeger Industries; president, Harnischfeger Industries Foundation
Kearney, Christopher J.: trustee, SPX Foundation
Koenemann, Carl F.: chief financial officer, executive vice president, Motorola Inc.
Lambe, James F.: senior vice president human resources, Nalco Chemical Co.; director, Nalco Foundation
Mack, Raymond Phillip: director, Arvin Foundation; vice president human resources, Arvin Industries, Inc.
McKenna, Andrew James: director, Aon Foundation
Moore, Patrick J.: vice president, Smurfit-Stone Container Corp.
Pehlke, Richard W.: vice president, treasurer, Ameritech Corp.
Piet, William M.: vice president, director, Wrigley Co. Foundation (Wm. Jr.); vice president corporate affairs, secretary, assistant to president, Wrigley Co. (Wm. Jr.)
Shapiro, Howard: executive vice president, general counsel, Playboy Enterprises Inc.; director, Playboy Foundation
Shiel, William A.: senior vice president facilities development, Walgreen Co.
Spindler, George S.: senior vice president law & corporate affairs, BP Amoco Corp.; chairman, director, BP Amoco Foundation
Stone, Jerome H.: vice president, secretary, treasurer, Stone Foundation
Stryker, Steven Charles: director, Shell Oil Co. Foundation

DePauw University

Baker, James Kendrick: chairman, director, Arvin Foundation; vice chairman, director, Arvin Industries, Inc.
Bickner, Bruce P.: chairman, chief executive officer, director, DeKalb Genetics Corp.
Coffin, Sarah R.: director, Fuller Co. Foundation (H.B.); vice president specialty group, Fuller Co. (H.B.)
Ellis, William H.: director, Piper Jaffray Companies Foundation
Ewing, Stephen E.: president, chief executive officer, director, Michigan Consolidated Gas Co.
Kendall, J. William: chairman, director, Arvin Foundation
Pulliam, Eugene Smith: vice president, director, Central Newspapers Foundation
Sanger, Stephen W.: chairman, trustee, General Mills Foundation; chairman, chief executive officer, director, General Mills, Inc.
Sharpe, Robert Francis, Jr.: senior vice president public affairs, general counsel, PepsiCo, Inc.
Solso, Theodore Matthew: president, chief operating officer, director, Cummins Engine Co., Inc.; director, Cummins Engine Foundation
Stewart, James Gathings: executive vice president, chief financial officer, CIGNA Corp.
Taylor, John I.: director, Zenith Electronics Corp.

DeVry Institute of Technology

Knauss, Dalton L.: trustee, Kemper Foundation (James S.)

Del Mar College

Jennings, James Burnett: president, Hunt Oil Co.

Denison College

Bemis, Richard A.: president, Bemis Family Foundation (F.K.); president, chief executive officer, director, Bemis Manufacturing Co.

Denison University

Bowen, William Gordon, PhD: trustee, Merck Co. Foundation
Daberko, David A.: chairman, chief executive officer, National City Corp.
Eisner, Michael Dammann: president, trustee, Disney Co. Foundation (Walt); chairman, chief executive officer, director, Disney Co. (Walt)
Esrey, William Todd: chairman, chief executive officer, Sprint Corp.
MacLeay, Thomas H.: president, chief operating officer, National Life of Vermont
McConnell, William Thompson: chairman, ceo, Park National Bank; chairman, Park National Corp. Foundation
McNamara, Kevin J.: president, director, Chemed Corp.; secretary, trustee, Chemed Foundation
Standen, Craig Clayton: senior vice president corporate development, Scripps Co. (E.W.)
Wehling, Robert Louis: global marketing, government relations officer, Procter & Gamble Co.; president, trustee, Procter & Gamble Fund

Denver University

Taylor, Andrew C.: president, chief executive officer, director, Enterprise Rent-A-Car Co.

Detroit Institute of Technology

Miller, Eugene A.: chairman, chief executive officer, Comerica Inc.

Dickinson College

Beaver, William S.: treasurer, vice president, Westvaco Corp.; trustee, Westvaco Foundation Trust
Curley, John J.: chairman, chief executive officer, director, Gannett Co., Inc.; chairman, Gannett Foundation

Dickinson School of Law

Yohe, Merrill A., Jr.: chairman contributions committee, AMP Inc.

Doane College

Weyers, Larry Lee: chief executive officer, chairman, director, Wisconsin Public Service Corp.; president, chief executive officer, Wisconsin Public Service Foundation, Inc.

Douglass College

Bauder, Lillian: vice president corporate affairs, Masco Corp.
Walker, Joan H.: senior vice president corporate communications, Ameritech Corp.

Drake University

Fish, Lawrence K.: trustee, Citizens Charitable Foundation; chairman, chief executive officer, Citizens Financial Group, Inc.
Hadley, Leonard Anson: chairman, chief executive officer, director, Maytag Corp.; president, trustee, Maytag Corp. Foundation
Hoak, Jon: trustee, NCR Foundation
Johnson, Norman E.: trustee, CLARCOR Foundation
Jorndt, Louis Daniel: president, chief executive officer, director, Walgreen Co.
Longfield, William H.: president, Bard Foundation (C.R.); chairman, chief executive officer, director, Bard, Inc. (C.R.)
Schiek, Fredrick A.: executive vice president, chief operating officer, Employers Mutual Casualty Co.
Sullivan, Laura P.: vice president, secretary, director, State Farm Companies Foundation; vice president, secretary, counsel, State Farm Mutual Automobile Insurance Co.
Turner, Fred L.: senior chairman, director, McDonald's Corp.

Draughons Business College

Walker, W. Paul: secretary, Boswell Foundation, Inc.; chief financial officer, secretary, treasurer, Independent Stave Co.

Drew University

Harding, Jack R.: president, chief executive officer, Cadence Designs Systems, Inc.
Shinn, George Latimer: director, New York Times Co. Foundation

Drexel Institute of Technology

Hafer, Fred Douglass: chairman, president, chief executive officer, GPU Inc.

Drexel University

Ayer, Ramani: chairman, president, chief executive officer, Hartford (The)
Baldassari, Dennis P.: president, chief operating officer, GPU Energy
Deering, Anthony W.: chairman, chief executive officer, Rouse Co.; chairman, president, trustee, Rouse Co. Foundation
Georges, John A.: director, International Paper Co.
Papso, Anna Mae: vice president, controller, West Co. Inc.
Sweeney, John J., III: vice president, CertainTeed Corp.

Drury College

Creach, Dale H.: vice president, director, MFA Foundation

Duke University

Allison, John Andrew, IV: chairman, chief executive officer, director, Branch Banking & Trust Co.
Berkley, Eugene Bertram: chairman, director, Tension Envelope Corp.; treasurer, Tension Envelope Foundation
Burrus, Robert Lewis, Jr.: trustee, Circuit City Foundation
Cambell, Lewis B.: chairman, chief executive officer, director, Textron Inc.
Cassidy, Samuel M.: director, Star Bank NA
Dozier, Ollin Kemp: treasurer, Universal Leaf Foundation
Durrett, Joseph P.: chief executive officer, Broderbund Software, Inc.
Eason, William Everette, Jr.: senior vice president, corporate secretary, general counsel, Scientific-Atlanta, Inc.
Farmer, Phillip W.: chairman, president, chief executive officer, Harris Corp.; president, trustee, Harris Foundation
Giering, John L.: senior vice president finance & administration, chief financial officer, NCR Corp.
Goode, David Ronald: chairman, president, chief executive officer, director, Norfolk Southern Corp.
Nichols, Kenwood C.: vice chairman, executive officer, Champion International Corp.
Ratcliffe, George Jackson, Jr.: trustee, Hubbell Foundation (Harvey); chairman, president, chief executive officer, Hubbell Inc.
Reed, William Garrard, Jr.: director, Matlock Foundation
Schoenholz, David A.: executive vice president, chief financial officer, Household International Inc.
Shepherd, Kathleen Shearen Maynard: director, Tribune New York Foundation
Smoot, Richard Leonard: chairman, PNC Bank
Wagoner, G. Richard, Jr.: president, chief executive officer, director, General Motors Corp.
Wilson, Gary Lee: chairman, director, Northwest Airlines, Inc.

Dunedin Teachers College

Little, William G.: chairman, president, chief executive officer, director, West Co. Inc.

Duquesne University

Argentine, Peter Dominic: executive vice president,

chief financial officer, Nestle U.S.A. Inc.

Breisinger, James R.: vice president, controller, Kennametal Foundation; vice president, controller, chief financial officer, Kennametal, Inc.

Davies, Charles R.: president, general counsel, director, GEICO Philanthropic Foundation

Edwards, Earnest Jonathan: director, Alcoa Foundation

Farley, James Bernard: chairman emeritus, trustee, Walter Industries Inc.

Gussin, Robert Zalmon, PhD: vice president science & technology, Johnson & Johnson; member corporate contributions committee, Johnson & Johnson Family of Companies Contribution Fund

Haggerty, Gretchen R.: vice president, treasurer, USX Corp.

Kelly, J. Peter: president, chief operating officer, director, LTV Corp.; trustee, LTV Foundation

Maloni, William R.: senior vice president policy & public affairs, Fannie Mae; director, Fannie Mae Foundation

Mesher, John R.: assistant secretary, CertainTeed Corp. Foundation

Parry, William E.: vice president, general counsel, Nalco Chemical Co.

Peconi, Maurice V.: member screening committee, PPG Industries Foundation

Pollock, E. Kears: director, PPG Industries Foundation; executive vice president, PPG Industries, Inc.

Dyke College

Curci, John V.: chief financial officer, Vesper Corp.; trustee, Vesper Foundation

Earlham College

Loose, John W.: trustee, Corning Inc. Foundation

Myers, Mark B.: senior vice president corporate research & technology, Xerox Corp.; trustee, Xerox Foundation

Taylor, Julian Howard: vice president, treasurer, director, Reynolds Metals Co. Foundation

Wagner, Thomas Joseph: chairman, CIGNA Foundation

East Carolina University

Scarbrough, Arlan Earl: vice president financial, Gulf Power Co.; trustee, Gulf Power Foundation

Williamson, Henry Gaston, Jr.: chief operating officer, Branch Banking & Trust Co.

East Central University

Nowell, Tommy Lynn: vice president finance, controller, Occidental Oil and Gas; treasurer, Occidental Oil and Gas Foundation

East Stroudsburg State University

Bennyhoff, George R.: senior vice president human resources, West Co. Inc.; chairman, trustee, West Foundation (Herman O.)

East Tennessee State University

Stinnette, Joe L., Jr.: director, Fireman's Fund Foundation; president, chief executive officer, director, Fireman's Fund Insurance Co.

East Texas State University

Simmons, Glenn Reuben: vice chairman, Contran Corp.

Eastern Kentucky University

Oliver, Orson: president, director, Mid-America Bank of Louisville

Eastern Michigan University

Janitz, John A.: president, chief executive officer, chairman, Textron Inc.

Jones, Ingrid Saunders: chairman, director, Coca-Cola Foundation

McGregor, Douglas J.: president, chief operating officer, director, Hanna Co. (M.A.)

Ecole Nationale D'Officiers De Marine

Dahan, Rene: senior vice president, Exxon Mobil Corp.

Ecole Normale Superieur

Delacote, Goery, PhD: director, Genentech Foundation for Biomedical Sciences

Ecole Polytechnique

Azoulay, Bernard: president, chief executive officer, Elf Atochem North America, Inc.

Ecole d'Hydrographie

Dahan, Rene: senior vice president, Exxon Mobil Corp.

Ecole des Beaux Arts

Buechner, Thomas Scharman: trustee, Corning Inc. Foundation

Edinburgh University

Coltman, David A.: senior vice president marketing, United Airlines Inc.

Education Institute

Levinson, Arthur David: president, chief executive officer, director, Genentech Inc.

Elizabethtown College

Moss, James H.: treasurer, York Federal Savings & Loan Foundation

Nation, Robert F.: former president, director, Harsco Corp.; trustee, Harsco Corp. Fund

Elmhurst

Meyers, Scott: vice president, treasurer, chief financial officer, Alliant Techsystems

Elmira College

Munder, Barbara A.: senior vice president new initiatives, McGraw-Hill Companies, Inc.

Elon College

Chandler, Wallace Lee: vice president, director, Universal Leaf Foundation

Emory University

Callaway, Ely Reeves, Jr.: chairman, Callaway Golf Co.

Denson, William Frank, III: president, Vulcan Materials Co. Foundation

Harkey, Robert Shelton: trustee, Delta Air Lines Foundation; senior vice president, general counsel, secretary, Delta Air Lines, Inc.

Henderson, George W., III: trustee, Burlington Industries Foundation; president, chief executive officer, director, Burlington Industries, Inc.

Herbert, Bart, Jr.: executive vice president, chief marketing officer, AEGON U.S.A. Inc.

Jobe, Warren Yancey: executive vice president, Georgia Power Co.; president, director, Georgia Power Foundation

Lacy, Alan J.: president credit, Sears, Roebuck and Co.

Levy, David: trustee, National Service Foundation

Moore, Virlyn B., Jr.: director, Pheonix Foundation

Spiegel, John William: member, SunTrust Bank Atlanta Foundation

West, Edward H.: chief financial officer, Delta Air Lines, Inc.

Emory University School of Law

Levy, David: trustee, National Service Foundation

Ward, Carol J.: secretary, compliance officer, CIGNA Corp.; secretary, CIGNA Foundation

Emporia State University

Taylor, Julian Howard: vice president, treasurer, director, Reynolds Metals Co. Foundation

Erasmus University (Netherlands) School of Economics

Ruding, Herman Onno: vice chairman, director, Citibank Corp.

Escola de Administration de Empresas de Fundacao Vargas

Reinhard, J. Pedro: executive vice president, chief financial officer, director, Dow Chemical Co.

Eton College

Coltman, David A.: senior vice president marketing, United Airlines Inc.

Evansville College

Critser, Gary P.: senior executive vice president, secretary, treasurer, director, Habig Foundation

Russell, Frank Eli: president, Central Newspapers Foundation; chairman, Central Newspapers, Inc.

Exeter University

Williams, David R.: trustee, Heinz Co. Foundation (H.J.); executive vice president, director, Heinz Co. (H.J.)

Fairfield University

Bigham, James John: executive vice president, chief financial officer, director, Continental Grain Co.

Pestillo, Peter John: executive chairman, Ford Motor Co.; trustee, Ford Motor Co. Fund

Sargent, Joseph Dudley: president, chief executive officer, director, Guardian Life Insurance Co. of America

Fairleigh Dickinson University

Brill, Ronald M.: executive vice president, chief administrative officer, director, Home Depot, Inc.

Buckwalter, Alan Roland, III: chief executive officer, Chase Bank of Texas; president, Chase Bank of Texas Foundation, Inc.

Doerfler, Ronald J.: senior vice president, chief financial officer, ABC; vice president, director, ABC Foundation

Dorsey, Jerry E.: executive vice president, chief operating officer, West Co. Inc.

Heagney, Lawrence: member advisory committee, contact, Milliken Foundation

Pribanic, Gerald J.: executive vice president, chief financial officer, Maytag Corp.; trustee, Maytag Corp. Foundation

Tumminello, Stephen C.: president, chief executive officer, director, Philips Electronics North America Corp.

Wendt, John R.: president, Maybelline, Inc.

Zenner, Patrick J.: trustee, Hoffmann-La Roche Foundation; president, chief executive officer, director, Hoffmann-La Roche Inc.

Fairmont State College

Westfall, David M.: senior vice president, chief financial officer, Consolidated Natural Gas Co.

Fashion Institute of Technology

Klein, Calvin Richard: president, Calvin Klein

Fenn College

Mandel, Jack N.: director, Premier Industrial Corp.

Finch Junior College

Chambers, Anne Cox: chairman, trustee, Cox Foundation (James M.)

Fisk University

Cole, Kenneth O.: vice president customer service, Memphis Light Gas & Water Division

Florida Institute of Technology

Neel, Curtis Dean, Jr.: trustee, Eckerd Corp. Foundation

Florida Southern College

Barnett, Hoyt R.: executive vice president, director, Publix Supermarkets

Gross, Murray: trustee, PerkinElmer Foundation; senior vice president, general counsel, clerk, PerkinElmer, Inc.

Florida State University

Hobgood, William P.: senior vice president, human resources, United Airlines Inc.

Kiernan, Donald E., Sr.: senior vice president, chief financial officer, treasurer, SBC Communications Inc.; director, SBC Foundation

McCook, Richard P.: vice president, Winn-Dixie Stores Foundation; vice president finance, chief financial officer, Winn-Dixie Stores Inc.

Fordham University

Ashley, James Wheeler: director, Globe Foundation

Broome, Burton Edward: vice president, controller, Transamerica Corp.; vice president, treasurer, Transamerica Foundation

Calderoni, Robert M.: chief financial officer, senior vice president finance, Avery Dennison Corp.

Connolly, Charles H.: senior vice president corporate affairs & investor relations, Whitman Corp.; president, Whitman Corp. Foundation

Devlin, James Richard: director, Sprint Foundation

Fino, Raymond M.: second vice president, Warner-Lambert Charitable Foundation; vice president human resources, Warner-Lambert Co.

Hohn, Harry George, Jr.: chairman, director, New York Life Foundation

Kentz, Frederick C., III: trustee, Hoffmann-La Roche Foundation; vice president, secretary, general counsel, Hoffmann-La Roche Inc.

Kurtz, Melvin H.: secretary, director, Chesebrough Foundation

Locher, John J.: treasurer, Barnes Group Foundation Inc.; vice president, treasurer, Barnes Group Inc.

McGovern, John Francis: chief financial officer, executive vice president, Georgia-Pacific Corp.; chairman, Georgia-Pacific Foundation

Melican, James Patrick, Jr.: executive vice president legal & external affairs, International Paper Co.; director, International Paper Co. Foundation

Nelson, Merlin Edward: chairman, director, IBJ Foundation

Paladino, Daniel R.: trustee, Bronfman Foundation/Joseph E. Seagram & Sons, Inc. Fund (Samuel); executive vice president, general counsel, secretary, Seagram & Sons, Inc. (Joseph E.)

Ruggiero, Anthony W.: executive vice president, chief financial officer, Olin Corp.

Scicutella, John Vincent: trustee, Chase Manhattan Foundation

Smith, Richard Donald: president, director, Chubb Corp.

Soden, Paul A.: senior vice president, secretary, general counsel, Reader's Digest Association, Inc. (The)

Stavropoulos, William S.: president, chief executive officer, director, Dow Chemical Co.

Wagar, James Lee: manager, Carter-Wallace Foundation

Fordham University School of Law

Khoury, Kenneth F.: secretary, Georgia-Pacific Foundation

Fort Hays State University

Richard, Shirley A.: vice president, director, APS Foundation, Inc.; executive vice president customer service marketing & corporate relations, Arizona Public Service Co.

Franklin and Marshall College

Baker, Calvin H.: vice president finance, chief financial officer, Wisconsin Energy Corp.; treasurer, director, Wisconsin Energy Corp. Foundation, Inc.

Harad, George Jay: chairman, chief executive officer, director, Boise Cascade Corp.

Hendler, Donald: assistant treasurer, Leviton Foundation New York

Sullivan, Kevin F.: member screening committee, PPG Industries Foundation

Freie University Berlin

Bryson, John E.: chairman, chief executive officer, Edison International

Furman University

Howes, William B.: chairman, chief executive officer, Inland Container Corp.; vice president, director, Inland Foundation, Inc.

Thompson, Robert L.: vice president public affairs, Springs Industries, Inc.

Gannon University

Lunger, Francis: chief financial officer, corporate vice president, Millipore Corp.

Gem Business College

Copenhaver, Don: director, MFA Foundation; president, chief executive officer, MFA Inc.

General Motors Institute

Butts, David Wayne: senior vice president, Illinois Power Co.

Snyder, Dale E.: senior vice president, technical services, Kohler Co.

Walker, Martin Dean: chairman, chief executive officer, director, Hanna Co. (M.A.)

George Mason University

Dahm, Anthony Edward: controller, Giant Food Inc.

George Washington University

Almeida, Richard: chairman, chief executive officer, Heller Financial, Inc.

Ballantyne, Richard Lee: vice president, general counsel, secretary, Harris Corp.; secretary, treasurer, Harris Foundation

Bright, Stanley J.: chairman, president, chief executive officer, director, MidAmerican Energy Holdings Co.

Carter, Marshall Nichols: chairman, chief executive officer, State Street Bank & Trust Co.

Davis, William E.: chairman, chief executive officer, Niagara Mohawk Holdings Inc.

Herres, Robert T.: chairman, chief executive officer, United Services Automobile Association

Herriman, M. Davis, Junior: senior vice president, chief merchandising officer, Giant Food Inc.

Hobgood, William P.: senior vice president, human resources, United Airlines Inc.

Knight, Merrill Donaldson, III: director, GEICO Philanthropic Foundation

Kucharski, John Michael: trustee, PerkinElmer Foundation; chairman, chief executive officer, director, PerkinElmer, Inc.

Manning, Kenneth Paul: president, Universal Foods Corp.; president, director, Universal Foods Foundation

Martore, Gracia C.: vice president investor relations, treasurer, Gannett Co., Inc.; assistant treasurer, Gannett Foundation

Powers, Paul Joseph: chairman, president, chief executive officer, director, Commercial Intertech Corp.; president, trustee, Commercial Intertech Foundation

Rogers, C. B., Jr.: chairman, Equifax Foundation; chairman, director, Equifax Inc.

Rutstein, David W.: secretary, Giant Food Foundation; senior vice president, general counsel, chief administrative officer, Giant Food Inc.

Salizzoni, Frank L.: vice chairman, Block Foundation (H&R); president, chief executive officer, director, Block, Inc. (H&R)

Schwartz, Peter A.: chief financial officer, consultant, Computer Associates International, Inc.

Smith, Donald Kaye: senior vice president, general counsel, director, GEICO Corp.

Watanabe, Jeffrey N.: director, Hawaiian Electric Industries Charitable Foundation

Wilks, David M.: vice president, New Century Energies Foundation

Wolff, Herbert Eric: secretary, director, First Hawaiian Foundation

George Washington University Law School

Devries, Robert K.: member administration committee, Nabisco Foundation Trust

Knight, Merrill Donaldson, III: director, GEICO Philanthropic Foundation

Moorhead, Thomas Leib, Esq.: vice president law, assistant secretary, Nordson Corp.; trustee, Nordson Corp. Foundation

Smith, Philip N., Jr.: secretary, Trace International Holdings, Inc. Foundation

Snow, John William: chairman, president, chief executive officer, CSX Corp.

Georgetown University

Bindley, Thomas L.: executive vice president finance & administration, Whitman Corp.; vice president, treasurer, Whitman Corp. Foundation

Brennan, Leo Joseph, Jr.: vice president, executive director, Ford Motor Co. Fund

Feller, Mimi A.: senior vice president public affairs & government relations, Gannett Co., Inc.; vice president, Gannett Foundation

Fischer, Richard Lawrence: director, Alcoa Foundation; executive vice president, chairman counsel, Alcoa Inc.

Guedry, James Walter: president, International Paper Co. Foundation

Kentz, Frederick C., III: trustee, Hoffmann-La Roche Foundation; vice president, secretary, general counsel, Hoffmann-La Roche Inc.

Kiener, Dan W.: member screening committee, PPG Industries Foundation

Klinedinst, Thomas John, Jr.: trustee, Star Bank NA, Cincinnati Foundation

Litvack, Sanford M.: senior executive vice president, chief corporate operations, director, Disney Co. (Walt)

McClimon, Timothy J.: executive director, AT&T Foundation

McDonough, Joseph E.: vice president finance,

chief financial officer, Analog Devices, Inc.
McGrath, Lee Upton: treasurer, Fuller Co. Foundation (H.B.); vice president, treasurer, Fuller Co. (H.B.); treasurer, Jostens Foundation Inc. (The)
McKenna, Matthew M.: treasurer, PepsiCo Foundation, Inc.; senior vice president, treasurer, PepsiCo, Inc.
McNally, Mark K.: senior vice president, general counsel, secretary, Aristech Chemical Corp.
McNeary, Joseph Allen: member grantmaking committee, Claiborne Foundation (Liz); senior vice president, Liz Claiborne, Inc.
O'Brien, John F.: trustee, McDonald & Co. Securities Foundation
Pestillo, Peter John: executive chairman, Ford Motor Co.; trustee, Ford Motor Co. Fund
Roche, George A.: chairman, president, Price Associates (T. Rowe)
Shaw, L. Edward, Jr.: general counsel, Aetna, Inc.; trustee, Chase Manhattan Foundation
Smith, Elizabeth Patience: director, Texaco Foundation; vice president investor relations & shareholder service, Texaco Inc.
Walsh, Michael J.: vice president, CertainTeed Corp.
Williams, William Joseph: trustee, Western-Southern Foundation, Inc.; chairman, director, Western & Southern Life Insurance Co.

Georgetown University Law Center

Bertrand, Frederic Howard: chairman, Central Vermont Public Service Corp.
Davies, Charles R.: president, general counsel, director, GEICO Philanthropic Foundation
Levy, David: trustee, National Service Foundation

Georgia Institute of Technology

Clayton, Jon Kerry: trustee, Fortis Foundation; executive vice president, Fortis, Inc.
Ecker, H. Allen: president subscriber systems, Scientific-Atlanta, Inc.
George, William Wallace: chief executive officer, chairman, Medtronic, Inc.
Hyatt, Kenneth Ernest: chairman, president, chief executive officer, director, Walter Industries Inc.
Jasse, Andre C., Jr.: trustee, Eastern Bank Charitable Foundation
Jones, David R.: principal, AGL Resources Inc.
Lacy, Alan J.: president credit, Sears, Roebuck and Co.
McCarthy, John Michael: vice president, Waffle House Foundation, Inc.
Necessary, Steven K.: senior vice president marketing, Scientific-Atlanta, Inc.
Saul, Julian D.: president, Shaw Industries Inc.
Spindler, George S.: senior vice president law & corporate affairs, BP Amoco Corp.; chairman, director, BP Amoco Foundation

Georgia State University

Altman, David R.: vice president corporate communications, Southern Co. Services Inc.
Dahlberg, Alfred William, III: chairman, president, chief executive officer, Southern Co. Services Inc.
Escarra, Vicki: executive vice president customer service, Delta Air Lines, Inc.
Hodges, Gene R.: director, Georgia Power Foundation
Hopkins, Wayne W.: vice president corporate communications, Tampa Electric Co.
Jacobson, Richard J.: vice president, treasurer, Cox Enterprises Inc.
Rawlins, Benjamin W., Jr.: chairman, chief executive officer, director, Union Planters Corp.
Redding, Peter Stoddard: trustee, Sherman-Standard Register Foundation; president, chief executive officer, director, Standard Register Co.
Reiman, Thomas Jay: senior vice president public policy, Ameritech Corp.
Wood, Edward Jenner: member, SunTrust Bank Atlanta Foundation
Zoffmann, Beth Clark: vice president, director, Georgia-Pacific Foundation

Gettysburg College

Helsby, Keith R.: treasurer, New York Stock Exchange Foundation, Inc.
Morgan, Edward L.: group senior vice president, Hartford (The)
Rogers, C. B., Jr.: chairman, Equifax Foundation; chairman, director, Equifax Inc.
Weigel, David V.: treasurer, MONY Life Insurance of New York (The)
Yohe, Merrill A., Jr.: chairman contributions committee, AMP Inc.

Glendale College

Anderson, Gordon M.: chairman, Santa Fe International Corp.

Golden Gate College

Rosenberg, Richard Morris: chairman, chief executive officer (retired), Bank of America

Golden Gate University

Beebe, Lydia I.: corporate secretary, Chevron Corp.
Phillips, Ped Wesley: vice president, Hanna Co. Foundation (M.A.)
Rosenberg, Richard Morris: chairman, chief executive officer (retired), Bank of America

Gonzaga University

Hannity, Vincent Thomas: vice president corporate communications & investor relations, Boise Cascade Corp.
Oliver, Walter Maurice: senior vice president human resources, Ameritech Corp.
Pederson, Jerrold P.: vice president, chief financial officer, director, Montana Power Co.; director, Montana Power Foundation
Redmond, Paul Anthony: chairman, chief executive officer, director, Avista Corporation

Gonzaga University Law School

Stanton, Philip H.: chief executive officer, director, Washington Trust Bank

Grinnell College

Farver, Joan Kuyper: chairman emeritus, director, Pella Corp.; director, Pella Rolscreen Foundation
Kelly, Janet L.: executive vice president corporate development, general counsel, secretary, Kellogg Co.
Zigas, Barry: senior vice president, Fannie Mae; director, Fannie Mae Foundation

Groton School

Milliken, Roger: chairman, chief executive officer, Milliken & Co.; member advisory committee, Milliken Foundation

Grove City College

Kasenter, Robert Albert: executive vice president human resources, Montgomery Ward & Co., Inc.; executive vice president, Montgomery Ward Foundation
Landin, Thomas Milton: vice president, director, CertainTeed Corp.; vice president, Norton Co. Foundation

Guilford College

Brewer, Oliver Gordon, Jr.: vice president finance, treasurer, IKON Office Solutions Foundation, Inc.
Trogdon, Dewey Leonard, Jr.: director, ABC Foundation; chairman, Cone Mills Corp.

Hamilton College

Connor, Walter Robert: director, Glaxo Wellcome Foundation
Gilbert, Glen S.: vice president advertising & social responsibility, GTE Corp.
Hand, Elbert O.: chairman, chief executive officer, director, Hartmarx Corp.
Jerrold, Douglas M.: vice president, Reynolds Metals Co. Foundation
Kaufman, Frank Joseph: senior vice president taxes, McGraw-Hill Companies, Inc.
McKenna, Matthew M.: treasurer, PepsiCo Foundation, Inc.; senior vice president, treasurer, PepsiCo, Inc.

Hamline University

Meyer, Jerome J.: chairman, chief executive officer, Tektronix, Inc.

Hampden-Sydney College

Druen, W. Sidney: director, Nationwide Insurance Enterprise Foundation

Hampton Institute

Fountain, W. Frank, Jr.: senior vice president government affairs, DaimlerChrysler Corp.; president, DaimlerChrysler Corp. Fund

Hampton University

Lewis, George Ralph: trustee, Kemper Foundation (James S.)

Hanover College

Gloyd, Lawrence Eugene: trustee, CLARCOR Foundation; chairman, chief executive officer, director, CLARCOR Inc.

Hartford Seminary

Jones, Russell H.: officer, Kaman Corp.

Harvard Business School

Caccamo, Aldo M.: vice president public affairs, Chevron Corp.
White, Gerald Andrew: director, Air Products Foundation

Harvard College

Alberts, Bruce Michael, PhD: director, Genentech Foundation for Biomedical Sciences
Cogan, John Francis, Jr.: president, chief executive officer, director, Pioneer Group
Davis, Edward J.: chief financial officer, vice president, treasurer, Wyman-Gordon Co.
Lehner, Philip: chairman, Leigh Fibers, Inc.; trustee, Orchard Foundation
O'Brien, John Francis, Jr.: president, chief executive officer, Allmerica Financial Corp.
Wilmers, Robert George: chairman, president, chief executive officer, Manufacturers & Traders Trust Co.

Harvard University

Ackerman, Philip Charles: senior vice president, director, National Fuel Gas Distribution Corp.
Alberts, Bruce Michael, PhD: director, Genentech Foundation for Biomedical Sciences
Alfiero, Salvatore Harry: founder, chairman, chief executive officer, director, Mark IV Industries; chairman, Mark IV Industries Foundation
Appell, Louis J., Jr.: president, Susquehanna-Pfaltzgraff Co.
Bachner, Robert L.: director, Wishnick Foundation (Robert I.)
Bacon, Kenneth J.: senior vice president, Fannie Mae; director, Fannie Mae Foundation
Baker, James Kendrick: chairman, director, Arvin Foundation; vice chairman, director, Arvin Industries, Inc.

Balloun, James S.: chairman, chief executive officer, president, National Service Industries, Inc.

Barnes, Wallace W.: director, Barnes Group Foundation Inc.

Batten, Frank, Sr.: chairman, director, Landmark Communications Foundation; chairman, Landmark Communications Inc.

Beaver, William S.: treasurer, vice president, Westvaco Corp.; trustee, Westvaco Foundation Trust

Becherer, Hans Walter: chairman, chief executive officer, director, Deere & Co.; director, Deere Foundation (John)

Beck, Edward W.: senior vice president, general counsel, secretary, director, Shaklee Corp.

Berwind, C. Graham, Jr.: chairman, president, chief executive officer, Berwind Group

Binder, Gordon M.: chairman, chief executive officer, director, Amgen, Inc.

Bindley, Thomas L.: executive vice president finance & administration, Whitman Corp.; vice president, treasurer, Whitman Corp. Foundation

Binswanger, David R.: president, chief executive officer, Binswanger Companies; treasurer, Binswanger Foundation

Block, Stephen A.: secretary, IFF Foundation Inc.

Bogomolny, Robert Lee: director, Searle Charitable Trust; senior vice president, general counsel, secretary, Searle & Co. (G.D.)

Booth, Chesleu Peter Washburn: senior vice president development, Corning Inc.; trustee, Corning Inc. Foundation

Bowman, Robert A.: president, chief operating officer, Starwood Hotels & Resorts Worldwide, Inc.

Brademas, John: chairman, Texaco Foundation

Brennan, John J.: chairman, chief executive officer, Vanguard Group; president, Vanguard Group Foundation

Bridgeland, James Ralph, Jr.: trustee, Star Bank NA, Cincinnati Foundation

Bridgewater, Bernard Adolphus, Jr.: member board control, Brown Shoe Co. Charitable Trust; chairman, president, chief executive officer, director, Brown Shoe Co., Inc.

Brooks, E. Richard 'Dick': chairman, chief executive officer, director, Central & South West Services

Brunetti, Wayne H.: vice chairman, president, chief operating officer, director, New Century Energies; president, chief executive officer, New Century Energies Foundation

Buchanan, William Hobart, Jr.: assistant secretary, Dun & Bradstreet Corp. Foundation, Inc.

Budney, Albert J., Jr.: president, director, Niagara Mohawk Holdings Inc.

Buechel, Kathleen W.: president, treasurer, Alcoa Foundation

Burg, H. Peter: president, chief operating officer, FirstEnergy Corp.

Burke, Daniel Barnett: vice president, treasurer, director, ABC Foundation

Burt, Robert Norcross: chairman, chief executive officer, director, FMC Corp.; director, FMC Foundation

Bush, Michael J.: vice president real estate, Giant Food Inc.

Cabot, John G. L.: vice chairman, Kinder Morgn

Call, Robert V., Jr.: chairman, trustee, Agrilink Foods/Pro-Fac Foundation

Campbell, Van C.: vice chairman, chief financial officer, chief administrative officer, director, Corning Inc.; trustee, Corning Inc. Foundation

Carter, John Douglas: executive vice president, director, Bechtel Group, Inc.

Carty, Donald J.: vice president, treasurer, AMR/American Airlines Foundation; president, chairman, chief executive officer, director, AMR Corp.

Castellini, Clateo: chairman, president, chief executive officer, Becton Dickinson & Co.

Chellgren, Paul Wilbur: chief executive officer, chairman, director, Ashland, Inc.; member, Ashland Inc. Foundation

Chenault, Kenneth Irvine: president, chief operating officer, director, American Express Co.; trustee, American Express Foundation

Clayton, Jon Kerry: trustee, Fortis Foundation; executive vice president, Fortis, Inc.

Cogan, Marshall Stuart: chairman, president, chief executive officer, director, Trace International Holdings, Inc.; director, Trace International Holdings, Inc. Foundation

Coker, Charles Westfield: trustee, Sonoco Foundation; vice president, Sonoco Products Co.

Collins, Duane E.: president, chief executive officer, director, Parker Hannifin Corp.; vice president, trustee, Parker Hannifin Foundation

Collins, Paul John: vice chairman, director, Citibank Corp.

Cook, John Rowland: trustee, Harcourt General Charitable Foundation; senior vice president, chief financial officer, Harcourt General, Inc.

Coolidge, E. David, III: vice president, Blair & Co. Foundation (William); chief executive officer, Blair & Co. (William); vice president, Pittway Corp. Charitable Foundation

Crenshaw, Gordon Lee, II: member, Universal Leaf Foundation; chairman emeritus, Universal Leaf Tobacco Co., Inc.

Critelli, Michael J.: vice president, secretary, general counsel, chairman, Pitney Bowes Inc.

Cutler, Richard M.: vice chairman, director, Putnam Investments

Danford, Philip C.: treasurer, Dun & Bradstreet Corp. Foundation, Inc.

David, George A. L.: chairman, president, chief executive officer, chief operating officer, United Technologies Corp.

Decherd, Robert William: chairman, president, chief executive officer, director, Belo Corp. (A.H.); chairman, trustee, Belo Corp. Foundation (A.H)

DiCamillo, Gary Thomas: chairman, chief executive officer, director, Polaroid Corp.

Dickson, Alan Thomas: president, Dickson Foundation; chairman, Ruddick Corp.

Doane, W. Allen: president, chief executive officer, director, Alexander & Baldwin, Inc.

Dozier, Ollin Kemp: treasurer, Universal Leaf Foundation

Dubes, Michael: membership, ReliaStar Foundation

Early, William Bernard: trustee, Jeld-wen Foundation; senior vice president, assistant secretary, director, Jeld-wen, Inc.

Edison, Bernard Alan: member, Edison Family Foundation

Ehrlich, M. Gordon: trustee, Orchard Foundation

Emmet, Robert: vice president financial planning, treasurer, Cleveland-Cliffs, Inc.

Ernst, Fred V.: president, director, MacMillan Bloedel Inc.

Esrey, William Todd: chairman, chief executive officer, Sprint Corp.

Ferland, E. James: chairman, president, chief executive officer, Public Service Electric & Gas Co.

Flanagan, David T.: president, chief executive officer, director, Central Maine Power Co.

Fligg, James E.: executive vice president, BP Amoco Corp.

Flood, Al: chairman, chief executive officer, CIBC Oppenheimer

Franklin, Barbara Hackman: director, Dow Chemical Co.

Fraumann, Willard George: president, director, partner, Kirkland & Ellis; president, Kirkland & Ellis Foundation

Furlaud, Richard Mortimer: interim chief executive officer, International Flavors & Fragrances Inc.

Gallagher, Richard S.: director, Badger Meter Foundation

Gallagher, Terence Joseph: secretary, director, Pfizer Foundation

Gamper, Albert R., Jr.: president, chief executive officer, director, CIT Group Foundation; president, chief executive officer, chairman, CIT Group, Inc. (The)

Gates, William Henry, III: co-founder, chairman, chief software architect, Microsoft Corp.

Gelb, Richard Lee: director, New York Times Co. Foundation

Geller, Eric P.: trustee, Harcourt General Charitable Foundation; senior vice president, general counsel, secretary, Harcourt General, Inc.

George, William Wallace: chief executive officer, chairman, Medtronic, Inc.

Gerstner, Louis Vincent, Jr.: chairman, chief executive officer, director, International Business Machines Corp.

Getz, Herbert A.: senior vice president, secretary, general counsel, Waste Management Inc.

Giertz, James R.: senior vice president, chief financial officer, Donaldson Co., Inc.; chief financial officer, vice president, Donaldson Foundation

Gilmartin, Raymond V.: chairman, president, chief executive officer, Merck & Co.; chairman, Merck Co. Foundation

Glickenhaus, Seth M.: general partner, Glickenhaus & Co.

Goldstein, Richard A.: president, chief executive officer, director, Lipton Co.

Gottwald, Thomas E.: president, chief operating officer, director, Ethyl Corp.

Graham, Donald Edward: chairman, chief executive officer, director, publisher, The Washington Post

Guthart, Leo A.: vice chairman, director, Pittway Corp.

Haas, Peter Edgar, Sr.: chairman executive committee, director, Levi Strauss & Co.

Haas, Robert Douglas: chairman, chief executive officer, director, Levi Strauss & Co.; president, Levi Strauss Foundation

Hamblett, Stephen: chairman, chief executive officer, publisher, Providence Journal-Bulletin Co.; trustee, Providence Journal Charitable Foundation

Hanower, L. David: assistant secretary, Burlington Resources Foundation

Harad, George Jay: chairman, chief executive officer, director, Boise Cascade Corp.

Harris, Edward D., Jr.: director, Genentech Foundation for Biomedical Sciences

Harris, King William: president, chief executive officer, Pittway Corp.; vice president, director, Pittway Corp. Charitable Foundation

Heineman, Benjamin Walter, Jr.: director, GE Fund

Henderson, James Alan: vice chairman, chief executive officer, director, Ameritech Corp.; chairman, director, Cummins Engine Foundation

Henn, Catherine Emily Campbell: president, Boston Globe Foundation

Herron, James Michael: secretary, director, Ryder System Charitable Foundation

Hiatt, Arnold Selig: chairman, director, Stride Rite Foundation

Hiersteiner, Walter L.: vice chairman, Tension Envelope Corp.; vice president, Tension Envelope Foundation

Hill, Kenneth D.: vice president, Sunoco Inc.

Hodgson, Thomas Richard: president, chief operating officer, director, Abbott Laboratories

Houghton, James Richardson: director, Corning Inc.; trustee, Corning Inc. Foundation
Huber, Richard Leslie: chairman, president, chief executive officer, director, Aetna, Inc.
Hubschman, Henry A.: director, GE Fund
Hudnut, Stewart Skinner: director, Illinois Tool Works Foundation
Huston, Edwin Allen: vice president, director, Ryder System Charitable Foundation; vice chairman, director, Ryder System, Inc.
James, George Barker, II: senior vice president, chief financial officer, Levi Strauss & Co.
Jannotta, Edgar D.: president, Blair & Co. Foundation (William); senior director, Blair & Co. (William)
Jenest, Jeffrey M.: senior vice president new business development, Playboy Enterprises Inc.; director, Playboy Foundation
Jewett, George Frederick, Jr.: trustee, Potlatch Foundation II
Jobe, Warren Yancey: executive vice president, Georgia Power Co.; president, director, Georgia Power Foundation
Johnson, Edward Crosby, III: president, Fidelity Foundation; chairman, president, chief executive officer, director, Fidelity Investments
Johnson, Samuel Curtis: chairman, director, president, Johnson & Son (S.C.); chairman, trustee, Johnson Wax Fund (S.C.)
Johnson, Scott W.: senior vice president, secretary, general counsel, Bemis Co., Inc.
Kamen, Harry Paul: chairman, president, chief executive officer, Metropolitan Life Insurance Co.
Kann, Peter Robert: chairman, chief executive officer, publisher, director, Dow Jones & Co., Inc.; member advisory committee, Dow Jones Foundation
Kasputys, Joseph Edward: chairman, trustee, Hitachi Foundation
Kaufman, Frank Joseph: senior vice president taxes, McGraw-Hill Companies, Inc.
Kelly, J. Peter: president, chief operating officer, director, LTV Corp.; trustee, LTV Foundation
Kemper, David Woods: chairman, president, chief executive officer, director, Commerce Bancshares, Inc.
Kemper, James Scott, Jr.: honorary chairman, Kemper Foundation (James S.)
Kemper, Jonathan McBride: director, Commerce Bancshares Foundation; vice chairman, Commerce Bancshares, Inc.
Kerr, William T.: chairman, chief executive officer, director, Meredith Corp.
Keyser, Richard Lee: chairman, chief executive officer, president, Grainger, Inc. (W.W.)
Kiely, W. Leo, III: president, chief operating officer, Coors Brewing Co.
Kinsolving, Augustus Blagden: director, ASARCO Foundation
Kissinger, Henry Alfred: director, CBS Foundation
Kreindler, Peter Michael: president, director, AlliedSignal Foundation Inc.; senior vice president, general counsel, secretary, AlliedSignal Inc.
Lasser, Lawrence Jay: president, chief executive officer, director, Putnam Investments; president, chief executive officer, Putnam Investors Fund
Law, L. William, Jr.: senior vice president, general counsel, secretary, Eastern Enterprises
Lawson, William Hogan, III: chairman, chief executive officer, director, Franklin Electric Co.; president, Franklin Electric, Edward J. Schaefer, and T. W. KehoeCharitable and Educational Foundation
Lee, Charles Robert: chairman, chief executive officer, director, GTE Corp.; chief executive officer, trustee, GTE Foundation
Levin, Michael Stuart: president, chief executive officer, Titan Industrial Corp.
Lipp, Robert Irving: chief executive officer, Citigroup; vice president, treasurer, trustee, Citigroup Foundation
Long, Robert R.: chairman, SunTrust Bank Atlanta
Loos, Henry J.: secretary, Charter Manufacturing Co. Foundation
Lower, H. Louis Gordon, II: vice president, trustee, Allstate Foundation
Mahoney, David L.: co-chief executive officer, McKesson-HBOC Corp.
Mark, Reuben: chairman, chief executive officer, Colgate-Palmolive Co.
Marshall, Siri M.: trustee, General Mills Foundation; senior vice president, general counsel, General Mills, Inc.
Martinez, Arthur C.: chairman, chief executive officer, president, Sears, Roebuck and Co.
Matheny, Edward Taylor, Junior: director, Block Foundation (H&R)
McClelland, William Craig: trustee, Union Camp Charitable Trust; chairman, chief executive officer, director, Union Camp Corp.
McMahon, Steve: director, Autodesk Foundation
McNealy, Scott G.: chairman, chief executive officer, director, Sun Microsystems Inc.
Meier, Stephen Charles: vice chairman, Times Mirror Co.
Melican, James Patrick, Jr.: executive vice president legal & external affairs, International Paper Co.; director, International Paper Co. Foundation
Meyer, Russell William, Jr.: chairman, chief executive officer, Cessna Aircraft Co.; president, Cessna Foundation, Inc.
Meyerson, Martin: director, Panasonic Foundation
Miller, Donn Biddle: president, chief executive officer, Pacific Mutual Life Insurance Co.
Milne, Garth Leroy: senior vice president, treasurer, Motorola Inc.
Mixon, A. Malachi, III: chairman, chief executive officer, Invacare Corp.; trustee, Invacare Foundation
Mullin, Leo Francis: chairman, president, chief executive officer, Delta Air Lines, Inc.
Naples, Ronald James: president, chief executive officer, director, Quaker Chemical Corp.
Necessary, Steven K.: senior vice president marketing, Scientific-Atlanta, Inc.
Nelson, Glen David, MD: vice chairman, Medtronic, Inc.
Nelson, John Martin: chairman, director, TJX Companies, Inc.
Newman, Andrew E.: member, Edison Family Foundation
Nunes, Geoffrey: chairman, Millipore Foundation (The)
O'Brien, John Francis, Jr.: president, chief executive officer, Allmerica Financial Corp.
Oldenburg, Richard Erik: chairman, Sotheby's Inc.
Ong, John Doyle: chairman board, director, Ameritech Corp.
Ostergard, Paul Michael: vice president, director corporate contributions, Citibank Corp.; president, Citigroup Foundation
Palmieri, Peter C.: vice chairman, chief credit officer, First Union National Bank, NA
Parker, Patrick Streeter: chairman, director, Parker Hannifin Corp.; president, trustee, Parker Hannifin Foundation
Patterson, Michael E.: vice chairman, Morgan & Co. Inc. (J.P.)
Peoples, D. Louis: vice chairman, chief executive officer, director, Orange & Rockland Utilities, Inc.
Pero, Perry R.: senior executive vice president, chief financial officer, Northern Trust Co.
Pitts, John Wilson: director, PACCAR Foundation
Pratt, Donald Henry: chairman, Butler Manufacturing Co.; vice president, trustee, Butler Manufacturing Co. Foundation
Price, David B., Jr.: vice president, Goodrich Foundation, Inc. (B.F.)
Pulitzer, Michael Edgar: chairman, president, chief executive officer, director, Pulitzer Publishing Co.; chairman, president, chief executive officer, Pulitzer Publishing Co. Foundation
Putnam, George, Jr.: chairman, president, chief executive officer, Putnam Investments
Raines, Franklin Delano: chairman, chief executive officer, Fannie Mae; director, Fannie Mae Foundation
Rasmuson, Edward B.: director, CIRI Foundation
Redstone, Sumner Murray: chairman, Viacom Inc.
Reid, James Sims, Jr.: chairman, director, Standard Products Co.; chairman, president, Standard Products Co. Charitable Foundation
Reyelts, Paul C.: vice president finance, chief financial officer, Valspar Corp.; vice president, assistant secretary, Valspar Foundation
Rice, William D.: senior vice president, chief financial officer, secretary, Agrilink Foods, Inc.; trustee, Agrilink Foods/Pro-Fac Foundation
Richards, John M.: chairman, chief executive officer, director, Potlatch Corp.; trustee, Potlatch Foundation II
Ridgley, Robert Louis: chairman, director, Northwest Natural Gas Co.
Riley, H. John, Jr.: chairman, president, chief executive officer, Cooper Industries Foundation; chairman, president, chief executive officer, director, Cooper Industries, Inc.
Ripley, Sidney Dillon, II: director emeritus, Hitachi Foundation
Robinson, E. B., Jr.: chairman, chief executive officer, director, Deposit Guaranty National Bank
Rock, Arthur: co-founder, chairman executive committee, director, Intel Corp.
Roe, John H.: chairman, director, Bemis Co., Inc.
Rogers, Desiree Glapion: vice president community affairs, Peoples Energy Corp.
Rogers, T. Gary: chairman, chief executive officer, director, Dreyer's Grand Ice Cream
Rompala, Richard M.: president, chief executive officer, director, chairman, Valspar Corp.; vice president, Valspar Foundation
Rosenberger, David M.: secretary, Tracy Fund (Emmet and Frances)
Rosenthal, Sol: counsel, Playboy Enterprises Inc.
Rothberg, Robert: vice president, general counsel, Cabot Corp.; director, Cabot Corp. Foundation
Ruckelshaus, William Doyle: chairman, director, Browning-Ferris Industries Inc.
Ryan, John Thomas, III: chairman, chief executive officer, Mine Safety Appliances Co.
Schacht, Henry Brewer: director, Cummins Engine Foundation
Schoenholz, David A.: executive vice president, chief financial officer, Household International Inc.
Schubach, John J.: senior vice president strategic management, Timken Co. (The); trustee, advisor, Timken Co. Charitable Trust (The)
Schwarz, H. Marshall: chairman, chief executive officer, United States Trust Co. of New York
Shapiro, Robert B.: chairman, president, chief executive officer, director, Monsanto Co.
Simmons, Hardwick: president, chief executive officer, director, Prudential Securities Inc.

Simpson, William H.: president, Susquehanna-Pfaltzgraff Co.; secretary, Susquehanna-Pfaltzgraff Foundation

Sims, Raymond J.: executive vice president, American General Finance Foundation

Smith, Frederick C.: chairman, trustee, Huffy Foundation, Inc.

Smith, Richard Alan: treasurer, director, Arvin Foundation; chairman, director, chief executive officer, Harcourt General, Inc.

Smith, Robert A.: trustee, Harcourt General Charitable Foundation; co-chief executive officer, director, president, Harcourt General, Inc.

Solso, Theodore Matthew: president, chief operating officer, director, Cummins Engine Co., Inc.; director, Cummins Engine Foundation

Sosland, Morton Irvin: director, Block Foundation (H&R)

Spaeth, Karl Henry: chairman, trustee, Quaker Chemical Foundation

Spina, David Anthony: president, chief operating officer, State Street Bank & Trust Co.

Spoon, Alan Gary: president, chief operating officer, director, The Washington Post

Stanley, Peter William: trustee, Hitachi Foundation

Stephens, James T.: president, director, Ebsco Industries, Inc.

Stoner, Richard Burkett, Jr.: director, Cummins Engine Foundation

Storch, Gerald L.: senior vice president strategic business, Dayton Hudson

Strickland, Robert Louis: vice president, Lowe's Charitable and Educational Foundation

Strickling, Lawrence E.: vice president, president public policy, Ameritech Corp.

Sullivan, Frank P.: vice president sales & marketing, Square D Co.; vice president, director, Square D Foundation

Sutton, Thomas C.: chairman, director, Pacific Mutual Charitable Foundation; chairman, chief executive officer, director, Pacific Mutual Life Insurance Co.

Taylor, Benjamin B.: director, Boston Globe Foundation

Taylor, William Osgood: chairman, chief executive officer, director, Boston Globe (The); chairman, director, Boston Globe Foundation; director, New York Times Co. Foundation

Thomas, Richard Lee: vice president, First National Bank of Chicago Foundation

Timken, William Robert, Jr.: chairman, president, chief executive officer, director, Timken Co. (The)

Tobias, Steven C.: vice chairman, chief operating officer, Norfolk Southern Corp.; director, Norfolk Southern Foundation

Toll, Daniel Roger: trustee, Kemper Foundation (James S.)

Ughetta, William Casper: trustee, Corning Inc. Foundation

Varet, Elizabeth Rosenwald: vice president, director, AMETEK Foundation; director, AMETEK, Inc.

Vitale, David J.: vice chairman, Bank One Corp.; vice president, director, First National Bank of Chicago Foundation

Wachtell, Herbert M.: senior partner, Wachtell, Lipton, Rosen & Katz; vice president, treasurer, Wachtell, Lipton, Rosen & Katz Foundation

Wagner, Harold A.: chairman, president, chief executive officer, director, Air Products and Chemicals, Inc.

Wagoner, G. Richard, Jr.: president, chief executive officer, director, General Motors Corp.

Watson, Solomon Brown, IV: vice president, New York Times Co. Foundation

Weber, Stephen Robert: director, Cowen Foundation

Weinberg, John Livingston: chairman, president, director, Goldman Sachs Foundation

Weinberger, Caspar Willard: chairman, Forbes Inc.

Welsh, Kelly Raymond: executive vice president, general counsel, Ameritech Corp.

Weyers, Larry Lee: chief executive officer, chairman, director, Wisconsin Public Service Corp.; president, chief executive officer, Wisconsin Public Service Foundation, Inc.

Whitehead, John Cunningham: chairman board, Goldman Sachs Foundation

Wiley, Deborah: vice chairman, Wiley & Sons (John)

Williams, Stephen E.: senior vice president, general counsel, Consolidated Natural Gas Co.; president, Consolidated Natural Gas System Foundation

Williams, William Joseph: trustee, Western-Southern Foundation, Inc.; chairman, director, Western & Southern Life Insurance Co.

Wilmers, Robert George: chairman, president, chief executive officer, Manufacturers & Traders Trust Co.

Wilson, James Lawrence: chairman, chief executive officer, director, Rohm & Haas Co.

Wilson, Stephen R.: executive vice president, chief financial officer, Reader's Digest Association, Inc. (The)

Wolff, Herbert Eric: secretary, director, First Hawaiian Foundation

Wolff, Jesse David: treasurer, director, Weil, Gotshal & Manges Foundation

Wood, Willis B., Jr.: chairman, chief executive officer, director, Pacific Enterprises

Zachem, Harry M.: chairman, trustee, Ashland Inc. Foundation

Zuckerman, Mortimer Benjamin: co-founder, chairman, co-publisher, director, Daily News

Harvard University Advanced Management Program

Barnes, Wallace W.: director, Barnes Group Foundation Inc.

Barnette, Curtis Handley: chairman, chief executive officer, director, Bethlehem Steel Corp.

Brothers, John Alfred 'Fred': trustee, Ashland Inc. Foundation

Calfee, William Rushton: trustee, Cleveland-Cliffs Foundation (The); executive vice president, commercial, Cleveland-Cliffs, Inc.

Daniels, John Hancock: chairman, Archer-Daniels-Midland Foundation

Grasso, Richard A.: chairman, chief executive officer, New York Stock Exchange, Inc.

Hall, Floyd: chairman, president, chief executive officer, director, Kmart Corp.

Howes, William B.: chairman, chief executive officer, Inland Container Corp.; vice president, director, Inland Foundation, Inc.

Ives, J. Atwood: chairman, chief executive officer, Boston Gas Co.; chairman, chief executive officer, trustee, Eastern Enterprises; trustee, Eastern Enterprises Foundation

Jacobsen, Thomas Herbert: chairman, president, chief executive officer, Mercantile Bank NA

Johnson, Norman E.: senior vice president technology, Weyerhaeuser Co.; trustee, Weyerhaeuser Co. Foundation

Kirby, William Joseph: vice president, director, FMC Foundation

McMillan, Howard Lamar, Jr.: president, chief operating officer, director, Deposit Guaranty National Bank

Messer, Chester R.: president, chief operating officer, Boston Gas Co.; trustee, Eastern Enterprises Foundation

Moffitt, Donald Eugene: chairman, director, CNF Transportation, Inc.

Rooney, Patrick W.: chairman, president, chief executive officer, director, Cooper Tire & Rubber Co.

Rosenzweig, Richard Stuart: executive vice president, director, Playboy Enterprises Inc.

Thompson, Sheldon Lee: senior vice president, chief administrative officer, Sunoco Inc.

Trogdon, Dewey Leonard, Jr.: director, ABC Foundation; chairman, Cone Mills Corp.

Harvard University Divinity School

Stockman, David A.: co-chairman, director, Collins & Aikman Corp.; president, director, Collins & Aikman Foundation

Harvard University Executive Management Program

Dunham, Archie W.: president, chief executive officer, Conoco, Inc.

Harvard University Graduate School of Business Administration

Ayotte, Robert C.: executive vice president, director, CertainTeed Corp.; vice president, director, Norton Co. Foundation

Bains, Harrison MacKellar, Jr.: vice president, treasurer, Bristol-Myers Squibb Co.; treasurer, Bristol-Myers Squibb Foundation Inc.

Ballmer, Steven Anthony: president, chief executive officer, director, Microsoft Corp.

Beghini, Victor Gene: trustee, USX Foundation, Inc.

Bell, Bradley John: vice president, treasurer, Whirlpool Corp.; treasurer, Whirlpool Foundation

Berkley, Eugene Bertram: chairman, director, Tension Envelope Corp.; treasurer, Tension Envelope Foundation

Bigham, James John: executive vice president, chief financial officer, director, Continental Grain Co.

Boyer, David Scott: president, chief executive officer, director, Teleflex Inc.

Brewer, Oliver Gordon, Jr.: vice president finance, treasurer, IKON Office Solutions Foundation, Inc.

Cabot, John G. L.: vice chairman, Kinder Morgn

Campbell, Edward Patrick: president, chief operating officer, drc, Nordson Corp.; trustee, Nordson Corp. Foundation

Clifton, Paul Hoot, Jr.: president, Colonial Life & Accident Insurance Co.

Dimon, James R.: trustee, Citigroup Foundation; president, chief operating officer, chief financial officer, Salomon Smith Barney

Ewing, Stephen E.: president, chief executive officer, director, Michigan Consolidated Gas Co.

Field, Benjamin R., III: senior vice president, chief financial officer, treasurer, Bemis Co., Inc.

Fish, Lawrence K.: trustee, Citizens Charitable Foundation; chairman, chief executive officer, Citizens Financial Group, Inc.

Gillis, Edwin J.: president, Lotus Development Corp.

Gross, Ronald Martin: chairman, president, director, Rayonier Foundation; chairman, president, chief executive officer, director, Rayonier Inc.

Haddock, John R.: board member, Ryder System Charitable Foundation; senior vice president marketing, Ryder System, Inc.

Hale, Roger Loucks: chairman, TENNANT Co.;

president, TENNANT Co. Foundation

Harris, Ralph A.: vice president corporate development, Campbell Soup Co.

Hattox, Brock Alan: director, National Service Foundation; executive vice president, chief financial officer, National Service Industries, Inc.

Hays, Thomas Chandler: chairman, chief executive officer, director, Fortune Brands, Inc.

Hernandez, William H.: director, PPG Industries Foundation; senior vice president, PPG Industries, Inc.

Howe, Stanley M.: president, HON Industries Charitable Foundation; chairman emeritus, director, HON Industries Inc.

Jackson, John E.: trustee, Nordson Corp. Foundation

Kerr, William T.: chairman, chief executive officer, director, Meredith Corp.

LaMantia, Charles Robert: president, chief executive officer, director, Little, Inc. (Arthur D.)

Magee, John Francis: chairman, director, Little, Inc. (Arthur D.)

Mullin, Leo Francis: chairman, president, chief executive officer, Delta Air Lines, Inc.

Murphy, Christopher J., III: president, chief executive officer, director, First Source Corp.; director, First Source Foundation

Nutter, Wallace L.: director, Rayonier Foundation

Osborne, Burl: president publishing division, director, Belo Corp. (A.H.); president, trustee, Belo Corp. Foundation (A.H.)

Puelicher, John A.: president, director, Marshall & Ilsley Foundation, Inc.

Rau, John E.: trustee, Chicago Title and Trust Co. Foundation

Reed, William Garrard, Jr.: director, Matlock Foundation

Reilly, Thomas E., Jr.: trustee, Reilly Foundation; chairman, chief executive officer, director, Reilly Industries, Inc.

Rice, William D.: senior vice president, chief financial officer, secretary, Agrilink Foods, Inc.; trustee, Agrilink Foods/Pro-Fac Foundation

Roche, George A.: chairman, president, Price Associates (T. Rowe)

Schermer, Lloyd G.: chairman, director, Lee Enterprises

Schmitt, Wolfgang Rudolph: chairman, chief executive officer, director, Rubbermaid Inc.

Stivers, William Charles: senior vice president, chief financial officer, treasurer, Weyerhaeuser Co.; treasurer, trustee, Weyerhaeuser Co. Foundation

Sulzberger, Arthur Ochs, Junior: director, chairman emeritus, New York Times Co.

Harvard University Law School

Cogan, John Francis, Jr.: president, chief executive officer, director, Pioneer Group

Goode, David Ronald: chairman, president, chief executive officer, director, Norfolk Southern Corp.

Grinstein, Gerald: director, PACCAR Inc.

Levine, Lawrence E.: secretary, Panasonic Foundation

Slovin, Bruce: president, director, Revlon Inc.

Tisch, Laurence Alan: chairman, co-chief executive officer, CBS Corp.; trustee, Loews Foundation

Harvard University School of Business

Hacker, Douglas A.: senior vice president finance, chief financial officer, United Airlines Inc.

Harvard University Senior Managers in Government

Hobgood, William P.: senior vice president, human resources, United Airlines Inc.

Hastings College

Hewitt, James Watt: vice president, treasurer, Abel Foundation

Haverford College

Gailey, John Robert, III: vice president, general counsel, secretary, West Co. Inc.

Pyke, John Secrest, Jr.: president, trustee, Hanna Co. Foundation (M.A.); vice president, secretary, general counsel, Hanna Co. (M.A.)

Spaeth, Karl Henry: chairman, trustee, Quaker Chemical Foundation

Whitehead, John Cunningham: chairman board, Goldman Sachs Foundation

Heidelberg College

Kelbley, Stephen Paul: executive vice president, Springs Industries, Inc.

Hendrix College

Murphy, R. Madison: chairman, director, Murphy Oil Corp.

High Point College

Berrier, Ronald G.: vice president, treasurer, assistant secretary, Thomasville Furniture Industries Inc.

Hillsdale College

Connor, Richard L.: president, publisher, Fort Worth Star-Telegram Inc.

Iott, Richard B.: president, chief executive officer, director, Seaway Food Town, Inc.

Hobart College

Setterstrom, William N.: chairman contributions committee, Northern Trust Co. Charitable Trust

Hofstra University

Brennan, Alice C.: vice president, secretary, Bristol-Myers Squibb Co.; secretary, Bristol-Myers Squibb Foundation Inc.

Connolly, Eugene Bernard, Jr.: chairman emeritus, USG Corp.

Larsen, Ralph Stanley: chairman, president, chief executive officer, director, Johnson & Johnson

Hope College

Suwyn, Mark A.: chairman, president, Louisiana-Pacific Foundation

Howard University

Jenifer, Franklyn Green: trustee, Texaco Foundation

Watson, Solomon Brown, IV: vice president, New York Times Co. Foundation

Hubart College

Brozyna, Jeffry H.: trustee

Hunter College

Copley, Helen K.: chairman, trustee, Copley Foundation (James S.); chairman, director, senior management board, Copley Press, Inc.

Sheehan, Jeremiah J.: chairman, director, Reynolds Metals Co. Foundation

Idaho State University

Humphrey, Neil Darwin: trustee, Commercial Intertech Foundation

Powell, Sandra Theresa: trustee, Potlatch Foundation II

Illinois College

Huston, Steve: secretary, Wrigley Co. Foundation (Wm. Jr.)

Illinois Institute of Technology

Condon, James Edward: treasurer, Hartmarx Charitable Foundation; vice president, treasurer, Hartmarx Corp.

Donovan, Thomas Roy: president, chief executive officer, Chicago Board of Trade

Grade, Jeffery T.: chairman, chief executive officer, director, Harnischfeger Industries; president, Harnischfeger Industries Foundation

Knauss, Dalton L.: trustee, Kemper Foundation (James S.)

Maatman, Gerald Leonard: chairman, president, trustee, Kemper Foundation (James S.); director, Kemper National Insurance Companies

Mitchell, John Francis: vice chairman, director, Motorola Inc.

Sanders, Wayne R.: chairman, chief executive officer, director, Kimberly-Clark Corp.

Schrickel, Patrick D.: vice president, Wisconsin Public Service Foundation, Inc.

Illinois State University

Perona, Dale F.: secretary, treasurer, True North Foundation

Schaffer, Donald J.: member contributions committee, GATX Corp.

Trosino, Vincent Joseph: assistant secretary, State Farm Companies Foundation; executive vice president, vice chairman, chief operating officer, director, State Farm Mutual Automobile Insurance Co.

Whaley, Ronald L.: foundation administrator, Solo Cup Foundation

Illinois Wesleyan University

Getz, Herbert A.: senior vice president, secretary, general counsel, Waste Management Inc.

Rust, Edward Barry, Jr.: chairman, president, director, State Farm Companies Foundation; chairman, president, chief executive officer, director, State Farm Mutual Automobile Insurance Co.

Indian Institute of Technology

Ayer, Ramani: chairman, president, chief executive officer, Hartford (The)

Indiana State University

Clabes, Judy G.: president, chief executive officer, Scripps Co. (E.W.); president, chief executive officer, trustee, member, Scripps Howard Foundation

Culp, E. Ronald: vice president public affairs, Sears, Roebuck and Co.; president, Sears, Roebuck and Co. Foundation

Gamron, W. Anthony: treasurer, director, Kimberly-Clark Foundation

Moffitt, Donald Eugene: chairman, director, CNF Transportation, Inc.

Indiana University

Albright, David L.: president, Campbell Soup Co.

Berey, Mark H.: senior vice president, chief financial officer, treasurer, Giant Food Inc.

Burns, Ron: chief financial officer, Grede Foundries

Carl, John L.: executive vice president, chief financial officer, BP Amoco Corp.; director, BP Amoco Foundation

Clark, John W.: president, Consumers Energy Foundation

Clayton, Joseph P.: president, chief executive officer, director, Frontier Corp.

Coffin, Sarah R.: director, Fuller Co. Foundation (H.B.); vice president specialty group, Fuller Co. (H.B.)

Cowan, James R.: vice president, director, Stonecutter Foundation; chairman, president, chief executive officer, director, Stonecutter Mills Corp.

Foley, Patricia A.: assistant secretary, Inland Container Corp.; secretary, treasurer, director, Inland Foundation, Inc.

Gamron, W. Anthony: treasurer, director, Kimberly-Clark Foundation

Graf, Alan B., Jr.: executive vice president, chief financial officer, FedEx Corp.

Griffin, Donald Wayne: chairman, president, chief executive officer, director, Olin Corp.; trustee, Olin Corp. Charitable Trust

Habig, Brian K.: director, Habig Foundation

Habig, Douglas A.: chairman, chief executive officer, director, Habig Foundation

Herr, Eric B.: president, chief operating officer, Autodesk Inc.

Hunt, V. William: director, Arvin Foundation; chief executive officer, chairman, president, director, Arvin Industries, Inc.

Hutton, Edward L.: chairman, chief executive officer, director, Chemed Corp.

Jenkins, Thomas A.: treasurer, trustee, Dayton Power and Light Co. Foundation

Kenney, Richard John: director, Consolidated Papers Foundation, Inc.; senior vice president finance, Consolidated Papers, Inc.

LaMacchia, John Thomas: trustee, Cincinnati Bell Foundation, Inc.; president, chief executive officer, director, Cincinnati Bell Inc.

Lang, Paul Louis: vice president, Illinois Power Co.

Lebedoff, Randy Miller: vice president, general counsel, McClatchy Co.; secretary, Star Tribune Foundation

Lodge, Robert W.: vice president, Carpenter Technology Corp. Foundation

Ludwick, John D.: vice president human resources, MGIC Investment Corp.

Meyer, Daniel Joseph: president, Milacron Foundation; chairman, president, chief executive officer, director, Milacron, Inc.

Meyer, W. Frederick: president, Arvin Foundation

Moffitt, Donald Eugene: chairman, director, CNF Transportation, Inc.

Morris, James Thomas: director, AUL Foundation Inc.

Pitts, Brenda S.: director, Cummins Engine Foundation

Powell, George Everett, III: president, chief executive officer, director, Yellow Corp.; trustee, Yellow Corp. Foundation

Rockey, Travis O.: vice president, director, Evening Post Publishing Co.

Russell, Frank Eli: president, Central Newspapers Foundation; chairman, Central Newspapers, Inc.

Sadler, Robert L.: president, vice chairman, director, Old Kent Bank

Sales, A. R.: director, Arvin Foundation; treasurer, Arvin Industries, Inc.

Sheley, Donald R., Junior: vice president finance, chief financial officer, Standard Products Co.; treasurer, trustee, Standard Products Co. Charitable Foundation

Shideler, Shirley Ann Williams: director, Central Newspapers Foundation

Thomasson, Dan King: vice president, trustee, Scripps Howard Foundation

Thyen, James C.: president, director, Habig Foundation

Tobias, Randall L.: chairman emeritus, Lilly & Co. (Eli)

Wagner, David J.: chairman, president, chief executive officer, Old Kent Bank; treasurer, Old Kent Foundation

Weil, Robert J.: vice president operations, McClatchy Co.; member, Star Tribune Foundation

Wentworth, Jack Roberts, Ph.D.: director, Habig Foundation

White, Walter Lucas: secretary, treasurer, trustee, Kemper Foundation (James S.)

Workman, John L.: executive vice president, Montgomery Ward & Co., Inc.; executive vice president, director, Montgomery Ward Foundation

Young, William D.: chief operating officer, Genentech Inc.

Indiana University of Pennsylvania

Alexander, John F.: trustee, PerkinElmer Foundation; senior vice president, chief financial officer, PerkinElmer, Inc.

Godlasky, Tom: executive vice president, chief investment officer, AmerUS Group

Madia, William J.: executive vice president, manager, Battelle Memorial Institute

Mesher, John R.: assistant secretary, CertainTeed Corp. Foundation

Institut voor Pictologie

Buechner, Thomas Scharman: trustee, Corning Inc. Foundation

Institute de Droit Compare

Shapiro, Isaac: chairman, secretary, trustee, Ise Cultural Foundation

Institute of Chartered Accountants Australia

Bible, Geoffrey Cyril: director, New York Stock Exchange Foundation, Inc.; chairman, chief executive officer, director, Philip Morris Companies Inc.

Institute of Chartered Accountants of England & Wales

Freeman, David: chairman, president, chief executive officer, director, Loctite Corp.

Institute of Paper Chemistry

Mead, George Wilson, II: president, director, Consolidated Papers Foundation, Inc.; chairman, director, Consolidated Papers, Inc.

Pottenger, Charles R.: group vice president pulp & paperboard group, Potlatch Corp.; trustee, Potlatch Foundation II

Iona College

Downes, Laurence M.: president, chief executive officer, director, chairman, New Jersey Natural Gas Co.; trustee, New Jersey Natural Gas Foundation

Gierer, Vincent A., Jr.: chairman, president, chief executive officer, director, UST Inc.

Lewis, George Ralph: trustee, Kemper Foundation (James S.)

McKenna, William John: director, chairman, Kellwood Co.; chairman, president, director, Kellwood Foundation

Ripp, Robert M.: chairman, chief executive officer, director, AMP Inc.

Robinson, Edward Joseph: president, chief operating officer, director, Avon Products, Inc.

Iowa Central Community College

Coughlin, Timothy C.: president, Riggs Bank NA

Iowa State University

Alton, Robert D., Jr.: chairman, president, chief executive officer, Hickory Tech Corp.; trustee, Hickory Tech Corp. Foundation

Baukol, Ronald O.: director, executive vice president, Minnesota Mining & Manufacturing Co.

Bolton, John Roger: senior vice president, Aetna Foundation; senior vice president corporate communications, Aetna, Inc.

Dubes, Michael: membership, ReliaStar Foundation

Garberding, Larry Gailbert: chief financial officer, executive vice president, Detroit Edison Co.; director, Detroit Edison Foundation

Giertz, James R.: senior vice president, chief financial officer, Donaldson Co., Inc.; chief financial officer, vice president, Donaldson Foundation

Holaday, G. Stephen: senior vice president, Alexander & Baldwin, Inc.

Howe, Stanley M.: president, HON Industries Charitable Foundation; chairman emeritus, director, HON Industries Inc.

Johnson, Charles S.: president, chief executive officer, chairman, Pioneer Hi-Bred International, Inc.

Kidder, C. Robert: chairman, president, chief executive officer, director, Borden, Inc.

Lasell, Raymond E.: secretary, director, HON Industries Charitable Foundation

Lawson, John K.: senior vice president, Deere & Co.; director, Deere Foundation (John)

Liddy, Richard A.: chairman, president, chief executive officer, GenAmerica Corp.

Taylor, Julian Howard: vice president, treasurer, director, Reynolds Metals Co. Foundation

Iowa State University of Science & Technology

Balloun, James S.: chairman, chief executive officer, president, National Service Industries, Inc.

Drury, David J.: chief executive officer, chairman, Principal Financial Group

Joos, David W.: president, chief executive officer electric, executive vice president, Consumers Energy Co.

Vondrasek, Frank Charles, Jr.: president, Madison Gas & Electric Foundation

Wetter, Larry V.: trustee, Jeld-wen Foundation; vice chairman, director, Jeld-wen, Inc.

Israeli Institute of Technology

Anderson, Basil L.: executive vice president, chief financial officer, Campbell Soup Co.

Jacksonville State University

Pope, G. Phillip: chief financial officer, Blue Cross & Blue Shield of Alabama; vice president, Caring Foundation

James Madison University

Damico, Joseph F.: director, Baxter Allegiance Foundation

Jamestown College

Unruh, James Arlen: director, Ameritech Foundation

John Carroll University

Breen, John Gerald: chairman, chief executive officer, director, Sherwin-Williams Co.; president, trustee, Sherwin-Williams Foundation

Mason, James L.: director public affairs, member contributions committee, Eaton Charitable Fund

John Marshall Law School

Huston, Steve: secretary, Wrigley Co. Foundation (Wm. Jr.)

Johns Hopkins University

Davis, Carolyne Kahle, PhD: trustee, Merck Co. Foundation

Hefty, Thomas R.: chairman, president, chief executive officer, United Wisconsin Services

Horan, Douglas S.: senior vice president, general counsel, Boston Edison Co.; trustee, Boston Edison Foundation

Magowan, Peter Alden: president, managing general partner, Safeway Inc.

Miller, Charles Daly: chairman, director, Avery Dennison Corp.; trustee, Whirlpool Foundation

Pierre, Percy A.: trustee, Hitachi Foundation

Roberts, Bert C., Jr.: chairman, MCI WorldCom, Inc.

Wiley, Bradford, II: chairman, director, Wiley & Sons (John)

Jones Law School

Farris, Banks H.: chairman, Alabama Power Foundation

McInnes, Duncan Joseph: executive vice president administration, chief administrative officer, Blount International, Inc.

Juniata College

Sease, Gene Elwood: director, Central Newspapers Foundation

Kalamazoo College

Carra, Phillip C.: director, Pharmacia & Upjohn Foundation; vice president public relations, Pharmacia & Upjohn, Inc.

Sikkema, Karen Ann: president, trustee, Unocal Foundation

Kansas State University

Chandler, Charles Q.: co-trustee, INTRUST Bank Charitable Trust; chairman, INTRUST Financial Corp.

Chandler, Charles Quarles, IV: co-trustee, INTRUST Bank Charitable Trust; president, director, INTRUST Financial Corp.

Cordes, Donald L.: secretary, Koch Foundation, Inc. (Fred C. and Mary R.)

Downey, Joseph L.: trustee, Dow Chemical Co.

Millenbruch, Gary Lee: executive vice president, chief financial officer, director, trustee, Bethlehem Steel Corp.

Staley, Warren R.: president, chief executive officer, Cargill Inc.; chairman, Excel Corp.

Kaufmaennissche Berufsschule

Pfeiffer, Eckhard A.: president, chief executive officer, director, Compaq Computer Corp.

Keio Gijyuka University

Ando, Tetsuo: chief financial officer, executive vice president, treasurer, Bridgestone/Firestone, Inc.

Itoh, Iwao: chairman, president, chief executive officer, New United Motor Manufacturing Inc.

Keller Graduate School of Management

Delo, Robert Paul: director, Chicago Tribune Foundation

Kemper Military School and College

Purvis, George Frank, Jr.: chairman, president, chief executive officer, director, Pan-American Life Insurance Co.

Kent State University

Brinzo, John S.: trustee, Cleveland-Cliffs Foundation (The); president, chief executive officer, Cleveland-Cliffs, Inc.

Dean, John W., III: vice president, treasurer, Rubbermaid Inc.

Ferry, Richard Michael: chairman, Pacific Mutual Life Insurance Co.

Gorman, Joseph T.: chairman, chief executive officer, TRW Inc.

Ong, John Doyle: chairman board, director, Ameritech Corp.

Skurek, John C.: vice president, treasurer, LTV Corp.; trustee, LTV Foundation

Kenyon College

Herr, Eric B.: president, chief operating officer, Autodesk Inc.

Little, Gene E.: trustee, advisor, Timken Co. Charitable Trust (The); secretary, treasurer, trustee, Timken Co. Educational Fund

Newman, Paul L.: president, Newman's Own Foundation

Thomas, Richard Lee: vice president, First National Bank of Chicago Foundation

King's College

Kampouris, Emmanuel Andrew: chairman, president, chief executive officer, director, American Standard Inc.

Kings Business College

Kulynych, Petro: chairman, treasurer, Lowe's Charitable and Educational Foundation

Meacham, William B.: director, Lance Foundation; vice president acquisitions & subsidiaries, director, Lance, Inc.

Knox College

Olson, Richard E.: chairman, chief executive officer, director, Champion International Corp.

Kumamoto University (Japan)

Ono, Masatoshi: chairman, chief executive officer, Bridgestone/Firestone, Inc.

LaSalle College

Barry, Richard Francis, III: director, Landmark Communications Foundation; vice chairman, Landmark Communications Inc.

McCarthy, Peter John: trustee, Elf Atochem North America Foundation; vice president public affairs, Elf Atochem North America, Inc.

Peterson, Donald Matthew: trustee, Trustmark Foundation; president, chief executive officer, director, Trustmark Insurance Co.

LaSalle University

Angelo, Robert A.: president, chief operating officer, York Federal Savings & Loan Association; secretary, York Federal Savings & Loan Foundation

Brennan, Michael J.: chief financial officer, senior vice president, Binswanger Companies

Campbell, W. Patrick: executive vice president corporate strategy & business development, Ameritech Corp.

Ervanian, Armen: vice president, Viad Corp. Fund

Pietrafitta, Clifford E.: vice president finance, treasurer, CSS Industries, Inc.

Lafayette College

Bukowick, Peter A.: president, chief operating officer, director, Alliant Techsystems

Graham, Richard William: president, chief executive officer, chief operating officer, director, Smurfit-Stone Container Corp.

Griffith, Alan Richard: vice chairman, Bank of New York Co., Inc.

Kline, Richard: president, Lehigh Portland Cement Co.

Manchester, Gilbert Mott: assistant secretary, Commercial Intertech Foundation

Muth, Robert James: president, director, ASARCO Foundation

Piergallini, Alfred A.: trustee, Gerber Foundation

Lake Forest College

Graham, William B.: chairman, director, Baxter Allegiance Foundation; chairman emeritus, Baxter International Inc.

Jacobsen, James C.: vice chairman, Kellwood Co.; vice president, director, Kellwood Foundation

Jacobsen, Thomas Herbert: chairman, president, chief executive officer, Mercantile Bank NA

Mathis, David B.: chairman, Kemper Foundation (James S.)

Lamar University

Page, Robert A.: chief financial officer, Tenneco Packaging

Lawrence University

Cianciola, Charles Sal: trustee, Chesapeake Corp. Foundation

Luke, John A., Jr.: chairman, president, chief executive officer, director, Westvaco Corp.

Mulford, David: chairman, Credit Suisse First Boston

Rust, Edward Barry, Jr.: chairman, president, director, State Farm Companies Foundation; chairman, president, chief executive officer, director, State Farm Mutual Automobile Insurance Co.

Schuh, Dale R.: president, chief executive officer, Sentry Insurance, A Mutual Co.

LeMoyne-Owen College

Cole, Kenneth O.: vice president customer service, Memphis Light Gas & Water Division

Lee Strasberg Actors Studio

Newman, Paul L.: president, Newman's Own Foundation

Lehigh University

Baxter, James G.: vice president, treasurer, Farber Foundation

Hecht, William F.: chairman, president, chief executive officer, Pennsylvania Power & Light

Hemelt, William J.: treasurer, director, APS Foundation, Inc.; controller, Arizona Public Service Co.

Kostecky, James Frank: executive director, Bethlehem Steel Corp.

Musser, Warren Van Dyke: chairman, chief executive officer, director, Safeguard Scientifics; president, director, Safeguard Scientifics Foundation

Neely, Walter Emerson: vice president, Humana Foundation

Sims, Raymond J.: executive vice president, American General Finance Foundation

Snyder, Frank Ronald, II: trustee,

Lewis & Clark College

Downing, Kathryn M.: executive vice president, Times Mirror Co.; vice chairman, Times Mirror Foundation

Lewis University

Dahm, Anthony Edward: controller, Giant Food Inc.

Lindenwood College

Kniffen, Jan Rogers: senior vice president, treasurer, May Department Stores Co.; vice president, secretary, treasurer, director, May Department Stores Computer Foundation (The)

Lindenwood University

Alton, Robert D., Jr.: chairman, president, chief executive officer, Hickory Tech Corp.; trustee, Hickory Tech Corp. Foundation

Linfield College

Eigsti, Roger Harry: chairman, chief executive officer, SAFECO Corp.

London School of Economics

Bilton, Stuart Douglas: president, chief executive officer, Chicago Title Corp.; trustee, Chicago Title and Trust Co. Foundation

Brown, Ronald C.: executive vice president, chief financial officer, Starwood Hotels & Resorts Worldwide, Inc.

Chookaszian, Dennis Haig: chairman, chief executive officer, CNA

Wurtzel, Alan Leon: chairman, Circuit City Foundation; chairman, trustee, Circuit City Stores, Inc.

Long Island University

DeCaro, Angelo: treasurer, director, Goldman Sachs Foundation

Gardner, James Richard: vice president, Pfizer Foundation

Johnsmeyer, William L.: trustee, Butler Manufacturing Co. Foundation

Osborne, Burl: president publishing division, director, Belo Corp. (A.H.); president, trustee, Belo Corp. Foundation (A.H.)

Yablon, Leonard Harold: secretary-treasurer, Forbes Foundation

Loras College

Kenney, Richard John: director, Consolidated Papers Foundation, Inc.; senior vice president finance, Consolidated Papers, Inc.

Louisiana College

McDivitt, Norris E.: vice president operations & engineering, Texas Gas Transmission Corp.

Louisiana State University

Armstrong, Malcolm: executive vice president operations, Delta Air Lines, Inc.

Bernard, Bruce E.: director, Shell Oil Co. Foundation

Brian, Pierre Leonce Thibaut: trustee, Air Products Foundation

Gilpin, Larry: executive vice president, Target Corp.; trustee, Target Foundation

Hemminghaus, Roger Roy: chairman, director, Ultramar Diamond Shamrock Corp.

Longwell, Harry J.: senior vice president, Exxon Mobil Corp.

Phares, Lynn Levisay: president, fund manager, director, ConAgra Foundation

Purvis, George Frank, Jr.: chairman, president, chief executive officer, director, Pan-American Life Insurance Co.

Raspino, Louis A., Jr.: senior vice president, chief financial officer, Louisiana Land & Exploration Co.; director, Louisiana Land & Exploration Co. Foundation

Terrill, James E.: executive vice president, United States Sugar Corp.

Woodward, Joanne Gignilliat: director, Newman's Own Foundation

Louisiana State University School of Banking

McMillan, Howard Lamar, Jr.: president, chief operating officer, director, Deposit Guaranty National Bank

Louisiana Tech University

Larance, Charles L.: vice president corporate relations, GenAmerica Corp.; president, GenAmerican Foundation

Lowell Technological Institute

McKone, Francis L.: president, chief executive officer, director, Albany International Corp.

Loyola College

Barrett, Allen M., Jr.: chairman, McCormick & Co. Inc.

Crooke, Edward A.: president, Baltimore Gas & Electric Foundation

Gans, Terry Alexander: vice president, advertising, Giant Food Inc.

Hanway, H. Edward: president, chief executive officer, CIGNA Corp.

Poindexter, Christian Herndon: chairman, Baltimore Gas & Electric Foundation; chairman, chief executive officer, director, Constellation Energy Group, Inc.

Loyola College Montreal

D'Alessandro, Dominic: president, chief executive officer, director, Manulife Financial

Loyola Marymount University

Gundhofer, Jerry A.: chairman, director, Star Bank NA; vice president, Star Bank NA, Cincinnati Foundation

Tambakeras, Markos I.: director, Honeywell Foundation

Loyola University

Bell, Wayne: secretary, Ralph's-Food 4 Less Foundation; senior counsel, assistant secretary, Ralph's Grocery Co.

Carroll, Philip Joseph: chairman, chief executive officer, Fluor Corp.; chairman, trustee, Fluor Foundation

Cosse, Steven Anthony: senior vice president, general counsel, Murphy Oil Corp.

Faust, F. Lee: vice president, CertainTeed Corp.

Forsythe, John G.: vice president tax and public affairs, Ecolab Inc.

Gauvreau, Paul Richard: treasurer, Pittway Corp. Charitable Foundation

Grundhofer, John Francis: president, chief executive officer, director, U.S. Bancorp

Julsrud, Christopher K.: vice president human resources, Morton International Inc.

Klein, Barbara A.: vice president, comptroller, Ameritech Corp.

Maher, Francesca M.: senior vice president, general counsel, secretary, United Airlines Inc.

Menzer, John: executive vice president, Wal-Mart Stores, Inc.

Moran, Harry J.: executive vice president, Sonoco Products Co.

Murdy, James L.: executive vice president finance and administration, chief financial officer, Allegheny Technologies Inc.; trustee, Allegheny Technologies Inc. Charitable Trust

O'Toole, Robert Joseph: director, Firstar Milwaukee Foundation; chairman, president, chief executive officer, director, Smith Corp. (A.O.); director, Smith Foundation, Inc. (A.O.)

Quinlan, Michael Robert: chairman executive committee, McDonald's Corp.; director, McDonald's Corp. Charitable Foundation

Raspino, Louis A., Jr.: senior vice president, chief financial officer, Louisiana Land & Exploration Co.; director, Louisiana Land & Exploration Co. Foundation

Loyola University Chicago

Koenemann, Carl F.: chief financial officer, executive vice president, Motorola Inc.

Mack, Raymond Phillip: director, Arvin Foundation; vice president human resources, Arvin Industries, Inc.

Luther College

McClimon, Timothy J.: executive director, AT&T Foundation

Scholtens, Jean A.: vice president, treasurer, Eastern Enterprises

Wangstad, Kristi Rollag: vice president public affairs, Alliant Techsystems; president, Alliant Techsystems Community Investment Foundation

Macalester College

Andersen, Anthony Lee: director, Fuller Co. Foundation (H.B.); chairman, director, Fuller Co. (H.B.)

Anderson, Lowell Carlton: chairman, director, Allianz Life Insurance Co. of North America

Beyer, Jeffrey C.: president, Farmers Group Safety Foundation

Malone College

Hopkins, Thomas E.: vice president human resources, Sherwin-Williams Co.; assistant secretary, trustee, Sherwin-Williams Foundation

Manchester College

Gochenaur, Jack A.: senior vice president administration & services, chief financial officer, Fortis Insurance Co.; president, trustee, Fortis Insurance Foundation

Winger, Charles Joseph (Chuck): vice president, chief financial officer, Cinergy Corp.

Manchester University

Sear, Timothy R. G.: trustee, Alcon Foundation; president, chief executive officer, Alcon Laboratories, Inc.

Manhattan College

Corbo, Vincent J.: president, chief executive officer, director, Hercules Inc.

Gallagher, Terence Joseph: secretary, director, Pfizer Foundation

Hunter, Robert D.: trustee, Chase Manhattan Foundation

Nelson, Robert N.: treasurer, Trace International Holdings, Inc. Foundation

Peterson, Charles T.: chief financial officer, managing director, S.G. Cowen

Mankato State University

Andreas, David Lowell: chairman, director, National City Bank Foundation; chairman, chief executive officer, National City Bank of Minneapolis

Malmberg, David Curtis: director, National City Bank of Minneapolis

Nagorske, Lynn A.: executive vice president, chief financial officer, treasurer, TCF National Bank Minnesota

Marietta College

Knicely, Howard V.: president, TRW Foundation

Ray, Terry D.: vice president business development, Eastern Enterprises

Marist College

Heasley, Philip G.: president, chief operating officer, U.S. Bancorp

McGowan, W. Brian: chairman, Grace Foundation Inc.

Marquette University

Bauer, Chris Michael: president, Firstar Milwaukee Foundation

Becker, John A.: president, chief operating officer, director, Firstar Bank Milwaukee NA; vice chairman, Firstar Milwaukee Foundation

Black, Natalie A.: group vice president interiors, general counsel, director, Kohler Co.

Brostowitz, James M.: treasurer, Harley-Davidson Foundation

Burleigh, William Robert: president, chief executive officer, director, Scripps Co. (E.W.); member, Scripps Howard Foundation

Graff, Stephen Ney: director, Bucyrus-Erie Foundation

Hobbs, Richard F.: vice president administration, Universal Foods Corp.; vice president, director, Universal Foods Foundation

Keyes, James Henry: advisor, Johnson Controls Foundation; president, Johnson Controls Inc.

Klein, Barbara A.: vice president, comptroller, Ameritech Corp.

Kucharski, John Michael: trustee, PerkinElmer Foundation; chairman, chief executive officer, director, PerkinElmer, Inc.

Larson, Wayne E.: trustee, Ladish Co. Foundation

Liebler, Arthur C.: vice president communications, DaimlerChrysler Corp.; trustee, DaimlerChrysler Corp. Fund

McCarragher, Bernard John: chairman, director, Menasha Corp.; chairman, Menasha Corp. Foundation

Remmel, Jerry G.: chief financial officer, vice president, treasurer, Wisconsin Energy Corp.
Sanders, Wayne R.: chairman, chief executive officer, director, Kimberly-Clark Corp.
Schuenke, Donald John: director, Freddie Mac
Shiel, William A.: senior vice president facilities development, Walgreen Co.
Shiely, John Stephen: president, chief operating officer, director, Briggs & Stratton Corp.; vice president, director, Briggs & Stratton Corp. Foundation
Wenzler, Joseph P.: secretary, treasurer, WICOR Foundation; senior vice president, chief financial officer, WICOR, Inc.

Marquette University Law School

Larson, Wayne E.: trustee, Ladish Co. Foundation

Marshall University

Osborne, Burl: president publishing division, director, Belo Corp. (A.H.); president, trustee, Belo Corp. Foundation (A.H.)

Marycrest College

Marty, Mary: assistant treasurer, Boston Globe Foundation

Maryknoll College

Cody, Thomas Gerald: executive vice president legal & human resources, Federated Department Stores, Inc.

Massachusetts Institute of Technology

Baukol, Ronald O.: director, executive vice president, Minnesota Mining & Manufacturing Co.
Benenson, James, Jr.: chairman, president, director, Vesper Corp.; trustee, Vesper Foundation
Blanchard, J. A., III: president, chief executive officer, director, Deluxe Corp.
Bodman, Samuel Wright, III: chairman, chief executive officer, director, Cabot Corp.; president, director, Cabot Corp. Foundation
Brian, Pierre Leonce Thibaut: trustee, Air Products Foundation
Campbell, Robert Henderson: chairman, chief executive officer, Sunoco Inc.
Carp, Daniel A.: president, chief operating officer, director, Eastman Kodak Co.
Condit, Philip Murray: chairman, chief executive officer, director, Boeing Co.
Deavenport, Earnest W., Jr.: chairman, chief executive officer, director, Eastman Chemical Co.
Engel, Joel Stanley: vice president technology, Ameritech Corp.
Fiorina, Carleton S.: president, chief executive officer, director, Hewlett-Packard Co.
Fites, Donald Vester: director, Caterpillar Foundation
Gray, Charles Agustus: vice president technology, Cabot Corp.; director, Cabot Corp. Foundation
Hale, Roger W.: chairman, chief executive officer, director, LG&E Energy Corp.; president, LG&E Energy Foundation
Harris, William W.: director, Pittway Corp. Charitable Foundation
Hatsopoulos, George Nicholas: founder, chairman, chief executive officer, director, Thermo Electron Corp.; committee member, Thermo Electron Foundation
Heuchling, Theodore Paul: trustee, Little Foundation (Arthur D.)
Howard, James Joseph, III: chairman, president, chief executive officer, director, Northern States Power Co.
Howison, George Everett: vice president, Burlington Resources Foundation
Koch, Charles de Ganahl: chairman, chief executive officer, director, president, Koch Industries, Inc.
Koch, David Hamilton: director, Koch Foundation, Inc. (Fred C. and Mary R.)
Kresa, Kent: chairman, president, chief executive officer, director, Northrop Grumman Corp.
Lhota, William J.: executive vice president, American Electric Power
Lohman, Gordon Russell: trustee, Amsted Industries Foundation; director, Amsted Industries Inc.
McCormick, William Thomas, Jr.: chairman, chief executive officer, director, Consumers Energy Co.; chairman, Consumers Energy Foundation
McKee, Robert E., III: executive vice president corporate strategy & development, du Pont de Nemours & Co. (E.I.)
Mead, Dana George: chairman, chief executive officer, director, Tenneco Automotive
Mee, Michael F.: senior vice president, chief financial officer, Bristol-Myers Squibb Co.
Nayak, P. Ranganath: trustee, Little Foundation (Arthur D.); senior vice president, Little, Inc. (Arthur D.)
Reed, John Shepard: co-chairman, Citibank Corp.
Richards, Thomas E.: executive vice president communications information products sector, Ameritech Corp.
Satre, Philip Glen: chairman, president, chief executive officer, director, Promus Hotel Corp.
Shaffer, Oren G.: executive vice president, chief financial officer, Ameritech Corp.
Simmons, Richard Paul: chairman, president, chief executive officer, Allegheny Technologies Inc.
Spoon, Alan Gary: president, chief operating officer, director, The Washington Post
Standish, J. Spencer: chairman, director, Albany International Corp.
Stata, Ray S.: chairman, chief executive officer, director, Analog Devices, Inc.
Stevens, Philip Ashworth: vice president, trustee, National Machinery Foundation, Inc.
Swanson, Robert A.: director, Genentech Foundation for Biomedical Sciences
Tyson, Laura D'Andrea: director, Ameritech Foundation
Wolf, Thomas W.: trustee, York Federal Savings & Loan Foundation

Massachusetts Institute of Technology Sloan School of Management

Hough, Lawrence Alan: president, chief executive officer, Student Loan Marketing Association

McGill University

Black, Lennox K.: president, Teleflex Foundation; chairman, director, Teleflex Inc.
Bronfman, Edgar Miles: chairman, trustee, Bronfman Foundation/Joseph E. Seagram & Sons, Inc. Fund (Samuel); chairman, Seagram & Sons, Inc. (Joseph E.)
D'Alessandro, Dominic: president, chief executive officer, director, Manulife Financial
DeSimone, Livio Diego: chairman, chief executive officer, Minnesota Mining & Manufacturing Co.
Pitts, John Wilson: director, PACCAR Foundation
Roth, John: president, chief executive officer, chief operating officer, director, Nortel
Thoman, G. Richard: president, chief operating officer, Xerox Corp.
Zuckerman, Mortimer Benjamin: co-founder, chairman, co-publisher, director, Daily News

Memphis State University

Kelley, John C., Jr.: president Memphis Banking Group, First Tennessee National Corp.

Menlo College

Copley, David C.: president, trustee, Copley Foundation (James S.); president, chief executive officer, director, senior management board, Copley Press, Inc.

Mercer University

Reiman, Thomas Jay: senior vice president public policy, Ameritech Corp.

Merrimack College

Doherty, Leonard Edward: member advisory committee, admin officer, Dow Jones Foundation
Powers, Paul Joseph: chairman, president, chief executive officer, director, Commercial Intertech Corp.; president, trustee, Commercial Intertech Foundation

Miami University

Armstrong, C. Michael: chairman, chief executive officer, AT&T Corp.
Bersticker, Albert C.: chairman, director, chief executive officer, Ferro Corp.; president, trustee, Ferro Foundation
Burrell, Richard L.: senator vice president finance, secretary, treasurer, Barry Corp. (R.G.); treasurer, Barry Foundation
Gans, Terry Alexander: vice president, advertising, Giant Food Inc.
Hayden, Joseph Page, Jr.: trustee, Star Bank NA, Cincinnati Foundation
Hines, B. E.: secretary, Duriron Foundation
Joslin, Roger Scott: treasurer, State Farm Companies Foundation
Lison, Stephen A.: vice president, trustee, SPX Foundation
Medford, Dale L.: vice president corporate finance, chief financial officer, Reynolds & Reynolds Co.
Perez, Arnaldo: assistant vice president, secretary, Arison Foundation; vice president, general counsel, secretary, Carnival Corp.
Stallkamp, William J.: member corporate review committee, Mellon Financial Corp.
Stein, James C.: president, chief operating officer, Fluor Corp.; trustee, Fluor Foundation
Wiksten, Barry Frank: president, CIGNA Foundation

Michigan Institute of Technology

Ford, William Clay, Jr.: chairman, Ford Motor Co.

Michigan School of Mines

Anderson, Charles D.: trustee, Anderson Foundation

Michigan State University

Beale, Susan M.: director, Detroit Edison Foundation
Borman, Paul: president, director, Borman Fund (The); chairman, Borman's Inc.
Buchholz, William E.: vice president, chief financial officer, Nalco Chemical Co.
Butler, John D.: executive vice president, chief human resources officer, Textron Inc.
Byrd, Richard Hays: treasurer, Borden Foundation, Inc.
Cornelius, James M.: director, AUL Foundation Inc.
Creek, Wallace W.: secretary, General Motors Foundation
Crull, Timm F.: retired chairman, Nestle U.S.A. Inc.
Davis, Dwight D.: president, chief operating officer

Ennest, John William: chief financial officer, Citizens Bank-Flint

Evans, Gorton M., Jr.: president, chief executive officer, director, Consolidated Papers, Inc.

Ewing, Stephen E.: president, chief executive officer, director, Michigan Consolidated Gas Co.

Golub, Lewis: chairman, chief executive officer, director, Golub Corp.

Hehl, David K.: director, La-Z-Boy Inc.

Hinton, John R.: executive vice president administration, chief financial officer, Kellogg Co.; president, trustee, Kellogg Co. Twenty-Five Year Employees' Fund Inc.

Jones, Ingrid Saunders: chairman, director, Coca-Cola Foundation

Lytle, Gary R.: vice president federal relations, Ameritech Corp.

McClung, James Allen: vice president, director, FMC Foundation

Melican, James Patrick, Jr.: executive vice president legal & external affairs, International Paper Co.; director, International Paper Co. Foundation

Meuleman, Robert Joseph: director, AMCORE Foundation

Nern, Christopher C.: vice president, general counsel, Detroit Edison Co.; director, Detroit Edison Foundation

Oesterreicher, James E.: chairman, chief executive officer, director, Penney Co., Inc. (J.C.)

Pilon, Lawrence James: senior vice president human resources, Whitman Corp.

Porter, Edward A.: vice president, general counsel, secretary, Walter Industries Inc.

Radcliffe, R. Stephen: executive vice president, American United Life Insurance Co.

Ranck, Bruce E.: president, chief executive officer, director, Browning-Ferris Industries Inc.

Ratner, Albert Benjamin: trustee, Forest City Enterprises Charitable Foundation, Inc.; co-chairman, director, Forest City Enterprises, Inc.

Schafer, Glenn Stanley: president, director, Pacific Mutual Life Insurance Co.

Scheid, Steven L.: executive vice president, chief financial officer, Schwab & Co., Inc. (Charles)

Stockman, David A.: co-chairman, director, Collins & Aikman Corp.; president, director, Collins & Aikman Foundation

Sutton, Howard: trustee, Steelcase Foundation

Valade, Gary C.: executive vice president, chief financial officer, DaimlerChrysler Corp.; trustee, DaimlerChrysler Corp. Fund

Walker, Martin Dean: chairman, chief executive officer, director, Hanna Co. (M.A.)

Wardeberg, George E.: president, WICOR Foundation; president, chief executive officer, director, WICOR, Inc.

Zemsky, Howard: president, Russer Foods; trustee, Russer Foods/Zemsky Family Trust

Michigan Technological Institute

Opie, John D.: vice chairman, executive officer, director, General Electric Co.

Middlebury College

Brown, Stephen Lee: chairman, chief executive officer, director, Hancock Financial Services (John)

Calise, Nicholas James: vice president, associate general counsel, secretary, BFGoodrich Co.; secretary, Goodrich Foundation, Inc. (B.F.)

Mark, Reuben: chairman, chief executive officer, Colgate-Palmolive Co.

Martin, John E.: chairman, chief executive officer, Taco Bell Corp.; chairman, Taco Bell Foundation

Merdek, Andrew Austin: vice president legal affairs, secretary, Cox Enterprises Inc.; secretary, Cox Foundation (James M.)

Painter, Alan Sproul: vice president, executive director, AlliedSignal Foundation Inc.

Steinhauser, Carolyn E.: trustee, York Federal Savings & Loan Foundation

Midland Lutheran College

Sturgeon, John: president, chief operating officer, Mutual of Omaha Insurance Co.

Midwestern University

Quinn, David W.: executive vice president, chief financial officer, director, Centex Corp.

Mills College

Hill, Bonnie Guiton: vice president, Times Mirror Co.; president, chief executive officer, Times Mirror Foundation

Millsaps College

Ray, John Thomas, Jr.: president, director, Fuller Co. Foundation (H.B.)

Mineral Area College

Koupal, Carl M., Jr.: trustee, Western Resources Foundation; executive vice president, chief administrative officer, Western Resources Inc.

Minnesota Deluth College

Senkler, Robert L.: president, director, Minnesota Mutual Foundation; chairman, president, chief executive officer, Minnesota Mutual Life Insurance Co.

Minnesota University

Nelson, Glen David, MD: vice chairman, Medtronic, Inc.

Mississippi College

Ebbers, Bernard J.: president, chief executive officer, director, MCI WorldCom, Inc.

Mississippi State University

De Nicola, Paul J.: president, chief executive officer, Southern Co. Services Inc.

Deavenport, Earnest W., Jr.: chairman, chief executive officer, director, Eastman Chemical Co.

Holliman, Wilbert G. 'Mickey': chairman, president, chief executive officer, director, Furniture Brands International, Inc.

May, T. Michael: president, Hawaiian Electric Co., Inc.; director, Hawaiian Electric Industries Charitable Foundation

Missouri School of Mines & Metallurgy

Bailey, Keith E.: chairman, president, director, chief executive officer, Texas Gas Transmission Corp.; president, director, Williams Companies Foundation (The)

Missouri State University

Jones, Raymond E.: secretary, director, Shelter Insurance Foundation; executive vice president, secretary, Shelter Mutual Insurance Co.

Mitchell College

Marsh, Harold N., III: treasurer, Fireman's Fund Foundation

Monmouth College

Pate, James Leonard: chairman, chief executive officer, director, Pennzoil-Quaker State Co.

Montana State University

Cromer, Richard F.: executive vice president, chief operating officer energy supply division, Montana Power Co.; director, Montana Power Foundation

Zimmerman, Michael E.: vice president, general counsel, Montana Power Co.

Monticello College

Humphreys, Ethel Mae Craig: president, Craig Foundation (E.L.); chairman, chief executive officer, Tamko Roofing Products

Morehouse College

Moten, John, Junior: vice president community relations, Laclede Gas Co.

Morgan State University

Fierce, Hughlyn F.: trustee, Chase Manhattan Foundation

Graves, Earl Gilbert: director, Aetna Foundation

Mount Holyoke College

Foley, Cheryl M.: vice president, secretary, general counsel, Cinergy Corp.; vice president, secretary, director, Cinergy Foundation

Mount Saint Mary's College

Amoss, George B.: vice president finance, chief financial officer, CertainTeed Corp.; chief financial officer, CertainTeed Corp. Foundation

Norris, Paul J.: chairman, president, chief executive officer, director, Grace & Co. (W.R.); director, Grace Foundation Inc.

Mount Senario College

Bonkoski, Kenneth John: controller, Menasha Corp.; treasurer, Menasha Corp. Foundation

Munich University

Becherer, Hans Walter: chairman, chief executive officer, director, Deere & Co.; director, Deere Foundation (John)

Murray State University

Knue, Paul Frederick: trustee, Scripps Howard Foundation

National War College

Johnson, Hansford Tillman: trustee, USAA Foundation, A Charitable Trust

Naval Nuclear Power School

McNeill, Corbin Asahel, Jr.: president, chief executive officer, director, chairman, PECO Energy Co.

Neighborhood Playhouse Dramatic School

Woodward, Joanne Gignilliat: director, Newman's Own Foundation

Netherlands School of Business

de Vink, Lodewijk J. R.: director, Warner-Lambert Charitable Foundation; president, chief operating officer, director, Warner-Lambert Co.

New England School of Law

Halperin, Richard E.: president, Revlon Foundation Inc.

Kendrick, William J.: vice president public affairs, Air Products and Chemicals, Inc.; chairman, Air Products Foundation

New Hampshire College

Marsh, David E.: chief financial officer, Central Maine Power Co.

New Jersey Institute of Technology

Caccamo, Aldo M.: vice president public affairs, Chevron Corp.

Devlin, James Richard: director, Sprint Foundation

New Mexico State University

Apodaca, Clara: trustee, Hitachi Foundation

New York Law School

Glickenhaus, Seth M.: general partner, Glickenhaus & Co.

Heagney, Lawrence: member advisory committee, contact, Milliken Foundation

Plumeri, Joseph James, II: president, Citigroup

Trencher, Lewis J.: chairman, director, Thompson Co. Fund (J. Walter); chief operating officer, director, Thompson Co. (J. Walter)

New York University

Black, Daniel James: treasurer, Carter-Wallace Foundation; president, chief operating officer, director, Carter-Wallace, Inc.

Boyle, Richard James: vice chairman, director, Chase Manhattan Bank, NA; trustee, Chase Manhattan Foundation

Breslawsky, Marc C.: president, chief operating officer, Pitney Bowes Inc.

Brine, Kevin R.: trustee, Bernstein & Co. Foundation, Inc. (Sanford C.)

Brown, Donald P.: executive vice president, treasurer, director, Slant/Fin Corp.; treasurer, director, Slant/Fin Foundation

Cantor, Bernard Gerald: president, director, Cantor, Fitzgerald Foundation; chairman, director, Cantor, Fitzgerald Securities Corp.

Cline, Robert Stanley: chairman, chief executive officer, director, Airborne Freight Corp.

Dubin, Melvin: chairman, Slant/Fin Corp.; president, director, Slant/Fin Foundation

Esposito, Michael Patrick, Jr.: trustee, Chase Manhattan Foundation

Evanson, Paul John: president, treasurer, director, FPL Group Foundation, Inc.

Falk, Harvey L.: member grantmaking committee, Claiborne Foundation (Liz); president, vice chairman, Liz Claiborne, Inc.

Farnsworth, Philip Richeson: secretary, ABC

Faust, F. Lee: vice president, CertainTeed Corp.

Fierce, Hughlyn F.: trustee, Chase Manhattan Foundation

Fine, Roger Seth: vice president, general counsel, Johnson & Johnson; president, Johnson & Johnson Family of Companies Contribution Fund

Gallagher, Terence Joseph: secretary, director, Pfizer Foundation

Giaramita, Phillip S.: vice president corporate communications, International Paper Co.; president, director, International Paper Co. Foundation

Goldstone, Steven F.: chairman, chief executive officer, director, Reynolds Tobacco (R.J.); chairman, RJR Nabisco Foundation

Golub, Harvey: chairman, chief executive officer, director, American Express Co.; trustee, American Express Foundation

Hammerman, Stephen Lawrence: vice president, trustee, Merrill Lynch & Co. Foundation Inc.; vice chairman, general counsel, Merrill Lynch & Co., Inc.

Heimbold, Charles Andreas, Jr.: chairman, president, chief executive officer, Bristol-Myers Squibb Co.

Heisen, JoAnn Heffernan: vice president, chief information officer, Johnson & Johnson; treasurer, Johnson & Johnson Family of Companies Contribution Fund

Hohn, Harry George, Jr.: chairman, director, New York Life Foundation

Humphreys, David Craig: secretary-treasurer, Craig Foundation (E.L.); president, chief operating officer, director, Tamko Roofing Products

Jones, D. Paul, Jr.: chairman, chief executive officer, Compass Bank; trustee, Compass Bank Foundation

Joyce, William H.: chairman, president, chief executive officer, chief operating officer, Union Carbide Corp.

Karmel, Roberta S.: trustee, Kemper Foundation (James S.); partner, Kemper National Insurance Companies

Kenny, John J.: treasurer, Loews Corp.; secretary, treasurer, trustee, Loews Foundation

Kogan, Richard Jay: chairman, chief executive officer, Schering-Plough Corp.; trustee, member, Schering-Plough Foundation

Kroeber, C. Kent: chairman contributions committee, Interpublic Group of Companies, Inc.

Labrecque, Thomas Goulet: president, chief operating officer, director, Chase Manhattan Bank, NA; president, Chase Manhattan Foundation

Levine, Lawrence E.: secretary, Panasonic Foundation

Levine, Ralph: president, chief operating officer, director, Carter-Wallace, Inc.

Lipp, Robert Irving: chief executive officer, Citigroup; vice president, treasurer, trustee, Citigroup Foundation

Lipton, Martin: partner, Wachtell, Lipton, Rosen & Katz; president, Wachtell, Lipton, Rosen & Katz Foundation

Lopiano, John A.: senior vice president, Xerox Corp.; trustee, Xerox Foundation

Lyall, Katharine Culbert: trustee, Kemper Foundation (James S.)

Matis, Nina B.: director, Katten, Muchin & Zavis Foundation

Maurer, Jeffrey Stuart: president, chief operating officer, director, United States Trust Co. of New York

McAllister, Francis R.: vice president, director, ASARCO Foundation; president, chief executive officer, ASARCO Inc.

McKenna, William John: director, chairman, Kellwood Co.; chairman, president, director, Kellwood Foundation

McWilliams, D. Bradley: vice president, Cooper Industries Foundation; chief financial officer, senior vice president finance, Cooper Industries, Inc.

Mirsky, Susan: vice president, director, Thompson Co. Fund (J. Walter)

O'Hare, Dean Raymond: chairman, Chubb Corp.

Paladino, Daniel R.: trustee, Bronfman Foundation/Joseph E. Seagram & Sons, Inc. Fund (Samuel); executive vice president, general counsel, secretary, Seagram & Sons, Inc. (Joseph E.)

Poses, Frederick M.: director, AlliedSignal Foundation Inc.; president, chief operating officer, AlliedSignal Inc.

Raskin, Fred C.: president, chief operating officer, Eastern Enterprises; trustee, Eastern Enterprises Foundation

Redgrave, Martyn R.: executive vice president, chief financial officer, Carlson Companies, Inc.

Rein, Catherine Amelia: director, MetLife Foundation; vice president, Metropolitan Life Insurance Co.

Ripp, Robert M.: chairman, chief executive officer, director, AMP Inc.

Roth, Michael I.: chairman, chief executive officer, director, MONY Group (The); director, MONY Life Insurance of New York (The)

Rukeyser, Robert James: senior vice president corporate affairs, Fortune Brands, Inc.

Russack, Richard A.: president, Burlington Northern Santa Fe Foundation

Schoon, Susan Wylie: trustee, Chase Manhattan Foundation

Schuman, Allan L.: president, chief executive officer, director, chairman, Ecolab Inc.

Schwartz, Barry K.: chairman, chief executive officer, director, Calvin Klein

Shepherd, Kathleen Shearen Maynard: director, Tribune New York Foundation

Strickland, Carol A.: chairman corporate contributions committee, U.S. Trust Corp. Foundation

Tisch, Laurence Alan: chairman, co-chief executive officer, CBS Corp.; trustee, Loews Foundation

Travaille, Hubert Duane: president, trustee, Potlatch Foundation II

Trencher, Lewis J.: chairman, director, Thompson Co. Fund (J. Walter); chief operating officer, director, Thompson Co. (J. Walter)

Wachtell, Herbert M.: senior partner, Wachtell, Lipton, Rosen & Katz; vice president, treasurer, Wachtell, Lipton, Rosen & Katz Foundation

Wagar, James Lee: manager, Carter-Wallace Foundation

Weill, Richard L.: president, MBIA Inc.

Wendt, John R.: president, Maybelline, Inc.

New York University Leonard N. Stern School of Business

Locher, John J.: treasurer, Barnes Group Foundation Inc.; vice president, treasurer, Barnes Group Inc.

Munder, Barbara A.: senior vice president new initiatives, McGraw-Hill Companies, Inc.

Travaglianti, Edward: chairman, chief executive officer, European American Bank

New York University School of Law

McLaughlin, Michael John: secretary, New York Life Foundation; senior vice president, deputy general counsel, New York Life Insurance Co.

Niagara University

Kennedy, Bernard Joseph: chairman, president, chief executive officer, director, National Fuel Gas Distribution Corp.

Noonan, Timothy J.: president, chief operating officer, director, Rite Aid Corp.

Riordan, Gerald R.: director, Ryder System Charitable Foundation

Nichols College

Lovejoy, Joseph Ensign: chairman, director, Ensign-Bickford Industries

Nordhein-Westfalen (Germany)

Mueller, Gerd Dieter: executive vice president, chief financial officer, director, chief administrative officer, Bayer Corp.; president, Bayer Foundation

North Carolina State College

Dickson, Alan Thomas: president, Dickson Foundation; chairman, Ruddick Corp.

North Carolina State University

Amick, Michael: executive vice president forest products & industrial packaging, International Paper Co.

Bush, Norman: vice president, Fort James Corp.

Causey, Jerry L.: director, Consolidated Natural Gas System Foundation

Ellis, William Edward, Jr.: secretary, Barry Foundation

Foster, Kent B.: president, director, GTE Corp.; trustee, GTE Foundation

Gill, John A.: senior vice president, FirstEnergy Corp.

Guin, James M.: vice president human resources & public relations, Burlington Industries, Inc.

Peterson, William E.: general counsel, Sierra Pacific Resources

Rhodes, James Thomas: president, chief executive officer, director, Dominion Resources, Inc.

Risinger, James A.: chairman, chief executive officer, Old National Bank Evansville

Spilman, Robert H.: chairman, chief executive officer, Bassett Furniture Industries; chairman, director, Bassett Furniture Industries Fdn.

Womack, Robert R.: chairman, chief executive officer, director, Zurn Industries, Inc.

Woolard, Edgar Smith, Jr.: director, du Pont de Nemours & Co. (E.I.)

North Dakota State University

Bernauer, David W.: president, chief operating officer, Walgreen Co.

Estenson, Noel Keith: president, chief executive officer, Cenex Harvest States

Kalainov, Sam Charles: chairman, president, chief executive officer, AmerUS Group

Watson, Noel G.: vice president, director, Jacobs Engineering Foundation; president, chief executive officer, director, Jacobs Engineering Group

North Georgia College

Eidson, Julian W.: vice president, controller, Scientific-Atlanta, Inc.

Heldreth, Nick E.: vice president human resources corporate relations, Harris Corp.

North Staffordshire College Technology

Kampouris, Emmanuel Andrew: chairman, president, chief executive officer, director, American Standard Inc.

North Texas State University

Bowlin, Michael Ray: chairman, director, ARCO Foundation; chairman, chief executive officer, director, Atlantic Richfield Co.

Braham, W. Martin: trustee, Delta Air Lines Foundation

Flood, Joan Moore: assistant treasurer, Trace International Holdings, Inc. Foundation

Northeast Missouri State University

Anderson, William J.: assistant secretary, Pella Corp.; secretary, Pella Rolscreen Foundation

Northeastern State University

Fleshman, Betty R.: secretary, Potlatch Corp.

Northeastern University

Aley, Paul Nathaniel: president, director, National Machinery Co.; president, National Machinery Foundation, Inc.

Convisser, Theodora S.: trustee, Boston Edison Foundation

Donnelly, James Charles: vice president, director, WICOR Foundation; vice president, WICOR, Inc.

Fair, Russell B.: vice president pharmacy operations, Giant Food Inc.

Fishman, Jerald G.: president, chief executive officer, director, Analog Devices, Inc.

Flake, Floyd Harold: director, Fannie Mae Foundation

Hjerpe, William M.: director, Honeywell Foundation

Horan, Douglas S.: senior vice president, general counsel, Boston Edison Co.; trustee, Boston Edison Foundation

Keough, William H.: senior vice president, chief financial officer, Pioneer Group

Lesser, Richard G.: executive vice president, chief operating officer, director, TJX Companies, Inc.; chief operating officer, director, TJX Foundation, Inc.

Long, Francis A.: executive vice president, chief operating officer, director, Pennsylvania Power & Light

Messer, Chester R.: president, chief operating officer, Boston Gas Co.; trustee, Eastern Enterprises Foundation

Pullo, Robert W.: chairman, chief executive officer, director, York Federal Savings & Loan Association; president, trustee, York Federal Savings & Loan Foundation

Reed, Cynthia: assistant secretary, Hasbro Charitable Trust Inc.; senior vice president, general counsel, Hasbro, Inc.

Northern Arizona University

Pulatie, David L.: senior vice president human resources, Phelps Dodge Corp.

Snider, Timothy R.: senior vice president, Phelps Dodge Corp.

Northern Illinois University

Brown, Joseph Warner, Jr.: chairman, chief executive officer, MBIA Inc.

Flaherty, Gerald S.: trustee, Caterpillar Foundation; group president, Caterpillar Inc.

Jokiel, Peter E.: senior vice president, chief financial officer, CNA

Kopp, David C.: assistant secretary, CIGNA Foundation

Northwest Missouri State University

Porter, James T.: director, Honeywell Foundation; vice president, chief administrative officer, Honeywell International Inc.

Northwestern College

Zylstra, Stanley James: chairman, director, Land O'Lakes, Inc.

Northwestern Polytechnic Institute

Weatherstone, Dennis: trustee, Merck Co. Foundation

Northwestern University

Adler, Ira R.: executive vice president, chief financial officer, Tucson Electric Power Co.

Ashley, James Wheeler: director, Globe Foundation

Bachmann, John W.: managing partner, Jones & Co. (Edward D.); chairman, Jones & Co. Foundation (Edward D.)

Berey, Mark H.: senior vice president, chief financial officer, treasurer, Giant Food Inc.

Besser, John Edward: director, Barnes Group Foundation Inc.; senior vice president finance & law, Barnes Group Inc.

Bottorff, Dennis C.: chairman, president, chief executive officer, director, First American Corp.

Brendsel, Leland C.: chairman, chief executive officer, director, Freddie Mac; director, Freddie Mac Foundation

Burdett, Kathleen: vice president, chief financial officer, Dexter Corp.; vice president, Dexter Corp. Foundation

Carpenter, William M.: chief executive officer, director, chairman, Bausch & Lomb Inc.

Chabraja, Nicholas D.: chairman, chief executive officer, director, General Dynamics Corp.

Chandler, Charles Quarles, IV: co-trustee, INTRUST Bank Charitable Trust; president, director, INTRUST Financial Corp.

Chookaszian, Dennis Haig: chairman, chief executive officer, CNA

Cole, Franklin Alan: chairman, Aon Foundation

Compton, Ronald E.: chairman, president, Aetna Foundation

Davis, Walter Stewart: secretary, treasurer, Grede Foundation

Denny, Charles W.: president, chief executive officer, director, Square D Co.

Forsythe, John G.: vice president tax and public affairs, Ecolab Inc.

Gallagher, Richard S.: director, Badger Meter Foundation

Galvin, Christopher B.: director, Motorola Foundation; president, chief executive officer, director, Motorola Inc.

Hatsopoulos, John Nicholas: retired president, Thermo Electron Corp.; committee member, Thermo Electron Foundation

Herron, James Michael: secretary, director, Ryder System Charitable Foundation

Hobor, Nancy A.: vice president communications & investor relations, Morton International Inc.

Holmes, David Richard: chief executive officer, chief operating officer, director, Reynolds & Reynolds Co.

Huston, Steve: secretary, Wrigley Co. Foundation (Wm. Jr.)

Iverson, Francis Kenneth: chairman, director, Nucor Corp.; director, Nucor Foundation

Kalaher, Richard A.: president, American Standard Foundation; vice president, secretary, general counsel, American Standard Inc.

Keyes, James Henry: advisor, Johnson Controls Foundation; president, Johnson Controls Inc.

LeBoeuf, Raymond W.: director, PPG Industries Foundation; director, chairman, chief executive officer, PPG Industries, Inc.

Liska, Paul J.: executive vice president, chief financial officer, Saint Paul Companies Inc.

Longfield, William H.: president, Bard Foundation (C.R.); chairman, chief executive officer, director, Bard, Inc. (C.R.)

Lux, Clifton L.: director, Globe Foundation

McConnell, William Thompson: chairman, ceo, Park National Bank; chairman, Park National Corp. Foundation

Meister, Paul M.: vice president, treasurer, Winthrop Foundation

Morgan, Glenn R.: executive vice president, chief financial officer, Hartmarx Corp.

Morris, Michael H.: secretary, director, Sun Microsystems Foundation, Inc.

Moseley, Colin: director, Matlock Foundation; chairman, chief executive officer, Simpson Investment Co.

Mutz, John M.: vice president, Cinergy Corp.; director, Cinergy Foundation

Pearce, Harry J.: vice chairman, General Motors Corp.

Pearl, Melvin E.: treasurer, director, Katten, Muchin & Zavis Foundation

Piet, William M.: vice president, director, Wrigley Co. Foundation (Wm. Jr.); vice president corporate affairs, secretary, assistant to president, Wrigley Co. (Wm. Jr.)

Pollard, Charles William, Jr.: chairman, director, ServiceMaster Co.; president, director, ServiceMaster Foundation

Powell, George Everett, Jr.: trustee, Yellow Corp. Foundation

Preston, James Edward: vice president, director, Avon Products Foundation, Inc.; chairman, chief executive officer, director, Avon Products, Inc.

Rosenzweig, Richard Stuart: executive vice president, director, Playboy Enterprises Inc.

Ryan, Patrick G.: chairman, president, chief executive officer, Aon Corp.; president, Aon Foundation

Schadt, James Phillip: chairman, president, chief executive officer, director, Reader's Digest Association, Inc. (The); chairman, director, Reader's Digest Foundation

Schaffer, Donald J.: member contributions committee, GATX Corp.
Schuchardt, Daniel Norman: secretary, treasurer, FMC Foundation
Shiely, John Stephen: president, chief operating officer, director, Briggs & Stratton Corp.; vice president, director, Briggs & Stratton Corp. Foundation
Simpson, Louis Allen: president, chief executive officer capital operations, director, GEICO Corp.
Standen, Craig Clayton: senior vice president corporate development, Scripps Co. (E.W.)
Stone, Jerome H.: vice president, secretary, treasurer, Stone Foundation
Stone, Marvin N.: director, Stone Foundation
Taylor, John I.: director, Zenith Electronics Corp.
Warner, John Andrew, III: director, Telcordia Technologies
Wayman, Robert P.: executive vice president finance & administration, chief financial officer, Hewlett-Packard Co.
Ziegler, R. Douglas: advisor, Johnson Controls Foundation

Northwestern University Kellogg Graduate School of Business Administration

Palmer, Denise: vice president, strategy & finance, Chicago Tribune Co.; treasurer, Chicago Tribune Foundation
Stryker, Steven Charles: director, Shell Oil Co. Foundation

Northwestern University Kellogg Graduate School of Management

Galvin, Christopher B.: director, Motorola Foundation; president, chief executive officer, director, Motorola Inc.

Northwestern University National Graduate Trust School

Oliver, Orson: president, director, Mid-America Bank of Louisville

Norwich University

Bertrand, Frederic Howard: chairman, Central Vermont Public Service Corp.
Keyser, F. Ray, Jr.: chairman, director, Central Vermont Public Service Corp.

Notre Dame College

Kearney, Christopher J.: trustee, SPX Foundation

Oakland University

Feldhouse, Lynn Alexandra: vice president, secretary, DaimlerChrysler Corp. Fund
Pawley, Dennis K.: executive vice president manufacturing, DaimlerChrysler Corp.

Oberlin College

Barnett, Robert L.: director, Ameritech Foundation
Greenfield, Jerry: cofounder, vice chairman, Ben & Jerry's Homemade Inc.
Shapira, David S.: trustee, Giant Eagle Foundation; chairman, chief executive officer, director, Giant Eagle Inc.
Wurtzel, Alan Leon: chairman, Circuit City Foundation; chairman, trustee, Circuit City Stores, Inc.

Occidental College

Meier, Stephen Charles: vice chairman, Times Mirror Co.

Ohio Northern University

Rish, Stephen A.: vice president, corporate public involvement, Nationwide Insurance Co.; president, Nationwide Insurance Enterprise Foundation

Ohio State University

Aley, Paul Nathaniel: president, director, National Machinery Co.; president, National Machinery Foundation, Inc.
Bero, Robert D.: president, chief executive officer, Menasha Corp.
Biehl, George C.: senior vice president, chief financial officer, corporate secretary, director, Southwest Gas Corp.; trustee, Southwest Gas Corp. Foundation
Blaine, Gregory W.: chief operating officer, True North Communications, Inc.; president, director, True North Foundation
Blouch, Gerald B.: president, chief operating officer, Invacare Corp.; trustee, Invacare Foundation
Bolton, John Roger: senior vice president, Aetna Foundation; senior vice president corporate communications, Aetna, Inc.
Ecker, H. Allen: president subscriber systems, Scientific-Atlanta, Inc.
Elbert, Paul A.: president, chief executive officer natural gas, Consumers Energy Co.
Gherlein, Gerald Lee: member contributions committee, Eaton Charitable Fund
Giering, John L.: senior vice president finance & administration, chief financial officer, NCR Corp.
Graber, Don R.: chairman, president, chief executive officer, director, Huffy Corp.; trustee, Huffy Foundation, Inc.
Gross, Ronald Martin: chairman, president, director, Rayonier Foundation; chairman, president, chief executive officer, director, Rayonier Inc.
Gruber, David P.: president, chief executive officer, director, Wyman-Gordon Co.; chairman, vice president, director, Wyman-Gordon Foundation
Johnson, Charles M.: vice chairman, Wells Fargo & Co.
Lhota, William J.: executive vice president, American Electric Power
Lowrie, William G.: president, deputy chief executive officer, director, BP Amoco Corp.
Martin, Richard J.: executive vice president public relations employee communications, AT&T Corp.; chairman, trustee, AT&T Foundation
Oakley, Robert Alan: executive vice president, chief financial officer, Nationwide Insurance Enterprise Foundation
Ong, John Doyle: chairman board, director, Ameritech Corp.
Parsons, Stuart N.: secretary, treasurer, director, Park National Corp. Foundation
Ridgway, Ronald H.: senior vice president, Pulitzer Publishing Co.; secretary, treasurer, director, Pulitzer Publishing Co. Foundation
Riethman, Robert B.: chief financial officer, Monarch Machine Tool Co.; treasurer, secretary, Monarch Machine Tool Co. Foundation
Rohr, James Edward: chief executive officer, president, director, PNC Financial Services Group
Roub, Bryan Roger: trustee, Harris Foundation
Sandman, Dan D.: senior vice president human resources, secretary, general counsel, USX Corp.; trustee, USX Foundation, Inc.
Stevens, Philip Ashworth: vice president, trustee, National Machinery Foundation, Inc.
Zacks, Gordon Benjamin: chairman, president, chief executive officer, director, Barry Corp. (R.G.); president, Barry Foundation

Ohio University

Brown, Richard Harris: chairman, chief executive officer, director, EDS Corp.
Burner, David L.: chairman, president, chief executive officer, director, BFGoodrich Co.
Carp, Daniel A.: president, chief operating officer, director, Eastman Kodak Co.
DiGirolamo, Vincent A.: executive vice president, vice chairman, National City Bank of Cleveland
Grasley, Michael Howard: senior vice president, Shell Oil Co.; member executive committee, director, Shell Oil Co. Foundation
Grealis, William J.: vice president, Cinergy Corp.; director, Cinergy Foundation
Marcum, Kenneth William: treasurer, Commercial Intertech Foundation
Parisi, Franklin Joseph: chairman, Star Tribune Foundation
Post, David A.: vice president, Equifax Foundation; corporate vice president, chief financial officer, Equifax Inc.

Ohio Wesleyan University

Gherlein, Gerald Lee: member contributions committee, Eaton Charitable Fund
Miller, Donn Biddle: president, chief executive officer, Pacific Mutual Life Insurance Co.
Moll, Curtis E.: treasurer, trustee, Jochum-Moll Foundation (The)
Roub, Bryan Roger: trustee, Harris Foundation
Simpson, Louis Allen: president, chief executive officer capital operations, director, GEICO Corp.

Oklahoma City University

Conant, Colleen Christner: branch manager, Scripps Co. (E.W.); trustee, Scripps Howard Foundation
Gaylord, Edward Lewis: chairman, chief executive officer, director, publisher, Oklahoma Publishing Co.; trustee, Oklahoma Foundation (The)

Oklahoma State University

Allen, W. Wayne: chairman, chief executive officer, director, Phillips Petroleum Co.
Jones, Lewis B.: vice president, partner, USX Corp.
McDaniel, Tom J.: vice chairman, director, Kerr-McGee Corp.
Strecker, A. M.: vice president, director, Oklahoma Gas & Electric Co. Foundation

Old Dominion University

Ellenberger, Richard G.: president, chief executive officer, director, Cincinnati Bell Inc.
Haislip, Wallace G.: senior vice president finance, chief financial officer, treasurer, Scientific-Atlanta, Inc.

Oregon State University

Ashwill, Terry M.: vice president, director, True North Foundation
Costley, Gary E.: chairman, president, chief executive officer, director, International Multifoods Corp.
Emmerson, George: director, Sierra Pacific Foundation; vice president, Sierra Pacific Industries
Johnson, Norman E.: senior vice president technology, Weyerhaeuser Co.; trustee, Weyerhaeuser Co. Foundation
Larson, Peter N.: chairman, chief executive officer, director, Brunswick Corp.
Laurance, Dale R.: director, Occidental Petroleum Charitable Foundation; president, senior operations officer, director, Occidental Petroleum Corp.
Martin, Lauralee: chief financial officer, Heller Financial, Inc.
McKennon, Keith Robert: chairman, president, PacifiCorp; member, PacifiCorp Foundation

Osgoode Hall Law School

Brown, Ronald C.: executive vice president, chief financial officer, Starwood

Hotels & Resorts Worldwide, Inc.

Ottawa University

Brown, Michael: president, Foundation of the Litton Industries; president, chief operating officer, Litton Industries, Inc.

Otterbein College

Schmitt, Wolfgang Rudolph: chairman, chief executive officer, director, Rubbermaid Inc.

Oxford University

Brademas, John: chairman, Texaco Foundation

Chellgren, Paul Wilbur: chief executive officer, chairman, director, Ashland, Inc.; member, Ashland Inc. Foundation

Hudnut, Stewart Skinner: director, Illinois Tool Works Foundation

Kampouris, Emmanuel Andrew: chairman, president, chief executive officer, director, American Standard Inc.

Kerr, William T.: chairman, chief executive officer, director, Meredith Corp.

Kinsolving, Augustus Blagden: director, ASARCO Foundation

Magowan, Peter Alden: president, managing general partner, Safeway Inc.

Miller, Joseph Irwin: director associate, Cummins Engine Co., Inc.; director, Cummins Engine Foundation

Mulford, David: chairman, Credit Suisse First Boston

Raines, Franklin Delano: chairman, chief executive officer, Fannie Mae; director, Fannie Mae Foundation

Romeril, Barry D.: executive vice president, chief financial officer, Xerox Corp.

Spaeth, Karl Henry: chairman, trustee, Quaker Chemical Foundation

Oxford University Balliol College

Heineman, Benjamin Walter, Jr.: director, GE Fund

Oxford University Worcester College

Kemper, David Woods: chairman, president, chief executive officer, director, Commerce Bancshares, Inc.

Pace University

Alegi, August Paul: director, GEICO Philanthropic Foundation

Auguste, MacDonald: treasurer, Rayonier Foundation

Boudreau, Donald L.: vice president, trustee, Chase Manhattan Foundation

Bundschuh, George August William: director, New York Life Foundation

Catlow, Walter S.: executive vice president, Ameritech Corp.

Eckstein, Marie N.: trustee, Dow Corning Foundation

Grasso, Richard A.: chairman, chief executive officer, New York Stock Exchange, Inc.

Hudnut, Stewart Skinner: director, Illinois Tool Works Foundation

Noha, Edward J.: director, CNA Foundation

O'Hare, Dean Raymond: chairman, Chubb Corp.

Prendergast, G. Joseph: director, Wachovia Foundation, Inc. (The)

Upbin, Hal Jay: president, chief executive officer, director, Kellwood Co.

Pacific Union College

Bainum, Stewart William, Jr.: chairman, Manor Care Health SVS, Inc.

Paper Science & Technology

Olson, Richard E.: chairman, chief executive officer, director, Champion International Corp.

Pennsylvania State University

Beghini, Victor Gene: trustee, USX Foundation, Inc.

Clarke, Thomas E.: president, chief operating officer, Nike, Inc.

Daley, Leo J.: vice president, treasurer, Air Products and Chemicals, Inc.

Dugan, Allan E.: senior vice president corporate strategic service, Xerox Corp.; trustee, Xerox Foundation

Edgerton, Brenda Evans: vice president business development, Campbell Soup Co.; treasurer, trustee, Campbell Soup Foundation

Franklin, Barbara Hackman: director, Dow Chemical Co.

Goode, R. Ray: director, Ryder System Charitable Foundation

Griffin, James B.: director, Ryder System Charitable Foundation

Grubb, Edgar Harold: executive vice president, chief financial officer, Transamerica Corp.; director, Transamerica Foundation

Heilala, John A.: trustee, Vulcan Materials Co. Foundation

Joyce, William H.: chairman, president, chief executive officer, chief operating officer, Union Carbide Corp.

Kirby, William Joseph: vice president, director, FMC Foundation

Laffon, Polk, IV: vice president corporate relations, corporate secretary, Knight Ridder

Leininger, Jeffrey L.: vice chairman specialized commercial banking, Mellon Financial Corp.

Louis, Kenneth C.: president, chief operating officer, director, Ameritas Life Insurance Corp.

Mattson, Eric Leonard: senior vice president, chief financial officer, Baker Hughes Inc.

Morgan, James McClay: member executive committee, director, Shell Oil Co. Foundation

Myers, Mark B.: senior vice president corporate research & technology, Xerox Corp.; trustee, Xerox Foundation

Phillips, Ped Wesley: vice president, Hanna Co. Foundation (M.A.)

Pribanic, Gerald J.: executive vice president, chief financial officer, Maytag Corp.; trustee, Maytag Corp. Foundation

Rein, Catherine Amelia: director, MetLife Foundation; vice president, Metropolitan Life Insurance Co.

Robin, Kenneth H.: senior vice president, general counsel, Household International Inc.

Salizzoni, Frank L.: vice chairman, Block Foundation (H&R); president, chief executive officer, director, Block, Inc. (H&R)

Stecko, Paul T.: president, director, Tenneco Packaging

Toner, Jeffrey M.: trustee, Kingsbury Fund

Wardrop, Richard M., Jr.: chairman, chief executive officer, director, AK Steel Corp.

Wiesner, Carol A.: treasurer, director, Foundation of the Litton Industries

Wolf, Gregory H.: president, chief operating officer, director, Humana, Inc.

Pennsylvania University

Goldstone, Steven F.: chairman, chief executive officer, director, Reynolds Tobacco (R.J.); chairman, RJR Nabisco Foundation

Pepperdine University

Mitchell, Warren I.: president, director, Southern California Gas Co.

Schwartz, Richard: chairman, president, chief executive officer, director, Alliant Techsystems

Wood, Willis B., Jr.: chairman, chief executive officer, director, Pacific Enterprises

Phillips Exeter Academy

Daniels, John Hancock: chairman, Archer-Daniels-Midland Foundation

Ottaway, James Haller, Jr.: senior vice president, director, Dow Jones & Co., Inc.; member advisory committee, Dow Jones Foundation

Pine Manor College

Wiley, Deborah: vice chairman, Wiley & Sons (John)

Pittsburgh Theological Seminary

Sease, Gene Elwood: director, Central Newspapers Foundation

Polytechnic Institute

Jacobs, Joseph J.: president, director, Jacobs Engineering Foundation; chairman, director, Jacobs Engineering Group

Polytechnic Institute Brooklyn

D'Amato, Anthony S.: chairman, Borden Foundation, Inc.

Engel, Joel Stanley: vice president technology, Ameritech Corp.

Matthews, Craig Gerard: president, chief operating officer, Brooklyn Union

Polytechnic University

Martinez, Arthur C.: chairman, chief executive officer, president, Sears, Roebuck and Co.

Pomona College

Disney, Roy Edward: trustee, Disney Co. Foundation (Walt); vice chairman, director, Disney Co. (Walt)

Fukunaga, Mark H.: chairman, director, Servco Foundation; chief executive officer, chairman, Servco Pacific

Mandel, Morton Leon: deputy chairman, Premier Industrial Corp.; trustee, Premier Industrial Foundation

Neal, Philip Mark: president, chief executive officer, director, Avery Dennison Corp.

Sasaki, Robert K.: director, Alexander & Baldwin Foundation

Scripps, Charles Edward: chairman executive committee, director, vice president, Scripps Co. (E.W.); member, Scripps Howard Foundation

Scripps, Edward Wyllis, II: member, Scripps Howard Foundation

Portland State University

Kirchhof, Anton Conrad: corporate secretary, general counsel, Louisiana-Pacific Corp.; secretary, Louisiana-Pacific Foundation

O'Brien, Richard T.: executive vice president, chief operating officer, PacifiCorp; member, PacifiCorp Foundation

Shafer, Douglas C.: trustee, Tektronix Foundation; president, America operations, Tektronix, Inc.

Presbyterian College

Kofol, Milan: vice president, treasurer, Reader's Digest Association, Inc. (The); treasurer, Reader's Digest Foundation

Sloan, Albert Frazier: director, Lance Foundation

Staton, Robert Emmett: president, Colonial Life & Accident Insurance Co.

Princeton University

Atwater, Horace Brewster, Jr.: trustee, Merck Co. Foundation

Baker, John Daniel, II: president, chief executive officer, director, Florida Rock Industries; vice president, Florida Rock Industries Foundation

Bewley, Peter D.: vice president, secretary, Clorox Co. Foundation

Blanchard, J. A., III: president, chief executive officer, director, Deluxe Corp.

Blankley, Walter Elwood: president, director, AMETEK Foundation; chairman, director, AMETEK, Inc.

Bowen, William Gordon, PhD: trustee, Merck Co. Foundation

Bradford, James C., Jr.: president, Bradford and Co. Foundation (J.C.); senior partner, Bradford & Co. (J.C.)

Buchanan, William Hobart, Jr.: assistant secretary, Dun & Bradstreet Corp. Foundation, Inc.

Budney, Albert J., Jr.: president, director, Niagara Mohawk Holdings Inc.

Buechner, Thomas Scharman: trustee, Corning Inc. Foundation

Burt, Robert Norcross: chairman, chief executive officer, director, FMC Corp.; director, FMC Foundation

Byck, Joseph S.: vice president, Union Carbide Foundation

Campbell, Robert Henderson: chairman, chief executive officer, Sunoco Inc.

Canning, John Beckman: secretary, Rayonier Foundation

Coker, Charles Westfield: trustee, Sonoco Foundation; vice president, Sonoco Products Co.

Condit, Philip Murray: chairman, chief executive officer, director, Boeing Co.

Connor, Walter Robert: director, Glaxo Wellcome Foundation

Coors, William K.: chairman, president, director, Coors Brewing Co.

Corbo, Vincent J.: president, chief executive officer, director, Hercules Inc.

Cutchins, Clifford Armstrong, IV: president, Fort James Corp.; chairman, director, Fort James Foundation (The)

Davis, William L.: chairman, chief executive officer, director, Donnelley & Sons Co. (R.R.)

Douglas, Paul W.: director, Phelps Dodge Foundation

Elliott, Anson Wright: vice president, trustee, Chase Manhattan Foundation

Fisher, Robert J.: vice president, Gap Foundation/ Gap Inc. Community Relations

Forbes, Christopher 'Kip': vice president, Forbes Foundation; vice chairman, corporate secretary, director, Forbes Inc.

Forbes, Malcolm Stevenson, Jr.: president, Forbes Foundation

Ford, William Clay, Jr.: chairman, Ford Motor Co.

Furlaud, Richard Mortimer: interim chief executive officer, International Flavors & Fragrances Inc.

Gardner, James Richard: vice president, Pfizer Foundation

Gifford, Charles Kilvert: trustee, BankBoston Charitable Foundation; chairman, chief executive officer, BankBoston Corp.

Greenwald, Gerald: chairman, chief executive officer, director, United Airlines Inc.

Hacker, Douglas A.: senior vice president finance, chief financial officer, United Airlines Inc.

Hamilton, Peter Bannerman: director, Brunswick Foundation; trustee, Kemper Foundation (James S.)

Henderson, James Alan: vice chairman, chief executive officer, director, Ameritech Corp.; chairman, director, Cummins Engine Foundation

Hockaday, Irvine O., Jr.: president, chief executive officer, director, Hallmark Cards Inc.

Hoyt, Charles Orcutt: director, Carter-Wallace Foundation; chairman executive committee, director, Carter-Wallace, Inc.

Hoyt, Henry Hamilton, Jr.: president, Carter-Wallace Foundation; chairman, chief executive officer, director, Carter-Wallace, Inc.

Hudnut, Stewart Skinner: director, Illinois Tool Works Foundation

Jannotta, Edgar D.: president, Blair & Co. Foundation (William); senior director, Blair & Co. (William)

Johnson, James A.: chairman, chief executive officer, director, Fannie Mae; chairman, Fannie Mae Foundation

Kurtz, Larry: trustee, McKesson Foundation

Lemberg, Thomas Michael: clerk, Lotus Development Corp.; secretary, Polaroid Foundation

Levinson, Arthur David: president, chief executive officer, director, Genentech Inc.

Lewis, Peter Benjamin: chairman, president, chief executive officer, director, Progressive Corp.

Mahoney, David L.: co-chief executive officer, McKesson-HBOC Corp.

Manigault, Peter: chairman, Evening Post Publishing Co.; president, Post and Courier Foundation

Maritz, William Edward: chairman, chief executive officer, president, Maritz Inc.

McClelland, William Craig: trustee, Union Camp Charitable Trust; chairman, chief executive officer, director, Union Camp Corp.

Melrose, Kendrick B.: chairman, co-president, chief executive officer, director, Toro Co.; director, Toro Foundation

Milliken, Minot King: member advisory committee, Milliken Foundation

Newlin, William Rankin: trustee, Kennametal Foundation

Nunes, Geoffrey: chairman, Millipore Foundation (The)

Osborne, Richard de Jongh: director, ASARCO Foundation; chairman, chief executive officer, director, ASARCO Inc.

Pfund, William H.: trustee, Rubbermaid Foundation

Pollnow, Charles F., Jr.: treasurer, director, Matlock Foundation; chief financial officer, Simpson Investment Co.

Redgrave, Martyn R.: executive vice president, chief financial officer, Carlson Companies, Inc.

Rosenberger, David M.: secretary, Tracy Fund (Emmet and Frances)

Rosenthal, Sol: counsel, Playboy Enterprises Inc.

Ruckelshaus, William Doyle: chairman, director, Browning-Ferris Industries Inc.

Schrader, Thomas F.: vice president, director, WICOR Foundation

Simpson, Louis Allen: president, chief executive officer capital operations, director, GEICO Corp.

Sullivan, Austin Padraic, Junior: trustee, General Mills Foundation; senior vice president corporate relations, General Mills, Inc.

Toll, Daniel Roger: trustee, Kemper Foundation (James S.)

Torgerson, William T.: managing, Potomac Electric Power Co.

Ughetta, William Casper: trustee, Corning Inc. Foundation

Van Cleve, William Moore: member public policy committee, Emerson Charitable Trust; partner, Emerson Electric Co.

Warner, John Andrew, III: director, Telcordia Technologies

Weinberg, John Livingston: chairman, president, director, Goldman Sachs Foundation

Wynne, John Oliver: president, director, Landmark Communications Foundation; president, chief executive officer, Landmark Communications Inc.

Princeton University Woodrow Wilson School of International Public Affairs

Hardis, Stephen Roger: chairman, chief executive officer, director, Eaton Corp.

Providence College

Dascoli, D. Paul: chief financial officer, vice president, Thomasville Furniture Industries Inc.

Fiondella, Robert William: chairman, president, chief executive officer, Phoenix Home Life Mutual Insurance Co.

Flaherty, Walter J.: chief financial officer, senior vice president, Eastern Enterprises; trustee, Eastern Enterprises Foundation

Ryan, Arthur Frederick: trustee, Chase Manhattan Foundation; chairman, chief executive officer, Prudential Insurance Co. of America

Sutton, Howard: president, Providence Journal Charitable Foundation

Purdue University

Armstrong, Neil A.: trustee, Milacron Foundation; director, Milacron, Inc.

Bares, William G.: chairman, president, chief executive officer, Lubrizol Corp. (The); trustee, Lubrizol Foundation (The)

Bescherer, Edwin A., Jr.: trustee, Dun & Bradstreet Corp. Foundation, Inc.

Binder, Gordon M.: chairman, chief executive officer, director, Amgen, Inc.

Campbell, Cheryl Nichols: operation service advisory group, Cincinnati Bell Inc.

Carl, John L.: executive vice president, chief financial officer, BP Amoco Corp.; director, BP Amoco Foundation

Cole, Robert A.: chief financial officer, senior vice president, American General Finance; senior vice president, chief financial officer, director, American General Finance Foundation

Davies, Richard Warren: trustee, Hubbell Foundation (Harvey)

Dora, James E.: director, AUL Foundation Inc.

Engibous, Thomas James: director, Texas Instruments Foundation; president, chief executive officer, chairman, director, Texas Instruments Inc.

Gardner, Jeff: chief financial officer, ALLTEL Corp.

Geier, Peter E.: vice chairman, Huntington Bancshares Inc.

Graham, Patricia Albjerg, PhD: trustee, Hitachi Foundation

Haddock, Ronald Wayne: president, chief executive officer, director, FINA; president, FINA Foundation

Hemminghaus, Roger Roy: chairman, director, Ultramar Diamond Shamrock Corp.

Higginbotham, A. Leon, Jr.: director, New York Times Co. Foundation

Hodgson, Thomas Richard: president, chief operating officer, director, Abbott Laboratories

Hoffer, Robert A., Jr.: trustee, Hoffer Foundation; vice president, Hoffer Plastics Corp.

Iverson, Francis Kenneth: chairman, director, Nucor Corp.; director, Nucor Foundation

Jenkins, Thomas A.: treasurer, trustee, Dayton Power and Light Co. Foundation

Jennings, James Burnett: president, Hunt Oil Co.

Johnsmeyer, William L.: trustee, Butler Manufacturing Co. Foundation

Kraft, Richard A.: president, director, Panasonic Foundation

Lawson, William Hogan, III: chairman, chief executive officer, director, Franklin Electric Co.; president, Franklin Electric, Edward J. Schaefer, and T. W. KehoeCharitable and Educational Foundation

Lucky, Robert Wendell: corporate vice president, Telcordia Technologies

McKee, E. Marie: senior vice president, Corning Inc.; chairman, trustee, Corning Inc. Foundation

McNeeley, Robert D.: president, director, Reilly Industries, Inc.

Meyer, Daniel Joseph: president, Milacron Foundation; chairman, president, chief executive officer, director, Milacron, Inc.

Muehlbauer, James Herman: vice president, director, Koch Foundation

Neel, Curtis Dean, Jr.: trustee, Eckerd Corp. Foundation

Oakley, Robert Alan: executive vice president, chief financial officer, Nationwide Insurance Enterprise Foundation
Parsons, Susan E.: secretary, treasurer, Koch Enterprises, Inc.; secretary, treasurer, director, Koch Foundation
Rhodes, James Thomas: president, chief executive officer, director, Dominion Resources, Inc.
Semler, Jerry D.: chairman, president, chief executive officer, director, American United Life Insurance Co.; chairman, director, AUL Foundation Inc.
Sharpe, Robert Francis, Jr.: senior vice president public affairs, general counsel, PepsiCo, Inc.
Vaughn, John: vice president unit development & strategy, Ameritech Corp.
Walton, Jon David: trustee, Allegheny Technologies Inc. Charitable Trust
Young, William D.: chief operating officer, Genentech Inc.

Queene University Kingston

Carty, Donald J.: vice president, treasurer, AMR/American Airlines Foundation; president, chairman, chief executive officer, director, AMR Corp.

Queens College

Barad, Jill Elikann: director, Mattel Foundation; chairman, chief executive officer, director, Mattel Inc.
Light, Walter Frederick: trustee, Air Products Foundation
Margolis, Jay M.: member grantmaking committee, Claiborne Foundation (Liz)

Queens University

Goodes, Melvin Russell: chairman, chief executive officer, director, Ameritech Corp.
Skilling, Raymond Inwood: executive vice president, chief counsel, director, Aon Corp.; director, Aon Foundation

Quincy University

Stephan, Richard C.: vice president, controller, director, Viad Corp. Fund

Radcliffe College

Karmel, Roberta S.: trustee, Kemper Foundation (James S.); partner, Kemper National Insurance Companies

Reed College

Jobs, Steven Paul: interim chief executive officer, Apple Computer, Inc.

Regis College

Kelly, Richard C.: executive vice president, chief financial officer, New Century Energies; treasurer, New Century Energies Foundation

Rensselaer Polytechnic Institute

Alfiero, Salvatore Harry: founder, chairman, chief executive officer, director, Mark IV Industries; chairman, Mark IV Industries Foundation
Bozzone, Robert P.: vice chairman, director, Allegheny Technologies Inc.; trustee, Allegheny Technologies Inc. Charitable Trust
Buhrmaster, Robert C.: president, chief executive officer, director, chairman, Jostens, Inc.
DiCamillo, Gary Thomas: chairman, chief executive officer, director, Polaroid Corp.
Manning, Kenneth Paul: president, Universal Foods Corp.; president, director, Universal Foods Foundation
McKone, Francis L.: president, chief executive officer, director, Albany International Corp.
Mitropoulis, Iris: chairman, Kingsbury Corp.
Snyder, Dale E.: senior vice president, technical services, Kohler Co.
Zuendt, William F.: president, chief executive officer, Wells Fargo & Co.

Rhode Island Institute of Technology

Carp, Daniel A.: president, chief operating officer, director, Eastman Kodak Co.

Rhodes College

Bryan, John Henry: chairman, Sara Lee Corp.; director, Sara Lee Foundation
Hollingsworth, John Mark: assistant secretary, Simmons Foundation, Inc. (Harold)
Morris, Herman, Jr.: president, chief executive officer, Memphis Light Gas & Water Division

Rice University

Draper, Ernest Linn, Jr.: chairman, president, chief executive officer, director, American Electric Power
Zimmerman, James M.: chairman, chief executive officer, director, Federated Department Stores, Inc.

Richmond College

Wagner, J. Wilt: director, Reynolds Metals Co. Foundation

Rider College

Alexander, John F.: trustee, PerkinElmer Foundation; senior vice president, chief financial officer, PerkinElmer, Inc.
Burenga, Kenneth L.: president, chief operating officer, director, Dow Jones & Co., Inc.

Rochester Institute Technology

Hermance, Frank S.: president, chief executive officer, director, AMETEK, Inc.
Kober, Roger W.: chairman, chief executive officer, director, Rochester Gas & Electric Corp.

Rockhurst College

Forsythe, Donald George: vice president corporate relations, Sprint Corp.; executive director, Sprint Foundation
Murphy, James W.: senior vice president corporate finance, American United Life Insurance Co.; treasurer, AUL Foundation Inc.
Panettiere, John Michael: president, chief executive officer, director, chairman, Blount International, Inc.

Rollins College

Ackerman, F. Duane: president, chief executive officer, BellSouth Corp.

Roosevelt University

Bangs, Lawrence N.: group executive, Household International Inc.
Burrus, Clark D.: vice president, director, First National Bank of Chicago Foundation
Elam, Lloyd Charles, MD: trustee, Merck Co. Foundation
Mahoney, Robert W.: chairman, president, chief executive officer, director, Diebold, Inc.
Rogala, Judith A.: member, Butler Manufacturing Co. Foundation
Williams, Edward Joseph: president, director, Harris Bank Foundation
Zona, Richard A.: vice chairman commercial banking & institutional finance, U.S. Bancorp

Rose-Hulman Institute Technology

Holland, Willard R.: chairman, chief executive officer, FirstEnergy Corp.

Royal Naval College

Black, Lennox K.: president, Teleflex Foundation; chairman, director, Teleflex Inc.

Royal Naval Engineering College

Walker, Grahame: chairman, chief executive officer, Dexter Corp.; president, Dexter Corp. Foundation

Rutgers University

Ackerman, Roger G.: trustee, Corning Inc. Foundation
Bell, Wayne: secretary, Ralph's-Food 4 Less Foundation; senior counsel, assistant secretary, Ralph's Grocery Co.
Cook, John Rowland: trustee, Harcourt General Charitable Foundation; senior vice president, chief financial officer, Harcourt General, Inc.
D'Andrade, Hugh Alfred: trustee, member, Schering-Plough Foundation
Edgerton, Brenda Evans: vice president business development, Campbell Soup Co.; treasurer, trustee, Campbell Soup Foundation
Gamper, Albert R., Jr.: president, chief executive officer, director, CIT Group Foundation; president, chief executive officer, chairman, CIT Group, Inc. (The)
Graham, John Gourlay: chief financial officer, senior vice president, GPU Energy
Hubschman, Henry A.: director, GE Fund
Jerrold, Douglas M.: vice president, Reynolds Metals Co. Foundation
Koeppe, Alfred C.: senior vice president corporate services & external affairs, Public Service Electric & Gas Foundation
Leininger, Jeffrey L.: vice chairman specialized commercial banking, Mellon Financial Corp.
Marcus, Bernard: chairman, director, Home Depot, Inc.
Matthews, Craig Gerard: president, chief operating officer, Brooklyn Union
McGregor, Douglas A.: trustee, Rouse Co. Foundation
Renyi, Thomas A.: president, chief executive officer, director, Bank of New York Co., Inc.
Walker, Joan H.: senior vice president corporate communications, Ameritech Corp.
Wells, James M., III: president, Crestar Finance Corp.
Wobst, Frank: chairman, chief executive officer, director, Huntington Bancshares Inc.
Wolff, Herbert Eric: secretary, director, First Hawaiian Foundation

Rutgers University Graduate School of Business

Codey, Lawrence R.: president, chief operating officer, Public Service Electric & Gas Co.

Rutgers University Stonier Graduate School of Banking

Allison, John Andrew, IV: chairman, chief executive officer, director, Branch Banking & Trust Co.
Cusick, Thomas A.: chairman, TCF National Bank Minnesota
DiGirolamo, Vincent A.: executive vice president, vice chairman, National City Bank of Cleveland
Khoury, Kenneth F.: secretary, Georgia-Pacific Foundation
Risinger, James A.: chairman, chief executive officer, Old National Bank Evansville
Sadler, Robert L.: president, vice chairman, director, Old Kent Bank
Yancey, James D.: vice chairman, director, president, chief operating officer, Synovus Financial Corp.

Ryerson Polytechnic Institute

Kitchen, Michael B.: president, chief executive officer, director, CUNA Mutual Group; secretary, treasurer, executive officer, CUNA Mutual Group Foundation, Inc.

Sacred Heart University

Gorman, Maureen V.: vice president, GTE Foundation

Iraola, Manuel J.: senior vice president, director, Phelps Dodge Corp.

Maffucci, David G.: senior vice president, chief financial officer, Bowater Inc.

Saint Bonaventure University

Emling, John: vice president, Barden Corp.; trustee, Barden Foundation, Inc.

Saint Cloud State College

McClimon, Timothy J.: executive director, AT&T Foundation

Saint Francis College

Cristallo, Peter P.: associate senior vice president human resources & administration, NEC America, Inc.

Dugan, Brendan J.: president, European American Bank

MacDonald, J. Randall: senior vice president human resources administration, GTE Corp.; trustee, GTE Foundation

Travaglianti, Edward: chairman, chief executive officer, European American Bank

Saint John's University

Amsterdam, Jack: secretary, treasurer, Leviton Foundation New York; chairman, treasurer, director, Leviton Manufacturing Co. Inc.

Black, Daniel James: treasurer, Carter-Wallace Foundation; president, chief operating officer, director, Carter-Wallace, Inc.

Cody, Thomas Gerald: executive vice president legal & human resources, Federated Department Stores, Inc.

Evanson, Paul John: president, treasurer, director, FPL Group Foundation, Inc.

Heine, Spencer H.: executive vice president, secretary, Montgomery Ward & Co., Inc.; president, Montgomery Ward Foundation

Larini, Ernest J.: chief financial officer, Warner-Lambert Charitable Foundation; vice president, chief financial officer, Warner-Lambert Co.

Mason, W. Bruce: chairman, chief executive officer, director, True North Communications, Inc.

Mattison, Robert Mayer: director, Graco Foundation; vice president, general counsel, secretary, Graco, Inc.

Maurer, Jeffrey Stuart: president, chief operating officer, director, United States Trust Co. of New York

McGowan, W. Brian: chairman, Grace Foundation Inc.

Needleman, Harry: secretary, Cantor, Fitzgerald Foundation; executive vice president, general counsel, Cantor, Fitzgerald Securities Corp.

Reuter, Carol Joan: chief executive officer, director, New York Life Foundation; vice president, New York Life Insurance Co.

Schamberger, John P.: member advisory board, Blue Bell Foundation; president, chairman jeanswear coalition, Blue Bell, Inc.

Schiro, James J.: chairman, senior partner, PricewaterhouseCoopers

Thornton, John T.: executive vice president, chief financial officer, Norwest Corp.; treasurer, Norwest Foundation

Saint John's University School of Law

Kenny, John J.: treasurer, Loews Corp.; secretary, treasurer, trustee, Loews Foundation

Saint Joseph's College

Boyer, David Scott: president, chief executive officer, director, Teleflex Inc.

Johnston, William E., Junior: president, chief operating officer, director, Morton International Inc.

Tuerff, James R.: president, director, American General Finance

Saint Joseph's Seminary

Conklin, Thomas J.: senior vice president, secretary, MONY Group (The); director, MONY Life Insurance of New York (The)

Saint Joseph's University

Agger, James Harrington: senior vice president, secretary, general counsel, Air Products and Chemicals, Inc.; director, Air Products Foundation

Donches, Steven G.: vice president public affairs, Bethlehem Steel Corp.; president, Bethlehem Steel Foundation

Heumann, Stephen Michael: vice president, treasurer, West Co. Inc.

Saint Lawrence University

Phillips, Richard B.: vice president, Crane Foundation

Scott, David J.: secretary, United Distillers & Vintners North America

Saint Leo College

Mullen, Dennis M.: president, chief executive officer, director, Agrilink Foods, Inc.

Saint Louis University

Ball, James Herington: senior vice president, general counsel, director, Nestle U.S.A. Inc.

Barrett, M. Patricia: vice president corporate communications, Ameren Corp.

Habig, Douglas A.: chairman, chief executive officer, director, Habig Foundation

Kniffen, Jan Rogers: senior vice president, treasurer, May Department Stores Co.; vice president, secretary, treasurer, director, May Department Stores Computer Foundation (The)

Mueller, Charles William: chairman, president, chief executive officer, Ameren Corp.; trustee, Ameren Corp. Charitable Trust

O'Connor, Edward J.: secretary, director, Smith Foundation, Inc. (A.O.)

Wadlington, Cuba, Jr.: vice president, Williams

Saint Mary Lake College

Corby, Francis Michael, Jr.: executive vice president finance & administration, chief financial officer, Harnischfeger Industries; treasurer, Harnischfeger Industries Foundation

Saint Mary's College

Coughlan, Gary Patrick: chief financial officer, senior vice president finance, Abbott Laboratories; director, Abbott Laboratories Fund

Raclin, Ernestine Morris: chairman emeritus, director, First Source Corp.; chairman, director, First Source Foundation

Saint Mary's University

Greehey, William Eugene: chairman, chief executive officer, director, Valero Energy Corp.

Saint Norbert College

Bittner, D. P.: treasurer, assistant secretary, Wisconsin Public Service Foundation, Inc.

Terry, Richard Edward: chairman, chief executive officer, director, Peoples Energy Corp.

Saint Paul Academy

Daniels, John Hancock: chairman, Archer-Daniels-Midland Foundation

Saint Paul's College

Wilson, Rita P.: director, Sears, Roebuck and Co. Foundation

Saint Peter's College

Codey, Lawrence R.: president, chief operating officer, Public Service Electric & Gas Co.

Lockwood, Glenn C.: senior vice president, chief financial officer, New Jersey Natural Gas Co.; treasurer, New Jersey Natural Gas Foundation

Sullivan, Thomas John: vice president, director,

Saint Thomas College

Commes, Thomas Allen: president, chief operating officer, director, Sherwin-Williams Co.; assistant secretary, trustee, Sherwin-Williams Foundation

Schoenecker, Guy: president, chief executive officer, Business Improvement; president, Schoeneckers Foundation

Saint Vincent College

Boyer, Herbert Wayne, PhD: chairman, president, director, Genentech Foundation for Biomedical Sciences; co-founder, director, Genentech Inc.

Salem College

Goodwin, James E.: president, chief operating officer, director, United Airlines Inc.

Salem State College

Davies, Richard Warren: trustee, Hubbell Foundation (Harvey)

Salmon P. Chase College of Law

Koziar, Stephen F., Jr.: president, trustee, Dayton Power and Light Co. Foundation

Lakin, Thomas J.: regional chairman, Star Bank NA; president, Star Bank NA, Cincinnati Foundation

San Francisco State University

Darling, Robert Edward, Jr.: chairman, Ensign-Bickford Foundation

San Jose State University

Barbakow, Jeffrey C.: chairman, chief executive officer, director, Tenet Healthcare Corp.

Beall, Donald Ray: director, Rockwell International Corp.

Choate, Jerry D.: chairman, chief executive officer, director, Allstate Foundation

Jacobi, Peter A.: president, Levi Strauss & Co.; vice president, Levi Strauss Foundation

Previte, Richard: president, chief operating officer, director, Advanced Micro Devices, Inc.

Sarah Lawrence College

Gumprecht, Pamela (Howard): trustee, Scripps Howard Foundation

Scripps College

Mersereau, Susan M.: trustee, Weyerhaeuser Co. Foundation

Seattle Pacific University

Blount, Winton Malcolm, Jr.: chairman, Blount International, Inc.

Habegger, Gary L.: vice president human resources, BFGoodrich Co.; president, Goodrich Foundation, Inc. (B.F.)

Seidman Graduate School

Metzger, Michael D.: vice president, chief financial officer, JSJ Corp.

Seton Hall University

Archinaco, Frank A.: director, PPG Industries Foundation; executive vice president, PPG Industries, Inc.
Codey, Lawrence R.: president, chief operating officer, Public Service Electric & Gas Co.
Koeppe, Alfred C.: senior vice president corporate services & external affairs, Public Service Electric & Gas Foundation
Larson, Peter N.: chairman, chief executive officer, director, Brunswick Corp.
Sullivan, Thomas John: vice president, director,

Shippensburg University of Pennsylvania

Welty, John Rider: secretary, Carpenter Technology Corp. Foundation

Siebel Institute of Technology

Busch, August Adolphus, III: chairman, president, chief executive officer, Anheuser-Busch Companies, Inc.

Simmons Colorado Graduate School of Management

Morby, Jacqueline C.: managing partner, Pacific Mutual Life Insurance Co.

Simpson College

Johnson, Charles B.: executive vice president operation, Cessna Aircraft Co.; trustee, Cessna Foundation, Inc.
Reed, James M.: trustee, Union Camp Charitable Trust; vice chairman, chief financial officer, director, Union Camp Corp.

Skidmore College

Brennan, Alice C.: vice president, secretary, Bristol-Myers Squibb Co.; secretary, Bristol-Myers Squibb Foundation Inc.
Strickland, Carol A.: chairman corporate contributions committee, U.S. Trust Corp. Foundation

Smith College

Lebedoff, Randy Miller: vice president, general counsel, McClatchy Co.; secretary, Star Tribune Foundation
Matis, Nina B.: director, Katten, Muchin & Zavis Foundation
Mirsky, Susan: vice president, director, Thompson Co. Fund (J. Walter)
Nelson, Marilyn Carlson: chairman, chief executive officer, president, Carlson Companies, Inc.
Tyson, Laura D'Andrea: director, Ameritech Foundation

Smithdeal College of Law

Chandler, Wallace Lee: vice president, director, Universal Leaf Foundation

Sorbonne University

Bergerac, Michel Christian: director, CBS Foundation

South Dakota State University

Dubois, Everett D.: treasurer, Burlington Resources Foundation; senior vice president, treasurer, Burlington Resources, Inc.

South Texas College of Law

Sykora, Donald D.: director, Reliant Energy Inc.

South Texas University

Martin, Bobby L.: member, Wal-Mart Foundation

Southeastern Louisiana University

Cosse, Steven Anthony: senior vice president, general counsel, Murphy Oil Corp.

Southern Illinois University

Dabney, Donna C.: secretary, Reynolds Metals Co. Foundation
Dabney, Fred E., II: executive director, Royal & SunAlliance Insurance Foundation, Inc.; vice president corporate communications, Royal & SunAlliance USA, Inc.
Howard, David P.: vice president, chief financial officer, treasurer, Furniture Brands International, Inc.
Kniffen, Jan Rogers: senior vice president, treasurer, May Department Stores Co.; vice president, secretary, treasurer, director, May Department Stores Computer Foundation (The)
Levan, B. W.: vice president, director, Shell Oil Co. Foundation
Wheatley, Bruce C.: vice president, Commercial Intertech Foundation

Southern Methodist University

Atkins, Sarah Humphreys: vice president, Craig Foundation (E.L.)
Duchossois, Craig J.: director, Duchossois Foundation; president, director, Duchossois Industries Inc.
Flood, Joan Moore: assistant treasurer, Trace International Holdings, Inc. Foundation
Hall, Floyd: chairman, president, chief executive officer, director, Kmart Corp.
Hall, William Austin: president, Hallmark Corporate Foundation
Hollingsworth, John Mark: assistant secretary, Simmons Foundation, Inc. (Harold)
Huey, Ward L., Jr.: president broadcast division, vice chairman, director, Belo Corp. (A.H.); vice president, trustee, Belo Corp. Foundation (A.H.)
Hunt, Ray Lee: chairman, chief executive officer, director, Hunt Oil Co.
Keith, Susan Stewart: assistant secretary, assistant treasurer, Halliburton Foundation, Inc.
Matthews, Clark J., II: president, chief executive officer, director, 7-Eleven, Inc.
Moll, Curtis E.: treasurer, trustee, Jochum-Moll Foundation (The)
Nye, Erle Allen: chairman, chief executive officer, director, TU Electric Co.
Pfeiffer, Eckhard A.: president, chief executive officer, director, Compaq Computer Corp.
Rosane, Edwin L.: president, USAA Life Insurance Co.
Rust, Edward Barry, Jr.: chairman, president, director, State Farm Companies Foundation; chairman, president, chief executive officer, director, State Farm Mutual Automobile Insurance Co.
Schlumberger, Pierre Marcel: director, Schlumberger Foundation
Skinner, Claire Corson: chairman, chief executive officer, Coachmen Industries, Inc.
Steward, H. Leighton: chairman, chief executive officer, president, Louisiana Land & Exploration Co.; director, Louisiana Land & Exploration Co. Foundation
Tyson, John H.: chairman, chief executive officer, president, director, Tyson Foods Inc.; trustee, Tyson Foundation, Inc.

Southern University

Stewart, Joseph Melvin: senior vice president corporate affairs, Kellogg Co.; trustee, Kellogg Co. Twenty-Five Year Employees' Fund Inc.

Southwest Missouri State University

Glass, David Dayne: trustee, Wal-Mart Foundation; director, Wal-Mart Stores, Inc.

Southwest Texas Junior College

Evans, Richard W., Jr.: chairman, chief executive officer, Frost National Bank

Southwest Texas State University

Baish, Richard Owen: senior vice president, director, El Paso Energy Foundation

Spring Hill College

Donovan, Dianne Francys: director, Chicago Tribune Foundation

Stanford University

Agnich, Richard John: director, Texas Instruments Foundation; senior vice president, secretary, general counsel, Texas Instruments Inc.
Allison, Herbert Monroe, Jr.: vice president, trustee, Merrill Lynch & Co. Foundation Inc.; president, chief operating officer, Merrill Lynch & Co., Inc.
Atwater, Horace Brewster, Jr.: trustee, Merck Co. Foundation
Bacon, Kenneth J.: senior vice president, Fannie Mae; director, Fannie Mae Foundation
Barrett, Craig R.: president, chief operating officer, director, Intel Corp.
Bechtel, Riley Peart: chairman, Bechtel Foundation; chairman, chief executive officer, director, Bechtel Group, Inc.
Belcher, Donald D.: chairman, president, chief executive officer, director, Banta Corp.; vice president, director, Banta Corp. Foundation
Bewley, Peter D.: vice president, secretary, Clorox Co. Foundation
Black, Natalie A.: group vice president interiors, general counsel, director, Kohler Co.
Brazier, Robert George: president, chief operating officer, director, Airborne Freight Corp.
Brinegar, Claude Stout: trustee, Unocal Foundation
Bryson, John E.: chairman, chief executive officer, Edison International
Buckwalter, Alan Roland, III: chief executive officer, Chase Bank of Texas; president, Chase Bank of Texas Foundation, Inc.
Bush, Michael J.: vice president real estate, Giant Food Inc.
Callaway, Lee: vice president public relations, Pacific Gas and Electric Co.
Carter, George Kent: vice president, treasurer, Chevron Corp.
Carter, John Douglas: executive vice president, director, Bechtel Group, Inc.
Ching, Meredith J.: senior vice president, director, chairman HI committee, Alexander & Baldwin Foundation; vice president government & community relations, Alexander & Baldwin, Inc.
Cool, Judd R.: senior vice president human resources, Allegheny Technologies Inc.
Davisson, Ralph M.: trustee, Potlatch Foundation II
Denning, Steven A.: vice president, General Atlantic Partners II LP
Diekman, Susan: executive director, AirTouch Communications Foundation
Downing, Kathryn M.: executive vice president, Times Mirror Co.; vice chairman, Times Mirror Foundation
Early, William Bernard: trustee, Jeld-wen Foundation; senior vice president, assistant secretary, director, Jeld-wen, Inc.
Farman, Richard Donald: chairman, chief executive officer, Pacific Enterprises
Fiorina, Carleton S.: president, chief executive officer, director, Hewlett-Packard Co.
Fisher, Robert J.: vice president, Gap Foundation/ Gap Inc. Community Relations
Franke, William Augustus: chairman, president, chief executive officer, America West Airlines, Inc.; director, Phelps Dodge Foundation
Friedewald, William Thomas, MD: director, MetLife Foundation

Gaylord, Edward Lewis: chairman, chief executive officer, director, publisher, Oklahoma Publishing Co.; trustee, Oklahoman Foundation (The)

Ginn, Samuel L.: chairman, director, AirTouch Communications Foundation; chairman, chief executive officer, director, Vodafone AirTouch Plc

Graves, Ronald Norman: secretary, Simplot Foundation (J.R.)

Gust, Anne B.: executive vice president, chief administrative officer, Gap, Inc.

Hannity, Vincent Thomas: vice president corporate communications & investor relations, Boise Cascade Corp.

Heiner, Clyde Mont: executive vice president, Questar Corp.

Holmes, David Richard: chief executive officer, chief operating officer, director, Reynolds & Reynolds Co.

Hough, Lawrence Alan: president, chief executive officer, Student Loan Marketing Association

James, George Barker, II: senior vice president, chief financial officer, Levi Strauss & Co.

Jenest, Jeffrey M.: senior vice president new business development, Playboy Enterprises Inc.; director, Playboy Foundation

Johnson, Charles M.: vice chairman, Wells Fargo & Co.

Johnson, Hansford Tillman: trustee, USAA Foundation, A Charitable Trust

Jordan, William M.: president, chief executive officer, chairman, director, Duriron Co., Inc.; president, Duriron Foundation

Kelley, John B.: vice president investor relations, Alexander & Baldwin, Inc.

Knight, Philip Hampson: chairman, chief executive officer, Nike, Inc.

Kovacevich, Richard M.: chairman, president, chief executive officer, Norwest Corp.; director, Norwest Foundation

Ledgett, Ronald A.: executive vice president, Boston Edison Co.; trustee, Boston Edison Foundation

Lucas, Donald Leo: chairman, Cadence Designs Systems, Inc.

Magowan, Peter Alden: president, managing general partner, Safeway Inc.

Mattson, Bradford C.: executive vice president exterior building products, CertainTeed Corp.

Maughan, Deryck C.: director, New York Stock Exchange Foundation, Inc.; co-chairman, co-chief executive officer, Salomon Smith Barney

McCoy, John Bonnet: president, chief executive officer, Ameritech Corp.

Meyerson, Ivan D.: vice president, general counsel, McKesson-HBOC Corp.

Miller, William Irwin: director, Cummins Engine Foundation

Minami, Wayne K.: director, Hawaiian Electric Industries Charitable Foundation

Moe, James D.: corporate vice president, general counsel, secretary, Cargill Inc.

Moore, William B.: senior vice president, secretary, general counsel, Whitman Corp.; secretary, Whitman Corp. Foundation

Morby, Jacqueline C.: managing partner, Pacific Mutual Life Insurance Co.

Neal, Philip Mark: president, chief executive officer, director, Avery Dennison Corp.

Owens, Jack Byron: executive vice president, general counsel, Gallo Winery, Inc. (E&J)

Painter, Alan Sproul: vice president, executive director, AlliedSignal Foundation Inc.

Penglase, Frank Dennis: vice president, treasurer,

Peoples, D. Louis: vice chairman, chief executive officer, director, Orange & Rockland Utilities, Inc.

Pigott, Charles McGee: president, director, PACCAR Foundation; chairman emeritus, director, PACCAR Inc.

Piper, Addison Lewis: director, Piper Jaffray Companies Foundation; chairman, chief executive officer, director, U.S. Bancorp Piper Jaffray

Pollnow, Charles F., Jr.: treasurer, director, Matlock Foundation; chief financial officer, Simpson Investment Co.

Rand, Addison Barry: executive vice president operations, Xerox Corp.; trustee, Xerox Foundation

Reilly, Thomas E., Jr.: trustee, Reilly Foundation; chairman, chief executive officer, director, Reilly Industries, Inc.

Reinhard, J. Pedro: executive vice president, chief financial officer, director, Dow Chemical Co.

Reising, Richard P.: senior vice president, general counsel, secretary, Archer-Daniels-Midland Co.; secretary, Archer-Daniels-Midland Foundation

Richards, John M.: chairman, chief executive officer, director, Potlatch Corp.; trustee, Potlatch Foundation II

Satre, Philip Glen: chairman, president, chief executive officer, director, Promus Hotel Corp.

Savedge, Henry S., Jr.: executive vice president, chief financial officer, director, Reynolds Metals Co.; executive vice president, director, Reynolds Metals Co. Foundation

Schurz, James Montgomery: president, Schurz Communications Foundation

Schwab, Charles R.: chairman, co-chief executive officer, director, Schwab & Co., Inc. (Charles); chairman, Schwab Corp. Foundation (Charles)

Shannon, Michael E.: chairman, chief financial officer, chief administration officer, director, Ecolab Inc.

Shapira, David S.: trustee, Giant Eagle Foundation; chairman, chief executive officer, director, Giant Eagle Inc.

Snell, Richard: chairman, president, chief executive officer, director, Arizona Public Service Co.

Stanton, Philip H.: chief executive officer, director, Washington Trust Bank

Steere, William Campbell, Jr.: chairman, chief executive officer, director, Pfizer Inc.

Stinson, Kenneth E.: member contributions committee, Kiewit Companies Foundation; chairman, chief executive officer, director, Kiewit Sons' Inc. (Peter)

Stivers, William Charles: senior vice president, chief financial officer, treasurer, Weyerhaeuser Co.; treasurer, trustee, Weyerhaeuser Co. Foundation

Stratton, Frederick Prescott, Jr.: chairman, chief executive officer, director, Briggs & Stratton Corp.; president, director, Briggs & Stratton Corp. Foundation

Timken, Ward Jackson: vice president, director, officer, Timken Co. (The); vice president, Timken Co. Charitable Trust (The); president, Timken Co. Educational Fund

Timken, William Robert, Jr.: chairman, president, chief executive officer, director, Timken Co. (The)

Ukropina, James R.: partner, Pacific Mutual Life Insurance Co.

Wagner, Harold A.: chairman, president, chief executive officer, director, Air Products and Chemicals, Inc.

Westfall, David M.: senior vice president, chief financial officer, Consolidated Natural Gas Co.

Wilbur, Brayton, Jr.: president, chief executive officer, Wilbur-Ellis Co. & Connell Brothers Co.; president, Wilbur Foundation (Brayton)

Wurtele, C. Angus: president, Valspar Foundation

Young, Robert Harris: president, chief executive officer, Central Vermont Public Service Corp.

ZoBell, Karl: vice president, trustee, Copley Foundation (James S.)

Zuendt, William F.: president, chief executive officer, Wells Fargo & Co.

d'Alessio, Jon W.: trustee, McKesson Foundation

Stanford University Executive Management Program

Dunham, Archie W.: president, chief executive officer, Conoco, Inc.

Stanford University Executive Program

Hovind, David J.: president, director, PACCAR Inc.

Tumminello, Stephen C.: president, chief executive officer, director, Philips Electronics North America Corp.

Ulrich, Robert J.: chairman, chief executive officer, director, Dayton Hudson; chairman, trustee, Target Foundation

Stanford University Graduate School of Business Administration

Ballmer, Steven Anthony: president, chief executive officer, director, Microsoft Corp.

Ives, J. Atwood: chairman, chief executive officer, Boston Gas Co.; chairman, chief executive officer, trustee, Eastern Enterprises; trustee, Eastern Enterprises Foundation

Kemper, David Woods: chairman, president, chief executive officer, director, Commerce Bancshares, Inc.

Lucas, Donald Leo: chairman, Cadence Designs Systems, Inc.

McNealy, Scott G.: chairman, chief executive officer, director, Sun Microsystems Inc.

Minton, Dwight Church: chairman, director, Church & Dwight Co., Inc.

Stanford University School of Law

Kirchhof, Anton Conrad: corporate secretary, general counsel, Louisiana-Pacific Corp.; secretary, Louisiana-Pacific Foundation

State University of New Jersey

Thompson, Donald L.: chairman, chief executive officer, Hunt Manufacturing Co.

State University of New York

Ackerman, Philip Charles: senior vice president, director, National Fuel Gas Distribution Corp.

Alm, John Richard: director, Coca-Cola Foundation

Dickoff, Gil A.: treasurer, Crane Foundation

Gardner, Gary E.: vice president human resources & public affairs, Valspar Corp.; vice president, assistant treasurer, Valspar Foundation

Lichtenberger, Horst William: chairman, chief executive officer, Praxair

Slizewski, Bea B.: vice president corporate communications, Agrilink Foods, Inc.

State University of New York Buffalo

Drexler, Millard S.: trustee, Gap Foundation/Gap Inc. Community Relations; president, chief executive officer, director, Gap, Inc.

Ringler, James M.: chairman, president, chief executive officer, director, Premark International Inc.

Weiser, Irving: chairman, president, chief executive officer, Dain Bosworth Inc.

State University of New York Graduate School of Business Administration

Bryan, John Henry: chairman, Sara Lee Corp.; director, Sara Lee Foundation

Stetson University

Davis, Andrew Dano: vice president, director, Winn-Dixie Stores Foundation; vice president, Winn-Dixie Stores Inc.

Stevens Institute of Technology

Howe, Wesley Jackson: chairman emeritus, director, Becton Dickinson & Co.

Schlauch, Walter F.: group vice president, National Starch & Chemical Co.

Stonehill College

Lemieux, Joseph Henry: chairman, chief executive officer, director, Owens-Illinois Inc.

Somers, Daniel E.: senior executive vice president, chief financial officer, AT&T Corp.

Suffolk University

Donnelly, James Charles: vice president, director, WICOR Foundation; vice president, WICOR, Inc.

McCahon, Jane W.: vice president corporate relations, Eastern Enterprises

Rosenberg, Richard Morris: chairman, chief executive officer (retired), Bank of America

Sussex University (England)

Welsh, Kelly Raymond: executive vice president, general counsel, Ameritech Corp.

Sweet Briar College

Blanke, Gail Ann: vice president, Avon Products Foundation, Inc.

Syracuse University

Almeida, Richard: chairman, chief executive officer, Heller Financial, Inc.

Barrett, Robert E.: executive vice president, UST Inc.

Davis, Carolyne Kahle, PhD: trustee, Merck Co. Foundation

Griffin, Donald Wayne: chairman, president, chief executive officer, director, Olin Corp.; trustee, Olin Corp. Charitable Trust

Heisen, JoAnn Heffernan: vice president, chief information officer, Johnson & Johnson; treasurer, Johnson & Johnson Family of Companies Contribution Fund

Hergenhan, Joyce: director, president, GE Fund

McNeill, Corbin Asahel, Jr.: president, chief executive officer, director, chairman, PECO Energy Co.

Raskin, Fred C.: president, chief operating officer, Eastern Enterprises; trustee, Eastern Enterprises Foundation

Riley, H. John, Jr.: chairman, president, chief executive officer, Cooper Industries Foundation; chairman, president, chief executive officer, director, Cooper Industries, Inc.

Rock, Arthur: co-founder, chairman executive committee, director, Intel Corp.

Technology University Aachen

Otto, Peter: president, Lehigh Portland Cement Co.

Temple University

Beatt, Bruce H.: secretary, Dexter Corp. Foundation

Campanaro, Leonard A.: treasurer, Harsco Corp. Fund

Edgerton, Brenda Evans: vice president business development, Campbell Soup Co.; treasurer, trustee, Campbell Soup Foundation

Gailey, John Robert, III: vice president, general counsel, secretary, West Co. Inc.

Gasich, Anthony F.: vice president administration, Farmers Group, Inc.; contributions officer, Farmers Group Safety Foundation

Haskin, Donald Lee: vice president, PNC Bank

Hill, Kenneth D.: vice president, Sunoco Inc.

Klein, David M.: vice president, Hartford (The)

Lavigne, Louis J., Jr.: executive vice president, chief financial officer, Genentech Inc.

McCarthy, Peter John: trustee, Elf Atochem North America Foundation; vice president public affairs, Elf Atochem North America, Inc.

Preston, James Edward: vice president, director, Avon Products Foundation, Inc.; chairman, chief executive officer, director, Avon Products, Inc.

Robin, Kenneth H.: senior vice president, general counsel, Household International Inc.

Tarola, Robert M.: senior vice president, chief financial officer, Grace & Co. (W.R.)

Tennessee Technical Institute

Stonecipher, Harry C.: president, chief operating officer, director, Boeing Co.

Texas A&M University

Barnes, W. Michael: senior vice president finance & planning, chief financial officer, Rockwell International Corp.; member trust committee, Rockwell International Corp. Trust

Bonsignore, Michael Robert: director, Honeywell Foundation; chairman, chief executive officer, director, Honeywell International Inc.

Bradford, William Edward: chairman, director, Halliburton Co.

Cloud, Bruce Benjamin, Sr.: vice chairman, director, Zachry Co. (H.B.)

Davis, Donald H., Jr.: president, chief executive officer, chairman, Rockwell International Corp.; chairman trust committee, Rockwell International Corp. Trust

Hanna, William W.: president, chief operating officer, director, Koch Industries, Inc.

Larsen, Terrence A.: chairman, chief executive officer, First Union Bank; chairman, First Union Regional Foundation

Maxwell, Harold C.: director, Temple-Inland Foundation

McGregor, Mark: vice president, treasurer, Storage Technology Corp.

Nye, Erle Allen: chairman, chief executive officer, director, TU Electric Co.

Wilks, David M.: vice president, New Century Energies Foundation

Zachry, Henry Bartell, Jr.: chairman, Zachry Co. (H.B.); trustee, Zachry Foundation (The)

Texas Christian University

Roach, John Vinson, II: chairman, director, Tandy Corp.

Simmons, Glenn Reuben: vice chairman, Contran Corp.

Texas Technology University

Benninger, Edward Charles, Jr.: president, chief financial officer, Valero Energy Corp.

Brooks, E. Richard 'Dick': chairman, chief executive officer, director, Central & South West Services

Cash, R. D.: chairman, president, chief executive officer, director, Questar Corp.

Eisman, Paul: senior vice president refining Southwest, Ultramar Diamond Shamrock Corp.

Helton, Bill D.: chairman, New Century Energies Foundation

Johnson, James Lawrence: chairman emeritus, Walter Industries Inc.

Morgensen, Jerry L.: president, chief executive officer, director, Hensel Phelps Construction Co.; director, Hensel Phelps Foundation

Whitacre, Edward E., Jr.: chairman, director, chief executive officer, SBC Communications Inc.

Texas Woman's University

Flood, Joan Moore: assistant treasurer, Trace International Holdings, Inc. Foundation

The Hague Academy of International Law

Heimbold, Charles Andreas, Jr.: chairman, president, chief executive officer, Bristol-Myers Squibb Co.

Thiel College

Pitorak, Larry John: senior vice president finance, treasurer, chief financial officer, Sherwin-Williams Co.; secretary, treasurer, trustee, Sherwin-Williams Foundation

Thomas More College

FitzGibbon, David J.: president, chief executive officer, Bardes Corp.

Tokyo University

Kanai, Tsutomu: president, Hitachi Foundation

Toledo

Sheets, Thomas R.: vice president, general counsel, Southwest Gas Corp.; trustee, Southwest Gas Corp. Foundation

Towson State University

Rowe, Thomas E.: chairman, director, Fireman's Fund Foundation; director, Fireman's Fund Insurance Co.

Trinity College

Baird, Dugald Euan: chairman, president, chief executive officer, Schlumberger Ltd. (USA)

Baker, Robert Woodward: executive vice president, AMR Corp.

Becherer, Hans Walter: chairman, chief executive officer, director, Deere & Co.; director, Deere Foundation (John)

Block, William, Jr.: president, trustee, Blade Foundation; president, director, Toledo Blade Co.

Bronfman, Charles Rosner: trustee, Bronfman Foundation/Joseph E. Seagram & Sons, Inc. Fund (Samuel)

Gildersleeve, Elizabeth T.: chairman, Chubb Foundation

Trinity University

Jennings, James Burnett: president, Hunt Oil Co.

Troy State University

Anderson, Judy M.: vice president, corporate secretary, Georgia Power Co.; executive director, secretary, assistant treasurer, Georgia Power Foundation

Tufts University

Cummings, William S.: chairman, Cummings Properties Management

Dimon, James R.: trustee, Citigroup Foundation; president, chief operating officer, chief financial officer, Salomon Smith Barney

Duff, Andrew S.: president, U.S. Bancorp Piper Jaffray

Flaws, James B.: senior vice president, chief financial officer, treasurer, Corning Inc.; trustee, Corning Inc. Foundation

Freedman, Allen Royal: trustee, Fortis Foundation; chairman, chief executive officer, president, Fortis, Inc.

Keyser, F. Ray, Jr.: chairman, director, Central Vermont Public Service Corp.

Loeb, Jerome Thomas: chairman, director, May Department Stores Co.; president, director, May Department Stores Computer Foundation (The)

Manzi, James Paul: president, director, Lotus Development Corp.

McGraw, Harold Whittlesey 'Terry', III: chairman, president, chief executive officer, McGraw-Hill Companies, Inc.

Peet, Creighton Houck: vice president, director, Cowen Foundation

Price, Timothy: president, chief executive officer, director, MCI WorldCom, Inc.

Resnick, Alan H.: treasurer, Bausch & Lomb Foundation, Inc.; vice president, treasurer, Bausch & Lomb Inc.

Schoch, Steven J.: vice president, treasurer, Times Mirror Co.; treasurer, chief financial officer, Times Mirror Foundation

Shepherd, Kathleen Shearen Maynard: director, Tribune New York Foundation

Sulzberger, Arthur Ochs, Junior: director, chairman emeritus, New York Times Co.

Syron, Richard F.: chairman, chief executive officer, director, American Stock Exchange, Inc.

Thoman, G. Richard: president, chief operating officer, Xerox Corp.

Williams, Karen Hastie: director, Fannie Mae Foundation

Wilson, Eric L.: director, Hensel Phelps Foundation

Tufts University Fletcher School of Law & Diplomacy

Naples, Ronald James: president, chief executive officer, director, Quaker Chemical Corp.

Wiksten, Barry Frank: president, CIGNA Foundation

Tulane University

Carroll, Philip Joseph: chairman, chief executive officer, Fluor Corp.; chairman, trustee, Fluor Foundation

Cavanaugh, William, III: chairman, president, chief executive officer, Carolina Power & Light Co.; president, CP&L Foundation

Deming, Claiborne P.: president, chief executive officer, director, Murphy Oil Corp.

Farnsworth, Philip Richeson: secretary, ABC

Habig, Thomas L.: vice chairman, director, Habig Foundation

Harden, Glen: executive vice president, chief financial officer, Carolina Power & Light Co.; treasurer, CP& L Foundation

Reily, Robert D.: vice president, director, Reily & Co., Inc. (William B.); president, director, Reily Foundation

Reily, William Boatner, III: president, chief executive officer, director, Reily & Co., Inc. (William B.); director, Reily Foundation

Thawerbhoy, Nazim G.: controller, Jacobs Engineering Foundation

Tulane University Law School

Deming, Claiborne P.: president, chief executive officer, director, Murphy Oil Corp.

Tulane University Newcomb College

Brown, JoBeth Goode: trustee, Anheuser-Busch Companies, Inc.

Union College

Castellani, John: executive vice president, Tenneco Automotive

Gilmartin, Raymond V.: chairman, president, chief executive officer, Merck & Co.; chairman, Merck Co. Foundation

Kalaher, Richard A.: president, American Standard Foundation; vice president, secretary, general counsel, American Standard Inc.

Penny, Roger Pratt: president, chief operating officer, director, Bethlehem Steel Corp.

Russack, Richard A.: president, Burlington Northern Santa Fe Foundation

United College (Canada)

Leatherdale, Douglas West: chairman, chief executive officer, president, Saint Paul Companies Inc.

United States Air Force Academy

Jackson, John E.: trustee, Nordson Corp. Foundation

Johnson, Hansford Tillman: trustee, USAA Foundation, A Charitable Trust

Lacy, William Howard: president, MGIC Investment Corp.

Pearce, Harry J.: vice chairman, General Motors Corp.

Rosane, Edwin L.: president, USAA Life Insurance Co.

Simpson, William H.: president, Susquehanna-Pfaltzgraff Co.; secretary, Susquehanna-Pfaltzgraff Foundation

United States Air Force Institute of Technology

Borman, Marlene: vice president, director, Borman Fund (The)

United States Army War College

Gardner, James Richard: vice president, Pfizer Foundation

Wolff, Herbert Eric: secretary, director, First Hawaiian Foundation

United States Maritime Academy

Hofmann, Kenneth H.: president, director, Hofmann Co.; president, Hofmann Foundation

United States Merchant Marine Academy

Kulynych, Petro: chairman, treasurer, Lowe's Charitable and Educational Foundation

Zaccaria, Adrian: president, chief operating officer, director, Bechtel Group, Inc.

United States Military Academy

Carter, Marshall Nichols: chairman, chief executive officer, State Street Bank & Trust Co.

Dozier, Ollin Kemp: treasurer, Universal Leaf Foundation

Gardner, James Richard: vice president, Pfizer Foundation

Jarman, Richard Sinclair: executive vice president, Butler Manufacturing Co.; trustee, Butler Manufacturing Co. Foundation

Lopiano, John A.: senior vice president, Xerox Corp.; trustee, Xerox Foundation

Mead, Dana George: chairman, chief executive officer, director, Tenneco Automotive

Moorhead, Thomas Leib, Esq.: vice president law, assistant secretary, Nordson Corp.; trustee, Nordson Corp. Foundation

Naples, Ronald James: president, chief executive officer, director, Quaker Chemical Corp.

Schaefer, George A., Jr.: president, Fifth Third Bancorp

Zadel, C. William: chairman, president, chief executive officer, Millipore Corp.; trustee, Millipore Foundation (The)

United States Naval Academy

Bonsignore, Michael Robert: director, Honeywell Foundation; chairman, chief executive officer, director, Honeywell International Inc.

Buxton, Charles Ingraham, II: chairman, Federated Mutual Insurance Co.; president, Federated Mutual Insurance Foundation

Davis, William E.: chairman, chief executive officer, Niagara Mohawk Holdings Inc.

Herres, Robert T.: chairman, chief executive officer, United Services Automobile Association

Keyser, Richard Lee: chairman, chief executive officer, president, Grainger, Inc. (W.W.)

Marshall, Joseph W.: chairman, chief executive officer, Idaho Power Co.

McGehee, Robert B.: executive vice president, general counsel, Carolina Power & Light Co.; trustee, CP&L Foundation

McNeill, Corbin Asahel, Jr.: president, chief executive officer, director, chairman, PECO Energy Co.

Orser, William Stanley: executive vice president energy supply, Carolina Power & Light Co.

Poindexter, Christian Herndon: chairman, Baltimore Gas & Electric Foundation; chairman, chief executive officer, director, Constellation Energy Group, Inc.

Reinemund, Steve S.: chairman, chief executive officer, Frito-Lay, Inc.

Schievelbein, Thomas C.: executive vice president, Newport News Shipbuilding

Wilson, Stephen R.: executive vice president, chief financial officer, Reader's Digest Association, Inc. (The)

United States Navy Post Graduate School

Carter, Marshall Nichols: chairman, chief executive officer, State Street Bank & Trust Co.

United Theology Seminary

Flake, Floyd Harold: director, Fannie Mae Foundation

University Catolica del Ecuador

McGrath, Lee Upton: treasurer, Fuller Co. Foundation (H.B.); vice president, treasurer, Fuller Co. (H.B.)

University College Dublin

O'Reilly, David J.: chairman, chief executive officer, Chevron Corp.

University College of Dublin

O'Reilly, F. Anthony John: chairman, trustee, Heinz Co. Foundation (H.J.); chairman, director, Heinz Co. (H.J.)

University Colorado Boulder School Marketing

Simpson, Andrea Lynn: president

University Maryland

Amoss, George B.: vice president finance, chief financial officer, CertainTeed Corp.; chief financial officer, CertainTeed Corp. Foundation

Norris, Paul J.: chairman, president, chief executive officer, director, Grace & Co. (W.R.); director, Grace Foundation Inc.

University Michigan

Pilon, Lawrence James: senior vice president human resources, Whitman Corp.

University Minnesota

Mee, Michael F.: senior vice president, chief financial officer, Bristol-Myers Squibb Co.

University Toronto

Dugan, Allan E.: senior vice president corporate strategic service, Xerox Corp.; trustee, Xerox Foundation

University of Akron

Bridgeland, James Ralph, Jr.: trustee, Star Bank NA, Cincinnati Foundation

Grealis, William J.: vice president, Cinergy Corp.; director, Cinergy Foundation

Little, Gene E.: trustee, advisor, Timken Co. Charitable Trust (The); secretary, treasurer, trustee, Timken Co. Educational Fund

Ong, John Doyle: chairman board, director, Ameritech Corp.

Scheurer, Charles B.: director, Diebold, Inc.

Weigand, George C.: vice president, trustee, Rubbermaid Foundation; chief financial officer, senior vice president, Rubbermaid Inc.

University of Alabama

Bakane, John L.: president, chief executive officer, director, Cone Mills Corp.

Beattie, Art P.: vice president, secretary, treasurer, Alabama Power Co.; treasurer, Alabama Power Foundation

Blount, Winton Malcolm, Jr.: chairman, Blount International, Inc.

Bowden, Travis J.: chairman, president, chief executive officer, director, Gulf Power Co.

Franklin, H. Allen: president, chief executive officer, Georgia Power Co.

Hardy, Gene M.: director, La-Z-Boy Foundation

Horsley, Richard David: vice chairman, executive financial officer, director, Regions Financial Corp.

James, Donald M.: chairman, Vulcan Materials Co. Foundation

Jones, D. Paul, Jr.: chairman, chief executive officer, Compass Bank; trustee, Compass Bank Foundation

McInnes, Duncan Joseph: executive vice president administration, chief administrative officer, Blount International, Inc.

Moore, Jackson W.: president, director, Union Planters Corp.

Powell, Jerry W.: secretary, general counsel, Compass Bank; secretary, Compass Bank Foundation

Robinson, J. William: president, director, Piedmont Charitable Foundation

University of Alabama Law School

Stephens, Elton Bryson: founder, chairman, Ebsco Industries, Inc.

University of Alaska

O'Brien, James E.: director, Schoeneckers Foundation

University of Arizona

Bame, Tracy L.: manager community affairs, Phelps Dodge Foundation

Boeckmann, Alan: trustee, Fluor Foundation

Busch, August Adolphus, III: chairman, president, chief executive officer, Anheuser-Busch Companies, Inc.

Campbell, George Leroy: vice president public affairs, Florida Power Corp.

De Schutter, Richard U.: director, Searle Charitable Trust; chairman, chief executive officer, Searle & Co. (G.D.)

Felsinger, Donald E.: president, chief executive officer, Sempra Energy

Gottlieb, Richard Douglas: president, chief executive officer, director, Lee Enterprises

Hazen, Paul Mandeville: chairman, chief executive officer, director, Wells Fargo & Co.

Leonis, John Michael: chairman, director, Litton Industries, Inc.

Loftin, Nancy Carol: secretary, director, APS Foundation, Inc.; vice president, general counsel, Arizona Public Service Co.

Meredith, Edwin Thomas, III: chairman executive committee, Meredith Corp.

Niebla, J. Fernando: chairman, chief executive officer, Pacific Mutual Life Insurance Co.

Parfet, Donald R.: president, Pharmacia & Upjohn Foundation; senior vice president associated business, Pharmacia & Upjohn, Inc.

Peru, Ramiro G.: senior vice president, chief financial officer, Phelps Dodge Corp.

Pulido, Mark A.: president, chief executive officer, director, chairman, McKesson-HBOC Corp.

Timken, Ward Jackson: vice president, director, officer, Timken Co. (The); vice president, Timken Co. Charitable Trust (The); president, Timken Co. Educational Fund

University of Arkansas

Blair, James Burton: trustee, Tyson Foundation, Inc.

Carter, Paul R.: executive vice president, Wal-Mart Stores, Inc.

Ford, Joseph 'Joe': chairman, chief executive officer, president, ALLTEL Corp.

Gasich, Anthony F.: vice president administration, Farmers Group, Inc.; contributions officer, Farmers Group Safety Foundation

Tyson, Donald John: senior chairman, Tyson Foods Inc.

Walton, S. Robson: member, Wal-Mart Foundation; chairman, director, Wal-Mart Stores, Inc.

Wray, Donald E.: president, chief operating officer, director, Tyson Foods Inc.

University of Baltimore

Angelo, Robert A.: president, chief operating officer, York Federal Savings & Loan Association; secretary, York Federal Savings & Loan Foundation

Oseroff, Stephen L.: vice president real estate, Giant Food Inc.

University of Birmingham

Haddock, John R.: board member, Ryder System Charitable Foundation; senior vice president marketing, Ryder System, Inc.

University of Bombay

Patel, Homi Burjor: president, chief operating officer, director, Hartmarx Corp.

University of Bonn

Hansmeyer, Herbert F.: chairman, Fireman's Fund Insurance Co.

University of Bradford

O'Reilly, F. Anthony John: chairman, trustee, Heinz Co. Foundation (H.J.); chairman, director, Heinz Co. (H.J.)

University of Bridgeport

DeLuca, Fred: vice president, Subway Sandwich Shops, Inc.

University of British Columbia

Langbo, Arnold Gordon: chairman, chief executive officer, director, Kellogg Co.

Tysoe, Ronald W.: vice chairman, director, Federated Department Stores, Inc.; member, Scripps Howard Foundation

University of Brussels

Guedry, James Walter: president, International Paper Co. Foundation

University of Buffalo

Lippes, Gerald Sanford: secretary, Mark IV Industries Foundation

Rich, Robert E., Sr.: president, treasurer, Rich Family Foundation; founder, chairman, director, Rich Products Corp.

University of California

Alpert, Janet A.: president, chief operating officer, director, LandAmerica Financial Services; trustee, LandAmerica Foundation

Bains, Harrison MacKellar, Jr.: vice president, treasurer, Bristol-Myers Squibb Co.; treasurer, Bristol-Myers Squibb Foundation Inc.

Broome, Burton Edward: vice president, controller, Transamerica Corp.; vice president, treasurer, Transamerica Foundation

Fisher, Donald George: president, Gap Foundation/Gap Inc. Community Relations; founder, chairman, director, Gap, Inc.

Guertin, Timothy E.: vice president, Varian Medical Systems, Inc.

Lacey, David C.: executive vice president, chief financial officer, Storage Technology Corp.; chief financial officer, director, StorageTek Foundation

Levy, Richard M.: president, chief executive officer, Varian Medical Systems, Inc.

Lundhagen, E. Wayne: treasurer, KN Energy Foundation

Moore, Gordon E., PhD: cofounder, chairman emeritus, director, Intel Corp.; trustee, Intel Foundation

Nakamura, Alyson J.: secretary, Alexander & Baldwin Foundation

Shaffer, Oren G.: executive vice president, chief financial officer, Ameritech Corp.

Tran, Khanh T.: senior vice president, chief financial officer, director, Pacific Mutual Life Insurance Co.

Watanabe, Jeffrey N.: director, Hawaiian Electric Industries Charitable Foundation

Work, David F.: senior vice president shared service, BP Amoco Corp.; director, BP Amoco Foundation

University of California at Berkeley

Berry, William S.: director, Rayonier Foundation

Burns, Mitchell Anthony: president, director, Ryder System Charitable Foundation; chairman, president, chief executive officer, Ryder System, Inc.

Clarke, Robert F.: chairman, president, chief executive officer, director, Hawaiian Electric Co., Inc.; president, director, Hawaiian Electric Industries Charitable Foundation

Condit, Philip Murray: chairman, chief executive officer, director, Boeing Co.

Cronk, William F., III: president, director, Dreyer's Grand Ice Cream

Grove, Andrew S.: chairman, Intel Corp.

Haas, Peter Edgar, Sr.: chairman executive committee, director, Levi Strauss & Co.

Haas, Robert Douglas: chairman, chief executive officer, director, Levi Strauss & Co.; president, Levi Strauss Foundation

Hazen, Paul Mandeville: chairman, chief executive officer, director, Wells Fargo & Co.

Hill, Bonnie Guiton: vice president, Times Mirror Co.; president, chief executive officer, Times Mirror Foundation

Hill, Steven Richard: senior vice president human resources, Weyerhaeuser Co.; trustee, Weyerhaeuser Co. Foundation

Johnson, Norman E.: senior vice president technology, Weyerhaeuser Co.; trustee, Weyerhaeuser Co. Foundation

Keller, Thomas M.: president, Fortis Insurance Co.

Klitten, Martin R.: vice president, chief financial officer, Chevron Corp.

Lacey, David C.: executive vice president, chief financial officer, Storage Technology Corp.; chief financial officer, director, StorageTek Foundation

McNeill, Corbin Asahel, Jr.: president, chief executive officer, director, chairman, PECO Energy Co.

Meyerson, Ivan D.: vice president, general counsel, McKesson-HBOC Corp.

Posey, Warren M., Jr.: treasurer, Armstrong Foundation

Reid, Frederick W.: executive vice president, chief marketing officer, Delta Air Lines, Inc.

Rogers, T. Gary: chairman, chief executive officer, director, Dreyer's Grand Ice Cream

Sasaki, Robert K.: director, Alexander & Baldwin Foundation

d'Alessio, Jon W.: trustee, McKesson Foundation

University of California, Davis

Bechtel, Riley Peart: chairman, Bechtel Foundation; chairman, chief executive officer, director, Bechtel Group, Inc.

Edwards, David M.: vice president finance, chief financial officer, GATX Corp.

Satre, Philip Glen: chairman, president, chief executive officer, director, Promus Hotel Corp.

University of California, Los Angeles

Bainum, Stewart William, Jr.: chairman, Manor Care Health SVS, Inc.

Beall, Donald Ray: director, Rockwell International Corp.

Bell, Wayne: secretary, Ralph's-Food 4 Less Foundation; senior counsel, assistant secretary, Ralph's Grocery Co.

Bergerac, Michel Christian: director, CBS Foundation

Bourns, Gordon L.: president, trustee, Bourns Foundation; chairman, Bourns, Inc.

Ching, Meredith J.: senior vice president, director, chairman HI committee, Alexander & Baldwin Foundation; vice president government & community relations, Alexander & Baldwin, Inc.

Coughlan, Gary Patrick: chief financial officer, senior vice president finance, Abbott Laboratories; director, Abbott Laboratories Fund

Dye, Donald H.: president, chief executive officer, Callaway Golf Co.

Falberg, Kathryn E.: senior vice president finance, chief financial officer, Amgen, Inc.

Folick, Jeffrey M.: member, PacifiCare Health System Foundation

Harden, Oleta J.: secretary, New Jersey Natural Gas Foundation

Hartshorn, Terry O'Dell: chairman, PacifiCare Health System Foundation

Henley, Jeffrey O.: executive vice president, chief financial officer, director, Oracle Corp.

Hill, Steven Richard: senior vice president human resources, Weyerhaeuser Co.; trustee, Weyerhaeuser Co. Foundation

Hoops, Alan R.: member, PacifiCare Health System Foundation

Masin, Michael Terry: vice chairman, president international, director, GTE Corp.; trustee, GTE Foundation

McFerson, Dimon Richard: chairman, chief executive officer, Nationwide Insurance Co.; chairman, chief executive officer, trustee, Nationwide Insurance Enterprise Foundation; chairman, chief executive officer, Wausau Insurance Companies

Resnick, Stewart A.: chairman, chief executive officer, Franklin Mint (The)

Womack, Robert R.: chairman, chief executive officer, director, Zurn Industries, Inc.

Wyne, Jon R.: senior vice president, treasurer, Bayer Corp.; treasurer, Bayer Foundation

University of California, San Diego

Ostler, Clyde W.: vice chairman, Wells Fargo & Co.

University of California, Santa Barbara

Henley, Jeffrey O.: executive vice president, chief financial officer, director, Oracle Corp.

Steere, William Campbell, Jr.: chairman, chief executive officer, director, Pfizer Inc.

Wyne, Jon R.: senior vice president, treasurer, Bayer Corp.; treasurer, Bayer Foundation

University of Central Florida

Harmon, Sam W.: senior vice president human resources, GenCorp; trustee, GenCorp Foundation

University of Charleston

Goode, R. Ray: director, Ryder System Charitable Foundation

Koenig, Brian C.: senior vice president human resources, Scientific-Atlanta, Inc.

University of Chicago

Anderson, Basil L.: executive vice president, chief financial officer, Campbell Soup Co.

Baker, Calvin H.: vice president finance, chief financial officer, Wisconsin Energy Corp.; treasurer, director, Wisconsin Energy Corp. Foundation, Inc.

Berg, Thomas C.: vice president, general counsel, secretary, Amsted Industries Inc.

Browning, Peter C.: chief executive officer, president, director, Sonoco Products Co.

Bruce, Peter Wayne: director, Badger Meter Foundation

Chookaszian, Dennis Haig: chairman, chief executive officer, CNA

Condon, James Edward: treasurer, Hartmarx Charitable Foundation; vice president, treasurer, Hartmarx Corp.

Crane, David W.: trustee, Crane & Co. Fund; chief financial officer, Crane & Co., Inc.

Davis, Erroll Brown, Jr.: president, chief executive officer, director, Wisconsin Power & Light Co.

Donnelley, James R.: vice chairman, Donnelley & Sons Co. (R.R.)

Donovan, Dianne Francys: director, Chicago Tribune Foundation

Elam, Lloyd Charles, MD: trustee, Merck Co. Foundation

Ellison, Lawrence J.: chairman, chief executive officer, director, president, Oracle Corp.

Else, Robert K.: director, Hickory Tech Corp.; secretary, Hickory Tech Corp. Foundation

Francis, Cheryl A.: executive vice president, chief financial officer, Donnelley & Sons Co. (R.R.)

Franklin, Marc Scott: senior vice president strategic planning, Pacific Mutual Life Insurance Co.

Fukunaga, Mark H.: chairman, director, Servco Foundation; chief executive officer, chairman, Servco Pacific

Gauvreau, Paul Richard: treasurer, Pittway Corp. Charitable Foundation

Geissinger, Frederick: chairman, chief executive officer, prs, American General Finance

Geissinger, Frederick Wallace: chairman, chief executive officer, president, director, American General Finance Foundation

Gidwitz, Gerald S.: chairman, Curtis Industries, Inc. (Helene)

Goodes, Melvin Russell: chairman, chief executive officer, director, Ameritech Corp.

Graham, Katharine Meyer: chairman executive committee, director, The Washington Post

Graham, William B.: chairman, director, Baxter Allegiance Foundation; chairman emeritus, Baxter International Inc.

Hasch, J. Bruce: president, chief operating officer, director, Peoples Energy Corp.

Higbee, David M.: secretary, Williams; secretary, treasurer, Williams Companies Foundation (The)

Hobor, Nancy A.: vice president communications & investor relations, Morton International Inc.

Jacobsen, Thomas Herbert: chairman, president, chief executive officer, Mercantile Bank NA

Johnson, David Willis: chairman, director, Campbell Soup Co.

Johnson, Kenneth James: vice president, controller, director, Motorola Inc.

Johnston, William E., Junior: president, chief operating officer, director, Morton International Inc.

King, Reatha Clark: director, Fuller Co. Foundation (H.B.); president, executive director, General Mills Foundation

Klein, Bruce A.: trustee, CLARCOR Foundation; chief financial officer, CLARCOR Inc.

Lester, Susan E.: executive vice president, chief financial officer, U.S. Bancorp

Lyon, Wayne Barton: president, chief operating officer, director, Masco Corp.

Marks, Michael J.: vice president, general counsel, secretary, Alexander & Baldwin, Inc.

Mason, W. Bruce: chairman, chief executive officer, director, True North Communications, Inc.

Matthews, Westina Lomax: secretary, trustee, Merrill Lynch & Co. Foundation Inc.; senior director, first vice president corporate respons, Merrill Lynch & Co., Inc.

McGrath, Lee Upton: treasurer, Fuller Co. Foundation (H.B.); vice president, treasurer, Fuller Co. (H.B.); treasurer, Jostens Foundation Inc. (The)

Melrose, Kendrick B.: chairman, co-president, chief executive officer, director, Toro Co.; director, Toro Foundation

Mersereau, Susan M.: trustee, Weyerhaeuser Co. Foundation

Ostler, Clyde W.: vice chairman, Wells Fargo & Co.

Piergallini, Alfred A.: trustee, Gerber Foundation

Pollay, Richard L.: vice chairman, director, Chicago Title Corp.; trustee, Chicago Title and Trust Co. Foundation

Rudnick, Alan A.: vice president, general counsel, corporate secretary, CSX Corp.

Schueppert, George Louis: chief financial officer, executive vice president, Outboard Marine Corp.

Sheehan, Jeremiah J.: chairman, director, Reynolds Metals Co. Foundation

Sheley, Donald R., Junior: vice president finance, chief financial officer, Standard Products Co.; treasurer, trustee, Standard Products Co. Charitable Foundation

Shepard, Donald James: chairman, president, chief executive officer, AEGON U.S.A. Inc.

Sherman, Saul S.: vice chairman, director, Trace International Holdings, Inc.

Shoemate, Charles Richard: chairman, president, chief executive officer, Bestfoods

Skilling, Raymond Inwood: executive vice president, chief counsel, director, Aon Corp.; director, Aon Foundation

Sopranos, Orpheus Javaras: corporate vice president, Amsted Industries Inc.

Springer, Denis E.: senior vice president, chief financial officer, Burlington Northern Santa Fe Corp.; director, Burlington Northern Santa Fe Foundation

Sullivan, Frank P.: vice president sales & marketing, Square D Co.; vice president, director, Square D Foundation

Vitale, David J.: vice chairman, Bank One Corp.; vice president, director, First National Bank of Chicago Foundation

Wagner, Thomas Joseph: chairman, CIGNA Foundation

Workman, John L.: executive vice president, Montgomery Ward & Co., Inc.; executive vice president, director, Montgomery Ward Foundation

Yeomans, Janet L.: treasurer, director, 3M Foundation

Zadel, C. William: chairman, president, chief executive officer, Millipore Corp.; trustee, Millipore Foundation (The)

Zavis, Michael W.: managing partner, Katten, Muchin & Zavis; president, director, Katten, Muchin & Zavis Foundation

Zeffren, Eugene: executive vice president, Curtis Industries, Inc. (Helene)

University of Chicago Graduate School of Business Administration

Allardyce, Fred A.: director, American Standard Foundation; senior vice president medical products sector, American Standard Inc.

University of Chicago Law School

Crook, Donald Martin: secretary, Kimberly-Clark Foundation

Hanower, L. David: assistant secretary, Burlington Resources Foundation

Oran, Stuart I.: director, United Airlines Foundation; senior vice president international, United Airlines Inc.

University of Cincinnati

Barrett, John F.: trustee, Western-Southern Foundation, Inc.; president, chief executive officer, director, Western & Southern Life Insurance Co.

Blake, Ronald L.: president general business services, Ameritech Corp.; director, Ameritech Foundation

Brown, Ronald D.: assistant treasurer, Milacron Foundation

Brumm, Paul Michael: executive vice president, chief financial officer, Fifth Third Bancorp

Cardy, Robert Willard: chairman, president, chief executive officer, director, Carpenter Technology Corp.; president, Carpenter Technology Corp. Foundation

Cassidy, Samuel M.: director, Star Bank NA

Dolan, Ronald J.: trustee, Ohio National Foundation; senior vice president, chief financial officer, director, Ohio National Life Insurance Co.

Dunlap, F. Thomas, Jr.: secretary, director, Intel Foundation

Granzow, Paul H.: chairman, director, Standard Register Co.

Gross, Randall A.: trustee, York Federal Savings & Loan Foundation

Lakin, Thomas J.: regional chairman, Star Bank NA; president, Star Bank NA, Cincinnati Foundation

Lyon, Wayne Barton: president, chief operating officer, director, Masco Corp.

Michaels, Jack D.: secretary, HON Industries Charitable Foundation; chairman, president, chief executive officer, director, HON Industries Inc.

Molen, Richard L.: chairman, chief executive officer, director, Huffy Corp.; trustee, Huffy Foundation, Inc.

Randolph, Jackson Harold: chairman, Cinergy Corp.; chairman, director, Cinergy Foundation

Sheafer, William L.: vice president, treasurer, Cinergy Corp.; treasurer, director, Cinergy Foundation

Smoot, Richard Leonard: chairman, PNC Bank

Stewart, S. Jay: chairman, chief executive officer, director, Morton International Inc.

Stonebraker, Barbara J.: executive vice president, Cincinnati Bell Foundation, Inc.; senior vice president, Cincinnati Bell Inc.

Taulbee, Richard: assistant treasurer, Western-Southern Foundation, Inc.; vice president, Western & Southern Life Insurance Co.

Voet, Paul C.: trustee, Chemed Foundation

University of Cincinnati Law School

Hayden, Joseph Page, Jr.: trustee, Star Bank NA, Cincinnati Foundation

University of Cologne

Hansmeyer, Herbert F.: chairman, Fireman's Fund Insurance Co.

Mueller, Gerd Dieter: executive vice president, chief financial officer, director, chief administrative officer, Bayer Corp.; president, Bayer Foundation

Reinhard, J. Pedro: executive vice president, chief financial officer, director, Dow Chemical Co.

University of Colorado

Brendsel, Leland C.: chairman, chief executive officer, director, Freddie Mac; director, Freddie Mac Foundation

Hoak, Jon: trustee, NCR Foundation

Hock, Delwin D.: chairman, New Century Energies

Hoffmann, Richard W.: general counsel, Employers Mutual Casualty Co.

Johnson, Hansford Tillman: trustee, USAA Foundation, A Charitable Trust

Kelly, Richard C.: executive vice president, chief financial officer, New Century Energies; treasurer, New Century Energies Foundation

Sissel, George A.: chairman, president, chief executive officer, director, Ball Corp.

Smoot, Richard Leonard: chairman, PNC Bank

Utley, Edward Harold: vice chairman, president, GEICO Corp.; chairman, director, GEICO Philanthropic Foundation

Weiss, David E.: chairman, president, chief executive officer, director, Storage Technology Corp.

Wells, James M., III: president, Crestar Finance Corp.

Whisler, J. Steven: chairman, president, chief executive officer, Phelps Dodge Corp.

White, Britton, Jr.: vice president, El Paso Energy Foundation

Wise, William Allen: chairman, president, chief executive officer, director, El Paso Energy Co.; chairman, director, El Paso Energy Foundation

University of Connecticut

Alpert, Janet A.: president, chief operating officer, director, LandAmerica Financial Services; trustee, LandAmerica Foundation

Ballantyne, Richard Lee: vice president, general counsel, secretary, Harris Corp.; secretary, treasurer, Harris Foundation

Harms, Carol J.: vice president, treasurer, Montgomery Ward & Co., Inc.; senior vice president, Montgomery Ward Foundation

Jones, Russell H.: officer, Kaman Corp.

Litvack, Sanford M.: senior executive vice president, chief corporate operations, director, Disney Co. (Walt)

Long, Michael Thomas: director, Ensign-Bickford Foundation

Martin, Lauralee: chief financial officer, Heller Financial, Inc.

Nickerson, Lucille M.: secretary, Aetna Foundation; vice president, corporate secretary, Aetna, Inc.

Orr, Charles Lee: president, chief executive officer, Shaklee Corp.

Wright, Elease E.: director, Aetna Foundation

University of Connecticut School of Law

Fiondella, Robert William: chairman, president, chief executive officer, Phoenix Home Life Mutual Insurance Co.

Hershman, Linda D.: vice president, Southern New England Telephone Co.

University of Dallas

Braham, W. Martin: trustee, Delta Air Lines Foundation

Flood, Joan Moore: assistant treasurer, Trace International Holdings, Inc. Foundation

Larsen, Terrence A.: chairman, chief executive officer, First Union Bank; chairman, First Union Regional Foundation

University of Dayton

Abdoo, Richard A.: chairman, president, chief executive officer, Wisconsin Energy Corp.; president, director, Wisconsin Energy Corp. Foundation, Inc.

Brown, Ronald D.: assistant treasurer, Milacron Foundation

Hill, Allen M.: president, chief executive officer, Dayton Power and Light Co.

Klesse, William R.: executive vice president operations, Ultramar Diamond Shamrock Corp.

Koziar, Stephen F., Jr.: president, trustee, Dayton Power and Light Co. Foundation

Lester, Susan E.: executive vice president, chief financial officer, U.S. Bancorp

Matthews, Westina Lomax: secretary, trustee, Merrill Lynch & Co. Foundation Inc.; senior director, first vice president corporate respons, Merrill Lynch & Co., Inc.

Palmer, Denise: vice president, strategy & finance, Chicago Tribune Co.; treasurer, Chicago Tribune Foundation

Palmieri, Peter C.: vice chairman, chief credit officer, First Union National Bank, NA

University of Delaware

Bohling, John A.: senior vice president, PacifiCorp; board member, PacifiCorp Foundation

Lovett, John Robert: director, Air Products Foundation

Shanks, David C.: trustee, Little Foundation (Arthur D.); vice president human resources, Little, Inc. (Arthur D.)

Sparks, Walter Alvon, Jr.: director, GEICO Philanthropic Foundation

Stoveken, James E., Jr.: senior vice president, Westvaco Corp.; trustee, Westvaco Foundation Trust

Townsend, David L.: vice president administration, Walter Industries Inc.

University of Delhi

Pinto, Michael P.: executive vice president, chief financial officer, Manufacturers & Traders Trust Co.

University of Denver

Adler, Ira R.: executive vice president, chief financial officer, Tucson Electric Power Co.

Andreas, David Lowell: chairman, director, National City Bank Foundation; chairman, chief executive officer, National City Bank of Minneapolis

Boesel, Stephen W.: vice president, secretary, treasurer, Price Associates Foundation (T. Rowe)

Carpenter, Marshall L.: vice president, chief financial officer, MTS Systems Corp.

Coors, Peter Hanson: vice president, director, Coors Brewing Co.

Hawes, Alexander Boyd, Jr.: treasurer, Boston Globe Foundation

Holland, William Ray: vice president, director, United Dominion Foundation; chairman, chief executive officer, director, United Dominion Industries, Ltd.

Humphrey, Neil Darwin: trustee, Commercial Intertech Foundation
Kennedy, James Cox: chairman, chief executive officer, director, Cox Enterprises Inc.; trustee, Cox Foundation (James M.)
Landin, Thomas Milton: vice president, director, CertainTeed Corp.; vice president, Norton Co. Foundation
MacLeay, Thomas H.: president, chief operating officer, National Life of Vermont
Unruh, James Arlen: director, Ameritech Foundation
Wheatley, Bruce C.: vice president, Commercial Intertech Foundation

University of Denver College of Law

Whisler, J. Steven: chairman, president, chief executive officer, Phelps Dodge Corp.

University of Detroit

Abdoo, Richard A.: chairman, president, chief executive officer, Wisconsin Energy Corp.; president, director, Wisconsin Energy Corp. Foundation, Inc.
Boyer, David Scott: president, chief executive officer, director, Teleflex Inc.
Brune, David A.: secretary, treasurer, Baltimore Gas & Electric Foundation
Capo, Thomas Patrick: senior vice president, treasurer, DaimlerChrysler Corp.
Cusick, Thomas A.: chairman, TCF National Bank Minnesota
Ennest, John William: chief financial officer, Citizens Bank-Flint
Farrell, W. James: chairman, chief executive officer, Illinois Tool Works, Inc.
Schafer, Glenn Stanley: president, director, Pacific Mutual Life Insurance Co.

University of Dubuque

Dammerman, Dennis Dean: vice chairman, director, General Electric Co.

University of Durham (England)

Freeman, David: chairman, president, chief executive officer, director, Loctite Corp.

University of Durham Kings

Naylor, Michael E.: senior vice president operations, Rubbermaid Inc.

University of Erlangen

Wobst, Frank: chairman, chief executive officer, director, Huntington Bancshares Inc.

University of Evansville

Griffin, Donald Wayne: chairman, president, chief executive officer, director, Olin Corp.; trustee, Olin Corp. Charitable Trust
Hinton, Michael R.: president, chief operating officer, director, Old National Bank Evansville
Lauderdale, Gary D.: senior vice president, general manager, Texas Gas Transmission Corp.
Ralph, E. Jack: vice president finance, controller, Texas Gas Transmission Corp.

University of Findlay

Rooney, Patrick W.: chairman, president, chief executive officer, director, Cooper Tire & Rubber Co.

University of Florida

Anderson, Girard F.: chairman, chief executive officer, president, Tampa Electric Co.
Baker, John Daniel, II: president, chief executive officer, director, Florida Rock Industries; vice president, Florida Rock Industries Foundation
Brunetti, Wayne H.: vice chairman, president, chief operating officer, director, New Century Energies; president, chief executive officer, New Century Energies Foundation
Chandler, William Everett: senior vice president finance, secretary, chief financial officer, Hunt Manufacturing Co.
Clarke, Thomas E.: president, chief operating officer, Nike, Inc.
Cook, J. Michael: chairman, chief executive officer, Deloitte & Touche; chairman, Deloitte & Touche Foundation
Grasley, Michael Howard: senior vice president, Shell Oil Co.; member executive committee, director, Shell Oil Co. Foundation
Rockey, Travis O.: vice president, director, Evening Post Publishing Co.
Wagner, J. Wilt: director, Reynolds Metals Co. Foundation

University of Georgia

Amos, Daniel P.: president, chief executive officer, director, AFLAC Inc.
Barron, Donald Ray: president, director, Atlantic Investment Co.
Blanchard, James Hubert: chairman, chief executive officer, Synovus Financial Corp.
Bowdoin, William R., Jr.: first vice president, SunTrust Bank Atlanta; secretary, SunTrust Bank Atlanta Foundation
Correll, Alston Dayton 'Pete', Jr.: chairman, president, chief executive officer, director, Georgia-Pacific Corp.; director, Georgia-Pacific Foundation
Everett, Malcolm E., III: director, First Union Foundation
Greene, Donald Ray: assistant vice president, Coca-Cola Co.; president, director, Coca-Cola Foundation
Herman, William A., III: secretary, treasurer, director, Morris Communications Corp.
Moore, Virlyn B., Jr.: director, Pheonix Foundation
Morris, William Shivers, III: founder, chairman, chief executive officer, director, Morris Communications Corp.; trustee, Stauffer Communications Foundation
Rowell, Harry Brown, Jr.: trustee, Hubbell Foundation (Harvey)

University of Georgia Savings & Loan League Executive Training Program

Fitzgerald, William Allingham: chairman, director, Commercial Federal Corp.

University of Ghent

Fonteyne, Herman J.: president, chief executive officer, director, Ensign-Bickford Industries

University of Goettingen

Wobst, Frank: chairman, chief executive officer, director, Huntington Bancshares Inc.

University of Grenoble

O'Brien, William J., III: trustee, DaimlerChrysler Corp. Fund

University of Hartford

Daddario, Richard M.: chief financial officer, MONY Life Insurance of New York (The)
Dillon, John T.: chairman, chief executive officer, director, International Paper Co.
Gareau, Joseph H.: executive vice president, chief investment officer, Hartford (The)

University of Hawaii

Bates, George E.: treasurer
Campbell, Cheryl Nichols: operation service advisory group, Cincinnati Bell Inc.
Dods, Walter Arthur, Jr.: president, director, First Hawaiian Foundation; chairman, chief executive officer, director, First Hawaiian, Inc.
Johnson, Lawrence M.: president, Pacific Century Financial Corp.
Karr, Howard Henry: treasurer, director, First Hawaiian Foundation
Nakagawa, Jean H.: vice president, director, Servco Foundation
Nakamura, Alyson J.: secretary, Alexander & Baldwin Foundation
Pang, Gerald M.: director, First Hawaiian Foundation

University of Hawaii at Manoa

Wellman, Thomas A.: controller, assistant treasurer, Alexander & Baldwin, Inc.

University of Houston

Barun, Kenneth Lee: president, director, McDonald's Corp. Charitable Foundation
Jordan, William M.: president, chief executive officer, chairman, director, Duriron Co., Inc.; president, Duriron Foundation
Rosilier, Glenn D.: executive vice president, chief financial officer, Central & South West Services
Sykora, Donald D.: director, Reliant Energy Inc.
Wheeler, Joyce W.: secretary, Royal & SunAlliance Insurance Foundation, Inc.; vice president, corporate secretary, Royal & SunAlliance USA, Inc.

University of Idaho

Beebe, Stephen A.: president, chief executive officer, director, Simplot Co. (J.R.)
Dahl, Richard J.: president, Pacific Century Financial Corp.
Graves, Ronald Norman: secretary, Simplot Foundation (J.R.)
Hanks, Stephen G.: president, Morrison Knudsen Corp. Foundation, Inc.
Michael, Gary Glenn: chairman, chief executive officer, director, Albertson's Inc.
Olson, A. Craig: senior vice president finance, chief financial officer, Albertson's Inc.

University of Illinois

Altenbaumer, Larry F.: senior vice president, chief financial officer, Illinois Power Co.
Anderson, Basil L.: executive vice president, chief financial officer, Campbell Soup Co.
Bell, Bradley John: vice president, treasurer, Whirlpool Corp.; treasurer, Whirlpool Foundation
Berry, Ilona M.: secretary, First National Bank of Chicago Foundation
Butts, David Wayne: senior vice president, Illinois Power Co.
Chelberg, Bruce Stanley: chairman, chief executive officer, director, Whitman Corp.; director, Whitman Corp. Foundation
Cole, Franklin Alan: chairman, Aon Foundation
Creek, Wallace W.: secretary, General Motors Foundation
Dargene, Carl J.: director, AMCORE Foundation
Davis, Dwight D.: president, chief operating officer
Elam, Lloyd Charles, MD: trustee, Merck Co. Foundation
Elbert, Paul A.: president, chief executive officer natural gas, Consumers Energy Co.
Ellison, Lawrence J.: chairman, chief executive officer, director, president, Oracle Corp.
Else, Robert K.: director, Hickory Tech Corp.; secretary, Hickory Tech Corp. Foundation
England, Joseph Walker: chairman, director, Deere Foundation (John)

Fisher, George Myles Cordell: chairman, president, chief executive officer, director, Eastman Kodak Co.
Gaiswinkler, Robert Sigfried: chairman, director, First Financial Bank; director, First Financial Foundation
Georges, John A.: director, International Paper Co.
Hefner, Hugh Marston: founder, chairman emeritus, Playboy Enterprises Inc.
Howat, Bruce Bradshaw, Jr.: secretary, corporate counsel, Ameritech Corp.
Jacobsen, James C.: vice chairman, Kellwood Co.; vice president, director, Kellwood Foundation
Johnson, Kenneth James: vice president, controller, director, Motorola Inc.
Joslin, Roger Scott: treasurer, State Farm Companies Foundation
Kniffen, Jan Rogers: senior vice president, treasurer, May Department Stores Co.; vice president, secretary, treasurer, director, May Department Stores Computer Foundation (The)
Kopp, David C.: assistant secretary, CIGNA Foundation
Kraiss, Glenn S.: executive vice president store operations, Walgreen Co.
Kurczewski, Walter W.: vice president, secretary, general counsel, Square D Co.; president, director, Square D Foundation
Lambe, James F.: senior vice president human resources, Nalco Chemical Co.; director, Nalco Foundation
LeBoeuf, Raymond W.: director, PPG Industries Foundation; director, chairman, chief executive officer, PPG Industries, Inc.
Levan, B. W.: vice president, director, Shell Oil Co. Foundation
Lindsay, David J.: trustee, CLARCOR Foundation; vice president, CLARCOR Inc.
Magliochetti, Joseph M.: president, chief executive officer, director, Dana Corp.; president, director, Dana Corp. Foundation
Medvin, Harvey Norman: executive vice president, treasurer, chief financial officer, Aon Corp.; treasurer, Aon Foundation
Moore, William B.: senior vice president, secretary, general counsel, Whitman Corp.; secretary, Whitman Corp. Foundation
Mrozek, Ernest J.: executive vice president, chief financial officer, ServiceMaster Co.
Nalbach, Kay C.: president, Hartmarx Charitable Foundation
Olschwang, Alan P., Esq.: secretary, Mitsubishi Electric America Foundation
Rauman, Thomas R.: chief financial officer, DeKalb Genetics Corp.; treasurer, director, DeKalb Genetics Foundation
Rose, Wayne Myron: treasurer, director, Quanex Foundation
Sanders, Walter Jeremiah, III: chairman, chief executive officer, director, Advanced Micro Devices, Inc.
Shapiro, Howard: executive vice president, general counsel, Playboy Enterprises Inc.; director, Playboy Foundation
Staheli, Donald L.: chairman, director, Continental Grain Co.; vice president, director, Continental Grain Foundation
Strobel, Pamela B.: senior vice president, general counsel, Commonwealth Edison Co.
Stroup, Stanley Stephenson: executive vice president, general counsel, Norwest Corp.
Teets, John William: president, chief executive officer, director, Viad Corp. Fund
Tomlinson, Joseph Ernest: vice president, treasurer, controller, Inland Container Corp.; vice president, director, Inland Foundation, Inc.
Vujovich, Christine M.: director, Habig Foundation
Welch, John Francis, Jr.: chairman, chief executive officer, director, General Electric Co.
Wilson, Cleo Francine: executive director, Playboy Foundation

University of Indiana

Carver, Martin Gregory: chairman, president, chief executive officer, Bandag, Inc.
Pate, James Leonard: chairman, chief executive officer, director, Pennzoil-Quaker State Co.

University of Indiana Savings & Loan League Executive Training Program

Fitzgerald, William Allingham: chairman, director, Commercial Federal Corp.

University of Iowa

Andreas, Lowell Willard: chairman audit committee, member executive & finance committee, Archer-Daniels-Midland Co.
Baird, Patrick S.: chief operating officer, chief financial officer, AEGON U.S.A. Inc.
Brooks, Roger Kay: chairman, AmerUS Group
Carver, Martin Gregory: chairman, president, chief executive officer, Bandag, Inc.
Connor, James Richard: executive director, Kemper Foundation (James S.)
Davidson, Park R.: trustee, Burlington Industries Foundation
Ellis, James D.: director, SBC Foundation
Forsythe, Donald George: vice president corporate relations, Sprint Corp.; executive director, Sprint Foundation
Hadley, Leonard Anson: chairman, chief executive officer, director, Maytag Corp.; president, trustee, Maytag Corp. Foundation
Hiersteiner, Walter L.: vice chairman, Tension Envelope Corp.; vice president, Tension Envelope Foundation
Johnson, Norman E.: trustee, CLARCOR Foundation
Killinger, Kerry Kent: chairman, president, chief executive officer, director, Washington Mutual, Inc.
Kolsrud, Douglas C.: executive vice president, chief investment officer, AEGON U.S.A. Inc.
Lichtenberger, Horst William: chairman, chief executive officer, Praxair
Pomerantz, Marvin Alvin: trustee, Mid-American Foundation
Roberts, John Kenneth, Jr.: president, chief executive officer, director, Pan-American Life Insurance Co.
Schoon, Susan Wylie: trustee, Chase Manhattan Foundation
Stone, Lawrence Mynatt: chairman, publisher, Rutledge Hill Press; secretary, treasurer, Rutledge Hill Press Foundation
Stryker, Steven Charles: director, Shell Oil Co. Foundation
Tiedens, George R.: group president power systems, Kohler Co.

University of Iowa Law School

Davidson, Park R.: trustee, Burlington Industries Foundation
Kelley, Bruce Gunn: vice president, director, Employers Mutual Charitable Foundation

University of Kansas

Beebe, Lydia I.: corporate secretary, Chevron Corp.
Cordes, Donald L.: secretary, Koch Foundation, Inc. (Fred C. and Mary R.)
Crane, Russell L.: director, PPG Industries Foundation; senior vice president, PPG Industries, Inc.
Crook, Donald Martin: secretary, Kimberly-Clark Foundation
Eaton, Robert James: co-chairman, president, chief executive officer, DaimlerChrysler Corp.
Holland, John J.: president, chief executive officer, director, Butler Manufacturing Co.
Huey, John W.: vice president administration, Butler Manufacturing Co.; trustee, Butler Manufacturing Co. Foundation
Humphreys, Ethel Mae Craig: president, Craig Foundation (E.L.); chairman, chief executive officer, Tamko Roofing Products
Kangas, Edward A.: chairman, chief executive officer, Deloitte & Touche
Laurance, Dale R.: director, Occidental Petroleum Charitable Foundation; president, senior operations officer, director, Occidental Petroleum Corp.
McClung, James Allen: vice president, director, FMC Foundation
Miller, Larry C.: vice president finance, chief financial officer, Butler Manufacturing Co.; treasurer, Butler Manufacturing Co. Foundation
Panettiere, John Michael: president, chief executive officer, director, chairman, Blount International, Inc.
Spangler, Phillip A.: vice president, treasurer, Yellow Corp.; treasurer, secretary, Yellow Corp. Foundation
Stauffer, John H.: trustee, Stauffer Communications Foundation
Stauffer, Stanley Howard: chairman, Stauffer Communications Foundation
Strandjord, Mary Jeannine: director, Sprint Foundation

University of Kentucky

Allen, Barry K.: president regulatory & wholesale operation, Ameritech Corp.
Chellgren, Paul Wilbur: chief executive officer, chairman, director, Ashland, Inc.; member, Ashland Inc. Foundation
Clabes, Judy G.: president, chief executive officer, Scripps Co. (E.W.); president, chief executive officer, trustee, member, Scripps Howard Foundation
Gilpin, Larry: executive vice president, Target Corp.; trustee, Target Foundation
Grasley, Michael Howard: senior vice president, Shell Oil Co.; member executive committee, director, Shell Oil Co. Foundation
Griffith, Beverly H.: general counsel, Texas Gas Transmission Corp.
McDonald, James F.: president, chief executive officer, Scientific-Atlanta, Inc.
Moore, John E.: executive vice president human resources, Cessna Aircraft Co.; vice president, Cessna Foundation, Inc.
O'Donnell, James P.: treasurer, ConAgra Foundation
Oliver, Orson: president, director, Mid-America Bank of Louisville
Osborne, Burl: president publishing division, director, Belo Corp. (A.H.); president, trustee, Belo Corp. Foundation (A.H.)
Rogers, James E., Jr.: vice chairman, president, chief executive officer, Cinergy Corp.; vice chairman, director, Cinergy Foundation
Routt, J. Robert: vice president, controller, Scripps Co. (E.W.); trustee, Scripps Howard Foundation
Zachem, Harry M.: chairman, trustee, Ashland Inc. Foundation

University of London

Sodhani, Arvind: corp. vice president, treasurer, Intel Corp.; treasurer, Intel Foundation
Wolf, Thomas W.: trustee, York Federal Savings & Loan Foundation

University of London Kings College

Flanagan, David T.: president, chief executive officer, director, Central Maine Power Co.

Maughan, Deryck C.: director, New York Stock Exchange Foundation, Inc.; co-chairman, co-chief executive officer, Salomon Smith Barney

University of Louisville

Doucette, James Willard: vice president, treasurer, Humana Foundation

Graham, Thomas Carlisle: trustee, AK Steel Foundation

Harreld, Michael Neal: president, chief executive officer, PNC Bank Kentucky Inc.

Hobgood, William P.: senior vice president, human resources, United Airlines Inc.

Jones, David Allen: chairman, chief executive officer, director, Humana Foundation; co-founder, chairman, director, Humana, Inc.

Klein, Bruce A.: trustee, CLARCOR Foundation; chief financial officer, CLARCOR Inc.

Nicholas, Jon O.: vice president, trustee, Maytag Corp. Foundation

Reynolds, Randolph Nicklas: vice chairman, executive officer, director, Reynolds Metals Co.; director, Reynolds Metals Co. Foundation

University of Louisville Law School

Harreld, Michael Neal: president, chief executive officer, PNC Bank Kentucky Inc.

University of Louvain

Fonteyne, Herman J.: president, chief executive officer, director, Ensign-Bickford Industries

University of Lowell

Mitropoulis, Iris: chairman, Kingsbury Corp.

University of Madrid

Ostergard, Paul Michael: vice president, director corporate contributions, Citibank Corp.; president, Citigroup Foundation

University of Maine

Correll, Alston Dayton 'Pete', Jr.: chairman, president, chief executive officer, director, Georgia-Pacific Corp.; director, Georgia-Pacific Foundation

Ferland, E. James: chairman, president, chief executive officer, Public Service Electric & Gas Co.

Magee, John Francis: chairman, director, Little, Inc. (Arthur D.)

Mundy, Donna T.: vice president, trustee, UNUM Foundation; senior vice president, UnumProvident

University of Manchester

Barnette, Curtis Handley: chairman, chief executive officer, director, Bethlehem Steel Corp.

University of Manitoba

Hunkin, John: president, CIBC Oppenheimer

Melnuk, Paul D.: president, chief executive officer, Clark Refining & Marketing

University of Maryland

Colgan, Celeste: vice president, secretary, Halliburton Foundation, Inc.

Crooke, Edward A.: president, Baltimore Gas & Electric Foundation

Davis, Ruth Margaret: trustee, Air Products Foundation

Dingman, Michael David: partner, director, Winthrop Foundation

Hale, Roger W.: chairman, chief executive officer, director, LG&E Energy Corp.; president, LG&E Energy Foundation

Jenifer, Franklyn Green: trustee, Texaco Foundation

Macrie, Sari: vice president investor relations, Ameritech Corp.

Mathews, Odonna: vice president consumer affairs, Giant Food Inc.

Nees, Kenneth L.: senior vice president, secretary, Sony Electronics; president, assistant secretary, director, Sony U.S.A. Foundation Inc.

Redding, Peter Stoddard: trustee, Sherman-Standard Register Foundation; president, chief executive officer, director, Standard Register Co.

Smith, Donald Kaye: senior vice president, general counsel, director, GEICO Corp.

Smith, Philip N., Jr.: secretary, Trace International Holdings, Inc. Foundation

Strickling, Lawrence E.: vice president, president public policy, Ameritech Corp.

Torgerson, William T.: managing, Potomac Electric Power Co.

Wasserman, David Sherman: vice president, treasurer, Harris Corp.; trustee, Harris Foundation

Wolff, Herbert Eric: secretary, director, First Hawaiian Foundation

do Carmo, Winston G.: vice president human resources, Giant Food Inc.

University of Massachusetts

Emmett, Denis L.: chief financial officer, Erving Industries

Gareau, Joseph H.: executive vice president, chief investment officer, Hartford (The)

Goldstein, Richard A.: president, chief executive officer, director, Lipton Co.

Hjerpe, William M.: director, Honeywell Foundation

Smith, John Francis, Jr.: chairman, General Motors Corp.

Welch, John Francis, Jr.: chairman, chief executive officer, director, General Electric Co.

University of Miami

Arison, M. Micky: trustee, Arison Foundation; chairman, president, chief executive officer, Carnival Corp.

Falla, Enrique Crabb: senior consult, director, Dow Chemical Co.

Humphreys, David Craig: secretary-treasurer, Craig Foundation (E.L.); president, chief operating officer, director, Tamko Roofing Products

Kelleher, L. J.: vice president, FPL Group Foundation, Inc.

Komansky, David H.: trustee, vice president, Merrill Lynch & Co. Foundation Inc.; chairman, chief executive officer, Merrill Lynch & Co., Inc.

Leviton, Harold: president, Leviton Foundation New York; president, chief executive officer, Leviton Manufacturing Co. Inc.

Pieper, Richard R.: chairman, chief executive officer, director, Pieper Power Electric Co.; secretary, Pieper Power Electric Foundation

Riordan, Gerald R.: director, Ryder System Charitable Foundation

Rubin, Donald S.: senior vice president investor relations, McGraw-Hill Companies, Inc.

University of Michigan

Adderley, Terence E.: chairman, president, chief executive officer, director, Kelly Services; president, director, Kelly Services Foundation

Ballentine, Richard O.: vice president, secretary, general counsel, Butler Manufacturing Co.; secretary, Butler Manufacturing Co. Foundation

Battaglia, Thomas S.: director, American Standard Foundation

Bauder, Lillian: vice president corporate affairs, Masco Corp.

Bayless, Charles Edward: chairman, president, chief executive officer, director, Illinois Power Co.

Beale, Susan M.: director, Detroit Edison Foundation

Berry, William S.: director, Rayonier Foundation

Bloch, Henry Wollman: chairman, Block Foundation (H&R); chairman, director, Block, Inc. (H&R)

Brooks, E. Richard 'Dick': chairman, chief executive officer, director, Central & South West Services

Buckler, Robert J.: director, Detroit Edison Foundation

Carson, David Ellis Adams: chairman, chief executive officer, Peoples Bank

Cohen, Maryjo Rose: president, chief executive officer, director, National Presto Industries, Inc.; vice president, treasurer, trustee, Presto Foundation

Dolan, Ronald J.: trustee, Ohio National Foundation; senior vice president, chief financial officer, director, Ohio National Life Insurance Co.

Erb, Frederick A.: president, Erb Foundation

Ferguson, Ronald Eugene: chairman, president, chief executive officer, director, General Reinsurance Corp.

Fraumann, Willard George: president, director, partner, Kirkland & Ellis; president, Kirkland & Ellis Foundation

Getz, Bert A.: chairman, Globe Corp.; president, director, Globe Foundation

Getz, Bert A., Jr.: executive vice president, Globe Corp.; vice president, Globe Foundation

Gherlein, Gerald Lee: member contributions committee, Eaton Charitable Fund

Greene, John Frederick: executive vice president exploration & production, director, Louisiana Land & Exploration Co.

Gussin, Robert Zalmon, PhD: vice president science & technology, Johnson & Johnson; member corporate contributions committee, Johnson & Johnson Family of Companies Contribution Fund

Gust, Anne B.: executive vice president, chief administrative officer, Gap, Inc.

Habegger, Gary L.: vice president human resources, BFGoodrich Co.; president, Goodrich Foundation, Inc. (B.F.)

Hackett, James P.: trustee, Steelcase Foundation; president, chief executive officer, Steelcase Inc.

Hockaday, Irvine O., Jr.: president, chief executive officer, director, Hallmark Cards Inc.

Hodgson, Thomas Richard: president, chief operating officer, director, Abbott Laboratories

Hogans, Mack L.: chairman, president, trustee, Weyerhaeuser Co. Foundation

Hunting, David Dyer, Jr.: trustee, Steelcase Foundation; director, Steelcase Inc.

Jenkins, James Robert: trustee, Dow Corning Foundation

Kaye, Diane L.: vice president, secretary, general counsel, Federal-Mogul Corp.

Kelley, John B.: vice president investor relations, Alexander & Baldwin, Inc.

Kelly, Richard C.: executive vice president, chief financial officer, New Century Energies; treasurer, New Century Energies Foundation

Kidder, C. Robert: chairman, president, chief executive officer, director, Borden, Inc.

Kittredge, Robert P.: chairman, chief executive officer, director, Fabri-Kal Corp.; president, Fabri-Kal Foundation

Kurczewski, Walter W.: vice president, secretary, general counsel, Square D Co.; president, director, Square D Foundation

Lewis, Frances Aaronson: trustee, Circuit City Foundation

Lippes, Gerald Sanford: secretary, Mark IV Industries Foundation

Lodge, Robert W.: vice president, Carpenter Technology Corp. Foundation

Loomans, Leslie Louis: treasurer, director, Detroit Edison Foundation

Marcus, Stephen Howard: chairman, chief executive officer, Marcus Corp.; president, director, Marcus Corp. Foundation

McGregor, Douglas J.: president, chief operating officer, director, Hanna Co. (M.A.)

Meijer, Douglas: co-chairman, director, chief executive officer, Meijer, Inc.

Meister, Paul M.: vice president, treasurer, Winthrop Foundation

Miller, Donn Biddle: president, chief executive officer, Pacific Mutual Life Insurance Co.

Morris, Michael H.: secretary, director, Sun Microsystems Foundation, Inc.

Ostergard, Paul Michael: vice president, director corporate contributions, Citibank Corp.; president, Citigroup Foundation

Parfet, Donald R.: president, Pharmacia & Upjohn Foundation; senior vice president associated business, Pharmacia & Upjohn, Inc.

Pierre, Percy A.: trustee, Hitachi Foundation

Porter, Edward A.: vice president, general counsel, secretary, Walter Industries Inc.

Radcliffe, R. Stephen: executive vice president, American United Life Insurance Co.

Resnick, Myron J.: vice president, treasurer, trustee, Allstate Foundation

Ridder, Paul Anthony: chairman, chief executive officer, director, Knight Ridder

Sanger, Stephen W.: chairman, trustee, General Mills Foundation; chairman, chief executive officer, director, General Mills, Inc.

Schweitzer, Peter A.: president, Thompson Co. (J. Walter)

Sikkema, Karen Ann: president, trustee, Unocal Foundation

Sodhani, Arvind: corp. vice president, treasurer, Intel Corp.; treasurer, Intel Foundation

Stewart, James Gathings: executive vice president, chief financial officer, CIGNA Corp.

Stroup, Stanley Stephenson: executive vice president, general counsel, Norwest Corp.

Tisch, Preston Robert: chairman, director, CBS Foundation; co-chairman, co-chief executive officer, director, CNA; trustee, Loews Foundation

Tooker, Eric S.: secretary, Central Newspapers Foundation; corporate secretary, vice president, general counsel, Central Newspapers, Inc.

Tracy, Emmet E., Jr.: president, chief executive officer, director, Alma Piston Co.; president, Tracy Fund (Emmet and Frances)

Travaille, Hubert Duane: president, trustee, Potlatch Foundation II

Ursu, John Joseph: director, 3M Foundation; general counsel, senior vice president legal affairs, Minnesota Mining & Manufacturing Co.

Wander, Herbert S.: secretary, director, Katten, Muchin & Zavis Foundation

Wege, Peter M.: trustee, Steelcase Foundation; vice chairman, director, Steelcase Inc.

Westin, David: vice president, director, ABC Foundation

Westover, Frank Thomas: senior vice president, Whitman Corp.; director, Whitman Corp. Foundation

Wild, Heidi Karin: trustee

Wolf, Philip C.: senior vice president, general counsel, secretary, Cyprus Amax Minerals Co.

University of Michigan Law School

Bickner, Bruce P.: chairman, chief executive officer, director, DeKalb Genetics Corp.

Kennedy, Bernard Joseph: chairman, president, chief executive officer, director, National Fuel Gas Distribution Corp.

University of Milwaukee

Kuester, Dennis J.: president, Marshall & Ilsley Corp.

University of Minnesota

Benson, John W.: executive vice president health care, Minnesota Mining & Manufacturing Co.

Burnham, Duane Lee: chairman, chief executive officer, director, Abbott Laboratories

Carlson, Curtis Leroy: chairman, director, Carlson Companies, Inc.; president, treasurer, Carlson Family Foundation (Curtis L.)

Cohen, Melvin Samuel: chairman, National Presto Industries, Inc.; chairman, president, trustee, Presto Foundation

Dewane, John Richard: director, Honeywell Foundation

DiMarco, James F.: senior vice president, Johnson & Son (S.C.)

Engh, Rolf: senior vice president, general counsel, secretary, Valspar Corp.; secretary, Valspar Foundation

Fritze, Steven L.: vice president, treasurer, Ecolab Inc.

Hale, James Thomas: senior vice president, general counsel, secretary, Dayton Hudson; trustee, Target Foundation

Hubbard, Stanley S.: chairman, president, chief executive officer, Hubbard Broadcasting, Inc.; president, Hubbard Foundation

Jacobson, Lyle Gordon: treasurer, Hickory Tech Corp. Foundation

Johnson, James A.: chairman, chief executive officer, director, Fannie Mae; chairman, Fannie Mae Foundation

Johnson, Scott W.: senior vice president, secretary, general counsel, Bemis Co., Inc.

King, Roger Leo: vice president, officer, Graco, Inc.

Kunin, Myron: chairman, director, Regis Corp.; president, Regis Foundation

Linnell, Norman C.: general counsel, secretary, Donaldson Co., Inc.; trustee, Donaldson Foundation

Mattison, Robert Mayer: director, Graco Foundation; vice president, general counsel, secretary, Graco, Inc.

Mead, Susan W. A.: vice president, ReliaStar Financial Corp.; director, ReliaStar Foundation

Meyer, Jerome J.: chairman, chief executive officer, Tektronix, Inc.

Mitau, Lee R.: executive vice president, general counsel, secretary, U.S. Bancorp

Moe, James D.: corporate vice president, general counsel, secretary, Cargill Inc.

Neville, James Morton: member board control, Ralston Purina Trust Fund

O'Brien, James E.: director, Schoeneckers Foundation

O'Hare, Don R.: director, Hamilton Sundstrand Corp.; president, director, Sundstrand Corp. Foundation

Pottenger, Charles R.: group vice president pulp & paperboard group, Potlatch Corp.; trustee, Potlatch Foundation II

Powell, Cornelius Patrick: president, Air Products Foundation

Prohofsky, Dennis E.: secretary, Minnesota Mutual Foundation; senior vice president, general counsel, secretary, Minnesota Mutual Life Insurance Co.

Pulido, Mark A.: president, chief executive officer, director, chairman, McKesson-HBOC Corp.

Raymond, Lee R.: chairman, president, chief executive officer, Exxon Mobil Corp.

Schubert, Rolf B.: director, Fuller Co. Foundation (H.B.)

Setzner, Leah Manning: vice president, general counsel, corporate secretary, Illinois Power Co.

Sheahan, Mark: treasurer, Graco Foundation

Sissel, George A.: chairman, president, chief executive officer, director, Ball Corp.

Thompson, Sheldon Lee: senior vice president, chief administrative officer, Sunoco Inc.

Tuominen, William: senior vice president, chief technology & environment officer, Ecolab Inc.

Ulrich, Robert J.: chairman, chief executive officer, director, Dayton Hudson; chairman, trustee, Target Foundation

Van Benschoten, David: treasurer, General Mills Foundation

Van Dyke, William Grant: chairman, president, chief executive officer, director, Donaldson Co., Inc.

Wright, Donald Franklin: director, Times Mirror Foundation

Wright, Michael William: chairman, president, chief executive officer, director, SuperValu, Inc.

University of Minnesota Law School

Schoenecker, Guy: president, chief executive officer, Business Improvement; president, Schoeneckers Foundation

University of Minnesota, Duluth

Senkler, Robert L.: president, director, Minnesota Mutual Foundation; chairman, president, chief executive officer, Minnesota Mutual Life Insurance Co.

University of Mississippi

Griffith, Beverly H.: general counsel, Texas Gas Transmission Corp.

Hattox, Brock Alan: director, National Service Foundation; executive vice president, chief financial officer, National Service Industries, Inc.

Lackey, S. Allen: director, Shell Oil Co. Foundation

McMillan, Howard Lamar, Jr.: president, chief operating officer, director, Deposit Guaranty National Bank

Quin, Joseph Marvin: trustee, Ashland Inc. Foundation

University of Missouri

Bailey, Keith E.: chairman, president, director, chief executive officer, Texas Gas Transmission Corp.; president, director, Williams Companies Foundation (The)

Ball, James Herington: senior vice president, general counsel, director, Nestle U.S.A. Inc.

Donovan, Dianne Francys: director, Chicago Tribune Foundation

Ellis, James D.: director, SBC Foundation

Gunther, Donald J.: director, Bechtel Group, Inc.

Haubein, Robert H., Jr.: director, Georgia Power Foundation

Herron, James Michael: secretary, director, Ryder System Charitable Foundation

Holman, Carl Ray: chairman, chief executive officer, director, Mallinckrodt Chemical, Inc.

Jarman, Richard Sinclair: executive vice president, Butler Manufacturing Co.; trustee, Butler Manufacturing Co. Foundation

Matheny, Edward Taylor, Junior: director, Block Foundation (H&R)

Offutt, James A.: director, Shelter Insurance Foundation

Phillips, Rosalind Ann: secretary, GEICO Philanthropic Foundation

Price, Charles H., II: director, New York Times Co. Foundation

Price, David B., Jr.: vice president, Goodrich Foundation, Inc. (B.F.)
Reising, Richard P.: senior vice president, general counsel, secretary, Archer-Daniels-Midland Co.; secretary, Archer-Daniels-Midland Foundation
Rubenstein, Leonard Mark: executive vice president investment, director, GenAmerica Corp.; vice president, director, GenAmerican Foundation
Shourd, Roy Ray: president, Schlumberger Foundation
Strandjord, Mary Jeannine: director, Sprint Foundation
Toft, Richard Paul: chairman, Chicago Title Corp.; trustee, Chicago Title and Trust Co. Foundation

University of Missouri Law School

Koupal, Carl M., Jr.: trustee, Western Resources Foundation; executive vice president, chief administrative officer, Western Resources Inc.

University of Missouri, Columbia

Boswell, John Joseph: president, Boswell Foundation, Inc.; chairman, Independent Stave Co.
Duello, J. Donald: president, treasurer, director, Shelter Insurance Foundation
Koupal, Carl M., Jr.: trustee, Western Resources Foundation; executive vice president, chief administrative officer, Western Resources Inc.

University of Missouri, Kansas City

Stinnett, J. Daniel: director, Commerce Bancshares Foundation

University of Montana

Dickey, Boh A.: president, chief operating officer, SAFECO Corp.
Gannon, Robert P.: chairman, president, director, chief executive officer, Montana Power Co.; president, director, Montana Power Foundation
Zimmerman, Michael E.: vice president, general counsel, Montana Power Co.

University of Montana Law School

Cain, Alan F.: director, Montana Power Foundation

University of Montevallo

Denson, William Frank, III: president, Vulcan Materials Co. Foundation

University of Munich

Mueller, Gerd Dieter: executive vice president, chief financial officer, director, chief administrative officer, Bayer Corp.; president, Bayer Foundation

University of Nebraska

Anderson, Eugene Karl: vice president, Contran Corp.; treasurer, Simmons Foundation, Inc. (Harold)
Arth, Lawrence Joseph: vice president, director, Ameritas Charitable Foundation; chairman, chief executive officer, director, Ameritas Life Insurance Corp.
Davis, John B., MD: director, Physicians Mutual Insurance Co. Foundation
Hall, Larry D.: chairman, president, chief executive officer, director, Kinder Morgn; president, director, KN Energy Foundation
Hasch, J. Bruce: president, chief operating officer, director, Peoples Energy Corp.
Hewitt, James Watt: vice president, treasurer, Abel Foundation
Martin, JoAnn M.: controller, Ameritas Charitable Foundation; senior vice president, partner, chief financial officer, Ameritas Life Insurance Corp.
Mattson, Bradford C.: executive vice president exterior building products, CertainTeed Corp.
McConnell, Richard Lynn: senior vice president, director research, Pioneer Hi-Bred International, Inc.
McCown, J. Ross: vice president, secretary, Abel Foundation
Peterson, Robert L.: chairman, chief executive officer, director, IBP
Phares, Lynn Levisay: president, fund manager, director, ConAgra Foundation
Tyner, Neal Edward: treasurer, director, Ameritas Charitable Foundation
Weill, Richard L.: president, MBIA Inc.

University of Neuchatel (Switzerland)

Williams, Karen Hastie: director, Fannie Mae Foundation

University of Nevada

Rupley, Theodore J.: president, chief executive officer, director, Allmerica Financial Corp.

University of New Hampshire

Farrington, Hugh G.: president, chief executive officer, director, Hannaford Brothers Co.
Gullotti, Russell A.: chairman, president, chief executive officer, National Computer Systems, Inc.
Messer, Chester R.: president, chief operating officer, Boston Gas Co.; trustee, Eastern Enterprises Foundation
Norwood, Ralph M.: treasurer, Polaroid Foundation
Sabbag, Allen L.: president, Meredith Corp.
Toner, Jeffrey M.: trustee, Kingsbury Fund

University of New Haven

Ferland, E. James: chairman, president, chief executive officer, Public Service Electric & Gas Co.
Thurston, Samuel E.: senior vice president distribution, Giant Food Inc.

University of New Mexico

Jorndt, Louis Daniel: president, chief executive officer, director, Walgreen Co.
Rogala, Judith A.: member, Butler Manufacturing Co. Foundation

University of New South Wales

Fligg, James E.: executive vice president, BP Amoco Corp.

University of North Carolina

Allison, John Andrew, IV: chairman, chief executive officer, director, Branch Banking & Trust Co.
Anderson, Ivan Verner, Jr.: president, chief executive officer, Evening Post Publishing Co.; vice president, Post and Courier Foundation
Atwood, Robert T.: executive vice president, chief financial officer, First Union Corp.; director, First Union Foundation
Campbell, Cole C.: editor, Pulitzer Publishing Co.; director, Pulitzer Publishing Co. Foundation
Cowan, James R.: vice president, director, Stonecutter Foundation; chairman, president, chief executive officer, director, Stonecutter Mills Corp.
Cowan, Keith O.: vice president corporate development, BellSouth Corp.
Cox, Daniel T.: executive vice president, Aon Corp.
Denny, Dwight D.: director, Ryder System Charitable Foundation
Ellis, William Edward, Jr.: secretary, Barry Foundation
Grise, Cheryl W.: senior vice president, chief administrative officer, Northeast Utilities
Henderson, George W., III: trustee, Burlington Industries Foundation; president, chief executive officer, director, Burlington Industries, Inc.
Herring, Leonard Gray: vice president, Lowe's Charitable and Educational Foundation
Hill, Frank Trent, Jr.: trustee, Sonoco Foundation; vice president, chief financial officer, Sonoco Products Co.
Hinshaw, Juanita H.: vice president, treasurer, Monsanto Co.; treasurer, Monsanto Fund
Horner, Donald G.: vice president, director, First Hawaiian Foundation
Hupfer, Charles J.: trustee, Sonoco Foundation
Jobe, Warren Yancey: executive vice president, Georgia Power Co.; president, director, Georgia Power Foundation
Jones, D. Michael: senior vice president, general counsel, Reynolds Metals Co.; vice president, director, Reynolds Metals Co. Foundation
Little, William Norris: vice chairman, director, Shaw Industries Inc.
McDowell, J. Walter: president, chief executive officer, director, Wachovia Bank of North Carolina NA; director, Wachovia Foundation, Inc. (The)
McLendon, Charles A.: trustee, Burlington Industries Foundation
Reed, Scott Eldridge: senior executive vice president, chief financial officer, Branch Banking & Trust Co.
Sloan, Albert Frazier: director, Lance Foundation
Street, Gordon P., Jr.: chairman, president, chief executive officer, director, North American Royalties; trustee, North American Royalties Foundation
Strickland, Robert Louis: vice president, Lowe's Charitable and Educational Foundation
Thompson, G. Kennedy: president, chief operating officer, First Union Corp.; member, First Union Foundation
Trogdon, Dewey Leonard, Jr.: director, ABC Foundation; chairman, Cone Mills Corp.
Walker, Thomas P.: secretary, Stonecutter Foundation
Wells, James M., III: president, Crestar Finance Corp.
Williamson, Henry Gaston, Jr.: chief operating officer, Branch Banking & Trust Co.
Wood, Edward Jenner: member, SunTrust Bank Atlanta Foundation
von Glahn, William G.: senior vice president, general counsel, Williams; director, Williams Companies Foundation (The)

University of North Carolina Law School

Atwood, Robert T.: executive vice president, chief financial officer, First Union Corp.; director, First Union Foundation

University of North Carolina, Charlotte

Hupfer, Charles J.: trustee, Sonoco Foundation

University of North Dakota

Bohn, Karen M.: president, Piper Jaffray Companies Foundation; chief executive officer, U.S. Bancorp Piper Jaffray
Grenz, M. Kay: director, 3M Foundation; vice president human resources, Minnesota Mining & Manufacturing Co.
Ruelle, Mark A.: senior vice president, chief financial officer, Sierra Pacific Resources
Setzner, Leah Manning: vice president, general counsel, corporate secretary, Illinois Power Co.

University of Northern Florida

Bragin, David H.: treasurer, assistant secretary, director, Winn-Dixie Stores Foundation

University of Northern Iowa

Polark, Roger L.: senior vice president, chief financial officer, Walgreen Co.

University of Notre Dame

Beargie, William T.: trustee, Lubrizol Foundation (The)

Brennan, Leo Joseph, Jr.: vice president, executive director, Ford Motor Co. Fund

Bueche, Wendell Francis: director, Marshall & Ilsley Foundation, Inc.

Campbell, Edward Patrick: president, chief operating officer, drc, Nordson Corp.; trustee, Nordson Corp. Foundation

Castellini, Daniel J.: senior vice president finance & administration, chief financial officer, Scripps Co. (E.W.); treasurer, Scripps Howard Foundation

Cushwa, Charles Benton, III: trustee, Commercial Intertech Foundation

Cushwa, William Wallace: director, Commercial Intertech Corp.; trustee, Commercial Intertech Foundation

Earley, Anthony Francis, Jr.: president, chief operating officer, Detroit Edison Co.; director, Detroit Edison Foundation

Esposito, Michael Patrick, Jr.: trustee, Chase Manhattan Foundation

Friedewald, William Thomas, MD: director, MetLife Foundation

Gannon, Robert P.: chairman, president, director, chief executive officer, Montana Power Co.; president, director, Montana Power Foundation

Goodyear, William M.: trustee, Bank of America Foundation

Hagale, John E.: vice president finance, Burlington Resources Foundation

Iverson, Kenneth A.: vice president, corporate secretary, Ecolab Inc.

Koch, Robert Louis, II: president, chief executive officer, director, Koch Enterprises, Inc.; president, director, Koch Foundation

Larini, Ernest J.: chief financial officer, Warner-Lambert Charitable Foundation; vice president, chief financial officer, Warner-Lambert Co.

Liska, Paul J.: executive vice president, chief financial officer, Saint Paul Companies Inc.

Long, Michael Thomas: director, Ensign-Bickford Foundation

Loughrey, F. Joseph: group president worldwide operations & technology, vice president, Cummins Engine Co., Inc.; director, Cummins Engine Foundation

Lozano, Ignacio Eugenio, Jr.: chairman, Pacific Mutual Life Insurance Co.

Mallardi, Michael Patrick: senior vice president, ABC; vice president, director, ABC Foundation

McKenna, Andrew James: director, Aon Foundation

McMahon, Steve: director, Autodesk Foundation

Meuleman, Robert Joseph: director, AMCORE Foundation

Murphy, Christopher J., III: president, chief executive officer, director, First Source Corp.; director, First Source Foundation

Parry, William E.: vice president, general counsel, Nalco Chemical Co.

Pierre, Percy A.: trustee, Hitachi Foundation

Rohr, James Edward: chief executive officer, president, director, PNC Financial Services Group

Ryan, John Thomas, III: chairman, chief executive officer, Mine Safety Appliances Co.

Shannon, Michael E.: chairman, chief financial officer, chief administration officer, director, Ecolab Inc.

Shiely, John Stephen: president, chief operating officer, director, Briggs & Stratton Corp.; vice president, director, Briggs & Stratton Corp. Foundation

Skinner, Claire Corson: chairman, chief executive officer, Coachmen Industries, Inc.

Springer, Denis E.: senior vice president, chief financial officer, Burlington Northern Santa Fe Corp.; director, Burlington Northern Santa Fe Foundation

Stinson, Kenneth E.: member contributions committee, Kiewit Companies Foundation; chairman, chief executive officer, director, Kiewit Sons' Inc. (Peter)

Sullivan, James Norman: vice chairman, director, Chevron Corp.

Sutton, Howard: president, Providence Journal Charitable Foundation

Thyen, Ronald J.: senior executive vice president, director, Habig Foundation; senior executive vice president, chief operating officer director, Kimball International, Inc.

Vaughn, John: vice president unit development & strategy, Ameritech Corp.

Wareham, James Lyman: president, AK Steel Corp.

University of Oklahoma

Dunham, Archie W.: president, chief executive officer, Conoco, Inc.

Durrett, William E.: senior chairman, American Fidelity Corp.; president, American Fidelity Corp. Founders Fund

Foster, Charles E.: director, SBC Foundation

McDaniel, Tom J.: vice chairman, director, Kerr-McGee Corp.

Moore, Steven: president, Oklahoma Gas & Electric Co. Foundation

Page, Barbara B.: trustee, Golub Foundation

Rainbolt, Harold E.: vice president, secretary, SBC Foundation

University of Oregon

Countryman, Gary Lee: chairman, Liberty Mutual Insurance Group

Ellis, William H.: director, Piper Jaffray Companies Foundation

Knight, Philip Hampson: chairman, chief executive officer, Nike, Inc.

Nelson, Merlin Edward: chairman, director, IBJ Foundation

Quesnel, Gregory L.: president, chief executive officer, director, CNF Transportation, Inc.

Shafer, Douglas C.: trustee, Tektronix Foundation; president, America operations, Tektronix, Inc.

University of Oregon Law School

Davisson, Ralph M.: trustee, Potlatch Foundation II

University of Ottawa

Adam, J. Marc: president, director, 3M Foundation; vice president marketing, Minnesota Mining & Manufacturing Co.

University of Paris

Buechner, Thomas Scharman: trustee, Corning Inc. Foundation

Shapiro, Isaac: chairman, secretary, trustee, Ise Cultural Foundation

University of Pavia

Caccini, Gianpaolo: chairman, chief executive officer, director, CertainTeed Corp.; chairman, CertainTeed Corp. Foundation; chairman, chief executive officer, director, Norton Co.; president, director, Norton Co. Foundation

University of Pennsylvania

Agger, James Harrington: senior vice president, secretary, general counsel, Air Products and Chemicals, Inc.; director, Air Products Foundation

Binyon, Bryan A.: treasurer, American General Finance Foundation

Block, Allan James: vice president, trustee, Blade Foundation; director, Toledo Blade Co.

Bowman, Robert A.: president, chief operating officer, Starwood Hotels & Resorts Worldwide, Inc.

Buxton, Charles Ingraham, II: chairman, Federated Mutual Insurance Co.; president, Federated Mutual Insurance Foundation

Campbell, Cheryl Nichols: operation service advisory group, Cincinnati Bell Inc.

Cohen, Joseph M.: president, director, Cowen Foundation; chairman, chief executive officer, S.G. Cowen

Cole, Lewis George: director, AMETEK Foundation

Corwin, Laura J.: secretary, New York Times Co. Foundation

Deering, Anthony W.: chairman, chief executive officer, Rouse Co.; chairman, president, trustee, Rouse Co. Foundation

Denlea, Leo Edward, Jr.: retired chairman, president, chief executive officer, director, Farmers Group, Inc.; vice president, Farmers Group Safety Foundation

Donahue, Jeffrey H.: senior vice president, chief financial officer, Rouse Co.

Durrett, Joseph P.: chief executive officer, Broderbund Software, Inc.

Evans, Robert Sheldon: chairman, chief executive officer, Crane Co.; chairman, president, director, Crane Foundation

Farber, Jack: chairman, president, director, CSS Industries, Inc.; president, Farber Foundation

Fountain, W. Frank, Jr.: senior vice president government affairs, DaimlerChrysler Corp.; president, DaimlerChrysler Corp. Fund

Gittis, Howard: director, Revlon Foundation Inc.

Glynn, Gary Allen: president, USX Corp.; vice president, USX Foundation, Inc.

Graham, Richard William: president, chief executive officer, chief operating officer, director, Smurfit-Stone Container Corp.

Grass, Martin Lehrman: chairman, chief executive officer, director, Rite Aid Corp.

Hammerman, Stephen Lawrence: vice president, trustee, Merrill Lynch & Co. Foundation Inc.; vice chairman, general counsel, Merrill Lynch & Co., Inc.

Hassenfeld, Alan Geoffrey: president, Hasbro Charitable Trust Inc.; chairman, chief executive officer, Hasbro, Inc.

Heimbold, Charles Andreas, Jr.: chairman, president, chief executive officer, Bristol-Myers Squibb Co.

Higgs, John H.: director, IBJ Foundation

Hill, Kenneth D.: vice president, Sunoco Inc.

Kamen, Harry Paul: chairman, president, chief executive officer, Metropolitan Life Insurance Co.

Kelson, Richard B.: director, Alcoa Foundation

Kiely, W. Leo, III: president, chief operating officer, Coors Brewing Co.

Klein, Bertram W.: chairman, director, Bank of Louisville Charities

Latzer, Richard Neal: vice president, director, Transamerica Foundation

Lipton, Martin: partner, Wachtell, Lipton, Rosen & Katz; president, Wachtell, Lipton, Rosen & Katz Foundation

MacElree, Jane Cox: member advisory committee, Dow Jones Foundation

Matherne, Louis K.: treasurer, Chesapeake Corp.

McDonough, Joseph E.: vice president finance, chief financial officer, Analog Devices, Inc.

Meyerson, Martin: director, Panasonic Foundation

Morie, G. Glen: secretary, treasurer, PACCAR Foundation

Paumgarten, Nicholas Biddle: managing director, Scripps Co. (E.W.); member, Scripps Howard Foundation

Peet, Creighton Houck: vice president, director, Cowen Foundation

Perelman, Ronald Owen: director, Revlon Foundation Inc.

Pinto, Michael P.: executive vice president, chief financial officer, Manufacturers & Traders Trust Co.

Platt, Lewis Emmett: chairman, Hewlett-Packard Co.

Pottruck, David Steven: president, chief executive officer, director, Schwab & Co., Inc. (Charles)

Resnick, Myron J.: vice president, treasurer, trustee, Allstate Foundation

Reynolds, William Gray, Jr.: vice president government relations & public affairs, Reynolds Metals Co.; director, Reynolds Metals Co. Foundation

Rutstein, David W.: secretary, Giant Food Foundation; senior vice president, general counsel, chief administrative officer, Giant Food Inc.

Schwebel, Joseph M.: president, director, Schwebel Baking Co.; trustee, Schwebel Family Foundation

Stone, Roger Warren: chairman, president, chief executive officer, director, Stone Container Corp.; president, Stone Foundation

Subin, Robert: senior vice president, Campbell Soup Co.

Tisch, Laurence Alan: chairman, co-chief executive officer, CBS Corp.; trustee, Loews Foundation

Vagelos, Pindaros Roy: trustee, Prudential Insurance Co. of America

Voet, Paul C.: trustee, Chemed Foundation

Wasserman, David Sherman: vice president, treasurer, Harris Corp.; trustee, Harris Foundation

Weber, Stephen Robert: director, Cowen Foundation

Weizenbaum, Norman: trustee, Giant Eagle Foundation

Wolfe, Kenneth L.: chairman, chief executive officer, director, Hershey Foods Corp.

Zavis, Michael W.: managing partner, Katten, Muchin & Zavis; president, director, Katten, Muchin & Zavis Foundation

Zuckerman, Mortimer Benjamin: co-founder, chairman, co-publisher, director, Daily News

University of Pennsylvania School of Law

Gittis, Howard: director, Revlon Foundation Inc.

Wiley, S. Donald: vice chairman, trustee, Heinz Co. Foundation (H.J.)

University of Pennsylvania Wharton School

Baker, Robert Woodward: executive vice president, AMR Corp.

Black, Sherry Salway: trustee, Hitachi Foundation

Colman, Robert L.: executive vice president human resources, Delta Air Lines, Inc.

Crandall, Robert Lloyd: director, AMR Corp.

DiSilvestro, Anthony P.: vice president, treasurer, Campbell Soup Co.; treasurer, Campbell Soup Foundation

Doucette, James Willard: vice president, treasurer, Humana Foundation

Foti, Samuel J.: president, chief operating officer, director, MONY Group (The); director, MONY Life Insurance of New York (The)

Grum, Clifford J.: director, Temple-Inland Foundation; director, chairman, chief executive officer, Temple-Inland Inc.

Hernandez, Robert M.: vice chairman, chief financial officer, director, USX Corp.; trustee, USX Foundation, Inc.

Hernandez, William H.: director, PPG Industries Foundation; senior vice president, PPG Industries, Inc.

Heumann, Stephen Michael: vice president, treasurer, West Co. Inc.

Hipp, William Hayne: president, chief executive officer, director, Liberty Corp.; chairman, president, director, Liberty Corp. Foundation

Hirsch, Laurence E.: chairman, chief executive officer, director, Centex Corp.

Kofol, Milan: vice president, treasurer, Reader's Digest Association, Inc. (The); treasurer, Reader's Digest Foundation

Luke, John A., Jr.: chairman, president, chief executive officer, director, Westvaco Corp.

McGraw, Harold Whittlesey 'Terry', III: chairman, president, chief executive officer, McGraw-Hill Companies, Inc.

Miglio, Daniel Joseph: chairman, president, director, chief executive officer, Southern New England Telephone Co.

O'Leary, Thomas Howard: chairman, Burlington Resources Foundation

Perelman, Ronald Owen: director, Revlon Foundation Inc.

Posey, Warren M., Jr.: treasurer, Armstrong Foundation

Ross, Arthur: senior vice president, Central National-Gottesman; director, Central National-Gottesman Foundation

Roub, Bryan Roger: trustee, Harris Foundation

Smart, George M.: trustee, Commercial Intertech Foundation

Smucker, Timothy Paul: chairman, director, Smucker Co. (JM)

Taylor, Frederick B.: vice chairman, chief investment officer, United States Trust Co. of New York

Tisch, James S.: president, chief executive officer, director, CNA

Wilson, Gary Lee: chairman, director, Northwest Airlines, Inc.

University of Pittsburgh

Argentine, Peter Dominic: executive vice president, chief financial officer, Nestle U.S.A. Inc.

Beall, Donald Ray: director, Rockwell International Corp.

Bijur, Peter I.: chairman, chief executive officer, Texaco Inc.

Blystone, John B.: chairman, president, chief executive officer, director, SPX Corp.

Boyer, Herbert Wayne, PhD: chairman, president, director, Genentech Foundation for Biomedical Sciences; co-founder, director, Genentech Inc.

Davidson, George A., Jr.: chairman, chief executive officer, director, Consolidated Natural Gas Co.

Fischer, Richard Lawrence: director, Alcoa Foundation; executive vice president, chairman counsel, Alcoa Inc.

Glancy, John E.: corporate executive vice president, chairman, Telcordia Technologies

Godlasky, Tom: executive vice president, chief investment officer, AmerUS Group

Gregg, Walter Emmor, Junior: senior executive vice president finance & administration, PNC Financial Services Group

Hernandez, Robert M.: vice chairman, chief financial officer, director, USX Corp.; trustee, USX Foundation, Inc.

Hershman, Linda D.: vice president, Southern New England Telephone Co.

Howard, James Joseph, III: chairman, president, chief executive officer, director, Northern States Power Co.

Kelson, Richard B.: director, Alcoa Foundation

Lison, Stephen A.: vice president, trustee, SPX Foundation

Massaro, Anthony A.: president, chief executive officer, chairman, chief operating officer, Lincoln Electric Co.

McNally, Mark K.: senior vice president, general counsel, secretary, Aristech Chemical Corp.

Moravitz, Edward: trustee, Giant Eagle Foundation

Newlin, William Rankin: trustee, Kennametal Foundation

Richards, Thomas E.: executive vice president communications information products sector, Ameritech Corp.

Sease, Gene Elwood: director, Central Newspapers Foundation

Smith, Raymond W.: chairman, chief executive officer, director, Bell Atlantic Corp.

Stallkamp, William J.: member corporate review committee, Mellon Financial Corp.

Stecko, Paul T.: president, director, Tenneco Packaging

Usher, Thomas J.: chairman, chief executive officer, USX Corp.; chairman board trustees, USX Foundation, Inc.

VanderRoest, Stan: trustee, treasurer, Gerber Foundation; vice president, comptroller, controller, Gerber Products Co.

Yasinsky, John B.: chairman, president, chief executive officer, GenCorp

University of Pittsburgh Law School

Kasenter, Robert Albert: executive vice president human resources, Montgomery Ward & Co., Inc.; executive vice president, Montgomery Ward Foundation

University of Pittsburgh School of Business Administration

Koch, Robert Louis, II: president, chief executive officer, director, Koch Enterprises, Inc.; president, director, Koch Foundation

University of Portland

Guerrero, Anthony R., Jr.: director, First Hawaiian Foundation

Quesnel, Gregory L.: president, chief executive officer, director, CNF Transportation, Inc.

Walsh, Michael J.: vice president, CertainTeed Corp.

University of Puerto Rico

Iraola, Manuel J.: senior vice president, director, Phelps Dodge Corp.

University of Puget Sound

Kelly, John F.: chairman, chief executive officer, director, Alaska Airlines, Inc.

Liljebeck, Roy C.: executive vice president, chief financial officer, Airborne Freight Corp.

McDade, Sandy D.: secretary, Weyerhaeuser Co.; assistant secretary legal affairs, Weyerhaeuser Co. Foundation

University of Redlands

Bains, Harrison MacKellar, Jr.: vice president, treasurer, Bristol-Myers Squibb Co.; treasurer, Bristol-Myers Squibb Foundation Inc.

Dye, Donald H.: president, chief executive officer, Callaway Golf Co.

University of Rhode Island

Ayotte, Robert C.: executive vice president, director, CertainTeed Corp.; vice president, director, Norton Co. Foundation

Crandall, Robert Lloyd: director, AMR Corp.

Klein, David M.: vice president, Hartford (The)

Lemieux, Joseph Henry: chairman, chief executive officer, director, Owens-Illinois Inc.

Verrecchia, Alfred J.: treasurer, trustee, Hasbro Charitable Trust Inc.; executive, director, Hasbro, Inc.

University of Richmond

Baker, Leslie Mayo, Jr.: president, chief executive officer, chairman, Wachovia Bank of North Carolina NA; chairman, Wachovia Foundation, Inc. (The)

Burrus, Robert Lewis, Jr.: trustee, Circuit City Foundation

Gottwald, Bruce Cobb: chairman, chief executive officer, director, Ethyl Corp.

Savedge, Henry S., Jr.: executive vice president, chief financial officer, director, Reynolds Metals Co.; executive vice president, director, Reynolds Metals Co. Foundation

University of Richmond TC Williams School of Law

Causey, John Paul, Jr.: senior vice president, secretary, general counsel, Chesapeake Corp.; chairman, trustee, Chesapeake Corp. Foundation

University of Rochester

Anderson, Mark Bo: senior vice president, European American Bank

Besser, John Edward: director, Barnes Group Foundation Inc.; senior vice president finance & law, Barnes Group Inc.

Rich, Robert E., Jr.: secretary, Rich Family Foundation; president, director, Rich Products Corp.

University of Rome

Balzer, Giorgio: chairman, chief executive officer, Business Men's Assurance Co. of America

University of Saint Thomas

Rosilier, Glenn D.: executive vice president, chief financial officer, Central & South West Services

Schoenecker, Larry: director, Schoeneckers Foundation

University of San Diego Law School

Mansour, N. Ned: president, director, Mattel Inc.

University of San Francisco

Dreyfus, Branton B.: director, Alexander & Baldwin Foundation

Lang, Rudolph E., Jr.: senior vice president, chief financial officer, Litton Industries, Inc.

Levinson, Arthur David: president, chief executive officer, director, Genentech Inc.

Phair, Joseph Baschon: corporate secretary, general counsel, vice president, Varian Medical Systems, Inc.

Rinehart, Charles Robert: chairman, chief executive officer, director, Washington Mutual, Inc.

University of Santa Clara

Dunlap, F. Thomas, Jr.: secretary, director, Intel Foundation

Rhein, Timothy James: president, chief executive officer, APL Ltd.

University of Saskatchewan

Smith, W. Keith: senior vice chairman, member corporate review committee, director, Mellon Financial Corp.

University of Scranton

Montrone, Paul Michael: vice president, partner, Winthrop Foundation

University of Sidney

Johnson, David Willis: chairman, director, Campbell Soup Co.

University of South Carolina

Anderson, Ivan Verner, Jr.: president, chief executive officer, Evening Post Publishing Co.; vice president, Post and Courier Foundation

Chandler, J. Harold: chairman, president, chief executive officer, Provident Companies, Inc.

Clifton, Paul Hoot, Jr.: president, Colonial Life & Accident Insurance Co.

Dargene, Carl J.: director, AMCORE Foundation

DeLoach, Harris E., Junior: executive vice president, director, Sonoco Products Co.

Elliott, R. Keith: chief executive officer, president, Hercules Inc.

Peterson, William E.: general counsel, Sierra Pacific Resources

Shelley, James Herbert: chairman, Sonoco Foundation

Staton, Robert Emmett: president, Colonial Life & Accident Insurance Co.

University of South Dakota

Coughlin, Timothy C.: president, Riggs Bank NA

Gustafson, James E.: president, chief operating officer, Saint Paul Companies Inc.

McClain, Terry James: director, Valmont Foundation; senior vice president, chief financial officer, Valmont Industries, Inc.

Zylstra, Stanley James: chairman, director, Land O'Lakes, Inc.

University of South Florida

Hult, Frank A.: vice president, controller, chief accounting officer, Walter Industries Inc.

University of Southern California

Anderson, Gordon M.: chairman, Santa Fe International Corp.

Armstrong, Neil A.: trustee, Milacron Foundation; director, Milacron, Inc.

Barbakow, Jeffrey C.: chairman, chief executive officer, director, Tenet Healthcare Corp.

Coulter, Patrick C. G.: president, Bell Atlantic Foundation; senior vice president corporate communications, Gulfstream Aerospace Corp.

Deutsch, Carl: president, Deutsch Foundation

Fluor, John Robert, II: president, trustee, Fluor Corp.

Foster, Kent B.: president, director, GTE Corp.; trustee, GTE Foundation

Groman, Arthur: president, Occidental Petroleum Charitable Foundation

Grundhofer, John Francis: president, chief executive officer, director, U.S. Bancorp

Haskell, Robert G.: president, director, Pacific Mutual Charitable Foundation; senior vice president public affairs, Pacific Mutual Life Insurance Co.

Horner, Donald G.: vice president, director, First Hawaiian Foundation

Irani, Raymond Reza: director, Occidental Petroleum Charitable Foundation; chairman, director, chief executive officer, Occidental Petroleum Corp.

Klitten, Martin R.: vice president, chief financial officer, Chevron Corp.

Lachman, Marguerite Leanne: trustee, Chicago Title and Trust Co. Foundation

Maffie, Michael O.: president, chief executive officer, director, Southwest Gas Corp.; trustee, Southwest Gas Corp. Foundation

Mansour, N. Ned: president, director, Mattel Inc.

Markkula, Armas Clifford, Jr.: chairman, director, Apple Computer, Inc.

McFerson, Dimon Richard: chairman, chief executive officer, Nationwide Insurance Co.; chairman, chief executive officer, trustee, Nationwide Insurance Enterprise Foundation; chairman, chief executive officer, Wausau Insurance Companies

McKenna, William P.: vice president finance, chief financial officer, treasurer, Bourns, Inc.

Mulholland, Charles Bradley: executive vice president, director, Alexander & Baldwin Foundation; executive vice president, Alexander & Baldwin, Inc.

Mullane, Donald A.: executive vice president, Bank of America; chairman, Bank of America Foundation

Niebla, J. Fernando: chairman, chief executive officer, Pacific Mutual Life Insurance Co.

Prince, Charles O., III: senior vice president, general counsel, secretary, Citigroup; secretary, trustee, Citigroup Foundation

Rollans, James Ora: senior vice president, chief administrative officer, chief financial officer, Fluor Corp.; trustee, Fluor Foundation

Simpson, Andrea Lynn: president

Stivers, William Charles: senior vice president, chief financial officer, treasurer, Weyerhaeuser Co.; treasurer, trustee, Weyerhaeuser Co. Foundation

University of Southern California Law School

Ukropina, James R.: partner, Pacific Mutual Life Insurance Co.

University of Southern Florida

Bragin, David H.: treasurer, assistant secretary, director, Winn-Dixie Stores Foundation

University of Southern Mississippi

Cooper, Janis Campbell: vice president, Maytag Corp. Foundation

Scarbrough, Arlan Earl: vice president financial, Gulf Power Co.; trustee, Gulf Power Foundation

University of Stuttgart

Hinrichs, Horst: vice chairman, director, American Standard Inc.

University of Sydney

Johnson, David Willis: chairman, director, Campbell Soup Co.

University of Tennessee

Beattie, Art P.: vice president, secretary, treasurer, Alabama Power Co.; treasurer, Alabama Power Foundation

Berlik, Leonard J.: vice president, National Starch & Chemical Co.

Holliday, Charles O., Jr.: chairman, chief executive officer, director, du Pont de Nemours & Co. (E.I.)

Reese, Terry W.: assistant treasurer, Vulcan Materials Co. Foundation

University of Texas

Agnich, Richard John: director, Texas Instruments Foundation; senior vice president, secretary, general counsel, Texas Instruments Inc.

Austin, H. Brent: executive vice president, chief financial officer, El Paso Energy Co.; vice president, treasurer, director, El Paso Energy Foundation

Baish, Richard Owen: senior vice president, director, El Paso Energy Foundation

Carr, Cassandra Colvin: director, SBC Foundation

Cloninger, Kriss, III: executive vice president, chief financial officer, treasurer, AFLAC Inc.

Easterly, David E.: president, chief operating officer, Cox Enterprises Inc.

Evans, Richard W., Jr.: chairman, chief executive officer, Frost National Bank

Gleaves, James Leslie: assistant treasurer, American General Finance Foundation

Godfrey, Cullen Michael: vice president, FINA Foundation

Harvey, A. Mosby, Jr.: secretary, HON Industries

Charitable Foundation; vice president, secretary, general counsel, HON Industries Inc.

Hurford, Gary Thomas: president, director, Hunt Oil Co.

Jastrow, Kenneth M., II: director, Temple-Inland Foundation

Jewell, George Hiram: director, Schlumberger Foundation

Johnson, Murray Lloyd, Jr.: secretary, trustee, Zachry Foundation (The)

Marsh, R. Bruce: general tax counsel, Chevron Corp.

McGehee, Robert B.: executive vice president, general counsel, Carolina Power & Light Co.; trustee, CP&L Foundation

McWilliams, D. Bradley: vice president, Cooper Industries Foundation; chief financial officer, senior vice president finance, Cooper Industries, Inc.

Mooney, Edward J., Jr.: chairman, president, chief executive officer, director, Nalco Chemical Co.

Moroney, James McQueen, Jr.: trustee, Belo Corp. Foundation (A.H.)

Mulva, James J.: president, chief operating officer, director, Phillips Petroleum Co.

Parrish, Jere Paul: president, chairman executive committee, director, Shell Oil Co. Foundation

Rice, Liston Michael, Jr.: president, director public affairs, Texas Instruments Foundation

Simmons, Harold Clark: chairman, director, Simmons Foundation, Inc. (Harold)

Skiles, Win: vice president, Texas Instruments Foundation; senior vice president, Texas Instruments Inc.

Wishnick, William: president, director, Wishnick Foundation (Robert I.)

Wynia, Ann: director, Fuller Co. Foundation (H.B.)

University of Texas Graduate School of Business

Gleaves, James Leslie: assistant treasurer, American General Finance Foundation

University of Texas at Dallas

Wiley, Michael E.: president, ARCO Foundation

University of Texas, Austin

Temple, Arthur, III: director, Temple-Inland Foundation

University of Tokyo

Condit, Philip Murray: chairman, chief executive officer, director, Boeing Co.

Tsutsumi, Senji: vice president, trustee, Ise Cultural Foundation

University of Toledo

Everingham, Lyle J.: trustee, Milacron Foundation

Marohn, William D.: vice chairman, director, Whirlpool Corp.

Nagy, Charles F.: treasurer, Standard Products Co.; trustee, Standard Products Co. Charitable Foundation

Pike, Robert William: vice president, secretary, Allstate Foundation; senior vice president, secretary, general counsel, director, Allstate Insurance Co.

Snow, John William: chairman, president, chief executive officer, CSX Corp.

Zampetis, Theodore K.: president, chief operating officer, director, Standard Products Co.

University of Toronto

Coyne, William E.: senior vice president, Minnesota Mining & Manufacturing Co.

Sutton, Thomas C.: chairman, director, Pacific Mutual Charitable Foundation; chairman, chief executive officer, director, Pacific Mutual Life Insurance Co.

University of Tulsa

Nowell, Tommy Lynn: vice president finance, controller, Occidental Oil and Gas; treasurer, Occidental Oil and Gas Foundation

Wiley, Michael E.: president, ARCO Foundation

Wood, Willis B., Jr.: chairman, chief executive officer, director, Pacific Enterprises

University of Utah

Bohling, John A.: senior vice president, PacifiCorp; board member, PacifiCorp Foundation

Eccles, Spencer Fox: chairman, chief executive officer, director, First Security Bank of Idaho NA

Hanks, Stephen G.: president, Morrison Knudsen Corp. Foundation, Inc.

Herbert, Bart, Jr.: executive vice president, chief marketing officer, AEGON U.S.A. Inc.

Marriott, J. Willard, Jr.: chairman, chief executive officer, Marriott International Inc.

McAllister, Francis R.: vice president, director, ASARCO Foundation; president, chief executive officer, ASARCO Inc.

Merrell, Pamela K.: secretary, Montana Power Co.; vice president, secretary, Montana Power Foundation

Milne, Garth Leroy: senior vice president, treasurer, Motorola Inc.

Norberg, Jaron B.: vice president, director, APS Foundation, Inc.; director, Arizona Public Service Co.

Parks, Stephen E.: vice president, treasurer, chief financial officer, Questar Corp.

University of Utah Law School

Merrell, Pamela K.: secretary, Montana Power Co.; vice president, secretary, Montana Power Foundation

University of Vermont

Berwind, C. Graham, Jr.: chairman, president, chief executive officer, Berwind Group

Burke, Daniel Barnett: vice president, treasurer, director, ABC Foundation

Glynn, Gary Allen: president, USX Corp.; vice president, USX Foundation, Inc.

Thompson, Donald L.: chairman, chief executive officer, Hunt Manufacturing Co.

University of Vienna

Leube, Helmut: trustee,

University of Virginia

Bakane, John L.: president, chief executive officer, director, Cone Mills Corp.

Baker, Leslie Mayo, Jr.: president, chief executive officer, chairman, Wachovia Bank of North Carolina NA; chairman, Wachovia Foundation, Inc. (The)

Barry, Richard Francis, III: director, Landmark Communications Foundation; vice chairman, Landmark Communications Inc.

Batten, Frank, Sr.: chairman, director, Landmark Communications Foundation; chairman, Landmark Communications Inc.

Bukowick, Peter A.: president, chief operating officer, director, Alliant Techsystems

Connolly, Gerald Edward: trustee, Reinhart Family Foundation (D. B. and Marjorie)

Coyne, William E.: senior vice president, Minnesota Mining & Manufacturing Co.

Crenshaw, Gordon Lee, II: member, Universal Leaf Foundation; chairman emeritus, Universal Leaf Tobacco Co., Inc.

Cutchins, Clifford Armstrong, IV: president, Fort James Corp.; chairman, director, Fort James Foundation (The)

Dabney, Donna C.: secretary, Reynolds Metals Co. Foundation

David, George A. L.: chairman, president, chief executive officer, chief operating officer, United Technologies Corp.

Davis, Edward J.: chief financial officer, vice president, treasurer, Wyman-Gordon Co.

Dickson, Thomas W.: vice president, Dickson Foundation

Druen, W. Sidney: director, Nationwide Insurance Enterprise Foundation

Emerson, Frederick George: vice president, secretary, director, Viad Corp. Fund

Fox, Joseph Carter: chairman, president, chief executive officer, Chesapeake Corp.

Freedman, Allen Royal: trustee, Fortis Foundation; chairman, chief executive officer, president, Fortis, Inc.

Frierson, Daniel K.: chairman, chief executive officer, Dixie Group, Inc. (The); president, trustee, Dixie Yarns Foundation, Inc.

Gottwald, Bruce Cobb: chairman, chief executive officer, director, Ethyl Corp.

Guedry, James Walter: president, International Paper Co. Foundation

James, Donald M.: chairman, Vulcan Materials Co. Foundation

Lowden, Francis V., III: secretary, Universal Leaf Foundation

Matherne, Louis K.: treasurer, Chesapeake Corp.

McCarthy, John Michael: vice president, Waffle House Foundation, Inc.

McKamey, William: general manager, director, Public Service Co. of Oklahoma

Merdek, Andrew Austin: vice president legal affairs, secretary, Cox Enterprises Inc.; secretary, Cox Foundation (James M.)

Murphy, Christopher J., III: president, chief executive officer, director, First Source Corp.; director, First Source Foundation

Norwood, Ralph M.: treasurer, Polaroid Foundation

Prendergast, Michael J.: vice president, chief financial officer, Aristech Chemical Corp.

Quin, Joseph Marvin: trustee, Ashland Inc. Foundation

Ratcliffe, George Jackson, Jr.: trustee, Hubbell Foundation (Harvey); chairman, president, chief executive officer, Hubbell Inc.

Reinemund, Steve S.: chairman, chief executive officer, Frito-Lay, Inc.

Reynolds, William Gray, Jr.: vice president government relations & public affairs, Reynolds Metals Co.; director, Reynolds Metals Co. Foundation

Schievelbein, Thomas C.: executive vice president, Newport News Shipbuilding

Sharp, Richard L.: trustee, Circuit City Foundation; chairman, chief executive officer, director, Circuit City Stores, Inc.

Snow, John William: chairman, president, chief executive officer, CSX Corp.

Sommer, Charles S.: member board control, Ralston Purina Trust Fund

Tilghman, Richard Granville: chairman, chief executive officer, Crestar Foundation

Trogdon, Dewey Leonard, Jr.: director, ABC Foundation; chairman, Cone Mills Corp.

Tyler, Kenneth Scott, Jr.: president, chief executive officer, Furniture Brands International, Inc.

Valentine, E. Massey: trustee, Chesapeake Corp. Foundation

Wynne, John Oliver: president, director, Landmark Communications Foundation; president, chief executive officer, Landmark Communications Inc.

University of Virginia Darden School of Business Administration

Watjen, Thomas R.: vice chairman, chief financial officer, Provident Companies, Inc.

University of Virginia School of Law

Cowan, Keith O.: vice president corporate development, BellSouth Corp.

Prendergast, Michael J.: vice president, chief financial officer, Aristech Chemical Corp.

University of Wales

Williams, John A.: president, chief executive officer, Louisiana Land & Exploration Co.; director, Louisiana Land & Exploration Co. Foundation

University of Washington

Almy, Richard E.: executive vice president, chief operating officer, director, Walter Industries Inc.

Benson, John W.: executive vice president health care, Minnesota Mining & Manufacturing Co.

Buxton, Winslow Hurlbert: chairman, president, chief executive officer, director, Pentair Inc.

Campbell, Phyllis J.: president private financial services, US Bank, Washington

Elam, Lloyd Charles, MD: trustee, Merck Co. Foundation

Hogans, Mack L.: chairman, president, trustee, Weyerhaeuser Co. Foundation

Hoops, Alan R.: member, PacifiCare Health System Foundation

Hovind, David J.: president, director, PACCAR Inc.

Kerr, William T.: chairman, chief executive officer, director, Meredith Corp.

Levinson, Arthur David: president, chief executive officer, director, Genentech Inc.

Meurer, Thomas E.: senior vice president administration, Hunt Oil Co.

Neale, Gary L.: chairman, president, chief executive officer, Northern Indiana Public Service Co.

Nutter, Wallace L.: director, Rayonier Foundation

Olesen, Douglas Eugene, PhD: president, chief executive officer, Battelle Memorial Institute

Stavropoulos, William S.: president, chief executive officer, director, Dow Chemical Co.

Wiborg, James Hooker: director, PACCAR Foundation

University of Waterloo

Bertran, David R.: senior vice president manufacturing & logistics, Nalco Chemical Co.; director, Nalco Foundation

University of West Florida

Labrato, Ronnie R.: secretary, Gulf Power Foundation

Wright, Samuel G.: trustee, Eckerd Corp. Foundation

University of Western Ontario

Kreh, Gordon W.: president, chief executive officer, director, Hartford Steam Boiler Inspection & Insurance Co.

Smith, W. Keith: senior vice chairman, member corporate review committee, director, Mellon Financial Corp.

Thrasher, F. Martin: senior vice president, Campbell Soup Co.

University of Windsor

Lawless, Robert J.: chairman, president, chief executive officer, chief operating officer, director, McCormick & Co. Inc.

University of Wisconsin

Bachmann, Richard Arthur: vice president, secretary, treasurer, director, Louisiana Land & Exploration Co. Foundation

Bartz, Carol A.: director, Autodesk Foundation; chairman, chief executive officer, Autodesk Inc.

Bauer, Chris Michael: president, Firstar Milwaukee Foundation

Bilton, Stuart Douglas: president, chief executive officer, Chicago Title Corp.; trustee, Chicago Title and Trust Co. Foundation

Brine, Kevin R.: trustee, Bernstein & Co. Foundation, Inc. (Sanford C.)

Bruce, Peter Wayne: director, Badger Meter Foundation

Brunner, Vernon A.: executive vice president marketing, Walgreen Co.

Burd, Steven A.: president, chief executive officer, chairman, director, Safeway Inc.

Burlingame, John Hunter: executive partner, Scripps Co. (E.W.)

Chazen, Jerome A.: trustee, Claiborne Foundation (Liz); co-founder, chairman, director, Liz Claiborne, Inc.

Collins, Duane E.: president, chief executive officer, director, Parker Hannifin Corp.; vice president, trustee, Parker Hannifin Foundation

Collins, Paul John: vice chairman, director, Citibank Corp.

Connor, James Richard: executive director, Kemper Foundation (James S.)

Critelli, Michael J.: vice president, secretary, general counsel, chairman, Pitney Bowes Inc.

Darehshori, Nader Farhang: chairman, president, chief executive officer, Houghton Mifflin Co.

Dewane, John Richard: director, Honeywell Foundation

Dix, Ronald H.: director, Badger Meter Foundation; vice president administration & human resources, Badger Meter, Inc.

Eckert, Ralph John: trustee, Trustmark Foundation

Feaster, Joyce: assistant treasurer, assistant secretary, Wisconsin Energy Corp. Foundation, Inc.

Fluno, Jere David: vice chairman, Grainger, Inc. (W.W.)

Forster, Peter Hans: chairman, director, Dayton Power and Light Co.

Gherty, John E.: president, chief executive officer, Land O'Lakes, Inc.

Gonring, Matthew P.: vice president, trustee, USG Foundation

Grainger, David William: senior chairman, Grainger, Inc. (W.W.)

Grigg, Richard R.: vice president, Wisconsin Energy Corp.; director, Wisconsin Energy Corp. Foundation, Inc.

Hefty, Thomas R.: chairman, president, chief executive officer, United Wisconsin Services

Hegel, Garrett R.: chief financial officer, Compass Bank; president, Compass Bank Foundation

Hinton, John R.: executive vice president administration, chief financial officer, Kellogg Co.; president, trustee, Kellogg Co. Twenty-Five Year Employees' Fund Inc.

Hobbs, Richard F.: vice president administration, Universal Foods Corp.; vice president, director, Universal Foods Foundation

Hultgren, Dennis N.: director, Appleton Papers Inc.

Jacobs, Bruce E.: vice president, director, Grede Foundation; president, director, Grede Foundries

Jacobs, Burleigh Edmund: president, director, Grede Foundation; chairman, Grede Foundries; director, Marshall & Ilsley Foundation, Inc.

Kerckhove, George H.: vice president, chief financial officer, American Standard Inc.

Kleinfeldt, Richard C.: vice president financial, chief financial officer, director, Giddings & Lewis

Kress, George F.: honorary chairman, director, Green Bay Packaging; president, Kress Foundation (George)

Kress, James F.: chairman, director, Green Bay Packaging

Krzos, Joseph T.: treasurer, Madison Gas & Electric Foundation

Ladish, John: trustee, Ladish Co. Foundation

Lehman, Michael E.: director, Sun Microsystems Foundation, Inc.

Lemke, Carl R.: secretary, Consolidated Papers Foundation, Inc.

Lesar, David J.: president, chief operating officer, Halliburton Co.; trustee, Halliburton Foundation, Inc.

Levin, Michael Stuart: president, chief executive officer, Titan Industrial Corp.

Lubar, Sheldon B.: chairman, Ameritech Corp.; director, Firstar Milwaukee Foundation

Marcus, Stephen Howard: chairman, chief executive officer, Marcus Corp.; president, director, Marcus Corp. Foundation

Mebane, David Cummins: chairman, president, chief executive officer, director, Madison Gas & Electric Co.; vice president, Madison Gas & Electric Foundation

Notebaert, Richard C.: chairman, chief executive officer, Ameritech Corp.; director, Ameritech Foundation

Omachinski, David L.: chief financial officer, treasurer, vice president, Oshkosh B'Gosh, Inc.

Pearl, Melvin E.: treasurer, director, Katten, Muchin & Zavis Foundation

Piano, Phyllis J.: president, Cooper Industries Foundation; vice president public affairs, Cooper Industries, Inc.

Puelicher, John A.: president, director, Marshall & Ilsley Foundation, Inc.

Randall, James R.: president, director, Archer-Daniels-Midland Co.

Raymond, Lee R.: chairman, president, chief executive officer, Exxon Mobil Corp.

Rupple, Brenton H.: director, Bucyrus-Erie Foundation

Salinger, Robert M.: secretary, First Financial Foundation

Schrickel, Patrick D.: vice president, Wisconsin Public Service Foundation, Inc.

Schueppert, George Louis: chief financial officer, executive vice president, Outboard Marine Corp.

Taylor, Philip E.: president, JSJ Corp.

Terry, Richard Edward: chairman, chief executive officer, director, Peoples Energy Corp.

Thies, Richard Henry: assistant treasurer, Madison Gas & Electric Foundation

Van Himbergen, Thomas: director, Deluxe Corp. Foundation

Ver Hagen, Jan Karol: president, United Dominion Industries, Ltd.

Wachtel, Michael D.: president, Oshkosh B'Gosh Foundation Inc.; chief operating officer, Oshkosh B'Gosh, Inc.

Wenzel, Fred William: chairman emeritus, Kellwood Co.

Wenzler, Joseph P.: secretary, treasurer, WICOR Foundation; senior vice president, chief financial officer, WICOR, Inc.

Whitwam, David Ray: chairman, president, chief executive officer, director, Whirlpool Corp.

Winter, William Bergford: president, Bucyrus-Erie Co.; chairman, president, director, Bucyrus-Erie Foundation

Wynia, Ann: director, Fuller Co. Foundation (H.B.)

Zech, Ronald H.: chairman, president, chief executive officer, chief operating officer, GATX Corp.

Ziemer, James L.: president, Harley-Davidson Foundation

Zimmerman, S. LaNette: senior vice president human resources, Chicago Title Corp.; trustee, Chicago Title and Trust Co. Foundation

Zutz, Denise M.: member advisory board, Johnson Controls Foundation

University of Wisconsin Law School

Hefty, Thomas R.: chairman, president, chief executive officer, United Wisconsin Services

University of Wisconsin School of Bank Administration

Miller, Eugene A.: chairman, chief executive officer, Comerica Inc.

University of Wisconsin, Madison

Amato, Anthony J.: senior vice president, Wisconsin Power & Light Co.; president, director, Wisconsin Power & Light Foundation, Inc.

Henseler, Gerald A.: executive vice president, chief financial officer, director, Banta Corp.; president, Banta Corp. Foundation

University of Wisconsin, Manitowoc

Muchin, Allan B.: chairman, Katten, Muchin & Zavis; director, Katten, Muchin & Zavis Foundation

University of Wisconsin, Milwaukee

Fitzsimonds, Roger Leon: chairman, Firstar Milwaukee Foundation

Lacy, William Howard: president, MGIC Investment Corp.

Willis, Gordon A.: assistant treasurer, assistant secretary, Wisconsin Energy Corp. Foundation, Inc.

University of Wisconsin, Oshkosh

Bittner, D. P.: treasurer, assistant secretary, Wisconsin Public Service Foundation, Inc.

University of Wisconsin, Stout

Davis, Dwight D.: president, chief operating officer

University of Wisconsin, Whitewater

Meeusen, Richard A.: vice president, chief financial officer, treasurer, Badger Meter, Inc.

University of Witwatersrand

Tambakeras, Markos I.: director, Honeywell Foundation

University of Wyoming

Cheney, Richard B.: chief executive officer, Halliburton Co.; president, Halliburton Foundation, Inc.

Colgan, Celeste: vice president, secretary, Halliburton Foundation, Inc.

Trujillo, Solomon D.: president, US West Foundation; president, chief executive officer, US West, Inc.

University of the Pacific

Binyon, Bryan A.: treasurer, American General Finance Foundation

Fleming, Richard Harrison: chief financial officer, senior vice president, USG Corp.; treasurer, trustee, USG Foundation

University of the South

Atkins, Sarah Humphreys: vice president, Craig Foundation (E.L.)

Humphreys, David Craig: secretary-treasurer, Craig Foundation (E.L.); president, chief operating officer, director, Tamko Roofing Products

Shaw, Robert E.: chairman, chief executive officer, Shaw Industries Inc.

White, Thomas A. H.: vice president corporate relations, Provident Companies, Inc.

Upsala College

Graham, John Gourlay: chief financial officer, senior vice president, GPU Energy

Ursinus College

Bloom, Geoffrey B.: chairman, chief executive officer, director, Wolverine World Wide

Lovett, John Robert: director, Air Products Foundation

Utah State University

King, Richard L.: president, chief operating officer, Albertson's Inc.

Staheli, Donald L.: chairman, director, Continental Grain Co.; vice president, director, Continental Grain Foundation

ZoBell, Karl: vice president, trustee, Copley Foundation (James S.)

Utica College

Whitelaw, Essie M.: president, chief operating officer, United Wisconsin Services; vice president, United Wisconsin Services Foundation

Valdosta State College

Ratcliffe, David M.: chief financial officer, treasurer, director, Georgia Power Co.

Valparaiso University

Fites, Donald Vester: director, Caterpillar Foundation

Hessler, David J.: secretary, trustee, Jochum-Moll Foundation (The); president, partner, MTD Products Inc.

Pehlke, Richard W.: vice president, treasurer, Ameritech Corp.

Walton, Jon David: trustee, Allegheny Technologies Inc. Charitable Trust

Zech, Ronald H.: chairman, president, chief executive officer, chief operating officer, GATX Corp.

Vanderbilt University

Bottorff, Dennis C.: chairman, president, chief executive officer, director, First American Corp.

Callaway, Lee: vice president public relations, Pacific Gas and Electric Co.

Carr, Cassandra Colvin: director, SBC Foundation

Colman, Robert L.: executive vice president human resources, Delta Air Lines, Inc.

Cox, Daniel T.: executive vice president, Aon Corp.

Dickson, Rush S., III: vice president, Dickson Foundation

Edwards, John Kenneth: executive president, group president power generation, Cummins Engine Co., Inc.; director, Cummins Engine Foundation

Moore, Jackson W.: president, director, Union Planters Corp.

Morris, Herman, Jr.: president, chief executive officer, Memphis Light Gas & Water Division

Rawlins, Benjamin W., Jr.: chairman, chief executive officer, director, Union Planters Corp.

Rosson, William Mimms: chairman, Conwood Co. LP

Smith, Richard C.: chief executive officer, director, Telcordia Technologies

Stinnett, J. Daniel: director, Commerce Bancshares Foundation

Turner, Cal, Jr.: chairman, chief executive officer, director, Dollar General Corp.

White, Thomas A. H.: vice president corporate relations, Provident Companies, Inc.

Wilson, James Lawrence: chairman, chief executive officer, director, Rohm & Haas Co.

Wise, William Allen: chairman, president, chief executive officer, director, El Paso Energy Co.; chairman, director, El Paso Energy Foundation

Wolf, Philip C.: senior vice president, general counsel, secretary, Cyprus Amax Minerals Co.

Vassar College

Beatt, Bruce H.: secretary, Dexter Corp. Foundation

Graham, Katharine Meyer: chairman executive committee, director, The Washington Post

Ingram, Martha R.: chairman, director, Ingram Industries Inc.

McNamara, Anne H.: senior vice president, general counsel, AMR Corp.

Victoria Jubilee Technology Institute Bombay

Nayak, P. Ranganath: trustee, Little Foundation (Arthur D.); senior vice president, Little, Inc. (Arthur D.)

Villanova University

Albright, David L.: president, Campbell Soup Co.

Archinaco, Frank A.: director, PPG Industries Foundation; executive vice president, PPG Industries, Inc.

Bettacchi, Robert J.: senior vice president, Grace & Co. (W.R.)

Brennan, Michael J.: chief financial officer, senior vice president, Binswanger Companies

Danford, Philip C.: treasurer, Dun & Bradstreet Corp. Foundation, Inc.

Denlea, Leo Edward, Jr.: retired chairman, president, chief executive officer, director, Farmers Group, Inc.; vice president, Farmers Group Safety Foundation

Furey, John J.: corporate secretary, corporate counsel, Campbell Soup Co.

Harkins, James F., Jr.: treasurer, CertainTeed Corp. Foundation

Heimbold, Charles Andreas, Jr.: chairman, president, chief executive officer, Bristol-Myers Squibb Co.

Janitz, John A.: president, chief executive officer, chairman, Textron Inc.

Kostecky, James Frank: executive director, Bethlehem Steel Corp.

Labrecque, Thomas Goulet: president, chief operating officer, director, Chase Manhattan Bank, NA; president, Chase Manhattan Foundation

Mahoney, Robert W.: chairman, president, chief executive officer, director, Diebold, Inc.

McGuinn, Martin Gregory: chairman, chief executive officer, Mellon Financial Corp.

Orr, James F., III: president, trustee, UNUM Foundation; chairman, Unum-Provident

Overbaugh, Joseph C.: director, AMP Foundation

Trosino, Vincent Joseph: assistant secretary, State Farm Companies Foundation; executive vice president, vice chairman, chief operating officer, director, State Farm Mutual Automobile Insurance Co.

White, Gerald Andrew: director, Air Products Foundation

Villanova University Law School

Hirsch, Laurence E.: chairman, chief executive officer, director, Centex Corp.

Vincennes University

Sheley, Donald R., Junior: vice president finance, chief financial officer, Standard Products Co.; treasurer, trustee, Standard Products Co. Charitable Foundation

Virginia Commonwealth University

DeRusha, William Charles: chairman, chief executive officer, Heilig-Meyers Co.

Virginia Military Institute

Adams, John B., Junior: chairman, president, chief executive officer, Dominion Resources, Inc.

Gottwald, Bruce Cobb: chairman, chief executive officer, director, Ethyl Corp.

Gottwald, Thomas E.: president, chief operating officer, director, Ethyl Corp.

Watjen, Thomas R.: vice chairman, chief financial officer, Provident Companies, Inc.

Virginia Polytechnic Institute & State University

Ambler, John Doss: vice president, Texaco Inc.

Ballengee, Jerry Hunter: president, chief operating officer, director, Union Camp Corp.

Brothers, John Alfred 'Fred': trustee, Ashland Inc. Foundation

Lorch, George A.: chairman, chief executive officer, director, Armstrong World Industries, Inc.

Madia, William J.: executive vice president, manager, Battelle Memorial Institute

Virginia State University

Edwards, Earnest Jonathan: director, Alcoa Foundation

Virginia Tech

Vaughn, Donald C.: vice chairman, Halliburton Co.

Wabash College

Bachmann, John W.: managing partner, Jones & Co. (Edward D.); chairman, Jones & Co. Foundation (Edward D.)

Bowerman, Charles L.: executive vice president, director, Phillips Petroleum Co.

Meyer, W. Frederick: president, Arvin Foundation

Spiegel, John William: member, SunTrust Bank Atlanta Foundation

Wagner College

Walters, John Alexander: trustee, Alcon Foundation

Wake Forest University

Disher, J. William: director, Lance Foundation; chairman, Lance, Inc.

Lay, Terry: president, Lee, Lee Apparel Co.

Reed, Scott Eldridge: senior executive vice president, chief financial officer, Branch Banking & Trust Co.

Sharpe, Robert Francis, Jr.: senior vice president public affairs, general counsel, PepsiCo, Inc.

Thompson, G. Kennedy: president, chief operating officer, First Union Corp.; member, First Union Foundation

Warden, William C., Jr.: secretary, Lowe's Charitable and Educational Foundation

Waseda University

Sugizaki, Teruyuki: director, Toshiba America Foundation

Washburn University

Cocklin, Kim Roland: senior vice president, Texas Gas Transmission Corp.

de Vink, Lodewijk J. R.: director, Warner-Lambert Charitable Foundation; president, chief operating officer, director, Warner-Lambert Co.

Washington & Lee University

Block, William, Jr.: president, trustee, Blade Foundation; president, director, Toledo Blade Co.

Dickson, Rush S., III: vice president, Dickson Foundation

Duchossois, Richard Louis: secretary, Duchossois Foundation; chairman, chief executive officer, director, Duchossois Industries Inc.

Farnsworth, Philip Richeson: secretary, ABC

Fox, Joseph Carter: chairman, president, chief executive officer, Chesapeake Corp.

Frost, Thomas C., Senior: chairman, Frost National Bank

Harrell, Henry Howze: director, Universal Leaf Foundation; chairman, chief executive officer, director, Universal Leaf Tobacco Co., Inc.

Hipp, William Hayne: president, chief executive officer, director, Liberty Corp.; chairman, president, director, Liberty Corp. Foundation

Moore, John E.: executive vice president human resources, Cessna Aircraft Co.; vice president, Cessna Foundation, Inc.

Peck, Arthur John, Jr.: secretary, vice president, Corning Inc.; secretary, Corning Inc. Foundation

White, James M., III: general counsel, Universal Leaf Foundation; senior vice president, general counsel, assistant secretary, Universal Leaf Tobacco Co., Inc.

Washington & Lee University Law School

Adams, John B.. Junior: chairman, president, chief executive officer, Dominion Resources, Inc.

Washington State University

Campbell, Phyllis J.: president private financial services, US Bank, Washington

Cool, Judd R.: senior vice president human resources, Allegheny Technologies Inc.

Suwyn, Mark A.: chairman, president, Louisiana-Pacific Foundation

Zeffren, Eugene: executive vice president, Curtis Industries, Inc. (Helene)

Washington University

Barrett, M. Patricia: vice president corporate communications, Ameren Corp.

Brown, JoBeth Goode: trustee, Anheuser-Busch Companies, Inc.

Essman, Alyn V.: chairman, chief executive officer, CPI Corp.

Foster, Charles E.: director, SBC Foundation

Geller, Eric P.: trustee, Harcourt General Charitable Foundation; senior vice president, general counsel, secretary, Harcourt General, Inc.

Heilala, John A.: trustee, Vulcan Materials Co. Foundation

Herron, James Michael: secretary, director, Ryder System Charitable Foundation

Hotchner, Aaron Edward: vice president, director, executive, Newman's Own Foundation; vice president, treasurer, Newman's Own Inc.

Jaudes, Robert Christian: chairman, trustee, Laclede Gas Charitable Trust

Loeb, Jerome Thomas: chairman, director, May Department Stores Co.; president, director, May Department Stores Computer Foundation (The)

Margolin, Abraham E.: director, Tension Envelope Foundation

Rubenstein, Leonard Mark: executive vice president investment, director, GenAmerica Corp.; vice president, director, GenAmerican Foundation

Schoening, Robert Walters: senior vice president information systems, Giant Food Inc.

Schuchardt, Daniel Norman: secretary, treasurer, FMC Foundation

Seiffert, Ron J.: vice chairman, Huntington Bancshares Inc.

Stupp, Robert P.: president, director, Stupp Brothers Bridge & Iron Co.; trustee, Stupp Brothers Bridge & Iron Co. Foundation

Van Cleve, William Moore: member public policy committee, Emerson Charitable Trust; partner, Emerson Electric Co.

Wadlington, Cuba, Jr.: vice president, Williams

Wendlandt, Gary Edward: executive vice president, chief investment officer, Massachusetts Mutual Life Insurance Co.

von Glahn, William G.: senior vice president, general counsel, Williams; director, Williams Companies Foundation (The)

Waverly College

Bible, Geoffrey Cyril: director, New York Stock Exchange Foundation, Inc.; chairman, chief executive officer, director, Philip Morris Companies Inc.

Wayne State University

Anderson, Eugene Karl: vice president, Contran Corp.; treasurer, Simmons Foundation, Inc. (Harold)

Cooper, William Allen: chairman, director, TCF National Bank Minnesota

Coughlan, Gary Patrick: chief financial officer, senior vice president finance, Abbott Laboratories; director, Abbott Laboratories Fund

Feldhouse, Lynn Alexandra: vice president, secretary, DaimlerChrysler Corp. Fund

Fryling, Victor J.: director, Consumers Energy Foundation

Greenwald, Gerald: chairman, chief executive officer, director, United Airlines Inc.

Liebler, Arthur C.: vice president communications, DaimlerChrysler Corp.; trustee, DaimlerChrysler Corp. Fund

McClain, Terry James: director, Valmont Foundation; senior vice president, chief financial officer, Valmont Industries, Inc.

McKinnon, Thomas E.: director, Ryder System Charitable Foundation; executive vice president human resources, Ryder System, Inc.

Nern, Christopher C.: vice president, general counsel, Detroit Edison Co.; director, Detroit Edison Foundation

Pond, Byron O.: chairman, chief executive officer, director, Arvin Industries, Inc.

Powell, Cornelius Patrick: president, Air Products Foundation

Webster University

Osler, Randy W.: president, Sprint/United Telephone

Wellesley College

Bowles, Crandall Close: president, chief executive officer, chairman, director, Springs Industries, Inc.

Henn, Catherine Emily Campbell: president, Boston Globe Foundation

Martore, Gracia C.: vice president investor relations, treasurer, Gannett Co., Inc.; assistant treasurer, Gannett Foundation

Reed, Cynthia: assistant secretary, Hasbro Charitable Trust Inc.; senior vice president, general counsel, Hasbro, Inc.

Rogers, Desiree Glapion: vice president community affairs, Peoples Energy Corp.

Wesleyan University

Binswanger, Frank G., Jr.: co-chairman, director, Binswanger Companies

Binswanger, John K.: co-chairman, director, Binswanger Companies; chairman, Binswanger Foundation

Denny, Charles W.: president, chief executive officer, director, Square D Co.

Exley, Charles Errol, Jr.: trustee, Merck Co. Foundation

Harris, William W.: director, Pittway Corp. Charitable Foundation

Nelson, John Martin: chairman, director, TJX Companies, Inc.

Orr, Charles Lee: president, chief executive officer, Shaklee Corp.
Pew, Robert Cunningham, II: trustee, Steelcase Foundation
Polin, Jane Louise: manager, comptroller, GE Fund
Prendergast, G. Joseph: director, Wachovia Foundation, Inc. (The)
Taylor, Frederick B.: vice chairman, chief investment officer, United States Trust Co. of New York
Typermass, Arthur G.: senior vice president, treasurer, Metropolitan Life Insurance Co.
Work, David F.: senior vice president shared service, BP Amoco Corp.; director, BP Amoco Foundation
Zilkha, Ezra Khedouri: president, treasurer, Zilkha Foundation, Inc.; president, Zilkha & Sons

West Chester University

Sweeney, John J., III: vice president, CertainTeed Corp.

West Minster College

Bridgewater, Bernard Adolphus, Jr.: member board control, Brown Shoe Co. Charitable Trust; chairman, president, chief executive officer, director, Brown Shoe Co., Inc.
Panettiere, John Michael: president, chief executive officer, director, chairman, Blount International, Inc.
Wiley, S. Donald: vice chairman, trustee, Heinz Co. Foundation (H.J.)

West Texas State University

Klesse, William R.: executive vice president operations, Ultramar Diamond Shamrock Corp.

West Virginia Institute of Technology

Bayless, Charles Edward: chairman, president, chief executive officer, director, Illinois Power Co.

West Virginia University

Barnette, Curtis Handley: chairman, chief executive officer, director, Bethlehem Steel Corp.
Bayless, Charles Edward: chairman, president, chief executive officer, director, Illinois Power Co.
Hiner, Glen Harold, Jr.: chairman, chief executive officer, director, Owens Corning
Knicely, Howard V.: president, TRW Foundation
Koenig, Brian C.: senior vice president human resources, Scientific-Atlanta, Inc.
Stewart, S. Jay: chairman, chief executive officer, director, Morton International Inc.
Williams, Stephen E.: senior vice president, general counsel, Consolidated Natural Gas Co.; president, Consolidated Natural Gas System Foundation

Westchester Community College

Shepherd, Kathleen Shearen Maynard: director, Tribune New York Foundation

Western Carolina University

Kiser, Gerald L.: president, chief operating officer, director, La-Z-Boy Inc.

Western Connecticut State College

Conklin, Thomas J.: senior vice president, secretary, MONY Group (The); director, MONY Life Insurance of New York (The)

Western Illinois University

Feller, Robert J.: vice president, Shelter Mutual Insurance Co.
Hodnik, David F.: president, chief executive officer, Ace Hardware Corp.
Rauman, Thomas R.: chief financial officer, DeKalb Genetics Corp.; treasurer, director, DeKalb Genetics Foundation
Shoemate, Charles Richard: chairman, president, chief executive officer, Bestfoods

Western Kentucky University

Gilpin, Larry: executive vice president, Target Corp.; trustee, Target Foundation
Guillaume, Raymond Kendrick: vice chairman, chief executive officer, Mid-America Bank of Louisville
Ralph, E. Jack: vice president finance, controller, Texas Gas Transmission Corp.

Western Michigan University

Carra, Phillip C.: director, Pharmacia & Upjohn Foundation; vice president public relations, Pharmacia & Upjohn, Inc.
Derry, R. Michael: vice president, HON Industries Charitable Foundation
McKinnon, Thomas E.: director, Ryder System Charitable Foundation; executive vice president human resources, Ryder System, Inc.
Metzger, Michael D.: vice president, chief financial officer, JSJ Corp.
Schaeffer, Wayne G.: community president, Citizens Bank-Flint
Schweitzer, Peter A.: president, Thompson Co. (J. Walter)
Wild, Heidi Karin: trustee

Western New England College

Pajak, John Joseph: president, chief operating officer, Massachusetts Mutual Life Insurance Co.
Trask, Robert B.: clerk; president, chief operating officer, director, Country Curtains, Inc.; clerk, trustee, High Meadow Foundation

Western State University

Grise, Cheryl W.: senior vice president, chief administrative officer, Northeast Utilities
Weidemeyer, Thomas H.: senior vice president, director, United Parcel Service of America Inc.; trustee, UPS Foundation

Wheaton College

Andreas, Dwayne Orville: chairman, chief executive officer, Archer-Daniels-Midland Co.
Andreas, Lowell Willard: chairman audit committee, member executive & finance committee, Archer-Daniels-Midland Co.
Pollard, Charles William, Jr.: chairman, director, ServiceMaster Co.; president, director, ServiceMaster Foundation
Soderquist, Donald G.: trustee, Wal-Mart Foundation; senior vice chairman, director, Wal-Mart Stores, Inc.

Wheeling Jesuit College

Yasinsky, John B.: chairman, president, chief executive officer, GenCorp

Wheeling Jesuit University

Cassidy, M. Sharon: assistant secretary, USX Foundation, Inc.

Whitman College

McDade, Sandy D.: secretary, Weyerhaeuser Co.; assistant secretary legal affairs, Weyerhaeuser Co. Foundation

Whittier College

Tran, Khanh T.: senior vice president, chief financial officer, director, Pacific Mutual Life Insurance Co.

Whitworth College

Oliver, Walter Maurice: senior vice president human resources, Ameritech Corp.

Wichita State University

Cocklin, Kim Roland: senior vice president, Texas Gas Transmission Corp.
Corson, Keith Daniel: president, chief operating officer, Coachmen Industries, Inc.
Hay, Gary W.: vice chairman, Cessna Aircraft Co.; trustee, Cessna Foundation, Inc.
Moore, William B.: director, Western Resources Foundation; executive vice president, chief financial officer, treasurer, Western Resources Inc.
Pratt, Donald Henry: chairman, Butler Manufacturing Co.; vice president, trustee, Butler Manufacturing Co. Foundation
Vance, Robert L.: trustee, Tektronix Foundation

Widener University

Daley, Leo J.: vice president, treasurer, Air Products and Chemicals, Inc.
Hanway, H. Edward: president, chief executive officer, CIGNA Corp.

Wilberforce University

Flake, Floyd Harold: director, Fannie Mae Foundation

Wilkes University

Montague, William Patrick: president, chief operating officer, director, Mark IV Industries; president, Mark IV Industries Foundation

Willamette University Law School

Wendt, Roderick C.: trustee, Jeld-wen Foundation; president, director, Jeld-wen, Inc.

William Mitchell College of Law

Bonvino, Frank W.: vice president, secretary, general counsel, International Multifoods Corp.
Engh, Rolf: senior vice president, general counsel, secretary, Valspar Corp.; secretary, Valspar Foundation
Prohofsky, Dennis E.: secretary, Minnesota Mutual Foundation; senior vice president, general counsel, secretary, Minnesota Mutual Life Insurance Co.
Sheahan, Mark: treasurer, Graco Foundation

Williams College

Barnes, Wallace W.: director, Barnes Group Foundation Inc.
Bronfman, Edgar Miles: chairman, trustee, Bronfman Foundation/Joseph E. Seagram & Sons, Inc. Fund (Samuel); chairman, Seagram & Sons, Inc. (Joseph E.)
Calfee, William Rushton: trustee, Cleveland-Cliffs Foundation (The); executive vice president, commercial, Cleveland-Cliffs, Inc.
Coolidge, E. David, III: vice president, Blair & Co. Foundation (William); chief executive officer, Blair & Co. (William); vice president, Pittway Corp. Charitable Foundation
Draper, Ernest Linn, Jr.: chairman, president, chief executive officer, director, American Electric Power
Field, Benjamin R., III: senior vice president, chief financial officer, treasurer, Bemis Co., Inc.
Kennedy, George Danner: trustee, Kemper Foundation (James S.)
Lipp, Robert Irving: chief executive officer, Citigroup; vice president, treasurer, trustee, Citigroup Foundation
McCoy, John Bonnet: president, chief executive officer, Ameritech Corp.
Parker, Patrick Streeter: chairman, director, Parker Hannifin Corp.; president, trustee, Parker Hannifin Foundation

Piper, Addison Lewis: director, Piper Jaffray Companies Foundation; chairman, chief executive officer, director, U.S. Bancorp Piper Jaffray

Pullo, Robert W.: chairman, chief executive officer, director, York Federal Savings & Loan Association; president, trustee, York Federal Savings & Loan Foundation

Rich, Robert E., Jr.: secretary, Rich Family Foundation; president, director, Rich Products Corp.

Roe, John H.: chairman, director, Bemis Co., Inc.

Wilson Junior College

Ervanian, Armen: vice president, Viad Corp. Fund

Winthrop College

Moser, Robert W.: executive vice president, Springs Industries, Inc.

Rockey, Travis O.: vice president, director, Evening Post Publishing Co.

Wisconsin State University

Bachmann, Richard Arthur: vice president, secretary, treasurer, director, Louisiana Land & Exploration Co. Foundation

Wittenberg University

Ballentine, Richard O.: vice president, secretary, general counsel, Butler Manufacturing Co.; secretary, Butler Manufacturing Co. Foundation

Ludwick, John D.: vice president human resources, MGIC Investment Corp.

Wofford College

Chandler, J. Harold: chairman, president, chief executive officer, Provident Companies, Inc.

Woodrow Wilson College

Ratcliffe, David M.: chief financial officer, treasurer, director, Georgia Power Co.

Worcester College

Murdoch, Rupert P.: chairman, Fox Entertainment Group

Worcester Polytechnic Institute

Allaire, Paul Arthur: chairman, chief executive officer, chairman executive committee, Xerox Corp.; president, Xerox Foundation

Wright State University

Lansaw, Judy W.: secretary, trustee, Dayton Power and Light Co. Foundation

Xavier University

Ballengee, Jerry Hunter: president, chief operating officer, director, Union Camp Corp.

Barnett, Robert L.: director, Ameritech Foundation

Berlik, Leonard J.: vice president, National Starch & Chemical Co.

Burrell, Richard L.: senator vice president finance, secretary, treasurer, Barry Corp. (R.G.); treasurer, Barry Foundation

Castellini, Daniel J.: senior vice president finance & administration, chief financial officer, Scripps Co. (E.W.); treasurer, Scripps Howard Foundation

Cox, Phillip R.: director, Cinergy Foundation

Lautenbach, Terry Robert: trustee, Air Products Foundation

Leser, Lawrence Arthur: chairman, director, Scripps Co. (E.W.); member, Scripps Howard Foundation

Molen, Richard L.: chairman, chief executive officer, director, Huffy Corp.; trustee, Huffy Foundation, Inc.

O'Donnell, James P.: treasurer, ConAgra Foundation

Schaefer, George A., Jr.: president, Fifth Third Bancorp

Sheafer, William L.: vice president, treasurer, Cinergy Corp.; treasurer, director, Cinergy Foundation

Thyen, James C.: president, director, Habig Foundation

Viviano, Joseph P.: president, court, Hershey Foods Corp.

Yale College

Grinstein, Gerald: director, PACCAR Inc.

Yale University

Akers, John Fellows: director, New York Times Co.

Allardyce, Fred A.: director, American Standard Foundation; senior vice president medical products sector, American Standard Inc.

Allison, Herbert Monroe, Jr.: vice president, trustee, Merrill Lynch & Co. Foundation Inc.; president, chief operating officer, Merrill Lynch & Co., Inc.

Barnes, Wallace W.: director, Barnes Group Foundation Inc.

Barnette, Curtis Handley: chairman, chief executive officer, director, Bethlehem Steel Corp.

Beard, Anson McCook, Jr.: director, NASDAQ Stock Market Educational Foundation

Beck, Edward W.: senior vice president, general counsel, secretary, director, Shaklee Corp.

Benenson, James, Jr.: chairman, president, director, Vesper Corp.; trustee, Vesper Foundation

Block, John Robinson: vice president, trustee, Blade Foundation

Block, Stephen A.: secretary, IFF Foundation Inc.

Block, William: vice president, trustee, Blade Foundation; chairman, director, Toledo Blade Co.

Bryson, John E.: chairman, chief executive officer, Edison International

Carbone, Anthony J.: vice chairman, director, Dow Chemical Co.

Cole, Lewis George: director, AMETEK Foundation

Corwin, Laura J.: secretary, New York Times Co. Foundation

Crane, Lansing E.: chairman, president, Crane & Co., Inc.

Daniels, John Hancock: chairman, Archer-Daniels-Midland Foundation

Davis, John B., MD: director, Physicians Mutual Insurance Co. Foundation

Demere, Robert H.: president, Colonial Foundation; chairman, Colonial Oil Industries, Inc.

Ehrlich, M. Gordon: trustee, Orchard Foundation

Elliott, David Holland: consultant, chairman executive committee, MBIA Inc.

Emmet, Robert: vice president financial planning, treasurer, Cleveland-Cliffs, Inc.

Forstmann, Theodore J.: chairman, Gulfstream Aerospace Corp.

Fretthold, Timothy Jon: executive vice president, general counsel, director, Ultramar Diamond Shamrock Corp.

Friedewald, William Thomas, MD: director, MetLife Foundation

Gelb, Richard Lee: director, New York Times Co. Foundation

Gorman, Joseph T.: chairman, chief executive officer, TRW Inc.

Groman, Arthur: president, Occidental Petroleum Charitable Foundation

Hamilton, Peter Bannerman: director, Brunswick Foundation; trustee, Kemper Foundation (James S.)

Harris, Irving Brooks: chairman executive committee, director, Pittway Corp.; chairman, director, Pittway Corp. Charitable Foundation

Harris, Richard Neison: chairman, director, Pittway Corp.; president, director, Pittway Corp. Charitable Foundation

Heineman, Benjamin Walter, Jr.: director, GE Fund

Higginbotham, A. Leon, Jr.: director, New York Times Co. Foundation

Horton, Alan M.: senior vice president newspapers, Scripps Co. (E.W.)

Hutchings, Peter Lounsbery: president, Guardian Life Insurance Co. of America

Ingersoll, Robert Stephen: chairman, director, Panasonic Foundation

Ives, J. Atwood: chairman, chief executive officer, Boston Gas Co.; chairman, chief executive officer, trustee, Eastern Enterprises; trustee, Eastern Enterprises Foundation

Jones, David Allen: chairman, chief executive officer, director, Humana Foundation; co-founder, chairman, director, Humana, Inc.

Keller, Thomas M.: president, Fortis Insurance Co.

Kelly, Janet L.: executive vice president corporate development, general counsel, secretary, Kellogg Co.

Kemper, James M., Jr.: director, Commerce Bancshares Foundation; chairman, president, director, Commerce Bancshares, Inc.

Kemper, James Scott, Jr.: honorary chairman, Kemper Foundation (James S.)

Kinsolving, Augustus Blagden: director, ASARCO Foundation

Kohler, Herbert Vollrath, Jr.: chairman, president, director, Kohler Co.

Laffon, Polk, IV: vice president corporate relations, corporate secretary, Knight Ridder

Lang, Robert Todd: chairman, director, Weil, Gotshal & Manges Foundation

Lawrence, Robert Ashton: director, New York Times Co. Foundation

Lemberg, Thomas Michael: clerk, Lotus Development Corp.; secretary, Polaroid Foundation

Lower, H. Louis Gordon, II: vice president, trustee, Allstate Foundation

Lynch, Charles Allen: chairman, director, Pacific Mutual Life Insurance Co.

Manfredi, John Frederick: member administration committee, Nabisco Foundation Trust

Manoogian, Richard Alexander: chairman, chief executive officer, director, Masco Corp.

Marshall, Siri M.: trustee, General Mills Foundation; senior vice president, general counsel, General Mills, Inc.

Mead, George Wilson, II: president, director, Consolidated Papers Foundation, Inc.; chairman, director, Consolidated Papers, Inc.

Meyer, Russell William, Jr.: chairman, chief executive officer, Cessna Aircraft Co.; president, Cessna Foundation, Inc.

Miller, Joseph Irwin: director associate, Cummins Engine Co., Inc.; director, Cummins Engine Foundation

Miller, William Irwin: director, Cummins Engine Foundation

Milliken, Gerrish H., Jr.: member advisory committee, Milliken Foundation

Milliken, Roger: chairman, chief executive officer, Milliken & Co.; member advisory committee, Milliken Foundation

Minami, Wayne K.: director, Hawaiian Electric Industries Charitable Foundation

Minton, Dwight Church: chairman, director, Church & Dwight Co., Inc.

Moritz, Charles Worthington: chairman, director, Dun & Bradstreet Corp.

Nelson, Merlin Edward: chairman, director, IBJ Foundation

Nichols, Wade Hampton, III: vice president, Revlon Foundation Inc.; executive vice president, general counsel, Revlon Inc.

O'Brien, William J., III: trustee, DaimlerChrysler Corp. Fund

Ottaway, James Haller, Jr.: senior vice president, director, Dow Jones & Co., Inc.; member advisory committee, Dow Jones Foundation

Peck, Arthur John, Jr.: secretary, vice president, Corning Inc.; secretary, Corning Inc. Foundation

Pepper, John E., Jr.: chairman executive committee, Procter & Gamble Co.

Ripley, Sidney Dillon, II: director emeritus, Hitachi Foundation

Rockefeller, Frederic Lincoln: trustee, Cranston Foundation

Rosett, Richard Nathaniel: trustee, Kemper Foundation (James S.)

Schacht, Henry Brewer: director, Cummins Engine Foundation

Schlumberger, Pierre Marcel: director, Schlumberger Foundation

Schwartz, Peter A.: chief financial officer, consultant, Computer Associates International, Inc.

Shaw, L. Edward, Jr.: general counsel, Aetna, Inc.; trustee, Chase Manhattan Foundation

Shuster, George Whitcomb: trustee, Cranston Foundation; president, chief executive officer, director, Cranston Print Works Co.

Smith, Frederick Wallace: chairman, president, chief executive officer, director, FedEx Corp.

Smith, Richard C.: chief executive officer, director, Telcordia Technologies

Stephens, James T.: president, director, Ebsco Industries, Inc.

Stevens, Gregory W.: vice president, treasurer, Phelps Dodge Corp.

Stoner, Richard Burkett, Jr.: director, Cummins Engine Foundation

Stratton, Frederick Prescott, Jr.: chairman, chief executive officer, director, Briggs & Stratton Corp.; president, director, Briggs & Stratton Corp. Foundation

Stupski, Lawrence J.: president, vice chairman, chief operating officer, director, Schwab & Co., Inc. (Charles); chief financial officer, secretary, Schwab Corp. Foundation (Charles)

Wander, Herbert S.: secretary, director, Katten, Muchin & Zavis Foundation

Ward, Carol J.: secretary, compliance officer, CIGNA Corp.; secretary, CIGNA Foundation

Warner, Douglas Alexander, III: chairman, president, chief executive officer, director, Morgan & Co. Inc. (J.P.)

Weyerhaeuser, George Hunt: director, Weyerhaeuser Co.; trustee, Weyerhaeuser Co. Foundation

Wheeler, Thomas Beardsley: chairman, chief executive officer, Massachusetts Mutual Life Insurance Co.

Wilbur, Brayton, Jr.: president, chief executive officer, Wilbur-Ellis Co. & Connell Brothers Co.; president, Wilbur Foundation (Brayton)

Williams, Eugene Flewellyn, Jr.: member public policy committee, Emerson Charitable Trust

Wolfe, Kenneth L.: chairman, chief executive officer, director, Hershey Foods Corp.

Wright, James O.: president, director, Badger Meter Foundation; chairman, director, Badger Meter, Inc.; director, Marshall & Ilsley Foundation, Inc.

Wrigley, William: chairman, director, Wrigley Co. Foundation (Wm. Jr.); president, chief executive officer, director, Wrigley Co. (Wm. Jr.)

Wurtele, C. Angus: president, Valspar Foundation

Wurtzel, Alan Leon: chairman, Circuit City Foundation; chairman, trustee, Circuit City Stores, Inc.

Yale University Divinity School

Muth, Robert James: president, director, ASARCO Foundation

Yale University Law School

Shuster, George Whitcomb: trustee, Cranston Foundation; president, chief executive officer, director, Cranston Print Works Co.

Tucker, Don Eugene: trustee, Commercial Intertech Foundation

Yale University School of Drama

Darling, Robert Edward, Jr.: chairman, Ensign-Bickford Foundation

Newman, Paul L.: president, Newman's Own Foundation

York University

Hunkin, John: president, CIBC Oppenheimer

McNally, Alan G.: chairman, chief executive officer, Harris Trust & Savings Bank

Youngstown State University

Bezik, Cynthia B.: senior vice president, finance, Cleveland-Cliffs, Inc.

Marshall, Betty J.: senior vice president, Shoney's Inc.

university of Pittsburg

Cassidy, M. Sharon: assistant secretary, USX Foundation, Inc.

university of San Francisco

Phair, Joseph Baschon: corporate secretary, general counsel, vice president, Varian Medical Systems, Inc.

OFFICERS AND DIRECTORS BY CORPORATE AFFILIATIONS

Lists individuals by corporations to which they belong.

121 Southwest Salmon Street Corp.
Miller, Fred D.: vice president public affairs, Portland General Electric Co.

150 Corp.
Reed, Scott Eldridge: senior executive vice president, chief financial officer, Branch Banking & Trust Co.

169 East 69th Corp.
Vogel, Howard Stanley: tax counsel, Texaco Foundation

1740 Advisors Inc.
Daddario, Richard M.: chief financial officer, MONY Life Insurance of New York (The)
Weigel, David V.: treasurer, MONY Life Insurance of New York (The)

1st Chicago NBD
Baker, James Kendrick: chairman, director, Arvin Foundation; vice chairman, director, Arvin Industries, Inc.

1st National Bank Lawrence
Hall, Donald Joyce: chairman board, director, Hallmark Cards Inc.; chairman, Hallmark Corporate Foundation

1st Source Bank
Murphy, Christopher J., III: president, chief executive officer, director, First Source Corp.; director, First Source Foundation
Raclin, Ernestine Morris: chairman emeritus, director, First Source Corp.; chairman, director, First Source Foundation

1st Source Capital Corp.
Murphy, Christopher J., III: president, chief executive officer, director, First Source Corp.; director, First Source Foundation

1st Source Industry Inc.
Murphy, Christopher J., III: president, chief executive officer, director, First Source Corp.; director, First Source Foundation

2426-4152 Quebec Inc.
Jacobsen, James C.: vice chairman, Kellwood Co.; vice president, director, Kellwood Foundation

299 Cleaning Service Co.
Fisher, Lawrence: partner, Fisher Brothers Cleaning Services; director, Fisher Brothers Foundation, Inc.

3555 Intermediate Corp.
Zilkha, Ezra Khedouri: president, treasurer, Zilkha Foundation, Inc.; president, Zilkha & Sons

3Com Corp.
Zuendt, William F.: president, chief executive officer, Wells Fargo & Co.

3D Industries Inc.
Wendt, Roderick C.: trustee, Jeld-wen Foundation; president, director, Jeld-wen, Inc.

3rd Avenue Television Inc.
Huey, Ward L., Jr.: president broadcast division, vice chairman, director, Belo Corp. (A.H.); vice president, trustee, Belo Corp. Foundation (A.H.)

77 Water Street Inc.
Leatherdale, Douglas West: chairman, chief executive officer, president, Saint Paul Companies Inc.

78 Inc.
Allbritton, Joe Lewis: chairman, chief executive officer, Riggs Bank NA

A & B Hawaii Inc.
Dods, Walter Arthur, Jr.: president, director, First Hawaiian Foundation; chairman, chief executive officer, director, First Hawaiian, Inc.
Marks, Michael J.: vice president, general counsel, secretary, Alexander & Baldwin, Inc.
Wellman, Thomas A.: controller, assistant treasurer, Alexander & Baldwin, Inc.

A & B Properties Inc.
Nakamura, Alyson J.: secretary, Alexander & Baldwin Foundation
Wellman, Thomas A.: controller, assistant treasurer, Alexander & Baldwin, Inc.

A Schulman Inc.
Holland, Willard R.: chairman, chief executive officer, FirstEnergy Corp.

A&B Development Co. (California)
Sasaki, Robert K.: director, Alexander & Baldwin Foundation

A&B Hawaii Inc.
Ching, Meredith J.: senior vice president, director, chairman HI committee, Alexander & Baldwin Foundation; vice president government & community relations, Alexander & Baldwin, Inc.

A&B-HI
Holaday, G. Stephen: senior vice president, Alexander & Baldwin, Inc.
Sasaki, Robert K.: director, Alexander & Baldwin Foundation

A. Duda & Sons
Goode, R. Ray: director, Ryder System Charitable Foundation

A.H. Belo Corp.
Enrico, Roger A.: chairman, PepsiCo Foundation, Inc.; chairman, chief executive officer, director, PepsiCo, Inc.
Hamblett, Stephen: chairman, chief executive officer, publisher, Providence Journal-Bulletin Co.; trustee, Providence Journal Charitable Foundation
Moroney, James McQueen, Jr.: trustee, Belo Corp. Foundation (A.H.)

A.S. Tomich Construction Co.
Tomich, Rosemary: director, Occidental Petroleum Charitable Foundation

AAR Corp.
Jannotta, Edgar D.: president, Blair & Co. Foundation (William); senior director, Blair & Co. (William)

ABB Power T & D Co. Inc.
Janson, Peter S.: president, chief executive officer, ABB Inc.

AC Nielsen Corp.
Griffin, Donald Wayne: chairman, president, chief executive officer, director, Olin Corp.; trustee, Olin Corp. Charitable Trust
Hays, Thomas Chandler: chairman, chief executive officer, director, Fortune Brands, Inc.

ACCO World Corp.
Rukeyser, Robert James: senior vice president corporate affairs, Fortune Brands, Inc.

ACE Insurance Agency Inc.
Hodnik, David F.: president, chief executive officer, Ace Hardware Corp.

ACE Ltd.
Ripp, Robert M.: chairman, chief executive officer, director, AMP Inc.
Springer, Denis E.: senior vice president, chief financial officer, Burlington Northern Santa Fe Corp.; director, Burlington Northern Santa Fe Foundation

ACM Aviation Inc.
Markkula, Armas Clifford, Jr.: chairman, director, Apple Computer, Inc.

AEGON United States of America Investment Management
Kolsrud, Douglas C.: executive vice president, chief investment officer, AEGON U.S.A. Inc.

AEP Energy Services Inc.
Draper, Ernest Linn, Jr.: chairman, president, chief executive officer, director, American Electric Power

AEP Industries Inc.
Kidder, C. Robert: chairman, president, chief executive officer, director, Borden, Inc.

AEP Investment Inc.
Draper, Ernest Linn, Jr.: chairman, president, chief executive officer, director, American Electric Power

AF Murch Co.
Smucker, Timothy Paul: chairman, director, Smucker Co. (JM)

AFLAC Inc.
Otake, Yoshiki: chairman, AFLAC Inc.

AG Communications Systems Corp.
Esstman, Michael B.: trustee, GTE Foundation

AGL Investment Inc.
Jones, David R.: principal, AGL Resources Inc.

AGL Resources Inc.
Bankston, Ralph: director community affairs, AGL Resources Inc.
Jones, David R.: principal, AGL Resources Inc.

AII Acquisition Corp.
Murdy, James L.: executive vice president finance and administration, chief financial officer, Allegheny Technologies Inc.; trustee, Allegheny Technologies Inc. Charitable Trust
Walton, Jon David: trustee, Allegheny Technologies Inc. Charitable Trust

AIL Systems Inc.
Armstrong, Neil A.: trustee, Milacron Foundation; director, Milacron, Inc.

AK Steel Corp.
Georges, John A.: director, International Paper Co.
Hill, Bonnie Guiton: vice president, Times Mirror Co.; president, chief executive officer, Times Mirror Foundation
Wareham, James Lyman: president, AK Steel Corp.

AK Steel Holding Corp.
Georges, John A.: director, International Paper Co.
Leser, Lawrence Arthur: chairman, director, Scripps Co. (E.W.); member, Scripps Howard Foundation
Preheim, Randall F.: president, trustee, AK Steel Foundation

ALCOA Inc.
Schacht, Henry Brewer: director, Cummins Engine Foundation

AMAI Corp.
Louis, Kenneth C.: president, chief operating officer, director, Ameritas Life Insurance Corp.

AMAL Corp.
Arth, Lawrence Joseph: vice president, director, Ameritas Charitable Foundation; chairman, chief executive officer, director, Ameritas Life Insurance Corp.

AMCORE Bank Rockford
Dargene, Carl J.: director, AMCORE Foundation

AMCORE Financial Inc.
Gloyd, Lawrence Eugene: trustee, CLARCOR Foundation; chairman, chief executive officer, director, CLARCOR Inc.
Meuleman, Robert Joseph: director, AMCORE Foundation

AMP Inc.
Franklin, Barbara Hackman: director, Dow Chemical Co.
Magliochetti, Joseph M.: president, chief executive officer, director, Dana Corp.; president, director, Dana Corp. Foundation
Meyer, Jerome J.: chairman, chief executive officer, Tektronix, Inc.

AMP Investments Inc.
Ripp, Robert M.: chairman, chief executive officer, director, AMP Inc.

AMR Corp.
Graves, Earl Gilbert: director, Aetna Foundation

AMR Eagle Inc.
Baker, Robert Woodward: executive vice president, AMR Corp.

AMR Training Consult Group
Carty, Donald J.: vice president, treasurer, AMR/American Airlines Foundation; president, chairman, chief executive officer, director, AMR Corp.

ANB Financial Corp.
Dods, Walter Arthur, Jr.: president, director, First Hawaiian Foundation; chairman, chief executive officer, director, First Hawaiian, Inc.

AO Irkutsk Energo
Rogers, James E., Jr.: vice chairman, president, chief executive officer, Cinergy Corp.; vice chairman, director, Cinergy Foundation

AO Smith Corp.
Schuenke, Donald John: director, Freddie Mac
Smith, Arthur O.: president, Smith Foundation, Inc. (A.O.)

AON Corp.
Cole, Franklin Alan: chairman, Aon Foundation
Jannotta, Edgar D.: president, Blair & Co. Foundation (William); senior director, Blair & Co. (William)
McKenna, Andrew James: director, Aon Foundation
Notebaert, Richard C.: chairman, chief executive officer, Ameritech Corp.; director, Ameritech Foundation
Turner, Fred L.: senior chairman, director, McDonald's Corp.

AON Group Inc.
Ryan, Patrick G.: chairman, president, chief executive officer, Aon Corp.; president, Aon Foundation

AON Risk Services Companies
Ryan, Patrick G.: chairman, president, chief executive officer, Aon Corp.; president, Aon Foundation

AON Warranty Group
Ryan, Patrick G.: chairman, president, chief executive officer, Aon Corp.; president, Aon Foundation

AP Green Industries Inc.
Toll, Daniel Roger: trustee, Kemper Foundation (James S.)

APL Land Transport Services
Rhein, Timothy James: president, chief executive officer, APL Ltd.
Stuebgen, William J.: vice president, controller, chief acct officer, APL Ltd.

AR Mexican Holdings Inc.
Kinsolving, Augustus Blagden: director, ASARCO Foundation

AR Public Service Co.
Snell, Richard: chairman, president, chief executive officer, director, Arizona Public Service Co.

ARC Reins Corp.
Broome, Burton Edward: vice president, controller, Transamerica Corp.; vice president, treasurer, Transamerica Foundation

ARCO International Oil & Gas Co.
Bowlin, Michael Ray: chairman, director, ARCO Foundation; chairman, chief executive officer, director, Atlantic Richfield Co.

ARCO Toys
Barad, Jill Elikann: director, Mattel Foundation; chairman, chief executive officer, director, Mattel Inc.

ASARCO Exploration Co.
Osborne, Richard de Jongh: director, ASARCO Foundation; chairman, chief executive officer, director, ASARCO Inc.

ASARCO Inc.
Ong, John Doyle: chairman board, director, Ameritech Corp.

ASARCO Inc. Oil & Gas Co.
Muth, Robert James: president, director, ASARCO Foundation

ASARCO International Corp.
Osborne, Richard de Jongh: director, ASARCO Foundation; chairman, chief executive officer, director, ASARCO Inc.

AT&T Broadband Internet Services
Armstrong, C. Michael: chairman, chief executive officer, AT&T Corp.

AT&T Corp.
Fisher, George Myles Cordell: chairman, president, chief executive officer, director, Eastman Kodak Co.
Fites, Donald Vester: director, Caterpillar Foundation
Haas, Peter Edgar, Sr.: chairman executive committee, director, Levi Strauss & Co.
Larsen, Ralph Stanley: chairman, president, chief executive officer, director, Johnson & Johnson
Schacht, Henry Brewer: director, Cummins Engine Foundation
Weill, Sanford I.: chairman, chief executive officer, Citibank Corp.; chairman, Citigroup Foundation

ATD Tools Corp.
Anderson, Charles D.: trustee, Anderson Foundation

AUSA Holding Co.
Baird, Patrick S.: chief operating officer, chief financial officer, AEGON U.S.A. Inc.

Abbott Laboratories
Fuller, Harry Laurance: co-chairman, director, BP Amoco Corp.
Jones, David Allen: chairman, chief executive officer, director, Humana Foundation; co-founder, chairman, director, Humana, Inc.
Rand, Addison Barry: executive vice president operations, Xerox Corp.; trustee, Xerox Foundation

Abbott-Northwestern Hospital
George, William Wallace: chief executive officer, chairman, Medtronic, Inc.

Abiomed Inc.
O'Brien, John Francis, Jr.: president, chief executive officer, Allmerica Financial Corp.

Able Body Corp.
Hillenbrand, John A., II: director, Cinergy Foundation

Acacia National Life
Martin, JoAnn M.: controller, Ameritas Charitable Foundation; senior vice president, partner, chief financial officer, Ameritas Life Insurance Corp.

Ace Ltd.
Staley, Robert Wayne: vice chairman Asia Pacific, Emerson Electric Co.

Acorn Fund
Harris, Irving Brooks: chairman executive committee, director, Pittway Corp.; chairman, director, Pittway Corp. Charitable Foundation

Acushnet Co.
Hays, Thomas Chandler: chairman, chief executive officer, director, Fortune Brands, Inc.
Rukeyser, Robert James: senior vice president corporate affairs, Fortune Brands, Inc.

Adac Laboratories
Shea, Edmund H., Jr.: secretary, Shea Co. Foundation (J. F.); executive vice president, Shea Co. (John F.)

Adams Martin & Nelson Inc.
Nelson, Marilyn Carlson: chairman, chief executive officer, president, Carlson Companies, Inc.

Adaptive Engineering Lab Inc.
Connolly, Gerald Edward: trustee, Reinhart Family Foundation (D. B. and Marjorie)

Adforce Inc.
Gallagher, Terence Joseph: secretary, director, Pfizer Foundation

Adhesive & Sealant Council
Ray, John Thomas, Jr.: president, director, Fuller Co. Foundation (H.B.)

Adjustment Services Inc.
Sturgeon, John: president, chief operating officer, Mutual of Omaha Insurance Co.

Adolph Coors Co.
Sanders, Wayne R.: chairman, chief executive officer, director, Kimberly-Clark Corp.

Advanced Telecommunications Corp.
Ford, Joseph 'Joe': chairman, chief executive officer, president, ALLTEL Corp.

Advanta Corp.
Naples, Ronald James: president, chief executive officer, director, Quaker Chemical Corp.

Advest Group
Fiondella, Robert William: chairman, president, chief executive officer, Phoenix Home Life Mutual Insurance Co.

Adwin Equipment Co.
McNeill, Corbin Asahel, Jr.: president, chief executive officer, director, chairman, PECO Energy Co.

Aeltus Investment Management
Kim, John Y.: director, Aetna Foundation

Aerojet-General Corp.
Yasinsky, John B.: chairman, president, chief executive officer, GenCorp

Aeroquip-Vickers Inc.
Goode, David Ronald: chairman, president, chief executive officer, director, Norfolk Southern Corp.
Timken, William Robert, Jr.: chairman, president, chief executive officer, director, Timken Co. (The)

Aerospace Corp.
Davis, Ruth Margaret: trustee, Air Products Foundation
Pierre, Percy A.: trustee, Hitachi Foundation

Aetna Inc.
Franklin, Barbara Hackman: director, Dow Chemical Co.
Graves, Earl Gilbert: director, Aetna Foundation
Greenwald, Gerald: chairman, chief executive officer, director, United Airlines Inc.

Aetna Life & Casualty Co. Inc.
Barnes, Wallace W.: director, Barnes Group Foundation Inc.
Graves, Earl Gilbert: director, Aetna Foundation
Huber, Richard Leslie: chairman, president, chief executive officer, director, Aetna, Inc.

Aetna Life Insurance Co.
Compton, Ronald E.: chairman, president, Aetna Foundation

Affiliated Publications Inc.
Henn, Catherine Emily Campbell: president, Boston Globe Foundation
Lewis, Russell T.: president, chief operating officer, New York Times Co.
Watson, Solomon Brown, IV: vice president, New York Times Co. Foundation

Affiliated Publishers Inc.
Sulzberger, Arthur Ochs, Sr.: director, New York Times Co.; chairman, director, New York Times Co. Foundation

Agency Management Services
Chookaszian, Dennis Haig: chairman, chief executive officer, CNA

Agricola Inc.
Shaw, Robert E.: chairman, chief executive officer, Shaw Industries Inc.

Agrilink Foods Inc.
Rice, William D.: senior vice president, chief financial officer, secretary, Agrilink Foods, Inc.; trustee, Agrilink Foods/Pro-Fac Foundation

Agrilink Foods, Inc.
Ford, Virginia: trustee, Agrilink Foods/Pro-Fac Foundation

Aiesec USA
Levin, Michael Stuart: president, chief executive officer, Titan Industrial Corp.

Air Holding Co.
Arison, M. Micky: trustee, Arison Foundation; chairman, president, chief executive officer, Carnival Corp.

Air Products & Chemicals Inc.
Davis, Ruth Margaret: trustee, Air Products Foundation
Lautenbach, Terry Robert: trustee, Air Products Foundation

AirKaman Jacksonville Inc.
Kaman, Charles Huron: chairman, president, chief executive officer, director, Kaman Corp.

AirTouch Communications Inc.
Bartz, Carol A.: director, Autodesk Foundation; chairman, chief executive officer, Autodesk Inc.
Hazen, Paul Mandeville: chairman, chief executive officer, director, Wells Fargo & Co.
Rock, Arthur: co-founder, chairman executive committee, director, Intel Corp.
Schwab, Charles R.: chairman, co-chief executive officer, director, Schwab & Co., Inc. (Charles); chairman, Schwab Corp. Foundation (Charles)

Airborne Freight Corp.
Rosenberg, Richard Morris: chairman, chief executive officer (retired), Bank of America

Airplanes Ltd.
Franke, William Augustus: chairman, president, chief executive officer, America West Airlines, Inc.; director, Phelps Dodge Foundation

Airplanes United States Trust
Franke, William Augustus: chairman, president, chief executive officer, America West Airlines, Inc.; director, Phelps Dodge Foundation

Airport Inn Developers
Dora, James E.: director, AUL Foundation Inc.

Alabama Property Co.
Harris, Elmer Beseler: president, chief executive officer, director, Alabama Power Co.

AlabamaBancorp
Stephens, Elton Bryson: founder, chairman, Ebsco Industries, Inc.

Alaska Air Group Inc.
Kelly, John F.: chairman, chief executive officer, director, Alaska Airlines, Inc.

Albany International Canada
McKone, Francis L.: president, chief executive officer, director, Albany International Corp.

Alberta Northeast Inc.
Catell, Robert Barry: chairman, chief executive officer, Brooklyn Union

Alberto-Culver Co.
Muchin, Allan B.: chairman, Katten, Muchin & Zavis; director, Katten, Muchin & Zavis Foundation

Alcon Puerto Rico Inc.
Sear, Timothy R. G.: trustee, Alcon Foundation; president, chief executive officer, Alcon Laboratories, Inc.

Alexander & Baldwin Inc.
Denlea, Leo Edward, Jr.: retired chairman, president, chief executive officer, director, Farmers Group, Inc.; vice president, Farmers Group Safety Foundation
Dods, Walter Arthur, Jr.: president, director, First Hawaiian Foundation; chairman, chief executive officer, director, First Hawaiian, Inc.
Sasaki, Robert K.: director, Alexander & Baldwin Foundation

Aliquippa Southern Railway Co.
Kelly, J. Peter: president, chief operating officer, director, LTV Corp.; trustee, LTV Foundation

All American Homes North Carolina
Corson, Keith Daniel: president, chief operating officer, Coachmen Industries, Inc.

Allamerica Financial Life Insurance and Annuity Co.
O'Brien, John Francis, Jr.: president, chief executive officer, Allmerica Financial Corp.

Allbritton 2600 Carlyle Inc.
Allbritton, Joe Lewis: chairman, chief executive officer, Riggs Bank NA

Alleghany Asset Management Inc.
Bilton, Stuart Douglas: president, chief executive officer, Chicago Title Corp.; trustee, Chicago Title and Trust Co. Foundation
Toft, Richard Paul: chairman, Chicago Title Corp.; trustee, Chicago Title and Trust Co. Foundation

Allegheny Ludlum Corp.
Bozzone, Robert P.: vice chairman, director, Allegheny Technologies Inc.; trustee, Allegheny Technologies Inc. Charitable Trust
McClelland, William Craig: trustee, Union Camp Charitable Trust; chairman, chief executive officer, director, Union Camp Corp.
Rohr, James Edward: chief executive officer, president, director, PNC Financial Services Group

Allegheny Teledyne Inc.
McClelland, William Craig: trustee, Union Camp Charitable Trust; chairman, chief executive officer, director, Union Camp Corp.
Queenan, Charles J., Jr.: trustee, Tippins Foundation
Rohr, James Edward: chief executive officer, president, director, PNC Financial Services Group

Allegiance Healthcare Corp.
Damico, Joseph F.: director, Baxter Allegiance Foundation

Allendale Insurance Co.
Harad, George Jay: chairman, chief executive officer, director, Boise Cascade Corp.

Allendale Mutual Insurance Co.
Carty, Donald J.: vice president, treasurer, AMR/American Airlines Foundation; president, chairman, chief executive officer, director, AMR Corp.

Allergan Inc.
Boyer, Herbert Wayne, PhD: chairman, president, director, Genentech Foundation for Biomedical Sciences; co-founder, director, Genentech Inc.

Allfino Inc.
Allbritton, Joe Lewis: chairman, chief executive officer, Riggs Bank NA

Alliance America Insurance Co.
Countryman, Gary Lee: chairman, Liberty Mutual Insurance Group

Kelley, Bruce Gunn: vice president, director, Employers Mutual Charitable Foundation

Alliant Health System Inc.
Hower, Frank Beard, Jr.: vice chairman, Anthem Foundation, Inc.

Alliant Industries Inc.
Davis, Erroll Brown, Jr.: president, chief executive officer, director, Wisconsin Power & Light Co.

Allianz America Corp.
Hansmeyer, Herbert F.: chairman, Fireman's Fund Insurance Co.

Allianz Life Insurance Co. North America
Rowe, Thomas E.: chairman, director, Fireman's Fund Foundation; director, Fireman's Fund Insurance Co.

Allied Life Financial Corp.
Miller, David O.: chairman, Employers Insurance of Wausau, A Mutual Co.; trustee, Nationwide Insurance Enterprise Foundation; chairman, Wausau Insurance Companies

Allied Products Corp.
Sherman, Saul S.: vice chairman, director, Trace International Holdings, Inc.

AlliedSignal Inc.
Becherer, Hans Walter: chairman, chief executive officer, director, Deere & Co.; director, Deere Foundation (John)

Carter, Marshall Nichols: chairman, chief executive officer, State Street Bank & Trust Co.

Allina Health System Inc.
George, William Wallace: chief executive officer, chairman, Medtronic, Inc.

Piper, Addison Lewis: director, Piper Jaffray Companies Foundation; chairman, chief executive officer, director, U.S. Bancorp Piper Jaffray

Allmerica Financial Corp.
O'Brien, John Francis, Jr.: president, chief executive officer, Allmerica Financial Corp.

Rupley, Theodore J.: president, chief executive officer, director, Allmerica Financial Corp.

Allmerica Property & Casualty Companies Inc.
O'Brien, John Francis, Jr.: president, chief executive officer, Allmerica Financial Corp.

Allnewsco Inc.
Allbritton, Joe Lewis: chairman, chief executive officer, Riggs Bank NA

Allstate Corp.
Gary, Robert W.: vice president, trustee, Allstate Foundation

Liddy, Edward M.: vice president, trustee, Allstate Foundation; president, chief operating officer, director, Allstate Insurance Co.

Sylla, Casey J.: senior vice president, chief investment officer, Allstate Insurance Co.

Allstate Indemnity Co.
Choate, Jerry D.: chairman, chief executive officer, director, Allstate Foundation

Gary, Robert W.: vice president, trustee, Allstate Foundation

Liddy, Edward M.: vice president, trustee, Allstate Foundation; president, chief operating officer, director, Allstate Insurance Co.

Lower, H. Louis Gordon, II: vice president, trustee, Allstate Foundation

Pike, Robert William: vice president, secretary, Allstate Foundation; senior vice president, secretary, general counsel, director, Allstate Insurance Co.

Sylla, Casey J.: senior vice president, chief investment officer, Allstate Insurance Co.

Allstate Insurance Co.
Choate, Jerry D.: chairman, chief executive officer, director, Allstate Foundation

Lower, H. Louis Gordon, II: vice president, trustee, Allstate Foundation

Pike, Robert William: vice president, secretary, Allstate Foundation; senior vice president, secretary, general counsel, director, Allstate Insurance Co.

Allstate Insurance Co. Ltd. (United Kingdom)
Resnick, Myron J.: vice president, treasurer, trustee, Allstate Foundation

Allstate Motor Club Inc.
Choate, Jerry D.: chairman, chief executive officer, director, Allstate Foundation

Gary, Robert W.: vice president, trustee, Allstate Foundation

Liddy, Edward M.: vice president, trustee, Allstate Foundation; president, chief operating officer, director, Allstate Insurance Co.

Alltrista Corp.
Molen, Richard L.: chairman, chief executive officer, director, Huffy Corp.; trustee, Huffy Foundation, Inc.

Allwin Inc.
Allbritton, Joe Lewis: chairman, chief executive officer, Riggs Bank NA

Alpine Lace Brands Inc.
Gherty, John E.: president, chief executive officer, Land O'Lakes, Inc.

Alstrip Inc.
Bozzone, Robert P.: vice chairman, director, Allegheny Technologies Inc.; trustee, Allegheny Technologies Inc. Charitable Trust

Altair International
Jacobsen, James C.: vice chairman, Kellwood Co.; vice president, director, Kellwood Foundation

Altamont Gas Transmission
Wise, William Allen: chairman, president, chief executive officer, director, El Paso Energy Co.; chairman, director, El Paso Energy Foundation

Altana Exploration Co.
Senechal, Ellen M.: treasurer, Montana Power Co.

Alumax Inc.
Brown, Harold, PhD: chairman, Mattel Foundation

Aluminum Co. North America
Gorman, Joseph T.: chairman, chief executive officer, TRW Inc.

AmSouth Bancorp
Chandler, J. Harold: chairman, president, chief executive officer, Provident Companies, Inc.

Harris, Elmer Beseler: president, chief executive officer, director, Alabama Power Co.

Amcast Industries Corp.
Blankley, Walter Elwood: president, director, AMETEK Foundation; chairman, director, AMETEK, Inc.

Forster, Peter Hans: chairman, director, Dayton Power and Light Co.

Amdahl Inc.
Ellison, Lawrence J.: chairman, chief executive officer, director, president, Oracle Corp.

Amer US Savings Bank
Brooks, Roger Kay: chairman, AmerUS Group

AmerUS Life Holdings Inc.
Kalainov, Sam Charles: chairman, president, chief executive officer, AmerUS Group

Amerada Hess Corp.
Johnson, William R.: president, chief executive officer, Heinz Co. (H.J.)

Ameren Corp.
Liddy, Richard A.: chairman, president, chief executive officer, GenAmerica Corp.

Lohman, Gordon Russell: trustee, Amsted Industries Foundation; director, Amsted Industries Inc.

Ameribanc Inc.
Jacobsen, Thomas Herbert: chairman, president, chief executive officer, Mercantile Bank NA

America & Efird Mills Inc.
Dickson, Alan Thomas: president, Dickson Foundation; chairman, Ruddick Corp.

Dickson, Rush Stuart: chairman, Dickson Foundation

America Airlines Inc.
Carty, Donald J.: vice president, treasurer, AMR/American Airlines Foundation; president, chairman, chief executive officer, director, AMR Corp.

Williams, Eugene Flewellyn, Jr.: member public policy committee, Emerson Charitable Trust

America Bechtel Inc.
Bechtel, Riley Peart: chairman, Bechtel Foundation; chairman, chief executive officer, director, Bechtel Group, Inc.

Zaccaria, Adrian: president, chief operating officer, director, Bechtel Group, Inc.

America Brands Inc.
Lohman, Gordon Russell: trustee, Amsted Industries Foundation; director, Amsted Industries Inc.

America Casualty Excess Ltd.

Hernandez, Robert M.: vice chairman, chief financial officer, director, USX Corp.; trustee, USX Foundation, Inc.

America Electric Power Service Corp.

Draper, Ernest Linn, Jr.: chairman, president, chief executive officer, director, American Electric Power

America Express Co.

Furlaud, Richard Mortimer: interim chief executive officer, International Flavors & Fragrances Inc.

America Family Corp.

Amos, Daniel P.: president, chief executive officer, director, AFLAC Inc.

America Greetings Corp.

Ratner, Albert Benjamin: trustee, Forest City Enterprises Charitable Foundation, Inc.; co-chairman, director, Forest City Enterprises, Inc.

America Home Products Corp.

Wrigley, William: chairman, director, Wrigley Co. Foundation (Wm. Jr.); president, chief executive officer, director, Wrigley Co. (Wm. Jr.)

America Insurance Co. Inc.

Stinnette, Joe L., Jr.: director, Fireman's Fund Foundation; president, chief executive officer, director, Fireman's Fund Insurance Co.

America Management System Inc.

Spoon, Alan Gary: president, chief operating officer, director, The Washington Post

America Manufacturings Mutual Insurance Co.

White, Walter Lucas: secretary, treasurer, trustee, Kemper Foundation (James S.)

America Motorists Insurance Co.

Maatman, Gerald Leonard: chairman, president, trustee, Kemper Foundation (James S.); director, Kemper National Insurance Companies

White, Walter Lucas: secretary, treasurer, trustee, Kemper Foundation (James S.)

America National Bank & Trust Co. Chicago

Cole, Franklin Alan: chairman, Aon Foundation

America National Canada Co.

Gidwitz, Ronald J.: president, chief executive officer, Curtis Industries, Inc. (Helene)

Kennedy, George Danner: trustee, Kemper Foundation (James S.)

America Online Inc.

Raines, Franklin Delano: chairman, chief executive officer, Fannie Mae; director, Fannie Mae Foundation

America Phoenix Corp.

Fiondella, Robert William: chairman, president, chief executive officer, Phoenix Home Life Mutual Insurance Co.

America Precision Industries Inc.

Kennedy, Bernard Joseph: chairman, president, chief executive officer, director, National Fuel Gas Distribution Corp.

America Recreation Products Inc.

Jacobsen, James C.: vice chairman, Kellwood Co.; vice president, director, Kellwood Foundation

Upbin, Hal Jay: president, chief executive officer, director, Kellwood Co.

America Security Insurance Co.

Freedman, Allen Royal: trustee, Fortis Foundation; chairman, chief executive officer, president, Fortis, Inc.

America Standard Sanitaryware Thailand Ltd.

Kampouris, Emmanuel Andrew: chairman, president, chief executive officer, director, American Standard Inc.

America Stock Exchange Inc.

Paton, Leland B.: president capital marketings, director, member executive committee, Prudential Securities Inc.

America United Life Insurance Co.

Dora, James E.: director, AUL Foundation Inc.

American & Foreign Insurance Co.

Kline, Philip E.: treasurer, director, Royal & SunAlliance Insurance Foundation, Inc.

American Airlines Fuel Corp.

Baker, Robert Woodward: executive vice president, AMR Corp.

American Airlines Inc.

Britton, Robert A.: secretary, manager, AMR/American Airlines Foundation

American Arbitration Association

Rosenthal, Sol: counsel, Playboy Enterprises Inc.

American Automobile Association Michigan

Bauer, Chris Michael: president, Firstar Milwaukee Foundation

American Automobile Insurance Co.

Hansmeyer, Herbert F.: chairman, Fireman's Fund Insurance Co.

Rowe, Thomas E.: chairman, director, Fireman's Fund Foundation; director, Fireman's Fund Insurance Co.

Stinnette, Joe L., Jr.: director, Fireman's Fund Foundation; president, chief executive officer, director, Fireman's Fund Insurance Co.

American Business Products Inc.

Ackerman, F. Duane: president, chief executive officer, BellSouth Corp.

McDonald, James F.: president, chief executive officer, Scientific-Atlanta, Inc.

American Casualty Reading Pennsylvania

Chookaszian, Dennis Haig: chairman, chief executive officer, CNA

Jokiel, Peter E.: senior vice president, chief financial officer, CNA

Sharkey, William Henry, Jr.: director, CNA Foundation

American Century Companies Inc.

Pratt, Donald Henry: chairman, Butler Manufacturing Co.; vice president, trustee, Butler Manufacturing Co. Foundation

American Civil Liberties Union Illinois Chapter

Wilson, Cleo Francine: executive director, Playboy Foundation

American Council Life Insurance

Hipp, William Hayne: president, chief executive officer, director, Liberty Corp.; chairman, president, director, Liberty Corp. Foundation

American Enterprises Holdings Inc.

Clark, Howard Longstreth, Jr.: vice chairman, Walter Industries Inc.

American Fidelity Assurance Co.

Rex, John: president, American Fidelity Corp.; treasurer, American Fidelity Corp. Founders Fund

American Fidelity Securities

Rex, John: president, American Fidelity Corp.; treasurer, American Fidelity Corp. Founders Fund

American Film Marketing Association

Rosenthal, Sol: counsel, Playboy Enterprises Inc.

American Gas Association

Harper, James J.: vice president, controller, Eastern Enterprises

American General Finance Corp.

Geissinger, Frederick: chairman, chief executive officer, prs, American General Finance

American General Property Insurance Co.

Tuerff, James R.: president, director, American General Finance

American Government Income Fund

Ellis, William H.: director, Piper Jaffray Companies Foundation

American Heritage Life

Ackerman, F. Duane: president, chief executive officer, BellSouth Corp.

American Horizon Property Casualty Insurance Co.

Resnick, Myron J.: vice president, treasurer, trustee, Allstate Foundation

American Insurance Co. Inc.

Black, Gary E.: president, director, Fireman's Fund Foundation; president claims division, director, Fireman's Fund Insurance Co.

Hansmeyer, Herbert F.: chairman, Fireman's Fund Insurance Co.

Rowe, Thomas E.: chairman, director, Fireman's Fund Foundation; director, Fireman's Fund Insurance Co.

American International Group Inc.

Rupley, Theodore J.: president, chief executive officer, director, Allmerica Financial Corp.

American Liberty Insurance Co.

Kelley, Bruce Gunn: vice president, director, Employers Mutual Charitable Foundation

American Life Insurance Co.

Hower, Frank Beard, Jr.: vice chairman, Anthem Foundation, Inc.

American Manufacturer Mutual Insurance Co.

Mathis, David B.: chairman, Kemper Foundation (James S.)

American Medical Security Group

Whitelaw, Essie M.: president, chief operating officer, United Wisconsin Services; vice president, United Wisconsin Services Foundation

American Motorists Insurance Co.

Chain, John T., Junior: trustee, Kemper Foundation (James S.); president, Kemper National Insurance Companies

Hamilton, Peter Bannerman: director, Brunswick Foundation; trustee, Kemper Foundation (James S.)

Knauss, Dalton L.: trustee, Kemper Foundation (James S.)

Mathis, David B.: chairman, Kemper Foundation (James S.)

Rosett, Richard Nathaniel: trustee, Kemper Foundation (James S.)

Toll, Daniel Roger: trustee, Kemper Foundation (James S.)

American Mutual Holding Corp.

Kalainov, Sam Charles: chairman, president, chief executive officer, AmerUS Group

American National Bank

Vitale, David J.: vice chairman, Bank One Corp.; vice president, director, First National Bank of Chicago Foundation

American National Bank Tr Chicago

Vitale, David J.: vice chairman, Bank One Corp.; vice president, director, First National Bank of Chicago Foundation

American Overseas Ltd.

Elkins, Lloyd Edwin, Junior: vice president, Chevron Corp.

American Piping Boiler Co.

Hanks, Stephen G.: president, Morrison Knudsen Corp. Foundation, Inc.

American President Lines Ltd.

Rhein, Timothy James: president, chief executive officer, APL Ltd.

American Protection Industries

Resnick, Lynda Rae: vice chairman, co-owner, Franklin Mint (The)

American Society of Corporate Secretaries

Gailey, John Robert, III: vice president, general counsel, secretary, West Co. Inc.

American Specialty Retailing Group

Chemerow, David I.: executive vice president, chief financial officer, Playboy Enterprises Inc.

American Standard Co. Inc.

Poses, Frederick M.: director, AlliedSignal Foundation Inc.; president, chief operating officer, AlliedSignal Inc.

American United Life Insurance Co.

Cornelius, James M.: director, AUL Foundation Inc.

Riggs, William R.: director, AUL Foundation Inc.

American Yearbook Co.

Buhrmaster, Robert C.: president, chief executive officer, director, chairman, Jostens, Inc.

Amerisource Health Corp.

Gozon, Richard C.: executive vice president pulp paper & packaging, Weyerhaeuser Co.; trustee, Weyerhaeuser Co. Foundation

Amerisure Companies

Miller, Eugene A.: chairman, chief executive officer, Comerica Inc.

Ameritas Investment Advisors Inc.

Arth, Lawrence Joseph: vice president, director, Ameritas Charitable Foundation; chairman, chief executive officer, director, Ameritas Life Insurance Corp.

Louis, Kenneth C.: president, chief operating officer, director, Ameritas Life Insurance Corp.

Ameritas Life Insurance Corp.

Abel, James P.: president, Abel Foundation; president, director, NEBCO Evans

Getz, Bert A.: chairman, Globe Corp.; president, director, Globe Foundation

Getz, Bert A., Jr.: executive vice president, Globe Corp.; vice president, Globe Foundation

Ameritas Managed Dental Plan Inc.

Louis, Kenneth C.: president, chief operating officer, director, Ameritas Life Insurance Corp.

Ameritas Marketing Group

Martin, JoAnn M.: controller, Ameritas Charitable Foundation; senior vice president, partner, chief financial officer, Ameritas Life Insurance Corp.

Ameritas Variable Life Insurance Co.

Louis, Kenneth C.: president, chief operating officer, director, Ameritas Life Insurance Corp.

Martin, JoAnn M.: controller, Ameritas Charitable Foundation; senior vice president, partner, chief financial officer, Ameritas Life Insurance Corp.

Ameritech Corp.

Goodes, Melvin Russell: chairman, chief executive officer, director, Ameritech Corp.

Henderson, James Alan: vice chairman, chief executive officer, director, Ameritech Corp.; chairman, director, Cummins Engine Foundation

Howard, James Joseph, III: chairman, president, chief executive officer, director, Northern States Power Co.

Lubar, Sheldon B.: chairman, Ameritech Corp.; director, Firstar Milwaukee Foundation

Martinez, Arthur C.: chairman, chief executive officer, president, Sears, Roebuck and Co.

McCoy, John Bonnet: president, chief executive officer, Ameritech Corp.

Ong, John Doyle: chairman board, director, Ameritech Corp.

Rand, Addison Barry: executive vice president operations, Xerox Corp.; trustee, Xerox Foundation

Tyson, Laura D'Andrea: director, Ameritech Foundation

Unruh, James Arlen: director, Ameritech Foundation

Ameritech Service Inc.

Cooper, Robert N.: president, Ameritech Michigan

Ameritech Services Inc. Delaware

Lebherz, Kent A.: president, Ameritech Indiana

Ametek Aerospace Products

Blankley, Walter Elwood: president, director, AMETEK Foundation; chairman, director, AMETEK, Inc.

Ametek Inc.

Cole, Lewis George: director, AMETEK Foundation

Friedlaender, Helmut N.: director, AMETEK Foundation

Varet, Elizabeth Rosenwald: vice president, director, AMETEK Foundation; director, AMETEK, Inc.

Amfed Financial Inc.

Stroup, Stanley Stephenson: executive vice president, general counsel, Norwest Corp.

Amgen Inc.

Choate, Jerry D.: chairman, chief executive officer, director, Allstate Foundation

Amgen International Inc.

Binder, Gordon M.: chairman, chief executive officer, director, Amgen, Inc.

Amoco Chemical Co.

Sosa, Enrique J.: trustee, Dow Chemical Co. Foundation

Amoco Oil Co.

Ford, W. Douglas: executive vice president, BP Amoco Corp.

Amoco Production Co.

Work, David F.: senior vice president shared service, BP Amoco Corp.; director, BP Amoco Foundation

Ampal Corp.

Krueger, Harvey M.: trustee, Barry Foundation

Amsted Industries Inc.

Terry, Richard Edward: chairman, chief executive officer, director, Peoples Energy Corp.

Amurcon Corp.

Erb, Frederick A.: president, Erb Foundation

Amurol Confections Co.

Wrigley, William, Jr.: vice president, director, Wrigley Co. Foundation (Wm. Jr.)

Anaheim Sports Inc.

Eisner, Michael Dammann: president, trustee, Disney Co. Foundation (Walt); chairman, chief executive officer, director, Disney Co. (Walt)

Ancast Industries Corp.

Baker, James Kendrick: chairman, director, Arvin Foundation; vice chairman, director, Arvin Industries, Inc.

Anchor Glass Container Corp.

Walter, James W.: trustee, Walter Foundation; chairman emeritus, founder, director, Walter Industries Inc.

Andersen Corp.

Hulings, Mary Andersen: vice president, Bayport Foundation

Andersen Laboratories Inc.

Cottrell, G. Walton: senior vice president, chief financial officer, Carpenter Technology Corp.

Andersen Windows

Hulings, Mary Andersen: vice president, Bayport Foundation

Anderson Lumber Co.

Eccles, Spencer Fox: chairman, chief executive officer, director, First Security Bank of Idaho NA

Andersons Inc.

Barrett, John F.: trustee, Western-Southern Foundation, Inc.; president, chief executive officer, director, Western & Southern Life Insurance Co.

Andrew Corp.

Fluno, Jere David: vice chairman, Grainger, Inc. (W.W.)

Andrews Group Inc.

Slovin, Bruce: president, director, Revlon Inc.

Angelica Corp.

Mueller, Charles William: chairman, president, chief executive officer, Ameren Corp.; trustee, Ameren Corp. Charitable Trust

Anheuser-Busch Companies Inc.

Edison, Bernard Alan: member, Edison Family Foundation

Kelly, John F.: chairman, chief executive officer, director, Alaska Airlines, Inc.

Knight, Charles Field: chairman, chief executive officer, Emerson Electric Co.

Taylor, Andrew C.: president, chief executive officer, director, Enterprise Rent-A-Car Co.

Warner, Douglas Alexander, III: chairman, president, chief executive officer, director, Morgan & Co. Inc. (J.P.)

Whitacre, Edward E., Jr.: chairman, director, chief executive officer, SBC Communications Inc.

Anicom Inc.

Reiman, Thomas Jay: senior vice president public policy, Ameritech Corp.

Ann Taylor Stores

Drexler, Millard S.: trustee, Gap Foundation/Gap Inc. Community Relations; president, chief executive officer, director, Gap, Inc.

Ansys Inc.

Morby, Jacqueline C.: managing partner, Pacific Mutual Life Insurance Co.

Anthem Companies Inc.

Frick, David R.: chairman, Anthem Foundation, Inc.

Anthem Health Indiana

Purcell, Nancy L.: secretary, Anthem Foundation, Inc.

Anthem Insurance Companies

Hower, Frank Beard, Jr.: vice chairman, Anthem Foundation, Inc.

Purcell, Nancy L.: secretary, Anthem Foundation, Inc.

Anthem Life Insurance Co.

Frick, David R.: chairman, Anthem Foundation, Inc.

Apco Argentina Inc.

Bailey, Keith E.: chairman, president, director, chief executive officer, Texas Gas Transmission Corp.; president, director, Williams Companies Foundation (The)

Appalachian Power Co.

Draper, Ernest Linn, Jr.: chairman, president, chief executive officer, director, American Electric Power

Lhota, William J.: executive vice president, American Electric Power

Apple Computer Inc.

Ellison, Lawrence J.: chairman, chief executive officer, director, president, Oracle Corp.

Woolard, Edgar Smith, Jr.: director, du Pont de Nemours & Co. (E.I.)

Applied Industrial Technologies Inc.

Bares, William G.: chairman, president, chief executive officer, Lubrizol Corp. (The); trustee, Lubrizol Foundation (The)

Appomattox Vermont Corp.

Young, Robert Harris: president, chief executive officer, Central Vermont Public Service Corp.

Aptagroup

Guthart, Leo A.: vice chairman, director, Pittway Corp.

Aquarian Co.

Ratcliffe, George Jackson, Jr.: trustee, Hubbell Foundation (Harvey); chairman, president, chief executive officer, Hubbell Inc.

Aquila Biopharmaceuticals Inc.

Nelson, John Martin: chairman, director, TJX Companies, Inc.

Ar Mexican Explorations Inc.

Osborne, Richard de Jongh: director, ASARCO Foundation; chairman, chief executive officer, director, ASARCO Inc.

Aramark Corp.

Preston, James Edward: vice president, director, Avon Products Foundation, Inc.; chairman, chief executive officer, director, Avon Products, Inc.

Aramark Uniform Services

Rogala, Judith A.: member, Butler Manufacturing Co. Foundation

Arch Coal Inc.

Chellgren, Paul Wilbur: chief executive officer, chairman, director, Ashland, Inc.; member, Ashland Inc. Foundation

Quin, Joseph Marvin: trustee, Ashland Inc. Foundation

Archorbank SSB

Omachinski, David L.: chief financial officer, treasurer, vice president, Oshkosh B'Gosh, Inc.

Arctic AK Fisheries Corp.

Tyson, John H.: chairman, chief executive officer, president, director, Tyson Foods Inc.; trustee, Tyson Foundation, Inc.

Arden Fabrics Ltd.

Jacobsen, James C.: vice chairman, Kellwood Co.; vice president, director, Kellwood Foundation

Argonaut Group Inc.

Rock, Arthur: co-founder, chairman executive committee, director, Intel Corp.

Aristotle Corp.

Miglio, Daniel Joseph: chairman, president, director, chief executive officer, Southern New England Telephone Co.

Arizona Daily Star

Pulitzer, Michael Edgar: chairman, president, chief executive officer, director, Pulitzer Publishing Co.; chairman, president, chief executive officer, Pulitzer Publishing Co. Foundation

Arkwright Insurance Co.

Frank, Stephen E.: president, chief operating officer, director, Edison International

Luke, John A., Jr.: chairman, president, chief executive officer, director, Westvaco Corp.

Arkwright Mutual Insurance Co.

Aylesworth, William Andrew: treasurer, Texas Instruments Foundation; chief financial officer, treasurer, Texas Instruments Inc.

Luke, John A., Jr.: chairman, president, chief executive officer, director, Westvaco Corp.

Arlington International Racecourse Ltd.

Duchossois, Richard Louis: secretary, Duchossois Foundation; chairman, chief executive officer, director, Duchossois Industries Inc.

Arlington Management Services

Duchossois, Richard Louis: secretary, Duchossois Foundation; chairman, chief executive officer, director, Duchossois Industries Inc.

Armar All Products Corp.

d'Alessio, Jon W.: trustee, McKesson Foundation

Armour International Co.

Teets, John William: president, chief executive officer, director, Viad Corp. Fund

Armstrong World Industries Inc.

Campbell, Van C.: vice chairman, chief financial officer, chief administrative officer, director, Corning Inc.; trustee, Corning Inc. Foundation

Arnold Distributors Inc.

Hessler, David J.: secretary, trustee, Jochum-Moll Foundation (The); president, partner, MTD Products Inc.

Moll, Curtis E.: treasurer, trustee, Jochum-Moll Foundation (The)

Arrow Specicalty Co.

Lyon, Wayne Barton: president, chief operating officer, director, Masco Corp.

Arrowhead Holdings Corp.

Benenson, James, Jr.: chairman, president, director, Vesper Corp.; trustee, Vesper Foundation

Curci, John V.: chief financial officer, Vesper Corp.; trustee, Vesper Foundation

Art Stamping Inc.

Bridgeland, James Ralph, Jr.: trustee, Star Bank NA, Cincinnati Foundation

Arthur Anderson & Co.

Dagley, Larry J.: senior vice president, chief financial officer, Pacific Enterprises

Arthur D Little Inc.

Heuchling, Theodore Paul: trustee, Little Foundation (Arthur D.)

Arthur Rock & Co.

Rock, Arthur: co-founder, chairman executive committee, director, Intel Corp.

Arthur Treacher's Inc.

Bookshester, Dennis S.: chairman, chief executive officer, Playboy Enterprises Inc.

Arts Education Council

Moten, John, Junior: vice president community relations, Laclede Gas Co.

Arundel Corp.

Baker, Edward L.: chairman, director, Florida Rock Industries; president, Florida Rock Industries Foundation

Arvin Industries Inc.

Kendall, J. William: chairman, director, Arvin Foundation

Ashland Coal Inc.

Quin, Joseph Marvin: trustee, Ashland Inc. Foundation

Ashland Inc.

Farley, James Bernard: chairman emeritus, trustee, Walter Industries Inc.

Ashwright Inc.

Shuster, George Whitcomb: trustee, Cranston Foundation; president, chief executive officer, director, Cranston Print Works Co.

Assoc Electric & Gas Insurance Services Ltd.

Farman, Richard Donald: chairman, chief executive officer, Pacific Enterprises

Kennedy, Bernard Joseph: chairman, president, chief executive officer, director, National Fuel Gas Distribution Corp.

Associate First Bank of Neenah

Cianciola, Charles Sal: trustee, Chesapeake Corp. Foundation

Associated Indemnity Corp.

Hansmeyer, Herbert F.: chairman, Fireman's Fund Insurance Co.

Pollard, David R.: director, Fireman's Fund Foundation; officer, Fireman's Fund Insurance Co.

Rowe, Thomas E.: chairman, director, Fireman's Fund Foundation; director, Fireman's Fund Insurance Co.

Associated Industries Florida

Campbell, George Leroy: vice president public affairs, Florida Power Corp.

Associated Industries Massachusetts

Bettacchi, Robert J.: senior vice president, Grace & Co. (W.R.)

Associated Industries Vermont

Young, Robert Harris: president, chief executive officer, Central Vermont Public Service Corp.

Astec Industries Inc.

Frierson, Daniel K.: chairman, chief executive officer, Dixie Group, Inc. (The); president, trustee, Dixie Yarns Foundation, Inc.

Astor Products Inc.

Bragin, David H.: treasurer, assistant secretary, director, Winn-Dixie Stores Foundation

Astronet Corp.

Olschwang, Alan P., Esq.: secretary, Mitsubishi Electric America Foundation

Atchison, Topeka & Santa Fe Railroad Co.

Springer, Denis E.: senior vice president, chief financial officer, Burlington Northern Santa Fe Corp.; director, Burlington Northern Santa Fe Foundation

Athena Assurance Co.

Leatherdale, Douglas West: chairman, chief executive officer, president, Saint Paul Companies Inc.

Athens Newspapers Co.

Morris, William Shivers, III: founder, chairman, chief executive officer, director, Morris Communications Corp.; trustee, Stauffer Communications Foundation

Athens Newspapers Inc.

Herman, William A., III: secretary, treasurer, director, Morris Communications Corp.

Morris, William Shivers, IV: president, director, Morris Communications Corp.; trustee, Stauffer Communications Foundation

Atlanta Exploration Co.

Pederson, Jerrold P.: vice president, chief financial officer, director, Montana Power Co.; director, Montana Power Foundation

Atlanta Freightliner Truck Sales Service

Hebe, James L.: chairman, president, chief executive officer, Freightliner Corp.

Atlanta Toyota Inc.

Cogan, Marshall Stuart: chairman, president, chief executive officer, director, Trace International Holdings, Inc.; director, Trace International Holdings, Inc. Foundation

Atlantic Health Group Inc.

Bewley, Peter D.: vice president, secretary, Clorox Co. Foundation

Atlantic Health System

Longfield, William H.: president, Bard Foundation (C.R.); chairman, chief executive officer, director, Bard, Inc. (C.R.)

Atlantic Monthly Co.

Zuckerman, Mortimer Benjamin: co-founder, chairman, co-publisher, director, Daily News

Atlantic Mutual Companies

Kogan, Richard Jay: chairman, chief executive officer, Schering-Plough Corp.; trustee, member, Schering-Plough Foundation

Schwarz, H. Marshall: chairman, chief executive officer, United States Trust Co. of New York

Atlantic Resources

O'Reilly, F. Anthony John: chairman, trustee, Heinz Co. Foundation (H.J.); chairman, director, Heinz Co. (H.J.)

Atlantic Richfield Co.

Kresa, Kent: chairman, president, chief executive officer, director, Northrop Grumman Corp.

Langbo, Arnold Gordon: chairman, chief executive officer, director, Kellogg Co.

Atlas Copco North America

Pratt, Donald Henry: chairman, Butler Manufacturing Co.; vice president, trustee, Butler Manufacturing Co. Foundation

Atrion Corp.

Stupp, John P., Jr.: executive vice president, chief operating officer, director, Stupp Brothers Bridge & Iron Co.; trustee, Stupp Brothers Bridge & Iron Co. Foundation

Atwater McMillian

Leatherdale, Douglas West: chairman, chief executive officer, president, Saint Paul Companies Inc.

Audubon Metals LLC

Koch, Robert Louis, II: president, chief executive officer, director, Koch Enterprises, Inc.; president, director, Koch Foundation

Audubon Printers Ink Ltd.

Decherd, Robert William: chairman, president, chief executive officer, director, Belo Corp. (A.H.); chairman, trustee, Belo Corp. Foundation (A.H.)

Auergesellschaft GmbH

Ryan, John Thomas, III: chairman, chief executive officer, Mine Safety Appliances Co.

Augusta Chronicle

Morris, William Shivers, III: founder, chairman, chief executive officer, director, Morris Communications Corp.; trustee, Stauffer Communications Foundation

Aurora Health Care Inc.

Bechtold, Ned W.: director, Firstar Milwaukee Foundation

Austin Powder Co.

True, David: partner, True Oil Co.

Autodesk Inc.

Starkweather, Kendall N.: director, Autodesk Foundation

Autoimmune Inc.

D'Andrade, Hugh Alfred: trustee, member, Schering-Plough Foundation

Automated Office Solutions

Parsons, Susan E.: secretary, treasurer, Koch Enterprises, Inc.; secretary, treasurer, director, Koch Foundation

Automatic Data Processing Corp.

Krueger, Harvey M.: trustee, Barry Foundation

Automatic Data Processing Inc.

Tisch, Laurence Alan: chairman, co-chief executive officer, CBS Corp.; trustee, Loews Foundation

Avanti Industries Inc.

Wendt, Richard L.: trustee, Jeld-wen Foundation; chief executive officer, chairman, Jeld-wen, Inc.

Avatar Holdings Inc.

Meyerson, Martin: director, Panasonic Foundation

Avco Corp.

Cambell, Lewis B.: chairman, chief executive officer, director, Textron Inc.

Avent Inc.

Gamron, W. Anthony: treasurer, director, Kimberly-Clark Foundation

Avery Dennison Corp.

Ferry, Richard Michael: chairman, Pacific Mutual Life Insurance Co.

Avery Dennison Decorative Films

Miller, Charles Daly: chairman, director, Avery Dennison Corp.; trustee, Whirlpool Foundation

Avery Dennison Office Privates Co.

Neal, Philip Mark: president, chief executive officer, director, Avery Dennison Corp.

Avnet Inc.

Lawrence, James A.: chief financial officer, executive vice president, General Mills, Inc.

Avon Energy Partners PLC

Graham, John Gourlay: chief financial officer, senior vice president, GPU Energy

Avon International Advisory Council
Nelson, Merlin Edward: chairman, director, IBJ Foundation

Avon International Operations
Preston, James Edward: vice president, director, Avon Products Foundation, Inc.; chairman, chief executive officer, director, Avon Products, Inc.

Avon-Lomalinda Inc.
Preston, James Edward: vice president, director, Avon Products Foundation, Inc.; chairman, chief executive officer, director, Avon Products, Inc.

Awawego Delivery Inc.
Cline, Robert Stanley: chairman, chief executive officer, director, Airborne Freight Corp.

Axx Trend Techs Inc.
Morby, Jacqueline C.: managing partner, Pacific Mutual Life Insurance Co.

Azalea Development Co.
Herman, William A., III: secretary, treasurer, director, Morris Communications Corp.

Aztar Corp.
Snell, Richard: chairman, president, chief executive officer, director, Arizona Public Service Co.

B I Holdings Corp.
Blount, Winton Malcolm, Jr.: chairman, Blount International, Inc.

B Sky B
Murdoch, Rupert P.: chairman, Fox Entertainment Group

B&D Associates
Dora, James E.: director, AUL Foundation Inc.

B.F. Goodrich Co.
Davidson, George A., Jr.: chairman, chief executive officer, director, Consolidated Natural Gas Co.

O'Leary, Thomas Howard: chairman, Burlington Resources Foundation

Olesen, Douglas Eugene, PhD: president, chief executive officer, Battelle Memorial Institute

Ong, John Doyle: chairman board, director, Ameritech Corp.

Osborne, Richard de Jongh: director, ASARCO Foundation; chairman, chief executive officer, director, ASARCO Inc.

B.F. Performance Freedom Chem Co.
Price, David B., Jr.: vice president, Goodrich Foundation, Inc. (B.F.)

Vinney, Les C.: senior vice president, chief financial officer, BFGoodrich Co.

B.F. Performance Materials
Price, David B., Jr.: vice president, Goodrich Foundation, Inc. (B.F.)

B.F. Processing Corp.
Kidder, C. Robert: chairman, president, chief executive officer, director, Borden, Inc.

B.R. Guest Ltd.
Rich, Robert E., Sr.: president, treasurer, Rich Family Foundation; founder, chairman, director, Rich Products Corp.

BAT Industries PLC
Denlea, Leo Edward, Jr.: retired chairman, president, chief executive officer, director, Farmers Group, Inc.; vice president, Farmers Group Safety Foundation

BB&T Corp.
Reed, Scott Eldridge: senior executive vice president, chief financial officer, Branch Banking & Trust Co.

BB&T Financial Corp.
Allison, John Andrew, IV: chairman, chief executive officer, director, Branch Banking & Trust Co.

Williamson, Henry Gaston, Jr.: chief operating officer, Branch Banking & Trust Co.

BB&T Financial Corp. of SC
Reed, Scott Eldridge: senior executive vice president, chief financial officer, Branch Banking & Trust Co.

Williamson, Henry Gaston, Jr.: chief operating officer, Branch Banking & Trust Co.

BB&T Savings Corp.
Reed, Scott Eldridge: senior executive vice president, chief financial officer, Branch Banking & Trust Co.

BC Sugar Refinery Ltd.
Pitts, John Wilson: director, PACCAR Foundation

BC Telecommunications Co.
Johnson, James Lawrence: chairman emeritus, Walter Industries Inc.

BC Telephone Co. Ltd.
Pitts, John Wilson: director, PACCAR Foundation

BCP Management Inc.
Byrd, Richard Hays: treasurer, Borden Foundation, Inc.

BEC Energy
Alden, Alison: senior vice president sales, service, human resources, Boston Edison Co.; trustee, Boston Edison Foundation

Countryman, Gary Lee: chairman, Liberty Mutual Insurance Group

Gifford, Charles Kilvert: trustee, BankBoston Charitable Foundation; chairman, chief executive officer, BankBoston Corp.

BFI Disposal System North America
Ranck, Bruce E.: president, chief executive officer, director, Browning-Ferris Industries Inc.

BGD5 Ltd. Partnership
Piper, Addison Lewis: director, Piper Jaffray Companies Foundation; chairman, chief executive officer, director, U.S. Bancorp Piper Jaffray

BGE Energy Projects & Services
Crooke, Edward A.: president, Baltimore Gas & Electric Foundation

BHP Hawaii Inc.
Kurren, Faye Watanabe: president, Tesoro Hawaii

BJC Health System
Mueller, Charles William: chairman, president, chief executive officer, Ameren Corp.; trustee, Ameren Corp. Charitable Trust

BLP Group Inc.
Morby, Jacqueline C.: managing partner, Pacific Mutual Life Insurance Co.

BMC Real Estate Inc.
Pratt, Donald Henry: chairman, Butler Manufacturing Co.; vice president, trustee, Butler Manufacturing Co. Foundation

BNY Mortgage Co. Inc.
Renyi, Thomas A.: president, chief executive officer, director, Bank of New York Co., Inc.

BOC Group
Baird, Dugald Euan: chairman, president, chief executive officer, Schlumberger Ltd. (USA)

BP America Inc.
Gorman, Joseph T.: chairman, chief executive officer, TRW Inc.

BP Amoco Corp.
Beall, Donald Ray: director, Rockwell International Corp.

Bryan, John Henry: chairman, Sara Lee Corp.; director, Sara Lee Foundation

Davis, Erroll Brown, Jr.: president, chief executive officer, director, Wisconsin Power & Light Co.

Knight, Charles Field: chairman, chief executive officer, Emerson Electric Co.

Martinez, Arthur C.: chairman, chief executive officer, president, Sears, Roebuck and Co.

Solso, Theodore Matthew: president, chief operating officer, director, Cummins Engine Co., Inc.; director, Cummins Engine Foundation

BSI Inc.
Koch, David Andrew: president, Graco Foundation; chairman, director, Graco, Inc.

BTG Inc.
Davis, Ruth Margaret: trustee, Air Products Foundation

Babcock & Wilcox Co.
Tetrault, Roger E.: chairman, chief executive officer, director, McDermott Inc.

Babcock Lumber Co.
Queenan, Charles J., Jr.: trustee, Tippins Foundation

Badger Meter Inc.
Manning, Kenneth Paul: president, Universal Foods Corp.; president, director, Universal Foods Foundation

Schuenke, Donald John: director, Freddie Mac

Strobel, Pamela B.: senior vice president, general counsel, Commonwealth Edison Co.

Badger Service Co.
Abdoo, Richard A.: chairman, president, chief executive officer, Wisconsin Energy Corp.; president, director, Wisconsin Energy Corp. Foundation, Inc.

Baird Finance Corp.
Purcell, Paul E.: president, Baird & Co. (Robert W.)

Baker Hughes Inc.
Beghini, Victor Gene: trustee, USX Foundation, Inc.

Riley, H. John, Jr.: chairman, president, chief executive officer, Cooper Industries Foundation; chairman, president, chief executive officer, director, Cooper Industries, Inc.

Baker Investments Ltd.
Baker, Edward L.: chairman, director, Florida Rock Industries; president, Florida Rock Industries Foundation

Baker, Knapp & Tubbs
Black, Natalie A.: group vice president interiors, general counsel, director, Kohler Co.

Baldwin & Lyons Inc.
Bilton, Stuart Douglas: president, chief executive officer, Chicago Title Corp.; trustee, Chicago Title and Trust Co. Foundation

Baldwin Filters Inc.

Johnson, Norman E.: trustee, CLARCOR Foundation

Baldwin Hardware Corp.

Lyon, Wayne Barton: president, chief operating officer, director, Masco Corp.

Manoogian, Richard Alexander: chairman, chief executive officer, director, Masco Corp.

Ball Aerospace & Technology Corp.

Sissel, George A.: chairman, president, chief executive officer, director, Ball Corp.

Ball-Foster Glass Container Co. LLC

Harkins, James F., Jr.: treasurer, CertainTeed Corp. Foundation

Baltimore Aircoil Co. Inc.

Lohman, Gordon Russell: trustee, Amsted Industries Foundation; director, Amsted Industries Inc.

Banana Republic Inc.

Drexler, Millard S.: trustee, Gap Foundation/Gap Inc. Community Relations; president, chief executive officer, director, Gap, Inc.

Fisher, Donald George: president, Gap Foundation/Gap Inc. Community Relations; founder, chairman, director, Gap, Inc.

Banc One Corp.

Dorrance, Bennett: vice chairman, director, Campbell Soup Co.

Exley, Charles Errol, Jr.: trustee, Merck Co. Foundation

Steward, H. Leighton: chairman, chief executive officer, president, Louisiana Land & Exploration Co.; director, Louisiana Land & Exploration Co. Foundation

Stratton, Frederick Prescott, Jr.: chairman, chief executive officer, director, Briggs & Stratton Corp.; president, director, Briggs & Stratton Corp. Foundation

BancBoston Capital Corp.

Gifford, Charles Kilvert: trustee, BankBoston Charitable Foundation; chairman, chief executive officer, BankBoston Corp.

BancBoston Ventures Inc.

Swihart, Susannah: trustee, BankBoston Charitable Foundation

Banco Santander

Kamen, Harry Paul: chairman, president, chief executive officer, Metropolitan Life Insurance Co.

Bancwest Corp.

Tsui, John K.: director, First Hawaiian Foundation

Bandag Inc.

Jannotta, Edgar D.: president, Blair & Co. Foundation (William); senior director, Blair & Co. (William)

Bank America

Trujillo, Solomon D.: president, US West Foundation; president, chief executive officer, US West, Inc.

Bank America Illinois

Getz, Bert A.: chairman, Globe Corp.; president, director, Globe Foundation

Getz, Bert A., Jr.: executive vice president, Globe Corp.; vice president, Globe Foundation

Bank American FSB

Coulter, David A.: president, director, Bank of America

Bank Bentonville

Glass, David Dayne: trustee, Wal-Mart Foundation; director, Wal-Mart Stores, Inc.

Bank Boston NA

Gifford, Charles Kilvert: trustee, BankBoston Charitable Foundation; chairman, chief executive officer, BankBoston Corp.

Bank Hawaii

Johnson, Lawrence M.: president, Pacific Century Financial Corp.

Bank New England

Fish, Lawrence K.: trustee, Citizens Charitable Foundation; chairman, chief executive officer, Citizens Financial Group, Inc.

Bank New York Co. Inc.

D'Amato, Anthony S.: chairman, Borden Foundation, Inc.

Griffith, Alan Richard: vice chairman, Bank of New York Co., Inc.

Kogan, Richard Jay: chairman, chief executive officer, Schering-Plough Corp.; trustee, member, Schering-Plough Foundation

Luke, John A., Jr.: chairman, president, chief executive officer, director, Westvaco Corp.

Rein, Catherine Amelia: director, MetLife Foundation; vice president, Metropolitan Life Insurance Co.

Renyi, Thomas A.: president, chief executive officer, director, Bank of New York Co., Inc.

Bank Oklahoma Tulsa

Bailey, Keith E.: chairman, president, director, chief executive officer, Texas Gas Transmission Corp.; president, director, Williams Companies Foundation (The)

Bank One

Holmes, David Richard: chief executive officer, chief operating officer, director, Reynolds & Reynolds Co.

Bank One Arizona NA

Snell, Richard: chairman, president, chief executive officer, director, Arizona Public Service Co.

Bank One Corp.

Bryan, John Henry: chairman, Sara Lee Corp.; director, Sara Lee Foundation

Lowrie, William G.: president, deputy chief executive officer, director, BP Amoco Corp.

Manoogian, Richard Alexander: chairman, chief executive officer, director, Masco Corp.

McCormick, William Thomas, Jr.: chairman, chief executive officer, director, Consumers Energy Co.; chairman, Consumers Energy Foundation

Reilly, Thomas E., Jr.: trustee, Reilly Foundation; chairman, chief executive officer, director, Reilly Industries, Inc.

Thomas, Richard Lee: vice president, First National Bank of Chicago Foundation

Bank One Dayton NA

Forster, Peter Hans: chairman, director, Dayton Power and Light Co.

Bank One Kentucky Corp.

Hower, Frank Beard, Jr.: vice chairman, Anthem Foundation, Inc.

Bank One Youngstown Ohio

Tucker, Don Eugene: trustee, Commercial Intertech Foundation

Bank Tokyo Mitsubishi Trust Co.

Shapiro, Isaac: chairman, secretary, trustee, Ise Cultural Foundation

BankAmerica Corp.

Coker, Charles Westfield: trustee, Sonoco Foundation; vice president, Sonoco Products Co.

Crull, Timm F.: retired chairman, Nestle U.S.A. Inc.

Dickson, Alan Thomas: president, Dickson Foundation; chairman, Ruddick Corp.

Guinn, Donald Eugene: chairman emeritus, Pacific Mutual Life Insurance Co.

BankAmerica NA

Barad, Jill Elikann: director, Mattel Foundation; chairman, chief executive officer, director, Mattel Inc.

BankBoston NA

Wheeler, Thomas Beardsley: chairman, chief executive officer, Massachusetts Mutual Life Insurance Co.

Bankers Life Holding Inc.

Rogers, James E., Jr.: vice chairman, president, chief executive officer, Cinergy Corp.; vice chairman, director, Cinergy Foundation

Bankers Life Insurance New York

Sease, Gene Elwood: director, Central Newspapers Foundation

Bankers Trust Co.

Kalainov, Sam Charles: chairman, president, chief executive officer, AmerUS Group

Thoman, G. Richard: president, chief operating officer, Xerox Corp.

Bankers Trust New York Corp.

O'Reilly, F. Anthony John: chairman, trustee, Heinz Co. Foundation (H.J.); chairman, director, Heinz Co. (H.J.)

Bankers United Life Assurance Co.

Kolsrud, Douglas C.: executive vice president, chief investment officer, AEGON U.S.A. Inc.

Banncock Center Corp.

Hock, Delwin D.: chairman, New Century Energies

Banta Corp.

Richelsen, Raymond C.: director, 3M Foundation; executive vice president, Minnesota Mining & Manufacturing Co.

Banta Healthcare Products Inc.

Henseler, Gerald A.: executive vice president, chief financial officer, director, Banta Corp.; president, Banta Corp. Foundation

Barbara Franklin Enterprises

Franklin, Barbara Hackman: director, Dow Chemical Co.

Barnes Group Inc.

Fiondella, Robert William: chairman, president, chief executive officer, Phoenix Home Life Mutual Insurance Co.

Barnett Bank Tampa

Hyatt, Kenneth Ernest: chairman, president, chief executive officer, director, Walter Industries Inc.

Baseline Financial Service

Kasputys, Joseph Edward: chairman, trustee, Hitachi Foundation

Baseview Products Inc.

Farmer, Phillip W.: chairman, president, chief executive officer, Harris

Corp.; president, trustee, Harris Foundation

Basic Electronics Manufacturing Corp.

Kleinfeldt, Richard C.: vice president financial, chief financial officer, director, Giddings & Lewis

Basic Resources Inc.

Nye, Erle Allen: chairman, chief executive officer, director, TU Electric Co.

Basic Vegetable Products Inc.

James, George Barker, II: senior vice president, chief financial officer, Levi Strauss & Co.

Bassett Bedding

Sloan, Albert Frazier: director, Lance Foundation

Bassett Furniture Industries Inc.

Dickson, Alan Thomas: president, Dickson Foundation; chairman, Ruddick Corp.

McGlothlin, James W.: chief executive officer, United Coal Co. Charitable Foundation; chairman, chief executive officer, United Co.

Sloan, Albert Frazier: director, Lance Foundation

Bassett Furniture Industries North Carolina

Dickson, Alan Thomas: president, Dickson Foundation; chairman, Ruddick Corp.

Bassett Tables

Sloan, Albert Frazier: director, Lance Foundation

Bath Manufacturing

Moser, Robert W.: executive vice president, Springs Industries, Inc.

Battle Mountain Gold Co.

Wise, William Allen: chairman, president, chief executive officer, director, El Paso Energy Co.; chairman, director, El Paso Energy Foundation

Bausch & Lomb Inc.

DeSole, Domenico: president, chief executive officer, Gucci America Inc.

Linen, Jonathan S.: vice chairman, American Express Co.; trustee, American Express Foundation

Wolfe, Kenneth L.: chairman, chief executive officer, director, Hershey Foods Corp.

Baxter International Inc.

Ingram, Martha R.: chairman, director, Ingram Industries Inc.

Knight, Charles Field: chairman, chief executive officer, Emerson Electric Co.

Turner, Fred L.: senior chairman, director, McDonald's Corp.

Baybanks Inc.

Gifford, Charles Kilvert: trustee, BankBoston Charitable Foundation; chairman, chief executive officer, BankBoston Corp.

Bayer AG

Wehmeier, Helge H.: president, chief executive officer, director, Bayer Corp.

Baymont Inns Suites

Marcus, Stephen Howard: chairman, chief executive officer, Marcus Corp.; president, director, Marcus Corp. Foundation

Bcbsm Inc.

Bohn, Karen M.: president, Piper Jaffray Companies Foundation; chief executive officer, U.S. Bancorp Piper Jaffray

Bea Systems

Bartz, Carol A.: director, Autodesk Foundation; chairman, chief executive officer, Autodesk Inc.

Bear Creek Corp.

Beck, Edward W.: senior vice president, general counsel, secretary, director, Shaklee Corp.

Bearings Inc.

Bares, William G.: chairman, president, chief executive officer, Lubrizol Corp. (The); trustee, Lubrizol Foundation (The)

Beatrice Home Fashions

Gindi, Sam: trustee, Century 21 Associates Foundation

Bechtel Americas

Gunther, Donald J.: director, Bechtel Group, Inc.

Bechtel Construction Operations Inc.

Bechtel, Riley Peart: chairman, Bechtel Foundation; chairman, chief executive officer, director, Bechtel Group, Inc.

Zaccaria, Adrian: president, chief operating officer, director, Bechtel Group, Inc.

Bechtel Corp.

Gunther, Donald J.: director, Bechtel Group, Inc.

Zaccaria, Adrian: president, chief operating officer, director, Bechtel Group, Inc.

Bechtel Energy Corp.

Bechtel, Riley Peart: chairman, Bechtel Foundation; chairman, chief executive officer, director, Bechtel Group, Inc.

Bechtel Enterprises Inc.

Carter, John Douglas: executive vice president, director, Bechtel Group, Inc.

Bechtel Financial Services Co.

Bechtel, Riley Peart: chairman, Bechtel Foundation; chairman, chief executive officer, director, Bechtel Group, Inc.

Bechtel Group Inc.

Warner, Douglas Alexander, III: chairman, president, chief executive officer, director, Morgan & Co. Inc. (J.P.)

Bechtel International Inc.

Bechtel, Riley Peart: chairman, Bechtel Foundation; chairman, chief executive officer, director, Bechtel Group, Inc.

Zaccaria, Adrian: president, chief operating officer, director, Bechtel Group, Inc.

Bechtel Leasing Services Inc.

Bechtel, Riley Peart: chairman, Bechtel Foundation; chairman, chief executive officer, director, Bechtel Group, Inc.

Zaccaria, Adrian: president, chief operating officer, director, Bechtel Group, Inc.

Bechtel Operating Services Corp.

Bechtel, Riley Peart: chairman, Bechtel Foundation; chairman, chief executive officer, director, Bechtel Group, Inc.

Bechtel Overseas Corp.

Bechtel, Riley Peart: chairman, Bechtel Foundation; chairman, chief executive officer, director, Bechtel Group, Inc.

Zaccaria, Adrian: president, chief operating officer, director, Bechtel Group, Inc.

Bechtel Power Corp.

Bechtel, Riley Peart: chairman, Bechtel Foundation; chairman, chief executive officer, director, Bechtel Group, Inc.

Bechtel Systems Infrastructure

Zaccaria, Adrian: president, chief operating officer, director, Bechtel Group, Inc.

Beckman Bros

Canning, John Beckman: secretary, Rayonier Foundation

Beckman Coulter Inc.

Wilson, Dennis K.: vice president finance, chief financial officer, Beckman Coulter, Inc.

Beckman Instruments

Davis, Carolyne Kahle, PhD: trustee, Merck Co. Foundation

Becor Western Inc.

Wright, James O.: president, director, Badger Meter Foundation; chairman, director, Badger Meter, Inc.; director, Marshall & Ilsley Foundation, Inc.

Bee Chemical Co.

Johnston, William E., Junior: president, chief operating officer, director, Morton International Inc.

Belk Brothers Co.

Belk, John Montgomery: member board advisors, Belk Foundation; chairman, Belk-Simpson Department Stores

Belk Center Inc.

Belk, John Montgomery: member board advisors, Belk Foundation; chairman, Belk-Simpson Department Stores

Belk Department Store, Greensboro NC

Belk, John Montgomery: member board advisors, Belk Foundation; chairman, Belk-Simpson Department Stores

Belk Department Store, Rock Hill

Robinson, Leroy: member board advisors, Belk Foundation

Belk Enterprises Inc.

Belk, John Montgomery: member board advisors, Belk Foundation; chairman, Belk-Simpson Department Stores

Belk-Gallant, La Grange Georgia

Belk, John Montgomery: member board advisors, Belk Foundation; chairman, Belk-Simpson Department Stores

Robinson, Leroy: member board advisors, Belk Foundation

Belk-Hudson Inc. Spartanburg SC

Belk, John Montgomery: member board advisors, Belk Foundation; chairman, Belk-Simpson Department Stores

Belk-Hudson-Leggett

Belk, John Montgomery: member board advisors, Belk Foundation; chairman, Belk-Simpson Department Stores

Bell Atlantic Corp.

O'Brien, Thomas H., Jr.: chairman, chief executive officer, PNC Financial Services Group

Pfeiffer, Eckhard A.: president, chief executive officer, director, Compaq Computer Corp.

de Vink, Lodewijk J. R.: director, Warner-Lambert Charitable Foundation; president, chief operating officer, director, Warner-Lambert Co.

Bell Atlantic Maryland

Smith, Raymond W.: chairman, chief executive officer, director, Bell Atlantic Corp.

Bell Helicopter Textron Inc.

Cambell, Lewis B.: chairman, chief executive officer, director, Textron Inc.

Bell Sports Inc.

Kiely, W. Leo, III: president, chief operating officer, Coors Brewing Co.

BellSouth Corp.

Blanchard, James Hubert: chairman, chief executive officer, Synovus Financial Corp.

Mullin, Leo Francis: chairman, president, chief executive officer, Delta Air Lines, Inc.

Stavropoulos, William S.: president, chief executive officer, director, Dow Chemical Co.

Willis, Patricia: president, BellSouth Foundation

Belle Fouche Pipeline Co.

True, Jean Durland: trustee, True Foundation; partner, True Oil Co.

Bellemead Development Corp.

O'Hare, Dean Raymond: chairman, Chubb Corp.

Beloit Corp.

Grade, Jeffery T.: chairman, chief executive officer, director, Harnischfeger Industries; president, Harnischfeger Industries Foundation

Bemis Co. Inc.

Buxton, Winslow Hurlbert: chairman, president, chief executive officer, director, Pentair Inc.

Wurtele, C. Angus: president, Valspar Foundation

Bend Millwork System Inc.

Early, William Bernard: trustee, Jeld-wen Foundation; senior vice president, assistant secretary, director, Jeld-wen, Inc.

Wendt, Richard L.: trustee, Jeld-wen Foundation; chief executive officer, chairman, Jeld-wen, Inc.

Wendt, Roderick C.: trustee, Jeld-wen Foundation; president, director, Jeld-wen, Inc.

Wetter, Larry V.: trustee, Jeld-wen Foundation; vice chairman, director, Jeld-wen, Inc.

Beneficial California Inc.

Aldinger, William F., III: chairman, chief executive officer, director, Household International Inc.

Benefitamerica Inc.

Staton, Robert Emmett: president, Colonial Life & Accident Insurance Co.

Bennett-Ebsco Subscription Services

Stephens, Elton Bryson: founder, chairman, Ebsco Industries, Inc.

Bentley College

Cawley, Michael J.: vice president risk management, Eastern Enterprises

Benz Oil Inc.

Jacobs, Burleigh Edmund: president, director, Grede Foundation; chairman, Grede Foundries; director, Marshall & Ilsley Foundation, Inc.

Beringer Wine Estates

Franke, William Augustus: chairman, president, chief executive officer, America West Airlines, Inc.; director, Phelps Dodge Foundation

Berkel & Co. Contractors Inc.

Reintjes, Robert J., Sr.: director, Butler Manufacturing Co.; member, Butler Manufacturing Co. Foundation

Berkeley Management Corp.

Countryman, Gary Lee: chairman, Liberty Mutual Insurance Group

Berkley Co.

Pomerantz, Marvin Alvin: trustee, Mid-American Foundation

Berkshire Gas Co., Inc.

Trask, Robert B.: president, chief operating officer, director, Country Curtains, Inc.; clerk, trustee, High Meadow Foundation

Berkshire Hathaway Inc.

Scott, Walter, Jr.: member contributions committee, Kiewit Companies Foundation

Berkshire Health Systems

Trask, Robert B.: president, chief operating officer, director, Country Curtains, Inc.; clerk, trustee, High Meadow Foundation

Berkshire Life Insurance Co.

Standish, J. Spencer: chairman, director, Albany International Corp.

Berwick Industries Inc.

Farber, Jack: chairman, president, director, CSS Industries, Inc.; president, Farber Foundation

Bessemer Securities Corp.

Gelb, Richard Lee: director, New York Times Co. Foundation

Bestfoods

Castellini, Clateo: chairman, president, chief executive officer, Becton Dickinson & Co.

Bethesda Research Laboratories

Alberts, Bruce Michael, PhD: director, Genentech Foundation for Biomedical Sciences

Bethlehem Steel Corp.

Kamen, Harry Paul: chairman, president, chief executive officer, Metropolitan Life Insurance Co.

Beverly Enterprises

Davis, Carolyne Kahle, PhD: trustee, Merck Co. Foundation

Ford, Joseph 'Joe': chairman, chief executive officer, president, ALLTEL Corp.

Bindley Western Industries Inc.

Koch, Robert Louis, II: president, chief executive officer, director, Koch Enterprises, Inc.; president, director, Koch Foundation

Binghampton Press Co. Inc.

Curley, John J.: chairman, chief executive officer, director, Gannett Co., Inc.; chairman, Gannett Foundation

Binswanger International

Binswanger, David R.: president, chief executive officer, Binswanger Companies; treasurer, Binswanger Foundation

Binswanger, Frank G., Jr.: co-chairman, director, Binswanger Companies

Binswanger International Ltd.

Binswanger, Frank G., III: secretary, Binswanger Foundation

Binswanger Management Corp.

Binswanger, David R.: president, chief executive officer, Binswanger Companies; treasurer, Binswanger Foundation

Binswanger, Frank G., III: secretary, Binswanger Foundation

Binswanger, Frank G., Jr.: co-chairman, director, Binswanger Companies

Binswanger, John K.: co-chairman, director, Binswanger Companies; chairman, Binswanger Foundation

Brennan, Michael J.: chief financial officer, senior vice president, Binswanger Companies

Biosym Technologies Inc.

Booth, Chesleu Peter Washburn: senior vice president development, Corning Inc.; trustee, Corning Inc. Foundation

Biotechnology Development Corp.

Bogomolny, Robert Lee: director, Searle Charitable Trust; senior vice president, general counsel, secretary, Searle & Co. (G.D.)

Bird Electronic Corp.

Hessler, David J.: secretary, trustee, Jochum-Moll Foundation (The); president, partner, MTD Products Inc.

Bird Inc.

Hilyard, James E.: president, CertainTeed Corp.; director, CertainTeed Corp. Foundation

Mattson, Bradford C.: executive vice president exterior building products, CertainTeed Corp.

Bird Technologies Group Inc.

Hessler, David J.: secretary, trustee, Jochum-Moll Foundation (The); president, partner, MTD Products Inc.

Birmingham Airport Authority

McMahon, John J., Jr.: trustee, McWane Foundation; chairman, president, chief executive officer, treasurer, McWane Inc.

Birmingham Steel Corp.

McGlothlin, James W.: chief executive officer, United Coal Co. Charitable Foundation; chairman, chief executive officer, United Co.

Osborne, Richard de Jongh: director, ASARCO Foundation; chairman, chief executive officer, director, ASARCO Inc.

Bison Baseball Inc.

Rich, Robert E., Sr.: president, treasurer, Rich Family Foundation; founder, chairman, director, Rich Products Corp.

Black & Decker Corp.

Willes, Mark Hinckley: chairman, president, chief executive officer, Times Mirror Co.; chairman, Times Mirror Foundation

Black Box Corp.

Newlin, William Rankin: trustee, Kennametal Foundation

Black Hills Trucking Inc.

True, David: partner, True Oil Co.

True, Diemer: partner, True Oil Co.

Blackhawk Coal Co.

Draper, Ernest Linn, Jr.: chairman, president, chief executive officer, director, American Electric Power

Blackrock Group

Hirsch, Laurence E.: chairman, chief executive officer, director, Centex Corp.

Blackstone Group

Stockman, David A.: co-chairman, director, Collins & Aikman Corp.; president, director, Collins & Aikman Foundation

Blade Broadcasting Co.

Block, Allan James: vice president, trustee, Blade Foundation; director, Toledo Blade Co.

Blade Communication

Block, John Robinson: vice president, trustee, Blade Foundation

Bliss-Salem Inc.

Wareham, James Lyman: president, AK Steel Corp.

Block Financial Corp.

Salizzoni, Frank L.: vice chairman, Block Foundation (H&R); president, chief executive officer, director, Block, Inc. (H&R)

Block HR Group Inc.

Salizzoni, Frank L.: vice chairman, Block Foundation (H&R); president, chief executive officer, director, Block, Inc. (H&R)

Bloomington Unlimited

Johnson, James Lawrence: chairman emeritus, Walter Industries Inc.

Blount Industries Power Equipment Group

Blount, Winton Malcolm, Jr.: chairman, Blount International, Inc.

Blue Circle Industries PLC

Walters, Peter: chairman, SmithKline Beecham Corp.

Blue Cross & Blue Shield Minnesota

Bohn, Karen M.: president, Piper Jaffray Companies Foundation; chief executive officer, U.S. Bancorp Piper Jaffray

Blue Cross & Blue Shield Oregon

Cameron, Gerry B.: chairman, director, U.S. Bancorp

Blue Cross & Blue Shield United

Siewert, Penny: vice president regional services, United Wisconsin Services; vice president, secretary, treasurer, United Wisconsin Services Foundation

Blue Cross & Blue Shield United Wisconsin

Granoff, Mark Howard: vice president, United Wisconsin Services Foundation

Hefty, Thomas R.: chairman, president, chief executive officer, United Wisconsin Services

Blue Ridge Airport

Spilman, Robert H.: chairman, chief executive officer, Bassett Furniture Industries; chairman, director, Bassett Furniture Industries Fdn.

Blue Ridge Industrial Sup Co.

McGlothlin, James W.: chief executive officer, United Coal Co. Charitable Foundation; chairman, chief executive officer, United Co.

Blue Ridge Industrial Supply Co.

Bell, Wayne L.: secretary, United Coal Co. Charitable Foundation

Bluegrass Coca-Cola Bottling Co.

Alm, John Richard: director, Coca-Cola Foundation

Bluet Investment Co. Ltd.

Jacobsen, James C.: vice chairman, Kellwood Co.; vice president, director, Kellwood Foundation

Boeing Co.

Duberstein, Kenneth: director, Cinergy Foundation

Pigott, Charles McGee: president, director, PACCAR Foundation; chairman emeritus, director, PACCAR Inc.

Platt, Lewis Emmett: chairman, Hewlett-Packard Co.

Weyerhaeuser, George Hunt: director, Weyerhaeuser Co.; trustee, Weyerhaeuser Co. Foundation

Boeing Corinth Co.

Condit, Philip Murray: chairman, chief executive officer, director, Boeing Co.

Boeing Corp.

Bryson, John E.: chairman, chief executive officer, Edison International

Vagelos, Pindaros Roy: trustee, Prudential Insurance Co. of America

Boiler Inspection & Insurance Co. Canada

Kreh, Gordon W.: president, chief executive officer, director, Hartford Steam Boiler Inspection & Insurance Co.

Boise Cascade Corp.

Carroll, Philip Joseph: chairman, chief executive officer, Fluor Corp.; chairman, trustee, Fluor Foundation

Michael, Gary Glenn: chairman, chief executive officer, director, Albertson's Inc.

Bolt Beranek & Newman

Hatsopoulos, George Nicholas: founder, chairman, chief executive officer, director, Thermo Electron Corp.; committee member, Thermo Electron Foundation

Boney Wilson Sons Inc.

Bowne, Garrett D., IV: treasurer, Hannaford Charitable Foundation

Farrington, Hugh G.: president, chief executive officer, director, Hannaford Brothers Co.

Borden Chemical Co.

D'Amato, Anthony S.: chairman, Borden Foundation, Inc.

Borden Chemical Inc.

Kidder, C. Robert: chairman, president, chief executive officer, director, Borden, Inc.

Borden Chemicals Plastics

Draper, Ernest Linn, Jr.: chairman, president, chief executive officer, director, American Electric Power

Borden Foods Corp.

Kidder, C. Robert: chairman, president, chief executive officer, director, Borden, Inc.

Borg-Warner Automotive Inc.

Rau, John E.: trustee, Chicago Title and Trust Co. Foundation

Boston Edison Co.

Countryman, Gary Lee: chairman, Liberty Mutual Insurance Group

Gifford, Charles Kilvert: trustee, BankBoston Charitable Foundation; chairman, chief executive officer, BankBoston Corp.

Boston Gas Co.

Flaherty, Walter J.: chief financial officer, senior vice president, Eastern Enterprises; trustee, Eastern Enterprises Foundation

Boston Globe Publishing

Taylor, William Osgood: chairman, chief executive officer, director, Boston Globe (The); chairman, director, Boston Globe Foundation; director, New York Times Co. Foundation

Boston Group Holdings Inc.

Smith, W. Keith: senior vice chairman, member corporate review committee, director, Mellon Financial Corp.

Boston Medical Center

Cogan, John Francis, Jr.: president, chief executive officer, director, Pioneer Group

Boston Safe Deposit & Trust Co.

Smith, W. Keith: senior vice chairman, member corporate review committee, director, Mellon Financial Corp.

Boulder Publishing Inc.

Conant, Colleen Christner: branch manager, Scripps Co. (E.W.); trustee, Scripps Howard Foundation

Boundary Gas Inc.

Catell, Robert Barry: chairman, chief executive officer, Brooklyn Union

Bourns Inc.

MacBeth, Anita L.: trustee, Bourns Foundation

Bowater Inc.

Pate, James Leonard: chairman, chief executive officer, director, Pennzoil-Quaker State Co.

Bowne & Co. Inc.

Schwarz, H. Marshall: chairman, chief executive officer, United States Trust Co. of New York

Boyd Gaming Corp.

Maffie, Michael O.: president, chief executive officer, director, Southwest Gas Corp.; trustee, Southwest Gas Corp. Foundation

Bracknell Corp.

Melnuk, Paul D.: president, chief executive officer, Clark Refining & Marketing

Bradley Paper Co.

Russell, Frank Eli: president, Central Newspapers Foundation; chairman, Central Newspapers, Inc.

Brake Supply Co.

Koch, Robert Louis, II: president, chief executive officer, director, Koch Enterprises, Inc.; president, director, Koch Foundation

Muehlbauer, James Herman: vice president, director, Koch Foundation

Branch Banking & Trust Co.

Allison, John Andrew, IV: chairman, chief executive officer, director, Branch Banking & Trust Co.

Brandrud Furniture Inc.

Wiborg, James Hooker: director, PACCAR Foundation

Brass Craft Manufacturing Co.

Lyon, Wayne Barton: president, chief operating officer, director, Masco Corp.

Bretlin Inc.

Frierson, Daniel K.: chairman, chief executive officer, Dixie Group, Inc. (The); president, trustee, Dixie Yarns Foundation, Inc.

Klein, Starr T.: secretary, treasurer, trustee, Dixie Yarns Foundation, Inc.

Bridgeport Machines Inc.

Fried, Eliot M.: managing director, Walter Industries Inc.

Briggs & Stratton Corp.

O'Toole, Robert Joseph: director, Firstar Milwaukee Foundation; chairman, president, chief executive officer, director, Smith Corp. (A.O.); director,

Smith Foundation, Inc. (A.O.)

Rogers, C. B., Jr.: chairman, Equifax Foundation; chairman, director, Equifax Inc.

Brinker International Inc.

Carty, Donald J.: vice president, treasurer, AMR/American Airlines Foundation; president, chairman, chief executive officer, director, AMR Corp.

Oesterreicher, James E.: chairman, chief executive officer, director, Penney Co., Inc. (J.C.)

Bristol Caribbean Inc.

Gelb, Richard Lee: director, New York Times Co. Foundation

Bristol-Myers Squibb Co.

Cambell, Lewis B.: chairman, chief executive officer, director, Textron Inc.

Gerstner, Louis Vincent, Jr.: chairman, chief executive officer, director, International Business Machines Corp.

Brit Pharma Group

Leschly, Jan: chief executive officer, SmithKline Beecham Corp.

Brita Products Co.

Rose, Karen M.: vice president, treasurer, Clorox Co.

British Columbia Forest Products Ltd.

Correll, Alston Dayton 'Pete', Jr.: chairman, president, chief executive officer, director, Georgia-Pacific Corp.; director, Georgia-Pacific Foundation

British Columbia Telecommunications

Masin, Michael Terry: vice chairman, president international, director, GTE Corp.; trustee, GTE Foundation

Broadcaster Press Inc.

Herman, William A., III: secretary, treasurer, director, Morris Communications Corp.

Morris, William Shivers, III: founder, chairman, chief executive officer, director, Morris Communications Corp.; trustee, Stauffer Communications Foundation

Morris, William Shivers, IV: president, director, Morris Communications Corp.; trustee, Stauffer Communications Foundation

Broadmoor Hotel Inc.

Gaylord, Edward Lewis: chairman, chief executive officer, director, publisher, Oklahoma Publishing Co.; trustee, Oklahoman Foundation (The)

Broadmoor Housing Inc.

Rein, Catherine Amelia: director, MetLife Foundation; vice president, Metropolitan Life Insurance Co.

Brothers Investment Co.

Belk, John Montgomery: member board advisors, Belk Foundation; chairman, Belk-Simpson Department Stores

Brown & Root Inc.

Colgan, Celeste: vice president, secretary, Halliburton Foundation, Inc.

Brown & Sharpe Manufacturing Co.

Nelson, John Martin: chairman, director, TJX Companies, Inc.

Brown Group Inc.

Maritz, William Edward: chairman, chief executive officer, president, Maritz Inc.

Toll, Daniel Roger: trustee, Kemper Foundation (James S.)

Brown Shoe Co. Inc.

Fromm, Ronald A.: vice president, Brown Shoe Co., Inc.

Liddy, Richard A.: chairman, president, chief executive officer, GenAmerica Corp.

Browning-Ferris Industries Colorado

Ranck, Bruce E.: president, chief executive officer, director, Browning-Ferris Industries Inc.

Browning-Ferris Industries Inc.

Grinstein, Gerald: director, PACCAR Inc.

Bruce Cloud Equipment Co. Inc.

Cloud, Bruce Benjamin, Sr.: vice chairman, director, Zachry Co. (H.B.)

Brunswick Corp.

Bleustein, Jeffrey L.: president, chief executive officer, director, Harley-Davidson Co.

Kennedy, George Danner: trustee, Kemper Foundation (James S.)

Brunswick Pulp & Paper Co.

Correll, Alston Dayton 'Pete', Jr.: chairman, president, chief executive officer, director, Georgia-Pacific Corp.; director, Georgia-Pacific Foundation

Brush Wellman Inc.

Bersticker, Albert C.: chairman, director, chief executive officer, Ferro Corp.; president, trustee, Ferro Foundation

Burner, David L.: chairman, president, chief executive officer, director, BFGoodrich Co.

Buckeye Discount Inc.

Iott, Richard B.: president, chief executive officer, director, Seaway Food Town, Inc.

Iott, Wallace D.: chairman, director, Seaway Food Town, Inc.

Bucon Inc.

Pratt, Donald Henry: chairman, Butler Manufacturing Co.; vice president, trustee, Butler Manufacturing Co. Foundation

Bud's Warehouse Outlets

Soderquist, Donald G.: trustee, Wal-Mart Foundation; senior vice chairman, director, Wal-Mart Stores, Inc.

Budgetel Inns Inc.

Marcus, Stephen Howard: chairman, chief executive officer, Marcus Corp.; president, director, Marcus Corp. Foundation

Buell Motorcycle Co.

Bleustein, Jeffrey L.: president, chief executive officer, director, Harley-Davidson Co.

Buena Vista Home Entertainment

Litvack, Sanford M.: senior executive vice president, chief corporate operations, director, Disney Co. (Walt)

Buffalo Niagara Partnership

Wilmers, Robert George: chairman, president, chief executive officer, Manufacturers & Traders Trust Co.

Builders Engr Co.

Stupp, Robert P.: president, director, Stupp Brothers Bridge & Iron Co.; trustee, Stupp Brothers Bridge & Iron Co. Foundation

Bulova Corp.

Tisch, Laurence Alan: chairman, co-chief executive officer, CBS Corp.; trustee, Loews Foundation

Tisch, Preston Robert: chairman, director, CBS Foundation; co-chairman, co-chief executive officer, director, CNA; trustee, Loews Foundation

Bulova Watch Corp.

Tisch, Preston Robert: chairman, director, CBS Foundation; co-chairman, co-chief executive officer, director, CNA; trustee, Loews Foundation

Burlington Northern Santa Fe Corp.

Springer, Denis E.: senior vice president, chief financial officer, Burlington Northern Santa Fe Corp.; director, Burlington Northern Santa Fe Foundation

Whisler, J. Steven: chairman, president, chief executive officer, Phelps Dodge Corp.

Whitacre, Edward E., Jr.: chairman, director, chief executive officer, SBC Communications Inc.

Burlington Research Hydrocarb

Dubois, Everett D.: treasurer, Burlington Resources Foundation; senior vice president, treasurer, Burlington Resources, Inc.

Burlington Resources Inc.

LaMacchia, John Thomas: trustee, Cincinnati Bell Foundation, Inc.; president, chief executive officer, director, Cincinnati Bell Inc.

McDonald, James F.: president, chief executive officer, Scientific-Atlanta, Inc.

Scott, Walter, Jr.: member contributions committee, Kiewit Companies Foundation

Steward, H. Leighton: chairman, chief executive officer, president, Louisiana Land & Exploration Co.; director, Louisiana Land & Exploration Co. Foundation

Williams, John A.: president, chief executive officer, Louisiana Land & Exploration Co.; director, Louisiana Land & Exploration Co. Foundation

Busch Mechanical Services Inc.

Brown, JoBeth Goode: trustee, Anheuser-Busch Companies, Inc.

Busch Media Group Inc.

Busch, August Adolphus, III: chairman, president, chief executive officer, Anheuser-Busch Companies, Inc.

Bush Boake Allen Inc.

Reed, James M.: trustee, Union Camp Charitable Trust; vice chairman, chief financial officer, director, Union Camp Corp.

Bush Brothers

Costley, Gary E.: chairman, president, chief executive officer, director, International Multifoods Corp.

Bushnell Horace Memorial Hall Corp.

Darling, Robert Edward, Jr.: chairman, Ensign-Bickford Foundation

Business Leases Inc.

Whaley, Ronald L.: foundation administrator, Solo Cup Foundation

Business Mens Assurance Co.

Hall, Donald Joyce: chairman board, director, Hallmark Cards Inc.; chairman, Hallmark Corporate Foundation

Kemper, David Woods: chairman, president, chief executive officer, director, Commerce Bancshares, Inc.

Butler Manufacturing Co.

Christensen, Gary M.: president, Pella Corp.; president, director, Pella Rolscreen Foundation

Haw, C. L. William: member, Butler Manufacturing Co. Foundation

Novello, Robert J.: chairman, Butler Manufacturing Co.; member, Butler Manufacturing Co. Foundation

Reintjes, Robert J., Sr.: director, Butler Manufacturing Co.; member, Butler Manufacturing Co. Foundation

Buttrey Food & Drug Stores Co.

Michael, Gary Glenn: chairman, chief executive officer, director, Albertson's Inc.

Byrne Plywood Co.

Erb, Frederick A.: president, Erb Foundation

C Tri Inc.

Gaylord, Edward Lewis: chairman, chief executive officer, director, publisher, Oklahoma Publishing Co.; trustee, Oklahoman Foundation (The)

C&S/Sovran Corp.

Bottorff, Dennis C.: chairman, president, chief executive officer, director, First American Corp.

C-SPAN

Block, Allan James: vice president, trustee, Blade Foundation; director, Toledo Blade Co.

CANEBSCO Subscription Services Ltd.

Stephens, Elton Bryson: founder, chairman, Ebsco Industries, Inc.

CBS Corp.

Leschly, Jan: chief executive officer, SmithKline Beecham Corp.

Schacht, Henry Brewer: director, Cummins Engine Foundation

CBS Inc.

Bergerac, Michel Christian: director, CBS Foundation

CCB & Trust Co.

Roessler-Alsoa, Ernest C.: president, chief executive officer, director, CCB Financial Corp.

CCC Holdings Inc.

Lipp, Robert Irving: chief executive officer, Citigroup; vice president, treasurer, trustee, Citigroup Foundation

CDI Corp.

Blankley, Walter Elwood: president, director, AMETEK Foundation; chairman, director, AMETEK, Inc.

CDS International

Mueller, Gerd Dieter: executive vice president, chief financial officer, director, chief administrative officer, Bayer Corp.; president, Bayer Foundation

CENEX Inc.

Glanzer, Aaron: trustee, Cenex Harvest States Foundation

Harris, Fred: trustee, Cenex Harvest States Foundation

Johnson, Douglas: trustee, Cenex Harvest States Foundation

Traphagen, Richard: trustee, Cenex Harvest States Foundation

CEO Venture Fund

Newlin, William Rankin: trustee, Kennametal Foundation

CF Industries Inc.

Copenhaver, Don: director, MFA Foundation; president, chief executive officer, MFA Inc.

Gherty, John E.: president, chief executive officer, Land O'Lakes, Inc.

CHC International Inc.

Arison, M. Micky: trustee, Arison Foundation; chairman, president, chief executive officer, Carnival Corp.

CIBC Subs

Flood, Al: chairman, chief executive officer, CIBC Oppenheimer

CIES

Golub, Lewis: chairman, chief executive officer, director, Golub Corp.

CIGNA Corp.

Campbell, Robert Henderson: chairman, chief executive officer, Sunoco Inc.

Larson, Peter N.: chairman, chief executive officer, director, Brunswick Corp.

Shoemate, Charles Richard: chairman, president, chief executive officer, Bestfoods

Zilkha, Ezra Khedouri: president, treasurer, Zilkha Foundation, Inc.; president, Zilkha & Sons

CIGNA Mutual Funds

Jones, Russell H.: officer, Kaman Corp.

CIT Group/ Commercial Services Inc.

Pollicino, Joseph Anthony: executive vice chairman, CIT Group Foundation; vice chairman, director, CIT Group, Inc. (The)

CIT Group/Credit Finance

Pollicino, Joseph Anthony: executive vice chairman, CIT Group Foundation; vice chairman, director, CIT Group, Inc. (The)

CMB-Sonoco Europe

Moran, Harry J.: executive vice president, Sonoco Products Co.

CMS Energy Corp.

Pierre, Percy A.: trustee, Hitachi Foundation

Yasinsky, John B.: chairman, president, chief executive officer, GenCorp

CMS Enterprises Co.

McCormick, William Thomas, Jr.: chairman, chief executive officer, director, Consumers Energy Co.; chairman, Consumers Energy Foundation

CNA Casualty California

Chookaszian, Dennis Haig: chairman, chief executive officer, CNA

Jokiel, Peter E.: senior vice president, chief financial officer, CNA

CNA Financial Corp.

Bush, Antoinette Cook: partner, CNA

Chookaszian, Dennis Haig: chairman, chief executive officer, CNA

Noha, Edward J.: director, CNA Foundation

Thomas, Richard Lee: vice president, First National Bank of Chicago Foundation

Tisch, James S.: president, chief executive officer, director, CNA

Tisch, Laurence Alan: chairman, co-chief executive officer, CBS Corp.; trustee, Loews Foundation

Tisch, Preston Robert: chairman, director, CBS Foundation; co-chairman, co-chief executive officer, director, CNA; trustee, Loews Foundation

CNB Bancshares

Koch, Robert Louis, II: president, chief executive officer, director, Koch Enterprises, Inc.; president, director, Koch Foundation

CNG Power Co.

Williams, Stephen E.: senior vice president, general counsel, Consolidated Natural Gas Co.; president, Consolidated Natural Gas System Foundation

CNG Storage Service Co.

Williams, Stephen E.: senior vice president, general counsel, Consolidated Natural Gas Co.; president, Consolidated Natural Gas System Foundation

CNO&TP Railroad

Street, Gordon P., Jr.: chairman, president, chief executive officer, director, North American Royalties; trustee, North American Royalties Foundation

CR Bard Inc.

Breslawsky, Marc C.: president, chief operating officer, Pitney Bowes Inc.

CRC Industries Inc.

Berwind, C. Graham, Jr.: chairman, president, chief executive officer, Berwind Group

CRC Leasing & Management Inc.

Carlson, Curtis Leroy: chairman, director, Carlson Companies, Inc.; president, treasurer, Carlson Family Foundation (Curtis L.)

CRSS Constructors Inc.

Watson, Noel G.: vice president, director, Jacobs Engineering Foundation; president, chief executive officer, director, Jacobs Engineering Group

CSW Credit Inc.

Rosilier, Glenn D.: executive vice president, chief financial officer, Central & South West Services

CSX Corp.

Brinegar, Claude Stout: trustee, Unocal Foundation

Burrus, Robert Lewis, Jr.: trustee, Circuit City Foundation

Gottwald, Bruce Cobb: chairman, chief executive officer, director, Ethyl Corp.

McGlothlin, James W.: chief executive officer, United Coal Co. Charitable Foundation; chairman, chief executive officer, United Co.

CSX Transportation

Snow, John William: chairman, president, chief executive officer, CSX Corp.

CT Natural Gas Corp.

Fonteyne, Herman J.: president, chief executive officer, director, Ensign-Bickford Industries

CUB Foods Green Bay Inc.

Wright, Michael William: chairman, president, chief executive officer, director, SuperValu, Inc.

CUMIS General Insurance Co.

Kitchen, Michael B.: president, chief executive officer, director, CUNA Mutual Group; secretary, treasurer, executive officer, CUNA Mutual Group Foundation, Inc.

CUMIS Life Insurance Co.

Kitchen, Michael B.: president, chief executive officer, director, CUNA Mutual Group; secretary, treasurer, executive officer, CUNA Mutual Group Foundation, Inc.

CUNA Mutual Insurance Group

Wilson, Larry: president, director, CUNA Mutual Group Foundation, Inc.

CUNA Mutual Insurance Society

Springer, Neil A.: vice president, director, CUNA Mutual Group Foundation, Inc.

CV Energy Resources
Young, Robert Harris: president, chief executive officer, Central Vermont Public Service Corp.

CVD Inc.
Johnston, William E., Junior: president, chief operating officer, director, Morton International Inc.

CVS Corp.
Joyce, William H.: chairman, president, chief executive officer, chief operating officer, Union Carbide Corp.
Lautenbach, Terry Robert: trustee, Air Products Foundation

Cable & Wireless PLC
Brown, Richard Harris: chairman, chief executive officer, director, EDS Corp.

Cabot Corp.
Cabot, John G. L.: vice chairman, Kinder Morgn
Hiatt, Arnold Selig: chairman, director, Stride Rite Foundation
O'Brien, John Francis, Jr.: president, chief executive officer, Allmerica Financial Corp.

Cadence Design Systems Inc.
Bartz, Carol A.: director, Autodesk Foundation; chairman, chief executive officer, Autodesk Inc.

CalEnergy Co. Inc.
Scott, Walter, Jr.: member contributions committee, Kiewit Companies Foundation

Cala Co.
Golleher, George C: president, Ralph's-Food 4 Less Foundation; chief executive officer, Ralph's Grocery Co.

Cala Foods Inc.
Golleher, George C: president, Ralph's-Food 4 Less Foundation; chief executive officer, Ralph's Grocery Co.

California Newspapers Inc.
McCorkindale, Douglas H.: vice chairman, president, Gannett Co., Inc.; president, Gannett Foundation

California Water Service Co.
Harris, Edward D., Jr.: director, Genentech Foundation for Biomedical Sciences

Callaway Editions Inc.
Callaway, Ely Reeves, Jr.: chairman, Callaway Golf Co.

Callaway Golf Co.
Duffy, John: director, Callaway Golf Co. Foundation

Calstart
Felsinger, Donald E.: president, chief executive officer, Sempra Energy
Mitchell, Warren I.: president, director, Southern California Gas Co.

Caltex Pacific Indonesia
Elkins, Lloyd Edwin, Junior: vice president, Chevron Corp.

Caltex Petroleum Corp.
Caccamo, Aldo M.: vice president public affairs, Chevron Corp.
Elkins, Lloyd Edwin, Junior: vice president, Chevron Corp.

Calvin Klein Jeanswear Co.
Schwartz, Barry K.: chairman, chief executive officer, director, Calvin Klein

Calvin Klein Sport
Klein, Calvin Richard: president, Calvin Klein

Camax Systems Inc.
Malmberg, David Curtis: director, National City Bank of Minneapolis

Cambridge Associates
Zilkha, Ezra Khedouri: president, treasurer, Zilkha Foundation, Inc.; president, Zilkha & Sons

Cambridge Trust Co.
Bettacchi, Robert J.: senior vice president, Grace & Co. (W.R.)

Campbell Investment Co.
Anderson, Basil L.: executive vice president, chief financial officer, Campbell Soup Co.
Harris, Ralph A.: vice president corporate development, Campbell Soup Co.
Lord, Gerald S.: vice president, controller, Campbell Soup Co.

Campbell Soup Co.
Dorrance, Bennett: vice chairman, director, Campbell Soup Co.
Foster, Kent B.: president, director, GTE Corp.; trustee, GTE Foundation
Golub, Harvey: chairman, chief executive officer, director, American Express Co.; trustee, American Express Foundation
Rydin, Craig: trustee, Campbell Soup Foundation
Stewart, Donald M.: director, New York Times Co. Foundation

Campbell Soup Co. International Grocery Europe/Canada
Thrasher, F. Martin: senior vice president, Campbell Soup Co.

Campbell's Fresh Inc.
Lanning, Donald R.: vice president grocery operations, Campbell Soup Co.

Canada Trust
Pitts, John Wilson: director, PACCAR Foundation

Canadian Airlines
Crandall, Robert Lloyd: director, AMR Corp.

Canadian Niagara Power
Davis, William E.: chairman, chief executive officer, Niagara Mohawk Holdings Inc.

Canadian Northern Shield Insurance Co.
Kitchen, Michael B.: president, chief executive officer, director, CUNA Mutual Group; secretary, treasurer, executive officer, CUNA Mutual Group Foundation, Inc.

Canadian Recreation Products
Jacobsen, James C.: vice chairman, Kellwood Co.; vice president, director, Kellwood Foundation

Canadian Salt Co. Ltd.
Johnston, William E., Junior: president, chief operating officer, director, Morton International Inc.

Canadian-Montana Gas Co. Ltd.
Gannon, Robert P.: chairman, president, director, chief executive officer, Montana Power Co.; president, director, Montana Power Foundation
Pederson, Jerrold P.: vice president, chief financial officer, director, Montana Power Co.; director, Montana Power Foundation

Canji Inc.
Wyszomierski, Jack L.: trustee, member, Schering-Plough Foundation

Cantel Industries Inc.
Slovin, Bruce: president, director, Revlon Inc.

Canton Sales & Storage Co.
Cohen, Maryjo Rose: president, chief executive officer, director, National Presto Industries, Inc.; vice president, treasurer, trustee, Presto Foundation
Cohen, Melvin Samuel: chairman, National Presto Industries, Inc.; chairman, president, trustee, Presto Foundation

Canyon Ranch
Blank, Arthur M.: president, chief executive officer, director, Home Depot, Inc.

Cape Publishing Inc.
McCorkindale, Douglas H.: vice chairman, president, Gannett Co., Inc.; president, Gannett Foundation

Capital Formation Inc.
Dillon, John T.: chairman, chief executive officer, director, International Paper Co.

Capital Gazette Newspapers Inc.
Barry, Richard Francis, III: director, Landmark Communications Foundation; vice chairman, Landmark Communications Inc.

Capital Marine Supply Inc.
Raskin, Fred C.: president, chief operating officer, Eastern Enterprises; trustee, Eastern Enterprises Foundation

Capital Security Insurance
Baird, Patrick S.: chief operating officer, chief financial officer, AEGON U.S.A. Inc.

Capitol Aggregates Inc. Delaware
Ebrom, Charles E.: director, vice president, Zachry Co. (H.B.); treasurer, trustee, Zachry Foundation (The)

Capitol Cement Corp.
Burrus, Robert Lewis, Jr.: trustee, Circuit City Foundation

Capitol Mortgage Bankers Inc.
Jastrow, Kenneth M., II: director, Temple-Inland Foundation

Capitol South Urdan Redev Corp.
McCoy, John Bonnet: president, chief executive officer, Ameritech Corp.

Carba Realty Inc.
Reed, Scott Eldridge: senior executive vice president, chief financial officer, Branch Banking & Trust Co.

Carborundum Specialty CP
Borst, Stephen L.: assistant secretary, CertainTeed Corp.

Carborundum Specialty Products
Amoss, George B.: vice president finance, chief financial officer, CertainTeed Corp.; chief financial officer, CertainTeed Corp. Foundation
Ayotte, Robert C.: executive vice president, director, CertainTeed Corp.; vice president, director, Norton Co. Foundation
Harkins, James F., Jr.: treasurer, CertainTeed Corp. Foundation

Cardinal Health Inc.
McCoy, John Bonnet: president, chief executive officer, Ameritech Corp.

Cardinal Operating Co.
Draper, Ernest Linn, Jr.: chairman, president, chief executive officer, director, American Electric Power
Lhota, William J.: executive vice president, American Electric Power

Cargill Inc.
Bonsignore, Michael Robert: director, Honeywell Foundation; chairman, chief executive officer, director, Honeywell International Inc.
DeSimone, Livio Diego: chairman, chief executive officer, Minnesota Mining & Manufacturing Co.
Johnson, Samuel Curtis: chairman, director, president, Johnson & Son (S.C.); chairman, trustee, Johnson Wax Fund (S.C.)
Kovacevich, Richard M.: chairman, president, chief executive officer, Norwest Corp.; director, Norwest Foundation
Wright, Michael William: chairman, president, chief executive officer, director, SuperValu, Inc.

Carl Zeiss Inc.
Shapiro, Isaac: chairman, secretary, trustee, Ise Cultural Foundation

Carlson Co. Inc.
Nelson, Glen David, MD: vice chairman, Medtronic, Inc.

Carlson Holdings Inc.
Carlson, Curtis Leroy: chairman, director, Carlson Companies, Inc.; president, treasurer, Carlson Family Foundation (Curtis L.)
Nelson, Glen David, MD: vice chairman, Medtronic, Inc.
Nelson, Marilyn Carlson: chairman, chief executive officer, president, Carlson Companies, Inc.
Redgrave, Martyn R.: executive vice president, chief financial officer, Carlson Companies, Inc.

Carlson Hospitality Group
Carlson, Curtis Leroy: chairman, director, Carlson Companies, Inc.; president, treasurer, Carlson Family Foundation (Curtis L.)

Carlson Leasing Inc.
Carlson, Curtis Leroy: chairman, director, Carlson Companies, Inc.; president, treasurer, Carlson Family Foundation (Curtis L.)

Carlson Marketing Group Inc.
Carlson, Curtis Leroy: chairman, director, Carlson Companies, Inc.; president, treasurer, Carlson Family Foundation (Curtis L.)

Carlson Properties Inc.
Carlson, Curtis Leroy: chairman, director, Carlson Companies, Inc.; president, treasurer, Carlson Family Foundation (Curtis L.)

Carlson Real Estate Co. Inc.
Carlson, Curtis Leroy: chairman, director, Carlson Companies, Inc.; president, treasurer, Carlson Family Foundation (Curtis L.)

Carlson Travel Group
Carlson, Curtis Leroy: chairman, director, Carlson Companies, Inc.; president, treasurer, Carlson Family Foundation (Curtis L.)

Carlspan SRL
Baker, James Kendrick: chairman, director, Arvin Foundation; vice chairman, director, Arvin Industries, Inc.

Carlyle Capital LP
Leatherdale, Douglas West: chairman, chief executive officer, president, Saint Paul Companies Inc.

Carmax Auto Superstores Inc.
Sharp, Richard L.: trustee, Circuit City Foundation; chairman, chief executive officer, director, Circuit City Stores, Inc.

Carnation Corp.
Crull, Timm F.: retired chairman, Nestle U.S.A. Inc.

Carnegie Body Co.
Hessler, David J.: secretary, trustee, Jochum-Moll Foundation (The); president, partner, MTD Products Inc.

Carnegie Foundation Advancement Teaching
Lyall, Katharine Culbert: trustee, Kemper Foundation (James S.)

Carnival Cruise Lines
Arison, M. Micky: trustee, Arison Foundation; chairman, president, chief executive officer, Carnival Corp.

Carolina Medicorp Inc.
Baker, Leslie Mayo, Jr.: president, chief executive officer, chairman, Wachovia Bank of North Carolina NA; chairman, Wachovia Foundation, Inc. (The)

Carolina Power & Light Co.
Baker, Leslie Mayo, Jr.: president, chief executive officer, chairman, Wachovia Bank of North Carolina NA; chairman, Wachovia Foundation, Inc. (The)
Coker, Charles Westfield: trustee, Sonoco Foundation; vice president, Sonoco Products Co.

Carolina Power Co.
McKee, E. Marie: senior vice president, Corning Inc.; chairman, trustee, Corning Inc. Foundation

Carpentar Advanced Ceramics
Welty, John Rider: secretary, Carpenter Technology Corp. Foundation

Carpenter Technology Corp.
Lawless, Robert J.: chairman, president, chief executive officer, chief operating officer, director, McCormick & Co. Inc.
Wolfe, Kenneth L.: chairman, chief executive officer, director, Hershey Foods Corp.

Carriage House Fruit Co.
Reading, Anthony John: president, trustee, Tomkins Corp. Foundation; president, chief executive officer, Tomkins Industries, Inc.

Carriage Industries Inc.
Frierson, Daniel K.: chairman, chief executive officer, Dixie Group, Inc. (The); president, trustee, Dixie Yarns Foundation, Inc.
Klein, Starr T.: secretary, treasurer, trustee, Dixie Yarns Foundation, Inc.

Carrol Reed Ski Shops
Gorman, Leon A.: president, chief executive officer, Bean, Inc. (L.L.)

Carter Holt Harvey Ltd.
Dillon, John T.: chairman, chief executive officer, director, International Paper Co.

Casa Di Bertacchi Corp.
Rich, Robert E., Jr.: secretary, Rich Family Foundation; president, director, Rich Products Corp.
Rich, Robert E., Sr.: president, treasurer, Rich Family Foundation; founder, chairman, director, Rich Products Corp.

Casco Cable Televising Inc.
Appell, Louis J., Jr.: president, Susquehanna-Pfaltzgraff Co.

Case Corp.
Hodgson, Thomas Richard: president, chief operating officer, director, Abbott Laboratories
Mead, Dana George: chairman, chief executive officer, director, Tenneco Automotive

Catamount Energy Corp.
Young, Robert Harris: president, chief executive officer, Central Vermont Public Service Corp.

Caterpillar Inc.
Dillon, John T.: chairman, chief executive officer, director, International Paper Co.
Goode, David Ronald: chairman, president, chief executive officer, director, Norfolk Southern Corp.
Knight, Charles Field: chairman, chief executive officer, Emerson Electric Co.
Magowan, Peter Alden: president, managing general partner, Safeway Inc.

Caterpillar Paving Products
Flaherty, Gerald S.: trustee, Caterpillar Foundation; group president, Caterpillar Inc.

Cawley Sheerin Wynne & Co.
O'Reilly, F. Anthony John: chairman, trustee, Heinz Co. Foundation (H.J.); chairman, director, Heinz Co. (H.J.)

Cedar Coal Co.
Draper, Ernest Linn, Jr.: chairman, president, chief executive officer, director, American Electric Power

Cedars Bank
Jacobs, Joseph J.: president, director, Jacobs Engineering Foundation; chairman, director, Jacobs Engineering Group

Cedel (Luxembourg)
Carter, Marshall Nichols: chairman, chief executive officer, State Street Bank & Trust Co.
Douglass, Robert Royal: trustee, Chase Manhattan Foundation

Cedel SA
Urkowitz, Michael: senior vice president, Chase Manhattan Bank, NA; trustee, Chase Manhattan Foundation

Celadon
Hilyard, James E.: president, CertainTeed Corp.; director, CertainTeed Corp. Foundation

CellStar Corp.
Johnson, James Lawrence: chairman emeritus, Walter Industries Inc.

Celsius Energy Co.
Cash, R. D.: chairman, president, chief executive officer, director, Questar Corp.

Cen Trust Bank NA
Randolph, Jackson Harold: chairman, Cinergy Corp.; chairman, director, Cinergy Foundation

Cen-Tex Holdings Inc.
Jacobsen, James C.: vice chairman, Kellwood Co.;

vice president, director, Kellwood Foundation

Cenex/Land O Lakes Agronomy Co.

Gherty, John E.: president, chief executive officer, Land O'Lakes, Inc.

Cengo Construction Corp.

Golub, Lewis: chairman, chief executive officer, director, Golub Corp.

Cenro Corp.

Wallach, Ira D.: chairman, Central National-Gottesman; executive vice president, Central National-Gottesman Foundation

Centel Corp.

Esrey, William Todd: chairman, chief executive officer, Sprint Corp.

Strandjord, Mary Jeannine: director, Sprint Foundation

CenterCore

Musser, Warren Van Dyke: chairman, chief executive officer, director, Safeguard Scientifics; president, director, Safeguard Scientifics Foundation

Centerior Energy Corp.

Bersticker, Albert C.: chairman, director, chief executive officer, Ferro Corp.; president, trustee, Ferro Foundation

Commes, Thomas Allen: president, chief operating officer, director, Sherwin-Williams Co.; assistant secretary, trustee, Sherwin-Williams Foundation

Centerior Service Co.

Burg, H. Peter: president, chief operating officer, FirstEnergy Corp.

Centex Construction Products

Hirsch, Laurence E.: chairman, chief executive officer, director, Centex Corp.

Centra Health Inc.

Tyler, Kenneth Scott, Jr.: president, chief executive officer, Furniture Brands International, Inc.

Central Appalachian Coal Co.

Draper, Ernest Linn, Jr.: chairman, president, chief executive officer, director, American Electric Power

Central Distributors Inc.

Golub, Lewis: chairman, chief executive officer, director, Golub Corp.

Central Houston Inc.

Riley, H. John, Jr.: chairman, president, chief executive officer, Cooper Industries Foundation; chairman, president, chief executive officer, director, Cooper Industries, Inc.

Central Illinois Public Service Co

Lohman, Gordon Russell: trustee, Amsted Industries Foundation; director, Amsted Industries Inc.

Central Life Assurance Co.

Brooks, Roger Kay: chairman, AmerUS Group

Central ME Power Co.

Gorman, Leon A.: president, chief executive officer, Bean, Inc. (L.L.)

Central Maine Power Co.

Marsh, David E.: chief financial officer, Central Maine Power Co.

Central Newspaper Inc.

Pulliam, Eugene Smith: vice president, director, Central Newspapers Foundation

Central Newspapers Inc.

Franke, William Augustus: chairman, president, chief executive officer, America West Airlines, Inc.; director, Phelps Dodge Foundation

Snell, Richard: chairman, president, chief executive officer, director, Arizona Public Service Co.

Central Newsprint

Russell, Frank Eli: president, Central Newspapers Foundation; chairman, Central Newspapers, Inc.

Central Ohio Coal Co.

Draper, Ernest Linn, Jr.: chairman, president, chief executive officer, director, American Electric Power

Central Studies Distributing Service Inc.

Smith, Arthur O.: president, Smith Foundation, Inc. (A.O.)

Central Telephone Co.

Strandjord, Mary Jeannine: director, Sprint Foundation

Central Telephone Co. Illinois

Esrey, William Todd: chairman, chief executive officer, Sprint Corp.

Central Vermont Public Services Corp.

Bertrand, Frederic Howard: chairman, Central Vermont Public Service Corp.

Century 21 Inc.

Gindi, Sam: trustee, Century 21 Associates Foundation

Century Leasing & Liquidating Inc.

Cohen, Maryjo Rose: president, chief executive officer, director, National Presto Industries, Inc.; vice president, treasurer, trustee, Presto Foundation

Cohen, Melvin Samuel: chairman, National Presto Industries, Inc.; chairman, president, trustee, Presto Foundation

Cerestar USA

Hausmann, Carl L.: chairman, president, chief executive officer, Central Soya Co.

Ceridian Corp.

Chabraja, Nicholas D.: chairman, chief executive officer, director, General Dynamics Corp.

Davis, Ruth Margaret: trustee, Air Products Foundation

Lewis, George Ralph: trustee, Kemper Foundation (James S.)

Walsh, Paul S.: chairman, president, chief executive officer, Pillsbury Co.; director, Pillsbury Co. Foundation

CertainTeed Corp.

Meyerson, Martin: director, Panasonic Foundation

Cessna Finance Corp.

Meyer, Russell William, Jr.: chairman, chief executive officer, Cessna Aircraft Co.; president, Cessna Foundation, Inc.

Chaco Energy Co.

Nye, Erle Allen: chairman, chief executive officer, director, TU Electric Co.

Chamberlain Group Inc.

Duchossois, Craig J.: director, Duchossois Foundation; president, director, Duchossois Industries Inc.

Duchossois, Richard Louis: secretary, Duchossois Foundation; chairman, chief executive officer, director, Duchossois Industries Inc.

Chamberlain Manufacturing Corp.

Duchossois, Richard Louis: secretary, Duchossois Foundation; chairman, chief executive officer, director, Duchossois Industries Inc.

Champion International Corp.

Bossidy, Lawrence Arthur: chairman, director, AlliedSignal Foundation Inc.; chairman, chief executive officer, director, AlliedSignal Inc.

Channel Industries Gas Co.

Wise, William Allen: chairman, president, chief executive officer, director, El Paso Energy Co.; chairman, director, El Paso Energy Foundation

Chaparral Steel Co.

Belk, John Montgomery: member board advisors, Belk Foundation; chairman, Belk-Simpson Department Stores

Chapman Machine Co. Inc.

Barnes, Thomas O.: secretary, Barnes Group Foundation Inc.

Charles Schwab Corp.

Fisher, Donald George: president, Gap Foundation/Gap Inc. Community Relations; founder, chairman, director, Gap, Inc.

Herringer, Frank Casper: president, chief executive officer, director, chairman, Transamerica Corp.; vice chairman, director, Transamerica Foundation

Pottruck, David Steven: president, chief executive officer, director, Schwab & Co., Inc. (Charles)

Charlotte Belk Inc.

Belk, John Montgomery: member board advisors, Belk Foundation; chairman, Belk-Simpson Department Stores

Robinson, Leroy: member board advisors, Belk Foundation

Charlottetown Inc.

Deering, Anthony W.: chairman, chief executive officer, Rouse Co.; chairman, president, trustee, Rouse Co. Foundation

Donahue, Jeffrey H.: senior vice president, chief financial officer, Rouse Co.

Chase Bank

Golub, Lewis: chairman, chief executive officer, director, Golub Corp.

Kissinger, Henry Alfred: director, CBS Foundation

Chase Bank Texas

Kennedy, James Cox: chairman, chief executive officer, director, Cox Enterprises Inc.; trustee, Cox Foundation (James M.)

Sanders, Wayne R.: chairman, chief executive officer, director, Kimberly-Clark Corp.

Chase Elastomer Midwest

Walker, Martin Dean: chairman, chief executive officer, director, Hanna Co. (M.A.)

Chase InfoServ International

Urkowitz, Michael: senior vice president, Chase Manhattan Bank, NA; trustee, Chase Manhattan Foundation

Chase Lincoln First Bank NA

Campbell, Van C.: vice chairman, chief financial officer, chief administrative

officer, director, Corning Inc.; trustee, Corning Inc. Foundation

Rice, William D.: senior vice president, chief financial officer, secretary, Agrilink Foods, Inc.; trustee, Agrilink Foods/Pro-Fac Foundation

Chase Manhattan Bank

Becherer, Hans Walter: chairman, chief executive officer, director, Deere & Co.; director, Deere Foundation (John)

Burns, Mitchell Anthony: president, director, Ryder System Charitable Foundation; chairman, president, chief executive officer, Ryder System, Inc.

Goodes, Melvin Russell: chairman, chief executive officer, director, Ameritech Corp.

Chase Manhattan Bank NA Inc.

Ackerman, Philip Charles: senior vice president, director, National Fuel Gas Distribution Corp.

Fuller, Harry Laurance: co-chairman, director, BP Amoco Corp.

Schacht, Henry Brewer: director, Cummins Engine Foundation

Chase Manhattan Corp.

Becherer, Hans Walter: chairman, chief executive officer, director, Deere & Co.; director, Deere Foundation (John)

Burns, Mitchell Anthony: president, director, Ryder System Charitable Foundation; chairman, president, chief executive officer, Ryder System, Inc.

Fuller, Harry Laurance: co-chairman, director, BP Amoco Corp.

Goodes, Melvin Russell: chairman, chief executive officer, director, Ameritech Corp.

Schacht, Henry Brewer: director, Cummins Engine Foundation

Stivers, William Charles: senior vice president, chief financial officer, treasurer, Weyerhaeuser Co.; treasurer, trustee, Weyerhaeuser Co. Foundation

Chase Manhattan Overseas Banking

Esposito, Michael Patrick, Jr.: trustee, Chase Manhattan Foundation

Evans, John B.: assistant secretary, assistant treasurer, Chase Manhattan Foundation

Fierce, Hughlyn F.: trustee, Chase Manhattan Foundation

Chatham Towing Co.

Demere, Robert H.: president, Colonial Foundation; chairman, Colonial Oil Industries, Inc.

Chattanooga Gas Co.

Jones, David R.: principal, AGL Resources Inc.

Chattanooga Times Co.

Sulzberger, Arthur Ochs, Sr.: director, New York Times Co.; chairman, director, New York Times Co. Foundation

Chaus

Krueger, Harvey M.: trustee, Barry Foundation

Chemed Corp.

Voet, Paul C.: trustee, Chemed Foundation

Chemfirst Inc.

Fligg, James E.: executive vice president, BP Amoco Corp.

Chemical Bank

Leser, Lawrence Arthur: chairman, director, Scripps Co. (E.W.); member, Scripps Howard Foundation

Chemical Bank & Trust Co.

Stavropoulos, William S.: president, chief executive officer, director, Dow Chemical Co.

Chemical Banking Corp.

Stivers, William Charles: senior vice president, chief financial officer, treasurer, Weyerhaeuser Co.; treasurer, trustee, Weyerhaeuser Co. Foundation

Chemical Finance Corp.

Stavropoulos, William S.: president, chief executive officer, director, Dow Chemical Co.

Chemung Canal Trust Co.

Ughetta, William Casper: trustee, Corning Inc. Foundation

Cherry Corp.

Denny, Charles W.: president, chief executive officer, director, Square D Co.

Chesapeake Corp.

Tilghman, Richard Granville: chairman, chief executive officer, Crestar Foundation

Viviano, Joseph P.: president, court, Hershey Foods Corp.

Chesebrough-Ponds Manufacturing

Phillips, Robert M.: president, Unilever Home & Personal Care U.S.A.

Chesebrough-Ponds U.S.A. Co.

Kurtz, Melvin H.: secretary, director, Chesebrough Foundation

Chesterton Blumenauer Binswanger

Binswanger, John K.: co-chairman, director, Binswanger Companies; chairman, Binswanger Foundation

Chevron Corp.

Pigott, Charles McGee: president, director, PACCAR Foundation; chairman emeritus, director, PACCAR Inc.

Weyerhaeuser, George Hunt: director, Weyerhaeuser Co.; trustee, Weyerhaeuser Co. Foundation

Chevron Services Co.

Elkins, Lloyd Edwin, Junior: vice president, Chevron Corp.

Cheyenne Light Fuel Power Co.

Helton, Bill D.: chairman, New Century Energies Foundation

Hock, Delwin D.: chairman, New Century Energies

Chicago Bears Football Club

McKenna, Andrew James: director, Aon Foundation

Chicago Board Options Exchange

Paton, Leland B.: president capital marketings, director, member executive committee, Prudential Securities Inc.

Chicago Bridge Iron Co.

Ballengee, Jerry Hunter: president, chief operating officer, director, Union Camp Corp.

Neale, Gary L.: chairman, president, chief executive officer, Northern Indiana Public Service Co.

Chicago Milwaukee Corp.

Zilkha, Ezra Khedouri: president, treasurer, Zilkha Foundation, Inc.; president, Zilkha & Sons

Chicago National League Baseball Club

McKenna, Andrew James: director, Aon Foundation

Chicago Stock Exchange

Fluno, Jere David: vice chairman, Grainger, Inc. (W.W.)

Chicago Title & Trust Co.

Bilton, Stuart Douglas: president, chief executive officer, Chicago Title Corp.; trustee, Chicago Title and Trust Co. Foundation

Mac Kimm, Margaret (Pontius) 'Mardie': trustee, Chicago Title and Trust Co. Foundation

Chicago Title Corp.

Lachman, Marguerite Leanne: trustee, Chicago Title and Trust Co. Foundation

Chicago Title Insurance Co.

Mac Kimm, Margaret (Pontius) 'Mardie': trustee, Chicago Title and Trust Co. Foundation

Toft, Richard Paul: chairman, Chicago Title Corp.; trustee, Chicago Title and Trust Co. Foundation

Chicago Transit Authority

Burrus, Clark D.: vice president, director, First National Bank of Chicago Foundation

Chicago Tube & Iron Co.

Ashley, James Wheeler: director, Globe Foundation

Child Welfare League America

Fleming, Richard Harrison: chief financial officer, senior vice president, USG Corp.; treasurer, trustee, USG Foundation

Children's Edition Inc.

McCorkindale, Douglas H.: vice chairman, president, Gannett Co., Inc.; president, Gannett Foundation

Childrens Memorial Hospital

McKenna, Andrew James: director, Aon Foundation

Chinet Co.

Schuit, Alexander J.: president, chief executive officer, chief financial officer, Van Leer Holding

Chittenden Trust Co.

Bertrand, Frederic Howard: chairman, Central Vermont Public Service Corp.

Chrysler Canada Ltd.

Capo, Thomas Patrick: senior vice president, treasurer, DaimlerChrysler Corp.

Chrysler Corp.

Kresa, Kent: chairman, president, chief executive officer, director, Northrop Grumman Corp.

Magowan, Peter Alden: president, managing general partner, Safeway Inc.

Chrysler Financial Corp.

Capo, Thomas Patrick: senior vice president, treasurer, DaimlerChrysler Corp.

Chubb & Son Inc.

O'Hare, Dean Raymond: chairman, Chubb Corp.

Chubb Corp.

Hoag, David H.: chairman, president, chief executive officer, director, LTV Corp.; trustee, LTV Foundation

O'Hare, Dean Raymond: chairman, Chubb Corp.

Small, Lawrence Malcolm: president, chief operating officer, Fannie Mae; director, Fannie Mae Foundation

Zimmerman, James M.: chairman, chief executive officer, director, Federated Department Stores, Inc.

Chubb Insurance Co. Canada

O'Hare, Dean Raymond: chairman, Chubb Corp.

Churchill Downs Inc.

Hower, Frank Beard, Jr.: vice chairman, Anthem Foundation, Inc.

Cimarron Coal Co.

Gaylord, Edward Lewis: chairman, chief executive officer, director, publisher, Oklahoma Publishing Co.; trustee, Oklahoman Foundation (The)

Cincinnati Bell Inc.

Barrett, John F.: trustee, Western-Southern Foundation, Inc.; president, chief executive officer, director, Western & Southern Life Insurance Co.

Cox, Phillip R.: director, Cinergy Foundation

Meyer, Daniel Joseph: president, Milacron Foundation; chairman, president, chief executive officer, director, Milacron, Inc.

Cincinnati Bell Telephone Co.

Ellenberger, Richard G.: president, chief executive officer, director, Cincinnati Bell Inc.

Cincinnati Financial Corp.

Randolph, Jackson Harold: chairman, Cinergy Corp.; chairman, director, Cinergy Foundation

Cincinnati Gas & Electric Co. Inc.

Grealis, William J.: vice president, Cinergy Corp.; director, Cinergy Foundation

Cincinnati Gas Electric Co.

Randolph, Jackson Harold: chairman, Cinergy Corp.; chairman, director, Cinergy Foundation

Cincinnati Milacron Inc.

Stonecipher, Harry C.: president, chief operating officer, director, Boeing Co.

Cincinnati Milacron Marketing Co.

Meyer, Daniel Joseph: president, Milacron Foundation; chairman, president, chief executive officer, director, Milacron, Inc.

Cincinnati Milocron Marketing Co.

Kasting, Barbara Glenn: assistant secretary, Milacron Foundation; vice president human resources, Milacron, Inc.

Cincinnati New Orleans Texas Railway

Wolf, Henry C.: vice chairman, chief financial officer, Norfolk Southern Corp.; vice president finance, Norfolk Southern Foundation

Cincinnati, New Orleans, Texas Railway

Goode, David Ronald: chairman, president, chief executive officer, director, Norfolk Southern Corp.

Cinergy Corp.

Armstrong, Neil A.: trustee, Milacron Foundation; director, Milacron, Inc.

Baker, James Kendrick: chairman, director, Arvin Foundation; vice chairman, director, Arvin Industries, Inc.

Cox, Phillip R.: director, Cinergy Foundation

Duberstein, Kenneth: director, Cinergy Foundation

Hillenbrand, John A., II: director, Cinergy Foundation

Juilfs, George C.: director, Cinergy Foundation

Cinergy Marketing & Trading LLC

Ludlow, Madaleine W.: vice president, chief financial officer, Cinergy Corp.

Circuit City Stores Inc.

Snow, John William: chairman, president, chief executive officer, CSX Corp.

Villanueva, Edward: trustee, Circuit City Foundation

Cisco Systems Inc.

Bartz, Carol A.: director, Autodesk Foundation; chairman, chief executive officer, Autodesk Inc.

Sarin, Arun: director, AirTouch Communications Foundation; president, chief operating officer, vice chairman, vice president, Vodafone AirTouch Plc

Citibank NA

Shapiro, Robert B.: chairman, president, chief executive officer, director, Monsanto Co.

Citicorp

Mark, Reuben: chairman, chief executive officer, Colgate-Palmolive Co.

Ruding, Herman Onno: vice chairman, director, Citibank Corp.

Shapiro, Robert B.: chairman, president, chief executive officer, director, Monsanto Co.

Woolard, Edgar Smith, Jr.: director, du Pont de Nemours & Co. (E.I.)

Citigroup

Thomas, Franklin Augustine: director, CBS Foundation

Citigroup Inc.

Armstrong, C. Michael: chairman, chief executive officer, AT&T Corp.

Masin, Michael Terry: vice chairman, president international, director, GTE Corp.; trustee, GTE Foundation

Maughan, Deryck C.: director, New York Stock Exchange Foundation, Inc.; co-chairman, co-chief executive officer, Salomon Smith Barney

Plumeri, Joseph James, II: president, Citigroup

Rhodes, William Reginald: vice chairman, Citibank Corp.

Shapiro, Robert B.: chairman, president, chief executive officer, director, Monsanto Co.

Citizen Publishing Co.

McCorkindale, Douglas H.: vice chairman, president, Gannett Co., Inc.; president, Gannett Foundation

Citizens Bank Massachusetts

Fish, Lawrence K.: trustee, Citizens Charitable Foundation; chairman, chief executive officer, Citizens Financial Group, Inc.

Citizens Bank Michigan

Schaeffer, Wayne G.: community president, Citizens Bank-Flint

Citizens Corp.

O'Brien, John Francis, Jr.: president, chief executive officer, Allmerica Financial Corp.

Citizens Financial Group Inc.

Cambell, Lewis B.: chairman, chief executive officer, director, Textron Inc.

Citizens Insurance Co. of America

O'Brien, John Francis, Jr.: president, chief executive officer, Allmerica Financial Corp.

Citizens National Bank Evansville

Muehlbauer, James Herman: vice president, director, Koch Foundation

Citizens State Bank Waterville

Nelson, Marilyn Carlson: chairman, chief executive officer, president, Carlson Companies, Inc.

City Forest Corp.

McCarragher, Bernard John: chairman, director, Menasha Corp.; chairman, Menasha Corp. Foundation

City National Bank Pittsburgh

Kemper, David Woods: chairman, president, chief executive officer, director, Commerce Bancshares, Inc.

City Savings Bank

Trask, Robert B.: president, chief operating officer, director, Country Curtains, Inc.; clerk, trustee, High Meadow Foundation

Civic Bancorp

Cronk, William F., III: president, director, Dreyer's Grand Ice Cream

Civic Center Corp.

Busch, August Adolphus, III: chairman, president, chief executive officer, Anheuser-Busch Companies, Inc.

Clarcor Inc.

Adam, J. Marc: president, director, 3M Foundation; vice president marketing, Minnesota Mining & Manufacturing Co.

Claridge Israel Inc.

Bronfman, Charles Rosner: trustee, Bronfman Foundation/Joseph E. Seagram & Sons, Inc. Fund (Samuel)

Clark USA

Melnuk, Paul D.: president, chief executive officer, Clark Refining & Marketing

Clark United States of America Inc.

Stockman, David A.: co-chairman, director, Collins & Aikman Corp.; president, director, Collins & Aikman Foundation

Clayton Acquisition Co.

James, George Barker, II: senior vice president, chief financial officer, Levi Strauss & Co.

Cleret Inc.

Hebert, William L.: assistant secretary, treasurer, Louisiana-Pacific Foundation

Cleveland Electric Illuminating

Holland, Willard R.: chairman, chief executive officer, FirstEnergy Corp.

Cleveland Gear Co.

Curci, John V.: chief financial officer, Vesper Corp.; trustee, Vesper Foundation

Cliffs Resources Inc.

Bezik, Cynthia B.: senior vice president, finance, Cleveland-Cliffs, Inc.

Cloister Spring Water Co.

Mohn, Richard E.: chairman, director, Sovereign Bank; director, Sovereign Bank Foundation

Clorox Co.

Matschullat, Robert W.: trustee, Bronfman Foundation/Joseph E. Seagram & Sons, Inc. Fund (Samuel); vice chairman, chief financial officer, Seagram & Sons, Inc. (Joseph E.)

Clorox International Co. Inc.

Rose, Karen M.: vice president, treasurer, Clorox Co.

Sullivan, G. Craig: chairman, president, chief executive officer, director, Clorox Co.; chairman, Clorox Co. Foundation

Clow Corp.

McMahon, John J., Jr.: trustee, McWane Foundation; chairman, president, chief executive officer, treasurer, McWane Inc.

Coachmen Industries Georgia

Corson, Keith Daniel: president, chief operating officer, Coachmen Industries, Inc.

Skinner, Claire Corson: chairman, chief executive officer, Coachmen Industries, Inc.

Coast Coast Advertising

Porter, Edward A.: vice president, general counsel, secretary, Walter Industries Inc.

Coast To Coast Advertising

Fjelstul, Dean M.: senior vice president, chief financial officer, Walter Industries Inc.

Coca-Cola Bottling Co. Consolidated

Belk, John Montgomery: member board advisors, Belk Foundation; chairman, Belk-Simpson Department Stores

Coca-Cola Co.

Beale, Michelle: director, Coca-Cola Foundation

Coca-Cola Enterprises Inc.

Humann, L. Phillip: member, SunTrust Bank Atlanta Foundation

Cohr Inc.

Simpson, Louis Allen: president, chief executive officer capital operations, director, GEICO Corp.

Coinstar Inc.

Ruckelshaus, William Doyle: chairman, director, Browning-Ferris Industries Inc.

Colfax Country RV Sales Inc.

Corson, Keith Daniel: president, chief operating officer, Coachmen Industries, Inc.

Colgate-Palmolive Co.

Ferguson, Ronald Eugene: chairman, president, chief executive officer, director, General Reinsurance Corp.

Johnson, David Willis: chairman, director, Campbell Soup Co.

Kogan, Richard Jay: chairman, chief executive officer, Schering-Plough Corp.; trustee, member, Schering-Plough Foundation

Colker and Newlin Management Association

Newlin, William Rankin: trustee, Kennametal Foundation

College Fund Advisory

Moten, John, Junior: vice president community relations, Laclede Gas Co.

Collins & Aikman Group Inc.

Stockman, David A.: co-chairman, director, Collins & Aikman Corp.; president, director, Collins & Aikman Foundation

Collins Aikman Plastics Inc.

Stockman, David A.: co-chairman, director, Collins & Aikman Corp.; president, director, Collins & Aikman Foundation

Collins International Service Co.

Walker, Martin Dean: chairman, chief executive officer, director, Hanna Co. (M.A.)

Cologne Life Reinsurance Co.

Toft, Richard Paul: chairman, Chicago Title Corp.; trustee, Chicago Title and Trust Co. Foundation

Colomet Inc.

Draper, Ernest Linn, Jr.: chairman, president, chief executive officer, director, American Electric Power

Colonial Bancorp Inc.

Griebel, R. Nelson: vice chairman, BankBoston Charitable Foundation; president, chief executive officer, director, BankBoston-Connecticut Region

Wilson, Bruce A.: senior vice president, BankBoston-Connecticut Region

Colonial Co. Inc.

Staton, Robert Emmett: president, Colonial Life & Accident Insurance Co.

Colonial Insurance Co. California

Miller, David O.: chairman, Employers Insurance of Wausau, A Mutual Co.; trustee, Nationwide Insurance Enterprise Foundation; chairman, Wausau Insurance Companies

Shisler, Arden L.: trustee, Nationwide Insurance Enterprise Foundation

Colonial Interstate

Demere, Robert H.: president, Colonial Foundation; chairman, Colonial Oil Industries, Inc.

Colonial Life Insurance Co. North America

O'Hare, Dean Raymond: chairman, Chubb Corp.

Colonial Marine Industries

Demere, Robert H.: president, Colonial Foundation; chairman, Colonial Oil Industries, Inc.

Colonial Terminals

Demere, Robert H.: president, Colonial Foundation; chairman, Colonial Oil Industries, Inc.

Colony Savings Bank

Hershman, Linda D.: vice president, Southern New England Telephone Co.

Colorado Board Room

Duncan, Ian: trustee, Tomkins Corp. Foundation; deputy chairman, managing director finance, Tomkins Industries, Inc.

Colt Energy Inc.

Powell, George Everett, Jr.: trustee, Yellow Corp. Foundation

Coltec Industries Inc.

Holland, William Ray: vice president, director, United Dominion Foundation; chairman, chief executive officer, director, United Dominion Industries, Ltd.

Columbia Casualty Co.

Jokiel, Peter E.: senior vice president, chief financial officer, CNA

Columbia Casualty Corp.

Chookaszian, Dennis Haig: chairman, chief executive officer, CNA

Columbia Forest Products Inc.

Wendt, Richard L.: trustee, Jeld-wen Foundation; chief executive officer, chairman, Jeld-wen, Inc.

Columbia Gas Systems Inc.

Olesen, Douglas Eugene, PhD: president, chief executive officer, Battelle Memorial Institute

Columbia Gear Co.

Curci, John V.: chief financial officer, Vesper Corp.; trustee, Vesper Foundation

Columbia Health System Inc.

Kasten, G. Frederick, Jr.: trustee, Baird & Co. Foundation (Robert W.); chairman, chief executive officer, director, Baird & Co. (Robert W.)

Wigdale, James B.: vice president, Marshall & Ilsley Corp.; vice president, director, Marshall & Ilsley Foundation, Inc.

Columbia Law School

Shapiro, Isaac: chairman, secretary, trustee, Ise Cultural Foundation

Columbia Mall Inc.

Deering, Anthony W.: chairman, chief executive officer, Rouse Co.; chairman, president, trustee, Rouse Co. Foundation

Columbia Management Inc.

Deering, Anthony W.: chairman, chief executive officer, Rouse Co.; chairman, president, trustee, Rouse Co. Foundation

Columbus Bank & Trust Co.

Amos, Daniel P.: president, chief executive officer, director, AFLAC Inc.

Blanchard, James Hubert: chairman, chief executive officer, Synovus Financial Corp.

Columbus Life Insurance Co. Ohio

Williams, William Joseph: trustee, Western-Southern Foundation, Inc.; chairman, director, Western & Southern Life Insurance Co.

Columbus Southern Power Co.

Draper, Ernest Linn, Jr.: chairman, president, chief executive officer, director, American Electric Power

Lhota, William J.: executive vice president, American Electric Power

Comair Holdings Inc.

Forster, Peter Hans: chairman, director, Dayton Power and Light Co.

Comair Inc.

Murphy, Christopher J., III: president, chief executive officer, director, First Source Corp.; director, First Source Foundation

Combined Communications Corp.

McCorkindale, Douglas H.: vice chairman, president, Gannett Co., Inc.; president, Gannett Foundation

Combined Communications Corp. Oklahoma Inc.

McCorkindale, Douglas H.: vice chairman, president, Gannett Co., Inc.; president, Gannett Foundation

Combined Insurance Co.

Medvin, Harvey Norman: executive vice president, treasurer, chief financial officer, Aon Corp.; treasurer, Aon Foundation

Ryan, Patrick G.: chairman, president, chief executive officer, Aon Corp.; president, Aon Foundation

Skilling, Raymond Inwood: executive vice president, chief counsel, director, Aon Corp.; director, Aon Foundation

Combustion Engineering Inc.

Whitwam, David Ray: chairman, president, chief executive officer, director, Whirlpool Corp.

Comcast United Kingdom Cable Partners Ltd.

Romeril, Barry D.: executive vice president, chief financial officer, Xerox Corp.

Comerica Bank

Bauder, Lillian: vice president corporate affairs, Masco Corp.

Miller, Eugene A.: chairman, chief executive officer, Comerica Inc.

Walker, Martin Dean: chairman, chief executive officer, director, Hanna Co. (M.A.)

Comerica Inc.

Lyon, Wayne Barton: president, chief operating officer, director, Masco Corp.

Walker, Martin Dean: chairman, chief executive officer, director, Hanna Co. (M.A.)

Commerce Bancshares Inc.

Bloch, Henry Wollman: chairman, Block Foundation (H&R); chairman, director, Block, Inc. (H&R)

Kemper, James M., Jr.: director, Commerce Bancshares Foundation; chairman, president, director, Commerce Bancshares, Inc.

Commerce Bank NA

Hall, Donald Joyce: chairman board, director, Hallmark Cards Inc.; chairman, Hallmark Corporate Foundation

Stinnett, J. Daniel: director, Commerce Bancshares Foundation

Weaver, Warren W.: chairman, Commerce Bancshares, Inc.

Commerce Bank Saint Joseph

Kemper, James M., Jr.: director, Commerce Bancshares Foundation; chairman, president, director, Commerce Bancshares, Inc.

Commerce Bank Saint Louis

Kemper, David Woods: chairman, president, chief executive officer, director, Commerce Bancshares, Inc.

Commerce Holdings Inc.

Nelson, John Martin: chairman, director, TJX Companies, Inc.

Commercial Bank San Francisco

Robinson, John H.: treasurer, secretary, Carter Star Telegram Employees Fund (Amon G.)

Commercial Carriers Inc.

West, Randall E.: director, Ryder System Charitable Foundation

Commercial Credit Co.

Lipp, Robert Irving: chief executive officer, Citigroup; vice president, treasurer, trustee, Citigroup Foundation

Commercial Federal Bank

Fitzgerald, William Allingham: chairman, director, Commercial Federal Corp.

Commercial Federal Bank Omaha

O'Donnell, James P.: treasurer, ConAgra Foundation

Commercial Federal Service

Fitzgerald, William Allingham: chairman, director, Commercial Federal Corp.

Commercial Intertech Corp.

Cushwa, Charles Benton, III: trustee, Commercial Intertech Foundation

Galvin, John: trustee, Commercial Intertech Foundation

Humphrey, Neil Darwin: trustee, Commercial Intertech Foundation

McDonough, Gerald C.: trustee, Commercial Intertech Foundation

Smart, George M.: trustee, Commercial Intertech Foundation

Tucker, Don Eugene: trustee, Commercial Intertech Foundation

Commercial Metals Co.

Massaro, Anthony A.: president, chief executive officer, chairman, chief operating officer, Lincoln Electric Co.

Commercial Metals Corp.

Hirsch, Laurence E.: chairman, chief executive officer, director, Centex Corp.

Commercial Realty Resources Corp.

Harden, Oleta J.: secretary, New Jersey Natural Gas Foundation

Commercial Shearing Inc.

Cushwa, William Wallace: director, Commercial Intertech Corp.; trustee, Commercial Intertech Foundation

Commercial Union Corp.

Darehshori, Nader Farhang: chairman, president, chief executive officer, Houghton Mifflin Co.

Commonwealth Edison Co.

Jannotta, Edgar D.: president, Blair & Co. Foundation (William); senior director, Blair & Co. (William)

Strobel, Pamela B.: senior vice president, general counsel, Commonwealth Edison Co.

Commonwealth General Corp.

Everingham, Lyle J.: trustee, Milacron Foundation

Compania Anonima Nacional Telefonos de Venezuela

Masin, Michael Terry: vice chairman, president international, director, GTE Corp.; trustee, GTE Foundation

Companion Life Insurance Co.

Sturgeon, John: president, chief operating officer, Mutual of Omaha Insurance Co.

Weekly, John William: chairman, chief executive officer, Mutual of Omaha Insurance Co.

Compaq Computer Corp.

Larson, Peter N.: chairman, chief executive officer, director, Brunswick Corp.

Compass Bank

Jones, D. Paul, Jr.: chairman, chief executive officer, Compass Bank; trustee, Compass Bank Foundation

Compass Brokerage Inc.

Powell, Jerry W.: secretary, general counsel, Compass Bank; secretary, Compass Bank Foundation

Compass International Service Corp.

Clark, Howard Longstreth, Jr.: vice chairman, Walter Industries Inc.

Compcare Health Services

Whitelaw, Essie M.: president, chief operating officer, United Wisconsin Services; vice president, United Wisconsin Services Foundation

Compcare Health Services Insurance Corp.

Hefty, Thomas R.: chairman, president, chief executive officer, United Wisconsin Services

CompuCom System

Musser, Warren Van Dyke: chairman, chief executive officer, director, Safeguard Scientifics; president, director, Safeguard Scientifics Foundation

CompuServe Inc.

Bloch, Henry Wollman: chairman, Block Foundation (H&R); chairman, director, Block, Inc. (H&R)

Computer Associates International Inc.

Grasso, Richard A.: chairman, chief executive officer, New York Stock Exchange, Inc.

Computer Holdings Corp.

Fjelstul, Dean M.: senior vice president, chief financial officer, Walter Industries Inc.

Hyatt, Kenneth Ernest: chairman, president, chief executive officer, director, Walter Industries Inc.

Computer Task Group Inc.

Elliott, R. Keith: chief executive officer, president, Hercules Inc.

Computerized Business Systems

Orscheln, Donald W.: director, chairman, Orscheln Co.; secretary, Orscheln Industries Foundation, Inc.

Orscheln, Gerald A.: president, Orscheln Industries Foundation, Inc.

Orscheln, William L.: treasurer, Orscheln Industries Foundation, Inc.

Comsource, Inc.

Koch, Robert Louis, II: president, chief executive officer, director, Koch Enterprises, Inc.; president, director, Koch Foundation

Con-Way Truckload Services

Moffitt, Donald Eugene: chairman, director, CNF Transportation, Inc.

ConAgra Inc.

Bay, Mogens C.: chairman, chief executive officer, Valmont Industries, Inc.

Scott, Walter, Jr.: member contributions committee, Kiewit Companies Foundation

Stinson, Kenneth E.: member contributions committee, Kiewit Companies Foundation; chairman, chief executive officer, director, Kiewit Sons' Inc. (Peter)

Concepts Direct Inc.

Burrus, Robert Lewis, Jr.: trustee, Circuit City Foundation

Concert PLC

Romeril, Barry D.: executive vice president, chief financial officer, Xerox Corp.

Concrete Industries Inc.

Abel, James P.: president, Abel Foundation; president, director, NEBCO Evans

Conergics Corp.

Reading, Anthony John: president, trustee, Tomkins Corp. Foundation; president, chief executive officer, Tomkins Industries, Inc.

Conesville Coal Preparation Co.

Draper, Ernest Linn, Jr.: chairman, president, chief executive officer, director, American Electric Power

Conexant Systems Inc.
Beall, Donald Ray: director, Rockwell International Corp.

Conference Board
Wehmeier, Helge H.: president, chief executive officer, director, Bayer Corp.

Conference Board Inc.
DeSimone, Livio Diego: chairman, chief executive officer, Minnesota Mining & Manufacturing Co.

Congress Financial Corp.
Coltman, Charles L., III: vice chairman, First Union Regional Foundation

Connect Oklahoma Inc.
Gaylord, Edward K., II: trustee, Oklahoman Foundation (The)

Connecticut Innovations Inc.
Barnes, Wallace W.: director, Barnes Group Foundation Inc.

Connecticut Valley Electric Co.
Young, Robert Harris: president, chief executive officer, Central Vermont Public Service Corp.

Connell Bros Co. Ltd.
Wilbur, Brayton, Jr.: president, chief executive officer, Wilbur-Ellis Co. & Connell Brothers Co.; president, Wilbur Foundation (Brayton)

Connetics Corp.
Ruvane, Joseph J., Jr.: director, Glaxo Wellcome Foundation

Conoco Inc.
Rhodes, William Reginald: vice chairman, Citibank Corp.
Thomas, Franklin Augustine: director, CBS Foundation

Conopco Inc.
McCall, James W.: president, director, Chesebrough Foundation

Conrail Inc.
Brinegar, Claude Stout: trustee, Unocal Foundation
Burke, Daniel Barnett: vice president, treasurer, director, ABC Foundation

Consolidated Computer Center
McConnell, William Thompson: chairman, ceo, Park National Bank; chairman, Park National Corp. Foundation

Consolidated Delivery Logistics
Hanson, Jon F.: trustee, Prudential Foundation

Consolidated Edison Co. New York Inc.
Davis, Ruth Margaret: trustee, Air Products Foundation

Consolidated Freightways Corp. DE
Moffitt, Donald Eugene: chairman, director, CNF Transportation, Inc.

Consolidated Natural Gas Co.
Simmons, Richard Paul: chairman, president, chief executive officer, Allegheny Technologies Inc.

Consolidated Papers Inc.
Shiely, John Stephen: president, chief operating officer, director, Briggs & Stratton Corp.; vice president, director, Briggs & Stratton Corp. Foundation

Consolidated Rail Corp.
Brinegar, Claude Stout: trustee, Unocal Foundation
Burke, Daniel Barnett: vice president, treasurer, director, ABC Foundation

Consolidated Water Power Co.
Mead, George Wilson, II: president, director, Consolidated Papers Foundation, Inc.; chairman, director, Consolidated Papers, Inc.

Constellation Biogas Inc.
Poindexter, Christian Herndon: chairman, Baltimore Gas & Electric Foundation; chairman, chief executive officer, director, Constellation Energy Group, Inc.

Constellation Energy Corp.
Ruszin, Thomas E., Jr.: assistant secretary, assistant treasurer, Baltimore Gas & Electric Foundation; treasurer, Constellation Energy Group, Inc.
Torgerson, William T.: managing, Potomac Electric Power Co.

Constellation Energy Group Inc.
Crooke, Edward A.: president, Baltimore Gas & Electric Foundation

Constellation Investments Inc.
Poindexter, Christian Herndon: chairman, Baltimore Gas & Electric Foundation; chairman, chief executive officer, director, Constellation Energy Group, Inc.

Constellation Properties Inc.
Poindexter, Christian Herndon: chairman, Baltimore Gas & Electric Foundation; chairman, chief executive officer, director, Constellation Energy Group, Inc.

Construction Machinery Inc.
Floerchinger, Craig A.: director, CIRI Foundation; vice president, Cook Inlet Region

Constructors Inc.
Abel, James P.: president, Abel Foundation; president, director, NEBCO Evans
Abel, John C.: director, Abel Foundation

Consumer Programs Inc.
Essman, Alyn V.: chairman, chief executive officer, CPI Corp.

Consumer Protection Quality Healthcare Industry
Montrone, Paul Michael: vice president, partner, Winthrop Foundation

Consumer's Press
Gottlieb, Richard Douglas: president, chief executive officer, director, Lee Enterprises

Consumers Energy
Yasinsky, John B.: chairman, president, chief executive officer, GenCorp

Contel Cellular Inc.
Walter, James W.: trustee, Walter Foundation; chairman emeritus, founder, director, Walter Industries Inc.

Continental Airlines Inc.
McCorkindale, Douglas H.: vice chairman, president, Gannett Co., Inc.; president, Gannett Foundation
Williams, Karen Hastie: director, Fannie Mae Foundation

Continental Assurance Canada
Sharkey, William Henry, Jr.: director, CNA Foundation

Continental Assurance Co.
Chookaszian, Dennis Haig: chairman, chief executive officer, CNA
Jokiel, Peter E.: senior vice president, chief financial officer, CNA

Continental Can Co.
Fino, Raymond M.: second vice president, Warner-Lambert Charitable Foundation; vice president human resources, Warner-Lambert Co.

Continental Casualty Canada
Sharkey, William Henry, Jr.: director, CNA Foundation

Continental Casualty Co.
Jokiel, Peter E.: senior vice president, chief financial officer, CNA

Continental Corp.
Chookaszian, Dennis Haig: chairman, chief executive officer, CNA
Jokiel, Peter E.: senior vice president, chief financial officer, CNA

Continental Energy Services Inc.
Cromer, Richard F.: executive vice president, chief operating officer energy supply division, Montana Power Co.; director, Montana Power Foundation
Merrell, Pamela K.: secretary, Montana Power Co.; vice president, secretary, Montana Power Foundation
Senechal, Ellen M.: treasurer, Montana Power Co.

Continental Illinois Venture Del
Coulter, David A.: president, director, Bank of America
Goodyear, William M.: trustee, Bank of America Foundation

Continental Insurance Canada
Sharkey, William Henry, Jr.: director, CNA Foundation

Continental Insurance Co. New Jersey
Chookaszian, Dennis Haig: chairman, chief executive officer, CNA
Jokiel, Peter E.: senior vice president, chief financial officer, CNA
Sharkey, William Henry, Jr.: director, CNA Foundation

Continental Life & Accident Co.
Simplot, John Richard: chairman, founder, Simplot Co. (J.R.); president, Simplot Foundation (J.R.)

Continental Loss Adjusting Services
Jokiel, Peter E.: senior vice president, chief financial officer, CNA
Noha, Edward J.: director, CNA Foundation

Continental Materials Corp.
Gidwitz, Ronald J.: president, chief executive officer, Curtis Industries, Inc. (Helene)

Continuum Co.
Anderson, Lowell Carlton: chairman, director, Allianz Life Insurance Co. of North America

Contract Transportation System Co.
Pitorak, Larry John: senior vice president finance, treasurer, chief financial officer, Sherwin-Williams Co.; secretary, treasurer, trustee, Sherwin-Williams Foundation

Contractors Supplies Inc.

Temple, Arthur, III: director, Temple-Inland Foundation

Convergys Corp.

Barrett, John F.: trustee, Western-Southern Foundation, Inc.; president, chief executive officer, director, Western & Southern Life Insurance Co.

Conwood Capital Corp.

Rosson, William Mimms: chairman, Conwood Co. LP

Cook Inlet Region Inc.

English, William D.: director, CIRI Foundation

Leask, Janie: director, CIRI Foundation

Cooper Industries Inc.

Grum, Clifford J.: director, Temple-Inland Foundation; director, chairman, chief executive officer, Temple-Inland Inc.

Ong, John Doyle: chairman board, director, Ameritech Corp.

Cooper Tire & Rubber Co.

Pond, Byron O.: chairman, chief executive officer, director, Arvin Industries, Inc.

Coors Brewing Co.

Coors, Peter Hanson: vice president, director, Coors Brewing Co.

Coors Distribution Co.

Kiely, W. Leo, III: president, chief operating officer, Coors Brewing Co.

Copley News Service

Copley, Helen K.: chairman, trustee, Copley Foundation (James S.); chairman, director, senior management board, Copley Press, Inc.

Copley Press Inc.

De Bakcsy, Alex: vice president, trustee, Copley Foundation (James S.)

Cordant Technology Inc.

Lesar, David J.: president, chief operating officer, Halliburton Co.; trustee, Halliburton Foundation, Inc.

Cordillera Communications Inc.

Rockey, Travis O.: vice president, director, Evening Post Publishing Co.

Core Industries

Drury, Robert E.: president, director, United Dominion Foundation

CoreStates Bank NA

Coltman, Charles L., III: vice chairman, First Union Regional Foundation

Larsen, Terrence A.: chairman, chief executive officer, First Union Bank; chairman, First Union Regional Foundation

CoreStates Financial Corp.

Cardy, Robert Willard: chairman, president, chief executive officer, director, Carpenter Technology Corp.; president, Carpenter Technology Corp. Foundation

Coresource Inc.

Gramm, Frank G., III: trustee, Trustmark Foundation

Peterson, Donald Matthew: trustee, Trustmark Foundation; president, chief executive officer, director, Trustmark Insurance Co.

Corion Corp.

Shanks, David C.: trustee, Little Foundation (Arthur D.); vice president human resources, Little, Inc. (Arthur D.)

Corn Products International Inc.

Gross, Ronald Martin: chairman, president, director, Rayonier Foundation; chairman, president, chief executive officer, director, Rayonier Inc.

Corning Consumer Products Co.

Kidder, C. Robert: chairman, president, chief executive officer, director, Borden, Inc.

Corning Enterprises Inc.

Gosnell, M. Ann: assistant secretary, Corning Inc. Foundation

Corning Inc.

Rein, Catherine Amelia: director, MetLife Foundation; vice president, Metropolitan Life Insurance Co.

Ruding, Herman Onno: vice chairman, director, Citibank Corp.

Corning Inc. Foreign Sales Corp.

Peck, Arthur John, Jr.: secretary, vice president, Corning Inc.; secretary, Corning Inc. Foundation

Corning International Corp.

Ackerman, Roger G.: trustee, Corning Inc. Foundation

Booth, Chesleu Peter Washburn: senior vice president development, Corning Inc.; trustee, Corning Inc. Foundation

Campbell, Van C.: vice chairman, chief financial officer, chief administrative officer, director, Corning Inc.; trustee, Corning Inc. Foundation

Peck, Arthur John, Jr.: secretary, vice president, Corning Inc.; secretary, Corning Inc. Foundation

Ughetta, William Casper: trustee, Corning Inc. Foundation

Corning Laboratory Services Inc.

Campbell, Van C.: vice chairman, chief financial officer, chief administrative officer, director, Corning Inc.; trustee, Corning Inc. Foundation

Cornwall & Stevens Co. Inc.

Frew, Burdette L.: president, director, MFA Foundation

Corp. Insurance & Reinsurance Co. Ltd.

Brewer, Oliver Gordon, Jr.: vice president finance, treasurer, IKON Office Solutions Foundation, Inc.

Coster Co.

Gidwitz, Ronald J.: president, chief executive officer, Curtis Industries, Inc. (Helene)

Cotton Studies Life Insurance Co.

Wood, Edward Jenner: member, SunTrust Bank Atlanta Foundation

Coty Corp.

Larson, Peter N.: chairman, chief executive officer, director, Brunswick Corp.

Coulter Pham Inc.

Lucas, Donald Leo: chairman, Cadence Designs Systems, Inc.

Country Curtains Inc.

Fitzpatrick, John H.: president, High Meadow Foundation; president, director, Housatonic Curtain Co.

Country Curtains Mail Order Inc.

Fitzpatrick, Jane P.: chairman, chief executive officer, treasurer, Country Curtains, Inc.; chairman, High Meadow Foundation

Trask, Robert B.: president, chief operating officer, director, Country Curtains, Inc.; clerk, trustee, High Meadow Foundation

Country Curtains Retail Inc.

Trask, Robert B.: president, chief operating officer, director, Country Curtains, Inc.; clerk, trustee, High Meadow Foundation

Courier Broadway Corp.

McCorkindale, Douglas H.: vice chairman, president, Gannett Co., Inc.; president, Gannett Foundation

Courier Corp.

Donahue, Richard King: vice chairman, Nike, Inc.

Courier-Journal & Louisville Times Co.

McCorkindale, Douglas H.: vice chairman, president, Gannett Co., Inc.; president, Gannett Foundation

Cousins Properties Inc.

Courts, Richard Winn, II: chairman, director, Atlantic Investment Co.

Covance Inc.

MacDonald, J. Randall: senior vice president human resources administration, GTE Corp.; trustee, GTE Foundation

Ughetta, William Casper: trustee, Corning Inc. Foundation

Coventry Health Care Inc.

Drury, David J.: chief executive officer, chairman, Principal Financial Group

Graf, Thomas J.: chief actuary, Principal Financial Group

Cox Communications Inc.

Easterly, David E.: president, chief operating officer, Cox Enterprises Inc.

Kennedy, James Cox: chairman, chief executive officer, director, Cox Enterprises Inc.; trustee, Cox Foundation (James M.)

Cox Enterprises Inc.

Anthony, Barbara Cox: chairman, Cox Foundation (James M.)

Blank, Arthur M.: president, chief executive officer, director, Home Depot, Inc.

Chambers, Anne Cox: chairman, trustee, Cox Foundation (James M.)

Cox Radio Inc.

Kennedy, James Cox: chairman, chief executive officer, director, Cox Enterprises Inc.; trustee, Cox Foundation (James M.)

Craigie Inc.

Reed, Scott Eldridge: senior executive vice president, chief financial officer, Branch Banking & Trust Co.

Crane Co.

Minton, Dwight Church: chairman, director, Church & Dwight Co., Inc.

Queenan, Charles J., Jr.: trustee, Tippins Foundation

Cranston International Sales Corp.

Mandeville, Robert: trustee, Cranston Foundation; chief financial officer, secretary, treasurer, Cranston Print Works Co.

Cranston Print Works Co.

Rockefeller, Frederic Lincoln: trustee, Cranston Foundation

Cranston Trucking Co.

Mandeville, Robert: trustee, Cranston Foundation;

chief financial officer, secretary, treasurer, Cranston Print Works Co.

Crawford & Co.

Wood, Edward Jenner: member, SunTrust Bank Atlanta Foundation

Cray Research Inc.

DeSimone, Livio Diego: chairman, chief executive officer, Minnesota Mining & Manufacturing Co.

Credit Suisse First Boston Corp.

Corti, Mario A.: senior vice president, chief administrative officer, Nestle U.S.A. Inc.

Stalder, Ruedi: trustee, Credit Suisse First Boston Foundation Trust

Crestar Bank

Tilghman, Richard Granville: chairman, chief executive officer, Crestar Foundation

Wells, James M., III: president, Crestar Finance Corp.

Crestar Financial Corp.

Fox, Joseph Carter: chairman, president, chief executive officer, Chesapeake Corp.

Hill, Bonnie Guiton: vice president, Times Mirror Co.; president, chief executive officer, Times Mirror Foundation

Crestar Financial Services Corp.

Williams, Karen Hastie: director, Fannie Mae Foundation

Crestar Mortgage Corp.

Wells, James M., III: president, Crestar Finance Corp.

Criterion Casualty Insurance Co.

Smith, Donald Kaye: senior vice president, general counsel, director, GEICO Corp.

Cub Cadet Corp.

Moll, Curtis E.: treasurer, trustee, Jochum-Moll Foundation (The)

Cullen/Frost Bankers Inc.

Frost, Thomas C., Senior: chairman, Frost National Bank

Culp Inc.

Norton, Patrick H.: chairman, director, La-Z-Boy Inc.

Cummins Americas Inc.

Solso, Theodore Matthew: president, chief operating officer, director, Cummins Engine Co., Inc.; director, Cummins Engine Foundation

Cummins Engine Co. Inc.

Johnson, James A.: chairman, chief executive officer, director, Fannie Mae; chairman, Fannie Mae Foundation

Miller, William Irwin: director, Cummins Engine Foundation

Ruckelshaus, William Doyle: chairman, director, Browning-Ferris Industries Inc.

Schacht, Henry Brewer: director, Cummins Engine Foundation

Thomas, Franklin Augustine: director, CBS Foundation

Wilson, James Lawrence: chairman, chief executive officer, director, Rohm & Haas Co.

Cuno Inc.

Powers, Paul Joseph: chairman, president, chief executive officer, director, Commercial Intertech Corp.; president, trustee, Commercial Intertech Foundation

Curtis Squire Inc.

Kunin, Myron: chairman, director, Regis Corp.; president, Regis Foundation

Curwood Inc.

Wulf, Gene C.: vice president, controller, Bemis Co. Foundation

Cushwa Small Business Development Center

Cushwa, Charles Benton, III: trustee, Commercial Intertech Foundation

Custer Pharmacy Inc.

Iott, Wallace D.: chairman, director, Seaway Food Town, Inc.

Cuyahoga Valley Railway Co. Inc.

Kelly, J. Peter: president, chief operating officer, director, LTV Corp.; trustee, LTV Foundation

Cyber Mark LLC

Geier, Peter E.: vice chairman, Huntington Bancshares Inc.

Cylinck Corp.

Harris, William W.: director, Pittway Corp. Charitable Foundation

Cylinder City Inc.

Powers, Paul Joseph: chairman, president, chief executive officer, director, Commercial Intertech Corp.; president, trustee, Commercial Intertech Foundation

Shields, Shirley M.: secretary, Commercial Intertech Foundation

Cylink Corp.

Guthart, Leo A.: vice chairman, director, Pittway Corp.

Cyprus Amax Minerals Co.

Solso, Theodore Matthew: president, chief operating officer, director, Cummins Engine Co., Inc.; director, Cummins Engine Foundation

Cyprus Miami Mining Corp.

Wolf, Philip C.: senior vice president, general counsel, secretary, Cyprus Amax Minerals Co.

Cytel Corp.

Mahoney, David L.: co-chief executive officer, McKesson-HBOC Corp.

D Diamond Sports Inc.

Hubbard Rominski, Kathryn: corporate secretary, Hubbard Broadcasting, Inc.; director, Hubbard Foundation

DIY Home Warehouse

Erb, Frederick A.: president, Erb Foundation

DNAX Research Institute Molecular Cell Biology

Kogan, Richard Jay: chairman, chief executive officer, Schering-Plough Corp.; trustee, member, Schering-Plough Foundation

DPL Inc.

Forster, Peter Hans: chairman, director, Dayton Power and Light Co.

Holmes, David Richard: chief executive officer, chief operating officer, director, Reynolds & Reynolds Co.

Koziar, Stephen F., Jr.: president, trustee, Dayton Power and Light Co. Foundation

Lansaw, Judy W.: secretary, trustee, Dayton Power and Light Co. Foundation

DQE Inc.

Bozzone, Robert P.: vice chairman, director, Allegheny Technologies Inc.; trustee, Allegheny Technologies Inc. Charitable Trust

DS Splitter Inc.

Hemminghaus, Roger Roy: chairman, director, Ultramar Diamond Shamrock Corp.

DST Corp.

Strandjord, Mary Jeannine: director, Sprint Foundation

DTE Energy Co.

Bauder, Lillian: vice president corporate affairs, Masco Corp.

Beale, Susan M.: director, Detroit Edison Foundation

Miller, Eugene A.: chairman, chief executive officer, Comerica Inc.

Dade Lease Management Inc.

Turner, Cal, Jr.: chairman, chief executive officer, director, Dollar General Corp.

Daily News Publishing Co. Inc.

McCorkindale, Douglas H.: vice chairman, president, Gannett Co., Inc.; president, Gannett Foundation

DaimlerChrysler

Thoman, G. Richard: president, chief operating officer, Xerox Corp.

DaimlerChrysler Aviation Inc.

Valade, Gary C.: executive vice president, chief financial officer, DaimlerChrysler Corp.; trustee, DaimlerChrysler Corp. Fund

Dain Bosworth

Weiser, Irving: chairman, president, chief executive officer, Dain Bosworth Inc.

Dain Rauscher Corp.

Civello, Nelson D.: director, Dain Bosworth Foundation

Dakota Dunes Development Co.

Bright, Stanley J.: chairman, president, chief executive officer, director, MidAmerican Energy Holdings Co.

Dal-Tile International Inc.

Lorch, George A.: chairman, chief executive officer, director, Armstrong World Industries, Inc.

Dallas Compressor Co.

Watson, Steven L.: vice president, secretary, Contran Corp.; vice president, secretary, director, Simmons Foundation, Inc. (Harold)

Dallas Morning News

Osborne, Burl: president publishing division, director, Belo Corp. (A.H.); president, trustee, Belo Corp. Foundation (A.H.)

Damark International

Cusick, Thomas A.: chairman, TCF National Bank Minnesota

Dames & Moore Group

Clarke, Robert F.: chairman, president, chief executive officer, director, Hawaiian Electric Co., Inc.; president, director, Hawaiian Electric Industries Charitable Foundation

Dana Corp.

Hiner, Glen Harold, Jr.: chairman, chief executive officer, director, Owens Corning

Danaven

Magliochetti, Joseph M.: president, chief executive officer, director, Dana Corp.; president, director, Dana Corp. Foundation

Daniel Boone Underwriters LLC

Jones, Raymond E.: secretary, director, Shelter Insurance Foundation; executive vice president, secretary, Shelter Mutual Insurance Co.

Lehr, Gustav J.: vice president, director, Shelter Insurance Foundation; chairman, director, Shelter Mutual Insurance Co.

Dapha Ltd.

Black, Natalie A.: group vice president interiors, general counsel, director, Kohler Co.

Darden Restaurants Inc.

Atwater, Horace Brewster, Jr.: trustee, Merck Co. Foundation

Burke, Daniel Barnett: vice president, treasurer, director, ABC Foundation

Darling Associates Garden Design

Darling, Robert Edward, Jr.: chairman, Ensign-Bickford Foundation

Data Resources

Marron, Donald Baird: chairman, chief executive officer, director, Paine Webber; trustee, Paine Webber Foundation

Data-Track Account Services Inc.

Ackerman, Philip Charles: senior vice president, director, National Fuel Gas Distribution Corp.

David Dart Inc.

Jacobsen, James C.: vice chairman, Kellwood Co.; vice president, director, Kellwood Foundation

David J. Joseph Co.

Bridgeland, James Ralph, Jr.: trustee, Star Bank NA, Cincinnati Foundation

David L. Babson Acquisition Co., Inc.

Wheeler, Thomas Beardsley: chairman, chief executive officer, Massachusetts Mutual Life Insurance Co.

David L. Babson Co., Inc.

Wendlandt, Gary Edward: executive vice president, chief investment officer, Massachusetts Mutual Life Insurance Co.

Davidson & Associates Inc.

Miller, Charles Daly: chairman, director, Avery Dennison Corp.; trustee, Whirlpool Foundation

Davidson Textron Inc.

Cambell, Lewis B.: chairman, chief executive officer, director, Textron Inc.

Davis & Kuelthau

Davis, Walter Stewart: secretary, treasurer, Grede Foundation

Dayco Distributing Inc.

Lippes, Gerald Sanford: secretary, Mark IV Industries Foundation

Dayco Products Inc.

Montague, William Patrick: president, chief operating officer, director, Mark IV Industries; president, Mark IV Industries Foundation

Dayton Hudson Corp.

Butzer, Bart: president, Mervyn's California

DeSimone, Livio Diego: chairman, chief executive officer, Minnesota Mining & Manufacturing Co.

Enrico, Roger A.: chairman, PepsiCo Foundation, Inc.; chairman, chief executive officer, director, PepsiCo, Inc.

George, William Wallace: chief executive officer, chairman, Medtronic, Inc.

Hale, Roger Loucks: chairman, TENNANT Co.; president, TENNANT Co. Foundation

Kovacevich, Richard M.: chairman, president, chief executive officer, Norwest Corp.; director, Norwest Foundation

Sanger, Stephen W.: chairman, trustee, General Mills Foundation; chairman, chief executive officer, director, General Mills, Inc.

Trujillo, Solomon D.: president, US West Foundation; president, chief executive officer, US West, Inc.

DeKalb Energy Co.

Bickner, Bruce P.: chairman, chief executive officer, director, DeKalb Genetics Corp.

DeMaria Electro Optics Inc.

Barnes, Wallace W.: director, Barnes Group Foundation Inc.

DeSoto Inc.

Simmons, Glenn Reuben: vice chairman, Contran Corp.

Dean Foods Co.

Getz, Bert A.: chairman, Globe Corp.; president, director, Globe Foundation

Getz, Bert A., Jr.: executive vice president, Globe Corp.; vice president, Globe Foundation

McKenna, Andrew James: director, Aon Foundation

Dean Witter Reynolds Inc.

Kidder, C. Robert: chairman, president, chief executive officer, director, Borden, Inc.

Dean Witter, Discover & Co.

Rogers, C. B., Jr.: chairman, Equifax Foundation; chairman, director, Equifax Inc.

Decibel Instruments Inc.

Pottruck, David Steven: president, chief executive officer, director, Schwab & Co., Inc. (Charles)

Deep South Products Inc.

Bragin, David H.: treasurer, assistant secretary, director, Winn-Dixie Stores Foundation

Deere & Co.

Hadley, Leonard Anson: chairman, chief executive officer, director, Maytag Corp.; president, trustee, Maytag Corp. Foundation

Deere Credit Inc.

Becherer, Hans Walter: chairman, chief executive officer, director, Deere & Co.; director, Deere Foundation (John)

England, Joseph Walker: chairman, director, Deere Foundation (John)

Deere Marketing Services Inc.

Becherer, Hans Walter: chairman, chief executive officer, director, Deere & Co.; director, Deere Foundation (John)

Lawson, John K.: senior vice president, Deere & Co.; director, Deere Foundation (John)

Deerfield Urethane Inc.

Wyne, Jon R.: senior vice president, treasurer, Bayer Corp.; treasurer, Bayer Foundation

Del Webb Corp.

Maffie, Michael O.: president, chief executive officer, director, Southwest Gas Corp.; trustee, Southwest Gas Corp. Foundation

Dell Computer Corp.

Carty, Donald J.: vice president, treasurer, AMR/ American Airlines Foundation; president, chairman, chief executive officer, director, AMR Corp.

Delphi Automotive Systems Corp.

Labrecque, Thomas Goulet: president, chief operating officer, director, Chase Manhattan Bank, NA; president, Chase Manhattan Foundation

Delsan Industries Inc.

Hiner, Glen Harold, Jr.: chairman, chief executive officer, director, Owens Corning

Delta Air Lines

Broadhead, James Lowell: chairman, president, chief executive officer, director, Florida Power & Light Co.; chief executive officer, director, FPL Group Foundation, Inc.

Fisher, George Myles Cordell: chairman, president, chief executive officer, director, Eastman Kodak Co.

Goode, David Ronald: chairman, president, chief executive officer, director, Norfolk Southern Corp.

Grinstein, Gerald: director, PACCAR Inc.

Deltic Timber Co.

Murphy, R. Madison: chairman, director, Murphy Oil Corp.

Deluxe Corp.

MacMillan, Whitney: member contributions committee, Cargill Inc.

Dentsply International Inc.

Smith, W. Keith: senior vice chairman, member corporate review committee, director, Mellon Financial Corp.

Denver Chemical

Wagar, James Lee: manager, Carter-Wallace Foundation

Deposit Guaranty Corp.

McMillan, Howard Lamar, Jr.: president, chief operating officer, director, Deposit Guaranty National Bank

Robinson, E. B., Jr.: chairman, chief executive officer, director, Deposit Guaranty National Bank

Depositors Corp.

Gorman, Leon A.: president, chief executive officer, Bean, Inc. (L.L.)

Depository Trust Co.

Ryan, Arthur Frederick: trustee, Chase Manhattan Foundation; chairman, chief executive officer, Prudential Insurance Co. of America

Derby International Corp.

Nelson, Merlin Edward: chairman, director, IBJ Foundation

Des Moines International Airport

Kalainov, Sam Charles: chairman, president, chief executive officer, AmerUS Group

Des Moines Register & Tribune Co.

Chapple, Thomas Leslie: senior vice president, general counsel, secretary, Gannett Co., Inc.; secretary, Gannett Foundation

Curley, John J.: chairman, chief executive officer, director, Gannett Co., Inc.; chairman, Gannett Foundation

McCorkindale, Douglas H.: vice chairman, president, Gannett Co., Inc.; president, Gannett Foundation

Desert Sun Publishing Co. Inc.

McCorkindale, Douglas H.: vice chairman, president,

Gannett Co., Inc.; president, Gannett Foundation

Destec Energy Inc.

Carr, Cassandra Colvin: director, SBC Foundation

Reinhard, J. Pedro: executive vice president, chief financial officer, director, Dow Chemical Co.

Detroit Edison Co.

Adderley, Terence E.: chairman, president, chief executive officer, director, Kelly Services; president, director, Kelly Services Foundation

Bauder, Lillian: vice president corporate affairs, Masco Corp.

Miller, Eugene A.: chairman, chief executive officer, Comerica Inc.

Detroit Lions Inc.

Ford, William Clay, Jr.: chairman, Ford Motor Co.

Detroit News Inc.

Chapple, Thomas Leslie: senior vice president, general counsel, secretary, Gannett Co., Inc.; secretary, Gannett Foundation

Curley, John J.: chairman, chief executive officer, director, Gannett Co., Inc.; chairman, Gannett Foundation

McCorkindale, Douglas H.: vice chairman, president, Gannett Co., Inc.; president, Gannett Foundation

Deutsch Fastener Corp.

Deutsch, Carl: president, Deutsch Foundation

Dial Corp.

Ford, Joseph 'Joe': chairman, chief executive officer, president, ALLTEL Corp.

Guinn, Donald Eugene: chairman emeritus, Pacific Mutual Life Insurance Co.

Diamond Offshore Drilling Inc.

Tisch, James S.: president, chief executive officer, director, CNA

Diamond Shamrock Refining & Marketing Co.

Hemminghaus, Roger Roy: chairman, director, Ultramar Diamond Shamrock Corp.

Klesse, William R.: executive vice president operations, Ultramar Diamond Shamrock Corp.

Diamond Shamrock Stations

Hemminghaus, Roger Roy: chairman, director, Ultramar Diamond Shamrock Corp.

Diebold Inc.

Timken, William Robert, Jr.: chairman, president, chief executive officer, director, Timken Co. (The)

Dietzgen Corp.

Weyerhaeuser, George Hunt: director, Weyerhaeuser Co.; trustee, Weyerhaeuser Co. Foundation

Digital Gene Techs

Jacobs, Joseph J.: president, director, Jacobs Engineering Foundation; chairman, director, Jacobs Engineering Group

Digital Solutions Inc.

Koeppe, Alfred C.: senior vice president corporate services & external affairs, Public Service Electric & Gas Foundation

Dimon Inc.

Dickson, Rush Stuart: chairman, Dickson Foundation

Diplom Ltd.

Jacobsen, James C.: vice chairman, Kellwood Co.; vice president, director, Kellwood Foundation

Direct Marketing Association

Trask, Robert B.: president, chief operating officer, director, Country Curtains, Inc.; clerk, trustee, High Meadow Foundation

Directors Guild of America

Rosenthal, Sol: counsel, Playboy Enterprises Inc.

Disney Enterprises Inc.

Disney, Roy Edward: trustee, Disney Co. Foundation (Walt); vice chairman, director, Disney Co. (Walt)

Eisner, Michael Dammann: president, trustee, Disney Co. Foundation (Walt); chairman, chief executive officer, director, Disney Co. (Walt)

Litvack, Sanford M.: senior executive vice president, chief corporate operations, director, Disney Co. (Walt)

Disneyland International

Eisner, Michael Dammann: president, trustee, Disney Co. Foundation (Walt); chairman, chief executive officer, director, Disney Co. (Walt)

Distrigas Massachusetts Corp.

Cabot, John G. L.: vice chairman, Kinder Morgn

Diversatek Inc.

Connolly, Gerald Edward: trustee, Reinhart Family Foundation (D. B. and Marjorie)

Dixie Building Supplies Inc.

Fjelstul, Dean M.: senior vice president, chief financial officer, Walter Industries Inc.

Porter, Edward A.: vice president, general counsel, secretary, Walter Industries Inc.

Dixie Group Inc.

Frierson, Daniel K.: chairman, chief executive officer, Dixie Group, Inc. (The); president, trustee, Dixie Yarns Foundation, Inc.

Dixie Packers Inc.

Bragin, David H.: treasurer, assistant secretary, director, Winn-Dixie Stores Foundation

Dofasco Inc.

Coyne, William E.: senior vice president, Minnesota Mining & Manufacturing Co.

Dole Food Co. Inc.

Ferry, Richard Michael: chairman, Pacific Mutual Life Insurance Co.

Dolgencorp Inc.

Turner, Cal, Jr.: chairman, chief executive officer, director, Dollar General Corp.

Dollar Tree Stores

Wurtzel, Alan Leon: chairman, Circuit City Foundation; chairman, trustee, Circuit City Stores, Inc.

Domaine Mumm Inc.

Bronfman, Samuel, II: president, trustee, Bronfman Foundation/Joseph E. Seagram & Sons, Inc. Fund (Samuel)

Dome Corp.

Poindexter, Christian Herndon: chairman, Baltimore Gas & Electric Foundation; chairman, chief executive officer, director, Constellation Energy Group, Inc.

Dominion Bankshares Corp.

McGlothlin, James W.: chief executive officer, United Coal Co. Charitable Foundation; chairman, chief executive officer, United Co.

Reynolds, Randolph Nicklas: vice chairman, executive officer, director, Reynolds Metals Co.; director, Reynolds Metals Co. Foundation

Dominion Energy Inc.

Spilman, Robert H.: chairman, chief executive officer, Bassett Furniture Industries; chairman, director, Bassett Furniture Industries Fdn.

Dominion National Bank

Reynolds, Randolph Nicklas: vice chairman, executive officer, director, Reynolds Metals Co.; director, Reynolds Metals Co. Foundation

Dominion Resources Inc.

Spilman, Robert H.: chairman, chief executive officer, Bassett Furniture Industries; chairman, director, Bassett Furniture Industries Fdn.

Donaldson Co. Inc.

Bonsignore, Michael Robert: director, Honeywell Foundation; chairman, chief executive officer, director, Honeywell International Inc.

Grundhofer, John Francis: president, chief executive officer, director, U.S. Bancorp

Sanger, Stephen W.: chairman, trustee, General Mills Foundation; chairman, chief executive officer, director, General Mills, Inc.

Donaldson Lufkin & Jenrette Inc.

Sanders, Walter Jeremiah, III: chairman, chief executive officer, director, Advanced Micro Devices, Inc.

Donaldson Lufkin Jenrette Mcht Banking Partners

Johnson, David Willis: chairman, director, Campbell Soup Co.

Dorinco Reinsurance Co.

Reinhard, J. Pedro: executive vice president, chief financial officer, director, Dow Chemical Co.

Double G Coatings

Penny, Roger Pratt: president, chief operating officer, director, Bethlehem Steel Corp.

Dow Chemical Europe SA

Butler, Andrew J.: trustee, Dow Chemical Co.

Dow Corning Corp.

Ackerman, Roger G.: trustee, Corning Inc. Foundation

Campbell, Van C.: vice chairman, chief financial officer, chief administrative officer, director, Corning Inc.; trustee, Corning Inc. Foundation

Falla, Enrique Crabb: senior consult, director, Dow Chemical Co.

Garrity, Norman E.: executive vice president, director, Corning Inc.; trustee, Corning Inc. Foundation

Stavropoulos, William S.: president, chief executive officer, director, Dow Chemical Co.

Dow Elanco

Downey, Joseph L.: trustee, Dow Chemical Co.

Reinhard, J. Pedro: executive vice president, chief financial officer, director, Dow Chemical Co.

Dow Jones & Co. Inc.

Cook, Jane Bancroft: chairman emeritus, Dow Jones Foundation

Golub, Harvey: chairman, chief executive officer, director, American Express Co.; trustee, American Express Foundation

Hockaday, Irvine O., Jr.: president, chief executive officer, director, Hallmark Cards Inc.

MacElree, Jane Cox: member advisory committee, Dow Jones Foundation

Steere, William Campbell, Jr.: chairman, chief executive officer, director, Pfizer Inc.

Dow Jones Telerate Inc.
Burenga, Kenneth L.: president, chief operating officer, director, Dow Jones & Co., Inc.

Drayton Co.
Gaiswinkler, Robert Sigfried: chairman, director, First Financial Bank; director, First Financial Foundation

Drexel Heritage Furnishings
Lyon, Wayne Barton: president, chief operating officer, director, Masco Corp.

Dreyfus Corp.
Ross, Arthur: senior vice president, Central National-Gottesman; director, Central National-Gottesman Foundation
Syron, Richard F.: chairman, chief executive officer, director, American Stock Exchange, Inc.

Dreyfus Fund
Hiatt, Arnold Selig: chairman, director, Stride Rite Foundation

Druen Dietrich Reynolds & Koogler
Druen, W. Sidney: director, Nationwide Insurance Enterprise Foundation

Dual Inc.
Pierre, Percy A.: trustee, Hitachi Foundation

Duane Reade Inc.
Johnson, David Willis: chairman, director, Campbell Soup Co.

Duchossois Communication Co.
Duchossois, Richard Louis: secretary, Duchossois Foundation; chairman, chief executive officer, director, Duchossois Industries Inc.

Dudley R. Cloud & Son Construction
Cloud, Bruce Benjamin, Sr.: vice chairman, director, Zachry Co. (H.B.)

Duke Energy Corp.
Esrey, William Todd: chairman, chief executive officer, Sprint Corp.

Duke Power Co.
Ford, Joseph 'Joe': chairman, chief executive officer, president, ALLTEL Corp.

Duke Realty Investments Inc.
Rogers, James E., Jr.: vice chairman, president, chief executive officer, Cinergy Corp.; vice chairman, director, Cinergy Foundation

Duluth & Northeastern Railroad Co.
Powell, Sandra Theresa: trustee, Potlatch Foundation II
Zuehlke, Gerald L.: treasurer, Potlatch Corp.

Duluth & Northeastern Rr Co.
Fleshman, Betty R.: secretary, Potlatch Corp.

Dun & Bradstreet Corp.
McKinnell, Henry A., PhD: president, chief operating officer, Pfizer Inc.
Quinlan, Michael Robert: chairman executive committee, McDonald's Corp.; director, McDonald's Corp. Charitable Foundation

Dun & Bradstreet Holdings Inc.
Buchanan, William Hobart, Jr.: assistant secretary, Dun & Bradstreet Corp. Foundation, Inc.

Dunhams Athleisure Corp.
Chemerow, David I.: executive vice president, chief financial officer, Playboy Enterprises Inc.

Duns Investing Corp.
Buchanan, William Hobart, Jr.: assistant secretary, Dun & Bradstreet Corp. Foundation, Inc.

Duquense Light Co.
Bozzone, Robert P.: vice chairman, director, Allegheny Technologies Inc.; trustee, Allegheny Technologies Inc. Charitable Trust

Duracell International Inc.
Edwards, Earnest Jonathan: director, Alcoa Foundation

Durco International Inc.
Molen, Richard L.: chairman, chief executive officer, director, Huffy Corp.; trustee, Huffy Foundation, Inc.

E.I. du Pont de Nemours and Co.
Weill, Sanford I.: chairman, chief executive officer, Citibank Corp.; chairman, Citigroup Foundation

E.W. Scripps Co.
Burlingame, John Hunter: executive partner, Scripps Co. (E.W.)
Meyer, Daniel Joseph: president, Milacron Foundation; chairman, president, chief executive officer, director, Milacron, Inc.
Paumgarten, Nicholas Biddle: managing director, Scripps Co. (E.W.); member, Scripps Howard Foundation
Tysoe, Ronald W.: vice chairman, director, Federated Department Stores, Inc.; member, Scripps Howard Foundation

EDI Leasing Co. LP
Bachmann, John W.: managing partner, Jones & Co. (Edward D.); chairman, Jones & Co. Foundation (Edward D.)

EFCO Inc.
Hessler, David J.: secretary, trustee, Jochum-Moll Foundation (The); president, partner, MTD Products Inc.

EFTEC North America LLC
Ray, John Thomas, Jr.: president, director, Fuller Co. Foundation (H.B.)

EG&G Holdings Inc.
Kucharski, John Michael: trustee, PerkinElmer Foundation; chairman, chief executive officer, director, PerkinElmer, Inc.

EG&G Technical Services
Johnson, Hansford Tillman: trustee, USAA Foundation, A Charitable Trust

EGT
Elam, Lloyd Charles, MD: trustee, Merck Co. Foundation

EI du Pont de Nemours & Co.
Dunham, Archie W.: president, chief executive officer, Conoco, Inc.
Mac Kimm, Margaret (Pontius) 'Mardie': trustee, Chicago Title and Trust Co. Foundation
McKee, Robert E., III: executive vice president corporate strategy & development, du Pont de Nemours & Co. (E.I.)

EMI America
Gersh, Gary: president, chief executive officer, EMI Music Publishing

EV International Inc.
Woolard, Edgar Smith, Jr.: director, du Pont de Nemours & Co. (E.I.)

EVI Weatherford Inc.
Lubar, Sheldon B.: chairman, Ameritech Corp.; director, Firstar Milwaukee Foundation

Eagle Carriers
Demere, Robert H.: president, Colonial Foundation; chairman, Colonial Oil Industries, Inc.

Easco Aluminum
Little, Gene E.: trustee, advisor, Timken Co. Charitable Trust (The); secretary, treasurer, trustee, Timken Co. Educational Fund

Easco Inc.
Little, Gene E.: trustee, advisor, Timken Co. Charitable Trust (The); secretary, treasurer, trustee, Timken Co. Educational Fund

East Barnet Hydroelectric
Young, Robert Harris: president, chief executive officer, Central Vermont Public Service Corp.

East Maui Irrigation Co.
Sasaki, Robert K.: director, Alexander & Baldwin Foundation

East River Housing Corp.
Gross, Murray: trustee, PerkinElmer Foundation; senior vice president, general counsel, clerk, PerkinElmer, Inc.

Eastern Enterprises Vol Associates
Cawley, Michael J.: vice president risk management, Eastern Enterprises

Eastern Heights Bank
Grenz, M. Kay: director, 3M Foundation; vice president human resources, Minnesota Mining & Manufacturing Co.

Eastman Kodak Co.
Tyson, Laura D'Andrea: director, Ameritech Foundation

Eaton Corp.
Armstrong, Neil A.: trustee, Milacron Foundation; director, Milacron, Inc.
Critelli, Michael J.: vice president, secretary, general counsel, chairman, Pitney Bowes Inc.

Eaton Vance Corp.
Cabot, John G. L.: vice chairman, Kinder Morgn
Nelson, John Martin: chairman, director, TJX Companies, Inc.

Ebsco Employee Savings & Profit Sharing Trust
Stephens, Elton Bryson: founder, chairman, Ebsco Industries, Inc.

Echelon Corp.
Markkula, Armas Clifford, Jr.: chairman, director, Apple Computer, Inc.
Rock, Arthur: co-founder, chairman executive committee, director, Intel Corp.

Eclipsys Corp.
Denning, Steven A.: vice president, General Atlantic Partners II LP

Ecolab Inc.
Howard, James Joseph, III: chairman, president, chief executive officer, director, Northern States Power Co.

Economic Development Partnership Alabama
Jones, D. Paul, Jr.: chairman, chief executive officer, Compass Bank; trustee, Compass Bank Foundation

Ecuatoriana de Sal Y Productos Quimicos California

Johnston, William E., Junior: president, chief operating officer, director, Morton International Inc.

Edison Brothers Apparel Stores

Newman, Andrew E.: member, Edison Family Foundation

Edison Electric Inst

Hale, Roger W.: chairman, chief executive officer, director, LG&E Energy Corp.; president, LG&E Energy Foundation

Edison Illuminating Co. Detroit

Beale, Susan M.: director, Detroit Edison Foundation

Edison International

Frank, Stephen E.: president, chief operating officer, director, Edison International

Sutton, Thomas C.: chairman, director, Pacific Mutual Charitable Foundation; chairman, chief executive officer, director, Pacific Mutual Life Insurance Co.

Edison Mission Energy

Bryson, John E.: chairman, chief executive officer, Edison International

Edward Don & Co.

Schulman, David R.: director, Katten, Muchin & Zavis Foundation

Edward W. Scripps Trust

Scripps, Charles Edward: chairman executive committee, director, vice president, Scripps Co. (E.W.); member, Scripps Howard Foundation

Ehrlich Manufacturing Co. Inc.

Ehrlich, M. Gordon: trustee, Orchard Foundation

Eighty-Eight Oil Co.

True, David: partner, True Oil Co.

True, Diemer: partner, True Oil Co.

El Dorado Investment Co.

Snell, Richard: chairman, president, chief executive officer, director, Arizona Public Service Co.

El Morro Corrugated Box Corp.

Tomlinson, Joseph Ernest: vice president, treasurer, controller, Inland Container Corp.; vice president, director, Inland Foundation, Inc.

El Paso Energy Corp.

Baish, Richard Owen: senior vice president, director, El Paso Energy Foundation

El Paso Gas Marketing Co.

Wise, William Allen: chairman, president, chief executive officer, director, El Paso Energy Co.; chairman, director, El Paso Energy Foundation

El Paso Natural Gas Co.

Richards, Joel, III: vice president, El Paso Energy Foundation

White, Britton, Jr.: vice president, El Paso Energy Foundation

Wise, William Allen: chairman, president, chief executive officer, director, El Paso Energy Co.; chairman, director, El Paso Energy Foundation

El Paso Tennessee Pipeline Co.

Richards, Joel, III: vice president, El Paso Energy Foundation

White, Britton, Jr.: vice president, El Paso Energy Foundation

El Paso Times

McCorkindale, Douglas H.: vice chairman, president, Gannett Co., Inc.; president, Gannett Foundation

Electric Energy Inc.

Mueller, Charles William: chairman, president, chief executive officer, Ameren Corp.; trustee, Ameren Corp. Charitable Trust

Electric Power Research Institute

Dahlberg, Alfred William, III: chairman, president, chief executive officer, Southern Co. Services Inc.

Electronic Data Systems Corp.

Cheney, Richard B.: chief executive officer, Halliburton Co.; president, Halliburton Foundation, Inc.

Eaton, Robert James: co-chairman, president, chief executive officer, DaimlerChrysler Corp.

Hunt, Ray Lee: chairman, chief executive officer, director, Hunt Oil Co.

Kidder, C. Robert: chairman, president, chief executive officer, director, Borden, Inc.

Smith, John Francis, Jr.: chairman, General Motors Corp.

Sosa, Enrique J.: trustee, Dow Chemical Co. Foundation

Eleven-Fifty Corp.

McCorkindale, Douglas H.: vice chairman, president, Gannett Co., Inc.; president, Gannett Foundation

Elizabeth Arden Interamerica

Phillips, Robert M.: president, Unilever Home & Personal Care U.S.A.

Elwyn Institute

Campbell, Robert Henderson: chairman, chief executive officer, Sunoco Inc.

Emco Ltd. London & Canada

Lyon, Wayne Barton: president, chief operating officer, director, Masco Corp.

Emerson Electric Co.

Busch, August Adolphus, III: chairman, president, chief executive officer, Anheuser-Busch Companies, Inc.

Van Cleve, William Moore: member public policy committee, Emerson Charitable Trust; partner, Emerson Electric Co.

Whitacre, Edward E., Jr.: chairman, director, chief executive officer, SBC Communications Inc.

Williams, Eugene Flewellyn, Jr.: member public policy committee, Emerson Charitable Trust

Emerson Electric Overseas Finance Corp.

Tamke, George W.: president, chief operating officer, director, Emerson Electric Co.

Emery Air Freight Corp.

Moffitt, Donald Eugene: chairman, director, CNF Transportation, Inc.

Emery Distr System

Quesnel, Gregory L.: president, chief executive officer, director, CNF Transportation, Inc.

Employees Mutual Savings Building Loan

Remmel, Jerry G.: chief financial officer, vice president, treasurer, Wisconsin Energy Corp.

Willis, Gordon A.: assistant treasurer, assistant secretary, Wisconsin Energy Corp. Foundation, Inc.

Employers Insurance of Wausau Mutual Co.

Druen, W. Sidney: director, Nationwide Insurance Enterprise Foundation

Employers Modern Life Co.

Kelley, Bruce Gunn: vice president, director, Employers Mutual Charitable Foundation

Employers Reins Corp.

Bossidy, Lawrence Arthur: chairman, director, AlliedSignal Foundation Inc.; chairman, chief executive officer, director, AlliedSignal Inc.

En. Able LLC

Aaronson, Morton C.: vice president, Kinder Morgn; director, KN Energy Foundation

Encycle Inc.

Osborne, Richard de Jongh: director, ASARCO Foundation; chairman, chief executive officer, director, ASARCO Inc.

Energy Corp. America

Coors, Peter Hanson: vice president, director, Coors Brewing Co.

Energy Inc.

Randolph, Jackson Harold: chairman, Cinergy Corp.; chairman, director, Cinergy Foundation

Energy Insurance Mutual

Burg, H. Peter: president, chief operating officer, FirstEnergy Corp.

Loomans, Leslie Louis: treasurer, director, Detroit Edison Foundation

Enershop Inc.

Rosilier, Glenn D.: executive vice president, chief financial officer, Central & South West Services

Enertech Associates International Inc.

Randolph, Jackson Harold: chairman, Cinergy Corp.; chairman, director, Cinergy Foundation

Engelhard Corp.

Watson, Douglas G.: chairman, Novartis US Foundation

Engineer and Fabricators Co.

Franke, William Augustus: chairman, president, chief executive officer, America West Airlines, Inc.; director, Phelps Dodge Foundation

England/Corsair Inc.

Norton, Patrick H.: chairman, director, La-Z-Boy Inc.

Engraph Corp.

Moran, Harry J.: executive vice president, Sonoco Products Co.

Enmark Stations

Demere, Robert H.: president, Colonial Foundation; chairman, Colonial Oil Industries, Inc.

Enron Corp.

Meyer, Jerome J.: chairman, chief executive officer, Tektronix, Inc.

Enserch Corp.

Bridgewater, Bernard Adolphus, Jr.: member board control, Brown Shoe Co. Charitable Trust; chairman, president, chief executive officer, director, Brown Shoe Co., Inc.

Enserch Exploration Inc.

Bridgewater, Bernard Adolphus, Jr.: member board control, Brown Shoe Co. Charitable Trust; chairman, president, chief executive officer, director, Brown Shoe Co., Inc.

Ensign-Bickford Co.

Fonteyne, Herman J.: president, chief executive officer, director, Ensign-Bickford Industries

Long, Michael Thomas: director, Ensign-Bickford Foundation

Ensign-Bickford Haz-Pros Inc.

Fonteyne, Herman J.: president, chief executive officer, director, Ensign-Bickford Industries

Long, Michael Thomas: director, Ensign-Bickford Foundation

Ensign-Bickford Industries

Darling, Robert Edward, Jr.: chairman, Ensign-Bickford Foundation

Ensign-Bickford Realty Corp.

Fonteyne, Herman J.: president, chief executive officer, director, Ensign-Bickford Industries

Long, Michael Thomas: director, Ensign-Bickford Foundation

Entech Inc.

Gannon, Robert P.: chairman, president, director, chief executive officer, Montana Power Co.; president, director, Montana Power Foundation

Pederson, Jerrold P.: vice president, chief financial officer, director, Montana Power Co.; director, Montana Power Foundation

Senechal, Ellen M.: treasurer, Montana Power Co.

Zimmerman, Michael E.: vice president, general counsel, Montana Power Co.

Enterprise Coffee & Supply Co.

Taylor, Andrew C.: president, chief executive officer, director, Enterprise Rent-A-Car Co.

Enterprise Diversified Holdings Inc.

Ferland, E. James: chairman, president, chief executive officer, Public Service Electric & Gas Co.

Enterprise Leasing Co. Denver

Taylor, Andrew C.: president, chief executive officer, director, Enterprise Rent-A-Car Co.

Entrada Industries Inc.

Heiner, Clyde Mont: executive vice president, Questar Corp.

Parks, Stephen E.: vice president, treasurer, chief financial officer, Questar Corp.

Envirite Corp.

Black, Lennox K.: president, Teleflex Foundation; chairman, director, Teleflex Inc.

Envoy Corp.

Hirsch, Laurence E.: chairman, chief executive officer, director, Centex Corp.

Epitope Inc.

Donahue, Richard King: vice chairman, Nike, Inc.

Equifax Canada

Rogers, C. B., Jr.: chairman, Equifax Foundation; chairman, director, Equifax Inc.

Equifax Credit Information Services

Rogers, C. B., Jr.: chairman, Equifax Foundation; chairman, director, Equifax Inc.

Equifax Inc.

Dahlberg, Alfred William, III: chairman, president, chief executive officer, Southern Co. Services Inc.

Humann, L. Phillip: member, SunTrust Bank Atlanta Foundation

Equifax Marketing Decision Systems

Rogers, C. B., Jr.: chairman, Equifax Foundation; chairman, director, Equifax Inc.

Equifax Payment Services Inc.

Rogers, C. B., Jr.: chairman, Equifax Foundation; chairman, director, Equifax Inc.

Equinox Vermont Corp.

Young, Robert Harris: president, chief executive officer, Central Vermont Public Service Corp.

Equitable Companies Inc.

Esrey, William Todd: chairman, chief executive officer, Sprint Corp.

Equitable Resources Inc.

Rohr, James Edward: chief executive officer, president, director, PNC Financial Services Group

Shapira, David S.: trustee, Giant Eagle Foundation; chairman, chief executive officer, director, Giant Eagle Inc.

Equitable of Iowa Companies

Rehm, Jack Daniel: chairman emeritus, director, Meredith Corp.

Equities Inc.

Chelberg, Bruce Stanley: chairman, chief executive officer, director, Whitman Corp.; director, Whitman Corp. Foundation

Ergo Science Corp.

Hunt, Ray Lee: chairman, chief executive officer, director, Hunt Oil Co.

Eskimo Pie Corp.

Reynolds, Randolph Nicklas: vice chairman, executive officer, director, Reynolds Metals Co.; director, Reynolds Metals Co. Foundation

Estee Lauder Companies Inc.

Vagelos, Pindaros Roy: trustee, Prudential Insurance Co. of America

Esterline Technologies Corp.

Meyer, Jerome J.: chairman, chief executive officer, Tektronix, Inc.

Euroclear

Carter, Marshall Nichols: chairman, chief executive officer, State Street Bank & Trust Co.

Evans Inc.

Bookshester, Dennis S.: chairman, chief executive officer, Playboy Enterprises Inc.

Evanston Hospital Corp.

Kelly, Janet L.: executive vice president corporate development, general counsel, secretary, Kellogg Co.

Evansville Courier Co. Inc.

Burleigh, William Robert: president, chief executive officer, director, Scripps Co. (E.W.); member, Scripps Howard Foundation

Scripps, Charles Edward: chairman executive committee, director, vice president, Scripps Co. (E.W.); member, Scripps Howard Foundation

Evenflo & Spalding Holdings

Tokarz, Michael T.: founding partner, Walter Industries Inc.

Everen Capital Corp.

Esrey, William Todd: chairman, chief executive officer, Sprint Corp.

Exel Ltd.

Esposito, Michael Patrick, Jr.: trustee, Chase Manhattan Foundation

Exeter International Corp.

Nelson, Merlin Edward: chairman, director, IBJ Foundation

Exton Square Inc.

Deering, Anthony W.: chairman, chief executive officer, Rouse Co.; chairman, president, trustee, Rouse Co. Foundation

Donahue, Jeffrey H.: senior vice president, chief financial officer, Rouse Co.

ExxonMobil Corp.

Esrey, William Todd: chairman, chief executive officer, Sprint Corp.

Heimbold, Charles Andreas, Jr.: chairman, president, chief executive officer, Bristol-Myers Squibb Co.

Houghton, James Richardson: director, Corning Inc.; trustee, Corning Inc. Foundation

Johnson, Samuel Curtis: chairman, director, president, Johnson & Son (S.C.); chairman, trustee, Johnson Wax Fund (S.C.)

King, Reatha Clark: director, Fuller Co. Foundation (H.B.); president, executive director, General Mills Foundation

Nelson, Marilyn Carlson: chairman, chief executive officer, president, Carlson Companies, Inc.

F A I Trading Co. Inc.

Ray, John Thomas, Jr.: president, director, Fuller Co. Foundation (H.B.)

F C Henderson Inc.

Ratner, Albert Benjamin: trustee, Forest City Enterprises Charitable Foundation, Inc.; co-chairman, director, Forest City Enterprises, Inc.

F-P Technology Holding Corp.

Montague, William Patrick: president, chief operating officer, director, Mark IV Industries; president, Mark IV Industries Foundation

FB Beattie & Co. Inc.

Eigsti, Roger Harry: chairman, chief executive officer, SAFECO Corp.

FD Engineers & Constructors

Rollans, James Ora: senior vice president, chief administrative officer, chief financial officer, Fluor Corp.; trustee, Fluor Foundation

FDL Reserve Bank

Koch, David Andrew: president, Graco Foundation; chairman, director, Graco, Inc.

FDX Corp.

Walsh, Paul S.: chairman, president, chief executive officer, Pillsbury Co.; director, Pillsbury Co. Foundation

FFS Inc.

Wurtele, C. Angus: president, Valspar Foundation

FH Center Inc.

Dods, Walter Arthur, Jr.: president, director, First Hawaiian Foundation; chairman, chief executive

officer, director, First Hawaiian, Inc.

Karr, Howard Henry: treasurer, director, First Hawaiian Foundation

FHB Mortgage Co. Inc.

Dods, Walter Arthur, Jr.: president, director, First Hawaiian Foundation; chairman, chief executive officer, director, First Hawaiian, Inc.

FHB Properties Inc.

Dods, Walter Arthur, Jr.: president, director, First Hawaiian Foundation; chairman, chief executive officer, director, First Hawaiian, Inc.

FHL Lease Holding Co. Inc.

Dods, Walter Arthur, Jr.: president, director, First Hawaiian Foundation; chairman, chief executive officer, director, First Hawaiian, Inc.

FHL SPC One Inc.

Dods, Walter Arthur, Jr.: president, director, First Hawaiian Foundation; chairman, chief executive officer, director, First Hawaiian, Inc.

FI Instruments Inc.

Hatsopoulos, George Nicholas: founder, chairman, chief executive officer, director, Thermo Electron Corp.; committee member, Thermo Electron Foundation

FINA Natural Gas Co.

Godfrey, Cullen Michael: vice president, FINA Foundation

FINA Oil & Chemical Co.

Haddock, Ronald Wayne: president, chief executive officer, director, FINA; president, FINA Foundation

FINASERVE Inc.

Godfrey, Cullen Michael: vice president, FINA Foundation

FM Global Insurance

Luke, John A., Jr.: chairman, president, chief executive officer, director, Westvaco Corp.

O'Toole, Robert Joseph: director, Firstar Milwaukee Foundation; chairman, president, chief executive officer, director, Smith Corp. (A.O.); director, Smith Foundation, Inc. (A.O.)

FMC Canada Ltd.

McClung, James Allen: vice president, director, FMC Foundation

FMC Corp.

Bridgewater, Bernard Adolphus, Jr.: member board control, Brown Shoe Co. Charitable Trust; chairman, president, chief executive officer, director, Brown Shoe Co., Inc.

Mooney, Edward J., Jr.: chairman, president, chief executive officer, director, Nalco Chemical Co.

FMC Gold Co.

Burt, Robert Norcross: chairman, chief executive officer, director, FMC Corp.; director, FMC Foundation

FMC Nederland BV

McClung, James Allen: vice president, director, FMC Foundation

FMR Corp.

Lawrence, Robert Ashton: director, New York Times Co. Foundation

FP Technologies Holding Corp.

Lippes, Gerald Sanford: secretary, Mark IV Industries Foundation

FPL Group Inc.

Evanson, Paul John: president, treasurer, director, FPL Group Foundation, Inc.

FRP Properties

Baker, Edward L.: chairman, director, Florida Rock Industries; president, Florida Rock Industries Foundation

Baker, John Daniel, II: president, chief executive officer, director, Florida Rock Industries; vice president, Florida Rock Industries Foundation

FW Woolworth Co.

Mac Kimm, Margaret (Pontius) 'Mardie': trustee, Chicago Title and Trust Co. Foundation

Preston, James Edward: vice president, director, Avon Products Foundation, Inc.; chairman, chief executive officer, director, Avon Products, Inc.

Facilities/Tech Support Group

Thyen, Ronald J.: senior executive vice president, director, Habig Foundation; senior executive vice president, chief operating officer director, Kimball International, Inc.

Fairbanks Trucking Inc.

Gallo, Joseph E.: co-president, Gallo Foundation

Falls City Industries Inc.

Hower, Frank Beard, Jr.: vice chairman, Anthem Foundation, Inc.

Family Care Services Metropolitan Chicago

Fleming, Richard Harrison: chief financial officer, senior vice president, USG Corp.; treasurer, trustee, USG Foundation

Fansteel

Evans, Robert Sheldon: chairman, chief executive officer, Crane Co.; chairman, president, director, Crane Foundation

Fargo Manufacturing Co. Inc.

Rowell, Harry Brown, Jr.: trustee, Hubbell Foundation (Harvey)

Farm City Insurance Co.

Kelley, Bruce Gunn: vice president, director, Employers Mutual Charitable Foundation

Farmer Insurance Co. Oregon

Denlea, Leo Edward, Jr.: retired chairman, president, chief executive officer, director, Farmers Group, Inc.; vice president, Farmers Group Safety Foundation

Farmers Insurance Exchange Farmers Group

Feinstein, Martin D.: chairman, chief executive officer, Farmers Group, Inc.

Farmers Insurance Group Companies

Denlea, Leo Edward, Jr.: retired chairman, president, chief executive officer, director, Farmers Group, Inc.; vice president, Farmers Group Safety Foundation

Farval Lubrication Systems

Curci, John V.: chief financial officer, Vesper Corp.; trustee, Vesper Foundation

Federal Home Loan Bank Seattle

Killinger, Kerry Kent: chairman, president, chief executive officer, director, Washington Mutual, Inc.

Federal Home Loan Mortgage Corp.

McCoy, John Bonnet: president, chief executive officer, Ameritech Corp.

Schuenke, Donald John: director, Freddie Mac

Federal Insurance Co.

O'Hare, Dean Raymond: chairman, Chubb Corp.

Federal Life Insurance Co.

Buxton, Charles Ingraham, II: chairman, Federated Mutual Insurance Co.; president, Federated Mutual Insurance Foundation

Federal National Mortgage Association

Friedman, Stephen James: senior advisor, Goldman Sachs Group

Gaiswinkler, Robert Sigfried: chairman, director, First Financial Bank; director, First Financial Foundation

Williams, Karen Hastie: director, Fannie Mae Foundation

Federal Publishing Inc.

McCorkindale, Douglas H.: vice chairman, president, Gannett Co., Inc.; president, Gannett Foundation

Federal Reserve Bank Atlanta

Jones, D. Paul, Jr.: chairman, chief executive officer, Compass Bank; trustee, Compass Bank Foundation

Robinson, E. B., Jr.: chairman, chief executive officer, director, Deposit Guaranty National Bank

Federal Reserve Bank Boston

Brown, Stephen Lee: chairman, chief executive officer, director, Hancock Financial Services (John)

Federal Reserve Bank Chicago

Martinez, Arthur C.: chairman, chief executive officer, president, Sears, Roebuck and Co.

Federal Reserve Bank Cleveland

Daberko, David A.: chairman, chief executive officer, National City Corp.

Federal Reserve Bank Cleveland/ Pittsburgh

Ryan, John Thomas, III: chairman, chief executive officer, Mine Safety Appliances Co.

Federal Reserve Bank Minneapolis

Howard, James Joseph, III: chairman, president, chief executive officer, director, Northern States Power Co.

Federal Reserve Bank New York

Gelb, Richard Lee: director, New York Times Co. Foundation

Labrecque, Thomas Goulet: president, chief operating officer, director, Chase Manhattan Bank, NA; president, Chase Manhattan Foundation

Steere, William Campbell, Jr.: chairman, chief executive officer, director, Pfizer Inc.

Federal Reserve Bank San Antonio

Hemminghaus, Roger Roy: chairman, director, Ultramar Diamond Shamrock Corp.

Federal Service Insurance Co.

Buxton, Charles Ingraham, II: chairman, Federated Mutual Insurance Co.; president, Federated Mutual Insurance Foundation

Federated Department Stores Inc.

Everingham, Lyle J.: trustee, Milacron Foundation

Graves, Earl Gilbert: director, Aetna Foundation

Federated Metals Corp.

Gonzalez, Carmen D.: assistant secretary, ASARCO Foundation

Osborne, Richard de Jongh: director, ASARCO Foundation; chairman, chief executive officer, director, ASARCO Inc.

Federation Barge Lines Inc.

Raskin, Fred C.: president, chief operating officer, Eastern Enterprises; trustee, Eastern Enterprises Foundation

Federation Insurance Co.

Small, Lawrence Malcolm: president, chief operating officer, Fannie Mae; director, Fannie Mae Foundation

Federation National Mortgage Association

Raines, Franklin Delano: chairman, chief executive officer, Fannie Mae; director, Fannie Mae Foundation

Federation Reserve Bank Atlanta

Jones, David R.: principal, AGL Resources Inc.

Federation Reserve Bank Boston

Taylor, William Osgood: chairman, chief executive officer, director, Boston Globe (The); chairman, director, Boston Globe Foundation; director, New York Times Co. Foundation

Federation Reserve Bank Chicago

Keyes, James Henry: advisor, Johnson Controls Foundation; president, Johnson Controls Inc.

Federation Reserve Bank New York

Wilmers, Robert George: chairman, president, chief executive officer, Manufacturers & Traders Trust Co.

Federation Reserve Bank Richmond

Sheehan, Jeremiah J.: chairman, director, Reynolds Metals Co. Foundation

Federation Reserve Bank Saint Louis

Jacobsen, Thomas Herbert: chairman, president, chief executive officer, Mercantile Bank NA

Mueller, Charles William: chairman, president, chief executive officer, Ameren Corp.; trustee, Ameren Corp. Charitable Trust

Fellows Corp.

Mitropoulis, Iris: chairman, Kingsbury Corp.

Ferro Enamel Espanola SA

Bersticker, Albert C.: chairman, director, chief executive officer, Ferro Corp.; president, trustee, Ferro Foundation

Ferro Far East Ltd. Hong Kong

Bersticker, Albert C.: chairman, director, chief executive officer, Ferro Corp.; president, trustee, Ferro Foundation

Ferro Southeast Asia PTE Ltd. Singapore

Bersticker, Albert C.: chairman, director, chief executive officer, Ferro Corp.; president, trustee, Ferro Foundation

Fesk

Koch, Robert Louis, II: president, chief executive officer, director, Koch Enterprises, Inc.; president, director, Koch Foundation

Fiber-Resin Corp.

Ray, John Thomas, Jr.: president, director, Fuller Co. Foundation (H.B.)

Fibreboard Corp.

James, George Barker, II: senior vice president, chief financial officer, Levi Strauss & Co.

Fibredyne Inc.

Wardeberg, George E.: president, WICOR Foundation; president, chief executive officer, director, WICOR, Inc.

Fidelity Life Association

Hamilton, Peter Bannerman: director, Brunswick Foundation; trustee, Kemper Foundation (James S.)

Mathis, David B.: chairman, Kemper Foundation (James S.)

Randall, Kenneth A.: trustee, Kemper Foundation (James S.)

Fiduciary Counseling Inc.

Cogan, John Francis, Jr.: president, chief executive officer, director, Pioneer Group

Fiduciary Trust Co. International

Geier, Philip Henry, Jr.: chairman, president, chief executive officer, Interpublic Group of Companies, Inc.

Field Tech Inc.

Haase, Bronson J.: president, chief executive officer, Ameritech Wisconsin

Schrader, Thomas F.: vice president, director, WICOR Foundation

Wardeberg, George E.: president, WICOR Foundation; president, chief executive officer, director, WICOR, Inc.

Fifth Third Bancorp

Barrett, John F.: trustee, Western-Southern Foundation, Inc.; president, chief executive officer, director, Western & Southern Life Insurance Co.

Schaefer, George A., Jr.: president, Fifth Third Bancorp

Fifth Third Bank

Barrett, John F.: trustee, Western-Southern Foundation, Inc.; president, chief executive officer, director, Western & Southern Life Insurance Co.

Keating, Michael K.: executive vice president, counsel, secretary, Fifth Third Bancorp

Pitorak, Larry John: senior vice president finance, treasurer, chief financial officer, Sherwin-Williams Co.; secretary, treasurer, trustee, Sherwin-Williams Foundation

Rogers, James E., Jr.: vice chairman, president, chief executive officer, Cinergy Corp.; vice chairman, director, Cinergy Foundation

Fifty Associates

Lawrence, Robert Ashton: director, New York Times Co. Foundation

Fiji Forbes Inc.

Yablon, Leonard Harold: secretary-treasurer, Forbes Foundation

Filemark Corp.

Jasse, Andre C., Jr.: trustee, Eastern Bank Charitable Foundation

Film Services Hawaii

Fukunaga, Mark H.: chairman, director, Servco Foundation; chief executive officer, chairman, Servco Pacific

Films for the Humanities Science

Golkin, Perry: member, Walter Industries Inc.

Finance Executive Institute

Edwards, David M.: vice president finance, chief financial officer, GATX Corp.

Tran, Khanh T.: senior vice president, chief financial officer, director, Pacific Mutual Life Insurance Co.

Financial Executive Institute

Harper, James J.: vice president, controller, Eastern Enterprises

Schoenholz, David A.: executive vice president, chief financial officer, Household International Inc.

Fingerhut Co. Inc.

Hubbard, Stanley S.: chairman, president, chief executive officer, Hubbard Broadcasting, Inc.; president, Hubbard Foundation

Finova Group Inc.

Teets, John William: president, chief executive officer, director, Viad Corp. Fund

Fire Creek Oil Co.

True, Diemer: partner, True Oil Co.

Fire Insurance Exchange

Gasich, Anthony F.: vice president administration, Farmers Group, Inc.; contributions officer, Farmers Group Safety Foundation

Fire Lite Alarms Inc.

Zermuehlen, William: secretary, Pittway Corp. Charitable Foundation

Firemans Fund Insurance Co. Ohio

Hansmeyer, Herbert F.: chairman, Fireman's Fund Insurance Co.

Stinnette, Joe L., Jr.: director, Fireman's Fund Foundation; president, chief executive officer, director, Fireman's Fund Insurance Co.

Firemans Insurance Newark New Jersey

Sharkey, William Henry, Jr.: director, CNA Foundation

Firemens Insurance Newark New Jersey

Chookaszian, Dennis Haig: chairman, chief executive officer, CNA

Jokiel, Peter E.: senior vice president, chief financial officer, CNA

First AUSA Life Insurance Co.

Kolsrud, Douglas C.: executive vice president, chief investment officer, AEGON U.S.A. Inc.

First Alabama Bancshares Inc.

Horsley, Richard David: vice chairman, executive financial officer, director, Regions Financial Corp.

First Allamerica Life Insurance Co.

O'Brien, John Francis, Jr.: president, chief executive officer, Allmerica Financial Corp.

First America National Bank Nashville

Turner, Cal, Jr.: chairman, chief executive officer, director, Dollar General Corp.

First American Bank

Butts, David Wayne: senior vice president, Illinois Power Co.

First American Corp.

Deavenport, Earnest W., Jr.: chairman, chief executive officer, director, Eastman Chemical Co.

Ingram, Martha R.: chairman, director, Ingram Industries Inc.
Turner, Cal, Jr.: chairman, chief executive officer, director, Dollar General Corp.

First Ameritas Life Insurance Corp.
Martin, JoAnn M.: controller, Ameritas Charitable Foundation; senior vice president, partner, chief financial officer, Ameritas Life Insurance Corp.

First Ameritas Life Insurance Corp. New York
Louis, Kenneth C.: president, chief operating officer, director, Ameritas Life Insurance Corp.

First Bank & Trust East Texas
Temple, Arthur, III: director, Temple-Inland Foundation

First Bank Montana National Association
Zona, Richard A.: vice chairman commercial banking & institutional finance, U.S. Bancorp

First Bankcard Systems Inc.
Rogers, C. B., Jr.: chairman, Equifax Foundation; chairman, director, Equifax Inc.

First Brands Corp.
Minton, Dwight Church: chairman, director, Church & Dwight Co., Inc.

First Capital Corp. Chicago
Berry, Ilona M.: secretary, First National Bank of Chicago Foundation

First Capital Investment Corp. Madison
Mebane, David Cummins: chairman, president, chief executive officer, director, Madison Gas & Electric Co.; vice president, Madison Gas & Electric Foundation

First Charleston Corp.
Allbritton, Joe Lewis: chairman, chief executive officer, Riggs Bank NA

First Chicago Capital Markets, Asia, Ltd.
Ingersoll, Robert Stephen: chairman, director, Panasonic Foundation

First Chicago Equity Capital
Sissel, George A.: chairman, president, chief executive officer, director, Ball Corp.

First Chicago Futures Inc.
Berry, Ilona M.: secretary, First National Bank of Chicago Foundation

First Chicago NBD Corp.
McKenna, Andrew James: director, Aon Foundation

First Chicago NBD Inc.
McCormick, William Thomas, Jr.: chairman, chief executive officer, director, Consumers Energy Co.; chairman, Consumers Energy Foundation

First Chicago National Processing
Berry, Ilona M.: secretary, First National Bank of Chicago Foundation

First Colony Corp.
Gottwald, Bruce Cobb: chairman, chief executive officer, director, Ethyl Corp.

First Commerce Corp.
Purvis, George Frank, Jr.: chairman, president, chief executive officer, director, Pan-American Life Insurance Co.
Steward, H. Leighton: chairman, chief executive officer, president, Louisiana Land & Exploration Co.; director, Louisiana Land & Exploration Co. Foundation

First Community Bank of Tifton
Yancey, James D.: vice chairman, director, president, chief operating officer, Synovus Financial Corp.

First Energy Corp.
Powers, Paul Joseph: chairman, president, chief executive officer, director, Commercial Intertech Corp.; president, trustee, Commercial Intertech Foundation

First Federal Capital Corp.
Mebane, David Cummins: chairman, president, chief executive officer, director, Madison Gas & Electric Co.; vice president, Madison Gas & Electric Foundation

First Federal Michigan
Borman, Paul: president, director, Borman Fund (The); chairman, Borman's Inc.

First Federal Savings & Loan Association
Johnson, James Lawrence: chairman emeritus, Walter Industries Inc.

First Federal Savings Bank Madison/LaCrosse
Mebane, David Cummins: chairman, president, chief executive officer, director, Madison Gas & Electric Co.; vice president, Madison Gas & Electric Foundation

First Fidelity Bancorp
Ferland, E. James: chairman, president, chief executive officer, Public Service Electric & Gas Co.
Meyerson, Martin: director, Panasonic Foundation
Palmieri, Peter C.: vice chairman, chief credit officer, First Union National Bank, NA

First Fin Bank
Salinger, Robert M.: secretary, First Financial Foundation

First Fin Corp.
Gaiswinkler, Robert Sigfried: chairman, director, First Financial Bank; director, First Financial Foundation
Salinger, Robert M.: secretary, First Financial Foundation

First Fin Savings Association
Gaiswinkler, Robert Sigfried: chairman, director, First Financial Bank; director, First Financial Foundation

First Financial Fund Inc.
Simmons, Hardwick: president, chief executive officer, director, Prudential Securities Inc.

First Fortis Life Insurance Co.
Freedman, Allen Royal: trustee, Fortis Foundation; chairman, chief executive officer, president, Fortis, Inc.

First Hawaii Bank
Karr, Howard Henry: treasurer, director, First Hawaiian Foundation

First Hawaiian Bank
Dods, Walter Arthur, Jr.: president, director, First Hawaiian Foundation; chairman, chief executive officer, director, First Hawaiian, Inc.
Horner, Donald G.: vice president, director, First Hawaiian Foundation
Wolff, Herbert Eric: secretary, director, First Hawaiian Foundation
Yao, Lily K.: director, First Hawaiian, Inc.

First Hawaiian Creditcorp Inc.
Dods, Walter Arthur, Jr.: president, director, First Hawaiian Foundation; chairman, chief executive officer, director, First Hawaiian, Inc.
Horner, Donald G.: vice president, director, First Hawaiian Foundation

First Hawaiian Insurance Inc.
Dods, Walter Arthur, Jr.: president, director, First Hawaiian Foundation; chairman, chief executive officer, director, First Hawaiian, Inc.

First Hawaiian Leasing Inc.
Dods, Walter Arthur, Jr.: president, director, First Hawaiian Foundation; chairman, chief executive officer, director, First Hawaiian, Inc.
Horner, Donald G.: vice president, director, First Hawaiian Foundation
Tsui, John K.: director, First Hawaiian Foundation
Wolff, Herbert Eric: secretary, director, First Hawaiian Foundation

First Industrial Realty Corp.
Rau, John E.: trustee, Chicago Title and Trust Co. Foundation

First Ing Life Insurance of New York
Christopher, Stephen: president, chief operating officer, Security Life of Denver Insurance Co.

First Insurance Co. Hawaii Ltd.
Dods, Walter Arthur, Jr.: president, director, First Hawaiian Foundation; chairman, chief executive officer, director, First Hawaiian, Inc.

First Interstate Bancorp
Stivers, William Charles: senior vice president, chief financial officer, treasurer, Weyerhaeuser Co.; treasurer, trustee, Weyerhaeuser Co. Foundation

First Liberty Insurance Corp.
Countryman, Gary Lee: chairman, Liberty Mutual Insurance Group
Kelly, Edmund F.: president, chief executive officer, Liberty Mutual Insurance Group

First Maryland Bancorp
Crooke, Edward A.: president, Baltimore Gas & Electric Foundation

First Merchants Bank NA
Sissel, George A.: chairman, president, chief executive officer, director, Ball Corp.

First Midwest Bank Corp. Inc.
Chelberg, Bruce Stanley: chairman, chief executive officer, director, Whitman Corp.; director, Whitman Corp. Foundation
England, Joseph Walker: chairman, director, Deere Foundation (John)

First Mississippi Corp.
Fligg, James E.: executive vice president, BP Amoco Corp.

First Morris Bank
Baldassari, Dennis P.: president, chief operating officer, GPU Energy

First National Bancshares Corp.

Henseler, Gerald A.: executive vice president, chief financial officer, director, Banta Corp.; president, Banta Corp. Foundation

First National Bank Altavista

Tyler, Kenneth Scott, Jr.: president, chief executive officer, Furniture Brands International, Inc.

First National Bank Boston

Countryman, Gary Lee: chairman, Liberty Mutual Insurance Group

Gifford, Charles Kilvert: trustee, BankBoston Charitable Foundation; chairman, chief executive officer, BankBoston Corp.

First National Bank Chicago

McKenna, Andrew James: director, Aon Foundation

Thomas, Richard Lee: vice president, First National Bank of Chicago Foundation

Vitale, David J.: vice chairman, Bank One Corp.; vice president, director, First National Bank of Chicago Foundation

First National Bank Commerce

Purvis, George Frank, Jr.: chairman, president, chief executive officer, director, Pan-American Life Insurance Co.

Steward, H. Leighton: chairman, chief executive officer, president, Louisiana Land & Exploration Co.; director, Louisiana Land & Exploration Co. Foundation

First National Bank Dayton

Glaser, Gary A.: president, chief executive officer, National City Bank of Columbus

First National Bank Fox Valley

Bero, Robert D.: president, chief executive officer, Menasha Corp.

Smith, Oliver C.: chairman, Menasha Corp. Foundation

First National Bank Maryland Inc.

Crooke, Edward A.: president, Baltimore Gas & Electric Foundation

First National Bank Pratt

Chandler, Charles Quarles, IV: co-trustee, INTRUST Bank Charitable Trust; president, director, INTRUST Financial Corp.

First National Bank Rogers AR

Soderquist, Donald G.: trustee, Wal-Mart Foundation; senior vice chairman, director, Wal-Mart Stores, Inc.

First National Insurance Co. America

Eigsti, Roger Harry: chairman, chief executive officer, SAFECO Corp.

First Omni Bank NA

Fitzsimmons, Thomas D.: treasurer, First Maryland Foundation

First Quadrant Corp.

Brown, Joseph Warner, Jr.: chairman, chief executive officer, MBIA Inc.

First Security Corp.

Simplot, John Richard: chairman, founder, Simplot Co. (J.R.); president, Simplot Foundation (J.R.)

First Security Insurance Inc.

Eccles, Spencer Fox: chairman, chief executive officer, director, First Security Bank of Idaho NA

First Tennessee Bank NA Corp.

Street, Gordon P., Jr.: chairman, president, chief executive officer, director, North American Royalties; trustee, North American Royalties Foundation

First Tennessee National Corp.

Street, Gordon P., Jr.: chairman, president, chief executive officer, director, North American Royalties; trustee, North American Royalties Foundation

First Trust National Association

Zona, Richard A.: vice chairman commercial banking & institutional finance, U.S. Bancorp

First Union Bank Savannah

Demere, Robert H.: president, Colonial Foundation; chairman, Colonial Oil Industries, Inc.

First Union Corp.

Dickson, Rush Stuart: chairman, Dickson Foundation

Herring, Leonard Gray: vice president, Lowe's Charitable and Educational Foundation

Larsen, Terrence A.: chairman, chief executive officer, First Union Bank; chairman, First Union Regional Foundation

Reynolds, Randolph Nicklas: vice chairman, executive officer, director, Reynolds Metals Co.; director, Reynolds Metals Co. Foundation

Trogdon, Dewey Leonard, Jr.: director, ABC Foundation; chairman, Cone Mills Corp.

First Union Corp. Georgia

Demere, Robert H.: president, Colonial Foundation; chairman, Colonial Oil Industries, Inc.

First Union National Bank Charlotte

Disher, J. William: director, Lance Foundation; chairman, Lance, Inc.

First United Bancshares Inc.

Murphy, R. Madison: chairman, director, Murphy Oil Corp.

First Wachovia Corp.

Iverson, Francis Kenneth: chairman, director, Nucor Corp.; director, Nucor Foundation

First Wisconsin National Bank Milwaukee

Becker, John A.: president, chief operating officer, director, Firstar Bank Milwaukee NA; vice chairman, Firstar Milwaukee Foundation

FirstEnergy Corp.

Smart, George M.: trustee, Commercial Intertech Foundation

FirstEnergy Services Corp.

Holland, Willard R.: chairman, chief executive officer, FirstEnergy Corp.

Firstar Bank

Vondrasek, Frank Charles, Jr.: president, Madison Gas & Electric Foundation

Firstar Bank Corp.

Lubar, Sheldon B.: chairman, Ameritech Corp.; director, Firstar Milwaukee Foundation

Firstar Bank Milwaukee NA

Fitzsimonds, Roger Leon: chairman, Firstar Milwaukee Foundation

Lacy, William Howard: president, MGIC Investment Corp.

Firstar Bank NA

O'Toole, Robert Joseph: director, Firstar Milwaukee Foundation; chairman, president, chief executive officer, director, Smith Corp. (A.O.); director, Smith Foundation, Inc. (A.O.)

Firstar Corp.

Lacy, William Howard: president, MGIC Investment Corp.

Manning, Kenneth Paul: president, Universal Foods Corp.; president, director, Universal Foods Foundation

O'Toole, Robert Joseph: director, Firstar Milwaukee Foundation; chairman, president, chief executive officer, director, Smith Corp. (A.O.); director, Smith Foundation, Inc. (A.O.)

Firstar Trust Co.

Fitzsimonds, Roger Leon: chairman, Firstar Milwaukee Foundation

Manning, Kenneth Paul: president, Universal Foods Corp.; president, director, Universal Foods Foundation

Schrader, Thomas F.: vice president, director, WICOR Foundation

Fisher Scientific International Inc.

Dingman, Michael David: partner, director, Winthrop Foundation

Fision Systems Corp.

Hardis, Stephen Roger: chairman, chief executive officer, director, Eaton Corp.

Fitzpatrick Companies Inc.

Fitzpatrick, Jane P.: chairman, chief executive officer, treasurer, Country Curtains, Inc.; chairman, High Meadow Foundation

Fitzpatrick Retail & Realty Co. Inc.

Fitzpatrick, John H.: president, High Meadow Foundation; president, director, Housatonic Curtain Co.

Trask, Robert B.: president, chief operating officer, director, Country Curtains, Inc.; clerk, trustee, High Meadow Foundation

Fitzwilton PLC

O'Reilly, F. Anthony John: chairman, trustee, Heinz Co. Foundation (H.J.); chairman, director, Heinz Co. (H.J.)

Flagler System Inc.

Kennedy, James Cox: chairman, chief executive officer, director, Cox Enterprises Inc.; trustee, Cox Foundation (James M.)

FleetBoston Financial Corp.

Countryman, Gary Lee: chairman, Liberty Mutual Insurance Group

Gifford, Charles Kilvert: trustee, BankBoston Charitable Foundation; chairman, chief executive officer, BankBoston Corp.

Swihart, Susannah: trustee, BankBoston Charitable Foundation

Wheeler, Thomas Beardsley: chairman, chief executive officer, Massachusetts Mutual Life Insurance Co.

Flextronics International

Sharp, Richard L.: trustee, Circuit City Foundation; chairman, chief executive officer, director, Circuit City Stores, Inc.

Flight Proficiency Service Inc.

Simmons, Glenn Reuben: vice chairman, Contran Corp.

Watson, Steven L.: vice president, secretary, Contran Corp.; vice president, secretary, director, Simmons Foundation, Inc. (Harold)

Flint Electric Membership Corp.

Wellborn, Sam M.: president, Synovus Charitable Trust

Florida East Coast Industries Inc.

Fairbanks, J. Nelson: president, chief executive officer, director, United States Sugar Corp.

Florida Gannett Broadcasting

Chapple, Thomas Leslie: senior vice president, general counsel, secretary, Gannett Co., Inc.; secretary, Gannett Foundation

Florida Publishing Co.

Morris, William Shivers, III: founder, chairman, chief executive officer, director, Morris Communications Corp.; trustee, Stauffer Communications Foundation

Flowserve Corp.

Rollans, James Ora: senior vice president, chief administrative officer, chief financial officer, Fluor Corp.; trustee, Fluor Foundation

Fluke Corp.

Condit, Philip Murray: chairman, chief executive officer, director, Boeing Co.

Fluor Corp.

Bowers, Betty H.: trustee, Fluor Foundation

O'Hare, Dean Raymond: chairman, Chubb Corp.

Stein, James C.: president, chief operating officer, Fluor Corp.; trustee, Fluor Foundation

Fluor Daniel Caribbean Inc.

Rollans, James Ora: senior vice president, chief administrative officer, chief financial officer, Fluor Corp.; trustee, Fluor Foundation

Fluor Daniel Inc.

Rollans, James Ora: senior vice president, chief administrative officer, chief financial officer, Fluor Corp.; trustee, Fluor Foundation

Foamex

Cogan, Marshall Stuart: chairman, president, chief executive officer, director, Trace International Holdings, Inc.; director, Trace International Holdings, Inc. Foundation

Foamex Capital Corp.

Cogan, Marshall Stuart: chairman, president, chief executive officer, director, Trace International Holdings, Inc.; director, Trace International Holdings, Inc. Foundation

Foamex International Inc.

Smith, Philip N., Jr.: secretary, Trace International Holdings, Inc. Foundation

Food Distributors International

Wright, Michael William: chairman, president, chief executive officer, director, SuperValu, Inc.

Food Town Inc.

Iott, Richard B.: president, chief executive officer, director, Seaway Food Town, Inc.

Foote Cone Belding

Mason, W. Bruce: chairman, chief executive officer, director, True North Communications, Inc.

Foote Cone Belding Advertising

Boland, Jack: vice president, director, True North Foundation

Foote Cone Belding Communications Inc.

Balousek, John B.: president, director, True North Communications, Inc.; vice president, director, True North Foundation

Footstar Inc.

Lautenbach, Terry Robert: trustee, Air Products Foundation

Forbes Europe

Yablon, Leonard Harold: secretary-treasurer, Forbes Foundation

Force One Inc.

Jacobsen, James C.: vice chairman, Kellwood Co.; vice president, director, Kellwood Foundation

Ford Motor Co.

Dingman, Michael David: partner, director, Winthrop Foundation

Hockaday, Irvine O., Jr.: president, chief executive officer, director, Hallmark Cards Inc.

Foremost Corp. America

Pew, Robert Cunningham, II: trustee, Steelcase Foundation

Forest City Enterprises Inc.

Esposito, Michael Patrick, Jr.: trustee, Chase Manhattan Foundation

Forest City Management Inc.

Ratner, Albert Benjamin: trustee, Forest City Enterprises Charitable Foundation, Inc.; co-chairman, director, Forest City Enterprises, Inc.

Forest City Trading Group Inc.

Ratner, Albert Benjamin: trustee, Forest City Enterprises Charitable Foundation, Inc.; co-chairman, director, Forest City Enterprises, Inc.

Formica Corp.

Lyon, Wayne Barton: president, chief operating officer, director, Masco Corp.

Fort Collins Newspapers Inc.

McCorkindale, Douglas H.: vice chairman, president, Gannett Co., Inc.; president, Gannett Foundation

Fort James Corp.

Coughlan, Gary Patrick: chief financial officer, senior vice president finance, Abbott Laboratories; director, Abbott Laboratories Fund

Sharp, Richard L.: trustee, Circuit City Foundation; chairman, chief executive officer, director, Circuit City Stores, Inc.

Fort James Europe NV

Cutchins, Clifford Armstrong, IV: president, Fort James Corp.; chairman, director, Fort James Foundation (The)

Fort James Operating Co.

Cutchins, Clifford Armstrong, IV: president, Fort James Corp.; chairman, director, Fort James Foundation (The)

Girvan, Daniel J.: senior vice president, director, Fort James Corp.; director, Fort James Foundation (The)

Fortis Capital Corp.

Freedman, Allen Royal: trustee, Fortis Foundation; chairman, chief executive officer, president, Fortis, Inc.

Fortis Capital Fund Inc.

Freedman, Allen Royal: trustee, Fortis Foundation; chairman, chief executive officer, president, Fortis, Inc.

Fortis Income Portfolios Inc.

Freedman, Allen Royal: trustee, Fortis Foundation; chairman, chief executive officer, president, Fortis, Inc.

Fortis Insurance Co.

Gochenaur, Jack A.: senior vice president administration & services, chief financial officer, Fortis Insurance Co.; president, trustee, Fortis Insurance Foundation

Fortis Money Fund Inc.

Freedman, Allen Royal: trustee, Fortis Foundation; chairman, chief executive officer, president, Fortis, Inc.

Fortune Brands Inc.

Lohman, Gordon Russell: trustee, Amsted Industries Foundation; director, Amsted Industries Inc.

Fortune Brands International Corp.

Rukeyser, Robert James: senior vice president corporate affairs, Fortune Brands, Inc.

Foster Wheeler Corp.

Ferland, E. James: chairman, president, chief executive officer, Public Service Electric & Gas Co.

Four Seasons Nursing Centers

Bainum, Stewart William, Jr.: chairman, Manor Care Health SVS, Inc.

Four Star International Inc.

Slovin, Bruce: president, director, Revlon Inc.

Four-Ten Corp.

Piet, William M.: vice president, director, Wrigley Co. Foundation (Wm. Jr.); vice president corporate affairs, secretary, assistant to president, Wrigley Co. (Wm. Jr.)

Fourteen Fifty Partner Emporio Armani

Forte, Gabriella: president, chief operating officer, Calvin Klein

Fox Cities Bank

Omachinski, David L.: chief financial officer, treasurer, vice president, Oshkosh B'Gosh, Inc.

Fox Valley Press Inc.

Copley, David C.: president, trustee, Copley Foundation (James S.); president, chief executive officer, director, senior management board, Copley Press, Inc.

Copley, Helen K.: chairman, trustee, Copley Foundation (James S.); chairman, director, senior management board, Copley Press, Inc.

Crouch, Robert F.: vice president, trustee, Copley Foundation (James S.)

Dwyer, Dean P.: vice president finance, treasurer, senior management board, Copley Press, Inc.

Fox Valley Steel Wire Co.

Simmons, Glenn Reuben: vice chairman, Contran Corp.

Franklin Real Estate Co.

Draper, Ernest Linn, Jr.: chairman, president, chief executive officer, director, American Electric Power

Franklin Square Agency Overseas Inc.

Stephens, Elton Bryson: founder, chairman, Ebsco Industries, Inc.

Freeport-McMoRan Copper & Gold Inc.

Putnam, George, Jr.: chairman, president, chief executive officer, Putnam Investments

Freeport-McMoRan Copper Gold Inc.

Kissinger, Henry Alfred: director, CBS Foundation

Freeport-McMoRan Inc.

Putnam, George, Jr.: chairman, president, chief executive officer, Putnam Investments

Freeway Easy Living Country

Corson, Keith Daniel: president, chief operating officer, Coachmen Industries, Inc.

Freight Services

McConnell, William Thompson: chairman, ceo, Park National Bank; chairman, Park National Corp. Foundation

Freightliner Market Development Corp.

Hebe, James L.: chairman, president, chief executive officer, Freightliner Corp.

Fremont Group LLC

Bechtel, Riley Peart: chairman, Bechtel Foundation; chairman, chief executive officer, director, Bechtel Group, Inc.

Fremont Investors Inc.

Bechtel, Riley Peart: chairman, Bechtel Foundation; chairman, chief executive officer, director, Bechtel Group, Inc.

Frigoscandia Inc.

Schuchardt, Daniel Norman: secretary, treasurer, FMC Foundation

Frontier Corp.

Edgerton, Brenda Evans: vice president business development, Campbell Soup Co.; treasurer, trustee, Campbell Soup Foundation

McCorkindale, Douglas H.: vice chairman, president, Gannett Co., Inc.; president, Gannett Foundation

Frontier Information Technology

Clayton, Joseph P.: president, chief executive officer, director, Frontier Corp.

Fruit of Loom

Bookshester, Dennis S.: chairman, chief executive officer, Playboy Enterprises Inc.

Fuel Resources Development Co.

Hock, Delwin D.: chairman, New Century Energies

Fuel Resources Inc.

Catell, Robert Barry: chairman, chief executive officer, Brooklyn Union

Fuji America Holdings Inc.

Almeida, Richard: chairman, chief executive officer, Heller Financial, Inc.

Fuji Xerox Co. Ltd.

Allaire, Paul Arthur: chairman, chief executive officer, chairman executive committee, Xerox Corp.; president, Xerox Foundation

Romeril, Barry D.: executive vice president, chief financial officer, Xerox Corp.

Thoman, G. Richard: president, chief operating officer, Xerox Corp.

Fulton Iron Works International

Stupp, Robert P.: president, director, Stupp Brothers Bridge & Iron Co.; trustee, Stupp Brothers Bridge & Iron Co. Foundation

Fund America Companies Inc.

Clark, Howard Longstreth, Jr.: vice chairman, Walter Industries Inc.

Furniture Brands International Inc.

Kincaid, Brent B.: president, chief executive officer, Furniture Brands International, Inc.

Suter, Albert E.: senior vice chairman, chief administrative officer, director, Emerson Electric Co.

Furon Co.

Ranck, Bruce E.: president, chief executive officer, director, Browning-Ferris Industries Inc.

Furrow

Hall, William Austin: president, Hallmark Corporate Foundation

Fusion Systems Corp.

Dillon, Adrian T.: executive vice president, chief financial officer, planning officer, Eaton Corp.

Future Value Ventures Inc.

Remmel, Jerry G.: chief financial officer, vice president, treasurer, Wisconsin Energy Corp.

GAMA

Younts, Rosemary: senior vice president communications, GenCorp

GATX Capital Corp.

Edwards, David M.: vice president finance, chief financial officer, GATX Corp.

Zech, Ronald H.: chairman, president, chief executive officer, chief operating officer, GATX Corp.

GATX Corp.

Cole, Franklin Alan: chairman, Aon Foundation

GATX Terminals Corp.

Edwards, David M.: vice president finance, chief financial officer, GATX Corp.

GB Distributors

Gindi, Abraham: trustee, Century 21 Associates Foundation

GC Co. Inc.

Smith, Richard Alan: treasurer, director, Arvin Foundation; chairman, director, chief executive officer, Harcourt General, Inc.

GE Fin Services Inc.

Dammerman, Dennis Dean: vice chairman, director, General Electric Co.

GEICO General Insurance Co.

Smith, Donald Kaye: senior vice president, general counsel, director, GEICO Corp.

GFS Realty Inc.

Bush, Michael J.: vice president real estate, Giant Food Inc.

GKN Westland Inc.

Battaglia, Thomas S.: director, American Standard Foundation

GP Corp.

Rosson, William Mimms: chairman, Conwood Co. LP

GPP Inc.

Tracy, Emmet E., Jr.: president, chief executive officer, director, Alma Piston Co.; president, Tracy Fund (Emmet and Frances)

GPU Inc.

Rein, Catherine Amelia: director, MetLife Foundation; vice president, Metropolitan Life Insurance Co.

GPU Nuclear Corp.

Hafer, Fred Douglass: chairman, president, chief executive officer, GPU Inc.

GSL Corp.

Eigsti, Roger Harry: chairman, chief executive officer, SAFECO Corp.

GST Inc.

Leshin, Arthur: senior vice president, chief financial officer, Gucci America Inc.

Stroup, Stanley Stephenson: executive vice president, general counsel, Norwest Corp.

GTE California Inc.

Dods, Walter Arthur, Jr.: president, director, First Hawaiian Foundation; chairman, chief executive officer, director, First Hawaiian, Inc.

GTE Data Services Inc.

Esstman, Michael B.: trustee, GTE Foundation

Foster, Kent B.: president, director, GTE Corp.; trustee, GTE Foundation

GTE Hawaiian Telephone Co. Inc.

Dods, Walter Arthur, Jr.: president, director, First Hawaiian Foundation; chairman, chief executive officer, director, First Hawaiian, Inc.

GTE Management Corp.

McGraw, Harold Whittlesey 'Terry', III: chairman, president, chief executive officer, McGraw-Hill Companies, Inc.

GTE Northwest Inc.

Dods, Walter Arthur, Jr.: president, director, First Hawaiian Foundation; chairman, chief executive officer, director, First Hawaiian, Inc.

GTS Duratk Inc.

Brothers, John Alfred 'Fred': trustee, Ashland Inc. Foundation

GUD Holdings Ltd.

Gloyd, Lawrence Eugene: trustee, CLARCOR Foundation; chairman, chief executive officer, director, CLARCOR Inc.

Gables Residental Trust

Martin, Lauralee: chief financial officer, Heller Financial, Inc.

Gadsden Times Inc.

Sulzberger, Arthur Ochs, Sr.: director, New York Times Co.; chairman, director, New York Times Co. Foundation

Gage Marketing Group LLC

Gage, Barbara C: director, Carlson Companies, Inc.; president, Carlson Family Foundation (Curtis L.)

Gaillardia Residential Community

Gaylord, Edward Lewis: chairman, chief executive officer, director, publisher, Oklahoma Publishing Co.; trustee, Oklahoman Foundation (The)

Gallaher Ltd.

Hays, Thomas Chandler: chairman, chief executive officer, director, Fortune Brands, Inc.

Gandalf Techs

Musser, Warren Van Dyke: chairman, chief executive officer, director, Safeguard Scientifics; president, director, Safeguard Scientifics Foundation

Gannett Broadcasting Division

McCorkindale, Douglas H.: vice chairman, president, Gannett Co., Inc.; president, Gannett Foundation

Gannett Co. Inc.
Williams, Karen Hastie: director, Fannie Mae Foundation

Gannett Co. Inc. DE
Chapple, Thomas Leslie: senior vice president, general counsel, secretary, Gannett Co., Inc.; secretary, Gannett Foundation

Gannett Direct Marketing Services Inc.
McCorkindale, Douglas H.: vice chairman, president, Gannett Co., Inc.; president, Gannett Foundation

Gannett International
McCorkindale, Douglas H.: vice chairman, president, Gannett Co., Inc.; president, Gannett Foundation

Gannett International Communication Inc.
McCorkindale, Douglas H.: vice chairman, president, Gannett Co., Inc.; president, Gannett Foundation

Gannett Massachusetts Broadcasting Inc.
McCorkindale, Douglas H.: vice chairman, president, Gannett Co., Inc.; president, Gannett Foundation

Gannett Media Technologies International
McCorkindale, Douglas H.: vice chairman, president, Gannett Co., Inc.; president, Gannett Foundation

Gannett National Newspaper Sales Inc.
McCorkindale, Douglas H.: vice chairman, president, Gannett Co., Inc.; president, Gannett Foundation

Gannett News Media
McCorkindale, Douglas H.: vice chairman, president, Gannett Co., Inc.; president, Gannett Foundation

Gannett News Service
McCorkindale, Douglas H.: vice chairman, president, Gannett Co., Inc.; president, Gannett Foundation

Gannett Newspaper Division
McCorkindale, Douglas H.: vice chairman, president, Gannett Co., Inc.; president, Gannett Foundation

Gannett Outdoor Co. Texas
McCorkindale, Douglas H.: vice chairman, president, Gannett Co., Inc.; president, Gannett Foundation

Gannett Pacific Corp.
McCorkindale, Douglas H.: vice chairman, president, Gannett Co., Inc.; president, Gannett Foundation

Gannett Retail Advertising Group
McCorkindale, Douglas H.: vice chairman, president, Gannett Co., Inc.; president, Gannett Foundation

Gannett River Saint Publishing Corp.
McCorkindale, Douglas H.: vice chairman, president, Gannett Co., Inc.; president, Gannett Foundation

Gannett Satellite Information Network
Curley, John J.: chairman, chief executive officer, director, Gannett Co., Inc.; chairman, Gannett Foundation

McCorkindale, Douglas H.: vice chairman, president, Gannett Co., Inc.; president, Gannett Foundation

Gannett Supply Corp.
McCorkindale, Douglas H.: vice chairman, president, Gannett Co., Inc.; president, Gannett Foundation

Gannett TG Subsidiary Inc.
McCorkindale, Douglas H.: vice chairman, president, Gannett Co., Inc.; president, Gannett Foundation

Gannett Telemktg Inc.
McCorkindale, Douglas H.: vice chairman, president, Gannett Co., Inc.; president, Gannett Foundation

Gannett Television
McCorkindale, Douglas H.: vice chairman, president, Gannett Co., Inc.; president, Gannett Foundation

Gannett Texas Broadcasting Inc.
McCorkindale, Douglas H.: vice chairman, president, Gannett Co., Inc.; president, Gannett Foundation

Garden Saint Life Insurance Co.
Smith, Donald Kaye: senior vice president, general counsel, director, GEICO Corp.

Gargoyles Inc.
Ruckelshaus, William Doyle: chairman, director, Browning-Ferris Industries Inc.

Garnett Direct Marketing Service
Curley, John J.: chairman, chief executive officer, director, Gannett Co., Inc.; chairman, Gannett Foundation

Gas Energy Inc.
Catell, Robert Barry: chairman, chief executive officer, Brooklyn Union

Gates Corp.
Duncan, Ian: trustee, Tomkins Corp. Foundation; deputy chairman, managing director finance, Tomkins Industries, Inc.

Gates McDonald Co.
Druen, W. Sidney: director, Nationwide Insurance Enterprise Foundation

Gateway Inc.
Carey, Chase: chief executive officer, chairman, Fox Entertainment Group

Gauley River Management Corp.
Young, Robert Harris: president, chief executive officer, Central Vermont Public Service Corp.

Gaylord Broadcasting Co.
Gaylord, Edward Lewis: chairman, chief executive officer, director, publisher, Oklahoma Publishing Co.; trustee, Oklahoman Foundation (The)

Gaylord Container Corp.
Hawkins, David B.: trustee, Mid-American Foundation

Johnson, Charles S.: president, chief executive officer, chairman, Pioneer Hi-Bred International, Inc.

Gaylord Entertainment Co.
Everest, Christine Gaylord: trustee, Oklahoman Foundation (The)

Gaylord, Edward K., II: trustee, Oklahoman Foundation (The)

Gaylord, Edward Lewis: chairman, chief executive officer, director, publisher, Oklahoma Publishing Co.; trustee, Oklahoman Foundation (The)

Gayno Inc.
Gaylord, Edward Lewis: chairman, chief executive officer, director, publisher, Oklahoma Publishing Co.; trustee, Oklahoman Foundation (The)

Gear Products Inc.
Blount, Winton Malcolm, Jr.: chairman, Blount International, Inc.

Geffen Records Inc.
Gersh, Gary: president, chief executive officer, EMI Music Publishing

Geisel-Seuss Enterprises Inc.
ZoBell, Karl: vice president, trustee, Copley Foundation (James S.)

Gen Tek Inc.
Montrone, Paul Michael: vice president, partner, Winthrop Foundation

GenRad Inc.
Gullotti, Russell A.: chairman, president, chief executive officer, National Computer Systems, Inc.

Genentech Ltd. Japan
Swanson, Robert A.: director, Genentech Foundation for Biomedical Sciences

General America Corp.
Eigsti, Roger Harry: chairman, chief executive officer, SAFECO Corp.

General America Life Insurance Co.
Busch, August Adolphus, III: chairman, president, chief executive officer, Anheuser-Busch Companies, Inc.

Edison, Bernard Alan: member, Edison Family Foundation

General American Investment Management Co.
Rubenstein, Leonard Mark: executive vice president investment, director, GenAmerica Corp.; vice president, director, GenAmerican Foundation

General American Transportation Corp.
Edwards, David M.: vice president finance, chief financial officer, GATX Corp.

General Chemical Group Inc.
Meister, Paul M.: vice president, treasurer, Winthrop Foundation

Montrone, Paul Michael: vice president, partner, Winthrop Foundation

General Electric Capital Corp.
Dammerman, Dennis Dean: vice chairman, director, General Electric Co.

General Electric Capital Services
Welch, John Francis, Jr.: chairman, chief executive officer, director, General Electric Co.

General Electric Co.
Atwater, Horace Brewster, Jr.: trustee, Merck Co. Foundation

Warner, Douglas Alexander, III: chairman, president, chief executive officer, director, Morgan & Co. Inc. (J.P.)

General Electric Communications & Services
Bossidy, Lawrence Arthur: chairman, director, AlliedSignal Foundation Inc.; chairman, chief executive officer, director, AlliedSignal Inc.

General Electric Financial Services
Bossidy, Lawrence Arthur: chairman, director, AlliedSignal Foundation Inc.; chairman, chief executive officer, director, AlliedSignal Inc.

General Electric Industries & Power System
Bossidy, Lawrence Arthur: chairman, director, AlliedSignal Foundation

Inc.; chairman, chief executive officer, director, AlliedSignal Inc.

General Electric Investment Corp.

Bossidy, Lawrence Arthur: chairman, director, AlliedSignal Foundation Inc.; chairman, chief executive officer, director, AlliedSignal Inc.

General Electric Lighting

Bossidy, Lawrence Arthur: chairman, director, AlliedSignal Foundation Inc.; chairman, chief executive officer, director, AlliedSignal Inc.

General Electric Motors

Bossidy, Lawrence Arthur: chairman, director, AlliedSignal Foundation Inc.; chairman, chief executive officer, director, AlliedSignal Inc.

General Electric S&S Long Term Fund

Cosgrove, Michael J.: treasurer, GE Fund

General Hotels Corp.

Dora, James E.: director, AUL Foundation Inc.

General Insurance Co. America

Eigsti, Roger Harry: chairman, chief executive officer, SAFECO Corp.

General Mills Inc.

DeSimone, Livio Diego: chairman, chief executive officer, Minnesota Mining & Manufacturing Co.

Esrey, William Todd: chairman, chief executive officer, Sprint Corp.

Gilmartin, Raymond V.: chairman, president, chief executive officer, Merck & Co.; chairman, Merck Co. Foundation

Wurtele, C. Angus: president, Valspar Foundation

General Motors Acceptance Corp.

Smith, John Francis, Jr.: chairman, General Motors Corp.

General Motors Corp.

Bryan, John Henry: chairman, Sara Lee Corp.; director, Sara Lee Foundation

Fisher, George Myles Cordell: chairman, president, chief executive officer, director, Eastman Kodak Co.

Marriott, J. Willard, Jr.: chairman, chief executive officer, Marriott International Inc.

Pfeiffer, Eckhard A.: president, chief executive officer, director, Compaq Computer Corp.

Weatherstone, Dennis: trustee, Merck Co. Foundation

General Reinsurance Corp.

Li, Victor Hao: director, Hawaiian Electric Industries Charitable Foundation

McGuinn, Martin Gregory: chairman, chief executive officer, Mellon Financial Corp.

General Reinsurance Service Corp.

Gustafson, James E.: president, chief operating officer, Saint Paul Companies Inc.

General Signal Corp.

Campbell, Van C.: vice chairman, chief financial officer, chief administrative officer, director, Corning Inc.; trustee, Corning Inc. Foundation

General Tel & Electric Corp.

Walter, James W.: trustee, Walter Foundation; chairman emeritus, founder, director, Walter Industries Inc.

Generali Assicurazioni Generali SPA

Balzer, Giorgio: chairman, chief executive officer, Business Men's Assurance Co. of America

Genesis Health Ventures Inc.

Freedman, Allen Royal: trustee, Fortis Foundation; chairman, chief executive officer, president, Fortis, Inc.

Geneva Pharmaceuticals Inc.

Watson, Douglas G.: chairman, Novartis US Foundation

Genicom Corp.

Burrus, Robert Lewis, Jr.: trustee, Circuit City Foundation

Genovese Drug Stores Inc.

McKenna, William John: director, chairman, Kellwood Co.; chairman, president, director, Kellwood Foundation

Gens Component Engineering Co.

Powers, Paul Joseph: chairman, president, chief executive officer, director, Commercial Intertech Corp.; president, trustee, Commercial Intertech Foundation

Gentek Inc.

Meister, Paul M.: vice president, treasurer, Winthrop Foundation

Genuine Parts Co.

Courts, Richard Winn, II: chairman, director, Atlantic Investment Co.

Geon Co.

Baker, James Kendrick: chairman, director, Arvin Foundation; vice chairman, director, Arvin Industries, Inc.

Ong, John Doyle: chairman board, director, Ameritech Corp.

Georgetown Communications Inc.

Anderson, Ivan Verner, Jr.: president, chief executive officer, Evening Post Publishing Co.; vice president, Post and Courier Foundation

Georgia Power Co.

Morris, William Shivers, III: founder, chairman, chief executive officer, director, Morris Communications Corp.; trustee, Stauffer Communications Foundation

Prendergast, G. Joseph: director, Wachovia Foundation, Inc. (The)

Georgia-Pacific Corp.

Fites, Donald Vester: director, Caterpillar Foundation

Goode, David Ronald: chairman, president, chief executive officer, director, Norfolk Southern Corp.

Giant Eagle Inc.

Chait, Gerald: trustee, Giant Eagle Foundation

Weizenbaum, Norman: trustee, Giant Eagle Foundation

Giant Maryland Inc.

Oseroff, Stephen L.: vice president real estate, Giant Food Inc.

Thurston, Samuel E.: senior vice president distribution, Giant Food Inc.

Gibbs Aluminum Die Casting Corp.

Koch, Robert Louis, II: president, chief executive officer, director, Koch Enterprises, Inc.; president, director, Koch Foundation

Muehlbauer, James Herman: vice president, director, Koch Foundation

Gibraltar Steel Corp.

Lippes, Gerald Sanford: secretary, Mark IV Industries Foundation

Montague, William Patrick: president, chief operating officer, director, Mark IV Industries; president, Mark IV Industries Foundation

Giddings & Lewis Corp.

Becker, John A.: president, chief operating officer, director, Firstar Bank Milwaukee NA; vice chairman, Firstar Milwaukee Foundation

Giddings & Lewis Electronics Ltd.

Kleinfeldt, Richard C.: vice president financial, chief financial officer, director, Giddings & Lewis

Gilead Sciences Inc.

Moore, Gordon E., PhD: cofounder, chairman emeritus, director, Intel Corp.; trustee, Intel Foundation

Gillette Co.

DeGraan, Edward F.: president, Duracell International

Glacier Gas Co.

Cromer, Richard F.: executive vice president, chief operating officer energy supply division, Montana Power Co.; director, Montana Power Foundation

Glacier Park Inc.

Emerson, Frederick George: vice president, secretary, director, Viad Corp. Fund

Gleason Corp.

Montague, William Patrick: president, chief operating officer, director, Mark IV Industries; president, Mark IV Industries Foundation

Gleason Reel Corp.

Davies, Richard Warren: trustee, Hubbell Foundation (Harvey)

Rowell, Harry Brown, Jr.: trustee, Hubbell Foundation (Harvey)

Glenbrook Life Annuity Co.

Lower, H. Louis Gordon, II: vice president, trustee, Allstate Foundation

Resnick, Myron J.: vice president, treasurer, trustee, Allstate Foundation

Global Government Plus Fund Inc.

McCorkindale, Douglas H.: vice chairman, president, Gannett Co., Inc.; president, Gannett Foundation

Global Marine Inc.

Powers, Paul Joseph: chairman, president, chief executive officer, director, Commercial Intertech Corp.; president, trustee, Commercial Intertech Foundation

Global Surety & Insurance Co.

Stinson, Kenneth E.: member contributions committee, Kiewit Companies Foundation; chairman, chief executive officer, director, Kiewit Sons' Inc. (Peter)

Globe Corp.

Ashley, James Wheeler: director, Globe Foundation

Lux, Clifton L.: director, Globe Foundation

Globe SPLty Products Inc.

Henn, Catherine Emily Campbell: president, Boston Globe Foundation

Goddard Technology Corp.

Reed, Scott Eldridge: senior executive vice president, chief financial officer, Branch Banking & Trust Co.

Gold Points Corp.

Carlson, Curtis Leroy: chairman, director, Carlson Companies, Inc.; president, treasurer, Carlson Family Foundation (Curtis L.)

Golden Enterprises Inc.

Jones, D. Paul, Jr.: chairman, chief executive officer, Compass Bank; trustee, Compass Bank Foundation

Goldman Sachs & Co.

Cohen, Jonathan L.: secretary, director, Goldman Sachs Foundation

McCarthy, Michael D.: director, Goldman Sachs Foundation

Goldman Sachs Group Inc.

Weinberg, John Livingston: chairman, president, director, Goldman Sachs Foundation

Golf Digest/Tennis Inc.

Kerr, William T.: chairman, chief executive officer, director, Meredith Corp.

Golub Service Stations Inc.

Golub, Lewis: chairman, chief executive officer, director, Golub Corp.

Goodyear Tire & Rubber Co.

Breen, John Gerald: chairman, chief executive officer, director, Sherwin-Williams Co.; president, trustee, Sherwin-Williams Foundation

Walker, Martin Dean: chairman, chief executive officer, director, Hanna Co. (M.A.)

Goulds Pumps Inc.

Ballengee, Jerry Hunter: president, chief operating officer, director, Union Camp Corp.

Government Employees Fin Corp.

Smith, Donald Kaye: senior vice president, general counsel, director, GEICO Corp.

Government Employees Insurance Co.

Phillips, Rosalind Ann: secretary, GEICO Philanthropic Foundation

Governor's Square Inc.

Deering, Anthony W.: chairman, chief executive officer, Rouse Co.; chairman, president, trustee, Rouse Co. Foundation

Donahue, Jeffrey H.: senior vice president, chief financial officer, Rouse Co.

Grace Pacific Corp.

Dods, Walter Arthur, Jr.: president, director, First Hawaiian Foundation; chairman, chief executive officer, director, First Hawaiian, Inc.

Watanabe, Jeffrey N.: director, Hawaiian Electric Industries Charitable Foundation

Graco Inc.

Baukol, Ronald O.: director, executive vice president, Minnesota Mining & Manufacturing Co.

Van Dyke, William Grant: chairman, president, chief executive officer, director, Donaldson Co., Inc.

Graham Resources Inc.

Leatherdale, Douglas West: chairman, chief executive officer, president, Saint Paul Companies Inc.

Grainger Caribe Inc.

Fluno, Jere David: vice chairman, Grainger, Inc. (W.W.)

Grand Forks Herald

Jones, Ross: senior vice president, chief financial officer, Knight Ridder

Grand Junction Newspapers

Easterly, David E.: president, chief operating officer, Cox Enterprises Inc.

Grand Ole Opry Tour Inc.

Gaylord, Edward Lewis: chairman, chief executive officer, director, publisher, Oklahoma Publishing Co.; trustee, Oklahoman Foundation (The)

Grand Trunk Corp.

Keyser, F. Ray, Jr.: chairman, director, Central Vermont Public Service Corp.

Grand Union Co.

Hall, Floyd: chairman, president, chief executive officer, director, Kmart Corp.

Great Cumberland Investments Ltd.

Allbritton, Joe Lewis: chairman, chief executive officer, Riggs Bank NA

Great Interactive Software Corp.

Denning, Steven A.: vice president, General Atlantic Partners II LP

Great Lakes Corp.

Nichols, Mack G.: president, chief executive officer, director, Mallinckrodt Chemical, Inc.

Great Lakes National Bank

Nagorske, Lynn A.: executive vice president, chief financial officer, treasurer, TCF National Bank Minnesota

Great Northern Nekoosa Corp.

Correll, Alston Dayton 'Pete', Jr.: chairman, president, chief executive officer, director, Georgia-Pacific Corp.; director, Georgia-Pacific Foundation

Great Western Finance Corp.

Miller, Charles Daly: chairman, director, Avery Dennison Corp.; trustee, Whirlpool Foundation

Greater Norfolk Corp.

Wolf, Henry C.: vice chairman, chief financial officer, Norfolk Southern Corp.; vice president finance, Norfolk Southern Foundation

Greater Rochester Health System Inc.

Dugan, Allan E.: senior vice president corporate strategic service, Xerox Corp.; trustee, Xerox Foundation

Grede Foundries Inc.

Kellner, Jack F.: director, board member, Marshall & Ilsley Foundation, Inc.

Wright, James O.: president, director, Badger Meter Foundation; chairman, director, Badger Meter, Inc.; director, Marshall & Ilsley Foundation, Inc.

Green Bay Packaging Inc.

Wigdale, James B.: vice president, Marshall & Ilsley Corp.; vice president, director, Marshall & Ilsley Foundation, Inc.

Green Mountain Bank

Young, Robert Harris: president, chief executive officer, Central Vermont Public Service Corp.

Greenfield Industries Inc.

Newlin, William Rankin: trustee, Kennametal Foundation

Greenland Garments Ltd.

Jacobsen, James C.: vice chairman, Kellwood Co.; vice president, director, Kellwood Foundation

Greensboro Daily News & Record

Barry, Richard Francis, III: director, Landmark Communications Foundation; vice chairman, Landmark Communications Inc.

Batten, Frank, Sr.: chairman, director, Landmark Communications Foundation; chairman, Landmark Communications Inc.

Greenspring Co.

Piper, Addison Lewis: director, Piper Jaffray Companies Foundation; chairman, chief executive officer, director, U.S. Bancorp Piper Jaffray

Greenvale Marketing Corp.

Dubin, Melvin: chairman, Slant/Fin Corp.; president, director, Slant/Fin Foundation

Greycas Inc.

Teets, John William: president, chief executive officer, director, Viad Corp. Fund

Greyhound Transportation Leasing Co.

Emerson, Frederick George: vice president, secretary, director, Viad Corp. Fund

Ervanian, Armen: vice president, Viad Corp. Fund

Stephan, Richard C.: vice president, controller, director, Viad Corp. Fund

Teets, John William: president, chief executive officer, director, Viad Corp. Fund

Group Lotus

Eaton, Robert James: co-chairman, president, chief executive officer, DaimlerChrysler Corp.

Groupe Schneider NA

Denny, Charles W.: president, chief executive officer, director, Square D Co.

Gruber's Food Town Inc.

Iott, Richard B.: president, chief executive officer, director, Seaway Food Town, Inc.

Iott, Wallace D.: chairman, director, Seaway Food Town, Inc.

Grucon Corp.

Davis, Walter Stewart: secretary, treasurer, Grede Foundation

Gryphon Holdings Inc.

Douglass, Robert Royal: trustee, Chase Manhattan Foundation

Elliott, David Holland: consultant, chairman executive committee, MBIA Inc.

Gryphon Inc.

Douglass, Robert Royal: trustee, Chase Manhattan Foundation

Guam Publications Inc.

McCorkindale, Douglas H.: vice chairman, president, Gannett Co., Inc.; president, Gannett Foundation

Guarantee Reserve Life Insurance Co.

Pearl, Melvin E.: treasurer, director, Katten, Muchin & Zavis Foundation

Guaranty Federal Bank FSB

Grum, Clifford J.: director, Temple-Inland Foundation; director, chairman, chief executive officer, Temple-Inland Inc.

Jastrow, Kenneth M., II: director, Temple-Inland Foundation

Temple, Arthur, III: director, Temple-Inland Foundation

Guaranty National Mortgage Corp.

Gaiswinkler, Robert Sigfried: chairman, director, First Financial Bank; director, First Financial Foundation

Gucci Timepieces

Leshin, Arthur: senior vice president, chief financial officer, Gucci America Inc.

Guest Services Inc.

Franklin, Barbara Hackman: director, Dow Chemical Co.

Guidant Corp.

Falla, Enrique Crabb: senior consult, director, Dow Chemical Co.

Gulf Power Co.

De Nicola, Paul J.: president, chief executive officer, Southern Co. Services Inc.

Gulf Resources & Chemical Corp.

Slovin, Bruce: president, director, Revlon Inc.

Gulfcoast Easy Living Country

Corson, Keith Daniel: president, chief operating officer, Coachmen Industries, Inc.

Gull Lake Marine Center Inc.

Parfet, Donald R.: president, Pharmacia & Upjohn Foundation; senior vice president associated business, Pharmacia & Upjohn, Inc.

Gulton Industries Inc.

Lippes, Gerald Sanford: secretary, Mark IV Industries Foundation

Montague, William Patrick: president, chief operating officer, director, Mark IV Industries; president, Mark IV Industries Foundation

Gum Tech International Inc.

Hemelt, William J.: treasurer, director, APS Foundation, Inc.; controller, Arizona Public Service Co.

H & R Block

Hale, Roger W.: chairman, chief executive officer, director, LG&E Energy Corp.; president, LG&E Energy Foundation

H B Zachry Co.

Zachry, Henry Bartell, Jr.: chairman, Zachry Co. (H.B.); trustee, Zachry Foundation (The)

H John Heinz III Sch Pub Policy & Management

Block, William: vice president, trustee, Blade Foundation; chairman, director, Toledo Blade Co.

H Plan Inc.

Neely, Walter Emerson: vice president, Humana Foundation

H&R Block Inc.

Sosland, Morton Irvin: director, Block Foundation (H&R)

H. P. Environmental Service LLC

Wilson, Eric L.: director, Hensel Phelps Foundation

H.P. Environmental Service LLC

Morgensen, Jerry L.: president, chief executive officer, director, Hensel Phelps Construction Co.; director, Hensel Phelps Foundation

HB DeViney Co. Inc.

Smucker, Timothy Paul: chairman, director, Smucker Co. (JM)

HB Fuller Automotive Products Inc.

Ray, John Thomas, Jr.: president, director, Fuller Co. Foundation (H.B.)

HB Fuller Co.

King, Reatha Clark: director, Fuller Co. Foundation (H.B.); president, executive director, General Mills Foundation

Mitau, Lee R.: executive vice president, general counsel, secretary, U.S. Bancorp

HB Fuller Co. International Inc.

Ray, John Thomas, Jr.: president, director, Fuller Co. Foundation (H.B.)

HBD Industries

Evans, Robert Sheldon: chairman, chief executive officer, Crane Co.; chairman, president, director, Crane Foundation

HC Prange Co.

Kress, James F.: chairman, director, Green Bay Packaging

HCR Manor Care Inc.

Lemieux, Joseph Henry: chairman, chief executive officer, director, Owens-Illinois Inc.

Longfield, William H.: president, Bard Foundation (C.R.); chairman, chief executive officer, director, Bard, Inc. (C.R.)

HCS Inc.

Simmons, Richard Paul: chairman, president, chief executive officer, Allegheny Technologies Inc.

HEI Diversified Inc.

Clarke, Robert F.: chairman, president, chief executive officer, director, Hawaiian Electric Co., Inc.; president, director, Hawaiian Electric Industries Charitable Foundation

HI Community Reinvestment Corp.

Johnson, Lawrence M.: president, Pacific Century Financial Corp.

HJ Heinz Co.

Johnson, Samuel Curtis: chairman, director, president, Johnson & Son (S.C.); chairman, trustee, Johnson Wax Fund (S.C.)

Wiley, S. Donald: vice chairman, trustee, Heinz Co. Foundation (H.J.)

Zimmerman, James M.: chairman, chief executive officer, director, Federated Department Stores, Inc.

HLR Service Corp.

Zenner, Patrick J.: trustee, Hoffmann-La Roche Foundation; president, chief executive officer, director, Hoffmann-La Roche Inc.

HMO Minnesota

Czajkowski, Andrew P.: chief executive officer, Blue Cross & Blue Shield of Minnesota; chairman, director, Blue Cross & Blue Shield of Minnesota Foundation Inc.

HRE Properties

Douglass, Robert Royal: trustee, Chase Manhattan Foundation

HSB Group Inc.

Ferland, E. James: chairman, president, chief executive officer, Public Service Electric & Gas Co.

HVL Inc.

Morby, Jacqueline C.: managing partner, Pacific Mutual Life Insurance Co.

Hale & Dorr

Cogan, John Francis, Jr.: president, chief executive officer, director, Pioneer Group

Halliburton Co.

Crandall, Robert Lloyd: director, AMR Corp.

Hunt, Ray Lee: chairman, chief executive officer, director, Hunt Oil Co.

Halmode Apparel Inc.

Jacobsen, James C.: vice chairman, Kellwood Co.; vice president, director, Kellwood Foundation

McKenna, William John: director, chairman, Kellwood Co.; chairman, president, director, Kellwood Foundation

Hammermill Paper Co.

Graham, Thomas Carlisle: trustee, AK Steel Foundation

McClelland, William Craig: trustee, Union Camp Charitable Trust; chairman, chief executive officer, director, Union Camp Corp.

Handy & Harman

Tetrault, Roger E.: chairman, chief executive officer, director, McDermott Inc.

Hanendale Mall Inc.

Deering, Anthony W.: chairman, chief executive officer, Rouse Co.; chairman, president, trustee, Rouse Co. Foundation

Hannaford Brothers

Strickland, Robert Louis: vice president, Lowe's Charitable and Educational Foundation

Hannaford Trucking Co.

Bowne, Garrett D., IV: treasurer, Hannaford Charitable Foundation

Fritzson, Paul A.: president, director, Hannaford Brothers Co.

Hodge, Ronald C.: director, Hannaford Charitable Foundation

Hanover Insurance Co. Inc.

O'Brien, John Francis, Jr.: president, chief executive officer, Allmerica Financial Corp.

Hanson PLC (London)

Price, Charles H., II: director, New York Times Co. Foundation

Harbor Holdings Inc.

Weekly, John William: chairman, chief executive officer, Mutual of Omaha Insurance Co.

Harcourt General Inc.

Countryman, Gary Lee: chairman, Liberty Mutual Insurance Group

Geller, Eric P.: trustee, Harcourt General Charitable Foundation; senior vice president, general counsel, secretary, Harcourt General, Inc.

Martin, Lynn M.: director, Ameritech Foundation

Hardaway Co.

Blanchard, James Hubert: chairman, chief executive officer, Synovus Financial Corp.

Harley-Davidson Holding Co.

Bleustein, Jeffrey L.: president, chief executive officer, director, Harley-Davidson Co.

Harley-Davidson Inc.

Allen, Barry K.: president regulatory & wholesale operation, Ameritech Corp.

Brostowitz, James M.: treasurer, Harley-Davidson Foundation

Harley-Davidson Motor Co.

Bleustein, Jeffrey L.: president, chief executive officer, director, Harley-Davidson Co.

Harley-Davidson Transportation Co.

Brostowitz, James M.: treasurer, Harley-Davidson Foundation

Ziemer, James L.: president, Harley-Davidson Foundation

Harnischfeger Corp.

Corby, Francis Michael, Jr.: executive vice president finance & administration, chief financial officer, Harnischfeger Industries; treasurer, Harnischfeger Industries Foundation

Kohler, Herbert Vollrath, Jr.: chairman, president, director, Kohler Co.

Harnischfeger International Corp.

Grade, Jeffery T.: chairman, chief executive officer, director, Harnischfeger Industries; president, Harnischfeger Industries Foundation

Harold C Simmons Family Trust

Simmons, Harold Clark: chairman, director, Simmons Foundation, Inc. (Harold)

Harrahs Entertainment Co.

Farley, James Bernard: chairman emeritus, trustee, Walter Industries Inc.

Harris Bank-Oakbrook Terrace

Terry, Richard Edward: chairman, chief executive officer, director, Peoples Energy Corp.

Harris Realty

Harris, Irving Brooks: chairman executive committee, director, Pittway Corp.; chairman, director, Pittway Corp. Charitable Foundation

Harris Technical Services Corp.

Roub, Bryan Roger: trustee, Harris Foundation

Wasserman, David Sherman: vice president, treasurer, Harris Corp.; trustee, Harris Foundation

Harris Teeter Inc.

Dickson, Alan Thomas: president, Dickson Foundation; chairman, Ruddick Corp.

Dickson, Rush Stuart: chairman, Dickson Foundation

Harris Trust & Savings Bank

McNally, Alan G.: chairman, chief executive officer, Harris Trust & Savings Bank

Terry, Richard Edward: chairman, chief executive officer, director, Peoples Energy Corp.

Harrisburg Television Inc.

Allbritton, Joe Lewis: chairman, chief executive officer, Riggs Bank NA

Harry David Co.

Beck, Edward W.: senior vice president, general counsel, secretary, director, Shaklee Corp.

Harsco Corp.

Nation, Robert F.: former president, director, Harsco Corp.; trustee, Harsco Corp. Fund

Viviano, Joseph P.: president, court, Hershey Foods Corp.

Hart Schaffner & Marx

Condon, James Edward: treasurer, Hartmarx Charitable Foundation; vice president, treasurer, Hartmarx Corp.

Morgan, Glenn R.: executive vice president, chief financial officer, Hartmarx Corp.

Patel, Homi Burjor: president, chief operating officer, director, Hartmarx Corp.

Hartford Accident Indemnity Co.

Ayer, Ramani: chairman, president, chief executive officer, Hartford (The)

Hartford Action Plan Infant Health

Goodman, Helen G.: senior vice president, Hartford (The)

Hartford Casualty Insurance Co.

Ayer, Ramani: chairman, president, chief executive officer, Hartford (The)

Hartford Financial Services Group Inc.

Goodman, Helen G.: senior vice president, Hartford (The)

Hartford Fire Insurance Co.

Ayer, Ramani: chairman, president, chief executive officer, Hartford (The)

Hartford Steam Boiler Inspection & Insurance Co.

Ferland, E. James: chairman, president, chief executive officer, Public Service Electric & Gas Co.

Hartle Marine Corp.

Raskin, Fred C.: president, chief operating officer, Eastern Enterprises; trustee, Eastern Enterprises Foundation

Harvard Corp.

Houghton, James Richardson: director, Corning Inc.; trustee, Corning Inc. Foundation

Hasbro Global operations

Verrecchia, Alfred J.: treasurer, trustee, Hasbro Charitable Trust Inc.; executive, director, Hasbro, Inc.

Hasbro Inc.

Tisch, Preston Robert: chairman, director, CBS Foundation; co-chairman, co-chief executive officer, director, CNA; trustee, Loews Foundation

Hatco Corp.

Connolly, Gerald Edward: trustee, Reinhart Family Foundation (D. B. and Marjorie)

Hathaway Corp.

Hock, Delwin D.: chairman, New Century Energies

Haverty Furniture Companies Inc.

Humann, L. Phillip: member, SunTrust Bank Atlanta Foundation

Hawaii Electric Co. Inc.

Clarke, Robert F.: chairman, president, chief executive officer, director, Hawaiian Electric Co., Inc.; president, director, Hawaiian Electric Industries Charitable Foundation

Hawaii Electric Industries Inc.

Li, Victor Hao: director, Hawaiian Electric Industries Charitable Foundation

Hawaii Electric Light Co.

Clarke, Robert F.: chairman, president, chief executive officer, director, Hawaiian Electric Co., Inc.; president, director, Hawaiian Electric Industries Charitable Foundation

Hawaii Energy Resources Inc.

Kurren, Faye Watanabe: president, Tesoro Hawaii

Hawaiian Electric Industries Inc.

Stender, Oswald K.: director, Hawaiian Electric Industries Charitable Foundation

Watanabe, Jeffrey N.: director, Hawaiian Electric Industries Charitable Foundation

Hawaiian Electric Light Co.

May, T. Michael: president, Hawaiian Electric Co., Inc.; director, Hawaiian Electric Industries Charitable Foundation

Health Care & Retirement Corp.

Lemieux, Joseph Henry: chairman, chief executive officer, director, Owens-Illinois Inc.

Health One

Coyne, William E.: senior vice president, Minnesota Mining & Manufacturing Co.

Healthsource Inc.

Chandler, J. Harold: chairman, president, chief executive officer, Provident Companies, Inc.

Heartland Development Corp.

Davis, Erroll Brown, Jr.: president, chief executive officer, director, Wisconsin Power & Light Co.

Lyall, Katharine Culbert: trustee, Kemper Foundation (James S.)

Heartland Partners

Flaherty, Gerald S.: trustee, Caterpillar Foundation; group president, Caterpillar Inc.

Zilkha, Ezra Khedouri: president, treasurer, Zilkha Foundation, Inc.; president, Zilkha & Sons

Heekin Can Co. Inc.

Leser, Lawrence Arthur: chairman, director, Scripps Co. (E.W.); member, Scripps Howard Foundation

Heilig-Meyers Co.

Burrus, Robert Lewis, Jr.: trustee, Circuit City Foundation

Meyers, Hyman: trustee, Circuit City Foundation

Heisklberger Zement AG

Hirsch, Laurence E.: chairman, chief executive officer, director, Centex Corp.

Helene Curtis Inc.

Gidwitz, Ronald J.: president, chief executive officer, Curtis Industries, Inc. (Helene)

Heller International Inc.

Almeida, Richard: chairman, chief executive officer, Heller Financial, Inc.

Helmsman Insurance Agency Inc.

Gilvar, Barry S.: secretary, Liberty Mutual Insurance Group

Helmsman Management Services Inc.

Countryman, Gary Lee: chairman, Liberty Mutual Insurance Group

Henderson Gleaner

Decherd, Robert William: chairman, president, chief executive officer, director, Belo Corp. (A.H.); chairman, trustee, Belo Corp. Foundation (A.H.)

Henley Group Inc.

Montrone, Paul Michael: vice president, partner, Winthrop Foundation

Henry Ford Health System

Ford, William Clay, Jr.: chairman, Ford Motor Co.

Henry Ford Health Systems

Valade, Gary C.: executive vice president, chief financial officer, DaimlerChrysler Corp.; trustee,

DaimlerChrysler Corp. Fund

Henry Ford Hospital
Manoogian, Richard Alexander: chairman, chief executive officer, director, Masco Corp.

Henry Heide Inc.
Wolfe, Kenneth L.: chairman, chief executive officer, director, Hershey Foods Corp.

Hensel Phelps Environmental Services
Carrico, Stephen J.: director, Hensel Phelps Foundation

Herider Farms Inc.
Edgerton, Brenda Evans: vice president business development, Campbell Soup Co.; treasurer, trustee, Campbell Soup Foundation

Herman Miller
Pollard, Charles William, Jr.: chairman, director, ServiceMaster Co.; president, director, ServiceMaster Foundation

Herman Miller Inc.
Chandler, J. Harold: chairman, president, chief executive officer, Provident Companies, Inc.

Hershey Foods Corp.
Campbell, Robert Henderson: chairman, chief executive officer, Sunoco Inc.

Graham, Thomas Carlisle: trustee, AK Steel Foundation

Hill, Bonnie Guiton: vice president, Times Mirror Co.; president, chief executive officer, Times Mirror Foundation

Hershey Trust Co.
Wolfe, Kenneth L.: chairman, chief executive officer, director, Hershey Foods Corp.

Hertz Corp.
Pestillo, Peter John: executive chairman, Ford Motor Co.; trustee, Ford Motor Co. Fund

Hewlett Packard Co.
Condit, Philip Murray: chairman, chief executive officer, director, Boeing Co.

Hickory Point Bank & Trust
Reising, Richard P.: senior vice president, general counsel, secretary, Archer-Daniels-Midland Co.; secretary, Archer-Daniels-Midland Foundation

Hickory Technology Corp.
Else, Robert K.: director, Hickory Tech Corp.; secretary, Hickory Tech Corp. Foundation

Jacobson, Lyle Gordon: treasurer, Hickory Tech Corp. Foundation

Kearney, R. Wynn, Jr.: director, Hickory Tech Corp.; trustee, Hickory Tech Corp. Foundation

Highland Bank
Stephens, Elton Bryson: founder, chairman, Ebsco Industries, Inc.

Highland Land & Minerals
Ackerman, Philip Charles: senior vice president, director, National Fuel Gas Distribution Corp.

Highlands Insurance Co.
Blurton, Jerry Halbert: treasurer, Halliburton Foundation, Inc.

Lesar, David J.: president, chief operating officer, Halliburton Co.; trustee, Halliburton Foundation, Inc.

Highlands Underwriters Insurance Co.
Blurton, Jerry Halbert: treasurer, Halliburton Foundation, Inc.

Hilb Rogal Hamilton
Ukrop, Robert S.: president, chief operating officer, director, Ukrop Foundation; president, chief operating officer, Ukrop's Super Markets

Hill n Dale Farms Inc.
Duchossois, Craig J.: director, Duchossois Foundation; president, director, Duchossois Industries Inc.

Duchossois, Richard Louis: secretary, Duchossois Foundation; chairman, chief executive officer, director, Duchossois Industries Inc.

Hillenbrand Industries
Hillenbrand, John A., II: director, Cinergy Foundation

Hilltop National Bank
True, Diemer: partner, True Oil Co.

Hilltop National Bank Mountain Plaza
True, David: partner, True Oil Co.

True, Diemer: partner, True Oil Co.

Hiniker Co.
Gidwitz, Gerald S.: chairman, Curtis Industries, Inc. (Helene)

Hipotronics Inc.
Davies, Richard Warren: trustee, Hubbell Foundation (Harvey)

Hitachi Seisakujo Co. Ltd.
Kanai, Tsutomu: president, Hitachi Foundation

Holga Inc.
Michaels, Jack D.: secretary, HON Industries Charitable Foundation; chairman, president, chief executive officer, director, HON Industries Inc.

Holiday Holding Corp.
Bleustein, Jeffrey L.: president, chief executive officer, director, Harley-Davidson Co.

Holiday Inn North
Dora, James E.: director, AUL Foundation Inc.

Hollinger International Inc.
Andreas, Dwayne Orville: chairman, chief executive officer, Archer-Daniels-Midland Co.

Kissinger, Henry Alfred: director, CBS Foundation

Hollingsworth & Voge Co.
Cabot, John G. L.: vice chairman, Kinder Morgn

Holly Farms Corp.
Blair, James Burton: trustee, Tyson Foundation, Inc.

Hollywood Records Inc.
Eisner, Michael Dammann: president, trustee, Disney Co. Foundation (Walt); chairman, chief executive officer, director, Disney Co. (Walt)

Holm Industries Inc.
Zampetis, Theodore K.: president, chief operating officer, director, Standard Products Co.

Holset Engineering Co. Ltd. UK
Stoner, Richard Burkett, Jr.: director, Cummins Engine Foundation

Home Depot United States of America Inc.
Blank, Arthur M.: president, chief executive officer, director, Home Depot, Inc.

Home Insurance Co.
Douglass, Robert Royal: trustee, Chase Manhattan Foundation

Home Properties New York
Kober, Roger W.: chairman, chief executive officer, director, Rochester Gas & Electric Corp.

Home Savings & Loan Co.
Cushwa, Charles Benton, III: trustee, Commercial Intertech Foundation

Home Savings of America FSB
Rinehart, Charles Robert: chairman, chief executive officer, director, Washington Mutual, Inc.

Honda North America
Amemiya, Koichi: president, chief executive officer, director, American Honda Motor Co., Inc.

Honeywell Electronics Corp.
Bonsignore, Michael Robert: director, Honeywell Foundation; chairman, chief executive officer, director, Honeywell International Inc.

Honeywell Inc.
Howard, James Joseph, III: chairman, president, chief executive officer, director, Northern States Power Co.

Rand, Addison Barry: executive vice president operations, Xerox Corp.; trustee, Xerox Foundation

Wright, Michael William: chairman, president, chief executive officer, director, SuperValu, Inc.

Hong Kong Telecom
Brown, Richard Harris: chairman, chief executive officer, director, EDS Corp.

Hoosier State Press
Russell, Frank Eli: president, Central Newspapers Foundation; chairman, Central Newspapers, Inc.

Hope Cattle Co.
Tomich, Rosemary: director, Occidental Petroleum Charitable Foundation

Horizon Air Industries Inc.
Kelly, John F.: chairman, chief executive officer, director, Alaska Airlines, Inc.

Horizon Energy Development Inc.
Ackerman, Philip Charles: senior vice president, director, National Fuel Gas Distribution Corp.

Horizon Health Corp.
Longfield, William H.: president, Bard Foundation (C.R.); chairman, chief executive officer, director, Bard, Inc. (C.R.)

Horsham Corp.
Melnuk, Paul D.: president, chief executive officer, Clark Refining & Marketing

Hotel Columbus
Blanchard, James Hubert: chairman, chief executive officer, Synovus Financial Corp.

Houghton Mifflin Co.
Magee, John Francis: chairman, director, Little, Inc. (Arthur D.)

Putnam, George, Jr.: chairman, president, chief executive officer, Putnam Investments

Housatonic Curtain Co. Inc.

Brown, JoAnn Fitzpatrick: director, High Meadow Foundation

Fitzpatrick, Jane P.: chairman, chief executive officer, treasurer, Country Curtains, Inc.; chairman, High Meadow Foundation

Trask, Robert B.: president, chief operating officer, director, Country Curtains, Inc.; clerk, trustee, High Meadow Foundation

Household Bank FSB

Kelly, Colin P.: senior vice president human resources, Household International Inc.

Household Commercial Financial Services

Aldinger, William F., III: chairman, chief executive officer, director, Household International Inc.

Household Finance Corp.

Schoenholz, David A.: executive vice president, chief financial officer, Household International Inc.

Household International Inc.

Lorch, George A.: chairman, chief executive officer, director, Armstrong World Industries, Inc.

Stewart, S. Jay: chairman, chief executive officer, director, Morton International Inc.

Houston Financial Services Ltd.

Allbritton, Joe Lewis: chairman, chief executive officer, Riggs Bank NA

Houston Freightliner Inc.

Hebe, James L.: chairman, president, chief executive officer, Freightliner Corp.

Hoxan Corp.

Kampouris, Emmanuel Andrew: chairman, president, chief executive officer, director, American Standard Inc.

Hubbell Inc.

Brooks, E. Richard 'Dick': chairman, chief executive officer, director, Central & South West Services

Meyer, Daniel Joseph: president, Milacron Foundation; chairman, president, chief executive officer, director, Milacron, Inc.

Hubbell Lighting Inc.

Davies, Richard Warren: trustee, Hubbell Foundation (Harvey)

Hudson Foods Inc.

Tyson, John H.: chairman, chief executive officer, president, director, Tyson Foods Inc.; trustee, Tyson Foundation, Inc.

Hudsons Bay Co.

D'Alessandro, Dominic: president, chief executive officer, director, Manulife Financial

Huffy Corp.

Rooney, Patrick W.: chairman, president, chief executive officer, director, Cooper Tire & Rubber Co.

Viviano, Joseph P.: president, court, Hershey Foods Corp.

Hugh M Woods

Hall, William Austin: president, Hallmark Corporate Foundation

Hughes Electronics Corp.

Armstrong, C. Michael: chairman, chief executive officer, AT&T Corp.

Pfeiffer, Eckhard A.: president, chief executive officer, director, Compaq Computer Corp.

Smith, John Francis, Jr.: chairman, General Motors Corp.

Humana Health Insurance Co. NV

Doucette, James Willard: vice president, treasurer, Humana Foundation

Humana Health Insurance NV Inc.

Neely, Walter Emerson: vice president, Humana Foundation

Humana Health Plan Inc.

Bauernfeind, George G.: vice president, Humana Foundation

Doucette, James Willard: vice president, treasurer, Humana Foundation

Murray, James E.: chief operating officer, senior vice president, Humana Foundation

Neely, Walter Emerson: vice president, Humana Foundation

Humana Health Plan Texas

Bauernfeind, George G.: vice president, Humana Foundation

Doucette, James Willard: vice president, treasurer, Humana Foundation

Neely, Walter Emerson: vice president, Humana Foundation

Wolf, Gregory H.: president, chief operating officer, director, Humana, Inc.

Humana Inc.

Neely, Walter Emerson: vice president, Humana Foundation

Humana Kansas City Inc.

Wolf, Gregory H.: president, chief operating officer, director, Humana, Inc.

Hunt Co.

Farber, Jack: chairman, president, director, CSS Industries, Inc.; president, Farber Foundation

Hunt Graphics America Corp.

Chandler, William Everett: senior vice president finance, secretary, chief financial officer, Hunt Manufacturing Co.

Hunt Manufacturing Co.

Belcher, Donald D.: chairman, president, chief executive officer, director, Banta Corp.; vice president, director, Banta Corp. Foundation

Hunt Overseas Oil Inc.

Meurer, Thomas E.: senior vice president administration, Hunt Oil Co.

Huntington Bancshares Inc.

Lhota, William J.: executive vice president, American Electric Power

Smucker, Timothy Paul: chairman, director, Smucker Co. (JM)

Huntington Leasing Co.

Seiffert, Ron J.: vice chairman, Huntington Bancshares Inc.

Huntington National Bank

Molen, Richard L.: chairman, chief executive officer, director, Huffy Corp.; trustee, Huffy Foundation, Inc.

Seiffert, Ron J.: vice chairman, Huntington Bancshares Inc.

Huntington Trust Co.

Wobst, Frank: chairman, chief executive officer, director, Huntington Bancshares Inc.

Huntsman Corp.

Hiner, Glen Harold, Jr.: chairman, chief executive officer, director, Owens Corning

Hutchinson Techs Inc.

Rosett, Richard Nathaniel: trustee, Kemper Foundation (James S.)

Hybritech Inc.

Wareham, John P.: president, chief executive officer, director, Beckman Coulter, Inc.

Wilson, Dennis K.: vice president finance, chief financial officer, Beckman Coulter, Inc.

Hydrocarbons Dow Resources

Reinhard, J. Pedro: executive vice president, chief financial officer, director, Dow Chemical Co.

Hypro Corp.

Wardeberg, George E.: president, WICOR Foundation; president, chief executive officer, director, WICOR, Inc.

I Bahcall Industries

Rosenzweig, Richard Stuart: executive vice president, director, Playboy Enterprises Inc.

I Fushion Holdings LLC

Recanati, Michael A.: executive vice president, director, OSG Foundation

I-70 East Inn Devel

Dora, James E.: director, AUL Foundation Inc.

IBM Corp.

Knight, Charles Field: chairman, chief executive officer, Emerson Electric Co.

IC Equities Inc.

Moore, William B.: senior vice president, secretary, general counsel, Whitman Corp.; secretary, Whitman Corp. Foundation

ICI Inc.

Montrone, Paul Michael: vice president, partner, Winthrop Foundation

ICI Mutual Insurance Co.

Brennan, John J.: chairman, chief executive officer, Vanguard Group; president, Vanguard Group Foundation

Cogan, John Francis, Jr.: president, chief executive officer, director, Pioneer Group

Keyser, F. Ray, Jr.: chairman, director, Central Vermont Public Service Corp.

ICN Pharmaceuticals

Bergerac, Michel Christian: director, CBS Foundation

ICO South Corp.

Gates, William Henry, III: co-founder, chairman, chief software architect, Microsoft Corp.

ICS CommunicationS

Carey, Chase: chief executive officer, chairman, Fox Entertainment Group

ID Energy Research Co.

Keen, J. LaMont: vice president, chief financial officer, Idaho Power Co.

IDB Bankholding Corp. Ltd.

Recanati, Raphael: president, director, OSG Foundation

IDEX Corp.

Tokarz, Michael T.: founding partner, Walter Industries Inc.

IDS Bond Fund Inc.

Golub, Harvey: chairman, chief executive officer, director, American Express Co.; trustee, American Express Foundation

IDS Discovery Fund Inc.

Golub, Harvey: chairman, chief executive officer, director, American Express Co.; trustee, American Express Foundation

IDS Extra Income Fund Inc.

Golub, Harvey: chairman, chief executive officer, director, American Express Co.; trustee, American Express Foundation

IDS Mutual Fund Group

Weill, Sanford I.: chairman, chief executive officer, Citibank Corp.; chairman, Citigroup Foundation

Wurtele, C. Angus: president, Valspar Foundation

IES Utilities

Davis, Erroll Brown, Jr.: president, chief executive officer, director, Wisconsin Power & Light Co.

IMC Global Inc.

Bueche, Wendell Francis: director, Marshall & Ilsley Foundation, Inc.

Mathis, David B.: chairman, Kemper Foundation (James S.)

Thomas, Richard Lee: vice president, First National Bank of Chicago Foundation

IMC Global Operation Delaware

Bueche, Wendell Francis: director, Marshall & Ilsley Foundation, Inc.

IMCERA

Kennedy, George Danner: trustee, Kemper Foundation (James S.)

INA Corp.

Rohrkemper, Paul H.: treasurer, CIGNA Corp.; vice president, treasurer, CIGNA Foundation

INB Finance Corp.

Baker, James Kendrick: chairman, director, Arvin Foundation; vice chairman, director, Arvin Industries, Inc.

INB National Bank

Habig, Douglas A.: chairman, chief executive officer, director, Habig Foundation

INCESA

Kampouris, Emmanuel Andrew: chairman, president, chief executive officer, director, American Standard Inc.

IP Timberlands Ltd.

Guedry, James Walter: president, International Paper Co. Foundation

ITT Destinations Inc.

Bowman, Robert A.: president, chief operating officer, Starwood Hotels & Resorts Worldwide, Inc.

ITT Systems & Sciences Corp.

Kaman, Charles Huron: chairman, president, chief executive officer, director, Kaman Corp.

IWC Resources Corp.

Semler, Jerry D.: chairman, president, chief executive officer, director, American United Life Insurance Co.; chairman, director, AUL Foundation Inc.

Ideal Industries Inc.

Pehlke, Richard W.: vice president, treasurer, Ameritech Corp.

Ideal Refractories SAI

Kampouris, Emmanuel Andrew: chairman, president, chief executive officer, director, American Standard Inc.

Illinois Emcasco Insurance Co.

Kelley, Bruce Gunn: vice president, director, Employers Mutual Charitable Foundation

Illinois Energy Partners

Bayless, Charles Edward: chairman, president, chief executive officer, director, Illinois Power Co.

Illinois State Bank E Alton

Griffin, Donald Wayne: chairman, president, chief executive officer, director, Olin Corp.; trustee, Olin Corp. Charitable Trust

Illinois Tool Works Inc.

Flury, L. Richard: executive vice president, BP Amoco Corp.

Kennedy, George Danner: trustee, Kemper Foundation (James S.)

Illinova Corp.

Altenbaumer, Larry F.: senior vice president, chief financial officer, Illinois Power Co.

Setzner, Leah Manning: vice president, general counsel, corporate secretary, Illinois Power Co.

Illinova Generating Co.

Bayless, Charles Edward: chairman, president, chief executive officer, director, Illinois Power Co.

Ilsco Corp.

Cudlip, Brittain B.: chairman, Bardes Corp.

FitzGibbon, David J.: president, chief executive officer, Bardes Corp.

Imation Corp.

George, William Wallace: chief executive officer, chairman, Medtronic, Inc.

Imation Enterprises Inc.

Pulido, Mark A.: president, chief executive officer, director, chairman, McKesson-HBOC Corp.

Imperial Holly Corp.

Grinstein, Gerald: director, PACCAR Inc.

Inacom Corp.

Bay, Mogens C.: chairman, chief executive officer, Valmont Industries, Inc.

Inagua Transports Inc.

Johnston, William E., Junior: president, chief operating officer, director, Morton International Inc.

Indala Corp.

Galvin, Christopher B.: director, Motorola Foundation; president, chief executive officer, director, Motorola Inc.

Koenemann, Carl F.: chief financial officer, executive vice president, Motorola Inc.

Independence Savings Bank

Catell, Robert Barry: chairman, chief executive officer, Brooklyn Union

Independence Square Properties

Brodie, Nancy S.: executive vice president, chief financial officer, Penn Mutual Life Insurance Co.

Independent Newspapers PLC

O'Reilly, F. Anthony John: chairman, trustee, Heinz Co. Foundation (H.J.); chairman, director, Heinz Co. (H.J.)

Independent Soy Processors

Andreas, Dwayne Orville: chairman, chief executive officer, Archer-Daniels-Midland Co.

Indiana Business Modernization & Technology Corp.

Habig, Douglas A.: chairman, chief executive officer, director, Habig Foundation

Indiana Franklin Realty Co.

Draper, Ernest Linn, Jr.: chairman, president, chief executive officer, director, American Electric Power

Indiana Michigan Power Co.

Lhota, William J.: executive vice president, American Electric Power

Indiana-Kentucky Electric Corp.

Draper, Ernest Linn, Jr.: chairman, president, chief executive officer, director, American Electric Power

Indianapolis Life Insurance Co.

Sease, Gene Elwood: director, Central Newspapers Foundation

Indianapolis News

Pulliam, Eugene Smith: vice president, director, Central Newspapers Foundation

Indianapolis Newspapers Inc.

Gillivray, Thomas K.: treasurer, Central Newspapers, Inc.

Russell, Frank Eli: president, Central Newspapers Foundation; chairman, Central Newspapers, Inc.

Indianapolis Power & Light Co.

Daniels, Mitchell E., Jr.: chairman, treasurer, Lilly Foundation (Eli)

Indianapolis Star

Pulliam, Eugene Smith: vice president, director, Central Newspapers Foundation

Industrial Bank Japan Trust Co.

Nelson, Merlin Edward: chairman, director, IBJ Foundation

Industrial Maintenance Corp.

Schuman, Allan L.: president, chief executive officer, director, chairman, Ecolab Inc.

Industries Bank Japan Trust Co.

Higgs, John H.: director, IBJ Foundation

Industries Insurance Corp.

Corby, Francis Michael, Jr.: executive vice president finance & administration, chief financial officer, Harnischfeger Industries; treasurer, Harnischfeger Industries Foundation

Infinet Co.

Barry, Richard Francis, III: director, Landmark Communications Foundation; vice chairman, Landmark Communications Inc.

Ingram Customer Systems Inc.

Ingram, Martha R.: chairman, director, Ingram Industries Inc.

Ingram Industries

Bottorff, Dennis C.: chairman, president, chief executive officer, director, First American Corp.

Ingram Micro Inc.

Davis, Donald H., Jr.: president, chief executive officer, chairman, Rockwell International Corp.; chairman trust committee, Rockwell International Corp. Trust

Ingram, Martha R.: chairman, director, Ingram Industries Inc.

Inland Paperboard Packaging

Jastrow, Kenneth M., II: director, Temple-Inland Foundation

Maxwell, Harold C.: director, Temple-Inland Foundation

Inland Steel Industries Inc.

Henderson, James Alan: vice chairman, chief executive officer, director, Ameritech Corp.; chairman,

director, Cummins Engine Foundation

Innowave Inc.

Sturgeon, John: president, chief operating officer, Mutual of Omaha Insurance Co.

Weekly, John William: chairman, chief executive officer, Mutual of Omaha Insurance Co.

Inquirer & Mirror Inc.

Ottaway, James Haller, Jr.: senior vice president, director, Dow Jones & Co., Inc.; member advisory committee, Dow Jones Foundation

Inroads Fairfield Westchester Counties Inc.

Smith, Elizabeth Patience: director, Texaco Foundation; vice president investor relations & shareholder service, Texaco Inc.

Institute America

Felsinger, Donald E.: president, chief executive officer, Sempra Energy

Insurance Counselors Inc.

Phillips, Rosalind Ann: secretary, GEICO Philanthropic Foundation

Integra National Bank

Newlin, William Rankin: trustee, Kennametal Foundation

Intel Corp.

Pottruck, David Steven: president, chief executive officer, director, Schwab & Co., Inc. (Charles)

Intel Puerto Rico Ltd.

Moore, Gordon E., PhD: cofounder, chairman emeritus, director, Intel Corp.; trustee, Intel Foundation

Inter Atlantic Securities

Esposito, Michael Patrick, Jr.: trustee, Chase Manhattan Foundation

Inter Leaf Inc.

Lopiano, John A.: senior vice president, Xerox Corp.; trustee, Xerox Foundation

InterFirst Bank NA

Hemminghaus, Roger Roy: chairman, director, Ultramar Diamond Shamrock Corp.

Interactive Light

Stolar, Bernie: trustee, Sega Foundation

Interfinancial Inc.

Freedman, Allen Royal: trustee, Fortis Foundation; chairman, chief executive officer, president, Fortis, Inc.

International Bechtel S De RL

Zaccaria, Adrian: president, chief operating officer, director, Bechtel Group, Inc.

International Business Machines Corp.

Chenault, Kenneth Irvine: president, chief operating officer, director, American Express Co.; trustee, American Express Foundation

International Center New York Inc.

Hatsopoulos, George Nicholas: founder, chairman, chief executive officer, director, Thermo Electron Corp.; committee member, Thermo Electron Foundation

International Disposal Corp. California

Ranck, Bruce E.: president, chief executive officer, director, Browning-Ferris Industries Inc.

International Distillers Vintners

Seremet, Peter M.: president, United Distillers & Vintners North America

International Financial Conference

Jones, D. Paul, Jr.: chairman, chief executive officer, Compass Bank; trustee, Compass Bank Foundation

International Herald Tribune

Graham, Katharine Meyer: chairman executive committee, director, The Washington Post

Spoon, Alan Gary: president, chief operating officer, director, The Washington Post

International Imaging Materials Inc.

Montague, William Patrick: president, chief operating officer, director, Mark IV Industries; president, Mark IV Industries Foundation

International Insurance Seminars Inc.

Purvis, George Frank, Jr.: chairman, president, chief executive officer, director, Pan-American Life Insurance Co.

International MDL Service

Harris, Edward D., Jr.: director, Genentech Foundation for Biomedical Sciences

International Multifoods Corp.

Rehm, Jack Daniel: chairman emeritus, director, Meredith Corp.

International Paper Co.

Bijur, Peter I.: chairman, chief executive officer, Texaco Inc.

Eaton, Robert James: cochairman, president, chief executive officer, DaimlerChrysler Corp.

Graham, Thomas Carlisle: trustee, AK Steel Foundation

McClelland, William Craig: trustee, Union Camp Charitable Trust; chairman, chief executive officer, director, Union Camp Corp.

Sheehan, Jeremiah J.: chairman, director, Reynolds Metals Co. Foundation

Shoemate, Charles Richard: chairman, president, chief executive officer, Bestfoods

International Paper Realty Corp.

Guedry, James Walter: president, International Paper Co. Foundation

International Reinsurance Co.

Purvis, George Frank, Jr.: chairman, president, chief executive officer, director, Pan-American Life Insurance Co.

International Telecharge

Bergerac, Michel Christian: director, CBS Foundation

International Women's Apparel

Condon, James Edward: treasurer, Hartmarx Charitable Foundation; vice president, treasurer, Hartmarx Corp.

Interstate Broadcasting Co.

Sulzberger, Arthur Ochs, Sr.: director, New York Times Co.; chairman, director, New York Times Co. Foundation

Interstate Energy Corp.

Lyall, Katharine Culbert: trustee, Kemper Foundation (James S.)

Interstate Fire & Casualty Co.

Pollard, David R.: director, Fireman's Fund Foundation; officer, Fireman's Fund Insurance Co.

Interstate Land Corp.

Heiner, Clyde Mont: executive vice president, Questar Corp.

Interstate Power Co.

Davis, Erroll Brown, Jr.: president, chief executive officer, director, Wisconsin Power & Light Co.

Interstate Stations

Demere, Robert H.: president, Colonial Foundation; chairman, Colonial Oil Industries, Inc.

Intertate National Corp.

Black, Gary E.: president, director, Fireman's Fund Foundation; president claims division, director, Fireman's Fund Insurance Co.

Intrust Bank NA

Koch, Charles de Ganahl: chairman, chief executive officer, director, president, Koch Industries, Inc.

Moore, William B.: director, Western Resources Foundation; executive vice president, chief financial officer, treasurer, Western Resources Inc.

Intrust Finance Corp.

Koch, Charles de Ganahl: chairman, chief executive officer, director, president, Koch Industries, Inc.

Investors Syndicate Development Corp.

Golub, Harvey: chairman, chief executive officer, director, American Express Co.; trustee, American Express Foundation

Ipalco Enterprises

Daniels, Mitchell E., Jr.: chairman, treasurer, Lilly Foundation (Eli)

Irvine Apartment Community Inc.

Grundhofer, John Francis: president, chief executive officer, director, U.S. Bancorp

Irwin Financial Corp.

Miller, Joseph Irwin: director associate, Cummins Engine Co., Inc.; director, Cummins Engine Foundation

Solso, Theodore Matthew: president, chief operating officer, director, Cummins Engine Co., Inc.; director, Cummins Engine Foundation

Irwin Management Co. Inc.

Miller, William Irwin: director, Cummins Engine Foundation

Isco Holding Co. Inc.

Boswell, John Joseph: president, Boswell Foundation, Inc.; chairman, Independent Stave Co.

Itron Inc.

Redmond, Paul Anthony: chairman, chief executive officer, director, Avista Corporation

Ivax Corp.

Krueger, Harvey M.: trustee, Barry Foundation

Ivy International Ltd.

Jacobsen, James C.: vice chairman, Kellwood Co.; vice president, director, Kellwood Foundation

J W Windo Components Inc.

Porter, Edward A.: vice president, general counsel,

secretary, Walter Industries Inc.

J. M. Huber Corp.
Tumminello, Stephen C.: president, chief executive officer, director, Philips Electronics North America Corp.

J. Ray McDermott S.A.
Tetrault, Roger E.: chairman, chief executive officer, director, McDermott Inc.

J. W. Teets Enterprise LLC
Teets, John William: president, chief executive officer, director, Viad Corp. Fund

J.A. Jones Inc.
Franklin, Barbara Hackman: director, Dow Chemical Co.
Holland, William Ray: vice president, director, United Dominion Foundation; chairman, chief executive officer, director, United Dominion Industries, Ltd.

J.D. Edwards & Co.
Allen, Richard E.: vice president finance, chief financial officer, Edwards Enterprise Software (J.D.)

JBB Worldwide Inc.
Rukeyser, Robert James: senior vice president corporate affairs, Fortune Brands, Inc.

JC Penney Co. Inc.
Burns, Mitchell Anthony: president, director, Ryder System Charitable Foundation; chairman, president, chief executive officer, Ryder System, Inc.
Foster, Kent B.: president, director, GTE Corp.; trustee, GTE Foundation

JKW Management Corp.
Jacobson, Lyle Gordon: treasurer, Hickory Tech Corp. Foundation

JL Clark Inc.
Johnson, Norman E.: trustee, CLARCOR Foundation

JLA Partners Inc.
Allbritton, Joe Lewis: chairman, chief executive officer, Riggs Bank NA

JLK Direct Distribution
Newlin, William Rankin: trustee, Kennametal Foundation

JM Smucker Co.
Graham, Richard William: president, chief executive officer, chief operating officer, director, Smurfit-Stone Container Corp.

JM Smucker Co. Inc.
Wrigley, William, Jr.: vice president, director, Wrigley Co. Foundation (Wm. Jr.)

JP Morgan & Co. Inc.
Allaire, Paul Arthur: chairman, chief executive officer, chairman executive committee, Xerox Corp.; president, Xerox Foundation
Bechtel, Riley Peart: chairman, Bechtel Foundation; chairman, chief executive officer, director, Bechtel Group, Inc.
Houghton, James Richardson: director, Corning Inc.; trustee, Corning Inc. Foundation
Raymond, Lee R.: chairman, president, chief executive officer, Exxon Mobil Corp.

JSCE Inc.
Smurfit, Michael William J.: chairman, Smurfit-Stone Container Corp.

JSJ Corp.
Lawson, William Hogan, III: chairman, chief executive officer, director, Franklin Electric Co.; president, Franklin Electric, Edward J. Schaefer, and T. W. KehoeCharitable and Educational Foundation
Richardson, John P.: trust, JSJ Foundation

JST Oregon
Bowen, William Gordon, PhD: trustee, Merck Co. Foundation

JW Confecciones
Jacobsen, James C.: vice chairman, Kellwood Co.; vice president, director, Kellwood Foundation

JW Window Components Inc.
Almy, Richard E.: executive vice president, chief operating officer, director, Walter Industries Inc.

Fjelstul, Dean M.: senior vice president, chief financial officer, Walter Industries Inc.

JWI Holdings Corp.
Almy, Richard E.: executive vice president, chief operating officer, director, Walter Industries Inc.
Hyatt, Kenneth Ernest: chairman, president, chief executive officer, director, Walter Industries Inc.

JWL Holdings Corp.
Fjelstul, Dean M.: senior vice president, chief financial officer, Walter Industries Inc.

Jackson Sales & Storage Co.
Cohen, Maryjo Rose: president, chief executive officer, director, National Presto Industries, Inc.; vice president, treasurer, trustee, Presto Foundation
Cohen, Melvin Samuel: chairman, National Presto Industries, Inc.; chairman, president, trustee, Presto Foundation

Jacobs Applied Technology Inc.
Markley, William C., III: secretary, director, Jacobs Engineering Foundation
Watson, Noel G.: vice president, director, Jacobs Engineering Foundation; president, chief executive officer, director, Jacobs Engineering Group

Jacobs Engineering Group Inc.
Laurance, Dale R.: director, Occidental Petroleum Charitable Foundation; president, senior operations officer, director, Occidental Petroleum Corp.

Jacobs Engineering Group Ohio
Watson, Noel G.: vice president, director, Jacobs Engineering Foundation; president, chief executive officer, director, Jacobs Engineering Group

James Benenson & Co. Inc.
Benenson, James, Jr.: chairman, president, director, Vesper Corp.; trustee, Vesper Foundation

James River Corp. Virginia
Gottwald, Bruce Cobb: chairman, chief executive officer, director, Ethyl Corp.

James River Paper Co. Inc.
Cutchins, Clifford Armstrong, IV: president, Fort James Corp.; chairman, director, Fort James Foundation (The)

Jamont NV
Cutchins, Clifford Armstrong, IV: president, Fort James Corp.; chairman, director, Fort James Foundation (The)

Janney Montgomery Scott
Chappell, Robert E.: chairman, chief executive officer, Penn Mutual Life Insurance Co.

Jansport Inc.
Pugh, Lawrence R.: chairman, director, Blue Bell, Inc.

Japanese Weekend Inc.
Mikulak, John P.: vice president, director, CertainTeed Corp.

Jasper Corp.
Wentworth, Jack Roberts, Ph.D.: director, Habig Foundation

Jaymar-Ruby Inc.
Hand, Elbert O.: chairman, chief executive officer, director, Hartmarx Corp.
Patel, Homi Burjor: president, chief operating officer, director, Hartmarx Corp.

Jefferson Bankshares Inc.
Harrell, Henry Howze: director, Universal Leaf Foundation; chairman, chief executive officer, director, Universal Leaf Tobacco Co., Inc.

Jefferson Insurance Co. of New York
Hansmeyer, Herbert F.: chairman, Fireman's Fund Insurance Co.

Jefferson Pilot Corp.
Henderson, George W., III: trustee, Burlington Industries Foundation; president, chief executive officer, director, Burlington Industries, Inc.

Jefferson Pilot Life Insurance Co.
Henderson, George W., III: trustee, Burlington Industries Foundation; president, chief executive officer, director, Burlington Industries, Inc.

Jefferson Smurfit Corp. United States
Smurfit, Michael William J.: chairman, Smurfit-Stone Container Corp.

Jefferson-Pilot Corp.
Spilman, Robert H.: chairman, chief executive officer, Bassett Furniture Industries; chairman, director, Bassett Furniture Industries Fdn.

Jersey Central Power & Light Co.
Graham, John Gourlay: chief financial officer, senior vice president, GPU Energy

Jim Walter Computer Service
Fjelstul, Dean M.: senior vice president, chief financial officer, Walter Industries Inc.

Jim Walter Homes Inc.
Hyatt, Kenneth Ernest: chairman, president, chief executive officer, director, Walter Industries Inc.
Michael, Robert W.: senior vice president, group executive, Walter Industries Inc.

Jim Walter Resources Inc.
Porter, Edward A.: vice president, general counsel, secretary, Walter Industries Inc.

Jitney Jungle America
Ebbers, Bernard J.: president, chief executive officer, director, MCI WorldCom, Inc.

Jobaro Corp.
Allbritton, Joe Lewis: chairman, chief executive officer, Riggs Bank NA

John Deere & Co.
Johnson, Samuel Curtis: chairman, director, president, Johnson & Son (S.C.); chairman, trustee, Johnson Wax Fund (S.C.)

John Deere Capital Corp.

Becherer, Hans Walter: chairman, chief executive officer, director, Deere & Co.; director, Deere Foundation (John)

England, Joseph Walker: chairman, director, Deere Foundation (John)

John Deere Credit Co.

Becherer, Hans Walter: chairman, chief executive officer, director, Deere & Co.; director, Deere Foundation (John)

John Deere Industries Equipment Co.

Becherer, Hans Walter: chairman, chief executive officer, director, Deere & Co.; director, Deere Foundation (John)

John H. Harland Co.

McMahon, John J., Jr.: trustee, McWane Foundation; chairman, president, chief executive officer, treasurer, McWane Inc.

John Hancock

Syron, Richard F.: chairman, chief executive officer, director, American Stock Exchange, Inc.

John Hancock Mutual Life Insurance Co.

Bodman, Samuel Wright, III: chairman, chief executive officer, director, Cabot Corp.; president, director, Cabot Corp. Foundation

Fish, Lawrence K.: trustee, Citizens Charitable Foundation; chairman, chief executive officer, Citizens Financial Group, Inc.

Magee, John Francis: chairman, director, Little, Inc. (Arthur D.)

Syron, Richard F.: chairman, chief executive officer, director, American Stock Exchange, Inc.

John Hancock Subsidiaries Inc.

Brown, Stephen Lee: chairman, chief executive officer, director, Hancock Financial Services (John)

John Nuveen & Co. Inc.

Leatherdale, Douglas West: chairman, chief executive officer, president, Saint Paul Companies Inc.

Johnson & Johnson

Langbo, Arnold Gordon: chairman, chief executive officer, director, Kellogg Co.

Mullin, Leo Francis: chairman, president, chief executive officer, Delta Air Lines, Inc.

Schacht, Henry Brewer: director, Cummins Engine Foundation

Snow, John William: chairman, president, chief executive officer, CSX Corp.

Johnson & Johnson International

Larsen, Ralph Stanley: chairman, president, chief executive officer, director, Johnson & Johnson

Johnson Bank

Johnson, Samuel Curtis: chairman, director, president, Johnson & Son (S.C.); chairman, trustee, Johnson Wax Fund (S.C.)

Johnson Controls Inc.

Barnett, Robert L.: director, Ameritech Foundation

Lacy, William Howard: president, MGIC Investment Corp.

Ziegler, R. Douglas: advisor, Johnson Controls Foundation

Johnson International Inc.

Johnson, Samuel Curtis: chairman, director, president, Johnson & Son (S.C.); chairman, trustee, Johnson Wax Fund (S.C.)

Johnson Smith Pence Densborn Wright Health

Stoner, Richard Burkett, Jr.: director, Cummins Engine Foundation

Johnson Wax Fund

Johnson, Samuel Curtis: chairman, director, president, Johnson & Son (S.C.); chairman, trustee, Johnson Wax Fund (S.C.)

Johnson Worldwide Associates Inc.

Johnson, Samuel Curtis: chairman, director, president, Johnson & Son (S.C.); chairman, trustee, Johnson Wax Fund (S.C.)

Johnston Coca-Cola Bottling Group

Alm, John Richard: director, Coca-Cola Foundation

Jones & Babson Inc.

Balzer, Giorgio: chairman, chief executive officer, Business Men's Assurance Co. of America

Jones Apparel Group Inc.

Gittis, Howard: director, Revlon Foundation Inc.

Jones Financial Co. LTD

Bachmann, John W.: managing partner, Jones & Co. (Edward D.); chairman, Jones & Co. Foundation (Edward D.)

Jostens Direct Inc.

Buhrmaster, Robert C.: president, chief executive officer, director, chairman, Jostens, Inc.

Jostens Inc.

Zona, Richard A.: vice chairman commercial banking & institutional finance, U.S. Bancorp

Jostens Photography Inc.

Buhrmaster, Robert C.: president, chief executive officer, director, chairman, Jostens, Inc.

Joy Tech

Corby, Francis Michael, Jr.: executive vice president finance & administration, chief financial officer, Harnischfeger Industries; treasurer, Harnischfeger Industries Foundation

Jundt Growth Fund

Hall, Floyd: chairman, president, chief executive officer, director, Kmart Corp.

Justin Industries Inc.

Roach, John Vinson, II: chairman, director, Tandy Corp.

K-III Prime Corp.

Golkin, Perry: member, Walter Industries Inc.

K-Mart Corp.

Falla, Enrique Crabb: senior consult, director, Dow Chemical Co.

K-Promotions Inc.

Carlson, Curtis Leroy: chairman, director, Carlson Companies, Inc.; president, treasurer, Carlson Family Foundation (Curtis L.)

KATV Television Inc.

Allbritton, Joe Lewis: chairman, chief executive officer, Riggs Bank NA

KCAC Inc.

Tulley, Herbert B.: vice president, chief financial officer, treasurer, Wilbur-Ellis Co. & Connell Brothers Co.; secretary, treasurer, Wilbur Foundation (Brayton)

KCCI Television Inc.

Pulitzer, Michael Edgar: chairman, president, chief executive officer, director, Pulitzer Publishing Co.; chairman, president, chief executive officer, Pulitzer Publishing Co. Foundation

KCTZ Communications Inc.

Anderson, Ivan Verner, Jr.: president, chief executive officer, Evening Post Publishing Co.; vice president, Post and Courier Foundation

KETV Television Inc.

Pulitzer, Michael Edgar: chairman, president, chief executive officer, director, Pulitzer Publishing Co.; chairman, president, chief executive officer, Pulitzer Publishing Co. Foundation

Ridgway, Ronald H.: senior vice president, Pulitzer Publishing Co.; secretary, treasurer, director, Pulitzer Publishing Co. Foundation

KETZ Communications Inc.

Rockey, Travis O.: vice president, director, Evening Post Publishing Co.

KIVI

Anderson, Ivan Verner, Jr.: president, chief executive officer, Evening Post Publishing Co.; vice president, Post and Courier Foundation

KKLT-FM

Pulitzer, Michael Edgar: chairman, president, chief executive officer, director, Pulitzer Publishing Co.; chairman, president, chief executive officer, Pulitzer Publishing Co. Foundation

KLAS-TV Las Vegas

Batten, Frank, Sr.: chairman, director, Landmark Communications Foundation; chairman, Landmark Communications Inc.

KMS Group Inc.

Poindexter, Christian Herndon: chairman, Baltimore Gas & Electric Foundation; chairman, chief executive officer, director, Constellation Energy Group, Inc.

KN Energy Inc.

Haines, Jordan L.: trustee, Cessna Foundation, Inc.

KO Transmission Co.

Foley, Cheryl M.: vice president, secretary, general counsel, Cinergy Corp.; vice president, secretary, director, Cinergy Foundation

KPAX Communications Inc.

Anderson, Ivan Verner, Jr.: president, chief executive officer, Evening Post Publishing Co.; vice president, Post and Courier Foundation

KPMG Peat Marwick

Dolanski, A. P.: trustee, KPMG Peat Marwick Foundation

KPNX Broadcasting Co.

Chapple, Thomas Leslie: senior vice president, general counsel, secretary, Gannett Co., Inc.; secretary, Gannett Foundation

McCorkindale, Douglas H.: vice chairman, president, Gannett Co., Inc.; president, Gannett Foundation

KRTV Communications Inc.

Anderson, Ivan Verner, Jr.: president, chief executive

officer, Evening Post Publishing Co.; vice president, Post and Courier Foundation

KTAR-AM

Pulitzer, Michael Edgar: chairman, president, chief executive officer, director, Pulitzer Publishing Co.; chairman, president, chief executive officer, Pulitzer Publishing Co. Foundation

KTRK TV Inc.

Westin, David: vice president, director, ABC Foundation

KTUL Television Inc.

Allbritton, Joe Lewis: chairman, chief executive officer, Riggs Bank NA

KTVQ Communications Inc.

Anderson, Ivan Verner, Jr.: president, chief executive officer, Evening Post Publishing Co.; vice president, Post and Courier Foundation

Rockey, Travis O.: vice president, director, Evening Post Publishing Co.

KVUE-TV Inc.

Chapple, Thomas Leslie: senior vice president, general counsel, secretary, Gannett Co., Inc.; secretary, Gannett Foundation

Curley, John J.: chairman, chief executive officer, director, Gannett Co., Inc.; chairman, Gannett Foundation

McCorkindale, Douglas H.: vice chairman, president, Gannett Co., Inc.; president, Gannett Foundation

KWD Holdings

Jacobsen, James C.: vice chairman, Kellwood Co.; vice president, director, Kellwood Foundation

KXLF Communications Inc.

Anderson, Ivan Verner, Jr.: president, chief executive officer, Evening Post Publishing Co.; vice president, Post and Courier Foundation

Rockey, Travis O.: vice president, director, Evening Post Publishing Co.

Kahului Trucking Storage

Wellman, Thomas A.: controller, assistant treasurer, Alexander & Baldwin, Inc.

Kaiser Permanente Inc.

Ridgley, Robert Louis: chairman, director, Northwest Natural Gas Co.

Kaman Aerospace Corp.

Garneau, Robert M.: chief financial officer, Kaman Corp.

Jones, Russell H.: officer, Kaman Corp.

Kaman, Charles Huron: chairman, president, chief executive officer, director, Kaman Corp.

Kaman Diversified Technical Corp.

Garneau, Robert M.: chief financial officer, Kaman Corp.

Kaman Electro Magnetics Corp.

Kaman, Charles Huron: chairman, president, chief executive officer, director, Kaman Corp.

Kaman Industrial Technology Corp.

Jones, Russell H.: officer, Kaman Corp.

Kaman Industries Tech

Kaman, Charles Huron: chairman, president, chief executive officer, director, Kaman Corp.

Kaman Music Corp.

Jones, Russell H.: officer, Kaman Corp.

Kaman, Charles Huron: chairman, president, chief executive officer, director, Kaman Corp.

Kamehamela Investment Corp.

Stender, Oswald K.: director, Hawaiian Electric Industries Charitable Foundation

Kanawha Valley Power Co.

Draper, Ernest Linn, Jr.: chairman, president, chief executive officer, director, American Electric Power

Kansas City Royals Baseball Club

Glass, David Dayne: trustee, Wal-Mart Foundation; director, Wal-Mart Stores, Inc.

Kansas City Southern Industries

Sosland, Morton Irvin: director, Block Foundation (H&R)

KartoffelSoft Inc.

Harad, George Jay: chairman, chief executive officer, director, Boise Cascade Corp.

Katten Muchin & Zavis

Matis, Nina B.: director, Katten, Muchin & Zavis Foundation

Katun Corp.

Dugan, Allan E.: senior vice president corporate strategic service, Xerox Corp.; trustee, Xerox Foundation

Kaufman & Broad Home Corp.

Irani, Raymond Reza: director, Occidental Petroleum Charitable Foundation; chairman, director, chief executive officer, Occidental Petroleum Corp.

Johnson, James A.: chairman, chief executive officer, director, Fannie Mae; chairman, Fannie Mae Foundation

Rinehart, Charles Robert: chairman, chief executive officer, director, Washington Mutual, Inc.

Keating Corp.

Moran, Harry J.: executive vice president, Sonoco Products Co.

Keeler & Long Inc.

LeBoeuf, Raymond W.: director, PPG Industries Foundation; director, chairman, chief executive officer, PPG Industries, Inc.

Keithley Instruments Inc.

Bachman, Brian R.: senior vice president, member contributions committee, Eaton Charitable Fund; senior vice president semiconductor & specialty systems, Eaton Corp.

Kellogg Caribbean Corp.

Hinton, John R.: executive vice president administration, chief financial officer, Kellogg Co.; president, trustee, Kellogg Co. Twenty-Five Year Employees' Fund Inc.

Kellogg Co.

Fiorina, Carleton S.: president, chief executive officer, director, Hewlett-Packard Co.

Smucker, Timothy Paul: chairman, director, Smucker Co. (JM)

Kellogg International

Langbo, Arnold Gordon: chairman, chief executive officer, director, Kellogg Co.

Kellogg Sales Co.

Clark, Richard McCourt: senior vice president, general counsel, secretary, Kellogg Co.; vice president, trustee, Kellogg Co. Twenty-Five Year Employees' Fund Inc.

Hinton, John R.: executive vice president administration, chief financial officer, Kellogg Co.; president, trustee, Kellogg Co. Twenty-Five Year Employees' Fund Inc.

Kellogg U.S.A. Inc.

Langbo, Arnold Gordon: chairman, chief executive officer, director, Kellogg Co.

Kellogg United States of America Inc.

Hinton, John R.: executive vice president administration, chief financial officer, Kellogg Co.; president, trustee, Kellogg Co. Twenty-Five Year Employees' Fund Inc.

Thomason, Donald W.: executive vice president service & technology, Kellogg Co.; trustee, Kellogg Co. Twenty-Five Year Employees' Fund Inc.

Kellwood Acquisitions Co.

Jacobsen, James C.: vice chairman, Kellwood Co.; vice president, director, Kellwood Foundation

Kellwood Asia Ltd.

Jacobsen, James C.: vice chairman, Kellwood Co.; vice president, director, Kellwood Foundation

Kellwood Haiti

Jacobsen, James C.: vice chairman, Kellwood Co.; vice president, director, Kellwood Foundation

Kellwood Honduras

Jacobsen, James C.: vice chairman, Kellwood Co.; vice president, director, Kellwood Foundation

Kelso & Co.

Shinn, George Latimer: director, New York Times Co. Foundation

Kemper Corp.

Mathis, David B.: chairman, Kemper Foundation (James S.)

Randall, Kenneth A.: trustee, Kemper Foundation (James S.)

Kemper Income Capital Prese

Mathis, David B.: chairman, Kemper Foundation (James S.)

Kemper Insurance Co.

Lyall, Katharine Culbert: trustee, Kemper Foundation (James S.)

Kemper Insurance Companies

Karmel, Roberta S.: trustee, Kemper Foundation (James S.); partner, Kemper National Insurance Companies

Kemper National Insurance Co.

Hamilton, Peter Bannerman: director, Brunswick Foundation; trustee, Kemper Foundation (James S.)

Kemper National Insurance Companies

Kennedy, George Danner: trustee, Kemper Foundation (James S.)

Toll, Daniel Roger: trustee, Kemper Foundation (James S.)

Kemper Sports Inc.

Kemper, James Scott, Jr.: honorary chairman, Kemper Foundation (James S.)

Kennametal Inc.

Newlin, William Rankin: trustee, Kennametal Foundation

Kentucky Bank & Trust

Zachem, Harry M.: chairman, trustee, Ashland Inc. Foundation

Kentucky Connector Corp.

Cudlip, Brittain B.: chairman, Bardes Corp.
FitzGibbon, David J.: president, chief executive officer, Bardes Corp.

Kentucky Electric Steel

Quin, Joseph Marvin: trustee, Ashland Inc. Foundation

Kentucky Power Co.

Draper, Ernest Linn, Jr.: chairman, president, chief executive officer, director, American Electric Power
Lhota, William J.: executive vice president, American Electric Power

Kenwood Products

Hall, Floyd: chairman, president, chief executive officer, director, Kmart Corp.

Kerford Limestone Inc.

Abel, John C.: director, Abel Foundation

Kerr-McGee Corp.

Bradford, William Edward: chairman, director, Halliburton Co.
Rompala, Richard M.: president, chief executive officer, director, chairman, Valspar Corp.; vice president, Valspar Foundation

Kesi INC

Hebe, James L.: chairman, president, chief executive officer, Freightliner Corp.

Ketchikan Pulp Co.

Hebert, William L.: assistant secretary, treasurer, Louisiana-Pacific Foundation

Key Bank

Burg, H. Peter: president, chief operating officer, FirstEnergy Corp.

Key Bank Corp.

Hardis, Stephen Roger: chairman, chief executive officer, director, Eaton Corp.

Key Bank NA

Moll, Curtis E.: treasurer, trustee, Jochum-Moll Foundation (The)

Key Corp.

Hardis, Stephen Roger: chairman, chief executive officer, director, Eaton Corp.

Key Trust Co.

Ashley, James Wheeler: director, Globe Foundation

KeyCorp

Bares, William G.: chairman, president, chief executive officer, Lubrizol Corp. (The); trustee, Lubrizol Foundation (The)
Bersticker, Albert C.: chairman, director, chief executive officer, Ferro Corp.; president, trustee, Ferro Foundation
Commes, Thomas Allen: president, chief operating officer, director, Sherwin-Williams Co.; assistant secretary, trustee, Sherwin-Williams Foundation
McGregor, Douglas J.: president, chief operating officer, director, Hanna Co. (M.A.)

Keyser Crowley Meub Zayden Kulig & Sullivan PC

Keyser, F. Ray, Jr.: chairman, director, Central Vermont Public Service Corp.

Keyspan Energy Corp.

Catell, Robert Barry: chairman, chief executive officer, Brooklyn Union

Keystone Consolidated Industries

Simmons, Glenn Reuben: vice chairman, Contran Corp.

Keystone Custodian Funds

Keyser, F. Ray, Jr.: chairman, director, Central Vermont Public Service Corp.

Kidder Peabody & Co. Inc.

Bossidy, Lawrence Arthur: chairman, director, AlliedSignal Foundation Inc.; chairman, chief executive officer, director, AlliedSignal Inc.

Kiel Center Corp.

Mueller, Charles William: chairman, president, chief executive officer, Ameren Corp.; trustee, Ameren Corp. Charitable Trust

Kiewit Coal Properties Inc.

Scott, Walter, Jr.: member contributions committee, Kiewit Companies Foundation

Kiewit Construction Co.

Stinson, Kenneth E.: member contributions committee, Kiewit Companies Foundation; chairman, chief executive officer, director, Kiewit Sons' Inc. (Peter)

Kiewit Construction Group Inc.

Stinson, Kenneth E.: member contributions committee, Kiewit Companies Foundation; chairman, chief executive officer, director, Kiewit Sons' Inc. (Peter)

Kiewit Diversified Group Inc.

Stinson, Kenneth E.: member contributions committee, Kiewit Companies Foundation; chairman, chief executive officer, director, Kiewit Sons' Inc. (Peter)

Kiewit Industrial Co.

Stinson, Kenneth E.: member contributions committee, Kiewit Companies Foundation; chairman, chief executive officer, director, Kiewit Sons' Inc. (Peter)

Kiewit Mining Group Inc.

Scott, Walter, Jr.: member contributions committee, Kiewit Companies Foundation

Kiewit Western Co.

Stinson, Kenneth E.: member contributions committee, Kiewit Companies Foundation; chairman, chief executive officer, director, Kiewit Sons' Inc. (Peter)

Kimball Electronics Inc.

Vujovich, Christine M.: director, Habig Foundation

Kimball Inc.

Schneider, Robert F.: officer, Habig Foundation; executive vice president, chief financial officer, assistant treasurer, Kimball International, Inc.
Vujovich, Christine M.: director, Habig Foundation

Kimball International Inc.

Graf, Alan B., Jr.: executive vice president, chief financial officer, FedEx Corp.
Vujovich, Christine M.: director, Habig Foundation
Wentworth, Jack Roberts, Ph.D.: director, Habig Foundation

Kimberly-Clark

Larson, Peter N.: chairman, chief executive officer, director, Brunswick Corp.

Kimberly-Clark Corp.

Collins, Paul John: vice chairman, director, Citibank Corp.
Decherd, Robert William: chairman, president, chief executive officer, director, Belo Corp. (A.H.); chairman, trustee, Belo Corp. Foundation (A.H.)
Schmitt, Wolfgang Rudolph: chairman, chief executive officer, director, Rubbermaid Inc.
Tobias, Randall L.: chairman emeritus, Lilly & Co. (Eli)

Kingsburg Industries Inc.

Toner, Jeffrey M.: trustee, Kingsbury Fund

Kingsbury Industries Inc.

Cookson, John Simmons: vice president finance, treasurer, assistant secretary, Kingsbury Corp.; trustee, Kingsbury Fund
Koontz, James L.: president, chief executive officer, director, Kingsbury Corp.; trustee, Kingsbury Fund

Kingsport Power Co.

Draper, Ernest Linn, Jr.: chairman, president, chief executive officer, director, American Electric Power
Lhota, William J.: executive vice president, American Electric Power

Kirkpatrick Pettis Inc.

Weekly, John William: chairman, chief executive officer, Mutual of Omaha Insurance Co.

Kirkpatrick Pettis Smith Polian Inc.

Sturgeon, John: president, chief operating officer, Mutual of Omaha Insurance Co.

Knight-Ridder Inc.

Tobias, Randall L.: chairman emeritus, Lilly & Co. (Eli)
Weinberg, John Livingston: chairman, president, director, Goldman Sachs Foundation

Knoll Inc.

Schacht, Henry Brewer: director, Cummins Engine Foundation

Knox

Hall, William Austin: president, Hallmark Corporate Foundation

Knutson Mortgage Corp.

Jastrow, Kenneth M., II: director, Temple-Inland Foundation

Koch Engineering Company Inc.

Koch, David Hamilton: director, Koch Foundation, Inc. (Fred C. and Mary R.)

Koch Industries Inc.

Koch, Charles de Ganahl: chairman, chief executive officer, director, president, Koch Industries, Inc.

Kohler Interiors Group Ltd.

Black, Natalie A.: group vice president interiors, general counsel, director, Kohler Co.

Kollmorgen Corp.

Fishman, Jerald G.: president, chief executive officer, director, Analog Devices, Inc.

Komag Inc.

Barrett, Craig R.: president, chief operating officer, director, Intel Corp.

Kraft Co. Georgia

Correll, Alston Dayton 'Pete', Jr.: chairman, president, chief executive officer, director, Georgia-Pacific Corp.; director, Georgia-Pacific Foundation

Kroger Co.

Everingham, Lyle J.: trustee, Milacron Foundation
LaMacchia, John Thomas: trustee, Cincinnati Bell

Foundation, Inc.; president, chief executive officer, director, Cincinnati Bell Inc.

Liddy, Edward M.: vice president, trustee, Allstate Foundation; president, chief operating officer, director, Allstate Insurance Co.

O'Leary, Thomas Howard: chairman, Burlington Resources Foundation

Kronos

Simmons, Harold Clark: chairman, director, Simmons Foundation, Inc. (Harold)

Kronos Data Systems Inc.

McWilliams, D. Bradley: vice president, Cooper Industries Foundation; chief financial officer, senior vice president finance, Cooper Industries, Inc.

Kronos Inc.

McWilliams, D. Bradley: vice president, Cooper Industries Foundation; chief financial officer, senior vice president finance, Cooper Industries, Inc.

Krueger International

Kress, James F.: chairman, director, Green Bay Packaging

Krueger International Inc.

Kuester, Dennis J.: president, Marshall & Ilsley Corp.

Kukui'ula Development Co., Inc.

Sasaki, Robert K.: director, Alexander & Baldwin Foundation

Kulicke Soffa Industries

Zadel, C. William: chairman, president, chief executive officer, Millipore Corp.; trustee, Millipore Foundation (The)

L & W Supply Corp.

Roller, Donald E.: executive vice president, USG Corp.; vice president, USG Foundation

LA Business Advisors

Rinehart, Charles Robert: chairman, chief executive officer, director, Washington Mutual, Inc.

LA CitiCorp.

Armstrong, C. Michael: chairman, chief executive officer, AT&T Corp.

LDDS Communications

Ford, Joseph 'Joe': chairman, chief executive officer, president, ALLTEL Corp.

LEXCO Ltd.

Countryman, Gary Lee: chairman, Liberty Mutual Insurance Group

LG&E Energy Corp.

McNamara, Anne H.: senior vice president, general counsel, AMR Corp.

LIMRA International

Semler, Jerry D.: chairman, president, chief executive officer, director, American United Life Insurance Co.; chairman, director, AUL Foundation Inc.

LM Institutional Fund Advisors 1 Inc.

Simpson, Louis Allen: president, chief executive officer capital operations, director, GEICO Corp.

LM Insurance Corp.

Countryman, Gary Lee: chairman, Liberty Mutual Insurance Group

LSI Logic Corp.

Keyes, James Henry: advisor, Johnson Controls Foundation; president, Johnson Controls Inc.

La Jolla Bank & Trust Co.

ZoBell, Karl: vice president, trustee, Copley Foundation (James S.)

La Mirada Product Co. Inc.

Roller, Donald E.: executive vice president, USG Corp.; vice president, USG Foundation

La-Z-Boy Chair Co.

Hehl, David K.: director, La-Z-Boy Inc.

LaSalle National Bank

Connolly, Eugene Bernard, Jr.: chairman emeritus, USG Corp.

Rau, John E.: trustee, Chicago Title and Trust Co. Foundation

Lab Holdings Inc.

Kemper, David Woods: chairman, president, chief executive officer, director, Commerce Bancshares, Inc.

Lab Safety Supply Inc.

Fluno, Jere David: vice chairman, Grainger, Inc. (W.W.)

Keyser, Richard Lee: chairman, chief executive officer, president, Grainger, Inc. (W.W.)

Lacey Manufacturing Co. Division

Moore, Robert P.: trustee, Barden Foundation, Inc.

Laclede Development Co.

Yaeger, Douglas H.: chairman, trustee, Laclede Gas Charitable Trust

Laclede Gas Co.

Stupp, Robert P.: president, director, Stupp Brothers Bridge & Iron Co.; trustee, Stupp Brothers Bridge & Iron Co. Foundation

Laclede Gas Division

Jaudes, Robert Christian: chairman, trustee, Laclede Gas Charitable Trust

Laclede Gas Family Service Inc.

Yaeger, Douglas H.: chairman, trustee, Laclede Gas Charitable Trust

Laclede Landing Development Corp.

Maritz, William Edward: chairman, chief executive officer, president, Maritz Inc.

Laclede Pipeline Co.

Yaeger, Douglas H.: chairman, trustee, Laclede Gas Charitable Trust

Ladd Petroleum Corp.

Bossidy, Lawrence Arthur: chairman, director, AlliedSignal Foundation Inc.; chairman, chief executive officer, director, AlliedSignal Inc.

Ladish Malting Co.

Ladish, John: trustee, Ladish Co. Foundation

Lafayette Pharmaceutical Inc.

Rollans, James Ora: senior vice president, chief administrative officer, chief financial officer, Fluor Corp.; trustee, Fluor Foundation

Laidlaw Environmental Service Inc.

Wareham, James Lyman: president, AK Steel Corp.

Lake Area Disposal Inc.

Ranck, Bruce E.: president, chief executive officer, director, Browning-Ferris Industries Inc.

Lakeland Ledger Publishing

Sulzberger, Arthur Ochs, Sr.: director, New York Times Co.; chairman, director, New York Times Co. Foundation

Lakey Hitchcock Clinic

Keyser, F. Ray, Jr.: chairman, director, Central Vermont Public Service Corp.

Lamons Metal Gasket Co.

Manoogian, Richard Alexander: chairman, chief executive officer, director, Masco Corp.

Lance Inc.

Dickson, Alan Thomas: president, Dickson Foundation; chairman, Ruddick Corp.

Holland, William Ray: vice president, director, United Dominion Foundation; chairman, chief executive officer, director, United Dominion Industries, Ltd.

Land O'Lakes Inc.

Wojchik, Larry: chairman, Land O'Lakes Foundation

Landing Holdings Inc.

Larson, Wayne E.: trustee, Ladish Co. Foundation

Landmark Communications Inc.

Henderson, James Alan: vice chairman, chief executive officer, director, Ameritech Corp.; chairman, director, Cummins Engine Foundation

Landmark Graphics Corp.

Cheney, Richard B.: chief executive officer, Halliburton Co.; president, Halliburton Foundation, Inc.

Latona Associates

Montrone, Paul Michael: vice president, partner, Winthrop Foundation

Lawrenceburg Gas Co.

Foley, Cheryl M.: vice president, secretary, general counsel, Cinergy Corp.; vice president, secretary, director, Cinergy Foundation

Randolph, Jackson Harold: chairman, Cinergy Corp.; chairman, director, Cinergy Foundation

Lawyers Title Insurance Co.

Chandler, Wallace Lee: vice president, director, Universal Leaf Foundation

Lazard Special Equities Fund

Ross, Arthur: senior vice president, Central National-Gottesman; director, Central National-Gottesman Foundation

Lazy Lane Farms Inc.

Allbritton, Joe Lewis: chairman, chief executive officer, Riggs Bank NA

Ledger

Sulzberger, Arthur Ochs, Sr.: director, New York Times Co.; chairman, director, New York Times Co. Foundation

Lee Community Development Corp.

Trask, Robert B.: president, chief operating officer, director, Country Curtains, Inc.; clerk, trustee, High Meadow Foundation

Lee Engineering Co.
Drury, Robert E.: president, director, United Dominion Foundation

Lee Enterprises Inc.
Newman, Andrew E.: member, Edison Family Foundation

Lee Ming & Co. Ltd.
Jacobsen, James C.: vice chairman, Kellwood Co.; vice president, director, Kellwood Foundation

Legg Mason Institutional Fund Advisors II
Tarola, Robert M.: senior vice president, chief financial officer, Grace & Co. (W.R.)

Leggett Realty South Boston Virginia
Belk, John Montgomery: member board advisors, Belk Foundation; chairman, Belk-Simpson Department Stores

Lehigh Portland Cement Co.
Otto, Peter: president, Lehigh Portland Cement Co.

Lehigh Valley Partnership
Barnette, Curtis Handley: chairman, chief executive officer, director, Bethlehem Steel Corp.

Lehman Brothers Holdings Inc.
Akers, John Fellows: director, New York Times Co.

Lend-A-Hand Inc.
McCorkindale, Douglas H.: vice chairman, president, Gannett Co., Inc.; president, Gannett Foundation

Lennox International Inc.
Anderson, David H.: vice chairman, trustee, Lennox Foundation

Brown, David V.: secretary, trustee, Lennox Foundation

Leo Burnett Worldwide Inc.
Fizdale, Richard B.: chairman, chief executive officer, director, Burnett Co. (Leo)

Leslie's Poolmart Inc.
Laurance, Dale R.: director, Occidental Petroleum Charitable Foundation; president, senior operations officer, director, Occidental Petroleum Corp.

Level 3 Communications Inc.
Scott, Walter, Jr.: member contributions committee, Kiewit Companies Foundation

Levi Strauss & Co.
Jacobi, Peter A.: president, Levi Strauss & Co.; vice president, Levi Strauss Foundation

Leviton Manufacturing Co. Inc.
Leviton, Shirley: treasurer, Leviton Foundation New York

Lexmark International Group
Hardis, Stephen Roger: chairman, chief executive officer, director, Eaton Corp.

Lexmark International Inc.
Walker, Martin Dean: chairman, chief executive officer, director, Hanna Co. (M.A.)

Liana Ltd.
Reinhard, J. Pedro: executive vice president, chief financial officer, director, Dow Chemical Co.

Liberty Finance Corp.
Countryman, Gary Lee: chairman, Liberty Mutual Insurance Group

Liberty Insurance Co.
Gilvar, Barry S.: secretary, Liberty Mutual Insurance Group

Liberty Insurance Co. Massachusetts Ltd.
Countryman, Gary Lee: chairman, Liberty Mutual Insurance Group

Liberty Insurance Corp.
Gilvar, Barry S.: secretary, Liberty Mutual Insurance Group

Liberty International Insurance Agency
Countryman, Gary Lee: chairman, Liberty Mutual Insurance Group

Liberty Life Assurance Co. Boston
Gilvar, Barry S.: secretary, Liberty Mutual Insurance Group

Liberty Mutual Bermuda Ltd.
Countryman, Gary Lee: chairman, Liberty Mutual Insurance Group

Liberty Mutual Equity Corp.
Gilvar, Barry S.: secretary, Liberty Mutual Insurance Group

Liberty Mutual Fire Insurance Co.
Countryman, Gary Lee: chairman, Liberty Mutual Insurance Group

Gilvar, Barry S.: secretary, Liberty Mutual Insurance Group

Liberty Mutual Insurance Group
Countryman, Gary Lee: chairman, Liberty Mutual Insurance Group

Liberty Property Trust
Lachman, Marguerite Leanne: trustee, Chicago Title and Trust Co. Foundation

Life Imaging System
Coyne, William E.: senior vice president, Minnesota Mining & Manufacturing Co.

Life Insurance Council New York
Fiondella, Robert William: chairman, president, chief executive officer, Phoenix Home Life Mutual Insurance Co.

Life Investors Insurance America
Baird, Patrick S.: chief operating officer, chief financial officer, AEGON U.S.A. Inc.

Life Investors Insurance of America
Kolsrud, Douglas C.: executive vice president, chief investment officer, AEGON U.S.A. Inc.

Life Management Institute
Martin, JoAnn M.: controller, Ameritas Charitable Foundation; senior vice president, partner, chief financial officer, Ameritas Life Insurance Corp.

Life Office Management Association
Tran, Khanh T.: senior vice president, chief financial officer, director, Pacific Mutual Life Insurance Co.

Life Technologies Inc.
Burdett, Kathleen: vice president, chief financial officer, Dexter Corp.; vice president, Dexter Corp. Foundation

Life Techs Inc.
Alberts, Bruce Michael, PhD: director, Genentech Foundation for Biomedical Sciences

Beatt, Bruce H.: secretary, Dexter Corp. Foundation

Walker, Grahame: chairman, chief executive officer, Dexter Corp.; president, Dexter Corp. Foundation

Life Virginia Series Funds
Chandler, Wallace Lee: vice president, director, Universal Leaf Foundation

Lifeline Systems Inc.
Kasputys, Joseph Edward: chairman, trustee, Hitachi Foundation

Liliuokalani Trust
Alm, Robert: director, First Hawaiian Foundation

Lilly Industries Inc.
Cornelius, James M.: director, AUL Foundation Inc.

Reilly, Thomas E., Jr.: trustee, Reilly Foundation; chairman, chief executive officer, director, Reilly Industries, Inc.

Lincoln Electric Holdings
Massaro, Anthony A.: president, chief executive officer, chairman, chief operating officer, Lincoln Electric Co.

Lincoln Gateway Shopping Center Inc.
Louis, Kenneth C.: president, chief operating officer, director, Ameritas Life Insurance Corp.

Martin, JoAnn M.: controller, Ameritas Charitable Foundation; senior vice president, partner, chief financial officer, Ameritas Life Insurance Corp.

Lincoln National (China) Inc.
Womack, C. Suzanne: director, Lincoln Financial Group

Lincoln National Convertible Securities Fund
Toll, Daniel Roger: trustee, Kemper Foundation (James S.)

Lincoln National Corp.
Kavetas, Harry L.: chief financial officer, executive vice president, director, Eastman Kodak Co.

Lachman, Marguerite Leanne: trustee, Chicago Title and Trust Co. Foundation

Lincoln National Income Fund
Toll, Daniel Roger: trustee, Kemper Foundation (James S.)

Lincoln National Management Service
Womack, C. Suzanne: director, Lincoln Financial Group

Linville Resorts Inc.
Dickson, Alan Thomas: president, Dickson Foundation; chairman, Ruddick Corp.

Little Tikes Co.
Dean, John W., III: vice president, treasurer, Rubbermaid Inc.

Litton System Inc.
Lang, Rudolph E., Jr.: senior vice president, chief

financial officer, Litton Industries, Inc.

Wiesner, Carol A.: treasurer, director, Foundation of the Litton Industries

Litton Systems Inc.

Leonis, John Michael: chairman, director, Litton Industries, Inc.

Liz Claiborne Cosemetics Inc.

Falk, Harvey L.: member grantmaking committee, Claiborne Foundation (Liz); president, vice chairman, Liz Claiborne, Inc.

Liz Claiborne Foreign Holdings Inc.

Falk, Harvey L.: member grantmaking committee, Claiborne Foundation (Liz); president, vice chairman, Liz Claiborne, Inc.

Liz Claiborne Retail Group

McNeary, Joseph Allen: member grantmaking committee, Claiborne Foundation (Liz); senior vice president, Liz Claiborne, Inc.

Lobon Policy Association

Crane, Russell L.: director, PPG Industries Foundation; senior vice president, PPG Industries, Inc.

Local Initiatives Support Corp.

Coulter, David A.: president, director, Bank of America

Gorelick, Jamie Shona: vice chairman, Fannie Mae

Lockheed Martin Corp.

Ukropina, James R.: partner, Pacific Mutual Life Insurance Co.

Loctite Corp.

Barnes, Wallace W.: director, Barnes Group Foundation Inc.

Loews Corp.

Brademas, John: chairman, Texaco Foundation

Chookaszian, Dennis Haig: chairman, chief executive officer, CNA

Noha, Edward J.: director, CNA Foundation

Loftin Equipment Co. Inc.

Loftin, Nancy Carol: secretary, director, APS Foundation, Inc.; vice president, general counsel, Arizona Public Service Co.

Logistics Management Institute

Mead, Dana George: chairman, chief executive officer, director, Tenneco Automotive

Lois/USA

Hatsopoulos, John Nicholas: retired president, Thermo Electron Corp.; committee member, Thermo Electron Foundation

Lollytogs

Gindi, Sam: trustee, Century 21 Associates Foundation

Loma Linda Corp.

Hower, Frank Beard, Jr.: vice chairman, Anthem Foundation, Inc.

Lone Star Industries Inc.

Wentworth, Jack Roberts, Ph.D.: director, Habig Foundation

Loomis Sayles Mutual Funds

Lautenbach, Terry Robert: trustee, Air Products Foundation

Loral Space & Communications Ltd.

Gittis, Howard: director, Revlon Foundation Inc.

Lord, Sullivan, Yoder, Worthington, Ohio, ZeeMed Services

Burrell, Richard L.: senator vice president finance, secretary, treasurer, Barry Corp. (R.G.); treasurer, Barry Foundation

Los Angeles Times

Willes, Mark Hinckley: chairman, president, chief executive officer, Times Mirror Co.; chairman, Times Mirror Foundation

Wright, Donald Franklin: director, Times Mirror Foundation

Lotus Development Corp.

Gillis, Edwin J.: president, Lotus Development Corp.

Loudoun Mutual Industry Co.

Adams, John B., Junior: chairman, president, chief executive officer, Dominion Resources, Inc.

Louis Harris & Assoc Inc.

McCorkindale, Douglas H.: vice chairman, president, Gannett Co., Inc.; president, Gannett Foundation

Louis Harris International Inc.

McCorkindale, Douglas H.: vice chairman, president, Gannett Co., Inc.; president, Gannett Foundation

Louisiana Land Exploration Co.

Williams, John A.: president, chief executive officer, Louisiana Land & Exploration Co.; director, Louisiana Land & Exploration Co. Foundation

Louisiana-Pacific Corp.

Dunham, Archie W.: president, chief executive officer, Conoco, Inc.

Hill, Bonnie Guiton: vice president, Times Mirror Co.; president, chief executive officer, Times Mirror Foundation

Louisville Gas & Electric Co.

McNamara, Anne H.: senior vice president, general counsel, AMR Corp.

Louisville Shopping Center

Deering, Anthony W.: chairman, chief executive officer, Rouse Co.; chairman, president, trustee, Rouse Co. Foundation

Lowe's Co. Inc.

Browning, Peter C.: chief executive officer, president, director, Sonoco Products Co.

Lowe's Companies Employee Stock Ownership Plan

Herring, Leonard Gray: vice president, Lowe's Charitable and Educational Foundation

Lowes Companies

Belk, John Montgomery: member board advisors, Belk Foundation; chairman, Belk-Simpson Department Stores

Lowes Home Centers Inc.

Belk, John Montgomery: member board advisors, Belk Foundation; chairman, Belk-Simpson Department Stores

Lozano Communications

Lozano, Ignacio Eugenio, Jr.: chairman, Pacific Mutual Life Insurance Co.

Lubar & Co.

Lubar, Sheldon B.: chairman, Ameritech Corp.; director, Firstar Milwaukee Foundation

Lubrizol Corp.

Hoag, David H.: chairman, president, chief executive officer, director, LTV Corp.; trustee, LTV Foundation

Lubys Cafeterias Inc.

Hemminghaus, Roger Roy: chairman, director, Ultramar Diamond Shamrock Corp.

Lucent Technologies Inc.

Allaire, Paul Arthur: chairman, chief executive officer, chairman executive committee, Xerox Corp.; president, Xerox Foundation

Thomas, Franklin Augustine: director, CBS Foundation

Ludowici Roof Tile Inc.

Hilyard, James E.: president, CertainTeed Corp.; director, CertainTeed Corp. Foundation

Lukens Inc.

Gross, Ronald Martin: chairman, president, director, Rayonier Foundation; chairman, president, chief executive officer, director, Rayonier Inc.

Lumberjack

Hall, William Austin: president, Hallmark Corporate Foundation

Lumbermens Mutual Casualty Co.

Mathis, David B.: chairman, Kemper Foundation (James S.)

Lumbermens Mutual Insurance Co.

Rosett, Richard Nathaniel: trustee, Kemper Foundation (James S.)

Lynch Corp.

Bell, Bradley John: vice president, treasurer, Whirlpool Corp.; treasurer, Whirlpool Foundation

Lynch Telephone Corp.

Evanson, Paul John: president, treasurer, director, FPL Group Foundation, Inc.

Lynx Technologys

Hall, Floyd: chairman, president, chief executive officer, director, Kmart Corp.

M & I First National Leasing

Kellner, Jack F.: director, board member, Marshall & Ilsley Foundation, Inc.

M & I Marshall & Ilsley Bank

Bueche, Wendell Francis: director, Marshall & Ilsley Foundation, Inc.

Wigdale, James B.: vice president, Marshall & Ilsley Corp.; vice president, director, Marshall & Ilsley Foundation, Inc.

M & T Bank Corp.

Lammert, Richard A.: secretary, director, M&T Charitable Foundation

M Wile & Co.

Patel, Homi Burjor: president, chief operating officer, director, Hartmarx Corp.

M&I Capital Markets Group

Wigdale, James B.: vice president, Marshall & Ilsley Corp.; vice president, director, Marshall & Ilsley Foundation, Inc.

M&I Data Services Inc.

Kuester, Dennis J.: president, Marshall & Ilsley Corp.

M&I First National Leasing

Wigdale, James B.: vice president, Marshall & Ilsley Corp.; vice president, director, Marshall & Ilsley Foundation, Inc.

M&I Mortgage Corp.

Wigdale, James B.: vice president, Marshall & Ilsley Corp.; vice president, director, Marshall & Ilsley Foundation, Inc.

M.A. Hanna Co.

Hoag, David H.: chairman, president, chief executive officer, director, LTV Corp.; trustee, LTV Foundation

MBIA Inc.

Elliott, David Holland: consultant, chairman executive committee, MBIA Inc.

MBIA Insurance Corp.

Weill, Richard L.: president, MBIA Inc.

MCI Research Inc.

Price, Timothy: president, chief executive officer, director, MCI WorldCom, Inc.

MCI Telecommunication Corp.

Roberts, Bert C., Jr.: chairman, MCI WorldCom, Inc.

MCI Telecommunications Group

Price, Timothy: president, chief executive officer, director, MCI WorldCom, Inc.

MCM Electronics Inc.

Mandel, Morton Leon: deputy chairman, Premier Industrial Corp.; trustee, Premier Industrial Foundation

MCN Energy Group Inc.

Ewing, Stephen E.: president, chief executive officer, director, Michigan Consolidated Gas Co.

MCP Co. Inc.

Kellner, Jack F.: director, board member, Marshall & Ilsley Foundation, Inc.

MD Ventures Inc.

Phillips, Rosalind Ann: secretary, GEICO Philanthropic Foundation

MEH Corp.

Adler, Ira R.: executive vice president, chief financial officer, Tucson Electric Power Co.

MF Worldwide

Meister, Paul M.: vice president, treasurer, Winthrop Foundation

MFA Oil Co.

Caspall, Ken: director, MFA Foundation

Creach, Dale H.: vice president, director, MFA Foundation

MFS Communications Co.

Stinson, Kenneth E.: member contributions committee, Kiewit Companies Foundation; chairman, chief executive officer, director, Kiewit Sons' Inc. (Peter)

MG Taylor Corp.

Darling, Robert Edward, Jr.: chairman, Ensign-Bickford Foundation

MGIC Holdings Corp.

Lacy, William Howard: president, MGIC Investment Corp.

MGIC Investment Corp.

Lubar, Sheldon B.: chairman, Ameritech Corp.; director, Firstar Milwaukee Foundation

MGIC Investor Services Corp.

Lacy, William Howard: president, MGIC Investment Corp.

MGIC Mortgage Insurance Corp.

Lauer, J. Michael: executive vice president, chief financial officer, MGIC Investment Corp.

MGIC Mortgage Marketing Corp.

Lacy, William Howard: president, MGIC Investment Corp.

MI Marshall Ilsley Bank

Shiely, John Stephen: president, chief operating officer, director, Briggs & Stratton Corp.; vice president, director, Briggs & Stratton Corp. Foundation

MIP Agency Inc.

Carlson, Curtis Leroy: chairman, director, Carlson Companies, Inc.; president, treasurer, Carlson Family Foundation (Curtis L.)

MML Series Investors Fund/ Institute

Wendlandt, Gary Edward: executive vice president, chief investment officer, Massachusetts Mutual Life Insurance Co.

MNC Finance Inc.

Bramble, Frank P.: president, chief executive officer, director, First Maryland Bancorp; president, trustee, First Maryland Foundation

MS Securities Services Inc.

Beard, Anson McCook, Jr.: director, NASDAQ Stock Market Educational Foundation

MSCH Co.

Nichols, Mack G.: president, chief executive officer, director, Mallinckrodt Chemical, Inc.

MSX International Inc.

Manoogian, Richard Alexander: chairman, chief executive officer, director, Masco Corp.

MTD Products Inc.

Hessler, David J.: secretary, trustee, Jochum-Moll Foundation (The); president, partner, MTD Products Inc.

MTS Inc.

Gullotti, Russell A.: chairman, president, chief executive officer, National Computer Systems, Inc.

MacLean Fogg Co.

Hodgson, Thomas Richard: president, chief operating officer, director, Abbott Laboratories

MacMillan Bathurst

Ernst, Fred V.: president, director, MacMillan Bloedel Inc.

Macromedia Inc.

Lucas, Donald Leo: chairman, Cadence Designs Systems, Inc.

Madison Newspapers Inc.

Gottlieb, Richard Douglas: president, chief executive officer, director, Lee Enterprises

Madrona Investment Group LLC

Ruckelshaus, William Doyle: chairman, director, Browning-Ferris Industries Inc.

Mafco Consolidated Group Inc.

Perelman, Ronald Owen: director, Revlon Foundation Inc.

Maine Electric Power Co.

Flanagan, David T.: president, chief executive officer, director, Central Maine Power Co.

Mallinckrodt Chemical Inc.

Nichols, Mack G.: president, chief executive officer, director, Mallinckrodt Chemical, Inc.

Mallinckrodt Group Inc.

Toll, Daniel Roger: trustee, Kemper Foundation (James S.)

Mallinckrodt Inc.

Davis, William L.: chairman, chief executive officer, director, Donnelley & Sons Co. (R.R.)

Karmel, Roberta S.: trustee, Kemper Foundation (James S.); partner, Kemper National Insurance Companies

Nichols, Mack G.: president, chief executive officer, director, Mallinckrodt Chemical, Inc.

Manhattan Industries

Krueger, Harvey M.: trustee, Barry Foundation

Manheim Auctions Inc.

Kennedy, James Cox: chairman, chief executive officer, director, Cox Enterprises Inc.; trustee, Cox Foundation (James M.)

Manitoba Telecom Services Inc.

Sawchuck, Arthur: chairman, director, Manulife Financial

Mankato Citizens Tel Co.

Alton, Robert D., Jr.: chairman, president, chief executive officer, Hickory Tech Corp.; trustee, Hickory Tech Corp. Foundation

Else, Robert K.: director, Hickory Tech Corp.; secretary, Hickory Tech Corp. Foundation

Holdrege, James H.: director, Hickory Tech Corp.; trustee, Hickory Tech Corp. Foundation

Jacobson, Lyle Gordon: treasurer, Hickory Tech Corp. Foundation

Kirklin, Starr J.: director, Hickory Tech Corp.; trustee, Hickory Tech Corp. Foundation

Taylor, Brett M., Junior: director, Hickory Tech Corp.; president, Hickory Tech Corp. Foundation

Manor Healthcare Corp.

Bainum, Stewart William, Jr.: chairman, Manor Care Health SVS, Inc.

Mansun North Inc.

Nation, Robert F.: former president, director, Harsco Corp.; trustee, Harsco Corp. Fund

Manufacturers & Traders Trust Co

Pinto, Michael P.: executive vice president, chief financial officer, Manufacturers & Traders Trust Co.

Manufacturers Alliance Productivity & Innovation Inc.

Blankley, Walter Elwood: president, director, AMETEK Foundation; chairman, director, AMETEK, Inc.

Manufacturers Railway Co.

Busch, August Adolphus, III: chairman, president, chief executive officer, Anheuser-Busch Companies, Inc.

Williams, Eugene Flewellyn, Jr.: member public policy committee, Emerson Charitable Trust

Mapco Inc.

Bailey, Keith E.: chairman, president, director, chief executive officer, Texas Gas Transmission Corp.; president, director, Williams Companies Foundation (The)

Marathon Oil Co.

Graham, Thomas Carlisle: trustee, AK Steel Foundation

Marathon Petroleum Sakhalin

Beghini, Victor Gene: trustee, USX Foundation, Inc.

Marc Plz Corp.

Marcus, Stephen Howard: chairman, chief executive officer, Marcus Corp.; president, director, Marcus Corp. Foundation

Marco Sales Inc.

Koch, Robert Louis, II: president, chief executive officer, director, Koch Enterprises, Inc.; president, director, Koch Foundation

Maremont Corp.

Pond, Byron O.: chairman, chief executive officer, director, Arvin Industries, Inc.

Marietta RV WInc.

Corson, Keith Daniel: president, chief operating officer, Coachmen Industries, Inc.

Marine Midland Banks Inc.

Alfiero, Salvatore Harry: founder, chairman, chief executive officer, director, Mark IV Industries; chairman, Mark IV Industries Foundation

Kennedy, Bernard Joseph: chairman, president, chief executive officer, director, National Fuel Gas Distribution Corp.

Marine Midland Trust Co.

Rich, Robert E., Sr.: president, treasurer, Rich Family Foundation; founder, chairman, director, Rich Products Corp.

Marion Merrell Dow Inc.

Stavropoulos, William S.: president, chief executive officer, director, Dow Chemical Co.

Maritime Overseas Corp.

Recanati, Michael A.: executive vice president, director, OSG Foundation

Maritz Corp. Services

Maritz, William Edward: chairman, chief executive officer, president, Maritz Inc.

Mark IV Industries

Lippes, Gerald Sanford: secretary, Mark IV Industries Foundation

Market Facts Inc.

Wentworth, Jack Roberts, Ph.D.: director, Habig Foundation

Market Street Restoration Corp.

Peck, Arthur John, Jr.: secretary, vice president, Corning Inc.; secretary, Corning Inc. Foundation

MarketSpan Corp.

Catell, Robert Barry: chairman, chief executive officer, Brooklyn Union

Marley Co.

Drury, Robert E.: president, director, United Dominion Foundation

Marmaxx Group

Lesser, Richard G.: executive vice president, chief operating officer, director, TJX Companies, Inc.; chief operating officer, director, TJX Foundation, Inc.

Marriott International Inc.

Small, Lawrence Malcolm: president, chief operating officer, Fannie Mae; director, Fannie Mae Foundation

Marsh & McLennan Companies Inc.

Lasser, Lawrence Jay: president, chief executive officer, director, Putnam Investments; president, chief executive officer, Putnam Investors Fund

Ong, John Doyle: chairman board, director, Ameritech Corp.

Putnam, George, Jr.: chairman, president, chief executive officer, Putnam Investments

Marshall & Huschart Machinery Co. Indiana

Kleinfeldt, Richard C.: vice president financial, chief financial officer, director, Giddings & Lewis

Marshall & Ilsley Bank

Jacobs, Burleigh Edmund: president, director, Grede Foundation; chairman, Grede Foundries; director, Marshall & Ilsley Foundation, Inc.

Kuester, Dennis J.: president, Marshall & Ilsley Corp.

Wardeberg, George E.: president, WICOR Foundation; president, chief executive officer, director, WICOR, Inc.

Wigdale, James B.: vice president, Marshall & Ilsley Corp.; vice president, director, Marshall & Ilsley Foundation, Inc.

Wright, James O.: president, director, Badger Meter Foundation; chairman, director, Badger Meter, Inc.; director, Marshall & Ilsley Foundation, Inc.

Marshall & Ilsley Corp.

Abdoo, Richard A.: chairman, president, chief executive officer, Wisconsin Energy Corp.; president, director, Wisconsin Energy Corp. Foundation, Inc.

Bueche, Wendell Francis: director, Marshall & Ilsley Foundation, Inc.

Jacobs, Burleigh Edmund: president, director, Grede Foundation; chairman, Grede Foundries; director, Marshall & Ilsley Foundation, Inc.

Kellner, Jack F.: director, board member, Marshall & Ilsley Foundation, Inc.

Kress, James F.: chairman, director, Green Bay Packaging

Lyall, Katharine Culbert: trustee, Kemper Foundation (James S.)

O'Hare, Don R.: director, Hamilton Sundstrand Corp.; president, director, Sundstrand Corp. Foundation

Wright, James O.: president, director, Badger Meter Foundation; chairman, director, Badger Meter, Inc.; director, Marshall & Ilsley Foundation, Inc.

Marshall's Inc.

Lesser, Richard G.: executive vice president, chief operating officer, director, TJX Companies, Inc.; chief operating officer, director, TJX Foundation, Inc.

Martin Marietta Materials Inc.

Reed, James M.: trustee, Union Camp Charitable Trust; vice chairman, chief financial officer, director, Union Camp Corp.

Martin's Food South Burlington Inc.

Bowne, Garrett D., IV: treasurer, Hannaford Charitable Foundation

Martins Foods of South Burlington Inc.

Farrington, Hugh G.: president, chief executive officer, director, Hannaford Brothers Co.

Marvel Group Inc.

Manoogian, Richard Alexander: chairman, chief executive officer, director, Masco Corp.

MassMutual Corp. Investors Inc.

Pajak, John Joseph: president, chief operating officer, Massachusetts Mutual Life Insurance Co.

Wendlandt, Gary Edward: executive vice president, chief investment officer, Massachusetts Mutual Life Insurance Co.

Massachusetts Capital Resource Co.

O'Brien, John Francis, Jr.: president, chief executive officer, Allmerica Financial Corp.

Massachusetts Electric Co.

Housen, Charles B.: chairman, president, chief executive officer, director, Erving Industries; president, director, Housen Foundation

Massachusetts Finance Services Co.

Ives, J. Atwood: chairman, chief executive officer, Boston Gas Co.; chairman, chief executive officer, trustee, Eastern Enterprises; trustee, Eastern Enterprises Foundation

Massachusetts Mutual Life Insurance Co.

Ackerman, Roger G.: trustee, Corning Inc. Foundation

Gifford, Charles Kilvert: trustee, BankBoston Charitable Foundation; chairman, chief executive officer, BankBoston Corp.

Lubar, Sheldon B.: chairman, Ameritech Corp.; director, Firstar Milwaukee Foundation

Master Card United States

Urkowitz, Michael: senior vice president, Chase Manhattan Bank, NA; trustee, Chase Manhattan Foundation

Master Lock Co.

Hays, Thomas Chandler: chairman, chief executive officer, director, Fortune Brands, Inc.

MasterBrand Industries Inc.

Rukeyser, Robert James: senior vice president corporate affairs, Fortune Brands, Inc.

MasterCard Inc.

Fish, Lawrence K.: trustee, Citizens Charitable Foundation; chairman, chief executive officer, Citizens Financial Group, Inc.

MasterCard International Inc.

McGuinn, Martin Gregory: chairman, chief executive officer, Mellon Financial Corp.

Matritech

Zadel, C. William: chairman, president, chief executive officer, Millipore Corp.; trustee, Millipore Foundation (The)

Matson Navigation Co. Inc.

Denlea, Leo Edward, Jr.: retired chairman, president, chief executive officer, director, Farmers Group, Inc.; vice president, Farmers Group Safety Foundation

Dods, Walter Arthur, Jr.: president, director, First Hawaiian Foundation; chairman, chief executive

officer, director, First Hawaiian, Inc.

Matsushita Electric Corp. America

Kraft, Richard A.: president, director, Panasonic Foundation

Levine, Lawrence E.: secretary, Panasonic Foundation

Matthews International Corp.

Stallkamp, William J.: member corporate review committee, Mellon Financial Corp.

Maurice's Inc.

Brenninkmeyer, Roland M.: president, chief executive officer, director, American Retail Group; president, director, Humanitas Foundation

Maxicare Health Plans Inc.

Brinegar, Claude Stout: trustee, Unocal Foundation

Maxium Service Television

Huey, Ward L., Jr.: president broadcast division, vice chairman, director, Belo Corp. (A.H.); vice president, trustee, Belo Corp. Foundation (A.H.)

May Department Stores Co.

Quinlan, Michael Robert: chairman executive committee, McDonald's Corp.; director, McDonald's Corp. Charitable Foundation

Whitacre, Edward E., Jr.: chairman, director, chief executive officer, SBC Communications Inc.

Maytag Appliances

Nicholas, Jon O.: vice president, trustee, Maytag Corp. Foundation

Maytag Corp.

Clark, Howard Longstreth, Jr.: vice chairman, Walter Industries Inc.

Kerr, William T.: chairman, chief executive officer, director, Meredith Corp.

McClure Newspapers Inc.

McCorkindale, Douglas H.: vice chairman, president, Gannett Co., Inc.; president, Gannett Foundation

McDermott Inc.

Tetrault, Roger E.: chairman, chief executive officer, director, McDermott Inc.

McDermott Will & Emery

Ashley, James Wheeler: director, Globe Foundation

McDonald & Co. Securities

O'Brien, John F.: trustee, McDonald & Co. Securities Foundation

McDonald Co. Investments

Clutterbuck, Robert T.: president, McDonald & Co. Securities, Inc.

McDonald Co. Investments Delaware

Summers, William B., Jr.: trustee, McDonald & Co. Securities Foundation; chairman, chief executive officer, president, McDonald & Co. Securities, Inc.

McDonald's Corp.

McKenna, Andrew James: director, Aon Foundation

Stone, Roger Warren: chairman, president, chief executive officer, director, Stone Container Corp.; president, Stone Foundation

McDonald's Restaurant Operations

Quinlan, Michael Robert: chairman executive committee, McDonald's Corp.; director, McDonald's Corp. Charitable Foundation

Turner, Fred L.: senior chairman, director, McDonald's Corp.

McDonald's Restaurants Arizona

Quinlan, Michael Robert: chairman executive committee, McDonald's Corp.; director, McDonald's Corp. Charitable Foundation

McDonald's Restaurants Colorado

Quinlan, Michael Robert: chairman executive committee, McDonald's Corp.; director, McDonald's Corp. Charitable Foundation

Turner, Fred L.: senior chairman, director, McDonald's Corp.

McDonald's Restaurants Illinois

Quinlan, Michael Robert: chairman executive committee, McDonald's Corp.; director, McDonald's Corp. Charitable Foundation

McDonald's Restaurants Missouri

Quinlan, Michael Robert: chairman executive committee, McDonald's Corp.; director, McDonald's Corp. Charitable Foundation

McDonald's Restaurants New Jersey

Quinlan, Michael Robert: chairman executive committee, McDonald's Corp.; director, McDonald's Corp. Charitable Foundation

Turner, Fred L.: senior chairman, director, McDonald's Corp.

McDonnell Douglas Corp.

Bridgewater, Bernard Adolphus, Jr.: member board control, Brown Shoe Co. Charitable Trust; chairman, president, chief executive officer, director, Brown Shoe Co., Inc.

McGrath Rentcorp

Zech, Ronald H.: chairman, president, chief executive officer, chief operating officer, GATX Corp.

McGraw-Hill Fin Services Co.

McGraw, Harold Whittlesey 'Terry', III: chairman, president, chief executive officer, McGraw-Hill Companies, Inc.

McGuire Furniture Co.

Black, Natalie A.: group vice president interiors, general counsel, director, Kohler Co.

McKesson Corp.

Pottruck, David Steven: president, chief executive officer, director, Schwab & Co., Inc. (Charles)

McKesson Corp. DE

Mahoney, David L.: co-chief executive officer, McKesson-HBOC Corp.

McLane Co. Inc.

Menzer, John: executive vice president, Wal-Mart Stores, Inc.

McMoran Oil & Gas Inc.

Putnam, George, Jr.: chairman, president, chief executive officer, Putnam Investments

Mead Corp.

Breen, John Gerald: chairman, chief executive officer, director, Sherwin-Williams Co.; president, trustee, Sherwin-Williams Foundation

Wilson, James Lawrence: chairman, chief executive officer, director, Rohm & Haas Co.

Mead Timber Co.

Correll, Alston Dayton 'Pete', Jr.: chairman, president, chief executive officer, director, Georgia-Pacific Corp.; director, Georgia-Pacific Foundation

Meadville Corp.

Gabel, Ivan H.: trustee, Merit Gasoline Foundation; president, chief executive officer, Merit Oil Corp.

Medalcraft Mint Inc.

Connolly, Gerald Edward: trustee, Reinhart Family Foundation (D. B. and Marjorie)

Media One Group

Crandall, Robert Lloyd: director, AMR Corp.

Media One Group Inc.

Simpson, Louis Allen: president, chief executive officer capital operations, director, GEICO Corp.

Mediastream Inc.

Jones, Ross: senior vice president, chief financial officer, Knight Ridder

Medical Information Bureau

MacLeay, Thomas H.: president, chief operating officer, National Life of Vermont

Medimart Inc.

Pulido, Mark A.: president, chief executive officer, director, chairman, McKesson-HBOC Corp.

Medirisk Inc.

Cowan, Keith O.: vice president corporate development, BellSouth Corp.

MedImmune Inc.

Franklin, Barbara Hackman: director, Dow Chemical Co.

Medovations

Connolly, Gerald Edward: trustee, Reinhart Family Foundation (D. B. and Marjorie)

Medtronic Bio-Medicus Inc.

George, William Wallace: chief executive officer, chairman, Medtronic, Inc.

Nelson, Glen David, MD: vice chairman, Medtronic, Inc.

Medtronic Inc.

Chellgren, Paul Wilbur: chief executive officer, chairman, director, Ashland, Inc.; member, Ashland Inc. Foundation

Medusa Cement Corp.

Minton, Dwight Church: chairman, director, Church & Dwight Co., Inc.

Medusa Corp.

Evans, Robert Sheldon: chairman, chief executive officer, Crane Co.; chairman, president, director, Crane Foundation

Minton, Dwight Church: chairman, director, Church & Dwight Co., Inc.

Meijer Companies Ltd.

Meijer, Douglas: co-chairman, director, chief executive officer, Meijer, Inc.

Meijer, Hendrik G.: co-chairman, director, Meijer, Inc

Melbank, Tweed, Hadly & McCloy

Douglass, Robert Royal: trustee, Chase Manhattan Foundation

Mellon Bank Corp.

Shapira, David S.: trustee, Giant Eagle Foundation; chairman, chief executive officer, director, Giant Eagle Inc.

Stallkamp, William J.: member corporate review committee, Mellon Financial Corp.

Mellon Bank NA

Graham, Thomas Carlisle: trustee, AK Steel Foundation

McGuinn, Martin Gregory: chairman, chief executive officer, Mellon Financial Corp.

Shapira, David S.: trustee, Giant Eagle Foundation; chairman, chief executive officer, director, Giant Eagle Inc.

Mellon First Business Bank

Ferry, Richard Michael: chairman, Pacific Mutual Life Insurance Co.

Mellon National Corp.

Graham, Thomas Carlisle: trustee, AK Steel Foundation

Memorial Healthcare System

Ranck, Bruce E.: president, chief executive officer, director, Browning-Ferris Industries Inc.

Menasha Transport, Inc.

Bero, Robert D.: president, chief executive officer, Menasha Corp.

Menlo Logistics Inc.

Moffitt, Donald Eugene: chairman, director, CNF Transportation, Inc.

Merastar Insurance Co.

Smith, Donald Kaye: senior vice president, general counsel, director, GEICO Corp.

Merc Institute

Eccles, Spencer Fox: chairman, chief executive officer, director, First Security Bank of Idaho NA

Mercantile Acquisition Corp.

Jacobsen, Thomas Herbert: chairman, president, chief executive officer, Mercantile Bank NA

Mercantile Bancorp Inc.

Hall, William Austin: president, Hallmark Corporate Foundation

Price, Charles H., II: director, New York Times Co. Foundation

Mercantile Bank Saint Louis NA

Graham, Richard William: president, chief executive officer, chief operating officer, director, Smurfit-Stone Container Corp.

Jacobsen, Thomas Herbert: chairman, president, chief executive officer, Mercantile Bank NA

Mercantile Bank Topeka

Stauffer, John H.: trustee, Stauffer Communications Foundation

Mercantile Bankshares Corp.

Grass, Martin Lehrman: chairman, chief executive officer, director, Rite Aid Corp.

Poindexter, Christian Herndon: chairman, Baltimore Gas & Electric Foundation; chairman, chief executive officer, director, Constellation Energy Group, Inc.

Shepard, Donald James: chairman, president, chief executive officer, AEGON U.S.A. Inc.

Mercantile National Bank Indiana

Neale, Gary L.: chairman, president, chief executive officer, Northern Indiana Public Service Co.

Mercantile Safe Deposit Trust Co.

Shepard, Donald James: chairman, president, chief executive officer, AEGON U.S.A. Inc.

Merchants Mutual Insurance Co.

Kennedy, Bernard Joseph: chairman, president, chief executive officer, director, National Fuel Gas Distribution Corp.

Merck & Co. Inc.

Bossidy, Lawrence Arthur: chairman, director, AlliedSignal Foundation Inc.; chairman, chief executive officer, director, AlliedSignal Inc.

Bowen, William Gordon, PhD: trustee, Merck Co. Foundation

Davis, Carolyne Kahle, PhD: trustee, Merck Co. Foundation

Elam, Lloyd Charles, MD: trustee, Merck Co. Foundation

Exley, Charles Errol, Jr.: trustee, Merck Co. Foundation

Fiorina, Carleton S.: president, chief executive officer, director, Hewlett-Packard Co.

Weatherstone, Dennis: trustee, Merck Co. Foundation

Mercury Fin

Chookaszian, Dennis Haig: chairman, chief executive officer, CNA

Meridian Bancorp Inc.

Hafer, Fred Douglass: chairman, president, chief executive officer, GPU Inc.

Meridian Managed Care Inc.

Formisano, Roger: vice president, United Wisconsin Services Foundation

Hefty, Thomas R.: chairman, president, chief executive officer, United Wisconsin Services

Meridian Oil Inc.

Dubois, Everett D.: treasurer, Burlington Resources Foundation; senior vice president, treasurer, Burlington Resources, Inc.

Meridian Oil Marketing Inc.

Howison, George Everett: vice president, Burlington Resources Foundation

Meridian Resources Corp.

Formisano, Roger: vice president, United Wisconsin Services Foundation

Hefty, Thomas R.: chairman, president, chief executive officer, United Wisconsin Services

Meridian Sport Holdings DE Corp.

Perelman, Ronald Owen: director, Revlon Foundation Inc.

Meridian Sports Inc.

Slovin, Bruce: president, director, Revlon Inc.

Merit Distribution Services

Menzer, John: executive vice president, Wal-Mart Stores, Inc.

Merit Oil Co.

Laubach, David A.: trustee, Merit Gasoline Foundation

Merit Oil Connecticut Inc.

Gabel, Ivan H.: trustee, Merit Gasoline Foundation; president, chief executive officer, Merit Oil Corp.

Laubach, David A.: trustee, Merit Gasoline Foundation

Merit Oil Corp.

Harting, Robert M.: executive director, trustee, Merit Gasoline Foundation

Merit Oil Maryland Inc.

Gabel, Ivan H.: trustee, Merit Gasoline Foundation; president, chief executive officer, Merit Oil Corp.

Harting, Robert M.: executive director, trustee, Merit Gasoline Foundation

Laubach, David A.: trustee, Merit Gasoline Foundation

Meritor Automotive Inc.

Beall, Donald Ray: director, Rockwell International Corp.

Walker, Martin Dean: chairman, chief executive officer, director, Hanna Co. (M.A.)

Merrill Lynch Derivatives Products Inc.

Wendlandt, Gary Edward: executive vice president, chief investment officer, Massachusetts Mutual Life Insurance Co.

Merrill Lynch International Financial Corp.

Allison, Herbert Monroe, Jr.: vice president, trustee, Merrill Lynch & Co. Foundation Inc.; president, chief operating officer, Merrill Lynch & Co., Inc.

Merrill Lynch Pierce Fenner & Smith

Allison, Herbert Monroe, Jr.: vice president, trustee, Merrill Lynch & Co. Foundation Inc.; president, chief operating officer, Merrill Lynch & Co., Inc.

Steffens, John Laundon: executive vice president, Merrill Lynch & Co., Inc.

Met Life Insurance Co.

Barnette, Curtis Handley: chairman, chief executive officer, director, Bethlehem Steel Corp.

Metricom Corp.

Cline, Robert Stanley: chairman, chief executive officer, director, Airborne Freight Corp.

Metro Edison Co.

Hafer, Fred Douglass: chairman, president, chief executive officer, GPU Inc.

Metro Structures

Gidwitz, Gerald S.: chairman, Curtis Industries, Inc. (Helene)

Metropolitan Edison Co.

Graham, John Gourlay: chief financial officer, senior vice president, GPU Energy

Metropolitan Life Insurance Co.

Houghton, James Richardson: director, Corning Inc.; trustee, Corning Inc. Foundation

Metropolitan Life Portfolios

Lawrence, Robert Ashton: director, New York Times Co. Foundation

Metropolitan Resources Inc.

Ebrom, Charles E.: director, vice president, Zachry Co. (H.B.); treasurer, trustee, Zachry Foundation (The)

Metropolitan Series Fund

Lawrence, Robert Ashton: director, New York Times Co. Foundation

Metropower Inc.

Hinson, Ronnie T.: president, Pieper Power Electric Co.

Mexico Desarrollo Industries Minero SA

McAllister, Francis R.: vice president, director, ASARCO Foundation; president, chief executive officer, ASARCO Inc.

Mfrs & Traders Trust Co.

Sadler, Robert E., Jr.: chief executive officer, M&T Charitable Foundation; executive vice president, Manufacturers & Traders Trust Co.

Wilmers, Robert George: chairman, president, chief executive officer, Manufacturers & Traders Trust Co.

Miami Heat

Arison, M. Micky: trustee, Arison Foundation; chairman, president, chief executive officer, Carnival Corp.

Miami Power Corp.

Foley, Cheryl M.: vice president, secretary, general counsel, Cinergy Corp.; vice president, secretary, director, Cinergy Foundation

Randolph, Jackson Harold: chairman, Cinergy Corp.; chairman, director, Cinergy Foundation

Miami Valley Development Co.

Koziar, Stephen F., Jr.: president, trustee, Dayton Power and Light Co. Foundation

Michcon Gathering Co.

Ewing, Stephen E.: president, chief executive officer, director, Michigan Consolidated Gas Co.

Michiana Easy Livin' Country

Corson, Keith Daniel: president, chief operating officer, Coachmen Industries, Inc.

Skinner, Claire Corson: chairman, chief executive officer, Coachmen Industries, Inc.

Michigan Canada & Tube Inc.

Smurfit, Michael William J.: chairman, Smurfit-Stone Container Corp.

Michigan First

Marohn, William D.: vice chairman, director, Whirlpool Corp.

Michigan Gas Storage Co.

Elbert, Paul A.: president, chief executive officer natural gas, Consumers Energy Co.

Microflect Co. Inc.

Egan, Thomas P., Jr.: officer, Valmont Foundation

Micron Tech

Simplot, Donald J.: vice president, Simplot Foundation (J.R.)

Simplot, John Richard: chairman, founder, Simplot Co. (J.R.); president, Simplot Foundation (J.R.)

Microsoft Corp.

Barad, Jill Elikann: director, Mattel Foundation; chairman, chief executive officer, director, Mattel Inc.

Reed, William Garrard, Jr.: director, Matlock Foundation

Mid-America Bancorp

Oliver, Orson: president, director, Mid-America Bank of Louisville

Mid-America Bancorp/Bank Louisville

Klein, Bertram W.: chairman, director, Bank of Louisville Charities

Mid-America Bank of Louisville

Guillaume, Raymond Kendrick: vice chairman, chief executive officer, Mid-America Bank of Louisville

Mid-America Group Ltd.

Pomerantz, Marvin Alvin: trustee, Mid-American Foundation

Mid-American Capital Co.

Bright, Stanley J.: chairman, president, chief executive officer, director, MidAmerican Energy Holdings Co.

Mid-Atlantic Acceptance Co. Ltd.

Schuchardt, Daniel Norman: secretary, treasurer, FMC Foundation

Mid-Century Insurance Co.

Denlea, Leo Edward, Jr.: retired chairman, president, chief executive officer, director, Farmers Group, Inc.; vice president, Farmers Group Safety Foundation

Mid-Ocean Ltd.

Evans, Robert Sheldon: chairman, chief executive officer, Crane Co.; chairman, president, director, Crane Foundation

Mid-State Holdings Corp.

Fjelstul, Dean M.: senior vice president, chief financial officer, Walter Industries Inc.

Hyatt, Kenneth Ernest: chairman, president, chief executive officer, director, Walter Industries Inc.

Mid-State Homes Inc.

Fjelstul, Dean M.: senior vice president, chief financial officer, Walter Industries Inc.

Hyatt, Kenneth Ernest: chairman, president, chief executive officer, director, Walter Industries Inc.

MidAm

Donovan, Thomas Roy: president, chief executive officer, Chicago Board of Trade

MidAmerica Energy Holdings Co.

Scott, Walter, Jr.: member contributions committee, Kiewit Companies Foundation

MidState Holdings Corp.

Porter, Edward A.: vice president, general counsel, secretary, Walter Industries Inc.

Midamerican Energy Corp.

Bright, Stanley J.: chairman, president, chief executive officer, director, MidAmerican Energy Holdings Co.

Midcal

Gallo, Joseph E.: co-president, Gallo Foundation

Midland Bank

Walters, Peter: chairman, SmithKline Beecham Corp.

Midland Enterprise Inc.

Raskin, Fred C.: president, chief operating officer, Eastern Enterprises; trustee, Eastern Enterprises Foundation

Midland Mutual Life Insurance Co.

Wobst, Frank: chairman, chief executive officer, director, Huntington Bancshares Inc.

Midlands Electricity PLC

Graham, John Gourlay: chief financial officer, senior vice president, GPU Energy

Midwest Capital Group Inc.

Bright, Stanley J.: chairman, president, chief executive officer, director, MidAmerican Energy Holdings Co.

Midwest Clearing Corp.

Fluno, Jere David: vice chairman, Grainger, Inc. (W.W.)

Midwest Express Airlines Inc.

Stratton, Frederick Prescott, Jr.: chairman, chief executive officer, director, Briggs & Stratton Corp.; president, director, Briggs & Stratton Corp. Foundation

Weekly, John William: chairman, chief executive officer, Mutual of Omaha Insurance Co.

Midwest Express Holdings Inc.

Stratton, Frederick Prescott, Jr.: chairman, chief executive officer, director, Briggs & Stratton Corp.; president, director, Briggs & Stratton Corp. Foundation

Midwest Grain Products Inc.

Reintjes, Robert J., Sr.: director, Butler Manufacturing Co.; member, Butler Manufacturing Co. Foundation

Midwest Securities Trust Co.

Fluno, Jere David: vice chairman, Grainger, Inc. (W.W.)

Milacron Inc.

Franklin, Barbara Hackman: director, Dow Chemical Co.

Meyer, Daniel Joseph: president, Milacron Foundation; chairman, president, chief executive officer, director, Milacron, Inc.

Milacron International Marketing Co.

Meyer, Daniel Joseph: president, Milacron Foundation; chairman, president, chief executive officer, director, Milacron, Inc.

Milacron Marketing Co.

Meyer, Daniel Joseph: president, Milacron Foundation; chairman, president, chief executive officer, director, Milacron, Inc.

Mileage Plus Inc.

Maher, Francesca M.: senior vice president, general counsel, secretary, United Airlines Inc.

Mill Haven Co. Inc.

Herman, William A., III: secretary, treasurer, director, Morris Communications Corp.

Milwaukee Land Co.

Zilkha, Ezra Khedouri: president, treasurer, Zilkha Foundation, Inc.; president, Zilkha & Sons

Minerals Technologies Inc.

Meister, Paul M.: vice president, treasurer, Winthrop Foundation

Steere, William Campbell, Jr.: chairman, chief executive officer, director, Pfizer Inc.

Minergy Corp.

Abdoo, Richard A.: chairman, president, chief executive officer, Wisconsin Energy Corp.; president, director, Wisconsin Energy Corp. Foundation, Inc.

Minimed Sylmar

Davis, Carolyne Kahle, PhD: trustee, Merck Co. Foundation

Minnesota Harbor Service Inc.

Raskin, Fred C.: president, chief operating officer, Eastern Enterprises; trustee, Eastern Enterprises Foundation

Minnesota Marketing

Grundhofer, John Francis: president, chief executive officer, director, U.S. Bancorp

Minnesota Mining & MFG Co. Canada

DeSimone, Livio Diego: chairman, chief executive officer, Minnesota Mining & Manufacturing Co.

Minnesota Mutual Life Insurance Co.

Grundhofer, John Francis: president, chief executive officer, director, U.S. Bancorp

Miracle Hill Golf & Tennis Center

Davis, John B., MD: director, Physicians Mutual Insurance Co. Foundation

Mirel & Alegi

Alegi, August Paul: director, GEICO Philanthropic Foundation

Miscellaneous Hospitality Development Corp.

Robinson, E. B., Jr.: chairman, chief executive officer, director, Deposit Guaranty National Bank

Mission Group Inc.

Bryson, John E.: chairman, chief executive officer, Edison International

Mission Supply Co.

Spangler, Phillip A.: vice president, treasurer, Yellow Corp.; treasurer, secretary, Yellow Corp. Foundation

Missouri Cooperage Co. Inc.

Boswell, John Joseph: president, Boswell Foundation, Inc.; chairman, Independent Stave Co.

Missouri Natural Gas Division

Jaudes, Robert Christian: chairman, trustee, Laclede Gas Charitable Trust

Mitchell Co.

Cowan, James R.: vice president, director, Stonecutter Foundation; chairman, president, chief executive officer, director, Stonecutter Mills Corp.

Walker, Thomas P.: secretary, Stonecutter Foundation

Mitsubishi Consumer Electric America

Olschwang, Alan P., Esq.: secretary, Mitsubishi Electric America Foundation

Mitsubishi Electric Auto American

Iwamoto, Yasul: director, Mitsubishi Electric America Foundation

Mitsubishi Electronics America

Savage, John: president, director, Mitsubishi Electric America Foundation

Mobile Corp.

Fites, Donald Vester: director, Caterpillar Foundation

Modagrafics Inc.

Bookshester, Dennis S.: chairman, chief executive officer, Playboy Enterprises Inc.

Modine Manufacturing Co.

Kuester, Dennis J.: president, Marshall & Ilsley Corp.

Neale, Gary L.: chairman, president, chief executive officer, Northern Indiana Public Service Co.

Mojave Pipeline Co.

Baish, Richard Owen: senior vice president, director, El Paso Energy Foundation

Molex Inc.

Jannotta, Edgar D.: president, Blair & Co. Foundation (William); senior director, Blair & Co. (William)

Monogram General Agency Texas

Dammerman, Dennis Dean: vice chairman, director, General Electric Co.

Monongahela Connecting Railway Co.

Kelly, J. Peter: president, chief operating officer, director, LTV Corp.; trustee, LTV Foundation

Monsanto Co.

De Schutter, Richard U.: director, Searle Charitable Trust; chairman, chief executive officer, Searle & Co. (G.D.)

Reed, John Shepard: co-chairman, Citibank Corp.

Ruckelshaus, William Doyle: chairman, director, Browning-Ferris Industries Inc.

Montana Power Co.

Cain, Alan F.: director, Montana Power Foundation

Lehrkind, Carl, III: director, Montana Power Foundation

Monterey Canning Co.

Bragin, David H.: treasurer, assistant secretary, director, Winn-Dixie Stores Foundation

Monterey Peninsula Herald

Block, John Robinson: vice president, trustee, Blade Foundation

Montgomery Capital Assoc

Rogers, T. Gary: chairman, chief executive officer, director, Dreyer's Grand Ice Cream

Montgomery Ward Co. Inc.

Dammerman, Dennis Dean: vice chairman, director, General Electric Co.

Montgomery Ward Holding Corp.

Goddu, Roger V.: chairman, chief executive officer, director, Montgomery Ward & Co., Inc.

Workman, John L.: executive vice president, Montgomery Ward & Co., Inc.; executive vice president, director, Montgomery Ward Foundation

Monticello Insurance Co.

Hansmeyer, Herbert F.: chairman, Fireman's Fund Insurance Co.

Monumental General Administrator

Herbert, Bart, Jr.: executive vice president, chief marketing officer, AEGON U.S.A. Inc.

Mony Life Insurance American AZ Corp.

Daddario, Richard M.: chief financial officer, MONY Life Insurance of New York (The)

Mony Life Insurance of America Arizona Corp.

Foti, Samuel J.: president, chief operating officer, director, MONY Group (The); director, MONY Life Insurance of New York (The)

Roth, Michael I.: chairman, chief executive officer, director, MONY Group (The); director, MONY Life Insurance of New York (The)

Moore Medical Corp.

Slovin, Bruce: president, director, Revlon Inc.

More Window Ways Inc.

Trask, Robert B.: president, chief operating officer, director, Country Curtains, Inc.; clerk, trustee, High Meadow Foundation

Morfecor California

Johnston, William E., Junior: president, chief operating officer, director, Morton International Inc.

Morgan Group Inc.

Bell, Bradley John: vice president, treasurer, Whirlpool Corp.; treasurer, Whirlpool Foundation

Morgan Guaranty Trust Co.

Atwater, Horace Brewster, Jr.: trustee, Merck Co. Foundation

Raymond, Lee R.: chairman, president, chief executive officer, Exxon Mobil Corp.

Morgan Guaranty Trust Co. New York

Allaire, Paul Arthur: chairman, chief executive officer, chairman executive committee, Xerox Corp.; president, Xerox Foundation

Morgan Products

Holland, William Ray: vice president, director, United Dominion Foundation; chairman, chief executive officer, director, United Dominion Industries, Ltd.

Morgan Stanley Dean Witter Co.

Kidder, C. Robert: chairman, president, chief executive officer, director, Borden, Inc.

Knight, Charles Field: chairman, chief executive officer, Emerson Electric Co.

Morgan Stanley Group Inc.

Burke, Daniel Barnett: vice president, treasurer, director, ABC Foundation

Morris Farm Center Inc.

Copenhaver, Don: director, MFA Foundation; president, chief executive officer, MFA Inc.

Jobe, G. David: director, MFA Foundation; senior vice president, MFA Inc.

Morrison Knudsen Corp.

Simplot, John Richard: chairman, founder, Simplot Co. (J.R.); president, Simplot Foundation (J.R.)

Morrison Knudsen Corp. Delaware Corp.

Hanks, Stephen G.: president, Morrison Knudsen Corp. Foundation, Inc.

Morrison Products Inc.

Knicely, Howard V.: president, TRW Foundation

Mortgage Guaranty Insurance Corp.

Lacy, William Howard: president, MGIC Investment Corp.

Lauer, J. Michael: executive vice president, chief financial officer, MGIC Investment Corp.

Schuenke, Donald John: director, Freddie Mac

Mortgage Guaranty Reinsurance Corp.

Lauer, J. Michael: executive vice president, chief financial officer, MGIC Investment Corp.

Morton International GmbH

Johnston, William E., Junior: president, chief operating officer, director, Morton International Inc.

Morton International Inc.

Farrell, W. James: chairman, chief executive officer, Illinois Tool Works, Inc.

Keyser, Richard Lee: chairman, chief executive officer, president, Grainger, Inc. (W.W.)

Mooney, Edward J., Jr.: chairman, president, chief executive officer, director, Nalco Chemical Co.

Stone, Roger Warren: chairman, president, chief executive officer, director, Stone Container Corp.; president, Stone Foundation

Morton International Ltd.

Johnston, William E., Junior: president, chief operating officer, director, Morton International Inc.

Morwal Investments

Walker, Martin Dean: chairman, chief executive officer, director, Hanna Co. (M.A.)

Motor Imports

Fukunaga, Mark H.: chairman, director, Servco Foundation; chief executive officer, chairman, Servco Pacific

Motorola Cellular Service Inc.

Koenemann, Carl F.: chief financial officer, executive vice president, Motorola Inc.

Motorola Communication International

Johnson, Kenneth James: vice president, controller, director, Motorola Inc.

Motorola Inc.

Fuller, Harry Laurance: co-chairman, director, BP Amoco Corp.

Pepper, John E., Jr.: chairman executive committee, Procter & Gamble Co.

Motorola de Puerto Rico Inc.

Galvin, Christopher B.: director, Motorola Foundation; president, chief executive officer, director, Motorola Inc.

Movado Group Inc.

Bush, Michael J.: vice president real estate, Giant Food Inc.

Mrs. Smith's Frozen Foods Co.

Langbo, Arnold Gordon: chairman, chief executive officer, director, Kellogg Co.

Mulberry Resources Inc.

Daniels, John Hancock: chairman, Archer-Daniels-Midland Foundation

Multifoods Distribution Group Inc.

Bonvino, Frank W.: vice president, secretary, general counsel, International Multifoods Corp.

Costley, Gary E.: chairman, president, chief executive officer, director, International Multifoods Corp.

Multimedia Inc.

Curley, John J.: chairman, chief executive officer, director, Gannett Co., Inc.; chairman, Gannett Foundation

LaMacchia, John Thomas: trustee, Cincinnati Bell Foundation, Inc.; president, chief executive officer, director, Cincinnati Bell Inc.

Muncie Newspapers Inc.

Russell, Frank Eli: president, Central Newspapers Foundation; chairman, Central Newspapers, Inc.

Municipal Bond Insurance Association Corp.

Elliott, David Holland: consultant, chairman executive committee, MBIA Inc.

Murphy Oil USA Inc.

Cosse, Steven Anthony: senior vice president, general counsel, Murphy Oil Corp.

Murray Inc.

Duncan, Ian: trustee, Tomkins Corp. Foundation; deputy chairman, managing director finance, Tomkins Industries, Inc.

Reading, Anthony John: president, trustee, Tomkins Corp. Foundation; president, chief executive officer, Tomkins Industries, Inc.

Mus Co. Inc.

Hall, Floyd: chairman, president, chief executive officer, director, Kmart Corp.

Musicland Stores Corp.

Wright, Michael William: chairman, president, chief executive officer, director, SuperValu, Inc.

Mutual America

Earley, Anthony Francis, Jr.: president, chief operating officer, Detroit Edison Co.; director, Detroit Edison Foundation

Mutual Benefit Life Insurance Co.

Hall, Donald Joyce: chairman board, director, Hallmark Cards Inc.; chairman, Hallmark Corporate Foundation

Mutual Insurance Co. Ltd.

McCorkindale, Douglas H.: vice chairman, president, Gannett Co., Inc.; president, Gannett Foundation

Mutual Life Insurance Co.

Johnson, James Lawrence: chairman emeritus, Walter Industries Inc.

Mutual Life Insurance Co. of New York

Weigel, David V.: treasurer, MONY Life Insurance of New York (The)

Mutual New York

Farley, James Bernard: chairman emeritus, trustee, Walter Industries Inc.

Mutual Omaha Investor Services Inc.

Weekly, John William: chairman, chief executive officer, Mutual of Omaha Insurance Co.

Mutual Omaha Marketing Corp.

Sturgeon, John: president, chief operating officer, Mutual of Omaha Insurance Co.

Mutual Reinsurance Bureau

Schiek, Fredrick A.: executive vice president, chief operating officer, Employers Mutual Casualty Co.

Mutual Service Casualty Insurance Co.

Frew, Burdette L.: president, director, MFA Foundation

NALAC Fin Plans

Anderson, Lowell Carlton: chairman, director, Allianz Life Insurance Co. of North America

NAPA Auto Parts

Courts, Richard Winn, II: chairman, director, Atlantic Investment Co.

NAPP Systems Inc.

Gottlieb, Richard Douglas: president, chief executive officer, director, Lee Enterprises

NASouth Dakota Regulation Inc.

Hill, Bonnie Guiton: vice president, Times Mirror Co.; president, chief executive officer, Times Mirror Foundation

NBD Bancorp Inc.

Adderley, Terence E.: chairman, president, chief executive officer, director, Kelly Services; president, director, Kelly Services Foundation

NBD Bank NA

Adderley, Terence E.: chairman, president, chief executive officer, director, Kelly Services; president, director, Kelly Services Foundation

NC International Home Furnishings Center

Spilman, Robert H.: chairman, chief executive officer, Bassett Furniture Industries; chairman, director, Bassett Furniture Industries Fdn.

NCNB Corp.

Coker, Charles Westfield: trustee, Sonoco Foundation; vice president, Sonoco Products Co.

Spilman, Robert H.: chairman, chief executive officer, Bassett Furniture Industries; chairman, director, Bassett Furniture Industries Fdn.

NCR Corp.

Burnham, Duane Lee: chairman, chief executive officer, director, Abbott Laboratories

Hoak, Jon: trustee, NCR Foundation

Holmes, David Richard: chief executive officer, chief operating officer, director, Reynolds & Reynolds Co.

Stavropoulos, William S.: president, chief executive officer, director, Dow Chemical Co.

NEC U.S.A. Inc.

Sugiyama, Mineo: chairman, president, NEC Foundation of America

NIPSCO Development Co. Inc.

Neale, Gary L.: chairman, president, chief executive officer, Northern Indiana Public Service Co.

NIPSCO Industries Management Services Co.

Johnson, Owen C., Jr.: vice president human resources, Northern Indiana Public Service Co.

NJP Insertco Inc.

Bero, Robert D.: president, chief executive officer, Menasha Corp.

NJR Energy Corp.

Harden, Oleta J.: secretary, New Jersey Natural Gas Foundation

NL Industries Inc.

Simmons, Glenn Reuben: vice chairman, Contran Corp.

Simmons, Harold Clark: chairman, director, Simmons Foundation, Inc. (Harold)

NRD LLC

Lippes, Gerald Sanford: secretary, Mark IV Industries Foundation

NRD, LLC

Montague, William Patrick: president, chief operating officer, director, Mark IV Industries; president, Mark IV Industries Foundation

NV Morton International SA

Johnston, William E., Junior: president, chief operating officer, director, Morton International Inc.

NWNL Management Corp.

Dubes, Michael: membership, ReliaStar Foundation

NWashington Inc.
Wilson, Gary Lee: chairman, director, Northwest Airlines, Inc.

NYNEX Corp.
Brademas, John: chairman, Texaco Foundation

NYP Holdings Inc.
Murdoch, Rupert P.: chairman, Fox Entertainment Group

Nabisco Inc.
Chain, John T., Junior: trustee, Kemper Foundation (James S.); president, Kemper National Insurance Companies
Goldstone, Steven F.: chairman, chief executive officer, director, Reynolds Tobacco (R.J.); chairman, RJR Nabisco Foundation

Nabors Industries Inc.
Hurford, Gary Thomas: president, director, Hunt Oil Co.

Naegele Co. Inc.
Carlson, Curtis Leroy: chairman, director, Carlson Companies, Inc.; president, treasurer, Carlson Family Foundation (Curtis L.)

Nalco Chemical Co.
Kelly, Burnett S.: vice president, Dow Corning Corp.

Nashua Corp.
Kucharski, John Michael: trustee, PerkinElmer Foundation; chairman, chief executive officer, director, PerkinElmer, Inc.
Orr, James F., III: president, trustee, UNUM Foundation; chairman, Unum-Provident

National Automatic Pipeline Oper Inc.
Cohen, Maryjo Rose: president, chief executive officer, director, National Presto Industries, Inc.; vice president, treasurer, trustee, Presto Foundation

National Bancorp of AK
Rasmuson, Edward B.: director, CIRI Foundation

National Bank Indianapolis
Cornelius, James M.: director, AUL Foundation Inc.

National Bank of South Carolina
Yancey, James D.: vice chairman, director, president, chief operating officer, Synovus Financial Corp.

National Broadcasting Co. Inc.
Atwater, Horace Brewster, Jr.: trustee, Merck Co. Foundation
Opie, John D.: vice chairman, executive officer, director, General Electric Co.
Welch, John Francis, Jr.: chairman, chief executive officer, director, General Electric Co.

National City Bank
Andreas, Lowell Willard: chairman audit committee, member executive & finance committee, Archer-Daniels-Midland Co.
Breen, John Gerald: chairman, chief executive officer, director, Sherwin-Williams Co.; president, trustee, Sherwin-Williams Foundation
Collins, Duane E.: president, chief executive officer, director, Parker Hannifin Corp.; vice president, trustee, Parker Hannifin Foundation
Zampetis, Theodore K.: president, chief operating officer, director, Standard Products Co.

National City Bank Cleveland
Daberko, David A.: chairman, chief executive officer, National City Corp.

National City Bank Indiana
Sease, Gene Elwood: director, Central Newspapers Foundation

National City Bank Kalamazoo
Daberko, David A.: chairman, chief executive officer, National City Corp.

National City Bank Minneapolis
Malmberg, David Curtis: director, National City Bank of Minneapolis

National City Bank Pennsylvania
Daberko, David A.: chairman, chief executive officer, National City Corp.
DiGirolamo, Vincent A.: executive vice president, vice chairman, National City Bank of Cleveland
Newlin, William Rankin: trustee, Kennametal Foundation

National City Bank of Minneapolis
Andreas, David Lowell: chairman, director, National City Bank Foundation; chairman, chief executive officer, National City Bank of Minneapolis

National City Bank, Pittsburgh
Daberko, David A.: chairman, chief executive officer, National City Corp.

National City Banking Division
Glaser, Gary A.: president, chief executive officer, National City Bank of Columbus

National City Corp.
Collins, Duane E.: president, chief executive officer, director, Parker Hannifin Corp.; vice president, trustee, Parker Hannifin Foundation
Glaser, Gary A.: president, chief executive officer, National City Bank of Columbus
Lemieux, Joseph Henry: chairman, chief executive officer, director, Owens-Illinois Inc.
Stitle, Stephen A.: chairman, National City Bank of Cleveland

National City Lines Inc.
Anderson, Eugene Karl: vice president, Contran Corp.; treasurer, Simmons Foundation, Inc. (Harold)
Simmons, Glenn Reuben: vice chairman, Contran Corp.
Watson, Steven L.: vice president, secretary, Contran Corp.; vice president, secretary, director, Simmons Foundation, Inc. (Harold)

National City Northwest
Lemieux, Joseph Henry: chairman, chief executive officer, director, Owens-Illinois Inc.

National Convenience Stores Inc.
Fretthold, Timothy Jon: executive vice president, general counsel, director, Ultramar Diamond Shamrock Corp.
Hemminghaus, Roger Roy: chairman, director, Ultramar Diamond Shamrock Corp.
Klesse, William R.: executive vice president operations, Ultramar Diamond Shamrock Corp.

National Defense Corp.
Cohen, Maryjo Rose: president, chief executive officer, director, National Presto Industries, Inc.; vice president, treasurer, trustee, Presto Foundation
Cohen, Melvin Samuel: chairman, National Presto Industries, Inc.; chairman, president, trustee, Presto Foundation

National Diversified Fin
Gaiswinkler, Robert Sigfried: chairman, director, First Financial Bank; director, First Financial Foundation

National Enterprises Inc.
Webb, Charles B., Jr.: vice chairman, United States Sugar Corp.

National Equity Investments Corp.
Gaiswinkler, Robert Sigfried: chairman, director, First Financial Bank; director, First Financial Foundation

National Equity Real Estate Corp.
Gaiswinkler, Robert Sigfried: chairman, director, First Financial Bank; director, First Financial Foundation

National Equity Securities
Gaiswinkler, Robert Sigfried: chairman, director, First Financial Bank; director, First Financial Foundation

National Fire Insurance Co. Hartford
Noha, Edward J.: director, CNA Foundation

National Fire Insurance Hartford
Chookaszian, Dennis Haig: chairman, chief executive officer, CNA

National Fuel Gas Distr Corp.
Ackerman, Philip Charles: senior vice president, director, National Fuel Gas Distribution Corp.
Kennedy, Bernard Joseph: chairman, president, chief executive officer, director, National Fuel Gas Distribution Corp.

National Fuel Gas Supply Corp.
Ackerman, Philip Charles: senior vice president, director, National Fuel Gas Distribution Corp.
Kennedy, Bernard Joseph: chairman, president, chief executive officer, director, National Fuel Gas Distribution Corp.

National Health Care Affiliates Inc.
Alfiero, Salvatore Harry: founder, chairman, chief executive officer, director, Mark IV Industries; chairman, Mark IV Industries Foundation

National Health Laboratories Inc.
Perelman, Ronald Owen: director, Revlon Foundation Inc.

National Holding Investment Co.
Cohen, Maryjo Rose: president, chief executive officer, director, National Presto Industries, Inc.; vice president, treasurer, trustee, Presto Foundation
Cohen, Melvin Samuel: chairman, National Presto Industries, Inc.; chairman, president, trustee, Presto Foundation

National Insurance Wholesalers
Leatherdale, Douglas West: chairman, chief executive officer, president, Saint Paul Companies Inc.

National Legal Pub Interest
Elliott, David Holland: consultant, chairman executive committee, MBIA Inc.

National Life Insurance Co.

Bertrand, Frederic Howard: chairman, Central Vermont Public Service Corp.

National Pipeline Co.

Cohen, Maryjo Rose: president, chief executive officer, director, National Presto Industries, Inc.; vice president, treasurer, trustee, Presto Foundation

National Reinsurance Corp.

Gustafson, James E.: president, chief operating officer, Saint Paul Companies Inc.

National Sanitary Supply Co.

Hutton, Edward L.: chairman, chief executive officer, director, Chemed Corp.

McNamara, Kevin J.: president, director, Chemed Corp.; secretary, trustee, Chemed Foundation

National Service Industries Inc.

Kennedy, James Cox: chairman, chief executive officer, director, Cox Enterprises Inc.; trustee, Cox Foundation (James M.)

Marcus, Bernard: chairman, director, Home Depot, Inc.

National Standard Co.

Sheley, Donald R., Junior: vice president finance, chief financial officer, Standard Products Co.; treasurer, trustee, Standard Products Co. Charitable Foundation

National Surety Corp.

Hansmeyer, Herbert F.: chairman, Fireman's Fund Insurance Co.

Rowe, Thomas E.: chairman, director, Fireman's Fund Foundation; director, Fireman's Fund Insurance Co.

National Tire Battery

Lacy, Alan J.: president credit, Sears, Roebuck and Co.

Martinez, Arthur C.: chairman, chief executive officer, president, Sears, Roebuck and Co.

National Westminster Bank USA

Walters, Peter: chairman, SmithKline Beecham Corp.

Nations Bank Corp.

Suter, Albert E.: senior vice chairman, chief administrative officer, director, Emerson Electric Co.

Nations Energy Corp.

Adler, Ira R.: executive vice president, chief financial officer, Tucson Electric Power Co.

NationsBank Corp.

Bridgewater, Bernard Adolphus, Jr.: member board control, Brown Shoe Co. Charitable Trust; chairman, president, chief executive officer, director, Brown Shoe Co., Inc.

Dickson, Alan Thomas: president, Dickson Foundation; chairman, Ruddick Corp.

Snow, John William: chairman, president, chief executive officer, CSX Corp.

NationsBank Virginia NA

Rhodes, James Thomas: president, chief executive officer, director, Dominion Resources, Inc.

Nationsbank Inc.

Meyer, Russell William, Jr.: chairman, chief executive officer, Cessna Aircraft Co.; president, Cessna Foundation, Inc.

Nationwide Advisory Services

Druen, W. Sidney: director, Nationwide Insurance Enterprise Foundation

Fuellgraf, Charles Louis, Jr.: trustee, Nationwide Insurance Enterprise Foundation

Miller, David O.: chairman, Employers Insurance of Wausau, A Mutual Co.; trustee, Nationwide Insurance Enterprise Foundation; chairman, Wausau Insurance Companies

Shisler, Arden L.: trustee, Nationwide Insurance Enterprise Foundation

Nationwide Beef Inc.

Muchin, Allan B.: chairman, Katten, Muchin & Zavis; director, Katten, Muchin & Zavis Foundation

Nationwide Corp.

Druen, W. Sidney: director, Nationwide Insurance Enterprise Foundation

Shisler, Arden L.: trustee, Nationwide Insurance Enterprise Foundation

Woodward, Robert J., Jr.: executive vice president, chief investment officer, Nationwide Insurance Enterprise Foundation

Nationwide Financial Services

Fuellgraf, Charles Louis, Jr.: trustee, Nationwide Insurance Enterprise Foundation

Miller, David O.: chairman, Employers Insurance of Wausau, A Mutual Co.; trustee, Nationwide Insurance Enterprise Foundation; chairman, Wausau Insurance Companies

Shisler, Arden L.: trustee, Nationwide Insurance Enterprise Foundation

Woodward, Robert J., Jr.: executive vice president, chief investment officer, Nationwide Insurance Enterprise Foundation

Nationwide Financial Services Inc.

Druen, W. Sidney: director, Nationwide Insurance Enterprise Foundation

Nationwide General Insurance Co.

Fuellgraf, Charles Louis, Jr.: trustee, Nationwide Insurance Enterprise Foundation

Miller, David O.: chairman, Employers Insurance of Wausau, A Mutual Co.; trustee, Nationwide Insurance Enterprise Foundation; chairman, Wausau Insurance Companies

Shisler, Arden L.: trustee, Nationwide Insurance Enterprise Foundation

Nationwide Health Properties Inc.

Miller, Charles Daly: chairman, director, Avery Dennison Corp.; trustee, Whirlpool Foundation

Nationwide Insurance Companies

Fuellgraf, Charles Louis, Jr.: trustee, Nationwide Insurance Enterprise Foundation

Nationwide Life Insurance Co.

Miller, David O.: chairman, Employers Insurance of Wausau, A Mutual Co.; trustee, Nationwide Insurance Enterprise Foundation; chairman, Wausau Insurance Companies

Shisler, Arden L.: trustee, Nationwide Insurance Enterprise Foundation

Nationwide Mutual Fire Insurance Co.

Fuellgraf, Charles Louis, Jr.: trustee, Nationwide Insurance Enterprise Foundation

Miller, David O.: chairman, Employers Insurance of Wausau, A Mutual Co.; trustee, Nationwide Insurance Enterprise Foundation; chairman, Wausau Insurance Companies

Shisler, Arden L.: trustee, Nationwide Insurance Enterprise Foundation

Woodward, Robert J., Jr.: executive vice president, chief investment officer, Nationwide Insurance Enterprise Foundation

Nationwide Mutual Insurance Co.

Druen, W. Sidney: director, Nationwide Insurance Enterprise Foundation

Fuellgraf, Charles Louis, Jr.: trustee, Nationwide Insurance Enterprise Foundation

Miller, David O.: chairman, Employers Insurance of Wausau, A Mutual Co.; trustee, Nationwide Insurance Enterprise Foundation; chairman, Wausau Insurance Companies

Woodward, Robert J., Jr.: executive vice president, chief investment officer, Nationwide Insurance Enterprise Foundation

Naturalite

Rutledge, Ronald E.: executive, Butler Manufacturing Co.

Navistar International Corp.

Correnti, John D.: president, chief executive officer, director, Nucor Corp.

Neiman Marcus

Geller, Eric P.: trustee, Harcourt General Charitable Foundation; senior vice president, general counsel, secretary, Harcourt General, Inc.

Neiman Marcus Group Helmsman Management Services

Countryman, Gary Lee: chairman, Liberty Mutual Insurance Group

Neiman Marcus Group Inc.

Ives, J. Atwood: chairman, chief executive officer, Boston Gas Co.; chairman, chief executive officer, trustee, Eastern Enterprises; trustee, Eastern Enterprises Foundation

Skoda, Daniel: president, Marshall Field's

Smith, Richard Alan: treasurer, director, Arvin Foundation; chairman, director, chief executive officer, Harcourt General, Inc.

Smith, Robert A.: trustee, Harcourt General Charitable Foundation; co-chief executive officer, director, president, Harcourt General, Inc.

Nellcor Puritan Bennett Inc.

Nichols, Mack G.: president, chief executive officer, director, Mallinckrodt Chemical, Inc.

Nestle Holdings Inc.

Ball, James Herington: senior vice president, general counsel, director, Nestle U.S.A. Inc.

Crull, Timm F.: retired chairman, Nestle U.S.A. Inc.

Nestle United States of America Beverage Division

Argentine, Peter Dominic: executive vice president, chief financial officer, Nestle U.S.A. Inc.

Nestles Frozen Food Co.

Ball, James Herington: senior vice president, general counsel, director, Nestle U.S.A. Inc.

Network Horizons Inc.

Alton, Robert D., Jr.: chairman, president, chief executive officer, Hickory Tech Corp.; trustee, Hickory Tech Corp. Foundation

Network Imaging Corp.

Ripp, Robert M.: chairman, chief executive officer, director, AMP Inc.

Neuman Health Services

Hanson, Jon F.: trustee, Prudential Foundation

New Century Energies Inc.

Hemminghaus, Roger Roy: chairman, director, Ultramar Diamond Shamrock Corp.

Wilks, David M.: vice president, New Century Energies Foundation

New Century Enterprises

Helton, Bill D.: chairman, New Century Energies Foundation

New Century Services

Wilks, David M.: vice president, New Century Energies Foundation

New Century Services Inc.

Helton, Bill D.: chairman, New Century Energies Foundation

New Discovery Inc.

Hofmann, Kenneth H.: president, director, Hofmann Co.; president, Hofmann Foundation

Shaw, Albert T.: president, Hofmann Co.; director, Hofmann Foundation

New England Electric System

Kucharski, John Michael: trustee, PerkinElmer Foundation; chairman, chief executive officer, director, PerkinElmer, Inc.

New England Guaranty Insurance Co.

Bertrand, Frederic Howard: chairman, Central Vermont Public Service Corp.

New England Investment Companies LP

Kamen, Harry Paul: chairman, president, chief executive officer, Metropolitan Life Insurance Co.

New England Mail Order Association

Trask, Robert B.: president, chief operating officer, director, Country Curtains, Inc.; clerk, trustee, High Meadow Foundation

New Era of Networks

Kasputys, Joseph Edward: chairman, trustee, Hitachi Foundation

New Horizons Madonna Hall

Cudlip, Brittain B.: chairman, Bardes Corp.

Cummings, William S.: chairman, Cummings Properties Management

New Jersey Business & Industry

Howe, Wesley Jackson: chairman emeritus, director, Becton Dickinson & Co.

New Jersey Energy Co.

Downes, Laurence M.: president, chief executive officer, director, chairman, New Jersey Natural Gas Co.; trustee, New Jersey Natural Gas Foundation

New Jersey Manufacturers Insurance Co.

Howe, Wesley Jackson: chairman emeritus, director, Becton Dickinson & Co.

New Jersey Natural Energy Co.

Downes, Laurence M.: president, chief executive officer, director, chairman, New Jersey Natural Gas Co.; trustee, New Jersey Natural Gas Foundation

Harden, Oleta J.: secretary, New Jersey Natural Gas Foundation

New Jersey Natural Gas Co.

Downes, Laurence M.: president, chief executive officer, director, chairman, New Jersey Natural Gas Co.; trustee, New Jersey Natural Gas Foundation

New Jersey Resources Corp.

Kononowitz, Thomas J.: vice president, New Jersey Natural Gas Foundation

New Jersey Utilities Association

Baldassari, Dennis P.: president, chief operating officer, GPU Energy

New Morgan Landfill Co.

Ranck, Bruce E.: president, chief executive officer, director, Browning-Ferris Industries Inc.

New World Television

Gittis, Howard: director, Revlon Foundation Inc.

New York Life Equity Corp.

Gammill, Lee Morgan, Jr.: director, New York Life Foundation; vice chairman, director, New York Life Insurance Co.

New York Life Insurance

Broadhead, James Lowell: chairman, president, chief executive officer, director, Florida Power & Light Co.; chief executive officer, director, FPL Group Foundation, Inc.

New York Life Insurance & Annuity Corp.

Gammill, Lee Morgan, Jr.: director, New York Life Foundation; vice chairman, director, New York Life Insurance Co.

New York Life Insurance Co.

Douglas, Paul W.: director, Phelps Dodge Foundation

Foster, Kent B.: president, director, GTE Corp.; trustee, GTE Foundation

Gelb, Richard Lee: director, New York Times Co. Foundation

Hohn, Harry George, Jr.: chairman, director, New York Life Foundation

New York Life Realty Corp.

Gammill, Lee Morgan, Jr.: director, New York Life Foundation; vice chairman, director, New York Life Insurance Co.

New York Life Securities Corp.

Gammill, Lee Morgan, Jr.: director, New York Life Foundation; vice chairman, director, New York Life Insurance Co.

New York Mercantile Exchange

Wise, William Allen: chairman, president, chief executive officer, director, El Paso Energy Co.; chairman, director, El Paso Energy Foundation

New York Stock Exchange Inc.

Ayer, Ramani: chairman, president, chief executive officer, Hartford (The)

Jannotta, Edgar D.: president, Blair & Co. Foundation (William); senior director, Blair & Co. (William)

Komansky, David H.: trustee, vice president, Merrill Lynch & Co. Foundation Inc.; chairman, chief executive officer, Merrill Lynch & Co., Inc.

Larsen, Ralph Stanley: chairman, president, chief executive officer, director, Johnson & Johnson

Mark, Reuben: chairman, chief executive officer, Colgate-Palmolive Co.

Maughan, Deryck C.: director, New York Stock Exchange Foundation, Inc.; co-chairman, co-chief executive officer, Salomon Smith Barney

O'Reilly, F. Anthony John: chairman, trustee, Heinz Co. Foundation (H.J.); chairman, director, Heinz Co. (H.J.)

Paton, Leland B.: president capital marketings, director, member executive committee, Prudential Securities Inc.

New York Subways Advertising Co. Inc.

McCorkindale, Douglas H.: vice chairman, president, Gannett Co., Inc.; president, Gannett Foundation

New York Times Co.

Lawrence, Robert Ashton: director, New York Times Co. Foundation

Price, Charles H., II: director, New York Times Co. Foundation

Taylor, William Osgood: chairman, chief executive officer, director, Boston Globe (The); chairman, director, Boston Globe Foundation; director, New York Times Co. Foundation

New York Times Co. Inc.

Gelb, Richard Lee: director, New York Times Co. Foundation

Sulzberger, Judith P., MD: director, New York Times Co. Foundation

New York University Medical Center

Steere, William Campbell, Jr.: chairman, chief executive officer, director, Pfizer Inc.

Newaygo Timber Co. Ltd.

Mead, George Wilson, II: president, director, Consolidated Papers Foundation, Inc.; chairman, director, Consolidated Papers, Inc.

Newbridge Latin American LLP

Franke, William Augustus: chairman, president, chief executive officer, America West Airlines, Inc.; director, Phelps Dodge Foundation

Newhall Land & Farming Co.

Sutton, Thomas C.: chairman, director, Pacific Mutual Charitable Foundation; chairman, chief executive officer, director, Pacific Mutual Life Insurance Co.

Zilkha, Ezra Khedouri: president, treasurer, Zilkha Foundation, Inc.; president, Zilkha & Sons

Newmans Own Inc.

Gerard, Jamie K.: attorney, Newman's Own Foundation

Newport News Shipbuilding & Drydock

Mead, Dana George: chairman, chief executive officer, director, Tenneco Automotive

News Publishing Co. Inc.

Jones, Ross: senior vice president, chief financial officer, Knight Ridder

News-Press Publishing Co.

McCorkindale, Douglas H.: vice chairman, president, Gannett Co., Inc.; president, Gannett Foundation

Newspaper First
Ridder, Paul Anthony: chairman, chief executive officer, director, Knight Ridder

Newspaper Services America Inc.
Geier, Philip Henry, Jr.: chairman, president, chief executive officer, Interpublic Group of Companies, Inc.

NiSource Inc.
Morris, James Thomas: director, AUL Foundation Inc.

Niagara Fire Insurance Co.
Chookaszian, Dennis Haig: chairman, chief executive officer, CNA

Sharkey, William Henry, Jr.: director, CNA Foundation

Niagara Mohawk Power Corp.
Alfiero, Salvatore Harry: founder, chairman, chief executive officer, director, Mark IV Industries; chairman, Mark IV Industries Foundation

Hill, Bonnie Guiton: vice president, Times Mirror Co.; president, chief executive officer, Times Mirror Foundation

Niagara Recycling Inc.
Ranck, Bruce E.: president, chief executive officer, director, Browning-Ferris Industries Inc.

Nicolet Instrument Corp.
Kelleher, Paul F.: committee member, Thermo Electron Foundation

Nicor Inc.
Rau, John E.: trustee, Chicago Title and Trust Co. Foundation

Toll, Daniel Roger: trustee, Kemper Foundation (James S.)

Nike International Ltd.
Clarke, Thomas E.: president, chief operating officer, Nike, Inc.

Knight, Philip Hampson: chairman, chief executive officer, Nike, Inc.

Nittany Printing & Publishing Co. Inc.
Jones, Ross: senior vice president, chief financial officer, Knight Ridder

Nokia Corp.
Collins, Paul John: vice chairman, director, Citibank Corp.

Noran Instrument Inc.
Aghababian, Robert V.: committee member, Thermo Electron Foundation

Kelleher, Paul F.: committee member, Thermo Electron Foundation

Nord Resources Corp.
Frydryk, Karl S.: trustee, Monarch Machine Tool Co. Foundation

Nordic-America Travel Inc.
Carlson, Curtis Leroy: chairman, director, Carlson Companies, Inc.; president, treasurer, Carlson Family Foundation (Curtis L.)

Nordson Corp.
Hardis, Stephen Roger: chairman, chief executive officer, director, Eaton Corp.

Nordstrom Inc.
Condit, Philip Murray: chairman, chief executive officer, director, Boeing Co.

Ruckelshaus, William Doyle: chairman, director, Browning-Ferris Industries Inc.

Norfolk & Western RY Co.
Wolf, Henry C.: vice chairman, chief financial officer, Norfolk Southern Corp.; vice president finance, Norfolk Southern Foundation

Norfolk Southern Properties
Wolf, Henry C.: vice chairman, chief financial officer, Norfolk Southern Corp.; vice president finance, Norfolk Southern Foundation

Norfolk Southern Railway Co.
Tobias, Steven C.: vice chairman, chief operating officer, Norfolk Southern Corp.; director, Norfolk Southern Foundation

Wolf, Henry C.: vice chairman, chief financial officer, Norfolk Southern Corp.; vice president finance, Norfolk Southern Foundation

Norfolk Virginian-Pilot & Ledger Star
Batten, Frank, Sr.: chairman, director, Landmark Communications Foundation; chairman, Landmark Communications Inc.

Norris Cylinder Co.
Manoogian, Richard Alexander: chairman, chief executive officer, director, Masco Corp.

Nortel (Northern Telecom)
Schuenke, Donald John: director, Freddie Mac

North America Finance Corp.
Carlson, Curtis Leroy: chairman, director, Carlson Companies, Inc.; president, treasurer, Carlson Family Foundation (Curtis L.)

North America Publs Inc.
Morris, William Shivers, III: founder, chairman, chief executive officer, director, Morris Communications Corp.; trustee, Stauffer Communications Foundation

North American Green Inc.
Koch, Robert Louis, II: president, chief executive officer, director, Koch Enterprises, Inc.; president, director, Koch Foundation

North American Resources Co.
Gannon, Robert P.: chairman, president, director, chief executive officer, Montana Power Co.; president, director, Montana Power Foundation

Pederson, Jerrold P.: vice president, chief financial officer, director, Montana Power Co.; director, Montana Power Foundation

Senechal, Ellen M.: treasurer, Montana Power Co.

Zimmerman, Michael E.: vice president, general counsel, Montana Power Co.

North Atlantic Life Insurance Co.
Hale, James Thomas: senior vice president, general counsel, secretary, Dayton Hudson; trustee, Target Foundation

North Shore Gas Co.
Hasch, J. Bruce: president, chief operating officer, director, Peoples Energy Corp.

Terry, Richard Edward: chairman, chief executive officer, director, Peoples Energy Corp.

North Star Mall Inc.
Deering, Anthony W.: chairman, chief executive officer, Rouse Co.; chairman, president, trustee, Rouse Co. Foundation

Donahue, Jeffrey H.: senior vice president, chief financial officer, Rouse Co.

McGregor, Douglas A.: trustee, Rouse Co. Foundation

North Star Steel Co.
Thayer, Tyrone K.: corp. vice president, Cargill Inc.

North Trust Corp.
Burnham, Duane Lee: chairman, chief executive officer, director, Abbott Laboratories

Northbrook Property & Casualty Insurance
Choate, Jerry D.: chairman, chief executive officer, director, Allstate Foundation

Northeast Asphalt Inc.
Bechtold, Ned W.: director, Firstar Milwaukee Foundation

Northern Illinois Gas Co.
Toll, Daniel Roger: trustee, Kemper Foundation (James S.)

Northern Life Insurance Co.
Turner, John Gosney: chairman, chief executive officer, director, ReliaStar Financial Corp.; director, ReliaStar Foundation

Northern Studies Power Co.
Ferrari, Giannantonio A.: director, Honeywell Foundation; president, chief operating officer, director, Honeywell International Inc.

Kovacevich, Richard M.: chairman, president, chief executive officer, Norwest Corp.; director, Norwest Foundation

Leatherdale, Douglas West: chairman, chief executive officer, president, Saint Paul Companies Inc.

Schuman, Allan L.: president, chief executive officer, director, chairman, Ecolab Inc.

Northern Telecom Ltd.
Schuenke, Donald John: director, Freddie Mac

Northern Trust Corp.
Mooney, Edward J., Jr.: chairman, president, chief executive officer, director, Nalco Chemical Co.

Northfield Laboratories Inc.
Chelberg, Bruce Stanley: chairman, chief executive officer, director, Whitman Corp.; director, Whitman Corp. Foundation

Northrop Grumman Corp.
Chain, John T., Junior: trustee, Kemper Foundation (James S.); president, Kemper National Insurance Companies

Rosenberg, Richard Morris: chairman, chief executive officer (retired), Bank of America

Northstar Investment Management Corp.
Turner, John Gosney: chairman, chief executive officer, director, ReliaStar Financial Corp.; director, ReliaStar Foundation

Northwest Central Pipeline Co.
Bailey, Keith E.: chairman, president, director, chief executive officer, Texas Gas Transmission Corp.; president, director, Williams Companies Foundation (The)

Northwest Electric Light & Power Association

Keen, J. LaMont: vice president, chief financial officer, Idaho Power Co.

Northwest Pipeline Corp.

Bailey, Keith E.: chairman, president, director, chief executive officer, Texas Gas Transmission Corp.; president, director, Williams Companies Foundation (The)

Northwest Publications Inc.

Jones, Ross: senior vice president, chief financial officer, Knight Ridder

Tobias, Randall L.: chairman emeritus, Lilly & Co. (Eli)

Northwestern Membership Hospital

Shapiro, Robert B.: chairman, president, chief executive officer, director, Monsanto Co.

Northwestern Memorial Hospital

Martinez, Arthur C.: chairman, chief executive officer, president, Sears, Roebuck and Co.

Northwestern Mutual Life Insurance Co.

Graff, Stephen Ney: director, Bucyrus-Erie Foundation

Graham, Patricia Albjerg, PhD: trustee, Hitachi Foundation

Wright, James O.: president, director, Badger Meter Foundation; chairman, director, Badger Meter, Inc.; director, Marshall & Ilsley Foundation, Inc.

Northwestern Resources Co.

Senechal, Ellen M.: treasurer, Montana Power Co.

Northwood Pulp & Timber Ltd.

Correll, Alston Dayton 'Pete', Jr.: chairman, president, chief executive officer, director, Georgia-Pacific Corp.; director, Georgia-Pacific Foundation

Northwoods RV Country Inc.

Corson, Keith Daniel: president, chief operating officer, Coachmen Industries, Inc.

Norton

Meyerson, Martin: director, Panasonic Foundation

Norton Chemical Process Products Corp.

Ayotte, Robert C.: executive vice president, director, CertainTeed Corp.; vice president, director, Norton Co. Foundation

Norton Co.

Amoss, George B.: vice president finance, chief financial officer, CertainTeed Corp.; chief financial officer, CertainTeed Corp. Foundation

Caccini, Gianpaolo: chairman, chief executive officer, director, CertainTeed Corp.; chairman, CertainTeed Corp. Foundation; chairman, chief executive officer, director, Norton Co.; president, director, Norton Co. Foundation

Harkins, James F., Jr.: treasurer, CertainTeed Corp. Foundation

Norton Performance Plastics

Ayotte, Robert C.: executive vice president, director, CertainTeed Corp.; vice president, director, Norton Co. Foundation

Harkins, James F., Jr.: treasurer, CertainTeed Corp. Foundation

Norwest Bank

Hadley, Leonard Anson: chairman, chief executive officer, director, Maytag Corp.; president, trustee, Maytag Corp. Foundation

Hewitt, James Watt: vice president, treasurer, Abel Foundation

Hultgren, Dennis N.: director, Appleton Papers Inc.

Norwest Bank Iowa NA

Pomerantz, Marvin Alvin: trustee, Mid-American Foundation

Rehm, Jack Daniel: chairman emeritus, director, Meredith Corp.

Norwest Bank Minnesota NA

Thornton, John T.: executive vice president, chief financial officer, Norwest Corp.; treasurer, Norwest Foundation

Norwest Bank Nevada

Maffie, Michael O.: president, chief executive officer, director, Southwest Gas Corp.; trustee, Southwest Gas Corp. Foundation

Norwest Corp.

Blanchard, J. A., III: president, chief executive officer, director, Deluxe Corp.

Wright, Michael William: chairman, president, chief executive officer, director, SuperValu, Inc.

Norwest Financial Service

Stroup, Stanley Stephenson: executive vice president, general counsel, Norwest Corp.

Norwest Ltd. Inc.

Thornton, John T.: executive vice president, chief financial officer, Norwest Corp.; treasurer, Norwest Foundation

Norwest Nova Inc.

Thornton, John T.: executive vice president, chief financial officer, Norwest Corp.; treasurer, Norwest Foundation

Norwest Venture Capital Management Inc.

Thornton, John T.: executive vice president, chief financial officer, Norwest Corp.; treasurer, Norwest Foundation

Nova Care Inc.

Bewley, Peter D.: vice president, secretary, Clorox Co. Foundation

Marshall, Siri M.: trustee, General Mills Foundation; senior vice president, general counsel, General Mills, Inc.

Nova Chemicals Inc.

Holaday, G. Stephen: senior vice president, Alexander & Baldwin, Inc.

Nuclear Electric Initiatives Ltd.

Graham, John Gourlay: chief financial officer, senior vice president, GPU Energy

Nucor Bearing Products

Iverson, Francis Kenneth: chairman, director, Nucor Corp.; director, Nucor Foundation

NutraSweet Kelco Co. Inc.

Shapiro, Robert B.: chairman, president, chief executive officer, director, Monsanto Co.

O'Sullivan Corp.

Burrus, Robert Lewis, Jr.: trustee, Circuit City Foundation

OGE Energy Corp.

Durrett, William E.: senior chairman, American Fidelity Corp.; president, American Fidelity Corp. Founders Fund

OPUBCO Development Co.

Gaylord, Edward Lewis: chairman, chief executive officer, director, publisher, Oklahoma Publishing Co.; trustee, Oklahoman Foundation (The)

OPUBCO International Ltd.

Gaylord, Edward Lewis: chairman, chief executive officer, director, publisher, Oklahoma Publishing Co.; trustee, Oklahoman Foundation (The)

OPUBCO Properties Inc.

Gaylord, Edward Lewis: chairman, chief executive officer, director, publisher, Oklahoma Publishing Co.; trustee, Oklahoman Foundation (The)

OPUBCO Resources Inc.

Gaylord, Edward Lewis: chairman, chief executive officer, director, publisher, Oklahoma Publishing Co.; trustee, Oklahoman Foundation (The)

ORMEC

Rosett, Richard Nathaniel: trustee, Kemper Foundation (James S.)

Oahu Transit Service Inc.

Guerrero, Anthony R., Jr.: director, First Hawaiian Foundation

Oak Hill Sportswear Corp.

Slovin, Bruce: president, director, Revlon Inc.

Oakleys Catering LLC

Parfet, Donald R.: president, Pharmacia & Upjohn Foundation; senior vice president associated business, Pharmacia & Upjohn, Inc.

Observer Transportation Co.

Jones, Ross: senior vice president, chief financial officer, Knight Ridder

Occidental Chemical Holding Corp.

Laurance, Dale R.: director, Occidental Petroleum Charitable Foundation; president, senior operations officer, director, Occidental Petroleum Corp.

Occidental Petrochemicals Inc.

Laurance, Dale R.: director, Occidental Petroleum Charitable Foundation; president, senior operations officer, director, Occidental Petroleum Corp.

Occidental Petroleum Corp.

Groman, Arthur: president, Occidental Petroleum Charitable Foundation

Laurance, Dale R.: director, Occidental Petroleum Charitable Foundation; president, senior operations officer, director, Occidental Petroleum Corp.

Tomich, Rosemary: director, Occidental Petroleum Charitable Foundation

Oceanic Cablevision

Dods, Walter Arthur, Jr.: president, director, First Hawaiian Foundation; chairman, chief executive officer, director, First Hawaiian, Inc.

Office Exptl Research Development Incentives

Pierre, Percy A.: trustee, Hitachi Foundation

Oglebay Norton Co.

Bares, William G.: chairman, president, chief executive officer, Lubrizol Corp. (The); trustee, Lubrizol Foundation (The)

Bersticker, Albert C.: chairman, director, chief executive officer, Ferro Corp.; president, trustee, Ferro Foundation

Ohanui Corp.

Sasaki, Robert K.: director, Alexander & Baldwin Foundation

Ohio CAP Insurance Co. Ltd.

Klinedinst, Thomas John, Jr.: trustee, Star Bank NA, Cincinnati Foundation

Ohio Citizens Bank

Lemieux, Joseph Henry: chairman, chief executive officer, director, Owens-Illinois Inc.

Ohio Edison Co.

Holland, Willard R.: chairman, chief executive officer, FirstEnergy Corp.

Powers, Paul Joseph: chairman, president, chief executive officer, director, Commercial Intertech Corp.; president, trustee, Commercial Intertech Foundation

Smart, George M.: trustee, Commercial Intertech Foundation

Ohio National Financial Services

Burleigh, William Robert: president, chief executive officer, director, Scripps Co. (E.W.); member, Scripps Howard Foundation

Ohio Power Co.

Draper, Ernest Linn, Jr.: chairman, president, chief executive officer, director, American Electric Power

Lhota, William J.: executive vice president, American Electric Power

Ohio River Co.

Raskin, Fred C.: president, chief operating officer, Eastern Enterprises; trustee, Eastern Enterprises Foundation

Ohio Valley Electric Corp.

Draper, Ernest Linn, Jr.: chairman, president, chief executive officer, director, American Electric Power

Lhota, William J.: executive vice president, American Electric Power

Oil Dynamics

Lawson, William Hogan, III: chairman, chief executive officer, director, Franklin Electric Co.; president, Franklin Electric, Edward J. Schaefer, and T. W. KehoeCharitable and Educational Foundation

Oil-Dri Corp. America

Jannotta, Edgar D.: president, Blair & Co. Foundation (William); senior director, Blair & Co. (William)

Oklahoma Gas & Electric Co.

Strecker, A. M.: vice president, director, Oklahoma Gas & Electric Co. Foundation

Oklahoma Press Publishing Co.

McCorkindale, Douglas H.: vice chairman, president, Gannett Co., Inc.; president, Gannett Foundation

Old Kent Bank

Pierre, Percy A.: trustee, Hitachi Foundation

Wagner, David J.: chairman, president, chief executive officer, Old Kent Bank; treasurer, Old Kent Foundation

Old Kent Financial Corp.

Meijer, Hendrik G.: co-chairman, director, Meijer, Inc.

Pew, Robert Cunningham, II: trustee, Steelcase Foundation

Pierre, Percy A.: trustee, Hitachi Foundation

Olin Asahi Interconnect Tech

Rompala, Richard M.: president, chief executive officer, director, chairman, Valspar Corp.; vice president, Valspar Foundation

Olin Corp.

Ratcliffe, George Jackson, Jr.: trustee, Hubbell Foundation (Harvey); chairman, president, chief executive officer, Hubbell Inc.

Rompala, Richard M.: president, chief executive officer, director, chairman, Valspar Corp.; vice president, Valspar Foundation

Oliver Rubber Co.

Zampetis, Theodore K.: president, chief operating officer, director, Standard Products Co.

Olsten Milwaukee Inc.

Loos, Henry J.: secretary, Charter Manufacturing Co. Foundation

Omaha Airport Authority

Weekly, John William: chairman, chief executive officer, Mutual of Omaha Insurance Co.

Omaha Indemnity Co.

Sturgeon, John: president, chief operating officer, Mutual of Omaha Insurance Co.

Omaha Property & Casualty Insurance Co.

Weekly, John William: chairman, chief executive officer, Mutual of Omaha Insurance Co.

Omega Health System

Murphy, Christopher J., III: president, chief executive officer, director, First Source Corp.; director, First Source Foundation

Omnicare

Hutton, Edward L.: chairman, chief executive officer, director, Chemed Corp.

McNamara, Kevin J.: president, director, Chemed Corp.; secretary, trustee, Chemed Foundation

On-Point Tech Systems

Robinson, John H.: treasurer, secretary, Carter Star Telegram Employees Fund (Amon G.)

Oneok Inc.

Fricke, Howard R.: president, director, Security Benefit Life Insurance Co.; trustee, Security Benefit Life Insurance Co. Charitable Trust

Onix Systems Inc.

Kelleher, Paul F.: committee member, Thermo Electron Foundation

Ontario Power Generation Inc.

Sawchuck, Arthur: chairman, director, Manulife Financial

Opinac Energy

Davis, William E.: chairman, chief executive officer, Niagara Mohawk Holdings Inc.

Oppenheimer Acquisition Corp.

Wendlandt, Gary Edward: executive vice president, chief investment officer, Massachusetts Mutual Life Insurance Co.

Wheeler, Thomas Beardsley: chairman, chief executive officer, Massachusetts Mutual Life Insurance Co.

Opportunity Capital Partners

Coulter, David A.: president, director, Bank of America

Opryland USA Inc.

Gaylord, Edward Lewis: chairman, chief executive officer, director, publisher, Oklahoma Publishing Co.; trustee, Oklahoman Foundation (The)

Option Care Inc.

Stone, Roger Warren: chairman, president, chief executive officer, director, Stone Container Corp.; president, Stone Foundation

Opus United States Corp.

Bechtold, Ned W.: director, Firstar Milwaukee Foundation

Oracle Corp.

Lucas, Donald Leo: chairman, Cadence Designs Systems, Inc.

Orange & Rockland Utilities Inc.

Hanson, Jon F.: trustee, Prudential Foundation

Orbital Sciences Corp.

Salizzoni, Frank L.: vice chairman, Block Foundation (H&R); president, chief executive officer, director, Block, Inc. (H&R)

Orbseal LLC

Orscheln, Donald W.: director, chairman, Orscheln Co.; secretary, Orscheln Industries Foundation, Inc.

Orscheln, Gerald A.: president, Orscheln Industries Foundation, Inc.

Ore-Ida Foods Inc.

O'Reilly, F. Anthony John: chairman, trustee, Heinz Co. Foundation (H.J.); chairman, director, Heinz Co. (H.J.)

Orscheln Co.

Orscheln, William L.: treasurer, Orscheln Industries Foundation, Inc.

Oryx Energy Co.

Thompson, Robert L.: vice president public affairs, Springs Industries, Inc.

Oshkosh Truck Corporation

Hebe, James L.: chairman, president, chief executive officer, Freightliner Corp.

Ottaway Newspapers Inc.

Burenga, Kenneth L.: president, chief operating officer, director, Dow Jones & Co., Inc.

Ottaway, James Haller, Jr.: senior vice president, director, Dow Jones & Co., Inc.; member advisory committee, Dow Jones Foundation

Outboard Marine Corp.

Marriott, J. Willard, Jr.: chairman, chief executive officer, Marriott International Inc.

Overnite Corp.

Suggs, Leo H.: director, chairman, chief executive officer, Overnite Transportation Co.

Overseas Bechtel Inc.

Bechtel, Riley Peart: chairman, Bechtel Foundation; chairman, chief executive officer, director, Bechtel Group, Inc.

Overseas Shipholding Group Inc.

Fribourg, Michel: chairman emeritus, director, Continental Grain Co.; president, director, Continental Grain Foundation

Oversees Partner Ltd.

Clanin, Robert J.: senior vice president, chief financial officer, treasurer, director, United Parcel Service of America Inc.

Owens & Minor Inc.

Rogers, James E., Jr.: vice chairman, president, chief executive officer, Cinergy Corp.; vice chairman, director, Cinergy Foundation

Ukrop, James E.: vice chairman, chief executive officer, director, Ukrop Foundation; vice chairman, chief executive officer, Ukrop's Super Markets

Owensboro Messenger Inquirer

Decherd, Robert William: chairman, president, chief executive officer, director, Belo Corp. (A.H.); chairman, trustee, Belo Corp. Foundation (A.H.)

Oxford Industries Inc.

Rogers, C. B., Jr.: chairman, Equifax Foundation; chairman, director, Equifax Inc.

Shaw, Robert E.: chairman, chief executive officer, Shaw Industries Inc.

Wood, Edward Jenner: member, SunTrust Bank Atlanta Foundation

Oxford University Press

Brademas, John: chairman, Texaco Foundation

Oximetrix De Puerto Rico Inc.

Burnham, Duane Lee: chairman, chief executive officer, director, Abbott Laboratories

P H Glatfelter Co.

Smoot, Richard Leonard: chairman, PNC Bank

PACCAR Inc.

Pitts, John Wilson: director, PACCAR Foundation

Reed, William Garrard, Jr.: director, Matlock Foundation

Wagner, Harold A.: chairman, president, chief executive officer, director, Air Products and Chemicals, Inc.

Wiborg, James Hooker: director, PACCAR Foundation

PC Service Inc.

Watanabe, Jeffrey N.: director, Hawaiian Electric Industries Charitable Foundation

PCA International Inc.

Dickson, Rush Stuart: chairman, Dickson Foundation

PECO Energy Co.

Elliott, R. Keith: chief executive officer, president, Hercules Inc.

Subin, Robert: senior vice president, Campbell Soup Co.

PFL Life Insurance Co.

Kolsrud, Douglas C.: executive vice president, chief investment officer, AEGON U.S.A. Inc.

PG Pub Co.

Block, John Robinson: vice president, trustee, Blade Foundation

PG Publishing Co.

Block, Allan James: vice president, trustee, Blade Foundation; director, Toledo Blade Co.

Block, William: vice president, trustee, Blade Foundation; chairman, director, Toledo Blade Co.

PG&E Corp.

Coulter, David A.: president, director, Bank of America

PH Glatfelter Co.

Chappell, Robert E.: chairman, chief executive officer, Penn Mutual Life Insurance Co.

PHH Corp.

Shepard, Donald James: chairman, president, chief executive officer, AEGON U.S.A. Inc.

PIMCO Advisor LP

Schafer, Glenn Stanley: president, director, Pacific Mutual Life Insurance Co.

PK Lumber

Robinette, Gary: president, Erb Lumber Co.

PM Group Life Insurance Co.

Carmichael, David R.: senior vice president, general counsel, director, Pacific Mutual Life Insurance Co.

Sutton, Thomas C.: chairman, director, Pacific Mutual Charitable Foundation; chairman, chief executive officer, director, Pacific Mutual Life Insurance Co.

PMI

Liddy, Edward M.: vice president, trustee, Allstate Foundation; president, chief operating officer, director, Allstate Insurance Co.

PMI Group Inc.

Liddy, Edward M.: vice president, trustee, Allstate Foundation; president, chief operating officer, director, Allstate Insurance Co.

PNC Bancorp Inc.

Gregg, Walter Emmor, Junior: senior executive vice president finance & administration, PNC Financial Services Group

PNC Bank Corp.

Chellgren, Paul Wilbur: chief executive officer, chairman, director, Ashland, Inc.; member, Ashland Inc. Foundation

Gregg, Walter Emmor, Junior: senior executive vice president finance & administration, PNC Financial Services Group

Hale, Roger W.: chairman, chief executive officer, director, LG&E Energy Corp.; president, LG&E Energy Foundation

McClelland, William Craig: trustee, Union Camp Charitable Trust; chairman, chief executive officer, director, Union Camp Corp.

Randolph, Jackson Harold: chairman, Cinergy Corp.; chairman, director, Cinergy Foundation

Simmons, Richard Paul: chairman, president, chief executive officer, Allegheny Technologies Inc.

Usher, Thomas J.: chairman, chief executive officer, USX Corp.; chairman board trustees, USX Foundation, Inc.

Wehmeier, Helge H.: president, chief executive officer, director, Bayer Corp.

PNC Bank Kentucky Inc.

Chellgren, Paul Wilbur: chief executive officer, chairman, director, Ashland, Inc.; member, Ashland Inc. Foundation

PNC Bank National Association

Rohr, James Edward: chief executive officer, president, director, PNC Financial Services Group

PNC Bridge Capital Inc.

Gregg, Walter Emmor, Junior: senior executive vice president finance & administration, PNC Financial Services Group

PNC Corp.

Randolph, Jackson Harold: chairman, Cinergy Corp.; chairman, director, Cinergy Foundation

PNC Fin Corp.

McClelland, William Craig: trustee, Union Camp Charitable Trust; chairman, chief executive officer, director, Union Camp Corp.

PNC Mortgage Bank National Association

Rohr, James Edward: chief executive officer, president, director, PNC Financial Services Group

PNC Venture Corp.

Gregg, Walter Emmor, Junior: senior executive vice president finance & administration, PNC Financial Services Group

PP&G Industries Inc.

Davis, Erroll Brown, Jr.: president, chief executive officer, director, Wisconsin Power & Light Co.

Usher, Thomas J.: chairman, chief executive officer, USX Corp.; chairman board trustees, USX Foundation, Inc.

Whitwam, David Ray: chairman, president, chief executive officer, director, Whirlpool Corp.

PP&L Global

Hecht, William F.: chairman, president, chief executive officer, Pennsylvania Power & Light

PS Colorado Credit Corp.

Hock, Delwin D.: chairman, New Century Energies

PSB Bancshares

Moore, Jackson W.: president, director, Union Planters Corp.

PSCO

Helton, Bill D.: chairman, New Century Energies Foundation

PSEG Energy Technologies Inc.

Ferland, E. James: chairman, president, chief executive officer, Public Service Electric & Gas Co.

PSI Energy Argentina Inc.

Foley, Cheryl M.: vice president, secretary, general counsel, Cinergy Corp.; vice president, secretary, director, Cinergy Foundation

PSI Energy Inc.

Foley, Cheryl M.: vice president, secretary, general counsel, Cinergy Corp.; vice president, secretary, director, Cinergy Foundation

Mutz, John M.: vice president, Cinergy Corp.; director, Cinergy Foundation

PSI Resources Inc.

Mutz, John M.: vice president, Cinergy Corp.; director, Cinergy Foundation

PSR Investments Inc.

Hock, Delwin D.: chairman, New Century Energies

PXRE Corp.

Fiondella, Robert William: chairman, president, chief executive officer, Phoenix Home Life Mutual Insurance Co.

Pacer Infotec Inc.

Niebla, J. Fernando: chairman, chief executive officer, Pacific Mutual Life Insurance Co.

PacifiCare California

Bowlus, Brad A.: member, PacifiCare Health System Foundation

PacifiCare Life Health Insurance

Hartshorn, Terry O'Dell: chairman, PacifiCare Health System Foundation

PacifiCare Operation Inc.

Bowlus, Brad A.: member, PacifiCare Health System Foundation

PacifiCare Operations

Hartshorn, Terry O'Dell: chairman, PacifiCare Health System Foundation

PacifiCare Oregon

Hoops, Alan R.: member, PacifiCare Health System Foundation

Pacific & Southern Co. Inc.

McCorkindale, Douglas H.: vice chairman, president, Gannett Co., Inc.; president, Gannett Foundation

Pacific America Income Shares Inc.

Bryson, John E.: chairman, chief executive officer, Edison International

Simpson, Louis Allen: president, chief executive officer capital operations, director, GEICO Corp.

Pacific Basin Economic Council

Tambakeras, Markos I.: director, Honeywell Foundation

Pacific Coast Beverage Distribution

Gallo, Joseph E.: co-president, Gallo Foundation

Pacific Coast Gas Association

Felsinger, Donald E.: president, chief executive officer, Sempra Energy

Pacific Electricord Co.

Amsterdam, Jack: secretary, treasurer, Leviton Foundation New York; chairman, treasurer, director, Leviton Manufacturing Co. Inc.

Leviton, Harold: president, Leviton Foundation New York; president, chief executive officer, Leviton Manufacturing Co. Inc.

Pacific Enterprises

Lozano, Ignacio Eugenio, Jr.: chairman, Pacific Mutual Life Insurance Co.

Pacific Finance Asset Management Corp.

Sutton, Thomas C.: chairman, director, Pacific Mutual Charitable Foundation; chairman, chief executive officer, director, Pacific Mutual Life Insurance Co.

Pacific Gas & Electric Co.

Coulter, David A.: president, director, Bank of America

Pacific Guardian Life Insurance Co.

Dods, Walter Arthur, Jr.: president, director, First Hawaiian Foundation; chairman, chief executive officer, director, First Hawaiian, Inc.

Pacific Industry Co. Inc.

Gareau, Joseph H.: executive vice president, chief investment officer, Hartford (The)

Pacific Life Corp.

Morby, Jacqueline C.: managing partner, Pacific Mutual Life Insurance Co.

Pacific Life Insurance Co.

Carmichael, David R.: senior vice president, general counsel, director, Pacific Mutual Life Insurance Co.

Ferry, Richard Michael: chairman, Pacific Mutual Life Insurance Co.

Lozano, Ignacio Eugenio, Jr.: chairman, Pacific Mutual Life Insurance Co.

Miller, Donn Biddle: president, chief executive officer, Pacific Mutual Life Insurance Co.

Ukropina, James R.: partner, Pacific Mutual Life Insurance Co.

Pacific Lifecorp

Sutton, Thomas C.: chairman, director, Pacific Mutual Charitable Foundation; chairman, chief executive officer, director, Pacific Mutual Life Insurance Co.

Pacific Magazines & Printing Ltd.

Donnelley, James R.: vice chairman, Donnelley & Sons Co. (R.R.)

Pacific Media Inc.

McCorkindale, Douglas H.: vice chairman, president, Gannett Co., Inc.; president, Gannett Foundation

Pacific Mutual

Ukropina, James R.: partner, Pacific Mutual Life Insurance Co.

Pacific Mutual Distributors

Milfs, Audrey L.: secretary, Pacific Mutual Charitable Foundation; vice president, corporate secretary, director, Pacific Mutual Life Insurance Co.

Sutton, Thomas C.: chairman, director, Pacific Mutual Charitable Foundation; chairman, chief executive officer, director, Pacific Mutual Life Insurance Co.

Pacific Mutual Life Insurance Co.

Miller, Charles Daly: chairman, director, Avery Dennison Corp.; trustee, Whirlpool Foundation

Pacific One Bank

Dods, Walter Arthur, Jr.: president, director, First Hawaiian Foundation; chairman, chief executive officer, director, First Hawaiian, Inc.

Pacific One Bank NA

Dods, Walter Arthur, Jr.: president, director, First Hawaiian Foundation; chairman, chief executive officer, director, First Hawaiian, Inc.

Pacific One Dealer Center Inc.

Dods, Walter Arthur, Jr.: president, director, First Hawaiian Foundation; chairman, chief executive officer, director, First Hawaiian, Inc.

Pacific Studies Industries, Inc.

James, George Barker, II: senior vice president, chief financial officer, Levi Strauss & Co.

Pacific Telesis Group

Hazen, Paul Mandeville: chairman, chief executive officer, director, Wells Fargo & Co.

Pacificare Behavioral Health

Folick, Jeffrey M.: member, PacifiCare Health System Foundation

Packaging Fulfillment Specialists

Belcher, Donald D.: chairman, president, chief executive officer, director, Banta Corp.; vice president, director, Banta Corp. Foundation

Paco Pharmaceutical Services

Gailey, John Robert, III: vice president, general counsel, secretary, West Co. Inc.

Page Koch Europe Ltd.

Muehlbauer, James Herman: vice president, director, Koch Foundation

Pagoda Trading Co. Inc.

Fromm, Ronald A.: vice president, Brown Shoe Co., Inc.

PaineWebber Inc.

Grano, Joseph J., Jr.: president, Paine Webber

Palm Beach National Golf & Country Club

Rich, Robert E., Sr.: president, treasurer, Rich Family Foundation; founder, chairman, director, Rich Products Corp.

PanEnergy Corp.

Esrey, William Todd: chairman, chief executive officer, Sprint Corp.

Panarem Inc.

Roberts, John Kenneth, Jr.: president, chief executive officer, director, Pan-American Life Insurance Co.

Panasonic Technologies Inc.

Takahashi, Ted: vice president, finance, Matsushita Electric Corp. of America; vice president, Panasonic Foundation

Pandesic LLC

Barrett, Craig R.: president, chief operating officer, director, Intel Corp.

Panhandle Eastern Corp.

Esrey, William Todd: chairman, chief executive officer, Sprint Corp.

Paper Magic Group Inc.

Farber, Jack: chairman, president, director, CSS Industries, Inc.; president, Farber Foundation

Parametric Technology Corp.

Gillis, Edwin J.: president, Lotus Development Corp.

Paramus Park Inc.

Deering, Anthony W.: chairman, chief executive officer, Rouse Co.; chairman, president, trustee, Rouse Co. Foundation

Park Bank

Davis, Walter Stewart: secretary, treasurer, Grede Foundation

Park National Bank

McConnell, William Thompson: chairman, ceo, Park National Bank; chairman, Park National Corp. Foundation

Park Saint Corp.

Syron, Richard F.: chairman, chief executive officer, director, American Stock Exchange, Inc.

Parker-Hannifin Corp.

Breen, John Gerald: chairman, chief executive officer, director, Sherwin-Williams Co.; president, trustee, Sherwin-Williams Foundation

Ortino, Hector R.: president, chief executive officer, director, Ferro Corp.; vice president, trustee, Ferro Foundation

Schmitt, Wolfgang Rudolph: chairman, chief executive officer, director, Rubbermaid Inc.

Parker/Hunter

Newlin, William Rankin: trustee, Kennametal Foundation

Parks-Belk Co. Northern Virginia

Belk, John Montgomery: member board advisors, Belk Foundation; chairman, Belk-Simpson Department Stores

Parkwood Corp.

Mandel, Morton Leon: deputy chairman, Premier Industrial Corp.; trustee, Premier Industrial Foundation

Parmatech Corp.

Cottrell, G. Walton: senior vice president, chief financial officer, Carpenter Technology Corp.

Welty, John Rider: secretary, Carpenter Technology Corp. Foundation

Pat Ryan & Associates

Ryan, Patrick G.: chairman, president, chief executive officer, Aon Corp.; president, Aon Foundation

Patagonia Inc.

Chouinard, Yvon: owner, principal, Patagonia Inc.

Pathmark Assurance Co.

Louis, Kenneth C.: president, chief operating officer, director, Ameritas Life Insurance Corp.

Martin, JoAnn M.: controller, Ameritas Charitable Foundation; senior vice president, partner, chief financial officer, Ameritas Life Insurance Corp.

Paul Harris Stores Inc.

Morris, James Thomas: director, AUL Foundation Inc.

Paul Hastings Janofsky & Walker

Eason, William Everette, Jr.: senior vice president, corporate secretary, general counsel, Scientific-Atlanta, Inc.

Payless Cashways Inc.

Hall, William Austin: president, Hallmark Corporate Foundation

Lyon, Wayne Barton: president, chief operating officer, director, Masco Corp.

Payless Shoe Source Inc.

Fricke, Howard R.: president, director, Security Benefit Life Insurance Co.; trustee, Security Benefit Life Insurance Co. Charitable Trust

Pelican Co.

Browning, Peter C.: chief executive officer, president, director, Sonoco Products Co.

Pella Corp.

Farver, Charles: treasurer, director, Pella Rolscreen Foundation

Howe, Stanley M.: president, HON Industries Charitable Foundation; chairman emeritus, director, HON Industries Inc.

Penn Insurance & Annuity Co.

Brodie, Nancy S.: executive vice president, chief financial officer, Penn Mutual Life Insurance Co.

Penn Mutual Life Insurance Co.

Meyerson, Martin: director, Panasonic Foundation

Penn Virginia Corp.

Black, Lennox K.: president, Teleflex Foundation; chairman, director, Teleflex Inc.

Penns Southwest

Ryan, John Thomas, III: chairman, chief executive officer, Mine Safety Appliances Co.

Pennsylvania Electric Association

Baldassari, Dennis P.: president, chief operating officer, GPU Energy

Pennsylvania Electric Co.

Graham, John Gourlay: chief financial officer, senior vice president, GPU Energy

Hafer, Fred Douglass: chairman, president, chief executive officer, GPU Inc.

Pennsylvania Power Co.

Holland, Willard R.: chairman, chief executive officer, FirstEnergy Corp.

Pennzoil Exploration Products Co.

Pate, James Leonard: chairman, chief executive officer, director, Pennzoil-Quaker State Co.

Pensacola News-Journal Inc.

Chapple, Thomas Leslie: senior vice president, general counsel, secretary, Gannett Co., Inc.; secretary, Gannett Foundation

McCorkindale, Douglas H.: vice chairman, president, Gannett Co., Inc.; president, Gannett Foundation

Pentair, Inc.

Kissling, Walter: director, Fuller Co. (H.B.)

Pentzer Corp.

Redmond, Paul Anthony: chairman, chief executive officer, director, Avista Corporation

Penwest Ltd.

Wiborg, James Hooker: director, PACCAR Foundation

People's Bank & Trust

Bowman, Robert A.: president, chief operating officer, Starwood Hotels & Resorts Worldwide, Inc.

Peoples Energy Corp.

Toft, Richard Paul: chairman, Chicago Title Corp.; trustee, Chicago Title and Trust Co. Foundation

Peoples Energy Service Corp.

Terry, Richard Edward: chairman, chief executive officer, director, Peoples Energy Corp.

Peoples Energy Services Corp.

Hasch, J. Bruce: president, chief operating officer, director, Peoples Energy Corp.

Peoples Gas Co.

Anderson, Girard F.: chairman, chief executive officer, president, Tampa Electric Co.

Peoples Gas, Light & Coke Co.

Hasch, J. Bruce: president, chief operating officer, director, Peoples Energy Corp.

Rogers, Desiree Glapion: vice president community affairs, Peoples Energy Corp.

Terry, Richard Edward: chairman, chief executive officer, director, Peoples Energy Corp.

Peoples Insurance Agency

Klein, Bruce A.: trustee, CLARCOR Foundation; chief financial officer, CLARCOR Inc.

Peoples Light Theatre Co. Inc.

Rohrkemper, Paul H.: treasurer, CIGNA Corp.; vice president, treasurer, CIGNA Foundation

Peoples Mutual Holdings

Biggs, James: president, Peoples Bank

Carson, David Ellis Adams: chairman, chief executive officer, Peoples Bank

Peoria Journal Star Inc.

Copley, David C.: president, trustee, Copley Foundation (James S.); president, chief executive officer, director, senior management board, Copley Press, Inc.

Copley, Helen K.: chairman, trustee, Copley Foundation (James S.); chairman, director, senior management board, Copley Press, Inc.

Dwyer, Dean P.: vice president finance, treasurer, senior management board, Copley Press, Inc.

Pep Boys

Black, Lennox K.: president, Teleflex Foundation; chairman, director, Teleflex Inc.

Pepsi Cola Bottling Co.

Enrico, Roger A.: chairman, PepsiCo Foundation, Inc.; chairman, chief executive officer, director, PepsiCo, Inc.

PepsiCo

Akers, John Fellows: director, New York Times Co.

Hunt, Ray Lee: chairman, chief executive officer, director, Hunt Oil Co.

Raines, Franklin Delano: chairman, chief executive officer, Fannie Mae; director, Fannie Mae Foundation

Reinemund, Steve S.: chairman, chief executive officer, Frito-Lay, Inc.

Vagelos, Pindaros Roy: trustee, Prudential Insurance Co. of America

PepsiCo Inc.

Thomas, Franklin Augustine: director, CBS Foundation

PepsiCo Worldwide Beverages

Enrico, Roger A.: chairman, PepsiCo Foundation, Inc.; chairman, chief executive officer, director, PepsiCo, Inc.

Perfecseal Inc.

Wulf, Gene C.: vice president, controller, Bemis Co. Foundation

Perfin Corp.

Allbritton, Joe Lewis: chairman, chief executive officer, Riggs Bank NA

Pericomp Corp.

Jasse, Andre C., Jr.: trustee, Eastern Bank Charitable Foundation

Perry Drug Stores Inc.

Grass, Martin Lehrman: chairman, chief executive officer, director, Rite Aid Corp.

PetSmart Inc.

Kovacevich, Richard M.: chairman, president, chief executive officer, Norwest Corp.; director, Norwest Foundation

Peter Kiewit Sons De Corp.

Stinson, Kenneth E.: member contributions committee, Kiewit Companies Foundation; chairman, chief executive officer, director, Kiewit Sons' Inc. (Peter)

Petrie Stores Corp.

Tisch, Laurence Alan: chairman, co-chief executive officer, CBS Corp.; trustee, Loews Foundation

Petrofina DE Inc.

Godfrey, Cullen Michael: vice president, FINA Foundation

Petroleum/ Chemical Environmental Services

Fretthold, Timothy Jon: executive vice president, general counsel, director, Ultramar Diamond Shamrock Corp.

Pfaltzgraff Co.

Appell, Louis J., Jr.: president, Susquehanna-Pfaltzgraff Co.

Finlayson, John L.: vice president finance & administration, Susquehanna-Pfaltzgraff Co.

Pfaltzgraff Outlet Co.

Appell, Louis J., Jr.: president, Susquehanna-Pfaltzgraff Co.

Finlayson, John L.: vice president finance & administration, Susquehanna-Pfaltzgraff Co.

Simpson, William H.: president, Susquehanna-Pfaltzgraff Co.; secretary, Susquehanna-Pfaltzgraff Foundation

Pfizer Inc.

Burns, Mitchell Anthony: president, director, Ryder System Charitable Foundation; chairman, president, chief executive officer, Ryder System, Inc.

Kamen, Harry Paul: chairman, president, chief executive officer, Metropolitan Life Insurance Co.

Labrecque, Thomas Goulet: president, chief operating officer, director, Chase Manhattan Bank, NA; president, Chase Manhattan Foundation

Mead, Dana George: chairman, chief executive officer, director, Tenneco Automotive

Raines, Franklin Delano: chairman, chief executive officer, Fannie Mae; director, Fannie Mae Foundation

Phar-Mor Inc.

Shapira, David S.: trustee, Giant Eagle Foundation; chairman, chief executive officer, director, Giant Eagle Inc.

Pharmaceutical Marketing Services Inc.

Davis, Carolyne Kahle, PhD: trustee, Merck Co. Foundation

Pharmaceutical Research & Management America

Gilmartin, Raymond V.: chairman, president, chief executive officer, Merck & Co.; chairman, Merck Co. Foundation

Pharmacia and Upjohn Inc.

Brown, Richard Harris: chairman, chief executive officer, director, EDS Corp.

Phelps Dodge Corp.

Burt, Robert Norcross: chairman, chief executive officer, director, FMC Corp.; director, FMC Foundation

Douglas, Paul W.: director, Phelps Dodge Foundation

Dunham, Archie W.: president, chief executive officer, Conoco, Inc.

Franke, William Augustus: chairman, president, chief executive officer, America West Airlines, Inc.; director, Phelps Dodge Foundation

Hazen, Paul Mandeville: chairman, chief executive officer, director, Wells Fargo & Co.

Knowles, Marie L.: executive vice president, chief financial officer, Atlantic Richfield Co.

Phelps Program Management

Carrico, Stephen J.: director, Hensel Phelps Foundation

Phelps Program Management LLC

Wilson, Eric L.: director, Hensel Phelps Foundation

Phico Group Inc.

Nation, Robert F.: former president, director, Harsco Corp.; trustee, Harsco Corp. Fund

Phico Insurance Co.

Nation, Robert F.: former president, director, Harsco Corp.; trustee, Harsco Corp. Fund

Phico Service Co.

Nation, Robert F.: former president, director, Harsco Corp.; trustee, Harsco Corp. Fund

Philadelphia Electric Co.

McNeill, Corbin Asahel, Jr.: president, chief executive officer, director, chairman, PECO Energy Co.

Philadelphia National Bank

Campbell, Robert Henderson: chairman, chief executive officer, Sunoco Inc.

Philip Morris Companies Inc.

Murdoch, Rupert P.: chairman, Fox Entertainment Group

Reed, John Shepard: co-chairman, Citibank Corp.

Phillips Gas Co.

Mulva, James J.: president, chief operating officer, director, Phillips Petroleum Co.

Phillips Gross & Aaron Pennsylvania

Gross, Bert M.: assistant secretary, Regis Foundation

Phillips Petroleum Co.

Tobias, Randall L.: chairman emeritus, Lilly & Co. (Eli)

Phillips-Van Heusen Corp.

Lagomasino, Maria Elena: trustee, Chase Manhattan Foundation

Phoenix Charter Oak Trust

Fiondella, Robert William: chairman, president, chief executive officer, Phoenix Home Life Mutual Insurance Co.

Phoenix Health System

Elam, Lloyd Charles, MD: trustee, Merck Co. Foundation

Phoenix Home Life Mutual Insurance Co.

Alfiero, Salvatore Harry: founder, chairman, chief executive officer, director, Mark IV Industries; chairman, Mark IV Industries Foundation

Browning, Peter C.: chief executive officer, president, director, Sonoco Products Co.

Phoenix Insurance Co.

Lipp, Robert Irving: chief executive officer, Citigroup; vice president, treasurer, trustee, Citigroup Foundation

Phoenix Investment Council Ltd.

Fiondella, Robert William: chairman, president, chief executive officer, Phoenix Home Life Mutual Insurance Co.

Phoenix Newspapers Inc.

Pulliam, Eugene Smith: vice president, director, Central Newspapers Foundation

Russell, Frank Eli: president, Central Newspapers Foundation; chairman, Central Newspapers, Inc.

Photo Corp. of America

Sloan, Albert Frazier: director, Lance Foundation

Physicians Life Insurance Co.

Lempka, Arnold W., MD: chairman, director, Physicians Mutual Insurance Co.; director, Physicians Mutual Insurance Co. Foundation

Physicians Mutual Insurance Canada

Woodbury, John D., MD: director, Physicians Mutual Insurance Co. Foundation

Physicians Mutual Insurance Co.

Davis, John B., MD: director, Physicians Mutual Insurance Co. Foundation

Hamsa, William R., MD: director, assistant secretary, Physicians Mutual Insurance Co. Foundation

McFadden, Harry W., Jr. MD: assistant treasurer, director, Physicians Mutual Insurance Co. Foundation

Pickands Mather

Bezik, Cynthia B.: senior vice president, finance, Cleveland-Cliffs, Inc.

Piedmont-Forrest Corp.

Anderson, Judy M.: vice president, corporate secretary, Georgia Power Co.; executive director, secretary, assistant treasurer, Georgia Power Foundation

Dahlberg, Alfred William, III: chairman, president, chief executive officer, Southern Co. Services Inc.

Pierce National Life Insurance Co.

Allbritton, Joe Lewis: chairman, chief executive officer, Riggs Bank NA

Hipp, William Hayne: president, chief executive officer, director, Liberty Corp.; chairman, president, director, Liberty Corp. Foundation

Piercing Pagoda Florida

Russ, Gina S.: assistant secretary, Ryder System Charitable Foundation

Pimco Advisor LP

Sutton, Thomas C.: chairman, director, Pacific Mutual Charitable Foundation; chairman, chief executive officer, director, Pacific Mutual Life Insurance Co.

Pioneer Capital Corp.

Cogan, John Francis, Jr.: president, chief executive officer, director, Pioneer Group

Pioneer Press Inc.

Jones, Ross: senior vice president, chief financial officer, Knight Ridder

Pioneering Management Corp.

Cogan, John Francis, Jr.: president, chief executive officer, director, Pioneer Group

Piper Jaffray & Hopwood Inc.

Piper, Addison Lewis: director, Piper Jaffray Companies Foundation; chairman, chief executive officer, director, U.S. Bancorp Piper Jaffray

Piper Jaffray Inc.

Cich, Brenda M.: secretary, Piper Jaffray Companies Foundation

Piper Trust Co.

Piper, Addison Lewis: director, Piper Jaffray Companies Foundation; chairman, chief executive officer, director, U.S. Bancorp Piper Jaffray

Pitchfork Land & Cattle Co.

Williams, Eugene Flewellyn, Jr.: member public policy committee, Emerson Charitable Trust

Pitney Bowes Inc.

Keyes, James Henry: advisor, Johnson Controls Foundation; president, Johnson Controls Inc.

Roth, Michael I.: chairman, chief executive officer, director, MONY Group (The); director, MONY Life Insurance of New York (The)

Pittsburgh Corning Corp.

Ackerman, Roger G.: trustee, Corning Inc. Foundation

Campbell, Van C.: vice chairman, chief financial officer, chief administrative officer, director, Corning Inc.; trustee, Corning Inc. Foundation

Kiener, Dan W.: member screening committee, PPG Industries Foundation

Pittsburgh National Leasing Corp.

Gregg, Walter Emmor, Junior: senior executive vice president finance & administration, PNC Financial Services Group

Pittsburgh Post Gazette

Block, William: vice president, trustee, Blade Foundation; chairman, director, Toledo Blade Co.

Pittsburgh Post-Gazette

Block, John Robinson: vice president, trustee, Blade Foundation

Pittsburgh Post-Gazette-Sun-Telegraph

Block, William: vice president, trustee, Blade Foundation; chairman, director, Toledo Blade Co.

Block, William, Jr.: president, trustee, Blade Foundation; president, director, Toledo Blade Co.

Pittston Co.

Ackerman, Roger G.: trustee, Corning Inc. Foundation

Broadhead, James Lowell: chairman, president, chief executive officer, director, Florida Power & Light Co.; chief executive officer, director, FPL Group Foundation, Inc.

Grinstein, Gerald: director, PACCAR Inc.

Gross, Ronald Martin: chairman, president, director, Rayonier Foundation; chairman, president, chief executive officer, director, Rayonier Inc.

Spilman, Robert H.: chairman, chief executive officer, Bassett Furniture Industries; chairman, director, Bassett Furniture Industries Fdn.

Pittway Corp.

Coolidge, E. David, III: vice president, Blair & Co. Foundation (William); chief executive officer, Blair & Co. (William); vice president, Pittway Corp. Charitable Foundation

Harris, William W.: director, Pittway Corp. Charitable Foundation

Pittway International Ltd.

Zermuehlen, William: secretary, Pittway Corp. Charitable Foundation

Pixar

Jobs, Steven Paul: interim chief executive officer, Apple Computer, Inc.

Plaid Clothing Co. Inc.

Patel, Homi Burjor: president, chief operating officer, director, Hartmarx Corp.

Plasti-Line

Clark, Howard Longstreth, Jr.: vice chairman, Walter Industries Inc.

Plastic Research & Development Corp.

Stephens, James T.: president, director, Ebsco Industries, Inc.

Playboy Enterprises Inc.

Bookshester, Dennis S.: chairman, chief executive officer, Playboy Enterprises Inc.

Chemerow, David I.: executive vice president, chief financial officer, Playboy Enterprises Inc.

Rosenthal, Sol: counsel, Playboy Enterprises Inc.

Playboy Jazz Festivals

Rosenzweig, Richard Stuart: executive vice president, director, Playboy Enterprises Inc.

Playboy Magazine

Hefner, Hugh Marston: founder, chairman emeritus, Playboy Enterprises Inc.

Plaza Communications Inc.

Rollans, James Ora: senior vice president, chief administrative officer, chief financial officer, Fluor Corp.; trustee, Fluor Foundation

Plaza Fin Services Co.

Phillips, Rosalind Ann: secretary, GEICO Philanthropic Foundation

Plymouth Meeting Mall Inc.

Deering, Anthony W.: chairman, chief executive officer, Rouse Co.; chairman, president, trustee, Rouse Co. Foundation

Pocahontas Land Corp.

Wolf, Henry C.: vice chairman, chief financial officer, Norfolk Southern Corp.; vice president finance, Norfolk Southern Foundation

Poco Graphite Inc.

Chessum, Darrell D.: treasurer, Unocal Foundation

Pola Cosmetics

Fukunaga, Mark H.: chairman, director, Servco Foundation; chief executive officer, chairman, Servco Pacific

Polaroid Corp.

Lemberg, Thomas Michael: clerk, Lotus Development Corp.; secretary, Polaroid Foundation

Loose, John W.: trustee, Corning Inc. Foundation

Pool Energy Services Co.

Sykora, Donald D.: director, Reliant Energy Inc.

Portland General Electric Co.

Meyer, Jerome J.: chairman, chief executive officer, Tektronix, Inc.

Post Properties Inc.

Blank, Arthur M.: president, chief executive officer, director, Home Depot, Inc.

Potlatch Corp.

Rosenberg, Richard Morris: chairman, chief executive officer (retired), Bank of America

Potomac Capital Investment Corp.

Simpson, Louis Allen: president, chief executive officer capital operations, director, GEICO Corp.

Powell Industries Inc.

Sykora, Donald D.: director, Reliant Energy Inc.

Power Control Technologies

Meister, Paul M.: vice president, treasurer, Winthrop Foundation

Power Corp. Canada

Bronfman, Charles Rosner: trustee, Bronfman Foundation/Joseph E. Seagram & Sons, Inc. Fund (Samuel)

Praxair Inc.

LeBoeuf, Raymond W.: director, PPG Industries Foundation; director, chairman, chief executive officer, PPG Industries, Inc.

Ratcliffe, George Jackson, Jr.: trustee, Hubbell Foundation (Harvey); chairman, president, chief executive officer, Hubbell Inc.

Precision Castparts Corp.

Graber, Don R.: chairman, president, chief executive officer, director, Huffy Corp.; trustee, Huffy Foundation, Inc.

Preferred Life Insurance Co. New York

Anderson, Lowell Carlton: chairman, director, Allianz Life Insurance Co. of North America

Premark International Inc.

Davis, Ruth Margaret: trustee, Air Products Foundation

Elam, Lloyd Charles, MD: trustee, Merck Co. Foundation

Farrell, W. James: chairman, chief executive officer, Illinois Tool Works, Inc.

Premier Industries Corp.

Mandel, Jack N.: director, Premier Industrial Corp.

Premiums International Ltd.

Carlson, Curtis Leroy: chairman, director, Carlson Companies, Inc.; president, treasurer, Carlson Family Foundation (Curtis L.)

President Trustees Colby

Pugh, Lawrence R.: chairman, director, Blue Bell, Inc.

Presto Export Ltd.

Cohen, Maryjo Rose: president, chief executive officer, director, National Presto Industries, Inc.; vice president, treasurer, trustee, Presto Foundation

Cohen, Melvin Samuel: chairman, National Presto Industries, Inc.; chairman, president, trustee, Presto Foundation

Presto Manufacturing Co.

Cohen, Maryjo Rose: president, chief executive officer, director, National Presto Industries, Inc.; vice president, treasurer, trustee, Presto Foundation

Cohen, Melvin Samuel: chairman, National Presto Industries, Inc.; chairman, president, trustee, Presto Foundation

Prestolite Wire Corp.

Montrone, Paul Michael: vice president, partner, Winthrop Foundation

Preview Travel Inc.

Pottruck, David Steven: president, chief executive officer, director, Schwab & Co., Inc. (Charles)

Pri Pak Inc.

Hillenbrand, John A., II: director, Cinergy Foundation

Price Chopper Oper Co. Massachusetts

Golub, Lewis: chairman, chief executive officer, director, Golub Corp.

Price River Coal Co. Inc.

Draper, Ernest Linn, Jr.: chairman, president, chief executive officer, director, American Electric Power

Pride Petroleum Services Inc.

Bickner, Bruce P.: chairman, chief executive officer, director, DeKalb Genetics Corp.

Primark Holding Corp.

Kasputys, Joseph Edward: chairman, trustee, Hitachi Foundation

Prime Source Corp.

Wiborg, James Hooker: director, PACCAR Foundation

Primedia Inc.

Golkin, Perry: member, Walter Industries Inc.

Tokarz, Michael T.: founding partner, Walter Industries Inc.

Primergy Corp.

Grigg, Richard R.: vice president, Wisconsin Energy Corp.; director, Wisconsin

Energy Corp. Foundation, Inc.

Prin Finance Group Inc.

Davis, Ruth Margaret: trustee, Air Products Foundation

Prin Preservation Mutual Funds

Eckert, Ralph John: trustee, Trustmark Foundation

Prin Preservation Portfolios

Ziegler, R. Douglas: advisor, Johnson Controls Foundation

Principal Financial Group

Drury, David J.: chief executive officer, chairman, Principal Financial Group

Kerr, William T.: chairman, chief executive officer, director, Meredith Corp.

Principal Financial Groupp

Graf, Thomas J.: chief actuary, Principal Financial Group

Principal Financial Services

Drury, David J.: chief executive officer, chairman, Principal Financial Group

Principal Life Insurance Co.

Graf, Thomas J.: chief actuary, Principal Financial Group

Griswell, Barry: president, Principal Financial Group

Principal Mutual Holding Co.

Drury, David J.: chief executive officer, chairman, Principal Financial Group

Principal Mutual Life Insurance Co.

Kerr, William T.: chairman, chief executive officer, director, Meredith Corp.

Printing Group Inc.

Shapiro, Isaac: chairman, secretary, trustee, Ise Cultural Foundation

Private Export Funding Corp.

Rohr, James Edward: chief executive officer, president, director, PNC Financial Services Group

Procter & Gamble Co.

Beall, Donald Ray: director, Rockwell International Corp.

Cheney, Richard B.: chief executive officer, Halliburton Co.; president, Halliburton Foundation, Inc.

Gorman, Joseph T.: chairman, chief executive officer, TRW Inc.

Lee, Charles Robert: chairman, chief executive officer, director, GTE Corp.; chief executive officer, trustee, GTE Foundation

Light, Walter Frederick: trustee, Air Products Foundation

Martin, Lynn M.: director, Ameritech Foundation

Smith, John Francis, Jr.: chairman, General Motors Corp.

Proctor & Gamble

Pritchard, Marc S.: president, Procter & Gamble Cosmetics Foundation

Professional Data Solutions

Menzer, John: executive vice president, Wal-Mart Stores, Inc.

Progressive America Life Insurance Co.

Lewis, Peter Benjamin: chairman, president, chief executive officer, director, Progressive Corp.

Progressive Companies

Hardis, Stephen Roger: chairman, chief executive officer, director, Eaton Corp.

Progressive County Mutual Insurance Co.

Lewis, Peter Benjamin: chairman, president, chief executive officer, director, Progressive Corp.

Progressive Distributor Inc.

Bowne, Garrett D., IV: treasurer, Hannaford Charitable Foundation

Progressive Distributors Inc.

Farrington, Hugh G.: president, chief executive officer, director, Hannaford Brothers Co.

Progressive Max Insurance Co.

Lewis, Peter Benjamin: chairman, president, chief executive officer, director, Progressive Corp.

Promus Hotel Corp.

Roth, Michael I.: chairman, chief executive officer, director, MONY Group (The); director, MONY Life Insurance of New York (The)

Protection Mutual Insurance Co.

O'Toole, Robert Joseph: director, Firstar Milwaukee Foundation; chairman, president, chief executive officer, director, Smith Corp. (A.O.); director, Smith Foundation, Inc. (A.O.)

Stivers, William Charles: senior vice president, chief financial officer, treasurer, Weyerhaeuser Co.; treasurer, trustee, Weyerhaeuser Co. Foundation

Protective Life Corp.

Dahlberg, Alfred William, III: chairman, president, chief executive officer, Southern Co. Services Inc.

McMahon, John J., Jr.: trustee, McWane Foundation; chairman, president, chief executive officer, treasurer, McWane Inc.

Provident Life & Accident Insurance Co.

Pollard, Charles William, Jr.: chairman, director, ServiceMaster Co.; president, director, ServiceMaster Foundation

Street, Gordon P., Jr.: chairman, president, chief executive officer, director, North American Royalties; trustee, North American Royalties Foundation

Provident Life Insurance

Reinemund, Steve S.: chairman, chief executive officer, Frito-Lay, Inc.

Providian Financial Corp.

Everingham, Lyle J.: trustee, Milacron Foundation

Weinberg, John Livingston: chairman, president, director, Goldman Sachs Foundation

Prudential Allocation Fund

McCorkindale, Douglas H.: vice chairman, president, Gannett Co., Inc.; president, Gannett Foundation

Prudential Capital & Investment Services

Simmons, Hardwick: president, chief executive officer, director, Prudential Securities Inc.

Prudential Equity Income Fund

McCorkindale, Douglas H.: vice chairman, president, Gannett Co., Inc.; president, Gannett Foundation

Prudential Global Genesis Fund

McCorkindale, Douglas H.: vice chairman, president, Gannett Co., Inc.; president, Gannett Foundation

Prudential Insurance Co. America

Davis, Carolyne Kahle, PhD: trustee, Merck Co. Foundation

Enrico, Roger A.: chairman, PepsiCo Foundation, Inc.; chairman, chief executive officer, director, PepsiCo, Inc.

Unruh, James Arlen: director, Ameritech Foundation

Vagelos, Pindaros Roy: trustee, Prudential Insurance Co. of America

Prudential Insurance Co. American

Hiner, Glen Harold, Jr.: chairman, chief executive officer, director, Owens Corning

Prudential Insurance Co. North America

Hanson, Jon F.: trustee, Prudential Foundation

Vagelos, Pindaros Roy: trustee, Prudential Insurance Co. of America

Prudential Insurance of America Inc.

Scicutella, John Vincent: trustee, Chase Manhattan Foundation

Prudential Multi-Sector Fund Inc.

McCorkindale, Douglas H.: vice chairman, president, Gannett Co., Inc.; president, Gannett Foundation

Prudential Municipal Bond Fund

McCorkindale, Douglas H.: vice chairman, president, Gannett Co., Inc.; president, Gannett Foundation

Prudential Mutual Group

McCorkindale, Douglas H.: vice chairman, president, Gannett Co., Inc.; president, Gannett Foundation

Prudential Natural Resources Fund Inc.

McCorkindale, Douglas H.: vice chairman, president, Gannett Co., Inc.; president, Gannett Foundation

Prudential Securities Group Inc.

Paton, Leland B.: president capital marketings, director, member executive committee, Prudential Securities Inc.

Simmons, Hardwick: president, chief executive officer, director, Prudential Securities Inc.

Public Broadcasting System

Meyer, Russell William, Jr.: chairman, chief executive officer, Cessna Aircraft Co.; president, Cessna Foundation, Inc.

Public Employees Benefit Service

Druen, W. Sidney: director, Nationwide Insurance Enterprise Foundation

Public Service Co. Colorado

Brunetti, Wayne H.: vice chairman, president, chief operating officer, director, New Century Energies; president, chief executive officer, New Century Energies Foundation

Helton, Bill D.: chairman, New Century Energies Foundation

Public Service Co. NC

Matthews, B. Frank, II: member board advisors, Belk Foundation

Public Service Co. New Hampshire

MacKenzie, Hugh C.: president retail business group, Northeast Utilities

Public Service Colorado

Wilks, David M.: vice president, New Century Energies Foundation

Public Service Electric & Gas Co.

Ferland, E. James: chairman, president, chief executive officer, Public Service Electric & Gas Co.

Gilmartin, Raymond V.: chairman, president, chief executive officer, Merck & Co.; chairman, Merck Co. Foundation

Public Service Enterprise Group Inc.

Codey, Lawrence R.: president, chief operating officer, Public Service Electric & Gas Co.

Gilmartin, Raymond V.: chairman, president, chief executive officer, Merck & Co.; chairman, Merck Co. Foundation

Public Service Resources Corp.

Ferland, E. James: chairman, president, chief executive officer, Public Service Electric & Gas Co.

Puget Sound Energy Co.

Campbell, Phyllis J.: president private financial services, US Bank, Washington

Pulitzer Broadcasting Co.

Pulitzer, Michael Edgar: chairman, president, chief executive officer, director, Pulitzer Publishing Co.; chairman, president, chief executive officer, Pulitzer Publishing Co. Foundation

Pulitzer Community Newspapers

Pulitzer, Michael Edgar: chairman, president, chief executive officer, director, Pulitzer Publishing Co.; chairman, president, chief executive officer, Pulitzer Publishing Co. Foundation

Pulitzer Ventures Inc.

Pulitzer, Michael Edgar: chairman, president, chief executive officer, director, Pulitzer Publishing Co.; chairman, president, chief executive officer, Pulitzer Publishing Co. Foundation

Pulse Communications Inc.

Davies, Richard Warren: trustee, Hubbell Foundation (Harvey)

Rowell, Harry Brown, Jr.: trustee, Hubbell Foundation (Harvey)

Purolator Products Co.

Lippes, Gerald Sanford: secretary, Mark IV Industries Foundation

Montague, William Patrick: president, chief operating officer, director, Mark IV Industries; president, Mark IV Industries Foundation

Putnam Advisory Co. Inc.

Burke, Robert W.: president, chief executive officer, Putnam Investors Fund

Putnam Advisory Co., Inc.

Lasser, Lawrence Jay: president, chief executive officer, director, Putnam Investments; president, chief executive officer, Putnam Investors Fund

Putnam, George, Jr.: chairman, president, chief executive officer, Putnam Investments

Putnam American Government

Lasser, Lawrence Jay: president, chief executive officer, director, Putnam Investments; president, chief executive officer, Putnam Investors Fund

Putnam Convertible Income Growth Trust

Lasser, Lawrence Jay: president, chief executive officer, director, Putnam Investments; president, chief executive officer, Putnam Investors Fund

Putnam Finance Services Co. Inc.

Putnam, George, Jr.: chairman, president, chief executive officer, Putnam Investments

Putnam High Income Convertible

Lasser, Lawrence Jay: president, chief executive officer, director, Putnam Investments; president, chief executive officer, Putnam Investors Fund

Putnam Income Fund

Lasser, Lawrence Jay: president, chief executive officer, director, Putnam Investments; president, chief executive officer, Putnam Investors Fund

Putnam Investment Management Inc.

Lasser, Lawrence Jay: president, chief executive officer, director, Putnam Investments; president, chief executive officer, Putnam Investors Fund

Putnam, George, Jr.: chairman, president, chief executive officer, Putnam Investments

Putnam Investors Fund

Lasser, Lawrence Jay: president, chief executive officer, director, Putnam Investments; president, chief executive officer, Putnam Investors Fund

Putnam Mutual Funds

Lasser, Lawrence Jay: president, chief executive officer, director, Putnam Investments; president, chief executive officer, Putnam Investors Fund

Putnam New York Tax Exempt Fund

Lasser, Lawrence Jay: president, chief executive officer, director, Putnam Investments; president, chief executive officer, Putnam Investors Fund

Q'west Communication International Inc.

Haines, Jordan L.: trustee, Cessna Foundation, Inc.

QVC Network

Musser, Warren Van Dyke: chairman, chief executive officer, director, Safeguard Scientifics; president, director, Safeguard Scientifics Foundation

Quad Graphics Inc.

Shiely, John Stephen: president, chief operating officer, director, Briggs & Stratton Corp.; vice president, director, Briggs & Stratton Corp. Foundation

Quaker Chemical Corp.

Black, Lennox K.: president, Teleflex Foundation; chairman, director, Teleflex Inc.

Chappell, Robert E.: chairman, chief executive officer, Penn Mutual Life Insurance Co.

Delattre, Edwin J.: trustee, Quaker Chemical Foundation

Quaker Oats Co.

Chenault, Kenneth Irvine: president, chief operating officer, director, American Express Co.; trustee, American Express Foundation

Farrell, W. James: chairman, chief executive officer, Illinois Tool Works, Inc.

Quaker State Corp.

McClelland, William Craig: trustee, Union Camp Charitable Trust; chairman, chief executive officer, director, Union Camp Corp.

Quaker State Oil Refining Corp.

McClelland, William Craig: trustee, Union Camp Charitable Trust; chairman, chief executive officer, director, Union Camp Corp.

Quality Bakers America Corp.

Schwebel, Joseph M.: president, director, Schwebel Baking Co.; trustee, Schwebel Family Foundation

Quality Dining Inc.

Murphy, Christopher J., III: president, chief executive officer, director, First Source Corp.; director, First Source Foundation

Quality Inks Inc.

Whaley, Ronald L.: foundation administrator, Solo Cup Foundation

Quantum Health Resources Inc.

Lucas, Donald Leo: chairman, Cadence Designs Systems, Inc.

Quest Diagnostics Inc.

Campbell, Van C.: vice chairman, chief financial officer, chief administrative officer, director, Corning Inc.; trustee, Corning Inc. Foundation

Questar Corp.

Michael, Gary Glenn: chairman, chief executive officer, director, Albertson's Inc.

Questar Energy Services Inc.

Cash, R. D.: chairman, president, chief executive officer, director, Questar Corp.

Questar Gas Co.

Michael, Gary Glenn: chairman, chief executive officer, director, Albertson's Inc.

Questar Gas Management Co.

Cash, R. D.: chairman, president, chief executive officer, director, Questar Corp.

Questar InfoComm Inc.

Heiner, Clyde Mont: executive vice president, Questar Corp.

Parks, Stephen E.: vice president, treasurer, chief financial officer, Questar Corp.

Questar Pipeline Co.

Cash, R. D.: chairman, president, chief executive officer, director, Questar Corp.

Parks, Stephen E.: vice president, treasurer, chief financial officer, Questar Corp.

Questar Synfuels Corp.

Heiner, Clyde Mont: executive vice president, Questar Corp.

Questor Gas Co.

Parks, Stephen E.: vice president, treasurer, chief financial officer, Questar Corp.

Quixx Corp.

Helton, Bill D.: chairman, New Century Energies Foundation

RA Brown Agency Ltd.

Stephens, Elton Bryson: founder, chairman, Ebsco Industries, Inc.

RCA/NBC

Brademas, John: chairman, Texaco Foundation

RES Holding Corp.

Stockman, David A.: co-chairman, director, Collins & Aikman Corp.; president, director, Collins & Aikman Foundation

RG Barry Corp.

Krueger, Harvey M.: trustee, Barry Foundation

RGI Group Inc.

Gittis, Howard: director, Revlon Foundation Inc.

RH Donnelley Corp.

Buchanan, William Hobart, Jr.: assistant secretary, Dun & Bradstreet Corp. Foundation, Inc.

RHM Holdings United States of America Inc.

Reading, Anthony John: president, trustee, Tomkins Corp. Foundation; president, chief executive officer, Tomkins Industries, Inc.

RHP Inc.

Dods, Walter Arthur, Jr.: president, director, First Hawaiian Foundation; chairman, chief executive officer, director, First Hawaiian, Inc.

RJ Reynolds Tobacco Holdings Inc.

Viviano, Joseph P.: president, court, Hershey Foods Corp.

RJR Nabisco Holdings Corp.

Rickard, David: chief financial officer, Reynolds Tobacco (R.J.)

RJR Nabisco Holdings Inc.

Chain, John T., Junior: trustee, Kemper Foundation (James S.); president, Kemper National Insurance Companies

RJR Nabisco Inc.

Chain, John T., Junior: trustee, Kemper Foundation (James S.); president, Kemper National Insurance Companies

Goldstone, Steven F.: chairman, chief executive officer, director, Reynolds Tobacco (R.J.); chairman, RJR Nabisco Foundation

RLC Industries

Ford, Kenneth W.: chairman, Roseburg Forest Products Co.

RMI Titanium Co.

Armstrong, Neil A.: trustee, Milacron Foundation; director, Milacron, Inc.

ROP Aviation

Halperin, Richard E.: president, Revlon Foundation Inc.

RPM Inc.

Ratner, Albert Benjamin: trustee, Forest City Enterprises Charitable Foundation, Inc.; co-chairman, director, Forest City Enterprises, Inc.

RR Donnelley & Sons Co.

Lorch, George A.: chairman, chief executive officer, director, Armstrong World Industries, Inc.

RRH Corp.

Hunt, Ray Lee: chairman, chief executive officer, director, Hunt Oil Co.

Rabbit Software Corp.

Musser, Warren Van Dyke: chairman, chief executive officer, director, Safeguard Scientifics; president, director, Safeguard Scientifics Foundation

Race Rock Holdings

Newman, Andrew E.: member, Edison Family Foundation

Radian Corp.

Kreh, Gordon W.: president, chief executive officer, director, Hartford Steam Boiler Inspection & Insurance Co.

Radiant System Inc.

Balloun, James S.: chairman, chief executive officer, president, National Service Industries, Inc.

Radio Metroplex Inc.

Appell, Louis J., Jr.: president, Susquehanna-Pfaltzgraff Co.

Radisson Group Inc.

Carlson, Curtis Leroy: chairman, director, Carlson Companies, Inc.; president, treasurer, Carlson Family Foundation (Curtis L.)

Radisson Hotel Corp.

Carlson, Curtis Leroy: chairman, director, Carlson Companies, Inc.; president, treasurer, Carlson Family Foundation (Curtis L.)

Radisson Minneapolis Corp.

Carlson, Curtis Leroy: chairman, director, Carlson Companies, Inc.; president, treasurer, Carlson Family Foundation (Curtis L.)

Radisson Missouri Corp.

Carlson, Curtis Leroy: chairman, director, Carlson Companies, Inc.; president, treasurer, Carlson Family Foundation (Curtis L.)

Radisson Moscow Corp.

Carlson, Curtis Leroy: chairman, director, Carlson Companies, Inc.; president, treasurer, Carlson Family Foundation (Curtis L.)

Radnor Venture Ptnr

Musser, Warren Van Dyke: chairman, chief executive officer, director, Safeguard Scientifics; president, director, Safeguard Scientifics Foundation

Rainbow Resources

Bailey, Keith E.: chairman, president, director, chief executive officer, Texas Gas Transmission Corp.; president, director, Williams Companies Foundation (The)

Rainier Bancorp

Broffman, Peter: executive director, Intel Foundation

Ralcorp Holdings Inc.

Kemper, David Woods: chairman, president, chief executive officer, director, Commerce Bancshares, Inc.

Ralston Purina Co.

Liddy, Richard A.: chairman, president, chief executive officer, GenAmerica Corp.

Ramco Manufacturing Co.

Reynolds, Randolph Nicklas: vice chairman, executive officer, director, Reynolds Metals Co.; director, Reynolds Metals Co. Foundation

Ramsey Insurance Co.

Leatherdale, Douglas West: chairman, chief executive officer, president, Saint Paul Companies Inc.

Rand Corp.

Reed, John Shepard: co-chairman, Citibank Corp.

Ranier Ice & Cold Storage

Cline, Robert Stanley: chairman, chief executive officer, director, Airborne Freight Corp.

Rank Xerox Ltd.

Allaire, Paul Arthur: chairman, chief executive officer, chairman executive committee, Xerox Corp.; president, Xerox Foundation

Rauscher Pierce Refinances Inc.

Weiser, Irving: chairman, president, chief executive officer, Dain Bosworth Inc.

Rayonier Forest Resources

Nutter, Wallace L.: director, Rayonier Foundation

Rayonier Forest Resources Co.

Griffin, Donald Wayne: chairman, president, chief executive officer, director, Olin Corp.; trustee, Olin Corp. Charitable Trust

Gross, Ronald Martin: chairman, president, director, Rayonier Foundation; chairman, president, chief executive officer, director, Rayonier Inc.

Rayonier Inc.

Fredericksen, Jay A.: vice president, Rayonier Foundation

Griffin, Donald Wayne: chairman, president, chief executive officer, director, Olin Corp.; trustee, Olin Corp. Charitable Trust

Rayonier New Zealand

Berry, William S.: director, Rayonier Foundation

Rayonier Timberlands LP

Auguste, MacDonald: treasurer, Rayonier Foundation

Griffin, Donald Wayne: chairman, president, chief executive officer, director, Olin Corp.; trustee, Olin Corp. Charitable Trust

Raytheon Co.

Piano, Phyllis J.: president, Cooper Industries Foundation; vice president public affairs, Cooper Industries, Inc.

Re Corp.

Huber, Richard Leslie: chairman, president, chief executive officer, director, Aetna, Inc.

Readers Digest Association Inc.

Preston, James Edward: vice president, director, Avon Products Foundation, Inc.; chairman, chief executive officer, director, Avon Products, Inc.

Readers Digest Latinoamerica SA

Soden, Paul A.: senior vice president, secretary, general counsel, Reader's Digest Association, Inc. (The)

Readers Digest Publishing Inc.

Schadt, James Phillip: chairman, president, chief executive officer, director, Reader's Digest Association, Inc. (The); chairman, director, Reader's Digest Foundation

Readers Digest Sales & Services Inc.

Jones, Ross: senior vice president, chief financial officer, Knight Ridder

Real Estate Delivery Inc.

Dods, Walter Arthur, Jr.: president, director, First Hawaiian Foundation; chairman, chief executive officer, director, First Hawaiian, Inc.

Real Estate Industries Group

Hazen, Paul Mandeville: chairman, chief executive officer, director, Wells Fargo & Co.

Realtor Information Network

Sabbag, Allen L.: president, Meredith Corp.

Realty Co. Pennsylvania Inc.

Hecht, William F.: chairman, president, chief executive officer, Pennsylvania Power & Light

Recovery Engineering Inc.

Gherty, John E.: president, chief executive officer, Land O'Lakes, Inc.

Recovery Services International

Bergsteinsson, Paul: assistant treasurer, CIGNA Foundation

Red Circle Transport Co.

Raskin, Fred C.: president, chief operating officer, Eastern Enterprises; trustee, Eastern Enterprises Foundation

Red Lion Inc.

Fitzpatrick, Jane P.: chairman, chief executive officer, treasurer, Country Curtains, Inc.; chairman, High Meadow Foundation

Red River Broadcasting Corp.

Kunin, Myron: chairman, director, Regis Corp.; president, Regis Foundation

Red Roof Inns Inc.

Rogala, Judith A.: member, Butler Manufacturing Co. Foundation

Red Spot Paint & Varnish Co. Inc.

Muehlbauer, James Herman: vice president, director, Koch Foundation

Redem Corp.

James, George Barker, II: senior vice president, chief financial officer, Levi Strauss & Co.

Reebok International Ltd.

Lesser, Richard G.: executive vice president, chief operating officer, director, TJX Companies, Inc.; chief operating officer, director, TJX Foundation, Inc.

Nunes, Geoffrey: chairman, Millipore Foundation (The)

Reference Press

Berkley, Eugene Bertram: chairman, director, Tension Envelope Corp.; treasurer, Tension Envelope Foundation

Berkley, William S.: president, chief executive officer, director, Tension Envelope Corp.; director, Tension Envelope Foundation

Regal-Beloit Corp.

Coleman, J. Reed: trustee, Kemper Foundation (James S.)

Graff, Stephen Ney: director, Bucyrus-Erie Foundation

Kasten, G. Frederick, Jr.: trustee, Baird & Co. Foundation (Robert W.); chairman, chief executive officer, director, Baird & Co. (Robert W.)

Regence Group

Cameron, Gerry B.: chairman, director, U.S. Bancorp

Regeneron Pharmaceuticals Inc.

Vagelos, Pindaros Roy: trustee, Prudential Insurance Co. of America

Regis Collection Inc.

Kunin, Myron: chairman, director, Regis Corp.; president, Regis Foundation

Regl Industries Development Corp.

McGuinn, Martin Gregory: chairman, chief executive officer, Mellon Financial Corp.

Rehabilitation Hospital Pacific

Watanabe, Jeffrey N.: director, Hawaiian Electric Industries Charitable Foundation

Reily Foods Co.

Herrmann, Harold M.: chief financial officer, Reily & Co., Inc. (William B.)

Reins Co.

Howe, Wesley Jackson: chairman emeritus, director, Becton Dickinson & Co.

Reinsurance Group America Inc.

Edison, Bernard Alan: member, Edison Family Foundation

ReliaStar Bankers Security Life Insurance Co.

Turner, John Gosney: chairman, chief executive officer, director, ReliaStar Financial Corp.; director, ReliaStar Foundation

ReliaStar Financial Corp.

Howard, James Joseph, III: chairman, president, chief executive officer, director, Northern States Power Co.

Koch, David Andrew: president, Graco Foundation; chairman, director, Graco, Inc.

Nelson, Glen David, MD: vice chairman, Medtronic, Inc.

ReliaStar Life Insurance Co.

Turner, John Gosney: chairman, chief executive officer, director, ReliaStar Financial Corp.; director, ReliaStar Foundation

ReliaStar United Services Life Insurance Co.

Turner, John Gosney: chairman, chief executive officer, director, ReliaStar Financial Corp.; director, ReliaStar Foundation

Reminger & Reminger Co.

Gorman, Joseph T.: chairman, chief executive officer, TRW Inc.

Renaissance Reinsurance

Liska, Paul J.: executive vice president, chief financial officer, Saint Paul Companies Inc.

Reno Newspapers Inc.

McCorkindale, Douglas H.: vice chairman, president, Gannett Co., Inc.; president, Gannett Foundation

Republic Airlines Inc.

Purvis, George Frank, Jr.: chairman, president, chief executive officer, director, Pan-American Life Insurance Co.

Resolute Reins Co.

Smith, Donald Kaye: senior vice president, general counsel, director, GEICO Corp.

Resource Partners Inc.

Kidder, C. Robert: chairman, president, chief executive officer, director, Borden, Inc.

Restaurant Suntory USA Inc.

Dods, Walter Arthur, Jr.: president, director, First Hawaiian Foundation; chairman, chief executive officer, director, First Hawaiian, Inc.

Reuters Founders Share Co. Ltd.

Graham, Katharine Meyer: chairman executive committee, director, The Washington Post

Revlon Consumer Products Corp.

Gittis, Howard: director, Revlon Foundation Inc.

Revlon Inc.

Kissinger, Henry Alfred: director, CBS Foundation

Slovin, Bruce: president, director, Revlon Inc.

Reynolds & Reynolds Co.

Walker, Martin Dean: chairman, chief executive officer, director, Hanna Co. (M.A.)

Reynolds International Service Co.

Reynolds, Randolph Nicklas: vice chairman, executive officer, director, Reynolds Metals Co.; director, Reynolds Metals Co. Foundation

Reynolds Metals Co.

Joyce, William H.: chairman, president, chief executive officer, chief operating officer, Union Carbide Corp.

Ringler, James M.: chairman, president, chief executive officer, director, Premark International Inc.

Rhode Island Monthly Communication

Sutton, Howard: president, Providence Journal Charitable Foundation

Rich Communications Corp.

Rich, David A.: executive director, Rich Family Foundation; vice president, secretary, director, Rich Products Corp.

Rich Food Holdings

Harris, Grace: member scholarship committee, Circuit City Foundation

Richfood Holdings Inc.

Ukrop, James E.: vice chairman, chief executive officer, director, Ukrop Foundation; vice chairman, chief executive officer, Ukrop's Super Markets

Villanueva, Edward: trustee, Circuit City Foundation

Richland Development Corp.

Pate, James Leonard: chairman, chief executive officer, director, Pennzoil-Quaker State Co.

Richmond Renaissance Inc.

Burrus, Robert Lewis, Jr.: trustee, Circuit City Foundation

Richmond Virginia Electric & Power Co.

Spilman, Robert H.: chairman, chief executive officer, Bassett Furniture Industries; chairman, director, Bassett Furniture Industries Fdn.

Riggs Asia Ltd.

Allbritton, Joe Lewis: chairman, chief executive officer, Riggs Bank NA

Rights Exchange Inc.

Lippes, Gerald Sanford: secretary, Mark IV Industries Foundation

Riley Roumell

Tracy, Emmet E., Jr.: president, chief executive officer, director, Alma Piston

Co.; president, Tracy Fund (Emmet and Frances)

Risk Capital Reinsurance Co.
Esposito, Michael Patrick, Jr.: trustee, Chase Manhattan Foundation

Rite Aid Connecticut Inc.
Grass, Martin Lehrman: chairman, chief executive officer, director, Rite Aid Corp.

Rite Aid Corp.
Tisch, Preston Robert: chairman, director, CBS Foundation; co-chairman, co-chief executive officer, director, CNA; trustee, Loews Foundation

Rite Aid Corp. Kentucky
Grass, Martin Lehrman: chairman, chief executive officer, director, Rite Aid Corp.
Noonan, Timothy J.: president, chief operating officer, director, Rite Aid Corp.

Rite Aid Florida Inc.
Grass, Martin Lehrman: chairman, chief executive officer, director, Rite Aid Corp.

Rite Aid Idaho Inc.
Noonan, Timothy J.: president, chief operating officer, director, Rite Aid Corp.

Rite Aid Indiana Inc.
Grass, Martin Lehrman: chairman, chief executive officer, director, Rite Aid Corp.

Rite Aid New Hampshire Inc.
Noonan, Timothy J.: president, chief operating officer, director, Rite Aid Corp.

Rite Aid New Jersey Inc.
Grass, Martin Lehrman: chairman, chief executive officer, director, Rite Aid Corp.

Rite Aid Pennsylvania Inc.
Noonan, Timothy J.: president, chief operating officer, director, Rite Aid Corp.

Rite Aid Rome Distribution Center
Grass, Martin Lehrman: chairman, chief executive officer, director, Rite Aid Corp.

River Fleets Inc.
Raskin, Fred C.: president, chief operating officer, Eastern Enterprises; trustee, Eastern Enterprises Foundation

River Pipeline Co.
Godfrey, Cullen Michael: vice president, FINA Foundation

River Terminal Railway Co.
Kelly, J. Peter: president, chief operating officer, director, LTV Corp.; trustee, LTV Foundation

Riverbend Bancshares Inc.
Griffin, Donald Wayne: chairman, president, chief executive officer, director, Olin Corp.; trustee, Olin Corp. Charitable Trust

Riverton Investment Corp.
Burrus, Robert Lewis, Jr.: trustee, Circuit City Foundation

Road System Inc.
Moffitt, Donald Eugene: chairman, director, CNF Transportation, Inc.

Roanoke Times & World-News
Batten, Frank, Sr.: chairman, director, Landmark Communications Foundation; chairman, Landmark Communications Inc.

Robert A. Cline Co.
Bridgeland, James Ralph, Jr.: trustee, Star Bank NA, Cincinnati Foundation

Robert L. Cristofaro MD
Nelson, John Martin: chairman, director, TJX Companies, Inc.

Robert Morris Associates
Baker, Leslie Mayo, Jr.: president, chief executive officer, chairman, Wachovia Bank of North Carolina NA; chairman, Wachovia Foundation, Inc. (The)
Wobst, Frank: chairman, chief executive officer, director, Huntington Bancshares Inc.

Robert Scott David Brooks Outlet Stores Inc.
Jacobsen, James C.: vice chairman, Kellwood Co.; vice president, director, Kellwood Foundation

Robinson Nugent Inc.
Previte, Richard: president, chief operating officer, director, Advanced Micro Devices, Inc.

Roche Carolina Inc.
Kentz, Frederick C., III: trustee, Hoffmann-La Roche Foundation; vice president, secretary, general counsel, Hoffmann-La Roche Inc.
Zenner, Patrick J.: trustee, Hoffmann-La Roche Foundation; president, chief executive officer, director, Hoffmann-La Roche Inc.

Roche Diagnostics System
Kentz, Frederick C., III: trustee, Hoffmann-La Roche Foundation; vice president, secretary, general counsel, Hoffmann-La Roche Inc.

Roche Molecular System Inc.
Kentz, Frederick C., III: trustee, Hoffmann-La Roche Foundation; vice president, secretary, general counsel, Hoffmann-La Roche Inc.
Zenner, Patrick J.: trustee, Hoffmann-La Roche Foundation; president, chief executive officer, director, Hoffmann-La Roche Inc.

Rochester Gas & Electric Corp.
Dugan, Allan E.: senior vice president corporate strategic service, Xerox Corp.; trustee, Xerox Foundation

Rock Tenn Co.
Spiegel, John William: member, SunTrust Bank Atlanta Foundation

Rockcliffe Research & Technology Inc.
Light, Walter Frederick: trustee, Air Products Foundation

Rockford Pro - America
Meuleman, Robert Joseph: director, AMCORE Foundation

Rockwell International Corp.
McCormick, William Thomas, Jr.: chairman, chief executive officer, director, Consumers Energy Co.; chairman, Consumers Energy Foundation
Shapiro, Robert B.: chairman, president, chief executive officer, director, Monsanto Co.

Rofan Services Inc.
Reinhard, J. Pedro: executive vice president, chief financial officer, director, Dow Chemical Co.

Rogers Corp.
Barnes, Wallace W.: director, Barnes Group Foundation Inc.

Rohm & Haas Co.
Burke, Daniel Barnett: vice president, treasurer, director, ABC Foundation
Graves, Earl Gilbert: director, Aetna Foundation
Henderson, James Alan: vice chairman, chief executive officer, director, Ameritech Corp.; chairman, director, Cummins Engine Foundation
Keyser, Richard Lee: chairman, chief executive officer, president, Grainger, Inc. (W.W.)

Roll Coater Inc.
Baker, James Kendrick: chairman, director, Arvin Foundation; vice chairman, director, Arvin Industries, Inc.

Roseburg Lumber Co.
Ford, Kenneth W.: chairman, Roseburg Forest Products Co.

Rosepointe Housing
Kunin, Myron: chairman, director, Regis Corp.; president, Regis Foundation

Roto-Rooter
McNamara, Kevin J.: president, director, Chemed Corp.; secretary, trustee, Chemed Foundation

Rouge Industries Inc.
Pestillo, Peter John: executive chairman, Ford Motor Co.; trustee, Ford Motor Co. Fund

Rouge Steel Co.
Pestillo, Peter John: executive chairman, Ford Motor Co.; trustee, Ford Motor Co. Fund

Roundy's Inc.
Rupple, Brenton H.: director, Bucyrus-Erie Foundation

Rouse Co.
Casey, Jeremiah E.: chairman, First Maryland Bancorp; chairman, trustee, First Maryland Foundation

Rouse Co. Colorado Inc.
Deering, Anthony W.: chairman, chief executive officer, Rouse Co.; chairman, president, trustee, Rouse Co. Foundation

Rouse Co. Florida Inc.
Deering, Anthony W.: chairman, chief executive officer, Rouse Co.; chairman, president, trustee, Rouse Co. Foundation

Rouse Co. Illinois Inc.
Deering, Anthony W.: chairman, chief executive officer, Rouse Co.; chairman, president, trustee, Rouse Co. Foundation

Rouse Co. Massachusetts Inc.
Deering, Anthony W.: chairman, chief executive officer, Rouse Co.; chairman, president, trustee, Rouse Co. Foundation
Donahue, Jeffrey H.: senior vice president, chief financial officer, Rouse Co.

Rouse Co. Michigan Inc.
Deering, Anthony W.: chairman, chief executive officer, Rouse Co.; chairman, president, trustee, Rouse Co. Foundation

Rouse Co. New Jersey Inc.
Donahue, Jeffrey H.: senior vice president, chief financial officer, Rouse Co.

Rouse Co. Ohio Inc.
Deering, Anthony W.: chairman, chief executive officer, Rouse Co.; chairman, president, trustee, Rouse Co. Foundation

Rouse Co. Oregon Inc.

Deering, Anthony W.: chairman, chief executive officer, Rouse Co.; chairman, president, trustee, Rouse Co. Foundation

Rouse Co. Owings Mills Inc.

Deering, Anthony W.: chairman, chief executive officer, Rouse Co.; chairman, president, trustee, Rouse Co. Foundation

Donahue, Jeffrey H.: senior vice president, chief financial officer, Rouse Co.

McGregor, Douglas A.: trustee, Rouse Co. Foundation

Rouse Co. Saint Louis Inc.

Deering, Anthony W.: chairman, chief executive officer, Rouse Co.; chairman, president, trustee, Rouse Co. Foundation

Rouse Co. Texas Inc.

Deering, Anthony W.: chairman, chief executive officer, Rouse Co.; chairman, president, trustee, Rouse Co. Foundation

Rouse Hotel Management Inc.

Donahue, Jeffrey H.: senior vice president, chief financial officer, Rouse Co.

Rouse Management Service Corp.

Deering, Anthony W.: chairman, chief executive officer, Rouse Co.; chairman, president, trustee, Rouse Co. Foundation

Donahue, Jeffrey H.: senior vice president, chief financial officer, Rouse Co.

Rouse Marshalltown Center

Deering, Anthony W.: chairman, chief executive officer, Rouse Co.; chairman, president, trustee, Rouse Co. Foundation

Donahue, Jeffrey H.: senior vice president, chief financial officer, Rouse Co.

Rouse Missouri Holding Co.

Deering, Anthony W.: chairman, chief executive officer, Rouse Co.; chairman, president, trustee, Rouse Co. Foundation

Rouse Philadelphia Inc.

Deering, Anthony W.: chairman, chief executive officer, Rouse Co.; chairman, president, trustee, Rouse Co. Foundation

Donahue, Jeffrey H.: senior vice president, chief financial officer, Rouse Co.

Rouse-Milwaukee Inc.

Deering, Anthony W.: chairman, chief executive officer, Rouse Co.; chairman, president, trustee, Rouse Co. Foundation

Rouse-Oakwood Shopping Center

Deering, Anthony W.: chairman, chief executive officer, Rouse Co.; chairman, president, trustee, Rouse Co. Foundation

Rouse-Tampa Inc.

Deering, Anthony W.: chairman, chief executive officer, Rouse Co.; chairman, president, trustee, Rouse Co. Foundation

Donahue, Jeffrey H.: senior vice president, chief financial officer, Rouse Co.

Rouse-Teachers Properties Inc.

McGregor, Douglas A.: trustee, Rouse Co. Foundation

Royal Group Inc.

Wheeler, Joyce W.: secretary, Royal & SunAlliance Insurance Foundation, Inc.; vice president, corporate secretary, Royal & SunAlliance USA, Inc.

Royal Surplus Lines Insurance Co.

Wheeler, Joyce W.: secretary, Royal & SunAlliance Insurance Foundation, Inc.; vice president, corporate secretary, Royal & SunAlliance USA, Inc.

Rubbermaid Cleaning Products

Weigand, George C.: vice president, trustee, Rubbermaid Foundation; chief financial officer, senior vice president, Rubbermaid Inc.

Rubbermaid Commercial Products

Dean, John W., III: vice president, treasurer, Rubbermaid Inc.

Weigand, George C.: vice president, trustee, Rubbermaid Foundation; chief financial officer, senior vice president, Rubbermaid Inc.

Rubbermaid Cortland Inc.

Carroll, Charles A.: president, chief operating officer, director, Rubbermaid Inc.

Dean, John W., III: vice president, treasurer, Rubbermaid Inc.

Schmitt, Wolfgang Rudolph: chairman, chief executive officer, director, Rubbermaid Inc.

Rubbermaid Specialty Products Inc.

Carroll, Charles A.: president, chief operating officer, director, Rubbermaid Inc.

Ruddick Corp.

Dickson, Alan Thomas: president, Dickson Foundation; chairman, Ruddick Corp.

Dickson, Rush Stuart: chairman, Dickson Foundation

Ruppman Marketing Inc.

Gloyd, Lawrence Eugene: trustee, CLARCOR Foundation; chairman, chief executive officer, director, CLARCOR Inc.

Russell Lands Co.

Jones, D. Paul, Jr.: chairman, chief executive officer, Compass Bank; trustee, Compass Bank Foundation

Rutland Regional Medical Center

Young, Robert Harris: president, chief executive officer, Central Vermont Public Service Corp.

Ryan Builders Inc.

Ryan, Patrick G.: chairman, president, chief executive officer, Aon Corp.; president, Aon Foundation

Ryan Companies United States Inc.

Ryan, Patrick G.: chairman, president, chief executive officer, Aon Corp.; president, Aon Foundation

Ryan Insurance Group DE

Medvin, Harvey Norman: executive vice president, treasurer, chief financial officer, Aon Corp.; treasurer, Aon Foundation

Ryan Properties Inc.

Ryan, Patrick G.: chairman, president, chief executive officer, Aon Corp.; president, Aon Foundation

Ryan Warranty Services

Medvin, Harvey Norman: executive vice president, treasurer, chief financial officer, Aon Corp.; treasurer, Aon Foundation

Ryder Energy Distr Corp.

Burns, Mitchell Anthony: president, director, Ryder System Charitable Foundation; chairman, president, chief executive officer, Ryder System, Inc.

Ryder Puerto Rico Inc.

Denny, Dwight D.: director, Ryder System Charitable Foundation

Ryder Student Transportation Services

Mulkey, Larry S.: director, Ryder System Charitable Foundation

Ryder System Inc.

Georges, John A.: director, International Paper Co.

Martin, Lynn M.: director, Ameritech Foundation

Willes, Mark Hinckley: chairman, president, chief executive officer, Times Mirror Co.; chairman, Times Mirror Foundation

Ryder Truck Rental Inc.

Burns, Mitchell Anthony: president, director, Ryder System Charitable Foundation; chairman, president, chief executive officer, Ryder System, Inc.

S&K Famous Brands Inc.

Burrus, Robert Lewis, Jr.: trustee, Circuit City Foundation

S&S Land & Cattle Co.

Stivers, William Charles: senior vice president, chief financial officer, treasurer, Weyerhaeuser Co.; treasurer, trustee, Weyerhaeuser Co. Foundation

SAFECO Corp.

Campbell, Phyllis J.: president private financial services, US Bank, Washington

Cline, Robert Stanley: chairman, chief executive officer, director, Airborne Freight Corp.

Reed, William Garrard, Jr.: director, Matlock Foundation

Weyerhaeuser, George Hunt: director, Weyerhaeuser Co.; trustee, Weyerhaeuser Co. Foundation

SAFECO Credit Co. Inc.

Eigsti, Roger Harry: chairman, chief executive officer, SAFECO Corp.

SAFECO Mutual Funds

Dickey, Boh A.: president, chief operating officer, SAFECO Corp.

SAFECO National Insurance Co.

Eigsti, Roger Harry: chairman, chief executive officer, SAFECO Corp.

SAIC

Simpson, Louis Allen: president, chief executive officer capital operations, director, GEICO Corp.

SB Decking Inc.

Spaeth, Karl Henry: chairman, trustee, Quaker Chemical Foundation

SB Foot Tanning Co.

Goggin, Joseph P.: treasurer, Red Wing Shoe Co. Foundation

SBC Cable Co.

Appell, Louis J., Jr.: president, Susquehanna-Pfaltzgraff Co.

Finlayson, John L.: vice president finance & administration, Susquehanna-Pfaltzgraff Co.

SBC Communications Inc.

Caldwell, Royce S.: director, SBC Foundation

Knight, Charles Field: chairman, chief executive officer, Emerson Electric Co.

Notebaert, Richard C.: chairman, chief executive officer, Ameritech Corp.; director, Ameritech Foundation

SBC Corp.

Rosenberg, Richard Morris: chairman, chief executive officer (retired), Bank of America

SC Johnson & Co. Inc.

Wright, Michael William: chairman, president, chief executive officer, director, SuperValu, Inc.

SCANA Corp.

Hipp, William Hayne: president, chief executive officer, director, Liberty Corp.; chairman, president, director, Liberty Corp. Foundation

SCI Holdings Inc.

Harris, Elmer Beseler: president, chief executive officer, director, Alabama Power Co.

SDL Inc.

Myers, Mark B.: senior vice president corporate research & technology, Xerox Corp.; trustee, Xerox Foundation

SEI Holdings Inc.

Franklin, H. Allen: president, chief executive officer, Georgia Power Co.

SENCO Products Inc.

Juilfs, George C.: director, Cinergy Foundation

SHURflo Pump Manufacturing Co.

Wardeberg, George E.: president, WICOR Foundation; president, chief executive officer, director, WICOR, Inc.

SHV North America Inc.

Bridgeland, James Ralph, Jr.: trustee, Star Bank NA, Cincinnati Foundation

SKF U.S.A. Inc.

Salizzoni, Frank L.: vice chairman, Block Foundation (H&R); president, chief executive officer, director, Block, Inc. (H&R)

SKI Realty Inc.

Gelb, Richard Lee: director, New York Times Co. Foundation

SLH Corp.

Kemper, David Woods: chairman, president, chief executive officer, director, Commerce Bancshares, Inc.

SPS

Helton, Bill D.: chairman, New Century Energies Foundation

SPX Corp.

Coffin, Sarah R.: director, Fuller Co. Foundation (H.B.); vice president specialty group, Fuller Co. (H.B.)

SRJ Financial Group Inc.

Yablon, Leonard Harold: secretary-treasurer, Forbes Foundation

SSDS Inc.

Davis, Ruth Margaret: trustee, Air Products Foundation

SVB & T Corp.

Habig, Thomas L.: vice chairman, director, Habig Foundation

Saab Automobile

Eaton, Robert James: co-chairman, president, chief executive officer, DaimlerChrysler Corp.

Sabre Group Holdings Inc.

McNamara, Anne H.: senior vice president, general counsel, AMR Corp.

Saco Defense Inc.

Duchossois, Craig J.: director, Duchossois Foundation; president, director, Duchossois Industries Inc.

Safe Driver Motor Club Inc.

Phillips, Rosalind Ann: secretary, GEICO Philanthropic Foundation

Utley, Edward Harold: vice chairman, president, GEICO Corp.; chairman, director, GEICO Philanthropic Foundation

Safeguard Insurance Co.

Wheeler, Joyce W.: secretary, Royal & SunAlliance Insurance Foundation, Inc.; vice president, corporate secretary, Royal & SunAlliance USA, Inc.

Safety-Kleen Corp.

Jannotta, Edgar D.: president, Blair & Co. Foundation (William); senior director, Blair & Co. (William)

Safeway Inc.

Hazen, Paul Mandeville: chairman, chief executive officer, director, Wells Fargo & Co.

Magowan, Peter Alden: president, managing general partner, Safeway Inc.

Saginaw Bay Lateral Co.

Ewing, Stephen E.: president, chief executive officer, director, Michigan Consolidated Gas Co.

Saint Charles Inc.

Shiely, John Stephen: president, chief operating officer, director, Briggs & Stratton Corp.; vice president, director, Briggs & Stratton Corp. Foundation

Saint Clair Energy Corp.

Beale, Susan M.: director, Detroit Edison Foundation

Saint Cloud Newspapers Inc.

McCorkindale, Douglas H.: vice chairman, president, Gannett Co., Inc.; president, Gannett Foundation

Saint James Holding Co. Bermuda Ltd.

Countryman, Gary Lee: chairman, Liberty Mutual Insurance Group

Saint Louis Board Election Commission

Moten, John, Junior: vice president community relations, Laclede Gas Co.

Saint Louis Post Dispatch

Ridgway, Ronald H.: senior vice president, Pulitzer Publishing Co.; secretary, treasurer, director, Pulitzer Publishing Co. Foundation

Saint Louis Refrigerator Car Co.

Williams, Eugene Flewellyn, Jr.: member public policy committee, Emerson Charitable Trust

Saint Louis Refrigerator Co.

Busch, August Adolphus, III: chairman, president, chief executive officer, Anheuser-Busch Companies, Inc.

Saint Louis Southwest Railway Co.

Starzel, Robert F.: president, Union Pacific Foundation

Saint Paul Co.s Inc.

Duberstein, Kenneth: director, Cinergy Foundation

Saint Paul Companies Inc.

Bonsignore, Michael Robert: director, Honeywell Foundation; chairman, chief executive officer, director, Honeywell International Inc.

Nelson, Glen David, MD: vice chairman, Medtronic, Inc.

Saint Paul Finance Group Inc.

Leatherdale, Douglas West: chairman, chief executive officer, president, Saint Paul Companies Inc.

Saint Wisconsin Savings & Loan

Gaiswinkler, Robert Sigfried: chairman, director, First Financial Bank; director, First Financial Foundation

Saint-Gobain Advanced Materials Corp.

Ayotte, Robert C.: executive vice president, director, CertainTeed Corp.; vice president, director, Norton Co. Foundation

Saint-Gobain Corp.

Amoss, George B.: vice president finance, chief financial officer, CertainTeed Corp.; chief financial officer, CertainTeed Corp. Foundation

Caccini, Gianpaolo: chairman, chief executive officer, director, CertainTeed Corp.; chairman, CertainTeed Corp. Foundation; chairman, chief executive officer, director, Norton Co.; president, director, Norton Co. Foundation

Harkins, James F., Jr.: treasurer, CertainTeed Corp. Foundation

Mattson, Bradford C.: executive vice president exterior building products, CertainTeed Corp.

Mesher, John R.: assistant secretary, CertainTeed Corp. Foundation

Sweeney, John J., III: vice president, CertainTeed Corp.

Saint-Gobain Industrial Ceramics

Ayotte, Robert C.: executive vice president, director, CertainTeed Corp.; vice president, director, Norton Co. Foundation

Saison Group

Tsutsumi, Senji: vice president, trustee, Ise Cultural Foundation

Salem County Sampler Inc.

McCorkindale, Douglas H.: vice chairman, president, Gannett Co., Inc.; president, Gannett Foundation

Salem Mall Inc.

Deering, Anthony W.: chairman, chief executive officer, Rouse Co.; chairman, president, trustee, Rouse Co. Foundation

Donahue, Jeffrey H.: senior vice president, chief financial officer, Rouse Co.

Salinas Newspapers Inc.

McCorkindale, Douglas H.: vice chairman, president, Gannett Co., Inc.; president, Gannett Foundation

Salomon Brothers Inc.

Maughan, Deryck C.: director, New York Stock Exchange Foundation, Inc.; co-chairman, co-chief executive officer, Salomon Smith Barney

Salomon Forex Inc.

Maughan, Deryck C.: director, New York Stock Exchange Foundation, Inc.; co-chairman, co-chief executive officer, Salomon Smith Barney

Salomon Inc.

Andreas, Dwayne Orville: chairman, chief executive officer, Archer-Daniels-Midland Co.

Samcor Glass Ltd.

Booth, Chesleu Peter Washburn: senior vice president development, Corning Inc.; trustee, Corning Inc. Foundation

Samsung Corning Co. Inc.

Booth, Chesleu Peter Washburn: senior vice president development, Corning Inc.; trustee, Corning Inc. Foundation

Samuel Mills Damon Estate

Dods, Walter Arthur, Jr.: president, director, First Hawaiian Foundation; chairman, chief executive officer, director, First Hawaiian, Inc.

San Diego Gas Electric Co.

Mitchell, Warren I.: president, director, Southern California Gas Co.

San Diego Union-Tribune

Copley, David C.: president, trustee, Copley Foundation (James S.); president, chief executive officer, director, senior management board, Copley Press, Inc.

San Francisco Reinsurance Co.

Hansmeyer, Herbert F.: chairman, Fireman's Fund Insurance Co.

Rowe, Thomas E.: chairman, director, Fireman's Fund Foundation; director, Fireman's Fund Insurance Co.

Sanchez Computer Associates

Musser, Warren Van Dyke: chairman, chief executive officer, director, Safeguard Scientifics; president, director, Safeguard Scientifics Foundation

Sangre de Cristo Ranches

Yablon, Leonard Harold: secretary-treasurer, Forbes Foundation

Santa Catalina Island Co.

Piet, William M.: vice president, director, Wrigley Co. Foundation (Wm. Jr.); vice president corporate affairs, secretary, assistant to president, Wrigley Co. (Wm. Jr.)

Wrigley, William: chairman, director, Wrigley Co. Foundation (Wm. Jr.); president, chief executive officer, director, Wrigley Co. (Wm. Jr.)

Santa Fe Energy Resources Inc.

Greehey, William Eugene: chairman, chief executive officer, director, Valero Energy Corp.

Santa Fe Minerals Inc.

Springer, Denis E.: senior vice president, chief financial officer, Burlington Northern Santa Fe Corp.; director, Burlington Northern Santa Fe Foundation

Santa Fe Pacific Pipelines Inc.

Springer, Denis E.: senior vice president, chief financial officer, Burlington Northern Santa Fe Corp.; director, Burlington Northern Santa Fe Foundation

Sara Lee Corp.

Allaire, Paul Arthur: chairman, chief executive officer, chairman executive committee, Xerox Corp.; president, Xerox Foundation

Burnham, Duane Lee: chairman, chief executive officer, director, Abbott Laboratories

Coker, Charles Westfield: trustee, Sonoco Foundation; vice president, Sonoco Products Co.

Thomas, Richard Lee: vice president, First National Bank of Chicago Foundation

Sargasso Mutual

MacLeay, Thomas H.: president, chief operating officer, National Life of Vermont

Prohofsky, Dennis E.: secretary, Minnesota Mutual Foundation; senior vice president, general counsel, secretary, Minnesota Mutual Life Insurance Co.

Savannah Foods & IDS Inc.

Reed, James M.: trustee, Union Camp Charitable Trust; vice chairman, chief financial officer, director, Union Camp Corp.

Save Mart Supermarkets

Busch, August Adolphus, III: chairman, president, chief executive officer, Anheuser-Busch Companies, Inc.

Saville System

Blanchard, J. A., III: president, chief executive officer, director, Deluxe Corp.

Sawtooth Communications Inc.

Rockey, Travis O.: vice president, director, Evening Post Publishing Co.

Scantron Corp.

Dollar, William Michael: vice president, treasurer, chief financial officer, Harland Co. (John H.)

Schering-Plough Corp.

Becherer, Hans Walter: chairman, chief executive officer, director, Deere & Co.; director, Deere Foundation (John)

Scholastic Corp.

Brademas, John: chairman, Texaco Foundation

Schroder Mortgage Associates

Lachman, Marguerite Leanne: trustee, Chicago Title and Trust Co. Foundation

Schutte & Koerting Inc.

Varet, Elizabeth Rosenwald: vice president, director, AMETEK Foundation; director, AMETEK, Inc.

Schwab Holding Inc.

Schwab, Charles R.: chairman, co-chief executive officer, director, Schwab & Co., Inc. (Charles); chairman, Schwab Corp. Foundation (Charles)

Stupski, Lawrence J.: president, vice chairman, chief operating officer, director, Schwab & Co., Inc. (Charles); chief financial officer, secretary, Schwab Corp. Foundation (Charles)

Scitex Corp. Ltd.

Melican, James Patrick, Jr.: executive vice president legal & external affairs, International Paper Co.; director, International Paper Co. Foundation

Suwyn, Mark A.: chairman, president, Louisiana-Pacific Foundation

Scotsman Industries Inc.

Kennedy, George Danner: trustee, Kemper Foundation (James S.)

Scott Paper Co.

Meyerson, Martin: director, Panasonic Foundation

Scott Tobacco Co.

Rosson, William Mimms: chairman, Conwood Co. LP

Scottsdale Insurance Co.

Druen, W. Sidney: director, Nationwide Insurance Enterprise Foundation

Miller, David O.: chairman, Employers Insurance of Wausau, A Mutual Co.; trustee, Nationwide Insurance Enterprise Foundation; chairman, Wausau Insurance Companies

Shisler, Arden L.: trustee, Nationwide Insurance Enterprise Foundation

Scripps Howard Broadcasting Co.

Gardner, Frank: senior vice president, Scripps Co. (E.W.)

Scripps, Charles Edward: chairman executive committee, director, vice president, Scripps Co. (E.W.); member, Scripps Howard Foundation

Scripps Howard Newspapers

Burleigh, William Robert: president, chief executive officer, director, Scripps Co. (E.W.); member, Scripps Howard Foundation

Sea-Land Service

Snow, John William: chairman, president, chief executive officer, CSX Corp.

Seafield Capital Corp.

Kemper, David Woods: chairman, president, chief executive officer, director, Commerce Bancshares, Inc.

Seagram Co. Ltd.

Bronfman, Edgar Miles: chairman, trustee, Bronfman Foundation/Joseph E. Seagram & Sons, Inc. Fund (Samuel); chairman, Seagram & Sons, Inc. (Joseph E.)

Brown, Richard Harris: chairman, chief executive officer, director, EDS Corp.

Sacks, David G.: trustee, Bronfman Foundation/Joseph E. Seagram & Sons, Inc. Fund (Samuel)

Sealed Air Corp.

Codey, Lawrence R.: president, chief operating officer, Public Service Electric & Gas Co.

Freeman, David: chairman, president, chief executive officer, director, Loctite Corp.

Sealtest Foods

Fino, Raymond M.: second vice president, Warner-Lambert Charitable Foundation; vice president human resources, Warner-Lambert Co.

Sealy Corp.

Hefner, Christie Ann: chairman, chief executive officer, Playboy Enterprises Inc.; director, Playboy Foundation

Sears, Roebuck & Co.

Correll, Alston Dayton 'Pete', Jr.: chairman, president, chief executive officer, director, Georgia-Pacific Corp.; director, Georgia-Pacific Foundation

Farrell, W. James: chairman, chief executive officer, Illinois Tool Works, Inc.

Notebaert, Richard C.: chairman, chief executive officer, Ameritech Corp.; director, Ameritech Foundation

Rogers, C. B., Jr.: chairman, Equifax Foundation; chairman, director, Equifax Inc.

Ryan, Patrick G.: chairman, president, chief executive officer, Aon Corp.; president, Aon Foundation

Seattle First National Bank

Cline, Robert Stanley: chairman, chief executive officer, director, Airborne Freight Corp.

Seattle Times Co.

Pigott, Charles McGee: president, director, PACCAR Foundation; chairman emeritus, director, PACCAR Inc.

Ridder, Paul Anthony: chairman, chief executive officer, director, Knight Ridder

Seaview Hotel Corp.

Andreas, Dwayne Orville: chairman, chief executive officer, Archer-Daniels-Midland Co.

Sebro Plastics Inc.

DeLoach, Harris E., Junior: executive vice president, director, Sonoco Products Co.

Second Corp.

Barron, Donald Ray: president, director, Atlantic Investment Co.

Sectional Die Co.

Hessler, David J.: secretary, trustee, Jochum-Moll Foundation (The); president, partner, MTD Products Inc.

Sectional Stamping Inc.

Hessler, David J.: secretary, trustee, Jochum-Moll Foundation (The); president, partner, MTD Products Inc.

Secure Futures Inc.

Fitzgerald, William Allingham: chairman, director, Commercial Federal Corp.

Securities Trust Co. New Jersey

Fluno, Jere David: vice chairman, Grainger, Inc. (W.W.)

Security Benefit Group Inc.

Fricke, Howard R.: president, director, Security Benefit Life Insurance Co.; trustee, Security Benefit Life Insurance Co. Charitable Trust

Hanna, William W.: president, chief operating officer, director, Koch Industries, Inc.

Security Capital Group Inc.

Bodman, Samuel Wright, III: chairman, chief executive officer, director, Cabot Corp.; president, director, Cabot Corp. Foundation

Security Distributor Inc. Co. LLC

Fricke, Howard R.: president, director, Security Benefit Life Insurance Co.; trustee, Security Benefit Life Insurance Co. Charitable Trust

Security Equity Life Insurance Co.

Liddy, Richard A.: chairman, president, chief executive officer, GenAmerica Corp.

Security Management

Fricke, Howard R.: president, director, Security Benefit Life Insurance Co.; trustee, Security Benefit Life Insurance Co. Charitable Trust

Security Offshore Insurance Ltd.

Keen, J. LaMont: vice president, chief financial officer, Idaho Power Co.

Security Savings Bank

Ford, Joseph 'Joe': chairman, chief executive officer, president, ALLTEL Corp.

Security Trust Co.

Bilton, Stuart Douglas: president, chief executive officer, Chicago Title Corp.; trustee, Chicago Title and Trust Co. Foundation

Sedona Publishing Co.

Getz, George F.: president, Globe Corp.; secretary, director, Globe Foundation

Sega America Inc.

Toyoda, Shinobu: trustee, Sega Foundation

Sega Enterprises

Rosen, David: trustee, Sega Foundation

Seinau-Fisher Studios Inc.

Bridgeland, James Ralph, Jr.: trustee, Star Bank NA, Cincinnati Foundation

Sejak Corp.

Wallach, Ira D.: chairman, Central National-Gottesman; executive vice president, Central National-Gottesman Foundation

Sematech

Barrett, Craig R.: president, chief operating officer, director, Intel Corp.

Sempra Energy

Lozano, Ignacio Eugenio, Jr.: chairman, Pacific Mutual Life Insurance Co.

Sensormatic Electronics Corp.

Ray, John Thomas, Jr.: president, director, Fuller Co. Foundation (H.B.)

Sentinel Group Funds

Farman, Richard Donald: chairman, chief executive officer, Pacific Enterprises

Sentry Fund Inc.

Lohr, William J. (Bill): vice president finance, Sentry Insurance, A Mutual Co.; treasurer, Sentry Insurance Foundation Inc.

Sentry Insurance

Lawson, William Hogan, III: chairman, chief executive officer, director, Franklin Electric Co.; president, Franklin Electric, Edward J. Schaefer, and T. W. KehoeCharitable and Educational Foundation

Sentry Insurance Co.

Davis, Erroll Brown, Jr.: president, chief executive officer, director, Wisconsin Power & Light Co.

Puelicher, John A.: president, director, Marshall & Ilsley Foundation, Inc.

Sentry Life Insurance Co.

Lohr, William J. (Bill): vice president finance, Sentry Insurance, A Mutual Co.; treasurer, Sentry Insurance Foundation Inc.

Schuh, Dale R.: president, chief executive officer, Sentry Insurance, A Mutual Co.

Sequoia Ventures Inc.

Bechtel, Riley Peart: chairman, Bechtel Foundation; chairman, chief executive officer, director, Bechtel Group, Inc.

Servco Fin Corp.

Nakagawa, Jean H.: vice president, director, Servco Foundation

Service Motors

Fukunaga, Mark H.: chairman, director, Servco Foundation; chief executive officer, chairman, Servco Pacific

ServiceMaster Co.

Reinemund, Steve S.: chairman, chief executive officer, Frito-Lay, Inc.

Servicemaster-Consumer Services

Soderquist, Donald G.: trustee, Wal-Mart Foundation; senior vice chairman, director, Wal-Mart Stores, Inc.

Shade Information System

Kress, James F.: chairman, director, Green Bay Packaging

Shamrock Holdings Inc.

Disney, Roy Edward: trustee, Disney Co. Foundation (Walt); vice chairman, director, Disney Co. (Walt)

Shareholder Fitness Mania Inc.

Suwyn, Mark A.: chairman, president, Louisiana-Pacific Foundation

Shaw Investments Inc.

Shaw, Robert E.: chairman, chief executive officer, Shaw Industries Inc.

Shearson Lehman Brothers Holdings Inc.

Furlaud, Richard Mortimer: interim chief executive officer, International Flavors & Fragrances Inc.

Shelter Financial Services

Cox, Robert T.: director, Shelter Insurance Foundation

Lenox, John W.: director, Shelter Insurance Foundation; president, chief executive officer, director, Shelter Mutual Insurance Co.

Offutt, James A.: director, Shelter Insurance Foundation

Shelter General Insurance Co.

Duello, J. Donald: president, treasurer, director, Shelter Insurance Foundation

Lehr, Gustav J.: vice president, director, Shelter Insurance Foundation; chairman, director, Shelter Mutual Insurance Co.

Lenox, John W.: director, Shelter Insurance Foundation; president, chief executive officer, director, Shelter Mutual Insurance Co.

Offutt, James A.: director, Shelter Insurance Foundation

Shelter Media Arizona Inc.

McCorkindale, Douglas H.: vice chairman, president, Gannett Co., Inc.; president, Gannett Foundation

Shelter Media Communication Inc.

McCorkindale, Douglas H.: vice chairman, president, Gannett Co., Inc.; president, Gannett Foundation

Shenandoah Life Insurance Co.

Wolf, Henry C.: vice chairman, chief financial officer, Norfolk Southern Corp.; vice president finance, Norfolk Southern Foundation

Sherman Wire Caldwell Inc.

Simmons, Glenn Reuben: vice chairman, Contran Corp.

Sherwin-Williams Co.

Collins, Duane E.: president, chief executive officer, director, Parker Hannifin Corp.; vice president, trustee, Parker Hannifin Foundation

Mahoney, Robert W.: chairman, president, chief executive officer, director, Diebold, Inc.

Mixon, A. Malachi, III: chairman, chief executive officer, Invacare Corp.; trustee, Invacare Foundation

Moll, Curtis E.: treasurer, trustee, Jochum-Moll Foundation (The)

Shiloh Corp.

Hessler, David J.: secretary, trustee, Jochum-Moll Foundation (The); president, partner, MTD Products Inc.

Zampetis, Theodore K.: president, chief operating officer, director, Standard Products Co.

Shivers Trading & Operating Co.

Morris, William Shivers, III: founder, chairman, chief executive officer, director, Morris Communications Corp.; trustee, Stauffer Communications Foundation

Morris, William Shivers, IV: president, director, Morris Communications Corp.; trustee, Stauffer Communications Foundation

Shivers Trading Operating Co.

Herman, William A., III: secretary, treasurer, director, Morris Communications Corp.

Shoney's
Bottorff, Dennis C.: chairman, president, chief executive officer, director, First American Corp.

Shoneys Inc.
Turner, Cal, Jr.: chairman, chief executive officer, director, Dollar General Corp.
Yancey, James D.: vice chairman, director, president, chief operating officer, Synovus Financial Corp.

Shop'n Save Massachusetts Inc.
Bowne, Garrett D., IV: treasurer, Hannaford Charitable Foundation
Farrington, Hugh G.: president, chief executive officer, director, Hannaford Brothers Co.

Siebel Systems, Inc.
Schwab, Charles R.: chairman, co-chief executive officer, director, Schwab & Co., Inc. (Charles); chairman, Schwab Corp. Foundation (Charles)

Siecor Corp.
Ughetta, William Casper: trustee, Corning Inc. Foundation

Siera Energy Co.
Malquist, Malyn K.: chairman, Sierra Pacific Resources

Sierra Designs Acquisition Corp.
Jacobsen, James C.: vice chairman, Kellwood Co.; vice president, director, Kellwood Foundation

Sierra Pacific Power Co.
Donnelley, James R.: vice chairman, Donnelley & Sons Co. (R.R.)
Malquist, Malyn K.: chairman, Sierra Pacific Resources
Ruelle, Mark A.: senior vice president, chief financial officer, Sierra Pacific Resources

Sierra Pacific Resources
Donnelley, James R.: vice chairman, Donnelley & Sons Co. (R.R.)
Peterson, William E.: general counsel, Sierra Pacific Resources

Sierra Water Development
Malquist, Malyn K.: chairman, Sierra Pacific Resources

Sigcorp Inc.
Koch, Robert Louis, II: president, chief executive officer, director, Koch Enterprises, Inc.; president, director, Koch Foundation

Sigma-Aldrich Corp.
Newman, Andrew E.: member, Edison Family Foundation

Signature Resorts Inc.
Kiely, W. Leo, III: president, chief operating officer, Coors Brewing Co.

Silicon Graphics
Shapiro, Robert B.: chairman, president, chief executive officer, director, Monsanto Co.

Simco Inc.
Draper, Ernest Linn, Jr.: chairman, president, chief executive officer, director, American Electric Power

Simplot Canada
Graves, Ronald Norman: secretary, Simplot Foundation (J.R.)

Simplot Fin Corp.
Simplot, Donald J.: vice president, Simplot Foundation (J.R.)

Simplot Livestock Co.
Graves, Ronald Norman: secretary, Simplot Foundation (J.R.)

Sintokagio Ltd.
Montrone, Paul Michael: vice president, partner, Winthrop Foundation

Sioux Falls Newspapers Inc.
McCorkindale, Douglas H.: vice chairman, president, Gannett Co., Inc.; president, Gannett Foundation

Skyline Corp.
Lawson, William Hogan, III: chairman, chief executive officer, director, Franklin Electric Co.; president, Franklin Electric, Edward J. Schaefer, and T. W. KehoeCharitable and Educational Foundation
McKenna, Andrew James: director, Aon Foundation

Skyport Industrial Park
Higgs, John H.: director, IBJ Foundation

Slant/Fin-Hidron Ltd.
Dubin, Melvin: chairman, Slant/Fin Corp.; president, director, Slant/Fin Foundation

Sloan Valve Co.
Jannotta, Edgar D.: president, Blair & Co. Foundation (William); senior director, Blair & Co. (William)

Smackover-Shell Ltd. Partnership
Bernard, Bruce E.: director, Shell Oil Co. Foundation

Smart & Final Inc.
Crull, Timm F.: retired chairman, Nestle U.S.A. Inc.

Smart Shirts Lanka Ltd.
Jacobsen, James C.: vice chairman, Kellwood Co.; vice president, director, Kellwood Foundation

Smart Shirts Ltd.
Jacobsen, James C.: vice chairman, Kellwood Co.; vice president, director, Kellwood Foundation

Smart Shirts Manufacturer Ltd.
Jacobsen, James C.: vice chairman, Kellwood Co.; vice president, director, Kellwood Foundation

SmartEnergy Services
Young, Robert Harris: president, chief executive officer, Central Vermont Public Service Corp.

Smith Corona Corp.
Rosett, Richard Nathaniel: trustee, Kemper Foundation (James S.)

Smith County Bank
Day, Frank R.: chairman, Trustmark National Bank

Smith Fiberglass Products Inc.
O'Toole, Robert Joseph: director, Firstar Milwaukee Foundation; chairman, president, chief executive officer, director, Smith Corp. (A.O.); director, Smith Foundation, Inc. (A.O.)

Smith Investment Co.
Smith, Arthur O.: president, Smith Foundation, Inc. (A.O.)

SmithKline Beecham International Co.
Leschly, Jan: chief executive officer, SmithKline Beecham Corp.

SmithKline Beecham PLC
Allaire, Paul Arthur: chairman, chief executive officer, chairman executive committee, Xerox Corp.; president, Xerox Foundation

Smithfield Foods Inc.
Burrus, Robert Lewis, Jr.: trustee, Circuit City Foundation

Smucker Quality Beverages
Smucker, Timothy Paul: chairman, director, Smucker Co. (JM)

Snap-On Inc.
Chelberg, Bruce Stanley: chairman, chief executive officer, director, Whitman Corp.; director, Whitman Corp. Foundation
Hadley, Leonard Anson: chairman, chief executive officer, director, Maytag Corp.; president, trustee, Maytag Corp. Foundation
Michaels, Jack D.: secretary, HON Industries Charitable Foundation; chairman, president, chief executive officer, director, HON Industries Inc.

Snap-On Tools Inc.
Chelberg, Bruce Stanley: chairman, chief executive officer, director, Whitman Corp.; director, Whitman Corp. Foundation
Mead, George Wilson, II: president, director, Consolidated Papers Foundation, Inc.; chairman, director, Consolidated Papers, Inc.

Snorac Inc.
Taylor, Andrew C.: president, chief executive officer, director, Enterprise Rent-A-Car Co.

Society National Bank
Moll, Curtis E.: treasurer, trustee, Jochum-Moll Foundation (The)

Solar Aluminum Technology Services
McNeeley, Robert D.: president, director, Reilly Industries, Inc.

Solar Press
Stone, Jerome H.: vice president, secretary, treasurer, Stone Foundation

Solid Visions Inc.
Liljebeck, Roy C.: executive vice president, chief financial officer, Airborne Freight Corp.

Solo Cup Co.
Whaley, Ronald L.: foundation administrator, Solo Cup Foundation

Solutia Inc.
Ruckelshaus, William Doyle: chairman, director, Browning-Ferris Industries Inc.

Somerville
Hall, William Austin: president, Hallmark Corporate Foundation

Sonic Corp.
Rainbolt, Harold E.: vice president, secretary, SBC Foundation

Sonoca Latin America
Moran, Harry J.: executive vice president, Sonoco Products Co.

Sonoco Products Co.
Dickson, Alan Thomas: president, Dickson Foundation; chairman, Ruddick Corp.

Sonopal
Shelley, James Herbert: chairman, Sonoco Foundation

Sony Corp. America
Burak, Howard Paul: secretary, director, Sony U.S.A. Foundation Inc.

Sony Corp. Japan
Morita, Masaaki: chairman, director, Sony U.S.A. Foundation Inc.

Sony Music Entertainment Inc.
Burak, Howard Paul: secretary, director, Sony U.S.A. Foundation Inc.

Sony Software Corp.

Kawai, Tadasu: director, Sony U.S.A. Foundation Inc.

Sony Trans Communication

Morita, Masaaki: chairman, director, Sony U.S.A. Foundation Inc.

South Asia Garments Ltd.

Jacobsen, James C.: vice chairman, Kellwood Co.; vice president, director, Kellwood Foundation

South Construction Co. Inc.

Foley, Cheryl M.: vice president, secretary, general counsel, Cinergy Corp.; vice president, secretary, director, Cinergy Foundation

South Shore Community Services, Inc.

Sasaki, Robert K.: director, Alexander & Baldwin Foundation

SouthTrust Corp.

Franklin, H. Allen: president, chief executive officer, Georgia Power Co.

Southeastern Electric Exchange

Dahlberg, Alfred William, III: chairman, president, chief executive officer, Southern Co. Services Inc.

Southeastern Newspaper Corp.

Herman, William A., III: secretary, treasurer, director, Morris Communications Corp.

Morris, William Shivers, III: founder, chairman, chief executive officer, director, Morris Communications Corp.; trustee, Stauffer Communications Foundation

Southeastern Newspapers Corp.

Morris, William Shivers, IV: president, director, Morris Communications Corp.; trustee, Stauffer Communications Foundation

Southern Appalachian Coal Co.

Draper, Ernest Linn, Jr.: chairman, president, chief executive officer, director, American Electric Power

Southern California Edison Co.

Bryson, John E.: chairman, chief executive officer, Edison International

Higgins, Thomas: vice president corporate contributions, Edison International

Southern California Gas Co.

Lozano, Ignacio Eugenio, Jr.: chairman, Pacific Mutual Life Insurance Co.

Southern Co. Inc.

De Nicola, Paul J.: president, chief executive officer, Southern Co. Services Inc.

Franklin, H. Allen: president, chief executive officer, Georgia Power Co.

Harris, Elmer Beseler: president, chief executive officer, director, Alabama Power Co.

Jobe, Warren Yancey: executive vice president, Georgia Power Co.; president, director, Georgia Power Foundation

Lesar, David J.: president, chief operating officer, Halliburton Co.; trustee, Halliburton Foundation, Inc.

Morris, William Shivers, III: founder, chairman, chief executive officer, director, Morris Communications Corp.; trustee, Stauffer Communications Foundation

Southern Co. Services Inc.

Dahlberg, Alfred William, III: chairman, president, chief executive officer, Southern Co. Services Inc.

Harris, Elmer Beseler: president, chief executive officer, director, Alabama Power Co.

Southern Electric Generating Co.

Franklin, H. Allen: president, chief executive officer, Georgia Power Co.

Harris, Elmer Beseler: president, chief executive officer, director, Alabama Power Co.

Jobe, Warren Yancey: executive vice president, Georgia Power Co.; president, director, Georgia Power Foundation

Southern Electronic Generating Co.

Dahlberg, Alfred William, III: chairman, president, chief executive officer, Southern Co. Services Inc.

Hutchins, William Bruce, III: director, Alabama Power Foundation

Southern Energy Homes

Evanson, Paul John: president, treasurer, director, FPL Group Foundation, Inc.

Southern Energy Resources Inc.

Franklin, H. Allen: president, chief executive officer, Georgia Power Co.

Harris, Elmer Beseler: president, chief executive officer, director, Alabama Power Co.

Southern Graphics System Inc.

Taylor, Julian Howard: vice president, treasurer, director, Reynolds Metals Co. Foundation

Southern Heritage Insurance Co.

Smith, Donald Kaye: senior vice president, general counsel, director, GEICO Corp.

Southern Indiana Gas & Electric Co.

Koch, Robert Louis, II: president, chief executive officer, director, Koch Enterprises, Inc.; president, director, Koch Foundation

Southern Indiana Minerals, Inc.

Koch, Robert Louis, II: president, chief executive officer, director, Koch Enterprises, Inc.; president, director, Koch Foundation

Southern Indiana Properties, Inc.

Koch, Robert Louis, II: president, chief executive officer, director, Koch Enterprises, Inc.; president, director, Koch Foundation

Southern Mills Inc.

Courts, Richard Winn, II: chairman, director, Atlantic Investment Co.

Southern New England Telecom Corp.

Hershman, Linda D.: vice president, Southern New England Telephone Co.

Southern Ohio Coal Co.

Draper, Ernest Linn, Jr.: chairman, president, chief executive officer, director, American Electric Power

Southern Peru Copper Corp.

Kinsolving, Augustus Blagden: director, ASARCO Foundation

McAllister, Francis R.: vice president, director, ASARCO Foundation; president, chief executive officer, ASARCO Inc.

Muth, Robert James: president, director, ASARCO Foundation

Osborne, Richard de Jongh: director, ASARCO Foundation; chairman, chief executive officer, director, ASARCO Inc.

Whisler, J. Steven: chairman, president, chief executive officer, Phelps Dodge Corp.

Southern Precision Corp.

Fjelstul, Dean M.: senior vice president, chief financial officer, Walter Industries Inc.

Porter, Edward A.: vice president, general counsel, secretary, Walter Industries Inc.

Southern-Republic Airlines

Purvis, George Frank, Jr.: chairman, president, chief executive officer, director, Pan-American Life Insurance Co.

Southgate USA Management Co.

Ratner, Albert Benjamin: trustee, Forest City Enterprises Charitable Foundation, Inc.; co-chairman, director, Forest City Enterprises, Inc.

Southland Publishing Co.

McCorkindale, Douglas H.: vice chairman, president, Gannett Co., Inc.; president, Gannett Foundation

Southwest Bell Corp.

Busch, August Adolphus, III: chairman, president, chief executive officer, Anheuser-Busch Companies, Inc.

Knight, Charles Field: chairman, chief executive officer, Emerson Electric Co.

Southwest Bell Mobile Systems

Ellis, James D.: director, SBC Foundation

Foster, Charles E.: director, SBC Foundation

Kiernan, Donald E., Sr.: senior vice president, chief financial officer, treasurer, SBC Communications Inc.; director, SBC Foundation

Southwest Bell Telephone Co.

Caldwell, Royce S.: director, SBC Foundation

Foster, Charles E.: director, SBC Foundation

Kiernan, Donald E., Sr.: senior vice president, chief financial officer, treasurer, SBC Communications Inc.; director, SBC Foundation

Whitacre, Edward E., Jr.: chairman, director, chief executive officer, SBC Communications Inc.

Southwest Newspapers Corp.

Morris, William Shivers, III: founder, chairman, chief executive officer, director, Morris Communications Corp.; trustee, Stauffer Communications Foundation

Southwest Oregon Publishing Co.

Pulitzer, Michael Edgar: chairman, president, chief executive officer, director, Pulitzer Publishing Co.; chairman, president, chief executive officer, Pulitzer Publishing Co. Foundation

Southwest Public Service Co.

Hemminghaus, Roger Roy: chairman, director, Ultramar Diamond Shamrock Corp.

Southwest Tobacco Co. Inc.

Crenshaw, Gordon Lee, II: member, Universal Leaf Foundation; chairman emeritus, Universal Leaf Tobacco Co., Inc.

Southwestern Public Service Co.

Helton, Bill D.: chairman, New Century Energies Foundation

Southwire Co.

Alfiero, Salvatore Harry: founder, chairman, chief executive officer, director, Mark IV Industries; chairman, Mark IV Industries Foundation

Denny, Charles W.: president, chief executive officer, director, Square D Co.

Space Industries

Baker, James Kendrick: chairman, director, Arvin Foundation; vice chairman, director, Arvin Industries, Inc.

Span Instruments Inc.

Zadel, C. William: chairman, president, chief executive officer, Millipore Corp.; trustee, Millipore Foundation (The)

Specialty Steel Industry North America

Cardy, Robert Willard: chairman, president, chief executive officer, director, Carpenter Technology Corp.; president, Carpenter Technology Corp. Foundation

Spectro Alloys Corp.

Wurtele, C. Angus: president, Valspar Foundation

Speidel Newspapers Inc.

Curley, John J.: chairman, chief executive officer, director, Gannett Co., Inc.; chairman, Gannett Foundation

McCorkindale, Douglas H.: vice chairman, president, Gannett Co., Inc.; president, Gannett Foundation

Spicer SA

Magliochetti, Joseph M.: president, chief executive officer, director, Dana Corp.; president, director, Dana Corp. Foundation

Springs Industries Inc.

Akers, John Fellows: director, New York Times Co.

Coker, Charles Westfield: trustee, Sonoco Foundation; vice president, Sonoco Products Co.

Springs Valley Bank & Trust Co.

Habig, Douglas A.: chairman, chief executive officer, director, Habig Foundation

Thyen, Ronald J.: senior executive vice president, director, Habig Foundation; senior executive vice president, chief operating officer director, Kimball International, Inc.

Sprint Corp.

Hockaday, Irvine O., Jr.: president, chief executive officer, director, Hallmark Cards Inc.

Sprint International Caribbean Inc.

Strandjord, Mary Jeannine: director, Sprint Foundation

Sprint United Management Co.

Esrey, William Todd: chairman, chief executive officer, Sprint Corp.

Strandjord, Mary Jeannine: director, Sprint Foundation

Sprout Venture Capital Group

Martinez, Arthur C.: chairman, chief executive officer, president, Sears, Roebuck and Co.

Square D Co.

Knauss, Dalton L.: trustee, Kemper Foundation (James S.)

St-Gobain Corp.

Meyerson, Martin: director, Panasonic Foundation

Sta-Rite Industries Inc.

Schrader, Thomas F.: vice president, director, WICOR Foundation

Wardeberg, George E.: president, WICOR Foundation; president, chief executive officer, director, WICOR, Inc.

Standard & Poors Compustat Services Inc.

Kaufman, Frank Joseph: senior vice president taxes, McGraw-Hill Companies, Inc.

McGraw, Harold Whittlesey 'Terry', III: chairman, president, chief executive officer, McGraw-Hill Companies, Inc.

Standard & Poors Corp.

Kaufman, Frank Joseph: senior vice president taxes, McGraw-Hill Companies, Inc.

Standard & Poors Securities Inc.

McGraw, Harold Whittlesey 'Terry', III: chairman, president, chief executive officer, McGraw-Hill Companies, Inc.

Standard Co. Inc.

Herrmann, Harold M.: chief financial officer, Reily & Co., Inc. (William B.)

Standard Insurance Co.

Meyer, Jerome J.: chairman, chief executive officer, Tektronix, Inc.

Standard Products (Canada) Ltd.

Zampetis, Theodore K.: president, chief operating officer, director, Standard Products Co.

Standard Products Co.

Moll, Curtis E.: treasurer, trustee, Jochum-Moll Foundation (The)

Standard Products International

Zampetis, Theodore K.: president, chief operating officer, director, Standard Products Co.

Standard Shares

Harris, Richard Neison: chairman, director, Pittway Corp.; president, director, Pittway Corp. Charitable Foundation

Stanley Works

Lorch, George A.: chairman, chief executive officer, director, Armstrong World Industries, Inc.

Staples Inc.

Anderson, Basil L.: executive vice president, chief financial officer, Campbell Soup Co.

Star Banc Cincinnati

Bridgeland, James Ralph, Jr.: trustee, Star Bank NA, Cincinnati Foundation

Star Banc Corp.

Benhase, Daniel B.: executive vice president, Star Bank NA; treasurer, Star Bank NA, Cincinnati Foundation

Bridgeland, James Ralph, Jr.: trustee, Star Bank NA, Cincinnati Foundation

Browning, Laurance LeWright, Jr.: member public policy committee, Emerson Charitable Trust; director, Emerson Electric Co.

Cassidy, Samuel M.: director, Star Bank NA

Gundhofer, Jerry A.: chairman, director, Star Bank NA; vice president, Star Bank NA, Cincinnati Foundation

Hayden, Joseph Page, Jr.: trustee, Star Bank NA, Cincinnati Foundation

Klinedinst, Thomas John, Jr.: trustee, Star Bank NA, Cincinnati Foundation

Meyer, Daniel Joseph: president, Milacron Foundation; chairman, president, chief executive officer, director, Milacron, Inc.

Star Bank NA

Browning, Laurance LeWright, Jr.: member public policy committee, Emerson Charitable Trust; director, Emerson Electric Co.

Hayden, Joseph Page, Jr.: trustee, Star Bank NA, Cincinnati Foundation

Star Bank NA Association

Klinedinst, Thomas John, Jr.: trustee, Star Bank NA, Cincinnati Foundation

Star City Pty Ltd.

Satre, Philip Glen: chairman, president, chief executive officer, director, Promus Hotel Corp.

Star Energy Inc.

Catell, Robert Barry: chairman, chief executive officer, Brooklyn Union

Star Marketing & Admin

Peterson, Donald Matthew: trustee, Trustmark Foundation; president, chief executive officer, director, Trustmark Insurance Co.

Star Publishing Co.

Pulitzer, Michael Edgar: chairman, president, chief executive officer, director, Pulitzer Publishing Co.; chairman, president, chief executive officer, Pulitzer Publishing Co. Foundation

Ridgway, Ronald H.: senior vice president, Pulitzer Publishing Co.; secretary, treasurer, director, Pulitzer Publishing Co. Foundation

Star Tribune Cowles Media Co.

Lebedoff, Randy Miller: vice president, general counsel, McClatchy Co.; secretary, Star Tribune Foundation

Star-Kist Foods

O'Reilly, F. Anthony John: chairman, trustee, Heinz Co. Foundation (H.J.); chairman, director, Heinz Co. (H.J.)

StarKist Foods Inc.

Williams, David R.: trustee, Heinz Co. Foundation (H.J.); executive vice president, director, Heinz Co. (H.J.)

State Auto Financial Corp.

Lhota, William J.: executive vice president, American Electric Power

State Farm Annuity & Life Insurance Co.

Joslin, Roger Scott: treasurer, State Farm Companies Foundation

Sullivan, Laura P.: vice president, secretary, director, State Farm Companies Foundation; vice president, secretary, counsel, State Farm Mutual Automobile Insurance Co.

State Farm Balanced Fund Inc.

Joslin, Roger Scott: treasurer, State Farm Companies Foundation

State Farm Fire & Casualty Co.

Rust, Edward Barry, Jr.: chairman, president, director, State Farm Companies Foundation; chairman, president, chief executive officer, director, State Farm Mutual Automobile Insurance Co.

Sullivan, Laura P.: vice president, secretary, director, State Farm Companies Foundation; vice president, secretary, counsel, State Farm Mutual Automobile Insurance Co.

State Farm Fire Casualty Co.

Trosino, Vincent Joseph: assistant secretary, State Farm Companies Foundation; executive vice president, vice chairman, chief operating officer, director, State Farm Mutual Automobile Insurance Co.

State Farm General Insurance Co.

Rust, Edward Barry, Jr.: chairman, president, director, State Farm Companies Foundation; chairman, president, chief executive officer, director, State Farm Mutual Automobile Insurance Co.

Sullivan, Laura P.: vice president, secretary, director, State Farm Companies Foundation; vice president, secretary, counsel, State Farm Mutual Automobile Insurance Co.

Trosino, Vincent Joseph: assistant secretary, State Farm Companies Foundation; executive vice president, vice chairman, chief operating officer, director, State Farm Mutual Automobile Insurance Co.

State Farm Growth Fund Inc.

Joslin, Roger Scott: treasurer, State Farm Companies Foundation

State Farm Indemnity Co.

Sullivan, Laura P.: vice president, secretary, director, State Farm Companies Foundation; vice president, secretary, counsel, State Farm Mutual Automobile Insurance Co.

State Farm Insurance Companies

Rust, Edward Barry, Jr.: chairman, president, director, State Farm Companies Foundation; chairman, president, chief executive officer, director, State Farm Mutual Automobile Insurance Co.

State Farm Interim Fund Inc.

Joslin, Roger Scott: treasurer, State Farm Companies Foundation

State Farm International Services

Trosino, Vincent Joseph: assistant secretary, State Farm Companies Foundation; executive vice president, vice chairman, chief operating officer, director, State Farm Mutual Automobile Insurance Co.

State Farm International Services Inc.

Rust, Edward Barry, Jr.: chairman, president, director, State Farm Companies Foundation; chairman, president, chief executive officer, director, State Farm Mutual Automobile Insurance Co.

State Farm Investment Management Corp.

Rust, Edward Barry, Jr.: chairman, president, director, State Farm Companies Foundation; chairman, president, chief executive officer, director, State Farm Mutual Automobile Insurance Co.

Trosino, Vincent Joseph: assistant secretary, State Farm Companies Foundation; executive vice president, vice chairman, chief operating officer, director, State Farm Mutual Automobile Insurance Co.

State Farm Life & Accident Assurance Co.

Joslin, Roger Scott: treasurer, State Farm Companies Foundation

Sullivan, Laura P.: vice president, secretary, director, State Farm Companies Foundation; vice president, secretary, counsel, State Farm Mutual Automobile Insurance Co.

Trosino, Vincent Joseph: assistant secretary, State Farm Companies Foundation; executive vice president, vice chairman, chief operating officer, director, State Farm Mutual Automobile Insurance Co.

State Farm Life & Annuity Co.

Rust, Edward Barry, Jr.: chairman, president, director, State Farm Companies Foundation; chairman, president, chief executive officer, director, State Farm Mutual Automobile Insurance Co.

Trosino, Vincent Joseph: assistant secretary, State Farm Companies Foundation; executive vice president, vice chairman, chief operating officer, director, State Farm Mutual Automobile Insurance Co.

State Farm Life Co.

Trosino, Vincent Joseph: assistant secretary, State Farm Companies Foundation; executive vice president, vice chairman, chief operating officer, director, State Farm Mutual Automobile Insurance Co.

State Farm Life Insurance Co.

Joslin, Roger Scott: treasurer, State Farm Companies Foundation

Rust, Edward Barry, Jr.: chairman, president, director, State Farm Companies Foundation; chairman, president, chief executive officer, director, State Farm Mutual Automobile Insurance Co.

Sullivan, Laura P.: vice president, secretary, director, State Farm Companies Foundation; vice president, secretary, counsel, State Farm Mutual Automobile Insurance Co.

Trosino, Vincent Joseph: assistant secretary, State Farm Companies Foundation; executive vice president, vice chairman, chief operating officer, director, State Farm Mutual Automobile Insurance Co.

State Farm Lloyds Inc.

Sullivan, Laura P.: vice president, secretary, director, State Farm Companies Foundation; vice president, secretary, counsel, State Farm Mutual Automobile Insurance Co.

State Farm Mutual Insurance Co.

Trosino, Vincent Joseph: assistant secretary, State Farm Companies Foundation; executive vice president, vice chairman, chief operating officer, director, State Farm Mutual Automobile Insurance Co.

State Life Insurance Co.

Semler, Jerry D.: chairman, president, chief executive officer, director, American United Life Insurance Co.; chairman, director, AUL Foundation Inc.

State Mutual Life Assurance Co.

O'Brien, John Francis, Jr.: president, chief executive officer, Allmerica Financial Corp.

State Street Bank & Trust Co.

Kucharski, John Michael: trustee, PerkinElmer Foundation; chairman, chief executive officer, director, PerkinElmer, Inc.

LaMantia, Charles Robert: president, chief executive officer, director, Little, Inc. (Arthur D.)

State Street Boston Corp.

Carter, Marshall Nichols: chairman, chief executive officer, State Street Bank & Trust Co.

Kucharski, John Michael: trustee, PerkinElmer Foundation; chairman, chief executive officer, director, PerkinElmer, Inc.

LaMantia, Charles Robert: president, chief executive officer, director, Little, Inc. (Arthur D.)

Spina, David Anthony: president, chief operating officer, State Street Bank & Trust Co.

State Street Corp.

Carter, Marshall Nichols: chairman, chief executive officer, State Street Bank & Trust Co.

Darehshori, Nader Farhang: chairman, president, chief executive officer, Houghton Mifflin Co.

Gruber, David P.: president, chief executive officer, director, Wyman-Gordon Co.; chairman, vice president, director, Wyman-Gordon Foundation

Spina, David Anthony: president, chief operating officer, State Street Bank & Trust Co.

State Street Exchange Fund

Lawrence, Robert Ashton: director, New York Times Co. Foundation

Statesman-Journal Co.

McCorkindale, Douglas H.: vice chairman, president, Gannett Co., Inc.; president, Gannett Foundation

Station WDPR-FM

Holmes, David Richard: chief executive officer, chief operating officer, director, Reynolds & Reynolds Co.

Stauffer Communications Inc.

Herman, William A., III: secretary, treasurer, director, Morris Communications Corp.

Morris, William Shivers, III: founder, chairman, chief executive officer, director, Morris Communications Corp.; trustee, Stauffer Communications Foundation

Morris, William Shivers, IV: president, director, Morris Communications Corp.; trustee, Stauffer Communications Foundation

Steelcase North American

Hackett, James P.: trustee, Steelcase Foundation; president, chief executive officer, Steelcase Inc.

Stein Roe Farnham

Kelly, Janet L.: executive vice president corporate development, general counsel, secretary, Kellogg Co.

Sterling Plumbing Group Inc.

Black, Natalie A.: group vice president interiors, general counsel, director, Kohler Co.

Kohler, Herbert Vollrath, Jr.: chairman, president, director, Kohler Co.

Stockery & Yale Inc.

Nelson, John Martin: chairman, director, TJX Companies, Inc.

Stockton Newspapers Inc.

McCorkindale, Douglas H.: vice chairman, president, Gannett Co., Inc.; president, Gannett Foundation

Stone Container Corp.

Aldinger, William F., III: chairman, chief executive officer, director, Household International Inc.

Kennedy, George Danner: trustee, Kemper Foundation (James S.)

Stone, Jerome H.: vice president, secretary, treasurer, Stone Foundation

Stonecutter Mills Corp.

Tanner, K. S., Jr.: director, Stonecutter Foundation

Storage Technology Corp.

Chandler, J. Harold: chairman, president, chief executive officer, Provident Companies, Inc.

Kerr, William T.: chairman, chief executive officer, director, Meredith Corp.

Stormedia Inc.
Lunger, Francis: chief financial officer, corporate vice president, Millipore Corp.

Stouffer Corp.
Corti, Mario A.: senior vice president, chief administrative officer, Nestle U.S.A. Inc.

Stupp Corp.
Stupp, Robert P.: president, director, Stupp Brothers Bridge & Iron Co.; trustee, Stupp Brothers Bridge & Iron Co. Foundation

Stupp Metals
Stupp, Robert P.: president, director, Stupp Brothers Bridge & Iron Co.; trustee, Stupp Brothers Bridge & Iron Co. Foundation

Subway Equipment Leasing Corp.
DeLuca, Fred: vice president, Subway Sandwich Shops, Inc.

Sugar Monitor Co.
Elbert, Paul A.: president, chief executive officer natural gas, Consumers Energy Co.

Sumitomo Bank Capital Markets
Okada, Natsuo: president, Sumitomo Bank; president, director, Sumitomo Bank Global Foundation

Summersville Hydro Corp.
Young, Robert Harris: president, chief executive officer, Central Vermont Public Service Corp.

Summit Communication
Strickland, Robert Louis: vice president, Lowe's Charitable and Educational Foundation

Sun America Inc.
Aldinger, William F., III: chairman, chief executive officer, director, Household International Inc.

Sun Bank Tampa Bay
Anderson, Girard F.: chairman, chief executive officer, president, Tampa Electric Co.

Sun Co. Inc.
Shanks, David C.: trustee, Little Foundation (Arthur D.); vice president human resources, Little, Inc. (Arthur D.)

Sun Co. San Bernardino California
McCorkindale, Douglas H.: vice chairman, president, Gannett Co., Inc.; president, Gannett Foundation

Sun Enterprises Inc.
Nation, Robert F.: former president, director, Harsco Corp.; trustee, Harsco Corp. Fund

Sun Federal
Bartz, Carol A.: director, Autodesk Foundation; chairman, chief executive officer, Autodesk Inc.

Sun Microsystems Inc.
Fisher, Robert J.: vice president, Gap Foundation/ Gap Inc. Community Relations

Sun Motor Cars Inc.
Nation, Robert F.: former president, director, Harsco Corp.; trustee, Harsco Corp. Fund

Sun Resources Inc.
Gaylord, Edward Lewis: chairman, chief executive officer, director, publisher, Oklahoma Publishing Co.; trustee, Oklahoman Foundation (The)

SunAmerica Inc.
Williams, Karen Hastie: director, Fannie Mae Foundation

SunTrust Bank, Chattanooga, NA
Frierson, Daniel K.: chairman, chief executive officer, Dixie Group, Inc. (The); president, trustee, Dixie Yarns Foundation, Inc.

SunTrust Banks Georgia Inc.
Courts, Richard Winn, II: chairman, director, Atlantic Investment Co.
Humann, L. Phillip: member, SunTrust Bank Atlanta Foundation
Spiegel, John William: member, SunTrust Bank Atlanta Foundation

SunTrust Banks Inc.
Correll, Alston Dayton 'Pete', Jr.: chairman, president, chief executive officer, director, Georgia-Pacific Corp.; director, Georgia-Pacific Foundation
Dahlberg, Alfred William, III: chairman, president, chief executive officer, Southern Co. Services Inc.
Humann, L. Phillip: member, SunTrust Bank Atlanta Foundation

Sunbeam Corp.
Gittis, Howard: director, Revlon Foundation Inc.

Sunbury Textile Mills Inc.
Lyon, Wayne Barton: president, chief operating officer, director, Masco Corp.

Suncor Development Co.
Snell, Richard: chairman, president, chief executive officer, director, Arizona Public Service Co.

Sundance Homes Inc.
Bookshester, Dennis S.: chairman, chief executive officer, Playboy Enterprises Inc.

Sundstrand Corp.
Grinstein, Gerald: director, PACCAR Inc.

Sunlite Plastics Inc.
Connolly, Gerald Edward: trustee, Reinhart Family Foundation (D. B. and Marjorie)

Sunrise Development Co.
Ratner, Albert Benjamin: trustee, Forest City Enterprises Charitable Foundation, Inc.; co-chairman, director, Forest City Enterprises, Inc.

Sunshine Mining Ref Co.
Shaffer, Oren G.: executive vice president, chief financial officer, Ameritech Corp.

Sunsource LP
Brewer, Oliver Gordon, Jr.: vice president finance, treasurer, IKON Office Solutions Foundation, Inc.

Sunstrand Corp.
Abdoo, Richard A.: chairman, president, chief executive officer, Wisconsin Energy Corp.; president, director, Wisconsin Energy Corp. Foundation, Inc.

Suntec Industries Inc.
Klein, Bruce A.: trustee, CLARCOR Foundation; chief financial officer, CLARCOR Inc.

Suntory Resort Inc.
Watanabe, Jeffrey N.: director, Hawaiian Electric Industries Charitable Foundation

Suntory Resorts Inc.
Dods, Walter Arthur, Jr.: president, director, First Hawaiian Foundation; chairman, chief executive officer, director, First Hawaiian, Inc.

Suntrust Bank Northwest Georgia N.A.
Bowdoin, William R., Jr.: first vice president, SunTrust Bank Atlanta; secretary, SunTrust Bank Atlanta Foundation

Super Rite Foods
Grass, Martin Lehrman: chairman, chief executive officer, director, Rite Aid Corp.

Super Steel Products Corp.
Kuester, Dennis J.: president, Marshall & Ilsley Corp.

SuperValu Transportation Inc.
Wright, Michael William: chairman, president, chief executive officer, director, SuperValu, Inc.

Supercuts Inc.
Kunin, Myron: chairman, director, Regis Corp.; president, Regis Foundation

Susquehanna Cable Co.
Finlayson, John L.: vice president finance & administration, Susquehanna-Pfaltzgraff Co.

Susquehanna Media Co.
Appell, Louis J., Jr.: president, Susquehanna-Pfaltzgraff Co.
Finlayson, John L.: vice president finance & administration, Susquehanna-Pfaltzgraff Co.

Susquehanna Pfalzgraff Co.
Simpson, William H.: president, Susquehanna-Pfaltzgraff Co.; secretary, Susquehanna-Pfaltzgraff Foundation

Susquehanna Radio Corp.
Appell, Louis J., Jr.: president, Susquehanna-Pfaltzgraff Co.
Finlayson, John L.: vice president finance & administration, Susquehanna-Pfaltzgraff Co.

Sybron Corp.
Hardis, Stephen Roger: chairman, chief executive officer, director, Eaton Corp.

Synorris Fin Corp.
Amos, Daniel P.: president, chief executive officer, director, AFLAC Inc.

Synovus Data Corp.
Blanchard, James Hubert: chairman, chief executive officer, Synovus Financial Corp.

System & Computer Tech
Freedman, Allen Royal: trustee, Fortis Foundation; chairman, chief executive officer, president, Fortis, Inc.

Systematics Information Services
Ford, Joseph 'Joe': chairman, chief executive officer, president, ALLTEL Corp.

T N Technology INC
Blaine, Gregory W.: chief operating officer, True North Communications, Inc.; president, director, True North Foundation

T Rowe Price Associates
Strickland, Robert Louis: vice president, Lowe's Charitable and Educational Foundation

T Rowe Price New Era Fund Inc.
Roche, George A.: chairman, president, Price Associates (T. Rowe)

T. Rowe Price Associates Inc.

Miller, Mary J.: vice president, trustee, Price Associates Foundation (T. Rowe)

TCF Fin Corp.

Cooper, William Allen: chairman, director, TCF National Bank Minnesota

Cusick, Thomas A.: chairman, TCF National Bank Minnesota

Nagorske, Lynn A.: executive vice president, chief financial officer, treasurer, TCF National Bank Minnesota

TCF National Bank Minnesota

Cusick, Thomas A.: chairman, TCF National Bank Minnesota

TCF finance Insurance Agency

Cooper, William Allen: chairman, director, TCF National Bank Minnesota

TFF Study Group

Thomas, Franklin Augustine: director, CBS Foundation

TFX Engineering

Black, Lennox K.: president, Teleflex Foundation; chairman, director, Teleflex Inc.

TGI Fridays Inc.

Carlson, Curtis Leroy: chairman, director, Carlson Companies, Inc.; president, treasurer, Carlson Family Foundation (Curtis L.)

TJ International Inc.

King, Richard L.: president, chief operating officer, Albertson's Inc.

TJX Co. Inc.

O'Brien, John Francis, Jr.: president, chief executive officer, Allmerica Financial Corp.

TMC Global Inc.

Mathis, David B.: chairman, Kemper Foundation (James S.)

TRINOVirginia Corp.

Spilman, Robert H.: chairman, chief executive officer, Bassett Furniture Industries; chairman, director, Bassett Furniture Industries Fdn.

TRP Finance Inc.

Roche, George A.: chairman, president, Price Associates (T. Rowe)

TRW Inc.

Martin, Lynn M.: director, Ameritech Foundation

Ong, John Doyle: chairman board, director, Ameritech Corp.

TSC Holdings Inc.

Crull, Timm F.: retired chairman, Nestle U.S.A. Inc.

TU Electric

Nye, Erle Allen: chairman, chief executive officer, director, TU Electric Co.

TV AlabamaInc.

Allbritton, Joe Lewis: chairman, chief executive officer, Riggs Bank NA

TWA

Bachmann, John W.: managing partner, Jones & Co. (Edward D.); chairman, Jones & Co. Foundation (Edward D.)

TXU

Oesterreicher, James E.: chairman, chief executive officer, director, Penney Co., Inc. (J.C.)

Taco Bell Corp.

Martin, John E.: chairman, chief executive officer, Taco Bell Corp.; chairman, Taco Bell Foundation

Taco Caliente Inc.

Martin, John E.: chairman, chief executive officer, Taco Bell Corp.; chairman, Taco Bell Foundation

Tacoma Moving Storage Co.

Wiborg, James Hooker: director, PACCAR Foundation

Take Control

Hefty, Thomas R.: chairman, president, chief executive officer, United Wisconsin Services

Talbots Inc.

Willes, Mark Hinckley: chairman, president, chief executive officer, Times Mirror Co.; chairman, Times Mirror Foundation

Talley Industries Inc.

Cottrell, G. Walton: senior vice president, chief financial officer, Carpenter Technology Corp.

Lodge, Robert W.: vice president, Carpenter Technology Corp. Foundation

Welty, John Rider: secretary, Carpenter Technology Corp. Foundation

Talley Manufacturing Technology Inc.

Cottrell, G. Walton: senior vice president, chief financial officer, Carpenter Technology Corp.

Lodge, Robert W.: vice president, Carpenter Technology Corp. Foundation

Welty, John Rider: secretary, Carpenter Technology Corp. Foundation

Tamarkin Co. Inc.

Chait, Gerald: trustee, Giant Eagle Foundation

Moravitz, Edward: trustee, Giant Eagle Foundation

Porter, Charles W.: trustee, Giant Eagle Foundation

Weizenbaum, Norman: trustee, Giant Eagle Foundation

Tamko Ennis Inc.

Humphreys, David Craig: secretary-treasurer, Craig Foundation (E.L.); president, chief operating officer, director, Tamko Roofing Products

Tamko Roofing Products Inc.

Atkins, Sarah Humphreys: vice president, Craig Foundation (E.L.)

Tampa Electric Co.

Anderson, Girard F.: chairman, chief executive officer, president, Tampa Electric Co.

Hopkins, Wayne W.: vice president corporate communications, Tampa Electric Co.

Target Corp.

Hall, Donald Joyce: chairman board, director, Hallmark Cards Inc.; chairman, Hallmark Corporate Foundation

Johnson, James A.: chairman, chief executive officer, director, Fannie Mae; chairman, Fannie Mae Foundation

Tata Honeywell, INC

Tambakeras, Markos I.: director, Honeywell Foundation

Tax Executives Institute

Harper, James J.: vice president, controller, Eastern Enterprises

Taylor Bros

Rosson, William Mimms: chairman, Conwood Co. LP

Taylor Made Co.

Golub, Lewis: chairman, chief executive officer, director, Golub Corp.

Teal Aviation Inc.

Dickson, Alan Thomas: president, Dickson Foundation; chairman, Ruddick Corp.

Teberebie Goldfields Ltd.

Cogan, John Francis, Jr.: president, chief executive officer, director, Pioneer Group

Tech Leaders Management

Musser, Warren Van Dyke: chairman, chief executive officer, director, Safeguard Scientifics; president, director, Safeguard Scientifics Foundation

Technical Council Greater Philadelphia

Blankley, Walter Elwood: president, director, AMETEK Foundation; chairman, director, AMETEK, Inc.

Technology Solutions Co.

Waltrip, William H.: chairman, director, Bausch & Lomb Inc.

Teddington Co. Ltd.

Peck, Arthur John, Jr.: secretary, vice president, Corning Inc.; secretary, Corning Inc. Foundation

Tejas Holdings LLC

Timken, William Robert, Jr.: chairman, president, chief executive officer, director, Timken Co. (The)

Tektronix Inc.

Cameron, Gerry B.: chairman, director, U.S. Bancorp

Tele-Flora

Resnick, Lynda Rae: vice chairman, co-owner, Franklin Mint (The)

Tele-Trip Co.

Sturgeon, John: president, chief operating officer, Mutual of Omaha Insurance Co.

Tele-Trip Inc.

Weekly, John William: chairman, chief executive officer, Mutual of Omaha Insurance Co.

Telecom New Zealand Ltd.

Pehlke, Richard W.: vice president, treasurer, Ameritech Corp.

Telecommunications Inc.

Roche, George A.: chairman, president, Price Associates (T. Rowe)

Teleconnect Co.

Roberts, Bert C., Jr.: chairman, MCI WorldCom, Inc.

Teledesic Corp.

Gates, William Henry, III: co-founder, chairman, chief software architect, Microsoft Corp.

Telephone & Data System

Wander, Herbert S.: secretary, director, Katten, Muchin & Zavis Foundation

Telerate Holdings Inc.

Burenga, Kenneth L.: president, chief operating officer, director, Dow Jones & Co., Inc.

Television 12 Jacksonville Inc.

McCorkindale, Douglas H.: vice chairman, president, Gannett Co., Inc.; president, Gannett Foundation

Temple-Inland Financial Services Inc.

Jastrow, Kenneth M., II: director, Temple-Inland Foundation

Temple, Arthur, III: director, Temple-Inland Foundation

Temple-Inland Mortgage Corp.

Jastrow, Kenneth M., II: director, Temple-Inland Foundation

Tenneco Inc.

McCoy, John Bonnet: president, chief executive officer, Ameritech Corp.

Tenneco Packaging Inc.

Page, Robert A.: chief financial officer, Tenneco Packaging

Stecko, Paul T.: president, director, Tenneco Packaging

Tennessee Gas Pipeline Co.

Mead, Dana George: chairman, chief executive officer, director, Tenneco Automotive

Wise, William Allen: chairman, president, chief executive officer, director, El Paso Energy Co.; chairman, director, El Paso Energy Foundation

Tension Envelope Corp.

Margolin, Abraham E.: director, Tension Envelope Foundation

Tension Envelope Corp. New York

Berkley, Eugene Bertram: chairman, director, Tension Envelope Corp.; treasurer, Tension Envelope Foundation

Terminal Railroad Association Saint Louis

Tobias, Steven C.: vice chairman, chief operating officer, Norfolk Southern Corp.; director, Norfolk Southern Foundation

Tesoro South Pacific Petro Co.

Kurren, Faye Watanabe: president, Tesoro Hawaii

Tessco Technology Inc.

Grass, Martin Lehrman: chairman, chief executive officer, director, Rite Aid Corp.

Tetragenics Co.

Pederson, Jerrold P.: vice president, chief financial officer, director, Montana Power Co.; director, Montana Power Foundation

Senechal, Ellen M.: treasurer, Montana Power Co.

Teva Pharmaceuticals Industries Ltd.

Harris, Irving Brooks: chairman executive committee, director, Pittway Corp.; chairman, director, Pittway Corp. Charitable Foundation

Texaco Inc.

Brademas, John: chairman, Texaco Foundation

Jenifer, Franklyn Green: trustee, Texaco Foundation

Price, Charles H., II: director, New York Times Co. Foundation

Steere, William Campbell, Jr.: chairman, chief executive officer, director, Pfizer Inc.

Wrigley, William: chairman, director, Wrigley Co. Foundation (Wm. Jr.); president, chief executive officer, director, Wrigley Co. (Wm. Jr.)

Texaco Overseas Holdings Inc.

Oelkers, Robert C.: director, Texaco Foundation

Texas Commerce Bancshares Inc.

Wise, William Allen: chairman, president, chief executive officer, director, El Paso Energy Co.; chairman, director, El Paso Energy Foundation

Texas Commerce Bank

Ranck, Bruce E.: president, chief executive officer, director, Browning-Ferris Industries Inc.

Wise, William Allen: chairman, president, chief executive officer, director, El Paso Energy Co.; chairman, director, El Paso Energy Foundation

Texas Gas

Lauderdale, Gary D.: senior vice president, general manager, Texas Gas Transmission Corp.

Texas Instruments Inc.

Carp, Daniel A.: president, chief operating officer, director, Eastman Kodak Co.

Goode, David Ronald: chairman, president, chief executive officer, director, Norfolk Southern Corp.

Texas Instruments Phillipines

Engibous, Thomas James: director, Texas Instruments Foundation; president, chief executive officer, chairman, director, Texas Instruments Inc.

Texas Oil & Gas Corp.

Graham, Thomas Carlisle: trustee, AK Steel Foundation

Texas Trust Savings Bank FSB

Quinn, David W.: executive vice president, chief financial officer, director, Centex Corp.

Texas Utilities Australia Pty Ltd.

Nye, Erle Allen: chairman, chief executive officer, director, TU Electric Co.

Texas Utilities Co.

Oesterreicher, James E.: chairman, chief executive officer, director, Penney Co., Inc. (J.C.)

Texas Utilities Communications Inc.

Nye, Erle Allen: chairman, chief executive officer, director, TU Electric Co.

Textile Clothing Tech Corp.

Patel, Homi Burjor: president, chief operating officer, director, Hartmarx Corp.

Textron Financial Corp.

Cambell, Lewis B.: chairman, chief executive officer, director, Textron Inc.

Textron Inc.

Dickson, Rush Stuart: chairman, Dickson Foundation

Fish, Lawrence K.: trustee, Citizens Charitable Foundation; chairman, chief executive officer, Citizens Financial Group, Inc.

Mead, Dana George: chairman, chief executive officer, director, Tenneco Automotive

Snow, John William: chairman, president, chief executive officer, CSX Corp.

Walker, Martin Dean: chairman, chief executive officer, director, Hanna Co. (M.A.)

Wheeler, Thomas Beardsley: chairman, chief executive officer, Massachusetts Mutual Life Insurance Co.

The Dixie Group Inc.

Klein, Starr T.: secretary, treasurer, trustee, Dixie Yarns Foundation, Inc.

The Gap Inc.

Fisher, Doris F.: treasurer, Gap Foundation/Gap Inc. Community Relations

Schwab, Charles R.: chairman, co-chief executive officer, director, Schwab & Co., Inc. (Charles); chairman, Schwab Corp. Foundation (Charles)

The Geon Co.

Brothers, John Alfred 'Fred': trustee, Ashland Inc. Foundation

The Good Guys Inc.

Martin, John E.: chairman, chief executive officer, Taco Bell Corp.; chairman, Taco Bell Foundation

The Houston Exploration Co.

Catell, Robert Barry: chairman, chief executive officer, Brooklyn Union

The Musicland Group

Wright, Michael William: chairman, president, chief executive officer, director, SuperValu, Inc.

The National Machinery Co.

Kalnow, Carl F.: trustee, National Machinery Foundation, Inc.

The Pepper Companies

Connolly, Eugene Bernard, Jr.: chairman emeritus, USG Corp.

The Post & Courier

Anderson, Ivan Verner, Jr.: president, chief executive officer, Evening Post Publishing Co.; vice president, Post and Courier Foundation

The Sabre Group

Crandall, Robert Lloyd: director, AMR Corp.

The Williams Co. Inc.

Higgins, Patricia L.: director, Alcoa Foundation

Thermedics Inc.

Hatsopoulos, George Nicholas: founder, chairman, chief executive officer, director, Thermo Electron Corp.; committee member, Thermo Electron Foundation

Hatsopoulos, John Nicholas: retired president, Thermo Electron Corp.; committee member, Thermo Electron Foundation

Kelleher, Paul F.: committee member, Thermo Electron Foundation

Thermo Cardiosys

Hatsopoulos, George Nicholas: founder, chairman, chief executive officer, director, Thermo Electron Corp.; committee member, Thermo Electron Foundation

Hatsopoulos, John Nicholas: retired president, Thermo Electron Corp.; committee member, Thermo Electron Foundation

Thermo Ecotek Corp.

Hatsopoulos, George Nicholas: founder, chairman, chief executive officer, director, Thermo Electron Corp.; committee member, Thermo Electron Foundation

Thermo Electron Corp.

Bodman, Samuel Wright, III: chairman, chief executive officer, director, Cabot Corp.; president, director, Cabot Corp. Foundation

Syron, Richard F.: chairman, chief executive officer, director, American Stock Exchange, Inc.

Thermo Fibertek Inc.

Hatsopoulos, George Nicholas: founder, chairman, chief executive officer, director, Thermo Electron Corp.; committee member, Thermo Electron Foundation

Hatsopoulos, John Nicholas: retired president, Thermo Electron Corp.; committee member, Thermo Electron Foundation

Kelleher, Paul F.: committee member, Thermo Electron Foundation

Thermo Instrument System Inc.

Hatsopoulos, George Nicholas: founder, chairman,

chief executive officer, director, Thermo Electron Corp.; committee member, Thermo Electron Foundation

Hatsopoulos, John Nicholas: retired president, Thermo Electron Corp.; committee member, Thermo Electron Foundation

Kelleher, Paul F.: committee member, Thermo Electron Foundation

Thermo Optek Corp.

Hatsopoulos, George Nicholas: founder, chairman, chief executive officer, director, Thermo Electron Corp.; committee member, Thermo Electron Foundation

Kelleher, Paul F.: committee member, Thermo Electron Foundation

Thermo Power Corp.

Hatsopoulos, George Nicholas: founder, chairman, chief executive officer, director, Thermo Electron Corp.; committee member, Thermo Electron Foundation

Hatsopoulos, John Nicholas: retired president, Thermo Electron Corp.; committee member, Thermo Electron Foundation

Thermo Process System

Hatsopoulos, George Nicholas: founder, chairman, chief executive officer, director, Thermo Electron Corp.; committee member, Thermo Electron Foundation

Thermo Remediation Inc.

Kelleher, Paul F.: committee member, Thermo Electron Foundation

ThermoTrex Corp.

Hatsopoulos, George Nicholas: founder, chairman, chief executive officer, director, Thermo Electron Corp.; committee member, Thermo Electron Foundation

Kelleher, Paul F.: committee member, Thermo Electron Foundation

Thermoquest Inc.

Hatsopoulos, George Nicholas: founder, chairman, chief executive officer, director, Thermo Electron Corp.; committee member, Thermo Electron Foundation

Thiokol Corp.

Armstrong, Neil A.: trustee, Milacron Foundation; director, Milacron, Inc.

Thomas & Betts Corp.

Waltrip, William H.: chairman, director, Bausch & Lomb Inc.

Thomas E Wood Inc.

Klinedinst, Thomas John, Jr.: trustee, Star Bank NA, Cincinnati Foundation

Thomas Group Inc.

Chain, John T., Junior: trustee, Kemper Foundation (James S.); president, Kemper National Insurance Companies

Thomas Industries Inc.

Davis, Walter Stewart: secretary, treasurer, Grede Foundation

Gloyd, Lawrence Eugene: trustee, CLARCOR Foundation; chairman, chief executive officer, director, CLARCOR Inc.

Massaro, Anthony A.: president, chief executive officer, chairman, chief operating officer, Lincoln Electric Co.

Thomas Nelson Inc.

Turner, Cal, Jr.: chairman, chief executive officer, director, Dollar General Corp.

Thrall Car Manufacturing Co.

Duchossois, Craig J.: director, Duchossois Foundation; president, director, Duchossois Industries Inc.

Duchossois, Richard Louis: secretary, Duchossois Foundation; chairman, chief executive officer, director, Duchossois Industries Inc.

Tidi Products Inc.

Henseler, Gerald A.: executive vice president, chief financial officer, director, Banta Corp.; president, Banta Corp. Foundation

Time Insurance Co.

Freedman, Allen Royal: trustee, Fortis Foundation; chairman, chief executive officer, president, Fortis, Inc.

Time Warner Inc.

Greenwald, Gerald: chairman, chief executive officer, director, United Airlines Inc.

Mark, Reuben: chairman, chief executive officer, Colgate-Palmolive Co.

Times Herald Co. Inc.

Chapple, Thomas Leslie: senior vice president, general counsel, secretary, Gannett Co., Inc.; secretary, Gannett Foundation

McCorkindale, Douglas H.: vice chairman, president, Gannett Co., Inc.; president, Gannett Foundation

Times Mirror Co.

Armstrong, C. Michael: chairman, chief executive officer, AT&T Corp.

Beall, Donald Ray: director, Rockwell International Corp.

Bryson, John E.: chairman, chief executive officer, Edison International

Times Mirror Magazines Inc.

Wright, Donald Franklin: director, Times Mirror Foundation

Times Printing Co.

Sulzberger, Arthur Ochs, Sr.: director, New York Times Co.; chairman, director, New York Times Co. Foundation

Times-World Corp.

Barry, Richard Francis, III: director, Landmark Communications Foundation; vice chairman, Landmark Communications Inc.

Timken Co.

Luke, John A., Jr.: chairman, president, chief executive officer, director, Westvaco Corp.

Mahoney, Robert W.: chairman, president, chief executive officer, director, Diebold, Inc.

Walker, Martin Dean: chairman, chief executive officer, director, Hanna Co. (M.A.)

Timken Latrobe Steel

Timken, William Robert, Jr.: chairman, president, chief executive officer, director, Timken Co. (The)

Tipton Lakes Co.

Miller, William Irwin: director, Cummins Engine Foundation

Titan Holding

Murphy, Christopher J., III: president, chief executive officer, director, First Source Corp.; director, First Source Foundation

Tokheim Corp.

Baker, James Kendrick: chairman, director, Arvin Foundation; vice chairman, director, Arvin Industries, Inc.

Tomkins Corp.

Reading, Anthony John: president, trustee, Tomkins Corp. Foundation; president, chief executive officer, Tomkins Industries, Inc.

Tomkins Industries Inc.

Duncan, Ian: trustee, Tomkins Corp. Foundation; deputy chairman, managing director finance, Tomkins Industries, Inc.

Tomkins Plc.

Reading, Anthony John: president, trustee, Tomkins Corp. Foundation; president, chief executive officer, Tomkins Industries, Inc.

Tonkawa Inc.

Carlson, Curtis Leroy: chairman, director, Carlson Companies, Inc.; president, treasurer, Carlson Family Foundation (Curtis L.)

Toolpushers Supply Co.

True, David: partner, True Oil Co.

True, Diemer: partner, True Oil Co.

Topeka-Capital Journal

Stauffer, John H.: trustee, Stauffer Communications Foundation

Topps Co.

Bergerac, Michel Christian: director, CBS Foundation

Toro Co.

Baukol, Ronald O.: director, executive vice president, Minnesota Mining & Manufacturing Co.

Buhrmaster, Robert C.: president, chief executive officer, director, chairman, Jostens, Inc.

Buxton, Winslow Hurlbert: chairman, president, chief executive officer, director, Pentair Inc.

George, William Wallace: chief executive officer, chairman, Medtronic, Inc.

Toshiba America Information Systems Inc.

Nishida, Atsutoshi: director, Toshiba America Foundation

Yasui, Toshihide: director, Toshiba America Foundation

Toshiba International Corp.

Sugizaki, Teruyuki: director, Toshiba America Foundation

Total System Service Inc.

Blanchard, James Hubert: chairman, chief executive officer, Synovus Financial Corp.

Total System Services Inc.

Yancey, James D.: vice chairman, director, president, chief operating officer, Synovus Financial Corp.

Touch America Inc.

Pederson, Jerrold P.: vice president, chief financial officer, director, Montana Power Co.; director, Montana Power Foundation

Senechal, Ellen M.: treasurer, Montana Power Co.

Zimmerman, Michael E.: vice president, general counsel, Montana Power Co.

Touchstar Technologies LLC

Bailey, Keith E.: chairman, president, director, chief executive officer, Texas Gas Transmission Corp.; president, director, Williams Companies Foundation (The)

Tower Group International

McGraw, Harold Whittlesey 'Terry', III: chairman, president, chief executive officer, McGraw-Hill Companies, Inc.

Tower Life Insurance

Ebrom, Charles E.: director, vice president, Zachry Co. (H.B.); treasurer, trustee, Zachry Foundation (The)

Toyota Motor Credit Corp.

Gieszl, Yale: executive vice president, Toyota Motor Sales U.S.A., Inc.

Ishizaka, Yoshio: president, chief executive officer, Toyota Motor Sales U.S.A., Inc.; president, Toyota U.S.A. Foundation

West, Doug: senior vice president, coordinating officer, Toyota U.S.A. Foundation

Toyota Motor Insurance Services

Gieszl, Yale: executive vice president, Toyota Motor Sales U.S.A., Inc.

Toys R Us

Mark, Reuben: chairman, chief executive officer, Colgate-Palmolive Co.

Trader Publishing Co. Landmark Television Inc.

Barry, Richard Francis, III: director, Landmark Communications Foundation; vice chairman, Landmark Communications Inc.

Tradewind Turbines Corp.

Barnes, Wallace W.: director, Barnes Group Foundation Inc.

Trans America Insurance Corp. California

Herringer, Frank Casper: president, chief executive officer, director, chairman, Transamerica Corp.; vice chairman, director, Transamerica Foundation

TransAmerica Assurance Co.

Latzer, Richard Neal: vice president, director, Transamerica Foundation

TransAmerica Business Technical Corp.

Grubb, Edgar Harold: executive vice president, chief financial officer, Transamerica Corp.; director, Transamerica Foundation

TransAmerica Cash Reserve Inc.

Latzer, Richard Neal: vice president, director, Transamerica Foundation

TransAmerica Corp.

Matschullat, Robert W.: trustee, Bronfman Foundation/Joseph E. Seagram & Sons, Inc. Fund (Samuel); vice chairman, chief financial officer, Seagram & Sons, Inc. (Joseph E.)

Moore, Gordon E., PhD: cofounder, chairman emeritus, director, Intel Corp.; trustee, Intel Foundation

Schwab, Charles R.: chairman, co-chief executive officer, director, Schwab & Co., Inc. (Charles); chairman, Schwab Corp. Foundation (Charles)

TransAmerica Fin Corp.

Herringer, Frank Casper: president, chief executive officer, director, chairman, Transamerica Corp.; vice chairman, director, Transamerica Foundation

TransAmerica Finance Corp.

Grubb, Edgar Harold: executive vice president, chief financial officer, Transamerica Corp.; director, Transamerica Foundation

TransAmerica Home First Corp.

Broome, Burton Edward: vice president, controller, Transamerica Corp.; vice president, treasurer, Transamerica Foundation

TransAmerica Income Shares

Latzer, Richard Neal: vice president, director, Transamerica Foundation

TransAmerica Insurance Corp. California

Grubb, Edgar Harold: executive vice president, chief financial officer, Transamerica Corp.; director, Transamerica Foundation

TransAmerica Insurance Group

Latzer, Richard Neal: vice president, director, Transamerica Foundation

TransAmerica Leasing Inc.

Herringer, Frank Casper: president, chief executive officer, director, chairman, Transamerica Corp.; vice chairman, director, Transamerica Foundation

TransAmerica Life & Annuity Co.

Latzer, Richard Neal: vice president, director, Transamerica Foundation

TransAmerica Occidental Life Insurance Co.

Grubb, Edgar Harold: executive vice president, chief financial officer, Transamerica Corp.; director, Transamerica Foundation

Herringer, Frank Casper: president, chief executive officer, director, chairman, Transamerica Corp.; vice chairman, director, Transamerica Foundation

Latzer, Richard Neal: vice president, director, Transamerica Foundation

Transcend Services Inc.

Lucas, Donald Leo: chairman, Cadence Designs Systems, Inc.

Transco Energy Co.

Bailey, Keith E.: chairman, president, director, chief executive officer, Texas Gas Transmission Corp.; president, director, Williams Companies Foundation (The)

Dagley, Larry J.: senior vice president, chief financial officer, Pacific Enterprises

Higbee, David M.: secretary, Williams; secretary, treasurer, Williams Companies Foundation (The)

Transcontinental Insurance Canada New York

Chookaszian, Dennis Haig: chairman, chief executive officer, CNA

Transcontinental Insurance Co. New York

Jokiel, Peter E.: senior vice president, chief financial officer, CNA

Sharkey, William Henry, Jr.: director, CNA Foundation

Tisch, Laurence Alan: chairman, co-chief executive officer, CBS Corp.; trustee, Loews Foundation

Tisch, Preston Robert: chairman, director, CBS Foundation; co-chairman, co-chief executive officer, director, CNA; trustee, Loews Foundation

Transfinancial Holdings Inc.

Devlin, James Richard: director, Sprint Foundation

Transit Management Tucson

Burns, Mitchell Anthony: president, director, Ryder System Charitable Foundation; chairman, president, chief executive officer, Ryder System, Inc.

Transmission Products

Cutchins, Clifford Armstrong, IV: president, Fort James Corp.; chairman, director, Fort James Foundation (The)

Transok Inc.

Brooks, E. Richard 'Dick': chairman, chief executive officer, director, Central & South West Services

Transportation Corp. Am

Duchossois, Richard Louis: secretary, Duchossois Foundation; chairman, chief executive officer, director, Duchossois Industries Inc.

Transportation Insurance Co.

Chookaszian, Dennis Haig: chairman, chief executive officer, CNA

Jokiel, Peter E.: senior vice president, chief financial officer, CNA

Sharkey, William Henry, Jr.: director, CNA Foundation

Transtar Inc.

Usher, Thomas J.: chairman, chief executive officer, USX Corp.; chairman board trustees, USX Foundation, Inc.

Transtream Inc.

Light, Walter Frederick: trustee, Air Products Foundation

Transworld Airlines Inc.

Jacobsen, Thomas Herbert: chairman, president, chief executive officer, Mercantile Bank NA

Travel Channel

Batten, Frank, Sr.: chairman, director, Landmark Communications Foundation; chairman, Landmark Communications Inc.

Wynne, John Oliver: president, director, Landmark Communications Foundation; president, chief executive officer, Landmark Communications Inc.

Travelers Group Inc.

Masin, Michael Terry: vice chairman, president international, director, GTE Corp.; trustee, GTE Foundation

Plumeri, Joseph James, II: president, Citigroup

Treasury Management Association

Tran, Khanh T.: senior vice president, chief financial officer, director, Pacific Mutual Life Insurance Co.

Tredegar Industries

Gottwald, Bruce Cobb: chairman, chief executive officer, director, Ethyl Corp.

Tremco Autobody Technologies

Vinney, Les C.: senior vice president, chief financial officer, BFGoodrich Co.

Trend Venture Corp.

Rainbolt, Harold E.: vice president, secretary, SBC Foundation

Tri-State Improvement Co.

Foley, Cheryl M.: vice president, secretary, general counsel, Cinergy Corp.; vice president, secretary, director, Cinergy Foundation

Randolph, Jackson Harold: chairman, Cinergy Corp.; chairman, director, Cinergy Foundation

Tri-W Corp.

Jacobsen, James C.: vice chairman, Kellwood Co.; vice president, director, Kellwood Foundation

TriCord System Inc.

Lucas, Donald Leo: chairman, Cadence Designs Systems, Inc.

Triad International Maint Corp.

Kasputys, Joseph Edward: chairman, trustee, Hitachi Foundation

Tribros Investment Co.

Gidwitz, Gerald S.: chairman, Curtis Industries, Inc. (Helene)

Tribune Co.

McKenna, Andrew James: director, Aon Foundation

Ryan, Patrick G.: chairman, president, chief executive officer, Aon Corp.; president, Aon Foundation

Tricon Global Restaurants Inc.

Dimon, James R.: trustee, Citigroup Foundation; president, chief operating officer, chief financial officer, Salomon Smith Barney

Ulrich, Robert J.: chairman, chief executive officer, director, Dayton Hudson; chairman, trustee, Target Foundation

Weinberg, John Livingston: chairman, president, director, Goldman Sachs Foundation

Trilateral Commission

Wehmeier, Helge H.: president, chief executive officer, director, Bayer Corp.

Trimac Corp.

Sawchuck, Arthur: chairman, director, Manulife Financial

Trinity Industries Inc.

Grum, Clifford J.: director, Temple-Inland Foundation; director, chairman, chief executive officer, Temple-Inland Inc.

Trinova Corp.

Goode, David Ronald: chairman, president, chief executive officer, director, Norfolk Southern Corp.

Trion Inc.

Hill, Frank Trent, Jr.: trustee, Sonoco Foundation; vice president, chief financial officer, Sonoco Products Co.

Triple Crown Service

Tobias, Steven C.: vice chairman, chief operating officer, Norfolk Southern Corp.; director, Norfolk Southern Foundation

Trizec Corp.

Melnuk, Paul D.: president, chief executive officer, Clark Refining & Marketing

True Drilling Co.

True, David: partner, True Oil Co.

True, Diemer: partner, True Oil Co.

True Geothermal Energy Co.

True, David: partner, True Oil Co.

True, Diemer: partner, True Oil Co.

True North Communications Inc.

Ashwill, Terry M.: vice president, director, True North Foundation

Boland, Jack: vice president, director, True North Foundation

Perona, Dale F.: secretary, treasurer, True North Foundation

True North Technologies

Balousek, John B.: president, director, True North Communications, Inc.; vice president, director, True North Foundation

True Ranches

True, David: partner, True Oil Co.

True, Diemer: partner, True Oil Co.

Trust Co. Bank

Dahlberg, Alfred William, III: chairman, president, chief executive officer, Southern Co. Services Inc.

Trust Co. New Jersey

Codey, Lawrence R.: president, chief operating officer, Public Service Electric & Gas Co.

Trust Co. West

Masin, Michael Terry: vice chairman, president international, director, GTE Corp.; trustee, GTE Foundation

Trust Corp. Mortgage Inc.

Murphy, Christopher J., III: president, chief executive officer, director, First Source Corp.; director, First Source Foundation

Trust Pipe Line Co.

Godfrey, Cullen Michael: vice president, FINA Foundation

Trustco Inc.

Peterson, Donald Matthew: trustee, Trustmark Foundation; president, chief executive officer, director, Trustmark Insurance Co.

Trustmark Corp.

Day, Frank R.: chairman, Trustmark National Bank

Trustmark Insurance Co. Mutual

Eckert, Ralph John: trustee, Trustmark Foundation

Peterson, Donald Matthew: trustee, Trustmark Foundation; president, chief executive officer, director, Trustmark Insurance Co.

Trustmark Life Insurance Co.

Batten, Richard D.: trustee, Trustmark Foundation

Gramm, Frank G., III: trustee, Trustmark Foundation

Peterson, Donald Matthew: trustee, Trustmark Foundation; president, chief executive officer, director, Trustmark Insurance Co.

Tucson Resources Inc.

Adler, Ira R.: executive vice president, chief financial officer, Tucson Electric Power Co.

Tupperware Corp. Inc.

Davis, Ruth Margaret: trustee, Air Products Foundation

Elam, Lloyd Charles, MD: trustee, Merck Co. Foundation

Grum, Clifford J.: director, Temple-Inland Foundation; director, chairman, chief executive officer, Temple-Inland Inc.

Turner Granzow & Hollenkamp

Granzow, Paul H.: chairman, director, Standard Register Co.

Tuscarora Inc.

Leininger, Jeffrey L.: vice chairman specialized commercial banking, Mellon Financial Corp.

Twin City Fire Insurance Co.

Ayer, Ramani: chairman, president, chief executive officer, Hartford (The)

Twin Disc Inc.

Powers, Paul Joseph: chairman, president, chief executive officer, director, Commercial Intertech Corp.; president, trustee, Commercial Intertech Foundation

Wardeberg, George E.: president, WICOR Foundation; president, chief executive officer, director, WICOR, Inc.

Tyson Export Sales Inc.

Blair, James Burton: trustee, Tyson Foundation, Inc.

Tyson Seafood Group

Wray, Donald E.: president, chief operating officer, director, Tyson Foods Inc.

UAL Corp.

Hacker, Douglas A.: senior vice president finance, chief financial officer, United Airlines Inc.

UAW-Ford National Programs

Pestillo, Peter John: executive chairman, Ford Motor Co.; trustee, Ford Motor Co. Fund

UCOM Inc.

Strandjord, Mary Jeannine: director, Sprint Foundation

UGI Corp.

Gozon, Richard C.: executive vice president pulp paper & packaging, Weyerhaeuser Co.; trustee, Weyerhaeuser Co. Foundation

UGI Utilities Inc.

Gozon, Richard C.: executive vice president pulp paper & packaging, Weyerhaeuser Co.; trustee, Weyerhaeuser Co. Foundation

UMB Bank

McDaniel, Tom J.: vice chairman, director, Kerr-McGee Corp.

UMB Fin Corp.

McKenna, William John: director, chairman, Kellwood Co.; chairman, president, director, Kellwood Foundation

UMB Financial Services

McDaniel, Tom J.: vice chairman, director, Kerr-McGee Corp.

UMB Mortgage Co.

Margolin, Abraham E.: director, Tension Envelope Foundation

UPS Airlines

Weidemeyer, Thomas H.: senior vice president, director, United Parcel Service of America Inc.; trustee, UPS Foundation

US Bancorp

Campbell, Phyllis J.: president private financial services, US Bank, Washington

Redmond, Paul Anthony: chairman, chief executive officer, director, Avista Corporation

US Bank NA

Zona, Richard A.: vice chairman commercial banking & institutional finance, U.S. Bancorp

US Corrulite Corp.

Fairbanks, J. Nelson: president, chief executive officer, director, United States Sugar Corp.

Terrill, James E.: executive vice president, United States Sugar Corp.

US Industries Inc.

Price, Charles H., II: director, New York Times Co. Foundation

US News & World Report

Zuckerman, Mortimer Benjamin: co-founder, chairman, co-publisher, director, Daily News

US Satellite Broadcasting Co. Inc.

Hubbard, Stanley S.: chairman, president, chief executive officer, Hubbard Broadcasting, Inc.; president, Hubbard Foundation

US Trust Co. of New York

Douglas, Paul W.: director, Phelps Dodge Foundation

US Trust Corp.

Strickland, Carol A.: chairman corporate contributions committee, U.S. Trust Corp. Foundation

Taylor, Frederick B.: vice chairman, chief investment officer, United States Trust Co. of New York

US West Inc.

Nelson, Marilyn Carlson: chairman, chief executive officer, president, Carlson Companies, Inc.

USA South African Business Council

Tambakeras, Markos I.: director, Honeywell Foundation

USA Today

Wehling, Robert Louis: global marketing, government relations officer, Procter & Gamble Co.; president, trustee, Procter & Gamble Fund

USA Today International Corp.

McCorkindale, Douglas H.: vice chairman, president, Gannett Co., Inc.; president, Gannett Foundation

USA Weekend Inc.

McCorkindale, Douglas H.: vice chairman, president, Gannett Co., Inc.; president, Gannett Foundation

USAA

Herres, Robert T.: chairman, chief executive officer, United Services Automobile Association

USAA Capital Corp.

Robles, Josue: chief financial officer, United Services Automobile Association

USAA General Indemnity Co.

Herres, Robert T.: chairman, chief executive officer, United Services Automobile Association

USAirways Group Inc.

Smith, Raymond W.: chairman, chief executive officer, director, Bell Atlantic Corp.

USG Corp.

Barnett, Robert L.: director, Ameritech Foundation

Ford, W. Douglas: executive vice president, BP Amoco Corp.

USI Insurance Service Corp.

Klinedinst, Thomas John, Jr.: trustee, Star Bank NA, Cincinnati Foundation

UST Enterprise Inc.

Barrett, Robert E.: executive vice president, UST Inc.

USX Corp.

Armstrong, Neil A.: trustee, Milacron Foundation; director, Milacron, Inc.

Beghini, Victor Gene: trustee, USX Foundation, Inc.

Lee, Charles Robert: chairman, chief executive officer, director, GTE Corp.; chief executive officer, trustee, GTE Foundation

Snow, John William: chairman, president, chief executive officer, CSX Corp.

Wilhelm, Paul J.: trustee, USX Foundation, Inc.

UTILX Corp.

Bright, Stanley J.: chairman, president, chief executive officer, director, MidAmerican Energy Holdings Co.

Ultramar Diamond Shamrock Corp.

Bradford, William Edward: chairman, director, Halliburton Co.

Ultramar Diamond Shamrock Refining & Marketing Co.

Fretthold, Timothy Jon: executive vice president, general counsel, director, Ultramar Diamond Shamrock Corp.

Ultramar Energy Inc.

Havens, Christopher: senior vice president, Ultramar Diamond Shamrock Corp.

Ultramar Inc.

Eisman, Paul: senior vice president refining Southwest, Ultramar Diamond Shamrock Corp.

Klesse, William R.: executive vice president operations, Ultramar Diamond Shamrock Corp.

Underwriters Laboratories

Maatman, Gerald Leonard: chairman, president, trustee, Kemper Foundation (James S.); director, Kemper National Insurance Companies

Uni-Flange Holdings Inc.

Agness, Terry D.: president, director, Ford Meter Box Co.; director, Honeywell Foundation

UniHealth America

Hartshorn, Terry O'Dell: chairman, PacifiCare Health System Foundation

UniSource Energy Corp.

Adler, Ira R.: executive vice president, chief financial officer, Tucson Electric Power Co.

Unicom Corp.

Jannotta, Edgar D.: president, Blair & Co. Foundation (William); senior director, Blair & Co. (William)

Strobel, Pamela B.: senior vice president, general counsel, Commonwealth Edison Co.

Thomas, Richard Lee: vice president, First National Bank of Chicago Foundation

Unilever Home & Personal Care North America

Phillips, Robert M.: president, Unilever Home & Personal Care U.S.A.

Union Bancal Corp.

Niebla, J. Fernando: chairman, chief executive officer, Pacific Mutual Life Insurance Co.

Union Bank

Farman, Richard Donald: chairman, chief executive officer, Pacific Enterprises

Union Camp Corp.

Sheehan, Jeremiah J.: chairman, director, Reynolds Metals Co. Foundation

Union Carbide Corp.

Ringler, James M.: chairman, president, chief executive officer, director, Premark International Inc.

Union Central Life Insurance Co.

Leser, Lawrence Arthur: chairman, director, Scripps Co. (E.W.); member, Scripps Howard Foundation

Union Federal Savings Bank

Muehlbauer, James Herman: vice president, director, Koch Foundation

Union Light Heat & Power Co.

Randolph, Jackson Harold: chairman, Cinergy Corp.; chairman, director, Cinergy Foundation

Union Mutual Fire Insurance Co.

Bertrand, Frederic Howard: chairman, Central Vermont Public Service Corp.

Keyser, F. Ray, Jr.: chairman, director, Central Vermont Public Service Corp.

Union Oil Co. California

Herringer, Frank Casper: president, chief executive officer, director, chairman, Transamerica Corp.; vice chairman, director, Transamerica Foundation

Sikkema, Karen Ann: president, trustee, Unocal Foundation

Union Pacific Corp.

Cheney, Richard B.: chief executive officer, Halliburton Co.; president, Halliburton Foundation, Inc.

Eccles, Spencer Fox: chairman, chief executive officer, director, First Security Bank of Idaho NA

Union Pacific Railroad Co.

Cheney, Richard B.: chief executive officer, Halliburton Co.; president, Halliburton Foundation, Inc.

Union Planters National Bank

Moore, Jackson W.: president, director, Union Planters Corp.

Rawlins, Benjamin W., Jr.: chairman, chief executive officer, director, Union Planters Corp.

Union Tribune Publishing Co.

Copley, Helen K.: chairman, trustee, Copley Foundation (James S.); chairman, director, senior management board, Copley Press, Inc.

Uniseal Inc.

Koch, Robert Louis, II: president, chief executive officer, director, Koch Enterprises, Inc.; president, director, Koch Foundation

Muehlbauer, James Herman: vice president, director, Koch Foundation

Unisource Worldwide Inc.

Countryman, Gary Lee: chairman, Liberty Mutual Insurance Group

Mead, Dana George: chairman, chief executive officer, director, Tenneco Automotive

Unisys Corp.

Goodes, Melvin Russell: chairman, chief executive officer, director, Ameritech Corp.

Huston, Edwin Allen: vice president, director, Ryder System Charitable Foundation; vice chairman, director, Ryder System, Inc.

United Air Specialists Inc.

Gloyd, Lawrence Eugene: trustee, CLARCOR Foundation; chairman, chief executive officer, director, CLARCOR Inc.

United Airlines Inc.

Goodwin, James E.: president, chief operating officer, director, United Airlines Inc.

Hobgood, William P.: senior vice president, human resources, United Airlines Inc.

Maher, Francesca M.: senior vice president, general counsel, secretary, United Airlines Inc.

Oran, Stuart I.: director, United Airlines Foundation; senior vice president international, United Airlines Inc.

United Auto Group Inc.

Cogan, Marshall Stuart: chairman, president, chief executive officer, director, Trace International Holdings, Inc.; director, Trace International Holdings, Inc. Foundation

Smith, Philip N., Jr.: secretary, Trace International Holdings, Inc. Foundation

United Aviation Fuels Corp. Del

Maher, Francesca M.: senior vice president, general counsel, secretary, United Airlines Inc.

United Central Industrial Sup Co.

McGlothlin, James W.: chief executive officer, United Coal Co. Charitable Foundation; chairman, chief executive officer, United Co.

United Cities Gas Co.

Ballengee, Jerry Hunter: president, chief operating officer, director, Union Camp Corp.

United Dental Care Inc.

Longfield, William H.: president, Bard Foundation (C.R.); chairman, chief executive officer, director, Bard, Inc. (C.R.)

United Dominion Holdings Inc.

Drury, Robert E.: president, director, United Dominion Foundation

Holland, William Ray: vice president, director, United Dominion Foundation; chairman, chief executive officer, director, United Dominion Industries, Ltd.

United Dominion Industries Ltd.

Dickson, Rush Stuart: chairman, Dickson Foundation

Ver Hagen, Jan Karol: president, United Dominion Industries, Ltd.

United Energy Corp.

Bell, Wayne L.: secretary, United Coal Co. Charitable Foundation

Fowlkes, J. Thomas: president, United Coal Co. Charitable Foundation

United Family Life Insurance Co.

Freedman, Allen Royal: trustee, Fortis Foundation; chairman, chief executive officer, president, Fortis, Inc.

United Financial Adjusting Co.

Lewis, Peter Benjamin: chairman, president, chief executive officer, director, Progressive Corp.

United HealthCare Corp.

Johnson, James A.: chairman, chief executive officer, director, Fannie Mae; chairman, Fannie Mae Foundation

Leatherdale, Douglas West: chairman, chief executive officer, president, Saint Paul Companies Inc.

United Heartland Inc.

Formisano, Roger: vice president, United Wisconsin Services Foundation

Hefty, Thomas R.: chairman, president, chief executive officer, United Wisconsin Services

United Illuminating Co.

Breslawsky, Marc C.: president, chief operating officer, Pitney Bowes Inc.

Carson, David Ellis Adams: chairman, chief executive officer, Peoples Bank

United Jeep Eagle Chrysler Plymouth

Cogan, Marshall Stuart: chairman, president, chief executive officer, director, Trace International Holdings, Inc.; director, Trace International Holdings, Inc. Foundation

United Meridian Corp.

Murdy, James L.: executive vice president finance and administration, chief financial officer, Allegheny Technologies Inc.; trustee, Allegheny Technologies Inc. Charitable Trust

United Metro Materials Inc.

Stinson, Kenneth E.: member contributions committee, Kiewit Companies Foundation; chairman, chief executive officer, director, Kiewit Sons' Inc. (Peter)

United Missouri Bank

Lay, Terry: president, Lee, Lee Apparel Co.

United Missouri Bank Saint Louis

McKenna, William John: director, chairman, Kellwood Co.; chairman, president, director, Kellwood Foundation

United Nissan Inc.

Cogan, Marshall Stuart: chairman, president, chief executive officer, director, Trace International Holdings, Inc.; director, Trace International Holdings, Inc. Foundation

United Oil Minerals Inc.

Fowlkes, J. Thomas: president, United Coal Co. Charitable Foundation

McGlothlin, James W.: chief executive officer, United Coal Co. Charitable Foundation; chairman, chief executive officer, United Co.

United Omaha Life Insurance Co.

Sturgeon, John: president, chief operating officer, Mutual of Omaha Insurance Co.

Weekly, John William: chairman, chief executive officer, Mutual of Omaha Insurance Co.

United Parcel Service Inc. Ohio

Weidemeyer, Thomas H.: senior vice president, director, United Parcel Service of America Inc.; trustee, UPS Foundation

United States Bancorp

Ahlers, Linda: president, department store division, Dayton Hudson; trustee, Target Foundation

Coors, Peter Hanson: vice president, director, Coors Brewing Co.

Hale, Roger Loucks: chairman, TENNANT Co.; president, TENNANT Co. Foundation

United States Financial Group Inc.

Yablon, Leonard Harold: secretary-treasurer, Forbes Foundation

United States Pipe Foundry Co. Inc.

Porter, Edward A.: vice president, general counsel, secretary, Walter Industries Inc.

United States Piper Jaffray Inc.

Bohn, Karen M.: president, Piper Jaffray Companies Foundation; chief executive officer, U.S. Bancorp Piper Jaffray

Piper, Addison Lewis: director, Piper Jaffray Companies Foundation; chairman, chief executive officer, director, U.S. Bancorp Piper Jaffray

Roesler, Deborah K.: chief financial officer, U.S. Bancorp Piper Jaffray

United States Satellite Broadcasting Co.

Hubbard, Karen H.: trustee, Hubbard Foundation

United States Surgical Corp.

Romeril, Barry D.: executive vice president, chief financial officer, Xerox Corp.

United States Telecom Inc.

Strandjord, Mary Jeannine: director, Sprint Foundation

United States West Inc.

Barrett, Craig R.: president, chief operating officer, director, Intel Corp.

Harad, George Jay: chairman, chief executive officer, director, Boise Cascade Corp.

United States of America Allied Irish Bank PLC

Casey, Jeremiah E.: chairman, First Maryland Bancorp; chairman, trustee, First Maryland Foundation

United States of America Networks Inc.

Bronfman, Edgar Miles, Jr.: trustee, Bronfman Foundation/Joseph E. Seagram & Sons, Inc. Fund (Samuel); president, chief executive officer, Seagram & Sons, Inc. (Joseph E.)

United States of America Today

McCorkindale, Douglas H.: vice chairman, president, Gannett Co., Inc.; president, Gannett Foundation

United States of America Today Information Network

McCorkindale, Douglas H.: vice chairman, president, Gannett Co., Inc.; president, Gannett Foundation

United Technologies Corp.

Lee, Charles Robert: chairman, chief executive officer, director, GTE Corp.; chief executive officer, trustee, GTE Foundation

Wagner, Harold A.: chairman, president, chief executive officer, director, Air Products and Chemicals, Inc.

United Telecommunications Inc.

Esrey, William Todd: chairman, chief executive officer, Sprint Corp.

Forsythe, Donald George: vice president corporate relations, Sprint Corp.; executive director, Sprint Foundation

Hall, Donald Joyce: chairman board, director, Hallmark Cards Inc.; chairman, Hallmark Corporate Foundation

Strandjord, Mary Jeannine: director, Sprint Foundation

United Vacations Inc.

Maher, Francesca M.: senior vice president, general counsel, secretary, United Airlines Inc.

United Water Mid-Atlantic Utilities

Codey, Lawrence R.: president, chief operating officer, Public Service Electric & Gas Co.

United Water New Jersey

Hanson, Jon F.: trustee, Prudential Foundation

United Water Resources Inc.

Codey, Lawrence R.: president, chief operating officer, Public Service Electric & Gas Co.

Hanson, Jon F.: trustee, Prudential Foundation

United Wisconsin Insurance Co.

Formisano, Roger: vice president, United Wisconsin Services Foundation

Granoff, Mark Howard: vice president, United Wisconsin Services Foundation

Hefty, Thomas R.: chairman, president, chief executive officer, United Wisconsin Services

United Wisconsin Life Insurance

Formisano, Roger: vice president, United Wisconsin Services Foundation

Granoff, Mark Howard: vice president, United Wisconsin Services Foundation

Hefty, Thomas R.: chairman, president, chief executive officer, United Wisconsin Services

United Wisconsin Service

Granoff, Mark Howard: vice president, United Wisconsin Services Foundation

United Wisconsin Services

Abdoo, Richard A.: chairman, president, chief executive officer, Wisconsin Energy Corp.; president, director, Wisconsin Energy Corp. Foundation, Inc.

Formisano, Roger: vice president, United Wisconsin Services Foundation

United World Life Insurance Co.

Sturgeon, John: president, chief operating officer, Mutual of Omaha Insurance Co.

Weekly, John William: chairman, chief executive officer, Mutual of Omaha Insurance Co.

Universal Corp.

Sheehan, Jeremiah J.: chairman, director, Reynolds Metals Co. Foundation

Towers, Thomas R.: president, director, Universal Leaf Foundation

Universal Foods Corp.

Keyes, James Henry: advisor, Johnson Controls Foundation; president, Johnson Controls Inc.

Whitelaw, Essie M.: president, chief operating officer, United Wisconsin Services; vice president, United Wisconsin Services Foundation

Zaar, Carl L.: secretary, treasurer, director, Universal Foods Foundation

Universal Health Services

Meyerson, Martin: director, Panasonic Foundation

Universal Hospital Service

Bohn, Karen M.: president, Piper Jaffray Companies Foundation; chief executive officer, U.S. Bancorp Piper Jaffray

Universal Resources Corp.

Cash, R. D.: chairman, president, chief executive officer, director, Questar Corp.

Parks, Stephen E.: vice president, treasurer, chief financial officer, Questar Corp.

University Bancshares Inc.

Allbritton, Joe Lewis: chairman, chief executive officer, Riggs Bank NA

Unocal Corp.

Herringer, Frank Casper: president, chief executive officer, director, chairman, Transamerica Corp.; vice chairman, director, Transamerica Foundation

Upgrade Corp. Am

Lippes, Gerald Sanford: secretary, Mark IV Industries Foundation

Utelcom Inc.

Strandjord, Mary Jeannine: director, Sprint Foundation

Utex Textiles

Jacobsen, James C.: vice chairman, Kellwood Co.; vice president, director, Kellwood Foundation

UtiliCorp. United Inc.

Hockaday, Irvine O., Jr.: president, chief executive officer, director, Hallmark Cards Inc.

Utilities Mutual Insurance Co.

Davis, William E.: chairman, chief executive officer, Niagara Mohawk Holdings Inc.

Graham, John Gourlay: chief financial officer, senior vice president, GPU Energy

Hafer, Fred Douglass: chairman, president, chief executive officer, GPU Inc.

Utility Constructors Inc.

Kennedy, Bernard Joseph: chairman, president, chief executive officer, director, National Fuel Gas Distribution Corp.

VF Corp.

Laws, Donald P.: member advisory committee, Blue Bell Foundation

Lay, Terry: president, Lee, Lee Apparel Co.

VF Inc.

Iott, Richard B.: president, chief executive officer, director, Seaway Food Town, Inc.

VP Inc.

Iott, Wallace D.: chairman, director, Seaway Food Town, Inc.

Vacco Industries Inc.

Osborne, Richard de Jongh: director, ASARCO Foundation; chairman, chief executive officer, director, ASARCO Inc.

Vail Resorts Inc.

Tisch, James S.: president, chief executive officer, director, CNA

Valcor Inc.

Simmons, Glenn Reuben: vice chairman, Contran Corp.

Simmons, Harold Clark: chairman, director, Simmons Foundation, Inc. (Harold)

Valenite Inc.

Meyer, Daniel Joseph: president, Milacron Foundation; chairman, president, chief executive officer, director, Milacron, Inc.

Valero Natural Gas Co.

Benninger, Edward Charles, Jr.: president, chief financial officer, Valero Energy Corp.

Valhi Group Inc.

Anderson, Eugene Karl: vice president, Contran Corp.; treasurer, Simmons Foundation, Inc. (Harold)

Simmons, Glenn Reuben: vice chairman, Contran Corp.

Valhi Inc.

Anderson, Eugene Karl: vice president, Contran Corp.; treasurer, Simmons Foundation, Inc. (Harold)

Simmons, Glenn Reuben: vice chairman, Contran Corp.

Valley City Steel Co.

Hessler, David J.: secretary, trustee, Jochum-Moll Foundation (The); president, partner, MTD Products Inc.

Moll, Curtis E.: treasurer, trustee, Jochum-Moll Foundation (The)

Valley Forge Life Insurance Co.

Chookaszian, Dennis Haig: chairman, chief executive officer, CNA

Jokiel, Peter E.: senior vice president, chief financial officer, CNA

Sharkey, William Henry, Jr.: director, CNA Foundation

Valley Health Plan

Formisano, Roger: vice president, United Wisconsin Services Foundation

Hefty, Thomas R.: chairman, president, chief executive officer, United Wisconsin Services

Valley Vinters Inc.

Gallo, Joseph E.: co-president, Gallo Foundation

Valspar Corp.

George, William Wallace: chief executive officer, chairman, Medtronic, Inc.

Vanguard Group Investment Companies

Wilson, James Lawrence: chairman, chief executive officer, director, Rohm & Haas Co.

Vanity Fair Intimates Inc.

Pugh, Lawrence R.: chairman, director, Blue Bell, Inc.

Vantageparts

Quesnel, Gregory L.: president, chief executive officer, director, CNF Transportation, Inc.

Vantis

Previte, Richard: president, chief operating officer, director, Advanced Micro Devices, Inc.

Varian Associates Inc.

Davis, Ruth Margaret: trustee, Air Products Foundation

Lautenbach, Terry Robert: trustee, Air Products Foundation

Moore, Gordon E., PhD: cofounder, chairman emeritus, director, Intel Corp.; trustee, Intel Foundation

Vectra Technologies Inc.

Draper, Ernest Linn, Jr.: chairman, president, chief executive officer, director, American Electric Power

Venator Group Inc.

Geier, Philip Henry, Jr.: chairman, president, chief executive officer, Interpublic Group of Companies, Inc.

Mac Kimm, Margaret (Pontius) 'Mardie': trustee, Chicago Title and Trust Co. Foundation

Preston, James Edward: vice president, director, Avon Products Foundation, Inc.; chairman, chief executive officer, director, Avon Products, Inc.

Ventura Industries

Mitropoulis, Iris: chairman, Kingsbury Corp.

Venture Corp.

Gaiswinkler, Robert Sigfried: chairman, director, First Financial Bank; director, First Financial Foundation

Veritas Corp.

Louis, Kenneth C.: president, chief operating officer, director, Ameritas Life Insurance Corp.

Vermont Electric Power Corp.

Keyser, F. Ray, Jr.: chairman, director, Central Vermont Public Service Corp.

Vernon Co.

Rehm, Jack Daniel: chairman emeritus, director, Meredith Corp.

Vestal Manufacturing Co.

Fjelstul, Dean M.: senior vice president, chief financial officer, Walter Industries Inc.

Porter, Edward A.: vice president, general counsel, secretary, Walter Industries Inc.

Vetrotex CertainTeed Corp.

Harkins, James F., Jr.: treasurer, CertainTeed Corp. Foundation

Mattson, Bradford C.: executive vice president exterior building products, CertainTeed Corp.

Viacom Inc.

Miller, Ken: trustee, Credit Suisse First Boston Foundation Trust

Viad Corp.

Ervanian, Armen: vice president, Viad Corp. Fund

Stephan, Richard C.: vice president, controller, director, Viad Corp. Fund

Teets, John William: president, chief executive officer, director, Viad Corp. Fund

Viad Corp. Subsidiaries
Emerson, Frederick George: vice president, secretary, director, Viad Corp. Fund

Viatel Inc.
Graham, John Gourlay: chief financial officer, senior vice president, GPU Energy

Viatro Corp.
O'Brien, John F.: trustee, McDonald & Co. Securities Foundation

Victory Funds Mutual Funds Group
Campbell, Edward Patrick: president, chief operating officer, drc, Nordson Corp.; trustee, Nordson Corp. Foundation

Vigilant Insurance Co.
O'Hare, Dean Raymond: chairman, Chubb Corp.

Village Cross Keys Inc.
Deering, Anthony W.: chairman, chief executive officer, Rouse Co.; chairman, president, trustee, Rouse Co. Foundation
Donahue, Jeffrey H.: senior vice president, chief financial officer, Rouse Co.

Vinyl-Metal Laminators Institute
Baker, James Kendrick: chairman, director, Arvin Foundation; vice chairman, director, Arvin Industries, Inc.

Vion Pharmaceuticals Inc.
Bergerac, Michel Christian: director, CBS Foundation

Virginia Electric & Power Co.
Adams, John B., Junior: chairman, president, chief executive officer, Dominion Resources, Inc.

Virginia Metal Industries
Bell, Wayne L.: secretary, United Coal Co. Charitable Foundation
Clarke, Lois A.: treasurer, United Coal Co. Charitable Foundation; executive vice president finance, chief financial officer, United Co.
McGlothlin, James W.: chief executive officer, United Coal Co. Charitable Foundation; chairman, chief executive officer, United Co.

Virginia Retirement System
Dozier, Ollin Kemp: treasurer, Universal Leaf Foundation

Visalia Newspapers Inc.
McCorkindale, Douglas H.: vice chairman, president, Gannett Co., Inc.; president, Gannett Foundation

Vision Service Plan California
Stevens, Philip Ashworth: vice president, trustee, National Machinery Foundation, Inc.

Viskase Companies Inc.
Page, Gregory R.: president, chief executive officer, Excel Corp.

Vistawall Architectural Products
Rutledge, Ronald E.: executive, Butler Manufacturing Co.

Visual Productions Inc.
Battaglia, Thomas S.: director, American Standard Foundation

Vitalink Pharmacy Services
Bainum, Stewart William, Jr.: chairman, Manor Care Health SVS, Inc.

Vons Companies Inc.
Magowan, Peter Alden: president, managing general partner, Safeway Inc.

Vulcan Materials Co.
DeSimone, Livio Diego: chairman, chief executive officer, Minnesota Mining & Manufacturing Co.
McGregor, Douglas J.: president, chief operating officer, director, Hanna Co. (M.A.)

W R Family Associates
Varet, Elizabeth Rosenwald: vice president, director, AMETEK Foundation; director, AMETEK, Inc.

WC Bradley Co.
Blanchard, James Hubert: chairman, chief executive officer, Synovus Financial Corp.

WDCI Inc.
Sasaki, Robert K.: director, Alexander & Baldwin Foundation

WDSU Television Inc.
Pulitzer, Michael Edgar: chairman, president, chief executive officer, director, Pulitzer Publishing Co.; chairman, president, chief executive officer, Pulitzer Publishing Co. Foundation

WESH Television Inc.
Pulitzer, Michael Edgar: chairman, president, chief executive officer, director, Pulitzer Publishing Co.; chairman, president, chief executive officer, Pulitzer Publishing Co. Foundation
Ridgway, Ronald H.: senior vice president, Pulitzer Publishing Co.; secretary, treasurer, director, Pulitzer Publishing Co. Foundation

WFMY Television Corp.
McCorkindale, Douglas H.: vice chairman, president, Gannett Co., Inc.; president, Gannett Foundation

WGBH
Gifford, Charles Kilvert: trustee, BankBoston Charitable Foundation; chairman, chief executive officer, BankBoston Corp.

WGBH Channel 2
Koch, David Hamilton: director, Koch Foundation, Inc. (Fred C. and Mary R.)

WI Electric Power Co.
Stratton, Frederick Prescott, Jr.: chairman, chief executive officer, director, Briggs & Stratton Corp.; president, director, Briggs & Stratton Corp. Foundation

WI Energy Corp.
Stratton, Frederick Prescott, Jr.: chairman, chief executive officer, director, Briggs & Stratton Corp.; president, director, Briggs & Stratton Corp. Foundation
Willis, Gordon A.: assistant treasurer, assistant secretary, Wisconsin Energy Corp. Foundation, Inc.

WI Gas Co.
Winter, William Bergford: president, Bucyrus-Erie Co.; chairman, president, director, Bucyrus-Erie Foundation

WI Natural Gas Co.
Willis, Gordon A.: assistant treasurer, assistant secretary, Wisconsin Energy Corp. Foundation, Inc.

WICOR
Whitelaw, Essie M.: president, chief operating officer, United Wisconsin Services; vice president, United Wisconsin Services Foundation

WICOR Energy
Wardeberg, George E.: president, WICOR Foundation; president, chief executive officer, director, WICOR, Inc.

WICOR Inc.
Bueche, Wendell Francis: director, Marshall & Ilsley Foundation, Inc.
Haase, Bronson J.: president, chief executive officer, Ameritech Wisconsin
Schrader, Thomas F.: vice president, director, WICOR Foundation
Winter, William Bergford: president, Bucyrus-Erie Co.; chairman, president, director, Bucyrus-Erie Foundation

WM Financial Inc.
Killinger, Kerry Kent: chairman, president, chief executive officer, director, Washington Mutual, Inc.

WNA Carthage Inc.
Jasse, Andre C., Jr.: trustee, Eastern Bank Charitable Foundation

WNET-TV
Steere, William Campbell, Jr.: chairman, chief executive officer, director, Pfizer Inc.

WPBT Channel 2
Huston, Edwin Allen: vice president, director, Ryder System Charitable Foundation; vice chairman, director, Ryder System, Inc.

WPS Resources Corp.
Bemis, Richard A.: president, Bemis Family Foundation (F.K.); president, chief executive officer, director, Bemis Manufacturing Co.

WQEW-AM
Sulzberger, Arthur Ochs, Sr.: director, New York Times Co.; chairman, director, New York Times Co. Foundation

WQXR-FM
Sulzberger, Arthur Ochs, Sr.: director, New York Times Co.; chairman, director, New York Times Co. Foundation

WRB Inc.
Cudlip, Brittain B.: chairman, Bardes Corp.
Cummings, William S.: chairman, Cummings Properties Management

WS Griffith & Co. Inc.
Fiondella, Robert William: chairman, president, chief executive officer, Phoenix Home Life Mutual Insurance Co.

WSET Inc.
Allbritton, Joe Lewis: chairman, chief executive officer, Riggs Bank NA

WTVF-Nashville
Batten, Frank, Sr.: chairman, director, Landmark Communications Foundation; chairman, Landmark Communications Inc.

WW Grainger Inc.
Turner, Fred L.: senior chairman, director, McDonald's Corp.

WWL TV Inc.
Huey, Ward L., Jr.: president broadcast division, vice chairman, director, Belo Corp. (A.H.); vice president, trustee, Belo Corp. Foundation (A.H.)

Wachovia Bank & Trust
Browning, Peter C.: chief executive officer, president,

director, Sonoco Products Co.

Wachovia Bank & Trust Co.

Iverson, Francis Kenneth: chairman, director, Nucor Corp.; director, Nucor Foundation

Kulynych, Petro: chairman, treasurer, Lowe's Charitable and Educational Foundation

Wachovia Bank NC NA

Baker, Leslie Mayo, Jr.: president, chief executive officer, chairman, Wachovia Bank of North Carolina NA; chairman, Wachovia Foundation, Inc. (The)

Wachovia Bank South Carolina

Anderson, Ivan Verner, Jr.: president, chief executive officer, Evening Post Publishing Co.; vice president, Post and Courier Foundation

Wachovia Bank of Georgia, NA

Ackerman, F. Duane: president, chief executive officer, BellSouth Corp.

Wachovia Corp.

Balloun, James S.: chairman, chief executive officer, president, National Service Industries, Inc.

Henderson, George W., III: trustee, Burlington Industries Foundation; president, chief executive officer, director, Burlington Industries, Inc.

Hipp, William Hayne: president, chief executive officer, director, Liberty Corp.; chairman, president, director, Liberty Corp. Foundation

Iverson, Francis Kenneth: chairman, director, Nucor Corp.; director, Nucor Foundation

McDowell, J. Walter: president, chief executive officer, director, Wachovia Bank of North Carolina NA; director, Wachovia Foundation, Inc. (The)

Reynolds, William Gray, Jr.: vice president government relations & public affairs, Reynolds Metals Co.; director, Reynolds Metals Co. Foundation

Waddington North America

Jasse, Andre C., Jr.: trustee, Eastern Bank Charitable Foundation

Wal-Mart International Division

Martin, Bobby L.: member, Wal-Mart Foundation

Wal-Mart Stores

Iverson, Francis Kenneth: chairman, director, Nucor Corp.; director, Nucor Foundation

Walbridge Coatings

Penny, Roger Pratt: president, chief operating officer, director, Bethlehem Steel Corp.

Walgreen Co.

Howard, James Joseph, III: chairman, president, chief executive officer, director, Northern States Power Co.

McNally, Alan G.: chairman, chief executive officer, Harris Trust & Savings Bank

Wall Saint Journal

Burenga, Kenneth L.: president, chief operating officer, director, Dow Jones & Co., Inc.

Walmart Stores Inc.

Friedman, Stephen James: senior advisor, Goldman Sachs Group

Walnut Hill Properties Inc.

Cudlip, Brittain B.: chairman, Bardes Corp.

Cummings, William S.: chairman, Cummings Properties Management

Walt Disney Co.

Lozano, Ignacio Eugenio, Jr.: chairman, Pacific Mutual Life Insurance Co.

Watson, Raymond L.: vice chairman, Pacific Mutual Life Insurance Co.

Wilson, Gary Lee: chairman, director, Northwest Airlines, Inc.

Walter Industries Inc.

Clark, Howard Longstreth, Jr.: vice chairman, Walter Industries Inc.

Golkin, Perry: member, Walter Industries Inc.

Johnson, James Lawrence: chairman emeritus, Walter Industries Inc.

Tokarz, Michael T.: founding partner, Walter Industries Inc.

Walters Art Gallery

Shepard, Donald James: chairman, president, chief executive officer, AEGON U.S.A. Inc.

Warnaco Group Inc.

Resnick, Stewart A.: chairman, chief executive officer, Franklin Mint (The)

Warner-Lambert Co.

Burt, Robert Norcross: chairman, chief executive officer, director, FMC Corp.; director, FMC Foundation

Georges, John A.: director, International Paper Co.

Washington Gas Light Co.

Williams, Karen Hastie: director, Fannie Mae Foundation

Washington Irrigation & Development Co.

Redmond, Paul Anthony: chairman, chief executive officer, director, Avista Corporation

Washington Mutual Inc.

Eigsti, Roger Harry: chairman, chief executive officer, SAFECO Corp.

Washington Mutual Savings Bank

Killinger, Kerry Kent: chairman, president, chief executive officer, director, Washington Mutual, Inc.

Washington Post Co.

Burke, Daniel Barnett: vice president, treasurer, director, ABC Foundation

O'Reilly, F. Anthony John: chairman, trustee, Heinz Co. Foundation (H.J.); chairman, director, Heinz Co. (H.J.)

Washington Square Capital Inc.

Turner, John Gosney: chairman, chief executive officer, director, ReliaStar Financial Corp.; director, ReliaStar Foundation

Washington Trust Bank

Stanton, Philip H.: chief executive officer, director, Washington Trust Bank

Washington Water Power Co.

Kelly, John F.: chairman, chief executive officer, director, Alaska Airlines, Inc.

Washovia Bank NA

Henderson, George W., III: trustee, Burlington Industries Foundation; president, chief executive officer, director, Burlington Industries, Inc.

Waste Management Inc.

Montrone, Paul Michael: vice president, partner, Winthrop Foundation

Watermark Books

Jacobs, Bruce E.: vice president, director, Grede Foundation; president, director, Grede Foundries

Watermark Press

Crull, Timm F.: retired chairman, Nestle U.S.A. Inc.

Jacobs, Bruce E.: vice president, director, Grede Foundation; president, director, Grede Foundries

Watermark West Rare Books

Jacobs, Bruce E.: vice president, director, Grede Foundation; president, director, Grede Foundries

Watson Healthcare Inc.

Gregg, Walter Emmor, Junior: senior executive vice president finance & administration, PNC Financial Services Group

Wausau Insurance Companies

Fuellgraf, Charles Louis, Jr.: trustee, Nationwide Insurance Enterprise Foundation

Wausau Preferred Health Insurance Co.

Miller, David O.: chairman, Employers Insurance of Wausau, A Mutual Co.; trustee, Nationwide Insurance Enterprise Foundation; chairman, Wausau Insurance Companies

Wave Technologies International Inc.

Kemper, David Woods: chairman, president, chief executive officer, director, Commerce Bancshares, Inc.

Weather Channel

Barry, Richard Francis, III: director, Landmark Communications Foundation; vice chairman, Landmark Communications Inc.

Batten, Frank, Sr.: chairman, director, Landmark Communications Foundation; chairman, Landmark Communications Inc.

Wynne, John Oliver: president, director, Landmark Communications Foundation; president, chief executive officer, Landmark Communications Inc.

Weatherford International Inc.

Greehey, William Eugene: chairman, chief executive officer, director, Valero Energy Corp.

Lubar, Sheldon B.: chairman, Ameritech Corp.; director, Firstar Milwaukee Foundation

Weigert Co. SA

Wrigley, William: chairman, director, Wrigley Co. Foundation (Wm. Jr.); president, chief executive officer, director, Wrigley Co. (Wm. Jr.)

Weldwood Can Ltd.

Olson, Richard E.: chairman, chief executive officer, director, Champion International Corp.

Wellman Inc.

Rogers, James E., Jr.: vice chairman, president, chief executive officer, Cinergy Corp.; vice chairman, director, Cinergy Foundation

Wells Fargo

Blanchard, J. A., III: president, chief executive officer, director, Deluxe Corp.

Wells Fargo & Co.

Bowlin, Michael Ray: chairman, director, ARCO Foundation; chairman, chief executive officer, director, Atlantic Richfield Co.

Wells Fargo Bank NA

Aldinger, William F., III: chairman, chief executive officer, director, Household International Inc.

Zuendt, William F.: president, chief executive officer, Wells Fargo & Co.

Wesbanco

Wareham, James Lyman: president, AK Steel Corp.

West Co. Inc.

Longfield, William H.: president, Bard Foundation (C.R.); chairman, chief executive officer, director, Bard, Inc. (C.R.)

West Co. of Puerto Rico

Little, William G.: chairman, president, chief executive officer, director, West Co. Inc.

West Harrison Gas & Electric Co.

Foley, Cheryl M.: vice president, secretary, general counsel, Cinergy Corp.; vice president, secretary, director, Cinergy Foundation

Randolph, Jackson Harold: chairman, Cinergy Corp.; chairman, director, Cinergy Foundation

West Hollywood Marketing Corp.

Rosenzweig, Richard Stuart: executive vice president, director, Playboy Enterprises Inc.

West Virginia Power Co.

Draper, Ernest Linn, Jr.: chairman, president, chief executive officer, director, American Electric Power

Westborn Service Center Inc.

Zampetis, Theodore K.: president, chief operating officer, director, Standard Products Co.

Western Auto Supply Co.

Martinez, Arthur C.: chairman, chief executive officer, president, Sears, Roebuck and Co.

Western Energy Co.

Pederson, Jerrold P.: vice president, chief financial officer, director, Montana Power Co.; director, Montana Power Foundation

Senechal, Ellen M.: treasurer, Montana Power Co.

Western Industries Inc.

Kellner, Jack F.: director, board member, Marshall & Ilsley Foundation, Inc.

Western National Corp.

Buckwalter, Alan Roland, III: chief executive officer, Chase Bank of Texas; president, Chase Bank of Texas Foundation, Inc.

Western Paper & Manufacturing Co.

Granzow, Paul H.: chairman, director, Standard Register Co.

Western Resources Inc.

Chandler, Charles Q.: co-trustee, INTRUST Bank Charitable Trust; chairman, INTRUST Financial Corp.

Chandler, Charles Quarles, IV: co-trustee, INTRUST Bank Charitable Trust; president, director, INTRUST Financial Corp.

Meyer, Russell William, Jr.: chairman, chief executive officer, Cessna Aircraft Co.; president, Cessna Foundation, Inc.

Westfield Investments Inc.

Allbritton, Joe Lewis: chairman, chief executive officer, Riggs Bank NA

Westinghouse Electric Corp.

Smith, Raymond W.: chairman, chief executive officer, director, Bell Atlantic Corp.

Westmoreland Coal Co.

Black, Lennox K.: president, Teleflex Foundation; chairman, director, Teleflex Inc.

Westvaco Corp.

Bodman, Samuel Wright, III: chairman, chief executive officer, director, Cabot Corp.; president, director, Cabot Corp. Foundation

Westvaco Development Corp.

Beaver, William S.: treasurer, vice president, Westvaco Corp.; trustee, Westvaco Foundation Trust

Wexpro Co.

Cash, R. D.: chairman, president, chief executive officer, director, Questar Corp.

Parks, Stephen E.: vice president, treasurer, chief financial officer, Questar Corp.

Weyco Group Inc.

Stratton, Frederick Prescott, Jr.: chairman, chief executive officer, director, Briggs & Stratton Corp.; president, director, Briggs & Stratton Corp. Foundation

Weyerhaeuser Co.

Ingram, Martha R.: chairman, director, Ingram Industries Inc.

Ruckelshaus, William Doyle: chairman, director, Browning-Ferris Industries Inc.

Weyerhaeuser Real Estate Co.

Stivers, William Charles: senior vice president, chief financial officer, treasurer, Weyerhaeuser Co.; treasurer, trustee, Weyerhaeuser Co. Foundation

Wheeling Power Co.

Draper, Ernest Linn, Jr.: chairman, president, chief executive officer, director, American Electric Power

Lhota, William J.: executive vice president, American Electric Power

Wheeling-Pitts Corp.

Wareham, James Lyman: president, AK Steel Corp.

Whirlpool Corp.

Langbo, Arnold Gordon: chairman, chief executive officer, director, Kellogg Co.

Whirlpool Financial Corp. DE

Bell, Bradley John: vice president, treasurer, Whirlpool Corp.; treasurer, Whirlpool Foundation

White Clover Dairy

Omachinski, David L.: chief financial officer, treasurer, vice president, Oshkosh B'Gosh, Inc.

White Marsh Mall Inc.

Deering, Anthony W.: chairman, chief executive officer, Rouse Co.; chairman, president, trustee, Rouse Co. Foundation

Whitman Corp.

Sharpe, Robert Francis, Jr.: senior vice president public affairs, general counsel, PepsiCo, Inc.

Whitman Leasing Inc.

Chelberg, Bruce Stanley: chairman, chief executive officer, director, Whitman Corp.; director, Whitman Corp. Foundation

Moore, William B.: senior vice president, secretary, general counsel, Whitman Corp.; secretary, Whitman Corp. Foundation

Westover, Frank Thomas: senior vice president, Whitman Corp.; director, Whitman Corp. Foundation

Whitney Holding Corp.

Roberts, John Kenneth, Jr.: president, chief executive officer, director, Pan-American Life Insurance Co.

Wichita Baseball Inc.

Rich, Robert E., Sr.: president, treasurer, Rich Family Foundation; founder, chairman, director, Rich Products Corp.

Will Rogers Bank

Chandler, Charles Quarles, IV: co-trustee, INTRUST Bank Charitable Trust; president, director, INTRUST Financial Corp.

Willamette Industries Inc.

Buxton, Winslow Hurlbert: chairman, president, chief executive officer, director, Pentair Inc.

Prendergast, G. Joseph: director, Wachovia Foundation, Inc. (The)

William E Coutts Co. Ltd.

Hall, Donald Joyce: chairman board, director, Hallmark Cards Inc.; chairman, Hallmark Corporate Foundation

William Harris & Co.

Harris, Irving Brooks: chairman executive committee, director, Pittway Corp.; chairman, director, Pittway Corp. Charitable Foundation

William Harris Investors

Harris, Irving Brooks: chairman executive committee, director, Pittway Corp.; chairman, director, Pittway Corp. Charitable Foundation

Williamette Sales Co.

Moffitt, Donald Eugene: chairman, director, CNF Transportation, Inc.

Williams Colorado Solutions

Bailey, Keith E.: chairman, president, director, chief executive officer, Texas Gas Transmission Corp.; president, director, Williams Companies Foundation (The)

Williams Communications Stations LLC

Higbee, David M.: secretary, Williams; secretary, treasurer, Williams Companies Foundation (The)

Williams Energy Ventures Inc.

Higbee, David M.: secretary, Williams; secretary, treasurer, Williams Companies Foundation (The)

Williams Gas Pipeline-Central

Lauderdale, Gary D.: senior vice president, general manager, Texas Gas Transmission Corp.

Williams Holdings Delaware

Bailey, Keith E.: chairman, president, director, chief executive officer, Texas Gas Transmission Corp.; president, director, Williams Companies Foundation (The)

Williams Information Services Corp.

Bailey, Keith E.: chairman, president, director, chief executive officer, Texas Gas Transmission Corp.; president, director, Williams Companies Foundation (The)

Williams-Sonoma Inc.

Drexler, Millard S.: trustee, Gap Foundation/Gap Inc. Community Relations; president, chief executive officer, director, Gap, Inc.

Willis Corroon Group LLC

Viault, Raymond: vice chairman, director, General Mills, Inc.

Windmill Inns America Inc.

Wendt, Richard L.: trustee, Jeld-wen Foundation; chief executive officer, chairman, Jeld-wen, Inc.

Wendt, Roderick C.: trustee, Jeld-wen Foundation; president, director, Jeld-wen, Inc.

Windsor Coal Co.

Draper, Ernest Linn, Jr.: chairman, president, chief executive officer, director, American Electric Power

Windsor Locks

Long, Michael Thomas: director, Ensign-Bickford Foundation

Windward Capital Partner LP

Georges, John A.: director, International Paper Co.

Winn-Dixie Atlanta Inc.

Bragin, David H.: treasurer, assistant secretary, director, Winn-Dixie Stores Foundation

Winthrop Resources Corp.

Nagorske, Lynn A.: executive vice president, chief financial officer, treasurer, TCF National Bank Minnesota

Reyelts, Paul C.: vice president finance, chief financial officer, Valspar Corp.; vice president, assistant secretary, Valspar Foundation

Wisconsin Electric Power Co.

Abdoo, Richard A.: chairman, president, chief executive officer, Wisconsin Energy Corp.; president, director, Wisconsin Energy Corp. Foundation, Inc.

Feaster, Joyce: assistant treasurer, assistant secretary, Wisconsin Energy Corp. Foundation, Inc.

Wisconsin Energy Corp.

Baker, Calvin H.: vice president finance, chief financial officer, Wisconsin Energy Corp.; treasurer, director, Wisconsin Energy Corp. Foundation, Inc.

Grigg, Richard R.: vice president, Wisconsin Energy Corp.; director, Wisconsin Energy Corp. Foundation, Inc.

Wisconsin Gas Co.

Bueche, Wendell Francis: director, Marshall & Ilsley Foundation, Inc.

Haase, Bronson J.: president, chief executive officer, Ameritech Wisconsin

Wardeberg, George E.: president, WICOR Foundation; president, chief executive officer, director, WICOR, Inc.

Wisconsin Michigan Investment Corp.

Abdoo, Richard A.: chairman, president, chief executive officer, Wisconsin Energy Corp.; president, director, Wisconsin Energy Corp. Foundation, Inc.

Wisconsin Natural Gas Co.

Feaster, Joyce: assistant treasurer, assistant secretary, Wisconsin Energy Corp. Foundation, Inc.

Remmel, Jerry G.: chief financial officer, vice president, treasurer, Wisconsin Energy Corp.

Wright, James O.: president, director, Badger Meter Foundation; chairman, director, Badger Meter, Inc.; director, Marshall & Ilsley Foundation, Inc.

Wisconsin Paper Group

Bonkoski, Kenneth John: controller, Menasha Corp.; treasurer, Menasha Corp. Foundation

Wisconsin Paper Products Co.

Loos, Henry J.: secretary, Charter Manufacturing Co. Foundation

Wisconsin Power & Light Co.

Davis, Erroll Brown, Jr.: president, chief executive officer, director, Wisconsin Power & Light Co.

Wisconsin Public Service Resources Corp.

Schrickel, Patrick D.: vice president, Wisconsin Public Service Foundation, Inc.

Wisland SA

Peck, Arthur John, Jr.: secretary, vice president, Corning Inc.; secretary, Corning Inc. Foundation

Wispark Corp.

Abdoo, Richard A.: chairman, president, chief executive officer, Wisconsin Energy Corp.; president, director, Wisconsin Energy Corp. Foundation, Inc.

Baker, Calvin H.: vice president finance, chief financial officer, Wisconsin Energy Corp.; treasurer, director, Wisconsin Energy Corp. Foundation, Inc.

Witco Corp.

Brinberg, Simeon: director, Wishnick Foundation (Robert I.)

Hohn, Harry George, Jr.: chairman, director, New York Life Foundation

Wishnick, William: president, director, Wishnick Foundation (Robert I.)

Witech Corp.

Abdoo, Richard A.: chairman, president, chief executive officer, Wisconsin Energy Corp.; president, director, Wisconsin Energy Corp. Foundation, Inc.

Wolf Distributing Co. Allentown

Wolf, Thomas W.: trustee, York Federal Savings & Loan Foundation

Wolverine Tube Corp.

Ver Hagen, Jan Karol: president, United Dominion Industries, Ltd.

Woodbridge Center Inc.

Donahue, Jeffrey H.: senior vice president, chief financial officer, Rouse Co.

McGregor, Douglas A.: trustee, Rouse Co. Foundation

Woodhead Industries Inc.

Denny, Charles W.: president, chief executive officer, director, Square D Co.

Woodward Governor Co.

Gloyd, Lawrence Eugene: trustee, CLARCOR Foundation; chairman, chief executive officer, director, CLARCOR Inc.

World Trade Center New Orleans

Greene, John Frederick: executive vice president exploration & production, director, Louisiana Land & Exploration Co.

Worthington Indiana Inc.

Blystone, John B.: chairman, president, chief executive officer, director, SPX Corp.

Wrigley (Cayman) Ltd.

Wrigley, William: chairman, director, Wrigley Co. Foundation (Wm. Jr.); president, chief executive officer, director, Wrigley Co. (Wm. Jr.)

Wrigley Chewing Gum Co. Ltd. China

Wrigley, William: chairman, director, Wrigley Co. Foundation (Wm. Jr.); president, chief executive officer, director, Wrigley Co. (Wm. Jr.)

Wrigley Co. (Thailand) Ltd.

Wrigley, William: chairman, director, Wrigley Co. Foundation (Wm. Jr.); president, chief executive officer, director, Wrigley Co. (Wm. Jr.)

Wrigley Co. Ltd. HK

Wrigley, William: chairman, director, Wrigley Co. Foundation (Wm. Jr.); president, chief executive officer, director, Wrigley Co. (Wm. Jr.)

Wrigley Co. Ltd. Japan

Wrigley, William: chairman, director, Wrigley Co. Foundation (Wm. Jr.); president, chief executive officer, director, Wrigley Co. (Wm. Jr.)

Wrigley Co. Ltd. NZ

Wrigley, William: chairman, director, Wrigley Co. Foundation (Wm. Jr.); president, chief executive officer, director, Wrigley Co. (Wm. Jr.)

Wrigley Co. Ltd. UK

Wrigley, William: chairman, director, Wrigley Co. Foundation (Wm. Jr.); president, chief executive officer, director, Wrigley Co. (Wm. Jr.)

Wrigley Co. Propriety Ltd. Australia

Wrigley, William: chairman, director, Wrigley Co. Foundation (Wm. Jr.); president, chief executive officer, director, Wrigley Co. (Wm. Jr.)

Wrigley Co. SA Spain

Wrigley, William: chairman, director, Wrigley Co. Foundation (Wm. Jr.); president, chief executive officer, director, Wrigley Co. (Wm. Jr.)

Wrigley Gmb H

Wrigley, William: chairman, director, Wrigley Co. Foundation (Wm. Jr.); president, chief executive officer, director, Wrigley Co. (Wm. Jr.)

Wrigley Phillipines Inc.

Wrigley, William: chairman, director, Wrigley Co. Foundation (Wm. Jr.); president, chief executive officer, director, Wrigley Co. (Wm. Jr.)

Wrigley Poland SPZOO

Wrigley, William: chairman, director, Wrigley Co. Foundation (Wm. Jr.); president, chief executive officer, director, Wrigley Co. (Wm. Jr.)

Wrigley Romania SRL

Wrigley, William: chairman, director, Wrigley Co. Foundation (Wm. Jr.); president, chief executive officer, director, Wrigley Co. (Wm. Jr.)

Wrigley T.O.O. Russia

Wrigley, William: chairman, director, Wrigley Co. Foundation (Wm. Jr.); president, chief executive officer, director, Wrigley Co. (Wm. Jr.)

Wrigley de Mexico SA

Wrigley, William: chairman, director, Wrigley Co. Foundation (Wm. Jr.); president, chief executive officer, director, Wrigley Co. (Wm. Jr.)

Wrigley doo Slovenia
Wrigley, William: chairman, director, Wrigley Co. Foundation (Wm. Jr.); president, chief executive officer, director, Wrigley Co. (Wm. Jr.)

Writers Guild America
Rosenthal, Sol: counsel, Playboy Enterprises Inc.

Wyman-Gordon Co.
Riley, H. John, Jr.: chairman, president, chief executive officer, Cooper Industries Foundation; chairman, president, chief executive officer, director, Cooper Industries, Inc.

Wyman-Gordon Forgings Inc.
Gruber, David P.: president, chief executive officer, director, Wyman-Gordon Co.; chairman, vice president, director, Wyman-Gordon Foundation

Whitney, Wallace F., Jr.: secretary, treasurer, Wyman-Gordon Foundation

Wyman-Gordon Inv Castings
Gruber, David P.: president, chief executive officer, director, Wyman-Gordon Co.; chairman, vice president, director, Wyman-Gordon Foundation

Whitney, Wallace F., Jr.: secretary, treasurer, Wyman-Gordon Foundation

Xerox Corp.
Larsen, Ralph Stanley: chairman, president, chief executive officer, director, Johnson & Johnson

Pepper, John E., Jr.: chairman executive committee, Procter & Gamble Co.

Xerox Credit Corp.
Romeril, Barry D.: executive vice president, chief financial officer, Xerox Corp.

Xerox Financial Services Inc.
Allaire, Paul Arthur: chairman, chief executive officer, chairman executive committee, Xerox Corp.; president, Xerox Foundation

Romeril, Barry D.: executive vice president, chief financial officer, Xerox Corp.

Xerox Printing Co.
Allaire, Paul Arthur: chairman, chief executive officer, chairman executive committee, Xerox Corp.; president, Xerox Foundation

Xtek Inc.
Burleigh, William Robert: president, chief executive officer, director, Scripps Co. (E.W.); member, Scripps Howard Foundation

Y-F Service Corp.
Angelo, Robert A.: president, chief operating officer, York Federal Savings & Loan Association; secretary, York Federal Savings & Loan Foundation

Moss, James H.: treasurer, York Federal Savings & Loan Foundation

Pullo, Robert W.: chairman, chief executive officer, director, York Federal Savings & Loan Association; president, trustee, York Federal Savings & Loan Foundation

YGK Inc.
Randolph, Jackson Harold: chairman, Cinergy Corp.; chairman, director, Cinergy Foundation

Yankee Group Research Inc.
Kasputys, Joseph Edward: chairman, trustee, Hitachi Foundation

Yellow Corp.
Carr, Cassandra Colvin: director, SBC Foundation

Yellowstone Country Food & Beverage
Lehrkind, Carl, III: director, Montana Power Foundation

Yemen Hunt Oil Co.
Hunt, Ray Lee: chairman, chief executive officer, director, Hunt Oil Co.

Meurer, Thomas E.: senior vice president administration, Hunt Oil Co.

York Federal Savings & Loan Association
Dotzel, Cynthia A., CPA: trustee, York Federal Savings & Loan Foundation

Erdos, Robert W.: trustee, York Federal Savings & Loan Foundation

Gross, Randall A.: trustee, York Federal Savings & Loan Foundation

Mills, Paul D.: trustee, York Federal Savings & Loan Foundation

Steinhauser, Carolyn E.: trustee, York Federal Savings & Loan Foundation

Wolf, Thomas W.: trustee, York Federal Savings & Loan Foundation

York Financial Corp.
Moss, James H.: treasurer, York Federal Savings & Loan Foundation

Pullo, Robert W.: chairman, chief executive officer, director, York Federal Savings & Loan Association; president, trustee, York Federal Savings & Loan Foundation

Wolf, Thomas W.: trustee, York Federal Savings & Loan Foundation

York International Corp.
Gambill, Malcolm W.: president, trustee, Harsco Corp. Fund

McDonough, Gerald C.: trustee, Commercial Intertech Foundation

Yorkshire Electricity Group
Draper, Ernest Linn, Jr.: chairman, president, chief executive officer, director, American Electric Power

Yosemite Insurance Co.
Geissinger, Frederick: chairman, chief executive officer, prs, American General Finance

Young Brothers Ltd.
Clarke, Robert F.: chairman, president, chief executive officer, director, Hawaiian Electric Co., Inc.; president, director, Hawaiian Electric Industries Charitable Foundation

Young Radiator Co.
Loos, Henry J.: secretary, Charter Manufacturing Co. Foundation

Zachry Inc.
Ebrom, Charles E.: director, vice president, Zachry Co. (H.B.); treasurer, trustee, Zachry Foundation (The)

Zeneca Inc.
Montrone, Paul Michael: vice president, partner, Winthrop Foundation

Zenith Electronics Corp.
Connolly, Eugene Bernard, Jr.: chairman emeritus, USG Corp.

Zeno Air Inc.
Wrigley, William: chairman, director, Wrigley Co. Foundation (Wm. Jr.); president, chief executive officer, director, Wrigley Co. (Wm. Jr.)

Ziegler Asset Management Co.
Ziegler, R. Douglas: advisor, Johnson Controls Foundation

Zions Corp.
Eccles, Spencer Fox: chairman, chief executive officer, director, First Security Bank of Idaho NA

Zoll Medical
Zadel, C. William: chairman, president, chief executive officer, Millipore Corp.; trustee, Millipore Foundation (The)

Zurich Group
Mead, Dana George: chairman, chief executive officer, director, Tenneco Automotive

OFFICERS AND DIRECTORS BY NONPROFIT AFFILIATIONS

Lists individuals by nonprofit organizations to which they belong.

10th District Federal Reserve Bank
Hockaday, Irvine O., Jr.: president, chief executive officer, director, Hallmark Cards Inc.

14th Street Business Improvement District
Hutchings, Peter Lounsbery: president, Guardian Life Insurance Co. of America

1st Hawaiian Foundation
Karr, Howard Henry: treasurer, director, First Hawaiian Foundation

1st Hawaiian Inc.
Pang, Gerald M.: director, First Hawaiian Foundation

360 Degree Committee Inc.
Price, Charles H., II: director, New York Times Co. Foundation

4th Jud. Cir. Association South Carolina
DeLoach, Harris E., Junior: executive vice president, director, Sonoco Products Co.

500 Festival Associate
Sease, Gene Elwood: director, Central Newspapers Foundation

A/Knox Art Gallery
Wilmers, Robert George: chairman, president, chief executive officer, Manufacturers & Traders Trust Co.

AIA
Milliken, Roger: chairman, chief executive officer, Milliken & Co.; member advisory committee, Milliken Foundation

AIAA
Condit, Philip Murray: chairman, chief executive officer, director, Boeing Co.

Hatsopoulos, George Nicholas: founder, chairman, chief executive officer, director, Thermo Electron Corp.; committee member, Thermo Electron Foundation

AICPCU
Choate, Jerry D.: chairman, chief executive officer, director, Allstate Foundation

AIME
Hill, George Richard: president, trustee, Lubrizol Foundation (The)

APEC Satellite Communication Committee
Dewane, John Richard: director, Honeywell Foundation

ARA Services
Preston, James Edward: vice president, director, Avon Products Foundation, Inc.; chairman, chief executive officer, director, Avon Products, Inc.

ARC
Buckwalter, Alan Roland, III: chief executive officer, Chase Bank of Texas; president, Chase Bank of Texas Foundation, Inc.

Gorman, Maureen V.: vice president, GTE Foundation

King, Reatha Clark: director, Fuller Co. Foundation (H.B.); president, executive director, General Mills Foundation

Polin, Jane Louise: manager, comptroller, GE Fund

Randolph, Jackson Harold: chairman, Cinergy Corp.; chairman, director, Cinergy Foundation

ARC Cincinnati Chapter
Standen, Craig Clayton: senior vice president corporate development, Scripps Co. (E.W.)

ARC Greater Greater New York
Ostergard, Paul Michael: vice president, director corporate contributions, Citibank Corp.; president, Citigroup Foundation

ARC, Wilson County Chapter
Williamson, Henry Gaston, Jr.: chief operating officer, Branch Banking & Trust Co.

ASYMCA
Wolff, Herbert Eric: secretary, director, First Hawaiian Foundation

ATLA
Margolin, Abraham E.: director, Tension Envelope Foundation

Abbott-Northwestern Hospital
Piper, Addison Lewis: director, Piper Jaffray Companies Foundation; chairman, chief executive officer, director, U.S. Bancorp Piper Jaffray

Academy Arts & Sciences
Grove, Andrew S.: chairman, Intel Corp.

Kemper, David Woods: chairman, president, chief executive officer, director, Commerce Bancshares, Inc.

Academy Basic Education
Davis, Walter Stewart: secretary, treasurer, Grede Foundation

Academy Educational Development
Brademas, John: chairman, Texaco Foundation

Academy Fin
Weill, Sanford I.: chairman, chief executive officer, Citibank Corp.; chairman, Citigroup Foundation

Academy Natural Science
Thompson, Sheldon Lee: senior vice president, chief administrative officer, Sunoco Inc.

Academy Squires
Bloch, Henry Wollman: chairman, Block Foundation (H&R); chairman, director, Block, Inc. (H&R)

Academy Television Arts & Sciences
Rosenthal, Sol: counsel, Playboy Enterprises Inc.

Accountants Coalition Liability Reform
Schiro, James J.: chairman, senior partner, PricewaterhouseCoopers

Acorn Fund
Guthart, Leo A.: vice chairman, director, Pittway Corp.

Acquisition Committee National Gallery Art
Resnick, Lynda Rae: vice chairman, co-owner, Franklin Mint (The)

Actors Equity - Canada
Darling, Robert Edward, Jr.: chairman, Ensign-Bickford Foundation

Actors Theatre Board
Hower, Frank Beard, Jr.: vice chairman, Anthem Foundation, Inc.

Actuarial Society Greater New York
Hutchings, Peter Lounsbery: president, Guardian Life Insurance Co. of America

Actuaries Club Boston
Brown, Stephen Lee: chairman, chief executive officer, director, Hancock Financial Services (John)

Adhesive Manufacturer Association
Ray, John Thomas, Jr.: president, director, Fuller Co. Foundation (H.B.)

Adrian College
Valade, Gary C.: executive vice president, chief financial officer, DaimlerChrysler Corp.; trustee, DaimlerChrysler Corp. Fund

Adv Comm Trade Policy Negotiations
Fites, Donald Vester: director, Caterpillar Foundation

Advertising Council
Graves, Earl Gilbert: director, Aetna Foundation

Wehling, Robert Louis: global marketing, government relations officer, Procter & Gamble Co.; president, trustee, Procter & Gamble Fund

Advertising Women New York
Dinerstein, Martha L.: managing director, head marketing & corporate communications, United States Trust Co. of New York

Advisory Council Rev Estimates State Virginia
Sheehan, Jeremiah J.: chairman, director, Reynolds Metals Co. Foundation

Advisory Council Stanford University Business School
Bartz, Carol A.: director, Autodesk Foundation; chairman, chief executive officer, Autodesk Inc.

Advocates Highway & Auto Safety
Maatman, Gerald Leonard: chairman, president, trustee, Kemper Foundation (James S.); director, Kemper National Insurance Companies

Advocates Nursing Home Reform
Carey, Kathryn Ann: foundation manager, American Honda Foundation

Aerospace Industries Association

Farmer, Phillip W.: chairman, president, chief executive officer, Harris Corp.; president, trustee, Harris Foundation

Kresa, Kent: chairman, president, chief executive officer, director, Northrop Grumman Corp.

Leonis, John Michael: chairman, director, Litton Industries, Inc.

Aerospace Institute America

Burner, David L.: chairman, president, chief executive officer, director, BFGoodrich Co.

Affinity Group Japanese Philanthropy

Carey, Kathryn Ann: foundation manager, American Honda Foundation

African-American Institute

Rhodes, William Reginald: vice chairman, Citibank Corp.

Agency Offs Round Table

Dubes, Michael: membership, ReliaStar Foundation

Agent Orange Asst Fund

Watson, Solomon Brown, IV: vice president, New York Times Co. Foundation

Agricultural Roundtable

Fites, Donald Vester: director, Caterpillar Foundation

Ahahui Koa Anuenue

Dods, Walter Arthur, Jr.: president, director, First Hawaiian Foundation; chairman, chief executive officer, director, First Hawaiian, Inc.

Air Conditioning Refrigeration Institute

Kerckhove, George H.: vice president, chief financial officer, American Standard Inc.

Air Force Association

Dewane, John Richard: director, Honeywell Foundation

Leonis, John Michael: chairman, director, Litton Industries, Inc.

Stauffer, Stanley Howard: chairman, Stauffer Communications Foundation

Air Transport Association

Franke, William Augustus: chairman, president, chief executive officer, America West Airlines, Inc.; director, Phelps Dodge Foundation

Harkey, Robert Shelton: trustee, Delta Air Lines Foundation; senior vice president, general counsel, secretary, Delta Air Lines, Inc.

Aircraft Owners & Pilots Association

Carey, Kathryn Ann: foundation manager, American Honda Foundation

Dewane, John Richard: director, Honeywell Foundation

Akron Art Museum

Holland, Willard R.: chairman, chief executive officer, FirstEnergy Corp.

Alabama Chamber of Commerce

Blount, Winton Malcolm, Jr.: chairman, Blount International, Inc.

Alabama Council Economic Education

Harris, Elmer Beseler: president, chief executive officer, director, Alabama Power Co.

Alabama State Bar

Denson, William Frank, III: president, Vulcan Materials Co. Foundation

Alan Guttmacher Institute

Smith, Frederick C.: chairman, trustee, Huffy Foundation, Inc.

Alarm Industries Research Education Foundation

Guthart, Leo A.: vice chairman, director, Pittway Corp.

Albany Academy

Standish, J. Spencer: chairman, director, Albany International Corp.

Albert Einstein College of Medicine

Millstein, Ira M.: partner, Weil, Gotshal & Manges Corp.; president, director, Weil, Gotshal & Manges Foundation

Albertson College Idaho

Graves, Ronald Norman: secretary, Simplot Foundation (J.R.)

Marshall, Joseph W.: chairman, chief executive officer, Idaho Power Co.

Albion College

Langbo, Arnold Gordon: chairman, chief executive officer, director, Kellogg Co.

Alche

Thompson, Sheldon Lee: senior vice president, chief administrative officer, Sunoco Inc.

Alcohol & Drug Addiction Services Cuyahoga

O'Brien, John F.: trustee, McDonald & Co. Securities Foundation

Alexander S. Onassis Public Benefit Foundation

Brademas, John: chairman, Texaco Foundation

Allegheny Conference

Rohr, James Edward: chief executive officer, president, director, PNC Financial Services Group

Allegheny Conference Community Development

Block, William: vice president, trustee, Blade Foundation; chairman, director, Toledo Blade Co.

Allegheny Conference on Community Development

Wehmeier, Helge H.: president, chief executive officer, director, Bayer Corp.

Allegheny County Bar Association

Gregg, Walter Emmor, Junior: senior executive vice president finance & administration, PNC Financial Services Group

McGuinn, Martin Gregory: chairman, chief executive officer, Mellon Financial Corp.

Newlin, William Rankin: trustee, Kennametal Foundation

Walton, Jon David: trustee, Allegheny Technologies Inc. Charitable Trust

Allegheny-Singer Research Institute

Queenan, Charles J., Jr.: trustee, Tippins Foundation

Allen Stevenson School

Evans, Robert Sheldon: chairman, chief executive officer, Crane Co.; chairman, president, director, Crane Foundation

Alliance American Insurers

Buxton, Charles Ingraham, II: chairman, Federated Mutual Insurance Co.; president, Federated Mutual Insurance Foundation

Rupley, Theodore J.: president, chief executive officer, director, Allmerica Financial Corp.

Alliance for Childrens Rights

Ball, James Herington: senior vice president, general counsel, director, Nestle U.S.A. Inc.

Alliance for Downtown New York

Douglass, Robert Royal: trustee, Chase Manhattan Foundation

Alliance for Education

Killinger, Kerry Kent: chairman, president, chief executive officer, director, Washington Mutual, Inc.

Nelson, John Martin: chairman, director, TJX Companies, Inc.

Alliance for Healthcare Reform

Gilmartin, Raymond V.: chairman, president, chief executive officer, Merck & Co.; chairman, Merck Co. Foundation

Alliance for Quality Education

Hipp, William Hayne: president, chief executive officer, director, Liberty Corp.; chairman, president, director, Liberty Corp. Foundation

Alliance for Telecommunication Industry Solutions

Engel, Joel Stanley: vice president technology, Ameritech Corp.

Alliance of American Insurers

Schiek, Fredrick A.: executive vice president, chief operating officer, Employers Mutual Casualty Co.

Aloha Council

Dods, Walter Arthur, Jr.: president, director, First Hawaiian Foundation; chairman, chief executive officer, director, First Hawaiian, Inc.

Aloha Council Boy Scouts America

Simpson, Andrea Lynn: president

Alpha Delta Phi

Polin, Jane Louise: manager, comptroller, GE Fund

Alpha Epsilon Chi

Cloud, Bruce Benjamin, Sr.: vice chairman, director, Zachry Co. (H.B.)

Alpha Gamma Delta

True, Jean Durland: trustee, True Foundation; partner, True Oil Co.

Alpha Phi

Simpson, Andrea Lynn: president

Alpha Phi Omega

Hill, George Richard: president, trustee, Lubrizol Foundation (The)

Sease, Gene Elwood: director, Central Newspapers Foundation

Welty, John Rider: secretary, Carpenter Technology Corp. Foundation

Alpha Psi Omega

Sease, Gene Elwood: director, Central Newspapers Foundation

Alpha Tau Omega

Matthews, Clark J., II: president, chief executive officer, director, 7-Eleven, Inc.

Stephens, Elton Bryson: founder, chairman, Ebsco Industries, Inc.

Alumni Council of Pennsylvania State University

Franklin, Barbara Hackman: director, Dow Chemical Co.

Alverno College

Bruce, Peter Wayne: director, Badger Meter Foundation

Ambassador Roundtable

Hays, Thomas Chandler: chairman, chief executive officer, director, Fortune Brands, Inc.

America AICE

Hilyard, James E.: president, CertainTeed Corp.; director, CertainTeed Corp. Foundation

America Bar Association

Ursu, John Joseph: director, 3M Foundation; general counsel, senior vice president legal affairs, Minnesota Mining & Manufacturing Co.

America China Society

Gerstner, Louis Vincent, Jr.: chairman, chief executive officer, director, International Business Machines Corp.

America Community Bankers

Fitzgerald, William Allingham: chairman, director, Commercial Federal Corp.

America Institute CPA

Gregg, Walter Emmor, Junior: senior executive vice president finance & administration, PNC Financial Services Group

America Iron Steel Engineers

Usher, Thomas J.: chairman, chief executive officer, USX Corp.; chairman board trustees, USX Foundation, Inc.

America Iron Steel Institute

Usher, Thomas J.: chairman, chief executive officer, USX Corp.; chairman board trustees, USX Foundation, Inc.

America Jewish Committee

Dubin, Stephen Victor: vice president, secretary, Farber Foundation

America Production Control Society

Hilyard, James E.: president, CertainTeed Corp.; director, CertainTeed Corp. Foundation

America Society

Luke, John A., Jr.: chairman, president, chief executive officer, director, Westvaco Corp.

Thoman, G. Richard: president, chief operating officer, Xerox Corp.

America Society Corp. Secretary

Gregg, Walter Emmor, Junior: senior executive vice president finance & administration, PNC Financial Services Group

American Academy Arts & Letters

Ripley, Sidney Dillon, II: director emeritus, Hitachi Foundation

American Academy Medicine Directors

Nelson, Glen David, MD: vice chairman, Medtronic, Inc.

American Academy Pediatrics

Harris, Irving Brooks: chairman executive committee, director, Pittway Corp.; chairman, director, Pittway Corp. Charitable Foundation

American Academy Science

Boyer, Herbert Wayne, PhD: chairman, president, director, Genentech Foundation for Biomedical Sciences; co-founder, director, Genentech Inc.

American Academy of Actuaries

Brown, Joseph Warner, Jr.: chairman, chief executive officer, MBIA Inc.

Brown, Stephen Lee: chairman, chief executive officer, director, Hancock Financial Services (John)

Drury, David J.: chief executive officer, chairman, Principal Financial Group

Eckert, Ralph John: trustee, Trustmark Foundation

Hutchings, Peter Lounsbery: president, Guardian Life Insurance Co. of America

Peterson, Donald Matthew: trustee, Trustmark Foundation; president, chief executive officer, director, Trustmark Insurance Co.

Rinehart, Charles Robert: chairman, chief executive officer, director, Washington Mutual, Inc.

Roberts, John Kenneth, Jr.: president, chief executive officer, director, Pan-American Life Insurance Co.

Stewart, James Gathings: executive vice president, chief financial officer, CIGNA Corp.

Sutton, Thomas C.: chairman, director, Pacific Mutual Charitable Foundation; chairman, chief executive officer, director, Pacific Mutual Life Insurance Co.

American Academy of Arts & Sciences

Brademas, John: chairman, Texaco Foundation

Connor, Walter Robert: director, Glaxo Wellcome Foundation

Graham, Katharine Meyer: chairman executive committee, director, The Washington Post

Gussin, Robert Zalmon, PhD: vice president science & technology, Johnson & Johnson; member corporate contributions committee, Johnson & Johnson Family of Companies Contribution Fund

Harris, Irving Brooks: chairman executive committee, director, Pittway Corp.; chairman, director, Pittway Corp. Charitable Foundation

Hatsopoulos, George Nicholas: founder, chairman, chief executive officer, director, Thermo Electron Corp.; committee member, Thermo Electron Foundation

Johnson, Edward Crosby, III: president, Fidelity Foundation; chairman, president, chief executive officer, director, Fidelity Investments

Kissinger, Henry Alfred: director, CBS Foundation

Lucky, Robert Wendell: corporate vice president, Telcordia Technologies

Meyerson, Martin: director, Panasonic Foundation

Miller, Joseph Irwin: director associate, Cummins Engine Co., Inc.; director, Cummins Engine Foundation

Millstein, Ira M.: partner, Weil, Gotshal & Manges Corp.; president, director, Weil, Gotshal & Manges Foundation

Shinn, George Latimer: director, New York Times Co. Foundation

Vagelos, Pindaros Roy: trustee, Prudential Insurance Co. of America

American Advertising Federation

Liebler, Arthur C.: vice president communications, DaimlerChrysler Corp.; trustee, DaimlerChrysler Corp. Fund

Sutton, Howard: trustee, Steelcase Foundation

American Air Music

Carroll, Philip Joseph: chairman, chief executive officer, Fluor Corp.; chairman, trustee, Fluor Foundation

American Ambassadors Chmns Council

Chambers, Anne Cox: chairman, trustee, Cox Foundation (James M.)

American Antiquarian Society

Graham, Donald Edward: chairman, chief executive officer, director, publisher, The Washington Post

American Apparel Association

Haas, Robert Douglas: chairman, chief executive officer, director, Levi Strauss & Co.; president, Levi Strauss Foundation

American Apparel Manufacturer Association

Morgan, Glenn R.: executive vice president, chief financial officer, Hartmarx Corp.

American Arbitration Association

Barnes, Wallace W.: director, Barnes Group Foundation Inc.

Bridgeland, James Ralph, Jr.: trustee, Star Bank NA, Cincinnati Foundation

Devlin, James Richard: director, Sprint Foundation

Fine, Roger Seth: vice president, general counsel, Johnson & Johnson; president, Johnson & Johnson Family of Companies Contribution Fund

Marshall, Siri M.: trustee, General Mills Foundation; senior vice president, general counsel, General Mills, Inc.

Olschwang, Alan P., Esq.: secretary, Mitsubishi Electric America Foundation

Walsh, Michael J.: vice president, CertainTeed Corp.

Walton, Jon David: trustee, Allegheny Technologies Inc. Charitable Trust

Watson, Solomon Brown, IV: vice president, New York Times Co. Foundation

American Assembly

Block, William: vice president, trustee, Blade Foundation; chairman, director, Toledo Blade Co.

American Association Advancement Science

Alberts, Bruce Michael, PhD: director, Genentech Foundation for Biomedical Sciences

Bradford, William Edward: chairman, director, Halliburton Co.

Davis, Ruth Margaret: trustee, Air Products Foundation

Graham, Patricia Albjerg, PhD: trustee, Hitachi Foundation

Hill, George Richard: president, trustee, Lubrizol Foundation (The)

Ripley, Sidney Dillon, II: director emeritus, Hitachi Foundation

Ross, Arthur: senior vice president, Central National-Gottesman; director, Central National-Gottesman Foundation

Swanson, Robert A.: director, Genentech Foundation for Biomedical Sciences

Weinberg, John Livingston: chairman, president, director, Goldman Sachs Foundation

American Association Advertising Agencies

Mason, W. Bruce: chairman, chief executive officer, director, True North Communications, Inc.

Schweitzer, Peter A.: president, Thompson Co. (J. Walter)

American Association Blacks Energy

Davis, Erroll Brown, Jr.: president, chief executive officer, director, Wisconsin Power & Light Co.

American Association Family & Consumer Sciences

Cooper, Janis Campbell: vice president, Maytag Corp. Foundation

American Association Museums

Manoogian, Richard Alexander: chairman, chief executive officer, director, Masco Corp.

American Association Petroleum Geologists

Bradford, William Edward: chairman, director, Halliburton Co.

Greene, John Frederick: executive vice president exploration & production, director, Louisiana Land & Exploration Co.

Jennings, James Burnett: president, Hunt Oil Co.

American Association Publishers

Downing, Kathryn M.: executive vice president, Times Mirror Co.; vice chairman, Times Mirror Foundation

Schadt, James Phillip: chairman, president, chief executive officer, director, Reader's Digest Association, Inc. (The); chairman, director, Reader's Digest Foundation

American Association Rhodes Scholars

Kinsolving, Augustus Blagden: director, ASARCO Foundation

American Association University Professors

Connor, James Richard: executive director, Kemper Foundation (James S.)

Hutton, Edward L.: chairman, chief executive officer, director, Chemed Corp.

Stanley, Peter William: trustee, Hitachi Foundation

American Australian Association

Osborne, Richard de Jongh: director, ASARCO Foundation; chairman, chief executive officer, director, ASARCO Inc.

American Automobile Manufacturers Association

Eaton, Robert James: co-chairman, president, chief executive officer, DaimlerChrysler Corp.

Smith, John Francis, Jr.: chairman, General Motors Corp.

American Bakers Association

Johnson, David Willis: chairman, director, Campbell Soup Co.

Schwebel, Joseph M.: president, director, Schwebel Baking Co.; trustee, Schwebel Family Foundation

American Bankers Association

Allison, John Andrew, IV: chairman, chief executive officer, director, Branch Banking & Trust Co.

Cameron, Gerry B.: chairman, director, U.S. Bancorp

Dods, Walter Arthur, Jr.: president, director, First Hawaiian Foundation; chairman, chief executive officer, director, First Hawaiian, Inc.

Eccles, Spencer Fox: chairman, chief executive officer, director, First Security Bank of Idaho NA

Elliott, Anson Wright: vice president, trustee, Chase Manhattan Foundation

Glaser, Gary A.: president, chief executive officer, National City Bank of Columbus

Hower, Frank Beard, Jr.: vice chairman, Anthem Foundation, Inc.

McCoy, John Bonnet: president, chief executive officer, Ameritech Corp.

McMillan, Howard Lamar, Jr.: president, chief operating officer, director, Deposit Guaranty National Bank

Murphy, Christopher J., III: president, chief executive officer, director, First Source Corp.; director, First Source Foundation

Rohr, James Edward: chief executive officer, president, director, PNC Financial Services Group

Ryan, Arthur Frederick: trustee, Chase Manhattan Foundation; chairman, chief executive officer, Prudential Insurance Co. of America

Sadler, Robert L.: president, vice chairman, director, Old Kent Bank

Tilghman, Richard Granville: chairman, chief executive officer, Crestar Foundation

American Bankers Council

Baker, Leslie Mayo, Jr.: president, chief executive officer, chairman, Wachovia Bank of North Carolina NA; chairman, Wachovia Foundation, Inc. (The)

American Bar Association

Agger, James Harrington: senior vice president, secretary, general counsel, Air Products and Chemicals, Inc.; director, Air Products Foundation

Agnich, Richard John: director, Texas Instruments Foundation; senior vice president, secretary, general counsel, Texas Instruments Inc.

Anderson, Judy M.: vice president, corporate secretary, Georgia Power Co.; executive director, secretary, assistant treasurer, Georgia Power Foundation

Ballantyne, Richard Lee: vice president, general counsel, secretary, Harris Corp.; secretary, treasurer, Harris Foundation

Barnes, Wallace W.: director, Barnes Group Foundation Inc.

Barnette, Curtis Handley: chairman, chief executive officer, director, Bethlehem Steel Corp.

Bayless, Charles Edward: chairman, president, chief executive officer, director, Illinois Power Co.

Bechtel, Riley Peart: chairman, Bechtel Foundation; chairman, chief executive officer, director, Bechtel Group, Inc.

Beck, Edward W.: senior vice president, general counsel, secretary, director, Shaklee Corp.

Besser, John Edward: director, Barnes Group Foundation Inc.; senior vice president finance & law, Barnes Group Inc.

Bickner, Bruce P.: chairman, chief executive officer, director, DeKalb Genetics Corp.

Black, Natalie A.: group vice president interiors, general counsel, director, Kohler Co.

Blair, James Burton: trustee, Tyson Foundation, Inc.

Bogomolny, Robert Lee: director, Searle Charitable Trust; senior vice president, general counsel, secretary, Searle & Co. (G.D.)

Bonvino, Frank W.: vice president, secretary, general counsel, International Multifoods Corp.

Bridgeland, James Ralph, Jr.: trustee, Star Bank NA, Cincinnati Foundation

Brown, JoBeth Goode: trustee, Anheuser-Busch Companies, Inc.

Buchanan, William Hobart, Jr.: assistant secretary, Dun & Bradstreet Corp. Foundation, Inc.

Burak, Howard Paul: secretary, director, Sony U.S.A. Foundation Inc.

Burlingame, John Hunter: executive partner, Scripps Co. (E.W.)

Burrus, Robert Lewis, Jr.: trustee, Circuit City Foundation

Calise, Nicholas James: vice president, associate general counsel, secretary, BFGoodrich Co.; secretary, Goodrich Foundation, Inc. (B.F.)

Canning, John Beckman: secretary, Rayonier Foundation

Carter, John Douglas: executive vice president, director, Bechtel Group, Inc.

Cassidy, M. Sharon: assistant secretary, USX Foundation, Inc.

Chabraja, Nicholas D.: chairman, chief executive officer, director, General Dynamics Corp.

Chapple, Thomas Leslie: senior vice president, general counsel, secretary, Gannett Co., Inc.; secretary, Gannett Foundation

Chenault, Kenneth Irvine: president, chief operating officer, director, American Express Co.; trustee, American Express Foundation

Clark, Richard McCourt: senior vice president, general counsel, secretary, Kellogg Co.; vice president, trustee, Kellogg Co. Twenty-Five Year Employees' Fund Inc.

Cocklin, Kim Roland: senior vice president, Texas Gas Transmission Corp.

Cody, Thomas Gerald: executive vice president legal & human resources, Federated Department Stores, Inc.

Cogan, John Francis, Jr.: president, chief executive officer, director, Pioneer Group

Cole, Lewis George: director, AMETEK Foundation

Colton, S. David: senior vice president, general counsel, Phelps Dodge Corp.

Connolly, Gerald Edward: trustee, Reinhart Family Foundation (D. B. and Marjorie)

Coyle, Dennis Patrick: secretary, director, FPL Group Foundation, Inc.

Crook, Donald Martin: secretary, Kimberly-Clark Foundation

Cutchins, Clifford Armstrong, IV: president, Fort James Corp.; chairman, director, Fort James Foundation (The)

D'Andrade, Hugh Alfred: trustee, member, Schering-Plough Foundation

Dabney, Donna C.: secretary, Reynolds Metals Co. Foundation

DeLoach, Harris E., Junior: executive vice president, director, Sonoco Products Co.

Denson, William Frank, III: president, Vulcan Materials Co. Foundation

Devlin, James Richard: director, Sprint Foundation

Donahue, Richard King: vice chairman, Nike, Inc.

Douglass, Robert Royal: trustee, Chase Manhattan Foundation

Dubin, Stephen Victor: vice president, secretary, Farber Foundation

Earley, Anthony Francis, Jr.: president, chief operating officer, Detroit Edison Co.; director, Detroit Edison Foundation

Ehrlich, M. Gordon: trustee, Orchard Foundation

Fine, Roger Seth: vice president, general counsel, Johnson & Johnson; president, Johnson & Johnson Family of Companies Contribution Fund

Flood, Joan Moore: assistant treasurer, Trace International Holdings, Inc. Foundation

Forster, Peter Hans: chairman, director, Dayton Power and Light Co.
Franke, William Augustus: chairman, president, chief executive officer, America West Airlines, Inc.; director, Phelps Dodge Foundation
Gallagher, Richard S.: director, Badger Meter Foundation
Gallagher, Terence Joseph: secretary, director, Pfizer Foundation
Gherlein, Gerald Lee: member contributions committee, Eaton Charitable Fund
Gherty, John E.: president, chief executive officer, Land O'Lakes, Inc.
Godfrey, Cullen Michael: vice president, FINA Foundation
Goode, David Ronald: chairman, president, chief executive officer, director, Norfolk Southern Corp.
Graves, Ronald Norman: secretary, Simplot Foundation (J.R.)
Gregg, Walter Emmor, Junior: senior executive vice president finance & administration, PNC Financial Services Group
Gross, Murray: trustee, PerkinElmer Foundation; senior vice president, general counsel, clerk, PerkinElmer, Inc.
Hall, Larry D.: chairman, president, chief executive officer, director, Kinder Morgn; president, director, KN Energy Foundation
Harkey, Robert Shelton: trustee, Delta Air Lines Foundation; senior vice president, general counsel, secretary, Delta Air Lines, Inc.
Heineman, Benjamin Walter, Jr.: director, GE Fund
Herron, James Michael: secretary, director, Ryder System Charitable Foundation
Hewitt, James Watt: vice president, treasurer, Abel Foundation
Hoak, Jon: trustee, NCR Foundation
Hoffmann, Richard W.: general counsel, Employers Mutual Casualty Co.
Hudnut, Stewart Skinner: director, Illinois Tool Works Foundation
Huston, Steve: secretary, Wrigley Co. Foundation (Wm. Jr.)
Jewell, George Hiram: director, Schlumberger Foundation
Johnson, Murray Lloyd, Jr.: secretary, trustee, Zachry Foundation (The)
Kalaher, Richard A.: president, American Standard Foundation; vice president, secretary, general counsel, American Standard Inc.
Karmel, Roberta S.: trustee, Kemper Foundation (James S.); partner, Kemper National Insurance Companies
Kelson, Richard B.: director, Alcoa Foundation
Kennedy, Bernard Joseph: chairman, president, chief executive officer, director, National Fuel Gas Distribution Corp.
Keyser, F. Ray, Jr.: chairman, director, Central Vermont Public Service Corp.
Kinsolving, Augustus Blagden: director, ASARCO Foundation
Kurtz, Melvin H.: secretary, director, Chesebrough Foundation
LaMacchia, John Thomas: trustee, Cincinnati Bell Foundation, Inc.; president, chief executive officer, director, Cincinnati Bell Inc.
Lambe, James F.: senior vice president human resources, Nalco Chemical Co.; director, Nalco Foundation
Landin, Thomas Milton: vice president, director, CertainTeed Corp.; vice president, Norton Co. Foundation
Lang, Robert Todd: chairman, director, Weil, Gotshal & Manges Foundation
Larson, Wayne E.: trustee, Ladish Co. Foundation
Levy, David: trustee, National Service Foundation
Long, Michael Thomas: director, Ensign-Bickford Foundation
Loos, Henry J.: secretary, Charter Manufacturing Co. Foundation
Maher, Francesca M.: senior vice president, general counsel, secretary, United Airlines Inc.
Margolin, Abraham E.: director, Tension Envelope Foundation
Masin, Michael Terry: vice chairman, president international, director, GTE Corp.; trustee, GTE Foundation
Matthews, Clark J., II: president, chief executive officer, director, 7-Eleven, Inc.
McClimon, Timothy J.: executive director, AT&T Foundation
McCorkindale, Douglas H.: vice chairman, president, Gannett Co., Inc.; president, Gannett Foundation
McDaniel, Tom J.: vice chairman, director, Kerr-McGee Corp.
McGuinn, Martin Gregory: chairman, chief executive officer, Mellon Financial Corp.
McLaughlin, Michael John: secretary, New York Life Foundation; senior vice president, deputy general counsel, New York Life Insurance Co.
Melican, James Patrick, Jr.: executive vice president legal & external affairs, International Paper Co.; director, International Paper Co. Foundation
Merdek, Andrew Austin: vice president legal affairs, secretary, Cox Enterprises Inc.; secretary, Cox Foundation (James M.)
Merrell, Pamela K.: secretary, Montana Power Co.; vice president, secretary, Montana Power Foundation
Meyer, Russell William, Jr.: chairman, chief executive officer, Cessna Aircraft Co.; president, Cessna Foundation, Inc.
Millstein, Ira M.: partner, Weil, Gotshal & Manges Corp.; president, director, Weil, Gotshal & Manges Foundation
Morie, G. Glen: secretary, treasurer, PACCAR Foundation
Morris, Herman, Jr.: president, chief executive officer, Memphis Light Gas & Water Division
Murphy, Christopher J., III: president, chief executive officer, director, First Source Corp.; director, First Source Foundation
Muth, Robert James: president, director, ASARCO Foundation
Neville, James Morton: member board control, Ralston Purina Trust Fund
Newlin, William Rankin: trustee, Kennametal Foundation
Nye, Erle Allen: chairman, chief executive officer, director, TU Electric Co.
Olschwang, Alan P., Esq.: secretary, Mitsubishi Electric America Foundation
Owens, Jack Byron: executive vice president, general counsel, Gallo Winery, Inc. (E&J)
Pike, Robert William: vice president, secretary, Allstate Foundation; senior vice president, secretary, general counsel, director, Allstate Insurance Co.
Pollock, E. Kears: director, PPG Industries Foundation; executive vice president, PPG Industries, Inc.
Powell, Jerry W.: secretary, general counsel, Compass Bank; secretary, Compass Bank Foundation
Purvis, George Frank, Jr.: chairman, president, chief executive officer, director, Pan-American Life Insurance Co.
Pyke, John Secrest, Jr.: president, trustee, Hanna Co. Foundation (M.A.); vice president, secretary, general counsel, Hanna Co. (M.A.)
Redstone, Sumner Murray: chairman, Viacom Inc.
Resnick, Myron J.: vice president, treasurer, trustee, Allstate Foundation
Robin, Kenneth H.: senior vice president, general counsel, Household International Inc.
Rosenthal, Sol: counsel, Playboy Enterprises Inc.
Rudnick, Alan A.: vice president, general counsel, corporate secretary, CSX Corp.
Russell, Frank Eli: president, Central Newspapers Foundation; chairman, Central Newspapers, Inc.
Rust, Edward Barry, Jr.: chairman, president, director, State Farm Companies Foundation; chairman, president, chief executive officer, director, State Farm Mutual Automobile Insurance Co.
Salinger, Robert M.: secretary, First Financial Foundation
Satre, Philip Glen: chairman, president, chief executive officer, director, Promus Hotel Corp.
Shapiro, Isaac: chairman, secretary, trustee, Ise Cultural Foundation
Sharpe, Robert Francis, Jr.: senior vice president public affairs, general counsel, PepsiCo, Inc.
Sheahan, Mark: treasurer, Graco Foundation
Sissel, George A.: chairman, president, chief executive officer, director, Ball Corp.
Skilling, Raymond Inwood: executive vice president, chief counsel, director, Aon Corp.; director, Aon Foundation
Skinner, Claire Corson: chairman, chief executive officer, Coachmen Industries, Inc.
Smith, Donald Kaye: senior vice president, general counsel, director, GEICO Corp.
Snell, Richard: chairman, president, chief executive officer, director, Arizona Public Service Co.
Soden, Paul A.: senior vice president, secretary, general counsel, Reader's Digest Association, Inc. (The)
Stroup, Stanley Stephenson: executive vice president, general counsel, Norwest Corp.
Sullivan, Laura P.: vice president, secretary, director, State Farm Companies Foundation; vice president, secretary, counsel, State Farm Mutual Automobile Insurance Co.
Sullivan, Thomas John: vice president, director,
Ughetta, William Casper: trustee, Corning Inc. Foundation
Ukropina, James R.: partner, Pacific Mutual Life Insurance Co.
Van Cleve, William Moore: member public policy committee, Emerson Charitable Trust; partner, Emerson Electric Co.
Vogel, Howard Stanley: tax counsel, Texaco Foundation
Wagner, Thomas Joseph: chairman, CIGNA Foundation
Wallach, Ira D.: chairman, Central National-Gottesman; executive vice president, Central National-Gottesman Foundation
Walton, Jon David: trustee, Allegheny Technologies Inc. Charitable Trust
Wander, Herbert S.: secretary, director, Katten, Muchin & Zavis Foundation
Ward, Carol J.: secretary, compliance officer, CIGNA Corp.; secretary, CIGNA Foundation
Wasserman, David Sherman: vice president, treasurer, Harris Corp.; trustee, Harris Foundation
Watson, Solomon Brown, IV: vice president, New York Times Co. Foundation
Weinberger, Caspar Willard: chairman, Forbes Inc.
Welsh, Kelly Raymond: executive vice president, general counsel, Ameritech Corp.
Welty, John Rider: secretary, Carpenter Technology Corp. Foundation
Williams, Karen Hastie: director, Fannie Mae Foundation
Wolff, Jesse David: treasurer, director, Weil, Gotshal & Manges Foundation
Zavis, Michael W.: managing partner, Katten, Muchin & Zavis; president, director, Katten, Muchin & Zavis Foundation

ZoBell, Karl: vice president, trustee, Copley Foundation (James S.)

American Bar Foundation

Burrus, Robert Lewis, Jr.: trustee, Circuit City Foundation

Gorelick, Jamie Shona: vice chairman, Fannie Mae

Hewitt, James Watt: vice president, treasurer, Abel Foundation

Jewell, George Hiram: director, Schlumberger Foundation

Karmel, Roberta S.: trustee, Kemper Foundation (James S.); partner, Kemper National Insurance Companies

Newlin, William Rankin: trustee, Kennametal Foundation

American Board Trial Advocates

Donahue, Richard King: vice chairman, Nike, Inc.

American Business Conference

Hatsopoulos, George Nicholas: founder, chairman, chief executive officer, director, Thermo Electron Corp.; committee member, Thermo Electron Foundation

Manoogian, Richard Alexander: chairman, chief executive officer, director, Masco Corp.

Syron, Richard F.: chairman, chief executive officer, director, American Stock Exchange, Inc.

Wurtele, C. Angus: president, Valspar Foundation

American Cablevision Indianapolis

Sease, Gene Elwood: director, Central Newspapers Foundation

American Century Mutual Funds

Strandjord, Mary Jeannine: director, Sprint Foundation

American Chamber of Commerce

Fierce, Hughlyn F.: trustee, Chase Manhattan Foundation

American Chamber of Commerce Brussels

Bonsignore, Michael Robert: director, Honeywell Foundation; chairman, chief executive officer, director, Honeywell International Inc.

American Chemical Society

Alberts, Bruce Michael, PhD: director, Genentech Foundation for Biomedical Sciences

Byck, Joseph S.: vice president, Union Carbide Foundation

D'Amato, Anthony S.: chairman, Borden Foundation, Inc.

Hemminghaus, Roger Roy: chairman, director, Ultramar Diamond Shamrock Corp.

Hill, George Richard: president, trustee, Lubrizol Foundation (The)

Lovett, John Robert: director, Air Products Foundation

Moten, John, Junior: vice president community relations, Laclede Gas Co.

Stewart, S. Jay: chairman, chief executive officer, director, Morton International Inc.

Swanson, Robert A.: director, Genentech Foundation for Biomedical Sciences

Vagelos, Pindaros Roy: trustee, Prudential Insurance Co. of America

American Cinematheque

Rosenzweig, Richard Stuart: executive vice president, director, Playboy Enterprises Inc.

American Civil Liberties Union Illinois Chapter

Hefner, Christie Ann: chairman, chief executive officer, Playboy Enterprises Inc.; director, Playboy Foundation

American College

Gammill, Lee Morgan, Jr.: director, New York Life Foundation; vice chairman, director, New York Life Insurance Co.

Hohn, Harry George, Jr.: chairman, director, New York Life Foundation

American College Lawyers

Matis, Nina B.: director, Katten, Muchin & Zavis Foundation

American College Physician Executives

Nelson, Glen David, MD: vice chairman, Medtronic, Inc.

American College Physicians

Harris, Edward D., Jr.: director, Genentech Foundation for Biomedical Sciences

American College Surgeons

Lempka, Arnold W., MD: chairman, director, Physicians Mutual Insurance Co.; director, Physicians Mutual Insurance Co. Foundation

American College Tax Counsel

Gallagher, Richard S.: director, Badger Meter Foundation

Jewell, George Hiram: director, Schlumberger Foundation

American College Trial Lawyers

Blair, James Burton: trustee, Tyson Foundation, Inc.

Chabraja, Nicholas D.: chairman, chief executive officer, director, General Dynamics Corp.

Donahue, Richard King: vice chairman, Nike, Inc.

American College Trust & Estate Counsel

Gallagher, Richard S.: director, Badger Meter Foundation

ZoBell, Karl: vice president, trustee, Copley Foundation (James S.)

American Compensation Association

Mack, Raymond Phillip: director, Arvin Foundation; vice president human resources, Arvin Industries, Inc.

Nikka, Joanne: trustee, Millipore Foundation (The)

American Concrete Paving Association

Cloud, Bruce Benjamin, Sr.: vice chairman, director, Zachry Co. (H.B.)

American Corp. Counsel Association

Hoffmann, Richard W.: general counsel, Employers Mutual Casualty Co.

Jeremiah, Barbara S.: director, Alcoa Foundation

Jones, D. Michael: senior vice president, general counsel, Reynolds Metals Co.; vice president, director, Reynolds Metals Co. Foundation

Kelson, Richard B.: director, Alcoa Foundation

American Corporate Counsel Association

Beck, Edward W.: senior vice president, general counsel, secretary, director, Shaklee Corp.

Bogomolny, Robert Lee: director, Searle Charitable Trust; senior vice president, general counsel, secretary, Searle & Co. (G.D.)

Calise, Nicholas James: vice president, associate general counsel, secretary, BFGoodrich Co.; secretary, Goodrich Foundation, Inc. (B.F.)

Causey, John Paul, Jr.: senior vice president, secretary, general counsel, Chesapeake Corp.; chairman, trustee, Chesapeake Corp. Foundation

Clark, Richard McCourt: senior vice president, general counsel, secretary, Kellogg Co.; vice president, director, trustee, Kellogg Co. Twenty-Five Year Employees' Fund Inc.

Dabney, Donna C.: secretary, Reynolds Metals Co. Foundation

Graves, Ronald Norman: secretary, Simplot Foundation (J.R.)

Kirchhof, Anton Conrad: corporate secretary, general counsel, Louisiana-Pacific Corp.; secretary, Louisiana-Pacific Foundation

Larson, Wayne E.: trustee, Ladish Co. Foundation

Long, Michael Thomas: director, Ensign-Bickford Foundation

Mattison, Robert Mayer: director, Graco Foundation; vice president, general counsel, secretary, Graco, Inc.

Merdek, Andrew Austin: vice president legal affairs, secretary, Cox Enterprises Inc.; secretary, Cox Foundation (James M.)

Morie, G. Glen: secretary, treasurer, PACCAR Foundation

Neville, James Morton: member board control, Ralston Purina Trust Fund

Olschwang, Alan P., Esq.: secretary, Mitsubishi Electric America Foundation

Parry, William E.: vice president, general counsel, Nalco Chemical Co.

Powell, Jerry W.: secretary, general counsel, Compass Bank; secretary, Compass Bank Foundation

Pyke, John Secrest, Jr.: president, trustee, Hanna Co. Foundation (M.A.); vice president, secretary, general counsel, Hanna Co. (M.A.)

Sharpe, Robert Francis, Jr.: senior vice president public affairs, general counsel, PepsiCo, Inc.

Shiely, John Stephen: president, chief operating officer, director, Briggs & Stratton Corp.; vice president, director, Briggs & Stratton Corp. Foundation

Smith, Donald Kaye: senior vice president, general counsel, director, GEICO Corp.

Sullivan, Laura P.: vice president, secretary, director, State Farm Companies Foundation; vice president, secretary, counsel, State Farm Mutual Automobile Insurance Co.

Ughetta, William Casper: trustee, Corning Inc. Foundation

Wagner, Thomas Joseph: chairman, CIGNA Foundation

Walton, Jon David: trustee, Allegheny Technologies Inc. Charitable Trust

Ward, Carol J.: secretary, compliance officer, CIGNA Corp.; secretary, CIGNA Foundation

Watson, Solomon Brown, IV: vice president, New York Times Co. Foundation

Welty, John Rider: secretary, Carpenter Technology Corp. Foundation

American Corporate Secretarys Association

Barnette, Curtis Handley: chairman, chief executive officer, director, Bethlehem Steel Corp.

American Council Arts

Brademas, John: chairman, Texaco Foundation

Greene, Donald Ray: assistant vice president, Coca-Cola Co.; president, director, Coca-Cola Foundation

Ostergard, Paul Michael: vice president, director corporate contributions, Citibank Corp.; president, Citigroup Foundation

American Council Capital Formation

Drury, David J.: chief executive officer, chairman, Principal Financial Group

Hatsopoulos, George Nicholas: founder, chairman, chief executive officer, director, Thermo Electron Corp.; committee member, Thermo Electron Foundation

Lucas, Donald Leo: chairman, Cadence Designs Systems, Inc.

Rehm, Jack Daniel: chairman emeritus, director, Meredith Corp.

American Council Education

Brademas, John: chairman, Texaco Foundation

Forsyth, John D.: president, chief executive officer, Blue Cross & Blue Shield of Iowa

Stanley, Peter William: trustee, Hitachi Foundation

American Council Germany

Raymond, Lee R.: chairman, president, chief executive officer, Exxon Mobil Corp.

American Council Life Insurance

Bertrand, Frederic Howard: chairman, Central Vermont Public Service Corp.

Brown, Stephen Lee: chairman, chief executive officer, director, Hancock Financial Services (John)

Chookaszian, Dennis Haig: chairman, chief executive officer, CNA

Eckert, Ralph John: trustee, Trustmark Foundation

Kalainov, Sam Charles: chairman, president, chief executive officer, AmerUS Group

Kamen, Harry Paul: chairman, president, chief executive officer, Metropolitan Life Insurance Co.

O'Brien, John Francis, Jr.: president, chief executive officer, Allmerica Financial Corp.

Peterson, Donald Matthew: trustee, Trustmark Foundation; president, chief executive officer, director, Trustmark Insurance Co.

Roth, Michael I.: chairman, chief executive officer, director, MONY Group (The); director, MONY Life Insurance of New York (The)

Semler, Jerry D.: chairman, president, chief executive officer, director, American United Life Insurance Co.; chairman, director, AUL Foundation Inc.

Tuerff, James R.: president, director, American General Finance

Turner, John Gosney: chairman, chief executive officer, director, ReliaStar Financial Corp.; director, ReliaStar Foundation

Weekly, John William: chairman, chief executive officer, Mutual of Omaha Insurance Co.

American Council Life Insurance Tax Steering Committee

Drury, David J.: chief executive officer, chairman, Principal Financial Group

American Council Life Insurers

Hoffmann, Richard W.: general counsel, Employers Mutual Casualty Co.

American Craft Council

Copley, David C.: president, trustee, Copley Foundation (James S.); president, chief executive officer, director, senior management board, Copley Press, Inc.

American Defense Preparedness Association

Dewane, John Richard: director, Honeywell Foundation

Kresa, Kent: chairman, president, chief executive officer, director, Northrop Grumman Corp.

American Economic Association

Abdoo, Richard A.: chairman, president, chief executive officer, Wisconsin Energy Corp.; president, director, Wisconsin Energy Corp. Foundation, Inc.

Bowen, William Gordon, PhD: trustee, Merck Co. Foundation

Lyall, Katharine Culbert: trustee, Kemper Foundation (James S.)

Rosett, Richard Nathaniel: trustee, Kemper Foundation (James S.)

American Electronics Association

Leonis, John Michael: chairman, director, Litton Industries, Inc.

Levy, Richard M.: president, chief executive officer, Varian Medical Systems, Inc.

Malmberg, David Curtis: director, National City Bank of Minneapolis

American Energy Partners Ltd.

Buckwalter, Alan Roland, III: chief executive officer, Chase Bank of Texas; president, Chase Bank of Texas Foundation, Inc.

American Enterprise Institute

Blount, Winton Malcolm, Jr.: chairman, Blount International, Inc.

Golub, Harvey: chairman, chief executive officer, director, American Express Co.; trustee, American Express Foundation

Rust, Edward Barry, Jr.: chairman, president, director, State Farm Companies Foundation; chairman, president, chief executive officer, director, State Farm Mutual Automobile Insurance Co.

Schadt, James Phillip: chairman, president, chief executive officer, director, Reader's Digest Association, Inc. (The); chairman, director, Reader's Digest Foundation

American European Chamber of Commerce

Dugan, Allan E.: senior vice president corporate strategic service, Xerox Corp.; trustee, Xerox Foundation

American Express Credit Corp.

Goeltz, Richard Karl: vice chairman, chief financial officer, American Express Co.

American Family Home Insurance Co.

Hayden, Joseph Page, Jr.: trustee, Star Bank NA, Cincinnati Foundation

American Federation Arts

Cantor, Bernard Gerald: president, director, Cantor, Fitzgerald Foundation; chairman, director, Cantor, Fitzgerald Securities Corp.

Manoogian, Richard Alexander: chairman, chief executive officer, director, Masco Corp.

American Federation Clinical Research

Gussin, Robert Zalmon, PhD: vice president science & technology, Johnson & Johnson; member corporate contributions committee, Johnson & Johnson Family of Companies Contribution Fund

American Film Institute

Rosenzweig, Richard Stuart: executive vice president, director, Playboy Enterprises Inc.

American Fin SVCs Association

Binyon, Bryan A.: treasurer, American General Finance Foundation

American Finance Association

Oakley, Robert Alan: executive vice president, chief financial officer, Nationwide Insurance Enterprise Foundation

American Footwear Industry Association

Hiatt, Arnold Selig: chairman, director, Stride Rite Foundation

American Forest & Paper Association

Fox, Joseph Carter: chairman, president, chief executive officer, Chesapeake Corp.

Harad, George Jay: chairman, chief executive officer, director, Boise Cascade Corp.

Kenney, Richard John: director, Consolidated Papers Foundation, Inc.; senior vice president finance, Consolidated Papers, Inc.

Luke, John A., Jr.: chairman, president, chief executive officer, director, Westvaco Corp.

Mead, George Wilson, II: president, director, Consolidated Papers Foundation, Inc.; chairman, director, Consolidated Papers, Inc.

Pomerantz, Marvin Alvin: trustee, Mid-American Foundation

Stivers, William Charles: senior vice president, chief financial officer, treasurer, Weyerhaeuser Co.; treasurer, trustee, Weyerhaeuser Co. Foundation

Stone, Roger Warren: chairman, president, chief executive officer, director, Stone Container Corp.; president, Stone Foundation

American Forest Foundation

Luke, John A., Jr.: chairman, president, chief executive officer, director, Westvaco Corp.

American Foundation Counsel Services

Kress, George F.: honorary chairman, director, Green Bay Packaging; president, Kress Foundation (George)

American Friends University College Oxford Inc.

Chellgren, Paul Wilbur: chief executive officer, chairman, director, Ashland, Inc.; member, Ashland Inc. Foundation

American Frozen Food Institute

Langbo, Arnold Gordon: chairman, chief executive officer, director, Kellogg Co.

American Furniture Manufacturer Association

Spilman, Robert H.: chairman, chief executive officer, Bassett Furniture Industries; chairman, director, Bassett Furniture Industries Fdn.

American Gas Association

Ackerman, Philip Charles: senior vice president, director, National Fuel Gas Distribution Corp.

Banks, Peter L.: vice president external affairs, AGL Resources Inc.

Catell, Robert Barry: chairman, chief executive officer, Brooklyn Union

Davis, Erroll Brown, Jr.: president, chief executive officer, director, Wisconsin Power & Light Co.

Downes, Laurence M.: president, chief executive officer, director, chairman, New Jersey Natural Gas Co.; trustee, New Jersey Natural Gas Foundation

Farman, Richard Donald: chairman, chief executive officer, Pacific Enterprises

Ferland, E. James: chairman, president, chief executive officer, Public Service Electric & Gas Co.
Hock, Delwin D.: chairman, New Century Energies
Kennedy, Bernard Joseph: chairman, president, chief executive officer, director, National Fuel Gas Distribution Corp.
Lang, Paul Louis: vice president, Illinois Power Co.
Matthews, Craig Gerard: president, chief operating officer, Brooklyn Union
McCormick, William Thomas, Jr.: chairman, chief executive officer, director, Consumers Energy Co.; chairman, Consumers Energy Foundation
McNeill, Corbin Asahel, Jr.: president, chief executive officer, director, chairman, PECO Energy Co.
Messer, Chester R.: president, chief operating officer, Boston Gas Co.; trustee, Eastern Enterprises Foundation
Mitchell, Warren I.: president, director, Southern California Gas Co.
Neale, Gary L.: chairman, president, chief executive officer, Northern Indiana Public Service Co.
Ruelle, Mark A.: senior vice president, chief financial officer, Sierra Pacific Resources
Terry, Richard Edward: chairman, chief executive officer, director, Peoples Energy Corp.
Thies, Richard Henry: assistant treasurer, Madison Gas & Electric Foundation
Wise, William Allen: chairman, president, chief executive officer, director, El Paso Energy Co.; chairman, director, El Paso Energy Foundation
Wood, Willis B., Jr.: chairman, chief executive officer, director, Pacific Enterprises

American Graduate School International Management

Bible, Geoffrey Cyril: director, New York Stock Exchange Foundation, Inc.; chairman, chief executive officer, director, Philip Morris Companies Inc.
McClung, James Allen: vice president, director, FMC Foundation
Snell, Richard: chairman, president, chief executive officer, director, Arizona Public Service Co.

American Ground Water Trust

Lawson, William Hogan, III: chairman, chief executive officer, director, Franklin Electric Co.; president, Franklin Electric, Edward J. Schaefer, and T. W. KehoeCharitable and Educational Foundation

American Guild Musical Artists

Darling, Robert Edward, Jr.: chairman, Ensign-Bickford Foundation

American Hardware Manufacturer Association

Gloyd, Lawrence Eugene: trustee, CLARCOR Foundation; chairman, chief executive officer, director, CLARCOR Inc.

American Heart Association

Friedewald, William Thomas, MD: director, MetLife Foundation
Gussin, Robert Zalmon, PhD: vice president science & technology, Johnson & Johnson; member corporate contributions committee, Johnson & Johnson Family of Companies Contribution Fund

American Heart Association Tulsa Metropolitan Division

Nowell, Tommy Lynn: vice president finance, controller, Occidental Oil and Gas; treasurer, Occidental Oil and Gas Foundation

American Helicopter Society

Kaman, Charles Huron: chairman, president, chief executive officer, director, Kaman Corp.

American Hellenic Chamber of Commerce

Kampouris, Emmanuel Andrew: chairman, president, chief executive officer, director, American Standard Inc.

American Historical Association

Graham, Patricia Albjerg, PhD: trustee, Hitachi Foundation
Stanley, Peter William: trustee, Hitachi Foundation

American Horse Show Association

Kohler, Herbert Vollrath, Jr.: chairman, president, director, Kohler Co.

American Hospital of Paris Foundation

Eisner, Michael Dammann: president, trustee, Disney Co. Foundation (Walt); chairman, chief executive officer, director, Disney Co. (Walt)

American Humane Association

Carey, Kathryn Ann: foundation manager, American Honda Foundation

American Institute Aeronautics & Astronautics

Beall, Donald Ray: director, Rockwell International Corp.
Condit, Philip Murray: chairman, chief executive officer, director, Boeing Co.
Davis, Ruth Margaret: trustee, Air Products Foundation
Kaman, Charles Huron: chairman, president, chief executive officer, director, Kaman Corp.
Kresa, Kent: chairman, president, chief executive officer, director, Northrop Grumman Corp.
Leonis, John Michael: chairman, director, Litton Industries, Inc.

American Institute Architects

Hall, Donald Joyce: chairman board, director, Hallmark Cards Inc.; chairman, Hallmark Corporate Foundation
Miller, Joseph Irwin: director associate, Cummins Engine Co., Inc.; director, Cummins Engine Foundation

American Institute Association

Chookaszian, Dennis Haig: chairman, chief executive officer, CNA

American Institute Baking

Schwebel, Joseph M.: president, director, Schwebel Baking Co.; trustee, Schwebel Family Foundation

American Institute Banking

Glaser, Gary A.: president, chief executive officer, National City Bank of Columbus
Wobst, Frank: chairman, chief executive officer, director, Huntington Bancshares Inc.

American Institute CPA's

Siegel, Samuel: vice chairman, secretary, treasurer, chief financial officer, director, Nucor Corp.; director, Nucor Foundation

American Institute CPAs

Breisinger, James R.: vice president, controller, Kennametal Foundation; vice president, controller, chief financial officer, Kennametal, Inc.
Broome, Burton Edward: vice president, controller, Transamerica Corp.; vice president, treasurer, Transamerica Foundation
Chookaszian, Dennis Haig: chairman, chief executive officer, CNA
Cook, J. Michael: chairman, chief executive officer, Deloitte & Touche; chairman, Deloitte & Touche Foundation
Cooper, William Allen: chairman, director, TCF National Bank Minnesota
Dahm, Anthony Edward: controller, Giant Food Inc.
Delo, Robert Paul: director, Chicago Tribune Foundation
Doerfler, Ronald J.: senior vice president, chief financial officer, ABC; vice president, director, ABC Foundation
Doherty, Leonard Edward: member advisory committee, admin officer, Dow Jones Foundation
Eigsti, Roger Harry: chairman, chief executive officer, SAFECO Corp.
Fluno, Jere David: vice chairman, Grainger, Inc. (W.W.)
Garberding, Larry Gailbert: chief financial officer, executive vice president, Detroit Edison Co.; director, Detroit Edison Foundation
Gierer, Vincent A., Jr.: chairman, president, chief executive officer, director, UST Inc.
Graff, Stephen Ney: director, Bucyrus-Erie Foundation
Grubb, Edgar Harold: executive vice president, chief financial officer, Transamerica Corp.; director, Transamerica Foundation
Harper, James J.: vice president, controller, Eastern Enterprises
Hegel, Garrett R.: chief financial officer, Compass Bank; president, Compass Bank Foundation
Hobbs, Richard F.: vice president administration, Universal Foods Corp.; vice president, director, Universal Foods Foundation
Hock, Delwin D.: chairman, New Century Energies
Karr, Howard Henry: treasurer, director, First Hawaiian Foundation
Keyes, James Henry: advisor, Johnson Controls Foundation; president, Johnson Controls Inc.
Knight, Philip Hampson: chairman, chief executive officer, Nike, Inc.
Lindenauer, Arthur: executive vice president, chief financial officer, Schlumberger Ltd. (USA)
Maffucci, David G.: senior vice president, chief financial officer, Bowater Inc.
Marcum, Kenneth William: treasurer, Commercial Intertech Foundation
Martin, JoAnn M.: controller, Ameritas Charitable Foundation; senior vice president, partner, chief financial officer, Ameritas Life Insurance Corp.
McCook, Richard P.: vice president, Winn-Dixie Stores Foundation; vice president finance, chief financial officer, Winn-Dixie Stores Inc.
McFerson, Dimon Richard: chairman, chief executive officer, Nationwide Insurance Co.; chairman, chief executive officer, trustee, Nationwide Insurance Enterprise Foundation; chairman, chief executive officer, Wausau Insurance Companies
Medford, Dale L.: vice president corporate finance, chief financial officer, Reynolds & Reynolds Co.
Menzer, John: executive vice president, Wal-Mart Stores, Inc.
Meyer, Daniel Joseph: president, Milacron Foundation; chairman, president, chief executive officer, director, Milacron, Inc.
Montague, William Patrick: president, chief operating officer, director, Mark IV Industries; president, Mark IV Industries Foundation
Moss, James H.: treasurer, York Federal Savings & Loan Foundation

Mrozek, Ernest J.: executive vice president, chief financial officer, ServiceMaster Co.
Norwood, Ralph M.: treasurer, Polaroid Foundation
Olson, A. Craig: senior vice president finance, chief financial officer, Albertson's Inc.
Omachinski, David L.: chief financial officer, treasurer, vice president, Oshkosh B'Gosh, Inc.
Overbaugh, Joseph C.: director, AMP Foundation
Powell, Sandra Theresa: trustee, Potlatch Foundation II
Prosser, John Warren, Jr.: treasurer, director, Jacobs Engineering Foundation; senior vice president finance & administration, treasurer, Jacobs Engineering Group
Robinson, Edward Joseph: president, chief operating officer, director, Avon Products, Inc.
Rosilier, Glenn D.: executive vice president, chief financial officer, Central & South West Services
Roth, Michael I.: chairman, chief executive officer, director, MONY Group (The); director, MONY Life Insurance of New York (The)
Roub, Bryan Roger: trustee, Harris Foundation
Russell, Frank Eli: president, Central Newspapers Foundation; chairman, Central Newspapers, Inc.
Scarbrough, Arlan Earl: vice president financial, Gulf Power Co.; trustee, Gulf Power Foundation
Schaeffer, Wayne G.: community president, Citizens Bank-Flint
Schaffer, Donald J.: member contributions committee, GATX Corp.
Schara, Charles Gerard: treasurer, GEICO Corp.; assistant treasurer, director, GEICO Philanthropic Foundation
Schiro, James J.: chairman, senior partner, PricewaterhouseCoopers
Schoenholz, David A.: executive vice president, chief financial officer, Household International Inc.
Sopranos, Orpheus Javaras: corporate vice president, Amsted Industries Inc.
Sparks, Walter Alvon, Jr.: director, GEICO Philanthropic Foundation
Springer, Denis E.: senior vice president, chief financial officer, Burlington Northern Santa Fe Corp.; director, Burlington Northern Santa Fe Foundation
Stephan, Richard C.: vice president, controller, director, Viad Corp. Fund
Strandjord, Mary Jeannine: director, Sprint Foundation
Sweeney, John J., III: vice president, CertainTeed Corp.
Tarola, Robert M.: senior vice president, chief financial officer, Grace & Co. (W.R.)
Trask, Robert B.: clerk; president, chief operating officer, director, Country Curtains, Inc.; clerk, trustee, High Meadow Foundation
Tumminello, Stephen C.: president, chief executive officer, director, Philips Electronics North America Corp.
Upbin, Hal Jay: president, chief executive officer, director, Kellwood Co.
VanderRoest, Stan: trustee, treasurer, Gerber Foundation; vice president, comptroller, controller, Gerber Products Co.
Wellman, Thomas A.: controller, assistant treasurer, Alexander & Baldwin, Inc.
Winger, Charles Joseph (Chuck): vice president, chief financial officer, Cinergy Corp.

American Institute Chartered Property & Casualty Underwriters

Brown, Joseph Warner, Jr.: chairman, chief executive officer, MBIA Inc.

American Institute Chemical Engineers

Hemminghaus, Roger Roy: chairman, director, Ultramar Diamond Shamrock Corp.
Hill, George Richard: president, trustee, Lubrizol Foundation (The)
LaMantia, Charles Robert: president, chief executive officer, director, Little, Inc. (Arthur D.)
Lovett, John Robert: director, Air Products Foundation
Pollock, E. Kears: director, PPG Industries Foundation; executive vice president, PPG Industries, Inc.
Stewart, S. Jay: chairman, chief executive officer, director, Morton International Inc.
White, Gerald Andrew: director, Air Products Foundation

American Institute Chemists

Hill, George Richard: president, trustee, Lubrizol Foundation (The)

American Institute Industrial Engineer

Neel, Curtis Dean, Jr.: trustee, Eckerd Corp. Foundation

American Institute Management

Cloud, Bruce Benjamin, Sr.: vice chairman, director, Zachry Co. (H.B.)

American Institute Mining & Metallurgical Engineers

Iverson, Francis Kenneth: chairman, director, Nucor Corp.; director, Nucor Foundation

American Institute Mining Engineers

Whisler, J. Steven: chairman, president, chief executive officer, Phelps Dodge Corp.

American Institute Mining Metallurgical Petroleum Engineers

Muth, Robert James: president, director, ASARCO Foundation

American Institute Planners

Meyerson, Martin: director, Panasonic Foundation

American Institute Property & Liability Underwriters

Buxton, Charles Ingraham, II: chairman, Federated Mutual Insurance Co.; president, Federated Mutual Insurance Foundation
Countryman, Gary Lee: chairman, Liberty Mutual Insurance Group
Rust, Edward Barry, Jr.: chairman, president, director, State Farm Companies Foundation; chairman, president, chief executive officer, director, State Farm Mutual Automobile Insurance Co.

American Institute Steel Construction

Stupp, Robert P.: president, director, Stupp Brothers Bridge & Iron Co.; trustee, Stupp Brothers Bridge & Iron Co. Foundation

American Institute of CPA's

Carpenter, Marshall L.: vice president, chief financial officer, MTS Systems Corp.
Hanway, H. Edward: president, chief executive officer, CIGNA Corp.
Jobe, Warren Yancey: executive vice president, Georgia Power Co.; president, director, Georgia Power Foundation

American Institute of Certified Public Accountant

Schafer, Glenn Stanley: president, director, Pacific Mutual Life Insurance Co.

American Insurance Association

Ayer, Ramani: chairman, president, chief executive officer, Hartford (The)
Leatherdale, Douglas West: chairman, chief executive officer, president, Saint Paul Companies Inc.
O'Hare, Dean Raymond: chairman, Chubb Corp.

American Intellectual Property Law Association

Pollock, E. Kears: director, PPG Industries Foundation; executive vice president, PPG Industries, Inc.

American Irish Foundation

O'Reilly, F. Anthony John: chairman, trustee, Heinz Co. Foundation (H.J.); chairman, director, Heinz Co. (H.J.)

American Iron & Steel Engineers

Penny, Roger Pratt: president, chief operating officer, director, Bethlehem Steel Corp.

American Iron & Steel Institute

Barnette, Curtis Handley: chairman, chief executive officer, director, Bethlehem Steel Corp.
Bezik, Cynthia B.: senior vice president, finance, Cleveland-Cliffs, Inc.
Brinzo, John S.: trustee, Cleveland-Cliffs Foundation (The); president, chief executive officer, Cleveland-Cliffs, Inc.
Graham, Thomas Carlisle: trustee, AK Steel Foundation
Lichtenberger, Horst William: chairman, chief executive officer, Praxair
Millenbruch, Gary Lee: executive vice president, chief financial officer, director, trustee, Bethlehem Steel Corp.
Penny, Roger Pratt: president, chief operating officer, director, Bethlehem Steel Corp.
Wareham, James Lyman: president, AK Steel Corp.

American Jewish Committee

Bronfman, Edgar Miles: chairman, trustee, Bronfman Foundation/Joseph E. Seagram & Sons, Inc. Fund (Samuel); chairman, Seagram & Sons, Inc. (Joseph E.)
Harris, Irving Brooks: chairman executive committee, director, Pittway Corp.; chairman, director, Pittway Corp. Charitable Foundation
Loeb, Jerome Thomas: chairman, director, May Department Stores Co.; president, director, May Department Stores Computer Foundation (The)
Margolin, Abraham E.: director, Tension Envelope Foundation

American Jewish Congress

Bronfman, Edgar Miles: chairman, trustee, Bronfman Foundation/Joseph E. Seagram & Sons, Inc. Fund (Samuel); chairman, Seagram & Sons, Inc. (Joseph E.)
Margolin, Abraham E.: director, Tension Envelope Foundation

American Judicature Society

Barnes, Wallace W.: director, Barnes Group Foundation Inc.
Barnette, Curtis Handley: chairman, chief executive officer, director, Bethlehem Steel Corp.
Johnson, Murray Lloyd, Jr.: secretary, trustee, Zachry Foundation (The)
Margolin, Abraham E.: director, Tension Envelope Foundation

Matthews, Clark J., II: president, chief executive officer, director, 7-Eleven, Inc.
Purvis, George Frank, Jr.: chairman, president, chief executive officer, director, Pan-American Life Insurance Co.
Redstone, Sumner Murray: chairman, Viacom Inc.
Walsh, Michael J.: vice president, CertainTeed Corp.

American Kentucky Bankers Association

Hower, Frank Beard, Jr.: vice chairman, Anthem Foundation, Inc.

American Law Institute

Barnette, Curtis Handley: chairman, chief executive officer, director, Bethlehem Steel Corp.
Bruce, Peter Wayne: director, Badger Meter Foundation
Ehrlich, M. Gordon: trustee, Orchard Foundation
Gallagher, Richard S.: director, Badger Meter Foundation
Gorelick, Jamie Shona: vice chairman, Fannie Mae
Heineman, Benjamin Walter, Jr.: director, GE Fund
Karmel, Roberta S.: trustee, Kemper Foundation (James S.); partner, Kemper National Insurance Companies
Lipton, Martin: partner, Wachtell, Lipton, Rosen & Katz; president, Wachtell, Lipton, Rosen & Katz Foundation
McGuinn, Martin Gregory: chairman, chief executive officer, Mellon Financial Corp.
Melican, James Patrick, Jr.: executive vice president legal & external affairs, International Paper Co.; director, International Paper Co. Foundation
Newlin, William Rankin: trustee, Kennametal Foundation
Owens, Jack Byron: executive vice president, general counsel, Gallo Winery, Inc. (E&J)

American Legion

Brademas, John: chairman, Texaco Foundation
Calise, Nicholas James: vice president, associate general counsel, secretary, BFGoodrich Co.; secretary, Goodrich Foundation, Inc. (B.F.)
Kalainov, Sam Charles: chairman, president, chief executive officer, AmerUS Group
Keyser, F. Ray, Jr.: chairman, director, Central Vermont Public Service Corp.

American Life Convention

Purvis, George Frank, Jr.: chairman, president, chief executive officer, director, Pan-American Life Insurance Co.

American Management Association

Bettacchi, Robert J.: senior vice president, Grace & Co. (W.R.)
Blount, Winton Malcolm, Jr.: chairman, Blount International, Inc.
Borman, Marlene: vice president, director, Borman Fund (The)
Cloud, Bruce Benjamin, Sr.: vice chairman, director, Zachry Co. (H.B.)
Elliott, R. Keith: chief executive officer, president, Hercules Inc.
Gierer, Vincent A., Jr.: chairman, president, chief executive officer, director, UST Inc.
Hinshaw, Juanita H.: vice president, treasurer, Monsanto Co.; treasurer, Monsanto Fund
Holmes, David Richard: chief executive officer, chief operating officer, director, Reynolds & Reynolds Co.
Johnson, Kenneth James: vice president, controller, director, Motorola Inc.
Moritz, Charles Worthington: chairman, director, Dun & Bradstreet Corp.
Rinehart, Charles Robert: chairman, chief executive officer, director, Washington Mutual, Inc.
Skinner, Claire Corson: chairman, chief executive officer, Coachmen Industries, Inc.
Standish, J. Spencer: chairman, director, Albany International Corp.
Teets, John William: president, chief executive officer, director, Viad Corp. Fund
Voet, Paul C.: trustee, Chemed Foundation
Weiser, Irving: chairman, president, chief executive officer, Dain Bosworth Inc.
Zacks, Gordon Benjamin: chairman, president, chief executive officer, director, Barry Corp. (R.G.); president, Barry Foundation

American Marketing Association

Nakagawa, Jean H.: vice president, director, Servco Foundation
Paton, Leland B.: president capital marketings, director, member executive committee, Prudential Securities Inc.
Rosenzweig, Richard Stuart: executive vice president, director, Playboy Enterprises Inc.
Simpson, Andrea Lynn: president
Sutton, Howard: trustee, Steelcase Foundation
Wentworth, Jack Roberts, Ph.D.: director, Habig Foundation

American Mathematical Society

Davis, Ruth Margaret: trustee, Air Products Foundation

American Medical Association

Elam, Lloyd Charles, MD: trustee, Merck Co. Foundation
Lempka, Arnold W., MD: chairman, director, Physicians Mutual Insurance Co.; director, Physicians Mutual Insurance Co. Foundation
Lyon, Wayne Barton: president, chief operating officer, director, Masco Corp.
Nelson, Glen David, MD: vice chairman, Medtronic, Inc.

American Morgan Horse Association

Kohler, Herbert Vollrath, Jr.: chairman, president, director, Kohler Co.

American Museum Britain

Forbes, Christopher 'Kip': vice president, Forbes Foundation; vice chairman, corporate secretary, director, Forbes Inc.

American Museum Natural History

Heimbold, Charles Andreas, Jr.: chairman, president, chief executive officer, Bristol-Myers Squibb Co.
Johnson, Samuel Curtis: chairman, director, president, Johnson & Son (S.C.); chairman, trustee, Johnson Wax Fund (S.C.)
Koch, David Hamilton: director, Koch Foundation, Inc. (Fred C. and Mary R.)
Reed, John Shepard: co-chairman, Citibank Corp.
Ross, Arthur: senior vice president, Central National-Gottesman; director, Central National-Gottesman Foundation

American Museum Natural History & Planetarium Authority

Graves, Earl Gilbert: director, Aetna Foundation

American Music Theatre Festival

Landin, Thomas Milton: vice president, director, CertainTeed Corp.; vice president, Norton Co. Foundation

American Naturalists Society

Ripley, Sidney Dillon, II: director emeritus, Hitachi Foundation

American Newspaper Editors

Klugman, Craig: editor, Journal-Gazette Co.

American Newspaper Publishers Association

Block, William: vice president, trustee, Blade Foundation; chairman, director, Toledo Blade Co.
Connor, Richard L.: president, publisher, Fort Worth Star-Telegram Inc.
Morris, William Shivers, III: founder, chairman, chief executive officer, director, Morris Communications Corp.; trustee, Stauffer Communications Foundation
Ottaway, James Haller, Jr.: senior vice president, director, Dow Jones & Co., Inc.; member advisory committee, Dow Jones Foundation
Wright, Donald Franklin: director, Times Mirror Foundation

American Newspaper Publishers Association Foundation

Pulliam, Eugene Smith: vice president, director, Central Newspapers Foundation

American Nuclear Energy Council

McNeill, Corbin Asahel, Jr.: president, chief executive officer, director, chairman, PECO Energy Co.

American Nuclear Society

Joos, David W.: president, chief executive officer electric, executive vice president, Consumers Energy Co.
McNeill, Corbin Asahel, Jr.: president, chief executive officer, director, chairman, PECO Energy Co.

American Ornithologists Union

Ripley, Sidney Dillon, II: director emeritus, Hitachi Foundation

American Orthopsychiatric Association

Harris, Irving Brooks: chairman executive committee, director, Pittway Corp.; chairman, director, Pittway Corp. Charitable Foundation

American Paper Institute

Mead, George Wilson, II: president, director, Consolidated Papers Foundation, Inc.; chairman, director, Consolidated Papers, Inc.

American Petroleum Institute

Bailey, Keith E.: chairman, president, director, chief executive officer, Texas Gas Transmission Corp.; president, director, Williams Companies Foundation (The)
Bijur, Peter I.: chairman, chief executive officer, Texaco Inc.
Brinegar, Claude Stout: trustee, Unocal Foundation
Brothers, John Alfred 'Fred': trustee, Ashland Inc. Foundation
Campbell, Robert Henderson: chairman, chief executive officer, Sunoco Inc.
Carl, John L.: executive vice president, chief financial officer, BP Amoco Corp.; director, BP Amoco Foundation
Carroll, Philip Joseph: chairman, chief executive officer, Fluor Corp.; chairman, trustee, Fluor Foundation

Chellgren, Paul Wilbur: chief executive officer, chairman, director, Ashland, Inc.; member, Ashland Inc. Foundation

Dunham, Archie W.: president, chief executive officer, Conoco, Inc.

Elkins, Lloyd Edwin, Junior: vice president, Chevron Corp.

Fuller, Harry Laurance: co-chairman, director, BP Amoco Corp.

Greene, John Frederick: executive vice president exploration & production, director, Louisiana Land & Exploration Co.

Haddock, Ronald Wayne: president, chief executive officer, director, FINA; president, FINA Foundation

Hemminghaus, Roger Roy: chairman, director, Ultramar Diamond Shamrock Corp.

Hunt, Ray Lee: chairman, chief executive officer, director, Hunt Oil Co.

Lowrie, William G.: president, deputy chief executive officer, director, BP Amoco Corp.

Marsh, R. Bruce: general tax counsel, Chevron Corp.

McDaniel, Tom J.: vice chairman, director, Kerr-McGee Corp.

McKee, Robert E., III: executive vice president corporate strategy & development, du Pont de Nemours & Co. (E.I.)

Mulva, James J.: president, chief operating officer, director, Phillips Petroleum Co.

Nowell, Tommy Lynn: vice president finance, controller, Occidental Oil and Gas; treasurer, Occidental Oil and Gas Foundation

O'Reilly, David J.: chairman, chief executive officer, Chevron Corp.

Pate, James Leonard: chairman, chief executive officer, director, Pennzoil-Quaker State Co.

Raymond, Lee R.: chairman, president, chief executive officer, Exxon Mobil Corp.

Shourd, Roy Ray: president, Schlumberger Foundation

American Pharmaceutical Association

Graham, William B.: chairman, director, Baxter Allegiance Foundation; chairman emeritus, Baxter International Inc.

American Philatelic Society

Doucette, James Willard: vice president, treasurer, Humana Foundation

American Philosophical Association

Connor, Walter Robert: director, Glaxo Wellcome Foundation

American Philosophical Society

Alberts, Bruce Michael, PhD: director, Genentech Foundation for Biomedical Sciences

Connor, Walter Robert: director, Glaxo Wellcome Foundation

Meyerson, Martin: director, Panasonic Foundation

Miller, Joseph Irwin: director associate, Cummins Engine Co., Inc.; director, Cummins Engine Foundation

Ripley, Sidney Dillon, II: director emeritus, Hitachi Foundation

Vagelos, Pindaros Roy: trustee, Prudential Insurance Co. of America

American Physics Society

Moore, Gordon E., PhD: cofounder, chairman emeritus, director, Intel Corp.; trustee, Intel Foundation

American Plastics Council

Deavenport, Earnest W., Jr.: chairman, chief executive officer, director, Eastman Chemical Co.

Haddock, Ronald Wayne: president, chief executive officer, director, FINA; president, FINA Foundation

Joyce, William H.: chairman, president, chief executive officer, chief operating officer, Union Carbide Corp.

American Political Science Association

Kissinger, Henry Alfred: director, CBS Foundation

American Portland Cement Alliance

Brozyna, Jeffry H.: trustee

American Portland Cement Association

Kline, Richard: president, Lehigh Portland Cement Co.

American Press Institute

Copley, Helen K.: chairman, trustee, Copley Foundation (James S.); chairman, director, senior management board, Copley Press, Inc.

American Production & Inventory Control Society

Keyser, Richard Lee: chairman, chief executive officer, president, Grainger, Inc. (W.W.)

American Promise - Alliance for Youth

Gorelick, Jamie Shona: vice chairman, Fannie Mae

American Psychiatric Association

Elam, Lloyd Charles, MD: trustee, Merck Co. Foundation

American Psychological Society

Levinson, Donald M.: director, CIGNA Corp.

American Public Radio Minneapolis

Miller, William Irwin: director, Cummins Engine Foundation

American Public Works Association

Thies, Richard Henry: assistant treasurer, Madison Gas & Electric Foundation

American Quarter Horse Association

Carey, Kathryn Ann: foundation manager, American Honda Foundation

American Red Cross

Moffitt, Donald Eugene: chairman, director, CNF Transportation, Inc.

Nakagawa, Jean H.: vice president, director, Servco Foundation

Wolff, Jesse David: treasurer, director, Weil, Gotshal & Manges Foundation

American Red Cross Greater New York City

Schwarz, H. Marshall: chairman, chief executive officer, United States Trust Co. of New York

American Rheumatism Association

Harris, Edward D., Jr.: director, Genentech Foundation for Biomedical Sciences

American Rose Society

Hewitt, James Watt: vice president, treasurer, Abel Foundation

American Royal Association

Hall, Donald Joyce: chairman board, director, Hallmark Cards Inc.; chairman, Hallmark Corporate Foundation

Margolin, Abraham E.: director, Tension Envelope Foundation

American School Classical Studies Athens

Ottaway, James Haller, Jr.: senior vice president, director, Dow Jones & Co., Inc.; member advisory committee, Dow Jones Foundation

American School Foodsvc Association Foundation

Stewart, Joseph Melvin: senior vice president corporate affairs, Kellogg Co.; trustee, Kellogg Co. Twenty-Five Year Employees' Fund Inc.

American Schools Oriental Research

Meyerson, Martin: director, Panasonic Foundation

American Service Metals

Hatsopoulos, George Nicholas: founder, chairman, chief executive officer, director, Thermo Electron Corp.; committee member, Thermo Electron Foundation

American Society Biochemistry & Molecular Biology

Alberts, Bruce Michael, PhD: director, Genentech Foundation for Biomedical Sciences

American Society Biological Chemists

Vagelos, Pindaros Roy: trustee, Prudential Insurance Co. of America

American Society CPAs

Hegel, Garrett R.: chief financial officer, Compass Bank; president, Compass Bank Foundation

American Society Cell Biology

Alberts, Bruce Michael, PhD: director, Genentech Foundation for Biomedical Sciences

American Society Certified Life Underwriters

Oakley, Robert Alan: executive vice president, chief financial officer, Nationwide Insurance Enterprise Foundation

American Society Chartered Life Underwriters

Dubes, Michael: membership, ReliaStar Foundation

American Society Civil Engineers

Stupp, Robert P.: president, director, Stupp Brothers Bridge & Iron Co.; trustee, Stupp Brothers Bridge & Iron Co. Foundation

American Society Clinical Pharmacology & Therapeutics

Gussin, Robert Zalmon, PhD: vice president science & technology, Johnson & Johnson; member corporate contributions committee, Johnson & Johnson Family of Companies Contribution Fund

American Society Clubs

Wheeler, Thomas Beardsley: chairman, chief executive officer, Massachusetts Mutual Life Insurance Co.

American Society Corporate Executives

Davis, Erroll Brown, Jr.: president, chief executive officer, director, Wisconsin Power & Light Co.

Goode, David Ronald: chairman, president, chief executive officer, director, Norfolk Southern Corp.

Mead, Dana George: chairman, chief executive officer, director, Tenneco Automotive

Pepper, John E., Jr.: chairman executive committee, Procter & Gamble Co.

Smith, John Francis, Jr.: chairman, General Motors Corp.

American Society Engineering

Raymond, Lee R.: chairman, president, chief executive officer, Exxon Mobil Corp.

American Society Mechanical Engineers

Blankley, Walter Elwood: president, director, AMETEK Foundation; chairman, director, AMETEK, Inc.

Hatsopoulos, George Nicholas: founder, chairman, chief executive officer, director, Thermo Electron Corp.; committee member, Thermo Electron Foundation

Joos, David W.: president, chief executive officer electric, executive vice president, Consumers Energy Co.

Muehlbauer, James Herman: vice president, director, Koch Foundation

American Society Metals

Griffin, Donald Wayne: chairman, president, chief executive officer, director, Olin Corp.; trustee, Olin Corp. Charitable Trust

Iverson, Francis Kenneth: chairman, director, Nucor Corp.; director, Nucor Foundation

American Society Microbiology

Alberts, Bruce Michael, PhD: director, Genentech Foundation for Biomedical Sciences

Swanson, Robert A.: director, Genentech Foundation for Biomedical Sciences

American Society Nephrology

Gussin, Robert Zalmon, PhD: vice president science & technology, Johnson & Johnson; member corporate contributions committee, Johnson & Johnson Family of Companies Contribution Fund

American Society Newspaper Editors

Block, John Robinson: vice president, trustee, Blade Foundation

Block, William: vice president, trustee, Blade Foundation; chairman, director, Toledo Blade Co.

Burleigh, William Robert: president, chief executive officer, director, Scripps Co. (E.W.); member, Scripps Howard Foundation

Connor, Richard L.: president, publisher, Fort Worth Star-Telegram Inc.

Graham, Katharine Meyer: chairman executive committee, director, The Washington Post

Knue, Paul Frederick: trustee, Scripps Howard Foundation

Osborne, Burl: president publishing division, director, Belo Corp. (A.H.); president, trustee, Belo Corp. Foundation (A.H.)

Ottaway, James Haller, Jr.: senior vice president, director, Dow Jones & Co., Inc.; member advisory committee, Dow Jones Foundation

Pulliam, Eugene Smith: vice president, director, Central Newspapers Foundation

Thomasson, Dan King: vice president, trustee, Scripps Howard Foundation

American Society Pharmacology & Experimental Therapeutics

Gussin, Robert Zalmon, PhD: vice president science & technology, Johnson & Johnson; member corporate contributions committee, Johnson & Johnson Family of Companies Contribution Fund

American Society Royal Botanical Garden

Raymond, Lee R.: chairman, president, chief executive officer, Exxon Mobil Corp.

American Society Testing & Materials

Stupp, Robert P.: president, director, Stupp Brothers Bridge & Iron Co.; trustee, Stupp Brothers Bridge & Iron Co. Foundation

American Society Women Accountants

Bezik, Cynthia B.: senior vice president, finance, Cleveland-Cliffs, Inc.

American Society of Corporate Secretaries

Agnich, Richard John: director, Texas Instruments Foundation; senior vice president, secretary, general counsel, Texas Instruments Inc.

Ballantyne, Richard Lee: vice president, general counsel, secretary, Harris Corp.; secretary, treasurer, Harris Foundation

Barnette, Curtis Handley: chairman, chief executive officer, director, Bethlehem Steel Corp.

Beck, Edward W.: senior vice president, general counsel, secretary, director, Shaklee Corp.

Brennan, Alice C.: vice president, secretary, Bristol-Myers Squibb Co.; secretary, Bristol-Myers Squibb Foundation Inc.

Brown, JoBeth Goode: trustee, Anheuser-Busch Companies, Inc.

Buchanan, William Hobart, Jr.: assistant secretary, Dun & Bradstreet Corp. Foundation, Inc.

Calise, Nicholas James: vice president, associate general counsel, secretary, BFGoodrich Co.; secretary, Goodrich Foundation, Inc. (B.F.)

Canning, John Beckman: secretary, Rayonier Foundation

Causey, John Paul, Jr.: senior vice president, secretary, general counsel, Chesapeake Corp.; chairman, trustee, Chesapeake Corp. Foundation

Clark, Richard McCourt: senior vice president, general counsel, secretary, Kellogg Co.; vice president, trustee, Kellogg Co. Twenty-Five Year Employees' Fund Inc.

Conklin, Thomas J.: senior vice president, secretary, MONY Group (The); director, MONY Life Insurance of New York (The)

Crook, Donald Martin: secretary, Kimberly-Clark Foundation

Dabney, Donna C.: secretary, Reynolds Metals Co. Foundation

Dubin, Stephen Victor: vice president, secretary, Farber Foundation

Emerson, Frederick George: vice president, secretary, director, Viad Corp. Fund

Gallagher, Terence Joseph: secretary, director, Pfizer Foundation

Gherlein, Gerald Lee: member contributions committee, Eaton Charitable Fund

Gross, Murray: trustee, PerkinElmer Foundation; senior vice president, general counsel, clerk, PerkinElmer, Inc.

Herron, James Michael: secretary, director, Ryder System Charitable Foundation

Kirchhof, Anton Conrad: corporate secretary, general counsel, Louisiana-Pacific Corp.; secretary, Louisiana-Pacific Foundation

Levy, David: trustee, National Service Foundation

Lippes, Gerald Sanford: secretary, Mark IV Industries Foundation

Martin, Dezora M.: corporate secretary, Norfolk Southern Corp.; secretary, Norfolk Southern Foundation

McDade, Sandy D.: secretary, Weyerhaeuser Co.; assistant secretary legal affairs, Weyerhaeuser Co. Foundation

McGuinn, Martin Gregory: chairman, chief executive officer, Mellon Financial Corp.

McInnes, Duncan Joseph: executive vice president administration, chief administrative officer, Blount International, Inc.

Merdek, Andrew Austin: vice president legal affairs, secretary, Cox Enterprises Inc.; secretary, Cox Foundation (James M.)

Merrell, Pamela K.: secretary, Montana Power Co.; vice president, secretary, Montana Power Foundation

Moore, William B.: senior vice president, secretary, general counsel, Whitman Corp.; secretary, Whitman Corp. Foundation

Morie, G. Glen: secretary, treasurer, PACCAR Foundation

Nalbach, Kay C.: president, Hartmarx Charitable Foundation

Neville, James Morton: member board control, Ralston Purina Trust Fund

Phillips, Rosalind Ann: secretary, GEICO Philanthropic Foundation

Pyke, John Secrest, Jr.: president, trustee, Hanna Co. Foundation (M.A.); vice president, secretary, general counsel, Hanna Co. (M.A.)

Siegel, Samuel: vice chairman, secretary, treasurer, chief financial officer, director, Nucor Corp.; director, Nucor Foundation

Sissel, George A.: chairman, president, chief executive officer, director, Ball Corp.

Strickland, Carol A.: chairman corporate contributions committee, U.S. Trust Corp. Foundation

Walton, Jon David: trustee, Allegheny Technologies Inc. Charitable Trust

Ward, Carol J.: secretary, compliance officer, CIGNA Corp.; secretary, CIGNA Foundation

Wolff, Herbert Eric: secretary, director, First Hawaiian Foundation

American Society of Planning Officials

Meyerson, Martin: director, Panasonic Foundation

American Statistical Association

Bush, Norman: vice president, Fort James Corp.

American Swiss Foundation

Ball, James Herington: senior vice president, general counsel, director, Nestle U.S.A. Inc.

American Technician Society

Bronfman, Edgar Miles: chairman, trustee, Bronfman Foundation/Joseph E. Seagram & Sons, Inc. Fund (Samuel); chairman, Seagram & Sons, Inc. (Joseph E.)

American Textile Manufacturer Association

Bakane, John L.: president, chief executive officer, director, Cone Mills Corp.

American Textile Manufacturer Institute

Milliken, Roger: chairman, chief executive officer, Milliken & Co.; member advisory committee, Milliken Foundation

Rockefeller, Frederic Lincoln: trustee, Cranston Foundation

American Trial Lawyers Association

Walsh, Michael J.: vice president, CertainTeed Corp.

American Trucking Association

Herron, James Michael: secretary, director, Ryder

System Charitable Foundation

American Women in Radio & Television

Blanke, Gail Ann: vice president, Avon Products Foundation, Inc.

American Women's Economic Development Corp.

Clemente, Constantine Louis: chairman, Pfizer Foundation; executive vice president corporate affairs, secretary, corporate counsel, Pfizer Inc.

American Youth Foundation

Maritz, William Edward: chairman, chief executive officer, president, Maritz Inc.

Americas Society

Rhodes, William Reginald: vice chairman, Citibank Corp.

Americas Utility Fund

Cutchins, Clifford Armstrong, IV: president, Fort James Corp.; chairman, director, Fort James Foundation (The)

Ams Society

Osborne, Richard de Jongh: director, ASARCO Foundation; chairman, chief executive officer, director, ASARCO Inc.

Ams for the Arts

Polin, Jane Louise: manager, comptroller, GE Fund

Amwell Valley Conservancy

Tobias, Randall L.: chairman emeritus, Lilly & Co. (Eli)

Amyotrophic Lateral Sclerosis Association

Griffith, Alan Richard: vice chairman, Bank of New York Co., Inc.

Phillips, Ellyn C.: executive director, Charlestein Foundation (Julius and Ray)

Ancient Accepted Scottish Rite

Russell, Frank Eli: president, Central Newspapers Foundation; chairman, Central Newspapers, Inc.

Ancient Free Accepted Masons

Stupp, Robert P.: president, director, Stupp Brothers Bridge & Iron Co.; trustee, Stupp Brothers Bridge & Iron Co. Foundation

Ann Arbor Chamber of Commerce

Forsyth, John D.: president, chief executive officer, Blue Cross & Blue Shield of Iowa

Anti-Defamation League B'nai B'rith

Margolin, Abraham E.: director, Tension Envelope Foundation

Resnick, Myron J.: vice president, treasurer, trustee, Allstate Foundation

Arch Funds Inc.

Carr, Cassandra Colvin: director, SBC Foundation

Archdiocese Communications Comm

Shepherd, Kathleen Shearen Maynard: director, Tribune New York Foundation

Archdiocese Saint Louis

McKenna, William John: director, chairman, Kellwood Co.; chairman, president, director, Kellwood Foundation

Arden Hill Hospital Foundation

Ottaway, James Haller, Jr.: senior vice president, director, Dow Jones & Co., Inc.; member advisory committee, Dow Jones Foundation

Arden Theatre Co.

Smith, Raymond W.: chairman, chief executive officer, director, Bell Atlantic Corp.

Area Progress Council

Holmes, David Richard: chief executive officer, chief operating officer, director, Reynolds & Reynolds Co.

Arizona Bar Association

Snell, Richard: chairman, president, chief executive officer, director, Arizona Public Service Co.

Arizona Cities in Schools Inc.

Dewane, John Richard: director, Honeywell Foundation

Arizona State University School Business

Franke, William Augustus: chairman, president, chief executive officer, America West Airlines, Inc.; director, Phelps Dodge Foundation

Arkansas Bar Association

Blair, James Burton: trustee, Tyson Foundation, Inc.

Arnot Art Museum Arts Southern Finger Lakes

Buechner, Thomas Scharman: trustee, Corning Inc. Foundation

Arrowhead Ranch

Lawson, John K.: senior vice president, Deere & Co.; director, Deere Foundation (John)

Art Institute

Martinez, Arthur C.: chairman, chief executive officer, president, Sears, Roebuck and Co.

Art Institute of Chicago

Bryan, John Henry: chairman, Sara Lee Corp.; director, Sara Lee Foundation

Art Lending Library

Redstone, Sumner Murray: chairman, Viacom Inc.

Art Paine Center & Arboretum

Omachinski, David L.: chief financial officer, treasurer, vice president, Oshkosh B'Gosh, Inc.

Arthur Page Society

Hobor, Nancy A.: vice president communications & investor relations, Morton International Inc.

Arthur R Metz Foundation

Getz, Bert A.: chairman, Globe Corp.; president, director, Globe Foundation

Arthur R. Metz Foundation

Getz, Bert A., Jr.: executive vice president, Globe Corp.; vice president, Globe Foundation

Arts & Education Council

Knight, Charles Field: chairman, chief executive officer, Emerson Electric Co.

Arts & Education Council Greater Saint Louis

Bachmann, John W.: managing partner, Jones & Co. (Edward D.); chairman, Jones & Co. Foundation (Edward D.)

Arts Business Council

Thompson, Sheldon Lee: senior vice president, chief administrative officer, Sunoco Inc.

Arts Fund

Bachmann, Richard Arthur: vice president, secretary, treasurer, director, Louisiana Land & Exploration Co. Foundation

Arts Inc. New York

Wehmeier, Helge H.: president, chief executive officer, director, Bayer Corp.

Asbury Theological Seminary

Amos, Paul Shelby: cofounder, chairman, director, AFLAC Inc.

Ashley Hall

Anderson, Ivan Verner, Jr.: president, chief executive officer, Evening Post Publishing Co.; vice president, Post and Courier Foundation

Ingram, Martha R.: chairman, director, Ingram Industries Inc.

Asia Foundation

Wilbur, Brayton, Jr.: president, chief executive officer, Wilbur-Ellis Co. & Connell Brothers Co.; president, Wilbur Foundation (Brayton)

Asia Pacific Economic Council

Dewane, John Richard: director, Honeywell Foundation

Asia Society

Franklin, Barbara Hackman: director, Dow Chemical Co.

Ross, Arthur: senior vice president, Central National-Gottesman; director, Central National-Gottesman Foundation

Aspen Institute

Brademas, John: chairman, Texaco Foundation

Hockaday, Irvine O., Jr.: president, chief executive officer, director, Hallmark Cards Inc.

Kann, Peter Robert: chairman, chief executive officer, publisher, director, Dow Jones & Co., Inc.; member advisory committee, Dow Jones Foundation

Koch, David Hamilton: director, Koch Foundation, Inc. (Fred C. and Mary R.)

Trujillo, Solomon D.: president, US West Foundation; president, chief executive officer, US West, Inc.

Whitwam, David Ray: chairman, president, chief executive officer, director, Whirlpool Corp.

Asphalt Roofing Manufacturing Association

Hilyard, James E.: president, CertainTeed Corp.; director, CertainTeed Corp. Foundation

Associate Churches Owatonna

Buxton, Charles Ingraham, II: chairman, Federated Mutual Insurance Co.; president, Federated Mutual Insurance Foundation

Associate Industry MA

Shanks, David C.: trustee, Little Foundation (Arthur D.); vice president human resources, Little, Inc. (Arthur D.)

Associated Colleges Indiana

Baker, James Kendrick: chairman, director, Arvin

Foundation; vice chairman, director, Arvin Industries, Inc.

Associated Press

Anderson, Ivan Verner, Jr.: president, chief executive officer, Evening Post Publishing Co.; vice president, Post and Courier Foundation

Easterly, David E.: president, chief operating officer, Cox Enterprises Inc.

Associated Press Managing Editors Association

Knue, Paul Frederick: trustee, Scripps Howard Foundation

Associates California Institute Technology

Wright, Donald Franklin: director, Times Mirror Foundation

Association American Medicine Colleges Council Teaching Hospitals

Forsyth, John D.: president, chief executive officer, Blue Cross & Blue Shield of Iowa

Association American RRs

Goode, David Ronald: chairman, president, chief executive officer, director, Norfolk Southern Corp.

Tobias, Steven C.: vice chairman, chief operating officer, Norfolk Southern Corp.; director, Norfolk Southern Foundation

Association American Universities

Forsyth, John D.: president, chief executive officer, Blue Cross & Blue Shield of Iowa

Lyall, Katharine Culbert: trustee, Kemper Foundation (James S.)

Association Asian Studies

Stanley, Peter William: trustee, Hitachi Foundation

Association Bank Holding Companies

McCoy, John Bonnet: president, chief executive officer, Ameritech Corp.

Association Bar City NYK

Kalaher, Richard A.: president, American Standard Foundation; vice president, secretary, general counsel, American Standard Inc.

Association Bar New York City

Buchanan, William Hobart, Jr.: assistant secretary, Dun & Bradstreet Corp. Foundation, Inc.

Burak, Howard Paul: secretary, director, Sony U.S.A. Foundation Inc.

Calise, Nicholas James: vice president, associate general counsel, secretary, BFGoodrich Co.; secretary, Goodrich Foundation, Inc. (B.F.)

Calise, William Joseph, Junior: senior vice president, secretary, general counsel, Rockwell International Corp.

Clark, Richard McCourt: senior vice president, general counsel, secretary, Kellogg Co.; vice president, trustee, Kellogg Co. Twenty-Five Year Employees' Fund Inc.

Cole, Lewis George: director, AMETEK Foundation

Furlaud, Richard Mortimer: interim chief executive officer, International Flavors & Fragrances Inc.

Guedry, James Walter: president, International Paper Co. Foundation

Hammerman, Stephen Lawrence: vice president, trustee, Merrill Lynch & Co. Foundation Inc.; vice chairman, general counsel, Merrill Lynch & Co., Inc.

Heimbold, Charles Andreas, Jr.: chairman, president, chief executive officer, Bristol-Myers Squibb Co.

Herron, James Michael: secretary, director, Ryder System Charitable Foundation

Karmel, Roberta S.: trustee, Kemper Foundation (James S.); partner, Kemper National Insurance Companies

Melican, James Patrick, Jr.: executive vice president legal & external affairs, International Paper Co.; director, International Paper Co. Foundation

Newlin, William Rankin: trustee, Kennametal Foundation

Olschwang, Alan P., Esq.: secretary, Mitsubishi Electric America Foundation

Pyke, John Secrest, Jr.: president, trustee, Hanna Co. Foundation (M.A.); vice president, secretary, general counsel, Hanna Co. (M.A.)

Shapiro, Isaac: chairman, secretary, trustee, Ise Cultural Foundation

Shaw, L. Edward, Jr.: general counsel, Aetna, Inc.; trustee, Chase Manhattan Foundation

Ughetta, William Casper: trustee, Corning Inc. Foundation

Watson, Solomon Brown, IV: vice president, New York Times Co. Foundation

Association Broadcast Executives Texas

Huey, Ward L., Jr.: president broadcast division, vice chairman, director, Belo Corp. (A.H.); vice president, trustee, Belo Corp. Foundation (A.H.)

Association California Insurance Companies

Pike, Robert William: vice president, secretary, Allstate Foundation; senior vice president, secretary, general counsel, director, Allstate Insurance Co.

Rupley, Theodore J.: president, chief executive officer, director, Allmerica Financial Corp.

Association Chartered Accts U.S.

Williams, David R.: trustee, Heinz Co. Foundation (H.J.); executive vice president, director, Heinz Co. (H.J.)

Association Chartered Accts UK

Williams, David R.: trustee, Heinz Co. Foundation (H.J.); executive vice president, director, Heinz Co. (H.J.)

Association Electrical Companies Texas

Brooks, E. Richard 'Dick': chairman, chief executive officer, director, Central & South West Services

Helton, Bill D.: chairman, New Century Energies Foundation

Association Energy Engineers

Moten, John, Junior: vice president community relations, Laclede Gas Co.

Association General Counsel

Barnette, Curtis Handley: chairman, chief executive officer, director, Bethlehem Steel Corp.

Jones, D. Michael: senior vice president, general counsel, Reynolds Metals Co.; vice president, director, Reynolds Metals Co. Foundation

Melican, James Patrick, Jr.: executive vice president legal & external affairs, International Paper Co.; director, International Paper Co. Foundation

Ursu, John Joseph: director, 3M Foundation; general counsel, senior vice president legal affairs, Minnesota Mining & Manufacturing Co.

Association Government Boards, Colleges & Universities

Hassenfeld, Alan Geoffrey: president, Hasbro Charitable Trust Inc.; chairman, chief executive officer, Hasbro, Inc.

Association Grads U.S. Military Academy

Naples, Ronald James: president, chief executive officer, director, Quaker Chemical Corp.

Association Grads W Point

Mead, Dana George: chairman, chief executive officer, director, Tenneco Automotive

Association International Petroleum Negotiators

Jennings, James Burnett: president, Hunt Oil Co.

Association Investment Management & Research

Condon, James Edward: treasurer, Hartmarx Charitable Foundation; vice president, treasurer, Hartmarx Corp.

Doucette, James Willard: vice president, treasurer, Humana Foundation

Glynn, Gary Allen: president, USX Corp.; vice president, USX Foundation, Inc.

Sweeney, John J., III: vice president, CertainTeed Corp.

Association Iron & Steel Engineers

Wareham, James Lyman: president, AK Steel Corp.

Association Life Insurance Council

Hohn, Harry George, Jr.: chairman, director, New York Life Foundation

Purvis, George Frank, Jr.: chairman, president, chief executive officer, director, Pan-American Life Insurance Co.

Resnick, Myron J.: vice president, treasurer, trustee, Allstate Foundation

Association Maximum Service Telecasters

Hubbard, Stanley S.: chairman, president, chief executive officer, Hubbard Broadcasting, Inc.; president, Hubbard Foundation

Association National Advertisers

Sutton, Howard: trustee, Steelcase Foundation

Wehling, Robert Louis: global marketing, government relations officer, Procter & Gamble Co.; president, trustee, Procter & Gamble Fund

Association Naval Aviation

Leonis, John Michael: chairman, director, Litton Industries, Inc.

Schievelbein, Thomas C.: executive vice president, Newport News Shipbuilding

Association Oil Pipelines

Bailey, Keith E.: chairman, president, director, chief executive officer, Texas Gas Transmission Corp.; president, director, Williams Companies Foundation (The)

Association Oilwell Drilling Contractors

Bradford, William Edward: chairman, director, Halliburton Co.

Association Professional Engineers

Light, Walter Frederick: trustee, Air Products Foundation

Association Professional Engineers Ontario

Roth, John: president, chief executive officer, chief operating officer, director, Nortel

Association Reserve City Bankers

Allbritton, Joe Lewis: chairman, chief executive officer, Riggs Bank NA

Glaser, Gary A.: president, chief executive officer, National City Bank of Columbus

Hower, Frank Beard, Jr.: vice chairman, Anthem Foundation, Inc.

Robinson, E. B., Jr.: chairman, chief executive officer, director, Deposit Guaranty National Bank

Wobst, Frank: chairman, chief executive officer, director, Huntington Bancshares Inc.

Association Texas Colleges Universitys

Pierre, Percy A.: trustee, Hitachi Foundation

Association U.S. Army

Dewane, John Richard: director, Honeywell Foundation

Griffin, Donald Wayne: chairman, president, chief executive officer, director, Olin Corp.; trustee, Olin Corp. Charitable Trust

Kresa, Kent: chairman, president, chief executive officer, director, Northrop Grumman Corp.

Leonis, John Michael: chairman, director, Litton Industries, Inc.

Wolff, Herbert Eric: secretary, director, First Hawaiian Foundation

Association for Corporate Growth

Shiely, John Stephen: president, chief operating officer, director, Briggs & Stratton Corp.; vice president, director, Briggs & Stratton Corp. Foundation

d'Alessio, Jon W.: trustee, McKesson Foundation

Association of Corporate Counsel

Chapple, Thomas Leslie: senior vice president, general counsel, secretary, Gannett Co., Inc.; secretary, Gannett Foundation

Association of Edison Illuminating Companies

Davis, Erroll Brown, Jr.: president, chief executive officer, director, Wisconsin Power & Light Co.

Davis, William E.: chairman, chief executive officer, Niagara Mohawk Holdings Inc.

Ferland, E. James: chairman, president, chief executive officer, Public Service Electric & Gas Co.

Hock, Delwin D.: chairman, New Century Energies

Holland, Willard R.: chairman, chief executive officer, FirstEnergy Corp.

Mueller, Charles William: chairman, president, chief executive officer, Ameren Corp.; trustee, Ameren Corp. Charitable Trust

Association of Iron & Mettallurgical Engineers

Wareham, James Lyman: president, AK Steel Corp.

Athens College

Connor, Walter Robert: director, Glaxo Wellcome Foundation

Athens College (Greece)

Brademas, John: chairman, Texaco Foundation

Atlanta Action Forum

Correll, Alston Dayton 'Pete', Jr.: chairman, president, chief executive officer, director, Georgia-Pacific Corp.; director, Georgia-Pacific Foundation

Atlanta Arts Alliance

Chambers, Anne Cox: chairman, trustee, Cox Foundation (James M.)

Atlanta Bar Association

Harkey, Robert Shelton: trustee, Delta Air Lines Foundation; senior vice president, general counsel, secretary, Delta Air Lines, Inc.

Sharpe, Robert Francis, Jr.: senior vice president public affairs, general counsel, PepsiCo, Inc.

Atlanta Chamber of Commerce

Correll, Alston Dayton 'Pete', Jr.: chairman, president, chief executive officer, director, Georgia-Pacific Corp.; director, Georgia-Pacific Foundation

Mullin, Leo Francis: chairman, president, chief executive officer, Delta Air Lines, Inc.

Atlanta Opera

Escarra, Vicki: executive vice president customer service, Delta Air Lines, Inc.

Atlanta Symphony Orchestra

Correll, Alston Dayton 'Pete', Jr.: chairman, president, chief executive officer, director, Georgia-Pacific Corp.; director, Georgia-Pacific Foundation

Atlantic Council U.S.

Herres, Robert T.: chairman, chief executive officer, United Services Automobile Association

Auburn-Cord-Duesenberg Museum

Adderley, Terence E.: chairman, president, chief executive officer, director, Kelly Services; president, director, Kelly Services Foundation

Auditorium Theatre Council

Gidwitz, Gerald S.: chairman, Curtis Industries, Inc. (Helene)

Audubon Institute Aquarium Americas

Bachmann, Richard Arthur: vice president, secretary, treasurer, director, Louisiana Land & Exploration Co. Foundation

Audubon Society

Ackerman, Philip Charles: senior vice president, director, National Fuel Gas Distribution Corp.

Manigault, Peter: chairman, Evening Post Publishing Co.; president, Post and Courier Foundation

Augusta College Foundation

Morris, William Shivers, III: founder, chairman, chief executive officer, director, Morris Communications Corp.; trustee, Stauffer Communications Foundation

Augustana College

Carver, Martin Gregory: chairman, president, chief executive officer, Bandag, Inc.

Aurora University

Resnick, Myron J.: vice president, treasurer, trustee, Allstate Foundation

Austin College

Agnich, Richard John: director, Texas Instruments Foundation; senior vice president, secretary, general counsel, Texas Instruments Inc.

Grum, Clifford J.: director, Temple-Inland Foundation; director, chairman, chief executive officer, Temple-Inland Inc.

Authors Guild

Hotchner, Aaron Edward: vice president, director, executive, Newman's Own Foundation; vice president, treasurer, Newman's Own Inc.

Authors Guild Foundation

Hotchner, Aaron Edward: vice president, director, executive, Newman's Own Foundation; vice president, treasurer, Newman's Own Inc.

Automobile Club Southern California

Miller, Donn Biddle: president, chief executive officer, Pacific Mutual Life Insurance Co.

Automotive Original Equipment Manufacturers Association

Magliochetti, Joseph M.: president, chief executive officer, director, Dana Corp.; president, director, Dana Corp. Foundation

Automotive Safety Foundation

Moffitt, Donald Eugene: chairman, director, CNF Transportation, Inc.

Automotive Service Indiana Association

Magliochetti, Joseph M.: president, chief executive officer, director, Dana Corp.; president, director, Dana Corp. Foundation

AvMed

Goode, R. Ray: director, Ryder System Charitable Foundation

Aviation Hall of Fame

Kaman, Charles Huron: chairman, president, chief executive officer, director, Kaman Corp.

Aviation Safety Commission

Meyer, Russell William, Jr.: chairman, chief executive officer, Cessna Aircraft Co.; president, Cessna Foundation, Inc.

B'nai B'rith Anti-Defamation League New York

Bronfman, Edgar Miles: chairman, trustee, Bronfman Foundation/Joseph E. Seagram & Sons, Inc. Fund (Samuel); chairman, Seagram & Sons, Inc. (Joseph E.)

B'nai B'rith International Trust

Bronfman, Edgar Miles: chairman, trustee, Bronfman Foundation/Joseph E. Seagram & Sons, Inc. Fund (Samuel); chairman, Seagram & Sons, Inc. (Joseph E.)

BB&T Center Leadership Development

Williamson, Henry Gaston, Jr.: chief operating officer, Branch Banking & Trust Co.

BRT Employee Relations Committee

Knicely, Howard V.: president, TRW Foundation

Babson College Corp.

Enrico, Roger A.: chairman, PepsiCo Foundation, Inc.; chairman, chief executive officer, director, PepsiCo, Inc.

Bald Peak Chamber of Commerce

Marriott, J. Willard, Jr.: chairman, chief executive officer, Marriott International Inc.

Baltimore Museum Art

Forbes, Christopher 'Kip': vice president, Forbes Foundation; vice chairman, corporate secretary, director, Forbes Inc.

Baltimore Symphony Orchestra

Shepard, Donald James: chairman, president, chief executive officer, AEGON U.S.A. Inc.

Bank Administration Institute

Stroup, Stanley Stephenson: executive vice president, general counsel, Norwest Corp.

Bank Marketing Association

Dods, Walter Arthur, Jr.: president, director, First Hawaiian Foundation; chairman, chief executive officer, director, First Hawaiian, Inc.

Bankers Association

Bottorff, Dennis C.: chairman, president, chief executive officer, director, First American Corp.

Bankers Association Foreign Trade

Rhodes, William Reginald: vice chairman, Citibank Corp.

Bankers Roundtable

Allison, John Andrew, IV: chairman, chief executive officer, director, Branch Banking & Trust Co.

Bauer, Chris Michael: president, Firstar Milwaukee Foundation

Cameron, Gerry B.: chairman, director, U.S. Bancorp

Daberko, David A.: chairman, chief executive officer, National City Corp.

Eccles, Spencer Fox: chairman, chief executive officer, director, First Security Bank of Idaho NA

Fitzsimonds, Roger Leon: chairman, Firstar Milwaukee Foundation

Jacobsen, Thomas Herbert: chairman, president, chief executive officer, Mercantile Bank NA

Kemper, David Woods: chairman, president, chief executive officer, director, Commerce Bancshares, Inc.

McCoy, John Bonnet: president, chief executive officer, Ameritech Corp.

McGuinn, Martin Gregory: chairman, chief executive officer, Mellon Financial Corp.

Miller, Eugene A.: chairman, chief executive officer, Comerica Inc.

Rhodes, William Reginald: vice chairman, Citibank Corp.

Rohr, James Edward: chief executive officer, president, director, PNC Financial Services Group

Tilghman, Richard Granville: chairman, chief executive officer, Crestar Foundation

Warner, Douglas Alexander, III: chairman, president, chief executive officer, director, Morgan & Co. Inc. (J.P.)

Baptist Health System

Goode, R. Ray: director, Ryder System Charitable Foundation

Baptist Hospital

Purvis, George Frank, Jr.: chairman, president, chief executive officer, director, Pan-American Life Insurance Co.

Baptist Hospital Fund Sponsor Board

Hubbard, Stanley S.: chairman, president, chief executive officer, Hubbard Broadcasting, Inc.; president, Hubbard Foundation

Baptist Medical Center

Ford, Joseph 'Joe': chairman, chief executive officer, president, ALLTEL Corp.

Bar Association Metropolitan Saint Louis

Brown, JoBeth Goode: trustee, Anheuser-Busch Companies, Inc.

Herron, James Michael: secretary, director, Ryder System Charitable Foundation

Van Cleve, William Moore: member public policy committee, Emerson Charitable Trust; partner, Emerson Electric Co.

Barat College

Peterson, Donald Matthew: trustee, Trustmark Foundation; president, chief executive officer, director, Trustmark Insurance Co.

Bard College

Resnick, Stewart A.: chairman, chief executive officer, Franklin Mint (The)

Barnard College

Ross, Arthur: senior vice president, Central National-Gottesman; director, Central National-Gottesman Foundation

Barnes-Jewish Hospital

Loeb, Jerome Thomas: chairman, director, May Department Stores Co.; president, director, May Department Stores Computer Foundation (The)

Barnes-Jewish Inc./ Christian Health Services

Loeb, Jerome Thomas: chairman, director, May Department Stores Co.; president, director, May Department Stores Computer Foundation (The)

Barry University

Mandel, Jack N.: director, Premier Industrial Corp.

Bartholomew County United Way

Sales, A. R.: director, Arvin Foundation; treasurer, Arvin Industries, Inc.

Basketball Hall Fame

Wheeler, Thomas Beardsley: chairman, chief executive officer, Massachusetts Mutual Life Insurance Co.

Battelle Memorial Institute

McCoy, John Bonnet: president, chief executive officer, Ameritech Corp.

Battle Creek Health Systems

Stewart, Joseph Melvin: senior vice president corporate affairs, Kellogg Co.; trustee, Kellogg Co. Twenty-Five Year Employees' Fund Inc.

Bay Area Community

Haas, Robert Douglas: chairman, chief executive officer, director, Levi Strauss & Co.; president, Levi Strauss Foundation

Bay Area Council

Coulter, David A.: president, director, Bank of America

Haas, Robert Douglas: chairman, chief executive officer, director, Levi Strauss & Co.; president, Levi Strauss Foundation

Moffitt, Donald Eugene: chairman, director, CNF Transportation, Inc.

Bay Area General Counsel Group

Beck, Edward W.: senior vice president, general counsel, secretary, director, Shaklee Corp.

Phair, Joseph Baschon: corporate secretary, general counsel, vice president, Varian Medical Systems, Inc.

Baylor College Medicine

Carroll, Philip Joseph: chairman, chief executive officer, Fluor Corp.; chairman, trustee, Fluor Foundation

Bazelon Center Mental Health Law

Gorelick, Jamie Shona: vice chairman, Fannie Mae

Bellevue University

Weekly, John William: chairman, chief executive officer, Mutual of Omaha Insurance Co.

Benchmark Group

Cameron, Gerry B.: chairman, director, U.S. Bancorp

Benevolent Protectorate Elks

Hall, Larry D.: chairman, president, chief executive officer, director, Kinder Morgn; president, director, KN Energy Foundation

Howe, Stanley M.: president, HON Industries Charitable Foundation; chairman emeritus, director, HON Industries Inc.

Berks Business Education Coalition

Hafer, Fred Douglass: chairman, president, chief executive officer, GPU Inc.

Berkshire Community College

Trask, Robert B.: clerk; president, chief operating officer, director, Country Curtains, Inc.; clerk, trustee, High Meadow Foundation

Berkshire Theatre Festival

Trask, Robert B.: clerk; president, chief operating officer, director, Country Curtains, Inc.; clerk, trustee, High Meadow Foundation

Berlitz International Inc.

Brademas, John: chairman, Texaco Foundation

Beta Alpha Psi

Hutchins, William Bruce, III: director, Alabama Power Foundation

Beta Gamma Sigma

Alpert, Janet A.: president, chief operating officer, director, LandAmerica Financial Services; trustee, LandAmerica Foundation

Anderson, Ivan Verner, Jr.: president, chief executive officer, Evening Post Publishing Co.; vice president, Post and Courier Foundation

Chookaszian, Dennis Haig: chairman, chief executive officer, CNA

Connor, James Richard: executive director, Kemper Foundation (James S.)

Guthart, Leo A.: vice chairman, director, Pittway Corp.

Hutchins, William Bruce, III: director, Alabama Power Foundation

Kaman, Charles Huron: chairman, president, chief executive officer, director, Kaman Corp.

Lewis, Frances Aaronson: trustee, Circuit City Foundation

Miller, Joseph Irwin: director associate, Cummins Engine Co., Inc.; director, Cummins Engine Foundation

Randolph, Jackson Harold: chairman, Cinergy Corp.; chairman, director, Cinergy Foundation

Rosett, Richard Nathaniel: trustee, Kemper Foundation (James S.)

Sales, A. R.: director, Arvin Foundation; treasurer, Arvin Industries, Inc.

Smith, John Francis, Jr.: chairman, General Motors Corp.

Voet, Paul C.: trustee, Chemed Foundation

Wentworth, Jack Roberts, Ph.D.: director, Habig Foundation
Wild, Heidi Karin: trustee
Williamson, Henry Gaston, Jr.: chief operating officer, Branch Banking & Trust Co.

Beta Theta Pi
Barnette, Curtis Handley: chairman, chief executive officer, director, Bethlehem Steel Corp.
Hewitt, James Watt: vice president, treasurer, Abel Foundation
Ukropina, James R.: partner, Pacific Mutual Life Insurance Co.

Beth Israel Hospital
Ehrlich, M. Gordon: trustee, Orchard Foundation

Beth Israel/ Deaconess Medical Center
Lasser, Lawrence Jay: president, chief executive officer, director, Putnam Investments; president, chief executive officer, Putnam Investors Fund

Bethesda Hospital
Hinshaw, Juanita H.: vice president, treasurer, Monsanto Co.; treasurer, Monsanto Fund

Better Business Bureau New York Inc.
Burenga, Kenneth L.: president, chief operating officer, director, Dow Jones & Co., Inc.

Beverly Hills Bar Association
Rosenthal, Sol: counsel, Playboy Enterprises Inc.

Beverly Hills Chamber of Commerce
Rosenzweig, Richard Stuart: executive vice president, director, Playboy Enterprises Inc.

Big Brothers Greater Los Angeles
Disney, Roy Edward: trustee, Disney Co. Foundation (Walt); vice chairman, director, Disney Co. (Walt)

Big Brotherss/Big Sisters
Gloyd, Lawrence Eugene: trustee, CLARCOR Foundation; chairman, chief executive officer, director, CLARCOR Inc.

Big Shoulders Fund
Graham, William B.: chairman, director, Baxter Allegiance Foundation; chairman emeritus, Baxter International Inc.
Terry, Richard Edward: chairman, chief executive officer, director, Peoples Energy Corp.

Bild-Werk Fravenau Germany
Buechner, Thomas Scharman: trustee, Corning Inc. Foundation

Bio Technology Industry Organization
Levinson, Arthur David: president, chief executive officer, director, Genentech Inc.

Birmingham Chamber of Commerce
Stephens, Elton Bryson: founder, chairman, Ebsco Industries, Inc.

Blood Bank Hawaii
Dods, Walter Arthur, Jr.: president, director, First Hawaiian Foundation; chairman, chief executive officer, director, First Hawaiian, Inc.

Blue Ribbon Panel Future Healthcare Hawaii
Dods, Walter Arthur, Jr.: president, director, First Hawaiian Foundation; chairman, chief executive officer, director, First Hawaiian, Inc.

Board of Professional Responsibility
Morris, Herman, Jr.: president, chief executive officer, Memphis Light Gas & Water Division

Boards Global Business Management Council
Smith, John Francis, Jr.: chairman, General Motors Corp.

Bombay Natural History Society
Ripley, Sidney Dillon, II: director emeritus, Hitachi Foundation

Bond Market Association
Civello, Nelson D.: director, Dain Bosworth Foundation

Boston Adult Literacy Fund
Taylor, William Osgood: chairman, chief executive officer, director, Boston Globe (The); chairman, director, Boston Globe Foundation; director, New York Times Co. Foundation

Boston Arts Festival
Redstone, Sumner Murray: chairman, Viacom Inc.

Boston Bar Association
Cogan, John Francis, Jr.: president, chief executive officer, director, Pioneer Group
Redstone, Sumner Murray: chairman, Viacom Inc.

Boston Chamber of Commerce
Gifford, Charles Kilvert: trustee, BankBoston Charitable Foundation; chairman, chief executive officer, BankBoston Corp.

Boston College
Syron, Richard F.: chairman, chief executive officer, director, American Stock Exchange, Inc.

Boston College School of Management
Ives, J. Atwood: chairman, chief executive officer, Boston Gas Co.; chairman, chief executive officer, trustee, Eastern Enterprises; trustee, Eastern Enterprises Foundation
LaMantia, Charles Robert: president, chief executive officer, director, Little, Inc. (Arthur D.)

Boston Coordinating Committee
Brown, Stephen Lee: chairman, chief executive officer, director, Hancock Financial Services (John)

Boston Estate Planning & Business Council
Ehrlich, M. Gordon: trustee, Orchard Foundation

Boston Estate Planning & Business Counsel
Cogan, John Francis, Jr.: president, chief executive officer, director, Pioneer Group

Boston Life Underwriters Association
Brown, Stephen Lee: chairman, chief executive officer, director, Hancock Financial Services (John)

Boston Municipal Research Bureau
Syron, Richard F.: chairman, chief executive officer, director, American Stock Exchange, Inc.

Boston Museum Fine Arts
Johnson, Edward Crosby, III: president, Fidelity Foundation; chairman, president, chief executive officer, director, Fidelity Investments
Redstone, Sumner Murray: chairman, Viacom Inc.

Boston Museum Science
Flaherty, Walter J.: chief financial officer, senior vice president, Eastern Enterprises; trustee, Eastern Enterprises Foundation
Hatsopoulos, George Nicholas: founder, chairman, chief executive officer, director, Thermo Electron Corp.; committee member, Thermo Electron Foundation
Redstone, Sumner Murray: chairman, Viacom Inc.

Boston Plan for Excellence in Public Schools
Gifford, Charles Kilvert: trustee, BankBoston Charitable Foundation; chairman, chief executive officer, BankBoston Corp.

Boston Private Industries Council
Gifford, Charles Kilvert: trustee, BankBoston Charitable Foundation; chairman, chief executive officer, BankBoston Corp.

Boston Probate & Estate Planning Forum
Cogan, John Francis, Jr.: president, chief executive officer, director, Pioneer Group

Boston Public Library
Taylor, William Osgood: chairman, chief executive officer, director, Boston Globe (The); chairman, director, Boston Globe Foundation; director, New York Times Co. Foundation

Boston Public Library Foundation
LaMantia, Charles Robert: president, chief executive officer, director, Little, Inc. (Arthur D.)
Taylor, William Osgood: chairman, chief executive officer, director, Boston Globe (The); chairman, director, Boston Globe Foundation; director, New York Times Co. Foundation

Boston Symphony Orchestra
Cogan, John Francis, Jr.: president, chief executive officer, director, Pioneer Group

Boston Tax Forum
Ehrlich, M. Gordon: trustee, Orchard Foundation

Boston Underwriters Association
Wheeler, Thomas Beardsley: chairman, chief executive officer, Massachusetts Mutual Life Insurance Co.

Boston University Medical Center
Magee, John Francis: chairman, director, Little, Inc. (Arthur D.)

Botanic Garden
Carroll, Philip Joseph: chairman, chief executive officer, Fluor Corp.; chairman, trustee, Fluor Foundation

Bowdoin College
Gorman, Leon A.: president, chief executive officer, Bean, Inc. (L.L.)
Magee, John Francis: chairman, director, Little, Inc. (Arthur D.)

Boy Scouts America
Dods, Walter Arthur, Jr.: president, director, First Hawaiian Foundation; chairman, chief executive

officer, director, First Hawaiian, Inc.
Graves, Earl Gilbert: director, Aetna Foundation
Herres, Robert T.: chairman, chief executive officer, United Services Automobile Association
Jacobsen, Thomas Herbert: chairman, president, chief executive officer, Mercantile Bank NA
Marriott, J. Willard, Jr.: chairman, chief executive officer, Marriott International Inc.
McCoy, John Bonnet: president, chief executive officer, Ameritech Corp.
Moffitt, Donald Eugene: chairman, director, CNF Transportation, Inc.
Moore, Jackson W.: president, director, Union Planters Corp.
Ughetta, William Casper: trustee, Corning Inc. Foundation
Whitacre, Edward E., Jr.: chairman, director, chief executive officer, SBC Communications Inc.

Boy Scouts America Aloha Council
Wolff, Herbert Eric: secretary, director, First Hawaiian Foundation

Boy Scouts America Baltimore Area Council
Poindexter, Christian Herndon: chairman, Baltimore Gas & Electric Foundation; chairman, chief executive officer, director, Constellation Energy Group, Inc.

Boy Scouts America Birmingham Area Council
Harris, Elmer Beseler: president, chief executive officer, director, Alabama Power Co.

Boy Scouts America Chicago Area Council
Chookaszian, Dennis Haig: chairman, chief executive officer, CNA

Boy Scouts America Circle Ten Council
Brooks, E. Richard 'Dick': chairman, chief executive officer, director, Central & South West Services

Boy Scouts America Crossroads Council
Sease, Gene Elwood: director, Central Newspapers Foundation

Boy Scouts America East Carolina Council
Williamson, Henry Gaston, Jr.: chief operating officer, Branch Banking & Trust Co.

Boy Scouts America Greater New York Council
Gardner, James Richard: vice president, Pfizer Foundation

Boy Scouts America Lehigh Valley
Penny, Roger Pratt: president, chief operating officer, director, Bethlehem Steel Corp.

Boy Scouts America Mount Diablo Council
Cronk, William F., III: president, director, Dreyer's Grand Ice Cream

Boy Scouts America New Orleans Council
Bachmann, Richard Arthur: vice president, secretary, treasurer, director, Louisiana Land & Exploration Co. Foundation

Boy Scouts America New York Council
Whitehead, John Cunningham: chairman board, Goldman Sachs Foundation

Boy Scouts America Saint Louis Area Council
Jacobsen, Thomas Herbert: chairman, president, chief executive officer, Mercantile Bank NA

Boy Scouts America Sam Houston Area Council
Tuerff, James R.: president, director, American General Finance

Boys & Girls Clubs America
Gidwitz, Ronald J.: president, chief executive officer, Curtis Industries, Inc. (Helene)
Kennedy, George Danner: trustee, Kemper Foundation (James S.)
Nye, Erle Allen: chairman, chief executive officer, director, TU Electric Co.

Boys & Girls Clubs Minneapolis
Dubes, Michael: membership, ReliaStar Foundation

Boys & Girls Clubs of American
Carroll, Philip Joseph: chairman, chief executive officer, Fluor Corp.; chairman, trustee, Fluor Foundation

Boys Club America
Andreas, Dwayne Orville: chairman, chief executive officer, Archer-Daniels-Midland Co.

Boys Club Mpls
Carlson, Curtis Leroy: chairman, director, Carlson Companies, Inc.; president, treasurer, Carlson Family Foundation (Curtis L.)

Boys Harbor
Mirsky, Susan: vice president, director, Thompson Co. Fund (J. Walter)

Boys Hope
McKenna, William John: director, chairman, Kellwood Co.; chairman, president, director, Kellwood Foundation

Bradley Hospital
Verrecchia, Alfred J.: treasurer, trustee, Hasbro Charitable Trust Inc.; executive, director, Hasbro, Inc.

Bradley International Airport Committee
Long, Michael Thomas: director, Ensign-Bickford Foundation

Bradley University
Flaherty, Gerald S.: trustee, Caterpillar Foundation; group president, Caterpillar Inc.

Brandeis National Womens Comm
Hefner, Christie Ann: chairman, chief executive officer, Playboy Enterprises Inc.; director, Playboy Foundation

Brandeis School
Laufer, Harry: president, chief executive officer, partner, director, Associated Food Stores; director, Associated Food Stores Charitable Foundation

Brandeis University
Hefner, Christie Ann: chairman, chief executive officer, Playboy Enterprises Inc.; director, Playboy Foundation
Margolin, Abraham E.: director, Tension Envelope Foundation
Redstone, Sumner Murray: chairman, Viacom Inc.

Branford College
Miller, Joseph Irwin: director associate, Cummins Engine Co., Inc.; director, Cummins Engine Foundation

Bretton Woods Committee
Carroll, Philip Joseph: chairman, chief executive officer, Fluor Corp.; chairman, trustee, Fluor Foundation
Dunham, Archie W.: president, chief executive officer, Conoco, Inc.
Franklin, Barbara Hackman: director, Dow Chemical Co.
Golub, Harvey: chairman, chief executive officer, director, American Express Co.; trustee, American Express Foundation
Rhodes, William Reginald: vice chairman, Citibank Corp.

Brigham Young University
Burns, Mitchell Anthony: president, director, Ryder System Charitable Foundation; chairman, president, chief executive officer, Ryder System, Inc.

Bristol Historical Society
Barnes, Wallace W.: director, Barnes Group Foundation Inc.

British Columbia Premier's Advisory Council
Langbo, Arnold Gordon: chairman, chief executive officer, director, Kellogg Co.

British Institute Management
O'Reilly, F. Anthony John: chairman, trustee, Heinz Co. Foundation (H.J.); chairman, director, Heinz Co. (H.J.)

British Ornithologists Union
Ripley, Sidney Dillon, II: director emeritus, Hitachi Foundation

Broadcast Fin Management Association
Doerfler, Ronald J.: senior vice president, chief financial officer, ABC; vice president, director, ABC Foundation

Broadcast Pioneers
Hubbard, Stanley S.: chairman, president, chief executive officer, Hubbard Broadcasting, Inc.; president, Hubbard Foundation

Broadcast Pioneers Library
Hubbard, Stanley S.: chairman, president, chief executive officer, Hubbard Broadcasting, Inc.; president, Hubbard Foundation

Broadcasters Foundation
Hubbard, Stanley S.: chairman, president, chief executive officer, Hubbard Broadcasting, Inc.; president, Hubbard Foundation

Brookings Institute
Whitehead, John Cunningham: chairman board, Goldman Sachs Foundation

Brookings Institution
Haas, Robert Douglas: chairman, chief executive officer, director, Levi Strauss & Co.; president, Levi Strauss Foundation
Labrecque, Thomas Goulet: president, chief operating officer, director, Chase Manhattan Bank, NA; president, Chase Manhattan Foundation
Schacht, Henry Brewer: director, Cummins Engine Foundation
Zilkha, Ezra Khedouri: president, treasurer, Zilkha Foundation, Inc.; president, Zilkha & Sons

Brooklyn Chamber of Commerce
Matthews, Craig Gerard: president, chief operating officer, Brooklyn Union

Brooklyn Institute Arts & Science

Buechner, Thomas Scharman: trustee, Corning Inc. Foundation

Brooklyn Law School

Karmel, Roberta S.: trustee, Kemper Foundation (James S.); partner, Kemper National Insurance Companies

Brooklyn Museum

Hall, Floyd: chairman, president, chief executive officer, director, Kmart Corp.

Brooklyn Museum Art

Forbes, Christopher 'Kip': vice president, Forbes Foundation; vice chairman, corporate secretary, director, Forbes Inc.

Brooklyn Philharmonic

Matthews, Craig Gerard: president, chief operating officer, Brooklyn Union

Brother Rice High School

Brennan, Leo Joseph, Jr.: vice president, executive director, Ford Motor Co. Fund

Brown University

Rhodes, William Reginald: vice chairman, Citibank Corp.

Small, Lawrence Malcolm: president, chief operating officer, Fannie Mae; director, Fannie Mae Foundation

Brunswick School

McGraw, Harold Whittlesey 'Terry', III: chairman, president, chief executive officer, McGraw-Hill Companies, Inc.

Bryan Memorial Hospital Foundation

Hewitt, James Watt: vice president, treasurer, Abel Foundation

Bryant College

Hassenfeld, Alan Geoffrey: president, Hasbro Charitable Trust Inc.; chairman, chief executive officer, Hasbro, Inc.

Lemieux, Joseph Henry: chairman, chief executive officer, director, Owens-Illinois Inc.

Bryant Park Restoration Corp.

Ross, Arthur: senior vice president, Central National-Gottesman; director, Central National-Gottesman Foundation

Buffalo Bill Historical Center

Griffin, Donald Wayne: chairman, president, chief executive officer, director, Olin Corp.; trustee, Olin Corp. Charitable Trust

Buffalo Chamber of Commerce

Penny, Roger Pratt: president, chief operating officer, director, Bethlehem Steel Corp.

Buffalo Fine Arts Academy

Lippes, Gerald Sanford: secretary, Mark IV Industries Foundation

Buffalo Sabres Hockey Club

Rich, Robert E., Jr.: secretary, Rich Family Foundation; president, director, Rich Products Corp.

Buffalo Society Natural Sciences

Ackerman, Philip Charles: senior vice president, director, National Fuel Gas Distribution Corp.

Bureau Government Research New Orleans

Purvis, George Frank, Jr.: chairman, president, chief executive officer, director, Pan-American Life Insurance Co.

Bus Higher Education Forum

Burns, Mitchell Anthony: president, director, Ryder System Charitable Foundation; chairman, president, chief executive officer, Ryder System, Inc.

Bus Institutional Furniture Manufacturer Association

Howe, Stanley M.: president, HON Industries Charitable Foundation; chairman emeritus, director, HON Industries Inc.

Bus Software Alliance

Lemberg, Thomas Michael: clerk, Lotus Development Corp.; secretary, Polaroid Foundation

Business & Professional Advertisers Association

Sutton, Howard: trustee, Steelcase Foundation

Business Advisory Council Federal Reports

Gallagher, Terence Joseph: secretary, director, Pfizer Foundation

Business Committee Arts

Bronfman, Edgar Miles: chairman, trustee, Bronfman Foundation/Joseph E. Seagram & Sons, Inc. Fund (Samuel); chairman, Seagram & Sons, Inc. (Joseph E.)

Bryan, John Henry: chairman, Sara Lee Corp.; director, Sara Lee Foundation

Cantor, Bernard Gerald: president, director, Cantor, Fitzgerald Foundation; chairman, director, Cantor, Fitzgerald Securities Corp.

Marron, Donald Baird: chairman, chief executive officer, director, Paine Webber; trustee, Paine Webber Foundation

Business Council

Becherer, Hans Walter: chairman, chief executive officer, director, Deere & Co.; director, Deere Foundation (John)

Bechtel, Riley Peart: chairman, Bechtel Foundation; chairman, chief executive officer, director, Bechtel Group, Inc.

Bijur, Peter I.: chairman, chief executive officer, Texaco Inc.

Blount, Winton Malcolm, Jr.: chairman, Blount International, Inc.

Bryan, John Henry: chairman, Sara Lee Corp.; director, Sara Lee Foundation

Burns, Mitchell Anthony: president, director, Ryder System Charitable Foundation; chairman, president, chief executive officer, Ryder System, Inc.

Daniels, John Hancock: chairman, Archer-Daniels-Midland Foundation

Eaton, Robert James: co-chairman, president, chief executive officer, DaimlerChrysler Corp.

Engibous, Thomas James: director, Texas Instruments Foundation; president, chief executive officer, chairman, director, Texas Instruments Inc.

Fites, Donald Vester: director, Caterpillar Foundation

Gelb, Richard Lee: director, New York Times Co. Foundation

Gilmartin, Raymond V.: chairman, president, chief executive officer, Merck & Co.; chairman, Merck Co. Foundation

Gorman, Joseph T.: chairman, chief executive officer, TRW Inc.

Henderson, James Alan: vice chairman, chief executive officer, director, Ameritech Corp.; chairman, director, Cummins Engine Foundation

Hiner, Glen Harold, Jr.: chairman, chief executive officer, director, Owens Corning

Ingersoll, Robert Stephen: chairman, director, Panasonic Foundation

Johnson, Samuel Curtis: chairman, director, president, Johnson & Son (S.C.); chairman, trustee, Johnson Wax Fund (S.C.)

Labrecque, Thomas Goulet: president, chief operating officer, director, Chase Manhattan Bank, NA; president, Chase Manhattan Foundation

Larsen, Ralph Stanley: chairman, president, chief executive officer, director, Johnson & Johnson

Marriott, J. Willard, Jr.: chairman, chief executive officer, Marriott International Inc.

Miller, Joseph Irwin: director associate, Cummins Engine Co., Inc.; director, Cummins Engine Foundation

Milliken, Roger: chairman, chief executive officer, Milliken & Co.; member advisory committee, Milliken Foundation

Ong, John Doyle: chairman board, director, Ameritech Corp.

Pigott, Charles McGee: president, director, PACCAR Foundation; chairman emeritus, director, PACCAR Inc.

Raymond, Lee R.: chairman, president, chief executive officer, Exxon Mobil Corp.

Reed, John Shepard: co-chairman, Citibank Corp.

Schacht, Henry Brewer: director, Cummins Engine Foundation

Steere, William Campbell, Jr.: chairman, chief executive officer, director, Pfizer Inc.

Tobias, Randall L.: chairman emeritus, Lilly & Co. (Eli)

Warner, Douglas Alexander, III: chairman, president, chief executive officer, director, Morgan & Co. Inc. (J.P.)

Welch, John Francis, Jr.: chairman, chief executive officer, director, General Electric Co.

Weyerhaeuser, George Hunt: director, Weyerhaeuser Co.; trustee, Weyerhaeuser Co. Foundation

Business Council Alabama

Jones, D. Paul, Jr.: chairman, chief executive officer, Compass Bank; trustee, Compass Bank Foundation

Business Council International Understanding Inc.

Raymond, Lee R.: chairman, president, chief executive officer, Exxon Mobil Corp.

Business Council National Issues

D'Alessandro, Dominic: president, chief executive officer, director, Manulife Financial

Flood, Al: chairman, chief executive officer, CIBC Oppenheimer

Business Council New York State

Kennedy, Bernard Joseph: chairman, president, chief executive officer, director, National Fuel Gas Distribution Corp.

Wilmers, Robert George: chairman, president, chief executive officer, Manufacturers & Traders Trust Co.

Business Council for a Sustainable Energy Future

Catell, Robert Barry: chairman, chief executive officer, Brooklyn Union

Business Enterprise Trust

Schacht, Henry Brewer: director, Cummins Engine Foundation

Business Higher Education Forum

Gorman, Joseph T.: chairman, chief executive officer, TRW Inc.

Labrecque, Thomas Goulet: president, chief operating officer, director, Chase Manhattan Bank, NA; president, Chase Manhattan Foundation

Business Improvement Distribution Task Force New York City Partnership/ Chamber of Commerce

Schiro, James J.: chairman, senior partner, PricewaterhouseCoopers

Business Marketing Corp.

Graves, Earl Gilbert: director, Aetna Foundation

Business Products Industry Association

Rukeyser, Robert James: senior vice president corporate affairs, Fortune Brands, Inc.

Business Roundtable

Barnette, Curtis Handley: chairman, chief executive officer, director, Bethlehem Steel Corp.

Becherer, Hans Walter: chairman, chief executive officer, director, Deere & Co.; director, Deere Foundation (John)

Bechtel, Riley Peart: chairman, Bechtel Foundation; chairman, chief executive officer, director, Bechtel Group, Inc.

Bijur, Peter I.: chairman, chief executive officer, Texaco Inc.

Bossidy, Lawrence Arthur: chairman, director, AlliedSignal Foundation Inc.; chairman, chief executive officer, director, AlliedSignal Inc.

Bryan, John Henry: chairman, Sara Lee Corp.; director, Sara Lee Foundation

Burns, Mitchell Anthony: president, director, Ryder System Charitable Foundation; chairman, president, chief executive officer, Ryder System, Inc.

Burt, Robert Norcross: chairman, chief executive officer, director, FMC Corp.; director, FMC Foundation

Eaton, Robert James: co-chairman, president, chief executive officer, DaimlerChrysler Corp.

Engibous, Thomas James: director, Texas Instruments Foundation; president, chief executive officer, chairman, director, Texas Instruments Inc.

Farmer, Phillip W.: chairman, president, chief executive officer, Harris Corp.; president, trustee, Harris Foundation

Fites, Donald Vester: director, Caterpillar Foundation

Gerstner, Louis Vincent, Jr.: chairman, chief executive officer, director, International Business Machines Corp.

Gilmartin, Raymond V.: chairman, president, chief executive officer, Merck & Co.; chairman, Merck Co. Foundation

Golub, Harvey: chairman, chief executive officer, director, American Express Co.; trustee, American Express Foundation

Goode, David Ronald: chairman, president, chief executive officer, director, Norfolk Southern Corp.

Gorman, Joseph T.: chairman, chief executive officer, TRW Inc.

Hays, Thomas Chandler: chairman, chief executive officer, director, Fortune Brands, Inc.

Henderson, James Alan: vice chairman, chief executive officer, director, Ameritech Corp.; chairman, director, Cummins Engine Foundation

Hewitt, James Watt: vice president, treasurer, Abel Foundation

Hiner, Glen Harold, Jr.: chairman, chief executive officer, director, Owens Corning

Kirby, William Joseph: vice president, director, FMC Foundation

Labrecque, Thomas Goulet: president, chief operating officer, director, Chase Manhattan Bank, NA; president, Chase Manhattan Foundation

Larsen, Ralph Stanley: chairman, president, chief executive officer, director, Johnson & Johnson

Lee, Charles Robert: chairman, chief executive officer, director, GTE Corp.; chief executive officer, trustee, GTE Foundation

Marriott, J. Willard, Jr.: chairman, chief executive officer, Marriott International Inc.

Montrone, Paul Michael: vice president, partner, Winthrop Foundation

Mooney, Edward J., Jr.: chairman, president, chief executive officer, director, Nalco Chemical Co.

Moritz, Charles Worthington: chairman, director, Dun & Bradstreet Corp.

Platt, Lewis Emmett: chairman, Hewlett-Packard Co.

Raymond, Lee R.: chairman, president, chief executive officer, Exxon Mobil Corp.

Reed, John Shepard: co-chairman, Citibank Corp.

Rust, Edward Barry, Jr.: chairman, president, director, State Farm Companies Foundation; chairman, president, chief executive officer, director, State Farm Mutual Automobile Insurance Co.

Satre, Philip Glen: chairman, president, chief executive officer, director, Promus Hotel Corp.

Sheehan, Jeremiah J.: chairman, director, Reynolds Metals Co. Foundation

Smith, Raymond W.: chairman, chief executive officer, director, Bell Atlantic Corp.

Steere, William Campbell, Jr.: chairman, chief executive officer, director, Pfizer Inc.

Sullivan, Austin Padraic, Junior: trustee, General Mills Foundation; senior vice president corporate relations, General Mills, Inc.

Vagelos, Pindaros Roy: trustee, Prudential Insurance Co. of America

Wehling, Robert Louis: global marketing, government relations officer, Procter & Gamble Co.; president, trustee, Procter & Gamble Fund

Welch, John Francis, Jr.: chairman, chief executive officer, director, General Electric Co.

Weyerhaeuser, George Hunt: director, Weyerhaeuser Co.; trustee, Weyerhaeuser Co. Foundation

Wiksten, Barry Frank: president, CIGNA Foundation

Business Roundtable Apartment Social Service

Berkley, Eugene Bertram: chairman, director, Tension Envelope Corp.; treasurer, Tension Envelope Foundation

Business Roundtable Ohio

Ong, John Doyle: chairman board, director, Ameritech Corp.

Business Roundtable Policy Comm

Smith, John Francis, Jr.: chairman, General Motors Corp.

Business School Canisius College

Kennedy, Bernard Joseph: chairman, president, chief executive officer, director, National Fuel Gas Distribution Corp.

Business School Columbia University

Montrone, Paul Michael: vice president, partner, Winthrop Foundation

Business Social Responsibility

Hiatt, Arnold Selig: chairman, director, Stride Rite Foundation

Business Task Force Education Inc.

Purvis, George Frank, Jr.: chairman, president, chief executive officer, director, Pan-American Life Insurance Co.

Business-Industry Politcal Action Committee

Castellani, John: executive vice president, Tenneco Automotive

Butler Institute American Art

Tucker, Don Eugene: trustee, Commercial Intertech Foundation

CAP

Scripps, Charles Edward: chairman executive committee, director, vice president, Scripps Co. (E.W.); member, Scripps Howard Foundation

CARE Foundation Minneapolis

Piper, Addison Lewis: director, Piper Jaffray Companies Foundation; chairman, chief executive officer, director, U.S. Bancorp Piper Jaffray

CASA

Chenault, Kenneth Irvine: president, chief operating officer, director, American Express Co.; trustee, American Express Foundation

CCIC

Schiek, Fredrick A.: executive vice president, chief operating officer, Employers Mutual Casualty Co.

CGF Health Care System

Lippes, Gerald Sanford: secretary, Mark IV Industries Foundation

CHIPS Same Day Settlement New York Clearing House

Ryan, Arthur Frederick: trustee, Chase Manhattan Foundation; chairman, chief executive officer, Prudential Insurance Co. of America

CLO Roundtable

Ursu, John Joseph: director, 3M Foundation; general counsel, senior vice president legal affairs, Minnesota Mining & Manufacturing Co.

CPA Society

Delo, Robert Paul: director, Chicago Tribune Foundation

CPAs Pub Interest

Schueppert, George Louis: chief financial officer, executive vice president, Outboard Marine Corp.

CaP Cure

Resnick, Lynda Rae: vice chairman, co-owner, Franklin Mint (The)

California Bar Association

Beck, Edward W.: senior vice president, general counsel, secretary, director, Shaklee Corp.

Bell, Wayne: secretary, Ralph's-Food 4 Less Foundation; senior counsel, assistant secretary, Ralph's Grocery Co.

Bryson, John E.: chairman, chief executive officer, Edison International

Carter, John Douglas: executive vice president, director, Bechtel Group, Inc.

Olschwang, Alan P., Esq.: secretary, Mitsubishi Electric America Foundation

Rosenthal, Sol: counsel, Playboy Enterprises Inc.

Satre, Philip Glen: chairman, president, chief executive officer, director, Promus Hotel Corp.

Stroup, Stanley Stephenson: executive vice president, general counsel, Norwest Corp.

Weinberger, Caspar Willard: chairman, Forbes Inc.
ZoBell, Karl: vice president, trustee, Copley Foundation (James S.)

California Business Roundtable
Bechtel, Riley Peart: chairman, Bechtel Foundation; chairman, chief executive officer, director, Bechtel Group, Inc.
Haas, Robert Douglas: chairman, chief executive officer, director, Levi Strauss & Co.; president, Levi Strauss Foundation
Moffitt, Donald Eugene: chairman, director, CNF Transportation, Inc.

California Chamber of Commerce
Bartz, Carol A.: director, Autodesk Foundation; chairman, chief executive officer, Autodesk Inc.

California Citizens Compensation Commission
Brinegar, Claude Stout: trustee, Unocal Foundation

California Community Foundation
Ferry, Richard Michael: chairman, Pacific Mutual Life Insurance Co.

California Economic Development Corp.
Jacobs, Joseph J.: president, director, Jacobs Engineering Foundation; chairman, director, Jacobs Engineering Group

California Institute Arts
Eisner, Michael Dammann: president, trustee, Disney Co. Foundation (Walt); chairman, chief executive officer, director, Disney Co. (Walt)

California Institute Technology
Ferry, Richard Michael: chairman, Pacific Mutual Life Insurance Co.
Moore, Gordon E., PhD: co-founder, chairman emeritus, director, Intel Corp.; trustee, Intel Foundation
Rock, Arthur: co-founder, chairman executive committee, director, Intel Corp.
Rosenberg, Richard Morris: chairman, chief executive officer (retired), Bank of America

California Medical Center Foundation
Wood, Willis B., Jr.: chairman, chief executive officer, director, Pacific Enterprises

California Newspaper Publishers Association
Copley, Helen K.: chairman, trustee, Copley Foundation (James S.); chairman, director, senior management board, Copley Press, Inc.

California Pacific Medical Center
Herringer, Frank Casper: president, chief executive officer, director, chairman, Transamerica Corp.; vice chairman, director, Transamerica Foundation
James, George Barker, II: senior vice president, chief financial officer, Levi Strauss & Co.

California Pollution Control Financing Authority
Bryson, John E.: chairman, chief executive officer, Edison International

California Press Association
Copley, Helen K.: chairman, trustee, Copley Foundation (James S.); chairman, director, senior management board, Copley Press, Inc.

California Press Institute
Copley, Helen K.: chairman, trustee, Copley Foundation (James S.); chairman, director, senior management board, Copley Press, Inc.

California Society CPA's
Broome, Burton Edward: vice president, controller, Transamerica Corp.; vice president, treasurer, Transamerica Foundation

California State Employees Pension Fund
James, George Barker, II: senior vice president, chief financial officer, Levi Strauss & Co.

California Water Rights Law Review Committee
Bryson, John E.: chairman, chief executive officer, Edison International

Calvary Hospital Fund
Gallagher, Terence Joseph: secretary, director, Pfizer Foundation

Camping Education Foundation
Maritz, William Edward: chairman, chief executive officer, president, Maritz Inc.

Can Manufacturers Institute
Sissel, George A.: chairman, president, chief executive officer, director, Ball Corp.

Canada Academy Engineering
Light, Walter Frederick: trustee, Air Products Foundation

Canadian Council Aboriginal Business
McNally, Alan G.: chairman, chief executive officer, Harris Trust & Savings Bank

Canadian Institute Chartered Accts
Melnuk, Paul D.: president, chief executive officer, Clark Refining & Marketing

Canadian Pulp Paper Association
McKone, Francis L.: president, chief executive officer, director, Albany International Corp.

Canadian-American Committee
Langbo, Arnold Gordon: chairman, chief executive officer, director, Kellogg Co.

Cancer Therapy Research Center
Johnson, Hansford Tillman: trustee, USAA Foundation, A Charitable Trust

Canterbury School
Copley, David C.: president, trustee, Copley Foundation (James S.); president, chief executive officer, director, senior management board, Copley Press, Inc.

Capital Cities Community Minorities Intern Program
Connor, Richard L.: president, publisher, Fort Worth Star-Telegram Inc.

Capital Fund Breast Cancer Research
D'Alessandro, Dominic: president, chief executive officer, director, Manulife Financial

Capital University
Olesen, Douglas Eugene, PhD: president, chief executive officer, Battelle Memorial Institute

Cardinal Ritter Institute
McKenna, William John: director, chairman, Kellwood Co.; chairman, president, director, Kellwood Foundation

Caribbean/Latin American Action
Landin, Thomas Milton: vice president, director, CertainTeed Corp.; vice president, Norton Co. Foundation

Carl Sandburg College
Nicholas, Jon O.: vice president, trustee, Maytag Corp. Foundation

Carleton College
Leatherdale, Douglas West: chairman, chief executive officer, president, Saint Paul Companies Inc.

Carleton University
Light, Walter Frederick: trustee, Air Products Foundation

Carlson School of Management
Turner, John Gosney: chairman, chief executive officer, director, ReliaStar Financial Corp.; director, ReliaStar Foundation

Carnegie Commission Science Technology & Government
Brademas, John: chairman, Texaco Foundation

Carnegie Endowment
Gorelick, Jamie Shona: vice chairman, Fannie Mae

Carnegie Endowment National Commission American & New World
Brademas, John: chairman, Texaco Foundation

Carnegie Hall
Armstrong, C. Michael: chairman, chief executive officer, AT&T Corp.
Collins, Paul John: vice chairman, director, Citibank Corp.
Golub, Harvey: chairman, chief executive officer, director, American Express Co.; trustee, American Express Foundation
Masin, Michael Terry: vice chairman, president international, director, GTE Corp.; trustee, GTE Foundation

Carnegie Hall Society Inc.
Weill, Sanford I.: chairman, chief executive officer, Citibank Corp.; chairman, Citigroup Foundation

Carnegie Institute
Alberts, Bruce Michael, PhD: director, Genentech Foundation for Biomedical Sciences
Graham, Thomas Carlisle: trustee, AK Steel Foundation

Carnegie Mellon University
Davis, Erroll Brown, Jr.: president, chief executive officer, director, Wisconsin Power & Light Co.
Hilyard, James E.: president, CertainTeed Corp.; director, CertainTeed Corp. Foundation
Pollock, E. Kears: director, PPG Industries Foundation; executive vice president, PPG Industries, Inc.
Rohr, James Edward: chief executive officer, president, director, PNC Financial Services Group
Wehmeier, Helge H.: president, chief executive officer, director, Bayer Corp.

Carnegie Museum Art
McGuinn, Martin Gregory: chairman, chief executive officer, Mellon Financial Corp.

Caron Foundation
Hafer, Fred Douglass: chairman, president, chief executive officer, GPU Inc.

Carter Amon Museum Western Art
Tatum, Nenetta Carter: president, Carter Star Telegram Employees Fund (Amon G.)

Carter Center
Correll, Alston Dayton 'Pete', Jr.: chairman, president, chief executive officer, director, Georgia-Pacific Corp.; director, Georgia-Pacific Foundation

Case Western Reserve University
Daberko, David A.: chairman, chief executive officer, National City Corp.
Parker, Patrick Streeter: chairman, director, Parker Hannifin Corp.; president, trustee, Parker Hannifin Foundation
Pyke, John Secrest, Jr.: president, trustee, Hanna Co. Foundation (M.A.); vice president, secretary, general counsel, Hanna Co. (M.A.)

Casper Area Chamber of Commerce
True, Jean Durland: trustee, True Foundation; partner, True Oil Co.

Casualty Actuarial Society
Rinehart, Charles Robert: chairman, chief executive officer, director, Washington Mutual, Inc.

Catalyst
Bryan, John Henry: chairman, Sara Lee Corp.; director, Sara Lee Foundation
Cook, J. Michael: chairman, chief executive officer, Deloitte & Touche; chairman, Deloitte & Touche Foundation
Engibous, Thomas James: director, Texas Instruments Foundation; president, chief executive officer, chairman, director, Texas Instruments Inc.

Catalyst for Women Inc.
Allaire, Paul Arthur: chairman, chief executive officer, chairman executive committee, Xerox Corp.; president, Xerox Foundation
Fuller, Harry Laurance: co-chairman, director, BP Amoco Corp.
Starrett, Cam: executive vice president human resources & corporate relations, Nestle U.S.A. Inc.

Cate School
James, George Barker, II: senior vice president, chief financial officer, Levi Strauss & Co.
Simpson, Louis Allen: president, chief executive officer capital operations, director, GEICO Corp.

Catherine Booth Home
Randolph, Jackson Harold: chairman, Cinergy Corp.; chairman, director, Cinergy Foundation

Catholic Charities
Ferry, Richard Michael: chairman, Pacific Mutual Life Insurance Co.

Catholic Charities Chicago
McKenna, Andrew James: director, Aon Foundation

Catholic Foundation Southwestern Indiana
Koch, Robert Louis, II: president, chief executive officer, director, Koch Enterprises, Inc.; president, director, Koch Foundation
Muehlbauer, James Herman: vice president, director, Koch Foundation

Catholic High School
Barry, Richard Francis, III: director, Landmark Communications Foundation; vice chairman, Landmark Communications Inc.

Catholic University America
Davis, Ruth Margaret: trustee, Air Products Foundation
Kaman, Charles Huron: chairman, president, chief executive officer, director, Kaman Corp.

Cato Institute
Koch, David Hamilton: director, Koch Foundation, Inc. (Fred C. and Mary R.)
Margolin, Abraham E.: director, Tension Envelope Foundation

Center College
Hower, Frank Beard, Jr.: vice chairman, Anthem Foundation, Inc.

Center Economic Policy Development
Ridder, Paul Anthony: chairman, chief executive officer, director, Knight Ridder

Center International Commercial Dispute Resolution
Dods, Walter Arthur, Jr.: president, director, First Hawaiian Foundation; chairman, chief executive officer, director, First Hawaiian, Inc.

Center International-American Relations
Bronfman, Edgar Miles: chairman, trustee, Bronfman Foundation/Joseph E. Seagram & Sons, Inc. Fund (Samuel); chairman, Seagram & Sons, Inc. (Joseph E.)

Center Literacy
Haskin, Donald Lee: vice president, PNC Bank

Center National Policy
Brademas, John: chairman, Texaco Foundation

Center Neurologic Diseases
Johnson, Edward Crosby, III: president, Fidelity Foundation; chairman, president, chief executive officer, director, Fidelity Investments

Center New West
Trujillo, Solomon D.: president, US West Foundation; president, chief executive officer, US West, Inc.

Center Park Conservancy
Millstein, Ira M.: partner, Weil, Gotshal & Manges Corp.; president, director, Weil, Gotshal & Manges Foundation

Center Policy Research
Hatsopoulos, George Nicholas: founder, chairman, chief executive officer, director, Thermo Electron Corp.; committee member, Thermo Electron Foundation

Center Public
Marshall, Siri M.: trustee, General Mills Foundation; senior vice president, general counsel, General Mills, Inc.

Center Resource Management
Elkins, Lloyd Edwin, Junior: vice president, Chevron Corp.

Center Strategic & International Studies
Gerstner, Louis Vincent, Jr.: chairman, chief executive officer, director, International Business Machines Corp.
Gorman, Joseph T.: chairman, chief executive officer, TRW Inc.
Pepper, John E., Jr.: chairman executive committee, Procter & Gamble Co.
Zuckerman, Mortimer Benjamin: co-founder, chairman, co-publisher, director, Daily News

Center Study International Business Law
Karmel, Roberta S.: trustee, Kemper Foundation (James S.); partner, Kemper National Insurance Companies

Center Workforce Preparation & Quality Education
Kennedy, George Danner: trustee, Kemper Foundation (James S.)

Center for Clean Air Policy
Davis, William E.: chairman, chief executive officer, Niagara Mohawk Holdings Inc.

Center for Visual History
Meyerson, Martin: director, Panasonic Foundation

Center of Intuitive & Outsider Art
Wilson, Cleo Francine: executive director, Playboy Foundation

Centerary College
Longfield, William H.: president, Bard Foundation (C.R.); chairman, chief executive officer, director, Bard, Inc. (C.R.)

Central Atlanta Progress
Correll, Alston Dayton 'Pete', Jr.: chairman, president, chief executive officer, director, Georgia-Pacific Corp.; director, Georgia-Pacific Foundation

Central Newspaper Federation
Sease, Gene Elwood: director, Central Newspapers Foundation

Central Newspapers Foundation
Russell, Frank Eli: president, Central Newspapers Foundation; chairman, Central Newspapers, Inc.

Central Park Community Fund
Ross, Arthur: senior vice president, Central National-Gottesman; director, Central National-Gottesman Foundation

Central Park Conservancy
Collins, Paul John: vice chairman, director, Citibank Corp.
Labrecque, Thomas Goulet: president, chief operating officer, director, Chase Manhattan Bank, NA; president, Chase Manhattan Foundation
Ross, Arthur: senior vice president, Central National-Gottesman; director, Central National-Gottesman Foundation

Central Pennsylvania Savings Loan League
Pullo, Robert W.: chairman, chief executive officer, director, York Federal Savings & Loan Association; president, trustee, York Federal Savings & Loan Foundation

Central Vermont Economic Development Corp.

Bertrand, Frederic Howard: chairman, Central Vermont Public Service Corp.

Centre College

Chellgren, Paul Wilbur: chief executive officer, chairman, director, Ashland, Inc.; member, Ashland Inc. Foundation

Centurion Foundation

Grasso, Richard A.: chairman, chief executive officer, New York Stock Exchange, Inc.

Century Association

Benenson, James, Jr.: chairman, president, director, Vesper Corp.; trustee, Vesper Foundation

Buechner, Thomas Scharman: trustee, Corning Inc. Foundation

Connor, Walter Robert: director, Glaxo Wellcome Foundation

Kerr, William T.: chairman, chief executive officer, director, Meredith Corp.

Shinn, George Latimer: director, New York Times Co. Foundation

Certified Fin Planner

Dubes, Michael: membership, ReliaStar Foundation

Chamber of Commerce California State

Wood, Willis B., Jr.: chairman, chief executive officer, director, Pacific Enterprises

Chamber of Commerce Greater New Orleans Area

Purvis, George Frank, Jr.: chairman, president, chief executive officer, director, Pan-American Life Insurance Co.

Chamber of Commerce Wheeling

Wareham, James Lyman: president, AK Steel Corp.

Charleston Symphony Orchestra

Anderson, Ivan Verner, Jr.: president, chief executive officer, Evening Post Publishing Co.; vice president, Post and Courier Foundation

Chartered Financial Analysts

Latzer, Richard Neal: vice president, director, Transamerica Foundation

Meuleman, Robert Joseph: director, AMCORE Foundation

Chatham College

Morby, Jacqueline C.: managing partner, Pacific Mutual Life Insurance Co.

Chem Marketing Association

Stewart, S. Jay: chairman, chief executive officer, director, Morton International Inc.

Chemical Manufacturers Association

Bersticker, Albert C.: chairman, director, chief executive officer, Ferro Corp.; president, trustee, Ferro Foundation

Brothers, John Alfred 'Fred': trustee, Ashland Inc. Foundation

Chellgren, Paul Wilbur: chief executive officer, chairman, director, Ashland, Inc.; member, Ashland Inc. Foundation

Deavenport, Earnest W., Jr.: chairman, chief executive officer, director, Eastman Chemical Co.

Elliott, R. Keith: chief executive officer, president, Hercules Inc.

Fligg, James E.: executive vice president, BP Amoco Corp.

Grasley, Michael Howard: senior vice president, Shell Oil Co.; member executive committee, director, Shell Oil Co. Foundation

Griffin, Donald Wayne: chairman, president, chief executive officer, director, Olin Corp.; trustee, Olin Corp. Charitable Trust

Lichtenberger, Horst William: chairman, chief executive officer, Praxair

Lovett, John Robert: director, Air Products Foundation

Minton, Dwight Church: chairman, director, Church & Dwight Co., Inc.

Mooney, Edward J., Jr.: chairman, president, chief executive officer, director, Nalco Chemical Co.

Ong, John Doyle: chairman board, director, Ameritech Corp.

Pollock, E. Kears: director, PPG Industries Foundation; executive vice president, PPG Industries, Inc.

Stewart, S. Jay: chairman, chief executive officer, director, Morton International Inc.

Wehmeier, Helge H.: president, chief executive officer, director, Bayer Corp.

Wilson, James Lawrence: chairman, chief executive officer, director, Rohm & Haas Co.

Chemical Specialties Manufacturing Association

Forsythe, John G.: vice president tax and public affairs, Ecolab Inc.

Chesapeake Bay Foundation

Griffith, Alan Richard: vice chairman, Bank of New York Co., Inc.

Chi Psi

Herring, Leonard Gray: vice president, Lowe's Charitable and Educational Foundation

Johnson, Samuel Curtis: chairman, director, president, Johnson & Son (S.C.); chairman, trustee, Johnson Wax Fund (S.C.)

Pew, Robert Cunningham, II: trustee, Steelcase Foundation

Chicago Area Central Comm

Terry, Richard Edward: chairman, chief executive officer, director, Peoples Energy Corp.

Chicago Association Commerce Industry

Donovan, Thomas Roy: president, chief executive officer, Chicago Board of Trade

Chicago Athletic Association

Connolly, Charles H.: senior vice president corporate affairs & investor relations, Whitman Corp.; president, Whitman Corp. Foundation

Chicago Bar Association

Ashley, James Wheeler: director, Globe Foundation

Chabraja, Nicholas D.: chairman, chief executive officer, director, General Dynamics Corp.

Dubin, Stephen Victor: vice president, secretary, Farber Foundation

Huston, Steve: secretary, Wrigley Co. Foundation (Wm. Jr.)

Olschwang, Alan P., Esq.: secretary, Mitsubishi Electric America Foundation

Resnick, Myron J.: vice president, treasurer, trustee, Allstate Foundation

Skilling, Raymond Inwood: executive vice president, chief counsel, director, Aon Corp.; director, Aon Foundation

Wander, Herbert S.: secretary, director, Katten, Muchin & Zavis Foundation

Welsh, Kelly Raymond: executive vice president, general counsel, Ameritech Corp.

Zavis, Michael W.: managing partner, Katten, Muchin & Zavis; president, director, Katten, Muchin & Zavis Foundation

Chicago Board Options Exchange

Simmons, Hardwick: president, chief executive officer, director, Prudential Securities Inc.

Chicago Central Area Comm

Donovan, Thomas Roy: president, chief executive officer, Chicago Board of Trade

Chicago Chamber of Commerce

Terry, Richard Edward: chairman, chief executive officer, director, Peoples Energy Corp.

Chicago Children's Museum

Rogers, Desiree Glapion: vice president community affairs, Peoples Energy Corp.

Chicago Comm

Stone, Roger Warren: chairman, president, chief executive officer, director, Stone Container Corp.; president, Stone Foundation

Chicago Community Trust

Mac Kimm, Margaret (Pontius) 'Mardie': trustee, Chicago Title and Trust Co. Foundation

Chicago Council Fgn Relationss

Burnham, Duane Lee: chairman, chief executive officer, director, Abbott Laboratories

Chicago Council Foreign Relations

Bryan, John Henry: chairman, Sara Lee Corp.; director, Sara Lee Foundation

Hodgson, Thomas Richard: president, chief operating officer, director, Abbott Laboratories

Ingersoll, Robert Stephen: chairman, director, Panasonic Foundation

Stone, Roger Warren: chairman, president, chief executive officer, director, Stone Container Corp.; president, Stone Foundation

Chicago Council Lawyers

Ashley, James Wheeler: director, Globe Foundation

Welsh, Kelly Raymond: executive vice president, general counsel, Ameritech Corp.

Chicago Council Urban Affairs

Williams, Edward Joseph: president, director, Harris Bank Foundation

Chicago Crime Commission

Gidwitz, Gerald S.: chairman, Curtis Industries, Inc. (Helene)

Chicago Education Television Association

Harris, Irving Brooks: chairman executive committee, director, Pittway Corp.; chairman, director, Pittway Corp. Charitable Foundation

Chicago Graduate School

Browning, Peter C.: chief executive officer, president, director, Sonoco Products Co.

Chicago Horticultural Society

Coughlan, Gary Patrick: chief financial officer, senior vice president finance, Abbott Laboratories; director, Abbott Laboratories Fund

Graham, William B.: chairman, director, Baxter Allegiance Foundation; chairman emeritus, Baxter International Inc.

Chicago Metropolitan Planning Commission

Toll, Daniel Roger: trustee, Kemper Foundation (James S.)

Chicago Mortgage Attorneys Association

Resnick, Myron J.: vice president, treasurer, trustee, Allstate Foundation

Chicago Museum Science & Industry

Terry, Richard Edward: chairman, chief executive officer, director, Peoples Energy Corp.

Chicago Network

Hefner, Christie Ann: chairman, chief executive officer, Playboy Enterprises Inc.; director, Playboy Foundation

Chicago Orchestral Association

Kennedy, George Danner: trustee, Kemper Foundation (James S.)

Chicago Pediatric Society

Harris, Irving Brooks: chairman executive committee, director, Pittway Corp.; chairman, director, Pittway Corp. Charitable Foundation

Chicago Rehabilitation Institute

Fuller, Harry Laurance: co-chairman, director, BP Amoco Corp.

Chicago Symphony Orchestra

Kennedy, George Danner: trustee, Kemper Foundation (James S.)

Stone, Roger Warren: chairman, president, chief executive officer, director, Stone Container Corp.; president, Stone Foundation

Chicago United

Terry, Richard Edward: chairman, chief executive officer, director, Peoples Energy Corp.

Chicago United Church

Connolly, Charles H.: senior vice president corporate affairs & investor relations, Whitman Corp.; president, Whitman Corp. Foundation

Chicago Urban League

Bryan, John Henry: chairman, Sara Lee Corp.; director, Sara Lee Foundation

Resnick, Myron J.: vice president, treasurer, trustee, Allstate Foundation

Terry, Richard Edward: chairman, chief executive officer, director, Peoples Energy Corp.

Chicago Youth Centers

McNally, Alan G.: chairman, chief executive officer, Harris Trust & Savings Bank

Chicago Youth Programs

Almeida, Richard: chairman, chief executive officer, Heller Financial, Inc.

Chicagoland Chamber of Commerce

Gidwitz, Ronald J.: president, chief executive officer, Curtis Industries, Inc. (Helene)

Chief Executives Organization

Duchossois, Richard Louis: secretary, Duchossois Foundation; chairman, chief executive officer, director, Duchossois Industries Inc.

Franke, William Augustus: chairman, president, chief executive officer, America West Airlines, Inc.; director, Phelps Dodge Foundation

Kampouris, Emmanuel Andrew: chairman, president, chief executive officer, director, American Standard Inc.

Zacks, Gordon Benjamin: chairman, president, chief executive officer, director, Barry Corp. (R.G.); president, Barry Foundation

Chief Naval Operations Executive Panel Washington

Kresa, Kent: chairman, president, chief executive officer, director, Northrop Grumman Corp.

Childcare Group

Agnich, Richard John: director, Texas Instruments Foundation; senior vice president, secretary, general counsel, Texas Instruments Inc.

Children Protective Services Greater Cincinnati

Campbell, Cheryl Nichols: operation service advisory group, Cincinnati Bell Inc.

Children of the Night

Rosenzweig, Richard Stuart: executive vice president, director, Playboy Enterprises Inc.

Children's Heart Link

Andreas, David Lowell: chairman, director, National City Bank Foundation; chairman, chief executive officer, National City Bank of Minneapolis

Children's Museum Atlanta

Banks, Peter L.: vice president external affairs, AGL Resources Inc.

Children's Research and Education Institute Inc.

Harris, William W.: director, Pittway Corp. Charitable Foundation

Childrens Cancer Research Foundation

Redstone, Sumner Murray: chairman, Viacom Inc.

Childrens Discovery Center

Simpson, Andrea Lynn: president

Childrens Home Society Minnesota

Weiser, Irving: chairman, president, chief executive officer, Dain Bosworth Inc.

Childrens Hospital

Cody, Thomas Gerald: executive vice president legal & human resources, Federated Department Stores, Inc.

Childrens Hospital Buffalo

Lippes, Gerald Sanford: secretary, Mark IV Industries Foundation

Childrens Hospital Foundation

Cline, Robert Stanley: chairman, chief executive officer, director, Airborne Freight Corp.

Childrens Hospital Inc.

Geier, Peter E.: vice chairman, Huntington Bancshares Inc.

Childrens Hospital Medical Center

Cody, Thomas Gerald: executive vice president legal & human resources, Federated Department Stores, Inc.

Childrens Hospital Medical Center Akron

Holland, Willard R.: chairman, chief executive officer, FirstEnergy Corp.

Childrens Hospital Philadelphia

Naples, Ronald James: president, chief executive officer, director, Quaker Chemical Corp.

Childrens Hospital Pittsburgh

Murdy, James L.: executive vice president finance and administration, chief financial officer, Allegheny Technologies Inc.; trustee, Allegheny Technologies Inc. Charitable Trust

Childrens Hospital Wisconsin

Shiely, John Stephen: president, chief operating officer, director, Briggs & Stratton Corp.; vice president, director, Briggs & Stratton Corp. Foundation

Childrens Medical Center

Redding, Peter Stoddard: trustee, Sherman-Standard Register Foundation; president, chief executive officer, director, Standard Register Co.

Childrens Memorial Hospital & Medical Center

Kennedy, George Danner: trustee, Kemper Foundation (James S.)

Childrens Memorial Medical Center

McKenna, Andrew James: director, Aon Foundation

Childrens Miracle Network

Barad, Jill Elikann: director, Mattel Foundation; chairman, chief executive officer, director, Mattel Inc.

Childrens Presbyterian Healthcare Center

Oesterreicher, James E.: chairman, chief executive officer, director, Penney Co., Inc. (J.C.)

China American Society

Masin, Michael Terry: vice chairman, president international, director, GTE Corp.; trustee, GTE Foundation

Chocolate Manufacturer Association

Viviano, Joseph P.: president, court, Hershey Foods Corp.

Christ Church Endowment Fund

Pepper, John E., Jr.: chairman executive committee, Procter & Gamble Co.

Christian Businessmens Association

Teets, John William: president, chief executive officer, director, Viad Corp. Fund

Christian Cable

Necessary, Steven K.: senior vice president marketing, Scientific-Atlanta, Inc.

Christian Democratic Alliance

Ruding, Herman Onno: vice chairman, director, Citibank Corp.

Christian Theological Seminary

Miller, William Irwin: director, Cummins Engine Foundation

Chrysler Corp. Fund
Valade, Gary C.: executive vice president, chief financial officer, DaimlerChrysler Corp.; trustee, DaimlerChrysler Corp. Fund

Chrysler Museum
Barry, Richard Francis, III: director, Landmark Communications Foundation; vice chairman, Landmark Communications Inc.

Cincinnati Art Museum
Pepper, John E., Jr.: chairman executive committee, Procter & Gamble Co.

Cincinnati Bar Association
Bridgeland, James Ralph, Jr.: trustee, Star Bank NA, Cincinnati Foundation

Cincinnati Better Business Bureau
Klinedinst, Thomas John, Jr.: trustee, Star Bank NA, Cincinnati Foundation

Cincinnati Business Committee
Pepper, John E., Jr.: chairman executive committee, Procter & Gamble Co.

Cincinnati Chamber of Commerce
LaMacchia, John Thomas: trustee, Cincinnati Bell Foundation, Inc.; president, chief executive officer, director, Cincinnati Bell Inc.

Cincinnati Council World Affairs
Pepper, John E., Jr.: chairman executive committee, Procter & Gamble Co.

Cincinnati Institute Fine Arts
Bridgeland, James Ralph, Jr.: trustee, Star Bank NA, Cincinnati Foundation

Cincinnati Medicine Institute
Pepper, John E., Jr.: chairman executive committee, Procter & Gamble Co.

Cincinnati Museum Association
Rogers, James E., Jr.: vice chairman, president, chief executive officer, Cinergy Corp.; vice chairman, director, Cinergy Foundation

Cincinnati Opera
Bridgeland, James Ralph, Jr.: trustee, Star Bank NA, Cincinnati Foundation

Cincinnati Youth Collaborative
Pepper, John E., Jr.: chairman executive committee, Procter & Gamble Co.
Wehling, Robert Louis: global marketing, government relations officer, Procter & Gamble Co.; president, trustee, Procter & Gamble Fund

Circle City Foundation
Lewis, Frances Aaronson: trustee, Circuit City Foundation

Cities Schs
Chambers, Anne Cox: chairman, trustee, Cox Foundation (James M.)

Citizens Crime Commission
Landin, Thomas Milton: vice president, director, CertainTeed Corp.; vice president, Norton Co. Foundation

Citizens Scholarship Foundation America
Feldhouse, Lynn Alexandra: vice president, secretary, DaimlerChrysler Corp. Fund

Citizens for Sound Economy
Koch, David Hamilton: director, Koch Foundation, Inc. (Fred C. and Mary R.)

City College Chicago
Gidwitz, Ronald J.: president, chief executive officer, Curtis Industries, Inc. (Helene)

City Trust Kansas City
Margolin, Abraham E.: director, Tension Envelope Foundation

City of Owatonna
Kraus, Rick: administrator, Federated Mutual Insurance Foundation

Citymeals Wheels
Tisch, Preston Robert: chairman, director, CBS Foundation; co-chairman, co-chief executive officer, director, CNA; trustee, Loews Foundation

Civic Council Greater Kansas City
Hall, Donald Joyce: chairman board, director, Hallmark Cards Inc.; chairman, Hallmark Corporate Foundation

Civic Light Opera
Rohr, James Edward: chief executive officer, president, director, PNC Financial Services Group

Civic Progress
Jacobsen, Thomas Herbert: chairman, president, chief executive officer, Mercantile Bank NA
Mueller, Charles William: chairman, president, chief executive officer, Ameren Corp.; trustee, Ameren Corp. Charitable Trust

Civic Progress Dialogue
Moten, John, Junior: vice president community relations, Laclede Gas Co.

Claremont Graduate University
Trujillo, Solomon D.: president, US West Foundation; president, chief executive officer, US West, Inc.

Claremont University Center
Barad, Jill Elikann: director, Mattel Foundation; chairman, chief executive officer, director, Mattel Inc.
Bryson, John E.: chairman, chief executive officer, Edison International

Claremont University Graduate School
Wright, Donald Franklin: director, Times Mirror Foundation

Clark Atlanta University
King, Reatha Clark: director, Fuller Co. Foundation

(H.B.); president, executive director, General Mills Foundation

Clearport School
McNeary, Joseph Allen: member grantmaking committee, Claiborne Foundation (Liz); senior vice president, Liz Claiborne, Inc.

Cleveland Bar Association
Burlingame, John Hunter: executive partner, Scripps Co. (E.W.)
Calise, Nicholas James: vice president, associate general counsel, secretary, BFGoodrich Co.; secretary, Goodrich Foundation, Inc. (B.F.)
Meyer, Russell William, Jr.: chairman, chief executive officer, Cessna Aircraft Co.; president, Cessna Foundation, Inc.

Cleveland Cliffs Iron Co.
Bezik, Cynthia B.: senior vice president, finance, Cleveland-Cliffs, Inc.

Cleveland Clinic Foundation
Gorman, Joseph T.: chairman, chief executive officer, TRW Inc.

Cleveland Clinic Inc.
Hardis, Stephen Roger: chairman, chief executive officer, director, Eaton Corp.

Cleveland Institute Art
Gorman, Joseph T.: chairman, chief executive officer, TRW Inc.

Cleveland Jewish Welfare Foundation
Mandel, Jack N.: director, Premier Industrial Corp.

Cleveland Museum Art
Cantor, Bernard Gerald: president, director, Cantor, Fitzgerald Foundation; chairman, director, Cantor, Fitzgerald Securities Corp.

Cleveland Orchestra
Burlingame, John Hunter: executive partner, Scripps Co. (E.W.)

Cleveland Playhouse
Gorman, Joseph T.: chairman, chief executive officer, TRW Inc.
Mandel, Jack N.: director, Premier Industrial Corp.

Cleveland Scholarship Program Inc.
Burner, David L.: chairman, president, chief executive officer, director, BFGoodrich Co.

Cleveland State University
Seiffert, Ron J.: vice chairman, Huntington Bancshares Inc.

Cleveland Tomorrow
Bersticker, Albert C.: chairman, director, chief executive officer, Ferro Corp.; president, trustee, Ferro Foundation
Daberko, David A.: chairman, chief executive officer, National City Corp.
Gorman, Joseph T.: chairman, chief executive officer, TRW Inc.
Hardis, Stephen Roger: chairman, chief executive officer, director, Eaton Corp.
Holland, Willard R.: chairman, chief executive officer, FirstEnergy Corp.

Cleveland YMCA
Collins, Duane E.: president, chief executive officer, director, Parker Hannifin Corp.; vice president, trustee, Parker Hannifin Foundation

Clothing Manufacturer Association America
Patel, Homi Burjor: president, chief operating officer, director, Hartmarx Corp.

Coal Industries Advisory Board
Goode, David Ronald: chairman, president, chief executive officer, director, Norfolk Southern Corp.

Coalition Drug-Free Hawaii
Dods, Walter Arthur, Jr.: president, director, First Hawaiian Foundation; chairman, chief executive officer, director, First Hawaiian, Inc.

Coalition Service Industry
O'Hare, Dean Raymond: chairman, Chubb Corp.
Reed, John Shepard: co-chairman, Citibank Corp.

Coalition of Education Initiatives
Wehling, Robert Louis: global marketing, government relations officer, Procter & Gamble Co.; president, trustee, Procter & Gamble Fund

Coker College
Browning, Peter C.: chief executive officer, president, director, Sonoco Products Co.

Cold Spring Harbor Laboratory
Warner, Douglas Alexander, III: chairman, president, chief executive officer, director, Morgan & Co. Inc. (J.P.)

Colgate Darden Graduate School
Baker, Leslie Mayo, Jr.: president, chief executive officer, chairman, Wachovia Bank of North Carolina NA; chairman, Wachovia Foundation, Inc. (The)

College Board
Raymond, Lee R.: chairman, president, chief executive officer, Exxon Mobil Corp.
Stanley, Peter William: trustee, Hitachi Foundation

College Entrance Examination Board
Stewart, Donald M.: director, New York Times Co. Foundation

College Holy Cross
Clark, Richard McCourt: senior vice president, general counsel, secretary, Kellogg Co.; vice president, trustee, Kellogg Co. Twenty-Five Year Employees' Fund Inc.
Rehm, Jack Daniel: chairman emeritus, director, Meredith Corp.

College Saint Thomas
Koch, David Andrew: president, Graco Foundation; chairman, director, Graco, Inc.

College William & Mary
Batten, Frank, Sr.: chairman, director, Landmark Communications Foundation; chairman, Landmark Communications Inc.
Plumeri, Joseph James, II: president, Citigroup

College Yr in Athens
Hatsopoulos, George Nicholas: founder, chairman, chief executive officer, director, Thermo Electron Corp.; committee member, Thermo Electron Foundation

Colonial Williamsburg Foundation
Tilghman, Richard Granville: chairman, chief executive officer, Crestar Foundation
Tobias, Randall L.: chairman emeritus, Lilly & Co. (Eli)

Colorado Alliance Business
Hall, Larry D.: chairman, president, chief executive officer, director, Kinder Morgn; president, director, KN Energy Foundation
Hock, Delwin D.: chairman, New Century Energies

Colorado Association Commerce & Industry
Hall, Larry D.: chairman, president, chief executive officer, director, Kinder Morgn; president, director, KN Energy Foundation

Colorado Bar Association
Hall, Larry D.: chairman, president, chief executive officer, director, Kinder Morgn; president, director, KN Energy Foundation
Sissel, George A.: chairman, president, chief executive officer, director, Ball Corp.
Wise, William Allen: chairman, president, chief executive officer, director, El Paso Energy Co.; chairman, director, El Paso Energy Foundation

Colorado Forum
Hock, Delwin D.: chairman, New Century Energies

Colorado Public Expenditures Council
Kelly, Richard C.: executive vice president, chief financial officer, New Century Energies; treasurer, New Century Energies Foundation

Colorado Society
Hock, Delwin D.: chairman, New Century Energies

Columbia Energy Group
Olesen, Douglas Eugene, PhD: president, chief executive officer, Battelle Memorial Institute

Columbia Health System Inc.
Fitzsimonds, Roger Leon: chairman, Firstar Milwaukee Foundation
Ladish, John: trustee, Ladish Co. Foundation

Columbia Presbyterian Hospital
Golub, Harvey: chairman, chief executive officer, director, American Express Co.; trustee, American Express Foundation

Columbia Seminary
Robinson, E. B., Jr.: chairman, chief executive officer, director, Deposit Guaranty National Bank

Columbia University
Kaden, Ellen O.: trustee, Campbell Soup Foundation
Sulzberger, Arthur Ochs, Sr.: director, New York Times Co.; chairman, director, New York Times Co. Foundation

Columbia University Business School
Cook, J. Michael: chairman, chief executive officer, Deloitte & Touche; chairman, Deloitte & Touche Foundation
Geier, Philip Henry, Jr.: chairman, president, chief executive officer, Interpublic Group of Companies, Inc.
Montrone, Paul Michael: vice president, partner, Winthrop Foundation

Columbia University Center Law Economic Studies
Millstein, Ira M.: partner, Weil, Gotshal & Manges Corp.; president, director, Weil, Gotshal & Manges Foundation

Columbia University Graduate School Business
Evans, Robert Sheldon: chairman, chief executive officer, Crane Co.; chairman, president, director, Crane Foundation

Columbia University Law School Alumni Association
Canning, John Beckman: secretary, Rayonier Foundation

Columbia University School Engineering
LaMantia, Charles Robert: president, chief executive officer, director, Little, Inc. (Arthur D.)

Columbia University School International & Public Affairs
Bronfman, Edgar Miles: chairman, trustee, Bronfman Foundation/Joseph E. Seagram & Sons, Inc. Fund (Samuel); chairman, Seagram & Sons, Inc. (Joseph E.)

Columbia University Teachers College
Schwarz, H. Marshall: chairman, chief executive officer, United States Trust Co. of New York

Columbus Area Chamber of Commerce
Baker, James Kendrick: chairman, director, Arvin Foundation; vice chairman, director, Arvin Industries, Inc.

Columbus Area Growth Foundation
McCoy, John Bonnet: president, chief executive officer, Ameritech Corp.

Columbus Bar Association
Druen, W. Sidney: director, Nationwide Insurance Enterprise Foundation

Columbus Chamber of Commerce
Brothers, John Alfred 'Fred': trustee, Ashland Inc. Foundation
McCoy, John Bonnet: president, chief executive officer, Ameritech Corp.

Columbus Children's Hospital
Brothers, John Alfred 'Fred': trustee, Ashland Inc. Foundation

Columbus Economic Development Board
Sales, A. R.: director, Arvin Foundation; treasurer, Arvin Industries, Inc.

Columbus Museum Art
Brothers, John Alfred 'Fred': trustee, Ashland Inc. Foundation
Glaser, Gary A.: president, chief executive officer, National City Bank of Columbus
Olesen, Douglas Eugene, PhD: president, chief executive officer, Battelle Memorial Institute
Seiffert, Ron J.: vice chairman, Huntington Bancshares Inc.

Columbus Regional Hospital Foundation
Sales, A. R.: director, Arvin Foundation; treasurer, Arvin Industries, Inc.

Combined Health Appeal
Grise, Cheryl W.: senior vice president, chief administrative officer, Northeast Utilities

Combined Jewish Philanthropies Greater Boston
Redstone, Sumner Murray: chairman, Viacom Inc.

Comm 200
Hefner, Christie Ann: chairman, chief executive officer, Playboy Enterprises Inc.; director, Playboy Foundation

Commerical Development Association

Stewart, S. Jay: chairman, chief executive officer, director, Morton International Inc.

Commit, Inc.

Koch, Robert Louis, II: president, chief executive officer, director, Koch Enterprises, Inc.; president, director, Koch Foundation

Committee 100

Townsend, David L.: vice president administration, Walter Industries Inc.

Committee 200

Bartz, Carol A.: director, Autodesk Foundation; chairman, chief executive officer, Autodesk Inc.

Committee Civil Rights

Kaden, Ellen O.: trustee, Campbell Soup Foundation

Committee Federal Regulation Securities

Lang, Robert Todd: chairman, director, Weil, Gotshal & Manges Foundation

Committee Monetary Union Europe

Ruding, Herman Onno: vice chairman, director, Citibank Corp.

Committee for Economic Development

Becherer, Hans Walter: chairman, chief executive officer, director, Deere & Co.; director, Deere Foundation (John)

Brademas, John: chairman, Texaco Foundation

Brown, Stephen Lee: chairman, chief executive officer, director, Hancock Financial Services (John)

Bryan, John Henry: chairman, Sara Lee Corp.; director, Sara Lee Foundation

Carroll, Philip Joseph: chairman, chief executive officer, Fluor Corp.; chairman, trustee, Fluor Foundation

Daniels, John Hancock: chairman, Archer-Daniels-Midland Foundation

Ferland, E. James: chairman, president, chief executive officer, Public Service Electric & Gas Co.

Gelb, Richard Lee: director, New York Times Co. Foundation

Gilmartin, Raymond V.: chairman, president, chief executive officer, Merck & Co.; chairman, Merck Co. Foundation

Gorman, Joseph T.: chairman, chief executive officer, TRW Inc.

Graham, Thomas Carlisle: trustee, AK Steel Foundation

James, George Barker, II: senior vice president, chief financial officer, Levi Strauss & Co.

Kangas, Edward A.: chairman, chief executive officer, Deloitte & Touche

Kasputys, Joseph Edward: chairman, trustee, Hitachi Foundation

O'Reilly, F. Anthony John: chairman, trustee, Heinz Co. Foundation (H.J.); chairman, director, Heinz Co. (H.J.)

Roth, Michael I.: chairman, chief executive officer, director, MONY Group (The); director, MONY Life Insurance of New York (The)

Schacht, Henry Brewer: director, Cummins Engine Foundation

Shoemate, Charles Richard: chairman, president, chief executive officer, Bestfoods

Commonwealth Fund Commission on Womens Health

Heimbold, Charles Andreas, Jr.: chairman, president, chief executive officer, Bristol-Myers Squibb Co.

Commonwealth University

Lewis, Frances Aaronson: trustee, Circuit City Foundation

Communication Economic Development New York

Hipp, William Hayne: president, chief executive officer, director, Liberty Corp.; chairman, president, director, Liberty Corp. Foundation

Community Alliance Foundation

Koch, Robert Louis, II: president, chief executive officer, director, Koch Enterprises, Inc.; president, director, Koch Foundation

Community Cancer Center Building Fund, Johnson Memorial

Fiondella, Robert William: chairman, president, chief executive officer, Phoenix Home Life Mutual Insurance Co.

Community Economic Development

Hohn, Harry George, Jr.: chairman, director, New York Life Foundation

Community Foundation Southeastern Michigan

Manoogian, Richard Alexander: chairman, chief executive officer, director, Masco Corp.

Community Foundations Fairfield County

Hays, Thomas Chandler: chairman, chief executive officer, director, Fortune Brands, Inc.

Community Hospital Indianapolis

Sease, Gene Elwood: director, Central Newspapers Foundation

Community School

Maritz, William Edward: chairman, chief executive officer, president, Maritz Inc.

Community Society

Lucky, Robert Wendell: corporate vice president, Telcordia Technologies

Competitive Wisconsin Inc.

Davis, Erroll Brown, Jr.: president, chief executive officer, director, Wisconsin Power & Light Co.

Fitzsimonds, Roger Leon: chairman, Firstar Milwaukee Foundation

Graff, Stephen Ney: director, Bucyrus-Erie Foundation

Competitiveness Policy Council

Gorman, Joseph T.: chairman, chief executive officer, TRW Inc.

Computer Law Forum

Ballantyne, Richard Lee: vice president, general counsel, secretary, Harris Corp.; secretary, treasurer, Harris Foundation

Computer Museum

Lucky, Robert Wendell: corporate vice president, Telcordia Technologies

Computer Systems Policy Project

Platt, Lewis Emmett: chairman, Hewlett-Packard Co.

Unruh, James Arlen: director, Ameritech Foundation

Concord Coalition

Hatsopoulos, George Nicholas: founder, chairman, chief executive officer, director, Thermo Electron Corp.; committee member, Thermo Electron Foundation

Conference Board

Becherer, Hans Walter: chairman, chief executive officer, director, Deere & Co.; director, Deere Foundation (John)

Bettacchi, Robert J.: senior vice president, Grace & Co. (W.R.)

Bijur, Peter I.: chairman, chief executive officer, Texaco Inc.

Blount, Winton Malcolm, Jr.: chairman, Blount International, Inc.

Browning, Peter C.: chief executive officer, president, director, Sonoco Products Co.

Carr, Cassandra Colvin: director, SBC Foundation

Cook, J. Michael: chairman, chief executive officer, Deloitte & Touche; chairman, Deloitte & Touche Foundation

Gelb, Richard Lee: director, New York Times Co. Foundation

Gorman, Joseph T.: chairman, chief executive officer, TRW Inc.

Gorman, Maureen V.: vice president, GTE Foundation

Haas, Robert Douglas: chairman, chief executive officer, director, Levi Strauss & Co.; president, Levi Strauss Foundation

Kalaher, Richard A.: president, American Standard Foundation; vice president, secretary, general counsel, American Standard Inc.

LaMantia, Charles Robert: president, chief executive officer, director, Little, Inc. (Arthur D.)

Marriott, J. Willard, Jr.: chairman, chief executive officer, Marriott International Inc.

Miller, Joseph Irwin: director associate, Cummins Engine Co., Inc.; director, Cummins Engine Foundation

Moffitt, Donald Eugene: chairman, director, CNF Transportation, Inc.

O'Reilly, F. Anthony John: chairman, trustee, Heinz Co. Foundation (H.J.); chairman, director, Heinz Co. (H.J.)

Ong, John Doyle: chairman board, director, Ameritech Corp.

Schacht, Henry Brewer: director, Cummins Engine Foundation

Sheehan, Jeremiah J.: chairman, director, Reynolds Metals Co. Foundation

Weinberg, John Livingston: chairman, president, director, Goldman Sachs Foundation

Whitwam, David Ray: chairman, president, chief executive officer, director, Whirlpool Corp.

Wiksten, Barry Frank: president, CIGNA Foundation

Conference Board & Economic

Hays, Thomas Chandler: chairman, chief executive officer, director, Fortune Brands, Inc.

Conference Board Canada

DeSimone, Livio Diego: chairman, chief executive officer, Minnesota Mining & Manufacturing Co.

Conference Board Council Financial Executive

Hernandez, William H.: director, PPG Industries Foundation; senior vice president, PPG Industries, Inc.

Conference Board Council Financial Executives

Kelson, Richard B.: director, Alcoa Foundation

Conference Board Inc.

Coughlan, Gary Patrick: chief financial officer, senior vice president finance, Abbott Laboratories; director, Abbott Laboratories Fund

Gilmartin, Raymond V.: chairman, president, chief

executive officer, Merck & Co.; chairman, Merck Co. Foundation

Sanger, Stephen W.: chairman, trustee, General Mills Foundation; chairman, chief executive officer, director, General Mills, Inc.

Shoemate, Charles Richard: chairman, president, chief executive officer, Bestfoods

Conference Board New York

Farley, James Bernard: chairman emeritus, trustee, Walter Industries Inc.

Howard, James Joseph, III: chairman, president, chief executive officer, director, Northern States Power Co.

Conference Boards Council Financial Executives

Mee, Michael F.: senior vice president, chief financial officer, Bristol-Myers Squibb Co.

Connecticut Academy Science & Engineering

Kaman, Charles Huron: chairman, president, chief executive officer, director, Kaman Corp.

Connecticut Bar Association

Barnes, Wallace W.: director, Barnes Group Foundation Inc.

Barnette, Curtis Handley: chairman, chief executive officer, director, Bethlehem Steel Corp.

Calise, Nicholas James: vice president, associate general counsel, secretary, BFGoodrich Co.; secretary, Goodrich Foundation, Inc. (B.F.)

Clark, Richard McCourt: senior vice president, general counsel, secretary, Kellogg Co.; vice president, trustee, Kellogg Co. Twenty-Five Year Employees' Fund Inc.

Fiondella, Robert William: chairman, president, chief executive officer, Phoenix Home Life Mutual Insurance Co.

Long, Michael Thomas: director, Ensign-Bickford Foundation

Connecticut Business & Industry Association

Barnes, Wallace W.: director, Barnes Group Foundation Inc.

Fiondella, Robert William: chairman, president, chief executive officer, Phoenix Home Life Mutual Insurance Co.

Kaman, Charles Huron: chairman, president, chief executive officer, director, Kaman Corp.

Walker, Grahame: chairman, chief executive officer, Dexter Corp.; president, Dexter Corp. Foundation

Connecticut Children's Center Campaign Our Children

Fiondella, Robert William: chairman, president, chief executive officer, Phoenix Home Life Mutual Insurance Co.

Connecticut Joint Council Economic Education

Miglio, Daniel Joseph: chairman, president, director, chief executive officer, Southern New England Telephone Co.

Connecticut Society Professional Engineers

Kaman, Charles Huron: chairman, president, chief executive officer, director, Kaman Corp.

Connectivity Technologies Inc.

Kelbley, Stephen Paul: executive vice president, Springs Industries, Inc.

Conservative International

Eisner, Michael Dammann: president, trustee, Disney Co. Foundation (Walt); chairman, chief executive officer, director, Disney Co. (Walt)

Resnick, Lynda Rae: vice chairman, co-owner, Franklin Mint (The)

Consolidated Civic Foundation

Mead, George Wilson, II: president, director, Consolidated Papers Foundation, Inc.; chairman, director, Consolidated Papers, Inc.

Consortium Financing Higher Education

Stanley, Peter William: trustee, Hitachi Foundation

Consult Contractors Council America

Cloud, Bruce Benjamin, Sr.: vice chairman, director, Zachry Co. (H.B.)

Consumer Advisory Council

Williams, Edward Joseph: president, director, Harris Bank Foundation

Consumer Bankers Association

Aldinger, William F., III: chairman, chief executive officer, director, Household International Inc.

Consumer Electronics Manufacturers Association

Taylor, John I.: director, Zenith Electronics Corp.

Contemporary Museum

Dods, Walter Arthur, Jr.: president, director, First Hawaiian Foundation; chairman, chief executive officer, director, First Hawaiian, Inc.

Cook Inlet Tribal Council

Huhndorf, Roy M.: president, CIRI Foundation

Cooper-Hewitt Museum

Ross, Arthur: senior vice president, Central National-Gottesman; director, Central National-Gottesman Foundation

Copper Development Association

Osborne, Richard de Jongh: director, ASARCO Foundation; chairman, chief executive officer, director, ASARCO Inc.

Whisler, J. Steven: chairman, president, chief executive officer, Phelps Dodge Corp.

Cornell University

Johnson, Samuel Curtis: chairman, director, president, Johnson & Son (S.C.); chairman, trustee, Johnson Wax Fund (S.C.)

Lee, Charles Robert: chairman, chief executive officer, director, GTE Corp.; chief executive officer, trustee, GTE Foundation

Platt, Lewis Emmett: chairman, Hewlett-Packard Co.

Cornell University Council

Cottrell, G. Walton: senior vice president, chief financial officer, Carpenter Technology Corp.

Cornell University Johnson Graduate School Management

Johnson, Samuel Curtis: chairman, director, president, Johnson & Son (S.C.); chairman, trustee, Johnson Wax Fund (S.C.)

Weill, Sanford I.: chairman, chief executive officer, Citibank Corp.; chairman, Citigroup Foundation

Cornell University Medicine College

Cook, J. Michael: chairman, chief executive officer, Deloitte & Touche; chairman, Deloitte & Touche Foundation

Weill, Sanford I.: chairman, chief executive officer, Citibank Corp.; chairman, Citigroup Foundation

Cornerstones

Apodaca, Clara: trustee, Hitachi Foundation

Corning Classic Charities Inc.

Peck, Arthur John, Jr.: secretary, vice president, Corning Inc.; secretary, Corning Inc. Foundation

Corning Glass Works Foundation

Campbell, Van C.: vice chairman, chief financial officer, chief administrative officer, director, Corning Inc.; trustee, Corning Inc. Foundation

Ughetta, William Casper: trustee, Corning Inc. Foundation

Corning Museum Glass

Ackerman, Roger G.: trustee, Corning Inc. Foundation

Buechner, Thomas Scharman: trustee, Corning Inc. Foundation

Houghton, James Richardson: director, Corning Inc.; trustee, Corning Inc. Foundation

Peck, Arthur John, Jr.: secretary, vice president, Corning Inc.; secretary, Corning Inc. Foundation

Ughetta, William Casper: trustee, Corning Inc. Foundation

Corp. Commn Edn Technology

Redstone, Sumner Murray: chairman, Viacom Inc.

Corp. Counsel Association

Salinger, Robert M.: secretary, First Financial Foundation

Corp. Engineers Quebec

Light, Walter Frederick: trustee, Air Products Foundation

Corporate Council Arts

Cline, Robert Stanley: chairman, chief executive officer, director, Airborne Freight Corp.

Corporate Council Association Greater Atlanta

Harkey, Robert Shelton: trustee, Delta Air Lines Foundation; senior vice president, general counsel, secretary, Delta Air Lines, Inc.

Corporate International Trade

Kalainov, Sam Charles: chairman, president, chief executive officer, AmerUS Group

Cosmetic Toiletry Fragrance Association

Preston, James Edward: vice president, director, Avon Products Foundation, Inc.; chairman, chief executive officer, director, Avon Products, Inc.

Council 100

Gloyd, Lawrence Eugene: trustee, CLARCOR Foundation; chairman, chief executive officer, director, CLARCOR Inc.

Council Aid Education

Brademas, John: chairman, Texaco Foundation

Council Americas

Kinsolving, Augustus Blagden: director, ASARCO Foundation

Luke, John A., Jr.: chairman, president, chief executive officer, director, Westvaco Corp.
Osborne, Richard de Jongh: director, ASARCO Foundation; chairman, chief executive officer, director, ASARCO Inc.
Rhodes, William Reginald: vice chairman, Citibank Corp.

Council BBBs

Feldhouse, Lynn Alexandra: vice president, secretary, DaimlerChrysler Corp. Fund

Council Better Louisiana

Purvis, George Frank, Jr.: chairman, president, chief executive officer, director, Pan-American Life Insurance Co.

Council Communication Economic Development

Bronfman, Edgar Miles: chairman, trustee, Bronfman Foundation/Joseph E. Seagram & Sons, Inc. Fund (Samuel); chairman, Seagram & Sons, Inc. (Joseph E.)

Council Competitiveness

Allaire, Paul Arthur: chairman, chief executive officer, chairman executive committee, Xerox Corp.; president, Xerox Foundation
Gorman, Joseph T.: chairman, chief executive officer, TRW Inc.

Council Fashion Designers America

Klein, Calvin Richard: president, Calvin Klein

Council Fgn Relations

Mulford, David: chairman, Credit Suisse First Boston

Council Financial Executives

Barnes, W. Michael: senior vice president finance & planning, chief financial officer, Rockwell International Corp.; member trust committee, Rockwell International Corp. Trust
Coughlan, Gary Patrick: chief financial officer, senior vice president finance, Abbott Laboratories; director, Abbott Laboratories Fund
Dammerman, Dennis Dean: vice chairman, director, General Electric Co.

Council Foreign Relations

Allaire, Paul Arthur: chairman, chief executive officer, chairman executive committee, Xerox Corp.; president, Xerox Foundation
Armstrong, C. Michael: chairman, chief executive officer, AT&T Corp.
Becherer, Hans Walter: chairman, chief executive officer, director, Deere & Co.; director, Deere Foundation (John)
Bijur, Peter I.: chairman, chief executive officer, Texaco Inc.
Bowen, William Gordon, PhD: trustee, Merck Co. Foundation
Bronfman, Edgar Miles: chairman, trustee, Bronfman Foundation/Joseph E. Seagram & Sons, Inc. Fund (Samuel); chairman, Seagram & Sons, Inc. (Joseph E.)
Chambers, Anne Cox: chairman, trustee, Cox Foundation (James M.)
Coughlan, Gary Patrick: chief financial officer, senior vice president finance, Abbott Laboratories; director, Abbott Laboratories Fund
Douglass, Robert Royal: trustee, Chase Manhattan Foundation
Franklin, Barbara Hackman: director, Dow Chemical Co.
Furlaud, Richard Mortimer: interim chief executive officer, International Flavors & Fragrances Inc.
Gelb, Richard Lee: director, New York Times Co. Foundation
Gerstner, Louis Vincent, Jr.: chairman, chief executive officer, director, International Business Machines Corp.
Gorelick, Jamie Shona: vice chairman, Fannie Mae
Gorman, Joseph T.: chairman, chief executive officer, TRW Inc.
Graham, Katharine Meyer: chairman executive committee, director, The Washington Post
Haas, Robert Douglas: chairman, chief executive officer, director, Levi Strauss & Co.; president, Levi Strauss Foundation
Huber, Richard Leslie: chairman, president, chief executive officer, director, Aetna, Inc.
Ingersoll, Robert Stephen: chairman, director, Panasonic Foundation
Kissinger, Henry Alfred: director, CBS Foundation
Kogan, Richard Jay: chairman, chief executive officer, Schering-Plough Corp.; trustee, member, Schering-Plough Foundation
Labrecque, Thomas Goulet: president, chief operating officer, director, Chase Manhattan Bank, NA; president, Chase Manhattan Foundation
Levin, Michael Stuart: president, chief executive officer, Titan Industrial Corp.
Luke, John A., Jr.: chairman, president, chief executive officer, director, Westvaco Corp.
Marron, Donald Baird: chairman, chief executive officer, director, Paine Webber; trustee, Paine Webber Foundation
Masin, Michael Terry: vice chairman, president international, director, GTE Corp.; trustee, GTE Foundation
Mead, Dana George: chairman, chief executive officer, director, Tenneco Automotive
Meyerson, Martin: director, Panasonic Foundation
Nelson, Merlin Edward: chairman, director, IBJ Foundation
Osborne, Richard de Jongh: director, ASARCO Foundation; chairman, chief executive officer, director, ASARCO Inc.
Raymond, Lee R.: chairman, president, chief executive officer, Exxon Mobil Corp.
Rhodes, William Reginald: vice chairman, Citibank Corp.
Ripley, Sidney Dillon, II: director emeritus, Hitachi Foundation
Ross, Arthur: senior vice president, Central National-Gottesman; director, Central National-Gottesman Foundation
Ryan, John Thomas, III: chairman, chief executive officer, Mine Safety Appliances Co.
Schacht, Henry Brewer: director, Cummins Engine Foundation
Shapiro, Isaac: chairman, secretary, trustee, Ise Cultural Foundation
Stanley, Peter William: trustee, Hitachi Foundation
Stockman, David A.: co-chairman, director, Collins & Aikman Corp.; president, director, Collins & Aikman Foundation
Thoman, G. Richard: president, chief operating officer, Xerox Corp.
Tisch, Laurence Alan: chairman, co-chief executive officer, CBS Corp.; trustee, Loews Foundation
Weinberg, John Livingston: chairman, president, director, Goldman Sachs Foundation
Whitehead, John Cunningham: chairman board, Goldman Sachs Foundation
Wilbur, Brayton, Jr.: president, chief executive officer, Wilbur-Ellis Co. & Connell Brothers Co.; president, Wilbur Foundation (Brayton)
Wilmers, Robert George: chairman, president, chief executive officer, Manufacturers & Traders Trust Co.
Zilkha, Ezra Khedouri: president, treasurer, Zilkha Foundation, Inc.; president, Zilkha & Sons
Zuckerman, Mortimer Benjamin: co-founder, chairman, co-publisher, director, Daily News

Council Foreign Relations Chicago

Welsh, Kelly Raymond: executive vice president, general counsel, Ameritech Corp.

Council Foundations

Carey, Kathryn Ann: foundation manager, American Honda Foundation

Council Jewish Federations

Wander, Herbert S.: secretary, director, Katten, Muchin & Zavis Foundation

Council LaRaza

Trujillo, Solomon D.: president, US West Foundation; president, chief executive officer, US West, Inc.

Council Medicine College Wisconsin

Bueche, Wendell Francis: director, Marshall & Ilsley Foundation, Inc.

Council Michigan Foundations

Feldhouse, Lynn Alexandra: vice president, secretary, DaimlerChrysler Corp. Fund

Council Support Higher Education

Robinson, E. B., Jr.: chairman, chief executive officer, director, Deposit Guaranty National Bank

Council for Canadian Unity

Flood, Al: chairman, chief executive officer, CIBC Oppenheimer

County Lawyers Association

Dubin, Stephen Victor: vice president, secretary, Farber Foundation

Court Appointed Special Advocates

Schafer, Glenn Stanley: president, director, Pacific Mutual Life Insurance Co.

Covenant House

Bachmann, Richard Arthur: vice president, secretary, treasurer, director, Louisiana Land & Exploration Co. Foundation

Craft & Folk Art Museum

Rosenzweig, Richard Stuart: executive vice president, director, Playboy Enterprises Inc.

Cranbrook Educational Community

Miller, Eugene A.: chairman, chief executive officer, Comerica Inc.

Cranbrook Kingswood Schools

Lyon, Wayne Barton: president, chief operating officer, director, Masco Corp.

Credit Comml France

Hohn, Harry George, Jr.: chairman, director, New York Life Foundation

Creighton University

Feller, Mimi A.: senior vice president public affairs & government relations, Gannett Co., Inc.; vice president, Gannett Foundation
Rohde, Bruce: vice chairman, chief executive officer, ConAgra, Inc.
Scott, Walter, Jr.: member contributions committee, Kiewit Companies Foundation

Crouse-Irving Memorial Hospital

Davis, William E.: chairman, chief executive officer, Niagara Mohawk Holdings Inc.

Cultural Trust

Rohr, James Edward: chief executive officer, president, director, PNC Financial Services Group

Culver Education Foundation

Batten, Frank, Sr.: chairman, director, Landmark Communications Foundation; chairman, Landmark Communications Inc.

Henderson, James Alan: vice chairman, chief executive officer, director, Ameritech Corp.; chairman, director, Cummins Engine Foundation

Cumberland Co. Training Resource Center

Hebert, William L.: assistant secretary, treasurer, Louisiana-Pacific Foundation

Cystic Fibrosis Foundation

Maritz, William Edward: chairman, chief executive officer, president, Maritz Inc.

DC Bar Association

Barnette, Curtis Handley: chairman, chief executive officer, director, Bethlehem Steel Corp.

Bell, Wayne: secretary, Ralph's-Food 4 Less Foundation; senior counsel, assistant secretary, Ralph's Grocery Co.

Bryson, John E.: chairman, chief executive officer, Edison International

Rutstein, David W.: secretary, Giant Food Foundation; senior vice president, general counsel, chief administrative officer, Giant Food Inc.

Smith, Donald Kaye: senior vice president, general counsel, director, GEICO Corp.

Walsh, Michael J.: vice president, CertainTeed Corp.

DC College Access

Gorelick, Jamie Shona: vice chairman, Fannie Mae

DIY Research Institute

DiCamillo, Gary Thomas: chairman, chief executive officer, director, Polaroid Corp.

DNA New Alternative Working Group

Kresa, Kent: chairman, president, chief executive officer, director, Northrop Grumman Corp.

DPL Inc.

Hill, Allen M.: president, chief executive officer, Dayton Power and Light Co.

DPQA University AR

Martin, Bobby L.: member, Wal-Mart Foundation

DS & RH Gottesman Foundation

Wallach, Ira D.: chairman, Central National-Gottesman; executive vice president, Central National-Gottesman Foundation

DT Watson Rehabilitation Hospital

Gregg, Walter Emmor, Junior: senior executive vice president finance & administration, PNC Financial Services Group

Dade County Bar Association

Herron, James Michael: secretary, director, Ryder System Charitable Foundation

Dade County Youth Fair & Expo

Goode, R. Ray: director, Ryder System Charitable Foundation

Dairy Institute California

Cronk, William F., III: president, director, Dreyer's Grand Ice Cream

Dallas Advertising League

Huey, Ward L., Jr.: president broadcast division, vice chairman, director, Belo Corp. (A.H.); vice president, trustee, Belo Corp. Foundation (A.H.)

Dallas Arboretum

Haddock, Ronald Wayne: president, chief executive officer, director, FINA; president, FINA Foundation

Dallas Bar Association

Agnich, Richard John: director, Texas Instruments Foundation; senior vice president, secretary, general counsel, Texas Instruments Inc.

Crook, Donald Martin: secretary, Kimberly-Clark Foundation

Godfrey, Cullen Michael: vice president, FINA Foundation

Matthews, Clark J., II: president, chief executive officer, director, 7-Eleven, Inc.

Nye, Erle Allen: chairman, chief executive officer, director, TU Electric Co.

Dallas Bar Foundation

Godfrey, Cullen Michael: vice president, FINA Foundation

Dallas Chamber of Commerce

Haddock, Ronald Wayne: president, chief executive officer, director, FINA; president, FINA Foundation

Nye, Erle Allen: chairman, chief executive officer, director, TU Electric Co.

Dallas Citizens Council

Engibous, Thomas James: director, Texas Instruments Foundation; president, chief executive officer, chairman, director, Texas Instruments Inc.

Haddock, Ronald Wayne: president, chief executive officer, director, FINA; president, FINA Foundation

Raymond, Lee R.: chairman, president, chief executive officer, Exxon Mobil Corp.

Dallas Committee Foreign Relations

Nye, Erle Allen: chairman, chief executive officer, director, TU Electric Co.

Raymond, Lee R.: chairman, president, chief executive officer, Exxon Mobil Corp.

Dallas Foundation

Huey, Ward L., Jr.: president broadcast division, vice chairman, director, Belo Corp. (A.H.); vice president, trustee, Belo Corp. Foundation (A.H.)

Nye, Erle Allen: chairman, chief executive officer, director, TU Electric Co.

Dallas Morning News Energy Board

Haddock, Ronald Wayne: president, chief executive officer, director, FINA; president, FINA Foundation

Dallas Museum Art

Godfrey, Cullen Michael: vice president, FINA Foundation

Dallas Opera

Haddock, Ronald Wayne: president, chief executive officer, director, FINA; president, FINA Foundation

Dallas Symphony Association

Brooks, E. Richard 'Dick': chairman, chief executive officer, director, Central & South West Services

Dallas Together Forum

Haddock, Ronald Wayne: president, chief executive officer, director, FINA; president, FINA Foundation

Nye, Erle Allen: chairman, chief executive officer, director, TU Electric Co.

Dallas Un Board

Haddock, Ronald Wayne: president, chief executive officer, director, FINA; president, FINA Foundation

Dalton School New York

Tisch, James S.: president, chief executive officer, director, CNA

Dana Farber Cancer Institute

Countryman, Gary Lee: chairman, Liberty Mutual Insurance Group

Redstone, Sumner Murray: chairman, Viacom Inc.

Danforth Foundation

Vagelos, Pindaros Roy: trustee, Prudential Insurance Co. of America

Darden School Foundation

Spilman, Robert H.: chairman, chief executive officer, Bassett Furniture Industries; chairman, director, Bassett Furniture Industries Fdn.

Darlington County Bar Association

DeLoach, Harris E., Junior: executive vice president, director, Sonoco Products Co.

Darlington County Community in School

Browning, Peter C.: chief executive officer, president, director, Sonoco Products Co.

Dartmouth College

Masin, Michael Terry: vice chairman, president international, director, GTE Corp.; trustee, GTE Foundation

Dartmouth College Amos Tuck School Business Administration

Cohen, Jonathan L.: secretary, director, Goldman Sachs Foundation

Davenport College Business

Sadler, Robert L.: president, vice chairman, director, Old Kent Bank

Davidson College

Herring, Leonard Gray: vice president, Lowe's Charitable and Educational Foundation

Dayton Bar Association

Forster, Peter Hans: chairman, director, Dayton Power and Light Co.

Dayton Business Committee Area Progress Council

Holmes, David Richard: chief executive officer, chief operating officer, director, Reynolds & Reynolds Co.

De La Salle Institute

Donovan, Thomas Roy: president, chief executive officer, Chicago Board of Trade

De Paul University College Commerce

Coughlan, Gary Patrick: chief financial officer, senior vice president finance, Abbott Laboratories; director, Abbott Laboratories Fund

De Paul University Government Assistance Project
Schueppert, George Louis: chief financial officer, executive vice president, Outboard Marine Corp.

DePaul University
McNally, Alan G.: chairman, chief executive officer, Harris Trust & Savings Bank

Terry, Richard Edward: chairman, chief executive officer, director, Peoples Energy Corp.

DePauw University
Sharpe, Robert Francis, Jr.: senior vice president public affairs, general counsel, PepsiCo, Inc.

DeWitt Wallace Fund For Memorial Sloan Kettering Cancer Center
Weinberg, John Livingston: chairman, president, director, Goldman Sachs Foundation

Deaconess Hospital
Muehlbauer, James Herman: vice president, director, Koch Foundation

Deafness Research Foundation
Hoyt, Henry Hamilton, Jr.: president, Carter-Wallace Foundation; chairman, chief executive officer, director, Carter-Wallace, Inc.

Dealer Bank Association
Robinson, E. B., Jr.: chairman, chief executive officer, director, Deposit Guaranty National Bank

Deerfield Academy Alumni Association
Hassenfeld, Alan Geoffrey: president, Hasbro Charitable Trust Inc.; chairman, chief executive officer, Hasbro, Inc.

Defenders Wildlife
Martinez, Arthur C.: chairman, chief executive officer, president, Sears, Roebuck and Co.

Defense Institute Initiative Steering Committee
Gorman, Joseph T.: chairman, chief executive officer, TRW Inc.

Defense Orientation Conference Association
Stauffer, Stanley Howard: chairman, Stauffer Communications Foundation

Defense Policy Advisory Committee Trade
Armstrong, C. Michael: chairman, chief executive officer, AT&T Corp.

Defense Science Board
Kresa, Kent: chairman, president, chief executive officer, director, Northrop Grumman Corp.

Delta Kappa Epsilon
Pulliam, Eugene Smith: vice president, director, Central Newspapers Foundation

Purvis, George Frank, Jr.: chairman, president, chief executive officer, director, Pan-American Life Insurance Co.

Delta Mu Delta
Brumm, Paul Michael: executive vice president, chief financial officer, Fifth Third Bancorp

Sadler, Robert L.: president, vice chairman, director, Old Kent Bank

Delta Sigma Pi
Connor, James Richard: executive director, Kemper Foundation (James S.)

Randolph, Jackson Harold: chairman, Cinergy Corp.; chairman, director, Cinergy Foundation

Delta Sigma Theta
King, Reatha Clark: director, Fuller Co. Foundation (H.B.); president, executive director, General Mills Foundation

Delta Upsilon
Gaiswinkler, Robert Sigfried: chairman, director, First Financial Bank; director, First Financial Foundation

Democrat Leadership Council
Sullivan, Austin Padraic, Junior: trustee, General Mills Foundation; senior vice president corporate relations, General Mills, Inc.

Denison University
Bowen, William Gordon, PhD: trustee, Merck Co. Foundation

Eisner, Michael Dammann: president, trustee, Disney Co. Foundation (Walt); chairman, chief executive officer, director, Disney Co. (Walt)

Department Aeronautics & Astronautics Corp.
Kresa, Kent: chairman, president, chief executive officer, director, Northrop Grumman Corp.

Department Energy
Hill, George Richard: president, trustee, Lubrizol Foundation (The)

Des Moines Arts Center
Kelley, Bruce Gunn: vice president, director, Employers Mutual Charitable Foundation

Detroit Funders Collaborative
Feldhouse, Lynn Alexandra: vice president, secretary, DaimlerChrysler Corp. Fund

Detroit Institute Arts
Brennan, Leo Joseph, Jr.: vice president, executive director, Ford Motor Co. Fund

Detroit Institute Arts Founder Society
Manoogian, Richard Alexander: chairman, chief executive officer, director, Masco Corp.

Detroit Medical Center
Miller, Eugene A.: chairman, chief executive officer, Comerica Inc.

Detroit Renaissance Inc.
Eaton, Robert James: co-chairman, president, chief executive officer, DaimlerChrysler Corp.

Manoogian, Richard Alexander: chairman, chief executive officer, director, Masco Corp.

Smith, John Francis, Jr.: chairman, General Motors Corp.

Detroit Symphony Orchestra
Eaton, Robert James: co-chairman, president, chief executive officer, DaimlerChrysler Corp.

Detroit Symphony Orchestra Hall Inc.
Miller, Eugene A.: chairman, chief executive officer, Comerica Inc.

Detroit Zoological Society
Brennan, Leo Joseph, Jr.: vice president, executive director, Ford Motor Co. Fund

Diggers Hotline
Thies, Richard Henry: assistant treasurer, Madison Gas & Electric Foundation

Dinamo Ovia
Usher, Thomas J.: chairman, chief executive officer, USX Corp.; chairman board trustees, USX Foundation, Inc.

Direct Marketing Association
Moritz, Charles Worthington: chairman, director, Dun & Bradstreet Corp.

Directors Guild American West
Disney, Roy Edward: trustee, Disney Co. Foundation (Walt); vice chairman, director, Disney Co. (Walt)

Discovery Museum Bridgeport
Sargent, Joseph Dudley: president, chief executive officer, director, Guardian Life Insurance Co. of America

District of Columbia Bar Association
Ruckelshaus, William Doyle: chairman, director, Browning-Ferris Industries Inc.

Donors Forum Wisconsin
Gallagher, Richard S.: director, Badger Meter Foundation

Downtown Association
Kinsolving, Augustus Blagden: director, ASARCO Foundation

Osborne, Richard de Jongh: director, ASARCO Foundation; chairman, chief executive officer, director, ASARCO Inc.

Downtown Cincinnati Inc.
Wehling, Robert Louis: global marketing, government relations officer, Procter & Gamble Co.; president, trustee, Procter & Gamble Fund

Downtown Dayton Partnership
Holmes, David Richard: chief executive officer, chief operating officer, director, Reynolds & Reynolds Co.

Downtown Medical Center
Lippes, Gerald Sanford: secretary, Mark IV Industries Foundation

Downtown-Lower Manhattan Association
Douglass, Robert Royal: trustee, Chase Manhattan Foundation

Dr Seuss Foundation
ZoBell, Karl: vice president, trustee, Copley Foundation (James S.)

Drake University
Drury, David J.: chief executive officer, chairman, Principal Financial Group

Kalainov, Sam Charles: chairman, president, chief executive officer, AmerUS Group

Pomerantz, Marvin Alvin: trustee, Mid-American Foundation

Rehm, Jack Daniel: chairman emeritus, director, Meredith Corp.

Dramatists Guild
Hotchner, Aaron Edward: vice president, director, executive, Newman's Own Foundation; vice president, treasurer, Newman's Own Inc.

Drew University
Shinn, George Latimer: director, New York Times Co. Foundation

Drexel University
McNeill, Corbin Asahel, Jr.: president, chief executive officer, director, chairman, PECO Energy Co.

Drucker Center Claremont Graduate School

Bachmann, John W.: managing partner, Jones & Co. (Edward D.); chairman, Jones & Co. Foundation (Edward D.)

Drug Use is Life Abuse

Rinehart, Charles Robert: chairman, chief executive officer, director, Washington Mutual, Inc.

Drugs Dont Work Leadership Council

Cook, J. Michael: chairman, chief executive officer, Deloitte & Touche; chairman, Deloitte & Touche Foundation

Ducks Unlimited Inc.

Coors, Peter Hanson: vice president, director, Coors Brewing Co.

Duke University

Goode, David Ronald: chairman, president, chief executive officer, director, Norfolk Southern Corp.

Tobias, Randall L.: chairman emeritus, Lilly & Co. (Eli)

Duke University Fuqua School Business

Goode, David Ronald: chairman, president, chief executive officer, director, Norfolk Southern Corp.

Labrecque, Thomas Goulet: president, chief operating officer, director, Chase Manhattan Bank, NA; president, Chase Manhattan Foundation

Duke University Law School

Burrus, Robert Lewis, Jr.: trustee, Circuit City Foundation

Dumbarton Oaks Research Library

Brademas, John: chairman, Texaco Foundation

Duty Free Shoppers Advisory Board

Dods, Walter Arthur, Jr.: president, director, First Hawaiian Foundation; chairman, chief executive officer, director, First Hawaiian, Inc.

ETV Endowment Board

Anderson, Ivan Verner, Jr.: president, chief executive officer, Evening Post Publishing Co.; vice president, Post and Courier Foundation

Eaglebrook School

Evans, Robert Sheldon: chairman, chief executive officer, Crane Co.; chairman, president, director, Crane Foundation

Earthwatch

Koch, David Hamilton: director, Koch Foundation, Inc. (Fred C. and Mary R.)

East Carolina University

Williamson, Henry Gaston, Jr.: chief operating officer, Branch Banking & Trust Co.

East West Center

Johnson, Lawrence M.: president, Pacific Century Financial Corp.

East-West Center Foundation

Dods, Walter Arthur, Jr.: president, director, First Hawaiian Foundation; chairman, chief executive officer, director, First Hawaiian, Inc.

Easter Seal Society Brevard County

Roub, Bryan Roger: trustee, Harris Foundation

Easter Seal Society Milwaukee

Larson, Peggy: manager, Ameritech Wisconsin

Economic Alliance Michigan

Eaton, Robert James: co-chairman, president, chief executive officer, DaimlerChrysler Corp.

Economic Club Indianapolis

Sease, Gene Elwood: director, Central Newspapers Foundation

Economic College Chicago

Greenwald, Gerald: chairman, chief executive officer, director, United Airlines Inc.

Economic Development

Stone, Roger Warren: chairman, president, chief executive officer, director, Stone Container Corp.; president, Stone Foundation

Economic Development Board

Castellini, Clateo: chairman, president, chief executive officer, Becton Dickinson & Co.

Economic Development Corp. Grand Rapids

Pew, Robert Cunningham, II: trustee, Steelcase Foundation

Economic Education

Dillon, John T.: chairman, chief executive officer, director, International Paper Co.

Edinburgh W Wide Investment Trust

Coltman, David A.: senior vice president marketing, United Airlines Inc.

Edison Electric Institute

Bayless, Charles Edward: chairman, president, chief executive officer, director, Illinois Power Co.

Brooks, E. Richard 'Dick': chairman, chief executive officer, director, Central & South West Services

Burg, H. Peter: president, chief operating officer, FirstEnergy Corp.

Campbell, George Leroy: vice president public affairs, Florida Power Corp.

Dahlberg, Alfred William, III: chairman, president, chief executive officer, Southern Co. Services Inc.

Davis, Erroll Brown, Jr.: president, chief executive officer, director, Wisconsin Power & Light Co.

Davis, William E.: chairman, chief executive officer, Niagara Mohawk Holdings Inc.

Felsinger, Donald E.: president, chief executive officer, Sempra Energy

Ferland, E. James: chairman, president, chief executive officer, Public Service Electric & Gas Co.

Harris, Elmer Beseler: president, chief executive officer, director, Alabama Power Co.

Hecht, William F.: chairman, president, chief executive officer, Pennsylvania Power & Light

Hock, Delwin D.: chairman, New Century Energies

Holland, Willard R.: chairman, chief executive officer, FirstEnergy Corp.

Howard, James Joseph, III: chairman, president, chief executive officer, director, Northern States Power Co.

McCormick, William Thomas, Jr.: chairman, chief executive officer, director, Consumers Energy Co.; chairman, Consumers Energy Foundation

Mueller, Charles William: chairman, president, chief executive officer, Ameren Corp.; trustee, Ameren Corp. Charitable Trust

Pederson, Jerrold P.: vice president, chief financial officer, director, Montana Power Co.; director, Montana Power Foundation

Peoples, D. Louis: vice chairman, chief executive officer, director, Orange & Rockland Utilities, Inc.

Rogers, James E., Jr.: vice chairman, president, chief executive officer, Cinergy Corp.; vice chairman, director, Cinergy Foundation

Rosilier, Glenn D.: executive vice president, chief financial officer, Central & South West Services

Ruelle, Mark A.: senior vice president, chief financial officer, Sierra Pacific Resources

Vondrasek, Frank Charles, Jr.: president, Madison Gas & Electric Foundation

Edison Institute

Ford, William Clay, Jr.: chairman, Ford Motor Co.

Edison International

Miller, Charles Daly: chairman, director, Avery Dennison Corp.; trustee, Whirlpool Foundation

Education Excellence Partnership

Wehling, Robert Louis: global marketing, government relations officer, Procter & Gamble Co.; president, trustee, Procter & Gamble Fund

Educational Enhancement Partnership

Timken, Ward Jackson: vice president, director, officer, Timken Co. (The); vice president, Timken Co. Charitable Trust (The); president, Timken Co. Educational Fund

Edward W. Scripps Trust

Burlingame, John Hunter: executive partner, Scripps Co. (E.W.)

Eisenhower Exchange Fellowships

Wagner, Thomas Joseph: chairman, CIGNA Foundation

Eiteljorg Museum

Russell, Frank Eli: president, Central Newspapers Foundation; chairman, Central Newspapers, Inc.

Electric Power Research Institute

Davis, Erroll Brown, Jr.: president, chief executive officer, director, Wisconsin Power & Light Co.

Howard, James Joseph, III: chairman, president, chief executive officer, director, Northern States Power Co.

Peoples, D. Louis: vice chairman, chief executive officer, director, Orange & Rockland Utilities, Inc.

Electronic Industries Association

Farmer, Phillip W.: chairman, president, chief executive officer, Harris Corp.; president, trustee, Harris Foundation

Elfun

Bossidy, Lawrence Arthur: chairman, director, AlliedSignal Foundation Inc.; chairman, chief executive officer, director, AlliedSignal Inc.

Elmhurst College

Bertran, David R.: senior vice president manufacturing & logistics, Nalco Chemical Co.; director, Nalco Foundation

Elon College

Baker, Leslie Mayo, Jr.: president, chief executive officer, chairman, Wachovia Bank of North Carolina NA; chairman, Wachovia Foundation, Inc. (The)

Elsa Wild Animal Appeal
Carey, Kathryn Ann: foundation manager, American Honda Foundation

Embry Riddle Aero University Curriculum Committee
Dewane, John Richard: director, Honeywell Foundation

Emergency Committee American Trade
Raymond, Lee R.: chairman, president, chief executive officer, Exxon Mobil Corp.

Emerson Hospital
Magee, John Francis: chairman, director, Little, Inc. (Arthur D.)

Emory Business School
Leschly, Jan: chief executive officer, SmithKline Beecham Corp.

Emory Museum Art & Archaeology
Chambers, Anne Cox: chairman, trustee, Cox Foundation (James M.)

Emory University
Harkey, Robert Shelton: trustee, Delta Air Lines Foundation; senior vice president, general counsel, secretary, Delta Air Lines, Inc.

Emory University Carter Center
Brademas, John: chairman, Texaco Foundation

Empire State College Foundation
Golub, Lewis: chairman, chief executive officer, director, Golub Corp.

Empire State Electric Energy Research Corp.
Peoples, D. Louis: vice chairman, chief executive officer, director, Orange & Rockland Utilities, Inc.

Empire State Electric Energy Resources
Kober, Roger W.: chairman, chief executive officer, director, Rochester Gas & Electric Corp.

Employee Stock Ownership Association
Strickland, Robert Louis: vice president, Lowe's Charitable and Educational Foundation

Employees Compensation Appeals Board
Walsh, Michael J.: vice president, CertainTeed Corp.

Employers Group
Mitchell, Warren I.: president, director, Southern California Gas Co.

Employers Mutual
Schiek, Fredrick A.: executive vice president, chief operating officer, Employers Mutual Casualty Co.

Employers Resource Association
Klinedinst, Thomas John, Jr.: trustee, Star Bank NA, Cincinnati Foundation

Employment Policy Foundation
Crane, Russell L.: director, PPG Industries Foundation; senior vice president, PPG Industries, Inc.

Energy Institute Americas
Dunham, Archie W.: president, chief executive officer, Conoco, Inc.

Engineering Institute Canada
Light, Walter Frederick: trustee, Air Products Foundation

Engineering Society Baltimore
Poindexter, Christian Herndon: chairman, Baltimore Gas & Electric Foundation; chairman, chief executive officer, director, Constellation Energy Group, Inc.

Engineering Society Detroit
Eaton, Robert James: co-chairman, president, chief executive officer, DaimlerChrysler Corp.

English Speaking Union
Sease, Gene Elwood: director, Central Newspapers Foundation

Enston Home
Anderson, Ivan Verner, Jr.: president, chief executive officer, Evening Post Publishing Co.; vice president, Post and Courier Foundation

Enterprise Foundation
Roth, Michael I.: chairman, chief executive officer, director, MONY Group (The); director, MONY Life Insurance of New York (The)

Zigas, Barry: senior vice president, Fannie Mae; director, Fannie Mae Foundation

Enterprise Group
Roth, Michael I.: chairman, chief executive officer, director, MONY Group (The); director, MONY Life Insurance of New York (The)

Envelope Manufacturer Association America
Berkley, Eugene Bertram: chairman, director, Tension Envelope Corp.; treasurer, Tension Envelope Foundation

Environmental Defense Fund
Chouinard, Yvon: owner, principal, Patagonia Inc.

Episcopal Community Services
Smoot, Richard Leonard: chairman, PNC Bank

Epsilon Tau Sigma
Bertrand, Frederic Howard: chairman, Central Vermont Public Service Corp.

Equipment Manufacturer Institute
Becherer, Hans Walter: chairman, chief executive officer, director, Deere & Co.; director, Deere Foundation (John)

Fites, Donald Vester: director, Caterpillar Foundation

Equipment Manufacturers Institute
Magliochetti, Joseph M.: president, chief executive officer, director, Dana Corp.; president, director, Dana Corp. Foundation

Erick Hawkins Dance Foundation
Levin, Michael Stuart: president, chief executive officer, Titan Industrial Corp.

Erickson Institute
Harris, Irving Brooks: chairman executive committee, director, Pittway Corp.; chairman, director, Pittway Corp. Charitable Foundation

Erie County Bar Association
Kennedy, Bernard Joseph: chairman, president, chief executive officer, director, National Fuel Gas Distribution Corp.

Lippes, Gerald Sanford: secretary, Mark IV Industries Foundation

Erie County Chapter ARC
Kennedy, Bernard Joseph: chairman, president, chief executive officer, director, National Fuel Gas Distribution Corp.

Eta Kappa Nu
Allaire, Paul Arthur: chairman, chief executive officer, chairman executive committee, Xerox Corp.; president, Xerox Foundation

Sissel, George A.: chairman, president, chief executive officer, director, Ball Corp.

Ethics Resource Center
Gilmartin, Raymond V.: chairman, president, chief executive officer, Merck & Co.; chairman, Merck Co. Foundation

European Academy Arts Science
Lucky, Robert Wendell: corporate vice president, Telcordia Technologies

European Academy Arts Science & Letters
Meyerson, Martin: director, Panasonic Foundation

European Center Chemical Manufacturing Federation
Butler, Andrew J.: trustee, Dow Chemical Co.

European Molecular Biology Organization
Alberts, Bruce Michael, PhD: director, Genentech Foundation for Biomedical Sciences

Evanston Hospital
Burt, Robert Norcross: chairman, chief executive officer, director, FMC Corp.; director, FMC Foundation

Carl, John L.: executive vice president, chief financial officer, BP Amoco Corp.; director, BP Amoco Foundation

Graham, William B.: chairman, director, Baxter Allegiance Foundation; chairman emeritus, Baxter International Inc.

Toll, Daniel Roger: trustee, Kemper Foundation (James S.)

Evanston Hospital Corp.
Keyser, Richard Lee: chairman, chief executive officer, president, Grainger, Inc. (W.W.)

Mathis, David B.: chairman, Kemper Foundation (James S.)

Evanston Northwestern Healthcare
Burnham, Duane Lee: chairman, chief executive officer, director, Abbott Laboratories

Evansville Chamber of Commerce
Koch, Robert Louis, II: president, chief executive officer, director, Koch Enterprises, Inc.; president, director, Koch Foundation

Evansville Industry Foundation Inc.
Muehlbauer, James Herman: vice president, director, Koch Foundation

Evansville Museum Arts & Science
Koch, Robert Louis, II: president, chief executive officer, director, Koch Enterprises, Inc.; president, director, Koch Foundation

Evenston Northwestern Healthcare
McNally, Alan G.: chairman, chief executive officer, Harris Trust & Savings Bank

Executive Council Foreign Diplomats
O'Reilly, F. Anthony John: chairman, trustee, Heinz Co. Foundation (H.J.); chairman, director, Heinz Co. (H.J.)

Executive Women International
Nalbach, Kay C.: president, Hartmarx Charitable Foundation

Eye Foundation
Matheny, Edward Taylor, Junior: director, Block Foundation (H&R)

FBA
Rogers, James E., Jr.: vice chairman, president, chief executive officer, Cinergy Corp.; vice chairman, director, Cinergy Foundation

FOCAS
Copley, David C.: president, trustee, Copley Foundation (James S.); president, chief executive officer, director, senior management board, Copley Press, Inc.

Fairfield University
Dammerman, Dennis Dean: vice chairman, director, General Electric Co.

Fairhaven Retirement Corp.
Connor, James Richard: executive director, Kemper Foundation (James S.)

Fairleigh Dickinson University
Tumminello, Stephen C.: president, chief executive officer, director, Philips Electronics North America Corp.

Family Focus Inc.
Harris, Irving Brooks: chairman executive committee, director, Pittway Corp.; chairman, director, Pittway Corp. Charitable Foundation

Family Service Society New Orleans
Purvis, George Frank, Jr.: chairman, president, chief executive officer, director, Pan-American Life Insurance Co.

Fannie Mae National Advisory Council
Rinehart, Charles Robert: chairman, chief executive officer, director, Washington Mutual, Inc.

Farm Foundation
Fites, Donald Vester: director, Caterpillar Foundation

Fathers Day/ Mothers Day Council
Margolis, Jay M.: member grantmaking committee, Claiborne Foundation (Liz)

Fed Bar Association
Barnette, Curtis Handley: chairman, chief executive officer, director, Bethlehem Steel Corp.
Hewitt, James Watt: vice president, treasurer, Abel Foundation
Hoak, Jon: trustee, NCR Foundation
Ruckelshaus, William Doyle: chairman, director, Browning-Ferris Industries Inc.

Fed Bar Council
Burak, Howard Paul: secretary, director, Sony U.S.A. Foundation Inc.

Fed City Council
Allbritton, Joe Lewis: chairman, chief executive officer, Riggs Bank NA
Rutstein, David W.: secretary, Giant Food Foundation; senior vice president, general counsel, chief administrative officer, Giant Food Inc.
Smith, Donald Kaye: senior vice president, general counsel, director, GEICO Corp.

Fed Communications Bar Association
Devlin, James Richard: director, Sprint Foundation

Fed Energy Bar Association
Kennedy, Bernard Joseph: chairman, president, chief executive officer, director, National Fuel Gas Distribution Corp.

Fed Savings & Loan Advisory Comm
Gaiswinkler, Robert Sigfried: chairman, director, First Financial Bank; director, First Financial Foundation

Federal American Society Experimental Biology
Alberts, Bruce Michael, PhD: director, Genentech Foundation for Biomedical Sciences

Federal Energy Bar Association
Hall, Larry D.: chairman, president, chief executive officer, director, Kinder Morgn; president, director, KN Energy Foundation
Jeremiah, Barbara S.: director, Alcoa Foundation

Federal National Mortgage Association
McCoy, John Bonnet: president, chief executive officer, Ameritech Corp.

Federal Reserve Bank New York
Brademas, John: chairman, Texaco Foundation

Federation Bar Association
Margolin, Abraham E.: director, Tension Envelope Foundation

Federation Employment & Guidance Service
Tisch, James S.: president, chief executive officer, director, CNA

Federation Executive Institute
Hegel, Garrett R.: chief financial officer, Compass Bank; president, Compass Bank Foundation

Federation Greek Industries
Kampouris, Emmanuel Andrew: chairman, president, chief executive officer, director, American Standard Inc.

Federation Home Loan Bank San Francisco
Rinehart, Charles Robert: chairman, chief executive officer, director, Washington Mutual, Inc.

Federation National Medals Science & Technology
Bartz, Carol A.: director, Autodesk Foundation; chairman, chief executive officer, Autodesk Inc.

Federation National Mortgage Association
Duberstein, Kenneth: director, Cinergy Foundation

Fidelco Guide Dog Foundation Inc.
Garneau, Robert M.: chief financial officer, Kaman Corp.
Kaman, Charles Huron: chairman, president, chief executive officer, director, Kaman Corp.

Fiduciary Trust International South
Herron, James Michael: secretary, director, Ryder System Charitable Foundation

Field Museum Natural History
Gidwitz, Ronald J.: president, chief executive officer, Curtis Industries, Inc. (Helene)
Kirby, William Joseph: vice president, director, FMC Foundation
Ryan, Patrick G.: chairman, president, chief executive officer, Aon Corp.; president, Aon Foundation

Field Papers
McClimon, Timothy J.: executive director, AT&T Foundation

Fin Accounting Foundation
Cook, J. Michael: chairman, chief executive officer, Deloitte & Touche; chairman, Deloitte & Touche Foundation
Dammerman, Dennis Dean: vice chairman, director, General Electric Co.

Fin Executives Research Foundation
White, Gerald Andrew: director, Air Products Foundation

Fin Management Association
Oakley, Robert Alan: executive vice president, chief financial officer, Nationwide Insurance Enterprise Foundation

Fin Managers Society
Moss, James H.: treasurer, York Federal Savings & Loan Foundation

Finance Executive Institute
Raskin, Fred C.: president, chief operating officer, Eastern Enterprises; trustee, Eastern Enterprises Foundation
Wellman, Thomas A.: controller, assistant treasurer, Alexander & Baldwin, Inc.

Financial Analysts Federation
Arth, Lawrence Joseph: vice president, director, Ameritas Charitable Foundation; chairman, chief executive officer, director, Ameritas Life Insurance Corp.
Gleaves, James Leslie: assistant treasurer, American General Finance Foundation

Financial Executive Institute
Hutchins, William Bruce, III: director, Alabama Power Foundation
Omachinski, David L.: chief financial officer, treasurer, vice president, Oshkosh B'Gosh, Inc.
Schafer, Glenn Stanley: president, director, Pacific Mutual Life Insurance Co.
Winger, Charles Joseph (Chuck): vice president, chief financial officer, Cinergy Corp.

Financial Executives Institute
Alexander, John F.: trustee, PerkinElmer Foundation; senior vice president, chief financial officer, PerkinElmer, Inc.
Alm, John Richard: director, Coca-Cola Foundation
Aylesworth, William Andrew: treasurer, Texas Instruments Foundation; chief financial officer, treasurer, Texas Instruments Inc.
Bains, Harrison MacKellar, Jr.: vice president, treasurer, Bristol-Myers Squibb Co.; treasurer, Bristol-Myers Squibb Foundation Inc.
Bakane, John L.: president, chief executive officer, director, Cone Mills Corp.

Bescherer, Edwin A., Jr.: trustee, Dun & Bradstreet Corp. Foundation, Inc.
Bezik, Cynthia B.: senior vice president, finance, Cleveland-Cliffs, Inc.
Brennan, John J.: chairman, chief executive officer, Vanguard Group; president, Vanguard Group Foundation
Broome, Burton Edward: vice president, controller, Transamerica Corp.; vice president, treasurer, Transamerica Foundation
Brumm, Paul Michael: executive vice president, chief financial officer, Fifth Third Bancorp
Buchholz, William E.: vice president, chief financial officer, Nalco Chemical Co.
Burrell, Richard L.: senator vice president finance, secretary, treasurer, Barry Corp. (R.G.); treasurer, Barry Foundation
Carl, John L.: executive vice president, chief financial officer, BP Amoco Corp.; director, BP Amoco Foundation
Carpenter, Marshall L.: vice president, chief financial officer, MTS Systems Corp.
Carr, Cassandra Colvin: director, SBC Foundation
Carter, George Kent: vice president, treasurer, Chevron Corp.
Chandler, William Everett: senior vice president finance, secretary, chief financial officer, Hunt Manufacturing Co.
Corby, Francis Michael, Jr.: executive vice president finance & administration, chief financial officer, Harnischfeger Industries; treasurer, Harnischfeger Industries Foundation
Cottrell, G. Walton: senior vice president, chief financial officer, Carpenter Technology Corp.
Coughlan, Gary Patrick: chief financial officer, senior vice president finance, Abbott Laboratories; director, Abbott Laboratories Fund
Daley, Leo J.: vice president, treasurer, Air Products and Chemicals, Inc.
Dammerman, Dennis Dean: vice chairman, director, General Electric Co.
Downes, Laurence M.: president, chief executive officer, director, chairman, New Jersey Natural Gas Co.; trustee, New Jersey Natural Gas Foundation
Dozier, Ollin Kemp: treasurer, Universal Leaf Foundation
Edwards, Earnest Jonathan: director, Alcoa Foundation
Francis, Cheryl A.: executive vice president, chief financial officer, Donnelley & Sons Co. (R.R.)
Fritze, Steven L.: vice president, treasurer, Ecolab Inc.
Gierer, Vincent A., Jr.: chairman, president, chief executive officer, director, UST Inc.
Glynn, Gary Allen: president, USX Corp.; vice president, USX Foundation, Inc.
Grubb, Edgar Harold: executive vice president, chief financial officer, Transamerica Corp.; director, Transamerica Foundation
Hardy, Gene M.: director, La-Z-Boy Foundation
Hemelt, William J.: treasurer, director, APS Foundation, Inc.; controller, Arizona Public Service Co.
Henley, Jeffrey O.: executive vice president, chief financial officer, director, Oracle Corp.
Hernandez, William H.: director, PPG Industries Foundation; senior vice president, PPG Industries, Inc.
Heumann, Stephen Michael: vice president, treasurer, West Co. Inc.
Howison, George Everett: vice president, Burlington Resources Foundation
Johnson, James Lawrence: chairman emeritus, Walter Industries Inc.
Johnson, Kenneth James: vice president, controller, director, Motorola Inc.
Karr, Howard Henry: treasurer, director, First Hawaiian Foundation
Kelson, Richard B.: director, Alcoa Foundation
Keough, William H.: senior vice president, chief financial officer, Pioneer Group
Kiener, Dan W.: member screening committee, PPG Industries Foundation
Klitten, Martin R.: vice president, chief financial officer, Chevron Corp.
Lavigne, Louis J., Jr.: executive vice president, chief financial officer, Genentech Inc.
LeBoeuf, Raymond W.: director, PPG Industries Foundation; director, chairman, chief executive officer, PPG Industries, Inc.
Leatherdale, Douglas West: chairman, chief executive officer, president, Saint Paul Companies Inc.
Lee, Charles Robert: chairman, chief executive officer, director, GTE Corp.; chief executive officer, trustee, GTE Foundation
Lord, Gerald S.: vice president, controller, Campbell Soup Co.
Maffucci, David G.: senior vice president, chief financial officer, Bowater Inc.
McClain, Terry James: director, Valmont Foundation; senior vice president, chief financial officer, Valmont Industries, Inc.
McCook, Richard P.: vice president, Winn-Dixie Stores Foundation; vice president finance, chief financial officer, Winn-Dixie Stores Inc.
McGovern, John Francis: chief financial officer, executive vice president, Georgia-Pacific Corp.; chairman, Georgia-Pacific Foundation
Medford, Dale L.: vice president corporate finance, chief financial officer, Reynolds & Reynolds Co.
Menzer, John: executive vice president, Wal-Mart Stores, Inc.
Metzger, Michael D.: vice president, chief financial officer, JSJ Corp.
Millenbruch, Gary Lee: executive vice president, chief financial officer, director, trustee, Bethlehem Steel Corp.
Morgan, Glenn R.: executive vice president, chief financial officer, Hartmarx Corp.
Moss, James H.: treasurer, York Federal Savings & Loan Foundation
Mrozek, Ernest J.: executive vice president, chief financial officer, ServiceMaster Co.
Murphy, James W.: senior vice president corporate finance, American United Life Insurance Co.; treasurer, AUL Foundation Inc.
Neal, Philip Mark: president, chief executive officer, director, Avery Dennison Corp.
Oakley, Robert Alan: executive vice president, chief financial officer, Nationwide Insurance Enterprise Foundation
Olson, A. Craig: senior vice president finance, chief financial officer, Albertson's Inc.
Ortino, Hector R.: president, chief executive officer, director, Ferro Corp.; vice president, trustee, Ferro Foundation
Pehlke, Richard W.: vice president, treasurer, Ameritech Corp.
Penglase, Frank Dennis: vice president, treasurer,
Prosser, John Warren, Jr.: treasurer, director, Jacobs Engineering Foundation; senior vice president finance & administration, treasurer, Jacobs Engineering Group
Roessler-Alsoa, Ernest C.: president, chief executive officer, director, CCB Financial Corp.
Rosilier, Glenn D.: executive vice president, chief financial officer, Central & South West Services
Roub, Bryan Roger: trustee, Harris Foundation
Sales, A. R.: director, Arvin Foundation; treasurer, Arvin Industries, Inc.
Schaeffer, Wayne G.: community president, Citizens Bank-Flint
Schaffer, Donald J.: member contributions committee, GATX Corp.
Shaffer, Oren G.: executive vice president, chief financial officer, Ameritech Corp.
Shannon, Michael E.: chairman, chief financial officer, chief administration officer, director, Ecolab Inc.
Siegel, Samuel: vice chairman, secretary, treasurer, chief financial officer, director, Nucor Corp.; director, Nucor Foundation
Smith, W. Keith: senior vice chairman, member corporate review committee, director, Mellon Financial Corp.
Snyder, Frank Ronald, II: trustee,
Sparks, Walter Alvon, Jr.: director, GEICO Philanthropic Foundation
Spoon, Alan Gary: president, chief operating officer, director, The Washington Post
Springer, Denis E.: senior vice president, chief financial officer, Burlington Northern Santa Fe Corp.; director, Burlington Northern Santa Fe Foundation
Stephan, Richard C.: vice president, controller, director, Viad Corp. Fund
Strandjord, Mary Jeannine: director, Sprint Foundation
Sullivan, Thomas John: vice president, director,
Thawerbhoy, Nazim G.: controller, Jacobs Engineering Foundation
Tomlinson, Joseph Ernest: vice president, treasurer, controller, Inland Container Corp.; vice president, director, Inland Foundation, Inc.
Wasserman, David Sherman: vice president, treasurer, Harris Corp.; trustee, Harris Foundation
White, Gerald Andrew: director, Air Products Foundation
Williams, David R.: trustee, Heinz Co. Foundation (H.J.); executive vice president, director, Heinz Co. (H.J.)
d'Alessio, Jon W.: trustee, McKesson Foundation

Financial Executives Institute Officers Conference Group

Kelson, Richard B.: director, Alcoa Foundation

Financial Executives Research Foundation

Roub, Bryan Roger: trustee, Harris Foundation

Financial Womens Association

Dinerstein, Martha L.: managing director, head marketing & corporate communications, United States Trust Co. of New York
Heisen, JoAnn Heffernan: vice president, chief information officer, Johnson & Johnson; treasurer, Johnson & Johnson Family of Companies Contribution Fund
Karmel, Roberta S.: trustee, Kemper Foundation (James S.); partner, Kemper National Insurance Companies

Fine Arts Fund

Wehling, Robert Louis: global marketing, government relations officer, Procter & Gamble Co.; president, trustee, Procter & Gamble Fund

Fine Arts Society San Diego

Cantor, Bernard Gerald: president, director, Cantor, Fitzgerald Foundation; chairman, director, Cantor, Fitzgerald Securities Corp.

First Cavalry Division Association

Wolff, Herbert Eric: secretary, director, First Hawaiian Foundation

First United Methodist Church

Fites, Donald Vester: director, Caterpillar Foundation

Fisk University

Clemente, Constantine Louis: chairman, Pfizer Foundation; executive vice president corporate affairs, secretary, corporate counsel, Pfizer Inc.

Fletcher School Law & Diplomacy

Naples, Ronald James: president, chief executive officer, director, Quaker Chemical Corp.

Flexographic Technology Association

Berkley, Eugene Bertram: chairman, director, Tension Envelope Corp.; treasurer, Tension Envelope Foundation

Florida Bar Association

Herron, James Michael: secretary, director, Ryder System Charitable Foundation

Loos, Henry J.: secretary, Charter Manufacturing Co. Foundation

Florida Chamber of Commerce

Ridder, Paul Anthony: chairman, chief executive officer, director, Knight Ridder

Florida Grand Opera

Herron, James Michael: secretary, director, Ryder System Charitable Foundation

Florida Institute CPAs

McCook, Richard P.: vice president, Winn-Dixie Stores Foundation; vice president finance, chief financial officer, Winn-Dixie Stores Inc.

Florida Institute Technology

Heldreth, Nick E.: vice president human resources corporate relations, Harris Corp.

Florida Institute of Technology

Farmer, Phillip W.: chairman, president, chief executive officer, Harris Corp.; president, trustee, Harris Foundation

Florida RV Trade Association

Skinner, Claire Corson: chairman, chief executive officer, Coachmen Industries, Inc.

Florida Society Blind

Mandel, Jack N.: director, Premier Industrial Corp.

Food & Drug Law Institute

Bogomolny, Robert Lee: director, Searle Charitable Trust; senior vice president, general counsel, secretary, Searle & Co. (G.D.)

Clark, Richard McCourt: senior vice president, general counsel, secretary, Kellogg Co.; vice president, trustee, Kellogg Co. Twenty-Five Year Employees' Fund Inc.

Food Marketing Government Affairs & Communications Division

Scher, Barry F.: vice president public affairs, Giant Food Inc.

Food Marketing Institute

Golub, Lewis: chairman, chief executive officer, director, Golub Corp.

Mathews, Odonna: vice president consumer affairs, Giant Food Inc.

Scher, Barry F.: vice president public affairs, Giant Food Inc.

Wright, Michael William: chairman, president, chief executive officer, director, SuperValu, Inc.

Food Safety Council

Bains, Harrison MacKellar, Jr.: vice president, treasurer, Bristol-Myers Squibb Co.; treasurer, Bristol-Myers Squibb Foundation Inc.

Fordham Prep School

Melican, James Patrick, Jr.: executive vice president legal & external affairs, International Paper Co.; director, International Paper Co. Foundation

Fordham University

Soden, Paul A.: senior vice president, secretary, general counsel, Reader's Digest Association, Inc. (The)

Foreign Policy Association

Andreas, Dwayne Orville: chairman, chief executive officer, Archer-Daniels-Midland Co.

Bronfman, Edgar Miles: chairman, trustee, Bronfman Foundation/Joseph E. Seagram & Sons, Inc. Fund (Samuel); chairman, Seagram & Sons, Inc. (Joseph E.)

Rhodes, William Reginald: vice chairman, Citibank Corp.

Ross, Arthur: senior vice president, Central National-Gottesman; director, Central National-Gottesman Foundation

Foreign Policy Research Institute

Meyerson, Martin: director, Panasonic Foundation

Naples, Ronald James: president, chief executive officer, director, Quaker Chemical Corp.

Forsyth County Bar Association

Sharpe, Robert Francis, Jr.: senior vice president public affairs, general counsel, PepsiCo, Inc.

Forward Arts Foundation

Chambers, Anne Cox: chairman, trustee, Cox Foundation (James M.)

Foster Parents Plan

Hassenfeld, Alan Geoffrey: president, Hasbro Charitable Trust Inc.; chairman, chief executive officer, Hasbro, Inc.

Foundation Drug-Free Pennsylvania

Hafer, Fred Douglass: chairman, president, chief executive officer, GPU Inc.

Foundation Health Enhancement

Chookaszian, Dennis Haig: chairman, chief executive officer, CNA

Foundation Independent Higher Education

Gorman, Maureen V.: vice president, GTE Foundation

Hohn, Harry George, Jr.: chairman, director, New York Life Foundation

Foundation Tri-State Community

Chellgren, Paul Wilbur: chief executive officer, chairman, director, Ashland, Inc.; member, Ashland Inc. Foundation

Foundation Womens Resources

Carr, Cassandra Colvin: director, SBC Foundation

Foundation for International Exchange of Science & Cultural Information

Meyerson, Martin: director, Panasonic Foundation

Founders Circle of Music Center

Rosenzweig, Richard Stuart: executive vice president, director, Playboy Enterprises Inc.

Franciscan Health Systems West

Stivers, William Charles: senior vice president, chief financial officer, treasurer, Weyerhaeuser Co.; treasurer, trustee, Weyerhaeuser Co. Foundation

Franciscan U.S. Department of Health and Human Services Systems Ohio Valley

Klinedinst, Thomas John, Jr.: trustee, Star Bank NA, Cincinnati Foundation

Franklin College

Thomasson, Dan King: vice president, trustee, Scripps Howard Foundation

Franklin Institute

Unruh, James Arlen: director, Ameritech Foundation

Franklin University

Glaser, Gary A.: president, chief executive officer, National City Bank of Columbus

Fraternal Order Eagles

Anderson, Charles D.: trustee, Anderson Foundation

Fred Hutchinson Cancer Research Center

Alberts, Bruce Michael, PhD: director, Genentech Foundation for Biomedical Sciences

Free Accepted Masons

Dubin, Stephen Victor: vice president, secretary, Farber Foundation

Fuellgraf, Charles Louis, Jr.: trustee, Nationwide Insurance Enterprise Foundation

Hall, Larry D.: chairman, president, chief executive officer, director, Kinder Morgn; president, director, KN Energy Foundation

Millenbruch, Gary Lee: executive vice president, chief financial officer, director, trustee, Bethlehem Steel Corp.

Russell, Frank Eli: president, Central Newspapers Foundation; chairman, Central Newspapers, Inc.

Free Library Philadelphia Federation

Naples, Ronald James: president, chief executive officer, director, Quaker Chemical Corp.

Freedom Trail Foundation

Taylor, William Osgood: chairman, chief executive officer, director, Boston Globe (The); chairman, director, Boston Globe Foundation; director, New York Times Co. Foundation

Freedoms Foundation

Scripps, Charles Edward: chairman executive committee, director, vice president, Scripps Co. (E.W.); member, Scripps Howard Foundation

French Institute

Ripley, Sidney Dillon, II: director emeritus, Hitachi Foundation

Fresh Start Women's Foundation

Bame, Tracy L.: manager community affairs, Phelps Dodge Foundation

Friendly Exchange
Beyer, Jeffrey C.: president, Farmers Group Safety Foundation

Friends Law Library Congress
Downing, Kathryn M.: executive vice president, Times Mirror Co.; vice chairman, Times Mirror Foundation

Friends Milwaukee Public Museum
Graff, Stephen Ney: director, Bucyrus-Erie Foundation

Friends New Jersey State Museum
Forbes, Christopher 'Kip': vice president, Forbes Foundation; vice chairman, corporate secretary, director, Forbes Inc.

Friends of Art
Hall, Donald Joyce: chairman board, director, Hallmark Cards Inc.; chairman, Hallmark Corporate Foundation

Friends of International Center
Copley, Helen K.: chairman, trustee, Copley Foundation (James S.); chairman, director, senior management board, Copley Press, Inc.

Friends of Sakonnet Lighthouse
Hawes, Alexander Boyd, Jr.: treasurer, Boston Globe Foundation

Friends of Statue of Liberty National Monument/Ellis Island
Grasso, Richard A.: chairman, chief executive officer, New York Stock Exchange, Inc.

Friendship House
Kohler, Herbert Vollrath, Jr.: chairman, president, director, Kohler Co.

Frontiers America
Elam, Lloyd Charles, MD: trustee, Merck Co. Foundation

Ft Lauderdale Art Museum
Huston, Edwin Allen: vice president, director, Ryder System Charitable Foundation; vice chairman, director, Ryder System, Inc.

Ft. Worth Academy
Connor, Richard L.: president, publisher, Fort Worth Star-Telegram Inc.

Fund Legal Aid Society
Hale, James Thomas: senior vice president, general counsel, secretary, Dayton Hudson; trustee, Target Foundation

O'Brien, James E.: director, Schoeneckers Foundation

Funhdsy
Graves, Ronald Norman: secretary, Simplot Foundation (J.R.)

Furniture Factories Marketing Association
Spilman, Robert H.: chairman, chief executive officer, Bassett Furniture Industries; chairman, director, Bassett Furniture Industries Fdn.

GM President Council
Armstrong, C. Michael: chairman, chief executive officer, AT&T Corp.

Garfield F Childs Memorial Fund
Lewis, Frances Aaronson: trustee, Circuit City Foundation

Garth Fagan Dance Theatre
Rand, Addison Barry: executive vice president operations, Xerox Corp.; trustee, Xerox Foundation

Gas Industry Studies
Wise, William Allen: chairman, president, chief executive officer, director, El Paso Energy Co.; chairman, director, El Paso Energy Foundation

Gas Research Institute
Catell, Robert Barry: chairman, chief executive officer, Brooklyn Union

Hall, Larry D.: chairman, president, chief executive officer, director, Kinder Morgn; president, director, KN Energy Foundation

Mitchell, Warren I.: president, director, Southern California Gas Co.

Gateway Music
Block, William: vice president, trustee, Blade Foundation; chairman, director, Toledo Blade Co.

Gen Agents & Managers Association
Dubes, Michael: membership, ReliaStar Foundation

Gen Aviation Manufacturer Association
Meyer, Russell William, Jr.: chairman, chief executive officer, Cessna Aircraft Co.; president, Cessna Foundation, Inc.

Gen Merchandise Advisory Council
Martin, Bobby L.: member, Wal-Mart Foundation

General Aviation Manufacturers Association
Dewane, John Richard: director, Honeywell Foundation

General Douglas MacArthur Memorial Foundation
Goode, David Ronald: chairman, president, chief executive officer, director, Norfolk Southern Corp.

General Services Board Alcoholic Anonymous
Glynn, Gary Allen: president, USX Corp.; vice president, USX Foundation, Inc.

Genetics Society America
Alberts, Bruce Michael, PhD: director, Genentech Foundation for Biomedical Sciences

George Bush Presidential Foundation
Allbritton, Joe Lewis: chairman, chief executive officer, Riggs Bank NA

George C Marshall Foundation
Mead, Dana George: chairman, chief executive officer, director, Tenneco Automotive

George School Comm
Muth, Robert James: president, director, ASARCO Foundation

George Washington University
Graham, Katharine Meyer: chairman executive committee, director, The Washington Post

Georgetown University
O'Reilly, F. Anthony John: chairman, trustee, Heinz Co. Foundation (H.J.); chairman, director, Heinz Co. (H.J.)

Georgetown University Law School
Owens, Jack Byron: executive vice president, general counsel, Gallo Winery, Inc. (E&J)

Georgia Bar Association
Eason, William Everette, Jr.: senior vice president, corporate secretary, general counsel, Scientific-Atlanta, Inc.

Harkey, Robert Shelton: trustee, Delta Air Lines Foundation; senior vice president, general counsel, secretary, Delta Air Lines, Inc.

Georgia Chamber of Commerce
Correll, Alston Dayton 'Pete', Jr.: chairman, president, chief executive officer, director, Georgia-Pacific Corp.; director, Georgia-Pacific Foundation

Georgia Council Economic Education
Clanin, Robert J.: senior vice president, chief financial officer, treasurer, director, United Parcel Service of America Inc.

Georgia Department of Human Resources
Davis, James K.: senior vice president corporate relations, Georgia Power Co.; director, Georgia Power Foundation

Georgia Research Alliance
Correll, Alston Dayton 'Pete', Jr.: chairman, president, chief executive officer, director, Georgia-Pacific Corp.; director, Georgia-Pacific Foundation

Mullin, Leo Francis: chairman, president, chief executive officer, Delta Air Lines, Inc.

Geothermal-Interisland Cable Project
Dods, Walter Arthur, Jr.: president, director, First Hawaiian Foundation; chairman, chief executive officer, director, First Hawaiian, Inc.

Gillette Children's Specialty Healthcare
Grenz, M. Kay: director, 3M Foundation; vice president human resources, Minnesota Mining & Manufacturing Co.

Gilmore International Keyboard Festival
Clark, Richard McCourt: senior vice president, general counsel, secretary, Kellogg Co.; vice president, trustee, Kellogg Co. Twenty-Five Year Employees' Fund Inc.

Langbo, Arnold Gordon: chairman, chief executive officer, director, Kellogg Co.

Girl Scouts U.S.
Wolff, Herbert Eric: secretary, director, First Hawaiian Foundation

Girl Scouts U.S. Council Hawaii
Simpson, Andrea Lynn: president

Give Kids the World
Hall, Floyd: chairman, president, chief executive officer, director, Kmart Corp.

Glass Ceiling Commission
Graves, Earl Gilbert: director, Aetna Foundation

Glass Pkg Institute
Lemieux, Joseph Henry: chairman, chief executive officer, director, Owens-Illinois Inc.

Glenayre Technologies Inc.
Kelbley, Stephen Paul: executive vice president, Springs Industries, Inc.

Glenwood School Boys

Vitale, David J.: vice chairman, Bank One Corp.; vice president, director, First National Bank of Chicago Foundation

Global Climate Coalition

Caccamo, Aldo M.: vice president public affairs, Chevron Corp.

Glyndeburne Arts Trust

Collins, Paul John: vice chairman, director, Citibank Corp.

Golden Key

Connor, James Richard: executive director, Kemper Foundation (James S.)

Golden Key National Honor Society

Bloch, Henry Wollman: chairman, Block Foundation (H&R); chairman, director, Block, Inc. (H&R)

Good Shepherd Services

Dugan, Brendan J.: president, European American Bank

O'Leary, David C.: chairman, trustee, Credit Suisse First Boston Foundation Trust

Goodman Theatre

Hefner, Christie Ann: chairman, chief executive officer, Playboy Enterprises Inc.; director, Playboy Foundation

Goodwill Industries

Moll, Curtis E.: treasurer, trustee, Jochum-Moll Foundation (The)

Schrader, Thomas F.: vice president, director, WICOR Foundation

Goodwill Industries San Antonio

Ebrom, Charles E.: director, vice president, Zachry Co. (H.B.); treasurer, trustee, Zachry Foundation (The)

Gordon College Foundation Inc.

Banks, Peter L.: vice president external affairs, AGL Resources Inc.

Gov Economic Advisory Council

Wurtzel, Alan Leon: chairman, Circuit City Foundation; chairman, trustee, Circuit City Stores, Inc.

Government Business Council

Carroll, Philip Joseph: chairman, chief executive officer, Fluor Corp.; chairman, trustee, Fluor Foundation

Government Cuomo's Task Force on Pension Fund Investment

Millstein, Ira M.: partner, Weil, Gotshal & Manges Corp.; president, director, Weil, Gotshal & Manges Foundation

Governments Advisory Council on Revenue Estimates

Goode, David Ronald: chairman, president, chief executive officer, director, Norfolk Southern Corp.

Governments Business Advisory Council New York

Tisch, Preston Robert: chairman, director, CBS Foundation; co-chairman, co-chief executive officer, director, CNA; trustee, Loews Foundation

Governments Commission Jobs & Economic Development

Pew, Robert Cunningham, II: trustee, Steelcase Foundation

Governments Education Council Ohio

Pepper, John E., Jr.: chairman executive committee, Procter & Gamble Co.

Governments Education Management Council

Wehling, Robert Louis: global marketing, government relations officer, Procter & Gamble Co.; president, trustee, Procter & Gamble Fund

Governments Human Investment Council

Smith, Frederick C.: chairman, trustee, Huffy Foundation, Inc.

Governments Task Force Future Mental Health Illinois

Harris, Irving Brooks: chairman executive committee, director, Pittway Corp.; chairman, director, Pittway Corp. Charitable Foundation

Governor Business Council

Haddock, Ronald Wayne: president, chief executive officer, director, FINA; president, FINA Foundation

Governor School & Business Alliance Task Force

Marron, Donald Baird: chairman, chief executive officer, director, Paine Webber; trustee, Paine Webber Foundation

Grad School Business University

Donovan, Thomas Roy: president, chief executive officer, Chicago Board of Trade

Graduate Institute Coop Leadership

Gherty, John E.: president, chief executive officer, Land O'Lakes, Inc.

Graduate Management Admissions Council

Wentworth, Jack Roberts, Ph.D.: director, Habig Foundation

Grand Rapids Chamber of Commerce

Pew, Robert Cunningham, II: trustee, Steelcase Foundation

Grant/Riverside Methodist Hospital Foundation

Glaser, Gary A.: president, chief executive officer, National City Bank of Columbus

Great Books Foundation

Schueppert, George Louis: chief financial officer, executive vice president, Outboard Marine Corp.

Great Hartford Chamber of Commerce

Barnes, Wallace W.: director, Barnes Group Foundation Inc.

Great Lakes Museum Science Environment

Woods, Jacqueline F.: president, Ameritech Ohio

Greater Baltimore Committee

DiCamillo, Gary Thomas: chairman, chief executive officer, director, Polaroid Corp.

Greater Buffalo Partnership

Kennedy, Bernard Joseph: chairman, president, chief executive officer, director, National Fuel Gas Distribution Corp.

Greater Cincinnati Chamber of Commerce

Barrett, John F.: trustee, Western-Southern Foundation, Inc.; president, chief executive officer, director, Western & Southern Life Insurance Co.

Schaefer, George A., Jr.: president, Fifth Third Bancorp

Wehling, Robert Louis: global marketing, government relations officer, Procter & Gamble Co.; president, trustee, Procter & Gamble Fund

Greater Cleveland Bar Association

Gherlein, Gerald Lee: member contributions committee, Eaton Charitable Fund

Greater Cleveland Growth Association

Bersticker, Albert C.: chairman, director, chief executive officer, Ferro Corp.; president, trustee, Ferro Foundation

Burner, David L.: chairman, president, chief executive officer, director, BFGoodrich Co.

Collins, Duane E.: president, chief executive officer, director, Parker Hannifin Corp.; vice president, trustee, Parker Hannifin Foundation

Daberko, David A.: chairman, chief executive officer, National City Corp.

Hardis, Stephen Roger: chairman, chief executive officer, director, Eaton Corp.

Holland, Willard R.: chairman, chief executive officer, FirstEnergy Corp.

O'Brien, John F.: trustee, McDonald & Co. Securities Foundation

Greater Columbus Chamber of Commerce

Wobst, Frank: chairman, chief executive officer, director, Huntington Bancshares Inc.

Greater Dallas Crime Commission

Godfrey, Cullen Michael: vice president, FINA Foundation

Greater Denver Chamber of Commerce

Hock, Delwin D.: chairman, New Century Energies

Greater Des Moines Chamber of Commerce

Brooks, Roger Kay: chairman, AmerUS Group

Kalainov, Sam Charles: chairman, president, chief executive officer, AmerUS Group

Kramer, Mary Elizabeth: vice president, Wellmark Foundation

Greater Des Moines Committee

Pomerantz, Marvin Alvin: trustee, Mid-American Foundation

Rehm, Jack Daniel: chairman emeritus, director, Meredith Corp.

Greater Des Moines Sports Authority

Kelley, Bruce Gunn: vice president, director, Employers Mutual Charitable Foundation

Greater Detroit Chamber of Commerce

McCormick, William Thomas, Jr.: chairman, chief executive officer, director, Consumers Energy Co.; chairman, Consumers Energy Foundation

Greater Hartford Arts Council

Besser, John Edward: director, Barnes Group Foundation Inc.; senior vice president finance & law, Barnes Group Inc.

Greater Hartford Chamber of Commerce

Fiondella, Robert William: chairman, president, chief executive officer, Phoenix Home Life Mutual Insurance Co.

Long, Michael Thomas: director, Ensign-Bickford Foundation

Greater Jamaica Development Corp.

Matthews, Craig Gerard: president, chief operating officer, Brooklyn Union

Greater Kansas City Chamber of Commerce

Bloch, Henry Wollman: chairman, Block Foundation (H&R); chairman, director, Block, Inc. (H&R)

Greater Kansas City Community Foundation

Kemper, Jonathan McBride: director, Commerce Bancshares Foundation; vice chairman, Commerce Bancshares, Inc.

Sosland, Morton Irvin: director, Block Foundation (H&R)

Greater Little Rock Chamber of Commerce

Ford, Joseph 'Joe': chairman, chief executive officer, president, ALLTEL Corp.

Greater Milwaukee Committee

Bauer, Chris Michael: president, Firstar Milwaukee Foundation

Greater Minneapolis Chamber of Commerce

Anderson, Lowell Carlton: chairman, director, Allianz Life Insurance Co. of North America

Nelson, Glen David, MD: vice chairman, Medtronic, Inc.

Greater Minneapolis Metropolitan Housing Corp.

Porter, James T.: director, Honeywell Foundation; vice president, chief administrative officer, Honeywell International Inc.

Greater Peoria Airport Authority

Flaherty, Gerald S.: trustee, Caterpillar Foundation; group president, Caterpillar Inc.

Greater Philadelphia Chamber of Commerce

Larsen, Terrence A.: chairman, chief executive officer, First Union Bank; chairman, First Union Regional Foundation

Thompson, Sheldon Lee: senior vice president, chief administrative officer, Sunoco Inc.

Greater Philadelphia First Corp.

Naples, Ronald James: president, chief executive officer, director, Quaker Chemical Corp.

Unruh, James Arlen: director, Ameritech Foundation

Greater Pittsburgh Chamber of Commerce

Newlin, William Rankin: trustee, Kennametal Foundation

Greater Pittsburgh Council Boy Scouts America

Rohr, James Edward: chief executive officer, president, director, PNC Financial Services Group

Greater Portland Chamber of Commerce

Gorman, Leon A.: president, chief executive officer, Bean, Inc. (L.L.)

Greater Saint Louis Area

Busch, August Adolphus, III: chairman, president, chief executive officer, Anheuser-Busch Companies, Inc.

Greater Tampa Chamber of Commerce

Townsend, David L.: vice president administration, Walter Industries Inc.

Greater Washington Board Trade

Allbritton, Joe Lewis: chairman, chief executive officer, Riggs Bank NA

Greater Washington Board Trade Legislative Bureau

Smith, Donald Kaye: senior vice president, general counsel, director, GEICO Corp.

Greater Washington Research Center

Rutstein, David W.: secretary, Giant Food Foundation; senior vice president, general counsel, chief administrative officer, Giant Food Inc.

Williams, Karen Hastie: director, Fannie Mae Foundation

Greater Yellowstone Coalition

Minton, Dwight Church: chairman, director, Church & Dwight Co., Inc.

Greenpeace

Carey, Kathryn Ann: foundation manager, American Honda Foundation

Greenville Chamber of Commerce

Hipp, William Hayne: president, chief executive officer, director, Liberty Corp.; chairman, president, director, Liberty Corp. Foundation

Greenville-Spartanburg Airport Comm

Milliken, Roger: chairman, chief executive officer, Milliken & Co.; member advisory committee, Milliken Foundation

Grinnell College

Kelly, Janet L.: executive vice president corporate development, general counsel, secretary, Kellogg Co.

Stewart, Donald M.: director, New York Times Co. Foundation

Grocery Manufacturer America

Bryan, John Henry: chairman, Sara Lee Corp.; director, Sara Lee Foundation

Gerstner, Louis Vincent, Jr.: chairman, chief executive officer, director, International Business Machines Corp.

Johnson, David Willis: chairman, director, Campbell Soup Co.

Langbo, Arnold Gordon: chairman, chief executive officer, director, Kellogg Co.

Mark, Reuben: chairman, chief executive officer, Colgate-Palmolive Co.

Minton, Dwight Church: chairman, director, Church & Dwight Co., Inc.

O'Reilly, F. Anthony John: chairman, trustee, Heinz Co. Foundation (H.J.); chairman, director, Heinz Co. (H.J.)

Pepper, John E., Jr.: chairman executive committee, Procter & Gamble Co.

Shoemate, Charles Richard: chairman, president, chief executive officer, Bestfoods

Sullivan, Austin Padraic, Junior: trustee, General Mills Foundation; senior vice president corporate relations, General Mills, Inc.

Viviano, Joseph P.: president, court, Hershey Foods Corp.

Wrigley, William: chairman, director, Wrigley Co. Foundation (Wm. Jr.); president, chief executive officer, director, Wrigley Co. (Wm. Jr.)

Grocery Manufacturer Association

Viviano, Joseph P.: president, court, Hershey Foods Corp.

Grocery Manufacturers America Inc.

Lawless, Robert J.: chairman, president, chief executive officer, chief operating officer, director, McCormick & Co. Inc.

Grocery Products Manufacturer Canada

Langbo, Arnold Gordon: chairman, chief executive officer, director, Kellogg Co.

Group 30

Carter, Marshall Nichols: chairman, chief executive officer, State Street Bank & Trust Co.

Guggenheim Museum

Klein, Calvin Richard: president, Calvin Klein

Koch, David Hamilton: director, Koch Foundation, Inc. (Fred C. and Mary R.)

Guild Lyric Opera Chicago

Hudnut, Stewart Skinner: director, Illinois Tool Works Foundation

Gunderson Medicine Foundation

Kerckhove, George H.: vice president, chief financial officer, American Standard Inc.

Guthrie Healthcare Sys.

Peck, Arthur John, Jr.: secretary, vice president, Corning Inc.; secretary, Corning Inc. Foundation

Guthrie Theater Foundation

Sanger, Stephen W.: chairman, trustee, General Mills Foundation; chairman, chief executive officer, director, General Mills, Inc.

Gwinnett Ballet Theatre

Necessary, Steven K.: senior vice president marketing, Scientific-Atlanta, Inc.

HRB Management Inc.

Bloch, Henry Wollman: chairman, Block Foundation (H&R); chairman, director, Block, Inc. (H&R)

Habitat Humanity Endowment Committee

Dewane, John Richard: director, Honeywell Foundation

Hall Westwood Hebrew Home

Gindi, Abraham: trustee, Century 21 Associates Foundation

Gindi, Sam: trustee, Century 21 Associates Foundation

Hanahavoli School

Simpson, Andrea Lynn: president

Hands Net Inc.

Zigas, Barry: senior vice president, Fannie Mae; director, Fannie Mae Foundation

Hardware Group Association

Gloyd, Lawrence Eugene: trustee, CLARCOR Foundation; chairman, chief executive officer, director, CLARCOR Inc.

Hardware Marketing Council

DiCamillo, Gary Thomas: chairman, chief executive officer, director, Polaroid Corp.

Harpeth Hall School

Ingram, Martha R.: chairman, director, Ingram Industries Inc.

Hartford Ballet

Huber, Richard Leslie: chairman, president, chief executive officer, director, Aetna, Inc.

Hartford County Bar Association

Long, Michael Thomas: director, Ensign-Bickford Foundation

Hartley House

McGraw, Harold Whittlesey 'Terry', III: chairman, president, chief executive officer, McGraw-Hill Companies, Inc.

Hartsville Chamber of Commerce

DeLoach, Harris E., Junior: executive vice president, director, Sonoco Products Co.

Harvard Alumni Association

O'Brien, John Francis, Jr.: president, chief executive officer, Allmerica Financial Corp.

Harvard Business School

Gilmartin, Raymond V.: chairman, president, chief executive officer, Merck & Co.; chairman, Merck Co. Foundation

Harvard Business School Alumni Association

Naples, Ronald James: president, chief executive officer, director, Quaker Chemical Corp.

Harvard Business School Club Chicago

Rogers, Desiree Glapion: vice president community affairs, Peoples Energy Corp.

Harvard College

O'Brien, John Francis, Jr.: president, chief executive officer, Allmerica Financial Corp.

Harvard Law School

Redstone, Sumner Murray: chairman, Viacom Inc.

Harvard University

Brademas, John: chairman, Texaco Foundation

Gilmartin, Raymond V.: chairman, president, chief executive officer, Merck & Co.; chairman, Merck Co. Foundation

Osborne, Burl: president publishing division, director, Belo Corp. (A.H.); president, trustee, Belo Corp. Foundation (A.H.)

Harvard University Alumni Association

Bridgeland, James Ralph, Jr.: trustee, Star Bank NA, Cincinnati Foundation

Harvard University Business School

Lee, Charles Robert: chairman, chief executive officer, director, GTE Corp.; chief executive officer, trustee, GTE Foundation

Schacht, Henry Brewer: director, Cummins Engine Foundation

Harvard University Business School Association

Lawson, William Hogan, III: chairman, chief executive officer, director, Franklin Electric Co.; president, Franklin Electric, Edward J. Schaefer, and T. W. KehoeCharitable and Educational Foundation

Harvard University Graduate School Business Administration Associates

O'Reilly, F. Anthony John: chairman, trustee, Heinz Co. Foundation (H.J.); chairman, director, Heinz Co. (H.J.)

Harvard University John F Kennedy School Government

Graves, Earl Gilbert: director, Aetna Foundation

Hatsopoulos, George Nicholas: founder, chairman, chief executive officer, director, Thermo Electron Corp.; committee member, Thermo Electron Foundation

Higginbotham, A. Leon, Jr.: director, New York Times Co. Foundation

Harvard University Law School

Ehrlich, M. Gordon: trustee, Orchard Foundation

Harvard University Law School Association

Bridgeland, James Ralph, Jr.: trustee, Star Bank NA, Cincinnati Foundation

Redstone, Sumner Murray: chairman, Viacom Inc.

Harvey Mudd College

Wood, Willis B., Jr.: chairman, chief executive officer, director, Pacific Enterprises

Hastings College Foundation

Daugherty, Robert B.: president, Valmont Foundation; director, Valmont Industries, Inc.

Scott, Walter, Jr.: member contributions committee, Kiewit Companies Foundation

Haverford College

Whitehead, John Cunningham: chairman board, Goldman Sachs Foundation

Hawaii Army Museum Society

Wolff, Herbert Eric: secretary, director, First Hawaiian Foundation

Hawaii Bankers Association

Dods, Walter Arthur, Jr.: president, director, First Hawaiian Foundation; chairman, chief executive officer, director, First Hawaiian, Inc.

Hawaii Baptist Academy

Nakagawa, Jean H.: vice president, director, Servco Foundation

Hawaii Business Roundtable

Dods, Walter Arthur, Jr.: president, director, First Hawaiian Foundation; chairman, chief executive officer, director, First Hawaiian, Inc.

Hawaii Chamber of Commerce

Dods, Walter Arthur, Jr.: president, director, First Hawaiian Foundation; chairman, chief executive officer, director, First Hawaiian, Inc.

Wild, Heidi Karin: trustee

Hawaii Comm Foreign Relations

Wolff, Herbert Eric: secretary, director, First Hawaiian Foundation

Hawaii Economic Association

Nakagawa, Jean H.: vice president, director, Servco Foundation

Hawaii Employers Council

Dods, Walter Arthur, Jr.: president, director, First Hawaiian Foundation; chairman, chief executive officer, director, First Hawaiian, Inc.

Hawaii Jaycees

Simpson, Andrea Lynn: president

Hawaii Maritime Center

Dods, Walter Arthur, Jr.: president, director, First Hawaiian Foundation; chairman, chief executive officer, director, First Hawaiian, Inc.

Hawaii Open

Dods, Walter Arthur, Jr.: president, director, First Hawaiian Foundation; chairman, chief executive officer, director, First Hawaiian, Inc.

Hawaii Pacific University

Johnson, Lawrence M.: president, Pacific Century Financial Corp.

Hawaii Public Television

Simpson, Andrea Lynn: president

Hawaii Society Corp. Planners

Nakagawa, Jean H.: vice president, director, Servco Foundation

Hawaii Strategic Development Corp.

Simpson, Andrea Lynn: president

Hawaii Visitors Bureau

Dods, Walter Arthur, Jr.: president, director, First Hawaiian Foundation; chairman, chief executive officer, director, First Hawaiian, Inc.

Hawken School

Daberko, David A.: chairman, chief executive officer, National City Corp.

Health Industry Manufacturers Association

George, William Wallace: chief executive officer, chairman, Medtronic, Inc.

Longfield, William H.: president, Bard Foundation (C.R.); chairman, chief executive officer, director, Bard, Inc. (C.R.)

Health Insurance Association America

Drury, David J.: chief executive officer, chairman, Principal Financial Group

Eckert, Ralph John: trustee, Trustmark Foundation

Peterson, Donald Matthew: trustee, Trustmark Foundation; president, chief executive officer, director, Trustmark Insurance Co.

Purvis, George Frank, Jr.: chairman, president, chief executive officer, director, Pan-American Life Insurance Co.

Turner, John Gosney: chairman, chief executive officer, director, ReliaStar Financial Corp.; director, ReliaStar Foundation
Wheeler, Thomas Beardsley: chairman, chief executive officer, Massachusetts Mutual Life Insurance Co.

Healthcare Leadership Council
Burnham, Duane Lee: chairman, chief executive officer, director, Abbott Laboratories
Gilmartin, Raymond V.: chairman, president, chief executive officer, Merck & Co.; chairman, Merck Co. Foundation

Hebrew Academy Kansas City
Margolin, Abraham E.: director, Tension Envelope Foundation

Hebrew University
Mandel, Jack N.: director, Premier Industrial Corp.
Meyerson, Martin: director, Panasonic Foundation

Heidelberg College
Stevens, Philip Ashworth: vice president, trustee, National Machinery Foundation, Inc.

Helicopter Association International
Kaman, Charles Huron: chairman, president, chief executive officer, director, Kaman Corp.

Hennepin County Bar Association
Hale, James Thomas: senior vice president, general counsel, secretary, Dayton Hudson; trustee, Target Foundation
Mattison, Robert Mayer: director, Graco Foundation; vice president, general counsel, secretary, Graco, Inc.
Neville, James Morton: member board control, Ralston Purina Trust Fund

Hennepin County Medicine Association
Nelson, Glen David, MD: vice chairman, Medtronic, Inc.

Henrico Doctors Hospital
Cutchins, Clifford Armstrong, IV: president, Fort James Corp.; chairman, director, Fort James Foundation (The)

Henry M. Jackson Foundation
Grinstein, Gerald: director, PACCAR Inc.

Heritage Foundation
Franklin, Barbara Hackman: director, Dow Chemical Co.
Margolin, Abraham E.: director, Tension Envelope Foundation

High Meadow Foundation Inc.
Trask, Robert B.: clerk; president, chief operating officer, director, Country Curtains, Inc.; clerk, trustee, High Meadow Foundation

High Museum Art
Chambers, Anne Cox: chairman, trustee, Cox Foundation (James M.)

Highway Users Federation Safety Mobility
Choate, Jerry D.: chairman, chief executive officer, director, Allstate Foundation
Moffitt, Donald Eugene: chairman, director, CNF Transportation, Inc.

Hillside Trust
Bridgeland, James Ralph, Jr.: trustee, Star Bank NA, Cincinnati Foundation

Hiram College
DiGirolamo, Vincent A.: executive vice president, vice chairman, National City Bank of Cleveland

Hispanic Americans Business Community
Trujillo, Solomon D.: president, US West Foundation; president, chief executive officer, US West, Inc.

Hispanics in Philanthropy
Apodaca, Clara: trustee, Hitachi Foundation

Hist Society West Pennsylvania
McGuinn, Martin Gregory: chairman, chief executive officer, Mellon Financial Corp.

Historic Richmond Foundation
Burrus, Robert Lewis, Jr.: trustee, Circuit City Foundation

Historical Society Western Pennsylvania
Block, William: vice president, trustee, Blade Foundation; chairman, director, Toledo Blade Co.

Hockey International
Langbo, Arnold Gordon: chairman, chief executive officer, director, Kellogg Co.

Hole in the Wall Gang Camp
Hotchner, Aaron Edward: vice president, director, executive, Newman's Own Foundation; vice president, treasurer, Newman's Own Inc.
Rukeyser, Robert James: senior vice president corporate affairs, Fortune Brands, Inc.

Hollings Cancer Center
Coker, Charles Westfield: trustee, Sonoco Foundation; vice president, Sonoco Products Co.

Hollins College
Goode, David Ronald: chairman, president, chief executive officer, director, Norfolk Southern Corp.

Holy Cross College
Cantor, Bernard Gerald: president, director, Cantor, Fitzgerald Foundation; chairman, director, Cantor, Fitzgerald Securities Corp.

Honolulu Advertising Federation
Simpson, Andrea Lynn: president

Honolulu Press Club
Dods, Walter Arthur, Jr.: president, director, First Hawaiian Foundation; chairman, chief executive officer, director, First Hawaiian, Inc.

Hoosiers for Higher Education
Koch, Robert Louis, II: president, chief executive officer, director, Koch Enterprises, Inc.; president, director, Koch Foundation

Hoover Institute
Andreas, Dwayne Orville: chairman, chief executive officer, Archer-Daniels-Midland Co.
Moffitt, Donald Eugene: chairman, director, CNF Transportation, Inc.

Horatio Alger Association
Grundhofer, John Francis: president, chief executive officer, director, U.S. Bancorp

Horticultural Society New York
Benenson, James, Jr.: chairman, president, director, Vesper Corp.; trustee, Vesper Foundation

Hospital for Sick Children
Flood, Al: chairman, chief executive officer, CIBC Oppenheimer

Houston Arts Fund
Gleaves, James Leslie: assistant treasurer, American General Finance Foundation

Houston Symphony
Buckwalter, Alan Roland, III: chief executive officer, Chase Bank of Texas; president, Chase Bank of Texas Foundation, Inc.

Howard University
Graves, Earl Gilbert: director, Aetna Foundation

Hugh O'Brian Youth Foundation
Bonsignore, Michael Robert: director, Honeywell Foundation; chairman, chief executive officer, director, Honeywell International Inc.
Ferry, Richard Michael: chairman, Pacific Mutual Life Insurance Co.
O'Reilly, F. Anthony John: chairman, trustee, Heinz Co. Foundation (H.J.); chairman, director, Heinz Co. (H.J.)

Human Race Theatre
Redding, Peter Stoddard: trustee, Sherman-Standard Register Foundation; president, chief executive officer, director, Standard Register Co.

Human Resources Council
Heldreth, Nick E.: vice president human resources corporate relations, Harris Corp.

Human Resources Management Association
Koenig, Brian C.: senior vice president human resources, Scientific-Atlanta, Inc.

Human Resources Planning Society
Grenz, M. Kay: director, 3M Foundation; vice president human resources, Minnesota Mining & Manufacturing Co.
Nicholas, Jon O.: vice president, trustee, Maytag Corp. Foundation

Human Resources Policy Institute
MacDonald, J. Randall: senior vice president human resources administration, GTE Corp.; trustee, GTE Foundation

Human Resources Roundtable Group
Grenz, M. Kay: director, 3M Foundation; vice president human resources, Minnesota Mining & Manufacturing Co.

Humane Society U.S.
Carey, Kathryn Ann: foundation manager, American Honda Foundation

Hundred Years Association New York
Bronfman, Edgar Miles: chairman, trustee, Bronfman Foundation/Joseph E. Seagram & Sons, Inc. Fund (Samuel); chairman, Seagram & Sons, Inc. (Joseph E.)

IEEE
Lucky, Robert Wendell: corporate vice president, Telcordia Technologies

INROADS
Bottorff, Dennis C.: chairman, president, chief executive officer, director, First American Corp.
Grenz, M. Kay: director, 3M Foundation; vice president human resources, Minnesota Mining & Manufacturing Co.
Hock, Delwin D.: chairman, New Century Energies

INROADS/ Columbus

Olesen, Douglas Eugene, PhD: president, chief executive officer, Battelle Memorial Institute

Idaho Bar Association

Graves, Ronald Norman: secretary, Simplot Foundation (J.R.)

Idaho Society Certified Public Accountants

Powell, Sandra Theresa: trustee, Potlatch Foundation II

Illinois Bar Association

Ashley, James Wheeler: director, Globe Foundation

Chelberg, Bruce Stanley: chairman, chief executive officer, director, Whitman Corp.; director, Whitman Corp. Foundation

Dubin, Stephen Victor: vice president, secretary, Farber Foundation

Hudnut, Stewart Skinner: director, Illinois Tool Works Foundation

Olschwang, Alan P., Esq.: secretary, Mitsubishi Electric America Foundation

Pike, Robert William: vice president, secretary, Allstate Foundation; senior vice president, secretary, general counsel, director, Allstate Insurance Co.

Resnick, Myron J.: vice president, treasurer, trustee, Allstate Foundation

Rust, Edward Barry, Jr.: chairman, president, director, State Farm Companies Foundation; chairman, president, chief executive officer, director, State Farm Mutual Automobile Insurance Co.

Skilling, Raymond Inwood: executive vice president, chief counsel, director, Aon Corp.; director, Aon Foundation

Stroup, Stanley Stephenson: executive vice president, general counsel, Norwest Corp.

Wander, Herbert S.: secretary, director, Katten, Muchin & Zavis Foundation

Zavis, Michael W.: managing partner, Katten, Muchin & Zavis; president, director, Katten, Muchin & Zavis Foundation

Illinois Business Roundtable

Burt, Robert Norcross: chairman, chief executive officer, director, FMC Corp.; director, FMC Foundation

Illinois CPAs Society

Chookaszian, Dennis Haig: chairman, chief executive officer, CNA

Sopranos, Orpheus Javaras: corporate vice president, Amsted Industries Inc.

Illinois Chamber of Commerce

Griffin, Donald Wayne: chairman, president, chief executive officer, director, Olin Corp.; trustee, Olin Corp. Charitable Trust

Illinois Competitive Access Reimbursement Equity Program

Harris, Irving Brooks: chairman executive committee, director, Pittway Corp.; chairman, director, Pittway Corp. Charitable Foundation

Illinois Council Economic Education

Gloyd, Lawrence Eugene: trustee, CLARCOR Foundation; chairman, chief executive officer, director, CLARCOR Inc.

Terry, Richard Edward: chairman, chief executive officer, director, Peoples Energy Corp.

Illinois Department Children & Family Services Training Institute

Harris, Irving Brooks: chairman executive committee, director, Pittway Corp.; chairman, director, Pittway Corp. Charitable Foundation

Illinois Development Fin Authority

Zavis, Michael W.: managing partner, Katten, Muchin & Zavis; president, director, Katten, Muchin & Zavis Foundation

Illinois General Assembly

Harris, Irving Brooks: chairman executive committee, director, Pittway Corp.; chairman, director, Pittway Corp. Charitable Foundation

Illinois Institute Technology

Lohman, Gordon Russell: trustee, Amsted Industries Foundation; director, Amsted Industries Inc.

Illinois Leadership Council Agricultural Education

Donovan, Thomas Roy: president, chief executive officer, Chicago Board of Trade

Illinois Life & Health Insurance Guaranty Association

Eckert, Ralph John: trustee, Trustmark Foundation

Illinois Life Insurance Council

Peterson, Donald Matthew: trustee, Trustmark Foundation; president, chief executive officer, director, Trustmark Insurance Co.

Illinois Manufacturer Association

Gidwitz, Gerald S.: chairman, Curtis Industries, Inc. (Helene)

Gloyd, Lawrence Eugene: trustee, CLARCOR Foundation; chairman, chief executive officer, director, CLARCOR Inc.

Graham, William B.: chairman, director, Baxter Allegiance Foundation; chairman emeritus, Baxter International Inc.

Illinois State Society CPAs

Menzer, John: executive vice president, Wal-Mart Stores, Inc.

Illinois State University College Business

Johnson, James Lawrence: chairman emeritus, Walter Industries Inc.

Illinois Wesleyan University

Rust, Edward Barry, Jr.: chairman, president, director, State Farm Companies Foundation; chairman, president, chief executive officer, director, State Farm Mutual Automobile Insurance Co.

Ind Academy

Miller, Joseph Irwin: director associate, Cummins Engine Co., Inc.; director, Cummins Engine Foundation

Independence Hall Association

Wiksten, Barry Frank: president, CIGNA Foundation

Independent Colleges & Universities

Anderson, Ivan Verner, Jr.: president, chief executive officer, Evening Post Publishing Co.; vice president, Post and Courier Foundation

Independent Colleges Indiana

Koch, Robert Louis, II: president, chief executive officer, director, Koch Enterprises, Inc.; president, director, Koch Foundation

Independent Colleges Southern California

Neal, Philip Mark: president, chief executive officer, director, Avery Dennison Corp.

Independent Insurance Agents Association Ohio

Klinedinst, Thomas John, Jr.: trustee, Star Bank NA, Cincinnati Foundation

Independent Order Sons Malta

Gallagher, Terence Joseph: secretary, director, Pfizer Foundation

Lucas, Donald Leo: chairman, Cadence Designs Systems, Inc.

Independent Sector

Belk, Judy: vice president, secretary, Levi Strauss Foundation

Indiana Association CPA's

Russell, Frank Eli: president, Central Newspapers Foundation; chairman, Central Newspapers, Inc.

Indiana Association Colleges

Russell, Frank Eli: president, Central Newspapers Foundation; chairman, Central Newspapers, Inc.

Indiana Association Credit Management

Russell, Frank Eli: president, Central Newspapers Foundation; chairman, Central Newspapers, Inc.

Indiana Bar Association

Murphy, Christopher J., III: president, chief executive officer, director, First Source Corp.; director, First Source Foundation

Ruckelshaus, William Doyle: chairman, director, Browning-Ferris Industries Inc.

Russell, Frank Eli: president, Central Newspapers Foundation; chairman, Central Newspapers, Inc.

Shideler, Shirley Ann Williams: director, Central Newspapers Foundation

Sissel, George A.: chairman, president, chief executive officer, director, Ball Corp.

Indiana Business Higher Education Forum

Koch, Robert Louis, II: president, chief executive officer, director, Koch Enterprises, Inc.; president, director, Koch Foundation

Indiana Center Philanthropy

Baker, James Kendrick: chairman, director, Arvin Foundation; vice chairman, director, Arvin Industries, Inc.

Indiana Chamber of Commerce

Baker, James Kendrick: chairman, director, Arvin Foundation; vice chairman, director, Arvin Industries, Inc.

Koch, Robert Louis, II: president, chief executive officer, director, Koch Enterprises, Inc.; president, director, Koch Foundation

Sease, Gene Elwood: director, Central Newspapers Foundation

Sissel, George A.: chairman, president, chief executive officer, director, Ball Corp.

Indiana Institute Technology

Lawson, William Hogan, III: chairman, chief executive officer, director, Franklin Electric Co.; president, Franklin Electric, Edward J. Schaefer, and T. W. KehoeCharitable and Educational Foundation

Indiana Law Enforcement Training Academy

Sease, Gene Elwood: director, Central Newspapers Foundation

Indiana Producers Association

Haddock, Ronald Wayne: president, chief executive officer, director, FINA; president, FINA Foundation

Indiana Repertory Theatre

Cornelius, James M.: director, AUL Foundation Inc.

Indiana Scholarship Commission

Sease, Gene Elwood: director, Central Newspapers Foundation

Indiana Society Council

Walters, Peter: chairman, SmithKline Beecham Corp.

Indiana University

Sales, A. R.: director, Arvin Foundation; treasurer, Arvin Industries, Inc.

Indiana University Foundation

Tobias, Randall L.: chairman emeritus, Lilly & Co. (Eli)

Indiana University President Advisory Council

Koch, Robert Louis, II: president, chief executive officer, director, Koch Enterprises, Inc.; president, director, Koch Foundation

Indiana University School Business Deans Advisory Council

Carl, John L.: executive vice president, chief financial officer, BP Amoco Corp.; director, BP Amoco Foundation

Indianapolis Bar Association

Ruckelshaus, William Doyle: chairman, director, Browning-Ferris Industries Inc.

Russell, Frank Eli: president, Central Newspapers Foundation; chairman, Central Newspapers, Inc.

Shideler, Shirley Ann Williams: director, Central Newspapers Foundation

Indianapolis Chamber of Commerce

Sease, Gene Elwood: director, Central Newspapers Foundation

Indianapolis Corp. Community Council

Tobias, Randall L.: chairman emeritus, Lilly & Co. (Eli)

Indianapolis Museum Art

Cornelius, James M.: director, AUL Foundation Inc.

Tobias, Randall L.: chairman emeritus, Lilly & Co. (Eli)

Indianapolis Zoological Society

Mutz, John M.: vice president, Cinergy Corp.; director, Cinergy Foundation

Indus Technology Institute

Eaton, Robert James: co-chairman, president, chief executive officer, DaimlerChrysler Corp.

Industrial Relations Research Association

Bowen, William Gordon, PhD: trustee, Merck Co. Foundation

Industrial Safety Equipment Association

Ryan, John Thomas, III: chairman, chief executive officer, Mine Safety Appliances Co.

Industries Sector Advisory Comm Paper Products for Trade Policy Matters

Melican, James Patrick, Jr.: executive vice president legal & external affairs, International Paper Co.; director, International Paper Co. Foundation

Inform

Matthews, Craig Gerard: president, chief operating officer, Brooklyn Union

Information Industry Association

Munder, Barbara A.: senior vice president new initiatives, McGraw-Hill Companies, Inc.

Inland Daily Press Association

Stauffer, Stanley Howard: chairman, Stauffer Communications Foundation

Inland Press Associates

Block, William: vice president, trustee, Blade Foundation; chairman, director, Toledo Blade Co.

Inland Press Association

Stauffer, John H.: trustee, Stauffer Communications Foundation

Inroads Wisconsin

Graff, Stephen Ney: director, Bucyrus-Erie Foundation

Ins Institute America

Brown, Joseph Warner, Jr.: chairman, chief executive officer, MBIA Inc.

Institute Advanced Study

Kann, Peter Robert: chairman, chief executive officer, publisher, director, Dow Jones & Co., Inc.; member advisory committee, Dow Jones Foundation

Institute Certified Management Accountants

Pribanic, Gerald J.: executive vice president, chief financial officer, Maytag Corp.; trustee, Maytag Corp. Foundation

Institute Chartered Accountants

D'Alessandro, Dominic: president, chief executive officer, director, Manulife Financial

Institute Chemical Engineers (UK)

Lovett, John Robert: director, Air Products Foundation

Institute Contemporary Art

Meyerson, Martin: director, Panasonic Foundation

Institute Contemporary Art Boston

Fish, Lawrence K.: trustee, Citizens Charitable Foundation; chairman, chief executive officer, Citizens Financial Group, Inc.

Institute Defense Analysts

Davis, Ruth Margaret: trustee, Air Products Foundation

Institute Directors Inc.

O'Reilly, F. Anthony John: chairman, trustee, Heinz Co. Foundation (H.J.); chairman, director, Heinz Co. (H.J.)

Institute East-West Studies

Rhodes, William Reginald: vice chairman, Citibank Corp.

Wallach, Ira D.: chairman, Central National-Gottesman; executive vice president, Central National-Gottesman Foundation

Institute Electrical & Electronics Engineers

Dingman, Michael David: partner, director, Winthrop Foundation

Engel, Joel Stanley: vice president technology, Ameritech Corp.

Engibous, Thomas James: director, Texas Instruments Foundation; president, chief executive officer, chairman, director, Texas Instruments Inc.

Fisher, George Myles Cordell: chairman, president, chief executive officer, director, Eastman Kodak Co.

Grove, Andrew S.: chairman, Intel Corp.

Hatsopoulos, George Nicholas: founder, chairman, chief executive officer, director, Thermo Electron Corp.; committee member, Thermo Electron Foundation

Joyce, William H.: chairman, president, chief executive officer, chief operating officer, Union Carbide Corp.

LaMacchia, John Thomas: trustee, Cincinnati Bell Foundation, Inc.; president, chief executive officer, director, Cincinnati Bell Inc.

Moore, Gordon E., PhD: co-founder, chairman emeritus, director, Intel Corp.; trustee, Intel Foundation

Mueller, Charles William: chairman, president, chief executive officer, Ameren Corp.; trustee, Ameren Corp. Charitable Trust

Pierre, Percy A.: trustee, Hitachi Foundation

Platt, Lewis Emmett: chairman, Hewlett-Packard Co.

Poindexter, Christian Herndon: chairman, Baltimore Gas & Electric Foundation; chairman, chief executive officer, director, Constellation Energy Group, Inc.

Institute Entrepreneurial Leadership Inc.

Berkley, Eugene Bertram: chairman, director, Tension Envelope Corp.; treasurer, Tension Envelope Foundation

Institute Gas Technology

Kennedy, Bernard Joseph: chairman, president, chief executive officer, director, National Fuel Gas Distribution Corp.

Messer, Chester R.: president, chief operating officer, Boston Gas Co.; trustee, Eastern Enterprises Foundation

Mitchell, Warren I.: president, director, Southern California Gas Co.

Terry, Richard Edward: chairman, chief executive officer, director, Peoples Energy Corp.

Institute Global Ethics

Baker, James Kendrick: chairman, director, Arvin Foundation; vice chairman, director, Arvin Industries, Inc.

Institute Human Origins

Koch, David Hamilton: director, Koch Foundation, Inc. (Fred C. and Mary R.)

Institute Humane Studies

Koch, Charles de Ganahl: chairman, chief executive officer, director, president, Koch Industries, Inc.

Institute Internal Auditors

Schara, Charles Gerard: treasurer, GEICO Corp.; assistant treasurer, director, GEICO Philanthropic Foundation

Institute International Economics

David, George A. L.: chairman, president, chief executive officer, chief operating officer, United Technologies Corp.

Polin, Jane Louise: manager, comptroller, GE Fund

Institute International Finance Inc.

Coulter, David A.: president, director, Bank of America

Rhodes, William Reginald: vice chairman, Citibank Corp.

Institute International Studies

Ginn, Samuel L.: chairman, director, AirTouch Communications Foundation; chairman, chief executive officer, director, Vodafone AirTouch Plc

Institute Judicial Administration

Kaden, Ellen O.: trustee, Campbell Soup Foundation

Lipton, Martin: partner, Wachtell, Lipton, Rosen & Katz; president, Wachtell, Lipton, Rosen & Katz Foundation

Institute Living

Kaman, Charles Huron: chairman, president, chief executive officer, director, Kaman Corp.

Institute Makers Explosives

Long, Michael Thomas: director, Ensign-Bickford Foundation

Institute Medicine

Elam, Lloyd Charles, MD: trustee, Merck Co. Foundation

Vagelos, Pindaros Roy: trustee, Prudential Insurance Co. of America

Institute Mining & Metallurgy Engineers

Wareham, James Lyman: president, AK Steel Corp.

Institute Navigation

Leonis, John Michael: chairman, director, Litton Industries, Inc.

Institute Newspaper Contrs & Fin Offs

Doherty, Leonard Edward: member advisory committee, admin officer, Dow Jones Foundation

Russell, Frank Eli: president, Central Newspapers Foundation; chairman, Central Newspapers, Inc.

Institute Newspaper Fin Executives

Doerfler, Ronald J.: senior vice president, chief financial officer, ABC; vice president, director, ABC Foundation

Institute Paper Chemistry

Mead, George Wilson, II: president, director, Consolidated Papers Foundation, Inc.; chairman, director, Consolidated Papers, Inc.

Institute Paper Science Technology

Ballengee, Jerry Hunter: president, chief operating officer, director, Union Camp Corp.

Harad, George Jay: chairman, chief executive officer, director, Boise Cascade Corp.

Luke, John A., Jr.: chairman, president, chief executive officer, director, Westvaco Corp.

Institute Petroleum

Bijur, Peter I.: chairman, chief executive officer, Texaco Inc.

Institute Research on Higher Education Fels Center

Meyerson, Martin: director, Panasonic Foundation

Institute Textile Technology

Milliken, Roger: chairman, chief executive officer, Milliken & Co.; member advisory committee, Milliken Foundation

Institute for Management Sciences

Magee, John Francis: chairman, director, Little, Inc. (Arthur D.)

Institute of Management Accountant

Parsons, Susan E.: secretary, treasurer, Koch Enterprises, Inc.; secretary, treasurer, director, Koch Foundation

Institute of Management Accountants

Daley, Leo J.: vice president, treasurer, Air Products and Chemicals, Inc.

Edwards, Earnest Jonathan: director, Alcoa Foundation

Hernandez, William H.: director, PPG Industries Foundation; senior vice president, PPG Industries, Inc.

Johnson, Kenneth James: vice president, controller, director, Motorola Inc.

Reese, Terry W.: assistant treasurer, Vulcan Materials Co. Foundation

Sullivan, Thomas John: vice president, director,

Trask, Robert B.: clerk; president, chief operating officer, director, Country Curtains, Inc.; clerk, trustee, High Meadow Foundation

Wellman, Thomas A.: controller, assistant treasurer, Alexander & Baldwin, Inc.

Insurance Economics Society America

Purvis, George Frank, Jr.: chairman, president, chief executive officer, director, Pan-American Life Insurance Co.

Insurance Ed Foundation

Beyer, Jeffrey C.: president, Farmers Group Safety Foundation

Insurance Information Institute

Herres, Robert T.: chairman, chief executive officer, United Services Automobile Association

Rupley, Theodore J.: president, chief executive officer, director, Allmerica Financial Corp.

Insurance Institute America

Ayer, Ramani: chairman, president, chief executive officer, Hartford (The)

Rupley, Theodore J.: president, chief executive officer, director, Allmerica Financial Corp.

Rust, Edward Barry, Jr.: chairman, president, director, State Farm Companies Foundation; chairman, president, chief executive officer, director, State Farm Mutual Automobile Insurance Co.

Insurance Institute Highway Safety

Choate, Jerry D.: chairman, chief executive officer, director, Allstate Foundation

Herres, Robert T.: chairman, chief executive officer, United Services Automobile Association

Sullivan, Laura P.: vice president, secretary, director, State Farm Companies Foundation; vice president, secretary, counsel, State Farm Mutual Automobile Insurance Co.

Insurance Institute Property Loss Reduction

Dabney, Fred E., II: executive director, Royal & SunAlliance Insurance Foundation, Inc.; vice president corporate communications, Royal & SunAlliance USA, Inc.

Insurance Marketing Communication Association

Dabney, Fred E., II: executive director, Royal & SunAlliance Insurance Foundation, Inc.; vice president corporate communications, Royal & SunAlliance USA, Inc.

Insurance Marketplace Standards Association

Roth, Michael I.: chairman, chief executive officer, director, MONY Group (The); director, MONY Life Insurance of New York (The)

Insurance Public Relations Council

Dabney, Fred E., II: executive director, Royal & SunAlliance Insurance Foundation, Inc.; vice president corporate communications, Royal & SunAlliance USA, Inc.

Insurance Service Office

Chookaszian, Dennis Haig: chairman, chief executive officer, CNA

Inter-American Press Association

Copley, Helen K.: chairman, trustee, Copley Foundation (James S.); chairman, director, senior management board, Copley Press, Inc.

Interlochen Center Arts

Valade, Gary C.: executive vice president, chief financial officer, DaimlerChrysler Corp.; trustee, DaimlerChrysler Corp. Fund

International Accounting Standards Committee

Cook, J. Michael: chairman, chief executive officer, Deloitte & Touche; chairman, Deloitte & Touche Foundation

International Air Transport Association

Mullin, Leo Francis: chairman, president, chief executive officer, Delta Air Lines, Inc.

International Association Corp. Real Estate

Ervanian, Armen: vice president, Viad Corp. Fund

International Association Defense Counsel

Johnson, Murray Lloyd, Jr.: secretary, trustee, Zachry Foundation (The)

International Association Insurance Council

Knight, Merrill Donaldson, III: director, GEICO Philanthropic Foundation

International Association Universities

Meyerson, Martin: director, Panasonic Foundation

International Association of Business Communications

Blanke, Gail Ann: vice president, Avon Products Foundation, Inc.

Dabney, Fred E., II: executive director, Royal & SunAlliance Insurance Foundation, Inc.; vice president corporate communications, Royal & SunAlliance USA, Inc.

Gorman, Maureen V.: vice president, GTE Foundation

International Astronautical Federation

Armstrong, Neil A.: trustee, Milacron Foundation; director, Milacron, Inc.

International Bar Association

Burak, Howard Paul: secretary, director, Sony U.S.A. Foundation Inc.

Carter, John Douglas: executive vice president, director, Bechtel Group, Inc.

Cogan, John Francis, Jr.: president, chief executive officer, director, Pioneer Group

Kalaher, Richard A.: president, American Standard Foundation; vice president, secretary, general counsel, American Standard Inc.

International Cap Markets Advisory Committee

Grasso, Richard A.: chairman, chief executive officer, New York Stock Exchange, Inc.

International Center Disabled

Zilkha, Ezra Khedouri: president, treasurer, Zilkha Foundation, Inc.; president, Zilkha & Sons

International Center Journalists

Taylor, William Osgood: chairman, chief executive officer, director, Boston Globe (The); chairman, director, Boston Globe Foundation; director, New York Times Co. Foundation

International Center for Companies of the Food Trade and Industry

Wright, Michael William: chairman, president, chief executive officer, director, SuperValu, Inc.

International Communications Forum

Engel, Joel Stanley: vice president technology, Ameritech Corp.

International Copper Association

Muth, Robert James: president, director, ASARCO Foundation

Osborne, Richard de Jongh: director, ASARCO Foundation; chairman, chief executive officer, director, ASARCO Inc.

International Council Shopping Centers

Shiel, William A.: senior vice president facilities development, Walgreen Co.

International Council of Museum Foundations

Ripley, Sidney Dillon, II: director emeritus, Hitachi Foundation

International Crisis Group

Taylor, William Osgood: chairman, chief executive officer, director, Boston Globe (The); chairman, director, Boston Globe Foundation; director, New York Times Co. Foundation

International Development Research Council

Ervanian, Armen: vice president, Viad Corp. Fund

International Executive Service Corps

Burke, Daniel Barnett: vice president, treasurer, director, ABC Foundation

Goodes, Melvin Russell: chairman, chief executive officer, director, Ameritech Corp.

Whitehead, John Cunningham: chairman board, Goldman Sachs Foundation

International Federation Periodical Press

Kerr, William T.: chairman, chief executive officer, director, Meredith Corp.

International Food Information Council

Gould, John T., Jr.: vice president, Unilever Foundation; director corporate affairs, Unilever United States, Inc.

International Franchise Association

Menzer, John: executive vice president, Wal-Mart Stores, Inc.

International House

Heimbold, Charles Andreas, Jr.: chairman, president, chief executive officer, Bristol-Myers Squibb Co.

Whitehead, John Cunningham: chairman board, Goldman Sachs Foundation

International House Center

Meyerson, Martin: director, Panasonic Foundation

International Institute Kidney Diseases UCLA

Rosenzweig, Richard Stuart: executive vice president, director, Playboy Enterprises Inc.

International Institute Strategic Studies

Ross, Arthur: senior vice president, Central National-Gottesman; director, Central National-Gottesman Foundation

International Iron & Steel Institute

Barnette, Curtis Handley: chairman, chief executive officer, director, Bethlehem Steel Corp.

Wareham, James Lyman: president, AK Steel Corp.

International Life Science Institute Nutrition Foundation

O'Reilly, F. Anthony John: chairman, trustee, Heinz Co. Foundation (H.J.); chairman, director, Heinz Co. (H.J.)

International Literacy Institute

Meyerson, Martin: director, Panasonic Foundation

International Mass Retail Association

Soderquist, Donald G.: trustee, Wal-Mart Foundation; senior vice chairman, director, Wal-Mart Stores, Inc.

International Material Management Society

Neel, Curtis Dean, Jr.: trustee, Eckerd Corp. Foundation

International Newspaper Fin Executives

Doherty, Leonard Edward: member advisory committee, admin officer, Dow Jones Foundation

Spoon, Alan Gary: president, chief operating officer, director, The Washington Post

International Patent & Trademark Association

Kurtz, Melvin H.: secretary, director, Chesebrough Foundation

International Petroleum Association

Bradford, William Edward: chairman, director, Halliburton Co.

International Platform Association

Sease, Gene Elwood: director, Central Newspapers Foundation

International Press Institute

Block, William: vice president, trustee, Blade Foundation; chairman, director, Toledo Blade Co.

Morris, William Shivers, III: founder, chairman, chief executive officer, director, Morris Communications Corp.; trustee, Stauffer Communications Foundation

International Public Relations Association

Simpson, Andrea Lynn: president

International Public Relations Council

Bloch, Henry Wollman: chairman, Block Foundation (H&R); chairman, director, Block, Inc. (H&R)

International Radio & Television Society

Doerfler, Ronald J.: senior vice president, chief financial officer, ABC; vice president, director, ABC Foundation

Hubbard, Stanley S.: chairman, president, chief executive officer, Hubbard Broadcasting, Inc.; president, Hubbard Foundation

International Rescue Committee

Whitehead, John Cunningham: chairman board, Goldman Sachs Foundation

International Society Explosive Engineers

Long, Michael Thomas: director, Ensign-Bickford Foundation

International Society Securities Administration

Carter, Marshall Nichols: chairman, chief executive officer, State Street Bank & Trust Co.

International Tennis Hall of Fame

Geier, Philip Henry, Jr.: chairman, president, chief executive officer, Interpublic Group of Companies, Inc.

International Trade & Investment Task Force

Gorman, Joseph T.: chairman, chief executive officer, TRW Inc.

International Trade Administration

Purvis, George Frank, Jr.: chairman, president, chief

executive officer, director, Pan-American Life Insurance Co.

International Wild Waterfowl Association

Ripley, Sidney Dillon, II: director emeritus, Hitachi Foundation

International Womens Forum

Brown, JoBeth Goode: trustee, Anheuser-Busch Companies, Inc.

Francis, Cheryl A.: executive vice president, chief financial officer, Donnelley & Sons Co. (R.R.)

Franklin, Barbara Hackman: director, Dow Chemical Co.

Interracial Council Business Opportunity

Graves, Earl Gilbert: director, Aetna Foundation

Interstate Natural Gas Association America

Bailey, Keith E.: chairman, president, director, chief executive officer, Texas Gas Transmission Corp.; president, director, Williams Companies Foundation (The)

Farman, Richard Donald: chairman, chief executive officer, Pacific Enterprises

Hall, Larry D.: chairman, president, chief executive officer, director, Kinder Morgn; president, director, KN Energy Foundation

Kennedy, Bernard Joseph: chairman, president, chief executive officer, director, National Fuel Gas Distribution Corp.

Wise, William Allen: chairman, president, chief executive officer, director, El Paso Energy Co.; chairman, director, El Paso Energy Foundation

Intl Bar Association

Davis, Walter Stewart: secretary, treasurer, Grede Foundation

Intl Institute Strategic Studies

Zuckerman, Mortimer Benjamin: co-founder, chairman, co-publisher, director, Daily News

Intl Peace Academy

Wallach, Ira D.: chairman, Central National-Gottesman; executive vice president, Central National-Gottesman Foundation

Investment Co. Institute

Cogan, John Francis, Jr.: president, chief executive officer, director, Pioneer Group

Keough, William H.: senior vice president, chief financial officer, Pioneer Group

Lasser, Lawrence Jay: president, chief executive officer, director, Putnam Investments; president, chief executive officer, Putnam Investors Fund

Investor Relations Institute

Smith, Elizabeth Patience: director, Texaco Foundation; vice president investor relations & shareholder service, Texaco Inc.

Iona College

Link, James F.: treasurer, Texaco Foundation

Robinson, Edward Joseph: president, chief operating officer, director, Avon Products, Inc.

Iowa Bar Association

Kelley, Bruce Gunn: vice president, director, Employers Mutual Charitable Foundation

Sullivan, Laura P.: vice president, secretary, director, State Farm Companies Foundation; vice president, secretary, counsel, State Farm Mutual Automobile Insurance Co.

Iowa Business Council

Hadley, Leonard Anson: chairman, chief executive officer, director, Maytag Corp.; president, trustee, Maytag Corp. Foundation

Rehm, Jack Daniel: chairman emeritus, director, Meredith Corp.

Iowa College Foundation

Hadley, Leonard Anson: chairman, chief executive officer, director, Maytag Corp.; president, trustee, Maytag Corp. Foundation

Lawson, John K.: senior vice president, Deere & Co.; director, Deere Foundation (John)

Iowa Insurance Hall Fame

Brooks, Roger Kay: chairman, AmerUS Group

Iowa Life Health Insurance Association

Drury, David J.: chief executive officer, chairman, Principal Financial Group

Iowa Management Association

Kramer, Mary Elizabeth: vice president, Wellmark Foundation

Iowa Public Employees Retirement Systems

Kelley, Bruce Gunn: vice president, director, Employers Mutual Charitable Foundation

Iowa State University Foundation

Lawson, John K.: senior vice president, Deere & Co.; director, Deere Foundation (John)

Iowa Technological Transfer Council

Hadley, Leonard Anson: chairman, chief executive officer, director, Maytag Corp.; president, trustee, Maytag Corp. Foundation

Iowa Wesleyan College

Howe, Stanley M.: president, HON Industries Charitable Foundation; chairman emeritus, director, HON Industries Inc.

Irish Management Institute

O'Reilly, F. Anthony John: chairman, trustee, Heinz Co. Foundation (H.J.); chairman, director, Heinz Co. (H.J.)

Irvine Medical Center

Rollans, James Ora: senior vice president, chief administrative officer, chief financial officer, Fluor Corp.; trustee, Fluor Foundation

Isabella Stewart Gardner Museum

Bodman, Samuel Wright, III: chairman, chief executive officer, director, Cabot Corp.; president, director, Cabot Corp. Foundation

Hiatt, Arnold Selig: chairman, director, Stride Rite Foundation

Isadore Newman School

Bachmann, Richard Arthur: vice president, secretary, treasurer, director, Louisiana Land & Exploration Co. Foundation

Isamu Noguchi Federation

Shapiro, Isaac: chairman, secretary, trustee, Ise Cultural Foundation

JP Morgan International Advisory Council

Bechtel, Riley Peart: chairman, Bechtel Foundation; chairman, chief executive officer, director, Bechtel Group, Inc.

Jackson Chamber of Commerce

McMillan, Howard Lamar, Jr.: president, chief operating officer, director, Deposit Guaranty National Bank

Robinson, E. B., Jr.: chairman, chief executive officer, director, Deposit Guaranty National Bank

Jackson Hole Group

Nelson, Glen David, MD: vice chairman, Medtronic, Inc.

Jacob L. and Ella C. Louse Foundation

Matheny, Edward Taylor, Junior: director, Block Foundation (H&R)

Jacobs Applied Technology Inc.

Prosser, John Warren, Jr.: treasurer, director, Jacobs Engineering Foundation; senior vice president finance & administration, treasurer, Jacobs Engineering Group

Jacobs Constructors California

Prosser, John Warren, Jr.: treasurer, director, Jacobs Engineering Foundation; senior vice president finance & administration, treasurer, Jacobs Engineering Group

Jacobs Engineering Foundation

Prosser, John Warren, Jr.: treasurer, director, Jacobs Engineering Foundation; senior vice president finance & administration, treasurer, Jacobs Engineering Group

Jacobs Engineering Group Ohio

Prosser, John Warren, Jr.: treasurer, director, Jacobs Engineering Foundation; senior vice president finance & administration, treasurer, Jacobs Engineering Group

James C Copley Charitable Foundation

ZoBell, Karl: vice president, trustee, Copley Foundation (James S.)

James Madison University

Harrell, Henry Howze: director, Universal Leaf Foundation; chairman, chief executive officer, director, Universal Leaf Tobacco Co., Inc.

Jamestown College

Unruh, James Arlen: director, Ameritech Foundation

Jamestown Foundation

Gidwitz, Gerald S.: chairman, Curtis Industries, Inc. (Helene)

Japan Society

Gerstner, Louis Vincent, Jr.: chairman, chief executive officer, director, International Business Machines Corp.

Ingersoll, Robert Stephen: chairman, director, Panasonic Foundation

Shapiro, Isaac: chairman, secretary, trustee, Ise Cultural Foundation

Japan-American Institute of Management Science

Dods, Walter Arthur, Jr.: president, director, First Hawaiian Foundation; chairman, chief executive officer, director, First Hawaiian, Inc.

Japan-American Society

McClung, James Allen: vice president, director, FMC Foundation

Japan-American Society Indiana

Sease, Gene Elwood: director, Central Newspapers Foundation

Japan-Hawaii Economic Council

Dods, Walter Arthur, Jr.: president, director, First Hawaiian Foundation; chairman, chief executive officer, director, First Hawaiian, Inc.

Japanese Cultural Center Hawaii

Dods, Walter Arthur, Jr.: president, director, First Hawaiian Foundation; chairman, chief executive officer, director, First Hawaiian, Inc.

Jason Foundation for Education

Raymond, Lee R.: chairman, president, chief executive officer, Exxon Mobil Corp.

Jaycees Franklin

Upbin, Hal Jay: president, chief executive officer, director, Kellwood Co.

Jerusalem Foundation

Hassenfeld, Alan Geoffrey: president, Hasbro Charitable Trust Inc.; chairman, chief executive officer, Hasbro, Inc.

Jesuit Secondary Education Association

Cody, Thomas Gerald: executive vice president legal & human resources, Federated Department Stores, Inc.

Jewish Federation Greater Kansas City

Margolin, Abraham E.: director, Tension Envelope Foundation

Jewish Federation Metropolitan Chicago

Wander, Herbert S.: secretary, director, Katten, Muchin & Zavis Foundation

Jewish Hospital Saint Louis

Loeb, Jerome Thomas: chairman, director, May Department Stores Co.; president, director, May Department Stores Computer Foundation (The)

Jewish Philanthropies, Inc.

Lippes, Gerald Sanford: secretary, Mark IV Industries Foundation

Jewish United Fund

Wander, Herbert S.: secretary, director, Katten, Muchin & Zavis Foundation

Jobs Massachusetts

Brown, Stephen Lee: chairman, chief executive officer, director, Hancock Financial Services (John)

Jobs for Americas Grads

Conaty, William J.: director, GE Fund

John Burroughs School

Maritz, William Edward: chairman, chief executive officer, president, Maritz Inc.

John Carroll University

Reid, James Sims, Jr.: chairman, director, Standard Products Co.; chairman, president, Standard Products Co. Charitable Foundation

John F. Kennedy Library Foundation

Redstone, Sumner Murray: chairman, Viacom Inc.

John F. Kennedy Medical Center

Tumminello, Stephen C.: president, chief executive officer, director, Philips Electronics North America Corp.

John F. Kennedy Profile Courage Award Committee

Redstone, Sumner Murray: chairman, Viacom Inc.

John F. Kennedy School Government

Stewart, Donald M.: director, New York Times Co. Foundation

John Hopkins University

Poindexter, Christian Herndon: chairman, Baltimore Gas & Electric Foundation; chairman, chief executive officer, director, Constellation Energy Group, Inc.

John Michael Kohler Arts Center

Kohler, Herbert Vollrath, Jr.: chairman, president, director, Kohler Co.

John Tracy Clinic for the Hearing Impaired

Kresa, Kent: chairman, president, chief executive officer, director, Northrop Grumman Corp.

Johns Hopkins Health System Corp./Johns Hopkins Hospital

Shepard, Donald James: chairman, president, chief executive officer, AEGON U.S.A. Inc.

Johns Hopkins School Medicine

Armstrong, C. Michael: chairman, chief executive officer, AT&T Corp.

Johns Hopkins University

Shepard, Donald James: chairman, president, chief executive officer, AEGON U.S.A. Inc.

Snow, John William: chairman, president, chief executive officer, CSX Corp.

Joint Center Political Economic Studies

Hill, Bonnie Guiton: vice president, Times Mirror Co.; president, chief executive officer, Times Mirror Foundation

Joint Venture Silicon Valley Network Board

Coulter, David A.: president, director, Bank of America

Platt, Lewis Emmett: chairman, Hewlett-Packard Co.

Joslyn Art Museum

Scott, Walter, Jr.: member contributions committee, Kiewit Companies Foundation

Judge Advisory General Association

Wolff, Jesse David: treasurer, director, Weil, Gotshal & Manges Foundation

Judge Advocates Association

Calise, Nicholas James: vice president, associate general counsel, secretary, BFGoodrich Co.; secretary, Goodrich Foundation, Inc. (B.F.)

Junior Achievement

Gifford, Charles Kilvert: trustee, BankBoston Charitable Foundation; chairman, chief executive officer, BankBoston Corp.

Herres, Robert T.: chairman, chief executive officer, United Services Automobile Association

Lowrie, William G.: president, deputy chief executive officer, director, BP Amoco Corp.

Standen, Craig Clayton: senior vice president corporate development, Scripps Co. (E.W.)

Junior Achievement Cincinnati

Campbell, Cheryl Nichols: operation service advisory group, Cincinnati Bell Inc.

Junior Achievement Michigan Valley

Loeb, Jerome Thomas: chairman, director, May Department Stores Co.; president, director, May Department Stores Computer Foundation (The)

Junior Achievement Mid-America

Bloch, Henry Wollman: chairman, Block Foundation (H&R); chairman, director, Block, Inc. (H&R)

Junior Achievement Mississippi Valley

Suter, Albert E.: senior vice chairman, chief administrative officer, director, Emerson Electric Co.

Junior Achievement National Board

Loeb, Jerome Thomas: chairman, director, May Department Stores Co.; president, director, May Department Stores Computer Foundation (The)

Suter, Albert E.: senior vice chairman, chief administrative officer, director, Emerson Electric Co.

Junior Achievement New York

Ostergard, Paul Michael: vice president, director corporate contributions, Citibank Corp.; president, Citigroup Foundation

Junior League

Campbell, Cheryl Nichols: operation service advisory group, Cincinnati Bell Inc.

Juvenile Diabetes Foundation International

Bowles, Crandall Close: president, chief executive officer, chairman, director, Springs Industries, Inc.

KETC

Maritz, William Edward: chairman, chief executive officer, president, Maritz Inc.

KETC Education Television

Gaiswinkler, Robert Sigfried: chairman, director, First Financial Bank; director, First Financial Foundation

KIDSPAC

Harris, William W.: director, Pittway Corp. Charitable Foundation

KQED

James, George Barker, II: senior vice president, chief financial officer, Levi Strauss & Co.

Kansas Bar Association

Meyer, Russell William, Jr.: chairman, chief executive officer, Cessna Aircraft Co.; president, Cessna Foundation, Inc.

Kansas Chamber of Commerce & Industry

Stauffer, Stanley Howard: chairman, Stauffer Communications Foundation

Kansas City Area Health Planning Council

Bloch, Henry Wollman: chairman, Block Foundation (H&R); chairman, director, Block, Inc. (H&R)

Kansas City Art Institute

Powell, George Everett, Jr.: trustee, Yellow Corp. Foundation

Kansas City Bar Association

Matheny, Edward Taylor, Junior: director, Block Foundation (H&R)

Kansas City Chamber of Commerce

Hall, Donald Joyce: chairman board, director, Hallmark Cards Inc.; chairman, Hallmark Corporate Foundation

Powell, George Everett, Jr.: trustee, Yellow Corp. Foundation

Stauffer, John H.: trustee, Stauffer Communications Foundation

Kansas City Minority Suppliers Development Council

Hall, Donald Joyce: chairman board, director, Hallmark Cards Inc.; chairman, Hallmark Corporate Foundation

Kansas City Public Television

Powell, George Everett, III: president, chief executive officer, director, Yellow Corp.; trustee, Yellow Corp. Foundation

Kansas City Symphony

Bloch, Henry Wollman: chairman, Block Foundation (H&R); chairman, director, Block, Inc. (H&R)

Hall, Donald Joyce: chairman board, director, Hallmark Cards Inc.; chairman, Hallmark Corporate Foundation

Kansas Press Association

Stauffer, John H.: trustee, Stauffer Communications Foundation

Stauffer, Stanley Howard: chairman, Stauffer Communications Foundation

Kansas University Lawrence

Strandjord, Mary Jeannine: director, Sprint Foundation

Kapiolani Medical Center

Simpson, Andrea Lynn: president

Kappa Alpha

Hemminghaus, Roger Roy: chairman, director, Ultramar Diamond Shamrock Corp.

Miglio, Daniel Joseph: chairman, president, director, chief executive officer, Southern New England Telephone Co.

Kappa Sigma Alumni Association

Van Dyke, William Grant: chairman, president, chief executive officer, director, Donaldson Co., Inc.

Keep America Beautiful

Fites, Donald Vester: director, Caterpillar Foundation

Keep America Beautiful Inc.

Correll, Alston Dayton 'Pete', Jr.: chairman, president, chief executive officer, director, Georgia-Pacific Corp.; director, Georgia-Pacific Foundation

Kendall School Art & Design

Bloom, Geoffrey B.: chairman, chief executive officer, director, Wolverine World Wide

Kennedy Center

Bloch, Henry Wollman: chairman, Block Foundation (H&R); chairman, director, Block, Inc. (H&R)

Kennedy Center Corp. Fund Board

Goode, David Ronald: chairman, president, chief executive officer, director, Norfolk Southern Corp.

Kennedy Center for Performing Arts

Ingram, Martha R.: chairman, director, Ingram Industries Inc.

Kennedy Krieger Institute

Lawless, Robert J.: chairman, president, chief executive officer, chief operating officer, director, McCormick & Co. Inc.

Kent County Memorial Hospital

Shuster, George Whitcomb: trustee, Cranston Foundation; president, chief executive officer, director, Cranston Print Works Co.

Kentucky & Tennessee District Export Council

Hower, Frank Beard, Jr.: vice chairman, Anthem Foundation, Inc.

Kentucky Bar Association

Guillaume, Raymond Kendrick: vice chairman, chief executive officer, Mid-America Bank of Louisville

Rogers, James E., Jr.: vice chairman, president, chief executive officer, Cinergy Corp.; vice chairman, director, Cinergy Foundation

Kentucky Center Arts Endowment Fund

Guillaume, Raymond Kendrick: vice chairman, chief executive officer, Mid-America Bank of Louisville

Kentucky Independent College Fund

Hower, Frank Beard, Jr.: vice chairman, Anthem Foundation, Inc.

Kenyon College

McCoy, John Bonnet: president, chief executive officer, Ameritech Corp.

Kettering University

Knicely, Howard V.: president, TRW Foundation

Keuka College

Rosett, Richard Nathaniel: trustee, Kemper Foundation (James S.)

Keystone Center

McKennon, Keith Robert: chairman, president, PacifiCorp; member, PacifiCorp Foundation

Kiddies Camp Corp.

Kohler, Herbert Vollrath, Jr.: chairman, president, director, Kohler Co.

Kids Fund

Harris, William W.: director, Pittway Corp. Charitable Foundation

Kids Help Phone

McNally, Alan G.: chairman, chief executive officer, Harris Trust & Savings Bank

Kids in Distressed Situations

Goddu, Roger V.: chairman, chief executive officer, director, Montgomery Ward & Co., Inc.

Lay, Terry: president, Lee, Lee Apparel Co.

King County United Way

Mersereau, Susan M.: trustee, Weyerhaeuser Co. Foundation

Kiwanis International

Jacobson, Lyle Gordon: treasurer, Hickory Tech Corp. Foundation

O'Brien, James E.: director, Schoeneckers Foundation

Thyen, James C.: president, director, Habig Foundation

Kiwanis Minneapolis

O'Brien, James E.: director, Schoeneckers Foundation

Knight Foundation

Osborne, Burl: president publishing division, director, Belo Corp. (A.H.); president, trustee, Belo Corp. Foundation (A.H.)

Knights of Columbus

Habig, Thomas L.: vice chairman, director, Habig Foundation

Omachinski, David L.: chief financial officer, treasurer, vice president, Oshkosh B'Gosh, Inc.

Trask, Robert B.: clerk; president, chief operating officer, director, Country Curtains, Inc.; clerk, trustee, High Meadow Foundation

Knox College

Fites, Donald Vester: director, Caterpillar Foundation

Koc University

Meyerson, Martin: director, Panasonic Foundation

Kutztown University Foundation

Hafer, Fred Douglass: chairman, president, chief executive officer, GPU Inc.

LOMA

Murphy, James W.: senior vice president corporate finance, American United Life Insurance Co.; treasurer, AUL Foundation Inc.

LP Advisory Comm

Coulter, David A.: president, director, Bank of America

La Jolla Museum Contemp Art

Copley, Helen K.: chairman, trustee, Copley Foundation (James S.); chairman, director, senior management board, Copley Press, Inc.

La Jolla Playhouse

Copley, David C.: president, trustee, Copley Foundation (James S.); president, chief executive officer, director, senior management board, Copley Press, Inc.

La Jolla Town Council

Copley, Helen K.: chairman, trustee, Copley Foundation (James S.); chairman, director, senior management board, Copley Press, Inc.

LaCoste School Arts

Chambers, Anne Cox: chairman, trustee, Cox Foundation (James M.)

LaRoche College

Edwards, Earnest Jonathan: director, Alcoa Foundation

Labor Policy Association

Conaty, William J.: director, GE Fund

Heldreth, Nick E.: vice president human resources corporate relations, Harris Corp.

Kirby, William Joseph: vice president, director, FMC Foundation

Knicely, Howard V.: president, TRW Foundation

MacDonald, J. Randall: senior vice president human resources administration, GTE Corp.; trustee, GTE Foundation

Richards, Joel, III: vice president, El Paso Energy Foundation

Lafayette College

Griffith, Alan Richard: vice chairman, Bank of New York Co., Inc.

Lake Forest Academy

Stone, Roger Warren: chairman, president, chief executive officer, director,

Stone Container Corp.; president, Stone Foundation

Lake Forest Graduate School Management

Connolly, Eugene Bernard, Jr.: chairman emeritus, USG Corp.

Keyser, Richard Lee: chairman, chief executive officer, president, Grainger, Inc. (W.W.)

Peterson, Donald Matthew: trustee, Trustmark Foundation; president, chief executive officer, director, Trustmark Insurance Co.

Lake Forest Hospital

Peterson, Donald Matthew: trustee, Trustmark Foundation; president, chief executive officer, director, Trustmark Insurance Co.

Lakeland College

Bemis, Peter F.: vice president, Bemis Family Foundation (F.K.)

Lambda Alpha

ZoBell, Karl: vice president, trustee, Copley Foundation (James S.)

Latin School of Chicago

Almeida, Richard: chairman, chief executive officer, Heller Financial, Inc.

Latrobe Chamber of Commerce

Meyer, Russell William, Jr.: chairman, chief executive officer, Cessna Aircraft Co.; president, Cessna Foundation, Inc.

Lauder Institute of Management & International Studies

Meyerson, Martin: director, Panasonic Foundation

Law Society Ireland

O'Reilly, F. Anthony John: chairman, trustee, Heinz Co. Foundation (H.J.); chairman, director, Heinz Co. (H.J.)

Lawrence University

Belcher, Donald D.: chairman, president, chief executive officer, director, Banta Corp.; vice president, director, Banta Corp. Foundation

Kohler, Herbert Vollrath, Jr.: chairman, president, director, Kohler Co.

Luke, John A., Jr.: chairman, president, chief executive officer, director, Westvaco Corp.

Mulford, David: chairman, Credit Suisse First Boston

Lead Industry Association

Muth, Robert James: president, director, ASARCO Foundation

Leadership Akron

Holland, Willard R.: chairman, chief executive officer, FirstEnergy Corp.

Leadership Atlanta

Eason, William Everette, Jr.: senior vice president, corporate secretary, general counsel, Scientific-Atlanta, Inc.

Leadership Cleveland

Bersticker, Albert C.: chairman, director, chief executive officer, Ferro Corp.; president, trustee, Ferro Foundation

Hardis, Stephen Roger: chairman, chief executive officer, director, Eaton Corp.

O'Brien, John F.: trustee, McDonald & Co. Securities Foundation

Leadership Council Southwest Illinois

Griffin, Donald Wayne: chairman, president, chief executive officer, director, Olin Corp.; trustee, Olin Corp. Charitable Trust

Leadership Giving Comm

Forsyth, John D.: president, chief executive officer, Blue Cross & Blue Shield of Iowa

Leadership Pennsylvania

Hafer, Fred Douglass: chairman, president, chief executive officer, GPU Inc.

Leadership Tampa Alumni

Townsend, David L.: vice president administration, Walter Industries Inc.

Leadership Tri State

Chellgren, Paul Wilbur: chief executive officer, chairman, director, Ashland, Inc.; member, Ashland Inc. Foundation

Learning National Advisory Board

Whitacre, Edward E., Jr.: chairman, director, chief executive officer, SBC Communications Inc.

Legal Aid Society

Watson, Solomon Brown, IV: vice president, New York Times Co. Foundation

Legal Assistance Association

Bell, Wayne: secretary, Ralph's-Food 4 Less Foundation; senior counsel, assistant secretary, Ralph's Grocery Co.

Lehigh University

Barnette, Curtis Handley: chairman, chief executive officer, director, Bethlehem Steel Corp.

Hecht, William F.: chairman, president, chief executive officer, Pennsylvania Power & Light

Lewis Ginter Botanical Garden

Harrell, Henry Howze: director, Universal Leaf Foundation; chairman, chief executive officer, director, Universal Leaf Tobacco Co., Inc.

Lewis Gintor Botanical Garden

Gottwald, Bruce Cobb: chairman, chief executive officer, director, Ethyl Corp.

Liberty Science Center

Baldassari, Dennis P.: president, chief operating officer, GPU Energy

Library Congress James Madison National Council

Smith, Raymond W.: chairman, chief executive officer, director, Bell Atlantic Corp.

Licensing Executives Society

Ballantyne, Richard Lee: vice president, general counsel, secretary, Harris Corp.; secretary, treasurer, Harris Foundation

Life & Health Insurance Medical Research Fund

Turner, John Gosney: chairman, chief executive officer, director, ReliaStar Financial Corp.; director, ReliaStar Foundation

Life Community Association

Mead, Susan W. A.: vice president, ReliaStar Financial Corp.; director, ReliaStar Foundation

Life Insurance Advisory Association

Larance, Charles L.: vice president corporate relations, GenAmerica Corp.; president, GenAmerican Foundation

Life Insurance Association America

Brown, Stephen Lee: chairman, chief executive officer, director, Hancock Financial Services (John)

Life Insurance Association of Massachusetts

O'Brien, John Francis, Jr.: president, chief executive officer, Allmerica Financial Corp.

Life Insurance Council

Roth, Michael I.: chairman, chief executive officer, director, MONY Group (The); director, MONY Life Insurance of New York (The)

Life Insurance Council New York

Hohn, Harry George, Jr.: chairman, director, New York Life Foundation

Life Insurance Marketing & Research Association

Dubes, Michael: membership, ReliaStar Foundation

Life Insurance Marketing & Research Association International

Gammill, Lee Morgan, Jr.: director, New York Life Foundation; vice chairman, director, New York Life Insurance Co.

Life Insurance Marketing & Research Institute

Sargent, Joseph Dudley: president, chief executive officer, director, Guardian Life Insurance Co. of America

Life Management Institute

Killinger, Kerry Kent: chairman, president, chief executive officer, director, Washington Mutual, Inc.

Schafer, Glenn Stanley: president, director, Pacific Mutual Life Insurance Co.

Life Management Institute Society Houston

Tuerff, James R.: president, director, American General Finance

Life Office Management Association

Eigsti, Roger Harry: chairman, chief executive officer, SAFECO Corp.

Hohn, Harry George, Jr.: chairman, director, New York Life Foundation

Sargent, Joseph Dudley: president, chief executive officer, director, Guardian Life Insurance Co. of America

Life Underwriters Training Council

Gammill, Lee Morgan, Jr.: director, New York Life Foundation; vice chairman, director, New York Life Insurance Co.

Lighthouse

Munder, Barbara A.: senior vice president new initiatives, McGraw-Hill Companies, Inc.

Lincoln Bar Association

Hewitt, James Watt: vice president, treasurer, Abel Foundation

Lincoln Center Consolidated Corporate Fund

Schiro, James J.: chairman, senior partner, PricewaterhouseCoopers

Lincoln Center Corporate Leadership Committee
Rhodes, William Reginald: vice chairman, Citibank Corp.

Lincoln Center Performing Arts
Bible, Geoffrey Cyril: director, New York Stock Exchange Foundation, Inc.; chairman, chief executive officer, director, Philip Morris Companies Inc.
Gelb, Richard Lee: director, New York Times Co. Foundation
Gerstner, Louis Vincent, Jr.: chairman, chief executive officer, director, International Business Machines Corp.

Lincoln Center Theater
Whitehead, John Cunningham: chairman board, Goldman Sachs Foundation

Lincoln Center for the Performing Arts
Enrico, Roger A.: chairman, PepsiCo Foundation, Inc.; chairman, chief executive officer, director, PepsiCo, Inc.

Lincoln Chamber of Commerce
Arth, Lawrence Joseph: vice president, director, Ameritas Charitable Foundation; chairman, chief executive officer, director, Ameritas Life Insurance Corp.

Lincoln Laboratories, MIT
Pierre, Percy A.: trustee, Hitachi Foundation

Lincoln Rose Society
Hewitt, James Watt: vice president, treasurer, Abel Foundation

Lindsey Wilson College
Turner, Cal, Jr.: chairman, chief executive officer, director, Dollar General Corp.

Little League Center
Fiondella, Robert William: chairman, president, chief executive officer, Phoenix Home Life Mutual Insurance Co.

Livraison Valeurs Mobilieres
Carter, Marshall Nichols: chairman, chief executive officer, State Street Bank & Trust Co.

Local Initiatives Support Corp.
Brendsel, Leland C.: chairman, chief executive officer, director, Freddie Mac; director, Freddie Mac Foundation

Loews Foundation
Kenny, John J.: treasurer, Loews Corp.; secretary, treasurer, trustee, Loews Foundation

Logan Circle Association
Darling, Robert Edward, Jr.: chairman, Ensign-Bickford Foundation

Long Island Research Institute
Guthart, Leo A.: vice chairman, director, Pittway Corp.

Long Range Strategy Task Force
Haddock, Ronald Wayne: president, chief executive officer, director, FINA; president, FINA Foundation

Long Wharf Theatre
Gorman, Maureen V.: vice president, GTE Foundation

Los Angeles Area Chamber of Commerce
Farman, Richard Donald: chairman, chief executive officer, Pacific Enterprises

Los Angeles Area Council Boy Scouts America
Wright, Donald Franklin: director, Times Mirror Foundation

Los Angeles Copyright Society
Rosenthal, Sol: counsel, Playboy Enterprises Inc.

Los Angeles County Bar Association
Bell, Wayne: secretary, Ralph's-Food 4 Less Foundation; senior counsel, assistant secretary, Ralph's Grocery Co.
Rosenthal, Sol: counsel, Playboy Enterprises Inc.
Ukropina, James R.: partner, Pacific Mutual Life Insurance Co.

Los Angeles County Museum Art
Resnick, Lynda Rae: vice chairman, co-owner, Franklin Mint (The)

Los Angeles County Music Center
Rosenzweig, Richard Stuart: executive vice president, director, Playboy Enterprises Inc.

Los Angeles Music Center
Kresa, Kent: chairman, president, chief executive officer, director, Northrop Grumman Corp.

Los Angeles Public Affairs Officers Association
Rosenzweig, Richard Stuart: executive vice president, director, Playboy Enterprises Inc.

Los Angeles Society Prevention Cruelty Animals
Carey, Kathryn Ann: foundation manager, American Honda Foundation

Los Angeles World Affairs Council
Kresa, Kent: chairman, president, chief executive officer, director, Northrop Grumman Corp.
Wood, Willis B., Jr.: chairman, chief executive officer, director, Pacific Enterprises

Louisiana Association Legal Research Life Insurance Companies
Purvis, George Frank, Jr.: chairman, president, chief executive officer, director, Pan-American Life Insurance Co.

Louisville Area Chamber of Commerce
Jones, David Allen: chairman, chief executive officer, director, Humana Foundation; co-founder, chairman, director, Humana, Inc.

Louisville Chamber of Commerce
Hower, Frank Beard, Jr.: vice chairman, Anthem Foundation, Inc.

Loyola Marymount University
Simpson, Louis Allen: president, chief executive officer capital operations, director, GEICO Corp.

Lycee Francaise
Zilkha, Ezra Khedouri: president, treasurer, Zilkha Foundation, Inc.; president, Zilkha & Sons

Lyric Opera Chicago
Burnham, Duane Lee: chairman, chief executive officer, director, Abbott Laboratories
Gidwitz, Ronald J.: president, chief executive officer, Curtis Industries, Inc. (Helene)
Graham, William B.: chairman, director, Baxter Allegiance Foundation; chairman emeritus, Baxter International Inc.
Kennedy, George Danner: trustee, Kemper Foundation (James S.)

M.D. Anderson Cancer Center
Wise, William Allen: chairman, president, chief executive officer, director, El Paso Energy Co.; chairman, director, El Paso Energy Foundation

MG Transport Service Inc.
Hayden, Joseph Page, Jr.: trustee, Star Bank NA, Cincinnati Foundation

MacDowell Colony
Chambers, Anne Cox: chairman, trustee, Cox Foundation (James M.)

Machinery & Allied Products Institute
Hale, Roger Loucks: chairman, TENNANT Co.; president, TENNANT Co. Foundation
Powers, Paul Joseph: chairman, president, chief executive officer, director, Commercial Intertech Corp.; president, trustee, Commercial Intertech Foundation
Roub, Bryan Roger: trustee, Harris Foundation

Madison Gas & Electric Foundation Madison
Mebane, David Cummins: chairman, president, chief executive officer, director, Madison Gas & Electric Co.; vice president, Madison Gas & Electric Foundation

Magazine Group
Ottaway, James Haller, Jr.: senior vice president, director, Dow Jones & Co., Inc.; member advisory committee, Dow Jones Foundation

Magazine Publishers American
Kerr, William T.: chairman, chief executive officer, director, Meredith Corp.

Magazine Publishers Association
Graves, Earl Gilbert: director, Aetna Foundation
Hefner, Christie Ann: chairman, chief executive officer, Playboy Enterprises Inc.; director, Playboy Foundation
Rehm, Jack Daniel: chairman emeritus, director, Meredith Corp.
Schadt, James Phillip: chairman, president, chief executive officer, director, Reader's Digest Association, Inc. (The); chairman, director, Reader's Digest Foundation

Magee-Women's Hospital
LeBoeuf, Raymond W.: director, PPG Industries Foundation; director, chairman, chief executive officer, PPG Industries, Inc.

Mahoney Institute Neuroscis
Meyerson, Martin: director, Panasonic Foundation

Mahoning County Bar Association
Tucker, Don Eugene: trustee, Commercial Intertech Foundation

Maine Audubon Society
Gorman, Leon A.: president, chief executive officer, Bean, Inc. (L.L.)

Makua Auxiliary

Copley, Helen K.: chairman, trustee, Copley Foundation (James S.); chairman, director, senior management board, Copley Press, Inc.

Maliotis Foundation

Hatsopoulos, George Nicholas: founder, chairman, chief executive officer, director, Thermo Electron Corp.; committee member, Thermo Electron Foundation

Management Education Council

Resnick, Stewart A.: chairman, chief executive officer, Franklin Mint (The)

Manhattan Institute

Flake, Floyd Harold: director, Fannie Mae Foundation

Manhattan Institute Public Policy Research

Elliott, Anson Wright: vice president, trustee, Chase Manhattan Foundation

Mankato University College of Business Advisory Council

Andreas, David Lowell: chairman, director, National City Bank Foundation; chairman, chief executive officer, National City Bank of Minneapolis

Manufacturer Alliance

Farmer, Phillip W.: chairman, president, chief executive officer, Harris Corp.; president, trustee, Harris Foundation

Flaherty, Gerald S.: trustee, Caterpillar Foundation; group president, Caterpillar Inc.

Heldreth, Nick E.: vice president human resources corporate relations, Harris Corp.

McClung, James Allen: vice president, director, FMC Foundation

Powers, Paul Joseph: chairman, president, chief executive officer, director, Commercial Intertech Corp.; president, trustee, Commercial Intertech Foundation

Manufacturer Alliance Productivity & Innovation

Ballantyne, Richard Lee: vice president, general counsel, secretary, Harris Corp.; secretary, treasurer, Harris Foundation

Burt, Robert Norcross: chairman, chief executive officer, director, FMC Corp.; director, FMC Foundation

Gruber, David P.: president, chief executive officer, director, Wyman-Gordon Co.; chairman, vice president, director, Wyman-Gordon Foundation

Phillips, Richard B.: vice president, Crane Foundation

Riley, H. John, Jr.: chairman, president, chief executive officer, Cooper Industries Foundation; chairman, president, chief executive officer, director, Cooper Industries, Inc.

Manufacturer Alliance Productivity & Innovation Human Resources Council

Mack, Raymond Phillip: director, Arvin Foundation; vice president human resources, Arvin Industries, Inc.

Manufacturer Association Berks County

Hafer, Fred Douglass: chairman, president, chief executive officer, GPU Inc.

Manufacturer Association Delaware Valley

Landin, Thomas Milton: vice president, director, CertainTeed Corp.; vice president, Norton Co. Foundation

Manufacturers Alliance

Keyes, James Henry: advisor, Johnson Controls Foundation; president, Johnson Controls Inc.

Manufacturers Alliance Financial Council

Roub, Bryan Roger: trustee, Harris Foundation

Manufacturing Association

Wareham, James Lyman: president, AK Steel Corp.

Maple Center

Rosenzweig, Richard Stuart: executive vice president, director, Playboy Enterprises Inc.

March Dimes

Johnson, Hansford Tillman: trustee, USAA Foundation, A Charitable Trust

Marconi International Fellowship Council

Meyerson, Martin: director, Panasonic Foundation

Marine Biology Laboratory

Alberts, Bruce Michael, PhD: director, Genentech Foundation for Biomedical Sciences

Marion County Sheriffs Merit Board

Sease, Gene Elwood: director, Central Newspapers Foundation

Mark Twain House

Ayer, Ramani: chairman, president, chief executive officer, Hartford (The)

Huber, Richard Leslie: chairman, president, chief executive officer, director, Aetna, Inc.

Markey Foundation

Alberts, Bruce Michael, PhD: director, Genentech Foundation for Biomedical Sciences

Marquette University

Becker, John A.: president, chief operating officer, director, Firstar Bank Milwaukee NA; vice chairman, Firstar Milwaukee Foundation

Sanders, Wayne R.: chairman, chief executive officer, director, Kimberly-Clark Corp.

Marshall University Foundation

Chellgren, Paul Wilbur: chief executive officer, chairman, director, Ashland, Inc.; member, Ashland Inc. Foundation

Maryland Academy Science

DiCamillo, Gary Thomas: chairman, chief executive officer, director, Polaroid Corp.

Poindexter, Christian Herndon: chairman, Baltimore Gas & Electric Foundation; chairman, chief executive officer, director, Constellation Energy Group, Inc.

Maryland Bar Association

Rudnick, Alan A.: vice president, general counsel, corporate secretary, CSX Corp.

Maryland Board Trade

Smith, Donald Kaye: senior vice president, general counsel, director, GEICO Corp.

Maryland Retailers Association

Scher, Barry F.: vice president public affairs, Giant Food Inc.

Marymount College

Boudreau, Donald L.: vice president, trustee, Chase Manhattan Foundation

Smith, Elizabeth Patience: director, Texaco Foundation; vice president investor relations & shareholder service, Texaco Inc.

Marymount University

Feller, Mimi A.: senior vice president public affairs & government relations, Gannett Co., Inc.; vice president, Gannett Foundation

Masons

Carlson, Curtis Leroy: chairman, director, Carlson Companies, Inc.; president, treasurer, Carlson Family Foundation (Curtis L.)

Dubin, Stephen Victor: vice president, secretary, Farber Foundation

Keyser, F. Ray, Jr.: chairman, director, Central Vermont Public Service Corp.

Russell, Frank Eli: president, Central Newspapers Foundation; chairman, Central Newspapers, Inc.

Stauffer, Stanley Howard: chairman, Stauffer Communications Foundation

Massachusetts Association Life Underwriters

Wheeler, Thomas Beardsley: chairman, chief executive officer, Massachusetts Mutual Life Insurance Co.

Massachusetts Bankers Association

Lukowski, Stanley J.: president, Eastern Bank

Massachusetts Bar Association

Cogan, John Francis, Jr.: president, chief executive officer, director, Pioneer Group

Donahue, Richard King: vice chairman, Nike, Inc.

Ehrlich, M. Gordon: trustee, Orchard Foundation

Geller, Eric P.: trustee, Harcourt General Charitable Foundation; senior vice president, general counsel, secretary, Harcourt General, Inc.

Redstone, Sumner Murray: chairman, Viacom Inc.

Watson, Solomon Brown, IV: vice president, New York Times Co. Foundation

Massachusetts Business Roundtable

Ives, J. Atwood: chairman, chief executive officer, Boston Gas Co.; chairman, chief executive officer, trustee, Eastern Enterprises; trustee, Eastern Enterprises Foundation

LaMantia, Charles Robert: president, chief executive officer, director, Little, Inc. (Arthur D.)

Massachusetts General Hospital

Countryman, Gary Lee: chairman, Liberty Mutual Insurance Group

Massachusetts General Hospital Corp.

Redstone, Sumner Murray: chairman, Viacom Inc.

Massachusetts Governments Council Growth & Technology

Morby, Jacqueline C.: managing partner, Pacific Mutual Life Insurance Co.

Massachusetts Governor's Council

LaMantia, Charles Robert: president, chief executive

officer, director, Little, Inc. (Arthur D.)

Massachusetts Governor's Council Economic Growth Technology

Bettacchi, Robert J.: senior vice president, Grace & Co. (W.R.)

Massachusetts Historical Society

Johnson, Edward Crosby, III: president, Fidelity Foundation; chairman, president, chief executive officer, director, Fidelity Investments

Massachusetts Institute Technology

Alberts, Bruce Michael, PhD: director, Genentech Foundation for Biomedical Sciences

Bodman, Samuel Wright, III: chairman, chief executive officer, director, Cabot Corp.; president, director, Cabot Corp. Foundation

Brademas, John: chairman, Texaco Foundation

Hatsopoulos, George Nicholas: founder, chairman, chief executive officer, director, Thermo Electron Corp.; committee member, Thermo Electron Foundation

Kresa, Kent: chairman, president, chief executive officer, director, Northrop Grumman Corp.

Reed, John Shepard: co-chairman, Citibank Corp.

Swanson, Robert A.: director, Genentech Foundation for Biomedical Sciences

Massachusetts Institute Technology Sloan School Management

Heisen, JoAnn Heffernan: vice president, chief information officer, Johnson & Johnson; treasurer, Johnson & Johnson Family of Companies Contribution Fund

Massachusetts Institute Technology Society Senior Executives

Sissel, George A.: chairman, president, chief executive officer, director, Ball Corp.

Massachusetts Institute Technology Visiting Committee on Political Science

Mead, Dana George: chairman, chief executive officer, director, Tenneco Automotive

Massachusetts Risk Insurance Management Society

Cawley, Michael J.: vice president risk management, Eastern Enterprises

Masters Foxhounds Association America

Daniels, John Hancock: chairman, Archer-Daniels-Midland Foundation

Maumee Valley Historical Society

Block, William: vice president, trustee, Blade Foundation; chairman, director, Toledo Blade Co.

Maxium Service TV Association

Huey, Ward L., Jr.: president broadcast division, vice chairman, director, Belo Corp. (A.H.); vice president, trustee, Belo Corp. Foundation (A.H.)

Maxwell School Citizenship Public Affairs

Heisen, JoAnn Heffernan: vice president, chief information officer, Johnson & Johnson; treasurer, Johnson & Johnson Family of Companies Contribution Fund

Mayo Foundation

Atwater, Horace Brewster, Jr.: trustee, Merck Co. Foundation

Johnson, Samuel Curtis: chairman, director, president, Johnson & Son (S.C.); chairman, trustee, Johnson Wax Fund (S.C.)

Mayor Peter's Hartford Americorps

Fiondella, Robert William: chairman, president, chief executive officer, Phoenix Home Life Mutual Insurance Co.

Mayor's Commission Children

Campbell, Cheryl Nichols: operation service advisory group, Cincinnati Bell Inc.

Wehling, Robert Louis: global marketing, government relations officer, Procter & Gamble Co.; president, trustee, Procter & Gamble Fund

Mayor's Economic Advisory Council

Pullo, Robert W.: chairman, chief executive officer, director, York Federal Savings & Loan Association; president, trustee, York Federal Savings & Loan Foundation

McCall School business/Queens College

Browning, Peter C.: chief executive officer, president, director, Sonoco Products Co.

McCarter Theatre Princeton New Jersey

Schiro, James J.: chairman, senior partner, PricewaterhouseCoopers

McLean County Association Commerce Industries

Johnson, James Lawrence: chairman emeritus, Walter Industries Inc.

Medical American Health Systems

Forster, Peter Hans: chairman, director, Dayton Power and Light Co.

Medical Center DEast

Woolard, Edgar Smith, Jr.: director, du Pont de Nemours & Co. (E.I.)

Medical College Ohio

Block, Allan James: vice president, trustee, Blade Foundation; director, Toledo Blade Co.

Medical College Wisconsin

Fitzsimonds, Roger Leon: chairman, Firstar Milwaukee Foundation

Wigdale, James B.: vice president, Marshall & Ilsley Corp.; vice president, director, Marshall & Ilsley Foundation, Inc.

Medical Education Foundation

Murphy, Christopher J., III: president, chief executive officer, director, First Source Corp.; director, First Source Foundation

Medical Science Center

DiCamillo, Gary Thomas: chairman, chief executive officer, director, Polaroid Corp.

Medical University South Carolina

Davis, Carolyne Kahle, PhD: trustee, Merck Co. Foundation

Memorial Dr Trust

LaMantia, Charles Robert: president, chief executive officer, director, Little, Inc. (Arthur D.)

Memorial Health Care

Nelson, John Martin: chairman, director, TJX Companies, Inc.

Memorial Park Committee

Gallagher, Richard S.: director, Badger Meter Foundation

Memorial Sloan Kettering Hospital

Koch, David Hamilton: director, Koch Foundation, Inc. (Fred C. and Mary R.)

Memorial Sloan-Kettering Cancer Center

Geier, Philip Henry, Jr.: chairman, president, chief executive officer, Interpublic Group of Companies, Inc.

Gelb, Richard Lee: director, New York Times Co. Foundation

Marron, Donald Baird: chairman, chief executive officer, director, Paine Webber; trustee, Paine Webber Foundation

Reed, John Shepard: co-chairman, Citibank Corp.

Smith, John Francis, Jr.: chairman, General Motors Corp.

Steere, William Campbell, Jr.: chairman, chief executive officer, director, Pfizer Inc.

Warner, Douglas Alexander, III: chairman, president, chief executive officer, director, Morgan & Co. Inc. (J.P.)

Memphis Development Network Foundation

Moore, Jackson W.: president, director, Union Planters Corp.

Menninger Foundation

Stauffer, Stanley Howard: chairman, Stauffer Communications Foundation

Mennonite Hospital

Johnson, James Lawrence: chairman emeritus, Walter Industries Inc.

Menorah Medical Center Foundation

Bloch, Henry Wollman: chairman, Block Foundation (H&R); chairman, director, Block, Inc. (H&R)

Menorah Medicine Center

Margolin, Abraham E.: director, Tension Envelope Foundation

Mercantile Bank National Association

Jacobsen, Thomas Herbert: chairman, president, chief executive officer, Mercantile Bank NA

Merce Cunningham Dance Foundation

McClimon, Timothy J.: executive director, AT&T Foundation

Mercury Health Systems

Brumm, Paul Michael: executive vice president, chief financial officer, Fifth Third Bancorp

Mercy Housing

Kelly, Richard C.: executive vice president, chief financial officer, New Century Energies; treasurer, New Century Energies Foundation

Mercy Housing Inc.

Zigas, Barry: senior vice president, Fannie Mae; director, Fannie Mae Foundation

Methodist Hospital of Indiana

Reilly, Thomas E., Jr.: trustee, Reilly Foundation; chairman, chief executive officer, director, Reilly Industries, Inc.

Methodist Medical Center

Fites, Donald Vester: director, Caterpillar Foundation

Metropolitan Airports Public Foundation Advisory Board

Hubbard, Stanley S.: chairman, president, chief executive officer, Hubbard Broadcasting, Inc.; president, Hubbard Foundation

Metropolitan Atlanta Olympic Games Authority

Eason, William Everette, Jr.: senior vice president, corporate secretary, general counsel, Scientific-Atlanta, Inc.

Metropolitan Development Association

Roth, Michael I.: chairman, chief executive officer, director, MONY Group (The); director, MONY Life Insurance of New York (The)

Metropolitan Economic Development Association

Bonsignore, Michael Robert: director, Honeywell Foundation; chairman, chief executive officer, director, Honeywell International Inc.

Metropolitan Kansas City Bar ASN

Margolin, Abraham E.: director, Tension Envelope Foundation

Metropolitan Milwaukee Association

Whitelaw, Essie M.: president, chief operating officer, United Wisconsin Services; vice president, United Wisconsin Services Foundation

Wigdale, James B.: vice president, Marshall & Ilsley Corp.; vice president, director, Marshall & Ilsley Foundation, Inc.

Metropolitan Milwaukee Association Commerce

Fitzsimonds, Roger Leon: chairman, Firstar Milwaukee Foundation

Metropolitan Milwaukee Chamber of Commerce

Graff, Stephen Ney: director, Bucyrus-Erie Foundation

Metropolitan Museum Art

Cantor, Bernard Gerald: president, director, Cantor, Fitzgerald Foundation; chairman, director, Cantor, Fitzgerald Securities Corp.

Chambers, Anne Cox: chairman, trustee, Cox Foundation (James M.)

Houghton, James Richardson: director, Corning Inc.; trustee, Corning Inc. Foundation

Kissinger, Henry Alfred: director, CBS Foundation

Klein, Calvin Richard: president, Calvin Klein

Resnick, Lynda Rae: vice chairman, co-owner, Franklin Mint (The)

Sulzberger, Arthur Ochs, Sr.: director, New York Times Co.; chairman, director, New York Times Co. Foundation

Tisch, Laurence Alan: chairman, co-chief executive officer, CBS Corp.; trustee, Loews Foundation

Metropolitan Museum Business Committee

Rhodes, William Reginald: vice chairman, Citibank Corp.

Metropolitan Opera

Bijur, Peter I.: chairman, chief executive officer, Texaco Inc.

Metropolitan Opera Association

Montrone, Paul Michael: vice president, partner, Winthrop Foundation

Metropolitan Pier & Exposition Authority

Welsh, Kelly Raymond: executive vice president, general counsel, Ameritech Corp.

Metropolitan Planning Council Chicago

Kirby, William Joseph: vice president, director, FMC Foundation

Metropolitan United Way Louisville

Guillaume, Raymond Kendrick: vice chairman, chief executive officer, Mid-America Bank of Louisville

Meyer Friedman Institute

Haas, Robert Douglas: chairman, chief executive officer, director, Levi Strauss & Co.; president, Levi Strauss Foundation

Miami Beach Chamber of Commerce

Coyle, Dennis Patrick: secretary, director, FPL Group Foundation, Inc.

Miami University

Armstrong, C. Michael: chairman, chief executive officer, AT&T Corp.

Miami University Ohio

Hayden, Joseph Page, Jr.: trustee, Star Bank NA, Cincinnati Foundation

Miami Valley Ohio Boy Scouts

Correll, Alston Dayton 'Pete', Jr.: chairman, president, chief executive officer, director, Georgia-Pacific Corp.; director, Georgia-Pacific Foundation

Michael Reese Foundation

Wander, Herbert S.: secretary, director, Katten, Muchin & Zavis Foundation

Michigan 4-H Council

Brennan, Leo Joseph, Jr.: vice president, executive director, Ford Motor Co. Fund

Michigan Bar Association

Clark, Richard McCourt: senior vice president, general counsel, secretary, Kellogg Co.; vice president, trustee, Kellogg Co. Twenty-Five Year Employees' Fund Inc.

Michigan Chamber of Commerce

Earley, Anthony Francis, Jr.: president, chief operating officer, Detroit Edison Co.; director, Detroit Edison Foundation

Michigan Colleges Foundation

Clark, Richard McCourt: senior vice president, general counsel, secretary, Kellogg Co.; vice president, trustee, Kellogg Co. Twenty-Five Year Employees' Fund Inc.

Valade, Gary C.: executive vice president, chief financial officer, DaimlerChrysler Corp.; trustee, DaimlerChrysler Corp. Fund

Michigan Corporate Volunteer Council

Feldhouse, Lynn Alexandra: vice president, secretary, DaimlerChrysler Corp. Fund

Michigan General Counsel Association

Clark, Richard McCourt: senior vice president, general counsel, secretary, Kellogg Co.; vice president, trustee, Kellogg Co. Twenty-Five Year Employees' Fund Inc.

Michigan Historical Society

Brennan, Leo Joseph, Jr.: vice president, executive director, Ford Motor Co. Fund

Michigan Leaders Health Care Group

Eaton, Robert James: co-chairman, president, chief executive officer, DaimlerChrysler Corp.

Michigan Nature Conservancy

Ford, William Clay, Jr.: chairman, Ford Motor Co.

Michigan State University Eli Broad College Business Alumni Association

Valade, Gary C.: executive vice president, chief financial officer, DaimlerChrysler Corp.; trustee, DaimlerChrysler Corp. Fund

Michigan Strategic Fund

Pew, Robert Cunningham, II: trustee, Steelcase Foundation

Michigan Womens Foundation

Feldhouse, Lynn Alexandra: vice president, secretary, DaimlerChrysler Corp. Fund

Micron Delta Epsilon

Hutchins, William Bruce, III: director, Alabama Power Foundation

Mid-American Coalition Health Care

Bloch, Henry Wollman: chairman, Block Foundation (H&R); chairman, director, Block, Inc. (H&R)

Mid-American Comm

Stone, Roger Warren: chairman, president, chief executive officer, director, Stone Container Corp.; president, Stone Foundation

Mid-Atlantic Committee for International Business

Bueche, Wendell Francis: director, Marshall & Ilsley Foundation, Inc.

Mid-Continent Oil Gas Association

Marsh, R. Bruce: general tax counsel, Chevron Corp.

Mid-Peninsula Young Men's Christian Association

Platt, Lewis Emmett: chairman, Hewlett-Packard Co.

MidIowa Council Boy Scouts America

Kelley, Bruce Gunn: vice president, director, Employers Mutual Charitable Foundation

Middlebury College

Bijur, Peter I.: chairman, chief executive officer, Texaco Inc.

Middlesex General University Hospital

Harris, Edward D., Jr.: director, Genentech Foundation for Biomedical Sciences

Midwest Gas Association

Hall, Larry D.: chairman, president, chief executive officer, director, Kinder Morgn; president, director, KN Energy Foundation

Terry, Richard Edward: chairman, chief executive officer, director, Peoples Energy Corp.

Thies, Richard Henry: assistant treasurer, Madison Gas & Electric Foundation

Midwest Pension Conference

Russell, Frank Eli: president, Central Newspapers Foundation; chairman, Central Newspapers, Inc.

Midwest Research Committee for Economic Development

Esrey, William Todd: chairman, chief executive officer, Sprint Corp.

Midwest Research Institute

Bloch, Henry Wollman: chairman, Block Foundation (H&R); chairman, director, Block, Inc. (H&R)

Hall, Donald Joyce: chairman board, director, Hallmark Cards Inc.; chairman, Hallmark Corporate Foundation

Hockaday, Irvine O., Jr.: president, chief executive officer, director, Hallmark Cards Inc.

Powell, George Everett, III: president, chief executive officer, director, Yellow Corp.; trustee, Yellow Corp. Foundation

Powell, George Everett, Jr.: trustee, Yellow Corp. Foundation

Stauffer, Stanley Howard: chairman, Stauffer Communications Foundation

Milken Family Foundation

Resnick, Lynda Rae: vice chairman, co-owner, Franklin Mint (The)

Millbrook Research Field Center

Furlaud, Richard Mortimer: interim chief executive officer, International Flavors & Fragrances Inc.

Million Dollar Round Table

Wheeler, Thomas Beardsley: chairman, chief executive officer, Massachusetts Mutual Life Insurance Co.

Million Dollar Round Table Foundation

Hohn, Harry George, Jr.: chairman, director, New York Life Foundation

Mills College

Ginn, Samuel L.: chairman, director, AirTouch Communications Foundation; chairman, chief executive officer, director, Vodafone AirTouch Plc

Grubb, Edgar Harold: executive vice president, chief financial officer, Transamerica Corp.; director, Transamerica Foundation

Millsaps College

Robinson, E. B., Jr.: chairman, chief executive officer, director, Deposit Guaranty National Bank

Milton Academy

Schwarz, H. Marshall: chairman, chief executive officer, United States Trust Co. of New York

Milwaukee Bar Association

Bruce, Peter Wayne: director, Badger Meter Foundation

Davis, Walter Stewart: secretary, treasurer, Grede Foundation

Loos, Henry J.: secretary, Charter Manufacturing Co. Foundation

Milwaukee Boys & Girls Club

Fitzsimonds, Roger Leon: chairman, Firstar Milwaukee Foundation

Milwaukee Financial Analysts

Meuleman, Robert Joseph: director, AMCORE Foundation

Milwaukee Public Library Foundation

Bauer, Chris Michael: president, Firstar Milwaukee Foundation

Milwaukee School Engineering

Shiely, John Stephen: president, chief operating officer, director, Briggs & Stratton Corp.; vice president, director, Briggs & Stratton Corp. Foundation

Milwaukee World Festival Inc.

Bauer, Chris Michael: president, Firstar Milwaukee Foundation

Mining Metallurgical Society America

Whisler, J. Steven: chairman, president, chief executive officer, Phelps Dodge Corp.

Minneapolis American Friends Jamaica

Hubbard, Stanley S.: chairman, president, chief executive officer, Hubbard Broadcasting, Inc.; president, Hubbard Foundation

Minneapolis Chamber of Commerce

Dewane, John Richard: director, Honeywell Foundation

Minneapolis Coalition Educational Reform & Accountability

Johnson, Scott W.: senior vice president, secretary, general counsel, Bemis Co., Inc.

Minneapolis College of Art & Design

Andreas, David Lowell: chairman, director, National City Bank Foundation; chairman, chief executive officer, National City Bank of Minneapolis

Minneapolis Institute Arts

Marshall, Siri M.: trustee, General Mills Foundation; senior vice president, general counsel, General Mills, Inc.

Minneapolis Junior League

Andreas, David Lowell: chairman, director, National City Bank Foundation; chairman, chief executive officer, National City Bank of Minneapolis

Minnesota Bar Association

Johnson, Scott W.: senior vice president, secretary, general counsel, Bemis Co., Inc.

Mattison, Robert Mayer: director, Graco Foundation; vice president, general counsel, secretary, Graco, Inc.

Neville, James Morton: member board control, Ralston Purina Trust Fund

Stroup, Stanley Stephenson: executive vice president, general counsel, Norwest Corp.

Minnesota Business Partnership

Gherty, John E.: president, chief executive officer, Land O'Lakes, Inc.

Grundhofer, John Francis: president, chief executive officer, director, U.S. Bancorp

Hale, Roger Loucks: chairman, TENNANT Co.; president, TENNANT Co. Foundation

Hubbard, Stanley S.: chairman, president, chief executive officer, Hubbard Broadcasting, Inc.; president, Hubbard Foundation

Piper, Addison Lewis: director, Piper Jaffray Companies Foundation; chairman, chief executive officer, director, U.S. Bancorp Piper Jaffray

Minnesota Center for Corporate Responsibility

Andreas, David Lowell: chairman, director, National City Bank Foundation; chairman, chief executive officer, National City Bank of Minneapolis

Minnesota Chamber of Commerce

Sullivan, Austin Padraic, Junior: trustee, General Mills Foundation; senior vice president corporate relations, General Mills, Inc.

Minnesota Continuing Legal Education

Hale, James Thomas: senior vice president, general counsel, secretary, Dayton Hudson; trustee, Target Foundation

Minnesota Corp. Counsel Association

Mattison, Robert Mayer: director, Graco Foundation; vice president, general counsel, secretary, Graco, Inc.

Minnesota Department Human Services

Wynia, Ann: director, Fuller Co. Foundation (H.B.)

Minnesota Executives Organization

Hubbard, Stanley S.: chairman, president, chief executive officer, Hubbard Broadcasting, Inc.; president, Hubbard Foundation

Minnesota Institute of the Arts

George, William Wallace: chief executive officer, chairman, Medtronic, Inc.

Minnesota Insurance Federation

Buxton, Charles Ingraham, II: chairman, Federated Mutual Insurance Co.; president, Federated Mutual Insurance Foundation

Minnesota Insurance Information Service

Buxton, Charles Ingraham, II: chairman, Federated Mutual Insurance Co.; president, Federated Mutual Insurance Foundation

Minnesota Medical Foundation

Coyne, William E.: senior vice president, Minnesota Mining & Manufacturing Co.

Minnesota Meetings

Carlson, Curtis Leroy: chairman, director, Carlson

Companies, Inc.; president, treasurer, Carlson Family Foundation (Curtis L.)

Minnesota Newspapers Association

Lebedoff, Randy Miller: vice president, general counsel, McClatchy Co.; secretary, Star Tribune Foundation

Minnesota Orchestra Association

Bonsignore, Michael Robert: director, Honeywell Foundation; chairman, chief executive officer, director, Honeywell International Inc.

Shannon, Michael E.: chairman, chief financial officer, chief administration officer, director, Ecolab Inc.

Minnesota Society CPA's

Alm, John Richard: director, Coca-Cola Foundation

Carpenter, Marshall L.: vice president, chief financial officer, MTS Systems Corp.

Minnesota State Bar Association

Bonvino, Frank W.: vice president, secretary, general counsel, International Multifoods Corp.

Minnesota Thunder Pro Soccer

George, William Wallace: chief executive officer, chairman, Medtronic, Inc.

Minnesota Trade Office

Bonsignore, Michael Robert: director, Honeywell Foundation; chairman, chief executive officer, director, Honeywell International Inc.

Miriam Hospital

Hassenfeld, Alan Geoffrey: president, Hasbro Charitable Trust Inc.; chairman, chief executive officer, Hasbro, Inc.

Misericordia College

Connor, Richard L.: president, publisher, Fort Worth Star-Telegram Inc.

Mission Health Systems Inc.

Hinton, Michael R.: president, chief operating officer, director, Old National Bank Evansville

Mississippi Bankers Association

McMillan, Howard Lamar, Jr.: president, chief operating officer, director, Deposit Guaranty National Bank

Mississippi College

Ebbers, Bernard J.: president, chief executive officer, director, MCI WorldCom, Inc.

Missouri Bar Association

Ball, James Herington: senior vice president, general counsel, director, Nestle U.S.A. Inc.

Besser, John Edward: director, Barnes Group Foundation Inc.; senior vice president finance & law, Barnes Group Inc.

Brown, JoBeth Goode: trustee, Anheuser-Busch Companies, Inc.

Herron, James Michael: secretary, director, Ryder System Charitable Foundation

Hotchner, Aaron Edward: vice president, director, executive, Newman's Own Foundation; vice president, treasurer, Newman's Own Inc.

Margolin, Abraham E.: director, Tension Envelope Foundation

Matheny, Edward Taylor, Junior: director, Block Foundation (H&R)

Missouri Botanical Gardens

Kemper, David Woods: chairman, president, chief executive officer, director, Commerce Bancshares, Inc.

Maritz, William Edward: chairman, chief executive officer, president, Maritz Inc.

Missouri Military Academy

Gaiswinkler, Robert Sigfried: chairman, director, First Financial Bank; director, First Financial Foundation

Missouri Womens Forum

Brown, JoBeth Goode: trustee, Anheuser-Busch Companies, Inc.

Modern Language Association

Hall, Larry D.: chairman, president, chief executive officer, director, Kinder Morgn; president, director, KN Energy Foundation

Monell Chemical Senses Center

Meyerson, Martin: director, Panasonic Foundation

Mont Pelerin Society

Rosett, Richard Nathaniel: trustee, Kemper Foundation (James S.)

Montefiore Home Aged

Mandel, Jack N.: director, Premier Industrial Corp.

Montgomery Bell Academy

Bradford, James C., Jr.: president, Bradford and Co. Foundation (J.C.); senior partner, Bradford & Co. (J.C.)

Montreal Museum Fine Arts

Light, Walter Frederick: trustee, Air Products Foundation

Morehouse College

Minton, Dwight Church: chairman, director, Church & Dwight Co., Inc.

Small, Lawrence Malcolm: president, chief operating officer, Fannie Mae; director, Fannie Mae Foundation

Morehouse School of Medicine

Platt, Lewis Emmett: chairman, Hewlett-Packard Co.

Morgan State University

Poindexter, Christian Herndon: chairman, Baltimore Gas & Electric Foundation; chairman, chief executive officer, director, Constellation Energy Group, Inc.

Morris County Fire Police Training Academy

Painter, Alan Sproul: vice president, executive director, AlliedSignal Foundation Inc.

Motion Picture Pioneers

Redstone, Sumner Murray: chairman, Viacom Inc.

Motor Equipment Manufacturers Association

Magliochetti, Joseph M.: president, chief executive officer, director, Dana Corp.; president, director, Dana Corp. Foundation

Mound City Bar Association

Van Cleve, William Moore: member public policy committee, Emerson Charitable Trust; partner, Emerson Electric Co.

Mount Sinai Medical Center

Mirsky, Susan: vice president, director, Thompson Co. Fund (J. Walter)

Mount Sinai Medical Center New York

Tisch, James S.: president, chief executive officer, director, CNA

Mountain Sts Legal Foundation

Graves, Ronald Norman: secretary, Simplot Foundation (J.R.)

Mt Union College

Mahoney, Robert W.: chairman, president, chief executive officer, director, Diebold, Inc.

Multnomah County Bar Association

Walsh, Michael J.: vice president, CertainTeed Corp.

Municipal Theatre Association

Mueller, Charles William: chairman, president, chief executive officer, Ameren Corp.; trustee, Ameren Corp. Charitable Trust

Museum Arts Association

Gorman, Joseph T.: chairman, chief executive officer, TRW Inc.

Museum City New York

Forbes, Christopher 'Kip': vice president, Forbes Foundation; vice chairman, corporate secretary, director, Forbes Inc.

Museum Contemporary Art

Rogers, Desiree Glapion: vice president community affairs, Peoples Energy Corp.

Rosenzweig, Richard Stuart: executive vice president, director, Playboy Enterprises Inc.

Museum Delta Kappa Epsilon Foundation

Geier, Philip Henry, Jr.: chairman, president, chief executive officer, Interpublic Group of Companies, Inc.

Museum Fine Arts

Carroll, Philip Joseph: chairman, chief executive officer, Fluor Corp.; chairman, trustee, Fluor Foundation

Cogan, John Francis, Jr.: president, chief executive officer, director, Pioneer Group

Forbes, Christopher 'Kip': vice president, Forbes Foundation; vice chairman, corporate secretary, director, Forbes Inc.

Ives, J. Atwood: chairman, chief executive officer, Boston Gas Co.; chairman, chief executive officer, trustee, Eastern Enterprises; trustee, Eastern Enterprises Foundation

Lasser, Lawrence Jay: president, chief executive officer, director, Putnam Investments; president, chief executive officer, Putnam Investors Fund

Museum Flight

Condit, Philip Murray: chairman, chief executive officer, director, Boeing Co.

Museum Modern Art

Chambers, Anne Cox: chairman, trustee, Cox Foundation (James M.)

Klein, Calvin Richard: president, Calvin Klein

Marron, Donald Baird: chairman, chief executive officer, director, Paine Webber; trustee, Paine Webber Foundation

Masin, Michael Terry: vice chairman, president international, director, GTE Corp.; trustee, GTE Foundation

Oldenburg, Richard Erik: chairman, Sotheby's Inc.

Rehm, Jack Daniel: chairman emeritus, director, Meredith Corp.

Weill, Sanford I.: chairman, chief executive officer, Citibank Corp.; chairman, Citigroup Foundation

Museum Photog Arts

Copley, David C.: president, trustee, Copley Foundation (James S.); president, chief executive officer, director, senior management board, Copley Press, Inc.

Museum Science & Industry

Burnham, Duane Lee: chairman, chief executive officer, director, Abbott Laboratories

Fluno, Jere David: vice chairman, Grainger, Inc. (W.W.)

Gidwitz, Ronald J.: president, chief executive officer, Curtis Industries, Inc. (Helene)

McKenna, Andrew James: director, Aon Foundation

Rogers, Desiree Glapion: vice president community affairs, Peoples Energy Corp.

Stewart, S. Jay: chairman, chief executive officer, director, Morton International Inc.

Museum Science Boston

DiCamillo, Gary Thomas: chairman, chief executive officer, director, Polaroid Corp.

Museum of Art

Chellgren, Paul Wilbur: chief executive officer, chairman, director, Ashland, Inc.; member, Ashland Inc. Foundation

Music Mt Lebanon

Walton, Jon David: trustee, Allegheny Technologies Inc. Charitable Trust

Musical Arts Association

Hardis, Stephen Roger: chairman, chief executive officer, director, Eaton Corp.

Musical Arts Association Cleveland

Reid, James Sims, Jr.: chairman, director, Standard Products Co.; chairman, president, Standard Products Co. Charitable Foundation

Mutual Fund Education Alliance

Brennan, John J.: chairman, chief executive officer, Vanguard Group; president, Vanguard Group Foundation

NAA

King, Reatha Clark: director, Fuller Co. Foundation (H.B.); president, executive director, General Mills Foundation

NAACP

Graves, Earl Gilbert: director, Aetna Foundation

Williams, Karen Hastie: director, Fannie Mae Foundation

NACD

Franklin, Barbara Hackman: director, Dow Chemical Co.

NAE

Lucky, Robert Wendell: corporate vice president, Telcordia Technologies

NAM

Blount, Winton Malcolm, Jr.: chairman, Blount International, Inc.

Harad, George Jay: chairman, chief executive officer, director, Boise Cascade Corp.

NASA Aeronautics Advisory Comm

Dewane, John Richard: director, Honeywell Foundation

NCAA

Chenault, Kenneth Irvine: president, chief operating officer, director, American Express Co.; trustee, American Express Foundation

NCASI

Luke, John A., Jr.: chairman, president, chief executive officer, director, Westvaco Corp.

NRC Board Science Technology Economic Policy

Hatsopoulos, George Nicholas: founder, chairman, chief executive officer, director, Thermo Electron Corp.; committee member, Thermo Electron Foundation

NSF International

Loomans, Leslie Louis: treasurer, director, Detroit Edison Foundation

Nashville Academy Medicine

Elam, Lloyd Charles, MD: trustee, Merck Co. Foundation

Nashville Area Chamber of Commerce

Ingram, Martha R.: chairman, director, Ingram Industries Inc.

Nashville Chamber of Commerce

Bottorff, Dennis C.: chairman, president, chief executive officer, director, First American Corp.

Nashville Community Foundation

Ingram, Martha R.: chairman, director, Ingram Industries Inc.

Nassau County Bar Association

Dubin, Stephen Victor: vice president, secretary, Farber Foundation

National 4-H Council

Beach, Roger C.: chairman, chief executive officer, director, Unocal Corp.

Lowrie, William G.: president, deputy chief executive officer, director, BP Amoco Corp.

National AID South Foundation

Hohn, Harry George, Jr.: chairman, director, New York Life Foundation

National Academy Arts & Sciences

Davis, Ruth Margaret: trustee, Air Products Foundation

National Academy Education

Graham, Patricia Albjerg, PhD: trustee, Hitachi Foundation

Meyerson, Martin: director, Panasonic Foundation

National Academy Engineering

Allaire, Paul Arthur: chairman, chief executive officer, chairman executive committee, Xerox Corp.; president, Xerox Foundation

Armstrong, Neil A.: trustee, Milacron Foundation; director, Milacron, Inc.

Davis, Ruth Margaret: trustee, Air Products Foundation

Eaton, Robert James: cochairman, president, chief executive officer, DaimlerChrysler Corp.

Engel, Joel Stanley: vice president technology, Ameritech Corp.

Grove, Andrew S.: chairman, Intel Corp.

Hatsopoulos, George Nicholas: founder, chairman, chief executive officer, director, Thermo Electron Corp.; committee member, Thermo Electron Foundation

Hill, George Richard: president, trustee, Lubrizol Foundation (The)

Joyce, William H.: chairman, president, chief executive officer, chief operating officer, Union Carbide Corp.

Kaman, Charles Huron: chairman, president, chief executive officer, director, Kaman Corp.

Moore, Gordon E., PhD: cofounder, chairman emeritus, director, Intel Corp.; trustee, Intel Foundation

Raymond, Lee R.: chairman, president, chief executive officer, Exxon Mobil Corp.

Welch, John Francis, Jr.: chairman, chief executive officer, director, General Electric Co.

National Academy Human Resources

Conaty, William J.: director, GE Fund

Kirby, William Joseph: vice president, director, FMC Foundation

Knicely, Howard V.: president, TRW Foundation

National Academy Public Administration

Davis, Ruth Margaret: trustee, Air Products Foundation

National Academy Sciences

Boyer, Herbert Wayne, PhD: chairman, president, director, Genentech Foundation for Biomedical Sciences; co-founder, director, Genentech Inc.

Brademas, John: chairman, Texaco Foundation

Harris, Irving Brooks: chairman executive committee, director, Pittway Corp.; chairman, director, Pittway Corp. Charitable Foundation

Ripley, Sidney Dillon, II: director emeritus, Hitachi Foundation

Vagelos, Pindaros Roy: trustee, Prudential Insurance Co. of America

National Academy Sciences Institute Medicine

Davis, Carolyne Kahle, PhD: trustee, Merck Co. Foundation

National Academy Television Arts Sciences Private Industry Council

Shepherd, Kathleen Shearen Maynard: director, Tribune New York Foundation

National Academy of Engineering

Barrett, Craig R.: president, chief operating officer, director, Intel Corp.

National Action Council Minorities Engineering

Carroll, Philip Joseph: chairman, chief executive officer, Fluor Corp.; chairman, trustee, Fluor Foundation

National Advertisers

Blanke, Gail Ann: vice president, Avon Products Foundation, Inc.

National Advisor Board Science & Technology

Roth, John: president, chief executive officer, chief operating officer, director, Nortel

National Advisory Committee Fighting Back

Brademas, John: chairman, Texaco Foundation

National Alliance Business

Goodes, Melvin Russell: chairman, chief executive officer, director, Ameritech Corp.

Gorman, Maureen V.: vice president, GTE Foundation

MacDonald, J. Randall: senior vice president human resources administration, GTE Corp.; trustee, GTE Foundation

Pepper, John E., Jr.: chairman executive committee, Procter & Gamble Co.

Wurtzel, Alan Leon: chairman, Circuit City Foundation; chairman, trustee, Circuit City Stores, Inc.

National American Wholesale Growers Association Inc.

Wright, Michael William: chairman, president, chief executive officer, director, SuperValu, Inc.

National Asphalt Paving Association

Cloud, Bruce Benjamin, Sr.: vice chairman, director, Zachry Co. (H.B.)

National Association Accts

Bezik, Cynthia B.: senior vice president, finance, Cleveland-Cliffs, Inc.

Gregg, Walter Emmor, Junior: senior executive vice president finance & administration, PNC Financial Services Group

Hernandez, William H.: director, PPG Industries Foundation; senior vice president, PPG Industries, Inc.

Hutchins, William Bruce, III: director, Alabama Power Foundation

Johnson, James Lawrence: chairman emeritus, Walter Industries Inc.

Maffucci, David G.: senior vice president, chief financial officer, Bowater Inc.

Reese, Terry W.: assistant treasurer, Vulcan Materials Co. Foundation

Shaffer, Oren G.: executive vice president, chief financial officer, Ameritech Corp.

Sullivan, Thomas John: vice president, director,

National Association Black Accountants

Edwards, Earnest Jonathan: director, Alcoa Foundation

National Association Business Economists

Murphy, Christopher J., III: president, chief executive officer, director, First Source Corp.; director, First Source Foundation

Ruelle, Mark A.: senior vice president, chief financial officer, Sierra Pacific Resources

National Association Chain Drug Stores

Neel, Curtis Dean, Jr.: trustee, Eckerd Corp. Foundation

National Association College & University Attorneys

Walsh, Michael J.: vice president, CertainTeed Corp.

National Association Corp. Directors

Millstein, Ira M.: partner, Weil, Gotshal & Manges Corp.; president, director, Weil, Gotshal & Manges Foundation

National Association Corp. Treas

Carr, Cassandra Colvin: director, SBC Foundation

National Association Corrosion Engineers

Bailey, Keith E.: chairman, president, director, chief executive officer, Texas Gas Transmission Corp.; president, director, Williams Companies Foundation (The)

National Association HMO Regulators

Doucette, James Willard: vice president, treasurer, Humana Foundation

National Association Health Underwriters

Peterson, Donald Matthew: trustee, Trustmark Foundation; president, chief executive officer, director, Trustmark Insurance Co.

National Association Independent Insurers

Herres, Robert T.: chairman, chief executive officer, United Services Automobile Association

Pike, Robert William: vice president, secretary, Allstate Foundation; senior vice president, secretary, general counsel, director, Allstate Insurance Co.

National Association Latino Elected Off Education Fund

Stanley, Peter William: trustee, Hitachi Foundation

National Association Life Underwriters

Dubes, Michael: membership, ReliaStar Foundation

Gammill, Lee Morgan, Jr.: director, New York Life Foundation; vice chairman, director, New York Life Insurance Co.

Kalainov, Sam Charles: chairman, president, chief executive officer, AmerUS Group

Larance, Charles L.: vice president corporate relations, GenAmerica Corp.; president, GenAmerican Foundation

Peterson, Donald Matthew: trustee, Trustmark Foundation; president, chief executive officer, director, Trustmark Insurance Co.

Sargent, Joseph Dudley: president, chief executive officer, director, Guardian Life Insurance Co. of America

National Association Manufacturer

Ackerman, Roger G.: trustee, Corning Inc. Foundation

Browning, Peter C.: chief executive officer, president, director, Sonoco Products Co.

Bueche, Wendell Francis: director, Marshall & Ilsley Foundation, Inc.

Campbell, George Leroy: vice president public affairs, Florida Power Corp.

Carver, Martin Gregory: chairman, president, chief executive officer, Bandag, Inc.

Ferrari, Giannantonio A.: director, Honeywell Foundation; president, chief operating officer, director, Honeywell International Inc.

Fites, Donald Vester: director, Caterpillar Foundation

Gloyd, Lawrence Eugene: trustee, CLARCOR Foundation; chairman, chief executive officer, director, CLARCOR Inc.

Gonring, Matthew P.: vice president, trustee, USG Foundation

Hadley, Leonard Anson: chairman, chief executive officer, director, Maytag Corp.; president, trustee, Maytag Corp. Foundation

Hecht, William F.: chairman, president, chief executive officer, Pennsylvania Power & Light

Howe, Stanley M.: president, HON Industries Charitable Foundation; chairman emeritus, director, HON Industries Inc.

Iverson, Francis Kenneth: chairman, director, Nucor Corp.; director, Nucor Foundation

Kohler, Herbert Vollrath, Jr.: chairman, president, director, Kohler Co.

Mead, Dana George: chairman, chief executive officer, director, Tenneco Automotive

Melican, James Patrick, Jr.: executive vice president legal & external affairs, International Paper Co.; director, International Paper Co. Foundation

Mueller, Gerd Dieter: executive vice president, chief financial officer, director, chief administrative officer, Bayer Corp.; president, Bayer Foundation

Mulva, James J.: president, chief operating officer, director, Phillips Petroleum Co.

Pestillo, Peter John: executive chairman, Ford Motor Co.; trustee, Ford Motor Co. Fund

Powers, Paul Joseph: chairman, president, chief executive officer, director, Commercial Intertech Corp.; president, trustee, Commercial Intertech Foundation

Shannon, Michael E.: chairman, chief financial officer, chief administration officer, director, Ecolab Inc.

Tumminello, Stephen C.: president, chief executive officer, director, Philips Electronics North America Corp.

Zachem, Harry M.: chairman, trustee, Ashland Inc. Foundation

National Association Manufacturers

Dugan, Allan E.: senior vice president corporate strategic service, Xerox Corp.; trustee, Xerox Foundation

Iraola, Manuel J.: senior vice president, director, Phelps Dodge Corp.

Keyes, James Henry: advisor, Johnson Controls Foundation; president, Johnson Controls Inc.

Kiely, W. Leo, III: president, chief operating officer, Coors Brewing Co.

McDaniel, Tom J.: vice chairman, director, Kerr-McGee Corp.

Sissel, George A.: chairman, president, chief executive officer, director, Ball Corp.

Wood, Willis B., Jr.: chairman, chief executive officer, director, Pacific Enterprises

National Association Over-the-Counter Companies

Strickland, Robert Louis: vice president, Lowe's Charitable and Educational Foundation

National Association Publically Traded Companies

Murphy, Christopher J., III: president, chief executive officer, director, First Source Corp.; director, First Source Foundation

National Association Retail Druggists

Goodes, Melvin Russell: chairman, chief executive officer, director, Ameritech Corp.

National Association Securities Dealers

Bachmann, John W.: managing partner, Jones & Co. (Edward D.); chairman, Jones & Co. Foundation (Edward D.)

Bartz, Carol A.: director, Autodesk Foundation; chairman, chief executive officer, Autodesk Inc.

Bradford, James C., Jr.: president, Bradford and Co. Foundation (J.C.); senior partner, Bradford & Co. (J.C.)

Cogan, John Francis, Jr.: president, chief executive officer, director, Pioneer Group

Murphy, Christopher J., III: president, chief executive officer, director, First Source Corp.; director, First Source Foundation

National Association Security Dealers

Kamen, Harry Paul: chairman, president, chief executive officer, Metropolitan Life Insurance Co.

National Association State Universities & Land-Grant Colleges

Forsyth, John D.: president, chief executive officer, Blue Cross & Blue Shield of Iowa

National Association Stock Plan Professionals

Martin, Dezora M.: corporate secretary, Norfolk Southern Corp.; secretary, Norfolk Southern Foundation

National Association Theatre Owners

Redstone, Sumner Murray: chairman, Viacom Inc.

National Association Underwater Instituteructors

Bonsignore, Michael Robert: director, Honeywell Foundation; chairman, chief executive officer, director, Honeywell International Inc.

National Association for State Court

Kinsolving, Augustus Blagden: director, ASARCO Foundation

National Association of Corporate Treasurers

Bains, Harrison MacKellar, Jr.: vice president, treasurer, Bristol-Myers Squibb Co.; treasurer, Bristol-Myers Squibb Foundation Inc.

Cottrell, G. Walton: senior vice president, chief financial officer, Carpenter Technology Corp.

Daley, Leo J.: vice president, treasurer, Air Products and Chemicals, Inc.

Hinshaw, Juanita H.: vice president, treasurer, Monsanto Co.; treasurer, Monsanto Fund

Lord, Gerald S.: vice president, controller, Campbell Soup Co.

Overbaugh, Joseph C.: director, AMP Foundation

Pehlke, Richard W.: vice president, treasurer, Ameritech Corp.

Sales, A. R.: director, Arvin Foundation; treasurer, Arvin Industries, Inc.

d'Alessio, Jon W.: trustee, McKesson Foundation

National Bankers Association

Williams, Edward Joseph: president, director, Harris Bank Foundation

National Bar Association

Morris, Herman, Jr.: president, chief executive officer, Memphis Light Gas & Water Division

Williams, Karen Hastie: director, Fannie Mae Foundation

National Board Professional Teaching Standards

Alberts, Bruce Michael, PhD: director, Genentech Foundation for Biomedical Sciences

National Boy Scouts America

Jacobsen, Thomas Herbert: chairman, president, chief executive officer, Mercantile Bank NA

National Breast Cancer Research Foundation

Bartz, Carol A.: director, Autodesk Foundation; chairman, chief executive officer, Autodesk Inc.

National Building Museum

Small, Lawrence Malcolm: president, chief operating officer, Fannie Mae; director, Fannie Mae Foundation

National Bureau Economic Research

Hatsopoulos, George Nicholas: founder, chairman, chief executive officer, director, Thermo Electron Corp.; committee member, Thermo Electron Foundation

National Business Higher Education Forum

Farman, Richard Donald: chairman, chief executive officer, Pacific Enterprises

National Cable Television Association

Wynne, John Oliver: president, director, Landmark Communications Foundation; president, chief executive officer, Landmark Communications Inc.

National Center Clinical Infant Programs

Harris, Irving Brooks: chairman executive committee, director, Pittway Corp.; chairman, director, Pittway Corp. Charitable Foundation

National Center State Courts

Fine, Roger Seth: vice president, general counsel, Johnson & Johnson; president, Johnson & Johnson Family of Companies Contribution Fund

National Chamber of Commerce

Moffitt, Donald Eugene: chairman, director, CNF Transportation, Inc.

National Coal Council

Hill, George Richard: president, trustee, Lubrizol Foundation (The)

National Coalition Against Censorship

Wilson, Cleo Francine: executive director, Playboy Foundation

National Coalition Crime Delinquency

Hefner, Christie Ann: chairman, chief executive officer, Playboy Enterprises Inc.; director, Playboy Foundation

National Collection Fine Arts

Buechner, Thomas Scharman: trustee, Corning Inc. Foundation

National Commission Against Drunk Driving

Beyer, Jeffrey C.: president, Farmers Group Safety Foundation

Kennedy, George Danner: trustee, Kemper Foundation (James S.)

National Commission Future Regis College

Coors, Peter Hanson: vice president, director, Coors Brewing Co.

National Committee Drunk Drivers

Kelley, Bruce Gunn: vice president, director, Employers Mutual Charitable Foundation

National Committee Science Education Standards Assesment

Alberts, Bruce Michael, PhD: director, Genentech Foundation for Biomedical Sciences

National Committee Student Financial Assistance

Brademas, John: chairman, Texaco Foundation

National Committee on U.S.-China Relations

Franklin, Barbara Hackman: director, Dow Chemical Co.

National Community Support Law Enforcement

Gorelick, Jamie Shona: vice chairman, Fannie Mae

National Conference Bar Foundations

Shideler, Shirley Ann Williams: director, Central Newspapers Foundation

National Conference Christians & Jews

Mandel, Jack N.: director, Premier Industrial Corp.

National Contract Management Association

Williams, Karen Hastie: director, Fannie Mae Foundation

National Corp. Fund Dance

James, George Barker, II: senior vice president, chief financial officer, Levi Strauss & Co.

National Council Economic Education

Goodes, Melvin Russell: chairman, chief executive officer, director, Ameritech Corp.

Gould, John T., Jr.: vice president, Unilever Foundation; director corporate affairs, Unilever United States, Inc.

National Council Farmer Coops

Gherty, John E.: president, chief executive officer, Land O'Lakes, Inc.

National Council Housing Industries

Whitwam, David Ray: chairman, president, chief executive officer, director, Whirlpool Corp.

National Council Paper Industry Air & Stream Improvement

Harad, George Jay: chairman, chief executive officer, director, Boise Cascade Corp.

Nutter, Wallace L.: director, Rayonier Foundation

National Council Savings Institutions

Gaiswinkler, Robert Sigfried: chairman, director, First Financial Bank; director, First Financial Foundation

National Council of Laraza

Reinemund, Steve S.: chairman, chief executive officer, Frito-Lay, Inc.

National Down Syndrome Society

Maatman, Gerald Leonard: chairman, president, trustee, Kemper Foundation (James S.); director, Kemper National Insurance Companies

National Electrical Contractors Association

Fuellgraf, Charles Louis, Jr.: trustee, Nationwide Insurance Enterprise Foundation

National Electrical Manufacturers Association

Ferrari, Giannantonio A.: director, Honeywell Foundation; president, chief operating officer, director, Honeywell International Inc.

National Endowment Arts

McClimon, Timothy J.: executive director, AT&T Foundation

National Environmental Education & Training Foundation

Minton, Dwight Church: chairman, director, Church & Dwight Co., Inc.

National Executive Service Corps

Mark, Reuben: chairman, chief executive officer, Colgate-Palmolive Co.

National Flag Foundation

Rohr, James Edward: chief executive officer, president, director, PNC Financial Services Group

National Fluid Power Association

Powers, Paul Joseph: chairman, president, chief executive officer, director, Commercial Intertech Corp.; president, trustee, Commercial Intertech Foundation

National Food Processors Association

Page, Barbara B.: trustee, Golub Foundation

Rice, William D.: senior vice president, chief financial officer, secretary, Agrilink Foods, Inc.; trustee, Agrilink Foods/Pro-Fac Foundation

National Food Products Association

Johnson, David Willis: chairman, director, Campbell Soup Co.

National Football Foundation

Hanson, Jon F.: trustee, Prudential Foundation

National Foreign Language Center

Stanley, Peter William: trustee, Hitachi Foundation

National Foreign Trade Council

Fites, Donald Vester: director, Caterpillar Foundation

National Foundation Advancement Arts

Chellgren, Paul Wilbur: chief executive officer, chairman, director, Ashland, Inc.; member, Ashland Inc. Foundation

National Freight Transportation Association

Goode, David Ronald: chairman, president, chief executive officer, director, Norfolk Southern Corp.

National Furniture Manufacturer Association

Spilman, Robert H.: chairman, chief executive officer, Bassett Furniture Industries; chairman, director, Bassett Furniture Industries Fdn.

National Futures Association

Donovan, Thomas Roy: president, chief executive officer, Chicago Board of Trade

National Gallery

Resnick, Stewart A.: chairman, chief executive officer, Franklin Mint (The)

National Gallery Art

Bryan, John Henry: chairman, Sara Lee Corp.; director, Sara Lee Foundation

Gorman, Maureen V.: vice president, GTE Foundation

Graham, Katharine Meyer: chairman executive committee, director, The Washington Post

National Gas Transmission Employee Relations Group

Richards, Joel, III: vice president, El Paso Energy Foundation

National Geographic Society

Allbritton, Joe Lewis: chairman, chief executive officer, Riggs Bank NA

Marriott, J. Willard, Jr.: chairman, chief executive officer, Marriott International Inc.

National Grain Car Council

Goode, David Ronald: chairman, president, chief executive officer, director, Norfolk Southern Corp.

National Heathcare Affil

Lippes, Gerald Sanford: secretary, Mark IV Industries Foundation

National Historical Fire Foundation

Getz, Bert A.: chairman, Globe Corp.; president, director, Globe Foundation

Getz, Bert A., Jr.: executive vice president, Globe Corp.; vice president, Globe Foundation

Lux, Clifton L.: director, Globe Foundation

National History Museum

Berkley, Eugene Bertram: chairman, director, Tension Envelope Corp.; treasurer, Tension Envelope Foundation

National Housing Trust

Zigas, Barry: senior vice president, Fannie Mae; director, Fannie Mae Foundation

National Individuals Advancement Council

Coors, Peter Hanson: vice president, director, Coors Brewing Co.

National Institute Foodservice Industry

Teets, John William: president, chief executive officer, director, Viad Corp. Fund

National Institute Music Theater

Darling, Robert Edward, Jr.: chairman, Ensign-Bickford Foundation

National Investor Relations Institute

Downes, Laurence M.: president, chief executive officer, director, chairman, New Jersey Natural Gas Co.; trustee, New Jersey Natural Gas Foundation

Forsythe, Donald George: vice president corporate relations, Sprint Corp.; executive director, Sprint Foundation

Gardner, James Richard: vice president, Pfizer Foundation

Hobor, Nancy A.: vice president communications & investor relations, Morton International Inc.

Medford, Dale L.: vice president corporate finance, chief financial officer, Reynolds & Reynolds Co.

Pehlke, Richard W.: vice president, treasurer, Ameritech Corp.

Rollans, James Ora: senior vice president, chief administrative officer, chief financial officer, Fluor Corp.; trustee, Fluor Foundation

Smith, Elizabeth Patience: director, Texaco Foundation; vice president investor relations & shareholder service, Texaco Inc.

Townsend, David L.: vice president administration, Walter Industries Inc.

National Italian American Foundation

Grasso, Richard A.: chairman, chief executive officer, New York Stock Exchange, Inc.

National Journalism Society

Parisi, Franklin Joseph: chairman, Star Tribune Foundation

National Judicial College

Satre, Philip Glen: chairman, president, chief executive officer, director, Promus Hotel Corp.

National League Nursing

Davis, Carolyne Kahle, PhD: trustee, Merck Co. Foundation

National Legal Aid & Defender Association

Kaden, Ellen O.: trustee, Campbell Soup Foundation

National Legal Center Public Interest

Barnette, Curtis Handley: chairman, chief executive officer, director, Bethlehem Steel Corp.

DeSimone, Livio Diego: chairman, chief executive officer, Minnesota Mining & Manufacturing Co.

Gorelick, Jamie Shona: vice chairman, Fannie Mae

McKennon, Keith Robert: chairman, president, PacifiCorp; member, PacifiCorp Foundation

National Management Association

Hutchins, William Bruce, III: director, Alabama Power Foundation

National Meat Canners

Page, Barbara B.: trustee, Golub Foundation

National Medicine Association

Elam, Lloyd Charles, MD: trustee, Merck Co. Foundation

National Merit Scholarship Board

Fisher, George Myles Cordell: chairman, president, chief executive officer, director, Eastman Kodak Co.

National Mining Association

Brinzo, John S.: trustee, Cleveland-Cliffs Foundation (The); president, chief executive officer, Cleveland-Cliffs, Inc.

Osborne, Richard de Jongh: director, ASARCO Foundation; chairman, chief executive officer, director, ASARCO Inc.

National Minority Supplier Development Council

Berkley, Eugene Bertram: chairman, director, Tension Envelope Corp.; treasurer, Tension Envelope Foundation

National Minority Supplier Development Council Inc.

David, George A. L.: chairman, president, chief executive officer, chief operating officer, United Technologies Corp.

Martinez, Arthur C.: chairman, chief executive officer, president, Sears, Roebuck and Co.

National Multiple Sclerosis Society

Kangas, Edward A.: chairman, chief executive officer, Deloitte & Touche

National Museum Natural History

Rogers, Desiree Glapion: vice president community affairs, Peoples Energy Corp.

National Museum of Naval Aviation

Kaman, Charles Huron: chairman, president, chief executive officer, director, Kaman Corp.

National Mutual Insurance Companies Board

Druen, W. Sidney: director, Nationwide Insurance Enterprise Foundation

National Natural Gas Vehicle Coalition

Hock, Delwin D.: chairman, New Century Energies

National Newspaper Association

Copley, David C.: president, trustee, Copley Foundation (James S.); president, chief executive officer, director, senior management board, Copley Press, Inc.

National Nuclear Accrediting board

Orser, William Stanley: executive vice president energy supply, Carolina Power & Light Co.

National Ocean Industry Association

Bradford, William Edward: chairman, director, Halliburton Co.

National Opera Institute

Darling, Robert Edward, Jr.: chairman, Ensign-Bickford Foundation

National Organization Disability

Pew, Robert Cunningham, II: trustee, Steelcase Foundation

National Paint & Coatings Association

Pollock, E. Kears: director, PPG Industries Foundation; executive vice president, PPG Industries, Inc.

Wurtele, C. Angus: president, Valspar Foundation

National Parenting Association

Gherty, John E.: president, chief executive officer, Land O'Lakes, Inc.

National Park Foundation

Gorelick, Jamie Shona: vice chairman, Fannie Mae

National Parks & Conservation Association

Berkley, Eugene Bertram: chairman, director, Tension Envelope Corp.; treasurer, Tension Envelope Foundation

National Petroleum Council

Bijur, Peter I.: chairman, chief executive officer, Texaco Inc.

Carroll, Philip Joseph: chairman, chief executive officer, Fluor Corp.; chairman, trustee, Fluor Foundation

Farman, Richard Donald: chairman, chief executive officer, Pacific Enterprises

Haddock, Ronald Wayne: president, chief executive officer, director, FINA; president, FINA Foundation

Hemminghaus, Roger Roy: chairman, director, Ultramar Diamond Shamrock Corp.

Kennedy, Bernard Joseph: chairman, president, chief executive officer, director, National Fuel Gas Distribution Corp.

Pate, James Leonard: chairman, chief executive officer, director, Pennzoil-Quaker State Co.

Raymond, Lee R.: chairman, president, chief executive officer, Exxon Mobil Corp.

Terry, Richard Edward: chairman, chief executive officer, director, Peoples Energy Corp.

Wise, William Allen: chairman, president, chief executive officer, director, El Paso Energy Co.; chairman, director, El Paso Energy Foundation

National Petroleum Refiners Association

Chellgren, Paul Wilbur: chief executive officer, chairman, director, Ashland, Inc.; member, Ashland Inc. Foundation

Fligg, James E.: executive vice president, BP Amoco Corp.

Haddock, Ronald Wayne: president, chief executive officer, director, FINA; president, FINA Foundation

Mooney, Edward J., Jr.: chairman, president, chief executive officer, director, Nalco Chemical Co.

National Planning Association

Lee, Charles Robert: chairman, chief executive officer, director, GTE Corp.; chief executive officer, trustee, GTE Foundation

National Press Foundation

Gould, John T., Jr.: vice president, Unilever Foundation; director corporate affairs, Unilever United States, Inc.

National Republican Senatorial Committee

Zacks, Gordon Benjamin: chairman, president, chief executive officer, director, Barry Corp. (R.G.); president, Barry Foundation

National Retail Federation

Loeb, Jerome Thomas: chairman, director, May Department Stores Co.; president, director, May Department Stores Computer Foundation (The)

Martinez, Arthur C.: chairman, chief executive officer, president, Sears, Roebuck and Co.

National Retail Merchants Association

Menzer, John: executive vice president, Wal-Mart Stores, Inc.

National Roofing Contractors Association

Hilyard, James E.: president, CertainTeed Corp.; director, CertainTeed Corp. Foundation

National Science Resource Center Smithsonian Institute

Alberts, Bruce Michael, PhD: director, Genentech Foundation for Biomedical Sciences

National Security Industry Association

Schievelbein, Thomas C.: executive vice president, Newport News Shipbuilding

National Security Telecommunications Advisory Committee

Armstrong, C. Michael: chairman, chief executive officer, AT&T Corp.

National Shooting Sports Foundation

Griffin, Donald Wayne: chairman, president, chief executive officer, director, Olin Corp.; trustee, Olin Corp. Charitable Trust

National Skills Studies Board

Wurtzel, Alan Leon: chairman, Circuit City Foundation; chairman, trustee, Circuit City Stores, Inc.

National Society Professional Engineers

Bailey, Keith E.: chairman, president, director, chief executive officer, Texas Gas Transmission Corp.; president, director, Williams Companies Foundation (The)

Borman, Marlene: vice president, director, Borman Fund (The)

Muehlbauer, James Herman: vice president, director, Koch Foundation

National Sporting Library

Daniels, John Hancock: chairman, Archer-Daniels-Midland Foundation

National Supplier Development Council

Graves, Earl Gilbert: director, Aetna Foundation

National Symphony Orchestra

Rogers, James E., Jr.: vice chairman, president, chief executive officer, Cinergy Corp.; vice chairman, director, Cinergy Foundation

National Tile Roofing Manufacturer Association

Hilyard, James E.: president, CertainTeed Corp.; director, CertainTeed Corp. Foundation

National Urban League

Burns, Mitchell Anthony: president, director, Ryder System Charitable Foundation; chairman, president, chief executive officer, Ryder System, Inc.

Carroll, Philip Joseph: chairman, chief executive officer, Fluor Corp.; chairman, trustee, Fluor Foundation

Hill, Bonnie Guiton: vice president, Times Mirror Co.; president, chief executive officer, Times Mirror Foundation

Martinez, Arthur C.: chairman, chief executive officer, president, Sears, Roebuck and Co.

National Venture Capital Organization

Morby, Jacqueline C.: managing partner, Pacific Mutual Life Insurance Co.

National Wholesale Druggists Association

Goodes, Melvin Russell: chairman, chief executive officer, director, Ameritech Corp.

National Women's Economic Alliance Foundation

Franklin, Barbara Hackman: director, Dow Chemical Co.

National Womens Economic Alliance

Bryan, John Henry: chairman, Sara Lee Corp.; director, Sara Lee Foundation

National Womens Law Center

Gorelick, Jamie Shona: vice chairman, Fannie Mae

National Youth Information Network

Berkley, Eugene Bertram: chairman, director, Tension Envelope Corp.; treasurer, Tension Envelope Foundation

Natural Disaster Coalition

Joslin, Roger Scott: treasurer, State Farm Companies Foundation

Natural Gas Council

Wise, William Allen: chairman, president, chief executive officer, director, El Paso Energy Co.; chairman, director, El Paso Energy Foundation

Natural Gas Vehicle Coalition

Mitchell, Warren I.: president, director, Southern California Gas Co.

Nature Conservancy

Anderson, Ivan Verner, Jr.: president, chief executive officer, Evening Post Publishing Co.; vice president, Post and Courier Foundation

Correll, Alston Dayton 'Pete', Jr.: chairman, president, chief executive officer, director, Georgia-Pacific Corp.; director, Georgia-Pacific Foundation

Nature Conservancy Hawaii

Dods, Walter Arthur, Jr.: president, director, First Hawaiian Foundation; chairman, chief executive officer, director, First Hawaiian, Inc.

Nature Conservancy Indiana Chapter Butler University

Rogers, James E., Jr.: vice chairman, president, chief executive officer, Cinergy Corp.; vice chairman, director, Cinergy Foundation

Nature Conservancy Nebraska Saint Chapter

Hewitt, James Watt: vice president, treasurer, Abel Foundation

Nature Conservatory

Johnson, Samuel Curtis: chairman, director, president, Johnson & Son (S.C.); chairman, trustee, Johnson Wax Fund (S.C.)

Naval Academy Endowment Trust

Marriott, J. Willard, Jr.: chairman, chief executive officer, Marriott International Inc.

Naval Architects & Marine Engineers

Hemminghaus, Roger Roy: chairman, director, Ultramar Diamond Shamrock Corp.

Naval Aviation Museum Foundation

Kresa, Kent: chairman, president, chief executive officer, director, Northrop Grumman Corp.

Naval Helicopter Association

Kaman, Charles Huron: chairman, president, chief executive officer, director, Kaman Corp.

Leonis, John Michael: chairman, director, Litton Industries, Inc.

Naval Reserve Association

Calise, Nicholas James: vice president, associate general counsel, secretary, BFGoodrich Co.; secretary, Goodrich Foundation, Inc. (B.F.)

Navy League

Kresa, Kent: chairman, president, chief executive officer, director, Northrop Grumman Corp.

Wild, Heidi Karin: trustee

Navy League U.S.

Calise, Nicholas James: vice president, associate general counsel, secretary, BFGoodrich Co.; secretary, Goodrich Foundation, Inc. (B.F.)

Griffin, Donald Wayne: chairman, president, chief executive officer, director, Olin Corp.; trustee, Olin Corp. Charitable Trust

Kaman, Charles Huron: chairman, president, chief executive officer, director, Kaman Corp.

Nebraska Bar Association

Hall, Larry D.: chairman, president, chief executive officer, director, Kinder Morgn; president, director, KN Energy Foundation

Hewitt, James Watt: vice president, treasurer, Abel Foundation

Nebraska Health Systems

Bay, Mogens C.: chairman, chief executive officer, Valmont Industries, Inc.

Nebraska Rose Society

Hewitt, James Watt: vice president, treasurer, Abel Foundation

Neighborhood Housing Services America

Matthews, Craig Gerard: president, chief operating officer, Brooklyn Union

Williams, Edward Joseph: president, director, Harris Bank Foundation

Neighborhood Progress

Daberko, David A.: chairman, chief executive officer, National City Corp.

Nelson-Atkins Museum Art

Bloch, Henry Wollman: chairman, Block Foundation (H&R); chairman, director, Block, Inc. (H&R)

Hall, Donald Joyce: chairman board, director, Hallmark Cards Inc.; chairman, Hallmark Corporate Foundation

Nevada Bar Association

Satre, Philip Glen: chairman, president, chief executive officer, director, Promus Hotel Corp.

New American Schools Development Corp.

Baker, James Kendrick: chairman, director, Arvin Foundation; vice chairman, director, Arvin Industries, Inc.

Gerstner, Louis Vincent, Jr.: chairman, chief executive officer, director, International Business Machines Corp.

Gorman, Joseph T.: chairman, chief executive officer, TRW Inc.

Graves, Earl Gilbert: director, Aetna Foundation

Lee, Charles Robert: chairman, chief executive officer, director, GTE Corp.; chief executive officer, trustee, GTE Foundation

Raymond, Lee R.: chairman, president, chief executive officer, Exxon Mobil Corp.

New England Air Museum

Garneau, Robert M.: chief financial officer, Kaman Corp.

New England Aquarium

Bodman, Samuel Wright, III: chairman, chief executive officer, director, Cabot Corp.; president, director, Cabot Corp. Foundation

DiCamillo, Gary Thomas: chairman, chief executive officer, director, Polaroid Corp.

Magee, John Francis: chairman, director, Little, Inc. (Arthur D.)

New England Bar Association

Donahue, Richard King: vice chairman, Nike, Inc.

New England Conservatory Music

Fish, Lawrence K.: trustee, Citizens Charitable Foundation; chairman, chief executive officer, Citizens Financial Group, Inc.

New England Financial

Kamen, Harry Paul: chairman, president, chief executive officer, Metropolitan Life Insurance Co.

New England Gas Association

Messer, Chester R.: president, chief operating officer, Boston Gas Co.; trustee, Eastern Enterprises Foundation

New England Historic Genealogical Society

Cabot, John G. L.: vice chairman, Kinder Morgn

New England Intercollegiate Sailing Association

Spoon, Alan Gary: president, chief operating officer, director, The Washington Post

New England Medical Center

Redstone, Sumner Murray: chairman, Viacom Inc.

New England Rheumatism Association

Harris, Edward D., Jr.: director, Genentech Foundation for Biomedical Sciences

New Germany Fund

Goeltz, Richard Karl: vice chairman, chief financial officer, American Express Co.

New Haven Symphony Orch

Miglio, Daniel Joseph: chairman, president, director, chief executive officer, Southern New England Telephone Co.

New Hope Project Inc.

Schrader, Thomas F.: vice president, director, WICOR Foundation

New Jersey Bar Association

Graham, John Gourlay: chief financial officer, senior vice president, GPU Energy

Sullivan, Thomas John: vice president, director,

New Jersey Center Performing Arts

Vagelos, Pindaros Roy: trustee, Prudential Insurance Co. of America

New Jersey Chamber of Commerce

Howe, Wesley Jackson: chairman emeritus, director, Becton Dickinson & Co.

New Jersey Council Humanities

Shinn, George Latimer: director, New York Times Co. Foundation

New Jersey Institute Technology

Devlin, James Richard: director, Sprint Foundation

New Jersey Partnership

O'Hare, Dean Raymond: chairman, Chubb Corp.

New Jersey Society CPAs

Doherty, Leonard Edward: member advisory committee, admin officer, Dow Jones Foundation

New Orleans Association Life Underwriters

Purvis, George Frank, Jr.: chairman, president, chief executive officer, director,

Pan-American Life Insurance Co.

New Orleans Geological Society

Greene, John Frederick: executive vice president exploration & production, director, Louisiana Land & Exploration Co.

New Orleans Philharmonic Symphony Society

Purvis, George Frank, Jr.: chairman, president, chief executive officer, director, Pan-American Life Insurance Co.

New Visions Public Schools

Labrecque, Thomas Goulet: president, chief operating officer, director, Chase Manhattan Bank, NA; president, Chase Manhattan Foundation

New World School Arts

Herron, James Michael: secretary, director, Ryder System Charitable Foundation

New York Academy Medicine

Hyman, Morton Peter: vice president, director, OSG Foundation; president, director, Overseas Shipholding Group Inc.

New York Bar Association

Kurtz, Melvin H.: secretary, director, Chesebrough Foundation

Olschwang, Alan P., Esq.: secretary, Mitsubishi Electric America Foundation

New York Botanical Garden

Bijur, Peter I.: chairman, chief executive officer, Texaco Inc.

Chambers, Anne Cox: chairman, trustee, Cox Foundation (James M.)

Steere, William Campbell, Jr.: chairman, chief executive officer, director, Pfizer Inc.

New York Botanical Garden Society Cincinnati

Benenson, James, Jr.: chairman, president, director, Vesper Corp.; trustee, Vesper Foundation

New York Chamber of Commerce

Golub, Harvey: chairman, chief executive officer, director, American Express Co.; trustee, American Express Foundation

New York City Ballet

Allaire, Paul Arthur: chairman, chief executive officer, chairman executive committee, Xerox Corp.; president, Xerox Foundation

New York City Bar Association

McClimon, Timothy J.: executive director, AT&T Foundation

Wallach, Ira D.: chairman, Central National-Gottesman; executive vice president, Central National-Gottesman Foundation

New York City Partnership

Catell, Robert Barry: chairman, chief executive officer, Brooklyn Union

Cook, J. Michael: chairman, chief executive officer, Deloitte & Touche; chairman, Deloitte & Touche Foundation

Gerstner, Louis Vincent, Jr.: chairman, chief executive officer, director, International Business Machines Corp.

Golub, Harvey: chairman, chief executive officer, director, American Express Co.; trustee, American Express Foundation

Marron, Donald Baird: chairman, chief executive officer, director, Paine Webber; trustee, Paine Webber Foundation

Raymond, Lee R.: chairman, president, chief executive officer, Exxon Mobil Corp.

Rhodes, William Reginald: vice chairman, Citibank Corp.

New York City Partnership Inc.

Gelb, Richard Lee: director, New York Times Co. Foundation

New York City Partnership Policy Center

Millstein, Ira M.: partner, Weil, Gotshal & Manges Corp.; president, director, Weil, Gotshal & Manges Foundation

New York City Police Foundation

Gelb, Richard Lee: director, New York Times Co. Foundation

Grasso, Richard A.: chairman, chief executive officer, New York Stock Exchange, Inc.

New York City Salvation Army

Urkowitz, Michael: senior vice president, Chase Manhattan Bank, NA; trustee, Chase Manhattan Foundation

New York Clearing House Association

Labrecque, Thomas Goulet: president, chief operating officer, director, Chase Manhattan Bank, NA; president, Chase Manhattan Foundation

Warner, Douglas Alexander, III: chairman, president, chief executive officer, director, Morgan & Co. Inc. (J.P.)

New York Co. Lawyers Association

Wallach, Ira D.: chairman, Central National-Gottesman; executive vice president, Central National-Gottesman Foundation

New York Convention & Visit Bureau

Tisch, Preston Robert: chairman, director, CBS Foundation; co-chairman, co-chief executive officer, director, CNA; trustee, Loews Foundation

New York Energy Research & Development Authority

Catell, Robert Barry: chairman, chief executive officer, Brooklyn Union

New York Gas Group

Ackerman, Philip Charles: senior vice president, director, National Fuel Gas Distribution Corp.

Catell, Robert Barry: chairman, chief executive officer, Brooklyn Union

New York Historical Society

Forbes, Christopher 'Kip': vice president, Forbes Foundation; vice chairman, corporate secretary, director, Forbes Inc.

New York Human Research Planners

Mirsky, Susan: vice president, director, Thompson Co. Fund (J. Walter)

New York Junior League

Dinerstein, Martha L.: managing director, head marketing & corporate communications, United States Trust Co. of New York

New York Landmarks Conservancy

Ross, Arthur: senior vice president, Central National-Gottesman; director, Central National-Gottesman Foundation

New York Law Journal

Douglass, Robert Royal: trustee, Chase Manhattan Foundation

New York Patent Law Association

Kurtz, Melvin H.: secretary, director, Chesebrough Foundation

New York Personnel Management Association

Conklin, Thomas J.: senior vice president, secretary, MONY Group (The); director, MONY Life Insurance of New York (The)

Mirsky, Susan: vice president, director, Thompson Co. Fund (J. Walter)

New York Presbyterian Hospital

Rhodes, William Reginald: vice chairman, Citibank Corp.

New York Public Library

Gerstner, Louis Vincent, Jr.: chairman, chief executive officer, director, International Business Machines Corp.

Tisch, Laurence Alan: chairman, co-chief executive officer, CBS Corp.; trustee, Loews Foundation

New York Racing Association

Gelb, Richard Lee: director, New York Times Co. Foundation

Schwartz, Barry K.: chairman, chief executive officer, director, Calvin Klein

New York Regional Association

Gorman, Maureen V.: vice president, GTE Foundation

New York Serda Board

Catell, Robert Barry: chairman, chief executive officer, Brooklyn Union

New York Society CPA's

Robinson, Edward Joseph: president, chief operating officer, director, Avon Products, Inc.

New York Society Security Analysts

Glynn, Gary Allen: president, USX Corp.; vice president, USX Foundation, Inc.

Weill, Sanford I.: chairman, chief executive officer, Citibank Corp.; chairman, Citigroup Foundation

New York State Arts Council

Lippes, Gerald Sanford: secretary, Mark IV Industries Foundation

New York State Bankers Association

Wilmers, Robert George: chairman, president, chief executive officer, Manufacturers & Traders Trust Co.

New York State Bar Association

Ackerman, Philip Charles: senior vice president, director, National Fuel Gas Distribution Corp.

Buchanan, William Hobart, Jr.: assistant secretary, Dun & Bradstreet Corp. Foundation, Inc.

Burak, Howard Paul: secretary, director, Sony U.S.A. Foundation Inc.

Calise, Nicholas James: vice president, associate general counsel, secretary, BFGoodrich Co.; secretary, Goodrich Foundation, Inc. (B.F.)

Chapple, Thomas Leslie: senior vice president, general counsel, secretary, Gannett Co., Inc.; secretary, Gannett Foundation

Clark, Richard McCourt: senior vice president, general counsel, secretary, Kellogg Co.; vice president, trustee, Kellogg Co.

Twenty-Five Year Employees' Fund Inc.

Cole, Lewis George: director, AMETEK Foundation

Douglass, Robert Royal: trustee, Chase Manhattan Foundation

Dubin, Stephen Victor: vice president, secretary, Farber Foundation

Gallagher, Terence Joseph: secretary, director, Pfizer Foundation

Hyman, Morton Peter: vice president, director, OSG Foundation; president, director, Overseas Shipholding Group Inc.

Kennedy, Bernard Joseph: chairman, president, chief executive officer, director, National Fuel Gas Distribution Corp.

Lippes, Gerald Sanford: secretary, Mark IV Industries Foundation

McClimon, Timothy J.: executive director, AT&T Foundation

McGuinn, Martin Gregory: chairman, chief executive officer, Mellon Financial Corp.

McLaughlin, Michael John: secretary, New York Life Foundation; senior vice president, deputy general counsel, New York Life Insurance Co.

Millstein, Ira M.: partner, Weil, Gotshal & Manges Corp.; president, director, Weil, Gotshal & Manges Foundation

Muth, Robert James: president, director, ASARCO Foundation

Shapiro, Isaac: chairman, secretary, trustee, Ise Cultural Foundation

Soden, Paul A.: senior vice president, secretary, general counsel, Reader's Digest Association, Inc. (The)

Ughetta, William Casper: trustee, Corning Inc. Foundation

New York State Business Council

Catell, Robert Barry: chairman, chief executive officer, Brooklyn Union

Golub, Lewis: chairman, chief executive officer, director, Golub Corp.

New York State Society Public Accountants

Schiro, James J.: chairman, senior partner, PricewaterhouseCoopers

New York State Urban Development Corp.

Graves, Earl Gilbert: director, Aetna Foundation

New York Stock Exchange Inc.

Bible, Geoffrey Cyril: director, New York Stock Exchange Foundation, Inc.; chairman, chief executive officer, director, Philip Morris Companies Inc.

Brademas, John: chairman, Texaco Foundation

Hammerman, Stephen Lawrence: vice president, trustee, Merrill Lynch & Co. Foundation Inc.; vice chairman, general counsel, Merrill Lynch & Co., Inc.

New York University

Brademas, John: chairman, Texaco Foundation

Lipton, Martin: partner, Wachtell, Lipton, Rosen & Katz; president, Wachtell, Lipton, Rosen & Katz Foundation

McClimon, Timothy J.: executive director, AT&T Foundation

Tisch, Laurence Alan: chairman, co-chief executive officer, CBS Corp.; trustee, Loews Foundation

Tisch, Preston Robert: chairman, director, CBS Foundation; co-chairman, co-chief executive officer, director, CNA; trustee, Loews Foundation

New York University Downtown Hospital

Chenault, Kenneth Irvine: president, chief operating officer, director, American Express Co.; trustee, American Express Foundation

New York University Hospital

Koch, David Hamilton: director, Koch Foundation, Inc. (Fred C. and Mary R.)

New York University Law School

Lipton, Martin: partner, Wachtell, Lipton, Rosen & Katz; president, Wachtell, Lipton, Rosen & Katz Foundation

New York University Medical Center

Bijur, Peter I.: chairman, chief executive officer, Texaco Inc.

Chenault, Kenneth Irvine: president, chief operating officer, director, American Express Co.; trustee, American Express Foundation

Small, Lawrence Malcolm: president, chief operating officer, Fannie Mae; director, Fannie Mae Foundation

New York University Stern School Business

Kogan, Richard Jay: chairman, chief executive officer, Schering-Plough Corp.; trustee, member, Schering-Plough Foundation

New York Womens Forum

Lachman, Marguerite Leanne: trustee, Chicago Title and Trust Co. Foundation

New York Zoological Society

Bergerac, Michel Christian: director, CBS Foundation

Newark Area Chamber of Commerce

McConnell, William Thompson: chairman, ceo, Park National Bank; chairman, Park National Corp. Foundation

Newark Museum

Forbes, Christopher 'Kip': vice president, Forbes Foundation; vice chairman, corporate secretary, director, Forbes Inc.

Newcomen Society

Barnes, Wallace W.: director, Barnes Group Foundation Inc.

Hewitt, James Watt: vice president, treasurer, Abel Foundation

Kaman, Charles Huron: chairman, president, chief executive officer, director, Kaman Corp.

Strickland, Robert Louis: vice president, Lowe's Charitable and Educational Foundation

Wobst, Frank: chairman, chief executive officer, director, Huntington Bancshares Inc.

Newcomen Society North America

Blount, Winton Malcolm, Jr.: chairman, Blount International, Inc.

Newspaper Advertising Bureau

Gottlieb, Richard Douglas: president, chief executive officer, director, Lee Enterprises

Leser, Lawrence Arthur: chairman, director, Scripps Co. (E.W.); member, Scripps Howard Foundation

Russell, Frank Eli: president, Central Newspapers Foundation; chairman, Central Newspapers, Inc.

Newspaper Association America

Anderson, Ivan Verner, Jr.: president, chief executive officer, Evening Post Publishing Co.; vice president, Post and Courier Foundation

Batten, Frank, Sr.: chairman, director, Landmark Communications Foundation; chairman, Landmark Communications Inc.

Copley, Helen K.: chairman, trustee, Copley Foundation (James S.); chairman, director, senior management board, Copley Press, Inc.

Curley, John J.: chairman, chief executive officer, director, Gannett Co., Inc.; chairman, Gannett Foundation

Decherd, Robert William: chairman, president, chief executive officer, director, Belo Corp. (A.H.); chairman, trustee, Belo Corp. Foundation (A.H.)

Easterly, David E.: president, chief operating officer, Cox Enterprises Inc.

Gottlieb, Richard Douglas: president, chief executive officer, director, Lee Enterprises

Lebedoff, Randy Miller: vice president, general counsel, McClatchy Co.; secretary, Star Tribune Foundation

McCorkindale, Douglas H.: vice chairman, president, Gannett Co., Inc.; president, Gannett Foundation

Osborne, Burl: president publishing division, director, Belo Corp. (A.H.); president, trustee, Belo Corp. Foundation (A.H.)

Ottaway, James Haller, Jr.: senior vice president, director, Dow Jones & Co., Inc.; member advisory committee, Dow Jones Foundation

Sulzberger, Arthur Ochs, Junior: director, chairman emeritus, New York Times Co.

Watson, Solomon Brown, IV: vice president, New York Times Co. Foundation

Newspaper Association American Legal Affairs Committee

Merdek, Andrew Austin: vice president legal affairs, secretary, Cox Enterprises Inc.; secretary, Cox Foundation (James M.)

Newton Chamber of Commerce

Hadley, Leonard Anson: chairman, chief executive officer, director, Maytag Corp.; president, trustee, Maytag Corp. Foundation

Newton First Un Methodist Church

Hadley, Leonard Anson: chairman, chief executive officer, director, Maytag Corp.; president, trustee, Maytag Corp. Foundation

Next Century Schools Foundation

Gerstner, Louis Vincent, Jr.: chairman, chief executive officer, director, International Business Machines Corp.

Next Door Foundation

Bauer, Chris Michael: president, Firstar Milwaukee Foundation

Nexus

Kramer, Mary Elizabeth: vice president, Wellmark Foundation

Niagara University

Kennedy, Bernard Joseph: chairman, president, chief executive officer, director, National Fuel Gas Distribution Corp.

Nieman Foundation

Osborne, Burl: president publishing division, director, Belo Corp. (A.H.); president, trustee, Belo Corp. Foundation (A.H.)

Nina Mason Pulliam Charitable Trust

Russell, Frank Eli: president, Central Newspapers Foundation; chairman, Central Newspapers, Inc.

Ninety-Nines

Carey, Kathryn Ann: foundation manager, American Honda Foundation

Nocturnal Adoration Society

Cloud, Bruce Benjamin, Sr.: vice chairman, director, Zachry Co. (H.B.)

Non Profit Facilities Fund

Childress, Jan C.: vice president, Brooklyn Union

Norfolk Academy

Barry, Richard Francis, III: director, Landmark Communications Foundation; vice chairman, Landmark Communications Inc.

Wynne, John Oliver: president, director, Landmark Communications Foundation; president, chief executive officer, Landmark Communications Inc.

Norfolk Bar Association

Goode, David Ronald: chairman, president, chief executive officer, director, Norfolk Southern Corp.

Norfolk State University

Campbell, Cole C.: editor, Pulitzer Publishing Co.; director, Pulitzer Publishing Co. Foundation

North Adams State College Foundation

Trask, Robert B.: clerk; president, chief operating officer, director, Country Curtains, Inc.; clerk, trustee, High Meadow Foundation

North American Consortium Free Market Study

Bronfman, Edgar Miles: chairman, trustee, Bronfman Foundation/Joseph E. Seagram & Sons, Inc. Fund (Samuel); chairman, Seagram & Sons, Inc. (Joseph E.)

North American Electrical Reliability Council

Brooks, E. Richard 'Dick': chairman, chief executive officer, director, Central & South West Services

North American Society Corporate Planning

Gardner, James Richard: vice president, Pfizer Foundation

North Carolina Bar Association

Sharpe, Robert Francis, Jr.: senior vice president public affairs, general counsel, PepsiCo, Inc.

North Carolina Performing Arts Center

Atwood, Robert T.: executive vice president, chief financial officer, First Union Corp.; director, First Union Foundation

North Carolina State University

Woolard, Edgar Smith, Jr.: director, du Pont de Nemours & Co. (E.I.)

North Central College

Lambe, James F.: senior vice president human resources, Nalco Chemical Co.; director, Nalco Foundation

North Hennepin Community College

Wynia, Ann: director, Fuller Co. Foundation (H.B.)

Northampton County Bar Association

Barnette, Curtis Handley: chairman, chief executive officer, director, Bethlehem Steel Corp.

Northeast Corporate Counsel Association Inc.

Ballantyne, Richard Lee: vice president, general counsel, secretary, Harris Corp.; secretary, treasurer, Harris Foundation

Northeastern University

Countryman, Gary Lee: chairman, Liberty Mutual Insurance Group

Northern California Grantmakers

Haas, Peter Edgar, Sr.: chairman executive committee, director, Levi Strauss & Co.

Northern Life

Dubes, Michael: membership, ReliaStar Foundation

Northern Lights Institute

Muth, Robert James: president, director, ASARCO Foundation

Northfield Mt Hermon School

Rhodes, William Reginald: vice chairman, Citibank Corp.

Northwestern Healthcare Network, Inc.

Toll, Daniel Roger: trustee, Kemper Foundation (James S.)

Northwestern Memorial Corp.

Lowrie, William G.: president, deputy chief executive officer, director, BP Amoco Corp.

Northwestern University

Burnham, Duane Lee: chairman, chief executive officer, director, Abbott Laboratories

Chookaszian, Dennis Haig: chairman, chief executive officer, CNA

Gifford, Charles Kilvert: trustee, BankBoston Charitable Foundation; chairman, chief executive officer, BankBoston Corp.

Gonring, Matthew P.: vice president, trustee, USG Foundation

Goode, David Ronald: chairman, president, chief executive officer, director, Norfolk Southern Corp.

Ryan, Patrick G.: chairman, president, chief executive officer, Aon Corp.; president, Aon Foundation

Schadt, James Phillip: chairman, president, chief executive officer, director, Reader's Digest Association, Inc. (The); chairman, director, Reader's Digest Foundation

Northwestern University Associates

Donovan, Thomas Roy: president, chief executive officer, Chicago Board of Trade

Stewart, S. Jay: chairman, chief executive officer, director, Morton International Inc.

Northwestern University Kellogg Graduate School Business Management

Baker, James Kendrick: chairman, director, Arvin Foundation; vice chairman, director, Arvin Industries, Inc.

Brendsel, Leland C.: chairman, chief executive officer, director, Freddie Mac; director, Freddie Mac Foundation

Burnham, Duane Lee: chairman, chief executive officer, director, Abbott Laboratories

Choate, Jerry D.: chairman, chief executive officer, director, Allstate Foundation

Langbo, Arnold Gordon: chairman, chief executive officer, director, Kellogg Co.

Martin, Lynn M.: director, Ameritech Foundation

Martinez, Arthur C.: chairman, chief executive officer, president, Sears, Roebuck and Co.

McNally, Alan G.: chairman, chief executive officer, Harris Trust & Savings Bank

Northwestern University Medill School Journalism

Hobor, Nancy A.: vice president communications & investor relations, Morton International Inc.

Northwestern University Transportation Center

Moffitt, Donald Eugene: chairman, director, CNF Transportation, Inc.

Norton Kosair Childrens Hospital Inc.

Hower, Frank Beard, Jr.: vice chairman, Anthem Foundation, Inc.

Norwalk Connecticut Hospital

Schadt, James Phillip: chairman, president, chief executive officer, director, Reader's Digest Association, Inc. (The); chairman, director, Reader's Digest Foundation

Notre Dame College Arts and Letters

Murphy, Christopher J., III: president, chief executive officer, director, First Source Corp.; director, First Source Foundation

Nuclear Energy Institute

Davis, William E.: chairman, chief executive officer, Niagara Mohawk Holdings Inc.

Ferland, E. James: chairman, president, chief executive officer, Public Service Electric & Gas Co.

Hecht, William F.: chairman, president, chief executive officer, Pennsylvania Power & Light

Holland, Willard R.: chairman, chief executive officer, FirstEnergy Corp.

Howard, James Joseph, III: chairman, president, chief executive officer, director, Northern States Power Co.

Orser, William Stanley: executive vice president energy supply, Carolina Power & Light Co.

Nuclear Management Resources Council

Hock, Delwin D.: chairman, New Century Energies

Nuclear Utility Management Resources Council

McNeill, Corbin Asahel, Jr.: president, chief executive officer, director, chairman, PECO Energy Co.

Occupl Physicians Scholarship Fund

Raymond, Lee R.: chairman, president, chief executive officer, Exxon Mobil Corp.

Ocicats International

Carey, Kathryn Ann: foundation manager, American Honda Foundation

Office Press

Trujillo, Solomon D.: president, US West Foundation; president, chief executive officer, US West, Inc.

Office Technology Assessment

Bonsignore, Michael Robert: director, Honeywell Foundation; chairman, chief executive officer, director, Honeywell International Inc.

Officers Conference Group

Dammerman, Dennis Dean: vice chairman, director, General Electric Co.

Shaffer, Oren G.: executive vice president, chief financial officer, Ameritech Corp.

Ohio Bankers Association

McConnell, William Thompson: chairman, ceo, Park National Bank; chairman, Park National Corp. Foundation

Ohio Bar Association

Bridgeland, James Ralph, Jr.: trustee, Star Bank NA, Cincinnati Foundation
Calise, Nicholas James: vice president, associate general counsel, secretary, BFGoodrich Co.; secretary, Goodrich Foundation, Inc. (B.F.)
Druen, W. Sidney: director, Nationwide Insurance Enterprise Foundation
Forster, Peter Hans: chairman, director, Dayton Power and Light Co.
Gherlein, Gerald Lee: member contributions committee, Eaton Charitable Fund
Meyer, Russell William, Jr.: chairman, chief executive officer, Cessna Aircraft Co.; president, Cessna Foundation, Inc.
Ong, John Doyle: chairman board, director, Ameritech Corp.
Pike, Robert William: vice president, secretary, Allstate Foundation; senior vice president, secretary, general counsel, director, Allstate Insurance Co.
Rudnick, Alan A.: vice president, general counsel, corporate secretary, CSX Corp.
Tucker, Don Eugene: trustee, Commercial Intertech Foundation

Ohio Business Roundtable

Holland, Willard R.: chairman, chief executive officer, FirstEnergy Corp.
Olesen, Douglas Eugene, PhD: president, chief executive officer, Battelle Memorial Institute

Ohio Chamber of Commerce

Druen, W. Sidney: director, Nationwide Insurance Enterprise Foundation
Olesen, Douglas Eugene, PhD: president, chief executive officer, Battelle Memorial Institute

Ohio Dominican College

Brothers, John Alfred 'Fred': trustee, Ashland Inc. Foundation
Seiffert, Ron J.: vice chairman, Huntington Bancshares Inc.

Ohio Electric Utility Institute

Holland, Willard R.: chairman, chief executive officer, FirstEnergy Corp.

Ohio Governments Education Management Council

Gorman, Joseph T.: chairman, chief executive officer, TRW Inc.

Ohio Historic Society

Ong, John Doyle: chairman board, director, Ameritech Corp.

Ohio Newspaper Association

Block, William, Jr.: president, trustee, Blade Foundation; president, director, Toledo Blade Co.

Ohio School Development Corp.

Wehling, Robert Louis: global marketing, government relations officer, Procter & Gamble Co.; president, trustee, Procter & Gamble Fund

Ohio Society CPA's

Roub, Bryan Roger: trustee, Harris Foundation

Ohio State University

Brothers, John Alfred 'Fred': trustee, Ashland Inc. Foundation

Ohio State University Foundation

Olesen, Douglas Eugene, PhD: president, chief executive officer, Battelle Memorial Institute

Ohio Steel Industry Advisory Commission

Wareham, James Lyman: president, AK Steel Corp.

Ohio Telephone Association

Stonebraker, Barbara J.: executive vice president, Cincinnati Bell Foundation, Inc.; senior vice president, Cincinnati Bell Inc.

Ohio Wesleyan University

Simpson, Louis Allen: president, chief executive officer capital operations, director, GEICO Corp.

Oklahoma Chamber of Commerce

Gaylord, Edward Lewis: chairman, chief executive officer, director, publisher, Oklahoma Publishing Co.; trustee, Oklahoman Foundation (The)

Old Dominion University Education Foundation

Barry, Richard Francis, III: director, Landmark Communications Foundation; vice chairman, Landmark Communications Inc.

Old Newsboys Goodfellow Association

Block, William, Jr.: president, trustee, Blade Foundation; president, director, Toledo Blade Co.

Omaha/Lincoln Society

Arth, Lawrence Joseph: vice president, director, Ameritas Charitable Foundation; chairman, chief executive officer, director, Ameritas Life Insurance Corp.

Omega Psi Phi

Graves, Earl Gilbert: director, Aetna Foundation

Omicron Delta Epsilon

Voet, Paul C.: trustee, Chemed Foundation
Williamson, Henry Gaston, Jr.: chief operating officer, Branch Banking & Trust Co.

Omicron Delta Kappa

Bridgewater, Bernard Adolphus, Jr.: member board control, Brown Shoe Co. Charitable Trust; chairman, president, chief executive officer, director, Brown Shoe Co., Inc.
Burrus, Robert Lewis, Jr.: trustee, Circuit City Foundation
Harrell, Henry Howze: director, Universal Leaf Foundation; chairman, chief executive officer, director, Universal Leaf Tobacco Co., Inc.
Ostergard, Paul Michael: vice president, director corporate contributions, Citibank Corp.; president, Citigroup Foundation
Purvis, George Frank, Jr.: chairman, president, chief executive officer, director, Pan-American Life Insurance Co.
Stephens, Elton Bryson: founder, chairman, Ebsco Industries, Inc.

Ontario Association Professional Engineering

Bertran, David R.: senior vice president manufacturing & logistics, Nalco Chemical Co.; director, Nalco Foundation

Ontario Jobs and Investment Board

Sawchuck, Arthur: chairman, director, Manulife Financial

Opera America

Darling, Robert Edward, Jr.: chairman, Ensign-Bickford Foundation

Operations Research America

Magee, John Francis: chairman, director, Little, Inc. (Arthur D.)

Opportunities Centers America

Coors, Peter Hanson: vice president, director, Coors Brewing Co.

Opportunity Partners

O'Brien, James E.: director, Schoeneckers Foundation

Orchard Park Chamber of Commerce

Penny, Roger Pratt: president, chief operating officer, director, Bethlehem Steel Corp.

Orchestra Association Chicago Symphony Orchestra

Burt, Robert Norcross: chairman, chief executive officer, director, FMC Corp.; director, FMC Foundation

Orchestra Association Chicago Symphony Orhcestra

Martinez, Arthur C.: chairman, chief executive officer, president, Sears, Roebuck and Co.

Orchestral Association

Fuller, Harry Laurance: co-chairman, director, BP Amoco Corp.
Graham, William B.: chairman, director, Baxter Allegiance Foundation; chairman emeritus, Baxter International Inc.

Order Coif

Brown, JoBeth Goode: trustee, Anheuser-Busch Companies, Inc.
Connolly, Gerald Edward: trustee, Reinhart Family Foundation (D. B. and Marjorie)
Hale, James Thomas: senior vice president, general counsel, secretary, Dayton Hudson; trustee, Target Foundation
Hyman, Morton Peter: vice president, director, OSG Foundation; president, director, Overseas Shipholding Group Inc.
Jewell, George Hiram: director, Schlumberger Foundation
Merdek, Andrew Austin: vice president legal affairs, secretary, Cox Enterprises Inc.; secretary, Cox Foundation (James M.)
Neville, James Morton: member board control, Ralston Purina Trust Fund
Owens, Jack Byron: executive vice president, general counsel, Gallo Winery, Inc. (E&J)
Russell, Frank Eli: president, Central Newspapers Foundation; chairman, Central Newspapers, Inc.
Satre, Philip Glen: chairman, president, chief executive officer, director, Promus Hotel Corp.
Sissel, George A.: chairman, president, chief executive officer, director, Ball Corp.

Order Daedalians

Johnson, Hansford Tillman: trustee, USAA Foundation, A Charitable Trust

Order Malta

Lucas, Donald Leo: chairman, Cadence Designs Systems, Inc.

Order Omega
Connor, James Richard: executive director, Kemper Foundation (James S.)

Oregon Bar Association
Bryson, John E.: chairman, chief executive officer, Edison International
Walsh, Michael J.: vice president, CertainTeed Corp.

Oregon Business Council
Cameron, Gerry B.: chairman, director, U.S. Bancorp
Meyer, Jerome J.: chairman, chief executive officer, Tektronix, Inc.

Oregon Industrial College Foundation Inc.
Cameron, Gerry B.: chairman, director, U.S. Bancorp

Organization American Historians
Connor, James Richard: executive director, Kemper Foundation (James S.)

Organization Developmental Network
Heldreth, Nick E.: vice president human resources corporate relations, Harris Corp.

Organization Professional Journalists
Osborne, Burl: president publishing division, director, Belo Corp. (A.H.); president, trustee, Belo Corp. Foundation (A.H.)

Organization Women Leaders
Nakagawa, Jean H.: vice president, director, Servco Foundation

Otterbein College
Schmitt, Wolfgang Rudolph: chairman, chief executive officer, director, Rubbermaid Inc.

Ounce Prevention Fund
Harris, Irving Brooks: chairman executive committee, director, Pittway Corp.; chairman, director, Pittway Corp. Charitable Foundation

Outward Bound Colorado
Coors, Peter Hanson: vice president, director, Coors Brewing Co.

Outward Bound School Hurricane Island
Gorman, Leon A.: president, chief executive officer, Bean, Inc. (L.L.)

Overseas Development Council
Graham, Katharine Meyer: chairman executive committee, director, The Washington Post
Nelson, Merlin Edward: chairman, director, IBJ Foundation

Oxford Law Society
Kampouris, Emmanuel Andrew: chairman, president, chief executive officer, director, American Standard Inc.

PEN
Hotchner, Aaron Edward: vice president, director, executive, Newman's Own Foundation; vice president, treasurer, Newman's Own Inc.

PICPA
Hanway, H. Edward: president, chief executive officer, CIGNA Corp.

PNC Bank National Association
Smoot, Richard Leonard: chairman, PNC Bank

PSA Municipal Securities Division
Civello, Nelson D.: director, Dain Bosworth Foundation

Pace University
Boudreau, Donald L.: vice president, trustee, Chase Manhattan Foundation
Bundschuh, George August William: director, New York Life Foundation
Upbin, Hal Jay: president, chief executive officer, director, Kellwood Co.

Pacific Asian Affairs Council
Nakagawa, Jean H.: vice president, director, Servco Foundation
Wolff, Herbert Eric: secretary, director, First Hawaiian Foundation

Pacific Coast Gas Association
Farman, Richard Donald: chairman, chief executive officer, Pacific Enterprises
Mitchell, Warren I.: president, director, Southern California Gas Co.
Richards, Joel, III: vice president, El Paso Energy Foundation
Wood, Willis B., Jr.: chairman, chief executive officer, director, Pacific Enterprises

Pacific International Center High-Tech Research
Dods, Walter Arthur, Jr.: president, director, First Hawaiian Foundation; chairman, chief executive officer, director, First Hawaiian, Inc.

Pacific Peace Foundation
Dods, Walter Arthur, Jr.: president, director, First Hawaiian Foundation; chairman, chief executive officer, director, First Hawaiian, Inc.

Pacific Rim Bankers Program
Cameron, Gerry B.: chairman, director, U.S. Bancorp

Pacific Rim Finance Center Graduate School Business, University Washington
Stivers, William Charles: senior vice president, chief financial officer, treasurer, Weyerhaeuser Co.; treasurer, trustee, Weyerhaeuser Co. Foundation

Pacific Studies Actuarial Club
Sutton, Thomas C.: chairman, director, Pacific Mutual Charitable Foundation; chairman, chief executive officer, director, Pacific Mutual Life Insurance Co.

Pacific Studies Advisory Board
Coulter, David A.: president, director, Bank of America

Packaging Education Foundation
Ray, John Thomas, Jr.: president, director, Fuller Co. Foundation (H.B.)

Palmetto Business Forum
Coker, Charles Westfield: trustee, Sonoco Foundation; vice president, Sonoco Products Co.

Panasonic Foundation
Ingersoll, Robert Stephen: chairman, director, Panasonic Foundation
Meyerson, Martin: director, Panasonic Foundation

Paper Industry Management Association
Ballengee, Jerry Hunter: president, chief operating officer, director, Union Camp Corp.

Parents As Teachers National Center
Van Cleve, William Moore: member public policy committee, Emerson Charitable Trust; partner, Emerson Electric Co.

Park Cities Baptist Church
Brooks, E. Richard 'Dick': chairman, chief executive officer, director, Central & South West Services

Park School
Taylor, Benjamin B.: director, Boston Globe Foundation

Partnership Drug Free America
Burke, Daniel Barnett: vice president, treasurer, director, ABC Foundation

Patent & Trademark Off
Kurtz, Melvin H.: secretary, director, Chesebrough Foundation

Pee Dee Area County Boy Scouts America
Browning, Peter C.: chief executive officer, president, director, Sonoco Products Co.

Pen Bar Association
Gregg, Walter Emmor, Junior: senior executive vice president finance & administration, PNC Financial Services Group

Pennsylvania Association Savings Institute
Pullo, Robert W.: chairman, chief executive officer, director, York Federal Savings & Loan Association; president, trustee, York Federal Savings & Loan Foundation

Pennsylvania Bar Association
Angelo, Robert A.: president, chief operating officer, York Federal Savings & Loan Association; secretary, York Federal Savings & Loan Foundation
Barnette, Curtis Handley: chairman, chief executive officer, director, Bethlehem Steel Corp.
Dubin, Stephen Victor: vice president, secretary, Farber Foundation
McGuinn, Martin Gregory: chairman, chief executive officer, Mellon Financial Corp.
Newlin, William Rankin: trustee, Kennametal Foundation
Walton, Jon David: trustee, Allegheny Technologies Inc. Charitable Trust
Welty, John Rider: secretary, Carpenter Technology Corp. Foundation

Pennsylvania Business Roundtable
Barnette, Curtis Handley: chairman, chief executive officer, director, Bethlehem Steel Corp.
Kelson, Richard B.: director, Alcoa Foundation
Rohr, James Edward: chief executive officer, president, director, PNC Financial Services Group
Unruh, James Arlen: director, Ameritech Foundation

Pennsylvania Chamber Business & Industry
Barnette, Curtis Handley: chairman, chief executive officer, director, Bethlehem Steel Corp.
McGuinn, Martin Gregory: chairman, chief executive officer, Mellon Financial Corp.
Walton, Jon David: trustee, Allegheny Technologies Inc. Charitable Trust

Pennsylvania Economic League
Kelson, Richard B.: director, Alcoa Foundation

Pennsylvania Electric Association

Hafer, Fred Douglass: chairman, president, chief executive officer, GPU Inc.

Pennsylvania Gas Association

Ackerman, Philip Charles: senior vice president, director, National Fuel Gas Distribution Corp.

Pennsylvania Horse Breeders Association

Mills, Paul D.: trustee, York Federal Savings & Loan Foundation

Pennsylvania Institute CPAs

Gregg, Walter Emmor, Junior: senior executive vice president finance & administration, PNC Financial Services Group

Pennsylvania Self Insurers Association

Welty, John Rider: secretary, Carpenter Technology Corp. Foundation

Pennsylvania Society

Barnette, Curtis Handley: chairman, chief executive officer, director, Bethlehem Steel Corp.

Pennsylvania Southwest Association

Newlin, William Rankin: trustee, Kennametal Foundation

Pension Benefit Guaranty Capital

Cassidy, M. Sharon: assistant secretary, USX Foundation, Inc.

People American Way

Wallach, Ira D.: chairman, Central National-Gottesman; executive vice president, Central National-Gottesman Foundation

Peoples Gas & Light Co.

Terry, Richard Edward: chairman, chief executive officer, director, Peoples Energy Corp.

Peoria Chamber of Commerce

Fites, Donald Vester: director, Caterpillar Foundation

Performance Space 122

McClimon, Timothy J.: executive director, AT&T Foundation

Periodical & Book Association America

Rosenzweig, Richard Stuart: executive vice president, director, Playboy Enterprises Inc.

Pers Roundtable

Kirby, William Joseph: vice president, director, FMC Foundation

Petroleum Accts Society

Nowell, Tommy Lynn: vice president finance, controller, Occidental Oil and Gas; treasurer, Occidental Oil and Gas Foundation

Petroleum Equipment Suppliers Association

Bradford, William Edward: chairman, director, Halliburton Co.

Petroleum Investors Relations Association

Smith, Elizabeth Patience: director, Texaco Foundation; vice president investor relations & shareholder service, Texaco Inc.

Pfeiffer College

Herring, Leonard Gray: vice president, Lowe's Charitable and Educational Foundation

Pharmaceutical Manufacturer Association

Goodes, Melvin Russell: chairman, chief executive officer, director, Ameritech Corp.

Graham, William B.: chairman, director, Baxter Allegiance Foundation; chairman emeritus, Baxter International Inc.

Steere, William Campbell, Jr.: chairman, chief executive officer, director, Pfizer Inc.

Pharmaceutical Research & Manufacturer America

Bogomolny, Robert Lee: director, Searle Charitable Trust; senior vice president, general counsel, secretary, Searle & Co. (G.D.)

Leschly, Jan: chief executive officer, SmithKline Beecham Corp.

Steere, William Campbell, Jr.: chairman, chief executive officer, director, Pfizer Inc.

Pharmaceutical Research & Manufacturer Association America

Kogan, Richard Jay: chairman, chief executive officer, Schering-Plough Corp.; trustee, member, Schering-Plough Foundation

Pharmaceutical Research & Manufacturer Financial for Infectious Diseases

Leschly, Jan: chief executive officer, SmithKline Beecham Corp.

Pharmacy Research Manufacturer America

Levinson, Arthur David: president, chief executive officer, director, Genentech Inc.

Phi Alpha Delta

Bridgewater, Bernard Adolphus, Jr.: member board control, Brown Shoe Co. Charitable Trust; chairman, president, chief executive officer, director, Brown Shoe Co., Inc.

Smith, Donald Kaye: senior vice president, general counsel, director, GEICO Corp.

Stephens, Elton Bryson: founder, chairman, Ebsco Industries, Inc.

Welty, John Rider: secretary, Carpenter Technology Corp. Foundation

Phi Alpha Theta

Barnette, Curtis Handley: chairman, chief executive officer, director, Bethlehem Steel Corp.

Connor, James Richard: executive director, Kemper Foundation (James S.)

Ong, John Doyle: chairman board, director, Ameritech Corp.

Voet, Paul C.: trustee, Chemed Foundation

Phi Beta Kappa

Alberts, Bruce Michael, PhD: director, Genentech Foundation for Biomedical Sciences

Barnette, Curtis Handley: chairman, chief executive officer, director, Bethlehem Steel Corp.

Bowen, William Gordon, PhD: trustee, Merck Co. Foundation

Brademas, John: chairman, Texaco Foundation

Brinegar, Claude Stout: trustee, Unocal Foundation

Brooks, Roger Kay: chairman, AmerUS Group

Bryson, John E.: chairman, chief executive officer, Edison International

Connor, James Richard: executive director, Kemper Foundation (James S.)

Connor, Walter Robert: director, Glaxo Wellcome Foundation

Esrey, William Todd: chairman, chief executive officer, Sprint Corp.

Graham, Patricia Albjerg, PhD: trustee, Hitachi Foundation

Graham, William B.: chairman, director, Baxter Allegiance Foundation; chairman emeritus, Baxter International Inc.

Haas, Robert Douglas: chairman, chief executive officer, director, Levi Strauss & Co.; president, Levi Strauss Foundation

Hale, James Thomas: senior vice president, general counsel, secretary, Dayton Hudson; trustee, Target Foundation

Harad, George Jay: chairman, chief executive officer, director, Boise Cascade Corp.

Hardis, Stephen Roger: chairman, chief executive officer, director, Eaton Corp.

Harrell, Henry Howze: director, Universal Leaf Foundation; chairman, chief executive officer, director, Universal Leaf Tobacco Co., Inc.

Hefner, Christie Ann: chairman, chief executive officer, Playboy Enterprises Inc.; director, Playboy Foundation

Heineman, Benjamin Walter, Jr.: director, GE Fund

Herringer, Frank Casper: president, chief executive officer, director, chairman, Transamerica Corp.; vice chairman, director, Transamerica Foundation

Hudnut, Stewart Skinner: director, Illinois Tool Works Foundation

Jewell, George Hiram: director, Schlumberger Foundation

Kasputys, Joseph Edward: chairman, trustee, Hitachi Foundation

Kissinger, Henry Alfred: director, CBS Foundation

Lemberg, Thomas Michael: clerk, Lotus Development Corp.; secretary, Polaroid Foundation

Lyall, Katharine Culbert: trustee, Kemper Foundation (James S.)

Magee, John Francis: chairman, director, Little, Inc. (Arthur D.)

Matheny, Edward Taylor, Junior: director, Block Foundation (H&R)

Merdek, Andrew Austin: vice president legal affairs, secretary, Cox Enterprises Inc.; secretary, Cox Foundation (James M.)

Meyerson, Martin: director, Panasonic Foundation

Miller, Joseph Irwin: director associate, Cummins Engine Co., Inc.; director, Cummins Engine Foundation

Nelson, Merlin Edward: chairman, director, IBJ Foundation

Ong, John Doyle: chairman board, director, Ameritech Corp.

Ostergard, Paul Michael: vice president, director corporate contributions, Citibank Corp.; president, Citigroup Foundation

Owens, Jack Byron: executive vice president, general counsel, Gallo Winery, Inc. (E&J)

Robinson, E. B., Jr.: chairman, chief executive officer, director, Deposit Guaranty National Bank

Rosenthal, Sol: counsel, Playboy Enterprises Inc.

Rosett, Richard Nathaniel: trustee, Kemper Foundation (James S.)

Shaw, L. Edward, Jr.: general counsel, Aetna, Inc.; trustee, Chase Manhattan Foundation

Simmons, Harold Clark: chairman, director, Simmons Foundation, Inc. (Harold)

Stanley, Peter William: trustee, Hitachi Foundation

Strickland, Robert Louis: vice president, Lowe's Charitable and Educational Foundation

Toll, Daniel Roger: trustee, Kemper Foundation (James S.)

Voet, Paul C.: trustee, Chemed Foundation

Wander, Herbert S.: secretary, director, Katten, Muchin & Zavis Foundation

Wehling, Robert Louis: global marketing, government relations officer, Procter & Gamble Co.; president, trustee, Procter & Gamble Fund

Phi Delta Kappa

Connor, James Richard: executive director, Kemper Foundation (James S.)

Davis, Carolyne Kahle, PhD: trustee, Merck Co. Foundation

Sease, Gene Elwood: director, Central Newspapers Foundation

Phi Delta Phi

Barnette, Curtis Handley: chairman, chief executive officer, director, Bethlehem Steel Corp.

Graham, William B.: chairman, director, Baxter Allegiance Foundation; chairman emeritus, Baxter International Inc.

Hewitt, James Watt: vice president, treasurer, Abel Foundation

Jewell, George Hiram: director, Schlumberger Foundation

Neville, James Morton: member board control, Ralston Purina Trust Fund

Purvis, George Frank, Jr.: chairman, president, chief executive officer, director, Pan-American Life Insurance Co.

Russell, Frank Eli: president, Central Newspapers Foundation; chairman, Central Newspapers, Inc.

Phi Delta Theta

Stauffer, John H.: trustee, Stauffer Communications Foundation

Stauffer, Stanley Howard: chairman, Stauffer Communications Foundation

Phi Eta Sigma

Connor, James Richard: executive director, Kemper Foundation (James S.)

Hodgson, Thomas Richard: president, chief operating officer, director, Abbott Laboratories

Randolph, Jackson Harold: chairman, Cinergy Corp.; chairman, director, Cinergy Foundation

Voet, Paul C.: trustee, Chemed Foundation

Phi Kappa Phi

Brothers, John Alfred 'Fred': trustee, Ashland Inc. Foundation

Connor, James Richard: executive director, Kemper Foundation (James S.)

Davis, Ruth Margaret: trustee, Air Products Foundation

Gardner, James Richard: vice president, Pfizer Foundation

Hemminghaus, Roger Roy: chairman, director, Ultramar Diamond Shamrock Corp.

Hill, George Richard: president, trustee, Lubrizol Foundation (The)

Hyman, Morton Peter: vice president, director, OSG Foundation; president, director, Overseas Shipholding Group Inc.

Satre, Philip Glen: chairman, president, chief executive officer, director, Promus Hotel Corp.

Wolff, Herbert Eric: secretary, director, First Hawaiian Foundation

Phi Kappa Psi

Magee, John Francis: chairman, director, Little, Inc. (Arthur D.)

Phi Lambda Upsilon

Hemminghaus, Roger Roy: chairman, director, Ultramar Diamond Shamrock Corp.

Phil High School Academy

Wilson, James Lawrence: chairman, chief executive officer, director, Rohm & Haas Co.

Philadelphia Bar Association

Dubin, Stephen Victor: vice president, secretary, Farber Foundation

Philadelphia Council on World Affairs

Hilyard, James E.: president, CertainTeed Corp.; director, CertainTeed Corp. Foundation

Philadelphia Liberty Medal

Meyerson, Martin: director, Panasonic Foundation

Philadelphia Museum Art

Naples, Ronald James: president, chief executive officer, director, Quaker Chemical Corp.

Resnick, Lynda Rae: vice chairman, co-owner, Franklin Mint (The)

Philadelphia Orchestra Association

Smoot, Richard Leonard: chairman, PNC Bank

Thompson, Sheldon Lee: senior vice president, chief administrative officer, Sunoco Inc.

Philanthropic Adv SVC

Feldhouse, Lynn Alexandra: vice president, secretary, DaimlerChrysler Corp. Fund

Phillip Exeter Academy

Ottaway, James Haller, Jr.: senior vice president, director, Dow Jones & Co., Inc.; member advisory committee, Dow Jones Foundation

Phoenix Body Positive

Bame, Tracy L.: manager community affairs, Phelps Dodge Foundation

Phoenix House Foundation Inc.

Heimbold, Charles Andreas, Jr.: chairman, president, chief executive officer, Bristol-Myers Squibb Co.

Pi Alpha Delta

Matthews, Clark J., II: president, chief executive officer, director, 7-Eleven, Inc.

Pi Gamma Mu

Pate, James Leonard: chairman, chief executive officer, director, Pennzoil-Quaker State Co.

Pi Kappa Alpha

Strickland, Robert Louis: vice president, Lowe's Charitable and Educational Foundation

Pi Tau Sigma

Hatsopoulos, George Nicholas: founder, chairman, chief executive officer, director, Thermo Electron Corp.; committee member, Thermo Electron Foundation

Kaman, Charles Huron: chairman, president, chief executive officer, director, Kaman Corp.

Urkowitz, Michael: senior vice president, Chase Manhattan Bank, NA; trustee, Chase Manhattan Foundation

Pierpont Morgan Library

Warner, Douglas Alexander, III: chairman, president, chief executive officer, director, Morgan & Co. Inc. (J.P.)

Pilchuck School

Buechner, Thomas Scharman: trustee, Corning Inc. Foundation

Pine Tree County Boy Scouts

Gorman, Leon A.: president, chief executive officer, Bean, Inc. (L.L.)

Pittsburgh Ballet Theatre

Pollock, E. Kears: director, PPG Industries Foundation; executive vice president, PPG Industries, Inc.

Pittsburgh Childrens Museum

Peconi, Maurice V.: member screening committee, PPG Industries Foundation

Pittsburgh High Technology Council

Newlin, William Rankin: trustee, Kennametal Foundation

Pittsburgh Symphony Society

Wehmeier, Helge H.: president, chief executive officer, director, Bayer Corp.

Pittsburgh Theological Seminary

McClelland, William Craig: trustee, Union Camp Charitable Trust; chairman, chief executive officer, director, Union Camp Corp.

Pittsburgh Youth Golf Foundation

Walton, Jon David: trustee, Allegheny Technologies Inc. Charitable Trust

Pittsburgh Zoo

Leggett, Richard B.: member screening committee, PPG Industries Foundation

Planning Executives Institute

Nakagawa, Jean H.: vice president, director, Servco Foundation

Planning Forum

Bezik, Cynthia B.: senior vice president, finance, Cleveland-Cliffs, Inc.

Cushwa, William Wallace: director, Commercial Intertech Corp.; trustee, Commercial Intertech Foundation

Gardner, James Richard: vice president, Pfizer Foundation

Ruelle, Mark A.: senior vice president, chief financial officer, Sierra Pacific Resources

Playhouse Square Foundation

DiGirolamo, Vincent A.: executive vice president, vice chairman, National City Bank of Cleveland

Hardis, Stephen Roger: chairman, chief executive officer, director, Eaton Corp.

Poly University

Matthews, Craig Gerard: president, chief operating officer, Brooklyn Union

Polytech University

Martinez, Arthur C.: chairman, chief executive officer, president, Sears, Roebuck and Co.

Pomona College

Neal, Philip Mark: president, chief executive officer, director, Avery Dennison Corp.

Port New Orleans

Purvis, George Frank, Jr.: chairman, president, chief executive officer, director, Pan-American Life Insurance Co.

Portland Chamber of Commerce

Walsh, Michael J.: vice president, CertainTeed Corp.

Practicing Law Institute

Karmel, Roberta S.: trustee, Kemper Foundation (James S.); partner, Kemper National Insurance Companies

Prairie School

Johnson, Samuel Curtis: chairman, director, president, Johnson & Son (S.C.); chairman, trustee, Johnson Wax Fund (S.C.)

Prep for Prep

Lipton, Martin: partner, Wachtell, Lipton, Rosen & Katz; president,

Wachtell, Lipton, Rosen & Katz Foundation

Presbytarian Hospital
Burke, Daniel Barnett: vice president, treasurer, director, ABC Foundation

Presbyterian Healthcare Center North
Oesterreicher, James E.: chairman, chief executive officer, director, Penney Co., Inc. (J.C.)

Presbyterian Hospital Foundation
Browning, Peter C.: chief executive officer, president, director, Sonoco Products Co.

Presbyterian Hospital Plano
Oesterreicher, James E.: chairman, chief executive officer, director, Penney Co., Inc. (J.C.)

President Advisory Committee Trade Policy & Negotiations
Eaton, Robert James: co-chairman, president, chief executive officer, DaimlerChrysler Corp.

Golub, Harvey: chairman, chief executive officer, director, American Express Co.; trustee, American Express Foundation

President Association
Gloyd, Lawrence Eugene: trustee, CLARCOR Foundation; chairman, chief executive officer, director, CLARCOR Inc.

President Association Advertising Council New York
Standen, Craig Clayton: senior vice president corporate development, Scripps Co. (E.W.)

President Commission Small & Minority Business
Graves, Earl Gilbert: director, Aetna Foundation

President Commission White House Fellows
Naples, Ronald James: president, chief executive officer, director, Quaker Chemical Corp.

President Commission White House Fellowships West Point Society
Mead, Dana George: chairman, chief executive officer, director, Tenneco Automotive

President Committee Arts & Humanities
Bryan, John Henry: chairman, Sara Lee Corp.; director, Sara Lee Foundation

Golub, Harvey: chairman, chief executive officer, director, American Express Co.; trustee, American Express Foundation

Marron, Donald Baird: chairman, chief executive officer, director, Paine Webber; trustee, Paine Webber Foundation

President National Security Telecommunications Advisory Committee
Lee, Charles Robert: chairman, chief executive officer, director, GTE Corp.; chief executive officer, trustee, GTE Foundation

Unruh, James Arlen: director, Ameritech Foundation

President Private Sector Survey Cost Control
Hutton, Edward L.: chairman, chief executive officer, director, Chemed Corp.

President's Circle
Rosenzweig, Richard Stuart: executive vice president, director, Playboy Enterprises Inc.

President's Export Council
Armstrong, C. Michael: chairman, chief executive officer, AT&T Corp.

Gorman, Joseph T.: chairman, chief executive officer, TRW Inc.

Mullin, Leo Francis: chairman, president, chief executive officer, Delta Air Lines, Inc.

Presidents Interchange Executive Alumni Association
Beach, Roger C.: chairman, chief executive officer, director, Unocal Corp.

Presidents Leadership Committee, University Colorado
Coors, Peter Hanson: vice president, director, Coors Brewing Co.

Press Association
Hall, Larry D.: chairman, president, chief executive officer, director, Kinder Morgn; president, director, KN Energy Foundation

Primus Capital Fund
Mixon, A. Malachi, III: chairman, chief executive officer, Invacare Corp.; trustee, Invacare Foundation

Prince Wales Business Leaders Forum
DeSimone, Livio Diego: chairman, chief executive officer, Minnesota Mining & Manufacturing Co.

Gorman, Joseph T.: chairman, chief executive officer, TRW Inc.

Princeton
Greenwald, Gerald: chairman, chief executive officer, director, United Airlines Inc.

Princeton Medical Center
Heisen, JoAnn Heffernan: vice president, chief information officer, Johnson & Johnson; treasurer, Johnson & Johnson Family of Companies Contribution Fund

Princeton University
Maritz, William Edward: chairman, chief executive officer, president, Maritz Inc.

Princeton University Art Museum
Forbes, Christopher 'Kip': vice president, Forbes Foundation; vice chairman, corporate secretary, director, Forbes Inc.

Princeton University Center International Studies
Gardner, James Richard: vice president, Pfizer Foundation

Princeton University Department Mechanical & Aerospace Engineering
Condit, Philip Murray: chairman, chief executive officer, director, Boeing Co.

Princeton University School Engineering & Applied Science
Burt, Robert Norcross: chairman, chief executive officer, director, FMC Corp.; director, FMC Foundation

Priority Health
Ozark, Edward L.: trustee, JSJ Foundation

Private Export Funding Corp.
Rhodes, William Reginald: vice chairman, Citibank Corp.

Private Industry Council
Shepherd, Kathleen Shearen Maynard: director, Tribune New York Foundation

Private Sector Councils
Smith, Raymond W.: chairman, chief executive officer, director, Bell Atlantic Corp.

Private Sector Councils CFPs
Kelson, Richard B.: director, Alcoa Foundation

Proctor's Theater
Golub, Lewis: chairman, chief executive officer, director, Golub Corp.

Professional Examination Service
Christopher, Stephen: president, chief operating officer, Security Life of Denver Insurance Co.

Project Encor
Klinedinst, Thomas John, Jr.: trustee, Star Bank NA, Cincinnati Foundation

Project Hope
Clemente, Constantine Louis: chairman, Pfizer Foundation; executive vice president corporate affairs, secretary, corporate counsel, Pfizer Inc.

Gilmartin, Raymond V.: chairman, president, chief executive officer, Merck & Co.; chairman, Merck Co. Foundation

Project Orbis International
Carter, Marshall Nichols: chairman, chief executive officer, State Street Bank & Trust Co.

Project Pride Living
Goddu, Roger V.: chairman, chief executive officer, director, Montgomery Ward & Co., Inc.

Project Shelter Pro-Am
Raymond, Lee R.: chairman, president, chief executive officer, Exxon Mobil Corp.

Project Smart School
Grasso, Richard A.: chairman, chief executive officer, New York Stock Exchange, Inc.

Proprietary Association
Goodes, Melvin Russell: chairman, chief executive officer, director, Ameritech Corp.

Prospect Park Alliance
Matthews, Craig Gerard: president, chief operating officer, Brooklyn Union

Psi Upsilon
Neville, James Morton: member board control, Ralston Purina Trust Fund

Public Affairs Council
Campbell, George Leroy: vice president public affairs, Florida Power Corp.

Gould, John T., Jr.: vice president, Unilever Foundation; director corporate affairs, Unilever United States, Inc.

Landin, Thomas Milton: vice president, director, CertainTeed Corp.; vice president, Norton Co. Foundation

Rosenzweig, Richard Stuart: executive vice president, director, Playboy Enterprises Inc.

Public Affairs Research Council Alabama

Harris, Elmer Beseler: president, chief executive officer, director, Alabama Power Co.

Public Comm Task Force

Haddock, Ronald Wayne: president, chief executive officer, director, FINA; president, FINA Foundation

Public Relations Seminar

Hobor, Nancy A.: vice president communications & investor relations, Morton International Inc.

Parisi, Franklin Joseph: chairman, Star Tribune Foundation

Public Relations Seminars New York

Wiksten, Barry Frank: president, CIGNA Foundation

Public Relations Society America

Barrett, Allen M., Jr.: chairman, McCormick & Co. Inc.

Carey, Kathryn Ann: foundation manager, American Honda Foundation

Connolly, Charles H.: senior vice president corporate affairs & investor relations, Whitman Corp.; president, Whitman Corp. Foundation

Cooper, Janis Campbell: vice president, Maytag Corp. Foundation

Coulter, Patrick C. G.: president, Bell Atlantic Foundation; senior vice president corporate communications, Gulfstream Aerospace Corp.

Dabney, Fred E., II: executive director, Royal & SunAlliance Insurance Foundation, Inc.; vice president corporate communications, Royal & SunAlliance USA, Inc.

Gorman, Maureen V.: vice president, GTE Foundation

Gould, John T., Jr.: vice president, Unilever Foundation; director corporate affairs, Unilever United States, Inc.

Liebler, Arthur C.: vice president communications, DaimlerChrysler Corp.; trustee, DaimlerChrysler Corp. Fund

Scher, Barry F.: vice president public affairs, Giant Food Inc.

Simpson, Andrea Lynn: president

Townsend, David L.: vice president administration, Walter Industries Inc.

Public Securities Association

Civello, Nelson D.: director, Dain Bosworth Foundation

Public Service Sta KCET-TV

Farman, Richard Donald: chairman, chief executive officer, Pacific Enterprises

Public Utility Report Inc.

Matthews, Craig Gerard: president, chief operating officer, Brooklyn Union

Public Utility Reports Inc.

Kennedy, Bernard Joseph: chairman, president, chief executive officer, director, National Fuel Gas Distribution Corp.

Pulp and Paper Industry

Olson, Richard E.: chairman, chief executive officer, director, Champion International Corp.

Punahou School

Dods, Walter Arthur, Jr.: president, director, First Hawaiian Foundation; chairman, chief executive officer, director, First Hawaiian, Inc.

Purdue University

Hodgson, Thomas Richard: president, chief operating officer, director, Abbott Laboratories

Koch, Robert Louis, II: president, chief executive officer, director, Koch Enterprises, Inc.; president, director, Koch Foundation

Sales, A. R.: director, Arvin Foundation; treasurer, Arvin Industries, Inc.

Purdue University Engineering

Engibous, Thomas James: director, Texas Instruments Foundation; president, chief executive officer, chairman, director, Texas Instruments Inc.

Queen Elizabeth Hospital Foundation

McNally, Alan G.: chairman, chief executive officer, Harris Trust & Savings Bank

Queens College

Barad, Jill Elikann: director, Mattel Foundation; chairman, chief executive officer, director, Mattel Inc.

Queens University

Carty, Donald J.: vice president, treasurer, AMR/American Airlines Foundation; president, chairman, chief executive officer, director, AMR Corp.

Goodes, Melvin Russell: chairman, chief executive officer, director, Ameritech Corp.

RF Boyd Medicine Society

Elam, Lloyd Charles, MD: trustee, Merck Co. Foundation

Radcliffe College

Taylor, Benjamin B.: director, Boston Globe Foundation

Ramsey County Ice Arena Committee

Hubbard, Stanley S.: chairman, president, chief executive officer, Hubbard Broadcasting, Inc.; president, Hubbard Foundation

Raymond Clapper Foundation

Thomasson, Dan King: vice president, trustee, Scripps Howard Foundation

Read for Literacy

Block, William, Jr.: president, trustee, Blade Foundation; president, director, Toledo Blade Co.

Reading Hospital & Medical Center

Cardy, Robert Willard: chairman, president, chief executive officer, director, Carpenter Technology Corp.; president, Carpenter Technology Corp. Foundation

Hafer, Fred Douglass: chairman, president, chief executive officer, GPU Inc.

Real Estate Board New York

Geissinger, Frederick Wallace: chairman, chief executive officer, president, director, American General Finance Foundation

Recordings for Blind

Heisen, JoAnn Heffernan: vice president, chief information officer, Johnson & Johnson; treasurer, Johnson & Johnson Family of Companies Contribution Fund

Recreation Unlimited

Glaser, Gary A.: president, chief executive officer, National City Bank of Columbus

Recreational Vehicle Industry Association

Skinner, Claire Corson: chairman, chief executive officer, Coachmen Industries, Inc.

Region 2020 Inc.

Jones, D. Paul, Jr.: chairman, chief executive officer, Compass Bank; trustee, Compass Bank Foundation

Regional Airport Authority Louisville & Jefferson County

Hower, Frank Beard, Jr.: vice chairman, Anthem Foundation, Inc.

Regional Commerce & Growth Association

Mueller, Charles William: chairman, president, chief executive officer, Ameren Corp.; trustee, Ameren Corp. Charitable Trust

Regional Commerce Growth Association

Maritz, William Edward: chairman, chief executive officer, president, Maritz Inc.

Regional Performing Arts Center

Haskin, Donald Lee: vice president, PNC Bank

Regional Plan Association

Matthews, Craig Gerard: president, chief operating officer, Brooklyn Union

Schiro, James J.: chairman, senior partner, PricewaterhouseCoopers

Regis Accounting Advisory Committee

Kelly, Richard C.: executive vice president, chief financial officer, New Century Energies; treasurer, New Century Energies Foundation

Registered Professional Engineers

Joos, David W.: president, chief executive officer electric, executive vice president, Consumers Energy Co.

Regulatory Affairs Council

Stroup, Stanley Stephenson: executive vice president, general counsel, Norwest Corp.

Rehabilitation Hospital Pacific

Dods, Walter Arthur, Jr.: president, director, First Hawaiian Foundation; chairman, chief executive officer, director, First Hawaiian, Inc.

Rehabilitation Institute

Jarman, Richard Sinclair: executive vice president, Butler Manufacturing Co.; trustee, Butler Manufacturing Co. Foundation

Rehabilitation Institute Chicago

Burt, Robert Norcross: chairman, chief executive officer, director, FMC Corp.; director, FMC Foundation

Rensselaer Alumni Association

DiCamillo, Gary Thomas: chairman, chief executive officer, director, Polaroid Corp.

Republic National Lawyers Association

Smith, Donald Kaye: senior vice president, general counsel, director, GEICO Corp.

Republican Leadership Council

Rupley, Theodore J.: president, chief executive officer, director, Allmerica Financial Corp.

Republican Senatorial Inner Circle

Strickland, Robert Louis: vice president, Lowe's Charitable and Educational Foundation

Research Board

Lawson, John K.: senior vice president, Deere & Co.; director, Deere Foundation (John)

Research Mental Health Foundation

Margolin, Abraham E.: director, Tension Envelope Foundation

Reserve Officers Association

Calise, Nicholas James: vice president, associate general counsel, secretary, BFGoodrich Co.; secretary, Goodrich Foundation, Inc. (B.F.)

Rhodes College

Blount, Winton Malcolm, Jr.: chairman, Blount International, Inc.

Rice University

Pate, James Leonard: chairman, chief executive officer, director, Pennzoil-Quaker State Co.

Rich Foundation

Rich, David A.: executive director, Rich Family Foundation; vice president, secretary, director, Rich Products Corp.

Richmond Bar Association

Burrus, Robert Lewis, Jr.: trustee, Circuit City Foundation

White, James M., III: general counsel, Universal Leaf Foundation; senior vice president, general counsel, assistant secretary, Universal Leaf Tobacco Co., Inc.

Richmond Chamber of Commerce

Lewis, Frances Aaronson: trustee, Circuit City Foundation

Richmond Childrens Museum

Burrus, Robert Lewis, Jr.: trustee, Circuit City Foundation

Richmond Management Roundtable

Sheehan, Jeremiah J.: chairman, director, Reynolds Metals Co. Foundation

Richmond Public School Board

Lewis, Frances Aaronson: trustee, Circuit City Foundation

Richmond Renaissance Inc.

Tilghman, Richard Granville: chairman, chief executive officer, Crestar Foundation

Risk & Insurance Management Society

Ozark, Edward L.: trustee, JSJ Foundation

Riverdale Country School

Paton, Leland B.: president capital marketings, director, member executive committee, Prudential Securities Inc.

Riverside Hospital Foundation

Olesen, Douglas Eugene, PhD: president, chief executive officer, Battelle Memorial Institute

Roanoke Bar Association

Goode, David Ronald: chairman, president, chief executive officer, director, Norfolk Southern Corp.

Robert Morris Associates

Hower, Frank Beard, Jr.: vice chairman, Anthem Foundation, Inc.

Murphy, Christopher J., III: president, chief executive officer, director, First Source Corp.; director, First Source Foundation

Robert Morris College

LeBoeuf, Raymond W.: director, PPG Industries Foundation; director, chairman, chief executive officer, PPG Industries, Inc.

Mueller, Gerd Dieter: executive vice president, chief financial officer, director, chief administrative officer, Bayer Corp.; president, Bayer Foundation

Robert W. Woodruff Arts Center

Correll, Alston Dayton 'Pete', Jr.: chairman, president, chief executive officer, director, Georgia-Pacific Corp.; director, Georgia-Pacific Foundation

Mullin, Leo Francis: chairman, president, chief executive officer, Delta Air Lines, Inc.

Robert Wood Johnson University Hospital

Fine, Roger Seth: vice president, general counsel, Johnson & Johnson; president, Johnson & Johnson Family of Companies Contribution Fund

Rochester New York Philharmonic Orchestra

Rand, Addison Barry: executive vice president operations, Xerox Corp.; trustee, Xerox Foundation

Rockefeller Archives Center

Furlaud, Richard Mortimer: interim chief executive officer, International Flavors & Fragrances Inc.

Rockefeller University

O'Reilly, F. Anthony John: chairman, trustee, Heinz Co. Foundation (H.J.); chairman, director, Heinz Co. (H.J.)

Whitehead, John Cunningham: chairman board, Goldman Sachs Foundation

Rockford Chamber of Commerce

Meuleman, Robert Joseph: director, AMCORE Foundation

Rockwell Museum

Buechner, Thomas Scharman: trustee, Corning Inc. Foundation

Peck, Arthur John, Jr.: secretary, vice president, Corning Inc.; secretary, Corning Inc. Foundation

Rocky Mountain Oil & Gas Association

True, Jean Durland: trustee, True Foundation; partner, True Oil Co.

Rollins College

Ackerman, F. Duane: president, chief executive officer, BellSouth Corp.

Ronald McDonald House Idaho

Graves, Ronald Norman: secretary, Simplot Foundation (J.R.)

Ronald Reagan Presidential Library

Binder, Gordon M.: chairman, chief executive officer, director, Amgen, Inc.

Roosevelt University

Gidwitz, Gerald S.: chairman, Curtis Industries, Inc. (Helene)

Kirby, William Joseph: vice president, director, FMC Foundation

Rose-Hulman Institute Technology

Holland, Willard R.: chairman, chief executive officer, FirstEnergy Corp.

Rotary International

Cosse, Steven Anthony: senior vice president, general counsel, Murphy Oil Corp.

Cushwa, Charles Benton, III: trustee, Commercial Intertech Foundation

DeLoach, Harris E., Junior: executive vice president, director, Sonoco Products Co.

Helton, Bill D.: chairman, New Century Energies Foundation

Hultgren, Dennis N.: director, Appleton Papers Inc.

Kramer, Mary Elizabeth: vice president, Wellmark Foundation

Nicholas, Jon O.: vice president, trustee, Maytag Corp. Foundation

Omachinski, David L.: chief financial officer, treasurer, vice president, Oshkosh B'Gosh, Inc.

Rich, David A.: executive director, Rich Family Foundation; vice president, secretary, director, Rich Products Corp.

Round Table

Haddock, Ronald Wayne: president, chief executive officer, director, FINA; president, FINA Foundation

Royal Aeronautical Society

Condit, Philip Murray: chairman, chief executive officer, director, Boeing Co.

Kaman, Charles Huron: chairman, president, chief executive officer, director, Kaman Corp.

Royal Economic Society

Pate, James Leonard: chairman, chief executive officer, director, Pennzoil-Quaker State Co.

Royal Institute British Architects

Miller, Joseph Irwin: director associate, Cummins Engine Co., Inc.; director, Cummins Engine Foundation

Royal Society Arts

Bijur, Peter I.: chairman, chief executive officer, Texaco Inc.

Meyerson, Martin: director, Panasonic Foundation

O'Reilly, F. Anthony John: chairman, trustee, Heinz Co. Foundation (H.J.); chairman, director, Heinz Co. (H.J.)

Royal Swedish Academy Engineering Science

Swanson, Robert A.: director, Genentech Foundation for Biomedical Sciences

Royal Television Society London

Hubbard, Stanley S.: chairman, president, chief executive officer, Hubbard Broadcasting, Inc.; president, Hubbard Foundation

Rubber Manufacturer Association

Ong, John Doyle: chairman board, director, Ameritech Corp.

Rush-Presbyterian-Saint Lukes Medical Center

Bryan, John Henry: chairman, Sara Lee Corp.; director, Sara Lee Foundation

Hefner, Christie Ann: chairman, chief executive officer, Playboy Enterprises Inc.; director, Playboy Foundation

Hodgson, Thomas Richard: president, chief operating officer, director, Abbott Laboratories

Ryan, Patrick G.: chairman, president, chief executive officer, Aon Corp.; president, Aon Foundation

Stewart, S. Jay: chairman, chief executive officer, director, Morton International Inc.

Russell Sage College

Golub, Lewis: chairman, chief executive officer, director, Golub Corp.

S Broward Jewish Federation

Mandel, Jack N.: director, Premier Industrial Corp.

S.S. Huebner Foundation Insurance Education

Purvis, George Frank, Jr.: chairman, president, chief executive officer, director, Pan-American Life Insurance Co.

SBC Community Inc.

Busch, August Adolphus, III: chairman, president, chief executive officer, Anheuser-Busch Companies, Inc.

Sabriyas Castle Fun Foundation

Armstrong, C. Michael: chairman, chief executive officer, AT&T Corp.

Saint Alphonsus Regional Medical Center

Marshall, Joseph W.: chairman, chief executive officer, Idaho Power Co.

Saint Barnabas Medical Center

Kogan, Richard Jay: chairman, chief executive officer, Schering-Plough Corp.; trustee, member, Schering-Plough Foundation

Saint Croix Valley Youth Center

Hubbard, Stanley S.: chairman, president, chief executive officer, Hubbard Broadcasting, Inc.; president, Hubbard Foundation

Saint Edward High School

O'Brien, John F.: trustee, McDonald & Co. Securities Foundation

Saint Elizabeth College

Painter, Alan Sproul: vice president, executive director, AlliedSignal Foundation Inc.

Saint Francis Community Hospital

Stivers, William Charles: senior vice president, chief financial officer, treasurer, Weyerhaeuser Co.; treasurer, trustee, Weyerhaeuser Co. Foundation

Saint Francis Hospital

Choate, Jerry D.: chairman, chief executive officer, director, Allstate Foundation

Sease, Gene Elwood: director, Central Newspapers Foundation

Saint Francis Hospital Medical Center

Fiondella, Robert William: chairman, president, chief executive officer, Phoenix Home Life Mutual Insurance Co.

Saint Johns Health Center

Ferry, Richard Michael: chairman, Pacific Mutual Life Insurance Co.

Saint Joseph County Bar Association

Murphy, Christopher J., III: president, chief executive officer, director, First Source Corp.; director, First Source Foundation

Saint Joseph Hospital Foundation

Tuerff, James R.: president, director, American General Finance

Saint Joseph Infant Maternity Home

LaMacchia, John Thomas: trustee, Cincinnati Bell Foundation, Inc.; president, chief executive officer, director, Cincinnati Bell Inc.

Saint Joseph Medical Center

Disney, Roy Edward: trustee, Disney Co. Foundation (Walt); vice chairman, director, Disney Co. (Walt)

Saint Josephs College

Tuerff, James R.: president, director, American General Finance

Saint Katherines-Saint Marks School

Becherer, Hans Walter: chairman, chief executive officer, director, Deere & Co.; director, Deere Foundation (John)

Saint Louis Bar Association

Neville, James Morton: member board control, Ralston Purina Trust Fund

Saint Louis Boy Scouts America

Busch, August Adolphus, III: chairman, president, chief executive officer, Anheuser-Busch Companies, Inc.

Saint Louis Childrens Hospital

Mueller, Charles William: chairman, president, chief executive officer, Ameren Corp.; trustee, Ameren Corp. Charitable Trust

Van Cleve, William Moore: member public policy committee, Emerson Charitable Trust; partner, Emerson Electric Co.

Saint Louis County Bar Association

Van Cleve, William Moore: member public policy committee, Emerson Charitable Trust; partner, Emerson Electric Co.

Saint Louis Regional Conv Sports Complex Authority

Carr, Cassandra Colvin: director, SBC Foundation

Saint Louis Roundtable

Moten, John, Junior: vice president community relations, Laclede Gas Co.

Saint Louis Science Center

Loeb, Jerome Thomas: chairman, director, May Department Stores Co.; president, director, May Department Stores Computer Foundation (The)

Suter, Albert E.: senior vice chairman, chief administrative officer, director, Emerson Electric Co.

Van Cleve, William Moore: member public policy committee, Emerson Charitable Trust; partner, Emerson Electric Co.

Saint Louis Symphony Orchestra

Kemper, David Woods: chairman, president, chief executive officer, director, Commerce Bancshares, Inc.

Saint Louis Symphony Society

Bachmann, John W.: managing partner, Jones & Co. (Edward D.); chairman, Jones & Co. Foundation (Edward D.)

Jacobsen, Thomas Herbert: chairman, president, chief executive officer, Mercantile Bank NA

Saint Louis University

McKenna, William John: director, chairman, Kellwood Co.; chairman, president, director, Kellwood Foundation

Pulitzer, Michael Edgar: chairman, president, chief executive officer, director, Pulitzer Publishing Co.; chairman, president, chief executive officer, Pulitzer Publishing Co. Foundation

Saint Louis Zoo Friends

Brown, JoBeth Goode: trustee, Anheuser-Busch Companies, Inc.

Saint Luke's Medical Center

Bauer, Chris Michael: president, Firstar Milwaukee Foundation

Bechtold, Ned W.: director, Firstar Milwaukee Foundation

Saint Lukes Foundation

Bloch, Henry Wollman: chairman, Block Foundation (H&R); chairman, director, Block, Inc. (H&R)

Saint Lukes Hospital

Bloch, Henry Wollman: chairman, Block Foundation (H&R); chairman, director, Block, Inc. (H&R)

Maritz, William Edward: chairman, chief executive officer, president, Maritz Inc.

Penny, Roger Pratt: president, chief operating officer, director, Bethlehem Steel Corp.

Saint Marys Hill Hospital Curative Foundation

Bruce, Peter Wayne: director, Badger Meter Foundation

Saint Marys Medical Center

Hinton, Michael R.: president, chief operating officer, director, Old National Bank Evansville

Saint Norbert College

Terry, Richard Edward: chairman, chief executive officer, director, Peoples Energy Corp.

Saint Paul Corp. National and Community Service

King, Reatha Clark: director, Fuller Co. Foundation (H.B.); president, executive director, General Mills Foundation

Saint Paul's School

Tarola, Robert M.: senior vice president, chief financial officer, Grace & Co. (W.R.)

Saint Petersburg Historical Society

Campbell, George Leroy: vice president public affairs, Florida Power Corp.

Saint Vincent Hospital

Harris, Elmer Beseler: president, chief executive officer, director, Alabama Power Co.

Saint Vincent de Paul Development Council

Phair, Joseph Baschon: corporate secretary, general counsel, vice president, Varian Medical Systems, Inc.

Saint Vincent de Paul Society

Copley, David C.: president, trustee, Copley Foundation (James S.); president, chief executive officer, director, senior

management board, Copley Press, Inc.

Saint Xavier College

Connolly, Charles H.: senior vice president corporate affairs & investor relations, Whitman Corp.; president, Whitman Corp. Foundation

Saint Xavier University

Terry, Richard Edward: chairman, chief executive officer, director, Peoples Energy Corp.

Salvation Army

Carroll, Philip Joseph: chairman, chief executive officer, Fluor Corp.; chairman, trustee, Fluor Foundation

Fites, Donald Vester: director, Caterpillar Foundation

Matthews, Craig Gerard: president, chief operating officer, Brooklyn Union

Purvis, George Frank, Jr.: chairman, president, chief executive officer, director, Pan-American Life Insurance Co.

Rohr, James Edward: chief executive officer, president, director, PNC Financial Services Group

Russell, Frank Eli: president, Central Newspapers Foundation; chairman, Central Newspapers, Inc.

Scripps, Charles Edward: chairman executive committee, director, vice president, Scripps Co. (E.W.); member, Scripps Howard Foundation

Salvation Army Advisory

Moten, John, Junior: vice president community relations, Laclede Gas Co.

Salvation Army Business Advisor Board

Brumm, Paul Michael: executive vice president, chief financial officer, Fifth Third Bancorp

Salvation Army Dallas County

Nye, Erle Allen: chairman, chief executive officer, director, TU Electric Co.

Salvation Army Greater Cleveland

Burner, David L.: chairman, president, chief executive officer, director, BFGoodrich Co.

Salvation Army Houston

Buckwalter, Alan Roland, III: chief executive officer, Chase Bank of Texas; president, Chase Bank of Texas Foundation, Inc.

Salzburg Seminar Board

Meyerson, Martin: director, Panasonic Foundation

Samford University

Harris, Elmer Beseler: president, chief executive officer, director, Alabama Power Co.

San Antonio Chamber of Commerce

Cloud, Bruce Benjamin, Sr.: vice chairman, director, Zachry Co. (H.B.)

Hemminghaus, Roger Roy: chairman, director, Ultramar Diamond Shamrock Corp.

San Antonio Livestock Association

Cloud, Bruce Benjamin, Sr.: vice chairman, director, Zachry Co. (H.B.)

San Diego Aerospace Museum

Copley, David C.: president, trustee, Copley Foundation (James S.); president, chief executive officer, director, senior management board, Copley Press, Inc.

San Diego Automotive Museum

Copley, David C.: president, trustee, Copley Foundation (James S.); president, chief executive officer, director, senior management board, Copley Press, Inc.

San Diego Council Literacy

Copley, Helen K.: chairman, trustee, Copley Foundation (James S.); chairman, director, senior management board, Copley Press, Inc.

San Diego Crew Classic Foundation

Copley, David C.: president, trustee, Copley Foundation (James S.); president, chief executive officer, director, senior management board, Copley Press, Inc.

San Diego Hall Science

Copley, David C.: president, trustee, Copley Foundation (James S.); president, chief executive officer, director, senior management board, Copley Press, Inc.

Copley, Helen K.: chairman, trustee, Copley Foundation (James S.); chairman, director, senior management board, Copley Press, Inc.

San Diego Historical Society

Copley, David C.: president, trustee, Copley Foundation (James S.); president, chief executive officer, director, senior management board, Copley Press, Inc.

San Diego Kind Corp.

Copley, David C.: president, trustee, Copley Foundation (James S.); president, chief executive officer, director, senior management board, Copley Press, Inc.

San Diego Museum Art

Copley, David C.: president, trustee, Copley Foundation (James S.); president, chief executive officer, director, senior management board, Copley Press, Inc.

San Diego Opera Association

Copley, Helen K.: chairman, trustee, Copley Foundation (James S.); chairman, director, senior management board, Copley Press, Inc.

San Diego Society Financial Analysts

Simpson, Louis Allen: president, chief executive officer capital operations, director, GEICO Corp.

San Diego Society Natural History

Copley, Helen K.: chairman, trustee, Copley Foundation (James S.); chairman, director, senior management board, Copley Press, Inc.

San Diego Symphony Association

Copley, Helen K.: chairman, trustee, Copley Foundation (James S.); chairman, director, senior management board, Copley Press, Inc.

San Diego Zoological Society

Copley, Helen K.: chairman, trustee, Copley Foundation (James S.); chairman, director, senior management board, Copley Press, Inc.

San Francisco AID South Foundation

Haas, Robert Douglas: chairman, chief executive officer, director, Levi Strauss & Co.; president, Levi Strauss Foundation

San Francisco Academy

Caccamo, Aldo M.: vice president public affairs, Chevron Corp.

San Francisco Art Institute

Coulter, David A.: president, director, Bank of America

San Francisco Ballet Association

James, George Barker, II: senior vice president, chief financial officer, Levi Strauss & Co.

Swanson, Robert A.: director, Genentech Foundation for Biomedical Sciences

San Francisco Bar Association

Beck, Edward W.: senior vice president, general counsel, secretary, director, Shaklee Corp.

Carter, John Douglas: executive vice president, director, Bechtel Group, Inc.

San Francisco Chamber of Commerce

Beck, Edward W.: senior vice president, general counsel, secretary, director, Shaklee Corp.

Caccamo, Aldo M.: vice president public affairs, Chevron Corp.

Carter, John Douglas: executive vice president, director, Bechtel Group, Inc.

San Francisco Commission Foreign Relations

James, George Barker, II: senior vice president, chief financial officer, Levi Strauss & Co.

San Francisco Conservatory Music

Beck, Edward W.: senior vice president, general counsel, secretary, director, Shaklee Corp.

San Francisco Foundation

Haas, Peter Edgar, Sr.: chairman executive committee, director, Levi Strauss & Co.

San Francisco Friends Urban Forest

Caccamo, Aldo M.: vice president public affairs, Chevron Corp.

San Francisco Museum Modern Art

Rock, Arthur: co-founder, chairman executive committee, director, Intel Corp.

Swanson, Robert A.: director, Genentech Foundation for Biomedical Sciences

San Francisco Symphony

Rosenberg, Richard Morris: chairman, chief executive officer (retired), Bank of America

San Francisco Yale Alumni Association

Beck, Edward W.: senior vice president, general counsel, secretary, director, Shaklee Corp.

Santa Barbara Museum Art

Luton, Barbara B.: executive director, Tenet Healthcare Foundation

Santa Clara County Manufacturing Group

Sanders, Walter Jeremiah, III: chairman, chief executive officer, director, Advanced Micro Devices, Inc.

Saratoga Performing Arts Center

Golub, Lewis: chairman, chief executive officer, director, Golub Corp.

Scabbard & Blade

Strickland, Robert Louis: vice president, Lowe's Charitable and Educational Foundation

Scholarships Scholars Inc.

Poindexter, Christian Herndon: chairman, Baltimore Gas & Electric Foundation; chairman, chief executive officer, director, Constellation Energy Group, Inc.

School American Ballet

Geier, Philip Henry, Jr.: chairman, president, chief executive officer, Interpublic Group of Companies, Inc.

School Management Yale University

Thoman, G. Richard: president, chief operating officer, Xerox Corp.

Schumberger

McCormick, William Thomas, Jr.: chairman, chief executive officer, director, Consumers Energy Co.; chairman, Consumers Energy Foundation

Science Apparatus Manufacturing Association

Platt, Lewis Emmett: chairman, Hewlett-Packard Co.

Science Museum Minnesota

Coyne, William E.: senior vice president, Minnesota Mining & Manufacturing Co.

Science Place

Nye, Erle Allen: chairman, chief executive officer, director, TU Electric Co.

Science Research Associatess

Graham, Patricia Albjerg, PhD: trustee, Hitachi Foundation

Scripps Clinic & Research Foundation

Copley, David C.: president, trustee, Copley Foundation (James S.); president, chief executive officer, director, senior management board, Copley Press, Inc.

Scripps Howard Broadcasting Co.

Standen, Craig Clayton: senior vice president corporate development, Scripps Co. (E.W.)

Scripps Memorial Hospital Auxiliary

Copley, Helen K.: chairman, trustee, Copley Foundation (James S.); chairman, director, senior management board, Copley Press, Inc.

Sea-Space Symposium

Bonsignore, Michael Robert: director, Honeywell Foundation; chairman, chief executive officer, director, Honeywell International Inc.

Seamen's Church Institute of Los Angeles

Dreyfus, Branton B.: director, Alexander & Baldwin Foundation

Seattle Chamber of Commerce

Eigsti, Roger Harry: chairman, chief executive officer, SAFECO Corp.

Killinger, Kerry Kent: chairman, president, chief executive officer, director, Washington Mutual, Inc.

Seattle Repertory Theatre

Eigsti, Roger Harry: chairman, chief executive officer, SAFECO Corp.

Killinger, Kerry Kent: chairman, president, chief executive officer, director, Washington Mutual, Inc.

Second Financial Reporting Institute

Broome, Burton Edward: vice president, controller, Transamerica Corp.; vice president, treasurer, Transamerica Foundation

Second Harvest

Scher, Barry F.: vice president public affairs, Giant Food Inc.

Second Harvest National Food Bank Network

Stewart, Joseph Melvin: senior vice president corporate affairs, Kellogg Co.; trustee, Kellogg Co. Twenty-Five Year Employees' Fund Inc.

Second Stage Theatre

McClimon, Timothy J.: executive director, AT&T Foundation

Securities Industry Association

Bachmann, John W.: managing partner, Jones & Co. (Edward D.); chairman, Jones & Co. Foundation (Edward D.)

Hammerman, Stephen Lawrence: vice president, trustee, Merrill Lynch & Co. Foundation Inc.; vice chairman, general counsel, Merrill Lynch & Co., Inc.

Paton, Leland B.: president capital marketings, director, member executive committee, Prudential Securities Inc.

Piper, Addison Lewis: director, Piper Jaffray Companies Foundation; chairman, chief executive officer, director, U.S. Bancorp Piper Jaffray

Securities Industry Institute

Paton, Leland B.: president capital marketings, director, member executive committee, Prudential Securities Inc.

Securities Regulation Institute

Cook, J. Michael: chairman, chief executive officer, Deloitte & Touche; chairman, Deloitte & Touche Foundation

Security Analysts San Francisco

Latzer, Richard Neal: vice president, director, Transamerica Foundation

Seeds of Hope Foundation

Coors, Peter Hanson: vice president, director, Coors Brewing Co.

Select Congressional Committee World Hunger

James, George Barker, II: senior vice president, chief financial officer, Levi Strauss & Co.

Selective Service Board

Davis, Erroll Brown, Jr.: president, chief executive officer, director, Wisconsin Power & Light Co.

Semiconductor Industry Association

Sanders, Walter Jeremiah, III: chairman, chief executive officer, director, Advanced Micro Devices, Inc.

Senate Monmouth College

Pate, James Leonard: chairman, chief executive officer, director, Pennzoil-Quaker State Co.

Senior PGA Tour

McCoy, John Bonnet: president, chief executive officer, Ameritech Corp.

Senior Personnel Association

Koenig, Brian C.: senior vice president human resources, Scientific-Atlanta, Inc.

Service Corp. Ret Executives

Jones, D. Paul, Jr.: chairman, chief executive officer, Compass Bank; trustee, Compass Bank Foundation

Services Policy Advisory Committee

Trujillo, Solomon D.: president, US West Foundation; president, chief executive officer, US West, Inc.

Settlement Music School

Haskin, Donald Lee: vice president, PNC Bank

Sewickley YMCA

Gregg, Walter Emmor, Junior: senior executive vice president finance & administration, PNC Financial Services Group

Shadyside Hospital

Rohr, James Edward: chief executive officer, president, director, PNC Financial Services Group

Shakespeare Theatre Co.

Hough, Lawrence Alan: president, chief executive officer, Student Loan Marketing Association

Sheboygan Chamber of Commerce

Kohler, Herbert Vollrath, Jr.: chairman, president, director, Kohler Co.

Shriners

Russell, Frank Eli: president, Central Newspapers Foundation; chairman, Central Newspapers, Inc.

Siena College

Standish, J. Spencer: chairman, director, Albany International Corp.

Sigma Alpha Epsilon

Russell, Frank Eli: president, Central Newspapers Foundation; chairman, Central Newspapers, Inc.

Sigma Alpha Mu

Tisch, Preston Robert: chairman, director, CBS Foundation; co-chairman, co-chief executive officer, director, CNA; trustee, Loews Foundation

Sigma Chi

Brown, Richard Harris: chairman, chief executive officer, director, EDS Corp.

George, William Wallace: chief executive officer, chairman, Medtronic, Inc.

Hayden, Joseph Page, Jr.: trustee, Star Bank NA, Cincinnati Foundation

Marriott, J. Willard, Jr.: chairman, chief executive officer, Marriott International Inc.

Matheny, Edward Taylor, Junior: director, Block Foundation (H&R)

Sissel, George A.: chairman, president, chief executive officer, director, Ball Corp.

Sigma Delta Chi

Batten, Frank, Sr.: chairman, director, Landmark Communications Foundation; chairman, Landmark Communications Inc.

Forsythe, Donald George: vice president corporate relations, Sprint Corp.; executive director, Sprint Foundation

Stauffer, Stanley Howard: chairman, Stauffer Communications Foundation

Sigma Iota Epsilon

Sadler, Robert L.: president, vice chairman, director, Old Kent Bank

Sigma Phi Epsilon

Carlson, Curtis Leroy: chairman, director, Carlson Companies, Inc.; president, treasurer, Carlson Family Foundation (Curtis L.)

Henley, Jeffrey O.: executive vice president, chief financial officer, director, Oracle Corp.

Knight, Charles Field: chairman, chief executive officer, Emerson Electric Co.

Smith, Donald Kaye: senior vice president, general counsel, director, GEICO Corp.

Sigma Pi Phi

Chapple, Thomas Leslie: senior vice president, general counsel, secretary, Gannett Co., Inc.; secretary, Gannett Foundation

Graves, Earl Gilbert: director, Aetna Foundation

Sigma Pi Sigma

Davis, Ruth Margaret: trustee, Air Products Foundation

Hill, George Richard: president, trustee, Lubrizol Foundation (The)

Sigma Tau

Sissel, George A.: chairman, president, chief executive officer, director, Ball Corp.

Sigma Theta Tau

Davis, Carolyne Kahle, PhD: trustee, Merck Co. Foundation

Sigma Xi

Batten, Frank, Sr.: chairman, director, Landmark Communications Foundation; chairman, Landmark Communications Inc.

Brinegar, Claude Stout: trustee, Unocal Foundation

Engel, Joel Stanley: vice president technology, Ameritech Corp.

Graham, William B.: chairman, director, Baxter Allegiance Foundation; chairman emeritus, Baxter International Inc.

Hatsopoulos, George Nicholas: founder, chairman, chief executive officer, director, Thermo Electron Corp.; committee member, Thermo Electron Foundation

Hill, George Richard: president, trustee, Lubrizol Foundation (The)

Pierre, Percy A.: trustee, Hitachi Foundation

Signature Learning Center Inc.

Koch, Robert Louis, II: president, chief executive officer, director, Koch Enterprises, Inc.; president, director, Koch Foundation

Silicon Valley Association General Counsel

Phair, Joseph Baschon: corporate secretary, general counsel, vice president, Varian Medical Systems, Inc.

Sinai Hospital

Ruding, Herman Onno: vice chairman, director, Citibank Corp.

Sinclair Community College Foundation

Smith, Frederick C.: chairman, trustee, Huffy Foundation, Inc.

Singapore-U.S. Business Council

Raymond, Lee R.: chairman, president, chief executive officer, Exxon Mobil Corp.

Sloan-Kettering Cancer Center

Gerstner, Louis Vincent, Jr.: chairman, chief executive officer, director, International Business Machines Corp.

Sloan-Kettering Institute Cancer Research

Gelb, Richard Lee: director, New York Times Co. Foundation

Small Arms Ammunition Manufacturer

Griffin, Donald Wayne: chairman, president, chief executive officer, director, Olin Corp.; trustee, Olin Corp. Charitable Trust

Smithsall Woods Foundation Inc.

Banks, Peter L.: vice president external affairs, AGL Resources Inc.

Smithsonian Institute

Bowen, William Gordon, PhD: trustee, Merck Co. Foundation

Johnson, Samuel Curtis: chairman, director, president, Johnson & Son (S.C.); chairman, trustee, Johnson Wax Fund (S.C.)

Manoogian, Richard Alexander: chairman, chief executive officer, director, Masco Corp.

Ripley, Sidney Dillon, II: director emeritus, Hitachi Foundation

Rogers, Desiree Glapion: vice president community affairs, Peoples Energy Corp.

Smithsonian Institute National Board

Brademas, John: chairman, Texaco Foundation

Haas, Peter Edgar, Sr.: chairman executive committee, director, Levi Strauss & Co.

Schermer, Lloyd G.: chairman, director, Lee Enterprises

Smithsonian Institute National Museum Natural History

Spoon, Alan Gary: president, chief operating officer, director, The Washington Post

Smokeless Tobacco Council

Rosson, William Mimms: chairman, Conwood Co. LP

Soap & Detergent Association

Mark, Reuben: chairman, chief executive officer, Colgate-Palmolive Co.

Pepper, John E., Jr.: chairman executive committee, Procter & Gamble Co.

Society Actuaries

Brooks, Roger Kay: chairman, AmerUS Group

Brown, Stephen Lee: chairman, chief executive officer, director, Hancock Financial Services (John)

Eckert, Ralph John: trustee, Trustmark Foundation

Hutchings, Peter Lounsbery: president, Guardian Life Insurance Co. of America

Levine, Kenneth M.: executive vice president, chief investment officer, director, MONY Group (The); director, MONY Life Insurance of New York (The)

Roberts, John Kenneth, Jr.: president, chief executive officer, director, Pan-American Life Insurance Co.

Senkler, Robert L.: president, director, Minnesota Mutual Foundation; chairman, president, chief executive officer, Minnesota Mutual Life Insurance Co.

Stewart, James Gathings: executive vice president, chief financial officer, CIGNA Corp.

Sutton, Thomas C.: chairman, director, Pacific Mutual Charitable Foundation; chairman, chief executive officer, director, Pacific Mutual Life Insurance Co.

Society American Military Engineers

Harris, Elmer Beseler: president, chief executive officer, director, Alabama Power Co.

Johnson, Hansford Tillman: trustee, USAA Foundation, A Charitable Trust

Society Automotive Engineers

Condit, Philip Murray: chairman, chief executive officer, director, Boeing Co.

Eaton, Robert James: co-chairman, president, chief executive officer, DaimlerChrysler Corp.

Fites, Donald Vester: director, Caterpillar Foundation

Janitz, John A.: president, chief executive officer, chairman, Textron Inc.

Naylor, Michael E.: senior vice president operations, Rubbermaid Inc.

Pollock, E. Kears: director, PPG Industries Foundation; executive vice president, PPG Industries, Inc.

Society Biochemistry & Molecular Biology

Levinson, Arthur David: president, chief executive officer, director, Genentech Inc.

Society Biological Chemical

Boyer, Herbert Wayne, PhD: chairman, president, director, Genentech Foundation for Biomedical Sciences; co-founder, director, Genentech Inc.

Society Cable Telecommunications Engineers

Necessary, Steven K.: senior vice president marketing, Scientific-Atlanta, Inc.

Society Chartered Property & Casualty Underwriters

Brown, Joseph Warner, Jr.: chairman, chief executive officer, MBIA Inc.

Lewis, Peter Benjamin: chairman, president, chief executive officer, director, Progressive Corp.

Oakley, Robert Alan: executive vice president, chief financial officer, Nationwide Insurance Enterprise Foundation

Society Chemical Industry

Chellgren, Paul Wilbur: chief executive officer, chairman, director, Ashland, Inc.; member, Ashland Inc. Foundation

Deavenport, Earnest W., Jr.: chairman, chief executive officer, director, Eastman Chemical Co.

Fligg, James E.: executive vice president, BP Amoco Corp.

Grasley, Michael Howard: senior vice president, Shell Oil Co.; member executive committee, director, Shell Oil Co. Foundation

LaMantia, Charles Robert: president, chief executive officer, director, Little, Inc. (Arthur D.)

Lovett, John Robert: director, Air Products Foundation

McKennon, Keith Robert: chairman, president, PacifiCorp; member, PacifiCorp Foundation

Stewart, S. Jay: chairman, chief executive officer, director, Morton International Inc.

Society Exploration Geophysicists

Jennings, James Burnett: president, Hunt Oil Co.

Society Explorational Test Pilots

Armstrong, Neil A.: trustee, Milacron Foundation; director, Milacron, Inc.

Society Financial Analysts
Killinger, Kerry Kent: chairman, president, chief executive officer, director, Washington Mutual, Inc.

Society Flight Test Engineers
Kresa, Kent: chairman, president, chief executive officer, director, Northrop Grumman Corp.

Society Gas Lighting
Catell, Robert Barry: chairman, chief executive officer, Brooklyn Union

Society Human Resources Management
Heldreth, Nick E.: vice president human resources corporate relations, Harris Corp.

Knicely, Howard V.: president, TRW Foundation

Kramer, Mary Elizabeth: vice president, Wellmark Foundation

Nicholas, Jon O.: vice president, trustee, Maytag Corp. Foundation

Phillips, Richard B.: vice president, Crane Foundation

Society Information Display
Davis, Ruth Margaret: trustee, Air Products Foundation

Society International Business Fellows
Jones, D. Paul, Jr.: chairman, chief executive officer, Compass Bank; trustee, Compass Bank Foundation

Society International Treasurers
Daley, Leo J.: vice president, treasurer, Air Products and Chemicals, Inc.

Society Manufacturing Engineers
Beall, Donald Ray: director, Rockwell International Corp.

Muehlbauer, James Herman: vice president, director, Koch Foundation

Pollock, E. Kears: director, PPG Industries Foundation; executive vice president, PPG Industries, Inc.

Society Mayflower Descendants
Blanke, Gail Ann: vice president, Avon Products Foundation, Inc.

Society Microbiology
Levinson, Arthur David: president, chief executive officer, director, Genentech Inc.

Society Petroleum Engineers
Bradford, William Edward: chairman, director, Halliburton Co.

Elkins, Lloyd Edwin, Junior: vice president, Chevron Corp.

Lowrie, William G.: president, deputy chief executive officer, director, BP Amoco Corp.

McKee, Robert E., III: executive vice president corporate strategy & development, du Pont de Nemours & Co. (E.I.)

Mooney, Edward J., Jr.: chairman, president, chief executive officer, director, Nalco Chemical Co.

Wood, Willis B., Jr.: chairman, chief executive officer, director, Pacific Enterprises

Society Plastics Engineers
Joyce, William H.: chairman, president, chief executive officer, chief operating officer, Union Carbide Corp.

Naylor, Michael E.: senior vice president operations, Rubbermaid Inc.

Society Plastics Industry
Sullivan, Kevin F.: member screening committee, PPG Industries Foundation

Society Professional Journalists
Block, John Robinson: vice president, trustee, Blade Foundation

Block, William: vice president, trustee, Blade Foundation; chairman, director, Toledo Blade Co.

Coulter, Patrick C. G.: president, Bell Atlantic Foundation; senior vice president corporate communications, Gulfstream Aerospace Corp.

Haskin, Donald Lee: vice president, PNC Bank

Hubbard, Stanley S.: chairman, president, chief executive officer, Hubbard Broadcasting, Inc.; president, Hubbard Foundation

Pulliam, Eugene Smith: vice president, director, Central Newspapers Foundation

Society Satellite Professionals International
Hubbard, Stanley S.: chairman, president, chief executive officer, Hubbard Broadcasting, Inc.; president, Hubbard Foundation

Society Sloan Fellows
Condit, Philip Murray: chairman, chief executive officer, director, Boeing Co.

Society Social Political Science
Pate, James Leonard: chairman, chief executive officer, director, Pennzoil-Quaker State Co.

Society Study Evolution
Ripley, Sidney Dillon, II: director emeritus, Hitachi Foundation

Society of Consumer Affairs Professionals
Mathews, Odonna: vice president consumer affairs, Giant Food Inc.

Software Pubs Association
Lemberg, Thomas Michael: clerk, Lotus Development Corp.; secretary, Polaroid Foundation

Sons American Revolution
Sulzberger, Arthur Ochs, Sr.: director, New York Times Co.; chairman, director, New York Times Co. Foundation

Soup Kitchen
Whitwam, David Ray: chairman, president, chief executive officer, director, Whirlpool Corp.

South Carolina Bar Association
DeLoach, Harris E., Junior: executive vice president, director, Sonoco Products Co.

South Carolina Business & Industry Policy Education Committee
Shelley, James Herbert: chairman, Sonoco Foundation

South Carolina Foundation Independent Colleges
Milliken, Roger: chairman, chief executive officer, Milliken & Co.; member advisory committee, Milliken Foundation

South Carolina Historical Society
Anderson, Ivan Verner, Jr.: president, chief executive officer, Evening Post Publishing Co.; vice president, Post and Courier Foundation

South Carolina Press Association
Anderson, Ivan Verner, Jr.: president, chief executive officer, Evening Post Publishing Co.; vice president, Post and Courier Foundation

South Carolina Research Authority
Hipp, William Hayne: president, chief executive officer, director, Liberty Corp.; chairman, president, director, Liberty Corp. Foundation

South Carolina Textile Manufacturer Association
Milliken, Roger: chairman, chief executive officer, Milliken & Co.; member advisory committee, Milliken Foundation

South Miami Hospital
Goode, R. Ray: director, Ryder System Charitable Foundation

Southeast Electric Exchange
Harris, Elmer Beseler: president, chief executive officer, director, Alabama Power Co.

Southeastern Newspaper Publisher's Association
Morris, William Shivers, III: founder, chairman, chief executive officer, director, Morris Communications Corp.; trustee, Stauffer Communications Foundation

Southern California ACLU
Rosenzweig, Richard Stuart: executive vice president, director, Playboy Enterprises Inc.

Southern California Association Philanthropy
Carey, Kathryn Ann: foundation manager, American Honda Foundation

Southern Center International Studies
Blount, Winton Malcolm, Jr.: chairman, Blount International, Inc.

Southern Christian Leadership Conference
Graves, Earl Gilbert: director, Aetna Foundation

Southern Gas Association
Bailey, Keith E.: chairman, president, director, chief executive officer, Texas Gas Transmission Corp.; president, director, Williams Companies Foundation (The)

Richards, Joel, III: vice president, El Paso Energy Foundation

Wadlington, Cuba, Jr.: vice president, Williams

Southern Illinois University
Nicholas, Jon O.: vice president, trustee, Maytag Corp. Foundation

Southern Methodist University
Engibous, Thomas James: director, Texas Instruments Foundation; president, chief executive officer, chairman, director, Texas Instruments Inc.

Huey, Ward L., Jr.: president broadcast division, vice chairman, director, Belo Corp. (A.H.); vice president, trustee, Belo Corp. Foundation (A.H.)

Raymond, Lee R.: chairman, president, chief executive officer, Exxon Mobil Corp.

Southern Methodist University Meadows School Arts

Huey, Ward L., Jr.: president broadcast division, vice chairman, director, Belo Corp. (A.H.); vice president, trustee, Belo Corp. Foundation (A.H.)

Southern New England Telephone Co. Political Action Comm

Miglio, Daniel Joseph: chairman, president, director, chief executive officer, Southern New England Telephone Co.

Southern Newspaper Publishers Association

Anderson, Ivan Verner, Jr.: president, chief executive officer, Evening Post Publishing Co.; vice president, Post and Courier Foundation

Easterly, David E.: president, chief operating officer, Cox Enterprises Inc.

Gaylord, Edward Lewis: chairman, chief executive officer, director, publisher, Oklahoma Publishing Co.; trustee, Oklahoman Foundation (The)

Morris, William Shivers, III: founder, chairman, chief executive officer, director, Morris Communications Corp.; trustee, Stauffer Communications Foundation

Osborne, Burl: president publishing division, director, Belo Corp. (A.H.); president, trustee, Belo Corp. Foundation (A.H.)

Southern Newspaper Publishers Association Foundation

Batten, Frank, Sr.: chairman, director, Landmark Communications Foundation; chairman, Landmark Communications Inc.

Southern Research Institute

Harris, Elmer Beseler: president, chief executive officer, director, Alabama Power Co.

Southwest Area Commerce & Industry Association

Hays, Thomas Chandler: chairman, chief executive officer, director, Fortune Brands, Inc.

Southwest Illinois Industry Association

Griffin, Donald Wayne: chairman, president, chief executive officer, director, Olin Corp.; trustee, Olin Corp. Charitable Trust

Southwest Legal Foundation

Agnich, Richard John: director, Texas Instruments Foundation; senior vice president, secretary, general counsel, Texas Instruments Inc.

Godfrey, Cullen Michael: vice president, FINA Foundation

Southwest Museum

Wood, Willis B., Jr.: chairman, chief executive officer, director, Pacific Enterprises

Southwest Research Institute

Whitacre, Edward E., Jr.: chairman, director, chief executive officer, SBC Communications Inc.

Zachry, Henry Bartell, Jr.: chairman, Zachry Co. (H.B.); trustee, Zachry Foundation (The)

Sovereign Military Order Malta

McKenna, William John: director, chairman, Kellwood Co.; chairman, president, director, Kellwood Foundation

Spanish Institute

Ross, Arthur: senior vice president, Central National-Gottesman; director, Central National-Gottesman Foundation

Spanish Repertory Theatre

Small, Lawrence Malcolm: president, chief operating officer, Fannie Mae; director, Fannie Mae Foundation

Special Olympics Colorado

Coors, Peter Hanson: vice president, director, Coors Brewing Co.

Special Olympics International

Fiondella, Robert William: chairman, president, chief executive officer, Phoenix Home Life Mutual Insurance Co.

Spelman College

Brademas, John: chairman, Texaco Foundation

Splash Club

Cronk, William F., III: president, director, Dreyer's Grand Ice Cream

Spokane County Bar Association

Stanton, Philip H.: chief executive officer, director, Washington Trust Bank

Sponsors Performing Arts Center

Wilbur, Brayton, Jr.: president, chief executive officer, Wilbur-Ellis Co. & Connell Brothers Co.; president, Wilbur Foundation (Brayton)

Springfield College

Wheeler, Thomas Beardsley: chairman, chief executive officer, Massachusetts Mutual Life Insurance Co.

Stamford Center Arts

Rukeyser, Robert James: senior vice president corporate affairs, Fortune Brands, Inc.

Stamford Hospital Foundation

Lee, Charles Robert: chairman, chief executive officer, director, GTE Corp.; chief executive officer, trustee, GTE Foundation

Stamford Symphony Orchestra

Canning, John Beckman: secretary, Rayonier Foundation

Kurtz, Melvin H.: secretary, director, Chesebrough Foundation

Stanford Athletic Board

Satre, Philip Glen: chairman, president, chief executive officer, director, Promus Hotel Corp.

Stanford Business School Association

Carter, George Kent: vice president, treasurer, Chevron Corp.

Stanford Graduate Business Alumni Association

Lucas, Donald Leo: chairman, Cadence Designs Systems, Inc.

Stanford University

McCoy, John Bonnet: president, chief executive officer, Ameritech Corp.

Stanley, Peter William: trustee, Hitachi Foundation

Ukropina, James R.: partner, Pacific Mutual Life Insurance Co.

Stanford University Alumni Association

Bryson, John E.: chairman, chief executive officer, Edison International

Carter, George Kent: vice president, treasurer, Chevron Corp.

Lucas, Donald Leo: chairman, Cadence Designs Systems, Inc.

Satre, Philip Glen: chairman, president, chief executive officer, director, Promus Hotel Corp.

Stanford University College Engineering

Eaton, Robert James: co-chairman, president, chief executive officer, DaimlerChrysler Corp.

Stanford University Graduate School Business

Bechtel, Riley Peart: chairman, Bechtel Foundation; chairman, chief executive officer, director, Bechtel Group, Inc.

Ives, J. Atwood: chairman, chief executive officer, Boston Gas Co.; chairman, chief executive officer, trustee, Eastern Enterprises; trustee, Eastern Enterprises Foundation

Wurtele, C. Angus: president, Valspar Foundation

Stanford University Hospital

James, George Barker, II: senior vice president, chief financial officer, Levi Strauss & Co.

Stanford University Law School

Bechtel, Riley Peart: chairman, Bechtel Foundation; chairman, chief executive officer, director, Bechtel Group, Inc.

Stanford University School Medicine

Harris, Edward D., Jr.: director, Genentech Foundation for Biomedical Sciences

Star of India Auxiliary

Copley, Helen K.: chairman, trustee, Copley Foundation (James S.); chairman, director, senior management board, Copley Press, Inc.

State Fair Texas

Huey, Ward L., Jr.: president broadcast division, vice chairman, director, Belo Corp. (A.H.); vice president, trustee, Belo Corp. Foundation (A.H.)

State Health Center Foundation

Strandjord, Mary Jeannine: director, Sprint Foundation

State SOC CPAs

Upbin, Hal Jay: president, chief executive officer, director, Kellwood Co.

State of Arizona Governor's Technical Commission

Dewane, John Richard: director, Honeywell Foundation

Stauffer Communications Foundation

Stauffer, Stanley Howard: chairman, Stauffer Communications Foundation

Steadman-Hawkins Sports Medicine

Graves, Earl Gilbert: director, Aetna Foundation

Steamship Association of Southern California

Dreyfus, Branton B.: director, Alexander & Baldwin Foundation

Stern Grove Festival Association

James, George Barker, II: senior vice president, chief financial officer, Levi Strauss & Co.

Stevens Institute Technology

Howe, Wesley Jackson: chairman emeritus, director, Becton Dickinson & Co.

Storm King Art Center

Ottaway, James Haller, Jr.: senior vice president, director, Dow Jones & Co., Inc.; member advisory committee, Dow Jones Foundation

Student Loan Funding Resource

Brown, Ronald D.: assistant treasurer, Milacron Foundation

Student Loan Marketing Association

Rohr, James Edward: chief executive officer, president, director, PNC Financial Services Group

Students Free Enterprise

Hopkins, Thomas E.: vice president human resources, Sherwin-Williams Co.; assistant secretary, trustee, Sherwin-Williams Foundation

Study National Needs Biomed & Behavioral Research

Brademas, John: chairman, Texaco Foundation

Success by Six

Dewane, John Richard: director, Honeywell Foundation

Summer Pop Concerts

Purvis, George Frank, Jr.: chairman, president, chief executive officer, director, Pan-American Life Insurance Co.

Summerbridge

Bachmann, Richard Arthur: vice president, secretary, treasurer, director, Louisiana Land & Exploration Co. Foundation

Summit Education Initiative

Burner, David L.: chairman, president, chief executive officer, director, BFGoodrich Co.

Sustainable Energy Future

Wood, Willis B., Jr.: chairman, chief executive officer, director, Pacific Enterprises

Swedish America Hosp Foundation

Meuleman, Robert Joseph: director, AMCORE Foundation

Swedish Council America

Carlson, Curtis Leroy: chairman, director, Carlson Companies, Inc.; president, treasurer, Carlson Family Foundation (Curtis L.)

Swedish-American Chamber of Commerce Honors Comm

Carlson, Curtis Leroy: chairman, director, Carlson Companies, Inc.; president, treasurer, Carlson Family Foundation (Curtis L.)

Syracuse Research Corp.

Engel, Joel Stanley: vice president technology, Ameritech Corp.

TN-Tombigbee Waterway Authority Economic Pension Comm

Stephens, Elton Bryson: founder, chairman, Ebsco Industries, Inc.

TV Academy Arts & Sciences Foundation

Redstone, Sumner Murray: chairman, Viacom Inc.

TV Bureau Advertising

Huey, Ward L., Jr.: president broadcast division, vice chairman, director, Belo Corp. (A.H.); vice president, trustee, Belo Corp. Foundation (A.H.)

Taft School

Miller, William Irwin: director, Cummins Engine Foundation

Task Force Hedge Funds

Lang, Robert Todd: chairman, director, Weil, Gotshal & Manges Foundation

Tau Beta Pi

Allaire, Paul Arthur: chairman, chief executive officer, chairman executive committee, Xerox Corp.; president, Xerox Foundation

Brothers, John Alfred 'Fred': trustee, Ashland Inc. Foundation

Davis, Ruth Margaret: trustee, Air Products Foundation

Hemminghaus, Roger Roy: chairman, director, Ultramar Diamond Shamrock Corp.

Hodgson, Thomas Richard: president, chief operating officer, director, Abbott Laboratories

Maatman, Gerald Leonard: chairman, president, trustee, Kemper Foundation (James S.); director, Kemper National Insurance Companies

Pierre, Percy A.: trustee, Hitachi Foundation

Schacht, Henry Brewer: director, Cummins Engine Foundation

Urkowitz, Michael: senior vice president, Chase Manhattan Bank, NA; trustee, Chase Manhattan Foundation

White, Gerald Andrew: director, Air Products Foundation

Tax Executives Institute

Marsh, R. Bruce: general tax counsel, Chevron Corp.

Reese, Terry W.: assistant treasurer, Vulcan Materials Co. Foundation

Russell, Frank Eli: president, Central Newspapers Foundation; chairman, Central Newspapers, Inc.

Wasserman, David Sherman: vice president, treasurer, Harris Corp.; trustee, Harris Foundation

Tea Council Canada

Langbo, Arnold Gordon: chairman, chief executive officer, director, Kellogg Co.

Tech Association Pulp & Paper Industry

Ballengee, Jerry Hunter: president, chief operating officer, director, Union Camp Corp.

McKone, Francis L.: president, chief executive officer, director, Albany International Corp.

Tech Center Silicon Valley

Swanson, Robert A.: director, Genentech Foundation for Biomedical Sciences

Tel Aviv University Museum Diaspora

Mandel, Jack N.: director, Premier Industrial Corp.

Telecommunication Network

Levinson, Arthur David: president, chief executive officer, director, Genentech Inc.

Telephone Pioneers America

Campbell, Cheryl Nichols: operation service advisory group, Cincinnati Bell Inc.

Temple Israel

Weiser, Irving: chairman, president, chief executive officer, Dain Bosworth Inc.

Temple University Accounting Advisory Board

Tarola, Robert M.: senior vice president, chief financial officer, Grace & Co. (W.R.)

Temple University School Podiatric Medicine Foundation

Thompson, Sheldon Lee: senior vice president, chief administrative officer, Sunoco Inc.

Temple Woodruff Foundation

Mandel, Jack N.: director, Premier Industrial Corp.

Tennessee Performing Arts Center

Ingram, Martha R.: chairman, director, Ingram Industries Inc.

Tennis Hall Fame

Zuckerman, Mortimer Benjamin: co-founder, chairman, co-publisher, director, Daily News

Texas Association General Contractors

Cloud, Bruce Benjamin, Sr.: vice chairman, director, Zachry Co. (H.B.)

Texas Bar Association

Agnich, Richard John: director, Texas Instruments Foundation; senior vice president, secretary, general counsel, Texas Instruments Inc.

Allbritton, Joe Lewis: chairman, chief executive officer, Riggs Bank NA

Flood, Joan Moore: assistant treasurer, Trace International Holdings, Inc. Foundation

Matthews, Clark J., II: president, chief executive officer, director, 7-Eleven, Inc.

Texas Board Legal Specialization

Godfrey, Cullen Michael: vice president, FINA Foundation

Texas Chamber of Commerce

Brooks, E. Richard 'Dick': chairman, chief executive officer, director, Central & South West Services

Texas Childrens Hospital

Jewell, George Hiram: director, Schlumberger Foundation

Texas Christian University

Roach, John Vinson, II: chairman, director, Tandy Corp.

Texas Congress Extension Service

Cloud, Bruce Benjamin, Sr.: vice chairman, director, Zachry Co. (H.B.)

Texas Council Economic Education

Brooks, E. Richard 'Dick': chairman, chief executive officer, director, Central & South West Services

Texas Good Roads-Transportation Association

Cloud, Bruce Benjamin, Sr.: vice chairman, director, Zachry Co. (H.B.)

Texas Gov's Business Council

Wise, William Allen: chairman, president, chief executive officer, director, El Paso Energy Co.; chairman, director, El Paso Energy Foundation

Texas Hotmix Paving Association
Cloud, Bruce Benjamin, Sr.: vice chairman, director, Zachry Co. (H.B.)

Texas Medical Center
Carroll, Philip Joseph: chairman, chief executive officer, Fluor Corp.; chairman, trustee, Fluor Foundation

Texas Mid-Continent Oil & Gas Association
Bradford, William Edward: chairman, director, Halliburton Co.

Texas Research League
Brooks, E. Richard 'Dick': chairman, chief executive officer, director, Central & South West Services

Texas Society Professional Engineers
Cloud, Bruce Benjamin, Sr.: vice chairman, director, Zachry Co. (H.B.)

Texas State Bar Association
Godfrey, Cullen Michael: vice president, FINA Foundation
Nye, Erle Allen: chairman, chief executive officer, director, TU Electric Co.
Rust, Edward Barry, Jr.: chairman, president, director, State Farm Companies Foundation; chairman, president, chief executive officer, director, State Farm Mutual Automobile Insurance Co.

Texas State Technology College Foundation
Cloud, Bruce Benjamin, Sr.: vice chairman, director, Zachry Co. (H.B.)

Texas Technology University & Health Science
Whitacre, Edward E., Jr.: chairman, director, chief executive officer, SBC Communications Inc.

Texas Transportation Institute
Cloud, Bruce Benjamin, Sr.: vice chairman, director, Zachry Co. (H.B.)

Textile Distr Association
Rockefeller, Frederic Lincoln: trustee, Cranston Foundation

Textile Institute
Milliken, Roger: chairman, chief executive officer, Milliken & Co.; member advisory committee, Milliken Foundation

Thacher School
Bechtel, Riley Peart: chairman, Bechtel Foundation; chairman, chief executive officer, director, Bechtel Group, Inc.

Theatre Committees Group
McClimon, Timothy J.: executive director, AT&T Foundation

Theatre Owners America
Redstone, Sumner Murray: chairman, Viacom Inc.

Theta Chi
Bertrand, Frederic Howard: chairman, Central Vermont Public Service Corp.
Tobias, Randall L.: chairman emeritus, Lilly & Co. (Eli)

Theta Delta Chi
Scripps, Charles Edward: chairman executive committee, director, vice president, Scripps Co. (E.W.); member, Scripps Howard Foundation

Thiel College
Pitorak, Larry John: senior vice president finance, treasurer, chief financial officer, Sherwin-Williams Co.; secretary, treasurer, trustee, Sherwin-Williams Foundation

Thomas Rivera Policy Institute
Trujillo, Solomon D.: president, US West Foundation; president, chief executive officer, US West, Inc.

Thompson Island Outward Bound Educational Center
Magee, John Francis: chairman, director, Little, Inc. (Arthur D.)

Thrift Institute Advisory Council
Rinehart, Charles Robert: chairman, chief executive officer, director, Washington Mutual, Inc.

Thunderbird Graduate School International Management Global Council
Iraola, Manuel J.: senior vice president, director, Phelps Dodge Corp.

Thunderbird-America Graduate School International Management
Zachem, Harry M.: chairman, trustee, Ashland Inc. Foundation

Thyssen-Bornemisza Group
Armstrong, C. Michael: chairman, chief executive officer, AT&T Corp.

Tiffany Foundation
Buechner, Thomas Scharman: trustee, Corning Inc. Foundation

Tifts University
Cummings, William S.: chairman, Cummings Properties Management

Tilton School
Connor, Richard L.: president, publisher, Fort Worth Star-Telegram Inc.

Times Square Business Improvement District
Sulzberger, Arthur Ochs, Junior: director, chairman emeritus, New York Times Co.

Tinker Foundation
Osborne, Richard de Jongh: director, ASARCO Foundation; chairman, chief executive officer, director, ASARCO Inc.

Toledo Museum Art
Block, William, Jr.: president, trustee, Blade Foundation; president, director, Toledo Blade Co.

Toledo Symphony
Block, William, Jr.: president, trustee, Blade Foundation; president, director, Toledo Blade Co.

Toledo Symphony Orchestra
Hiner, Glen Harold, Jr.: chairman, chief executive officer, director, Owens Corning

Tomas Rivera Policy Institute
Decherd, Robert William: chairman, president, chief executive officer, director, Belo Corp. (A.H.); chairman, trustee, Belo Corp. Foundation (A.H.)

Tomorrow
Bottorff, Dennis C.: chairman, president, chief executive officer, director, First American Corp.

Top Tower
Stauffer, John H.: trustee, Stauffer Communications Foundation

Towle Trust Fund
James, George Barker, II: senior vice president, chief financial officer, Levi Strauss & Co.

Town Hall California
Barad, Jill Elikann: director, Mattel Foundation; chairman, chief executive officer, director, Mattel Inc.
Neal, Philip Mark: president, chief executive officer, director, Avery Dennison Corp.
Rosenzweig, Richard Stuart: executive vice president, director, Playboy Enterprises Inc.

Trade Policy & Negotiations
Barnette, Curtis Handley: chairman, chief executive officer, director, Bethlehem Steel Corp.

Trading Stamp Institute America
Carlson, Curtis Leroy: chairman, director, Carlson Companies, Inc.; president, treasurer, Carlson Family Foundation (Curtis L.)

TransAfrica Forum
Graves, Earl Gilbert: director, Aetna Foundation

Transit Construction Authority
Hock, Delwin D.: chairman, New Century Energies

Transit Management Tucson
Huston, Edwin Allen: vice president, director, Ryder System Charitable Foundation; vice chairman, director, Ryder System, Inc.

Transportation Research Board Executive Committee
Goode, David Ronald: chairman, president, chief executive officer, director, Norfolk Southern Corp.

Travelfest
Berkley, Eugene Bertram: chairman, director, Tension Envelope Corp.; treasurer, Tension Envelope Foundation

Treasury Management Association
Doucette, James Willard: vice president, treasurer, Humana Foundation

Tri-County Scholarship Fund
Painter, Alan Sproul: vice president, executive director, AlliedSignal Foundation Inc.

Tri-Regional Com.
Wise, William Allen: chairman, president, chief executive officer, director, El Paso Energy Co.; chairman, director, El Paso Energy Foundation

Trident United Way
Anderson, Ivan Verner, Jr.: president, chief executive officer, Evening Post Publishing Co.; vice president, Post and Courier Foundation

Trilateral Commission
Andreas, Dwayne Orville: chairman, chief executive officer, Archer-Daniels-Midland Co.
Brademas, John: chairman, Texaco Foundation
Gorman, Joseph T.: chairman, chief executive officer, TRW Inc.
Haas, Robert Douglas: chairman, chief executive officer, director, Levi Strauss & Co.; president, Levi Strauss Foundation
Houghton, James Richardson: director, Corning Inc.; trustee, Corning Inc. Foundation
Labrecque, Thomas Goulet: president, chief operating officer, director, Chase Manhattan Bank,

NA; president, Chase Manhattan Foundation
Raymond, Lee R.: chairman, president, chief executive officer, Exxon Mobil Corp.
Ruding, Herman Onno: vice chairman, director, Citibank Corp.

Trinity University
Herres, Robert T.: chairman, chief executive officer, United Services Automobile Association

Truman Medicine Center
Margolin, Abraham E.: director, Tension Envelope Foundation

Trust Public Land
Nelson, Merlin Edward: chairman, director, IBJ Foundation

Tufts University
Cudlip, Brittain B.: chairman, Bardes Corp.

Tulane University Center for Bioenvironmental Research
Carroll, Philip Joseph: chairman, chief executive officer, Fluor Corp.; chairman, trustee, Fluor Foundation

Tustin Public School Foundation
Rinehart, Charles Robert: chairman, chief executive officer, director, Washington Mutual, Inc.

Twin Cities Society Security Analysts
Leatherdale, Douglas West: chairman, chief executive officer, president, Saint Paul Companies Inc.

U.S. Air Force Civilian Advisory
Wild, Heidi Karin: trustee

U.S. Army Aviation Museum
Blount, Winton Malcolm, Jr.: chairman, Blount International, Inc.

U.S. Army Museum Society
Wolff, Herbert Eric: secretary, director, First Hawaiian Foundation

U.S. Asian Business Council
Knight, Philip Hampson: chairman, chief executive officer, Nike, Inc.

U.S. Chamber of Commerce
Blount, Winton Malcolm, Jr.: chairman, Blount International, Inc.
Campbell, George Leroy: vice president public affairs, Florida Power Corp.
Goode, David Ronald: chairman, president, chief executive officer, director, Norfolk Southern Corp.
Marriott, J. Willard, Jr.: chairman, chief executive officer, Marriott International Inc.

U.S. Commission Constellation System
Meyerson, Martin: director, Panasonic Foundation

U.S. Council International Business
Baukol, Ronald O.: director, executive vice president, Minnesota Mining & Manufacturing Co.
Clemente, Constantine Louis: chairman, Pfizer Foundation; executive vice president corporate affairs, secretary, corporate counsel, Pfizer Inc.
Cook, J. Michael: chairman, chief executive officer, Deloitte & Touche; chairman, Deloitte & Touche Foundation
Knicely, Howard V.: president, TRW Foundation
Schiro, James J.: chairman, senior partner, PricewaterhouseCoopers

U.S. Department Commerce
Dewane, John Richard: director, Honeywell Foundation

U.S. Holocaust Memorial Council
Small, Lawrence Malcolm: president, chief operating officer, Fannie Mae; director, Fannie Mae Foundation

U.S. Humane Society
Copley, David C.: president, trustee, Copley Foundation (James S.); president, chief executive officer, director, senior management board, Copley Press, Inc.

U.S. Information Agency
Rehm, Jack Daniel: chairman emeritus, director, Meredith Corp.

U.S. Naval Academy Alumni Association
Bonsignore, Michael Robert: director, Honeywell Foundation; chairman, chief executive officer, director, Honeywell International Inc.

U.S. Naval Academy Foundation
Batten, Frank, Sr.: chairman, director, Landmark Communications Foundation; chairman, Landmark Communications Inc.
Herres, Robert T.: chairman, chief executive officer, United Services Automobile Association

U.S. Naval Academy Sailing Squadron
Disney, Roy Edward: trustee, Disney Co. Foundation (Walt); vice chairman, director, Disney Co. (Walt)

U.S. Naval Institute
Calise, Nicholas James: vice president, associate general counsel, secretary, BFGoodrich Co.; secretary, Goodrich Foundation, Inc. (B.F.)

U.S. Navy League
Dewane, John Richard: director, Honeywell Foundation

U.S. Supreme Court Bar Association
Neville, James Morton: member board control, Ralston Purina Trust Fund

U.S. Telephone Association
Miglio, Daniel Joseph: chairman, president, director, chief executive officer, Southern New England Telephone Co.
Stonebraker, Barbara J.: executive vice president, Cincinnati Bell Foundation, Inc.; senior vice president, Cincinnati Bell Inc.

U.S. Trade Report
Bonsignore, Michael Robert: director, Honeywell Foundation; chairman, chief executive officer, director, Honeywell International Inc.
Reed, John Shepard: co-chairman, Citibank Corp.

U.S.-Japan Business Council
Cook, J. Michael: chairman, chief executive officer, Deloitte & Touche; chairman, Deloitte & Touche Foundation
Eaton, Robert James: co-chairman, president, chief executive officer, DaimlerChrysler Corp.
Smith, John Francis, Jr.: chairman, General Motors Corp.
Usher, Thomas J.: chairman, chief executive officer, USX Corp.; chairman board trustees, USX Foundation, Inc.

US-USSR Trade Economic Council
Bonsignore, Michael Robert: director, Honeywell Foundation; chairman, chief executive officer, director, Honeywell International Inc.
Bronfman, Edgar Miles: chairman, trustee, Bronfman Foundation/Joseph E. Seagram & Sons, Inc. Fund (Samuel); chairman, Seagram & Sons, Inc. (Joseph E.)

USMA Association Graduates
Gardner, James Richard: vice president, Pfizer Foundation

USO
Wolff, Herbert Eric: secretary, director, First Hawaiian Foundation

Un Arts Fund/ Metropolitan Arts Council
Stephens, Elton Bryson: founder, chairman, Ebsco Industries, Inc.

Un Jewish Appeal
Zacks, Gordon Benjamin: chairman, president, chief executive officer, director, Barry Corp. (R.G.); president, Barry Foundation

Un Scenic Artists
Darling, Robert Edward, Jr.: chairman, Ensign-Bickford Foundation

Un Techs Pacific
Ingersoll, Robert Stephen: chairman, director, Panasonic Foundation

Underground Railroad Freedom Center
Cody, Thomas Gerald: executive vice president legal & human resources, Federated Department Stores, Inc.

Unilaw
O'Brien, James E.: director, Schoeneckers Foundation

Union College
Golub, Lewis: chairman, chief executive officer, director, Golub Corp.

Union Insurance Co. of Providence
Schiek, Fredrick A.: executive vice president, chief operating officer, Employers Mutual Casualty Co.

Union Public Schools Education Foundation
Nowell, Tommy Lynn: vice president finance, controller, Occidental Oil and Gas; treasurer, Occidental Oil and Gas Foundation

United Center Community Economic Development Fund
Maher, Francesca M.: senior vice president, general counsel, secretary, United Airlines Inc.

United Jewish Appeal Federation
Bronfman, Edgar Miles: chairman, trustee, Bronfman Foundation/Joseph E. Seagram & Sons, Inc. Fund (Samuel); chairman, Seagram & Sons, Inc. (Joseph E.)
Tisch, Laurence Alan: chairman, co-chief executive officer, CBS Corp.; trustee, Loews Foundation

United Jewish Appeal Federation New York
Tisch, James S.: president, chief executive officer, director, CNA

United Nations Association
Ross, Arthur: senior vice president, Central National-Gottesman; director, Central National-Gottesman Foundation

United Nations Association USA

Whitehead, John Cunningham: chairman board, Goldman Sachs Foundation

United Negro College Fund

Bloch, Henry Wollman: chairman, Block Foundation (H&R); chairman, director, Block, Inc. (H&R)

Correll, Alston Dayton 'Pete', Jr.: chairman, president, chief executive officer, director, Georgia-Pacific Corp.; director, Georgia-Pacific Foundation

Gilmartin, Raymond V.: chairman, president, chief executive officer, Merck & Co.; chairman, Merck Co. Foundation

Labrecque, Thomas Goulet: president, chief operating officer, director, Chase Manhattan Bank, NA; president, Chase Manhattan Foundation

Luke, John A., Jr.: chairman, president, chief executive officer, director, Westvaco Corp.

Raymond, Lee R.: chairman, president, chief executive officer, Exxon Mobil Corp.

United Performing Arts Fund

Gallagher, Richard S.: director, Badger Meter Foundation

United States Air Force

Lucky, Robert Wendell: corporate vice president, Telcordia Technologies

United States Business School Prague

Rosett, Richard Nathaniel: trustee, Kemper Foundation (James S.)

United States Chamber of Commerce

DeSimone, Livio Diego: chairman, chief executive officer, Minnesota Mining & Manufacturing Co.

United States Commn Civil Rights

Higginbotham, A. Leon, Jr.: director, New York Times Co. Foundation

United States Energy Association

Dunham, Archie W.: president, chief executive officer, Conoco, Inc.

United States National Academy Engineering

Condit, Philip Murray: chairman, chief executive officer, director, Boeing Co.

United States National Council International Management Center Budapest

Rhodes, William Reginald: vice chairman, Citibank Corp.

United States Pacific Economic Corp. Council

Wagner, Thomas Joseph: chairman, CIGNA Foundation

United States Semiconductor Industry Association

Barrett, Craig R.: president, chief operating officer, director, Intel Corp.

United States Supreme Court Historical Society

Margolin, Abraham E.: director, Tension Envelope Foundation

United States Tel Association

Lytle, Gary R.: vice president federal relations, Ameritech Corp.

United States-ASEAN Council Business Technology

David, George A. L.: chairman, president, chief executive officer, chief operating officer, United Technologies Corp.

United States-China Business Council

Franklin, Barbara Hackman: director, Dow Chemical Co.

Gorman, Joseph T.: chairman, chief executive officer, TRW Inc.

United States-Egyptian President Council

Rhodes, William Reginald: vice chairman, Citibank Corp.

United States-Korea Business Council

Usher, Thomas J.: chairman, chief executive officer, USX Corp.; chairman board trustees, USX Foundation, Inc.

United States-Russia Business Council

Marriott, J. Willard, Jr.: chairman, chief executive officer, Marriott International Inc.

Rhodes, William Reginald: vice chairman, Citibank Corp.

United Way

Gifford, Charles Kilvert: trustee, BankBoston Charitable Foundation; chairman, chief executive officer, BankBoston Corp.

Rohr, James Edward: chief executive officer, president, director, PNC Financial Services Group

United Way Ada County

Graves, Ronald Norman: secretary, Simplot Foundation (J.R.)

United Way America

Cook, J. Michael: chairman, chief executive officer, Deloitte & Touche; chairman, Deloitte & Touche Foundation

Harris, Elmer Beseler: president, chief executive officer, director, Alabama Power Co.

Lewis, Frances Aaronson: trustee, Circuit City Foundation

Meyer, Russell William, Jr.: chairman, chief executive officer, Cessna Aircraft Co.; president, Cessna Foundation, Inc.

Polin, Jane Louise: manager, comptroller, GE Fund

Raymond, Lee R.: chairman, president, chief executive officer, Exxon Mobil Corp.

Reuter, Carol Joan: chief executive officer, director, New York Life Foundation; vice president, New York Life Insurance Co.

Ridder, Paul Anthony: chairman, chief executive officer, director, Knight Ridder

Rosenberg, Richard Morris: chairman, chief executive officer (retired), Bank of America

United Way Bay Area Campaign

Beck, Edward W.: senior vice president, general counsel, secretary, director, Shaklee Corp.

United Way Chicago County

Carl, John L.: executive vice president, chief financial officer, BP Amoco Corp.; director, BP Amoco Foundation

United Way Cincinnati

Wehling, Robert Louis: global marketing, government relations officer, Procter & Gamble Co.; president, trustee, Procter & Gamble Fund

United Way Franklin

Olesen, Douglas Eugene, PhD: president, chief executive officer, Battelle Memorial Institute

United Way Greater Saint Louis

Loeb, Jerome Thomas: chairman, director, May Department Stores Co.; president, director, May Department Stores Computer Foundation (The)

Mueller, Charles William: chairman, president, chief executive officer, Ameren Corp.; trustee, Ameren Corp. Charitable Trust

United Way Jackson

McMillan, Howard Lamar, Jr.: president, chief operating officer, director, Deposit Guaranty National Bank

United Way Lake County Illinois

Peterson, Donald Matthew: trustee, Trustmark Foundation; president, chief executive officer, director, Trustmark Insurance Co.

United Way Massachusetts Bay

Ives, J. Atwood: chairman, chief executive officer, Boston Gas Co.; chairman, chief executive officer, trustee, Eastern Enterprises; trustee, Eastern Enterprises Foundation

Lasser, Lawrence Jay: president, chief executive officer, director, Putnam Investments; president, chief executive officer, Putnam Investors Fund

United Way Metropolitan Dallas

Brooks, E. Richard 'Dick': chairman, chief executive officer, director, Central & South West Services

United Way Michigan

Forsyth, John D.: president, chief executive officer, Blue Cross & Blue Shield of Iowa

United Way New York City

Golub, Harvey: chairman, chief executive officer, director, American Express Co.; trustee, American Express Foundation

Sargent, Joseph Dudley: president, chief executive officer, director, Guardian Life Insurance Co. of America

Schwarz, H. Marshall: chairman, chief executive officer, United States Trust Co. of New York

United Way Ohio

Smith, Frederick C.: chairman, trustee, Huffy Foundation, Inc.

United Way Services

Gorman, Joseph T.: chairman, chief executive officer, TRW Inc.

United Way South Hampton

Barry, Richard Francis, III: director, Landmark Communications Foundation; vice chairman, Landmark Communications Inc.

United Way Southeast Michigan

Eaton, Robert James: co-chairman, president, chief executive officer, DaimlerChrysler Corp.

Feldhouse, Lynn Alexandra: vice president, secretary, DaimlerChrysler Corp. Fund

United Way Southwest Indiana

Muehlbauer, James Herman: vice president, director, Koch Foundation

United Way Toledo

Block, William, Jr.: president, trustee, Blade Foundation; president, director, Toledo Blade Co.

United Way Tri-State

Hohn, Harry George, Jr.: chairman, director, New York Life Foundation

United Way Upper Ohio Valley

Wareham, James Lyman: president, AK Steel Corp.

United Way Wichita & Sedgwick County

Meyer, Russell William, Jr.: chairman, chief executive officer, Cessna Aircraft Co.; president, Cessna Foundation, Inc.

United Way of Phoenix

Dewane, John Richard: director, Honeywell Foundation

United Way of Saint Louis

Busch, August Adolphus, III: chairman, president, chief executive officer, Anheuser-Busch Companies, Inc.

United World College New Mexico

Meyerson, Martin: director, Panasonic Foundation

University Alabama

Blount, Winton Malcolm, Jr.: chairman, Blount International, Inc.

Jones, D. Paul, Jr.: chairman, chief executive officer, Compass Bank; trustee, Compass Bank Foundation

Moore, Jackson W.: president, director, Union Planters Corp.

University Albany Foundation

Standish, J. Spencer: chairman, director, Albany International Corp.

University Arizona Keller Business School

Dewane, John Richard: director, Honeywell Foundation

University Arkansas

Blair, James Burton: trustee, Tyson Foundation, Inc.

University Arts

Naples, Ronald James: president, chief executive officer, director, Quaker Chemical Corp.

University Buffalo Council

Lippes, Gerald Sanford: secretary, Mark IV Industries Foundation

University California Berkeley

Broome, Burton Edward: vice president, controller, Transamerica Corp.; vice president, treasurer, Transamerica Foundation

University California Berkeley Alumni Council

Cronk, William F., III: president, director, Dreyer's Grand Ice Cream

University California Irvine School Management

Sutton, Thomas C.: chairman, director, Pacific Mutual Charitable Foundation; chairman, chief executive officer, director, Pacific Mutual Life Insurance Co.

University California Los Angeles Board Medicine Science

Eisner, Michael Dammann: president, trustee, Disney Co. Foundation (Walt); chairman, chief executive officer, director, Disney Co. (Walt)

University California Los Angeles Chancellor's Associates

Rosenzweig, Richard Stuart: executive vice president, director, Playboy Enterprises Inc.

University California San Diego Graduate School International Relations

Coulter, David A.: president, director, Bank of America

University California, Santa Barbara

Lucky, Robert Wendell: corporate vice president, Telcordia Technologies

University Central Florida

Heldreth, Nick E.: vice president human resources corporate relations, Harris Corp.

University Chicago

Bryan, John Henry: chairman, Sara Lee Corp.; director, Sara Lee Foundation

Graham, Katharine Meyer: chairman executive committee, director, The Washington Post

Harris, Irving Brooks: chairman executive committee, director, Pittway Corp.; chairman, director, Pittway Corp. Charitable Foundation

Ingersoll, Robert Stephen: chairman, director, Panasonic Foundation

Ong, John Doyle: chairman board, director, Ameritech Corp.

University Chicago School Business

Johnson, David Willis: chairman, director, Campbell Soup Co.

University Chicago School Social Services

Zavis, Michael W.: managing partner, Katten, Muchin & Zavis; president, director, Katten, Muchin & Zavis Foundation

University Cincinnati

Bridgeland, James Ralph, Jr.: trustee, Star Bank NA, Cincinnati Foundation

University Cincinnati Foundation

LaMacchia, John Thomas: trustee, Cincinnati Bell Foundation, Inc.; president, chief executive officer, director, Cincinnati Bell Inc.

University Cincinnati Medical Center Fund

LaMacchia, John Thomas: trustee, Cincinnati Bell Foundation, Inc.; president, chief executive officer, director, Cincinnati Bell Inc.

University Circle Inc.

Daberko, David A.: chairman, chief executive officer, National City Corp.

University Colorado Foundation

Wise, William Allen: chairman, president, chief executive officer, director, El Paso Energy Co.; chairman, director, El Paso Energy Foundation

University Connecticut School Business

Grise, Cheryl W.: senior vice president, chief administrative officer, Northeast Utilities

University Corp. for Advanced Internet Development

Bowen, William Gordon, PhD: trustee, Merck Co. Foundation

University Dallas

Moroney, James McQueen, Jr.: trustee, Belo Corp. Foundation (A.H.)

University Dubuque

Dammerman, Dennis Dean: vice chairman, director, General Electric Co.

University Evansville

Hinton, Michael R.: president, chief operating officer, director, Old National Bank Evansville

University Florida School Business

Cook, J. Michael: chairman, chief executive officer, Deloitte & Touche; chairman, Deloitte & Touche Foundation

University Georgia Foundation

Correll, Alston Dayton 'Pete', Jr.: chairman, president, chief executive officer, director, Georgia-Pacific Corp.; director, Georgia-Pacific Foundation

University Hartford American Leadership Forum

Kaman, Charles Huron: chairman, president, chief executive officer, director, Kaman Corp.

University Hawaii

Yao, Lily K.: director, First Hawaiian, Inc.

University Hawaii Alumni Association

Wild, Heidi Karin: trustee

University Health Care System Government Comm

Bachmann, Richard Arthur: vice president, secretary, treasurer, director, Louisiana Land & Exploration Co. Foundation

University Health Care Systems

Bersticker, Albert C.: chairman, director, chief executive officer, Ferro Corp.; president, trustee, Ferro Foundation

University Hospital Cleveland

Daberko, David A.: chairman, chief executive officer, National City Corp.

University Idaho Business School

Graves, Ronald Norman: secretary, Simplot Foundation (J.R.)

University Illinois Chicago

Coughlan, Gary Patrick: chief financial officer, senior vice president finance, Abbott Laboratories; director, Abbott Laboratories Fund

University Illinois College Commerce & Business Administration

Rust, Edward Barry, Jr.: chairman, president, director, State Farm Companies Foundation; chairman, president, chief

executive officer, director, State Farm Mutual Automobile Insurance Co.

University Illinois College of Engineering

Engel, Joel Stanley: vice president technology, Ameritech Corp.

University Iowa Foundation

Hadley, Leonard Anson: chairman, chief executive officer, director, Maytag Corp.; president, trustee, Maytag Corp. Foundation

University Iowa School Business

Carver, Martin Gregory: chairman, president, chief executive officer, Bandag, Inc.

Hadley, Leonard Anson: chairman, chief executive officer, director, Maytag Corp.; president, trustee, Maytag Corp. Foundation

University Kansas Business School

Kangas, Edward A.: chairman, chief executive officer, Deloitte & Touche

University Kansas City

Bloch, Henry Wollman: chairman, Block Foundation (H&R); chairman, director, Block, Inc. (H&R)

University Kentucky

Chellgren, Paul Wilbur: chief executive officer, chairman, director, Ashland, Inc.; member, Ashland Inc. Foundation

Disney, Roy Edward: trustee, Disney Co. Foundation (Walt); vice chairman, director, Disney Co. (Walt)

University Kentucky Business Partnership Foundation

Rogers, James E., Jr.: vice chairman, president, chief executive officer, Cinergy Corp.; vice chairman, director, Cinergy Foundation

University Louisville

Hower, Frank Beard, Jr.: vice chairman, Anthem Foundation, Inc.

University Massachusetts Medical Center Foundation Inc.

Nelson, John Martin: chairman, director, TJX Companies, Inc.

University Medicine Dentistry New Jersey

Fine, Roger Seth: vice president, general counsel, Johnson & Johnson; president, Johnson & Johnson Family of Companies Contribution Fund

University Miami

Burns, Mitchell Anthony: president, director, Ryder System Charitable Foundation; chairman, president, chief executive officer, Ryder System, Inc.

Goode, R. Ray: director, Ryder System Charitable Foundation

University Michigan

Ridder, Paul Anthony: chairman, chief executive officer, director, Knight Ridder

University Michigan College Engineering

Eaton, Robert James: cochairman, president, chief executive officer, DaimlerChrysler Corp.

University Michigan Global Leadership

Bonsignore, Michael Robert: director, Honeywell Foundation; chairman, chief executive officer, director, Honeywell International Inc.

University Michigan Medical Center

Davis, Carolyne Kahle, PhD: trustee, Merck Co. Foundation

University Michigan School Business Administration

White, Bernard Joseph: director, Cummins Engine Foundation

University Minnesota

Carlson, Curtis Leroy: chairman, director, Carlson Companies, Inc.; president, treasurer, Carlson Family Foundation (Curtis L.)

Nelson, Glen David, MD: vice chairman, Medtronic, Inc.

University Minnesota Alumni Association

Wright, Donald Franklin: director, Times Mirror Foundation

University Minnesota Carlson School Management

Mee, Michael F.: senior vice president, chief financial officer, Bristol-Myers Squibb Co.

University Minnesota Curtis L Carlson School Management

Carlson, Curtis Leroy: chairman, director, Carlson Companies, Inc.; president, treasurer, Carlson Family Foundation (Curtis L.)

University Minnesota Foundation

Carlson, Curtis Leroy: chairman, director, Carlson Companies, Inc.; president, treasurer, Carlson Family Foundation (Curtis L.)

DeSimone, Livio Diego: chairman, chief executive officer, Minnesota Mining & Manufacturing Co.

Hubbard, Stanley S.: chairman, president, chief executive officer, Hubbard Broadcasting, Inc.; president, Hubbard Foundation

University Minnesota Law School Alumni Association

Neville, James Morton: member board control, Ralston Purina Trust Fund

University Mississippi Alumni Association

McMillan, Howard Lamar, Jr.: president, chief operating officer, director, Deposit Guaranty National Bank

University Montevallo

Denson, William Frank, III: president, Vulcan Materials Co. Foundation

University Nebraska Foundation

Hewitt, James Watt: vice president, treasurer, Abel Foundation

University New England

Countryman, Gary Lee: chairman, Liberty Mutual Insurance Group

University North Carolina

Herring, Leonard Gray: vice president, Lowe's Charitable and Educational Foundation

University North Carolina Chapel Hill

Anderson, Ivan Verner, Jr.: president, chief executive officer, Evening Post Publishing Co.; vice president, Post and Courier Foundation

Burns, Mitchell Anthony: president, director, Ryder System Charitable Foundation; chairman, president, chief executive officer, Ryder System, Inc.

Strickland, Robert Louis: vice president, Lowe's Charitable and Educational Foundation

University Notre Dame

Brademas, John: chairman, Texaco Foundation

McKenna, Andrew James: director, Aon Foundation

University Notre Dame Alumni Clubs Greater Hartford

Long, Michael Thomas: director, Ensign-Bickford Foundation

University Notre Dame College Business Administration

Johnson, David Willis: chairman, director, Campbell Soup Co.

University Notre Dame College Engineering

Earley, Anthony Francis, Jr.: president, chief operating officer, Detroit Edison Co.; director, Detroit Edison Foundation

University Pennsylvania

Bowman, Robert A.: president, chief operating officer, Starwood Hotels & Resorts Worldwide, Inc.

Heimbold, Charles Andreas, Jr.: chairman, president, chief executive officer, Bristol-Myers Squibb Co.

Meyerson, Martin: director, Panasonic Foundation

Pottruck, David Steven: president, chief executive officer, director, Schwab & Co., Inc. (Charles)

Resnick, Lynda Rae: vice chairman, co-owner, Franklin Mint (The)

Vagelos, Pindaros Roy: trustee, Prudential Insurance Co. of America

University Pennsylvania Foundation

Meyerson, Martin: director, Panasonic Foundation

University Pennsylvania Graduate School Fine Arts

Ross, Arthur: senior vice president, Central National-Gottesman; director, Central National-Gottesman Foundation

University Pennsylvania Institute Law & Economics

Resnick, Myron J.: vice president, treasurer, trustee, Allstate Foundation

Wagner, Thomas Joseph: chairman, CIGNA Foundation

University Pennsylvania Law School

Heimbold, Charles Andreas, Jr.: chairman, president, chief executive officer, Bristol-Myers Squibb Co.

University Pennsylvania Medical Center

Davis, Carolyne Kahle, PhD: trustee, Merck Co. Foundation

University Pennsylvania Press

Meyerson, Martin: director, Panasonic Foundation

University Pennsylvania School Arts & Sciences

Hassenfeld, Alan Geoffrey: president, Hasbro Charitable Trust Inc.; chairman, chief executive officer, Hasbro, Inc.

University Pennsylvania Wharton School

Hirsch, Laurence E.: chairman, chief executive officer, director, Centex Corp.

Zuckerman, Mortimer Benjamin: co-founder, chairman, co-publisher, director, Daily News

University Pennsylvania Wharton School Business

Kangas, Edward A.: chairman, chief executive officer, Deloitte & Touche

Resnick, Stewart A.: chairman, chief executive officer, Franklin Mint (The)

Stone, Roger Warren: chairman, president, chief executive officer, director, Stone Container Corp.; president, Stone Foundation

Thompson, Sheldon Lee: senior vice president, chief administrative officer, Sunoco Inc.

Unruh, James Arlen: director, Ameritech Foundation

University Pittsburgh

O'Reilly, F. Anthony John: chairman, trustee, Heinz Co. Foundation (H.J.); chairman, director, Heinz Co. (H.J.)

Usher, Thomas J.: chairman, chief executive officer, USX Corp.; chairman board trustees, USX Foundation, Inc.

University Pittsburgh Joseph M. Katz Graduate School of Business

Graham, Thomas Carlisle: trustee, AK Steel Foundation

University Pittsburgh Law School Board Visitors

Kelson, Richard B.: director, Alcoa Foundation

University Pittsburgh Medical Center

McGuinn, Martin Gregory: chairman, chief executive officer, Mellon Financial Corp.

University Radio Foundation

Dabney, Fred E., II: executive director, Royal & SunAlliance Insurance Foundation, Inc.; vice president corporate communications, Royal & SunAlliance USA, Inc.

University Richmond

Burrus, Robert Lewis, Jr.: trustee, Circuit City Foundation

University Richmond Claiborne Robins School Business

Sheehan, Jeremiah J.: chairman, director, Reynolds Metals Co. Foundation

University Rochester

Dugan, Allan E.: senior vice president corporate strategic service, Xerox Corp.; trustee, Xerox Foundation

University Saint Thomas

Howard, James Joseph, III: chairman, president, chief executive officer, director, Northern States Power Co.

Hubbard, Stanley S.: chairman, president, chief executive officer, Hubbard Broadcasting, Inc.; president, Hubbard Foundation

University San Diego President Club

Copley, David C.: president, trustee, Copley Foundation (James S.); president, chief executive officer, director, senior management board, Copley Press, Inc.

University Santa Clara

Lucas, Donald Leo: chairman, Cadence Designs Systems, Inc.

University Southern California

Wood, Willis B., Jr.: chairman, chief executive officer, director, Pacific Enterprises

University Southern California Alumni Association

Simpson, Andrea Lynn: president

University Southern California Business School

Armstrong, C. Michael: chairman, chief executive officer, AT&T Corp.

University Southern California College Business Administration Business Partnership Foundation

Anderson, Ivan Verner, Jr.: president, chief executive officer, Evening Post Publishing Co.; vice president, Post and Courier Foundation

University Southern Indiana Foundation

Muehlbauer, James Herman: vice president, director, Koch Foundation

University Texas

Wise, William Allen: chairman, president, chief executive officer, director, El Paso Energy Co.; chairman, director, El Paso Energy Foundation

University Utah

Hill, George Richard: president, trustee, Lubrizol Foundation (The)

University Utah Business College

Eccles, Spencer Fox: chairman, chief executive officer, director, First Security Bank of Idaho NA

University Vermont

Graves, Earl Gilbert: director, Aetna Foundation

University Virginia

Frank, Stephen E.: president, chief operating officer, director, Edison International

University Virginia Colgate Business School

Batten, Frank, Sr.: chairman, director, Landmark Communications Foundation; chairman, Landmark Communications Inc.

University Virginia Colgate Business School Foundation

Barry, Richard Francis, III: director, Landmark Communications Foundation; vice chairman, Landmark Communications Inc.

University Wisconsin - Milwaukee Foundation

Bauer, Chris Michael: president, Firstar Milwaukee Foundation

University Wisconsin Alumni Advisory Council

Dewane, John Richard: director, Honeywell Foundation

University Wisconsin Foundation

Fluno, Jere David: vice chairman, Grainger, Inc. (W.W.)

Raymond, Lee R.: chairman, president, chief executive officer, Exxon Mobil Corp.

University Wisconsin Madison

Lyall, Katharine Culbert: trustee, Kemper Foundation (James S.)

University Wisconsin Research Park Corp.

Mebane, David Cummins: chairman, president, chief executive officer, director, Madison Gas & Electric Co.; vice president, Madison Gas & Electric Foundation

University Wisconsin School Business

Bartz, Carol A.: director, Autodesk Foundation; chairman, chief executive officer, Autodesk Inc.

Fitzsimonds, Roger Leon: chairman, Firstar Milwaukee Foundation

University Wyoming Institute Environment & Natural Resources & Policy

Kirby, William Joseph: vice president, director, FMC Foundation

Ruckelshaus, William Doyle: chairman, director, Browning-Ferris Industries Inc.

Universitys Research Association

Joyce, William H.: chairman, president, chief executive officer, chief operating officer, Union Carbide Corp.

Up With People

Coors, Peter Hanson: vice president, director, Coors Brewing Co.

Urban Affairs Coalition

Larsen, Terrence A.: chairman, chief executive officer, First Union Bank; chairman, First Union Regional Foundation

Urban Bankers Forum

Williams, Edward Joseph: president, director, Harris Bank Foundation

Urban Institute

Graham, Katharine Meyer: chairman executive committee, director, The Washington Post

Urban Land Foundation

Lachman, Marguerite Leanne: trustee, Chicago Title and Trust Co. Foundation

Urban Land Institute

Geissinger, Frederick: chairman, chief executive officer, prs, American General Finance

Geissinger, Frederick Wallace: chairman, chief executive officer, president, director, American General Finance Foundation

Lachman, Marguerite Leanne: trustee, Chicago Title and Trust Co. Foundation

Matis, Nina B.: director, Katten, Muchin & Zavis Foundation

Utah State Bar Association

Colton, S. David: senior vice president, general counsel, Phelps Dodge Corp.

Utilities Communicators International

Simpson, Andrea Lynn: president

Utilities State Government Association

Campbell, George Leroy: vice president public affairs, Florida Power Corp.

VP Fair Foundation

Maritz, William Edward: chairman, chief executive officer, president, Maritz Inc.

Valentine Museum

Burrus, Robert Lewis, Jr.: trustee, Circuit City Foundation

Valley Forge Military Academy & College

Buckwalter, Alan Roland, III: chief executive officer, Chase Bank of Texas; president, Chase Bank of Texas Foundation, Inc.

Valley Health Systems Inc.

Gilmartin, Raymond V.: chairman, president, chief executive officer, Merck & Co.; chairman, Merck Co. Foundation

Valley Hospital

Gilmartin, Raymond V.: chairman, president, chief executive officer, Merck & Co.; chairman, Merck Co. Foundation

Valparaiso Chamber of Commerce

Penny, Roger Pratt: president, chief operating officer, director, Bethlehem Steel Corp.

Valparaiso University

Fites, Donald Vester: director, Caterpillar Foundation

Van Cliburn Foundation

Roach, John Vinson, II: chairman, director, Tandy Corp.

Vanderbilt Law School

Moore, Jackson W.: president, director, Union Planters Corp.

Vanderbilt University

Bottorff, Dennis C.: chairman, president, chief executive officer, director, First American Corp.

Ingram, Martha R.: chairman, director, Ingram Industries Inc.

Wilson, James Lawrence: chairman, chief executive officer, director, Rohm & Haas Co.

Vanderbilt University Medical Center

Turner, Cal, Jr.: chairman, chief executive officer, director, Dollar General Corp.

Vassar College

Ingram, Martha R.: chairman, director, Ingram Industries Inc.

Venezuela-American Chamber of Commerce

Rhodes, William Reginald: vice chairman, Citibank Corp.

Vermont Bar Association

Bertrand, Frederic Howard: chairman, Central Vermont Public Service Corp.

Keyser, F. Ray, Jr.: chairman, director, Central Vermont Public Service Corp.

Vermont Business Roundtable

Bertrand, Frederic Howard: chairman, Central Vermont Public Service Corp.

Veterans Advisor Board

Watson, Solomon Brown, IV: vice president, New York Times Co. Foundation

Victorian Society America

Forbes, Christopher 'Kip': vice president, Forbes Foundation; vice chairman, corporate secretary, director, Forbes Inc.

Villa Julie College

Poindexter, Christian Herndon: chairman, Baltimore Gas & Electric Foundation; chairman, chief executive officer, director, Constellation Energy Group, Inc.

Village Shorewood Community Development Association

Bruce, Peter Wayne: director, Badger Meter Foundation

Villanova Law School

McGuinn, Martin Gregory: chairman, chief executive officer, Mellon Financial Corp.

Villanova University Law School

Hirsch, Laurence E.: chairman, chief executive officer, director, Centex Corp.

Vineyard Open Land Foundation

Lasser, Lawrence Jay: president, chief executive officer, director, Putnam Investments; president, chief executive officer, Putnam Investors Fund

Virginia Bankers Association

Tilghman, Richard Granville: chairman, chief executive officer, Crestar Foundation

Virginia Bar Association

Burrus, Robert Lewis, Jr.: trustee, Circuit City Foundation

Cutchins, Clifford Armstrong, IV: president, Fort James Corp.; chairman, director, Fort James Foundation (The)

Druen, W. Sidney: director, Nationwide Insurance Enterprise Foundation

Goode, David Ronald: chairman, president, chief executive officer, director, Norfolk Southern Corp.

Murphy, Christopher J., III: president, chief executive officer, director, First Source Corp.; director, First Source Foundation

Rudnick, Alan A.: vice president, general counsel, corporate secretary, CSX Corp.

Snow, John William: chairman, president, chief executive officer, CSX Corp.

Virginia Business Council

Goode, David Ronald: chairman, president, chief executive officer, director, Norfolk Southern Corp.

Sheehan, Jeremiah J.: chairman, director, Reynolds Metals Co. Foundation

Tilghman, Richard Granville: chairman, chief executive officer, Crestar Foundation

Virginia Business Higher Education Council

Goode, David Ronald: chairman, president, chief executive officer, director, Norfolk Southern Corp.

Virginia Commonwealth Foundation

Reynolds, Randolph Nicklas: vice chairman, executive officer, director, Reynolds Metals Co.; director, Reynolds Metals Co. Foundation

Virginia Commonwealth University

Dozier, Ollin Kemp: treasurer, Universal Leaf Foundation

Virginia Commonwealth University School Engineering Foundation

Sheehan, Jeremiah J.: chairman, director, Reynolds Metals Co. Foundation

Virginia Council Economic Education

Gottwald, Bruce Cobb: chairman, chief executive officer, director, Ethyl Corp.

Virginia Environmental Endowment

Lewis, Frances Aaronson: trustee, Circuit City Foundation

Virginia Foundation Independent Colleges

Goode, David Ronald: chairman, president, chief executive officer, director, Norfolk Southern Corp.

Sheehan, Jeremiah J.: chairman, director, Reynolds Metals Co. Foundation

Spilman, Robert H.: chairman, chief executive officer, Bassett Furniture Industries; chairman, director, Bassett Furniture Industries Fdn.

Tilghman, Richard Granville: chairman, chief executive officer, Crestar Foundation

Virginia Institute of Marine Science

Wolf, Henry C.: vice chairman, chief financial officer, Norfolk Southern Corp.; vice president finance, Norfolk Southern Foundation

Virginia Law Foundation

Burrus, Robert Lewis, Jr.: trustee, Circuit City Foundation

Virginia Manufacturers Association

Spilman, Robert H.: chairman, chief executive officer, Bassett Furniture Industries; chairman, director, Bassett Furniture Industries Fdn.

Virginia Military Institute

Gottwald, Bruce Cobb: chairman, chief executive officer, director, Ethyl Corp.

Virginia Museum

Burrus, Robert Lewis, Jr.: trustee, Circuit City Foundation

Virginia Museum Fine Arts

Lewis, Frances Aaronson: trustee, Circuit City Foundation

Virginia Music Foundation

Tilghman, Richard Granville: chairman, chief executive officer, Crestar Foundation

Virginia Neurol Institute

Weinberg, John Livingston: chairman, president, director, Goldman Sachs Foundation

Virginia Retail Merchants Association

Lewis, Frances Aaronson: trustee, Circuit City Foundation

Virginia State Bar Association

White, James M., III: general counsel, Universal Leaf Foundation; senior vice president, general counsel, assistant secretary, Universal Leaf Tobacco Co., Inc.

Virginia State Board Education

Lewis, Frances Aaronson: trustee, Circuit City Foundation

Wurtzel, Alan Leon: chairman, Circuit City Foundation; chairman, trustee, Circuit City Stores, Inc.

Visiting Nurse Foundation Inc.

Resnick, Alan H.: treasurer, Bausch & Lomb Foundation, Inc.; vice president, treasurer, Bausch & Lomb Inc.

Viterbo College

Connolly, Gerald Edward: trustee, Reinhart Family Foundation (D. B. and Marjorie)

Vitoria Theater Association

Redding, Peter Stoddard: trustee, Sherman-Standard Register Foundation; president, chief executive officer, director, Standard Register Co.

Vocational Resources Inc.

Cain, Alan F.: director, Montana Power Foundation

Voices Illinois Children

Williams, Edward Joseph: president, director, Harris Bank Foundation

Volunteer Lawyers Arts

McClimon, Timothy J.: executive director, AT&T Foundation

Voters Choice

Hefner, Christie Ann: chairman, chief executive officer, Playboy Enterprises Inc.; director, Playboy Foundation

WDC

O'Hare, Dean Raymond: chairman, Chubb Corp.

WGBH Public Broadcasting

LaMantia, Charles Robert: president, chief executive officer, director, Little, Inc. (Arthur D.)

WHYY Philadelphia

Wiksten, Barry Frank: president, CIGNA Foundation

WI Bar Association

Davis, Walter Stewart: secretary, treasurer, Grede Foundation

Salinger, Robert M.: secretary, First Financial Foundation

WI Manufacturing & Commerce

Davis, Erroll Brown, Jr.: president, chief executive officer, director, Wisconsin Power & Light Co.

WKND Greater Hartford Initiative

Fiondella, Robert William: chairman, president, chief executive officer, Phoenix Home Life Mutual Insurance Co.

WLVT-TV

Barnette, Curtis Handley: chairman, chief executive officer, director, Bethlehem Steel Corp.

WMVS Education Television

Gaiswinkler, Robert Sigfried: chairman, director, First Financial Bank; director, First Financial Foundation

WOSU Education Television

Gaiswinkler, Robert Sigfried: chairman, director, First Financial Bank; director, First Financial Foundation

WTTW Channel 11

Rogers, Desiree Glapion: vice president community affairs, Peoples Energy Corp.

WV Bar Association

Barnette, Curtis Handley: chairman, chief executive officer, director, Bethlehem Steel Corp.

WVIZ Public Television

Gherlein, Gerald Lee: member contributions committee, Eaton Charitable Fund

Wabash College

Bachmann, John W.: managing partner, Jones & Co. (Edward D.); chairman, Jones & Co. Foundation (Edward D.)

Wadsworth Atheneum

Besser, John Edward: director, Barnes Group Foundation Inc.; senior vice president finance & law, Barnes Group Inc.

David, George A. L.: chairman, president, chief executive officer, chief operating officer, United Technologies Corp.

Wake Forest University

Meyer, Russell William, Jr.: chairman, chief executive officer, Cessna Aircraft Co.; president, Cessna Foundation, Inc.

Sharpe, Robert Francis, Jr.: senior vice president public affairs, general counsel, PepsiCo, Inc.

Walker Art Center

Atwater, Horace Brewster, Jr.: trustee, Merck Co. Foundation

Liska, Paul J.: executive vice president, chief financial officer, Saint Paul Companies Inc.

Walker Home Children

Cogan, John Francis, Jr.: president, chief executive officer, director, Pioneer Group

Wang Center Performing Arts

Brown, Stephen Lee: chairman, chief executive officer, director, Hancock Financial Services (John)

Washburn University Endowment Association

Stauffer, Stanley Howard: chairman, Stauffer Communications Foundation

Washington & Lee University

Lewis, Frances Aaronson: trustee, Circuit City Foundation

Washington Bar Association

Franke, William Augustus: chairman, president, chief executive officer, America West Airlines, Inc.; director, Phelps Dodge Foundation

Stanton, Philip H.: chief executive officer, director, Washington Trust Bank

Williams, Karen Hastie: director, Fannie Mae Foundation

Washington Board Trade

Larance, Charles L.: vice president corporate relations, GenAmerica Corp.; president, GenAmerican Foundation

Washington County Bar Association

Bertrand, Frederic Howard: chairman, Central Vermont Public Service Corp.

Washington Crossing Foundation

Copley, Helen K.: chairman, trustee, Copley Foundation (James S.); chairman, director, senior management board, Copley Press, Inc.

Washington DC Bar Association

Landin, Thomas Milton: vice president, director, CertainTeed Corp.; vice president, Norton Co. Foundation

Rogers, James E., Jr.: vice chairman, president, chief executive officer, Cinergy Corp.; vice chairman, director, Cinergy Foundation

Washington DC Court Appeals

Weinberger, Caspar Willard: chairman, Forbes Inc.

Washington Daffodil Society

Darling, Robert Edward, Jr.: chairman, Ensign-Bickford Foundation

Washington Legal Clinic for Homeless

Gorelick, Jamie Shona: vice chairman, Fannie Mae

Washington Metropolitan Area Corporate Counsel Association

Rutstein, David W.: secretary, Giant Food Foundation; senior vice president, general counsel, chief administrative officer, Giant Food Inc.

Washington Metropolitan Board Trade

Rutstein, David W.: secretary, Giant Food Foundation; senior vice president, general counsel, chief administrative officer, Giant Food Inc.

Washington Opera

Smith, Donald Kaye: senior vice president, general counsel, director, GEICO Corp.

Washington Philosophical Society

Davis, Ruth Margaret: trustee, Air Products Foundation

Washington Roundtable

Cline, Robert Stanley: chairman, chief executive officer, director, Airborne Freight Corp.

Killinger, Kerry Kent: chairman, president, chief executive officer, director, Washington Mutual, Inc.

Washington School Employes Credit Union

Kurack, Sandra: vice president, trustee, PEMCO Foundation

Washington Society CPA's

Jones, D. Michael: senior vice president, general counsel, Reynolds Metals

Co.; vice president, director, Reynolds Metals Co. Foundation

Washington State Business Roundtable

Weyerhaeuser, George Hunt: director, Weyerhaeuser Co.; trustee, Weyerhaeuser Co. Foundation

Washington University

Bridgewater, Bernard Adolphus, Jr.: member board control, Brown Shoe Co. Charitable Trust; chairman, president, chief executive officer, director, Brown Shoe Co., Inc.

Kemper, David Woods: chairman, president, chief executive officer, director, Commerce Bancshares, Inc.

Knight, Charles Field: chairman, chief executive officer, Emerson Electric Co.

Maritz, William Edward: chairman, chief executive officer, president, Maritz Inc.

Newman, Andrew E.: member, Edison Family Foundation

Van Cleve, William Moore: member public policy committee, Emerson Charitable Trust; partner, Emerson Electric Co.

Washington University School Law

Herron, James Michael: secretary, director, Ryder System Charitable Foundation

Waste Not

Bame, Tracy L.: manager community affairs, Phelps Dodge Foundation

Water Quality Association

DiCamillo, Gary Thomas: chairman, chief executive officer, director, Polaroid Corp.

Watson Institute International Studies

Rhodes, William Reginald: vice chairman, Citibank Corp.

Waverly Children's Home

Lay, Terry: president, Lee, Lee Apparel Co.

Wayne State University Alumni Association

Feldhouse, Lynn Alexandra: vice president, secretary, DaimlerChrysler Corp. Fund

Weizmann Institute Science

Bronfman, Edgar Miles: chairman, trustee, Bronfman Foundation/Joseph E. Seagram & Sons, Inc. Fund (Samuel); chairman, Seagram & Sons, Inc. (Joseph E.)

Wellesley College

Darehshori, Nader Farhang: chairman, president, chief executive officer, Houghton Mifflin Co.

Wendell P Clark Memorial Association

Cogan, John Francis, Jr.: president, chief executive officer, director, Pioneer Group

Wendy Will Care Federation

Graham, William B.: chairman, director, Baxter Allegiance Foundation; chairman emeritus, Baxter International Inc.

Wesley Hospital Endowment Association

Meyer, Russell William, Jr.: chairman, chief executive officer, Cessna Aircraft Co.; president, Cessna Foundation, Inc.

Wesleyan Associates

Johnson, James Lawrence: chairman emeritus, Walter Industries Inc.

Wesleyan University

Zilkha, Ezra Khedouri: president, treasurer, Zilkha Foundation, Inc.; president, Zilkha & Sons

West Point Society New York

Gardner, James Richard: vice president, Pfizer Foundation

Mead, Dana George: chairman, chief executive officer, director, Tenneco Automotive

West Virginia Manufacturing Association

Wareham, James Lyman: president, AK Steel Corp.

West Virginia University College Business Economics

Knicely, Howard V.: president, TRW Foundation

Westchester Education Coalition

Smith, Elizabeth Patience: director, Texaco Foundation; vice president investor relations & shareholder service, Texaco Inc.

Western Energy Supply Transmission Associates

Hock, Delwin D.: chairman, New Century Energies

Western Insurance Information Service

Beyer, Jeffrey C.: president, Farmers Group Safety Foundation

Western Kentucky University National Alumni Association

Guillaume, Raymond Kendrick: vice chairman, chief executive officer, Mid-America Bank of Louisville

Western Michigan Alumni Association

Wild, Heidi Karin: trustee

Western Pension Conference

Kirchhof, Anton Conrad: corporate secretary, general counsel, Louisiana-Pacific Corp.; secretary, Louisiana-Pacific Foundation

Western Regional Council

Hock, Delwin D.: chairman, New Century Energies

Western Studies Petroleum Association

O'Reilly, David J.: chairman, chief executive officer, Chevron Corp.

Westminster Chapel of Bellevue

Eigsti, Roger Harry: chairman, chief executive officer, SAFECO Corp.

Westminster College

Walton, Jon David: trustee, Allegheny Technologies Inc. Charitable Trust

Wharton School Finance

Kiely, W. Leo, III: president, chief operating officer, Coors Brewing Co.

Wheaton College

Pollard, Charles William, Jr.: chairman, director, ServiceMaster Co.; president, director, ServiceMaster Foundation

Wheeling Hospital

Wareham, James Lyman: president, AK Steel Corp.

White House Conference Children Youth

Raines, Franklin Delano: chairman, chief executive officer, Fannie Mae; director, Fannie Mae Foundation

White House Correspondents Association

Thomasson, Dan King: vice president, trustee, Scripps Howard Foundation

White House Fellows Association

Mulford, David: chairman, Credit Suisse First Boston

White Memorial Foundation

Ripley, Sidney Dillon, II: director emeritus, Hitachi Foundation

Whitehead Institute

Koch, David Hamilton: director, Koch Foundation, Inc. (Fred C. and Mary R.)

Whitehead Institution

Soden, Paul A.: senior vice president, secretary, general counsel, Reader's Digest Association, Inc. (The)

Whitney Museum American Art

Chambers, Anne Cox: chairman, trustee, Cox Foundation (James M.)

Geier, Philip Henry, Jr.: chairman, president, chief executive officer, Interpublic Group of Companies, Inc.

Klein, Calvin Richard: president, Calvin Klein

O'Reilly, F. Anthony John: chairman, trustee, Heinz Co. Foundation (H.J.); chairman, director, Heinz Co. (H.J.)

Wichita Chamber of Commerce

Meyer, Russell William, Jr.: chairman, chief executive officer, Cessna Aircraft Co.; president, Cessna Foundation, Inc.

Wildlife Conservation Society

Cohen, Jonathan L.: secretary, director, Goldman Sachs Foundation

Wildlife Legislative Fund

Coors, Peter Hanson: vice president, director, Coors Brewing Co.

Wildlife Management Institute

Griffin, Donald Wayne: chairman, president, chief executive officer, director, Olin Corp.; trustee, Olin Corp. Charitable Trust

Wilkes-Barre Chamber of Commerce

Connor, Richard L.: president, publisher, Fort Worth Star-Telegram Inc.

Will Rogers Memorial Fund

Redstone, Sumner Murray: chairman, Viacom Inc.

Willamette University

Meyer, Jerome J.: chairman, chief executive officer, Tektronix, Inc.

William Allen White Foundation

Stauffer, Stanley Howard: chairman, Stauffer Communications Foundation

William Mitchell of College Law

Stroup, Stanley Stephenson: executive vice president, general counsel, Norwest Corp.

Winston Churchill Memorial Trust

Weinberger, Caspar Willard: chairman, Forbes Inc.

Winterthur Museum Gardens
Woolard, Edgar Smith, Jr.: director, du Pont de Nemours & Co. (E.I.)

Wisconsin Alumni Research Foundation
Raymond, Lee R.: chairman, president, chief executive officer, Exxon Mobil Corp.

Wisconsin Association Manufacturing & Commerce
Fitzsimonds, Roger Leon: chairman, Firstar Milwaukee Foundation

Wisconsin Bar Association
Bruce, Peter Wayne: director, Badger Meter Foundation
Loos, Henry J.: secretary, Charter Manufacturing Co. Foundation

Wisconsin Institute CPA's
Graff, Stephen Ney: director, Bucyrus-Erie Foundation

Wisconsin Policy Research Institute
Fitzsimonds, Roger Leon: chairman, Firstar Milwaukee Foundation

Wisconsin Utilities Association
Schrader, Thomas F.: vice president, director, WICOR Foundation

Wofford College
Milliken, Roger: chairman, chief executive officer, Milliken & Co.; member advisory committee, Milliken Foundation

Wolf Trap Foundation
Zuckerman, Mortimer Benjamin: co-founder, chairman, co-publisher, director, Daily News

Women Cable TV
Necessary, Steven K.: senior vice president marketing, Scientific-Atlanta, Inc.

Women's First Healthcare
Heisen, JoAnn Heffernan: vice president, chief information officer, Johnson & Johnson; treasurer, Johnson & Johnson Family of Companies Contribution Fund

Women's Forum New York
Blanke, Gail Ann: vice president, Avon Products Foundation, Inc.

Women's Forum Washington
Franklin, Barbara Hackman: director, Dow Chemical Co.

Women's Research Education Institute
Heisen, JoAnn Heffernan: vice president, chief information officer, Johnson & Johnson; treasurer, Johnson & Johnson Family of Companies Contribution Fund

Womens Bar Association
Gorelick, Jamie Shona: vice chairman, Fannie Mae

Womens Economic Roundtable
Dinerstein, Martha L.: managing director, head marketing & corporate communications, United States Trust Co. of New York

Woodrow Wilson Center International Scholars
Andreas, Dwayne Orville: chairman, chief executive officer, Archer-Daniels-Midland Co.
Brademas, John: chairman, Texaco Foundation

Woodrow Wilson College Law
Moore, Virlyn B., Jr.: director, Pheonix Foundation

Woodrow Wilson National Fellowship Foundation
Connor, James Richard: executive director, Kemper Foundation (James S.)
Simpson, Louis Allen: president, chief executive officer capital operations, director, GEICO Corp.

Woodruff Arts Center
Harkey, Robert Shelton: trustee, Delta Air Lines Foundation; senior vice president, general counsel, secretary, Delta Air Lines, Inc.

Woods Hole Oceanographic Institute
Magee, John Francis: chairman, director, Little, Inc. (Arthur D.)

Woodward Academy
Eason, William Everette, Jr.: senior vice president, corporate secretary, general counsel, Scientific-Atlanta, Inc.

Wooster College
Walton, S. Robson: member, Wal-Mart Foundation; chairman, director, Wal-Mart Stores, Inc.

Worcester Art Music
Nelson, John Martin: chairman, director, TJX Companies, Inc.

Worcester Performing Arts School
Whitney, Wallace F., Jr.: secretary, treasurer, Wyman-Gordon Foundation

Worcester Polytech Institute
Nelson, John Martin: chairman, director, TJX Companies, Inc.
O'Brien, John Francis, Jr.: president, chief executive officer, Allmerica Financial Corp.

World Affairs Council
Armstrong, C. Michael: chairman, chief executive officer, AT&T Corp.
James, George Barker, II: senior vice president, chief financial officer, Levi Strauss & Co.

World Affairs Council Philadelphia
Hanway, H. Edward: president, chief executive officer, CIGNA Corp.

World Affairs Council Town Hall
Leonis, John Michael: chairman, director, Litton Industries, Inc.

World Business Council
Hubbard, Stanley S.: chairman, president, chief executive officer, Hubbard Broadcasting, Inc.; president, Hubbard Foundation
Musser, Warren Van Dyke: chairman, chief executive officer, director, Safeguard Scientifics; president, director, Safeguard Scientifics Foundation

World Council Churches
Brademas, John: chairman, Texaco Foundation

World Cup USA Inc.
Kissinger, Henry Alfred: director, CBS Foundation

World Economic Forum
Schiro, James J.: chairman, senior partner, PricewaterhouseCoopers
Standish, J. Spencer: chairman, director, Albany International Corp.
Trujillo, Solomon D.: president, US West Foundation; president, chief executive officer, US West, Inc.

World Firms General Council
Schiro, James J.: chairman, senior partner, PricewaterhouseCoopers

World Jewish Congress
Bronfman, Edgar Miles: chairman, trustee, Bronfman Foundation/Joseph E. Seagram & Sons, Inc. Fund (Samuel); chairman, Seagram & Sons, Inc. (Joseph E.)
Margolin, Abraham E.: director, Tension Envelope Foundation

World President Organization
Koch, Robert Louis, II: president, chief executive officer, director, Koch Enterprises, Inc.; president, director, Koch Foundation

World Press Freedom Comm
Ottaway, James Haller, Jr.: senior vice president, director, Dow Jones & Co., Inc.; member advisory committee, Dow Jones Foundation

World Resources Institute
Bryson, John E.: chairman, chief executive officer, Edison International
Burt, Robert Norcross: chairman, chief executive officer, director, FMC Corp.; director, FMC Foundation

World Trade Organization Task Force Member
Platt, Lewis Emmett: chairman, Hewlett-Packard Co.

World Travel Tourism Council
Golub, Harvey: chairman, chief executive officer, director, American Express Co.; trustee, American Express Foundation
Marriott, J. Willard, Jr.: chairman, chief executive officer, Marriott International Inc.

World Wildlife Foundation USA
Ottaway, James Haller, Jr.: senior vice president, director, Dow Jones & Co., Inc.; member advisory committee, Dow Jones Foundation

World Wildlife Fund
Ripley, Sidney Dillon, II: director emeritus, Hitachi Foundation

Writers Guild America
Disney, Roy Edward: trustee, Disney Co. Foundation (Walt); vice chairman, director, Disney Co. (Walt)
Hotchner, Aaron Edward: vice president, director, executive, Newman's Own Foundation; vice president, treasurer, Newman's Own Inc.

Xavier University
Cody, Thomas Gerald: executive vice president legal & human resources, Federated Department Stores, Inc.
Hayden, Joseph Page, Jr.: trustee, Star Bank NA, Cincinnati Foundation
Lautenbach, Terry Robert: trustee, Air Products Foundation
Leser, Lawrence Arthur: chairman, director, Scripps Co. (E.W.); member, Scripps Howard Foundation

Viviano, Joseph P.: president, court, Hershey Foods Corp.

YM-YWHA New York

Wallach, Kenneth L.: vice president, Central National-Gottesman Foundation

YMCA

Holmes, David Richard: chief executive officer, chief operating officer, director, Reynolds & Reynolds Co.

Meyer, Jerome J.: chairman, chief executive officer, Tektronix, Inc.

Purvis, George Frank, Jr.: chairman, president, chief executive officer, director, Pan-American Life Insurance Co.

YMCA Anne Arundel County

Poindexter, Christian Herndon: chairman, Baltimore Gas & Electric Foundation; chairman, chief executive officer, director, Constellation Energy Group, Inc.

YMCA Chicago

Fligg, James E.: executive vice president, BP Amoco Corp.

YMCA Greater Houston

Tuerff, James R.: president, director, American General Finance

YMCA Greater Philadelphia

Landin, Thomas Milton: vice president, director, CertainTeed Corp.; vice president, Norton Co. Foundation

YMCA Metropolitan Chicago

Maher, Francesca M.: senior vice president, general counsel, secretary, United Airlines Inc.

YMCA Metropolitan Milwaukee

Winter, William Bergford: president, Bucyrus-Erie Co.; chairman, president, director, Bucyrus-Erie Foundation

YMCA Metropolitan Phoenix & Sun Valley

Snell, Richard: chairman, president, chief executive officer, director, Arizona Public Service Co.

YMCA Montgomery

Blount, Winton Malcolm, Jr.: chairman, Blount International, Inc.

YMCA United States of America

Platt, Lewis Emmett: chairman, Hewlett-Packard Co.

YWCA

Copley, Helen K.: chairman, trustee, Copley Foundation (James S.); chairman, director, senior management board, Copley Press, Inc.

Yachad Inc.

Zigas, Barry: senior vice president, Fannie Mae; director, Fannie Mae Foundation

Yale Alumni Association

Manoogian, Richard Alexander: chairman, chief executive officer, director, Masco Corp.

Yale Corp.

Pepper, John E., Jr.: chairman executive committee, Procter & Gamble Co.

Schacht, Henry Brewer: director, Cummins Engine Foundation

Yale Library Association

Daniels, John Hancock: chairman, Archer-Daniels-Midland Foundation

Yale School Management

Armstrong, C. Michael: chairman, chief executive officer, AT&T Corp.

Pepper, John E., Jr.: chairman executive committee, Procter & Gamble Co.

Yale University Art Gallery

Manoogian, Richard Alexander: chairman, chief executive officer, director, Masco Corp.

Yale University Law Journal

Bryson, John E.: chairman, chief executive officer, Edison International

Yale University Law School Association

Wander, Herbert S.: secretary, director, Katten, Muchin & Zavis Foundation

Yale University School Management

Grasso, Richard A.: chairman, chief executive officer, New York Stock Exchange, Inc.

York Area Chamber of Commerce

Gross, Randall A.: trustee, York Federal Savings & Loan Foundation

York Area Enterprise Development Committee

Pullo, Robert W.: chairman, chief executive officer, director, York Federal Savings & Loan Association; president, trustee, York Federal Savings & Loan Foundation

York City School District Authority

Angelo, Robert A.: president, chief operating officer, York Federal Savings & Loan Association; secretary, York Federal Savings & Loan Foundation

York County Bar Association

Angelo, Robert A.: president, chief operating officer, York Federal Savings & Loan Association; secretary, York Federal Savings & Loan Foundation

York County Industrial Development Corp.

Pullo, Robert W.: chairman, chief executive officer, director, York Federal Savings & Loan Association; president, trustee, York Federal Savings & Loan Foundation

York Township Water Sewer Authority

Pullo, Robert W.: chairman, chief executive officer, director, York Federal Savings & Loan Association; president, trustee, York Federal Savings & Loan Foundation

York University

McNally, Alan G.: chairman, chief executive officer, Harris Trust & Savings Bank

Young Audiences

Polin, Jane Louise: manager, comptroller, GE Fund

Young Men's Christian Association Greater New York

Grasso, Richard A.: chairman, chief executive officer, New York Stock Exchange, Inc.

Young President Association

Voet, Paul C.: trustee, Chemed Foundation

Young President Organization

Coors, Peter Hanson: vice president, director, Coors Brewing Co.

Graves, Earl Gilbert: director, Aetna Foundation

Hefner, Christie Ann: chairman, chief executive officer, Playboy Enterprises Inc.; director, Playboy Foundation

Kampouris, Emmanuel Andrew: chairman, president, chief executive officer, director, American Standard Inc.

Koch, Robert Louis, II: president, chief executive officer, director, Koch Enterprises, Inc.; president, director, Koch Foundation

McCoy, John Bonnet: president, chief executive officer, Ameritech Corp.

Murphy, Christopher J., III: president, chief executive officer, director, First Source Corp.; director, First Source Foundation

Powell, George Everett, III: president, chief executive officer, director, Yellow Corp.; trustee, Yellow Corp. Foundation

Robinson, E. B., Jr.: chairman, chief executive officer, director, Deposit Guaranty National Bank

Rogers, James E., Jr.: vice chairman, president, chief executive officer, Cinergy Corp.; vice chairman, director, Cinergy Foundation

Rohr, James Edward: chief executive officer, president, director, PNC Financial Services Group

Satre, Philip Glen: chairman, president, chief executive officer, director, Promus Hotel Corp.

Weiser, Irving: chairman, president, chief executive officer, Dain Bosworth Inc.

Youngstown Area Chamber of Commerce

Powers, Paul Joseph: chairman, president, chief executive officer, director, Commercial Intertech Corp.; president, trustee, Commercial Intertech Foundation

Tucker, Don Eugene: trustee, Commercial Intertech Foundation

Youth Understanding

Whitehead, John Cunningham: chairman board, Goldman Sachs Foundation

Zeta Psi

Lucas, Donald Leo: chairman, Cadence Designs Systems, Inc.

Moritz, Charles Worthington: chairman, director, Dun & Bradstreet Corp.

Zoological Society India

Ripley, Sidney Dillon, II: director emeritus, Hitachi Foundation

Zoological Society San Diego

Copley, David C.: president, trustee, Copley Foundation (James S.); president, chief executive officer, director, senior management board, Copley Press, Inc.

Officers And Directors By Club Affiliations

Lists individuals by clubs to which they belong.

100 Club

Disney, Roy Edward: trustee, Disney Co. Foundation (Walt); vice chairman, director, Disney Co. (Walt)

100 Club Jackson

McMillan, Howard Lamar, Jr.: president, chief operating officer, director, Deposit Guaranty National Bank

1925 F Street Club

Franklin, Barbara Hackman: director, Dow Chemical Co.

Graham, Katharine Meyer: chairman executive committee, director, The Washington Post

200 Club

Dods, Walter Arthur, Jr.: president, director, First Hawaiian Foundation; chairman, chief executive officer, director, First Hawaiian, Inc.

25 Year Club

Haddock, Ronald Wayne: president, chief executive officer, director, FINA; president, FINA Foundation

25 Year Petroleum Industries Club

Carroll, Philip Joseph: chairman, chief executive officer, Fluor Corp.; chairman, trustee, Fluor Foundation

33 Club

Howe, Stanley M.: president, HON Industries Charitable Foundation; chairman emeritus, director, HON Industries Inc.

Actuaries Des Moines Club

Brooks, Roger Kay: chairman, AmerUS Group

Advertising Los Angeles Club

Carey, Kathryn Ann: foundation manager, American Honda Foundation

Ahepa Club

Brademas, John: chairman, Texaco Foundation

Akron City Club

Calise, Nicholas James: vice president, associate general counsel, secretary, BFGoodrich Co.; secretary, Goodrich Foundation, Inc. (B.F.)

Holland, Willard R.: chairman, chief executive officer, FirstEnergy Corp.

Algonquin Club

Brown, Stephen Lee: chairman, chief executive officer, director, Hancock Financial Services (John)

Countryman, Gary Lee: chairman, Liberty Mutual Insurance Group

Allegheny Club

O'Reilly, F. Anthony John: chairman, trustee, Heinz Co. Foundation (H.J.); chairman, director, Heinz Co. (H.J.)

Allegheny Country Club

Newlin, William Rankin: trustee, Kennametal Foundation

Alpha Delta Phi

Peressinni, William E.: senior vice president, chief financial officer, PacifiCorp; treasurer, PacifiCorp Foundation

Alta Club

Eccles, Spencer Fox: chairman, chief executive officer, director, First Security Bank of Idaho NA

America Club

Johnson, Samuel Curtis: chairman, director, president, Johnson & Son (S.C.); chairman, trustee, Johnson Wax Fund (S.C.)

American Legion Club

Barnes, Wallace W.: director, Barnes Group Foundation Inc.

Buxton, Charles Ingraham, II: chairman, Federated Mutual Insurance Co.; president, Federated Mutual Insurance Foundation

American Yacht Club

Holmes, David Richard: chief executive officer, chief operating officer, director, Reynolds & Reynolds Co.

Annabels Club

O'Reilly, F. Anthony John: chairman, trustee, Heinz Co. Foundation (H.J.); chairman, director, Heinz Co. (H.J.)

Annandale Golf Club

Ukropina, James R.: partner, Pacific Mutual Life Insurance Co.

Apawanis Club

Paton, Leland B.: president capital marketings, director, member executive committee, Prudential Securities Inc.

Arcola Country Club

Howe, Wesley Jackson: chairman emeritus, director, Becton Dickinson & Co.

Argyle Club

Schlumberger, Pierre Marcel: director, Schlumberger Foundation

Arid Club

Harad, George Jay: chairman, chief executive officer, director, Boise Cascade Corp.

Arizona Club

Franke, William Augustus: chairman, president, chief executive officer, America West Airlines, Inc.; director, Phelps Dodge Foundation

Army-Navy Country Club

Landin, Thomas Milton: vice president, director, CertainTeed Corp.; vice president, Norton Co. Foundation

Arsenal Golf Club

Becherer, Hans Walter: chairman, chief executive officer, director, Deere & Co.; director, Deere Foundation (John)

Arts Chicago Club

Simpson, Louis Allen: president, chief executive officer capital operations, director, GEICO Corp.

Athenaeum Club

Wiksten, Barry Frank: president, CIGNA Foundation

Athletic Club

Brumm, Paul Michael: executive vice president, chief financial officer, Fifth Third Bancorp

Tobias, Randall L.: chairman emeritus, Lilly & Co. (Eli)

Atlanta Country Club

McGovern, John Francis: chief financial officer, executive vice president, Georgia-Pacific Corp.; chairman, Georgia-Pacific Foundation

Augusta National Golf Club

Houghton, James Richardson: director, Corning Inc.; trustee, Corning Inc. Foundation

Milliken, Roger: chairman, chief executive officer, Milliken & Co.; member advisory committee, Milliken Foundation

Avenel Golf Club

Marriott, J. Willard, Jr.: chairman, chief executive officer, Marriott International Inc.

Bachelor San Diego Club

Copley, David C.: president, trustee, Copley Foundation (James S.); president, chief executive officer, director, senior management board, Copley Press, Inc.

Bald Peak Colony Club

Montrone, Paul Michael: vice president, partner, Winthrop Foundation

Baltusrol Golf Club

Longfield, William H.: president, Bard Foundation (C.R.); chairman, chief executive officer, director, Bard, Inc. (C.R.)

Bankers Club

Carter, George Kent: vice president, treasurer, Chevron Corp.

Carter, John Douglas: executive vice president, director, Bechtel Group, Inc.

Cody, Thomas Gerald: executive vice president legal & human resources, Federated Department Stores, Inc.

Ginn, Samuel L.: chairman, director, AirTouch Communications Foundation; chairman, chief executive officer, director, Vodafone AirTouch Plc

Hayden, Joseph Page, Jr.: trustee, Star Bank NA, Cincinnati Foundation

Hutton, Edward L.: chairman, chief executive officer, director, Chemed Corp.

LaMacchia, John Thomas: trustee, Cincinnati Bell Foundation, Inc.; president, chief executive officer, director, Cincinnati Bell Inc.

Randolph, Jackson Harold: chairman, Cinergy Corp.; chairman, director, Cinergy Foundation

Rogers, James E., Jr.: vice chairman, president, chief executive officer, Cinergy Corp.; vice chairman, director, Cinergy Foundation

Bankers San Francisco Club

Mullane, Donald A.: executive vice president, Bank of America; chairman, Bank of America Foundation

Bassett Country Club

Spilman, Robert H.: chairman, chief executive officer, Bassett Furniture Industries; chairman, director, Bassett Furniture Industries Fdn.

Bath & Tennis Club

Graham, William B.: chairman, director, Baxter Allegiance Foundation; chairman emeritus, Baxter International Inc.

Bayville Golf Club

Goode, David Ronald: chairman, president, chief executive officer, director, Norfolk Southern Corp.

Beachmont Country Club

Mandel, Jack N.: director, Premier Industrial Corp.

Bel-Air Bay Club

Hays, Thomas Chandler: chairman, chief executive officer, director, Fortune Brands, Inc.

Belle Meade Country Club

Bottorff, Dennis C.: chairman, president, chief executive officer, director, First American Corp.

Bradford, James C., Jr.: president, Bradford and Co. Foundation (J.C.); senior partner, Bradford & Co. (J.C)

Bellerive Country Club

McKenna, William John: director, chairman, Kellwood Co.; chairman, president, director, Kellwood Foundation

Bellport Bay Yacht Club

Cohen, Jonathan L.: secretary, director, Goldman Sachs Foundation

Belmont Country Club

Block, John Robinson: vice president, trustee, Blade Foundation

Berkshire Country Club

Hafer, Fred Douglass: chairman, president, chief executive officer, GPU Inc.

Bethlehem Club

Barnette, Curtis Handley: chairman, chief executive officer, director, Bethlehem Steel Corp.

Big Eddy Club

Amos, Paul Shelby: cofounder, chairman, director, AFLAC Inc.

Bighorn Country Club

Lucas, Donald Leo: chairman, Cadence Designs Systems, Inc.

Birmingham Country Club

Denson, William Frank, III: president, Vulcan Materials Co. Foundation

Birmingham Press Club

Stephens, Elton Bryson: founder, chairman, Ebsco Industries, Inc.

Blackhawk Country Club

Ginn, Samuel L.: chairman, director, AirTouch Communications Foundation; chairman, chief executive officer, director, Vodafone AirTouch Plc

Blind Brook Club

Cook, J. Michael: chairman, chief executive officer, Deloitte & Touche; chairman, Deloitte & Touche Foundation

Mead, Dana George: chairman, chief executive officer, director, Tenneco Automotive

Blind Brook Country Club

Andreas, Dwayne Orville: chairman, chief executive officer, Archer-Daniels-Midland Co.

Clark, Howard Longstreth, Jr.: vice chairman, Walter Industries Inc.

Douglass, Robert Royal: trustee, Chase Manhattan Foundation

Lee, Charles Robert: chairman, chief executive officer, director, GTE Corp.; chief executive officer, trustee, GTE Foundation

Moritz, Charles Worthington: chairman, director, Dun & Bradstreet Corp.

Schadt, James Phillip: chairman, president, chief executive officer, director, Reader's Digest Association, Inc. (The); chairman, director, Reader's Digest Foundation

Bloomfield Hills Country Club

Lyon, Wayne Barton: president, chief operating officer, director, Masco Corp.

Bloomfield Open Hunt Club

Brennan, Leo Joseph, Jr.: vice president, executive director, Ford Motor Co. Fund

Blooming Grove Hunting & Fishing Club

Barnette, Curtis Handley: chairman, chief executive officer, director, Bethlehem Steel Corp.

Bloomington Country Club

Johnson, James Lawrence: chairman emeritus, Walter Industries Inc.

Blue Hills Country Club

Strandjord, Mary Jeannine: director, Sprint Foundation

Blue Key Club

Connor, James Richard: executive director, Kemper Foundation (James S.)

Blue Mound Country Club

Davis, Walter Stewart: secretary, treasurer, Grede Foundation

Gaiswinkler, Robert Sigfried: chairman, director, First Financial Bank; director, First Financial Foundation

Board Room New York City Club

O'Reilly, F. Anthony John: chairman, trustee, Heinz Co. Foundation (H.J.); chairman, director, Heinz Co. (H.J.)

Bob Olink Golf Club

Jacobsen, Thomas Herbert: chairman, president, chief executive officer, Mercantile Bank NA

Boca Bay Pass Club

Hayden, Joseph Page, Jr.: trustee, Star Bank NA, Cincinnati Foundation

Boca Rio Country Club

Zavis, Michael W.: managing partner, Katten, Muchin & Zavis; president, director, Katten, Muchin & Zavis Foundation

Bogey Club

Bachmann, John W.: managing partner, Jones & Co. (Edward D.); chairman, Jones & Co. Foundation (Edward D.)

Jacobsen, Thomas Herbert: chairman, president, chief executive officer, Mercantile Bank NA

Mueller, Charles William: chairman, president, chief executive officer, Ameren Corp.; trustee, Ameren Corp. Charitable Trust

Van Cleve, William Moore: member public policy committee, Emerson Charitable Trust; partner, Emerson Electric Co.

Bohemian Club

Dingman, Michael David: partner, director, Winthrop Foundation

Gammill, Lee Morgan, Jr.: director, New York Life Foundation; vice chairman, director, New York Life Insurance Co.

Ingersoll, Robert Stephen: chairman, director, Panasonic Foundation

James, George Barker, II: senior vice president, chief financial officer, Levi Strauss & Co.

Kissinger, Henry Alfred: director, CBS Foundation

Weinberger, Caspar Willard: chairman, Forbes Inc.

Wilbur, Brayton, Jr.: president, chief executive officer, Wilbur-Ellis Co. & Connell Brothers Co.; president, Wilbur Foundation (Brayton)

Bond Club

Cohen, Jonathan L.: secretary, director, Goldman Sachs Foundation

Paton, Leland B.: president capital marketings, director, member executive committee, Prudential Securities Inc.

Simmons, Hardwick: president, chief executive officer, director, Prudential Securities Inc.

Boone Valley Golf Club

Loeb, Jerome Thomas: chairman, director, May Department Stores Co.; president, director, May Department Stores Computer Foundation (The)

Boothbay Harbor Yacht Club

Brinegar, Claude Stout: trustee, Unocal Foundation

Brae Burn Country Club

DiCamillo, Gary Thomas: chairman, chief executive officer, director, Polaroid Corp.

Briar Club

Buckwalter, Alan Roland, III: chief executive officer, Chase Bank of Texas; president, Chase Bank of Texas Foundation, Inc.

Broadmoor Golf Club

Gaylord, Edward Lewis: chairman, chief executive officer, director, publisher, Oklahoma Publishing Co.; trustee, Oklahoman Foundation (The)

Brook Club

Kerr, William T.: chairman, chief executive officer, director, Meredith Corp.

Kissinger, Henry Alfred: director, CBS Foundation

Masin, Michael Terry: vice chairman, president international, director, GTE Corp.; trustee, GTE Foundation

Montrone, Paul Michael: vice president, partner, Winthrop Foundation

Price, Charles H., II: director, New York Times Co. Foundation

Spilman, Robert H.: chairman, chief executive officer, Bassett Furniture Industries; chairman, director, Bassett Furniture Industries Fdn.

Brook Hollow Golf Club

Haddock, Ronald Wayne: president, chief executive officer, director, FINA; president, FINA Foundation

Brookline Country Club

Houghton, James Richardson: director, Corning Inc.; trustee, Corning Inc. Foundation

Bryn Mawr Country Club

Zavis, Michael W.: managing partner, Katten, Muchin & Zavis; president, director, Katten, Muchin & Zavis Foundation

Bucks Harbor Yacht Club

Benenson, James, Jr.: chairman, president, director, Vesper Corp.; trustee, Vesper Foundation

Buffalo Canoe Club

Kennedy, Bernard Joseph: chairman, president, chief executive officer, director, National Fuel Gas Distribution Corp.

Buffalo Soccer Club

Penny, Roger Pratt: president, chief operating officer, director, Bethlehem Steel Corp.

Bull & Bear Club

Burrus, Robert Lewis, Jr.: trustee, Circuit City Foundation

Bulls Eye Club

Kenney, Richard John: director, Consolidated Papers Foundation, Inc.; senior vice president finance, Consolidated Papers, Inc.

Burlingame Country Club

Wilbur, Brayton, Jr.: president, chief executive officer, Wilbur-Ellis Co. & Connell Brothers Co.; president, Wilbur Foundation (Brayton)

Burning Tree Club

Marriott, J. Willard, Jr.: chairman, chief executive officer, Marriott International Inc.

McCorkindale, Douglas H.: vice chairman, president, Gannett Co., Inc.; president, Gannett Foundation

Usher, Thomas J.: chairman, chief executive officer, USX Corp.; chairman board trustees, USX Foundation, Inc.

Butterfield Country Club

Quinlan, Michael Robert: chairman executive committee, McDonald's Corp.; director, McDonald's Corp. Charitable Foundation

California Club

Farman, Richard Donald: chairman, chief executive officer, Pacific Enterprises

Masin, Michael Terry: vice chairman, president international, director, GTE Corp.; trustee, GTE Foundation

Simpson, Louis Allen: president, chief executive officer capital operations, director, GEICO Corp.

Ukropina, James R.: partner, Pacific Mutual Life Insurance Co.

Wood, Willis B., Jr.: chairman, chief executive officer, director, Pacific Enterprises

California Yacht Club

Disney, Roy Edward: trustee, Disney Co. Foundation (Walt); vice chairman, director, Disney Co. (Walt)

Capital City Club

Eason, William Everette, Jr.: senior vice president, corporate secretary, general counsel, Scientific-Atlanta, Inc.

Capital Hill Club

Campbell, George Leroy: vice president public affairs, Florida Power Corp.

Kasputys, Joseph Edward: chairman, trustee, Hitachi Foundation

Landin, Thomas Milton: vice president, director, CertainTeed Corp.; vice president, Norton Co. Foundation

Carlton Club London

Skilling, Raymond Inwood: executive vice president, chief counsel, director, Aon Corp.; director, Aon Foundation

Carriage Club

Bloch, Henry Wollman: chairman, Block Foundation (H&R); chairman, director, Block, Inc. (H&R)

Cascade Country Club

Sadler, Robert L.: president, vice chairman, director, Old Kent Bank

Casino Club

Graham, William B.: chairman, director, Baxter Allegiance Foundation; chairman emeritus, Baxter International Inc.

Skilling, Raymond Inwood: executive vice president, chief counsel, director, Aon Corp.; director, Aon Foundation

Casper Country Club

True, Jean Durland: trustee, True Foundation; partner, True Oil Co.

Castalia Trout Club

Ong, John Doyle: chairman board, director, Ameritech Corp.

Castle Harbor Yacht Club

Hilyard, James E.: president, CertainTeed Corp.; director, CertainTeed Corp. Foundation

Castle Pines Golf Club

Price, Charles H., II: director, New York Times Co. Foundation

Catawba Island Club

O'Brien, John F.: trustee, McDonald & Co. Securities Foundation

Causeway Club

Heimbold, Charles Andreas, Jr.: chairman, president, chief executive officer, Bristol-Myers Squibb Co.

Center Club

Wood, Willis B., Jr.: chairman, chief executive officer, director, Pacific Enterprises

Central Park Tennis Club

Eigsti, Roger Harry: chairman, chief executive officer, SAFECO Corp.

Century Association

Douglass, Robert Royal: trustee, Chase Manhattan Foundation

Century Boston Club

Harad, George Jay: chairman, chief executive officer, director, Boise Cascade Corp.

Century Club

Forbes, Christopher 'Kip': vice president, Forbes Foundation; vice chairman, corporate secretary, director, Forbes Inc.

Hotchner, Aaron Edward: vice president, director, executive, Newman's Own Foundation; vice president, treasurer, Newman's Own Inc.

Kissinger, Henry Alfred: director, CBS Foundation

Meyerson, Martin: director, Panasonic Foundation

Weinberger, Caspar Willard: chairman, Forbes Inc.

Century Country Club

Tisch, Preston Robert: chairman, director, CBS Foundation; co-chairman, co-chief executive officer, director, CNA; trustee, Loews Foundation

Weill, Sanford I.: chairman, chief executive officer, Citibank Corp.; chairman, Citigroup Foundation

Champions Golf Club

Carroll, Philip Joseph: chairman, chief executive officer, Fluor Corp.; chairman, trustee, Fluor Foundation

Chapoquoit Yacht Club

Wheeler, Thomas Beardsley: chairman, chief executive officer, Massachusetts Mutual Life Insurance Co.

Chatmoss Country Club

Spilman, Robert H.: chairman, chief executive officer, Bassett Furniture Industries; chairman, director, Bassett Furniture Industries Fdn.

Chemists Club

Kampouris, Emmanuel Andrew: chairman, president, chief executive officer, director, American Standard Inc.

Cherokee Town & Country Club

Spiegel, John William: member, SunTrust Bank Atlanta Foundation

Chesapeake Bay Yacht Club Association

Hilyard, James E.: president, CertainTeed Corp.; director, CertainTeed Corp. Foundation

Chevy Chase Club

Simpson, Louis Allen: president, chief executive officer capital operations, director, GEICO Corp.

Chicago Club

Almeida, Richard: chairman, chief executive officer, Heller Financial, Inc.

Becherer, Hans Walter: chairman, chief executive officer, director, Deere & Co.; director, Deere Foundation (John)

Bridgewater, Bernard Adolphus, Jr.: member board control, Brown Shoe Co. Charitable Trust; chairman, president, chief executive officer, director, Brown Shoe Co., Inc.

Chelberg, Bruce Stanley: chairman, chief executive officer, director, Whitman Corp.; director, Whitman Corp. Foundation

Fligg, James E.: executive vice president, BP Amoco Corp.

Fuller, Harry Laurance: co-chairman, director, BP Amoco Corp.

Graham, William B.: chairman, director, Baxter Allegiance Foundation; chairman emeritus, Baxter International Inc.

Hodgson, Thomas Richard: president, chief operating officer, director, Abbott Laboratories

Ingersoll, Robert Stephen: chairman, director, Panasonic Foundation

Kennedy, George Danner: trustee, Kemper Foundation (James S.)

Keyser, Richard Lee: chairman, chief executive officer, president, Grainger, Inc. (W.W.)

Kirby, William Joseph: vice president, director, FMC Foundation

Knight, Charles Field: chairman, chief executive officer, Emerson Electric Co.

McNally, Alan G.: chairman, chief executive officer, Harris Trust & Savings Bank

Patel, Homi Burjor: president, chief operating officer, director, Hartmarx Corp.

Rosett, Richard Nathaniel: trustee, Kemper Foundation (James S.)

Schadt, James Phillip: chairman, president, chief executive officer, director, Reader's Digest Association, Inc. (The); chairman, director, Reader's Digest Foundation

Skilling, Raymond Inwood: executive vice president, chief counsel, director, Aon Corp.; director, Aon Foundation

Terry, Richard Edward: chairman, chief executive officer, director, Peoples Energy Corp.

Toll, Daniel Roger: trustee, Kemper Foundation (James S.)

Chicago Country Club

Stewart, S. Jay: chairman, chief executive officer, director, Morton International Inc.

Chicago Golf Club

Fuller, Harry Laurance: co-chairman, director, BP Amoco Corp.

Chippance Golf Club

Barnes, Wallace W.: director, Barnes Group Foundation Inc.

Cincinnati Commercial Club

Burleigh, William Robert: president, chief executive officer, director, Scripps Co. (E.W.); member, Scripps Howard Foundation

Cincinnati Country Club

Burleigh, William Robert: president, chief executive officer, director, Scripps Co. (E.W.); member, Scripps Howard Foundation

Hays, Thomas Chandler: chairman, chief executive officer, director, Fortune Brands, Inc.

Klinedinst, Thomas John, Jr.: trustee, Star Bank NA, Cincinnati Foundation

Randolph, Jackson Harold: chairman, Cinergy Corp.; chairman, director, Cinergy Foundation

Cincinnati Literacy Club

Bridgeland, James Ralph, Jr.: trustee, Star Bank NA, Cincinnati Foundation

Burleigh, William Robert: president, chief executive officer, director, Scripps Co. (E.W.); member, Scripps Howard Foundation

City Athletic Club

Margolis, Jay M.: member grantmaking committee, Claiborne Foundation (Liz)

City Bunker Hill Club

Mullane, Donald A.: executive vice president, Bank of America; chairman, Bank of America Foundation

Wright, Donald Franklin: director, Times Mirror Foundation

City Club

Mahoney, David L.: co-chief executive officer, McKesson-HBOC Corp.

Roach, John Vinson, II: chairman, director, Tandy Corp.

City London Club

Skilling, Raymond Inwood: executive vice president, chief counsel, director, Aon Corp.; director, Aon Foundation

Cleveland Racquet Club

Lewis, Peter Benjamin: chairman, president, chief executive officer, director, Progressive Corp.

Cleveland Skating Club

Breen, John Gerald: chairman, chief executive officer, director, Sherwin-Williams Co.; president, trustee, Sherwin-Williams Foundation

Cleveland Yacht Club

O'Brien, John F.: trustee, McDonald & Co. Securities Foundation

Pyke, John Secrest, Jr.: president, trustee, Hanna Co. Foundation (M.A.); vice president, secretary, general counsel, Hanna Co. (M.A.)

Clifton Club

Pyke, John Secrest, Jr.: president, trustee, Hanna Co. Foundation (M.A.); vice president, secretary, general counsel, Hanna Co. (M.A.)

Club 30

Hall, Larry D.: chairman, president, chief executive officer, director, Kinder Morgn; president, director, KN Energy Foundation

Club International

Fligg, James E.: executive vice president, BP Amoco Corp.

Coldstream Country Club

Brumm, Paul Michael: executive vice president, chief financial officer, Fifth Third Bancorp

Colonial Country Club

Roach, John Vinson, II: chairman, director, Tandy Corp.

Colony Club

Wheeler, Thomas Beardsley: chairman, chief executive officer, Massachusetts Mutual Life Insurance Co.

Columbia Club

Russell, Frank Eli: president, Central Newspapers Foundation; chairman, Central Newspapers, Inc.

Sease, Gene Elwood: director, Central Newspapers Foundation

Tobias, Randall L.: chairman emeritus, Lilly & Co. (Eli)

Columbia Country Club

Smith, Donald Kaye: senior vice president, general counsel, director, GEICO Corp.

Columbia Tower Club

Condit, Philip Murray: chairman, chief executive officer, director, Boeing Co.

Columbus Club

Brothers, John Alfred 'Fred': trustee, Ashland Inc. Foundation

Plumeri, Joseph James, II: president, Citigroup

Commede Club

Mandel, Jack N.: director, Premier Industrial Corp.

Commerce Club

Correll, Alston Dayton 'Pete', Jr.: chairman, president, chief executive officer, director, Georgia-Pacific Corp.; director, Georgia-Pacific Foundation

Harkey, Robert Shelton: trustee, Delta Air Lines Foundation; senior vice president, general counsel, secretary, Delta Air Lines, Inc.

Morris, William Shivers, III: founder, chairman, chief executive officer, director, Morris Communications Corp.; trustee, Stauffer Communications Foundation

Commercial Club

Brown, Stephen Lee: chairman, chief executive officer, director, Hancock Financial Services (John)

Graham, William B.: chairman, director, Baxter Allegiance Foundation; chairman emeritus, Baxter International Inc.

Harris, Irving Brooks: chairman executive committee, director, Pittway Corp.; chairman, director, Pittway Corp. Charitable Foundation

Ingersoll, Robert Stephen: chairman, director, Panasonic Foundation

Pepper, John E., Jr.: chairman executive committee, Procter & Gamble Co.

Stone, Roger Warren: chairman, president, chief executive officer, director, Stone Container Corp.; president, Stone Foundation

Terry, Richard Edward: chairman, chief executive officer, director, Peoples Energy Corp.

Toll, Daniel Roger: trustee, Kemper Foundation (James S.)

Commercial Club Chicago

Lachman, Marguerite Leanne: trustee, Chicago Title and Trust Co. Foundation

McNally, Alan G.: chairman, chief executive officer, Harris Trust & Savings Bank

Stewart, S. Jay: chairman, chief executive officer, director, Morton International Inc.

Commercial Club Colorado

Choate, Jerry D.: chairman, chief executive officer, director, Allstate Foundation

Commerical Club Chicago

Keyser, Richard Lee: chairman, chief executive officer, president, Grainger, Inc. (W.W.)

Commonwealth Cinicinnati Club

Cody, Thomas Gerald: executive vice president legal & human resources, Federated Department Stores, Inc.

Commonwealth Club

Bridgeland, James Ralph, Jr.: trustee, Star Bank NA, Cincinnati Foundation

Broome, Burton Edward: vice president, controller, Transamerica Corp.; vice president, treasurer, Transamerica Foundation

Burrus, Robert Lewis, Jr.: trustee, Circuit City Foundation

Cutchins, Clifford Armstrong, IV: president, Fort James Corp.; chairman, director, Fort James Foundation (The)

Graham, William B.: chairman, director, Baxter Allegiance Foundation; chairman emeritus, Baxter International Inc.

Harrell, Henry Howze: director, Universal Leaf Foundation; chairman, chief executive officer, director, Universal Leaf Tobacco Co., Inc.

Hayden, Joseph Page, Jr.: trustee, Star Bank NA, Cincinnati Foundation

LaMacchia, John Thomas: trustee, Cincinnati Bell Foundation, Inc.; president, chief executive officer, director, Cincinnati Bell Inc.

Luke, John A., Jr.: chairman, president, chief executive officer, director, Westvaco Corp.

Pepper, John E., Jr.: chairman executive committee, Procter & Gamble Co.

Spilman, Robert H.: chairman, chief executive officer, Bassett Furniture Industries; chairman, director, Bassett Furniture Industries Fdn.

Tilghman, Richard Granville: chairman, chief executive officer, Crestar Foundation

Wehling, Robert Louis: global marketing, government relations officer, Procter & Gamble Co.; president, trustee, Procter & Gamble Fund

Commonwealth Club Boston

Hatsopoulos, George Nicholas: founder, chairman, chief executive officer, director, Thermo Electron Corp.; committee member, Thermo Electron Foundation

Commonwelth Club Chicago

Keyser, Richard Lee: chairman, chief executive officer, president, Grainger, Inc. (W.W.)

Communal Chicago Club

Donovan, Thomas Roy: president, chief executive officer, Chicago Board of Trade

Concord Country Club

Magee, John Francis: chairman, director, Little, Inc. (Arthur D.)

Confrerie des Chevaliers du Tastevin Club

Disney, Roy Edward: trustee, Disney Co. Foundation (Walt); vice chairman, director, Disney Co. (Walt)

Conway Farms Golf Club

Peterson, Donald Matthew: trustee, Trustmark Foundation; president, chief executive officer, director, Trustmark Insurance Co.

Coral Ridge Country Club

Huston, Edwin Allen: vice president, director, Ryder System Charitable Foundation; vice chairman, director, Ryder System, Inc.

Cordillera Club

Calise, Nicholas James: vice president, associate general counsel, secretary, BFGoodrich Co.; secretary, Goodrich Foundation, Inc. (B.F.)

Cornell Club

Johnson, Samuel Curtis: chairman, director, president, Johnson & Son (S.C.); chairman, trustee, Johnson Wax Fund (S.C.)

Weill, Sanford I.: chairman, chief executive officer, Citibank Corp.; chairman, Citigroup Foundation

Corning Country Club

Houghton, James Richardson: director, Corning Inc.; trustee, Corning Inc. Foundation

Ughetta, William Casper: trustee, Corning Inc. Foundation

Coronado Club

Buckwalter, Alan Roland, III: chief executive officer, Chase Bank of Texas; president, Chase Bank of Texas Foundation, Inc.

Coronado Country Club

Jewell, George Hiram: director, Schlumberger Foundation

Cosmopolitan Club

Graham, Katharine Meyer: chairman executive committee, director, The Washington Post

Gumprecht, Pamela (Howard): trustee, Scripps Howard Foundation

Cosmos Club

Meyerson, Martin: director, Panasonic Foundation

Country Club

Magee, John Francis: chairman, director, Little, Inc. (Arthur D.)

Parker, Patrick Streeter: chairman, director, Parker Hannifin Corp.; president, trustee, Parker Hannifin Foundation

Country Club Buffalo

Kennedy, Bernard Joseph: chairman, president, chief executive officer, director, National Fuel Gas Distribution Corp.

Country Club Columbus

Amos, Paul Shelby: cofounder, chairman, director, AFLAC Inc.

Country Club Hudson

Calise, Nicholas James: vice president, associate general counsel, secretary, BFGoodrich Co.; secretary, Goodrich Foundation, Inc. (B.F.)

Country Club Lincoln

Hewitt, James Watt: vice president, treasurer, Abel Foundation

Country Club New Canaan

Bijur, Peter I.: chairman, chief executive officer, Texaco Inc.

Country Club North

Redding, Peter Stoddard: trustee, Sherman-Standard Register Foundation; president, chief executive officer, director, Standard Register Co.

Country Club Rockies

Piper, Addison Lewis: director, Piper Jaffray Companies Foundation; chairman, chief executive officer, director, U.S. Bancorp Piper Jaffray

Country Club Virginia

Burrus, Robert Lewis, Jr.: trustee, Circuit City Foundation

Dozier, Ollin Kemp: treasurer, Universal Leaf Foundation

Harrell, Henry Howze: director, Universal Leaf Foundation; chairman, chief executive officer, director, Universal Leaf Tobacco Co., Inc.

Tilghman, Richard Granville: chairman, chief executive officer, Crestar Foundation

Crane Creek Country Club

Harad, George Jay: chairman, chief executive officer, director, Boise Cascade Corp.

Crestwicke Country Club

Johnson, James Lawrence: chairman emeritus, Walter Industries Inc.

Creve Coeur Club

Fites, Donald Vester: director, Caterpillar Foundation

Crooked Stick Golf Club

Pulliam, Eugene Smith: vice president, director, Central Newspapers Foundation

Rogers, James E., Jr.: vice chairman, president, chief executive officer, Cinergy Corp.; vice chairman, director, Cinergy Foundation

Tomlinson, Joseph Ernest: vice president, treasurer, controller, Inland Container Corp.; vice president, director, Inland Foundation, Inc.

Cruising Club American

Dingman, Michael David: partner, director, Winthrop Foundation

Crystal Downs Club

Knight, Charles Field: chairman, chief executive officer, Emerson Electric Co.

Cumberland Club

Bottorff, Dennis C.: chairman, president, chief executive officer, director, First American Corp.

Cypress Hunt Club

Meyer, Russell William, Jr.: chairman, chief executive officer, Cessna Aircraft Co.; president, Cessna Foundation, Inc.

Cypress Point Club

Herringer, Frank Casper: president, chief executive officer, director, chairman, Transamerica Corp.; vice chairman, director, Transamerica Foundation

McCoy, John Bonnet: president, chief executive officer, Ameritech Corp.

Price, Charles H., II: director, New York Times Co. Foundation

Ridder, Paul Anthony: chairman, chief executive officer, director, Knight Ridder

Wilbur, Brayton, Jr.: president, chief executive officer, Wilbur-Ellis Co. & Connell Brothers Co.; president, Wilbur Foundation (Brayton)

Dallas Country Club

Huey, Ward L., Jr.: president broadcast division, vice chairman, director, Belo Corp. (A.H.); vice president, trustee, Belo Corp. Foundation (A.H.)

Dallas Petroleum Club

Haddock, Ronald Wayne: president, chief executive officer, director, FINA; president, FINA Foundation

Darien Country Club

Hays, Thomas Chandler: chairman, chief executive officer, director, Fortune Brands, Inc.

Standen, Craig Clayton: senior vice president corporate development, Scripps Co. (E.W.)

Dayton Country Club

Holmes, David Richard: chief executive officer, chief operating officer, director, Reynolds & Reynolds Co.

Redding, Peter Stoddard: trustee, Sherman-Standard Register Foundation; president, chief executive officer, director, Standard Register Co.

DeBordieu Country Club

Browning, Peter C.: chief executive officer, president, director, Sonoco Products Co.

DeMolay Club

Matthews, Clark J., II: president, chief executive officer, director, 7-Eleven, Inc.

DePauw University Alumni Club

Baker, James Kendrick: chairman, director, Arvin Foundation; vice chairman, director, Arvin Industries, Inc.

Deep Run Hunt Club

Harrell, Henry Howze: director, Universal Leaf Foundation; chairman, chief executive officer, director, Universal Leaf Tobacco Co., Inc.

Des Moines Club

Brooks, Roger Kay: chairman, AmerUS Group

Hadley, Leonard Anson: chairman, chief executive officer, director, Maytag Corp.; president, trustee, Maytag Corp. Foundation

Kelley, Bruce Gunn: vice president, director, Employers Mutual Charitable Foundation

Kerr, William T.: chairman, chief executive officer, director, Meredith Corp.

Desert Forest Golf Club

Ingersoll, Robert Stephen: chairman, director, Panasonic Foundation

Desert Mountain Club

Hall, Larry D.: chairman, president, chief executive officer, director, Kinder Morgn; president, director, KN Energy Foundation

Ingersoll, Robert Stephen: chairman, director, Panasonic Foundation

Desert Mountain Country Club

Franke, William Augustus: chairman, president, chief executive officer, America West Airlines, Inc.; director, Phelps Dodge Foundation

Detroit Adcraft Club

Liebler, Arthur C.: vice president communications, DaimlerChrysler Corp.; trustee, DaimlerChrysler Corp. Fund

Detroit Golf Club

Liebler, Arthur C.: vice president communications, DaimlerChrysler Corp.; trustee, DaimlerChrysler Corp. Fund

Double Eagle Chamber of Commerce

Meyer, Russell William, Jr.: chairman, chief executive officer, Cessna Aircraft Co.; president, Cessna Foundation, Inc.

Double Eagle Club

Usher, Thomas J.: chairman, chief executive officer, USX Corp.; chairman board trustees, USX Foundation, Inc.

Doubles Club

Blanke, Gail Ann: vice president, Avon Products Foundation, Inc.

Geier, Philip Henry, Jr.: chairman, president, chief executive officer, Interpublic Group of Companies, Inc.

Downtown Athletic Club

Cohen, Jonathan L.: secretary, director, Goldman Sachs Foundation

Drones Club

Glynn, Gary Allen: president, USX Corp.; vice president, USX Foundation, Inc.

Duquesne Club

Abrew, Frederick H.: chairman, president, chief executive officer, director, Equitable Resources, Inc.

Calise, William Joseph, Junior: senior vice president, secretary, general counsel, Rockwell International Corp.

Graham, Thomas Carlisle: trustee, AK Steel Foundation

Gregg, Walter Emmor, Junior: senior executive vice president finance & administration, PNC Financial Services Group

Newlin, William Rankin: trustee, Kennametal Foundation

O'Reilly, F. Anthony John: chairman, trustee, Heinz Co. Foundation (H.J.); chairman, director, Heinz Co. (H.J.)

Rohr, James Edward: chief executive officer, president, director, PNC Financial Services Group

Smith, W. Keith: senior vice chairman, member corporate review committee, director, Mellon Financial Corp.

Usher, Thomas J.: chairman, chief executive officer, USX Corp.; chairman board trustees, USX Foundation, Inc.

Walton, Jon David: trustee, Allegheny Technologies Inc. Charitable Trust

East Bank Club

Chookaszian, Dennis Haig: chairman, chief executive officer, CNA

East Lake Gulf Club

Goode, David Ronald: chairman, president, chief executive officer, director, Norfolk Southern Corp.

Echo Lake Country Club

Longfield, William H.: president, Bard Foundation (C.R.); chairman, chief executive officer, director, Bard, Inc. (C.R.)

Economic Club

Barnes, Wallace W.: director, Barnes Group Foundation Inc.

Cook, J. Michael: chairman, chief executive officer, Deloitte & Touche; chairman, Deloitte & Touche Foundation

Duchossois, Richard Louis: secretary, Duchossois Foundation; chairman, chief executive officer, director, Duchossois Industries Inc.

Hays, Thomas Chandler: chairman, chief executive officer, director, Fortune Brands, Inc.

Hodgson, Thomas Richard: president, chief operating officer, director, Abbott Laboratories

Hutton, Edward L.: chairman, chief executive officer, director, Chemed Corp.

Ingersoll, Robert Stephen: chairman, director, Panasonic Foundation

Kirby, William Joseph: vice president, director, FMC Foundation

Moritz, Charles Worthington: chairman, director, Dun & Bradstreet Corp.

Osborne, Richard de Jongh: director, ASARCO Foundation; chairman, chief executive officer, director, ASARCO Inc.

Rogers, Desiree Glapion: vice president community affairs, Peoples Energy Corp.

Skilling, Raymond Inwood: executive vice president, chief counsel, director, Aon Corp.; director, Aon Foundation

Stone, Roger Warren: chairman, president, chief executive officer, director, Stone Container Corp.; president, Stone Foundation

Terry, Richard Edward: chairman, chief executive officer, director, Peoples Energy Corp.

Toll, Daniel Roger: trustee, Kemper Foundation (James S.)

Wander, Herbert S.: secretary, director, Katten, Muchin & Zavis Foundation

Williams, Edward Joseph: president, director, Harris Bank Foundation

Economic Club Chicago

Chookaszian, Dennis Haig: chairman, chief executive officer, CNA

Coughlan, Gary Patrick: chief financial officer, senior vice president finance, Abbott Laboratories; director, Abbott Laboratories Fund

McNally, Alan G.: chairman, chief executive officer, Harris Trust & Savings Bank

Peterson, Donald Matthew: trustee, Trustmark Foundation; president, chief executive officer, director, Trustmark Insurance Co.

Schueppert, George Louis: chief financial officer, executive vice president, Outboard Marine Corp.

Stewart, S. Jay: chairman, chief executive officer, director, Morton International Inc.

Economic Club Detroit

Smith, John Francis, Jr.: chairman, General Motors Corp.

Economic Club Indianapolis

Tobias, Randall L.: chairman emeritus, Lilly & Co. (Eli)

Economic Club New York

Andreas, Dwayne Orville: chairman, chief executive officer, Archer-Daniels-Midland Co.

Franklin, Barbara Hackman: director, Dow Chemical Co.

Glynn, Gary Allen: president, USX Corp.; vice president, USX Foundation, Inc.

Heisen, JoAnn Heffernan: vice president, chief information officer, Johnson & Johnson; treasurer, Johnson & Johnson Family of Companies Contribution Fund

Kampouris, Emmanuel Andrew: chairman, president, chief executive officer, director, American Standard Inc.

Mee, Michael F.: senior vice president, chief financial officer, Bristol-Myers Squibb Co.

Economic Club Washington

Franklin, Barbara Hackman: director, Dow Chemical Co.

El Paso Country Club

Wise, William Allen: chairman, president, chief executive officer, director, El Paso Energy Co.; chairman, director, El Paso Energy Foundation

Eldorado Country Club

Jewell, George Hiram: director, Schlumberger Foundation

Price, Charles H., II: director, New York Times Co. Foundation

Elizabethan Club

Daniels, John Hancock: chairman, Archer-Daniels-Midland Foundation

Elk River Club

Strickland, Robert Louis: vice president, Lowe's Charitable and Educational Foundation

Elkridge Club

DiCamillo, Gary Thomas: chairman, chief executive officer, director, Polaroid Corp.

Elks Club

Barnes, Wallace W.: director, Barnes Group Foundation Inc.

Cianciola, Charles Sal: trustee, Chesapeake Corp. Foundation

Hall, Larry D.: chairman, president, chief executive officer, director, Kinder Morgn; president, director, KN Energy Foundation

Howe, Stanley M.: president, HON Industries Charitable Foundation; chairman emeritus, director, HON Industries Inc.

Kress, George F.: honorary chairman, director, Green Bay Packaging; president, Kress Foundation (George)

Kulynych, Petro: chairman, treasurer, Lowe's Charitable and Educational Foundation

Tyson, Donald John: senior chairman, Tyson Foods Inc.

Emerald Hills Country Club

Mandel, Jack N.: director, Premier Industrial Corp.

Evansville Country Club

Koch, Robert Louis, II: president, chief executive officer, director, Koch Enterprises, Inc.; president, director, Koch Foundation

Muehlbauer, James Herman: vice president, director, Koch Foundation

Everglades Club

Graham, William B.: chairman, director, Baxter Allegiance Foundation; chairman emeritus, Baxter International Inc.

Executive Club

Duchossois, Richard Louis: secretary, Duchossois Foundation; chairman, chief executive officer, director, Duchossois Industries Inc.

Peterson, Donald Matthew: trustee, Trustmark Foundation; president, chief executive officer, director, Trustmark Insurance Co.

Executive Club Chicago

Chookaszian, Dennis Haig: chairman, chief executive officer, CNA

Donovan, Thomas Roy: president, chief executive officer, Chicago Board of Trade

Executives Club Chicago

McNally, Alan G.: chairman, chief executive officer, Harris Trust & Savings Bank

Explorers Club

Koch, David Hamilton: director, Koch Foundation, Inc. (Fred C. and Mary R.)

Sulzberger, Arthur Ochs, Sr.: director, New York Times Co.; chairman, director, New York Times Co. Foundation

Fair Oaks Country Club

Hemminghaus, Roger Roy: chairman, director, Ultramar Diamond Shamrock Corp.

Fairfield Country Club

Schadt, James Phillip: chairman, president, chief executive officer, director, Reader's Digest Association, Inc. (The); chairman, director, Reader's Digest Foundation

Fairfield County Hunt Club

Schadt, James Phillip: chairman, president, chief executive officer, director, Reader's Digest Association, Inc. (The); chairman, director, Reader's Digest Foundation

Fairlane Club

Lyon, Wayne Barton: president, chief operating officer, director, Masco Corp.

Farmington Country Club

Barnes, Wallace W.: director, Barnes Group Foundation Inc.

Federal City Club

Donahue, Richard King: vice chairman, Nike, Inc.

Firestone Country Club

Holland, Willard R.: chairman, chief executive officer, FirstEnergy Corp.

Shaffer, Oren G.: executive vice president, chief financial officer, Ameritech Corp.

Flint Hills National Club

Meyer, Russell William, Jr.: chairman, chief executive officer, Cessna Aircraft Co.; president, Cessna Foundation, Inc.

Forest Hills Country Club

Carr, Cassandra Colvin: director, SBC Foundation

Forsyth Club

Strickland, Robert Louis: vice president, Lowe's Charitable and Educational Foundation

Fort Orange Club

Standish, J. Spencer: chairman, director, Albany International Corp.

Fort Wayne Country Club

Lawson, William Hogan, III: chairman, chief executive officer, director, Franklin Electric Co.; president, Franklin Electric, Edward J. Schaefer, and T. W. KehoeCharitable and Educational Foundation

Fort Worth Country Club

Roach, John Vinson, II: chairman, director, Tandy Corp.

Forum Club

Burrus, Robert Lewis, Jr.: trustee, Circuit City Foundation

Harrell, Henry Howze: director, Universal Leaf Foundation; chairman, chief executive officer, director, Universal Leaf Tobacco Co., Inc.

Fox Chapel Golf Club

Graham, Thomas Carlisle: trustee, AK Steel Foundation

O'Reilly, F. Anthony John: chairman, trustee, Heinz Co. Foundation (H.J.); chairman, director, Heinz Co. (H.J.)

Friars Club

Andreas, Dwayne Orville: chairman, chief executive officer, Archer-Daniels-Midland Co.

Klinedinst, Thomas John, Jr.: trustee, Star Bank NA, Cincinnati Foundation

Garden of Gods Club

Stauffer, Stanley Howard: chairman, Stauffer Communications Foundation

Georgetown Club

Brinegar, Claude Stout: trustee, Unocal Foundation

Landin, Thomas Milton: vice president, director, CertainTeed Corp.; vice president, Norton Co. Foundation

Wise, William Allen: chairman, president, chief executive officer, director, El Paso Energy Co.; chairman, director, El Paso Energy Foundation

Georgetown University Club

Walsh, Michael J.: vice president, CertainTeed Corp.

Georgian Club

Eason, William Everette, Jr.: senior vice president, corporate secretary, general counsel, Scientific-Atlanta, Inc.

Glen View Club

McNally, Alan G.: chairman, chief executive officer, Harris Trust & Savings Bank

Glen View Golf Club

Kirby, William Joseph: vice president, director, FMC Foundation

Knight, Charles Field: chairman, chief executive officer, Emerson Electric Co.

Glenview Country Club

Suter, Albert E.: senior vice chairman, chief administrative officer, director, Emerson Electric Co.

Golden Valley Country Club

Mattison, Robert Mayer: director, Graco Foundation; vice president, general counsel, secretary, Graco, Inc.

Grandfather Golf Club & Country Club

Spilman, Robert H.: chairman, chief executive officer, Bassett Furniture Industries; chairman, director, Bassett Furniture Industries Fdn.

Great Lakes Cruising Club

Kress, George F.: honorary chairman, director, Green Bay Packaging; president, Kress Foundation (George)

Greenwich City Club

Mead, Dana George: chairman, chief executive officer, director, Tenneco Automotive

Greenwich Country Club

Cook, J. Michael: chairman, chief executive officer, Deloitte & Touche; chairman, Deloitte & Touche Foundation

Mead, Dana George: chairman, chief executive officer, director, Tenneco Automotive

Gridiron Society Club

Thomasson, Dan King: vice president, trustee, Scripps Howard Foundation

Grolier Club

Daniels, John Hancock: chairman, Archer-Daniels-Midland Foundation

Forbes, Christopher 'Kip': vice president, Forbes Foundation; vice chairman, corporate secretary, director, Forbes Inc.

Gulfstream PC Club

Levin, Michael Stuart: president, chief executive officer, Titan Industrial Corp.

Hacienda Golf Club

Mullane, Donald A.: executive vice president, Bank of America; chairman, Bank of America Foundation

Wood, Willis B., Jr.: chairman, chief executive officer, director, Pacific Enterprises

Harbor Club

Goode, David Ronald: chairman, president, chief executive officer, director, Norfolk Southern Corp.

Wynne, John Oliver: president, director, Landmark Communications Foundation; president, chief executive officer, Landmark Communications Inc.

Harmonie Club

Hyman, Morton Peter: vice president, director, OSG Foundation; president, director, Overseas Shipholding Group Inc.

Weill, Sanford I.: chairman, chief executive officer, Citibank Corp.; chairman, Citigroup Foundation

Zuckerman, Mortimer Benjamin: co-founder, chairman, co-publisher, director, Daily News

Harrison Lake Country Club

Baker, James Kendrick: chairman, director, Arvin Foundation; vice chairman, director, Arvin Industries, Inc.

Hartford Club

Walker, Grahame: chairman, chief executive officer, Dexter Corp.; president, Dexter Corp. Foundation

Hartsville Country Club

Shelley, James Herbert: chairman, Sonoco Foundation

Harvard Business School Chicago Club

Hodgson, Thomas Richard: president, chief operating officer, director, Abbott Laboratories

Keyser, Richard Lee: chairman, chief executive officer, president, Grainger, Inc. (W.W.)

Harvard Business School Club

Kasputys, Joseph Edward: chairman, trustee, Hitachi Foundation

Toll, Daniel Roger: trustee, Kemper Foundation (James S.)

Harvard Business School Minnesota Club

Dubes, Michael: membership, ReliaStar Foundation

Harvard Business School Philadelphia Club

Naples, Ronald James: president, chief executive officer, director, Quaker Chemical Corp.

Harvard Club

Bridgeland, James Ralph, Jr.: trustee, Star Bank NA, Cincinnati Foundation

DiCamillo, Gary Thomas: chairman, chief executive officer, director, Polaroid Corp.

Guthart, Leo A.: vice chairman, director, Pittway Corp.

Houghton, James Richardson: director, Corning Inc.; trustee, Corning Inc. Foundation

Huber, Richard Leslie: chairman, president, chief executive officer, director, Aetna, Inc.

James, George Barker, II: senior vice president, chief financial officer, Levi Strauss & Co.

Kirby, William Joseph: vice president, director, FMC Foundation

Lawson, William Hogan, III: chairman, chief executive officer, director, Franklin Electric Co.; president, Franklin Electric, Edward J. Schaefer, and T. W. KehoeCharitable and Educational Foundation

Ostergard, Paul Michael: vice president, director corporate contributions, Citibank Corp.; president, Citigroup Foundation

Paton, Leland B.: president capital marketings, director, member executive committee, Prudential Securities Inc.

Redstone, Sumner Murray: chairman, Viacom Inc.

Robinson, E. B., Jr.: chairman, chief executive officer, director, Deposit Guaranty National Bank

Weinberger, Caspar Willard: chairman, Forbes Inc.

Zuckerman, Mortimer Benjamin: co-founder, chairman, co-publisher, director, Daily News

Heights Casino Club

McNeary, Joseph Allen: member grantmaking committee, Claiborne Foundation (Liz); senior vice president, Liz Claiborne, Inc.

Hillcrest Country Club

Groman, Arthur: president, Occidental Petroleum Charitable Foundation

Rosenberg, Richard Morris: chairman, chief executive officer (retired), Bank of America

Hiwan Country Club

Hall, Larry D.: chairman, president, chief executive officer, director, Kinder Morgn; president, director, KN Energy Foundation

Homestead Country Club

Berkley, Eugene Bertram: chairman, director, Tension Envelope Corp.; treasurer, Tension Envelope Foundation

Honolulu Country Club

Dods, Walter Arthur, Jr.: president, director, First Hawaiian Foundation; chairman, chief executive officer, director, First Hawaiian, Inc.

Wolff, Herbert Eric: secretary, director, First Hawaiian Foundation

Hop Meadow Country Club

Long, Michael Thomas: director, Ensign-Bickford Foundation

Hound Ears Club

Strickland, Robert Louis: vice president, Lowe's Charitable and Educational Foundation

Houston Club

Bradford, William Edward: chairman, director, Halliburton Co.

Buckwalter, Alan Roland, III: chief executive officer, Chase Bank of Texas; president, Chase Bank of Texas Foundation, Inc.

Houston Country Club

Jewell, George Hiram: director, Schlumberger Foundation

Hundred Club

Bottorff, Dennis C.: chairman, president, chief executive officer, director, First American Corp.

Hunting Hills Country Club

Goode, David Ronald: chairman, president, chief executive officer, director, Norfolk Southern Corp.

Spilman, Robert H.: chairman, chief executive officer, Bassett Furniture Industries; chairman, director, Bassett Furniture Industries Fdn.

Hurlingham Club

Geier, Philip Henry, Jr.: chairman, president, chief executive officer, Interpublic Group of Companies, Inc.

Hyde Golf Club

Hayden, Joseph Page, Jr.: trustee, Star Bank NA, Cincinnati Foundation

Hyde Park Country Club

Cody, Thomas Gerald: executive vice president legal & human resources, Federated Department Stores, Inc.

India House Club

Cohen, Jonathan L.: secretary, director, Goldman Sachs Foundation

O'Hare, Dean Raymond: chairman, Chubb Corp.

Indian Creek Country Club

Andreas, Dwayne Orville: chairman, chief executive officer, Archer-Daniels-Midland Co.

Ridder, Paul Anthony: chairman, chief executive officer, director, Knight Ridder

Indian Hill Club

Ingersoll, Robert Stephen: chairman, director, Panasonic Foundation

Kennedy, George Danner: trustee, Kemper Foundation (James S.)

Toll, Daniel Roger: trustee, Kemper Foundation (James S.)

Indian Hills Country Club

Bridgewater, Bernard Adolphus, Jr.: member board control, Brown Shoe Co. Charitable Trust; chairman, president, chief executive officer, director, Brown Shoe Co., Inc.

Graham, William B.: chairman, director, Baxter Allegiance Foundation; chairman emeritus, Baxter International Inc.

Indianapolis Athletic Club

Russell, Frank Eli: president, Central Newspapers Foundation; chairman, Central Newspapers, Inc.

Indianapolis Kiwanis Club

Sease, Gene Elwood: director, Central Newspapers Foundation

Interlochen Country Club

Dubes, Michael: membership, ReliaStar Foundation

Johnson, Scott W.: senior vice president, secretary, general counsel, Bemis Co., Inc.

Inverness Club

Hiner, Glen Harold, Jr.: chairman, chief executive officer, director, Owens Corning

Lemieux, Joseph Henry: chairman, chief executive officer, director, Owens-Illinois Inc.

Ivy Hills Country Club

Standen, Craig Clayton: senior vice president corporate development, Scripps Co. (E.W.)

Jackson Country Club

Robinson, E. B., Jr.: chairman, chief executive officer, director, Deposit Guaranty National Bank

Jackson Hole Golf & Tennis Club

Lucas, Donald Leo: chairman, Cadence Designs Systems, Inc.

Jefferson Club

Guillaume, Raymond Kendrick: vice chairman, chief executive officer, Mid-America Bank of Louisville

Jesters

Carlson, Curtis Leroy: chairman, director, Carlson Companies, Inc.; president, treasurer, Carlson Family Foundation (Curtis L.)

Jockey Club

Duchossois, Richard Louis: secretary, Duchossois Foundation; chairman, chief executive officer, director, Duchossois Industries Inc.

John Gardiners Tennis Ranch

Bloch, Henry Wollman: chairman, Block Foundation (H&R); chairman, director, Block, Inc. (H&R)

Johns Island Club

Moritz, Charles Worthington: chairman, director, Dun & Bradstreet Corp.

Schadt, James Phillip: chairman, president, chief executive officer, director, Reader's Digest Association, Inc. (The); chairman, director, Reader's Digest Foundation

Smith, Donald Kaye: senior vice president, general counsel, director, GEICO Corp.

Standish, J. Spencer: chairman, director, Albany International Corp.

Junior League Owensboro Club

Griffith, Beverly H.: general counsel, Texas Gas Transmission Corp.

Jupiter Island

Clark, Howard Longstreth, Jr.: vice chairman, Walter Industries Inc.

Kansas City Club

Margolin, Abraham E.: director, Tension Envelope Foundation

Kansas City Country Club

Bloch, Henry Wollman: chairman, Block Foundation (H&R); chairman, director, Block, Inc. (H&R)

Esrey, William Todd: chairman, chief executive officer, Sprint Corp.

Kemper, David Woods: chairman, president, chief executive officer, director, Commerce Bancshares, Inc.

Price, Charles H., II: director, New York Times Co. Foundation

Kansas City Racquet Club

Bloch, Henry Wollman: chairman, Block Foundation (H&R); chairman, director, Block, Inc. (H&R)

Kent Country Club

Pew, Robert Cunningham, II: trustee, Steelcase Foundation

Kentuckians New York Club

Guillaume, Raymond Kendrick: vice chairman, chief executive officer, Mid-America Bank of Louisville

Kenwood Country Club

LaMacchia, John Thomas: trustee, Cincinnati Bell Foundation, Inc.; president, chief executive officer, director, Cincinnati Bell Inc.

Meyer, Daniel Joseph: president, Milacron Foundation; chairman, president, chief executive officer, director, Milacron, Inc.

Standen, Craig Clayton: senior vice president corporate development, Scripps Co. (E.W.)

Kildare Street Club

O'Reilly, F. Anthony John: chairman, trustee, Heinz Co. Foundation (H.J.); chairman, director, Heinz Co. (H.J.)

Kiwanis Club

Williamson, Henry Gaston, Jr.: chief operating officer, Branch Banking & Trust Co.

Zylstra, Stanley James: chairman, director, Land O'Lakes, Inc.

Kiwanis Club Birmingham

Denson, William Frank, III: president, Vulcan Materials Co. Foundation

Knickerbocker Club

Andreas, Dwayne Orville: chairman, chief executive officer, Archer-Daniels-Midland Co.

Zilkha, Ezra Khedouri: president, treasurer, Zilkha Foundation, Inc.; president, Zilkha & Sons

Knights of Columbus

Herman, William A., III: secretary, treasurer, director, Morris Communications Corp.

Riethman, Robert B.: chief financial officer, Monarch Machine Tool Co.; treasurer, secretary, Monarch Machine Tool Co. Foundation

Knollwood Club
Hodgson, Thomas Richard: president, chief operating officer, director, Abbott Laboratories

Knollwood Golf Club
Maatman, Gerald Leonard: chairman, president, trustee, Kemper Foundation (James S.); director, Kemper National Insurance Companies

L'Hirondelle Club
DiCamillo, Gary Thomas: chairman, chief executive officer, director, Polaroid Corp.

LA Press Club
Copley, Helen K.: chairman, trustee, Copley Foundation (James S.); chairman, director, senior management board, Copley Press, Inc.

La Cita Country Club
Roub, Bryan Roger: trustee, Harris Foundation

La Jolla Beach & Tennis Club
ZoBell, Karl: vice president, trustee, Copley Foundation (James S.)

La Jolla Country Club
Dingman, Michael David: partner, director, Winthrop Foundation

La Quinta Country Club
Stauffer, Stanley Howard: chairman, Stauffer Communications Foundation

Ladue Racquet Club
Neville, James Morton: member board control, Ralston Purina Trust Fund

Lagunitas Country Club
Gammill, Lee Morgan, Jr.: director, New York Life Foundation; vice chairman, director, New York Life Insurance Co.

Lake Shore Country Club
Stone, Roger Warren: chairman, president, chief executive officer, director, Stone Container Corp.; president, Stone Foundation

Lauderdale Yacht Club
Huston, Edwin Allen: vice president, director, Ryder System Charitable Foundation; vice chairman, director, Ryder System, Inc.

Laurel Valley Country Club
Graham, Thomas Carlisle: trustee, AK Steel Foundation

Usher, Thomas J.: chairman, chief executive officer, USX Corp.; chairman board trustees, USX Foundation, Inc.

Laurel Valley Golf Club
Goode, David Ronald: chairman, president, chief executive officer, director, Norfolk Southern Corp.

Houghton, James Richardson: director, Corning Inc.; trustee, Corning Inc. Foundation

Kampouris, Emmanuel Andrew: chairman, president, chief executive officer, director, American Standard Inc.

Lee, Charles Robert: chairman, chief executive officer, director, GTE Corp.; chief executive officer, trustee, GTE Foundation

Newlin, William Rankin: trustee, Kennametal Foundation

Lawrence Beach Club
Blanke, Gail Ann: vice president, Avon Products Foundation, Inc.

Legal Club
Welsh, Kelly Raymond: executive vice president, general counsel, Ameritech Corp.

Lemon Bay Golf Club
Hayden, Joseph Page, Jr.: trustee, Star Bank NA, Cincinnati Foundation

Les Ambassadeurs Club
O'Reilly, F. Anthony John: chairman, trustee, Heinz Co. Foundation (H.J.); chairman, director, Heinz Co. (H.J.)

Lincoln Country Club
Arth, Lawrence Joseph: vice president, director, Ameritas Charitable Foundation; chairman, chief executive officer, director, Ameritas Life Insurance Corp.

Links Club New York
McCoy, John Bonnet: president, chief executive officer, Ameritech Corp.

Linville Golf Club
Spilman, Robert H.: chairman, chief executive officer, Bassett Furniture Industries; chairman, director, Bassett Furniture Industries Fdn.

Litchfield Country Club
Kerr, William T.: chairman, chief executive officer, director, Meredith Corp.

Loblolly Bay Yacht Club
Barnette, Curtis Handley: chairman, chief executive officer, director, Bethlehem Steel Corp.

Log Cabin Club
Bridgewater, Bernard Adolphus, Jr.: member board control, Brown Shoe Co. Charitable Trust; chairman, president, chief executive officer, director, Brown Shoe Co., Inc.

Busch, August Adolphus, III: chairman, president, chief executive officer, Anheuser-Busch Companies, Inc.

Knight, Charles Field: chairman, chief executive officer, Emerson Electric Co.

Suter, Albert E.: senior vice chairman, chief administrative officer, director, Emerson Electric Co.

Lone Pine Golf Club
Barnett, Hoyt R.: executive vice president, director, Publix Supermarkets

Long Cove Club
Paton, Leland B.: president capital marketings, director, member executive committee, Prudential Securities Inc.

Long Meadow Country Club
Wheeler, Thomas Beardsley: chairman, chief executive officer, Massachusetts Mutual Life Insurance Co.

Longboat Key Club
Bueche, Wendell Francis: director, Marshall & Ilsley Foundation, Inc.

Longwood Club
Fish, Lawrence K.: trustee, Citizens Charitable Foundation; chairman, chief executive officer, Citizens Financial Group, Inc.

Los Angeles Country Club
Farman, Richard Donald: chairman, chief executive officer, Pacific Enterprises

Kresa, Kent: chairman, president, chief executive officer, director, Northrop Grumman Corp.

Simpson, Louis Allen: president, chief executive officer capital operations, director, GEICO Corp.

Los Angeles Yacht Club
Disney, Roy Edward: trustee, Disney Co. Foundation (Walt); vice chairman, director, Disney Co. (Walt)

Lost Tree Club
Pew, Robert Cunningham, II: trustee, Steelcase Foundation

Lotos Club
Minton, Dwight Church: chairman, director, Church & Dwight Co., Inc.

Louisville Boat Club
Guillaume, Raymond Kendrick: vice chairman, chief executive officer, Mid-America Bank of Louisville

Lyford Cay Club
Dingman, Michael David: partner, director, Winthrop Foundation

Gammill, Lee Morgan, Jr.: director, New York Life Foundation; vice chairman, director, New York Life Insurance Co.

Montrone, Paul Michael: vice president, partner, Winthrop Foundation

O'Reilly, F. Anthony John: chairman, trustee, Heinz Co. Foundation (H.J.); chairman, director, Heinz Co. (H.J.)

Mackinac Island Yacht Club
Kress, George F.: honorary chairman, director, Green Bay Packaging; president, Kress Foundation (George)

Manhasset Bay Yacht Club
Black, Daniel James: treasurer, Carter-Wallace Foundation; president, chief operating officer, director, Carter-Wallace, Inc.

Marco Polo Club
Griffith, Alan Richard: vice chairman, Bank of New York Co., Inc.

Marks London Club
O'Reilly, F. Anthony John: chairman, trustee, Heinz Co. Foundation (H.J.); chairman, director, Heinz Co. (H.J.)

Maryland Club
DiCamillo, Gary Thomas: chairman, chief executive officer, director, Polaroid Corp.

Mashomack Fish & Game Preserve Club
Levin, Michael Stuart: president, chief executive officer, Titan Industrial Corp.

Masons Club
Bowerman, Charles L.: executive vice president, director, Phillips Petroleum Co.

Brademas, John: chairman, Texaco Foundation

Buxton, Charles Ingraham, II: chairman, Federated Mutual Insurance Co.; president, Federated Mutual Insurance Foundation

Eckert, Ralph John: trustee, Trustmark Foundation

Gloyd, Lawrence Eugene: trustee, CLARCOR Foundation; chairman, chief executive officer, director, CLARCOR Inc.

Jamison, Zean, Jr.: director, Lance Foundation; director human resources, Lance, Inc.

Kelley, Bruce Gunn: vice president, director, Employers Mutual Charitable Foundation

Levine, Lawrence E.: secretary, Panasonic Foundation

Redstone, Sumner Murray: chairman, Viacom Inc.

Smith, Donald Kaye: senior vice president, general counsel, director, GEICO Corp.

Wentworth, Jack Roberts, Ph.D.: director, Habig Foundation

Meadow Brook Club

Warner, Douglas Alexander, III: chairman, president, chief executive officer, director, Morgan & Co. Inc. (J.P.)

Meadow Club

Zilkha, Ezra Khedouri: president, treasurer, Zilkha Foundation, Inc.; president, Zilkha & Sons

Media Club

Kniffen, Jan Rogers: senior vice president, treasurer, May Department Stores Co.; vice president, secretary, treasurer, director, May Department Stores Computer Foundation (The)

Memphis Country Club

Moore, Jackson W.: president, director, Union Planters Corp.

Menlo Circus Club

James, George Barker, II: senior vice president, chief financial officer, Levi Strauss & Co.

Lucas, Donald Leo: chairman, Cadence Designs Systems, Inc.

Mercer Island Country Club

Eigsti, Roger Harry: chairman, chief executive officer, SAFECO Corp.

Meridian Hills Country Club

Rogers, James E., Jr.: vice chairman, president, chief executive officer, Cinergy Corp.; vice chairman, director, Cinergy Foundation

Russell, Frank Eli: president, Central Newspapers Foundation; chairman, Central Newspapers, Inc.

Tobias, Randall L.: chairman emeritus, Lilly & Co. (Eli)

Metedeconk Country Club

Longfield, William H.: president, Bard Foundation (C.R.); chairman, chief executive officer, director, Bard, Inc. (C.R.)

Metro Breakfast Club

Dubes, Michael: membership, ReliaStar Foundation

Metro Club

Black, Daniel James: treasurer, Carter-Wallace Foundation; president, chief operating officer, director, Carter-Wallace, Inc.

Chelberg, Bruce Stanley: chairman, chief executive officer, director, Whitman Corp.; director, Whitman Corp. Foundation

Glynn, Gary Allen: president, USX Corp.; vice president, USX Foundation, Inc.

Goode, David Ronald: chairman, president, chief executive officer, director, Norfolk Southern Corp.

Graham, Katharine Meyer: chairman executive committee, director, The Washington Post

Marriott, J. Willard, Jr.: chairman, chief executive officer, Marriott International Inc.

Mead, Dana George: chairman, chief executive officer, director, Tenneco Automotive

Millstein, Ira M.: partner, Weil, Gotshal & Manges Corp.; president, director, Weil, Gotshal & Manges Foundation

Ong, John Doyle: chairman board, director, Ameritech Corp.

Randolph, Jackson Harold: chairman, Cinergy Corp.; chairman, director, Cinergy Foundation

Robinson, Edward Joseph: president, chief operating officer, director, Avon Products, Inc.

Sulzberger, Arthur Ochs, Sr.: director, New York Times Co.; chairman, director, New York Times Co. Foundation

Williams, Edward Joseph: president, director, Harris Bank Foundation

Metro DC Club

Kissinger, Henry Alfred: director, CBS Foundation

Metro Denver Executives Club

Coors, Peter Hanson: vice president, director, Coors Brewing Co.

Metro Opera Association

Glynn, Gary Allen: president, USX Corp.; vice president, USX Foundation, Inc.

Metropolitan Club

Blanke, Gail Ann: vice president, Avon Products Foundation, Inc.

Block, Allan James: vice president, trustee, Blade Foundation; director, Toledo Blade Co.

Hayden, Joseph Page, Jr.: trustee, Star Bank NA, Cincinnati Foundation

Mulford, David: chairman, Credit Suisse First Boston

Muth, Robert James: president, director, ASARCO Foundation

Rogers, James E., Jr.: vice chairman, president, chief executive officer, Cinergy Corp.; vice chairman, director, Cinergy Foundation

Simpson, Louis Allen: president, chief executive officer capital operations, director, GEICO Corp.

Mid-America Club

Fligg, James E.: executive vice president, BP Amoco Corp.

Fuller, Harry Laurance: co-chairman, director, BP Amoco Corp.

Kirby, William Joseph: vice president, director, FMC Foundation

Lowrie, William G.: president, deputy chief executive officer, director, BP Amoco Corp.

Sopranos, Orpheus Javaras: corporate vice president, Amsted Industries Inc.

Terry, Richard Edward: chairman, chief executive officer, director, Peoples Energy Corp.

Mid-Day Club

Harris, Irving Brooks: chairman executive committee, director, Pittway Corp.; chairman, director, Pittway Corp. Charitable Foundation

Mid-Ocean Club

McCorkindale, Douglas H.: vice chairman, president, Gannett Co., Inc.; president, Gannett Foundation

Paton, Leland B.: president capital marketings, director, member executive committee, Prudential Securities Inc.

Milbrook Golf and Tennis Club

Levin, Michael Stuart: president, chief executive officer, Titan Industrial Corp.

Mill Reef Club

Brothers, John Alfred 'Fred': trustee, Ashland Inc. Foundation

Mill Valley Tennis Club

Gammill, Lee Morgan, Jr.: director, New York Life Foundation; vice chairman, director, New York Life Insurance Co.

Milwaukee Club

Connolly, Gerald Edward: trustee, Reinhart Family Foundation (D. B. and Marjorie)

Davis, Walter Stewart: secretary, treasurer, Grede Foundation

Graff, Stephen Ney: director, Bucyrus-Erie Foundation

Kress, George F.: honorary chairman, director, Green Bay Packaging; president, Kress Foundation (George)

Milwaukee Country Club

Bauer, Chris Michael: president, Firstar Milwaukee Foundation

Bueche, Wendell Francis: director, Marshall & Ilsley Foundation, Inc.

Fitzsimonds, Roger Leon: chairman, Firstar Milwaukee Foundation

Winter, William Bergford: president, Bucyrus-Erie Co.; chairman, president, director, Bucyrus-Erie Foundation

Milwaukee Order of World Wars

Buxton, Charles Ingraham, II: chairman, Federated Mutual Insurance Co.; president, Federated Mutual Insurance Foundation

Milwaukee Yacht Club

Connolly, Gerald Edward: trustee, Reinhart Family Foundation (D. B. and Marjorie)

Minikahda Club

Carlson, Curtis Leroy: chairman, director, Carlson Companies, Inc.; president, treasurer, Carlson Family Foundation (Curtis L.)

George, William Wallace: chief executive officer, chairman, Medtronic, Inc.

Shannon, Michael E.: chairman, chief financial officer, chief administration officer, director, Ecolab Inc.

Minneapolis Athletic Club

Buxton, Charles Ingraham, II: chairman, Federated Mutual Insurance Co.; president, Federated Mutual Insurance Foundation

Minneapolis Club

Anderson, Lowell Carlton: chairman, director, Allianz Life Insurance Co. of North America

Andreas, David Lowell: chairman, director, National City Bank Foundation; chairman, chief executive officer, National City Bank of Minneapolis

Carlson, Curtis Leroy: chairman, director, Carlson Companies, Inc.; president, treasurer, Carlson Family Foundation (Curtis L.)

Daniels, John Hancock: chairman, Archer-Daniels-Midland Foundation

Johnson, Scott W.: senior vice president, secretary, general counsel, Bemis Co., Inc.

Piper, Addison Lewis: director, Piper Jaffray Companies Foundation; chairman, chief executive officer, director, U.S. Bancorp Piper Jaffray

Shannon, Michael E.: chairman, chief financial officer, chief administration officer, director, Ecolab Inc.

Weiser, Irving: chairman, president, chief executive officer, Dain Bosworth Inc.

Wurtele, C. Angus: president, Valspar Foundation

Minnesota Club

George, William Wallace: chief executive officer, chairman, Medtronic, Inc.

Leatherdale, Douglas West: chairman, chief executive officer, president, Saint Paul Companies Inc.

Shannon, Michael E.: chairman, chief financial officer, chief administration officer, director, Ecolab Inc.

Mission Hills Country Club

Bueche, Wendell Francis: director, Marshall & Ilsley Foundation, Inc.

Esrey, William Todd: chairman, chief executive officer, Sprint Corp.

Matheny, Edward Taylor, Junior: director, Block Foundation (H&R)

Missouri Athletic Club

Mueller, Charles William: chairman, president, chief executive officer, Ameren Corp.; trustee, Ameren Corp. Charitable Trust

Monroe Club

Ashley, James Wheeler: director, Globe Foundation

Montgomery Club

Harris, Elmer Beseler: president, chief executive officer, director, Alabama Power Co.

Morris County Golf Club

Shinn, George Latimer: director, New York Times Co. Foundation

Mount Royal Club

Light, Walter Frederick: trustee, Air Products Foundation

Mountain Brook Country Club

Stephens, Elton Bryson: founder, chairman, Ebsco Industries, Inc.

Mountain Oyster Club

Pulitzer, Michael Edgar: chairman, president, chief executive officer, director, Pulitzer Publishing Co.; chairman, president, chief executive officer, Pulitzer Publishing Co. Foundation

Mt Hawley Country Club

Fites, Donald Vester: director, Caterpillar Foundation

Muirfield Country Club

Brothers, John Alfred 'Fred': trustee, Ashland Inc. Foundation

Nantucket Golf Club

Clark, Howard Longstreth, Jr.: vice chairman, Walter Industries Inc.

National Arts Club

Forbes, Christopher 'Kip': vice president, Forbes Foundation; vice chairman, corporate secretary, director, Forbes Inc.

National Golf The Links America Club

Moritz, Charles Worthington: chairman, director, Dun & Bradstreet Corp.

National Press Club

Gould, John T., Jr.: vice president, Unilever Foundation; director corporate affairs, Unilever United States, Inc.

Graham, Katharine Meyer: chairman executive committee, director, The Washington Post

Thomasson, Dan King: vice president, trustee, Scripps Howard Foundation

National Space Club

Kresa, Kent: chairman, president, chief executive officer, director, Northrop Grumman Corp.

Nebraska Club

Hewitt, James Watt: vice president, treasurer, Abel Foundation

New Canaan Field Club

Buchanan, William Hobart, Jr.: assistant secretary, Dun & Bradstreet Corp. Foundation, Inc.

New Orleans Country Club

Steward, H. Leighton: chairman, chief executive officer, president, Louisiana Land & Exploration Co.; director, Louisiana Land & Exploration Co. Foundation

New York Athletic Club

James, George Barker, II: senior vice president, chief financial officer, Levi Strauss & Co.

Robinson, Edward Joseph: president, chief operating officer, director, Avon Products, Inc.

New York Economic Club

Graves, Earl Gilbert: director, Aetna Foundation

New York Yacht Club

Benenson, James, Jr.: chairman, president, director, Vesper Corp.; trustee, Vesper Foundation

Dingman, Michael David: partner, director, Winthrop Foundation

Kinsolving, Augustus Blagden: director, ASARCO Foundation

Kress, George F.: honorary chairman, director, Green Bay Packaging; president, Kress Foundation (George)

Levin, Michael Stuart: president, chief executive officer, Titan Industrial Corp.

Steere, William Campbell, Jr.: chairman, chief executive officer, director, Pfizer Inc.

Noonday Club

Busch, August Adolphus, III: chairman, president, chief executive officer, Anheuser-Busch Companies, Inc.

Kniffen, Jan Rogers: senior vice president, treasurer, May Department Stores Co.; vice president, secretary, treasurer, director, May Department Stores Computer Foundation (The)

Neville, James Morton: member board control, Ralston Purina Trust Fund

Van Cleve, William Moore: member public policy committee, Emerson Charitable Trust; partner, Emerson Electric Co.

Norfolk Yacht Club & Country Club

Goode, David Ronald: chairman, president, chief executive officer, director, Norfolk Southern Corp.

North Shore Country Club

Connolly, Gerald Edward: trustee, Reinhart Family Foundation (D. B. and Marjorie)

Peterson, Donald Matthew: trustee, Trustmark Foundation; president, chief executive officer, director, Trustmark Insurance Co.

Northland Country Club

Carlson, Curtis Leroy: chairman, director, Carlson Companies, Inc.; president, treasurer, Carlson Family Foundation (Curtis L.)

Northmoor Country Club

Wander, Herbert S.: secretary, director, Katten, Muchin & Zavis Foundation

Oak Hills Country Club

McCorkindale, Douglas H.: vice chairman, president, Gannett Co., Inc.; president, Gannett Foundation

Oakbrook Handball-Racquetball Club

Quinlan, Michael Robert: chairman executive committee, McDonald's Corp.; director, McDonald's Corp. Charitable Foundation

Oakmont Country Club

Usher, Thomas J.: chairman, chief executive officer, USX Corp.; chairman board trustees, USX Foundation, Inc.

Oakwood Country Club

Berkley, Eugene Bertram: chairman, director, Tension Envelope Corp.; treasurer, Tension Envelope Foundation

Bloch, Henry Wollman: chairman, Block Foundation (H&R); chairman, director, Block, Inc. (H&R)

Oakwood Golf & Country Club

Margolin, Abraham E.: director, Tension Envelope Foundation

Ocean Reef Club

Carlson, Curtis Leroy: chairman, director, Carlson Companies, Inc.; president, treasurer, Carlson Family Foundation (Curtis L.)

Oglethorpe Club

Morris, William Shivers, III: founder, chairman, chief executive officer, director, Morris Communications Corp.; trustee, Stauffer Communications Foundation

Old Baldy Club

Jewell, George Hiram: director, Schlumberger Foundation

Wise, William Allen: chairman, president, chief executive officer, director, El Paso Energy Co.; chairman, director, El Paso Energy Foundation

Old Elm Club

Graham, William B.: chairman, director, Baxter Allegiance Foundation; chairman emeritus, Baxter International Inc.

Ingersoll, Robert Stephen: chairman, director, Panasonic Foundation

Old Warson Country Club

Kemper, David Woods: chairman, president, chief executive officer, director, Commerce Bancshares, Inc.

Neville, James Morton: member board control, Ralston Purina Trust Fund

Suter, Albert E.: senior vice chairman, chief administrative officer, director, Emerson Electric Co.

Olympic Club

Carter, John Douglas: executive vice president, director, Bechtel Group, Inc.

Herringer, Frank Casper: president, chief executive officer, director, chairman, Transamerica Corp.; vice chairman, director, Transamerica Foundation

Phair, Joseph Baschon: corporate secretary, general counsel, vice president, Varian Medical Systems, Inc.

Orchard Lake Country Club

Lyon, Wayne Barton: president, chief operating officer, director, Masco Corp.

Order Coif

Salinger, Robert M.: secretary, First Financial Foundation

Oregon Golf Club

Meyer, Jerome J.: chairman, chief executive officer, Tektronix, Inc.

Orinda Country Club

Redding, Peter Stoddard: trustee, Sherman-Standard Register Foundation; president, chief executive officer, director, Standard Register Co.

Oswego Club

Peressinni, William E.: senior vice president, chief financial officer, PacifiCorp; treasurer, PacifiCorp Foundation

Otsego Ski Club

Brennan, Leo Joseph, Jr.: vice president, executive director, Ford Motor Co. Fund

Ottawa Shooting Club

Ong, John Doyle: chairman board, director, Ameritech Corp.

Outrigger Canoe Club

Simpson, Andrea Lynn: president

Overseas Press Club

Gould, John T., Jr.: vice president, Unilever Foundation; director corporate

affairs, Unilever United States, Inc.

Sulzberger, Arthur Ochs, Sr.: director, New York Times Co.; chairman, director, New York Times Co. Foundation

Thomasson, Dan King: vice president, trustee, Scripps Howard Foundation

Owatonna Country Club

Buxton, Charles Ingraham, II: chairman, Federated Mutual Insurance Co.; president, Federated Mutual Insurance Foundation

Oxford University Club

Kampouris, Emmanuel Andrew: chairman, president, chief executive officer, director, American Standard Inc.

PRI Golf Club

Wild, Heidi Karin: trustee

Pacific Club

Simpson, Andrea Lynn: president

Pacific-Union Club

Gammill, Lee Morgan, Jr.: director, New York Life Foundation; vice chairman, director, New York Life Insurance Co.

Ginn, Samuel L.: chairman, director, AirTouch Communications Foundation; chairman, chief executive officer, director, Vodafone AirTouch Plc

Herringer, Frank Casper: president, chief executive officer, director, chairman, Transamerica Corp.; vice chairman, director, Transamerica Foundation

James, George Barker, II: senior vice president, chief financial officer, Levi Strauss & Co.

Weinberger, Caspar Willard: chairman, Forbes Inc.

Wilbur, Brayton, Jr.: president, chief executive officer, Wilbur-Ellis Co. & Connell Brothers Co.; president, Wilbur Foundation (Brayton)

Palm Bay Club

Carlson, Curtis Leroy: chairman, director, Carlson Companies, Inc.; president, treasurer, Carlson Family Foundation (Curtis L.)

Paradise Valley Country Club

Franke, William Augustus: chairman, president, chief executive officer, America West Airlines, Inc.; director, Phelps Dodge Foundation

Snell, Richard: chairman, president, chief executive officer, director, Arizona Public Service Co.

Pelham Country Club

Geissinger, Frederick Wallace: chairman, chief executive officer, president, director, American General Finance Foundation

Pelican Nest Golf Club

Peterson, Donald Matthew: trustee, Trustmark Foundation; president, chief executive officer, director, Trustmark Insurance Co.

Pendennis Club

Guillaume, Raymond Kendrick: vice chairman, chief executive officer, Mid-America Bank of Louisville

Peninsular Club

Pew, Robert Cunningham, II: trustee, Steelcase Foundation

Pennsylvania Club

Block, Allan James: vice president, trustee, Blade Foundation; director, Toledo Blade Co.

Pepper Pike Club

Breen, John Gerald: chairman, chief executive officer, director, Sherwin-Williams Co.; president, trustee, Sherwin-Williams Foundation

Parker, Patrick Streeter: chairman, director, Parker Hannifin Corp.; president, trustee, Parker Hannifin Foundation

Pepper Pike Country Club

Gherlein, Gerald Lee: member contributions committee, Eaton Charitable Fund

Persimmon Woods Golf Club

Loeb, Jerome Thomas: chairman, director, May Department Stores Co.; president, director, May Department Stores Computer Foundation (The)

Petroleum Club

Bradford, William Edward: chairman, director, Halliburton Co.

Greene, John Frederick: executive vice president exploration & production, director, Louisiana Land & Exploration Co.

Haddock, Ronald Wayne: president, chief executive officer, director, FINA; president, FINA Foundation

Hemminghaus, Roger Roy: chairman, director, Ultramar Diamond Shamrock Corp.

True, Jean Durland: trustee, True Foundation; partner, True Oil Co.

Philadelphia Club

Meyerson, Martin: director, Panasonic Foundation

Spaeth, Karl Henry: chairman, trustee, Quaker Chemical Foundation

Phoenix Country Club

Franke, William Augustus: chairman, president, chief executive officer, America West Airlines, Inc.; director, Phelps Dodge Foundation

Snell, Richard: chairman, president, chief executive officer, director, Arizona Public Service Co.

Piedmont City Club

Strickland, Robert Louis: vice president, Lowe's Charitable and Educational Foundation

Pine Valley Club

Meyer, Russell William, Jr.: chairman, chief executive officer, Cessna Aircraft Co.; president, Cessna Foundation, Inc.

Pine Valley Country Club

Moritz, Charles Worthington: chairman, director, Dun & Bradstreet Corp.

Pine Valley Golf Club

Goodes, Melvin Russell: chairman, chief executive officer, director, Ameritech Corp.

McCorkindale, Douglas H.: vice chairman, president, Gannett Co., Inc.; president, Gannett Foundation

Rehm, Jack Daniel: chairman emeritus, director, Meredith Corp.

Ridder, Paul Anthony: chairman, chief executive officer, director, Knight Ridder

Pinnacle Club

Morris, William Shivers, III: founder, chairman, chief executive officer, director, Morris Communications Corp.; trustee, Stauffer Communications Foundation

Pittsburgh Golf Club

O'Reilly, F. Anthony John: chairman, trustee, Heinz Co. Foundation (H.J.); chairman, director, Heinz Co. (H.J.)

Pittsburgh Press Club

O'Reilly, F. Anthony John: chairman, trustee, Heinz Co. Foundation (H.J.); chairman, director, Heinz Co. (H.J.)

Plainfield Country Club

Goodes, Melvin Russell: chairman, chief executive officer, director, Ameritech Corp.

Plaza Club

Hemminghaus, Roger Roy: chairman, director, Ultramar Diamond Shamrock Corp.

Wolff, Herbert Eric: secretary, director, First Hawaiian Foundation

Point O Woods Club

Whitwam, David Ray: chairman, president, chief executive officer, director, Whirlpool Corp.

Polo Club

Zilkha, Ezra Khedouri: president, treasurer, Zilkha Foundation, Inc.; president, Zilkha & Sons

Pool & Yacht Club

Anderson, Lowell Carlton: chairman, director, Allianz Life Insurance Co. of North America

Port Royal Club

Wheeler, Thomas Beardsley: chairman, chief executive officer, Massachusetts Mutual Life Insurance Co.

Portage Country Club

Holland, Willard R.: chairman, chief executive officer, FirstEnergy Corp.

Ong, John Doyle: chairman board, director, Ameritech Corp.

Shaffer, Oren G.: executive vice president, chief financial officer, Ameritech Corp.

Prestwood Club

Shelley, James Herbert: chairman, Sonoco Foundation

Princess Anne Country Club

Goode, David Ronald: chairman, president, chief executive officer, director, Norfolk Southern Corp.

Princeton Club

Buchanan, William Hobart, Jr.: assistant secretary, Dun & Bradstreet Corp. Foundation, Inc.

Connor, Walter Robert: director, Glaxo Wellcome Foundation

Hutton, Edward L.: chairman, chief executive officer, director, Chemed Corp.

Ughetta, William Casper: trustee, Corning Inc. Foundation

Van Cleve, William Moore: member public policy committee, Emerson Charitable Trust; partner, Emerson Electric Co.

Vogel, Howard Stanley: tax counsel, Texaco Foundation

Provost Club

Dewane, John Richard: director, Honeywell Foundation

Pyramid Club

Naples, Ronald James: president, chief executive officer, director, Quaker Chemical Corp.

Quail Hollow Country Club

Browning, Peter C.: chief executive officer, president, director, Sonoco Products Co.

Iverson, Francis Kenneth: chairman, director, Nucor Corp.; director, Nucor Foundation

Quaker Ridge Golf Club

Millstein, Ira M.: partner, Weil, Gotshal & Manges Corp.; president, director, Weil, Gotshal & Manges Foundation

Queen City Club

Bridgeland, James Ralph, Jr.: trustee, Star Bank

NA, Cincinnati Foundation

Burleigh, William Robert: president, chief executive officer, director, Scripps Co. (E.W.); member, Scripps Howard Foundation

Cody, Thomas Gerald: executive vice president legal & human resources, Federated Department Stores, Inc.

Hayden, Joseph Page, Jr.: trustee, Star Bank NA, Cincinnati Foundation

Hutton, Edward L.: chairman, chief executive officer, director, Chemed Corp.

Klinedinst, Thomas John, Jr.: trustee, Star Bank NA, Cincinnati Foundation

LaMacchia, John Thomas: trustee, Cincinnati Bell Foundation, Inc.; president, chief executive officer, director, Cincinnati Bell Inc.

Pepper, John E., Jr.: chairman executive committee, Procter & Gamble Co.

Randolph, Jackson Harold: chairman, Cinergy Corp.; chairman, director, Cinergy Foundation

Rogers, James E., Jr.: vice chairman, president, chief executive officer, Cinergy Corp.; vice chairman, director, Cinergy Foundation

Wehling, Robert Louis: global marketing, government relations officer, Procter & Gamble Co.; president, trustee, Procter & Gamble Fund

Quogue Beach Club

Kampouris, Emmanuel Andrew: chairman, president, chief executive officer, director, American Standard Inc.

Quogue Field Club

Kerr, William T.: chairman, chief executive officer, director, Meredith Corp.

Racine Country Club

Johnson, Samuel Curtis: chairman, director, president, Johnson & Son (S.C.); chairman, trustee, Johnson Wax Fund (S.C.)

Racquet & Tennis Club

Clark, Howard Longstreth, Jr.: vice chairman, Walter Industries Inc.

Koch, David Hamilton: director, Koch Foundation, Inc. (Fred C. and Mary R.)

Minton, Dwight Church: chairman, director, Church & Dwight Co., Inc.

Zilkha, Ezra Khedouri: president, treasurer, Zilkha Foundation, Inc.; president, Zilkha & Sons

Racquet Club

Benenson, James, Jr.: chairman, president, director, Vesper Corp.; trustee, Vesper Foundation

Guthart, Leo A.: vice chairman, director, Pittway Corp.

Kemper, David Woods: chairman, president, chief executive officer, director, Commerce Bancshares, Inc.

Naples, Ronald James: president, chief executive officer, director, Quaker Chemical Corp.

Racquet Club Chicago

Skilling, Raymond Inwood: executive vice president, chief counsel, director, Aon Corp.; director, Aon Foundation

Rainier Club

Condit, Philip Murray: chairman, chief executive officer, director, Boeing Co.

Rosenberg, Richard Morris: chairman, chief executive officer (retired), Bank of America

Rams Hill Country Club

Ginn, Samuel L.: chairman, director, AirTouch Communications Foundation; chairman, chief executive officer, director, Vodafone AirTouch Plc

Raveneaux Country Club

Bradford, William Edward: chairman, director, Halliburton Co.

Reform Club

Kerr, William T.: chairman, chief executive officer, director, Meredith Corp.

Resnick, Myron J.: vice president, treasurer, trustee, Allstate Foundation

Rensselaer Polytechnic Institute Club

DiCamillo, Gary Thomas: chairman, chief executive officer, director, Polaroid Corp.

River Club

Baker, Edward L.: chairman, director, Florida Rock Industries; president, Florida Rock Industries Foundation

Bloch, Henry Wollman: chairman, Block Foundation (H&R); chairman, director, Block, Inc. (H&R)

Bridgewater, Bernard Adolphus, Jr.: member board control, Brown Shoe Co. Charitable Trust; chairman, president, chief executive officer, director, Brown Shoe Co., Inc.

Clark, Howard Longstreth, Jr.: vice chairman, Walter Industries Inc.

Collins, Paul John: vice chairman, director, Citibank Corp.

Esrey, William Todd: chairman, chief executive officer, Sprint Corp.

Furlaud, Richard Mortimer: interim chief executive officer, International Flavors & Fragrances Inc.

Geier, Philip Henry, Jr.: chairman, president, chief executive officer, Interpublic Group of Companies, Inc.

Heimbold, Charles Andreas, Jr.: chairman, president, chief executive officer, Bristol-Myers Squibb Co.

Houghton, James Richardson: director, Corning Inc.; trustee, Corning Inc. Foundation

Kemper, David Woods: chairman, president, chief executive officer, director, Commerce Bancshares, Inc.

Kissinger, Henry Alfred: director, CBS Foundation

Koch, David Hamilton: director, Koch Foundation, Inc. (Fred C. and Mary R.)

Matheny, Edward Taylor, Junior: director, Block Foundation (H&R)

McCook, Richard P.: vice president, Winn-Dixie Stores Foundation; vice president finance, chief financial officer, Winn-Dixie Stores Inc.

Shinn, George Latimer: director, New York Times Co. Foundation

Warner, Douglas Alexander, III: chairman, president, chief executive officer, director, Morgan & Co. Inc. (J.P.)

River Oaks Country Club

Buckwalter, Alan Roland, III: chief executive officer, Chase Bank of Texas; president, Chase Bank of Texas Foundation, Inc.

Carroll, Philip Joseph: chairman, chief executive officer, Fluor Corp.; chairman, trustee, Fluor Foundation

Wise, William Allen: chairman, president, chief executive officer, director, El Paso Energy Co.; chairman, director, El Paso Energy Foundation

Rivers Club

Newlin, William Rankin: trustee, Kennametal Foundation

Riverside Yacht Club

Heimbold, Charles Andreas, Jr.: chairman, president, chief executive officer, Bristol-Myers Squibb Co.

Roaring Gap Club

Strickland, Robert Louis: vice president, Lowe's Charitable and Educational Foundation

Rock Island Club

Becherer, Hans Walter: chairman, chief executive officer, director, Deere & Co.; director, Deere Foundation (John)

Rockaway Hunt Club

Blanke, Gail Ann: vice president, Avon Products Foundation, Inc.

Rockefeller Center Club

Calise, William Joseph, Junior: senior vice president, secretary, general counsel, Rockwell International Corp.

Rockford Country Club

Meuleman, Robert Joseph: director, AMCORE Foundation

Rolling Rock Club

Brothers, John Alfred 'Fred': trustee, Ashland Inc. Foundation

Graham, Thomas Carlisle: trustee, AK Steel Foundation

Houghton, James Richardson: director, Corning Inc.; trustee, Corning Inc. Foundation

O'Reilly, F. Anthony John: chairman, trustee, Heinz Co. Foundation (H.J.); chairman, director, Heinz Co. (H.J.)

Ong, John Doyle: chairman board, director, Ameritech Corp.

Shannon, Michael E.: chairman, chief financial officer, chief administration officer, director, Ecolab Inc.

Usher, Thomas J.: chairman, chief executive officer, USX Corp.; chairman board trustees, USX Foundation, Inc.

Walton, Jon David: trustee, Allegheny Technologies Inc. Charitable Trust

Rotary Club

Baker, James Kendrick: chairman, director, Arvin Foundation; vice chairman, director, Arvin Industries, Inc.

Blount, Winton Malcolm, Jr.: chairman, Blount International, Inc.

Bright, Stanley J.: chairman, president, chief executive officer, director, MidAmerican Energy Holdings Co.

Buxton, Charles Ingraham, II: chairman, Federated Mutual Insurance Co.; president, Federated Mutual Insurance Foundation

Coker, Charles Westfield: trustee, Sonoco Foundation; vice president, Sonoco Products Co.

Dubes, Michael: membership, ReliaStar Foundation

Harris, Elmer Beseler: president, chief executive officer, director, Alabama Power Co.

Howe, Stanley M.: president, HON Industries Charitable Foundation; chairman emeritus, director, HON Industries Inc.

Hyatt, Kenneth Ernest: chairman, president, chief executive officer, director, Walter Industries Inc.

Johnson, James Lawrence: chairman emeritus, Walter Industries Inc.

Jones, D. Paul, Jr.: chairman, chief executive officer, Compass Bank; trustee, Compass Bank Foundation

Kalainov, Sam Charles: chairman, president, chief executive officer, AmerUS Group

Kelley, Bruce Gunn: vice president, director, Employers Mutual Charitable Foundation

Killinger, Kerry Kent: chairman, president, chief executive officer, director, Washington Mutual, Inc.

Klinedinst, Thomas John, Jr.: trustee, Star Bank NA, Cincinnati Foundation

Lakin, Thomas J.: regional chairman, Star Bank NA;

president, Star Bank NA, Cincinnati Foundation

McCarthy, John Michael: vice president, Waffle House Foundation, Inc.

Salinger, Robert M.: secretary, First Financial Foundation

Simpson, Andrea Lynn: president

Sissel, George A.: chairman, president, chief executive officer, director, Ball Corp.

Smith, Donald Kaye: senior vice president, general counsel, director, GEICO Corp.

Wolff, Herbert Eric: secretary, director, First Hawaiian Foundation

Rotary International Club

Aley, Paul Nathaniel: president, director, National Machinery Co.; president, National Machinery Foundation, Inc.

Carver, Martin Gregory: chairman, president, chief executive officer, Bandag, Inc.

Donehue, J. Douglas: managing director, Post and Courier Foundation

Hadley, Leonard Anson: chairman, chief executive officer, director, Maytag Corp.; president, trustee, Maytag Corp. Foundation

McCarragher, Bernard John: chairman, director, Menasha Corp.; chairman, Menasha Corp. Foundation

Round Hill Club

Douglass, Robert Royal: trustee, Chase Manhattan Foundation

Round Hill Country Club

Clark, Howard Longstreth, Jr.: vice chairman, Walter Industries Inc.

Round Table Club

Van Cleve, William Moore: member public policy committee, Emerson Charitable Trust; partner, Emerson Electric Co.

Royal Palm Tennis Club

Herron, James Michael: secretary, director, Ryder System Charitable Foundation

Rye Racquet Club

Tisch, Preston Robert: chairman, director, CBS Foundation; co-chairman, co-chief executive officer, director, CNA; trustee, Loews Foundation

Saddle & Cycle Club

Harris, Irving Brooks: chairman executive committee, director, Pittway Corp.; chairman, director, Pittway Corp. Charitable Foundation

Saint Clair Country Club

Mueller, Charles William: chairman, president, chief executive officer, Ameren Corp.; trustee, Ameren Corp. Charitable Trust

Saint Francis Yacht Club

Disney, Roy Edward: trustee, Disney Co. Foundation (Walt); vice chairman, director, Disney Co. (Walt)

Saint Louis Club

Bachmann, John W.: managing partner, Jones & Co. (Edward D.); chairman, Jones & Co. Foundation (Edward D.)

Carr, Cassandra Colvin: director, SBC Foundation

Kemper, David Woods: chairman, president, chief executive officer, director, Commerce Bancshares, Inc.

McKenna, William John: director, chairman, Kellwood Co.; chairman, president, director, Kellwood Foundation

Mueller, Charles William: chairman, president, chief executive officer, Ameren Corp.; trustee, Ameren Corp. Charitable Trust

Suter, Albert E.: senior vice chairman, chief administrative officer, director, Emerson Electric Co.

Saint Louis Country Club

Bridgewater, Bernard Adolphus, Jr.: member board control, Brown Shoe Co. Charitable Trust; chairman, president, chief executive officer, director, Brown Shoe Co., Inc.

Busch, August Adolphus, III: chairman, president, chief executive officer, Anheuser-Busch Companies, Inc.

Jacobsen, Thomas Herbert: chairman, president, chief executive officer, Mercantile Bank NA

Kemper, David Woods: chairman, president, chief executive officer, director, Commerce Bancshares, Inc.

Knight, Charles Field: chairman, chief executive officer, Emerson Electric Co.

Pulitzer, Michael Edgar: chairman, president, chief executive officer, director, Pulitzer Publishing Co.; chairman, president, chief executive officer, Pulitzer Publishing Co. Foundation

Van Cleve, William Moore: member public policy committee, Emerson Charitable Trust; partner, Emerson Electric Co.

Saint Stephen's Green Club

O'Reilly, F. Anthony John: chairman, trustee, Heinz Co. Foundation (H.J.); chairman, director, Heinz Co. (H.J.)

Sakonnet Golf Club

Osborne, Richard de Jongh: director, ASARCO Foundation; chairman, chief executive officer, director, ASARCO Inc.

Salesmanship Club Dallas

Huey, Ward L., Jr.: president broadcast division, vice chairman, director, Belo Corp. (A.H.); vice president, trustee, Belo Corp. Foundation (A.H.)

Salmagundi Club

Forbes, Christopher 'Kip': vice president, Forbes Foundation; vice chairman, corporate secretary, director, Forbes Inc.

Salt Lake Country Club

Eccles, Spencer Fox: chairman, chief executive officer, director, First Security Bank of Idaho NA

San Diego Yacht Club

Dingman, Michael David: partner, director, Winthrop Foundation

Disney, Roy Edward: trustee, Disney Co. Foundation (Walt); vice chairman, director, Disney Co. (Walt)

San Francisco Golf Club

Herringer, Frank Casper: president, chief executive officer, director, chairman, Transamerica Corp.; vice chairman, director, Transamerica Foundation

San Francisco Press Club

Copley, Helen K.: chairman, trustee, Copley Foundation (James S.); chairman, director, senior management board, Copley Press, Inc.

Sanctuary Golf Club

Lautenbach, Terry Robert: trustee, Air Products Foundation

Sand Creek Club

Penny, Roger Pratt: president, chief operating officer, director, Bethlehem Steel Corp.

Sand Hills Golf Club

Lucas, Donald Leo: chairman, Cadence Designs Systems, Inc.

Sands Point Golf Club

Black, Daniel James: treasurer, Carter-Wallace Foundation; president, chief operating officer, director, Carter-Wallace, Inc.

Saucon Valley Country Club

Barnette, Curtis Handley: chairman, chief executive officer, director, Bethlehem Steel Corp.

Penny, Roger Pratt: president, chief operating officer, director, Bethlehem Steel Corp.

Scarsdale Golf Club

Rehm, Jack Daniel: chairman emeritus, director, Meredith Corp.

Soden, Paul A.: senior vice president, secretary, general counsel, Reader's Digest Association, Inc. (The)

Schuyler Meadows Country Club

Standish, J. Spencer: chairman, director, Albany International Corp.

Sciotto Country Club

Brothers, John Alfred 'Fred': trustee, Ashland Inc. Foundation

Wobst, Frank: chairman, chief executive officer, director, Huntington Bancshares Inc.

Scottish Rite Club

Smith, Donald Kaye: senior vice president, general counsel, director, GEICO Corp.

Seal Harbor Club

Douglass, Robert Royal: trustee, Chase Manhattan Foundation

Seawanhaka Corinthian Yacht Club

Minton, Dwight Church: chairman, director, Church & Dwight Co., Inc.

Seminole Club

Clark, Howard Longstreth, Jr.: vice chairman, Walter Industries Inc.

Graham, William B.: chairman, director, Baxter Allegiance Foundation; chairman emeritus, Baxter International Inc.

Seminole Golf Club

McCoy, John Bonnet: president, chief executive officer, Ameritech Corp.

Shades Valley Rotary Club

Stephens, Elton Bryson: founder, chairman, Ebsco Industries, Inc.

Sheboygan Economic Club

Kohler, Herbert Vollrath, Jr.: chairman, president, director, Kohler Co.

Shenandoah Club

Goode, David Ronald: chairman, president, chief executive officer, director, Norfolk Southern Corp.

Shoreacres Club

Hodgson, Thomas Richard: president, chief operating officer, director, Abbott Laboratories

Shoreby Club

Burlingame, John Hunter: executive partner, Scripps Co. (E.W.)

Shriners Club

Buxton, Charles Ingraham, II: chairman, Federated Mutual Insurance Co.; president, Federated Mutual Insurance Foundation

Carlson, Curtis Leroy: chairman, director, Carlson Companies, Inc.; president, treasurer, Carlson Family Foundation (Curtis L.)

Kulynych, Petro: chairman, treasurer, Lowe's Charitable and Educational Foundation

Vondrasek, Frank Charles, Jr.: president, Madison Gas & Electric Foundation

Sigma Delta Chi
Thomasson, Dan King: vice president, trustee, Scripps Howard Foundation

Simsbury Farms Men's Club
Long, Michael Thomas: director, Ensign-Bickford Foundation

Sioux City Country Club
Peterson, Robert L.: chairman, chief executive officer, director, IBP

Sitzmarker Ski Club
Ackerman, Philip Charles: senior vice president, director, National Fuel Gas Distribution Corp.
Kennedy, Bernard Joseph: chairman, president, chief executive officer, director, National Fuel Gas Distribution Corp.

Skokie Country Club
DiCamillo, Gary Thomas: chairman, chief executive officer, director, Polaroid Corp.
Sopranos, Orpheus Javaras: corporate vice president, Amsted Industries Inc.

Skyline Club
Rogers, James E., Jr.: vice chairman, president, chief executive officer, Cinergy Corp.; vice chairman, director, Cinergy Foundation
Russell, Frank Eli: president, Central Newspapers Foundation; chairman, Central Newspapers, Inc.
Sease, Gene Elwood: director, Central Newspapers Foundation

Sleepy Hollow Country Club
Kennedy, George Danner: trustee, Kemper Foundation (James S.)

Sloane Club
Geier, Philip Henry, Jr.: chairman, president, chief executive officer, Interpublic Group of Companies, Inc.

Somerset Club
Magee, John Francis: chairman, director, Little, Inc. (Arthur D.)

Southport Yacht Club
Brinegar, Claude Stout: trustee, Unocal Foundation

Spee Club
Kann, Peter Robert: chairman, chief executive officer, publisher, director, Dow Jones & Co., Inc.; member advisory committee, Dow Jones Foundation

Spring Brook Country Club
Kampouris, Emmanuel Andrew: chairman, president, chief executive officer, director, American Standard Inc.

Springdale Hall Club
Daniels, John Hancock: chairman, Archer-Daniels-Midland Foundation

Springs Club
Maatman, Gerald Leonard: chairman, president, trustee, Kemper Foundation (James S.); director, Kemper National Insurance Companies

Standard Club
Harris, Irving Brooks: chairman executive committee, director, Pittway Corp.; chairman, director, Pittway Corp. Charitable Foundation
Stone, Roger Warren: chairman, president, chief executive officer, director, Stone Container Corp.; president, Stone Foundation
Wander, Herbert S.: secretary, director, Katten, Muchin & Zavis Foundation
Zavis, Michael W.: managing partner, Katten, Muchin & Zavis; president, director, Katten, Muchin & Zavis Foundation

Stanford Buck Club
Lucas, Donald Leo: chairman, Cadence Designs Systems, Inc.

Stanwich Club
Lee, Charles Robert: chairman, chief executive officer, director, GTE Corp.; chief executive officer, trustee, GTE Foundation

Stevens Point Country Club
Salinger, Robert M.: secretary, First Financial Foundation

Summit Club
Harris, Elmer Beseler: president, chief executive officer, director, Alabama Power Co.
Stephens, Elton Bryson: founder, chairman, Ebsco Industries, Inc.

Summit Fort Wayne Club
Lawson, William Hogan, III: chairman, chief executive officer, director, Franklin Electric Co.; president, Franklin Electric, Edward J. Schaefer, and T. W. KehoeCharitable and Educational Foundation

Sun Valley Ski Club
Kress, George F.: honorary chairman, director, Green Bay Packaging; president, Kress Foundation (George)

Sweetwater Country Club
Buckwalter, Alan Roland, III: chief executive officer, Chase Bank of Texas; president, Chase Bank of Texas Foundation, Inc.

Swinley Forest Golf Club
Price, Charles H., II: director, New York Times Co. Foundation

TPC of Michigan Club
Lyon, Wayne Barton: president, chief operating officer, director, Masco Corp.

Tarratine Club
Houghton, James Richardson: director, Corning Inc.; trustee, Corning Inc. Foundation

Tavern Club
Stone, Roger Warren: chairman, president, chief executive officer, director, Stone Container Corp.; president, Stone Foundation

Tchefuncta Country Club
Carroll, Philip Joseph: chairman, chief executive officer, Fluor Corp.; chairman, trustee, Fluor Foundation

Terrapin Club
Smith, Donald Kaye: senior vice president, general counsel, director, GEICO Corp.

Teton Pines Club
Lucas, Donald Leo: chairman, Cadence Designs Systems, Inc.

The Casino
Almeida, Richard: chairman, chief executive officer, Heller Financial, Inc.

The Club
Stephens, Elton Bryson: founder, chairman, Ebsco Industries, Inc.

The Links Club
Andreas, Dwayne Orville: chairman, chief executive officer, Archer-Daniels-Midland Co.
Barnette, Curtis Handley: chairman, chief executive officer, director, Bethlehem Steel Corp.
Clark, Howard Longstreth, Jr.: vice chairman, Walter Industries Inc.
Daniels, John Hancock: chairman, Archer-Daniels-Midland Foundation
Dingman, Michael David: partner, director, Winthrop Foundation
Esrey, William Todd: chairman, chief executive officer, Sprint Corp.
Furlaud, Richard Mortimer: interim chief executive officer, International Flavors & Fragrances Inc.
Gammill, Lee Morgan, Jr.: director, New York Life Foundation; vice chairman, director, New York Life Insurance Co.
Goode, David Ronald: chairman, president, chief executive officer, director, Norfolk Southern Corp.
Graham, William B.: chairman, director, Baxter Allegiance Foundation; chairman emeritus, Baxter International Inc.
Hiner, Glen Harold, Jr.: chairman, chief executive officer, director, Owens Corning
Luke, John A., Jr.: chairman, president, chief executive officer, director, Westvaco Corp.
Milliken, Roger: chairman, chief executive officer, Milliken & Co.; member advisory committee, Milliken Foundation
Moritz, Charles Worthington: chairman, director, Dun & Bradstreet Corp.
O'Hare, Dean Raymond: chairman, Chubb Corp.
O'Reilly, F. Anthony John: chairman, trustee, Heinz Co. Foundation (H.J.); chairman, director, Heinz Co. (H.J.)
Ong, John Doyle: chairman board, director, Ameritech Corp.
Warner, Douglas Alexander, III: chairman, president, chief executive officer, director, Morgan & Co. Inc. (J.P.)
Wheeler, Thomas Beardsley: chairman, chief executive officer, Massachusetts Mutual Life Insurance Co.
Whitehead, John Cunningham: chairman board, Goldman Sachs Foundation

Thunderbird Country Club
Lee, Charles Robert: chairman, chief executive officer, director, GTE Corp.; chief executive officer, trustee, GTE Foundation

Tokeneke Club
Hays, Thomas Chandler: chairman, chief executive officer, director, Fortune Brands, Inc.

Toledo Club
Block, Allan James: vice president, trustee, Blade Foundation; director, Toledo Blade Co.
Block, William, Jr.: president, trustee, Blade Foundation; president, director, Toledo Blade Co.
Hiner, Glen Harold, Jr.: chairman, chief executive officer, director, Owens Corning

Toledo Press Club
Block, William, Jr.: president, trustee, Blade Foundation; president, director, Toledo Blade Co.

Top Tower Club
Stauffer, Stanley Howard: chairman, Stauffer Communications Foundation

Topeka Country Club
Stauffer, John H.: trustee, Stauffer Communications Foundation
Stauffer, Stanley Howard: chairman, Stauffer Communications Foundation

Town Point Club
Goode, David Ronald: chairman, president, chief executive officer, director, Norfolk Southern Corp.

Transpacific Yacht Club

Disney, Roy Edward: trustee, Disney Co. Foundation (Walt); vice chairman, director, Disney Co. (Walt)

Travelers Club

Zilkha, Ezra Khedouri: president, treasurer, Zilkha Foundation, Inc.; president, Zilkha & Sons

Tri State Athletic Club

Koch, Robert Louis, II: president, chief executive officer, director, Koch Enterprises, Inc.; president, director, Koch Foundation

Tuxedo Club

Glynn, Gary Allen: president, USX Corp.; vice president, USX Foundation, Inc.

Twin City Club

Strickland, Robert Louis: vice president, Lowe's Charitable and Educational Foundation

Union Club

Breen, John Gerald: chairman, chief executive officer, director, Sherwin-Williams Co.; president, trustee, Sherwin-Williams Foundation

Burlingame, John Hunter: executive partner, Scripps Co. (E.W.)

Dingman, Michael David: partner, director, Winthrop Foundation

Kerr, William T.: chairman, chief executive officer, director, Meredith Corp.

Ong, John Doyle: chairman board, director, Ameritech Corp.

Parker, Patrick Streeter: chairman, director, Parker Hannifin Corp.; president, trustee, Parker Hannifin Foundation

Pyke, John Secrest, Jr.: president, trustee, Hanna Co. Foundation (M.A.); vice president, secretary, general counsel, Hanna Co. (M.A.)

Union League Club

Donahue, Richard King: vice chairman, Nike, Inc.

Milliken, Roger: chairman, chief executive officer, Milliken & Co.; member advisory committee, Milliken Foundation

O'Reilly, F. Anthony John: chairman, trustee, Heinz Co. Foundation (H.J.); chairman, director, Heinz Co. (H.J.)

Ong, John Doyle: chairman board, director, Ameritech Corp.

Toll, Daniel Roger: trustee, Kemper Foundation (James S.)

Wiksten, Barry Frank: president, CIGNA Foundation

Union League Club Chicago

Williams, Edward Joseph: president, director, Harris Bank Foundation

Union League Club New York

Franklin, Barbara Hackman: director, Dow Chemical Co.

Union League Club Philadelphia

Landin, Thomas Milton: vice president, director, CertainTeed Corp.; vice president, Norton Co. Foundation

University Club

Bauer, Chris Michael: president, Firstar Milwaukee Foundation

Black, Daniel James: treasurer, Carter-Wallace Foundation; president, chief operating officer, director, Carter-Wallace, Inc.

Booth, Chesleu Peter Washburn: senior vice president development, Corning Inc.; trustee, Corning Inc. Foundation

Brumm, Paul Michael: executive vice president, chief financial officer, Fifth Third Bancorp

Burak, Howard Paul: secretary, director, Sony U.S.A. Foundation Inc.

Druen, W. Sidney: director, Nationwide Insurance Enterprise Foundation

Farnsworth, Philip Richeson: secretary, ABC

Graff, Stephen Ney: director, Bucyrus-Erie Foundation

Hayden, Joseph Page, Jr.: trustee, Star Bank NA, Cincinnati Foundation

Houghton, James Richardson: director, Corning Inc.; trustee, Corning Inc. Foundation

Hutton, Edward L.: chairman, chief executive officer, director, Chemed Corp.

Johnson, Samuel Curtis: chairman, director, president, Johnson & Son (S.C.); chairman, trustee, Johnson Wax Fund (S.C.)

Kemper, David Woods: chairman, president, chief executive officer, director, Commerce Bancshares, Inc.

Luke, John A., Jr.: chairman, president, chief executive officer, director, Westvaco Corp.

Mead, Dana George: chairman, chief executive officer, director, Tenneco Automotive

Montrone, Paul Michael: vice president, partner, Winthrop Foundation

Morris, William Shivers, III: founder, chairman, chief executive officer, director, Morris Communications Corp.; trustee, Stauffer Communications Foundation

Peressinni, William E.: senior vice president, chief financial officer, PacifiCorp; treasurer, PacifiCorp Foundation

Pew, Robert Cunningham, II: trustee, Steelcase Foundation

Redstone, Sumner Murray: chairman, Viacom Inc.

Sadler, Robert L.: president, vice chairman, director, Old Kent Bank

Shannon, Michael E.: chairman, chief financial officer, chief administration officer, director, Ecolab Inc.

Sopranos, Orpheus Javaras: corporate vice president, Amsted Industries Inc.

Steere, William Campbell, Jr.: chairman, chief executive officer, director, Pfizer Inc.

Terry, Richard Edward: chairman, chief executive officer, director, Peoples Energy Corp.

Tobias, Randall L.: chairman emeritus, Lilly & Co. (Eli)

Ughetta, William Casper: trustee, Corning Inc. Foundation

Wentworth, Jack Roberts, Ph.D.: director, Habig Foundation

Whitehead, John Cunningham: chairman board, Goldman Sachs Foundation

Winter, William Bergford: president, Bucyrus-Erie Co.; chairman, president, director, Bucyrus-Erie Foundation

University Club Dublin

O'Reilly, F. Anthony John: chairman, trustee, Heinz Co. Foundation (H.J.); chairman, director, Heinz Co. (H.J.)

University Club Hartford

Miglio, Daniel Joseph: chairman, president, director, chief executive officer, Southern New England Telephone Co.

University Club New York

Griffith, Alan Richard: vice chairman, Bank of New York Co., Inc.

Patel, Homi Burjor: president, chief operating officer, director, Hartmarx Corp.

University Club New York City

Dozier, Ollin Kemp: treasurer, Universal Leaf Foundation

University Club Pennsylvania

Meyerson, Martin: director, Panasonic Foundation

University Club Texas

Gleaves, James Leslie: assistant treasurer, American General Finance Foundation

University Club Washington

Barnette, Curtis Handley: chairman, chief executive officer, director, Bethlehem Steel Corp.

Thomasson, Dan King: vice president, trustee, Scripps Howard Foundation

University Houston Club

Bradford, William Edward: chairman, director, Halliburton Co.

University of Pennsylvania of Greater Hartford Club

Miglio, Daniel Joseph: chairman, president, director, chief executive officer, Southern New England Telephone Co.

Useppa Island Club

Hayden, Joseph Page, Jr.: trustee, Star Bank NA, Cincinnati Foundation

Valley Brook Country Club

Walton, Jon David: trustee, Allegheny Technologies Inc. Charitable Trust

Vantana Country Club

Gaiswinkler, Robert Sigfried: chairman, director, First Financial Bank; director, First Financial Foundation

Variety Iowa Club

Dubes, Michael: membership, ReliaStar Foundation

Variety Southern California Club

Rosenzweig, Richard Stuart: executive vice president, director, Playboy Enterprises Inc.

Ventana Canyon

Piper, Addison Lewis: director, Piper Jaffray Companies Foundation; chairman, chief executive officer, director, U.S. Bancorp Piper Jaffray

Vesper Club

Landin, Thomas Milton: vice president, director, CertainTeed Corp.; vice president, Norton Co. Foundation

Vesper Country Club

Donahue, Richard King: vice chairman, Nike, Inc.

Veterans Foreign Wars

Buxton, Charles Ingraham, II: chairman, Federated Mutual Insurance Co.; president, Federated Mutual Insurance Foundation

Viking Beach Club

Cianciola, Charles Sal: trustee, Chesapeake Corp. Foundation

Vintage Club

Lucas, Donald Leo: chairman, Cadence Designs Systems, Inc.

Virginia Country Club

Cutchins, Clifford Armstrong, IV: president, Fort James Corp.; chairman, director, Fort James Foundation (The)

Virginia Golf Club

Goode, David Ronald: chairman, president, chief executive officer, director, Norfolk Southern Corp.

Waialae Country Club

Wolff, Herbert Eric: secretary, director, First Hawaiian Foundation

Wakonda Golf Club

Kerr, William T.: chairman, chief executive officer, director, Meredith Corp.

Rehm, Jack Daniel: chairman emeritus, director, Meredith Corp.

Washington Golf & Country Club

Thomasson, Dan King: vice president, trustee, Scripps Howard Foundation

Waterfront Golf Club

Spilman, Robert H.: chairman, chief executive officer, Bassett Furniture Industries; chairman, director, Bassett Furniture Industries Fdn.

Wee Burn Country Club

Lautenbach, Terry Robert: trustee, Air Products Foundation

Moritz, Charles Worthington: chairman, director, Dun & Bradstreet Corp.

Wellesley Club

Rogers, Desiree Glapion: vice president community affairs, Peoples Energy Corp.

Western Racquet Club

Winter, William Bergford: president, Bucyrus-Erie Co.; chairman, president, director, Bucyrus-Erie Foundation

Westmoor Country Club

Bauer, Chris Michael: president, Firstar Milwaukee Foundation

Bueche, Wendell Francis: director, Marshall & Ilsley Foundation, Inc.

Corby, Francis Michael, Jr.: executive vice president finance & administration, chief financial officer, Harnischfeger Industries; treasurer, Harnischfeger Industries Foundation

Westmoreland Country Club

Chookaszian, Dennis Haig: chairman, chief executive officer, CNA

Westwood Country Club

Loeb, Jerome Thomas: chairman, director, May Department Stores Co.; president, director, May Department Stores Computer Foundation (The)

O'Brien, John F.: trustee, McDonald & Co. Securities Foundation

Roub, Bryan Roger: trustee, Harris Foundation

Wexford Plantation Club

Ostergard, Paul Michael: vice president, director corporate contributions, Citibank Corp.; president, Citigroup Foundation

White's Club

Price, Charles H., II: director, New York Times Co. Foundation

Wianno Club

DiCamillo, Gary Thomas: chairman, chief executive officer, director, Polaroid Corp.

Wichita Club

Meyer, Russell William, Jr.: chairman, chief executive officer, Cessna Aircraft Co.; president, Cessna Foundation, Inc.

Wichita Country Club

Meyer, Russell William, Jr.: chairman, chief executive officer, Cessna Aircraft Co.; president, Cessna Foundation, Inc.

Williams Club

Barnes, Wallace W.: director, Barnes Group Foundation Inc.

Willow Point Golf & Country Club

Denson, William Frank, III: president, Vulcan Materials Co. Foundation

Willowbend Club

DiCamillo, Gary Thomas: chairman, chief executive officer, director, Polaroid Corp.

Wilson Country Club

Williamson, Henry Gaston, Jr.: chief operating officer, Branch Banking & Trust Co.

Winged Foot Country Club

Robinson, Edward Joseph: president, chief operating officer, director, Avon Products, Inc.

Winged Foot Golf Club

Shaw, L. Edward, Jr.: general counsel, Aetna, Inc.; trustee, Chase Manhattan Foundation

Wolferts Roost Country Club

Standish, J. Spencer: chairman, director, Albany International Corp.

Womens Athletic Club

Mac Kimm, Margaret (Pontius) 'Mardie': trustee, Chicago Title and Trust Co. Foundation

Womens City Club

Bezik, Cynthia B.: senior vice president, finance, Cleveland-Cliffs, Inc.

Womens National Republican Club

Franklin, Barbara Hackman: director, Dow Chemical Co.

Womens Rotary Club

Shideler, Shirley Ann Williams: director, Central Newspapers Foundation

Woodhill Country Club

Daniels, John Hancock: chairman, Archer-Daniels-Midland Foundation

Piper, Addison Lewis: director, Piper Jaffray Companies Foundation; chairman, chief executive officer, director, U.S. Bancorp Piper Jaffray

Woodstock Club

Tobias, Randall L.: chairman emeritus, Lilly & Co. (Eli)

Woodway Country Club

Johnson, James Lawrence: chairman emeritus, Walter Industries Inc.

World Trade Center Club

Douglass, Robert Royal: trustee, Chase Manhattan Foundation

World Trade Club

Chelberg, Bruce Stanley: chairman, chief executive officer, director, Whitman Corp.; director, Whitman Corp. Foundation

Ginn, Samuel L.: chairman, director, AirTouch Communications Foundation; chairman, chief executive officer, director, Vodafone AirTouch Plc

Yale Club

Barnes, Wallace W.: director, Barnes Group Foundation Inc.

Barnette, Curtis Handley: chairman, chief executive officer, director, Bethlehem Steel Corp.

Block, John Robinson: vice president, trustee, Blade Foundation

Ingersoll, Robert Stephen: chairman, director, Panasonic Foundation

Minton, Dwight Church: chairman, director, Church & Dwight Co., Inc.

Pepper, John E., Jr.: chairman executive committee, Procter & Gamble Co.

Wheeler, Thomas Beardsley: chairman, chief executive officer, Massachusetts Mutual Life Insurance Co.

Yeamans Hall Club

Milliken, Roger: chairman, chief executive officer, Milliken & Co.; member advisory committee, Milliken Foundation

Yorick Club

Donahue, Richard King: vice chairman, Nike, Inc.

York Club

Light, Walter Frederick: trustee, Air Products Foundation

MASTER INDEX

Arranges alphabetically and by page number, all foundations profiled in this directory.

B

C

D

E

F

G

H

I

J

N

O

P

Master Index

Q

R

S

T

U

V

W

X

Y

MW01195955

PREHISTORIC WORLD

Prehistoric World

Copyright © 2024 by Applesauce Press Book Publishers LLC.

This is an officially licensed book by Cider Mill Press Book Publishers LLC.

All rights reserved under the Pan-American and International Copyright Conventions.

No part of this book may be reproduced in whole or in part, scanned, photocopied, recorded, distributed in any printed or electronic form, or reproduced in any manner whatsoever, or by any information storage and retrieval system now known or hereafter invented, without express written permission of the publisher, except in the case of brief quotations embodied in critical articles and reviews.

The scanning, uploading, and distribution of this book via the internet or via any other means without permission of the publisher is illegal and punishable by law. Please support authors' rights, and do not participate in or encourage piracy of copyrighted materials.

13-Digit ISBN: 978-1-40034-373-7
10-Digit ISBN: 1-40034-373-9

This book may be ordered by mail from the publisher.
Please include $5.99 for postage and handling. Please support your local bookseller first!

Books published by Cider Mill Press Book Publishers are available at special discounts for bulk purchases in the United States by corporations, institutions, and other organizations. For more information, please contact the publisher.

Cider Mill Press Book Publishers
"Where good books are ready for press"
501 Nelson Place
Nashville, Tennessee 37214

cidermillpress.com

Printed in China

Typography: Depot New, DIN, Gipsiero
All vectors used under official license from Shutterstock.com

24 25 26 27 28 TYC 5 4 3 2 1
First Edition

MESSAPICETUS GREGARIUS

ESSENTIAL FACTS: All modern beaked whales represent a single lineage of the family which became highly adapted for deep diving, with most specializing in eating cephalopods and other invertebrates. Another, older lineage consists of long-snouted, dolphin-like beaked whales that were adapted to hunt fish closer to the surface. Their elongated, slender snouts have jaws lined with well-developed teeth adapted for piercing and holding prey. The disappearance of these long-snouted beaked whales coincides with the radiation of oceanic dolphins (Delphinidae) during the Late Miocene and Pliocene, leaving the more highly specialized diving beaked whales as the sole representatives of the family.

The Social Messapicetus is perhaps the most well-studied member of the long-snouted beaked whales. Its neck was more flexible than those of modern beaked whales due to a lower degree of fusion between the cervical (neck) vertebrae. This, combined with the slender snout, is similar to the morphology seen among modern freshwater dolphins, suggesting a similar hunting method involving rapid sideways sweeps of the head while snapping their jaws into masses of small fishes. One individual of this species seemingly died while feeding on a school of an ancient species of sardine. The fact that this whale died with undigested fish preserved within the chest cavity while being surrounded by other fish of the same species suggests that the animal died during a hunt, perhaps predator and prey alike were exposed to an aquatic toxin.

SEE ENTRY ON PAGE 794

ACROPHYSETER DEINODON

NAME MEANING: Terrible toothed acute sperm whale

AGE: Late Miocene (8.5–6.7 MYA)

DISTRIBUTION: Pacific Ocean

SIZE: 13–15 feet (4–4.5 meters)

DIET: Marine hypercarnivore

ESSENTIAL FACTS: The genus name describes the short, upturned snout. With its robust and recurved teeth, it probably hunted the diverse assemblage of marine mammals it is known to have coexisted with. Interestingly, it had two nostrils unlike modern sperm whales with the left being five times larger than the right.

LIVYATAN MELVILLEI

NAME MEANING: Herman Melville's Leviathan

AGE: Late Miocene (9.9–5 MYA)

DISTRIBUTION: Worldwide

SIZE: 44–57 feet (13.5–17.5 meters)

DIET: Marine hypercarnivore

SEE MORE ON PAGES 800–801

MONODONTIDAE

Monodontidae is a family containing only two modern species: the Beluga (*Delphinapterus leucas*) and the Narwhal (*Monodon monoceros*), both of which inhabit the cold waters of the Arctic. The monodontids are one of the youngest groups of cetaceans to evolve, having a record dating back to the Late Miocene with a distribution that included the warmer waters farther south. They are characterized by lack of a dorsal fin and reduced dentitions with small, rounded heads.

DENEBOLA BRACHYCEPHALA

NAME MEANING: Short-headed Denebola

AGE: Late Miocene

DISTRIBUTION: Pacific Ocean

SIZE: Unknown

DIET: Marine hypercarnivore

ESSENTIAL FACTS: Denebola is the earliest known member of Monodontidae, its fossils being known from Baja California. The genus name is derived from the name of a star, which is in the constellation Cygnus in the Milky Way.

BOHASKAIA MONODONTOIDES

NAME MEANING: David J. Bohaska's Monodon-like (whale)

AGE: Early Pliocene (3.8–2.9 MYA)

DISTRIBUTION: Atlantic Ocean

SIZE: Unknown

DIET: Marine hypercarnivore

ESSENTIAL FACTS: This species was described in 2012 from a nearly complete skull originally collected in 1969 in Virginia. Together with Denebola (*Denebola brachycephala*), its presence in warmer latitudes demonstrate that the modern, cold-adapted monodontids must have evolved relatively recently, possibly during the Pleistocene.

ODOBENOCETOPS PERUVIANUS

NAME MEANING: Tooth-walking whale from Peru

AGE: Late Miocene

DISTRIBUTION: Pacific Ocean

SIZE: 10–13 feet (3–4 meters)

DIET: Marine hypercarnivore

SEE MORE ON PAGES 802–803

LIVYATAN MELVILLEI

ESSENTIAL FACTS: The discoverers of this whale originally named it the English word *Leviathan*, after the sea monster mentioned in the Bible. However, upon realization that the name had been used as a synonym for the American Mastodon (*Mammut americanum*), the animal was renamed Livyatan, the original Hebrew pronunciation of the word. The species name *mellvillei* is a direct reference to author Herman Melville, whose book *Moby-Dick* featured an aggressive sperm whale as its antagonist. Livyatan has the largest known distribution of all the known fossil sperm whales, showing definitively that the species had a near global presence inhabiting the Pacific, Atlantic, and Indian Oceans, its fossils being discovered on North America, South America, Africa, and Australia.

Livyatan is the one of the largest known sperm whales, second only to the modern sperm whale (*Physeter macrocephalus*). It is distinguished from other sperm whales by its particularly large basin that spanned the length of the snout, implying a particularly large melon and spermaceti organ. Its snout was thick and robust and the back of the skull was very wide, indicating the presence of massive jaw muscles and a powerful bite. Its teeth measured 1.2 feet (36.2 centimeters) in length, the largest teeth of any known animal with the exception of tusks. These teeth occluded with each other in a shearing action, which allowed them to take bites out of large carcasses. This species coexisted and probably competed directly with the great shark Megalodon (*Otodus megalodon*), hunting many of the same prey items which included large baleen whales.

SEE ENTRY ON PAGE 798

ODOBENOCETOPS PERUVIANUS

ESSENTIAL FACTS: Odobenocetops is sometimes placed within its own family, Odobenocetopsidae, but it has long been recognized as a close relative of the monodontids. By far the most unusual looking of all the whales, the shortened skull of Odobenocetops was downturned at a sharp angle and was broad and flattened at the tip of the snout. By far its most notable feature is its large, asymmetric tusks which emerge from sheath-like structures in the premaxillae. Aside from the tusks, the skull was completely toothless. The nostrils are located at the highest point of the skull. Odobenocetops shows a trend over time toward losing the melon, being highly reduced to the point of being vestigial in earlier forms to being fully absent in later forms. Perhaps to compensate, the eyes are relatively large and set high on the skull to enable them to watch for predators as they searched for food at the ocean floor.

The morphology of the Odobenocetops skull suggests a feeding behavior similar to that of the modern walrus (*Odobenus rosmarus*), being a specialized molluscivore that extracts its prey from their shells via suction. The skulls downturned shape was suited to probe the seafloor for its preferred prey. Relying strictly on their tactile sense to locate prey, the flattened area at the front of the skull supported complex facial muscles and sensitive whiskers which they would use to feel around and pick them up once detected. To increase its efficiency, the neck has a wide range of head motion, even greater than that of the beluga (*Delphinapterus leucas*) which is known for its flexible neck. The tusks faced backward so they would not get in the way as the whales searched for food; the relatively fragile nature of these tusks indicates that they did not function as combat weapons.

SEE ENTRY ON PAGE 799

EURHINODELPHINIDAE

Eurhinodelphinids are characterized by their pointed snouts which, in most species, exceed the length of their lower jaw resembling the snout of a swordfish. Their jaws are lined with numerous thin, pointed teeth. How these animals used their skulls is not fully understood. The group is known to have lived from the Early to Late Miocene.

MACRODELPHINUS KELLOGGI

NAME MEANING: Kellogg's long dolphin

AGE: Late Oligocene

DISTRIBUTION: Pacific Ocean

SIZE: 23 feet (7 meters)

DIET: Marine hypercarnivore

ESSENTIAL FACTS: This species was the largest of the eurhinodelphinid, about the size of a killer whale (*Orcinus orca*). Unlike many of its relatives, its upper and lower jaws are thought to have been of equal length.

EURHINODELPHIS LONGIROSTRIS

NAME MEANING: Long-snouted well-nosed dolphin

AGE: Middle Miocene

DISTRIBUTION: Atlantic Ocean

SIZE: 6.6 feet (2 meters)

DIET: Marine hypercarnivore

ESSENTIAL FACTS: This species was one of the smaller members of the family. Like swordfishes, these animals may have swung their heads into schooling fish in order to stun multiple individuals at a time before swallowing them.

XIPHIACETUS BOSSI

NAME MEANING: Norman H. Boss' sword whale

AGE: Middle Miocene (14 MYA)

DISTRIBUTION: Atlantic Ocean

SIZE: 10 feet (3 meters)

DIET: Marine hypercarnivore

ESSENTIAL FACTS: One of the larger eurhinodelphinids, its fossils are known from the eastern coast of North America, especially from Calvert Cliffs in Maryland. When first described in 1925, it was considered to be a species of *Eurhinodelphis*.

PHOCOENIDAE

Although similar to dolphins in general appearance, porpoises are more closely related to monodontids. The eight modern species alive today are among the smallest of the toothed whales, characterized by their flattened or spade-shaped teeth. They first appear in the fossil record during the Middle Miocene.

NUMATAPHOCOENA YAMASHITAI

NAME MEANING: Shigeru Yamashita's porpoise from Numata Town

AGE: Pliocene

DISTRIBUTION: Pacific Ocean

SIZE: 7.2–8.2 feet (2.2–2.5 meters)

DIET: Marine hypercarnivore

ESSENTIAL FACTS: The axial skeleton is significantly different from that of modern porpoises, having a reduced number of vertebrae and a long humerus relative to the radius ulna. The reason for this unique morphology is currently not understood.

HABOROPHOCOENA TOYOSHIMAI

NAME MEANING: Sadao Toyoshima's porpoise from Haboro Town

AGE: Pliocene

DISTRIBUTION: Pacific Ocean

SIZE: 6.6 feet (2 meters)

DIET: Marine hypercarnivore

ESSENTIAL FACTS: Toyoshima's Porpoise is known from a nearly complete skull and jaw discovered in northwestern Hokkaido, Japan. Typical of porpoises, its mouth was full of tiny, blunt teeth.

SEMIROSTUM CERUTTII

NAME MEANING: Richard A. Cerutti's half-snout

AGE: Pliocene (3.1–2.6 MYA)

DISTRIBUTION: Pacific Ocean

SIZE: 6.6 feet (2 meters)

DIET: Marine hypercarnivore

ESSENTIAL FACTS: This species was an unusual porpoise with a greatly enlarged mandibular symphysis that extends far beyond the snout. This structure appears to have been very sensitive to touch and may have been used to skim-feeding on the seafloor in a manner similar to that of birds of the genus *Rynchops*.

NORTH AMERICA

FLORIDA MUSEUM OF NATURAL HISTORY

Despite being an extremely fossiliferous state, Florida lacks a Mesozoic fossil record after being submerged by the Atlantic Ocean until the Late Eocene. Instead, the state boasts an impressive record of Cenozoic mammals, particularly from the Miocene and Pleistocene, and the Florida Museum of Natural History serves as a repository for the many Florida fossil sites. The fossil hall, called Florida Fossils: Evolution of Life and Land, takes museum visitors on a path that begins in the Late Eocene when the state was just starting to emerge from the ocean, and ends in the Pleistocene when humans were starting to interact with now extinct animals. Included in the exhibit are mounted skeletons of the horses Archaeohippus blackbergi and Parahippus leonensis, the otter Enhydritherium terranovae, the scimitar toothed cat Xenosmilus hodsonae, the sloth Thinobadistes segnis, and the camel Hemiauchenia macrocephala.

LA BREA TAR PITS AND MUSEUM

Located in the heart of metropolitan Los Angeles, California, the La Brea Tar Pits and Museum was built next to the famous La Brea Tar Pits, which remains an active paleontological research site. Formerly called the George C. Page Museum, the building serves as a repository for the many thousands of fossils that have been recovered from the asphalt and the collection continues to grow. The museum features an exhibit hall which tells the story of the tar pits and presents skeletal mounts and artistic reconstructions of the animals that have been found within them. The fossil site is viewable to the public, and guided tours are offered to allow the public to see the process of excavating the fossils from the asphalt.

DENVER MUSEUM OF NATURE AND SCIENCE

The Denver Museum's Prehistoric Journey exhibit features numerous fossils and skeletal mounts arranged in chronological order spanning almost 4 billion years of Earth's history. The Cenozoic stretch of this exhibit features a huge variety of extinct mammals, mostly from western North America, that includes various brontotheres, entelodonts, oreodonts, and proboscideans.

GRAY FOSSIL SITE AND MUSEUM

Situated right next to the Gray Fossil Site, the museum was built in 2007 and is owned by East Tennessee State University. Fossils collected from outside are carried inside to the prep lab, where specimens are prepared behind glass in full view of museum visitors, allowing them to see the work involved in preparing fossils for use in display and research. Included among the animals featured are the tapir Tapirus polkensis, the rhino Teleoceras aepysoma, the panda Pristinailurus bristoli, and the badger Arctomeles dimolodontus. Over the last few years, crews at the Gray Fossil Site have been excavating and preparing a nearly complete mastodon skeleton.

MAMMOTH SITE

This museum in Hot Springs, South Dakota is built over an active paleontological site that is famous for yielding dozens of Columbian Mammoths (*Mammuthus columbi*) and Woolly Mammoths (*M. primigenius*). The skeletons of numerous Pleistocene animals can be excavated in full view of the public in the comfort of a climate-controlled environment, providing unique opportunities for education.

AGATE FOSSIL BEDS VISITOR CENTER & MUSEUM

Built near the Agate Fossil Beds in Harrison, Nebraska, the building features animals that lived in the area 20 million years ago during the Early Miocene. On permanent display in the front lobby are mounted skeletons of the entelodont *Daeodon shoshonensis*, the chalicothere *Moropus elatus*, and the bear-dog *Daphoenodon superbus* arranged in a way that shows hypothetical interactions between these species. Just beyond this point, visitors can view fossils of other iconic Agate Springs fauna, such as the camel *Stenomylus hitchcocki*.

CINCINNATI MUSEUM CENTER

The Cincinnati Museum's *Ice Age Gallery* features several unique exhibits that allow visitors to envision the state of Ohio as it was 23,000 years ago at the base of the Laurentide Ice Sheet. The beginning of the visit is marked by the mounted skeleton of a Long-Horned Bison (*Bison latifrons*). From there, visitors can walk through a maze-like cave exhibit which features examples of cave paleontology, including a partially articulated skeleton of a jaguar (*Panthera onca*) shown as it would be discovered in a cave deposit. Similarly, a glacier exhibit takes visitors on a journey through the inside of a glacier. Just outside the glacier exhibit is a simulated tundra environment with life-sized models of Dire Wolf (*Aenocyon dirus*), Saber-Toothed Cat (*Smilodon fatalis*), Jefferson's Ground Sloth (*Megalonyx jeffersoni*), Flat-Headed Peccary (*Platygonus compressus*), Woodland Muskox (*Bootherium bombifrons*), and Stag Moose (*Cervalces scotti*) whose fossils have all been discovered in the state. Skeletons of most of these animals are on display at the Cincinnati Municipal Airport.

ASHFALL FOSSIL BEDS VISITOR CENTER

Built over an active paleontological site in Royal, Nebraska, the *Hubbard Rhino Barn* contains numerous articulated complete skeletons of the rhino *Teleoceras major* and other animals still in their death poses. These animals died from inhaling volcanic ash and were subsequently buried in it about 12 million years ago. Built out of necessity due to the fragile nature of the skeletons in the ash bed, the facility allows paleontologists to excavate in a climate-controlled environment and visitors can view paleontological fieldwork in action during the summer excavations. The associated visitor center features interpretive displays, a fossil preparation laboratory that is viewable to the public, and regular educational programs.

FIELD MUSEUM OF NATURAL HISTORY

Found in Chicago, Illinois, the Field Museum's *Evolving Planet* exhibit displays life on earth over 4 billion years. The Cenozoic portion of this exhibit features fossils and mounted skeletons of many extinct mammals including the pantodont *Barylambda faberi*, the uintathere *Eobasileus cornutus*, the bears *Arctodus simus* and *Ursus spelea*, and the sloths *Pronothrotherium typicum* and *Megatherium americanum*.

SMITHSONIAN NATIONAL MUSEUM OF NATURAL HISTORY

The Smithsonian's previous hall of fossils opened in 1911 in Washington, DC, and closed in 2014 for renovation. The updated David H. Koch Hall of Fossils features many more specimens and a more interactive museum experience. The *Deep Time* exhibit starts 4.6 billion years ago and ends in the future with a number of touchable fossils. The many fossil mammal skeletal mounts include everything from the squirrel *Protosciurus jeffersoni* to the early whale *Basilosaurus cetoides*. Other mounts include chalicotheres, brontotheres, rhinos, and the deer *Megaloceras giganteus*.

AMERICAN MUSEUM OF NATURAL HISTORY

Located in New York, New York, the American Museum of Natural History's Lila Acheson Wallace Wing of Mammals and Their Extinct Relatives has two dedicated fossil mammal exhibits that together highlight the evolution and great diversity of mammals throughout the group's history. The *Hall of Primitive Mammals* traces the lower branches of the evolutionary tree of mammals back to their Paleozoic and Mesozoic forebearers and shows how key mammalian features emerged over time. Mammalian groups represented in this hall include monotremes, multituberculates, triconodonts, and xenarthrans. The second mammal exhibit, the *Paul and Irma Milstein Hall of Advanced Mammals*, features extinct relatives of modern mammals from the later Cenozoic such as mammoths, mastodons, saber-toothed cats, camels, and ground sloths. Among the many skeletal mounts on display are the wombat *Phascolonus gigas*, the glyptodont *Panochthus frenzelianus*, the sloth *Lestodon armatus*, the cat *Smilodon fatalis*, and the deer *Megaloceras giganteus*.

RAYMOND M. ALF MUSEUM OF PALEONTOLOGY

The *Hall of Life* exhibit showcases life on our planet over its 4.6 billion-year history from oldest to youngest, with wall-sized murals that depict ancient environments and a timeline of important events of life on earth. Among the mammalian fossils on display are those of brontotheres, rhinos, and nimravids including a complete mounted skeleton of *Dinictis felina*. The *Hall of Footprints* is a unique collection of fossil tracks and trackways that is among the largest of its kind in the United States. Among the many displays in this exhibit is a mounted skeleton of the bear-dog *Amphicyon ingens*. Visitors to the museum (located in Claremont, California) can also witness the inner workings of the fossil preparation lab and the collections room for a complete experience of the paleontological process.

UNIVERSITY OF NEBRASKA STATE MUSEUM

Founded in 1871, this museum focuses heavily on the natural history of Nebraska. The Paleontology of Nebraska exhibits are located in the main floor. The Elephant Hall contains skeletons and models of proboscideans from various ages and is famous for having the largest Columbian Mammoth (*Mammuthus columbi*) skeleton known to date, which has been nicknamed Archie. A life-sized statue of Archie stands outside the museum entrance. Other notable displays include an interactive *Barbourfelis fricki* skull and skeletal mounts of extinct camels, deer, canids, and many others.

ROYAL ONTARIO MUSEUM

Located in Toronto, Ontario, this museum features an extensive fossil hall with numerous mounted skeletons of animals that lived from the Paleozoic to the Cenozoic Era. This includes dozens of fossil mammal skulls and skeletons including an impressive assortment of South American species including pampatheres, glyptodonts, sloths, toxodonts, and machraucheniids. They also have a substantial collection of megafauna from the North American Pleistocene and a variety of species from earlier in the Cenozoic such as brontotheres and nimravids.

SOUTH AMERICA

MUSEO DE LA PLATA

Located in La Plata, Argentina, the La Plata Museum first opened its doors in 1888. The front of the building is distinctive for having twin sculptures of *Smilodon populator* on either side of the front stairway as if to guard the museum entrance. The museum's reputation comes largely from its collection of large mammal fossils from the Pampas region of northern Argentina including mounted skeletons of *Smilodon populator*, *Megatherium americanum*, *Lestodon armatus*, and other sloths and glyptodonts.

BERNARDINO RIVADAVIA MUSEUM OF NATURAL SCIENCE

This museum, located in Buenos Aires, Argentina, was established in 1812. It has a Cenozoic paleontology hall that features iconic megafauna from Pleistocene South America like *Megatherium americanum* and various other sloths, the browsing horse *Hippidion principale*, *Machraucenia patachonica*, *Toxodon platensis*, and *Smilodon populator*.

EUROPE

NATURAL SCIENCE MUSEUM OF VALENCIA

Located in Valencia, Spain, this museum was created thanks to the engineer José Rodrigo Bolet, who did extensive work throughout South America, collecting numerous fossils during his travels there. He generously donated his extensive private collection which has become possibly the best European collection of fossils from the South American Pleistocene. Fossil mammals displayed within the museum include various species of ground sloths and glyptodonts, *Toxodon platensis*, and many others.

MUSEO NACIONAL DE CIENCIAS NATURALES

This museum in Madrid, Spain, was established in 1771. The building does not have fossil mammal displays, but it is notable for housing the original skeleton of *Megatherium americanum* brought over from South America in 1789. Other fossils include those of *Deinotherium giganteum* and the South American gomphothere *Cuvieronus hyodon*.

NATURMUSEUM SENCKENBERG

The Senckenberg Natural History Museum houses many of the fossil skeletons unearthed from the nearby Messel Pit, Germany's first UNESCO World Natural Heritage Site. Much of the research done on this unique fossil locality is carried out at this museum. An exhibit of human evolution features a cast of the famous *Australopiticus afarensis* specimen named Lucy, as well as reconstructions of several ancient human relatives. Skeletal mounts of the gomphothere *Gomphotherium angustidens* and various other denizens of prehistoric Europe are displayed here as well.

ASIA

PALEOZOOLOGICAL MUSEUM OF CHINA

This paleontology museum was established in 1929 in Beijing, China. The museum contains exhibition halls with specimens for public display, while the rest of the building is used for research purposes. Mammals are located on the third floor of the building with many skeletal mounts including proboscideans like *Stegodon zdanskyi* and *Platybelodon grangeri*, the paracerathere rhino *Juxia sharamurenense*, and the brontothere *Rhinoitan mongoliensis*. The museum also houses the Institute of Vertebrate Paleontology and Paleoanthropology of the Chinese Academy of Sciences.

NATIONAL MUSEUM OF NATURE AND SCIENCE, TOKYO

Located in the northeast corner of Ueno Park in Tokyo, Japan, this museum features many exceptional fossil mammals displays. Among them, an impressive variety of fossil whales including *Basilosaurus isis* and *Ambulocetus natans* are shown. Other skeletal mounts include the mesonychid *Sinonyx jiashanensis*, the palaeanodont *Ernanodon antelios*, the desmostylian *Paleoparadoxia tabatai*, the mylagaulid rodent *Ceratogaulus hatcheri*, and many others from around the world.

AUSTRALIA

WONAMBI FOSSIL CENTRE

Located at the Naracoorte Caves National Park in South Australia, the Wonambi Fossil Centre serves as the park's visitor center and is a functioning museum that features a simulated rainforest environment that would have covered the region 200,000 years ago. Many skeletal mounts and models depicting iconic Australian megafauna such as *Diprotodon optatum*, *Procoptodon goliah*, and *Thylacoleo carnifex* are on display. The park itself was recognized in 1994 for its extensive fossil record when the site was inscribed on the World Heritage List, along with Riversleigh. Visitors may take tours of four out of the twenty-eight caves, enabling them to see where and how these fossils are discovered. The others are kept away from the public eye to preserve their contents and are active sites of scientific research.

ROBERT BOESSENECKER

Dr. Robert Boessenecker is a paleontologist from Foster City, California. He acquired his bachelor's and master's degrees at Montana State University, where he majored in earth sciences and geology, respectively. He then traveled to New Zealand to attain his PhD at the University of Otago, continuing to major in geology.

Dr. Boessenecker's primary research interests are ancient marine mammals, with an emphasis in cetaceans and pinnipeds. More broadly, he studies marine vertebrate ecosystems from the Eocene to the Pleistocene. Among his many projects, he is currently working on a monograph reporting at least half a dozen new genera and species of "spear-toothed" waipatiid-grade dolphins from the Oligocene of South Carolina. Throughout his career he has named at least fourteen new genera and species of extinct cetaceans and pinnipeds and even an entire family, the Coronodontidae. Dr. Boessenecker served as a research fellow at the Mace Brown Museum of Natural History, located in Charleston, South Carolina, where he contributed significantly to the marine mammal collection. He is currently the Chief Paleontologist at the Charleston Center for Paleontology, Wando, South Carolina, a nonprofit privately funded paleontological research institute which he started himself in 2024.

DARIN A. CROFT

At the University of Iowa, Dr. Darin Croft earned his bachelor's in Interdepartmental Studies, a program that allows students to create their own major that can help them meet their career goals. He created an organismal biology major that focuses on ecology, evolution, and organism-level biology. He then obtained his master's and PhD at the University of Chicago, and after his graduation he would later return to the University of Iowa as a lecturer in the Department of Organismal Biology and Anatomy for three years. In the intervening time, he was a Post-Doctoral Research Scientist and Education Program Developer at the Field Museum in Chicago.

Dr. Croft is currently a Professor of Anatomy at the Case Western Reserve University in Cleveland, Ohio. He is also a research associate at the American Museum of Natural History, Carnegie Museum, Cleveland Museum of Natural History, and Field Museum. Dr. Croft's main research interest is Cenozoic mammals of South America, though he is also interested in mammal paleoecology and evolution in general as well as reconstructing habitats and paleoenvironments of Cenozoic sites in South America. He is actively involved in fieldwork, mainly in Bolivia and Chile. There, he investigates the mammals and paleoenvironments of Miocene sites to help constrain the timing of uplift of that portion of the Andes Mountains. He also investigates the evolutionary relationships of South American native ungulates in relation to other groups of mammals, as well as patterns in their diversity throughout the Cenozoic.

Dr. Croft also collaborates with many of his students on various projects related to his research. He is also part of a team studying dental topography in modern and extinct marsupials, and his research has been supported by the National

Science Foundation. Dr. Croft is also a prolific writer. He has published roughly ninety peer-reviewed articles and book chapters. His popular science book, *Horned Armadillos and Rafting Monkeys: The Fascinating Fossil Mammals of South America*, won a gold medal in the Independent Publisher Book Awards. He has co-edited a multi-author volume published by Springer in 2018 on reconstructing Cenozoic terrestrial ecosystems, and currently serves as the editor-in-chief of the *Journal of Mammalian Evolution*.

ADVAIT MAHESH JUKAR

Dr. Advait Mahesh Jukar grew up in Mumbai, a city of more than 20 million people on the west coast of India. He has lived in various parts of the United States since 2007 and generally considers Washington, DC, his home in the country. He obtained his bachelor's degree in biology at Reed College in Portland, Oregon, and his master's and PhD in Environmental Science and Policy at George Mason University in Fairfax, Virginia. Although his degrees were not in paleontology, his research has always focused on organismal biology, ecology, and paleontology.

Dr. Mahesh Jukar is currently the Lecturer of Paleontology at the University of Arizona in the Department of Geosciences. As a university professor, he finds teaching to be an incredibly fulfilling experience. Working with students, both undergraduate and graduate, has been a real joy for him. In addition, he is a Research Associate in the Department of Paleobiology at the Smithsonian's National Museum of Natural History and a Curatorial Affiliate in the Division of Vertebrate Paleontology at the Yale Peabody Museum.

Before becoming a lecturer at the University of Arizona, Dr. Mahesh Jukar was a Gaylord Donnelley Postdoctoral Associate at Yale University in the Department of Anthropology, and a Deep Time-Peter Buck Postdoctoral Fellow in the Department of Paleobiology at the Smithsonian's National Museum of Natural History. He is also involved in education and outreach at natural history museums, setting up of museum policies, and trying to bridge the world of natural history museums, paleontology, and conservation policy.

Dr. Mahesh Jukar's research and fieldwork is divided between India and North America. He is currently investigating the extinction of large mammals in both countries to understand how humans and the climate may have caused their extinctions. He was the first researcher to uncover the pattern of Ice Age extinctions in India. His interests broadly cover the ecology and evolution of herbivorous mammals and dinosaurs, with a particular soft spot for elephants and their extinct relatives. He has worked on the ecology and biogeography of extinct mammals in Asia over the last 20 million years. He is also sorting out the taxonomy of large mammals in India and has recently started a project to try to understand the process of dispersal and evolution of extinct elephant relatives in North America. He collaborates with colleagues across the world on these projects and on others relating to the paleoecology of dinosaurs, and even the life history of whales! His research has been featured in popular press articles and blogs. Dr. Mahesh Jukar has also helped develop museum exhibitions at the Smithsonian Institution, and at Yale, and his proudest achievement is the new Human Footprints Gallery at the renovated Yale Peabody Museum, which features extinct ice age megafauna, human evolution, and the impact of modern humans on ecosystems.

JULIE MEACHEN

Dr. Julie Meachen is an Associate Professor of Anatomy at Des Moines University and a research associate at the Natural History Museum of Los Angeles and the associated La Brea Tar Pits and Museum. Her formative years were spent in Tampa, Florida. As an undergraduate student, Dr. Meachen worked as a collections assistant in the Florida Museum of Natural History on the campus of the University of Florida. Her time at the museum is where she learned about paleontology. She would go on to obtain her bachelor's and master's degrees in zoology at the university and earned a PhD in Ecology and Evolutionary Biology at UCLA. During her time as a PhD student, she spent two summers at the Hagerman Fossil Beds National Monument.

Chief among Dr. Meachen's research interests is the end-Pleistocene extinction event: questioning if it occurred simultaneously over the whole of North America, its causes, and the speed at which it took place. She also studies Plio-Pleistocene carnivorans. Her current projects include the evolutionary relationships of Pleistocene canids, the forearm strength of *Smilodon fatalis*, and the consequences of the end-Pleistocene extinction, to name a few. She recently won the Raymond M. Alf award for excellence in paleontology in 2021. She is a National Geographic explorer, and she has served as the PI of the internationally recognized Natural Trap Cave fossil site since 2014.

HUGH GREGORY (GREG) MCDONALD

Dr. Greg McDonald attained his bachelor's degree at Idaho State University, his master's at University of Florida, and his PhD at University of Toronto, majoring in zoology and minoring in geology at each institution. He is now retired, but his last held position was Regional Paleontologist for Bureau of Land Management. Other positions he has held over his career include Senior Curator of the Museum Management Program for the National Park Service, Paleontology Program Coordinator for the Geologic Resources Division National Park Service, Paleontologist at the Hagerman Fossil Beds National Monument, Curator of Vertebrate Paleontology at the Cincinnati Museum of Natural History, and a Collection Manager of Vertebrate Paleontology at the Idaho Museum of Natural History.

Dr. McDonald's research interests center around Plio-Pleistocene mammals of the New World, with a particular emphasis on sloths and other xenarthrans. He has authored and co-authored several hundred research papers and has contributed significantly to our understanding of sloth evolution, biology, and paleoecology. Currently, he is studying sloths recovered from submerged cave deposits in the Yucatán. While working for the National Park Service he was a member of the team conducting the Special Resource Study that resulted in the Waco Mammoth Site becoming a national monument. He is an Honorary Member of the Society of Vertebrate Paleontology.

JENNY MCGUIRE

Dr. Jenny McGuire is an Associate Professor at the Georgia Institute of Technology. She earned her bachelor's degree at Duke University, where she dual-majored in biological anthropology and anatomy and Earth and oceanic sciences. For her PhD, she majored in Integrative Biology at UC Berkeley.

Dr. McGuire studies spatial ecology and conservation paleontology. She is interested in quantifying the extent to which climate controls the distribution of different plant and animal species (as opposed to, say, interspecific interactions). This can tell us which organisms will be most sensitive to climate change going forward. She is also interested in how

different species have been able to handle extremely arid conditions. Thus far, two PhD students have graduated from her lab. Dr. McGuire was involved in a recent special feature in PNAS entitled "The past as a lens for biodiversity conservation on a dynamically changing planet."

RACHEL NARDUCCI

Dr. Rachel Narducci is currently a collections manager of vertebrate paleontology at the Florida Museum of Natural History, located on the campus of University of Florida. From this facility, she has attained a bachelor's degree in anthropology and geology and a PhD in zoology. She has also worked as a fossil preparator, field site coordinator, and collections assistant during her time as a student.

Dr. Narducci grew up a short drive away from the Florida Museum in Interlachen, Florida. Animatronic dinosaurs, along with the films *Jurassic Park* and *The Land Before Time*, sparked her love of paleontology. To her, a trip to the museum was as exciting as a trip to Disney World, and her dreams later came true when she went on to work at the same museum! She is the first person in her family to receive a college degree. Her research interests are paleoneurology (the study of fossil brains), Florida's geological and paleontological history, and xenarthrans.

Dr. Narducci's current projects include describing the morphology of the cranial armor of pampatheres the endo- and intracranial anatomy of *Holmesina* and other xenarthrans, both living and extinct, using 3D geometric morphometrics. Other projects include the evolution of body size in sloths, descriptions of shark rostral nodes and of the Steinhatchee River fossil assemblage, porcupine range expansion during the Great American Biotic Interchange, and she is working on an anatomical identification guide for pampatheres based on articulated specimens from Haile 7G.

MELISSA PARDI

Dr. Melissa Pardi is the assistant curator of geology at the Illinois State Museum, a position she has held since 2020. Originally from Connecticut, she obtained her bachelor's and master's in geosciences at the Pennsylvania State University, and her PhD in biology at the University of New Mexico. The work that first introduced her to paleontology involved cave excavations and cave faunas still hold a special place in her heart.

Dr. Pardi is interested in the paleoecology and biogeography of late Quaternary mammals, everything from tiny shrews to giant mammoths, and her recent work revolves around how and why traits such as body size and diet vary within species. For her research, she relies primarily relies on records in databases and museum collections.

Prior to her position at Illinois State Museum, Dr. Pardi worked as a postdoc at Vanderbilt University where she worked with Larisa DeSantis on a project looking at extinct herbivore diets over space and time, which was supported by an NSF Earth Sciences Postdoctoral Research Fellowship. She currently works on projects that examine dietary variation in several extinct mammal species. Within mammoths and mastodons, she has a few ongoing projects using dietary proxies and morphological data to analyze variation in past diets under different environmental contexts. She is also exploring population-level variation in diets of extinct peccaries in the Midwest. Other ongoing projects involving carnivorans look at body size, morphology, and diet in Southern California and the Midwest. Her work involves numerous collaborators from several different institutions across the United States, including students.

Between 2022 and 2023 Melissa wrote two book chapters: one covering the paleoecological context for early hunter gatherers in the midcontinent (co-authored with Dr. Chris Widga) and the second featuring an update to an encyclopedia chapter on late Pleistocene North American vertebrate faunas (co-authored with Dr. Catalina Tomé). She is active in professional service, and serves on several different committees for education, outreach, and DEAI (Diversity, Equity, Accessibility, Inclusion) for the American Society of Mammalogists and the Society of Vertebrate Paleontology. Currently she is the secretary for the ASM and chairs their committee for student honoraria and travel awards. She has recently been nominated to serve as a US representative to the US National Committee for the International Quaternary Association.

JOSHUA XAVIER SAMUELS

Dr. Joshua Samuels attained his bachelor's degree from the College of Idaho, where he majored in biology. He would later go on to get his PhD from the University of California, Los Angeles. Josh's career in paleontology began as an undergraduate intern at Hagerman Fossil Beds National Monument in Idaho. He has served as the Chief of Paleontology / Museum Curator at John Day Fossil Beds National Monument in Oregon. Most recently, Dr. Samuels moved to East Tennessee, where he currently works as an associate professor at East Tennessee State University and a curator at the Gray Fossil Site and Museum.

Dr. Samuels' research is mainly focused on the paleoecology and evolution of mammals, primarily rodents and carnivorans, and their responses to environmental changes through time. More specifically, he is interested in how changes in climate, topography, and vegetation through the Cenozoic drove dietary and locomotor adaptations of mammals and major changes in communities. Ultimately, this research can help scholars understand how environmental changes impact species and ecosystems, both in the past and at present. His many current projects include the examination of how climate change and volcanic activity impacted mammal communities through time in Oregon, studies of fossil mammals from the Gray Fossil Site, and a study of the world's largest squirrel, the giant groundhog *Paenemarmota*. Dr. Samuels has published studies that describe how dietary and locomotor adaptations in rodents and lagomorphs changed through time; these small mammals are abundant and important parts of modern ecosystems, but they are often overlooked by scientists and the public. He has described twenty new species, including the smallest and earliest aquatic beaver, the earliest kangaroo rat (*Aurimys xeros*), the earliest wolverine (*Gulo sudorus*), a horned gopher (*Ceratogaulus cornutasagma*), and the last nonhuman primate in North America (*Ekgmowechashala zancanellai*).

Dr. Samuels encourages his students and others interested in paleontology to look at groups of animals which may be less charismatic than mammoths and saber-tooths but serve equally important roles within their respective ecosystems.

JULIA SCHAP

Julia Schap attended the University of Florida for her undergraduate studies, just two hours away from her hometown of Ormond Beach. While there, she majored in integrative biology. She later obtained her master's degree at East Tennessee State University, where she also worked as a graduate research assistant and as a collections and field crew intern. She has also worked at The Mammoth Site as an education and field intern. She is currently a PhD candidate and graduate research assistant at Georgia Institute of Technology with a major in biological sciences.

Schap studies rodent and lagomorph community dynamics and how these communities have shifted in abundances and functional traits through time in response to past climate change. With this information, paleontologists can work together with conservation practitioners to determine how best to protect these communities against modern and future climate change. Most of her work focuses on North American mammal communities, but she has recently worked on African mammal communities as well, to determine the trait-environment relationships and how dental traits can be used to estimate precipitation. One of her current research focuses is community responses to drought events. Most of her dissertation work looks at the small mammals from Natural Trap Cave, Wyoming, over the last 21,000 years, examining how the community changed in response to times of drought.

She is currently the co-chair of the Student Panel for the Conservation Paleobiology Network and was awarded the Presidential Fellowship at Georgia Institute of Technology. She has written six peer reviewed publications and a book chapter. Schap also hosts Fossil Friday, a weekly event where students from Georgia Tech and residents of Atlanta can pick and sort fossil material from Natural Trap Cave.

DR. RACHEL SHORT

Dr. Rachel Short grew up in Creve Coeur, Illinois, and pursued her undergraduate studies at Illinois Wesleyan University, where she majored in biology with a minor in psychology, spending the summers of 2009 and 2010 at Ashfall Fossil Beds in Nebraska. She earned her master's degree in geosciences at East Tennessee State University where, for her thesis, she described a new species of fossil rhino (*Teleoceras aepysoma*) from the Gray Fossil Site. She would later earn a PhD from the Department of Ecosystem Science and Management (now called Ecology and Conservation Biology) at Texas A&M University. Then, she worked as an NSF Postdoctoral Research Fellow co-hosted at Texas A&M University and Georgia Institute of Technology.

Dr. Short is currently an assistant professor in the Department of Natural Resource Management at South Dakota State University. As far as research interests, Rachel studies how mammals respond to climate change and human pressures. Most of her work focuses on functional traits related to how an animal lives and how those traits relate to environment: for example, how the calcaneum (heel bone) relates to the presence of vegetation cover in the habitats of carnivorans and artiodactyls. She uses fossils to study past communities of mammals so that scholars can better understand today's fauna and anticipate what future fauna might look like with continued climate change. Her recent work has included many modern studies that scholars can compare to the fossil record and to future climate projections. There has been a large amount of data collection in museums to expand this work.

Although most of her work has focused on hoofed mammals, Dr. Short's lab is starting to study carnivorans a bit more. Their goal is to build models of multiple taxonomic groups and functional traits to get a more complete view of the communities. Some of Dr. Short's postdoc research was recently published in a special feature of PNAS that focused on the importance of using the fossil record for informing modern and future conservation. In addition to all this, she has done descriptive, specimen-based paleontology. She has named four new species from the fossil record: the previously mentioned rhino from the Gray Fossil Site in Tennessee and three procyonids from Florida (*Procyon gipsoni*, *Procyon megalokolos*, and *Nasua mastodonta*).

DR. KATY SMITH

Dr. Katy Smith grew up in Milwaukee, Wisconsin. Her inspiration for becoming a paleontologist came from visiting the Milwaukee Public Museum as a child, igniting a passion to become a paleontologist for as long as she can remember. Immediately after graduating high school in 1998, she landed an internship at the Milwaukee Public Museum in the Geology Division. After this, she underwent undergraduate studies at Purdue University, where she would major in solid Earth science. She then obtained her master's degree at Michigan State University with a major in geological sciences. After obtaining her master's she took another internship at The Mammoth Site in Hot Springs, South Dakota, before attending the University of Michigan for her PhD.

She is currently an associate professor of Geology in the School of Earth, Environment, and Sustainability at Georgia Southern University and Curator of Paleontology at the Georgia Southern University Museum. She is also part of a team that's working on documenting fossil resources in the National Park lands of Georgia's coastal plain.

Katy's favorite extinct animals are the mastodons of North America. She is interested in exploring the differences between the sexes, in morphology, life history, and behavior of these animals. She tends to focus on tusks, which can record changes in growth rate, morphology, and other factors (for example, diet and seasonality of environment) throughout the life of the individual. She is also interested in documenting the differences between American Mastodons (*Mammut americanum*) and Pacific Mastodons (*M. pacificus*), both their tusk and body size and shape, sexual dimorphism, and behaviors. Recently, she has gone on a data-collecting trip to museums in Southern California, and she is collaborating with scientists at the Western Science Center to look at Pacific Mastodon tusks and skeletons. The archaeocetes of Georgia, like Georigacetus and Basilosaurus, are another interest of hers, studying the locomotion related to the land-to-sea transition in the former ant the paleoenvironmental and biogeographical distribution of the latter.

A passionate teacher, Katy is proud of the students she has mentored on research projects in paleontology since joining the faculty at Georgia Southern in 2010. She regularly teach courses on dinosaurs, Principles of Paleontology, and Historical Geology.

DR. CATALINA SUAREZ

Born in Colombia, Dr. Catalina Suarez obtained her degrees at the National University of Colombia and the La Plata National University. Currently, she is a postdoctoral researcher at the Argentinian Institute for Nivology, Glaciology and Environmental Sciences in Mendoza, Argentina. Prior to this, she has held numerous research and teaching positions at the Universidad del Rosario, the Smithsonian Tropical Research Institute, Colombian Geological Survey, and the National Scientific and Technical Research Council at La Plata Museum.

Dr. Suarez's research interests primarily focus on fossil mammals, especially metatherians. One of her current projects involves the evolution and phylogeny of thylacosmilid sparassodonts and describing new Paleogene marsupials from Colombia. She also studies climate and environmental changes across time and the radiations and extinctions linked to these events. Dr. Suarez has published several works about South American and Caribbean paleontology. In her doctoral dissertation she made a complete revision of the fossil metatherians from northern South America. Her most recent research about the redescription of the skull of the thylacosmilid Anachlysictis gracilis received coverage in numerous

science news outlets and viewed around the world. During her career, Dr. Suarez has participated in or led many fossil digs, mainly in Panama, Colombia, and Argentina. During some of these field expeditions she had the opportunity to train students and young scientists in paleontological field techniques, including students from the local communities.

DR. SUSUMU TOMIYA

Dr. Susumu Tomiya's family moved to the United States from Kuwana, Japan, while he was in high school. What was originally planned to be a one-year stay turned into nineteen years, during which time Susumu finished high school, college, graduate school, and two rounds of postdoctoral appointments! He attended Johns Hopkins University, where he majored in Earth and planetary sciences. He then completed his doctoral program in integrative biology at UC Berkeley. While there, he worked as a collections assistant at the Museums of Paleontology (UCMP) and Vertebrate Zoology (MVZ), also serving as a graduate student instructor. After obtaining his PhD, he remained at Berkeley for a semester to work as a part-time lecturer.

Dr. Tomiya is passionate about taking care of natural history collections that enable research on the dynamics of biodiversity. For his first postdoctoral scholar position he spent three years at the Field Museum, organizing and expanding a collection of vertebrate fossils from the Eocene Washakie Formation of Wyoming. This work has led to a monographic study that more than doubled the known diversity of mammalian carnivores from the formation and revealed a substantial loss of carnivores and primates during the middle Eocene of the central Rocky Mountains region, probably in response to loss of forests.

Susumu returned to Japan in 2018 where he now works as a program-specific assistant professor at Kyoto University. For his research, Dr. Tomiya is interested in finding out what drives large-scale patterns of evolution and extinction in mammals with particular focus carnivores. He and his colleagues are studying how vertebrate faunas respond to forest loss over evolutionary time, comparing what happened in the Eocene of North America and the Mio-Pliocene of Southeast Asia.

DR. JACK TSENG

Dr. Jack Tseng is currently a faculty member in the Department of Integrative Biology and a curator in the Museum of Paleontology at the University of California, Berkeley. It was from this same institution, less than two hours away from his hometown San Jose, that he undertook his studies majoring in integrative biology. As a grad student, he worked at the Natural History Museum of Los Angeles County, and he was a postdoctoral researcher at the American Museum of Natural History. Jack's primary interest is in the evolution of skulls and jaws in mammals; he studies the bones of fossil and living mammals and how they have adapted to different physical forces created during feeding and chewing. Most of his fieldwork is done in the United States, Mexico, and China with the goal of discovering new fossils that help us better understand the evolutionary story of mammals. He is currently building a database of the jaws of mammals and their relatives to study the evolutionary limits of jaw shape and function during and after the rise of mammals.

Hyenas hold a special place in Jack's heart as these are the animals that inspired him to pursue his research career. To that end, he has published on fossil hyenas from some of the highest and coldest places on earth: the running hyena *Chasmaporthetes gangsriensis* from the Himalayas and the closely related *C. ossifragus* from above the Arctic Circle in the Yukon Territory.

ABOUT THE AUTHOR AND ILLUSTRATOR

AARON WOODRUFF

Aaron Woodruff is a paleontologist interested in comparative ecomorphology in Cenozoic mammals, especially carnivores and ungulates. He obtained his master's degree at East Tennessee State University and currently works as a collections manager in vertebrate paleontology at the Florida Museum of Natural History. Much of his free time is spent making digital paleoart, mostly of animals from the Cenozoic Era, and a few of his reconstructions have been used in museum displays and educational media. He is passionate about science communication.

JULIUS CSOTONYI

Julius Csotonyi is one of the world's most high-profile and talented contemporary scientific illustrators. His considerable academic expertise informs his stunning, dynamic art. He has created life-size dinosaur murals for the Royal Ontario Museum and for the Dinosaur Hall at the Natural History Museum of Los Angeles County, as well as most of the artwork for the exhibit "Deep Time" in the David H. Koch Hall of Fossils at the Smithsonian National Museum of Natural History in Washington, DC. He lives in Canada.

His books include *Discovering Reptiles*, *Discovering Sharks*, *Discovering Bugs*, *The T. Rex Handbook*, *The Paleoart of Julius Csotonyi*, *Prehistoric Predators*, *Dino World*, *Discovering Birds*, and *Dinosaur World*.

EDITOR'S NOTE

Paleontologists are constantly making new discoveries. While this book was accurate at the time it was written, it's possible that new information will change or expand upon the facts presented here. That will be reflected in future editions as we continue to learn more about the amazing world of prehistoric mammals.

INDEX

TABLE OF CONTENTS

PREHISTORIC WORLD

OVER 1,200 INCREDIBLE MAMMALS & DISCOVERIES FROM THE MESOZOIC & CENOZOIC

ILLUSTRATED BY JULIUS CSOTONYI

WRITTEN BY AARON WOODRUFF

MAGERICYON ANCEPS

ESSENTIAL FACTS: Fossils of Spanish bear-dog are known only from Cerro de los Batallones, a late Miocene fossil site located in Madrid, Spain. A predator trap, the fossil remains of otherwise rare carnivorans are recorded in great abundance here. Prey animals occasionally would fall into the pit cave, and local predators would be drawn in expecting an easy meal, only to find themselves unable to escape. The site has yielded hundreds of Spanish bear-dog fossils, constituting one of the most complete and best-preserved samples of any bear-dog ever recorded. At least thirteen individuals, including both juveniles and adults, are recorded. The environment surrounding Cerro de los Batallones would have been a woodland habitat with patches of wooded grassland at the time of deposition.

The genus name is derived from Magerit, the original name of Madrid, in reference to the location of the sites of Batallones. The Spanish bear-dog was a hypercarnivore built for strength and the fast killing of prey in well-vegetated habitats. Its upper canines were large and moderately flattened with weakly serrated margins. The limbs were powerful and built for efficient terrestrial travel and immobilizing prey. The spine was remarkably strong along its length, with a particularly rigid lumbar region to resist high tensions generated from grappling with and subduing large prey. The tail was also long and muscular for balance and provided additional leverage during prey capture. Its diet consisted of medium- to large-sized antelopes, giraffids, horses, and juvenile rhinos.

SEE ENTRY ON PAGE 403

HAPLOCYONINAE

The haplocyonines were terrestrial bear-dogs with cursorial adaptations such as digitigrade feet and slender limb proportions.

HAPLOCYONOIDES MORDAX

NAME MEANING: Haplocyon-like biter

AGE: Early Miocene (20–17 MYA)

DISTRIBUTION: Eurasia

SIZE: About wolf-sized

DIET: Hypercarnivore

ESSENTIAL FACTS: Members of the genus Haplocyonoides had a digitigrade foot posture with cursorial adaptations, although probably not to the extent of modern canids or even contemporary hemicyonine bears.

GOBICYON MACROGNATHUS

NAME MEANING: Long-jawed Gobi dog

AGE: Middle Miocene (16–11 MYA)

DISTRIBUTION: Eurasia

SIZE: 220–365 pounds (100–165 kilograms)

DIET: Hypercarnivore

ESSENTIAL FACTS: The dentition of this bear-dog suggests that it was evolving a similar bone-breaking dentition seen among certain hyenas and canids. The post-carnassial molars are reduced while the pre-carnassial premolars are enlarged and strengthened.

TEMNOCYONINAE

Temnocyonines exhibited more extreme cursorial adaptations than the Eurasian haplocyonines, including digitigrade feet, slender limbs, and elongated distal limb segments. They filled the ecological roles of modern wolves and hunting dogs in North America from the Middle Oligocene to earliest Miocene. After this period they were replaced by hemicyonine bears, which migrated from Eurasia during the Early Miocene.

MAMMACYON OBTUSIDENS

NAME MEANING: Blunt-toothed nipple dog

AGE: Late Oligocene (26–23 MYA)

DISTRIBUTION: North America

SIZE: About wolf-sized

DIET: Hypercarnivore

ESSENTIAL FACTS: One of the oldest of the temnocyonines, this bear-dog had a wolflike body plan with elongated, slender yet sturdy limbs and narrow paws adapted for frequent or long-distance running. Its jaws, teeth, and neck were very durable and adapted to latch on to large, struggling animals.

DELOTROCHANTER ORYKTES

NAME MEANING: Digging evident runner

AGE: Early Miocene (23–20 MYA)

DISTRIBUTION: North America

SIZE: 140–176 pounds (65–80 kilograms)

DIET: Hypercarnivore

ESSENTIAL FACTS: This species has been compared to the modern spotted hyena (*Crocuta crocuta*) for its cursorial adaptations combined with its blunt premolars, presumably specialized for cracking bones during feeding. Known from the Agate Springs National Monument locality, it hunted medium- to large-sized mammals from gazelle-like camels to ox-sized rhinos.

TEMNOCYON FINGERUTI

NAME MEANING: Michael Fingerut's cutting dog

AGE: Early Miocene (23–20 MYA)

DISTRIBUTION: North America

SIZE: 40–80 pounds (18–36 kilograms)

DIET: Hypercarnivore

ESSENTIAL FACTS: Fingerut's Temnocyon is known from the John Day Fossil Beds in Oregon. It inhabited open woodland, savanna, and grassland environments where it hunted a variety of midsized ungulates, most frequently horses and camels.

THAUMASTOCYONINAE

Thaumastocyonines are heavily built hypercarnivores ranging from the size of a jaguar (*Panthera onca*) up to the size of the largest cats known to have lived, such as the American lion (*Panthera atrox*). They were ambush predators adapted to pounce on relatively large prey from cover and to wrestle prey to the ground.

YSENGRINIA AMERICANUS

NAME MEANING: American Ysengrinia

AGE: Early Miocene (23–20 MYA)

DISTRIBUTION: North America

SIZE: About jaguar-sized

DIET: Hypercarnivore

ESSENTIAL FACTS: American Ysengrinia was part of a larger biotic interchange of mammals between North America and Eurasia. This jaguar-sized bear-dog was a powerful ambush hunter, with a particularly broad skull and massive canines. Its diet included peccaries, oreodonts, medium-sized rhinos, and juvenile chalicotheres.

AMMITOCYON KAINOS

NAME MEANING: New dog of Ammit

AGE: Late Miocene (10–9 MYA)

DISTRIBUTION: Eurasia

SIZE: 510 pounds (231 kilograms)

DIET: Hypercarnivore

ESSENTIAL FACTS: Ammitocyon had the most robust postcranial skeleton of any bear-dog. It was an ambush predator that attacked prey by essentially leaping on it from cover and positioning it for a killing bite. It evolved a secondary carnassial pair consisting of the first upper molar (M1) and second lower molar (m2) to maximize the cutting surface.

AGNOTHERIUM ANTIQUUM

NAME MEANING: Ancient chaste beast

AGE: Late Miocene (10–9 MYA)

DISTRIBUTION: Eurasia

SIZE: 348–440 pounds (158–200 kilograms)

DIET: Hypercarnivore

ESSENTIAL FACTS: A lion-sized predator that inhabited woodland and savanna habitats, where it would ambush medium- to large-sized prey items such as horses, giraffids, tapirs, and antelopes.

CANIDAE

Canidae underwent much of its evolutionary history and diversification in North America. The first members of the family to appear during the Late Eocene were small predators that resembled mongoose or civets. Throughout the Oligocene and Early Miocene, they remained mostly small; none exceeded the size of a fox. The first larger-bodied canids began to appear during the Middle Miocene. Canids begin to appear in the Old World during the Late Miocene, where they begin replacing many of the doglike hyenas, and they enter South America during the Pliocene. Canids have slender limbs and digitigrade feet adapted for terrestrial travel, although a few are adept climbers. They generally have long snouts and large, triangular ears and are distinctive for their loss of the third upper molar (M3).

HESPEROCYONINAE

Hesperocyonines were small mesocarnivores and hypercarnivores that filled the ecological roles that foxes, civets, and small cats fill today. They were the first canids to evolve during the Late Eocene, and they became extinct by the Middle Miocene.

PROHESPEROCYON WILSONI

NAME MEANING: Wilson's before *Hesperocyon*

AGE: Late Eocene (37–36 MYA)

DISTRIBUTION: North America

SIZE: About mongoose-sized

DIET: Mesocarnivore

ESSENTIAL FACTS: Prohesperocyon is the oldest canid known to date, showing the characteristic lack of the third upper molars (M3). Compared to its miacid ancestors, it was likely more terrestrial with relatively longer limbs and narrower feet, although it was still an able climber.

HESPEROCYON GREGARIUS

NAME MEANING: Social western dog

AGE: Early Oligocene (35–30 MYA)

DISTRIBUTION: North America

SIZE: About mongoose-sized

DIET: Mesocarnivore

ESSENTIAL FACTS: Hesperocyon was one of the more common carnivorans in the fossil localities in which it occurs, implying high population densities and possible social behaviors. It may have occurred in small family groups which would opportunistically feed on small vertebrates and insects.

MESOCYON CORYPHAEUS

NAME MEANING: Top middle dog

AGE: Early Oligocene

DISTRIBUTION: North America

SIZE: About cat-sized

DIET: Hypercarnivore

ESSENTIAL FACTS: *Mesocyon* were little hypercarnivores that hunted a variety of small vertebrates such as rodents, lagomorphs, and small artiodactyls. Like cats, they had relatively short faces, robust canines, and a broad skull to deliver powerful bite forces through the canine teeth.

SUNKAHETANKA GERINGENSIS

NAME MEANING: Large-toothed dog from the Gering Formation

AGE: Middle Oligocene (30.8–26.3 MYA)

DISTRIBUTION: North America

SIZE: About coyote-sized

DIET: Hypercarnivore

ESSENTIAL FACTS: Descended from a species of *Mesocyon*, Sunkahetanka was larger overall with more robust jaws and teeth, with particularly large canines and carnassials. These adaptations suggest the ability to tackle larger prey items, perhaps regularly targeting animals their own size or slightly larger.

PHILOTROX CONDONI

NAME MEANING: Condon's (dog who) loves to gnaw

AGE: Middle Oligocene (30.8–26.3 MYA)

DISTRIBUTION: North America

SIZE: About coyote-sized

DIET: Hypercarnivore

ESSENTIAL FACTS: Like Sunkahetanka, Philotrox was a hypercarnivore with robust jaws adapted to kill prey quickly and efficiently.

ENHYDROCYON CRASSIDENS

NAME MEANING: Thick-toothed *Enhydra* dog

AGE: Middle Oligocene (30–27 MYA)

DISTRIBUTION: North America

SIZE: 22 pounds (10 kilograms)

DIET: Hypercarnivore

ESSENTIAL FACTS: The Thick-Toothed Dog had particularly deep and robust jaws that reminded its discoverers of the sea otter (*Enhydra lutris*). Ecologically, this species was probably more comparable to a wolverine (*Gulo gulo*), having a robust, short-legged body and powerful neck to match its crushing jaws.

OSBORNODON IAMENSIS

NAME MEANING: Osborn's dog from Lake Iamonia

AGE: Early Miocene (21–18 MYA)

DISTRIBUTION: North America

SIZE: About fox-sized

DIET: Hypocarnivore

ESSENTIAL FACTS: The most abundant carnivoran found at the Thomas Farm site in northern Florida. The dental morphology of the Lamonia Dog suggests that its diet consisted of a high percentage of plant matter, perhaps adapting its diet seasonally to take advantage of seasonal fruits.

BOROPHAGINAE

Borophaginae are sometimes referred to as "the bone-crushing dogs." This name is misleading, because only one lineage within this group developed the bone-cracking specializations observed among modern hyenas within the subfamily Hyaeninae. Most borophagines were more similar to modern canids like foxes and wolves. The first pack-hunting canids belong to this subfamily.

ARCHAEOCYON LEPTODUS

NAME MEANING: Slender-toothed ancient dog

AGE: Middle Oligocene (27 MYA)

DISTRIBUTION: North America

SIZE: About mongoose-sized

DIET: Mesocarnivore

ESSENTIAL FACTS: Similar in size to *Hesperocyon*, the grinding component of the dentition of Archaeocyon suggests that it was more dependent on plant matter than its earlier relative, although it was still an active predator that hunted rodents, small birds, and reptiles.

OTAROCYON COOKI

NAME MEANING: Cook's ear dog

AGE: Middle Oligocene (27 MYA)

DISTRIBUTION: North America

SIZE: 2.2–4.4 pounds (1–2 kilograms)

DIET: Hypocarnivore

ESSENTIAL FACTS: Cook's Otarocyon is strikingly similar to the modern fennec fox (*Vulpes zerda*), being small-bodied, having huge ears, and a hypocarnivorous diet. Like the fennec fox, it inhabited desert habitats where it foraged primarily at night, relying on its ears to detect small prey items.

PHLAOCYON LEUCOSTEUS

NAME MEANING: White-boned greedy dog

AGE: Middle Oligocene (28–27 MYA)

DISTRIBUTION: North America

SIZE: About raccoon-sized

DIET: Hypocarnivore

ESSENTIAL FACTS: Phlaocyon was part of a lineage of hypocarnivorous borophagines that were likely similar in ecology to modern raccoons (Procyonidae). Its dentition suggests that it mostly ate plants, with animal prey being hunted opportunistically as encountered instead of actively sought out.

AELURODON FEROX

NAME MEANING: Fierce cat tooth

AGE: Late Miocene (10 MYA)

DISTRIBUTION: North America

SIZE: About wolf-sized

DIET: Hypercarnivore

ESSENTIAL FACTS: Members of the genus *Aelurodon* are the first pack-hunting canids, replacing the older hemicyonine bears which dominated from the Early to Middle Miocene. As such, they were pursuit predators adapted to chase down fast-moving ungulates like horses.

EPICYON SAEVUS

NAME MEANING: Fierce top dog

AGE: Late Miocene (10 MYA)

DISTRIBUTION: North America

SIZE: 77–88 pounds (35–40 kilograms)

DIET: Hypercarnivore

ESSENTIAL FACTS: The Fierce Epicyon was a long-legged animal about the same size and build as the modern painted dog (*Lycaon pictus*). It lived in open woodlands and grasslands across North America, where it hunted small- to medium-sized ungulates.

EPICYON HAYDENI

NAME MEANING: Hayden's top dog

AGE: Late Miocene (10–9 MYA)

DISTRIBUTION: North America

SIZE: 220–420 pounds (100–190 kilograms)

DIET: Hypercarnivore

SEE MORE ON PAGES 416–417

BOROPHAGUS SECUNDUS

NAME MEANING: Second gluttonous eater

AGE: Late Miocene (7–5 MYA)

DISTRIBUTION: North America

SIZE: 66–88 pounds (30–40 kilograms)

DIET: Hypocarnivore

ESSENTIAL FACTS: Arguably the most famous Borophagines, members of *Borophagus* are often referred to as "bone-crushing dogs" or "hyena dogs" for their enlarged, blunt premolars that are analogous to those of hyenas. They were opportunistic foragers that specialized in scavenging from large carcasses.

CANINAE

Caninae is the subfamily which includes all modern canids. The group appears in the fossil record around the same time as the borophagines but remained ecologically restricted to smaller predator niches for much of the Oligocene and Miocene. Later in the Miocene they started to grow larger and more diverse, corresponding to a decline in borophagine diversity, and around this time they become the first canids to invade the Old World. The subfamily continued to diversify rapidly through the Pliocene, replacing most of the Old World hyenas and borophagines in North America, even expanding their range into South America.

LEPTOCYON VAFER

NAME MEANING: Variable slender dog

AGE: Early Oligocene (34 MYA)

DISTRIBUTION: North America

SIZE: 4.4 pounds (2 kilograms)

DIET: Mesocarnivore

ESSENTIAL FACTS: *Leptocyon* were small canids about the size of mongooses (Herpestidae) and were probably similar in ecology and behavior. They share many features with early borophagines, although they had relatively longer and narrower jaws. They fed mainly on insects and small vertebrates.

EPICYON HAYDENI

ESSENTIAL FACTS: Hayden's Epicyon is the largest canid known to have ever lived, about the size of a small lion (*Panthera leo*). Aside from being over four to five times larger, it differs from its contemporary relative, the Fierce Epicyon (*E. saevus*), in having proportionately more robust jaws and teeth, a broader skull, and an overall sturdier skeleton that was still adapted for long-distance pursuits. Its distribution is known to have encompassed nearly the entirety of the United States: east-to-west from Florida to California, and north-to-south from Idaho to Texas, and potentially into Mexico and Canada. Its habitat included savanna and open grassland.

Given the size difference between the two, both species of *Epicyon* avoided direct competition by focusing on slightly different prey items. The smaller Fierce Epicyon would have targeted smaller prey ranging from small pronghorns (Antilocapridae) around 44 pounds (20 kilograms) up to larger ungulates weighing as much as 440 pounds (200 kilograms), generally favoring prey in the middle of this range. With its larger size, stronger jaws and neck, and sturdier skeleton, Hayden's Epicyon more actively targeted larger ungulates weighing 440 pounds or more, with a diet that included horses, camels, smaller rhinos, and juvenile proboscideans.

SEE ENTRY ON PAGE 414

EUCYON DAVISI

NAME MEANING: Davis' true dog

AGE: Late Miocene (10 MYA)

DISTRIBUTION: North America

SIZE: 33 pounds (15 kilograms)

DIET: Mesocarnivore

ESSENTIAL FACTS: Davis' Eucyon is a particularly long-lived species that existed for several million years. Its ecology was like that of the modern coyote (*Canis latrans*). It may be ancestral to the modern South American canids. Another species of *Eucyon* became the first canid known outside of North America during the Late Miocene.

CYNOTHERIUM SARDOUS

NAME MEANING: Sardinian dog beast

AGE: Pleistocene to Holocene

DISTRIBUTION: Sardinia

SIZE: 22 pounds (10 kilograms)

DIET: Hypercarnivore

SEE MORE ON PAGES 420–421

DUSICYON AVUS

NAME MEANING: Ancestral foolish dog

AGE: Pleistocene to Holocene

DISTRIBUTION: South America

SIZE: About fox-sized

DIET: Hypercarnivore

ESSENTIAL FACTS: This species was the ecological equivalent of a jackal, mostly hunting small mammals and scavenging from the carcasses of larger ones. It became extinct as recently as 400 years ago, persisting until the time of first European contact. It is the ancestor of the recently extinct Falkland Island Wolf (*D. australis*).

PROTOCYON TROGLODYTES

NAME MEANING: Cave-dwelling first dog

AGE: Pleistocene

DISTRIBUTION: South America

SIZE: 55–82 pounds (25–37 kilograms)

DIET: Hypercarnivore

ESSENTIAL FACTS: Protocyon was a pack-hunting canid similar in morphology to the painted dog (*Lycaon pictus*). This species is known to have hunted medium- to large-sized mammals in lightly wooded and open habitats, with some dietary overlap with the Southern Smilodon (*Smilodon populator*).

AENOCYON DIRUS

NAME MEANING: Ominous terrible dog

AGE: Pleistocene to early Holocene (1 MYA–9,500 YA)

DISTRIBUTION: North America, South America

SIZE: 132–154 pounds (60–70 kilograms)

DIET: Hypercarnivore

SEE MORE ON PAGES 422–423

URSIDAE

The nine species of bear alive today are robust, plantigrade animals. Most of them are hypocarnivores which feed mostly on plant matter but will opportunistically take animal prey. Only the polar bear (*Ursus maritimus*) and sloth bear (*Melursus ursinus*) are the exception, the latter being secondarily hypercarnivorous and the former being a myrmecophagous mesocarnivore. The oldest bears which appear during the Late Eocene were raccoon-like animals whose carnassials retained a dedicated shearing surface (trigonid) which had started to become reduced in favor of an expanded grinding area (talonid). Also, the post-carnassial molars were broader than those of their ancestors, showing that although animal prey was still an important dietary component, they were becoming better equipped to handle plant matter.

CYNOTHERIUM SARDOUS

ESSENTIAL FACTS: The Sardinian Dhole was endemic to the islands of Sardinia and Corsica. It is thought to have descended from the larger pack-hunting canid *Xenocyon lycaonoides*, which itself is a close relative of the modern dhole (*Cuon alpinus*) and painted dog (*Lycaon pictus*). A 2021 genetic study showed that its closest modern relative is indeed the dhole, the two species having diverged less than 1 million years ago.

Because the small islands on which it lived lacked many larger ungulates its ancestors hunted on the mainland, the ancestors of the Sardinian Dhole needed to adapt to the hunt the smaller mammals on the island. The species shrank in overall body size, their jaws became longer and more slender, and the teeth became smaller to more efficiently catch smaller targets. Jaw musculature decreased and the sagittal crest was reduced. In 2022 it was found that the hearing of this species had become highly specialized to detect the high-pitched calls made by rodents and lagomorphs. The primary prey for Sardinian Dholes were the Sardinian Pika (*Prolagus sardus*), as well as Tyrrhenian Field Rat (*Rhagamys orthodon*), Tyrrhenian Vole (*Microtus henseli*), and various species of birds. Like other canids which specialize in small prey, small family groups would separate to hunt alone.

SEE ENTRY ON PAGE 418

AENOCYON DIRUS

ESSENTIAL FACTS: Although referred to commonly as the Dire Wolf, this species is only distantly related to true wolves of the genus *Canis*, having split from a common ancestor at least 5 million years ago. Dire Wolves were similar to gray wolves (*Canis lupus*) in overall size and morphology, although the former was somewhat more robust. The two species were contemporaneous, although the Dire Wolf seems to have been less cold-adapted and is not known to have occurred farther north than modern-day Alberta. Its range extended south as far as Argentina in South America.

Dire Wolves lived in family units and appear to have favored more open environments where they hunted prey items such as horses and juvenile bison. The species is famously the most numerous animal recovered from the La Brea Tar Pits in Los Angeles, California, where several individuals at a time were summoned by the distress calls of prey animals which had become stuck in the asphalt or by the odors of those which had already died. These Dire Wolves were in turn trapped themselves after attempting to feed upon these seemingly easy meals. Individuals spanning in age from weaned juveniles and elderly adults are known. Some specimens have been found with healed injuries that would have made it difficult or impossible for them to hunt for themselves, implying that like modern pack-hunting canids, wounded individuals were cared for by other members of the pack and allowed to feed from kills.

SEE ENTRY ON PAGE 419

EOARCTOS VORAX

NAME MEANING: Voracious dawn bear

AGE: Early Oligocene (32–31 MYA)

DISTRIBUTION: North America

SIZE: 9.4 pounds (4.3 kilograms)

DIET: Hypocarnivore

ESSENTIAL FACTS: A raccoon-like, scansorial animal described in 2023, Eoarctos appears to have fed heavily on hard objects such as mollusks. This conjecture is based on dental injuries observed among known specimens, some of which may have been fatal.

PARICTIS PRIMAEVUS

NAME MEANING: Ancient beside weasel

AGE: Early Oligocene (34–30 MYA)

DISTRIBUTION: North America

SIZE: About marten-sized

DIET: Hypocarvivore

ESSENTIAL FACTS: *Parictis* were small hypocarnivores that would have fed heavily on fruits and other soft plants, as well as insects and small vertebrates on occasion. Fossils of this species are frequently found in the badlands of western North America.

HEMICYONINAE

Sometimes referred to as "dog-bears" (not to be confused with "bear-dogs" of the family Amphicyonidae), these were specialized bears that evolved slender, digitigrade limbs and hypercarnivorous wolf-like dentition. After the extinction of hyaenodontids in the Late Oligocene, they evolved to fill the niches occupied today by pack-hunting canids such as wolves.

PHOBEROGALE SHARERI

NAME MEANING: Kevin Sharer's fearful polecat

AGE: Early Miocene (22–20 MYA)

DISTRIBUTION: North America

SIZE: About wolf-sized

DIET: Hypercarnivore

ESSENTIAL FACTS: The oldest hemicyonine in North America, its ancestors evolved in Eurasia in the Late Oligocene and migrated to North America early in the Miocene. It is known from a nearly complete skull found in Southern California.

PHOBEROCYON JOHNHENRYI

NAME MEANING: John Henry's fearful dog

AGE: Early Miocene (20–17 MYA)

DISTRIBUTION: North America

SIZE: 132–154 pounds (60–70 kilograms)

DIET: Hypercarnivore

ESSENTIAL FACTS: John Henry's Phoberocyon was a wolf-sized predator known from the Thomas Farm site in northern Florida. Its teeth and jaws are morphologically very similar to those of a Dire Wolf (*Aenocyon dirus*), and they fed on the various horses, camels, and small rhinos that were its contemporaries.

PLITHOCYON URSINUS

NAME MEANING: Bear-like stone dog

AGE: Middle Miocene (15–11 MYA)

DISTRIBUTION: North America

SIZE: About lion-sized

DIET: Hypercarnivore

ESSENTIAL FACTS: Compared to the older genus *Hemicyon*, these hemicyonines were even better adapted for cursoriality with larger carnassials. It was also one of the larger members of the subfamily approaching the size of a lioness.

HEMICYON SANSANIENSIS

NAME MEANING: Half dog from Sansan

AGE: Middle Miocene (16–11 MYA)

DISTRIBUTION: Eurasia

SIZE: About wolf-sized

DIET: Hypercarnivore

ESSENTIAL FACTS: One of the most famous members of the subfamily, this species is remarkably similar to specimens from North America (*H. ursinus*). This suggests a possible Holarctic distribution not unlike that of the modern gray wolf (*Canis lupus*).

URSAVINAE

The ursavines were early bears that lived from the Early to Late Miocene, inhabiting the continents of North America, Eurasia, Africa. They were long-tailed hypocarnivores that physically and ecologically would have been similar to raccoons (Procyonidae) or badgers (Mustelidae).

BALLUSIA ORIENTALIS

NAME MEANING: Eastern Ballusia

AGE: Early Miocene (20–18 MYA)

DISTRIBUTION: Eurasia

SIZE: About cat-sized

DIET: Mesocarnivore

ESSENTIAL FACTS: Known from a complete skeleton found in China, this animal had similar proportions to that of a fisher (*Pekania pennanti*) or wolverine (*Gulo gulo*). It had a generalized diet consisting of a variety of small animals and plants.

URSAVUS TEDFORDI

NAME MEANING: Tedford's bear ancestor

AGE: Late Miocene

DISTRIBUTION: Eurasia

SIZE: About wolf-sized

DIET: Mesocarnivore

ESSENTIAL FACTS: This was the largest species within *Ursavus* and the only one for which a complete skull is known. Compared to modern bears, Tedford's Ursavus had a longer body and tail with teeth more adapted for carnivory, although its diet consisted of a high proportion of plant matter.

AILUROPODINAE

The panda bear (*Ailuropoda melanoleuca*) is the last surviving member of this subfamily, and is also the most specialized, being adapted for a diet of bamboo. The lineage which led to the modern species evolved toward specialized plant-based diets, but many members were more mesocarnivorous and retained carnassials with a dedicated shearing function. These bears appear in the fossil record during the Middle Miocene and were distributed throughout Eurasia, North America, and Africa.

INDARCTOS ARCTOIDES

NAME MEANING: Bear-like Indian bear

AGE: Late Miocene (9–5 MYA)

DISTRIBUTION: Eurasia

SIZE: 90–400 pounds (41–182 kilograms)

DIET: Hypocarnivore

ESSENTIAL FACTS: This bear had broad, robust molars adapted for crushing plant matter but retained a functional shearing blade on the carnassial. It was similar in size and ecology to a modern black bear (*Ursus americanus*) with a primarily plant-based diet but would opportunistically take animal prey and carrion.

AGRIOTHERIUM AFRICANUM

NAME MEANING: African wild beast

AGE: Pliocene to Pleistocene

DISTRIBUTION: Africa, Eurasia

SIZE: 5 feet (1.8 meters) SH; 1,320 pounds (600 kilograms)

DIET: Mesocarnivore

SEE MORE ON PAGES 430–431

KRETZOIARCTOS BEATRIX

NAME MEANING: Beatriz Azanza's bear of Kretzoi

AGE: Middle Miocene

DISTRIBUTION: Eurasia

SIZE: 132 pounds (60 kilograms)

DIET: Hypocarnivore

ESSENTIAL FACTS: While it still retained a carnassial with a functioning shearing surface (trigonid), the post-carnassial molars were more complex and broader than other bears of the time, showing that it was becoming better adapted to feed on tough plants. It is a direct ancestor of the panda bear (*Ailuropoda melanoleuca*).

AILURARCTOS LUFENGENSIS

NAME MEANING: Cat bear from Lufeng

AGE: Late Miocene (7–5 MYA)

DISTRIBUTION: Eurasia

SIZE: 150–280 pounds (70–126 kilograms)

DIET: Hypocarnivore

ESSENTIAL FACTS: Like its modern descendant, the panda bear (*Ailuropoda melanoleuca*), the Lufeng Panda Bear was a bamboo specialist that inhabited the bamboo forests of what is now China. Already it possessed the strong jaws and durophagous teeth needed to crush bamboo stalks and the false thumb for gripping them.

TREMARCTINAE

Commonly referred to as "the short-faced bears," the tremarctines have been restricted to the New World throughout their evolutionary history, which is known to have started in the Late Miocene in North America and replaced the ailuropodine bears on the continent. When South America connected to North America during the Pliocene, they spread southward and radiated into several distinct species. Included among this group are some of the largest bears that have ever lived. A single surviving species, the spectacled bear (*Tremarctos ornatus*), continues to survive in South America. These bears are characterized by a secondary masseteric fossa in the lower jaw, which further strengthens the jaws and inspired the name of the genus *Tremarctos*, which means "hole bear." Another distinctive feature of these bears is their broad and deepened snouts from which they derive their common name.

PLIONARCTOS EDENSIS

NAME MEANING: Near bear from Eden

AGE: Late Miocene (10–5 MYA)

DISTRIBUTION: North America

SIZE: 90–400 pounds (41–182 kilograms)

DIET: Hypocarnivore

ESSENTIAL FACTS: The genus *Plionarctos* is the oldest among the tremarctines, with the Eden Bear being perhaps the best known among them. Its fossils are known from various localities from Florida, Tennessee, and Indiana, suggesting a wide distribution in the forests and woodlands of eastern North America.

ARCTOTHERIUM WINGEI

NAME MEANING: Winge's bear beast

AGE: Pleistocene

DISTRIBUTION: South America, North America

SIZE: 183 pounds (83 kilograms)

DIET: Hypocarnivore

ESSENTIAL FACTS: The smallest of the *Arctotherium* bears, it was distributed throughout South America and southern North America. Carbon isotope studies confirm that plant matter formed the bulk of the Winge's Bear diet and that it would have opportunistically hunted manageably sized prey items.

AGRIOTHERIUM AFRICANUM

ESSENTIAL FACTS: Bears have never had a strong presence in the African fossil record. Even today, no bears currently inhabit the continent since the extinction of the north African Atlas Bear (*Ursus arctos crowtheri*) in 1870. The African Bear, whose fossils have been discovered in modern-day South Africa, is the first definitive bear known to have been distributed south of the modern Sahara Desert.

The African Bear inhabited open woodland, savanna, grassland, and desert environments. Similar to the Giant Short-Faced Bear (*Arctodus simus*) and the South American Short-Faced Bear (*Arctotherium angustidens*), it had relatively long and slender limbs adapted to efficiently traverse large distances in search of food. Its jaws were wide and short, capable of generating tremendous bite forces. Isotope analyses confirm that it fed on a considerable amount of animal matter. Like modern bears, its skeleton was not particularly optimized for the active hunting of prey by pursuit or ambush, but it was still an effective opportunistic predator capable of securing its own kills. Likely prey included various ungulates, targeting mostly young, sick, or wounded individuals when it could get them. Given its large size, it was also capable of intimidating other predators into giving up their kills.

SEE ENTRY ON PAGE 428

ARCTOTHERIUM ANGUSTIDENS

NAME MEANING: Narrow-toothed bear beast

AGE: Pleistocene

DISTRIBUTION: South America

SIZE: 908–2,645 pounds (412–1,200 kilograms)

DIET: Mesocarnivore

SEE MORE ON PAGES 434–435

ARCTODUS PRISTINUS

NAME MEANING: Pristine bear tooth

AGE: Pleistocene

DISTRIBUTION: North America

SIZE: 293–880 pounds (133–400 kilograms)

DIET: Hypocarnivore

ESSENTIAL FACTS: Known as the Eastern Short-faced Bear or Lesser Short-faced Bear, this species is known from the eastern and southern United States. It was the size of a brown bear (*Ursus arctos*) and likely occupied the same ecological niche. Compared to its larger relative its teeth were smaller, its limbs were shorter, and its jaws were less robust.

ARCTODUS SIMUS

NAME MEANING: Short bear tooth

AGE: Pleistocene

DISTRIBUTION: North America

SIZE: 5.5 feet (1.6 meters) SH; 660–2,090 (300–950 kilograms)

DIET: Mesocarnivore

SEE MORE ON PAGES 436–437

TREMARCTOS FLORIDANUS

NAME MEANING: Hole bear from Florida

AGE: Pleistocene

DISTRIBUTION: North America

SIZE: 90–400 pounds (41–182 kilograms)

DIET: Hypocarnivore

ESSENTIAL FACTS: Florida Spectacled Bear fossils are most abundantly found in Florida, hence the name, but its range is also known to have extended to Tennessee in the north, New Mexico in the west, and Mexico in the south. A mounted skeleton is on permanent display at the Florida Museum of Natural History.

URSINAE

Ursine bears appear in the fossil record during the Middle Miocene in North America, although they remained relatively rare and small in size until the Pliocene. Much of their diversification seems to have taken place in Eurasia. Seven of the nine surviving species of bear belong to this subfamily. Compared to other bears, they are uniquely well-suited to the temperate regions of the north due to their ability to hibernate, during which they lower their metabolisms to survive extended periods of food shortage following a few months of binge-eating during the growing season.

AURORARCTOS TIRAWA

NAME MEANING: Dawn bear of Tirawa

AGE: Middle Miocene (15–12.5 MYA)

DISTRIBUTION: North America

SIZE: 22–44 pounds (10–20 kilograms)

DIET: Hypocarnivore

ESSENTIAL FACTS: This species is named after Tirawa, a creator god from Pawnee mythology. Aurorarctos is the oldest-known of the ursine bears and also the smallest. The presence of cavities in the teeth suggest that it frequently fed on sweet fruits and other food items high in carbohydrates.

ARCTOTHERIUM ANGUSTIDENS

ESSENTIAL FACTS: When the Panamanian Land Bridge formed, connecting North America and South America during the Pliocene, it enabled the transfer and intermixing of animals from both continents. This event is known as the Great American Biotic Interchange, which began earlier during the Late Miocene. Animals would island-hop in the shallow seaway that existed between the Americas, but the direct land connection greatly accelerated this event. Among carnivorans, the newly arrived dogs, cats, and bears underwent rapid adaptive radiations into numerous new species. The bear genus *Arctotherium* radiated into as many as many as five distinct species, the South American Short-faced Bear being the largest among them.

The South American Short-faced Bear is the earliest species of *Arctotherium* despite its great size, suggesting a gap in the fossil record for the genus. It was of similar size and proportion to other giant bears like the African Bear (*Agriotherium africanum*) and its northern contemporary the Giant Short-faced Bear (*Arctodus simus*). It was the largest terrestrial carnivoran to have ever inhabited South America and had a mostly carnivorous diet, likely consisting mostly of scavenged meat. It would opportunistically browse on edible plants that grew in the woodlands and grasslands in which it lived.

SEE ENTRY ON PAGE 432

ARCTODUS SIMUS

ESSENTIAL FACTS: The Giant Short-faced Bear is the larger of the two species of *Arctodus* and is known from more complete remains. It was widely distributed throughout North America, encompassing most of the United States and Canada, particularly the west, with its range extending from Alaska to Mexico. It would have favored open woodland and grassland environments and avoided especially dense forests. It had relatively long limbs adapted for swift and efficient long-distance travel. In fact, its overall skull, body, and limb proportions were broadly similar to those of hyenas. Its paws were also relatively narrow and slender for active running. Males were considerably larger than the females, and it is possible that female cubs remained at their mother's side for extended periods.

The Giant Short-faced Bear readily browsed on soft leaves and fruits when encountered, but it would preferentially feed on meat. Its diet consisted largely of scavenged carcasses; using its size it was able to intimidate smaller predators into giving up their kills the same way that modern brown bears are known to plunder carcasses from smaller gray wolves (*Canis lupus*) and cougars (*Puma concolor*). Puncture and gouge damage matching this bear's teeth have been identified on mammoth bones, demonstrating this bear's formidable bite force and effectiveness as a scavenger. It would have also brought down its own prey when the opportunity arose.

SEE ENTRY ON PAGE 432

PROTARCTOS ABSTRUSUS

NAME MEANING: Hidden before bear

AGE: Pliocene to Pleistocene (5–2 MYA)

DISTRIBUTION: North America

SIZE: 90–400 pounds (41–182 kilograms)

DIET: Hypocarnivore

ESSENTIAL FACTS: The presence of cavities in this bear's teeth, combined with its distribution in the High Arctic, suggest that it needed a high-calorie diet to build energy reserves in preparation for hibernation, making it among the first bears known to do so.

URSUS SPELEA

NAME MEANING: Cave bear

AGE: Pleistocene

DISTRIBUTION: Eurasia

SIZE: 495–1,320 pounds (225–600 kilograms)

DIET: Herbivore

SEE MORE ON PAGES 440–441

MUSTELIDAE

Mustelids are ecologically and morphologically the most diverse of all the carnivorans, its members including terrestrial, arboreal, cursorial, semiaquatic, and fossorial forms. Most are small-bodied and hypercarnivorous, with the largest modern species being less than 100 pounds (45 kilograms). The smallest modern carnivoran, the least weasel (*Mustela nivalis*), is a member of this family. The group first appears during the Late Eocene. During prehistory, mustelids were even more variable, with some growing to be as big as large canids or medium-sized cats.

OLIGOBUNINAE

Oligobuninae is a paraphyletic subfamily which includes the largest mustelids known to have ever lived, some growing to be the size of gray wolves (*Canis lupus*) or cougars (*Puma concolor*).

ZODIOLESTES DAIMONELIXENSIS

NAME MEANING: Little thief of the devil's corkscrews

AGE: Early Miocene (23–20 MYA)

DISTRIBUTION: North America

SIZE: 1–3 pounds (600–1,400 grams)

DIET: Hypercarnivore

ESSENTIAL FACTS: The Diamonelix Weasel had a predator-prey relationship with burrowing beavers of the genus *Palaeocastor*, similar to that which exists between the modern black-footed ferret (*Mustela nigripes*) and prairie dogs (*Cynomys*). After it ate its victims, this predator would take up residency in its burrows.

MEGALICTIS FEROX

NAME MEANING: Fierce great weasel

AGE: Early Miocene (22.7–18.5 MYA)

DISTRIBUTION: North America

SIZE: 130–220 pounds (60–100 kilograms)

DIET: Hypercarnivore

ESSENTIAL FACTS: The Fierce Megalictis was a jaguar-sized predator with a robust skeleton built to stalk, ambush, and grapple with relatively large prey items such as oreodonts, horses, and small rhinos. Its skull is notably similar to that of a big cat and could deliver powerful and precise killing bites.

URSUS SPELEA

ESSENTIAL FACTS: Cave Bears are named such because their fossils are frequently found in cave deposits. These bears appear to have utilized caves more frequently than the contemporaneous brown bears (*Ursus arctos*), which are more likely to excavate their own dens or renovate the burrows made by other animals to make use of for hibernation. Numerous skeletons of individuals that died during hibernation have been discovered, suggesting that this was a leading cause of mortality for the species. Because of the abundance of remains and reasonably complete material, we know more about this species' biology and life history than any other extinct bear. Cave Bear skeletons are frequently on display in museums across the world.

Compared to the brown bear, the Cave Bear skull was broader with a steep forehead, its cheek teeth are larger and wider, and its body was overall more stocky. Sexual dimorphism in this species is extreme even by bear standards, with males being as much as three times heavier than the females. Wear patterns on the teeth show that it fed almost exclusively on plant matter, with a tendency toward rather tough plants. Meat may have been more actively consumed just before hibernation as is typical of modern bears. Cave Bears were distributed throughout western Eurasia, inhabiting forested and mountainous environments and generally avoided open areas. The youngest known recorded Cave Bear fossils date to about 24,000 years ago.

SEE ENTRY ON PAGE 438

EKORUS EKAKERAN

NAME MEANING: Unknown

AGE: Late Miocene (6 MYA)

DISTRIBUTION: Africa

SIZE: 97 pounds (44 kilograms)

DIET: Hypercarnivore

ESSENTIAL FACTS: Ekorus is a cursorial mustelid the size of a large painted dog (*Lycaon pictus*) or small gray wolf (*Canis lupus*) and may have engaged in similar hunting behaviors. It inhabited forest and woodland habitats. Nearly complete skeletons have been found in the Lothagam site in Kenya.

EOMELLIVORA PIVETEAUI

NAME MEANING: Piveteau's dawn Mellivora

AGE: Late Miocene (11–9 MYA)

DISTRIBUTION: Africa

SIZE: 11–20 pounds (5–9 kilograms)

DIET: Hypercarnivore

ESSENTIAL FACTS: This species was among the many predators recovered from the Cerro de los Batallones locality in Madrid, Spain. Its limbs were adapted for cursoriality and its jaws and teeth were robust for handling relatively large prey similar to modern bush dogs (*Speothos venaticus*), which it closely matched in size.

ICTONYCHINAE

Formerly included among the Mustelinae, these mustelids are distributed on all continents except Australia and Antarctica and were more diverse in the prehistoric past, with a fossil record dating back to the Miocene. Members of the group are characterized by having some variation of black fur with white markings.

TRIGONICTIS MACRODON

NAME MEANING: Long-toothed triangular weasel

AGE: Pliocene to Pleistocene (3–1 MYA)

DISTRIBUTION: North America

SIZE: 2–6 kilograms (4–13 pounds)

DIET: Hypercarnivore

ESSENTIAL FACTS: The Long-Toothed Grison was a scansorial predator that fed on a variety of prey items such as rabbit, large rodents, and birds. It was widely distributed throughout the forests and woodlands of North America similar in size and proportions to a modern fisher (*Pekania pennanti*).

ENHYDRICTIS GALICTOIDES

NAME MEANING: Galictis-like otter weasel

AGE: Pleistocene

DISTRIBUTION: Sardinia, Corsica

SIZE: 22–30 pounds (10–15 kilograms)

DIET: Hypercarnivore

ESSENTIAL FACTS: Although only about the size of a lynx, it was one of the largest terrestrial predators on the small islands of Sardinia and Corsica, and the largest-known representative of its subfamily. Its main prey would have been small mammals such as the Sardinian Pika (*Prolagus sardous*).

MELINAE

Badgers are a Eurasian group of hypocarnivorous mustelids. They typically have wide bodies and short, powerful limbs with strong claws adapted for digging and long, tubular snouts for sniffing out food in the ground or under leaf litter. Despite their common names, the modern honey badger (*Mellivora capensis*) and American badger (*Taxidea taxus*) may not be true members of the subfamily, instead representing completely different mustelid lineages.

ARCTOMELES DIMOLODONTUS

NAME MEANING: Two millstone toothed bear-badger

AGE: Pliocene

DISTRIBUTION: North America

SIZE: 15–31 pounds (7–14 kilograms)

DIET: Hypocarnivore

ESSENTIAL FACTS: The Woodland Badger is one of the most common small carnivorans from the Gray Fossil Site in Tennessee and one of the few true badgers to invade North America. Its closest modern relative is the modern hog badger (*Arctonyx*) from Eurasia. The Woodland Badger's teeth were adapted for crush fruits and roots, and they would opportunistically catch small animals.

LUTRINAE

Otters are semiaquatic mustelids with long bodies set on short, powerful limbs with webbed digits. Their tails are long and muscular and are used to propel them through the water. These animals first appear during the Middle Miocene, and there are thirteen modern species distributed throughout every continent except Australia and Antarctica.

ENHYDRIODON SIVALENSIS

NAME MEANING: Otter tooth from Siwalik Hills

AGE: Late Miocene (10–5 MYA)

DISTRIBUTION: Eurasia

SIZE: 49–55 pounds (22–25 kilograms)

DIET: Aquatic hypercarnivore

ESSENTIAL FACTS: The Siwalik Otter is part of a subgroup of otters with bunodont carnassials adapted for crushing instead of shearing. Its primary prey included hard-shelled mollusks and crustaceans in addition to fish.

ENHYDRITHERIUM TERRANOVAE

NAME MEANING: Otter beast from the new land

AGE: Late Miocene (6.5–4.5 MYA)

DISTRIBUTION: North America

SIZE: 44–70 pounds (20–32 kilograms)

DIET: Aquatic hypercarnivore

SEE MORE ON PAGES 446–447

MEGALENHYDRIS BARBARICINA

NAME MEANING: Great otter from Barbaricina

AGE: Pleistocene

DISTRIBUTION: Sardinia

SIZE: About Leopard-sized

DIET: Aquatic hypercarnivore

ESSENTIAL FACTS: The Sardinian Giant Otter is one of the largest otters to have ever lived and the largest predator on the islands where it lived. Its flattened tail made it a swift and efficient swimmer that fed on large fish, mollusks, and crustaceans.

SARDOLUTRA ICHNUSAE

NAME MEANING: Trace Sardinian otter

AGE: Pleistocene

DISTRIBUTION: Sardinia

SIZE: About cat-sized

DIET: Aquatic hypercarnivore

ESSENTIAL FACTS: Formerly placed in the genus *Nesolutra*, meaning "island otter," this species is thought to have lived and hunted mostly in the sea, where it used its great speed and agility to chase down fish. It is the smallest of Sardinia's four otters.

ENHYDRITHERIUM TERRANOVAE

ESSENTIAL FACTS: Like the Siwalik Otter, Enhydritherium is part of a lineage of bunodont otters known almost exclusively from Eurasia and Africa. Its species name is derived from the Latin words *terra* and *novus*, meaning "land" and "new," respectively, which refer to the creature's origin. Its fossils have been found in California, Mexico, and Florida, in both freshwater and saltwater deposits. Previously thought to be a close relative of the modern sea otter (*Enhydra lutris*), Enhydritherium was more amphibious, as it was better adapted for movement over land than its seagoing relative. Its style of swimming also appears to have been less dependent on its hindlimbs for propulsion, and the jaws appear to have been more important for prey capture (and the forepaws less so).

A large otter the same size as the modern giant otter (*Pteronura brasiliensis*) from South America, Enhydritherium was one of the most formidable predators in the waterways in which it lived. Fish fossils found associated near the stomach region show that this species had a diet consisting of fish like that of modern river otters. Like its modern relative, Enhydritherium would have taken a variety of aquatic and terrestrial vertebrates opportunistically as encountered. A nearly complete skeleton based on a specimen from the Moss Acres Racetrack Site in Central Florida is on permanent display at the Florida Museum of Natural History.

SEE ENTRY ON PAGE 445

GULONINAE

The gulonine mustelids are mostly arboreal or scansorial predators, with the modern wolverine (*Gulo gulo*) being mostly terrestrial and adapted to traverse great distances in search of food, although it too is a skilled climber.

STHENICTIS CAMPESTRIS

NAME MEANING: Strong weasel of the fields

AGE: Late Miocene

DISTRIBUTION: North America

SIZE: About Fisher-sized

DIET: Hypercarnivore

ESSENTIAL FACTS: Members of the genus *Sthenictis* are among the more basal members of Guloninae and are distributed throughout North America and Eurasia. Like the modern tayra (*Eira barbara*) it had a long and flexible body and long limbs adapted for climbing and leaping.

PLESIOGULO BRACHYGNATHUS

NAME MEANING: Short jawed near Gulo

AGE: Late Miocene

DISTRIBUTION: Eurasia

SIZE: About dog-sized

DIET: Hypercarnivore

ESSENTIAL FACTS: A complete skeleton of this animal from the Shanghai Natural History Museum shows that its limbs were rather long and slender, resembling those of pursuit-hunting canids, and its canines are relatively robust. Its relationships within the subfamily Guloninae are uncertain.

GULO SUDORUS

NAME MEANING: Sweaty glutton

AGE: Pliocene

DISTRIBUTION: North America

SIZE: Unknown

DIET: Hypercarnivore

ESSENTIAL FACTS: This species is the oldest-known wolverine. It was discovered at the Gray Fossil Site in East Tennessee and described in 2018. The presence of this animal in a subtropical forest environment is in vast contrast to its modern, cold-adapted relative.

PROCYONIDAE

Procyonids are endemic to the New World and appear to have never crossed Beringia into Eurasia, perhaps due to competition from early bears, which were small raccoon-like hypocarnivores during their early history. Most are small hypocarnivores, the shearing function of the carnassials greatly reduced to being almost absent in some. A few, like the modern ringtail (*Bassariscus astutus*), are scansorial mesocarnivores. They first appear in the fossil record during the Early Miocene. Procyonids were the first carnivorans known to have inhabited South America, arriving there before the land connection between the two continents formed. Here, some species grew as large as modern bears.

CYNONASUA BREVIROSTRIS

NAME MEANING: Short-faced dog-coati

AGE: Late Miocene (7–5.5MYA)

DISTRIBUTION: South America

SIZE: 33–55 pounds (15–25 kilogram)

DIET: Mesocarnivore

ESSENTIAL FACTS: Cynonasua was the oldest known terrestrial member of Carnivora to have lived in South America, as well as the first North American immigrant in the Great American Biotic Interchange. Its ancestors reached the continent through small islands that existed between the two land masses before the Panamanian Land Bridge could form. It was about twice the size of the modern common raccoon (*Procyon lotor*) and had a more mesocarnivorous diet.

ARCTONASUA FLORIDANA

NAME MEANING: Bear *Nasua* from Florida

AGE: Late Miocene (11.5–8 MYA)

DISTRIBUTION: North America

SIZE: About badger-sized

DIET: Hypocarnivore

ESSENTIAL FACTS: Fossils of the Florida Arctonasua are known from the Love Bone Bed site in Central Florida. Compared to modern coatis (*Nasua*) it was noticeably larger and more robust and probably had an ecology similar to that of badgers. It had a varied diet consisting of plants and small animals.

CHAPALMALANIA ORTHOGNATHA

NAME MEANING: Straight jaws from Chapadmalal

AGE: Late Miocene to Pliocene (6–2 MYA)

DISTRIBUTION: South America

SIZE: 276–400 pounds (125–181 kilograms)

DIET: Hypocarnivore

ESSENTIAL FACTS: This is the largest-known procyonid the size of a black bear (*Ursus americanus*), and likely filled the same niche during the interval before bears became established in South America. It is named for the town of Chapadmalal in Argentina near where it was discovered.

PROCYON GIPSONI

NAME MEANING: Aaron Gipson's before dog

AGE: Pliocene

DISTRIBUTION: North America

SIZE: About raccoon-sized

DIET: Hypocarnivore

ESSENTIAL FACTS: Gipson's Raccoon was slightly larger than the modern common raccoon (*Procyon lotor*) but was otherwise morphologically similar in its dentition. The species is named in honor of Aaron Gipson, the discoverer and primary excavator of the Withlacoochee River 1A site where the species was discovered.

PROCYON MEGALOKOLOS

NAME MEANING: Large colossus before dog

AGE: Pliocene

DISTRIBUTION: North America

SIZE: 60 pounds (27 kilograms)

DIET: Hypocarnivore

ESSENTIAL FACTS: The Giant Raccoon was significantly larger than the modern common raccoon (*Procyon lotor*) and the contemporary Gipson's Raccoon (*Procyon gipsoni*). It opportunistically fed upon any small animals it could catch and readily took fruits and nuts.

NASUA MASTODONTA

NAME MEANING: Breast-toothed coati

AGE: Pliocene

DISTRIBUTION: North America

SIZE: 9–13 pounds (4–6 kilograms)

DIET: Hypocarnivore

ESSENTIAL FACTS: About the same size as the modern white-nosed coati (*Nasua narica*), it used its long snout and sensitive nose to hunt for insects, small vertebrates, fruits, and nuts hidden in the leaf-litter of the forests in which it lived.

AILURIDAE

The red panda (*Ailurus fulgens*) is the last-surviving member of this group and specializes in eating bamboo. The word "panda" is derived from the Nepalese term *nigalya poonya*, which means "bamboo-eater," a reference to the diets of the living red panda and the unrelated panda bear (*Ailuropoda melanoleuca*). Across their evolutionary history, pandas were much more diverse and included small- to medium-sized mesocarnivores and hypercarnivores. Molecular studies have shown that the group may be particularly close to procyonids. Indeed, the oldest species from the Late Oligocene have a striking resemblance to the modern ringtail (*Bassariscus astutus*), and similarities in cranial morphology between the two families have been noted.

AMPHICTIS ANTIQUA

NAME MEANING: Ancient double weasel

AGE: Early Miocene (23 MYA)

DISTRIBUTION: Eurasia

SIZE: About cat-sized

DIET: Mesocanivore

ESSENTIAL FACTS: One of the first pandas, this animal was morphologically similar to the modern ringtail (*Bassariscus astutus*). It was an opportunistic predator of various small vertebrates which it hunted both in the trees and on land. Fruits and berries were less frequently fed upon.

SIMOCYONINAE

Originally thought to be a type of canid and later considered to be procyonids, simocyonines were small to medium-sized hypercarnivorous pandas that were distributed throughout North America and Eurasia. Their fossil record is known from the Middle Miocene to the Early Pliocene.

SIMOCYON BATALLERI

NAME MEANING: Bataller's flat-nosed dog

AGE: Late Miocene (11–9 MYA)

DISTRIBUTION: Eurasia

SIZE: About leopard-sized

DIET: Hypercarnivore

SEE MORE ON PAGES 454–455

SIMOCYON PRIMIGENIUS

NAME MEANING: Firstborn flat-nosed dog

AGE: Late Miocene (8–6 MYA)

DISTRIBUTION: Eurasia

SIZE: About leopard-sized

DIET: Hypercarnivore

ESSENTIAL FACTS: Compared to Bataller's Simocyon, this species had a more domed, broader, and overall more robust skull with deeper jaws and larger teeth, indicating a much stronger bite and the ability to tackle larger prey. The postcranial skeleton is unknown but it may be inferred to be a powerful and agile predator of small- to medium-sized mammals.

AILURINAE

Ailurines were mostly small hypocarnivores represented by a single modern species. Their fossils are known from Eurasia and North America starting from the Middle Miocene onward. Most were hypocarnivores with robust molars with accessory cusps.

MAGERICTIS IMPERIALENIS

NAME MEANING: Imperial weasel of Madrid

AGE: Middle Miocene (11–9 MYA)

DISTRIBUTION: Eurasia

SIZE: About raccoon-sized

DIET: Mesocarnivore

ESSENTIAL FACTS: The earliest member of the subfamily Ailurinae, this species was discovered in Madrid, Spain, and probably had a lifestyle similar to that of modern raccoons (*Procyon*).

SIMOCYON BATALLERI

ESSENTIAL FACTS: Another of the otherwise rare predators known only from the Spanish fossil locality of Cerro de los Batallones (others including *Magericyon anceps*, *Ammitocyon kainos*, *Eomellivora piveteaui*, and *Indarctos arctoides* mentioned previously in this book), Bataller's Simocyon is known from at least two individuals represented by reasonably complete skeletons. Together with the North American Bristol's Panda, Bataller's Panda is one of only two fossil ailurids for which enough of the skeleton is known to create a full-body reconstruction. Before its discovery here, *Simocyon* fossils were known from fragmentary or incomplete remains from Eurasia and North America.

Bataller's Simocyon was slightly smaller than a leopard (*Panthera pardus*) but was comparable in general body proportions, explosively fast and agile with great climbing abilities. Adaptations such as powerful shoulder and lower back muscles, wide paws with dexterous forelimbs, recurved claws, and a counterbalancing tail enabled them to bolt up vertical surfaces with great speed. Bataller's Panda also possessed a proportionally smaller "false thumb" or "panda's thumb" than the red panda (*Ailurus fulgens*), a modified radial sesamoid bone that enhances the ability to grip tree trunks and thin branches. Its diet consisted of relatively small prey items such as rabbits, small ruminants, and juvenile pigs. By focusing on smaller prey, it was able to minimize competition with other medium-sized predators such as the similarly sized Ogygia Cat (*Promegantereon ogygia*).

SEE ENTRY ON PAGE 452

PRISTINAILURUS BRISTOLI

NAME MEANING: Larry Bristol's former Ailurus

AGE: Pliocene

DISTRIBUTION: North America

SIZE: 17–33 pounds (8–15 kilograms)

DIET: Mesocarnivore

SEE MORE ON PAGES 458–459

AMPHICYNODONTIDAE

Amphicynodontidae is a family of carnivorans which contains small- to medium-sized terrestrial and semiaquatic predators. These animals provide a link between early bears and pinnipeds, with some researchers believing them to be a subfamily within Ursidae. They are known to have lived from the Late Eocene to Early Miocene in North America and Eurasia.

AMPHICYNODON LEPTORHYNCHUS

NAME MEANING: Slender snouted double dog tooth

AGE: Early Oligocene (34–30 MYA)

DISTRIBUTION: Eurasia

SIZE: About marten-sized

DIET: Mesocarnivore

ESSENTIAL FACTS: A terrestrial predator that probably hunted invertebrates and small vertebrates in wetland and marsh environments similar to modern marsh mongoose (*Atilax paludinosus*).

KOLPONOMOS NEWPORTENSIS

NAME MEANING: Unknown

AGE: Early Miocene (20 MYA)

DISTRIBUTION: North America

SIZE: 130–176 pounds (60–80 kilograms)

DIET: Aquatic hypercarnivore

ESSENTIAL FACTS: A unique animal that inhabited the Pacific coast of North America, Kolponomus had powerful jaws and enlarged molars well-suited for a diet of hard-shelled mollusks, which it would pry from the seafloor and off rocks using its huge neck muscles.

SEMANTORIDAE

Semantorids were otter-like carnivorans adapted to a semiaquatic lifestyle in freshwater environments. With their elongated bodies, strong limbs, and long tails that could aid in propulsion, they were initially thought to be otters until researchers realized the creatures were early pinnipeds.

PUIJILA DARWINI

NAME MEANING: Charles Darwin's young sea mammal

AGE: Early Miocene (23–20 MYA)

DISTRIBUTION: North America

SIZE: About otter-sized

DIET: Aquatic hypercarnivore

ESSENTIAL FACTS: The genus name is an Inuktitut word for a "young seal," a reference to its status as the oldest-known pinniped. A complete skeleton of this animal discovered in Nunavut, Canada, is housed at the Canadian Museum of Nature in Ottawa, Ontario.

PRISTINAILURUS BRISTOLI

ESSENTIAL FACTS: Together with the Woodland Badger (*Arctomeles dimolodontus*), Bristol's Panda is the most commonly occurring small carnivoran found at the Gray Fossil Site. Several complete skeletons have been found, and much is known about its anatomy and paleobiology. Compared to the modern red panda (*Ailurus fulgens*), Bristol's Panda was much larger, more than twice the size. The skull was not as domed and lacked a sagittal crest, suggesting a relatively weaker bite. However, its snout was longer with larger incisors and canines. The upper carnassials were also longer with a more defined shearing surface, suggesting that it was not as dependent on plant matter as part of its diet. While it was still an agile and skillful climber, Bristol's Panda was more habitually terrestrial than the highly arboreal red panda, with proportionally shorter and more robust forelimbs and significantly longer hindlimbs.

With its broad paws featuring recurved semi-retractable claws along with a nimble body, Bristol's Panda was able to climb trees rapidly to exploit feeding opportunities or escape from threats on the ground. Its diet consisted of relatively small animals such as rodents and small birds, supplementing its diet with fruits. Males are known to have been considerably larger than the females.

SEE ENTRY ON PAGE 456

POTAMOTHERIUM VALLETONI

NAME MEANING: Valleton's river beast

AGE: Early Miocene (23–20 MYA)

DISTRIBUTION: Eurasia

SIZE: About otter-sized

DIET: Aquatic hypercarnivore

ESSENTIAL FACTS: Like modern pinnipeds, Valleton's Potamotherium possessed a dense array of long whiskers, which it used to track its prey through dark waters. Its sense of smell was poor while its hearing and vision were acute. It inhabited freshwater rivers and lakes like modern otters.

ENALIARCTIDAE

A family of transitional pinnipeds that had become better adapted for life in the ocean as opposed to freshwater ecosystems. It contains a single genus restricted to the early Miocene.

ENALIARCTOS EMLONGI

NAME MEANING: Douglas Emlong's sea bear

AGE: Early Miocene (23–22 MYA)

DISTRIBUTION: North America

SIZE: 200 pounds (90 kilograms)

DIET: Aquatic hypercarnivore

SEE MORE ON PAGES 462–463

DESMATOPHOCIDAE

Desmatophocids are directly descended from and contemporaneous to the enaliarctids, occurring in the fossil record from the Early to Late Miocene. Their fossils are mostly known from the north Pacific, particularly along the western coast of North America as well as Japan. They share similarities with both seals (Phocidae) and sea lions (Otariidae), especially in having large eyes that indicate a sight-based hunting method. They also possessed long and well-developed necks, which allowed flexible movements and quick direction changes when hunting and swimming. They also possessed unusually strong canines, thick jaws, and heavy skulls that indicate powerful bite forces.

ALLODESMUS GRACILIS

NAME MEANING: Slender other bond

AGE: Middle Miocene

DISTRIBUTION: Pacific Ocean

SIZE: 8 feet (2.4 meters) HBL; 790 pounds (360 kilograms)

DIET: Aquatic hypercarnivore

ESSENTIAL FACTS: Members of the genus *Allodesmus* were among the largest desmatophocids currently known, all specimens coming from California and Japan. They are also the most well-known members of the group, with complete skeletons on display at several museums.

ATOPOTARUS COURSENI

NAME MEANING: Coursen's strange seal

AGE: Middle Miocene

DISTRIBUTION: Pacific Ocean

SIZE: Unknown

DIET: Aquatic hypercarnivore

ESSENTIAL FACTS: The only known specimen of this animal is an incomplete articulated skeleton preserved in a slab of rock, consisting of most of the upper body. It is housed at the Natural History Museum of Los Angeles County and was discovered in 1952 by the Coursen family, on their property in Palos Verdes.

ENALIARCTOS EMLONGI

ESSENTIAL FACTS: Before the establishment of the Semantidae, enaliarctids were thought to have been the oldest pinnipeds. Among the more notable differences from the ancestral semantids, the tail had become greatly reduced in size while the limbs expanded into paddles, which became its sole source of propulsion and steering. The limbs of enaliarctids were still capable of lifting the weight of the body fully off the ground and walking, albeit in a slow and ungainly manner. Enaliarctids retained slicing carnassials, although the pre-carnassial premolars had become simplified and homodont. In fact these premolars trended toward the condition seen in modern pinnipeds, which typically have peg-shaped teeth designed to grip fishes and other slippery or soft-bodied animals. Like the semantids, enaliarctids' sense of smell was reduced, and they depended more on their vision, hearing, and tactile sensation to hunt, navigate their environment, and to communicate. They had enlarged eyes, dense whiskers, and a specialized inner ear for underwater hearing. Like walruses, they utilized both sets of limbs were employed in swimming.

Like modern pinnipeds, Emlong's Enaliarctos was highly sexually dimorphic, with males being noticeably larger than the females with more robust canines. This suggests that, like modern sea lions, females would congregate in breeding colonies known as *rookeries*, with males attempting to defend these groups from other males.

SEE ENTRY ON PAGE 460

DESMATOPHOCA OREGONENSIS

NAME MEANING: Linked seal from Oregon

AGE: Middle Miocene

DISTRIBUTION: Pacific Ocean

SIZE: Unknown

DIET: Aquatic hypercarnivore

ESSENTIAL FACTS: Only two species of *Desmatophoca* are known, both from the Astoria Foundation, which extends to both Washington State and Oregon in the United States. Little is known about these animals except that they resembled modern sea lions in much of their feeding and social behaviors.

ODOBENIDAE

Containing a single modern species, the walruses were far more diverse and widespread during prehistory, distributed throughout the Pacific Ocean. The type genus *Odobenus* translates to "tooth-walker," referencing its behavior of using its long tusks to haul itself out of the water. Most fossil walruses lacked tusks and would have looked and behaved more like sea lions. The family's decline in diversity appears to coincide with an increase in the diversity of fur seals and sea lions. Most fossil walruses are known from incomplete remains.

NANODOBENUS ARANDAI

NAME MEANING: Aranda's little Odobenus

AGE: Middle Miocene (16–15 MYA)

DISTRIBUTION: Pacific Ocean

SIZE: Unknown

DIET: Aquatic hypercarnivore

ESSENTIAL FACTS: Aranda's Dwarf Walrus is the smallest species of walrus known to date, and probably would have looked more like a small fur seal than a walrus. It is known only from a complete left dentary described in 2018.

PRONEOTHERIUM REPENNINGI

NAME MEANING: Repenning's before *Neotherium*

AGE: Early Miocene (20–15 MYA)

DISTRIBUTION: Pacific Ocean

SIZE: Unknown

DIET: Aquatic hypercarnivore

ESSENTIAL FACTS: Repenning's Walrus is only known from the Astoria Formation of Lincoln County, Oregon. Little of the skeleton has been found, but it is known from a complete lower jaw that resembles that of modern piscivorous pinnipeds.

PROTOTARIA PRIMIGENA

NAME MEANING: Original before *Otaria*

AGE: Middle Miocene (16–13 MYA)

DISTRIBUTION: Pacific Ocean

SIZE: Unknown

DIET: Aquatic hypercarnivore

ESSENTIAL FACTS: This species is known from a complete skull discovered in southwestern Japan and described in 1984. Its features are similar to those of *Enaliarctos*, such as the retention of shearing carnassials, though this species is notably more slender.

ARCHAEODOBENUS AKAMATSUI

NAME MEANING: Morio Akamatsu's ancient Odobenus

AGE: Late Miocene

DISTRIBUTION: Pacific Ocean

SIZE: 10 feet (3 meters) HBL; 1,042 pounds (473 kilograms)

DIET: Aquatic hypercarnivore

ESSENTIAL FACTS: A partial skeleton of this walrus was discovered in 1977 in Japan's Tobetsu Town, Hokkaido, and formally described in 2015. It was about the size of the largest modern sea lions.

NEOTHERIUM MIRUM

NAME MEANING: Wonderful new beast

AGE: Middle Miocene (15 MYA)

DISTRIBUTION: Pacific Ocean

SIZE: Unknown

DIET: Aquatic hypercarnivore

ESSENTIAL FACTS: This species was described in 1931 based on limb bones collected in California. The skull, which was described later, is relatively long and narrow and is indicative of a piscivorous diet.

TITANOTARIA ORANGENSIS

NAME MEANING: Giant *Otaria* from Oregon

AGE: Late Miocene (6–5 MYA)

DISTRIBUTION: Pacific Ocean

SIZE: 10 feet (3 meters) HBL; 1,200 pounds (540 kilograms)

DIET: Aquatic hypercarnivore

ESSENTIAL FACTS: Most of the skeleton of this species is known, yet only the skull and lower jaw is described in a 2018 study. The specimen was discovered in Orange County, California. Titanotaria grew to the size of the largest modern sea lions.

PONTOLIS BARRONI

NAME MEANING: Barron's great sea

AGE: Late Miocene (11.6–5 MYA)

DISTRIBUTION: Pacific Ocean

SIZE: 13 feet (4 meters) HBL; 4,400–8,800 pounds (2,000–4,000 kilograms)

DIET: Aquatic hypercarnivore

ESSENTIAL FACTS: Barron's Walrus is the largest fossil walrus yet known, being the size of a modern southern elephant seal (*Mirounga leonine*). It may have been adapted to hunt fish and squid at very deep depths.

PELAGIARCTOS THOMASI

NAME MEANING: Thomas' oceanic bear

AGE: Middle Miocene (16–13 MYA)

DISTRIBUTION: Pacific Ocean

SIZE: 7–10 feet (2.5–3 meters) HBL

DIET: Aquatic hypercarnivore

ESSENTIAL FACTS: Thomas' Walrus is unique among the family in being adapted to hunt large prey items. It had unusually robust and thick jaws with massive teeth. It may have been ecologically similar to the modern leopard seal (*Hydrurga leptonyx*), which hunts other marine mammals among other prey items.

IMAGOTARIA DOWNSI

NAME MEANING: Down's likeness of Otaria

AGE: Late Miocene (12–10 MYA)

DISTRIBUTION: Pacific Ocean

SIZE: 7–10 feet (2.5–3 meters)

DIET: Aquatic hypercarnivore

ESSENTIAL FACTS: Down's Walrus was the first member of the family to show enlarged upper canine teeth, although not nearly as long as those of the modern species. Also, its teeth indicate that it still depended on fish as its primary food source and not mollusks.

AIVUKUS CEDROSENSIS

NAME MEANING: Walrus from Cedros Island

AGE: Late Miocene (7–5 MYA)

DISTRIBUTION: Pacific Ocean

SIZE: 4,400 pounds (2,000 kilograms)

DIET: Aquatic hypercarnivore

ESSENTIAL FACTS: The genus name is derived from the Inuit word for walrus, *aivuk*. It was about the same size of the modern walrus (*Odobenus rosmarus*) and may have also been a molluscivore. However, it had not yet evolved tusks.

GOMPHOTARIA PUGNAX

NAME MEANING: Combative nail *Odobenus*

AGE: Late Miocene (7.2–5.3 MYA)

DISTRIBUTION: Pacific Ocean

SIZE: Unknown

DIET: Aquatic hypercarnivore

ESSENTIAL FACTS: The Nail Walrus was built much like a sea lion but was much larger. Both its upper and lower canines were enlarged instead of just the uppers. It seems to have been a molluscivore that relied on crushing their prey rather than sucking them out of their shells.

VALENICTUS IMPERIALENSIS

NAME MEANING: Imperial strong weasel

AGE: Pliocene

DISTRIBUTION: Pacific Ocean

SIZE: Unknown

DIET: Aquatic hypercarnivore

ESSENTIAL FACTS: This unusual walrus had large tusks similar to those of the modern species. However, the rest of its mouth was completely toothless.

OTARIIDAE

There are fifteen modern species of sea lions and fur seals, which are distinguished from seals (Phocidae) by their proportionally larger forelimbs used to propel themselves through the water. They are also able to turn their hindlimbs forward to walk, albeit in a slow waddling gait. This trait is unlike that of seals, which have backward-facing hindlimbs and must crawl on their bellies. Otariidae are sometimes referred to as the "eared seals" for their retention of highly reduced external ears. The name *Otaria* comes from the Greek word *otarion*, meaning "little ear." These pinnipeds appear during the Middle Miocene in the northern Pacific Ocean.

EOTARIA CRYPTA

NAME MEANING: Hidden dawn *Otaria*

AGE: Middle Miocene (17–15 MYA)

DISTRIBUTION: Pacific Ocean

SIZE: About otter-sized

DIET: Aquatic hypercarnivore

ESSENTIAL FACTS: The oldest-known fur seal, this species had previously been misidentified as a small walrus. It was a small pinniped only slightly larger than a sea otter (*Enhydra lutris*). Its teeth were intermediate in morphology between those of enaliarctids and later members of its family.

THALASSOLEON MEXICANUS

NAME MEANING: Mexican sea lion

AGE: Late Miocene (7–5 MYA)

DISTRIBUTION: Pacific Ocean

SIZE: 650–700 pounds (295–318 kilograms)

DIET: Aquatic hypercarnivore

ESSENTIAL FACTS: Like modern fur seals, these animals would have gathered in large colonies during breeding season and spent the rest of the year out in the open sea hunting moderately sized fish and squid.

PHOCIDAE

The seals are arguably better adapted to marine life than sea lions, which lack external ears and have an overall more streamlined body shape. Seals first appear in the fossil record during the Late Oligocene or Early Miocene in the Atlantic Ocean. Seals swim by using their hind flippers for propulsion, while their front flippers are mostly used for steering. Most members of the family are able to dive at considerable depths, some rivaling even the deepest-diving whales. The largest modern carnivoran, the southern elephant seal (*Mirounga leonine*), is a member of this family.

KAWAS BENEGASORUM

NAME MEANING: Benegas' elephant seal

AGE: Middle Miocene (14–12 MYA)

DISTRIBUTION: Pacific Ocean

SIZE: 6 feet (1.8 meters)

DIET: Aquatic hypercarnivore

ESSENTIAL FACTS: The genus name comes from the Tehuelche word for the elephant seal. Preserved stomach contents show that its diet was mostly piscivorous.

NANOPHOCA VITULINOIDES

NAME MEANING: Calf-like little seal

AGE: Middle Miocene

DISTRIBUTION: Atlantic Ocean

SIZE: 3 feet (1 meter) HBL

DIET: Aquatic hypercarnivore

ESSENTIAL FACTS: Long thought to be a close relative of the harbor seal (*Phoca vitulina*), a 2017 study highlighted the uniqueness of this seal and erected the genus *Nanophoca* for its tiny size compared to modern seals. Its front flippers appear to have been particularly flexible, implying some special use.

PRAEPUSA BOESKA

NAME MEANING: Boes' before *Pusa*

AGE: Late Miocene to Pliocene (6–3 MYA)

DISTRIBUTION: Atlantic Ocean

SIZE: 3 feet (1 meter)

DIET: Aquatic hypercarnivore

ESSENTIAL FACTS: Named after seals of the genus *Pusa*, this species is notable for being the smallest-known fossil seal. Its fossils have been found in the Netherlands.

ACROPHOCA LONGIROSTRIS

NAME MEANING: Long-snouted high seal

AGE: Late Miocene (7–5 MYA)

DISTRIBUTION: Pacific Ocean

SIZE: 5 feet (1.5 meters)

DIET: Aquatic hypercarnivore

ESSENTIAL FACTS: Having the overall appearance of a stretched-out seal, this species had a notably long and flexible neck, which inspired the name "Swan-Necked Seal." Its skull and body were also elongated, with teeth adapted for piercing. It is thought to have inhabited shallow nearshore waters.

SARCODECTES MAGNUS

NAME MEANING: Great flesh-biter

AGE: Pliocene

DISTRIBUTION: Atlantic Ocean

SIZE: 9.3 feet (2.83 meters)

DIET: Marine hypercarnivore

ESSENTIAL FACTS: Sarcodectes is the largest known extinct monachine seal, comparable to the modern leopard seal (*Hydrurga leptonyx*). Its dentition is unique, as it was adapted to shear flesh rather than to simply pierce as in most seals. Combined with its powerful jaws, it seems to have been adapted to attack relatively large prey items.

FELIFORMIA

The "cat-like carnivorans" are generally distinguishable from caniforms by their tendency to reduce the anterior premolars and posterior molars. This allowed for a lengthening of the carnassials, with more emphasis placed on the shearing component of the dentition. Having a reduced dentition often results in a shorter face and a stronger bite around the canine teeth. Most have claws that are semi-retractable or retractable for climbing or prey capture. Members tend to be mesocarnivorous or hypercarnivorous.

FEJFARICTIS VALECENSIS

NAME MEANING: Oldřich Fejfar's weasel from Valeč

AGE: Early Oligocene (30 MYA)

DISTRIBUTION: Eurasia

SIZE: About cat-sized

DIET: Hypocarnivore

ESSENTIAL FACTS: This species is known for a nearly complete jaw discovered in 2017 and was described in 2024. Based on the dentition, this animal was a small hypocarnivore that fed on fruits as well as small vertebrates. Its exact affinities with other feliforms are currently unknown.

NIMRAVIDAE

The nimravids are superficially cat-like carnivorans sometimes referred to as "false-cats." They branched off from a common ancestor with cats (Felidae) during the Middle Eocene and survived until the Late Miocene, being distributed throughout the Northern Hemisphere. To a modern observer a nimravid would have looked something like a cross between a cat and a gulonine mustelid. They had broad, shortened faces with sectoral dentition, retractable claws, with plantigrade or semi-digitigrade feet. Notably, included among the Nimravidae are the first saber toothed carnivorans.

NIMRAVINAE

Of all the nimravids, the nimravines show the most resemblance to modern cat species. They possess modestly sized upper canines with minimal, if any, flattening. Their fossils are common throughout the Middle Eocene to the Late Oligocene.

MAOFELIS CANTONENSIS

NAME MEANING: Maoming Basin cat from Canton

AGE: Late Eocene (40–36 MYA)

DISTRIBUTION: North America

SIZE: About lynx-sized

DIET: Hypercarnivore

ESSENTIAL FACTS: One of the oldest nimravids known from Asia, this species appears to exhibit the beginnings of sabertooth adaptations, with notable lengthening of the canines similar to that of the modern clouded leopard (*Neofelis nebulosa*).

DINICTIS FELINA

NAME MEANING: Double weasel cat

AGE: Late Eocene (37–34 MYA)

DISTRIBUTION: North America

SIZE: About lynx-sized

DIET: Hypercarnivore

ESSENTIAL FACTS: Dinictis grew to the size of a Eurasian lynx (*Lynx lynx*). One fossil records a violent interaction between this nimravid and the Horrid Hyaenodon (*Hyaenodon horridus*): a Dinictis skull with bite marks that match the teeth of the larger predator. This injury must have been fatal for the Dinictis, as these wounds show no signs of healing.

DINAELURUS CRASSUS

NAME MEANING: Thick double cat

AGE: Early Oligocene (30 MYA)

DISTRIBUTION: North America

SIZE: Unknown

DIET: Hypercarnivore

ESSENTIAL FACTS: Dinaelurus is unique among nimravids in its small, conical canines and its domed head with enlarged nasal passages. These features are also present in the cheetah (*Acinonyx jubatus*), and it has been inferred to have had similar hunting behaviors. Unfortunately, not enough postcranial remains are known to be able to confirm this hypothesis.

NIMRAVUS BRACHYOPS

NAME MEANING: Short-faced hunter

AGE: Oligocene (25 MYA)

DISTRIBUTION: North America

SIZE: 4 feet (120 centimeters) HBL

DIET: Hypercarnivore

ESSENTIAL FACTS: Two instances of violent confrontations involving this species are known from the fossil record. In one, a Nimravus skull has a healed puncture wound made by the upper canine of a Eusmilus. In the other, a Nimravus bit another individual in the arm so hard that its canine became stuck in its rival's humerus, killing both combatants.

POGONODON PLATYCOPIS

NAME MEANING: Flat knife beard tooth

AGE: Late Oligocene (25–23 MYA)

DISTRIBUTION: North America

SIZE: About jaguar-sized

DIET: Hypercarnivore

ESSENTIAL FACTS: Pogonodon is the largest nimravine known to date. It was a robust predator exhibiting moderate sabertooth adaptations. It would have hunted prey such as small rhinos and oreodonts of its time.

HOPLOPHOENINAE

The hoplophoenines are saber-toothed nimravids possessing elongated, laterally flattened upper canines that are matched in length by a protective flange on the lower jaw. Their forelimbs are more robust, enabling them to grapple and hold prey in position to land a killing bite to the neck.

EUSMILUS BIDENTATUS

NAME MEANING: Two-toothed true knife

AGE: Late Eocene to Early Oligocene (37–33 MYA)

DISTRIBUTION: Eurasia

SIZE: About leopard-sized

DIET: Hypercarnivore

ESSENTIAL FACTS: One of the more well-known nimravids from Eurasia, some of the best fossils from this species has been found in the Quercy phosphorite mines in France. Its sabertooth adaptations were particularly well-developed.

EUSMILUS ADELOS

NAME MEANING: Hidden true knife

AGE: Early Oligocene (34–32 MYA)

DISTRIBUTION: North America

SIZE: 245 pounds (111 kilograms)

DIET: Hypercarnivore

ESSENTIAL FACTS: This species was the largest hoplophoenine nimravid about the size of a jaguar (*Panthera onca*). A partial skeleton of this animal was discovered in Niobrara County, Wyoming, and was described in 2021. It was built to hunt quite large targes, such as rhinos, which at the time grew about the size of cattle.

HOPLOPHONEUS PRIMAEVUS

NAME MEANING: Ancient blade-wielding killer

AGE: Early Oligocene (34–30 MYA)

DISTRIBUTION: North America

SIZE: 350 pounds (160 kilograms)

DIET: Hypercarnivore

ESSENTIAL FACTS: This species was one of the better-known hoplophoenines, famed for its abundant skeletal material from the North American badlands. A fossil showing healed bite marks made by the saberteeth of another individual of the same species was found in Badlands National Park, South Dakota.

NANOSMILUS KURTENI

NAME MEANING: Kurten's little knife

AGE: Early Oligocene (34–30 MYA)

DISTRIBUTION: North America

SIZE: About bobcat-sized

DIET: Hypercarnivore

ESSENTIAL FACTS: Previously placed within the genus *Eusmilus*, this animal was one of the smallest saber-toothed predators to have ever lived. Despite being about the size of a bobcat (*Lynx rufus*), it was able to bring down prey items considerably longer than itself.

BARBOUROFELINAE

Barbourofelines occur from the Middle to Late Miocene. They were especially robust and heavily-built predators, with highly specialized skulls for delivering bites with their saberteeth. They were distributed throughout North America, Eurasia, and Africa.

SANSANOSMILUS PALMIDENS

NAME MEANING: Palm tooth knife from Sansan

AGE: Middle Miocene (14–11 MYA)

DISTRIBUTION: Eurasia

SIZE: 5 feet (1.5 meters) HBL; 176 pounds (80 kilograms)

DIET: Hypercarnivore

ESSENTIAL FACTS: This species is named for the Sansan paleontological site in France, where the best fossils of this species have been recovered. This leopard-sized predator was among the earliest-known barbourofelines, with moderately long saberteeth. It had a robust body with semi-plantigrade feet.

BARBOUROFELIS FRICKI

NAME MEANING: Frick's and Barbour's cat

AGE: Late Miocene (10–7 MYA)

DISTRIBUTION: North America

SIZE: 395–640 pounds (180–290 kilograms)

DIET: Hypercarnivore

SEE MORE ON PAGES 478–479

VIVERRIDAE

Viverrids are among the oldest of the feliform carnivorans, with a sparse fossil record dating back to the Late Eocene. Members of the group are generally cat- or fox-like in morphology, with unspecialized mesocarnivorous dentition and some having become adapted to hypocarnivory or hypercarnivory. Most are scansorial or arboreal forest-dwellers with retractable claws.

VIVERRA LEAKEYI

NAME MEANING: Leakey's ferret

AGE: Late Miocene

DISTRIBUTION: Africa

SIZE: 20–24 inches (50–60 centimeters) SH; 66–88 pounds (30–40 kilogram)

DIET: Hypercarnivore

ESSENTIAL FACTS: The dentition of Leakey's Civet is notably more sectoral than that of modern representatives of the genus, indicating a more actively carnivorous diet. It is also the largest viverrid known to date, about the size of a large dog.

BARBOUROFELIS FRICKI

ESSENTIAL FACTS: The first fossils of Frick's Barbourofelis, which included a beautifully complete skull and lower jaw as well as much of the skeleton, was collected in 1947 in Frontier County, Nebraska. It was not described until 1970. The genus was named in honor of American paleontologist Erwin Hinckley Barbour, who died a few days after the holotype was discovered, and the species after another paleontologist, Childs Frick.

In general, members of the genus *Barbourofelis* are powerfully built with physical attributes and movements comparable to that of a wolverine (*Gulo gulo*), only much larger. They are characterized, among other things, by the presence of a postorbital bar that fully encircles the eye in bone. They also exhibit extreme lengthening of the carnassials into even more efficient cutting tools. Frick's Barbourofelis is the last and largest species. Like the Saber-Toothed Cat (*Smilodon fatalis*), juveniles displayed a prolonged period of juvenile dependency and did not obtain their adult canines until they reached adult size. This suggests that these predators lived in small family units which worked together to secure prey far larger than themselves.

SEE ENTRY ON PAGE 477

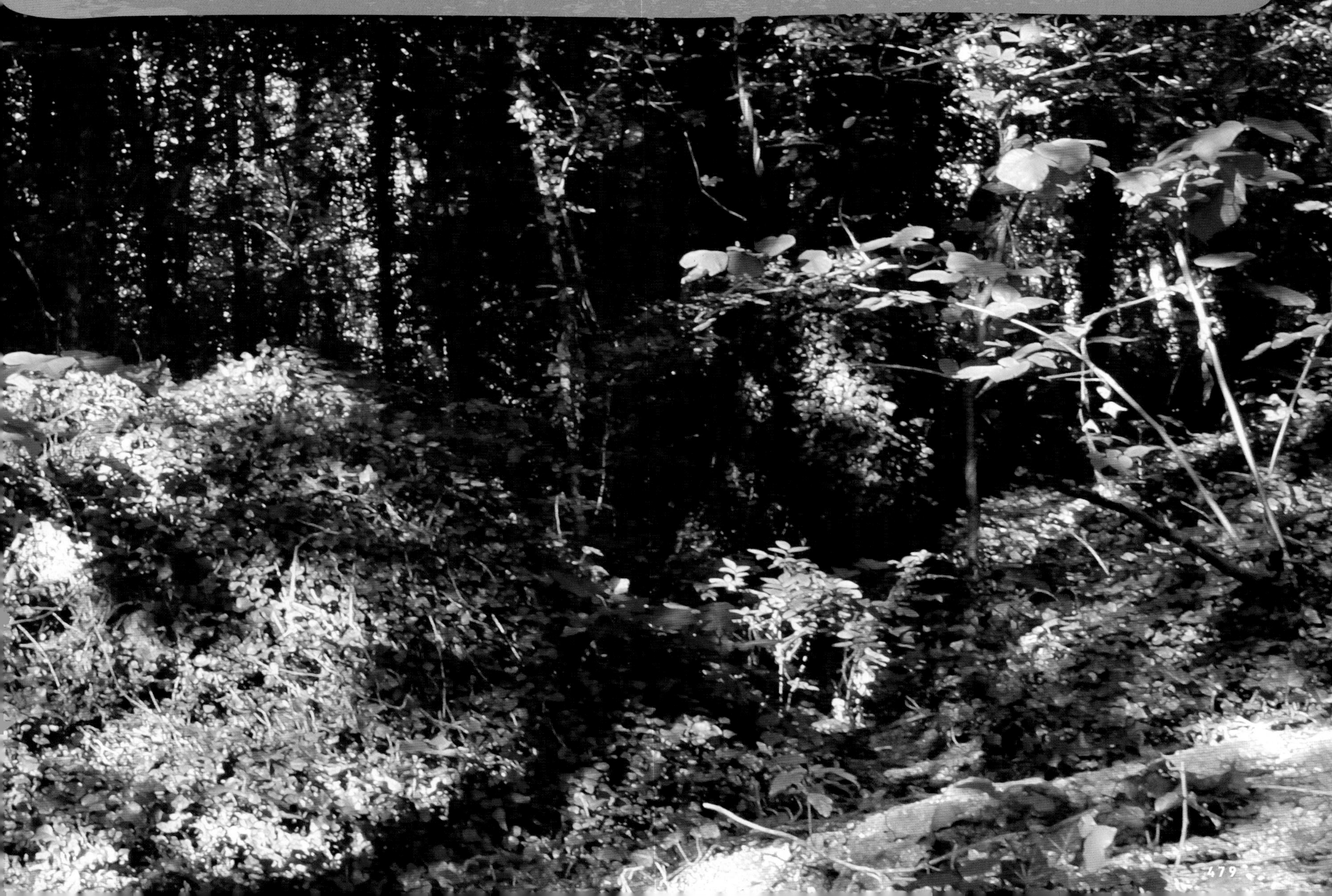

PERCROCUTIDAE

The percrocutids are a small group of hyena-like mesocarnivores that occur in the fossil record from the Middle Miocene to the Late Pliocene exclusively from Eurasia. They share many features in common with hyaenine hyenas, including robust premolars adapted for breaking bones, immensely powerful jaw muscles, forelimbs that were longer than the hindlimbs, and powerful neck and shoulder muscles. Though traditionally considered to be a distinct family, recent studies suggest that they should in fact be included among the Hyaenidae.

PERCROCUTA ABESSALOMI

NAME MEANING: Abessalom's pouch *Crocuta*

AGE: Middle Miocene

DISTRIBUTION: Eurasia

SIZE: 5 feet (1.5 meters) HBL; 155–200 pounds (70–90 kilograms)

DIET: Mesocarnivore

ESSENTIAL FACTS: Although capable of hunting its own prey, this species was a specialized scavenger that was able to make use of large carcasses even after most of the meat was gone. Its jaws and teeth were strong enough to break large bones to expose the nutritious marrow within.

DINOCROCUTA GIGANTEA

NAME MEANING: Giant terrible hyena

AGE: Late Miocene

DISTRIBUTION: Eurasia

SIZE: 6.2 feet (1.9) HBL; 440 pounds (200 kilograms)

DIET: Mesocarnivore

ESSENTIAL FACTS: This lion-sized animal was the largest of the percrocutids. While most of its meat would have come from scavenging, there is direct evidence of a failed predation attempt by this species; the skull of a female Wiman's Rhino (*Chilotherium wimani*) was found with healed bite wounds that match the jaws of Dinococuta.

HYAENIDAE

The evolution of Hyenas in the Old World mirrored that of canids in North America. The first hyenas appeared during the Early Miocene. They were mostly terrestrial animals that resembled mongooses or civets, with semi-retractable claws and retained the ability to climb trees. By the Middle Miocene, two distinct lineages of hyenas had emerged: the nimble-bodied dog-hyenas (Chasmaporthetiinae) and the robust bone-cracking hyenas (Hyaeninae). There are four surviving species of hyena. The highly specialized aardwolf (*Proteles cristatus*) is the last surviving member of the dog-like lineage, and the remaining three species belong to the bone-cracking group.

PROTICTITHERIUM CRASSUM

NAME MEANING: Thick before *Ictitherium*

AGE: Middle Miocene (16 MYA)

DISTRIBUTION: Eurasia

SIZE: 8–18 pounds (4–8 kilograms)

DIET: Mesocarnivore

ESSENTIAL FACTS: This species presented as a small, generalized hyena that would have been similar to a fox in its general ecology. It retained semi-retractable claws and was able to climb trees to escape danger. It would have hunted mostly on the ground, and its diet included small vertebrates, carrion, and fruits.

CHASMAPORTHETINAE

The dog-hyenas occupied the niches which today are filled by various canids like foxes, jackals, and wolves. They possessed relatively long, slender limbs and narrow paws adapted for active and sustained running. The group started to go into decline when canids began to colonize the Old World during the Late Miocene and continued to diversify there.

GANSUYAENA MEGALOTIS

NAME MEANING: Big-eared hyena from Gansu

AGE: Middle Miocene (15–12 MYA)

DISTRIBUTION: Eurasia

SIZE: About fox-sized

DIET: Mesocarnivore

ESSENTIAL FACTS: An early relative of the aardwolf (*Proteles cristatus*), the Big-Eared Hyena would have readily consumed small vertebrates and fruits. As its name suggests, its ears were large for detecting small prey among low vegetation.

ICTITHERIUM VIVERRINUM

NAME MEANING: Ferret-like weasel beast

AGE: Late Miocene (12–9 MYA)

DISTRIBUTION: Eurasia

SIZE: About coyote-sized

DIET: Mesocarnivore

ESSENTIAL FACTS: This hyena was an opportunistic predator that hunted a variety of small animals, occasionally taking larger prey in small groups, and would readily scavenge from carcasses while also consuming plant matter on occasion. Its closest modern ecological match was probably the jackal (*Lupulella*).

CHASMAPORTHETES OSSIFRAGUS

NAME MEANING: Bone-breaking chasm destroyer

AGE: Pliocene to Pleistocene

DISTRIBUTION: North America, Eurasia, Africa

SIZE: 40–80 pounds (18–36 kilograms)

DIET: Hypercarnivore

SEE MORE ON PAGES 484–485

HYAENINAE

The bone-crushing hyenas are specially adapted for scavenging, with large, broad skulls with enlarged, blunt premolars adapted to break open even very large bones. They were widespread throughout the Old World but never crossed into North America, possibly due to the presence of canids of the genus *Borophagus*.

ADCROCUTA EXIMIA

NAME MEANING: Extraordinary toward Crocuta

AGE: Late Miocene (10 MYA)

DISTRIBUTION: Eurasia, Africa

SIZE: 110–200 pounds (50–90 kilograms)

DIET: Mesocarnivore

ESSENTIAL FACTS: This species featured one of the first of the specialized bone-cracking hyenas, having evolved the tall forelimbs and shorter hindlimbs to facilitate long-distance jogging and carry large pieces of carcasses. Its premolars had become larger and stronger specifically to break bones.

PACHYCROCUTA BREVIROSTRIS

NAME MEANING: Short-faced thick *Crocuta*

AGE: Pliocene to Pleistocene

DISTRIBUTION: Eurasia, Africa

SIZE: 240 pounds (110 kilograms)

DIET: Hypocarnivore

SEE MORE ON PAGES 486–487

CHASMAPORTHETES OSSIFRAGUS

ESSENTIAL FACTS: The type genus of the subfamily Chasmaporthetiinae, members of the genus *Chasmaporthetes* have been referred to as the "Running Hyenas" or "Hunting Hyenas" due to their long and slender limbs, which were adapted for active pursuit hunting over great distances. The only hyena known to have inhabited North America, the American Hunting Hyena, is known to have lived from northwestern Canada to as far south as Texas, Florida, and Mexico. Furthermore, this species may be synonymous with the Eurasian Hunting Hyena (*C. lunensis*), thus representing a single wide-ranging species with an intercontinental distribution not unlike the modern gray wolf (*Canis lupus*).

The size and body proportions of the American Hunting Hyena suggest a lifestyle similar to that of the modern painted dog (*Lycaon pictus*). It hunted medium- to large-sized mammals in packs, which it would have chased to exhaustion before eating it alive. As with most of the dog-hyenas, this species' teeth do not show any adaptations for consistent bone-breaking. Rather, the dentition was highly sectoral, more like that of a cat, showing that these hyenas focused more on quickly stripping the flesh from carcasses. Favoring open grassland and lightly wooded habitats, potential prey items of the American Hunting Hyena included deer, camels, and horses.

SEE ENTRY ON PAGE 482

PACHYCROCUTA BREVIROSTRIS

ESSENTIAL FACTS: The Giant Short-Faced Hyena is the largest-known species of hyena and the most well-researched member of the genus *Pachycrocuta*. It grew to the size of a small lion (*Panthera leo*) with all the typical attributes of hyaenine hyenas. The skull was large, tall, and broad with massive, blunt premolars adapted for breaking large bones. The forelimbs were longer than the hindlimbs, giving the animal a sloping back. Powerful neck and shoulder muscles enabled these hyenas to carry large carcasses or pieces of carcasses for long distances.

The Giant Short-Faced Hyena's diet included fruits, and it would have opportunistically hunted small- to medium-sized mammals. However its primary source of nutrition would have been large carcasses of ungulates and proboscideans. It was able to feed on carcasses in varying stages of decomposition, consuming not just the flesh but also the bones, skin, and ligaments. Its stomach acids were strong enough to kill harmful pathogens found in rotting meat and fully digest bones, so much so that its dung would have had a high calcium content, appearing white and chalky. It would frequently scavenge from kills made by large canids and cats, likely able to challenge predators up to the size of Dirk-Toothed Cats (*Megantereon cultridens*) or Scimitar Cats (*Homotherium latidens*) in one-on-one confrontations relying on its loose skin, long fur, and large size for defense.

SEE ENTRY ON PAGE 483

STENOPLESICTIDAE

Stenoplesictids are a poorly understood group of small-bodied basal feliforms similar to modern linsangs (Prionodontidae). Their dentition shows that they were mesocarnivorous or hypercarnivorous and are potentially ancestral to other filiform groups like cats (Felidae) and nimravids (Nimravidae). They appear in the fossil record during the Eocene.

PALAEOPRIONODON LALANDI

NAME MEANING: Laland's ancient *Prionodon*

AGE: Middle Oligocene

DISTRIBUTION: Eurasia

SIZE: About cat-sized

DIET: Hypercarnivore

ESSENTIAL FACTS: This species is known for beautifully preserved specimens from Quercy, France. Its skull and teeth were similar to that of a genet (*Genetta*), and its diet consisted of small mammals, birds, insects, and possibly some fruits.

STENOPLESICTIS CAYLUXI

NAME MEANING: Cayluxi's narrow *Plesictis*

AGE: Early Oligocene (34–30 MYA)

DISTRIBUTION: Eurasia

SIZE: About cat-sized

DIET: Hypercarnivore

ESSENTIAL FACTS: A skull and several preserved dentaries of this species have been collected from Quercy and are housed at the Museum of Natural History in Paris. The teeth and jaws of this species are relatively robust.

MOGHRADICTIS NEDJEMA

NAME MEANING: Sweet weasel from Wadi Moghra

AGE: Early Miocene (23–20 MYA)

DISTRIBUTION: Africa

SIZE: About cat-sized

DIET: Hypercarnivore

ESSENTIAL FACTS: The species name comes from the ancient Egyptian word *nedjem*, which means "sweet one," and is also the name of the pet cat of Pharaoh Thutmosis III.

ASIAVORATOR GRACILIS

NAME MEANING: Slender Asian devourer

AGE: Early Oligocene (34–31 MYA)

DISTRIBUTION: Eurasia

SIZE: 8–13 pounds (3.6–5.6 kilograms)

DIET: Hypercarnivore

ESSENTIAL FACTS: The first fossils of Asiavorator were collected in the 1922 field season of the Central Asiatic Expeditions of the American Museum of Natural History and were described in 1995. The morphology of the limbs and teeth suggest that it was a scansorial mesocarnivore.

ANICTIS SIMPLICIDENS

NAME MEANING: Simple toothed non-weasel

AGE: Early Oligocene (33–28 MYA)

DISTRIBUTION: Eurasia

SIZE: About cat-sized

DIET: Hypercarnivore

ESSENTIAL FACTS: This species was another stenoplesicted from Quercy, France. It is known to have been contemporaneous with the smaller and less predatory Fejfarictis (*Fejfarictis valecensis*).

AFRICANICTIS MEINI

NAME MEANING: Pierre Mein's African weasel

AGE: Middle Miocene (17–16 MYA)

DISTRIBUTION: Africa

SIZE: About cat-sized

DIET: Hypercarnivore

ESSENTIAL FACTS: Mein's Africanictis and the larger Hyaena Africanictis (*A. hyaenoides*) are known from Arrisdrift, Namibia. These little predators appear to have been terrestrial with moderate cursorial capabilities, their limb proportions being comparable to those of foxes.

FELIDAE

All cats are hypercarnivores with highly sectoral cheek teeth. They have powerful jaws and shortened faces caused by the loss of the anterior premolars and the posterior molars. This shortening of the face enables a more efficient killing bite by directing the main force of the jaws to the canine teeth. Most species have curved, well-developed claws that are able to retract into protective sheathes to preserve the tips. The oldest cats appear in the fossil record during the Early Oligocene and have dominated the large-predator niches from the Late Miocene onward.

PROAILURUS LEMANENSIS

NAME MEANING: Leman's dawn cat

AGE: Middle Oligocene (30 MYA)

DISTRIBUTION: Eurasia

SIZE: 20 pounds (9 kilograms)

DIET: Hypercarnivore

ESSENTIAL FACTS: Regarded as the earliest known member of the cat family, the skeletal proportions of this animal suggest that it was an agile predator that would chase arboreal prey through the forest canopy, very much like the modern fossa (*Cryptoprocta ferox*) of Madagascar.

FELINAE

Felines are defined as cats that do not have an ossified hyoid bone in their throats, which allows them to purr but does not permit roaring. Most felines are small, less than 50 pounds (23 kilograms), although a few species have exceeded this threshold and evolved to fill midsized predator niches.

NAMAFELIS MINOR

NAME MEANING: Lesser Namibian cat

AGE: Middle Miocene (17.5–16 MYA)

DISTRIBUTION: Africa

SIZE: 20 pounds (9 kilograms)

DIET: Hypercarnivore

ESSENTIAL FACTS: One of the oldest cats known from Africa, Namafelis was a small predator that would have focused on rodents as its primary prey source, with the occasional inclusion of larger animals such as rabbits and hyraxes.

HYPERAILURICTIS INTREPIDUS

NAME MEANING: Fearless excessive cat

AGE: Middle Miocene (16–13 MYA)

DISTRIBUTION: North America

SIZE: About leopard-sized

DIET: Hypercarnivore

ESSENTIAL FACTS: One of the first cats to inhabit North America, this leopard-sized predator is known to have been distributed throughout the western United States.

LEPTOFELIS VALLESIENSIS

NAME MEANING: Vallesian slender cat

AGE: Late Miocene (11–9 MYA)

DISTRIBUTION: Eurasia

SIZE: 15–20 pounds (7–9 kilograms)

DIET: Hypercarnivore

ESSENTIAL FACTS: This species was similar to a modern serval (*Leptailurus serval*) or caracal (*Caracal caracal*), with its long and slender legs adapted for leaping. It likely hunted rodents and birds among tall grasses and bushes.

MIOPANTHERA LORTETI

NAME MEANING: Lortet's lesser *Panthera*

AGE: Late Miocene (10 MYA)

DISTRIBUTION: Eurasia

SIZE: About lynx-sized

DIET: Hypercarnivore

ESSENTIAL FACTS: Formerly placed in the genus *Pseudaelurus*, Lortet's Cat was about the size of a Eurasian lynx (*Lynx lynx*). It was a hunter of relatively small mammals like rodents, rabbits, and small artiodactyls.

PRATIFELIS MARTINI

NAME MEANING: Martin's field cat

AGE: Late Miocene

DISTRIBUTION: North America

SIZE: About leopard-sized

DIET: Hypercarnivore

ESSENTIAL FACTS: Martin's Field Cat was one of the oldest cats known to have lived in North America. It was about the size of a modern leopard (*Panthera pardus*) or cougar (*Puma concolor*), and like them it was a generalized predator that hunted a wide variety of small- to medium-sized prey.

MIRACINONYX TRUMANI

NAME MEANING: Truman's amazing Acinonyx

AGE: Pleistocene

DISTRIBUTION: North America

SIZE: 5 feet (180 centimeters) HBL; 150 pounds (70 kilograms)

DIET: Hypercarnivore

ESSENTIAL FACTS: This species is referred to as "the American Cheetah" for its superficial resemblance to the modern cheetah (*Acinonyx jubatus*). Its claws were retractable, however, and various lines of evidence suggest that it was not adapted to chase down its prey. Its closest modern relative is the cougar (*Puma concolor*).

ACINONYX PARDINENSIS

NAME MEANING: Non-moving claw from Pardin

AGE: Pliocene to Pleistocene

DISTRIBUTION: Eurasia

SIZE: 110–220 pounds (50–100 kilograms)

DIET: Hypercarnivore

ESSENTIAL FACTS: This species is commonly referred to as "the Giant Cheetah" for its superficial resemblance to the modern species, albeit twice the size. Like its namesake, it had elongated limbs and a flexible spine that undoubtedly enabled great agility. Its overall more robust skeleton suggests a markedly different hunting method, however.

LEOPARDUS VOROHUENSIS

NAME MEANING: Lion-Leopard from the Vorohué Formation

AGE: Pleistocene

DISTRIBUTION: South America

SIZE: About margay-sized

DIET: Hypercarnivore

ESSENTIAL FACTS: This species is the oldest-known cat of the genus *Leopardus*. It is likely that this species or a close relative migrated to South America and underwent an adaptive radiation in the continent, which lacked small cat-like predators at the time.

MACHAIRODONTINAE

Derived from the genus *Machairodus*, which means "dagger-tooth," the machairodonts are more commonly referred to as "the saber-toothed cats." These cats are characterized by their laterally flattened upper canines. Depending on the species or hunting method, these canines may be serrated along the edges or elongated beyond the extent seen in other cats. This elongation is accompanied by cranial adaptations, which allow the mouth to open wider. Usually, the upper canines are matched in length by a flange on the lower jaw against which they are sheathed.

YOSHI GAREVSKII

NAME MEANING: Risto Garevski's Yoshi

AGE: Late Miocene

DISTRIBUTION: Eurasia

SIZE: About cheetah-sized

DIET: Hypercarnivore

ESSENTIAL FACTS: The genus is named after the pet cat of Nikolai Spassov, one of the authors on the paper which described it. The skull is notably similar to that of a cheetah (*Acinonyx jubatus*), and it is hypothesized that this cat employed a similar high-speed hunting style.

DINOFELIS BARLOWI

NAME MEANING: Barlow's terrible cat

AGE: Pliocene to Pleistocene

DISTRIBUTION: Africa, Eurasia

SIZE: About jaguar-sized

DIET: Hypercarnivore

ESSENTIAL FACTS: This powerfully built, jaguar-sized cat is thought to have been a predator of early hominins such as *Australopithecus* and *Paranthropus*, although its primary prey items would have been medium- to large-sized ungulates. Its habitat was forest, woodland, and savanna.

MACHAIRODUS APHANISTUS

NAME MEANING: Unseen dagger tooth

AGE: Late Miocene

DISTRIBUTION: Africa, Eurasia

SIZE: 220–530 pounds (100–240 kilograms)

DIET: Hypercarnivore

ESSENTIAL FACTS: This cat was a large but agile predator with particularly good leaping capabilities and built very much like a modern tiger (*Panthera tigris*). It inhabited forest and open woodland habitats, where it hunted small- to medium-sized prey such as large deer, giraffids, and horses.

LOKOTUNJAILURUS EMAGERITUS

NAME MEANING: Clawed cat

AGE: Late Miocene (7 MYA)

DISTRIBUTION: Africa

SIZE: About wolf-sized

DIET: Hypercarnivore

ESSENTIAL FACTS: The oldest and smallest known scimitar-cat, this species had notable cursorial adaptations with long, slender legs and a relatively light skeleton. Like cheetahs (*Acinonyx jubatus*), its dewclaws were particularly large for tripping or holding onto its prey while it was running.

XENOSMILUS HODSONAE

NAME MEANING: Debra Hodson's strange knife

AGE: Late Pliocene to Early Pleistocene

DISTRIBUTION: North America, South America

SIZE: 6 feet (1.8 meters) HBL

DIET: Hypercarnivore

ESSENTIAL FACTS: Unlike other scimitar-toothed cats, which are cursorial, Xenosmilus was a heavily built animal that seems better suited to grapple with large prey items. With its serrated teeth, it was adapted to take bites out of prey while it was still struggling, causing death by blood loss.

HOMOTHERIUM LATIDENS

NAME MEANING: Wide-toothed same beast

AGE: Pliocene to Pleistocene

DISTRIBUTION: Eurasia, Africa, North America, South America

SIZE: 3.5 feet (1.1 meters) SH; 6 feet (1.8 meters) HBL; 420 pounds (190 kilograms)

DIET: Hypercarnivore

SEE MORE ON PAGES 498–499

PROMEGANTEREON OGYGIA

NAME MEANING: Before *Megantereon* from Ogygia

AGE: Late Miocene

DISTRIBUTION: Eurasia

SIZE: About leopard-sized

DIET: Hypercarnivore

ESSENTIAL FACTS: The Ogygia Cat was a nimble predator that hunted small- to medium-sized prey items from rabbits to antelopes.

MEGANTEREON CULTRIDENS

NAME MEANING: Knife-toothed great beast

AGE: Pliocene to Pleistocene

DISTRIBUTION: Eurasia, Africa, North America

SIZE: 200–330 pounds (90–150 kilograms)

DIET: Hypercarnivore

ESSENTIAL FACTS: This species was a widespread cat about the size and build of a modern jaguar (*Panthera onca*). It inhabited forests, woodlands, and savannas where it preyed on small- to large-sized ungulates and primates. There is also evidence of an aggressive interaction with Upright Man (*Homo erectus*): the cat's toothmarks on the ape's skull!

SMILODON FATALIS

NAME MEANING: Deadly knife tooth

AGE: Pleistocene to early Holocene (1 MYA–10,000 YA)

DISTRIBUTION: North America, South America

SIZE: 3–3.3 feet (90–100 centimeters) SH, 5–8 feet (1.5–1.8 meters) HBL, 352–617 pounds (160–280 kilograms)

DIET: Hypercarnivore

SEE MORE ON PAGES 500–501

SMILODON POPULATOR

NAME MEANING: Knife tooth that brings devastation

AGE: Pleistocene

DISTRIBUTION: South America

SIZE: 3.5–4 feet (1.1–1.2 meters) SH; 8 feet (2.5 meters) HBL; 485–960 pounds (220–436 kilograms)

DIET: Hypercarnivore

SEE MORE ON PAGES 502–503

PANTHERINAE

Pantherines are medium- to large-sized cats that are characterized by an ossified hyoid bone with elastic tendons that enables a wider range of vocalizations, most notably roars. The oldest pantherines occur in the fossil record in the Late Miocene.

HOMOTHERIUM LATIDENS

ESSENTIAL FACTS: The Scimitar Cat is potentially the most widely distributed large mammalian carnivore ever known. Specimens of *Homotherium* across Eurasia, Africa, and North America show minimal variation that falls within the range of modern animals with intercontinental distributions, suggesting that these animals represent a single wide-ranging species. Ancient DNA sequencing has shown that the scimitar-toothed cats (Homotherini) and dirk-toothed cats (Smilodontini) diverged about 18 million years ago.

The Scimitar Cat was a cursorial predator the size of a female lion (*Panthera leo*). Like lions, this cat lived and hunted in groups that actively targeted large mammals like horses and large bovids, as well as the juveniles of rhinos, proboscideans, and large sloths. With their serrated, blade-like teeth, Scimitar Cats were more efficient than lions at bringing down such prey items, cutting through their thick skin to sever blood vessels and tendons. A site called Friesenhahn Cave in Texas appears to have functioned as a multi-generational den-site which the local Scimitar Cats periodically used for shelter. Among other large prey items, the scattered remains of 400 juvenile mammoths and mastodons were found here, suggesting that after successful hunts the cats would dismember and carry pieces of their kills back to this cave to be consumed at leisure.

SEE ENTRY ON PAGE 496

SMILODON FATALIS

ESSENTIAL FACTS: Arguably the most famous of all fossil cats, the Saber-Toothed Cat is the second most common animal recovered from the La Brea Tar Pits after the Dire Wolf (*Aenocyon dirus*), with over 2,000 individuals recorded. This abundance is the reason this species is among the most well-studied and understood of all extinct carnivorans; much is known about the paleobiology and social behavior. The possibility that this cat formed some form of pack structure had long been speculated given the sheer volume of fossils uncovered from La Brea, which includes a range from very young juveniles to old adults. The presence of healed injuries and deformities on the skeletons of some individuals show that weakened individuals who were unable to hunt were allowed to feed from kills, a behavior observed among modern lions (*Panthera leo*).

There is minimal sexual dimorphism with Saber-Toothed Cats, a pattern which is typically present among carnivorans that exhibit monogamous breeding behavior or occur in mixed-sex groups. Juveniles also took longer to develop their adult dentition compared to more solitary cats of similar size, implying that a longer period of parental dependency was needed.

The Saber-Toothed Cat had a robust skeleton with particularly strong forelimbs and lower back, adaptations specialized for grappling with relatively large prey items. Its most notable feature, and the inspiration for both its common and scientific names, are its 8-inch (20-centimeter) upper canines, which are adapted to sever the neck arteries of their prey in a single bite, resulting in quick kills. Isotope studies have demonstrated that this cat may have preferred woodland habitats, where it would have hunted prey such as tapirs, large deer, llamas, musk oxen, and bison. This apparent preference for forest-dwelling prey shows that, although there was some overlap, Saber-Toothed Cats had minimal interspecific competition with Dire Wolves and Scimitar Cats (*Homotherium latidens*), which tended to hunt in more open environments.

SEE ENTRY ON PAGE 497

SMILODON POPULATOR

ESSENTIAL FACTS: The Southern Smilodon was described by Danish paleontologist, zoologist, and archeologist Peter Wilhelm Lund in 1842, making it the first of its genus known to science. In addition to being an overall larger animal, the Southern Smilodon has a more robust skeleton, with particularly sturdy forelimb bones compared to the more well-known cousin the Saber-Toothed Cat (*Smilodon fatalis*). The hindlimbs were slightly shorter but still strong and well-equipped for sudden bursts of energy. Overall, the body proportions are indicative of a predator that was not built for chasing prey in the way that lions (*Panthera leo*) and tigers (*P. tigris*) are known to do. Rather, they were highly adept at stalking prey as close as possible before pouncing on it within one or two bounds.

Southern Smilodon was a hunter of relatively large or slow-moving prey, most commonly targeting animals between 220–880 pounds (100–400 kilograms) but were able to handle prey as large as 2,200 pounds (1,000 kilograms) or more. The diet of this cat is relatively well-known, thanks to stable isotope analyses and was variable depending on region and the individual cat. Among its more common targets were the various types of medium-sized sloths and the juveniles of giants such as Panamerican Sloth (*Eremotherium laurillardi*) and Giant Sloth (*Megatherium americanum*). The large litoptern Macrauchenia (*Macrauchenia patachonica*) also appears to be a common target. Less common prey would have been the browsing horse Hippidion (*Hippidion principale*), juvenile gomphotheres, the large grazer Toxodon (*Toxodon platensis*), llamas, tapirs, pampatheres, and glypyodonts.

SEE ENTRY ON PAGE 497

PANTHERA BLYTHEAE

NAME MEANING: Paul and Heather Haaga's all-beast

AGE: Pliocene

DISTRIBUTION: Eurasia

SIZE: 60–80 pounds (27–37 kilograms)

DIET: Hypercarnivore

ESSENTIAL FACTS: This species is the oldest-known member of the genus *Panthera*. The only known specimen was smaller than any modern pantherine cat, closer in size to a clouded leopard (*Neofelis nebulosa*).

PANTHERA ATROX

NAME MEANING: Savage all-beast

AGE: Pleistocene

DISTRIBUTION: North America, South America

SIZE: 3.5–4 feet (1.1–1.2 meters) SH; 5.3–8.3 feet (1.6–2.5 meters) HBL; 518–880 pounds (235–400 kilograms)

DIET: Hypercarnivore

SEE MORE ON PAGES 506–507

PHOLIDOTAMORPHA

Pholidotamorphs are the group of mammals that includes the pangolins (Pholidota) and their extinct relatives, the palaeanodonts (Palaeanodonta). This group first appears during the Early Paleocene and show adaptations toward myrmecophagy: robust limbs and claws adapted for digging, and a reduced dentition with a sticky, protrusible tongue for gathering multiple small prey items per extension.

PALAEANODONTA

Like the pangolins, palaeanodonts were never very abundant in the fossil record. Many are known from relatively complete and articulated skeletons, suggesting that they were preserved in burrows. Members of this group, in fact, have skeletons that are highly specialized for digging. All species are characterized by short, very robust limbs, wedge-shaped heads with powerful neck muscles. Reduced incisors and a spout-like mandibular symphysis shows that these animals had protrusible tongues used in gathering colonial insects. All have prominent canine teeth.

ESCAVADODON ZYGUS

NAME MEANING: Yoked tooth of Escavada

AGE: Middle Paleocene (61–60 MYA)

DISTRIBUTION: North America

SIZE: About squirrel-sized

DIET: Myrmecophagous hypercarnivore

ESSENTIAL FACTS: This species is the oldest-known palaeanodont and the only member of the family Escavadodontidae. Although it had notable digging adaptations, these were less specialized than those of later palaeanodonts.

ERNANODONTIDAE

Ernanodonts were among the larger palaeanodonts with even more robust bodies that emphasize the fossorial adaptations observed in the rest of the group. There are currently only two described species from Asia during the Paleocene.

PANTHERA ATROX

ESSENTIAL FACTS: Commonly referred to as "the American Lion," this species was larger and more robust than true lions (*Panthera leo*) and may have been more solitary. Its relatively large skull and jaws show similarities to those of tigers (*P. tigris*) and jaguars (*P. onca*), suggesting a much stronger bite for its size. It was comparable in size to the Southern Smilodon (*Smilodon populator*) and may have been starting to adopt a similar ecological niche.

The American Lion was a young species, having diverged about 530,000 years ago. It was distributed throughout North America, with its range extending through South America to the west of the Andes Mountains where the Southern Smilodon appears to have been absent, instead inhabiting the lands east of the mountains. The American Lion's diet included medium- to large-sized herbivores such as deer, tapirs, horses, large bovids, and smaller sloths, as well as the juveniles of larger sloths and proboscideans. Dental microwear analyses have shown that they deliberately avoided biting bones when feeding, more like a cheetah (*Acinonyx jubatus*) but unlike modern lions, which are known to consume any bones small enough to be crunched in their jaws as they feed. Possible preserved pelt fragments of an American Lion found in a cave in Chile, and ancient rock art found in Argentina show that the coat was reddish in color on the back and became more yellowish in color on the sides and limbs.

At least 80 specimens have been located at Rancho La Brea, compared to the 2,000 Saber-Toothed Cat (*Smilodon fatalis*) and 4,000 Dire Wolves (*Aenocyon dirus*). This disparity in numbers suggests that the American Lion was less social than its contemporaries. The high degree of sexual dimorphism exhibited within this species is a feature that is typical of more solitary mammals or those in which males and females live separately from one another, hunting differently sized prey items to minimize competition for resources. Furthermore, male American Lions were highly territorial and were very aggressive toward each other, sometimes engaging in vicious battles over territory. Evidence for this behavior comes from the skulls of males which show bite damage inflicted by a member of the same species.

SEE ENTRY ON PAGE 504

ERNANODON ANTELIOS

NAME MEANING: Luminous sprout without teeth

AGE: Late Paleocene (62–56 MYA)

DISTRIBUTION: Asia

SIZE: 20 inches (50 centimeters) HBL

DIET: Myrmecophagous hypercarnivore

ESSENTIAL FACTS: One of the larger palaeanodonts, the skeleton of this animal is particularly well-adapted for fossoriality. The forelimb bones are massive with enlarged muscles and short, thick fingers with enlarged claws. Xenarthrous processes in the lower back provide stability. In life, the animal may have appeared somewhat top-heavy.

METACHEIROMYIDAE

Metacheiromyidae were a North American family of palaeanodonts that lived during the Paleocene and Eocene. Members of this family retained their post-canine dentition.

MYLANODON ROSEI

NAME MEANING: Kenneth Rose's molar without teeth

AGE: Late Paleocene (58–56 MYA)

DISTRIBUTION: North America

SIZE: Unknown

DIET: Myrmecophagous hypercarnivore

ESSENTIAL FACTS: The first juvenile dentition of a Paleocene-age palaeanodont is attributed to this species. Its fossils have been discovered in Clarks Fork Basin, Wyoming.

METACHEIROMYS MARSHI

NAME MEANING: Marsh's next to Cheiromys

AGE: Early Eocene (50–46.2 MYA)

DISTRIBUTION: North America

SIZE: 18 inches (45 centimeters) HBL

DIET: Myrmecophagous hypercarnivore

ESSENTIAL FACTS: This species is known for a complete skeleton. When it was first discovered, its bones were mistakenly thought to be of a primate similar to the aye-aye (*Daubentonia madagascariensis*), whose alternate genus name at the time was *Cheiromys*.

BRACHIANODON WESTORUM

NAME MEANING: Robert West's short without teeth

AGE: Middle Eocene (47–45 MYA)

DISTRIBUTION: North America

SIZE: Unknown

DIET: Myrmecophagous hypercarnivore

ESSENTIAL FACTS: This species was known from a nearly complete skeleton found in the Green River Basin in Wyoming. Unlike other metacheiromyids, the postcanine teeth retained an enamel coating and retained a distinct cusp morphology.

EPOICOTHERIIDAE

Epoicotheriidae were small, highly specialized diggers similar to moles (Talpidae), golden moles (Chrysochloridae), and marsupial moles (Notoryctidae). Possibly due to their specialization, they outlasted all other palaeanodont groups, occurring from the Late Paleocene into the Oligocene.

AMELOTABES SIMPSONI

NAME MEANING: George Simpson's enamel loss

AGE: Late Paleocene (58–56 MYA)

DISTRIBUTION: South America

SIZE: About mole-sized

DIET: Subterranean hypercarnivore

ESSENTIAL FACTS: The oldest known member of Epoicotheriidae, it is known from a nearly complete wedge-shaped skull that shows evidence of powerful neck muscles that would have helped when excavating burrows.

ALOCODONTULUM ATOPUM

NAME MEANING: Out of place tooth

AGE: Early Eocene (54–50 MYA)

DISTRIBUTION: North America

SIZE: About mole-sized

DIET: Subterranean hypercarnivore

ESSENTIAL FACTS: This species is most fossorially adapted mammal known from the Early Eocene of North America, with the oldest and most complete known skeleton referable to the family. It displays many of the fossorial adaptations present in later epoicotheriids, albeit less developed.

XENOCRANIUM PILEORIVALE

NAME MEANING: Strange skull from Hat Creek

AGE: Late Eocene (36–34 MYA)

DISTRIBUTION: North America

SIZE: About mole-sized

DIET: Hypercarnivore

ESSENTIAL FACTS: This mole-like animal had a distinctive wedge-shaped skull and upturned snout adapted to push dirt and the limbs were extremely robust. Its diet included a variety of subterranean invertebrates such as earthworms.

PHOLIDOTA

Early pangolins are very similar to palaeanodonts in overall skeletal anatomy, the one key difference being that the former are completely toothless. They may be directly descended from palaeanodonts after becoming specialized for a myrmecophagous diet. In addition to their toothless jaws, pangolins are characterized by their powerful forelimbs with long claws adapted for digging, a long tail that may be prehensile in more arboreal species, and having skin that is covered in large scales for protection. When threatened, pangolins roll themselves into balls which predators find difficult to penetrate.

EUROMANIS KREBSI

NAME MEANING: Krebs' European *Manis*

AGE: Middle Eocene (48–46 MYA)

DISTRIBUTION: Eurasia

SIZE: Unknown

DIET: Myrmecophagous hypercarnivore

ESSENTIAL FACTS: Complete and articulated skeletons of Krebs' Pangolin have been found at Messel Pit in Germany. It was formerly placed within the genus *Eomanis* until 2009.

EUROTAMANDUA JORESI

NAME MEANING: Jores' European Tamandua

AGE: Middle Eocene (48–46 MYA)

DISTRIBUTION: Eurasia

SIZE: About cat-sized

DIET: Myrmecophagous hypercarnivore

ESSENTIAL FACTS: When it was discovered, this species was misidentified as a European xenarthran due to its strong resemblance to modern anteaters of the genus *Tamandua*, and it was named accordingly. It was later recognized as an early pangolin, although it lacked the characteristic scales.

PATRIOMANIDAE

Patriomanidae were Eocene-age pangolins known from North America and Asia.

PATRIOMANIS AMERICANA

NAME MEANING: Father *Manis* from America

AGE: Late Eocene (37–34 MYA)

DISTRIBUTION: North America

SIZE: Unknown

DIET: Myrmecophagous hypercarnivore

ESSENTIAL FACTS: Known for a remarkably complete articulated skeleton, this species is the only pangolin known to have inhabited North America.

CRYPTOMANIS GOBIENSIS

NAME MEANING: Hidden *Manis* from the Gobi Desert

AGE: Late Eocene (42–40 MYA)

DISTRIBUTION: Eurasia

SIZE: 22 pounds (10 kilograms)

DIET: Myrmecophagous hypercarnivore

ESSENTIAL FACTS: The Hidden Pangolin differs from modern pangolins in having more robust upper limb elements and more slender hindfeet and tail. These features suggest that it was more of an active climber. Its name is in reference to the holotype being "hidden" in the collection of the American Museum of Natural History after its discovery in 1928. It was rediscovered and described in 2004.

EOMANIDAE

Members of this family are the oldest pangolins to preserve evidence of scale armor.

EOMANIS WALDI

NAME MEANING: Wald's dawn *Manis*

AGE: Middle Eocene (48–46 MYA)

DISTRIBUTION: Eurasia

SIZE: Unknown

DIET: Myrmecophagous hypercarnivore

ESSENTIAL FACTS: Despite its skull resembling those of modern pangolins in completely lacking teeth, gut contents observed in skeletons from Messel Pit show that its diet included plants as well as insects. These specimens also preserve scales similar to those of modern pangolins.

NECROMANIS FRANCONICA

NAME MEANING: Dead *Manis* from Franconia

AGE: Middle Miocene (16 MYA)

DISTRIBUTION: Eurasia

SIZE: Unknown

DIET: Myrmecophagous hypercarnivore

ESSENTIAL FACTS: A complete femur of this pangolin was found in the site of Can Cerda, Spain, and represents the earliest record of pangolins in the Iberian Peninsula. Its relationship with other fossil and modern pangolins is unknown.

MANIDAE

The only modern family of Pholidotamorpha, pangolins of the family Manidae are known from the Late Eocene and are distributed throughout Eurasia and Africa. There are eight modern species.

SMUTSIA OLTENIENSIS

NAME MEANING: Smuts' animal from Olt

AGE: Pleistocene

DISTRIBUTION: Eurasia

SIZE: 66 pounds (30 kilograms)

DIET: Myrmecophagous hypercarnivore

ESSENTIAL FACTS: The Olt Pangolin was very similar to its modern relatives, the giant pangolin (*S. gigantea*) and the ground pangolin (*S. temminckii*). Its fossils are known from the Oltet River valley of Romania.

MANIS PALAEOJAVANICA

NAME MEANING: Ancient Javan spirit

AGE: Pleistocene

DISTRIBUTION: Eurasia

SIZE: Unknown

DIET: Myrmecophagous hypercarnivore

ESSENTIAL FACTS: The Giant Asian Pangolin is one of the largest pangolin species known, being significantly larger than the largest modern species, the giant pangolin (*Smutsia gigantea*). Its fossils are discovered in Java and Malaysia.

EULIPOTYPHLA

The name Eulipotyphla means "truly fat and blind," possibly a reference to the generally rounded appearance and poor eyesight associated with moles. These animals were once included within the orders Insectivora or Lipotyphla alongside tenrecs, golden moles, and otter shrews. However, these are now understood to be part of the clade Afrotheria within the order Afrosoricida, and are thus unrelated, having evolved similar morphologies through convergent evolution. Eulipotyphla are a group of small, mostly insectivorous mammals that includes shrews (Soricidae), moles (Talpidae), and solenodons (Solenodontidae), among others. The earliest-known eulipotyphlan fossils are known from the Paleocene. However, molecular studies indicate that the order may have originated and began to diversify as early as 75 million years ago in the Late Cretaceous.

AMPHILEMURIDAE

Amphilemurids were a morphologically diverse group from the Eocene of North America and Eurasia. Many appear to have been cursorial animals, probably analogous to modern elephant shrews. At least one species, however, was a heavily-armored burrower.

MACROCRANION TUPAIODON

NAME MEANING: Treeshrew toothed big head

AGE: Early Eocene (48 MYA)

DISTRIBUTION: Eurasia

SIZE: About squirrel-sized

DIET: Mesocarnivore

ESSENTIAL FACTS: Known from complete skeletons from Messel Pit, we know that this species had a coat of woolly fur and a long, mobile snout. Short forelimbs and elongated hindlimbs show that it was a fast runner with particularly good leaping abilities. The morphology of its skull shows that it relied more on its sound, smell, and touch more than sight. The remains of fish, insects, and plant matter have been found in the stomach region.

MACROCRANION TENERUM

NAME MEANING: Delicate big head

AGE: Early Eocene (48 MYA)

DISTRIBUTION: Eurasia

SIZE: About mouse-sized

DIET: Mesocarnivore

ESSENTIAL FACTS: The smaller of the two species of *Macrocranion* to be found at Messel Pit, the Delicate Macrocranion was more slender of build. Its hindlimbs were much longer, its fur was also spikier, and ants have been found preserved in its stomach region.

PHOLIDOCERCUS HASSIACUS

NAME MEANING: Scaly tail from Hesse

AGE: Early Eocene (48 MYA)

DISTRIBUTION: Eurasia

SIZE: 1 foot (30 centimeters) HBL; 4 inches (10 centimeters) TL

DIET: Mesocarnivore

ESSENTIAL FACTS: An armored animal that combines features of hedgehogs and armadillos; its fur was spiny. Its head was covered by a helmet-like arrangement of scales, and the tail was covered with overlapping osteoderms down its entire length.

ZIONODON WALSHI

NAME MEANING: Stephen Walsh's Zion tooth

AGE: Early Eocene (45 MYA)

DISTRIBUTION: North America

SIZE: About squirrel-sized

DIET: Mesocarnivore

ESSENTIAL FACTS: One of two species from Utah, the genus being named for the homeland of the Latter-day Saints. The morphology of the forelimbs suggests moderate digging capabilities, while the hindlimbs are long and built for sprinting.

ERINACEIDAE

The Erinaceidae, the group which contains hedgehogs and gymnures, has the most well-known fossil record of any modern group of eulipotyphlans. They appear to have originated in North America during the Late Paleocene, although in modern times they occur only in Eurasia and Africa. Members of the group tend to be small mesocarnivores that feed on invertebrates and softer plants. Erinaceids are thought to have originated 64 million years ago.

LITOLESTES IGNOTUS

NAME MEANING: Strange smooth thief

AGE: Late Paleocene (55 MYA)

DISTRIBUTION: North America

SIZE: About rat-sized

DIET: Mesocarnivore

ESSENTIAL FACTS: The oldest-known erinaceid. Its fossils, mostly consisting of jaws and teeth, are known from Montana and Wyoming, suggesting that hedgehogs originated in North America despite being restricted to the Old World in modern times.

ERINACEINAE

The hedgehogs are prickly eulipotyphlans whose back and sides are covered in sharp quills. When threatened, hedgehogs roll themselves into a spiky ball for defense. They are known to have highly varied diets.

SILVACOLA ACARES

NAME MEANING: Small forest-dweller

AGE: Early Eocene (50 MYA)

DISTRIBUTION: North America

SIZE: 2–2.4 inches (5–6 centimeters) HBL

DIET: Mesocarnivore

ESSENTIAL FACTS: As referenced in its species name, it is the smallest erinaceid ever found, comparable in size to some of today's shrews. Its teeth suggest a mixed diet of both animal and plant matter for which it foraged on the forest floor.

GALERICINAE

Presently restricted to southeastern Asia, Gymnures were formerly diverse and widespread throughout Eurasia and North America with records in Africa during the Miocene. They are also known as hairy hedgehogs or moonrats.

EOGALERICIUS BUTLERI

NAME MEANING: Butler's dawn weasel

AGE: Middle Eocene (45 MYA)

DISTRIBUTION: Eurasia

SIZE: About

DIET: Mesocarnivore

ESSENTIAL FACTS: This species was the earliest member of the subfamily Galericinae, known from a partial skull and jaw found in Mongolia.

DEINOGALERIX KOENIGSWALDI

NAME MEANING: Koenigswald's terrible *Garerix*

AGE: Late Miocene (10–5 MYA)

DISTRIBUTION: Gargano Island

SIZE: 2 feet (60 centimeters)

DIET: Mesocarnivore

ESSENTIAL FACTS: The size of a small badger, this species was one of the largest-known eulipotyphlans matched only by Giant Solenodon (*Solenodon arredondoi*) of Cuba. It was the largest terrestrial mammalian carnivore on the former island of Gargano.

NESOPHONTIDAE

Known commonly as "the West Indian shrews," members of this family are endemic to the Caribbean islands. The family contains seven known species within the singular genus *Nesophontes*. They are known only from the Pleistocene and Holocene, having gone extinct as recently as 500 years ago. Their fossil and evolutionary history is unknown, although they appear to have diverged from the solenodons (Solenodontidae) about 40 million years ago.

NESOPHONTES HEMICINGULUS

NAME MEANING: Half-belted island murderer

AGE: Pleistocene to Holocene

DISTRIBUTION: Cayman Islands

SIZE: About rat-sized

DIET: Mesocarnivore

ESSENTIAL FACTS: The Cayman Nesophontes coexisted with the indigenous peoples of the Cayman Islands. They are thought to have become extinct after the arrival of rats and habitat destruction brought by European colonists in the sixteenth century.

SOLENODONTIDAE

Solenodons are venomous eulipotyphlans endemic to the Caribbean islands. The fossil record and evolutionary history of the family is unknown, although a possible relative was present on North America during the Oligocene.

SOLENODON ARREDONDOI

NAME MEANING: Arredondo's channel tooth

AGE: Pleistocene to Holocene

DISTRIBUTION: Cuba

SIZE: 2 feet (60 centimeters) HBL

DIET: Hypercarnivore

ESSENTIAL FACTS: The largest endemic mammalian predator on Cuba, the Giant Solenodon hunted many of the island's birds, reptiles, and amphibians. It coexisted with large predatory birds such as Cuban Giant Owl (*Ornimegalonyx oteroi*) and Suarez's Giant Eagle (*Gigantohierax suarezi*).

CHIROPTERA

The second largest mammalian order after the rodents (Rodentia), there are about 1,400 modern species of bats that account for 20 percent of all mammal species. These animals are one of three vertebrate groups that evolved powered flight, the others being pterosaurs and birds. They have lightweight skeletons with elongated arms and fingers which support a wing membrane; the name Chiroptera means "hand wing." The first bats in the fossil record occur during the Early Eocene and are fully recognizable as bats, complete with fully developed wings, the ability to echolocate, and had spread across all continents from North America and Eurasia to Australia. To date, no "transitional taxa" have been discovered that could link bats with another known mammalian group. Such an ancestor would have been an arboreal glider with a patagium stretching between its arms and legs.

ONYCHONYCTERIS FINNEYI

NAME MEANING: Bonnie Finney's clawed bat

AGE: Early Eocene (53–52 MYA)

DISTRIBUTION: North America

SIZE: 15 inches (37 centimeters) WS

DIET: Hypercarnivore

ESSENTIAL FACTS: This species is the most basal species of bat currently known. Claws are present on all five fingers; later bats would lose all but the thumb claw. Finney's Clawed Bat had not yet evolved the ability to echolocate, as evidenced by its small cochlea like that of diurnal, vision-oriented fruit bats.

ICARONYCTERIS GUNNELLI

NAME MEANING: Gregg Gunnell's Icarus bat

AGE: Early Eocene (53–52 MYA)

DISTRIBUTION: North America

SIZE: 15 inches (37 centimeters) WS

DIET: Hypercarnivore

ESSENTIAL FACTS: Both North American species of *Icaronycteris* are known from complete skeletons from the Green River Formation. They coexisted with Finney's Clawed Bat (*Onychonycteris finneyi*), but all finger claws are absent except for the thumb and index finger. They are the most well-known members of Icaronycteridae.

PALAEOCHIROPTERYX TUPAIODON

NAME MEANING: *Tupaia* toothed ancient hand wing

AGE: Middle Eocene (48–45 MYA)

DISTRIBUTION: Eurasia

SIZE: 0.24–0.35 ounces (7–10 grams); 9.8–12 inches (25–30 centimeters) WS

DIET: Hypercarnivore

SEE MORE ON PAGES 522–523

PALAEOCHIROPTERYX TUPAIODON

ESSENTIAL FACTS: Two species of *Palaeochiropteryx* account for 75 percent of the bat fossils found at Messel Pit in Germany, and are collectively the most common mammals from the site overall. The complete skeletons found here are exquisitely preserved and show evidence of fur, wing membranes, and stomach contents. Like other early bats, they retained claws on their index fingers in addition to their thumbs. They are the most well-known and well-studied bats in the family Palaeochiropterygidae.

The Treeshrew Bat shared its habitat with the slightly larger Spiegel's Bat (*P. spiegeli*). Analyses of the melanosomes preserved in the hairs of both species show that these bats were brown in color like most modern bats. They had broad wings adapted for hunting among the canopy of dense forests. Other bats found at Messel Pit have longer, narrower wings suggesting that they hunted above the canopy, partially explaining their relative lack of abundance. Preserved stomach contents indicate that the diet consisted mostly of moths and caddisflies. Enlarged cochlea indicates that *Palaeochiropteryx* and other early bats were able to echolocate.

SEE ENTRY ON PAGE 521

ARCHAEONYCTERIS POLLEX

NAME MEANING: Thumbed ancient bat

AGE: Middle Eocene (48–45 MYA)

DISTRIBUTION: Eurasia

SIZE: 0.24–0.35 ounces (7–10 grams)

DIET: Hypercarnivore

ESSENTIAL FACTS: Another of the bats found at Messel Pit, this species had longer, narrower wings than the more common *Palaeochiropteryx* species. These wings were adapted for fast flight above the forest canopy or over bodies of water, where this species would chase down fast-flying insects. It is the best-known species in the family Archaeonycteridae.

AUSTRALONYCTERIS CLARKAE

NAME MEANING: Elaine Clark's Australian bat

AGE: Early Eocene (55–54 MYA)

DISTRIBUTION: Australia

SIZE: Unknown

DIET: Hypercarnivore

ESSENTIAL FACTS: Clark's Bat is the oldest bat species known from Australia. The simultaneous presence of bats in North America, Eurasia, and Australia implies that bats had already been present for a long time and were capable of powered flight well before the Early Eocene.

HIPPOSIDERIDAE

There are over seventy modern species of Old-World, leaf-nosed bats. The oldest fossils attributed to the family are from the Middle Eocene of Europe. These bats are distinguished by an elaborate, fleshy nasal structure that assists in echolocation.

RIVERSLEIGHA WILLIAMSI

NAME MEANING: Stephan William's Riversleigh

AGE: Early Miocene (19 MYA)

DISTRIBUTION: Australia

SIZE: Unknown

DIET: Hypercarnivore

ESSENTIAL FACTS: William's Leaf-Nosed Bat was one of the largest bats found at Riversleigh, surpassed in size only by the ghost bats (*Macroderma*) from the site. Its robust teeth and powerful jaws were specialized to feed upon hard-shelled insects such as beetles.

XENORHINOS HALLI

NAME MEANING: Hall's strange nose

AGE: Early Miocene (19 MYA)

DISTRIBUTION: Australia

SIZE: Unknown

DIET: Hypercarnivore

ESSENTIAL FACTS: Hall's Bat is the second of two species of Old-World, leaf-nosed bat found at the Riversleigh World Heritage Area. Its genus name references its unusual shortened palate, broad rostrum, and other unique cranial proportions that other members of the family lack.

HIPPOSIDEROS BOUZIGUENSIS

NAME MEANING: Horseshoe from Bouzigues

AGE: Early Miocene (19 MYA)

DISTRIBUTION: Eurasia

SIZE: Unknown

DIET: Hypercarnivore

ESSENTIAL FACTS: The Bouzigues Roundleaf Bat had broad wings suited for maneuvering among the branches when hunting insects in forests.

MEGADERMATIDAE

The false vampire bats are so named because it was once believed that some of its members were sanguivorous (blood-feeding) like true vampire bats (*Desmodus*). They are relatively large compared to most other bats with massive, ridged ears and a prominent nose leaf that aids in echolocation. The family contains the only bats known to preferentially feed on small vertebrate prey, including other bats.

MACRODERMA GODTHELPI

NAME MEANING: Godthelp's long skin

AGE: Early Miocene (19 MYA)

DISTRIBUTION: Australia

SIZE: Unknown

DIET: Hypercarnivore

ESSENTIAL FACTS: Godthelp's Ghost Bat was a predatory bat that hunted small reptiles, birds, and mammals in the forests of Riversleigh. Compared to the ghost bat (*Macoderma gigas*), the only modern member of the genus, it was slightly smaller and had a longer face, suggesting a relatively weaker bite force.

MACRODERMA KOPPA

NAME MEANING: Koppa with long skin

AGE: Pliocene (5–2.5 MYA)

DISTRIBUTION: Australia

SIZE: 2.6–5.1 ounces (75–145 grams)

DIET: Hypercarnivore

ESSENTIAL FACTS: The Koppa Ghost Bat had powerful jaws with proportionally larger incisors and premolars than the modern species, possibly indicating a tendency toward larger prey items. It is named after a mythological cave spirit from native folklore known as the Koppa.

MOLOSSIDAE

The free-tailed bats are the fourth-largest family of bats containing 110 modern species. They have relatively robust bodies with relatively long, narrow wings that enable them to take advantage of tailwinds at altitudes over 10,000 feet. They are the only bats capable of flying at such heights. Thus, these bats have been compared to swifts and swallows, which are also notorious for high-altitude flying. Their fossil record extends back to the late Eocene.

TADARIDA STEHLINI

NAME MEANING: Stehlin's bat

AGE: Middle Miocene (16 MYA)

DISTRIBUTION: Eurasia

SIZE: 0.25–0.42 ounces (7–12 grams)

DIET: Hypercarnivore

ESSENTIAL FACTS: Like modern free-tailed bats, Stehlin's Free-tailed Bat flew at high heights, chasing fast-flying insects with its mouth opened wide. They were relatively proficient walkers and, unlike other bats, rested by clinging to vertical surfaces instead of by hanging upside down by their hindfeet.

MINIOPTERIDAE

Bent-winged bats are small bats typically weighing less than 20 grams. They have broad, short snouts with tall, bulbous craniums. Unlike other bats, they lack a tendon-locking mechanism in their toes. The name "bent-winged bat" refers to the group's ability to fold back an exceptionally long third finger when the wings are folded. This finger gives the bats long, narrow wings that enable high-speed flight in open environments.

MINIOPTERUS ZAPFEI

NAME MEANING: Helmuth Zapfe's small wing

AGE: Middle Miocene (16–13 MYA)

DISTRIBUTION: Eurasia

SIZE: 0.25–0.46 ounces (7–13 grams)

DIET: Hypercarnivore

ESSENTIAL FACTS: Zapfe's Bent-winged Bat have been recovered in France and described in 2002. Like many of its modern relatives, it may have taken part in seasonal long-distance migrations with dedicated summer and winter roosts. It was built to chase down fast-flying insects over water bodies.

MYSTACINIDAE

Despite the name, the New Zealand short-tailed bats originate in the Late Oligocene of Australia, becoming established in New Zealand by the Middle Miocene. Members of this family are unique among bats, because they forage for food exclusively on the ground rather than by air. They even have the ability to fold their wings into a leathery membrane so they can more efficiently walk and run. They tend to be either mesocarnivorous or hypocarnivorous with extremely varied diets.

ICAROPS PARADOX

NAME MEANING: Incredible Icarus

AGE: Late Oligocene to early Miocene (25–20 MYA)

DISTRIBUTION: Australia

SIZE: Unknown

DIET: Hypocarnivore

ESSENTIAL FACTS: The oldest known of the mystacinid bats, this species already had adaptations for terrestrial foraging as seen in their modern relatives on New Zealand. Its fossils have been found at the Riversleigh World Heritage Area.

VULCANOPS JENNYWORTHYAE

NAME MEANING: Jennifer Worthy's Vulcan bat

AGE: Early Miocene (19–16 MYA)

DISTRIBUTION: New Zealand

SIZE: 1.4 ounces (40 grams)

DIET: Hypocarnivore

SEE MORE ON PAGES 530–531

MYSTACINA MIOCENALIS

NAME MEANING: Moustache of the Miocene

AGE: Middle Miocene (19–16 MYA)

DISTRIBUTION: New Zealand

SIZE: 0.42–0.53 ounces (12–15 grams)

DIET: Hypocarnivore

ESSENTIAL FACTS: Virtually identical to its two modern relatives, this species coexisted with its larger relative, Vulcanops (*Vulcanops jennyworthyae*) in the St. Bathans fauna, where it foraged the forest floor for small invertebrates and softer plant parts.

PHYLLOSTOMIDAE

New-World leaf-nosed bats, as their name suggests, are endemic to North and South America. The fossil record for this group extends to about 30 million years ago in South America, and the group has attained a high degree of ecological diversity with almost two hundred modern species.

VULCANOPS JENNYWORTHYAE

ESSENTIAL FACTS: Vulcanops is the largest of the mystacinid bats, named in honor of Jennifer P. Worthy, the scientist who discovered the fossils of the species. Referring to New Zealand's tectonically active nature, the genus name is derived from Vulcan, the Roman god of fire and volcanoes. As with modern mystacinids, it had a broad diet that included invertebrates, carrion (dead animals), and fruits among other food items which it foraged for by crawling along the forest floor. Its broad molars confirm its hypocarnivorous habits.

Vulcanops is recorded from the Saint Bathans Fauna of central Otago, the only pre-Pleistocene Cenozoic terrestrial fauna of New Zealand. The site is an indicator of the past diversity of New Zealand with early examples of kiwi and moa (a flightless bird), a mekosuchine crocodile, several aquatic and terrestrial turtles, and even an unnamed species of terrestrial mammal. Called the "Saint Bathans mammal," the creature is known from scarce material including fragmentary jaws that indicate that it is a late-surviving member of one of the non-therian Mesozoic mammal lineages. Along with the Tuatara (*Sphenodon punctatus*), it was a relict whose ancestors inhabited New Zealand before it separated from other continents 80 million years ago and survived in isolation long after its relatives became extinct prior to the K/Pg mass extinction. The Saint Bathans Fauna suggests that small land mammals were a common component of New Zealand's fauna in the Miocene, with even bats being significantly more diverse than they are today.

SEE ENTRY ON PAGE 529

DESMODONTINAE

Vampire bats first appear in the fossil record during the Early Pleistocene. As the name suggests, members of this subfamily specialize in feeding on the blood of other animals, a feeding behavior known as hematophagy, with such animals being termed *sanguivores*. There are three modern species.

DESMODUS DRACULAE

NAME MEANING: Dracula's linked tooth

AGE: Pleistocene to Holocene (2.5 MYA–300 YA)

DISTRIBUTION: South America and North America

SIZE: 1.3–2.1 ounces (38–60 grams)

DIET: Sanguivore

SEE MORE ON PAGES 534–535

DESMODUS STOCKI

NAME MEANING: Stock's linked tooth

AGE: Late Pleistocene to Holocene (120,000–5,000 YA)

DISTRIBUTION: North America

SIZE: 1.3–2.1 ounces (38–60 grams)

DIET: Sanguivore

ESSENTIAL FACTS: Stock's Vampire Bat has the northernmost distribution of any known vampire bat, its range extending from Mexico in the south to Virginia in the north. At least 50 percent larger and more robust than the modern species (*D. rotundus*), it likely fed on the blood of Pleistocene megafauna (large animals).

DINOCERATA

Uintatheres lived from the Late Paleocene and survived until the Middle Eocene. They are some of the first large mammalian herbivores, with some growing to be as big as modern rhinos. Their fossils are known only from North America and Asia. Through the Eocene, they were gradually replaced by brontotheres (Brontotheriidae). All uintatheres have lost their upper incisors, suggesting the presence of a horny pad which occluded with the lower incisors, as seen among modern ruminants. The cheek teeth are brachydont and bilophodont for browsing. Most species had long upper canines that functioned as tusks.

PRODINOCERATIDAE

Prodinoceratids were medium-sized browsers that would have filled the niches that tapirs occupy today. They existed from the Late Paleocene to the Early Eocene.

PRODINOCERAS XINJIANGENSIS

NAME MEANING: Before *Dinoceras* from Xinjiang

AGE: Late Paleocene (57–55 MYA)

DISTRIBUTION: Eurasia

SIZE: 9.5 feet (2.9 meters) HBL; 400 pounds (182 kilograms)

DIET: Herbivore; browser

ESSENTIAL FACTS: This species is the oldest-known member of the group, occurring in both North America and Asia. This provides supporting evidence that a land connection existed between the two continents at the time.

DESMODUS DRACULAE

ESSENTIAL FACTS: Fossil and subfossil remains of Dracula's Bat are known from cave deposits in Argentina, Brazil, Venezuela, Belize, Bolivia, Ecuador, and Mexico. Despite its common name, the Giant Vampire Bat is about the same size as its more northern relative, Stock's Vampire Bat (*D. stocki*), both of which are at least 50 percent larger the modern common vampire bat (*D. rotundus*). Its wingspan has been estimated at around 20 inches (50 centimeters), compared to the 7-inch (18-centimeter) wingspan of the modern species. Interestingly, the two larger vampire bats' ranges do not appear to have overlapped, possibly being limited by specific climatic factors encountered at different latitudes.

A tooth from Buenos Aires, Argentina, that has been attributed to this species was dated to three hundred years ago, around the year 1650! Given the recency of its extinction, it has been speculated that the Giant Vampire Bat could be the inspiration for native folkloric accounts of particularly large bats that feed on blood. The species name, *draculae*, is a direct reference to Count Dracula. Likely prey would have included any of the various Pleistocene megafaunal mammals that it would have coexisted with. Like modern vampire bats, they would obtain blood meals by carefully sneaking toward sleeping animals during the night, often jumping directly on them when close enough. Then, using heat sensors located in the nose, they would detect blood vessels near the surface of the skin, using specialized upper incisors to open a small cut from which to drink a small amount of blood.

SEE ENTRY ON PAGE 532

UINTATHERIIDAE

Members of Uintatheriidae were the largest land mammals of their time, growing to be the size of rhinos. The most distinctive feature of these animals are their distinctive horns, which come in three pairs: a pair above the nose, a larger pair in front of the eyes, and the largest pair behind the eyes. These horns may have been covered in toughened skin like the ossicones of a giraffid. The limbs were more graviportal than those of prodinoceratids, and their legs and feet would have resembled those of elephants in life.

BATHYOPSIS FISSIDENS

NAME MEANING: Deep-looking cleft tooth

AGE: Early Eocene (55–50 MYA)

DISTRIBUTION: North America

SIZE: 660 pounds (300 kilograms)

DIET: Herbivore; browser

ESSENTIAL FACTS: This species was one of the smaller members of the family, comparable in size to its prodinoceratid ancestors. Nonetheless, it possessed a single pair of small nasal horns.

UINTATHERIUM ANCEPS

NAME MEANING: Double-headed beast of the Uintah Mountains

AGE: Early Eocene (55–50 MYA)

DISTRIBUTION: North America

SIZE: 5 feet (1.5 meters) SH; 13 feet (4 meters) HBL; 2 tons

DIET: Herbivore; browser

ESSENTIAL FACTS: This species is the best known of the uintatheres, thanks to numerous skeletal remains found in western North America. This iconic animal was the largest herbivore in its environment with no known predators of the time appearing capable of threatening one.

EOBASILEUS CORNUTUS

NAME MEANING: Horned dawn king

AGE: Middle Eocene (47–45 MYA)

DISTRIBUTION: North America

SIZE: 7 feet (2.1 meters) SH; 5,500 pounds (2,500 kilograms)

DIET: Herbivore; browser

ESSENTIAL FACTS: The largest of the uintatheres, during the late 1800s this species was at the center of a dispute which helped spark the famous Bone Wars between paleontologists Othniel Charles Marsh and Edward Drinker Cope.

GOBIATHERIUM MAJOR

NAME MEANING: Larger beast from the Gobi Desert

AGE: Middle Eocene (47–45 MYA)

DISTRIBUTION: Eurasia

SIZE: About rhino-sized

DIET: Herbivore; browser

ESSENTIAL FACTS: One of the last uintatheres, this animal lacked the horns and tusks of its relatives. Instead, this species evolved a long, low skull with a rounded structure at the end of its snout that may have been used to emit sounds. It also possessed distinctive flaring zygomatic arches.

MERIDIUNGULATA

The South American native ungulates, often abbreviated to SANUs, were a diverse, possibly polyphyletic group of herbivores that evolved in isolation on South America, when the landmass was an island. Fossil evidence shows that members of the group spread to Antarctica while it was still connected to South America but after it had separated from Africa and Australia. The earliest forms occur during the Early Paleocene, and the group undergoes a stark decline in diversity during the Late Miocene that corresponds with a diversification of xenarthrans and cavimorph rodents. Only a single species is known to have inhabited North America. The entire group became extinct by the Late Pleistocene or Early Holocene. While the evolutionary relationships between most lineages within this group are unclear, collagen analyses on the most recent litopterns and notoungulates has shown that at least these two groups are closely related to each other. Furthermore, the same study suggests that they share a common ancestor with perissodactyls.

MIOCLAENIDAE

The Mioclaenidae is a primarily North American and European group of ungulates. The presence of these animals in South America suggests that the family dispersed there from North America, probably by way of small islands in between the two landmasses. South American species are sometimes placed within their own family, Kollpaniidae, and are thought to be closely related to two other groups: Litopterna and Didolodontidae.

MOLINODUS SUAREZI

NAME MEANING: Mario Suarez Riglos' tooth from the El Molino Formation

AGE: Early Paleocene (65–64 MYA)

DISTRIBUTION: South America

SIZE: 8–12 inches (18–30 centimeters) HBL; 0.5–1 pound (250–500 grams)

DIET: Herbivore; browser

ESSENTIAL FACTS: Suarez's Molinodus had bunodont dentition and is thought to have had a primarily fruit-based diet, with the inclusion of seeds and softer leaves. It is notably the most abundant mammal from the Tiupampa fossil locality in Bolivia.

PYROTHERIA

Pyrotheres were medium- to large-sized herbivores that lived from the Late Paleocene to the Late Oligocene. The more basal members of this group had bunodont dentition adapted to feed on relatively tough but non-abrasive plants and potentially some animal matter. More derived forms evolved bilophodont dentition that are indicative of a specialized browsing diet of fibrous leaves and fruits. Some researchers consider Pyrotheria to include the Xenungulata, meaning "strange ungulates" based on similarities in dentition and anatomy. Potential affinities with uintatheres in the Northern Hemisphere and arsinoitheres in Africa have been proposed.

CARODNIA VIEIRAI

NAME MEANING: Jose Vieira da Silva's thunder

AGE: Early Eocene (53–50 MYA)

DISTRIBUTION: South America

SIZE: 5–6 feet (1.5–1.75 meters) HBL; 450–550 pounds (200–250 kilograms)

DIET: Herbivore; browser

ESSENTIAL FACTS: Carodnia is the largest South American herbivore known from its time. It was the size of a tapir and had a similar diet, consisting mainly of leaves and some fruits. It is the most well-known member of Carodniidae, represented by complete skeletal material.

COLOMBITHERIUM TOLIMENSE

NAME MEANING: Beast from Tolima, Colombia

AGE: Late Eocene (35–34 MYA)

DISTRIBUTION: South America

SIZE: About pig-sized

DIET: Herbivore

ESSENTIAL FACTS: This species is known only from a partial maxilla with a partial row of bunodont teeth. It has been tentatively placed within the family Colombitheriidae, along with the similarly incomplete species *Proticia venezuelensis*.

PYROTHERIIDAE

The pyrotheriids were large browsing herbivores that lived from the Middle Eocene to Late Oligocene. In life, these animals resembled a cross between a tapir and an elephant, with bilophodont dentition adapted for shredding fibrous leaves and retracted nasals, which indicate the presence of a well-developed proboscis.

BAGUATHERIUM JAUREGUII

NAME MEANING: Jauregui's beast from Bagua Grande

AGE: Early Oligocene (31 MYA)

DISTRIBUTION: South America

SIZE: Unknown

DIET: Herbivore; browser

ESSENTIAL FACTS: The fossils of Jauregui's Pyrothere were discovered in Peru near the town of Bagua Grande, after which it was named in 2006. It differs from the younger, larger, and better-known Romero's Pyrothere (*Pyrotherium romeroi*) in its smaller size and broader skull.

PYROTHERIUM ROMEROI

NAME MEANING: Antonio Romero's fire beast

AGE: Late Oligocene (27–26 MYA)

DISTRIBUTION: South America

SIZE: 6,000–7,000 pounds (2,721–3,175 kilograms)

DIET: Herbivore; browser

SEE MORE ON PAGES 542–543

ASTRAPOTHERIA

Astrapotheres are known from the Late Paleocene and survived until the Late Miocene. At least one species is known to have inhabited Antarctica during the Early Eocene. They were robust animals with graviportal skeletons, and many of them would have resembled small elephants, while the cheek teeth were notably similar to those of rhinos.

EOASTRAPOSTYLOPS RIOLORENSE

NAME MEANING: Dawn Astrapostylops from Rio Loro

AGE: Late Paleocene (56 MYA)

DISTRIBUTION: South America

SIZE: 1.5 feet (50 centimeters) HBL; 10 pounds (4 kilograms)

DIET: Herbivore

ESSENTIAL FACTS: Eoastrapostylops was very small compared to other astrapotheres and had not yet evolved the tusks or proboscis of later species. However, its teeth were very similar to those of *Trigonostylops*, suggesting a close relation. It is considered the sole member of its own family, Eoastrapostylopidae.

TRIGONOSTYLOPS WORTMANI

NAME MEANING: Jacob Wortman's triangular Notostylops

AGE: Late Eocene (38–37 MYA)

DISTRIBUTION: South America

SIZE: 45–90 pounds (20–40 kilograms)

DIET: Herbivore; browser

ESSENTIAL FACTS: The postcranial skeleton of Trigonostylops is mostly unknown, but the skull is well understood. It had powerful jaws with cheek teeth suited for a diet of hard foods like nuts or particularly fibrous leaves. Its canines were large and self-sharpening. It is the sole member of the family Trigonostylopidae.

ASTRAPOTHERIIDAE

Astrapotheriids first appear in the fossil record during the Late Eocene and are last known from the Late Miocene. Like the pyrotheres, they had retracted nasals with elephant-like proboscises. They were fairly diverse, ranging in size from that of a peccary to that of a rhino, and to a modern observer would have resembled a small elephant at a glance.

PYROTHERIUM ROMEROI

ESSENTIAL FACTS: Most of what we know about pyrotheres comes from a nearly complete skull of Romero's Pyrothere, found in southern Argentina in 1912. The skull measures 2.3 feet (72 centimeters) long. Among its more notable features, the nasal passage is located between the eyes and well-developed processes for muscle attachment are located around this opening. This is evidence that pyrotheres possessed a prehensile, elephant-like proboscis, which it would have used to gather food and potentially to drink. The upper and lower incisors are enlarged and protrude forward resembling tusks. Bilophodont cheek teeth show that the species were specialized browsers that fed mostly on leaves, twigs, and branches.

The postcranial skeleton of this animal is mostly unknown, but it can be inferred to have been the size of a large male white rhinoceros (*Ceratotherium simum*). The morphology of the ankle bones show that it would have had pillar-like legs adapted for supporting great weight, similar to the limbs of elephants. The great size of Romero's Pyrothere would have made the adults virtually immune to predation from predators such as the larger terror birds, sebecid crocodilians, and sparassodonts. The genus name *Pyrotherium*, meaning "fire beast," references the volcanic ash-bearing sediments in which its fossils were first discovered.

SEE ENTRY ON PAGE 540

ASTRAPOTHERIUM MAGNUM

NAME MEANING: Great lightning beast

AGE: Middle Miocene (18.5–15 MYA)

DISTRIBUTION: South America

SIZE: 8 feet (2.5 meters) HBL; 800–1,000 pounds (363–455 kilograms)

DIET: Herbivore; browser

ESSENTIAL FACTS: Astrapotherium was the size of a large tapir and likely shared many of its habits. The hindlimbs are notably weaker than the forelimbs, which has led to hypotheses that it was a semiaquatic animal that propelled itself through the water with its strong forelimbs, while the hindlimbs trailed behind, acting as a pair of rudders.

GRANASTRAPOTHERIUM SNORKI

NAME MEANING: Large Astrapotherium with a snorkel

AGE: Middle Miocene (13.5–11.5 MYA)

DISTRIBUTION: South America

SIZE: 11–13 feet (3.5–4 meters) HBL; 4,000–5,500 pounds (1,800–2,500 kilograms)

DIET: Herbivore; browser

ESSENTIAL FACTS: This species was the size of a white rhinoceros (*Ceratotherium simum*) with teeth that indicate a browsing diet of leaves, twigs, and fruit. Unlike other astrapotheres, Snork's Astrapothere lacked lower incisors. Males have notably longer and thicker tusks than females.

LITOPTERNA

In terms of longevity and morphological diversity litopterns are rivaled only by the notoungulates, to which they are closely related. Species within this group were comparable to chevrotains, duikers, gazelles, horses, and camels in their appearance. They are known to have lived throughout the Cenozoic from the early Paleocene all the way to the Holocene.

PROTOLIPTERNA ELLIPSODONTOIDES

NAME MEANING: First litoptern like Ellipsodon

AGE: Early Eocene (53–50 MYA)

DISTRIBUTION: South America

SIZE: 10–14 inches (25–35 centimeters) HBL; 1–3 pounds (500–1,500 grams)

DIET: Herbivore; browser

ESSENTIAL FACTS: Protolipterna was a small, fleet-footed browser that was likely similar in ecology to modern chevrotains (Tragulidae). The upper canines of adult males were long and tusk-like, most likely used during territorial disputes. It is currently the only species placed within the family Protolipternidae.

SPARNOTHERIODONTIDAE

Sparnotheriodonts were forest-dwelling browsers that lived during the Early to Late Eocene. Their fossils are known from southern South America and Antarctica. Most species are known only from jaws.

NOTIOLOFOS ARQUINOTIENSIS

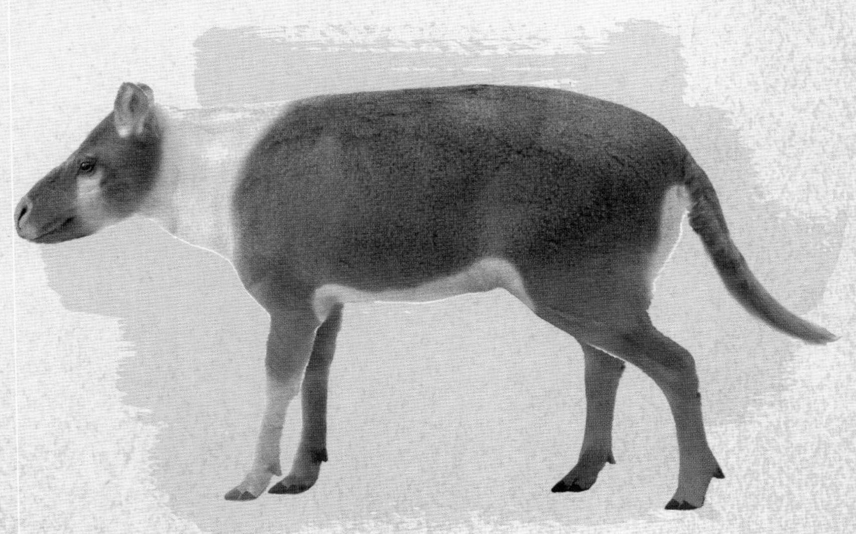

NAME MEANING: Southern crest from Archinotis

AGE: Eocene

DISTRIBUTION: Antarctica

SIZE: 880 pounds (400 kilograms)

DIET: Herbivore

ESSENTIAL FACTS: One of the largest litopterns of the Paleogene, this species was the larger of two species of Notiolofos, the other having an estimated body weight of 55–125 pounds (25–57 kilograms). Both species were among the few meridiungulates known to have inhabited Antarctica.

PROTEROTHERIIDAE

Proterotheres were small- to medium-sized herbivores that resembled horses (Equidae), with cursorial adaptations and a trend toward the reduction in number of digits. Many had a single pair of large tusk-like incisors, like those of hyraxes that show dimorphism. The cheek teeth were brachydont and adapted to feed on non-abrasive foods. Proterotheres become less diverse and abundant in the fossil record after the Late Miocene, but are known to have persisted until the Late Pleistocene.

DIADIAPHORUS MAJUSCULUS

NAME MEANING: Large one that carries through

AGE: Late Miocene (10–6.8 MYA)

DISTRIBUTION: South America

SIZE: 4 feet (120 centimeters) HBL; 150 pounds (70 kilograms)

DIET: Herbivore; browser

ESSENTIAL FACTS: Diadiaphorus was a sheep-sized herbivore that was built like a small horse. Each foot had three toes (only the middle toe would touch the ground) and ended in a large hoof, similar to hipparionine horses. Its brachydont molars suggest a primarily browsing diet.

THOATHERIUM MINUSCULUM

NAME MEANING: Tiny quick beast

AGE: Early Miocene (18–16 MYA)

DISTRIBUTION: South America

SIZE: 2.5 feet (75 centimeters)

DIET: Herbivore; browser

ESSENTIAL FACTS: *Thoatherium* were notable for being the only mammals aside from horses of the genus *Equus* to have evolved fully monodactyl feet, lacking even vestiges of the lateral digits. They were built like a small gazelles with their short, muscular torsos set on long, slender legs for swift running and quick changes in direction. Despite this mix of horse and gazelle-like features, their teeth suggest a browse-based diet.

MEGADOLODUS MOLARIFORMIS

NAME MEANING: Great didolodont with molariform teeth

AGE: Middle Miocene (13.5–11.8 MYA)

DISTRIBUTION: South America

SIZE: 3 feet (1 meter) HBL; 4–60 pounds (18–27 kilograms)

DIET: Herbivore

ESSENTIAL FACTS: At the time of its discovery in the 1950s, this animal was thought to have been a late-surviving didolodont. Additional fossils discovered in the 1980s confirmed that it was actually a litoptern.

NEOBRACHYTHERIUM ULLUMENSE

NAME MEANING: New *Brachytherium* from Valle de Ullum

AGE: Late Miocene (10–9 MYA)

DISTRIBUTION: South America

SIZE: 3 feet (1 meter) HBL; 35–40 pounds (16–18 kilograms)

DIET: Herbivore; browser

ESSENTIAL FACTS: Although this species had three toes on each foot, the two side toes were highly reduced and the feet were functionally monodactyl. The first fossils of this species were discovered at Valle de Ullum in San Juan, Argentina.

NEOLICAPHRIUM RECENS

NAME MEANING: Recent new Licaphrium

AGE: Pleistocene (1.2 MYA–11,000 YA)

DISTRIBUTION: South America

SIZE: 81 pounds (37 kilograms)

DIET: Herbivore; browser

ESSENTIAL FACTS: Discovered in Late Pleistocene deposits of Uruguay, this species is the last-known proterothere. It inhabited savanna and open woodland habitats, and isotopic analyses have shown that its diet consisted mainly of fruits and occasionally low-growing vegetation.

ADIANTHIDAE

Adianthids were small-bodied litopterns less than 50 pounds. In life they would have resembled chevrotains (Tragulidae) or small duikers (Bovidae). They lived from the Middle Eocene to the Middle Miocene when they were replaced by cavimorph rodents.

ADIANTHUS BUCATUS

NAME MEANING: Not Zeus' flower of the mouth

AGE: Early Miocene (20–16 MYA)

DISTRIBUTION: South America

SIZE: About cat-sized

DIET: Herbivore

ESSENTIAL FACTS: This species was one of the better-known and more specialized members of the group with molariform premolars that increase the surface area for grinding.

MACRAUCHENIIDAE

The macraucheniid skeleton at a glance resembles that of a camelid with their long necks and compact bodies. The limbs, however, are proportionally shorter and more robust, particularly in the distal segments. The family is first known from the Middle Eocene and survived until as recently as the Early Holocene. Starting in the Miocene, members of this family exhibit retracted nasals which has traditionally been interpreted as evidence for proboscises. Another possibility is that macraucheniids were evolving more complicated lip musculature, which could have played a role in visual communication, giving them particularly expressive faces.

CRAMAUCHENIINAE

The older of the two macraucheniid subfamilies, the Cramaucheniinae were small- to medium-sized herbivores that would have superficially resembled llamas. More derived species later in the group's evolution exhibited nasal retraction, though not to the extent seen in the Macrauheniinae. The group appears to have become extinct during the Late Miocene.

CRAMAUCHENIA NORMALIS

NAME MEANING: Normal *Macrauchenia*

AGE: Middle Oligocene (29–27 MYA)

DISTRIBUTION: South America

SIZE: About sheep-sized

DIET: Herbivore; browser

ESSENTIAL FACTS: Cramauchenia had a long skull with a marked sagittal crest, perhaps for breaking tough or fibrous plants. It lacked the retracted nasals, which later macrauchenids were well-known for and would have a more "conventional" deer-like face. A complete skull and jaw are on display at the Field Museum of Natural History in Chicago.

THEOSODON PATAGONICUM

NAME MEANING: God tooth from Patagonia

AGE: Early Miocene (18–17.5 MYA)

DISTRIBUTION: South America

SIZE: 6 feet (2 meters) HBL; 275–375 pounds (125–170 kilograms)

DIET: Herbivore; browser

ESSENTIAL FACTS: The nasal passages of this species are located halfway between the tip of the premaxilla, and the eye sockets opened upward rather than forward. In life it would have resembled a robust llama with the nose of a moose (*Alces alces*).

LLULLATARUCA SHOCKEYI

NAME MEANING: Bruce Shockey's false deer

AGE: Middle Miocene (13.8–11.8 MYA)

DISTRIBUTION: South America

SIZE: 80–110 pounds (35–50 kilograms)

DIET: Herbivore

ESSENTIAL FACTS: Described in 2018, Llullataruca is known for a complete lower jaw and some postcranial elements. The morphology of its bones suggests that it would have been similar in appearance to the earlier Cramauchenia.

MACRAUCHENIINAE

This subfamily contains the largest of the macraucheniids, with later forms growing as large as bison (*Bison*) or elands (*Taurotragus*). They were also the most recent members of the family, having originated in the Late Miocene and persisting long enough to be observed by the first humans in South America in the Holocene. They exhibit extreme retraction of the nasals, the openings for which migrated just behind the eyes. The skulls also feature a fully formed postorbital bar.

MICRAUCHENIA SALADENSIS

NAME MEANING: Small neck from Bahia Salado

AGE: Late Miocene (10–8 MYA)

DISTRIBUTION: South America

SIZE: 117–227 pounds (53–103 kilograms)

DIET: Herbivore

ESSENTIAL FACTS: The environment in which the sole known specimen would have lived was a coastal environment with dry-adapted woodland and shrubland vegetation. The species is known for incomplete skeletal elements found in Chile.

XENORHINOTHERIUM BAHIENSE

NAME MEANING: Strange-nosed beast rom Bahia

AGE: Pleistocene to Holocene

DISTRIBUTION: South America

SIZE: 2,070 pounds (940 kilograms)

DIET: Herbivore

ESSENTIAL FACTS: Xenorhinotherium was very similar to the more famous Macrauchenia, to which it was contemporary and differed in its smaller size. It lived recently enough to be observed by humans, and pictographs of it have been found in the Serranía de La Lindosa rock formation in Colombia.

MACRAUCHENIA PATACHONICA

NAME MEANING: Large llama from Patagonia

AGE: Pleistocene to Holocene

DISTRIBUTION: South America

SIZE: 10–11 feet (3–3.2 feet) HBL; 2,400 pounds (1,100 kilograms)

DIET: Herbivore; mixed feeder

SEE MORE ON PAGES 552–553

NOTOUNGULATA

Notoungulates are the most morphologically diverse group of meridiungulates, with representatives that resembled rabbits, peccaries, chalicotheres, cattle, and rhinos. The group first appears in the fossil record during the Early Paleocene and survive until the Early Holocene. Their diversity declined from the Middle Miocene onward, with only a few larger species remaining by the Late Pleistocene.

MACRAUCHENIA PATACHONICA

ESSENTIAL FACTS: Macrauchenia was described by Sir Richard Owen in 1838 from fossils recovered by Charles Darwin during his voyage on the *HMS Beagle* four years earlier. It has since become arguably the most famous of the South American native ungulates, due to its long history of being represented in the form of toys and in animation. Macrauchenia have traditionally been reconstructed with an elephant or tapir-like proboscis due to the nasals opening on top of the skull just behind and between the eyes. This interpretation has been challenged in recent years, with some researchers suggesting a more moose-like nose or a face with enlarged and highly mobile lips.

One of the last, largest, and most well-studied of the machraucheniids, Macrauchenia would have resembled a stocky camel at a glance. The limbs were relatively long with relatively short distal segments. Although it was undoubtedly able to move quite fast, the limbs seem to emphasize great agility despite its large size, an adaptation that may have evolved in its ancestors to evade bipedal terror birds (Phorusrhachidae). It was a mixed feeder that fed on both leaves from trees and bushes as well as grasses, likely adjusting its diet based on seasonality. It was widespread in South America, with fossils being found from sea level to altitudes up to 13,000 feet (4,000 meters). The primary predators of sub-adult and adult Macrauchenia were the Southern Smilodon (*Smilodon populator*), while juveniles were targeted by jaguars (*Panthera onca*).

SEE ENTRY ON PAGE 551

OLDFIELDTHOMASIIDAE

The type genus of the family, *Oldfieldthomasia*, is named for the English zoologist Oldfield Thomas. They were basal notoungulates about the size of marmots or hyraxes, likely occupying similar niches.

COLBERTIA MAGELLANICA

NAME MEANING: Edwin Colbert and Ferdinand Magellan

AGE: Early Eocene (53–50 MYA)

DISTRIBUTION: South America

SIZE: 12–20 inches (30–50 centimeters) HBL; 4–7 pounds (2–3 kilograms)

DIET: Herbivore; browser

ESSENTIAL FACTS: The most abundant notoungulate from the Itaborai locality, the species had a plantigrade stance and brachydont-lophodont teeth adapted for browsing on soft leaves, twigs, buds, and flowers. In life, it probably would have resembled a hyrax (Procaviidae).

NOTOSTYLOPSIDAE

Notostylopsids are known to have lived from the Late Paleocene to the Early Oligocene. They have skulls similar to those of wombats (Vombatidae). They had a distinctive dentition in which the first pair of upper incisors were relatively large and worked against the first incisors of the lower jaw, which would have become procumbent. There was a diastema between the canines and premolars.

NOTOSTYLOPS MURINUS

NAME MEANING: Rat-like southern pillar tooth

AGE: Middle Eocene (48–45 MYA)

DISTRIBUTION: South America

SIZE: 28–30 inches (70–75 centimeters) HBL;
15–25 pounds (7–11 kilograms)

DIET: Herbivore; browser

ESSENTIAL FACTS: The Murine Notostylops had a skull and dentition that was adapted to browse on tough, low-growing plants. Its skeleton was robust and may have been adapted for excavating burrows in which these animals would take shelter.

OTRHONIA MUEHLBERGI

NAME MEANING: Friedrich Muhlberg's animal from Otròn

AGE: Late Eocene (38–37 MYA)

DISTRIBUTION: South America

SIZE: 24–28 inches (60–70 centimeters) HBL;
13–20 pounds (6–9 kilograms)

DIET: Herbivore; browser

ESSENTIAL FACTS: Otrhonia was a small herbivore about the size of a raccoon with a diet that consisted of leaves and fruits. Compared to other notostylopsids, the skull was more elongated and the teeth more hypsodont.

ARCHAEOHYRACIDAE

Archaeohyracids were among the first South American mammals to evolve hypsodont cheek teeth, suggesting that they had begun to shift to a more graze-dominated diet in open, arid environments rather than a strictly browsing one in wetter environments. They had complete dentitions with teeth that were closely packed together without a diastema. Archaeohyracids are among the more poorly known families of notoungulates and may in fact be paraphyletic, consisting of a collection of animals related to mesotheres and hegetotheres. They are rare in most faunas, and postcranial skeletons are unknown. The group is known to have lived from the Middle Eocene to Late Oligocene.

ARCHAEOHYRAX PATAGONICUS

NAME MEANING: Ancient hyrax from Patagonia

AGE: Late Oligocene (29–25 MYA)

DISTRIBUTION: South America

SIZE: 18 inches (40 centimeters) HBL

DIET: Herbivore; mixed feeder

ESSENTIAL FACTS: The skull of this animal resembled that of a hyrax, only much more elongated. Its diet consisted mainly of leaves and fruits with the occasional inclusion of invertebrates. Fossils of it are known from Argentina and Bolivia.

PSEUDHYRAX EUTRACHYTHEROIDES

NAME MEANING: False hyrax similar to *Eutrachytherus*

AGE: Late Eocene (38–37 MYA)

DISTRIBUTION: South America

SIZE: 24–30 inches (65–75 centimeters) HBL;
15–20 pounds (7–9 kilograms)

DIET: Herbivore; grazer

ESSENTIAL FACTS: Its teeth were relatively hypsodont compared to other archaeohyracids, indicating a diet that included more abrasive plants such as grasses in addition to leaves.

ISOTEMNIDAE

The Isotemnidae family name means "equal cutting" in reference to the hypothesized function of the cheek teeth. Their teeth were brachydont and increased in size from front to back with no large spaces between them, resulting in a single continuous grinding surface.

THOMASHUXLEYA ROSTRATA

NAME MEANING: Thomas Huxley's snout

AGE: Middle Eocene (42–38 MYA)

DISTRIBUTION: South America

SIZE: 4.3–5 feet (1.3–1.5 meters) HBL; 150–200 pounds (70–90 kilograms)

DIET: Herbivore; browser

ESSENTIAL FACTS: Thomashuxleya was a medium-sized herbivore about the size of a bush pig (*Potamochoerus larvatus*) and is often reconstructed in paleoart to resemble a warthog (*Phacochoerus africanus*). It had tusk-like canines that would have been used for self-defense and in battles between males.

NOTOHIPPIDAE

The name *Notohippus* means "southern horse," referencing the upper incisors which resemble those of horses adapted for cropping vegetation. They had hypsodont cheek teeth with complex occlusal surfaces for grinding and shredding tough vegetation encountered at ground level. Their bodies were stocky, with relatively slender limbs for running. More basal forms had four-toed feet while others had three toes, with digits ending in claws rather than hooves.

EOMORPHIPPUS BONDI

NAME MEANING: Bond's dawn *Morphippus*

AGE: Early Oligocene (32–29 MYA)

DISTRIBUTION: South America

SIZE: About goat-sized

DIET: Herbivore; grazer

ESSENTIAL FACTS: Bond's Notohippid was described in 2018 based on fossils found in Chile. Its head was particularly robust with a shortened face, featuring notably enlarged incisors typical of the family.

MORPHIPPUS IMBRICATUS

NAME MEANING: Roofed slow horse

AGE: Late Oligocene (29–24 MYA)

DISTRIBUTION: South America

SIZE: About goat-sized

DIET: Herbivore; grazer

ESSENTIAL FACTS: This species was described in 1897 by Argentinian paleontologist Florentino Ameghino. It is known for a partial skull with a complete dentition without a diastema. Like other notohippids it was hypsodont with a robust body with slender legs for fast running.

RHYNCHIPPUS EQUINUS

NAME MEANING: Snout horse

AGE: Late Oligocene (28.4–24 MYA)

DISTRIBUTION: South America

SIZE: 3.3 feet (1 meter) HBL; 40 pounds (18 kilograms)

DIET: Herbivore; grazer

ESSENTIAL FACTS: This species consisted of small grazing herbivores with teeth resembling those of rhinos, being relatively large and hypsodont with complex ridges for shredding tough vegetation. It is the type species of its genus, described by Florentino Ameghino in 1897.

EURYGENIUM LATIROSTRIS

NAME MEANING: Wide jaws

AGE: Late Oligocene (28–24 MYA)

DISTRIBUTION: South America

SIZE: 2.7 feet (80 centimeters) HBL; 22 pounds (10 kilograms)

DIET: Herbivore; grazer

ESSENTIAL FACTS: The snout of this species was especially short and broad with wide zygomatic arches, hence its scientific name, which means "wide jaws" twice. Its limbs were also proportionally more robust than other notohippids, with four-toed feet instead of just three.

HOMALODOTHERIIDAE

The oldest homalodothere fossils have been unearthed from Eocene deposits, and the group became extinct during the Late Miocene. These herbivores had long limbs and clawed feet, similar to those of chalicotheres and palorchestids. They were specialized browsers able to feed on high vegetation that other herbivores their own size could not reach, standing up on their hindfeet and using their clawed forelimbs to pull leaves and branches close to their mouths.

HOMALODOTHERIUM CUNNINGHAMI

NAME MEANING: Cunningham's even-toothed beast

AGE: Middle Miocene (16.3–15.5 MYA)

DISTRIBUTION: South America

SIZE: 6.6 feet (2 meters) HBL; 660 pounds (300 kilograms)

DIET: Herbivore; browser

ESSENTIAL FACTS: The most well-known member of the family, Cunningham's Homalodothere had digitigrade forelimbs and plantigrade hindlimbs. It was adapted to stand on its hindfeet to reach high-growing leaves from trees similar to the chalicotheres (Chalicotheriidae) which lived on the other continents.

CHASICOTHERIUM ROTHI

NAME MEANING: Santiago Roth's beast from the Arroyo Chasico Formation

AGE: Late Miocene (10–9 MYA)

DISTRIBUTION: South America

SIZE: 7–8 feet (2.1–2.4 meters) HBL; 600–800 pounds (272–363 kilograms)

DIET: Herbivore; browser

ESSENTIAL FACTS: The last and possibly the largest known of the homalodotheres, this species was named after the Arroyo Chasicó fossil locality in Argentina in which its fossils were discovered.

LEONTINIIDAE

Leontiniids were medium- to large-sized herbivores that lived from the Middle Eocene to the Late Miocene. Early in their evolutionary history these animals lost their canines, developing in their place enlarged, caniniform incisors that functioned as true canines and were likely used as defensive weapons against predators and members of their own species. They appear to have been specialized browsers. Their hindfeet were notably short and probably plantigrade, as seen in the homalodotheres.

SCARRITTIA CANQUELENSIS

NAME MEANING: Scarritt from Canquel

AGE: Late Oligocene (28.4–23 MYA)

DISTRIBUTION: South America

SIZE: 6.6 feet (2 meters) HBL; 440 pounds (200 kilograms)

DIET: Herbivore; browser

ESSENTIAL FACTS: This species is known for a complete albeit flattened skeleton found in Argentina. It was a tapir-sized herbivore that inhabited moist environments where it browsed on leaves and fruits.

LEONTINIA GAUDRYI

NAME MEANING: Leontin and Gaudry

AGE: Late Oligocene (28–24 MYA)

DISTRIBUTION: South America

SIZE: About cow-sized

DIET: Herbivore; browser

ESSENTIAL FACTS: This species is known for a nearly complete skull, with thickened and elevated nasals that suggest the presence of a small nasal horn similar to that of early horned rhinos. It is the type genus and species of the family.

ANAYATHERIUM FORTIS

NAME MEANING: Federico Anaya's strong beast

AGE: Late Oligocene (27–26 MYA)

DISTRIBUTION: South America

SIZE: 6–8 feet (2–2.2 meters) HBL; 600–800 pounds (280–370 kilograms)

DIET: Herbivore; browser

ESSENTIAL FACTS: This creature was the larger of two species of *Anayatherium* found at the Salla fossil locality in Bolivia. The rarity of these animals at the site suggests that the habitat was not suitable for leontiniids, which are generally common whenever present. Further evidence comes from relatively young individuals with highly worn teeth, indicating they were forced to eat abrasive ground vegetation and not utilizing the browsing they were adapted for.

HUILATHERIUM PLURIPLICATUM

NAME MEANING: Beast of Huila with many pleats

AGE: Middle Miocene (15.9–11.8 MYA)

DISTRIBUTION: South America

SIZE: 1,540–1,760 pounds (700–800 kilograms)

DIET: Herbivore; browser

ESSENTIAL FACTS: The last known leontiniid and possibly also the largest, Huilatherium was a large animal about the size of a Sumatran rhino (*Dicerorhinus sumatrensis*). It was discovered in the La Venta locality in Colombia.

TOXODONTIDAE

Toxodonts were medium- to large-sized herbivores that filled the ecological roles which pigs, cattle, and rhinos fulfill elsewhere in the world. They typically had relatively long bodies on short limbs and most were browsers or mixed feeders. They appear in the fossil record during the late Oligocene to early Holocene, experiencing a sharp decline in diversity from the late Miocene into the Pliocene.

ADINOTHERIUM FERUM

NAME MEANING: Not terrible beast of iron

AGE: Middle Miocene (17.5–15 MYA)

DISTRIBUTION: South America

SIZE: 5 feet (1.5 meters) HBL; 260 pounds (120 kilograms)

DIET: Herbivore

ESSENTIAL FACTS: This species was a pig-sized herbivore with a relatively long body set on short, slender limbs. It had caniniform second incisors (I2), which were used to fight each other.

NESODON IMBRICATUS

NAME MEANING: Imbricated island teeth

AGE: Early Miocene (18–17.5 MYA)

DISTRIBUTION: South America

SIZE: 550–770 pounds (250–350 kilograms)

DIET: Herbivore; grazer

ESSENTIAL FACTS: Built like a small rhino, a number of studies done on this species have shown that they fed on a wide variety of plants, from grasses and shrubs to trees and bushes.

TRIGODON GAUDRYI

NAME MEANING: Gaudry's triangular tooth

AGE: Late Miocene (9–7 MYA)

DISTRIBUTION: South America

SIZE: 8–10 feet (2.5–3 meters) HBL; 1,300–1,750 pounds (600–800 kilograms)

DIET: Herbivore

ESSENTIAL FACTS: Trigodon is one of the only horned South American native ungulates. It possessed a prominent bump on the skull above and between its eyes with a roughened texture. This is believed to have supported a keratinous horn similar to those of rhinos (Rhinoceratinae).

TOXODON PLATENSIS

NAME MEANING: Bow tooth from La Plata River Basin

AGE: Pleistocene

DISTRIBUTION: South America

SIZE: 8–10 feet (2.5–3 meters) HBL; 1,000–2,000 pounds (454–908 kilograms)

DIET: Herbivore; graze-dominated mixed feeder

SEE MORE ON PAGES 564–565

MIXOTOXODON LARENSIS

NAME MEANING: Mixed *Toxodon* from Lare

AGE: Pleistocene

DISTRIBUTION: South America, North America

SIZE: 2,200–2,600 pounds (1,000–1,200 kilograms)

DIET: Herbivore

ESSENTIAL FACTS: Mixotoxodon had a broad distribution from Argentina to Texas, making it the only known meridiungulate known to have had a North American distribution. Its mouth was noticeably narrower than that of the closely related Toxodon, suggesting more of a browsing diet.

INTERATHERIIDAE

Interatheres were small herbivores that were ecologically comparable to creatures like marmots or rabbits. They are often among the more abundant mammals in the fossil sites in which they occur. They are characterized by enlarged first incisors and simplified hypselodont cheek teeth. The family originated in the Early Eocene and disappear from the fossil record by the Late Pliocene. Complete or nearly complete skeletons of interatheres have been found representing individuals that died within burrows.

TOXODON PLATENSIS

ESSENTIAL FACTS: The first remains of Toxodon were discovered by Charles Darwin in Argentina in 1833 during his famous voyage on the *HMS Beagle*. It is the first South American native ungulate to be described. Because he had nothing else to compare it to, Sir Richard Owen hypothesized that the animal must have been a relative to rodents, based on its large, hypselodont upper incisors for which he would derive the genus name in 1837. Owen also suspected a relationship to elephants and rhinos, though this is now known to be incorrect. Abundant skeletal material of Toxodon has since been unearthed, and it is the most well-studied of all the notoungulates.

Isotope studies show that Toxodons fed heavily on grasses but would also switch to browse whenever grass was scarce. Its forelimbs were shorter than its hindlimbs, and its head was supported by strong muscles and ligaments, which enabled it to keep its head in a lowered position for extended periods. The molars were also hypselodont to deal with rapid wear from particularly abrasive vegetation. It was distributed across much of South America and appears to have been very adaptable in terms of its habitat and local flora. Predators of Toxodon included large cats such as Southern Smilodon (*Smilodon populator*).

SEE ENTRY ON PAGE 563

NOTOPITHECUS ADAPINUS

NAME MEANING: Southern ape like *Adapis*

AGE: Middle Eocene (42–38 MYA)

DISTRIBUTION: South America

SIZE: 1 foot (30 centimeters) HBL; 2 pounds (800–1,000 grams)

DIET: Herbivore; browser

ESSENTIAL FACTS: This animal's name was coined in 1887 by Florentino Ameghino, who initially believed these animals to be a type of primate due to certain characteristics of the teeth. Later with the discovery of its limb bones, it was realized that it was an ungulate.

INTERATHERIUM RODENS

NAME MEANING: Between beast with gnawing teeth

AGE: Early Miocene (18–16 MYA)

DISTRIBUTION: South America

SIZE: 15 inches (38 centimeters) HBL; 2–7 pounds (1–3 kilograms)

DIET: Herbivore; grazer

ESSENTIAL FACTS: Members of *Interatherium* were built quite differently from other interatheres. The body proportions were somewhat squirrel-like, with a long body set on shortened legs. The head was robust with especially powerful chewing muscles. This may indicate a diet centered around particularly tough or fibrous foods.

PROTYPOTHERIUM ANTIQUUM

NAME MEANING: Ancient before *Typotherium*

AGE: Early Miocene (21–19 MYA)

DISTRIBUTION: South America

SIZE: About rabbit-sized

DIET: Herbivore

ESSENTIAL FACTS: The genus *Protypotherium* has many species attributed to it, spanning from the Early to Late Miocene. They were swift runners with slender, digitigrade limbs and long hindfeet similar to those of a rabbit or hare.

MIOCOCHILIUS ANOMOPODUS

NAME MEANING: Irregular-footed Cochilius from the Miocene

AGE: Middle Miocene (13.5–11.5 MYA)

DISTRIBUTION: South America

SIZE: 12–15 inches (30–38 centimeters) HBL; 24–30 pounds (11–13 kilograms)

DIET: Herbivore; grazer

ESSENTIAL FACTS: Miocochilius is built quite differently from other interatheres, having slender limbs and cloven hooves adapted for sudden bursts of speed. Morphologically or ecologically, it is perhaps most comparable to a peccary.

SANTIAGOROTHIA CHILIENSIS

NAME MEANING: Santiago Roth from Chile

AGE: Early Oligocene (33–31 MYA)

DISTRIBUTION: South America

SIZE: 20–26 inches (55–65 centimeters) HBL; 11–15 pounds (5–7 kilograms)

DIET: Herbivore; grazer

ESSENTIAL FACTS: One of the more common herbivores of the Tinguiririca fossil site, it is named after paleontologist Santiago Roth, in honor of his significant contributions to South American paleontology.

MESOTHERIIDAE

Mesotheres were semi-fossorial herbivores similar to modern wombats. It features notable digging adaptations that include strong claws and reinforcement of the elbow joint and pelvis. The first incisors are rodent-like, being enlarged, hypselodont, and have enamel only covering the anterior surface. All species have hypsodont cheek teeth, and later forms become hypselodont and covered by a thick layer of cementum. These adaptations show that they were adapted to feed on highly abrasive foods covered in silica. The oldest fossils are known from the Early Oligocene, and they appear to become extinct during the Pleistocene.

TRACHYTHERUS ALLOXUS

NAME MEANING: Abundant rough beast

AGE: Late Oligocene (27–26 MYA)

DISTRIBUTION: South America

SIZE: 3–3.3 feet (90–100 centimeters) HBL; 50–60 pounds (24–28 kilograms)

DIET: Herbivore; grazer

ESSENTIAL FACTS: The most completely known of all the mesotheres, this species provides a reference when scholars infer what other, less complete mesotheres may have looked like.

ALTITYPOTHERIUM CHUCALENSIS

NAME MEANING: *Typotherium* of Chucal, Altiplano

AGE: Early Miocene (18–17 MYA)

DISTRIBUTION: South America

SIZE: 2–2.5 feet (72–80 centimeters) HBL; 20–28 pounds (9–13 kilograms)

DIET: Herbivore; grazer

ESSENTIAL FACTS: Described in 2004 based on material recovered from the Chucal Fomation in northern Chile, it is one of the smaller species of mesotheres, barely larger than a marmot.

TYPOTHERIOPSIS CHASICOENSIS

NAME MEANING: Like *Typotherium* from Arroyo Chasico

AGE: Late Miocene (10–9 MYA)

DISTRIBUTION: South America

SIZE: 3–3.5 feet (1–1.2 meters) HBL; 50–75 pounds (22–33 kilograms)

DIET: Herbivore; grazer

ESSENTIAL FACTS: One of the larger mesotheres, Typotheriopsis had an exceptionally broad skull and thickened teeth, possibly indicating that roots and tubers comprised a particularly large proportion of its diet.

PLESIOTYPOTHERIUM ACHIRENSE

NAME MEANING: Near *Typotherium* from Achiri

AGE: Late Miocene (8–6 MYA)

DISTRIBUTION: South America

SIZE: About wombat-sized

DIET: Herbivore; grazer

ESSENTIAL FACTS: A partial adult skeleton of this species was discovered with several pathologies, such as the loss of its first lower molars (m1) due to a periodontal disease and bone tumors in its forelimbs. Surprisingly, these afflictions do not appear to have caused its death, and it lived a rather long life.

HYPSITHERIUM BOLIVIANUM

NAME MEANING: High beast from Bolivia

AGE: Pliocene (4–3 MYA)

DISTRIBUTION: South America

SIZE: About beaver-sized

DIET: Herbivore; grazer

ESSENTIAL FACTS: The genus name of this mesothere references its discovery in the eastern Andean Cordillera at about 10,500 feet (3,200 meters) above sea level.

MESOTHERIUM CRISTATUM

NAME MEANING: Crested middle beast

AGE: Pleistocene

DISTRIBUTION: South America

SIZE: 120–220 pounds (55–100 kilograms)

DIET: Herbivore; grazer

ESSENTIAL FACTS: The name Mesotherium was given due to the belief that these animals were intermediate between rodents and ungulates because of their rodent-like hypselodont incisors. They were among the largest of the mesotheres, growing to the size of sheep, and this particular species was also one of the last.

HEGETOTHERIIDAE

Hegetotheres are notable for their rabbit-like body proportions, likely filling a similar niches during South America's isolation. In addition to their cursorial adaptations, there is evidence that these animals were semi-fossorial and took shelter in burrows. The family first appear in the Late Oligocene and become extinct in the Late Pliocene.

HEGETOTHERIINAE

The cursorial adaptations within this subfamily are less developed than in the more derived pachyrukhines with relatively shorter hindlimbs. Their fossils are known mostly from the early to middle Miocene.

HEGETOTHERIUM MIRABILE

NAME MEANING: Unknown

AGE: Early Miocene (21–18 MYA)

DISTRIBUTION: South America

SIZE: About rabbit-sized

DIET: Herbivore

ESSENTIAL FACTS: This species was a rabbit-like animal with teeth adapted to graze on relatively tough plants like grasses. They were cursorial and may have lived in colonies. It is the type genus and species for the family, described in 1887 by Florentino Ameghino.

ETHEGOTHERIUM CARETTEI

NAME MEANING: Carette's *Hegetotherium*

AGE: Middle Miocene (18–14 MYA)

DISTRIBUTION: South America

SIZE: About rabbit-sized

DIET: Herbivore

ESSENTIAL FACTS: This species was described in 1947. It is only known from a skull and jaw found in Argentina, but it can be inferred that it was a rabbit-like animal like its more completely known relatives.

HEMIHEGETOTHERIUM TRILOBUS

NAME MEANING: Three-lobed half *Hegetotherium*

AGE: Middle Miocene (13–12 MYA)

DISTRIBUTION: South America

SIZE: 28–36 inches (70–90 centimeter); 20–38 pounds (9–17 kilogram)

DIET: Herbivore; mixed feeder

ESSENTIAL FACTS: This species was one of the more common animals from the Quebrada Honda site. It is distinguishable from other members of its genus by the presence of a trilobed third lower molar, hence its species name meaning "three lobes."

PACHYRUKHINAE

This subfamily is characterized by its specialized chewing apparatus similar to that of sciurimorph rodents, making them the only non-rodent mammals to have such an adaptation. This, combined with their hypselodont cheek teeth, suggests that they fed on ground-level vegetation. These animals had particularly rabbit-like skeletons with elongated hindlimbs that would have given them a bounding gait when running.

PROSOTHERIUM GARZONI

NAME MEANING: Garzon's before *Sotherium*

AGE: Late Oligocene (29–24 MYA)

DISTRIBUTION: South America

SIZE: About rabbit-sized

DIET: Herbivore

ESSENTIAL FACTS: This species is known for complete skeletons preserved inside the animals' burrows. Compared to the closely related genus *Pachyrukhos*, the femur of this animal was longer, the tibia and fibula unfused, the feet shorter. These features show it was less optimized for running.

PACHYRUKHOS MOYANI

NAME MEANING: Moyan's thick spine

AGE: Early Miocene (21–15.5 MYA)

DISTRIBUTION: South America

SIZE: 1 foot (30 centimeters) HBL

DIET: Herbivore; grazer

ESSENTIAL FACTS: The skull and skeletal anatomy of Moyan's Hegetothere was particularly rabbit-like, and likely moved in a similar fashion. Its hearing apparatus was also complex, and it may have possessed enlarged ears. It exhibits fusion of the tibia and fibula and elongation of the hindfeet, adaptations for cursoriality.

PAEDOTHERIUM TYPICUM

NAME MEANING: Typical child beast

AGE: Pliocene to Pleistocene (4.5–1.5 MYA)

DISTRIBUTION: South America

SIZE: 12–16 inches (30–40 centimeters) HBL; 2–4 pounds (1–2 kilograms)

DIET: Herbivore; grazer

ESSENTIAL FACTS: Fossils of this species are commonly found in collapsed burrows. Its skull was particularly rabbit-like. Several species of this genus coexisted during the Pliocene.

TREMACYLLUS IMPRESSUS

NAME MEANING: Unknown

AGE: Pleistocene

DISTRIBUTION: South America

SIZE: About hare-sized

DIET: Herbivore; grazer

ESSENTIAL FACTS: Together with hegetotheres of the genus *Paedotherium*, this species is among the last hegetotheres. These animals probably faced extinction due to competition pressure from rapidly breeding rabbits during the Great American Biotic Interchange.

PERISSODACTYLA

Perissodactyla is the order of mammalian herbivores which includes modern tapirs (Tapiridae), rhinos (Rhinoceratidae), and horses (Equidae). This group is characterized by having third digits on each foot, which are enlarged and reinforced to carry most of the body weight. As a result, families within this order independently lost the first and fifth digits (similar to your thumb and pinky finger, respectively). This reduced the number of functional digits down to at least three, as in modern rhinos and the hindfeet of tapirs. For this reason, perissodactyls are commonly referred to as the "odd-toed ungulates." The group first appears in the fossil record during the Early Paleocene. During the first half of the Cenozoic Era, perissodactyls dominated the medium- to large-sized herbivore niches, with a diversity unseen in the group today. Increasingly through the Miocene, perissodactyls experience a gradual decline that coincides with an increase in artiodactyl diversity. Today there are seventeen modern species of perissodactyls, compared to the 230 species of artiodactyl.

HYOPSODONTIDAE

At first glance hyopsodontids might appear to be related to rodents or hyraxes. However, analysis of the inner-ear morphology suggests a relation to the Perissodactyla, apparently having branched off very early in the group's history. They were small hypocarnivores that ranged from rat-sized to raccoon-sized. Their fossil record extends from the Early Paleocene to the Early Eocene.

HYPSODUS WORTMANI

NAME MEANING: Wortman's high tooth

AGE: Early Eocene (56–50 MYA)

DISTRIBUTION: North America

SIZE: About hyrax-sized

DIET: Hypocarnivore

ESSENTIAL FACTS: *Hypsodus* are sometimes referred to as "tube-sheep" for their elongated bodies and short legs. They were nocturnal foragers with an excellent sense of smell and a rudimentary form of echolocation used to find food in the dark, which included fruits, fungi, soft leaves, and invertebrates.

PHENACODONTIDAE

Phenacodonts were terrestrial animals that evolved during the Middle Paleocene and lasted until the Middle Eocene. Most had bunodont dentition, suggesting a hypocarnivorous diet that included large quantities of plants with the ready inclusion of small animal prey. Later species became more optimized for herbivory, with lophodont dentition to shred particularly tough plants to make digestion easier. In general, they were cat- to sheep-sized animals, some having long limbs adapted for cursoriality. They also had long tails for balance and five-toed feet with small hooves at the end of each digit. The middle (third) toe of each foot was the largest, and the first and fifth digits were becoming more reduced, foreshadowing the condition seen in later perissodactyls.

TETRACLAENODON PUERCENSIS

NAME MEANING: Four-cusped teeth from the Puercan

AGE: Late Paleocene (61–56 MYA)

DISTRIBUTION: North America

SIZE: About cat-sized

DIET: Hypocarnivore

ESSENTIAL FACTS: The extremities of this animal's digits were tipped in claws that were starting to appear more like hooves, and the first and fifth digits were unreduced and still functional in weight distribution. Its bunodont dentition suggests a mixed diet of softer plants like fruits and some animal matter such as insects.

PHENACODONTINAE

Members of Phenacodontinae are small- to medium-sized mammals with robust bodies and generalized dentitions able to deal with a wide range of foods, although plant matter would have formed the base of their diets. They may have filled the ecological niches filled by certain forest-dwelling pigs today.

PHENACODUS PRIMAEVUS

NAME MEANING: Ancient deceptive tooth

AGE: Late Paleocene

DISTRIBUTION: North America

SIZE: 5 feet (1.5 meters) HBL; 123 pounds (56 kilograms)

DIET: Herbivore; browser

ESSENTIAL FACTS: This sheep-sized animal is one of the largest of the phenacodonts. It was built somewhat like a pig with a relatively long body set on relatively short limbs. Its head was small with bunodont dentition for selective feeding on soft plant material, fungi, and the occasional small animal.

ECTOCION OSBORNIANUS

NAME MEANING: Osborn's sometimes Ectocyon

AGE: Late Paleocene (56–55 MYA)

DISTRIBUTION: North America

SIZE: About fox-sized

DIET: Herbivore; browser

ESSENTIAL FACTS: The teeth of this species and other members of its genus are intermediate between bunodont and lophodont (bunolophodont), showing that it was transitioning from a hypocarnivorous diet to a more herbivorous one.

MENISCOTHERIINAE

Meniscotheriines were more specialized for herbivory and cursoriality than other phenacodonts and are also relatively common in the fossil record, suggesting they had higher population densities and were potentially gregarious.

MENISCOTHERIUM CHAMENSE

NAME MEANING: Robust beast from the earth

AGE: Early Eocene (54–48 MYA)

DISTRIBUTION: North America

SIZE: 11–38 pounds (5–17 kilograms)

DIET: Herbivore; browser

ESSENTIAL FACTS: Among the phenacodonts, *Meniscotherium* were most specialized for herbivory. Its teeth have high and complex lophs for processing fibrous, low-growing leaves and fruits. Its hindlimbs were longer than the forelimbs, enabling rapid acceleration and agility when bounding through the forest undergrowth.

ANTHRACOBUNIDAE

Anthracobunids have a sparse fossil record. Most species are known only from fragmentary remains or isolated teeth, although a few well-preserved jaws are known. The group occurs in the fossil record from the Early to Middle Eocene and are geographically limited to the Indo-Pakistan landmass which, at the time these animals lived, was not yet fully connected to the rest of the Eurasian continent. They were semiaquatic herbivores that spent much of their time in water but fed on terrestrial plants that grew nearby. They are the most likely ancestors of the desmostylians.

ANTHRACOBUNE WARDI

NAME MEANING: Ward's coal mound

AGE: Middle Eocene

DISTRIBUTION: Eurasia

SIZE: About tapir-sized

DIET: Herbivore; browser

ESSENTIAL FACTS: Ward's Anthracobune is the largest-known anthracobunid, inhabiting marshy environments where it fed on soft aquatic plants and shoreline terrestrial vegetation. It is known for a nearly complete lower jaw and partial skull.

JOZARIA PALUSTRIS

NAME MEANING: Joazara Rest House in the marsh

AGE: Middle Eocene

DISTRIBUTION: Eurasia

SIZE: Unknown

DIET: Herbivore; browser

ESSENTIAL FACTS: Geological evidence shows that Jozaria inhabited brackish marsh environments, where it fed on soft aquatic plants. Its fossils are known from the Kuldana Formation of Kohat, Pakistan.

PILGRIMELLA PILGRIM

NAME MEANING: Guy Ellcock Pilgrim

AGE: Early Eocene

DISTRIBUTION: Eurasia

SIZE: Unknown

DIET: Herbivore; browser

ESSENTIAL FACTS: Known only from isolated teeth, this species was suggested to have been an artiodactyl, close to the ancestry of anthracotheres (Anthracotheriidae), in 1958. A 2008 study later confirmed that the animal was a basal perissodactyl outside of any of the more well-known families. It was finally placed among the Anthracobunidae in 2014.

OBERGFELLIA OCCIDENTALIS

NAME MEANING: See description

AGE: Middle Eocene

DISTRIBUTION: Eurasia

SIZE: About pig-sized

DIET: Herbivore; browser

ESSENTIAL FACTS: Obergfellia was named in honor of the paleontologists Friedlinde Obergfell and her husband A. Ranga Rao. Both were crucial in the initial discovery and description of the Kalakot fauna, the best-known Eocene land mammal fauna from India. Its species name, Latin for "west," honors Robert M. West, who discovered and described the holotype under the genus *Anthracobune*.

TAPIRIDAE

Tapirs are a long-lived family of forest-dwelling herbivores that first appear during the Early Eocene. All are adapted to a browsing diet, with none evolving the specializations for grazing or cursoriality seen in other perissodactyls.

HELALETINAE

Sometimes treated as a separate family, the Helaletidae, these early tapirs were mostly small-bodied herbivores known to have lived from the Early Eocene to the Early Oligocene. Ecologically, these animals would have been similar to modern duikers.

HELALETES NANUS

NAME MEANING: Small marsh-dweller

AGE: Early Eocene (54–50 MYA)

DISTRIBUTION: North America

SIZE: About fox-sized

DIET: Herbivore; browser

ESSENTIAL FACTS: One of the oldest tapirs, already this species had a greatly retracted nasal notch that opened one-third up the length of the skull. Rather than a proboscis, it possessed a semi-prehensile upper lip, similar to modern browsing rhinos, that enabled it to pull food within range of its front teeth.

HEPTODON CALCICULUS

NAME MEANING: Seven teeth from the limestone

AGE: Early Eocene (50.3–48.6 MYA)

DISTRIBUTION: North America

SIZE: 3.3 feet (1 meter) HBL; 40 pounds (18 kilograms)

DIET: Herbivore; browser

ESSENTIAL FACTS: Like its close relative, the Little Marsh Tapir (*Helaletes nanus*), this species inhabited the tropical rainforests that once covered North America, where it fed primarily on soft leaves, shoots, seeds, buds, and fruits. When threatened with predation its first defense would be to hide.

COLODON OCCIDENTALIS

NAME MEANING: Short tooth from the west

AGE: Early Oligocene

DISTRIBUTION: North America

SIZE: About pig-sized

DIET: Herbivore; browser

ESSENTIAL FACTS: Members of the genus *Colodon* were the first tapirs to have fully bilophodont cheek teeth like those of modern tapirs, suggesting a highly folivorous diet. They also possessed retracted nasals almost as extreme as those of modern tapirs, suggesting the presence of a true proboscis.

TAPIRINAE

The subfamily Tapirinae, which includes the modern tapirs, first appear in the fossil record during the Early Oligocene in Europe. There are four modern species: one inhabiting southeast Asia and the remaining three inhabiting the tropics of the New World, although in the prehistoric past they were also present in the temperate forests of the north. They are characterized by their highly retracted nasals and well-developed proboscises. These herbivores remained conservative in their morphology throughout their evolutionary history. The presence of tapirs in any given fossil locality is generally seen as an indicator of an ancient forest ecosystem.

PROTAPIRUS PRISCUS

NAME MEANING: Ancient before *Tapirus*

AGE: Late Oligocene (25–23 MYA)

DISTRIBUTION: Eurasia

SIZE: About pig-sized

DIET: Herbivore; browser

ESSENTIAL FACTS: Members of the genus *Protapirus* are sometimes considered the first "true" tapirs. However, their premolars were not as molariform and the nasals were not as retracted, showing that it had not yet developed the proboscis possessed by later species.

PARATAPIRUS INTERMEDIUS

NAME MEANING: Intermediate beside *Tapirus*

AGE: Late Oligocene (25 MYA)

DISTRIBUTION: Eurasia

SIZE: About tapir-sized

DIET: Herbivore; browser

ESSENTIAL FACTS: The scientific name of this species may reference its dentition, which is intermediate between that of older tapirs like *Protapirus* and modern tapirs of the genus *Tapirus*, with greater molarization of the premolars.

MIOTAPIRUS HARRISONENSIS

NAME MEANING: Lesser *Tapirus* from the Harrisonian

AGE: Early Miocene (20 MYA)

DISTRIBUTION: North America

SIZE: 6.8 feet (2 meters) HBL

DIET: Herbivore; browser

ESSENTIAL FACTS: A species virtually identical in overall form to modern tapirs, Miotapirus is named for the proposed North American Land Mammal Age, the Harrisonian. This period of geologic time would cover 24.8 to 20.6 million years ago when this tapir would have lived.

PLESIOTAPIRUS YAGII

NAME MEANING: Yagi's near *Tapirus*

AGE: Early Miocene

DISTRIBUTION: Eurasia

SIZE: About tapir-sized

DIET: Herbivore; browser

ESSENTIAL FACTS: Yagi's Tapir was first described in 1921, based on fragmentary material from Japan. More complete material was later collected in China in 1991, among which is a complete skull currently housed in Paleozoological Museum of China.

TAPIRUS POLKENSIS

NAME MEANING: Tapir from Polk County

AGE: Late Miocene to early Pliocene (7–4 MYA)

DISTRIBUTION: North America

SIZE: 3 feet (90 centimeters) SH; 276 pounds (125 kilograms)

DIET: Herbivore; browser

ESSENTIAL FACTS: Dwarf Tapir was a sheep-sized browser that inhabited the subtropical forests of eastern North America. It is the best known of all fossil tapirs, thanks to the huge number of specimens unearthed at the Gray Fossil Site in East Tennessee.

TAPIRUS WEBBI

NAME MEANING: David Webb's tapir

AGE: Late Miocene (9.5–8 MYA)

DISTRIBUTION: North America

SIZE: 880 pounds (400 kilograms)

DIET: Herbivore; browser

ESSENTIAL FACTS: So far, Webb's Tapir is only known to have lived in the state of Florida. Like the Dwarf Tapir (*Tapirus polkensis*), its limbs appear to have been relatively long compared to those of other tapirs. It may have been adapted to browse on leaves higher off the ground.

TAPIRUS AUGUSTUS

NAME MEANING: Majestic tapir

AGE: Pleistocene

DISTRIBUTION: Eurasia

SIZE: 1,373 pounds (623 kilograms)

DIET: Herbivore; browser

ESSENTIAL FACTS: Known to have inhabited the forests of southeast Asia, the Giant Tapir is the largest-known species of tapir, about the size of a small Sumatran Rhino (*Dicerorhinus sumatrensis*). It was formerly placed within its own genus, *Megatapirus*.

TAPIRUS VEROENSIS

NAME MEANING: Tapir from Vero

AGE: Pleistocene

DISTRIBUTION: North America

SIZE: 510 pounds (230 kilograms)

DIET: Herbivore; browser

ESSENTIAL FACTS: The first fossil remains of this tapir were discovered in Vero Beach, Florida, in 1915. It has since been found throughout the eastern and southern United States and, like the modern mountain tapir (*T. pinchaque*), may have grown a woolly winter coat to deal with cold temperatures.

LOPHIODONTIDAE

Lophiodonts are a poorly understood family of perissodactyls known only from the Eocene of Europe. They attained a modest diversity during the period, when the continent was a tropical archipelago. Although often compared to tapirs, they are thought to be close relatives of chalicotheres (Chalicotheriidae), though it is unknown whether these animals had hooves or claws.

LOPHIODON LAUTRICENSE

NAME MEANING: Crested tooth from Lautrec

AGE: Middle Eocene

DISTRIBUTION: Europe

SIZE: About pig-sized

DIET: Herbivore; browser

ESSENTIAL FACTS: Like other lophiodonts, this species was a robust herbivore with a long, muscular body set on relatively short legs. It would have resembled a short-legged tapir, although it lacked a proboscis. Its well-developed canines were used as weapons against predators or rivals.

CHALICOTHERIIDAE

The chalicotheres are an interesting family of perissodactyls, famous for having digits that ended in large, sturdy claws which were anchored to deep fissures in the third phalanges. Chalicothere claws were very strong and able to resist heavy impacts and tension. This suggests the animals evolved from ancestors that would dig up food items such as roots and tubers, later adapting them to hook onto overhanging branches to browse. Adult chalicotheres lacked canines and upper incisors with which to crop vegetation, likely possessing a long, prehensile tongue and muscular lips like those of giraffids that would pull food into their mouths. The family is known to have lived from the Middle Eocene to the Pleistocene.

SCHIZOTHERIINAE

Schizotheriines had a conventional digitigrade posture, walking on padded toes. To prevent wear and to allow unhindered movement, the tips of the claws were held above the ground when walking or running, thanks to tendons in the toes. Most schizotheriines were able to live in more open woodland and savanna environments, where their efficient gait enabled them to travel farther distances to exploit widely dispersed food sources. They typically had long necks and long, narrow skulls for browsing and could reach higher branches by balancing on their hindlimbs like goats. To withstand the weight of the body and facilitate an upright posture for extended periods, the lower back was shortened and reinforced by well-developed neural spines, which supported muscles and tendons. Furthermore, analysis of chalicothere teeth suggests that schizotheriines preferentially fed on more leaves and twigs, while chalicotheriines were ingesting more seeds and fruits in addition to leaves. This subfamily is known to have lived from the Late Eocene to the Pleistocene.

MOROPUS ELATUS

NAME MEANING: Lofty slow foot

AGE: Early Miocene (23–20 MYA)

DIET: Herbivore; browser

DISTRIBUTION: North America

SIZE: 8 feet (2.4 meters) SH; 12 feet (3.6 meters); 2,200–4,400 pounds (1,000–2000 kilograms)

SEE MORE ON PAGES 586–587

TYLOCEPHALONYX SKINNERI

NAME MEANING: Skinner's knob head claw

AGE: Middle Miocene (16–13 MYA)

DISTRIBUTION: North America

SIZE: 6 feet (1.8 meters) SH; 2,200 pounds (1,000 kilograms)

DIET: Herbivore; browser

ESSENTIAL FACTS: Male chalicotheres grew considerably larger than the females, possessing thickened and reinforced skull bones that imply a head-butting fighting style similar to that of giraffes (*Giraffa camelopardalis*). Skinner's Chalicothere takes this to the extreme, having a prominent domed skull similar to that of a pachycephalosaur.

ANCYLOTHERIUM HENNIGI

NAME MEANING: Hennig's hooked beast

AGE: Pliocene to Pleistocene (4–2 MYA)

DISTRIBUTION: Africa

SIZE: 5–6.6 feet (1.5–2 meters) SH; 990 pounds (450 kilograms)

DIET: Herbivore; browser

ESSENTIAL FACTS: One of the last of the schizotheriine chalicotheres, the Hennig's Chalicothere teeth were relatively hypsodont compared of other chalicotheres. This suggests the creature had a diet that included more tougher leaves or low-growing vegetation. Three-clawed footprints of this species have been found at the Laetoli site in Tanzania.

CHALICOTHERIINAE

The chalicotheriines walked on their knuckles to preserve their claws. They possessed thickened and well-developed second phalanges adapted for bearing weight. In the living animals, thickened skin pads would have covered the upper surface of the knuckles to cushion the digits, preventing abrasion. Modern gorillas and anteaters have the same adaptation, which is designed to protect either their touch-sensitive fingertips or pointed claw tips, respectively. Compared to the schizotheriines, chalicotheriines had shorter necks and much longer arms, suggesting they relied more on their forelimbs and inward-facing hands to hook branches and pull them toward their mouths. The short, yet powerful hindlimbs were well-suited for maintaining a sitting or squatting posture for extended periods of time, with pad-supporting bone on the ischium to act as a cushion. This stabilized the creature on its haunches while its torso stood fully vertical. This subfamily is known to have lived from the Middle Miocene to the Pleistocene.

ANISODON GRANDE

NAME MEANING: Big unequal teeth

AGE: Late Miocene

DISTRIBUTION: Eurasia

SIZE: 5 feet (1.5 meters) SH; (600 kilograms)

DIET: Herbivore; browser

ESSENTIAL FACTS: This species was formerly named *Chalicotherium grande*. Like other chalicotheriines, the Great Chalicothere lived in thickly forested environments where they could use their unique feeding strategy to full advantage.

MOROPUS ELATUS

ESSENTIAL FACTS: The Lofty Moropus is the most well-studied of all the chalicotheres. It was widespread throughout the open woodlands and savannas of North America, but the best and most abundant remains of this species come from the Agate Fossil Beds in Nebraska. The remains of 17 individuals were found together at this site in a confined space, suggesting these animals moved in small herds for protection against predators. These chalicotheres moved efficiently across their habitat, where they would browse on trees and bushes. When it stood up on its hindlimbs, this animal had a vertical reach rivaling that of a giraffe (*Giraffa camelopardalis*).

There is evidence of a possible predator-prey relationship between this animal and the Giant Entelodont (*Daeodon shoshonensis*). Bite marks matching the teeth of the entelodont have been found on the bones of the chalicothere. Whether or not these chalicotheres were actively hunted or scavenged is unknown, but either scenario is possible. Because of their large size and powerful claws that could be wielded in defense, adult Lofty Moropus would have had little to fear from all but the largest predators. Juveniles and subadults were vulnerable to attack from various species of bear-dog (Amphicyonidae), which had become quite diverse by the early Miocene; some like the Running Bear-Dog (*Delotrochanter oryktes*) were wolflike pack-hunters while others like the American Ysengrinia (*Ysengrinia americanus*) were powerful ambush-predators that attacked prey from cover.

SEE ENTRY ON PAGE 584

HESPEROTHERIUM SINENSE

NAME MEANING: Western beast from China

AGE: Pleistocene (1 MYA–700,000 YA)

DISTRIBUTION: Eurasia

SIZE: About gorilla-sized

DIET: Herbivore; browser

ESSENTIAL FACTS: One of the last-known chalicotheres, this species is known to have lived in modern-day China and potentially the rest of eastern and southern Asia.

BRONTOTHERIIDAE

Brontotheres, also known as titanotheres, were a family of rhino-like perissodactyls known to have lived from the Early to Late Eocene and were distributed across the Northern Hemisphere. They were the largest land mammals to have evolved during the Eocene, with later species growing to the size of small elephants. Brontotheres are characterized by a W-shaped shearing blade on their upper molars. Many members of the group developed bony nose horns, which grew from reinforced nasals. Most of the hornless species had relatively large canine teeth, which males would use to fight other males for territory or mates. Like tapirs, they had four toes on the forefeet and three toes on the hindfeet. Despite their rhino-like appearance, brontotheres are more closely related to horses (Equidae).

EOTITANOPS BOREALIS

NAME MEANING: Northern dawn titan-face

AGE: Early Eocene (54–50 MYA)

DISTRIBUTION: North America

SIZE: 1.5 feet (45 centimeters) SH; 40 pounds (18 kilograms)

DIET: Herbivore

ESSENTIAL FACTS: One of the earliest and smallest of the brontotheres, being about the size of a small dog. It would have looked similar to, albeit more robust, than the early horses and rhinos with which it coexisted.

PALAEOSYOPS ROBUSTUS

NAME MEANING: Robust ancient boar-face

AGE: Middle Eocene (50–46 MYA)

DISTRIBUTION: North America

SIZE: 1,322–1,763 pounds (600–800 kilograms)

DIET: Herbivore; browser

ESSENTIAL FACTS: A large perissodactyl for its time, about the size of a large wild ox (*Bos*), this browsing herbivore coexisted with rhino-sized uinatheres and would have been preyed upon by large mesonychians and oxyaenodonts.

SPHENOCOELUS HYOGNATHUS

NAME MEANING: Pig-jawed wedged-hollow

AGE: Middle Eocene (46.2–40 MYA)

DISTRIBUTION: North America

SIZE: 4 feet (1.2 meters) SH

DIET: Herbivore

ESSENTIAL FACTS: This brontothere had a notably elongated skull with a retracted nasal notch that opened just in front of the eyes. The nasal bone itself was long and thickened. This indicates the presence of a small proboscis, but their robust nature may also indicate these animals had a combat system based on head-shoving.

PROTITANOTHERIUM EMARGINATUM

NAME MEANING: Before *Titanotherium* with a notch

AGE: Middle Eocene

DISTRIBUTION: North America

SIZE: About ox-sized

DIET: Herbivore

ESSENTIAL FACTS: One of the earliest of the horned brontotheres, this species had a pair of small nasal horns set side by side.

RHINOTITAN MONGOLIENSIS

NAME MEANING: Nose giant from Mongolia

AGE: Late Eocene (37–34 MYA)

DISTRIBUTION: Eurasia

SIZE: About bison-sized

DIET: Herbivore

ESSENTIAL FACTS: The Mongolian Rhinotitan was a bison-sized animal that had sexually dimorphic horns. Because both sexes possessed horns, it is likely that these animals lived in mixed-sex herds in which males would occasionally engage each other in ritualized, low-risk battles to settle disputes.

MEGACEROPS COLORADENSIS

NAME MEANING: Great horn from Colorado

AGE: Late Eocene (38–34 MYA)

DISTRIBUTION: North America

SIZE: 8.2 feet (2.5 meters) SH; 15.2 feet (4.63 meters) HBL; 6,000–8,000 pounds (2,721–3,628 kilograms)

DIET: Herbivore

ESSENTIAL FACTS: This species was one of the last and most well-known of the North American brontotheres. Males had a single large, Y-shaped horn on their noses, while females had much smaller paired horns. They were the largest herbivores of their time, and adults are unlikely to have had any predators.

EMBOLOTHERIUM ANDREWSI

NAME MEANING: Andrews' battering ram beast

AGE: Late Eocene (37–34 MYA)

DISTRIBUTION: Eurasia

SIZE: About elephant-sized

DIET: Herbivore

ESSENTIAL FACTS: Andrews' Brontothere possessed a shallow nasal horn that was slightly curved upward toward the tip. Rather than functioning as a true horn, it has been hypothesized that this structure—with its concave, ventral surface—supported an enlarged nose that may have amplified the sounds of its vocalizations.

EMBOLOTHERIUM GRANGER

NAME MEANING: Granger's battering ram beast

AGE: Late Eocene (37–34 MYA)

DISTRIBUTION: Eurasia

SIZE: About elephant-sized

DIET: Herbivore

ESSENTIAL FACTS: The nasal horn of Granger's Brontothere was much deeper, rising halfway between the eyes and the back of the skull and having a straight profile. This resulted in the shape of the head being very distinctive from Andrews' Brontothere. Postcranial material for both species is scarce, but based on skull size they may have approached the size of elephants.

PALAEOTHERIIDAE

The palaeotheres were browsing herbivores that ranged from cat-sized to deer-sized. They are known to have lived from the Early Eocene to Early Oligocene. They were endemic to Eurasia, and their closest modern relatives are horses. Palaeotheres possessed brachydont dentition and relatively large canines.

HYRACOTHERIUM LEPORINUM

NAME MEANING: Slender-nosed hyrax beast

AGE: Early Eocene (55–50 MYA)

DISTRIBUTION: Eurasia

SIZE: 2.5 feet (78 centimeters) HBL; 20 pounds (9 kilograms)

DIET: North America

ESSENTIAL FACTS: Once thought to be an early horse, this animal is now thought to be closer to palaeotheres. They fed on soft leaves, fruits, shoots, and nuts. Other species have been placed within the genus *Hyracotherium*, but these are all now thought to have been early horses rather than palaeotheres.

PALAEOTHERIUM MAGNUM

NAME MEANING: Great ancient beast

AGE: Late Eocene

DISTRIBUTION: Eurasia

SIZE: 3.3 feet (1.43 meters) SH; 9.1 feet (2.8 meters) HBL

DIET: North America

ESSENTIAL FACTS: This species was one of the larger palaeotheres, having both the size and general body proportions of an okapi (*Okapia johnstoni*). It possessed a relatively long neck and limbs compared to other palaeotheres. It was a high-browser that inhabited forest and woodland habitats.

PLAGIOLOPHUS ANNECTENS

NAME MEANING: Connecting oblique crests

AGE: Late Eocene

DISTRIBUTION: Eurasia

SIZE: About tapir-sized

DIET: North America

ESSENTIAL FACTS: Dental microwear analyses performed on this species show they were selective feeders that browsed on relatively tough or fibrous leaves.

PROPALAEOTHERIUM HASSIACUM

NAME MEANING: Before *Palaeotherium* from Hassia

AGE: Middle Eocene (47–45 MYA)

DISTRIBUTION: Eurasia

SIZE: 1.5 feet (52 centimeters) SH

DIET: Herbivore; browser

ESSENTIAL FACTS: Complete skeletons with preserved gut contents of this animal from Messel Pit show that its diet consisted of soft leaves and fruits on or just above the forest floor, similar to the diet of modern chevrotains (Tragulidae). Its forelimbs were shorter than the hindlimbs, and the neck was notably short for feeding from the forest floor and low-growing plants.

EQUIDAE

Horses were present in both Europe and North America during the Early to Middle Eocene. After becoming extinct in Eurasia, the family underwent most of their evolution and diversification in North America. Horses would not enter the Old World again until the Early Miocene, after which they took part in waves of dispersal events throughout the Neogene. Horses are more cursorial than other perissodactyls, developing longer and more slender limbs and feet with reduced digits. Early horses had digitigrade feet with all three toes touching the ground. Later species would reduce the size of the lateral toes so that they didn't touch the ground. Most early horses were browsers that resembled chevrotains or deer, but during the Middle Miocene one lineage of horses became increasingly adapted to a grazing diet with more hypsodont teeth to resist abrasion.

SIFRHIPPUS SANDRAE

NAME MEANING: Sandra's zero horse

AGE: Early Eocene (56–50 MYA)

DISTRIBUTION: North America

SIZE: 8.5–12 pounds (3.9–5.5 kilograms)

DIET: Herbivore; browser

ESSENTIAL FACTS: The genus name of this species references its status as the oldest-known species of horse. Sandra's Horse was about the size of a large rabbit, with long hindlimbs for bounding through the forest undergrowth. It was originally thought to be a species of *Hyracotherium*.

EOHIPPUS ANGUSTIDENS

NAME MEANING: Narrow-toothed dawn horse

AGE: Early Eocene (54–50 MYA)

DISTRIBUTION: North America

SIZE: About fox-sized

DIET: Herbivore; browser

ESSENTIAL FACTS: This species was originally thought to be a species of *Hyracotherium*, to which it is rather similar in its ecomorphology. It possessed notably sharp and well-developed canines used to settle territorial disputes between individuals of the same species.

EUROHIPPUS MESSELENSIS

NAME MEANING: European horse from Messel Pit

AGE: Middle Eocene (48–45 MYA)

DISTRIBUTION: Eurasia

SIZE: About cat-sized

DIET: Herbivore; browser

ESSENTIAL FACTS: Before it was recognized as an early European horse, the Messel Horse was formerly considered to be a species of *Propaleotherium* in the family Palaeotheriidae. It features the most famous for a skeleton of a pregnant female individual found at Messel Pit, which was reported and described in 2015.

PLIOLOPHUS VULPICEPS

NAME MEANING: Fox-headed (with) more crests

AGE: Early Eocene

DISTRIBUTION: Eurasia

SIZE: About cat-sized

DIET: Herbivore; browser

ESSENTIAL FACTS: This species was described by Sir Richard Owen in 1858 based on a complete skull and mandible discovered in London, who later synonymized it with *Hyracotherium*. The genus was resurrected in 1994, and a second species from France was described in 2017.

PROTOROHIPPUS VENTICOLUM

NAME MEANING: Before Orohippus with a hollow belly

AGE: Early Eocene (55–50 MYA)

DISTRIBUTION: North America

SIZE: About fox-sized

DIET: Herbivore; browser

ESSENTIAL FACTS: This species is known for a complete skeleton found in the Green River Formation in the western United States.

OROHIPPUS PUMILLUS

NAME MEANING: Child mountain horse

AGE: Early Eocene (50 MYA)

DISTRIBUTION: North America

SIZE: About cat-sized

DIET: Herbivore; browser

ESSENTIAL FACTS: A complete skeleton of this species is on display at the American Museum of Natural History. This horse had a notably slender build with limbs adapted for jumping. Its teeth suggest that its diet consisted mostly of leaves and fruits.

ANCHITHERIINAE

Anchitheres were deer-like horses that were either browsers or browse-dominated mixed feeders. They underwent a significant radiation during the Late Oligocene and immigrated into Eurasia during the Early Miocene, becoming the first horses in the Old World since the Eocene. Compared to their Early Eocene ancestors, anchitheres were generally larger. They had longer limbs adapted for more sustained running and leaping, with fully tridactyl (three-toed) feet, the middle toe becoming notably larger and sturdier. Their necks and faces were longer, giving them more range when browsing. The premolars had also become fully molariform for more efficiently processing plant matter. They appear in the fossil record during the Late Eocene to survive until the Middle Pliocene.

MESOHIPPUS BARBOURI

NAME MEANING: Barbour's middle horse

AGE: Early Oligocene (32–30 MYA)

DISTRIBUTION: North America

SIZE: 2 feet (60 centimeters); 55–66 pounds (25–30 kilograms)

DIET: Herbivore; browser

ESSENTIAL FACTS: Members of the genus *Mesohippus* were the first fully tridactyl horses. They were goat-sized animals with faces lengthened by a diastema and the eyes were set farther back on the skull. Endocasts of the skull show that the brain was similar to that of modern horses.

MIOHIPPUS PRIMUS

NAME MEANING: First Miocene horse

AGE: Middle Oligocene (28 MYA)

DISTRIBUTION: North America

SIZE: 2.5 feet (75 centimeters) SH; 88–121 pounds (40–55 kilograms)

DIET: Herbivore; browser

ESSENTIAL FACTS: *Miohippus* averaged larger than *Mesohippus* in body size, with longer skulls and longer limbs. The genus was named by Othneil Charles Marsh in 1874, who mistakenly believed that the animal lived during the Miocene.

ARCHAEOHIPPUS BLACKBERGI

NAME MEANING: Blackberg's ancient horse

AGE: Early Miocene (18 MYA)

DISTRIBUTION: North America

SIZE: 22–66 pounds (10–30 kilograms)

DIET: Herbivore; browser

SEE MORE ON PAGES 598–599

ANCHITHERIUM CLARENCEI

NAME MEANING: Clarence's near beast

AGE: Early Miocene (18 MYA)

DISTRIBUTION: North America

SIZE: 3.3 feet (1 meter) SH

DIET: Herbivore; browser

ESSENTIAL FACTS: Clarence's Horse was about the size of a white-tailed deer (*Odocileus virginianus*). Its hindlimbs were slightly longer than the forelimbs, adapted for leaping over and around obstacles encountered in the forests. Its brachydont teeth and relatively long neck were adapted for a browsing diet.

HYPOHIPPUS OSBORNI

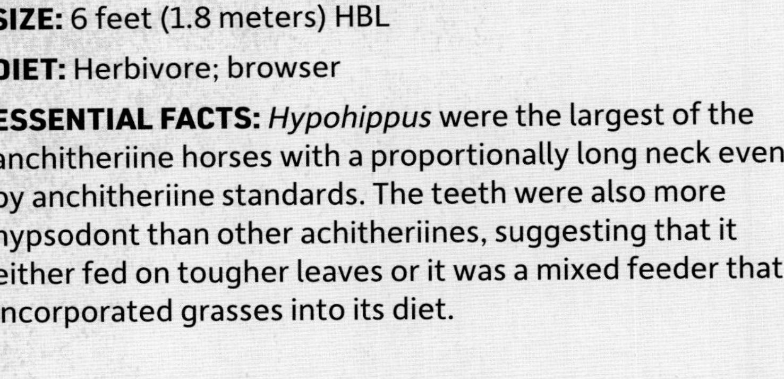

NAME MEANING: Osborn's under horse

AGE: Middle Miocene (15–10 MYA)

DISTRIBUTION: North America

SIZE: 6 feet (1.8 meters) HBL

DIET: Herbivore; browser

ESSENTIAL FACTS: *Hypohippus* were the largest of the anchitheriine horses with a proportionally long neck even by anchitheriine standards. The teeth were also more hypsodont than other achitheriines, suggesting that it either fed on tougher leaves or it was a mixed feeder that incorporated grasses into its diet.

EQUINAE

The equine horses developed more hypsodont teeth with complicated enamel ridges to process abrasive grasses and other ground-level plants and combat tooth wear. As these horses became more adapted to life in open mostly treeless habitats, their limbs became longer and better-suited to running at high speed for long distances to escape predators. In the process, the foot shifted from a digitigrade stance to an unguligrade stance. The central hoof grew larger while the lateral digits shrank and eventually no longer contacted the ground while the foot pads disappeared. There are two tribes within this subfamily: the three-toed Hipparionini and the one-toed Equini, to which all of the eight modern species of horse belong.

PARAHIPPUS LEONENSIS

NAME MEANING: Beside horse from Leon County

AGE: Early Miocene (18 MYA)

DISTRIBUTION: North America

SIZE: 2 feet (60 centimeters) SH; 3 feet (100 centimeters) HBL; 160 pounds (72.5 kilograms)

DIET: Herbivore; mixed feeder

ESSENTIAL FACTS: This species was the most abundant mid- to large-sized mammal recovered from the Thomas Farm site in central Florida. It is an early member of the equine lineage that would lead to the modern horses. It has been estimated that this species had an average lifespan of three to four years and a maximum life expectancy of nine years.

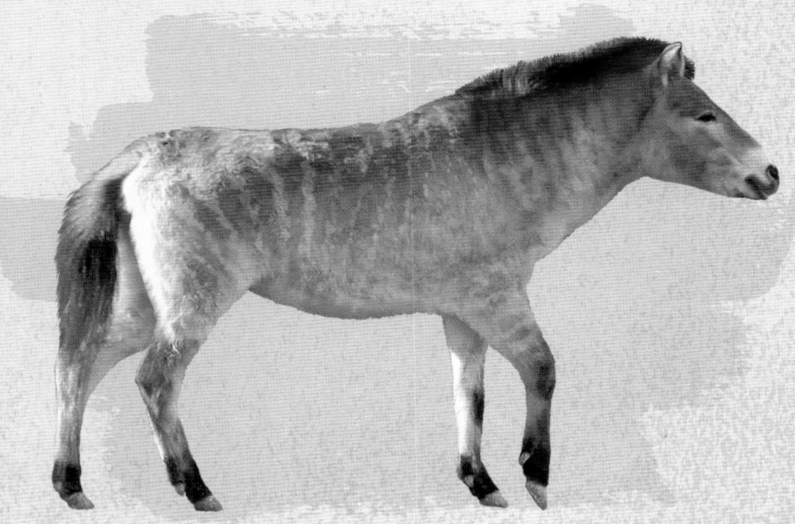

ARCHAEOHIPPUS BLACKBERGI

ESSENTIAL FACTS: Blackberg's Dwarf Horse is among one of the more common animals recovered from the Thomas Farm Site of Central Florida and is the second-most common of the four species of horse known from there. Hundreds of fossils have been recovered, making Thomas Farm the single greatest source for the entire genus. Outside of Florida, this species is also known definitively from Texas, with unconfirmed remains found in Delaware and South Dakota. It was about the size of modern small, forest-dwelling ungulates such as musk deer and likely occupied a similar niche. They possess simple, low-crowned teeth adapted for browsing on low-growing leaves and fruits. The legs were relatively long and slender, adapted for running and leaping through the woodlands and forests in which it lived.

The large volume of fossils recovered from Thomas Farm has allowed paleontologists to learn numerous aspects of the animal's life history. It has been estimated based on tooth eruption sequences that the average life expectancy would have been around five years, with an upper limit of perhaps seven years. A particularly high mortality rate among young adults has also been identified, possibly resulting from fatalities incurred from combat between males over access to territory and females. Male Blackberg's Horses have elongated and sharpened canine teeth, making such confrontations particularly risky for younger, less experienced males.

SEE ENTRY ON PAGE 596

MERYCHIPPUS INSIGNIS

NAME MEANING: Remarkable ruminating horse

AGE: Middle Miocene (16–10 MYA)

DISTRIBUTION: North America

SIZE: About deer-sized

DIET: Herbivore

ESSENTIAL FACTS: *Merychippus* were the first horses to develop a primarily grazing diet. They also shifted from a digitigrade stance to a more unguligrade condition. With its foot supported entirely by ligaments, the animal lost its foot pads, and the lateral toes were reduced in size.

EURYGNATHOHIPPUS WOLDEGABRIELI

NAME MEANING: Giday WoldeGabriel's wide-jawed horse

AGE: Pliocene (4–3 MYA)

DISTRIBUTION: Africa

SIZE: 485–710 pounds (220–332 kilograms)

DIET: Herbivore; grazer

ESSENTIAL FACTS: WoldeGabriel's Horse fossils were discovered in Ethiopia in 2001 and 2002, and the species was formerly described in 2013. It was the size of modern plains zebra (*Equus burchelli*) and likely had a similar niche, being adapted for cursoriality and having a diet consisting of coarse grasses.

HIPPOTHERIUM PRIMIGENIUM

NAME MEANING: Firstborn horse beast

AGE: Late Miocene (12–10 MYA)

DISTRIBUTION: Eurasia

SIZE: 4–5 feet (1.2–1.5 meters) SH; 7–8 feet (2.1–2.4 meters); 377–644 pounds (171–292 kilograms)

DIET: Herbivore; graze-dominated mixed feeder

ESSENTIAL FACTS: This species was a lightly built horse with a similar build to a deer. It was more adapted for leaping and springing through woodland habitats than for sustained running in open grassland. In many ways this species harkened back to the earlier anchitheriine horses.

NEOHIPPARION LEPTODE

NAME MEANING: Slender-footed new *Hipparion*

AGE: Late Miocene

DISTRIBUTION: North America

SIZE: 4.5–5 feet (1.4–1.5 meters) HBL

DIET: Herbivore; graze-dominated mixed feeder

ESSENTIAL FACTS: This species was another deer-like horse more adapted for bouncing than running, with strong hindlimbs and a long torso. A mounted skeleton of this horse is on display at the Natural History Museum of Los Angeles County, positioned as if being chased by Hayden's Epicyon (*Epicyon haydeni*).

NANNIPPUS AZTECUS

NAME MEANING: Aztec dwarf horse

AGE: Late Miocene

DISTRIBUTION: North America

SIZE: 90 pounds (40 kilograms)

DIET: Herbivore; grazer

ESSENTIAL FACTS: Members of the genus *Nannippus* were similar in size and build to small antelopes like gazelles. Fossils of the Aztec Horse are relatively common and are known from Texas, Oklahoma, Florida, and Mexico.

PSEUDHIPPARION SIMPSONI

NAME MEANING: Simpson's false horse

AGE: Late Miocene (7–5 MYA)

DISTRIBUTION: North America

SIZE: 90 pounds (40 kilograms)

DIET: Herbivore; grazer

ESSENTIAL FACTS: Simpson's Horse was a lightweight species built like a gazelle. The dentition of this species suggests that it was feeding on especially abrasive foods.

PROBOSCIDIPPARION PATER

NAME MEANING: Father proboscis horse

AGE: Pliocene to Pleistocene (5.5–1 MYA)

DISTRIBUTION: Eurasia

SIZE: 483–880 pounds (220–400 kilograms)

DIET: Herbivore; grazer

ESSENTIAL FACTS: This species was an unusual browsing hipparionine horse with retracted nasals that suggest the presence of a tapir-like proboscis. It was widespread in Eurasia, ranging from Britain to China and may also be the youngest hipparionine. Its preferred habitat was likely forest and woodland, where it would browse on a wide variety of plants.

HARINGTONHIPPUS FRANCISCI

NAME MEANING: Richard Harrington's horse

AGE: Pleistocene

DISTRIBUTION: North America

SIZE: 368–553 pounds (167–251 kilograms)

DIET: Herbivore; grazer

ESSENTIAL FACTS: Stilt-Legged Horse had a wide distribution, its fossils known from Alaska to Mexico. Described under the genus Equus in 1915, it was assigned the genus *Haringtonhippus* in 2017 due to differences in morphology. Its body proportions were similar to those of asses, with proportionally long and slender legs built for cursoriality.

EQUUS GIGANTEUS

NAME MEANING: Giant horse

AGE: Pliocene to Pleistocene

DISTRIBUTION: North America

SIZE: About bison-sized

DIET: Herbivore

ESSENTIAL FACTS: No complete skeletons of the Giant Horse are known, but known fossils are considerably larger than those of the largest modern draft horses. Estimates from known material scaled up from modern horses suggest an animal that grew about the size of a bison.

EQUUS SIMPLICIDENS

NAME MEANING: Simple-toothed horse

AGE: Pliocene to Pleistocene

DISTRIBUTION: North America

SIZE: 227–848 pounds (110–385 kilograms)

DIET: Herbivore; grazer

ESSENTIAL FACTS: The Hagerman Horse is the most abundant large mammal from the Hagerman Fossil Beds National Monument in Idaho, from which over 200 individuals have been collected. This accumulation may represent a mass death assemblage in which multiple animals were killed by a single catastrophic event.

EQUUS STENONIS

NAME MEANING: Narrow horse

AGE: Pliocene to Pleistocene

DISTRIBUTION: Eurasia

SIZE: 4.2–5 feet (1.3–1.5 meters) SH

DIET: Herbivore

ESSENTIAL FACTS: The Narrow Horse is the oldest one-toed horse known from Europe. Its limbs were relatively long but robust with a relatively long head, similar in proportion to the modern Grevy's zebra (*Equus grevyi*), and its closest modern relatives are thought to be zebras and asses.

EQUUS LAMBEI

NAME MEANING: Lambe's horse

AGE: Pleistocene

DISTRIBUTION: North America

SIZE: 4 feet (1.2 meters) SH

DIET: Herbivore; grazer

SEE MORE ON PAGES 604–605

EQUUS LAMBEI

ESSENTIAL FACTS: The Yukon Horse was abundant in North America's grasslands, ranging from Alaska to the southern United States. It potentially extended its range into Eurasia following the extensive open grassland biome known as Mammoth Steppe, which straddled both continents during glacial intervals. Abundant fossils collected from Beringia shows that it was a particularly common and successful species in this environment. A partial carcass of this species discovered in 1993 in the Yukon permafrost shows that the animal had blonde mane and tail hairs, light-colored body hairs, and dark-colored lower legs. This specimen is on display at the Yukon Beringia Interpretive Centre in Whitehorse, Yukon.

The Yukon Horse was relatively small and lightly built with proportionally long limbs, similar in form to the Tarpan horse breed, which has been speculated to represent a distinct, partly domesticated version of this species. Their social structure was similar to that of modern horses in which a dominant male (stallion) led a small herd of females and their offspring, defending them from other males. Other males without an established maternal herd instead formed bachelor herds. The primary predators of Yukon Horses were pack-hunting canids such as gray wolves (*Canis lupus*) in Eurasia and Dire Wolves (*Aenocyon dirus*) in North America.

SEE ENTRY ON PAGE 603

EQUUS NEOGEUS

NAME MEANING: New horse

AGE: Pleistocene

DISTRIBUTION: South America

SIZE: 5 feet (1.5 meters) SH; 880 pounds (400 kilograms)

DIET: Herbivore; grazer

ESSENTIAL FACTS: This horse inhabited the grassland and open woodlands of South America and was formerly placed in the genus *Amerihippus*. They were primarily grazers but could occasionally browse from bushes and low-hanging tree branches.

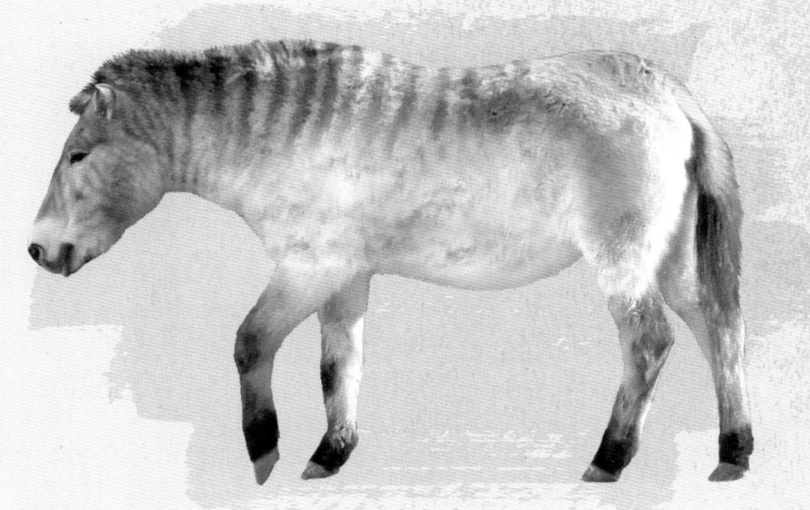

HIPPIDION PRINCIPALE

NAME MEANING: Chief little horse

AGE: Pleistocene

DISTRIBUTION: South America

SIZE: 500–800 pounds (227–363 kilograms)

DIET: Herbivore; browse-dominated mixed feeder

SEE MORE ON PAGES 608–609

RHINOCERATIDAE

Today Rhinoceratidae are limited to five modern species, all of which are endangered and distributed through Africa and southern Asia. Rhinos were once far more common, diverse, and widespread throughout Eurasia, Africa, and North America. Rhinos have proportionally large teeth, with hypsodont crowns and characteristic ridges on the upper cheek teeth that form the Pi Symbol. During the Middle to Late Eocene, rhinos became the first large mammals to become adapted to a graze-dominated diet, while the contemporary brontotheres were mostly browsers or browse-dominated mixed feeders. They did not colonize Africa until the Early Miocene, due to the abundance of large hyraxes and medium-sized proboscideans that were already established there. They were never known to have entered South America.

HYRACHYUS MINIMUS

NAME MEANING: Small hyrax-pig

AGE: Middle Eocene (48–45 MYA)

DISTRIBUTION: Eurasia

SIZE: About sheep-sized

DIET: Herbivore

ESSENTIAL FACTS: *Hyrachyus* was a widespread genus distributed throughout Eurasia and North America, one species even making it to Jamaica. They were fast runners despite being relatively robust. The Little Hyrachyus was a Eurasian species known for complete skeletons from Messel Pit.

HYRACODONTINAE

Far from the short-legged bulky animals we know today, hyracodonts were long-legged cursorial animals that likely had similar ecology and behaviors to horses or antelopes. They had a more hypsodont dentition than many of the contemporary herbivores, suggesting that they were grazers. This made them among the first to adapt to the expanding grassland habitats that were becoming common toward the later Eocene and into the Oligocene. The fossil record for hyracodonts extended from the Middle Eocene to the Late Oligocene, and they were distributed throughout the Northern Hemisphere. The group remains relatively under-researched group despite their uniqueness and relative abundance.

HYRACODON NEBRASKENSIS

NAME MEANING: Hyrax tooth from Nebraska

AGE: Late Eocene

DISTRIBUTION: North America

SIZE: About sheep-sized

DIET: Herbivore

ESSENTIAL FACTS: Numerous species of *Hyracodon* have been described, ranging from sheep-sized to horse-sized. They were likely gregarious and inhabited open woodland and grassland habitats. Their primary predators were nimravids and hyaenodontids.

HIPPIDION PRINCIPALE

ESSENTIAL FACTS: Part of a lineage of horses that originated in North America about 6 million years ago, *Hippidion* immigrated into South America during the Early Pleistocene. In addition to the Chief Hippidion, the type species of the genus, there appear to have been two other species during the Late Pleistocene of South America: Saldias' Hippidion (*H. saldiasi*), and Deville's Hippidion (*H. devillei*). Some of these horses have been referred to the genus *Onohippidium*, but this is likely to be synonymous with *Hippidion*.

Hippidion were robust and stocky horses with relatively short limbs. The most distinctive characteristic of these horses, however, was their extremely long nasal notches separating the long nasal bones from the rest of the skull. This structure made the reconstructed head of this horse rather deep and corresponded with a prehensile upper lip, which it used to browse from trees and bushes. The skull was narrower than those of grazing horses, like the contemporary New Horse (*Equus neogeus*) with the incisors arranged in a U-shaped pattern adapted for selective feeding. Furthermore, the teeth were less hypsodont than other horses, suggesting a less abrasive diet. Jaguars (*Panthera onca*) were among the primary predators of these horses.

SEE ENTRY ON PAGE 606

AMYNODONTINAE

Amynodonts are characterized by their formidable tusk-like canine teeth from which the type genus of the family *Amynodon* derives its name, "defensive tooth." Their fossil record extends from the Late Eocene to the Early Miocene of North America and Eurasia.

CADURCODON ARDYNENSIS

NAME MEANING: Cadurco's tooth from Ardyn

AGE: Early Oligocene (34–30 MYA)

DISTRIBUTION: Eurasia

SIZE: About tapir-sized

DIET: Herbivore; browser

ESSENTIAL FACTS: The extreme retraction of the nasals and the deep processes for muscle attachment on the face indicate the presence of a tapir-like proboscis, which these animals would use to browse from bushes and small trees. In life, they would have resembled short-faced tapirs and probably had similar behaviors.

METAMYNODON PLANIFRONS

NAME MEANING: Flat-headed

AGE: Early Oligocene

DISTRIBUTION: North America

SIZE: 13 feet (4 meters) HBL; 2 tons

DIET: Herbivore

SEE MORE ON PAGES 612–613

PARACERATHERIINAE

Paraceratheres were long-limbed and long-necked rhinos adapted for high-browsing, ranging in size from that of a large deer to that of the largest proboscideans. Their relatively short-lived fossil record covered the Middle Eocene to Late Oligocene, when they were replaced by proboscideans which immigrated from Africa. They appear to have been endemic to Eurasia with no evidence of having entered North America.

PAPPACERAS CONFLUENS

NAME MEANING: Grandfather without a horn with confluent teeth

AGE: Early Eocene (50–48 MYA)

DISTRIBUTION: Eurasia

SIZE: About deer-sized

DIET: Herbivore; browser

ESSENTIAL FACTS: *Pappaceras* were the oldest members of the group and were adapted to browsing in forested habitats. They were widely distributed throughout Eurasia.

FORSTERCOOPERIA TOTADENTATA

NAME MEANING: Clive Forster-Cooper with all teeth

AGE: Middle Eocene (47–42 MYA)

DISTRIBUTION: Eurasia

SIZE: About deer-sized

DIET: Herbivore

ESSENTIAL FACTS: The genus name of this species honors English paleontologist Clive Forster-Cooper, who had major contributions to the knowledge of paraceratheres.

METAMYNODON PLANIFRONS

ESSENTIAL FACTS: The type species for its genus, the Flat-Headed Metamynodon, was first described in 1887 by American paleontologists William Berryman Scott and Henry Fairfield Osborn. It was the largest species of its genus, being of the same size and build as the modern river hippopotamus (*Hippopotamus amphibius*). The body was broad, barrel-shaped, set on relatively slender but short and powerful limbs, which enabled the animal to walk and run through shallow water and soft substrates. The eyes, nostrils, and ears were located relatively high on the skull, enabling them to investigate things above the surface while the rest of the body remained hidden. Its fossils are often found in riverbed deposits, particularly in Badlands National Park in South Dakota, which have been nicknamed "the Metamynodon Beds."

The body proportions and paleoenvironmental evidence show that the Flat-Headed Metamynodon was an amphibious herbivore that was probably similar to the river hippopotamus in its ecology and behavior. It had hypsodont cheek teeth adapted for grazing, and these animals probably spent their days in the water, emerging during the cooler nights to graze on grasses and near-shore vegetation. The canines were massive even by the standards of amynodonts, and males would use these teeth in territorial conflicts with each other.

SEE ENTRY ON PAGE 610

JUXIA SHARAMURENENSE

NAME MEANING: Giant rhino from Shara Muren

AGE: Middle Eocene (48–41 MYA)

DISTRIBUTION: Eurasia

SIZE: 1,500–2,000 pounds (680–908 kilograms)

DIET: Herbivore; browser

ESSENTIAL FACTS: Juxia was a large browser the size of a moose (*Alces alces*) with the proportions of an okapi (*Okapia johnstoni*). Its long legs and neck allowed it to reach plants from up to 14 feet (4.26 meters) above the ground. A mounted skeleton is on display at Paleozoological Museum of China.

PARACERATHERIUM TRANSOURALICUM

NAME MEANING: Beside Aceratherium

AGE: Oligocene

DISTRIBUTION: Eurasia

SIZE: 15.7 feet (4.8 meters) SH; 24.3 feet (7.4 meters) HBL; 30,000–40,000 pounds (13,607–18,143 kilograms)

DIET: Herbivore; browser

SEE MORE ON PAGES 616–617

ELASMOTHERIINAE

Among the members of the Elasmotheriinae were the first horned rhinos. The subfamily first occurs during the Late Eocene as hornless browsers that ranged from pig-sized to ox-sized. By the Early Miocene, horned elasmotheriines begin to appear with small, paired nasal bumps at the tip of their snouts that were covered in keratin. In larger species that evolved later in the Miocene, the horn bases joined and expanded into one large, rugose structure from which a single massive horn grew. These big-horned elasmotheres of the Middle to Late Miocene grew to huge sizes matching or exceeding the largest modern rhinos and had also evolved complex, hypsodont cheek teeth adapted for purely grazing diets in open grasslands. Another feature of the group is the retention of a vestigial fifth metacarpal. Elasmotherines became extinct during the Late Pleistocene.

TRIGONIAS OSBORNI

NAME MEANING: Osborn's triangle

AGE: Late Eocene (35 MYA)

DISTRIBUTION: North America

SIZE: 7 feet (2.1 meters); 862 pounds (391 kilograms)

DIET: Herbivore

ESSENTIAL FACTS: Osborn's Trigonias was an ox-sized rhino that lived in forests and woodlands. They formed herds and had a mostly browsing diet. Like most elasmotheriines, they retained a vestigial fifth metacarpal.

SUBHYRACODON OCCIDENTALIS

NAME MEANING: Below Hyracodon from the west

AGE: Early Oligocene (33 MYA)

DISTRIBUTION: North America

SIZE: 8 feet (2.4 meters) HBL; 841 pounds (381 kilograms)

DIET: Herbivore

ESSENTIAL FACTS: This species was one of the better known and most common rhinos from the Early Oligocene of North America. Trackways from Toadstool Geologic Park in Nebraska shows that this rhino lived in herds. Bite marks that appear to match the teeth of Morton's Entelodont (*Archaeotherium mortoni*) suggest a predator-prey relationship between the two species.

DICERATHERIUM NIOBRARENSE

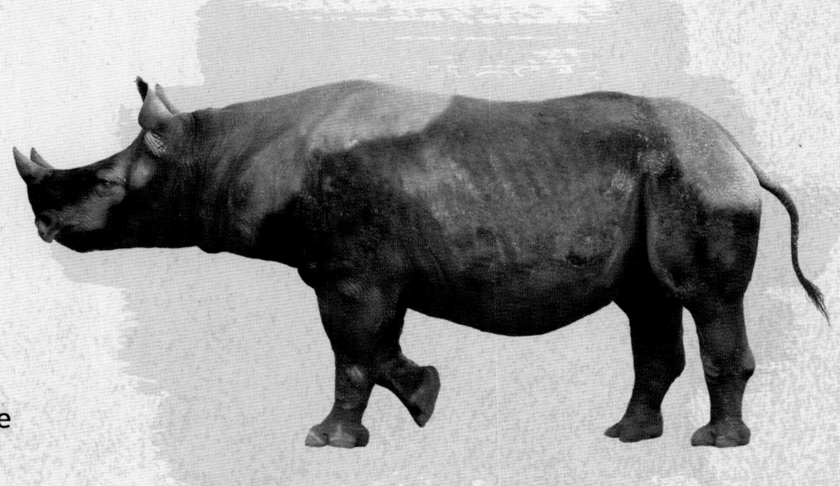

NAME MEANING: Two-horned beast from Niobrara

AGE: Early Miocene (23–20 MYA)

DISTRIBUTION: North America

SIZE: About ox-sized

DIET: Herbivore

ESSENTIAL FACTS: This species was named for Niobrara River in Nebraska, near which its fossils were discovered. As its genus name suggests, male Niobrara Rhinos had a pair of small nasal horns arranged side-by-side. It was among the earliest horned rhinos.

PARACERATHERIUM TRANSOURALICUM

ESSENTIAL FACTS: The most famous of the paractatheres, Paraceratherium may be the largest land mammal to have existed up to the time in which it lived. Previously referred to as Baluchitherium and Indricotherium since its description in 1922, no complete skeletons are known for this species, but enough material exists to reconstruct the life appearance of the animal. Paraceratherium were giant long-legged and long-necked herbivores that matched in size the largest known proboscideans. The limbs were columnar to support massive weight, although the body was relatively lightly built. There is evidence that males had thicker, slightly domed skulls which they used to fight each other in head-butting contests similar to modern giraffes (*Giraffa camelopardalis*).

Paraceratherium was a committed browser that fed primarily on tree foliage. Tooth wear analyses on its brachydont teeth confirm a diet of relatively soft leaves. The animal's long neck with large, strong muscles and wide range of motion enabled it to efficiently strip leaves from trees while in a stationary position. The structure of its nasals suggests the presence of prehensile upper lips, which were used to pull food toward the mouth. Its long legs not only extended its reach, but also aided the animal to travel large distances quickly and efficiently in search of food. The preferred habitat for Paraceratherium was mixed forest, woodland, and savanna.

SEE ENTRY ON PAGE 614

MENOCERAS ARIKARENSE

NAME MEANING: Crescent horns from the Arikareean

AGE: Early Miocene (23–20 MYA)

DISTRIBUTION: North America

SIZE: 5 feet (1.5 meters) HBL

DIET: Herbivore

ESSENTIAL FACTS: This species has been found at high densities at the Agate Springs Fossil Beds, suggesting that it was a gregarious animal that formed large herds. As many as 200 individuals have been identified from the locality. They were sexually dimorphic, with females being slightly smaller and lacking the paired nasal horns.

SINOTHERIUM LAGRELII

NAME MEANING: Lagreli's beast from China

AGE: Late Miocene to Pliocene (6–3 MYA)

DISTRIBUTION: Eurasia

SIZE: 4,000–6,000 pounds (1,814–2,721 kilograms)

DIET: Herbivore; grazer

ESSENTIAL FACTS: Lagreli's Rhino is the likely ancestor of *Elasmotherium*. It differs in its smaller size as well as its horn, which was not oriented as far back on the skull. It lived in semi-arid grassland habitats.

IRANOTHERIUM MORGANI

NAME MEANING: Morgan's beast from Iran

AGE: Late Miocene

DISTRIBUTION: Eurasia

SIZE: 8.2 feet (2.5 meters) SH; 13 feet (4 meters) HBL; 4,000–6,000 pounds (1,814–2,721 kilograms)

DIET: Herbivore; grazer

ESSENTIAL FACTS: Morgan's Rhino was a highly dimorphic species. The rugose bump from which the horn grew was much larger in males, which also had odd rugosities on the zygomatic arches unique to this species. It inhabited open grassland and had hypsodont teeth adapted for grazing.

PARELASMOTHERIUM LINXIAENSE

NAME MEANING: Beside Elasmotherium from the Linxia Basin

AGE: Late Miocene (11–10 MYA)

DISTRIBUTION: Eurasia

SIZE: 6.8 feet (2.1 meters) SH; 13 feet (4 meters) HBL; 3,530–5,070 pounds (1,600–2,300 kilograms)

DIET: Herbivore

ESSENTIAL FACTS: This rhino is known for its elongated skull featuring its massive, forward-pointing nasal horn. They were giant grazers about the size of the modern white rhino (*Ceratotherium simum*) with hypsodont teeth adapted for grazing.

ELASMOTHERIUM SIBIRICUM

NAME MEANING: Plate beast from Siberia

AGE: Pleistocene (1 MYA–39,000 YA)

DISTRIBUTION: Eurasia

DIET: Herbivore; grazer

SIZE: 8 feet (2.5 meters) SH; 15 feet (4.5 meters) HBL; 6,000–10,000 pounds (2,721–4,535 kilograms)

SEE MORE ON PAGES 620–621

ACERATHERIINAE

The name of the type genus for this subfamily *Aceratherium* translates to “beast without a horn,” alluding to the members of this group lacking the nasal horns seen among the elasmotheriines and rhinocerotines. Instead, aceratheres had self-sharpening, tusk-like lower incisors, which were used as offensive and defensive weapons. These teeth were much larger in males. Aceratheres appear in the fossil record during the Early Oligocene and become extinct during the Pliocene. They appear to have originated in Eurasia and became widely distributed throughout Africa and North America. Most species were relatively modest in body size, most not growing much larger than the modern Sumatran rhino (*Dicerorhinus sumatrensis*), the smallest of today’s rhinos.

ELASMOTHERIUM SIBIRICUM

ESSENTIAL FACTS: Several species of *Elasmotherium* are known to have lived from the Early Pliocene to Late Pleistocene. The last and largest of the species was the Siberian Elasmothere, which inhabited the arid, open steppes from eastern Europe to central Asia. It is sometimes referred to as the "Siberian Unicorn" for its large horn, which grew from a large bump in the middle of its head above the eyes. This horn is traditionally reconstructed in paleoart as a massive structure, sometimes matching or exceeding the shoulder height of the rhino to which it belonged. However, a 2021 study suggested perhaps the horn would have been smaller. The species was described in 1809 by German/Russian paleontologist Gotthelf Fischer von Waldheim based on a left lower jaw. Like other elasmotheres before it, it retained a vestigial fifth metacarpal in its forefoot.

The Siberian Elasmothere was a true giant, about as large as modern Asian elephants (*Elephas maximus*) and forest elephants (*Loxodonta cyclotis*). For its size it was surprisingly fleet-footed, with comparably slender limbs that could manage a gallop like modern rhinos. Like the contemporary Woolly Rhino (*Coelodona antiquitatus*) it is likely to have grown a thick coat for insulation during winter, which would have been shed during spring. The cheek teeth were hypselodont with complex enamel ridges adapted to process abrasive grasses encountered in semi-arid open ecosystems, where the wind often coats plants in minerals that can cause rapid tooth erosion. This rhino may have possessed squared-off lips like those of the modern white rhino (*Ceratotherium simum*) for bulk-feeding on multiple blades of grass at once.

SEE ENTRY ON PAGE 619

DIACERATHERIUM AURELIANENSE

NAME MEANING: Golden double *Aceratherium*

AGE: Late Oligocene (25 MYA)

DISTRIBUTION: Eurasia

SIZE: Unknown

DIET: Herbivore

ESSENTIAL FACTS: Members of the genus *Diaceratherium* are early relatives of the better-known genus *Teleoceras*. They have similar short, squat limb bones, though the shortening is not as extreme as that seen in its later relative. There are seven identified species.

FLORIDACERAS WHITEI

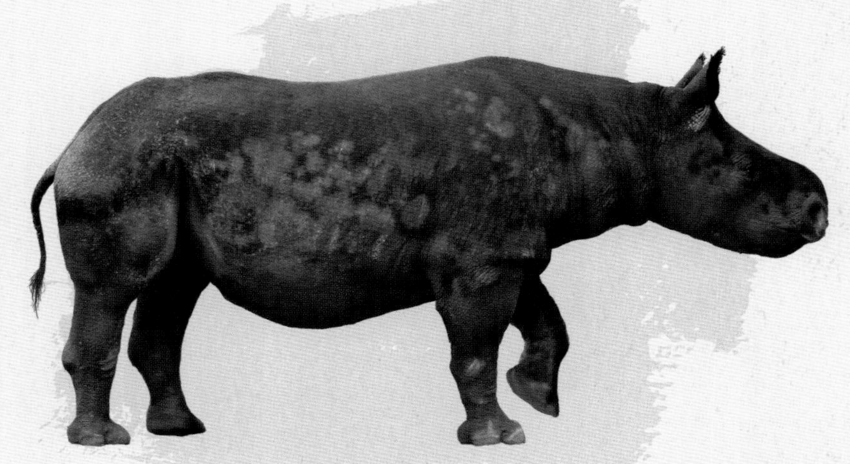

NAME MEANING: White's Florida horn

AGE: Early Miocene (18 MYA)

DISTRIBUTION: North America

SIZE: 1,760–3,090 pounds (800–1,400 kilograms)

DIET: Herbivore; browser

ESSENTIAL FACTS: White's Rhino is the largest animal found at the Thomas Farm Site in Central Florida. So far, the only other confirmed place where its fossils have been recovered are from Panama. It was comparable in size to a modern black rhino (*Diceras bicornis*) with brachydont teeth that suggest a similar browsing diet.

CHILOTHERIUM WIMANI

NAME MEANING: Wiman's lip beast

AGE: Late Miocene (10–8 MYA)

DISTRIBUTION: Eurasia

SIZE: 5–6 feet (1.5–1.8 meters) SH; 2,000–5,000 pounds (907–2,2267 kilograms)

DIET: Herbivore

ESSENTIAL FACTS: *Chilotherium* are known for their particularly large lower incisors. Other features include tridactyl feet and shortened metapodials, though not to the extent seen in *Teleoceras* rhinos. A skull of an adult female Wiman's Chilotherium was found with bite marks made by Dinocrocuta (*Dinocrocuta gigantea*).

ACERATHERIUM INCISIVUM

NAME MEANING: Hornless beast with incisors

AGE: Late Miocene

DISTRIBUTION: Eurasia

SIZE: (1.3 meters) SH; 7.5 feet (2.3 meters) HBL

DIET: Herbivore

ESSENTIAL FACTS: This animal was one of the more well-known species within the genus *Aceratherium*, known from reasonably complete skeletons. They were browsers that inhabited woodland habitats. Its species name describes large, tusk-like lower incisors which aceratherine rhinos are known for.

ACERORHINUS NELEUS

NAME MEANING: Without nose horn from the Neleus River

AGE: Late Miocene (9–5 MYA)

DISTRIBUTION: Eurasia

SIZE: Unknown

DIET: Herbivore; browser

ESSENTIAL FACTS: A species described in 2014 based on the well-preserved skull of an adult female specimen found in Greece. Its brachydont teeth show that it had a browsing diet.

APHELOPS MALACORHINUS

NAME MEANING: Soft nose and smooth face

AGE: Late Miocene (10–9 MYA)

DISTRIBUTION: North America

SIZE: 2,000 pounds (907 kilograms)

DIET: Herbivore

ESSENTIAL FACTS: This bison-sized rhino is known from several Late Miocene fossil sites in Florida. The demography of specimens recovered from the Love Bone Bed in Florida suggests that the species may have been gregarious animals, with males settling disputes using ritualized confrontations with low risk of mortality.

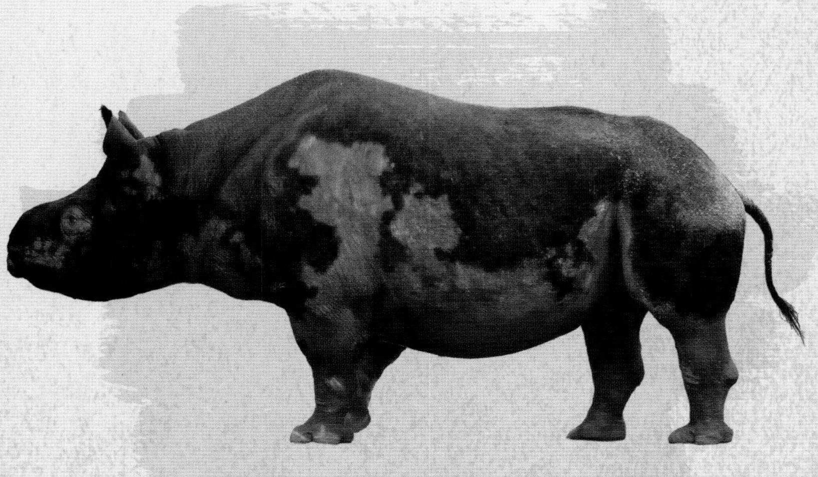

PROSANTORHINUS DOUVILLEI

NAME MEANING: Before *Santorhinus* from Germany

AGE: Middle Miocene

DISTRIBUTION: Eurasia

SIZE: 4.3 feet (1.3 meters) SH; 9.6 feet (2.9 meters) HBL; 1,100–2,200 pounds (500–1,000 kilograms)

DIET: Herbivore

ESSENTIAL FACTS: Douville's Rhino had the characteristic deep body and stubby legs of its better-known relatives *Teleoceras*. Unlike *Teleoceras*, however, they appear to have been browsers. This species was about the size of the modern Sumatran rhino (*Dicerorhinus sumatrensis*).

TELEOCERAS PROTERUM

NAME MEANING: Former complete horn

AGE: Late Miocene (10–8 MYA)

DISTRIBUTION: North America

SIZE: 1,350 pounds (615 kilograms)

SEE MORE ON PAGES 626–627

RHINOCEROTINAE

The remaining five modern species of modern rhinos belong to this subfamily. The group is named for the genus *Rhinoceros*, which means "nose horn," referencing the defining feature of these rhinos. Rhinoceratines most likely evolved from aceratheres during the Late Oligocene and enlarged and reinforced nasal bones, which have a rugose texture that serves as a base for a single nasal horn. From the one-horned rhinos, a lineage of two-horned rhinos diverged in the Early Miocene, which grow a smaller secondary horn above the eyes. Rhinoceratines seem to have been endemic to the Old World throughout their evolutionary history.

PROTACERATHERIUM MINUTUM

NAME MEANING: Small before *Aceratherium*

AGE: Late Oligocene (25 MYA)

DISTRIBUTION: Eurasia

SIZE: About ox-sized

DIET: Herbivore; browser

ESSENTIAL FACTS: One of the oldest of the rhinoceratine rhinos. This was a particularly lightly built species with good running abilities and brachydont dentition.

GAINDATHERIUM BROWNI

NAME MEANING: Brown's beast from Gaidakot

AGE: Early Miocene (23–20 MYA)

DISTRIBUTION: Eurasia

SIZE: Unknown

DIET: Herbivore

ESSENTIAL FACTS: Brown's Rhino is a possible ancestor of the modern genus *Rhinoceros*, with evidence of a single nasal horn on its nose. Its skull was longer and narrower however, with teeth that suggest a strictly browsing diet.

RUSINGACEROS LEAKEYI

NAME MEANING: Leakey's Rusinga Island horn

AGE: Early Miocene (18–17 MYA)

DISTRIBUTION: Africa

SIZE: 5 feet (1.5 meters) SH

DIET: Herbivore

ESSENTIAL FACTS: Formerly known as *Dicerorhinus leakeyi*. Its genus is named for Rusinga Island, Kenya, where its fossils have been found. Leakey's Rhino is the earliest-known two-horned rhino.

TELEOCERAS PROTERUM

ESSENTIAL FACTS: Members of the genus *Teleoceras* have famously short, stubby legs with compressed foot bones set under a long, barrel-shaped body. In the past it was assumed that these rhinos were semiaquatic like modern hippos. However, all evidence points to these animals being more terrestrial in their general habits, their permanently low-slung heads being suited for grazing on short grasses. Undoubtedly slow-moving, it is likely that these rhinos had especially thickened skin to defend against attacks from large predators, minimizing the damage inflicted by teeth and claws. The genus name *Teleoceras*, which means "complete horn" or "perfect horn," is misleading, as these rhinos lacked the structures necessary to grow horns.

Teleoceras were widespread in North America with several distinct species identified. Fossils of Archer Teleoceras are known from four fossil localities in Central Florida. Thousands of fossils are associated with several hundred individuals between them, suggesting that they were very common. A mounted skeleton of the species is on permanent display at the Florida Museum of Natural History. The Love Bone Bed site has a disproportionately high proportion of young male specimens. Scholars see this pattern as an indicator of aggressive territorial behavior in sexually mature males, during which younger, less experienced individuals are more likely to have suffered catastrophic injury. This may suggest that this species formed maternal herds fought over by mature males during breeding season, similar to what is seen among modern gregarious, sexually dimorphic artiodactyls. A mass death accumulation of the closely related Greater Teleoceras (*T. major*) at the Ashfall Fossil Beds in Nebraska preserves a large herd that was killed at once during a volcanic eruption, the demographics of which shows a higher number of adult females and juveniles to adult males.

SEE ENTRY ON PAGE 624

ABOUT APPLESAUCE PRESS

Good ideas ripen with time. From seed to harvest, Applesauce Press creates books with beautiful designs, creative formats, and kid-friendly information. Like our parent company, Cider Mill Press Book Publishers, our press bears fruit twice a year, publishing a new crop of titles each spring and fall.

"Where good books are ready for press"
501 Nelson Place
Nashville, Tennessee 37214

cidermillpress.com

INTRODUCTION

Since the beginning of the Age of Dinosaurs nearly 220 million years ago, mammals have been one of the most diverse groups of vertebrates, with species adapted to nearly all habitats, lifestyles, and diets. There are over 5,000 modern species, which together have a dominating presence in terrestrial and aquatic ecosystems—some have even taken to the sky! We ourselves are mammals. This variety is just the tip of the iceberg, representing a small sliver of geologic time. A large number of species lived and then went extinct throughout prehistory, a relative handful of which are recorded as fossils. Using the latest scientific research and by studying comparisons with modern species, scientists have been able to learn a lot about these animals. This book will explore those animals and their long evolutionary history with interesting facts about over 1,000 prehistoric species. Some of these, such as mammoths, sabertooths, and hominids may be familiar to most of us. However, there are many more obscure and poorly known species, some of which are brought to life through artwork for the first time in these pages.

MAMMALIAN CHARACTERISTICS

SKELETAL ANATOMY: characteristics that are readily visible from fossils

Lower Jaw

Mammals have fewer bones in the lower jaw compared to other animals. For example, in reptiles the jaw is made up of the dentary (which contains teeth), the coronoid, angular, splenial (the bone close to the tongue), surangular (the back of the jaw), and the articular, which forms a joint with the quadrate bone at the back of the skull. Among the therapsids, the group of reptiles from which mammals evolved, the dentary are expanded while other bones at the rear have been reduced. Possibly adapted to generate stronger bites, the complete loss of the posterior jaw bones is considered by most researchers to be the feature that separates true mammals from their mammaliform ancestors. In the skull, the quadrate bone experienced a similar decline in importance and is also absent in mammals, the jaw articulating with the squamosal instead.

Middle Ear

With the expansion of the dentary, the articular and quadrate bones reduced in size and eventually fully detached from the jaw. Rather than disappearing completely, these bones incorporated into the middle ear, forming a chain with the stapes, a small stirrup-shaped bone in the middle ear involved in the conduction of sound vibrations toward the inner ear. The quadrate and articular evolved into the incus and malleus bones, resulting in a greater ability to transfer and process sounds than other animals.

Tooth Replacement

Most vertebrates are polyphyodont, meaning they cycle through multiple sets of teeth throughout their lifespans. Mammals, in contrast, generally have only two sets of teeth; a deciduous (which means "shedding") juvenile set, often called "milk teeth," and a permanent adult set. This is known as diphyodont dentition (teeth pattern) and is unique to mammals. Because vertebrates grow and lose almost constantly and predictable across genera and families, mammalian teeth can be useful in determining the age of a given specimen. When manatees, elephants, and kangaroos replace teeth, new teeth erupt from the back of the jaw and old teeth are pushed out the front of the mouth. However, the total number of cheek teeth these animals get is fixed and corresponds to the number of deciduous and permanent teeth seen in more basal members of their lineages.

Occipital Condyle

The occipital condyle, the part of the skull which the atlas (the first neck vertebra) attaches, consists of a single knob in most tetrapods. Only in mammals does the occipital condyle consist of two knobs. It is unclear why this feature evolved; researchers think perhaps it may have been an adaptation to aid in prey-capture in early mammals.

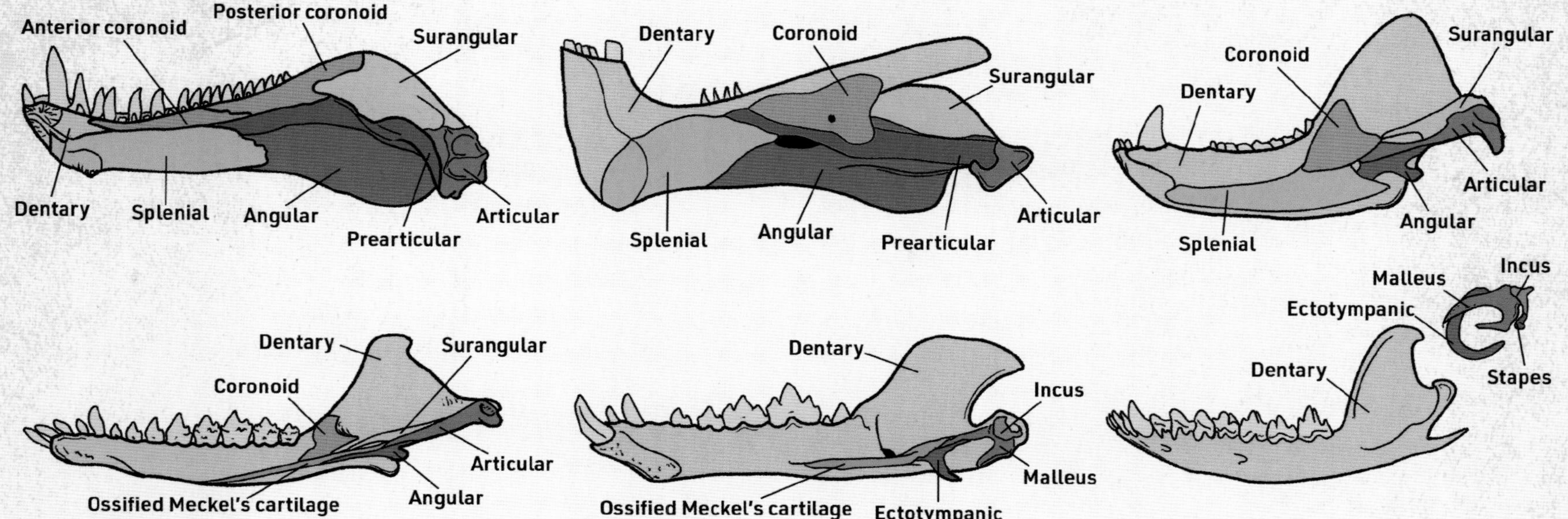

SOFT ANATOMY: characteristics that do not fossilize but whose presence, absence, functionality, or morphology can be inferred based on modern species.

Diaphragm

Mammals have an efficient respiratory system; they can draw air in and out of their lungs more forcibly and quickly by expanding and contracting their rib cage. Most reptiles breathe using the same muscles they use when they move around. This means most reptiles have to hold their breath during intense runs. The evolution of the diaphragm enabled mammals to maintain a constant flow of oxygen during intense activity, and they have a quicker recovery period afterward. This gives them a key advantage. Meanwhile, a four-chambered heart keeps oxygenated and deoxygenated blood separated to ensure that muscles and organs are well-supplied.

Endothermy

Endothermy (warm-bloodedness) is the ability of an organism to maintain a stable body temperature. They do this by releasing the heat generated by their internal bodily functions. They also have an insulating layer of hair, feathers, or blubber depending on the organism. It takes a lot of effort for these organisms to regulate their temperatures, so mammals must consume several times the calories as a similarly sized ectothermic (cold-blooded) organism to fuel their fast metabolisms. Not having to rely on the temperature of their environments has enabled mammals to remain active in and occupy even the coldest habitats.

Hair

All mammals have hair at some stage of their lives. In most mammals, the hair forms a dense covering that serves as insulation, trapping the body heat generated from metabolic activity near the skin; this is the same warming effect that you experience when you put on a layer of clothing or get under a blanket. Thicker, stiffer hairs known as whiskers (vibrissae) tend to be found in clusters on the face and intermittently over the entire body; they also help in sensory perception. Evidence for these specialized hairs in the form of foramina (openings) can be found in the skulls and jaws of fossil mammals. In some mammals, hair follicles may become thicker and wrapped in keratin (a protein), forming sharp, defensive quills or spines.

Rhinarium

Early in their evolutionary history, mammals evolved to be more reliant on their sense of smell to track down their prey and for communication within their species. Among other adaptations, most modern mammals and their Mesozoic ancestors have an area of hairless, often moist and wrinkled skin that surrounds their nostrils called the rhinarium. In most vertebrates, the premaxillae (small cranial bones at the tip of the upper jaw) extend upward to connect with the nasal bones, forming a bridge of bone that separates both nostrils on either side of the snout. The loss of the premaxilla-nasal bridge in mammals may have resulted from the nostrils

becoming located more toward the front, so that they completely face forward. This feature makes the presence of a rhinarium easy to see among fossil mammals. Furthermore, the rhinarium is highly sensitive to touch and provides a vital tactile sensory organ coupled with the whiskers, and is also able to detect wind direction to better assess the location of scents in the air. The structure of the rhinarium is formed entirely by cartilage, allowing the tip of the snout to move, which varies between groups. Modern mammals that possess rhinariums are typically those for which the sense of smell remains a vital means of communication and food acquisition.

Proboscis

In some mammal groups, the rhinarium often may be lost to increase flexibility of the lips and their ability to move around. In many herbivorous mammals, for example, the nostrils and upper lip have joined together into a singular unit used to pull food items closer to the mouth. This structure is shown by the presence of nasal bones, which are not flat against the premaxillae; instead, the nasal-premaxilla connection is reduced. This opens the nasal passage and causes the protruding nasals to form a shelf, where strong muscles can attach. In extreme cases, this feature gives rise to a proboscis (trunk), which is marked by extreme retraction of the nasal opening to just above the eyes, losing the connection with the premaxillae and gaining deep muscle attachment sites at the base.

Nasal Turbinates

Mammals have thin, scroll-like sheets of bone that fill the nasal cavity; this is usually seen in organisms that have a greater ability to breathe and perceive odors. Toward the front of the nasal passages, the turbinates (bony shelves in your nose that regulate air flow) are lined with mucous, which warms and moistens incoming air. Toward the back of the nasal passages, this covering transitions into a thin layer of soft tissue packed with olfactory (smell) receptor neurons to receive any odors from the air.

External Ears

Mammals tend to be more sensitive to airborne sounds than other animals. This is partly due to the presence of external ears (pinnae). Comprised of cartilage, these appendages funnel incoming sound energy into the ear canals and toward the eardrums. Often, sensitive hairs are present within the ears that pick up vibrations. Many mammals are able to swivel their ears in multiple directions in order to better pinpoint the source of a sound. In most mammals, these mobile ears are an important means of visual communication.

Lactation

Regardless of their method of reproduction, all mammals possess mammary glands which, in females, produce milk that nourishes newborn young until they are developed enough to eat solid foods. Indeed, this adaptation is where the word "mammal" comes from. In monotremes (mammals that lay eggs) and other archaic mammals, milk flows from pores in the skin. More derived mammals have nipples from which the young can feed.

MAMMALIAN TEETH

Mammalian teeth are incredibly diverse, more so than those of any other vertebrate group. Much information can be gathered about a mammal's age, diet, behavior, and taxonomic affiliation which can then be applied to extinct species. This section serves to introduce basic tooth terminology, morphology, and function.

Tooth Variety

Most mammals have heterodont dentition, possessing two or more different kinds of teeth that serve different functions during feeding. Most vertebrates are homodont, meaning that they have jaws lined with teeth that are all similar in shape and function. Heterodonty has been a defining feature for the mammalian lineage as far back as the Permian Period in their distinctly non-mammalian ancestors. It is worth noting that a few mammalian lineages have secondarily evolved homodont dentition due to certain feeding specializations. For example, odontocete cetaceans (toothed whales) like dolphins and sperm whales have jaws lined with uniformly conical teeth to help grip their prey captured underwater.

Primary Tooth Types

The incisors are the frontmost teeth rooted in the premaxilla bones of the skull and occlude (contact) with corresponding teeth at the front of the dentary. They are involved in pulling, clipping, or tearing manageable pieces of food before passing it further back. The canines are usually long, pointed teeth whose primary function is to pierce, usually by predators during the capture and killing of prey. The upper canines grow from the juncture of the premaxilla and the maxilla. The premolars are multi-rooted and may have multiple cuspids. Deciduous premolars are often much more complex than their

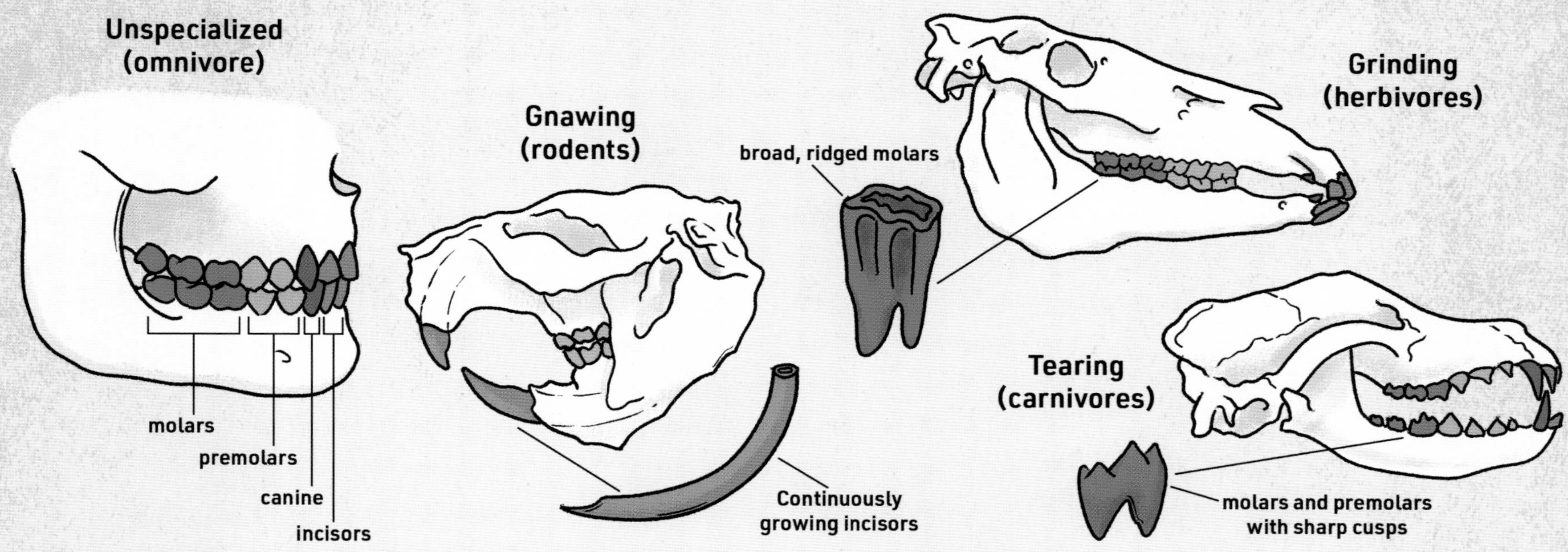

permanent replacements, with the posterior ones tending to resemble the adult molars. In predatory mammals, premolars are usually short and pointy for gripping prey items or may form secondary shearing surfaces. In herbivores, the premolars serve as an expansion of the grinding surface. The molars are the only teeth which do not have a deciduous counterpart. These teeth are most used for grinding and crushing, typically having the widest surface of all the teeth.

Secondary Tooth Types

Depending on the type of mammal and its dietary needs, the primary types of teeth mentioned above may be modified in any number of ways be it a change in shape or function, reduction in size or number, or even the complete loss of teeth. Non-predatory mammals, for example, usually have reduced or absent canines, although in some they are modified into tusks. Tusks are modified incisors or canines which can be seen protruding from the mouth when closed and used during intraspecies fights or defense against predators. Typically, the dentine of tusks is laid in a cross-hatching pattern and the enamel is reduced. In this condition, the teeth may be referred to as ivory. Some herbivores have also modified their canines to function as part of the incisor array and have adopted a similar morphology. In this condition they may be considered to be incisiform (resembling an incisor tooth). Similarly, a non-canine tooth (usually an incisor) that develops a more canine-like shape is said to be caniniform. Premolars which become modified to match the molars are described as being molariform. Mammals with plagiaulacoid dentition tend to have enlarged lower incisors usually followed by a wide diastema (gap in the tooth row) or occupied by a series of vestigial teeth, followed by a hypertrophied, blade-like premolar. Plagiaulacoid mammals include multituberculates, phalangeriform diprotodontians, and paucituberculates.

Dental Formulas

Dental formulas are a shorthand method to indicate the number of each kind of tooth in a particular type of mammal. For example, the dental formula for a human is I2/2, C1/1, P2/2, M3/3. The number above the line represents the teeth in the upper jaw, both sides; the number below the line represents the teeth in the lower jaw, both sides. The total number of teeth is found by multiplying each number by two. So for humans: I2/2, C1/1, P2/2, M3/3 = 32 teeth.

Crown Height

Mammalian cheek teeth may be either brachydont (low-crowned) or hypsodont (high-crowned). Brachydont teeth are typical of species whose diets consist of soft or non-abrasive food items. Hypsodont teeth, however, are more typical of mammals that encounter high amounts of minerals in their diets, due to regularly eating foods at or below ground level. Hypsodont cheek teeth remain rootless and continue to erupt over an extended period of time to counteract higher rates of tooth wear. Some mammals that encounter extreme levels of wear take things a step further and have evolved hypselodont teeth, whose roots never close, so they never stop growing.

Molar Specializations

- Zalambdodont: V-shaped crests, typical of small insectivores which specialize in relatively soft-bodied prey.
- Modern examples: marsupial moles, solenodons, tenrecs, golden moles
- Fossil examples: Zalamdodontidae
- Dilambdodont: similar to zalambdodont, except with a W-shaped ridge.
- Modern examples: shrews, moles, many insectivorous bats
- Fossil examples: various insectivorous Mesozoic mammals
- Bunodont: usually brachydont, square-shaped molar with four distinct, rounded cusps. Unspecialized, it is often a hypocarnivorous diet that often includes large amounts of plant matter with ready consumption of animal matter.
- Modern examples: pigs, some peccaries, primates
- Fossil examples: entelodont, helohyids
- Bilophodont: having straight, sharply angular transverse crests formed by the elongation and joining of two primary cusps on either side of the tooth. It is typical of browsing specialists that feed primarily on leaves. A similar condition, known as zygodonty, involves the inclusion of additional ridges.
- Modern examples: tapirs, manatees, kangaroos
- Fossil examples: mastodons, megatheriid sloths
- Lophodont: cusps link together to form into longer, more complex ridges called lophs. This morphology is typical of mammals which are specialist grazers or evolved from ancestors who were.
- Modern examples: horses, rhinos, most rodents
- Fossil examples: brontotheres, chalicotheres
- Selenodont: similar to lophodont dentition, but each ridge is derived from a single cusp and tend to form a crescent shape.
- Modern examples: ruminants, camels
- Fossil examples: protoceratids, some hyraxes
- Secodont: tooth has a single crest that forms a continuous, blade-like shearing surface which slides against a similar tooth from the opposing tooth row to function as a pair of shears.
- Modern examples: carnivorans, dasyurimorphans
- Fossil examples: oxyaenodonts, hyaenodonts, thylacoleonids, sparassodonts

Mammalian Diets

Animals are often categorized as carnivorous, omnivorous, and herbivorous based on their dietary behaviors. These generalizations are very broad, however, and do not account for how adaptable most animals are. For example, all herbivores are technically omnivores, as they will consume animal prey as a dietary supplement when the opportunity arises. A hypercarnivore is an animal whose diet consists of more than 70 percent animal matter. Hypercarnivores typically have a mouthful of teeth that emphasizes slicing or piercing with minimal, if any, surface area dedicated to grinding. Mesocarnivores have diets that consist of 50 percent to 70 percent animal matter, with a dentition in which the slicing component remains dominant but with defined crushing molars for dealing with plant matter. Hypocarnivores are animals for whom animal matter accounts for less than 50 percent of the overall diet. These typically have a teeth pattern that greatly emphasizes grinding and with a minimized slicing function.

Despite having a primarily plant-based diet, hypocarnivores generally retain the digestive systems of their more predatory ancestors, so they may not be able to extract all available nutrients from the plants they eat. So, for the purposes of this book, an herbivore will be defined as any animal whose primary source of nutrition is plant matter, with specialized dental and digestive adaptations to efficiently process it. Among herbivores there are browsers, which specialize in feeding on plants that grow above ground level. Grazers specialize in feeding on plants that grow on the ground and often have dental adaptations that counteract the abrasive grit (like dirt and sand) that often coats low-growing plants; the teeth are often hypsodont or hypselodont with complex lophs. Mixed-feeders have versatile diets and can feed on variable amounts of both graze and browse, depending on the species. More specialized herbivores may be further categorized as frugivorous (fruit-eating), granivorous (seed-eating), or folivorous (leaf-eating). Similarly, hypercarnivores may be categorized as piscivorous (fish-eating) or insectivorous (insect-eating).

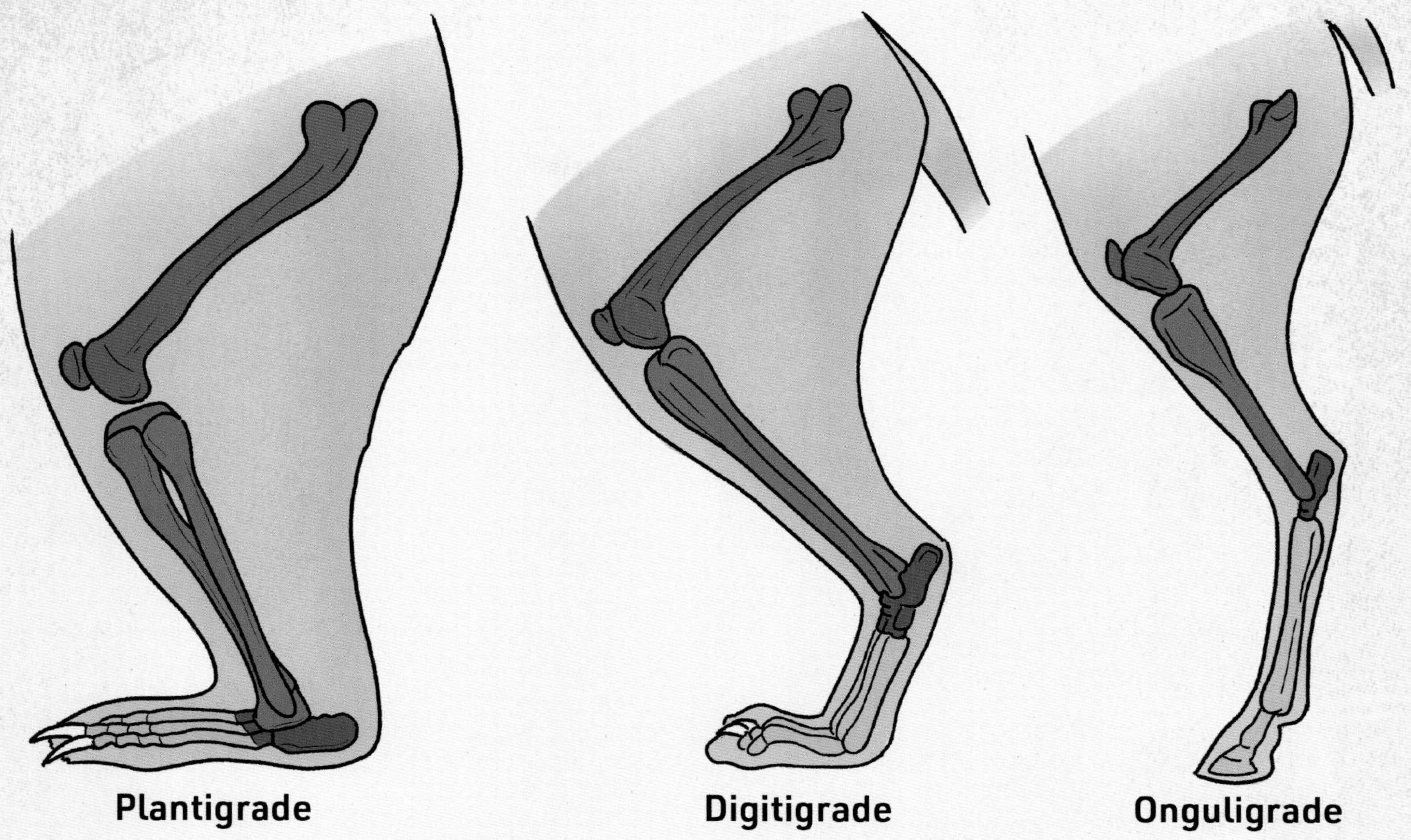

LOCOMOTOR ADAPTATIONS

Stances

The most basal (referring to characteristics possessed by an ancestral member of a group) limb structure in mammals is the plantigrade posture, in which the whole foot is planted on the ground. Some examples of plantigrade mammals are humans and other primates, bears, and opossums. Mammals that have this unspecialized foot posture are generally geared to a more ambulatory (walking) lifestyle. This is not to say that plantigrade animals are not fast runners, as many people who have been chased by bears have discovered! Rather, plantigrade mammals typically cannot maintain their top speeds for extended periods and do not run frequently. They tend to be better suited for sudden, short bursts of speed (sprinting) or running at intermediate speeds (jogging) for extended periods. Shortened metapodials (the bones that make up the palms of your hands and soles of your feet), reinforced and often enlarged calcanei (heel bones) and pisiform (wrist bones), support the body weight.

The digitigrade foot posture involves the raising of the wrists and ankles so that only the digits are in contact with the ground when standing or moving about. This functionally lengthens the limb and increases stride length, allowing for quicker and more efficient movement. Digitigrade animals often exhibit some ability to run or travel long distances, or evolved from ancestors that were. The calcaneus and pisiform are reduced in size, since they are no longer used for bearing weight. Metapodials are noticeably longer. Digitigrade mammals are very rare in the fossil record until the Cenozoic Era, implying that Mesozoic mammals were generally more sedentary and occupied relatively small home ranges.

The unguligrade stance involves walking on the very tips of the toes, which typically have highly modified distal phalanges ("unguals") covered by a hoof for protection. With few

exceptions, this foot type is typical of artiodactyls and perissodactyls, the even and odd toed "ungulates," respectively. Unguligrade mammals have a reduced number of functional digits down to two or one, which have extra wide and sturdy phalanges (finger and toe bones) to compensate for the reduction. The hooves not only protect the toe tips from damage, but also dig into the ground to provide instant traction when a minimal amount of extra force is applied to them, a useful feature for prey animals that must evade predators regularly.

Movement Specializations

- Arboreal: Climbing mammals generally have shoulder and ankle joints with a wide range of movement and broad hands and feet for gripping. More agile species have flexible spines and strong hindlimbs for leaping. Arboreal is typically used to define animals which spend most of their lives in trees, rarely descending to the ground.
- Scansorial: Mammals spend most of their time on the ground but are skillful climbers and will readily do so when necessary.
- Cursorial: Limbs are typically digitigrade or unguligrade with lengthening of the distal limb segments (forearm, shins, hands, and feet). The overall skeleton also tends to be relatively lightweight.
- Saltatorial: Movement by repeated jumping or hopping. Smaller forelimbs are typical due to lack of use as weight-bearing elements. The hindlimbs are greatly emphasized, with even further lengthening of the lower segments. The thighs are often short and muscular for shock absorption.
- Fossorial: Specialized for digging. Fossorial mammals tend to have short limbs with long, well-muscled bodies. The bones of the forelimb are usually hypertrophied (enlarged) with massive humeri and lengthened olecranon processes (elbows) of the ulna for greater muscle attachment for constantly moving soil and sand as they travel. In extreme cases, some mammals have greatly reduced eye sockets, suggesting they spent most or all of their lives underground where vision is effectively useless.
- Natatorial: Specialized for swimming. Similar to fossorial mammals, a long body is typically set over relatively short limbs. The feet are often enlarged with webbed digits for propulsion. Some also have flattened tails.
- Graviportal: Typical of very large mammals, the skeletons are adapted to handle great weight. The limbs tend to be shaped like columns, and galloping is difficult to impossible.
- Gliding: Gliding mammals are always arboreal, with extra-long limbs that support a skin membrane known as a patagium between them; this is used for gliding through the air for long distances.

MAMMAL EVOLUTION SUMMARIZED

Mammalian fossils are frustratingly scarce and fragmentary during the Mesozoic era, mostly being restricted to isolated teeth and jaw fragments. This results in numerous gaps in our knowledge of early mammal evolution, taxonomy, and biology. Nonetheless the first true mammals appear in the fossil record by the Late Triassic Period, having descended from a group of advanced therapsids called cynodonts. Because the dinosaurs had become well-established in the ecosystem by the time of their appearance, mammals were ecologically restricted to mostly small creatures; today we would associate these creatures with rodents and eulipotyphlans (shews, moles, and their relatives). This would remain mostly the same throughout the Mesozoic, although by the early Cretaceous Period, a few species had grown to the size of cats or badgers. Although they never achieved the great diversity that they would enjoy during the Cenozoic Era, by the Early Jurassic Period, Mesozoic mammals had achieved a broad assortment of morphotypes including specialized diggers, climbers, gliders, and swimmers.

Mesozoic mammals are thought to have been mostly nocturnal in their behavior. Known as the "nocturnal bottleneck hypothesis," this line of thinking may explain certain features shared among modern animals. Compared to other vertebrates, mammals often have superior senses of hearing, smell, and touch useful for locating food in complete darkness. Mammalian eyes retain traits that make them adapted to low-light conditions. The ability to discern colors is less important under low-light conditions, and this may explain why mammals, with the exception of haplorrhine primates, have limited color vision compared to birds and reptiles. An endothermic (warm-blooded) metabolism and insulating coat of hair would have enabled early mammals to maintain high activity rates in the cooler temperatures encountered at night.

The devastating consequences of the Chicxulub asteroid impact 66 million years ago negatively affected all animal groups, including mammals. Global fires sparked by extreme heat and the blocking of sunlight by airborne debris destroyed plant communities, resulting in near-complete ecosystem collapse in which there was not enough food to sustain large-bodied animals. No mammal larger than a house cat survived this mass extinction. At the beginning of the Cenozoic Era, mammals underwent an explosive adaptive radiation as they began to fill niches left vacant by the non-bird dinosaurs. Within a few thousand years into the Paleocene Epoch, mammals had far outgrown even their largest Mesozoic forerunners. And by the Eocene Epoch, nearly every modern mammalian order had arisen and were well established in the fossil record.

The Cenozoic Era is divided into seven subdivisions known as epochs. From oldest to youngest, those epochs are the Paleocene, Eocene, Oligocene, Miocene, Pliocene, Pleistocene, and Holocene. Throughout this time, mammals have a dominating presence in terrestrial (land) and marine (water) ecosystems across the planet, thus the Cenozoic Era is commonly referred to as the Age of Mammals.

*The data presented within the following section follows the standards set by Ansell in 1965 for the measurement of mammals: height at the shoulder (SH), head-and-body length (HBL), tail length (TL), and weight will be referenced when data is available or can be estimated.

*MYA = million years ago

In this book, mammals are divided into taxonomic groups. Taxonomy is the practice of classifying organisms.

The class Mammalia is composed of orders, broad groupings whose members evolved from a common ancestor and share a number of anatomical characteristics which unite them. These orders are further divided into families, which contain organisms that are more closely related to each other than they are to members from different orders.

In animals, family names always end in the Greek suffix -idae. Particularly diverse families, in turn, may be further subdivided into subfamilies, whose names end in the suffix -inae.

Each organism has both a genus and species name; this is a system known as binomial nomenclature. The genus name is always first, capitalized, and written in italics. The species name comes last, is lowercase, and is also italicized. A genus may have any number of species placed within it.

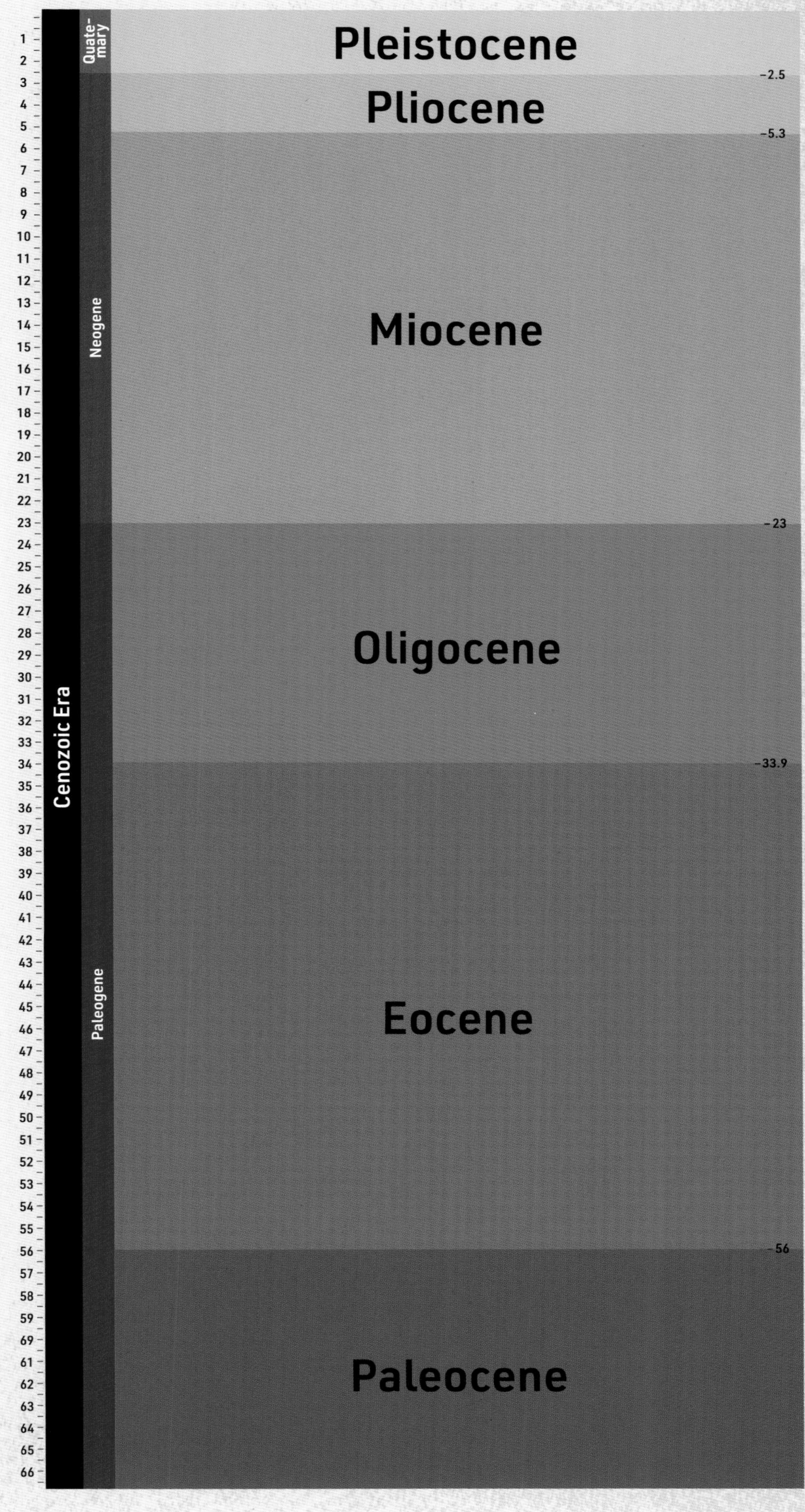

MAMMALIAFORMES

Mammaliaforms are a link between the mammal-like cynodonts and the more derived "true" mammals. These animals possess nearly all the defining features that are used to classify mammals; heterodont diphyodont dentition, fur, and lactation. The bones of the inner ear, however, had not yet fully detached from the dentary.

MORGANUCODONTA

Some researchers think the morganucodonts are the oldest mammals. The dentition is heterodont with clearly differentiated incisors, canines, premolars, and molars, and they developed a diphyodont system of tooth replacement. More basal members still retained a functional articular bone in the lower jaw. However, many of the more notable forms have a jaw joint comprising the dentary and squamosal bones, as is the case with all later mammalian lineages. An interclavicle is also present in the pectoral girdle, which is still present in monotremes but lost in therian mammals. They were endothermic, although they had significantly lower metabolisms than modern mammals of comparable size; this resulted in longer lifespans more like those of reptiles. Containing the families Morganucodontidae and Megazostrodontidae, members of this group were small-bodied predators that were the ecological equivalent to shrews and hedgehogs.

MEGAZOSTRODON RUDNERAE

NAME MEANING: Rudner's large girdle tooth

AGE: Late Triassic (201–199 MYA)

DISTRIBUTION: Africa

SIZE: 4–4.7 inches (10–12 centimeters) HBL

DIET: Hypercarnivore

ESSENTIAL FACTS: The areas of the brain dedicated to process sounds and smells are enlarged relative to the earlier cynodonts.

MORGANUCODON WATSONI

NAME MEANING: Watson's Glamorgan tooth

AGE: Early Jurassic (201.3–193 MYA)

DISTRIBUTION: Eurasia

SIZE: 4 inches (10 centimeters) HBL

DIET: Hypercarnivore; mostly insectivorous

ESSENTIAL FACTS: Dental microwear studies suggest its diet consisted of hard-shelled insects and small vertebrates. They are known to have had a lifespan of at least fourteen years.

HADROCODIUM WUI

NAME MEANING: Xiao-Chun Wu's heavy head

AGE: Early Jurassic (195 MYA)

DISTRIBUTION: Eurasia

SIZE: 1.9 inches (4.4 centimeters) HBL; 0.071 ounces (2 grams) One of the smallest Mesozoic mammaliforms, it was about the size of an Etruscan pygmy shrew (*Suncus etruscus*). It was known only from a nearly complete skull and jaw found in China which, notably, has completely lost the articular bone.

DIET: Hypercarnivore; insectivore

DOCODONTA

Docodonts are a group of advanced early mammaliforms that lived from the middle Jurassic to the early Cretaceous. They had more complex-shaped teeth than other early mammaliaforms—more comparable to those of modern mammals, actually, with variable piercing and crushing surfaces that enabled members of this group to adapt to a wider range of food types. Indeed, the group is known to have attained great ecological and morphological diversity, which includes everything from specialized climbers, diggers, and swimmers with a range of diets that includes hypercarnivores, mesocarnivores, and hypocarnivores.

MICRODOCODON GRACILIS

NAME MEANING: Slender, small docodon

AGE: Middle Jurassic (166 MYA)

DISTRIBUTION: Eurasia

SIZE: 1.7 inches (45 millimeters) HBL; 2.4 inches (60 millimeters) TL; 0.17–0.32 ounces (5–9 grams)

DIET: Hypercarnivore; insectivore

SEE MORE ON PAGES 20–21

AGILODOCODON SCANSORIUS

NAME MEANING: Climbing agile docodon

AGE: Middle Jurassic (164.7–161.2 MYA)

DISTRIBUTION: Eurasia

SIZE: 0.95–1.4 ounces (27–40 grams)

DIET: Hypocarnivore

SEE MORE ON PAGES 22–23

CASTOROCAUDA LUTRASIMILIS

NAME MEANING: Beaver tail; otter-like

AGE: Middle Jurassic (164–159 MYA)

DISTRIBUTION: Eurasia

SIZE: 1.1–1.8 pounds (500–800 grams)

DIET: Aquatic hypercarnivore

SEE MORE ON PAGES 24–25

DOCOFOSSOR BRACHYDACTYLUS

NAME MEANING: Short-fingered docodont

AGE: Middle Jurassic (160 MYA)

DISTRIBUTION: Eurasia

SIZE: 3.5 inches (9 centimeters) HBL; 0.32 ounces (9 grams)

DIET: Fossorial insectivore

SEE MORE ON PAGES 26–27

ALLOTHERIA

Allotheres, meaning "other beasts," are a clade of mammals that fulfilled the niches which, today, are filled by various species of rodents. Most notably, except in the very earliest forms, the first incisors are procumbent and hypselodont as seen in rodents and would have given their faces very much rodent-like appearances. They existed from the late Triassic and survived until midway through the Cenozoic Era.

MEGACONUS MAMMALIAFORMIS

NAME MEANING: Mammal-like big cones

AGE: Middle Jurassic (165 MYA)

DISTRIBUTION: Asia

SIZE: 8 inches (20 centimeters) HBL; 4 inches (10 centimeters) TL; 8.8 ounces (250 grams)

DIET: Herbivore

ESSENTIAL FACTS: Known from a complete skeleton with fur traces, Megaconus was a rat-sized herbivore with a lightly-built, generalized skeleton adapted for bursts of quick movements to escape predators. It appears to have had a hairless abdomen.

MICRODOCODON GRACILIS

ESSENTIAL FACTS: Resembling a shrew in size, morphology, and ecology, Microdocodon is known from a well-preserved, nearly complete skeleton found at the Daohugou locality in China. It is the smallest of the diverse community of docodontans found at Daohugou; these include *Agilodocodon scansorius*, *Castorocauda lutrasimilis*, and *Docofossor brachydactylus*.

Microdocodon is notable because it provides the earliest indirect evidence of lactation. The holotype skeleton of the animal also preserved an intact hyoid bone. The hyoid is an isolated bone in the throat, which serves as the anchor point for the muscles of the tongue. In mammals, this bone is particularly complex and is integral to making the necessary tongue movements involved in mastication (chewing) and, in newborns, to suckle during the first stage of their lives. The presence of this structure in Microdocodon implies that lactation evolved prior to the evolution of "true" mammals.

SEE ENTRY ON PAGE 18

BASAL EUTHERIANS

The Eutheria ("true beasts") is the clade to which the majority of modern mammals belong. Originating as far back as the Late Jurassic, the earliest members of the clade are distinguished by features like the lower tibia and metatarsals, as well as the reduction of the molar count down to M3/3. The base dental formula of modern eutherian groups is considered to be I3/3, C1/1, P4/4, M3/3. However, the earliest members of this group have extra incisors and premolars: I5/4 and P5. Another notable characteristic of early eutherians is the retention of epipubic bones. These bones function to stiffen the body during locomotion. Such stiffening is potentially harmful to more advanced eutherians, whose abdomens must expand to accommodate the growing young inside the placenta during pregnancy. Thus, epipubic bones were lost early in the history of eutherians. Researchers think these basal eutherians gave birth to extremely underdeveloped young after a very short gestation, similar to metatherians. This is reinforced by early eutharians having relatively narrow pelvic canals.

JURAMAIA SINENSIS

NAME MEANING: Chinese Jurassic mother

AGE: Late Jurassic (161–160 MYA)

DISTRIBUTION: Asia

SIZE: (7–10 centimeters) HBL

DIET: Mesocarnivore

ESSENTIAL FACTS: This is the oldest known eutherian mammal, known from western Liaoning, China. Its appearance in the fossil record sets the divergence date between metatherians and eutherians about 35 million years older than previously thought.

EOMAIA SCANSORIA

NAME MEANING: Scansorial dawn mother

AGE: Early Cretaceous (125 MYA)

DISTRIBUTION: Asia

SIZE: 4 inches (10 centimeters) HBL; 0.7–0.9 ounces (20–25 grams)

DIET: Mesocarnivore

ESSENTIAL FACTS: Previously the oldest eutherian prior to the discovery of Juramaia, the Eomaia is known from a complete skeleton with hair impressions. Its skeletal proportions show that it was a skillful and active climber.

COKOTHERIUM JIUFOTANGENSIS

NAME MEANING: Chuan-Kui Li's beast from the Jiufotang Formation

AGE: Early Cretaceous (120 MYA)

DISTRIBUTION: Asia

SIZE: About shrew-sized

DIET: Mesocarnivore

ESSENTIAL FACTS: Cokotherium has reduced the number of incisors down to I4/3, though it still retains a premolar count of P5/5. It is the only eutherian with direct preservation of an ossified meckelian cartilage, the cartilaginous bar which connects the inner ear ossicles to the jaw.

UKHAATHERIUM NESSOVI

NAME MEANING: Nessov's beast from Ukhaa Tolgod

AGE: Late Cretaceous (84–72 MYA)

DISTRIBUTION: Eurasia

SIZE: 1.13 ounces (32 grams)

DIET: Mesocarnivore

ESSENTIAL FACTS: Ukhaatherium was a shrew-sized predator from Mongolia known from nearly complete specimens. Structurally, it was very similar to a modern tenrec and probably would have had a very similar lifestyle hunting for invertebrates among the undergrowth.

ZALAMBDALESTIDAE

Zalambdalestids are a group of early eutherians known only from the continent of Asia during the late Cretaceous. It is currently unknown to which order they belong, but they represent a distinctive family with at least seven known genera. They possessed zalambdodont molars, as their name suggest, which suggest a primarily insectivorous diet. Members of the group show clear cursorial and saltatorial adaptations.

ZALAMBDALESTES LECHEI

NAME MEANING: Leche's zalambdodont thief

AGE: Late Cretaceous (70 MYA)

DISTRIBUTION: Eurasia

SIZE: 8 inches (20 centimeters) HBL

DIET: Hypercarnivore

ESSENTIAL FACTS: Leche's Zalambdalestes was a small insectivore that lived in what is now Mongolia. It was a swift and agile animal with a build similar to a rabbit, able to sprint away from danger in a series of great bounding leaps.

LEPTICTIDA

Leptictids are a group of basal eutherians that first appeared during the Late Cretaceous and underwent a modest radiation during the Paleocene. Members of this group are small mesocarnivores that became extinct during the Late Oligocene. They possessed the archaic therian premolar count of P5/5, showing that their ancestors diverged very early in the history of eutherian mammals.

GYPSONICTOPIDAE

The Gypsonictopidae were the earliest family of leptictids from the Late Cretaceous. Though believed to have gone extinct before the Cenezoic began, there is some evidence that the family survived into the Paleocene.

GYPSONICTOPS PETERSONI

NAME MEANING: Peterson's chalk weasel face

AGE: Late Cretaceous (66 MYA)

DISTRIBUTION: North America

SIZE: Unknown

DIET: Mesocarnivore

ESSENTIAL FACTS: Known only from teeth and jaw fossils, Peterson's Gypsonictops is one of the oldest-known leptictidians.

PSEUDORYNCHCOCYONIDAE

The Pseudorynchcocyonidae name means "false Rynchococyon." *Rynchococyon* is the genus to which elephant shrews belong, and leptictids in general are often reconstructed with short proboscises similar to those of elephant-shrews. These animals utilized bipedal (two-foot) locomotion; the forelimbs were greatly reduced while the hindlimbs were elongated. They also had a long counterbalancing tail, longer than the length of the body and comprised of up to forty vertebrae. Similar to sthenurine kangaroos, leptictids did not hop but instead took alternating strides.

LEPTICTIDIUM AUDERIENSE

NAME MEANING: Slender little weasel from Auderia

AGE: Early Eocene (48 MYA)

DISTRIBUTION: Eurasia

SIZE: 0.7–0.72 feet (21.5–22 centimeters) HBL; 1.1–1.2 feet (34–37.5 centimeters) TL

DIET: Mesocarnivore

ESSENTIAL FACTS: Three species of *Leptictidium* are known from the Messel Pit Fossil Site in Germany. The Auderian Leptictidium is the smallest of the three, known from several complete skeletons.

LEPTICTIDIUM NASUTUM

NAME MEANING: Big-nosed slender little weasel

AGE: Early Eocene (48 MYA)

DISTRIBUTION: Eurasia

SIZE: 1 foot (29.5–32.8 centimeters) HBL; 1.46–1.5 feet (44.5–45.4 centimeters) TL

DIET: Mesocarnivore

ESSENTIAL FACTS: This organism was intermediate in size between the other two Messel Pit leptictidiums.

LEPTICTIDIUM TOBIENI

NAME MEANING: Heinz Tobien's slender little weasel

AGE: Early Eocene (48 MYA)

DISTRIBUTION: Eurasia

SIZE: 1.2 feet (37.5 centimeters) HBL; 1.6 feet (50 centimeters) TL

DIET: Mesocarnivore

ESSENTIAL FACTS: Tobien's Leptictidium is the largest member of the genus. Compared to other leptictidiums from Messel Pit, its jaws were relatively more robust, suggesting that it fed on somewhat tougher foods than the other two contemporary species.

LEPTICTIDAE

Possibly the last surviving members of the group, fossils of these animals are most commonly found from western North America in sediments dating to the Late Eocene and Early Oligocene. Hindlimb proportions are built for high-speed sprinting on all fours instead of the bipedal locomotion displayed by pseudorynchcocyonids.

LEPTICTIS DAKOTENSIS

NAME MEANING: Slender weasel from Dakota

AGE: Late Eocene (35–30 MYA)

DISTRIBUTION: North America

SIZE: About the size of an elephant shrew

DIET: Mesocarnivore

ESSENTIAL FACTS: One of the last leptictids, it can be inferred that these animals were able to excavate underground dens in which to shelter, as evidenced by their remains have been found in burrow-like structures.

CIMOLESTA

Cimolesta is a poorly understood grouping of eutherians that originated in the Late Cretaceous and survived until the Late Eocene or Early Oligocene. This group has been thought to be ancestral to other mammalian orders such as pantodonts, carnivorans, hyaenodonts, and pangolins, though this has since been rejected.

CIMOLESTIDAE

Cimolestids were small, shrew-like predators that occurred mostly during the Late Cretaceous and were distributed throughout the Northern Hemisphere. Most members are known only from isolated teeth and partial jaws, but a few are known from more complete skull and skeletal material.

MAELESTES GOBIENSIS

NAME MEANING: See description

AGE: Late Cretaceous (75–71 MYA)

DISTRIBUTION: Eurasia

SIZE: About mouse-sized

DIET: Mesocarnivore

ESSENTIAL FACTS: *Mae* is the acronym for Mongolian Academy of Sciences-American Museum of Natural History Expeditions, while *lestes* is the Greek word for robber or thief. Discovered in what is now the Gobi Desert, it was a contemporary of such dinosaurs as *Velociraptor* and *Protoceratops*.

CIMOLESTES STIRTONI

NAME MEANING: Stirton's chalk thief

AGE: Late Cretaceous (69–66 MYA)

DISTRIBUTION: North America

SIZE: About weasel-sized

DIET: Mesocarnivore

ESSENTIAL FACTS: *Cimolestes* is the most well-known cimolestid genus, with five species spanning in age from Late Cretaceous to Early Paleocene. A complete skeleton attributed to *Cimolestes* shows that they were agile tree-dwellers with grasping toes and an exceptionally long prehensile tail.

PAROXYCLAENIDAE

Paroxyclaenids were arboreal herbivores that were probably analogous to modern tree squirrels. Skeletal features such as mobile elbow and shoulder joints, rotating ankles, and long tails are indicative of active and agile tree-dwellers. The group is known from the Eocene of Eurasia.

KOPIDODON MACROGNATHUS

NAME MEANING: Long jawed knife tooth

AGE: Early Eocene (48 MYA)

DISTRIBUTION: Eurasia

SIZE: 11–26 pounds (5–12 kilograms)

DIET: Herbivore; browser

ESSENTIAL FACTS: Several skeletons from Messel Pit preserving the fur outline of the body show that the living animal superficially resembled a large tree squirrel, complete with a long and bushy tail. Its skeleton shows that it was adapted to an arboreal or scansorial lifestyle, and it had particularly large canines.

MERIALUS MARTINAE

NAME MEANING: Martine Mons-Gillet from Meyreuil

AGE: Early Eocene (55–54 MYA)

DISTRIBUTION: Eurasia

SIZE: Unknown; about squirrel-sized

DIET: Herbivore; browser

ESSENTIAL FACTS: Merialus was discovered in Palette, France, in the 1980s along with several other paroxyclaenid species. The genus is named after Meyreuil, the Commune on which the fossil locality is situated. The species is dedicated to Martin Emons-Gillet, for her help during the Palette excavations.

PANTOLESTIDAE

Pantolestids were semiaquatic cimolestans from the Middle Paleocene to Late Eocene of North America and Europe. They were the ecological equivalents of river otters, with a number of notable adaptations for swimming. Most notably, they had powerful tails used to propel themselves through the water at great speeds and strong neck muscles to hold their heads up when swimming at the surface. Also like otters, they had strong forelimbs for digging underground dens next to bodies of water.

BISONALVEUS BROWNI

NAME MEANING: Brown's Bison Basin

AGE: Late Paleocene (60–56 MYA)

DISTRIBUTION: North America

SIZE: Unknown

DIET: Aquatic hypercarnivore

ESSENTIAL FACTS: This species is thought to have had a venomous bite. Special grooved canines have similar morphology to the incisors of solenodons, which deliver toxic saliva into their prey through these dental grooves during bites.

PALAEOSINOPA DIDELPHOIDES

NAME MEANING: Opossum-like ancient sinopa

AGE: Early Eocene (53.5–48.5 MYA)

DISTRIBUTION: North America

SIZE: 3 pounds (1.4 kilograms)

DIET: Aquatic hypercarnivore

ESSENTIAL FACTS: Known from the Green River Formation in Wyoming, skeletons of this organism have been found with fish remains in the abdominal region. This shows it was an aquatic predator and agile swimmer.

BUXOLESTES MINOR

NAME MEANING: Little thief from Bouxwiller

AGE: Early Eocene (48 MYA)

DISTRIBUTION: Eurasia

SIZE: About river otter-sized

DIET: Aquatic hypercarnivore

ESSENTIAL FACTS: Buxolestes is known from well-preserved complete skeletons found at Messel Pit in Germany. Even the fur outline of the body is recorded.

PANTODONTA

Among the pantodonts are the first mammals to grow to large sizes after the K/Pg mass extinction. Pantodonts were defining herbivores of Paleocene and Eocene faunas of North America and Eurasia, with a few even being known from South America and Antarctica. The group became extinct 34 million years ago at the end of the Eocene as perissodactyls became larger and more diverse.

ALCIDEDORBIGNYA INOPINATA

NAME MEANING: Alcide d'Orbigny the unexpected

AGE: Early Paleocene (64.5–64 MYA)

DISTRIBUTION: South America

SIZE: 10 inches (25 centimeters) HBL; 1 pound (500 grams)

DIET: Hypocarnivore

ESSENTIAL FACTS: The first and only pantodont known outside of the Northern Hemisphere, it is the most common mammal found at the Tiupampa fossil locality. It is the only member of the family Wangliidae.

HARPYODUS PROGRESSUS

NAME MEANING: Progressive hooked tooth

AGE: Early Paleocene (63 MYA)

DISTRIBUTION: Eurasia

SIZE: 10 inches (25 centimeters) HBL; 1 pound (500 grams)

DIET: Hypocarnivore

ESSENTIAL FACTS: The only member of the family Harpyodidae, this was a squirrel-sized pantodont with a generalized dentition suggesting a diet that included softer plant matter and invertebrates.

ARCHAEOLAMBDA MICRON

NAME MEANING: Small ancient lambda

AGE: Middle Paleocene (60 MYA)

DISTRIBUTION: Eurasia

SIZE: 15 pounds (7 kilograms)

DIET: Herbivore; browser

ESSENTIAL FACTS: A member of Archaeolambdidae, these were small pantodonts with clawed feet and a gracile skeleton. Members of this genus appear to have been scansorial, if not fully arboreal.

BEMALAMBDA PACHYOESTEUS

NAME MEANING: Thick boned raised lambda

AGE: Early Paleocene (63 MYA)

DISTRIBUTION: Eurasia

SIZE: 22 pounds (10 kilograms)

DIET: Herbivore; browser

ESSENTIAL FACTS: The type species for the family Bemalambdidae, Bemalambda had a robust skeleton with particularly powerful forelimbs, which suggest active digging behavior. Its broad skull, wide zygomatic arches, and deep jaws suggest that it fed on particularly tough, fibrous plants.

CYRIACOTHERIUM ARGYREUM

NAME MEANING: Silver Sunday beast

AGE: Early Paleocene (63 MYA)

DISTRIBUTION: North America

SIZE: About cat-sized

DIET: Herbivore; browser

ESSENTIAL FACTS: Cyriacotheriidae were small-bodied pantodonts known from western North America during the Paleocene. They are distinguished from other pantodonts in having molariform premolars, an adaptation which expanded the surface area for grinding. *Cyriacotherium* is the most well-known genus within this family.

CORYPHODON LOBATUS

NAME MEANING: Lobed peak-tooth

AGE: Middle Eocene (44–47 MYA)

DISTRIBUTION: North America

SIZE: 3–4 feet (1–1.2 meters) SH; 8-10 feet (2.5–3 meters) HBL; 800–1,500 pounds (363–700 kilograms)

DIET: Herbivore; browser

ESSENTIAL FACTS: The most well-known of the Coryphodontidae, members of the genus *Coryphodon* were widespread across the Northern Hemisphere and most were comparable in size to tapirs and hippos. They had a semiaquatic lifestyle, and adult males possessed enlarged tusk-like canines.

TITANOIDES PRIMAEVUS

NAME MEANING: Ancient giant-like

AGE: Late Paleocene (59–56 MYA)

DISTRIBUTION: North America

SIZE: 330–440 pounds (150–200 kilograms)

DIET: Hypocarnivore

ESSENTIAL FACTS: The only member of the family Titanoideidae, it has claws instead of hooves and may have been adapted digging, flipping over large rocks, and breaking open rotting logs in search of food the way modern bears are known to do.

BARYLAMBDA FABERI

NAME MEANING: Faber's heavy lambda

AGE: Late Paleocene (58–55 MYA)

DISTRIBUTION: North America

SIZE: 1,430 pounds (650 kilograms)

DIET: Herbivore; browser

SEE MORE ON PAGES 162–163

BARYLAMBDA FABERI

ESSENTIAL FACTS: The most well-known member of the Barylambdidae, it is known for complete skeletal material. The genus *Barylambda* has three described species which lived in North America during the middle Paleocene to earliest Eocene. All three are relatively large by pantodont standards, but Faber's Barylambda is the largest. An exceptional mounted skeleton of this animal is on display at the Field Museum in Chicago, Illinois. The genus name refers to its larger size compared to pantodonts of the genus *Pantolambda* (Pantolambdidae). Morphologically, these animals were vaguely similar to a megalonychid ground sloths.

Faber's Barylambda is one of the largest animals of its time, weighing about as much as a modern polar bear (*Ursus maritimus*). It was heavily built, with graviportal (the ability to bear great weight) limbs and five-toed plantigrade feet. In addition to feeding on all fours, it was also able to rear up on its hindlimbs to access foods higher than the height of its shoulders and well out of reach of other terrestrial herbivores. The tail was particularly massive and able to support its weight, acting as a third limb while the animal was browsing. Male individuals had large, well-developed canines which they would use to fight against each other during conflicts over territory or mates.

SEE ENTRY ON PAGE 161

PANTOLAMBDA BATHMODON

NAME MEANING: All lambda with stepped teeth

AGE: Early Paleocene (63–57 MYA)

DISTRIBUTION: North America

SIZE: 77–92 pounds (35–42 kilograms)

DIET: Herbivore; browser

SEE MORE ON PAGES 166–167

TILLODONTIA

Tillodonts are distinctive for having evolved a pair of enlarged second incisors for gnawing and cutting. Only the front surfaces of these teeth are covered by enamel. As the incisors grind against each other, the softer dentine on the rear of the teeth wears away faster, leaving the sharp enamel edge shaped like the blade of a chisel. In more derived tillodonts, these teeth are hypselodont (continuously growing). Because of the superficial resemblance of these teeth to the hypertrophied canines of taeniodonts, it was once believed that the two groups were closely related. However, this is now known not to be the case. Wear patterns on the cheek teeth suggest that they had a primarily herbivorous diet of tough or fibrous foods. Fossils are known from across the Northern Hemisphere, although they are most abundant in North America, which is thought to be where the group originated.

DELTATHERIUM FUNDAMINIS

NAME MEANING: Foundation delta beast

AGE: Early Eocene (50 MYA)

DISTRIBUTION: North America

SIZE: Unknown

DIET: Herbivore; browser

ESSENTIAL FACTS: An animal of uncertain affiliations, Deltatherium is commonly considered an early tillodont. It also shows characteristics seen among arctocyonids. Its upper canines were notably long, and a well-developed sagittal crest suggests a powerful bite.

ESTHONYCHIDAE

Esthonychids were derived tillodonts with strongly hypertrophied and hypselodont incisors.

AZYGONYX GUNNELLI

NAME MEANING: Gunnell's non-joining claw

AGE: Late Paleocene (56 MYA)

DISTRIBUTION: North America

SIZE: About cat-sized

DIET: Herbivore; browser

ESSENTIAL FACTS: Azygonyx is the oldest-known tillodont. Little postcranial material is known for this species, but what is known suggests that it was scansorial.

ESTHONYX BISULCATUS

NAME MEANING: Two-grooved sensitive claw

AGE: Early Eocene (55–50 MYA)

DISTRIBUTION: North America

SIZE: About cat-sized

DIET: Herbivore; browser

ESSENTIAL FACTS: Like Azygonyx, not much postcranial material is known for this species. What little is known, however, suggests that it was more terrestrially oriented and less of a climber than its close relative.

PANTOLAMBDA BATHMODON

ESSENTIAL FACTS: It is the most well-studied member of Pantolambdidae and one of the first larger-bodied browsing mammals. This particular species was nicknamed "ManBearPig" after the hybrid creature from the television series *South Park*, for its seemingly mixed assortment of features. It had five digits on its hands and feet, its reconstructed face has been described as "bearlike," and it had a long barrel-shaped body somewhat like that of a pig. It is also the oldest-known selenodont mammal, its cheek teeth having crescent-shaped ridges, a feature seen in many artiodactyls. This shows that this animal was a specialized herbivore adapted to shred tough or fibrous plant matter.

Much of the life history of this species has been deduced and was published in 2022 using paleohistology and geochemistry. The gestation period was estimated to be about 207 days and that weaning began between at one month after birth and concluded at around two months. At weaning, juveniles weighed around 20 pounds (9 kilograms). While Pantolambda had a longer gestation period than would be expected for an animal of its size, the period of juvenile dependency was greatly reduced, showing that the young were highly precocial (able to move independently almost immediately). Mortality among individuals appears to have been very high, with most individuals dying between ages 2 and 5, with the oldest known specimen being 11.

SEE ENTRY ON PAGE 164

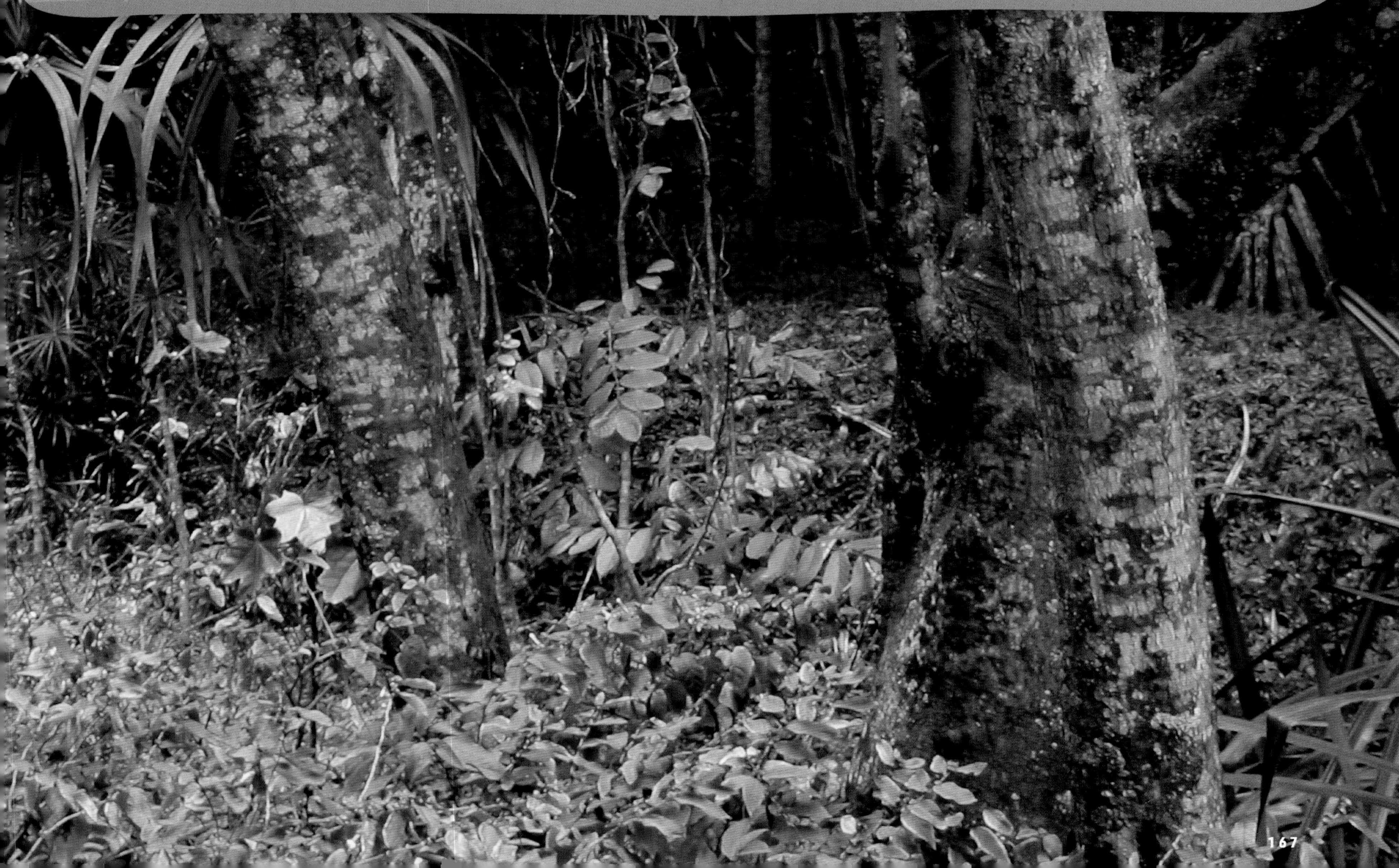

TROGOSUS HYRACOIDES

NAME MEANING: Hyrax-like gnawer

AGE: Middle Eocene (47–45 MYA)

DISTRIBUTION: North America

SIZE: 330 pounds (150 kilograms)

DIET: Herbivore; browser

ESSENTIAL FACTS: Trogosus was a very large tillodont about the size of a black bear (*Ursus americanus*). The postcranial skeleton is the most well-known of any tillodont. Its limb bones were stout and powerfully muscled, implying active digging or climbing behaviors.

TAENIODONTA

Taeniodonts are only known from North America and are very rare in the fossil record. The oldest representatives appear in the latest Cretaceous and they become extinct during the middle Eocene. All have powerful forelimbs and large claws for digging. Most have modified gnawing incisors and simplified cheek teeth for grinding particularly tough foods.

SCHOWALTERIA CLEMENSI

NAME MEANING: Schowalter Clemens

AGE: Late Cretaceous (70–66 MYA)

DISTRIBUTION: North America

SIZE: Unknown; raccoon to badger-sized

DIET: Herbivore; browser

ESSENTIAL FACTS: Schowalteria is one of the largest Mesozoic mammals known, and almost certainly the largest-known herbivorous mammal from that age. It is also the earliest-known representative of the Taeniodonta.

ONYCHODECTES TISONENSIS

NAME MEANING: Clawed biter from Tiso

AGE: Early Paleocene

DISTRIBUTION: North America

SIZE: About cat-sized

DIET: Hypocarnivore

ESSENTIAL FACTS: Onychodectes had robust limbs, in particular a powerful forearm, and a mobile hand. This suggests a certain propensity for digging and possibly climbing. It possessed some of the largest olfactory bulbs relative to any known mammal.

STYLINODONTIDAE

Stylinodont skulls are heavily built, with short faces and very robust jaws. The canines are enlarged and are hypselodont in more derived genera. The enamel on these canines is restricted to the anterior surface as in the second incisors of the tillodonts, resulting in a permanent chisel-like cutting surface through differential wear. The cheek teeth in later genera are also ever growing and reduced to simplified peg-like structures which lose their enamel early in life. In this attribute, they are similar to aardvarks (Orycteropodidae) and xenarthrans. In another similarity, their skeletons appear to have been adapted to digging, with compact bodies and particularly robust forelimbs with short digits ending in sturdy, laterally compressed claws. The broader claws on the hindfeet and long, heavy tails helped to stabilize them while digging.

WORTMANIA OTARIIDENS

NAME MEANING: Little-eared Wortman

AGE: Early Paleocene

DISTRIBUTION: North America

SIZE: About pig-sized

DIET: Herbivore; browser

ESSENTIAL FACTS: The earliest stylinodont, Wortmania already displayed many of the features that would characterize the family including recurved, laterally flattened claws for digging. Its jaws and teeth, though robust, were not as extreme as those of its later relatives.

PSITTACOTHERIUM MULTIFRAGUM

NAME MEANING: Many scented parrot beast

AGE: Early Paleocene (63–60 MYA)

DISTRIBUTION: North America

SIZE: 110 pounds (50 kilograms)

DIET: Herbivore; browser

ESSENTIAL FACTS: Psittacotherium had a lower jaw that was particularly deep at the anterior half, corresponding with the expanded lower canine roots, a distinctive feature of more derived stylinodonts.

STYLINODON MIRUS

NAME MEANING: Amazing stake tooth

AGE: Middle Eocene (45 MYA)

DISTRIBUTION: North America

SIZE: 180 pounds (80 kilograms)

DIET: Herbivore; browser

ESSENTIAL FACTS: Stylinodon was the best-known and last of the taeniodonts. All its teeth were hypselodont, and its cheek teeth were undifferentiated pegs probably adapted for chewing roots and tubers.

XENARTHRA

Xenarthrans represent a particularly ancient lineage of mammals, thought to have split off from other eutherians during the late Cretaceous or earliest Paleocene. The group underwent most of its evolutionary history in South America which had been an island continent for much of the Cenozoic, with species spreading to North America starting in the late Miocene. The name Xenarhra means "strange joints," a reference to members of this group having vertebrae with extra points of articulation that function to strengthen the lower back. This feature is not present in any other eutherian, although a similar adaptation evolved in the completely unrelated eutriconodont Spinolestes from the Early Cretaceous. The pelvis and sacrum are fused in xenarthrans, lending further back strength. The limb bones are generally very robust with large areas of muscle attachment and all have long, powerful claws. Taken together, all these features suggests that the common ancestor for all xenarthrans was highly fossorial. This unknown common ancestor may also have been a specialized ant and termite eater (myrmecophagous) with a simplified homodont-hypselodont dentition, a loss of enamel, and the loss of the incisors to allow for the passage of a protrusible tongue, all features which can be seen in modern aardvarks, for example. Although different xenarthran lineages have modified their teeth as they adapted to different diets, all retain this hypselodont and largely homodont pattern.

CINGULATA

The group which contains modern armadillos and their extinct relatives. The name cingulate translates to "the ones with armor," alluding to the key defining trait shared among all members of the group; an armored shell covering their back and sides, known as a carapace. Protective shields on the head and tail are also present. This armor is composed of networks of small bones called osteoderms, which are embedded in the skin and have a keratinized covering for added protection. The shape of these osteoderms and the armor that they form varies from family to family.

DASYPODIDAE

UTAETUS BUCCATUS

NAME MEANING: *Eutatus* cheeks

AGE: Middle Eocene (42–38 MYA)

DISTRIBUTION: South America

SIZE: 3–3.2 feet (30–36 centimeters) HBL; 4.4–6.6 pounds (2–3 kilograms)

DIET: Mesocarnivore

ESSENTIAL FACTS: The oldest armadillo to be known from a relatively complete skeleton, the organism's carapace (hard upper shell) consists of a series of movable transverse bands beginning at the neck and ending in a pelvic shield in the back.

STEGOTHERIUM TESSELLATUM

NAME MEANING: Mosaic roofed beast

AGE: Early Miocene (17.5–16.3 MYA)

DISTRIBUTION: South America

SIZE: Unknown

DIET: Myrmecophagous hypercarnivore

ESSENTIAL FACTS: The skull of this armadillo is more similar to the skulls of anteaters than to other cingulates, with an elongated snout, almost toothless jaws, and weak jaw musculature. These adaptations indicate that it was an ant and termite specialist.

PROEUTATUS OENOPHORUM

NAME MEANING: Basket-like before *Eutatus*

AGE: Early Miocene (20 MYA)

DISTRIBUTION: South America

SIZE: 11–13 pounds (5–6 kilograms)

DIET: Hypocarnivore

ESSENTIAL FACTS: Sturdy teeth and robust jaws with powerful chewing muscles indicate that this armadillo was among the most specialized for an herbivorous diet outside of pampatheres and glyptodonts.

DASYPUS BELLUS

NAME MEANING: Beautiful rough foot

AGE: Pleistocene (2.5 MYA–11,000 YA)

DISTRIBUTION: North America, South America

SIZE: 10–30 pounds (5–13 kilograms)

DIET: Mesocarnivore

ESSENTIAL FACTS: The Pretty Armadillo is morphologically similar to the modern nine-banded armadillo (*D. novemcinctus*) but about twice the size. Its fossils are known from Florida to New Mexico, and as far north as Indiana.

PELTEPHILIDAE

Peltephilids, referred to commonly as horned armadillos, have paired nasal horns formed by modified cranial osteoderms. Their exact function is uncertain, although similar structures evolved among North American rodents of the family Mylagaulidae (horned gophers) and are speculated to have been used for defense. The fossil record for this family extends from the early Eocene to the late Miocene.

RONWOLFFIA PACIFICA

NAME MEANING: Ronald Wolff from the Pacific

AGE: Late Oligocene (29–25 MYA)

DISTRIBUTION: South America

SIZE: Unknown

DIET: Hypocarnivore

ESSENTIAL FACTS: One of the oldest-known horned armadillos, it lived during a time when an increase in the diversity of xenarthrans and rodents is noted in the fossil record. This was also when meridiungulates experienced a slight drop in terms of sheer number of species, if not overall abundance.

PELTEPHILUS FEROX

NAME MEANING: Fierce small shield loving

AGE: Early Miocene (18–17.5 MYA)

DISTRIBUTION: South America

SIZE: 17–24 pounds (8–11 kilograms)

DIET: Hypocarnivore

ESSENTIAL FACTS: Studies have shown that the Fierce Horned Armadillo probably fed on tough foods such as underground tubers.

EPIPELTEPHILUS RECURVES

NAME MEANING: Bent over *Peltephilus*

AGE: Middle Miocene (11.8–10 MYA)

DISTRIBUTION: South America

SIZE: Unknown

DIET: Hypocarnivore

ESSENTIAL FACTS: Little is known about this species, other than that it is slightly larger than other horned armadillos and had even more robust jaws and teeth, indicating a greater reliance on tough foods.

PAMPATHERIIDAE

Pampatheres were large armadillos which appear in the South American fossil record from the Middle Miocene and survived into the Early Holocene. They are particularly well-represented in Pleistocene assemblages in North and South America. Pampatheres have three movable bands in their carapaces like those of Three-Banded Armadillos (*Tolypeutes*), which allow for flexibility at the spine and makes these animals faster and more nimble than their glyptodont cousins. The osteoderms are much larger and thicker proportionally than those of most armadillos (surpassed in thickness only by those of glyptodonts) and have a distinctive surface pattern: a large, smooth center surrounded by pits along the edges. They were herbivorous like glyptodonts with robust skulls and large, slightly lobed teeth. There is evidence that at least some species dug burrows in which to take shelter.

MACHLYDOTHERIUM ASPERUM

NAME MEANING: Unknown

AGE: Middle Eocene (48 MYA)

DISTRIBUTION: South America

SIZE: Unknown

DIET: Herbivore; grazer

ESSENTIAL FACTS: Although the teeth and osteoderms of this species is similar to those of pampatheres, its exact affinities are uncertain, and it is only tentatively placed within Pampatheriidae. If this placement is correct, then it would be the oldest-known pampathere.

SCIRROTHERIUM HONDAENSIS

NAME MEANING: Covered beast from Honda

AGE: Middle Miocene (13.8 MYA)

DISTRIBUTION: South America

SIZE: Unknown

DIET: Herbivore; grazer

ESSENTIAL FACTS: The Honda Pampathere is one of the earliest definitive pampatheres. It inhabited the middle Miocene forests and woodlands that covered the La Venta fossil locality in what is now Colombia.

HOLMESINA FLORIDANUS

NAME MEANING: Holmes from Florida

AGE: Pleistocene

DISTRIBUTION: North America

SIZE: 154–220 pounds (70–100 kilograms)

DIET: Herbivore; grazer

ESSENTIAL FACTS: Florida Pampathere fossils are abundant in Pleistocene-age fossil sites of its namesake state, known from complete skeletal material and articulated armor. A complete mounted skeleton is on permanent display at the Florida Museum of Natural History.

PAMPATHERIUM HUMBOLDTII

NAME MEANING: Humboldt's pampas beast

AGE: Pleistocene

DISTRIBUTION: South America

SIZE: 462 pounds (209.5 kilograms)

DIET: Herbivore; grazer

ESSENTIAL FACTS: One of the largest of the pampatheres, Humboldt's Pampathere appears to have fed on less abrasive plants than other pampatheres of the time. Its fossils are known from eastern South America.

PAMPATHERIUM MEXICANUM

NAME MEANING: Mexican pampas beast

AGE: Pleistocene

DISTRIBUTION: North America

SIZE: Unknown

DIET: Herbivore; grazer

ESSENTIAL FACTS: Mexican Pampathere is the only member of its genus known to have had a North American distribution, which extended at least as far north as Sonora, Mexico.

TONNICINCTUS MIRUS

NAME MEANING: Wonderful mobile bands of Eduardo P. Tonni

AGE: Pleistocene

DISTRIBUTION: South America

SIZE: Unknown

DIET: Herbivore; grazer

ESSENTIAL FACTS: Described in 2015, Tonni's Pampathere is one of the smallest of the pampatheres.

PACHYARMATHERIIDAE

Pachyarmatheres appear in the South American fossil record during the late Miocene and inhabited southern North America during the Pliocene and Pleistocene. The carapace is unlike that of other armadillos, being mostly composed almost entirely of small, thick, polygonal osteoderms that are solidly joined to one another like those of glyptodonts. Only two rows of wedge-shaped osteoderms separate the pectoral and pelvic shields and would have permitted moderate movement of the spine. These characteristics led to the early belief that it was an early-diverging glyptodont.

NEOGLYPTATELUS ORIGINALIS

NAME MEANING: Original new *Glyptatelus*

AGE: Late Miocene (9–7 MYA)

DISTRIBUTION: South America

SIZE: 20–24 inches (50–60 centimeters) HBL; 22–33 pounds (10–15 kilograms)

DIET: Hypercarnivore; possibly myrmecophagous

ESSENTIAL FACTS: The genus is named after the early glyptodont genus *Glyptatelus* to which the osteoderms bear a strong resemblance. More complete remains of these animals demonstrated that they form their own taxonomic grouping.

PACHYARMATHERIUM LEISEYI

NAME MEANING: Thick-armored beast from Leisey

AGE: Pliocene to Pleistocene (4.9 MYA–11,000 YA)

DISTRIBUTION: North America

SIZE: Unknown

DIET: Hypercarnivore; myrmecophagous

ESSENTIAL FACTS: The Leisey Armadillo is the most northerly distributed member of the family and the only one for which complete skull material is known. Named for the Leisey Shell Pit in Florida where it was first discovered, portions of the lower jaw are slender and completely lack teeth or tooth sockets, suggesting that it had a diet consisting of ants and termites like the modern giant armadillo (*Priodontes maximus*).

CHLAMYPHORIDAE

This is a morphologically and ecologically diverse assemblage of armadillos which encompasses all modern species except for the long-nosed armadillos (*Dasypus*).

EUPHRACTINAE

Euphractines are fossorial armadillos that excavate extensive burrows for shelter. Members of this group are covered in a coat of bristly hairs and are notably more predatory than other armadillo. Their diets include small vertebrates as well as insects and plant matter. The group has a history that extends back to the Middle Eocene.

MACROEUPHRACTUS OUTESI

NAME MEANING: Outes' large *Euphractus*

AGE: Pliocene (4.5–3.3 MYA)

DISTRIBUTION: South America

SIZE: 4 feet (125 centimeters) HBL; 200–220 pounds (90–100 kilograms)

DIET: Hypercarnivore

ESSENTIAL FACTS: Unique among xenarthrans, Outes's Armadillo was a hypercarnivore adapted to catch and consume quite large prey items, potentially close to its own size. The skull was robust with particularly strong temporalis muscles for delivering powerful bites and maintaining a solid grip. The jaws were filled with sturdy, sharply pointed teeth, the second pair of which are particularly long and resemble canines.

GLYPTODONTINAE

The name glyptodont means "carved tooth" in Greek, referring to their distinctive teeth which have a complex three-lobed shape. Their skulls were short and tall with particularly robust jaws adapted for chewing. The most notable characteristic of glyptodonts, however, were their tall, domed carapaces in which nearly all the osteoderms were thickened, hexagonal in shape, and solidly attached to one another. This resulted in a rigid shell more like that of a tortoise than the flexible shells of other armadillos. Due to this rigidity and great weight of the carapace, the thoracic vertebrae in glyptodonts fused together forming a "dorsal tube." The oldest glyptodonts appeared during the Late Eocene and survived until the latest Pleistocene and possibly into the Holocene.

PARAPROPALAEHOPLOPHORUS SEPTENTRIONALIS

NAME MEANING: Near *Propalaehoplophorus* from the north

AGE: Early Miocene (18–17.5 MYA)

DISTRIBUTION: South America

SIZE: 143–209 pounds (65–95 kilograms)

DIET: Herbivore

ESSENTIAL FACTS: It is among the oldest glyptodonts to be known from skeletal material. At the time in which this animal lived, the Chucal site in Argentina, in which its fossils were found, featured an open grassland habitat.

NEOSCLEROCALYPTUS ORNATUS

NAME MEANING: Adorned new hard covering

AGE: Pleistocene

DISTRIBUTION: South America

SIZE: 793 pounds (360 kilograms)

DIET: Herbivore; grazer

ESSENTIAL FACTS: One of the smaller glyptodonts of the Pleistocene, this species shows strong development of the front nasal sinuses, which may have enabled it to breathe particularly dry and dusty air.

DOEDICURUS CLAVICAUDATUS

NAME MEANING: Pestle tail / club tail

AGE: Pleistocene

DISTRIBUTION: South America

SIZE: 2,200–3,300 pounds (1,000–1,500 kilograms)

DIET: Herbivore; grazer

SEE MORE ON PAGES 180–181

PANOCHTHUS TUBERCULATUS

NAME MEANING: Humped hill

AGE: Pleistocene

DISTRIBUTION: South America

SIZE: 3,300 pounds (1,500 kilograms)

DIET: Herbivore; grazer

ESSENTIAL FACTS: This species is similar to Doedicurus in having a long, stiffened tail that could be wielded as a bludgeoning weapon against predators and rivals.

DOEDICURUS CLAVICAUDATUS

ESSENTIAL FACTS: Doedicurus is possibly the most famous of the glyptodonts and also one of the largest, weighing about as much as a small- to medium-sized car. Its most notable feature is its long tail which ends in a heavy, spiky tail club comparable to those seen in ankylosaurs. The base of the tail is flexible thanks to overlapping rings of armor, but the distal half of the tail is encased in a stiffened, solid mass of armor that has been compared to the handle of a mace or morning star. While almost certainly being applicable as an anti-predator defensive weapon, there is evidence that individuals used their tail clubs against each other during intraspecific confrontations. Specimens have been found with healed injuries to their carapaces, and a fatty hump directly underneath would have acted to cushion impacts.

Glyptodonts were once placed within their own family, Glyptodontidae. However, ancient DNA extracted from a 12,000-year-old specimen revealed a close relation to modern armadillos within the subfamilies Tolypeutinae and Chlamyphorinae within the family Chlamyphoridae. Thus, glyptodonts have been downgraded to subfamily status and placed among these armadillos.

SEE ENTRY ON PAGE 179

GLYPTOTHERIUM TEXANUM

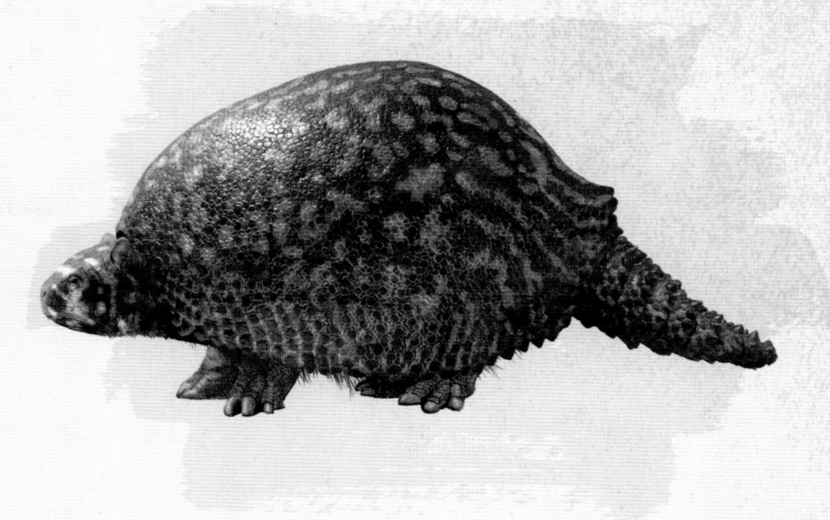

NAME MEANING: Carved beast from Texas

AGE: Pleistocene

DISTRIBUTION: North America

SIZE: 5 feet (1.5 meters) HBL

DIET: Herbivore; grazer

ESSENTIAL FACTS: The Northern Glyptodont was distributed throughout southern North America and was the smaller of the two known species of *Glyptotherium*.

GLYPTODON RETICULATUS

NAME MEANING: Net-like carved tooth

AGE: Pleistocene

DISTRIBUTION: South America

SIZE: 884–1,900 pounds (401–862 kilograms)

DIET: Herbivore; grazer

ESSENTIAL FACTS: Glyptodon was a particularly well-armored species, with pointed osteoderms lining the bottom edges of its carapace for added protection of its neck and abdomen. Damage to the carapace of one specimen shows that these animals used their short tails to fight each other.

PILOSA

The xenarthran order Pilosa includes the sloths and anteaters. The lineage originated in South America during the early Paleocene and attained a great diversity of ecomorphs throughout the Cenozoic, particularly the sloths. Anteaters were never very diverse or abundant without much of a presence in the fossil record. Sloths, on the other hand, were an important lineage of South American herbivores that gradually became more speciose from the Early Miocene onward. They ranged from small arboreal animals to giants that were South America's answer to rhinos and elephants on other continents. They are characterized by broad, barrel-shaped torsos that housed a large gut for digesting plant matter. The limbs are well-muscled and end in large claws. To preserve these claws, most sloths have shifted from a plantigrade stance to a pedolateral stance, a condition unique to sloths in which the feet are rotated inward so that the animal walks on the sides of the feet.

PSEUDOGLYPTODON SALLAENSIS

NAME MEANING: False *Glyptodon* from the Salla Formation

AGE: Early Oligocene (33–31 MYA)

DISTRIBUTION: South America

SIZE: 4 feet (115 centimeters) HBL; 65–90 pounds (30–40 kilograms)

DIET: Herbivore; grazer

ESSENTIAL FACTS: Despite being among the oldest recorded sloths, Pseudoglyptodon shows extremely derived traits, most notably having three-lobed molariform teeth specialized for grazing similar to those of glyptodonts. This feature makes it difficult to place among other sloths, and may indeed represent the only known member of its own family that diverged early in the group's evolutionary history.

MEGALOCNIDAE

Megalocnidae is a basal lineage of sloths that evolved in isolation on the Caribbean islands between North and South America. It is thought that the ancestors of these sloths arrived in the Caribbean from South America around the Eocene-Oligocene boundary about 33 million years ago, when there was a significant sea level drop caused by a glaciation episode.

MEGALOCNUS RODENS

NAME MEANING: Gnawing toothed great sloth

AGE: Pleistocene to Holocene (125,000–4,190 YA)

DISTRIBUTION: Cuba

SIZE: 440–595 pounds (200–270 kilograms)

DIET: Herbivore

ESSENTIAL FACTS: Megalocnus was the largest of the Caribbean sloths, being about the size of a large pig. On its initial discovery it was misidentified as a giant rodent due to its incisor-like caniniforms.

NEOCNUS DOUSMAN

NAME MEANING: Slow new sloth

AGE: Pleistocene to Holocene

DISTRIBUTION: Hispaniola

SIZE: 20 pounds (9 kilograms)

DIET: Herbivore

ESSENTIAL FACTS: Lesser Neocnus was about the size of modern tree sloths but was much more mobile and active. It was likely a scansorial animal that divided its time between the ground and the trees.

ACRATOCNUS YE

NAME MEANING: Yesterday's apex sloth

AGE: Pleistocene to Holocene

DISTRIBUTION: Hispaniola

SIZE: About badger-sized

DIET: Herbivore

ESSENTIAL FACTS: Yesterday's Acratocnus were terrestrial herbivores whose fossils are often recovered from cave deposits.

MEGALONYCHIDAE

Megalonychids originated in South America during the Early Oligocene and would go on to become the most widespread sloth family during the Late Miocene and through the Pleistocene. It was among the first xenarthrans to inhabit North America and some species spreading as far north as Alaska. As with the Caribbean sloths (Megalocnidae) and modern two-toed sloths (Choloepus), the first pair of upper and lower teeth are caniniform.

PLIOMETANASTES PROTISTUS

NAME MEANING: Very first Pliocene wanderer

AGE: Late Miocene (10.3–5 MYA)

DISTRIBUTION: North America

SIZE: About bear-sized

DIET: Herbivore; browser

ESSENTIAL FACTS: The Wandering Sloth was one of the first South American participants of the Great American Biotic Interchange. Its ancestors island-hopped across the Central American Seaway, and its known distribution encompassed Costa Rica, California, and Florida.

MEGALONYX JEFFERSONI

NAME MEANING: Thomas Jefferson's great claw

AGE: Pleistocene

DISTRIBUTION: North America

SIZE: 10 feet (3 meters) HBL; 2,200 pounds (1,000 kilograms)

DIET: Herbivore; browser

SEE MORE ON PAGES 186–187

SCELIDOTHERIIDAE

Scelidotheres were larger sloths that used to be considered a subfamily within the Mylodontidae. These sloths possessed notably narrow mouths and were selective mixed feeders for whom graze and browse were consumed at different proportions from species to species.

MEGALONYX JEFFERSONI

ESSENTIAL FACTS: Jefferson's Ground Sloth is an iconic animal of the Pleistocene. The discovery and description of its limb bones in the 1700s is regarded as the origin of vertebrate paleontology in the United States. When Thomas Jefferson first examined the fossil claw cores, he initially thought they belonged to a giant cat three times the size of a Lion (*Panthera leo*). The claw was later found to be that of an ox-sized sloth, which was named *Megalonyx jeffersoni*, or Jefferson's Ground Sloth, in honor of the third president.

Jefferson's Ground Sloth is the second ground sloth to be described after the Giant Ground Sloth (*Megatherium americanum*) and is also the largest-known member of the family Megalonychidae. It inhabited woodland and forest habitats throughout North America with a range extending from coast to coast and from Mexico to Alaska. They are particularly well-represented in the Midwestern United States. Its diet consisted of the leaves from various types of trees and bushes. A 2022 study centered around an adult specimen in association with two juveniles of different ages suggests that females would care for young from different birthing seasons at any given time as some modern herbivores are known to do. Its lifespan has been estimated to be around nineteen years on average, with a gestation of around fourteen months.

SEE ENTRY ON PAGE 185

CATONYX CUVIERI

NAME MEANING: Cuvier's downward claw

AGE: Pleistocene

DISTRIBUTION: South America

SIZE: 10 feet (3 meters) HBL

DIET: Herbivore; mixed feeder

ESSENTIAL FACTS: Cuvier's Sloth was the first of its genus to be described in 1839. It inhabited the savanna habitats of South America, where it browsed from bushes and low-hanging branches. Isotope studies have shown that these animals were a common prey item of the Southern Smilodon (*Smilodon populator*).

SCELIDOTHERIUM LEPTOCEPHALUM

NAME MEANING: Slender-headed leg beast

AGE: Pleistocene

DISTRIBUTION: South America

SIZE: 6.5 feet (2 meters) HBL

DIET: Herbivore; mixed feeder

ESSENTIAL FACTS: The type species of the family Scelidotheriidae, this species has a notably long and narrow mouth that suggests it was a very selective feeder. Stable isotopes show that they fed on a variety of plants in open environments.

SCELIDODON CHILIENSE

NAME MEANING: Leg tooth from Chili

AGE: Pleistocene to Holocene

DISTRIBUTION: South America

SIZE: 10 feet (3 meters) HBL

DIET: Herbivore; mixed feeder

ESSENTIAL FACTS: The Chilean Sloth is known to have inhabited more arid environments and was a generalist feeder whose diet likely included a variety of plants including leaves, fruits, flowers, and grasses.

MYLODONTIDAE

The mylodont record extends back to the Late Oligocene, and they became extinct during the Early Holocene. All mylodonts are terrestrial, robust sloths that appear to have been predominantly grazers or graze-dominated mixed feeders. Mylodonts are the only sloths known to have had osteoderms, though unlike those seen in armadillos, sloth osteoderms occur as network of small, irregularly shaped bones embedded within the skin.

THINOBADISTES SEGNIS

NAME MEANING: Slow beach walker

AGE: Late Miocene (10.3–5 MYA)

DISTRIBUTION: North America

SIZE: 2,090–2,350 pounds (948–1,066 kilograms)

DIET: Herbivore; grazer

ESSENTIAL FACTS: The earliest known mylodont sloth known from North America, its ancestors probably arrived via island-hopping in the Central American Seaway. Its fossils are known from the Late Miocene of Florida. A complete mounted skeleton is on permanent display at the Florida Museum of Natural History.

LESTODON ARMATUS

NAME MEANING: Armored robber tooth

AGE: Pleistocene

DISTRIBUTION: South America

SIZE: 3,600–4,100 pounds (1,632–1,859 kilograms)

DIET: Herbivore; grazer

ESSENTIAL FACTS: The largest-known of the mylodontid sloths, Lestodon was about the size of a river hippopotamus (*Hippopotamus amphibius*) or white rhinoceros (*Ceratotherium simum*). Much like these animals, it had a notably wide mouth adapted for bulk-grazing on short grasses.

MYLODON DARWINI

NAME MEANING: Darwin's molar tooth

AGE: Pleistocene to early Holocene (2.5 MYA–10,000 YA)

DISTRIBUTION: South America

SIZE: 10 feet (3 meters) HBL

DIET: Herbivore

SEE MORE ON PAGES 192–193

PARAMYLODON HARLANI

NAME MEANING: Harlan's beside Mylodon

AGE: Pleistocene

DISTRIBUTION: North America

SIZE: 4 feet (1.2 meters) SH; 7.2 feet (2.2 meters) HBL; 1,100 pounds (500 kilograms)

DIET: Herbivore; grazer

SEE MORE ON PAGES 194–195

NOTHROTHERIIDAE

Nothrotheres are characterized by their slender builds and long, narrow skulls adapted for selective browsing. The family originated in the Early Miocene and were originally placed as a subfamily within Megatheriidae. Most species were small- to medium-sized and many retained the ability to climb trees.

HAPALOPS RUETIMEYERI

NAME MEANING: Ruetimeyer's gentle face

AGE: Early Miocene (18–16 MYA)

DISTRIBUTION: South America

SIZE: 135 centimeters (4.5 feet) HBL; 45–135 pounds (20–60 kilograms)

DIET: Herbivore; browser

ESSENTIAL FACTS: Ruetimeyer's Sloth is known from remarkably complete specimens. These were scansorial sloths that were equally comfortable feeding in the trees and on the ground. Members of the genus are notably long-bodied, which combined with the long neck and tail gave them a stretched-out appearance.

LAKUKULLUS ANATISROSTRATUS

NAME MEANING: Duck-beaked wild animal of heights

AGE: Middle Miocene (13.8–11.8 MYA)

DISTRIBUTION: South America

SIZE: About ox-sized

DIET: Herbivore; browser

ESSENTIAL FACTS: Lakukullus is the largest-known of the nothrotheriid sloths, about the size of the largest examples of Jefferson's Ground Sloth (*Megalonyx jeffersoni*). Little of the skeleton is known, but it can be inferred that it was a mostly terrestrial browser.

PRONOTHROTHERIUM TYPICUM

NAME MEANING: Typical before *Nothrotherium*

AGE: Late Miocene (7–5.5 MYA)

DISTRIBUTION: South America

SIZE: 125 centimeters (4 feet) HBL; 110–220 pounds (50–100 kilograms)

DIET: Herbivore; browser

ESSENTIAL FACTS: The environment in which this animal lived was a mixture of mixed savanna and upland forests. It was built similarly to *Haplops*. A complete mounted skeleton of this species is on permanent display at the Field Museum in Chicago, Illinois.

MYLODON DARWINI

ESSENTIAL FACTS: Darwin's Ground Sloth is named in honor of Charles Darwin, who collected the first recorded fossils of the species during his voyage on the *HMS Beagle*. Its skull is notably longer and narrower than that of other mylodonts, suggesting a more mixed and selective diet. Unusually, the nasal bones are long and curve downward to fuse with the premaxillae, forming a bony nasal arch. Aside from this, postcranial skeletal elements of this species are much rarer.

Cave deposits, particularly the aptly named Cueva del Milodon (Mylodon Cave) in southern Chile, have yielded the most significant finds. The cool, dry, and stable environments of such sites have facilitated the preservation of soft tissue remains including hair, skin, and claw sheaths. Mummified pelts indicate that Darwin's Ground Sloth had a coat of reddish-brown fur with thickened skin containing a network of osteoderms. Feces have also been preserved in association with these sloth remains, showing that its diet consisted mostly of grasses with the inclusion of herbaceous plants. Stable isotope analyses conducted in 2021 also indicate that Darwin's Ground Sloth would opportunistically feed on animal matter, likely scavenging from found carcasses.

SEE ENTRY ON PAGE 190

PARAMYLODON HARLANI

ESSENTIAL FACTS: Named in honor of American paleontologist Richard Harlan, Harlan's Ground Sloth was distributed throughout North America, from Guatemala in the south to Alberta in the north, and from California to Florida west to east. Fossils of this species are particularly abundant at Rancho La Brea in California, where up to ninety individuals of various life stages have been excavated from the asphalt deposits. Studies of the Rancho La Brea sample have given us much of our current understanding of the anatomy and paleobiology of this species.

Harlan's Ground Sloths appear to have favored relatively open environments with minimal tree cover. Its minimal sexual dimorphism and abundance of its fossils relative to other sloths suggests that they lived in mixed-sex herds. Their diet consisted mostly of grasses and herbaceous plants. Preserved footprints of this species are known, demonstrating that these sloths exhibited relatively quick walking speeds. Like several other mylodonts, Harlan's Ground Sloth is known to have had osteoderms within its skin, which would have provided a degree of protection when attacked by such predators as Saber-Toothed Cats (*Smilodon fatalis*), Dire Wolves (*Aenocyon dirus*), and Scimitar Cats (*Homotherium latidens*).

SEE ENTRY ON PAGE 190

THALASSOCNUS NATANS

NAME MEANING: Swimming sea sloth

AGE: Late Miocene (9–7 MYA)

DISTRIBUTION: South America

SIZE: 125 centimeters (4 feet) HBL; 130–200 pounds (60–90 kilograms)

DIET: Marine herbivore

SEE MORE ON PAGES 198–199

NOTHROTHERIUM MAQUINENSE

NAME MEANING: Lazy beast from the Maquiné Grotto

AGE: Pleistocene

DISTRIBUTION: South America

SIZE: 110–155 pounds (50–70 kilograms)

DIET: Herbivore; browser

ESSENTIAL FACTS: A scansorial sloth known to have inhabited relatively arid environments of South America and fed on leaves and fruits. Isotope analyses show that this species was a regular prey item of jaguars (*Panthera onca*) and Southern Smilodon (*Smilodon populator*).

NOTHROTHERIOPS SHASTENSIS

NAME MEANING: Nothrotherium-like from Shasta

AGE: Pleistocene (2.6 MYA–11,000 YA)

DISTRIBUTION: North America

SIZE: 550 pounds (250 kilograms)

DIET: Herbivore; browser

SEE MORE ON PAGES 200–201

MEGATHERIIDAE

Megatheres were browsing specialists with hypsodont, bilophodont teeth for breaking and cutting leaves and twigs and large chewing muscles for processing fibrous foods. Included among them are the largest sloths to have ever lived, some rivaling elephants in terms of mass. The family appears in the fossil record during the Late Oligocene and became extinct early in the Holocene about 8,000 years ago.

DIABOLOTHERIUM NORDENSKIOLDI

NAME MEANING: Erland Nordenskioldi's beast of Casa del Diablo Cave

AGE: Pleistocene

DISTRIBUTION: South America

SIZE: Unknown

DIET: Herbivore; browser

ESSENTIAL FACTS: Diabolotherium is a relatively small member of a group that includes species the size of elephants and rhinos. Unlike other megatheres, Diabolotherium was adapted for active climbing, with notably long and slender limbs with a wide range of motion.

EREMOTHERIUM LAURILLARDI

NAME MEANING: Laurillard's steppe beast

AGE: Pleistocene

DISTRIBUTION: South America, North America

SIZE: 7 feet (2.2 meters) SH; 16.4 feet (5 meters) HBL; 6,600–14,400 pounds (3–6 tons)

DIET: Herbivore; browser

ESSENTIAL FACTS: About the size of the Giant Ground Sloth, Panamerican Ground Sloths lived in warmer, more tropical woodland and forest habitats of northern South America and southern North America.

THALASSOCNUS NATANS

ESSENTIAL FACTS: Modern tree sloths are surprisingly adept swimmers, and this was likely true for larger terrestrial sloths as well. The Sea Sloth, however, took this to the extreme, becoming the only xenarthran to have been adapted to a marine environment. Its fossils are known only from coastal deposits of western South America and are often associated with animals such as whales, dugongs, and sharks among other marine vertebrates.

Five "chronospecies" of *Thalossocnus* have been described which display gradual anatomical changes to make them more efficient underwater foragers. From oldest to youngest, these chronospecies are *T. antiquus*, *T. natans*, *T. littoralis*, *T. carolomartini*, and *T. yuacensis*. Over 4 million years their bones became denser in order to combat buoyancy, and their snouts became proportionally longer to more efficiently collect the sea grasses and seaweeds on which they fed. They also developed thick, muscular lips to better grip these food items. Their claws and forelimbs also became better adapted to anchor themselves to the seafloor and to rocks, so that they could avoid getting battered or swept away by waves. With time, they became able to venture farther from the shoreline into deeper waters.

SEE ENTRY ON PAGE 196

NOTHROTHERIOPS SHASTENSIS

ESSENTIAL FACTS: The Shasta Ground Sloth was one of the smaller of the Late Pleistocene ground sloths, often compared to a modern Black Bear (*Ursus americanus*) in size. It had a relatively slender build with a long, flexible neck and long arms. They seem to have had a habit of seeking out dry caves in which to take shelter. Because of this behavior, this species is one of three extinct sloths for which soft tissue has been preserved (the others being Darwin's Sloth and Jefferson's Sloth). Skin and hair preserved in Rampart Cave, Gypsum Cave, and Aden Crater show that this sloth possessed a coat of coarse, yellowish-brown colored fur, giving us a more complete picture of its life appearance than many other Pleistocene animals.

The diet of the Shasta Ground Sloth is well-known thanks to numerous dried dung samples recovered from Rampart Cave in Arizona. We know that this species browsed on a wide variety of desert plants such as yucca, desert globemallow, various types of cacti, and the leaves of the Joshua tree, to name just a few. In fact, this species likely had a crucial ecological role as a disperser of such plants, carrying the seeds over great distances before depositing them within a convenient bundle of fertilizer!

SEE ENTRY ON PAGE 196

MEGATHERIUM AMERICANUM

NAME MEANING: Great beast from America

AGE: Pleistocene

DISTRIBUTION: South America

SIZE: 7 feet (2.2 meters) SH; 16.4 feet (5 meters) HBL; 8,400–10,100 pounds (3.8–4.58 tons)

DIET: Herbivore; browser

SEE MORE ON PAGES 204–205

VERMILINGUA

Anteaters belong to the xenarthran suborder of Pilosa are known as Vermilingua, meaning "worm-tongue," in reference to the long, sticky tongues these animals use to collect the insects on which they feed. Sloths form the suborder Folivora, meaning "leaf-eaters." They are very rare in the fossil record, and it is unknown when the group may have diverged from sloths.

NEOTAMANDUA BOREALIS

NAME MEANING: Northern new *Tamandua*

AGE: Middle Miocene (13.5–11.5 MYA)

DISTRIBUTION: South America

SIZE: 1.5–3 feet (50–100 centimeters) HBL; 22–44 pounds (10–20 kilograms)

DIET: Myrmecophagous hypercarnivore

ESSENTIAL FACTS: This species, despite being morphologically similar to modern tamanduas, may be more closely related to the giant anteater (*Myrmecophaga tridactyla*).

PALAEOMYRMIDON INCOMTUS

NAME MEANING: Messy ancient *Myrmidon*

AGE: Late Miocene (9–6.8 MYA)

DISTRIBUTION: South America

SIZE: Unknown

DIET: Myrmecophagous hypercarnivore

ESSENTIAL FACTS: A relative of the modern silky anteater (*Cyclopes didactylus*) in the family Cyclopedidae, the Messy Anteater is the only known extinct member of this family.

AFROTHERIA

Afrotheria is a clade of mammals which originated in and underwent most of their evolutionary history in Africa, hence the name. The group originated during the Paleocene while the African continent was effectively a huge island. Distinguishing features include relatively high vertebral counts, internal testes in males, and relatively late eruption of the permanent dentition.

OCEPEIIDAE

Ocepeiidae was among the oldest afrotherians known only from the Paleocene of northern Africa. The few known members of this family were small herbivores or hypocarnivores. In life they probably would have vaguely resembled long-skulled hyraxes.

MEGATHERIUM AMERICANUM

ESSENTIAL FACTS: Also known as the Giant Ground Sloth, this species is the first fossil sloth to be discovered and formally described. The first fossils were discovered along the Lujan River in Argentina in 1788. These fossils were sent to Museo Nacional de Ciencias Naturales in Madrid the following year, where they were formally described by Georges Cuvier in 1796. This specimen is still housed within this museum. Ironically, the skeletons of giant mammals such as Giant Ground Sloths were the most popular museum exhibits prior to the discovery of giant dinosaurs.

As its common name suggests, the Giant Ground Sloth is possibly the largest known of all the sloths, being about the size of a modern Asian elephant (*Elephas maximus*). It was a selective browser with the narrowest mouth in proportion to any other sloth. Due to its great size, healthy adult individuals were likely immune to predation. Juveniles would have been vulnerable to attack from such animals as Southern Smilodon (*Smilodon populator*). Their preferred habitat is temperate woodlands and savanna environments.

SEE ENTRY ON PAGE 202

OCEPEIA DAOUIENSIS

NAME MEANING: Office Chérifien des Phosphates from the Grand Daoui

AGE: Paleocene (61–57 MYA)

DISTRIBUTION: Africa

SIZE: 5.5–19 pounds (2.5–8.5 kilograms)

DIET: Herbivore; browser

ESSENTIAL FACTS: The smaller of two species within the genus *Ocepeia*, this animal is thought to have had a generalized diet that included soft leaves, fruits, and potentially invertebrates.

ABDOUNODUS HAMDII

NAME MEANING: Hamdi's tooth from the Ouled Abdoun Basin

AGE: Paleocene (61–59 MYA)

DISTRIBUTION: Africa

SIZE: Unknown; about cat-sized

DIET: Herbivore; browser

ESSENTIAL FACTS: Known only from teeth and a nearly complete jaw, Abdounodus was morphologically similar to the closely related and contemporaneous *Ocepeia*.

AFROSORICIDA

Formerly thought to be close relatives of shrews, moles, and hedgehogs (Eulipotypla), afrosoricidans are now known to be afrorheres that evolved similar ecologies and appearances through convergent evolution. The name Afrosoricida means "African shrew." Based on molecular data, it is thought that the group originated in the Early Paleocene. Undoubtedly more diverse in prehistory, modern examples of the group include tenrecs (Tenrecidae) and golden moles (Chrysochloridae).

DILAMBDOGALE GHEERBRANTI

NAME MEANING: Emmanuel Gheerbrant's Dilambda weasel

AGE: Late Eocene (38–37 MYA)

DISTRIBUTION: Africa

SIZE: About shrew-sized

DIET: Mesocarnivore

ESSENTIAL FACTS: Dilambdogale is the oldest-known afrosoricidan, with a dentition that suggests its diet included small amounts of plant matter in addition to insects and small vertebrates.

PLESIORYCTEROPUS MADAGASCARIENSIS

NAME MEANING: Near Orycteropus from Madagascar

AGE: Pleistocene and Holocene

DISTRIBUTION: Africa

SIZE: 13–40 pounds (6–18 kilograms)

DIET: Hypercarnivore

ESSENTIAL FACTS: The common name for this species, Bibymalagasy, translates to "animal from Madagascar." The structure of the forelimb bones suggest that these were active diggers. They are thought to have been myrmecophagous, though the true diet is unknown. They potentially could have taken a wider range of prey from insects to small vertebrates.

ORYCTEROPODIDAE

Aardvarks have a sparse fossil record dating back to the Early Miocene, though the group is likely much older and descends from an ancestor close to tenrecs. The family shares homodont dentition consisting of simplified pegs that lack enamel and are hypselodont. Snouts are elongated with an excellent sense of smell and a long tongue that is used to gather insects. The forelimbs are adapted for burrowing.

MYORYCTEROPUS AFRICANUS

NAME MEANING: African muscle Orycteropus

AGE: Early Miocene (20–17 MYA)

DISTRIBUTION: Africa

SIZE: 1.3 feet (40 centimeters) SH; 2 feet (60 centimeters) HBL

DIET: Myrmecophagous hypercarnivore

ESSENTIAL FACTS: Myorycteropus was much smaller than the modern aardvark but had more robust forelimb elements, indicating that it had an even greater aptitude for digging.

LEPTORYCTEROPUS GUILIEMI

NAME MEANING: Guiliem's slender digging feet

AGE: Late Miocene (7.4–6.5 MYA)

DISTRIBUTION: Africa

SIZE: 0.8 feet (24 centimeters) SH; 1.3 feet (40 centimeters) HBL; 15–22 pounds (7–10 kilograms)

DIET: Myrmecophagous hypercarnivore

ESSENTIAL FACTS: Leptorycteropus was smaller and much more lightly built than the modern aardvark, with longer and less muscular limbs and a relatively shorter snout. Its overall build suggests it was less of a digger and more of a runner, likely relying on collecting ants and termites from the surface rather than digging them out directly.

HYRACOIDEA

The six species of modern hyraxes are rabbit-sized herbivores sometimes referred to as "dassies" or "conies." All are native to Africa and the Middle East. Hyraxes have a fossil record dating to the Early Eocene, and the group was much more diverse throughout the Cenozoic. An adaptive radiation during the Paleogene saw the introduction of generalized and small-bodied forms similar to modern species, large pig-like hypocarnivores, cursorial browsers, and massive herbivores the size of tapirs or small rhinos. Hyracoids remained the dominant terrestrial herbivores in Africa and Arabia until the Early Miocene, when competition from immigrating artiodactyls and perissodactyls led to a great reduction in the group's diversity and abundance.

DIMAITHERIUM PATNAIKI

NAME MEANING: Rajeev Patnaik's beast from Dimai

AGE: Late Eocene (37 MYA)

DISTRIBUTION: Africa

SIZE: About rabbit-sized

DIET: Herbivore

ESSENTIAL FACTS: Dimaitherium was one of the smaller hyraxes of the Late Eocene. The teeth of Patnaik's Hyrax suggest a more generalized diet of fruits, nuts, seeds, and perhaps some animal matter.

PROCAVIIDAE

The family to which all modern hyraxes belong, these tend to be relatively small bodied with good jumping and climbing capabilities.

GIGANTOHYRAX MAGUIREI

NAME MEANING: Maguire's giant hyrax

AGE: Pliocene (4–2.5 MYA)

DISTRIBUTION: Africa

SIZE: 26 pounds (12 kilograms)

DIET: Herbivore

ESSENTIAL FACTS: Maguire's Hyrax grew to about three times the size of the largest modern hyraxes. Its skeletal anatomy is most similar to that of modern tree hyraxes (*Dendrohyrax*), suggesting similar scansorial behaviors.

GENIOHYIDAE

Geniohyids had bunodont teeth very similar to those of peccaries (Tayassuidae) adapted for dealing with a varied diet of both hard and soft plants. They were ecologically analogous to pigs (Suidae).

GENIOHYUS MIRUS

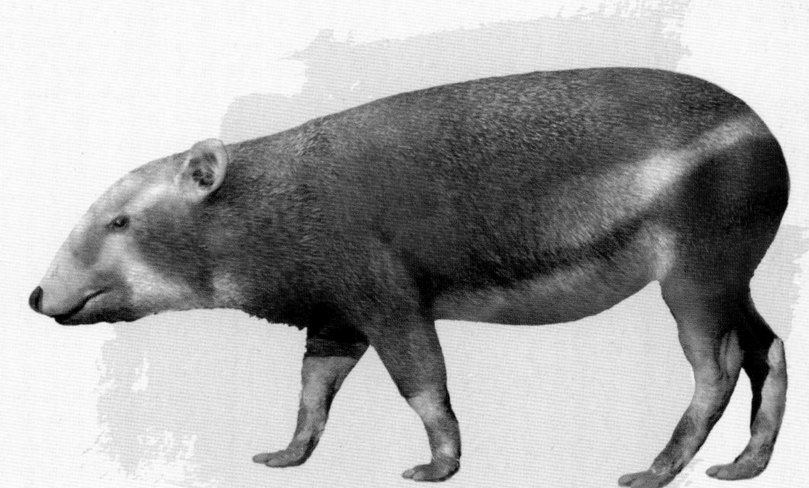

NAME MEANING: Wonderful jaw pig

AGE: Early Oligocene (34–28 MYA)

DISTRIBUTION: Africa

SIZE: 100 pounds (45 kilograms)

DIET: Herbivore

ESSENTIAL FACTS: Geniohyus is the best-known species of the genus *Geniohyus*, with the characteristic bunodont teeth for crushing foods such as tubers, fruits, and nuts.

BUNOHYRAX MAJOR

NAME MEANING: Larger mound hyrax

AGE: Early Oligocene (34–28 MYA)

DISTRIBUTION: Africa

SIZE: 526 pounds (239 kilograms)

DIET: Hypocarnivore

ESSENTIAL FACTS: Bunohyrax is the largest representative of its genus with even more inflated cusps on the molars and premolars possibly for dealing with particularly hard-shelled food items.

PACHYHYRAX CRASSIDENTATUS

NAME MEANING: Thick toothed thick hyrax

AGE: Early Oligocene (34–28 MYA)

DISTRIBUTION: Africa

SIZE: 330 pounds (150 kilograms)

DIET: Herbivore

ESSENTIAL FACTS: Pachyhyrax was the largest and most robust species of its genus. Its premolars were more molarized than those of other geniohyids, expanding the surface area of the grinding surface.

TITANOHYRACIDAE

The Titanohyracidae family contains the largest hyraxes known to date. Postcranial material is rare, but what little has been found suggests that these animals were relatively gracile (thin) animals with slender limbs adapted for cursoriality.

ANTILOHYRAX PECTIDENS

NAME MEANING: Comb-toothed antelope hyrax

AGE: Early Eocene (37 MYA)

DISTRIBUTION: Africa

SIZE: 55–77 pounds (25–35 kilograms)

DIET: Herbivore; browser

ESSENTIAL FACTS: Antilohyrax was a gazelle-like hyrax most notable for its elongated, slender limbs adapted for speed and agility. Its cheek teeth were adapted for shredding tough leaves. A lack of upper incisors suggests that the lower incisors occluded with a horny pad on the upper jaw as seen in ruminants.

TITANOHYRAX ULTIMUS

NAME MEANING: Ultimate giant hyrax

AGE: Early Oligocene (34–28 MYA)

DISTRIBUTION: Africa

SIZE: 1,300–2,900 pounds (600–1,300 kilograms)

DIET: Herbivore; browser

ESSENTIAL FACTS: Titanohyrax was the largest of six species of *Titanohyrax*, the smallest of which is estimated at 50 pounds (23 kilograms). The Ultimate Titanohyrax was one of the largest herbivores in its environment, surpassed only by contemporary arsinoitheres and early proboscideans.

PLIOHYRACIDAE

Pliohyracidae was the largest and most morphologically diverse family of hyraxes. The group originated in the Eocene and survived into the Pleistocene.

MICROHYRAX LAVOCATI

NAME MEANING: Lavocat's little hyrax

AGE: Early Eocene (55 MYA)

DISTRIBUTION: Africa

SIZE: 6–7 pounds (3 kilograms)

DIET: Herbivore

ESSENTIAL FACTS: One of the smallest known hyraxes, Lavocat's Hyrax was a scansorial animal that was equally at home on the ground and in the trees.

MEGALOHYRAX EOCAENUS

NAME MEANING: Great hyrax from the Eocene

AGE: Late Eocene (37–34 MYA)

DISTRIBUTION: Africa

SIZE: 5 feet (1.5 meters) HBL; 352 pounds (160 kilograms)

DIET: Herbivore

ESSENTIAL FACTS: Megalohyrax was a large hyrax with a heavily built body and a long skull.

THYROHYRAX MEYERI

NAME MEANING: Meyer's door hyrax

AGE: Late Eocene (37 MYA)

DISTRIBUTION: Africa

SIZE: 28 pounds (13 kilograms)

DIET: Herbivore

ESSENTIAL FACTS: Isotopic studies of Thyrohyrax's teeth have shown Meyer's Hyrax may have been semiaquatic, possibly comparable to the modern water chevrotain (*Hyemoschus aquaticus*). Its dentition was that of a browser which probably focused on softer leaves and fruits.

PLIOHYRAX GRAECUS

NAME MEANING: Near hyrax from Greece

AGE: Pliocene

DISTRIBUTION: Eurasia

SIZE: 5–5.3 feet (1.5–1.6 meters) HBL; 176–200 pounds (80–90 kilograms)

DIET: Herbivore

ESSENTIAL FACTS: This large hyrax was distributed through many European and Middle Eastern countries.

KVABEBIHYRAX KACHETHICUS

NAME MEANING: Hyrax from Kvabebi

AGE: Pliocene

DISTRIBUTION: Eurasia

SIZE: 5.3 feet (1.6 meters) HBL

DIET: Herbivore

ESSENTIAL FACTS: This was an unusual hyrax with certain adaptations indicative of a semiaquatic lifestyle. The eyes were set high on the head and the nasal passages were large and slightly retracted. It may have behaved something like a tapir.

PROHYRAX HENDEYI

NAME MEANING: Hendey's early hyrax

AGE: Middle Miocene (16 MYA)

DISTRIBUTION: Africa

SIZE: 20 pounds (9 kilograms)

DIET: Herbivore

ESSENTIAL FACTS: Over twice the size of the largest modern hyraxes, Hendey's Hyrax had relatively longer limbs and straighter limbs for quicker and more efficient terrestrial locomotion.

POSTSCHIZOTHERIUM CHARDINI

NAME MEANING: Chardin's after split beast

AGE: Pliocene to Pleistocene (3.5–2 MYA)

DISTRIBUTION: Eurasia

SIZE: 5 feet (1.5 meters) HBL; 176 pounds (80 kilograms)

DIET: Herbivore

ESSENTIAL FACTS: This pig-sized hyrax survived in eastern Asia long after other giant hyraxes had gone extinct. Its fossils have been found in Russia and China.

SIRENIA

Sirenians are the only modern herbivorous mammals fully adapted to an aquatic lifestyle. They originated in Africa during the Paleocene from an undetermined ancestor from within Afrotheria, but they may be particularly close to proboscideans. By the end of the Eocene, the group had become widely distributed in the shallow coastal waters, estuaries, rivers, and swamps throughout the tropics and subtropics. Among the more notable characteristics in commonly preserved fossils are their extremely dense and heavy pachyosteoscleric ribs which provide ballast, acting as a weight allowing them to forage for food on the seafloor without unwillingly floating to the surface.

PRORASTOMIDAE

Walking sirens are the oldest members of Sirenia with only two genera known, both from Jamaica. The presence of these animals in the North American island by the middle Eocene suggests that sirenians had appeared long before this point, potentially in the Late Paleocene or Early Eocene in their African homeland and spreading along the coasts and islands of the Atlantic Ocean.

PEZOSIREN PORTELLI

NAME MEANING: Portell's walking siren

AGE: Middle Eocene (49–46 MYA)

DISTRIBUTION: North America

SIZE: 6 feet (2 meters)

DIET: Marine herbivore

ESSENTIAL FACTS: Although able to move efficiently on land, Portell's Walking Manatee spent most of its time in the water. Like later sirenians, it had pachyosteoscleric ribs to provide ballast and neutral buoyancy. Its style of swimming would have been similar to that of an otter.

PRORASTOMUS SIRENOIDES

NAME MEANING: Siren-like prow mouth

AGE: Middle Eocene (40 MYA)

DISTRIBUTION: North America

SIZE: 5 feet (1.5 meters)

DIET: Marine herbivore

ESSENTIAL FACTS: The Prow-Mouthed Siren had a more developed sense of smell than other sirenians, suggesting that it relied more on olfactory communication. Its diet appears to have consisted of smaller plants.

PROTOSIRENIDAE

Compared to the prorastomids, the hindlimbs of protosirenids were smaller than the forelimbs and had a relatively weak connection with the pelvis, suggesting a limited capacity for terrestrial locomotion. Movement on land would have been reduced to a crawl or waddle, comparable to that of a seal or sea lion. The tail vertebrae were more robust, and the end may have supported a fluke.

SOBRARBESIREN CARDIELI

NAME MEANING: Cardiel's siren from Sobrarbe

AGE: Middle Eocene

DISTRIBUTION: Atlantic Ocean

SIZE: 9 feet (2.7 meters)

DIET: Marine herbivore

ESSENTIAL FACTS: Cardiel's Siren is the first well-known quadrupedal sirenian from Eurasia and the oldest from western Europe. At the time in which this animal lived, Europe was still a tropical archipelago.

PROTOSIREN FRAASI

NAME MEANING: Fraas' original siren

AGE: Middle Eocene (40 MYA)

DISTRIBUTION: Atlantic Ocean, Indian Ocean

SIZE: 9 feet (2.7 meters)

DIET: Marine herbivore

ESSENTIAL FACTS: Fraas's Siren was the first of five species of *Protosiren* to be described (the type species). It inhabited the shallow waters that once covered the Sahara Desert, where it coexisted with and probably occasionally hunted by the whale Basilosaurus.

DUGONGIDAE

Dugongs are fully aquatic sirenians that originated in the Early Oligocene. They are distinguished from the manatees (Trichechidae) by their fluked tails, which resemble those of cetaceans. The cheek teeth are also relatively simplified compared to those of manatees, and they have distinctly downturned mouths for feeding on seagrass.

HALITHERIUM SCHINZI

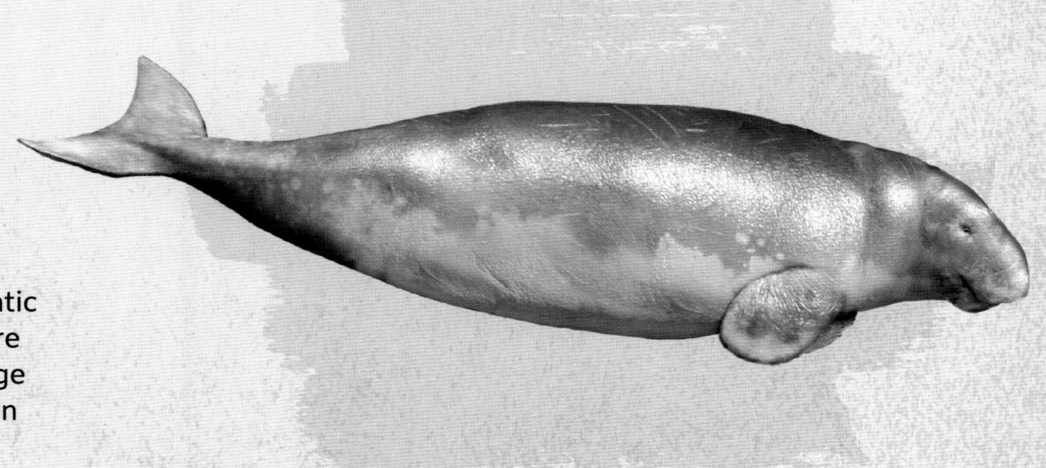

NAME MEANING: Schinz's ocean beast

AGE: Early Oligocene (37–6 MYA)

DISTRIBUTION: Atlantic Ocean

SIZE: 10 feet (3 meters)

DIET: Marine herbivore

ESSENTIAL FACTS: One of the oldest-known fully aquatic sirenians, the bones of this ocean beast's hindlimbs were present but would not have shown externally. Its rib cage was also broader than those of earlier sirens, showing an increased lung capacity.

METAXYTHERIUM FLORIDANUM

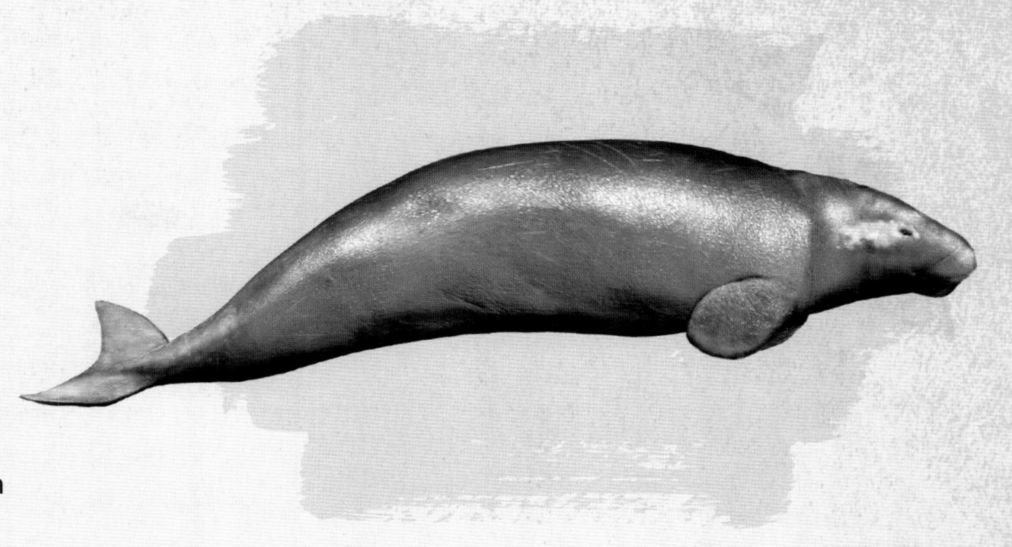

NAME MEANING: Intermediate beast from Florida

AGE: Middle to late Miocene (14–7 MYA)

DISTRIBUTION: Atlantic Ocean

SIZE: 10 feet (3 meters)

DIET: Marine herbivore

ESSENTIAL FACTS: During the Miocene, sea levels were higher than they are today, and much of Florida was underwater. The Floridian Dugong fossils are known from phosphate mines in the middle of the state.

RYTIODUS CAPGRANDI

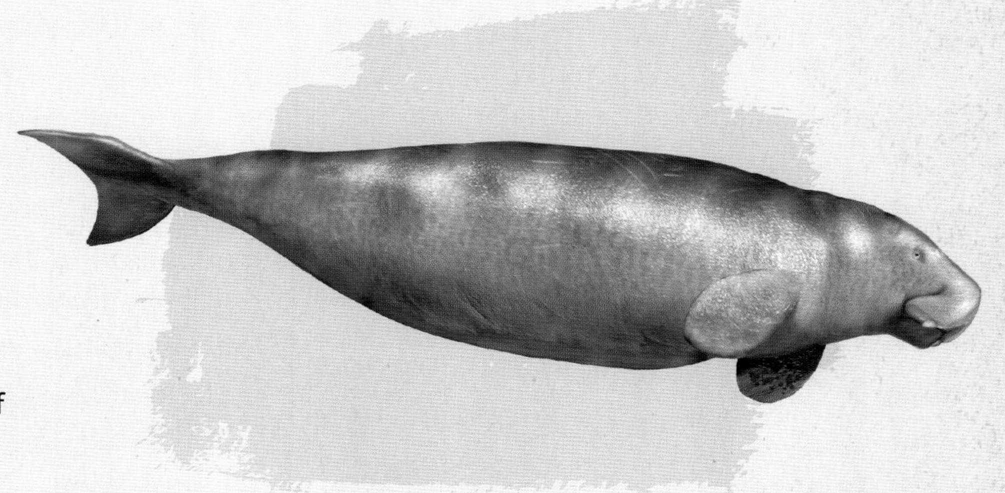

NAME MEANING: Capgrand's wrinkled tooth

AGE: Early Miocene (23–20 MYA)

DISTRIBUTION: Atlantic Ocean

SIZE: 20 feet (6 meters)

DIET: Marine herbivore

ESSENTIAL FACTS: Rytiodus was one of the largest sirenians. Apart from its size, the most notable feature of this species are its short, walrus-like tusks which it likely used to uplift food from the seafloor.

DUSISIREN JORDANI

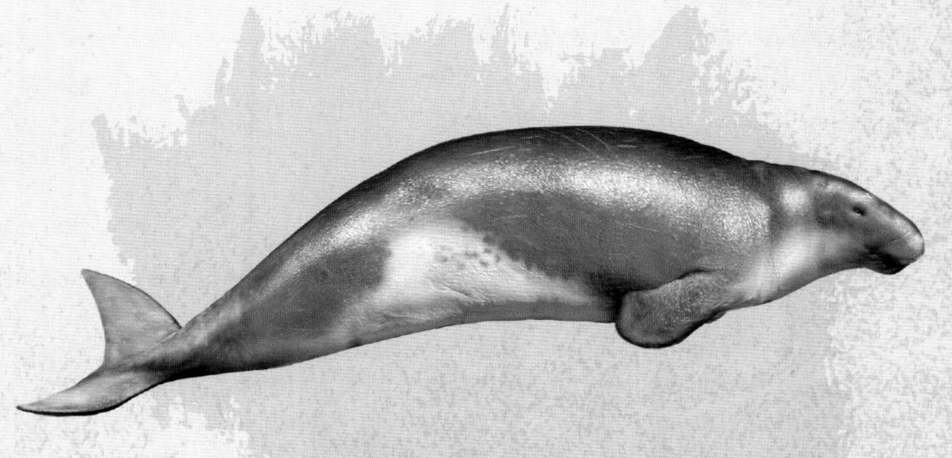

NAME MEANING: Jordan's foolish siren

AGE: Late Miocene

DISTRIBUTION: North Pacific Ocean

SIZE: 30 feet (9 meters)

DIET: Marine herbivore

ESSENTIAL FACTS: Jordan's Sea Cow is in the direct line of ancestry to the Steller's Sea Cow (*Hydrodamalis gigas*), showing adaptations to feed on kelp beds in cold waters. It may have been positively buoyant, unable to submerge completely.

HYDRODAMALIS CUESTAE

NAME MEANING: Water calf of the hills

AGE: Pliocene (3.6–2.6 MYA)

DISTRIBUTION: North Pacific Ocean

SIZE: 30 feet (9 meters)

DIET: Marine herbivore

ESSENTIAL FACTS: The direct ancestor of the Steller's Sea Cow (*Hydrodamalis gigas*), the Cuesta Sea Cow is known to have inhabited the kelp forests along the western coast of North America.

TRICHECHIDAE

Manatees are much rarer in the fossil record than dugongs, but they appear in the fossil record at about the same time. They have a conveyor belt–like system of tooth development, in which identical new molars are continually forming from the back of the tooth row, migrating forward and being discarded out the front when worn down. They have paddle-shaped tails and are slower and less agile swimmers compared to dugongs.

ANOMOTHERIUM LANGEWIESCHEI

NAME MEANING: Langewiesche's lawless beast

AGE: Late Oligocene

DISTRIBUTION: Atlantic Ocean

SIZE: 10 feet (3 meters)

DIET: Marine herbivore

ESSENTIAL FACTS: One of the oldest manatees, this species is known to have inhabited the warm waters that once covered Germany.

MIOSIREN KOCKI

NAME MEANING: Kock's lesser siren

AGE: Early Miocene

DISTRIBUTION: Atlantic Ocean

SIZE: 10 feet (3 meters)

DIET: Marine herbivore

ESSENTIAL FACTS: Kock's Manatee differs from the dugongs of the time in having the same tooth replacement system as modern manatees. Its teeth are relatively robust, suggesting a tougher diet.

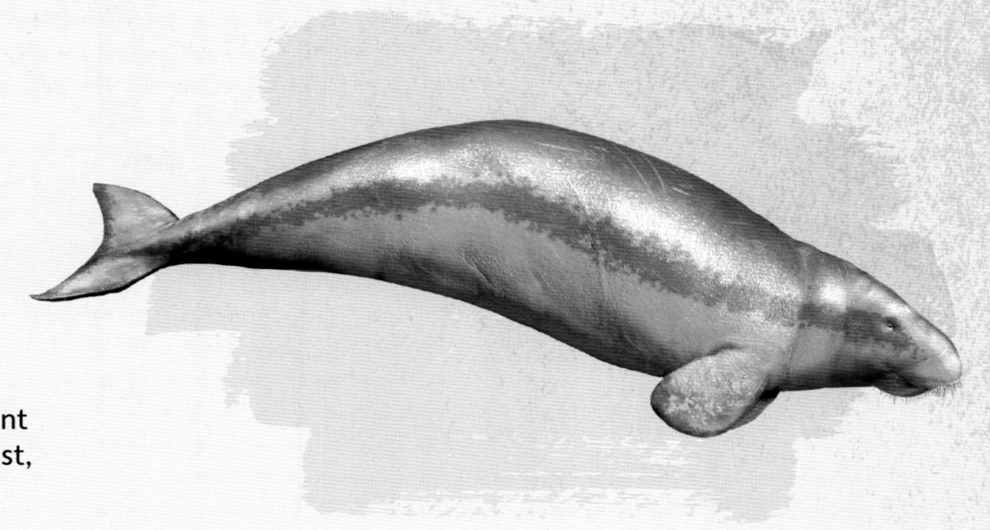

EMBRITHOPODA

Embrithopods are a group of midsized to large herbivores known to have occurred from the Early Eocene to Latest Oligocene. The name of the group means "heavy-foooted." Limited fossil remains and few known species means that little is known about their evolutionary history.

PALAEOAMASIIDAE

The ancestors of these animals likely evolved in Africa but eventually became isolated on islands in the Tethys Sea.

PALAEOAMASIA KANSUI

NAME MEANING: Kansu's ancient (animal) from Amasya

AGE: Middle Eocene (48–45 MYA)

DISTRIBUTION: Turkey

SIZE: About tapir-sized

DIET: Herbivore; browser

ESSENTIAL FACTS: Fossils of this animal have only been found in Turkey, which was an island during the Middle Eocene. The brachydont-bilophodont teeth of Kansu's Palaeomasia indicate a diet that consisted of soft leaves and possibly fruits.

HYPSAMASIA SENI

NAME MEANING: Sevket Sen's high (animal) from Amasya

AGE: Middle Eocene (48–45 MYA)

DISTRIBUTION: Turkey

SIZE: About rhino-sized

DIET: Herbivore; browser

ESSENTIAL FACTS: Also endemic to Turkey, Hypsamasia was larger than its contemporary relative Kansui's Palaeomasia with more hypsodont teeth adapted to handle tougher and more fibrous vegetation. It may have been the largest animal in its island environment.

CRIVADIATHERIUM MACKENNAI

NAME MEANING: Mackenn's beast from the Crivadia site

AGE: Late Eocene

DISTRIBUTION: Hateg, Romania

SIZE: About tapir-sized

DIET: Herbivore

ESSENTIAL FACTS: Likely evolving from island-hopping ancestors, Crivadiatherium fossils are known from the town of Hateg, Romania, which ironically was an island during the Late Cretaceous and Early Paleocene. Its teeth show more basal features than other known palaeomasiids despite occurring later.

ARSINOITHERIIDAE

Arsinoitheres were superficially rhino-like herbivores endemic to Africa and Arabia. The family contains a single genus with three species from the Late Eocene to Oligocene.

ARSINOITHERIUM ZITTELI

NAME MEANING: Karl Alfred Ritter von Zittel's beast of Pharoh Arsinoe

AGE: Late Eocene (36–34 MYA)

DISTRIBUTION: Africa

SIZE: 5.7 feet (1.75 meters) SH; 10 feet (3 meters) HBL; 2.5 tons

DIET: Herbivore

SEE MORE ON PAGES 224–225

PROBOSCIDEA

Early proboscideans of the Paleocene were small herbivores comparable in ecology to duikers or agoutis. Eocene forms were much larger, more the size of tapirs and had similar adaptations as semiaquatic browsers, including the development of a short proboscis to help pull food into the mouth. Late Eocene and Early Oligocene proboscideans grew to the size of modern hippos and rhinos. Truly giant forms in the range of modern species begin to appear from the Early Miocene onward.

ERITHERIUM AZZOUZORUM

NAME MEANING: Early beast from Ouled Azzouz village

AGE: Middle Paleocene (60 MYA)

DISTRIBUTION: Africa

SIZE: 8 inches (20 centimeters) SH; 11–13 pounds (5–6 kilograms)

DIET: Herbivore

ESSENTIAL FACTS: The oldest and smallest-known proboscidean, its cheek teeth were bunodont, and the eyes are set relatively far forward on the skull as is the case in other early proboscideans.

NUMIDOTHERIIDAE

Numidotheres were small- to medium-sized browsing herbivores that occurred from the Late Paleocene to earliest Oligocene. They were the first to develop bilophodont dentition for cutting fibrous leaves, a feature that would be inherited by later proboscideans. A few species also show the beginnings of short proboscises.

PHOSPHATHERIUM ESCUILLEI

NAME MEANING: François Escuillié's phosphate beast

AGE: Late Paleocene (56 MYA)

DISTRIBUTION: Africa

SIZE: 1 foot (30 centimeters) SH; 37 pounds (17 kilograms)

DIET: Herbivore; browser

ESSENTIAL FACTS: Unlike the older Eritherium, Phosphatherium had more zygodont molars, indicating a diet that was more browse-heavy, focused primarily on leaves and fruits.

ARSINOITHERIUM ZITTELI

ESSENTIAL FACTS: Zittel's Arsinoithere is the most well-known of the embrithropods and the only one known for complete skeletal material. It was a large animal about the size of a modern black rhino (*Diceros bicornis*). It lived in coastal swamps and heavily vegetated lowland forests of northern Africa and Arabia. Previously, this animal was thought to have been semiaquatic, spending most of its time in water but feeding on land like modern hippos. While almost certainly a capable swimmer, isotope studies have shown that it was actually more terrestrial in its general habits.

The most notable feature of Zittel's Arsinoithere are its giant set of paired horns on top of its head, starting behind the eyes and extending forward beyond its nose. Just behind these are a smaller pair of horns. The limbs are notably elephant-like and columnar in shape. It was most likely a selective browser. The dentition is a complete set of forty-four teeth with a particularly long grinding surface. The premolars are large and molariform, and even the incisors and canines develop flattened occlusal surfaces during the animal's life.

SEE ENTRY ON PAGE 222

NUMIDOTHERIUM KOHOLENSE

NAME MEANING: Numidia beast from El Kohol

AGE: Middle Eocene (46 MYA)

DISTRIBUTION: Africa

SIZE: 3–3.3 feet (90–100 centimeters) SH; 550–660 pounds (250–300 kilograms)

DIET: Herbivore; browser

ESSENTIAL FACTS: The structure of this animal's skull suggests the presence of a short proboscis that would have aided it when browsing. Numidotheres were the size of tapirs and likely had a similar lifestyle.

MOERITHERIIDAE

Moeritheres were semiaquatic browsers from the late Eocene of Africa. The family contains a single genus with five described species.

MOERITHERIUM LYONSI

NAME MEANING: Lyon's Lake Moeris beast

AGE: Late Eocene (37–35 MYA)

DISTRIBUTION: Africa

SIZE: 2.3 feet (70 centimeters) SH; 518 pounds (235 kilograms)

DIET: Herbivore

ESSENTIAL FACTS: Lyon's Moeritherium was a semi-aquatic animal that would have spent most of its time in water but fed mostly on land like a tapir or pygmy hippo. It had a flexible upper lip instead of a true proboscis. Its elongated body and stubby limbs made it vaguely resemble early sirenians such as *Pezosiren*.

BARYTHERIIDAE

Barytheres were the first giant proboscideans to appear in the fossil record and were the largest animals of their time, outsizing the contemporary arsinoitheres which were themselves as big as rhinos.

BARYTHERIUM GRAVE

NAME MEANING: Grav's heavy beast

AGE: Early Oligocene (35–30 MYA)

DISTRIBUTION: Africa

SIZE: 6–6.5 feet (1.8–2 meters) SH

DIET: Herbivore

ESSENTIAL FACTS: Unlike later proboscideans which have either four or two incisor tusks, Barytherium has eight tusk-like incisors more similar to those of hippos. It was about the size of a river hippopotamus (*Hippopotamus amphibius*) and was probably comparable in its ecology. Isotope analysis of its teeth demonstrate that Barytherium spent much of its time in water.

DEINOTHERIIDAE

Deinotheres were giant proboscideans that occurred from the Late Oligocene to Early Pleistocene. They were high-browsing specialists that replaced the paracerathere rhinos that dominated the giant-browser niches during the Oligocene. The most notable feature of the family are their downward-curving tusks, which inspired the nickname "hoe-tusker" due to early interpretations of these tusks being used for digging. Throughout their long history, deinotheres changed very little from species to species, alluding to their great success and efficiency in their particular niche.

DEINOTHERIUM GIGANTEUM

NAME MEANING: Giant terrible beast

AGE: Late Miocene to Pleistocene

DISTRIBUTION: Eurasia, Africa

SIZE: 12–13 feet (3.63–4 meters); 8–12 tons

DIET: Herbivore; browser

SEE MORE ON PAGES 230–231

PALAEOMASTODONTIDAE

Palaeomastodonts looked very much like small gomphotheres. They differ in having smaller teeth and a normal diphyodont system of tooth replacement in which new teeth arose vertically from the skull or lower jaw as is the case for most mammals.

PHIOMIA SERRIDENS

NAME MEANING: Saw-toothed (animal) from Faiyum

AGE: Early Oligocene (35–30 MYA)

DISTRIBUTION: Africa

SIZE: 4.4 feet (1.34 meters) SH

DIET: Herbivore

ESSENTIAL FACTS: This was an ox-sized animal that resembled a smaller version of later "shovel-tusked" gomphotheres of the Miocene. It may have fed primarily on low-growing vegetation.

PALAEOMASTODON BEADNELLI

NAME MEANING: Beadnell's ancient mastodon

AGE: Early Oligocene (34–30 MYA)

DISTRIBUTION: Africa

SIZE: 7.2 feet (2.2 meters) SH

DIET: Herbivore

ESSENTIAL FACTS: Morphologically this organism was similar to Phioma but much larger. It was closer in size to a large rhino.

GOMPHOTHERIIDAE

Gomphotheres are distinguished from modern elephants in their tooth structure, having numerous rounded cusps. Early gomphotheres have long lower jaws with prominent lower tusks, while later gomphotheres feature a shorter face and smaller lower tusks. Many resemble modern elephants, but with larger heads and stockier bodies. The group first appeared in Africa during the Late Oligocene and became established throughout the Northern Hemisphere by the Middle Miocene. Then they spread to South America by the Late Pliocene, where they survived until the Early Holocene. Gomphotheres were the first proboscideans to evolve a system of tooth replacement that would be inherited by mastodons and elephants. Two large teeth are planted in each quadrant of the mouth at any given time, with new teeth erupting from the back, pushing the oldest and most worn teeth out through the front of the mouth.

GOMPHOTHERIUM STEINHEIMENSE

NAME MEANING: Nail beast from Steinheim

AGE: Middle Miocene

DISTRIBUTION: Eurasia

SIZE: 10.4 feet (3.17 meters) SH; 6.7 tons

DIET: Herbivore; grazer

ESSENTIAL FACTS: The Steinheim Gomphothere is the largest-known member of the genus and the earliest-known proboscidean to show a preference for grazing. Compared to other members of the genus, it exhibits a slight shortening of the face. This apparently started a trend, leading to such genera as *Tetralophodon*.

DEINOTHERIUM GIGANTEUM

ESSENTIAL FACTS: Like other deinotheres, these animals had proportionately longer necks with a greater range of motion, as well as limbs that were longer and more slender than those of other proboscideans. These features enabled them to reach higher and to travel more efficiently. Unlike later proboscideans, which have a back-to-front system of tooth replacement, deinotheres have a more conventional vertical system; adults have a dental formula of I 0/1, C 0/0, P 2/2, M 3/3. Like tapirs, the teeth were worn down very slowly, and many fossil specimens exhibit little or no obvious abrasion, a sign of a diet consisting almost exclusively of tree foliage that grew high above the ground. The peculiar hooked lower jaw and downward-pointing tusks may have been used to hook onto and break branches. The tusks appear on both males and females, and so were probably not wielded as weapons.

There are three universally agreed species of *Deinotherium* and three other tentative species that range in age from the Middle Miocene to the Middle Pleistocene. All are roughly the same size and have the same overall shape, suggesting that they occupied the same niche across different times and different regions. The last deinotheres survived in Africa until the Middle Pleistocene, where they coexisted with many modern mammals—including early human relatives.

SEE ENTRY ON PAGE 228

RHYNCHOTHERIUM FALCONERI

NAME MEANING: Falconer's snout beast

AGE: Late Miocene (6–5 MYA)

DISTRIBUTION: North America

SIZE: 5–6 feet (1.5–1.8 meters) SH; 2–3 tons

DIET: Herbivore

ESSENTIAL FACTS: Members of the genus are distinguished from *Gomphotherium* by their notably down-turned lower jaw and relatively small size. Falconer's Rynchothere was widely distributed through southern North America and appears particularly abundant in freshwater deposits.

AMEBELODON FRICKI

NAME MEANING: Frick's shovel-spear tooth

AGE: Late Miocene (5 MYA)

DISTRIBUTION: North America

SIZE: 4–6 tons

DIET: Herbivore

ESSENTIAL FACTS: Members of the genus *Amebelodon* and the closely related *Platybelodon* and *Konobelodon* had flattened lower tusks that inspired the nickname "shovel-tuskers." Researchers once thought these creatures used their tusks to dig up plants by the roots. This interpretation is now known to be false.

PLATYBELODON GRANGERI

NAME MEANING: Granger's flat-spear tooth

AGE: Middle Miocene

DISTRIBUTION: Eurasia

SIZE: 2–3 tons

DIET: Herbivore

ESSENTIAL FACTS: Like other shovel-tuskers, *Platybelodon* used their flattened lower tusks in conjunction with their proboscises to crop vegetation in bulk.

CHOEROLOPHODON PENTELICI

NAME MEANING: Pig crested tooth from Mount Pentelicus

AGE: Late Miocene (10–7 MYA)

DISTRIBUTION: Eurasia

SIZE: About ox-sized

DIET: Herbivore

ESSENTIAL FACTS: Members of the genus *Choerolophodon* were small by gomphothere standards, most species ranging from ox-sized to rhino-sized. This particular species was primarily a grazer but would opportunistically shift to browse under certain situations.

CUVIERONIUS HYODON

NAME MEANING: Georges Cuvier's high arch tooth

AGE: Pleistocene to Holocene

DISTRIBUTION: North America, South America

SIZE: 7.5 feet (2.3 meters) SH; 3–4 tons

DIET: Herbivore; graze-dominated mixed feeder

ESSENTIAL FACTS: This species was widely distributed throughout tropical and subtropical South America and had extended its range to the southern United States. They appear to go extinct in North America with the appearance of the Columbian Mammoth (*Mammuthus columbi*). They would continue to thrive in South America until the Early Holocene.

NOTIOMASTODON PLATENSIS

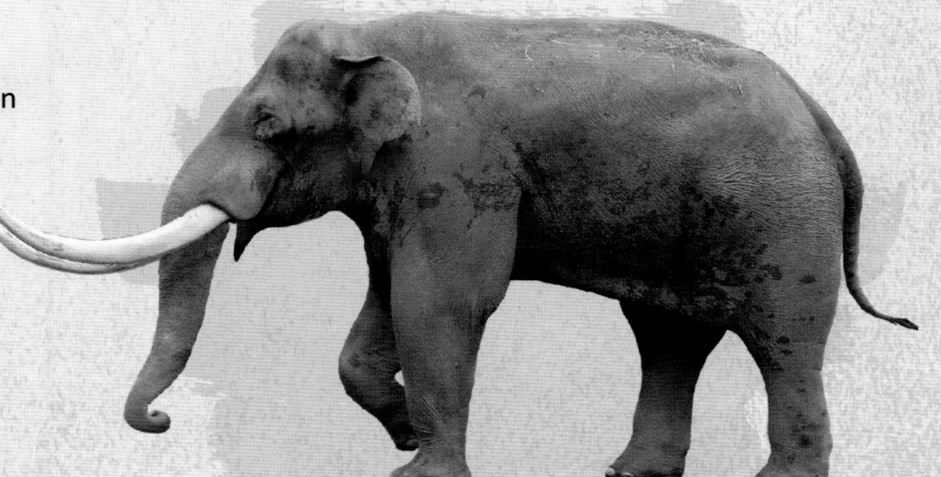

NAME MEANING: Southern mastodon from La Plata River Basin

AGE: Pleistocene to Holocene

DISTRIBUTION: South America

SIZE: 8.2–10 feet (2.5–3 meters) SH; 4–8 tons

DIET: Herbivore; browse-dominated mixed feeder

ESSENTIAL FACTS: Notiomastodon is the second of two gomphotheres to inhabit South America during the Pleistocene. They were adaptable mixed feeders that opportunistically shifted their feeding behaviors to fit local food conditions.

MAMMUTIDAE

The name mastodon means "nipple tooth." This refers to the supposedly nipple-like projections on the crowns of the molars. Compared to modern elephants, mastodons have larger heads and longer bodies with shorter legs. This would have made them slightly heavier than an elephant of the same shoulder height. Their teeth differ from those of gomphotheres in lacking accessory cuspules.

SINOMAMMUT TOBIENI

NAME MEANING: Tobien's Chinese mastodon

AGE: Middle Miocene (12–11 MYA)

DISTRIBUTION: Eurasia

SIZE: Unknown

DIET: Herbivore; browser

ESSENTIAL FACTS: Described in 2016, Tobien's Mastodon is only known for a lower jaw, which was nearly complete on its discovery. Sadly, most of the specimen has since been lost and only a portion of the right dentary remains.

ZYGOLOPHODON PROAVUS

NAME MEANING: Great-grandfather yoke-crested tooth

AGE: Middle Miocene (16–13 MYA)

DISTRIBUTION: North America

SIZE: Unknown; about the size of an Asian elephant (*Elephas maximus*)

DIET: Herbivore; browser

ESSENTIAL FACTS: Great-grandfather Mastodon is notable for being the first-known proboscidean from North America. Its probable ancestor, the Zurich Mastodon (*Z. turicensis*), crossed over from Asia earlier in the Miocene and became the largest mammal ever to have lived in the continent up to that point.

MAMMUT BORSONI

NAME MEANING: Borson's nipple

AGE: Late Miocene to early Pleistocene (6–2 MYA)

DISTRIBUTION: Eurasia

SIZE: 12.8–13.5 feet (3.9–4.1 meters) SH; 14 tons

DIET: Herbivore; browser

ESSENTIAL FACTS: Sometimes considered part of the genus *Zygolophodon*, Borson's Mastodon is the latest surviving mastodon in the Old World (Africa, Europe, and Asia) and possibly the largest mastodon known to have lived. This species had particularly long tusks measuring up to 16.5 feet (5 meters).

MAMMUT PACIFICUS

NAME MEANING: Pacific nipple

AGE: Pleistocene

DISTRIBUTION: North America

SIZE: 9.5–10.7 feet (2.9–3.25 meters) SH; 7–11 tons

DIET: Herbivore; browser

ESSENTIAL FACTS: This species was established in 2019 after several distinctions from the American Mastodon (*M. americanum*). Pacific Mastodons appear to have mostly inhabited western North America, while American Mastodons inhabited the east.

MAMMUT AMERICANUM

NAME MEANING: American nipple

AGE: Pleistocene

DISTRIBUTION: North America

SIZE: 9.5–10.7 feet (2.9–3.25 meters) SH; 7–11 tons

DIET: Herbivore

SEE MORE ON PAGES 236–237

MAMMUT AMERICANUM

ESSENTIAL FACTS: The first American Mastodon specimens were discovered in New York in 1705. Their geographic range extended from Honduras in the south and Alaska in the north, favoring moist forest and woodland habitats. Their presence appears to have been particularly strong east of the Mississippi River. The closely related Pacific Mastodon (*M. pacificus*) was more common in the drier woodlands and savannas to the west. The skull is long and low like that of other mastodons. The tusks are very long and strongly curved upward. Lower tusks are mostly absent, although they sometimes occur in juveniles.

They lived in maternal herds consisting of adult females and their offspring. Young males left these herds at puberty to form bachelor herds or live alone. They inhabited forest and woodland habitats, where they fed primarily on leaves from trees and occasionally fruits, such as pumpkins. There is evidence that mature males engaged in intense battles, with at least one specimen nicknamed the Buesching Mastodon having died when the tusk of a rival pierced the right side of its skull. Healthy adult individuals had little to fear from predators. However, there is evidence that humans occasionally killed and butchered them by driving them into traps in which it was difficult for the animal to fight back or escape. Juvenile American Mastodons are known to have been hunted by Scimitar Cats (*Homotherium latidens*).

SEE ENTRY ON PAGE 235

STEGODONTIDAE

Stegodonts appear during the Middle Miocene and survived until the Late Pleistocene in Africa and Eurasia. Their teeth are very similar to those of true elephants (Elephantidae) with multiple transverse crests running across them. But this is thought to have convergently evolved and not a case of one being ancestral to the other.

STEGODON ZDANSKYI

NAME MEANING: Zdansky's roofed tooth

AGE: Late Pliocene to Early Pleistocene

DISTRIBUTION: Eurasia

SIZE: 12 feet (3.6 meters) SH

DIET: Herbivore

ESSENTIAL FACTS: Like all members of the genus, Zdansky's Stegodon had very long tusks which were so close together that its trunk could not fit between them. Rather, the trunk would need to be hung over the tusks and draped over one side or the other when not in use.

STEGODON SONDAARI

NAME MEANING: Sondaar's roofed tooth

AGE: Pleistocene

DISTRIBUTION: Flores Island

SIZE: 3 feet (0.9 meters) SH

DIET: Herbivore; mixed feeder

ESSENTIAL FACTS: Sondaar's Stegodon was one of two species of dwarf stegodon that inhabited the island of Flores. It had a mixed diet consisting of a wide variety of plants and was small enough to have been hunted by Komodo dragons (*Varanus komodoensis*).

ELEPHANTIDAE

Elephantidae is the family to which all three species of modern elephant belong. This family first appeared in Africa during the Middle Miocene. Their teeth differ from those of gomphotheres and mastodons by having large, flat teeth with multiple parallel lophs that evolved to handle particularly abrasive grasses.

TETRALOPHODON LONGIROSTRIS

NAME MEANING: Long-snouted, four-crested tooth

AGE: Middle Miocene (16–10 MYA)

DISTRIBUTION: Eurasia

SIZE: 11.3 feet (3.45 meters) SH; 10 tons

DIET: Herbivore

ESSENTIAL FACTS: This species closely resembled its four-tusked gomphothere ancestors. Tooth wear analysis suggests that it chewed its food in a manner similar to that of modern elephants, using a forward-and-backward motion, something which gomphotheres did not do.

STEGOTETRABELODON SYRTICUS

NAME MEANING: Roofed, four-spear tooth from Sirt

AGE: Late Miocene (7–5.3 MYA)

DISTRIBUTION: Africa

SIZE: 13 feet (4 meters) SH; 11–13 tons

DIET: Herbivore

ESSENTIAL FACTS: The Sirt Elephant is most notable for its two pairs of downward-pointing tusks on the skull and lower jaw more exaggerated than those seen in the genus *Tetralophodon*. How it may have used these tusks is not understood.

ANANCUS ARVERNENSIS

NAME MEANING: King Anancus from Arverne

AGE: Pliocene to Pleistocene (5–1.6 MYA)

DISTRIBUTION: Eurasia

SIZE: 8–8.5 feet (2.5–2.6 meters) SH; 5–6 tons

DIET: Herbivore; browser

ESSENTIAL FACTS: The Arverne Elephant is known from remarkably complete fossils found in various sites in Europe. Its straight tusks could reach almost 10 feet (3 meters) long. It was formerly considered a type of gomphothere, but more recently it has been grouped among the true elephants.

PALAEOLOXODON ANTIQUUS

NAME MEANING: Ancient, ancient Loxodon

AGE: Pleistocene (1 MYA–30,000 YA)

DISTRIBUTION: Eurasia

SIZE: 12.5–13.8 feet (3.81–4.2 meters) SH; 11–15 tons

DIET: Herbivore

SEE MORE ON PAGES 242–243

PALAEOLOXODON FALCONERI

NAME MEANING: Hugh Falconer's ancient Loxodon

AGE: Pleistocene

DISTRIBUTION: Sicily and Malta

SIZE: 2.5–3.3 feet (0.8–1 meter) SH; 332–551 pounds (150–250 kilograms)

DIET: Herbivore; mixed feeder

SEE MORE ON PAGES 244–245

PALAEOLOXODON NAMADICUS

NAME MEANING: Ancient Loxodon from Namadi

AGE: Pleistocene

DISTRIBUTION: Eurasia

SIZE: 14.3–17.1 feet (4.35–5.2 meters) SH; 13–20 tons

DIET: Herbivore

ESSENTIAL FACTS: Apart from its overall larger size, it is distinguishable from the Straight-Tusked Elephant (*Palaeoloxodon antiquus*) by its proportionally longer and more slender limbs and more developed crests on the back of the head, which supported the neck muscles.

MAMMUTHUS PRIMIGENIUS

NAME MEANING: Firstborn mammoth

AGE: Pleistocene to Holocene

DISTRIBUTION: Eurasia, North America

SIZE: 7.5–11.5 feet (2.3–3.49 meters) SH; 3–8 tons

DIET: Herbivore

SEE MORE ON PAGES 246–247

MAMMUTHUS COLUMBI

NAME MEANING: Christopher Columbus' mammoth

AGE: Pleistocene

DISTRIBUTION: North America

SIZE: 12.2–13.8 feet (3.72–4.2 meters) SH; 10 tons

DIET: Herbivore

SEE MORE ON PAGES 248–249

PALAEOLOXODON ANTIQUUS

ESSENTIAL FACTS: The Straight-Tusked Elephant is a lesser-known cousin of its more famous cousins, the mammoths, with which it coexisted. Like mammoths, its closest modern relative is the Asian elephant (*Elephas maximus*), although it was closer in size and ecology to the African bush elephant (*Loxodonta africana*). Compared to the giant Namadi Elephant (*Palaeoloxodon namadicus*), it is an overall much smaller animal but possesses proportionately more robust limbs. The iconic tusks for which it is named could grow up to 13 feet (4 meters) in fully-grown males and were slightly curved in shape rather than being straight. It lived in the temperate and subtropical woodlands and savannas of Eurasia, with its range expanding and contracting with fluctuations in northern glaciers. Straight-Tusked Elephants are ancestral to several populations of dwarf elephants that became stranded on islands.

Straight-Tusked Elephants had a mixed diet that varied from season to season, sometimes being more graze-dominated and sometimes more browse-dominated. Stone tools have been found in association with some skeletons which show signs of butchery. This suggests these elephants were hunted by Neanderthals (*Homo neanderthalensis*) and potentially by modern humans (*H. sapiens*).

SEE ENTRY ON PAGE 240

PALAEOLOXODON FALCONERI

ESSENTIAL FACTS: Derived from giant mainland species, many types of dwarf elephant have existed, needing to downsize in order to maintain sustainable populations in a limited space. This phenomenon is known as insular dwarfism. At barely 1 meter (3 feet) tall at the shoulder, Falconer's Dwarf Elephant is among the smallest of these island variants. This tapir-sized elephant descended from Straight-Tusked Elephants (*P. antiquus*) from mainland Europe and arrived to the islands of Sicily and Malta during periods of low sea level. Compared to its mainland ancestor, it had a proportionately larger head, longer neck, longer torso, and more slender limbs.

Despite its diminutive size, Falconer's Elephant was the largest animal endemic to the islands on which it lived. Like its larger ancestor, it was an opportunistic mixed feeder. Studies have shown that it retained the slow growth rate and long lifespans of its ancestors, living to be as old as 68 years old. This is a typical age for giant elephants but highly unusual for a mammal of its size, which would typically be expected to live for 30 years or less. Similarly, sexual maturity was achieved at about 15 years of age.

SEE ENTRY ON PAGE 240

MAMMUTHUS COLUMBI

ESSENTIAL FACTS: Its range encompassed Canada, most of the United States, and as far south as Costa Rica. Their preferred habitat was open grasslands and savanna. It differed from its more arctic-adapted cousin the Woolly Mammoth in its larger size, longer tail, and in the shape of its skull. It was likely not as well insulated, given that much of its range was warmer year-round. However, it may have grown a seasonal winter coat during the fall and shed it during the onset of spring, given that much of its distribution still experienced pronounced winter seasons. A population of Columbian Mammoths became isolated on the Channel Islands off the coast of California during the Late Pleistocene, giving rise to the Pygmy Mammoth (*Mammuthus exilis*).

Adult Columbian Mammoths needed to consume 400 pounds (180 kilograms) of food a day with a diet comprising mostly of grasses and sedges, with other plants such as the leaves of various trees, bushes, and fruits being taken opportunistically. They were able to live as long as 60 to 70 years like modern elephants. There is evidence that humans would hunt them on occasion. Juveniles are known to have been opportunistically hunted by the Scimitar Cat (*Homotherium latidens*).

SEE ENTRY ON PAGE 241

EUARCHONTOGLIRES

Euarchontoglires is the clade that includes rodents and lagomorphs (Glires) along with the colugos, treeshrews, and primates (Euarchonta). The group may have diverged from other eutherians during the Middle to Late Cretaceous, with the oldest fossils dating to the Early Paleocene.

APATOTHERIA

Apatotheres are a distinctive group of mammals known to have lived in Europe and North America. Their fossils occur from the Paleocene to Oligocene. Containing a single family, the Apatemyidae, members of this group range from mouse-sized to beaver-sized. They were arboreal with specializations such as flexible ankle and shoulder joints, grasping digits which end in claws, and a long tail for balance. The skull is proportionately large compared to the otherwise slender skeleton. They have enlarged first incisors that resemble those of plesiadapiform primates. The other incisors, canines, and anterior premolars are reduced or absent to make room for these teeth, which were likely used to gnaw through bark to expose underlying plant exudates or insects.

APATEMYS CHARDINI

NAME MEANING: Chardin's deceptive mouse

AGE: Early Eocene (50–46 MYA)

DISTRIBUTION: North America

SIZE: 6 inches (15 centimeters) HBL; 8 inches (20 centimeters) TL

DIET: Mesocarnivore

ESSENTIAL FACTS: A complete skeleton of this species was found at Fossil Butte in southwestern Wyoming. The squirrel-like proportions and grasping digits of the animal show that it was well-adapted for quick and agile movement through the trees.

HETEROHYUS NANUS

NAME MEANING: Dwarf different pig

AGE: Middle Eocene (47 MYA)

DISTRIBUTION: Eurasia

SIZE: About squirrel-sized

DIET: Mesocarnivore

ESSENTIAL FACTS: Complete skeletons with soft tissue impressions are known from Messel Pit in Germany. It had particularly elongated second and third fingers like those of an aye-aye (*Daubentonia madagascariensis*) for picking grubs out of holes, which it would bore with its strong incisors.

SINCLAIRELLA DAKOTENSIS

NAME MEANING: Sinclair from Dakota

AGE: Middle Oligocene (29.75–28.8 MYA)

DISTRIBUTION: North America

SIZE: About cat-sized

DIET: Mesocarnivore

ESSENTIAL FACTS: This species was the last-surviving apatomyid in North America. Known for an exceptionally complete skull which is now lost, its upper incisors were especially long and caniniform.

LAGOMORPHA

Lagomorphs have a long history going back as far as the Late Paleocene. It is thought that the group originated in India, because the oldest known lagomorph fossils were found there and date to the Late Paleocene-Early Eocene, when India was still an island. There are two modern families with 110 species, all of which are small herbivores.

OCHOTONIDAE

The pikas currently inhabit the mountainous regions of western North America and Eurasia. They appear in the fossil record during the Oligocene. In general, pikas are built for traversing rocky terrain and are good jumpers with moderate digging capabilities, but they are not especially adapted for running.

OCHOTONA SPANGLE

NAME MEANING: Spangle's pika

AGE: Late Miocene (10–5 MYA)

DISTRIBUTION: North America

SIZE: 6 ounces (170 grams)

DIET: Herbivore

ESSENTIAL FACTS: Spangle's Pika is the oldest-known pika to inhabit North America. After it disappeared from the fossil record, pikas are not known from North America until the Pleistocene.

PROLAGUS IMPERIALIS

NAME MEANING: Before rabbit from Poggio Imperiale

AGE: Late Miocene to Pliocene (7–3 MYA)

DISTRIBUTION: Gargano Island (now part of Italy)

SIZE: 12 pounds (5 kilograms)

DIET: Herbivore

ESSENTIAL FACTS: One of two species of pika endemic to Gargano Island, the Imperial Pika was possibly the largest pika to have ever lived. It was about the size of the largest hares (*Lepus*).

PROLAGUS SARDUS

NAME MEANING: Before rabbit from Sardinia

AGE: Pleistocene to Holocene (800,000–1,200 YA)

DISTRIBUTION: Sardinia and Corsica

SIZE: 1–15.4 ounces (504–525 grams)

DIET: Herbivore

SEE MORE ON PAGES 254–255

LEPORIDAE

The first rabbits are known from the Late Eocene. Leporids possess unusual, perforated skulls. The function of these holes is currently not agreed upon by researchers, but they are present in even the earliest forms. They show a trend toward increasing cursoriality; early rabbits were built a lot like pikas and over time evolved elongated hindlimbs adapted to take great leaping strides.

PALAEOLAGUS HAYDENI

NAME MEANING: Hayden's ancient rabbit

AGE: Early Oligocene (34–30 MYA)

DISTRIBUTION: North America

SIZE: 9.8 inches (25 centimeters)

DIET: Herbivore

ESSENTIAL FACTS: Hayden's Rabbit was an extremely common rabbit, its fossils often greatly outnumbering other mammals of its time. It already possessed the hypselodont teeth and perforated skull that would be inherited by all later leporids, although it had not yet developed many cursorial specializations.

PROLAGUS SARDUS

ESSENTIAL FACTS: The Sardinian Pika was the last-surviving member of the genus *Prolagus*. After its ancestor arrived to Sardinia and Corsica during the Pliocene, the islands served as a refuge while their relatives on the mainland declined and eventually became extinct. Once established, these pikas thrived. Facing limited competition from larger herbivores, the species became abundant over nearly every habitat from sea level up to 2,624 feet (800 meters), while its hypsodont teeth enabled it to tackle a variety of plants. Numerous accumulations of fossil and subfossil remains indicate a rather high population density with many individuals surviving to reach old age, evidenced by the frequency of arthritis among these remains. Maximum life expectancy has been estimated at eight years.

Native predators of the Sardinian Pika included the Sardinian Dhole (*Cynotherium sardous*) and the Sardinian Weasel (*Enhydrictis galictoides*). When threatened, these pikas would retreat into burrows. There is evidence that once the first humans arrived on the islands 10,000 years ago, Sardinian Pikas became a welcome and regular food source. Perhaps due to sustainable hunting practices, pika populations remained stable for the next few thousand years. The arrival of the Romans about 2,000 years ago seems to have been the cause of this species' extinction between 800 BC and 600 AD. Their demise was due to destructive agricultural practices, the introduction of new predators, and competitors in the form of domesticated or otherwise invasive animals.

SEE ENTRY ON PAGE 253

SERENGETILAGUS PRAECAPENSIS

NAME MEANING: Serengeti rabbit from before the Cape

AGE: Late Miocene to Pliocene (7–2.6 MYA)

DISTRIBUTION: Africa

SIZE: 2.6–3.5 pounds (1.2–1.6 kilograms)

DIET: Herbivore

ESSENTIAL FACTS: This rabbit was the most abundant animal from the famous Laetoli sites in Tanzania. It was built similarly to modern rabbits of the genus *Oryctolagus*, with moderate cursorial adaptations and forelimbs adapted to burrowing.

AZTLANOLAGUS AGILIS

NAME MEANING: Agile rabbit from Aztlan

AGE: Pliocene to Pleistocene

DISTRIBUTION: North America

SIZE: 2.6–4.4 pounds (1.2–2 kilograms)

DIET: Herbivore

ESSENTIAL FACTS: The genus name of this rabbit refers to Aztlán, the legendary place of origin of the Nahua peoples as recorded in the mythological accounts of the Aztecs and other Nahua groups.

SYLVILAGUS LEONENSIS

NAME MEANING: Forest rabbit from Leon County

AGE: Pleistocene

DISTRIBUTION: North America

SIZE: 0.8–1.1 pounds (375–500 grams)

DIET: Herbivore

ESSENTIAL FACTS: This species was known as the Dwarf Cottontail for its small size compared to other cottontail rabbits of the genus *Sylvilagus*. It is likely to have favored areas with high shrub cover in which to hide from predators.

HYPOLAGUS PEREGRINUS

NAME MEANING: Wandering low rabbit

AGE: Pleistocene

DISTRIBUTION: Sicily

SIZE: 11 pounds (5 kilograms)

DIET: Herbivore

ESSENTIAL FACTS: Endemic to the island of Sicily, this rabbit had a notably more robust skeleton than other members of its genus, with limbs better suited for excavating burrows and for cursoriality.

ORYCTOLAGUS LACOSTI

NAME MEANING: Lacost's digging rabbit

AGE: Late Pliocene

DISTRIBUTION: Eurasia

SIZE: 24–30 inches (60–75 centimeters) HBL; 8.8–15.4 pounds (4–7 kilograms)

DIET: Herbivore

ESSENTIAL FACTS: This species was much larger than modern examples of the genus, being more the size of a hare (*Lepus*).

NESOLAGUS SINENSIS

NAME MEANING: Chinese island rabbit

AGE: Middle Pleistocene (1.6–1.2 MYA)

DISTRIBUTION: Eurasia

SIZE: 4 pounds (1.5 kilograms)

DIET: Herbivore

ESSENTIAL FACTS: The Chinese Striped Rabbit is an extinct relative of two east Asian rabbit species that were commonly referred to as the "striped rabbits," due to their bold black markings. The genus name refers to the modern Sumatran striped rabbit (*N. netscheri*), the type species which is endemic to the Indonesian island of Sumatra.

BRACHYLAGUS COLORADOENSIS

NAME MEANING: Short rabbit from Colorado

AGE: Pleistocene

DISTRIBUTION: North America

SIZE: 5 pounds (2 kilograms)

DIET: Herbivore

ESSENTIAL FACTS: The Colorado Rabbit is a slightly larger relative of the pygmy rabbit (*B. idahoensis*), the smallest modern rabbit species that weighs little more than 1 pound (about 500 grams). It appears to have evolved from a North American species of *Hypolagus*.

NURALAGUS REX

NAME MEANING: King rabbit from Minorca

AGE: Pliocene (5–3 MYA)

DISTRIBUTION: Minorca

SIZE: 18–26 pounds (8–12 kilograms)

DIET: Herbivore

ESSENTIAL FACTS: Nuralagus was an island species that evolved with minimal competition from larger herbivores. It is the largest leporid known to have ever lived. The genus name is derived from Nura, the ancient Phoenician name for the Mediterranean island of Minorca.

RODENTIA

Rodents are the most speciose (have the most species) of any modern mammal, with over 2,000 accepted modern species. This is due to most species being small in size and having rapid reproductive cycles. The group is characterized by the first incisors of the upper and lower jaws, which are hypselodont and have enamel covering only the front surface. Because of their teeth's ever-growing nature, rodents must continuously grind down their tips against each other, so they do not become overgrown. The name *rodent*, in fact, comes from the Latin word meaning "to gnaw." Due to their enamel coating, the front of the teeth are worn more slowly than the soft dentine in the back, causing permanently sharpened chisel-like tips. All rodents lack their second and third incisors, canines, and anterior premolars.

ANOMALUROMORPHA

Anomaluromorpha are characterized by a set of scales on the underside of the base of the tail, a unique attribute that inspires the group name, which is derived from the genus *Anomalurus*, meaning "odd tail." They are morphologically and ecologically comparable to squirrels (Sciuridae). They are superficially squirrel-like with the same arboreal habits. Modern anomaluromrphs are confined to the forests of central Africa, but the oldest fossils of this group are recorded from the Middle Eocene of Myanmar. Their first appearance in the African fossil record in the Late Eocene coincides with the arrival of other Asian immigrants, the hystricomorph rodents and haplorrhine primates.

PONDAUNGIMYS ANOMALUROPSIS

NAME MEANING: *Anomalurus*-like mouse from Pondaung

AGE: Middle Eocene (40 MYA)

DISTRIBUTION: Eurasia

SIZE: About squirrel-sized

DIET: Herbivore

ESSENTIAL FACTS: The oldest known anomaluromorph and one of only two species found outside of Africa, the other being *Downsimys margolisi* from the Oligocene of Pakistan. It is considered part of an extinct family called Nementchamyidae.

ANOMALURIDAE

Anomalures appear in the African fossil record during the Late Eocene and may have originated before this given their diversity at the time. Today the six surviving species are still restricted to the forests of central Africa. Members of this family have two rows of raised scales on the undersides of their tails, which is why they are commonly referred to as the "scaly-tailed squirrels." Despite possessing a patagium stretching between their front and hindlimbs, anomalures are not relatives of flying squirrels.

KABIRMYS QARUNENSIS

NAME MEANING: Big mouse from Birket Qarun

AGE: Late Eocene (37 MYA)

DISTRIBUTION: Africa

SIZE: 2.8–4.4 pounds (1.3–2 kilograms)

DIET: Herbivore

ESSENTIAL FACTS: The largest anomalure known from its time, the size of modern species examples of *Anomalurus*. Due to its relatively short humerus, it is probable that it had not yet evolved the gliding membrane possessed by modern species.

SHAZURUS MINUTUS

NAME MEANING: Small anomalous tail

AGE: Late Eocene (37 MYA)

DISTRIBUTION: Africa

SIZE: About mouse-sized

DIET: Herbivore

ESSENTIAL FACTS: Notably much smaller than its contemporary the Qarun Anomalure (*Kabirmys qarunensis*), it is overall one of the smallest anomalures yet known. It is surprisingly specialized for its early age, being similar in dental morphology to the modern genus *Anomalurus*.

ZENKERELLIDAE

Scaly-tails are squirrel-like rodents that were once placed within the family Anomaluridae. Zenkerellids are known only from Africa and have a fossil record dating back to the Early Oligocene, although they are estimated to have diverged from the Anomaluridae potentially as far back as 49 million years ago. There is only one known surviving species: the Cameroon scaly-tail (*Zenkerella insignis*).

PROZENKERELLA SAHARAENSIS

NAME MEANING: Before *Zenkerella* from the Sahara Desert

AGE: Early Oligocene (32–31 MYA)

DISTRIBUTION: Africa

SIZE: About squirrel-sized

DIET: Herbivore

ESSENTIAL FACTS: The oldest-known member of Zenkerellidae, it displays only slight differences in dental morphology from members of the genus *Zenkerella*.

ZENKERELLA WINTONI

NAME MEANING: Unknown

AGE: Early Miocene (20 MYA)

DISTRIBUTION: Africa

SIZE: About squirrel-sized

DIET: Herbivore

ESSENTIAL FACTS: Aside from being slightly smaller, Winton's Scaly-Tail is very similar to its modern relative. Its fossils have been found in Kenya and Uganda.

SCIUROMORPHA

This is possibly the oldest rodent suborder, appearing in the Paleocene. Members of this diverse group are adapted for a wide range of lifestyles, including terrestrial, scansorial, arboreal, and fossorial.

REITHROPARAMYS HUERFANENSIS

NAME MEANING: Channel Paramys from Huerfano County

AGE: Late Paleocene (57–55 MYA)

DISTRIBUTION: North America

SIZE: About squirrel-sized

DIET: Herbivore

ESSENTIAL FACTS: This species had a gracile skeleton adapted for leaping. It is sometimes placed within the Ischyromyidae but is also sometimes considered unique enough to be given its own family, Reithroparamyidae.

ISCHYROMYIDAE

Ischyromyidae is one of the earliest rodent families known in the fossil record, appearing in the fossil record during the late Paleocene of North America and in Europe during the Early Eocene. The family was particularly abundant and diverse during the Late Eocene to earliest Oligocene of North America, after which they rather quickly disappear and are replaced by true squirrels (Sciuridae).

PARAMYS ATAVUS

NAME MEANING: Ancestral near mouse

AGE: Late Paleocene (57–55 MYA)

DISTRIBUTION: North America

SIZE: About squirrel-sized

DIET: Herbivore

ESSENTIAL FACTS: One of the earliest-known ischyromyids, this species was a scansorial herbivore with similar proportions to those of modern tree squirrels.

AILURAVUS MACRURUS

NAME MEANING: Big-tailed cat-ancestor

AGE: Middle Eocene (48.6–45 MYA)

DISTRIBUTION: Eurasia

SIZE: 1.6 feet (50 centimeters) HBL; 2 feet (60 centimeters) TL

DIET: Herbivore

ESSENTIAL FACTS: Complete skeletons with soft tissue impressions of this animal have been found at Messel Pit in Germany. It had a bushy tail and preserved gut contents that show that its diet included soft leaves.

MASILLAMYS BEEGERI

NAME MEANING: Beeger's mouse from Messel

AGE: Middle Eocene (48.6–45 MYA)

DISTRIBUTION: Eurasia

SIZE: About squirrel-sized

DIET: Herbivore

ESSENTIAL FACTS: Another ischyromyid from Messel Pit, this species was smaller and shorter-legged than the marmot-sized Ailuravus and does not appear to have had the same fluffy tail. It may have been a scansorial fruit and seed eater. Members of the genus are notable in having developed the hystricomorphous jaw musculature.

ISCHYROMYS TYPUS

NAME MEANING: Typical strong mouse

AGE: Early Oligocene (34 to 32 MYA)

DISTRIBUTION: North America

SIZE: About squirrel-sized

DIET: Herbivore

ESSENTIAL FACTS: Known extensively from Early Oligocene deposits in Nebraska, this species had a lifestyle similar to that of modern ground squirrels.

MELDIMYS MUSAK

NAME MEANING: Pleasant mouse

AGE: Early Eocene (50 MYA)

DISTRIBUTION: Eurasia

SIZE: About squirrel-sized

DIET: Herbivore

ESSENTIAL FACTS: This species is the oldest rodent known from India. Another, slightly older species of *Meldimys* is known from France. This suggests that a land passage existed between India, which was an island at the time, and the main Eurasian landmass. Its species name is the Sanskrit word for “mouse.”

APLODONTIIDAE

This family is represented by a single surviving species, the Mountain Beaver (*Aplodontia rufa*), which lives in the Pacific Northwest of North America. Aplodontids were once very diverse and widespread, with fossils being found across the Northern Hemisphere, having apparently originated in North America during the Oligocene.

PROSCIURUS ALBICLIVUS

NAME MEANING: Before *Sciurus* from White Butte

AGE: Early Oligocene (34–30 MYA)

DISTRIBUTION: North America

SIZE: 2.2 pounds (1 kilogram)

DIET: Herbivore

ESSENTIAL FACTS: The largest species of its genus, its fossils have been found in North Dakota and Nebraska.

MYLAGAULIDAE

Mylagaulids are unique among rodents in that many species possessed paired horns on their heads. Hence, they are commonly known as "horned gophers." They mostly inhabited North America, but the group made incursions into Eurasia during the Middle Miocene. The fossil record for the family stretches back to the Oligocene, and they are last known from the Early Pliocene. They appear to be closely related to the aplodontidae. Members of this group have robust forelimbs with long claws adapted for digging.

TRILACCOGAULUS MONTANENSIS

NAME MEANING: Three-pitted bowel from Montana

AGE: Middle Oligocene (29 MYA)

DISTRIBUTION: North America

SIZE: About gopher-sized

DIET: Herbivore

ESSENTIAL FACTS: This species is the oldest member of Mylagaulidae. Horns had not evolved in this genus yet, so the animal would have looked like a robust marmot (*Marmota*).

LAMUGAULUS OLKHONENSIS

NAME MEANING: Lamu bowl from Olkhon island

AGE: Middle Miocene

DISTRIBUTION: Eurasia

SIZE: About gopher-sized

DIET: Herbivore

ESSENTIAL FACTS: Mylagaulids are a primarily North American group, but the discovery of Lamugaulus in eastern Siberia presents the third Asian record for the family. Prior to its discovery mylagaulids had been discovered in Kazakhstan and China.

MYLAGAULUS CORNUSAULAX

NAME MEANING: Horn-furrow molar bowl

AGE: Late Miocene (9–8 MYA)

DISTRIBUTION: North America

SIZE: About gopher-sized

DIET: Herbivore

ESSENTIAL FACTS: This species is unique among known mylagaulids in having nasal horns with large posterior furrows, from which its species name is derived.

CERATOGAULUS HATCHERI

NAME MEANING: Hatcher's horned bowl

AGE: Late Miocene (8–6 MYA)

DISTRIBUTION: North America

SIZE: 1 foot (30 centimeters)

DIET: Herbivore

SEE MORE ON PAGES 268–269

SCIURIDAE

Sciuridae is a large family with 275 modern species that include the squirrels, chipmunks, and marmots. They seem to have originated in North America and were widespread in the Northern Hemisphere by the Late Eocene.

PROTOSCIURUS JEFFERSONI

NAME MEANING: Jefferson's first squirrel

AGE: Late Eocene (38–34 MYA)

DISTRIBUTION: North America

SIZE: About squirrel-sized

DIET: Herbivore

ESSENTIAL FACTS: One of the oldest sciurids, Jefferson's Squirrel is known from a remarkably complete skeleton that was similar in proportions to that of modern tree squirrels, adapted to a scansorial lifestyle. It has also been called *Douglassciurus jeffersoni*.

PALAEOSCIURUS GOTI

NAME MEANING: Got's ancient *Sciurus*

AGE: Early Oligocene (30 MYA)

DISTRIBUTION: Eurasia

SIZE: About squirrel-sized

DIET: Herbivore

ESSENTIAL FACTS: An early ground squirrel that would have looked virtually identical to its modern counterparts, it is the oldest squirrel known to have inhabited Europe.

KUBWAXERUS PATTERSONI

NAME MEANING: Bryan Patterson's large dry squirrel

AGE: Late Miocene (7–5 MYA)

DISTRIBUTION: Africa

SIZE: 1.3 feet (40 centimeters) HBL; 3 pounds (1.4 kilograms)

DIET: Herbivore

ESSENTIAL FACTS: Patterson's Squirrel was very large by tree squirrel standards, with particularly deep incisors adapted to break open particularly large seeds, nuts, and fruits.

CERATOGAULUS HATCHERI

ESSENTIAL FACTS: Hatcher's Horned Gopher is the youngest-known member of Mylagaulidae, last occurring in the latest Miocene or earliest Pliocene. The complete skeleton is known, so a great deal can be inferred about its anatomy and potential behaviors. Like other horned gophers, it was a fossorial animal with a compact body, with massively developed forelimbs and giant spade-like forepaws with massive claws. Its eyes were reduced in size, and its vision was likely limited, a common adaptation of mammals which spend most of their lives underground.

The paired horns that grow between the nose and eyes are among the longest observed among the horned gophers. Much speculation has been given to explain how exactly these animals may have used these horns. Males and females both had horns, so it is unlikely that they functioned to attract mates or wield as weapons. The horns are also unsuited to function as digging tools given their shape and position. The most likely explanation may be that the horns acted as predator deterrents. When threatened, the animals may have retreated to their burrow before turning at the entrance so that their horns faced in the direction of the threat as they moved inside, thus preventing predators from biting them.

SEE ENTRY ON PAGE 266

PAENOMARMOTA BARBOURI

NAME MEANING: Barbour's almost-marmot

AGE: Pliocene (4.18–3.79 MYA)

DISTRIBUTION: North America

SIZE: 40 pounds (15 kilograms)

DIET: Herbivore

ESSENTIAL FACTS: Barbour's Marmot was the largest-known member of Sciuridae. It was able to excavate its own burrows in soft soils, thanks to its robust forelimbs and strong claws. But it would have spent most of its time on the surface.

GLIRIDAE

The glirids, commonly known as dormice, are a group of small-bodied arboreal rodents that originated in the Early Eocene. The fossil record for dormice is best known from Europe and the Middle East during the Miocene.

EOGLIRAVUS WILDI

NAME MEANING: Wild's dawn *Gliravus*

AGE: Middle Eocene (48.6–45 MYA)

DISTRIBUTION: Eurasia

SIZE: 0.53 ounces (15 grams)

DIET: Herbivore

ESSENTIAL FACTS: The oldest-known glirid, Wild's Dormouse is known from a complete skeleton from Messel Pit, which already displays the physical attributes typical of modern dormice. It was a swift and agile climber with curved claws and a bushy tail for balance. Its diet consisted of seeds, fruits, and buds.

LEITHIA MELITENSIS

NAME MEANING: Leith Adams from Malta

AGE: Pleistocene and Holocene

DISTRIBUTION: Sicily and Malta

SIZE: 2.2 pounds (1 kilogram)

DIET: Herbivore

SEE MORE ON PAGES 272–273

CASTORIMORPHA

Sometimes considered to be part of Sciuromorpha, castorimorphs include all the rodents that show morphological similarities of the skull and teeth with beavers (Castoridae).

HITONKALA ANDERSONTAU

NAME MEANING: Anderson's mouse

AGE: Early Miocene (20 MYA)

DISTRIBUTION: North America

SIZE: About squirrel-sized

DIET: Herbivore

ESSENTIAL FACTS: This species was a member of the Florentiamyidae, a group of rodents closely related to pocket gophers (Geomyidae). It is known for nearly complete skulls.

LEITHIA MELITENSIS

ESSENTIAL FACTS: Endemic to the islands of Sicily and Malta, the Maltese Dormouse is the largest known species of dormouse. The size of a small rabbit, it a giant among a family of rodents which typically range from 0.5–6.35 ounces (15–180 grams) in weight. Its size is the result of a phenomenon known as insular gigantism, when small animals in an isolated environment free of larger competitors evolve to exploit niches that would otherwise be occupied by larger animals. This radiation often occurs rapidly in evolutionary terms given the typically short generation times of smaller animals.

The jaws of the Maltese Dormouse were extremely robust and adapted for extensive chewing of abrasive plants. Like other dormice, it was an arboreal herbivore, but its diet likely consisted of particularly fibrous leaves. It coexisted alongside dwarfed versions of mainland animals such as the sheep-sized Falconer's Elephant (*Palaeoloxodon falconeri*), the ox-sized Maltese Dwarf Hippo (*Hippopotamus melitensis*), as well as the Giant Swan (*Cygnus falconeri*), which was another result of insular gigantism.

SEE ENTRY ON PAGE 271

HELISCOMYS OSTRANDERI

NAME MEANING: Ostrander's sun mouse

AGE: Late Eocene (35 MYA)

DISTRIBUTION: North America

SIZE: About mouse-sized

DIET: Herbivore

ESSENTIAL FACTS: This species is part of other pocket gopher–related rodents, the Heliscomyidae. It had robust cheek teeth adapted to handle tough foods.

EUTYPOMYIDAE

This family of rodents are closely related to beavers (Castoridae) and likely descended from ischyromyids. They were restricted to North America for much of their history but spread to Eurasia during the Miocene.

EUTYPOMYS THOMSONI

NAME MEANING: Thomson's true Typomys

AGE: Late Oligocene

DISTRIBUTION: North America

SIZE: 10–15 pounds (4.5–7 kilograms)

DIET: Herbivore

ESSENTIAL FACTS: The most well-known member of the family, this species shared several cranial characteristics in common with beavers and in life probably resembled a modern nutria (*Myocastor coypus*).

CASTORIDAE

Represented today by two semiaquatic species, early beavers were more terrestrial, with many being fossorial. Among other features, beavers are K-selected breeders, meaning that they produce a small number of offspring at a time which the parents invest much time and energy into raising to independence. Most rodents, in contrast, are r-selected breeders; they produce numerous offspring per litter with relatively minimal parental care and typically have very high mortality rates.

AGNOTOCASTOR PRAETEREADENS

NAME MEANING: Before smooth tooth pure beaver

AGE: Late Eocene (37–35 MYA)

DISTRIBUTION: North America

SIZE: About squirrel-sized

DIET: Herbivore; grazer

ESSENTIAL FACTS: The earliest beaver in the fossil record, this species had already developed higher crowned and more complex teeth than its ancestors, which it used to feed on tough or abrasive foods.

MIGMACASTOR PROCUMBODENS

NAME MEANING: Mixed beaver with flat-lying teeth

AGE: Early Miocene (23 MYA)

DISTRIBUTION: North America

SIZE: About gopher-sized

DIET: Herbivore; grazer

ESSENTIAL FACTS: A single nearly complete skull of this beaver has been found, which has similarities to modern rodents that engage in tooth-digging. It may not have been closely related to burrowing beavers within the subfamily Palaeocastorinae, having evolved fossorial adaptations independently.

PALAEOCASTORINAE

As the name suggests, the burrowing beavers were fossorial animals with specializations for digging. They were ecologically analogous to prairie dogs (*Cynomys*) and blesmols (Bathyergidae)

CAPACIKALA GRADATUS

NAME MEANING: Step large beaver

AGE: Late Oligocene

DISTRIBUTION: North America

SIZE: 1–3 pounds (0.5–1.5 kilogram)

DIET: Herbivore; grazer

ESSENTIAL FACTS: This species is known from several nearly complete skulls found at the John Day National Monument. It was a fossorial animal that would have excavated burrows using its incisors and claws.

PALAEOCASTOR FOSSOR

NAME MEANING: Digging ancient beaver

AGE: Early Miocene

DISTRIBUTION: North America

SIZE: 1–3 pounds (0.5–1.5 kilogram)

DIET: Herbivore; grazer

ESSENTIAL FACTS: This species is most well-known of the burrowing beavers, with complete skeletons having been found inside their vertical, twisting burrows which have been nicknamed daimonelix (devil's corkskrews). A predator-prey relationship is inferred between this species and the Daimonelix Weasel (*Zodiolestes daimonelixensis*).

EUHAPSIS PLATYCEPS

NAME MEANING: Flat-headed true curve

AGE: Late Oligocene (25 MYA)

DISTRIBUTION: North America

SIZE: About gopher-sized

DIET: Herbivore; grazer

ESSENTIAL FACTS: Like modern blesmols (Bathyergidae), these subterranean beavers excavated burrows with their teeth. The mouth closed behind the incisors so that they would not ingest dirt as they dug. The eyes were also greatly reduced in size due to their lack of exposure to light.

PARAEUHAPSIS ELLICOTTAE

NAME MEANING: Ellicott's beside Euhapsis

AGE: Early Miocene (20 MYA)

DISTRIBUTION: North America

SIZE: About gopher-sized

DIET: Herbivore; grazer

ESSENTIAL FACTS: This species featured same adaptations as *Euhapsis*, but with the addition of a horny pad on its nose which grew from a rugose patch of bone on the thickened nasals. This enabled them to push loose dirt out of the passageways of their burrows.

ANCHITHERIOMYS BUCEEI

NAME MEANING: Buc-ee's Anchitherium mouse

AGE: Middle Miocene (16–15 MYA)

DISTRIBUTION: North America

SIZE: 44–88 pounds (20–40 kilograms)

DIET: Herbivore

ESSENTIAL FACTS: The genus *Anchitheriomys* is so named because their fossils have frequently been found in association with the browsing horse *Anchitherium*. This particular species is named after Buc-ee's roadside travel centers, which popularized beavers in the state of Texas.

CASTORINAE

Castorines are semiaquatic beavers to which the two modern species belong. Aquatic adaptations include nostrils, eyes, and ears that have migrated to the top of the skull. The feet are large with webbed toes for propulsion.

PROPALAEOCASTOR IRTYSHENSIS

NAME MEANING: Before ancient Castor from the Irtysh River

AGE: Early Oligocene (30 MYA)

DISTRIBUTION: Eurasia

SIZE: Unknown

DIET: Herbivore

ESSENTIAL FACTS: The genus *Propalaeocastor* is poorly understood. However, the morphology of the few available bones shows that they were the earliest members of Castorinae. It is currently unknown if these beavers were semiaquatic.

STENEOFIBER ESSERI

NAME MEANING: Esser's narrow beaver

AGE: Early Miocene (20 MYA)

DISTRIBUTION: Eurasia

SIZE: (30 centimeters) HBL; 5 pounds (2 kilograms)

DIET: Herbivore

ESSENTIAL FACTS: Esser's Beaver is the oldest-known semiaquatic beaver, as indicated by the presence of combing-claws, which modern beavers use to waterproof their fur. They lived in small family units that inhabited burrows along the shores of the rivers and lakes in which it lived.

TROGONTHERIUM CUVIERI

NAME MEANING: Cuvier's gnawing beast

AGE: Late Pliocene to Pleistocene (3 MYA–40,000 YA)

DISTRIBUTION: Eurasia

SIZE: 77–146 pounds (35–66 kilograms)

DIET: Herbivore; grazer

ESSENTIAL FACTS: An unusual capybara-sized beaver with cursorial adaptations, its lower limbs were long and slender with an ankle joint that is similar to those of rabbits. They would likely travel some distance away from water to feed, but were able to flee quickly when threatened with predation.

CASTOROIDES OHIOENSIS

NAME MEANING: Beaver-like animal from Ohio

AGE: Pleistocene

DISTRIBUTION: North America

SIZE: 2 feet (60 centimeters) SH; 5 feet (150 centimeters) HBL; 176–276 pounds (80–125 kilograms)

DIET: Herbivore; grazer

SEE MORE ON PAGES 280–281

EOMYIDAE

Eomyids were squirrel-like rodents that are most closely related to New World (North and South America) pocket mice (Heteromyidae) and pocket gophers (Geomyidae) among modern rodent groups. They achieved their peak diversity during the Late Oligocene and Early Miocene. They first appear during the Middle Eocene in North America and survived there until the Late Miocene. In Eurasia, they appeared slightly later but lasted much longer, surviving to the beginning of the Pleistocene.

CASTOROIDES OHIOENSIS

ESSENTIAL FACTS: The first fossils of this animal were discovered in 1837 in a peat bog in Ohio, hence the species name *ohioensis*. After its initial discovery, *Castoroides* fossils were identified across North America and attributed to this species. During the 1960s it was noted that individuals found in South Carolina and Florida possessed slight but consistent differences in their tooth morphology compared to northern specimens. Thus, a new species was erected. The Northern Giant Beaver is now known to have inhabited the majority of the United States, particularly the more temperate zones, and Canada. The closely related Southern Giant Beaver (*C. dilophidus*) inhabited the warmer lands of southern North America. Both species inhabited wetland environments.

Compared to modern beavers (*Castor*), the hindlimbs were proportionally much longer and the tail was rounded in cross-section instead of being flattened. This shows it was a foot-propelled swimmer rather than a tail-propelled one. Its teeth were not built for gnawing into trees. Instead, they were suited for aquatic plants and also for grazing on grasses that grew near the water. Due to their large hindfeets, movement over moist, muddy ground would have been relatively efficient but movement on drier ground would have been somewhat slow, so they were unlikely to have ventured too far away from water. The robust incisors are notable for having a series of parallel ridges running down their length.

SEE ENTRY ON PAGE 279

ADJIDAUMO MINUTUS

NAME MEANING: Tiny Adjidaumo

AGE: Early Oligocene (30 MYA)

DISTRIBUTION: Eurasia

SIZE: About squirrel-sized

DIET: Herbivore

ESSENTIAL FACTS: The genus name for this species is the name of a squirrel in Henry Longfellow's epic poem *The Song of Hiawatha*. The name itself is derived from a word used by the North American Native tribe of Ojibwa, meaning "mouth-foremost." This refers to the fact that squirrels descend trees headfirst.

EOMYS QUERCI

NAME MEANING: Dawn mouse from Quercy

AGE: Early Oligocene (30 MYA)

DISTRIBUTION: Eurasia

SIZE: About squirrel-sized

DIET: Herbivore

ESSENTIAL FACTS: This species was the earliest known gliding rodent and the first eomyid known to have inhabited Europe. Unlike flying squirrels, its patagium is supported by a modified tendon which extends from the elbow.

APEOMYOIDES SAVAGEI

NAME MEANING: Donald Savage's Apeomys-like

AGE: Middle Miocene (16–15 MYA)

DISTRIBUTION: North America

SIZE: About squirrel-sized

DIET: Herbivore

ESSENTIAL FACTS: Compared to other eomyids, members of *Apeomyoides* had notably hypsodont teeth with thickened enamel, suggesting a diet of more abrasive foods.

HETEROMYIDAE

This family includes pocket mice (Perognathinae) and kangaroo rats (Dipodomyinae) with fifty-nine modern species. Heteromyids are known for excavating log and complex burrow systems like their close relatives, the pocket gophers (Geomyidae). The name "pocket mouse" references the presence of fur-lined cheek pouches in which food can be temporarily stored for later consumption. The family first appears during the Early Miocene.

PROHETEROMYS FLORIDANUS

NAME MEANING: Before *Heteromys* from Florida

AGE: Early Miocene (18 MYA)

DISTRIBUTION: North America

SIZE: About mouse-sized

DIET: Herbivore

ESSENTIAL FACTS: The most abundant small mammal from the Thomas Farm site, it seems to have lived in complex communal burrows like some of its modern relatives.

HARRYMYS MAGNUS

NAME MEANING: Harry's great mouse

AGE: Early Miocene (18 MYA)

DISTRIBUTION: North America

SIZE: About mouse-sized

DIET: Herbivore

ESSENTIAL FACTS: This species is another rodent from the Thomas Farm site. Anatomically, it's nearly identical to its contemporary relative but was about twice the size and much rarer.

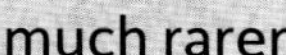

DIPODOMYINAE

Kangaroo-rats are adapted to saltatorial locomotion with the characteristic long hindlimbs and shortened forelimbs. They are nocturnal and inhabit arid habitats. They also have very large ears, which can be identified in the fossil record by an expanded auditory bulla.

AURIMYS XEROS

NAME MEANING: Ear mouse from dry habitats

AGE: Early Miocene (23 MYA)

DISTRIBUTION: North America

SIZE: 8–10 ounces (226–284 grams)

DIET: Herbivore

ESSENTIAL FACTS: This species is the oldest-known and largest-known kangaroo-rat, being one-third larger than the largest modern species. Known fossils of this species include a nearly complete skull and partial foot recovered from John Day Fossil Beds. Like modern kangaroo-rats, it appears to have had very large ears but does not appear to have been bipedal. Researchers infer this by the placement of the foramen magnum, the opening in the base of the skull that connects the spinal cord to the brain.

HYSTRICOMORPHA

Hystricomorph rodents originated in Africa or Eurasia during the Eocene, possibly from an ischyromyid ancestor. The group immigrated to South America late in the Late Eocene through a combination of island-hopping and rafting. They are the most ecologically diverse group that includes the largest rodents that have ever lived. Among the most distinctive features of hystricomorphs is the unique nature of the infraorbital foramen, the small hole beneath and slightly in front of the eyes in most mammals through which the facial nerves and vessels pass. In hystricomorphs, this passage is greatly enlarged to provide extra attachment for the jaw muscles.

PEDETIDAE

Springhares are bipedal rodents that move using saltatory locomotion. They are typically nocturnal and inhabit drier habitats. The oldest known springhares occur in the African fossil record in the early Miocene of Kenya and Uganda.

PARAPEDETES NAMAQUENSIS

NAME MEANING: Beside *Pedetes* from Namibia

AGE: Early Miocene (20 MYA)

DISTRIBUTION: Africa

SIZE: 1.1 pounds (500 grams)

DIET: Herbivore

ESSENTIAL FACTS: Much smaller than modern springhares, this early species was already highly specialized for saltatory locomotion, suggesting that the family had evolved much earlier.

MEGAPEDETES PENTADACTYLUS

NAME MEANING: Great *Pedetes* with five toes

AGE: Middle Miocene (16 MYA)

DISTRIBUTION: Africa

SIZE: 8–15 pounds (4–7 kilograms)

DIET: Herbivore

ESSENTIAL FACTS: This species is the largest-known member of the family. Like its modern relatives, it is likely to have been largely nocturnal in its behavior, resting in burrows by day and emerging at dusk to feed.

CTENODACTYLIDAE

Known commonly as gundis, this family is today restricted to Africa, although they originated in eastern Asia during the Eocene. They remained widespread for much of the Cenozoic and achieved their peak diversity during the Oligocene and Early Miocene. Members of the group could still be found in parts of Eurasia during the Pleistocene.

TAMQUAMMYS ROBUSTUS

NAME MEANING: Robust comparative mouse

AGE: Middle Eocene (55–50 MYA)

HOME: Eurasia

SIZE: About rat-sized

DIET: Herbivore

ESSENTIAL FACTS: The Robust Tamquammys appears to have been one of the more abundant rodents of its time. It was a generalized animal that could run and climb effectively but was not particularly specialized for either, similar to modern rats (*Rattus*).

DIATOMYIDAE

The family Diatomyidae is a Lazarus taxon: a species, genus, or (in this case) family that, at some point, was believed to have gone extinct only for living examples to be rediscovered later. Before the discovery of the sole surviving species, the Laotian Rock Rat (*Laonastes aenigmamus*), this family was thought to have been extinct since the Late Miocene. The oldest fossils for this group are known from the Early Oligocene, and they were once widespread, being found across Eurasia.

DIATOMYS SHANTUNGENSIS

NAME MEANING: Separate mouse from Shandong

AGE: Early Miocene (18 MYA)

DISTRIBUTION: Eurasia

SIZE: 9.8 inches (25 centimeters) HBL; 14 ounces (400 grams)

DIET: Herbivore

ESSENTIAL FACTS: This species is known from complete but flattened skeletons found in China. Like its modern relative, it was a terrestrial generalized herbivore that fed on leaves, grasses, and seeds, occasionally supplementing its diet with insects.

TSAGANOMYIDAE

Tsaganomyids are an extinct family known only from Asia during the Oligocene. They were fossorial rodents that share similar adaptations to the mole-rats (Bathyergidae), using their incisors and strong jaws to excavate burrows.

TSAGANOMYS ALTAICUS

NAME MEANING: Tsagaan mouse from the Altai Mountains

AGE: Middle Oligocene (28 MYA)

DISTRIBUTION: Eurasia

SIZE: About gopher-sized

DIET: Herbivore

ESSENTIAL FACTS: This species is the most well-known member of its family, thanks to complete skull material. This species excavated burrows by gnawing its way through soft substrates feeding on roots, tubers, and bulbs.

BATHYERGIDAE

Commonly known as mole-rats or blesmols, these fossorial rodents appear in the fossil record in the Early Miocene and were more widespread and diverse in the past. They mostly use their strong incisors to dig while using their forelimbs to push aside loose dirt. They have specialized lip muscles that close the mouth behind the incisors, so that they do not ingest dirt as they dig.

BATHYERGOIDES NEOTERTIARIUS

NAME MEANING: New third *Bathyergus*-like

AGE: Early Miocene (21 MYA)

DISTRIBUTION: Africa

SIZE: About gopher-sized

DIET: Herbivore

ESSENTIAL FACTS: The oldest known mole-rat discovered in Namibia, it is sometimes placed as the only member of the family Bathyergoididae.

HYSTRICIDAE

Old World porcupines are heavily built, terrestrial rodents that are covered in modified hairs called *quills* for protection. They first appeared during the Late Miocene and have always been widespread throughout Africa and Eurasia. Though they are not closely related to the New World porcupines (Erethizontide), both families evolved their spiky armor through convergent evolution.

HYSTRIX REFOSSA

NAME MEANING: Back trench porcupine

AGE: Pleistocene

DISTRIBUTION: Eurasia

SIZE: 33–90 pounds (15–40 kilograms)

DIET: Herbivore

ESSENTIAL FACTS: This species is 20 percent larger than its closest relative, the Indian Crested Porcupine (*H. indica*). It was widespread throughout Eurasia during the Pleistocene and likely a nocturnal forager that fed on a wide variety of plants.

PETROMURIDAE

Represented by a single living species, this family first appeared in the fossil record during the Early Miocene and do not appear to have ever been particularly diverse, based on the low number of described species.

PETROMUS ANTIQUUS

NAME MEANING: Ancient rock mouse

AGE: Pliocene

DISTRIBUTION: Africa

SIZE: About squirrel-sized

DIET: Herbivore; grazer

ESSENTIAL FACTS: This species is possibly the direct ancestor of the modern dassie rat (*P. typicus*), the only surviving member of the family. Like its modern relative, it fed mostly on grass and made its home among rocky outcrops.

THRYONOMYIDAE

The two modern species of cane rat (*Thyromys*) are the last surviving members of this family which originated during the Oligocene. Currently restricted to sub-Saharan Africa, the family was much more diverse and widespread during their history with fossils known from across Eurasia. They share a common ancestor with the dassie rats (Petromuridae).

MONAMYS SIMONSI

NAME MEANING: Mona Mohammed Shahin's mouse

AGE: Early Oligocene (30 MYA)

DISTRIBUTION: Africa

SIZE: Unknown

DIET: Herbivore

ESSENTIAL FACTS: Simon's Cane Rat is one of the earliest members of the group, discovered in early Oligocene deposits in Egypt.

EOCARDIIDAE

An extinct family named for their heart-shaped prisms on their teeth, the group may be ancestral to Caviidae.

EOCARDIA EXCAVATE

NAME MEANING: Hollowed-out dawn heart

AGE: Early Miocene (17.5–16.3 MYA)

DISTRIBUTION: South America

SIZE: 1 foot (30 centimeters) HBL

DIET: Herbivore

ESSENTIAL FACTS: Eocardia had long, slender legs adapted for sudden bursts of speed and agility. It was about the size of modern agoutis (*Dasyprocta*) and likely filled a similar niche.

CAVIIDAE

The most anatomically diverse group of living cavimorph rodents with nineteen modern species that includes guinea pigs and capybaras. Members of the family share certain features of their jaw structure and chewing muscles. They also have distinctive ever-growing cheek teeth composed of two or more lobes referred to as prisms.

GUIOMYS UNCIA

NAME MEANING: Maria Guiomar Vucetich's unique mouse

AGE: Middle Miocene (13–12 MYA)

DISTRIBUTION: South America

SIZE: 14–18 inches (35–45 centimeters) HBL; 2–3 pounds (1–1.5 kilograms)

DIET: Herbivore

ESSENTIAL FACTS: Guiomys is a basal member of Caviidae with the diagnostic cheek teeth of the family. They also possess a jaw structure intermediate between that of caviids and eocardiids.

NEOCHOERUS PINCKNEYI

NAME MEANING: Pinckney's new pig

AGE: Pleistocene

DISTRIBUTION: South America

SIZE: 200–250 pounds (90–113 kilograms)

DIET: Herbivore

ESSENTIAL FACTS: Pinckney's Capybara grew to be 40 to 50 percent heavier than the modern capybara (*Hydrochoerus hydrochaeris*) on average. Its fossils are known throughout the southern United States down through Central America and northern South America.

HYDROCHOERUS HESPEROTIGANITES

NAME MEANING: Western pancake water pig

AGE: Pleistocene (130,000–80,000 YA)

DISTRIBUTION: South America

SIZE: 77–160 pounds (35–73 kilograms)

DIET: Herbivore

ESSENTIAL FACTS: The Western Capybara is the only member of its genus known to have reached the United States, its fossils having been found in California. Its species name "western pancake" refers to the holotype skull which was badly crushed.

DASYPROCTIDAE

The dasyproctids include modern agoutis (*Dasyprocta*) and acouhis (*Myoprocta*). These rodents are highly cursorial with relatively long, slender legs for moving quickly through dense vegetation.

ANDEMYS TERMASI

NAME MEANING: Andes Mouse from Termas del Flaco

AGE: Early Oligocene (33–31 MYA)

DISTRIBUTION: South America

SIZE: 2.5–3.5 pounds (1.1–1.5 kilograms)

DIET: Herbivore; browser and frugivore

ESSENTIAL FACTS: Like modern members of its family, Andemys was probably a diurnal (active in the daytime) herbivore that fed on leaves, fruits, and nuts. They favored areas of dense bush cover in which to escape predators.

NEOREOMYS AUSTRALIS

NAME MEANING: Southern new mountain mouse

AGE: Early Miocene (18–16 MYA)

DISTRIBUTION: South America

SIZE: 6–11 pounds (3–5 kilograms)

DIET: Herbivore; grazer

ESSENTIAL FACTS: Neoreomys is well known, thanks to abundant skeletal material from the Santa Cruz and Pampa Castillo sites. Its exact family relationships are not fully understood, but most paleontologists tend to consider it a dasyproctid.

DINOMYIDAE

The sole modern representative of this family, the Pacarana (*Dinomys branickii*) is large by modern rodent standards weighing up to 33 pounds (15 kilograms). Fossil representatives of the family, however, include the largest rodents to have ever lived, some being as big as oxen.

TELICOMYS GIGANTEUS

NAME MEANING: Giant web mouse

AGE: Late Miocene (11.6–7.2 MYA)

DISTRIBUTION: South America

SIZE: 6.6 feet (2 meters) HBL; 440–1,100 pounds (200–500 kilograms)

DIET: Herbivore

ESSENTIAL FACTS: The Giant Telicomys is known to have lived in Brazil during the Late Miocene, inhabiting woodland and savanna habitats. It was the earliest of several species of large-sized South American rodents that competed directly with the notoungulates for the large herbivore niches.

JOSEPHOARTIGASIA MAGNA

NAME MEANING: Great José Artigas

AGE: Pliocene to Pleistocene

DISTRIBUTION: South America

SIZE: 560–1,270 pounds (254–576 kilograms)

DIET: Herbivore

ESSENTIAL FACTS: The larger of the two known species of *Josephoartigasia*, it lived in forest and woodland environments where it primarily browsed on leaves and fruits.

NEOEPIBLEMIDAE

This group of large-sized rodents lived in South America from Early Miocene and became extinct during the Pliocene about 3 million years ago.

NEOEPIBLEMA ACREENSIS

NAME MEANING: Unknown

AGE: Late Miocene (9–6.8 MYA)

DISTRIBUTION: South America

SIZE: 144–170 pounds (65.3–77.2 kilograms)

DIET: Herbivore

ESSENTIAL FACTS: A 2022 study looking at this postcranial anatomy suggests that neoepiblemids were built for powerful motions associated with bounding and swimming. This species seems to have inhabited wet environments.

PHOBEROMYS PATTERSONI

NAME MEANING: Patterson's fearful mouse

AGE: Late Miocene (9–6.8 MYA)

DISTRIBUTION: South America

SIZE: 6.6 feet (2 meters) HBL; 330–550 pounds (150–250 kilograms)

DIET: Herbivore

ESSENTIAL FACTS: Compared to other rodents such as *Telicomys* and *Josephoartigasia*, Patterson's Phoberomys may have been more of a grazer based on its more hypsodont teeth. It is thought to have inhabited wetland environments.

CHINCHILLIDAE

The family that includes the chinchillas and viscachas. There are seven modern species, all of which are gregarious animals known for excavating complex burrow systems and for their particularly dense fur. The group first appears during the Late Oligocene.

EOVISCACCIA FRASSINETTII

NAME MEANING: Daniel Frassinetti's dawn Viscaccia

AGE: Early Oligocene (33–31 MYA)

DISTRIBUTION: South America

SIZE: About hare-sized

DIET: Herbivore

ESSENTIAL FACTS: One of the oldest chinchillids known to have lived, it inhabited the grasslands of Argentina. It grazed in small groups that shared a communal network of burrows.

INCAMYS BOLIVIANUS

NAME MEANING: Bolivian Inca mouse

AGE: Late Oligocene (27–26 MYA)

DISTRIBUTION: South America

SIZE: Unknown

DIET: Herbivore

ESSENTIAL FACTS: The genus *Incamys* is named in honor of the Inca civilization, which inhabited the Andes Mountains. There are two described species.

PROLAGOSTOMUS AMPLUS

NAME MEANING: Abundant before *Lagostomus*

AGE: Late Miocene (9.5–9 MYA)

DISTRIBUTION: South America

SIZE: 14–18 inches (35–45 centimeters) HBL; 1–3 pounds (500–1,500 grams)

DIET: Herbivore

ESSENTIAL FACTS: The closest relative of this species is the Plains Viscachas (*Lagostomus maximus*). They lived in open environments where they mostly grazed on a variety of grasses and forbs.

ERETHIZONTIDAE

The fossil record for New World porcupines extends back to the Late Oligocene. They were similar to the Old World porcupines (Hystricidae) in having evolved long, sharp defensive quills. But it is believed those features evolved independently through convergent evolution. The family has nineteen modern species, most of them being arboreal forest-dwellers. They often have prehensile tails to aid in grasping branches and typically feed on soft plants.

EOPULULO WIGMOREI

NAME MEANING: John Wigmore's dawn porcupine

AGE: Late Eocene to Early Oligocene

DISTRIBUTION: South America

SIZE: Unknown

DIET: Herbivore

ESSENTIAL FACTS: The earliest-known New World porcupine, its name is derived from the indigenous Peruvian word for "porcupine."

STEIROMYS DUPLICATUS

NAME MEANING: Double keel mouse

AGE: Early Miocene (18–16 MYA)

DISTRIBUTION: South America

SIZE: 2–3 feet (60–90 centimeters) HBL; 22–35 pounds (10–16 kilograms)

DIET: Herbivore

ESSENTIAL FACTS: Double Steiromys is so named because it is twice the size of the closely related *S. dentatus*. Members of the genus differ from other New World porcupines in having larger chewing muscles, more robust incisors, and thicker enamel on its teeth suggesting a tendency to overall tougher and more abrasive foods and were probably more terrestrial.

ERETHIZON POYERI

NAME MEANING: Arthur Poyer's irritating animal

AGE: Late Pliocene to Early Pleistocene

DISTRIBUTION: North America

SIZE: 33 pounds (15 kilograms)

DIET: Herbivore

ESSENTIAL FACTS: Possibly ancestral to the modern North American Porcupine (*Erethizon dorsatum*), Poyer's Porcupine was smaller and more arboreal, possessing more dexterous feet and a long prehensile tail for gripping branches. Its fossils are known only from the Haile 7C site in Alachua County, Florida.

HEPTAXODONTIDAE

Despite not being closely related to hutias (Capromyinae), members of this family are commonly referred to as "giant hutias." Instead, these rodents are more closely related to chinchillas (Chinchillidae). Like their namesakes, they are endemic to the Caribbean islands. The ancestors of these rodents diverged from their ancestors on mainland South America during the Miocene and evolved into larger sizes.

AMBLYRHIZA INUNDATA

NAME MEANING: Flooded blunt root

AGE: Pleistocene

DISTRIBUTION: Anguilla, Saint Martin

SIZE: 110–440 pounds (50–200 kilograms)

DIET: Herbivore

ESSENTIAL FACTS: Blunt-toothed Giant Hutia is the largest-known species within Heptaxodontidae, being about the size of a pig. It rivaled some of the larger Caribbean sloths (Megalocnidae) in size.

CLIDOMYS OSBORNI

NAME MEANING: Osborn's key mouse

AGE: Pleistocene

DISTRIBUTION: Jamaica

SIZE: Unknown

DIET: Herbivore

ESSENTIAL FACTS: The least studied of the giant hutias, Osborn's Key Mouse fossils have been found in numerous cave deposits on the island of Jamaica.

ELASMODONTOMYS OBLIQUUS

NAME MEANING: Oblique plate-toothed mouse

AGE: Pleistocene to Holocene

DISTRIBUTION: Puerto Rico

SIZE: 29 pounds (13 kilograms)

DIET: Herbivore

ESSENTIAL FACTS: The Plate-toothed Giant Hutia was a terrestrial herbivore about the size of a North American Porcupine (*Erethizon dorsatum*). It survived well into the Holocene, coexisting with humans for about 2,000 years.

QUEMISIA GRAVIS

NAME MEANING: Unknown

AGE: Pleistocene to Holocene

DISTRIBUTION: Hispaniola

SIZE: About beaver-sized

DIET: Herbivore

ESSENTIAL FACTS: Twisted-toothed Mouse is named for the complex, maze-like ridges on its cheek teeth which in shares with other members of Heptaxodontidae. It is thought that it could have survived until the arrival of the Spanish.

MYOMORPHA

Myomorpha is the most specious of the rodent suborders with 1,524 modern species. This group includes rats, mice, gerbils, hamsters, lemmings, and voles and are distributed on all continents except Antarctica. Members of this group are overall very diminutive in size, with only a few extinct island species growing over 10 pounds (4 kilograms). The oldest known fossils of these animals are known from the Middle Eocene. They can be distinguished from other rodents in having lost their fourth premolars, giving them a dental formula of I1/1, C 0/0, P0/0, M3/3.

PLATACANTHOMYIDAE

These creates are known commonly as "oriental dormice" due to their superficial and behavioral resemblance to true dormice of the family Gliridae. The earliest fossils of these animals date back to the Early Miocene, but the family is believed to have diverged much earlier.

PLATACANTHOMYS DIANENSIS

NAME MEANING: Flat-spined mouse

AGE: Late Miocene (9 MYA)

DISTRIBUTION: Eurasia

SIZE: About rat-sized

DIET: Herbivore

ESSENTIAL FACTS: Discovered in Late Miocene deposits of China, this species is likely to have been similar in appearance and behavior to its living relative the Malabar spiny dormouse (*Platacanthomys lasiurus*), being an arboreal, nocturnal animal that fed mostly on fruits.

SPALACIDAE

Spalacids are fossorial rodents that evolved convergent adaptations with pocket gophers (Geomyidae), mole-rats (Bathyergidae), and palaeocastorine beavers (Castoridae). They are native to much of Eurasia and parts of Africa. Along with the oriental dormice (Platacanthomyidae), they are thought to be one of the oldest myomorph families to diverge.

TACHYORYCTES PLIOCAENICUS

NAME MEANING: Fast digger from the Pliocene

AGE: Pliocene

DISTRIBUTION: Africa

SIZE: About gopher-sized

DIET: Herbivore

ESSENTIAL FACTS: This species was discovered in the Hadar Formation of Ethiopia. Like modern members of the genus, it had fully functional eyes and external ears. It would spend most of the day in relatively simple burrows but emerge nightly to forage for food.

CRICETIDAE

With 608 modern species, the Cricetidae is one of the largest mammalian families, second only to the Muridae. It includes the hamsters, voles, lemmings, muskrats, and New World rats and mice. The earliest cricetids occur in the Early Oligocene and quickly became adapted to a wide range of habitats. They now occur in Eurasia and the Americas.

MELISSIODON SCHLOSSERI

NAME MEANING: Schlosser's honeycomb tooth

AGE: Early Miocene (23 MYA)

DISTRIBUTION: Eurasia

SIZE: About mouse-sized

DIET: Herbivore

ESSENTIAL FACTS: The genus *Melissodon* were distinctive hamsters that lived from the Early Oligocene to Early Miocene. They were arboreal or scansorial and fed on soft-bodied invertebrates and softer plant materials.

EUMYS ELEGANS

NAME MEANING: Elegant true mouse

AGE: Middle Oligocene (30 MYA)

DISTRIBUTION: North America

SIZE: About rat-sized

DIET: Herbivore

ESSENTIAL FACTS: This species was one of the most common rodents in North America during its time. Based on the morphology of its teeth, it is likely to have fed on relatively tough plants.

MURIDAE

With at least 1,383 modern species, Muridae is the largest mammalian family. The group includes rats, mice, and gerbils among others. Members occur naturally in Eurasia, Africa, and Australia, and in recent times they have been introduced by humans to the Americas. The fossil record of this group is not well-known, but the earliest representatives are Early Miocene in age.

KRITIMYS CATREUS

NAME MEANING: Cretan mouse of Catreus

AGE: Pleistocene

DISTRIBUTION: Crete

SIZE: 1.14 pounds (518 grams)

DIET: Herbivore

ESSENTIAL FACTS: Of the three species of *Kritimys* that evolved on the island of Crete in the Mediterranean, this species was the largest. Its closest modern relatives are thought to be soft-furred mice (*Praomys*).

MALPAISOMYS INSULARIS

NAME MEANING: Island badlands mouse

AGE: Pleistocene to Holocene

DISTRIBUTION: Canary Islands

SIZE: About rat-sized

DIET: Herbivore

ESSENTIAL FACTS: True to its name, the Lava Mouse made its home in the cracks and crevices in lava fields. It only became extinct after the arrival of Europeans in 1270, possibly from pressure from introduced rats.

CORYPHOMYS MUSSERI

NAME MEANING: Musser's summit mouse

AGE: Pleistocene to Holocene

DISTRIBUTION: Timor Island

SIZE: 13 pounds (6 kilograms)

DIET: Herbivore

ESSENTIAL FACTS: The Timor Giant Rat became extinct between 2,000 and 1,000 years ago for unknown reasons. They coexisted with humans for about 46,000 years and were probably hunted by them.

MIKROTIA MAGNA

NAME MEANING: Great sall ear

AGE: Late Miocene (12–6 MYA)

DISTRIBUTION: Gargano

SIZE: About beaver-sized

DIET: Herbivore

ESSENTIAL FACTS: The Great Mikrotia was the last and largest of three species of *Mikrotia* which evolved on Gargano Island, today part of the east coast of Italy. Their teeth were hypsodont for feeding on particularly tough or abrasive foods.

SPELAEOMYS FLORENSIS

NAME MEANING: Cave mouse of Flores

AGE: Pleistocene to Holocene

DISTRIBUTION: Flores

SIZE: 1.3–3.5 pounds (0.6–1.6 kilograms)

DIET: Herbivore

ESSENTIAL FACTS: The Flores Giant Rat is thought to have been an arboreal browser. It may have been hunted by the Flores Man (*Homo floresiensis*).

DIPODIDAE

Jerboas are bipedal desert-dwellers that exhibit extreme elongation of the hindlimbs and shortening of the forelimbs to a greater extent to springhares (Pedetidae) and kangaroo-rats (Dipodomyinae). They frequently move by saltation but are also capable of skipping and bipedal running. The oldest fossils date to the Middle Miocene.

ALLACTAGA FRU

NAME MEANING: Long-eared jerboa from Frunzovka

AGE: Late Miocene (9–8 MYA)

DISTRIBUTION: Eurasia

SIZE: About rabbit-sized

DIET: Herbivore

ESSENTIAL FACTS: The oldest-known of the five-toed jerboas, the presence of this species in Ukraine suggests that the region was much more arid than it is today during the Late Miocene. Like modern jerboas, it was primarily nocturnal and herbivorous.

SCANDENTIA

The treeshrews are an ancient family with the oldest-known fossils dating to the Middle Eocene. It is represented by two modern families, with twenty-two species restricted to southeastern Asia. Overall, these animals are small, arboreal hypocarnivores that vaguely resemble shrews or opossums. Members of the group have remained remarkably similar throughout their evolutionary history, with modern species being virtually identical to their ancient ancestors. They are very similar in form and function to the earliest primates such as *Purgatorius*.

EODENDROGALE PARVA

NAME MEANING: Little dawn tree polecat

AGE: Middle Eocene (47–45 MYA)

DISTRIBUTION: Eurasia

SIZE: About squirrel-sized

DIET: Mesocarnivore

ESSENTIAL FACTS: Although some researchers question its placement among Scandentia, this species is widely accepted to be the oldest-known species of treeshrew. Its fossils are known from Henan, China.

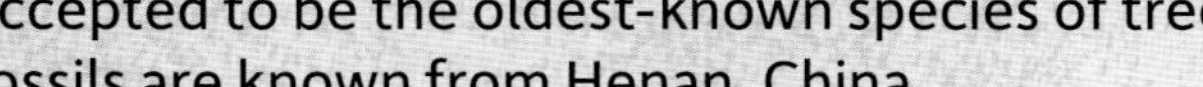

TUPAIA MIOCENICA

NAME MEANING: Squirrel from the Miocene

AGE: Early Miocene (18 MYA)

DISTRIBUTION: Eurasia

SIZE: About squirrel-sized

DIET: Mesocarnivore

ESSENTIAL FACTS: This species is known only from a few isolated teeth discovered in Thailand, which are nearly identical to those of modern examples of the genus. It was diurnal and arboreal, feeding on insects, small vertebrates, fruits, and seeds.

DERMOPTERA

Colugos are arboreal gliding mammals that share a common ancestry with treeshrews and primates, likely descending from an animal that resembled *Purgatorius*. Their fossil record dates back to the Paleocene. The incisor teeth take on a comb-like shape like that of strepsirrhine primates, adapted for grooming. There are two modern species restricted to southeast Asia.

PLANETETHERIUM MIRABILE

NAME MEANING: Wonderful wandering beast

AGE: Late Paleocene (56–55 MYA)

DISTRIBUTION: North America

SIZE: 10 inches (25 centimeters)

DIET: Herbivore

ESSENTIAL FACTS: The Wonderful Colugo is the oldest-known member of Dermoptera, already showing many distinguishing characteristics such as the toothcomb. Its body proportions suggest that it had the ability to glide like its modern relatives.

DERMOTHERIUM MAJOR

NAME MEANING: Greater skin beast

AGE: Late Eocene (37–35 MYA)

DISTRIBUTION: Eurasia

SIZE: About squirrel-sized

DIET: Herbivore

ESSENTIAL FACTS: Like its modern relatives, this species was arboreal and nocturnal, feeding on a variety of plants such as such as leaves, flowers, buds, and fruit.

PRIMATES

The name *primate* is derived from the Latin word *primus*, which means "prime" or "first." Primates are distinguished by several features, including a postorbital bar in the skull which completely surrounds the eyeballs with bone; in most mammals the back of the eye sockets are open, with a band of cartilage separating the eyes from the jaw musculature. Early primates became reliant on manual (hand) dexterity and tactile sensation when handling food, and thus evolved fingernails instead of claws; this increases the sensitivity at the ends of the digits at the cost of protection. Primates also have forward-facing eyes to increases depth perception when reaching for objects directly in front of them. Throughout their evolutionary history, primates appear to have been tied to the tropical and subtropical conditions, mostly avoiding areas which experience extreme cold winters, apart for a few exceptions which evolved adaptations to tolerate such conditions.

PLESIADAPIFORMES

Plesiadapiforms are an early offshoot of the primate lineage, having diverged from a common ancestor early in the Paleocene. They are considered by some researchers not to be true primates for lacking certain features that unite modern primate groups; they lack opposable thumbs, most have claws on the ends of their digits instead of fingernails, and the postorbital bar is absent. Many have rodent-like incisors adapted for gnawing, although they were not continuously growing. These teeth may have been an adaptation to access and feed on the fluids found within trees. Only members of the family Purgatoriidae lack this adaptation. They appear to have been quite diverse during their time with numerous families being attributed including Purgatoriidae, Carpolestidae, Paromomyidae, and Plesiadapidae. Plesiadapiforms coexisted with early strepsirrhine primates for a time, but eventually became extinct during the Middle Eocene.

PURGATORIUS UNIO

NAME MEANING: Pearl of Purgatory Hills

AGE: Early Paleocene (66–63 MYA)

DISTRIBUTION: North America

SIZE: 4 inches (10 centimeters) HBL; 4 inches (10 centimeters) TL; 1.3 ounces (37 grams)

DIET: Hypocarnivore

ESSENTIAL FACTS: Members of the genus *Purgatorius* are the oldest primates known to date, having appeared right after the K/Pg mass extinction. In life, they likely resembled modern tree shrews (Scandentia) and shared a similar ecology.

CARPOLESTES SIMPSONI

NAME MEANING: Simpson's fruit thief

AGE: Late Paleocene (58.7–56.8 MYA)

DISTRIBUTION: North America

SIZE: 3.5 ounces (100 grams)

DIET: Hypocarnivore

ESSENTIAL FACTS: This arboreal animal had evolved nails on its hindfeet and plagiaulacoid dentition similar to that seen in some herbivorous metatherians like possums (Phalangeriformes). The diet of Simpson's Carpolestes included fruits, seeds, and insects.

CHIROMYOIDES CAMPANICUS

NAME MEANING: Chiromys-like from Campania

AGE: Late Paleocene (56 MYA)

DISTRIBUTION: North America

SIZE: 10.6 ounces (300 grams)

DIET: Hypocarnivore

ESSENTIAL FACTS: This species was similar overall to *Plesiadapis* but much smaller and with deeper jaws similar to those of the animal which inspired its name, the aye-aye (*Daubentonia madagascariensis*). The aye-aye's original genus name was *Chiromys*.

SAXONELLA NAYLORI

NAME MEANING: Bruce Naylor's (animal) from Saxony

AGE: Late Paleocene (58.7–56.8 MYA)

DISTRIBUTION: North America

SIZE: Unknown

DIET: Herbivore; browser

ESSENTIAL FACTS: Members of *Saxonella* are first known from Germany and have since also been found in North America. The lower incisors of Naylor's Saxonella show wear patterns like those of the "toothcombs" found in modern strepsirrhines, suggesting that these teeth were used for grooming.

IGNACIUS GRAYBULLIANUS

NAME MEANING: Fire from the Graybullian

AGE: Early Eocene (55–50 MYA)

DISTRIBUTION: North America

SIZE: Unknown

DIET: Hypocarnivore

ESSENTIAL FACTS: The skeletal morphology of this species shows that they were particularly agile and skillful climbers, able to move from branch to branch with great bounding leaps.

PLESIADAPIS TRICUSPIDENS

NAME MEANING: Near Adapis with three-cusped teeth

AGE: Late Paleocene (58–55 MYA)

DISTRIBUTION: North America

SIZE: 11 pounds (5 kilograms)

DIET: Hypocarnivore

ESSENTIAL FACTS: This animal is the type species of the group Plesiadapiformes, with the typical rodent-like skull with chisel-like incisors. They appear to have been scansorial animals that underwent most of their activities on the ground but could readily climb trees.

STREPSIRRHINI

Strepsirrhines are true primates defined as possessing a moist rhinarium, leading to their being commonly known as the "wet-nosed primates." They also possess a specialized toothcomb and grooming claw for grooming purposes. The group first appear during the Early Eocene and were distributed throughout North America, Eurasia, and Africa.

ADAPIDAE

Adapids are a group of primates known exclusively from the Eocene in the Northern Hemisphere. Despite being arboreal, they were relatively slow climbers comparable to modern lorises (Lorisidae). Their hindlimbs are relatively short with highly mobile ankle joints enabling them to hang by their feet.

DARWINIUS MASILLAE

NAME MEANING: Charles Darwin from Messel

AGE: Middle Eocene (47 MYA)

DISTRIBUTION: Eurasia

SIZE: 9.4 inches (24 centimeters) HBL; 13.6 inches (34 centimeters) TL; 1.3–1.4 pounds (622–642 grams)

DIET: Herbivore

ESSENTIAL FACTS: This species is known from complete specimens from Messel Pit in Germany, which preserve soft tissue impressions such as the fur outline over the whole body. Preserved gut contents show that they fed on leaves, fruits, and seeds.

GODINOTIA NEGLECTA

NAME MEANING: Marc Godinot's neglected primate

AGE: Middle Eocene (49–47 MYA)

DISTRIBUTION: Eurasia

SIZE: 1 foot (30 centimeters) HBL

DIET: Hypocarnivore

ESSENTIAL FACTS: Godinotia is named after primate researcher Marc Godinot. Its fossils have been found in the Messel Pit, Germany.

AFRADAPIS LONGICRISTATUS

NAME MEANING: Long-crested African Adapis

AGE: Late Eocene (36–34 MYA)

DISTRIBUTION: Africa

SIZE: 4.5–7.2 pounds (2.1–3.3 kilograms)

DIET: Herbivore; browser

ESSENTIAL FACTS: Long-crested Adapis was an arboreal animal, but also a slow climber similar to modern lorises. Its zygodont teeth show that it had a folivorous diet of tough leaves.

EUROPOLEMUR KLATTI

NAME MEANING: Klatt's European lemur

AGE: Middle Eocene (49–47 MYA)

DISTRIBUTION: Eurasia

SIZE: 3.7 pounds (1.7 kilograms)

DIET: Herbivore

ESSENTIAL FACTS: This species is notable for its proportionally large hands, which among other features are indicative of an arboreal lifestyle. It is known for a complete skeleton found at Messel Pit.

LEPTADAPIS MAGNUS

NAME MEANING: Great slender Adapis

AGE: Late Eocene (37–34 MYA)

DISTRIBUTION: Eurasia

SIZE: 18.5–20 pounds (8.4–9 kilograms)

DIET: Herbivore; browser

ESSENTIAL FACTS: The Great Adapis is the largest member of its genus, with relatively small eyes. Its diet consisted mostly of leaves with the inclusion of some fruits. It had particularly expanded jaw muscles with tall sagittal and lambdoid crests.

ADAPIS PARISIENSIS

NAME MEANING: Without carpet from Paris

AGE: Late Eocene (40–37 MYA)

DISTRIBUTION: Eurasia

SIZE: 5 pounds (2 kilograms)

DIET: Herbivore; browser

ESSENTIAL FACTS: This species is among the best-known of the Eocene primates, known from several skulls and skeletal elements recovered from fissure infillings of Quercy in France.

NOTHARCTIDAE

Notharctids were ecologically and morphologically analogous to modern lemurs within the family Lemuridae. Like lemurs and other modern strepsirrhines but unlike adapids, they possess a grooming claw on the second digit of the hindfoot. Where adapids were slow climbers, notharctids are adapted for quicker and more nimble movements. Their long hindlimbs and flexible spines enabled great leaping capabilities.

CANTIUS FRUGIVORUS

NAME MEANING: Fruit-eater from Cantium

AGE: Early Eocene (55–50 MYA)

DISTRIBUTION: North America

SIZE: 6.2 pounds (2.8 kilograms)

DIET: Herbivore

ESSENTIAL FACTS: Based on the dental morphology of this species, it is believed to have had a primarily frugivorous diet. In life, it would have looked and moved very much like a modern-day lemur.

NOTHARCTUS TENEBROSUS

NAME MEANING: Dark false bear

AGE: Early Eocene (54–50 MYA)

DISTRIBUTION: North America

SIZE: 1.4 feet (40 centimeters) HBL; 9.2 pounds (4.2 kilograms)

DIET: Herbivore; browser

ESSENTIAL FACTS: This species is one of the most well-known members of the family, thanks to the discovery of complete skeletal material. Like other notharctids, they were acrobatic climbers built for leaping. They fed mostly on leaves.

SMILODECTES GRACILIS

NAME MEANING: Slender knife biter

AGE: Early Eocene (55 MYA)

DISTRIBUTION: North America

SIZE: 4.6 pounds (2.1 kilograms)

DIET: Herbivore

ESSENTIAL FACTS: Compared to other notharctids, *Smilodectes* had particularly short and rounded heads, with large eyes and reduced olfactory lobes showing that they were more visually oriented and less reliant on smell.

PELYCODUS JARROVII

NAME MEANING: Jarrovi's bowl tooth

AGE: Early Eocene (55–50 MYA)

DISTRIBUTION: North America

SIZE: 10 pounds (4.5 kilograms)

DIET: Herbivore

ESSENTIAL FACTS: Closely related to the genus *Cantius*, these animals were also arboreal and primarily frugivorous. It likely had a more inclusive diet that included softer leaves, seeds, and invertebrates.

HESPEROLEMUR ACTIUS

NAME MEANING: Western lemur from Actium

AGE: Middle Eocene (49–47 MYA)

DISTRIBUTION: North America

SIZE: 10 pounds (4.5 kilograms)

DIET: Herbivore

ESSENTIAL FACTS: This is another species closely related to the more well-known *Cantius*, distinguished by differences in the auditory bullae. The region in which it was discovered is thought to have been a forest refugia during a time when much of North America was giving way to open grassland.

MARCGODINOTIUS INDICUS

NAME MEANING: Marc Godinot from India

AGE: Early Eocene (52 MYA)

DISTRIBUTION: Eurasia

SIZE: 2.6 ounces (75 grams)

DIET: Herbivore

ESSENTIAL FACTS: This species is a member of the subfamily Asiadapinae, which are notable for their extreme small size, being comparable in size to modern mouse lemurs (*Microcebus*).

PRONYCTICEBUS NEGLECTUS

NAME MEANING: Neglected before *Nycticebus*

AGE: Late Eocene (40 MYA)

DISTRIBUTION: Eurasia

SIZE: 1.8 pounds (825 grams)

DIET: Herbivore

ESSENTIAL FACTS: Part of the subfamily Cercamoniinae, this species has relatively sharp-cusped teeth, suggesting a diet of insects and possibly fruits. Relatively large eye sockets are indicative of possible crepuscular or nocturnal habits.

SIVALADAPIDAE

Organisms in this group likely descended from notharctids in the Late Eocene and survived until the Late Miocene, mostly known from southern Asia. They are mostly known from jaws and isolated teeth, which resemble those of modern lemurs. They have molariform fourth premolars.

RAMADAPIS SAHNII

NAME MEANING: Ashok Sahni's *Adapis* from Ramnagar

AGE: Middle Miocene (14–11 MYA)

DISTRIBUTION: Eurasia

SIZE: 11 pounds (5 kilograms)

DIET: Herbivore

ESSENTIAL FACTS: This species is known from a single lower jaw that was notably similar to that of the modern ring-tailed lemur (*Lemur catta*).

SIAMOADAPIS MAEMOHENSIS

NAME MEANING: Siamese *Adapis* from Mae Moh

AGE: Middle Miocene (13 MYA)

DISTRIBUTION: Eurasia

SIZE: 6 inches (15 centimeters) HBL

DIET: Herbivore

ESSENTIAL FACTS: Four lower jaws of this animal were discovered in Mae Moh coal mine in Thailand in 2004. It was among the smallest of the sivaladapids.

SIVALADAPIS PALAEINDICUS

NAME MEANING: Ancient Indian *Adapis* from Siwalik

AGE: Middle Miocene (13.7–11.1 MYA)

DISTRIBUTION: Eurasia

SIZE: 5.7–7.5 pounds (2.6–3.4 kilograms)

DIET: Herbivore

ESSENTIAL FACTS: This animal is known to have had a highly folivorous diet, thanks to its specialized teeth adapted for shredding fibrous leaves. Its extinction may have been due to competition from incoming colobine monkeys during the Late Miocene.

EKGMOWECHASHALIDAE

The group originated in Asia and dispersed to North America in the Oligocene after other primates on the continent seem to have gone extinct.

EKGMOWECHASHALA ZANCANELLAI

NAME MEANING: Zancanella's little cat man

AGE: Late Oligocene (26 MYA)

DISTRIBUTION: North America

SIZE: 5 pounds (2.3 kilograms)

DIET: Hypocarnivore

ESSENTIAL FACTS: This species is the second youngest known species of nonhuman primate to have lived in continental North America. Its teeth, which resemble those of a raccoon (Procyonidae), suggest that it had a diet that consisted of soft fruits and perhaps invertebrates.

LEMUROIDEA

The lemurs are a surviving lineage of strepsirrhine primates that are thought to have originated in the Early Eocene on mainland Africa. These animals have since become extinct on the continent, but continued to survive on the island of Madagascar. There are 100 modern species all weighing less than 25 pounds (11.3 kilograms). But when humans arrived in Madagascar 2,000 years ago lemurs were much more diverse, with some species growing as large as the largest apes in Africa and Asia today.

ARCHAEOLEMURIDAE

Monkey lemurs, sometimes called baboon lemurs, are compared to the Old World monkeys due to convergences in morphological and locomotory features. Compared to modern lemurs, the limbs are relatively shorter, and the hands and feet are smaller, enabling more efficient terrestrial locomotion. They also had relatively large brains compared to the other extinct lemurs.

HADROPITHECUS STENOGNATHUS

NAME MEANING: Narrow-jawed heavy ape

AGE: Pleistocene to Holocene

DISTRIBUTION: Madagascar

SIZE: 60–77 pounds (27–35 kilograms)

DIET: Herbivore

ESSENTIAL FACTS: The Narrow-jawed Monkey Lemur had shortened face, robust jaws, and expanded molars adapted for chewing particularly tough foods. It lived in relatively open habitats.

ARCHAEOLEMUR EDWARDSI

NAME MEANING: Edward's ancient lemur

AGE: Pleistocene to Holocene

DISTRIBUTION: Madagascar

SIZE: 40–58 pounds (18.2–26.5 kilograms)

DIET: Hypocarnivore

ESSENTIAL FACTS: Edward's Monkey Lemur spent most of its time on the ground foraging for fruits, seeds, and small animals while readily taking to the trees when threatened by predators or to sleep.

DAUBENTONIIDAE

The Aye-Ayes are uniquely adapted lemurs that fulfill the ecological roles that woodpeckers occupy elsewhere in the world. In this regard, they are comparable to extinct mammals such as the metatherian Yalkaparidontids and the distantly related Apatemyids.

DAUBENTONIA ROBUSTA

NAME MEANING: Robust Daubenton

AGE: Pleistocene to Holocene

DISTRIBUTION: Madagascar

SIZE: 8–13.2 pounds (4–6 kilograms)

DIET: Mesocarnivore

ESSENTIAL FACTS: Giant Aye-Ayes were similar morphologically to the modern aye-aye (*D. madagascarensis*), but 2 to 2.5 times larger. Its diet would have consisted mostly of wood-boring insects, which it fished out of holes using elongated, thin fingers.

LEMURIDAE

The Lemuridae contains possibly the most iconic of the modern lemur species. These animals tend to be small and somewhat monkey-like in their postcranial anatomy, being built for great agility in the trees. They mainly feed on fruits, leaves, and nectar in varying proportions.

PACHYLEMUR INSIGNIS

NAME MEANING: Remarkable thick lemur

AGE: Pleistocene to Holocene

DISTRIBUTION: Madagascar

SIZE: 22 pounds (10 kilograms)

DIET: Herbivore; frugivore

ESSENTIAL FACTS: The two species of the genus *Pachylemur* were larger and more robust than modern ruffed lemurs (*Varecia*), and like them, they were fruit-specialists. They favored larger, harder, more fibrous fruits than those selected by their modern relatives.

MEGALADAPIDAE

For a time, the family Megaladapidae included the modern sporting lemurs (*Lepilemur*). These were small, arboreal, and nocturnal lemurs with folivorous diets. This relationship has now been dropped, and sporting lemurs are now placed within their own family, Lepilemuridae. Megaladapidae consists of three extinct species of the extinct genus *Megaladapis*, commonly referred to as "koala lemurs" for their highly specialized skeletons and folivorous diets.

MEGALADAPIS EDWARDSI

NAME MEANING: Edward's big Adapis

AGE: Pleistocene to Holocene

DISTRIBUTION: Madagascar

SIZE: 103–310 pounds (46.5–140 kilograms)

DIET: Herbivore; browser

SEE MORE ON PAGES 322–323

PALAEOPROPITHECIDAE

Sloth lemurs are so named for their arboreal suspensory locomotion (moving through trees), which would have been combined with modified brachiation or arm-swinging as exhibited by apes. The forelimbs are generally longer and more robust than the hindlimbs, and the proximal phalanges are highly curved, a weight-bearing adaptation that indicates that they actively hung from their hands.

ARCHAEOINDRIS FONTOYNONTII

NAME MEANING: Antoine Maurice Fontoynont's ancient Indri

AGE: Pleistocene to Holocene

DISTRIBUTION: Madagascar

SIZE: 331–538 pounds (150–244.1 kilograms)

DIET: Herbivore; browser

ESSENTIAL FACTS: Giant Sloth Lemur is the largest primate known to have evolved on Madagascar, comparable in size to a male gorilla. It inhabited mixed woodlands, bushlands, and savanna habitats where it fed mostly on leaves.

BABAKOTIA RADOFILAI

NAME MEANING: Jean Radofilao's Babakoto

AGE: Pleistocene to Holocene

DISTRIBUTION: Madagascar

SIZE: 35–45 pounds (16–20 kilograms)

DIET: Herbivore

ESSENTIAL FACTS: The genus name is derived from Babakoto, an alternate native Malagasy (the language of Madigascar) name for the Indri (*Indri indri*). Its fossils have only been found in limestone caves within the Ankarana Reserve in northern Madagascar which were mapped by French mathematician Jean Radofilao.

MESOPROPITHECUS GLOBICEPS

NAME MEANING: Round-headed middle ape

AGE: Pleistocene to Holocene

DISTRIBUTION: Madagascar

SIZE: 24 pounds (11 kilograms)

DIET: Herbivore; browser

ESSENTIAL FACTS: Like other members of its genus, the Round-Headed Sloth Lemur moved through the trees using suspensory locomotion. Its diet consisted mainly of leaves, fruits, and seeds.

MEGALADAPIS EDWARDSI

ESSENTIAL FACTS: Like other members of the genus, the skeletal morphology of Edward's Koala Lemur is highly specialized to a fully arboreal lifestyle much like that of a koala (*Phascolarctos cinereus*), albeit one about the size of a small male gorilla. Its arms were long and highly mobile with elongated fingers and toes for grasping. Its legs were splayed for grabbing wide tree trunks. These features made the animal a highly efficient climber that undoubtedly spent much of its life among the branches. However, these same proportions made it very slow and awkward on the ground and vulnerable to predators. They likely would only descend when they needed to drink or move to a different grove of trees.

The skull of Edward's Koala Lemur was rather odd by primate standards, having more in common with those of early perissodactyls or oreodonts. The snout was long, narrow, and deep with nasals that protruded past the premaxillae and curved downward, possibly indicating the presence of a semi-prehensile upper lip for browsing. The eyes were set more to the sides of head, giving it a wide field of vision but limiting depth perception. The upper canines are notably long and robust. Interestingly, the brain is relatively small compared to other lemurs, potentially indicating a rapid evolution from a smaller ancestor.

SEE ENTRY ON PAGE 320

PALAEOPROPITHECUS INGENS

NAME MEANING: Great ancient early ape

AGE: Pleistocene to Holocene

DISTRIBUTION: Madagascar

SIZE: 100–120 pounds (45–54 kilograms)

DIET: Herbivore; browser

ESSENTIAL FACTS: The Great Sloth Lemur was one of the larger sloth lemurs about the size of a chimpanzee (*Pan troglodytes*) and had a diet that consisted of leaves and fruits. Studies suggest that juveniles were weaned early and needed to forage for themselves with their first month.

LORISOIDEA

A group of nocturnal primates that are distributed throughout Africa and Asia, the earliest fossils of these animals come from Africa during the Eocene.

GALAGIDAE

Galagos are small, nocturnal primates that are endemic to Africa. Also known as "bush babies" or "nagapies," they are characterized by large eyes and ears adapted to hunting in the dark, and they have remarkable jumping abilities. They share a common ancestor with lorises (Lorisidae), and the two families likely diverged during the Middle Eocene. The earliest definitive galago fossils are Late Eocene in age.

SAHARAGALAGO MISRENSIS

NAME MEANING: Desert galago from Egypt

AGE: Late Eocene (40–37 MYA)

DISTRIBUTION: Africa

SIZE: 4.3 ounces (122 grams)

DIET: Mesocarnivore

ESSENTIAL FACTS: The Egyptian Galago is the oldest-known species of galago discovered from Fayum, Egypt. Today this region is covered by desert, hence the scientific name. During the Late Eocene, the region was much wetter and covered in woodland.

LAETOLIA SADIMANENSIS

NAME MEANING: From the Sadiman Volcano at Laetoli

AGE: Pliocene (4 to 3 MYA)

DISTRIBUTION: Africa

SIZE: Unknown

DIET: Mesocarnivore

ESSENTIAL FACTS: Originally considered part of the modern genus *Galago*, Laetoli Galago was found to be distinct enough to be given its own genus. It is the best-known galago from the Pliocene, although it is known only from teeth and jaws.

HAPLORRHINI

The name *haplorrhine* means "simple nose," in reference to the loss of the rhinarium. This absence means that the lower lip is no longer directly connected to the nose or gums, enabling a wider range of facial expressions in these animals which are often highly social. The group is sometimes also referred to as the "dry-nosed primates." Unlike strepsirrhines, haplorrhines have all lost the function of the terminal enzyme that manufactures vitamin C within their bodies and must obtain this nutrient from their diets. They have also lost the tapetum lucidum, a layer of reflective cells within the eyes that increase light intake, likely a result of evolving from ancestors that had become strictly diurnal and relied heavily on color vision. To compensate for the loss of the tapetum lucidum, secondarily nocturnal haplorrhines often have extremely large eyes to increase the size of the corneas and the number of rod cells to see in low light levels.

OMOMYIDAE

Omomyids are the earliest-known haplorrhines. They were all small-bodied animals that would have resembled modern tarsiers. They had notably large eyes, suggesting that they were primarily nocturnal, as well as a relatively globular brain case. The incisors are relatively large and procumbent with small canines. Rather than having the crested molars of adapids, the cheek teeth had sharp, pointed cusps suggesting highly insectivorous diets. The skeletal anatomy also suggests great leaping abilities.

TEILHARDINA MAGNOLIANA

NAME MEANING: Teilhard de Chardin of the Magnolia State

AGE: Late Paleocene (56 MYA)

DISTRIBUTION: North America

SIZE: 1 ounce (28 grams)

DIET: Hypocarnivore

ESSENTIAL FACTS: The oldest haplorrhine primate in North America, found in the state of Mississippi. This tiny animal was the size of Berthe's mouse lemur (*Microcebus berthae*), the smallest modern primate, and likely had a diet consisting of fruits, gums, and insects.

NECROLEMUR ANTIQUUS

NAME MEANING: Ancient death lemur

AGE: Middle Eocene (45 MYA)

DISTRIBUTION: North America

SIZE: 4–12 ounces (114–346 grams)

DIET: Hypocarnivore

ESSENTIAL FACTS: *Necrolemur* were small, lemur-like omomyids that were specially built for leaping. Based on their tooth morphology, their diet consisted of soft fruits, gums, and insects.

TARSIIDAE

Tarsiers are small, arboreal, nocturnal primates found in the forests of Asia with a fossil record dating back to the Eocene. They have huge eyes that are even larger than the brain in some species. Their fingers are especially long for grasping thin branches. The name "tarsier" comes from their uniquely elongated tarsal bones.

TARSIUS EOCAENUS

NAME MEANING: Eocene tarsier

AGE: Middle Eocene (45 MYA)

DISTRIBUTION: Eurasia

SIZE: Unknown

DIET: Hypocarnivore

ESSENTIAL FACTS: Although its placement within the genus *Tarsius* is uncertain, this is the oldest-known species of tarsier. It is known from five isolated teeth found in China.

PARAPITHECIDAE

Parapithecids lived from the Eocene through Oligocene of Africa, their fossils being mostly known from the Jebel Qatrani Formation of Egypt. Their skull and jaw morphology resembled that of tarsiers, and they are believed to have been ancestral to both Old World monkeys and New World monkeys.

APIDIUM PHIOMENSE

NAME MEANING: Little Apis from Fayoum

AGE: Middle Oligocene (30–28 MYA)

DISTRIBUTION: Africa

SIZE: Unknown

DIET: Frugivorous herbivore

ESSENTIAL FACTS: This species is the most well-represented parapithecid. It was an arboreal animal with a dentition indicative of a frugivorous diet. Its skeletal proportions point to it being an agile leaper.

BIRETIA FAYUMENSIS

NAME MEANING: From Bir el Ater and Fayoum

AGE: Late Eocene (37 MYA)

DISTRIBUTION: Africa

SIZE: 9.6 ounces (273 grams)

DIET: Mesocarnivore

ESSENTIAL FACTS: This species is the smaller of the two known species of the genus. What is known of the skull suggests that it had very large eyes in proportion to the rest of its head, a feature typical of nocturnal primates which lack a tapetum lucidum.

PARAPITHECUS GRANGERI

NAME MEANING: Granger's near ape

AGE: Late Eocene (40–34 MYA)

DISTRIBUTION: Africa

SIZE: Unknown

DIET: Herbivore

ESSENTIAL FACTS: Known from a nearly complete skull, this species is closely related to the contemporary Apidium but somewhat larger. Its relatively small eye sockets show that it was a diurnal animal.

CEBIDAE

The oldest families of New World monkeys, dating back to the Middle Oligocene. Their ancestors likely arrived in South America from Africa via a series of small islands that once existed between the two continents when the distance between them was much shorter. Cebids include the capuchin monkeys and the squirrel monkeys. They are typically arboreal and diurnal, with diets composed mainly of fruits and insects.

BRANISELLA BOLIVIANA

NAME MEANING: Leonardo Branisa from Bolivia

AGE: Late Oligocene (27–26 MYA)

DISTRIBUTION: South America

SIZE: 1.5 pounds (700–750 grams)

DIET: Hypocarnivore

ESSENTIAL FACTS: One of the oldest South American primates, the morphology of its teeth suggest that its diet likely centered around fruits with the possible inclusion of invertebrates and other small animals.

PANAMACEBUS TRANSITUS

NAME MEANING: Crossing long-tailed monkey from Panama

AGE: Early Miocene (21.1–20.76 MYA)

DISTRIBUTION: North America

SIZE: Unknown

DIET: Hypocarnivore

ESSENTIAL FACTS: This species has the distinction of being the last known nonhuman primate to have lived in North America, most likely entering the continent by island-hopping from South America. Its species name, the Latin word for “crossing,” is a direct reference to this intercontinental passage.

CEBINAE

The name "capuchin" monkey originated when Portuguese explorers in the fifteenth century observed the monkeys, and their brown fur color and rounded faces reminded them of the robes worn by the Order of Friars Minor Capuchin. These are the oldest New World monkeys known.

DOLICHOCEBUS GAIMANENSIS

NAME MEANING: Long Cebus from Gaiman

AGE: Early Miocene (21–17.5 MYA)

DISTRIBUTION: South America

SIZE: 5 pounds (2 kilograms)

DIET: Hypocarnivore

ESSENTIAL FACTS: This species is a possible link between more basal cebids and squirrel monkeys (*Saimiri*). The tooth morphology of this species suggests a close relationship with squirrel monkeys given their similarity.

KILLIKAIKE BLAKEI

NAME MEANING: Blake family's Killik Aike Norte site

AGE: Early Miocene (17.5–16.3 MYA)

DISTRIBUTION: South America

SIZE: Unknown

DIET: Hypocarnivore

ESSENTIAL FACTS: This species is known for the most well-preserved face of any extinct New World monkey. The back of the skull is absent in the specimen. The available material shows that Blake's Monkey had a relatively large brain.

ACRECEBUS FRAILEYI

NAME MEANING: Carl Frailey's Acre River monkey

AGE: Late Miocene (11.6–7.2 MYA)

DISTRIBUTION: South America

SIZE: 15 pounds (7 kilograms)

DIET: Herbivore

ESSENTIAL FACTS: Frailey's Monkey was about the size of modern woolly monkeys (*Lagothrix*). Its molars have weakly-developed crests, suggesting a diet that consisted primarily of fruit.

SAIMIRINAE

The squirrel monkeys are smaller than capuchins, the name Saimiri being derived from the Tupi words meaning "small monkey." The subfamily is first recorded during the middle Miocene, but all of the modern species appear to have arisen during the Pleistocene.

SAIMIRI ANNECTENS

NAME MEANING: Connecting small monkey

AGE: Middle Miocene (13.8–11.8 MYA)

DISTRIBUTION: South America

SIZE: 1.3–1.8 pounds (605–800 grams)

DIET: Hypocarnivore

ESSENTIAL FACTS: Formerly known as *Laventiana annectens*, the teeth of the Connecting Squirrel Monkey are very similar to those of the earlier Gaiman Monkey (*Dolichocebus gaimanensis*). The two demonstrate a gradual transition between capuchin monkeys and squirrel monkeys.

SAIMIRI FIELDSI

NAME MEANING: Fields' small monkey

AGE: Middle Miocene (13.8–11.8 MYA)

DISTRIBUTION: South America

SIZE: 1.6–1.8 pounds (768–840 grams)

DIET: Hypocarnivore

ESSENTIAL FACTS: Fields' Squirrel Monkey shows more derived *Saimiri* characteristics than its contemporary, the connecting squirrel monkey. Both species have been found in the "Monkey Beds" of the Honda Group, which is the richest site for fossil primates in South America.

CALLITRICHIDAE

The Callitrichidae is the family which includes the marmosets and tamarins, the smallest of the haplorrhine primates. They are arboreal and different species feed on varying proportions of insects, fruits, small vertebrates, and tree exudates. They are the only primates known to regularly produce twins, with males providing equal amounts of parental care. The group is known from South America during the Middle Miocene.

PATASOLA MAGDALENAE

NAME MEANING: Patasola from the Magdalena River

AGE: Middle Miocene (13.4–11.8 MYA)

DISTRIBUTION: South America

SIZE: 1 pound (480 grams)

DIET: Hypocarnivore

ESSENTIAL FACTS: The genus name for the Magdalena River Marmoset is the name of a forest spirit from Colombian folklore known as the Patasola. Its teeth were adapted to feed on insects and fruits.

MICODON KIOTENSIS

NAME MEANING: *Mico* tooth from Kiot

AGE: Middle Miocene (13.8–11.8 MYA)

DISTRIBUTION: South America

SIZE: 0.88 pounds (400 grams)

DIET: Hypocarnivore

ESSENTIAL FACTS: This early marmoset is one of many monkey species found at the Monkey Beds, which during the Middle Miocene was covered in seasonally dry forest.

AOTIDAE

Known as "night monkeys" or "owl monkeys" due to their large eyes and nocturnal habits, the family name is derived from the sole modern genus *Aotus*, which "means earless." This name refers to these monkeys' small ears that are difficult to see among their dense fur. All of them are small, weighing less than 3 pounds (1.4 kilograms). They are arboreal and mostly frugivorous, with eleven modern species.

AOTUS DINDENSIS

NAME MEANING: Earless (monkey) from the El Dinde site

AGE: Middle Miocene (13.8–11.8 MYA)

DISTRIBUTION: South America

SIZE: Unknown

DIET: Hypocarnivore

ESSENTIAL FACTS: Like its modern relatives, the El Dinde Night Monkey was a nocturnal forager that fed mostly on fruits, occasionally supplementing its diet with leaves and insects.

PITHECIIDAE

Pitheciids are a group of frugivorous monkeys characterized by their long, nonprehensile tails with thick, coarse fur covering much of their bodies. Their skulls and teeth are specialized for eating foods with thick, tough husks. Their stout, sharp-tipped, outwardly angled canines were helpful for splitting large fruits. The incisors are procumbent for scraping the flesh from fruits that are too large to fit in between the canines. Finally, the molars have low, broad cusps for breaking open hard seeds. All are arboreal and are powerful leapers. The family has a strong presence in the South American fossil record by the Middle Miocene. There are currently six genera with fifty-four species alive in modern times.

NUCIRUPTOR RUBRICAE

NAME MEANING: Nut breaker from the red beds

AGE: Middle Miocene (13.8–11.8 MYA)

DISTRIBUTION: South America

SIZE: 4.4 pounds (2 kilograms)

DIET: Hypocarnivore

ESSENTIAL FACTS: The genus name of the Nut-Breaker Monkey alludes to its diet, which would have included tough-shelled nuts and fruits. The species name references the El Cardón red beds of the Honda Group, in which it and many other monkey species were discovered.

CEBUPITHECIA SARMIENTOI

NAME MEANING: Sarmiento's long-tailed ape

AGE: Middle Miocene (13.8–11.8 MYA)

DISTRIBUTION: South America

SIZE: 3.5 pounds (1.6 kilograms)

DIET: Hypocarnivore

ESSENTIAL FACTS: The skeletal anatomy of Sarmiento's Monkey suggests that it may have moved somewhat differently than other New World monkeys. The tail was similar to that of other pitheciids in being nonprehensile but was more robust, possibly functioning as an anchor.

MIOCALLICEBUS VILLAVIEJAI

NAME MEANING: Miocene *Callicebus* from Villavieja

AGE: Middle Miocene (13.8–11.8 MYA)

DISTRIBUTION: South America

SIZE: 3.3 pounds (1.5 kilograms)

DIET: Herbivore

ESSENTIAL FACTS: This species is morphologically similar to but much larger than modern titis monkeys (*Callicebus*). Its diet would have consisted mostly of leaves with the occasional inclusion of various fruits.

ANTILLOTHRIX BERNENSIS

NAME MEANING: Antillian hair from Berne

AGE: Pleistocene to Holocene

DISTRIBUTION: Hispaniola

SIZE: Unknown

DIET: Hypocarnivore

ESSENTIAL FACTS: Hispaniola Monkey is thought to have gone extinct in the sixteenth century, likely due to disturbances caused by European colonizers after 1492.

INSULACEBUS TOUSSENTIANA

NAME MEANING: Toussaint Louverture's island monkey

AGE: Holocene

DISTRIBUTION: Hispaniola

SIZE: 9.1–12 pounds (4.1–5.4 kilograms)

DIET: Hypocarnivore

ESSENTIAL FACTS: The dental morphology of this and other Caribbean monkeys suggests that the ancestral population had been isolated for as long as 11 million years. Its species name honors Toussainte Louverture, a Haitian hero and a founding father of the nation.

XENOTHRIX MCGREGORI

NAME MEANING: McGregor's strange hair

AGE: Pleistocene to Holocene

DISTRIBUTION: Jamaica

SIZE: Unknown

DIET: Hypocarnivore

ESSENTIAL FACTS: DNA of the Jamaican Monkey has been analyzed and confirms a Middle Miocene split from South American monkeys. More specifically, xenotrichins appear to group among the titi monkeys (Callicebinae), with the genus *Cheracebus* being the closest modern relative.

ATELIDAE

The atelids are arboreal, mostly folivorous monkeys that includes the howler monkeys (*Alouatta*) and spider monkeys (*Ateles*). They are characterized by long, prehensile tails which have a hairless tactile pad on the underside of the distal end. The tail functions as a fifth limb when moving through the trees and are even able to hang by their tails for extended periods while feeding.

CHILECEBUS CARRASCOENSIS

NAME MEANING: Gabriel Carrasco's *Cebus* from Chile

AGE: Early Miocene (21–17.5 MYA)

DISTRIBUTION: South America

SIZE: 2.2 pounds (1 kilogram)

DIET: Herbivore

ESSENTIAL FACTS: CT scanning and 3D digital reconstruction of the inside of this monkey's skull show that it had a very complex brain. It was a diurnal animal with a reduced sense of smell but well-developed eyesight.

MOHANAMICO HERSHKOVITZI

NAME MEANING: Philip Hershkovitz's Mohan

AGE: Middle Miocene (13.8–11.8 MYA)

DISTRIBUTION: South America

SIZE: 2.2 pounds (1 kilogram)

DIET: Herbivore

ESSENTIAL FACTS: Hershkovitz's Monkey is named after Mohan, the god of the Magdalena River in Colombia. Its teeth are adapted to a primarily frugivorous diet.

STIRTONIA TATACOENSIS

NAME MEANING: Ruben Stirton from Tatacoa Desert

AGE: Middle Miocene (13 MYA)

DISTRIBUTION: South America

SIZE: 22 pounds (10 kilograms)

DIET: Herbivore

ESSENTIAL FACTS: The largest monkey to come from the Monkey Beds, it was morphologically very similar to modern howler monkeys (*Alouatta*) and had the same primarily folivorous diet.

SOLIMOEA ACRENSIS

NAME MEANING: From the Acre State in the Solimoes Formation

AGE: Late Miocene (11.6–7.2 MYA)

DISTRIBUTION: South America

SIZE: 12–18 pounds (5.4–8 kilograms)

DIET: Herbivore

ESSENTIAL FACTS: The oldest-known of the spider monkeys (Atelinae), the molar structure of this animal suggests that its diet consisted primarily of fruit.

CARTELLES COIMBRAFILHOI

NAME MEANING: Cástor Cartelle and Coimbra Filho

AGE: Pleistocene

DISTRIBUTION: South America

SIZE: 53 pounds (24 kilograms)

DIET: Herbivore

ESSENTIAL FACTS: This species is the largest known member of Atelidae. Because of its size, it is thought to have spent most of its life on the ground although it would have climbed trees regularly.

CAIPORA BAMBUIORUM

NAME MEANING: Grupo Bambui's forest inhabitant

AGE: Pleistocene

DISTRIBUTION: South America

SIZE: 45 pounds (20.5 kilograms)

DIET: Herbivore

ESSENTIAL FACTS: The genus name is derived from the *caipora*, a figure in Brazilian folklore. Despite its size it was an arboreal animal that would have very rarely descended to the forest floor.

PROTOPITHECUS BRASILIENSIS

NAME MEANING: First ape from Brazil

AGE: Pleistocene

DISTRIBUTION: South America

SIZE: 50 pounds (22.6 kilograms)

DIET: Herbivore

ESSENTIAL FACTS: Another large, arboreal monkey, this species was built very much like modern spider monkeys (*Ateles*), although its limb bones were twice as thick. The structure of its lower jaw shows that it had a vocal pouch that enabled it to howl in a similar fashion to howler monkeys (*Alouatta*).

PARALOUATTA VARONAI

NAME MEANING: Luis Varona's beside Alouatta

AGE: Pleistocene to Holocene

DISTRIBUTION: Cuba

SIZE: 19 pounds (8.4 kilograms)

DIET: Herbivore

ESSENTIAL FACTS: This ancestor of Varona's Monkey arrived in Cuba during the Early Miocene. Its skeleton shows that it was scansorial, able to move efficiently and feed mostly on the ground but able to readily climb trees likely to rest or escape predators.

OLIGOPITHECIDAE

The record for this family dates from the Late Eocene to the Early Oligocene. Due to their relatively simple molars and cusp arrangement, members of the group are thought to have been primarily insectivorous with the inclusion of some softer fruits.

OLIGOPITHECUS SAVAGEI

NAME MEANING: David Savage's small ape

AGE: Early Oligocene (34–30 MYA)

DISTRIBUTION: Africa

SIZE: 3.3 pounds (1.5 kilograms)

DIET: Hypocarnivore

ESSENTIAL FACTS: This species is known for a single lower jaw found in Egypt. It is similar in morphology to those of marmosets and tamarins (Callitrichidae), suggesting a similar diet consisting of insects and fruits.

CATOPITHECUS BROWNI

NAME MEANING: Mark Brown's below ape

AGE: Late Eocene (36–34 MYA)

DISTRIBUTION: Africa

SIZE: Unknown

DIET: Hypocarnivorous

ESSENTIAL FACTS: At the time in which this monkey lived, much of Egypt was covered in tropical coastal swamp. Its tooth morphology is indicative of a diet consisting of leaves and insects.

PLIOPITHECIDAE

Pliopithecids are an interesting group of monkeys that possess notably ape-like dental and skull morphology while retaining more archaic traits such as a relatively long snout.

ANAPITHECUS HERNYAKI

NAME MEANING: Gabor Hernyák's upward ape

AGE: Late Miocene (10 MYA)

DISTRIBUTION: Eurasia

SIZE: 33 pounds (15 kilograms)

DIET: Herbivore

ESSENTIAL FACTS: A gibbon-sized monkey whose fossils have been discovered in northern Hungary, its diet is known to have consisted of leaves and fruits.

EPIPLIOPITHECUS VINDOBONENSIS

NAME MEANING: Over Pliopithecus from Vindobona

AGE: Middle Miocene (15.5 MYA)

DISTRIBUTION: Eurasia

SIZE: About gibbon-sized

DIET: Herbivore

ESSENTIAL FACTS: This species is distinguished from other pliopithecids in differences in its dental morphology, and in certain aspects of its skull it is comparable to gibbons (*Hylobates*). Though now understood to be the result of convergent evolution, it was previously thought that this monkey was ancestral to gibbons by early researchers.

CERCOPITHECIDAE

Old World monkeys are a diverse collection of primates that includes twenty-four modern genera and 138 species. True to their common name, the family is restricted in distribution to Africa and Eurasia. Most likely originating in Africa, the group is known in the fossil record as far back as the Early Oligocene. Their potential divergence from their common ancestor with the New World monkeys is estimated to date back to between 45 and 55 million years ago. They differ from New World monkeys in having downward-facing nostrils, lack of prehensile tails, and a reduced number of premolars from three to two.

AEGYPTOPITHECUS ZEUXIS

NAME MEANING: Linking Egyptian ape

AGE: Early Oligocene (30.2–29.5 MYA)

DISTRIBUTION: Africa

SIZE: 13–18 pounds (6–8 kilograms)

DIET: Herbivore; frugivore

ESSENTIAL FACTS: This species is part of a group of early Old World monkeys that are sometimes placed within a separate family Propliopithicidae due to their notably basal characteristics. Nonetheless, they share many features in common with modern forms including their dental formula; I2/2, C1/1, P2/2, M3/3 = 32 teeth.

VICTORIAPITHECUS MACINNESI

NAME MEANING: MacInnes' Ape from Lake Victoria

AGE: Middle Miocene (17–15 MYA)

DISTRIBUTION: Africa

SIZE: 3–11 pounds (3–5 kilograms)

DIET: Herbivore; frugivore

SEE MORE ON PAGES 344–345

COLOBINAE

Colobine monkeys are arboreal and highly acrobatic monkeys distributed through the forests and woodlands of Africa. They are commonly referred to as "leaf monkeys" due to their almost exclusively folivorous diets and possess complex stomachs with which to process highly fibrous foods. The name *Colobus* is derived from the Greek word *colube*, meaning "cripple," a reference to the reduction or loss of the thumb in these monkeys. As a result, the hand is well-suited for use as a hook when moving through the trees, but makes the handling of food difficult.

MICROCOLOBUS TUGENENSIS

NAME MEANING: Small Colobus from the Tugen Hills

AGE: Late Miocene (10.5–8.5 MYA)

DISTRIBUTION: Africa

SIZE: 8.8–11 pounds (4–5 kilograms)

DIET: Herbivore; browser

ESSENTIAL FACTS: Regarded as the earliest-known colobine, its teeth were more bunodont, unlike later colobines which have functionally zygodont dentition adapted to shred fibrous leaves. This may indicate a less folivorous diet, perhaps being more reliant on fruits and seeds.

PARACOLOBUS CHEMERONI

NAME MEANING: Beside Colobus from the Chemeron Beds

AGE: Pliocene to Pleistocene (3–1 MYA)

DISTRIBUTION: Africa

SIZE: 66–110 pounds (30–50 kilograms)

DIET: Herbivore; browser

ESSENTIAL FACTS: Possibly the largest-known colobine monkeys, Chemeron Colobus is known from remarkably complete skeletons that show that it would have been agile in the trees despite its great size.

RHINOCOLOBUS TURKANAENSIS

NAME MEANING: Nose Colobus from Turkana

AGE: Pliocene to Pleistocene (3.4–1.5 MYA)

DISTRIBUTION: Africa

SIZE: 68 pounds (31 kilograms)

DIET: Herbivore; browser

ESSENTIAL FACTS: This species is a baboon-sized colobine with a noticeably short nose, similar to that of modern snub-nosed monkeys (*Rhinopithecus*) from Asia. Aside from this, its skeletal proportions are comparable to those of modern colobus monkeys, reflecting an arboreal lifestyle and folivorous diet.

MESOPITHECUS PENTELICI

NAME MEANING: Pentelic's middle ape

AGE: Late Miocene (7–5 MYA)

DISTRIBUTION: Eurasia

SIZE: 16 inches (40 centimeters) HBL

DIET: Herbivore; browser

ESSENTIAL FACTS: Pentelic's Monkey was widespread, with a distribution that stretched at least from modern-day Greece in the west and China in the east. They were equally at home foraging in the trees and on the ground, and were probably analogous to modern langur monkeys (*Semnopithecus*).

VICTORIAPITHECUS MACINNESI

ESSENTIAL FACTS: This species is one of the best known of all fossil monkeys, thanks to the discovery of thousands of specimens from Maboko Island in Lake Victoria, Kenya. As with most Old World monkeys and apes, Victoriapithecus adult males were larger than females on average and possessed proportionally longer canines. Its skeletal anatomy shows that it was a scansorial animal with a highly frugivorous diet. The presence of a well-developed sagittal crest shows that it had particularly strong jaw muscles that may have been used for breaking open particularly hard fruits and nuts. Cranial casts have shown that the brain was proportionally smaller yet about as complex as those of modern monkeys.

There are two frustrating gaps in the African monkey fossil record, which limit our understanding of the early evolution of these primates. Between the propliopithecine-grade monkeys of the Early Oligocene and victoriapithecine-grade monkeys of the Middle Miocene, there is a gap of about 15 million years, during which monkey fossils are mostly unknown. After this, monkey fossils become scarce again until the Late Miocene, with recognizable representatives of modern lineages being well documented. Due to this lack of fossils, the evolutionary affinities of Victoriapithecus are not understood, and it is typically placed within its own family, Victoriapithecidae.

SEE ENTRY ON PAGE 342

DOLICHOPITHECUS RUSCINENSIS

NAME MEANING: Long ape from Ruscin

AGE: Late Miocene to Pliocene (6–3 MYA)

DISTRIBUTION: Eurasia

SIZE: 26–66 pounds (12–30 kilograms)

DIET: Herbivore; browser

ESSENTIAL FACTS: This species was probably descended from *Mesopithecus* but larger, with a proportionally longer skull and canines and more adapted for a terrestrial lifestyle. Overall, these monkeys appear to have been morphologically closer to baboons (*Papio*) than to other colobines. They were the last colobine monkey known to have inhabited Europe.

PARAPRESBYTIS EOHANUMAN

NAME MEANING: Dawn Hanuman beside Presbytis

AGE: Pliocene (5–2 MYA)

DISTRIBUTION: Eurasia

SIZE: 66 pounds (30 kilograms)

DIET: Herbivore; browser

ESSENTIAL FACTS: A baboon-sized colobine similar to *Dolichopithecus* but with better climbing capabilities, its species name is a reference to Hanuman, a monkey deity from Hindu mythology.

CERCOPITHECINAE

This morphologically diverse subfamily includes vervet monkeys (*Chlorocebus*), macaques (*Macaca*), baboons (*Papio*), and geladas (*Theropithecus*) among others. Members of the group are commonly referred to as "the cheek-pouched monkeys" due to its members possessing pockets on the sides of their faces in which food can be collected and stored to be eaten at a later time. Most are scansorial, feeding and carrying out much of their daily activities mostly on the ground, but returning to the trees to sleep or escape predators.

THEROPITHECUS BRUMPTI

NAME MEANING: Brumpt's beast ape

AGE: Pliocene (3–2 MYA)

DISTRIBUTION: Africa

SIZE: 96.5 pounds (43.8 kilograms)

DIET: Herbivore; grazer

SEE MORE ON PAGES 348–349

THEROPITHECUS OSWALDI

NAME MEANING: Oswald's beast ape

AGE: Pleistocene

DISTRIBUTION: Africa, Eurasia

SIZE: 159 pounds (72 kilograms)

DIET: Herbivore; grazer

ESSENTIAL FACTS: Oswald's Gelada is the largest known species of monkey, with adult males of the species weighing as much as full grown men and standing as tall as one when reared up on its hindlimbs. Widely distributed throughout Africa, its remains are also known from Spain, making it the only known gelada to have lived outside of Africa.

DINOPITHECUS INGENS

NAME MEANING: Great terrible ape

AGE: Pleistocene (2.5–2 MYA)

DISTRIBUTION: Africa

SIZE: 64–101 pounds (29–46 kilograms)

DIET: Hypocarnivore

ESSENTIAL FACTS: The Great Baboon is about twice the size of the largest modern baboons. It is one of the largest Old World monkeys, surpassed in size only by Oswald's Gelada (*Theropithecus oswaldi*). Its diet likely consisted mostly of fruits and leaves, which was likely supplemented with invertebrates and smaller vertebrates.

THEROPITHECUS BRUMPTI

ESSENTIAL FACTS: The genus *Theropithicus*, of which the modern gelada baboon (*T. gelada*) is the last surviving member, are the only grazing monkeys. The cheek teeth were robust, and the jaw muscles were very strong, adapted to chew tough vegetation. They are terrestrial animals with small, sturdy fingers that allow them to selectively pluck short grasses and herbs for extended periods of time. When grazing, they move in a unique gait known as a "shuffle gait," in which they squat bipedally and move by sliding their feet without changing their posture. The skeletal characteristics of fossil geladas show that they shared these same habits and behaviors.

Brumpt's Gelada is over twice the size, had a proportionally longer face, and more extensive jaw musculature than its modern relative. Aside from these differences, the skeleton is very similar in proportions between the two species, with adaptations geared toward terrestrial locomotion and grazing. This species inhabited forested environments, with permanent access to water in the form of rivers, lakes, and marshes. Males were nearly twice the size of females with much larger canines. It can be inferred that, like the modern species, male Brumpt's Geladas were covered in very long, dense fur that would have protected them from the bites of other males during fights.

SEE ENTRY ON PAGE 347

HOMINOIDEA

The first apes appear in the fossil record during the Late Oligocene and descended from an unknown ancestor within the Old World monkeys (Cercophithecidae). They are distinguishable from monkeys most notably in their lack of a tail. Apes tend to be much larger and less agile than monkeys, moving through the trees using arm-swinging or modified brachiation.

PROCONSULIDAE

The first apes to appear in the fossil record, proconsulids are only known from Africa. The species ranged in size from that of a large monkey to a small gorilla. Their skeletons were still very monkey-like, and they had not yet developed the ability to hang from their arms for extended periods.

PROCONSUL AFRICANUS

NAME MEANING: Before Consul from Africa

AGE: Early Miocene (23–13 MYA)

DISTRIBUTION: Africa

SIZE: 1.5 feet (45 centimeters) SH; 7–22 pounds (3–10 kilograms)

DIET: Herbivore

ESSENTIAL FACTS: Named after a captive chimpanzee named Consul, members of the genus *Proconsul* retained monkey-like proportions. They were only recognizable as true apes by their lack of tails. In terms of their ecology and behavior, they were most analogous to modern macaques (*Macaca*).

RANGWAPITHECUS GORDONI

NAME MEANING: Gordon's ape from Rangwa

AGE: Early Miocene (23–20 MYA)

DISTRIBUTION: Eurasia

SIZE: 33 pounds (15 kilograms)

DIET: Herbivore

ESSENTIAL FACTS: This species was a little-known proconsulid that is only identified from isolated teeth and jaws. It was formerly considered to be a member of *Proconsul* before being given its own genus based on differences in dental morphology.

AFROPITHECUS TURKANENSIS

NAME MEANING: African ape from Turkana

AGE: Middle Miocene (18–16 MYA)

DISTRIBUTION: Africa

SIZE: About the size of a Bonobo (*Pan paniscus*)

DIET: Herbivore

ESSENTIAL FACTS: Afropithecus has notably thick enamel on its teeth compared to other early apes, possibly an early adaptation to deal with tougher foods such as hard-shelled fruits. It is considered by some to represent its own family, Afropithecidae.

DENDROPITHECIDAE

These small, gibbon-like apes are restricted to the Miocene and lived throughout Eurasia.

DENDROPITHECUS MACINNESI

NAME MEANING: MacInnes' tree ape

AGE: Early to middle Miocene (20–15 MYA)

DISTRIBUTION: Africa

SIZE: 2 feet (60 centimeters)

DIET: Herbivore

ESSENTIAL FACTS: Members of the genus *Dendropithecus* are comparable to modern gibbons (Hylobatidae) in size and morphology, although they were not closely related and were less efficient brachiators. Their diet consisted of fruits, flowers, and leaves.

OREOPITHECUS BAMBOLII

NAME MEANING: Bamboli's hill ape

AGE: Late Miocene (9–7 MYA)

DISTRIBUTION: Eurasia

SIZE: 66–77 pounds (30–35 kilograms)

DIET: Herbivore

ESSENTIAL FACTS: Well-known from fossils in northern Italy, Oreopithecus inhabited swampy habitats and had a skeleton adapted for suspensory locomotion. It was capable of bipedal locomotion, albeit not as efficient as that exhibited in more humanoid apes.

NYANZAPITHECUS PICKFORDI

NAME MEANING: Martin Pickford's ape from Nyanza

AGE: Middle Miocene

DISTRIBUTION: Africa

SIZE: 22 pounds (10 kilograms)

DIET: Herbivore

ESSENTIAL FACTS: Named for the Nyanza Province of Kenya in which it was discovered, Pickford's Ape was a small ape the size of a gibbon.

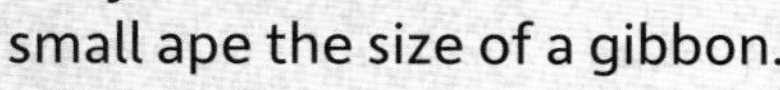

HOMINIDAE

The “great apes” are first known in the fossil record in the Middle or Late Miocene. A considerable amount of morphological diversity can be observed among the few modern species. Members of the family range from arboreal to terrestrial, with diets that may be generalized hypocarnivorous, folivorous, or frugivorous.

PONGINAE

Asian great apes originated during the Middle Miocene and were once diverse and distributed throughout Eurasia. Today they are restricted to a single genus which lives in southeast Asia.

SIVAPITHECUS INDICUS

NAME MEANING: Indian ape of Shiva

AGE: Late Miocene (12.5–10.5 MYA)

DISTRIBUTION: Eurasia

SIZE: 5 feet (1.5 meters) HBL

DIET: Herbivore

ESSENTIAL FACTS: Indian Sivapithecus had a distinctly orangutan-like face but had the body proportions more like that of a chimpanzee (*Pan troglodytes*). Much of its day would have been spent foraging on the ground, but they were still adept climbers. They fed on a wide variety of foods with their robust teeth.

GIGANTOPITHECUS BLACKI

NAME MEANING: Davidson Black's giant ape

AGE: Pleistocene (2 MYA–100,000 YA)

DISTRIBUTION: Eurasia

SIZE: 440–660 pounds (200–300 kilograms)

DIET: Herbivore

SEE MORE ON PAGES 356–357

HOMININAE

The three modern nonhuman species of African great apes are restricted to Africa. The group originated in the Late Miocene and were once distrusted over much of eastern Eurasia as well as Africa.

HISPANOPITHECUS LAIETANUS

NAME MEANING: Lucky Spanish ape

AGE: Late Miocene (11.5–9.5 MYA)

DISTRIBUTION: Eurasia

SIZE: 49–88 pounds (22–40 kilograms)

DIET: Herbivore

ESSENTIAL FACTS: An arboreal ape with strong hands and long arms adapted to suspensory locomotion, this species seems to have had a preference for softer foods, such as fruits and young leaves.

DRYOPITHECUS FONTANI

NAME MEANING: Monsieur Fontan's oak tree ape

AGE: Late Miocene (12.5–11.1 MYA)

DISTRIBUTION: Africa

SIZE: 97 pounds (44 kilograms)

DIET: Herbivore

ESSENTIAL FACTS: Much like modern chimpanzees (*Pan troglodytes*), Fontan's Ape had a varied diet that consisted of non-abrasive foods. Cavities in the teeth of some specimens indicate a high-sugar diet, suggesting the species frequently consumed ripened fruits.

KENYAPITHECUS WICKERI

NAME MEANING: Wicker's ape from Kenya

AGE: Middle Miocene (14 MYA)

DISTRIBUTION: Africa

SIZE: Unknown

DIET: Herbivore

ESSENTIAL FACTS: Wicker's Ape was once thought to have been a direct ancestor to the human lineage of apes (Hominini). Its robust teeth and jaws suggest that it fed on hard or fibrous foods.

CHORORAPITHECUS ABYSSINICUS

NAME MEANING: Abyssinian ape of the Chorora Formation

AGE: Late Miocene (10–8 MYA)

DISTRIBUTION: Africa

SIZE: About gorilla-sized

DIET: Herbivore

ESSENTIAL FACTS: The Abyssinian Ape is thought to be an early member of the gorilla lineage due to its teeth, which are virtually identical to those of gorillas apart from crown height.

GIGANTOPITHECUS BLACKI

ESSENTIAL FACTS: The first fossils of Black's Gigantopithecus to be described were several molars bought at a Chinese medicine shop in 1935 by anthropologist Ralph von Koenigswald, who immediately identified them as belonging to a large ape. Since then, several lower jaws and several thousand isolated teeth have been discovered from cave sites in southeast Asia. Sadly, no postcranial remains are known, but gnaw marks on surviving fossils suggests that most skeletal elements were consumed by local porcupines before they could fossilize. Early on, researchers thought this ape was closely related to hominine apes such as *Paranthropus* or *Australopithecus* until it was discovered to be closer to modern orangutans.

Black's Gigantopithecus is often depicted with gorilla-like body proportions. While this is highly plausible, this build is speculative due to the lack of postcranial remains. Body-size estimates have been obtained by comparing the molars to those of modern apes. Black's Gigantopithecus had strong jaws adapted for intensive chewing with molariform premolars to increase the grinding surface. The thick enamel on the teeth shows that they were adept at dealing with particularly tough, fibrous, or gritty foods. Isotope analyses suggest that they were generalist browsers that fed on a variety of plants, particularly the leaves and fruits from trees. Their diets were likely supplemented with seeds, tubers, and possibly bamboo. The preferred habitat for these apes was the subtropical forests of southern Asia. Given their great size, adults were probably exclusively terrestrial, though juveniles were potentially able to climb to flee from danger.

SEE ENTRY ON PAGE 354

ARDIPITHECUS RAMIDUS

NAME MEANING: Root ground ape

AGE: Pliocene (4.5–4.3 MYA)

DISTRIBUTION: Africa

SIZE: 77–132 pounds (35–60 kilograms)

DIET: Herbivore

ESSENTIAL FACTS: The oldest hominin ape, *Ardipithecus* were scansorial and would not have travelled too far from trees. They inhabited savanna habitats and would shift between a quadrupedal and bipedal stance, depending on the situation. They had not yet developed the bipedal adaptations displayed in *Australopithecus*. Among its more notable features are its vastly reduced canines.

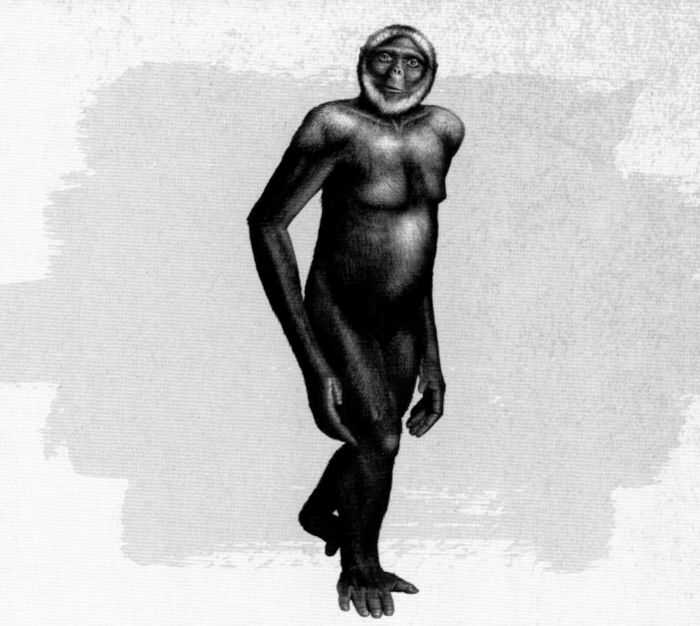

AUSTRALOPITHECUS AFARENSIS

NAME MEANING: Southern ape from afar

AGE: Pliocene (3.9–2.9 MYA)

DISTRIBUTION: Africa

SIZE: 3.5–5.5 feet (105–165 centimeters); 55–100 pounds (25–45 kilograms)

DIET: Hypocarnivore

ESSENTIAL FACTS: This species is the first ape to show adaptations for obligate bipedalism. There is direct evidence that they were preyed upon by big cats such as leopards (*Panthera pardus*) and Barlow's Dinofelis (*Dinofelis barlowi*).

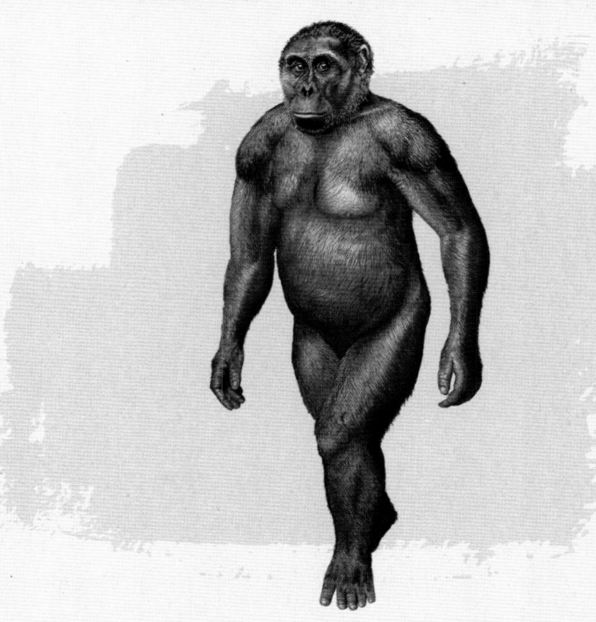

PARANTHROPUS BOISEI

NAME MEANING: Charles Boise's beside man

AGE: Pleistocene (2.5–1.15 MYA)

DISTRIBUTION: Africa

SIZE: 136 pounds (61.7 kilograms)

DIET: Herbivore

ESSENTIAL FACTS: Compared to members of *Australopithecus*, *Paranthropus* were much more heavily built, with a notably flattened face, broad skull, and powerful jaw muscles and teeth.

HOMO ERECTUS

NAME MEANING: Upright man

AGE: Pleistocene (2 MYA–100,000 YA)

DISTRIBUTION: Africa and Eurasia

SIZE: 5–6 feet (146–185 centimeters); 88–150 pounds (40–68 kilograms)

DIET: Hypocarnivore

SEE MORE ON PAGES 360–361

HOMO FLORESIENSIS

NAME MEANING: Flores man

AGE: Pleistocene to Holocene (190,000–50,000 YA)

DISTRIBUTION: Flores

SIZE: 3.3–4.5 feet (1–1.37 meter)

DIET: Hypocarnivore

SEE MORE ON PAGES 362–363

HOMO NEANDERTHALENSIS

NAME MEANING: Neander Valley man

AGE: Pleistocene (430,000–40,000 YA)

DISTRIBUTION: Eurasia

SIZE: 5–5.5 feet (150–168 centimeters); 146–171 pounds (66.4–77.6 kilograms)

DIET: Hypocarnivore

SEE MORE ON PAGES 364–365

HOMO ERECTUS

ESSENTIAL FACTS: Upright Man is known to have made several notable technological innovations during its time. Stone tools such as hand-axes became more efficient and their production more intricate, requiring more time and skill to produce than the stone tools of their ancestors. There is evidence that they butchered quite large mammals, though whether all of these were hunted, scavenged, or a mix of both is unclear. It may have also been the first hominin to learn how to use fire for warmth and to prepare food. Upright Man is also the first hominin known to have extended its range outside of Africa, with fossils uncovered from western Europe to southeast Asia where the species is last recorded.

Upright Man averaged smaller in overall size than modern humans; males trended larger than females. The skull was relatively low and flat, with a humanoid flattened face and prominent nose. The skeletal anatomy and preserved footprints indicate that its gait was identical to that of a modern human. Also like modern humans, the shoulder joint suggests that it was capable of throwing objects with great speed and precision and could wield larger handheld weapons. This behavior is notable for self-defense implications that may have developed to compensate for the reduction of the jaw musculature and canines. Upright Man is likely to have had a reduced hair covering with exposed skin, as indicated by the increased presence of melanin. This feature would have protected the skin from ultraviolet radiation and is a primary function of mammalian hair. An increase in melanin indicates that the skin needed to become darker due to increased sun exposure.

SEE ENTRY ON PAGE 359

HOMO FLORESIENSIS

ESSENTIAL FACTS: The Flores Man was nicknamed "the hobbit" by its discoverers after the fictional race popularized by J. R. R. Tolken's book *The Hobbit*. The first fossils of Flores Man were discovered in 2003 by a joint Australian and Indonesian team of archaeologists, who were working in Flores to search for the earliest evidence of human habitation. The expedition crews eventually found a nearly complete skeleton of this species in Liang Bua Cave, and more individuals would be discovered at this site continuing into the next year.

Flores Man is the smallest of the genus *Homo*, most likely descended from Upright Man (*H. erectus*), who had become isolated on the island of Flores and became smaller to adapt to its environment after it became isolated from the mainland. Compared to other humanoid species, the leg bones were proportionally more robust, with unusually long and flattened feet with a shortened first digit. Flores Man was proficient at crafting stone tools and weapons. Among other small animals, it is thought to have hunted the Flores Giant Rat (*Spelaeomys florensis*). They were themselves hunted by Komodo dragons (*Varanus komodoensis*) while juveniles were also at risk of attack from the Giant Stork (*Leptoptilos robustus*).

SEE ENTRY ON PAGE 359

HOMO NEANDERTHALENSIS

ESSENTIAL FACTS: Neanderthal Man was comparable in size to modern humans but were notably more robust and muscular, with thicker bones overall. Their skulls were larger with greater brain capacity. Their noses were enlarged to enable them to more efficiently thermoregulate in their cold environments. Aside from the obvious physical differences, Neanderthals were similar to modern humans in many ways. There is evidence that they could fashion clothing from animal hides, craft musical instruments from bones, engage in religious or ceremonial practices, and even build simple rafts and boats.

Neanderthals are thought to have had lower population densities than modern humans. Perhaps because of their strong bodies, their metabolic rates were notably higher on average than modern humans and they would have needed to consume more calories per day. In addition to feeding on a variety of plants and fungi, they are known to have occasionally hunted large herbivores including elephants and rhinos, although more common prey the size of wild boar (*Sus scrofa*) or red deer (*Cervus elaphus*) would have been more common. They hunted using strong thrusting spears with stone points. Traumatic injuries during hunts were not uncommon, and many Neanderthal skeletons famously show similar injury patterns to those of rodeo protection athletes and bullfighters, who frequently face attacks from large, aggressive ungulates. Unsurprisingly, there is also evidence based on the healing of particularly severe injuries that Neanderthals had a tradition of medical care.

SEE ENTRY ON PAGE 359

LAURASIATHERIA

The name Laurasiatheria means "Laurasian beasts," originating from the theory that the group originated on the Mesozoic northern supercontinent of Laurasia. Fossil evidence for this group date back to the Early Paleocene, but molecular data pushes the potential origin of several lineages in the Late Cretaceous. Today, laurasiatheres have a dominating presence in terrestrial and marine ecosystems.

PROTUNGULATUM DONNAE

NAME MEANING: Donna's first ungulate

AGE: Early Paleocene (66–63 MYA)

DISTRIBUTION: North America

SIZE: About cat-sized

DIET: Hypocarnivore

ESSENTIAL FACTS: An early hoofed mammal of uncertain affinities, this species may be close to the ancestry of artiodactyls and perissodactyls. *Protungulatum* were definitively known from the earliest Paleocene, with a possible presence in latest Cretaceous deposits. It was a digitigrade animal with hoofed toes and moderate cursorial abilities.

PERIPTYCHIDAE

A family of uncertain affiliations, members of this group are temporally restricted to the Paleocene and known mostly from North America. The family is characterized by their teeth, which have vertical striations on the enamel. Each of the five toes on their plantigrade feet ended in a small hoof.

PERIPTYCHUS CARINIDENS

NAME MEANING: Keel-toothed surrounded folds

AGE: Early Paleocene

DISTRIBUTION: North America

SIZE: 50 pounds (23 kilograms)

DIET: Herbivore

ESSENTIAL FACTS: The tooth grooves that characterize the Periptychidae are most pronounced in this species. Overall, the dentition is robust and suggests a diet of tough or fibrous foods. The musculature of its forelimbs indicate that it was a capable digger.

ECTOCONUS DITRIGONUS

NAME MEANING: Six-sided outside cone

AGE: Early Paleocene

DISTRIBUTION: North America

SIZE: About sheep-sized

DIET: Herbivore

ESSENTIAL FACTS: One of the larger herbivores of its time, this animal was a browser that lived in forested environments. It is known from complete skeletons. Predators of this animal included planocraniid crocodiles and mesonychids.

ARCTOCYONIA

Arctocyonids were raccoon and bear-like mammals that were restricted in age to the Paleocene and Earliest Eocene. They filled the ecological niches of raccoons or bears, being hypocarnivores that primarily fed on plant matter but would opportunistically take animal prey or carrion. There are three families, of which the Arctocyonidae is the most well-documented. Members of the family have plantigrade, five-toed feet and curved claws.

CHRIACUS PELVIDENS

NAME MEANING: Useful basin-tooth

AGE: Early Eocene

DISTRIBUTION: North America

SIZE: 15 pounds (7 kilograms)

DIET: Hypocarnivore

ESSENTIAL FACTS: This species was a raccoon-like animal with marked climbing adaptations such as highly mobile shoulder, elbow, and ankle joints and a tail that may have been semi-prehensile. Reconstructions of the brain show that it depended heavily on its sense of smell to locate food.

ARCTOCYON PRIMAEVUS

NAME MEANING: Ancestral bear dog

AGE: Late Paleocene

DISTRIBUTION: Eurasia

SIZE: 3–4 feet (1–1.2 meters) HBL

DIET: Hypocarnivore

ESSENTIAL FACTS: Physically, *Arctocyon* would have resembled a small bear with a long tail. While not particularly fleet-footed, it was a highly mobile animal that was a skilled climber and could excavate simple dens in which to shelter. The lower canines were notably long and used to display to other individuals and potential threats.

MESONYCHIA

Mesonychians were the first predatory mammals to grow to large sizes and take on the niches left vacant by theropod dinosaurs. They appeared in the Early Paleocene and quickly became widespread across the Northern Hemisphere. Throughout the Eocene the group went into steady decline in the face of mounting competition from oxaenodonts and hyaenodonts; it disappeared completely during the Early Oligocene.

Mesonychians appear to have originated and undergone much of their diversification in eastern Asia. Their teeth were not as adapted for slicing (sectoral) as other terrestrial mammalian predator groups. Instead they were more suited for gripping and tearing flesh. Later members of the group had digitigrade feet, with small hooves at the end of each digit. Their necks were short and powerful, and their torsos are relatively stiff like those of most ungulates. Most had long tails for balance when running and jumping. Scholars think Mesonychians share a common ancestor with artiodactyls.

EOCONODON CORYPHAEUS

NAME MEANING: Chief dawn cone tooth

AGE: Early Paleocene (66–63 MYA)

DISTRIBUTION: North America

SIZE: About cat-sized

DIET: Hypercarnivore

ESSENTIAL FACTS: Though tiny by today's standards, this cat-sized animal was one of the largest predators known for its time immediately following the extinction of the non-avian dinosaurs. Its narrow snout and strong jaw muscles were adapted to capture and hold on to small prey.

TRIISODON QUIVIRENSIS

NAME MEANING: Tree equal teeth from Quivira

AGE: Early Paleocene (63.3–61.7 MYA)

DISTRIBUTION: North America

SIZE: About wolf-sized

DIET: Hypercarnivore

ESSENTIAL FACTS: Known from partial skulls, these animals had relatively large, blunt skulls with tall sagittal crests that gave it a powerful bite.

HAPALODECTIDAE

Hapalodectids were small-bodied mesonychians mostly restricted to the Paleocene and only known from the east Asian fossil record. Unlike other mesonychians, their teeth appear specialized for shearing.

HAPALODECTES HETANGENSIS

NAME MEANING: Soft biter from He Tang Village

AGE: Middle Eocene (50–37 MYA)

DISTRIBUTION: Eurasia

SIZE: About cat-sized

DIET: Aquatic hypercarnivore

ESSENTIAL FACTS: This species is most known for having the most complete skull of any hapalodectid ever discovered. Unlike other mesonychians, a postorbital bar is present. The humerus of another species of *Hapalodectes* shows that, while being swift in short bursts, it was not as specialized for running as later mesonychids.

HAPALORESTES LOVEI

NAME MEANING: David Love's soft mountaineer

AGE: Middle Eocene (44–47 MYA)

DISTRIBUTION: North America

SIZE: 2.2–18 pounds (1–8 kilograms)

DIET: Hypercarnivore

ESSENTIAL FACTS: This fox-sized animal is the largest-known member of the group. The palate features pits into which the tips of the lower teeth fit when the jaws are closed. A similar feature is present in early cetaceans, which has led researchers to hypothesize that this animal was a semiaquatic predator.

MESONYCHIDAE

This was the most diverse family of mesonychians and the longest lasting, appearing in the Early Paleocene to the Early Oligocene. Members of this family became adapted for cursoriality with adaptations such as slender limbs, narrow paws, and four-toed digitigrade feet with hooves on the tips.

YANTANGLESTES CONEXUS

NAME MEANING: Connected thief from Yantang

AGE: Early Paleocene

DISTRIBUTION: Eurasia

SIZE: About cat-sized

DIET: Mesocarnivore

ESSENTIAL FACTS: Yantanglestes is the oldest-known member of mesonychidae. Its jaws were relatively slender and adapted to feeding on small prey items and possibly some plant matter.

ANKALAGON SAUROGNATHUS

NAME MEANING: Lizard-jawed Ancalagon

AGE: Early Paleocene (63–60 MYA)

DISTRIBUTION: North America

SIZE: 3 feet (90 centimeters) SH; 6 feet (1.8 meters) HBL; 220–375 pounds (100–170 kilograms)

DIET: Hypercarnivore

ESSENTIAL FACTS: The genus name refers to the dragon Ancalagon, a creature mentioned in *The Silmarillion* by J. R. R. Tolkien. Ankalagon is notable since it is one of the first large mammalian predators to evolve during the Cenozoic, being about the size of a Jaguar (Panthera onca).

DISSACUS PRAENUNTIUS

NAME MEANING: Unknown

AGE: Middle Paleocene (60 MYA)

DISTRIBUTION: North America

SIZE: About fox-sized

DIET: Mesocarnivore

ESSENTIAL FACTS: Analyses on the teeth of this species show that it was a mesocarnivore, mostly feeding on small mammals but would also supplement its diet with fruits and other edible plants.

DISSACUS EUROPAEUS

NAME MEANING: Unknown

AGE: Late Paleocene (58–57 MYA)

DISTRIBUTION: Eurasia

SIZE: (10–20 kilograms)

DIET: Hypercarnivore

ESSENTIAL FACTS: This species was only mesonychian known to have lived in Europe. It had more specialized cursorial adaptations than other *Dissacus* species and may have chased down prey in packs.

SINONYX JIASHANENSIS

NAME MEANING: Chinese claw from Jiashan

AGE: Late Paleocene (56 MYA)

DISTRIBUTION: Eurasia

SIZE: About wolf-sized

DIET: Hypercarnivore

ESSENTIAL FACTS: This species may have focused on relatively small prey with its low, narrow skull and long canines. Its sense of hearing appears to have been optimized to detect high-frequency sounds like those typically made by smaller mammals.

PACHYAENA OSSIFRAGA

NAME MEANING: Bone-breaking thick hyena

AGE: Late Paleocene (55 MYA)

DISTRIBUTION: North America

SIZE: 125.4 pounds (56.9 kilograms)

DIET: Hypercarnivore

ESSENTIAL FACTS: Despite being included in the genus *Pachyaena*, this wolf-sized species appears to be more closely related to other mesonychid genera such as *Synoplotherium*.

PACHYAENA GIGANTEA

NAME MEANING: Giant thick hyena

AGE: Early Eocene (54–50 MYA)

DISTRIBUTION: North America

SIZE: About lion-sized

DIET: Hypercarnivore

ESSENTIAL FACTS: One of the larger mesonychids, this Lion-sized predator had a robust skeleton but was still able to chase prey for considerable distances. It hunted medium- to large-sized herbivores such as pantodonts, uintatheres, and brontotheres.

SYNOPLOTHERIUM VORAX

NAME MEANING: Voracious fused armored beast

AGE: Early Eocene (50 MYA)

DISTRIBUTION: North America

SIZE: About wolf-sized

DIET: Hypercarnivore

ESSENTIAL FACTS: A complete mounted skeleton of this animal is on display at the Peabody Museum of Natural History. The skeleton shows a healed jaw fracture that would have impaired its ability to hunt for a time, suggesting that it may have lived in social groups. The individual survived to quite an old age, based on its tooth wear.

HARPAGOLESTES IMMANIS

NAME MEANING: Monstrous hooked thief

AGE: Middle Eocene (45–40 MYA)

DISTRIBUTION: Eurasia

SIZE: 330–660 pounds (150–300 kilograms)

DIET: Mesocarnivore

ESSENTIAL FACTS: Harpagolestes may have been a specialist scavenger similar to the Giant Short-Faced Hyena (*Pahycrocuta brevirostis*) of the Plio-Pleistocene. Its teeth are adapted for crushing and tend to exhibit heavy wear. In addition to carrion and live prey, Harpagolestes may have also eaten fruits.

MESONYX OBTUSIDENS

NAME MEANING: Blunt-toothed middle claw

AGE: Early Eocene (54–50 MYA)

DISTRIBUTION: North America

SIZE: 4.5–5 feet (1.25–1.5 meters) HBL; 110–120 pounds (50–55 kilograms)

DIET: Hypercarnivore

ESSENTIAL FACTS: This species was the first mesonychid to be named, described by Edward Drinker Cope in 1872. It was adapted to hunt small to medium-sized herbivores like early brontotheres, rhinos, and horses, all of which at the time were rather small and not much larger than sheep.

MONGOLONYX ROBUSTUS

NAME MEANING: Robust Mongolian claw

AGE: Late Eocene (40 MYA)

DISTRIBUTION: Eurasia

SIZE: About lion-sized

DIET: Hypercarnivore

ESSENTIAL FACTS: This species was one of the last and largest of the mesonychids about the size of a lion (*Panthera leo*) or tiger (*Panthera tigris*). It hunted some of the largest animals in its environment like rhinos and brontotheres.

MONGOLESTES HADRODENS

NAME MEANING: Thick toothed Mongolian thief

AGE: Early Oligocene (34–30 MYA)

DISTRIBUTION: Eurasia

SIZE: 440–880 pounds (200–400 kilograms)

DIET: Hypercarnivore

ESSENTIAL FACTS: This species was the youngest-known mesonychid and potentially also the largest. Its regular prey items would have been the many rhinos at the time which ranged from horse-sized to bison-sized.

OXYAENODONTA

The Oxyaenodonta is one of two extinct groups of predatory mammals (the other being Hyaenodonta) that was historically placed within the Creodonta. This grouping is now considered to be invalid as a proper taxonomic grouping, because the two do not appear to be particularly closely related to each other. Oxyaenodonts had a relatively low diversity and brief temporal span, containing a single family with a fossil record dating from the Late Paleocene to the Middle Eocene. Nonetheless, the group includes the largest and most specialized predatory mammals of the Early and Middle Eocene. Oxyaenodont skeletal morphology is often compared to those of mustelids and felids, being generally stocky and powerfully muscled. The legs are typically short and muscular with plantigrade or semi-plantigrade feet set underneath a relatively long body that ends with an elongated tail. This body type is unsuited for cursoriality, instead suggesting that these animals relied on ambush tactics to capture prey. Oxyaenodonts were all hypercarnivores with heavy, robust skulls and short faces.

TYTTHAENA LICHNA

NAME MEANING: Greedy little hyena

AGE: Late Paleocene (59–55 MYA)

DISTRIBUTION: North America

SIZE: 22 pounds (10 kilograms)

DIET: Hypercarnivore

ESSENTIAL FACTS: The oldest and smallest oxyaenid, it is one of two species within the subfamily Tytthaeninae, which is ancestral to all other oxyaenids. This little predator would have hunted small reptiles, birds, and mammals in the forest undergrowth.

OXYAENINAE

The oxyaenines were superficially cat-like oxyaenids that lived from the early to Late Eocene in North America and Eurasia. Included in this subfamily are the largest members of Oxyaenidae.

OXYAENA LUPINA

NAME MEANING: Wolf-like sharp hyena

AGE: Early Eocene (56–50 MYA)

DISTRIBUTION: North America

SIZE: 3.3 feet (1 meter) HBL; 45 pounds (20 kilograms)

DIET: Hypercarnivore

ESSENTIAL FACTS: This species was a small predator the size of an ocelot (*Leopardus pardalis*) or bobcat (*Lynx rufus*). It is known from complete skeletal material which shows that it was a quick and agile animal that hunted a variety of smaller animals, but was also capable of taking prey its own size or smaller.

PATRIOFELIS FEROX

NAME MEANING: Fierce father cat

AGE: Middle Eocene (50–45 MYA)

DISTRIBUTION: North America

SIZE: 4–6 feet (1.2–1.8 meters) HBL; 220–440 pounds (100–200 kilograms)

DIET: Hypercarnivore

SEE MORE ON PAGES 378–379

SARKASTODON MONGOLIENSIS

NAME MEANING: Flesh-tearing tooth from Mongolia

AGE: Late Eocene (45–40 MYA)

DISTRIBUTION: Eurasia

SIZE: 660–880 pounds (300–400 kilograms)

DIET: Hypercarnivore

ESSENTIAL FACTS: This species was the last and largest oxyaenid known only from a nearly complete skull found in the Gobi Desert in 1930. With its powerful jaws and teeth, it was built to bring down some of the largest herbivores of its time such as brontotheres and rhinos.

PALAEONICTINAE

Palaeonictines were particularly robust predators with compact bodies, heavy limbs, and plantigrade feet. They had powerful jaws with dentition that featured blunt-cusped premolars along with blade-like carnassials.

PALAEONICTIS OCCIDENTALIS

NAME MEANING: Western ancient weasel

AGE: Early Eocene (56.8–48.6 MYA)

DISTRIBUTION: North America

SIZE: 77 pounds (35 kilograms)

DIET: Hypercarnivore

ESSENTIAL FACTS: Western Palaeonictis was the size of a wolverine (*Gulo gulo*) and may have fulfilled a similar niche, having teeth that were equally suited for slicing flesh and breaking bones.

MACHAEROIDINAE

Machaeroidines were the first saber-toothed mammals to have evolved. They are known only from the Middle Eocene of North America, and are characterized by their long skulls with deep lower jaws and blade-like upper canines.

PATRIOFELIS FEROX

ESSENTIAL FACTS: Patriofelis is the last-known oxyaenine oxyaenodont from North America. The genus was established in 1870 by Joseph Leidy based on fossils from the Bridger Formation of Wyoming. Two species have been placed within the genus: *P. ulta* and *P. ferox*. However, because both "species" exhibit virtually identical morphology only differing in size, it is likely that the two should be synonymized into a single species. The differing sizes noted between the two could be attributed to individual or sexual variation.

The complete skeleton of Patriofelis is known. The animal was the size of a jaguar (*Panthera onca*) with relatively short but powerful limbs set under a long and well-muscled body. It was once believed that Patriofelis was a semiaquatic predator resembling a huge otter, a hypothesis which has been depicted in the paleoart of Charles R. Knight. Later studies have confirmed that these were terrestrial predators that were built to ambush and grapple with quite large prey items. In particular, the powerful forelimbs have a wide range of motion, and the lumbar region of the lower back was short and rigid to minimize the risk of damage from dragging down large prey items. Potential prey items included the brontotheres and rhinos of the time.

SEE ENTRY ON PAGE 376

MACHAEROIDES EOTHEN

NAME MEANING: Dagger-like from the east

AGE: Early Eocene (52.4–46.2 MYA)

DISTRIBUTION: North America

SIZE: 22–31 pounds (10–14 kilograms)

DIET: Hypercarnivore

ESSENTIAL FACTS: Despite being about as tall as a large house cat, Machaeroides had a robust skeleton that would have made it much heavier. It was built to handle prey items its own size or larger, such as the early horses and rhinos with which it coexisted.

APATAELURUS KAYI

NAME MEANING: Kay's deceptive cat

AGE: Middle Eocene

DISTRIBUTION: North America

SIZE: 66 pounds (30 kilograms)

DIET: Hypercarnivore

ESSENTIAL FACTS: This species is possibly the largest-known representative of the subfamily Machaeroidinae, estimated to be about the size of a large Eurasian lynx (*Lynx lynx*). It is known from a single lower jaw.

DIEGOAELURUS VANVALKENBURGHAE

NAME MEANING: Blaire Van Valkenburgh's San Diego cat

AGE: Middle Eocene (46.2–39.7 MYA)

DISTRIBUTION: North America

SIZE: 22–37 pounds (10–17 kilograms)

DIET: Hypercarnivore

ESSENTIAL FACTS: Described in 2022, the discovery of this species in southern California expands the known range of the Machaeroidinae; all other species were known only from Utah and Wyoming. It is also the youngest member of the group.

HYAENODONTA

Hyaenodonta was the second of the two mammalian predator groups once placed in the now-invalid order Creodonta. Compared to the oxyaenodonts, which are often compared to cats and mustelids, hyaenodonts are often described as being more similar to dogs (Canidae) or hyenas (Hyaenidae). Early members of the group tended to have long, slender bodies with semi-digitigrade or fully digitigrade feet. Some later species feature shorter torsos with often longer and more slender limbs adapted for cursoriality.

Hyaenodonts have notably larger skulls and teeth than carnivorans of comparable size. They were hypercarnivores with the molars forming a series of carnassials, which have a unique adaptation to combat tooth wear as they age. The upper and lower carnassials rotate sideways against each other throughout the adult life of the hyaenodont so that a long-term shearing surface is maintained.

The creatures are first known from the Early Paleocene and became mostly extinct from the Northern Hemisphere by the Early Miocene. Africa served as a stronghold for the group, with hyaenodonts maintaining a prominent presence in predator communities through much of the Miocene, even in the face of steadily increasing competition from carnivorans. African hyaenodonts made periodic incursions into southern Asia with the last species being recorded from the Late Miocene of India.

PYROCYON DIOCTETUS

NAME MEANING: Double eight-year fire dog

AGE: Early Eocene (55.8–50 MYA)

DISTRIBUTION: North America

SIZE: 5.7 pounds (2.6 kilograms)

DIET: Hypercarnivore

ESSENTIAL FACTS: This species was a small hyaenodont that may have been an active climber. Its genus name was inspired by the memory of the fires that burned in Yellowstone in the summer of 1988 when its fossils were discovered.

GALECYON MORDAX

NAME MEANING: Biting polecat dog

AGE: Early Eocene (56–50 MYA)

DISTRIBUTION: North America

SIZE: 11–17 pounds (5.2–7.9 kilograms)

DIET: Hypercarnivore

ESSENTIAL FACTS: This species was morphologically similar to *Prolimnocyon* but with limbs better suited for efficient terrestrial travel. Its jaws and canines were particularly robust for its size, suggesting that it was able to target prey items close to its own size.

TRITEMNODON AGILIS

NAME MEANING: Agile three cutting tooth

AGE: Middle Eocene (50.5–46.2 MYA)

DISTRIBUTION: North America

SIZE: About fox-sized

DIET: Hypercarnivore

ESSENTIAL FACTS: This species is known for a complete skeleton that was mounted at the American Museum of Natural History. It was particularly long-bodied with a proportionally large and robust head. Its overall proportions are that of an agile predator with possibly some moderate climbing abilities.

BOUALITOMIDAE

Boualitomidae was the earliest of the hyaenodonts known from Africa during the Middle Paleocene to Eocene. The early presence of these animals in Africa and the continued persistence of hyaenodonts overall (later in the Cenozoic after they had gone extinct elsewhere in the world) suggest the group originated on the continent and underwent much of their diversification there.

LAHIMIA SELLOUMI

NAME MEANING: Omar Selloum's carnivore

AGE: Middle Paleocene (61.6–59.2 MYA)

DISTRIBUTION: Africa

SIZE: About weasel-sized

DIET: Hypercarnivore

ESSENTIAL FACTS: This species was one of the oldest-known hyaenodonts, with especially tall and pointy teeth that suggest a primarily insectivorous diet.

BOUALITOMUS MAROCANENSIS

NAME MEANING: Bou Ali knife of Morocco

AGE: Early Eocene (54–52 MYA)

DISTRIBUTION: Africa

SIZE: About weasel-sized

DIET: Hypercarnivore

ESSENTIAL FACTS: This creature was another tiny insect hunter and the type genus for the family Boualitomidae. This species is named after the village Ouled Bou Ali, near where it was discovered.

PROVIVERRIDAE

The proviverrids are known only from Europe throughout the Eocene. They were ecologically similar to genets or civets (Viverridae) with long, low skulls featuring small teeth for dealing with relatively small prey items.

LESMESODON EDINGERI

NAME MEANING: Edinger's tooth from Messel

AGE: Middle Eocene (50.8–46.3 MYA)

DISTRIBUTION: Eurasia

SIZE: About marten-sized

DIET: Hypercarnivore

ESSENTIAL FACTS: Complete skeletons of this creature are known from the Messel Pit Fossil Site in Germany. These specimens include hair impressions, which show that Edinger's Lesmesodon had a particularly fluffy tail that resembled that of a fox.

PROVIVERRA TYPICA

NAME MEANING: Type before civet

AGE: Middle Eocene (46.3–41.2 MYA)

DISTRIBUTION: Eurasia

SIZE: About weasel-sized

DIET: Hypercarnivore

ESSENTIAL FACTS: It was once hypothesized that the hyaenodonts' extinction was partly due to the creature having small or less sophisticated brains compared to those of carnivorans. Endocasts taken from the skulls of Proviverra contradict this hypothesis, showing that the brain was actually rather highly developed.

LIMNOCYONIDAE

Limnocyonids were morphologically similar to the European Proviverridae, only being distributed through North America.

PROLIMNOCYON CHOWI

NAME MEANING: Minchen Chow's before Limnocyon

AGE: Late Paleocene (57–55 MYA)

DISTRIBUTION: North America

SIZE: About weasel-sized

DIET: Insectivorous hypercarnivore

ESSENTIAL FACTS: This creature was the oldest and smallest representative of the genus *Prolimnocyon*. It was an agile climber, adapted to feed on insects and small vertebrates in the trees and on the ground.

LIMNOCYON VERUS

NAME MEANING: True marsh dog

AGE: Middle Eocene

DISTRIBUTION: North America

SIZE: 2.2 pounds (1 kilogram)

DIET: Hypercarnivore

ESSENTIAL FACTS: For its small size, this species possessed a broad skull and deep jaws adapted for handling large prey.

SINOPIDAE

Sinopa were terrestrial predators that resembled foxes or civets. They are known only from Early to Middle Eocene deposits of North America and Eurasia.

SINOPA RAPAX

NAME MEANING: Greedy swift fox

AGE: Middle Eocene (50.3–46.2 MYA)

DISTRIBUTION: North America

SIZE: About fox-sized

DIET: Hypercarnivore

ESSENTIAL FACTS: *Sinopa* is one of the best-known members of the Sinopidae, represented by complete skeletal material. This species had moderately elongated and slender limbs, adapted for swift running though not for sustained distances. It would have hunted small mammals such as the early horses of the time.

HYAENODONTIDAE

Members of Hyaenodontidae are cursorial and ecologically analogous to modern pack-hunting canids and hyenas. They had slender limbs and narrow feet adapted for active and sustained pursuits.

HYAENODON MUSTELINUS

NAME MEANING: Weasel-like hyena tooth

AGE: Early Oligocene (34–30 MYA)

DISTRIBUTION: North America

SIZE: 8 inches (20 centimeters) SH; 1.6 feet (50 centimeters) HBL; 11 pounds (5 kilograms)

DIET: Hypercarnivore

ESSENTIAL FACTS: This cat-sized animal was one of the smallest of the genus *Hyaenodon* with the typical large head and robust jaws that characterize these animals. Like its larger relatives it had long limbs adapted for fast running.

HYAENODON CRUCIANS

NAME MEANING: Weasel-like hyena tooth

AGE: Early Oligocene (34–30 MYA)

DISTRIBUTION: North America

SIZE: 22–55 pounds (10–25 kilograms)

DIET: Hypercarnivore

ESSENTIAL FACTS: About the size of a dhole (*Cuon alpinus*), this species inhabited forests and woodlands and hunted small- to medium-sized prey items. It is known for abundant remains from western North America, including a beautifully preserved skull housed at the Royal Tyrrell Museum.

HYAENODON HORRIDUS

NAME MEANING: Horrible hyena tooth

AGE: Early Oligocene (34–30 MYA)

DISTRIBUTION: North America

SIZE: 27.5 – 31.5 inches (70–80 centimeters) SH; 88–130 pounds (40–60 kilograms)

DIET: Hypercarnivore

ESSENTIAL FACTS: The largest and most common North American species of *Hyaenodon*, the size of a gray wolf (*Canis lupus*), it hunted ungulates that were considerably larger than itself. *Hyaenodon* had an extended period of juvenile dependency, gaining their adult dentition after three or four years of age.

HYAENODON GIGAS

NAME MEANING: Giant hyena tooth

AGE: Late Eocene

DISTRIBUTION: Eurasia

SIZE: 330–660 pounds (150–300 kilograms)

DIET: Hypercarnivore

ESSENTIAL FACTS: This species is perhaps best known for its appearance in the documentary *Walking with Beasts*, where it is incorrectly stated as being "rhino-sized." It is the largest species of *Hyaenodon*, about the size of a lion (*Panthera leo*). Its prey included some of the larger rhinos and brontotheres of its time.

TERATODONTIDAE

Teratodontidae was perhaps the longest-lived family of hyaenodonts with a record extending from the Middle Eocene to Late Miocene. They were mostly restricted to Africa but also extended into Arabia and southern Asia.

EKWEECONFRACTUS AMORUI

NAME MEANING: Broken fox of the stones

AGE: Early Miocene (17 MYA)

DISTRIBUTION: Africa

SIZE: 33 pounds (15 kilograms)

DIET: Hypercarnivore

ESSENTIAL FACTS: This species is known from a single specimen found in Moruorot, Kenya: a nearly complete but partially crushed skull with an intact cranium. It is one of a handful of hyaenodonts for which the shape and structure of the brain is known.

DISSOPSALIS CARNIFEX

NAME MEANING: Executioner double scissors

AGE: Late Miocene (10–8.8 MYA)

DISTRIBUTION: Eurasia

SIZE: 44–88 pounds (20–40 kilograms)

DIET: Hypercarnivore

ESSENTIAL FACTS: The last-known hyaenodont, this predator is known from India and Pakistan and probably hunted smaller ungulates and rabbits.

HYAINAILOURIDAE

Hyainailurids are known in the fossil record from the Middle Eocene to Middle Miocene and includes some of the largest hyaenodonts known to have ever lived. They had slender yet powerfully muscled skeletons adapted for great bursts of speed and agility. Most had jaws and teeth adapted to hunt relatively large prey items, with enlarged canines and highly sectoral cheek teeth. At least one lineage, the Apterodontinae, were semiaquatic predators that resembled otters.

APTERODON MACROGNATHUS

NAME MEANING: Long-jawed without wing tooth

AGE: Late Eocene (39.6–36 MYA)

DISTRIBUTION: Africa

SIZE: About river otter-sized

DIET: Aquatic hypercarnivore

ESSENTIAL FACTS: Members of the genus Apterodon were otter-like animals with long skulls, shortened faces, elongated bodies, and short limbs. They chased fish and other aquatic prey through the water and would excavate dens in the shore when the ground was soft.

HYAINAILOURINAE

Hyainailourines were medium- to large-sized predators that occurred from the Middle Eocene to the Middle Miocene. The subfamily occurred throughout the Northern Hemisphere but originated and survived longer in Africa, with species occasionally immigrating into southern Eurasia. They were built to stalk and ambush prey rather than to chase it down, with short semi-digitigrade feet. They were ecologically replaced by bear dogs throughout the Miocene.

HEMIPSALODON GRANDIS

NAME MEANING: Great half-scissor tooth

AGE: Late Eocene (41–37 MYA)

DISTRIBUTION: North America

SIZE: About jaguar-sized

DIET: Hypercarnivore

ESSENTIAL FACTS: Compared to the closely-related Vieja Hemipsalodon (*H. viejaensis*), the skull of this species was much more robust. The skull featured proportionally larger canines, indicating a habitual preference for larger prey items, which would have included oreodonts and rhinos.

KERBEROS LANGEBADREA

NAME MEANING: Brigitte Lange-Badre's Cerberus

AGE: Late Eocene (40–37.8 MYA)

DISTRIBUTION: Eurasia

SIZE: About jaguar-sized

DIET: Hypercarnivore

ESSENTIAL FACTS: This species was described in 2015 and named after the mythical three-headed dog from Greek mythology. Kerberos is known for a complete skull, lower jaws, and lower limb elements. Its primary prey were medium to large-sized perissodactyls.

SIMBAKUBWA KUTOKAAFRIKA

NAME MEANING: Great lion of Africa

AGE: Early Miocene (23–22 MYA)

DISTRIBUTION: Africa

SIZE: 620–880 pounds (280–400 kilograms)

DIET: Hypercarnivore

ESSENTIAL FACTS: The body mass of Simbakubwa has been calculated to be up to 3,300 pounds (1,500 kilograms) by comparing its teeth to those of modern carnivorans. However, this figure is likely an overestimate. The canines were particularly massive and suggest the ability to take down quite large prey items.

MEGISTOTHERIUM OSTEOTHLASTES

NAME MEANING: Greatest bone-crushing beast

AGE: Early Miocene (19–14 MYA)

DISTRIBUTION: Africa

SIZE: 620–880 pounds (280–400 kilograms)

DIET: Hypercarnivore

ESSENTIAL FACTS: Known for a nearly complete, toothless skull that measures over 2 feet (66 centimeters) long, Megistotherium is one of the largest hyaenodonts alongside Simbakubwa. It may have hunted gomphotheres and rhinos in its environment.

CARNIVORA

Carnivorans, the group which includes cats (Felidae), dogs (Canidae), bears (Ursidae), hyenas (Hyaenidae), and many others, first appear in the fossil record during the Early Paleocene. Some scholars estimate the potential origin of the group may have been in the Late Cretaceous.

Carnivorans are possibly the most morphologically diverse group among modern mammals; members include terrestrial, arboreal, scansorial, fossorial, semiaquatic, and marine forms. They have a presence on all seven continents, making them the most widespread mammal group as well. The most diagnostic characteristic of the group is the position of the carnassial teeth, always comprising the last upper premolar and the first lower molar. In the ancestral condition, the pre-carnassial premolars are pointed for gripping prey, while the post-carnassial molars are more brachydont for grinding plant matter. The shearing and grinding aspects of the dentition may be expanded or reduced from species to species depending on diet. This is a key aspect in how carnivorans outlasted other predator groups.

The name *Carnivora*, meaning "flesh-eating," is misleading. Early carnivorans possessed a greater degree of dietary versatility than the contemporaneous oxyaenodonts and hyaenodonts. They were able to shift from being mesocarnivores to becoming more hypocarnivorous or hypercarnivorous and back again when conditions demanded it, making the group less vulnerable to extinction.

RAVENICTIS KRAUSEI

NAME MEANING: Krause's Ravenscrag weasel

AGE: Early Paleocene (66–63 MYA)

DISTRIBUTION: North America

SIZE: Unknown

DIET: Mesocarnivore

ESSENTIAL FACTS: Ravenictis is the oldest-known carnivoran. Known only from a single isolated tooth found in Ravenscrag, Saskatchewan, its family and paleobiology cannot be determined at this time.

MIACIDAE

The family Miacidae are thought to be a paraphyletic group, meaning that some of its members may be closer to other families than they are to each other. For example, in 2016 two species traditionally placed within Miacidae were found instead to be early bear-dogs (Amphicyonidae). In general, they were small-bodied animals that would have resembled the weasel-like marten or civet. Miacids were mostly arboreal or scansorial with semi-retractile claws, although a few were more terrestrial and show moderate fossorial adaptations. They had a generalized dentition, with the diagnostic carnassial composition of Carnivora.

GRACILOCYON WINKLERI

NAME MEANING: Winkler's gracile dog

AGE: Early Eocene (55 MYA)

DISTRIBUTION: North America

SIZE: About weasel-sized

DIET: Mesocarnivore

ESSENTIAL FACTS: The high, pointed cusps of this species' teeth suggest that its diet mostly consisted of insects and smaller vertebrates.

MESSELOGALE KESSLERI

NAME MEANING: Kessler's weasel from Messel

AGE: Middle Eocene (47–45 MYA)

DISTRIBUTION: Eurasia

SIZE: About marten-sized

DIET: Hypercarnivore

ESSENTIAL FACTS: The skull anatomy of Messelogale suggests a placement within the suborder Caniformia. The loss of the last molars indicates that it may have been more of a hypercarnivore. A complete skeleton of a juvenile individual has been recovered from Messel Pit.

VASSACYON TAXIDIOTUS

NAME MEANING: Travelling Wasatchian dog

AGE: Early Eocene (55–50 MYA)

DISTRIBUTION: Eurasia

SIZE: About weasel-sized

DIET: Mesocarnivore

ESSENTIAL FACTS: The Travelling Vassacyon is named for its discovery in France, while other members of its genus are known from North America.

TAPOCYON ROBUSTUS

NAME MEANING: Robust dog from Tapo Canyon

AGE: Middle Eocene (46–40 MYA)

DISTRIBUTION: North America

SIZE: 44 pounds (20 kilograms)

DIET: Hypercarnivore

ESSENTIAL FACTS: Tapocyon was the largest-known species of the miacids, the size of a coyote (*Canis latrans*). Despite having caniform characteristics, Tapocyon had a notably cat-like skull with a relatively short snout, robust canines, and slightly reduced premolars.

PAROODECTES FEISTI

NAME MEANING: Otto Feist's near Oodectes

AGE: Middle Eocene (48–46 MYA)

DISTRIBUTION: Eurasia

SIZE: About cat-sized

DIET: Mesocarnivore

ESSENTIAL FACTS: Paroodectes is known from complete skeletons found at Messel Pit. Its proportions are indicative of an agile climbing animal that may have hunted the early primates of the time.

DORMAALOCYON LATOURI

NAME MEANING: Latour's dog from Dormaal

AGE: Early Eocene (56–55 MYA)

DISTRIBUTION: Eurasia

SIZE: About marten-sized

DIET: Mesocarnivore

ESSENTIAL FACTS: Dormaalocyon was named after Dormaal Village in Belgium, where it was discovered. The anatomy of its ankle bones shows that it was mostly arboreal.

MIACIS PARVIVORUS

NAME MEANING: Small point

AGE: Middle Eocene (50–46 MYA)

DISTRIBUTION: North America

SIZE: About weasel-sized

DIET: Mesocarnivore

ESSENTIAL FACTS: With its long and flexible body and tail, retractable claws, and relatively long hindlimbs, Miacis was an arboreal predator that would have resembled modern ringtails (*Bassariscus astutus*), members of the raccoon family. Its diet consisted of small mammals, birds, reptiles, and fruits.

VULPAVUS OVATUS

NAME MEANING: Egg-shaped fox ancestor

AGE: Early Eocene

DISTRIBUTION: North America

SIZE: About marten-sized

DIET: Mesocarnivore

ESSENTIAL FACTS: Vulpavus was an agile tree-dweller with long limbs, large paws, and a relatively small, deep head. Its diet may have consisted of a high proportion of fruit along with small vertebrates, similar to that of modern palm civets (*Paradoxurus*).

VIVERRAVIDAE

Viverravidae were another ancestral group of carnivorans. They are regarded as a defined family which is characterized by the absence of the last molars. This characteristic is also possessed by the feliform carnivorans, and viverravids have been hypothesized to be ancestral to that suborder. Although the record for viverravids is slightly older than that of miacids, this derived characteristic suggests that the more generalized miacids may be the older lineage, with viverravids having branched away from them in the Early Paleocene. Their fossils have been found in North America and Eurasia, and they appear to have become extinct by the Late Eocene.

ICTIDOPAPPUS MUSTELINUS

NAME MEANING: Grandfather of weasels

AGE: Early Paleocene (63.8–60.9 MYA)

DISTRIBUTION: North America

SIZE: About weasel-sized

DIET: Mesocarnivore

ESSENTIAL FACTS: This species was one of the oldest-known carnivorans after Ravenictis. Members of the genus are known only from jaws and isolated teeth.

DIDYMICTIS PROTENUS

NAME MEANING: Forward double weasel

AGE: Early Eocene (55–50 MYA)

DISTRIBUTION: North America

SIZE: About civet-sized

DIET: Mesocarnivore

ESSENTIAL FACTS: While the species likely retained the ability to climb, its limbs suggest that the creature was terrestrial with a degree of cursoriality. Its snout was long and narrow with relatively powerful jaws. Overall, the animal may have borne a resemblance to a fox (*Vulpes*) or civet (*Viverra*).

VIVERRAVUS MINUTUS

NAME MEANING: Tiny civet ancestor

AGE: Early Eocene (55–50 MYA)

DISTRIBUTION: North America

SIZE: About marten-sized

DIET: Mesocarnivore

ESSENTIAL FACTS: The long, low skull of this animal indicates a preference for relatively small prey items.

CANIFORMIA

Broadly referred to as the "dog-like carnivorans," terrestrial members of the Caniformia group often have a mostly complete and generalized dentition, which enables a higher degree of dietary adaptability. They tend to have long faces and semi-retractable or non-retractable claws. Caniformia may be further subdivided into Musteloidea (weasel-like carnivorans), Arctoidea (bear-like carnivorans), and Pinnipedia (marine carnivorans such as seals, sea lions, walruses).

LONCHOCYON QIUI

NAME MEANING: Zhan-Xiang Qiu's spear dog

AGE: Late Eocene

DISTRIBUTION: Eurasia

SIZE: About wolf-sized

DIET: Hypercarnivore

ESSENTIAL FACTS: The lower jaw of Lonchocyon is similar to that of thaumastocyonine bear-dogs, with deep robust canines and blade-like carnassials. Overall, it was built to deliver devastating killing bites with its canines in a similar manner to a cat.

LYCOPHOCYON HUTCHISONI

NAME MEANING: Howard Hutchinson's twilight dog

AGE: Middle Eocene (43–40 MYA)

DISTRIBUTION: North America

SIZE: About marten-sized

DIET: Mesocarnivore

ESSENTIAL FACTS: Lycophocyon was a marten-like predator known for a partial skeleton, including much of the skull and limb elements. The limb anatomy of the creature shows that it was scansorial with plantigrade feet. In addition to small vertebrates, insects and plant matter made up a significant portion of its diet.

AMPHICYONIDAE

Amphicyonidae are commonly referred to as "bear-dogs" because the scientists who described them noted a combination of features possessed by both dogs (Canidae) and bears (Ursidae) within a single animal. The family was very diverse, ranging from raccoon-sized up to the size of big cats or bears. Many were mesocarnivores, most were hypercarnivores, and a few were hypocarnivores. Most had either plantigrade or semi-plantigrade hindfeet, and some were digitigrade and trended toward cursoriality. The oldest-known bear-dogs are known from the Middle Eocene of North America, and they appear in Eurasia shortly after. Bear-dogs are known in Africa starting in the Early Miocene, and they survived there until the Miocene-Pliocene boundary after the family had gone extinct elsewhere. The decline of bear-dogs began during the Late Miocene when they began to face mounting competition from large cats.

GUSTAFSONIA COGNITA

NAME MEANING: Known Eric Gustafson

AGE: Late Eocene (39 MYA)

DISTRIBUTION: North America

SIZE: About marten-sized

DIET: Mesocarnivore

ESSENTIAL FACTS: Gustafsonia was thought to be a member of Miacidae until 2016, when it was discovered this species had more in common with bear-dogs than with other early carnivorans. The genus is named after Eric Gustafson, who described the animal in 1986 under the now-invalid name *Miacis cognitus*.

ANGELARCTOCYON AUSTRALIS

NAME MEANING: Southern messenger bear-dog

AGE: Late Eocene (38.1–36.6 MYA)

DISTRIBUTION: North America

SIZE: About marten-sized

DIET: Mesocarnivore

ESSENTIAL FACTS: Formerly named *Miacis australis*, this species was renamed in the same 2016 paper as Gustofsonia. Both these animals are only known from singular skulls discovered in Texas.

GUANGXICYON SINOAMERICANUS

NAME MEANING: Chinese-American Guangxi dog

AGE: Late Eocene (37–35 MYA)

DISTRIBUTION: Eurasia

SIZE: About Bobcat-sized

DIET: Mesocarnivore

ESSENTIAL FACTS: This animal represents the oldest Asian record of Amphicyonidae. It had a notably shortened face with an unreduced dentition, robust jaws, and large canines. Despite its derived traits it is unknown to which subfamily it belongs.

PARADAPHOENUS TOOHEYI

NAME MEANING: Toohey's beside *Daphoenus*

AGE: Early Oligocene (33 MYA)

DISTRIBUTION: North America

SIZE: About cat-sized

DIET: Hypocarnivore

ESSENTIAL FACTS: Paradaphoenus was a small-bodied bear-dog similar in size and morphology to the early canids like *Hesperocyon* and *Archaeocyon*. It had broad, raccoon-like molars that suggest the species fed on considerable amounts of plant matter in addition to small animals.

DAPHOENINAE

Daphoenines were small- to medium-sized bear-dogs with post-cranial anatomy adapted for catlike stalk-and-pounce hunting behaviors. Their bodies were long and flexible with moderately elongated limbs and short, digitigrade feet.

DAPHOENODON SUPERBUS

NAME MEANING: Overbearing killing teeth

AGE: Early Miocene (23–20 MYA)

DISTRIBUTION: North America

SIZE: 154–220 pounds (70–100 kilograms)

DIET: Hypercarnivore

ESSENTIAL FACTS: Complete skeletal remains of this bear-dog have been found at Agate Springs National Monument. It was a quick and agile predator that hunted small- to medium-sized prey items such as the camels and horses of the time.

ADILOPHONTES BRACHYKOLOS

NAME MEANING: Short-legged fearless killer

AGE: Early Miocene (23–20 MYA)

DISTRIBUTION: North America

SIZE: About Leopard-sized

DIET: Hypercarnivore

ESSENTIAL FACTS: Armed with a robust skull with powerful jaws and relatively short and sturdy forelimbs, Adilophontes was built to dispatch relatively large prey items. Like other bear-dogs, males were significantly larger than the females, implying mostly solitary hunting behaviors.

BRACHYRHYNCHOCYON MONTANUS

NAME MEANING: Short-nosed dog from Montana

AGE: Early Oligocene (33 MYA)

DISTRIBUTION: North America

SIZE: About fox-sized

DIET: Mesocarnivore

ESSENTIAL FACTS: *Brachyrynchocyon* were small, lightly built bear-dogs that would have filled the niches which today are occupied by foxes. Their primary prey items were small mammals and birds, in addition to carrion and some plant matter.

DAPHOENICTIS TEDFORDI

NAME MEANING: Tedford's killing weasel

AGE: Early Oligocene (34–33 MYA)

DISTRIBUTION: North America

SIZE: About cat-sized

DIET: Hypercarnivore

ESSENTIAL FACTS: A small bear-dog with a notably cat-like hypercarnivorous dentition, Daphoenictis was adapted to hunt the many small rodents and lagomorphs with which it coexisted.

DAPHOENUS VETUS

NAME MEANING: Former killer

AGE: Early Oligocene (34–33 MYA)

DISTRIBUTION: North America

SIZE: About coyote-sized

DIET: Mesocarnivore

ESSENTIAL FACTS: One of the more common predators from the Early Oligocene deposits of western North America, Daphoenus was roughly the size of a coyote (*Canis latrans*). Its long, low skull shows a preference for relatively small prey items which it would stalk and pounce upon.

AMPHICYONINAE

Amphicyonines first appeared in Eurasia during the Late Eocene and begin to colonize North America during the Early Miocene. Early examples of this group were small predators that would have had a similar ecology to small cats or mustelids. As hyaenodonts went into decline during the Miocene, they grew ever larger and more robust, becoming the top predators of their ecosystems. However, they themselves began to go into decline during the Middle Miocene, when their niches began to be occupied by large cats.

CYNODICTIS PEIGNEI

NAME MEANING: Peigne's dog weasel

AGE: Early Oligocene (34–33 MYA)

DISTRIBUTION: Eurasia

SIZE: About cat-sized

DIET: Hypercarnivore

ESSENTIAL FACTS: The small bear-dogs of the genus *Cynodictis* were long-bodied animals with limbs adapted for sudden bursts of speed and agility. They fed on small mammals, birds, and reptiles.

CYNELOS CARONIAVORUS

NAME MEANING: Carrion-eating dog

AGE: Early Miocene (20–18 MYA)

DISTRIBUTION: North America

SIZE: About coyote-sized

DIET: Mesocarnivore

ESSENTIAL FACTS: The smaller of two species of bear-dog found at the Thomas Farm Site in northern Florida, this species is likely to have hunted prey items up to the size of Blackberg's Horse (*Archaeohippus blackbergi*) and would have readily fed on plant matter such as fruits and nuts.

AMPHICYON LONGIRAMUS

NAME MEANING: Long-branched ambiguous dog

AGE: Early Miocene (18–16 MYA)

DISTRIBUTION: North America

SIZE: About Lion-sized

DIET: Hypercarnivore

ESSENTIAL FACTS: The largest predator known to have lived at Thomas Farm, this species had a robust skeleton with a relatively long and narrow yet strong skull with huge canines. It likely fed on the medium- to large-sized herbivores in its woodland environment such as camels, horses, and rhinos.

AMPHICYON INGENS

NAME MEANING: Great ambiguous dog

AGE: Middle Miocene (16–13 MYA)

DISTRIBUTION: North America

SIZE: 4–4.4 feet (1.2–1.3 meters) SH; 8.5–10 feet (2.6–3 meters) HBL

DIET: Hypercarnivore

ESSENTIAL FACTS: Great Amphicyon was the largest member of the genus, matching the dimensions of the largest cats such as Southern Smilodon (*Smilodon populator*) and American lion (*Panthera atrox*). Apart from its great size, its most notable feature is its high sagittal crest, which would power an exceptionally strong bite.

ISCHYROCYON HYAENODUS

NAME MEANING: Hyena-toothed strong dog

AGE: Middle Miocene (14–10 MYA)

DISTRIBUTION: North America

SIZE: 352–660 pounds (160–300 kilograms)

DIET: Hypercarnivore

ESSENTIAL FACTS: As with the closely related *Amphicyon*, Ischyrocyon was an ambush predator that would stalk its prey in a manner similar to a big cat, before rushing from cover and colliding with it in several bounds. It fed on a variety of medium- to large-sized ungulates.

MYACYON DOJAMBIR

NAME MEANING: Wadi Maya dog of December

AGE: Middle Miocene (14–11 MYA)

DISTRIBUTION: Africa

SIZE: 330–550 pounds (150–250 kilograms)

DIET: Hypercarnivore

ESSENTIAL FACTS: Myacyon was a hypercarnivore with highly specialized shearing dentition, a shortened and vaguely cat-like face, and massive canines. Some size estimates have put it about as large as the Great Amphicyon (*Amphicyon ingens*) from North America.

TARTAROCYON CAZANAVEI

NAME MEANING: Alain Cazanave Tartaro dog

AGE: Middle Miocene (13–12 MYA)

DISTRIBUTION: Eurasia

SIZE: 440 pounds (200 kilograms)

DIET: Hypercarnivore

ESSENTIAL FACTS: The genus name *Tartarocyon* is inspired by a man-eating giant from southwestern French Pyrenees legend known as Tartaro. Its closest relatives appear to be bear-dogs of the genus *Cynelos*, although it grew much larger.

MAGERICYON ANCEPS

NAME MEANING: Trenchant dog of Madrid

AGE: Late Miocene (10–9 MYA)

DISTRIBUTION: Eurasia

SIZE: 264–420 pounds (120–190 kilograms)

DIET: Hypercarnivore

SEE MORE ON PAGES 404–405

BONISICYON ILLACABO

NAME MEANING: Louis de Bonis' dog of the end

AGE: Late Miocene (6.5–5.3 MYA)

DISTRIBUTION: Africa

SIZE: 44–66 pounds (20–30 kilograms)

DIET: Hypercarnivore

ESSENTIAL FACTS: Bonisicyon is the last-surviving bear-dog, disappearing just before the start of the Pliocene. The morphology of its carnassials shows that it was a hypercarnivore whose diet most likely included rodents, lagomorphs, and small antelopes in savanna environments.

AGILODOCODON SCANSORIUS

ESSENTIAL FACTS: Agilodocodon is the one of the earliest mammaliforms known to have evolved marked specializations to an arboreal lifestyle. It had elongated fingers and toes, each ending in a curved claw for gripping tree trunks. The wrist and ankle joints were very flexible; their feet were capable of a great degree of rotation. Like squirrels, this adaptation would have enabled them to grip the thinnest branches and to descend trees headfirst. The arm bones were slender and had a wide range of motion at the shoulder joint. The spine was more flexible than that of other docodonts and would have enabled powerful leaps for moving from branch to branch and making rapid ascents. Agilodocodon may have spent the majority of its life in the trees, so movement on the ground would have been relatively awkward and limited to brief ventures that were never more than a few leaps away from the nearest tree trunk.

The crushed skull of the only known Agilodocodon specimen is 2.7 centimeters long, with a well-preserved dentition. The dental formula is I4/4, C1/1, P6/6, M4/4, totaling 58 teeth. The dentition differs from that of other known docodonts, because it is more adapted to a hypocarnivorous diet. While other docodonts had simple peg-like incisors, Agilodocodon had spade-shaped and spatulate (broad, rounded) lower incisors that were morphologically similar to those of modern New World monkeys like marmosets, spider monkeys, and howler monkeys; these animals are known for using these teeth to peel tree bark in order to access the underlying gum and sap. Therefore, this type of tooth in Agilodocodon represents the earliest evidence for gumnivorous feeding behavior in the mammalian lineage. The molars, meanwhile, show characteristics similar to those of galagid and lorisid primates, whose diets consist of fruits, insects, and occasionally smaller vertebrates in addition to gums and saps.

SEE ENTRY ON PAGE 18

CASTOROCAUDA LUTRASIMILIS

ESSENTIAL FACTS: Castorocauda is known from a single partial skeleton discovered in China, which includes an incomplete skull and well-preserved lower jaws with intact dentition. It is the earliest-known mammaliform to show aquatic specializations, predating the next oldest by at least 100 million years. Its body was similar to that of a platypus, with a sprawling posture including broad, webbed feet for paddling through the water. By far its most notable feature, and the inspiration behind its name, is its flattened tail, which it would have used to propel itself swiftly through the water. Its pointed premolars are similar in morphology to those of seals and early whales, well adapted to catching fish and other aquatic animals. It was also the largest-known docodont and largest of all Jurassic mammaliforms.

Castorocauda is the earliest mammaliform to show evidence of a complete fur coating. Preserved as impressions surrounding the holotype skeleton, the animal had a dual-layer coat of protective guard hairs and insulating underfur, which would have kept it warm during and after dives. Like platypuses, the forelimbs appear to have been adapted to digging in soft substrates, and this animal probably excavated burrows along the banks of rivers and lakes in which to take shelter.

SEE ENTRY ON PAGE 18

DOCOFOSSOR BRACHYDACTYLUS

ESSENTIAL FACTS: The only fossil of Docofossor, a compressed skeleton with a complete skull and lower jaws, was discovered by farers in Hebei, China. Fur impressions are also visible around the specimen.

Docofossor is the earliest-known mammal to show fossorial specializations. Its skeletal structure and body proportions were similar to those of modern golden moles (Chrysochloridae). The number of phalanges of the hands and feet are reduced, due to the fusion of the proximal and medial segments, resulting in greater strength. The hands are larger than the feet, and the enlarged claws are spade-shaped for movement through the soil. A sprawling posture is useful for moving through narrow passageways. Typical of fossorial mammals, the olecranon (elbow) is expanded for the attachment of large arm muscles. All these adaptations would have enabled Docofossor to effectively swim through the ground. Similar to moles, the cheek teeth are hypsodont and adapted to catch and eat subterranean invertebrates.

SEE ENTRY ON PAGE 19

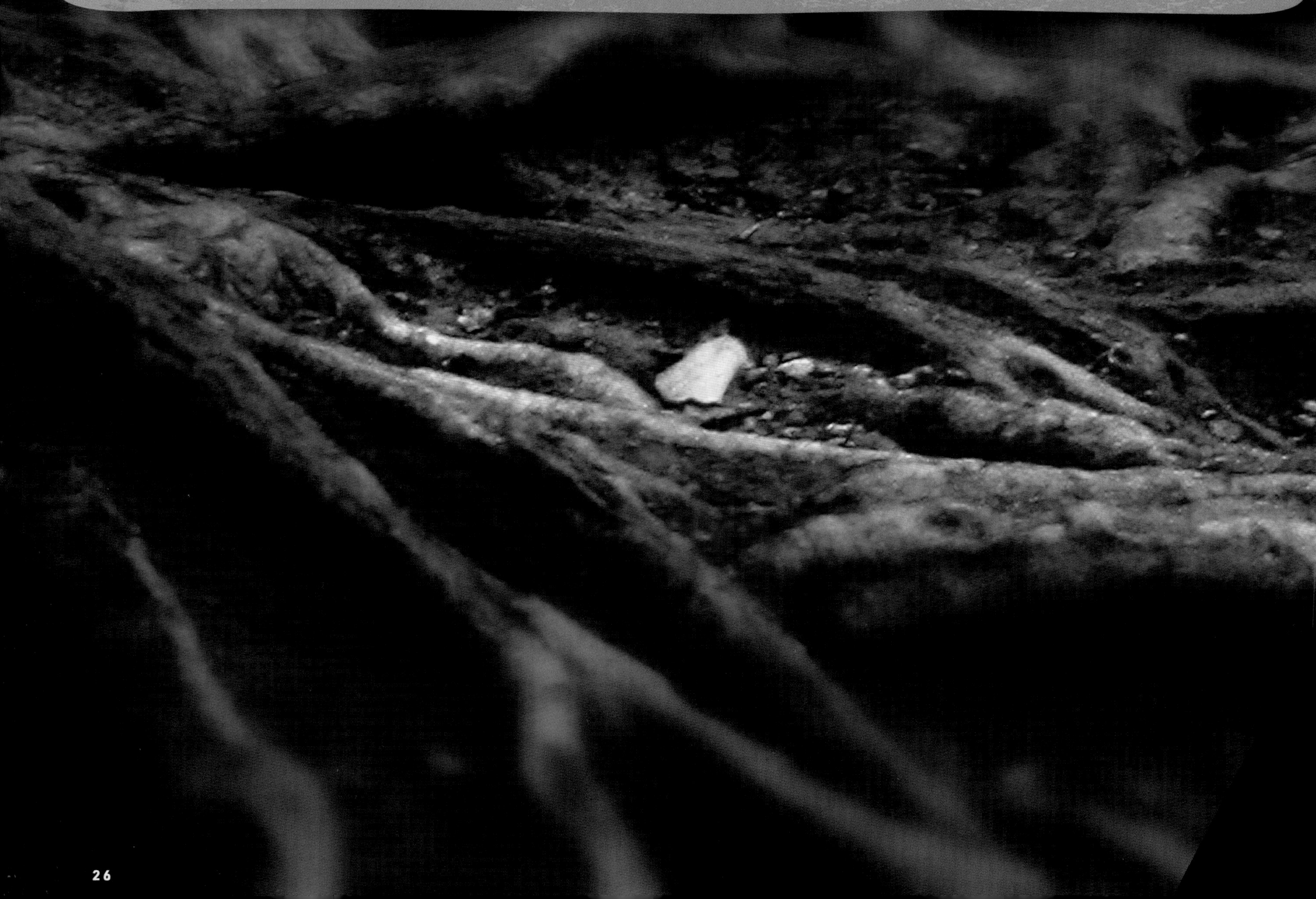

HARAMIYIDA

The group name is derived from the Arabic word *haramiya*, meaning "trickster." Haramiyidans are archaic members of Allotheria that originated during the late Triassic. They were highly specialized mammals with a new pattern of puncture-crushing occlusion that differs dramatically from the grinding or shearing mechanisms of other Early Mesozoic mammals. Early members of this group were shrew-like insectivores, while later forms evolved to resemble squirrels, possums, and sugar gliders.

HARAMIYAVIA CLEMMENSENI

NAME MEANING: Lars Clemmensen's trickster grandmother

AGE: Late Triassic (206–202 MYA)

DISTRIBUTION: North America

SIZE: Unknown

DIET: Mesocarnivore

ESSENTIAL FACTS: Discovered in Greenland, Haramiyavia is thought to have had a heavily insectivorous diet. Its name refers to its status as the oldest-known among the haramiyids.

CIFELLIODON WAHKARMOOSUCH

NAME MEANING: Richard Cifelli's tooth; yellow cat

AGE: Early Cretaceous (139–124 MYA)

DISTRIBUTION: North America

SIZE: 2–2.8 pounds (0.91–1.27 kilograms)

DIET: Hypocarnivore

ESSENTIAL FACTS: Cifelliodon is known for an exceptionally well-preserved skull, which is housed at the Natural History Museum of Utah.

MAIOPATAGIUM FURCULIFERUM

NAME MEANING: Mother skin membrane; similar fork

AGE: Middle Jurassic (165–153 MYA)

DISTRIBUTION: Asia

SIZE: (9 centimeters) HBL; (13 centimeters) TL

DIET: Herbivore

ESSENTIAL FACTS: Its species name references the fused interclavicle and clavicles that are similar to the furcula (wishbone) found in birds.

VILEVOLODON DIPLOMYLOS

NAME MEANING: Double grinding glider tooth

AGE: Middle Jurassic (161–160 MYA)

DISTRIBUTION: Asia

SIZE: About squirrel-sized

DIET: Herbivore

ESSENTIAL FACTS: The morphology of Vilevolodon's feet is similar to that of bats, suggesting it used an upside-down hanging behavior when roosting.

SHENSHOU LUI

NAME MEANING: Lu Jianhua's god animal

AGE: Middle Jurassic (160 MYA)

DISTRIBUTION: Asia

SIZE: 11 ounces (300 grams)

DIET: Herbivore

ESSENTIAL FACTS: Shenshou was an arboreal, squirrel-like animal with a light skeleton, a long prehensile (capable of grasping) tail, along with hands and feet adapted for clutching.

XIANSHOU LINGLONG

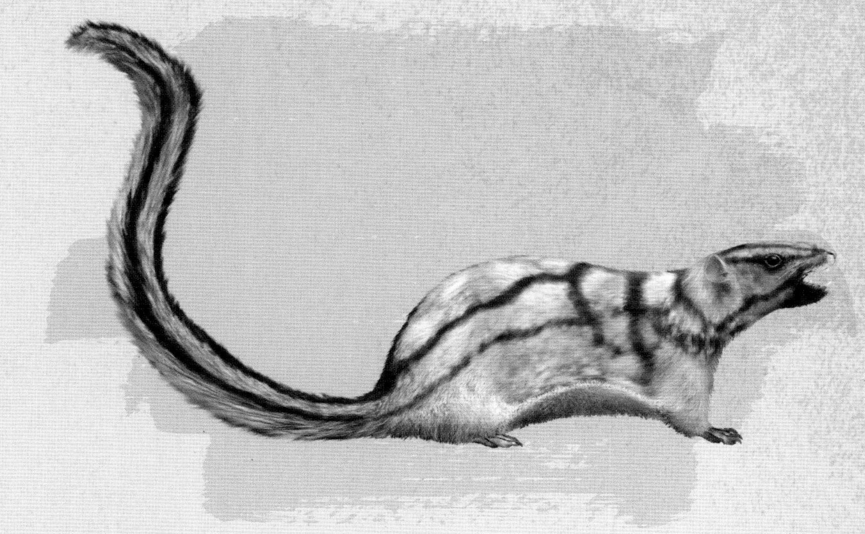

NAME MEANING: Exquisite immortal beast

AGE: Middle Jurassic (160 MYA)

DISTRIBUTION: Asia

SIZE: 2.9 ounces (83 grams)

DIET: Herbivore

ESSENTIAL FACTS: Direct evidence for a patagium has never been found with Xianshou, but it is very likely that it too was a glider just like *Maiopatagium* and *Vilevolodon*, as they shared similar morphology of the limbs and feet.

ARBOROHARAMIYA JENKINSI

NAME MEANING: Jenkins' tree trickster

AGE: Middle Jurassic (159 MYA)

DISTRIBUTION: Asia

SIZE: 12.5 ounces (354 grams)

DIET: Herbivore

ESSENTIAL FACTS: Despite being the largest known haramiyidan, Jenkins' Arborharamiya was still no bigger than today's eastern gray squirrel (*Sciurus carolinensis*).

GONDWANATHERIA

As their name suggests, gondwanatheres are known only from the southern supercontinent of Gondwana, the landmass formed by South America, Antarctica, Australia, Africa, India, and Madagascar, where fossils of these animals have been found. First appearing in the late Cretaceous, the group persisted in South America until the early Miocene, making them the last-surviving group of allotheres. Members of this group are specialized herbivores with deep, robust snouts and well-developed chewing muscles. Included among the group are some of the first mammals to develop grazing adaptations.

VINTANA SERTICHI

NAME MEANING: Joseph Sertich's luck

AGE: Late Cretaceous (66 MYA)

DISTRIBUTION: Madagascar

SIZE: 18 pounds (8.74 kilograms)

DIET: Herbivore

ESSENTIAL FACTS: Vintana is known for the first well-preserved skull of any gondwanathere, and its features reveal a relation between gondwanatheres, haramiyidans, and multituberculates. It is the largest Mesozoic mammal known from the Southern Hemisphere.

GONDWANATHERIUM PATAGONICUM

NAME MEANING: Patagonian beast of Gondwana

AGE: Late Cretaceous (72–66 MYA)

DISTRIBUTION: South America

SIZE: Unknown

DIET: Herbivore; grazer

ESSENTIAL FACTS: Gondwanatherium may be the first mammals to evolve grazing specializations; its cheek teeth were hypsodont and adapted to process tough, abrasive vegetation found at ground level. Its Cenozoic relative, Sudamerica, had similar dental morphology; that indicates they probably had a similar diet.

SUDAMERICA AMEGHINOI

NAME MEANING: Florentino Ameghino's South America

AGE: Middle Paleocene to Early Eocene (61–48.6 MYA)

DISTRIBUTION: South America

SIZE: Unknown

DIET: Herbivore; grazer

ESSENTIAL FACTS: Sudamerica is the last-known, officially recognized gondwanathere. Another animal, *Patagonia peregrina*, is from the late Miocene and lived in Argentina. It was originally thought to have been a metatherian, but recently researchers have suggested it was a sudamericid gondwanathere.

ADALATHERIUM HUI

NAME MEANING: Yaoming Hu's crazy beast

AGE: Late Cretaceous (70–66 MYA)

DISTRIBUTION: Madagascar

SIZE: 20 inches (52 centimeters) HBL; 4–11 pounds (1.7–5.2 kilograms)

DIET: Herbivore

ESSENTIAL FACTS: Its skeleton is the most complete of any Southern Hemisphere Mesozoic mammal and the second largest after Vintana.

MULTITUBERCULATA

Multituberculates were the most successful groups of mammals in terms of their longevity; the group originated by the Middle Jurassic (130 MYA), survived past the K/Pg mass extinction, and became extinct by the late Eocene. They achieved their peak diversity and abundance during the late Cretaceous and Paleocene, with about 150 described species from within this interval. Their method of reproduction is not known, although they were most likely egg-layers like modern monotremes. Multituberculates were mostly herbivorous and were ecologically and anatomically analogous to rodents such as mice, voles, and squirrels; they had chisel-shaped incisors separated by the cheek teeth by a diastema, or toothless gap along the tooth row. The name *multituberculate* refers to creatures having multiple rows of individual cusps on their cheek teeth. The order's gradual decline and eventual extinction by the end of the Eocene corresponds to the emergence of rodents during this epoch.

PLAGIAULAX BECKLESII

NAME MEANING: Beckles' oblique groove

AGE: Early Cretaceous

DISTRIBUTION: Europe

SIZE: Unknown

DIET: Herbivore

ESSENTIAL FACTS: Plagiaulax is known from a nearly complete dentary (lower jaw bone) discovered in Dorset, England. It was described in 1857, making it the first multituburculate to be described in scientific research.

PAULCHOFFATIA DELGADOI

NAME MEANING: Delgado's Paul Choffat

AGE: Late Jurassic (145 MYA)

DISTRIBUTION: Europe

SIZE: Unknown (probably rat-sized)

DIET: Herbivore

ESSENTIAL FACTS: This creature is type species which represents the family Paulchoffatiidae, a group that occurred from the late Jurassic to early Cretaceous of Europe. Most were found in Spain and Portugal.

SINOBAATAR LINGYUANENSIS

NAME MEANING: Chinese hero from Lingyuan City

AGE: Early Cretaceous (125 MYA)

DISTRIBUTION: Eurasia

SIZE: About mouse-sized

DIET: Herbivore

ESSENTIAL FACTS: Sinobaatar is one of two mammal species (the other being the symmetrodont Zhangheotherium) found preserved as stomach contents within the dinosaur *Sinosauropteryx prima*. This shows that mammals were preyed upon by dinosaurs.

BOFFIUS SPLENDIDUS

NAME MEANING: Unknown

AGE: Early Paleocene (65–62 MYA)

DISTRIBUTION: Eurasia

SIZE: 66 pounds (30 kilograms)

DIET: Herbivore

ESSENTIAL FACTS: Boffius is the only member of the family Boffiidae characterized by its large size compared to other multituberculates; it was about two-thirds the size of *Taeniolabis taoensis*. It was certainly a giant among the species from the early Paleocene Hainin locality in China, where it was found.

BARBATODON TRANSYLVANICUS

NAME MEANING: Transylvanian Bărbat River tooth

AGE: Late Cretaceous (66 MYA)

DISTRIBUTION: Eurasia

SIZE: Unknown

DIET: Hypercarnivore

SEE MORE ON PAGES 36–37

LITOVOI THOLOCEPHALOS

NAME MEANING: Dome-headed litovoi

AGE: Late Cretaceous (66 MYA)

DISTRIBUTION: Eurasia

SIZE: Unknown

DIET: Hypercarnivore

ESSENTIAL FACTS: Interestingly, Litovoi has undergone extreme brain size reduction, having one of the smallest brains in proportion to body size of any mammal. Despite this, its sense of smell appears to have been extremely well-developed. This species also had an unusual domed skull.

HAININA BELGICA

NAME MEANING: From Hainin, Belgium

AGE: Late Cretaceous (66 MYA)

DISTRIBUTION: Eurasia

SIZE: Unknown

DIET: Hypercarnivore

ESSENTIAL FACTS: When Hateg Island connected to the rest of Europe during the Paleocene, kogaionids that survived the K/Pg extinction experienced a short-lived expansion into the mainland, where they competed with other small insectivorous mammals. The last of the family, members of the genus *Hainina* are known from Belgium, Spain, and France.

PTILODUS MONTANUS

NAME MEANING: Montana short-haired

AGE: Middle Paleocene (63 MYA)

DISTRIBUTION: North America

SIZE: 23 ounces (650 grams)

DIET: Herbivore

ESSENTIAL FACTS: One of the largest members of the genus *Ptilodus*, the most well-known representatives of a family of arboreal squirrel-like multituberculates, the Ptilodontidae. The *Montana Ptilodus* is among the largest of this group yet known, being the size of an eastern gray squirrel (*Sciurus carolinensis*).

BAIOTOMEUS DOUGLASSI

NAME MEANING: Douglass' little cutter

AGE: Early Paleocene (65–62 MYA)

DISTRIBUTION: North America

SIZE: 7 ounces (200 grams)

DIET: Herbivore

ESSENTIAL FACTS: The postcranial skeleton is unknown, but it may be inferred that, like the closely related *Ptilodus*, the *Baiotomeus* were arboreal animals with grasping digits, sharp claws, rotating hindfeet, and prehensile tails.

PROCHETODON FOXI

NAME MEANING: Unknown

AGE: Late Paleocene

DISTRIBUTION: North America

SIZE: 7 ounces (200 grams)

DIET: Herbivore

ESSENTIAL FACTS: Members of the genus *Prochetodon* are the latest surviving representatives of the family Ptilodontidae.

BARBATODON TRANSYLVANICUS

ESSENTIAL FACTS: The Kogaionidae, a family of multituberculates that evolved in isolation on the late Cretaceous island of Hateg, a landmass which became Transylvania, Romania, in recent times. Like some shrews, kogaionids have tooth cusps coated with red, iron-pigmented enamel similar to what is observed within modern "red-toothed shrews" of the subfamily Soricinae. In these shrews, this adaptation extends the functional life of the tooth cusps so that they can deal with abrasive prey items on a regular basis. This suggests that, instead of being purely herbivorous or hypocarnivorous like other multituberculates, kogaionids trended more toward hypercarnivory; they probably consumed many hard-shelled insects or fossorial invertebrates like worms. These multituberculates represent the oldest record of iron-pigmented teeth in mammalian evolution.

The Transylvanian Barbatodon is the first mammal described from the Mesozoic of Romania. In addition to isolated teeth, it is known from a well-preserved partial skull and jaws which enabled the first description of the complete dentition for a kogaionid. The red enamel is particularly prominent in this species, suggesting that it specialized in feeding on particularly well-armored insects such as beetles or that it dug up subterranean invertebrates that would have been coated in abrasive minerals.

SEE ENTRY ON PAGE 34

CORRIEBAATAR MARYWALTERSAE

NAME MEANING: Mary Walters' hero of Corrie Williams

AGE: Early Cretaceous (125 MYA)

DISTRIBUTION: Australia

SIZE: Unknown

DIET: Herbivore

ESSENTIAL FACTS: Corriebaatar is the only member of the family Corriebaataridae and represents the first evidence of multituberculates in Australia.

MENISCOESSUS ROBUSTUS

NAME MEANING: Robust small crescent tooth

AGE: Late Cretaceous (66 MYA)

DISTRIBUTION: North America

SIZE: 7.3 pounds (3.3 kilograms)

DIET: Herbivore

ESSENTIAL FACTS: Members of the genus *Meniscoessus* are relatively large by multituberculate standards, with the Robust Meniscoessus being one of the largest. Its fossils are known from latest Cretaceous and possibly earliest Paleocene of the Hell Creek Formation in western North America.

CIMOLOMYS GRACILIS

NAME MEANING: Unknown

AGE: Late Cretaceous

DISTRIBUTION: North America

SIZE: 15 ounces (415 grams)

DIET: Herbivore

ESSENTIAL FACTS: Cimolomys is the type species of the genus described by Othniel Cherles Marsh in 1889. This species is known from a nearly complete skull.

YUBATAAR ZHONGYUANENSIS

NAME MEANING: Henan Province hero from Zhongyuan

AGE: Late Cretaceous (66 MYA)

DISTRIBUTION: Eurasia

SIZE: 3 pounds (1.4 kilograms)

DIET: Herbivore

ESSENTIAL FACTS: Yubataar is the largest known Mesozoic multituberculate and an early relative of the taeniolabids and lambdopsalids. It had the characteristic enlarged grinding molars of these later groups.

TAENIOLABIS TAOENSIS

NAME MEANING: Banded incisors from Taos

AGE: Early Paleocene

DISTRIBUTION: North America

SIZE: Up to 220 pounds (100 kilograms)

DIET: Herbivore; browser

SEE MORE ON PAGES 40–41

KIMBETOPSALIS SIMMONSAE

NAME MEANING: Nancy Simmons' Kimbeto Wash cutting shears

AGE: Early Paleocene

DISTRIBUTION: North America

SIZE: 44 pounds (20 kilograms)

DIET: Herbivore; browser

ESSENTIAL FACTS: The Kimbetopsalis was smaller than its relative *Taeniolabis*, but still relatively large by multituberculate standards. It was about the same size as a beaver.

TAENIOLABIS TAOENSIS

ESSENTIAL FACTS: Known only from North America, the Taeniolabididae includes the largest multituberculates known to have ever existed. These animals were among the first mammals to attain large body sizes after the K/Pg mass extinction, appearing in the fossil record just a few thousand years after. The genus *Taeniolabis* appears in the fossil record between 730,000 years and 2 million years after the extinction of the dinosaurs. The group became extinct by the end of the Paleocene.

Named for the town of Taos, New Mexico, the Taos Taeniolabis is an iconic Paleocene mammal from the Western Interior Seaway of North America and the type species of its family. It was named by Edward Drinker Cope in 1882, making it among the first early Cenozoic mammals to be described. It also holds the distinction of being not only the largest multituberculate known to date, but also the largest known non-therian mammal, which is a mammal unrelated to either placentals or marsupials. Although estimates of its mass have varied wildly, Taos Taeniolabis is about the size of a Giant Beaver (*Castoroides ohioensis*). The closely related Lambert's Taeniolabis (*T. lamberti*) is almost as big. These animals are considered to be the most specialized multituberculates, possessing particularly large, multi-cusped molars for grinding vegetation. They were browsing herbivores that fed on leaves and fruits in the dense forests in which they lived.

SEE ENTRY ON PAGE 39

LAMBDOPSALIS BULLA

NAME MEANING: Rounded lambda cutting shears

AGE: Late Paleocene

DISTRIBUTION: Eurasia

SIZE: Unknown

DIET: Herbivore

ESSENTIAL FACTS: Closely related to the North American taeniolabids, the Lambdopsalidae were an Asian lineage that persisted into the Eocene. Lambdopsalis itself is the only multituberculate to have preserved evidence of fur.

PROTOTHERIA

MONOTREMATA

Monotremes are the most ancient group of modern mammals. Their first definitive fossils date back to the Barremian stage of the Cretaceous period (126 MYA), with potential origins in the late Jurassic. Due to their early divergence, monotremes retain a number of traits from their reptilian ancestors. Most famously, females lay leathery eggs from which underdeveloped young hatch. They also have extra bones in the shoulder girdle, which more derived mammalian groups lack. They also have a reptile-like sprawling gait and the presence of a cloaca, an opening on the body which serves as a common exit point for the urinary, digestive, and reproductive tracts (the name "monotreme" is a reference to this, derived from the Greek words *monós* and *trêma*, meaning "one hole" or "one opening"). Monotremes appear to have been limited to the southern continents of Australia, Antarctica, and South America throughout their fossil history.

TEINOLOPHOS TRUSLERI

NAME MEANING: Peter Trusler's extended lophs

AGE: Early Cretaceous (123 MYA)

DISTRIBUTION: Australia

SIZE: Unknown

DIET: Possibly insectivore

ESSENTIAL FACTS: The earliest known monotreme known only from a partial left lower jaw with a single molar that resembles that of the later *Steropodon* and the platypus *Obdurodon*. A total length of nine centimeters has been tentatively estimated for this species, making it the smallest known monotreme.

STEROPODON GALMANI

NAME MEANING: Galman's lightning tooth

AGE: Middle Cretaceous (105–93 MYA)

DISTRIBUTION: Australia

SIZE: 16–20 inches (40–50 centimeters)

DIET: Mesocarnivore

ESSENTIAL FACTS: The Steropodon was the first Mesozoic mammal discovered from Australia. This species is known from a single jaw fragment containing three molars that resemble those of the Miocene platypus *Obdurodon*.

KOLLIKODON RITCHIEI

NAME MEANING: Alex Ritchie's bun tooth

AGE: Middle Cretaceous (99–96 MYA)

DISTRIBUTION: Australia

SIZE: Unknown, but slightly larger than *Steropodon*

DIET: Possibly molluscivore or herbivore

ESSENTIAL FACTS: Kollikodon had broad, robust molars that lacked cutting ridges; instead, it had four rounded cusps. Researchers believe perhaps it was a shellfish-eater or an herbivore that consumed hard foods like nuts and seeds.

PATAGORHYNCHUS PASCUALI

NAME MEANING: Rosendo Pascual's Patagonian nose

AGE: Late Cretaceous (70 MYA)

DISTRIBUTION: South America

SIZE: Unknown

DIET: Possibly aquatic hypercarnivore

ESSENTIAL FACTS: Described in 2023 based on a single molar and lower jaw fragment, this is the oldest known monotreme from South America. It was perhaps an early platypus, though this is yet to be confirmed.

ORNITHORYNCHIDAE

Platypuses are semiaquatic monotremes that seem to originate in the middle Paleocene and represented today by the Duck-Billed Platypus (*Ornithorynchus anatinus*). The most notable characteristic of the family is the sensitive, flattened rostrum resembling a duck's bill and is covered in electroreceptors and mechanoreceptors to aid in prey detection and navigation through dark waters. There seems to be a trend of tooth reduction among the family leading up to the modern species. The tail is broad and flat, and the feet are webbed for propulsion. Sharp spurs are present on the ankles of both sexes. Males are able to use spurs to deliver a potent venom used in conflict and defense, making the platypus one of the few venomous modern mammals.

MONOTREMATUM SUDAMERICANUM

NAME MEANING: South American monotreme

AGE: Middle Paleocene (61 MYA)

DISTRIBUTION: South America

SIZE: Unknown; about river otter–sized

DIET: Aquatic hypercarnivore

ESSENTIAL FACTS: The oldest and only platypus known outside of Australia. Its early presence in South America suggests that the family potentially originated there before dispersing to Australia through Antarctica while the continents were still linked.

OBDURODON DICKSONI

NAME MEANING: Dickson's lasting tooth

AGE: Early Miocene (20–15 MYA)

DISTRIBUTION: Australia

SIZE: Unknown; about river otter–sized

DIET: Aquatic hypercarnivore

SEE MORE ON PAGES 46–47

TACHYGLOSSIDAE

Echidnas are a family of terrestrial, insectivorous monotremes endemic to Australia and New Guinea; they first appeared during the Miocene. Distinguishing features include long, protrusible tongues with which to gather prey and hairs that have become modified into sharp quills for defense as seen in hedgehogs and porcupines. They are believed to have diverged from an aquatic ancestor within Ornithorynchidae at some point during the Middle or Late Neogene. Evidence of this relationship includes the retention of a beak-like rostrum that retains a degree of electroreception, ankle spurs, and several skeletal features which evolved first among platypuses for efficient movement through water.

MEGALIBGWILIA ROBUSTA

NAME MEANING: Robust, large Libgwil

AGE: Middle Miocene

DISTRIBUTION: Australia

SIZE: Similar to short-beaked echidna (*Tachyglossus aculeatus*)

DIET: Insectivore

ESSENTIAL FACTS: This is the oldest-known species of echidna and the only echidna known from the Miocene epoch. The genus name comes from the Greek word *mégas* (meaning "great) and the Wemba Wemba Aboriginal name *libgwil* for the modern short-beaked echidna, plus the Latin suffix *-ia*.

OBDURODON DICKSONI

ESSENTIAL FACTS: Obdurodon is commonly known as the "Riversleigh Platypus" because its fossils have been found in the Riversleigh World Heritage Area. It is known from an exceptionally well-preserved and complete skull and lower jaw. Unlike the modern species, which lose their teeth soon after birth, the Riversleigh Platypus and other members of their genus retained their teeth throughout life. Because of this, the genus name *Obdurodon* translates to "lasting tooth." The upper jaw had two premolars and two molars on each side, and the lower jaw had two molars and three molars on each side.

In comparison to the modern platypus, the skull of the Riversleigh Platypus was proportionally larger; its bill had a more spoon-like shape. Rather than having a V-shaped opening beginning at the tip of the bill, Riversleigh Platypus had an oval-shaped opening that was fully enclosed in bone. This could imply that the extinct species was less reliant on electroreception when locating prey, and more powerful jaws could suggest a different range of foraging behaviors. Researchers have also suggested that this species may have used its bill to dig in soft substrates. Its diet would have consisted of freshwater crustaceans, fish, and perhaps other aquatic vertebrates.

SEE ENTRY ON PAGE 45

MURRAYGLOSSUS HACKETTI

NAME MEANING: John Hackett's and Peter Murray's tongue

AGE: Pleistocene

DISTRIBUTION: Australia

SIZE: 2 feet (60 centimeters) SH, 3.3 feet (100 centimeters) HBL, 66 pounds (30 kilograms)

DIET: Insectivore

ESSENTIAL FACTS: Known commonly as "Hackett's Giant Echidna," this animal is the largest species of monotreme known to have ever lived. It had longer, straighter legs compared to other echidnas, which had possibly been adapted for traversing over greater distances.

AUSTRALOSPHENIDA

The Australosphenida is poorly understood grouping of mammals from the Middle Jurassic through Early Cretaceous of Gondwana. The group shows notable similarities to monotremes in terms of their southern distribution and certain dental characteristics. Some researchers believe that the two should be merged.

AUSKTRIBOSPHENIDAE

Members of this family are known from the Early Cretaceous of Australia and South America.

BISHOPS WHITMOREI

NAME MEANING: Barry Bishop and Frank Whitmore

AGE: Early Cretaceous (130–125 MYA)

DISTRIBUTION: Australia

SIZE: Unknown; about shrew-sized

DIET: Insectivore

ESSENTIAL FACTS: Known for a left dentary with almost the entire dentition, Bishops was one of eight candidates for Victoria's state fossil emblem in 2021.

AUSKTRIBOSPHENOS NYKTOS

NAME MEANING: Australian tribosphenic mammal of the night

AGE: Early Cretaceous (121–113 MYA)

DISTRIBUTION: Australia

SIZE: Unknown; about shrew-sized

DIET: Insectivore

ESSENTIAL FACTS: Ausktribosphenos is known only from a single right dentary with one premolar and three molars. The term *tribosphenic* describes a molar with three peaks, typically found among therian mammals.

SYMMETRODONTA

Symmetrodonts are a group of small, shrew-like Mesozoic mammals known mostly from the Early Cretaceous. They are known for the unique morphology of the upper molars, which have three large, pointed cusps arranged in a triangular arrangement. They're notable for sharing a number of anatomical traits with monotremes, such as a semi-erect sprawling posture, extra bones in the pectoral girdle, and ankle spurs that may have secreted venom. Traditionally there has been only one family, Spalacotheriidae, contained within this group with the possible inclusion of Zhangheotheriidae.

AKIDOLESTES CIFELLII

NAME MEANING: Richard Cifelli's pointed thief

AGE: Early Cretaceous (122 MYA)

DISTRIBUTION: Eurasia

SIZE: About shrew-sized

DIET: Hypercarnivore; mostly insectivorous

ESSENTIAL FACTS: The third symmetrodont to be known from a complete skeleton, it is interpreted to have been mostly terrestrial, although it had the ability to climb.

SPALACOTHERIUM TRICUSPIDENS

NAME MEANING: Mole beast with three-cusped teeth

AGE: Early Cretaceous (145–140 MYA)

DISTRIBUTION: Eurasia

SIZE: Unknown; about shrew-sized

DIET: Hypercarnivore; mostly insectivorous

ESSENTIAL FACTS: Spalacotherium is the type species of the family Spalacotheriidae.

SYMMETROLESTES PARVUS

NAME MEANING: Small symmetric thief

AGE: Early Cretaceous (130–113 MYA)

DISTRIBUTION: Eurasia

SIZE: Unknown

DIET: Hypercarnivore; mostly insectivorous

ESSENTIAL FACTS: Symmetrolestes is the only symmetrodont known from Japan, specifically coming from the Dinosaur Quarry in Kitadani Formation.

MAOTHERIUM SINENSIS

NAME MEANING: Chinese fur beast

AGE: Early Cretaceous (124.6 MYA)

DISTRIBUTION: Eurasia

SIZE: Mouse-sized

DIET: Hypercarnivore

ESSENTIAL FACTS: Discovered in Liaoning Province, China, the genus name of this species refers to the discovery of fur impressions around its nearly complete skeleton.

ZHANGHEOTHERIUM QUINQUECUSPIDENS

NAME MEANING: Zhang He's five-cusped beast

AGE: Early Cretaceous (125 MYA)

DISTRIBUTION: Eurasia

SIZE: Squirrel-sized

DIET: Hypercarnivore; mostly insectivorous

SEE MORE ON PAGES 52–53

THERIIMORPHA

ZHANGHEOTHERIUM QUINQUECUSPIDENS

ESSENTIAL FACTS: Zhangheotherium fossils are known from complete skeletons found in Jianshangou Valley in the Liaoning Province of northeastern China, some of which include fur impressions preserved around the bones. The dental formula is I3/3, C1/1, P2/2, M5/6. It differs from other symmetrodonts because they have two additional cusps, making five in total rather than the more typical three, the trait which inspired its specific name. The cusps are relatively robust, perhaps indicating that it may have fed on tough prey such as large, hard-shelled beetles.

Zhangheotherium was about the size of a squirrel or rat and shows several skeletal adaptations that indicate it was scansorial. The shoulder joint appears to have had a wider range of motion compared to other symmetrodonts (at least the ones for which post-cranial bones are known) and the limbs were also relatively long. This could indicate that it was a more active climber compared to its close relatives. There is direct fossil evidence that this species was occasionally hunted by the small theropod dinosaur Sinosauropteryx; researchers have found a pair of jaws from the animal found preserved in the stomach contents of the dinosaur.

SEE ENTRY ON PAGE 51

FRUITAFOSSOR WINDSCHEFFELI

NAME MEANING: Windscheffel's digger of Fruita, Colorado

AGE: Late Jurassic (150 MYA)

DISTRIBUTION: North America

SIZE: 0.2 ounces (6 grams)

DIET: Fossorial insectivore

SEE MORE ON PAGES 56–57

EUTRICONODONTA

Eutriconodonta were a group of mostly carnivorous mammals characterized by molar teeth with three main cusps on the crowns that are arranged in a row. Similar to monotremes, they possessed venomous spurs and sprawling limbs with the retention of extra bones in the pectoral girdle. They had a modern ear anatomy, the main difference from therian mammals (Metatheria and Eutheria) being that the ear ossicles (a small bone in the inner ear) were still somewhat connected to the jaw via the Meckel's cartilage. Included among this group are the largest Mesozoic mammals, some comparable in size to badgers. Successful though they were, it is believed that they may have been replaced by deltatheroidean metatherians in the later Cretaceous as the dominant mammalian predators.

TRICONODONTIDAE

Triconodonts lived from the Middle Jurassic to Late Cretaceous of Eurasia and North America, with a possible presence in South America and Africa.

TRICONODON MORDAX

NAME MEANING: Biting three-coned teeth

AGE: Early Cretaceous (145–140 MYA)

DISTRIBUTION: Europe

SIZE: 8–11 pounds (3.5–5 kilograms)

DIET: Hypercarnivore

ESSENTIAL FACTS: This was a cat-sized carnivore with powerful jaws and unique three-cusped teeth adapted for shearing. Endocasts of the skull show their sense of smell was well-developed.

ALTICONODON LINDOEI

NAME MEANING: Lindoe's high-coned teeth

AGE: Late Cretaceous (84.5–83.5 MYA)

DISTRIBUTION: North America

SIZE: Unknown

DIET: Hypercarnivore

ESSENTIAL FACTS: A late-surviving eutriconodont, Alticonodon had the most specialized shearing teeth among the group, suggesting that it was highly predatory. It existed during a time when most mammalian predator niches had been taken up by metatherians.

GOBICONODONTIDAE

Included among the gobiconodonts are the largest known Mesozoic mammals which had a strong presence in the small predator niches of the Middle Jurassic to Early Cretaceous.

FRUITAFOSSOR WINDSCHEFFELI

ESSENTIAL FACTS: This mammal was found in the Morrison Formation in the state of Colorado. Researchers nicknamed it "Popeye" because of its large forelimbs that were adapted to digging. The humerus (long, upper arm bone) is especially short and thick; its shape is similar to that of moles, showing that it dug with a similar "swimming" motion. The ulna (a bone in the forearm) has an expanded olecranon process (elbow) for increased muscle attachment. Large hands with stocky finger bones and thickened claws made effective spades for pushing aside soil and pebbles. The vertebral column also shows similarities to those of xenarthrans, which evolved from a fossorial ancestor; there are extra points of contact among the vertebra termed "xenarthrous processes," which make the spine more rigid.

The teeth bear a striking resemblance to those of modern armadillos and aardvarks: open-rooted, peg-shaped, and lacking enamel. This tooth type is most commonly found among mammals which feed on colonial insects (myrmecophagy). If the same was true for Fruitafossor, it would make it the earliest-known mammal to have had such a diet.

SEE ENTRY ON PAGE 54

SPINOLESTES XENARTHROSUS

NAME MEANING: Strange-jointed spiny thief

AGE: Early Cretaceous (125 MYA)

DISTRIBUTION: Europe

SIZE: 1.7–2.5 ounces (50–70 grams)

DIET: Hypercarnivore

ESSENTIAL FACTS: Spinolestes is known from an exquisitely preserved, complete skeleton from Spain and includes traces of soft tissue. The pelage (hair or fur) had thickened, stiffened guard hairs that formed small quills, making this the earliest-known prickly mammal. Its vertebrae were seemingly adapted to handle stresses involved in digging.

GOBICONODON OSTROMI

NAME MEANING: John Ostrom's Gobi Desert coned teeth

AGE: Middle Cretaceous (109–98 MYA)

DISTRIBUTION: North America

SIZE: 14 inches (35 centimeters) HBL

DIET: Hypercarnivore

ESSENTIAL FACTS: Gobiconodon is one of the largest and best-preserved members of the genus. It had an interesting feature for predatory mammals: the lower canines were greatly reduced and the front incisors were caniniform (formed like canine teeth) for stabbing.

REPENOMAMUS ROBUSTUS

NAME MEANING: Robust reptile-mammal

AGE: Early Cretaceous (125–123.2 MYA)

DISTRIBUTION: Asia

SIZE: 16 inches (41.2 centimeters) HBL; 8.8–13 pounds (4–6 kilograms)

DIET: Hypercarnivore

SEE MORE ON PAGES 60–61

REPENOMAMUS GIGANTICUS

NAME MEANING: Gigantic reptile-mammal

AGE: Early Cretaceous (125–123.2 MYA)

DISTRIBUTION: Asia

SIZE: 27 inches (68.2 centimeters) HBL; 14 inches (36.4 centimeters) TL; 26–31 pounds (12–14 kilograms)

DIET: Hypercarnivore

ESSENTIAL FACTS: True to its name, the Giant Repenomamus is believed to be the largest known Mesozoic mammal being about as large as an American badger (*Taxidea taxus*) and larger than some of the predatory dinosaurs with which it coexisted.

JEHOLODENTIDAE

Currently there are only two known species within this family, both of them small, long-bodied carnivores.

YANOCONODON ALLINI

NAME MEANING: Edgar Allin's coned teeth from the Yan Mountains

AGE: Early Cretaceous (122 MYA)

DISTRIBUTION: Asia

SIZE: 5 inches (13 centimeters) HBL

DIET: Hypercarnivore

ESSENTIAL FACTS: With its elongated body and sprawling limbs, the living animal would have had a striking resemblance to a furry lizard!

REPENOMAMUS ROBUSTUS

ESSENTIAL FACTS: One of the largest mammals of its time, the Robust Repenomamus was the size of a Tasmanian devil (*Sarcophillus harrisii*). It had a relatively elongated, powerfully built body set on short, robust sprawling limbs. The broad skull was similarly shaped like a reptile's, and it had powerful jaws ; its teeth were adapted for puncturing, tearing, and crushing. The dental formula I3/2, C1/1, P1/2, M5/5. Its fossils have been found in the Yixian Formation in China, a location famous for yielding exquisitely preserved remains of feathered dinosaurs. During the Early Cretaceous during which it lived, the area would have been covered in a moist forest habitat.

This species is most well-known for being the second line of direct evidence that Mesozoic mammals occasionally preyed on dinosaurs (the first being from the metatherian *Deltatheridium pretrituberculare*). One skeleton of a Robust Repenomamus included the disarticulated (separated) remains of a juvenile ceratopsian called *Psittacosaurus lujiatunensis* within its stomach cavity. Another remarkable find preserves the mammal locked in an apparent death struggle with an adult *P. lujiatunensis*. The mammal can be seen latching onto the much larger dinosaur with its jaws, hands, and feet.

SEE ENTRY ON PAGE 58

JEHOLODENS JENKINSI

NAME MEANING: Jenkins' teeth from Jehol

AGE: Early Cretaceous (125 MYA)

DISTRIBUTION: Asia

SIZE: (4 centimeters) HBL; (5 centimeters) TL

DIET: Hypercarnivore

ESSENTIAL FACTS: A virtually complete skull and skeleton of this animal are known from Liaoning, China. It had proportionally large eyes and was specialized for an arboreal (tree) lifestyle, with prehensile fingers and toes for grasping branches. It had forelimb proportions like that of modern climbing mammals, but its hindlimbs retained sprawling posture.

VOLATICOTHERINI

Volaticotheres were gliding eutriconodonts known from the Middle Jurassic to Early Cretaceous. These animals appear to have been fully carnivorous, with teeth adapted to deal with small animals. It has been speculated that later taxa (groups) could have been capable of fully powered flight similar to bats.

ARGENTOCONODON FARIASORUM

NAME MEANING: Ricardo Farias' Argentinian coned teeth

AGE: Middle Jurassic (179–178 MYA)

DISTRIBUTION: South America

SIZE: Unknown

DIET: Gliding hypercarnivore

ESSENTIAL FACTS: Argentoconodon is potentially the oldest known gliding mammal and one of only two eutriconodonts known from South America. Studies of its teeth and jaws suggests that it was a hunter of small vertebrate prey, as opposed to the insect-dominated diet of the more well-known Volaticotherium.

VOLATICOTHERIUM ANTIQUUM

NAME MEANING: Ancient gliding beast

AGE: Middle Jurassic (164 MYA)

DISTRIBUTION: Asia

SIZE: About squirrel-sized

DIET: Gliding hypercarnivore; insectivore

SEE MORE ON PAGES 64–65

ICHTHYOCONODON JAWOROWSKORUM

NAME MEANING: Jaworowska's fish(-eating) coned teeth

AGE: Early Cretaceous (145–140 MYA)

DISTRIBUTION: Africa

SIZE: Unknown

DIET: Gliding hypercarnivore; piscivore

ESSENTIAL FACTS: Ichthyoconodon is only known from two molar teeth which, while being morphologically similar to those of other volaticotheres, also show similarities to early piscivorous (animals that feed on fish) mammals. Combined with its discovery in marine deposits alongside various sea creatures, researchers think that Ichthyoconodon was a fish-hunting specialist, possibly capable of powered flight.

CLADOTHERIA

VOLATICOTHERIUM ANTIQUUM

ESSENTIAL FACTS: The only known fossil of Volaticotherium was recovered from the Daohugou Beds of Ningcheng County, Inner Mongolia, China. This fossil is an exceptionally well-preserved skeleton which retains traces of soft tissue, including a dense coat of fur and, crucially, the patagium (gliding membrane) which stretched between the limbs to the base of the tail. The hand was poorly preserved, so its anatomy is unknown. The digits of its hindfeet, however, are built for grasping and are ideal for climbing trees.

At the time of its discovery, Volaticotherium was the oldest-known gliding mammal, a distinction which has since been taken by fellow volaticothere Argetoconodon from South America, along with several gliding haramiyidans that are comparable in age or slightly older. The tail was flat and acted as a rudder for making midair direction changes and adjustments. The femur is similar in proportion to that of bats, built to resist flying stresses while making terrestrial locomotion extremely awkward. Volaticotherium was a carnivore with teeth adapted to puncturing and shearing. It is likely to have had a primarily insectivorous diet and perhaps agile enough to capture prey in flight. The teeth have backward-facing cusps; researchers assume this was for preventing the escape of captured prey.

SEE ENTRY ON PAGE 63

MERIDIOLESTIDA

Meridiolestidans appear to have been endemic to South America, first appearing in the fossil record in the Late Cretaceous; the group survived there until the Early Miocene. Evolutionarily, these mammals are related to metatherians and eutherians but do not belong to either group. Despite its scarce fossil record, known members of this group show significant variation, suggesting that they must have been quite diverse during their history.

CRONOPIO DENTIACUTUS

NAME MEANING: Sharp-toothed cronopio

AGE: Late Cretaceous (100–94 MYA)

DISTRIBUTION: South America

SIZE: Unknown; about squirrel-sized

DIET: Insectivore

ESSENTIAL FACTS: Cronopio is most notable for its elongated upper canine teeth that have earned it the nickname "saber-toothed squirrel." These teeth were probably used as weapons to settle territorial disputes.

REIGITHERIUM BUNODONTUM

NAME MEANING: Osvaldo A. Reig's beast with rounded teeth

AGE: Late Cretaceous (74–70 MYA)

DISTRIBUTION: South America

SIZE: Unknown; probably about rabbit-sized

DIET: Hypocarnivore

ESSENTIAL FACTS: Little is known about this species, although its robust cheek teeth suggest that it had a highly herbivorous diet.

PELIGROTHERIUM TROPICALIS

NAME MEANING: Tropical beast from Peligro

AGE: Early Paleocene (62–59 MYA)

DISTRIBUTION: South America

SIZE: 44 pounds (20 kilograms)

DIET: Hypocarnivore

ESSENTIAL FACTS: Peligrotherium was the largest known meridiolestid and the largest known mammal of the South American Early Paleocene. Despite its fierce looking canines and premolars, it was primarily herbivorous.

NECROLESTES PATAGONENSIS

NAME MEANING: Patagonian corpse robber

AGE: Early Miocene (18–16 MYA)

DISTRIBUTION: South America

SIZE: 6 inches (15 centimeters) HBL; 3–4 ounces (80–120 grams)

DIET: Fossorial insectivore

ESSENTIAL FACTS: The latest surviving meridiolestidan highly specialized to fossoriality, Necrolestes shares an unusual feature with modern African golden moles: the tendon for the muscle which flexes the wrist is ossified (turned to bone), effectively forming a third limb bone.

METATHERIA

The metatherians are commonly called "marsupials" due to their reproductive strategy; underdeveloped young are born after a short gestation and finish development in a special abdominal pouch known as the marsupium. There are two major clades: Deltatheroida and Marsupialiformes. Deltatheroida were small predatory metatherians with an Asian and North American distribution. Most became extinct at the end of the Cretaceous, although a few groups managed to survive into the Paleocene. The Marsupialiformes includes all modern marsupials and their fossil relatives. Unlike the deltatheroids, they achieved great ecological and morphological diversity during the Cenozoic, primarily distributed through southern continents of South America, Antarctica, Australia. Fossil metatherians are distinguishable from their eutherian counterparts by their dentition; the base metatherian dental formula is I5/4, C1/1, P3/3, M4/4, while eutherian mammals the layout is I3/3, C1/1, P4/4, M3/3. Well-developed epipubic bones, paired bony projections which extend forward from the pelvis, are often present These bony extensions were inherited from older mammalian groups, and were even present in non-mammalian cynodonts, although in some lineages like the sparassodonts they became primarily cartilaginous.

HERPETOTHERIIDAE

Herpetotheres are opossum-like metatherians that originated in North America in the Late Cretaceous and spread to Europe prior to the K/Pg mass extinction. They continued to persist in both hemispheres during the Cenozoic. Ironically, these animals became extinct in North America during the Early Miocene, and metatherians would not enter the continent again until the Pliocene, when opossums arrived from South America as part of the Great American Biotic Interchange. Herpetotherids persisted longer in Eurasia, their extinction seeming to coincide with a mid-Miocene cooling event.

MAASTRICHTIDELPHYS MEURISMETI

NAME MEANING: Meuris' and Smet's Maastrichtian opossum

AGE: Late Cretaceous (66 MYA)

DISTRIBUTION: Europe

SIZE: Unknown

DIET: Mesocarnivore

ESSENTIAL FACTS: This animal represents the first record of an opossum-like metatherian in Europe. This shows that these animals settled there at least 10 million years earlier than previously thought, most likely via a land route that once existed in the North Atlantic.

AMPHIPERATHERIUM FREQUENS

NAME MEANING: Frequent half-*Peratherium*

AGE: Middle Miocene (15 MYA)

DISTRIBUTION: Eurasia

SIZE: 6 inches (15 centimeters) HBL; 7 inches (17 centimeters) TL

DIET: Mesocarnivore

ESSENTIAL FACTS: The last of the herpetotheres and the last metatherian known to have lived in the Northern Hemisphere. The skeleton suggests that it was a scansorial animal that foraged on the ground but readily climbed trees.

HERPETOTHERIUM FUGAX

NAME MEANING: Fleeting creeping beast

AGE: Early Miocene (23–20 MYA)

DISTRIBUTION: North America

SIZE: 1.4–2.8 ounces (40–80 grams)

DIET: Mesocarnivore

ESSENTIAL FACTS: Members of this genus would have been ecologically similar to mouse opossums (*Marmosa*), meaning they were probably nocturnal arboreal animals that fed on insects and fruits.

PERATHERIUM AFRICANUS

NAME MEANING: African pouched beast

AGE: Late Oligocene

DISTRIBUTION: Australia

SIZE: Unknown

DIET: Mesocarnivore

ESSENTIAL FACTS: The African Peratherium has the distinction of being the first recognized metatherian from Africa. Discovered in Egypt, its ancestors migrated to the continent after the Tethys Sea receded at the end of the Eocene.

ASIATHERIIDAE

Sometimes called "Asian opossums," Asiatheres are a poorly known group of Asian metatherians that show a close relation to modern lineages, with several notable dental similarities.

ASIATHERIUM RESHETOVI

NAME MEANING: Yuri Reshetovi's Asian beast

AGE: Late Cretaceous (80 MYA)

DISTRIBUTION: Asia

SIZE: About mouse-sized

DIET: Mesocarnivore

ESSENTIAL FACTS: Known from an exceptionally complete skeleton found in Mongolia. The teeth of this mouse-sized animal are very similar to those of modern metatherians, suggesting a closer relation to them than to the contemporary deltatheridians.

ANATOLIADELPHYIDAE

Anatoliadelphyids are known for two described species that were endemic (native) to Turkey, which during the Middle Eocene was an island in the Tethys Sea known as Balkanatolia. The name *Anatolia* is the former name of Turkey.

ANATOLIADELPHYS MAASAE

NAME MEANING: Mary Maas' Anatolian opossum

AGE: Middle Eocene (44–43 MYA)

DISTRIBUTION: Turkey

SIZE: 6.6–8.8 pounds (3–4 kilograms)

DIET: Hypercarnivore

ESSENTIAL FACTS: Anatoliadelphys was a cat-sized predator with powerful, crushing jaws and teeth similar to those of the modern Tasmanian devil.

ORHANIYEIA NAUTA

NAME MEANING: Sailor from Orhaniye Basin

AGE: Middle Eocene (44–43 MYA)

DISTRIBUTION: Turkey

SIZE: 2.2–3 pounds (1–1.4 kilograms)

DIET: Hypercarnivore

ESSENTIAL FACTS: Like Anatoliadelpys, Orhaniyeia also had a durophagous (crushing) dentition. However, researchers believe that Orhaniyeia specialized in eating shelled mollusks.

DELTATHEROIDA

Deltatheres are an extinct group of basal metatherians that first appear in the fossil record during the Cretaceous. The group consists of mostly small animals that grew no larger than modern shrews or opossums and likely fulfilled similar niches. There are currently two recognized families: Pappotheriidae, which is only known from the early to late Cretaceous, and Deltatheridiidae, which lasted from the early Cretaceous and into the Paleocene. The group appears to have been restricted to North America and Eurasia, while all other metatherians were distributed throughout the southern continents.

DELTATHERIDIIDAE

Deltatheridiids were small, predatory metatherians which originated during the Early Cretaceous and persisted into the Cenozoic era.

DELTATHERIDIUM PRETRITUBERCULARE

NAME MEANING:

AGE: Late Cretaceous (75–70 MYA)

DISTRIBUTION: Eurasia

SIZE: 6 inches (15 centimeters) HBL

DIET: Hypercarnivore

ESSENTIAL FACTS: Deltatheridium was a small predator about the size of a least weasel (*Mustela nivalis*). Bite marks of this species have been found on the skull of a juvenile theropod called *Archaeornithoides deinosauriscus*, providing the first direct evidence that Mesozoic mammals occasionally hunted non-avian dinosaurs.

LOTHERIDIUM MENGI

NAME MEANING: Jin Meng's small beast from Luoyang

AGE: Late Cretaceous (75–70 MYA)

DISTRIBUTION: Eurasia

SIZE: Unknown

DIET: Hypercarnivore

ESSENTIAL FACTS: Lotheridium is known for the most complete, if somewhat crushed, skull of and deltatheridian. The skull was especially broad with particularly long canines.

GURBANODELTA KARA

NAME MEANING:

AGE: Late Paleocene (58.7–55.8 MYA)

DISTRIBUTION: Eurasia

SIZE: Unknown; about shrew-sized

DIET: Mesocarnivore

ESSENTIAL FACTS: Before its discovery in Late Paleocene deposits in China, researchers believed that all deltatheres became extinct during the K/Pg mass extinction event. In addition to being the youngest deltatheridian, it also the smallest known to date.

ARCHIMETATHERIA

This is a poorly known and understudied group of metatherians, once thought to be closely related to modern opossums. Members of this group are restricted to the Late Cretaceous, their fossils known mostly from North America (though a few Eurasian taxa are also recorded). Only two families are currently known.

ALPHADONTIDAE

Alphadontidae are a poorly-known family of metatherians from North America that lived during the Late Cretaceous.

ALPHADON MARSHI

NAME MEANING: Marsh's first tooth

AGE: Late Cretaceous (66 MYA)

DISTRIBUTION: North America

SIZE: Unknown

DIET: Mesocarnivore

ESSENTIAL FACTS: Unfortunately, not much is known about the postcranial skeleton. It is generally thought to have been similar to modern opossums in appearance.

STAGODONTIDAE

Stagodonts were some of the largest mammals of the Late Cretaceous and are thought to have been semiaquatic. They are known for having particularly robust and bulbous premolars, likely an adaptation for crushing hard shelled prey items.

DIDELPHODON VORAX

NAME MEANING: Voracious opossum tooth

AGE: Late Cretaceous (66 MYA)

DISTRIBUTION: North America

SIZE: 11 pounds (5.2 kilograms)

DIET: Hypercarnivore

ESSENTIAL FACTS: Didelphodon had a skull comparable to that of a Tasmanian Devil (*Sarcophilus harrisii*). It had strong jaws and crushing teeth, combined with an otter-like body seemingly built for swimming. These features suggest that it was a semiaquatic predator that hunted aquatic prey, with perhaps a preference for crustaceans and shelled mollusks.

DIDELPHIMORPHIA

An order of metatherians endemic to the Americas.

DIDELPHIDAE

The opossums are a diverse family of metatherians native to the Americas. The family first appears in the fossil record during the Early Miocene, and there are currently ninety-three species distributed mostly through South America. They are all small (no species growing much larger than a house cat), and most species are mesocarnivorous or hypocarnivorous. However, a few opossums during the Late Miocene developed more hypercarnivorous adaptations and were active predators of small vertebrates and filled the niches occupied by mongoose and weasels. The two species of the weasel-like lutrine opossums (*Lutreolina*) are the last members of this lineage.

THYLOPHOROPS LORENZINII

NAME MEANING: Silvio Lorenzini's pouch bearer

AGE: Late Pliocene (3 MYA)

DISTRIBUTION: South America

SIZE: 9.7–16 pounds (4.4–7.4 kilograms)

DIET: Hypercarnivore

ESSENTIAL FACTS: Lorenzini's Opossum is the largest known species of opossum, more than twice the size of the modern Virginia opossum (*Didelphis virginianus*). It was an active predator that could hunt such as agoutis and armadillos.

SPARASSOCYNUS DERIVATUS

NAME MEANING: Derived tearing dog

AGE: Pliocene (4.5–3.3 MYA)

DISTRIBUTION: South America

SIZE: 8–10 inches (20–25 centimeters) HBL; 12 ounces (350 grams)

DIET: Hypercarnivore

ESSENTIAL FACTS: This was a small predator a little larger than a modern least weasel (*Mustela nivalis*). Members of the genus have an expanded tympanic bulla, possibly indicating a heightened ability to detect and process sounds.

CAROLAMEGHINIIDAE

Carolameghiniidae were small marsupials that share several features in common with primates. These features include: strong dentaries, brachydont cheek teeth, and square-shaped molars with bunodont cusps. These adaptations are associated with a primarily frugivorous lifestyle. The family is known to have lived from the late Paleocene to early Oligocene. Their extinction appears to coincide with the global cooling trend that began at the Eocene-Oligocene boundary (extinction event).

CAROLAMEGHINIA MATER

NAME MEANING: Carlos Ameghino's mother

AGE: Middle Eocene (42–38 MYA)

DISTRIBUTION: South America

SIZE: 1.5–2.5 pounds (700–1200 grams)

DIET: Herbivore; frugivore

ESSENTIAL FACTS: No limb bones belonging to this species are known, but researchers believe that it was arboreal like most small, fruit-eating mammals.

PAUCITUBERCULATA

Known commonly as "shrew opossums," paucituberculates are a separate group only distantly related to true opossums (*Didelphimorpha*). Consisting of seven modern species, the group was much more diverse in prehistory, with four families: Abderitidae, Palaeothentidae, Pichipilidae, and Caenolestidae. Much of the order seems to have abruptly gone extinct at the end of the Middle Miocene around 12 million years ago, leaving only the lineage that would lead to the modern species (Caenolestidae). Their niches were largely occupied by small opossums (Didelphidae) and rodents.

RIOLESTES CAPRICORNICUS

NAME MEANING: Rio de Janeiro thief from the Southern Tropic of Capricorn

AGE: Late Paleocene (55 MYA)

DISTRIBUTION: South America

SIZE: Unknown

DIET: Mesocarnivore

ESSENTIAL FACTS: Riolestes is the oldest recognized member of Paucituberculata. It is known only from isolated teeth found at the Itaboraí Formation fossil locality in Rio de Janeiro, Brazil.

BARDALESTES HUNCO

NAME MEANING: Theif from La Barda

AGE: Early Eocene (53–50 MYA)

DISTRIBUTION: South America

SIZE: Unknown

DIET: Mesocarnivore

ESSENTIAL FACTS: Bardalestes is known only from a partial, well-preserved upper tooth row found at the La Barda locality at the Paso del Sapo Formation in Argentina.

PALAEOTHENTIDAE

The most diverse group of paucituberculates, palaeothentids were abundant during the Early to Middle Miocene and occupied a broad range of ecologic niches that includes specialized frugivores, insectivores, and mesocarnivores.

CARLOTHENTES CHUBUTENSIS

NAME MEANING: Carlos Ameghino's godhead from Chubut

AGE: Late Oligocene (29–25 MYA)

DISTRIBUTION: South America

SIZE: 2.2 pounds (1 kilogram)

DIET: Mesocarnivore

ESSENTIAL FACTS: Carlothentes is the largest paucituberculate known to date, about the size of a guinea pig.

PALAEOTHENTES LEMOINEI

NAME MEANING: Marie Lemoine's godhead

AGE: Early Miocene (17.5–16.3 MYA)

DISTRIBUTION: South America

SIZE: Unknown

DIET: Mesocarnivore

ESSENTIAL FACTS: Studies of the postcranial anatomy of Lemoine's Palaeothentes shows that it was a swift and agile animal with particularly good leaping abilities.

PALAEOTHENTES SERRATUS

NAME MEANING: Saw-like godhead

AGE: Middle Miocene (15.4–11.9 MYA)

DISTRIBUTION: South America

SIZE: 3.5 ounces (99 grams)

DIET: Mesocarnivore

ESSENTIAL FACTS: The Saw-Toothed Palaeothentes is thought to have been primarily insectivorous. Its name alludes to well-developed slicing premolars.

PALAEOTHENTES RELICTUS

NAME MEANING: Relict godhead

AGE: Middle Miocene (15.4–11.9 MYA)

DISTRIBUTION: South America

SIZE: 5 ounces (141.7 grams)

DIET: Hypocarnivore

ESSENTIAL FACTS: The Relict Palaeothentes had large, well-developed molars adapted for grinding. This feature suggests that it was mostly herbivorous, perhaps feeding heavily on seeds.

CHIMERALESTES AMBIGUOUS

NAME MEANING: Ambiguous chimera thief

AGE: Middle Miocene (15.4–11.9 MYA)

DISTRIBUTION: South America

SIZE: Unknown

DIET: Mesocarnivore

ESSENTIAL FACTS: Chimeralestes is named for its uncertain placement within Palaeothentidae.

ACDESTIS MADDENI

NAME MEANING: Unknown; Richard Madden's

AGE: Middle Miocene (15.4–11.9 MYA)

DISTRIBUTION: South America

SIZE: 1 pound (454 grams)

DIET: Mesocarnivore

ESSENTIAL FACTS: One of the larger shew opossums, Madden's Acdestis had a generalized diet that included insects, small vertebrates, fruits, and nuts. It is known for its relatively robust, short-faced skull with combination shearing and grinding dentition.

ABDERITIDAE

Unlike the palaeothentids, abderitids exhibit low species diversity.

ABDERITES MERIDIONALIS

NAME MEANING: Unknown; southern

AGE: Early Miocene (17.5–16.3 MYA)

DISTRIBUTION: South America

SIZE: 9.1 ounces (248 grams)

DIET: Herbivore; frugivore

ESSENTIAL FACTS: One of the larger paucituberculates, toothwear analysis has shown that this species was a specialized fruit-eater.

PITHICULITES MINIMUS

NAME MEANING: Unknown; minimal

AGE: Early Miocene (17.5–16.3 MYA)

DISTRIBUTION: South America

SIZE: 0.9 ounces (25 grams)

DIET: Mesocarnivore

ESSENTIAL FACTS: Based on tooth wear, this species seems to have been an opportunistic feeder that fed on a range of plant and animal matter.

SPARASSODONTA

First appearing during the Early Paleocene, sparassodonts were the dominant mammalian predators of South America during its period as an island continent through most of the Cenozoic Era. They were rivaled by phorusrhacid birds and sebecid crocodylomorphs in terrestrial predator guilds. The group became extinct during the Pliocene. The name *sparassodont* means "tearing tooth" or "rending tooth" because of the predatory dentition of these animals were adapted to shearing flesh.

PUCADELPHYS ANDINUS

NAME MEANING: Puca Group opossum from the Andes Mountains

AGE: Early Paleocene (64.5–64 MYA)

DISTRIBUTION: South America

SIZE: 4 inches (10 centimeters) HBL; 1 ounce (11–33 grams)

DIET: Mesocarnivore

ESSENTIAL FACTS: The accumulation of twenty-three individual skeletons gathered in a single place suggests that Pacudelphys had a gregarious lifestyle. Males had longer canines than the females, suggesting that they actively fought with each other. This animal is probably not a sparassodont, but its placement among the metatherian family tree is uncertain.

MAYULESTES FEROX

NAME MEANING: Fierce river thief

AGE: Early Paleocene (64.5–64 MYA)

DISTRIBUTION: South America

SIZE: 8 inches (18 centimeters) HBL; 7–10 ounces (200–275 grams)

DIET: Hypercarnivore

ESSENTIAL FACTS: Mayulestes is regarded by some researchers to be the earliest of the sparassodonts. It was small arboreal predator that is known from a significant portion of the skeleton, including a complete skull.

HONDADELPHIDAE

This is a family which contains only one known species.

HONDADELPHYS FIELDSI

NAME MEANING: Field's opossum from the Honda Group

AGE: Middle Miocene (17.5–15.5 MYA)

DISTRIBUTION: South America

SIZE: Unknown; about weasel-sized

DIET: Mesocarnivore

ESSENTIAL FACTS: Thought to be an opossum upon its original discovery, hence the name, it is now thought to be a small sparassodont. It is only known from a partial skull and lower jaw.

HATHLIACYNIDAE

Hathliacynids were smaller-bodied sparassodonts and are sometimes described as being "doglike" due to their long, slender snouts; this would have given them distinctively foxlike or jackal-like faces in life. Other sparassodonts, in contrast, tend to have deeper, shorter faces with less spacing between their premolars. Hathliacynids also have proportionately smaller slicing blades on their molars than other sparassodonts, hinting at a more mesocarnivorous diet.

CLADOSICTIS PATAGONICA

NAME MEANING: Patagonian branch weasel

AGE: Middle Miocene (17.5–15.5 MYA)

DISTRIBUTION: South America

SIZE: 20 pounds (9 kilograms)

DIET: Mesocarnivore

ESSENTIAL FACTS: Cladosictis was the most abundant sparassodont collected within the Santa Cruz Formation. The Patagonian Cladosictis was about the size of a fisher (*Pekania pennanti*) and likely filled a similar niche, being a scansorial predator that could hunt on the ground and in the trees, supplementing its diet with small amounts of plant matter.

ACYON MYCTODEROS

NAME MEANING: Long snouted non-dog

AGE: Middle Miocene (13–12 MYA)

DISTRIBUTION: South America

SIZE: 28 inches (70 centimeters) HBL, 28–38 pounds (13–17.5 kilograms)

DIET: Mesocarnivore

ESSENTIAL FACTS: Acyon was the largest known member of its family, and even then, it was no bigger than a large red fox (*Vulpes vulpes*) or African civet (*Civettictis civetta*). It is the largest mammalian predator known from the Quebrada Honda site in Bolivia and would have likely hunted the contemporary small mammals such as argyrolagid marsupial *Hondalagus altiplanensis*, the rodent *Guiomys uncia*, and the notoungulate *Hemihegatotherium trilobus*.

PROTHYLACINIDAE

Prothylacinidae is a collection of medium-sized predators that may not form a natural grouping, encompassing several unrelated species.

PROTHYLACINUS PATAGONICUS

NAME MEANING: Early thylacine from Patagonia

AGE: Middle Miocene (17.5–15.5 MYA)

DISTRIBUTION: South America

SIZE: 13–18 inches (35–45cm) SH; 39 inches (100 centimeters) HBL; 66–88 pounds (30–40 kilograms)

DIET: Hypercarnivore

ESSENTIAL FACTS: Prothylacinus would have done most of its hunting on the ground, but it was also an adept climber that could quickly escape into the trees when faced by larger predators.

DUKECYNUS MAGNUS

NAME MEANING: Big Duke dog

AGE: Middle Miocene (13.8–11.8 MYA)

DISTRIBUTION: South America

SIZE: 150 pounds (68 kilograms)

DIET: Hypercarnivore

ESSENTIAL FACTS: Named to honor Duke University paleontologists, Dukecynus was the largest-known prothylacinid, about the size of a leopard (*Panthera pardus*). It is known for an associated lower jaw and partial skull.

LYCOPSIS LONGIROSTRIS

NAME MEANING: Wolf-like; long-snouted

AGE: Middle Miocene (13.5–11.5 MYA)

DISTRIBUTION: South America

SIZE: Fox-sized

DIET: Hypercarnivore

ESSENTIAL FACTS: This exceptionally slender-snouted animal is known from a nearly complete skeleton, from which we can tell that it was a terrestrial ambush predator of relatively small prey items; the skeletal remains of a dinomyid rodent called *Scleromys colombianus* were found preserved in the stomach region. It was also likely a skillful climber.

BORHYAENIDAE

Borhyaenids were terrestrial sparassodonts known for their broad skulls and deep jaws for delivering extremely powerful bites.

AUSTRALOHYAENA ANTIQUA

NAME MEANING: Ancient southern hyena

AGE: Late Oligocene (25 MYA)

DISTRIBUTION: South America

SIZE: 150 pounds (70 kilograms)

DIET: Hypercarnivore

ESSENTIAL FACTS: Known only from isolated teeth and a nearly complete skull, this large predator had a shortened face with massive canines and a powerful bite. It was able to dispatch quite large prey in a manner similar to a big cat.

ARCTODICTIS SINCLAIRI

NAME MEANING: Sinclair's bear weasel

AGE: Early Miocene (21–17.5 MYA)

DISTRIBUTION: South America

SIZE: 3 feet (1 meter) HBL; 2.5 feet (70 centimeters) TL; 40 pounds (18.3 kilograms)

DIET: Hypercarnivore

ESSENTIAL FACTS: Sinclair's Arctodictis was about the size of a large bobcat (*Lynx rufus*). Its exceptionally powerful jaws were adapted to handle prey up to several times larger than itself.

BORHYAENA TUBERATA

NAME MEANING: Swollen flesh (eating) hyena

AGE: Early Miocene (18–16 MYA)

DISTRIBUTION: South America

SIZE: 3 feet (90 centimeters) HBL; 45–80 pounds (20–35 kilograms)

DIET: Hypercarnivore

ESSENTIAL FACTS: Though not built for long-distance running, its limbs were built for swift and efficient movement on the ground. Its hands and feet were proportionately longer than other sparassodonts, suggesting a semi-digitigrade (walking on toes) stance.

PROBORHYAENIDAE

The Proborhyaenidae includes the largest metatherian predators ever known. They lived from the Early Eocene to Late Oligocene and are characterized by reduced incisors and grooved canines that grew perpetually throughout life. This family is ancestral to the sabertoothed thylacosmilids.

CALLISTOE VINCEI

NAME MEANING: Martín Vince's Callisto

AGE: Early Eocene (50 MYA)

DISTRIBUTION: South America

SIZE: 50 pounds (23 kilograms)

DIET: Hypercanivore

ESSENTIAL FACTS: A small, agile predator with a slender body adapted for quick and efficient terrestrial locomotion. The shape of its claws suggest moderate digging capabilities, suggesting that it likely took shelter in burrows that it either dug itself or procured from other animals. It is known from an exceptionally intact skeleton.

ARMINIHERINGIA AUCETA

NAME MEANING: Unknown

AGE: Early Eocene (50 MYA)

DISTRIBUTION: South America

SIZE: 88–176 pounds (40–80 kilograms)

DIET: Hypercanivore

ESSENTIAL FACTS: The lower canines of this animal are exceptionally long and project forward, suggesting that it used a unique killing bite when dispatching prey. The body was sturdy with robust limbs. The carnassial (shearing) teeth rotated throughout life to maintain a continuous cutting surface.

PROBORHYAENA GIGANTEA

NAME MEANING: Giant early Borhyaena

AGE: Late Oligocene (27–26 MYA)

DISTRIBUTION: South America

SIZE: 660–880 pounds (300–400 kilograms)

DIET: Hypercanivore

ESSENTIAL FACTS: Proborhyaena is the largest metatherian carnivore known to date. Estimating its size from its 2-foot (60-centimeter) skull places it in the size range of the largest cats. This powerful animal was built to tackle some of the largest herbivores in its environment, potentially even juvenile pyrotheres.

PARABORHYAENA BOLIVIANA

NAME MEANING: Near Borhyaena; from Bolivia

AGE: Late Oligocene (27–26 MYA)

DISTRIBUTION: South America

SIZE: 5 feet (150 centimeters) HBL; 220–275 pounds (100–125 kilograms)

DIET: Hypercanivore

ESSENTIAL FACTS: Paraborhyaena was a smaller version of the contemporary, closely related Proborhyaena. This jaguar-sized animal would have hunted smaller, more manageable prey animals to minimize direct competition.

THYLACOSMILIDAE

Considered by some researchers to be a subfamily within the Proborhyaenidae, thylacosmilids retained the reduced incisors and ever-growing canines of their ancestors. These animals take these adaptations a step forward by developing true saberteeth, in which the upper canines are greatly elongated and blade-shaped with their length matched by a flange on the lower jaw. Members of this group never reached the large sizes of some later proborhyaenids.

EOMAKHAIRA MOLOSSUS

NAME MEANING: Dawn sword; molossus

AGE: Early Oligocene (33–31.5 MYA)

DISTRIBUTION: South America

SIZE: 20–22 pounds (9.5–10 kilograms)

DIET: Hypercarnivore

ESSENTIAL FACTS: The oldest and smallest known of the thylacosmilids.

ANACHLYSICTIS GRACILIS

NAME MEANING: Slender forward weasel

ERA: Middle Miocene (13.8–11.8MYA)

DISTRIBUTION: South America

SIZE: 3 feet (1 meter) HBL; 1.5 feet (50 centimeters) TL; 40–50 pounds (18–23 kilograms)

DIET: Hypercanivore

ESSENTIAL FACTS: Anachlysictis was a bobcat-sized carnivore that inhabited tropical rainforest habitats. Much of the skeleton is known, and it had a notably long and narrow snout that was more dog-like in morphology than cat-like.

PATAGOSMILUS GOINI

NAME MEANING: Francisco Goin's Patagonian knife

AGE: Middle Miocene (15.5–13.8MYA)

DISTRIBUTION: South America

SIZE: About lynx-sized

DIET: Hypercanivore

ESSENTIAL FACTS: Patagosmilus was similar in several ways to the later Thylacosmilus and may have been ancestral to it.

THYLACOSMILUS ATROX

NAME MEANING: Fierce pouched knife

AGE: Late Miocene to Pliocene (9–3 MYA)

DISTRIBUTION: South America

SIZE: 180–260 pounds (80–120 kilograms)

DIET: Hypercarnivore

SEE MORE ON PAGES 90–91

YALKAPARIDON COHENI

NAME MEANING: Barry Cohen's boomerang tooth

AGE: Early Miocene (25–20 MYA)

DISTRIBUTION: Australia

SIZE: Unknown; about possum-sized

DIET: Hypercarnivore; insectivore

SEE MORE ON PAGES 92–93

THYLACOSMILUS ATROX

ESSENTIAL FACTS: Discovered in 1926 and formally described in 1933, Thylacosmilus is the most famous of all the sparassodonts, commonly referred to as the "marsupial sabertooth." The weight of a small jaguar (*Panthera onca*), it was the largest mammalian carnivore known from South America at its time. It inhabited savanna, woodland, and forest habitats.

The sabertooth morphology of Thylacosmilus was the most specialized of any thylacosmilid and arguably even more so than many carnivoran sabertooths. The roots of the ever-growing upper canines grew in an arc extending over the eye sockets, which had the added effect of strengthening it. The upper canine crowns experience were sharpened through continuous grinding against the lower canines as the animal opened and shut its mouth. An intact premaxilla has never been preserved; this means the upper incisors are unknown, although there is evidence in the form of wear on the canines that they were present. Interestingly for a predatory mammal, the eyes are oriented more to the sides of the skull, rather than facing forward. This likely aided the animal's depth perception, though this is unlikely to have been too much of a hindrance for its likely hunting method. It was an ambush predator that relied on getting as close to its prey as possible before essentially leaping on its back from cover. To employ its specialized killing method, Thylacosmilus had several key adaptations for grappling with and stabilizing prey: the bones of its forelimbs are especially robust with large muscles, and the lumbar vertebrae are short and rigid to strengthen the lower back. Like other saber-toothed predators, its neck was relatively long with highly-developed musculature that allowed for powerful downward and backward motions of the head during the killing bite. The target for the killing bite were the arteries of the neck, which result in rapid loss of consciousness and death when severed.

SEE ENTRY ON PAGE 89

YALKAPARIDON COHENI

ESSENTIAL FACTS: Described in 1988, the genus *Yalkaparidon* contains two known species (*Y. coheni* and *Y. jonesi*) known from the Riversleigh World Heritage site in northwest Queensland. Numerous isolated teeth and jaws of these animals have been recovered, but only *Y. coheni* is known from a complete skull. These animals had large and ever-growing first incisors similar to those of rodents. These incisors, together with archaic features of the skull, led some researchers to believe that Yalkaparidon represents an early-branching lineage of diprotodontians. More commonly, however, the family Yalkaparidontidae is placed within its own order, Yalkaparidontia.

The genus name is based on the Waanyi Aboriginal word *yalkapari*, meaning "boomerang," a reference to the V-shaped zalambdodont arrangement of the molar crowns. This tooth type is shared by marsupial moles, solenodons, tenrecs, and golden moles among modern mammal groups like insectivorous mammals, whose diets center around soft-bodied invertebrates such as worms and insect larvae. This suggests that *Yalkaparidon* had a similar diet. The robust lower jaw and sturdy incisors, meanwhile, indicate that it actively gnawed on hard objects, seemingly contradicting the molars which did not serve a crushing function. With this combination of features, it is likely that Yalkaparidon was ecologically analogous to the modern aye-aye (*Daubentonia madagascariensis*) of Madagascar, which uses similarly hypertrophied incisors to gnaw openings in the bark and wood of trees in order to access insects hidden within.

SEE ENTRY ON PAGE 89

DASYUROMORPHA

The Dasyuromorpha is a group of predatory marsupials which comprises the families Dasyuridae, Thylacinidae, and Myrmecobiidae.

MALLEODECTES MIRABILIS

NAME MEANING: Extraordinary hammer biter

AGE: Middle Miocene (15 MYA)

DISTRIBUTION: Australia

SIZE: 2 pounds (896 grams)

DIET: Hypercarnivore; molluscivore

SEE MORE ON PAGES 96–97

DASYURIDAE

After the recently extinct Tasmanian Thylacine (*Thylacinus cynocephalus*), the dasyuridae includes the largest existing carnivorous metatherians, although they are still relatively small; the largest species, the Tasmanian devil (*Sarcophilus harrisii*), rarely exceeds ten kilograms in weight. Most species are small hypercarnivores ecologically analogous to shrews. The family is fairly diverse, with at least seventy modern species.

BARINYA WANGALA

NAME MEANING: Dreamtime quoll

AGE: Early Miocene (18 MYA)

DISTRIBUTION: Australia

SIZE: Unknown

DIET: Mesocarnivore

ESSENTIAL FACTS: Known from a nearly complete skull and numerous jaws and teeth collected from the Riversleigh World Heritage Area. It is the oldest definitive dasyurid and the only known member of the subfamily Barinyainae.

DASYURINAE

Members of this family rang in size from that of a shrew to that of a small fox. The fossil record for this group extends back to the Late Oligocene.

ARCHERIUM CHINCHILLAENSIS

NAME MEANING: Archer from Chinchilla

AGE: Early Pliocene (5–4 MYA)

DISTRIBUTION: Australia

SIZE: Unknown

DIET: Hypercarnivore

ESSENTIAL FACTS: Named for the Chinchilla Rifle Range where its fossils are known. Features of its teeth suggest that it inhabited relatively arid or lightly wooded areas with marked seasonality.

MALLEODECTES MIRABILIS

ESSENTIAL FACTS: Members of the genus *Malleodectes* are so unique in their dental morphology that they have were placed within their own family in 2016, the Malleodectidae. The name is derived from the Latin word *malleo* and the Greek *dectes*, meaning "hammer biter." The name refers to the animal's highly specialized dentition, specifically an enlarged third premolar with a flattened profile designed for crushing. Two species of Malleodectes were described in 2011; *M. mirablis* and *M. moenia*. The former of the two, the Extraordinary Malleodectes, was a ferret-sized animal that lived in what is now the Riversleigh World Heritage Site during the Middle Miocene.

The enlarged third premolars displayed by this genus is remarkably similar to a specialization observed in modern blue-tongued skinks (*Cyclodomorphus*). These lizards have heterodont dentitions with a particularly enlarged and blunt tooth near the end of the tooth row, which they use to feed on snails. This is a striking example of dental convergence and suggests that Malleodectes, which pre-date these skinks, were snail specialists whose dentition specifically evolved to crush snail shells. Because of this, these animals are commonly known as "marsupial skinks."

SEE ENTRY ON PAGE 94

DASYCERCUS WORBOYSI

NAME MEANING: Worboys' mulgara

AGE: Early Pliocene

DISTRIBUTION: Australia

SIZE: 7 ounces (200 grams)

DIET: Hypercarnivore

ESSENTIAL FACTS: Dasycercus was slightly larger than its modern relative, the crest-tailed mulgara (*Dasycercus cristicauda*). Worboy's Mulgara probably had the same unusual feeding method of eating prey from head to tail, gradually turning the skin back on itself.

DASYURUS DUNMALLI

NAME MEANING: Dunmall's quoll

AGE: Early Pliocene (5–4 MYA)

DISTRIBUTION: Australia

SIZE: About cat-sized

DIET: Hypercarnivore

ESSENTIAL FACTS: The oldest and only known extinct quoll. Among modern examples of the genus, it is most similar to the spotted-tailed quoll (*D. maculatus*) in terms of its dentition suggesting similar dietary habits.

GANBULANYI DJADJINGULI

NAME MEANING: Bone-eating quoll

AGE: Late Miocene (10 MYA)

DISTRIBUTION: Australia

SIZE: Unknown

DIET: Hypercarnivore

ESSENTIAL FACTS: The scientific name of this species alludes to its robust dentition similar to that of the modern Tasmanian devil (*Sarcophilis harrisii*) and was also probably an active carnivore that actively fed from large carcasses. The particularly strong premolars were useful in breaking bones.

GLAUCODON BALLARATENSIS

NAME MEANING: Blue-tooth from Ballarat

AGE: Pliocene (5–3 MYA)

DISTRIBUTION: Australia

SIZE: Unknown

DIET: Hypercarnivore

ESSENTIAL FACTS: The dentition of this animal has been described as being between a quoll and a Tasmanian devil, perhaps suggesting it could take relatively larger prey than the former but lacked the durophagous (ability to eat hard-shelled organisms) habits of the latter.

PHASCOGALINAE

A subfamily that includes antechinuses, dasyures, and phascogales. Members of this group are small, mostly insectivorous predators with a limited fossil record dating back to the Pliocene.

ANTECHINUS PUTEUS

NAME MEANING: Pit antechinus

AGE: Late Pleistocene

DISTRIBUTION: Australia

SIZE: Unknown; about mouse-sized

DIET: Hypercarnivore

ESSENTIAL FACTS: Like modern members of the genus, it was a generalized predator that fed on a variety of invertebrates, as well as small reptiles and mammals.

SMINTHOPSINAE

Sminthopsinae were small-bodied dasyurids similar in ecology to shrews. The group includes dunnarts, planigales, and ningauis, comprising almost thirty modern species. The fossil record is extremely sparse and limited to the Pliocene and Pleistocene.

SMINTHOPSIS FLORAVILLENSIS

NAME MEANING: Floraville dunnart

AGE: Pliocene or Pleistocene

DISTRIBUTION: Australia

SIZE: Unknown; about mouse-sized

DIET: Hypercarnivore

ESSENTIAL FACTS: Like its modern relatives, Floraville Dunnarts were mostly insectivorous but could occasionally tackle smaller vertebrates. It is the only known fossil dunnart.

THYLACINIDAE

The Tasmanian Thylacine (*Thylacinus cynocephalus*) was the last survivor of this family of marsupial carnivores whose fossil record dates back to the Oligocene. Members of this group were superficially canid-like in their morphology with elongated faces and slender limbs with narrow paws adapted for terrestrial locomotion. There is a naming trend with members of this family in which all generic names with *cinus*.

BABJCINUS TURNBULLI

NAME MEANING: Bill Turnbull's hunting thylacine

AGE: Late Oligocene (25 MYA)

DISTRIBUTION: Australia

SIZE: Unknown; about quoll-sized

DIET: Mesocarnivore

ESSENTIAL FACTS: The oldest, and one of the smallest known thylacines, the Babjcinus was about the size of a modern quoll.

NIMBACINUS DICKSONI

NAME MEANING: Dickson's little thylacine

AGE: Early Miocene (23–16 MYA)

DISTRIBUTION: Australia

SIZE: 1 foot (30 centimeters) SH; 20 inches (50 centimeters) HBL; 20 pounds (9 kilograms)

DIET: Hypercarnivore

SEE MORE ON PAGES 102–103

THYLACINUS POTENS

NAME MEANING: Powerful thylacine

AGE: Late Miocene (10–8 MYA)

DISTRIBUTION: Australia

SIZE: 5 feet (150 centimeters) HBL; 130–150 pounds (60–70 kilograms)

DIET: Hypercarnivore

ESSENTIAL FACTS: With its name meaning "Powerful Thylacine," this is the largest thylacine known to have lived. In addition to being over twice the size of the modern Tasmanian Thylacine (*Thylacinus cynocephalus*), its jaws were proportionately more robust suggesting that it also hunted relatively larger prey items matching or exceeding its own body mass.

NIMBACINUS DICKSONI

ESSENTIAL FACTS: The best fossils of this thylacine come from the Riversleigh World Heritage Area, with additional remains known from Bullock Creek in Australia's Northern Territory. The species was originally described on the basis of just its upper and lower jaws. Since this discovery, a nearly complete skeleton missing only the feet and tail was recovered not far from the initial discovery. It is the best-known fossil thylacinid and the most well-studied. The species has been commonly referred to as the "Riversleigh Thylacine" after the site of its discovery, and also "Dickinson's Thylacine."

The Riversleigh Thylacine is much smaller than its modern relative. However, pound for pound it was more powerfully built, with a notably broader skull and rostrum with more surface area for jaw muscle attachment. These traits suggest that unlike the Tasmanian Thylacine, which specialized in prey smaller than itself, the Riversleigh Thylacine was able to handle prey animals its own size or possibly even larger.

SEE ENTRY ON PAGE 101

NOTORYCTEMORPHA

Marsupial moles are a group of fossorial metatherians that convergently evolved along similar ecomorphological lines to that of moles (Talpidae) and golden moles (Chrysochloridae).

NARABORYCTES PHILCREASERI

NAME MEANING: Phil Creaser's drinking digger

AGE: Early Miocene (20 MYA)

DISTRIBUTION: Australia

SIZE: 7 ounces (200 grams)

DIET: Fossorial hypercarnivore

ESSENTIAL FACTS: The species name refers to the rainforest habitat of this animal. This differs from modern marsupial moles, which live in dryer, sandy habitats. This species hunted for worms beneath the leaf litter of what would become the Riversleigh World Heritage Area.

PERAMELEMORPHA

It is thought that bandicoots and bilbies share a common ancestry with diprotodontians because both groups display syndactyly, where the second and third toes are reduced and functionally fused together into a single unit.

YARALIDAE

The Yaralidae are a fully extinct family of bandicoots that lack the specializations found in all other bandicoots. The family appears to have been quite diverse at the Riversleigh World Heritage Area during the Late Oligocene, with species ranging from mouse-sized to hare-sized. They were extinct by the end of the Pliocene. Among other differences, they had relatively short snouts compared to those of thylacomyids and paramelids, suggesting that the lengthening of the skull occurred in more derived families as an adaptation for collecting invertebrates.

BULUNGU MUIRHEADAE

NAME MEANING: Muirhead's niece

AGE: Late Oligocene (25 MYA)

DISTRIBUTION: Australia

SIZE: 4.6 ounces (130 grams)

DIET: Mesocarnivore

ESSENTIAL FACTS: Muirhead's Bandicoot is the oldest fossil bandicoot known to date. Though not the smallest banditcoot overall, it is smaller than any of the modern species, comparable in size to a black rat (*Rattus rattus*)

YARLA BURCHFIELDI

NAME MEANING: Geoffrey Burchfield's root

AGE: Early Miocene (23 MYA)

DISTRIBUTION: Australia

SIZE: Mouse-sized

DIET: Mesocarnivore

ESSENTIAL FACTS: The name *Yarla* is derived from a Waanyi Aboriginal word meaning "the root of a tree," implying this species' place near the base of bandicoot evolution. It also has the distinction of being the smallest bandicoot known to date, living or extinct; it was no bigger than a mouse.

GALADI SPECIOSUS

NAME MEANING: Beautiful bandicoot

AGE: Late Oligocene to Early Miocene (25–20 MYA)

DISTRIBUTION: Australia

SIZE: 3.3 pounds (1.5 kilograms)

DIET: Mesocarnivore

ESSENTIAL FACTS: Members of the genus are known for their relatively large size compared to other bandicoots. They also had more robust skulls and slicing cheek teeth, suggesting a greater reliance on vertebrate prey.

PERAMELIDAE

Bandicoots of the family Peramelidae have a fossil history that dates back to the Middle Miocene. There are nine modern species, five of which have been driven to extinction in recent times due to human-caused disruptions of their ecosystems; namely, the deliberate introduction of cats and foxes to Australia. The various species may be found in a wide range of habitats, from wet forests to arid deserts, where they feed primarily on insects.

CRASH BANDICOOT

NAME MEANING: Literally, the video game character

AGE: Middle Miocene (15 MYA)

DISTRIBUTION: Australia

SIZE: 2.2 pounds (1 kilograms)

DIET: Mesocarnivore

ESSENTIAL FACTS: The species name directly references the main character of the video game franchise *Crash Bandicoot*. It is the oldest known representative of Peramelidae.

PERAMELES ALLINGHAMENSIS

NAME MEANING: Other badger from Allingham Creek

AGE: Early Pliocene (4 MYA)

DISTRIBUTION: Australia

SIZE: Rabbit-sized

DIET: Mesocarnivore

ESSENTIAL FACTS: Perameles is also known as the Bluff Downs Bandicoot, named after the Bluff Downs fossil site where it was discovered. Like modern members of the genus, much of its diet likely consisted of invertebrates with the occasional fruit or fungi.

THYLACOMYIDAE

Bilbies are desert-adapted animals with enlarged ears for dissipating heat. The evolution of this family seems to have coincided with the opening of forested habitats in the Early Neogene. At the time of European colonization there were two species alive in Australia, but one was driven to extinction.

LIYAMAYI DAYI

NAME MEANING: Robert Day's round tooth

AGE: Middle Miocene (15 MYA)

DISTRIBUTION: Australia

SIZE: 23 ounces (650 grams)

DIET: Mesocarnivore

ESSENTIAL FACTS: Day's Bilby is the oldest known species of bilby, having lived at the Riversleigh World Heritage Area during a time when much of Australia's forests were beginning to give way to more open, drier habitats.

ISCHNODON AUSTRALIS

NAME MEANING: Southern thin tooth

AGE: Early Pliocene (3.9 MYA)

DISTRIBUTION: Australia

SIZE: About rabbit-sized

DIET: Mesocarnivore

ESSENTIAL FACTS: The Thin-Toothed Bilby is the first fossil bandicoot to be discovered and named back in 1955. It was similar in many ways to modern bilbies of the genus *Macrotis*, and likely had a similar ecology.

POLYDOLOPIMORPHA

This is a diverse and long-lived order with a history spanning from the early Paleocene to the early Pleistocene of South America. There is also record of this group inhabiting Antarctica during the Eocene before the continent split from South America. They had a generalized bunodont dentition. Despite their clear abundance throughout the Cenozoic, their fossil record is very sparse, with most species known only from isolated teeth and partial jaws.

GROEBERIIDAE

Groeberiids were similar to rodents in several regards, most notably in their enlarged, chisel-shaped first incisors adapted to gnawing. They lived in South America during a period in which rodents had yet to diversify. Because of this, these small marsupials occupied many of these niches.

GROEBERIA MINOPRIOI

NAME MEANING: Unknown

AGE: Late Eocene (35 MYA)

DISTRIBUTION: South America

SIZE: 1–2 ounces (35–45 grams)

DIET: Herbivore

ESSENTIAL FACTS: The type species of the family Groeberiidae, this species had a deep, shortened skull and lower jaws that show that it was built for chewing. Unfortunately, the postcranial skeleton is not known.

KLOHNIA CHARRIERI

NAME MEANING: Charles Klohn and Reynaldo Cherrier

AGE: Early Oligocene (33–31 MYA)

DISTRIBUTION: South America

SIZE: 1–2 ounces (35–45 grams)

DIET: Herbivore

ESSENTIAL FACTS: Klohnia was a mouse-sized herbivore with teeth adapted to handle tough foods such as seeds, nuts, and hard fruits.

BONAPARTHERIIDAE

Bonapartheres are a poorly known group of metatherians that became extinct around the Eocene-Oligocene boundary.

EPIDOLOPS AMEGHINOI

NAME MEANING: Florentino Ameghino's upon trick

AGE: Early Eocene (53–50 MYA)

DISTRIBUTION: South America

SIZE: 9–12 inches (22–30 centimeters) HBL; 1 pound (500–600 grams)

DIET: Hypocarnivore

ESSENTIAL FACTS: No limb bones are known, but Epidolops is the only member of its family for which a well-preserved skull is known. It is believed to have been an arboreal animal with a diet of soft-bodied insects and fruits. The species is most known for its enlarged, serrated premolars.

ARGYROLAGIDAE

Argyrolagids were small, herbivorous metatherians that inhabited South America from the Late Oligocene to Early Pleistocene. Members of this group are morphologically similar to small, saltatorial mammals such as kangaroo rats, with shortened forelimbs and elongated hindlimbs with particularly emphasized lower legs and feet.

PROARGYROLAGUS BOLIVIANUS

NAME MEANING: Before Argyrolagus from Bolivia

AGE: Late Oligocene (27–25 MYA)

DISTRIBUTION: South America

SIZE: 2–3.4 ounces (58–95 grams)

DIET: Herbivore

ESSENTIAL FACTS: Proargyrolagus was the oldest-known member of Argyrolagidae, known from a nearly complete skull. Along with later members of the family, it appears to have possessed very dense whiskers and a highly mobile nose, suggesting it relied heavily on tactile sensation and smell when foraging and possibly nocturnality.

HONDALAGUS ALTIPLANENSIS

NAME MEANING: Honda rabbit from Altiplano

AGE: Middle Miocene (13–12 MYA)

DISTRIBUTION: South America

SIZE: 4–6 inches (10–15 centimeters) HBL; 1–2 ounces (20–50 grams)

DIET: Herbivore

ESSENTIAL FACTS: Hondalagus was one of the smaller argyrolagids, possessing hypsodont teeth adapted to eating seeds in open areas.

ARGYROLAGUS PALMERI

NAME MEANING: Palmer's silver sabbit

AGE: Early Pliocene (5.3–3.6 MYA)

DISTRIBUTION: South America

SIZE: 5.9–8 inches (15–20 centimeters) HBL

DIET: Herbivore

ESSENTIAL FACTS: An inhabitant of hot, arid regions, it had large eyes that suggest it was primarily nocturnal. Its teeth, meanwhile, appear well-suited to handle desert plants.

DIPROTODONTIA

Diprotodontia is a hugely diverse grouping of Australian metatherians. The earliest fossils date to Late Oligocene, although their origins surely lie much earlier, as multiple families are well established and differentiated by this time. Members of the order are mostly herbivores, although the common ancestor of these animals was probably a hypo-carnivore with plagiaulacoid dentition. Mesocarnivorous and hypercarnivorous taxa have also evolved among several lineages. The most notable uniting feature of this group and the one for which they are named are their procumbent first incisors on the upper and lower jaws. Members of this order also exhibit syndactyly, in which the reduced second and third digits are bound together by soft tissue into a single unit, giving the appearance of a single toe that bears two claws. There are three suborders: Phalangeriformes, Vombatiformes, and Macropodiformes.

PHALANGERIFORMES

Collectively known as possums, most members of this suborder are arboreal and nocturnal forest dwellers ranging in size from a mouse to a small monkey. Unfortunately, the fossil record for this group is somewhat sparse, as most taxa are known only from partial jaws and isolated teeth. The reclusive habits of many of the modern species results in most members of this very speciose group being poorly understood and rarely seen.

BURRAMYIDAE

The aptly named pygmy possums are tiny, nocturnal animals that feed on insects, seeds, fruits, nectar, and pollen. There are five modern species no larger than mice. The Mountain Pygmy Possum (*Burrayms parvus*) was first known from Pleistocene-age fossils discovered in 1895 and believed extinct until a living individual was found in 1966, making it a Lazarus taxon.

BURRAMYS BRUTYI

NAME MEANING: Arthur Bruty's mouse from Burra Town

AGE: Late Oligocene (25 MYA)

DISTRIBUTION: Australia

SIZE: 1.6 ounces (45 grams)

DIET: Hypocarnivore

ESSENTIAL FACTS: Bruty's Pygmy Possum is the oldest-known member of the family that inhabited rainforests of Oligocene Australia. Its diet consisted of insects, fruits, and seeds.

PILKIPILDRIDAE

Pilkipildridae is a completely extinct of very small possums. Their relation to other possum families is currently unknown, and its members are known from isolated teeth and partial jaws.

PILKIPILDRA HANDAE

NAME MEANING: Suzanne Hand's different possum

AGE: Late Oligocene (25 MYA)

DISTRIBUTION: Australia

SIZE: Mouse-sized

DIET: Hypocarnivore

ESSENTIAL FACTS: The morphology of the teeth of Hand's Possum suggests that it fed on fruits, nuts, and invertebrates.

DJILGARINGA GILLESPIAE

NAME MEANING: Anna Gillepsie's baby possum

AGE: Middle Miocene (14–12 MYA)

DISTRIBUTION: Australia

SIZE: About mouse-sized

DIET: Hypocarnivore

ESSENTIAL FACTS: The dentition of this animal, which includes prominent shearing premolars, suggests that it regularly fed on seeds and nuts, perhaps even supplementing its diet with insects.

ACROBATIDAE

Acrobatidae consists of two modern species, both are nocturnal mouse-sized animals that feed mainly on nectar. Fossils attributed to this family dating back to the Late Oligocene and early Miocene have been known for many years, but these have only recently been described.

DISTOECHURUS JEANESORUM

NAME MEANING: Doug and Ann Jeanes feathered tail

AGE: Late Oligocene (25 MYA)

DISTRIBUTION: Australia

SIZE: About mouse-sized

DIET: Herbivore

ESSENTIAL FACTS: Jeanes' Feather-Tailed Possum, like its modern relative (*D. pennatus*), was a nocturnal animal that fed mainly on nectar and pollen.

ACROBATES MAGICUS

NAME MEANING: Magic high climber

AGE: Early Miocene (18 MYA)

DISTRIBUTION: Australia

SIZE: About mouse-sized

DIET: Hypocarnivore

ESSENTIAL FACTS: The Magic Feathertail Glider is named for the children's book *Possum Magic* by Mem Fox. Like the modern feathertail glider (*A. pygmaeus*), they would have spent most of their time high in the trees feeding on arthropods and nectar during the night. It had the ability to glide great distances between trees.

PSEUDOCHEIRIDAE

Ringtail possums are small, arboreal herbivores that feed exclusively on leaves.

PILDRA ANTIQUUS

NAME MEANING: First possum

AGE: Late Oligocene

DISTRIBUTION: Australia

SIZE: Unknown

DIET: Herbivore

ESSENTIAL FACTS: Members of the genus are the oldest of the ringtail possums. Multiple species coexisted in the rainforests of Riversleigh.

MARLU KUTJAMARPENSIS

NAME MEANING: Kutjamarpu possum

AGE: Early Miocene

DISTRIBUTION: Australia

SIZE: Unknown

DIET: Herbivore; folivore

ESSENTIAL FACTS: Marlu is named for the Kutjamarpu Local Fauna in South Australia. It's known from several nearly complete jaws and isolated teeth.

PALJARA TIRARENSE

NAME MEANING: Small possum from Tirari Desert

AGE: Early Miocene

DISTRIBUTION: Australia

SIZE: Unknown

DIET: Herbivore

ESSENTIAL FACTS: When this animal was alive, the Tirari Desert in which its fossils were found was a lush, moist forest. Paljara coexisted with the larger Marlu.

PETAUROIDES STIRTONI

NAME MEANING: Stirton's glider

AGE: Early Pliocene (4 MYA)

DISTRIBUTION: Australia

SIZE: About house cat-sized

DIET: Herbivore

ESSENTIAL FACTS: Stirton's Greater Glider was likely a nocturnal animal able to glide considerable distances between trees like modern members of *Petauroides*. Eucalyptus leaves were likely a significant part of its diet.

PSEUDOKOALA ERLITA

NAME MEANING: Ancient false koala

AGE: Early Pliocene

DISTRIBUTION: Australia

SIZE: Unknown

DIET: Herbivore

ESSENTIAL FACTS: Pseudokoala was so named due to the koala-like morphology of its cheek teeth.

PETAURIDAE

The family, which includes wrist-winged gliders and trioks, are small, arboreal animals that inhabit Australian woodlands and forests

DACTYLOPSILA KAMBUAYAI

NAME MEANING: Kambuaya's high finger

AGE: Early Holocene (8,000 YA)

DISTRIBUTION: Australia

SIZE: About squirrel-sized

DIET: Hypercarnivore; insectivore

ESSENTIAL FACTS: The Ayamaru Triok is known from subfossil remains from cave deposits. Like its modern relatives it used an elongated fourth finger to locate and extract insect larvae from inside wood, a similar behavior can be observed in the aye-aye of Madagascar (*Daubentonia madagascariensis*).

DJALUDJANGI YADJANA

NAME MEANING: First heavy mouth

AGE: Early or Middle Miocene

DISTRIBUTION: Australia

SIZE: About squirrel-sized

DIET: Hypocarnivore

ESSENTIAL FACTS: Named for its large, relatively high-crowned third premolars and unreduced dentition.

MIRALINIDAE

Miralinidae is an extinct family known from the Miocene of Australia containing a handful of species between two genera. The group may be a link between ektopodontids and phalangerids.

DURUDAWIRI INSUSITATUS

NAME MEANING: Unusual littlest sister of the sun

AGE: Early Miocene (18 MYA)

DISTRIBUTION: Australia

SIZE: Unknown

DIET: Hypocarnivore

ESSENTIAL FACTS: The smallest member of its genus. The teeth of this animal were less specialized than those of the genus *Miralina*. Its diet likely consisted of invertebrates and softer plants.

MIRALINA DOYLEI

NAME MEANING: Steven Doyle's one who gives light

AGE: Late Oligocene (25 MYA)

DISTRIBUTION: Australia

SIZE: 2.6–10 pounds (1.2–4.5 kilograms)

DIET: Hypocarnivore

ESSENTIAL FACTS: Doyle's Miralina was about the size of a modern common brushtail possum (*Trichosurus vulpecula*) and was probably similar in much of its foraging behaviors.

EKTOPODONTIDAE

The family is characterized by their short faces and unusual, complex molars, which have numerous cusps in transverse (crosswise) rows that vaguely resemble the molars of some multituberculates. This could suggest these possums were adapted to feed on fibrous or abrasive foods. The family is known to have lived from the Late Oligocene to Early Pleistocene.

CHUNIA ILLUMINATA

NAME MEANING: Illuminating Chun-style

AGE: Late Oligocene (25 MYA)

DISTRIBUTION: Australia

SIZE: Unknown

DIET: Herbivore

ESSENTIAL FACTS: The genus name is a reference to the Chun style of pottery of the Sung Dynasty of China. Chun pottery exhibits numerous fine lines, much like the teeth of these animals.

DARCIUS DUGGANI

NAME MEANING: Bruce Darcy Duggan

AGE: Early Pliocene (5–4 MYA)

DISTRIBUTION: Australia

SIZE: Unknown

DIET: Herbivore

ESSENTIAL FACTS: This species is named after Bruce Darcy Duggan, who found the type specimen.

EKTOPODON STIRTONI

NAME MEANING: Stirton's strange tooth

AGE: Early Miocene (18 MYA)

DISTRIBUTION: Australia

SIZE: 2.9 pounds (1,300 grams)

DIET: Herbivore

ESSENTIAL FACTS: Like most ektopodontids, Stirton's Ektopodon is known only from isolated teeth and partial jaws. Enough material is present to know that these animals had exceptionally short faces.

PHALANGERIDAE

The Phalangeridae includes the brushtail possums and cuscuses, the largest possums alive today. Like ringtail possums, they specialize in eating leaves. The family has 29 modern species which occupy the niches that monkeys occupy in other parts of the world.

ARCHERUS JOHNTONIAE

NAME MEANING: Belonging to Michael Archer, as well as John and Toni Myers

AGE: Early to middle Miocene (18–12 MYA)

DISTRIBUTION: Australia

SIZE: 2.8 pounds (1.3 kilograms)

DIET: Herbivore

ESSENTIAL FACTS: Described in 2023, Archerus is one of the smallest-known phalangerids.

STRIGOCUSCUS REIDI

NAME MEANING: Neil Reid's thin cuscus

AGE: Middle Miocene

DISTRIBUTION: Australia

SIZE: Unknown

DIET: Herbivore

ESSENTIAL FACTS: The two modern species of *Strigocuscus* are found only on the Indonesian island of Sulawesi and some of its surrounding islands. Reid's Dwarf Cuscus inhabited the forests of mainland Australia. Like its modern relatives, it was likely a nocturnal folivore.

TRICHOSURUS DICKSONI

NAME MEANING: Martin Dickson's hairy tail

AGE: Middle Miocene (15 MYA)

DISTRIBUTION: Australia

SIZE: Cat-sized

DIET: Hypocarnivore

ESSENTIAL FACTS: Like modern examples of the genus *Trichosurus*, Dickson's Brushtail Possum was a scansorial hypocarnivore with a varied diet, equally comfortable foraging on the ground and in the trees. Its diet included leaves, fruits, flowers, seeds, insects, small vertebrates, and eggs.

VOMBATIFORMES

Although early members of this group were scansorial and resembled robust possums, vombatiformes are generally larger and more terrestrial. They are the least speciouse of the three driprotodontian subfamilies with only four species between two families. Included among this group are the wombats (Vombatidae) and koalas (Phascolarctidae).

NIMBADON LAVARACKORUM

NAME MEANING: Sue and Jim Lavarack's small tooth

AGE: Late Oligocene (25 MYA)

DISTRIBUTION: Australia

SIZE: 110 pounds (50 kilograms)

DIET: Herbivore; browser

ESSENTIAL FACTS: Nimbadon was a sheep-sized herbivore from Riversleigh. It was originally thought to have been a member of the Diprotodontidae, but now it seems to be regarded as a more basal vombatiform with no definitive family placement. These were arboreal browsing animals with large hands and feet with curved claws that could be raised off the ground when walking.

WYNYARDIIDAE

Wynyardiids were possum-like diprotodontians only known from the Late Oligocene and Early Miocene.

MURAMURA WILLIAMSI

NAME MEANING: David Williams' Muramura

AGE: Late Oligocene (25 MYA)

DISTRIBUTION: Australia

SIZE: 40 pounds (18 kilograms)

DIET: Herbivore; browser

ESSENTIAL FACTS: Named for a demigod from Diari Aboriginal legend, Muramura is known from several complete, articulated skeletons.

NAMILAMADETA SNIDERY

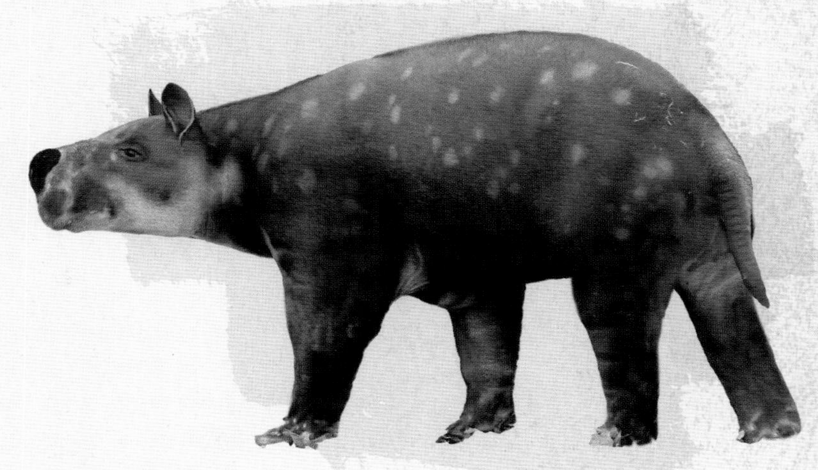

NAME MEANING: Edwin Snider's altered teeth

AGE: Late Oligocene (25 MYA)

DISTRIBUTION: Australia

SIZE: Unknown

DIET: Herbivore; browser

ESSENTIAL FACTS: Known for an almost complete skull and partial skeleton.

WYNYARDIA BASSIANA

NAME MEANING: From Wynyard near Bass Strait

AGE: Early Miocene (20 MYA)

DISTRIBUTION: Australia

SIZE: Unknown

DIET: Herbivore; browser

ESSENTIAL FACTS: At the time of its discovery in 1876, Wynyardia was the oldest marsupial identified in Australia. It is only known for a single partial skeleton.

PHASCOLARCTIDAE

Koalas are arboreal herbivores with a fossil history starting from the Late Oligocene and has only one species alive today. The name *Phascolarctos* translates to "pouched bear," for the modern species' resemblance to a teddy bear.

NIMIOKOALA GREYSTANESI

NAME MEANING: Greystanes High School excessive koala

AGE: Early Miocene (23–16 MYA)

DISTRIBUTION: Australia

SIZE: 9.8–11.8 pounds (25–30 centimeters) HBL; 7.7 pounds (3.5 kilograms)

DIET: Herbivore

SEE MORE ON PAGES 126–127

PHASCOLARCTOS STIRTONI

NAME MEANING: Ruben Stirton's pouched bear

AGE: Pleistocene (2 MYA–50,000 YA)

DISTRIBUTION: Australia

SIZE: 29 pounds (13 kilograms)

DIET: Herbivore

ESSENTIAL FACTS: Despite its common name, the Giant Koala is not that much larger than the modern koala (*P. cinereus*). It was an arboreal folivore (leaf eater) as well, but it is unknown if it was also a eucalyptus specialist or if it had a more varied diet that included other trees.

VOMBATIDAE

Wombats are robust, grazing diprotodontians represented by three modern species not exceeding 90 pounds (41 kilograms) in weight. The family is estimated to have diverged from other diprotodontians around 40 million years ago at the earliest, although the oldest definitive fossils appear during the late Oligocene about 25 million years ago. Members of the group are squat, robust semi-fossorial animals that dig complex burrows in which to shelter.

RHIZOPHASCOLONUS CROWCROFTI

NAME MEANING: Peter Crowcroft's root phascolonus

AGE: Early Miocene (23 MYA)

DISTRIBUTION: Australia

SIZE: Unknown

DIET: Herbivore; grazer

ESSENTIAL FACTS: Rhizophascolonus is the oldest-known wombat to be described. Unlike later wombats which have hypselodont teeth, Crowcroft's Wombat teeth had roots, suggesting that they had not yet adapted to handle more abrasive plants encountered out in the open, instead feeding on low-growing vegetation within forested environments.

WARENDJA WAKEFIELDI

NAME MEANING: Norman Wakefield's wombat

AGE: Pleistocene

DISTRIBUTION: Australia

SIZE: 22 pounds (10 kilograms)

DIET: Herbivore, grazer

ESSENTIAL FACTS: Wakefield's Wombat was relatively small by wombat standards, known for having slender and delicate features of its skull and lower jaw.

RAMSAYIA MAGNA

NAME MEANING: Ramsay's large (wombat)

AGE: Pleistocene

DISTRIBUTION: Australia

SIZE: 220 pounds (100 kilograms)

DIET: Herbivore; grazer

ESSENTIAL FACTS: Ramsay's Wombat was a large wombat species, second in size only to Phascolonus. It had a large, fleshy nose in real life.

NIMIOKOALA GREYSTANESI

ESSENTIAL FACTS: The Riversleigh Rainforest Koala is the oldest-known and smallest koala species. It inhabited the tropical rainforest that dominated much of western Australia during the Late Oligocene and Early Miocene. Its range would have shrunk as the Australian climate dried over the course of the Miocene and dense forests gave way to more open woodland and grassland.

The genus name "excessive koala" references the particularly complex molar morphology of this animal. This, along with its smaller size, suggest it would have been much more mobile and active than the modern koala (*Phascolarctos cinereus*) with a higher metabolism. Riversleigh Rainforest Koalas would have had a browsing diet that most likely included leaves and fruits from various types of trees. The snout of this animal was relatively long and resembled that of a possum. It also had eye sockets that were proportionally large, suggesting more nocturnal habits. The structure of the auditory bullae shows that it was sensitive to low frequency sounds and was probably extremely vocal, with males producing loud, guttural sounds to attract mates as the modern species does today.

SEE ENTRY ON PAGE 124

PHASCOLONUS GIGAS

NAME MEANING: Giant pouched ass

AGE: Pleistocene

DISTRIBUTION: Australia

SIZE: 3 feet (1 meter) SH; 5–6 feet (1.6–1.8 meters) HBL; 450–790 pounds (200–360 kilograms)

DIET: Herbivore; grazer

ESSENTIAL FACTS: The largest wombat known to have ever lived, Phascolonus was widespread throughout Australia and inhabited relatively open environments. It was probably not a burrower like modern wombats.

VOMBATUS HACKETTI

NAME MEANING: Winthrop Hackett's wombat

AGE: Pleistocene to early Holocene (2 MYA–10,000 YA)

DISTRIBUTION: Australia

SIZE: Slightly larger than modern common wombat (*Vombatus ursinus*)

DIET: Herbivore; grazer

ESSENTIAL FACTS: Hackett's Wombat is known to have lived in southern Australia and survived into the early Holocene. Like the smaller, closely related common wombat (*V. ursinus*) its burrowing activity helped to aid plant growth by turning and aerating the soil.

PALORCHESTIDAE

Compared to other diprotodontians, palorchestids have a number of unusual characteristics including large, robust forelimbs with strong claws. By comparison, the hindlimbs are relatively smaller. The skull has a long snout with greatly retracted nasals, suggesting the presence of a short proboscis, a muscular and mobile appendage formed by the fusion of the nose and upper lip. For this reason, palorchestids have been given the nickname "marsupial tapirs." The symphysis of the lower jaw is narrow and somewhat spout-shaped, suggesting the presence of a protrusible (able to be extended) tongue as seen in giraffids. Lastly, the jaw musculature was wombat-like and built for intensive chewing with hypsodont teeth. All these features combined show that palorchestids were the most specialized browsers among the diprotodontians, with a feeding strategy similar to that of chalicotheres: sitting or rearing up on their hindlimbs and using their strong arms and claws to anchor themselves and pull down branches.

PROPALORCHESTES NOVACULACEPHALUS

NAME MEANING: Razor-headed before Palorchestes

AGE: Middle Miocene

DISTRIBUTION: Australia

SIZE: 110 pounds (50 kilograms)

DIET: Herbivore; browser

ESSENTIAL FACTS: This species was a medium-sized browser about the size of a sheep. It is the oldest known member of Palorchestidae. Its nasals show considerable retraction but not to the same extent as its later relative.

PALORCHESTES AZAEL

NAME MEANING: Ancient leaper; species name meaning unknown

AGE: Pleistocene

DISTRIBUTION: Australia

SIZE: 8 feet (2.5 meters) HBL; 2,200 pounds (1,000 kilograms)

DIET: Herbivore; browser

ESSENTIAL FACTS: Researchers have interpreted Palorchestes as a solitary animal due to its relative scarcity in the fossil record. Analysis of its teeth, together with its long and narrow skull, suggest that it was a selective browser.

DIPROTODONTIDAE

Diprotodontids first appear in the fossil record in the Late Oligocene and became extinct at the end of the Pleistocene. These were the largest herbivores to live in Australia and would have filled similar niches that elephants, rhinos, hippos, and tapirs fill elsewhere in the world. Early representatives were midsized herbivores often compared to sheep in terms of their body size, while later species from the Pliocene and Pleistocene ranged from the size of an ox to the size of a rhino. Like elephants, many had large heads that were lightened by extensive sinus cavities.

SILVABESTIUS JOHNNILANDI

NAME MEANING: John Niland's forest beast

AGE: Late Oligocene (25 MYA)

DISTRIBUTION: Australia

SIZE: 132 pounds (60 kilograms)

DIET: Herbivore; browser

ESSENTIAL FACTS: Silvabestius was a sheep-sized herbivore from the Riversleigh World Heritage Area. The holotype is a complete skull with the lower jaws of a pouched juvenile. Its genus name translates to "Beast of the Forest," from the Latin words *silva* (meaning "forest") and *bestius* (meaning "beast").

PLAISIODON CENTRALIS

NAME MEANING: Central oblong tooth

AGE: Late Miocene (10 MYA)

DISTRIBUTION: Australia

SIZE: 4 feet (1.2 meters) SH; 8 feet (2.5 meters) HBL; 660 pounds (300 kilograms)

DIET: Herbivore; grazer

ESSENTIAL FACTS: This species is known for its particularly high-domed and robust skull with powerful jaw muscles. These features imply that it was specialized to feed on particularly tough, coarse plants.

HULITHERIUM TOMASETTI

NAME MEANING: Bernard Tomasetti's beast of the Huli people

AGE: Pleistocene

DISTRIBUTION: Australia

SIZE: 3 feet (1 meter) SH; 6 feet (2 meters) HBL; 165–440 pounds (75–200 kilograms)

DIET: Herbivore; browser

ESSENTIAL FACTS: A browser that fed on relatively soft plant matter, the limb anatomy of Hulitherium may suggest it had the ability to rear up on its hindlimbs to reach plants higher off the ground.

ZYGOMATURUS TRILOBUS

NAME MEANING: Three-lobed cheek arches

AGE: Pleistocene (1 MYA to 45,000 YA)

DISTRIBUTION: Australia

SIZE: 4.9 feet (1.5 meters) SH; 8.2 feet (2.5 meters) HBL; 1,100–1,500 pounds (500–700 kilograms)

DIET: Herbivore; browser

ESSENTIAL FACTS: Widely distributed throughout Australia, this species was the last and largest of its genus, which is characterized by its elevated nasals.

EURYZYGOMA DUNENSE

NAME MEANING: Wide cheek arches; species name unknown

AGE: Pliocene (5 to 3 MYA)

DISTRIBUTION: Australia

SIZE: 1,100 pounds (500 kilograms)

DIET: Herbivore; browser

ESSENTIAL FACTS: Euryzygoma is an ox-sized herbivore whose most notable feature is its unusual, flaring zygomatic arches (cheekbones). The reason for this feature is unclear, but it potentially played a role as a courtship display, given that it appears to be much more pronounced in males.

DIPROTODON OPTATUM

NAME MEANING: Two front teeth; species name unknown

AGE: Pleistocene (1.7 MYA–30,000 YA)

DISTRIBUTION: Australia

SIZE: 5.3–6 feet (1.6-1.8 meters) SH; 9–13 feet (2.75–4 meters); 5,000–7,533 pounds (2,272–3,417 kilograms)

DIET: Herbivore; browse-dominated mixed feeder

SEE MORE ON PAGES 132–133

DIPROTODON OPTATUM

ESSENTIAL FACTS: At about the size of a white rhino (*Ceratotherium simum*), Diprotodon is the largest metatherian known to have ever lived. Like elephants, it had several skeletal adaptations for dealing with its massive body weight, including upper limb elements that were long, straight, and had thickened walls. It is also the first fossil mammal to be described from Australia, by Richard Owen in 1838.

Much is known about the paleobiology of Diprotodon. It is the only metatherian living or extinct that is known to have undertaken seasonal migrations, most likely correlating to food and water availability. One study demonstrated that at least one individual made annual round trips of 120 miles (200 kilometers) along the Condamine River. Trackways found at Lake Callabonna and the Victorian Volcanic Plain Grasslands show their feet were curved inward so that they left kidney-shaped prints, and their stance was plantigrade with the wrist and ankle bones bearing most of the weight. They traveled in segregated herds; females and young formed large groups, and mature males were solitary or formed smaller, more fluid bachelor herds. This species is known to have occurred throughout Australia in almost every environment, although its preferred habitat appears to be grassland and open woodland. The narrow skull and bilophodont (having two crossways ridges or crests) cheek teeth which resemble those of a tapir suggest a browse-dominated diet consisting of leaves and twigs, with the occasional inclusion of grasses. The great size and strong jaws of Diprotodon made healthy adults virtually immune to predation by any of Australia's native predators.

SEE ENTRY ON PAGE 131

THYLACOLEONIDAE

The Thylacoleonidae are a family of predatory marsupials often referred to as "marsupial lions."

As a trend, all generic names within this family end with *leo*, the Latin word for "Lion." The family first appears in the fossil record during the Late Oligocene and lasts until the Late Pleistocene (25 MYA–40,000 YA). Thylacoleonids have a unique dentition among mammalian predators, with sturdy, canine-like incisors for stabbing prey and blade-like third premolars for shearing flesh. Most seem to have been arboreal or scansorial, and even the more actively terrestrial groups would have still been skillful climbers.

WAKALEO PITIKANTENSIS

NAME MEANING: Little lion from Lake Pitikanta

AGE: Late Oligocene (25 MYA)

DISTRIBUTION: Australia

SIZE: 20 pounds (9 kilograms)

DIET: Hypercarnivore

ESSENTIAL FACTS: Formerly named *Priscileo pitikantensis*, this is the smallest known species within its genus; it was about the size of a domestic cat. It is named for the Lake Pitikanta fossil site, from which the only known fossils have been found.

MICROLEO ATTENBOROUGHI

NAME MEANING: David Attenborough's tiny lion

AGE: Early Miocene (18 MYA)

DISTRIBUTION: Australia

SIZE: 21 ounces (600 grams)

DIET: Hypercarnivore

ESSENTIAL FACTS: Microleo was a forest-dweller that probably hunted small prey among the trees. Its genus name references its status as the smallest known thylacoleonid, while its species name honors British broadcaster and natural historian Sir David Attenborough, who has increased recognition of the Riversleigh World Heritage Area where the species was discovered.

THYLACOLEO CARNIFEX

NAME MEANING: Executioner pouched lion

AGE: Pleistocene

DISTRIBUTION: Australia

SIZE: 30 inches (75 centimeters) SH; 5 feet (150 centimeters) HBL; 220–362 pounds (100–164 kilograms)

DIET: Hypercarnivore

SEE MORE ON PAGES 136–137

MACROPODIFORMES

Macropodiformes are commonly known as kangaroos but are also referred to as macropods. The word macropod means "big foot" or "long foot." This refers to the elongated hindfeet of these animals, which most species use to engage in high-speed saltatorial (jumping) locomotion, although more basal species were quadrupedal.

BALBARIDAE

Balbarids are the most basal macropod family, still retaining functional canines and first digits on their hindfeet. They had zygodont dentition adapted for browsing. Much of the anatomy and movement would have been similar to that of rat-kangaroos (Hypsiprymnodontidae).

THYLACOLEO CARNIFEX

ESSENTIAL FACTS: This was last and most well-known of the thylacoleonids and the type species for the family. *Thylacoleo carnifex* was the largest carnivorous land mammal known to have existed in Australia, being the size of a jaguar (*Panthera onca*). It has a heavily built skeleton with particularly robust forelimbs. The first digits of the forepaws were enlarged and bore a powerful hooked claw, which was held above the ground to retain its sharpness. The muscular tail was used as an anchor, providing leverage when grappling with large prey items. Its hindlimbs were well suited for leaping and sudden bursts of speed.

Sir Richard Owen famously described this animal as "one of the fellest and most destructive of predatory beasts" when he examined its fossils back in 1859, even giving it the name *carnifex*, which means "executioner" or "butcher" in Latin. In some regards, his assessment is appropriate. For its size, this animal has the strongest bite of any mammal, living or extinct; it has been calculated that a 100-kilogram Marsupial Lion had a bite force comparable to that of a lion more than twice its weight. This, combined with its powerful skeleton built for strength and grappling, shows that this animal was a big game specialist that actively targeted prey as large or larger than itself. Possible prey items include large kangaroos and wombats, juvenile diprotodontids, and the dromornithid bird *Genyornis newtoni*, which it would have captured using ambush tactics and dispatched with a single bite to the head or neck. The first human inhabitants of Australia may have depicted this animal in their rock art, showing a large-headed animal with almost exaggerated forelimbs and vertical stripes running down the full length of its back, possibly hinting at its coat patterning.

SEE ENTRY ON PAGE 135

BALBAROO FANGAROO

NAME MEANING: Strange roo with fangs

AGE: Late Oligocene (25 MYA)

DISTRIBUTION: Australia

SIZE: About the size of a wallaby

DIET: Herbivore

ESSENTIAL FACTS: True to its name, Fangaroo and other members of its genus have enlarged upper canines. Like modern herbivores such as musk deer (Moschidae) and chevrotains (Tragulidae), it is likely that these animals, particularly the males, used their long canines against each other in territorial disputes.

GANAWAMAYA GILLESPIEAE

NAME MEANING: Anna Gillespie's long tooth

AGE: Late Oligocene (25 MYA)

DISTRIBUTION: Australia

SIZE: 5.5–11 pounds (2.5–5 kilograms)

DIET: Herbivore

ESSENTIAL FACTS: Much of the skeleton is known for this species, unlike others of its genus which are known from isolated teeth and jaws. Like other balbarids, it was a quadrupedal animal with robust forelimbs and an opposable first toe, which could indicate the ability to climb.

HYPSIPRYMNODONTIDAE

Rat-kangaroos were hypocarnivorous or mesocarnivorous macropods that lack multi-chambered stomachs, which most others in the group have. They have five-toed hind feet and engage in quadrupedal locomotion, galloping rather than hopping when they need to move quicky. There is only one surviving species. Their molars are bunodont and they have plagiaulacoid third premolars like the distantly related possums.

HYPSIPRYMNODON KARENBLACKAE

NAME MEANING: Karen Black's high rump tooth

AGE: Middle Miocene (15 MYA)

DISTRIBUTION: Australia

SIZE: 2.2 pounds (1 kilogram)

DIET: Hypocarnivore

ESSENTIAL FACTS: Slightly larger than the living musky rat-kangaroo (*H. moschatus*), Black's Rat-Kangaroo inhabited rainforests of eastern Australia, where it fed on a variety of foods including fruits, fungi, and invertebrates.

EKALTADETA IMA

NAME MEANING: Condemned powerful tooth

AGE: Late Oligocene (25 MYA)

DISTRIBUTION: Australia

SIZE: About wallaby-sized

DIET: Mesocarnivore

ESSENTIAL FACTS: The earliest-known of a lineage of highly predatory rat-kangaroos with sectoral dentition adapted for shearing flesh. The lower incisors were particularly long and appear to have been adapted for stabbing.

PROPLEOPUS OSCILLANS

NAME MEANING: Unknown

AGE: Pleistocene

DISTRIBUTION: Australia

SIZE: 155 pounds (70 kilograms)

DIET: Mesocarnivore

ESSENTIAL FACTS: Possibly the last and largest of the predatory rat-kangaroos, this species was about the size of a modern eastern gray kangaroo (*Macropus giganteus*). It's likely to have fed on animals up to the size of wallabies, supplementing its diet with eggs, fruits, and softer plants.

POTOROIDAE

The family includes the bettongs and potoroos. These are small rabbit or hare-sized kangaroos that may be ancestral to Macropodidae, sharing many similar features but in a less developed capacity. Potoroids feed on a wide variety of plant foods. However, most modern species are strongly fungivorous, primarily feeding on the fruiting bodies of fungi. These animals are important ecosystem engineers, as their digging activities help aerate the soil and improve drainage.

PALAEOPOTOROUS PRISCUS

NAME MEANING: First ancient potoroo

AGE: Late Oligocene (25 MYA)

DISTRIBUTION: Australia

SIZE: About rabbit-sized

DIET: Hypocarnivore

ESSENTIAL FACTS: As the oldest-known potoroid, little is known of its paleoecology or biology. It probably had a mixed diet of plants and fungi like other members of the family.

BORUNGABOODIE HATCHERI

NAME MEANING: Lindsay Hatcher's very large ground-rat

AGE: Pleistocene

DISTRIBUTION: Australia

SIZE: 22 pounds (10 kilograms)

DIET: Fungivore

ESSENTIAL FACTS: The largest of the bettongs, Borungaboodie was about 30 percent larger than the largest modern species, the rufous bettong (*Aepyprymnus rufescens*). The Giant Potoroo had relatively strong jaws and teeth seemingly adapted to eat hard foods such as nuts, roots, and tubers.

BETTONGIA MOYESI

NAME MEANING: Allan Moyes' small wallaby

AGE: Middle Miocene (15 MYA)

DISTRIBUTION: Australia

SIZE: About rabbit-sized

DIET: Fungivore

ESSENTIAL FACTS: Like modern bettongs, Moyes's Bettong was likely a nocturnal forager whose diet consisted mainly of truffles and other underground fungi and roots.

MACROPODIDAE

Most members of this specious family are nimble herbivores that occupy the niches that deer (Cervidae), antelopes and goats (Bovidae), and horses (Equidae) occupy in other parts of the world. One branch of this group became adapted to an arboreal lifestyle and are ecologically comparable to monkeys. Some fossil taxa were high-browsers that were Australia's answer to giraffes (Giraffidae) and camels (Camelidae).

MACROPODINAE

The most specious of the three subfamilies are what we tend to think about when we hear the word *kangaroo*. In addition to the numerous hopping taxa, the group includes tree-kangaroos (*Dendrolagus*), which are adapted for life in the trees.

CONGRUUS KITCHENERI

NAME MEANING: Kitchener's agreeable (animal)

AGE: Pleistocene

DISTRIBUTION: Australia

SIZE: 130 pounds (60 kilograms)

DIET: Herbivore; browser

ESSENTIAL FACTS: Kitchener's Kangaroo was a semi-arboreal browser, as evidenced by its highly mobile shoulder joints and overall robust forelimbs and curved claws. Its long skull and long, flexible neck increased its reach when browsing.

BOHRA PAULAE

NAME MEANING: Paula Kendall's Bohra

AGE: Pleistocene

DISTRIBUTION: Australia

SIZE: 110 pounds (50 kilograms)

DIET: Herbivore; browser

SEE MORE ON PAGES 144–145

NOMBE NOMBE

NAME MEANING: After the Nombe rock shelter

AGE: Pleistocene

DISTRIBUTION: Australia

SIZE: About wallaby-sized

DIET: Herbivore; browser

ESSENTIAL FACTS: Nombe is known to have lived in montane (mountainous) rainforests with thick undergrowth and a closed canopy. Its robust jaws and strong chewing muscles show that it fed on tough leaves from trees and shrubs. It was formerly described as *Protemnodon nombe* in 1982, before being placed in its own genus forty years later in 2022.

PROTEMNODON ANAK

NAME MEANING: First saw tooth

AGE: Pleistocene

DISTRIBUTION: Australia

SIZE: 242 pounds (110 kilograms)

DIET: Herbivore; mixed feeder

ESSENTIAL FACTS: Compared to its closest modern relatives of the genus *Macropus*, Protemnodon had longer and more robust arms with short, stubby fingers built for quadrupedal locomotion. It is one of the best-known and most widespread of all extinct kangaroos. Stable isotope analysis has shown that it may have had a mixed diet of both grazing and browsing.

LAGOSTROPHINAE

A group containing a single modern species, these kangaroos are closely related to the sthenurines, the two subfamilies probably branching away from each other during the late Miocene.

TROPOSODON MINOR

NAME MEANING: Little turning tooth

AGE: Pliocene to Pleistocene

DISTRIBUTION: Australia

SIZE: 110 pounds (50 kilograms)

DIET: Herbivore

ESSENTIAL FACTS: The Little Troposodon is a moderately sized kangaroo that shares a number of features in common with the modern banded hare-wallaby (*Lagostrophus fasciatus*) and with short-faced kangaroos (Sthenurinae). It was a browsing herbivore that may have also fed regularly on fungi.

BOHRA PAULAE

ESSENTIAL FACTS: Tree kangaroos are descended from rock-wallabies (*Petrogale*), a transition which likely took place during the late Miocene during a rainforest expansion. Rock-wallabies are extremely agile and capable of scaling near vertical slopes at surprising speeds, and some are even known to climb trees on occasion. Over time, one lineage of these animals evolved shorter hindlimbs and stronger arms specially adapted for climbing.

The name *Bohra* is the name of a legendary kangaroo from the folklore of the Euahlayi tribe of New South Wales. The genus contains seven species of which Paula's Bohra is the largest. This species was widespread through Australia's woodlands and forests and would have browsed on a variety of plants. Notably, the presence of this species and its close relatives in such areas as the now treeless Nullarbor Plain (literally "treeless plain" in Latin) is far removed from the current distributions of tree kangaroos, and serves as an indicator of the vastly different climate and vegetation over much of Australia in the recent past.

SEE ENTRY ON PAGE 142

STHENURINAE

Sthenurines are commonly known as the "short-faced kangaroos" due to species in this group having relatively short and deep skulls and jaws that supported well-developed chewing muscles. Other distinguishing features include forward-facing eyes and long, powerful arms with two extra-long fingers with large claws seemingly adapted for high browsing from trees. All digits of the hindfoot except the fourth are reduced or lost, with the last phalanx resembling a horse hoof. Short-faced kangaroos were not able to hop like their modern relatives; instead, they walked and ran using alternating strides like birds. The group includes some of the largest kangaroos to have ever lived.

HADRONOMAS PUCKRIDGI

NAME MEANING: Puckridge's heavy nomad

AGE: Late Miocene

DISTRIBUTION: Australia

SIZE: 220 pounds (100 kilograms)

DIET: Herbivore; browser

ESSENTIAL FACTS: This was the oldest-known of the short-faced kangaroos, as well as the largest kangaroo known from the late Miocene. Its skull is notably deeper than those of other kangaroos, but not to the extent of later sthenurines. It was probably not as well adapted to handle more fibrous plants.

STHENURUS STIRLINGI

NAME MEANING: Edward Stirling's strong tail

AGE: Pleistocene

DISTRIBUTION: Australia

SIZE: 530 pounds (240 kilograms)

DIET: Herbivore; browser

ESSENTIAL FACTS: Stirling's Sthenurus is one of the largest kangaroos known to have ever lived, tied with Goliath Procoptodon (*Procoptodon goliah*). There is evidence that these animals were occasionally hunted by humans.

SIMOSTHENURUS OCCIDENTALIS

NAME MEANING: Western short nosed sthenurus

AGE: Pleistocene

DISTRIBUTION: Australia

SIZE: 260 pounds (118 kilograms)

DIET: Herbivore; browser

ESSENTIAL FACTS: Fossils of this species from Tasmanian caves have yielded mtDNA which, among other things, revealed that the closet modern relatives of the sthenurines is the banded hare-wallaby (*Lagostrophus fasciatus*).

PROCOPTODON GOLIAH

NAME MEANING: Goliath front chopping tooth

AGE: Pleistocene

DISTRIBUTION: Australia

SIZE: 440–530 pounds (200–240 kilograms)

DIET: Herbivore; browser

SEE MORE ON PAGES 148–149

EUTHERIA

PROCOPTODON GOLIAH

ESSENTIAL FACTS: Probably the most famous of the short-faced kangaroos, the Giant Procoptodon inhabited areas of open woodland and savanna. Like other sthenurines, it was adapted for high browsing, feeding primarily from trees. Using its long arms and mobile shoulders, they were capable of reaching leaves and branches as high as twelve feet above the ground, pulling them back down toward its mouth. The species is characterized by an extremely deep, short face even by the standards of the subfamily.

The megafauna of Pleistocene Australia, including Giant Procoptodon, coexisted with humans on the continent for over 30,000 years, and evidence of this coexistence has been recorded in several unique ways. In a wilderness area called Arnhem Land in Northern Territory, ancient Aboriginal rock art has been found that depicts multiple now-extinct animals from Australia's ancient past. Among them is an image of what is thought to represent Giant Procoptodon. The art depicts a long-legged, bipedal animal with a relatively short, thick tail, shortened face, and long ears. Furthermore, there exists in native Australian oral tradition stories of very large, aggressive kangaroos which would attack men with the claws on their long arms, which has been interpreted as a possible surviving account of this species. Though it may have been more resilient than other megafauna species, Giant Procoptodon became extinct between 40,000 and 18,000 years ago.

SEE ENTRY ON PAGE 147

NESORHINUS HAYASAKI

NAME MEANING: Hayasaka's island nose

AGE: Pleistocene

DISTRIBUTION: Eurasia

SIZE: 2,244–3,682 pounds (1,018–1,670 kilograms)

DIET: Herbivore

ESSENTIAL FACTS: This animal was the larger of two species of *Nesorhinus* related to modern one-horned rhinos of the genus *Rhinoceros*. Its fossils have so far only been found on the island of Taiwan, which was connected to mainland China when this rhino lived. It lived in an open grassland habitat.

LARTETOTHERIUM SANSANIENSE

NAME MEANING: Édouard Lartet's beast from Sansan

AGE: Middle Miocene (16–13 MYA)

DISTRIBUTION: Eurasia

SIZE: About ox-sized

DIET: Herbivore

ESSENTIAL FACTS: The Lartet's Rhino was a browsing herbivore with a particularly long, low, and narrow skull. It had cursorial adaptations with relatively long, slender limbs and it had a single nasal horn, showing its relationship to the modern one-horned rhinos (*Rhinoceros*).

DIHOPLUS MEGARHINUS

NAME MEANING: Great nose with two weapons

AGE: Pliocene

DISTRIBUTION: Eurasia

SIZE: 8.2 feet (2.5 meters) SH; 23 feet (7 meters) HBL

DIET: Herbivore

ESSENTIAL FACTS: This animal was a widely distributed species with fossils found from Europe to China. It is sometimes placed in the genus *Pliorhinus* and appears to have been primarily a browser.

STEPHANORHINUS KIRCHBERGENSIS

NAME MEANING: King Stephan's nose from Kirchberg an der Jagst

AGE: Pleistocene

DISTRIBUTION: Eurasia

SIZE: 6 feet (1.8 meters) SH

DIET: Herbivore; browse-dominated mixed feeder

ESSENTIAL FACTS: Known as "the Merk's Rhino" or "Forest Rhino," this species inhabited open woodland and forest habitat and appears to have been a browse-dominated mixed feeder with a robust build. The common name is in honor of Karl Heinrich Merk, who first named the animal in 1784.

COELODONTA ANTIQUITATUS

NAME MEANING: Ancient hollow tooth

AGE: Pleistocene

DISTRIBUTION: Eurasia

SIZE: 4.8–5.2 feet (1.45–1.6 meters) SH; 10.5–11.8 feet (3.2–3.6 meters) HBL; 3,000–4,000 pounds (1,360–1,814 kilograms)

DIET: Herbivore; grazer

SEE MORE ON PAGES 630

DESMOSTYLIA

To modern observers, these animals would have appeared rather odd looking. The skull was vaguely hippo-like with forward-pointing incisors. Their feet were broad and paddle-like. They were adapted to graze on seaweeds and sea-grasses near the coast. These animals were marine herbivores that lived along the Pacific coast from the Early Oligocene to Late Miocene. The structure of their limbs and rib cage suggests that they were not capable of terrestrial locomotion. The closest relatives of these animals appear to be the semiaquatic anthracobunids, which would therefore place them among the Perissodactyla. The name Desmostylia means "bundle pillar," in reference to their unique shape of their molars. The decline and eventual extinction of these animals appears to match an increase in the diversity of dugongs (Dugongidae) throughout the Miocene. They primarily walked and ran along the sea floor, and swam mostly by paddling with their forelimbs.

COELODONTA ANTIQUITATUS

ESSENTIAL FACTS: Despite being sympatric with three other extinct rhinos, the Woolly Rhino is by far the most famous among them, known from multiple complete skeletons, cave paintings, and even carcasses preserved in bogs or permafrost. The species was distributed throughout northern Eurasia, where it inhabited grassland ecosystems. Its closest modern relative is the Sumatran Rhino (*Dicerorhinus sumatrensis*). The ancestor of the species is thought to have originated in the highlands of central Asia. The youngest remains have been reliably dated to 14,000 years ago.

The life appearance of the Woolly Rhino is well-known, thanks to the preservation of frozen carcasses found in permafrost and cave paintings made by ancient humans. During autumn these rhinos grew a two-layered coat for which the species derives its common name; these coats would be shed during spring as the weather warmed. Their long, coarse guard hairs were reddish-brown over most of the body, with a band of darker fur around its torso behind the shoulders. Beneath this lay a dense woolly undercoat for insulation. The Woolly Rhino possessed thick, squared lips similar to those of the modern white rhino (*Ceratotherium simum*) for bulk-feeding on the short grasses, which comprised most of its diet. The nasal horn grew up to 4.4 feet (1.35 meters) long, crescent-shaped, and laterally flattened. These rhinos used these nasal horns to sweep away snow to expose the underlying vegetation. The species would also opportunistically browse during winter when its preferred grasses and sedges were less abundant.

SEE ENTRY ON PAGE 629

DESMOSTYLIDAE

The more basal of the two families of desmostylians, this group is known to have lived from the Early Oligocene to the Late Miocene. They had narrow skulls and were active swimmers. They may have been adapted to feed in kelp forest ecosystems, which are known to have become established by the Early Oligocene.

CORNWALLIUS SOOKENSIS

NAME MEANING: Cornwall from the Chattian Sooke Formation

AGE: Late Oligocene (27–24 MYA)

DISTRIBUTION: Pacific Ocean

SIZE: Unknown

DIET: Marine herbivore

ESSENTIAL FACTS: The genus name was coined by paleontologist Oliver Hay in 1923 after Ira Cornwall, who described it as *Desmostylus sookensis* in 1922. First discovered in Vancouver Island, Canada, this species was distributed throughout the North American Pacific coast from Alaska to Baja California.

BEHEMOTOPS PROTEUS

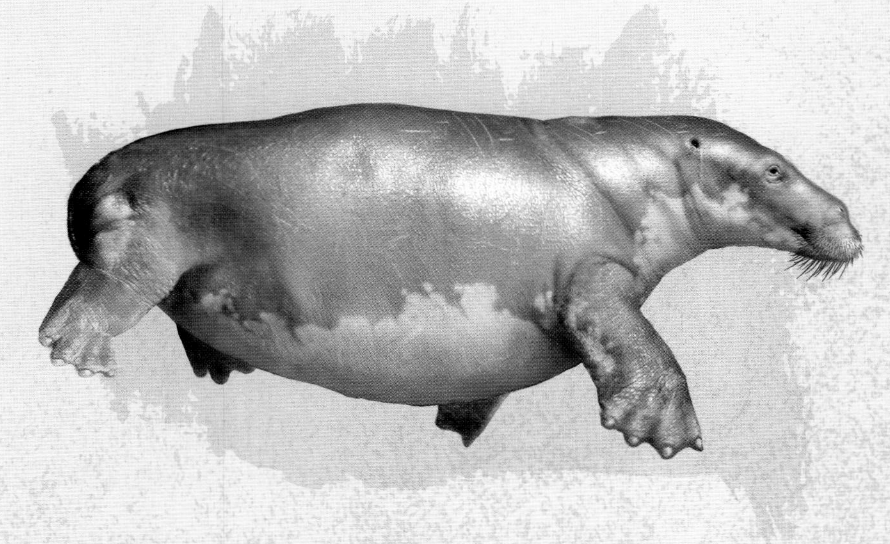

NAME MEANING: Behemoth-like Proteus

AGE: Early Oligocene

DISTRIBUTION: Pacific Ocean

SIZE: 10 feet (3 meters)

DIET: Marine herbivore

ESSENTIAL FACTS: One of the largest-known desmostylians, Proteus' Behemops had a particularly deep body with proportionally small hindlimbs compared to other desmostylians. It may have been adapted to float near the surface rather than walk along the seafloor as other desmostylians. The teeth resembled those of mastodons with ridges adapted to feed on kelp.

DESMOSTYLUS JAPONICUS

NAME MEANING: Bundle pillar from Japan

AGE: Miocene

DISTRIBUTION: Pacific Ocean

SIZE: 11 feet (3.3 meters) HBL; 2,000 pounds (910 kilograms)

DIET: Marine herbivore

ESSENTIAL FACTS: Its bones were less dense than those of other desmostylians, suggesting that it was an active swimmer that did not spend as much time at the seafloor. It was able to inhabit both salt and freshwater environments and may have been particularly fond of estuary ecosystems.

PALEOPARADOXIIDAE

The palaeoparadoxiids evolved larger hands and feet, enlarged noses, and elevated orbits. They had broad snouts adapted for bulk aquatic feeding. Such adaptations in these last desmostylians may have been means by which to compete against dougongs, which had been increasing in diversity throughout the Miocene.

ASHOROA LATICOSTA

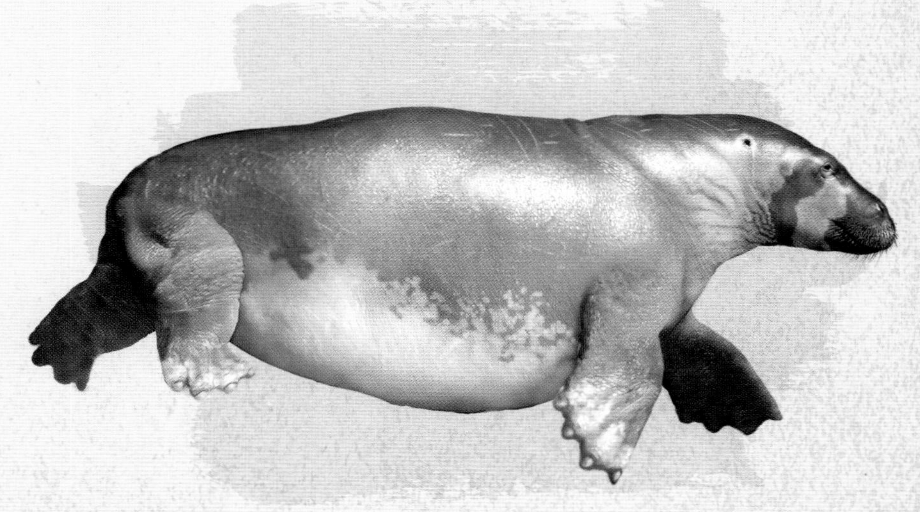

NAME MEANING: Broad-ribbed (animal) from Ashoro, Hokkaido

AGE: Early Oligocene (28–24 MYA)

DISTRIBUTION: Pacific Ocean

SIZE: 6.5 feet (2 meters)

DIET: Marine herbivore

ESSENTIAL FACTS: The genus is named for its type locality, and the species named for its dense, heavy ribs which would have helped them remain on the seafloor for extended periods. Ashoroa is the smallest-known desmostylian and also one of the oldest, although its derived features suggest the group's origins lie even earlier.

PALEOPARADOXIA TABATAI

NAME MEANING: Tabata's ancient paradox

AGE: Middle Miocene

DISTRIBUTION: Pacific Ocean

SIZE: 7 feet (2.15 meters) HBL; 1,283 pounds (582 kilograms)

DIET: Marine herbivore

ESSENTIAL FACTS: Tabata's Desmostylian inhabited deep, offshore waters along the Pacific coasts of Asia and North America, where it grazed on sea grasses at the seafloor. Its jaws were relatively broad with procumbent incisors similar to those of hippos.

NEOPARADOXIA CECILIALINA

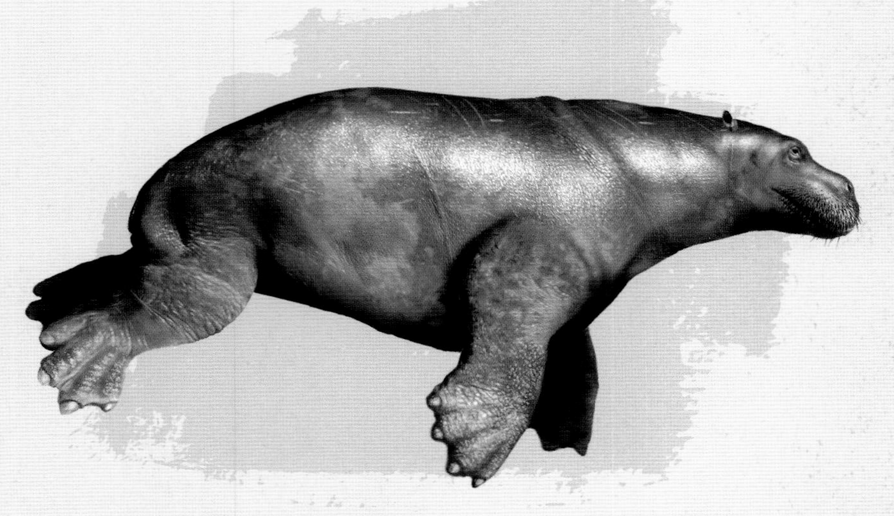

NAME MEANING: Cecilia and Alina's new paradox

AGE: Late Miocene (11–10 MYA)

DISTRIBUTION: Pacific Ocean

SIZE: 8 feet (2.4 meters)

DIET: Marine herbivore

ESSENTIAL FACTS: This species, discovered in the Monterey Formation in Southern California's Orange County, is known for a complete skeleton on display at the Natural History Museum of Los Angeles County. It had the most extreme adaptations of the palaeoparadoxiines.

ARTIODACTYLA

Artiodactyla is a diverse order of mammals which includes modern pigs (Suidae), peccaries (Tayassuidae), hippos (Hippopotamidae), deer (Cervidae), antelope (Bovidae), and giraffes (Giraffidae), among others. Members of this group are characterized by their feet; the main weight of the body is equally distributed through the third and fourth digits of each foot. As a result, animals within this group tend to reduce the number of functional toes from five to just four or two. For this reason, artiodactyls are commonly referred to as the "even-toed ungulates." The name Artiodactyla is derived from the Greek words *artios* and *daktulos*, meaning "even" and "finger," respectively. Cetaceans (whales, dolphins, and porpoises) evolved from early artiodactyls during the Eocene and are closely related to hippos, leading some authors to combine the Cetacea and Artiodactyla into a common order known as "Cetartiodactyla."

DICHOBUNIDAE

Dichobunids were a family that includes the oldest artiodactyls. They occur in the fossil record starting in the Early Eocene and become extinct by the Late Oligocene. Most species were small, not much larger than a house cat, and were generally built like chevrotains (Tragulidae) with long tails. The hindlimbs were much longer than the forelimbs, adapted for quick acceleration and leaping through the forests in which they lived. They had four or five hooved toes on their feet, with the third and fourth digits being the largest and bearing most of the weight.

DIACODEXIS PAKISTANENSIS

NAME MEANING: Across the book from Pakistan

AGE: Early Eocene (56–54 MYA)

DISTRIBUTION: Eurasia

SIZE: About cat-sized

DIET: Hypocarnivore

ESSENTIAL FACTS: Members of the genus *Diacodexis* are the oldest-known artiodactyls. They were hypocarnivores that fed on softer leaves and fruits, while also eating any small animals they could catch. They were built for sprinting and leaping through the dense forest undergrowth.

MESSELOBUNODON SCHAEFERI

NAME MEANING: Schaefer's rounded teeth from Messel

AGE: Middle Eocene (48–45 MYA)

DISTRIBUTION: Eurasia

SIZE: About cat-sized

DIET: Hypocarnivore

ESSENTIAL FACTS: Messelobunodon is named after Messel Pit in Germany, from which complete skeletons have been recovered. Preserved gut contents show that they fed on seeds, fruits, leaves, and mushrooms.

WHIPPOMORPHA

Whippomorpha is the group which contains the earliest artiodactyls and cetaceans. Traditionally, the families Hippopotamidae (hippos), Anthracotheriidae (anthracotheres), and Entelodontidae (entelodonts) have been placed within the Suina (pig-like artiodactyls) for morphological reasons. However, a 2009 study of artiodactyl phylogeny found that these three families, together with the Middle Eocene predator Andrewsarchus (*Andrewsarchus mongoliensis*), are much more closely related to Cetacea than to other artiodactyls. Barring the cetaceans, members of this group are the least derived among the artiodactyls, with a history dating back to the Early Eocene.

ANDREWSARCHUS MONGOLIENSIS

NAME MEANING: Roy Chapman Andrews' flesh (eater) from Mongolia

AGE: Middle Eocene (45–40 MYA)

DISTRIBUTION: Eurasia

SIZE: 2,000 pounds (907 kilograms)

DIET: Mesocarnivore

SEE MORE ON PAGES 638–639

RAOELLIDAE

Raoellids were broadly similar in form to their dichobunid ancestors but were more robust overall and adapted for a semi-aquatic lifestyle. They were directly ancestral to the cetaceans and are known to have lived from the Early to Middle Eocene.

INDOHYUS MAJOR

NAME MEANING: Greater pig from India

AGE: Early Eocene (50–48 MYA)

DISTRIBUTION: Eurasia

SIZE: About raccoon-sized

DIET: Hypocarnivore

ESSENTIAL FACTS: Indohyus would have fed mostly on land but would readily dive into water to feed on aquatic plants and small animals or to escape from predators. Its dense bones enabled it to walk and run along the bottom like a water chevrotain (*Hyemoschus aquaticus*).

HELOHYIDAE

Helohyids are a family of hypocarnivorous artiodactyls that lived from the middle to late Eocene. Powerful jaws, large canines, and bunodont molars characterize the group and they are closely related to entelodonts and andrewsarchids.

ACHAENODON ROBUSTUS

NAME MEANING: Robust ancient tooth

AGE: Middle Eocene (43–39 MYA)

DISTRIBUTION: North America

SIZE: 630 pounds (285 kilograms)

DIET: Hypocarnivore

SEE MORE ON PAGES 640–641

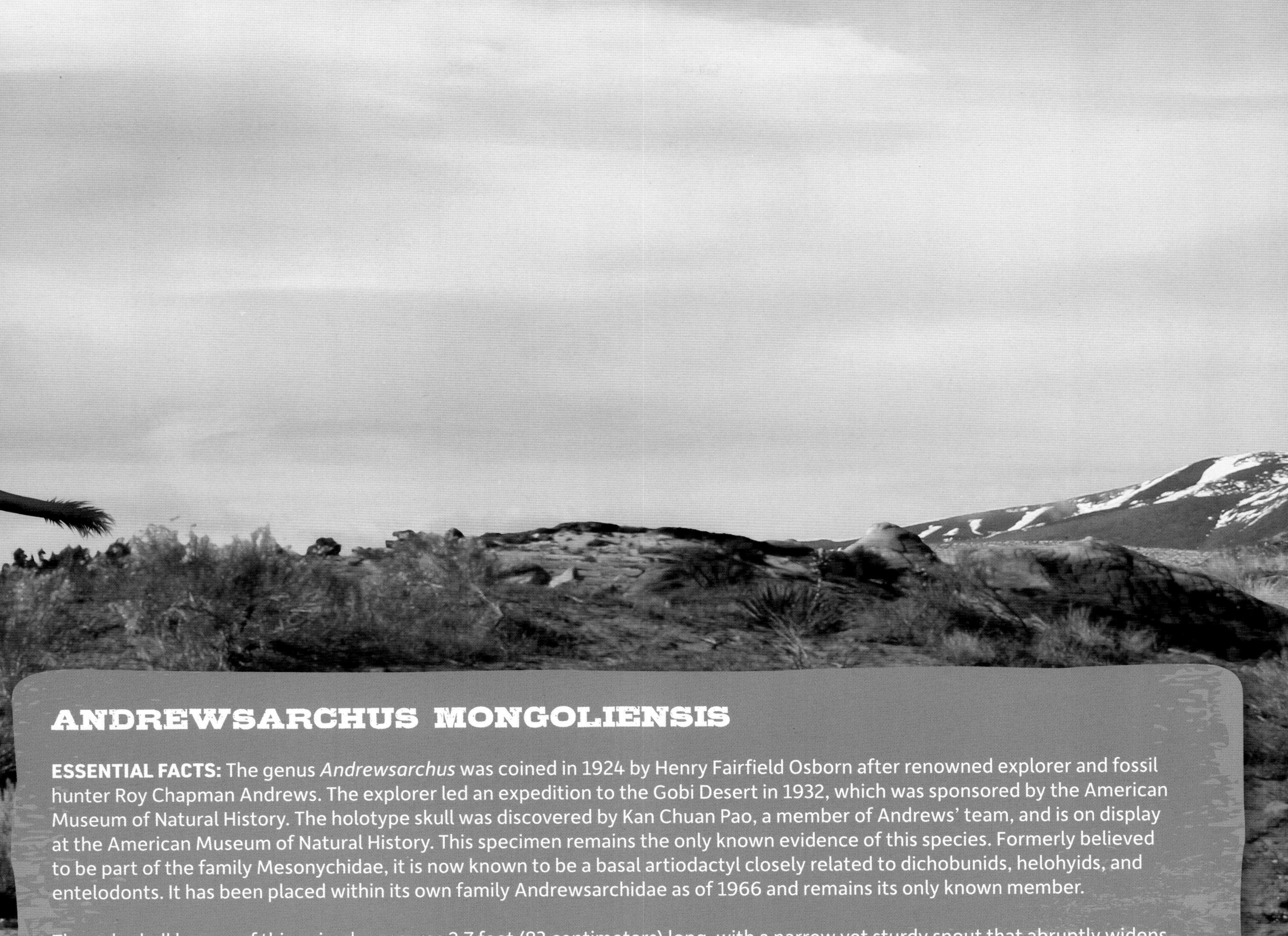

ANDREWSARCHUS MONGOLIENSIS

ESSENTIAL FACTS: The genus *Andrewsarchus* was coined in 1924 by Henry Fairfield Osborn after renowned explorer and fossil hunter Roy Chapman Andrews. The explorer led an expedition to the Gobi Desert in 1932, which was sponsored by the American Museum of Natural History. The holotype skull was discovered by Kan Chuan Pao, a member of Andrews' team, and is on display at the American Museum of Natural History. This specimen remains the only known evidence of this species. Formerly believed to be part of the family Mesonychidae, it is now known to be a basal artiodactyl closely related to dichobunids, helohyids, and entelodonts. It has been placed within its own family Andrewsarchidae as of 1966 and remains its only known member.

The only skull known of this animal measures 2.7 feet (83 centimeters) long, with a narrow yet sturdy snout that abruptly widens toward the rear to support massive jaw muscles. In general proportions, the skull is similar to that of entelodonts with robust incisors, canines, and premolars adapted for gripping, and crushing molars in the back. Lengthwise, the skull is comparable to that of the largest entelodonts such as Giant Entelodont (*Daeodon shoshonensis*). It can be inferred that the postcranial anatomy was similar, adapted to traveling long distances in search of food, be it carrion or edible plants.

SEE ENTRY ON PAGE 636

ACHAENODON ROBUSTUS

ESSENTIAL FACTS: The Robust Achaenodon is the largest of the helohyids. True to its name, it was a powerful and well-muscled animal, with body proportions comparable to that of a tapir with hindlimbs slightly longer than its forelimbs for propulsion. It had a large head that was supported by a short and powerful neck. The front of the snout was relatively narrow but quickly broadened toward the back by wide zygomatic arches which supported huge jaw muscles. Overall, the animal's skull resembled that of an entelodont, differing in the much shorter face and lack of ornamentation. The canines were massive, and premolars were triangular for gripping. The molars were bunodont and capable of processing a variety of plant and animal foods.

Robust Achaenodon was the size of a brown bear (*Ursus arctos*) and likely had a similar niche and diet, the skull and teeth being indicative of a diverse hypocarnivorous diet. It would have fed heavily on various types of plants found within its forest and woodland habitats and would occasionally scavenge the carcasses of other animals. With its strong jaws and canines, it was also capable of opportunistically taking live prey items, including quite large animals. Robust Achaenodon was the largest artiodactyl known up to its time. After its extinction nothing approaching its size would appear until the arrival of the entelodont genus *Archaeotherium* about 5 million years later.

SEE ENTRY ON PAGE 637

ENTELODONTIDAE

Entelodonts were predatory artiodactyls that were distributed across the Northern Hemisphere from the Late Eocene to the Early Miocene. They were characterized by large heads with powerful jaws, compact and muscular bodies, and two-toed feet with cloven hooves. The family is named for the genus *Entelodon*, whose name means "perfect tooth," in reference to their complete dentition. The incisors and canines are robust and conical, with triangular premolars adapted for gripping prey items and bunodont molars for crushing. The skull is supported by powerful neck muscles anchored in elevated neural spines on the thoracic vertebrae. Flanges protrude from the zygomatic arches, and strange protuberances grow from the lower jaw, serving as display structures.

BRACHYHYOPS WYOMINGENSIS

NAME MEANING: Short pig face from Wyoming

AGE: Late Eocene (40–37 MYA)

DISTRIBUTION: North America

SIZE: About coyote-sized

DIET: Mesocarnivore

ESSENTIAL FACTS: Compared to the later and better-known Morton's Entelodont (*Archaeotherium mortoni*), this species was a much smaller animal overall, with a proportionally shorter snout and deeper skull. It inhabited forest and woodland environments.

ARCHAEOTHERIUM MORTONI

NAME MEANING: Morton's ancient beast

AGE: Late Eocene to early Oligocene (35–28 MYA)

DISTRIBUTION: North America

SIZE: 4 feet (1.2 meters) SH; 6.5 feet (2 meters) HBL; 330–530 pounds (150–250 kilograms)

DIET: Mesocarnivore

SEE MORE ON PAGES 644–645

DAEODON SHOSHONENSIS

NAME MEANING: Hostile tooth from Shoshon

AGE: Early Miocene (23 MYA)

DISTRIBUTION: North America

SIZE: 5–6 feet (1.5–1.8 meters) SH; 1,653–2,000 pounds (750–907 kilograms)

DIET: Mesocarnivore

SEE MORE ON PAGES 646–647

ANTHRACOTHERIIDAE

The anthracotheres are an extinct group of herbivorous artiodactyls that appear in the fossil record during the Middle Eocene, possibly originating in Asia given the group's high diversity there. Anthracotheres became extinct in North America during the Late Miocene and survived in the Old World until the Late Pliocene. Ranging in morphology from piglike, tapir-like, and hippo-like, they typically had robust skeletons with relatively short limbs, large heads, and large canines. The dentition was brachydont and most species had specialized selenodont or bunoselenodont molars. Many species have been discovered in channel deposits, suggesting semiaquatic habits. In fact, hippos are believed to have descended from anthracotheres during the Late Miocene.

MICROBUNODONTINAE

Microbunodontines are small-bodied anthracotheres that occur from the Middle Eocene to Late Miocene of Eurasia. They are characterized by their slender limbs adapted for cursoriality, and adult males possessed large, laterally compressed canines similar to those of musk deer (Moschidae), suggesting that these animals were territorial and would fight each other for territory.

ARCHAEOTHERIUM MORTONI

ESSENTIAL FACTS: Morton's Entelodont is one of the best-known entelodonts, thanks to abundant fossil remains from western North America. The species exhibits sexual dimorphism, with males having larger cheek flanges and jaw protuberances than females. The species was named by Joseph Leidy in 1850.

Evidence of predatory behavior in Morton's Entelodont is well-documented. The bones of rhinos and other animals have been found with bite marks matching the dimensions of the entelodont's teeth. Modern predators will often store excess meat in caches, returning to it for later consumption. This behavior is documented in Morton's Entelodont. One discovery in the White River Formation near Douglas, Wyoming, has yielded multiple disarticulated skeletons of the sheep-sized Wilson's Camel (*Poebrotherium wilsoni*), all clustered together with bite marks to their skulls, necks, and upper thoracic vertebrae matching the size and spacing of the teeth of Morton's Entelodont. Furthermore, it seems that the predators preferred to feed on the muscular hind quarters of their prey before moving on to the rest of the carcass. Such selective feeding behavior is observed among modern predators when faced with an overabundance of prey. This discovery shows that the entelodonts were actively hunting and killing these camels as opposed to scavenging them. Because the teeth had no slicing function, carcasses would have to be pinned to the ground, and chunks of flesh would be torn away using its strong neck muscles and incisors.

SEE ENTRY ON PAGE 642

DAEODON SHOSHONENSIS

ESSENTIAL FACTS: The Giant Entelodont had a broad distribution throughout North America where it primarily inhabited grassland and open woodland habitats. Its fossils have been found in the states of California, Oregon, Texas, South Dakota, Wyoming, Nebraska, New Jersey, Mississippi, Alabama, South Carolina, and Florida. It is the largest-known of all entelodonts, about the size of a modern plains bison (*Bison bison*). Its massive three-foot (90 centimeter) skull amounted to as much as 25 percent of its total head-and-body length. Compared to the earlier Morton's Entelodont, its skull and teeth were even more robust, and its facial protuberances were reduced in size.

The best and most complete fossils of this species come from the Agate Springs Fossil Beds in Nebraska. From this locality, evidence of this entelodont's potential as a predator is well-known. Gouge and puncture damage matching the great teeth of this animal have been found on the broken bones of rhinos and chalicotheres. While these could have been the remains of scavenged carcasses, it was undoubtedly capable of tackling quite large prey items when it had the chance. The incisors, canines, and premolars often exhibit considerable amounts of wear, showing that it actively bit into bones during feeding or prey capture. In addition to animal matter, it is also likely to have browsed on edible plants that grew within its environment.

SEE ENTRY ON PAGE 643

ANTHRACOKERYX NADUONGENSIS

NAME MEANING: Coal horn from Na Duong

AGE: Middle Eocene (47–45 MYA)

DISTRIBUTION: Eurasia

SIZE: 45 pounds (20 kilograms)

DIET: Herbivore; browser

ESSENTIAL FACTS: The first fossils of this species are known from Na Duong, Vietnam, with additional material being found in China and Myanmar.

MICROBUNODON MINIMUM

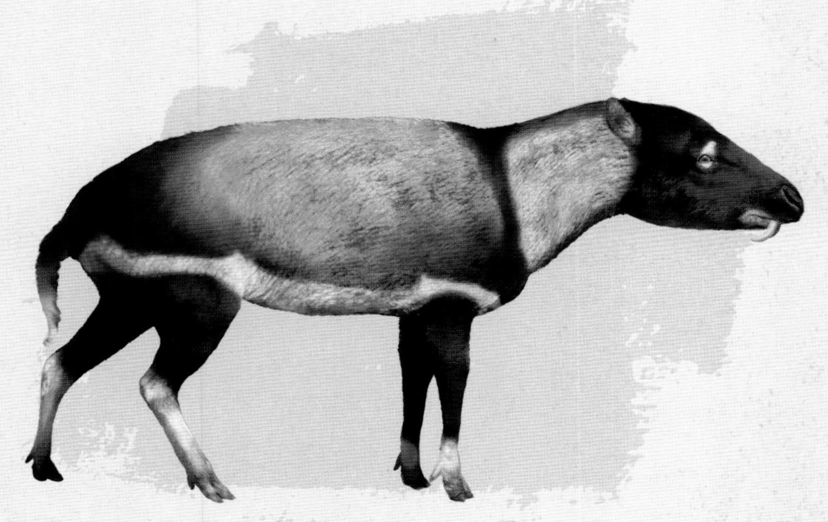

NAME MEANING: Small rounded teeth

AGE: Oligocene

DISTRIBUTION: Eurasia

SIZE: 45 pounds (20 kilograms)

DIET: Herbivore; browser

ESSENTIAL FACTS: Analysis of tooth wear shows that this species' diet consisted mainly of soft leaves and fruits. It was widespread throughout Europe's forests, this species' fossils are known from France, Germany, Switzerland, Austria, and Turkey.

BOTHRIODONTINAE

The bothriodontines may be a paraphyletic subfamily with its members being more closely related to other anthracothere subfamilies than they are to each other. A broad range of morphologies and diets are represented within the group, including small and large species with specialized browsers and grazers.

ELOMERYX ARMATUS

NAME MEANING: Armed marsh ruminant

AGE: Early Oligocene (34–30 MYA)

DISTRIBUTION: North America

SIZE: 5 feet (1.5 meters) HBL; 160–200 pounds (73–90 kilograms)

DIET: Herbivore; browser

ESSENTIAL FACTS: This species was a pig-sized animal with slender, digitigrade limbs adapted for moderate cursoriality. The males possessed long canines, which were serrated on the rear edges. Their preferred habitat seems to have been forests.

BOTHRIOGENYS FRAASI

NAME MEANING: Fraas' trench jaw

AGE: Early Oligocene (34–30 MYA)

DISTRIBUTION: Africa

SIZE: About pig-sized

DIET: Herbivore; browser

ESSENTIAL FACTS: Known for fossils collected from the Fayum Depression in Egypt, this species had an elongated, pig-like skull with a long, muscular body set on relatively short legs. It was a forest-dweller whose diet consisted mainly of leaves, fruits, nuts, and other plants. It is one of the first anthracotheres known to have entered Africa.

BOTHRIODON AMERICANUS

NAME MEANING: American trench teeth

AGE: Late Eocene (37–35 MYA)

DISTRIBUTION: North America

SIZE: About pig-sized

DIET: Herbivore; browser

ESSENTIAL FACTS: The genus *Bothriodon* was widespread throughout the Northern Hemisphere. The American Bothriodon was an animal of about the size and build of a wild boar (*Sus scrofa*) and may have had a similar diet.

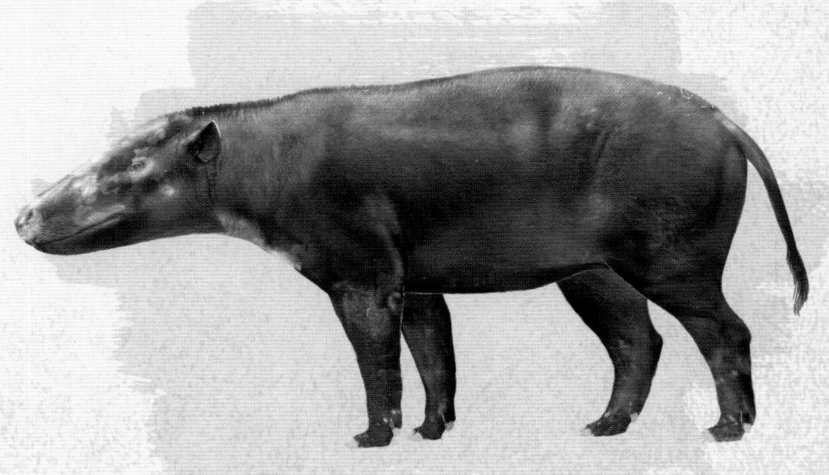

ANTHRACOTHERIINAE

This subfamily includes some of the largest of the anthracotheres, members of the group ranging from pig-sized to rhino-sized. Anthracotheriines are known to have lived from the Middle Eocene to Early Miocene.

HEPTACODON YEGUAENSIS

NAME MEANING: Seven teeth from the Yegua Formation

AGE: Late Eocene (42–38 MYA)

DISTRIBUTION: North America

SIZE: About pig-sized

DIET: Herbivore; browser

ESSENTIAL FACTS: The genus *Heptacodon* is endemic to North America. Several species have been described, of which the Yegua Heptacodon is the oldest. The animal featured a relatively short snout compared to other anthracotheres lacking a diastema.

PAENANTHRACOTHERIUM BERGERI

NAME MEANING: Berger's almost *Anthracotherium*

AGE: Early Oligocene (30 MYA)

DISTRIBUTION: Eurasia

SIZE: 2,900–3,300 pounds (1,300–1,500 kilograms)

DIET: Herbivore; browser

ESSENTIAL FACTS: Berger's Anthracothere is one of the largest members of the family, about the size of a river hippopotamus or Indian rhino (*Rhinoceros unicornis*), with a skull that was over 3 feet (1 meter) long. Its teeth are indicative of a primarily browsing diet and it lived in forested environments with access to standing water.

ANTHRACOTHERIUM MAGNUM

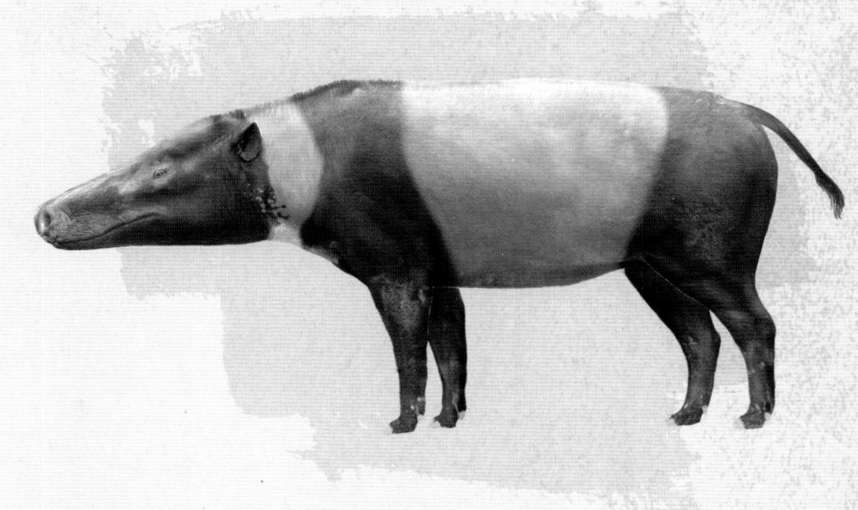

NAME MEANING: Great coal beast

AGE: Late Oligocene (25–23 MYA)

DISTRIBUTION: Eurasia

SIZE: 6.6 feet (2 meters) HBL; 550 pounds (250 kilograms)

DIET: Herbivore; browser

ESSENTIAL FACTS: The name *Anthracotherium* was coined due to the first fossils of these animals being collected from European coal mines. This species had a lifestyle comparable to that of a tapir (Tapiridae) or pygmy hippo (*Choeropsis liberiensis*), browsing on terrestrial and aquatic plants and escaping to the water when threatened.

HIPPOPOTAMIDAE

Hippos appear during the Late Miocene, apparently descending from anthracotheres (Anthracotheriidae) in Africa. They are semiaquatic herbivores with barrel-shaped bodies, naked skin, and relatively short yet slender limbs with four toes on each foot. During the Pliocene through Holocene hippos were widely distributed throughout Africa and Eurasia. Their heads are large with strong jaws that can open extremely wide, as well as long tusk-like canines that self-sharpen. There are two modern species: the river hippo (*Hippopotamus amphibius*) and the smaller and more docile pygmy hippo (*Choeropsis liberiensis*).

KENYAPOTAMUS CORYNDONI

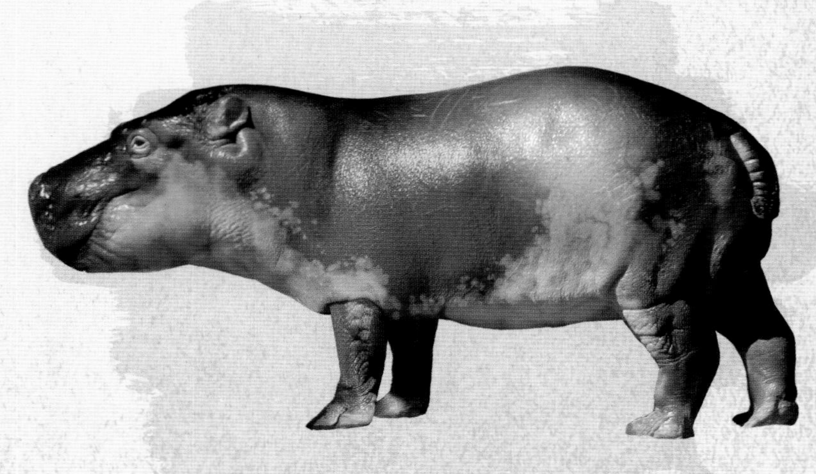

NAME MEANING: Coryndon's *Hippopotamus* from Kenya

AGE: Middle Mioocene (16–14 MYA)

DISTRIBUTION: Africa

SIZE: About tapir-sized

DIET: Herbivore; browser

ESSENTIAL FACTS: *Kenyapotamus* were the oldest hippos known to have lived and are placed within the subfamily Kenyapotaminae. Little is known about their paleoecology, but it can be inferred from their later relatives that they were partly aquatic browsers like the modern pygmy hippo (*Choeropsis liberiensis*).

HIPPOPOTOMINAE

Hippopotominae is the subfamily to which the two modern species evolve. The hippopotamines range from tapir-sized to rhino-sized and may be either terrestrial with a strong liking for water or semiaquatic, spending most of their lives in water only leaving to feed on land. The more terrestrial species tend to have eyes placed relatively lower on the skull and have more robust limb bones for active walking and running. More aquatic hippos have telescoped (high-set) eyes that enable them to peer above the water's surface while the rest of the body remains hidden.

ARCHAEOPOTAMUS LOTHAGAMENSIS

NAME MEANING: Ancient Hippopotamus from Lothagam

AGE: Late Miocene (8–6 MYA)

DISTRIBUTION: Africa

SIZE: 4 feet (1.2 meters) SH; 1,100 pounds (500 kilograms)

DIET: Herbivore; browser

ESSENTIAL FACTS: Lothagam Hippo is named for the Lothagam site in Kenya, where its fossils are known. It is the smallest member of its genus with a relatively slender skeleton. Compared to modern hippos the skull was long, low, and narrow with eyes placed relatively low, suggesting that it spent most of its time on land.

HEXAPROTODON SIVALENSIS

NAME MEANING: Six front teeth from Siwalik Hills

AGE: Pleistocene

DISTRIBUTION: Eurasia

SIZE: 10 feet (3 meters) HBL; 880–1,543 pounds (400–700 kilograms)

DIET: Herbivore; grazer

ESSENTIAL FACTS: Based on the elevated position of its eyes, the Indian Hippo is thought to have spent most of its time in water, mainly emerging onto land to graze. This species had long and spike-like incisors that made dangerous defensive weapons against the many big cats it shared its environment with.

SAOTHERIUM MINGOZ

NAME MEANING: Sao beast

AGE: Early Pliocene (5.3–4 MYA)

DISTRIBUTION: Africa

SIZE: 3.6 feet (1.1 meters) SH; 7.5 feet (2.3 meters) HBL

DIET: Herbivore; browser

ESSENTIAL FACTS: Named for a medieval civilization that once existed in the African country of Chad, the Sao Hippo is similar to the modern pygmy hippo (*Choeropsis liberiensis*), only somewhat larger. It would have spent most of its time on land, retreating to the water when threatened by predators.

HIPPOPOTAMUS ANTIQUUS

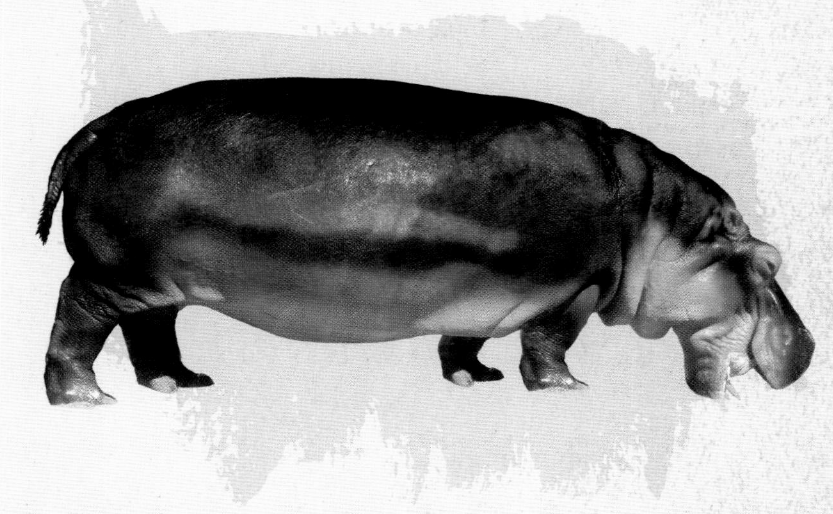

NAME MEANING: Ancient horse river

AGE: Pleistocene

DISTRIBUTION: Eurasia

SIZE: 7,700–9,300 pounds (3,500–4,200 kilograms)

DIET: Herbivore; grazer

ESSENTIAL FACTS: The European Hippo was about twice the size of the modern river hippo (*H. amphibius*), with a distribution that extended as far north as Britain. It may represent a northern variant of the similarly sized Gorgon-eyed Hippo (*H. gorgops*) from Africa.

HIPPOPOTAMUS MINOR

NAME MEANING: Lesser horse river

AGE: Pleistocene to Holocene

DISTRIBUTION: Cyprus

SIZE: 2.5 feet (76 centimeters) SH; 4 feet (120 centimeters) HBL; 440 pounds (200 kilograms)

DIET: Herbivore; browser

ESSENTIAL FACTS: Cyprus Dwarf Hippo is an insular variant of the modern river hippo (*H. amphibius*) that lived on the island of Cyprus in the Mediterranean Sea. It was more terrestrial than its living relative, with longer and more robust limbs suited to move over rough terrain. It may have been more of a browser.

HIPPOPOTAMUS MADAGASCARIENSIS

NAME MEANING: Horse river from Madagascar

AGE: Pleistocene and Holocene

DISTRIBUTION: Madagascar

SIZE: About tapir-sized

DIET: Herbivore

ESSENTIAL FACTS: One of several species of hippo that inhabited Madagascar, the Malagasy Dwarf Hippo was one of the largest terrestrial herbivores on the island. Its limbs were sturdy and slender for running on land, and it may have taken to water only to cool off. These extinct hippos are mentioned prominently in Malagasy folklore and may have become extinct as recently as 1500.

SUINA

The Suina, or "pig-like artiodactyls," contains the modern families Suidae (pigs) and Tayassuidae (peccaries). These animals are characterized by having relatively robust heads with specialized nasals that support a distinctive snout ending in a disc-shaped nose. Their bodies are often robust, and cursorial adaptations are minimal in most. They first originated in the Northern Hemisphere during the Early Oligocene. Members of this group may be either hypocarnivores or specialized herbivores.

DOLIOCHOERIDAE

Referred to in the past as "Old World peccaries," the doliochoerids may represent a common ancestor of both pigs and peccaries. They were small-bodied animals with long skulls and bunodont or lophodont dentition. Their fossils are known from the Early Oligocene to Late Miocene of Eurasia.

TAUCANAMO PYGMAEUM

NAME MEANING: Unknown

AGE: Early Miocene

DISTRIBUTION: Eurasia

SIZE: 26 pounds (12 kilograms)

DIET: Herbivore

ESSENTIAL FACTS: *Taucanamo* were small, peccary-like herbivores with high, lophodont cusps on their teeth adapted to a mostly browsing diet. They are notable for their particularly large premolars.

TAYASSUIDAE

Peccaries are superficially piglike in appearance and are sometimes incorrectly referred to as "wild pigs" or "New World pigs." Both pigs (Suidae) and peccaries possess relatively large heads with a cartilaginous nasal disc at the tip of the snout covered in tough, leathery skin. Peccaries differ from pigs in many ways, including having self-sharpening canines that are oriented vertically and are concealed by lips when the mouth is closed. Peccaries originated in North America during the Late Eocene and were endemic to the continent until the formation of the Isthmus of Panama during the Pliocene enabled passage into South America. There is no evidence they ever immigrated to the Old World. There are three modern species distributed throughout the New World subtropics and tropics. Peccaries have a full coat of bristly hairs, with an erectile mane running from the back of the head to the rump. They have compact bodies with longer, more slender limb proportions adapted for cursoriality. The tail is vestigial, barely visible within the fur of the animal, and the stomach is complex with two chambers. Modern peccaries are highly social and live in mixed herds that may number from five to several hundred individuals, depending on the species. Sexual dimorphism is weak, with negligible differences in body size between males and females, which form monogamous pairs.

PERCHOERUS MINOR

NAME MEANING: Lesser pouch pig

AGE: Late Eocene (37–35 MYA)

DISTRIBUTION: North America

SIZE: About cat-sized

DIET: Herbivore

ESSENTIAL FACTS: The Lesser Peccary is the oldest-known species of peccary. Like its later relatives, it was probably a social and diurnal animal that fed mostly on plant matter. Its fossils are relatively abundant in the badlands of western North America.

FLORIDACHOERUS OLSENI

NAME MEANING: Olsen's Florida pig

AGE: Early Miocene (18–17 MYA)

DISTRIBUTION: North America

SIZE: 35–60 pounds (16–27 kilograms)

DIET: Herbivore

ESSENTIAL FACTS: First described by David White in 1941 based on fossils recovered during 1930s field expeditions to the Thomas Farm Site, Olsen's Peccary is the oldest fossil peccary known from the state of Florida, with additional material known from Texas. Its cheek teeth are similar in morphology to that of the Plio-Pleistocene genus *Platygonus*.

PROSTHENNOPS SERUS

NAME MEANING: Late before strong face

AGE: Late Miocene

DISTRIBUTION: North America

SIZE: 35–60 pounds (16–27 kilograms)

DIET: Herbivore; mixed feeder

ESSENTIAL FACTS: This peccary had an elongated and robust skull that was adapted for browsing, approaching the morphology of the later genus *Mylohyus*. Thickened tooth enamel suggest a preference for particularly tough foods.

SKINNERHYUS SHERMERORUM

NAME MEANING: Morris Skinner's pig of the Shermer's

AGE: Middle Miocene (13.6–10.3 MYA)

DISTRIBUTION: North America

SIZE: 60–88 pounds (27–40 kilograms)

DIET: Herbivore

ESSENTIAL FACTS: This animal is known for a complete skull and lower jaw found by paleontologist Morris Skinner, after whom the genus is named. Skinner's Peccary is notable for its flaring, wing-like flanges extending from its zygomatic arches, which served as display structures.

MYLOHYUS NASUTUS

NAME MEANING: Big nosed molar pig

AGE: Pleistocene

DISTRIBUTION: North America

SIZE: 176 pounds (80 kilograms)

DIET: Herbivore

SEE MORE ON PAGES 658–659

PLATYGONUS COMPRESSUS

NAME MEANING: Compressed flat angle

AGE: Pleistocene

DISTRIBUTION: North America

SIZE: 88–98 pounds (40–45 kilograms)

DIET: Herbivore

SEE MORE ON PAGES 660–661

SUIDAE

The pigs are hypocarnivorous to herbivorous artiodactyls that inhabit the Old World. They appear to have originated in Asia during the Oligocene and have always been confined to the Old World. Pigs never entered the New World until humans brought the domesticated form of the wild boar (*Sus scrofa*) with them from Europe. Compared to peccaries, pigs have true canine tusks, which point sideways and remain visible when the mouth is closed. Their bodies are longer and more robust, their limbs are often shorter, and their tails are longer. They also tend to have a sparser covering of hair. Pigs possess characteristic teeth with multiple accessory cusps adapted for grinding tough foods.

MYLOHYUS NASUTUS

ESSENTIAL FACTS: Long-Nosed Peccaries were distributed throughout North America, where they favored woodland and forest habitats. Unlike the contemporary Flat-Headed Peccary (*Platygonus compressus*), Long-Nosed Peccary fossils are rarely found in cave deposits. The elongated snout for which it derives its common name is lengthened by a long diastema between the canines and front premolars, and the skull comprises about one-third of its total body length. Aside from its larger head, this peccary was also somewhat stilt-legged, its forelimbs slightly longer than its hindlimbs. Heightened thoracic spines serve as the origin for large muscles which support the head. The canines are also relatively small and enlarged, suggesting it had a better sense of hearing compared to other peccaries.

Long-Nosed Peccaries were adapted to browse on the leaves, flowers, fruits, and twigs of overhanging shrubs and trees. Equipped with a flexible neck, elongated skull, and long forelimbs, they were able to access foods higher off the ground than other peccaries. The bunodont cheek teeth are robust, with distinctive rounded cusps well-suited to handle woody plants. Although they shared the same distribution, Long-Nosed Peccaries are much less common in the fossil record than the Flat-Headed Peccary, possibly suggesting that they formed smaller social groups.

SEE ENTRY ON PAGE 657

PLATYGONUS COMPRESSUS

ESSENTIAL FACTS: Flat-Headed Peccary fossils are frequently found in Pleistocene-age cave deposits throughout the United States, particularly in the Midwest region. These cave sites often yield many hundreds of bones corresponding to dozens of individuals. Megenity Cave in Indiana currently stands out as the most prolific fossil peccary site in the world, with over 600 individuals recorded! Long-term usage of caves must have been an important aspect of this species' ecology. Modern peccaries will readily exploit caves as shelter from extreme temperatures and as communal nighttime dens.

Flat-Headed Peccaries lived throughout North America inhabiting grassland, savanna, and open woodland environments, with a preference for areas with bush cover and standing water sources. They fed on a wide range of foods but preferentially browsed on softer above-ground plants, their robust jaws and tall bilophodont teeth being adapted to shred leaves and break twigs. They would also selectively graze on certain types of ground-based plants such as forbs. Salt licks would have been visited regularly to compensate for their low-sodium diet. They may have also occasionally taken animal foods like insects and small vertebrates. Flat-Headed Peccaries were highly adapted to forage in relatively open environments. Compared to other peccaries, their eyes were larger and set higher and farther back on the skull, suggesting keen eyesight and a wide field of vision with which to scan their surroundings while feeding. The postcranial skeleton is also adapted for cursoriality.

SEE ENTRY ON PAGE 657

CAINOCHOERINAE

The cainochoerines are small, cursorial pigs that resemble peccaries in their morphology and were originally considered members of Tayassuidae. They are known to have lived from the Middle to Late Miocene.

ALBANOHYUS PYMAEUS

NAME MEANING: Dwarf white pig

AGE: Middle Miocene (16.9–11.1 MYA)

DISTRIBUTION: Eurasia

SIZE: 33 pounds (15 kilograms)

DIET: Hypocarnivore

ESSENTIAL FACTS: Like other cainochoerines, this species was a small, generalized herbivore whose diet consisted of various non-abrasive plants, seeds, and fruits. It may have lived in relatively large herds that were mostly diurnal.

CAINOCHOERUS AFRICANUS

NAME MEANING: New pig from Africa

AGE: Late Miocene (11.6–5.3 MYA)

DISTRIBUTION: Africa

SIZE: 33 pounds (15 kilograms)

DIET: Hypocarnivore

ESSENTIAL FACTS: Originally thought to be an African peccary based on the morphology of its premolars and body proportions, this species is now recognized as a peccary-like pig that achieved a similar morphology through convergent evolution.

HYOTHERIINAE

Hyotherines were small- to medium-sized pigs that were rather generalized in their morphology. They may be ancestral to modern pigs.

HYOTHERIUM MAJOR

NAME MEANING: Greater pig beast

AGE: Late Oligocene (25 MYA)

DISTRIBUTION: Eurasia

SIZE: 132 pounds (60 kilograms)

DIET: Hypocarnivore

ESSENTIAL FACTS: Like many modern pigs, *Hyotherium* possessed bunodont-brachydont teeth suited for a mixed diet of softer plant materials as well as small animals and carrion.

NGURUWE KIJIVIUM

NAME MEANING: Unknown

AGE: Early Miocene (20.4–16 MYA)

DISTRIBUTION: Africa

SIZE: 22–33 pounds (10–15 kilograms)

DIET: Hypocarnivore

ESSENTIAL FACTS: Members of the genus *Nguruwe* were relatively small pigs endemic to Africa. The genus name is the Swahili word for “pig.”

LISTRIODONTINAE

Listriodontines appeared during the Early Miocene in Eurasia and quickly spread to Africa. Their incisors were wide and short for cropping vegetation, a feature referenced in the name of the type genus *Listrodon*, which means "spade-tooth." They were relatively stilt-legged by pig standards, with elongated yet sturdy limbs. They were primarily browsers with bunolophodont or lophodont dentition adapted to specialized herbivorous diets.

KUBANOCHOERUS GIGAS

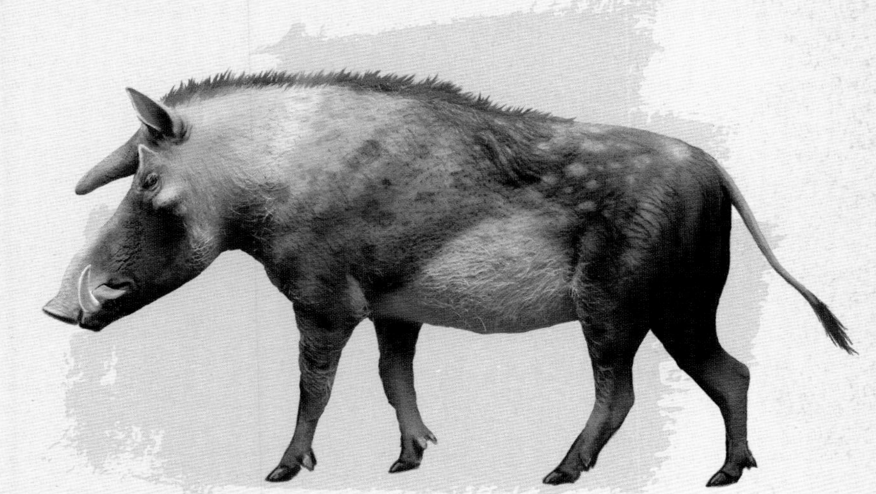

NAME MEANING: Unknown

AGE: Middle Miocene (14 MYA)

DISTRIBUTION: Eurasia

SIZE: 4 feet (1.2 meters) SH; 1,100 pounds (500 kilograms)

DIET: Herbivore

ESSENTIAL FACTS: The genus *Kubanochoerus* is characterized by a pair of small conical horns over the eyes, with males having a larger horn protruding forward from between the eyes. They had relatively long and slender limbs and were much larger than modern members of the family.

LISTRIODON SPLENDENS

NAME MEANING: Splendid spade-tooth

AGE: Middle Miocene (15–13 MYA)

DISTRIBUTION: Eurasia

SIZE: 660 pounds (300 kilograms)

DIET: Herbivore

ESSENTIAL FACTS: Like other listriodontines its cheek teeth were lophodont, somewhat resembling those of perissodactyls and adapted for finely shredding fibrous plant matter. Its diet consisted mostly of leaves, seeds, and fruits.

MEGALOCHOERUS HUMUNGOUS

NAME MEANING: Humungous big pig

AGE: Late Miocene (11–9 MYA)

DISTRIBUTION: Africa

SIZE: 6.6 feet (2 meters) SH; 2 tons

DIET: Herbivore

ESSENTIAL FACTS: The largest pig known to have ever lived, being about as heavy as a large modern black rhino (*Diceros bicornis*), This long-legged pig is the last and largest member of its genus. It had a browse-dominated diet, favoring forest and woodland habitats.

TETRACONODONTINAE

Tetraconodontines were distributed throughout Eurasia and Africa. They are characterized by thickened enameled teeth with conical premolars suggesting a diet of hard foods.

NYANZACHOERUS SYRTICUS

NAME MEANING: Nyanza Pig from Sirt

AGE: Late Miocene

DISTRIBUTION: Africa

SIZE: 660 pounds (300 kilograms)

DIET: Herbivore; browser

ESSENTIAL FACTS: This species is known from well-preserved skulls from the Lothagam site in Kenya. The skulls show strong sexual dimorphism, with males being much larger and having large lumps and crests on their faces with flaring zygomatic arches. This ornamentation likely functioned as a mating display. The tusks were relatively small, suggesting a relatively ritualized and non-violent form of conflict resolution.

NOTOCHOERUS EULIUS

NAME MEANING: Southern pig of Eulius

AGE: Pliocene

DISTRIBUTION: Africa

SIZE: 4 feet (1.2 meters) SH; 990 pounds (450 kilograms)

DIET: Herbivore; grazer

ESSENTIAL FACTS: This animal was a large pig with hypsodont teeth and a grass-dominated diet. It is known from reasonably complete fossils from the Koobi Fora Formation in Kenya.

TETRACONODON MAGNUM

NAME MEANING: Great four-coned teeth

AGE: Middle Miocene

DISTRIBUTION: Eurasia

SIZE: 660 pounds (300 kilograms)

DIET: Hypocarnivore

ESSENTIAL FACTS: Unique to the genus *Tetraconodon*, the last two pairs of premolars were extremely large and conical, adapted for crushing. The wear patterns on these premolars resemble those of hyenas, potentially alluding to an active scavenging behavior with the ability to process bones.

SUINAE

Suinae is the subfamily to which all modern pigs evolved. Most of these pigs have generalized hypocarnivorous diets with brachydont-bunodont dentition. Others, like the two tribes Hippohyini (horse-pigs) and the warthogs (Phacochoerini), are more herbivorous with hypsodont teeth.

HIPPOPOTAMODON MAJOR

NAME MEANING: Greater *Hippopotamus* tooth

AGE: Late Miocene (11–8 MYA)

DISTRIBUTION: Eurasia

SIZE: 440 pounds (200 kilograms)

DIET: Hypocarnivore

ESSENTIAL FACTS: This pig's skull is similar to that of a modern wild boar (*Sus scrofa*). It likely had a similarly versatile diet that included roots, tubers, fruits, nuts, leaves, which was supplemented with small animals and carrion. Its habitat was forest and woodland.

EUMAIOCHOERUS ETRUSCUS

NAME MEANING: True mother pig from Etruria

AGE: Late Miocene (11.6–7.2 MYA)

DISTRIBUTION: Eurasia

SIZE: 110 pounds (50 kilograms)

DIET: Hypocarnivore

ESSENTIAL FACTS: The Etruscan Pig is known from the modern county of Italy, which was a series of islands at the time in which it lived. It was a dwarf island species whose most likely ancestor was a species of *Microstonyx*.

MICROSTONYX MAJOR

NAME MEANING: Greater little sharp point

AGE: Late Miocene (11.6–7.2 MYA)

DISTRIBUTION: Eurasia

SIZE: 3.5 feet (1.1 meters)

DIET: Hypocarnivore

ESSENTIAL FACTS: A widespread generalist species, the Greater Microstonyx shows a high degree of morphological versatility with subtle regional variations across its range. This is similar to the modern wild boar (*Sus scrofa*) whose size and dentition can vary significantly due to regional food options, climate, and the presence or absence of other animals within its ecosystem.

CELEBOCHOERUS HEEKERENI

NAME MEANING: Heekeren's Celebes Island pig

AGE: Pleistocene

DISTRIBUTION: Eurasia

SIZE: 880 pounds (400 kilograms)

DIET: Herbivore

ESSENTIAL FACTS: Heekeren's Pig inhabited the island of Sulawesi in Indonesia, where it was one of the largest herbivores. The males have notably massive, heavy tusks that may be the largest in proportion to body size of any pig. This suggests a style of combat similar to that of modern warthogs (*Phacochoerus*).

KOLPOCHOERUS LIMNETES

NAME MEANING: Marsh breast pig

AGE: Pleistocene

DISTRIBUTION: Africa

SIZE: 220 pounds (100 kilograms)

DIET: Herbivore

ESSENTIAL FACTS: Like its closest modern relative, the giant forest hog (*Hylochoerus meinertzhageni*), the Marsh Pig was a large animal with massive zygomatic knobs and huge tusks with which males would use in tusk-grappling contests. This species seems to have shifted its diet and habitat preferences over time, from a woodland browser to a savanna grazer.

HIPPOHYUS SIVALENSIS

NAME MEANING: Horse pig from Siwalik Hills

AGE: Pliocene

DISTRIBUTION: Eurasia

SIZE: 440 pounds (200 kilograms)

DIET: Herbivore; grazer

ESSENTIAL FACTS: *Hippohyus* are notable for their hypsodont molars with wrinkled enamel; the wear patterns resemble those of horses. This indicates that they were specialized grazers that favored open grassland habitats. Fossils of these pigs are common in southern Asia, particularly in India.

METRIDIOCHOERUS ANDREWSI

NAME MEANING: Andrew's frightful pig

AGE: Pliocene and Pleistocene

DISTRIBUTION: Africa

SIZE: 660 pounds (300 kilograms)

DIET: Herbivore; grazer

ESSENTIAL FACTS: Like other members of the genus, Andrew's Giant Warthog had hypsodont teeth with particularly massive third molars adapted for grazing. Its grass-dominated diet was occasionally supplemented by scavenged meat as observed in modern warthogs (*Phacochoerus*).

TYLOPODA

Camels (Camelidae) are the sole modern representatives of the group Tylopoda, a group which branched away from other artiodactyls during the Middle Eocene. Extinct members of this group include the endemic European families Anoplotheriidae, Xiphodontidae, and Cainotheriidae and the endemic North American families Protoceratidae and Merycoidodontidae. The latter family were once erroneously placed within the Suina due to their common, yet inaccurate description of "ruminating hogs."

ANOPLOTHERIIDAE

Anoplotheriids are recorded from the Middle Eocene to Early Oligocene and are only known from Europe during the period where the region was a tropical archipelago, isolated from the rest of Eurasia. Members of this group are known to have varied substantially in size and morphology, most being terrestrial, while a few adapted to a more scansorial lifestyle. The smallest would have been about the size of a small goat, with the largest growing as big as large deer.

ANOPLOTHERIUM COMMUNE

NAME MEANING: Common unarmed beast

AGE: Late Eocene (37–34 MYA)

DISTRIBUTION: Eurasia

SIZE: 4 feet (1.2 meters) SH; 8.1 feet (2.5 meters) HBL; 597 pounds (271 kilograms)

DIET: Herbivore; browser

SEE MORE ON PAGES 672–673

DIPLOBUNE SECUNDARIA

NAME MEANING: Suder's double hill

AGE: Early Oligocene (34–30 MYA)

DISTRIBUTION: Eurasia

SIZE: 4 feet (1.2 meters) SH; 6.6 feet (2 meters) HBL; 290 pounds (130 kilograms)

DIET: Herbivore; browser

ESSENTIAL FACTS: Diplobune was the largest member of the genus, most of which are under 50 pounds (23 kilograms). Their mobile limbs and long digits ending in claw-like hooves suggest the ability to climb trees, where they would feed on leaves. Their second digit is slightly offset, functioning as a thumb and was held off the ground and backward when walking.

DACRYTHERIUM OVINUM

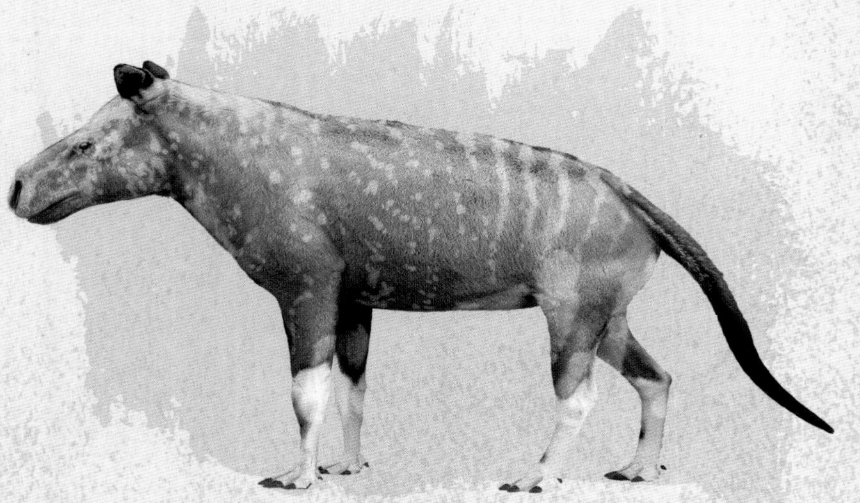

NAME MEANING: Sheep-like tear beast

AGE: Late Eocene (45–34 MYA)

DISTRIBUTION: Eurasia

SIZE: 30 pounds (14 kilograms)

DIET: Herbivore; browser

ESSENTIAL FACTS: *Darcytherium* were small, terrestrial herbivores about the size of goats. The genus name, meaning "tear beast," references the deep preorbital fossa in front of each eye that may have housed a scent gland.

AGRIOCHOERIDAE

Agriochoerids possessed claws instead of hooves and were adapted to a scansorial or arboreal lifestyle. Their feet were shorter and broader than those of their terrestrial ancestors, and their limbs had a wider range of motion. They had five-toed forefeet with atrophied first digits. Their deep jaws were suited for intensive chewing, and their diets consisted mainly of leaves with perhaps some fruits. They are known to have lived from the Late Eocene to the Early Miocene. Agriochoerids were formerly considered to be a subfamily within Merycoidodontidae.

PROTOREODON PARVUS

NAME MEANING: Small first *Oreodon*

AGE: Late Eocene (40–35 MYA)

DISTRIBUTION: North America

DIET: Herbivore; browser

SIZE: About squirrel-sized

ESSENTIAL FACTS: *Protoreodon* were small, lightly built herbivores. Scansorial in their general habits, they would spend much of their time feeding on the ground and could readily ascend trees to escape predators.

AGRIOCHOERUS ANTIQUUS

NAME MEANING: Ancient wild pig

AGE: Late Eocene (40–35 MYA)

DISTRIBUTION: North America

SIZE: 50 pounds (23 kilograms)

DIET: Herbivore; browser

ESSENTIAL FACTS: The largest and most well-known member of the family, this species was adapted to feed on leaves among the tree branches. A complete skeleton is on display at the American Museum of Natural History.

ANOPLOTHERIUM COMMUNE

ESSENTIAL FACTS: The first fossils of this animal were discovered in Montmarte in Paris, France, in 1804; more complete skeletons were found in 1807. Georges Cuvier, who described them, was so intrigued by the unfamiliar anatomy of the animal that he drew a skeletal and muscular reconstruction of it, making it among the first instances of paleoart, anatomical reconstructions based on fossil evidence. The description of this animal along with the Great Paleothere (*Palaeotherium magnum*) are recognized as critical moments that pioneered paleontology, helping to demonstrate the then-novel concept of extinction; both animals were found in older sediments and had no modern descendants. Cuvier's description of an endocast from a broken skull of Common Anoplothere is also the first instance of paleoneurology, the study of brain evolution.

By far the largest member of Anoplotheriidae, of which it is the type species, the Common Anoplothere grew to the size of a large deer like an elk (*Cervus canadensis*). Given that much of Europe was still underwater during the Late Eocene, it has been suggested that its large size may be the result of insular gigantism due to the absence of other large herbivores in the region. The feet were robust and unguligrade with two digits each. It is thought that these animals had the ability to rear up on their hindlimbs to reach higher plants, similar to modern goats using their strong pelvis and robust tail to support themselves in an upright position. Brachydont-selenodont dentition suggests a primarily folivorous diet. Possible footprints belonging to this species have also been recorded.

SEE ENTRY ON PAGE 670

MERYCOIDODONTIDAE

Commonly referred to as oreodonts, these were a diverse group of herbivores that were endemic to North America, with a history spanning from the Late Eocene to the earliest Pliocene. The name oreodont means "mountain tooth," referring to the shape of the molar cusps. The group has also been referred to as the "ruminating hogs" due to the pig-like morphology of some of the species. They ranged from rabbit-sized to sheep-sized. Their fossils are extremely common in parts of the White River Badlands, aptly called the "Oreodon Beds." They are characterized by their long tails, digitigrade feet, and robust jaws and well-developed sagittal crests adapted for intensive chewing.

OREONETINAE

The oreonetines represent the earliest stages of the explosive radiation of oreodonts in the Late Eocene and Early Oligocene. They were small-bodied oreodonts that may have been analogous to modern marmots.

OREONETES ANCEPS

NAME MEANING: Two-headed mountain-dweller

AGE: Late Eocene (38–34 MYA)

DISTRIBUTION: North America

SIZE: About marmot-sized

DIET: Herbivore; browser

ESSENTIAL FACTS: This species was larger than the closely related Douglass' Oreonetes (*Oreonetes douglassi*) with more robust and heavier premolars. Its fossils are known from western Montana and inhabited forest ecosystems.

BATHYGENYS ALPHA

NAME MEANING: First deep jaw

AGE: Early Oligocene (34–33 MYA)

DISTRIBUTION: North America

SIZE: About marmot-sized

DIET: Herbivore

ESSENTIAL FACTS: Members of the genus *Bathygenys* are the smallest oreodonts known. They fed primarily on non-abrasive plants and fruits.

LIMNETES PLATYCEPS

NAME MEANING: Flat-headed marsh-dweller

AGE: Late Eocene (36–34 MYA)

DISTRIBUTION: North America

SIZE: About beaver-sized

DIET: Hebivore

ESSENTIAL FACTS: The cheek teeth of *Limnetes* were relatively more hypsodont than other oreodontines, suggesting a more abrasive diet that included some grasses. The genus may have been ancestral to the leptauchenine oreodonts.

LEPTAUCHENIINAE

The leptauchenines were goat-like oreodonts which lived during the Late Oligocene. They had hypsodont teeth adapted for grazing on low-growing plants found in arid environments. Their fossils are often found in dune deposits, indicating that these were desert specialists. They had notably enlarged auditory bullae, suggesting particularly large external ears.

LEPTAUCHENIA DECORA

NAME MEANING: Elegant slender neck

AGE: Early Oligocene (34–30 MYA)

DISTRIBUTION: North America

SIZE: About goat-sized

DIET: Herbivore

ESSENTIAL FACTS: This species was adapted to arid and semi-arid conditions, its fossils often being found in dune deposits. Their hypsodont dentition enabled them to process plants coated in silica. Mass death accumulations of this have been unearthed; dozens of individuals died at the same time.

SESPIA CALIFORNICA

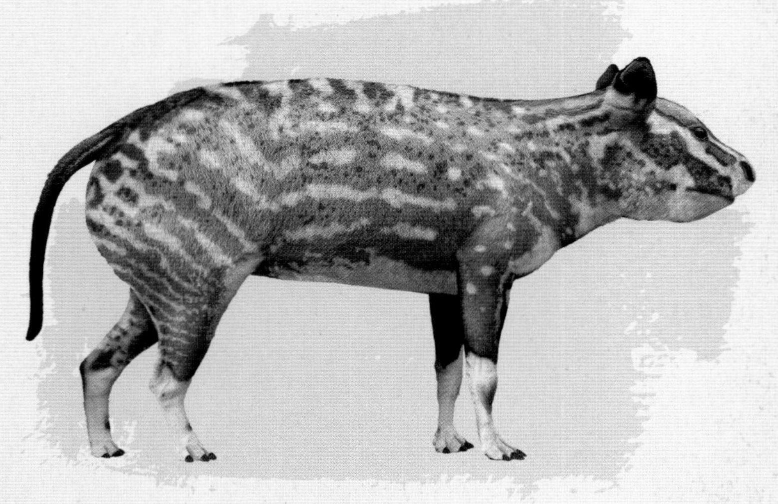

NAME MEANING: Sespe Creek from California

AGE: Late Oligocene

DISTRIBUTION: North America

SIZE: About hare-sized

DIET: Herbivore

ESSENTIAL FACTS: The smaller of the two species of Sespia, the California Sespia was a hare-sized herbivore that fed on the coarse vegetation of its dry environments. Their fossils are extremely common, suggesting possible colonial and burrowing habits.

MERYCOIDODONTINAE

Merycoidodontinae was a short-lived group of oredonts known from the Late Eocene to Early Oligocene. They were about the size of peccaries and probably occupied similar niches, seemingly going into decline at around the time peccaries (Tayassuidae) were becoming more common in the fossil record. They had proportionally large heads with robust jaws and teeth adapted to chew tough foods.

MERYCOIDODON CULBERTSONI

NAME MEANING: Culbertson's ruminating teeth

AGE: Late Eocene to Early Oligocene

DISTRIBUTION: North America

SIZE: 4.6 feet (1.4 meters)

DIET: About goat-sized

ESSENTIAL FACTS: This species featured somewhat piglike proportions with a long body set on short legs. Culbertson's Oreodont are consistently the most abundant oreodonts in the localities in which they occur, suggesting they lived in particularly large groups or had high population densities.

MINIOCHOERUS GRACILIS

NAME MEANING: Slender pointed pig

AGE: Early Oligocene (34–30 MYA)

DISTRIBUTION: North America

SIZE: About cat-sized

DIET: Herbivore; browser

ESSENTIAL FACTS: A small herbivore only a little larger than a house cat, this species' thin-enameled teeth suggest a diet of relatively softer foods such as younger leaves, fruits, and flowers. A mounted skeleton of this species is on display at the Natural History Museum of Los Angeles.

MESOREODON FLORIDENSIS

NAME MEANING: Middle mountain tooth from Florida

AGE: Early Miocene (23–20 MYA)

DISTRIBUTION: North America

SIZE: 1.5 feet (0.5 meters) SH; 3.5 feet (1.1 meters) HBL; 55 pounds (25 kilograms)

DIET: Herbivore; mixed feeder

ESSENTIAL FACTS: The Florida Mesoreodon is the only oreodont known from Florida for which a complete skeleton has been discovered. A cast of this species is on display at the Florida Museum of Natural History.

EPOREODON MAJOR

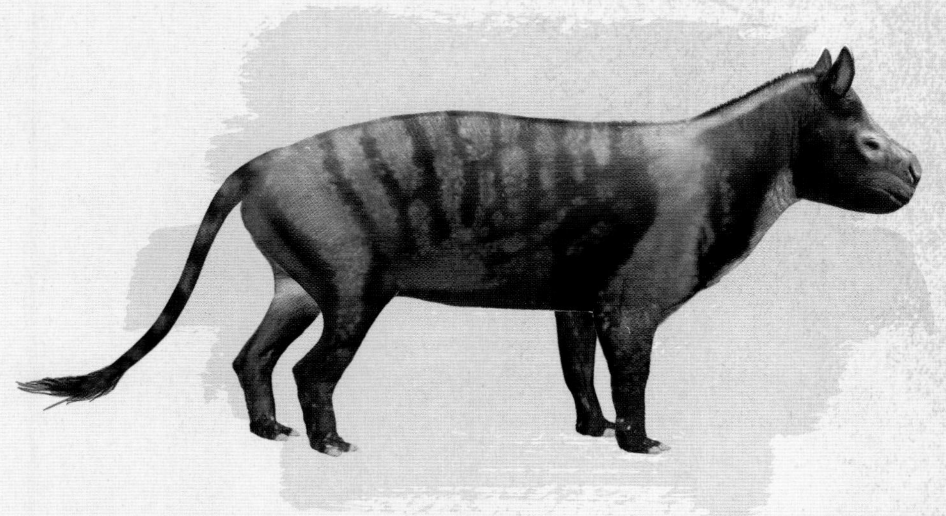

NAME MEANING: Over mountain tooth

AGE: Late Oligocene

DISTRIBUTION: North America

SIZE: About sheep-sized

DIET: Herbivore; browser

ESSENTIAL FACTS: *Eporeodon* were among the larger oreodonts of the Oligocene, dwarfing contemporary genera by a wide margin. They had relatively underdeveloped sagittal crests and brachydont dentition, which suggest a browsing diet limited to softer plants.

MERYCHYINAE

The Merychyinae subfamily includes the last and most specialized of all the oreodonts. Some members of this group attained piglike and tapir-like morphologies.

MERYCHYUS MAJOR

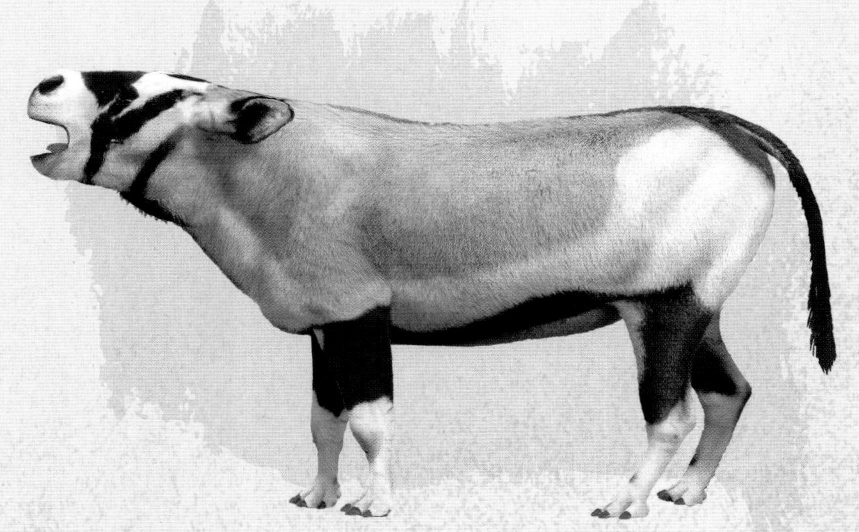

NAME MEANING: Greater ruminating pig

AGE: Middle Miocene (14–10 MYA)

DISTRIBUTION: North America

SIZE: About sheep-sized

DIET: Herbivore; mixed feeder

ESSENTIAL FACTS: The Greater Merychyus is known for having ossified vocal cords, similar to those of modern howler monkeys (*Alouatta*). This suggests that they communicated with similar loud, booming calls.

MERYCOCHOERUS MAGNUS

NAME MEANING: Great ruminating pig

AGE: Early Miocene (18 MYA)

DISTRIBUTION: North America

SIZE: About pig-sized

DIET: Herbivore; browser

ESSENTIAL FACTS: This species had a barrel-shaped body with relatively short legs and retracted nasals. This suggests the presence of a mobile upper lip, which aided in browsing. A pair of mounted skeletons are on display at the Denver Museum of Nature and Science.

PROMERYCOCHOERUS SUPERBUS

NAME MEANING: Suburb before Merycochoerus

AGE: Early Miocene

DISTRIBUTION: North America

SIZE: 3.3 feet (1 meter) HBL; 60 pounds (27 kilograms)

DIET: Herbivore; browser

ESSENTIAL FACTS: The Superb Oreodont had enlarged canines and flaring, thickened zygomatic arches, giving it a particularly wide head. Its extremely strong jaws were adapted to process tough foods such as roots and tubers.

BRACHYCRUS LATICEPS

NAME MEANING: Broad head short leg

AGE: Middle Miocene

DISTRIBUTION: North America

SIZE: 3.3 feet (1 meter) HBL, 50 pounds (23 kilograms)

DIET: Herbivore; browser

ESSENTIAL FACTS: This species was a distinctive oreodont with greatly retracted nasals similar to those of tapirs, suggesting the presence of a short proboscis. It was a forest-dwelling browser that fed on leaves, fruits, and nuts.

USTATOCHOERUS MAJOR

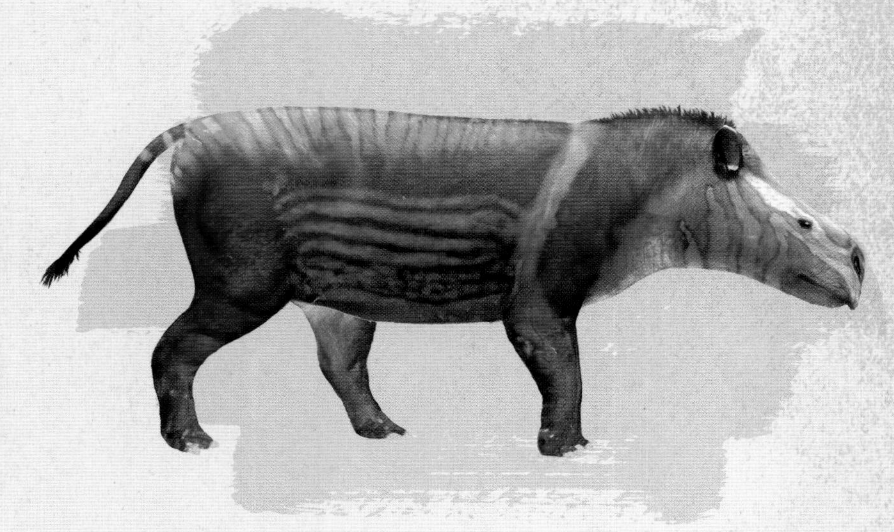

NAME MEANING: Unknown

AGE: Late Miocene (11–10 MYA)

DISTRIBUTION: North America

SIZE: About sheep-sized

DIET: Herbivore; browser

ESSENTIAL FACTS: This species was part of a subfamily of oreodonts called the Ustatochoerinae, which survived long after other oreodonts became extinct in the Middle Miocene. The teeth were more hypsodont than those of other oreodonts, adapted to feed on both abrasive and non-abrasive foods.

XIPHODONTIDAE

Xiphodonts are a family of small artiodactyls only known from Europe, occuring from the Late Eocene to Middle Oligocene. It is currently unknown whether they were distributed elsewhere. They superficially resembled camels with elongated legs, necks, and skulls adapted for high-browsing.

XIPHODON GRACILIS

NAME MEANING: Slender sword tooth

AGE: Late Eocene

DISTRIBUTION: Eurasia

SIZE: 22–44 pounds (10–20 kilograms)

DIET: Herbivore

ESSENTIAL FACTS: The Slender Xiphodon is the only xiphodontid to be represented by postcranial fossils. This species was morphologically very similar to early camelids like *Poebrotherium*. It was a folivore, whose brachydont-selenodont teeth were well-suited for the shredding of fibrous leaves.

CAINOTHERIIDAE

Cainotheres were small artiodactyls that resembled rabbits or chevrotains in overall size, morphology, and ecology. Their teeth were selenodont, and their feet were unguligrade like those of ruminants. However, they also had enlarged, rabbit-like ears possibly used to dissipate heat.

CAINOTHERIUM LATICURVATUM

NAME MEANING: Side-curved new beast

AGE: Early Miocene (23–20 MYA)

DISTRIBUTION: Eurasia

SIZE: About rabbit-sized

DIET: Herbivore

ESSENTIAL FACTS: To a modern observer, these little herbivores would have resembled a cross between a rabbit and a deer. It was adapted for explosive speed and agility to escape predators and had a mostly browsing diet.

CAMELIDAE

The only surviving members of the suborder Tylopoda, camels are characterized by their elongated necks and legs, which were originally adapted to traverse large expanses of open ground. Early in the group's evolutionary history, the lateral toes were completely lost, making the feet didactyl. In more derived groups, the third and fourth metapodials of each limb are fused into a single bone and branch at the distal end, forming a distinctive Y-shape. Other bones in the limbs are fused or reduced in the lower limbs.

The family originated in North America during the Middle Eocene and underwent most of their diversity there. Many camels are ecologically comparable to giraffids in the Old World, their typically long-necked and long-legged form initially evolving as a means to browse from trees and bushes. Other species became mixed feeders, and a few became specialist grazers. Camels only began to migrate to the Old World during the Late Miocene, and they entered South America during the Pliocene when the Isthmus of Panama formed. Interestingly, the family becomes extinct in North America by the Early Holocene along with horses. The five modern species are distributed through South America, central Asia, and northern Africa.

OROMERYCINAE

Sometimes considered as a distinct family, Oromerycidae, these were small herbivores that lived from the middle to late Eocene in North America. These animals already displayed adaptations for cursoriality that later camels would inherit such as a fused radius and ulna.

PROTYLOPUS PETERSONI

NAME MEANING: Peterson's before knob foot

AGE: Middle Eocene

DISTRIBUTION: North America

SIZE: 2.6 feet (80 centimeters) HBL; 57 pounds (26 kilograms)

DIET: Herbivore

ESSENTIAL FACTS: Unlike later camels, this species had unguligrade feet that retained the lateral digits, as well as unfused metapodials, radius-ulna, and tibia-fibula. They were forest browsers that fed on soft leaves and fruits.

EOTYLOPUS REEDI

NAME MEANING: Reed's dawn knob foot

AGE: Early Oligocene

DISTRIBUTION: North America

SIZE: About goat-sized

DIET: Herbivore

ESSENTIAL FACTS: This short-necked oromerycine a was adapted for cursoriality, with a fused radius and ulna to lighten the forelimb and absorb shock. This suggests that this species had become adapted to life on relatively hard and open ground.

POEBROTHERIINAE

Poebrotheriines are a small group of early camels from which all later subfamilies descend. Features such as fully didactyl feet and elongated limbs and neck vertebrae are features that would be inherited by all later camels. They occurred from the Late Eocene to Late Oligocene.

POEBROTHERIUM WILSONI

NAME MEANING: Wilson's grass (eating) beast

AGE: Late Eocene to early Oligocene (35–28 MYA)

DISTRIBUTION: North America

SIZE: 88–110 pounds (40–50 kilograms)

DIET: Herbivore

ESSENTIAL FACTS: Wilson's Camel is the most well-known species within the genus Poebrotherium. Despite its name, these camels would have consumed mostly leaves from low-hanging trees and bushes, with perhaps some forbs and fresh grasses. It is known to have been preyed upon by Morton's Entelodont (*Archaeotherium mortoni*).

FLORIDATRAGULINAE

Floridatragulines appear to have been restricted to the tropical and subtropical climates of southern North America during the Early Miocene. They share several features with more basal camels such as *Poebrotherium*, including unfused metapodials, unguligrade feet, and the presence of a postorbital process instead of the postorbital bar seen in all other camel lineages. They possessed brachydont dentition and elongated faces adapted to browsing.

AGUASCALIENTIA PANAMAENSIS

NAME MEANING: From Panama and Aguascalientes

AGE: Early Miocene (20 MYA)

DISTRIBUTION: North America

SIZE: About goat-sized

DIET: Herbivore; browser

ESSENTIAL FACTS: This camel is the larger of two species of *Aguascalientia* discovered during field excavations in Panama by the Florida Museum of Natural History and published in 2012. The genus is named after Aguascalientes, Mexico, where the first specimen was discovered.

FLORIDATRAGULUS DOLICHANTHEREUS

NAME MEANING: Long beast; Florida *Tragulus*

AGE: Early Miocene (18 MYA)

DISTRIBUTION: North America

SIZE: About deer-sized

DIET: Herbivore; browser

ESSENTIAL FACTS: The species name of this camel references its extremely elongated snout, most likely an adaptation for browsing from trees, further reinforced by its brachydont dentition. This species is currently only known from the Thomas Farm Site in Gilchrist County, Florida.

MIOLABINAE

Miolabinae is a poorly studied group of camels which originated in the Early Miocene and survived into the Pleistocene. They retained unfused metapodials.

CAPRICAMELUS GETTYI

NAME MEANING: Andrew R. Getty's goat-camel

AGE: Pleistocene

DISTRIBUTION: North America

SIZE: 200–310 pounds (90–140 kilograms)

DIET: Herbivore; graze-dominated mixed feeder

SEE MORE ON PAGES 686–687

STENOMYLINAE

Stenomylines were small, fleet-footed camels that evolved similar morphology to gazelles and pronghorns. Their short but muscular torsos and long limbs enabled them to run and jump at high speeds. They had pointed, unguligrade feet for traction and hypsodont teeth for feeding on gritty plants encountered in open, arid environments. They first appear during the Late Oligocene and become extinct during the Middle Miocene, when they appear to have been replaced by pronghorns (Antilocapridae).

STENOMYLUS HITCHCOCKI

NAME MEANING: Hitchcock's narrow molars

AGE: Early Miocene (23–20 MYA)

DISTRIBUTION: North America

SIZE: 24–28 inches (60–70 centimeters) SH; 33–55 pounds (15–25 kilograms)

DIET: Herbivore; grazer

ESSENTIAL FACTS: Hitchcock's Gazelle-Camel is known for numerous specimens found at Agate Springs Fossil Beds in Nebraska. The Stenomylus Quarry has yielded dozens of fossils of this species with individuals of all age groups, possibly representing a herd that died during a volcanic eruption.

CAPRICAMELUS GETTYI

ESSENTIAL FACTS: The last and most highly specialized of the miolabine camels adapted to live on dry, mountainous terrain. The most distinctive feature of Getty's Camel were its relatively short limbs, similar in proportion to those of modern Mountain Goats (*Oreamnos americanus*). As such, it was adapted to climb near-vertical rock faces and cliffs, with the agility to leap across short chasms and from one foothold to another. This morphological convergence is what inspired the genus name *Capricamelus*, which means "goat-camel." The species is named in recognition of Andrew R. Getty, whose support and interest aided in the study and description of this camel.

The Getty's Camel is known from nearly complete skeletons of an adult and a juvenile, along with the distal limb elements of at least fifteen other individuals. It possessed enlarged incisors and deep jaws for cropping and processing coarse vegetation encountered in their high-altitude environments. Most of their time would have been spent grazing on grasses, herbs, and sedges, and would occasionally browse the leaves from low-growing shrubs, conifers, and ferns. Like modern mountain-dwelling ungulates, it most likely engaged in seasonal migrations to lower and higher altitudes during the autumn and spring, respectively, in response to changing temperatures, snowfall, and food availability.

SEE ENTRY ON PAGE 685

BLICKOMYLUS MORONI

NAME MEANING: Blick Quarry molar from the Moroni Formation

AGE: Early Miocene (19–17 MYA)

DISTRIBUTION: North America

SIZE: 24–28 inches (60–70 centimeters) SH; 33–55 pounds (15–25 kilograms)

DIET: Herbivore; grazer

ESSENTIAL FACTS: Members of the genus *Blickomylus* are known for the elongation of the third molars. Moron's Gazelle-Camel is the first fossil vertebrate to be discovered in the Moroni Formation of Central Utah.

AEPYCAMELINAE

The aepycamelines are known for having particularly elongated necks and limbs, even by the standards of the family. They were high-browsers specialized in feeding on tree foliage, retaining the unguligrade feet of their ancestors.

OXYDACTYLUS CAMPESTRIS

NAME MEANING: Flat sharp digits

AGE: Early Miocene

DISTRIBUTION: North America

SIZE: 100–175 pounds (45–80 kilograms)

DIET: Herbivore

ESSENTIAL FACTS: The earliest of the giraffe-camel lineage, this species is known from the Agate Spring locality. Unlike the contemporary Hitchcock's Gazelle-Camel (*Stenomylus hitchcocki*), it was a browser that mostly fed on shrubs and low-hanging tree branches.

AEPYCAMELUS MAJOR

NAME MEANING: Greater high camel

AGE: Late Miocene (9.5–6 MYA)

DISTRIBUTION: North America

SIZE: 13 feet (4 meters) SH; 2,200 pounds (1,000 kilograms)

DIET: Herbivore; browser

SEE MORE ON PAGES 690–691

CAMELINAE

The camelines originated in the Early Miocene and are characterized by their fused metapodials and digitigrade feet. Included among this group are the tribes Lamini (llama-like camels) and Camelini (true camels). The transition from an unguligrade foot to a padded digitigrade one may have initially been an adaptation to aid in walking on soft substrates. This is the origin of the name Tylopoda, meaning "padded foot."

PROTOLABIS GRACILIS

NAME MEANING: Slender first forceps

AGE: Early Miocene (19–17 MYA)

DISTRIBUTION: North America

SIZE: About deer-sized

DIET: Herbivore

ESSENTIAL FACTS: One of the oldest members of the lineage which would lead to modern camels, this species had developed the fused, branching metapodials which characterize the group. Its teeth were slightly more hypsodont, indicating a more mixed-feeding dietary regime.

AEPYCAMELUS MAJOR

ESSENTIAL FACTS: Commonly referred to as "the Giraffe Camel," this species is the first of several species of giant camels that evolved to fill the high-browsing niche, which the modern giraffe (*Giraffa camelopardalis*) occupies in Africa today. The species was first described in 1901 under the name *Alticamelus*. In 1956 the name was changed to *Aepycamelus*, which similarly translates to "high camel," referencing the great size and obvious height of the animal. The species is definitively known only from several fossil sites in north-central Florida with additional material from Nebraska, implying a rather wide distribution across much of the United States. Its preferred habitat was grassland, savanna, and open woodland.

Although no singular complete skeleton of the Giraffe Camel has ever been found, the known material for this species translates to an animal with the size and reach of a modern giraffe, adapted to browse on tree foliage beyond the reach of other herbivores its own size. Its elongated limb bones gave the largest specimens a shoulder height of 13 feet (4 meters). Its similarly elongated neck vertebrae gave it a 6.6 foot (2 meter) neck. Combined with a long, narrow head, the largest adult males would have had a vertical reach of over 20 feet (6 meters). Using its long legs, it was able to travel quickly and efficiently across open ground to locate new feeding sites.

SEE ENTRY ON PAGE 689

NOTHOKEMAS FLORIDANUS

NAME MEANING: Bastard deer from Florida

AGE: Early Miocene (18 MYA)

DISTRIBUTION: North America

SIZE: Unknown

DIET: Herbivore

ESSENTIAL FACTS: Known only from the Thomas Farm Site in Gilchrist County, Florida, it was one of the largest camels of its time. This species was one of a poorly known lineage of camels that are characterized by their slightly down-curved snouts.

PROCAMELUS GRANDIS

NAME MEANING: Great before camel

AGE: Late Miocene (12–10 MYA)

DISTRIBUTION: North America

SIZE: 660 pounds (300 kilograms)

DIET: Herbivore

ESSENTIAL FACTS: The teeth of this llama-like camel were more hypsodont than its ancestors, suggesting that it may have been a mixed feeder capable of processing tougher plants. The shape of its toes also show that it possessed the characteristic foot pads seen in modern camels.

PALAEOLAMA MIRIFICA

NAME MEANING: Miraculous ancient llama

AGE: Pleistocene

DISTRIBUTION: North America, South America

SIZE: 440–660 pounds (200–300 kilograms)

DIET: Herbivore; browser

ESSENTIAL FACTS: As its common name suggests, the Stout-Legged Llama had relatively short and stout metapodials than other llamas, an adaptation for moving quickly through forested environments. Isotope analysis suggests it had an exclusively browse-based diet.

HEMIAUCHENIA MACROCEPHALA

NAME MEANING: Long-headed half llama

AGE: Pliocene to Pleistocene

DISTRIBUTION: North America

SIZE: 880 pounds (400 kilograms)

DIET: Herbivore; mixed feeder

SEE MORE ON PAGES 694–695

PARACAMELUS GIGAS

NAME MEANING: Giant beside camel

AGE: Late Miocene (7.5–6 MYA)

DISTRIBUTION: North America, Eurasia, Africa

SIZE: 660–1,520 pounds (300–690 kilograms)

DIET: Herbivore; mixed feeder

ESSENTIAL FACTS: About the size of modern dromedary camels (*Camelus dromedarius*) and Bactrian camels (*C. bactrianus*), this camel was adapted to travel far distances and feed on a wide variety of both graze and browse. This species was the first camel to immigrate the Old World.

MEGATYLOPUS GIGAS

NAME MEANING: Giant big padded foot

AGE: Late Miocene (7 MYA)

DISTRIBUTION: North America

SIZE: 14 feet (4.2 meters); 3,700 pounds (1,698 kilograms)

DIET: Herbivore; browser

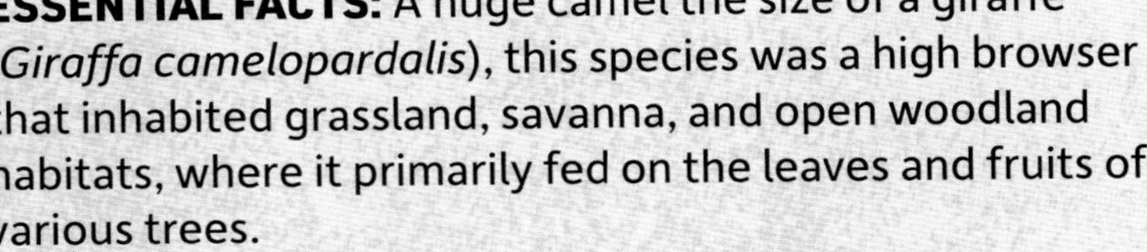

ESSENTIAL FACTS: A huge camel the size of a giraffe (*Giraffa camelopardalis*), this species was a high browser that inhabited grassland, savanna, and open woodland habitats, where it primarily fed on the leaves and fruits of various trees.

HEMIAUCHENIA MACROCEPHALA

ESSENTIAL FACTS: This animal is the last of several species of *Hemiauchenia* that have existed since the Late Miocene. The Large-Headed Llama was widely distributed throughout North America, with particularly abundant remains coming from Florida. The most complete skeleton known for this species was discovered near Lecanto in Citrus County. Strangely, when Cope named the llama in 1893, he did not have an intact skull to reference, so its common name may instead be a reference to the length of the mandible, which Cope stated was considerably longer than those of the modern guanaco (*Lama guanicoe*). Compared to modern llamas, this species was notably much larger.

While the Large-Headed Llama is known from much of southern North America, it is known as far north as the state of Idaho. Numerous studies conducted to determine the species' paleoecology have shown that it was a generalized mixed feeder whose diet consisted primarily of browse during winter and graze during summer. Overall, the species was highly versatile in regard to its diet and was able to adapt to local and seasonal conditions.

SEE ENTRY ON PAGE 693

TITANOTYLOPUS NEBRASKENSIS

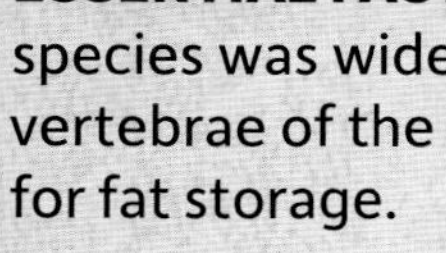

NAME MEANING: Giant padded foot from Nebraska

AGE: Pliocene to Pleistocene

DISTRIBUTION: North America

SIZE: 11–14 feet (3.4–4.2 meters) SH; 5,480 pounds (2,485 kilograms)

DIET: Herbivore; browser

ESSENTIAL FACTS: The last of the giant giraffe-sized camels, this species was widespread throughout North America. The thoracic vertebrae of the Nebraska Camel show evidence that it had a hump for fat storage.

CAMELOPS HESTERNUS

NAME MEANING: Camel face from yesterday

AGE: Pleistocene

DISTRIBUTION: North America

SIZE: 7.5 feet (2.3 meters) SH; 2,200 pounds (1,000 kilograms)

DIET: Herbivore

ESSENTIAL FACTS: Widely distributed throughout the savannas and grasslands of North America, Yesterday's Camel is well-known thanks to dozens of fossils collected from the La Brea Tar Pits in Los Angeles, California. It was a mixed feeder, whose diet would vary in the proportion of graze or browse based on seasonality.

PROTOCERATIDAE

The Protoceratidae are an extinct family of artiodactyls endemic to North America. The earliest known protoceratids appear in the fossil record during the Middle Eocene and became extinct during the Early Pliocene. The family achieved its peak diversity during the Late Eocene and in some cases were common elements of the fauna, although they were never as diverse or abundant as contemporary ungulate groups. At any given fossil locality there may be several species of horse and camel for every one protoceratid. Their relative lack of diversity, their brachydont dentition, and their general absence from higher latitudes together suggest that the family were specialized for life in subtropical or tropical forest and woodland environments. The dentition is bunoselenodont or selenodont, with molars that are wider from side to side than from front to back. They had relatively short legs and four functional toes on the forelimbs and two on the hindlimbs. As in camelids and ruminants, protoceratids undergo a trend toward the loss of their upper incisors and fusion of the lower leg bones, although they never achieved the level of modification seen in camels and ruminants.

LEPTOTRAGULINAE

The earliest protoceratids of the subfamily Leptotragulinae were small, hornless animals, most of them having previously been placed in other families such as Camellidae, Hypertragulidae, or Leptomerycidae. Males possessed elongated upper canines like chevrotains (Tragulidae) and musk deer (Moschidae).

TOROMERYX MARGINENSIS

NAME MEANING: Muscled ruminant from the margin

AGE: Middle Eocene (46–42 MYA)

DISTRIBUTION: North America

SIZE: About deer-sized

DIET: Herbivore

ESSENTIAL FACTS: One of the larger of the hornless protoceratids, Toromeryx had relatively thick-enameled teeth with bulbous cusps, suggesting a diet that included tougher food items. Its fossils are known from Texas, near its border with Mexico.

LEPTOREODON MARSHI

NAME MEANING: Marsh's slender mountain tooth

AGE: Late Eocene (40.4–37.2 MYA)

DISTRIBUTION: North America

SIZE: 45 pounds (20 kilograms)

DIET: Herbivore

ESSENTIAL FACTS: Described by Paleontologist Jacob L. Wortman in 1898, Marsh's Leptoreodon is known from reasonably complete skull and jaw material found in Utah. Like other early protoceratids, the males possessed elongated upper canines for fighting with each other.

HETEROMERYX DISPAR

NAME MEANING: Unequal different ruminant

AGE: Late Eocene (37.3–34 MYA)

DISTRIBUTION: North America

SIZE: 45 pounds (20 kilograms)

DIET: Herbivore

ESSENTIAL FACTS: Known from the states of Texas, South Dakota, and Nebraska, Heteromeryx is one of the few early protoceratids to be known from reasonably complete skull material.

LEPTOTRAGULUS MEDIUS

NAME MEANING: Middle slender Tragulus

AGE: Late Eocene (37.3–34 MYA)

DISTRIBUTION: North America

SIZE: 45 pounds (20 kilograms)

DIET: Herbivore; browser

ESSENTIAL FACTS: Despite its early age and hornless head, *Leptotragulus* had several traits that would be inherited by later horned protoceratids. Among them, its skull was broad and flattened, possibly an adaptation for head-shoving contests between males which would evolve into head-wrestling contests in their horned descendants.

PROTOCERATINAE

Protoceratines possess horn-like structures called ossicones, the bony cores of which are strongly textured with vascular grooves running along their lengths. These serve as tracks for blood vessels, which supply thickened skin which covers them, unlike true horns which have a keratinized covering. Giraffids are the only modern ungulates to possess ossicones. Like other "horned" artiodactyls, protoceratids have paired orbital horns, which are expansions of the frontal bones of the skull that protrude above each eye. Unique among other horned mammals, in addition to these paired appendages, protoceratids also possess a single horn on the nose known as the rostral or nasal horn.

PSEUDOPROTOCERAS LONGINARIS

NAME MEANING: Long-nosed false *Protoceras*

AGE: Late Eocene (37.3–34 MYA)

DISTRIBUTION: North America

SIZE: About goat-sized

DIET: Herbivore; browser

ESSENTIAL FACTS: This species is known for a complete, albeit crushed, skeleton of an adult female with an unborn fawn still in the womb. Members of the genus are known for being more hypsodont than other early protoceratids, suggesting that they tended to feed on coarser plants.

PROTOCERAS CELER

NAME MEANING: Swift first horn

AGE: Early Oligocene (33–30 MYA)

DISTRIBUTION: North America

SIZE: 3.3 feet (1 meter) HBL

DIET: Herbivore

ESSENTIAL FACTS: This animal was the oldest of the horned protoceratids and the type species for the family. Male specimens of Swift Protoceras possessed three pairs of blunt ossicones. They also retained the long canines of its ancestors.

PARATOCERAS MACADAMSI

NAME MEANING: MacAdams' beside horn

AGE: Middle Miocene (14–10 MYA)

DISTRIBUTION: North America

SIZE: About goat-sized

DIET: Herbivore

ESSENTIAL FACTS: MacAdams' Paratoceras is characterized by a short pair of ossicones on the snout, a larger pair above the eyes, and a single one in the back of the skull that branched into a Y-shape. It inhabited the humid forests of southern North America, where it browsed on soft vegetation.

SYNTHETOCERATINAE

Synthetocerotines diverged from the protoceratines during the Early Miocene. All are characterized by some form of branched rostral ossicone and long orbital ossicones in males. Both males and females have longer muzzles and nasal bones, reduced premolars, reduced canines, and more hypsodont molars. The subfamily is further subdivided into two tribes: the Kyptoceratini and Synthetoceratini.

SYNDYOCERAS COOKI

NAME MEANING: Cook's fused horn

AGE: Early Miocene (23–20 MYA)

DISTRIBUTION: North America

SIZE: 5.2 feet (1.6 meters) HBL; 155 pounds (70 kilograms)

DIET: Herbivore; browser

ESSENTIAL FACTS: Male Syndoceras possessed two pairs of ossicones: a fused, V-shaped pair on the nose and a larger, inward-curving pair just behind the eyes. Its limbs were relatively short and robust. A mounted skeleton of this species is on display at the Nebraska State Museum of Natural History.

SYNTHETOCERAS TRICORNATUS

NAME MEANING: Three-horned combined horn

AGE: Late Miocene (10–7 MYA)

DISTRIBUTION: North America

SIZE: 6.6 feet (2 meters); 330–440 pounds (150–200 kilograms)

DIET: Herbivore; browser

ESSENTIAL FACTS: One of the last and largest of the protoceratids, this species most distinctive feature is its lone nasal ossicone, which branches into a Y-shape. A shorter, thicker pair of inward-curving ossicones are situated behind the eyes. Its fossils are known from Texas, Florida, and Alabama.

KYPTOCERAS AMATORUM

NAME MEANING: Bent horn of the amateurs

AGE: Late Miocene to Early Pliocene (6–3 MYA)

DISTRIBUTION: North America

SIZE: About deer-sized

DIET: Herbivore; mixed feeder

SEE MORE ON PAGES 702–703

RUMINANTIA

Ruminants are named for the specialized method by which they digest food known as rumination. After mastication (chewing), food is swallowed and fermented in the first chamber of a four-sectioned stomach to be regurgitated, chewed again, and swallowed to be passed through the remaining stomach chambers. The name ruminant comes from the Latin word *rumunare* which means "to chew again." At present, the ruminants are the most diverse group of ungulates, comprising nearly two hundred modern species which include chevrotains (Tragulidae), musk deer (Moschidae), deer (Cervidae), pronghorns (Antilocapridae), giraffes (Giraffidae), and antelopes (Bovidae), along with several extinct families. Most ruminants lack upper incisors. Instead, they have a toughened pad which occludes with the lower incisors. The cuboid and navicular bones of the hindfoot have fused together, forming the cubonavicular bone. Additionally, many ruminant families have independently evolved paired horns or horn-like structures used for species identification, gender identification, and combat. The first true ruminants appear in the fossil record at the end of the Eocene and underwent a gradual increase in diversity from the Miocene onward.

TRAGULIDAE

The chevrotains, also known as the mouse-deer for their small size, are the most ancient group of modern ruminants. They have a fossil record that reaches back to the Late Eocene. Of the ten modern species, only one grows larger than 20 pounds (9 kilograms). They are all forest-dwelling browsers. Both sexes have prominent canines, although they are especially developed in males. As basal ruminants, chevrotains have several traits that were retained from a more piglike ancestor such as sharp premolars, foot anatomy, and aspects of their reproduction. The hindlimbs are longer than the forelimbs, and their spines are in a curved shape when at rest and act as a spring when running. Throughout the Cenozoic there have been many tragulid-like ruminant families (Hypertragulidae, Bachitheriidae, and Leptomerycidae), which are morphologically similar but have subtle differences.

KYPTOCERAS AMATORUM

ESSENTIAL FACTS: Described by David Webb in 1981, the species name *amatorum* means "of the amateurs," honoring the many contributions of amateur fossil collectors to Florida paleontology. The type specimen, a nearly complete skull, was discovered by amateur fossil collector Frank Garcia in Ruskin, Florida, who then donated it to the Florida Museum of Natural History. Kyptoceras fossils are so far only known from the southeastern United States, most having been found in phosphate mines in Central Florida, with forty-four specimens housed within the collections of the Florida Museum of Natural History. Additional material is also known from eastern North Carolina.

The morphology of Kyptoceras ossicones is notably different from those of other synthetoceratines. The nasal ossicones lack a supporting shaft as seen in Synthetoceras (*Synthetoceras tricornatus*), instead branching into a V-shaped structure near the base as in Syndoceras (*Syndyoceras cooki*). Unlike its relatives, whose nasal horns curve backward, those of Kyptoceras angled forward. The similarly forward-facing frontal horns are about 21 inches (53 centimeters) long, nearly twice the length as those of the similarly sized Synthetoceras. Kyptoceras teeth are more hypsodont than those of other protoceratids, suggesting that it had shifted from a strictly browsing diet and had become more of a mixed feeder. It is the last-known member of the family.

SEE ENTRY ON PAGE 701

DORCATHERIUM NAUI

NAME MEANING: Nau's gazelle beast

AGE: Early Miocene

DISTRIBUTION: Eurasia

SIZE: 20 pounds (9 kilograms)

DIET: Herbivore

ESSENTIAL FACTS: This animal was the type species of *Dorcatherium*, described in 1834. It is known from complete skeletal material which shows that it was virtually identical to modern chevrotains, being a small forest-dweller that fed on soft plants and small animals.

AFROTRAGULUS MORUOROTENSIS

NAME MEANING: African *Tragulus* from Moruorot

AGE: Early Miocene (17.5–16.8 MYA)

DISTRIBUTION: Eurasia

SIZE: About rabbit-sized

DIET: Herbivore

ESSENTIAL FACTS: This animal was the first African chevrotain not placed within the genus *Dorcatherium*, differing in its longer and more specialized molars adapted for shredding more fibrous plant matter.

HYPERTRAGULIDAE

Hypertragulids were early ruminants that resembled chevrotains (Tragulidae) living from the Late Eocene to Middle Miocene. They have only been found in North America. They retained five-toed (pentodactyl) forefeet, although the first digit is greatly reduced, and four-toed (tetradactyl) hindfeet. Unlike the tragulids, the skull had a postorbital process instead of a postorbital bar.

HYPERTRAGULUS CALCARATUS

NAME MEANING: Excessive goat of the limestone

AGE: Early Oligocene (34–30 MYA)

DISTRIBUTION: North America

SIZE: 20 pounds (9 kilograms)

DIET: Herbivore

ESSENTIAL FACTS: The teeth of this animal are not as hypsodont as seen in other members of the family, implying a softer diet. Sites containing multiple specimens together suggest group living. A complete mounted skeleton is on display at the American Museum of Natural History.

HYPISODUS MINIMUS

NAME MEANING: Little high teeth

AGE: Early Oligocene (34–30 MYA)

DISTRIBUTION: North America

SIZE: About rabbit-sized

DIET: Herbivore

ESSENTIAL FACTS: Smaller than most rabbits, this species is one of the smallest ruminants to have ever lived. Its snout was extremely narrow and shortened, and the molars were hypsodont, adapted for a highly selective diet of tougher plants. They had greatly enlarged auditory bullae, which translated to large external ears.

BACHITHERIIDAE

Bachitheres are small group of chevrotain-like ruminants known mostly from Europe. They are distinguished by a caniniform first lower premolars (P1), which acted with the sharp upper canines as formidable offensive weapons. The true lower canines are incisiform as in most other ruminants. Like other small, forest-dwelling ungulates, the hindlimbs were longer than the forelimbs to enable powerful leaps and sudden zig-zagging turns through the undergrowth.

BACHITHERIUM INSIGNE

NAME MEANING: Marked beast from Bach

AGE: Early Oligocene (34–30 MYA)

DISTRIBUTION: Eurasia

SIZE: 2 feet (60 centimeters) SH; 80 pounds (36 kilograms)

DIET: Herbivore; browser

ESSENTIAL FACTS: Members of the genus *Bachitherium* are the oldest ruminants known to have appeared in Europe. This species is named after the French locality of Bach, where the first fossils were discovered. This species is known from complete skeletons and is the largest-known member of the genus.

LEPTOMERYCIDAE

Leptomerycids are distinguished from hypertragulids in having broader snouts, complete postorbital bars, reduced canines, absent first premolars, and procumbent first lower incisors. The fibula is also reduced to a small proximal remnant fused to the tibia as in more derived ruminants. They were distributed throughout North America and Eurasia and occurred from the Late Eocene to Early Miocene.

LEPTOMERYX EVANSI

NAME MEANING: Evan's slender ruminant

AGE: Early Oligocene (34–30 MYA)

DISTRIBUTION: North America

SIZE: About cat-sized

DIET: Herbivore

ESSENTIAL FACTS: Leptomeryx are extremely common as fossils, sometimes represented by multiple individuals that died together. These numbers enable population and demographic studies have been able to be performed. The maximum lifespan for this species is estimated to have been eight years.

MOSCHIDAE

The musk deer are small, deer-like ruminants weighing less than 50 pounds (23 kilograms). The common name references the musk gland possessed by adult males located between their navel and genitals used to mark territory. Male musk deer have long canine tusks that resemble saberteeth, which they use to fight each other. The fossil record for the family dates back to the Early Miocene. They were distributed across Eurasia and North America, although today they are restricted to the former. There are seven modern species, all within the genus Moschus.

MICROMERYX FLOURENSIANUS

NAME MEANING: Little ruminant from Florence

AGE: Late Miocene (10–8 MYA)

DISTRIBUTION: Eurasia

SIZE: 12 pounds (5 kilograms)

DIET: Herbivore

ESSENTIAL FACTS: The legs of this tiny musk deer were extremely elongated and bult for running and leaping. It was similar in build to modern dik-diks (*Madoqua*) and likely had similar habits, inhabiting open woodland and savanna habitats relying on tall grass and shrubs for cover and food.

PARABLASTOMERYX FLORIDANUS

NAME MEANING: Beside *Blastomeryx* from Florida

AGE: Early Miocene (18 MYA)

DISTRIBUTION: North America

SIZE: 30 pounds (14 kilograms)

DIET: Herbivore

ESSENTIAL FACTS: This animal was the larger of the two species of musk deer found at the Thomas Farm Site in Central Florida. Like modern musk deer it was probably nocturnal and solitary, with male home ranges overlapping with those of several females.

MACHAEROMERYX GILCHRISTENSIS

NAME MEANING: Dagger (toothed) ruminant from Gilchrist County

AGE: Early Miocene (18 MYA)

DISTRIBUTION: North America

SIZE: 12 pounds (5 kilograms)

DIET: Herbivore

ESSENTIAL FACTS: The smaller of the two musk deer from Thomas Farm, members of the genus *Machaeromeryx* are known for their small size and particularly long upper canines.

LONGIROSTROMERYX CLARENDONENSIS

NAME MEANING: Long-snouted ruminant from the Clarendonian

AGE: Middle Miocene (14–10 MYA)

DISTRIBUTION: North America

SIZE: About deer-sized

DIET: Herbivore

ESSENTIAL FACTS: Musk deer of the genus *Longirostromeryx* were unusually large for the family, about the size of medium-sized deer. The Clarendonian Musk Deer is known from complete skeletons from the Ashfall Fossil Beds, representing animals that died during a volcanic eruption.

DROMOMERYCIDAE

Dromomerycids are a North American family of three-horned deer-like ruminants similar in many ways to the Old World Palaeomerycids. Their fossils are known from the Early Miocene to the Pliocene. Members of the family are characterized by paired unbranched ossicones above the eyes and a third appendage growing from the back of the skull.

DROMOMERYX BOREALIS

NAME MEANING: Northern running ruminant

AGE: Middle Miocene (16–14 MYA)

DISTRIBUTION: North America

SIZE: 396 pounds (180 kilograms)

DIET: Herbivore

ESSENTIAL FACTS: The Northern Dromomeryx inhabited wooded and forested environments, where it browsed on leaves, fruits, and flowers from trees and shrubs.

PEDIOMERYX HAMILTONI

NAME MEANING: Hamilton's child ruminant

AGE: Late Miocene

DISTRIBUTION: North America

SIZE: 848 pounds (385 kilograms)

DIET: Herbivore

ESSENTIAL FACTS: One of the last and largest of the dromomerycids, this species was about the size of a modern elk (*Cervus canadensis*) and inhabited woodland and savanna habitats, where it would intermittently graze on browse on various plants.

PALAEOMERYCIDAE

Palaeomerycids are an extinct family of large ruminants that lived in Eurasia from the Early to Late Miocene. They have features in common with musk deer (Moschidae) such as elongated upper canine tusks, and giraffes (Giraffidae) such as the presence of ossicones. Relatively little is known about these animals, but it is generally accepted that their closest modern relatives are giraffes and could be early-branching giraffids. Members of the family are characterized by flattened skulls with ornate head ornamentation consisting of paired ossicones over each eye and a more elaborate one at the back of the skull. The elaborate nature of these ossicones suggest that they were used more for display than for direct combat, with males perhaps relying more on their sharp canines when they needed to fight. Brachydont cheek teeth suggest that they were primarily browsers.

AMPELOMERYX GINSBURGI

NAME MEANING: Ginsburg's vessel beast

AGE: Middle Miocene

DISTRIBUTION: Eurasia

SIZE: 4 feet (1.2 meters) SH; 260–550 pounds (120–250 kilograms)

DIET: Herbivore

ESSENTIAL FACTS: Ampelomeryx had a flattened skull with triangular ossicones extending laterally over each eye, forming a kind of eye shade, along with an unpaired ossicone extending from the back of the skull that branched into a Y-shape.

XENOKERYX AMIDALAE

NAME MEANING: Padme Amidala's strange horn

AGE: Middle Miocene

DISTRIBUTION: Eurasia

SIZE: 4 feet (1.2 meters) SH; 260–550 pounds (120–250 kilograms)

DIET: Herbivore

ESSENTIAL FACTS: Formerly known as *Triceromeryx conquensis*, Xenokeryx had a third ossicone at the back of the skull that branched into a T-shape. The species name is inspired by the striking resemblance that the third ossicone bears to a hairstyle displayed by the character Padme Amidala in the film *Star Wars: Episode I—The Phantom Menace*.

CLIMACOCERATIDAE

Like the palaeomerycids, climacoceratids were closely related to giraffes and may represent an early-branching subfamily of giraffids. These were deer-like herbivores with elaborate ossicones that resemble antlers. They lived during the Early and Middle Miocene of Eurasia and Africa.

CLIMACOCERAS GENTRYI

NAME MEANING: Gentry's ladder horn

AGE: Early Miocene

DISTRIBUTION: Africa

SIZE: 5 feet (1.5 meters) SH

DIET: Herbivore

ESSENTIAL FACTS: Gentry's Climacoceras possessed ossicones with a crescent moon shape with three backward-pointing tines. The closely related African Climacoceras (*C. africanus*) had straighter ossicones that resembled a thorny branch with multiple small tines branching from a vertical beam.

GIRAFFIDAE

The giraffidae contains two modern species: the okapi (*Okapia johnstoni*) and giraffe (*Giraffa camelopardalis*), both with distributions limited to Africa. Despite this, giraffids are relative newcomers to the African continent, first appearing there during the Late Miocene after living in Eurasia since the Early Miocene. They are characterized by elongated legs and necks for high-browsing, a dark blue prehensile tongue for pulling leaves and branches towards their mouths, and skin-covered horn-like structures called ossicones.

PROLIBYTHERIINAE

A poorly known group of giraffids known for their particularly elaborate ossicones, they are known from the Early and Middle Miocene of Africa and Eurasia.

PROLIBYTHERIUM MAGNIERI

NAME MEANING: Magnier's before *Lybitherium*

AGE: Middle Miocene (17–16 MYA)

DISTRIBUTION: Africa

SIZE: 6 feet (1.8 meters)

DIET: Herbivore

ESSENTIAL FACTS: Males of this species had broad, flat ossicones shaped like butterfly wings, while those of females were much thinner and more horn-like. Given their shape, direct combat with these appendages may have been unlikely, instead functioning as display structures.

DISCOKERYX XIEZHI

NAME MEANING: Round-plated horned Xiezhi

AGE: Middle Miocene (17–16 MYA)

DISTRIBUTION: Eurasia

SIZE: About sheep-sized

DIET: Herbivore

ESSENTIAL FACTS: Unlike other giraffids, Discokeryx was optimized for headbutting, possessing a thick-boned skull with a disc-shaped growth in the middle of its head rather than the typical ossicones. To resist high impacts, the neck vertebrae were thick and sturdy. Examination of its tooth enamel suggests that it was a grazer of the open plains, unlike its browsing relatives.

SIVATHERIINAE

Sivatheres were large giraffes with robust, heavily built skeletons with bones matching those of oxen or buffalo in terms of thickness. They resembled stocky okapis and typically had more complicated ossicones than giraffines.

SHANSITHERIUM TAFELI

NAME MEANING: Tafel's beast from Shanxi

AGE: Late Miocene

DISTRIBUTION: Eurasia

SIZE: About moose-sized

DIET: Herbivore

ESSENTIAL FACTS: Tafel's Shanisitherium was a massive browser about the size of a moose (*Alces alces*) that once inhabited the forests of China. A complete mounted skeleton of this animal is on display at the Beijing Museum of Natural History.

DECENNATHERIUM REX

NAME MEANING: King tenth beast

AGE: Late Miocene (11.6–7.8 MYA)

DISTRIBUTION: Eurasia

SIZE: 4,400 pounds (2,000 kilograms)

DIET: Herbivore

ESSENTIAL FACTS: The King Decennatherium had two pairs of ossicones: a small pair just in front of the eyes and a large, backward-curving pair behind the eyes which had ridges running along their front surface. Described in 2012, it was one of the largest herbivores at the Cerro de los Batallones site in Spain.

HELLADOTHERIUM DUVERNOYI

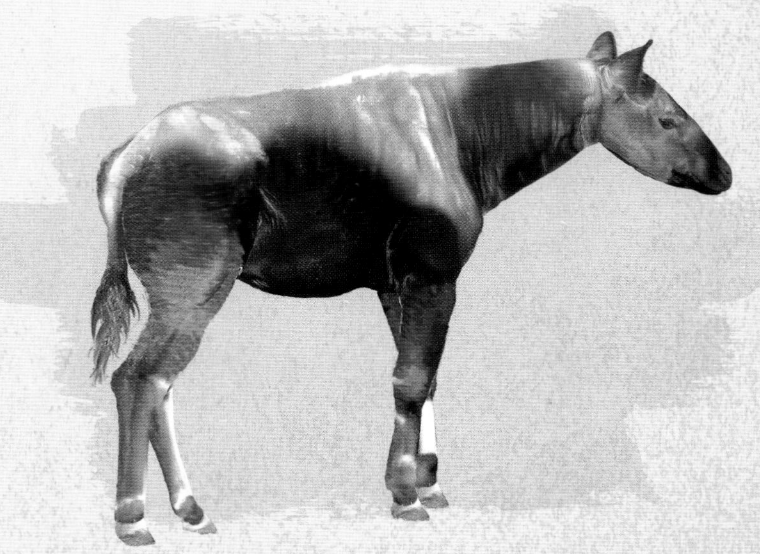

NAME MEANING: Guvernoy's Greek beast

AGE: Late Miocene

DISTRIBUTION: Eurasia

SIZE: About moose-sized

DIET: Herbivore

ESSENTIAL FACTS: Members of the genus *Helladotherium* lacked ossicones, and a live specimen may have resembled a short-necked camel. Like most giraffids, they were browsing specialists.

SIVATHERIUM GIGANTEUM

NAME MEANING: Moorish beast of Shiva

AGE: Pleistocene to Holocene

DISTRIBUTION: Eurasia, Africa

SIZE: 7.2 feet (2.2 meters) SH; 10 feet (3 meters) HBL; 2,760–3,000 pounds (1,250–1,360 kilograms)

DIET: Herbivore; mixed feeder

SEE MORE ON PAGES 716–717

GIRAFFINAE

The subfamily to which both modern species belong. Like most other giraffids they were browsing specialists with forelimbs longer than the hindlimbs.

GIRAFFOKERYX PUNJABIENSIS

NAME MEANING: Giraffe chief from Punjab

AGE: Middle Miocene (14–11 MYA)

DISTRIBUTION: Eurasia

SIZE: About ox-sized

DIET: Herbivore

ESSENTIAL FACTS: The two species of *Giraffokeryx*, of which the Punjab Giraffokeryx is the better known, are characterized by their skulls which bear four conical ossicones of equal length. Their fossils are known from southern Asia.

HONANOTHERIUM SCHLOSSERI

NAME MEANING: Schlosser's beast from Henan

AGE: Late Miocene

DISTRIBUTION: Eurasia

SIZE: About rhino-sized

DIET: Herbivore; browser

ESSENTIAL FACTS: Named for the province of Henan in China where its fossils were first found, this species inhabited woodland and savanna habitats where it selectively grazed on trees and shrubs. A complete skeleton is on display at the Henan Geological Museum.

ANTILOCAPRIDAE

The American Pronghorn (*Antilocapra americana*) is the sole surviving representative of the family Antilocapridae, known commonly as the pronghorns. The family appears in the fossil record during the Middle Miocene and became adapted to life as small- to medium-sized grazers adapted for cursoriality and life in open environments, convergently evolving similar morphologies to antilopine bovids. Throughout their evolutionary history, the family has remained restricted to the North American continent. Horn core morphology is the primary means of classifying fossil antilocaprids.

MERYCONDONTINAE

Merycondontines possess horn cores that are similar in appearance to antlers, having a burr at the base and branching off into several tines.

SIVATHERIUM GIGANTEUM

ESSENTIAL FACTS: Members of the genus *Sivatherium* are all very similar to each other, differing mainly in age and location. They are characterized by their large size and palmate ossicones that vaguely resemble the antlers of a moose (*Alces alces*). The first species to be described back in 1836 was the Giant Sivathere (*S. giganteum*) from the Pleistocene of India. The better-known Moorish Shivathere is slightly younger and is known to have been distributed through southern Asia and Africa.

Like other members of its genus, the Moorish Sivathere was a massive animal with a robust skeleton. It represents a culmination of a trend seen within the genus that involves the shortening of the metacarpals (hand bones) relative to the metatarsals (foot bones), possibly an adaptation for grazing. Additionally, their teeth were more hypsodont than those of other giraffes, indicating the shift from an exclusively browsing diet to a more mixed one that included substantial amounts of grazing. Rock art depicting this animal, found in the Sahara Desert and India, shows that this species was observed by humans in the regions about 8,000 years ago. There is even a figurine of an animal resembling a sivathere found in Iraq that is associated with the ancient Sumerian civilization—which, if correct, suggests a late survival up to 3,500 years ago for these animals!

SEE ENTRY ON PAGE 714

RAMOCEROS OSBORNI

NAME MEANING: Osborn's branched horn

AGE: Middle Miocene (13.6–10.3 MYA)

DISTRIBUTION: North America

SIZE: 22–44 pounds (10–20 kilograms)

DIET: Herbivore

ESSENTIAL FACTS: Osborn's Ramoceros was a small pronghorn with an unusual set of horns; they were asymmetrical and resembled deer antlers, with the left being several times larger than the right. A mounted skeleton of this species is on display at the American Museum of Natural History.

MERRIAMOCEROS CORONATUS

NAME MEANING: John Merriam's crowned horn

AGE: Middle Miocene (17.5–14.8 MYA)

DISTRIBUTION: North America

SIZE: About sheep-sized

DIET: Herbivore

ESSENTIAL FACTS: The most distinctive feature of Crowned Pronghorn are its horns, which have a short shaft that widens horizontally into a palmate shape, with numerous small tines running along the top edge. This shape inspired its species name. The genus name honors American paleontologist John C. Merriam, who described it in 1913 under the genus *Merycodus*.

COSORYX FURCATUS

NAME MEANING: Forked antelope

AGE: Pliocene

DISTRIBUTION: North America

SIZE: About goat-sized

DIET: Herbivore

ESSENTIAL FACTS: The Forked Pronghorn is named for its horns, which grow from a vertical main branch that splits into two small points. Its fossils are known from Nebraska.

ANTILOCAPRINAE

Compared to the Merycodontinae, the Antilocaprinae is more diverse and longer lived, the modern American Pronghorn (*Antilocapra americana*) being the last surviving member. In contrast to the bony, antler-like horns of the merycodontines, members of this subfamily have lost the burrs from the horn core shafts and have added a keratinous horn sheath. Its presence is revealed in fossil species by the lack of wear at the tips of the tines and the horn core having a texture similar to that of the modern species. Additionally, all have horn cores that are flattened in cross-section, highly hypsodont teeth, enlarged auditory bullae, and elongated metapodials with loss of the lateral digits.

OSBORNOCEROS OSBORNI

NAME MEANING: Henry Osborn's horn

AGE: Late Miocene (7–6 MYA)

DISTRIBUTION: North America

SIZE: About goat-sized

DIET: Herbivore

ESSENTIAL FACTS: Osborn's Pronghorn possessed unforked horn cores with distinctive slender, flattened, twisted shafts, which superficially similar the horns of a modern nyala antelope (*Tragelephus angasii*).

HAYOCEROS FALKENBACHI

NAME MEANING: Charles Falkenbach's horn from Hay Springs

AGE: Pleistocene

DISTRIBUTION: North America

SIZE: About goat-sized

DIET: Herbivore

ESSENTIAL FACTS: Falkenbach's Pronghorn possessed horns that split into two branches at the base. The front branch was shorter and flattened, while the back branch was longer and more pointed. The species name honors Charles Falkenbach, who discovered the first fossils for the species.

CAPROMERYX MINOR

NAME MEANING: Lesser goat ruminant

AGE: Pleistocene

DISTRIBUTION: North America

SIZE: 2 feet (60 centimeters) SH; 22 pounds (10 kilograms)

DIET: Herbivore

SEE MORE ON PAGES 722–723

HEXAMERYX SIMPSONI

NAME MEANING: Simpson's six horns

AGE: Late Miocene (7–5 MYA)

DISTRIBUTION: North America

SIZE: About goat-sized

DIET: Herbivore

ESSENTIAL FACTS: Simpson's Pronghorn had horns that branched into three points at the base, each being covered in its own sheath, giving the living animal a six-horned appearance. Its fossils are so far only known from the state of Florida.

TETRAMERYX SHULERI

NAME MEANING: Shuler's four (horned) ruminant

AGE: Pleistocene

DISTRIBUTION: North America

SIZE: 100–165 pounds (45–75 kilograms)

DIET: Herbivore

ESSENTIAL FACTS: One of five species in the genus *Tetrameryx*, Shuler's Pronghorn had horns that branched in two at the base; the front branch was shorter while the back branch was much taller. It was about the same size as the modern species but somewhat more heavily built.

STOCKOCEROS CONKLINGI

NAME MEANING: Conkling's horn of Chester Stock

AGE: Pleistocene

DISTRIBUTION: North America

SIZE: Herbivore; graze-dominated mixed feeder

DIET: Herbivore

ESSENTIAL FACTS: Conkling's Pronghorn possessed horn core was symmetrically forked into two branches of equal length and individually sheathed. Though its diet consisted mostly of grazed grasses it would switch to browse during the winter.

CERVIDAE

Deer are the second most diverse family of modern artiodactyls, with sixty-eight modern species. They are characterized from other ruminants by their unique head ornamentation called antlers: rapidly growing, highly mineralized bone that grows from the skull into shapes that are unique from one species to another, making them useful in the identification of fossil species. The first deer that appear during the Early Miocene lacked antlers. Instead, the males possessed elongated upper canine tusks. The Chinese Water Deer (*Hydropotes inermis*) is a late-surviving member of this lineage of early "fanged deer." Most deer are either browsers or browse-dominated mixed feeders, with only a few evolving into grazers.

CERVINAE

Cervines appear during the Middle Miocene and are mostly restricted to the Old World. They can be distinguished from capreolines by the loss of parts of the second and fifth metacarpals. The first members of the genus resembled modern muntjacs (*Muntiacus*), small deer from southeast Asia which possess long upper canines and short antlers which grew from elongated stalks or pedicles. Over time, members of the group grew in size and developed ever larger and more elaborate antlers, which corresponded with the reduction of the pedicle. They have always been highly diverse and appear to be better suited to the more temperate northern latitudes than bovids, which are more concentrated in the tropics and subtropics.

CAPROMERYX MINOR

ESSENTIAL FACTS: Members of the genus *Capromeryx*, also known as "the dwarf pronghorns," are first known in the fossil record during the Pliocene, with four confirmed species existing through to the Early Holocene. Interestingly, they appear to have evolved from a larger-bodied ancestor that became smaller over time to exploit new niches. Ecologically, they paralleled dwarf antelopes (Neotragini) of the genera *Raphicerus* and *Ourebia*. These small herbivores live their lives hidden among brush and tall grass, feeding on the surrounding plants which conceal them. Their first line of defense is to lie completely still to avoid detection, but when necessary they bolt from cover and flee with great speed and agility. Dwarf pronghorns are likely to have shown similar behaviors.

The Lesser Dwarf Pronghorn is best known from the La Brea Tar Pits of Los Angeles, California, which has yielded the most complete material for the species. Additional fossils are known from Texas. Both sexes had similarly shaped horns, which consist of two short, straight points that split at the base and are positioned parallel to each other rather than diverging. Its long-legged, lightweight skeleton made it very fast and agile, although its primary means of defense would have been to hide in tall grass. A likely factor that hastened its extinction may have been increased fire frequency toward the end of the Pleistocene linked to human activity, which would severely reduced the tall vegetation on which it depended, making them more vulnerable to predation and cutting their food supply.

SEE ENTRY ON PAGE 720

EUPROX FURCATUS

NAME MEANING: Forked

AGE: Middle Miocene

DISTRIBUTION: Eurasia

SIZE: 3.3 feet (1 meter) SH; 66–154 pounds (30–70 kilograms)

DIET: Herbivore; browser

ESSENTIAL FACTS: Members of the genus *Euprox* resembled modern muntjacs with short, two-pronged antlers with long upper canine tusks. They were the oldest deer known to possess a burr, the bony rim at the base of the antler. It inhabited tropical and subtropical forests where it fed on leaves and fruits.

HETEROPROX LARTETI

NAME MEANING: Lartet's different points

AGE: Middle Miocene (16–11 MYA)

DISTRIBUTION: Eurasia

SIZE: 3.3 feet (1 meter) SH; 77 pounds (35 kilograms)

DIET: Herbivore; browser

ESSENTIAL FACTS: Lartet's Heteroprox had short, two-pronged antlers that grew from tall pedicles. Its body proportions are similar to those of modern bovids within the subfamily Reduncinae, suggesting that it was semiaquatic. Its long hindlimbs and splayed hooves enabled it to swim efficiently and dash through shallow water.

DICROCERUS ELEGANS

NAME MEANING: Elegant forked horn

AGE: Middle Miocene

DISTRIBUTION: Eurasia

SIZE: 2.3 feet (70 centimeters) SH; 75 pounds (35 kilograms)

DIET: Herbivore

ESSENTIAL FACTS: A forest-dwelling browser with brachydont teeth adapted for browsing, it possessed two-pronged antlers that were longer than the pedicle with a burr at their bases.

HAPLOIDOCEROS MEDITERRANEUS

NAME MEANING: Mediterranean simple horn

AGE: Pleistocene

DISTRIBUTION: Eurasia

SIZE: 150–180 pounds (70–80 kilograms)

DIET: Herbivore; browse-dominated mixed feeder

ESSENTIAL FACTS: Fossils of the Mediterranean Deer possessed two-beamed antlers; the front beam pointed straight upward, while the rear beam was longer and curved backward and upward. Its skeleton shows adaptations for leaping, and it would have run with a bounding gait.

CROIZETOCEROS RAMOSUS

NAME MEANING: Branched crossing horn

AGE: Pliocene

DISTRIBUTION: Eurasia

SIZE: 130 pounds (60 kilograms)

DIET: Herbivore

ESSENTIAL FACTS: The antlers of this deer were complex, with four or five tines branching off from a central beam. It may have preferentially browsed on softer plants but would occasionally graze.

CANDIACERVUS CRETENSIS

NAME MEANING: Brilliant deer from Crete

AGE: Pleistocene

DISTRIBUTION: Crete

SIZE: About sheep-sized

DIET: Herbivore

ESSENTIAL FACTS: Several different species of this deer inhabited the island of Crete, ranging in size from 60 pounds (27 kilograms) to 540 pounds (245 kilograms). All have long, almost-straight antlers consisting of a single beam with a short prong near the base. The Cretan Candiacervus was the first species to be described.

SINOMEGACEROS PACHYOSTEUS

NAME MEANING: Thick-boned Chinese great horns

AGE: Pleistocene

DISTRIBUTION: Eurasia

SIZE: 440–880 pounds (200–400 kilograms)

DIET: Herbivore; grazer

ESSENTIAL FACTS: Several species of *Sinomegaceros* have been described from China, the most well-known being the Thick-boned Deer and Yabe's Deer (*S. yabei*). The former have antlers which split into two broad, flattened branches.

MEGALOCEROS GIGANTEUS

NAME MEANING: Gigantic big horns

AGE: Late Pleistocene to Holocene (500,000–7,700 YA)

DISTRIBUTION: Eurasia

SIZE: 7 feet (2.1 meters) SH; 990–1,540 pounds (450–700 kilograms)

DIET: Herbivore; graze-dominated mixed feeder

SEE MORE ON PAGES 728–729

CAPREOLINAE

Capreolinae appear during the Middle Miocene in Eurasia, although today most of the thirty-eight species are limited to the New World. Throughout their history they have ranged from small forest-dwelling browsers to giant grazers of the open plains.

LIBRALCES GALLICUS

NAME MEANING: Gallic balanced elk

AGE: Pliocene to Pleistocene

DISTRIBUTION: Eurasia

SIZE: 5 feet (1.5 meters) SH; 880 pounds (400 kilograms)

DIET: Herbivore

ESSENTIAL FACTS: The Gallic Deer possessed long antlers comprised of a single elongated beam with a palmate end spanning 6.6 feet (2 meters) tip-to-tip. It likely favored relatively open environments because its wide antler span would have made maneuvering through trees difficult.

TORONTOCEROS HYPOGAEUS

NAME MEANING: Toronto horn from underground

AGE: Late Pleistocene

DISTRIBUTION: North America

SIZE: Unknown; about the size of a Caribou

DIET: Herbivore

ESSENTIAL FACTS: This species was forest-dwelling deer, known from a single incomplete skeleton from Toronto, Ontario, of a male that died during the spring before his antlers had fully grown. It's closest modern relative is the caribou (*Rangifer tarandus*), but it had notably thicker and heavier antlers.

CERVALCES SCOTTI

NAME MEANING: William B. Scott's deer elk

AGE: Pleistocene

DISTRIBUTION: North America

SIZE: 6 feet (1.8 meters) SH; 8.2 feet (2.5 meters) HBL; 1,562 pounds (708.5 kilograms)

DIET: Herbivore; browser

ESSENTIAL FACTS: Commonly known as "the Stag Moose," this species had long legs that made it almost as tall as it was long, enabling it to browse from particularly high branches. Its antlers were very complex, with a sideways-pointing beam that branches into a palmate lower portion and a multi-tined upper portion.

MEGALOCEROS GIGANTEUS

ESSENTIAL FACTS: This species is often called "the Irish Elk" because the first described, most well-known, and best-preserved fossils have been found in Irish peat bogs. This species is perhaps the most well-known and most well-studied of all extinct deer species. Despite its name, Irish Elk were quite widespread throughout Eurasia north of the Himalayas and seemed to have avoided extensive open plains and dense forests. Stable isotope analysis suggests that it would have mostly grazed on grasses and forbs, occasionally supplementing its diet with browse from trees and shrubs encountered in open areas. Despite its size, the body proportions of the Irish Elk show that it was a capable runner that could rely on its speed to escape predators. The species survived well into the Holocene, with the youngest remains from western Russia dated to about 7,700 years ago.

The Irish Elk was one of the largest deer known to have ever lived, about the size of a moose (*Alces alces*) and surpassed only by the contemporary Broad-Fronted Moose (*Cervalces latifrons*). It did, however, possess the largest antlers of any deer. Fully mature males had an antler span of up to 12 feet (3.7 meters), each one weighing about 88 pounds (40 kilograms). Sexual dimorphism is marked, with males averaging 20 percent larger than the females. Based on exceptionally detailed cave paintings, we know that Irish Elk had a light-colored coat with a dark stripe running down the back. This stripe branched into two more stripes on either side, running from the shoulders to the thighs and downward from the shoulders, forming a collar-like marking around the base of the neck. There also appears to have been a dark chinstrap marking.

SEE ENTRY ON PAGE 726

CERVALCES LATIFRONS

NAME MEANING: Broad-fronted stag moose

AGE: Pleistocene

DISTRIBUTION: Eurasia

SIZE: 7–8 feet (2.1–2.4 meters) SH; 2,200–2,600 pounds (1,000–1,200 kilograms)

DIET: Herbivore

ESSENTIAL FACTS: The Broad-Fronted Moose was one of the largest deer to have ever lived, being in the size class of a large bull plains bison (*Bison bison*). Despite its impressive dimensions it is relatively poorly known. It likely had a primarily browsing diet like the closely related Stag Moose (*C. scotti*).

ODOCOILEUS LUCASI

NAME MEANING: Lucas' tooth hollow

AGE: Pleistocene

DISTRIBUTION: North America

SIZE: 600 pounds (270 kilograms)

DIET: Herbivore

ESSENTIAL FACTS: Formerly known as *Navahoceros fricki*, the Mountain Deer was significantly larger than modern members of its genus, with proportions that made it adept at traversing mountainous or rocky terrain. In fact, its fossils are common in the Rocky Mountains and Guadalupe Mountains.

MORENELAPHUS BRACHYCEROS

NAME MEANING: Morene's deer with short-horns

AGE: Pleistocene

DISTRIBUTION: South America

SIZE: 440 pounds (200 kilograms)

DIET: Herbivore

ESSENTIAL FACTS: The largest deer known to have lived in South America, it was a mixed feeder that inhabited savanna and grassland habitats.

BOVIDAE

The bovids are the most diverse family of artiodactyls with 143 species, most of which are endemic to Africa. The defining feature of this group are the paired horns on their heads, growing from a bony core surrounded by a thin layer of vascular tissue covered in keratin. The family first appears during the Early Miocene represented by small forest-dwelling browsers that resembled modern duikers. They were restricted to the Old World until the Pleistocene when bison, musk-oxen, and goat antelopes entered North America.

BOVINAE

The bovines are the oldest representatives of the family and also contains some of the largest species. The boselaphines (Boselaphini) were the first to appear and were highly diverse during the Miocene, but today is represented by just two surviving species: the Four-horned Antelope (*Tetracerus quadricornis*) and the Nilgai (*Boselaphus tragocamelus*). The spiral-horned antelopes (Tragelaphini) appear during the Middle Miocene. Today they are confined to Africa, but they are known in the fossil record from Eurasia, where they are thought to have originated. The wild cattle (Bovini) are robust, large-bodied antelopes which include the buffalo, oxen, and bison.

EOTRAGUS SANSANIENSIS

NAME MEANING: Dawn goat from Sansan

AGE: Early Miocene (20–18 MYA)

DISTRIBUTION: Eurasia

SIZE: 6.6–13.2 pounds (3–6 kilograms)

DIET: Herbivore

ESSENTIAL FACTS: *Eotragus* were the oldest of the boselaphines. They were small, forest-dwelling animals about the size of modern dik-diks (*Madoqua*). They had simple straight, small, conical horns typical of small forest-dwelling ruminants. Their brachydont teeth were adapted to feed on soft plants, fruits, and small animals.

KIPSIGICERUS LOBIDOTUS

NAME MEANING: Unknown

AGE: Middle Miocene

DISTRIBUTION: Africa

SIZE: About goat-sized

DIET: Herbivore; browser

ESSENTIAL FACTS: This species was a small, African boselaphine related to the modern four-horned antelope (*Tetracerus quadricornis*). The males possess small, highly compressed horns with additional horn-producing growth at the base of the main horn cores.

MIOTRAGOCERUS PANONNIAE

NAME MEANING: Lesser goat horn from Pannonia

AGE: Late Miocene (10–8 MYA)

DISTRIBUTION: Eurasia

SIZE: 3.3 feet (1 meter) SH; 176 pounds (80 kilograms)

DIET: Herbivore; browser

ESSENTIAL FACTS: The Panonnian Antelope was adapted for life in humid forests, where it primarily browsed on soft plants. Its body proportions are similar to those of modern semiaquatic antelopes such as the sitatunga (*Tragelaphus spekii*).

AUSTROPORTAX LATIFRONS

NAME MEANING: Broad-fronted southern antelope

AGE: Late Miocene (11–9 MYA)

DISTRIBUTION: Eurasia

SIZE: 660 pounds (300 kilograms)

DIET: Herbivore; browser

ESSENTIAL FACTS: This species was a large bovid for its time, of similar size and proportion to a small ox or buffalo. It inhabited woodland habitats where it was adapted to browsing. Its closest modern relative is the nilgai (*Boselaphus tragocamelus*), formerly placed under the genus *Portax*.

TRAGOPORTAX GAUDRYI

NAME MEANING: Gaudry's goat antelope

AGE: Late Miocene (10–8 MYA)

DISTRIBUTION: Eurasia

SIZE: About deer-sized

DIET: Herbivore

ESSENTIAL FACTS: This species had deer-like body proportions adapted for running and leaping through open forests. It was highly sexually dimorphic, with males being significantly larger than females with well-developed horns.

PELOROVIS OLDOWAYENSIS

NAME MEANING: Monster sheep from Oldoway Gorge

AGE: Pleistocene

DISTRIBUTION: Africa

SIZE: 5 feet (1.5 meters) SH; 1,763 pounds (800 kilograms)

DIET: Herbivore

ESSENTIAL FACTS: Despite being larger than the modern cape buffalo (*Syncerus caffer*), Oldoway Pelorovis had proportionally longer and more slender limbs adapted for fast running. The skull was also longer and angled downward reminiscent of alcelephines, suggesting a specialized diet of short grasses on open plains.

SYNCERAS ANTIQUUS

NAME MEANING: Ancient fused horn

AGE: Pleistocene and Holocene

DISTRIBUTION: Africa

SIZE: 6.1 feet (1.85 meters) SH; 10 feet (3 meters) HBL; 4,400 pounds (2,000 kilograms)

DIET: Herbivore; grazer

SEE MORE ON PAGES 734–735

SYNCERAS ANTIQUUS

ESSENTIAL FACTS: The Giant Buffalo is the largest bovid known to have lived in Africa, being more than twice the size of the modern Cape Buffalo (*S. caffer*) and matching more closely to larger specimens of white rhinos (*Ceratotherium simum*). Its massive horn cores spanned up to 10 feet (3 meters) from tip to tip and were even longer with the keratin sheath, the tips pointing straight upward or curved slightly inward in some individuals. Not only was it larger overall than its modern relative, but it was also more robust with stockier limb proportions. The Giant Buffalo's habitat was likely limited to open environments, as its long horns may have made navigating through wooded environments difficult. Isotopic and tooth wear evidence has shown this animal to have been a grazer.

A large amount of rock art depicting this species has been found across northern Africa, showing that they survived recently enough to have been observed by modern humans who appear to have been well-versed in the life history and behavior of this species. From these depictions, it can be inferred that Giant Buffalo lived in relatively large herds. Early humans seem to have hunted them occasionally, as there are also depictions of hunters attacking the buffalos with spears. The extinction of the Giant Buffalo may be attributed to changes in climate and environment, including the desertification of the Sahara which would have vastly reduced and fragmented its distribution. This was exacerbated by the rise of agriculture, expanding human civilizations, and increasing hunting pressures. The species survived as recently as 4,000 years ago.

SEE ENTRY ON PAGE 733

BOS PRIMIGENIUS

NAME MEANING: Firstborn ox

AGE: Pleistocene to Holocene

DISTRIBUTION: Eurasia, Africa

SIZE: 5–6 feet (1.5–1.8 meters) SH; 880–1,540 (400–700 kilograms)

DIET: Herbivore; graze-dominated mixed feeder

SEE MORE ON PAGES 738–739

BISON PRISCUS

NAME MEANING: Ancient Bison

AGE: Pleistocene

DISTRIBUTION: North America, Eurasia

SIZE: 2,000 pounds (900 kilograms)

DIET: Herbivore

SEE MORE ON PAGES 740–741

BISON ANTIQUUS

NAME MEANING: Ancient bison

AGE: Pleistocene to Holocene

DISTRIBUTION: North America

SIZE: 6 feet (1.8 meters) SH; 10 feet (3 meters) HBL; 3,501 pounds (1,588 kilograms)

DIET: Herbivore

ESSENTIAL FACTS: The Antique Bison was slightly larger than the modern plains bison (*B. bison*) with taller neural spines. This gave the animal a more pronounced humped back, which increased its overall height up to 7.4 feet (2.3 meters). Widespread throughout North America, it is known to have engaged in seasonal migrations.

BISON LATIFRONS

NAME MEANING: Broad-fronted bison

AGE: Pleistocene

DISTRIBUTION: North America

SIZE: 8.5 feet (2.3–2.5 meters) SH; 15.6 feet (4.7 meters) HBL; 4,400 pounds (2,000 kilograms)

DIET: Herbivore; graze-dominated mixed feeder

ESSENTIAL FACTS: The Long-Horned Bison is one of the largest bovids to have ever lived, matching the African Giant Buffalo (*Synceras antiquus*) in size. Apart from its large size, its horn cores spanned 8 feet (2.1 meters) from tip to tip. It would preferentially graze, but could switch to browse during winter months.

ANTILOPINAE

Antilopines are small- to medium-sized bovids adapted for cursoriality. Most are specialized grazers that inhabit open habitats, making use of their great speed to evade predation. They are widespread throughout Africa and Eurasia

GAZELLA PSOLEA

NAME MEANING: Unknown

AGE: Pliocene

DISTRIBUTION: Africa, Eurasia

SIZE: About goat-sized

DIET: Herbivore

ESSENTIAL FACTS: Distributed through the dry habitats of northern Africa and Arabia, this gazelle had an unusual skull that resembled that of the modern saiga (*Saiga tatarica*) with greatly retracted nasals and an enlarged nasal cavity. This suggests the presence of an enlarged nose that would warm and moisten dry, dusty air on inhalation.

BOS PRIMIGENIUS

ESSENTIAL FACTS: The Aurochs are the wild ancestor of today's domestic cattle. Formerly widespread throughout Eurasia and northern Africa, their preferred habitat was open woodland and savanna, seemingly avoiding deserts, mountains, extensive open grassland, and particularly dense forests. Males tended to be larger and darker colored than the females, as is typical of the genus Bos. Both sexes had a white muzzle and appear to have had a lighter-colored, saddle-shaped patch of fur on their backs. Older cattle breeds alive today still retain this coat patterning. The legs were proportionally longer and more slender than those of domestic cattle, with an overall more athletic build, better suited for cursoriality. The skull was also proportionally larger, longer, and bore large forward-curving horns.

Aurochs are famously well-represented in ancient European cave art from the Pleistocene, and in historic times they appear in reliefs, engravings, sculptures, and seals in ancient cultures from Mesopotamia to Egypt. They may have even been worshipped by the Minoan civilization. Despite its clear cultural significance, Aurochs gradually became extinct throughout its range due to habitat fragmentation caused by the rise of agriculture and may have been deliberately extirpated to reduce competition with domesticated cattle. South Asian populations appear to have gone extinct around 3,800 years ago, and northern African populations survived until Roman times. European populations lasted longer, but their decline coincides with the gradual clear-cutting of their habitats to make room for farmlands. The Romans are known to have captured many individuals for use in gladiatorial events. Aurochs hunting continued, although by the 13th century this became an exclusive right of nobility and royals. By the 18th century the species existed in small, isolated populations around Europe which gradually disappeared. The last known Aurochs survived until 1627.

SEE ENTRY ON PAGE 736

BISON PRISCUS

ESSENTIAL FACTS: The Steppe Bison was widespread throughout the open grasslands across the Northern Hemisphere, closely associated with the Mammoth Steppe ecosystem which straddled Eurasia and North America during glacial periods. It is believed to be ancestral to North American bison species, and its closest modern relative is the European bison (*B. bonasus*), differing in its overall larger size and larger horns.

The life appearance of this species is well-known thanks to its depictions in ancient cave art, suggesting that its coat was mostly reddish-brown in color with patches of darker fur on its back, throat, and chest. Frozen specimens have also been found in permafrost from northern Russia and Alaska. Most famously, a mostly complete 36,000-year-old carcass of a male specimen was discovered in Fairbanks, Alaska, in 1979. Nicknamed "Blue Babe" after Paul Bunyan's mythical giant ox, the specimen appears to have frozen quickly after death and subsequently buried by snowdrifts. Most of the fur was lost over time, but enough remains to confirm the accuracy of the cave painting depictions. Blue Babe was killed by a large cat, possibly an American Lion (*Panthera atrox*); the hindquarters were partially consumed, and claw and bite damage can be seen on the head and neck, which are consistent with big cat attacks. Blue Babe is on permanent display at the University of Alaska Museum of the North in Fairbanks.

SEE ENTRY ON PAGE 736

TYRRHENOTRAGUS GRACILLIMUS

NAME MEANING: Slender goat of the Tyrrhenian Sea

AGE: Late Miocene (10–8 MYA)

DISTRIBUTION: Baccinello

SIZE: About hare-sized

DIET: Herbivore; grazer

ESSENTIAL FACTS: This species was discovered in Baccinello, Italy, which was an island during the Late Miocene. The Tyrrhenian Dwarf Antelope was characterized by shortened metapodials and hypselodont teeth suggesting a specialized diet of abrasive vegetation.

ANTIDORCAS BONDI

NAME MEANING: Bond's opposite gazelle

AGE: Pliocene to Holocene

DISTRIBUTION: Africa

SIZE: About goat-sized

DIET: Herbivore; grazer

ESSENTIAL FACTS: Bond's Springbok was a specialized grazer with exceptionally hypsodont dentition suited for processing abrasive vegetation in arid, open grasslands. This is in stark contrast to the primarily browsing diet of the modern common springbok (*A. marsupialis*). It is known to have survived in South Africa until about 5,000 years ago.

REDUNCINAE

Reduncines first appear during the Late Miocene and are known for favoring well-watered habitats. The subfamily is confined to Africa today, but their Eurasian fossil record is slightly older than their African one, suggesting that they originated there.

MENELIKIA LYROCERA

NAME MEANING: Unknown

AGE: Pliocene to Pleistocene

DISTRIBUTION: Africa

SIZE: 3.3 feet (1 meter) SH; 88 pounds (40 kilograms)

DIET: Herbivore; browse-dominated mixed feeder

ESSENTIAL FACTS: Named for its curved, lyre-shaped horns, this species inhabited wetlands in eastern Africa, where it primarily fed on plants that grew in or near the water. Its fossils having been found in Ethiopia.

SIVACOBUS PATULICORNIS

NAME MEANING: Shiva's Kobus with spreading horns

AGE: Pliocene to Pleistocene

DISTRIBUTION: Eurasia

SIZE: Unknown

DIET: Herbivore

ESSENTIAL FACTS: Members of the genus *Sivacobus* are the only known reduncine to have lived outside of Africa. Like their African relatives they were associated with well-watered habitats.

CAPRINAE

Goat antelopes typically have relatively stocky bodies, and many are adapted to high altitudes. Sheep, goats, and musk-oxen are members of this group. They first appear during the Late Miocene, with early representatives resembling modern serow (*Capricornis*). They are among the only bovids to reach North America.

MYOTRAGUS BALEARICUS

NAME MEANING: Baleric mouse-goat

AGE: Pleistocene to Holocene

DISTRIBUTION: Mallorca, Menorca

SIZE: 1.6 feet (50 centimeters) SH; 51–71 pounds (23–32 kilograms)

DIET: Herbivore; browse-dominated mixed feeder

ESSENTIAL FACTS: This dwarfed island species had particularly short legs with partially fused foot bones, making it relatively slow-moving with a reduced ability to jump. Accompanied by reduced senses, it may have evolved with a relative absence of predators.

BOOTHERIUM BOMBIFRONS

NAME MEANING: High-fronted ox beast

AGE: Pleistocene

DISTRIBUTION: North America

SIZE: 934 pounds (423.5 kilograms)

DIET: Herbivore; mixed feeder

ESSENTIAL FACTS: The Woodland Muskox was taller, leaner, and more adapted for life in less frigid climates than its modern relative, the tundra muskox (*Ovibos moschatus*). Its distribution covered nearly the entire North American continent, absent only from Mexico and the southeastern states.

EUCERATHERIUM COLLINUM

NAME MEANING: True horned beast of the hills

AGE: Pleistocene

DISTRIBUTION: North America

SIZE: 1,339 pounds (607.5 kilograms)

DIET: Herbivore; browser

ESSENTIAL FACTS: The Shrub Ox diet is known thanks to preserved dung pellets found in cave deposits, showing that it was a browser that fed on various trees and shrubs with a particular liking for berries. It seems to have preferred relatively rugged terrain or elevated terrain.

MAKAPANIA BROOMI

NAME MEANING: Broom's (goat) from Makapansgat

AGE: Pliocene to Holocene

DISTRIBUTION: Africa

SIZE: 579 pounds (263 kilograms)

DIET: Herbivore

ESSENTIAL FACTS: Broom's Musk Ox represents the oldest and one of the few caprine bovid known to have occurred in Africa. Today, the Barbary sheep (*Ammotragus lervia*) is the only one native to the continent and is limited to the north of the Sahara. Fossils of the Broom's Musk Ox are known from cave deposits.

MEGALOVIS LATIFRONS

NAME MEANING: Broad-fronted great sheep

AGE: Pliocene to Pleistocene

DISTRIBUTION: Eurasia

SIZE: 1,000 pounds (454 kilograms)

DIET: Herbivore

ESSENTIAL FACTS: Despite being the size of an ox, the skull of this animal notably resembled that of a goral (*Nemorhaedus*). They were grazers that inhabited open environments on rocky or hilly terrain.

TSAIDAMOTHERIUM HEDINI

NAME MEANING: Sven Hedin's beast from the Qaidam Basin

AGE: Late Miocene

DISTRIBUTION: Eurasia

SIZE: About sheep-sized

DIET: Herbivore; grazer

ESSENTIAL FACTS: This species is best known for its unusual, uneven horns in which the left horn core is several times larger than the right. Its enlarged nasal passages would help warm and moisten incoming air during inhalation similar to the saiga (*Saiga tartarica*).

ALCELAPHINAE

Alcelaphines were large, cursorial grazing antelopes adapted to life on open country. They first appear during the Late Miocene. All ten of the modern species are confined to Africa.

DAMALISCUS HYPSODON

NAME MEANING: High-toothed deer

AGE: Pleistocene

DISTRIBUTION: Africa

SIZE: 88–168 pounds (40–76 kilograms)

DIET: Herbivore; grazer

ESSENTIAL FACTS: Described in 2012, the High-crowned Damalisk is one of the smallest alcelaphines known to have ever lived. As its name implies, the degree of hypsodonty exhibited in this species is even greater than that of its modern relatives, suggesting a specialized diet of abrasive plants in open arid grasslands.

DAMALBOREA ELISABETHAE

NAME MEANING: Elisabeth Vrba's deer of the north

AGE: Pliocene

DISTRIBUTION: Africa

SIZE: About deer-sized

DIET: Herbivore; grazer

ESSENTIAL FACTS: Elisabeth's Antelope was a medium-sized alcelaphine with almost straight, relatively thin horns. It's long-legged, lightly built body was adapted for fast running on flat, open terrain.

DAMALOPS PALAEINDICUS

NAME MEANING: Ancient Indian deer-like (antelope)

AGE: Pliocene to Pleistocene

DISTRIBUTION: Eurasia

SIZE: About deer-sized

DIET: Herbivore; grazer

ESSENTIAL FACTS: Known from the Siwalik Hills of India, this species is one of the few alcelaphines known from outside of Africa. Like its modern relatives, it was a cursorial animal adapted to life on the open plains, where it grazed on short grasses.

MEGALOTRAGUS PRISCUS

NAME MEANING: Ancient great goat

AGE: Pleistocene to Holocene

DISTRIBUTION: Africa

SIZE: 5 feet (1.5 meters) SH; 9.1 feet (2.8 meters) HBL; 660 pounds (300 kilograms)

DIET: Herbivore; grazer

ESSENTIAL FACTS: This species was built somewhat like modern wildebeests (*Connochaetes*) but much larger. The Ancient Megalotragus had a lack of inflation in its nasal region and much longer, curving horns compared to the other two species of its genus, and was also the latest-surviving member, with the youngest material dated to 7,500 years ago.

NUMIDOCAPRA CRASSICORNIS

NAME MEANING: Thick-horned Numidian goat

AGE: Pleistocene

DISTRIBUTION: Herbivore; grazer

SIZE: 550 pounds (250 kilograms)

DIET: Herbivore

ESSENTIAL FACTS: The largest member of its genus, this species had upright horns that curved forward. When first described in 1949, it was thought to have been a goat antelope within the subfamily Caprinae before it was later recognized as part of Alcelaphinae.

RUSINGORYX ATOPOCRANION

NAME MEANING: Rusinga Island antelope with disarranged skull

AGE: Pleistocene

DISTRIBUTION: Africa

SIZE: 286-550 pounds (130-250 kilograms)

DIET: Herbivore; grazer

ESSENTIAL FACTS: Formerly placed within the genus *Megalotragus*, the Bellowing Antelope is characterized by its highly domed nasals which amplified its vocalizations, similar to the crests of hadrosaurid dinosaurs. It was a specialized grazer that lived in arid grasslands.

HOPLITOMERYCIDAE

This family contains several species within the genus *Hoplitomeryx*, which evolved in isolation on the island of Gargano, today part of the eastern coast of Italy. The closest relatives of these animals is unknown, hence their placement within their own family, but they share features in common with musk deer (Moschdae) and boselaphine bovids (Bovidae).

HOPLITOMERYX MATTHEI

NAME MEANING: Matthe's heavily armed ruminant

AGE: Late Miocene

DISTRIBUTION: Gargano Island

SIZE: About goat-sized

DIET: Herbivore

ESSENTIAL FACTS: Commonly known as the Prongdeer, this unusual island ruminant possessed five horns on its head: a larger and shorter pair above the eyes, and a single horn in the middle of the skull just in front of the eyes. They also had elongated upper canines similar to those of musk deer (Moschidae).

CETACEA

Cetaceans are marine mammals that evolved from artiodactyls during the Early Eocene, their closest modern relatives being hippos (Hippopotamidae). This discovery has led some authors to lump the Cetacea and Artiodactyla into a single common order known as "Cetartiodactyla." Cetaceans themselves are the most diverse and the most specialized of all marine mammals, represented by thirteen modern families with almost ninety species between them. They range in size from the 3.3-foot (1-meter) long, 110-pound (50-kilogram) Hector's Dolphin (*Cephalorhynchus hectori*) to the 100-foot (30-meter) long, 418,874-pound (190,000-kilogram) blue whale (*Balaenoptera musculus*), the largest mammal known to have ever lived.

ARCHAEOCETI

The first whales belong to the clade archaeoceti, a group which lasted from the Early Eocene to the Early Oligocene. Contained within this group are the families Pakicetidae, Ambulocetidae, Remingtonocetidae, and Protocetidae, all of which are sometimes informally referred to as the "walking whales" because they retained well-developed limbs with webbed toes that enabled terrestrial locomotion to varying degrees of efficiency depending on the family. Members of these families filled the niches that otters and pinnipeds occupy today. Members of the family Basilosauridae were fully aquatic cetaceans and are directly ancestral to all of today's species.

PAKICETIDAE

The Early Eocene pakicetids were still very much tied to land and would have been ecologically comparable to modern otters. Their fossils are found in ancient river and lake deposits in India and Pakistan, but none found in marine environments, suggesting they were confined to freshwater ecosystems. They had osteosclerotic bones that provided ballast, enabling them to walk and run along the bottom without floating to the surface, switching to a foot-propelled swimming method when they needed to chase prey.

ICHTHYOLESTES PINFOLDI

NAME MEANING: Pionfold's fish thief

AGE: Early Eocene (50 MYA)

DISTRIBUTION: Eurasia

SIZE: 3.3 feet (1 meter) HBL

DIET: Aquatic hypercarnivore

ESSENTIAL FACTS: Although it is the first pakicetid to be described, this species was not recognized as a cetacean on its initial discovery, instead being placed among the Mesonychia. Its fossils have been found in river deposits in Pakistan and it utilized bottom-walking and swam with undulations of its spine and thrusts of its hindfeet.

PAKICETUS ATTOCKI

NAME MEANING: Pakistani whale from the Attock District

AGE: Early Eocene (50–48 MYA)

DISTRIBUTION: Eurasia

SIZE: 3.3 feet (1 meter) HBL

DIET: Aquatic hypercarnivore

SEE MORE ON PAGES 752–753

AMBULOCETIDAE

Ambulocetids were even more specialized for aquatic life, being the first cetaceans to be able to inhabit saltwater environments. Named for the genus *Ambulocetus*, which means "walking whale," these cetaceans would have spent most of their lives in water coming ashore only to breed, give birth, and rest. There are three species in three genera, all restricted to the Middle Eocene of Pakistan.

AMBULOCETUS NATANS

NAME MEANING: Swimming walking whale

AGE: Middle Eocene (48–47 MYA)

DISTRIBUTION: Eurasia

SIZE: 6.6 feet (2 meters) HBL; 3.3 feet (1 meter) TL; 660 pounds (300 kilograms)

DIET: Aquatic hypercarnivore

SEE MORE ON PAGES 754–755

REMINGTONOCETIDAE

The remingtonocetids appear to have lived exclusively in saltwater environments, their fossils being found in estuarine and marine environments and may have been ecologically comparable to seals. They are characterized by long, low bodies with short limbs. The skull makes up to one-third of the total head-and-body length, and the snout is particularly long and narrow with flattened teeth adapted for rapid snapping, similar to gharials. The nostrils were located at the tip of the snout. Despite having long tails, they were still foot-propelled swimmers that used undulations of the spine combined with powerful thrusts of the hindfeet. The swimming stroke was made even more efficient with fused sacrums, powerful muscles connecting to the pelvis and lumbar region, and mobile hip joints. They are known to have lived from the Early to Middle Eocene.

KUTCHICETUS MINIMUS

NAME MEANING: Little whale from Kachchh

AGE: Middle Eocene (46–43 MYA)

DISTRIBUTION: Eurasia

SIZE: 176–330 pounds (80–150 kilograms)

DIET: Marine hypercarnivore

ESSENTIAL FACTS: Kutchicetus is the smallest-known of the remingtonocetids, comparable in size to small seals of the genus *Pusa*. A mounted skeleton on display at the National Museum of Nature and Science, Tokyo.

PAKICETUS ATTOCKI

ESSENTIAL FACTS: The countries of India and Pakistan appear to have been the staging ground for early cetacean evolution, as most non-basilosaurid archaeocetes have been discovered in the region. Earliest of them all, the genus Pakicetus is named for the country of Pakistan, where its fossils were first discovered in 1980. Members of *Pakicetus* differed from raoellids like *Indohyus* in having an elongated, vaguely crocodilian-looking skull with conical incisors and triangular premolars adapted for piercing and gripping struggling prey; the diet was overall more carnivorous. The eyes were situated at the top of the skull, and the digits were splayed with webbing for propulsion. Aside from these differences, pakicetids inherited from their raoellid ancestors their specialized inner ear anatomy that enabled underwater hearing, osteosclerotic bones, and a diagnostic artiodactyl astragalus.

Based on the placement of its eyes, Attock's Pakicetus may have hunted by walking along the bottom, weighed down by its dense bones. When prey was spotted from its low vantage point, it would lunge upward to pursue it, swimming by combining up-and-down undulations of its spine with thrusts from its hindfeet as demonstrated by modern beavers (*Castor*) and the Russian desman (*Desmana moschata*). To steer, it would rely on movements of its head and neck and forelimbs. While still reasonably mobile on land, its broad feet and heavy bones would have made Attock's Pakicetus rather inefficient and unable to run at speed for long distances, making it unlikely to have ventured very far from the shoreline. A mounted skeleton is on display at the Canadian Museum of Nature.

SEE ENTRY ON PAGE 750

AMBULOCETUS NATANS

ESSENTIAL FACTS: Ambulocetus is known from a nearly complete skeleton discovered in 1992 in Pakistan. Compared to the earlier pakicetids, Ambulocetus had a larger and more robust skull and larger teeth for capturing relatively larger prey. The body was overall more robust with shorter legs which would have limited its movement on land. The hindlimbs were powerful and longer than the forelimbs, with particularly large feet serving as its primary means of propulsion. The living animal would have looked even more like a mammalian crocodile. Its eyes were still set on top of the skull as seen in the pakicetids, implying a similar hunting method.

Isotopic evidence shows that Ambulocetus was able to inhabit both freshwater and saltwater environments, perhaps most commonly occurring in mangroves and estuaries at the mouths of rivers and occasionally moving inland or out to sea, depending on the circumstance. It was a powerful aquatic predator armed with sturdy jaws and teeth. Its diet would have included larger fish such as catfish and small sharks, along with aquatic reptiles, and other aquatic mammals such as sirenians and anthracobunids. Ambulocetus is by far the most famous and well-known of the Ambulocetidae, first rising to prominence in its appearance in the 2001 documentary *Walking with Beasts*. Casts of the original holotype skeleton are featured in museum exhibits around the world.

SEE ENTRY ON PAGE 751

ANDREWSIPHIUS SLOANI

NAME MEANING: Robert E. Sloan's Andrews

AGE: Middle Eocene (47.8–41.2 MYA)

DISTRIBUTION: Eurasia

SIZE: 10.8 feet (3.3 meters)

DIET: Marine hypercarnivore

ESSENTIAL FACTS: Fossils of Andrewsiphius are known from India and Pakistan and include a nearly complete skull that is missing the end of the snout. Compared to Kuchicetus its teeth were more durable with stronger jaws and more robust tail vertebrae.

RAYANISTES AFER

NAME MEANING: African whale from Wadi El-Rayan

AGE: Middle Eocene (45–41 MYA)

DISTRIBUTION: Africa

SIZE: Unknown

DIET: Marine hypercarnivore

ESSENTIAL FACTS: The discovery of Rayanistes fossils in Egypt has broadened the known distribution of remingtonocetids, which are otherwise only known from India and Pakistan. It seems to have had a specialized mode of locomotion with particularly robust hindlimbs, an expanded ischium, and enhanced lumbar flexibility.

REMINGTONOCETUS HARUDIENSIS

NAME MEANING: Remington Kellogg's whale from the Harudi Formation

AGE: Middle Eocene (45–43.5 MYA)

DISTRIBUTION: Eurasia

SIZE: 437–500 pounds (198–227 kilograms)

DIET: Marine hypercarnivore

ESSENTIAL FACTS: The type genus of the family Remingtonocetidae, this animal is named after naturalist Remington Kellogg, who specialized in marine mammals. It is known for a complete skull, unique among its family, and may have utilized a different hunting method.

DALANISTES AHMEDI

NAME MEANING: From Dalana Nala and Basti Ahmed

AGE: Middle Eocene (48.6–40.4 MYA)

DISTRIBUTION: Eurasia

SIZE: 1,265–1,653 pounds (574–750 kilograms)

DIET: Marine hypercarnivore

ESSENTIAL FACTS: Known from India and Pakistan, Dalanites is the largest-known remingtonocetid. It is adapted to hunt in marine environments far from shore and had a particularly robust skull with strong jaws.

PROTOCETIDAE

Members of these families filled out the niches that seals and sea lions occupy today: spending most of their lives at sea and returning to land only to rest and breed. They are the first cetaceans known to have distributions outside of southern Asia and northern Africa, with fossils having been discovered in North America and South America. Overall, they were more robust than remingtonocetids with their nostrils located above the canines instead of at the tip.

MAIACETUS INUUS

NAME MEANING: Mother whale of Inuus

AGE: Middle Eocene (47.5 MYA)

DISTRIBUTION: Eurasia

SIZE: 8.5 feet (2.6 meters); 620–860 pounds (280–390 kilograms)

DIET: Marine hypercarnivore

ESSENTIAL FACTS: Maiacetus is named for a specimen of a pregnant female. The fetal skeleton inside is positioned for a headfirst birth, suggesting that these animals return to land to give birth. Modern cetaceans are born tailfirst to ensure the newborn does not drown during delivery. The species references Inuus, a Roman god of fecundity.

RODHOCETUS KASRANI

NAME MEANING: Rhodo whale of the Qaisrani

AGE: Middle Eocene (47–46 MYA)

DISTRIBUTION: Eurasia

SIZE: 6.6–9.8 feet (2–3 meters)

DIET: Marine hypercarnivore

ESSENTIAL FACTS: Rodhocetus had trunk and limb proportions similar to that of the Russian desman (*Desmana moschata*), a foot-powered swimmer using its tail mainly as a rudder. The species name honors the Qaisrani, the Baloch tribe inhabiting the type locality.

PEREGOCETUS PACIFICUS

NAME MEANING: Traveling whale that reached the Pacific Ocean

AGE: Middle Eocene (42.6 MYA)

DISTRIBUTION: South America

SIZE: 13.1 feet (4 meters)

DIET: Marine hypercarnivore

ESSENTIAL FACTS: Discovered in 2011 and described in 2019 in Peru, Peregocetus is the first walking whale known from the Pacific Ocean and the Southern Hemisphere. Its discovery shows that protocetids attained a near global distribution. The tail was flattened for added propulsion.

PROTOCETUS ATAVUS

NAME MEANING: Ancestral first whale

AGE: Middle Eocene (45–43.5 MYA)

DISTRIBUTION: Africa

SIZE: 8.2 feet (2.5 meters)

DIET: Marine hypercarnivore

ESSENTIAL FACTS: Protocetus is the first protocetid to be discovered and the type genus for the family, described in 1904 based on a skull found in Egypt. The postcranial skeleton is unknown, but it is likely to have been a foot-propelled swimmer like most other protocetids.

GEORGIACETUS VOGTLENSIS

NAME MEANING: Georgia whale of the Plant Vogtle

AGE: Middle Eocene (46–43 MYA)

DISTRIBUTION: North America

SIZE: 11.5 feet (3.5 meters)

DIET: Marine hypercarnivore

ESSENTIAL FACTS: Georgiacetus was discovered in 1983 during the construction of the nuclear power plant Plant Vogtle in Burke County, Georgia. Its fossils have since been found in Alabama and Mississippi. Its powerful jaws and teeth were adapted to seize, hold, and process relatively large prey items.

AEGICETUS GEHENNAE

NAME MEANING: Shield whale from Hell

AGE: Late Eocene (35 MYA)

DISTRIBUTION: Africa

SIZE: 1,960 pounds (890 kilograms)

DIET: Marine hypercarnivore

ESSENTIAL FACTS: Aegicetus had larger and more powerful vertebrae than other protocetids, showing that it was transitioning from a foot-propelled swimming method to a tail-propelled one. In fact, its ability to move on land was reduced, due to the lack of a firm sacroiliac joint and reduction of the hindfeet. It is known to have coexisted with basilosaurids.

BASILOSAURIDAE

Basilosaurids were the first fully aquatic cetaceans which possessed many of the key adaptations retained by all modern forms: streamlined bodies, forelimbs which had become modified into flippers, highly reduced hindlimbs, and powerful tails which ended with horizontal flukes for propulsion. As seen in protocetids, the nostrils were located above the canine. The modern whale groups, Odontoceti (toothed whales) and Mysteceti (baleen whales) diverged from basilosaurid ancestors around the Eocene-Oligocene boundary and all three suborders coexisted for a brief time. Indeed, early representatives of these groups shared several features with their basilosaurid contemporaries: most notably in having well-developed heterodont dentition.

TUTCETUS RAYANENSIS

NAME MEANING: King Tut's whale from Wadi El-Rayan

AGE: Late Eocene (41 MYA)

DISTRIBUTION: Atlantic Ocean

SIZE: 8.1 feet (2.5 meters); 398–412 pounds (180–187 kilograms)

DIET: Marine hypercarnivore

ESSENTIAL FACTS: Discovered in the Fayum Depression of Egypt and described in 2023, Tutcetus is the oldest and smallest member of Basilosauridae.

DORUDONTINAE

Dorudontines were small- to medium-sized stout-bodied cetaceans that were adapted to hunt in open ocean habitats. They were probably similar to modern dolphins (Delphinidae) in terms of their ecology and many of their behaviors.

DORUDON ATROX

NAME MEANING: Cruel spear tooth

AGE: Late Eocene (40–34 MYA)

DISTRIBUTION: Atlantic Ocean

SIZE: 16 feet (5 meters); 1–2 tons

DIET: Marine hypercarnivore

SEE MORE ON PAGES 762–763

CYNTHIACETUS MAXWELLI

NAME MEANING: Maxwell's and Cynthia's whale

AGE: Late Eocene (40–34 MYA)

DISTRIBUTION: Atlantic Ocean, Pacific Ocean

SIZE: 29.5 feet (9 meters)

DIET: Marine hypercarnivore

ESSENTIAL FACTS: Two species of *Cynthiacetus* are known from marine deposits in North America and South America, where they coexisted with Owen's Basilosaurus (*Basilosaurus cetoides*). The skull is similar in size to that of *Basilosaurus*, but it was notably much shorter due to its more compressed vertebrae.

ZYGORHIZA KOCHII

NAME MEANING: Kochi's yoke root

AGE: Late Eocene (39–34 MYA)

DISTRIBUTION: Atlantic Ocean

SIZE: 17 feet (5.2 meters); 7,388 ponds (3,351 kilograms)

DIET: Marine hypercarnivore

ESSENTIAL FACTS: Described in 1847, Zygorhiza is one of the first basilosaurids known from North America, second to Owen's Basilosaurus (*Basilosaurus cetoides*) described in 1839. The mounted specimen in the Macon Museum of Arts and Sciences in Macon, Georgia, is nicknamed "Ziggy."

SAGHACETUS OSIRIS

NAME MEANING: Osiris whale of the Qasr el Sagha Formation

AGE: Late Eocene (37.2–34 MYA)

DISTRIBUTION: Atlantic Ocean

SIZE: 13 feet (4 meters); 772–836 pounds (350–379 kilograms)

DIET: Marine hypercarnivore

ESSENTIAL FACTS: The genus is named after the Qasr el Sagha Formation, which is just a few kilometers away from the Wadi Al-Hitan (Valley of the Whales) fossil locality. The size of a bottlenose dolphin (*Tursiops truncates*), this whale is the smallest of the dorudontine basilosaurids with a proportionally long tail.

DORUDON ATROX

ESSENTIAL FACTS: Andrews' Dorudon was described by Charles William Andrews in 1906 based on abundant material from the Wadi Al-Hitan fossil site located in northern Egypt. Called "Valley of the Whales" in English, this locality is famous for its abundance of fossils of basilosaurid whales, most notably Andrews' Dorudon and Andrews' Basilosaurus (*Basilosaurus isis*), along with two other whale species, three sirenians, and the proboscidean Lyon's Moeritherium (*Moeritherium lyonsi*). During the time of deposition the site was a shallow sea environment with abundant sea grasses and a nearby mangrove. Much about the anatomy and paleobiology of these animals has been uncovered based on the findings from this site.

The size of a large dolphin, Andrews' Dorudon was a swift-swimming predator whose diet would have consisted mostly of fish, evidenced by preserved stomach contents found in the rib cages of some skeletons. It likely spent most of its time hunting in the open ocean but would return to shallow coastal waters to give birth to their young. In such areas, newborn individuals were vulnerable to predation from the much larger Andrews' Basilosaurus and sharks.

SEE ENTRY ON PAGE 760

BASILOSAURINAE

Basilosaurines are notably long-bodied basilosaurines with lengthened vertebrae, which would have given them a stretched out, almost serpentine appearance in life.

BASILOTERUS HUSSEINI

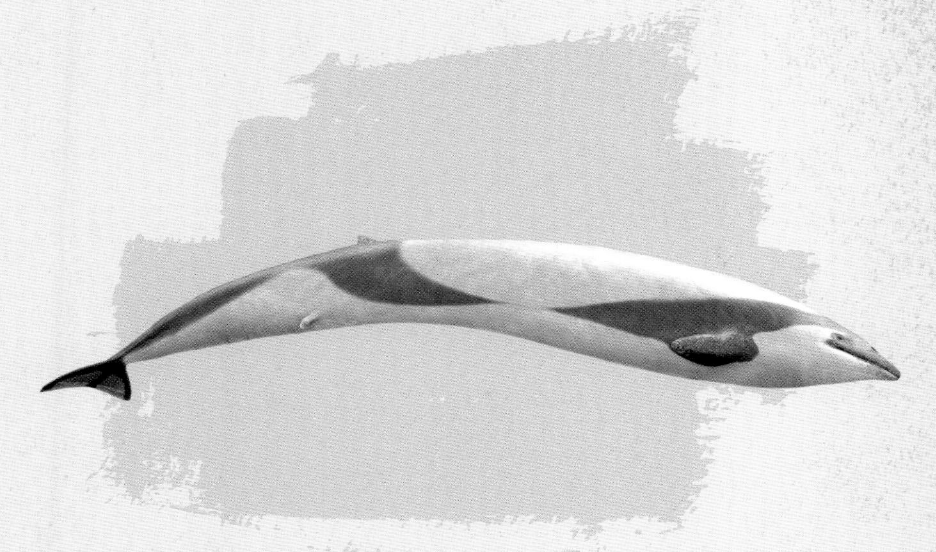

NAME MEANING: Taseer Hussain's other king

AGE: Early Eocene (40 MYA)

DISTRIBUTION: Eurasia

SIZE: Unknown

DIET: Marine hypercarnivore

ESSENTIAL FACTS: This species is known only from two isolated lumbar vertebrae that show similar elongation to the better-known genus *Basilosaurus*, which inspired the genus name. This morphological similarity implies a close relation between the two genera, however this remains inconclusive due to lack of skeletal material.

BASILOSAURUS ISIS

NAME MEANING: King lizard of Isis

AGE: Late Eocene (38–34 MYA)

DISTRIBUTION: Atlantic Ocean

SIZE: 49–59 feet (15–18 meters)

DIET: Marine hypercarnivore

SEE MORE ON PAGES 766–767

BASILOSAURUS CETOIDES

NAME MEANING: Whale-like king lizard

AGE: Late Eocene (38–34 MYA)

DISTRIBUTION: Atlantic Ocean

SIZE: 49–59 feet (15–18 meters)

DIET: Marine hypercarnivore

ESSENTIAL FACTS: Slightly younger than the more well-known Andrews' Basilosaurus (*B. isis*), Owen's Basilosaurus was described first by Sir Richard Owen in 1839. Its fossils are known from the southeastern United States, and the remains of large bony fish and sharks have been found among its stomach contents.

PACHYCETINAE

The Pachycetinae are named for the genus Pachycetus, which means "thick whale," a reference to the unusual dense bones of these whales. Pachycetines differ from dorudontines in having elongated posterior thoracic and lumbar vertebrae like those of *Basilosaurus*. However they differ from both basilosaurines and dorudontines in having pachy-osteosclerotic vertebrae with dense and thickly laminated cortical bone surrounding a cancellous core, very much like those of sirenians. Because of their dense vertebrae, pachycetines have been inferred to be slow swimmers that lived in shallow coastal waters much like sirenians, feeding on passing fish and mobile invertebrates.

PERUCETUS COLOSSUS

NAME MEANING: Colossal Peruvian whale

AGE: Late Eocene (39–37 MYA)

DISTRIBUTION: South America

SIZE: 55–66 feet (17–20 meters), 120,000–140,000 pounds (54,431–63,502 kilograms)

DIET: Marine hypercarnivore

ESSENTIAL FACTS: Described in 2023, Perucetus was among the heaviest animals known, with incredibly thick and dense bones. All that is known for this species are a few vertebrae, partial ribs, and a pelvis so its life appearance is speculative, but it is often reconstructed with a thick, manatee-like body.

BASILOSAURUS ISIS

ESSENTIAL FACTS: Described by Charles William Andrews in 1904 from material recovered from Wadi Al-Hitan. The species is named for the Egyptian goddess Isis. The abundant skeletal remains of this species provide a unique look into the predator's anatomy and behavior. Its fossils were also broadly distributed throughout northern Africa. Andrew's Basilosaurus had the characteristic elongated skeleton which characterizes the basilosaurines. Its bite force is among the strongest estimated for any mammal. The skull was asymmetrical like those of modern toothed-whales, implying an acute sense of hearing and a complex range of vocalizations. Males are known to have been 20 percent larger than the females.

Evidence of a predator-prey relationship between Andrews Basilosaurus and Andrews Dorudon (*Dorudon atrox*) is observed at the Egyptian fossil site of Wadi Al-Hitan. The site is believed to have been a calving ground for the smaller whale, which was opportunistically visited by local predators to hunt the juveniles. This inference is supported by the high number of subadult Andrews' Dorudon with toothmarks on their bones matching the teeth of Andrews' Basilosaurus. Newborn specimens measuring 4.9–6.5 feet (1.5–2 meters) long have also been found among the stomach contents of Andrews' Basilosaurus. Based on the placement of toothmarks, Andrews' Basilosaurus appears to have dispatched larger prey items with a bite to the head after attacking it from the side or from below. Other stomach contents include large bony fish and sharks.

SEE ENTRY ON PAGE 764

ANTAECETUS AITHAI

NAME MEANING: Aitha's whale of Antaios

AGE: Middle Eocene

DISTRIBUTION: Atlantic Ocean

SIZE: Unknown

DIET: Marine hypercarnivore

ESSENTIAL FACTS: Aitha's Whale is known from a skull and much of an associated axial skeleton discovered in Morrocco and described in 2015. Compared to *Pachycetus*, its skull is proportionally smaller and the teeth were also smaller and more gracile, implying a focus on relatively smaller prey items.

KEKENODONTIDAE

Kekenodonts are a late-surviving group of archaeocetes known from the Late Oligocene of New Zealand. Members within the group have been classified within Mysticeti and Odontoceti at various points, but they lack the defining characteristics of either group. Rather, these whales appear to be morphologically intermediate between basilosaurids and the early mysticetes.

KEKENODON ONAMATA

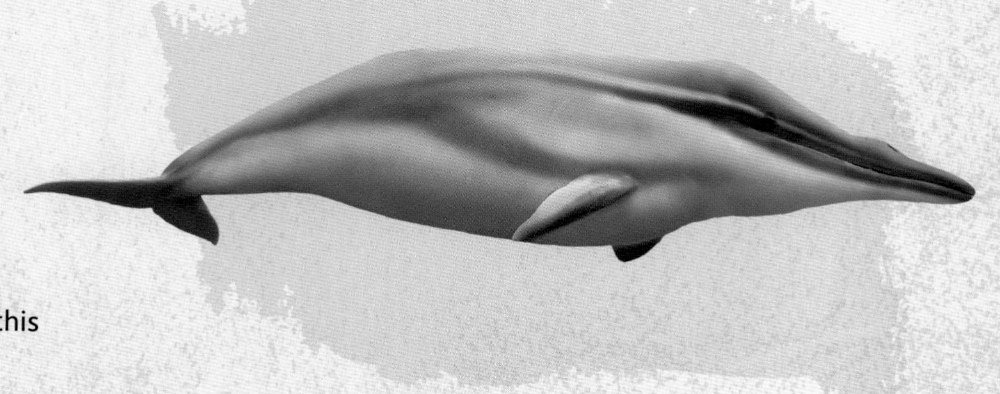

NAME MEANING: Seal tooth from long ago

AGE: Late Oligocene

DISTRIBUTION: Pacific Ocean

SIZE: 26–30 feet (8–9 meters)

DIET: Marine hypercarnivore

ESSENTIAL FACTS: Discovered in New Zealand and originally described in 1881, the full scientific name of this whale is derived from the Māori language.

TOHORAONEPU NIHOKAIWAIU

NAME MEANING: Sand whale with baby teeth

AGE: Late Oligocene

DISTRIBUTION: Pacific Ocean

SIZE: Unknown for adult

DIET: Marine hypercarnivore

ESSENTIAL FACTS: Derived from the Māori language, the species name references the deciduous teeth of the juvenile that was the holotype described in 2024. This discovery is the first record of diphyodonty in cetaceans later than the Eocene.

MYSTICETI

The Mysticeti contains the largest of all cetaceans and, indeed, the largest of all mammals. Mysticetes are unique among the cetaceans in that they feed by filtering small prey animals in bulk from the surrounding water using baleen plates: dual rows of keratin bristles that protrude down from either side of the palate, resembling a pair of massive brushes. When feeding, these whales take in large volumes of water that contain clusters of an intended prey item. The water is then pushed out the sides of the partially opened mouth by pressing the tongue against the palate, leaving the prey trapped against the baleen plates to be swallowed. The earliest mysticetes have been suggested to have employed suction-feeding as a precursor to filter-feeding, which involves the rapid expanding of the oral cavity, creating a pressure difference between the inside of the mouth and the surrounding water, pulling in nearby prey items. This technique is used by modern beaked whales, which are mostly toothless. All cetaceans are generally highly vocal animals, but mysticetes are known for producing complex vocalizations known as "songs" during breeding season. These songs vary in complexity from one species to another, may be heard for hundreds of kilometers away, and tend to be region specific: individuals of the same species from different parts of the ocean have noticeable dialects or accents.

LLANOCETIDAE

Llanocetids have similar heterodont dentition to that of archaeocetes, but the teeth and jaws were weaker and not suited to cutting prey. Compared to the contemporary basilosaurids, the skulls were flatter, broader, and capable of expansion upon opening. They relied on suction-feeding to pull in bulk quantities of relatively small prey items when opening their mouths before pushing out the excess water through the sides of the mouth while leaving the prey behind for swallowing. Although the teeth were reduced, they were heavily notched like those of the modern Crabeater Seal (*Lobodon carcinophaga*), adapted to trap prey in their mouths and sieve out the water. The nostrils had also begun to migrate farther back on the skull.

MYSTACODON SELENENSIS

NAME MEANING: Selene's mustached whale

AGE: Late Eocene (36.4 MYA)

DISTRIBUTION: South America

SIZE: 12–13 feet (3.8–4 meters)

DIET: Marine hypercarnivore

ESSENTIAL FACTS: This species is the oldest known mysticete. Based on the proportions of its forelimbs, Mystacodon is thought to have been a relatively slow-moving whale that fed at the seafloor, sifting through mouthfuls of sand for the small animals hidden within.

LLANOCETUS DENTICRENATUS

NAME MEANING: Llano's notch-toothed whale

AGE: Late Eocene (35 MYA)

DISTRIBUTION: Antarctica

SIZE: Unknown for adult

DIET: Marine hypercarnivore

ESSENTIAL FACTS: In addition to being one of the oldest, Llanocetus is the first of the truly large mysticetes. The only known material is of a juvenile specimen that measured an estimated 26 feet (8 meters) in life, already the size of the average adult minke whale (*Balaenoptera acutorostrata*)! The adult form was potentially much larger.

CORONODONTIDAE

Coronodontidae was an early offshoot of the baleen whale lineage. In general appearance, coronodontids were very similar to dorudontine basilosaurids, from which it most likely descended. The incisors were caniniform and adapted for gripping prey such as larger fish and cephalopods, and the cheek teeth retained the jagged triangular shape. At the same time, they had broad skulls that were capable of slight expansion, suggesting that they were capable of suction-feeding.

CORONODON HAVENSTEINI

NAME MEANING: Havenstein's crown tooth

AGE: Early Oligocene (30–25 MYA)

DISTRIBUTION: Atlantic Ocean

SIZE: 16 feet (4.9 meters); 2,540 pounds (1,150 kilograms)

DIET: Marine hypercarnivore

ESSENTIAL FACTS: Havenstein's Coronodon was described in 2017 based on fossils found in South Carolina. It was an active predator with suction-feeding capabilities. Two additional *Coronodon* species were described in 2023: Newton's Coronodon (*C. newtonorum*) and Flat-headed Coronodon (*C. planifrons*).

MAMMALODONTIDAE

Mammalodont fossils are so far only known from the Late Oligocene of Australia and New Zealand. They are characterized by their short, broad faces with widely spaced teeth that are reduced in number, although incisors, premolars, and molars were still recognizable. The cheek teeth retain their triangular, serrated shape from their basilosaurid ancestors.

MAMMALODON COLLIVERI

NAME MEANING: Stanley Colliver's mammal tooth

AGE: Late Oligocene (25.6–23.9 MYA)

DISTRIBUTION: Australia and New Zealand

SIZE: 10 feet (3 meters)

DIET: Marine hypercarnivore

ESSENTIAL FACTS: A small whale with a notably short, broad face with widely spaced teeth, this species may have fed by sifting small animals from the sand on the seafloor.

JANJUCETUS HUNDERI

NAME MEANING: Staumn Hunder's whale of Jan Juc

AGE: Late Oligocene (25 MYA)

DISTRIBUTION: Australia

SIZE: 11 feet (3.6 meters)

DIET: Marine hypercarnivore

ESSENTIAL FACTS: In contrast to other mysticetes, Janjucetus had strong jaws and sturdy teeth adapted to handle relatively large prey items. The species had relatively large eyes perhaps adapted to nocturnal hunting.

AETIOCETIDAE

Aetiocetids are the first whales to possess baleen, evidenced by the presence of paired grooves in the palate called "nutrient foramina," from which the baleen plates grow in modern mysticetes. These were used in combination with their still functional teeth. They are therefore the first mysticetes to accurately be called "baleen whales," the common term used for modern members of the suborder.

AETIOCETUS WELTONI

NAME MEANING: Bruce Welton's original whale

AGE: Late Oligocene (25–23 MYA)

DISTRIBUTION: Pacific Ocean

SIZE: 20 feet (6 meters)

DIET: Marine hypercarnivore; filter-feeder

ESSENTIAL FACTS: *Aetiocetus* retained widely spaced, weak teeth, but also possess nutrient foramina, indicating the presence of baleen. Thus, these whales represent the early transition from teeth to baleen.

FUCAIA BUELLI

NAME MEANING: Carl Buell from the Strait of Juan de Fuca

AGE: Early Oligocene (33–31 MYA)

DISTRIBUTION: North America; Pacific Ocean

SIZE: 10 feet (3 meters)

DIET: Marine hypercarnivore; filter-feeder

ESSENTIAL FACTS: Containing two species described in 2015, members of the genus *Fucaia* are among the smallest-known mysticetes, comparable in size to the smallest modern odontocetes. Both are known from western North America.

ASHOROCETUS EGUCHII

NAME MEANING: Kenichiro Eguchi's whale of Ashoro

AGE: Late Oligocene (30 MYA)

DISTRIBUTION: Pacific Ocean

SIZE: 26 feet (8 meters)

DIET: Marine hypercarnivore; filter-feeder

ESSENTIAL FACTS: Discovered in Hokkaido, Japan, near the town of Ashoro, this whale has been described as the most primitive of the aetiocetids.

EOMYSTICETIDAE

Eomysticetids are mostly known from the Late Oligocene of New Zealand, although at least one species has been identified from North America. Small tooth sockets are present in the skull and lower jaw, though it is possible that most or all teeth were lost during maturity. The skulls were less flexible than those of modern baleen whales but more flexible than those of earlier toothed mysticetes like the aetiocetids and llanocetids. The nostrils were also still positioned in front of the eyes.

EOMYSTICETUS WHITMOREI

NAME MEANING: Frank Whitmore's dawn mustached whale

AGE: Late Oligocene (24 MYA)

DISTRIBUTION: Atlantic Ocean

SIZE: 23 feet (7 meters)

DIET: Marine hypercarnivore; filter-feeder

ESSENTIAL FACTS: A five-foot (1.5-meter) skull and partial skeleton of this whale was discovered in the Chandler Bridge Formation of South Carolina in 1975 and described in 2002. The morphology of the forelimb and vertebrae still resembled those of archaeocetes.

TOHORAATA RAEKOHAO

NAME MEANING: Dawn whale with forehead holes

AGE: Late Oligocene (25 MYA)

DISTRIBUTION: New Zealand

SIZE: 26 feet (8 meters)

DIET: Marine hypercarnivore; filter-feeder

ESSENTIAL FACTS: Described in 2014, the discovery of this species confirmed the presence of eomysticetids in New Zealand. Derived from the Māori language, the genus name means "dawn whale," referencing the Greek translation of the genus *Eomysticetus*. The species name references the diagnostic pits in the frontal bones of this whale's skull.

TOKARAHIA KAUAEROA

NAME MEANING: Long jaw from Tokarahia

AGE: Late Oligocene (27.3–25.2 MYA)

DISTRIBUTION: New Zealand

SIZE: 26 feet (8 meters)

DIET: Marine hypercarnivore; filter-feeder

ESSENTIAL FACTS: The species name references the delicate, elongated skull and mandible of the holotype. Like other eomysticetids, this species was not able to employ the lunge-feeding strategy that modern balaenopterids use. Rather, it would rely on skim-feeding, passively swimming through concentrations of food with the mouth open.

YAMATOCETUS CANALICULATUS

NAME MEANING: Grooved whale of Yamato

AGE: Late Oligocene

DISTRIBUTION: Asia, Pacific Ocean

SIZE: Unknown

DIET: Marine hypercarnivore; filter-feeder

ESSENTIAL FACTS: A partial skeleton of Yamatocetus found in Kyushu, Japan, in 1981 and described in 2012. Based on its rigid rib cage, it was a surface dweller that relied on skim-feeding like modern right whales (Balaenidae) and its head was relatively blunt compared to other eomysticetids.

MATAPANUI WAIHAO

NAME MEANING: Large flat face from the Waihao river

AGE: Late Oligocene (28.1–27.3 MYA)

DISTRIBUTION: New Zealand

SIZE: 26 feet (8 meters)

DIET: Marine hypercarnivore; filter-feeder

ESSENTIAL FACTS: This species was discovered on Kokoamu Island, New Zealand. It was previously named *Matapa waihao* until it was discovered that the name Matapa was already in use by a genus of butterfly, necessitating a name change.

WAHAROA RUWHENUA

NAME MEANING: Long mouth of the shaking land

AGE: Late Oligocene (28.1–27.3 MYA)

DISTRIBUTION: New Zealand

SIZE: 16.4–19.7 feet (5–6 meters)

DIET: Marine hypercarnivore; filter-feeder

ESSENTIAL FACTS: This species is known for a juvenile skeleton described in 2015 in South Island, New Zealand. The species name references the locality in which it was discovered known as "The Earthquakes."

CETOTHERIIDAE

Cetotheres evolved during the Late Oligocene. The pygmy right whale (*Caperea marginata*) is the last surviving member of the family. Cetotheres were relatively small mysticetes that rarely exceeded 16 feet (5 meters) in length. They have osteoschlerotic skeletons for feeding on the seafloor with particularly broad and dense ribs like those seen in sirenians. Their tails are also relatively short, and the ear bone has a unique wrinkled texture.

CETOTHERIUM RIABININI

NAME MEANING: Riabinin's whale beast

AGE: Late Miocene

DISTRIBUTION: Atlantic Ocean

SIZE: 10 feet (3 meters)

DIET: Marine hypercarnivore; filter-feeder

ESSENTIAL FACTS: Riabinin's Cetothere is known for a virtually complete skeleton with a characteristic osteoschlerotic ribs and reduction of lumbar and caudal vertebrae, similar to those of sirenians. It was a benthic suction-feeder that would take mouthfuls of sand from the seafloor and sift out the small animals hidden within.

PISCOBALAENA NANA

NAME MEANING: Little whale from the Pisco Formation

AGE: Middle to late Miocene (11–5.3 MYA)

DISTRIBUTION: Atlantic Ocean, Pacific Ocean

SIZE: 16 feet (5 meters)

DIET: Marine hypercarnivore

ESSENTIAL FACTS: This species is named for the Pisco Formation of Peru, where the first fossils were collected. Additional material from the Bone Valley Formation in Florida shows that Piscobalaena was widely distributed through the Pacific and Atlantic Oceans. It is known for well-preserved material of juveniles and adults.

MIOCAPEREA PULCHRA

NAME MEANING: Beautiful less wrinkled

AGE: Late Miocene (11.6–7.2 MYA)

DISTRIBUTION: South America

SIZE: 10 feet (3 meters)

DIET: Marine hypercarnivore; filter-feeder

ESSENTIAL FACTS: Known for a beautifully preserved skull which inspired the species name, this species is a close relative of the modern pygmy right whale (*Caperea marginata*) within the subfamily Neobalaeninae, which may have diverged from other cetotheres during the Early Miocene.

HERPETOCETUS BRAMBLEI

NAME MEANING: Bramble's reptilian whale

AGE: Late Miocene

DISTRIBUTION: Pacific Ocean

SIZE: 14.7 feet (4.5 meters)

DIET: Marine hypercarnivore; filter-feeder

ESSENTIAL FACTS: Like other members of *Herpetocetus*, Bramble's Whale is a small whale with a long and slender body. They have been hypothesized to be benthic filter-feeders like grey whales (*Eschrichtius robustus*), by which they dive to the seafloor and roll on to their side, picking up mouthfuls of sand.

BALAENOPTERIDAE

Included among the rorqual whales is the largest animal known to have ever lived, the blue whale (*Balaenoptera musculus*). These whales are characterized by longitudinal folds of skin running from below the mouth to the chest that allow the throat to expand substantially during feeding, similar to the beak of a pelican. They are swift swimmers with streamlined body shapes and employ a feeding method known as lunge-feeding, in which they rush at high speed toward mass accumulations of small fishes or crustaceans (referred to as "bait balls"). The massive quantities of water they gulp with their expanding throat pouches is then pushed out through the baleen, trapping the prey inside their mouths. Lunge-feeding is achieved through separated dentaries and a unique sensory organ that specifically helps to coordinate the engulfment action.

INCAKUJIRA ANILLODEFUEGO

NAME MEANING: Inca whale from the Ring of Fire

AGE: Late Miocene (8–7.3 MYA)

DISTRIBUTION: South America; Pacific Ocean

SIZE: 20 feet (6 meters)

DIET: Marine hypercarnivore; filter-feeder

ESSENTIAL FACTS: This species was described in 2016 from fossils found in the Pisco Formation in Peru. The lunge-feeding capabilities of Incakujira were not as sophisticated as those of modern rorqual whales and they may have fed partly by skim-feeding.

ARCHAEBALAENOPTERA LIESSELENSIS

NAME MEANING: Ancient *Balaenoptera* from Leissel

AGE: Late Miocene to Pliocene

DISTRIBUTION: Atlantic Ocean

SIZE: 30 feet (10 meters)

DIET: Marine hypercarnivore; filter-feeder

ESSENTIAL FACTS: The largest species within the genus *Archaebalaenoptera*, it was described in 2020 from material discovered in Leissel, Netherlands. The morphology of the skull suggests that it could not lunge-feed, relying instead on skim-feeding.

PLESIOBALAENOPTERA QUARANTELLII

NAME MEANING: Raffaele Quarantelli's archaic *Balaenoptera*

AGE: Late Miocene (11–7 MYA)

DISTRIBUTION: Atlantic Ocean

SIZE: 30 feet (10 meters)

DIET: Marine hypercarnivore; filter-feeder

ESSENTIAL FACTS: The skull of Quarantelli's Whale suggests that it did not engage in lunge-feeding; its skull was uniquely wide relative to other rorquals, making it ideal for suction-feeding. Its fossils were discovered in the Stirone River in northern Italy.

PROTORORQUALUS CUVIERII

NAME MEANING: Cuvier's first rorqual

AGE: Pliocene (3.6–2.6 MYA)

DISTRIBUTION: Atlantic Ocean

SIZE: 20 feet (6 meters)

DIET: Marine hypercarnivore; filter-feeder

ESSENTIAL FACTS: Cuvier's Whale had relatively straight dentaries compared to the more bowed ones of modern forms. One of several basal rorquals from the Mediterranean Basin, it is thought that the region may have served as a refugia for more basal rorquals while the family continued to diversify elsewhere.

BALAENOPTERA BERTAE

NAME MEANING: Annalisa Berta whale fin

AGE: Pliocene (3.35–2.5 MYA)

DISTRIBUTION: Pacific Ocean

SIZE: 16–20 meters (5–6 meters)

DIET: Marine hypercarnivore; filter-feeder

ESSENTIAL FACTS: This species is known for an incomplete skull at the Purisima Formation in the San Francisco Bay Area in 2005. Berta's Whale may be the first rorqual to use the lunge-feeding behavior of the modern members of the family.

BALAENIDAE

The right whales are limited to four species today, but they were more diverse in prehistoric times. They are characterized by narrow, arched skulls, which gives them a deeply curved jawline that supports particularly long baleen. The fossil record for the group dates to the Early Miocene.

MORENOCETUS PARVUS

NAME MEANING: Little whale from Moreno

AGE: Early Miocene (20–16 MYA)

DISTRIBUTION: Pacific Ocean

SIZE: 17–18 feet (5.2–5.5 meters)

DIET: Marine hypercarnivore; filter-feeder

ESSENTIAL FACTS: Morenocetus is the oldest named species of right whale. Despite its early age, Morenocetus already displays the arched skull that characterizes modern right whales, albeit to a lesser extent.

BALAENULA ASTENSIS

NAME MEANING: Whale from Asti

AGE: Pliocene (5.3–2.5 MYA)

DISTRIBUTION: Atlantic Ocean

SIZE: 20–26 feet (6–8 meters)

DIET: Marine hypercarnivore; filter-feeder

ESSENTIAL FACTS: Members of *Balaenula* were morphologically identical to modern right whales with a deeply bowed skull and a robust body. They lived near the surface where they relied on skim-feeding.

ESCHRICHTIIDAE

The eschrichtiids have always been rare in the fossil record compared to other mysticetes, although the record dates back to the Miocene.

ARCHAESCHRICHTIUS RUGGIEROI

NAME MEANING: Livio Ruggiero's ancient *Eschrichtius*

AGE: Late Miocene (7–5 MYA)

DISTRIBUTION: Atlantic Ocean

SIZE: Unknown

DIET: Marine hypercarnivore; filter-feeder

ESSENTIAL FACTS: This species was the oldest-known eschrichtiid, discovered in Apuila, Italy, and described in 2006. It belongs to a family that has been identified from the Mediterranean Basin, showing that the family's distribution was much wider than it is today, the modern species being present only in the northern Pacific.

ESCHRICHTIOIDES GASTALDII

NAME MEANING: Bartolomeo Gastaldi's *Eschrichtius*-like whale

AGE: Early Pliocene

DISTRIBUTION: Atlantic Ocean

SIZE: Unknown

DIET: Marine hypercarnivore; filter-feeder

ESSENTIAL FACTS: Described in 1885 to the genus *Balaenoptera*, Gastaldi's Whale was renamed Eschrichtioides in 2008 when it was found to be closer to the modern grey whale (*Eschrichtius robustus*).

ESCHRICHTIUS AKISHIMAENSIS

NAME MEANING: Daniel Eschricht's (whale) from Akishima

AGE: Pleistocene (1.95–1.77 MYA)

DISTRIBUTION: Pacific Ocean

SIZE: 39 feet (12 meters)

DIET: Marine hypercarnivore; filter-feeder

ESSENTIAL FACTS: A nearly complete skeleton of the Akishima Whale was discovered in 1961 in a riverbed in Akishima, Tokyo, and described in 2017. Although it is morphologically very similar to the grey whale (*Eschrichtius robustus*), the two species can be distinguished by variations in the shape of the skull bones.

ODONTOCETI

The Odontoceti is the most diverse group of whales comprising seventy-three of the ninety modern species. Included within this group are the modern dolphins (Delphinidae), porpoises (Phocoenidae), beaked whales (Ziphiidae), sperm whales (Physeteridae), and narwhals (Monodontidae). As their common name suggests, the primary feature that distinguishes these whales from their filter-feeding relatives is the retention of teeth as adults. Another characteristic of this group is a type of sonar known as echolocation. At its simplest, echolocation in odontocetes occurs when repetitive clicking sounds produced in the airway are amplified by a special organ in the forehead known as the "melon," producing a focused beam of sound. These outgoing sound waves bounce off distant objects and the resulting echoes are then received through complex fatty tissues along the lower jaw en route to the middle ear, producing an accurate image of distant objects. Echolocation has been employed by toothed whales at least since the Early Oligocene and may have originated to locate prey buried in sediment, in murky water, at night, or in other areas of low visibility.

ANKYLORHIZA TIEDEMANI

NAME MEANING: Tiedeman's fused roots

AGE: Late Oligocene (29–23.5 MYA)

DISTRIBUTION:

SIZE: 16 feet (4.6 meters)

DIET: Marine hypercarnivore

SEE MORE ON PAGES 784–785

SQUALODONTIDAE

Squalodontids are more commonly referred to as "the shark-toothed dolphins." The name of the genus *Squalodon* comes from *Squalus*, a genus of dogfish sharks commonly known as "spurdogs" whose tooth shape bears a slight resemblance. The known fossil record for these animals dates from the Late Oligocene to Middle Miocene, and their closest modern relatives river dolphins in the family Platanistidae. Like other toothed whales, they had basined, asymmetric skulls indicating the presence of a melon and the ability to echolocate. They have long, narrow jaws with heterodont dentition resembling those of basilosaurid archaeocetes with differentiated conical incisors and canines and serrated, triangular premolars and molars adapted for grasping and cutting, respectively.

EOSQUALODON LANGEWIESCHEI

NAME MEANING: Langewiesche's dawn *Squalodon*

AGE: Late Oligocene (27–24 MYA)

DISTRIBUTION: Atlantic Ocean

SIZE: Unknown

DIET: Marine hypercarnivore

ESSENTIAL FACTS: It is known from incomplete skulls and sparse postcranial material discovered in Germany and Italy. It is very similar to the later genus *Squalodon* overall, and likely had a niche similar to that of modern dolphins.

PHOBERODON ARCTIROSTRIS

NAME MEANING: Bear-snouted fearful tooth

AGE: Early Miocene

DISTRIBUTION: Atlantic Ocean

SIZE: Unknown

DIET: Marine hypercarnivore

ESSENTIAL FACTS: This species was described in 1926 based on a nearly complete skull with associated postcrania. Like other squalodonts it was a gregarious open ocean predator whose diet consisted mainly of fishes, as well as cephalopods and crustaceans.

SQUALODON WHITMOREI

NAME MEANING: Whitmore's *Squalus* tooth

AGE: Middle Miocene

DISTRIBUTION: Atlantic Ocean

SIZE: 18 feet (5.5 meters)

DIET: Marine hypercarnivore

ESSENTIAL FACTS: The genus *Squalodon* was named by French naturalist Jean-Pierre Sylvestre de Grateloup in 1840, based on a jaw fragment which he thought to have come from the dinosaur *Iguanodon*. Later fossil discoveries would show that the animal was a toothed whale. Whitmore's Squalodon is the largest-known species in the genus.

ANKYLORHIZA TIEDEMANI

ESSENTIAL FACTS: Ankylorhiza is the most completely known of all the early toothed whales. Its relationships with other toothed whales are currently uncertain, as it appears to be part of a lineage that split off early in the radiation of the suborder. It is intermediate in morphology between basilosaurid archaeocetes and other odontocetes, still possessing heterodont dentition with discernable incisors and canines, although the premolars and molars are harder to tell apart. The forelimb also has relatively long forelimb bones with proportionally small hand bones. The first fossils of this whale were discovered in South Carolina in 1887 and placed in the genus *Squalodon*. With the later discovery of more complete material, a detailed 2020 study showed that it was distinct enough to warrant its own genus.

Ankylorhiza appears to have been a swift-swimming predator that was able to hunt relatively large prey items. Its large skull had enlarged attachment sites for powerful jaw muscles. The dentition was robust with the front teeth being adapted to pierce and grip. The teeth behind these are triangular and serrated, adapted for slicing carcasses into manageable pieces for swallowing. It was adapted to hunt relatively large prey items and may have opportunistically hunted fish, birds, reptiles, and other marine mammals. Ankylorhiza also possessed forward-pointing incisors that were probably employed during interspecific battles.

SEE ENTRY ON PAGE 782

XENOROPHIDAE

Xenorophids were small by cetacean standards, with a body length ranging from 4.1 feet (1.2 meters) to about 10–13 feet (3–4 meters). Their fossils are only known from Oligocene deposits in the southeastern United States. Xenorophids typically have long snouts with interlocking teeth and are among the first cetaceans known to have evolved adaptations for echolocation. Their ear bones are adapted for hearing high-frequency sounds for use in biosonar.

ALBERTOCETUS MEFFORDORUM

NAME MEANING: Mefford and Albert's whale

AGE: Early Oligocene (29 MYA)

DISTRIBUTION: Atlantic Ocean

SIZE: 6 feet (1.8 meters); 112–161 pounds (51–73 kilograms)

DIET: Marine hypercarnivore

ESSENTIAL FACTS: Albertocetus had an unusually large brain for an early whale, more similar to what is seen among modern toothed whales. The first specimens of this species were collected from a drainage ditch in the 1990s by undergraduate students at College of Charleston in South Carolina.

COTYLOCARA MACEI

NAME MEANING: Mace Brown's cavity head

AGE: Early Oligocene (28 MYA)

DISTRIBUTION: Atlantic Ocean

SIZE: Unknown

DIET: Marine hypercarnivore

ESSENTIAL FACTS: The first fossils of this species, a nearly complete skull and jaw with associated postcranial material, was discovered in a drainage ditch in the College Park Subdivision of Berkeley County, South Carolina.

ECHOVENATOR SANDERSI

NAME MEANING: Sanders' echo hunter

AGE: Late Oligocene (27 MYA)

DISTRIBUTION: Atlantic Ocean

SIZE: Unknown

DIET: Marine hypercarnivore

ESSENTIAL FACTS: Though it may not have been the oldest toothed whale to evolve the ability to echolocate, Echovenator is the first fossil whale for whom a focused study on the capacity for echolocation was conducted. Its genus name is a direct reference to this.

XENOROPHUS SLOANI

NAME MEANING: Sloan's strange snout

AGE: Late Oligocene (25 MYA)

DISTRIBUTION: Atlantic Ocean

SIZE: 8.5–10 feet (2.6–3 meters)

DIET: Marine hypercarnivore

ESSENTIAL FACTS: Sloan's Xenorophus is the first member of Xenorophidae to be described back in 1923 and is the type species for which the family is named. A second species has since been named as of 2023, exactly 100 years after the first.

INERMOROSTRUM XENOPS

NAME MEANING: Strange faced weaponless snout

AGE: Middle Oligocene (30 MYA)

DISTRIBUTION: Atlantic Ocean

SIZE: 3.3 feet (1 meter)

DIET: Marine hypercarnivore

ESSENTIAL FACTS: An unusual dwarfed, short-faced, toothless xenorophid adapted for suction-feeding soft-bodied prey such as squids. It is the oldest known to have possessed echolocation.

WAIPATIIDAE

Waipatiids are a group of small dolphin-like cetaceans that are known to have lived around the Pacific Ocean during the Late Oligocene. Their dentition is solely adapted for piercing with the teeth at the rear of the jaw, sometimes having faint cusps that would not be very effective for slicing.

WAIPATIA MAEREWHENUA

NAME MEANING: Maerewhenua River in Waipati

AGE: Late Oligocene (27–24 MYA)

DISTRIBUTION: Pacific Ocean

SIZE: Unknown

DIET: Marine hypercarnivore

ESSENTIAL FACTS: Discovered in New Zealand, Waipatia is the first waipatiid to be described back in 1994. It is known for a nearly complete skull with most of its teeth. Upon study its uniqueness among toothed whales was quickly recognized and it was placed in its own family.

URKUDELPHIS CHAWPIPACHA

NAME MEANING: Mountain dolphin from the equator

AGE: Late Oligocene (27–24 MYA)

DISTRIBUTION: Pacific Ocean

SIZE: Unknown

DIET: Marine hypercarnivore

ESSENTIAL FACTS: Known only from a juvenile skull discovered in Ecuador, its genus name is derived from the native Kichwa word *urku*, meaning "mountain," referencing its type locality of Montañita where it was discovered.

NIHOHAE MATAKOI

NAME MEANING: Pointed face with slashing teeth

AGE: Late Oligocene (25–25 MYA)

DISTRIBUTION: Pacific Ocean

SIZE: 10 feet (3 meters)

DIET: Marine hypercarnivore

ESSENTIAL FACTS: Described in 2023, Nihohae had a long snout with long front teeth that protruded from the jaws. It may have hunted in a manner similar to a sawfish, swinging its head from side to side to impale and slice nearby fish.

PLATANISTIDAE

Containing only two modern species, the Ganges river dolphin (*Platanista gangetica*) and Indus river dolphin (*P. minor*), this family was once much more widespread, distributed through the shallow coastal waters and estuaries around the world. Their fossil record dates to the Early Miocene and have been found on all continents accept Australia, Antarctica, and Africa. Platanistids are characterized by exceptionally long and narrow snouts for catching small and agile prey, along with small eyes for hunting in murky water. They also have wide salinity tolerances and are able to live in nearshore marine and estuarine environments, with the ability to travel up streams and rivers. It was once thought that modern members of Iniidae were part of this family as well. However, DNA evidence suggests these species are distinct lineages that obtained similar adaptations through convergent evolution.

DILOPHODELPHIS FORDYCEI

NAME MEANING: Fordyce's two-crested dolphin

AGE: Early Miocene

DISTRIBUTION: Pacific Ocean

SIZE: Unknown

DIET: Marine hypercarnivore

ESSENTIAL FACTS: Modern members of Platanistidae possess enlarged, inward-curving crests over its eyes that partially encase the melon, possibly serving to focus and amplify their echolocation calls. The scientific name of this species is a direct reference to this characteristic.

PREPOMATODELPHIS KORNEUBURGENSIS

NAME MEANING: Before *Pomatodelphis* from Korneuburg

AGE: Early Miocene

DISTRIBUTION: Atlantic Ocean

SIZE: Unknown

DIET: Marine hypercarnivore

ESSENTIAL FACTS: The Korneuburg River Dolphin is one of the smallest and oldest of the platanistids. It had a notably flattened snout and lacked the supraorbital crests that characterize the family and may represent a more basal lineage.

PACHYACANTHUS SUESSI

NAME MEANING: Suess' thick spines

AGE: Middle Miocene (16–15 MYA)

DISTRIBUTION: Atlantic Ocean

SIZE: Unknown

DIET: Marine hypercarnivore

ESSENTIAL FACTS: The Thick-Spined Dolphin exhibits pachyostosis of the neural spines on its postcervical vertebrae. This adaptation may have evolved to aid in hunting prey near the seafloor among seagrass beds. The deposits in which its fossils are found correspond to shallow waters with abundant seagrass.

POMATODELPHIS INAEQUALIS

NAME MEANING: Unequal river dolphin

AGE: Late Miocene (13.5–6.8 MYA)

DISTRIBUTION: Atlantic Ocean

SIZE: Unknown

DIET: Marine hypercarnivore

ESSENTIAL FACTS: Fossils of this species have been found in Alabama and Florida. Its jaws were relatively weak, and its teeth were small unlike those of modern piscivorous dolphins, possibly indicating a preference for soft-bodied prey like squids.

INIIDAE

Like the platanistids, modern members of the family have a number of adaptations that make them better able to navigate freshwater environments and the obstacles encountered therein. These include flexible necks, reduced or absent dorsal fins, and wide pectoral fins. The two modern species are restricted to the rivers of South America, but the family has had a presence throughout the Atlantic Ocean since their origin in the Miocene.

GONIODELPHIS HUDSONI

NAME MEANING: Hudson's angled dolphin

AGE: Late Miocene (14.9–8.7 MYA)

DISTRIBUTION: Atlantic Ocean

SIZE: Unknown

DIET: Marine hypercarnivore

ESSENTIAL FACTS: Discovered from phosphate mines in Polk County, Florida. Polk County was dry land during the Late Miocene but was close to the ocean, given higher sea levels at the time. Thus, Hudson's Dolphin may have inhabited rivers or brackish water at river mouths.

MEHERRINIA ISONI

NAME MEANING: Ronald Ison's (dolphin) from the Meherrin River

AGE: Late Miocene

DISTRIBUTION: Atlantic Ocean

SIZE: Unknown

DIET: Marine hypercarnivore

ESSENTIAL FACTS: Despite its fossils being found in the Meherrin River in North Carolina, the fossils appear to have eroded out of the ground from another location and deposited there by the current. It is unknown whether this species favored saltwater or freshwater.

ISTHMINIA PANAMENSIS

NAME MEANING: Isthmus of Panama

AGE: Late Miocene (6.1–5.8 MYA)

DISTRIBUTION: Pacific Ocean, Atlantic Ocean

SIZE: 9.4 feet (2.9 meters)

DIET: Marine hypercarnivore

ESSENTIAL FACTS: This species is known from a nearly complete skull found in Panama, which had not yet connected to South America at the time this species lived. Thus, the Panama Dolphin was able to swim freely between the Atlantic and Pacific Oceans. It may have favored coastal environments and estuaries.

DELPHINIDAE

Oceanic dolphins are the most diverse and speciose family of cetaceans with thirty-seven modern species, almost half of all modern cetaceans. They first appear in the fossil record during the Middle Miocene. Most species are relatively small, less than 15 feet (4.5 meters), and have primarily piscivorous diets. Some, like the killer whale (*Orinus orca*), are not only much larger but also have more robust jaws and teeth for tackling larger prey, including other marine mammals.

EODELPHINUS KABATENSIS

NAME MEANING: Dawn dolphin from

AGE: Late Miocene (13–8.5 MYA)

DISTRIBUTION: Pacific Ocean

SIZE: Unknown

DIET: Marine hypercarnivore

ESSENTIAL FACTS: Eodelphinus is the oldest-known member of the dolphin family. When first described in 1977 it was considered to be a relative of oceanic dolphins in the genus Stenella. This relationship was challenged in 2014, and the current genus name was assigned to highlight its uniqueness and age.

AUSTRALODELPHIS MIRUS

NAME MEANING: Strange southern dolphin

AGE: Pliocene (4.5–4 MYA)

DISTRIBUTION: Southern Ocean

SIZE: 11.5 feet (3.5 meters)

DIET: Marine hypercarnivore

ESSENTIAL FACTS: Australodelphis is the first Pliocene mammal from Antarctica to be described. It is unique for its toothless jaws and skull morphology resembling that of beaked whales (Ziphiidae), indicating that it relied on suction-feeding when hunting squid and small fish.

ZIPHIIDAE

Ziphiidae is currently the second largest family of cetaceans with twenty-two modern species, modern beaked whales. Beaked whales are the second largest family of cetaceans with twenty-four modern species, only three of which are reasonably well-studied. Modern examples of the family are small- to medium-sized whales that specialize in feeding on invertebrates at deep depths. Because of their diving habits they are one of the least-known groups of mammals. They are characterized by their elongated, streamlined bodies, dolphin-like snouts, and toothless jaws except for a pair of tusks found in adult males. Only the Shepherd's beaked whale (*Tasmacetus shepherdi*) retains teeth, although theirs are relatively small and weak. Modern beaked whales rely on suction-feeding to capture prey.

MICROBERARDIUS AFRICANUS

NAME MEANING: Little *Berardius* from Africa

AGE: Unknown

DISTRIBUTION: Atlantic Ocean, Indian Ocean

SIZE: 10 feet (3 meters)

DIET: Marine hypercarnivore

ESSENTIAL FACTS: One of 10 extinct species of beaked whale described in 2007 based on material recovered by trawling operations off the coast of South Africa. This species is notable for its small size, being about the size of one of the smaller dolphins.

MESSAPICETUS GREGARIUS

NAME MEANING: Social whale from Messapia

AGE: Late Miocene (11–9 MYA)

DISTRIBUTION: Pacific Ocean

SIZE: 15 feet (4.5 meters)

DIET: Marine hypercarnivore

SEE MORE ON PAGES 796–797

NINOZIPHIUS PLATYROSTRIS

NAME MEANING: Flat-snouted young Ziphius

AGE: Late Miocene (6–4 MYA)

DISTRIBUTION: Pacific Ocean

SIZE: Unkown

DIET: Marine hypercarnivore

ESSENTIAL FACTS: Discovered in Peru, like other long-snouted beaked whales, the skeleton of the Flat-Snouted Beaked Whale was not suited for deep-diving, instead being adapted to a mostly fish-based diet closer to the surface. Interestingly, the front of the jaws were toothless except for the two lower tusks.

PHYSETERIDAE

The sperm whales first appear during the Late Oligocene and achieved peak diversity during the Middle and Late Miocene. Their eyesight is relatively weak but is compensated for by an enhanced ability to echolocate. The melon is expanded and is paired by a "spermaceti organ," which contains a special waxy liquid called *spermaceti*, which serves to amplify and focus outgoing sounds. These features result in a deep head with a rectangular profile. Sperm whales are generally robust in build with many having proportionally large heads and strong jaws with enlarged, deeply rooted teeth for hunting large prey.

BRYGMOPHYSETER SHIGENSIS

NAME MEANING: Biting sperm whale of Shigamura

AGE: Middle Miocene (16–15 MYA)

DISTRIBUTION: Pacific Ocean

SIZE: 21–23 feet (6.5–7 meters)

DIET: Marine hypercarnivore

ESSENTIAL FACTS: Commonly known as the Biting Sperm Whale, this species is often compared to the modern killer whale (*Orcinus orca*) in terms of its ecology. However, its skeleton is more robust and its skull and teeth were proportionally much larger, suggesting that it was even more efficient at hunting larger prey.

AULOPHYSETER MORRICEI

NAME MEANING: Morrice's pipe whale

AGE: Middle to late Miocene (16–5.3 MYA)

DISTRIBUTION: Atlantic Ocean, Pacific Ocean

SIZE: 20 feet (6 meters); 2,400 pounds (1,100 kilograms)

DIET: Marine hypercarnivore

ESSENTIAL FACTS: This species had relatively narrow jaws and small teeth compared to the other sperm whales mentioned in this section, suggesting that it focused on relatively smaller prey, perhaps being more dependent on fish.

ZYGOPHYSETER VAROLAI

NAME MEANING: Angelo Varola's sperm whale

AGE: Late Miocene (11.6–7.2 MYA)

DISTRIBUTION: Atlantic Ocean

SIZE: 21–23 feet (6.5–7 meters)

DIET: Marine hypercarnivore

ESSENTIAL FACTS: The morphology of its skull suggests that it had a particularly bulbous forehead with a defined, pointed snout, similar to that seen in beaked whales. It has been referred to as the "Killer Sperm Whale" due to it being similar in size to the killer whale (*Orcinus orca*) but with larger teeth.